MARTINDALE-HUBBELL®

BAR REGISTER
OF
PREEMINENT
LAWYERS™
1997

VOLUME I

ALABAMA–MICHIGAN

EIGHTY-FIRST EDITION

MARTINDALE-HUBBELL
121 Chanlon Road
New Providence, NJ 07974
(908) 464-6800
Email: info@martindale.com
World Wide Web: http://www.martindale.com

Published by Martindale-Hubbell®, a member of the Reed Elsevier plc group

John R. Agel, Publisher
Carol D. Cooper, Vice President, Associate Publisher
Larry Thompson, Vice President, Sales
Edward J. Roycroft, Vice President, Sales Support
Dean Hollister, Vice President Database Production
Chuck Doscher, Vice President Production

International Standard Book Number: 1-56160-243-4

Printed and Bound in the United States of America
by World Color™ Book Services
Taunton, Massachusetts

ISBN 1 - 56160 - 243 - 4

9 781561 602438

TABLE OF CONTENTS

TABLE OF CONTENTS — *Continued*

FOREWORD

This year, we are pleased to publish the 81st edition of the **Martindale-Hubbell® Bar Register of Preeminent Lawyers**, which includes almost 27,000 listings representing the legal community's most highly regarded professionals.

The **Martindale-Hubbell Bar Register** lists only those sole practitioners and law firms who have received the highest (AV®) rating in the *Martindale-Hubbell® Law Directory*. These ratings are the result of confidential questionnaires sent to other practicing attorneys and members of the judiciary. The "A" rating is the highest legal ability rating, while the "V" signifies very high adherence to professional standards of conduct, ethics, reliability, and diligence.

The 1997 **Bar Register** provides information on firms excelling in 46 practice areas, including new sections on Aviation Law, Commercial Litigation, Constitutional Law, Energy Law, International Trade Law, and Mergers and Acquisitions.

Organized by practice area, then alphabetically by state and city, each entry in the **Bar Register** features complete contact information, names of associates and "of counsel", representative clients, and branch office locations.

In response to your requests for improved ease of handling, we are pleased to have redesigned the 1997 **Bar Register** into a two volume set. Divided geographically by state, this set is contained in an attractive slip-cover for shelf display while still maintaining the flexibility and portability of smaller volumes.

I hope you find this edition valuable as a source of information on the finest legal representation available, and I welcome your comments concerning the **Martindale-Hubbell Bar Register of Preeminent Lawyers**.

John R. Agel

John R. Agel
Publisher

USER'S GUIDE

The **MARTINDALE-HUBBELL BAR REGISTER OF PREEMINENT LAWYERS** is a two volume registry of firms and attorneys of significant stature. The 1997 Edition presents forty-six alphabetically sequenced practice area sections and an index to the firms listed in each practice area.

This **Subscriber Locator**, arranged alphabetically by subscriber name, will assist the user in identifying those practice areas and geographic location(s) where the subscriber lists.

A typical entry appears as follows:

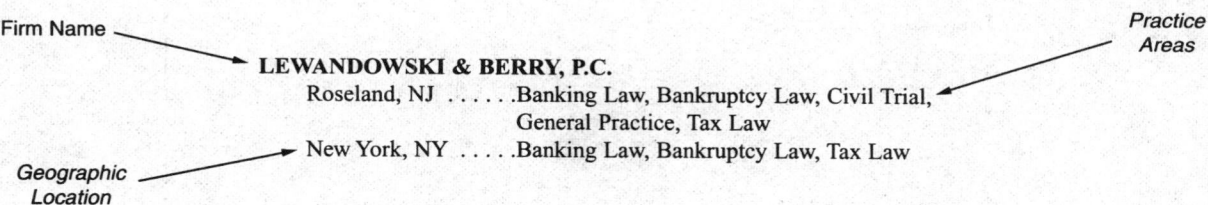

The **Practice Areas Section** clearly lists the practice area at the top of the page, along with the geographic location. Listings for the United States and Canada are arranged in alphabetic sequence by state (or Canadian province) and within state (or Canadian province) by city name and finally by listee name. For countries other than the United States and Canada, alphabetic country name is the major sequence, followed by city and then listee name.

A typical section entry appears as follows:

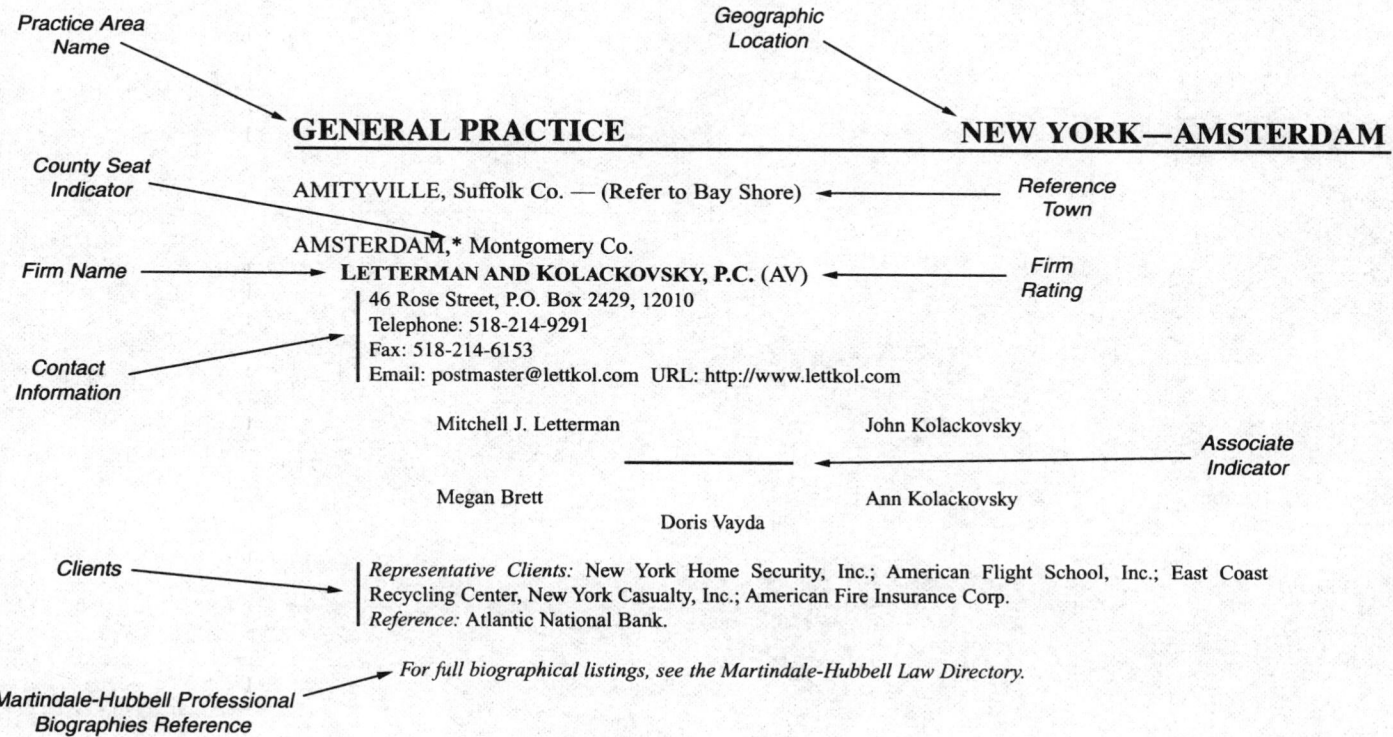

For additional help or explanation, please call Martindale-Hubbell Customer Relations, at (800) 526-4902.

INDEX SECTION

AABY, PUTNAM, ALBO & CAUSEY, A PROFESSIONAL SERVICES CORPORATION
Seattle, WA ....Workers Compensation

AARON, WILLIAM
Miami, FL ....Criminal Trial Practice

AARONS LAW FIRM, P.C.
Santa Fe, NM........................Criminal Trial Practice; Personal Injury

AARONSON & AARONSON
Encino, CA..............................Real Estate Law

ABBOT, MURPHY AND HARVEY, P.C.
Louisville, GA ....Business Law; General Practice

ABBOTT, C. MICHAEL, P.C.
Atlanta, GA ....Appellate Practice; Criminal Trial Practice

ABBOTT, NICHOLSON, QUILTER, ESSHAKI & YOUNGBLOOD, P.C.
Detroit, MI...........................Business Law; Civil Trial Practice; Employment Benefits Law; Labor and Employment Law; Municipal and Zoning Law; Probate, Trusts and Estate Planning; Real Estate Law

ABDO AND ABDO, P.A.
Minneapolis, MN...................Appellate Practice; Business Law; Civil Trial Practice; Environmental Law; General Practice; Probate, Trusts and Estate Planning; Real Estate Law; Securities Law; Sports and Entertainment Law

ABELE, CARLSON & SANDERSON, L.L.C.
St. Louis, MO........................Personal Injury; Product Liability Law; Workers Compensation

ABEL, MUSSER, SOKOLOSKY, MARES, BURCH, KOURI & GEORGE
Oklahoma City, OK................Civil Trial Practice; Personal Injury; Workers Compensation

ABELSON LAW FIRM, THE
Washington, DC...................Medical Malpractice; Personal Injury

ABEYTA-NELSON, P.C.
Yakima, WA............................Personal Injury

ABOWITZ AND RHODES, P.C.
Oklahoma City, OK................Civil Trial Practice; Insurance Defense; Personal Injury; Securities Law

ABRAHAM PRESSMAN & BAUER P.C.
Philadelphia, PA ....Civil Trial Practice

ABRAHAMS, KASLOW & CASSMAN
Omaha, NE ....General Practice

ABRAHAMS, LOEWENSTEIN, BUSHMAN & KAUFFMAN, P.C.
Philadelphia, PA ....General Practice

ABRAHAMSON, REED & ADLEY
Hammond, IN........................Civil Trial Practice; Commercial Litigation; Insurance Defense; Transportation Law

ABRAHAM, WATKINS, NICHOLS & FRIEND
Houston, TX ....General Practice; Medical Malpractice; Personal Injury

ABRAMOFF, NEUBERGER AND LINDER, LLP
Baltimore, MD ....Business Law; Real Estate Law

ABRAMS & MARTIN, P.C.
New York, NY.......................Administrative Law; Civil Trial Practice; Insurance Defense

ABRAMSON & FOX
Chicago, IL.............................Civil Trial Practice

ABRAMSON & FREEDMAN
Philadelphia, PA ....Administrative Law; Civil Trial Practice; Commercial Litigation

ABRAMSON & MAGIDSON, P.A.
Miami, FL ....Personal Injury

ABRAMSON, REIS, BROWN & DUGAN
Manchester, NH.....................Medical Malpractice; Personal Injury

ACKELS & ACKELS, L.L.P.
Dallas, TX...............................Civil Trial Practice; Criminal Trial Practice; Labor and Employment Law; Probate, Trusts and Estate Planning; Real Estate Law

ACKERMAN, JAMES H. LAW OFFICES OF
Long Beach, CA ....Admiralty/Maritime Law; General Practice

ACKERMAN, ALLAN A., P.C.
Chicago, IL.............................Appellate Practice; Criminal Trial Practice

ACKMAN, MAREK, BOYD AND WOODRUFF, LTD.
Kankakee, IL..........................Civil Trial Practice; General Practice; Insurance Defense; Medical Malpractice

---

Watseka, IL.............................General Practice

ADAMO & NEWMAN
Westerly, RI ....Criminal Trial Practice; Family Law; Personal Injury

ADAMS, WESTON
Columbia, SC ....General Practice

ADAMS & ADAMS
Miami, FL ....Civil Trial Practice; General Practice
Somerset, KY ....Banking Law; Commercial Litigation; Insurance Defense; Real Estate Law

ADAMS, BARFIELD, DUNAWAY & HANKINSON
Thomaston, GA ....General Practice

ADAMS, BROOKING, STEPNER, WOLTERMANN & DUSING
Covington, KY.......................Civil Trial Practice; General Practice; Insurance Defense; Personal Injury; Probate, Trusts and Estate Planning
Florence, KY ....Civil Trial Practice; General Practice; Insurance Defense; Personal Injury; Probate, Trusts and Estate Planning

ADAMS, COFFEY & DUESLER, L.L.P.
Beaumont, TX ....Insurance Defense

ADAMS, COOGLER, WATSON & MERKEL, P.A.
West Palm Beach, FL ....Civil Trial Practice

ADAMS & CRAMER
Shelbyville, IN........................General Practice

ADAMS, GILBERT T., A PROF. CORP., LAW OFFICES OF
Beaumont, TX ....Civil Trial Practice; Personal Injury

ADAMS & GRAHAM, L.L.P.
Harlingen, TX ....Appellate Practice; Civil Trial Practice; Insurance Defense; Medical Malpractice; Product Liability Law

ADAMS, HILL, REIS, ADAMS, HALL & SCHIEFFELIN
Orlando, FL ....Civil Trial Practice; General Practice; Health Care Law; Insurance Defense; Medical Malpractice

ADAMS, JOHNSTON & ORECK, A PROFESSIONAL LAW CORPORATION
New Orleans, LA ....Insurance Defense

ADAMS, JONES, ROBINSON AND MALONE, CHARTERED
Wichita, KS.............................Civil Trial Practice; Commercial Law; Natural Resources Law; Real Estate Law

ADAMS KLEEMEIER HAGAN HANNAH & FOUTS
Asheville, NC..........................Civil Trial Practice; General Practice; Labor and Employment Law; Real Estate Law
Greensboro, NC......................Civil Trial Practice; General Practice; Labor and Employment Law; Real Estate Law

ADAMS AND REESE
New Orleans, LA ....General Practice

ADAMS & SPEARS, P.A.
Orlando, FL ....Civil Trial Practice; Commercial Litigation; General Practice

ADAMS & WHITEAKER, P.C.
Nashville, TN..........................Commercial Law; Probate, Trusts and Estate Planning

ADANG, PETER J., P.C.
Albuquerque, NM...................Civil Trial Practice; Labor and Employment Law; Personal Injury

ADDISON, MICHAEL C.
Tampa, FL ....Antitrust Law; Civil Trial Practice; Construction Law; Product Liability Law; Securities Law

ADDUCI, MASTRIANI & SCHAUMBERG, L.L.P.
Washington, DC.....................Administrative Law; International Trade Law; Patent, Trademark, Copyright and Unfair Competition

ADELMAN, GETTLEMAN, MERENS, BERISH & CARTER, LTD.
Chicago, IL.............................Bankruptcy Law

ADELMAN LAVINE GOLD AND LEVIN, A PROFESSIONAL CORPORATION
Philadelphia, PA ....Bankruptcy Law

ADELMAN, ROBERT A., A LAW CORPORATION
Beverly Hills, CA ....Family Law

ADELSON, GOLDEN & LORIA, P.C.
Boston, MA ....Real Estate Law

ADERSON, FRANK & STEINER, A PROFESSIONAL CORPORATION
Pittsburgh, PA ....Administrative Law; Bankruptcy Law; Civil Trial Practice; Commercial Law; Family Law; Personal Injury; Probate, Trusts and Estate Planning; Product Liability Law

ADINAMIS & ADINAMIS, ATTORNEYS, A PROFESSIONAL CORPORATION
Indianapolis, IN ....Probate, Trusts and Estate Planning; Tax Law

ADKINS & ADKINS
Catlettsburg, KY....................Probate, Trusts and Estate Planning; Real Estate Law

ADKINS, KISE & DIACO, P.A.
Tampa, FL ....Commercial Litigation; Construction Law; Criminal Trial Practice

ADKINS, POTTS & SMETHURST, L.L.P.
Salisbury, MD ....Civil Trial Practice; Environmental Law; Municipal and Zoning Law; Real Estate Law

ADKISON NEED
Bloomfield Hills, MI ....Banking Law; Business Law; Commercial Litigation; Communications Law; Computer Law; General Practice; Land Use Law; Municipal and Zoning Law; Trademark, Copyright and Unfair Competition

ADLER, ALAN R.
Morristown, NJ......................Tax Law

ADLER, DAVID W.
Phoenix, AZ ....Family Law

ADOLPH & BINTINGER, P.S.
Seattle, WA ....Civil Trial Practice

ADVICE & COUNSEL INCORPORATED
San Francisco, CA ....Probate, Trusts and Estate Planning

AGAPAY, LEVYN & HALLING, A PROFESSIONAL CORPORATION
Los Angeles, CA ....Civil Trial Practice

AGNEW & BRUSAVICH
Los Angeles, CA ....Civil Trial Practice; Medical Malpractice; Personal Injury; Product Liability Law
Torrance, CA...........................Civil Trial Practice; Medical Malpractice; Personal Injury; Product Liability Law

AGNOLI, ROBERT G.
Springfield, MA.......................Probate, Trusts and Estate Planning

AHERIN, RICE & ANEGON, A PROFESSIONAL ASSOCIATION
Lewiston, ID ....Personal Injury

AHLERS, COONEY, DORWEILER, HAYNIE, SMITH & ALLBEE, P.C.
Des Moines, IA ....General Practice

AHMUTY, DEMERS & MCMANUS
New York, NY.........................Civil Trial Practice; Insurance Defense

AIKEN, KRAMER & CUMMINGS, INCORPORATED
Oakland, CA ....Business Law; Construction Law; Environmental Law; Probate, Trusts and Estate Planning; Real Estate Law

AIKIN, WENDY L., P.A.
Winter Park, FL......................Civil Trial Practice

AIKINS, MACAULAY & THORVALDSON
Winnipeg, MB, Canada...........Business Law; Civil Trial Practice; General Practice; Insurance Defense; Personal Injury; Probate, Trusts and Estate Planning; Tax Law

AINSWORTH, SULLIVAN, TRACY, KNAUF, WARNER & RUSLANDER
Albany, NY.............................General Practice

AIRD & BERLIS
Toronto, ON, Canada.............General Practice

AITKEN, SCHAUBLE, PATRICK, NEILL & RUFF
Pullman, WA...........................General Practice

AITKEN, WYLIE A., A LAW CORPORATION, LAW OFFICES OF
Santa Ana, CA ....Personal Injury

AJALAT, POLLEY & AYOOB
Los Angeles, CA ....Tax Law

AKIN, GUMP, STRAUSS, HAUER & FELD
Brussels, Belgium ....General Practice
Washington, DC......................General Practice
Austin, TX ....General Practice
Dallas, TX...............................General Practice
Houston, TX............................General Practice
San Antonio, TX......................General Practice

AKIN & TATE, L.L.C.
Cartersville, GA ....General Practice

AKINS, JEFFREY R.
San Antonio, TX......................Civil Trial Practice; Natural Resources Law

AKLUFI AND WYSOCKI
Riverside, CA ....General Practice

ALALA MULLEN HOLLAND & COOPER, P.A.
Gastonia, NC ....General Practice

ALBANESE, ALBANESE & FIORE LLP
Garden City, NY ....Banking Law; Civil Trial Practice; General Practice; Probate, Trusts and Estate Planning; Real Estate Law

ALBERT, BATES, WHITEHEAD & MCGAUGH, P.C.
Chicago, IL..............................Business Law; Civil Trial Practice; Labor and Employment Law

ALBERT, WARD & JOHNSON, P.C.
Greenwich, CT ....Civil Trial Practice; Construction Law; General Practice; Municipal and Zoning Law; Probate, Trusts and Estate Planning; Real Estate Law

ALBERT, WEILAND & GOLDEN
Costa Mesa, CA ....Bankruptcy Law; Real Estate Law

ALBRECHT, MAGUIRE, HEFFERN & GREGG, P.C.
Buffalo, NY ....Business Law; Civil Trial Practice; Employment Benefits Law; General Practice; Probate, Trusts and Estate Planning; Tax Law

ALBRIGHT BROWN & CAUDILL, LLC
Baltimore, MD ....Civil Trial Practice; Criminal Trial Practice

ALBRIGHT, STODDARD, WARNICK & ALBRIGHT, A PROFESSIONAL CORPORATION
Las Vegas, NV ....Appellate Practice; Bankruptcy Law; Civil Trial Practice; Commercial Law; Construction Law; Family Law; General Practice; Insurance Defense; Personal Injury; Probate, Trusts and Estate Planning; Real Estate Law

ALCANTARA & FRAME, ATTORNEYS AT LAW, A LAW CORPORATION
Honolulu, HI...........................Admiralty/Maritime Law; Insurance Defense; Product Liability Law

ALDEN ARONOVSKY & SAX
San Francisco, CA ....Civil Trial Practice; Environmental Law

ALDERMAN & ALDERMAN
Syracuse, NY...........................Family Law; Real Estate Law

ALDERSON, ONDOV, LEONARD, SWEEN & RIZZI, P.A.
Austin, MN ....General Practice

ALDRICH & BONNEFIN, P.L.C.
Irvine, CA................................Banking Law

ALDRICH LAW OFFICES
Minneapolis, MN ....Family Law

ALEMBIK & ALEMBIK
Atlanta, GA ....Family Law; Real Estate Law

ALEMBIK, FINE & CALLNER, P.A.
Atlanta, GA ....Business Law; Civil Trial Practice; Family Law; General Practice; Insurance Defense; Real Estate Law

ALEXANDER & ASSOCIATES
Houston, TX ....Civil Trial Practice; Family Law

ALEXANDER, BEARDEN, HAIRSTON & MARKS, LLP
Washington, DC......................Administrative Law; Communications Law; Employment Benefits Law; Environmental Law; Municipal Bond/Public Authority Financing; Municipal and Zoning Law; Real Estate Law; Tax Law; Trademark, Copyright and Unfair Competition

ALEXANDER, BEARDEN, HAIRSTON & MARKS, LLP
Silver Spring, MD ....Civil Trial Practice; Labor and Employment Law

ALEXANDER & CRABTREE, P.C.
Denver, CO ....Administrative Law; Business Law; Civil Trial Practice; Commercial Law; Employment Benefits Law; Insurance Defense

ALEXANDER, HOLBURN, BEAUDIN & LANG
Vancouver, BC, Canada...........General Practice; Insurance Defense; Labor and Employment Law

ALEXANDER LAW FIRM, THE
San Jose, CA ....Business Law; Civil Trial Practice; Environmental Law; Personal Injury; Product Liability Law

ALEXANDER & VANN
Thomasville, GA ....General Practice

ALFORD, E. GREGORY
San Diego, CA ....Family Law

ALFRED, JEAN-ROBERT
Christiansted, St. Croix, VI .....Civil Trial Practice; General Practice; Insurance Defense; Personal Injury; Probate, Trusts and Estate Planning; Real Estate Law

ALLABEN, MASSIE, VANDER WEYDEN & TIMMER
Grand Rapids, MI ....Civil Trial Practice; General Practice; Insurance Defense; Personal Injury

ALLAN & SHIPP, P.A.
St. Petersburg, FL...................Probate, Trusts and Estate Planning; Securities Law

ALLARD & FISH, A PROFESSIONAL CORPORATION
Detroit, MI............................Bankruptcy Law; Commercial Law; Tax Law

ALLEN, RICHARD E.
Augusta, GA ....Civil Trial Practice; Criminal Trial Practice

ALLEN, ALLEN, ALLEN & ALLEN, A PROFESSIONAL CORPORATION
Richmond, VA ....Personal Injury

ALLEN, ALLEN BOERNER & BREELAND
Brookhaven, MS.....................Banking Law; Civil Trial Practice; Commercial Law; Family Law; General Practice; Insurance Defense; Labor and Employment Law; Personal Injury; Probate, Trusts and Estate Planning; Real Estate Law

ALLEN, BRINTON & SIMMONS, P.A.
Jacksonville, FL ....Business Law; Civil Trial Practice

ALLEN & CLASSENS
Statesboro, GA........................General Practice

ALLEN, COOLEY & ALLEN
Lawrence, KS ....General Practice

ALLEN, DELL, FRANK & TRINKLE, P.A.
Tampa, FL ....Civil Trial Practice; General Practice

ALLEN, DYER, DOPPELT, MILBRATH & GILCHRIST
Orlando, FL ....Patent, Trademark, Copyright and Unfair Competition

ALLEN, GLENN K., A PROFESSIONAL ASSOCIATION
Jacksonville, FL ....Civil Trial Practice; Medical Malpractice; Personal Injury

ALLEN & GOOCH
Lafayette, LA ....Insurance Defense

ALLEN & HAROLD, P.L.C.
Manassas, VA ....Business Law; Commercial Law; Communications Law

ALLEN, JOHNSON, ALEXANDER & KARP, P.A.
Washington, DC.....................Civil Trial Practice; General Practice; Insurance Defense; Product Liability Law
Baltimore, MD ....Civil Rights; Civil Trial Practice; General Practice; Insurance Defense; Product Liability Law

ALLEN AND KIMBELL
Santa Barbara, CA ....General Practice

ALLEN, KNUDSEN & DEBOEST, P.A.
Fort Myers, FL ....Administrative Law; Civil Trial Practice; Probate, Trusts and Estate Planning; Real Estate Law

ALLEN LAW FIRM, A PROFESSIONAL CORPORATION
Little Rock, AR ....Banking Law; Civil Trial Practice; Insurance Defense; Securities Law

ALLEN LAW OFFICE
Lafayette, LA ....Personal Injury

ALLEN & MALLER, P.A.
St. Petersburg, FL...................General Practice

ALLEN, MATKINS, LECK, GAMBLE & MALLORY LLP
Irvine, CA...............................General Practice
Los Angeles, CA ....General Practice
San Diego, CA ....General Practice

ALLEN, NELSON & BOWERS
Elizabethton, TN....................Civil Trial Practice; General Practice

ALLEN AND PINNIX, P.A.
Raleigh, NC............................Administrative Law; Antitrust Law; Immigration and Naturalization; International Business Law

ALLEN, POLGAR, PROIETTI & FAGALDE
Merced, CA ....Civil Trial Practice; General Practice

ALLEN & PRICE, P.L.C.
Phoenix, AZ ....Antitrust Law; Civil Trial Practice; Health Care Law; Patent, Trademark, Copyright and Unfair Competition

ALLEN, RHODES, SOBELSOHN & JOHNSON, LLP
Santa Barbara, CA ....Insurance Defense

ALLEN, RHODES, SOBELSOHN & JOHNSON, LLP
Los Angeles, CA ....Insurance Defense

ALLEN, ROGERS AND VAHRENWALD
Fort Collins, CO ....General Practice

ALLEN, SCRUGGS, SOSSAMAN & THOMPSON, P.C.
Memphis, TN ....Business Law; Labor and Employment Law; Workers Compensation

ALLEN, VAUGHN, COBB & HOOD, P.A.
Gulfport, MS ....Banking Law; Civil Trial Practice; General Practice; Insurance Defense

ALLEN, YURASEK & MERKLIN
Marysville, OH ....General Practice

ALLEY AND ALLEY/FORD & HARRISON
Miami, FL ....Labor and Employment Law
Tampa, FL ....Civil Trial Practice; Labor and Employment Law

ALLEY, RAYMOND A., JR., P.A.
Tampa, FL ....Family Law

ALLGOOD, CHILDS, MEHRHOF AND MILLIANS, P.C.
Augusta, GA ....Insurance Defense; Workers Compensation

ALLISON, MACKENZIE, HARTMAN, SOUMBENIOTIS & RUSSELL, LTD.
Carson City, NV ....General Practice

ALLISON, YEAGER & BASSETT, L.L.P.
Austin, TX ....Criminal Trial Practice

ALLMAN SPRY LEGGETT & CRUMPLER, P.A.
Winston-Salem, NC ....General Practice

ALLOTT & MAKAR, A PROFESSIONAL CORPORATION
Denver, CO ....Immigration and Naturalization

ALLRED, BACON, HALFHILL, LANDAU & YOUNG, PC
Fairfax, VA ....General Practice

ALLRED, JOEL M., P.C.
Salt Lake City, UT..................Civil Trial Practice; Family Law; Medical Malpractice; Personal Injury; Product Liability Law

ALLRED LAW FIRM, THE
Jackson, MS ....Banking Law; Civil Trial Practice; Commercial Law; Environmental Law; Insurance Defense; Personal Injury; Product Liability Law

ALLSHOUSE, J. D. BUCKY, A PROFESSIONAL CORPORATION
Houston, TX ....Family Law

ALPERT, BARKER & CALCUTT, P.A.
Tampa, FL ....Civil Trial Practice; General Practice; Insurance Defense; Securities Law

ALPERT, BARR AND GROSS, A PROFESSIONAL LAW CORPORATION
Encino, CA.............................Business Law; Commercial Litigation; Family Law; Probate, Trusts and Estate Planning; Real Estate Law

ALSCHULER GROSSMAN & PINES LLP
Los Angeles, CA ....General Practice

AL-SHUBAIKI, TORKI A., LEGAL ADVISORS
Riyadh, Saudi Arabia...............General Practice

ALSPACH, THOMAS T.
Easton, MD............................Commercial Litigation; Health Care Law

ALSTON & BIRD
Atlanta, GA ....Antitrust Law; Banking Law; Civil Trial Practice; Communications Law; Environmental Law; General Practice; Health Care Law; Immigration and Naturalization; International Business Law; Labor and Employment Law; Municipal Bond/Public Authority Financing; Real Estate Law; Tax Law; Trademark, Copyright and Unfair Competition

ALSTON, HUNT, FLOYD & ING, ATTORNEYS AT LAW, A LAW CORPORATION
Honolulu, HI..........................Civil Trial Practice; Commercial Law; General Practice

ALSTON, RUTHERFORD & VAN SLYKE
Jackson, MS ....Antitrust Law; Civil Trial Practice; Communications Law; General Practice; Natural Resources Law; Tax Law

ALTHEIMER & GRAY
Chicago, IL.............................General Practice

ALTHOUSE & MCDONOUGH
Upland, CA ....Business Law; Civil Trial Practice; General Practice; Probate, Trusts and Estate Planning

ALTICK & CORWIN CO., L.P.A.
Dayton, OH............................Bankruptcy Law; General Practice; Probate, Trusts and Estate Planning

ALTMAN, JAMES J.
New Port Richey, FL ....Probate, Trusts and Estate Planning

ALTMAN, LAWRENCE J.
Chesterfield, MO ....Labor and Employment Law

ALTMAN & CALARDO CO., A LEGAL PROFESSIONAL ASSOCIATION
Cincinnati, OH ....Environmental Law

ALTMAN, GREER & DOUGHERTY
Lake Worth, FL ....Probate, Trusts and Estate Planning; Real Estate
Law

ALTMAN, KRITZER & LEVICK, P.C.
Atlanta, GA ....General Practice

ALVARADO, SMITH, VILLA & SANCHEZ, A PROFESSIONAL CORPORATION
Newport Beach, CA ....International Business Law

ALVERSON, TAYLOR, MORTENSEN, NELSON & SANDERS
Las Vegas, NV ....Administrative Law; Banking Law; Bankruptcy
Law; Business Law; Civil Trial Practice; Commercial
Law; Construction Law; Immigration and Naturalization;
Insurance Defense; International Business
Law; Medical Malpractice; Municipal Bond/Public
Authority Financing; Probate, Trusts and Estate
Planning; Real Estate Law

AMAN & LINS, P.A.
Tampa, FL ....Commercial Litigation

AMBROSE, WILSON, GRIMM & DURAND
Knoxville, TN ....Civil Trial Practice; General Practice; Insurance
Defense

AMELUNG, WULFF & WILLENBROCK, P.C.
St. Louis, MO ....Insurance Defense

AMENT, JOHN S. III
Jacksonville, TX ....Civil Trial Practice

AMER CUNNINGHAM BRENNAN CO., L.P.A.
Akron, OH ....Civil Trial Practice; Employment Benefits Law;
Personal Injury; Probate, Trusts and Estate
Planning; Tax Law

AMERLING & BURNS, A PROFESSIONAL ASSOCIATION
Portland, ME ....Civil Trial Practice; Commercial Law; Construction
Law; Environmental Law; General Practice;
Insurance Defense; Product Liability Law

AMES & AMES
Onancock, VA ....General Practice

AMIS, ROBERT W., P.L.L.C.
Plano, TX ....Employment Benefits Law; General Practice

AMLONG & AMLONG, P.A.
Fort Lauderdale, FL ....Family Law; Labor and Employment Law

AMSTER, ROTHSTEIN & EBENSTEIN
New York, NY ....Patent, Trademark, Copyright and Unfair Competition

ANAPOL, SCHWARTZ, WEISS AND COHAN, A PROFESSIONAL CORPORATION
Philadelphia, PA ....Civil Trial Practice; Commercial Litigation; Environmental
Law; Medical Malpractice; Personal Injury

ANCEL & DUNLAP
Indianapolis, IN ....Bankruptcy Law

ANDERSEN, BERKSHIRE, LAURITSEN & BROWER
Omaha, NE ....General Practice; Labor and Employment Law

ANDERSEN, DAVIDSON & TATE, P.C.
Lawrenceville, GA ....Banking Law; Business Law; Civil Trial Practice;
General Practice; Real Estate Law

ANDERSON, ADOLPH N. JR.
Providence, RI ....Probate, Trusts and Estate Planning

ANDERSON, CHARLES E.
Albuquerque, NM ....Business Law; Probate, Trusts and Estate Planning;
Tax Law

ANDERSON, JEFFREY C. LAW OFFICES OF
San Antonio, TX ....Medical Malpractice

ANDERSON, KENNETH G.
Jacksonville, FL ....Probate, Trusts and Estate Planning; Tax Law

ANDERSON, ABLON, LEWIS & GALE, LLP
Los Angeles, CA ....Commercial Litigation; Insurance Defense

ANDERSON, BRODY, LEVINSON, WEISER & HORWITZ, P.A.
Phoenix, AZ ....General Practice; Real Estate Law

ANDERSON & BROUSSARD
Lafayette, LA ....Personal Injury

ANDERSON, COE & KING, L.L.P.
Baltimore, MD ....Civil Trial Practice; Product Liability Law

ANDERSON, DANIEL & COXE
Wrightsville Beach, NC ....Insurance Defense

ANDERSON, GALLOWAY & LUCCHESE, A PROFESSIONAL CORPORATION
Walnut Creek, CA ....Civil Trial Practice; Insurance Defense; Medical
Malpractice; Product Liability Law

ANDERSON & GILBERT
St. Louis, MO ....Civil Trial Practice; General Practice

ANDERSON GREENFIELD & DOUGHERTY, LTD.
Philadelphia, PA ....Banking Law; Commercial Litigation; Labor and
Employment Law

ANDERSON, JOHNSON, LAWRENCE, BUTLER & BOCK
Fayetteville, NC ....Insurance Defense

ANDERSON & KARRENBERG, A PROFESSIONAL CORPORATION
Salt Lake City, UT ....Commercial Litigation

ANDERSON KILL & OLICK, L.L.P.
Washington, DC ....Civil Trial Practice; General Practice

ANDERSON KILL & OLICK, P.C.
New York, NY ....Antitrust Law; Civil Trial Practice

ANDERSON & KILPATRICK
Little Rock, AR ....Insurance Defense; Medical Malpractice; Product
Liability Law; Workers Compensation

ANDERSON & ORCUTT, P.A.
Tampa, FL ....Commercial Litigation

ANDERSON & QUINN
Rockville, MD ....Civil Trial Practice; Insurance Defense; Personal
Injury; Product Liability Law; Workers Compensation

ANDERSON, SHANNON, O'BRIEN, RICE & BERTZ
Stevens Point, WI ....General Practice

ANDERSON & SMITH, L.C.
Salt Lake City, UT ....Commercial Litigation; Construction Law

ANDERSON, SMITH, NULL, STOFER & MURPHREE, L.L.P.
Victoria, TX ....General Practice

ANDERSON, THOMAS T., P.C.
Indio, CA ....General Practice

ANDERSON, TIMOTHY G., P.A.
Tampa, FL ....Civil Trial Practice; Personal Injury; Product
Liability Law

ANDERSON, WALKER & REICHERT, P.C.
Macon, GA ....General Practice; Insurance Defense; Probate, Trusts
and Estate Planning; Tax Law

ANDERSON, ZEIGLER, DISHAROON, GALLAGHER & GRAY, PROFESSIONAL CORPORATION
Santa Rosa, CA ....General Practice

ANDORA, PALMISANO & GEANEY, A PROFESSIONAL CORPORATION
Elmwood Park, NJ ....Banking Law; Municipal and Zoning Law; Public
Utilities Law; Tax Law

ANDRADE & MUZI
Irvine, CA ....Admiralty/Maritime Law; Construction Law;
Insurance Defense; Labor and Employment Law

ANDREOS, GEORGE P., A PROFESSIONAL LAW CORPORATION
San Diego, CA ....Medical Malpractice; Personal Injury

ANDREWS, ANGUS G.
De Funiak Springs, FL ....General Practice

ANDREWS DAVIS LEGG BIXLER MILSTEN & PRICE, A PROFESSIONAL CORPORATION
Oklahoma City, OK ....Antitrust Law; Banking Law; Bankruptcy Law;
Civil Trial Practice; Employment Benefits Law;
Environmental Law; General Practice; Health Care
Law; Insurance Defense; Labor and Employment
Law; Natural Resources Law; Probate, Trusts and
Estate Planning; Real Estate Law; Securities Law;
Tax Law; Trademark, Copyright and Unfair Competition;
Transportation Law

ANDREWS & KURTH L.L.P.
Los Angeles, CA ....General Practice
Washington, DC ....General Practice
New York, NY ....General Practice
Dallas, TX ....General Practice
Houston, TX ....General Practice

ANDREWS, RANSFORD & PLOCHOCKI, LLP
Syracuse, NY............................Insurance Defense; Product Liability Law

ANDRUS, SCEALES, STARKE & SAWALL
Milwaukee, WI........................Patent, Trademark, Copyright and Unfair Competition

ANESI, FRANK J.
Durango, CO............................Commercial Law; General Practice; Real Estate Law

ANESI, OZMON & RODIN, LTD.
Chicago, IL..............................Civil Trial Practice; Personal Injury

ANGEL AND NEISTAT, A PROFESSIONAL CORPORATION
Los Angeles, CA ....Banking Law; Bankruptcy Law; Business Law; Civil Trial Practice

ANGINO & ROVNER, P.C.
Harrisburg, PA........................Civil Trial Practice; Medical Malpractice; Personal Injury

ANGLE, CARLSON, GOLDRICK & ROBERTS
Santa Barbara, CA...................Appellate Practice; Bankruptcy Law; Commercial Litigation; Family Law; Personal Injury; Probate, Trusts and Estate Planning; Real Estate Law

ANGLE, MURPHY, VALENTINO & CAMPBELL, P.C.
York, NE..................................General Practice

ANGONES, HUNTER, MCCLURE, LYNCH & WILLIAMS, P.A.
Miami, FL................................Civil Trial Practice; General Practice; Insurance Defense; Medical Malpractice

ANKELE, ICENOGLE, NORTON, WHITE & SETER, A PROFESSIONAL CORPORATION
Denver, CO ....Civil Trial Practice; Municipal and Zoning Law

ANNINO, DRAPER & MOORE, P.C.
Springfield, MA.......................Construction Law; Environmental Law; Health Care Law

ANSELL ZARO & GRIMM, A PROFESSIONAL CORPORATION
Eatontown, NJ ....Banking Law; Civil Trial Practice; General Practice

ANSPACH & DALTON
Chicago, IL..............................Environmental Law

ANSPACH, ROBERT M., ASSOCIATES
Toledo, OH ....Civil Trial Practice; Insurance Defense; Labor and Employment Law; Medical Malpractice; Product Liability Law

ANSTANDIG, MCDYER, BURDETTE & YURCON, P.C.
Pittsburgh, PA........................Civil Trial Practice; General Practice; Insurance Defense

ANTHENELLI & OTWAY
Salisbury, MD.........................General Practice

ANTHONY & CARLSON
Oakland, CA ....Civil Trial Practice; Labor and Employment Law; Medical Malpractice; Personal Injury

ANTHONY, SEIBERT AND DLOSKI
Mount Clemens, MI................Municipal and Zoning Law

ANTIN & TAYLOR
Los Angeles, CA ....Employment Benefits Law; Probate, Trusts and Estate Planning; Tax Law

ANTON, BRUCE
Dallas, TX...............................Criminal Trial Practice

ANTONELLI, TERRY, STOUT & KRAUS, LLP
Arlington, VA ....Patent, Trademark, Copyright and Unfair Competition

APFELBAUM, APFELBAUM & APFELBAUM
Sunbury, PA............................General Practice

APICELLA AND TRAPP
Cleveland, OH.........................Personal Injury

APKER, APKER, HAGGARD & KURTZ, P.C.
Phoenix, AZ ....Civil Trial Practice; Commercial Law; Natural Resources Law; Real Estate Law

APPEL, CHITWOOD & HARLEY
Atlanta, GA ....Securities Law

APPEL & YOST, LLP
Lancaster, PA..........................Business Law; Real Estate Law; Tax Law

APPLE AND APPLE, A PROFESSIONAL CORPORATION
Pittsburgh, PA ....Bankruptcy Law; Commercial Law

APRUZZESE, MCDERMOTT, MASTRO & MURPHY, A PROFESSIONAL CORPORATION
Liberty Corner, NJ...................Commercial Law; Labor and Employment Law
Newark, NJ ....Commercial Law; Labor and Employment Law

Springfield, NJ ....Commercial Law; Labor and Employment Law

ARAGON, BURLINGTON, WEIL & CROCKETT, P.A.
Miami, FL ....Civil Trial Practice

ARÁN CORREA & GUARCH, P.A.
Miami, FL ....Admiralty/Maritime Law

ARANSON & ASSOCIATES
Dallas, TX...............................Civil Trial Practice; Criminal Trial Practice; Family Law

ARBES, JAKE
Atlanta, GA ....Appellate Practice; Criminal Trial Practice

ARCHBALD & SPRAY
Santa Barbara, CA..................Civil Trial Practice; General Practice; Insurance Defense; Labor and Employment Law; Product Liability Law

ARENT FOX KINTNER PLOTKIN & KAHN
Washington, DC......................General Practice

ARESTY INTERNATIONAL LAW OFFICES
Boston, MA.............................International Business Law

ARESTY, JOEL M., P.A.
Miami, FL ....Bankruptcy Law

ARIANO, ANDERSON, BAZOS, HARDY & CASTILLO
Elgin, IL ....General Practice

ARKIN, HARRY L., & ASSOCIATES, P.C.
Denver, CO ....International Business Law; Probate, Trusts and Estate Planning

ARKIN SCHAFFER & KAPLAN LLP
New York, NY.........................Appellate Practice; Civil Trial Practice; Criminal Trial Practice

ARLEN, ROBERT M., P.A.
Boynton Beach, FL.................Probate, Trusts and Estate Planning; Tax Law

ARMBRECHT, JACKSON, DEMOUY, CROWE, HOLMES & REEVES, L.L.C.
Mobile, AL..............................Administrative Law; Admiralty/Maritime Law; Antitrust Law; Banking Law; Business Law; Civil Trial Practice; Employment Benefits Law; General Practice; Insurance Defense; Labor and Employment Law; Natural Resources Law; Securities Law; Tax Law

ARMSTRONG, E. ALAN
Atlanta, GA ....Civil Trial Practice

ARMSTRONG ALLEN PREWITT GENTRY JOHNSTON & HOLMES
Memphis, TN ....Antitrust Law; Banking Law; Bankruptcy Law; Civil Trial Practice; Commercial Law; Communications Law; Computer Law; Environmental Law; General Practice; Insurance Defense; Labor and Employment Law; Municipal Bond/Public Authority Financing; Personal Injury; Probate, Trusts and Estate Planning; Real Estate Law; Tax Law; Trademark, Copyright and Unfair Competition; Workers Compensation

ARMSTRONG & ARMSTRONG, P.A.
Smithfield, NC ....Family Law; Personal Injury

ARMSTRONG, DAN L., A PROFESSIONAL CORPORATION
El Paso, TX.............................Personal Injury

ARMSTRONG, DONOHUE & CEPPOS, CHARTERED
Rockville, MD..........................Civil Trial Practice; Criminal Trial Practice; Insurance Defense; Medical Malpractice; Personal Injury

ARMSTRONG, GARRISON, LAW CORPORATION
San Diego, CA ....Tax Law

ARMSTRONG LAW OFFICES
Edwardsville, IL.......................Medical Malpractice; Personal Injury; Product Liability Law

ARMSTRONG & MEJER, P.A.
Miami, FL ....Admiralty/Maritime Law; Civil Trial Practice; Insurance Defense

ARMSTRONG, TEASDALE, SCHLAFLY & DAVIS
Kansas City, MO.....................General Practice
St. Louis, MO..........................Antitrust Law; Civil Trial Practice; Environmental Law; General Practice; Labor and Employment Law; Tax Law

ARNETT, DRAPER & HAGOOD
Knoxville, TN ....Civil Trial Practice; General Practice; Labor and Employment Law

ARNEY, JOHN
Weatherford, OK ....General Practice; Probate, Trusts and Estate Planning; Real Estate Law

ARNOLD & ANDERSON
Atlanta, GA ....Labor and Employment Law

ARNOLD, ANDERSON & DOVE, P.L.L.P.
Minneapolis, MN ....Business Law; Civil Trial Practice; Family Law;
General Practice; Personal Injury; Real Estate Law

ARNOLD GALLAGHER SAYDACK PERCELL & ROBERTS, P.C.
Eugene, OR ....General Practice

ARNOLD, GROBMYER & HALEY, A PROFESSIONAL ASSOCIATION
Little Rock, AR ....Banking Law; Bankruptcy Law; Civil Trial Practice;
Commercial Law; General Practice; Probate, Trusts
and Estate Planning; Real Estate Law; Tax Law

ARNOLD, MATHENY & EAGAN, P.A.
Orlando, FL ....Civil Trial Practice; Commercial Litigation; Real
Estate Law

ARNOLD, PETTWAY & DIXON, L.L.P.
Monroe, LA ....Tax Law

ARNOLD & PORTER
Washington, DC.....................General Practice

ARNOLD, WHITE & DURKEE, A PROFESSIONAL CORPORATION
Menlo Park, CA ....Patent, Trademark, Copyright and Unfair Competition
Chicago, IL.............................Patent, Trademark, Copyright and Unfair Competition
Austin, TX ....Patent, Trademark, Copyright and Unfair Competition
Houston, TX ....Patent, Trademark, Copyright and Unfair Competition
Arlington, VA ....Patent, Trademark, Copyright and Unfair Competition

ARONBERG GOLDGEHN DAVIS & GARMISA
Chicago, IL.............................Banking Law; Civil Trial Practice; General Practice;
Insurance Defense; Probate, Trusts and Estate
Planning; Real Estate Law

ARONSOHN & WEINER
Hackensack, NJ......................Appellate Practice; Civil Trial Practice; Commercial
Law; Family Law

ARONSON, ROBERT H.
Chicago, IL.............................Criminal Trial Practice

ARRINGTON KIHLE GABERINO & DUNN, A PROFESSIONAL CORPORATION
Tulsa, OK...............................Banking Law; Bankruptcy Law; General Practice;
Public Utilities Law; Securities Law

ARSENEAULT & KROVATIN
Chatham, NJ..........................Appellate Practice; Civil Trial Practice; Criminal
Trial Practice

ARTER & HADDEN
Los Angeles, CA.....................General Practice
Washington, DC.....................General Practice
Cleveland, OH........................Antitrust Law; General Practice; Labor and
Employment Law; Tax Law
Columbus, OH ....General Practice

ARTHUR, PEARSON & MARTIN, LTD.
Arlington, VA ....Civil Trial Practice

ARTZ, WILLIAM E., A PROFESSIONAL CORPORATION
Arlington, VA ....Medical Malpractice; Personal Injury

ASBELL, COLEMAN & HO, P.A.
Naples, FL...............................Family Law

ASBILL, JUNKIN & MOFFITT, CHTD.
Washington, DC.....................Civil Trial Practice; Criminal Trial Practice

ASHBURN & MASON, A PROFESSIONAL CORPORATION
Anchorage, AK ....Civil Trial Practice

ASHBY & GEDDES
Wilmington, DE.....................Civil Trial Practice; General Practice

ASHCRAFT LAW FIRM, A PROFESSIONAL CORPORATION
Dallas, TX ....Labor and Employment Law

ASHEN, GOLANT & LIPPMAN
Los Angeles, CA.....................Patent, Trademark, Copyright and Unfair Competition

ASHFORD, GEORGE W. JR.
Honolulu, HI..........................Admiralty/Maritime Law; Business Law; Civil Trial
Practice; Commercial Law; Insurance Defense;
Personal Injury; Product Liability Law

ASHFORD & THOMAS, P.A.
Albuquerque, NM...................Commercial Litigation

ASHMORE, JOSEPH E., JR., P.C.
Dallas, TX...............................Banking Law; General Practice; Health Care Law;
Probate, Trusts and Estate Planning

ASHWORTH & MORAN
Laguna Niguel, CA ....Business Law

ASPERO & ASPERO, A PROFESSIONAL CORPORATION
Morristown, NJ......................Business Law; Probate, Trusts and Estate Planning;
Real Estate Law

ASPEY, WATKINS & DIESEL, P.L.L.C.
Cottonwood, AZ ....General Practice
Flagstaff, AZ...........................Business Law; Civil Trial Practice; Commercial Law;
Construction Law; Criminal Trial Practice; Family
Law; General Practice; Insurance Defense; Medical
Malpractice; Personal Injury; Probate, Trusts and
Estate Planning; Real Estate Law
Page, AZ.................................General Practice
Sedona, AZ.............................General Practice

ASTOR WEISS KAPLAN & ROSENBLUM
Philadelphia, PA ....Bankruptcy Law; Business Law; Family Law;
General Practice; Probate, Trusts and Estate
Planning; Real Estate Law

ASWAD & INGRAHAM
Binghamton, NY ....General Practice; Labor and Employment Law;
Medical Malpractice

ATCHLEY, RUSSELL, WALDROP & HLAVINKA, L.L.P.
Texarkana, TX ....Civil Trial Practice; General Practice

ATER WYNNE HEWITT DODSON & SKERRITT, LLP
Portland, OR ....General Practice

ATES & ASSOCIATES, A PROFESSIONAL LAW CORPORATION
New Orleans, LA ....General Practice

ATHERTON & ALLEN
Chula Vista, CA.....................General Practice; Probate, Trusts and Estate
Planning

ATHERTON & ATHERTON
Emporia, KS ....General Practice

ATKINSON & ATKINSON
Evanston, IL............................Health Care Law

ATKINSON, HASKINS, NELLIS, BOUDREAUX, HOLEMAN, PHIPPS & BRITTINGHAM
Tulsa, OK................................Appellate Practice; Aviation Law; Civil Rights; Civil
Trial Practice; Environmental Law; Insurance
Defense; Medical Malpractice; Personal Injury;
Product Liability Law

ATKINSON & KELSEY, P.A.
Albuquerque, NM...................Family Law

ATLAS & HALL, L.L.P.
McAllen, TX ....General Practice

ATLASS PROFESSIONAL CORPORATION
Denver, CO ....Probate, Trusts and Estate Planning; Tax Law

ATLEE & HALL
Lancaster, PA..........................Medical Malpractice; Personal Injury; Product
Liability Law

ATWOOD & CHERNY
Boston, MA.............................Civil Trial Practice; Family Law

ATWOOD, HAGER & ANDERSON
Bellingham, WA......................General Practice

ATWOOD, MALONE, TURNER & SABIN, A PROFESSIONAL ASSOCIATION
Roswell, NM...........................Insurance Defense; Medical Malpractice

AUERBACH, MARSHALL J., & ASSOCIATES, LTD.
Chicago, IL..............................Family Law

AUERBACH, PHILIP G., A PROFESSIONAL CORPORATION
Red Bank, NJ..........................Civil Trial Practice; Criminal Trial Practice; General
Practice; Medical Malpractice; Personal Injury;
Product Liability Law

AUGUST, COMITER, KULUNAS & SCHEPPS, P.A.
West Palm Beach, FL ....Probate, Trusts and Estate Planning; Tax Law

AULTMAN, TYNER, MCNEESE, RUFFIN & LAIRD, LTD., A PROFESSIONAL LAW CORPORATION
Columbia, MS ....Admiralty/Maritime Law; Civil Trial Practice;
Commercial Law; Environmental Law; General
Practice; Insurance Defense
Gulfport, MS...........................Admiralty/Maritime Law; Civil Trial Practice;
Commercial Law; Environmental Law; General
Practice; Insurance Defense
Hattiesburg, MS......................Admiralty/Maritime Law; Civil Trial Practice;
Commercial Law; Environmental Law; General
Practice; Insurance Defense

AUSLEY & MCMULLEN, P.A.
Tallahassee, FL ....General Practice

AUSLEY, THOMAS L., A PROFESSIONAL CORPORATION
Austin, TX ....Family Law

AUSTIN & ABRAMS, A PROFESSIONAL ASSOCIATION
Minneapolis, MN ....Civil Trial Practice; General Practice; Personal Injury

AUSTIN, HINDERAKER, HOPPER, STRAIT & BRATLAND, LLP
Watertown, SD ....General Practice

AUSTIN, PEIRCE & SMITH, P.C.
Aspen, CO ....Appellate Practice; Civil Trial Practice; General Practice; Municipal and Zoning Law; Real Estate Law

AUSTIN & PEPPERMAN
Leesburg, FL ....Civil Trial Practice; General Practice

AVERY & ASSOCIATES
San Francisco, CA ....Probate, Trusts and Estate Planning; Tax Law

AVERY, WHIGHAM & WINESETT, P.A.
Fort Myers, FL ....Probate, Trusts and Estate Planning

AVIS & AVIS, P.A.
North Palm Beach, FL ....Commercial Litigation; Family Law

AWALT & TROMPETER, LLP
Dallas, TX ....Civil Trial Practice; Patent, Trademark, Copyright and Unfair Competition

AWTREY AND PARKER, P.C.
Marietta, GA ....Civil Trial Practice; General Practice; Municipal Bond/Public Authority Financing; Personal Injury; Probate, Trusts and Estate Planning

AXE, JOHN R. AND ASSOCIATES
Grosse Pointe Farms, MI ....Municipal Bond/Public Authority Financing

AXLEY BRYNELSON
Madison, WI ....Civil Trial Practice; Commercial Law; General Practice; Insurance Defense; Medical Malpractice; Personal Injury

AYABE, CHONG, NISHIMOTO, SIA & NAKAMURA
Honolulu, HI ....Civil Trial Practice; Construction Law; General Practice; Insurance Defense; Medical Malpractice; Personal Injury; Real Estate Law

AYCOCK, HORNE & COLEMAN
Franklin, LA ....General Practice

AYRES, CLUSTER, CURRY, MCCALL & BRIGGS, P.A.
Ocala, FL ....General Practice

AYRES, JENKINS, GORDY & ALMAND, P.A.
Ocean City, MD ....Civil Trial Practice; Criminal Trial Practice

BABB & BRADSHAW, P.C.
Austin, TX ....General Practice

BABER & KALINOWSKI, P.C.
Fairfax, VA ....Securities Law

BABST, CALLAND, CLEMENTS AND ZOMNIR, A PROFESSIONAL CORPORATION
Pittsburgh, PA ....Commercial Law; Construction Law; Environmental Law

BACHMAN & LAPOINTE, P.C.
New Haven, CT ....Patent, Trademark, Copyright and Unfair Competition

BACHMANN, HESS, BACHMANN & GARDEN
Wheeling, WV ....General Practice; Insurance Defense; Personal Injury

BACKER, GLENN
New York, NY ....Civil Trial Practice

BACKER & BACKER, A PROFESSIONAL CORPORATION
Indianapolis, IN ....Commercial Law; Construction Law; Probate, Trusts and Estate Planning; Real Estate Law

BACKES & HILL
Trenton, NJ ....Civil Trial Practice; General Practice

BACON & MILLS, LLP
Los Angeles, CA ....Business Law; Insurance Defense

BADER & VILLANUEVA, P.C.
Denver, CO ....Civil Trial Practice

BADGER, DAVID R., P.A.
Charlotte, NC ....Bankruptcy Law

BADGER, DOLAN, PARKER & COHEN
Boston, MA ....Commercial Law; Insurance Defense; Product Liability Law

BADIAK WILL & MALOOF
New York, NY ....Admiralty/Maritime Law; Civil Trial Practice; General Practice

BAER MARKS & UPHAM LLP
New York, NY ....Civil Trial Practice; General Practice

BAGBY, WILLIAM R.
Lexington, KY ....Tax Law

BAGERT LAW FIRM, THE
New Orleans, LA ....Commercial Litigation; Criminal Trial Practice; Personal Injury

BAGGETT, MCCALL & BURGESS, A PROFESSIONAL LAW CORPORATION
Lake Charles, LA ....General Practice; Personal Injury

BAI, POLLOCK AND COYNE, P.C.
Bridgeport, CT ....Civil Trial Practice; Insurance Defense; Medical Malpractice; Personal Injury; Product Liability Law

BAILEY, BRUCE R. LAW OFFICES OF
Los Angeles, CA ....Tax Law

BAILEY & DIXON, L.L.P.
Raleigh, NC ....Civil Trial Practice; Insurance Defense; Personal Injury

BAILEY & DWYER
Mandeville, LA ....Admiralty/Maritime Law; General Practice; Insurance Defense; Product Liability Law; Workers Compensation

BAILEY & KORNBLUM
San Francisco, CA ....Medical Malpractice; Personal Injury; Product Liability Law

BAILEY LAW OFFICES
Milwaukee, WI ....Family Law

BAILEY, PATTERSON, CADDELL, HART & BAILEY, P.A.
Charlotte, NC ....Civil Trial Practice; Criminal Trial Practice; Personal Injury

BAILEY, PICKERING & STOCK
Fort Collins, CO ....Civil Trial Practice
Cheyenne, WY ....Civil Trial Practice; Personal Injury

BAILEY, RALPH, P.A.
Greenville, SC ....Patent, Trademark, Copyright and Unfair Competition

BAILEY & THOMAS, P.A.
Winston-Salem, NC ....Insurance Defense; Probate, Trusts and Estate Planning

BAIN, TROY E.
Shreveport, LA ....Civil Trial Practice; Medical Malpractice; Personal Injury

BAIN & MCRAE
Lillington, NC ....General Practice

BAINBRIDGE, MIMS, ROGERS & SMITH
Birmingham, AL ....Business Law; Civil Trial Practice; General Practice

BAIR, BORMANN, BAIR & GARRITY, PLLP
Mandan, ND ....Administrative Law; Personal Injury; Probate, Trusts and Estate Planning

BAIRD, BAIRD, BAIRD AND JONES, P.S.C.
Pikeville, KY ....General Practice

BAKER, J. NORMAN
Mountain View, CA ....Family Law

BAKER & BOTTS, L.L.P.
Washington, DC ....Administrative Law; Business Law; Civil Trial Practice; Commercial Law; Environmental Law; General Practice; Natural Resources Law; Patent, Trademark, Copyright and Unfair Competition; Tax Law; Trademark, Copyright and Unfair Competition
New York, NY ....Business Law; Civil Trial Practice; Commercial Law; General Practice; Tax Law
Austin, TX ....Administrative Law; Banking Law; Bankruptcy Law; Business Law; Civil Trial Practice; Commercial Law; Environmental Law; General Practice; Patent, Trademark, Copyright and Unfair Competition; Real Estate Law; Trademark, Copyright and Unfair Competition
Dallas, TX ....Administrative Law; Antitrust Law; Banking Law; Bankruptcy Law; Business Law; Civil Trial Practice; Commercial Law; General Practice; Labor and Employment Law; Patent, Trademark, Copyright and Unfair Competition; Personal Injury; Real Estate Law; Trademark, Copyright and Unfair Competition
Houston, TX ....Administrative Law; Admiralty/Maritime Law; Antitrust Law; Banking Law; Bankruptcy Law; Business Law; Civil Trial Practice; Commercial Law; Environmental Law; General Practice; Labor and Employment Law; Patent, Trademark, Copyright and Unfair Competition; Personal Injury; Probate, Trusts and Estate Planning; Real Estate Law; Tax Law

BAKER, CAMPBELL & PARSONS
Nashville, TN..................General Practice

BAKER & DANIELS
Fort Wayne, IN...............General Practice; Patent, Trademark, Copyright and Unfair Competition
Indianapolis, IN.............Bankruptcy Law; Civil Trial Practice; Computer Law; Environmental Law; General Practice; Labor and Employment Law; Land Use Law; Municipal Bond/Public Authority Financing; Patent, Trademark, Copyright and Unfair Competition; Real Estate Law; Tax Law
South Bend, IN..............General Practice; Patent, Trademark, Copyright and Unfair Competition

BAKER, DONELSON, BEARMAN & CALDWELL
Chattanooga, TN............General Practice; Health Care Law; Tax Law
Huntsville, TN...............General Practice
Johnson City, TN............Environmental Law; General Practice; Natural Resources Law
Knoxville, TN................Civil Trial Practice; Environmental Law; General Practice; Tax Law
Memphis, TN................Banking Law; Bankruptcy Law; Civil Trial Practice; Environmental Law; General Practice; Insurance Defense; Labor and Employment Law; Municipal Bond/Public Authority Financing; Patent, Trademark, Copyright and Unfair Competition; Tax Law
Nashville, TN................Civil Trial Practice; General Practice; Health Care Law; Tax Law

BAKER, DUBLIKAR, BECK, WILEY & GRIFFIN
Canton, OH..................Civil Trial Practice; Insurance Defense

BAKER & HOSTETLER
Long Beach, CA..............Admiralty/Maritime Law; General Practice
Los Angeles, CA.............Admiralty/Maritime Law; Bankruptcy Law; Civil Trial Practice; Environmental Law; General Practice; Labor and Employment Law; Real Estate Law; Trademark, Copyright and Unfair Competition
Denver, CO..................Civil Trial Practice; Environmental Law; General Practice
Washington, DC..............Administrative Law; Antitrust Law; Banking Law; Civil Trial Practice; Communications Law; Environmental Law; General Practice; Labor and Employment Law; Tax Law; Trademark, Copyright and Unfair Competition; Transportation Law
Orlando, FL.................Civil Trial Practice; Construction Law; General Practice; Municipal Bond/Public Authority Financing; Real Estate Law; Tax Law
Cleveland, OH...............Antitrust Law; Banking Law; Bankruptcy Law; Civil Trial Practice; Communications Law; Construction Law; Employment Benefits Law; Environmental Law; General Practice; Immigration and Naturalization; Labor and Employment Law; Municipal Bond/Public Authority Financing; Probate, Trusts and Estate Planning; Real Estate Law; Tax Law; Trademark, Copyright and Unfair Competition
Columbus, OH...............Bankruptcy Law; Civil Trial Practice; Employment Benefits Law; General Practice; Labor and Employment Law; Tax Law; Transportation Law
Houston, TX.................Civil Trial Practice; General Practice

BAKER AND JACOBSON, A PROFESSIONAL CORPORATION
Los Angeles, CA.............Bankruptcy Law; Civil Trial Practice; Real Estate Law

BAKER, JENKINS, JONES & DALY, P.A.
Ahoskie, NC.................Insurance Defense

BAKER, MANOCK & JENSEN, A PROFESSIONAL CORPORATION
Fresno, CA..................General Practice

BAKER, MAXHAM, JESTER & MEADOR, A PROFESSIONAL CORPORATION
San Diego, CA...............Patent, Trademark, Copyright and Unfair Competition

BAKER & MCKENZIE
Palo Alto, CA...............General Practice
San Diego, CA...............General Practice
San Francisco, CA...........General Practice
Washington, DC..............General Practice
Miami, FL...................General Practice
Chicago, IL.................General Practice
New York, NY................General Practice
Dallas, TX..................General Practice
Toronto, ON, Canada.........General Practice
Buenos Aires, Argentina.....General Practice
Melbourne, Victoria, Australia..................General Practice
Sydney, New South Wales, Australia..................General Practice
Brussels, Belgium...........General Practice
Santiago, Chile.............General Practice
Beijing (Peking), People's Republic of China...........General Practice

Prague, Czech Republic......General Practice
Cairo, Egypt................General Practice
Paris, France...............General Practice
Hong Kong, Hong Kong........General Practice
Budapest, Hungary...........General Practice
Milan, Italy................General Practice
Rome, Italy.................General Practice
Ciudad Juarez, Chihuahua, Mexico......................General Practice
Mexico, D.F., Mexico........General Practice
Monterrey, Nuevo León, Mexico......................General Practice
Tijuana, Baja California, Mexico......................General Practice
Moscow, Russia..............General Practice
St. Petersburg, Russia......General Practice
Singapore, Singapore........General Practice
Barcelona, Spain............General Practice
Madrid, Spain...............General Practice
Zürich, Switzerland.........General Practice
Taipei, Taiwan..............General Practice
Bangkok, Thailand...........General Practice
Kiev, Ukraine...............General Practice
Caracas, Venezuela..........General Practice
Valencia, Venezuela.........General Practice
Hanoi, Vietnam..............General Practice
Ho Chi Minh City, Vietnam...General Practice
Stockholm, Sweden...........General Practice
Almaty, Republic of Kazakstan..................General Practice
Warsaw, Poland..............General Practice

BAKER, OLSON, LECROY & DANIELIAN, A LAW CORPORATION
Glendale, CA................Civil Trial Practice; Immigration and Naturalization; Probate, Trusts and Estate Planning; Real Estate Law; Tax Law

BAKER STERCHI COWDEN & RICE, L.L.C.
Kansas City, MO.............Bankruptcy Law; Civil Trial Practice; Commercial Law; Construction Law; Environmental Law; Insurance Defense; Labor and Employment Law

BALCH & BINGHAM
Birmingham, AL..............General Practice

BALDOVIN, PAUL A., JR., P.A.
Boca Raton, FL..............Probate, Trusts and Estate Planning

BALDWIN RENNER & CLARK
Philadelphia, PA............Business Law
Wayne, PA...................Business Law; Securities Law

BALFOUR MOSS
Regina, SK, Canada..........Civil Trial Practice; Commercial Law; General Practice

BALISLE & ROBERSON, S.C.
Madison, WI.................Appellate Practice; Family Law; Probate, Trusts and Estate Planning

BALK, OXFELD, MANDELL & COHEN, A PROFESSIONAL CORPORATION
Newark, NJ..................Labor and Employment Law

BALLARD SPAHR ANDREWS & INGERSOLL
Denver, CO..................Civil Trial Practice; Commercial Law; Environmental Law; General Practice; Municipal Bond/Public Authority Financing; Natural Resources Law; Real Estate Law; Securities Law
Washington, DC..............General Practice; Municipal Bond/Public Authority Financing; Real Estate Law
Baltimore, MD...............Banking Law; Bankruptcy Law; Civil Trial Practice; Commercial Law; Real Estate Law
Philadelphia, PA............Antitrust Law; Banking Law; Bankruptcy Law; Civil Trial Practice; Commercial Law; Employment Benefits Law; Environmental Law; General Practice; Health Care Law; Labor and Employment Law; Municipal Bond/Public Authority Financing; Probate, Trusts and Estate Planning; Real Estate Law; Tax Law
Salt Lake City, UT..........Municipal Bond/Public Authority Financing; Real Estate Law

BALL, BALL, MATTHEWS & NOVAK, P.A.
Montgomery, AL..............Civil Trial Practice; General Practice

BALL, BARTON & HOFFMAN
Monticello, AR..............General Practice

BALL, EGGLESTON, BUMBLEBURG & MCBRIDE
Lafayette, IN...............Appellate Practice; Civil Trial Practice; General Practice; Insurance Defense; Municipal and Zoning Law; Personal Injury; Probate, Trusts and Estate Planning; Real Estate Law

BALL & MOURTON, LTD., PLLC
Fayetteville, AR............General Practice

BALLON STOLL BADER & NADLER, P.C.
New York, NY.........................General Practice

BAMBERGER & ABSHIER
Owensboro, KY.......................Bankruptcy Law; General Practice

BAMBERGER & FEIBLEMAN
Indianapolis, IN.......................Bankruptcy Law; Commercial Law; International Business Law

BAMBERGER, FOREMAN, OSWALD AND HAHN
Evansville, IN.........................Banking Law; Bankruptcy Law; Civil Trial Practice; General Practice; Health Care Law

BANDER, MICHAEL A., P.A.
Miami, FL..............................Immigration and Naturalization

BANDY, ROBERT M., P.C.
Tyler, TX..............................Bankruptcy Law; Probate, Trusts and Estate Planning; Tax Law

BANGEL, BANGEL & BANGEL, L.L.P.
Portsmouth, VA.......................Personal Injury

BANGS, MCCULLEN, BUTLER, FOYE & SIMMONS, L.L.P.
Rapid City, SD........................Civil Trial Practice; General Practice; Labor and Employment Law

BANGSER KLEIN ROCCA & BLUM LLP
New York, NY.........................General Practice

BANKS, CURRAN, KEEFE & SPOLZINO, LLP
Mount Kisco, NY.....................General Practice; Labor and Employment Law; Real Estate Law

BANKS & SACKS
Portland, OR..........................Commercial Litigation; Securities Law

BANKSTON & ASSOCIATES, P.C.
Houston, TX...........................Civil Trial Practice; Medical Malpractice; Personal Injury; Product Liability Law

BANNER & ALLEGRETTI, LTD.
Chicago, IL............................Patent, Trademark, Copyright and Unfair Competition

BANNER, BRILEY & WHITE, L.L.P.
Wichita Falls, TX.....................Commercial Law; Health Care Law

BANNER & WITCOFF, LTD.
Washington, DC.......................Patent, Trademark, Copyright and Unfair Competition; Trademark, Copyright and Unfair Competition

BANNIGAN & KELLY, P.A.
St. Paul, MN..........................Civil Trial Practice; Municipal and Zoning Law; Personal Injury

BANTA, COX & HENNESSY
Chicago, IL............................Labor and Employment Law

BANTA, HOYT, EVERALL & FARRINGTON, L.L.C.
Englewood, CO........................Civil Trial Practice; General Practice; Real Estate Law

BANTZ, GOSCH, CREMER, PETERSON & SOMMERS
Aberdeen, SD.........................Banking Law; Business Law; Insurance Defense

BANZET, BANZET & THOMPSON
Warrenton, NC........................General Practice

BARASH & STOERZBACH, P.C.
Galesburg, IL..........................General Practice

BARBAS, WEED, MORGAN & WHEELEY
Tampa, FL.............................Workers Compensation

BARBER, JAMES C. LAW OFFICES OF
Dallas, TX.............................Medical Malpractice; Personal Injury

BARBER, EMERSON, SPRINGER, ZINN & MURRAY, L.C.
Lawrence, KS.........................General Practice

BARBER, MCCASKILL, AMSLER, JONES & HALE, P.A.
Little Rock, AR.......................Commercial Law; General Practice; Health Care Law; Insurance Defense; Medical Malpractice; Personal Injury; Probate, Trusts and Estate Planning; Product Liability Law; Workers Compensation

BARBERA, CLAPPER, BEENER, RULLO & MELVIN
Somerset, PA.........................General Practice

BARBOSA GARCIA & BARNES
Los Angeles, CA......................Commercial Litigation; Municipal and Zoning Law

BARCE & RYAN
Fowler, IN.............................Civil Trial Practice; General Practice; Probate, Trusts and Estate Planning
Kentland, IN...........................Civil Trial Practice; General Practice; Probate, Trusts and Estate Planning

BARFORD, BURNS F. JR.
Valatie, NY............................General Practice; Probate, Trusts and Estate Planning; Real Estate Law

BARHAM & ARCENEAUX, A PROFESSIONAL LAW CORPORATION
New Orleans, LA.....................Appellate Practice; Civil Trial Practice

BARHAM, DOVER, BENNETT, MILLER, SHERWOOD & STONE
Valdosta, GA..........................Civil Trial Practice; General Practice

BARISH, MARVIN I., LAW OFFICES, A PROFESSIONAL CORPORATION
Philadelphia, PA......................Admiralty/Maritime Law; Civil Trial Practice; Medical Malpractice; Personal Injury; Transportation Law

BARKAN AND ROBON
Toledo, OH............................Banking Law; Bankruptcy Law; Civil Trial Practice; Commercial Law; Employment Benefits Law; Municipal and Zoning Law; Probate, Trusts and Estate Planning; Real Estate Law; Tax Law

BARKER, BROWN, BUSBY & SUTHERLAND, A PROFESSIONAL CORPORATION
Las Vegas, NV........................Civil Trial Practice; Insurance Defense

BARKER & ROMNEY, A PROFESSIONAL CORPORATION
Pasadena, CA.........................Civil Trial Practice; Real Estate Law

BARKER, THOMAS, MCCOLLOCH & WALTERS, A PROFESSIONAL LAW CORPORATION
San Diego, CA........................Commercial Litigation; Labor and Employment Law

BARLEY, SNYDER, SENFT & COHEN
Harrisburg, PA........................General Practice
Lancaster, PA.........................General Practice
York, PA...............................General Practice

BARLOW AND HARDTNER, L.C.
Shreveport, LA........................Administrative Law; Appellate Practice; Business Law; Civil Trial Practice; Commercial Law; Communications Law; Construction Law; Environmental Law; General Practice; Insurance Defense; Land Use Law; Natural Resources Law; Probate, Trusts and Estate Planning; Product Liability Law; Public Utilities Law; Real Estate Law; Tax Law; Transportation Law

BARLOW, JOHNSON, FLODMAN, SUTTER, GUENZEL & ESKE
Lincoln, NE...........................Civil Trial Practice; Family Law; General Practice; Insurance Defense; Labor and Employment Law; Probate, Trusts and Estate Planning

BARLOW & LANGE, P.C.
Troy, MI...............................Business Law; Civil Trial Practice; Health Care Law; Labor and Employment Law

BARNES, F. SMITH
Oklahoma City, OK...................Business Law; Probate, Trusts and Estate Planning

BARNES, ALFORD, STORK & JOHNSON, L.L.P.
Columbia, SC.........................Banking Law; General Practice; Insurance Defense; Medical Malpractice; Product Liability Law; Real Estate Law; Tax Law

BARNES & BATZLI, P.C.
Chesterfield, VA......................General Practice

BARNES, BROWNING, TANKSLEY & CASURELLA
Marietta, GA..........................Banking Law; Family Law; Medical Malpractice; Personal Injury; Probate, Trusts and Estate Planning; Product Liability Law

BARNES, CROSBY, FITZGERALD & ZEMAN, LLP
Irvine, CA.............................Construction Law; Employment Benefits Law; Real Estate Law

BARNES, KISSELLE, RAISCH, CHOATE, WHITTEMORE & HULBERT, P.C.
Detroit, MI............................Patent, Trademark, Copyright and Unfair Competition

BARNES & THORNBURG
Indianapolis, IN.......................General Practice

BARNETT, SCOTT F.
Tampa, FL.............................Probate, Trusts and Estate Planning

BARNETT, BARCLAY & SPRINGMANN, P.A.
Orlando, FL............................Criminal Trial Practice; Family Law

BARNETT, HANES, O'NEAL, DUFFEE & GARFIELD, LLC
Birmingham, AL.......................Civil Trial Practice; Family Law

BARNETT MACLEAN
Seattle, WA............................Bankruptcy Law

BARNETT • MATTICE
Fairfield, CA...........................Personal Injury

BARNETT & RUBIN, A PROFESSIONAL CORPORATION
Irvine, CA.............................Bankruptcy Law; Civil Trial Practice; Commercial Litigation; Real Estate Law

BARNEY, GROSSMAN, ROTH & DUBOW
Ithaca, NY..............................General Practice

BARNHART, KATHERINE L., P.C.
Royal Oak, MI........................Family Law

BARNHORST, SCHREINER & GOONAN, A PROFESSIONAL CORPORATION
San Diego, CA ....Business Law; Commercial Law

BARNWELL WHALEY PATTERSON & HELMS
Charleston, SC ....Civil Trial Practice; Construction Law; General Practice; Insurance Defense

BAROKAS & MARTIN
Seattle, WA ....Business Law; Construction Law

BARON, GALLAGHER & PERZLEY
Parsippany, NJ........................Banking Law; Land Use Law; Real Estate Law

BAROUSSE & CRATON
Crowley, LA.............................Civil Trial Practice; General Practice

BARR, BARR AND MCINTOSH
Charleston, SC ....Civil Trial Practice; Criminal Trial Practice

BARR, DUGAN, & ASSOCIATES
Redding, CA ....Aviation Law; Civil Trial Practice; Personal Injury; Product Liability Law

BARR, JOSEPH J., JR., A PROFESSIONAL CORPORATION
San Diego, CA ....Civil Trial Practice

BARR, MURMAN, TONELLI, HERZFELD & RUBIN
Tampa, FL ....Civil Trial Practice; Commercial Litigation; Insurance Defense; Personal Injury

BARRACK, RODOS & BACINE
Philadelphia, PA ....Antitrust Law; Securities Law

BARRET, HAYNES, MAY, CARTER AND ROARK, P.S.C.
Hazard, KY.............................General Practice

BARRETT BURKE WILSON CASTLE DAFFIN & FRAPPIER, L.L.P.
Dallas, TX................................Banking Law; Civil Trial Practice; Real Estate Law

BARRETT & DEACON
Jonesboro, AR ....Civil Trial Practice; General Practice; Insurance Defense

BARRETT & MCNAGNY
Fort Wayne, IN........................Banking Law; Bankruptcy Law; Civil Trial Practice; Environmental Law; General Practice; Transportation Law

BARRETT & WEBER, A LEGAL PROFESSIONAL ASSOCIATION
Cincinnati, OH ....Administrative Law; Municipal and Zoning Law; Probate, Trusts and Estate Planning; Real Estate Law

BARRICK, MCKAY & CATTANO, P.L.C.
Charlottesville, VA..................Commercial Litigation; Communications Law; Insurance Defense

BARRIGAR MOSS HAMMOND CASSAN & MACLEAN
Ottawa, ON, Canada ....Patent, Trademark, Copyright and Unfair Competition

BARRIOS, KINGSDORF & CASTEIX, L.L.P.
New Orleans, LA ....Business Law; Civil Trial Practice; Real Estate Law

BARRIS, SOTT, DENN & DRIKER, P.L.L.C.
Detroit, MI..............................Civil Trial Practice; Immigration and Naturalization; Real Estate Law

BARRON, VANCE JR.
Greensboro, NC.......................Civil Trial Practice; Medical Malpractice; Personal Injury

BARRON, PECK & BENNIE CO., A LEGAL PROFESSIONAL ASSOCIATION
Cincinnati, OH ....Civil Trial Practice; Real Estate Law

BARRON & STADFELD, P.C.
Boston, MA..............................Banking Law; Civil Trial Practice; Environmental Law; General Practice; Personal Injury; Real Estate Law

BARROW GADDIS GRIFFITH & GRIMM, A PROFESSIONAL CORPORATION
Tulsa, OK................................Bankruptcy Law; Business Law; Civil Trial Practice; Tax Law

BARROW, SIMS, MORROW, LEE & GARDNER, A PROFESSIONAL CORPORATION
Savannah, GA ....Insurance Defense

BARRY & MCMORAN, A PROFESSIONAL CORPORATION
Newark, NJ..............................Appellate Practice; Civil Trial Practice; Commercial Law; Criminal Trial Practice; Labor and Employment Law

BARRY, RICHARD, AND SHARON MAH
San Rafael, CA........................Family Law

BARSAMIAN, J. ALBERT
Albany, NY ....Administrative Law; Criminal Trial Practice; Labor and Employment Law

BARST & MUKAMAL
New York, NY........................Immigration and Naturalization

BARTELS & FEUREISEN
White Plains, NY ....General Practice

BARTHOLIC, ROBERT L.
Denver, CO ....Natural Resources Law; Probate, Trusts and Estate Planning; Real Estate Law; Transportation Law

BARTHOLOMEW, WASZNICKY & MOLINARO, LLP
Sacramento, CA ....Family Law

BARTIMUS, KAVANAUGH, FRICKLETON & PRESLEY, A PROFESSIONAL CORPORATION
Kansas City, MO ....Medical Malpractice; Personal Injury; Product Liability Law

BARTKO, ZANKEL, TARRANT & MILLER, PROFESSIONAL CORPORATION
San Francisco, CA ....Commercial Litigation; Real Estate Law

BARTLETT AND BARTLETT
Walden, NY ....General Practice

BARTLETT, MCDONOUGH, BASTONE & MONAGHAN, LLP
Mineola, NY ....Medical Malpractice; Personal Injury

BARTON, JOSEPH C. LAW OFFICES OF
San Francisco, CA ....Commercial Litigation

BARTON, KLUGMAN & OETTING
Los Angeles, CA ....Banking Law; Business Law; Civil Trial Practice; Insurance Defense; Probate, Trusts and Estate Planning; Tax Law

BARTON & SCHNEIDER, L.L.P.
San Antonio, TX......................Real Estate Law

BARTON AND STREVER, P.C.
Newport, OR............................Personal Injury

BASILE & LANE, L.L.P.
Los Angeles, CA ....Tax Law

BASILE & TESTA, A PROFESSIONAL CORPORATION
Vineland, NJ............................Civil Trial Practice; General Practice

BASKIN, JACKSON & HANSBARGER, A PROFESSIONAL CORPORATION
Falls Church, VA.....................General Practice

BASKINS & ROEDER
North Platte, NE ....General Practice

BASON, GEORGE FRANCIS JR.
Washington, DC.......................Bankruptcy Law

BASS, SHIRLEY A.
Portland, OR............................Probate, Trusts and Estate Planning

BASS, SUZANNE
Jacksonville, FL ....Criminal Trial Practice

BASS, BERRY & SIMS PLC
Nashville, TN ....Antitrust Law; Bankruptcy Law; Environmental Law; Health Care Law; Labor and Employment Law; Municipal Bond/Public Authority Financing; Securities Law; Tax Law

BASSETT & COPPLE, LLP
Roswell, NM............................Probate, Trusts and Estate Planning

BASSETT LAW FIRM
Fayetteville, AR ....Civil Trial Practice; General Practice

BASSFORD, LOCKHART, TRUESDELL & BRIGGS, P.A.
Minneapolis, MN ....Civil Trial Practice; Environmental Law; General Practice; Insurance Defense; Personal Injury

BASTEDO STEWART SMITH
Toronto, ON, Canada ....Family Law

BASTONE, LAWRENCE D.
Boston, MA.............................Immigration and Naturalization

BASYE & GOLDEN
San Mateo, CA........................Probate, Trusts and Estate Planning

BATCHELOR, JAMES K., A PROFESSIONAL CORPORATION
Orange, CA ....Family Law

BATES & CASEY
Fort Worth, TX ....Criminal Trial Practice

BATES MECKLER BULGER & TILSON
Chicago, IL..............................Civil Trial Practice; Commercial Law; Insurance Defense; Labor and Employment Law; Product Liability Law

BATHGATE, WEGENER & WOLF, P.C.
Lakewood, NJ ....General Practice

BATJER & WAGSTAFF, P.C.
Abilene, TX..............................General Practice; Insurance Defense

BATSEL, MCKINLEY, ITTERSAGEN, GUNDERSON & BERNTSSON, P.A.
Englewood, FL..........................Probate, Trusts and Estate Planning; Real Estate Law

BATTLE FOWLER LLP
New York, NY..........................General Practice

BATZAR & WEINBERG, A PROFESSIONAL CORPORATION
Rockville Centre, NY ....Bankruptcy Law; Commercial Law

BAUCUM AND STEED, P.C.
San Antonio, TX......................Real Estate Law

BAUDLER, BAUDLER, MAUS & BLAHNIK
Austin, MN..............................General Practice
Spring Valley, MN...................General Practice

BAUER, BERNARD K., CO., L.P.A.
Findlay, OH ....Personal Injury

BAUER, CRIDER & PELLEGRINO
Clearwater, FL ....Criminal Trial Practice
Tampa, FL ....Criminal Trial Practice

BAUER & DEITCH, P.C.
Atlanta, GA ....Civil Trial Practice; Commercial Law; Family Law

BAUER, RENTZEL, MILLARD & HARDWICK, L.L.P.
Dallas, TX................................Business Law; Civil Trial Practice; Commercial Law; Probate, Trusts and Estate Planning; Real Estate Law

BAUERSFELD, BURTON, HENDRICKS & VANDERHOOF, L.L.C.
Bethesda, MD ....Probate, Trusts and Estate Planning

BAUGHER, METTLER & SHELTON
Palm Beach, FL........................Probate, Trusts and Estate Planning; Real Estate Law; Tax Law

BAUMAN KUNKIS & CAVERA, P.C.
New York, NY..........................Personal Injury

BAUM & ASSOCIATES
Bloomfield Hills, MI...............Criminal Trial Practice

BAUMEISTER & SAMUELS, P.C.
New York, NY..........................Civil Trial Practice; Environmental Law; General Practice; Medical Malpractice; Personal Injury

BAUM, HEDLUND, ARISTEI, GUILFORD & DOWNEY, A PROFESSIONAL CORPORATION
Los Angeles, CA ....Civil Trial Practice; Personal Injury
Washington, DC.......................Civil Trial Practice; Personal Injury

BAVOL, BUSH & SISCO, P.A.
Tampa, FL ....Commercial Litigation; Medical Malpractice; Product Liability Law

BAVOSO, COFFILL & PLOTSKY
Port Jervis, NY ....Civil Trial Practice; Municipal and Zoning Law; Probate, Trusts and Estate Planning; Real Estate Law

BAXLEY, DILLARD, DAUPHIN & MCKNIGHT
Birmingham, AL ....Administrative Law; Criminal Trial Practice; Personal Injury

BAYER, KARL
Austin, TX ....Appellate Practice; Civil Trial Practice; Computer Law; Medical Malpractice; Patent, Trademark, Copyright and Unfair Competition; Personal Injury; Product Liability Law

BAYKO GIBSON CARNEGIE HAGAN SCHOONMAKER & MEYER LLP
Houston, TX ....Civil Trial Practice; General Practice; Labor and Employment Law

BAYLESS & STOKES
Houston, TX ....Civil Trial Practice; Commercial Law; Probate, Trusts and Estate Planning

BAYLOR, EVNEN, CURTISS, GRIMIT & WITT
Lincoln, NE..............................General Practice

BAYS, DEAVER, HIATT, LUNG & ROSE
Honolulu, HI ....Commercial Law; Construction Law; Real Estate Law

BEACH, BURCKE, HELFERS AND MITTLEMAN, L.L.C.
St. Louis, MO..........................Commercial Litigation; Family Law; Personal Injury; Probate, Trusts and Estate Planning

BEALE & HUMPHREY, P.S.C.
Louisville, KY ....General Practice

BEALL LAW OFFICE, INC.
Kingfisher, OK ....General Practice; Probate, Trusts and Estate Planning; Real Estate Law

BEAL, PRATT AND PRATT
Monmouth, IL ....General Practice

BEALS & QUINN
Portland, ME ....Insurance Defense

BEAL, SCHMIDT & DYER, P.C.
Tucson, AZ ....Medical Malpractice; Personal Injury; Product Liability Law

BEAM, BROBECK & WEST
Santa Ana, CA ....General Practice; Insurance Defense; Medical Malpractice; Product Liability Law

BEAN & GENTRY
Olympia, WA ....Business Law; Insurance Defense; Personal Injury

BEAN, KAUFFMAN & SPENCER
Buffalo, NY ....Patent, Trademark, Copyright and Unfair Competition

BEAN, KINNEY & KORMAN, A PROFESSIONAL CORPORATION
Arlington, VA ....Banking Law; Family Law; Personal Injury

BEARD, RUSSELL C. (RUSTY)
Abilene, TX..............................Commercial Litigation; Insurance Defense

BEARD, STEVEN L., P.C.
Marietta, GA............................Personal Injury

BEARMAN TALESNICK & CLOWDUS, PROFESSIONAL CORPORATION
Denver, CO ....Real Estate Law; Securities Law

BEASLEY, CASEY & ERBSTEIN
Philadelphia, PA ....General Practice

BEASLEY, WILSON, ALLEN, MAIN & CROW, P.C.
Montgomery, AL ....Personal Injury; Product Liability Law

BEATIE, KING & ABATE
New York, NY..........................Civil Trial Practice; Commercial Law; Environmental Law; Insurance Defense; Securities Law

BEATTIE PADOVANO
Montvale, NJ............................Civil Trial Practice; Commercial Law

BEATTY, THOMAS D.
Las Vegas, NV ....Civil Trial Practice; Criminal Trial Practice

BEATTY, CRAMP, KAUFFMAN & LINCKE
Media, PA ....General Practice; Insurance Defense; Medical Malpractice; Municipal and Zoning Law; Probate, Trusts and Estate Planning

BEAUREGARD & BURKE
New Bedford, MA ....Civil Trial Practice

BECK, PAUL A. & ASSOCIATES
Pittsburgh, PA ....Patent, Trademark, Copyright and Unfair Competition

BECK, DE CORSO, DALY, BARRERA & OH, A PROFESSIONAL LAW CORPORATION
Los Angeles, CA ....Administrative Law; Business Law; Criminal Trial Practice

BECKER ASSOCIATES
Chicago, IL...............................Civil Trial Practice; Commercial Litigation

BECKER, GLYNN, MELAMED & MUFFLY LLP
New York, NY..........................General Practice

BECKER LAW OFFICE
San Francisco, CA ....Bankruptcy Law

BECKER, STEVEN A., A PROFESSIONAL LAW CORPORATION
San Bernardino, CA.................Family Law

BECKERMAN & BECKERMAN
Rochester, NY..........................General Practice

BECKETT & WEBBER, P.C.
Urbana, IL................................Personal Injury

BECK & HALBERG
New York, NY.........................Admiralty/Maritime Law; Civil Trial Practice

BECKHAM & BECKHAM, P.A.
North Miami Beach, FL...........Appellate Practice; Transportation Law

BECKHAM, WALTER H., P.C.
Atlanta, GA ....Personal Injury

BECKLEY, JAMES E., & ASSOCIATES, P.C.
Wheaton, IL ....Securities Law

BECKLEY, JAMES F., P.A.
Albuquerque, NM ....Probate, Trusts and Estate Planning

BECKLEY & MADDEN
Harrisburg, PA........................Construction Law; General Practice; Labor and
Employment Law

BECKMAN, KELLY & SMITH
Hammond, IN..........................Civil Trial Practice; Commercial Law; Environmental Law

BECKMAN, LAWSON, SANDLER, SNYDER & FEDEROFF
Fort Wayne, IN......................Bankruptcy Law; General Practice; Labor and
Employment Law; Land Use Law; Real Estate Law

BECKMAN & MILLMAN, P.C.
New York, NY........................Business Law; Civil Trial Practice; General Practice;
Insurance Defense

BECKMANN & QUIRK, A PROFESSIONAL CORPORATION
San Antonio, TX....................Aviation Law; Civil Trial Practice; Construction
Law; Insurance Defense; Personal Injury

BECK, REDDEN & SECREST
Houston, TX ....General Practice

BECK & TRAVIS, P.C.
Montgomery, AL ....Criminal Trial Practice; General Practice; Personal
Injury

BEDFORD, KIRSCHNER AND VENKER, P.C.
Atlanta, GA ....Criminal Trial Practice; Medical Malpractice;
Personal Injury

BEECHER, RATHERT, ROBERTS, FIELD, WALKER & MORRIS, P.C.
Waterloo, IA ....General Practice

BEECHER, WAGNER, ROSE & KLEMEYER
Milford, PA ....General Practice; Municipal and Zoning Law

BEELER, JOSEPH, P.A.
Miami, FL ....Criminal Trial Practice

BEEMER & BEEMER
Clarks Summit, PA ....Civil Trial Practice

BEER & TOONE, P.C.
Phoenix, AZ ....General Practice

BEERS, ANDERSON, JACKSON & SMITH, P.C.
Montgomery, AL ....Civil Trial Practice; Insurance Defense

BEERS, MALLERS, BACKS & SALIN
Fort Wayne, IN......................Banking Law; General Practice; Labor and
Employment Law

BEERY & SPURLOCK CO., L.P.A.
Columbus, OH ....Transportation Law

BEGAM, LEWIS, MARKS & WOLFE, A PROF. ASSN. OF LAWYERS
Phoenix, AZ ....Civil Trial Practice; Medical Malpractice; Personal
Injury; Product Liability Law

BEGGS & LANE
Pensacola, FL..........................General Practice

BEGLEY, CARLIN & MANDIO
Bristol, PA...............................Civil Trial Practice; General Practice
Langhorne, PA ....Civil Trial Practice; General Practice

BEHLES-GIDDENS, P.A.
Albuquerque, NM ....Bankruptcy Law; Commercial Litigation

BEHRENDS & GENTRY
Peoria, IL.................................Business Law

BEIER HOWLETT, PROFESSIONAL CORPORATION
Bloomfield Hills, MI...............Commercial Litigation; Family Law; Probate, Trusts
and Estate Planning

BEIL, JACOB
Columbus, GA ....Commercial Law

BEIRNE, MAYNARD & PARSONS, L.L.P.
Houston, TX ....Civil Trial Practice; General Practice

BELANGER & PLIMPTON
Lovelock, NV ....General Practice

BELCHER, HENZIE & BIEGENZAHN, A PROFESSIONAL CORPORATION
Los Angeles, CA ....Aviation Law; General Practice; Insurance Defense;
Product Liability Law

BELDEN, ABBEY, WEITZENBERG & KELLY, A PROFESSIONAL CORPORATION
Santa Rosa, CA......................Banking Law; Bankruptcy Law; Business Law; Civil
Trial Practice; Commercial Law; Construction Law;
General Practice; Labor and Employment Law;
Medical Malpractice; Personal Injury; Probate,
Trusts and Estate Planning; Real Estate Law

BELDEN, BELDEN, PERSIN & JOHNSTON
Greensburg, PA ....General Practice

BELDOCK LEVINE & HOFFMAN LLP
New York, NY........................Civil Trial Practice; Criminal Trial Practice; Family
Law

BELES, ROBERT J.
Oakland, CA ....Criminal Trial Practice

BELES GROUP, THE
Seattle, WA ....International Business Law

BELGRADE AND O'DONNELL, A PROFESSIONAL CORPORATION
Chicago, IL.............................Admiralty/Maritime Law; Insurance Defense;
Transportation Law

BELIN LAMSON MCCORMICK ZUMBACH FLYNN, A PROFESSIONAL CORPORATION
Des Moines, IA ....Civil Trial Practice; General Practice

BELIN RAWLINGS & BADAL
Los Angeles, CA ....Business Law

BELKIN, BILLICK, HARROLD & WIENCEK
Cleveland, OH.........................Labor and Employment Law

BELLAMY, RUTENBERG, COPELAND, EPPS, GRAVELY & BOWERS, P.A.
Myrtle Beach, SC ....Appellate Practice; Business Law; Civil Trial
Practice; Commercial Law; General Practice;
Insurance Defense; Labor and Employment Law;
Personal Injury; Probate, Trusts and Estate
Planning; Product Liability Law; Real Estate Law

BELLAND, STANTON P., P.C.
Los Angeles, CA ....International Trade Law

BELLATTI, FAY, BELLATTI & BEARD
Jacksonville, IL ....General Practice

BELL, BOYD & LLOYD
Washington, DC......................Antitrust Law; Banking Law; Civil Trial Practice;
Communications Law; Construction Law; General
Practice; Patent, Trademark, Copyright and Unfair
Competition
Chicago, IL.............................Antitrust Law; Banking Law; Civil Trial Practice;
Construction Law; Environmental Law; General
Practice; Health Care Law; Labor and Employment
Law; Municipal Bond/Public Authority Financing;
Patent, Trademark, Copyright and Unfair Competition; Real Estate Law; Securities Law; Tax Law

BELL, COOPER & HYMAN, A PROFESSIONAL LAW CORPORATION
Baton Rouge, LA....................Insurance Defense

BELL, DAVIS & PITT, P.A.
Winston-Salem, NC ....General Practice

BELL, ORR, AYERS & MOORE, P.S.C.
Bowling Green, KY ....Banking Law; Civil Trial Practice; General Practice;
Product Liability Law; Real Estate Law

BELL, SCHUSTER & WHEELER, P.A.
Pensacola, FL..........................Insurance Defense; Medical Malpractice

BELL, SELTZER, PARK & GIBSON, PROFESSIONAL ASSOCIATION
Charlotte, NC..........................Patent, Trademark, Copyright and Unfair Competition
Raleigh, NC.............................Patent, Trademark, Copyright and Unfair Competition

BELL, STANLEY J., A PROFESSIONAL CORPORATION
San Francisco, CA ....Personal Injury

BELOVIN & FRANZBLAU
Bronx, NY...............................Medical Malpractice; Personal Injury; Product
Liability Law

BELSER & BELSER, P.A.
Columbia, SC ....Civil Trial Practice

BELSKY & ASSOCIATES
San Diego, CA ....Insurance Defense; Medical Malpractice; Personal
Injury

BELTZ, EDWARDS & SABO, L.L.P.
Colorado Springs, CO.............Business Law; Civil Trial Practice; Construction
Law; General Practice; Personal Injury; Probate,
Trusts and Estate Planning; Real Estate Law;
Securities Law; Workers Compensation

BENCKENSTEIN, NORVELL & NATHAN, L.L.P.
Beaumont, TX........................Civil Trial Practice; Insurance Defense; Patent,
Trademark, Copyright and Unfair Competition;
Personal Injury

BENCKENSTEIN & OXFORD, L.L.P.
Beaumont, TX.........................Admiralty/Maritime Law; Civil Trial Practice; Environmental Law; General Practice; Natural Resources Law

BENCOMO & ASSOCIATES
New Orleans, LA....................Personal Injury

BENDER, HAROLD J.
Charlotte, NC.........................Criminal Trial Practice

BENDER, LEVI & BUSS, S.C.
Watertown, WI.......................General Practice

BENDER, MICHAEL L., P.C.
Denver, CO ....Criminal Trial Practice

BENDURE & THOMAS
Detroit, MI.............................Appellate Practice; Civil Trial Practice; Tax Law

BENEFIELD & CORDA
Lakeland, FL...........................Personal Injury

BENESCH, KATHERINE LAW OFFICES OF
Lawrenceville, NJ....................Commercial Law; Health Care Law; Personal Injury

BENETAR BERNSTEIN SCHAIR & STEIN
New York, NY.........................Labor and Employment Law

BENETATOS, GEORGE G. LAW OFFICE OF
San Francisco, CA ....Civil Trial Practice

BENJAMIN & ASSOCIATES, P.C.
Denver, CO ....Banking Law; Real Estate Law

BENJAMIN & BENSON
Cambridge, MA ....Family Law

BENKWITH AND HEARD, A PROFESSIONAL CORPORATION
Montgomery, AL ....Banking Law

BENNAZAR-ZEQUEIRA, A.J., LAW OFFICES
San Juan, PR...........................Banking Law; Bankruptcy Law; Civil Trial Practice; General Practice; Insurance Defense; Real Estate Law; Trademark, Copyright and Unfair Competition

BENNETT AND ASSOCIATES, P.A.
Portland, ME ....Civil Trial Practice; General Practice; Labor and Employment Law; Personal Injury

BENNETT & BENNETT
Eaton, OH...............................Civil Trial Practice; Criminal Trial Practice; General Practice; Probate, Trusts and Estate Planning

BENNETT & BIGELOW, A PROFESSIONAL SERVICE CORPORATION
Seattle, WA ....Health Care Law

BENNETT & BLANCATO, L.L.P.
Winston-Salem, NC ....Construction Law; Insurance Defense; Medical Malpractice

BENNETT, BOEHNING, POYNTER & CLARY
Lafayette, IN...........................General Practice

BENNETT, BOWMAN, TRIPLETT & VITTITOW
Louisville, KY ....General Practice; Insurance Defense

BENNETT, BROWN, INGVALDSON, COATY & MCNEIL, P.A.
Minneapolis, MN....................Civil Trial Practice; Personal Injury; Real Estate Law

BENNETT & DILLON, L.L.P.
Topeka, KS..............................Administrative Law; Civil Trial Practice; Criminal Trial Practice; General Practice; Medical Malpractice; Transportation Law

BENNETT JONES VERCHERE
Calgary, AB, Canada...............Appellate Practice; Banking Law; Business Law; Civil Trial Practice; Commercial Law; Employment Benefits Law; Environmental Law; General Practice; Health Care Law; International Business Law; Medical Malpractice; Natural Resources Law; Probate, Trusts and Estate Planning; Public Utilities Law; Real Estate Law; Securities Law
Edmonton, AB, Canada ....General Practice
Ottawa, ON, Canada ....General Practice; Patent, Trademark, Copyright and Unfair Competition; Trademark, Copyright and Unfair Competition
Toronto, ON, Canada.............General Practice
Montreal, QU, Canada ....General Practice

BENNETT & KISTNER
Long Beach, CA......................Civil Trial Practice; Insurance Defense

BENNETT, LYTLE, WETZLER, MARTIN & PISHNY, L.C.
Prairie Village, KS ....General Practice

BENNETT, MAIN, FREDERICKSON & BAILEY, A PROFESSIONAL CORPORATION
Belle Fourche, SD ....Environmental Law; General Practice; Natural Resources Law; Probate, Trusts and Estate Planning

BENNETT, SAMUELSEN, REYNOLDS AND ALLARD, A PROFESSIONAL CORPORATION
Oakland, CA ....Civil Trial Practice; Insurance Defense; Personal Injury

BENNETT, WILLIAM P., A P.L.C.
Orange, CA ....Family Law

BENNINGTON JOHNSON & REEVE, A PROFESSIONAL CORPORATION
Denver, CO ....Commercial Law

BENSINGER, COTANT, MENKES & AARDEMA, P.C.
Gaylord, MI ....Civil Trial Practice; Insurance Defense
Grand Rapids, MI ....Insurance Defense
Marquette, MI.........................Insurance Defense

BENSON, ARTHUR A. II, & ASSOCIATES
Kansas City, MO ....Civil Rights; Constitutional Law

BENTHALL, DEEDRA
Danville, KY ....Personal Injury; Workers Compensation

BENTLEY, MOSHER, BABSON & LAMBERT, P.C.
Greenwich, CT ....Civil Trial Practice; Land Use Law; Probate, Trusts and Estate Planning

BENTON, ORR, DUVAL & BUCKINGHAM, A PROFESSIONAL CORPORATION
Ventura, CA ....Civil Trial Practice; General Practice

BERENBAUM, WEINSHIENK & EASON, P.C.
Denver, CO ....Banking Law; General Practice; Real Estate Law; Trademark, Copyright and Unfair Competition

BERENS & TATE, P.C.
Omaha, NE ....Business Law; Employment Benefits Law; General Practice; Labor and Employment Law; Workers Compensation

BERENSTEIN, MOORE, MOSER, BERENSTEIN & HEFFERNAN
Sioux City, IA ....General Practice; Probate, Trusts and Estate Planning; Tax Law

BERESKIN & PARR
Toronto, ON, Canada.............Business Law; Patent, Trademark, Copyright and Unfair Competition

BERG & ANDROPHY
Houston, TX ....Civil Trial Practice; Criminal Trial Practice

BERG, ZIEGLER, ANDERSON & PARKER, LLP
San Francisco, CA ....Civil Trial Practice; Commercial Litigation; Real Estate Law

BERGEN, JOSEPH B., AND FREDERICK S. BERGEN
Savannah, GA ....Personal Injury

BERGER, GARY D. LAW OFFICES OF
San Francisco, CA ....Probate, Trusts and Estate Planning

BERGER AND BERGER
Evansville, IN..........................Civil Trial Practice; Labor and Employment Law; Personal Injury; Product Liability Law

BERGER & CHAFETZ
Miami, FL ....Appellate Practice

BERGER & DAVIS, P.A.
Fort Lauderdale, FL................Business Law; Civil Trial Practice; Real Estate Law; Tax Law

BERGER & MONTAGUE, P.C.
Philadelphia, PA ....Antitrust Law; General Practice

BERGESON, ELIOPOULOS, GRADY & GRAY
San Jose, CA ....Antitrust Law; Civil Trial Practice; Commercial Litigation

BERGMAN & BARRETT
Princeton, NJ ....Civil Trial Practice; Commercial Law; Family Law

BERGMAN, HOROWITZ & REYNOLDS, P.C.
New Haven, CT ....Bankruptcy Law; Business Law; Commercial Law; Probate, Trusts and Estate Planning; Real Estate Law; Tax Law

BERGMAN & WEDNER, INC.
Los Angeles, CA......................Business Law; Civil Trial Practice; Construction Law; Labor and Employment Law; Real Estate Law

BERGSTEDT & MOUNT
Lake Charles, LA....................Admiralty/Maritime Law; Banking Law; Civil Trial Practice; General Practice; Insurance Defense; Real Estate Law

BERGSTROM, THOMAS A.
Malvern, PA............................Criminal Trial Practice

BERICK, PEARLMAN & MILLS, A LEGAL PROFESSIONAL ASSOCIATION
Cleveland, OH........................Banking Law; Business Law; General Practice; Real Estate Law; Securities Law; Tax Law

BERKE, ROBERT LAW OFFICES OF
Santa Monica, CA..................Criminal Trial Practice

BERKEMEYER & BARKS
Hermann, MO.........................General Practice

BERKEY, JON H., P.C.
Bloomfield Hills, MI...............Commercial Law; Real Estate Law

BERKMAN, GORDON, MURRAY & DEVAN
Cleveland, OH........................Civil Trial Practice; Criminal Trial Practice

BERKOWITZ, LEFKOVITS, ISOM & KUSHNER, A PROFESSIONAL CORPORATION
Birmingham, AL ....Antitrust Law; Business Law; Civil Trial Practice; General Practice; Health Care Law; Labor and Employment Law; Probate, Trusts and Estate Planning; Real Estate Law; Securities Law; Tax Law

BERLACK, ISRAELS & LIBERMAN LLP
New York, NY.....................Administrative Law; Bankruptcy Law; Civil Trial Practice; Employment Benefits Law; Tax Law

BERLAND, ALLAN M.
San Francisco, CA ....Real Estate Law

BERLINER, CORCORAN & ROWE, L.L.P.
Washington, DC.....................Business Law; International Business Law

BERLINER LAW OFFICES
Nevada City, CA.....................Civil Trial Practice

BERLINER ZISSER WALTER & GALLEGOS, P.C.
Denver, CO ....Securities Law

BERMAN, DAVID
Medford, MA ....Civil Trial Practice

BERMAN, BLANCHARD, MAUSNER & RESSER, A LAW CORPORATION
Los Angeles, CA ....Appellate Practice; Civil Trial Practice; Commercial Litigation; Computer Law; Probate, Trusts and Estate Planning; Trademark, Copyright and Unfair Competition

BERMAN, BOURNS & CURRIE, LLC
West Hartford, CT.................Family Law; General Practice; Probate, Trusts and Estate Planning; Real Estate Law

BERMAN, DELEVE, KUCHAN & CHAPMAN, L.C.
Kansas City, MO....................Bankruptcy Law; Commercial Law; Probate, Trusts and Estate Planning

BERMAN, GAUFIN, TOMSIC & SAVAGE, A PROFESSIONAL CORPORATION
Salt Lake City, UT.................Civil Trial Practice; Criminal Trial Practice

BERMAN, PALEY, GOLDSTEIN & KANNRY, LLP
New York, NY.......................Construction Law

BERMAN & WEISS
Palm Desert, CA ....Medical Malpractice; Personal Injury

BERMAN WOLFE & RENNERT, P.A.
Miami, FL ....Commercial Litigation; Securities Law

BERMAN & YOTIS, A PROFESSIONAL ASSOCIATION
Chicago, IL............................Banking Law; Business Law; Civil Trial Practice; Commercial Litigation; Labor and Employment Law; Personal Injury; Real Estate Law

BERNARD, JACK M.
Philadelphia, PA ....Civil Trial Practice; Commercial Litigation

BERNARD, CASSISA & ELLIOTT, A PROFESSIONAL LAW CORPORATION
Metairie, LA...........................General Practice

BERNARD, HAFFEY & BOHNERT CO., L.P.A.
Cleveland, OH........................Business Law; Civil Trial Practice; Criminal Trial Practice; General Practice

BERNAUER, THOMAS A., A PROFESSIONAL CORPORATION
Newport Beach, CA................Family Law

BERNKOPF, GOODMAN & BASEMAN, LLP
Boston, MA............................Business Law; General Practice; Real Estate Law

BERNSEN, JAMAIL & GOODSON, L.L.P.
Beaumont, TX........................Administrative Law; Admiralty/Maritime Law; Civil Trial Practice; Insurance Defense

BERNSTEIN & BERNSTEIN, P.A.
Charleston, SC ....Bankruptcy Law; Civil Trial Practice; Commercial Law

BERNSTEIN AND BERNSTEIN, P.C.
Pittsburgh, PA ....Bankruptcy Law; Commercial Law; Real Estate Law

BERNSTEIN, SHUR, SAWYER & NELSON, A PROFESSIONAL CORPORATION
Augusta, ME..........................General Practice

Kennebunk, ME......................General Practice
Portland, ME ....General Practice

BERNSTEIN, STAIR & MCADAMS
Knoxville, TN ....Civil Trial Practice; General Practice

BERRIGAN, PATRICK J., (P.L.C.)
Slidell, LA ....Commercial Litigation

BERRY, THOMAS A. & ASSOCIATES
Bloomington, IN ....Civil Trial Practice

BERRY, ABLES, TATUM, BAXTER, PARKER & HALL, P.C.
Huntsville, AL.........................Appellate Practice; Bankruptcy Law; Business Law; Civil Trial Practice; Commercial Law; Construction Law; Family Law; General Practice; Personal Injury; Probate, Trusts and Estate Planning; Real Estate Law; Tax Law

BERRY, ADAMS, QUACKENBUSH & DUNBAR, P.A.
Columbia, SC ....Immigration and Naturalization; International Business Law; Real Estate Law

BERRY & BERRY, A PROFESSIONAL CORPORATION
Oakland, CA ....General Practice

BERRY, CAPPER, DONALDSON & TULLEY
Crawfordsville, IN...................Family Law; General Practice; Municipal and Zoning Law; Personal Injury; Probate, Trusts and Estate Planning; Real Estate Law

BERRY, KELLEY, HANSEN & BURT
Lincoln, NE............................Appellate Practice; Criminal Trial Practice

BERRY AND OGLESBY
Franklin, TN ....General Practice

BERRY, SHOEMAKER & CLARK
Columbus, OH ....Civil Trial Practice; Commercial Litigation; Family Law; Labor and Employment Law; Personal Injury

BERRYHILL & WILLIAMS, P.A.
Fort Lauderdale, FL................General Practice

BERSCH & RHODES, P.C.
Roanoke, VA...........................Business Law; Employment Benefits Law; Personal Injury; Probate, Trusts and Estate Planning

BESS & DYSART, P.C.
Phoenix, AZ ....Civil Trial Practice; Environmental Law; Insurance Defense; Personal Injury; Product Liability Law

BESSEY, JOHN D.
Sacramento, CA ....Bankruptcy Law

BEST & ANDERSON, P.A.
Crystal River, FL....................Civil Trial Practice; Medical Malpractice; Personal Injury
Melbourne, FL ....Civil Trial Practice; Medical Malpractice; Personal Injury
Orlando, FL ....Civil Trial Practice; Environmental Law; Medical Malpractice; Personal Injury

BEST & BEST, P.L.C.
Norfolk, VA ....Commercial Law

BEST BEST & KRIEGER LLP
Riverside, CA ....General Practice

BEST KOEPPEL, A PROFESSIONAL LAW CORPORATION
New Orleans, LA....................Admiralty/Maritime Law; Insurance Defense

BEST, SHARP, HOLDEN, BEST, SULLIVAN & KEMPFERT, A PROFESSIONAL CORPORATION
Tulsa, OK...............................Civil Trial Practice; Insurance Defense; Medical Malpractice; Personal Injury; Workers Compensation

BETHEA, JORDAN & GRIFFIN, P.A.
Hilton Head Island, SC...........Probate, Trusts and Estate Planning; Tax Law

BETHELL, CALLAWAY, ROBERTSON, BEASLEY & COWAN
Fort Smith, AR.......................Civil Trial Practice; General Practice

BETTERMAN & PERRY
Omaha, NE ....Commercial Litigation

BETTS, PATTERSON & MINES, P.S.
Seattle, WA ....General Practice

BEUS, GILBERT & MORRILL, P.L.L.C.
Phoenix, AZ ....Banking Law; Commercial Litigation

BEVER, DYE, MUSTARD & BELIN, L.C.
Wichita, KS............................Probate, Trusts and Estate Planning; Tax Law

BEVERIDGE, DEGRANDI, WEILACHER & YOUNG, L.L.P.
Washington, DC......................Patent, Trademark, Copyright and Unfair Competition

BEVERIDGE & DIAMOND
San Francisco, CA ....General Practice
Washington, DC....................General Practice
New York, NY........................General Practice

BEWLEY & KODAY
Fort Wayne, IN......................Probate, Trusts and Estate Planning

BEWLEY, LASSLEBEN & MILLER
Whittier, CA............................Civil Trial Practice; General Practice; Probate, Trusts and Estate Planning

BIALAC, JAMES T.
Phoenix, AZ ....General Practice

BIALICK, STEVEN M. LAW OFFICE OF
Minneapolis, MN....................Personal Injury

BIANCO & MURPHY
San Francisco, CA ....Labor and Employment Law; Personal Injury

BIBLE, HANEY, HOY, TRACHOK & WADHAMS, A PROFESSIONAL CORPORATION
Las Vegas, NV ....Civil Trial Practice
Reno, NV ....Civil Trial Practice

BICKEL, BRUCE D.
Fresno, CA ....Probate, Trusts and Estate Planning

BICKEL & ASSOCIATES
San Francisco, CA ....Real Estate Law

BICKEL & BREWER
Dallas, TX................................Civil Trial Practice; General Practice

BICKFORD, PASLEY & FARABOUGH
Ardmore, OK ....Civil Trial Practice; General Practice; Workers Compensation

BIEBEL & FRENCH, A LEGAL PROFESSIONAL ASSOCIATION
Columbus, OH ....Patent, Trademark, Copyright and Unfair Competition
Dayton, OH............................Patent, Trademark, Copyright and Unfair Competition

BIEN & SUMMERS
San Francisco, CA ....Appellate Practice

BIENSTOCK & CLARK
Santa Monica, CA..................Civil Trial Practice
Miami, FL ....Civil Trial Practice

BIERI, BERNSTEIN & AMES
Detroit, MI..............................Real Estate Law

BIERMAN & BIERMAN, P.C.
Grinnell, IA..............................General Practice

BIERMAN, SHOHAT, LOEWY, PERRY & KLEIN, PROFESSIONAL ASSOCIATION
Miami, FL ....Appellate Practice; Criminal Trial Practice; General Practice; International Business Law

BIESER, GREER & LANDIS
Dayton, OH..............................Civil Trial Practice; General Practice

BIGGERS, BEASLEY, EARLE AND HIGHTOWER, P.C.
Dallas, TX................................Commercial Litigation

BIGGS AND BATTAGLIA
Wilmington, DE......................Civil Trial Practice; Criminal Trial Practice; General Practice

BIGHAM ENGLAR JONES & HOUSTON
New York, NY........................General Practice

BILLINGS, CUNNINGHAM, MORGAN & BOATWRIGHT, PROFESSIONAL ASSOCIATION
Orlando, FL ....Medical Malpractice; Personal Injury

BILLINGS & SOLOMON, P.C.
Houston, TX ....Admiralty/Maritime Law

BINGAMAN, HESS, COBLENTZ & BELL, A PROFESSIONAL CORPORATION
Reading, PA ....Banking Law; Bankruptcy Law; Civil Trial Practice; General Practice

BINGHAM, DANA & GOULD LLP
Hartford, CT ....General Practice
Washington, DC....................General Practice
Boston, MA..............................General Practice
London, England ....General Practice

BINNING, J. BOYD
Columbus, OH ....Personal Injury

BINSTOCK, SHELTON M. THE LAW OFFICES OF
Washington, DC....................Probate, Trusts and Estate Planning; Tax Law

BIRCH, DE JONGH, HINDELS & HALL
Charlotte Amalie, St.
Thomas, VI..............................Banking Law; General Practice; Real Estate Law

BIRCH, STEWART, KOLASCH & BIRCH, LLP
Falls Church, VA....................Patent, Trademark, Copyright and Unfair Competition

BIRD, ELIZABETH ANNE LAW OFFICES OF
San Francisco, CA ....Probate, Trusts and Estate Planning

BIRD, FRANCIS M. JR.
Atlanta, GA ....Business Law; General Practice; Probate, Trusts and Estate Planning

BIRD, BALLARD & STILL
Atlanta, GA ....Civil Trial Practice; Medical Malpractice; Personal Injury; Product Liability Law

BIRD & BIRD, A LAW CORPORATION
Torrance, CA............................Criminal Trial Practice

BIRDWELL, WILLIAM A. & ASSOCIATES
Portland, OR............................Patent, Trademark, Copyright and Unfair Competition

BIREN, MATTHEW B. F. & ASSOCIATES
Los Angeles, CA ....Personal Injury; Product Liability Law

BIRGE & MAYERS, P.C.
Denver, CO ....Commercial Law; Criminal Trial Practice; Securities Law

BIRKA-WHITE, DAVID M. LAW OFFICES OF
Alamo, CA ....Construction Law; Product Liability Law

BIRMINGHAM THORSON & BARNETT, P.C.
Seattle, WA ....Employment Benefits Law

BIRNDORF, THEODORE
Chicago, IL..............................Family Law

BISGYER, BERT NEIL LAW OFFICE OF
Washington, DC....................Labor and Employment Law

BISHOP, JAMES A. LAW OFFICES OF
Brunswick, GA........................General Practice

BISHOP, BARRY, HOWE, HANEY & RYDER, A PROFESSIONAL CORPORATION
San Francisco, CA ....Environmental Law; Insurance Defense; Probate, Trusts and Estate Planning; Real Estate Law

BISHOP & BISHOP
Ashdown, AR ....General Practice

BISHOP, COLVIN, JOHNSON & KENT
Birmingham, AL ....General Practice

BISHOP, E. THOMAS, P.C.
Dallas, TX................................Insurance Defense

BISHOP & HEINTZ, P.C.
Traverse City, MI....................Business Law; Patent, Trademark, Copyright and Unfair Competition

BISHOP, PAYNE, WILLIAMS & WERLEY, L.L.P.
Fort Worth, TX ....Civil Trial Practice; Real Estate Law

BISIGNANO & HARRISON, L.L.P.
Dallas, TX................................Business Law; Probate, Trusts and Estate Planning

BISK & LUTZ, L.L.P.
Houston, TX ....Commercial Law; Probate, Trusts and Estate Planning; Real Estate Law; Tax Law

BITTMAN, HOWARD
Boulder, CO ....Civil Trial Practice; Criminal Trial Practice; Family Law; Real Estate Law

BIVENS, HOFFMAN & FOWLER
Atlanta, GA ....Business Law; Civil Trial Practice; Family Law; Personal Injury; Probate, Trusts and Estate Planning; Tax Law

BLACHLY, TABOR, BOZIK & HARTMAN
Valparaiso, IN........................Civil Trial Practice; General Practice; Personal Injury; Probate, Trusts and Estate Planning; Real Estate Law

BLACK, A. CLIFTON
Orlando, FL ....Bankruptcy Law; Commercial Litigation

BLACKARD, WILLIAM R. JR.
Jacksonville, FL ....Probate, Trusts and Estate Planning; Tax Law

BLACK & BLACK
Port Arthur, TX......................General Practice

BLACK BOBANGO & MORGAN, A PROFESSIONAL CORPORATION
Memphis, TN ....Civil Trial Practice

BLACK COMPEAN HALL & LENNEMAN
Los Angeles, CA ....Appellate Practice; Civil Trial Practice; Insurance Defense

BLACK & GOTTLIEB
Phoenix, AZ ....Criminal Trial Practice

BLACK HELTERLINE
Portland, OR...........................Banking Law; Bankruptcy Law; Civil Trial Practice; Commercial Law; Environmental Law; General Practice; Immigration and Naturalization; Natural Resources Law; Real Estate Law; Tax Law

BLACKHURST, HORNECKER, HASSEN & ERVIN B. HOGAN
Medford, OR...........................General Practice

BLACK, MCCARTHY & ANEWALT, P.C.
Allentown, PA ....Civil Trial Practice; General Practice; Real Estate Law

BLACK, MCCUSKEY, SOUERS & ARBAUGH, A LEGAL PROFESSIONAL ASSOCIATION
Canton, OH...........................Civil Trial Practice; General Practice; Labor and Employment Law

BLACKMON, DROZD & SNELLINGS
Sacramento, CA ....Criminal Trial Practice

BLACK, NOLAND & READ, P.L.C.
Staunton, VA ....General Practice

BLACK, RICHARD A., P.C.
Phoenix, AZ ....Personal Injury

BLACK, SREBNICK & KORNSPAN, P.A.
Miami, FL ....Criminal Trial Practice

BLACKWELL & WHITE
Gulfport, MS...........................General Practice

BLACKWOOD, MATTHEWS & STEEL
Atlanta, GA ....Civil Trial Practice; Personal Injury; Product Liability Law

BLAIR, HOLLADAY AND PARSONS
Pell City, AL...........................Civil Trial Practice; General Practice; Insurance Defense

BLAIR, SCHAEFER, HUTCHISON & WOLFE, LLP
Vancouver, WA......................General Practice

BLAIR & STROUD
Batesville, AR ....General Practice

BLAKE, CASSELS & GRAYDON
Calgary, AB, Canada ....General Practice
Vancouver, BC, Canada...........General Practice
Ottawa, ON, Canada ....General Practice
Toronto, ON, Canada ....General Practice
London, England ....General Practice

BLAKE, KIRCHNER, SYMONDS, MACFARLANE, LARSON & SMITH, P.C.
Detroit, MI............................Insurance Defense; Medical Malpractice; Workers Compensation

BLAKENEY & ALEXANDER
Charlotte, NC.........................Civil Trial Practice; General Practice; Labor and Employment Law

BLALOCK, LANDERS, WALTERS AND VOGLER, P.A.
Bradenton, FL.........................Commercial Litigation; Probate, Trusts and Estate Planning; Real Estate Law

BLANCHARD, JENKINS & MILLER, P.A.
Raleigh, NC............................Aviation Law; Personal Injury; Product Liability Law

BLANCHARD, ROBERTSON, MITCHELL & CARTER, P.C.
Joplin, MO ....General Practice; Insurance Defense

BLANCHARD, WALKER, O'QUIN & ROBERTS, A PROFESSIONAL LAW CORPORATION
Shreveport, LA........................General Practice

BLANCHFIELD CORDLE & MOORE, P.A.
Charlotte, NC.........................Tax Law

BLANCO TACKABERY COMBS & MATAMOROS, P.A.
Winston-Salem, NC ....Bankruptcy Law; Commercial Law

BLANEY, MCMURTRY, STAPELLS, FRIEDMAN
Toronto, ON, Canada..............General Practice

BLANK, MARTIN H. JR.
Los Angeles, CA ....General Practice; Probate, Trusts and Estate Planning; Real Estate Law

BLANKE, NORDEN, BARMANN, KRAMER & BOHLEN, P.C.
Kankakee, IL...........................Commercial Law; General Practice; Health Care Law

BLANKENSHIP, DAVID B., ATTORNEY-AT-LAW, P.C.
Huntsville, AL.........................Family Law

BLANKINGSHIP & KEITH, A PROFESSIONAL CORPORATION
Fairfax, VA ....Civil Trial Practice

BLANK ROME COMISKY & MCCAULEY
Philadelphia, PA ....General Practice

BLANTON, RICE, SIDWELL & OTTINGER, LLC
Sikeston, MO..........................General Practice; Insurance Defense

BLASINGAME, BURCH, GARRARD, BRYANT & ASHLEY, P.C.
Athens, GA ....Civil Trial Practice; General Practice; Insurance Defense; Product Liability Law

BLATT, HAMMESFAHR & EATON
Chicago, IL.............................Commercial Litigation; Environmental Law; Insurance Defense

BLAUGRUND, GABEL, HERBERT & MESIROW
Dublin, OH ....Administrative Law; Appellate Practice; Business Law; Civil Trial Practice; Labor and Employment Law

BLAU, KRAMER, WACTLAR & LIEBERMAN, P.C.
Jericho, NY ....Real Estate Law; Securities Law

BLAZZARD, GRODD & HASENAUER, P.C.
Westport, CT..........................General Practice; Probate, Trusts and Estate Planning; Securities Law; Tax Law

BLEAKLEY PLATT & SCHMIDT
White Plains, NY ....Civil Trial Practice; General Practice

BLECHER & COLLINS, A PROFESSIONAL CORPORATION
Los Angeles, CA ....Antitrust Law; Appellate Practice; Business Law; Civil Trial Practice; Trademark, Copyright and Unfair Competition

BLEDSOE & BLEDSOE, P.L.L.C.
Charlotte, NC.........................General Practice

BLEDSOE, SCHMIDT & LIPPES, P.A.
Jacksonville, FL ....Civil Trial Practice

BLEIER LAW FIRM, THE
Sacramento, CA ....Civil Trial Practice; Commercial Law; Environmental Law; Real Estate Law

BLEIMAIER, JOHN KUHN
Princeton, NJ ....Immigration and Naturalization; International Business Law

BLESSEY, GERALD, & ASSOCIATES
Biloxi, MS..............................Civil Trial Practice; Municipal and Zoning Law

BLEUEL & MUIRHEAD
Ventura, CA ....Probate, Trusts and Estate Planning

BLEVINS, MICHAEL W.
Sayre, OK ....Civil Trial Practice

BLISH & CAVANAGH
Providence, RI........................Antitrust Law; Civil Trial Practice; Commercial Law; Commercial Litigation; Construction Law; Environmental Law; General Practice; Labor and Employment Law; Medical Malpractice

BLODNICK BLODNICK & ZELIN, P.C.
Roslyn Heights, NY ....General Practice

BLOND, BARTON S., P.C., LAW OFFICES OF
Kansas City, MO ....Family Law

BLOODWORTH LAW OFFICES
Poplar Bluff, MO ....General Practice

BLOOM & BUELL
Boston, MA............................Civil Trial Practice; General Practice; Health Care Law; Insurance Defense

BLOOM, DAVID B., A PROF. CORP., LAW OFFICES OF
Los Angeles, CA ....Banking Law; Bankruptcy Law; Business Law; Civil Trial Practice; Commercial Law; Construction Law; General Practice; International Business Law; Personal Injury; Real Estate Law; Sports and Entertainment Law

BLOOM & KRETEN
Sacramento, CA ....Patent, Trademark, Copyright and Unfair Competition
Towson, MD ....Patent, Trademark, Copyright and Unfair Competition

BLOOM & WITKIN
   Boston, MA ....Sports and Entertainment Law; Tax Law

BLOOSTON, MORDKOFSKY, JACKSON & DICKENS
   Washington, DC.....................Communications Law

BLOUNT, MARVIN K. JR.
   Greenville, NC ....Antitrust Law; Medical Malpractice; Personal Injury

BLUM, EDWARD L.
   Oakland, CA ....Commercial Law

BLUM, LORIN B. LAW OFFICES OF
   Oakland, CA ....Family Law

BLUMENFELD, ELI, LAW CORPORATION
   Beverly Hills, CA ....Tax Law

BLUM, YUMKAS, MAILMAN, GUTMAN & DENICK, P.A.
   Baltimore, MD ....General Practice

BLUNT, A. PAUL, P.C.
   Scottsdale, AZ ....Probate, Trusts and Estate Planning

BLUT, JEROME L., CHARTERED
   Las Vegas, NV ....Probate, Trusts and Estate Planning; Tax Law

BLYLER, WILLIAM E.
   Fort Lauderdale, FL ....General Practice

BOARD, JOHN
   Guymon, OK ....General Practice

BOARDMAN, SUHR, CURRY & FIELD
   Madison, WI ....Civil Trial Practice; General Practice; Personal Injury

BOBERSCHMIDT, MILLER, O'BRYAN & TURNER, A PROFESSIONAL ASSOCIATION
   Indianapolis, IN ....Business Law; Civil Trial Practice; Commercial Law; Family Law; Probate, Trusts and Estate Planning

BOBO, SPICER, CIOTOLI, FULFORD, BOCCHINO, DEBEVOISE & LE CLAINCHE, P.A.
   Orlando, FL ....Health Care Law; Medical Malpractice; Personal Injury
   West Palm Beach, FL ....Health Care Law; Medical Malpractice; Personal Injury

BOCCARDO LAW FIRM, THE
   San Jose, CA ....Business Law; Civil Trial Practice; Medical Malpractice; Personal Injury; Product Liability Law

BOCK, JOHN GORDON
   Houston, TX ....Civil Trial Practice; Family Law

BODDINGTON & BROWN, CHTD.
   Kansas City, KS.......................General Practice

BODELL, BOVÉ & VAN HORN
   Philadelphia, PA ....Product Liability Law

BODENHEIMER, BUSBEE, HUNTER & GRIFFITH
   Aiken, SC ....Civil Trial Practice; General Practice; Personal Injury; Probate, Trusts and Estate Planning; Real Estate Law; Tax Law

BODKER, RAMSEY & ANDREWS, A PROFESSIONAL CORPORATION
   Atlanta, GA ....Business Law; Civil Trial Practice; Commercial Law; Communications Law; Probate, Trusts and Estate Planning; Tax Law

BODMAN, LONGLEY & DAHLING LLP
   Cheboygan, MI ....Banking Law
   Detroit, MI.............................Administrative Law; Antitrust Law; Appellate Practice; Banking Law; Bankruptcy Law; Business Law; Civil Trial Practice; Commercial Law; Communications Law; Construction Law; Environmental Law; General Practice; Health Care Law; Labor and Employment Law; Municipal Bond/Public Authority Financing; Municipal and Zoning Law; Natural Resources Law; Probate, Trusts and Estate Planning; Product Liability Law; Real Estate Law; Securities Law; Tax Law; Trademark, Copyright and Unfair Competition

BODYFELT, MOUNT, STROUP & CHAMBERLAIN
   Portland, OR...........................Civil Trial Practice; Insurance Defense

BOEHL STOPHER & GRAVES
   Lexington, KY ....Civil Trial Practice; General Practice; Workers Compensation
   Louisville, KY ....Civil Trial Practice; General Practice; Workers Compensation
   Paducah, KY ....Civil Trial Practice; General Practice; Workers Compensation

BOEHM, KURTZ & LOWRY
   Cincinnati, OH ....Public Utilities Law

BOEHM, PEARLSTEIN & BRIGHT, LTD.
   Chicago, IL..............................Banking Law; Commercial Law; Real Estate Law

BOESCHE, MCDERMOTT & ESKRIDGE
   Tulsa, OK ....Banking Law; Bankruptcy Law; Civil Trial Practice; Commercial Litigation; Employment Benefits Law; Energy Law; General Practice; Health Care Law; International Business Law; International Trade Law; Mergers and Acquisitions; Natural Resources Law

BOGART, SUSAN
   Chicago, IL..............................Criminal Trial Practice; Labor and Employment Law

BOGATIN LAW FIRM, THE, PLC
   Memphis, TN ....Civil Trial Practice; General Practice; Health Care Law; International Business Law; Probate, Trusts and Estate Planning; Tax Law

BOGENSCHUTZ & DUTKO, P.A.
   Fort Lauderdale, FL ....Criminal Trial Practice

BOGGS, LOEHN & RODRIGUE
   New Orleans, LA ....Environmental Law; Health Care Law; Insurance Defense; Medical Malpractice

BOGIN, PATTERSON & BOHMAN
   Dayton, OH............................Bankruptcy Law; Business Law; Civil Trial Practice

BOGLE & GATES P.L.L.C.
   Seattle, WA ....General Practice

BOGOSLOW & JONES, P.A.
   Walterboro, SC........................General Practice

BOHANNON, BOHANNON & HANCOCK, P.C.
   Norfolk, VA ....Business Law

BOHN, BENNION & NILAND
   San Jose, CA ....Labor and Employment Law; Personal Injury; Product Liability Law

BOHRNSEN AND OWEN, P.S., THE LAW OFFICES OF
   Spokane, WA...........................Civil Trial Practice; Insurance Defense; Personal Injury

BOIVIN, JONES, UERLINGS, DIIACONI & ODEN, P.C.
   Klamath Falls, OR ....General Practice

BOKELMAN & BENJAMIN, A PROFESSIONAL LAW CORPORATION
   San Francisco, CA ....Medical Malpractice; Personal Injury

BOLLING, WALTER & GAWTHROP, A PROFESSIONAL CORPORATION
   Sacramento, CA ....Civil Trial Practice

BONAHOOM & BONAHOOM
   Fort Wayne, IN.......................Business Law; Probate, Trusts and Estate Planning; Real Estate Law

BONAPARTE & MIYAMOTO, A PROFESSIONAL LAW CORPORATION
   Los Angeles, CA ....Immigration and Naturalization

BONDURANT, MIXSON & ELMORE, LLP
   Atlanta, GA ....Antitrust Law; Appellate Practice; Civil Trial Practice; Criminal Trial Practice; Environmental Law; Personal Injury; Trademark, Copyright and Unfair Competition

BONDY & SCHLOSS LLP
   New York, NY........................General Practice

BONE, BILL, P.A., THE LAW OFFICE OF
   West Palm Beach, FL ....Personal Injury

BONINA & BONINA, P.C.
   Brooklyn, NY ....Civil Trial Practice; Medical Malpractice; Personal Injury; Product Liability Law

BONN, LUSCHER, PADDEN & WILKINS, CHARTERED
   Phoenix, AZ ....Appellate Practice; Business Law; Civil Trial Practice; Commercial Litigation; Health Care Law; Real Estate Law

BONNE, BRIDGES, MUELLER, O'KEEFE & NICHOLS, PROFESSIONAL CORPORATION
   Los Angeles, CA ....Medical Malpractice

BONNETT, FAIRBOURN, FRIEDMAN & BALINT, P.C.
   Phoenix, AZ ....Civil Trial Practice; Insurance Defense; Municipal and Zoning Law; Personal Injury; Real Estate Law; Securities Law

BONNEY, WEAVER, CORLEY & BENEFIELD
   Duncan, OK ....General Practice

BOOKHOLDER, BASSETT, GORNBEIN & COHEN, P.L.L.C.
   Troy, MI.................................Family Law; Probate, Trusts and Estate Planning

BOONE, RICHARD W. LAW OFFICES OF
Vienna, VA................................Health Care Law; Insurance Defense

BOONE, BEALE, CARPENTER & COSBY
Richmond, VA.........................Criminal Trial Practice; Personal Injury

BOONE, DAVID WM., P.C.
Atlanta, GA ....Civil Trial Practice; Medical Malpractice; Personal Injury

BOONE, KARLBERG AND HADDON
Missoula, MT ....General Practice

BOONE, SMITH, DAVIS, HURST & DICKMAN, A PROFESSIONAL CORPORATION
Tulsa, OK.................................Banking Law; General Practice; Health Care Law; Labor and Employment Law; Securities Law; Workers Compensation

BOOTH, MITCHELL B.
New York, NY.........................Probate, Trusts and Estate Planning

BOOTH, BATE, GRIECO AND BRIODY
Montclair, NJ...........................Probate, Trusts and Estate Planning

BOOTH, MITCHEL & STRANGE
Los Angeles, CA......................Insurance Defense

BOOTH PATTERSON, P.C.
Pontiac, MI ....Bankruptcy Law; Business Law; Civil Trial Practice; Environmental Law; Family Law; General Practice; Labor and Employment Law; Municipal and Zoning Law; Personal Injury; Probate, Trusts and Estate Planning; Real Estate Law

BOOTHBY & YINGST
Washington, DC......................Civil Trial Practice
Berrien Springs, MI.................Civil Trial Practice

BOOTHMAN, HEBERT & ELLER, P.C.
Ann Arbor, MI ....Civil Trial Practice; General Practice; Insurance Defense; Medical Malpractice
Detroit, MI..............................Civil Trial Practice; General Practice; Insurance Defense; Medical Malpractice

BORCHARD & WILLOUGHBY, A PROFESSIONAL CORPORATION
Irvine, CA.................................Appellate Practice; General Practice; Real Estate Law; Securities Law

BORDEN & ELLIOT
Toronto, ON, Canada..............Administrative Law; Admiralty/Maritime Law; Antitrust Law; Banking Law; Bankruptcy Law; Business Law; Civil Trial Practice; Commercial Law; Communications Law; Construction Law; Criminal Trial Practice; Employment Benefits Law; Environmental Law; Family Law; General Practice; Health Care Law; Immigration and Naturalization; Insurance Defense; International Business Law; Labor and Employment Law; Medical Malpractice; Municipal and Zoning Law; Natural Resources Law; Patent, Trademark, Copyright and Unfair Competition; Personal Injury; Probate, Trusts and Estate Planning; Real Estate Law; Securities Law; Tax Law

BORING & PILGER, P.C.
Vienna, VA..............................Appellate Practice; Business Law; Civil Trial Practice; Commercial Law; Commercial Litigation; Employment Benefits Law; Labor and Employment Law; Probate, Trusts and Estate Planning; Tax Law

BORINS, SETEL, SNITZER & BROWNSTEIN
Buffalo, NY ....General Practice; Probate, Trusts and Estate Planning

BOROD & KRAMER, P.C.
Memphis, TN ....Bankruptcy Law; Civil Trial Practice; General Practice; Securities Law

BOROWSKY, PHILIP, A PROF. CORP., LAW OFFICES OF
San Francisco, CA ....Civil Trial Practice

BORRE, PETERSON, FOWLER & REENS, P.C.
Grand Rapids, MI ....Banking Law; Bankruptcy Law; Business Law; Civil Trial Practice; Commercial Law; Commercial Litigation; Environmental Law; General Practice; Probate, Trusts and Estate Planning; Real Estate Law; Tax Law

BORRON & DELAHAYE, A PROFESSIONAL LAW CORPORATION
Plaquemine, LA.......................General Practice

BORRUS, GOLDIN & FOLEY, A PROFESSIONAL CORPORATION
New Brunswick, NJ ....General Practice

BORRUS, GOLDIN, FOLEY, VIGNUOLO, HYMAN & STAHL, A PROFESSIONAL CORPORATION
North Brunswick, NJ..............Civil Trial Practice; Criminal Trial Practice; Family Law; General Practice; Probate, Trusts and Estate Planning; Real Estate Law

BORTON, PETRINI & CONRON
Bakersfield, CA ....General Practice; Tax Law

BOSCO, JOSEPH A.
Washington, DC......................Business Law

BOSE MCKINNEY & EVANS
Indianapolis, IN ....Antitrust Law; Banking Law; Bankruptcy Law; Civil Trial Practice; Communications Law; Environmental Law; General Practice; Labor and Employment Law; Municipal Bond/Public Authority Financing; Public Utilities Law; Real Estate Law; Tax Law

BOS & GLAZIER, P.L.C.
Grand Rapids, MI ....Civil Trial Practice; Environmental Law; Insurance Defense

BOSSIN, PHYLLIS G., CO., L.P.A.
Cincinnati, OH ....Family Law

BOSSO, WILLIAMS, LEVIN, SACHS & BOOK, A PROFESSIONAL CORPORATION
Santa Cruz, CA ....General Practice

BOSTON, BATES & HOLT
Lawrenceburg, TN ....General Practice

BOSTON & CUNNINGHAM, P.C.
Houston, TX ....Medical Malpractice

BOSTON, WILLIAM C., & ASSOCIATES
Oklahoma City, OK.................Aviation Law; Commercial Law; Transportation Law

BOSWELL, SNYDER, TINTNER & PICCOLA
Harrisburg, PA........................Business Law; Civil Trial Practice; Labor and Employment Law; Probate, Trusts and Estate Planning; Real Estate Law

BOTTI, MARINACCIO & DELONGIS, LTD.
Oak Brook, IL..........................Civil Trial Practice; Commercial Litigation; Criminal Trial Practice; Family Law

BOTTS, R. DAVID
Atlanta, GA ....Criminal Trial Practice

BOTTUM & FELITON, A PROFESSIONAL CORPORATION
Los Angeles, CA......................Appellate Practice; Civil Trial Practice; Construction Law; Environmental Law; Insurance Defense; Labor and Employment Law; Medical Malpractice; Personal Injury; Transportation Law

BOUCHARD & MALLORY, P.A.
Manchester, NH......................Insurance Defense

BOUDREAU, PHILIP M.
Hyannis, MA...........................Probate, Trusts and Estate Planning

BOUDREAU & TRENTACOSTA, A PROFESSIONAL LAW CORPORATION
San Diego, CA ....Medical Malpractice; Personal Injury; Product Liability Law

BOUGHEY, GARVIE & BUSHNER
San Francisco, CA ....Admiralty/Maritime Law; Insurance Defense

BOUHAN, WILLIAMS & LEVY LLP
Savannah, GA ....General Practice

BOULT, CUMMINGS, CONNERS & BERRY, PLC
Nashville, TN ....General Practice

BOURGEOIS, DRESSER & WHITE
Worcester, MA........................Commercial Litigation

BOURNE, NOLL & KENYON, A PROFESSIONAL CORPORATION
Summit, NJ ....Banking Law; Commercial Law; General Practice; Probate, Trusts and Estate Planning; Real Estate Law; Tax Law

BOVIS, KYLE & BURCH
Atlanta, GA ....Business Law; Civil Trial Practice; Construction Law; Environmental Law; Insurance Defense

BOWEN, BRASSEY, GARDNER, WETHERELL & CRAWFORD
Boise, ID..................................Insurance Defense

BOWEN RILEY WARNOCK & JACOBSON, PLC
Nashville, TN ....Civil Trial Practice; Commercial Litigation; Patent, Trademark, Copyright and Unfair Competition; Trademark, Copyright and Unfair Competition

BOWEN & SIEGEL
Northampton, MA...................Real Estate Law

BOWERS, HARRISON, KENT & MILLER, LLP
Evansville, IN...........................Appellate Practice; Banking Law; Bankruptcy Law; Business Law; Civil Trial Practice; Commercial Law; General Practice; Labor and Employment Law; Land Use Law; Real Estate Law

BOWERS ORR & DOUGALL, L.L.P.
Columbia, SC ....Civil Trial Practice; Construction Law; Environmental Law; Insurance Defense; Product Liability Law

BOWLES RICE MCDAVID GRAFF & LOVE
Charleston, WV ....Civil Trial Practice; General Practice
Fairmont, WV ....Civil Trial Practice; General Practice
Martinsburg, WV ....Civil Trial Practice; General Practice
Morgantown, WV ....Civil Trial Practice; General Practice
Parkersburg, WV ....Civil Trial Practice; General Practice

BOWLING, BOWLING & ASSOCIATES
Memphis, TN ....Labor and Employment Law

BOWMAN, ANDREW B.
Westport, CT...........................Appellate Practice; Constitutional Law; Criminal Trial Practice

BOWMAN, ALAN DEXTER, P.A.
Newark, NJ ....Civil Trial Practice; Criminal Trial Practice

BOWMAN AND BROOKE
Minneapolis, MN ....Civil Trial Practice; Product Liability Law

BOWMAN, GEORGE, SCHEB, TOALE & MARSHALL, P.A.
Sarasota, FL ....General Practice; Probate, Trusts and Estate Planning

BOWMER, COURTNEY, BURLESON, NORMAND & MOORE
Temple, TX ....General Practice

BOXER, SANDOR T.
Los Angeles, CA ....Commercial Law

BOYAJIAN, HARRINGTON & RICHARDSON
Providence, RI.........................Bankruptcy Law; General Practice

BOYCE & BOYCE, A PROFESSIONAL ASSOCIATION
Newport, AR ....General Practice

BOYCE LAW FIRM
Newport, AR ....General Practice; Personal Injury

BOYCE, MURPHY, MCDOWELL & GREENFIELD
Sioux Falls, SD........................General Practice

BOYD & BOYD, P.C.
Hyannis, MA...........................Probate, Trusts and Estate Planning
Norfolk, VA ....General Practice

BOYD, PHILLIP LARRY, P.C.
Rogersville, TN ....Civil Trial Practice

BOYER, REYNOLDS & DEMARCO, LTD.
Providence, RI.........................Civil Trial Practice; Insurance Defense

BOYER, TANZLER & BOYER
Jacksonville, FL ....Civil Trial Practice

BOYER, WAYNE J., P.A.
Clearwater, FL ....Family Law

BOYES & FARINA, PROFESSIONAL ASSOCIATION
West Palm Beach, FL ....Probate, Trusts and Estate Planning

BOYLE & ANDERSON, P.C.
Auburn, NY ....General Practice; Immigration and Naturalization; Probate, Trusts and Estate Planning

BOYLE, CARTER & GAINES
Wilmington, NC......................Personal Injury

BOYLE, CHARLES A., & ASSOCIATES, LTD.
Chicago, IL..............................Personal Injury; Product Liability Law

BOYLE, CORDES & BROWN
De Kalb, IL ....General Practice

BOYLE, GOLDSMITH & BOLIN
Hennepin, IL............................General Practice

BRACEWELL & PATTERSON, L.L.P.
Houston, TX ....General Practice

BRACH, EICHLER, ROSENBERG, SILVER, BERNSTEIN, HAMMER & GLADSTONE, A PROFESSIONAL CORPORATION
Roseland, NJ............................Banking Law; Business Law; Civil Trial Practice; Commercial Litigation; Construction Law; General Practice; Health Care Law; Insurance Defense; Personal Injury; Real Estate Law; Tax Law

BRACKEN, CLYDE
Dallas, TX...............................Insurance Defense

BRACKEN & MARGOLIN
Islandia, NY ....Business Law; Civil Trial Practice; General Practice

BRADEN & OLSON
Lake Geneva, WI ....Civil Trial Practice; Personal Injury; Probate, Trusts and Estate Planning; Real Estate Law

BRADFORD, MICHAEL E.
Phoenix, AZ ....Insurance Defense; Medical Malpractice; Personal Injury

BRADFORD, PETER C.
Newport Beach, CA.................Probate, Trusts and Estate Planning

BRADFORD, COENEN & WELSH
Omaha, NE ....Civil Trial Practice; General Practice

BRADLEY, ARANT, ROSE & WHITE
Birmingham, AL ....Antitrust Law; Appellate Practice; Banking Law; Bankruptcy Law; Business Law; Civil Rights; Civil Trial Practice; Commercial Law; Communications Law; Computer Law; Construction Law; Employment Benefits Law; Environmental Law; Family Law; General Practice; Health Care Law; Immigration and Naturalization; Insurance Defense; International Business Law; Labor and Employment Law; Land Use Law; Municipal Bond/Public Authority Financing; Municipal and Zoning Law; Natural Resources Law; Patent, Trademark, Copyright and Unfair Competition; Personal Injury; Probate, Trusts and Estate Planning; Product Liability Law; Public Utilities Law; Real Estate Law; Securities Law; Tax Law; Trademark, Copyright and Unfair Competition; Transportation Law; Workers Compensation
Huntsville, AL.........................Civil Trial Practice; Communications Law; Environmental Law; General Practice; Insurance Defense; Labor and Employment Law; Personal Injury; Probate, Trusts and Estate Planning; Real Estate Law; Tax Law

BRADLEY & BRADLEY
Chicago, IL..............................Personal Injury; Probate, Trusts and Estate Planning; Workers Compensation

BRADLEY, CAMPBELL, CARNEY & MADSEN, PROFESSIONAL CORPORATION
Golden, CO ....Civil Trial Practice; General Practice; Labor and Employment Law; Real Estate Law

BRADLEY & MCCULLOCH, P.A.
Albuquerque, NM....................Insurance Defense

BRADSHAW, JOHN G., A PROFESSIONAL LAW CORPORATION
Santa Ana, CA ....Business Law; Probate, Trusts and Estate Planning

BRADSHAW, STEELE, COCHRANE & BERENS, L.C.
Cape Girardeau, MO ....General Practice

BRADY, BROOKS & O'CONNELL, LLP
Salamanca, NY........................Commercial Litigation; Personal Injury; Probate, Trusts and Estate Planning

BRADY HATHAWAY, PROFESSIONAL CORPORATION
Detroit, MI..............................Administrative Law; Admiralty/Maritime Law; Civil Trial Practice; General Practice; Immigration and Naturalization; Labor and Employment Law; Real Estate Law; Workers Compensation

BRAFMAN GILBERT & ROSS, P.C.
New York, NY.........................Criminal Trial Practice

BRAGG & BAKER, P.C.
Denver, CO ....Personal Injury

BRAMAN BARBACKI MOREAU, S.E.N.C.
Montreal, QU, Canada ....Business Law; Civil Trial Practice; Commercial Law; International Business Law; Tax Law

BRAMBLETT & PRATT
Camden, AR ....General Practice

BRAND & ALLEN
Greenfield, IN ....Bankruptcy Law; Criminal Trial Practice; Personal Injury

BRAND FARRAR DZIUBLA FREILICH & KOLSTAD, LLP
Los Angeles, CA ....International Business Law; International Trade Law; Land Use Law; Real Estate Law; Tax Law

BRANDON & SCHMIDT
Carbondale, IL ....Insurance Defense; Medical Malpractice

BRANDT AND BEESON, P.C.
Johnson City, TN.....................Business Law; Probate, Trusts and Estate Planning; Real Estate Law

BRANDT, HAUGHEY, PENBERTHY, LEWIS & HYLAND, P.A.
Moorestown, NJ.......................Banking Law; Civil Trial Practice; Environmental Law; Land Use Law; Personal Injury; Probate, Trusts and Estate Planning; Real Estate Law

BRANDT, LARRY C., P.A.
Walhalla, SC...........................Appellate Practice; Civil Trial Practice; General Practice; Medical Malpractice; Personal Injury; Product Liability Law

BRANDT, MILNES, REA & WISE
Pittsburgh, PA ....Business Law; Civil Trial Practice; Medical Malpractice

BRANHAM & DAY, P.C.
Nashville, TN..........................Civil Trial Practice; Personal Injury

BRANN & ISAACSON
Lewiston, ME..........................General Practice; Tax Law

BRANNEN, SEARCY & SMITH
Savannah, GA ....Civil Trial Practice; General Practice; Insurance Defense

BRANNEY, HILLYARD AND BARNHART, L.L.P.
Englewood, CO ....Personal Injury

BRANNON, BROWN, HALEY, ROBINSON & BULLOCK, P.A.
Lake City, FL...........................General Practice

BRANSON, FITZGERALD & HOWARD, A PROFESSIONAL CORPORATION
Redwood City, CA ....Insurance Defense

BRANSON, FRANK L., P.C., LAW OFFICES OF
Dallas, TX...............................Business Law; Civil Trial Practice; Medical Malpractice; Personal Injury

BRANTLEY & WILKERSON, P.C.
Montgomery, AL ....Communications Law; Health Care Law; Insurance Defense; Public Utilities Law

BRANTON & HALL, P.C.
San Antonio, TX.....................Aviation Law; Personal Injury; Product Liability Law

BRASCH & TAYLOR, L.L.P.
Harlingen, TX ....Family Law; Probate, Trusts and Estate Planning

BRASHEAR & GINN
Omaha, NE ....Bankruptcy Law; Business Law; Civil Trial Practice; Commercial Law; General Practice

BRASSEL & BALDWIN, P.A.
Annapolis, MD ....Civil Trial Practice

BRATTAIN & MINNIX
Indianapolis, IN ....Civil Trial Practice; General Practice

BRAUDE & MARGULIES, P.C.
Washington, DC......................Administrative Law; Civil Trial Practice; Construction Law

BRAULT, GRAHAM, SCOTT & BRAULT
Rockville, MD.........................Business Law; Civil Trial Practice; Commercial Law; General Practice; Insurance Defense; Medical Malpractice; Personal Injury; Product Liability Law

BRAULT, PALMER, GROVE, ZIMMERMAN, WHITE & MIMS
Fairfax, VA ....Civil Trial Practice; General Practice; Insurance Defense; Product Liability Law; Workers Compensation

BRAUN, RICHARD J. & ASSOCIATES
Nashville, TN..........................Antitrust Law; Criminal Trial Practice

BRAUN KENDRICK FINKBEINER, PLC
Ann Arbor, MI ....Banking Law; Commercial Law; Environmental Law; General Practice; Insurance Defense; Labor and Employment Law; Natural Resources Law; Personal Injury; Probate, Trusts and Estate Planning; Real Estate Law; Tax Law; Workers Compensation
Bay City, MI ....Banking Law; Bankruptcy Law; Environmental Law; General Practice; Labor and Employment Law; Natural Resources Law; Real Estate Law; Tax Law
Saginaw, MI ....Banking Law; Bankruptcy Law; Commercial Law; Environmental Law; General Practice; Insurance Defense; Labor and Employment Law; Natural Resources Law; Personal Injury; Probate, Trusts and Estate Planning; Real Estate Law; Tax Law; Workers Compensation

BRAUNLICH, RUSSOW & BRAUNLICH, A PROFESSIONAL CORPORATION
Monroe, MI ....Environmental Law; Insurance Defense; Labor and Employment Law; Municipal and Zoning Law; Personal Injury; Probate, Trusts and Estate Planning

BRAUNSTEIN & TODISCO, LLC
Fairfield, CT...........................Probate, Trusts and Estate Planning; Tax Law

BRAUWERMAN & ASSOCIATES, P.A.
Miami, FL ....Immigration and Naturalization

BRAY, GEIGER, RUDQUIST & NUSS
Stockton, CA...........................General Practice

BREAZEALE, SACHSE & WILSON, L.L.P.
Baton Rouge, LA ....Antitrust Law; Civil Trial Practice; General Practice; Labor and Employment Law; Municipal Bond/Public Authority Financing; Natural Resources Law

---

New Orleans, LA ....General Practice

BREEDEN, MACMILLAN & GREEN, P.L.C.
Norfolk, VA ....Civil Trial Practice; General Practice

BREGA & WINTERS, P.C.
Denver, CO ....Civil Trial Practice; Criminal Trial Practice; General Practice; Securities Law
Greeley, CO.............................Business Law; Civil Trial Practice; Probate, Trusts and Estate Planning; Real Estate Law

BREGEL, KERR, DAVIS & DANTES
Towson, MD ....Family Law

BREMER, WADE, NELSON, LOHR & COREY, LLP
Grand Rapids, MI ....Civil Trial Practice; Insurance Defense; Medical Malpractice; Personal Injury; Product Liability Law

BREMYER & WISE, P.A.
McPherson, KS ....General Practice

BRENMAN KEY & BROMBERG, P.C.
Denver, CO ....Business Law; Civil Trial Practice; Commercial Litigation; Mergers and Acquisitions; Real Estate Law; Securities Law; Tax Law

BRENNAN & COLLINS
Milwaukee, WI ....Insurance Defense

BRENNAN, HAYSKAR, JEFFERSON, WALKER & SCHWERER, PROFESSIONAL ASSOCIATION
Fort Pierce, FL........................Civil Trial Practice; General Practice

BRENNAN, ROBINS & DALEY, P.C.
Pittsburgh, PA ....Civil Trial Practice; Probate, Trusts and Estate Planning; Real Estate Law

BRENNAN, STEIL, BASTING & MACDOUGALL, S.C.
Janesville, WI ....General Practice

BRENNER, DOHNAL, EVANS & YOFFY, P.C.
Richmond, VA ....Commercial Litigation

BREON, O'DONNELL, MILLER, BROWN & DANNIS
San Francisco, CA ....Construction Law; Labor and Employment Law

BRESLIN AND BRESLIN, P.A.
Hackensack, NJ.......................Civil Trial Practice; Criminal Trial Practice; General Practice; Medical Malpractice; Personal Injury; Real Estate Law

BRESLOW & WALKER, LLP
New York, NY.........................Business Law; Securities Law

BREW, RICHARD DOUGLAS, A PROFESSIONAL LAW CORPORATION
Modesto, CA...........................Business Law; International Business Law; Trademark, Copyright and Unfair Competition

BREWER, R. KENT
Walnut Creek, CA ....Family Law

BREWER, CHARLES M., LTD.
Phoenix, AZ ....Civil Trial Practice; Personal Injury

BREWER & PRITCHARD, P.C.
Houston, TX ....Construction Law; Insurance Defense; Securities Law

BREWER, WORTEN, ROBINETT
Bartlesville, OK......................Civil Trial Practice; General Practice
Pawhuska, OK ....General Practice

BREWSTER, MORHOUS & CAMERON
Bluefield, WV ....General Practice

BREWSTER, SHALLCROSS AND DEANGELIS
Tulsa, OK................................Medical Malpractice

BRICE LEGAL GROUP, THE, P.C.
Dallas, TX...............................Civil Trial Practice

BRICKER & ECKLER
Columbus, OH ....Banking Law; Civil Trial Practice; Commercial Law; Environmental Law; General Practice; Labor and Employment Law; Municipal Bond/Public Authority Financing; Real Estate Law; Tax Law

BRICKFIELD, BURCHETTE & RITTS, P.C.
Washington, DC......................Administrative Law; Energy Law; Natural Resources Law; Public Utilities Law

BRICKLEMYER SMOLKER & BOLVES, P.A.
Tampa, FL ....Land Use Law; Real Estate Law

BRIDGERS, GILL & HOLMAN
Pensacola, FL..........................Insurance Defense; Product Liability Law; Workers Compensation

BRIDGES, TERRY LAW OFFICES OF
Riverside, CA ....Civil Trial Practice

BRIDGES, YOUNG, MATTHEWS & DRAKE PLC
Pine Bluff, AR..........................General Practice

BRIDGFORTH & BUNTIN
Southaven, MS ....General Practice; Real Estate Law

BRIERLY LAW OFFICE
Newton, IA ....General Practice

BRIERTON & JONES
San Diego, CA ....Probate, Trusts and Estate Planning

BRIGDEN & PETAJAN, S.C.
Milwaukee, WI ....Labor and Employment Law

BRIGHT, J. CONVERSE
Valdosta, GA ....Criminal Trial Practice; Personal Injury

BRIGHT AND BROWN
Glendale, CA..........................Business Law; Environmental Law

BRIGHT & LORIG, A PROFESSIONAL CORPORATION
Los Angeles, CA ....Antitrust Law; Patent, Trademark, Copyright and
Unfair Competition

BRILL, MOORE & WAGONER, P.C.
West Plains, MO ....General Practice

BRINKER, DOYEN & KOVACS, P.C.
St. Louis, MO..........................Insurance Defense

BRINKLEY, MCNERNEY, MORGAN, SOLOMON & TATUM, LLP
Fort Lauderdale, FL...............General Practice; Real Estate Law

BRINKS HOFER GILSON & LIONE, A PROFESSIONAL CORPORATION
Chicago, IL..............................General Practice

BRINK, SOBOLIK, SEVERSON, MALM & ALBRECHT, P.A.
Hallock, MN ....Civil Trial Practice; General Practice; Personal
Injury

BRINSON, ASKEW, BERRY, SEIGLER, RICHARDSON & DAVIS
Rome, GA ....Business Law; Civil Rights; Civil Trial Practice;
General Practice; Insurance Defense; Product
Liability Law

BRIONES LAW FIRM, A PROFESSIONAL ASSOCIATION
Farmington, NM....................General Practice

BRISCOE, JACK C. & ASSOCIATES
Philadelphia, PA ....Business Law; Civil Trial Practice; Probate, Trusts
and Estate Planning; Real Estate Law

BRISKMAN & BINION, P.C.
Mobile, AL...............................Civil Trial Practice; Criminal Trial Practice; Family
Law; Insurance Defense; Personal Injury

BRITT, HANKINS, SCHAIBLE & MOUGHAN
Philadelphia, PA ....Insurance Defense

BRITTAIN SLEDZ MORRIS & SLOVAK, A PROFESSIONAL CORPORATION
Chicago, IL..............................Employment Benefits Law; Labor and Employment
Law

BRITTON AND ADCOCK
Oklahoma City, OK................Banking Law; Business Law; Civil Trial Practice

BROAD AND CASSEL
Boca Raton, FL ....General Practice
Fort Lauderdale, FL...............General Practice
Miami, FL ....General Practice
Orlando, FL ....General Practice
Stuart, FL ....General Practice
Tallahassee, FL ....General Practice
Tampa, FL ....General Practice
West Palm Beach, FL ....General Practice

BROBECK, PHLEGER & HARRISON LLP
Los Angeles, CA ....General Practice
Newport Beach, CA................General Practice
Palo Alto, CA ....General Practice
San Diego, CA ....General Practice
San Francisco, CA ....General Practice
New York, NY.........................General Practice

BROCATO & BROCATO, L.L.P.
Beaumont, TX.........................Civil Trial Practice

BROCK, BROCK & BAGBY
Lexington, KY ....Civil Trial Practice; Family Law; General Practice;
Probate, Trusts and Estate Planning

BROCKINTON, BROCKINTON & KERR, P.A.
Charleston, SC ....General Practice

BROCK & PERSON, A PROFESSIONAL CORPORATION
San Antonio, TX.....................Insurance Defense; Personal Injury; Product
Liability Law; Workers Compensation

BRODERICK, NEWMARK & GRATHER, A PROFESSIONAL CORPORATION
Morristown, NJ......................Family Law; Labor and Employment Law; Land
Use Law

BRODERICK, THORNTON & PIERCE
Bowling Green, KY ....General Practice; Insurance Defense

BRODER, SHERRY P., A LAW CORPORATION, LAW OFFICE OF
Honolulu, HI ....Civil Trial Practice

BRODIE & PAWLUC
Stuart, FL ....Probate, Trusts and Estate Planning

BRODY AND OBER, P.C.
Southport, CT ....Business Law; Civil Trial Practice; Employment
Benefits Law; Probate, Trusts and Estate Planning;
Real Estate Law; Tax Law

BROENING, OBERG, WOODS, WILSON & CASS, P.C.
Phoenix, AZ ....Insurance Defense; Real Estate Law

BROGAN & STAFFORD, P.C.
Norfolk, NE ....General Practice

BROKER & O'KEEFE, PROFESSIONAL CORPORATION
Newport Beach, CA................Bankruptcy Law; Commercial Litigation

BROMBERG, ROBERT S.
Cincinnati, OH ....Tax Law

BROMBERG, ROSENTHAL & SIEGEL
Rockville, MD..........................General Practice

BROMBERG & SUNSTEIN
Boston, MA.............................Business Law; Civil Trial Practice; Patent,
Trademark, Copyright and Unfair Competition

BRONFIN & HELLER, L.L.C.
New Orleans, LA ....Bankruptcy Law

BRONSON, BRONSON & MCKINNON LLP
Los Angeles, CA ....Civil Trial Practice; General Practice
San Francisco, CA ....General Practice; Labor and Employment Law

BRONSTEIN, VAN VEEN & BRONSTEIN, P.C.
New York, NY.........................Family Law

BRONSTON, EDYTHE L. LAW OFFICES OF
Los Angeles, CA ....Bankruptcy Law

BROOCKS, BAKER & LANGE, L.L.P.
Houston, TX ....Appellate Practice; Bankruptcy Law; Civil Trial
Practice; Criminal Trial Practice; Personal Injury

BROOKES, LAWRENCE V.
San Francisco, CA ....Tax Law

BROOK, PIZZA & VAN LOON, L.L.P.
New Orleans, LA ....Business Law; Health Care Law; Natural Resources
Law

BROOKS, GARY L. AND ASSOCIATES
Oklahoma City, OK................Civil Trial Practice; Medical Malpractice; Personal
Injury; Product Liability Law

BROOKS & DISTLER
New York, NY.........................Sports and Entertainment Law

BROOKS, HENLEY & DRELL, P.C.
Casper, WY ....Civil Trial Practice; General Practice

BROOKS & KUSHMAN, P.C.
Southfield, MI ....Trademark, Copyright and Unfair Competition

BROOKS, MULCAHY, SANBORN & WILLIAMS
Springfield, MA.......................Insurance Defense

BROOKS, PIERCE, MCLENDON, HUMPHREY & LEONARD, L.L.P.
Greensboro, NC ....Civil Trial Practice; General Practice

BROOTEN, KENNETH E., JR., CHARTERED
Winter Park, FL......................Civil Trial Practice; Health Care Law; International
Trade Law

BROPHY, MILLS, SCHMOR, GERKING & BROPHY
Medford, OR...........................General Practice

BROSNAHAN, JOSEPH & SUGGS, P.A.
Minneapolis, MN ....Personal Injury

BROUDY & JACOBSON
New York, NY.........................General Practice

BROUJOS, GILROY & HOUSTON, P.C.
Carlisle, PA ....General Practice

BROUSSARD, DAVID & DAIGLE, A PROFESSIONAL LAW CORPORATION
Lafayette, LA ....Personal Injury

BROWDER & KENNEY, P.C.
Phoenix, AZ ....Insurance Defense

BROWDY AND NEIMARK
Washington, DC.....................Patent, Trademark, Copyright and Unfair Competition

BROWN, DOUGLAS C.
San Diego, CA ....Criminal Trial Practice

BROWN, KENT MASTERSON LAW OFFICES OF
Danville, KY..........................Appellate Practice; Civil Trial Practice

BROWN, THOMAS P. III
Bethesda, MD ....General Practice

BROWN AND AMODIO, A LEGAL PROFESSIONAL ASSOCIATION
Medina, OH ....General Practice

BROWN & BAIN
Palo Alto, CA ....General Practice; Patent, Trademark, Copyright and Unfair Competition
Phoenix, AZ ....Antitrust Law; Appellate Practice; Banking Law; Civil Trial Practice; Commercial Law; Communications Law; Environmental Law; General Practice; Labor and Employment Law; Patent, Trademark, Copyright and Unfair Competition; Product Liability Law; Public Utilities Law; Real Estate Law
Tucson, AZ ....General Practice

BROWN, BEMILLER, MURRAY & MCINTYRE
Mansfield, OH.........................General Practice; Insurance Defense

BROWN AND BROWN
St. Ignace, MI ....General Practice

BROWN & BROWN, P.C.
Newark, NJ ....Appellate Practice; Civil Trial Practice; Criminal Trial Practice; General Practice; Medical Malpractice; Personal Injury

BROWN, BROWN & BROWN, A PROFESSIONAL ASSOCIATION
Bel Air, MD ....Civil Trial Practice; Criminal Trial Practice; Family Law; Personal Injury; Probate, Trusts and Estate Planning; Real Estate Law

BROWN, BROWN, BROWN AND STOKES, L.L.P.
Albemarle, NC ....General Practice

BROWN CLARK & WALTERS, P.A.
Sarasota, FL ....Commercial Litigation; Construction Law

BROWN & CONNERY
Camden, NJ.............................Admiralty/Maritime Law; Civil Trial Practice; General Practice; Insurance Defense
Westmont, NJ ....Admiralty/Maritime Law; Civil Trial Practice; General Practice; Insurance Defense

BROWN, CRAIG M., INC.
San Jose, CA ....Appellate Practice; Business Law; Civil Trial Practice; Criminal Trial Practice

BROWN, CUMMINS & BROWN CO., L.P.A.
Cincinnati, OH ....Business Law; Civil Trial Practice; Health Care Law; Labor and Employment Law; Securities Law

BROWN, DOUGLAS & BROWN
St. Joseph, MO........................General Practice

BROWN, DREW, MASSEY & SULLIVAN
Casper, WY ....Administrative Law; Appellate Practice; Banking Law; Bankruptcy Law; Business Law; Civil Trial Practice; Commercial Law; Construction Law; Environmental Law; Family Law; General Practice; Insurance Defense; Labor and Employment Law; Natural Resources Law; Probate, Trusts and Estate Planning; Public Utilities Law; Real Estate Law; Tax Law

BROWN & GAVIN
Belleville, IL ....Admiralty/Maritime Law; Commercial Law; Commercial Litigation; Environmental Law

BROWN, GERBASE, CEBULL, FULTON, HARMAN & ROSS, P.C.
Billings, MT ....Environmental Law; General Practice; Insurance Defense; Labor and Employment Law; Medical Malpractice; Probate, Trusts and Estate Planning; Product Liability Law; Tax Law

BROWN & GREEN, P.A.
Orlando, FL ....Labor and Employment Law

BROWN, HARMON & ECKSTEIN, P.C.
Denver, CO ....Civil Trial Practice; Real Estate Law; Securities Law

BROWN, HAY & STEPHENS
Springfield, IL ....Business Law; General Practice

BROWN, HUDGENS, P.C.
Mobile, AL..............................Medical Malpractice; Product Liability Law

BROWN, JACOBSON, TILLINGHAST, LAHAN & KING, P.C.
Norwich, CT ....General Practice; Insurance Defense

BROWN, JEFFERIES AND BOULWARE
Barnwell, SC...........................General Practice

BROWN & KAROSEN
Bloomfield, NJ ....Probate, Trusts and Estate Planning

BROWN, KELLEHER, ZWICKEL & WILHELM
Windham, NY ....Civil Trial Practice; Patent, Trademark, Copyright and Unfair Competition; Real Estate Law

BROWN & KELLY, L.L.P.
Buffalo, NY ....Civil Trial Practice; Construction Law; General Practice; Insurance Defense; Probate, Trusts and Estate Planning

BROWN, KINSEY & FUNKHOUSER
Mason City, IA ....General Practice

BROWN & LIVINGSTON, P.C.
Statesboro, GA.........................Insurance Defense

BROWN, MALCOLM H., P.C.
Bismarck, ND ....Commercial Litigation

BROWN, MARTIN, HALLER & MCCLAIN
San Diego, CA ....Patent, Trademark, Copyright and Unfair Competition; Trademark, Copyright and Unfair Competition

BROWN, MCDONNELL & ROMAKER, A PROFESSIONAL LAW CORPORATION
San Diego, CA ....Admiralty/Maritime Law; Civil Trial Practice; Commercial Litigation; Real Estate Law

BROWN, PAINDIRIS & ZARELLA, LLP
Hartford, CT ....Criminal Trial Practice; General Practice

BROWN, PISTONE, HURLEY & VAN VLEAR, A PROFESSIONAL CORPORATION
Irvine, CA...............................Construction Law; Environmental Law; International Business Law; Natural Resources Law

BROWN RAYSMAN MILLSTEIN FELDER & STEINER LLP
New York, NY.........................Civil Trial Practice; General Practice

BROWN, ROSETA, LONG, MCCONVILLE, KILCULLEN & CARLSON
Eugene, OR ....Insurance Defense

BROWN, SCHLAGETER, CRAIG & SHINDLER
Toledo, OH ....General Practice

BROWN, SIMS, WISE & WHITE, A PROFESSIONAL CORPORATION
Houston, TX ....Admiralty/Maritime Law; Insurance Defense

BROWN & STADFELD
Boston, MA.............................Antitrust Law; General Practice

BROWN, TERRELL, HOGAN, ELLIS, MCCLAMMA & YEGELWEL, P.A.
Jacksonville, FL ....Medical Malpractice; Personal Injury

BROWN THOMPSON PRUITT & PETERSON, P.C. A PROFESSIONAL CORPORATION
Fort Worth, TX ....Insurance Defense; Probate, Trusts and Estate Planning; Real Estate Law

BROWN & VAN LEUVEN, P.A.
Orlando, FL ....Business Law; Construction Law

BROWN, WARD & HAYNES, P.A.
Waynesville, NC.......................General Practice

BROWN, WATT & BUCHANAN, P.A.
Biloxi, MS...............................Environmental Law; Product Liability Law; Transportation Law
Pascagoula, MS........................Environmental Law; Product Liability Law; Transportation Law

BROWN, WINFIELD & CANZONERI, INCORPORATED
Los Angeles, CA.......................General Practice

BROWN, WINICK, GRAVES, GROSS, BASKERVILLE, SCHOENEBAUM AND WALKER, P.L.C.
Des Moines, IA........................General Practice

BROWN & WOOD LLP
Washington, DC.......................General Practice
New York, NY.........................General Practice

BROWNFIELD, C. WILLIAM & ASSOCIATES
Columbus, OH ....Commercial Litigation

BROWNING BUSHMAN, A PROFESSIONAL CORPORATION
Houston, TX ....Patent, Trademark, Copyright and Unfair Competition

BROWNMARTIN, P.C.
Chicago, IL..............................Environmental Law

BROWNSTEIN HYATT FARBER & STRICKLAND, P.C.
Denver, CO ....Administrative Law; Business Law; Civil Trial Practice; Environmental Law; General Practice; Land Use Law; Municipal Bond/Public Authority Financing; Real Estate Law; Securities Law; Tax Law

BRUCKER, ALEX M., A LAW CORPORATION
Los Angeles, CA ....Employment Benefits Law

BRUCKNER & SYKES, L.L.P.
Houston, TX ....Labor and Employment Law

BRUDER, GENTILE & MARCOUX, L.L.P.
Washington, DC......................Administrative Law; Energy Law; Public Utilities Law

BRUINOOGE & ASSOCIATES
Rutherford, NJ.......................Land Use Law; Real Estate Law

BRUMBAUGH, GRAVES, DONOHUE & RAYMOND
New York, NY........................Patent, Trademark, Copyright and Unfair Competition; Trademark, Copyright and Unfair Competition

BRUNN & FLYNN, A PROFESSIONAL CORPORATION
Modesto, CA ....Civil Trial Practice; Insurance Defense; Probate, Trusts and Estate Planning; Real Estate Law

BRUNO, FREDERIC & ASSOCIATES
Minneapolis, MN....................Criminal Trial Practice

BRYAN CAVE LLP
St. Louis, MO...........................General Practice

BRYAN, NELSON, RANDOLPH AND WEATHERS, P.A.
Hattiesburg, MS......................Environmental Law; Insurance Defense; Medical Malpractice; Product Liability Law

BRYAN, NELSON, SCHROEDER, CASTIGLIOLA & BANAHAN
Pascagoula, MS ....Civil Trial Practice

BRYANT AND HIGBY, CHARTERED
Panama City, FL......................General Practice

BRYANT LAW OFFICES
Wilmington, OH......................General Practice

BRYANT, LOVLIEN & JARVIS
Bend, OR..................................General Practice

BRYCE, WILLIAM D.
Georgetown, TX ....General Practice

BRYDGES, MAHAN & O'BRIEN
Virginia Beach, VA ....Civil Trial Practice; Criminal Trial Practice; Personal Injury

BRYDGES RISEBOROUGH PETERSON FRANKE AND MORRIS
Chicago, IL..............................Appellate Practice; Civil Trial Practice; Insurance Defense; Personal Injury; Product Liability Law

BRYDON, SWEARENGEN & ENGLAND, PROFESSIONAL CORPORATION
Jefferson City, MO..................General Practice

BUCCI & CHAMBERS, L.C.
Charleston, WV......................Medical Malpractice; Personal Injury; Product Liability Law

BUCHALTER, NEMER, FIELDS & YOUNGER, A PROFESSIONAL CORPORATION
Los Angeles, CA ....Bankruptcy Law; Civil Trial Practice; Commercial Law; General Practice; Insurance Defense; Labor and Employment Law; Real Estate Law; Tax Law
Newport Beach, CA ....Civil Trial Practice; General Practice
San Francisco, CA ....Civil Trial Practice; General Practice

BUCHANAN INGERSOLL
Princeton, NJ ....Business Law; Commercial Law; General Practice; Trademark, Copyright and Unfair Competition
Aventura, FL...........................Bankruptcy Law; Civil Trial Practice; Commercial Law; Construction Law; General Practice; Insurance Defense; Probate, Trusts and Estate Planning; Real Estate Law; Tax Law
Tampa, FL ....Civil Trial Practice; General Practice; Health Care Law
Lexington, KY ....Environmental Law; General Practice; Natural Resources Law
Buffalo, NY ....Environmental Law; General Practice; Natural Resources Law
Harrisburg, PA.........................Administrative Law; Business Law; Civil Trial Practice; Commercial Law; Environmental Law; General Practice; Health Care Law; Labor and Employment Law; Natural Resources Law; Probate, Trusts and Estate Planning; Real Estate Law; Tax Law
Philadelphia, PA ....Administrative Law; Antitrust Law; Banking Law; Bankruptcy Law; Business Law; Commercial Law; Construction Law; Criminal Trial Practice; Environmental Law; General Practice; Labor and Employment Law; Natural Resources Law; Real Estate Law; Tax Law
Pittsburgh, PA ....Administrative Law; Admiralty/Maritime Law; Antitrust Law; Banking Law; Bankruptcy Law; Business Law; Civil Trial Practice; Commercial Law; Communications Law; Construction Law; Employment Benefits Law; Environmental Law; Family Law; General Practice; Health Care Law; Insurance Defense; Labor and Employment Law; Municipal Bond/Public Authority Financing; Municipal and Zoning Law; Natural Resources Law; Patent, Trademark, Copyright and Unfair Competition; Personal Injury; Probate, Trusts and Estate Planning; Real Estate Law; Tax Law; Trademark, Copyright and Unfair Competition

BUCHANAN, SILVER & BECKERING, P.L.C.
Grand Rapids, MI ....Civil Trial Practice; Commercial Litigation; Medical Malpractice; Personal Injury; Product Liability Law

BUCK & GORDON
Seattle, WA ....Environmental Law; Municipal and Zoning Law; Real Estate Law

BUCKINGHAM, HOLZAPFEL, ZEIHER, WALDOCK & SCHELL CO., L.P.A.
Sandusky, OH ....General Practice

BUCKLEY FIRM, THE, P.C.
Mission Viejo, CA...................Bankruptcy Law; Civil Trial Practice; General Practice; Real Estate Law

BUCKLEY KING & BLUSO, A LEGAL PROFESSIONAL ASSOCIATION
Cleveland, OH.........................Civil Trial Practice

BUCKLEY, MILLER & WRIGHT
Wilmington, OH......................General Practice; Insurance Defense; Probate, Trusts and Estate Planning; Real Estate Law

BUCKLEY, NAGLE, GENTRY, BRION, MCGUIRE & MORRIS
West Chester, PA.....................Business Law; Family Law; General Practice; Municipal and Zoning Law; Personal Injury; Real Estate Law

BUCKNER, LARA & SWINDELL, L.L.P.
Amarillo, TX...........................Civil Trial Practice

BUECHNER, HAFFER, O'CONNELL, MEYERS & HEALEY CO., L.P.A.
Cincinnati, OH ....Family Law; Probate, Trusts and Estate Planning

BUEHLER & BUEHLER
Lake Oswego, OR ....Insurance Defense

BUESSER, BUESSER, BLACK, LYNCH, FRYHOFF & GRAHAM, P.C.
Bloomfield Hills, MI...............General Practice

BUFALINI, DAVID A., P.S., INC.
Tacoma, WA ....Personal Injury

BUGBEE & CONKLE
Toledo, OH ....Workers Compensation

BUGG & WOLF, P.A.
Durham, NC ....Civil Trial Practice; Construction Law

BUIST, MOORE, SMYTHE & MCGEE, P.A.
Charleston, SC ....Admiralty/Maritime Law; Bankruptcy Law; Civil Trial Practice; Commercial Law; Environmental Law; General Practice; Insurance Defense; Labor and Employment Law; Real Estate Law

BULLARD, KORSHOJ, SMITH & JERNSTEDT, A PROFESSIONAL CORPORATION
Portland, OR...........................Labor and Employment Law

BULLEN, MOILANEN, KLAASEN & SWAN, P.C.
Jackson, MI.............................General Practice; Insurance Defense

BULL, HOUSSER & TUPPER
Vancouver, BC, Canada...........General Practice

BULMAN, DUNIE, BURKE & FELD, CHARTERED
Bethesda, MD ....General Practice

BUMGARDNER, HARDIN & ELLIS, A PROFESSIONAL CORPORATION
Springfield, NJ ....Appellate Practice; Civil Trial Practice; Commercial Litigation; Construction Law; Environmental Law; Health Care Law; Insurance Defense; Medical Malpractice; Product Liability Law; Transportation Law

BUMP AND BUMP
Chadron, NE...........................General Practice

BUNCH & BROCK
Lexington, KY ....Bankruptcy Law

BUNDA STUTZ & DEWITT
Toledo, OH ....Appellate Practice; Civil Trial Practice; Insurance Defense; Product Liability Law

BUNGER & ROBERTSON
Bloomington, IN ....Banking Law; Business Law; Civil Trial Practice; General Practice; Health Care Law; Insurance Defense; Personal Injury; Probate, Trusts and Estate Planning; Real Estate Law

BUONAURO, ROBERT J., P.A.
Orlando, FL ....Criminal Trial Practice

BURBIDGE AND MITCHELL
Salt Lake City, UT.................Civil Trial Practice; Product Liability Law

BURCH & CRACCHIOLO, P.A.
Phoenix, AZ ....Appellate Practice; Bankruptcy Law; Civil Trial
Practice; Commercial Law; Criminal Trial Practice;
Environmental Law; Family Law; General Practice;
Insurance Defense; Medical Malpractice; Personal
Injury; Probate, Trusts and Estate Planning;
Product Liability Law; Real Estate Law; Tax Law

BURCH, PORTER & JOHNSON
Memphis, TN ....General Practice

BURCHFIELD, PARK & HEDDON, P.C.
Brighton, MI ....Business Law; Civil Trial Practice

BURD & NAYLOR
Santa Ana, CA ....Bankruptcy Law

BURESH, KAPLAN, JANG, FELLER & AUSTIN
Berkeley, CA ....Insurance Defense

BURG & ELDREDGE, P.C.
Denver, CO ....Civil Trial Practice; Commercial Law; Insurance
Defense

BURGER, WILLIAM KENNERLY
Murfreesboro, TN ....Civil Trial Practice

BURGESS, RYAN & WAYNE
New York, NY ....Patent, Trademark, Copyright and Unfair Competition

BURGETT & ROBBINS
Jamestown, NY ....Civil Trial Practice; Family Law; General Practice;
Personal Injury; Product Liability Law

BURGE & WETTERMARK, P.C.
Birmingham, AL ....Personal Injury; Transportation Law

BURKE, FREDERICK A.
Durham, NC ....Business Law

BURKE & BURKE, LTD.
Chicago, IL ....Medical Malpractice; Personal Injury; Product
Liability Law

BURKE HORAN & MACRI
New York, NY ....Labor and Employment Law

BURKE, MURPHY, COSTANZA & CUPPY
Merrillville, IN ....Bankruptcy Law; Civil Trial Practice; Commercial
Law; Environmental Law; General Practice;
Insurance Defense; Labor and Employment Law;
Land Use Law; Municipal and Zoning Law; Real
Estate Law

**BURKE, SAKAI, MCPHEETERS, BORDNER, IWANAGA & ESTES,
ATTORNEYS AT LAW, A LAW CORPORATION**
Honolulu, HI ....General Practice

BURKE, THOMAS M., P.C., LAW OFFICES
St. Louis, MO..........................Personal Injury

BURKERT & HART
Fort Myers, FL ....Personal Injury

BURKETT AND ROSS
Dimmitt, TX ....General Practice

BURK LAW FIRM, THE, A PROFESSIONAL CORPORATION
Austin, TX ....Civil Trial Practice; Commercial Litigation

BURMAN & MANNING
Chicago, IL..............................Tax Law

BURNETT, LOUIS J., P.C.
Birmingham, MI......................Business Law; Commercial Law; Real Estate Law

BURNHAM & KLINEFELTER, P.C.
Anniston, AL ....Civil Trial Practice; General Practice

**BURNS, AMMIRATO, PALUMBO, MILAM & BARONIAN, A PROFESSIONAL
LAW CORPORATION**
Long Beach, CA.......................Medical Malpractice
Pasadena, CA ....Appellate Practice; Civil Trial Practice; Construction
Law; Insurance Defense; Medical Malpractice;
Product Liability Law

BURNS, BRYANT, HINCHEY, COX & ROCKEFELLER, P.A.
Dover, NH ....Insurance Defense; Medical Malpractice; Personal
Injury

BURNS, CUNNINGHAM & MACKEY, P.C.
Mobile, AL...............................Civil Trial Practice; Personal Injury; Product
Liability Law

BURNS, DOANE, SWECKER & MATHIS, L.L.P.
Alexandria, VA ....Patent, Trademark, Copyright and Unfair Competition; Trademark, Copyright and Unfair Compe-
tition

BURNS & LEVINSON LLP
Boston, MA..............................Civil Trial Practice; General Practice; Tax Law;
Workers Compensation

BURNS, MCDONALD, BRADFORD, PATRICK & TINSLEY, L.L.P.
Greenwood, SC ....Civil Trial Practice; General Practice

BURNS WALL SMITH AND MUELLER, A PROFESSIONAL CORPORATION
Denver, CO ....Business Law; General Practice; Natural Resources
Law

BURNSIDE DEES JOHNSTON & CHOISSER
Vandalia, IL.............................Civil Trial Practice; General Practice; Workers
Compensation

BURNSIDE, WALL, DANIEL, ELLISON & REVELL
Augusta, GA ....Civil Trial Practice; General Practice; Personal
Injury

BURR & FORMAN
Birmingham, AL ....Antitrust Law; Banking Law; Business Law; Civil
Trial Practice; Communications Law; Environmental
Law; General Practice; Labor and Employment
Law; Municipal Bond/Public Authority Financing;
Probate, Trusts and Estate Planning; Real Estate
Law; Tax Law
Huntsville, AL..........................Banking Law; Business Law; Probate, Trusts and
Estate Planning; Real Estate Law

BURRIS, MACMILLAN, PEARCE & MAYER, L.L.P.
Charlotte, NC..........................Real Estate Law

BURROUGHS, HEPLER, BROOM, MACDONALD & HEBRANK
Edwardsville, IL.......................Civil Trial Practice; General Practice; Probate,
Trusts and Estate Planning; Product Liability Law

BURSON, I. JACKSON, JR., A PROFESSIONAL LAW CORPORATION
Eunice, LA ....Insurance Defense; Product Liability Law

BURSTEIN & FASS L.L.P.
New York, NY.........................Appellate Practice; Civil Trial Practice; Criminal
Trial Practice; Family Law

BURSTEIN, HERTOGS, OLSEN & MCFARLAND, P.A.
Minneapolis, MN ....General Practice

BURT, WARREN B. & ASSOCIATES
Wilmington, DE......................Construction Law; Environmental Law; Insurance
Defense; Medical Malpractice; Personal Injury;
Product Liability Law

BURT & ASSOCIATES, P.C.
Portland, OR...........................General Practice; Tax Law

BURT & PUCILLO
West Palm Beach, FL ....Antitrust Law; Commercial Law; Environmental
Law; Securities Law

BURTON, R. NICHOLAS
Decatur, IL..............................Probate, Trusts and Estate Planning; Tax Law

BURTON & NORRIS
Pasadena, CA ....Appellate Practice; Civil Rights; Civil Trial Practice;
Medical Malpractice; Personal Injury

BURTON & SUE, L.L.P.
Greensboro, NC.......................Civil Trial Practice; Insurance Defense; Personal
Injury

BUSCH, ROBERT G.
Lakewood, CO ....General Practice

BUSCH AND BUSCH
North Brunswick, NJ..............General Practice; Insurance Defense; Personal Injury

BUSCH & TALBOTT, L.C.
Elkins, WV ....Civil Trial Practice; General Practice

BUSCHMANN, CARR & SHANKS, PROFESSIONAL CORPORATION
Indianapolis, IN ....Bankruptcy Law; Civil Trial Practice; Commercial
Law; Labor and Employment Law; Workers
Compensation

BUSH CRADDOCK & RENEKER, L.L.P.
Dallas, TX...............................Civil Trial Practice; Personal Injury

BUSH, HAUDER & ADKERSON
Dallas, TX ....Insurance Defense

BUSSART, WEST, ROSSETTI, PIAIA & TYLER, P.C.
Rock Springs, WY ....Civil Trial Practice; General Practice

BUTHOD & BUTHOD
Evansville, IN..........................Business Law; Natural Resources Law

BUTLER, JACK A. LAW OFFICES OF
Nashville, TN............................Personal Injury

BUTLER & BINION, L.L.P.
Washington, DC......................General Practice
Dallas, TX.............................General Practice
Houston, TX..........................General Practice
San Antonio, TX....................General Practice

BUTLER, CINCIONE, DICUCCIO, DRITZ & BARNHART
Columbus, OH.......................Civil Trial Practice; Medical Malpractice; Personal Injury; Probate, Trusts and Estate Planning; Workers Compensation

BUTLER, HICKY & LONG
Forrest City, AR.....................Civil Trial Practice; General Practice; Insurance Defense; Probate, Trusts and Estate Planning

BUTLER, SNOW, O'MARA, STEVENS & CANNADA, PLLC
Jackson, MS...........................General Practice

BUTLER, VINES AND BABB, P.L.L.C.
Knoxville, TN........................Environmental Law; General Practice; Insurance Defense; Medical Malpractice; Personal Injury

BUTLER, WOOTEN, OVERBY, CHEELEY, PEARSON & FRYHOFER
Atlanta, GA...........................Civil Trial Practice; Medical Malpractice; Personal Injury; Product Liability Law
Columbus, GA.......................Civil Trial Practice; Medical Malpractice; Personal Injury; Product Liability Law

BUTT, THORNTON & BAEHR, P.C.
Albuquerque, NM...................Civil Trial Practice; General Practice

BUTTERMORE, MULLEN, JEREMIAH AND PHILLIPS
Westfield, NJ..........................General Practice; Probate, Trusts and Estate Planning

BUTTERWICK, BRIGHT & O'LAUGHLIN, INC., A PROFESSIONAL LAW CORPORATION
Riverside, CA.........................General Practice

BUTZ, LUCAS & DUNN, A PROFESSIONAL CORPORATION
San Diego, CA........................Civil Trial Practice

BUTZBAUGH & DEWANE, P.L.C.
St. Joseph, MI........................General Practice; Insurance Defense; Labor and Employment Law; Probate, Trusts and Estate Planning; Real Estate Law; Tax Law

BUTZEL LONG, A PROFESSIONAL CORPORATION
Birmingham, MI....................Family Law
Detroit, MI............................Administrative Law; Antitrust Law; Appellate Practice; Business Law; Civil Trial Practice; Commercial Law; Communications Law; Constitutional Law; Construction Law; Employment Benefits Law; Environmental Law; General Practice; Health Care Law; Immigration and Naturalization; International Trade Law; Labor and Employment Law; Mergers and Acquisitions; Municipal and Zoning Law; Product Liability Law; Real Estate Law; Securities Law; Trademark, Copyright and Unfair Competition

BUZARD, A. VINCENT LAW FIRM OF
Rochester, NY........................Civil Trial Practice; General Practice; Personal Injury

BUZZELL & PINKSTON
Macon, GA............................Medical Malpractice; Personal Injury

BYE BOYD AGNEW, LTD.
Duluth, MN...........................General Practice

BYELAS, LESLIE
Westport, CT.........................Civil Trial Practice; Family Law; Real Estate Law

BYERS, FRITZ
Toledo, OH...........................Appellate Practice; Civil Trial Practice; Communications Law; Labor and Employment Law

BYERS CASGRAIN
Montreal, QU, Canada............General Practice

BYNUM, ARLEN DEAN SPIDER, P.C., LAW OFFICES OF
Dallas, TX..............................Insurance Defense

BYRD, BYRD, ERVIN, WHISNANT, MCMAHON & ERVIN, P.A.
Morganton, NC......................General Practice

BYRD, DAVIS AND EISENBERG, L.L.P.
Austin, TX.............................Aviation Law; Personal Injury

BYRNE & BENESCH, P.C.
Yuma, AZ...............................Real Estate Law

BYRNE, JAMES B., JR., P.A.
Longwood, FL........................Civil Trial Practice

BYRON & ROBERTS
Owingsville, KY.....................Civil Trial Practice; Probate, Trusts and Estate Planning; Real Estate Law

BYSSHE, FREDERICK H. JR., LAW OFFICES OF
Ventura, CA...........................Business Law; Civil Trial Practice; Medical Malpractice; Personal Injury; Product Liability Law

CABANISS & BURKE, P.A.
Orlando, FL...........................Civil Trial Practice; Product Liability Law

CABANISS, JOHNSTON, GARDNER, DUMAS & O'NEAL
Birmingham, AL....................Admiralty/Maritime Law; Civil Trial Practice; General Practice
Mobile, AL............................Civil Trial Practice; General Practice

CACACE, TUSCH & SANTAGATA
Stamford, CT..........................Civil Trial Practice; Municipal and Zoning Law; Real Estate Law

CACCIATORE, RONALD K., P.A.
Tampa, FL.............................Criminal Trial Practice

CACHERIS & TREANOR
Washington, DC.....................Criminal Trial Practice
Alexandria, VA......................Criminal Trial Practice

CADES SCHUTTE FLEMING & WRIGHT
Honolulu, HI.........................Banking Law; Civil Trial Practice; General Practice; Patent, Trademark, Copyright and Unfair Competition; Probate, Trusts and Estate Planning; Real Estate Law
Kailua-Kona, HI.....................Civil Trial Practice; General Practice

CADWALADER, WICKERSHAM & TAFT
New York, NY........................General Practice

CAFFERY, OUBRE, DUGAS & CAMPBELL, L.L.P.
New Iberia, LA.......................Energy Law; Insurance Defense

CAGE, HILL & NIEHAUS, L.L.P.
Houston, TX..........................Bankruptcy Law; Civil Trial Practice; Probate, Trusts and Estate Planning; Real Estate Law

CAGNEY, WILLIAM P., III, P.A.
Miami, FL..............................Appellate Practice; Civil Trial Practice; Criminal Trial Practice

CAHALANE, VINCENT P., P.C.
Brockton, MA.........................Civil Trial Practice; Construction Law; Insurance Defense; Personal Injury; Product Liability Law

CAHILL GORDON & REINDEL
Washington, DC.....................General Practice
New York, NY........................General Practice; Municipal Bond/Public Authority Financing
Paris, France..........................General Practice

CAHILL LAW OFFICES
Nevada, IA............................General Practice

CAHILL & MARQUART, P.A.
Moorhead, MN.......................General Practice
Fargo, ND..............................General Practice

CAHN WISHOD & LAMB, LLP
Melville, NY...........................General Practice

CAIN, HIBBARD, MYERS & COOK, A PROFESSIONAL CORPORATION
Pittsfield, MA.........................Commercial Law; Construction Law; Environmental Law; Health Care Law; Labor and Employment Law; Product Liability Law

CAIRNS, J. T. & ASSOCIATES
Los Angeles, CA.....................Bankruptcy Law; Commercial Litigation; Real Estate Law

CAIRNS, DOYLE, LANS, NICHOLAS & SONI, A LAW CORPORATION
Pasadena, CA.........................Banking Law; Bankruptcy Law; Civil Trial Practice; Environmental Law; Insurance Defense

CAKE & RHOADES, P.C.
Alexandria, VA......................Personal Injury

CALAFELL, RAY, JR., P.A.
Tampa, FL.............................Civil Trial Practice

CALAWAY, STEPHEN G.
Winston-Salem, NC................Real Estate Law

CALBOM & SCHWAB, P.S.C.
Moses Lake, WA.....................Personal Injury; Workers Compensation

CALDWELL, J. THOMAS LAW OFFICES OF
Ripley, TN.............................General Practice

CALDWELL, BERNER & CALDWELL
Woodstock, IL........................General Practice

CALDWELL & PACETTI
Palm Beach, FL.........................General Practice; Municipal Bond/Public Authority Financing

CALFEE, HALTER & GRISWOLD
Cleveland, OH..........................General Practice; Trademark, Copyright and Unfair Competition
Columbus, OH ....General Practice

CALHOUN, FAULK, WATKINS & CLOWER, L.L.C.
Troy, AL ....Civil Trial Practice; General Practice; Insurance Defense

CALHOUN, KADEMENOS & HEICHEL CO., L.P.A.
Mansfield, OH.........................General Practice

CALHOUN & STACY
Dallas, TX..............................Banking Law; Bankruptcy Law; Business Law; Civil Trial Practice; Commercial Law; Communications Law; Construction Law; Environmental Law; General Practice; Health Care Law; Insurance Defense; Labor and Employment Law; Medical Malpractice; Municipal and Zoning Law; Patent, Trademark, Copyright and Unfair Competition; Personal Injury; Probate, Trusts and Estate Planning; Product Liability Law; Real Estate Law; Transportation Law

CALKINS & CALKINS
Eugene, OR ....General Practice

CALLAGHAN & RUCKMAN
Summersville, WV ....General Practice

CALLAHAN & ASSOCIATES
Newport Beach, CA.................Appellate Practice; Bankruptcy Law; Civil Trial Practice; Commercial Litigation

CALLAHAN & BLAINE, A PROFESSIONAL LAW CORPORATION
Irvine, CA................................Business Law; Commercial Litigation; Construction Law; Environmental Law; General Practice; Patent, Trademark, Copyright and Unfair Competition; Real Estate Law

CALLAHAN & DEACON
Sacramento, CA ....Civil Trial Practice; Personal Injury

CALLAN, REGENSTREICH, KOSTER & BRADY
New York, NY.........................Civil Trial Practice; Insurance Defense; Medical Malpractice; Personal Injury

CALL, BARRETT & BURBANK, A PROFESSIONAL CORPORATION
Fairbanks, AK ....General Practice

CALLENDER, JOHN F.
Jacksonville, FL ....Civil Trial Practice

CALLISTER, NEBEKER & McCULLOUGH, A PROFESSIONAL CORPORATION
Salt Lake City, UT..................Antitrust Law; Banking Law; Bankruptcy Law; Business Law; Civil Trial Practice; Commercial Law; Employment Benefits Law; Environmental Law; General Practice; Municipal Bond/Public Authority Financing; Natural Resources Law; Personal Injury; Probate, Trusts and Estate Planning; Real Estate Law; Securities Law; Tax Law

CAMERON & HORNBOSTEL, L.L.P.
Washington, DC.....................Banking Law; International Business Law

CAMERON, MADDEN, PEARLSON, GALE & SELLARS
Long Beach, CA.......................Civil Trial Practice; Environmental Law; Family Law; Labor and Employment Law; Land Use Law; Real Estate Law; Tax Law

CAMERON, MARRIOTT, WALSH, HODGES & COLEMAN, P.A.
Orlando, FL ....Civil Trial Practice; Insurance Defense

CAMERON & MITTLEMAN
Providence, RI.........................Business Law; Health Care Law

CAMP & CAMP, P.A.
Fort Lauderdale, FL................Probate, Trusts and Estate Planning

CAMP CHURCH & ASSOCIATES
Vancouver, BC, Canada...........Administrative Law; Aviation Law; Commercial Litigation

CAMPBELL, DONALD J. & ASSOCIATES
Las Vegas, NV ....Criminal Trial Practice

CAMPBELL, ANDERSON, CASEY, SINK & JOHNSON, A PROF. CORP., THE LAW OFFICES OF
Santa Rosa, CA........................Insurance Defense

CAMPBELL, ARELLANO & RICH
Charlotte Amalie, St. Thomas, VI...............................Bankruptcy Law; Commercial Litigation

CAMPBELL, BLACK, CARNINE & HEDIN, P.C.
Mount Vernon, IL ....Civil Trial Practice; General Practice; Insurance Defense

CAMPBELL, DELONG, HAGWOOD & WADE, LLP
Greenville, MS........................General Practice; Insurance Defense

CAMPBELL, DILLE AND BARNETT
Puyallup, WA ....Civil Trial Practice

CAMPBELL KYLE PROFFITT
Carmel, IN ....General Practice
Noblesville, IN ....General Practice

CAMPBELL, LEA, MICHAEL, McCONNELL & PIGOT
Charlottetown, PE, Canada.....Administrative Law; Business Law; Civil Trial Practice; General Practice; Insurance Defense; Personal Injury

CAMPBELL & LEVINE, LLC
Pittsburgh, PA ....Bankruptcy Law; Commercial Law

CAMPBELL MAACK & SESSIONS, A PROFESSIONAL CORPORATION
Salt Lake City, UT..................Civil Trial Practice; General Practice

CAMPBELL, McCRANIE, SISTRUNK, ANZELMO & HARDY, P.C.
Metairie, LA............................Civil Trial Practice; Commercial Law

CAMPBELL, O'BRIEN & MISTELE, P.C.
Troy, MI..................................Business Law; General Practice

CAMPBELL & RIGGS, A PROFESSIONAL CORPORATION
Houston, TX ....Business Law; Probate, Trusts and Estate Planning; Real Estate Law

CAMPBELL & SNYDER, LLP
Albuquerque, NM...................Administrative Law; Business Law; Civil Trial Practice; Commercial Law

CAMPBELL, WARBURTON, FITZSIMMONS, SMITH, MENDELL & PASTORE, A PROFESSIONAL CORPORATION
San Jose, CA ....Civil Trial Practice; General Practice; Insurance Defense

CAMPBELL, WOODS, BAGLEY, EMERSON, McNEER & HERNDON
Charleston, WV.......................General Practice
Huntington, WV ....General Practice

CAMPEAU & THOMAS, A LAW CORPORATION
San Jose, CA ....Bankruptcy Law; Civil Trial Practice; Commercial Law

CAMPNEY & MURPHY
Vancouver, BC, Canada...........General Practice

CAMPOLI & CURLEY, A PROFESSIONAL CORPORATION
Pittsfield, MA..........................General Practice; Insurance Defense

CAMRUD, MADDOCK, OLSON & LARSON, LTD.
Grand Forks, ND ....General Practice

CANALES & SIMONSON, P.C.
Corpus Christi, TX ....Appellate Practice; Civil Trial Practice; Commercial Litigation; Criminal Trial Practice

CANDOR, YOUNGMAN, GIBSON AND GAULT
Williamsport, PA ....General Practice; Probate, Trusts and Estate Planning

CANGES, IWASHKO & BETHKE, A PROFESSIONAL CORPORATION
Denver, CO ....Civil Trial Practice; Criminal Trial Practice; Family Law

CANNIZZARO, FRASER & BRIDGES
Marysville, OH........................Bankruptcy Law; Workers Compensation

CANNON & BRUNS
Muncie, IN ....General Practice; Personal Injury; Probate, Trusts and Estate Planning

CANNON & DUNPHY, S.C.
Milwaukee, WI ....Personal Injury

CANNON & MEYER VON BREMEN, LLP
Albany, GA..............................Civil Trial Practice; Personal Injury; Real Estate Law

CANO, KRISTIN M.
Newport Beach, CA.................Business Law; Securities Law

CANSLER, LOCKHART, CAMPBELL, EVANS, BRYANT & GARLITZ, P.A.
Charlotte, NC...........................Insurance Defense

CANTEY & HANGER
Dallas, TX................................General Practice
Fort Worth, TX ....General Practice; Labor and Employment Law; Tax Law

CANTOR, ARKEMA & EDMONDS, A PROFESSIONAL CORPORATION
Richmond, VA ....Business Law

CANTRILL, SKINNER, SULLIVAN & KING
Boise, ID..................................General Practice; Insurance Defense

CAPEHART & SCATCHARD, P.A.
Mount Laurel, NJ ....General Practice

CAPERS, DUNBAR, SANDERS & BRUCKNER
Augusta, GA ....Banking Law; Civil Trial Practice; Construction Law; General Practice; Insurance Defense; Personal Injury; Real Estate Law

CAPITELLI & WICKER
New Orleans, LA ....Admiralty/Maritime Law; Civil Trial Practice; Criminal Trial Practice; Medical Malpractice; Personal Injury

CAPLIN & DRYSDALE, CHARTERED
Washington, DC....................Business Law; Civil Trial Practice; Criminal Trial Practice; Probate, Trusts and Estate Planning; Tax Law
New York, NY......................Business Law; Civil Trial Practice; Criminal Trial Practice; Probate, Trusts and Estate Planning

CAPRETZ & RADCLIFFE
Newport Beach, CA................Business Law; Civil Trial Practice; Commercial Law; General Practice

CAPSHAW, GOSS & BOWERS, L.L.P.
Dallas, TX........................Business Law; Commercial Litigation; Construction Law; Insurance Defense; Personal Injury

CAPUTO, JOHN A. & ASSOCIATES
Pittsburgh, PA ....Medical Malpractice; Personal Injury; Product Liability Law

CAPUTO, ANTHONY J., P.C.
White Plains, NY ....Civil Trial Practice

CARB, LURIA, COOK & KUFELD, LLP
New York, NY......................Civil Trial Practice; Probate, Trusts and Estate Planning; Real Estate Law

CARDELLI, SCHAEFER & MASON, P.C.
Royal Oak, MI.....................Civil Trial Practice; Commercial Law; Insurance Defense; Personal Injury; Product Liability Law

CARDENAS, WHITIS & STEPHEN, L.L.P.
McAllen, TX ....Bankruptcy Law; Probate, Trusts and Estate Planning; Real Estate Law

CARDOZO & CARDOZO
Modesto, CA.......................Insurance Defense; Labor and Employment Law; Personal Injury

CARELLA, BYRNE, BAIN, GILFILLAN, CECCHI, STEWART & OLSTEIN, A PROFESSIONAL CORPORATION
Roseland, NJ......................General Practice; Municipal Bond/Public Authority Financing; Patent, Trademark, Copyright and Unfair Competition

CAREY, AUSTIN, JR., P.C.
Hartford, CT ....Environmental Law

CAREY, O'MALLEY, WHITAKER & MANSON, P.A.
Tampa, FL ....Commercial Litigation; Construction Law

CARLBERG, GWENDOLYN JO M.
Alexandria, VA ....Family Law

CARLIN, BRADSHAW, THOMAS & YEATMAN L.L.P.
Bethesda, MD ....General Practice

CARLIN, HELLSTROM & BITTNER
Davenport, IA.....................General Practice

CARLIN, MADDOCK, FAY & CERBONE, P.C.
Florham Park, NJ..................Civil Trial Practice; Environmental Law; General Practice; Labor and Employment Law

CARLINER AND REMES, P.C.
Washington, DC....................Immigration and Naturalization

CARL, LEE & COSELLI, P.C.
Houston, TX ....Bankruptcy Law; Real Estate Law

CARLOCK, DAVID, P.C.
Dallas, TX........................Family Law

CARLSMITH BALL WICHMAN CASE & ICHIKI
Los Angeles, CA ....General Practice
Washington, DC....................General Practice
Hilo, HI..........................General Practice
Honolulu, HI......................General Practice; Land Use Law
Kailua-Kona, HI ....General Practice
Wailuku, HI ....General Practice
Agana, GU ....General Practice
Saipan, TT ....General Practice
Mexico, D.F., Mexico ....General Practice

CARLSON & BALES, A PROFESSIONAL ASSOCIATION
Miami, FL ....Commercial Law; Securities Law

CARLSON, DREWELOW & MCMAHON, P.S.
Wenatchee, WA.....................General Practice; Insurance Defense

CARLSON, HAMMOND & PADDOCK, L.L.C.
Denver, CO ....Environmental Law

CARLSON WENDLER & SANDERSON, P.C.
Edwardsville, IL..................Personal Injury

CARLTON, FIELDS, WARD, EMMANUEL, SMITH & CUTLER, P.A.
Orlando, FL ....General Practice
Pensacola, FL.....................General Practice
St. Petersburg, FL................General Practice
Tallahassee, FL ....General Practice
Tampa, FL ....General Practice
West Palm Beach, FL ....General Practice

CARLTON & SMITH, P.A.
Santa Fe, NM......................Commercial Litigation; Insurance Defense

CARMAN, CALLAHAN & INGHAM
Farmingdale, NY ....Commercial Law

CARMICHAEL & POWELL, PROFESSIONAL CORPORATION
Phoenix, AZ ....Administrative Law; Bankruptcy Law; Construction Law; Personal Injury; Real Estate Law

CARMODY & TORRANCE
New Haven, CT ....General Practice
Waterbury, CT ....General Practice

CARMOUCHE LAW FIRM, THE, A PROFESSIONAL CORPORATION
Lake Charles, LA..................Energy Law; Insurance Defense; Municipal Bond/Public Authority Financing; Product Liability Law; Real Estate Law; Workers Compensation

CARNAHAN, EVANS, CANTWELL & BROWN, P.C.
Springfield, MO...................General Practice

CARNEY BADLEY SMITH & SPELLMAN, A PROFESSIONAL SERVICES CORPORATION
Seattle, WA ....General Practice

CARNEY & BROTHERS, LTD.
Chicago, IL.......................Business Law; Civil Trial Practice; Commercial Litigation; Real Estate Law

CARON & STEVENS
Amsterdam, The Netherlands ....General Practice

CAROSELLI, SPAGNOLLI & BEACHLER, LLC
Pittsburgh, PA ....Civil Trial Practice

CARPENTER, BENNETT & MORRISSEY
Newark, NJ ....Admiralty/Maritime Law; Antitrust Law; Appellate Practice; Banking Law; Civil Trial Practice; Commercial Law; Employment Benefits Law; Environmental Law; General Practice; Health Care Law; Immigration and Naturalization; Labor and Employment Law; Personal Injury; Probate, Trusts and Estate Planning; Real Estate Law; Tax Law; Workers Compensation

CARPENTER & CHÁVEZ, LTD.
Albuquerque, NM...................Civil Trial Practice; Personal Injury; Product Liability Law

CARPENTER, COMEAU, MALDEGEN, NIXON & TEMPLEMAN
Santa Fe, NM......................Civil Trial Practice; Commercial Law; General Practice; Insurance Defense; Natural Resources Law

CARPENTER & KLATSKIN, P.C.
Denver, CO ....Commercial Law; Real Estate Law

CARPENTER & O'CONNOR
Knoxville, TN ....General Practice; Insurance Defense

CARPENTER, PAFFENBARGER, MEYERHOEFER & MCDANIEL
Norwalk, OH ....General Practice

CARPONELLI & KRUG, P.C.
Chicago, IL.......................Civil Trial Practice

CARR, FOUTS, HUNT & WOLFE, L.L.P.
Lubbock, TX.......................Appellate Practice; Commercial Law; Family Law; General Practice; Insurance Defense

CARR GOODSON LEE & WARNER, A PROFESSIONAL CORPORATION
Washington, DC....................Environmental Law; General Practice; Insurance Defense

CARR, KENNEDY, PETERSON & FROST, A LAW CORPORATION
Redding, CA ....Civil Trial Practice; General Practice

CARR, KOREIN, TILLERY, KUNIN, MONTROY & GLASS
East St. Louis, IL................Admiralty/Maritime Law; General Practice; Medical Malpractice

CARR, MCCLELLAN, INGERSOLL, THOMPSON & HORN, PROFESSIONAL CORPORATION
Burlingame, CA......................General Practice

CARR, TABB & POPE
Atlanta, GA ....Civil Trial Practice

CARRELL & RICE, A PROFESSIONAL CORPORATION
Richmond, VA ....Appellate Practice; Civil Trial Practice

CARRINGTON, COLEMAN, SLOMAN & BLUMENTHAL, L.L.P.
Dallas, TX..............................Antitrust Law; General Practice; Tax Law

CARROLL, GEORGE & PRATT
Rutland, VT ....Banking Law; Bankruptcy Law; Business Law; Criminal Trial Practice; Environmental Law; Family Law; General Practice; Health Care Law; Personal Injury; Probate, Trusts and Estate Planning; Real Estate Law; Securities Law

CARROLL, HEYD
Barrie, ON, Canada ....General Practice

CARROLL, KELLY & MURPHY
Providence, RI........................Civil Trial Practice; General Practice

CARRUTHERS & ROTH, P.A.
Greensboro, NC.....................Civil Trial Practice; General Practice

CARSON, CHARLES T.
Phoenix, AZ ....Insurance Defense

CARSON, LESLIE J. JR.
Philadelphia, PA ....Probate, Trusts and Estate Planning; Real Estate Law

CARSON & COIL, P.C.
Jefferson City, MO..................Appellate Practice; Civil Trial Practice; Family Law; Insurance Defense; Medical Malpractice; Personal Injury; Probate, Trusts and Estate Planning; Real Estate Law; Workers Compensation

CARSON FISCHER, P.L.C.
Birmingham, MI.....................Bankruptcy Law; Business Law; Civil Trial Practice; Commercial Law; Construction Law; Environmental Law; Family Law; Medical Malpractice; Municipal and Zoning Law; Personal Injury; Probate, Trusts and Estate Planning; Product Liability Law; Real Estate Law; Securities Law; Sports and Entertainment Law; Tax Law

CARSON, GUEMMER & NICHOLSON
Tampa, FL ....Insurance Defense

CARTER, LOUIS J.
Philadelphia, PA ....Public Utilities Law; Transportation Law

CARTER & ANSLEY
Atlanta, GA ....Business Law; Civil Trial Practice; General Practice

CARTER, CARLILE, NEALE & FRIEDMAN, P.A.
Boca Raton, FL ....Civil Trial Practice; Personal Injury; Probate, Trusts and Estate Planning; Real Estate Law

CARTER, HARROD & CUNNINGHAM
Athens, TN.............................Civil Trial Practice; Commercial Litigation; General Practice; Insurance Defense

CARTER, NOLAN, P.A.
Orlando, FL ....Medical Malpractice; Personal Injury

CARTER, SMITH, MERRIAM, ROGERS & TRAXLER, P.A. A PROFESSIONAL CORPORATION
Greenville, SC........................Commercial Litigation

CARTON, WITT, ARVANITIS & BARISCILLO
Asbury Park, NJ.....................Banking Law; Civil Trial Practice; General Practice
Manasquan, NJ.......................Banking Law; Civil Trial Practice; General Practice

CARTWRIGHT & ALEXANDER, INC.
San Francisco, CA ....Personal Injury; Product Liability Law

CARTWRIGHT, DRUKER & RYDEN
Marshalltown, IA....................General Practice

CARUANA, LANGAN, LORENZEN AND MENDELSOHN, P.A.
Miami, FL...............................Commercial Litigation

CARUSO, JAMES D.
Toledo, OH ....Personal Injury

CARUSO, BURLINGTON, BOHN & COMPIANI, P.A.
West Palm Beach, FL...............Appellate Practice

CASARINO, CHRISTMAN & SHALK
Wilmington, DE.....................Civil Trial Practice; Insurance Defense; Personal Injury; Product Liability Law; Workers Compensation

CASASSA AND RYAN
Hampton, NH.........................General Practice; Probate, Trusts and Estate Planning; Real Estate Law

CASE & DUSTERHOFF, LLP
Portland, OR..........................Insurance Defense

CASE & SILER, P.L.L.C.
Scottsdale, AZ.........................Probate, Trusts and Estate Planning

CASEY, DONALD C.
Alexandria, VA ....Patent, Trademark, Copyright and Unfair Competition

CASEY, JOHN F.
Columbus, OH ....Business Law

CASEY, GERRY, REED & SCHENK
San Diego, CA ....Civil Trial Practice; Personal Injury; Product Liability Law

CASEY, PATRICK A., P.A.
Santa Fe, NM..........................Civil Trial Practice; Personal Injury

CASKIE & FROST, A PROFESSIONAL CORPORATION
Lynchburg, VA ....General Practice

CASNER & EDWARDS, LLP
Boston, MA.............................Business Law; Civil Trial Practice; General Practice

CASPER AND CASPER
Middletown, OH.....................Personal Injury; Workers Compensation

CASPER & DE TOLEDO LLC
Stamford, CT...........................Labor and Employment Law; Personal Injury

CASSADY, FULLER & MARSH
Enterprise, AL.........................Civil Trial Practice; General Practice; Insurance Defense

CASSELL & STONE, L.L.P.
Dallas, TX...............................Business Law; Computer Law; Tax Law

CASSELS BROCK & BLACKWELL
Toronto, ON, Canada..............General Practice

CASSIDAY, BENJAMIN B. III
Honolulu, HI...........................Civil Trial Practice; Criminal Trial Practice

CASSIDAY, SCHADE & GLOOR
Chicago, IL..............................General Practice

CASSIDY, BRUCE G., & ASSOCIATES, P.A.
Philadelphia, PA ....Civil Trial Practice; Criminal Trial Practice; International Business Law; Medical Malpractice

CASSIDY & MUELLER
Peoria, IL.................................Civil Trial Practice; General Practice

CASSIDY, MYERS, COGAN, VOEGELIN & TENNANT, L.C.
Wheeling, WV ....Civil Trial Practice; Labor and Employment Law; Personal Injury

CASSIDY & VERGES, A PROFESSIONAL CORPORATION
San Francisco, CA ....Land Use Law; Real Estate Law

CASSIDY, WARNER, THURBER & LANE, A PROFESSIONAL CORPORATION
Santa Ana, CA ....Environmental Law; Insurance Defense; Product Liability Law

CASSTEVENS, HANNER, GUNTER & GORDON, P.A.
Charlotte, NC..........................General Practice

CASTELLO, WAYNE P.
Gainesville, FL ....Probate, Trusts and Estate Planning; Real Estate Law

CATALANO, FISHER, GREGORY & SULLIVAN, CHARTERED
Naples, FL...............................General Practice

CATALDO, PAUL A., & ASSOCIATES
Franklin, MA ....Criminal Trial Practice; Family Law

CATAPANO-FRIEDMAN, ROBERT S., P.C.
Albany, NY ....Employment Benefits Law

CATCHICK, JAMES M.
Grand Rapids, MI ....Civil Trial Practice

CATES & HOLLOWAY
Scottsdale, AZ.........................Patent, Trademark, Copyright and Unfair Competition

CATHEY & STRAIN
Cornelia, GA...........................Civil Trial Practice; Personal Injury; Product Liability Law

CATLETT & YANCEY, PLC
Little Rock, AR.......................Tax Law

CATRON, CATRON & SAWTELL, A PROFESSIONAL ASSOCIATION
Santa Fe, NM..........................Appellate Practice; Banking Law; Civil Trial Practice; Commercial Law; General Practice; Probate, Trusts and Estate Planning; Real Estate Law; Tax Law

CATTERTON, KEMP & DONOHUE
Rockville, MD..........................Criminal Trial Practice

CAUDLE & SPEARS, P.A.
Charlotte, NC..........................Civil Trial Practice; Commercial Litigation; Environmental Law; General Practice; Insurance Defense; Personal Injury

CAULFIELD, DAVIES & DONAHUE
Sacramento, CA......................Construction Law; Insurance Defense; Personal Injury; Product Liability Law

CAUSEY, CAYWOOD, TAYLOR, MCMANUS & BAILEY
Memphis, TN..........................Criminal Trial Practice; Family Law; General Practice; Probate, Trusts and Estate Planning

CAUTHEN, OLDHAM & KEOUGH, P.A.
Tavares, FL..........................Commercial Litigation; Personal Injury; Probate, Trusts and Estate Planning

CAYER, KILSTOFTE & CRATON, A PROFESSIONAL LAW CORPORATION
Long Beach, CA......................Banking Law; Civil Trial Practice; General Practice

CEARLEY LAW FIRM
Little Rock, AR......................Civil Trial Practice; General Practice

CENTER FOR EMPLOYMENT LAW, THE, P.C.
Roanoke, VA..........................Labor and Employment Law

CERRATO, DAWES, COLLINS, SAKER & BROWN, A PROFESSIONAL CORPORATION
Freehold, NJ..........................Banking Law; Civil Trial Practice; General Practice

CERTILMAN BALIN ADLER & HYMAN, LLP
East Meadow, NY..................Bankruptcy Law; Civil Trial Practice; General Practice; Municipal and Zoning Law; Probate, Trusts and Estate Planning; Real Estate Law; Securities Law; Tax Law

CERUSSI & SPRING, A PROFESSIONAL CORPORATION
White Plains, NY....................Civil Trial Practice; Insurance Defense; Personal Injury

CESARANO, MARILYN J. W., P.A.
Miami, FL..............................Family Law

CESARI AND MCKENNA
Boston, MA............................Antitrust Law; Patent, Trademark, Copyright and Unfair Competition; Trademark, Copyright and Unfair Competition

CETRULO, ROBERT C., P.S.C.
Covington, KY........................Civil Trial Practice

CHADBOURNE & PARKE LLP
Los Angeles, CA......................General Practice
Washington, DC......................General Practice
New York, NY..........................General Practice
London, England......................General Practice
Hong Kong, Hong Kong.........General Practice
Moscow, Russia......................General Practice

CHAFFE, MCCALL, PHILLIPS, TOLER & SARPY, L.L.P.
New Orleans, LA....................Admiralty/Maritime Law; General Practice; Labor and Employment Law; Natural Resources Law

CHAIKIN & KARP, P.C.
Bethesda, MD..........................Personal Injury

CHAIT AMYOT
Montreal, QU, Canada............Civil Trial Practice; Construction Law; General Practice; Real Estate Law

CHALAT • JUSTINO, P.C.
Denver, CO..............................Medical Malpractice; Personal Injury

CHALEFF & ENGLISH
Santa Monica, CA....................Criminal Trial Practice

CHALFIE, JAMES J., CO., L.P.A.
Cincinnati, OH........................General Practice; Probate, Trusts and Estate Planning

CHAMBERLAIN, NEATON & JOHNSON
Wayzata, MN..........................Civil Trial Practice

CHAMBERS, JOY S.
Alexandria, VA........................Probate, Trusts and Estate Planning

CHAMBERS, SALZMAN & BANNON, PROFESSIONAL ASSOCIATION
St. Petersburg, FL..................Admiralty/Maritime Law; Personal Injury; Product Liability Law; Workers Compensation

CHAMBLESS, HIGDON & CARSON
Macon, GA..............................Business Law; General Practice; Insurance Defense; Medical Malpractice

CHAMBLISS & BAHNER, PLLC
Chattanooga, TN....................Bankruptcy Law; Civil Trial Practice; Commercial Law; General Practice; Labor and Employment Law; Municipal Bond/Public Authority Financing; Probate, Trusts and Estate Planning; Real Estate Law; Tax Law

CHAMLEE, DUBUS & SIPPLE
Savannah, GA..........................Admiralty/Maritime Law; General Practice

CHAMPION, JAN
San Jose, CA..........................Civil Trial Practice; Medical Malpractice; Personal Injury; Product Liability Law

CHANCE & MADDOX
Calhoun, GA............................General Practice

CHANDLER AND BRITT
Buford, GA..............................General Practice

CHANDLER, GEORGE, LAW OFFICES OF
Lufkin, TX..............................Personal Injury

CHANDLER, TULLAR, UDALL & REDHAIR
Tucson, AZ..............................Civil Trial Practice; Commercial Law; General Practice; Insurance Defense; Natural Resources Law; Real Estate Law

CHANFRAU & CHANFRAU
Daytona Beach, FL..................Personal Injury

CHANIN, JOHN A. THE LAW OFFICES OF
Honolulu, HI............................Bankruptcy Law; Civil Trial Practice

CHAPIN & CHAPIN
Springfield, IL........................Probate, Trusts and Estate Planning

CHAPIN, FLEMING & WINET, A PROFESSIONAL CORPORATION
San Diego, CA........................Business Law; Civil Trial Practice; Commercial Law; Insurance Defense; Product Liability Law

CHAPLIN & CHAPLIN
Boston, MA............................General Practice
Orleans, MA............................General Practice

CHAPMAN AND CUTLER
Chicago, IL..............................General Practice; Municipal Bond/Public Authority Financing
Salt Lake City, UT..................General Practice

CHAPMAN & GLUCKSMAN, A PROFESSIONAL CORPORATION
Los Angeles, CA......................Construction Law; Insurance Defense

CHAPMAN, LEWIS & SWAN
Clarksdale, MS........................General Practice; Personal Injury

CHAPPELL, E. HUGH, JR., P.A.
Fort Lauderdale, FL................Personal Injury

CHAPPELL & MCGARTLAND, L.L.P.
Fort Worth, TX........................Civil Trial Practice; General Practice

CHAR SAKAMOTO ISHII & LUM
Honolulu, HI............................Business Law; General Practice

CHARFOOS, REITER, PETERSON, HOLMQUIST & PILCHAK, P.C.
Detroit, MI..............................Labor and Employment Law; Workers Compensation
Farmington Hills, MI..............Labor and Employment Law; Workers Compensation

CHARITON & KEISER
Wilkes-Barre, PA....................Civil Trial Practice; Commercial Law

CHARLSON & BREDEHOFT, P.C.
Reston, VA..............................Labor and Employment Law

CHARLSON, MARBEN & JORGENSON, P.A.
Thief River Falls, MN............General Practice

CHARTERS, HECK, O'DONNELL, PETRULIS & ZORZA, P.C.
Troy, MI..................................General Practice

CHARTIER, OGAN, BRADY, LUKAKIS, SHUTE & EMMA
Holyoke, MA............................General Practice

CHASE, EDWARD T., LAW OFFICES OF
New York, NY..........................Medical Malpractice; Personal Injury; Product Liability Law

CHATHAM, GERALD W. SR.
Hernando, MS..........................General Practice; Medical Malpractice

CHAZEN & CHAZEN
Englewood, NJ........................Civil Trial Practice; General Practice; Product Liability Law

CHEATHAM & ACKER, P.C.
West Bloomfield, MI............Civil Trial Practice; Environmental Law; Insurance Defense; Medical Malpractice; Product Liability Law

CHEEK, MICHAEL C.
Clearwater, FL.........Criminal Trial Practice

CHEEK, CHEEK & CHEEK
Oklahoma City, OK.........Insurance Defense; Personal Injury

CHEELEY, JOSEPH E., JR., P.C.
Buford, GA.........Family Law; Personal Injury

CHEN, WALSH, TECLER & MCCABE
Rockville, MD.........General Practice; Real Estate Law

CHERNAU, CHAFFIN & BURNSED
Nashville, TN.........Banking Law; Civil Trial Practice; Labor and Employment Law; Real Estate Law; Trademark, Copyright and Unfair Competition

CHERNOFF, VILHAUER, MCCLUNG & STENZEL
Portland, OR.........Patent, Trademark, Copyright and Unfair Competition

CHERRY, DAVIS, HARRISON, MONTEZ, WILLIAMS & BAIRD, P.C.
Waco, TX.........General Practice

CHERRY & FLYNN
Chicago, IL.........Antitrust Law; Business Law; Civil Trial Practice; Environmental Law; Municipal and Zoning Law; Trademark, Copyright and Unfair Competition

CHERWIN, GLICKMAN & THEISE, LLP
Boston, MA.........Business Law; Commercial Law; General Practice

CHESNUT & LIVINGSTON, P.C.
Doraville, GA.........General Practice

CHESNUTT, CHARLES R.
Dallas, TX.........Bankruptcy Law

CHESTER, PFAFF & BROTHERSON
Elkhart, IN.........Bankruptcy Law; Business Law; Commercial Law; Commercial Litigation; Criminal Trial Practice; Environmental Law; Family Law; General Practice; Labor and Employment Law; Land Use Law; Municipal and Zoning Law; Probate, Trusts and Estate Planning; Real Estate Law

CHESTER, WILLCOX AND SAXBE
Columbus, OH.........Bankruptcy Law; Business Law; Civil Trial Practice; Employment Benefits Law; International Business Law; Public Utilities Law; Real Estate Law

CHICKERING & GREGORY, A PROFESSIONAL CORPORATION
San Francisco, CA.........Civil Trial Practice; Tax Law

CHICOINE & HALLETT, P.S.
Seattle, WA.........Tax Law

CHIERICI, CHIERICI & SMITH, A PROFESSIONAL CORPORATION
Moorestown, NJ.........Appellate Practice; Civil Trial Practice; Commercial Litigation; Insurance Defense; Medical Malpractice; Personal Injury; Product Liability Law

CHILIVIS, COCHRAN, LARKINS & BEVER
Atlanta, GA.........Administrative Law; Criminal Trial Practice

CHING, YUEN & MORIKAWA
Honolulu, HI.........Banking Law; Real Estate Law; Tax Law

CHINNERY, CARL, & ASSOCIATES, P.C.
Lee's Summit, MO.........Business Law; Probate, Trusts and Estate Planning; Real Estate Law

CHINSKI, TOBI J. LAW OFFICES OF
Los Angeles, CA.........Probate, Trusts and Estate Planning

CHISM JACOBSON & JOHNSON, P.L.L.C.
Seattle, WA.........Commercial Law; Construction Law

CHOATE, HALL & STEWART
Boston, MA.........General Practice

CHODOS, DEBORAH
Los Angeles, CA.........Civil Trial Practice

CHOLETTE, PERKINS & BUCHANAN
Grand Rapids, MI.........Civil Trial Practice; General Practice; Insurance Defense; Product Liability Law

CHORCHES & NOVAK, P.C.
Wethersfield, CT.........Bankruptcy Law

CHOREY, TAYLOR & FEIL, A PROFESSIONAL CORPORATION
Atlanta, GA.........Administrative Law; Civil Trial Practice; Communications Law; General Practice; Real Estate Law

CHORNENKY, O. JOSEPH, P.C.
Phoenix, AZ.........Criminal Trial Practice

CHRISTENSEN, JAY D., AND ASSOCIATES
Pasadena, CA.........Health Care Law

CHRISTENSEN & JENSEN, A PROFESSIONAL CORPORATION
Salt Lake City, UT.........Insurance Defense; Medical Malpractice; Personal Injury; Product Liability Law

CHRISTENSEN, O'CONNOR, JOHNSON & KINDNESS, PLLC
Seattle, WA.........Patent, Trademark, Copyright and Unfair Competition

CHRISTIAN, SPARTZ, KEOGH & CHRISTIAN
Le Center, MN.........General Practice

CHRISTIANSEN & JACKNIN
West Palm Beach, FL.........Civil Trial Practice; Family Law

CHRISTIANSEN, JUBE & KEEGAN, A PROFESSIONAL CORPORATION
Shrewsbury, NJ.........General Practice

CHRISTIE & KANTOR
Virginia Beach, VA.........Criminal Trial Practice; Family Law

CHRISTIE, PABARUE, MORTENSEN AND YOUNG, A PROFESSIONAL CORPORATION
Philadelphia, PA.........Employment Benefits Law; Health Care Law; Insurance Defense

CHRISTOPHER, HAYS, WOJCIK & MAVRICOS
Worcester, MA.........Civil Trial Practice; Commercial Law; Commercial Litigation; Medical Malpractice

CHRISTOPHER & TAYLOR
Indianapolis, IN.........Civil Trial Practice

CHRISTOVICH AND KEARNEY, L.L.P.
New Orleans, LA.........Admiralty/Maritime Law; General Practice; Insurance Defense

CHUN, KERR, DODD, BEAMAN & WONG
Honolulu, HI.........General Practice

CHURCH, CHURCH, HITTLE & ANTRIM
Noblesville, IN.........General Practice; Municipal Bond/Public Authority Financing; Personal Injury

CHURCHILL, MANOLIS, FREEMAN, KLUDT & KAUFMAN
Huron, SD.........General Practice

CHURCHILL MCDONNELL & HATCH
Belleville, IL.........Insurance Defense; Product Liability Law

CIARDI, MASCHMEYER & KARALIS, P.C.
Philadelphia, PA.........Bankruptcy Law; Civil Trial Practice; Commercial Law; Commercial Litigation; Real Estate Law

CITY, HAYES, MEAGHER & DISSETTE, P.C.
Boston, MA.........Civil Trial Practice; Construction Law; Probate, Trusts and Estate Planning; Real Estate Law; Tax Law

CIVEROLO, GRALOW & HILL, A PROFESSIONAL ASSOCIATION
Albuquerque, NM.........Civil Trial Practice; General Practice; Insurance Defense

CLANCY, CALLAHAN & SMITH
Roseland, NJ.........Business Law; Civil Trial Practice; Commercial Law; Construction Law; Securities Law

CLAPP & MURPHY
North Attleboro, MA.........Real Estate Law

CLARK, BRUCE G. & ASSOCIATES
New York, NY.........Civil Trial Practice; Medical Malpractice

CLARK, BEVERLY, P.C.
Detroit, MI.........Family Law

CLARK & CARTER
Yuma, AZ.........Commercial Litigation; Insurance Defense; Personal Injury

CLARK, CHARLTON & MARTINO, A PROFESSIONAL ASSOCIATION
Tampa, FL.........Civil Trial Practice; Personal Injury

CLARK, DRUMMIE & COMPANY
Saint John, NB, Canada.........Administrative Law; Admiralty/Maritime Law; Banking Law; Bankruptcy Law; Civil Trial Practice; Commercial Law; Environmental Law; Family Law; General Practice; Insurance Defense; Labor and Employment Law; Municipal and Zoning Law; Personal Injury; Probate, Trusts and Estate Planning; Real Estate Law; Transportation Law

CLARKE, JOHNSON, PETERSON & MCLEAN, A PROFESSIONAL ASSOCIATION
Florence, SC.........Insurance Defense

CLARKE, JON B., P.C.
Denver, CO ....Bankruptcy Law; Real Estate Law

CLARKE SILVERGLATE WILLIAMS & MONTGOMERY
Miami, FL ....Admiralty/Maritime Law; Commercial Law; Employment Benefits Law; Personal Injury; Product Liability Law

CLARK, GAGLIARDI & MILLER, P.C.
White Plains, NY ....Civil Trial Practice; General Practice; Personal Injury

CLARK HILL P.L.C.
Detroit, MI...........................Administrative Law; Antitrust Law; Bankruptcy Law; Business Law; Civil Trial Practice; Commercial Law; Communications Law; Construction Law; Employment Benefits Law; Energy Law; Environmental Law; General Practice; Immigration and Naturalization; Labor and Employment Law; Probate, Trusts and Estate Planning; Product Liability Law; Real Estate Law; Securities Law; Tax Law; Transportation Law

CLARK, LADNER, FORTENBAUGH & YOUNG
Philadelphia, PA ....Admiralty/Maritime Law; General Practice

CLARK, LINDAUER, MCCLINTON, FETHERSTON, EDMONDS & LIPPOLD
Salem, OR ....General Practice

CLARK, MIZE & LINVILLE, CHARTERED
Salina, KS...............................General Practice

CLARK, NEWTON, HINSON & MCLEAN, L.L.P.
Wilmington, NC....................Admiralty/Maritime Law; Business Law; Civil Trial Practice; General Practice

CLARK, PERDUE, ROBERTS & SCOTT CO., L.P.A.
Columbus, OH ....Civil Trial Practice; Medical Malpractice; Personal Injury; Product Liability Law; Transportation Law

CLARK, QUINN, MOSES & CLARK
Indianapolis, IN ....Commercial Litigation; Environmental Law; Land Use Law; Municipal and Zoning Law; Public Utilities Law; Real Estate Law

CLARK & SCHOLNIK
Fort Lauderdale, FL ....General Practice; Real Estate Law

CLARKSON, FORTSON, WALSH & RHENEY, P.A.
Greenville, SC...........................Commercial Litigation; Construction Law; Insurance Defense

CLARK & STANT, P.C.
Virginia Beach, VA ....Civil Trial Practice; General Practice; Tax Law

CLARK & TREVITHICK, A PROFESSIONAL CORPORATION
Los Angeles, CA.....................Banking Law; Bankruptcy Law; Business Law; Civil Trial Practice; Commercial Law; Commercial Litigation; Environmental Law; General Practice; Insurance Defense; Labor and Employment Law; Probate, Trusts and Estate Planning; Product Liability Law; Real Estate Law; Securities Law; Tax Law

CLARK, WEST, KELLER, BUTLER & ELLIS
Dallas, TX................................Civil Trial Practice; Family Law; General Practice; Labor and Employment Law; Product Liability Law

CLARK WHARTON & BERRY
Greensboro, NC.....................Civil Trial Practice; General Practice; Insurance Defense; Securities Law

CLARK & WILLIAMS
Tulsa, OK................................Family Law; General Practice

CLARK, WILSON
Vancouver, BC, Canada...........Family Law; Patent, Trademark, Copyright and Unfair Competition

CLAUSEN MILLER, P.C.
Chicago, IL..............................General Practice
Wheaton, IL ....General Practice

CLAWSON & STAUBES, L.L.C.
Charleston, SC ....Bankruptcy Law; Civil Trial Practice

CLAYSON, MANN & YAEGER, A PROFESSIONAL LAW CORPORATION
Corona, CA ....Business Law; General Practice

CLEARY, DAVID L., ASSOCIATES, A PROF. CORP.
Rutland, VT ....Civil Trial Practice; Commercial Litigation; Construction Law; Insurance Defense; Medical Malpractice; Personal Injury; Product Liability Law

CLEARY, GOTTLIEB, STEEN & HAMILTON
Washington, DC.......................General Practice
New York, NY.........................General Practice
Brussels, Belgium ....General Practice
London, England ....General Practice
Paris, France...........................General Practice

Frankfurt/Main, Germany ......General Practice
Hong Kong, Hong Kong........General Practice
Tokyo, Japan ....General Practice

CLEMENS & SPENCER, A PROFESSIONAL CORPORATION
San Antonio, TX....................General Practice

CLEMENT & WHEATLEY, A PROFESSIONAL CORPORATION
Danville, VA ....General Practice

CLEMENTE, DICKSON & MUELLER, P.A.
Morristown, NJ.......................Civil Trial Practice; General Practice; Labor and Employment Law

CLEMENTS, MAHIN & COHEN
Cincinnati, OH ....Personal Injury; Workers Compensation

CLEMENTS, RICHARD R., A PROFESSIONAL CORPORATION
Signal Hill, CA........................Bankruptcy Law

CLEM, POLACKWICH, VOCELLE & TAYLOR
Vero Beach, FL ....Civil Trial Practice; Personal Injury; Real Estate Law

CLENDENEN, WILLIAM H., JR., A PROFESSIONAL CORPORATION
New Haven, CT ....Civil Trial Practice; General Practice

CLEVELAND, CARL W., & ASSOCIATES LLP
New Orleans, LA ....Civil Trial Practice

CLIFFORD, CLENDENIN & O'HALE, L.L.P.
Greensboro, NC ....Criminal Trial Practice; Personal Injury

CLIFFORD LAW OFFICES, P.C.
Chicago, IL..............................Civil Trial Practice; Commercial Litigation; Medical Malpractice; Personal Injury; Product Liability Law

CLINE, WILLIAMS, WRIGHT, JOHNSON & OLDFATHER
Lincoln, NE.............................General Practice

CLONTZ & COX
Mount Vernon, KY ....Criminal Trial Practice; General Practice

CLURE, EATON, BUTLER, MICHELSON, FERGUSON & MUNGER, P.A.
Duluth, MN ....Civil Trial Practice

CLYATT, CLYATT, WALLACE & DEVAUGHN, P.C.
Valdosta, GA ....Insurance Defense; Workers Compensation

COALE & VAN SUSTEREN, A PROFESSIONAL CORPORATION
Washington, DC......................Aviation Law; Civil Trial Practice; Personal Injury; Product Liability Law

COBB, SAM B. JR.
Tyler, TX.................................Natural Resources Law

COBB & SHEALY, P.A.
Dothan, AL..............................Civil Trial Practice; General Practice; Insurance Defense

COBB, STANTON L., P.A., LAW FIRM OF
Orlando, FL ....Family Law

COBRIN GITTES & SAMUEL
New York, NY........................Patent, Trademark, Copyright and Unfair Competition

COCHRAN & DAHL, P.C.
Phoenix, AZ ....Real Estate Law

CODDINGTON, HICKS & DANFORTH, A PROFESSIONAL CORPORATION
Redwood City, CA ....Civil Trial Practice

CODE HUNTER WITTMANN
Calgary, AB, Canada ....General Practice

COE, NORDWALL & LIEBMAN, LLP
Seattle, WA ....Immigration and Naturalization; Probate, Trusts and Estate Planning; Real Estate Law

COFER, WILLIAM L., P.A.
Winston-Salem, NC ....Criminal Trial Practice

COFFEY, COFFEY & GERAGHTY
Milwaukee, WI.......................Criminal Trial Practice

COFFMAN, COLEMAN, ANDREWS & GROGAN, PROFESSIONAL ASSOCIATION
Jacksonville, FL ....Labor and Employment Law

COFFMAN, DEFRIES & NOTHERN, A PROFESSIONAL ASSOCIATION
Topeka, KS..............................Tax Law

COGAVIN AND WAYSTACK
Boston, MA.............................Civil Trial Practice; Insurance Defense

COGBURN, JOHN M. JR.
Griffin, GA..............................Business Law; Probate, Trusts and Estate Planning

COGSWELL, WILTON W. III
Colorado Springs, CO..............Probate, Trusts and Estate Planning; Tax Law

COHAN, DAVID RODMAN, & ASSOCIATES, P.C.
Baltimore, MD........................Business Law

COHAN, SIMPSON, COWLISHAW & WULFF, L.L.P.
Dallas, TX..............................Insurance Defense

COHEN, ERNEST ALLEN
Tucson, AZ.............................Business Law; Labor and Employment Law

COHEN AND COTTON, P.C. A PROFESSIONAL CORPORATION
Phoenix, AZ............................Civil Trial Practice; Real Estate Law

COHEN/DAVID & ASSOCIATES, P.C.
Atlanta, GA............................Real Estate Law

COHEN, FEELEY & ORTWEIN, P.C.
Easton, PA.............................Personal Injury

COHEN AND FROMM, P.C.
Phoenix, AZ............................Family Law

COHEN, GETTINGS, DUNHAM & DAVIS, P.C.
Arlington, VA.........................Civil Trial Practice; Criminal Trial Practice

COHEN, GREENE & WASSERMAN, P.A.
Annapolis, MD........................Personal Injury

COHEN & GRIGSBY, P.C.
Pittsburgh, PA........................General Practice; International Business Law; Securities Law

COHEN, HENNESSEY & BIENSTOCK, P.C.
New York, NY.........................Family Law

COHEN, JAYSON & FOSTER, P.A., THE LAW FIRM OF
Tampa, FL..............................Civil Trial Practice; Criminal Trial Practice

COHEN, JULES S., P.A.
Orlando, FL............................Bankruptcy Law

COHEN & LEGON, P.A.
Miami, FL...............................Civil Trial Practice

COHEN & LEGON, P.C.
Washington, DC......................Civil Trial Practice

COHEN & LOMBARDO, P.C.
Buffalo, NY.............................Insurance Defense

COHEN & MARLOW
Greenwich, CT........................Family Law
New Haven, CT.......................Family Law
Stamford, CT...........................Family Law

COHEN MCGOVERN SHORALL & STEVENS, P.C.
Phoenix, AZ............................Insurance Defense

COHEN, MILSTEIN, HAUSFELD & TOLL, P.L.L.C.
Washington, DC......................Antitrust Law; Civil Rights; Commercial Litigation; Environmental Law; Labor and Employment Law; Natural Resources Law; Product Liability Law; Securities Law

COHEN, PETER A., P.A.
Miami, FL...............................Commercial Litigation; Probate, Trusts and Estate Planning

COHEN PRIMIANI & FOSTER, A PROFESSIONAL CORPORATION
Los Angeles, CA.....................Tax Law

COHEN & THURSTON, P.A.
Jacksonville, FL......................Bankruptcy Law

COHEN AND WOLF, P.C.
Bridgeport, CT........................General Practice

COHN, FREDERICK H.
New York, NY.........................Criminal Trial Practice

COHN LIFLAND PEARLMAN HERRMANN & KNOPF
Saddle Brook, NJ....................Appellate Practice; Bankruptcy Law; Civil Trial Practice; Commercial Law; Criminal Trial Practice; Family Law; Medical Malpractice; Personal Injury

COHN AND MARKS
Washington, DC......................Administrative Law; Communications Law; Immigration and Naturalization

COKER, JEAN C., P.A.
Jacksonville, FL......................Probate, Trusts and Estate Planning

COKER, MYERS, SCHICKEL & SORENSON, P.A.
Jacksonville, FL......................Insurance Defense; Medical Malpractice; Personal Injury

COLBY, MONET, DEMERS, DELAGE & CREVIER
Montreal, QU, Canada.............General Practice

COLE, DOROTHY A.
Escondido, CA........................Probate, Trusts and Estate Planning

COLE, LATHAM & JOINT, P.C.
Bath, NY................................Banking Law; Commercial Litigation; General Practice; Probate, Trusts and Estate Planning; Real Estate Law

COLELLA & KOLCZUN, P.L.L.
Lorain, OH.............................Business Law

COLEMAN, JOSEPH C.
Columbia, SC.........................Civil Trial Practice

COLEMAN, LARRY K.
Bradenton, FL.........................Family Law

COLEMAN, HULL & VAN VLIET, P.L.L.P.
Minneapolis, MN....................Construction Law

COLEMAN & RICHARDS, A PROFESSIONAL CORPORATION
Los Angeles, CA.....................Civil Trial Practice; Criminal Trial Practice

COLEMAN, RITCHIE & ROBERTSON
Twin Falls, ID........................General Practice

COLEMAN & STEVENS
Elizabethtown, KY..................General Practice; Insurance Defense

COLE, MOORE & BAKER
Bowling Green, KY.................Banking Law; Civil Trial Practice; General Practice

COLE, RAYWID & BRAVERMAN, L.L.P.
Washington, DC......................Communications Law

COLFER, WOOD, LYONS & WOOD
Mc Cook, NE..........................General Practice

COLINGO, WILLIAMS, HEIDELBERG, STEINBERGER & MCELHANEY, P.A.
Pascagoula, MS.......................Environmental Law; General Practice; Insurance Defense; Medical Malpractice; Personal Injury

COLLERAN, JAMES E. LAW OFFICES OF
Philadelphia, PA.....................Civil Trial Practice; Medical Malpractice; Personal Injury; Product Liability Law

COLLERAN, O'HARA & MILLS
Garden City, NY.....................General Practice; Labor and Employment Law

COLLEY, MICHAEL F., CO., L.P.A.
Columbus, OH........................Civil Trial Practice; General Practice; Medical Malpractice; Personal Injury; Product Liability Law

COLLIER, ARNETT, QUICK & COLEMAN
Elizabethtown, KY..................General Practice; Insurance Defense

COLLIER-MAGAR & KIRAGES, P.C.
Indianapolis, IN......................Commercial Litigation

COLLINS, BROWN, CALDWELL, BARKETT, ROSSWAY, GARAVAGLIA & MOORE, CHARTERED
Vero Beach, FL.......................Civil Trial Practice; Environmental Law; General Practice; Real Estate Law

COLLINS, BUCKLEY, SAUNTRY AND HAUGH, P.L.L.P.
St. Paul, MN..........................Family Law; General Practice; Insurance Defense; Personal Injury

COLLINS, COLLINS, MUIR & TRAVER
Pasadena, CA..........................Civil Trial Practice; Construction Law; Insurance Defense; Personal Injury; Product Liability Law

COLLINS, EINHORN, FARRELL & ULANOFF, A PROFESSIONAL CORPORATION
Southfield, MI........................Appellate Practice; Civil Trial Practice; Commercial Law; Environmental Law; Insurance Defense; Product Liability Law

COLLINS, GALLOWAY & SMITH
Mobile, AL.............................Insurance Defense

COLLINS, GEORGE W., INC., A PROFESSIONAL CORPORATION
Santa Monica, CA...................General Practice

COLLINS & LACY, P.C.
Columbia, SC.........................Civil Trial Practice; General Practice

COLLINS & SCHLOTHAUER
San Jose, CA..........................Insurance Defense; Medical Malpractice; Personal Injury; Product Liability Law

COLOMBO AND COLOMBO, P.C.
Bloomfield Hills, MI...............General Practice

COLQUHOUN & COLQUHOUN, A PROFESSIONAL CORPORATION
Morristown, NJ.......................Insurance Defense

COLSON, HICKS, EIDSON, COLSON & MATTHEWS
Miami, FL ....Commercial Law; General Practice; Personal Injury

COLUCCI & UMANS
New York, NY ....Patent, Trademark, Copyright and Unfair Competition

COMBS AND ISAAC
Prestonsburg, KY ....General Practice; Natural Resources Law

COMPTON & DULING, L.C.
Woodbridge, VA ....General Practice

COMPTON, PREWETT, THOMAS & HICKEY, P.A.
El Dorado, AR ....General Practice

COMPUTER LAW ADVISERS
Springfield, VA ....Business Law; Computer Law; Trademark, Copyright and Unfair Competition

CONANT WHITTENBURG FRENCH & SCHACHTER, P.C.
Amarillo, TX ....Bankruptcy Law; Civil Trial Practice; General Practice
Dallas, TX ....Civil Trial Practice; General Practice

CONANT WHITTENBURG FRENCH & SCHACHTER, S.C.
Milwaukee, WI ....Civil Trial Practice; General Practice

CONBOY, MCKAY, BACHMAN & KENDALL, LLP
Carthage, NY ....General Practice
Watertown, NY ....General Practice; Insurance Defense

CONDER & WANGSGARD, L.C.
Salt Lake City, UT ....Commercial Law; Criminal Trial Practice; Personal Injury

CONDO & MASTERMAN, P.C.
Vienna, VA ....Family Law

CONDON & FORSYTH
Washington, DC ....Insurance Defense; Labor and Employment Law; Product Liability Law

CONGALTON, JOHN S.
Seattle, WA ....Admiralty/Maritime Law; Personal Injury

CONKLIN, BENHAM, DUCEY, LISTMAN & CHUHRAN, P.C.
Detroit, MI ....Workers Compensation
Traverse City, MI ....Workers Compensation

CONLEY & CLEARY
Bradenton, FL ....Real Estate Law

CONLEY & HALEY
Bath, ME ....Civil Trial Practice; Environmental Law; General Practice; Labor and Employment Law; Personal Injury; Public Utilities Law

CONLEY & HAUSHALTER
Princeton, NJ ....Tax Law

CONLIFFE, SANDMANN & SULLIVAN
Louisville, KY ....General Practice; Probate, Trusts and Estate Planning

CONLIN, MCKENNEY & PHILBRICK, P.C.
Ann Arbor, MI ....Banking Law; Bankruptcy Law; General Practice; Real Estate Law

CONLIN, ROXANNE B., AND ASSOCIATES, P.C.
Des Moines, IA ....Employment Benefits Law; Medical Malpractice; Personal Injury

CONMY, FESTE, BOSSART, HUBBARD & CORWIN, LTD.
Fargo, ND ....Banking Law; Civil Trial Practice; General Practice; Personal Injury; Probate, Trusts and Estate Planning; Real Estate Law

CONNELL, FOLEY & GEISER
Roseland, NJ ....Civil Trial Practice; General Practice; Insurance Defense

CONNELL LIGHTBODY
Vancouver, BC, Canada ....General Practice

CONNELLY & SCHROEDER
Chicago, IL ....Aviation Law; Commercial Litigation; Medical Malpractice; Product Liability Law

CONNELLY, SHEEHAN & MORAN
Chicago, IL ....Labor and Employment Law

CONNELLY, SOUTAR & JACKSON
Toledo, OH ....Civil Trial Practice; Commercial Litigation; Medical Malpractice; Personal Injury

CONNER & OPIE
Great Bend, KS ....General Practice

CONNER & RILEY
Erie, PA ....Personal Injury

CONNER & WINTERS, A PROFESSIONAL CORPORATION
Oklahoma City, OK ....Antitrust Law; Civil Trial Practice; General Practice
Tulsa, OK ....Civil Trial Practice; General Practice; Natural Resources Law; Securities Law; Tax Law

CONNER & WINTERS, P.L.L.C.
Fayetteville, AR ....General Practice

CONNERTON & RAY
Washington, DC ....General Practice; Labor and Employment Law

CONNOLLY, BOVE, LODGE & HUTZ
Wilmington, DE ....Business Law; Commercial Law; General Practice; Patent, Trademark, Copyright and Unfair Competition; Probate, Trusts and Estate Planning

CONNOLLY, O'MALLEY, LILLIS, HANSEN & OLSON, L.L.P.
Des Moines, IA ....General Practice; Probate, Trusts and Estate Planning; Real Estate Law

CONNOR, BUNN, ROGERSON & WOODARD, P.L.L.C.
Wilson, NC ....General Practice

CONNOR, CULVER, BLAKE & GRIFFIN LLP
Irvine, CA ....Business Law; Construction Law

CONNOR, CURRAN & SCHRAM, P.C.
Hudson, NY ....General Practice

CONNOR & WEBER, P.C.
Philadelphia, PA ....Insurance Defense

CONNORS & CORCORAN, L.L.P.
Rochester, NY ....General Practice; Probate, Trusts and Estate Planning

CONNORS & FARRELL
Chatham, MA ....Admiralty/Maritime Law

CONNORS & VILARDO
Buffalo, NY ....Appellate Practice; Civil Trial Practice; Criminal Trial Practice

CONOUR • DOEHRMAN
Indianapolis, IN ....Civil Trial Practice; Medical Malpractice; Personal Injury

CONRAD, SCHERER & JENNE
Fort Lauderdale, FL ....Civil Trial Practice; General Practice; Insurance Defense; Medical Malpractice; Personal Injury

CONSTANGY, BROOKS & SMITH, LLC
Birmingham, AL ....Labor and Employment Law
Atlanta, GA ....Labor and Employment Law
Winston-Salem, NC ....Labor and Employment Law
Columbia, SC ....Labor and Employment Law
Nashville, TN ....Labor and Employment Law
Arlington, VA ....Labor and Employment Law

CONTANT, SCHERBY & ATKINS
Hackensack, NJ ....Banking Law; Commercial Law; Municipal and Zoning Law; Probate, Trusts and Estate Planning; Real Estate Law

CONTIGUGLIA & GIACONA
Auburn, NY ....General Practice; Probate, Trusts and Estate Planning; Real Estate Law

CONWAY, JACK K.
San Marino, CA ....Personal Injury

CONWAY, JOSEPH WM.
Pittsburgh, PA ....Civil Trial Practice

CONWAY & HALL, A LEGAL PROFESSIONAL ASSOCIATION
Dayton, OH ....General Practice

COOGAN, SMITH, BENNETT, MCGAHAN, LORINCZ & JACOBI
Attleboro, MA ....General Practice

COOK, H. CLAYTON JR.
Washington, DC ....Admiralty/Maritime Law; General Practice
McLean, VA ....Admiralty/Maritime Law; General Practice

COOK, ROBERT M.
Yuma, AZ ....Bankruptcy Law; Civil Trial Practice; Commercial Law

COOK AND BATISTA CO., L.P.A.
Lorain, OH ....General Practice

COOK & CONNELLY
Summerville, GA ....Civil Trial Practice; Criminal Trial Practice

COOKE & COOKE
Greensboro, NC......................General Practice

COOK & FRANKE, S.C.
Milwaukee, WI......................Admiralty/Maritime Law; General Practice; Tax Law

COOK & LEE, P.C.
Boulder, CO......................Civil Trial Practice; Medical Malpractice; Personal Injury; Product Liability Law

COOK, NOELL, TOLLEY & WIGGINS
Athens, GA......................Criminal Trial Practice; Medical Malpractice

COOK, TUCKER, NETTER & CLOONAN, P.C.
Kingston, NY......................General Practice; Insurance Defense

COOLEY, RONALD G.
Phoenix, AZ......................General Practice

COOLEY GODWARD LLP
Palo Alto, CA......................General Practice
San Francisco, CA......................General Practice

COOLEY, SHRAIR, P.C.
Springfield, MA......................General Practice; Labor and Employment Law

COOMBS & DUNLAP
Napa, CA......................General Practice

COONEY & CREW, P.C.
Portland, OR......................Business Law; Civil Trial Practice; Health Care Law; Insurance Defense; Labor and Employment Law; Medical Malpractice; Transportation Law

COONEY, MATTSON, LANCE, BLACKBURN, RICHARDS & O'CONNOR, P.A.
Fort Lauderdale, FL......................Medical Malpractice; Personal Injury

COOPER, C. JAMES JR.
Denver, CO......................Immigration and Naturalization

COOPER, JOHN KENNEDY
Roseland, NJ......................Civil Trial Practice; Commercial Law

COOPER, BECKMAN & TUERK, L.L.P.
Baltimore, MD......................Personal Injury

COOPER & COOPER
New Rochelle, NY......................Civil Trial Practice; Construction Law; General Practice; Insurance Defense; Medical Malpractice

COOPER, COPPINS & MONROE, P.A.
Tallahassee, FL......................Civil Trial Practice

COOPER, COX & BARLOW
Madison, IN......................General Practice

COOPER, DAVID J., A PROF. CORP., LAW OFFICES OF
West Bloomfield, MI......................Insurance Defense; Medical Malpractice

COOPER & DUNHAM LLP
New York, NY......................General Practice; Patent, Trademark, Copyright and Unfair Competition; Trademark, Copyright and Unfair Competition

COOPER, FREDERICK L., III, A PROFESSIONAL CORPORATION
Roswell, GA......................Computer Law

COOPER, HALL, WHITTUM AND SHILLABER, P.C.
Rochester, NH......................General Practice

COOPER, HEWITT & KATZ
Atlanta, GA......................Civil Trial Practice

COOPER, MARVIN A., P.C.
White Plains, NY......................Personal Injury

COOPER, MITCH, CRAWFORD, KUYKENDALL & WHATLEY, L.L.C.
Birmingham, AL......................Civil Trial Practice; Environmental Law; General Practice; Labor and Employment Law

COOPER & PRESTON
Parsons, WV......................Civil Trial Practice

COOPER, SPONG & DAVIS, P.C.
Portsmouth, VA......................Environmental Law; General Practice; Health Care Law

COOPERSMITH, HENRY J.
Costa Mesa, CA......................Probate, Trusts and Estate Planning

COOVER & COOVER
Corpus Christi, TX......................Family Law

COPELAND, DONALD F.
Norristown, PA......................Probate, Trusts and Estate Planning

COPELAND COOK TAYLOR & BUSH, A PROFESSIONAL ASSOCIATION
Jackson, MS......................Banking Law; Civil Trial Practice; Commercial Law; Insurance Defense; Natural Resources Law; Tax Law

COPELAND, LANDYE, BENNETT AND WOLF, LLP
Portland, OR......................Bankruptcy Law; Business Law; Environmental Law; Real Estate Law; Securities Law

COPP & BERALL, LLP
Hartford, CT......................Probate, Trusts and Estate Planning; Tax Law

COPPERSMITH & GORDON P.L.C.
Phoenix, AZ......................Antitrust Law; Business Law; Commercial Litigation; Health Care Law; Real Estate Law

COPPLE, CHAMBERLIN & BOEHM, P.C.
Phoenix, AZ......................Appellate Practice; Insurance Defense

CORBALLY, GARTLAND AND RAPPLEYEA
Poughkeepsie, NY......................Banking Law; Civil Trial Practice; General Practice; Municipal and Zoning Law; Real Estate Law

CORBAN & GUNN
Biloxi, MS......................General Practice

CORBETT, BERNARD R. LAW OFFICES OF
Alexandria, VA......................Business Law

CORBETT, CROCKETT & LECKRONE
Nashville, TN......................Commercial Law; Commercial Litigation; Real Estate Law; Tax Law

CORBETT & KANE, A PROFESSIONAL CORPORATION
Oakland, CA......................Labor and Employment Law
San Francisco, CA......................Labor and Employment Law

CORBIN, DICKINSON, DUVALL & KITCHEN
Jacksonville, FL......................General Practice; Labor and Employment Law

CORBITT, RINEER & JOHNSON, P.C.
Tulsa, OK......................Family Law

CORBOY & DEMETRIO, P.C.
Chicago, IL......................Civil Trial Practice; Medical Malpractice; Personal Injury

CORCORAN, PECKHAM & HAYES, P.C.
Newport, RI......................General Practice

CORETTE POHLMAN & KEBE, A PROFESSIONAL CORPORATION
Butte, MT......................General Practice

CORINBLIT & SELTZER, A PROFESSIONAL CORPORATION
Los Angeles, CA......................Antitrust Law; Business Law; Civil Trial Practice; General Practice; Securities Law

CORLEY, MONCUS & WARD, P.C.
Birmingham, AL......................Bankruptcy Law; General Practice; Probate, Trusts and Estate Planning; Real Estate Law; Securities Law

CORNELIUS & COLLINS
Nashville, TN......................Civil Trial Practice; General Practice

CORNELL AND GOLLUB
Boston, MA......................Civil Trial Practice; General Practice; Insurance Defense; Medical Malpractice

CORNWELL, GARY T.
Spicewood, TX......................Civil Trial Practice

CORS & BASSETT
Cincinnati, OH......................General Practice; Labor and Employment Law

CORSI, MARIO D.
Dover, OH......................General Practice

CORWIN, GREGG M. & ASSOCIATES
Minneapolis, MN......................Labor and Employment Law

CORWIN & MATTHEWS
Huntington, NY......................General Practice

CORY, MEREDITH, WITTER, ROUSH & CHENEY, A LEGAL PROFESSIONAL ASSOCIATION
Lima, OH......................General Practice

COSENTINO, SHEWMAKER & CHRISTOFENO
Elkhart, IN......................Civil Trial Practice

COSGRAVE, VERGEER & KESTER, L.L.P.
Portland, OR......................General Practice

COSGROVE, FLYNN & GASKINS, P.L.L.P.
Minneapolis, MN......................Civil Trial Practice; Insurance Defense; Product Liability Law

COSGROVE, MICHELIZZI, SCHWABACHER, WARD & BIANCHI, A PROFESSIONAL CORPORATION
Lancaster, CA......................General Practice

COSGROVE, WEBB & OMAN
Topeka, KS......................General Practice

COSHO, HUMPHREY, GREENER & WELSH, P.A.
Boise, ID................General Practice

COSTELLO COONEY & FEARON
Syracuse, NY..........Bankruptcy Law; Civil Trial Practice; General Practice; Health Care Law; Real Estate Law; Tax Law; Trademark, Copyright and Unfair Competition

COSTELLO, MARSH & WARD
Greensburg, PA................General Practice

COSTELLO, PORTER, HILL, HEISTERKAMP & BUSHNELL, LLP
Rapid City, SD................Civil Trial Practice; General Practice

COTKIN & COLLINS, A PROFESSIONAL CORPORATION
Los Angeles, CA................General Practice
Santa Ana, CA................General Practice

COTNEY, HUGH, P.A.
Jacksonville, FL................Criminal Trial Practice; Personal Injury

COTSIRILOS, JOHN G.
San Diego, CA................Criminal Trial Practice

COTTER, COTTER AND SOHON, P.C.
Bridgeport, CT................Insurance Defense; Workers Compensation

COTTINGHAM & PORTER, P.C.
Douglas, GA................General Practice

COUCH, WHITE, BRENNER, HOWARD & FEIGENBAUM, LLP
Albany, NY................General Practice

COUDERT BROTHERS
Washington, DC................General Practice
New York, NY................General Practice
Brussels, Belgium................General Practice
London, England................General Practice
Hong Kong, Hong Kong................General Practice
Tokyo, Japan................General Practice
Singapore, Singapore................General Practice

COUDERT FRÈRES
Paris, France................General Practice

COUGHLAN, SEMMER & LIPMAN
San Diego, CA................Civil Trial Practice; Commercial Litigation; Criminal Trial Practice

COUGHLIN & GERHART
Binghamton, NY................Civil Trial Practice; General Practice

COULOMBE & KOTTKE, A PROFESSIONAL CORPORATION
Costa Mesa, CA................Appellate Practice; Business Law; Civil Trial Practice; Commercial Law; Construction Law; Real Estate Law; Securities Law

COUNCIL, BARADEL, KOSMERL & NOLAN, P.A.
Annapolis, MD................General Practice

COUREY, ALBERS, KOSANDA & ZIMMER, P.A.
Minneapolis, MN................Probate, Trusts and Estate Planning

COUSENS, MARK H.
Southfield, MI................Labor and Employment Law

COUSINEAU, MCGUIRE & ANDERSON, CHARTERED
Minneapolis, MN................Insurance Defense

COUSINS AND JOHNSON, P.C.
Stratford, CT................Personal Injury; Workers Compensation

COUZENS, LANSKY, FEALK, ELLIS, ROEDER & LAZAR, P.C.
Farmington Hills, MI................Bankruptcy Law; Business Law; Civil Trial Practice; Commercial Law; General Practice; Probate, Trusts and Estate Planning; Tax Law

COVEY, ROBERTS, BUCHANAN & MCGRODDY
Katonah, NY................General Practice; Probate, Trusts and Estate Planning

COVINGTON & BURLING
Washington, DC................General Practice

COVINGTON & CROWE
Ontario, CA................Civil Trial Practice; Employment Benefits Law; Family Law; General Practice; Real Estate Law

COVINGTON, PATRICK, HAGINS & LEWIS, P.A.
Greenville, SC................Civil Trial Practice; Product Liability Law

COWAN, DENNIS K.
Redding, CA................Bankruptcy Law

COWAN, STUART M. LAW OFFICES OF
Honolulu, HI................Admiralty/Maritime Law; Civil Trial Practice; Personal Injury; Product Liability Law

COWAN & OWEN, P.C.
Richmond, VA................Business Law; Civil Trial Practice; General Practice; Insurance Defense; Product Liability Law

COWARD, HICKS & SILER, P.A.
Sylva, NC................General Practice

COWART, ROY N., P.C.
Warner Robins, GA................General Practice

COWLES & SHAUGHNESSY, P.A.
Jacksonville, FL................Personal Injury; Product Liability Law

COWLES & THOMPSON, A PROFESSIONAL CORPORATION
Dallas, TX................Civil Trial Practice; Commercial Law; General Practice; Insurance Defense; Municipal and Zoning Law
McKinney, TX................General Practice
Temple, TX................General Practice
Tyler, TX................General Practice

COWLEY & CHIDESTER
Rancho Santa Fe, CA................Probate, Trusts and Estate Planning

COWPERTHWAIT, LINDLEY M., JR., P.C.
Norristown, PA................Civil Trial Practice; Commercial Law; Medical Malpractice; Personal Injury; Product Liability Law

COX, JAMES S. & ASSOCIATES
Memphis, TN................Civil Trial Practice; Family Law; Personal Injury

COX BUCHANAN PADMORE & SHAKARCHY
New York, NY................General Practice

COX, COX & STOKES, P.C.
Wellsboro, PA................General Practice; Workers Compensation

COX DOWNIE
Halifax, NS, Canada................General Practice

COX & GOUDY
Minneapolis, MN................Civil Trial Practice; Commercial Law; Personal Injury

COX, MUSTAIN-WOOD, WALKER & SCHUMACHER, LLC
Littleton, CO................Family Law

COX & SMITH INCORPORATED
San Antonio, TX................Antitrust Law; Banking Law; Bankruptcy Law; Business Law; Civil Trial Practice; Computer Law; General Practice; Health Care Law; Labor and Employment Law; Natural Resources Law; Patent, Trademark, Copyright and Unfair Competition; Probate, Trusts and Estate Planning; Real Estate Law; Securities Law; Tax Law

COX, TAYLOR
Victoria, BC, Canada................General Practice

COX, ZWERNER, GAMBILL & SULLIVAN
Terre Haute, IN................Banking Law; Civil Trial Practice; General Practice; Insurance Defense; Probate, Trusts and Estate Planning; Real Estate Law

COY, GILBERT & GILBERT
Richmond, KY................General Practice

COYLE, JOHN J., JR., P.C.
Phillipsburg, NJ................Civil Trial Practice; Criminal Trial Practice; Personal Injury; Product Liability Law

COZEN AND O'CONNOR, A PROFESSIONAL CORPORATION
Philadelphia, PA................Civil Trial Practice; Commercial Law; General Practice; Insurance Defense; Personal Injury

CRABBE, BROWN, JONES, POTTS & SCHMIDT
Columbus, OH................Civil Trial Practice; General Practice; Insurance Defense

CRABTREE & CRABTREE
San Diego, CA................Probate, Trusts and Estate Planning

CRABTREE & GOFORTH
London, KY................General Practice; Insurance Defense

CRABTREE, SCHMIDT, ZEFF, JACOBS & FARRAR
Modesto, CA................General Practice

CRADDICK, CANDLAND & CONTI, PROFESSIONAL CORPORATION
Danville, CA................Insurance Defense; Medical Malpractice

CRAIG, RANDALL K. LAW OFFICES OF
Evansville, IN................Business Law; Probate, Trusts and Estate Planning; Tax Law

CRAIG & CRAIG
Mattoon, IL................Banking Law; Business Law; Civil Trial Practice; Commercial Law; Environmental Law; General Practice; Labor and Employment Law; Land Use Law; Medical Malpractice; Natural Resources Law; Probate, Trusts and Estate Planning; Product Liability Law; Public Utilities Law; Real Estate Law; Workers Compensation

CRAIG AND MACAULEY, PROFESSIONAL CORPORATION

Boston, MA..................Banking Law; Bankruptcy Law; Business Law; General Practice

CRAIG AND SHEPHERD

Chico, CA..................Business Law; Insurance Defense

CRAIGE, BRAWLEY, LIIPFERT, WALKER & SEARCY, L.L.P.

Winston-Salem, NC................General Practice; Probate, Trusts and Estate Planning

CRAIGHILL, MAYFIELD, FENWICK & CROMELIN

Washington, DC..................Probate, Trusts and Estate Planning

CRAMER & ANDERSON

Litchfield, CT..................General Practice

CRAMER, MULTHAUF & HAMMES

Waukesha, WI..................Business Law

CRANE, PAUL N.

Los Angeles, CA..................Business Law; Real Estate Law

CRANFILL, SUMNER & HARTZOG, L.L.P.

Raleigh, NC..................Insurance Defense; Personal Injury

CRASSWELLER, MAGIE, ANDRESEN, HAAG & PACIOTTI, P.A.

Duluth, MN..................Banking Law; Civil Trial Practice; General Practice; Insurance Defense; Real Estate Law

CRAVATH, SWAINE & MOORE

New York, NY..................General Practice

London, England..................General Practice

Hong Kong, Hong Kong.........General Practice

CRAWFORD, JOHN A. JR.

San Diego, CA..................Criminal Trial Practice

CRAWFORD, CROWE, BAINBRIDGE & HASKINS, P.A.

Tulsa, OK..................Antitrust Law; Civil Trial Practice; Constitutional Law; Energy Law; Family Law; General Practice; Securities Law

CRAWFORD & MCKINNEY

Houston, TX..................Personal Injury

CRAWFORD & REIMANN LLP

Los Angeles, CA..................Civil Trial Practice; Construction Law

CRAWFORD & RODDENBERY, P.A.

Lakeland, FL..................Insurance Defense; Personal Injury

CRAWFORD, THOMAS M., P.S.C.

Louisville, KY..................Personal Injury

CREMEN, FRANK J.

Las Vegas, NV..................Criminal Trial Practice

CREMINS & ASSOCIATES, P.C.

Fairfax, VA..................Civil Trial Practice; Health Care Law; Medical Malpractice

CRENSHAW, DUPREE & MILAM, L.L.P.

Lubbock, TX..................General Practice; Insurance Defense; Labor and Employment Law; Medical Malpractice; Personal Injury; Probate, Trusts and Estate Planning; Product Liability Law

CRENSHAW, WARE AND MARTIN, P.L.C.

Norfolk, VA..................Admiralty/Maritime Law; Banking Law; Business Law; Civil Trial Practice; Commercial Litigation; General Practice; Real Estate Law

CREW, BUCHANAN & LOWE

Dayton, OH..................Civil Trial Practice; Family Law; General Practice; Personal Injury; Real Estate Law

CREWS & HANCOCK, P.L.C.

Richmond, VA..................Business Law; Commercial Law; Health Care Law; Medical Malpractice

CREWS & KLEIN, P.C.

Charlotte, NC..................Insurance Defense

CRIBBS & MCFARLAND, A PROFESSIONAL CORPORATION

Arlington, TX..................General Practice

CRIM & BASSLER

Atlanta, GA..................Civil Trial Practice; Insurance Defense

CRISLIP, PHILIP & ASSOCIATES

Memphis, TN..................General Practice

CRISPE & CRISPE

Brattleboro, VT..................Business Law; Civil Trial Practice; General Practice; Personal Injury

CRIST, GRIFFITHS, SCHULZ & BIORN, A PROFESSIONAL CORPORATION

Palo Alto, CA..................Probate, Trusts and Estate Planning

CRISTE, VIRGINIA S. LAW OFFICES OF

Palm Desert, CA..................Family Law

CRISTE, PIPPIN & GOLDS

Palm Desert, CA..................Bankruptcy Law; Business Law; Civil Trial Practice; Real Estate Law

CRISWELL & CRISWELL, INC. A PROFESSIONAL CORPORATION

Durant, OK..................General Practice

CRITCHFIELD, CRITCHFIELD & JOHNSTON, LTD.

Millersburg, OH..................General Practice

Wooster, OH..................General Practice

CRITCHLEY, MICHAEL & ASSOCIATES

West Orange, NJ..................Civil Trial Practice

CRITTENDEN & CRITTENDEN, P.A.

Winter Haven, FL..................General Practice

CROCKETT, DAVID G., P.C.

Atlanta, GA..................Bankruptcy Law; Civil Trial Practice; Commercial Law; Real Estate Law

CROCKETT & MYERS, LTD. A PROFESSIONAL CORPORATION

Las Vegas, NV..................Business Law; Commercial Law; Commercial Litigation; Criminal Trial Practice; General Practice; Medical Malpractice; Personal Injury; Probate, Trusts and Estate Planning; Real Estate Law; Workers Compensation

CROLEY, DAVIDSON & HUIE

Knoxville, TN..................Real Estate Law

CRONIN, FRIED, SEKIYA, KEKINA & FAIRBANKS, ATTORNEYS AT LAW, A LAW CORPORATION

Honolulu, HI..................Admiralty/Maritime Law; Civil Trial Practice; Medical Malpractice; Personal Injury; Product Liability Law

CRONIN & STANEWICH

Phoenix, AZ..................Insurance Defense; Personal Injury; Product Liability Law

CROSBY, GUENZEL, DAVIS, KESSNER & KUESTER

Lincoln, NE..................General Practice

CROSS, JENKS, MERCER AND MAFFEI

Baraboo, WI..................General Practice

CROSS, MURPHY, SMUCK & HOUSTON

Washington, DC..................Probate, Trusts and Estate Planning; Tax Law

CROSSETT, EDGAR L., III, P.C.

Atlanta, GA..................Personal Injury

CROUCH & CROUCH

Arlington, VA..................General Practice

CROWDER & SCOGGINS, LTD.

Columbia, IL..................General Practice

CROWE & DUNLEVY, A PROFESSIONAL CORPORATION

Oklahoma City, OK................Antitrust Law; Civil Trial Practice; General Practice; Labor and Employment Law; Municipal Bond/ Public Authority Financing; Natural Resources Law; Tax Law

CROWE & SCOTT, A PROFESSIONAL ASSOCIATION

Phoenix, AZ..................Criminal Trial Practice

CROWELL & MORING LLP

Irvine, CA..................General Practice

Washington, DC..................General Practice

London, England..................General Practice

CROWELL & OWENS, L.L.C.

Alexandria, LA..................Business Law; Tax Law

CROWLEY, HAUGHEY, HANSON, TOOLE & DIETRICH, P.L.L.P.

Billings, MT..................Administrative Law; Banking Law; Bankruptcy Law; Business Law; Civil Trial Practice; Commercial Law; Criminal Trial Practice; Employment Benefits Law; Environmental Law; Family Law; General Practice; Health Care Law; Immigration and Naturalization; Insurance Defense; Labor and Employment Law; Medical Malpractice; Municipal Bond/Public Authority Financing; Natural Resources Law; Personal Injury; Probate, Trusts and Estate Planning; Product Liability Law; Public Utilities Law; Real Estate Law; Securities Law; Tax Law; Trademark, Copyright and Unfair Competition; Transportation Law; Workers Compensation

CRUMLEY, JOHN W., P.C.

Fort Worth, TX..................Probate, Trusts and Estate Planning; Real Estate Law

CRUMMY, DEL DEO, DOLAN, GRIFFINGER & VECCHIONE, A PROFESSIONAL CORPORATION
Newark, NJ.............................Antitrust Law; Bankruptcy Law; Environmental Law; General Practice; Health Care Law; Insurance Defense; Labor and Employment Law; Municipal and Zoning Law; Patent, Trademark, Copyright and Unfair Competition; Product Liability Law; Securities Law

CRUMPLER O'CONNOR & WYNNE
El Dorado, AR ....General Practice

CRUSE, FIRETAG & BOCK, P.C.
Phoenix, AZ ....Banking Law; Commercial Law; Real Estate Law

CRUSE, SCOTT, HENDERSON & ALLEN, L.L.P.
Houston, TX ....Civil Trial Practice; Medical Malpractice

CRYSTAL, HEYTOW & WARNICK, P.C.
Chicago, IL..............................Insurance Defense

CUCCIO AND CUCCIO
Hackensack, NJ......................General Practice

CUDDY BIXBY
Boston, MA.............................Business Law; Family Law; General Practice; Probate, Trusts and Estate Planning

CULBERTSON, THOMAS A.
Santa Ana, CA ....Civil Trial Practice

CULLEN, CARSNER, SEERDEN & CULLEN, L.L.P.
Victoria, TX ....General Practice; Insurance Defense; Medical Malpractice

CULLEN AND DYKMAN
Brooklyn, NY..........................General Practice; Probate, Trusts and Estate Planning
Garden City, NY ....Banking Law; General Practice

CULLEN LAW FIRM, LTD.
Minneapolis, MN....................Civil Trial Practice

CULP ELLIOTT & CARPENTER, P.L.L.C.
Charlotte, NC..........................Tax Law

CULVER, KNOWLTON, EVEN & FRANKS
Muskegon, MI..........................General Practice

CUMMING, CUMMING & ESARY
Griffin, GA..............................General Practice; Real Estate Law

CUMMING, HATCHETT & JORDAN, A PROFESSIONAL CORPORATION
Hampton, VA...........................General Practice

CUMMINS, BERNARD F.
Martinez, CA............................General Practice

CUNNINGHAM, BLACKBURN, FRANCIS, BROCK & CUNNINGHAM
Grand Island, NE ....General Practice

CUNNINGHAM, BOUNDS, YANCE, CROWDER & BROWN
Mobile, AL...............................Admiralty/Maritime Law; Civil Trial Practice; General Practice; Personal Injury; Product Liability Law

CUNNINGHAM DALMAN, P.C.
Holland, MI ....Banking Law; Business Law; Civil Trial Practice; Environmental Law; Family Law; General Practice; Insurance Defense; Personal Injury; Probate, Trusts and Estate Planning; Real Estate Law

CUNNINGHAM LAW FIRM
Phoenix, AZ ....Personal Injury

CUNNINGHAM LAW GROUP, P.A.
Tampa, FL ....Civil Trial Practice; General Practice; Medical Malpractice; Personal Injury; Product Liability Law

CURAN & TROY, P.C.
New York, NY.........................Civil Trial Practice; Insurance Defense

CURLEY & CURLEY, P.C.
Boston, MA..............................Civil Trial Practice; General Practice; Insurance Defense

CURRAN, DENNIS J.
Boston, MA..............................Civil Trial Practice; Personal Injury

CURRAN & PARRY
Las Vegas, NV ....Real Estate Law

CURRAN AND WATSON
Fullerton, CA...........................Criminal Trial Practice

CURRIE JOHNSON GRIFFIN GAINES & MYERS, PLLC
Jackson, MS ....Civil Trial Practice; General Practice; Insurance Defense; Medical Malpractice

CURRY, DOYLE, P.C.
Marshall, TX ....Aviation Law; Civil Trial Practice; Personal Injury

CURRY & SALZER
Toms River, NJ.......................Civil Trial Practice; General Practice; Medical Malpractice

CURTIS ALEXANDER & VARNER
Winter Haven, FL...................Commercial Litigation; Personal Injury

CURTIS, BRINCKERHOFF & BARRETT, P.C.
Stamford, CT...........................General Practice

CURTIS, MALLET-PREVOST, COLT & MOSLE
Washington, DC......................General Practice
New York, NY.........................Civil Trial Practice; Criminal Trial Practice; International Business Law; Tax Law
London, England ....General Practice
Paris, France............................General Practice

CURTIS, MORRIS & SAFFORD, P.C.
New York, NY.........................Patent, Trademark, Copyright and Unfair Competition

CURTIS WILDE & NEAL LAW OFFICES
Oshkosh, WI............................Civil Trial Practice; Personal Injury; Workers Compensation

CURTIS, ZAKLUKIEWICZ, VASILE, DEVINE & MCELHENNY
Merrick, NY............................Civil Trial Practice
Riverhead, NY ....Civil Trial Practice

CUSACK & STILES LLP
New York, NY.........................Labor and Employment Law; Tax Law

CUSTER & HILL, P.C.
Marietta, GA............................Family Law; General Practice; Probate, Trusts and Estate Planning

CUTHBERT LAW OFFICES, A PROFESSIONAL CORPORATION
Petersburg, VA........................Personal Injury

CUTLER, LAURENCE J.
Morristown, NJ.......................Family Law

CUTLER & NYLANDER, A PROFESSIONAL SERVICE CORPORATION
Seattle, WA ....Business Law; Commercial Law

CUTLER & STANFIELD, L.L.P.
Denver, CO ....Transportation Law
Washington, DC......................Aviation Law; Energy Law; Environmental Law; Municipal and Zoning Law; Natural Resources Law; Transportation Law

CUTRIGHT & CUTRIGHT
Chillicothe, OH ....General Practice; Probate, Trusts and Estate Planning; Real Estate Law

CUYLER BURK
Parsippany, NJ.........................Civil Trial Practice; Commercial Litigation; Insurance Defense

CYPERT, CROUCH, CLARK & HARWELL
Springdale, AR.........................Commercial Litigation; General Practice

CYRIL & CROWLEY
San Francisco, CA ....Civil Trial Practice; Product Liability Law

DAAR & NEWMAN, PROFESSIONAL CORPORATION
Los Angeles, CA ....General Practice; Insurance Defense

DAERR-BANNON, KATHLEEN L.
Philadelphia, PA ....Civil Trial Practice

DAHLGREN AND CLOSE
Washington, DC......................International Business Law

DAILEY, GARRETT C.
Oakland, CA ....Family Law

DAILY, WEST, CORE, COFFMAN & CANFIELD
Fort Smith, AR........................Civil Trial Practice; General Practice

DALE & EKE, PROFESSIONAL CORPORATION
Indianapolis, IN ....Civil Trial Practice; Probate, Trusts and Estate Planning; Real Estate Law; Tax Law

DALEIDEN, THOMPSON & TREMAINE, LTD.
Chicago, IL..............................General Practice

DALE & KLEIN, L.L.P.
McAllen, TX ....Civil Trial Practice; Family Law; Insurance Defense

DALE, ROSENBERG & MCLEAN
Nashville, TN..........................Business Law

D'ALESSANDRO & JACOVINO
Florham Park, NJ ....Civil Trial Practice; General Practice

DALEY, BLACK & MOREIRA
Halifax, NS, Canada ....General Practice

DALEY, ERISMAN & VAN OGTROP
Wilmington, DE.................Medical Malpractice; Personal Injury; Probate, Trusts and Estate Planning; Real Estate Law

DALLER GREENBERG & DIETRICH
Fort Washington, PA..............Civil Trial Practice; Insurance Defense; Product Liability Law

DALNEKOFF & MASON, P.A.
Annapolis, MD ....Civil Trial Practice

DALTON, TREASURE & MOWRER
Kennett, MO............................General Practice

DALY & LAVERY
Ossining, NY ....General Practice

D'AMATO & LYNCH
New York, NY.........................Civil Trial Practice; Insurance Defense

D'AMATO, PAUL R., P.C.
Atlantic City, NJ.....................Personal Injury
Linwood, NJ............................Civil Trial Practice; Personal Injury

DAMON & DAMON
Grand Rapids, MI ....Business Law

DAMON KEY BOCKEN LEONG KUPCHAK, ATTORNEYS AT LAW, A LAW CORPORATION
Honolulu, HI...........................General Practice

DAMRELL, NELSON, SCHRIMP, PALLIOS & LADINE, A PROFESSIONAL CORPORATION
Modesto, CA............................Civil Trial Practice; General Practice

DAMSEL & GELSTON, P.A.
West Palm Beach, FL..............Civil Trial Practice

DANFORTH, MEIERHENRY & MEIERHENRY, LLP
Sioux Falls, SD.......................Civil Trial Practice; Real Estate Law

DANIEL, E. BART
Charleston, SC ....Criminal Trial Practice

DANIEL & DANIEL
Pawleys Island, SC..................General Practice; Personal Injury

DANIEL, HARVILL, BATSON & NOLAN
Clarksville, TN........................General Practice

DANIEL, LAWSON, TUGGLE & JERLES
Perry, GA.................................General Practice

DANIEL & OBERMAN
Knoxville, TN ....Civil Trial Practice; Criminal Trial Practice

DANIELS, BARATTA & FINE
Los Angeles, CA......................Appellate Practice; Civil Trial Practice; Construction Law; Insurance Defense

DANIELS, KASHTAN & FORNARIS, P.A.
Miami, FL................................Construction Law; Insurance Defense

DANIELS, SANDERS, PIANOWSKI, HAMILTON & TODD
Elkhart, IN..............................Civil Trial Practice

DANIEL & SHOULTZ, L.L.P.
Dallas, TX................................Banking Law; Personal Injury

DANKENBRING, GREIMAN, OSTERHOLT & HOFFMANN, P.C.
St. Louis, MO..........................Real Estate Law; Tax Law; Trademark, Copyright and Unfair Competition

DANN, DORFMAN, HERRELL AND SKILLMAN, A PROFESSIONAL CORPORATION
Philadelphia, PA ....Computer Law; Patent, Trademark, Copyright and Unfair Competition

DANN PECAR NEWMAN & KLEIMAN, PROFESSIONAL CORPORATION
Indianapolis, IN ....Administrative Law; Banking Law; Bankruptcy Law; Business Law; Civil Trial Practice; Commercial Law; Commercial Litigation; Environmental Law; Family Law; General Practice; Land Use Law; Mergers and Acquisitions; Municipal Bond/Public Authority Financing; Municipal and Zoning Law; Personal Injury; Probate, Trusts and Estate Planning; Real Estate Law; Securities Law; Tax Law

DANNING, GILL, DIAMOND & KOLLITZ, LLP
Los Angeles, CA......................Bankruptcy Law

DANO * MILLER * RIES
Moses Lake, WA.....................General Practice; Probate, Trusts and Estate Planning

DANTIN & DANTIN
Columbia, MS ....General Practice

DANZIGER & MARKHOFF LLP
White Plains, NY ....Probate, Trusts and Estate Planning; Tax Law

DAPEER, ROSENBLIT & LITVAK, LLP
Beverly Hills, CA....................Civil Trial Practice; Commercial Law; Land Use Law; Municipal and Zoning Law; Real Estate Law

DARBY & DARBY, PROFESSIONAL CORPORATION
New York, NY.........................Patent, Trademark, Copyright and Unfair Competition

DARBY, PEELE, BOWDOIN & PAYNE
Lake City, FL...........................General Practice

DARCHE, GARY M.
Kew Gardens, NY ....Commercial Litigation

DARK, CLAYTON E. JR.
Lufkin, TX ....General Practice; Insurance Defense

DARLING, HALL & RAE
Los Angeles, CA......................Business Law; Civil Trial Practice; Probate, Trusts and Estate Planning; Real Estate Law

DART, ADAMSON & DONOVAN
Salt Lake City, UT...................Commercial Litigation; Construction Law; Family Law; Municipal and Zoning Law; Personal Injury; Real Estate Law

DASCHBACH, KELLY, COOPER & HOTCHKISS, PROFESSIONAL ASSOCIATION
Lebanon, NH ....General Practice

DAUGHERTY, DAVID H.
Huntington, WV ....Probate, Trusts and Estate Planning; Real Estate Law

DAUZAT, FALGOUST, CAVINESS & BIENVENU
Opelousas, LA..........................Insurance Defense

DAVENPORT, EVANS, HURWITZ & SMITH, L.L.P.
Sioux Falls, SD........................Banking Law; Bankruptcy Law; Business Law; Civil Trial Practice; General Practice; Insurance Defense; Personal Injury; Real Estate Law; Tax Law

DAVENPORT, FILES & KELLY, L.L.P.
Monroe, LA ....Criminal Trial Practice; General Practice; Insurance Defense

DAVID, ANTHONY P., A PROFESSIONAL CORPORATION
San Francisco, CA ....Commercial Litigation; Personal Injury

DAVID, HAGNER, KUNEY & KRUPIN, P.C.
Washington, DC.......................Business Law; General Practice

DAVIDOFF, PAUL F., A PROFESSIONAL CORPORATION
Kalamazoo, MI ....Bankruptcy Law

DAVIDSON, CALHOUN, MILLER & BUEHLER, P.C.
Columbus, GA ....Banking Law; General Practice; Probate, Trusts and Estate Planning; Tax Law

DAVIDSON, MEAUX, SONNIER, MCELLIGOTT & SWIFT
Lafayette, LA ....Aviation Law; Business Law; Civil Trial Practice; Commercial Litigation; General Practice; Insurance Defense

DAVIDSON, WIGGINS & CROWDER, P.C.
Tuscaloosa, AL ....Civil Trial Practice; General Practice; Insurance Defense

DAVID, THOMAS L., P.A.
Miami, FL ....General Practice

DAVIES, THOMAS I.
Austin, TX ....Real Estate Law

DAVIES, CANTRELL, HUMPHREYS & MCCOY
Nashville, TN ....General Practice

DAVIES MCFARLAND & CARROLL, P.C.
Pittsburgh, PA ....Civil Trial Practice; General Practice; Insurance Defense; Medical Malpractice; Product Liability Law; Workers Compensation

DAVIES, WARD & BECK
Toronto, ON, Canada...............Antitrust Law; Banking Law; Business Law; Civil Trial Practice; Commercial Law; Environmental Law; General Practice; Real Estate Law; Securities Law; Tax Law

DAVIS, JAMES J.
Boise, ID..................................Insurance Defense

DAVIS, ROBERT L.
Cincinnati, OH ....Personal Injury

DAVIS, STEPHEN J.
Minneapolis, MN ....Real Estate Law

DAVIS, BROWN, KOEHN, SHORS & ROBERTS, P.C.
Des Moines, IA......................General Practice; Patent, Trademark, Copyright and Unfair Competition; Tax Law

DAVIS, BROWNING & SCHNITKER
Madison, FL......................General Practice

DAVIS AND BUJOLD
Manchester, NH......................Patent, Trademark, Copyright and Unfair Competition

DAVIS & CANNON
Cheyenne, WY......................Civil Trial Practice; Construction Law; General Practice; Labor and Employment Law; Natural Resources Law
Sheridan, WY......................Civil Trial Practice; General Practice; Insurance Defense; Labor and Employment Law; Natural Resources Law; Probate, Trusts and Estate Planning; Real Estate Law

DAVIS & COMPANY
Vancouver, BC, Canada..........General Practice

DAVIS, COX & WRIGHT, PLC
Fayetteville, AR......................Civil Trial Practice; Commercial Law; Commercial Litigation; General Practice; Insurance Defense; Product Liability Law

DAVIS & DAVIS
Decatur, GA......................Civil Trial Practice; General Practice
New York, NY......................Insurance Defense
Austin, TX......................Administrative Law; Civil Trial Practice; General Practice; Health Care Law; Insurance Defense

DAVIS, DAVIS & KAAR
Milton, PA......................General Practice

DAVIS AND FAJEN, P.C.
Ann Arbor, MI......................Civil Trial Practice; General Practice

DAVIS FIRM, THE
Seattle, WA......................Personal Injury

DAVIS & FOX
Los Angeles, CA......................Business Law; Civil Trial Practice; Environmental Law; General Practice; Insurance Defense; Real Estate Law

DAVIS, GORDON, DONER & CHANDLER, P.A.
West Palm Beach, FL......................Civil Trial Practice; Personal Injury; Product Liability Law; Securities Law

DAVIS, GRAHAM & STUBBS LLP
Denver, CO......................General Practice
Washington, DC......................General Practice

DAVIS, GREGORY, CHRISTY & FOREHAND
Cordele, GA......................General Practice
Vienna, GA......................General Practice

DAVIS, HOWARD M., P.C.
West Orange, NJ......................Civil Trial Practice; General Practice

DAVIS & KUELTHAU, S.C.
Milwaukee, WI......................Admiralty/Maritime Law; Business Law; Environmental Law; Labor and Employment Law; Municipal Bond/Public Authority Financing; Probate, Trusts and Estate Planning; Real Estate Law; Tax Law

DAVIS & LOWE, P.C.
Phoenix, AZ......................Bankruptcy Law

DAVIS, MANNIX & MCGRATH
Chicago, IL......................Antitrust Law; Computer Law; Trademark, Copyright and Unfair Competition

DAVIS, MATTHEWS & QUIGLEY, P.C.
Atlanta, GA......................Civil Trial Practice; Family Law; General Practice; Real Estate Law; Tax Law

DAVIS & MURPHY
Westminster, MD......................General Practice

DAVIS, MURRELLE & LUMSDEN, P.A.
Beaufort, NC......................Admiralty/Maritime Law; Civil Trial Practice; Personal Injury

DAVIS POLK & WARDWELL
Washington, DC......................General Practice
New York, NY......................General Practice
London, England......................General Practice
Paris, France......................General Practice

DAVIS, PUNELLI, KEATHLEY & WILLARD
Newport Beach, CA......................Business Law; Civil Trial Practice; Environmental Law; General Practice; Real Estate Law

DAVIS, REBERKENNY & ABRAMOWITZ, A PROFESSIONAL CORPORATION
Cherry Hill, NJ......................Bankruptcy Law; Public Utilities Law

DAVIS, STURGES & TOMLINSON
Louisburg, NC......................General Practice; Insurance Defense

DAVIS & TAFF
Tallahassee, FL......................Banking Law; Personal Injury

DAVIS, TUPPER, GRIMSLEY & SEELHOFF
Beaufort, SC......................Insurance Defense; Medical Malpractice; Product Liability Law; Real Estate Law

DAVIS, UNREIN, HUMMER & BUCK, L.L.P.
Topeka, KS......................Civil Trial Practice; General Practice; Insurance Defense; Personal Injury

DAVIS & WEINSTEIN
Denver, CO......................Construction Law; Family Law; Real Estate Law

DAVIS & WILKERSON, P.C.
Austin, TX......................Civil Trial Practice; Commercial Litigation; Health Care Law; Insurance Defense; Labor and Employment Law; Medical Malpractice

DAVIS WRIGHT TREMAINE LLP
Bellevue, WA......................General Practice
Seattle, WA......................General Practice

DAVIS AND YOUNG CO., L.P.A.
Cleveland, OH......................General Practice; Insurance Defense; Medical Malpractice; Product Liability Law

DAWDA, MANN, MULCAHY & SADLER, P.L.C.
Bloomfield Hills, MI......................Business Law; Civil Trial Practice; Commercial Litigation; Environmental Law; Labor and Employment Law; Mergers and Acquisitions; Probate, Trusts and Estate Planning; Real Estate Law; Tax Law

DAWSON, JOHN B., JR., P.C.
Mineola, NY......................Probate, Trusts and Estate Planning

DAY, DAVID F. LAW OFFICES OF
Honolulu, HI......................Business Law; Commercial Law; Construction Law; International Business Law

DAY, BERRY & HOWARD
Hartford, CT......................General Practice
Stamford, CT......................General Practice
Boston, MA......................General Practice

DAY, EDWARDS, FEDERMAN, PROPESTER & CHRISTENSEN, P.C.
Oklahoma City, OK......................Banking Law; Bankruptcy Law; Business Law; Civil Trial Practice; Commercial Law; Construction Law; Environmental Law; General Practice; Health Care Law; Insurance Defense; International Business Law; Labor and Employment Law; Natural Resources Law; Real Estate Law; Securities Law

DAY, KETTERER, RALEY, WRIGHT & RYBOLT, LTD.
Canton, OH......................Business Law; General Practice; Insurance Defense

DAY & SAWDEY, A PROFESSIONAL CORPORATION
Grand Rapids, MI......................Bankruptcy Law; Civil Trial Practice; Commercial Law; Construction Law; Environmental Law; Real Estate Law

DEAN, MAX
Flint, MI......................Medical Malpractice

DEAN & GIBSON
Charlotte, NC......................Aviation Law; Civil Trial Practice; Commercial Litigation; Insurance Defense

DEAN, GIBSON, II, P.C.
Buford, GA......................General Practice

DEANER, DEANER, SCANN, CURTAS & MALAN
Las Vegas, NV......................General Practice; Real Estate Law

DEARTH, MARKHAM & JACK, CHARTERED
Parsons, KS......................General Practice

DEASEY, MAHONEY & BENDER, LTD.
Philadelphia, PA......................Civil Trial Practice; Insurance Defense

DEASON, CHARLES A. JR.
El Paso, TX......................Medical Malpractice; Personal Injury

DEATON, DAVISON & KESSINGER, A PROFESSIONAL CORPORATION
Ada, OK......................General Practice; Insurance Defense

DEBEVOISE & PLIMPTON
Washington, DC......................General Practice
New York, NY......................Banking Law; Civil Trial Practice; General Practice; Tax Law; Trademark, Copyright and Unfair Competition
London, England......................General Practice

DEBEVOISE & PLIMPTON — Continued

Paris, France.................................General Practice
Hong Kong, Hong Kong........General Practice
Budapest, Hungary ....General Practice

DE BLASIO, FIGMAN & EPSTEIN, P.C.
New York, NY........................Civil Trial Practice; Medical Malpractice; Personal Injury; Product Liability Law

DEBRUYN, JOHN LAW OFFICES
Denver, CO ....Probate, Trusts and Estate Planning; Tax Law

DEBUS & KAZAN, LTD.
Phoenix, AZ ....Criminal Trial Practice; Personal Injury

DECARO, DORAN, SICILIANO, GALLAGHER, SONNTAG & DEBLASIS
Lanham, MD..........................General Practice; Insurance Defense

DECAROLIS, PATRICK, JR., A PROFESSIONAL LAW CORPORATION
Los Angeles, CA ....Family Law

DECHERT PRICE & RHOADS
Washington, DC....................General Practice
Boston, MA...........................General Practice
Princeton, NJ ....General Practice
New York, NY.......................General Practice
Harrisburg, PA ....General Practice
Philadelphia, PA ....General Practice
Brussels, Belgium ....General Practice
London, England ....General Practice
Paris, France..........................General Practice

DECKELBAUM OGENS & FISCHER, CHARTERED
Washington, DC.....................Bankruptcy Law; Civil Trial Practice; Commercial Law; Family Law
Bethesda, MD ....Bankruptcy Law; Civil Trial Practice; Commercial Law; Family Law

DECKER & GUNTA, S.C.
Milwaukee, WI.......................Constitutional Law; Construction Law

DECOF & GRIMM, A PROFESSIONAL CORPORATION
Providence, RI........................Commercial Law; Medical Malpractice; Personal Injury

DECOTIIS, FITZPATRICK & GLUCK
Teaneck, NJ............................Civil Trial Practice; Environmental Law; Municipal Bond/Public Authority Financing; Municipal and Zoning Law; Public Utilities Law

DE CUIR & SOMACH, A PROFESSIONAL CORPORATION
Sacramento, CA ....Natural Resources Law

DEEGAN & DEEGAN, L.L.P.
Hempstead, NY......................General Practice; Insurance Defense

DEEHL, DAVID L. LAW OFFICES OF
Miami, FL ....Civil Trial Practice; Insurance Defense; Personal Injury

DEENER, FEINGOLD & STERN, A PROFESSIONAL CORPORATION
Hackensack, NJ.......................Administrative Law; Business Law; Civil Trial Practice; Commercial Law; General Practice; Probate, Trusts and Estate Planning; Tax Law

DEEP & WOMACK
Henderson, KY ....Civil Trial Practice; General Practice; Insurance Defense

DEETH WILLIAMS WALL
Toronto, ON, Canada..............Computer Law; Patent, Trademark, Copyright and Unfair Competition

DEFINO, MICHAEL G.
Media, PA ....Criminal Trial Practice

DEFOREST & KOSCELNIK
Pittsburgh, PA ....Civil Trial Practice; Commercial Law; Labor and Employment Law

DE GRANDPRÉ, GODIN
Montreal, QU, Canada ....General Practice

DEGRAVELLES, PALMINTIER & HOLTHAUS
Baton Rouge, LA....................Personal Injury

DE GROOT, KELLER & VINCENT
Grand Rapids, MI ....Bankruptcy Law; Civil Trial Practice; Commercial Law; Commercial Litigation; Personal Injury

DEGUERIN & DICKSON
Houston, TX ....Criminal Trial Practice

DEHAY & ELLISTON, L.L.P.
Dallas, TX...............................Personal Injury; Product Liability Law

DEHNER & ELLIS
Morehead, KY ....Banking Law; Insurance Defense; Probate, Trusts and Estate Planning

DEITCH & HAMILTON, A PROFESSIONAL CORPORATION
Austin, TX ....Bankruptcy Law; Civil Trial Practice; Commercial Law

DEKLE, PATRICK H., P.A.
Tampa, FL ....Civil Trial Practice; Medical Malpractice; Personal Injury

DE LA GARZA, BILL, & ASSOCIATES, P.C.
Houston, TX ....Family Law; Real Estate Law

DELANEY & BALCOMB, P.C.
Glenwood Springs, CO............General Practice

DELANEY AND O'CONNOR LLP
Syracuse, NY...........................Probate, Trusts and Estate Planning

DELANEY, WILES, HAYES, GERETY & ELLIS, INC.
Anchorage, AK.......................Environmental Law; General Practice; Insurance Defense; Medical Malpractice; Natural Resources Law; Product Liability Law

DELANEY, ZEMETIS, DONAHUE, DURHAM & NOONAN, P.C.
Wallingford, CT ....Civil Trial Practice; Construction Law; Personal Injury; Product Liability Law

DE LA PARTE, GILBERT & BALES, PROFESSIONAL ASSOCIATION
Tampa, FL ....Commercial Litigation; Environmental Law

DELGADO, ACOSTA & BRADEN, L.L.P.
El Paso, TX.............................General Practice

DELISIO MORAN GERAGHTY & ZOBEL, P.C.
Anchorage, AK ....Business Law; Civil Trial Practice

DEL SOLE & DEL SOLE
New Haven, CT ....Civil Trial Practice

DEL TORO & SANTANA
San Juan, PR ....Commercial Law; General Practice

DEMARS, GORDON, OLSON & SHIVELY
Lincoln, NE.............................Business Law; Insurance Defense; Labor and Employment Law

DE MARTINO FINKELSTEIN ROSEN & VIRGA
Washington, DC......................Business Law; Securities Law

DEMENT AND MARQUARDT, P.L.C.
Kalamazoo, MI ....Probate, Trusts and Estate Planning

DEMENT, VANDIVORT AND DEMENT
Sikeston, MO...........................Civil Trial Practice

DEMERSSEMAN JENSEN, L.L.P.
Rapid City, SD........................General Practice

DEMETRIOU, DEL GUERCIO, SPRINGER & MOYER, LLP
Los Angeles, CA ....Administrative Law; Business Law; Civil Trial Practice; Commercial Law; Environmental Law; Health Care Law; Natural Resources Law; Probate, Trusts and Estate Planning; Real Estate Law; Tax Law

DEMPSEY & ASSOCIATES, P.A.
Winter Park, FL......................Antitrust Law; Civil Trial Practice; Construction Law; Criminal Trial Practice; Labor and Employment Law

DEMUTH & DEMUTH
Denver, CO ....General Practice

DENIUS, FRANKLIN W.
Austin, TX ....Civil Trial Practice

DENLINGER, ROSENTHAL & GREENBERG
Cincinnati, OH ....Labor and Employment Law

DENMEAD & MALONEY
Columbus, OH ....Civil Trial Practice; General Practice; Personal Injury

DENNIN, TIMOTHY J., P.C.
New York, NY.........................Securities Law

DENNIS, CORRY, PORTER & GRAY
Atlanta, GA ....Civil Trial Practice; Insurance Defense; Personal Injury; Transportation Law

DENT & COOK, P.A.
Sarasota, FL ....Real Estate Law

DENTON, WILLIAM L.
Biloxi, MS................................Admiralty/Maritime Law; Personal Injury

DENTON & CARY
Bolivar, TN ....General Practice

DENTON & DENTON, LTD.
Las Vegas, NV ....Civil Trial Practice; General Practice; Natural Resources Law; Probate, Trusts and Estate Planning

DENTON & KEULER
Paducah, KY ....General Practice

DENTON & MERRITT, A PROFESSIONAL CORPORATION
Dallas, TX ....Real Estate Law

DE ORCHIS & PARTNERS
New York, NY ....Admiralty/Maritime Law; Civil Trial Practice; Insurance Defense

DEPEW AND GILLEN, L.L.C.
Wichita, KS ....Civil Trial Practice; Environmental Law; General Practice; Insurance Defense; Personal Injury

DERR, DAILEY J., P.A.
Durham, NC ....Construction Law

DERRYBERRY, GEORGE M.
Chattanooga, TN ....Civil Trial Practice; Labor and Employment Law

DESHAZO, GARY F. & ASSOCIATES
Austin, TX ....Civil Trial Practice

DESJARDINS DUCHARME STEIN MONAST
Montreal, QU, Canada ....General Practice
Quebec, QU, Canada ....General Practice

DESSEN, MOSES & SHEINOFF
Philadelphia, PA ....Civil Trial Practice

DESTEFANO & WARREN, P.C.
Philadelphia, PA ....Antitrust Law; Civil Trial Practice; Commercial Law; Commercial Litigation; Criminal Trial Practice

DESTRIBATS, CAMPBELL, DESANTIS, MAGEE & O'DONNELL
Trenton, NJ ....Civil Trial Practice; Medical Malpractice

DETISCH & CHRISTENSEN
San Diego, CA ....General Practice

DEUSCHLE AND ASSOCIATES, P.A.
Fort Lauderdale, FL ....Commercial Law

DEUTSCH & BLUMBERG, P.A.
Miami, FL ....Civil Trial Practice; Medical Malpractice; Personal Injury; Product Liability Law

DEUTSCH, DAVID M., CO., L.P.A.
Dayton, OH...........................Personal Injury; Product Liability Law

DEUTSCH, KERRIGAN & STILES, L.L.P.
New Orleans, LA ....Admiralty/Maritime Law; Antitrust Law; Commercial Law; Construction Law; Environmental Law; General Practice; Insurance Defense; Labor and Employment Law; Product Liability Law; Tax Law

DEUTSCH, LEVY & ENGEL, CHARTERED
Chicago, IL...........................Civil Trial Practice; Probate, Trusts and Estate Planning; Tax Law

DEUTSCH & RUBIN
Los Angeles, CA ....Family Law

DEUTSCH WILLIAMS BROOKS DERENSIS HOLLAND & DRACHMAN, P.C.
Boston, MA...........................Civil Trial Practice
Nantucket, MA ....Civil Trial Practice

DEVEAU, COLTON & MARQUIS
Atlanta, GA ....Patent, Trademark, Copyright and Unfair Competition

DEVEREUX, MURPHY, STRILER & BRICKEY, L.L.C.
St. Louis, MO.........................Commercial Litigation; Real Estate Law

DE VINE & KOHN
Southfield, MI ....Business Law; Construction Law; Probate, Trusts and Estate Planning; Tax Law

DEVINE, MILLIMET & BRANCH, PROFESSIONAL ASSOCIATION
Manchester, NH......................General Practice

DEVITT, THISTLE & DEVITT, P.A.
Delray Beach, FL ....Probate, Trusts and Estate Planning

DEVLIN, CITTADINO & SHAW, P.C.
Trenton, NJ ....Personal Injury; Workers Compensation

DEVLIN, JOHN GERARD, & ASSOCIATES, P.C.
Philadelphia, PA ....Civil Trial Practice; Environmental Law; Insurance Defense; Product Liability Law; Transportation Law

DEWEY BALLANTINE
Washington, DC......................General Practice
New York, NY ....General Practice; Municipal Bond/Public Authority Financing

DEWITT ROSS & STEVENS S.C.
Madison, WI ....General Practice; Patent, Trademark, Copyright and Unfair Competition

DEWOLF, WARD, O'DONNELL & GLATT, P.A.
Orlando, FL ....Civil Trial Practice; Commercial Litigation; Personal Injury

DEYOE, HEISSENBUTTEL & MATTIA
Wayne, NJ.............................Appellate Practice; Civil Trial Practice; Environmental Law; Family Law; General Practice; Insurance Defense; Medical Malpractice; Personal Injury; Product Liability Law

DIAMOND, HASSER & FROST
Mobile, AL.............................Admiralty/Maritime Law; Personal Injury; Product Liability Law

DIAMOND RASH GORDON & JACKSON, P.C.
El Paso, TX ....Civil Trial Practice; Municipal Bond/Public Authority Financing

DICE, MICHAEL R., AND COMPANY, L.L.C.
Denver, CO ....Probate, Trusts and Estate Planning

DICK & DICK
The Dalles, OR ....General Practice

DICKENSON, MURDOCH, REX AND SLOAN, CHARTERED
Boca Raton, FL ....Probate, Trusts and Estate Planning; Real Estate Law

DICKENSON, PEATMAN & FOGARTY, A PROFESSIONAL LAW CORPORATION
Napa, CA ....Business Law; General Practice; Land Use Law

DICKERSON, DICKERSON, LIEBERMAN & CONSUL
Las Vegas, NV ....Civil Trial Practice; Family Law; Personal Injury

DICKERSON, RICE, SPAETH, HEISSERER & SUMMERS, L.C.
Cape Girardeau, MO ....Business Law; Civil Trial Practice

DICKEY, H. ELDRIDGE JR.
Fort Worth, TX ....Business Law; Probate, Trusts and Estate Planning; Tax Law

DICK AND HARRIS
Chicago, IL.............................Patent, Trademark, Copyright and Unfair Competition; Trademark, Copyright and Unfair Competition

DICKIE, MCCAMEY & CHILCOTE
Wheeling, WV ....Patent, Trademark, Copyright and Unfair Competition
Pittsburgh, PA ....General Practice; Patent, Trademark, Copyright and Unfair Competition

DICKINSON & GIBBONS, P.A.
Sarasota, FL ....Civil Trial Practice; General Practice; Insurance Defense; Medical Malpractice; Probate, Trusts and Estate Planning; Real Estate Law

DICKINSON, MACKAMAN, TYLER & HAGEN, P.C.
Des Moines, IA ....Banking Law; General Practice; Labor and Employment Law; Probate, Trusts and Estate Planning; Tax Law

DICKINSON, WRIGHT, MOON, VAN DUSEN & FREEMAN
Washington, DC......................General Practice; Patent, Trademark, Copyright and Unfair Competition
Chicago, IL.............................General Practice
Bloomfield Hills, MI...............General Practice
Detroit, MI.............................Civil Trial Practice; Environmental Law; General Practice; Labor and Employment Law; Municipal Bond/Public Authority Financing; Patent, Trademark, Copyright and Unfair Competition
Grand Rapids, MI ....General Practice
Lansing, MI............................General Practice

DICKSTEIN & SCUTTI
Philadelphia, PA ....Civil Trial Practice; Criminal Trial Practice; Personal Injury

DICKSTEIN SHAPIRO MORIN & OSHINSKY LLP
Washington, DC......................General Practice

DIDAK & JACK
Los Angeles, CA ....Appellate Practice; Insurance Defense

DIDONATO & WINTERHALTER, P.C.
Philadelphia, PA ....Bankruptcy Law; Commercial Law

DIEHL CLAYTON & JACOBSEN
Newton, IA ....General Practice

DIEHL, STEINHEIMER, RIGGIO, HAYDEL & MORDAUNT, A PROFESSIONAL LAW CORPORATION
Stockton, CA............................Civil Trial Practice; General Practice

DIEPENBROCK & COSTA
Sacramento, CA ....Environmental Law; Insurance Defense

DIEPENBROCK, WULFF, PLANT & HANNEGAN, LLP
Sacramento, CA ....Business Law; Civil Trial Practice

DIETRICH, ZODY, HOWARD & VANDERROEST, P.C.
Kalamazoo, MI ....Business Law; Civil Trial Practice; Commercial Law; Insurance Defense; Probate, Trusts and Estate Planning

DIGGINS, JOHN J., P.C.
Dallas, TX..............................Civil Trial Practice; Personal Injury

DIKE, BRONSTEIN, ROBERTS & CUSHMAN, LLP
Boston, MA...........................Patent, Trademark, Copyright and Unfair Competition; Trademark, Copyright and Unfair Competition

DIKMAN AND DIKMAN
Jamaica, NY.........................Family Law; Personal Injury; Probate, Trusts and Estate Planning; Real Estate Law

DILL, MATTHEW T.
Wilmington, NC....................Probate, Trusts and Estate Planning

DILLARD, BOWER AND EAST
Waycross, GA ....Civil Trial Practice; Insurance Defense

DILLARD AND KATONA
Tappahannock, VA ....General Practice

DILLINGHAM CROSS, P.L.C.
Phoenix, AZ ....Bankruptcy Law

DILLON MCCANDLESS KING COULTER & GRAHAM, L.L.P.
Butler, PA............................General Practice

DILWORTH & BARRESE
Uniondale, NY ....Patent, Trademark, Copyright and Unfair Competition

DILWORTH, PAXSON, KALISH & KAUFFMAN, LLP
Harrisburg, PA......................General Practice
Philadelphia, PA ....General Practice; Municipal Bond/Public Authority Financing; Tax Law

DIMITRIOU, EMMANUEL H., P.C.
Reading, PA ....Criminal Trial Practice

DIMOCK STRATTON CLARIZIO
Toronto, ON, Canada.............Computer Law; Patent, Trademark, Copyright and Unfair Competition; Trademark, Copyright and Unfair Competition

DIMURO, GINSBERG & LIEBERMAN, P.C.
Alexandria, VA ....Commercial Litigation; General Practice

DINES, WILSON & GROSS, P.C.
Albuquerque, NM..................Commercial Litigation; Communications Law; Environmental Law; Insurance Defense; Labor and Employment Law; Product Liability Law

DINNIN & DUNN, P.C.
Troy, MI...............................Patent, Trademark, Copyright and Unfair Competition

DINSE, ERDMANN, KNAPP & MCANDREW, P.C.
Burlington, VT ....Civil Trial Practice; General Practice; Insurance Defense

DIORIO & FALZONE
Media, PA ....Civil Trial Practice; Family Law; Personal Injury

DI RENZO AND BOMIER
Neenah, WI ....Business Law; General Practice; Insurance Defense

DIRMANN, JAMES R., P.A.
Sarasota, FL ....Criminal Trial Practice

DITTMER, WOHLUST & WILKINS, P.A.
Maitland, FL ....Probate, Trusts and Estate Planning

DIVER, GRACH, QUADE & MASINI
Waukegan, IL.........................Civil Trial Practice; General Practice; Insurance Defense; Personal Injury

DIXON, SMITH & STAHL
Fairfax, VA ....Construction Law; Real Estate Law

DIXON AND SNOW, P.C.
Denver, CO ....Aviation Law; Commercial Litigation; Criminal Trial Practice; Family Law; Labor and Employment Law

DOAR, DRILL & SKOW, S.C.
New Richmond, WI...............Civil Trial Practice; Personal Injury

DOBSON & BROWN, P.A.
St. Augustine, FL....................Commercial Litigation; Environmental Law

DODD AND DENNIS, P.C.
Valdosta, GA ....Civil Trial Practice; Criminal Trial Practice; Family Law; Personal Injury

DODDS, KIDD, RYAN & MOORE
Little Rock, AR ....Personal Injury

DODGE, DAVID A., P.C.
Grand Rapids, MI ....Criminal Trial Practice

DOERING, STEVEN B.
Garnett, KS ....General Practice

DOERNER, SAUNDERS, DANIEL & ANDERSON
Tulsa, OK...............................General Practice; Labor and Employment Law; Natural Resources Law; Securities Law

DOFFERMYRE, SHIELDS, CANFIELD, KNOWLES & DEVINE
Atlanta, GA ....Civil Trial Practice; Personal Injury; Product Liability Law

DOGAN & ASSOCIATES
New York, NY.......................International Business Law

DOHERTY, MARY CUSHING
Norristown, PA......................Family Law

DOHERTY, SHERIDAN & GRIMALDI, L.L.P.
Fairfax, VA ....Insurance Defense; Probate, Trusts and Estate Planning

DOHERTY & VENEZIA, A PROFESSIONAL CORPORATION
Phoenix, AZ ....Insurance Defense; Workers Compensation

DOHERTY, WALLACE, PILLSBURY AND MURPHY, P.C.
Springfield, MA......................General Practice; Patent, Trademark, Copyright and Unfair Competition

DOK, LEVY & PERRIN
San Jose, CA ....Family Law

DOLACK, HANSLER, LORAN, ROWAN & RITCHIE, P.S.
Tacoma, WA ....General Practice

DOLAN AND DOLAN, P.A. A PROFESSIONAL CORPORATION
Newton, NJ ....General Practice

DOLD, SPATH & MCKELVIE, P.C.
Grosse Pointe, MI ....General Practice
Troy, MI...............................General Practice

DOLE, COALWELL & CLARK, P.C.
Roseburg, OR ....Civil Trial Practice; General Practice

DOLIN, NORMAN M.
Los Angeles, CA ....Family Law

DOLIN & ASSOCIATES, P.C.
Rochester, NY........................Labor and Employment Law

DOLLAR, LAIRD & SCOTT, L.L.P.
Monroe, LA ....Commercial Litigation

DOLLINGER, GONSKI, GROSSMAN, PERMUT & HIRSCHHORN
Carle Place, NY ....Civil Trial Practice; General Practice; Real Estate Law

DOMENGEAUX WRIGHT MOROUX & ROY, A PROFESSIONAL LAW CORPORATION
Lafayette, LA ....Admiralty/Maritime Law; Civil Trial Practice; Personal Injury; Product Liability Law

DOMESTICO & BARRY
Framingham, MA ....Civil Trial Practice; Commercial Litigation

DOMINA & COPPLE, P.C.
Norfolk, NE ....Banking Law; Civil Trial Practice; Insurance Defense; Personal Injury

DOMINICK, FLETCHER, YEILDING, WOOD & LLOYD, P.A.
Birmingham, AL ....Civil Trial Practice; General Practice; Real Estate Law; Tax Law

DOMINIK & STEIN
Miami, FL ....Patent, Trademark, Copyright and Unfair Competition
Tampa, FL ....Patent, Trademark, Copyright and Unfair Competition

DONAHOO, DONAHOO & BALL, P.A.
Jacksonville, FL ....Probate, Trusts and Estate Planning; Real Estate Law; Tax Law

DONAHUE & DONAHUE, ATTORNEYS, P.C.
Lowell, MA ....Business Law; General Practice; Insurance Defense

DONAHUE & WARENDA
Morrisville, PA ....Commercial Law

DONAU & BOLT
Tucson, AZ ....Criminal Trial Practice; Family Law

DONENFELD, JACK A., A LEGAL PROF. ASSN., LAW OFFICES OF
Cincinnati, OH ....Securities Law

DONNELLY, DANIEL
New York, NY ....Civil Trial Practice

DONNELLY, BALDWIN AND WILHITE, P.C.
Lebanon, MO ....General Practice

DONOHOE, LAWRENCE E. JR.
Lafayette, LA ....General Practice

DONOHOE, JAMESON & CARROLL, P.C.
Dallas, TX ....Banking Law; Bankruptcy Law; Business Law; Commercial Litigation; General Practice; Real Estate Law; Tax Law

DONOHUE, JAMES F.
White Plains, NY ....Criminal Trial Practice; Personal Injury

DONOHUE AND DONOHUE
Philadelphia, PA ....Administrative Law; International Trade Law

DONOHUE, SABO, VARLEY & ARMSTRONG, P.C.
Albany, NY ....Civil Trial Practice; Insurance Defense

DONOVAN, MARTIN K.
Providence, RI ....Civil Trial Practice; General Practice; Insurance Defense; Personal Injury

DONOVAN & DESJARDINS, PROFESSIONAL CORPORATION
Lancaster, NH ....General Practice

DONOVAN LEISURE NEWTON & IRVINE
New York, NY ....General Practice
Paris, France...........................General Practice

DONOVAN PARRY CARBIN MCDERMOTT & RADZIK
New York, NY ....Admiralty/Maritime Law

DONOVAN & ROBERTS, P.C.
Wheaton, IL ....Civil Trial Practice; Commercial Litigation; General Practice; Personal Injury

DONOVAN, ROSE, NESTER, SZEWCZYK & JOLEY, P.C.
Belleville, IL ....Civil Trial Practice; General Practice; Insurance Defense

DORAMUS, TRAUGER & NEY
Nashville, TN ....Business Law; Civil Trial Practice

DORAN BLACKMOND READY HAMILTON & WILLIAMS
South Bend, IN ....Civil Trial Practice; Commercial Law; Environmental Law; Insurance Defense; Personal Injury; Product Liability Law

DORAN & NOWALIS
Wilkes-Barre, PA ....Bankruptcy Law

DORF & DORF, A PROFESSIONAL CORPORATION
Rahway, NJ.............................Labor and Employment Law

DORFMAN & GRUBER
Freeport, NY ....Personal Injury

DORITY & MANNING, P.A.
Greenville, SC.........................Patent, Trademark, Copyright and Unfair Competition

DORMAN, DENNIS PAUL & ASSOCIATES
San Diego, CA ....Personal Injury

DORR, BAIRD AND LIGHTNER, A PROFESSIONAL CORPORATION
Springfield, MO.......................Civil Trial Practice; Insurance Defense

DORR, CARSON, SLOAN & BIRNEY, P.C.
Denver, CO ....Patent, Trademark, Copyright and Unfair Competition; Trademark, Copyright and Unfair Competition

DORSEY & WHITNEY LLP
Minneapolis, MN ....General Practice

DORTCH, WRIGHT & WRIGHT
Gadsden, AL...........................General Practice; Insurance Defense; Medical Malpractice

DORWART, FREDERIC
Tulsa, OK...............................Banking Law; Natural Resources Law

DÖSER AMERELLER NOACK
Berlin, Germany......................General Practice
Frankfurt/Main, Germany ......General Practice

DOSLAND, NORDHOUGEN, LILLEHAUG & JOHNSON, P.A.
Moorhead, MN ....Commercial Law; Real Estate Law

DOSS, OWEN L., P.C.
Chicago, IL.............................Family Law

DOSTART CLAPP STERRETT & COVENEY, LLP
San Diego, CA ....Business Law

DOTY & SHAPIRO, P.C.
Boulder, CO ....Business Law; Probate, Trusts and Estate Planning

DOUGHERTY, HESSIN, BEAVERS & GILBERT, A PROFESSIONAL CORPORATION
Oklahoma City, OK.................Patent, Trademark, Copyright and Unfair Competition

DOUGHERTY & HILDRE
San Diego, CA ....Admiralty/Maritime Law; Civil Trial Practice; Personal Injury; Product Liability Law

DOUGLAS, ALEXA, KOEPPEN & HURLEY
Valparaiso, IN ....General Practice

DOUGLAS & DOUGLAS
Concord, NH ....Civil Trial Practice

DOUGLAS, DOUGLAS & DOUGLAS
Carlisle, PA ....Civil Trial Practice; General Practice; Insurance Defense; Personal Injury

DOUGLAS & ELMS, INC.
San Antonio, TX.....................General Practice

DOUGLAS, WHITING, DENHAM & ROGERS
Portland, ME ....Insurance Defense

DOUMAR, CURTIS, CROSS, LAYSTROM & PERLOFF
Fort Lauderdale, FL.................Commercial Law; General Practice; Municipal Bond/Public Authority Financing

DOVER & DIXON, P.A.
Little Rock, AR ....General Practice

DOW, COGBURN & FRIEDMAN, P.C.
Houston, TX ....Real Estate Law

DOW, EINHAUS & MATTISON, P.A.
Owatonna, MN ....General Practice

DOW, LOHNES & ALBERTSON, PLLC
Washington, DC......................Antitrust Law; Communications Law; Computer Law; General Practice; Tax Law

DOWD & DOWD, LTD.
Chicago, IL.............................Appellate Practice; Civil Trial Practice; Insurance Defense; Product Liability Law

DOWDY, T. WILLIAM
Springfield, VA........................Real Estate Law

DOWELL, JAIRL P.
Amarillo, TX...........................Commercial Litigation

DOWLER, ROBERT W.
Fairfax, VA ....Civil Trial Practice

DOWLING, AARON & KEELER, INCORPORATED
Fresno, CA ....Business Law; Civil Trial Practice; Commercial Law; Environmental Law; General Practice; Health Care Law; Insurance Defense; Probate, Trusts and Estate Planning; Real Estate Law; Securities Law; Sports and Entertainment Law; Tax Law; Trademark, Copyright and Unfair Competition

DOWLING LAW FIRM, P.A.
Beaufort, SC ....Civil Trial Practice; General Practice

DOWNEY, BRAND, SEYMOUR & ROHWER
Sacramento, CA ....Environmental Law; General Practice; Natural Resources Law

DOWNEY & CLEVELAND
Marietta, GA...........................Civil Trial Practice; General Practice; Insurance Defense; Medical Malpractice; Personal Injury

DOWNING, RICHARD C., P.A.
Little Rock, AR ....Business Law; Commercial Litigation; Real Estate Law; Securities Law

DOWNS, JUDIN & STANFORD, A PROFESSIONAL CORPORATION
Dallas, TX..............................Civil Trial Practice; Insurance Defense; Labor and Employment Law

DOYLE, GARTLAND, NELSON & MCCLEERY, P.C.
Eugene, OR ....General Practice

DOYLE & HARRIS, A PROFESSIONAL CORPORATION
Tulsa, OK..................................Antitrust Law; Civil Trial Practice; Securities Law

DOYLE, LEWIS & WARNER
Toledo, OH ....Appellate Practice; Business Law; Civil Trial Practice; General Practice; Insurance Defense; Probate, Trusts and Estate Planning; Real Estate Law; Transportation Law

DOYLE & NELSON
Augusta, ME..............................General Practice; Probate, Trusts and Estate Planning

DOYLE, WINTHROP, OBERBILLIG & WEST, P.C.
Phoenix, AZ ....Health Care Law; Insurance Defense; Medical Malpractice

DRAKE & DRAKE
Cullman, AL ....Personal Injury; Workers Compensation

DRAKE, SOMMERS, LOEB, TARSHIS & CATANIA, P.C.
Newburgh, NY..........................General Practice

DRANOFF, SANFORD S.
Pearl River, NY ....Family Law; General Practice

DRANOFF-PERLSTEIN ASSOCIATES
Philadelphia, PA ....Civil Trial Practice; Personal Injury

DRAUGELIS & ASHTON, L.L.P.
Plymouth, MI..........................Civil Trial Practice; Insurance Defense; Personal Injury

DRAY, THOMSON & DYEKMAN, P.C.
Cheyenne, WY.........................Business Law; Insurance Defense

DREILING, BIEKER & HOFFMAN
Hays, KS ....General Practice

DRENDEL, TATNALL, HOFFMAN & MCCRACKEN, A PROFESSIONAL CORPORATION
Batavia, IL................................General Practice

DRENNAN, J. C.
Medford, OK...........................General Practice; Probate, Trusts and Estate Planning; Real Estate Law

DRESSER LAW OFFICE, P.C.
Sturgis, MI ....General Practice

DRESSLER, GOLDSMITH, MILNAMOW & KATZ, LTD.
Chicago, IL..............................Patent, Trademark, Copyright and Unfair Competition

DREW, COOPER & ANDING
Grand Rapids, MI ....Personal Injury

DREW ECKL & FARNHAM
Atlanta, GA ....Civil Rights; Civil Trial Practice; Commercial Law; Construction Law; General Practice; Insurance Defense; Labor and Employment Law; Medical Malpractice; Personal Injury; Product Liability Law

DREW, WARD, GRAF, COOGAN & GOEDDEL, A LEGAL PROFESSIONAL ASSOCIATION
Cincinnati, OH.........................Civil Trial Practice; Employment Benefits Law; Family Law; Probate, Trusts and Estate Planning; Tax Law

DREYER, BABICH, BUCCOLA & CALLAHAM
Sacramento, CA ....Personal Injury; Product Liability Law

DREYER BOYAJIAN LLP
Albany, NY..............................Civil Trial Practice; Criminal Trial Practice; Labor and Employment Law

DRIEBE & DRIEBE, P.C.
Jonesboro, GA ....Civil Trial Practice; General Practice; Personal Injury; Sports and Entertainment Law

DRIGGERS, SCHULTZ & HERBST, A PROFESSIONAL CORPORATION
Troy, MI..................................Business Law

DRINKER BIDDLE & REATH
Washington, DC.......................General Practice
Philadelphia, PA ....General Practice

DROLET, FREEMAN, COTTON, MACADDINO & NORRIS, P.C.
Bloomfield Hills, MI...............Real Estate Law

DROZD, DONALD L.
Laguna Beach, CA ....Probate, Trusts and Estate Planning

DRUMMOND & DRUMMOND
Portland, ME ....General Practice

DRUMMOND & DUCKWORTH
Newport Beach, CA................Patent, Trademark, Copyright and Unfair Competition

DRUMM, WINCHESTER & THORNTON
Sikeston, MO...........................Civil Trial Practice; General Practice

DRYDEN, GROSSHEIM & SUTTON
Beaumont, TX.........................Personal Injury

DRYSDALE, DON M. LAW OFFICES OF
Newport Beach, CA................International Business Law

DUANE, W. FORD
Orlando, FL ....Criminal Trial Practice

DUANE, MORRIS & HECKSCHER
Wilmington, DE......................General Practice
Cherry Hill, NJ ....General Practice
Newark, NJ ....General Practice
New York, NY.........................General Practice
Allentown, PA ....General Practice
Harrisburg, PA.........................General Practice
Philadelphia, PA ....Administrative Law; Bankruptcy Law; Environmental Law; General Practice; Health Care Law; Labor and Employment Law; Patent, Trademark, Copyright and Unfair Competition; Tax Law
Wayne, PA ....General Practice

DUANE AND SHANNON, P.C.
Richmond, VA ....Civil Trial Practice; Criminal Trial Practice; General Practice; Insurance Defense; Personal Injury; Product Liability Law

DUBITSKY, IRA L., P.A.
Miami, FL................................Family Law

DUBUISSON AND DUBUISSON
Opelousas, LA.........................General Practice

DUCKOR SPRADLING & METZGER, A LAW CORPORATION
San Diego, CA ....Civil Trial Practice; Commercial Law; Securities Law

DUDLEY, DUDLEY, WINDLE & STEVENS
El Paso, TX.............................Insurance Defense; Personal Injury

DUDLEY, GALUMBECK & SIMMONS
Tazewell, VA ....Civil Trial Practice; Criminal Trial Practice; Personal Injury

DUDLEY, TOPPER AND FEUERZEIG
Charlotte Amalie, St.
Thomas, VI..............................Business Law; Civil Trial Practice

DUÉ, CABALLERO, PERRY, PRICE & GUIDRY, (A PROFESSIONAL ASSOCIATION)
Baton Rouge, LA....................Personal Injury

DUFFIELD, MILLER, YOUNG, ADAMSON & ALFRED, P.C.
Green Valley, AZ....................Civil Trial Practice; General Practice
Tucson, AZ ....Civil Trial Practice; Commercial Law; Commercial Litigation; General Practice; Insurance Defense; Personal Injury; Probate, Trusts and Estate Planning; Real Estate Law; Tax Law

DUFFORD & BROWN, P.C.
Denver, CO ....Antitrust Law; Bankruptcy Law; Business Law; Civil Trial Practice; Commercial Law; Environmental Law; General Practice; Labor and Employment Law; Natural Resources Law; Real Estate Law; Trademark, Copyright and Unfair Competition

DUFFY, VIRGINIA M.
Jenkintown, PA ....Real Estate Law

DUFFY & GREEN
West Chester, PA....................Criminal Trial Practice; General Practice; Personal Injury

DUGAN, BRINKMANN, MAGINNIS AND PACE
Philadelphia, PA ....Civil Trial Practice

DUKE, GERSTEL, SHEARER & BREGANTE, LLP
Costa Mesa, CA ....Construction Law
San Diego, CA ....Construction Law
San Jose, CA ....Construction Law

DUKER BARRETT GRAVANTE & MARKEL LLP
New York, NY.........................Appellate Practice; Civil Trial Practice; Criminal Trial Practice

DUKES, DUKES, KEATING AND FANECA, P.A.
Gulfport, MS...........................Administrative Law; Admiralty/Maritime Law; Bankruptcy Law; Business Law; Civil Trial Practice; Commercial Law; Commercial Litigation; Construction Law; Environmental Law; General Practice; Insurance Defense; Labor and Employment Law; Land Use Law; Municipal and Zoning Law; Product Liability Law; Real Estate Law; Transportation Law; Workers Compensation

DULANY & LEAHY
Westminster, MD...................General Practice

DUMOUCHEL, DAVID F., P.C.
Detroit, MI...................Appellate Practice; Criminal Trial Practice

DUNAWAY & CROSS, A PROFESSIONAL CORPORATION
Washington, DC...................Administrative Law; Antitrust Law

DUNCAN & ALLEN
Washington, DC...................Energy Law; General Practice

DUNCAN, GREEN, BROWN, LANGENESS & ECKLEY, A PROFESSIONAL CORPORATION
Des Moines, IA...................General Practice

DUNCAN, JOHN A., A PROFESSIONAL CORPORATION
Orange, CA...................Probate, Trusts and Estate Planning

DUNCAN & RAINWATER, TRIAL LAWYERS, A PROF. ASSN.
Little Rock, AR...................Civil Trial Practice; Personal Injury

DUNCAN, THOMASSON & ACREE
La Grange, GA...................General Practice

DUNHAM, BOMAN & LESKERA
Belleville, IL...................Criminal Trial Practice; General Practice; Insurance Defense
Collinsville, IL...................Civil Trial Practice; Criminal Trial Practice; Insurance Defense
East St. Louis, IL...................Civil Trial Practice; Criminal Trial Practice; General Practice; Probate, Trusts and Estate Planning

DUNKLEY, BENNETT & CHRISTENSEN, P.A.
Minneapolis, MN...................Civil Trial Practice; Personal Injury

DUNLAP & BURDICK, A PROFESSIONAL LAW CORPORATION
Santa Cruz, CA...................Personal Injury; Product Liability Law

DUNLAP & CODDING, P.C.
Oklahoma City, OK...................Patent, Trademark, Copyright and Unfair Competition

DUNLAP & SEEGER, P.A.
Rochester, MN...................General Practice

DUNN, ABPLANALP & CHRISTENSEN, P.C.
Vail, CO...................Civil Trial Practice; General Practice; Real Estate Law

DUNN, ABRAHAM & SWAIN
Daytona Beach, FL...................Civil Trial Practice; Probate, Trusts and Estate Planning; Real Estate Law

DUNN, HAASE, SULLIVAN, MALLON, CHERNER & BROADT
Media, PA...................General Practice

DUNN, HUNDMAN, STANCZAK & WILLARD
Bloomington, IL...................General Practice

DUNN, KACAL, ADAMS, PAPPAS & LAW, A PROFESSIONAL CORPORATION
Houston, TX...................Civil Trial Practice

DUNN, LODISH & WIDOM, P.A.
Miami, FL...................Civil Trial Practice

DUNN, MACDONALD & COLEMAN, P.C.
Knoxville, TN...................General Practice; Insurance Defense

DUNN AND MILLER
Media, PA...................Civil Trial Practice

DUNN, NUTTER, MORGAN & SHAW
Texarkana, AR...................Civil Trial Practice; Commercial Litigation; General Practice; Medical Malpractice; Natural Resources Law; Product Liability Law

DUNN, ROGASKI, PREOVOLOS & WEBER
Vallejo, CA...................General Practice

DUNN & WEATHERED, P.C.
Corpus Christi, TX...................Appellate Practice; Insurance Defense; Product Liability Law

DUNNAM & DUNNAM, L.L.P.
Waco, TX...................Civil Trial Practice; Criminal Trial Practice; Family Law; General Practice; Real Estate Law

DUNNIGAN, KEITH D.
Westport, CT...................Aviation Law

DUNNINGS & FRAWLEY, P.C.
Lansing, MI...................Administrative Law; Civil Trial Practice; Criminal Trial Practice; Family Law; General Practice; Labor and Employment Law; Personal Injury; Workers Compensation

DUNTON RAINVILLE SENC
Montreal, QU, Canada...................Commercial Law; General Practice; Labor and Employment Law

DUNTON, SIMMONS & DUNTON
White Stone, VA...................Civil Trial Practice; General Practice

DUNWODY WHITE & LANDON, P.A.
Miami, FL...................Probate, Trusts and Estate Planning
Naples, FL...................Probate, Trusts and Estate Planning

DURANT & DURANT
Philadelphia, PA...................Civil Trial Practice; Criminal Trial Practice

DURBIN, LARIMORE & BIALICK, P.C.
Oklahoma City, OK...................Commercial Law; Insurance Defense; Real Estate Law

DURHAM, EDWARD D.
Montrose, CO...................Civil Trial Practice; Family Law; General Practice

DURHAM, EVANS, JONES & PINEGAR
Salt Lake City, UT...................Business Law; Civil Trial Practice; Real Estate Law; Securities Law

DURIE & LAWSON, P.A., LAW OFFICES OF
Orlando, FL...................Aviation Law; Civil Trial Practice; Medical Malpractice; Personal Injury; Product Liability Law

DURKIN & BOGGIA
Ridgefield Park, NJ...................Civil Trial Practice

DURLAND & DURLAND
Oklahoma City, OK...................Commercial Law; Energy Law; Medical Malpractice; Personal Injury; Securities Law

DURR AND KEINZ
Utica, NY...................General Practice; Personal Injury

DUSHOFF & MCCALL, A PROFESSIONAL CORPORATION
Phoenix, AZ...................Civil Trial Practice; Municipal and Zoning Law; Real Estate Law

DUTHIE & TATE
Durango, CO...................General Practice

DUTTON, BRAUN, STAACK, HELLMAN & IVERSEN, P.L.C.
Waterloo, IA...................General Practice

DUVALL & DUVALL, L.L.P.
Salisbury, MD...................Civil Trial Practice; Criminal Trial Practice; General Practice

DUVIN, CAHN & HUTTON, A LEGAL PROFESSIONAL ASSOCIATION
Cleveland, OH...................Civil Trial Practice; Employment Benefits Law; Labor and Employment Law

DWIGHT, ROYALL, HARRIS, KOEGEL & CASKEY
Washington, DC...................General Practice
New York, NY...................General Practice

DWORKIN, MICHAEL L.
San Mateo, CA...................Aviation Law; Transportation Law

DWORSKY, TAMARA L.
Scottsdale, AZ...................Probate, Trusts and Estate Planning

DWYER & CAMBRE, A PROFESSIONAL LAW CORPORATION
Metairie, LA...................Real Estate Law

DWYER, HUDDLESON & RAY, P.C.
Fort Collins, CO...................General Practice

DWYER IMANAKA SCHRAFF KUDO MEYER & FUJIMOTO, ATTORNEYS AT LAW, A LAW CORPORATION
Honolulu, HI...................Administrative Law; Banking Law; Bankruptcy Law; Business Law; Civil Trial Practice; Commercial Law; Construction Law; Environmental Law; Health Care Law; Insurance Defense; Labor and Employment Law; Municipal and Zoning Law; Natural Resources Law; Real Estate Law; Trademark, Copyright and Unfair Competition

DWYER, SMITH, GRIMM, GARDNER, LAZER, POHREN & ROGERS
Omaha, NE...................Bankruptcy Law; Civil Trial Practice; General Practice; Health Care Law; Personal Injury; Tax Law

DWYER, WHITE & SAPP
Atlanta, GA...................Medical Malpractice; Personal Injury

DYE, TUCKER, EVERITT, WHEALE & LONG, A PROFESSIONAL ASSOCIATION
Augusta, GA...................Civil Trial Practice; General Practice; Insurance Defense

DYER, ROBERT G. LAW OFFICES OF
San Diego, CA...................Admiralty/Maritime Law; Civil Trial Practice

DYER, GAROFALO, MANN & SCHULTZ, A LEGAL PROFESSIONAL ASSOCIATION
Dayton, OH...................Personal Injury

DYER & WHITE
Menlo Park, CA....................Civil Trial Practice; Labor and Employment Law; Personal Injury; Product Liability Law

DYKEMA GOSSETT PLLC
Washington, DC....................General Practice
Ann Arbor, MI ....General Practice
Bloomfield Hills, MI..............General Practice
Detroit, MI............................Antitrust Law; Civil Trial Practice; Environmental Law; General Practice; Health Care Law; International Business Law; Labor and Employment Law; Municipal Bond/Public Authority Financing; Patent, Trademark, Copyright and Unfair Competition; Personal Injury; Real Estate Law; Tax Law
Grand Rapids, MI ....General Practice
Lansing, MI..........................General Practice

DYMOND, LEWIS W., JR., A PROFESSIONAL CORPORATION
Aurora, CO ....Probate, Trusts and Estate Planning

EADINGTON, MERHAB & EADINGTON, A PROFESSIONAL CORPORATION
Newport Beach, CA................Business Law; General Practice

EAGLETON, EAGLETON AND HARRISON, INC.
Tulsa, OK..............................Business Law; Employment Benefits Law; Family Law; Probate, Trusts and Estate Planning; Tax Law

EAMES, DONALD E.
Skowhegan, ME ....General Practice; Probate, Trusts and Estate Planning

EAMES WILCOX
Detroit, MI............................Administrative Law; Bankruptcy Law; Civil Trial Practice; Commercial Law; Personal Injury; Probate, Trusts and Estate Planning; Transportation Law

EARDLEY LAW OFFICES, P.C.
Grand Rapids, MI ....Personal Injury

EARL, BLANK, KAVANAUGH & STOTTS, PROFESSIONAL ASSOCIATION
Miami, FL ....Environmental Law; Natural Resources Law
Sarasota, FL ....Environmental Law; Natural Resources Law

EARL, CURLEY & LAGARDE
Phoenix, AZ ....Land Use Law; Municipal and Zoning Law

EARLEY, JACK M.
Irvine, CA..............................Criminal Trial Practice; Environmental Law

EARLEY & DICKINSON, P.C.
Las Vegas, NV ....Civil Trial Practice; Construction Law; Insurance Defense; Medical Malpractice; Product Liability Law

EARLY, LENNON, PETERS & CROCKER, P.C.
Kalamazoo, MI ....Business Law; General Practice; Insurance Defense; Probate, Trusts and Estate Planning; Real Estate Law; Tax Law; Workers Compensation

EARNEST, FOSTER, EDER, LEVI & NORTHAM
Rushville, IN..........................Civil Trial Practice; General Practice; Probate, Trusts and Estate Planning

EASTMAN & SMITH LTD.
Toledo, OH ....Banking Law; Business Law; Civil Trial Practice; Environmental Law; General Practice; Health Care Law; Labor and Employment Law; Municipal and Zoning Law; Probate, Trusts and Estate Planning; Tax Law

EASTON, W. DOUGLAS LAW OFFICES OF
Costa Mesa, CA......................Medical Malpractice; Personal Injury

EATON AND COTTRELL, P.A.
Bay St. Louis, MS..................General Practice
Gulfport, MS..........................General Practice
Jackson, MS ....General Practice

EATON, PEABODY, BRADFORD & VEAGUE, P.A.
Bangor, ME............................Antitrust Law; Banking Law; Business Law; Civil Trial Practice; Environmental Law; General Practice; Health Care Law; Insurance Defense; Labor and Employment Law; Municipal Bond/Public Authority Financing; Municipal and Zoning Law; Personal Injury; Probate, Trusts and Estate Planning; Real Estate Law

EATON & ROMWEBER
Batesville, IN..........................General Practice
Versailles, IN..........................Civil Trial Practice; General Practice; Insurance Defense

EAVES, BARDACKE & BAUGH, P.A.
Albuquerque, NM....................Antitrust Law; Banking Law; Civil Trial Practice; Commercial Law; Commercial Litigation; Environmental Law; Insurance Defense

EBE & ASSOCIATES, P.C.
Austin, TX ....Appellate Practice; Civil Trial Practice; Commercial Litigation; Labor and Employment Law

EBERLE, BERLIN, KADING, TURNBOW & MCKLVEEN, CHARTERED
Boise, ID................................Antitrust Law; Civil Trial Practice; General Practice; Natural Resources Law; Securities Law; Tax Law

EBLING, SAMUEL C., A PROF. CORP., LAW OFFICES OF
St. Louis, MO........................Banking Law; Business Law; Construction Law; Real Estate Law; Securities Law

ECKBERG, LAMMERS, BRIGGS, WOLFF & VIERLING, P.L.L.P.
Stillwater, MN........................General Practice

ECKERT, JAMES D.
St. Petersburg, FL..................Civil Trial Practice

ECKERT SEAMANS CHERIN & MELLOTT
Washington, DC......................General Practice
Allentown, PA ....Patent, Trademark, Copyright and Unfair Competition
Harrisburg, PA ....General Practice
Philadelphia, PA ....Patent, Trademark, Copyright and Unfair Competition
Pittsburgh, PA ....General Practice; Patent, Trademark, Copyright and Unfair Competition

ECKERT & STINGL
Rhinelander, WI......................Appellate Practice; Civil Trial Practice; General Practice; Insurance Defense

ECKSTEIN, MICHAEL L., ATTY AT LAW, A PROF. CORP.
New Orleans, LA....................Business Law; Mergers and Acquisitions; Probate, Trusts and Estate Planning; Sports and Entertainment Law; Tax Law

EDDY, YOUNG, HOYT & DOWNS
Fredericton, NB, Canada.........Commercial Law

EDENFIELD & COX, P.C.
Statesboro, GA........................Civil Trial Practice

EDES & EDES, INC., A PROFESSIONAL CORPORATION
Concord, MA ....General Practice

EDGARTON, ST. PETER, PETAK, MASSEY & BULLON
Fond du Lac, WI ....General Practice

EDMONDS & CO., P.C.
New York, NY ....Business Law

EDMONSON, BIGGS, MOZINGO & HOLBROOK, P.A.
Jackson, MS ....Insurance Defense

EDMUNDS & WILLIAMS, P.C.
Lynchburg, VA ....General Practice

EDMUNDSON, TERANDO AND HOPKINS
Poplar Bluff, MO....................Criminal Trial Practice; Insurance Defense; Personal Injury

EDWARDS, CHARLES W.
Spencer, IN............................General Practice

EDWARDS, HARRY L.
Greenville, SC..........................Business Law

EDWARDS, STEPHEN B.
Austin, TX ....Antitrust Law; Criminal Trial Practice; Securities Law

EDWARDS & ANGELL
Providence, RI........................Antitrust Law; Civil Trial Practice; Communications Law; Environmental Law; General Practice; Labor and Employment Law; Municipal Bond/Public Authority Financing; Natural Resources Law; Tax Law; Trademark, Copyright and Unfair Competition

EDWARDS & ANTHOLIS
Morristown, NJ......................Tax Law

EDWARDS, BELK, HUNTER & KERR
El Paso, TX............................Banking Law

EDWARDS & KIRBY, L.L.P.
Raleigh, NC............................Medical Malpractice; Personal Injury

EDWARDS LAW FIRM
Billings, MT ....Personal Injury

EDWARDS, MORSE, OLSON, WAITE & WINTERTON, CHTD.
Las Vegas, NV ....Commercial Litigation; Probate, Trusts and Estate Planning; Real Estate Law; Tax Law

EDWARDS, RICK, INC.
Los Angeles, CA......................Civil Trial Practice

EDWARDS, SIEH, HATHAWAY, SMITH & GOODFRIEND, P.S.
Seattle, WA ....Appellate Practice

EDWARDS SINGER WOLK AND SPOENEMAN
St. Louis, MO........................General Practice

EDWARDS, SOOY & BYRON, A PROFESSIONAL CORPORATION
San Diego, CA ....Civil Trial Practice

EGAN, FLANAGAN AND COHEN, P.C.
Springfield, MA.....................General Practice

EGAN, THOMAS F., P.A.
Orlando, FL ....Criminal Trial Practice

EGERTON, MCAFEE, ARMISTEAD & DAVIS, P.C.
Knoxville, TN ....Banking Law; Civil Trial Practice; Health Care Law; Probate, Trusts and Estate Planning; Tax Law; Workers Compensation

EGGENBERGER, EGGENBERGER, MCKINNEY, WEBER & HOFMEISTER, P.C.
Detroit, MI.............................Business Law; Civil Trial Practice; Insurance Defense; Labor and Employment Law; Personal Injury; Probate, Trusts and Estate Planning

EGGER BETTS SHERWOOD AUSTIN TREACY, PLLC
Bellevue, WA..........................Probate, Trusts and Estate Planning; Tax Law

EGGER & HALLETT, PROFESSIONAL LAW CORPORATION
San Bernardino, CA................Workers Compensation

EGGERS, EGGERS & EGGERS
Boone, NC.............................General Practice

EGGERT, ERB, O'DONOHOE, FRYE AND VON AH, P.L.C.
Charles City, IA.....................General Practice

EGGUM, SUSAN K., P.C.
Portland, OR ....Civil Trial Practice; General Practice

EHLINGER & KRILL, S.C.
Milwaukee, WI ....Business Law; Civil Trial Practice; Health Care Law

EHMANN & HILLER, P.C.
Phoenix, AZ ....Probate, Trusts and Estate Planning; Tax Law

EHRENPREIS, RALPH, A PROFESSIONAL LAW CORPORATION
Los Angeles, CA ....Immigration and Naturalization

EHRLICH, FRAZER & FELDMAN
Garden City, NY ....Labor and Employment Law

EICH & FRANKLIN
Chicago, IL.............................Insurance Defense

EIDSON & ASSOCIATES, P.C.
Atlanta, GA ....Civil Trial Practice

EIKENBURG & STILES
Houston, TX ....General Practice

EINHORN, JONATHAN J.
New Haven, CT ....Civil Trial Practice; Personal Injury

EISEN & JOHNSTON
Sacramento, CA ....Appellate Practice

EISENBERG, ANDERSON, MICHALIK & LYNCH
New Britain, CT......................Labor and Employment Law

EISENBERG & KIRSCH
Liberty, NY ....Insurance Defense

EISENHART & EISENHART
Cambridge, NE ....General Practice

EISENHOWER & CARLSON
Tacoma, WA ....General Practice

EISENSTAT, GABAGE, BERMAN & FURMAN, A PROFESSIONAL CORPORATION
Vineland, NJ...........................Civil Trial Practice; General Practice; Insurance Defense

EISENSTEIN, GWEN M., P.C.
Dallas, TX ....Real Estate Law

EISFELDER, ROBERT W., P.C., LAW OFFICES OF
Los Angeles, CA ....Civil Trial Practice; Family Law

EISNER & HUBBARD, P.C.
New York, NY ....Labor and Employment Law

EKKER, KUSTER & MCCONNELL
Sharon, PA ....General Practice; Insurance Defense

EKMAN & BOHRER, P.S.
Seattle, WA ....Employment Benefits Law

ELAM & BURKE, A PROFESSIONAL ASSOCIATION
Boise, ID................................Antitrust Law; Banking Law; Bankruptcy Law; Business Law; Civil Trial Practice; Commercial Law; Environmental Law; General Practice; Insurance Defense; Labor and Employment Law; Municipal Bond/Public Authority Financing; Natural Resources Law; Probate, Trusts and Estate Planning; Real Estate Law; Securities Law; Tax Law; Workers Compensation

ELAM & GLASGOW
Union City, TN.......................General Practice; Insurance Defense

ELARBEE, THOMPSON & TRAPNELL
Atlanta, GA ....Employment Benefits Law; Labor and Employment Law

ELDEN LAW FIRM, THE
Chicago, IL.............................Business Law; Health Care Law

ELDERKIN, MARTIN, KELLY & MESSINA, P.C.
Erie, PA.................................Commercial Litigation; Labor and Employment Law

ELDER & KURZMAN, P.A.
Miami, FL ....Construction Law

ELENBAAS & SCHOEMAN
Fullerton, CA ....Civil Trial Practice; Labor and Employment Law

ELKINS & ASSOCIATES, A PROFESSIONAL LAW CORPORATION
New Orleans, LA ....Tax Law

ELKINS, JAMES W., P.A.
Naples, FL..............................General Practice; Probate, Trusts and Estate Planning; Real Estate Law; Tax Law

ELKUS, LAWRENCE M.
Southfield, MI ....Natural Resources Law; Probate, Trusts and Estate Planning

ELLENBOGEN & GOLDSTEIN, P.C.
New York, NY ....Family Law

ELLIN AND BAKER
Baltimore, MD ....Civil Trial Practice; Medical Malpractice; Personal Injury; Product Liability Law

ELLIOTT & BLACKBURN
Valdosta, GA ....Civil Trial Practice; General Practice

ELLIOTT & PARK
Portland, OR ....Commercial Litigation

ELLIOTT REIHNER SIEDZIKOWSKI & EGAN, P.C.
Blue Bell, PA..........................Civil Trial Practice; Commercial Law

ELLIS, RONALD D.
Torrance, CA...........................Commercial Law

ELLIS, BROWN & SHEILS, CHARTERED
Boise, ID................................Civil Trial Practice; Commercial Litigation; Workers Compensation

ELLIS, EASTERLIN, PEAGLER, GATEWOOD, HARPER & SKIPPER, P.C., A PROFESSIONAL CORPORATION
Americus, GA ....Bankruptcy Law; General Practice; Insurance Defense

ELLIS, HOOPER, WARLICK, MORGAN & HENRY
Jacksonville, NC......................General Practice

ELLIS LAW FIRM
Benton, AR ....Civil Trial Practice; General Practice; Insurance Defense

ELLIS, LI & MCKINSTRY, PLLC
Seattle, WA ....Commercial Litigation

ELLIS & MORGAN
Stillwater, OK ....Commercial Law; Probate, Trusts and Estate Planning

ELLIS, PAINTER, RATTERREE & BART LLP
Savannah, GA ....General Practice

ELLIS, SPENCER AND BUTLER
Hollywood, FL........................Civil Trial Practice; General Practice

ELLISON, HINKLE & BAYER, A PROFESSIONAL LAW CORPORATION
Ventura, CA ....Personal Injury

ELLMAN, BURKE, HOFFMAN & JOHNSON, A PROFESSIONAL CORPORATION
San Francisco, CA ....Land Use Law; Municipal and Zoning Law; Real Estate Law

ELLMANN & ELLMANN, P.C.
Ann Arbor, MI ....Bankruptcy Law; Labor and Employment Law

ELMAN & ASSOCIATES, A PROFESSIONAL CORPORATION
Media, PA..............................Patent, Trademark, Copyright and Unfair Competition

ELMAN & EHARDT, LTD.
Harvard, IL ....General Practice

ELMORE, ELMORE & WILLIAMS, P.A.
Asheville, NC ....Civil Trial Practice; Criminal Trial Practice; Family Law; Medical Malpractice; Personal Injury

ELROD, KATZ, PREEO, LOOK, MOISON & SILVERMAN, PROFESSIONAL CORPORATION
Denver, CO ....Business Law; Civil Trial Practice; Commercial Litigation; Probate, Trusts and Estate Planning; Real Estate Law; Tax Law

ELROD, LAWING & SHARPLESS, P.A.
Greensboro, NC ....Civil Trial Practice; General Practice; Medical Malpractice

ELSENER & CADENHEAD
Seminole, OK ....Civil Trial Practice; General Practice

ELSTEIN AND ELSTEIN, P.C.
Bridgeport, CT ....Business Law; Personal Injury; Real Estate Law

ELWOOD, O'DONOHOE, O'CONNOR & STOCHL
Cresco, IA ....General Practice
New Hampton, IA ....General Practice

ELY, CARY, WELCH & HICKMAN
Hannibal, MO ....General Practice

ELY, FRITZ & HOGAN
Costa Mesa, CA ....Civil Trial Practice; General Practice; Insurance Defense; Personal Injury; Product Liability Law

ELY AND TRUE
Batavia, OH ....Insurance Defense

EMENS, KEGLER, BROWN, HILL & RITTER
Columbus, OH ....Administrative Law; Banking Law; Bankruptcy Law; Business Law; Civil Trial Practice; Construction Law; Employment Benefits Law; Environmental Law; General Practice; Health Care Law; Immigration and Naturalization; Labor and Employment Law; Municipal and Zoning Law; Natural Resources Law; Patent, Trademark, Copyright and Unfair Competition; Probate, Trusts and Estate Planning; Real Estate Law; Tax Law; Trademark, Copyright and Unfair Competition

EMERSON & EMERSON, P.A.
Naples, FL...............................Commercial Law; Commercial Litigation; International Business Law

EMERY JAMIESON
Edmonton, AB, Canada ....Civil Trial Practice; General Practice; Patent, Trademark, Copyright and Unfair Competition

EMISON, DOOLITTLE, KOLB & ROELLGEN
Vincennes, IN..........................General Practice; Insurance Defense

EMMETT, COBB, WAITS & KESSENICH, A PROFESSIONAL LAW CORPORATION
New Orleans, LA ....Admiralty/Maritime Law; Medical Malpractice

EMROCH, WALTER H. & ASSOCIATES
Richmond, VA ....Personal Injury

ENFIELD BROWN & COLLINS
Salem, OR ....General Practice

ENGELBRECHT, MARCY M., P.A., LAW OFFICES OF
Cockeysville, MD....................Labor and Employment Law

ENGELS, PERTNOY, SOLOWSKY & ALLEN, P.A.
Miami, FL ....General Practice

ENGLAND & COHEN
Oxnard, CA ....General Practice

ENGLAND & MCKNIGHT
Atlanta, GA ....Civil Trial Practice; Criminal Trial Practice; Insurance Defense; Medical Malpractice; Personal Injury; Product Liability Law

ENGLAND, WHITFIELD, SCHRÖEDER & TREDWAY, L.L.P.
Oxnard, CA ....General Practice; Real Estate Law; Tax Law
Thousand Oaks, CA ....General Practice

ENGLE & BRIDE
Ventura, CA ....General Practice; Insurance Defense; Medical Malpractice

ENGLISH, LUCAS, PRIEST & OWSLEY
Bowling Green, KY ....Banking Law; Bankruptcy Law; Civil Trial Practice; Commercial Law; Criminal Trial Practice; Environmental Law; General Practice; Immigration and Naturalization; Labor and Employment Law; Medical Malpractice; Municipal Bond/Public Authority Financing; Natural Resources Law; Personal Injury; Probate, Trusts and Estate Planning; Real Estate Law; Tax Law

ENGLISH & VAN HORNE, P.C.
Detroit, MI..............................Immigration and Naturalization

ENGSTROM, LIPSCOMB & LACK, A PROFESSIONAL CORPORATION
Los Angeles, CA ....Civil Trial Practice; Commercial Litigation

ENSLEN, JOHNSTON & PINKSTON, L.L.C.
Wetumpka, AL........................Criminal Trial Practice; General Practice; Real Estate Law

ENTERPRISE LAW GROUP, INC.
Menlo Park, CA ....Business Law; Civil Trial Practice; Commercial Litigation

ENTIN & MARGULES, P.A.
Fort Lauderdale, FL...............Commercial Litigation; Criminal Trial Practice; Insurance Defense

ENWALL, MICHAEL R. LAW OFFICES OF
Boulder, CO ....Civil Trial Practice; Criminal Trial Practice

EPPS AND EPPS, LAW OFFICE OF
Johnson City, TN....................General Practice

EPSTEIN, SHERWIN L. & ASSOCIATES
Kansas City, MO ....Appellate Practice; Business Law; Civil Trial Practice; Municipal and Zoning Law; Real Estate Law

EPSTEIN, BARRY D., P.A.
Rochelle Park, NJ ....Civil Trial Practice

EPSTEIN BECKER & GREEN, P.C.
New York, NY ....General Practice

EPSTEIN, EDNA SELAN, THE LAW OFFICES OF
Chicago, IL..............................Civil Trial Practice; Labor and Employment Law

EPSTEIN FOGARTY COHEN & SELBY, LLC
Greenwich, CT ....General Practice

EPSTEIN & KOOPERSMITH
Mineola, NY............................Commercial Law; Commercial Litigation; Family Law; General Practice

EPSTEIN, SHAPIRO & EPSTEIN
Philadelphia, PA ....Tax Law

EPTING & HACKNEY
Chapel Hill, NC ....Civil Trial Practice; Family Law; General Practice; Personal Injury; Real Estate Law

ERICKSON, DAVIS, MURPHY, JOHNSON, GRIFFITH & WALSH, LTD.
Decatur, IL...............................General Practice; Insurance Defense

ERICKSON & SEDERSTROM, P.C.
Lincoln, NE.............................Civil Trial Practice; General Practice; Health Care Law; Insurance Defense; Labor and Employment Law; Municipal and Zoning Law; Personal Injury; Probate, Trusts and Estate Planning; Real Estate Law
Omaha, NE ....Civil Trial Practice; General Practice; Insurance Defense; Labor and Employment Law; Personal Injury; Probate, Trusts and Estate Planning; Tax Law

ERICKSON, THORPE & SWAINSTON, LTD.
Reno, NV ....Civil Trial Practice; Construction Law; General Practice; Insurance Defense; Labor and Employment Law; Medical Malpractice; Product Liability Law

ERICKSON, WEBB & SCOLTON
Jamestown, NY ....General Practice

ERICSSON RIDGEWAY, A PROFESSIONAL CORPORATION
Portland, OR...........................Insurance Defense

ERLACH, RAYMOND N. STELLA, LAW OFFICES OF
San Francisco, CA ....Business Law; Civil Trial Practice; Health Care Law

ERMAN, TEICHER, MILLER, ZUCKER & FREEDMAN, A PROFESSIONAL CORPORATION
Southfield, MI ....Bankruptcy Law

ERNSTROM & DRESTE, LLP
Rochester, NY.........................Construction Law

ERSKINE & ERSKINE
Worcester, MA ....Probate, Trusts and Estate Planning

ERVAIS, RONALD
Philadelphia, PA ....General Practice

ERVIN, VARN, JACOBS AND ERVIN
Tallahassee, FL ....Administrative Law; Business Law; General Practice

ERWIN, OTT, CLARK & CAMPBELL
York, ME ....Civil Trial Practice; Probate, Trusts and Estate Planning; Real Estate Law

ESDAILE, BARRETT & ESDAILE
Boston, MA.............................Civil Trial Practice; General Practice; Personal Injury

ESKIN & JACKSON
Santa Barbara, CA ....Criminal Trial Practice; Family Law

Ventura, CA ....Criminal Trial Practice; Family Law

ESLER, PETRIE & LINDIE, P.A.
Fort Lauderdale, FL ....Civil Trial Practice; General Practice; Insurance Defense; Personal Injury

ESPY, ALAN C., P.A.
West Palm Beach, FL ....Insurance Defense; Personal Injury

ESSEN, ESSEN, SUSANECK, CANET & LIPSON, P.A.
Miami, FL ....Criminal Trial Practice

ESTES, LEE LAW OFFICES OF
West Bloomfield, MI...............Civil Trial Practice; Insurance Defense

ESTES & HOYT, A PROFESSIONAL CORPORATION
San Diego, CA ....Bankruptcy Law; Civil Trial Practice

ETHEREDGE & STEUER, P.C.
Northampton, MA..................General Practice

ETHERIDGE, MOSER, GARNER AND BRUNER, P.A.
Laurinburg, NC.......................General Practice

ETIENNE & ASSOCIÉS, ETUDE
Geneva, Switzerland.................General Practice
Lausanne, Switzerland ....General Practice

ETNIRE, GEOFFREY C.
Pleasanton, CA........................Real Estate Law

EUBANK, HASSELL & ASSOC., P.A.
Daytona Beach, FL..................Insurance Defense; Medical Malpractice; Product Liability Law

EUBANKS, GARY, & ASSOCIATES, P.A.
Little Rock, AR ....Administrative Law; Medical Malpractice; Personal Injury; Product Liability Law

EUBANKS, HILYARD, RUMBLEY, MEIER & LENGAUER, A PROFESSIONAL ASSOCIATION
Orlando, FL ....General Practice

EVANS, JOHN F. Q.C.
Hamilton, ON, Canada............Civil Trial Practice

EVANS, ROGER
Dallas, TX ....Civil Trial Practice; Labor and Employment Law

EVANS & BURRELL
Philadelphia, PA ....Municipal Bond/Public Authority Financing

EVANS, CARTER, KUNES & BENNETT, P.A.
Charleston, SC ....Probate, Trusts and Estate Planning; Tax Law

EVANS & DIXON
St. Louis, MO..........................Admiralty/Maritime Law; General Practice; Insurance Defense

EVANS, GANDY, DANIEL & MOORE
Fort Worth, TX ....Criminal Trial Practice

EVANS ● IVORY, P.C.
Pittsburgh, PA ....Admiralty/Maritime Law; Medical Malpractice; Personal Injury; Product Liability Law

EVANS, JONES & REYNOLDS, A PROFESSIONAL CORPORATION
Nashville, TN ....General Practice

EVANS, KEANE LLP
Boise, ID..................................General Practice
Kellogg, ID ....General Practice

EVANS & MULLINIX, P.A.
Lenexa, KS...............................Bankruptcy Law; Civil Trial Practice; Commercial Law

EVANS, OSBORNE, KREIZMAN & BONNEY
Red Bank, NJ...........................Admiralty/Maritime Law; Civil Trial Practice; General Practice

EVANS & PETREE
Memphis, TN ....General Practice; Insurance Defense

EVANS, PORTNOY & QUINN
Pittsburgh, PA ....Medical Malpractice; Personal Injury

EVERETT, GASKINS, HANCOCK & STEVENS
Raleigh, NC.............................Administrative Law; Bankruptcy Law; Civil Trial Practice; Commercial Law; Communications Law; Construction Law; International Business Law

EVERETT & LUYMES, P.C.
Galva, IL.................................General Practice

EVERSOLE & RUDD, P.A.
Miami, FL ....Medical Malpractice; Personal Injury; Product Liability Law

EVERSON, WHITNEY, EVERSON & BREHM, S.C.
Green Bay, WI ....General Practice; Insurance Defense

EWEN, HILLIARD & BUSH
Louisville, KY ....Civil Trial Practice; General Practice; Insurance Defense

EWING & EWING, P.C.
Denver, CO ....Commercial Litigation; Personal Injury

EWING & HOBEROCK
Nevada, MO............................General Practice

EWING & JOHNSON, A PROFESSIONAL LAW CORPORATION
El Centro, CA ....General Practice

EYSTER, KEY, TUBB, WEAVER & ROTH
Decatur, AL ....General Practice; Insurance Defense; Medical Malpractice; Tax Law

FABOZZI, THIERBACH & CALEY
Orange, CA ....Banking Law; Bankruptcy Law; Commercial Law

FABRIS, BURGESS & RING, A PROFESSIONAL CORPORATION
San Francisco, CA ....General Practice

FADEL & BEYER
Cleveland, OH ....General Practice

FAEGRE & BENSON LLP
Denver, CO ....General Practice
Minneapolis, MN ....General Practice
London, England ....General Practice

FAERBER, HISSAM, CLIFF & PEREZ-BENITOA
Naples, FL...............................Criminal Trial Practice

FAGEL & HABER
Chicago, IL..............................Banking Law; Bankruptcy Law; Real Estate Law; Securities Law; Tax Law

FAIN, HARRY M.
Beverly Hills, CA.....................Family Law

FAIN, MAJOR & WILEY, P.C.
Atlanta, GA ....Civil Trial Practice; General Practice; Insurance Defense; Labor and Employment Law; Workers Compensation

FAIRCHILD, PRICE, THOMAS & HALEY, L.L.P.
Center, TX...............................General Practice; Insurance Defense; Real Estate Law

FAIRFIELD, FARROW, FLOWERS, PIERSON & STROTZ, P.C.
Albuquerque, NM....................Commercial Litigation; Construction Law; Real Estate Law

FAIRFIELD, STRAUSS, URITZ & KINIGSTEIN, A PROFESSIONAL CORPORATION
Ventura, CA ....Business Law; Civil Trial Practice; Environmental Law; Labor and Employment Law; Tax Law

FAIRFIELD AND WOODS, P.C.
Denver, CO ....Civil Trial Practice; General Practice; Real Estate Law

FAISANT, ROBIN D.
Menlo Park, CA.......................Land Use Law; Municipal and Zoning Law; Probate, Trusts and Estate Planning

FAISON & GILLESPIE
Durham, NC ....General Practice; Medical Malpractice

FAKES, ARTHUR, P.C.
Chicago, IL..............................International Business Law
Lombard, IL.............................Computer Law; International Business Law

FALCIANI, ANGELO J., P.A., A PROFESSIONAL CORPORATION
Woodbury, NJ.........................Civil Trial Practice; General Practice

FALK LAW FIRM, THE
Washington, DC.......................Administrative Law; Civil Trial Practice; Health Care Law; Insurance Defense; Labor and Employment Law; Medical Malpractice; Probate, Trusts and Estate Planning

FALK & SIEMER, LLP
Buffalo, NY ....General Practice

FANCHER, C. LARRY
La Habra, CA ....Family Law

FANNIN, TYLER & HAMILTON, P.A.
Jacksonville, FL ....Civil Trial Practice; General Practice; Insurance Defense

FANNING, HARPER & MARTINSON, A PROFESSIONAL CORPORATION
Dallas, TX ....Insurance Defense

FANT, PHILIP A.
San Francisco, CA ....Admiralty/Maritime Law

FARAGE AND MCBRIDE
Philadelphia, PA ....Medical Malpractice; Product Liability Law

FARBER, STEVEN G.
Santa Fe, NM........................Criminal Trial Practice; Personal Injury

FARBER, SEGALL & PAPPALARDO
White Plains, NY ....Commercial Litigation

FARHAT, STORY & KRAUS, P.C.
East Lansing, MI ....Appellate Practice; Business Law; Civil Trial Practice; Commercial Law; Criminal Trial Practice; Environmental Law; Family Law; General Practice; Health Care Law; Medical Malpractice; Personal Injury; Probate, Trusts and Estate Planning; Real Estate Law; Tax Law

FARISH, FARISH & ROMANI
West Palm Beach, FL ....Civil Trial Practice; Family Law; Personal Injury

FARLOW LAW FIRM, THE
Albuquerque, NM...................Civil Trial Practice; Insurance Defense; Personal Injury

FARMER, FARMER, KELLEY AND BROWN
London, KY ....Civil Trial Practice; General Practice; Insurance Defense; Medical Malpractice; Product Liability Law

FARMER, PRICE, HORNSBY & WEATHERFORD
Dothan, AL ....Personal Injury

FARMER & READY, A LAW CORPORATION
San Luis Obispo, CA ....Bankruptcy Law

FARMER & WATLINGTON
Yanceyville, NC ....General Practice

FARNAM LAW FIRM, THE
St. Louis, MO........................Tax Law

FARNSWORTH & VONBERG
Houston, TX ....Business Law; Commercial Law; Labor and Employment Law; Natural Resources Law

FARR, DAVIS & FITZE
Tunkhannock, PA ....Civil Trial Practice; General Practice; Real Estate Law

FARRELL, J. MICHAEL
Philadelphia, PA ....Civil Trial Practice

FARRELL, FARRELL & FARRELL, L.C.
Huntington, WV ....Commercial Litigation; Medical Malpractice; Product Liability Law

FARRELL, FARRELL & GINSBACH
Hot Springs, SD ....General Practice

FARRELL & LESLIE
Wallingford, CT ....Civil Trial Practice; General Practice; Personal Injury; Real Estate Law

FARRINGTON & CURTIS, P.C.
Springfield, MO.....................Civil Trial Practice; General Practice

FARRIS & GREEN, L.L.P.
Austin, TX ....Family Law

FARRIS, VAUGHAN, WILLS & MURPHY
Vancouver, BC, Canada..........General Practice

FARRIS, WARFIELD & KANADAY
Nashville, TN ....General Practice

FARRISH, JOHNSON & MASCHKA, P.L.L.P.
Mankato, MN ....Civil Trial Practice; General Practice; Insurance Defense

FARUKI GILLIAM & IRELAND
Dayton, OH...........................Civil Trial Practice; Commercial Litigation; Criminal Trial Practice; Environmental Law; Product Liability Law

FASKEN CAMPBELL GODFREY
Toronto, ON, Canada.............General Practice; Trademark, Copyright and Unfair Competition

FASKEN MARTINEAU
London, England ....General Practice

FASS, FLORENCE M.
Garden City, NY ....Family Law

FAULKNER, BANFIELD, DOOGAN & HOLMES, A PROFESSIONAL CORPORATION
Anchorage, AK ....General Practice

Juneau, AK ....General Practice
Seattle, WA ....General Practice

FAUST, HARRELSON, FULKER, MCCARTHY & SCHLEMMER
Troy, OH...............................General Practice

FAVOUR, MOORE & WILHELMSEN, A PROFESSIONAL ASSOCIATION
Prescott, AZ ....Appellate Practice; Business Law; Civil Trial Practice; Commercial Law; General Practice; Insurance Defense; Probate, Trusts and Estate Planning; Real Estate Law

FAVRET, DEMAREST, RUSSO & LUTKEWITTE, A PROFESSIONAL LAW CORPORATION
New Orleans, LA ....General Practice

FAW, FOLGER, JOHNSON & CAMPBELL, L.L.P.
Mount Airy, NC ....General Practice

FAY, SHARPE, BEALL, FAGAN, MINNICH & MCKEE
Cleveland, OH........................Patent, Trademark, Copyright and Unfair Competition

FEARER, NYE, AHLBERG & CHADWICK
Rochelle, IL ....General Practice

FECZKO AND SEYMOUR
Pittsburgh, PA ....Civil Trial Practice; Personal Injury; Probate, Trusts and Estate Planning

FEDERLEIN & KERANEN, P.C.
Bloomfield Hills, MI ....Commercial Litigation; Construction Law; Insurance Defense

FEDER & MILLS, A PROFESSIONAL CORPORATION
Los Angeles, CA ....Bankruptcy Law

FEENEY, DENA C., P.A.
Silver Spring, MD ....Probate, Trusts and Estate Planning

FEENEY KELLETT WIENNER & BUSH, PROFESSIONAL CORPORATION
Bloomfield Hills, MI ....Civil Trial Practice; Commercial Law; General Practice; Personal Injury; Product Liability Law; Securities Law

FEIKENS, VANDER MALE, STEVENS, BELLAMY & GILCHRIST, P.C.
Detroit, MI............................Banking Law; Business Law; Civil Trial Practice; Commercial Law; Commercial Litigation; General Practice; Health Care Law; Insurance Defense; Labor and Employment Law; Medical Malpractice; Probate, Trusts and Estate Planning; Product Liability Law

FEINBERG, KENNETH R. & ASSOCIATES
Washington, DC.....................Business Law; Civil Trial Practice; Commercial Law; Construction Law; Employment Benefits Law; General Practice; Insurance Defense; Labor and Employment Law; Medical Malpractice; Patent, Trademark, Copyright and Unfair Competition; Product Liability Law

FEINBERG & BARRY, P.C.
Chicago, IL............................Family Law

FEINGOLD, EUGENE M. LAW OFFICES OF
Munster, IN ....Civil Trial Practice; General Practice; Municipal and Zoning Law

FEINGOLD & NAPOLI, L.L.P.
New York, NY ....Tax Law

FEIRICH/MAGER/GREEN/RYAN
Carbondale, IL ....General Practice

FEIWELL & HANNOY, PROFESSIONAL CORPORATION
Indianapolis, IN ....Bankruptcy Law; Commercial Law; Real Estate Law; Sports and Entertainment Law

FELDER, RAOUL LIONEL, P.C., THE FIRM OF
New York, NY ....Civil Trial Practice; Family Law

FELDESMAN, TUCKER, LEIFER, FIDELL & BANK
Washington, DC.....................Family Law; Health Care Law

FELDHAKE, ROBERT J. LAW OFFICES OF
Costa Mesa, CA ....Commercial Litigation; General Practice

FELD, HYDE, LYLE & WERTHEIMER, P.C.
Birmingham, AL ....Probate, Trusts and Estate Planning

FELDMAN & FIORELLO
Wayne, NJ ....Appellate Practice; Civil Trial Practice; Construction Law; Family Law

FELDMAN, FRANDEN, WOODARD, FARRIS & TAYLOR
Tulsa, OK..............................Civil Trial Practice; Medical Malpractice

FELDMAN, JOEL H., P.A.
Boca Raton, FL ....Commercial Litigation; Family Law; Real Estate Law

FELDMAN, KIEFFER & HERMAN, LLP
Buffalo, NY ....Civil Trial Practice; Environmental Law; Health Care Law; Insurance Defense; Medical Malpractice

FELDMAN & KLEIDMAN
Fishkill, NY.............................Personal Injury

FELDMAN, WALDMAN & KLINE, A PROFESSIONAL CORPORATION
San Francisco, CA ....Bankruptcy Law; Business Law; Civil Trial Practice; Construction Law; General Practice; Probate, Trusts and Estate Planning; Real Estate Law; Tax Law

FELDSTEIN GRINBERG STEIN & MCKEE, A PROFESSIONAL CORPORATION
Pittsburgh, PA ....Business Law; Civil Trial Practice; Employment Benefits Law; Family Law; Health Care Law; Insurance Defense; Personal Injury

FELHABER, LARSON, FENLON & VOGT, PROFESSIONAL ASSOCIATION
Minneapolis, MN ....General Practice; Labor and Employment Law
St. Paul, MN ....General Practice

FELLERS, SNIDER, BLANKENSHIP, BAILEY & TIPPENS, A PROFESSIONAL CORPORATION
Oklahoma City, OK...............General Practice
Tulsa, OK................................General Practice

FELLHEIMER EICHEN BRAVERMAN & KASKEY, A PROFESSIONAL CORPORATION
Philadelphia, PA ....Banking Law; Bankruptcy Law; Business Law; Civil Trial Practice; General Practice; Real Estate Law; Securities Law; Tax Law

FELL, MCGARVEY, TRAURING & WILSON
Kokomo, IN............................General Practice; Insurance Defense; Probate, Trusts and Estate Planning

FELL & SPALDING
Philadelphia, PA ....Civil Trial Practice

FENDIG, MCLEMORE, TAYLOR, WHITWORTH & DURHAM, P.C.
Brunswick, GA........................Civil Trial Practice; General Practice; Insurance Defense; Product Liability Law

FENDLER, OSCAR
Blytheville, AR........................General Practice

FENDON, DON A., P.C.
Phoenix, AZ ....Workers Compensation

FENNEBRESQUE, CLARK, SWINDELL & HAY
Charlotte, NC..........................Banking Law; Business Law; Real Estate Law

FENNEMORE CRAIG, A PROFESSIONAL CORPORATION
Phoenix, AZ ....Administrative Law; Antitrust Law; Banking Law; Bankruptcy Law; Business Law; Civil Trial Practice; Commercial Law; Construction Law; Employment Benefits Law; Environmental Law; General Practice; Health Care Law; Insurance Defense; Labor and Employment Law; Medical Malpractice; Municipal and Zoning Law; Natural Resources Law; Patent, Trademark, Copyright and Unfair Competition; Personal Injury; Probate, Trusts and Estate Planning; Real Estate Law; Securities Law; Tax Law; Transportation Law
Scottsdale, AZ........................General Practice; Probate, Trusts and Estate Planning; Real Estate Law
Tucson, AZ ....General Practice; Labor and Employment Law

FENSTER AND FAERBER, PROFESSIONAL ASSOCIATION
Plantation, FL.........................Civil Trial Practice; Personal Injury

FENTON, CHAPMAN, FENTON, SMITH & KANE, P.A.
Bar Harbor, ME......................Civil Trial Practice; Environmental Law; General Practice; International Business Law; Patent, Trademark, Copyright and Unfair Competition; Personal Injury; Probate, Trusts and Estate Planning; Real Estate Law

FENZEL & PERRONE
New York, NY.........................Admiralty/Maritime Law

FERGUS & FERGUS, L.L.P.
Abilene, TX.............................Energy Law

FERGUSON, C. ROBERT
Claremont, CA ....Business Law; Civil Trial Practice; Land Use Law

FERGUSON, CASE, ORR, PATERSON & CUNNINGHAM
Ventura, CA ....Civil Trial Practice; Real Estate Law

FERGUSON, NEWBURN & WESTON, A PROFESSIONAL CORPORATION
La Jolla, CA............................Probate, Trusts and Estate Planning

FERGUSON, SCHETELICH, HEFFERNAN & MURDOCK, P.A.
Baltimore, MD ....Admiralty/Maritime Law; Construction Law; Criminal Trial Practice; Environmental Law; Insurance Defense; Probate, Trusts and Estate Planning; Tax Law; Transportation Law

FERGUSON, STEIN, WALLAS, ADKINS, GRESHAM & SUMTER, P.A.
Charlotte, NC..........................Civil Trial Practice; Criminal Trial Practice; Labor and Employment Law; Medical Malpractice; Personal Injury

FERGUSON & WIDMAYER, P.C.
Ann Arbor, MI ....Employment Benefits Law

FERNANDEZ, JOHN D., P.A.
Clearwater, FL ....Criminal Trial Practice; Personal Injury

FERRARA, FIORENZA, LARRISON, BARRETT & REITZ, P.C.
Syracuse, NY...........................Labor and Employment Law

FERRARO, RUSSELL J., JR. AND ASSOCIATES, P.A.
Stuart, FL................................Family Law

FERRELL & FERTEL, P.A.
Miami, FL ....Civil Trial Practice; Criminal Trial Practice

FERRERI & FOGLE
Lexington, KY ....Workers Compensation
Louisville, KY ....Workers Compensation

FERRERO, MIDDLEBROOKS & CARBO, P.A.
Fort Lauderdale, FL................Personal Injury

FERRIS & BRITTON, A PROFESSIONAL CORPORATION
San Diego, CA ....Antitrust Law; Banking Law; Business Law; Civil Trial Practice; Commercial Law; Communications Law; General Practice; Insurance Defense; Labor and Employment Law; Real Estate Law; Securities Law; Tax Law; Trademark, Copyright and Unfair Competition

FERRITER, SCOBBO, SIKORA, SINGAL, CARUSO & RODOPHELE, P.C.
Boston, MA.............................General Practice

FERRO LABELLA LOGERFO & ZUCKER, A PROFESSIONAL CORPORATION
Hackensack, NJ.......................Banking Law; Commercial Law

FERRO & LEHR, P.A.
Miami, FL ....Criminal Trial Practice; Medical Malpractice; Personal Injury

FERRUZZO & FERRUZZO
Santa Ana, CA ....Business Law; Environmental Law; Family Law; Labor and Employment Law; Probate, Trusts and Estate Planning; Tax Law

FETTER, KESSLER AND PERSING
Lewisburg, PA.........................General Practice

FETTERLY & GORDON, P.A.
Minneapolis, MN ....Civil Trial Practice; Insurance Defense; Personal Injury

FETTINGER, BLOOM & QUINLAN, P.C.
Alamogordo, NM ....General Practice

FEW & FEW, P.A.
Greenville, SC.........................Civil Trial Practice; Environmental Law; Personal Injury; Product Liability Law; Securities Law

FIDDLER, GONZÁLEZ & RODRÍGUEZ
San Juan, PR...........................Antitrust Law; Banking Law; Bankruptcy Law; Civil Trial Practice; Commercial Law; Environmental Law; General Practice; Immigration and Naturalization; Insurance Defense; Labor and Employment Law; Municipal Bond/Public Authority Financing; Real Estate Law; Tax Law; Trademark, Copyright and Unfair Competition

FIEGER, FIEGER & SCHWARTZ, A PROFESSIONAL CORPORATION
Southfield, MI ....Civil Trial Practice; Criminal Trial Practice; Medical Malpractice; Personal Injury; Product Liability Law

FIELD & FIELD, P.C.
Kalamazoo, MI ....Personal Injury

FIELD, GENTRY & BENJAMIN, P.C.
Kansas City, MO ....General Practice

FIELD GOLAN & SWIGER
Chicago, IL..............................Banking Law; Business Law; Commercial Litigation

FIELDING, BARRETT & TAYLOR, L.L.P.
Fort Worth, TX ....Municipal and Zoning Law

FIELD, RICHARDSON & WILHELMY
Walnut Creek, CA ....Construction Law; Real Estate Law

FIGARI & DAVENPORT
Dallas, TX...............................Civil Trial Practice; General Practice

FIKE, CASCIO & BOOSE
Somerset, PA...........................General Practice

FILDEW HINKS, P.L.L.C.
Detroit, MI............................Civil Trial Practice; General Practice; Real Estate Law; Tax Law

FILE, PAYNE, SCHERER & FILE
Beckley, WV............................General Practice; Insurance Defense

FILION, WAKELY & THORUP
Toronto, ON, Canada..............Employment Benefits Law

FILLEY, G. WILLIAM
San Francisco, CA..................Family Law

FINBURY & SULLIVAN, P.C.
Haverhill, MA........................Personal Injury

FINCH, MONTGOMERY & WRIGHT
Palo Alto, CA........................Probate, Trusts and Estate Planning

FINCK, KEVIN W. LAW OFFICES OF
San Francisco, CA..................Business Law; Commercial Law; International Business Law

FINE & HATFIELD
Evansville, IN........................Appellate Practice; Bankruptcy Law; Business Law; Civil Rights; Environmental Law; Health Care Law; Insurance Defense; Labor and Employment Law; Probate, Trusts and Estate Planning; Product Liability Law; Real Estate Law; Tax Law; Workers Compensation

FINE & MCDOWELL
Russellville, AL......................General Practice; Insurance Defense

FINE, RICHARD I., & ASSOCIATES, A PROF. CORP., LAW OFFICES OF
Los Angeles, CA......................Antitrust Law; International Business Law

FINER, KIM & STEARNS
Torrance, CA..........................Bankruptcy Law; Business Law; Civil Trial Practice; Environmental Law; General Practice; Probate, Trusts and Estate Planning; Real Estate Law

FINKBOHNER AND LAWLER, L.L.C.
Mobile, AL..............................Bankruptcy Law; Civil Trial Practice; Commercial Law; General Practice; Municipal and Zoning Law; Personal Injury; Product Liability Law

FINKEL ALTMAN & BAILEY, L.L.C.
Columbia, SC..........................Bankruptcy Law; Civil Trial Practice; Commercial Law; Criminal Trial Practice; Insurance Defense; Personal Injury

FINKEL GOLDSTEIN BERZOW & ROSENBLOOM
New York, NY........................Bankruptcy Law

FINKELSTEIN BRUCKMAN WOHL MOST & ROTHMAN, LLP
New York, NY........................Civil Trial Practice; Commercial Law; Family Law; General Practice; Health Care Law; Medical Malpractice

FINK & SWEET
Daytona Beach, FL..................Civil Trial Practice; General Practice

FINK ZAUSMER, P.C.
Farmington Hills, MI..............Environmental Law; Municipal and Zoning Law

FINLEY, WARREN
Laguna Beach, CA..................General Practice

FINLEY, ALT, SMITH, SCHARNBERG, MAY & CRAIG, P.C.
Des Moines, IA........................Appellate Practice; Banking Law; Business Law; Civil Trial Practice; Construction Law; Employment Benefits Law; General Practice; Health Care Law; Insurance Defense; Labor and Employment Law; Medical Malpractice; Personal Injury; Probate, Trusts and Estate Planning; Product Liability Law; Real Estate Law; Tax Law; Transportation Law; Workers Compensation

FINMAN, SHELDON E., P.A.
Fort Myers, FL........................Family Law

FINNEGAN, HENDERSON, FARABOW, GARRETT & DUNNER, L.L.P.
Washington, DC......................Patent, Trademark, Copyright and Unfair Competition; Trademark, Copyright and Unfair Competition

FINNEGAN, UNDERWOOD, RYAN & TIERNEY
Boston, MA..............................Administrative Law; Civil Trial Practice; Insurance Defense

FINNERTY & FINNERTY
Boston, MA..............................Insurance Defense; Product Liability Law

FIORE, OWEN G.
San Jose, CA..........................Probate, Trusts and Estate Planning; Tax Law

FIORENZA & HAYES, S.C.
Milwaukee, WI........................Banking Law; Business Law; Civil Trial Practice; Commercial Litigation; Criminal Trial Practice; Labor and Employment Law; Personal Injury; Probate, Trusts and Estate Planning; Real Estate Law

FIORETTI, MICHAEL D.
Philadelphia, PA......................Family Law

FISCHER, BESSETTE & MULDOWNEY, L.L.P.
Malone, NY............................General Practice

FISCHER, BROWN & GUNN, P.C.
Fort Collins, CO......................General Practice

FISCHER, HOWARD & FRANCIS, LLP
Fort Collins, CO......................Commercial Law; General Practice; Real Estate Law

FISCHETTE, OWEN & HELD
Jacksonville, FL......................Bankruptcy Law; Commercial Litigation

FISCHETTI, RONALD P.
New York, NY........................Criminal Trial Practice

FISCHL CULP MCMILLIN CHAFFIN & BAHNER
Ardmore, OK..........................General Practice

FISH & BENSON
Maplewood, NJ......................Civil Trial Practice; Environmental Law; Personal Injury; Product Liability Law

FISH & NEAVE
Palo Alto, CA..........................Patent, Trademark, Copyright and Unfair Competition
New York, NY........................Patent, Trademark, Copyright and Unfair Competition

FISH & RICHARDSON P.C.
Menlo Park, CA......................Patent, Trademark, Copyright and Unfair Competition
Washington, DC......................Patent, Trademark, Copyright and Unfair Competition
Boston, MA..............................Patent, Trademark, Copyright and Unfair Competition
New York, NY........................Patent, Trademark, Copyright and Unfair Competition
Houston, TX............................Patent, Trademark, Copyright and Unfair Competition

FISHEL, GRACE J.
St. Louis, MO..........................Patent, Trademark, Copyright and Unfair Competition

FISHER & BENDECK, P.A.
West Palm Beach, FL..............Family Law

FISHER, FISHER & BERGER
New York, NY........................Civil Trial Practice; General Practice

FISHER FISHER GAYLE CLINARD & CRAIG, P.A.
High Point, NC........................General Practice

FISHER, GALLAGHER & LEWIS, L.L.P.
Houston, TX............................International Business Law

FISHER, HERBERT F., PLLC, LAW OFFICES OF
New York, NY........................Real Estate Law

FISHER & HURST, LLP
San Francisco, CA..................Insurance Defense

FISHER LAW OFFICE
St. Joseph, MI........................Business Law; General Practice; Probate, Trusts and Estate Planning; Real Estate Law

FISHER AND MATTHEWS, P.A.
Altamonte Springs, FL............Civil Trial Practice
Orlando, FL............................Civil Trial Practice

FISHER, OLSON, DALEY & BATA, LTD.
Grand Forks, ND......................General Practice

FISHER, PATTERSON, SAYLER & SMITH, L.L.P.
Overland Park, KS..................Civil Rights; Civil Trial Practice; Commercial Law; Insurance Defense; Labor and Employment Law; Medical Malpractice; Product Liability Law
Topeka, KS..............................Appellate Practice; Civil Rights; Civil Trial Practice; Commercial Law; General Practice; Insurance Defense; Labor and Employment Law; Personal Injury; Product Liability Law

FISHER & PHILLIPS
Newport Beach, CA..................Labor and Employment Law
Redwood City, CA..................Labor and Employment Law
Fort Lauderdale, FL..................Labor and Employment Law
Atlanta, GA..............................Employment Benefits Law; Labor and Employment Law

FISHER & PORTER, A LAW CORPORATION
Long Beach, CA......................Admiralty/Maritime Law; Environmental Law; General Practice; Insurance Defense; Product Liability Law; Transportation Law

FISHER, ROBERT W., LLC
Atlanta, GA ....Tax Law

FISHER THURBER LLP
La Jolla, CA...........................Securities Law

FISHER WAYLAND COOPER LEADER & ZARAGOZA L.L.P
Washington, DC.....................Communications Law; General Practice

FITCH, EVEN, TABIN & FLANNERY
San Diego, CA ....Patent, Trademark, Copyright and Unfair Competition
Chicago, IL...........................Patent, Trademark, Copyright and Unfair Competition

FITCH, KING & CAFFENTZIS
New York, NY.......................International Trade Law

FITZGERALD, ABBOTT & BEARDSLEY LLP
Oakland, CA ....General Practice

FITZGERALD & ASSOCIATES
Palm Springs, CA ....Labor and Employment Law

FITZGERALD LAW OFFICES
Cheyenne, WY.......................Civil Trial Practice; Medical Malpractice; Personal Injury; Product Liability Law
Laramie, WY..........................Civil Trial Practice; Medical Malpractice; Personal Injury; Product Liability Law

FITZGIBBONS, JOHN M.
Sarasota, FL ....Criminal Trial Practice
Tampa, FL ....Criminal Trial Practice

FITZGIBBONS BROTHERS
Estherville, IA ....General Practice

FITZGIBBONS LAW OFFICES, P.L.C.
Casa Grande, AZ....................Criminal Trial Practice; General Practice; Personal Injury; Probate, Trusts and Estate Planning

FITZPATRICK, CELLA, HARPER & SCINTO
Washington, DC.....................Patent, Trademark, Copyright and Unfair Competition
New York, NY.......................Patent, Trademark, Copyright and Unfair Competition

FITZPATRICK, F. EMMETT, P.C.
Philadelphia, PA ....Appellate Practice; Civil Trial Practice; Commercial Law; Commercial Litigation; Computer Law; Criminal Trial Practice; General Practice; International Business Law; International Trade Law; Real Estate Law

FITZPATRICK & WATERMAN
Bayonne, NJ...........................General Practice; Municipal Bond/Public Authority Financing; Tax Law
Secaucus, NJ...........................General Practice; Municipal Bond/Public Authority Financing; Tax Law

FITZSIMMONS RINGLE & JACOBS, P.C.
Newark, NJ ....Civil Trial Practice; Criminal Trial Practice; Personal Injury; Product Liability Law

FIXEL & MAGUIRE
Tallahassee, FL ....Real Estate Law

FLACK, MCRAVEN & STEPHENS
Macomb, IL ....General Practice

FLAHERTY, COHEN, GRANDE, RANDAZZO & DOREN, P.C.
Buffalo, NY ....Labor and Employment Law

FLAHERTY, MEISLER & COURTNEY
Vernon, CT.............................Civil Trial Practice; Criminal Trial Practice; General Practice; Personal Injury

FLAHERTY, SENSABAUGH & BONASSO
Charleston, WV.......................Insurance Defense

FLAHIVE, OGDEN & LATSON, A PROFESSIONAL CORPORATION
Austin, TX ....Workers Compensation

FLANAGAN, BOOTH, UNGER & MOSES
Glendale, CA...........................Criminal Trial Practice; Personal Injury

FLANAGAN, LIEBERMAN, HOFFMAN & SWAIM
Dayton, OH............................Criminal Trial Practice; General Practice

FLANDERS, SONNESYN & STOVER, LLP
Longmont, CO ....General Practice

FLASTER, GREENBERG, WALLENSTEIN, RODERICK, SPIRGEL, ZUCKERMAN, SKINNER & KIRCHNER, P.C.
Cherry Hill, NJ ....Business Law; Probate, Trusts and Estate Planning; Real Estate Law; Tax Law

FLAXMAN, NEIL, PROFESSIONAL ASSOCIATION
Miami, FL...............................Administrative Law; Labor and Employment Law

FLECK, MATHER & STRUTZ, LTD.
Bismarck, ND ....Environmental Law; Health Care Law; Insurance Defense; Labor and Employment Law; Medical Malpractice; Natural Resources Law; Personal Injury; Tax Law

FLEHR, HOHBACH, TEST, ALBRITTON & HERBERT
San Francisco, CA ....Patent, Trademark, Copyright and Unfair Competition

FLEISCHMANN & FLEISCHMANN, L.L.P.
San Francisco, CA ....Business Law

FLEISSNER, COOPER, MARCUS & QUINN
Chattanooga, TN ....Civil Trial Practice; Insurance Defense; Labor and Employment Law; Product Liability Law

FLEMING, DONALD D., P.S.
Bellevue, WA..........................General Practice; Probate, Trusts and Estate Planning; Real Estate Law

FLEMING, HOVENKAMP & GRAYSON, P.C.
Houston, TX ....Aviation Law; Environmental Law; Personal Injury; Product Liability Law

FLEMING, PATTRIDGE & RUNNERSTROM, P.C.
Golden, CO ....General Practice

FLETCHER DEGROW
Port Huron, MI......................Civil Trial Practice; Environmental Law; General Practice; Health Care Law; Insurance Defense; Labor and Employment Law; Municipal and Zoning Law

FLETCHER, HARLEY & FLETCHER
Augusta, GA ....General Practice

FLETCHER, HEALD & HILDRETH, P.L.C.
Washington, DC.....................Communications Law
Arlington, VA ....General Practice

FLETCHER, SIBELL, MIGATZ & MULRY, P.C.
Manhasset, NY ....General Practice

FLETCHER, TILTON & WHIPPLE, P.C.
Worcester, MA........................General Practice

FLEURIET, SCHELL & PHILLIPS, L.L.P.
Harlingen, TX ....Civil Trial Practice

FLICKER & KERIN
Palo Alto, CA ....Business Law; Family Law; Real Estate Law

FLIGELTAUB, WILLIAM H.
Seattle, WA ....Criminal Trial Practice; Personal Injury

FLIPPIN, COLLINS, HUEY & WEBB
Milan, TN...............................General Practice

FLOOD JOHNSTON & MCSHANE, P.C.
New York, NY........................Civil Trial Practice; Environmental Law; Insurance Defense; Product Liability Law; Sports and Entertainment Law

FLORENCE & SMITH
Peekskill, NY..........................General Practice

FLORES, CASSO, ROMERO & PETTITT
McAllen, TX ....General Practice; Personal Injury; Product Liability Law

FLOURNOY, ROBERT E. III
Marietta, GA...........................Family Law

FLOYD, KEENER, CUSIMANO & ROBERTS, P.C.
Gadsden, AL............................Civil Trial Practice; Criminal Trial Practice; General Practice

FLOYD LAW FIRM, THE, PC
Surfside Beach, SC ....General Practice

FLUEGEL, HELSETH, MCLAUGHLIN, ANDERSON & BRUTLAG, CHARTERED
Elbow Lake, MN ....General Practice

FLYNN, DELICH & WISE
Long Beach, CA......................Admiralty/Maritime Law; Civil Trial Practice; Insurance Defense; International Business Law
San Francisco, CA ....Admiralty/Maritime Law; Civil Trial Practice; Insurance Defense; International Business Law; Patent, Trademark, Copyright and Unfair Competition

FLYNN MCKENNA WRIGHT & KARSH
Colorado Springs, CO.............Banking Law; Commercial Law; International Business Law; Real Estate Law; Tax Law

FLYNN, PALMER & TAGUE
Champaign, IL ....General Practice

FLYNN, PY & KRUSE, A LEGAL PROFESSIONAL ASSOCIATION
Sandusky, OH ....General Practice

FOGEL, FELDMAN, OSTROV, RINGLER & KLEVENS, A LAW CORPORATION
Santa Monica, CA....................Civil Trial Practice; Labor and Employment Law; Personal Injury

FOGEL, JO BENSON, P.A.
Rockville, MD........................Family Law

FOGEL AND LAMBER, PROFESSIONAL ASSOCIATION
Phoenix, AZ ....Appellate Practice; Business Law; Civil Trial Practice; Personal Injury

FOGG, FOGG & HANDLEY
El Reno, OK ....Civil Trial Practice; Personal Injury; Probate, Trusts and Estate Planning

FOLEY, COGNETTI & COMERFORD
Scranton, PA ....Insurance Defense

FOLEY & FOLEY
Palmyra, NY ....Medical Malpractice; Personal Injury

FOLEY, HOAG & ELIOT LLP
Washington, DC....................General Practice
Boston, MA ....General Practice; Labor and Employment Law; Tax Law

FOLEY & JUDELL, L.L.P.
New Orleans, LA ....Municipal Bond/Public Authority Financing

FOLEY & LARDNER
Washington, DC....................General Practice
Jacksonville, FL ....General Practice
Orlando, FL ....General Practice; Labor and Employment Law
Tallahassee, FL ....General Practice
Tampa, FL ....General Practice
West Palm Beach, FL.............General Practice
Chicago, IL............................General Practice
Annapolis, MD ....General Practice
Madison, WI ....General Practice
Milwaukee, WI.......................Antitrust Law; General Practice; Tax Law

FOLEY LARDNER WEISSBURG & ARONSON
Los Angeles, CA ....Health Care Law

FOLEY, MCLANE, NEALON, FOLEY & MCDONALD
Scranton, PA ....Medical Malpractice; Personal Injury; Product Liability Law

FOLEY, SMITH & MAHMOOD, P.C.
Huntsville, AL........................Immigration and Naturalization; International Business Law

FOLGER LEVIN & KAHN LLP
San Francisco, CA ....General Practice

FOLGER, TUCKER & HOWE
Madison, NC..........................General Practice

FOLIART, HUFF, OTTAWAY & CALDWELL, A PROFESSIONAL CORPORATION
Oklahoma City, OK................Civil Trial Practice; Insurance Defense; Medical Malpractice; Personal Injury; Workers Compensation

FOLKESTAD & FAZEKAS, P.C.
Castle Rock, CO ....General Practice; Municipal and Zoning Law; Real Estate Law

FONDA, GARRARD, HILBERMAN & DAVIS, A PROFESSIONAL CORPORATION
Los Angeles, CA ....Insurance Defense

FONVIELLE & HINKLE
Tallahassee, FL ....Medical Malpractice; Personal Injury; Product Liability Law

FORAN & SCHULTZ
Chicago, IL............................Civil Trial Practice; Construction Law; Criminal Trial Practice; Health Care Law; Trademark, Copyright and Unfair Competition

FORBES, THOMAS A.
Austin, TX ....Administrative Law; General Practice; Sports and Entertainment Law

FORBES & BOWMAN
Savannah, GA ....Labor and Employment Law; Product Liability Law

FORCENO, HANNON & ARANGIO
Philadelphia, PA ....Civil Trial Practice; Personal Injury; Product Liability Law

FORCHELLI, SCHWARTZ, MINEO & CARLINO
Mineola, NY...........................Land Use Law

FORD, BRYAN KENT
Dallas, TX ....Civil Trial Practice

FORD, JON R.
Enid, OK ....Family Law

FORD AND ASSOCIATES, P.C.
Gadsden, AL ....Civil Trial Practice; Commercial Law; General Practice; Insurance Defense

FORD, DOMNICK, WOLF & LOPEZ-ALBEAR, P.A.
Miami, FL ....Medical Malpractice

FORD & FERRARO, L.L.P.
Austin, TX ....Banking Law; Civil Trial Practice; Health Care Law; Insurance Defense

FORD & HARRISON
Los Angeles, CA ....Labor and Employment Law
Atlanta, GA ....Labor and Employment Law

FORD MARRIN ESPOSITO WITMEYER & GLESER, L.L.P.
New York, NY........................Civil Trial Practice; General Practice

FORDNEY, DUST & PRINE
Saginaw, MI ....Insurance Defense; Medical Malpractice

FORD, WALKER, HAGGERTY & BEHAR, PROFESSIONAL LAW CORPORATION
Long Beach, CA......................Civil Trial Practice; Commercial Litigation; Construction Law; General Practice; Insurance Defense; Product Liability Law

FORD YUNGBLUT WHITE & SALAZAR, P.C.
Dallas, TX ....General Practice

FOREMAN, ARCH, DODGE & VOLYN, P.S.
Wenatchee, WA ....Civil Trial Practice

FORMAN, MARTH, BLACK & ANGLE, P.A.
Greensboro, NC ....Business Law; Probate, Trusts and Estate Planning; Tax Law

FORMAN STERN, A PROFESSIONAL CORPORATION
Paramus, NJ...........................Appellate Practice; Bankruptcy Law; Civil Trial Practice; Commercial Law; Land Use Law; Personal Injury

FORSYTH, HOWE, O'DWYER, KALB & MURPHY, P.C.
Rochester, NY.........................Banking Law; Bankruptcy Law; Commercial Law; Real Estate Law

FORTINO, PLAXTON & MOSKAL
Alma, MI................................General Practice

FORTUNE, JOHNNY, P.A.
Fort Walton Beach, FL ....Probate, Trusts and Estate Planning

FORTUNO, ROBERT A., P.C.
Tucson, AZ ....Real Estate Law

FOSS, WHITTY, LITTLEFIELD & MCDANIEL, LLP
Coos Bay, OR ....General Practice

FOSSETT & BRUGGER, CHARTERED
Seabrook, MD.........................Civil Trial Practice; Real Estate Law

FOSTER ● JOHNSON HARRIS ● MCDONALD
Albuquerque, NM....................Business Law; Commercial Litigation

FOSTER, FOSTER, ALLEN & DURRENCE
Chattanooga, TN ....Civil Trial Practice; Construction Law; Environmental Law; General Practice; Insurance Defense; Medical Malpractice; Personal Injury; Real Estate Law

FOSTER, HELLER & KILGORE, P.C.
San Antonio, TX.....................Labor and Employment Law

FOSTER, MEADOWS & BALLARD, P.C.
Detroit, MI.............................Admiralty/Maritime Law; General Practice; Immigration and Naturalization; Insurance Defense; Labor and Employment Law; Probate, Trusts and Estate Planning; Product Liability Law; Real Estate Law; Transportation Law

FOSTER, O'KEEFE
Charlottetown, PE, Canada .....General Practice

FOSTER PEPPER & SHEFELMAN
Seattle, WA ....General Practice

FOSTER, PURDY, ALLAN, PETERSON & DAHLIN
Medford, OR ....General Practice

FOSTER, SWIFT, COLLINS & SMITH, P.C.
Lansing, MI............................Banking Law; Civil Trial Practice; Employment Benefits Law; Environmental Law; General Practice; Health Care Law; Immigration and Naturalization; Insurance Defense; International Business Law; Labor and Employment Law; Patent, Trademark, Copyright and Unfair Competition; Personal Injury; Probate, Trusts and Estate Planning; Real Estate Law; Transportation Law

FOSTER, WALDECK & LIND, LTD.
Minneapolis, MN ....Appellate Practice; Civil Trial Practice; Insurance Defense

FOSTER, WM. D., & ASSOCIATES
Minneapolis, MN ....Civil Trial Practice; Personal Injury

FOULSTON & SIEFKIN, L.L.P.
Dodge City, KS.....................Business Law; Civil Trial Practice; General Practice; Probate, Trusts and Estate Planning; Tax Law
Topeka, KS.........................Administrative Law; Business Law; Employment Benefits Law; Tax Law; Transportation Law
Wichita, KS........................Administrative Law; Antitrust Law; Banking Law; Bankruptcy Law; Business Law; Civil Trial Practice; Commercial Law; Construction Law; Employment Benefits Law; Environmental Law; General Practice; Health Care Law; Insurance Defense; International Business Law; Labor and Employment Law; Medical Malpractice; Natural Resources Law; Personal Injury; Probate, Trusts and Estate Planning; Real Estate Law; Securities Law; Tax Law; Trademark, Copyright and Unfair Competition

FOURNARIS, THEODORE J., PROFESSIONAL ASSOCIATION
Miami, FL ....Medical Malpractice; Personal Injury; Product Liability Law

FOUTS & MOORE, L.L.P.
Houston, TX ....Commercial Litigation

FOWLER, ADDAMS & RUNDLE
Carlisle, PA ....General Practice

FOWLER, MEASLE & BELL, L.L.P.
Lexington, KY ....Bankruptcy Law; General Practice; Insurance Defense

FOX, MAURICE F.
Denver, CO ....Real Estate Law

FOX, MICHAEL E. & ASSOCIATES
Chicago, IL........................Sports and Entertainment Law

FOX, WAYNE C.
Houston, TX ....Business Law; Civil Trial Practice; Real Estate Law

FOX AND FOX
Livingston, NJ....................Administrative Law; Banking Law; Civil Trial Practice; Commercial Law; General Practice; Probate, Trusts and Estate Planning; Real Estate Law; Tax Law

FOX & GROVE, CHARTERED
Chicago, IL........................Civil Trial Practice; Commercial Law; Labor and Employment Law

FOX, GROVE, ABBEY, ADAMS, BYELICK & KIERNAN
St. Petersburg, FL.................Insurance Defense

FOX & HORAN
New York, NY.......................International Business Law

FOX, OLDT & BROWN
Easton, PA ....Personal Injury; Probate, Trusts and Estate Planning

FOX, ROTHSCHILD, O'BRIEN & FRANKEL
Trenton, NJ ....Banking Law; General Practice
Philadelphia, PA ....General Practice; Real Estate Law; Tax Law

FOX, WOOD & WOOD
Maysville, KY ....General Practice

FRAMME MACAULAY & LEE LC
Richmond, VA ....Civil Trial Practice

FRANCIS, ARTHUR W., JR., A PROF. CORP., LAW OFFICES OF
Redondo Beach, CA ....Insurance Defense

FRANCIS & STARZYNSKI, P.A.
Albuquerque, NM....................Bankruptcy Law

FRANCZEK ● SULLIVAN ● MANN ● CREMENT ● HEIN ● RELIAS, P.C.
Chicago, IL........................Labor and Employment Law

FRANKE, RAINEY & SALLOUM, PLLC
Gulfport, MS.......................Admiralty/Maritime Law; Civil Trial Practice; Insurance Defense; Probate, Trusts and Estate Planning; Real Estate Law

FRANKE & SCHULTZ, A PROFESSIONAL CORPORATION
Kansas City, MO....................Civil Trial Practice; Insurance Defense

FRANKEL & ABRAMS
New York, NY.......................Civil Trial Practice; Criminal Trial Practice; General Practice

FRANK, JOHN J., PARTNERSHIP, THE
St. Louis, MO......................Personal Injury

FRANKLIN, CARDWELL & JONES
Houston, TX ....Civil Trial Practice; Medical Malpractice; Personal Injury

FRANKLIN AND HANCE, P.S.C.
Louisville, KY ....Civil Trial Practice; Medical Malpractice; Personal Injury

FRANKOVITCH & ANETAKIS
Weirton, WV ....General Practice

FRANKS, JON MICHAEL
Fort Worth, TX ....Family Law

FRANSCELL, STRICKLAND, ROBERTS & LAWRENCE, A PROFESSIONAL CORPORATION
Pasadena, CA ....Appellate Practice; Civil Rights; Civil Trial Practice; General Practice; Labor and Employment Law; Personal Injury

FRANSEN & HARDIN, A P.L.C.
New Orleans, LA ....Admiralty/Maritime Law

FRANTZ, MCCONNELL & SEYMOUR, LLP
Knoxville, TN ....Civil Trial Practice; Commercial Litigation; General Practice; Insurance Defense

FRASER, RICHARD A. III
New Orleans, LA ....General Practice

FRASER & BEATTY
Vancouver, BC, Canada..............General Practice
North York, ON, Canada.............General Practice
Ottawa, ON, Canada ....General Practice
Toronto, ON, Canada................General Practice

FRASER, STRYKER, VAUGHN, MEUSEY, OLSON, BOYER & BLOCH, P.C.
Omaha, NE ....Banking Law; Commercial Law; Environmental Law; General Practice; Insurance Defense; Labor and Employment Law; Real Estate Law; Tax Law

FRASER TREBILCOCK DAVIS & FOSTER, P.C.
Lansing, MI ....Banking Law; Civil Trial Practice; Employment Benefits Law; Environmental Law; General Practice; Health Care Law; Insurance Defense; Labor and Employment Law; Medical Malpractice; Probate, Trusts and Estate Planning; Product Liability Law; Real Estate Law

FRASSINETI AND GLOVER
Greensboro, NC ....Probate, Trusts and Estate Planning; Real Estate Law

FRATAR & KERN
Springfield, MA....................Municipal and Zoning Law; Probate, Trusts and Estate Planning; Real Estate Law

FRAZER, S. STEWART
Dallas, TX ....General Practice

FRAZIER & FRAZIER, ATTORNEYS AT LAW, P.A.
Jacksonville, FL ....Probate, Trusts and Estate Planning; Tax Law

FRAZIER & OXLEY, L.C.
Huntington, WV ....Banking Law; Probate, Trusts and Estate Planning; Tax Law

FREDERICKS, BARRY I.
Englewood Cliffs, NJ...............Civil Trial Practice; Patent, Trademark, Copyright and Unfair Competition

FREDERICKSON & HEINTSCHEL, CO., L.P.A.
Toledo, OH ....Bankruptcy Law; Civil Trial Practice; Probate, Trusts and Estate Planning

FREDERICKSON & YOUNG
Los Angeles, CA ....Civil Trial Practice

FREDRICKSON & JOHNSON, P.C.
Canon City, CO ....General Practice

FREDRIKSON & BYRON, P.A.
Minneapolis, MN ....Antitrust Law; General Practice; Labor and Employment Law; Sports and Entertainment Law

FREEARK, HARVEY, MENDILLO, DENNIS & WULLER, PROFESSIONAL CORPORATION
Belleville, IL ....Commercial Litigation; Insurance Defense

FREEBURG, JUDY & NETTELS
Pasadena, CA ....Civil Trial Practice; Environmental Law; Insurance Defense; Medical Malpractice

FREEDMAN, HOWARD J.
Cleveland, OH ....Business Law; Real Estate Law

FREEDMAN, BOYD, DANIELS, HOLLANDER, GUTTMANN & GOLDBERG, P.A.
Albuquerque, NM....................Civil Trial Practice; Criminal Trial Practice

FREEDMAN, GARY, LAW OFFICES OF
Santa Monica, CA..................Business Law; Civil Trial Practice

FREEDMAN, LEVY, KROLL & SIMONDS
Washington, DC.....................Environmental Law; General Practice; Natural
Resources Law; Securities Law

FREELAND & FREELAND
Oxford, MS..............................Banking Law; Bankruptcy Law; Civil Trial Practice;
Commercial Law; Commercial Litigation; Constitu-
tional Law; Insurance Defense; Product Liability
Law; Real Estate Law

FREEMAN, FREEMAN & SALZMAN, P.C.
Chicago, IL..............................Antitrust Law; Commercial Litigation; Securities
Law

FREEMAN & JENNER, P.C.
Aspen, CO.............................Medical Malpractice; Patent, Trademark, Copyright
and Unfair Competition; Personal Injury
Bethesda, MD.........................Medical Malpractice; Patent, Trademark, Copyright
and Unfair Competition; Personal Injury

FREEMAN, LOFTUS & MANLEY
New City, NY.........................Banking Law; Probate, Trusts and Estate Planning;
Real Estate Law

**FREER, MCGARRY, BODANSKY & RUBIN, A PROFESSIONAL
CORPORATION**
Washington, DC......................General Practice

FREID AND GOLDSMAN, A PROFESSIONAL LAW CORPORATION
Los Angeles, CA......................Family Law

FREILICH, HORNBAKER & ROSEN, P.C.
Los Angeles, CA.....................Patent, Trademark, Copyright and Unfair Competition

FREISHTAT & SANDLER
Baltimore, MD.........................Civil Trial Practice; Construction Law; Criminal
Trial Practice

FRENCH & STONE, P.C.
Boulder, CO............................Civil Trial Practice; Commercial Law; Personal
Injury

FRESE, NASH & TORPY, P.A.
Melbourne, FL.........................Commercial Litigation; Probate, Trusts and Estate
Planning

FREUD, JOHN S., P.A.
Miami, FL................................Insurance Defense

FREUND, FREEZE & ARNOLD, A LEGAL PROFESSIONAL ASSOCIATION
Dayton, OH.............................Appellate Practice; Civil Trial Practice; Commercial
Law; Construction Law; Insurance Defense; Medical
Malpractice; Product Liability Law

FRIDAY, ELDREDGE & CLARK
Little Rock, AR.......................Antitrust Law; Banking Law; Civil Trial Practice;
General Practice; Insurance Defense; Labor and
Employment Law; Municipal Bond/Public
Authority Financing; Personal Injury; Securities
Law; Tax Law

FRIED & ASSOCIATES, P.C.
Livonia, MI..............................Probate, Trusts and Estate Planning; Tax Law

FRIEDBERG, JOSEPH S., CHARTERED
Minneapolis, MN....................Criminal Trial Practice

FRIED, BIRD & CRUMPACKER, A PROFESSIONAL CORPORATION
Los Angeles, CA......................Banking Law; Real Estate Law

FRIED, FRANK, HARRIS, SHRIVER & JACOBSON
Washington, DC......................General Practice; Tax Law
New York, NY.........................General Practice
London, England....................General Practice
Paris, France...........................General Practice

FRIEDLANDER & FRIEDLANDER, P.C.
Arlington, VA..........................Business Law; Civil Trial Practice; Personal Injury;
Probate, Trusts and Estate Planning; Real Estate
Law

FRIEDLANDER, MISLER, FRIEDLANDER, SLOAN & HERZ
Washington, DC......................Banking Law; General Practice; Labor and
Employment Law

FRIEDLOB SANDERSON RASKIN PAULSON & TOURTILLOTT, LLC
Denver, CO.............................Business Law; Civil Trial Practice; Environmental
Law; Natural Resources Law; Securities Law

FRIEDMAN, AVERY S.
Cleveland, OH.........................Civil Rights

FRIEDMAN & ATHERTON
Boston, MA.............................Civil Trial Practice; Family Law; General Practice

FRIEDMAN & BABBITT CO., L.P.A.
Columbus, OH ....Family Law

FRIEDMAN & BABCOCK
Portland, ME ....Civil Trial Practice; Environmental Law; Health
Care Law; Insurance Defense; Personal Injury;
Product Liability Law

FRIEDMAN, C. MARSHALL, A PROFESSIONAL CORPORATION
St. Louis, MO..........................Civil Trial Practice

**FRIEDMAN, COLLARD, CUTTER & PANNETON, PROFESSIONAL
CORPORATION**
Sacramento, CA ....General Practice; Personal Injury

FRIEDMAN, DOMIANO & SMITH CO., L.P.A.
Cleveland, OH.........................Personal Injury; Product Liability Law

FRIEDMAN & KAPLAN LLP
New York, NY.........................Civil Trial Practice; Securities Law

FRIEDMAN, MELLITZ & NEWMAN, P.C.
Fairfield, CT ....Insurance Defense; Medical Malpractice; Personal
Injury; Workers Compensation

**FRIEDMAN, OLIVE, MCCUBBIN, SPALDING, BILTER & ROOSEVELT, A
PROFESSIONAL CORPORATION**
San Francisco, CA ....Probate, Trusts and Estate Planning

FRIEDMAN, ROSS & HERSH, A PROFESSIONAL CORPORATION
San Francisco, CA ....Civil Trial Practice

FRIEDMAN WEITZMAN & FRIEDMAN, A PROFESSIONAL CORPORATION
St. Louis, MO..........................Business Law; Family Law; Probate, Trusts and
Estate Planning

**FRIEDMAN, WITTENSTEIN & HOCHMAN, A PROFESSIONAL
CORPORATION**
New York, NY.........................General Practice

FRIEDRICH & FRIEDRICH, P.A.
Fort Lauderdale, FL...............Probate, Trusts and Estate Planning

FRIEND, KARL E.
Allentown, PA ....Bankruptcy Law
Reading, PA ....Bankruptcy Law

FRIERSON & WATSON
Stuart, FL................................Criminal Trial Practice; Personal Injury

FRIJOUF, RUST & PYLE, P.A.
Tampa, FL ....Patent, Trademark, Copyright and Unfair Competition

FRILOT, PARTRIDGE, KOHNKE & CLEMENTS, L.C.
New Orleans, LA ....Insurance Defense; Product Liability Law

FRIMET & ROGALSKI, P.C.
Southfield, MI ....Administrative Law; Health Care Law

FRINK, FOY, GAINEY & YOUNT, P.A.
Shallotte, NC...........................General Practice
Southport, NC.........................General Practice

FRISK, FRANK W., JR., P.C.
Washington, DC......................Administrative Law; Environmental Law; Municipal
and Zoning Law; Natural Resources Law

FRISTOE, TAYLOR & SCHULTZ, LTD., P.S.
Olympia, WA ....General Practice

FRITH, DOUGLAS K., & ASSOCIATES, P.C.
Martinsville, VA......................Civil Trial Practice; Criminal Trial Practice; Family
Law; Personal Injury

FROELICH & WEPRIN CO., LPA
Dayton, OH.............................Business Law; Real Estate Law

FROHNMAYER, DEATHERAGE, PRATT, JAMIESON & CLARKE, P.C.
Medford, OR..........................General Practice

FROIMSON, JEROME L.
Phoenix, AZ ....Labor and Employment Law

FROMMELT & EIDE, LTD.
Minneapolis, MN....................Business Law; Real Estate Law; Securities Law

FRONEFIELD AND DE FURIA
Media, PA ....Civil Trial Practice; General Practice; Insurance
Defense; Labor and Employment Law; Municipal
and Zoning Law; Probate, Trusts and Estate
Planning; Real Estate Law

FROSS ZELNICK LEHRMAN & ZISSU, P.C.
New York, NY.......................Trademark, Copyright and Unfair Competition

FROST & JACOBS
Cincinnati, OH ....Antitrust Law; Banking Law; Bankruptcy Law;
Civil Trial Practice; Commercial Law; Communica-
tions Law; Environmental Law; General Practice;
Health Care Law; Labor and Employment Law;
Patent, Trademark, Copyright and Unfair Compe-
tition; Real Estate Law; Tax Law

Middletown, OH ....General Practice

FROST, O'TOOLE & SAUNDERS, P.A.
Bartow, FL............................Civil Trial Practice; Commercial Litigation; General
Practice; Medical Malpractice; Personal Injury

FRUE LAW FIRM, THE, L.L.P.
Asheville, NC ....Civil Trial Practice; Probate, Trusts and Estate
Planning; Real Estate Law

FTHENAKIS & COLVIN
Palo Alto, CA ....Antitrust Law; Civil Trial Practice; Patent,
Trademark, Copyright and Unfair Competition

FUCHSBERG & FUCHSBERG
New York, NY.......................Civil Trial Practice; Medical Malpractice

FUENTES AND KREISCHER
Tampa, FL ....Real Estate Law

FUGATE, IVAN D.
Denver, CO ....Banking Law

FUGATE, LEE
Clearwater, FL ....Criminal Trial Practice

FUJIYAMA, DUFFY & FUJIYAMA, ATTORNEYS AT LAW, A LAW CORPORATION
Honolulu, HI...........................Civil Trial Practice; General Practice

FUKUNAGA MATAYOSHI HERSHEY & CHING
Honolulu, HI..........................Civil Trial Practice; Insurance Defense; Product
Liability Law

FULBRIGHT & JAWORSKI L.L.P.
Houston, TX ....General Practice

FULCHER, HAGLER, REED, HANKS & HARPER
Augusta, GA ....Business Law; Civil Trial Practice; General Practice;
Insurance Defense; Real Estate Law; Workers
Compensation

FULLER, W. SIDNEY
Andalusia, AL.........................General Practice

FULLER, BECTON, SLIFKIN & BELL, P.A.
Raleigh, NC............................Medical Malpractice; Personal Injury

FULLER & FULLER, P.C., LAW OFFICES OF
San Antonio, TX.....................Insurance Defense

FULLER & HENRY P.L.L.
Toledo, OH ....Civil Trial Practice; Environmental Law; General
Practice; Health Care Law; Insurance Defense;
Labor and Employment Law; Probate, Trusts and
Estate Planning; Real Estate Law; Tax Law

FULLER, JOHNSON & FARRELL, P.A.
Pensacola, FL..........................Civil Trial Practice; Product Liability Law
Tallahassee, FL ....Civil Trial Practice; Product Liability Law

FULLER, ROSENBERG, PALMER & BELIVEAU
Worcester, MA.........................Civil Trial Practice; Insurance Defense; Personal
Injury; Product Liability Law; Workers Compen-
sation

FULLER, SWINDLE & HOLSONBACK, P.A.
Tampa, FL ....Commercial Litigation; Probate, Trusts and Estate
Planning

FULLER, TUBB & POMEROY
Oklahoma City, OK.................Bankruptcy Law; Commercial Law; General
Practice; Probate, Trusts and Estate Planning

FULTON, RADMILA A.
San Diego, CA ....Bankruptcy Law

FULTON, THEODORE H. JR.
Fort Lauderdale, FL...............Probate, Trusts and Estate Planning

FULWIDER PATTON LEE & UTECHT, LLP
Los Angeles, CA..... ....Patent, Trademark, Copyright and Unfair Competition

FUNDERBURK & ANDREWS
Baton Rouge, LA....................Civil Trial Practice; General Practice; Insurance
Defense

FUNDERBURK & FUNDERBURK, L.L.P.
Houston, TX ....Civil Trial Practice; Insurance Defense; Product
Liability Law

FUNK & BOLTON, A PROFESSIONAL ASSOCIATION
Baltimore, MD ....Administrative Law; Appellate Practice; Insurance
Defense; Municipal Bond/Public Authority
Financing

FURBEE, AMOS, WEBB & CRITCHFIELD
Fairmont, WV ....Civil Trial Practice; Commercial Litigation;
Insurance Defense; Real Estate Law

Morgantown, WV ....General Practice

FUREY & FUREY, P.C.
Hempstead, NY.......................Civil Trial Practice

FURGANG & MILDE, L.L.P
New York, NY........................Patent, Trademark, Copyright and Unfair Competition

FURIA AND TURNER
Philadelphia, PA ....Civil Trial Practice; Personal Injury; Probate, Trusts
and Estate Planning; Product Liability Law; Real
Estate Law; Workers Compensation

FURR AND COHEN, P.A.
Boca Raton, FL ....Bankruptcy Law; Family Law

FURR AND HENSHAW
Myrtle Beach, SC ....Civil Trial Practice; Medical Malpractice; Personal
Injury

FUSCO & NEWBRAUGH, L.C.
Morgantown, WV ....Antitrust Law; Civil Trial Practice; Commercial
Litigation; General Practice; Health Care Law;
Mergers and Acquisitions; Securities Law

GABEL & HAIR
Jacksonville, FL ....Admiralty/Maritime Law; Civil Trial Practice;
Communications Law; General Practice; Workers
Compensation

GABLER & ASSOCIATES, P.C.
Pittsburgh, PA ....Employment Benefits Law

GABROY, ROLLMAN & BOSSÉ, P.C.
Tucson, AZ ....Civil Trial Practice; General Practice; Personal
Injury; Probate, Trusts and Estate Planning; Tax
Law

GADDIS, KIN & HERD, P.C.
Colorado Springs, CO.............Civil Trial Practice; Personal Injury; Probate, Trusts
and Estate Planning; Real Estate Law

GADSBY & HANNAH LLP
Boston, MA.............................Civil Trial Practice; General Practice

GAGER & PETERSON
Waterbury, CT ....General Practice

GAILOR & ASSOCIATES, P.L.L.C.
Raleigh, NC............................Family Law

GAINSBURGH, BENJAMIN, DAVID, MEUNIER, NORIEA & WARSHAUER
New Orleans, LA ....Admiralty/Maritime Law; Criminal Trial Practice;
Environmental Law; International Business Law;
Medical Malpractice; Personal Injury; Product
Liability Law

GAIR, GAIR, CONASON, STEIGMAN & MACKAUF
New York, NY........................Civil Trial Practice; General Practice; Medical
Malpractice; Personal Injury; Product Liability Law

GAITENS, TUCCERI & NICHOLAS, A PROFESSIONAL CORPORATION
Pittsburgh, PA ....Civil Trial Practice; Criminal Trial Practice; General
Practice; Insurance Defense; Medical Malpractice;
Personal Injury

GALARDI, LAWRENCE J.
Irvine, CA...............................Aviation Law; Civil Trial Practice; Construction
Law

GALATZ, EARL & BULLA
Las Vegas, NV ....Civil Trial Practice; Medical Malpractice; Personal
Injury; Product Liability Law

GALBUT & CONANT, A PROFESSIONAL CORPORATION
Phoenix, AZ ....Antitrust Law; Civil Trial Practice; Commercial
Litigation; Real Estate Law; Securities Law

GALFAND, BERGER, LURIE, BRIGHAM, JACOBS, SWAN JUREWICZ AND JENSEN, LTD.
Philadelphia, PA ....Personal Injury

GALLAGHER & ARCHAMBEAULT, A PROFESSIONAL CORPORATION
Glasgow, MT ....General Practice

GALLAGHER, EVELIUS & JONES
Baltimore, MD ....Health Care Law; Real Estate Law

GALLAGHER GALLAGHER & CALISTRO
New Haven, CT ....Appellate Practice; Civil Trial Practice; General
Practice

GALLAGHER GOSSEEN & FALLER
Garden City, NY ....Civil Trial Practice; Employment Benefits Law;
General Practice; Insurance Defense; Labor and
Employment Law; Personal Injury; Product
Liability Law

GALLAGHER, JOHN J., P.C., LAW OFFICES OF
Philadelphia, PA ....Business Law; Commercial Litigation; Personal
Injury; Product Liability Law; Public Utilities Law

GALLAGHER & JOSLYN
Oakbrook Terrace, IL..............Business Law; Civil Trial Practice; General Practice; Insurance Defense; Product Liability Law

GALLAGHER & LATHROP, A PROFESSIONAL CORPORATION
San Francisco, CA..................Patent, Trademark, Copyright and Unfair Competition

GALLAGHER, MAY & BURGOYNE
Baltimore, MD........................General Practice

GALLAGHER, REILLY AND LACHAT, P.C.
Philadelphia, PA....................Business Law; Civil Rights; Civil Trial Practice; General Practice; Insurance Defense; Medical Malpractice; Personal Injury; Product Liability Law; Transportation Law; Workers Compensation

GALLAGHER, WALKER & BIANCO
Stewart Manor, NY................Business Law; Insurance Defense; Medical Malpractice; Product Liability Law

GALLEGOS LAW FIRM, P.C.
Santa Fe, NM........................Antitrust Law; Civil Trial Practice; Natural Resources Law

GALLIGAN & NEWMAN
McMinnville, TN....................General Practice

GALLIGAN, TULLY, DOYLE & REID, P.C.
Des Moines, IA......................Medical Malpractice

GALLOP, JOHNSON & NEUMAN, L.C.
St. Louis, MO........................Civil Trial Practice; General Practice

GALLOWAY & GALLOWAY, P.A.
Gulfport, MS..........................General Practice

GALLOWAY, WIEGERS & HEENEY
Marysville, KS........................General Practice

GALLUCCI, HOPKINS & THEISEN, P.C.
Fort Wayne, IN......................Civil Rights; Labor and Employment Law

GALTON & HELM
Los Angeles, CA....................Civil Trial Practice; Health Care Law; Insurance Defense

GALVIN, GALVIN & LEENEY
Hammond, IN........................Banking Law; Civil Trial Practice; General Practice; Health Care Law; Insurance Defense; Medical Malpractice

GAMBERG, JAY M., P.A.
Hollywood, FL........................Bankruptcy Law

GAMBLE HARTSHORN ALDEN
Columbus, OH........................Civil Trial Practice; Health Care Law; Transportation Law

GAMBRELL & STOLZ, L.L.P.
Atlanta, GA............................Civil Trial Practice; General Practice

GAMMAGE & BURNHAM, P.L.C.
Phoenix, AZ............................Bankruptcy Law; General Practice; Health Care Law; Municipal and Zoning Law; Real Estate Law

GAMOT & FREEMAN
West Palm Beach, FL..............Civil Trial Practice; Family Law; Medical Malpractice; Personal Injury

GANDELOT, JON B., P.C.
Grosse Pointe Woods, MI.......Probate, Trusts and Estate Planning

GANDIN, SCHOTSKY, RAPPAPORT, GLASS & GREENE, LLP
Melville, NY............................Civil Trial Practice; Medical Malpractice; Personal Injury; Product Liability Law

GANDY, FRANCIS I. JR.
Corpus Christi, TX..................Civil Trial Practice

GANNAM & GNANN
Savannah, GA........................Immigration and Naturalization; Workers Compensation

GANNON, COTTRELL & WARD, P.C.
Alexandria, VA......................Civil Trial Practice; Family Law
Fairfax, VA............................Family Law

GARAN, LUCOW, MILLER, SEWARD & BECKER, P.C.
Ann Arbor, MI......................General Practice
Detroit, MI............................Civil Trial Practice; General Practice; Insurance Defense
Grand Blanc, MI....................General Practice
Mount Clemens, MI................General Practice
Port Huron, MI......................General Practice
Troy, MI................................General Practice

GARBARINI & SCHER, P.C.
New York, NY........................Civil Trial Practice; Insurance Defense; Medical Malpractice; Product Liability Law

GARCIA, JULIO A.
Laredo, TX............................Criminal Trial Practice; General Practice; Medical Malpractice

GARCIA, MANUEL D. LAW OFFICES OF
Honolulu, HI..........................International Business Law; Real Estate Law; Tax Law

GARCIA & FIELDS, P.A.
Tampa, FL..............................Family Law; Real Estate Law

GARDENAL, JOHN, A PROFESSIONAL CORPORATION
San Francisco, CA..................Medical Malpractice; Personal Injury; Product Liability Law

GARDERE & WYNNE, L.L.P.
Dallas, TX..............................General Practice

GARDINER, ROBERTS
Toronto, ON, Canada..............General Practice

GARDNER, CARTON & DOUGLAS
Chicago, IL............................General Practice

GARDNER, EWING & SOUZA
Louisville, KY........................Medical Malpractice

GARDNER, GARDNER & GARDNER LLP
Sedalia, MO............................General Practice

GARDNER, MIDDLEBROOKS, FLEMING & HAMILTON, P.C.
Mobile, AL............................Insurance Defense; Labor and Employment Law

GARDNER, WILKES, SHAHEEN & CANDELORA
Tampa, FL..............................Civil Trial Practice

GARFINKLE, MCLEMORE & WALKER, PLLC
Nashville, TN........................Bankruptcy Law; Personal Injury

GARGARO, WILLIAM J., JR., A PROFESSIONAL CORPORATION
Los Angeles, CA....................Medical Malpractice

GARIPPA AND DAVENPORT, A PROFESSIONAL CORPORATION
Montclair, NJ........................Real Estate Law; Tax Law

GARLAND AND DRUM, P.A.
Gastonia, NC..........................General Practice

GARLAND, SAMUEL & LOEB, P.C.
Atlanta, GA............................Appellate Practice; Civil Trial Practice; Criminal Trial Practice; Medical Malpractice; Personal Injury; Product Liability Law

GARLINGTON, LOHN & ROBINSON, PLLP
Missoula, MT..........................General Practice

GARMON & GOODMAN
Glasgow, KY..........................Bankruptcy Law; General Practice; Real Estate Law

GARNER, LOVELL & STEIN, P.C.
Amarillo, TX..........................Civil Trial Practice; Commercial Law; Personal Injury

GARNIER & GARNIER, P.C.
Falls Church, VA....................Product Liability Law

GAROFALO, HANSON, SCHREIBER & VANDLIK, CHARTERED
Chicago, IL............................Insurance Defense; Workers Compensation

GARRAHAN, BARBIERI & GARRAHAN, P.C.
Framingham, MA....................Real Estate Law

GARRETT & GARRETT, A PROF. CORP., LAW OFFICES
Bedford, VA............................General Practice

GARRETT & GILLIARD
Augusta, GA............................Appellate Practice; Criminal Trial Practice

GARRETT & JENSEN
Santa Ana, CA........................Insurance Defense; Personal Injury

GARRIGLE & PALM
Cherry Hill, NJ......................Appellate Practice; Civil Trial Practice; Environmental Law; Insurance Defense; Personal Injury; Product Liability Law

GARRISON PHELAN LEVIN-EPSTEIN & PENZEL, P.C.
New Haven, CT......................General Practice

GARTNER & YOUNG, A PROFESSIONAL CORPORATION
Los Angeles, CA....................Labor and Employment Law

GARVEY, TERENCE BRIAN
Gaithersburg, MD..................Bankruptcy Law

GARVEY, ANDERSON, JOHNSON, GABLER & GERACI, S.C.
Eau Claire, WI........................General Practice; Insurance Defense

GARVEY, SCHUBERT & BARER
Portland, OR............................General Practice
Seattle, WA ....Admiralty/Maritime Law; General Practice

GARVIN, DAVID M., P.A.
Miami, FL ....Criminal Trial Practice; Tax Law

GARVIN & MALONEY
St. Louis, MO...........................Business Law; Civil Trial Practice

GARVIN & TRIPP, A PROFESSIONAL ASSOCIATION
Fort Myers, FL ....Personal Injury

GARWOOD, MCKENNA, MCKENNA & WOLF, P.A.
Orlando, FL ....Labor and Employment Law

GASSMAN & CONETTA, P.A.
Clearwater, FL ....Probate, Trusts and Estate Planning

GASSMAN & FISHER, L.L.P.
Garden City, NY ....Family Law

GASTON & RUANE
Bridgeport, CT ....Criminal Trial Practice; Personal Injury

GATES LAW OFFICE
Columbia City, IN ....Probate, Trusts and Estate Planning

GATLIN, WOODS & CARLSON
Tallahassee, FL ....Administrative Law; Public Utilities Law

GATZKE, MISPAGEL & DILLON
Carlsbad, CA...........................Aviation Law; Civil Trial Practice; Environmental Law

GAULEY & CO.
Saskatoon, SK, Canada ....Civil Trial Practice; Commercial Law; General Practice

GAULT DAVISON, A PROFESSIONAL SERVICE CORPORATION
Flint, MI..............................Business Law; Civil Trial Practice; Commercial Law; Environmental Law; Labor and Employment Law; Probate, Trusts and Estate Planning

GAUNTLETT & ASSOCIATES
Irvine, CA..............................Antitrust Law; Appellate Practice; Business Law; Employment Benefits Law; Environmental Law; Insurance Defense; Labor and Employment Law; Patent, Trademark, Copyright and Unfair Competition

GAWTHROP, GREENWOOD & HALSTED, A PROFESSIONAL CORPORATION
West Chester, PA....................Business Law; General Practice; Municipal and Zoning Law; Probate, Trusts and Estate Planning

GAY & CHACKER, A PROFESSIONAL CORPORATION
Philadelphia, PA ....Personal Injury

GAY, HALL & DITORE
Sacramento, CA ....Civil Trial Practice

GAYLORD, MCNALLY, STRICKLAND AND SNYDER, L.L.P.
Greenville, NC ....General Practice

GEARHISER, PETERS, LOCKABY & TALLANT, PLLC
Chattanooga, TN ....Business Law; Civil Trial Practice; General Practice; Probate, Trusts and Estate Planning; Tax Law

GEBHARDT & KIEFER, P.C.
Clinton, NJ..............................General Practice

GEDNEY, SEAMAN & HILGENDORFF
Florham Park, NJ ....General Practice; Probate, Trusts and Estate Planning

GEESLIN, GEORGE M.
Atlanta, GA ....Bankruptcy Law

GEESLIN, JOSEPH D. JR.
Indianapolis, IN ....Tax Law

GEHLHAUSEN, JOHN, P.C.
Lamar, CO ....Civil Trial Practice; Personal Injury

GEHRING, ROBERT J., CO., L.P.A.
Cincinnati, OH ....Civil Trial Practice; Insurance Defense; Personal Injury

GEISTER & WHALEY, A PROFESSIONAL CORPORATION
Oklahoma City, OK................Civil Trial Practice

GELB & GELB
Boston, MA............................Civil Trial Practice; Family Law; Securities Law

GELBER, GELBER, INGERSOLL, KLEVANSKY & FARIS, A LAW CORPORATION
Honolulu, HI ....Business Law

GELERMAN, CASHMAN & DONAHUE
Dedham, MA ....General Practice

GELLERT & CUTLER, P.C.
Poughkeepsie, NY ....Banking Law; Civil Trial Practice; Employment Benefits Law; General Practice; Labor and Employment Law

GELMAN, NORRIS E.
Philadelphia, PA ....Appellate Practice; Criminal Trial Practice

GENDLER & SINGLETON, P.A.
Baltimore, MD ....Labor and Employment Law

GENERAL COUNSEL SERVICES, A PROFESSIONAL LAW CORPORATION
Oakland, CA ....Business Law

GENNET, KALLMANN, ANTIN & ROBINSON, A PROFESSIONAL CORPORATION
Parsippany, NJ ....Appellate Practice; Civil Trial Practice; Insurance Defense; Personal Injury

GENOVA, BURNS, TRIMBOLI & VERNOIA
Livingston, NJ.........................Administrative Law; Appellate Practice; Civil Trial Practice; Commercial Law; Environmental Law; Health Care Law; Insurance Defense; Labor and Employment Law

GENTILE & DICKLER
New York, NY ....General Practice

GENTILE, DOMINIC P., LTD.
Las Vegas, NV ....Appellate Practice; Civil Rights; Civil Trial Practice; Commercial Litigation; Communications Law; Constitutional Law; Criminal Trial Practice; Health Care Law; Municipal and Zoning Law; Probate, Trusts and Estate Planning

GENTRY, ELVIN L., P.C.
Colorado Springs, CO.............Criminal Trial Practice

GENTRY, TIPTON, KIZER & MCLEMORE, P.C.
Knoxville, TN ....Bankruptcy Law; General Practice; Tax Law

GEORGE, DONALDSON & FORD, L.L.P.
Austin, TX ....Appellate Practice; Civil Trial Practice

GEORGE, EDWARD P., JR., INC., A PROF. CORP.
Long Beach, CA......................Appellate Practice; Civil Trial Practice; Criminal Trial Practice; Personal Injury

GEORGE, GALLO & SULLIVAN, A LAW CORPORATION
Los Osos, CA ....Probate, Trusts and Estate Planning
San Luis Obispo, CA ....Business Law; Probate, Trusts and Estate Planning

GEORGE AND GEORGE, LTD., A PROFESSIONAL LAW CORPORATION
Baton Rouge, LA....................Admiralty/Maritime Law; Personal Injury

GEORGE, HARTZ, LUNDEEN, FLAGG & FULMER
Miami, FL ....Insurance Defense; Medical Malpractice

GEORGE & SHIELDS, LLP
Irvine, CA...............................Civil Trial Practice

GEORGESON, THOMPSON & ANGARAN, CHARTERED
Reno, NV ....Insurance Defense

GERAGHTY, O'LOUGHLIN & KENNEY, PROFESSIONAL ASSOCIATION
St. Paul, MN ....Civil Trial Practice; Construction Law; Insurance Defense; Labor and Employment Law; Medical Malpractice

GERAGHTY, PATRICK E., A PROFESSIONAL ASSOCIATION
Fort Myers, FL ....Civil Rights; Civil Trial Practice; Commercial Law; Personal Injury

GERAGOS & GERAGOS
Los Angeles, CA ....Criminal Trial Practice

GERALDS, MOLONEY & JONES
Lexington, KY ....General Practice; Insurance Defense; Real Estate Law

GERBER & GERBER
Blue Bell, PA..........................Business Law; Civil Trial Practice; Criminal Trial Practice; General Practice; Personal Injury

GERBER, RITCHEY & O'BANION
Sacramento, CA ....Patent, Trademark, Copyright and Unfair Competition

GERDES, MASON AND SIMPSON, L.L.P.
Charlotte, NC..........................Personal Injury

GERLING LAW OFFICES, PROFESSIONAL CORPORATION
Evansville, IN..........................Medical Malpractice; Personal Injury; Product Liability Law

GERMAN, GALLAGHER & MURTAGH, A PROFESSIONAL CORPORATION
Philadelphia, PA ....Antitrust Law; Civil Trial Practice; Commercial Law; Construction Law; Environmental Law; General Practice; Insurance Defense; Medical Malpractice; Product Liability Law; Transportation Law; Workers Compensation

GERMER & GERTZ, L.L.P.
Beaumont, TX..........................Business Law; Personal Injury

GERRISH & MCCREARY, P.C.
Memphis, TN..........................Banking Law

GERRITY, TIMOTHY D. & ASSOCIATES
Columbus, OH........................Family Law; Personal Injury

GERSON, GREKIN & WYNHOFF, ATTORNEYS AT LAW, A LAW CORPORATION
Honolulu, HI..........................Probate, Trusts and Estate Planning; Real Estate Law

GERSTEIN, COHEN & GRAYSON
Haddonfield, NJ......................General Practice

GERSTEIN, JOE W., P.C.
Doraville, GA........................General Practice

GERTNER & GERTNER
Columbus, OH........................Civil Trial Practice; Criminal Trial Practice; Personal Injury

GESS MATTINGLY & ATCHISON, P.S.C.
Lexington, KY........................Antitrust Law; General Practice; Labor and Employment Law

GESSLER, HUGHES & SOCOL, LTD.
Chicago, IL...........................Civil Trial Practice; Commercial Litigation; Health Care Law; Immigration and Naturalization; Insurance Defense; Labor and Employment Law; Medical Malpractice; Personal Injury; Sports and Entertainment Law

GETMAN LAW FIRM
Oneonta, NY..........................General Practice

GEX AND ARTIGUES
Waveland, MS........................Civil Trial Practice; Construction Law

GHERTY & GHERTY
Hudson, WI...........................Personal Injury

GHOLSON, HICKS & NICHOLS, A PROFESSIONAL ASSOCIATION
Columbus, MS........................General Practice

GIACOMINI & KNIEPS
Klamath Falls, OR ....General Practice

GIANAS, PETER T., P.C.
Tucson, AZ ....General Practice

GIANELLI & FORES, A PROFESSIONAL LAW CORPORATION
Modesto, CA..........................General Practice

GIAUQUE, CROCKETT, BENDINGER & PETERSON, A PROFESSIONAL CORPORATION
Salt Lake City, UT..................Antitrust Law; Commercial Law

GIBBES GRAVES MULLINS FERRIS HORTMAN & HARLOW, PLLC
Laurel, MS...........................General Practice

GIBBINS, WINCKLER & HARVEY, L.L.P.
Austin, TX ....Civil Trial Practice; Medical Malpractice; Personal Injury

GIBBONS, WILLIAM P.
Cleveland, OH........................Business Law

GIBBONS, BUCKLEY, SMITH, PALMER & PROUD, P.C.
Media, PA ....Insurance Defense

GIBBONS, SMITH, COHN & ARNETT, A PROFESSIONAL ASSOCIATION
Tampa, FL ....General Practice

GIBBS, JOSEPH A.
Indian Wells, CA ....Civil Trial Practice

GIBBS & BRUNS, L.L.P.
Houston, TX ....Civil Trial Practice; Commercial Law

GIBBS & HOLMES
Charleston, SC ....Labor and Employment Law

GIBBS AND SCHWARTZMAN
San Antonio, TX.....................Probate, Trusts and Estate Planning; Tax Law

GIBNEY, ANTHONY & FLAHERTY, LLP
New York, NY.......................General Practice; Tax Law

GIBSON & ASSOCIATES
Princeton, WV.......................Banking Law; Civil Trial Practice; Criminal Trial Practice; Medical Malpractice; Personal Injury; Product Liability Law

GIBSON, DEAL AND FLETCHER, P.C.
Norcross, GA ....General Practice

GIBSON, DUNN & CRUTCHER LLP
Los Angeles, CA ....General Practice

GIBSON, EVERETT B., LAW FIRM
Memphis, TN ....Civil Trial Practice

GIBSON, HAGLUND & JOHNSON
Irvine, CA.............................Securities Law

GIBSON, MCCLURE & WALLACE, L.L.P.
Dallas, TX............................Civil Trial Practice; Commercial Litigation; Insurance Defense

GIBSON, OCHSNER & ADKINS, LLP
Amarillo, TX.........................General Practice

GIBSON, RICHARD H., LAW OFFICES OF
Los Angeles, CA ....Banking Law; Bankruptcy Law

GIDIERE & HINTON
Montgomery, AL ....Commercial Litigation; Insurance Defense

GIDLEY, SARLI & MARUSAK
Providence, RI.......................Construction Law; General Practice; Health Care Law; Insurance Defense; Labor and Employment Law; Medical Malpractice; Municipal and Zoning Law; Personal Injury

GIESSEL, BARKER & LYMAN, INC.
Houston, TX ....Insurance Defense; Medical Malpractice

GIFFEN, JAMES KELLY
Knoxville, TN ....Banking Law; Bankruptcy Law; Real Estate Law

GIFFEN LEE
Kitchener, ON, Canada ....Appellate Practice; Bankruptcy Law; Business Law; Civil Trial Practice; Commercial Law; Employment Benefits Law; Family Law; Insurance Defense; Personal Injury; Probate, Trusts and Estate Planning; Product Liability Law

GIFFIN, WINNING, COHEN & BODEWES, P.C.
Springfield, IL ....Civil Trial Practice; General Practice; Insurance Defense

GIGNAC, SUTTS
Windsor, ON, Canada ....Civil Trial Practice; Commercial Law; Criminal Trial Practice; Family Law; General Practice; Insurance Defense; Labor and Employment Law; Medical Malpractice; Personal Injury

GIGNILLIAT, SAVITZ & BETTIS
Columbia, SC ....Employment Benefits Law; Labor and Employment Law

GILARDI & COOPER, P.A.
Pittsburgh, PA ....Civil Trial Practice; Personal Injury

GILBERT & COFFEY, P.C.
El Paso, TX...........................General Practice

GILBERT, HARRELL, GILBERT, SUMERFORD & MARTIN, P.C.
Brunswick, GA.......................Civil Trial Practice; General Practice; Insurance Defense

GILBERT, MCGLOAN, GILLIS
Saint John, NB, Canada ....Business Law; Civil Trial Practice; General Practice; Insurance Defense

GILBREATH LAW FIRM
Fort Smith, AR ....Medical Malpractice; Product Liability Law

GILCHRIST & RUTTER, PROFESSIONAL CORPORATION
Santa Monica, CA...................Business Law; Real Estate Law

GILCREASE, GLYNN W. JR., LAW OFFICES OF
Tempe, AZ ....Personal Injury

GILES, GERALD F.
Portsmouth, NH ....General Practice

GILES AND GILES
Sioux City, IA ....Bankruptcy Law; Family Law; General Practice

GILKERSON, GEORGE E., ATTORNEY-AT-LAW, P.C.
Lubbock, TX..........................Criminal Trial Practice; Family Law; Probate, Trusts and Estate Planning

GILKEY & STEPHENSON, P.A.
Albuquerque, NM...................Labor and Employment Law

GILLARY, RANDALL J., P.C.
Troy, MI..............................Commercial Litigation

GILL AND BALDWIN
Glendale, CA..........................Business Law; Civil Trial Practice; Construction Law; Probate, Trusts and Estate Planning

GILLESPIE & GOLDMAN
Fort Lauderdale, FL ....Civil Trial Practice; Personal Injury

GILLESPIE, HART, ALTIZER & WHITESELL, P.C.
Tazewell, VA ....General Practice

GILLESPIE, JAMES R., P.A.
Boise, ID ....General Practice

GILLESPIE, ROZEN, TANNER & WATSKY, P.C.
Dallas, TX...............................Labor and Employment Law
Fort Worth, TX ....Labor and Employment Law

GILLILAND, JOHN C. II, THE LAW OFFICE OF
Crestview Hills, KY ....Health Care Law; Labor and Employment Law

GILLILAND & HAYES, P.A. A PROFESSIONAL CORPORATION
Hutchinson, KS.........................General Practice

GILLIN, JACOBSON, ELLIS, LARSEN & DOYLE
Orinda, CA..............................Civil Trial Practice; Commercial Litigation; Patent, Trademark, Copyright and Unfair Competition; Personal Injury

GILLIS & ANGLEY
Hingham, MA ....General Practice

GILLIS & SLOGAR
Houston, TX ....Bankruptcy Law; Business Law; Civil Trial Practice; Commercial Law; Communications Law; Real Estate Law; Tax Law

GILL LAW FIRM, A PROFESSIONAL ASSOCIATION
Little Rock, AR ....Business Law; General Practice; Municipal Bond/ Public Authority Financing; Probate, Trusts and Estate Planning; Public Utilities Law; Tax Law

GILLOTTI, CAPRISTO & BECK, P.C.
Pittsburgh, PA ....Family Law

GILL PROFESSIONAL CORPORATION
Denver, CO ....Probate, Trusts and Estate Planning

GILMAN, MCLAUGHLIN & HANRAHAN
Boston, MA.............................General Practice

GILMAN & PANGIA
Washington, DC.......................Aviation Law; Transportation Law

GILMARTIN, POSTER & SHAFTO
New York, NY.........................Admiralty/Maritime Law; Civil Trial Practice; Real Estate Law

GILMER, SADLER, INGRAM, SUTHERLAND & HUTTON
Blacksburg, VA ....General Practice; Insurance Defense; Personal Injury
Pulaski, VA ....General Practice; Insurance Defense; Personal Injury

GILMORE, R. PATRICK
Chandler, OK ....Civil Trial Practice

GILMORE, AAFEDT, FORDE, ANDERSON & GRAY, P.A.
Minneapolis, MN ....Insurance Defense

GILMORE, REES & CARLSON, P.C.
Franklin, MA ....Probate, Trusts and Estate Planning

GILPIN, PAXSON & BERSCH
Houston, TX ....Real Estate Law

GILREATH, JAMES R., P.A.
Greenville, SC..........................Civil Trial Practice; Probate, Trusts and Estate Planning; Tax Law

GILSTRAP, WILLIAM G., P.C.
Albuquerque, NM.....................Personal Injury

GINGELL & JENKINS, P.C.
Silver Spring, MD ....General Practice

GINNINGS, C. MICHAEL
El Paso, TX..............................Business Law

GINSBERG, EUGENE S.
Garden City, NY ....Business Law; Construction Law; Labor and Employment Law; Real Estate Law

GINSBERG & BROOME
New York, NY.........................Civil Trial Practice; Medical Malpractice; Personal Injury; Product Liability Law

GINSBERG AND BRUSILOW, P.C.
Dallas, TX...............................Real Estate Law; Tax Law

GIOFFRE & GIOFFRE, P.C.
Purchase, NY ....General Practice; Probate, Trusts and Estate Planning; Real Estate Law

GIORDANO, A. ROBERT
White Plains, NY ....Probate, Trusts and Estate Planning

GIORDANO, HALLERAN & CIESLA, A PROFESSIONAL CORPORATION
Middletown, NJ ....General Practice

GIRARDI AND KEESE
Los Angeles, CA ....Civil Trial Practice; Commercial Litigation; Personal Injury; Product Liability Law

GISLASON, DOSLAND, HUNTER & MALECKI, P.L.L.P.
Mankato, MN ....Civil Trial Practice
Minneapolis, MN ....Civil Trial Practice
New Ulm, MN ....Civil Trial Practice; General Practice

GISRIEL & BRUSH, P.A.
Baltimore, MD ....Civil Trial Practice

GLANKLER BROWN, PLLC
Memphis, TN ....Antitrust Law; Banking Law; Bankruptcy Law; Business Law; Civil Trial Practice; Construction Law; Environmental Law; General Practice; Health Care Law; Insurance Defense; Medical Malpractice; Probate, Trusts and Estate Planning; Real Estate Law; Tax Law

GLASER & DEROS
Baltimore, MD ....Civil Trial Practice; Criminal Trial Practice

GLASER, SHANDELL & BLITZ
New York, NY.........................Medical Malpractice; Personal Injury

GLASGOW AND VEAZEY
Nashville, TN ....Insurance Defense

GLASS, JOSEPH G.
Louisville, KY ....General Practice

GLASS, MCCULLOUGH, SHERRILL & HARROLD
Atlanta, GA ....Business Law; Civil Trial Practice; General Practice; Immigration and Naturalization; International Business Law; Real Estate Law

GLASSCOCK, GARDY AND SAVAGE
Suffolk, VA.............................Municipal and Zoning Law; Personal Injury; Probate, Trusts and Estate Planning; Real Estate Law

GLASSER AND GLASSER, P.L.C.
Norfolk, VA ....Commercial Litigation

GLASSMAN, JETER, EDWARDS & WADE, P.C.
Memphis, TN ....Civil Trial Practice; Construction Law; Insurance Defense; Labor and Employment Law; Personal Injury; Product Liability Law

GLAST, PHILLIPS & MURRAY, P.C.
Dallas, TX...............................Business Law

GLAZER, LEONARD, P.C. & ASSOCIATES, LAW OFFICES OF
Boston, MA.............................Medical Malpractice; Personal Injury; Product Liability Law

GLEASON, BARLOW & BOHNE, P.A.
Melbourne, FL ....Commercial Litigation; Real Estate Law

GLEASON AND MCGUIRE
Chicago, IL.............................Insurance Defense

GLEAVES SWEARINGEN LARSEN POTTER SCOTT & SMITH
Eugene, OR ....General Practice

GLEICHER & REYNOLDS, P.C.
Detroit, MI..............................Medical Malpractice; Personal Injury; Product Liability Law

GLEISS, LOCANTE & KAFTAN
Sparta, WI ....General Practice

GLENN, MILLS & FISHER, P.A.
Durham, NC ....Civil Trial Practice; Personal Injury

GLENN MURPHY GRAY & STEPP, L.L.P.
Columbia, SC ....Civil Trial Practice; Criminal Trial Practice; General Practice; Personal Injury; Product Liability Law

GLENNON, GOODMAN & LUBELEY
Reston, VA..............................General Practice

GLICKMAN, SUGARMAN & KNEELAND
Worcester, MA.........................Civil Trial Practice; General Practice

GLOBENSKY, GLEISS, BITTNER & HYRNS, P.C.
St. Joseph, MI ....Civil Trial Practice; Medical Malpractice; Municipal and Zoning Law; Probate, Trusts and Estate Planning

GLOSSER & SHREVE
Pittsburgh, PA ....Bankruptcy Law

GLOVER, ANDERSON, CHANDLER & UZICK, L.L.P.
Houston, TX ....Appellate Practice; Insurance Defense; Medical Malpractice; Personal Injury; Product Liability Law

GLOVER & DAVIS, P.A.
Newnan, GA ....Bankruptcy Law; Business Law; Civil Trial Practice; Construction Law; General Practice; Municipal and Zoning Law; Personal Injury; Probate, Trusts and Estate Planning; Real Estate Law

GLOVER & VAN COTT, A PROFESSIONAL ASSOCIATION
Phoenix, AZ ....Commercial Litigation

GLOVSKY, TARLOW & MILBERG
Boston, MA.............................Business Law; Civil Trial Practice; Labor and
Employment Law

GODARD, WEST & ADELMAN, P.C.
Fairfax, VA ....Insurance Defense; Medical Malpractice

GODDARD & GODDARD, P.C.
Denver, CO ....Probate, Trusts and Estate Planning

GODFREY FIRM, THE, A PROFESSIONAL LAW CORPORATION
New Orleans, LA ....Civil Trial Practice; Municipal Bond/Public
Authority Financing; Public Utilities Law; Tax Law

GODFREY & KAHN, S.C.
Green Bay, WI ....General Practice
Madison, WI............................General Practice
Milwaukee, WI........................General Practice
Oshkosh, WI ....General Practice

GODFREY, NESHEK, WORTH & LEIBSLE, S.C.
Elkhorn, WI ....General Practice

GODFREY, VANDOVER & BURNS, INC., A PROFESSIONAL CORPORATION
St. Louis, MO...........................Insurance Defense

GODLOVE, MAYHALL, DZIALO, DUTCHER & ERWIN, A PROFESSIONAL CORPORATION
Lawton, OK ....General Practice

GODWIN & CARLTON, A PROFESSIONAL CORPORATION
Dallas, TX................................Banking Law; Bankruptcy Law; Civil Trial Practice;
Commercial Law; General Practice; Insurance
Defense; Labor and Employment Law; Probate,
Trusts and Estate Planning; Tax Law

GOEBEL, LOUIS E.
San Diego, CA ....Civil Trial Practice; General Practice

GOEDERT & HUNTINGTON
Oak Park, IL ....Business Law; Probate, Trusts and Estate Planning

GOEHRING, RUTTER & BOEHM, A PROFESSIONAL CORPORATION
Pittsburgh, PA ....Probate, Trusts and Estate Planning; Real Estate
Law; Tax Law

GOERING, ROBERTS, BERKMAN, RUBIN & BROGNA, P.C.
Tucson, AZ ....Civil Trial Practice; General Practice; Insurance
Defense; Medical Malpractice; Personal Injury

GOETZ, FITZPATRICK & FLYNN, L.L.P.
New York, NY.........................Civil Trial Practice; Construction Law; Real Estate
Law

GOFF AND GOFF
Ruston, LA ....Product Liability Law

GOICOECHEA & DI GRAZIA, LTD., A PROF. CORP., LAW OFFICES
Elko, NV ....Business Law; Civil Trial Practice; General Practice

GOLD, ESTELLA S.
Moorestown, NJ......................Civil Trial Practice; Insurance Defense

GOLD BENNETT & CERA LLP
San Francisco, CA ....Securities Law

GOLDBERG, FIELDMAN & LETHAM, P.C.
Washington, DC......................Energy Law

GOLDBERG, GOLDSTEIN & BUCKLEY, P.A.
Fort Myers, FL ....Commercial Law; Construction Law; General
Practice; Personal Injury

GOLDBERG, GRUENER, GENTILE, VOELKER & HOROHO, P.C.
Pittsburgh, PA ....Family Law

GOLDBERG & HALL
San Diego, CA ....Criminal Trial Practice

GOLDBERG, JAY, P.C.
New York, NY.........................Real Estate Law

GOLDBERG, JEFFREY M., & ASSOCIATES, LTD.
Chicago, IL...............................Aviation Law; Medical Malpractice; Product
Liability Law

GOLDBERG, KATZMAN & SHIPMAN, P.C.
Harrisburg, PA.........................Antitrust Law; Business Law; Civil Trial Practice;
Commercial Law; Criminal Trial Practice; Family
Law; General Practice; Insurance Defense; Medical
Malpractice; Municipal Bond/Public Authority
Financing; Municipal and Zoning Law; Personal
Injury; Probate, Trusts and Estate Planning;
Product Liability Law; Real Estate Law; Tax Law

GOLDBERG, KOHN, BELL, BLACK, ROSENBLOOM & MORITZ, LTD.
Chicago, IL...............................Real Estate Law

GOLDBERG, MUFSON & SPAR, A PROFESSIONAL CORPORATION
West Orange, NJ.....................Business Law; General Practice; Probate, Trusts and
Estate Planning; Tax Law

GOLDBERG & SIMPSON, P.S.C.
Louisville, KY ....Bankruptcy Law; Civil Trial Practice; Insurance
Defense; Securities Law

GOLDBERG, STINNETT, MEYERS & DAVIS, A PROFESSIONAL CORPORATION
San Francisco, CA ....Bankruptcy Law

GOLDBERG, YOUNG & GRAVENHORST, P.A., LAW OFFICES
Fort Lauderdale, FL................General Practice

GOLDBERGER AND DUBIN, P.C.
New York, NY.........................Appellate Practice; Criminal Trial Practice

GOLDBLATT, LIPKIN & COHEN, P.C.
Norfolk, VA..............................Bankruptcy Law; Commercial Law; Family Law;
Personal Injury; Probate, Trusts and Estate
Planning; Workers Compensation

GOLDEN, ROBERT E., P.C.
San Antonio, TX......................Civil Trial Practice

GOLDEN, TAYLOR & POTTERFIELD
Columbia, SC ....Civil Trial Practice; Family Law

GOLDEN, WEXLER & SARNESE, P.C.
Garden City, NY ....General Practice

GOLDFARB & FLEECE
New York, NY.........................Probate, Trusts and Estate Planning; Real Estate
Law

GOLDFEIN & JOSEPH, A PROFESSIONAL CORPORATION
Philadelphia, PA ....Civil Trial Practice; Commercial Litigation;
Insurance Defense; Medical Malpractice; Product
Liability Law; Workers Compensation

GOLDMAN, LAURENCE R.
Woodland Hills, CA ....Family Law

GOLDMAN ANTONETTI & CÓRDOVA
San Juan, PR ....Banking Law; Civil Trial Practice; Commercial Law;
Environmental Law; General Practice; Labor and
Employment Law; Municipal Bond/Public
Authority Financing; Natural Resources Law; Real
Estate Law; Tax Law

GOLDMAN & CURTIS
Lowell, MA ....Business Law; General Practice

GOLDMAN & GORDON, L.L.P.
Los Angeles, CA ....Bankruptcy Law; Civil Trial Practice; Commercial
Law; Real Estate Law

GOLDMAN & HAFETZ
New York, NY.........................Civil Trial Practice; Criminal Trial Practice

GOLDMAN & KAGON, LAW CORPORATION
Los Angeles, CA ....Family Law; General Practice; Real Estate Law

GOLDMAN & KAPLAN, LTD.
Phoenix, AZ ....Personal Injury; Probate, Trusts and Estate
Planning; Tax Law

GOLDMAN, KENNETH L., PROFESSIONAL CORPORATION
Los Angeles, CA ....Probate, Trusts and Estate Planning

GOLDMAN & VETTER, P.A.
Baltimore, MD ....Bankruptcy Law; Business Law

GOLDNER, SOMMERS, SCRUDDER & BASS
Atlanta, GA ....Civil Trial Practice; Commercial Law; Construction
Law; General Practice; Health Care Law; Insurance
Defense; Medical Malpractice; Personal Injury;
Product Liability Law; Workers Compensation

GOLD, ROTATORI & SCHWARTZ, L.P.A.
Cleveland, OH..........................Appellate Practice; Criminal Trial Practice; General
Practice

GOLDSMITH, EDWIN M. III
Philadelphia, PA ....Commercial Litigation

GOLDSMITH, HOWARD M., P.C.
Philadelphia, PA ....Family Law

GOLD & STANLEY, P.C. PROFESSIONAL CORPORATION
Alexandria, VA ....Bankruptcy Law; General Practice

GOLDSTEIN, BERTRAM M., & ASSOCIATES, P.A.
Baltimore, MD ....Product Liability Law

GOLDSTEIN, FLANZ & FISHMAN
Montreal, QU, Canada ....Banking Law; Bankruptcy Law; Civil Trial Practice;
Commercial Law; Real Estate Law

GOLDSTEIN, GOLDSTEIN AND HILLEY
San Antonio, TX.....................Criminal Trial Practice

GOLDSTEIN, KENNEDY & PETITO
Los Angeles, CA ....Labor and Employment Law

GOLDSTEIN & MCGRODER, LTD. A PROFESSIONAL CORPORATION
Phoenix, AZ ....Appellate Practice; Civil Trial Practice; Medical Malpractice; Personal Injury; Product Liability Law

GOLDSTEIN AND PECK, P.C.
Bridgeport, CT.........................General Practice
Westport, CT..........................General Practice

GOLDSTEIN & PHILLIPS, A PROFESSIONAL CORPORATION
San Francisco, CA ....Civil Trial Practice

GOLDSTEIN AND PRICE, L.C.
St. Louis, MO..........................Admiralty/Maritime Law

GOLDSTEIN, RICHARD S., P.C., LAW OFFICES OF
New York, NY.......................Immigration and Naturalization

GOLDSTEIN & RUBINTON, P.C.
Huntington, NY.....................Family Law; Municipal and Zoning Law; Personal Injury; Real Estate Law

GOLDSTEIN, STUART
Phoenix, AZ ....Personal Injury

GOLDSTEIN TILL & LITE
Newark, NJ ....Admiralty/Maritime Law; Appellate Practice; Civil Trial Practice; Commercial Law; Criminal Trial Practice; Environmental Law; Family Law; Personal Injury; Product Liability Law

GOLDSTEIN, WARREN A., A PROFESSIONAL LAW CORPORATION
New Orleans, LA ....Civil Trial Practice; General Practice

GOLDSTICK, WEINBERGER, FELDMAN & GROSSMAN, P.C.
New York, NY........................Real Estate Law

GOLD, WEEMS, BRUSER, SUES & RUNDELL, A PROFESSIONAL LAW CORPORATION
Alexandria, LA ....General Practice; Tax Law

GOLENBOCK, EISEMAN, ASSOR & BELL
New York, NY........................Civil Trial Practice; Commercial Law; General Practice

GOLLAHER & CHAMBERS, A PROFESSIONAL CORPORATION
Dallas, TX...............................Insurance Defense

GOLOB, MICHAEL H.
Farmington Hills, MI ....Civil Trial Practice; Commercial Law; Family Law

GOLOMB, DAVID B. LAW OFFICES OF
New York, NY........................Medical Malpractice; Personal Injury; Product Liability Law

GOMEZ, DAVID F., A PROFESSIONAL CORPORATION
Phoenix, AZ ....Civil Trial Practice; Labor and Employment Law

GOMPERS, MCCARTHY, HILL & MCCLURE
Wheeling, WV ....Civil Trial Practice; General Practice; Personal Injury

GONANO & HARRELL, CHARTERED
Fort Pierce, FL........................Land Use Law; Real Estate Law

GONZALEZ, ANTHONY F.
Tampa, FL ....Civil Rights; Employment Benefits Law

GONZALEZ & CESTERO
San Juan, PR...........................Commercial Law

GOODELL, DEVRIES, LEECH & GRAY, LLP
Baltimore, MD ....Insurance Defense; Medical Malpractice; Product Liability Law

GOODELL, STRATTON, EDMONDS & PALMER, L.L.P.
Topeka, KS..............................Civil Trial Practice; Communications Law; Environmental Law; General Practice; Health Care Law; Insurance Defense; Labor and Employment Law; Probate, Trusts and Estate Planning; Securities Law; Tax Law

GOODING, HUFFMAN, KELLEY & BECKER
Lima, OH ....Civil Trial Practice; Insurance Defense

GOODMAN, EARLE GARY
Los Angeles, CA ....Real Estate Law

GOODMAN CHESNOFF & KEACH, A PROFESSIONAL CORPORATION
Las Vegas, NV ....Appellate Practice; Constitutional Law; Criminal Trial Practice; Personal Injury; Sports and Entertainment Law

GOODMAN & CLARK
Arlington, TX ....Family Law

GOODMAN, EDEN, MILLENDER & BEDROSIAN
Detroit, MI ....Personal Injury

GOODMAN GARY & LICKSTEIN, P.C.
Vienna, VA..............................Business Law

GOODMAN & GOODMAN, A LEGAL PROFESSIONAL ASSOCIATION
Cincinnati, OH ....Family Law; Labor and Employment Law

GOODMAN, MCGUFFEY, AUST & LINDSEY
Atlanta, GA ....Civil Trial Practice; Insurance Defense

GOODMAN PHILLIPS & VINEBERG
Montreal, QU, Canada ....General Practice
Hong Kong, Hong Kong.........General Practice

GOODMAN, ROBERT U., P.L.C.
Shreveport, LA.......................Business Law; Civil Trial Practice; Commercial Law

GOODMAN WEISS MILLER GOLDFARB
Cleveland, OH........................Business Law; Civil Trial Practice; Labor and Employment Law; Securities Law

GOODSILL ANDERSON QUINN & STIFEL
Honolulu, HI...........................General Practice
Kailua-Kona, HI.....................General Practice

GOODSON, MANLEY & DURFEE, P.L.C.
Phoenix, AZ ....Business Law; General Practice; Probate, Trusts and Estate Planning

GOODWIN & GOODWIN
Charleston, WV......................Civil Trial Practice; General Practice; Insurance Defense; Municipal Bond/Public Authority Financing; Personal Injury
Parkersburg, WV....................General Practice
Ripley, WV.............................General Practice

GOODWIN, PROCTER & HOAR LLP
Boston, MA............................General Practice

GOOGASIAN FIRM, THE, P.C.
Bloomfield Hills, MI...............Commercial Litigation; Medical Malpractice; Personal Injury

GOOLD, PATTERSON, DEVORE & RONDEAU
Las Vegas, NV ....Commercial Law; General Practice; International Business Law; Real Estate Law

GORANSON, BAIN & LARSEN, L.C.
Dallas, TX...............................Family Law

GORDON, ALEXANDER IV
Easton, MD............................Bankruptcy Law

GORDON, J. HOUSTON
Covington, TN ....General Practice

GORDON, ARATA, MCCOLLAM & DUPLANTIS, L.L.P.
Baton Rouge, LA....................Natural Resources Law
Lafayette, LA ....Natural Resources Law
New Orleans, LA ....Environmental Law; General Practice; Natural Resources Law

GORDON, EDELSTEIN, KREPACK, GRANT, FELTON & GOLDSTEIN
Los Angeles, CA ....Construction Law; Medical Malpractice; Personal Injury; Product Liability Law; Workers Compensation

GORDON & EINSTEIN, LTD.
Chicago, IL..............................Business Law; Real Estate Law; Tax Law

GORDON, FEINBLATT, ROTHMAN, HOFFBERGER & HOLLANDER, LLC
Baltimore, MD ....General Practice

GORDON & HENESON, P.A.
Baltimore, MD ....Civil Trial Practice

GORDON LAW FIRM
Hartwell, GA ....Civil Trial Practice; General Practice; Real Estate Law

GORDON, MUIR AND FOLEY
Hartford, CT ....Banking Law; Civil Trial Practice; Commercial Law; Construction Law; General Practice; Insurance Defense; Medical Malpractice; Probate, Trusts and Estate Planning; Real Estate Law

GORDON, SIEGEL, MASTRO, MULLANEY, GORDON & GALVIN, P.C.
Schenectady, NY....................General Practice

GORDON, SILBERMAN, WIGGINS & CHILDS, A PROFESSIONAL CORPORATION
Birmingham, AL ....Banking Law; Bankruptcy Law; Business Law; Civil Rights; Civil Trial Practice; Commercial Law; Employment Benefits Law; General Practice; Labor and Employment Law; Personal Injury; Probate, Trusts and Estate Planning; Real Estate Law; Tax Law

GORDON, WILLIAM C., A PROFESSIONAL CORPORATION
Sausalito, CA............................Personal Injury

GOREN & GOREN, P.C.
Birmingham, MI....................Health Care Law; Medical Malpractice; Personal Injury

GORES & BLAIS, P.S.
Seattle, WA ....Probate, Trusts and Estate Planning

GORHAM & WALDREP, P.C.
Birmingham, AL ....Criminal Trial Practice; General Practice; Real Estate Law; Tax Law

GORMAN & ENRIGHT, P.C.
New Haven, CT ....Business Law; Commercial Law; Real Estate Law

GORMAN, WASZKIEWICZ, GORMAN & SCHMITT
Utica, NY ....General Practice

GORMLEY & COLUCCI, P.C.
Cambridge, MA ....Criminal Trial Practice; General Practice; Insurance Defense

GOSS, JAMES W., PROFESSONAL CORPORATION
Grosse Pointe Farms, MI ....Civil Trial Practice

GOTHA, FREDERICK
Pasadena, CA ....Patent, Trademark, Copyright and Unfair Competition

GOTT, YOUNG & BOGLE, P.A.
Wichita, KS ....General Practice

GOTTLIEB & PEARSON
Montreal, QU, Canada ....International Trade Law

GOUBEAUX & GOUBEAUX
Greenville, OH ....General Practice

GOUGH, SHANAHAN, JOHNSON & WATERMAN
Helena, MT ....General Practice

GOULD, COOKSEY, FENNELL, O'NEILL & MARINE, PROFESSIONAL ASSOCIATION
Vero Beach, FL ....Civil Trial Practice; General Practice

GOULD, KILLIAN & WYNNE
Hartford, CT ....Business Law; General Practice; Probate, Trusts and Estate Planning

GOULSTON & STORRS, A PROFESSIONAL CORPORATION
Boston, MA..............................General Practice

GOURVITZ, ELLIOT H., P.A.
Springfield, NJ ....Appellate Practice; Civil Trial Practice; Family Law

GOVERNALI, JOSEPH P.
White Plains, NY ....Family Law; General Practice

GOZIGIAN, WASHBURN & CLINTON
Cooperstown, NY ....General Practice

GRACE, JOHN PHILIP, P.C.
Phoenix, AZ ....Personal Injury

GRACEY, RUTH, HOWARD, TATE & SOWELL
Nashville, TN ....General Practice; Insurance Defense; Workers Compensation

GRAD, LOGAN & KLEWANS, P.C.
Alexandria, VA ....Business Law; Civil Trial Practice; Commercial Law; Criminal Trial Practice; Health Care Law; Labor and Employment Law; Probate, Trusts and Estate Planning

GRADY & ASSOCIATES, LEGAL PROFESSIONAL ASSOCIATION
Naples, FL................................Securities Law

GRAHAM, CLARK, JONES, BUILDER, PRATT & MARKS
Winter Park, FL......................Civil Trial Practice; Real Estate Law

GRAHAM, CURTIN & SHERIDAN, A PROFESSIONAL ASSOCIATION
Morristown, NJ......................General Practice

GRAHAM & DUNN, A PROFESSIONAL SERVICE CORPORATION
Seattle, WA ....General Practice

GRAHAM AND GRAHAM
Springfield, IL ....General Practice

GRAHAM & JAMES LLP
Los Angeles, CA ....General Practice
Palo Alto, CA ....General Practice
San Francisco, CA ....Admiralty/Maritime Law; General Practice
Washington, DC........................General Practice
Milan, Italy..............................General Practice

GRAHAM, MARJORIE GADARIAN, P.A.
Palm Beach Gardens, FL.........Appellate Practice

GRAHAM, MOLETTEIRE & TUTTLE, P.A.
Merritt Island, FL....................Personal Injury

GRAHAM, SMITH & LINDQUIST, L.L.P.
Dallas, TX ....Probate, Trusts and Estate Planning

GRANIK SILVERMAN CAMPBELL & HEKKER
New City, NY ....Employment Benefits Law

GRANNAN & MALOY, P.C.
Arlington, MA ....Probate, Trusts and Estate Planning; Real Estate Law

GRANT, BERNARD, LYONS & GADDIS, A PROFESSIONAL CORPORATION
Longmont, CO ....General Practice

GRANT, FRIDKIN & PEARSON, P.A.
Naples, FL................................Commercial Litigation; Probate, Trusts and Estate Planning; Real Estate Law

GRANT & LEATHERWOOD, P.A.
Greenville, SC..........................Civil Trial Practice; Construction Law; Product Liability Law

GRANT, ROGERS, MAUL & GRANT
Columbus, NE..........................General Practice

GRASSI & TOERING, P.L.C.
Troy, MI..................................Business Law; Civil Trial Practice; Probate, Trusts and Estate Planning

GRAVEL AND SHEA, A PROFESSIONAL CORPORATION
Burlington, VT ....Appellate Practice; Civil Trial Practice; Commercial Law; Environmental Law; General Practice; Municipal and Zoning Law; Probate, Trusts and Estate Planning; Real Estate Law; Tax Law

GRAVES AND ASSOCIATES
St. Catharines, ON, Canada ....Civil Trial Practice

GRAVES, DOUGHERTY, HEARON & MOODY, A PROFESSIONAL CORPORATION
Austin, TX ....Administrative Law; General Practice

GRAY CARY WARE & FREIDENRICH, A PROFESSIONAL CORPORATION
El Centro, CA ....General Practice
La Jolla, CA............................General Practice
Palo Alto, CA ....General Practice
San Diego, CA ....General Practice

GRAY, SOWLE & IACCO, A PROFESSIONAL CORPORATION
Mount Pleasant, MI................Medical Malpractice; Personal Injury

GRAY, YORK, DUFFY & RATTET
Los Angeles, CA ....Civil Trial Practice; Construction Law; Labor and Employment Law

GRAYSON, SMITH, STODGHILL & PRICE, P.C.
Greenville, SC..........................Real Estate Law

GRECO, MOLLIS & O'HARA, A PROFESSIONAL CORPORATION
Irvine, CA................................Business Law; Probate, Trusts and Estate Planning; Tax Law

GREELEY WALKER & KOWEN
Honolulu, HI............................Civil Trial Practice; Insurance Defense

GREEN, JOHN R.
Duncan, OK ....General Practice

GREEN, MARGO L. AND ASSOCIATES
St. Louis, MO..........................Family Law

GREEN, CHENEY AND HUGHES, LLP
Jackson, MS ....General Practice

GREEN LAW OFFICES
Boise, ID..................................General Practice

GREEN PARISH
Halifax, NS, Canada ....Civil Trial Practice; Commercial Law

GREEN, SCHAAF & MARGO, P.C.
St. Louis, MO..........................Business Law; Commercial Litigation; Securities Law

GREEN & SEIFTER, ATTORNEYS, P.C.
Syracuse, NY............................Tax Law

GREENAN, WALKER, TRAINOR & BILLMAN
Largo, MD ....Civil Trial Practice

GREENBAUM, ROWE, SMITH, RAVIN, DAVIS AND HIMMEL
Woodbridge, NJ ....Bankruptcy Law; Civil Trial Practice; General Practice; Real Estate Law; Tax Law

GREENBERG DAUBER AND EPSTEIN, A PROFESSIONAL CORPORATION
Newark, NJ ....Banking Law; Civil Trial Practice; Commercial Law; Criminal Trial Practice; General Practice; Tax Law

GREENBERG GLUSKER FIELDS CLAMAN & MACHTINGER LLP
Los Angeles, CA ....General Practice; Probate, Trusts and Estate Planning; Tax Law

GREENBERG, MAX E., TRAGER, TOPLITZ & HERBST
New York, NY........................Civil Trial Practice; Construction Law; Real Estate Law

GREENBERG & PARENTEAU, P.C.
New London, CT.................General Practice

GREENBERG & PLEBAN
St. Louis, MO.........................Criminal Trial Practice; Medical Malpractice; Personal Injury; Product Liability Law

GREENBERG, TRAURIG, HOFFMAN, LIPOFF, ROSEN & QUENTEL, P.A.
Miami, FL ....General Practice

GREENBLATT, JAY H., & ASSOCIATES, A PROF. CORP.
Vineland, NJ...........................Civil Trial Practice; General Practice; Insurance Defense; Personal Injury

GREENBURG, POSNER, POSNER & FEINMAN, LLP
White Plains, NY ....Commercial Law; Environmental Law; Probate, Trusts and Estate Planning; Real Estate Law

GREENE, BROILLET, TAYLOR, WHEELER & PANISH
Santa Monica, CA...................Personal Injury

GREENE AND LETTS
Chicago, IL.............................Labor and Employment Law

GREENE & MCQUILLAN CO., L.P.A.
Cleveland, OH........................Personal Injury

GREENE RADOVSKY MALONEY & SHARE, LLP
San Francisco, CA ....Real Estate Law; Tax Law

GREENE AND REID
Syracuse, NY..........................Insurance Defense; Personal Injury

GREENE & ZINNER, P.C.
White Plains, NY ....Commercial Litigation; General Practice

GREENEBAUM DOLL & MCDONALD PLLC
Louisville, KY ....Labor and Employment Law

GREENFELDER, MANDER, HANSON, MURPHY & DWYER
Dade City, FL.........................Criminal Trial Practice; Personal Injury

GREENFIELD AND MURPHY
New Haven, CT ....Civil Trial Practice; Family Law; General Practice

GREENFIELD, STANLEY, & ASSOCIATES
Pittsburgh, PA ....Civil Trial Practice; Criminal Trial Practice

GREENHAW & GREENHAW
Fayetteville, AR ....General Practice

GREENLEE, WINNER AND SULLIVAN, P.C.
Boulder, CO ....Patent, Trademark, Copyright and Unfair Competition

GREENMAN, GOLDBERG, RABY & MARTINEZ, PROFESSIONAL CORPORATION
Las Vegas, NV ....Civil Trial Practice; Personal Injury; Workers Compensation

GREENSPAN & GREENSPAN
White Plains, NY ....Civil Trial Practice; Criminal Trial Practice; Securities Law; Tax Law

GREENSPUN, PETER D., & ASSOCIATES, P.C.
Fairfax, VA ....Civil Trial Practice; Criminal Trial Practice; Personal Injury

GREENWALD, GREENWALD & POWERS
Milford, MA...........................Civil Trial Practice; Personal Injury; Real Estate Law

GREENWALD, HOFFMAN & MEYER
Glendale, CA...........................Business Law; Probate, Trusts and Estate Planning; Real Estate Law

GREENWALD, STEVEN I., P.A.
Boca Raton, FL ....Real Estate Law

GREER, BURNS & CRAIN, LTD.
Chicago, IL.............................Patent, Trademark, Copyright and Unfair Competition

GREER, HERZ & ADAMS, L.L.P.
Galveston, TX.........................Commercial Litigation; General Practice

GREESON, GRIFFIN & ASSOCIATES
Greensboro, NC......................Personal Injury

GREFE & SIDNEY, P.L.C.
Des Moines, IA ....Civil Trial Practice; General Practice; Insurance Defense; Probate, Trusts and Estate Planning; Tax Law

GREGG, HART & FARRIS
Batesville, AR ....Commercial Litigation; General Practice; Insurance Defense

GREGG, MIESZKUC, LEWIS & DAUGHTRY, P.C.
Houston, TX ....Civil Trial Practice; General Practice; Municipal and Zoning Law; Real Estate Law

GREGORIO, SAM N., A PROFESSIONAL LAW CORPORATION
Shreveport, LA ....Personal Injury

GREGORY, A. J. JR.
Natchitoches, LA ....Personal Injury

GREGORY, RAYMOND F. LAW OFFICES OF
New York, NY........................Civil Rights; Commercial Litigation; Labor and Employment Law

GREGORY, EASLEY, BLANKENSHIP AND COURTNEY
Murray, KY ....General Practice

GREGSON AND PIXLER, P.C.
Denver, CO ....Labor and Employment Law

GREINES, MARTIN, STEIN & RICHLAND
Beverly Hills, CA ....Appellate Practice

GRENADIER, DAVIS & SIMPSON, P.C.
Alexandria, VA ....Family Law

GRESHAM, DAVIS, GREGORY, WORTHY & MOORE, A PROFESSIONAL CORPORATION
San Antonio, TX.....................General Practice

GRESHIN, ZIEGLER & PRUZANSKY
Smithtown, NY ....Civil Trial Practice; Commercial Law; General Practice; Personal Injury; Probate, Trusts and Estate Planning

GREVE, CLIFFORD, WENGEL & PARAS, LLP
Sacramento, CA ....General Practice

GRIDER, HAL L.
Altus, OK...............................Civil Trial Practice

GRIEM, DAVID
Detroit, MI.............................Civil Trial Practice; Criminal Trial Practice
Mount Clemens, MI................Civil Trial Practice; Criminal Trial Practice

GRIER AND GRIER, P.A.
Charlotte, NC..........................Bankruptcy Law; Environmental Law

GRIFFIN COCHRANE & MARSHALL, A PROFESSIONAL CORPORATION
Atlanta, GA ....Construction Law

GRIFFIN, COOGAN & VENERUSO, P.C.
Bronxville, NY ....Real Estate Law; Tax Law

GRIFFIN & FLETCHER
Cincinnati, OH ....Real Estate Law

GRIFFIN & GOULKA
Boston, MA.............................Insurance Defense

GRIFFITH LAW OFFICES
Rome, NY ....Civil Trial Practice; General Practice; Personal Injury; Probate, Trusts and Estate Planning

GRIMBALL & CABANISS
Charleston, SC ....Civil Trial Practice; General Practice; Medical Malpractice

GRIMES GOEBEL GRIMES HAWKINS & GLADFELTER, P.A.
Bradenton, FL.........................Civil Trial Practice; Environmental Law; Family Law; General Practice; Land Use Law; Personal Injury; Probate, Trusts and Estate Planning; Real Estate Law

GRIMES, GRIMES, GRIMES & GRIMES
Philadelphia, PA ....General Practice

GRIMES & WARWICK
San Diego, CA ....Criminal Trial Practice

GRIMMER, EDWARD P.
Crown Point, IN ....Civil Trial Practice; Commercial Litigation

GRISI & RIEGLER
Akron, OH ....Personal Injury

GRISSIM & HODGES
Nashville, TN..........................Real Estate Law

GRISWOLD, LASALLE, COBB, DOWD & GIN, L.L.P.
Hanford, CA ....General Practice

GROGAN, GRAFFAM, MCGINLEY & LUCCHINO, P.C.
Pittsburgh, PA ....General Practice

GRONER AND GRONER, CHARTERED
Chevy Chase, MD..................Family Law

GROOM AND NORDBERG, CHARTERED
Washington, DC.....................Employment Benefits Law; Tax Law

GROSMAN & GROSMAN
Millburn, NJ...........................Family Law

GROSS, MCGINLEY, LABARRE & EATON, LLP
Allentown, PA ....Civil Trial Practice; Communications Law

GROSS, MINSKY, MOGUL & SINGAL, P.A.
Bangor, ME............................Banking Law; Bankruptcy Law; Civil Trial Practice;
Criminal Trial Practice; General Practice; Probate,
Trusts and Estate Planning; Real Estate Law

GROSS SHUMAN BRIZDLE & GILFILLAN, P.C.
Buffalo, NY ....General Practice

GROSSBART, ROBERT N., P.A.
Baltimore, MD ....Bankruptcy Law

GROSSMAN, J.B., P.A., LAW PRACTICE OF
Fort Lauderdale, FL................Administrative Law; Antitrust Law; Civil Trial
Practice; Commercial Law; Patent, Trademark,
Copyright and Unfair Competition; Securities Law

GROSSMAN LAW OFFICES, A LEGAL PROFESSIONAL ASSOCIATION
Columbus, OH ....Family Law

GROSSMAN, O'GRADY & MCGOLDRICK, P.C.
Scottsdale, AZ........................Insurance Defense; Personal Injury

GROVE, JASKIEWICZ AND COBERT
Washington, DC......................Health Care Law; Transportation Law

GROWHOSKI, CALLAHAN & KUZMESKI
Northampton, MA...................Civil Trial Practice; General Practice

GRUCCIO, PEPPER, GIOVINAZZI, DESANTO & FARNOLY, P.A., A PROFES-SIONAL CORPORATION
Vineland, NJ............................Banking Law; Bankruptcy Law; Civil Trial Practice;
General Practice; Insurance Defense; Labor and
Employment Law; Municipal and Zoning Law;
Personal Injury; Probate, Trusts and Estate
Planning

GRUEL, MILLS, NIMS AND PYLMAN
Grand Rapids, MI ....Civil Trial Practice; Commercial Law; Commercial
Litigation; Environmental Law; General Practice;
Health Care Law; Medical Malpractice; Personal
Injury

GRUND & BRESLAU, P.C.
Denver, CO ....Aviation Law; Commercial Law; Insurance Defense;
Product Liability Law; Real Estate Law

GRUND & STARKOPF, A PROFESSIONAL CORPORATION
Chicago, IL.............................Family Law

GRUNERT STOUT & BRUCH
Charlotte Amalie, St.
Thomas, VI..............................Aviation Law; Banking Law; Business Law; Civil
Rights; Civil Trial Practice; Commercial Law;
General Practice; Insurance Defense; International
Business Law; Personal Injury; Probate, Trusts and
Estate Planning; Real Estate Law; Tax Law

GRUNSKY, EBEY, FARRAR & HOWELL, A PROFESSIONAL CORPORATION
Watsonville, CA ....General Practice

GRZANKA GRIT
Grand Rapids, MI ....Insurance Defense

GUDMUNDSON, SIGGINS, STONE & SKINNER
San Francisco, CA ....Insurance Defense

GUEBERT & YEOMANS, P.C.
Albuquerque, NM...................Civil Trial Practice; Commercial Litigation;
Insurance Defense; Personal Injury; Product
Liability Law

GUEVARA, REBE, BAUMANN, COLDWELL & REEDMAN, L.L.P.
El Paso, TX............................Civil Trial Practice; Probate, Trusts and Estate
Planning; Real Estate Law

GUGLIELMO, MARKS, SCHUTTE, TERHOEVE & LOVE
Baton Rouge, LA....................Banking Law; Business Law; Commercial Law;
Commercial Litigation; General Practice; Insurance
Defense; Real Estate Law; Workers Compensation

GUICE, JUDY M., A PROFESSIONAL ASSOCIATION
Biloxi, MS...............................Admiralty/Maritime Law; Civil Trial Practice;
Personal Injury; Product Liability Law

GUIKEMA & HULBERT, P.C.
Grand Rapids, MI ....Commercial Litigation

GUILD, RUSSELL, GALLAGHER & FULLER, LTD.
Reno, NV ....Business Law; Civil Trial Practice; General Practice;
Insurance Defense; Probate, Trusts and Estate
Planning

GUILFOIL PETZALL & SHOEMAKE
St. Louis, MO.........................Commercial Law; Commercial Litigation; Mergers
and Acquisitions

GUION, STEVENS & RYBAK
Litchfield, CT ....General Practice

GULLAHORN & HARE, P.C.
Albertville, AL ....Banking Law; Civil Trial Practice; General Practice;
Municipal Bond/Public Authority Financing

GULLETT & COMBS
Hazard, KY.............................General Practice; Natural Resources Law; Personal
Injury

GUMP, RICHARD A., JR., P.C., LAW OFFICES OF
Dallas, TX..............................Immigration and Naturalization

GUNDLACH, LEE, EGGMANN, BOYLE & ROESSLER
Belleville, IL ....General Practice

GUNHUS, GRINNELL, KLINGER, SWENSON & GUY, LTD.
Moorhead, MN ....Civil Trial Practice; General Practice
Fargo, ND ....General Practice

GUNN & HICKMAN, P.C.
Danville, IL ....Civil Trial Practice; General Practice

GUNSTER, YOAKLEY, VALDES-FAULI & STEWART, PROFESSIONAL ASSOCIATION
West Palm Beach, FL ....General Practice

GUNTY & MCCARTHY
Chicago, IL.............................Environmental Law; Insurance Defense; Product
Liability Law

GURMAN, BLASK & FREEDMAN, CHARTERED
Washington, DC......................Communications Law

GURNEY & HANDLEY, P.A.
Orlando, FL ....Civil Trial Practice; General Practice

GUSTE, BARNETT & SHUSHAN, L.L.P.
New Orleans, LA ....General Practice

GUTGLASS ERICKSON & BONVILLE, S.C.
Milwaukee, WI........................Insurance Defense

GUTHERY & RICKLES, P.C.
Denver, CO ....General Practice; Tax Law

GUTMAN, GUTMAN & GUTMAN
Mineola, NY............................Bankruptcy Law; Commercial Law; Commercial
Litigation; Real Estate Law

GUY & GILBERT
Montreal, QU, Canada ....General Practice

GUY, LAMMERT & TOWNE
Akron, OH ....Bankruptcy Law; Commercial Law

GWILLIAM, IVARY, CHIOSSO, CAVALLI & BREWER, A PROFESSIONAL CORPORATION
Oakland, CA ....Labor and Employment Law; Personal Injury;
Product Liability Law

GWIN, LEWIS & PUNCHES, LLP
Natchez, MS...........................General Practice; Insurance Defense
Woodville, MS.........................General Practice

HAAS, THOMAS M.
Mobile, AL..............................Criminal Trial Practice

HAASIS, STEVEN R. LAW OFFICES OF
San Diego, CA ....Civil Trial Practice; Insurance Defense

HABANS, BOLOGNA & CARRIERE, A PROFESSIONAL LAW CORPORATION
New Orleans, LA ....Criminal Trial Practice; Environmental Law;
Insurance Defense

HABEDANK, CUMMING, BEST & SAVAGE
Sidney, MT ....General Practice

HABERNIGG, CHARLES H.
Portland, OR ....Civil Trial Practice; International Business Law;
Personal Injury

HABUSH, HABUSH, DAVIS & ROTTIER, S.C.
Appleton, WI ....Medical Malpractice; Personal Injury; Product
Liability Law
Green Bay, WI ....Medical Malpractice; Personal Injury; Product
Liability Law
Lake Geneva, WI ....Medical Malpractice; Personal Injury; Product
Liability Law

Madison, WI ....Medical Malpractice; Personal Injury; Product Liability Law

Milwaukee, WI ....Medical Malpractice; Personal Injury; Product Liability Law

Racine, WI ....Medical Malpractice; Personal Injury; Product Liability Law

Rhinelander, WI....................Medical Malpractice; Personal Injury; Product Liability Law

Waukesha, WI........................Medical Malpractice; Personal Injury; Product Liability Law

Wausau, WI............................Medical Malpractice; Personal Injury; Product Liability Law

HACKETT, BENJAMIN F. & ASSOCIATES
Edmond, OK ....Natural Resources Law

HACKETT, MAXWELL & PHILLIPS, P.L.L.C.
Troy, MI....................................Antitrust Law; Civil Trial Practice; Commercial Litigation; Communications Law; Transportation Law

HACKLER, HINKLE & HACKLER, CHARTERED
Olathe, KS.................................Health Care Law

HACKMAN MCCLARNON HULETT & CRACRAFT
Indianapolis, IN ....Administrative Law; General Practice; Real Estate Law

HACK, PIRO, O'DAY, MERKLINGER, WALLACE & MCKENNA, P.A.
Florham Park, NJ ....Bankruptcy Law; Civil Trial Practice; Environmental Law; General Practice; Insurance Defense; Medical Malpractice; Personal Injury; Probate, Trusts and Estate Planning; Product Liability Law; Real Estate Law; Workers Compensation

HADDAD, SUSAN CHRISTINE
Chicago, IL.................................Family Law

HADDAD, JOSEPHS, JACK, GAEBE & MARKARIAN
Miami, FL ....Civil Trial Practice; General Practice; Insurance Defense; Medical Malpractice; Product Liability Law

HADDLETON & COLLINS, P.C.
Hyannis, MA..............................Probate, Trusts and Estate Planning

HADDOCK PROFESSIONAL ASSOCIATION
Orlando, FL ....Business Law; Real Estate Law
Winter Park, FL........................Business Law; Real Estate Law

HADIPUTRANTO, HADINOTO & PARTNERS
Jakarta, Indonesia ....General Practice

HADLEY & HOUSE, P.C.
Bethesda, MD ....Business Law

HADSELL, LANDGRAF & LYNCH
Niles, MI ....General Practice

HAGEN, DYE, HIRSCHY & DILORENZO, P.C.
Portland, OR.............................Business Law; Commercial Law; Probate, Trusts and Estate Planning; Real Estate Law; Tax Law

HAGENBAUGH & MURPHY
Glendale, CA..............................Computer Law; Employment Benefits Law; Insurance Defense; Medical Malpractice; Patent, Trademark, Copyright and Unfair Competition

HAGGERTY, DONOHUE & MONAGHAN, A PROFESSIONAL ASSOCIATION
Summit, NJ ....Civil Trial Practice; Criminal Trial Practice; Environmental Law; General Practice; Insurance Defense; Personal Injury; Product Liability Law; Real Estate Law

HAGGERTY, MCDONNELL AND O'BRIEN
Scranton, PA ....General Practice

HAGOORT, NICHOLAS H., JR., P.A.
Boynton Beach, FL.................Probate, Trusts and Estate Planning

HAHN & HAHN
Pasadena, CA.............................General Practice

HAHN, MCCLURG, WATSON, GRIFFITH & BUSH, P.A.
Lakeland, FL..............................Commercial Litigation; General Practice; Probate, Trusts and Estate Planning; Real Estate Law

HAIGHT, BROWN & BONESTEEL
Santa Ana, CA ....Civil Trial Practice; General Practice; Insurance Defense; Personal Injury
Santa Monica, CA...................Banking Law; Civil Trial Practice; Commercial Law; Environmental Law; General Practice; Insurance Defense; Labor and Employment Law; Personal Injury

HAILEY, MCNAMARA, HALL, LARMANN & PAPALE, L.L.P.
Metairie, LA..............................Admiralty/Maritime Law; General Practice; Insurance Defense

HAIMS, JOHNSON, MACGOWAN & MCINERNEY
Oakland, CA ....Civil Trial Practice; Construction Law; Environmental Law; General Practice; Health Care Law; Insurance Defense; Personal Injury; Product Liability Law

HAINER, DEMOREST & BERMAN, P.C.
Troy, MI.....................................Business Law; Civil Trial Practice; Environmental Law; Labor and Employment Law

HAINES, MARTIN L., III, CHARTERED
North Palm Beach, FL ....Family Law

HALABY CROSS LIECHTY & SCHLUTER
Denver, CO ....Civil Trial Practice; General Practice; Insurance Defense

HALDEMAN & ASSOCIATES
Rockford, IL ....Civil Trial Practice

HALE, ASTON, SECKEL & TAUBENFELD, P.C.
Dallas, TX ....Bankruptcy Law; Commercial Litigation; Insurance Defense

HALE AND DORR
Washington, DC.......................General Practice
Boston, MA...............................General Practice
Manchester, NH.......................General Practice

HALE, FOGLEMAN & ROGERS
West Memphis, AR ....General Practice

HALE & HAMLIN
Ellsworth, ME..........................Civil Trial Practice; Probate, Trusts and Estate Planning; Real Estate Law

HALE, KINCAID & SKINNER, P.C.
Liberty, MO ....General Practice

HALE, LANE, PEEK, DENNISON, HOWARD, ANDERSON AND PEARL
Las Vegas, NV ....Administrative Law; Bankruptcy Law; Civil Trial Practice; Commercial Law; General Practice; Health Care Law; Probate, Trusts and Estate Planning; Real Estate Law; Tax Law
Reno, NV ....Bankruptcy Law; Civil Trial Practice; Commercial Law; General Practice; Health Care Law; Natural Resources Law; Probate, Trusts and Estate Planning; Real Estate Law; Tax Law

HALEY BADER & POTTS P.L.C.
Arlington, VA ....Communications Law; Trademark, Copyright and Unfair Competition

HALEY, PURCHIO, SAKAI & SMITH
Hayward, CA ....Civil Trial Practice; General Practice

HALFPENNY, HAHN, ROCHE & MARCHESE
Chicago, IL................................Antitrust Law

HALICZER, PETTIS & WHITE, P.A.
Fort Lauderdale, FL.................Appellate Practice; Civil Trial Practice; Insurance Defense; Medical Malpractice; Workers Compensation

HALIO & HALIO
Charleston, SC ....Civil Trial Practice

HALIW, SICILIANO AND MYCHALOWYCH
Farmington Hills, MI ....Business Law; Commercial Law; Insurance Defense

HALKIDES & MORGAN, A PROFESSIONAL CORPORATION
Redding, CA ....Insurance Defense

HALL, HARRY P.
Atlanta, GA ....Family Law

HALL, ANDREW, AND ASSOCIATES, P.A.
Miami, FL ....Civil Trial Practice; Commercial Law; Family Law; Personal Injury

HALL & BAILEY
Irvine, CA..................................Civil Trial Practice

HALL, BLOCH, GARLAND & MEYER
Macon, GA ....Banking Law; Business Law; Civil Trial Practice; General Practice; Insurance Defense; Personal Injury; Tax Law

HALL, DAVID W., ATTORNEY AT LAW, A LAW CORPORATION
Honolulu, HI............................Civil Trial Practice; Criminal Trial Practice

HALLENBECK, LASCELL, NORRIS & ZORN
Rochester, NY..........................Civil Trial Practice; Commercial Litigation; Medical Malpractice; Personal Injury; Product Liability Law

HALL, ESTILL, HARDWICK, GABLE, GOLDEN & NELSON, A PROFESSIONAL CORPORATION
Tulsa, OK..................................General Practice

HALL & EVANS, L.L.C.
Colorado Springs, CO.............General Practice
Denver, CO ....General Practice

HALL & HALL
Staten Island, NY ....Banking Law

HALL, LESTAGE & LANDRENEAU
De Ridder, LA ....General Practice; Insurance Defense

HALL AND LEWIS, P.C.
Mount Pleasant, MI................General Practice

HALLMARK, KEATING & ABBOTT, P.C.
Portland, OR..........................Insurance Defense

HALL, MONAHAN, ENGLE, MAHAN & MITCHELL
Leesburg, VA ....Civil Trial Practice; General Practice

HALLORAN, R. BARTLEY, P.C., LAW OFFICES OF
Hartford, CT ....Civil Trial Practice

HALLORAN & SAGE
Hartford, CT ....General Practice
Middletown, CT......................General Practice

HALL, PARTENHEIMER & KINKLE
Princeton, IN..........................General Practice; Natural Resources Law; Real
Estate Law

HALL, RENDER, KILLIAN, HEATH & LYMAN, PROFESSIONAL CORPORATION
Indianapolis, IN ....General Practice; Health Care Law; Medical
Malpractice; Probate, Trusts and Estate Planning

HALL AND SICKELS, P.C.
Reston, VA..............................General Practice; Personal Injury

HALLSTEAD, B. THOMAS, P.C.
San Antonio, TX.....................Business Law; Real Estate Law

HALSEY, DOUGLAS M., P.A.
Miami, FL ....Environmental Law

HALVERSON, LOWELL K. LAW OFFICES OF
Mercer Island, WA ....Family Law

HALVERSON & APPLEGATE, P.S.
Yakima, WA............................General Practice

HALVERSON, WATTERS, DOWNS, REYELTS & BATEMAN, LTD.
Duluth, MN ....General Practice; Insurance Defense

HAM, DONALD R.
Amarillo, TX...........................Probate, Trusts and Estate Planning

HAMADA, EDWIN C., P.C. THE LAW OFFICE OF
Boston, MA.............................Civil Trial Practice

HAMB & POFFENBARGER
Charleston, WV.......................General Practice; Municipal Bond/Public Authority
Financing; Real Estate Law

HAMEL, DESHAIES & GAGLIARDI
Amesbury, MA ....Business Law; Commercial Law; General Practice;
Personal Injury; Probate, Trusts and Estate
Planning

HAMILTON, BROOK, SMITH & REYNOLDS, P.C.
Lexington, MA.........................Patent, Trademark, Copyright and Unfair Competition

HAMILTON AND FAATZ, A PROFESSIONAL CORPORATION
Denver, CO ....Business Law; Civil Trial Practice; General Practice

HAMILTON, GIBSON, NICKELSEN, RUSH & MOORE
Honolulu, HI ....General Practice

HAMILTON, KRAMER, MYERS & CHEEK
Columbus, OH ....Insurance Defense

HAMILTON & LINDER
Meridian, MS ....General Practice; Personal Injury

HAMLIN & SASSER, P.A.
Boise, ID..................................Insurance Defense

HAMMER, HAMMER, CARRIGG & POTTERFIELD
Columbia, SC ....General Practice

HAMMER JACOBS & THROGMORTON
San Jose, CA ....Family Law

HAMMETT, HAROLD D.
Fort Worth, TX ....Appellate Practice; Commercial Litigation

HAMMETT & BAUS
New Orleans, LA ....Insurance Defense

HAMM, MILBY & RIDINGS
London, KY ....General Practice; Insurance Defense; Workers
Compensation

HAMMOND, CLARK AND WHITE
Loveland, CO ....General Practice

HAMMOND LAW OFFICE
Columbus, OH ....Commercial Litigation; Insurance Defense; Medical
Malpractice

HAMMOND, ZUETEL & CAHILL
Pasadena, CA ....Civil Trial Practice; Medical Malpractice

HAMPTON & HAMPTON
Pratt, KS ....General Practice

HAMPTON, ROYCE, ENGLEMAN & NELSON
Salina, KS ....General Practice

HAMRICK, BOWEN, NANNEY & DALTON, L.L.P.
Rutherfordton, NC ....General Practice

HANCOCK & ESTABROOK, LLP
Syracuse, NY ....General Practice; Municipal Bond/Public Authority
Financing; Tax Law

HANCOCK ROTHERT & BUNSHOFT LLP
San Francisco, CA ....General Practice

HANDLON, EASTMAN & DEWITT, P.C.
Midland, MI ....General Practice

HANDY & ROBINSON, P.C.
Fort Worth, TX ....Personal Injury

HANEN, ALEXANDER, JOHNSON & SPALDING, L.L.P.
Houston, TX ....Civil Trial Practice; Insurance Defense; Medical
Malpractice; Product Liability Law

HANES & SCHUTZ, P.C.
Colorado Springs, CO..............Civil Trial Practice; Patent, Trademark, Copyright
and Unfair Competition

HANES, SEVILA, SAUNDERS & MCCAHILL, A PROFESSIONAL CORPORATION
Leesburg, VA ....Civil Trial Practice; Family Law; General Practice;
Personal Injury

HANFT, FRIDE, O'BRIEN, HARRIES, SWELBAR & BURNS, P.A.
Duluth, MN ....Civil Trial Practice; General Practice; Insurance
Defense; Probate, Trusts and Estate Planning

HANIFY & KING, PROFESSIONAL CORPORATION
Boston, MA.............................Antitrust Law; Bankruptcy Law; Civil Trial
Practice; Commercial Law; Labor and Employment
Law; Product Liability Law

HANKIN, THEODORE M.
Newport Beach, CA.................Banking Law; Business Law; Probate, Trusts and
Estate Planning

HANLEY & DEJORAS, P.A.
Minneapolis, MN ....Criminal Trial Practice

HANLEY & PATCH
Irvine, CA................................Commercial Law

HANNA & GERDE
Lafayette, IN ....Civil Trial Practice; Municipal and Zoning Law;
Personal Injury

HANNA, KERNS & STRADER, A PROFESSIONAL CORPORATION
Portland, OR...........................Probate, Trusts and Estate Planning; Real Estate
Law; Tax Law

HANNA AND MORTON
Los Angeles, CA ....Civil Trial Practice; Environmental Law; General
Practice; Natural Resources Law; Probate, Trusts
and Estate Planning; Real Estate Law; Tax Law

HANNA & VAN ATTA
Palo Alto, CA ....Construction Law; Land Use Law; Real Estate Law

HANNA, YOUNG, UPRIGHT & CATINA, LLP
Stroudsburg, PA......................Probate, Trusts and Estate Planning; Tax Law

HANNAFAN, MICHAEL T., & ASSOCIATES, LTD.
Chicago, IL..............................Civil Trial Practice; Commercial Litigation

HANNOCH WEISMAN, A PROFESSIONAL CORPORATION
Roseland, NJ ....Banking Law; Bankruptcy Law; Business Law; Civil
Trial Practice; Commercial Law; Construction Law;
Criminal Trial Practice; Environmental Law; Family
Law; General Practice; International Business Law;
Labor and Employment Law; Product Liability
Law; Real Estate Law; Securities Law; Tax Law;
Trademark, Copyright and Unfair Competition;
Transportation Law

HANOVER & SCHNITZER
San Bernardino, CA...............Bankruptcy Law

HANOVER & TURNER
Kansas City, MO...................Medical Malpractice; Personal Injury; Product Liability Law

HANOVER, WALSH, JALENAK & BLAIR
Memphis, TN.........................Bankruptcy Law; Civil Trial Practice; General Practice; Immigration and Naturalization; Real Estate Law

HANSEN, JOEL F. & ASSOCIATES
Las Vegas, NV.......................Insurance Defense

HANSEN, BOYD, CULHANE & WATSON
Sacramento, CA.....................Appellate Practice; Business Law; Civil Trial Practice; Insurance Defense; Personal Injury; Real Estate Law

HANSEN, ENGLES & LOCHER, P.C.
Omaha, NE...........................Admiralty/Maritime Law; Appellate Practice; Banking Law; Bankruptcy Law; Civil Trial Practice; General Practice; Insurance Defense; Personal Injury; Product Liability Law; Workers Compensation

HANSEN & HUBBARD
Sturgis, SD.............................General Practice

HANSEN, MCCLINTOCK & RILEY
Des Moines, IA......................Civil Trial Practice; General Practice; Insurance Defense

HANSON, BRIDGETT, MARCUS, VLAHOS & RUDY, LLP
San Francisco, CA..................General Practice

HANSON, CURRAN, PARKS & WHITMAN
Providence, RI.......................Admiralty/Maritime Law; Appellate Practice; Civil Trial Practice; Environmental Law; General Practice; Insurance Defense; Labor and Employment Law

HANSON, EPPERSON & SMITH, A PROFESSIONAL CORPORATION
Salt Lake City, UT.................General Practice; Insurance Defense; Medical Malpractice

HANSON & HANSON
Mc Cook, NE.........................General Practice

HANSON, HASHEY
Fredericton, NB, Canada........Administrative Law; Appellate Practice; Banking Law; Bankruptcy Law; Civil Trial Practice; Commercial Law; Construction Law; Environmental Law; Family Law; General Practice; Insurance Defense; Labor and Employment Law; Real Estate Law; Tax Law
Saint John, NB, Canada..........Tax Law

HANSON, LULIC & KRALL
Minneapolis, MN....................Insurance Defense

HARALSON, KINERK & MOREY
Tucson, AZ.............................Civil Trial Practice; Medical Malpractice; Personal Injury

HARBEN & HARTLEY
Gainesville, GA......................General Practice; Labor and Employment Law

HARBINSON, CARLSON & TUNE, A PROFESSIONAL CORPORATION
San Francisco, CA..................Workers Compensation

HARBISON, KESSINGER, LISLE & BUSH
Lexington, KY........................General Practice

HARBOLD, R. CHRIS AND ASSOCIATES
Columbus, OH........................Family Law

HARDAWAY LAW FIRM, P.A.
Greenville, SC........................Patent, Trademark, Copyright and Unfair Competition

HARDIG, LEE AND GROVES, PROFESSIONAL ASSOCIATION
South Bend, IN......................Medical Malpractice; Personal Injury

HARDIG PARSONS & PEDERSEN
Bloomfield Hills, MI...............Business Law; Civil Trial Practice; Commercial Law; Family Law

HARDIMAN, OLSON & CARROLL, A LAW PARTNERSHIP
San Francisco, CA.................Insurance Defense

HARDIN, HAL D.
Nashville, TN.........................General Practice

HARDIN, COOK, LOPER, ENGEL & BERGEZ
Oakland, CA..........................Civil Trial Practice; Environmental Law; General Practice; Insurance Defense; Probate, Trusts and Estate Planning

HARDIN, DAWSON & TERRY
Fort Smith, AR.......................General Practice; Insurance Defense; Natural Resources Law

HARDING, BASS, FARGASON & BOOTH, L.L.P.
Lubbock, TX..........................General Practice

HARDT, FREDERICK W.
Moorestown, NJ.....................Land Use Law; Municipal and Zoning Law

HARDT LAW OFFICES, P.A.
Naples, FL..............................Civil Trial Practice; Commercial Litigation; Insurance Defense; Personal Injury

HARDWICK & ERICSON
Renton, WA...........................Personal Injury

HARDWICK, HAUSE & SEGREST
Dothan, AL............................Civil Trial Practice; General Practice

HARDY & BISSETT, P.A.
Miami, FL..............................Civil Trial Practice; General Practice; Personal Injury; Product Liability Law

HARDY ERICH BROWN & WILSON, A PROFESSIONAL CORPORATION
Sacramento, CA.....................Bankruptcy Law; Civil Trial Practice; Construction Law; Environmental Law; Insurance Defense; Labor and Employment Law; Medical Malpractice; Personal Injury; Product Liability Law; Real Estate Law

HARDY & JOHNS
Houston, TX...........................Civil Trial Practice; Commercial Law; Personal Injury

HARDY, TERRELL, BOSWELL & SIMS
Paducah, KY...........................General Practice

HARE, WYNN, NEWELL AND NEWTON
Birmingham, AL.....................Civil Trial Practice; Medical Malpractice; Personal Injury; Product Liability Law

HARGADON, LENIHAN, HARBOLT, & HERRINGTON
Louisville, KY........................Personal Injury

HARGRAVES, KARB, WILCOX & GALVANI
Framingham, MA....................Business Law; General Practice

HARGROVE, PESNELL & WYATT, A P.L.C.
Shreveport, LA.......................Civil Trial Practice; Natural Resources Law

HARHAI, STEPHEN J.
Denver, CO............................Family Law

HARKAVY, SHAINBERG, KOSTEN & KAPLAN
Memphis, TN.........................General Practice; Labor and Employment Law; Real Estate Law

HARKLEROAD & HERMANCE, A PROFESSIONAL CORPORATION
Atlanta, GA............................Administrative Law; Business Law; International Business Law

HARLAN, DENTON & FLORA, P.C.
Norfolk, VA...........................Civil Trial Practice; General Practice; Medical Malpractice; Personal Injury; Product Liability Law

HARLEY & BROWNE
New York, NY........................Civil Trial Practice; Medical Malpractice

HARLIN & PARKER, P.S.C.
Bowling Green, KY................Appellate Practice; Banking Law; Bankruptcy Law; Civil Trial Practice; Construction Law; General Practice; Insurance Defense; Medical Malpractice; Personal Injury; Probate, Trusts and Estate Planning; Product Liability Law; Real Estate Law

HARLLEE, PORGES, HAMLIN, KNOWLES, BALD & PROUTY, P.A.
Bradenton, FL........................Commercial Law; Commercial Litigation; Land Use Law; Probate, Trusts and Estate Planning

HARLOW, ADAMS & FRIEDMAN, P.C.
Milford, CT...........................Bankruptcy Law; General Practice; Real Estate Law

HARMAN, CLAYTOR, CORRIGAN & WELLMAN, A PROFESSIONAL CORPORATION
Richmond, VA........................Insurance Defense

HARMAN LAW FIRM, THE, P.C.
Albuquerque, NM...................Banking Law; Commercial Law; Computer Law; Construction Law

HARMAN, OWEN, SAUNDERS & SWEENEY, A PROFESSIONAL CORPORATION
Atlanta, GA............................Business Law; Insurance Defense

HARMATA LAW OFFICES
Sacramento, CA.....................Administrative Law; Construction Law; General Practice

HARMON, STEVEN L.
Riverside, CA ....Criminal Trial Practice

HARMON, SMITH, BRIDGES & WILBANKS
Atlanta, GA ....Civil Trial Practice; Commercial Law; Family Law; Probate, Trusts and Estate Planning

HARNESS, DICKEY & PIERCE, P.L.C.
Ann Arbor, MI ....Patent, Trademark, Copyright and Unfair Competition
Troy, MI..................................Patent, Trademark, Copyright and Unfair Competition

HARNEY LAW OFFICES, A LEGAL CORPORATION
Los Angeles, CA ....Aviation Law; Civil Trial Practice; Medical Malpractice; Personal Injury; Product Liability Law

HARNISCH & HOHAUSER, P.C.
Bingham Farms, MI ....Commercial Litigation; Criminal Trial Practice; Personal Injury

HARNISH, JENNEY, MITCHELL AND RESH
Waltham, MA ....General Practice; Probate, Trusts and Estate Planning; Real Estate Law

HARP & JOHNSON, P.C.
Columbus, GA ....Civil Trial Practice; Family Law

HARPER, FERGUSON & DAVIS
Louisville, KY ....Municipal Bond/Public Authority Financing

HARPER, HORNBAKER, ALTENHOFEN & OPAT, CHARTERED
Junction City, KS....................General Practice

HARPER, YOUNG, SMITH & MAURRAS, PLC
Fort Smith, AR......................Business Law; Commercial Litigation

HARRANG LONG GARY RUDNICK, P.C.
Eugene, OR ....General Practice

HARRAY, MASUDA & LINKER
Monterey, CA ....Appellate Practice; Civil Trial Practice; Employment Benefits Law; Insurance Defense

HARRELL AND HARRELL
Trenton, TN ....Criminal Trial Practice; Personal Injury

HARRIGAN, RUFF, SBARDELLATI & MOORE, A PROFESSIONAL CORPORATION
San Diego, CA ....General Practice

HARRINGTON, ROBERT L.
Portland, OR............................Patent, Trademark, Copyright and Unfair Competition

HARRINGTON, MALEY, GARDNER & SAYRE
Richmond, IN ....Banking Law; Construction Law; Personal Injury; Probate, Trusts and Estate Planning; Real Estate Law

HARRINGTON & MITCHELL, LTD.
Youngstown, OH ....Banking Law; Bankruptcy Law; General Practice

HARRINGTON, PORTER, ERMENTROUT & TOCK
Champaign, IL ....Real Estate Law

HARRINGTON & STULTZ
Eden, NC..................................General Practice
Wentworth, NC........................General Practice

HARRINGTON, THOMPSON, ACKER & HARRINGTON, LTD.
Chicago, IL..............................Civil Trial Practice; Personal Injury

HARRIS, BRANTLY
Houston, TX ....Civil Trial Practice

HARRIS, CADDELL & SHANKS, P.C.
Decatur, AL ....Civil Trial Practice; General Practice; Insurance Defense; Product Liability Law; Tax Law

HARRIS, CARTER, MAHOTA & MAZZA
Columbus, OH ....International Business Law; Product Liability Law

HARRIS, CLECKLER, BERG & ROGERS, P.C.
Birmingham, AL ....Civil Trial Practice; Insurance Defense; Medical Malpractice

HARRIS & COMPANY
Vancouver, BC, Canada..........Labor and Employment Law

HARRIS, DOWELL, FISHER & HARRIS, L.C.
St. Louis, MO.........................Labor and Employment Law

HARRIS, FEARS, DAVIS, LYNCH & MCDANIEL
Norfolk, VA ....Personal Injury

HARRIS & HARRIS
Austin, TX ....Administrative Law; Civil Trial Practice; Workers Compensation

HARRIS AND HARRIS, A PROFESSIONAL CORPORATION
Warrington, PA.......................Civil Trial Practice; Municipal and Zoning Law

HARRIS & HARRIS, P.C.
Kerrville, TX ....Civil Trial Practice

HARRIS & JAMES
Macon, GA ....General Practice

HARRIS, KUKEY & HELGESEN, P.A.
Palm Beach Gardens, FL........Real Estate Law

HARRIS, LAMBERT, HOWERTON & DORRIS
Marion, IL................................Criminal Trial Practice; Personal Injury

HARRIS, MIDYETTE, GEARY & DARBY, P.A.
Lakeland, FL............................General Practice

HARRIS & PALUMBO, A PROFESSIONAL CORPORATION
Phoenix, AZ ....Insurance Defense; Medical Malpractice; Personal Injury

HARRIS, SHELTON, DUNLAP AND COBB, L.L.P.C.
Memphis, TN ....General Practice

HARRIS, SHIELDS AND CREECH, P.A.
New Bern, NC ....Civil Trial Practice; Medical Malpractice

HARRIS & SMITH
Media, PA ....Criminal Trial Practice; General Practice; Personal Injury

HARRIS, TIM L., AND ASSOCIATES
Charlotte, NC...........................Medical Malpractice; Personal Injury; Workers Compensation
Gastonia, NC ....Medical Malpractice; Personal Injury
Monroe, NC ....Personal Injury

HARRIS, TRIMMER & THOMPSON
Reno, NV ....Environmental Law; Natural Resources Law

HARRIS, TUCKER & HARDIN, P.C.
Dallas, TX.................................Patent, Trademark, Copyright and Unfair Competition

HARRIS, WELSH & LUKMANN
Chesterton, IN ....General Practice

HARRISON, BRENNECKE, MOORE, SMAHA & MCKIBBEN
Marshalltown, IA.....................General Practice

HARRISON & HAYES
Spartanburg, SC.......................Civil Trial Practice; Personal Injury

HARRISON & JOHNSTON
Winchester, VA ....General Practice

HARRISON, ROBERT, & ASSOCIATES
Bloomfield Hills, MI................Civil Trial Practice; Criminal Trial Practice

HARRISON & WALL
Eastman, GA............................General Practice

HARRISS, HARTMAN, AARON, WHARTON, BOYD & SECORD, P.C.
Rossville, GA ....General Practice; Workers Compensation

HART & CALLEY, P.C.
Alexandria, VA ....Municipal and Zoning Law

HART AND HART
Benton, IL ....Civil Trial Practice; General Practice

HART & MCINTYRE
Atlanta, GA ....Medical Malpractice; Personal Injury

HARTE, WILLIAM J., LTD.
Chicago, IL...............................Civil Trial Practice; Commercial Law; Securities Law

HARTLEY, DENNIS W., P.C., PROFESSIONAL CORPORATION
Colorado Springs, CO..............Criminal Trial Practice

HARTLEY & WALL
Orlando, FL ....Civil Trial Practice; Commercial Litigation

HARTUNIAN, ARAM A., AND ASSOCIATES, A PROF. CORP.
Chicago, IL...............................Antitrust Law; Business Law

HARTWEG, MUELLER, TURNER, DRAZEWSKI & WOOD, P.C.
Bloomington, IL.......................Business Law; Commercial Law; General Practice; Probate, Trusts and Estate Planning; Real Estate Law; Tax Law

HARTZELL, GLIDDEN, TUCKER AND HARTZELL
Carthage, IL ....General Practice

HARTZOG CONGER & CASON, A PROFESSIONAL CORPORATION
Oklahoma City, OK................Banking Law; Civil Trial Practice; Commercial Law; General Practice; Health Care Law; Labor and Employment Law; Probate, Trusts and Estate Planning; Real Estate Law; Securities Law; Tax Law

HARTZOG, SILVA & DAVIES
Franklin, TN ....General Practice

HARVEY & BATTEY, P.A.
Beaufort, SC ....General Practice

HARVEY AND HARVEY, HARVEY & MUMFORD
Albany, NY ....Civil Trial Practice

HARVEY, PENNINGTON, HERTING & RENNEISEN, LTD.
Philadelphia, PA ....General Practice

HARWELL HOWARD HYNE GABBERT & MANNER, P.C.
Nashville, TN ....Health Care Law; Securities Law

HARWELL, PLANT & CHEATWOOD
Lawrenceburg, TN ....Insurance Defense

HARWOOD LLOYD
Hackensack, NJ.......................Civil Trial Practice; General Practice; Insurance Defense; Personal Injury

HASH, O'BRIEN & BARTLETT, PLLP
Kalispell, MT ....General Practice; Insurance Defense; Real Estate Law; Tax Law

HASKELL & PERRIN
Chicago, IL...............................Insurance Defense

HASKELL SLAUGHTER & YOUNG, L.L.C.
Birmingham, AL ....Antitrust Law; Banking Law; Business Law; Civil Trial Practice; Commercial Law; General Practice; Health Care Law; Labor and Employment Law; Municipal Bond/Public Authority Financing; Tax Law

Montgomery, AL ....Civil Trial Practice; General Practice; Labor and Employment Law

HASSENFELD & LEDERMAN
Boston, MA ....Commercial Law

HATCHER, STUBBS, LAND, HOLLIS & ROTHSCHILD
Columbus, GA ....Banking Law; Commercial Law; Employment Benefits Law; General Practice; Insurance Defense; Municipal Bond/Public Authority Financing; Probate, Trusts and Estate Planning; Real Estate Law; Tax Law

HATFIELD & LASSITER
Little Rock, AR ....Criminal Trial Practice; Tax Law

HATHAWAY, SPEIGHT & KUNZ
Cheyenne, WY.......................Civil Trial Practice; General Practice

HATTERY, SIMPSON & WEST
Galesburg, IL ....General Practice

HAUGEN AND NIKOLAI, P.A.
Minneapolis, MN....................International Business Law; Patent, Trademark, Copyright and Unfair Competition

HAUGH & HAUGH, P.C.
Charlottesville, VA..................Civil Trial Practice; Criminal Trial Practice

HAUPTMAN & RICHMOND, P.A.
West Orange, NJ....................Probate, Trusts and Estate Planning; Tax Law

HAWKINS, BLICK & FITZPATRICK
Palo Alto, CA ....Personal Injury
San Jose, CA ....Civil Trial Practice; Personal Injury

HAWKINS, DELAFIELD & WOOD
New York, NY.......................General Practice

HAWKINS, MOODY, BINGHAM, MILLER & ASSOCIATES, P.C.
Kingsport, TN........................Medical Malpractice; Personal Injury; Product Liability Law; Workers Compensation

HAWKINS & PARNELL
Atlanta, GA ....Civil Rights; Civil Trial Practice; Commercial Law; Environmental Law; General Practice; Municipal and Zoning Law; Product Liability Law; Sports and Entertainment Law; Transportation Law

HAWKINS, SCHNABEL, LINDAHL & BECK
Los Angeles, CA ....Civil Trial Practice; Insurance Defense

HAWLEY, HUDSON & HAWLEY
Mt. Vernon, IN......................Natural Resources Law

HAWLEY, NYSTEDT & FLETCHER, P.C.
Tucson, AZ ....Tax Law

HAWORTH, RIGGS, KUHN & HAWORTH
High Point, NC ....General Practice

HAWTHORNE, ACKERLY & DORRANCE
New Canaan, CT....................General Practice

HAYDEN AND MILLIKEN, P.A.
Miami, FL ....Admiralty/Maritime Law; Insurance Defense
Tampa, FL ....Admiralty/Maritime Law; Insurance Defense

HAYDEN, THOMAS C., JR., P.A.
La Plata, MD ....General Practice

HAYDUK, ANDREWS & HYPNAR, P.C.
Detroit, MI.............................Aviation Law; Civil Trial Practice; Insurance Defense; Probate, Trusts and Estate Planning; Product Liability Law

HAYES, J. MICHAEL
Buffalo, NY ....Civil Trial Practice; Personal Injury

HAYES, COOPER, CAMPBELL & PREST
Steubenville, OH ....General Practice

HAYES, DAVIS & DELLENBUSCH
Grand Rapids, MI ....Probate, Trusts and Estate Planning

HAYES, HARKEY, SMITH & CASCIO, L.L.P.
Monroe, LA ....Civil Trial Practice; General Practice; Insurance Defense; Medical Malpractice

HAYES & HAYES
Fort Wayne, IN......................Family Law

HAYES, PHILLIPS & MALONEY, P.C.
Denver, CO ....Municipal and Zoning Law

HAYGOOD, LYNCH, HARRIS & MELTON
Forsyth, GA ....General Practice
Monticello, GA ....General Practice

HAYNER, WILLIAM M. & ASSOCIATES
Dallas, TX..............................Personal Injury

HAYNES AND BOONE, L.L.P.
Dallas, TX..............................General Practice

HAYNES, FORD AND ROWE
Lewisburg, WV ....General Practice

HAYNES, HULL & RIEDER, P.A.
Tullahoma, TN.......................General Practice

HAYNES & SONTICH
Youngstown, OH ....Insurance Defense

HAYNSWORTH, BALDWIN, JOHNSON AND GREAVES, P.A.
Charlotte, NC.........................Labor and Employment Law
Greensboro, NC.....................Labor and Employment Law
Raleigh, NC............................Labor and Employment Law
Columbia, SC.........................Labor and Employment Law
Greenville, SC.........................Labor and Employment Law

HAYNSWORTH, BALDWIN, JOHNSON AND HARPER
Jacksonville, FL ....Labor and Employment Law
Tampa, FL ....Labor and Employment Law
Macon, GA ....Labor and Employment Law

HAYNSWORTH, MARION, MCKAY & GUÉRARD, L.L.P
Charleston, SC ....Administrative Law; Banking Law; Bankruptcy Law; Business Law; Civil Trial Practice; Construction Law; Employment Benefits Law; Environmental Law; General Practice; Health Care Law; Insurance Defense; Medical Malpractice; Municipal Bond/Public Authority Financing; Product Liability Law; Real Estate Law; Securities Law; Tax Law

Columbia, SC ....Administrative Law; Banking Law; Bankruptcy Law; Business Law; Civil Trial Practice; Construction Law; Employment Benefits Law; Environmental Law; General Practice; Insurance Defense; Medical Malpractice; Municipal Bond/Public Authority Financing; Product Liability Law; Public Utilities Law; Real Estate Law; Securities Law

Greenville, SC.........................Administrative Law; Banking Law; Bankruptcy Law; Business Law; Civil Trial Practice; Construction Law; Employment Benefits Law; Environmental Law; General Practice; Health Care Law; Insurance Defense; Medical Malpractice; Patent, Trademark, Copyright and Unfair Competition; Probate, Trusts and Estate Planning; Product Liability Law; Public Utilities Law; Real Estate Law; Securities Law; Tax Law; Workers Compensation

HAYNSWORTH, PERRY, BRYANT, MARION & JOHNSTONE
Greenville, SC.........................General Practice

HAYS, CHRISTOPHER LAW OFFICES OF
San Francisco, CA ....General Practice

HAYS, MCCONN, RICE & PICKERING
Houston, TX ....Banking Law; Civil Trial Practice; Insurance Defense

HAYTHE & CURLEY
New York, NY.........................Business Law

HAZELRIGG AND COX
Frankfort, KY ....Administrative Law

HAZEL & THOMAS, A PROFESSIONAL CORPORATION
Alexandria, VA ....General Practice
Falls Church, VA ....General Practice
Leesburg, VA ....General Practice
Manassas, VA ....General Practice
Richmond, VA ....General Practice

HAZLETT & WILKES
Tucson, AZ ....General Practice; Insurance Defense; Medical
Malpractice

HEAGNEY, LENNON & SLANE
Greenwich, CT ....General Practice

HEALY, JOHN PATRICK
Chicago, IL............................Civil Trial Practice; Personal Injury

HEALY & BAILLIE, LLP
Stamford, CT..........................Admiralty/Maritime Law; General Practice
New York, NY........................Admiralty/Maritime Law; General Practice

HEALY LAW FIRM
Tucson, AZ ....Medical Malpractice; Personal Injury; Product
Liability Law

HEALY & ROCHELEAU, P.C.
Worcester, MA........................Insurance Defense

HEARD, GOGGAN, BLAIR & WILLIAMS
San Antonio, TX.....................Business Law; Civil Trial Practice; Family Law;
International Business Law; Personal Injury

HEARD, LEVERETT, PHELPS, WEAVER & CAMPBELL
Elberton, GA..........................General Practice

HEARN, BRITTAIN & MARTIN, P.A.
Conway, SC............................Criminal Trial Practice; Family Law; Personal
Injury

HEARNE, EPPRIGHT & GEST, A PROFESSIONAL CORPORATION
Austin, TX ....Civil Trial Practice; General Practice

HEBB & GITLIN, A PROFESSIONAL CORPORATION
Hartford, CT ....Bankruptcy Law; General Practice

HEBERT, MOULEDOUX & BLAND, A PROFESSIONAL LAW CORPORATION
New Orleans, LA.....................Admiralty/Maritime Law; Commercial Law;
Environmental Law; General Practice; Workers
Compensation

HECKENKAMP, SIMHAUSER, WARD & ZERKLE
Springfield, IL ....General Practice

HECKSCHER, TEILLON, TERRILL & SAGER, A PROFESSIONAL CORPORATION
Philadelphia, PA ....Probate, Trusts and Estate Planning

HEDEEN, HUGHES, WETERING & KNESS
Worthington, MN...................General Practice

HEDGES & CALDWELL, A PROFESSIONAL CORPORATION
Los Angeles, CA.....................Commercial Litigation

HEDRICK, DEWBERRY & REGAN, P.A.
Jacksonville, FL ....Civil Trial Practice; Construction Law; Labor and
Employment Law

HEENAN BLAIKIE
Montreal, QU, Canada ....General Practice

HEENEY, ARMSTRONG & HEENEY
Rockville, MD........................Criminal Trial Practice

HEIDELBERG, SUTHERLAND AND MCKENZIE, PROFESSIONAL ASSOCIATION
Hattiesburg, MS......................Commercial Law; General Practice; Insurance
Defense; Medical Malpractice

HEIDELL, PITTONI, MURPHY & BACH, P.C.
New York, NY........................Insurance Defense; Medical Malpractice

HEIDMAN, REDMOND, FREDREGILL, PATTERSON, SCHATZ & PLAZA, L.L.P.
Sioux City, IA ....Civil Trial Practice; General Practice; Insurance
Defense

HEILIG, MCKENRY, FRAIM & LOLLAR, A PROFESSIONAL CORPORATION
Norfolk, VA ....General Practice

HEILIGENSTEIN & BADGLEY, PROFESSIONAL CORPORATION
Belleville, IL ....Personal Injury

HEIN, SMITH, BEREZIN, MALOOF, DAVIDSON & JACOBS
Hackensack, NJ......................Business Law; Civil Trial Practice; Commercial Law;
Employment Benefits Law; General Practice;
Insurance Defense; Medical Malpractice; Personal
Injury; Probate, Trusts and Estate Planning; Real
Estate Law; Tax Law; Workers Compensation

HEINRICH GORDON HARGROVE WEIHE & JAMES, P.A.
Fort Lauderdale, FL...............Civil Trial Practice; General Practice; Personal
Injury

HEINTZMAN, WARREN & WISE
Pittsburgh, PA ....Civil Trial Practice; Insurance Defense; Medical
Malpractice; Product Liability Law

HEISERMAN, ROBERT G., P.C.
Denver, CO ....Immigration and Naturalization

HEITLAND, ANN RAE
Flagstaff, AZ ....Civil Trial Practice

HELEIN & ASSOCIATES, P.C.
McLean, VA...........................Communications Law

HELLER, HOLMES & ASSOCIATES, P.C.
Mattoon, IL............................Civil Trial Practice; General Practice

HELLER, SHAPIRO, FRISONE & FERLEGER, LTD.
Chicago, IL............................Commercial Litigation

HELLER, STEPHEN H., A PROFESSIONAL CORPORATION
Encino, CA............................Personal Injury

HELLRING LINDEMAN GOLDSTEIN & SIEGAL
Newark, NJ ....Antitrust Law; Appellate Practice; Bankruptcy Law;
Civil Trial Practice; Commercial Law; Criminal Trial
Practice; Environmental Law; Family Law; General
Practice; Labor and Employment Law; Natural
Resources Law; Probate, Trusts and Estate
Planning; Real Estate Law; Securities Law; Tax Law

HELMKE, BEAMS, BOYER & WAGNER
Fort Wayne, IN......................General Practice; Municipal and Zoning Law;
Probate, Trusts and Estate Planning

HELMS, HANRAHAN & MYERS
Arcadia, CA ....Family Law; General Practice; Probate, Trusts and
Estate Planning

HELMSING, LYONS, SIMS & LEACH, P.C.
Mobile, AL.............................Civil Trial Practice; General Practice; Insurance
Defense; Personal Injury

HELSELL FETTERMAN LLP
Seattle, WA ....General Practice

HELWIG, NORMAN R., P.C.
Vail, CO................................Real Estate Law

HEMENWAY & BARNES
Boston, MA...........................Business Law; General Practice; Probate, Trusts and
Estate Planning

HEMER, BARKUS & CLARK
Glendale, CA.........................Medical Malpractice
Ontario, CA...........................Medical Malpractice

HEMPHILL, ROBERT D.
Dallas, TX.............................Civil Trial Practice; General Practice

HEMRY & HEMRY, P.C., THE LAW OFFICES OF
Oklahoma City, OK................Probate, Trusts and Estate Planning; Real Estate
Law

HENDEL, COLLINS & NEWTON, P.C.
Springfield, MA......................Banking Law; Bankruptcy Law; Commercial Law;
Real Estate Law

HENDERSON, RICHARD A. LAW OFFICES OF
Cohasset, MA.........................General Practice

HENDERSON, THOMAS W.
Newport Beach, CA................Probate, Trusts and Estate Planning

HENDERSON, FRANKLIN, STARNES & HOLT, PROFESSIONAL ASSOCIATION
Fort Myers, FL.......................Civil Trial Practice; General Practice; Insurance
Defense; Personal Injury; Probate, Trusts and Estate
Planning; Real Estate Law; Tax Law

HENDERSON, HANEMANN & MORRIS, A PROFESSIONAL LAW CORPORATION
Houma, LA ....Insurance Defense

HENDERSON & STURM
Davenport, IA........................Patent, Trademark, Copyright and Unfair Competition

HENDERSON, WOHLGEMUTH & BOHL, A PROFESSIONAL CORPORATION
Ventura, CA ....Insurance Defense

Woodland Hills, CA ....Insurance Defense

HENDREN AND ANDRAE
Jefferson City, MO.................General Practice; Insurance Defense

HENDREN LAW OFFICES
Oroville, CA ....Civil Trial Practice

HENDRICKS, LEWIS S.
Rockwell City, IA ....Probate, Trusts and Estate Planning

HENDRICKS & HENDRICKS
Coral Gables, FL ....Probate, Trusts and Estate Planning

HENDRICKSON, RAY
Irvine, CA..............................Family Law

HENDRY, LLOYD G., P.A., LAW OFFICES OF
Fort Myers, FL ....General Practice; Probate, Trusts and Estate
Planning; Real Estate Law

HENINGER AND HENINGER, PROFESSIONAL CORPORATION
Davenport, IA ....General Practice

HENNENHOEFER, JAMES A., A PROFESSIONAL CORPORATION
Vista, CA...............................Family Law

HENNIGAN, MERCER & BENNETT
Los Angeles, CA....................Antitrust Law; Bankruptcy Law; Civil Trial
Practice; Commercial Litigation; Securities Law

HENRY & BEAVER
Lebanon, PA ....Civil Trial Practice; General Practice

HENRY, BUCHANAN, HUDSON, SUBER & WILLIAMS, P.A.
Tallahassee, FL ....Civil Trial Practice; General Practice; Insurance
Defense

HENRY, MCCORD, BEAN & MILLER, P.L.L.C.
Tullahoma, TN........................General Practice

HENRY & PRICE LLC
Easton, MD.............................Municipal and Zoning Law; Probate, Trusts and
Estate Planning; Real Estate Law

HENSHALL, PENNINGTON & BRAKE
Chanute, KS ....General Practice

HENSHAW, TODD MAXWELL
Tulsa, OK................................Bankruptcy Law

HENSLEY, DUNN, ROSS & HOWARD
Horse Cave, KY......................General Practice

HENSON, JOHN P.
Greenwood, MS ....General Practice

HENSON, RICHARD W. LAW OFFICE OF
San Carlos, CA ....Probate, Trusts and Estate Planning

HENSON & EFRON, P.A.
Minneapolis, MN....................Commercial Litigation; Environmental Law; Family
Law; General Practice; Securities Law

HENSON & HENSON, L.L.P.
Greensboro, NC......................Civil Trial Practice; Insurance Defense; Personal
Injury

HENSON, HENSON, HENSON, MARSHALL & MILBURN
Shawnee, OK...........................General Practice

HENTHORN, HARRIS AND TAYLOR, P.C.
Crawfordsville, IN...................General Practice

HEPBURN WILLCOX HAMILTON & PUTNAM
Philadelphia, PA ....General Practice

HEPFORD, SWARTZ & MORGAN
Harrisburg, PA........................Administrative Law; Appellate Practice; Business
Law; Civil Trial Practice; Criminal Trial Practice;
Family Law; General Practice; Insurance Defense;
Medical Malpractice; Personal Injury; Probate,
Trusts and Estate Planning; Product Liability Law;
Real Estate Law

HERBERT & HERBERT
Glasgow, KY...........................Civil Trial Practice; Family Law; General Practice;
Real Estate Law

HERBERT, JOHN G., P.C.
Denver, CO ....Mergers and Acquisitions; Securities Law

HERBOLSHEIMER, LANNON, HENSON, DUNCAN AND REAGAN, P.C.
La Salle, IL.............................General Practice; Insurance Defense; Real Estate
Law

HERDEG & ASSOCIATES, P.A.
Wilmington, DE......................Probate, Trusts and Estate Planning

HERLOCKER, ROBERTS & ST. PETER, P.A.
Winfield, KS............................General Practice

HERMAN, HERMAN, KATZ & COTLAR, L.L.P.
New Orleans, LA ....General Practice

HERMANIES, MAJOR, CASTELLI & GOODMAN
Cincinnati, OH ....Civil Trial Practice; Medical Malpractice; Personal
Injury; Workers Compensation

HERMANN, CAHN & SCHNEIDER
Cleveland, OH.........................Civil Trial Practice; Family Law; Insurance Defense;
Personal Injury; Product Liability Law

HERNDON, COLEMAN, BRADING & MCKEE
Johnson City, TN....................General Practice

HERRERA, LONG & POUND, P.A.
Santa Fe, NM..........................Civil Trial Practice; Health Care Law; Insurance
Defense; Land Use Law; Municipal and Zoning
Law; Product Liability Law; Real Estate Law

HERRICK, STEWART T. & ASSOCIATES
Framingham, MA ....Civil Trial Practice; Criminal Trial Practice; General
Practice; Real Estate Law

HERRICK, ARY, COOK, COOK, COOK & COOK
Cherokee, IA ....General Practice

HERRICK, LANGDON & LANGDON
Des Moines, IA ....Civil Trial Practice; General Practice; Insurance
Defense

HERRIG & VOGT
Rancho Cordova, CA ....Construction Law
Kennewick, WA ....Construction Law

HERRIN & MORANO
Greenville, NC ....Insurance Defense

HERRING, D. JEFFERSON
Nashville, TN ....Probate, Trusts and Estate Planning; Tax Law

HERRMANN, LAWRENCE M.
Jackson Heights, NY ....Criminal Trial Practice

HERSCHBACH, TRACY, JOHNSON, BERTANI & WILSON
Joliet, IL ....Commercial Law; General Practice; Municipal and
Zoning Law; Real Estate Law

HERSHBERGER, PATTERSON, JONES & ROTH, L.C.
Wichita, KS.............................Administrative Law; Appellate Practice; Civil Trial
Practice; Commercial Law; Employment Benefits
Law; General Practice; Insurance Defense; Natural
Resources Law; Probate, Trusts and Estate
Planning; Real Estate Law

HERSHNER, HUNTER, ANDREWS, NEILL & SMITH, LLP
Eugene, OR ....General Practice

HERT & BAKER, A PROFESSIONAL CORPORATION
Stillwater, OK ....General Practice

HERTEN, BURSTEIN, SHERIDAN, CEVASCO, BOTTINELLI & LITT
Hackensack, NJ.......................Civil Trial Practice

HERTZBERG, RICHARD J.
Phoenix, AZ ....Civil Trial Practice; Criminal Trial Practice

HERZFELD & RUBIN, P.C.
New York, NY.........................General Practice

HERZOG, ENGSTROM & KOPLOVITZ, P.C.
Albany, NY.............................General Practice; Probate, Trusts and Estate
Planning

HERZOG, FISHER & GRAYSON, A LAW CORPORATION
Beverly Hills, CA....................Business Law; Commercial Litigation; Health Care
Law; Insurance Defense

HESLIN, THOMAS P.
Hartford, CT ....Civil Trial Practice

HESLIN & ROTHENBERG, P.C.
Albany, NY.............................Patent, Trademark, Copyright and Unfair Competition

HESS & ATCHISON
Mobile, AL..............................Criminal Trial Practice; Personal Injury

HESSIAN, MCKASY & SODERBERG, PROFESSIONAL ASSOCIATION
Minneapolis, MN ....Bankruptcy Law; Labor and Employment Law;
Municipal and Zoning Law; Real Estate Law

HESTERBERG & KELLER
Brooklyn, NY..........................Probate, Trusts and Estate Planning; Real Estate
Law

HESTER, GRADY, HESTER & GREENE
Elizabethtown, NC..................General Practice

HESTER, JON L., P.C., A PROFESSIONAL CORPORATION
Oklahoma City, OK................Family Law

HEWITT, JAMES W.
Lincoln, NE................General Practice

HEWLETT, COLLINS AND ALLARD
Wilmington, NC................Criminal Trial Practice

HEYL, ROYSTER, VOELKER & ALLEN, PROFESSIONAL CORPORATION
Edwardsville, IL................Insurance Defense
Peoria, IL................Insurance Defense
Rockford, IL................Insurance Defense
Springfield, IL................Insurance Defense
Urbana, IL................Insurance Defense

HICKEY & HICKEY
Kingston, ON, Canada............Health Care Law

HICKEY, MACKEY, EVANS, WALKER & STEWART
Cheyenne, WY................Banking Law; Civil Trial Practice; Commercial Law; Communications Law; Criminal Trial Practice; General Practice; Personal Injury

HICKMAN, SUMNERS, GOZA & GORE
New Albany, MS................General Practice; Insurance Defense

HICKS, ANDERSON & BLUM, P.A.
Miami, FL................Appellate Practice; General Practice

HICKS & HAVRILAK, P.C.
Fairfax, VA................Family Law

HICKS & LUCKY, A PROFESSIONAL CORPORATION
El Paso, TX................Medical Malpractice

HICKS, MALOOF & CAMPBELL, A PROFESSIONAL CORPORATION
Atlanta, GA................Bankruptcy Law; Business Law; Computer Law; Securities Law

HICKSON, DAVID L.
San Diego, CA................Probate, Trusts and Estate Planning

HIENTON, MINER, FRY & KURTZ, P.C.
Phoenix, AZ................Real Estate Law

HIERING, DUPIGNAC & STANZIONE, A PROFESSIONAL CORPORATION
Toms River, NJ................Civil Trial Practice; General Practice

HIERONYMUS, HODGDEN & HALLREN
Woodward, OK................General Practice

HIGBEE & ASSOCIATES, P.C.
Cedar City, UT................General Practice

HIGBIE, WESLEY R. LAW OFFICES OF
San Francisco, CA................Natural Resources Law

HIGGINS, CAVANAGH & COONEY
Providence, RI................Civil Trial Practice; General Practice; Insurance Defense

HIGGINS, ROBERTS, BEYERL & COAN, P.C.
Schenectady, NY................General Practice

HIGGS, FLETCHER & MACK LLP
San Diego, CA................Banking Law; Civil Trial Practice; General Practice

HIGH, STACK, LAZENBY, PALAHACH & DEL AMO
Miami, FL................General Practice

HIGH, SWARTZ, ROBERTS & SEIDEL
Norristown, PA................General Practice

HIGHLAND & ZANETTI
Southfield, MI................Appellate Practice; Insurance Defense; Labor and Employment Law; Medical Malpractice; Personal Injury; Product Liability Law

HIGHSAW, MAHONEY & CLARKE, P.C.
Washington, DC................Labor and Employment Law

HILBRECHT & ASSOCIATES, CHARTERED
Las Vegas, NV................Administrative Law; General Practice

HILBURN, CALHOON, HARPER, PRUNISKI & CALHOUN, LTD.
Little Rock, AR................Civil Trial Practice; General Practice; Labor and Employment Law; Securities Law; Tax Law; Transportation Law

HILL, JOHN E. LAW OFFICES OF
San Francisco, CA................Civil Trial Practice

HILL & BARLOW, A PROFESSIONAL CORPORATION
Boston, MA................General Practice

HILL & BEYER, A PROFESSIONAL LAW CORPORATION
Lafayette, LA................Admiralty/Maritime Law; Business Law; Civil Trial Practice; Environmental Law; General Practice; Insurance Defense; Labor and Employment Law; Product Liability Law

HILL AND BLEIBERG
Atlanta, GA................Medical Malpractice; Personal Injury; Product Liability Law

HILL, EVANS, DUNCAN, JORDAN & DAVIS
Greensboro, NC................Civil Trial Practice; General Practice

HILL, FARRER & BURRILL LLP
Los Angeles, CA................Appellate Practice; Civil Trial Practice; General Practice; Labor and Employment Law; Real Estate Law; Tax Law

HILL & HILL, ATTYS. AT LAW, A PROF. CORP.
Houston, TX................General Practice

HILL, HILL, CARTER, FRANCO, COLE & BLACK, P.C.
Montgomery, AL................Civil Trial Practice; General Practice

HILLIS CLARK MARTIN & PETERSON, A PROFESSIONAL SERVICE CORPORATION
Seattle, WA................General Practice

HILLIX, BREWER, HOFFHAUS, WHITTAKER & WRIGHT, L.L.C.
Kansas City, MO................General Practice

HILL & PARKER, A PROFESSIONAL CORPORATION
Houston, TX................Civil Trial Practice

HILL AND PONTON, PROFESSIONAL ASSOCIATION
Orlando, FL................Civil Trial Practice; Personal Injury

HIMROD, ROBERT M.
Los Angeles, CA................Probate, Trusts and Estate Planning

HINCKLEY, ALLEN & SNYDER
Boston, MA................General Practice
Providence, RI................General Practice

HINDS, COWAN, STRANGE, GEER & LUMPKIN
Georgetown, SC................General Practice

HINDS, ROBERT T., JR. AND ASSOCIATES, P.C.
Denver, CO................Family Law

HINKLE, COX, EATON, COFFIELD & HENSLEY, L.L.P.
Albuquerque, NM................General Practice
Roswell, NM................General Practice
Santa Fe, NM................General Practice
Amarillo, TX................General Practice
Midland, TX................Banking Law; Civil Trial Practice; Commercial Law; General Practice; Natural Resources Law

HINKLE GIBBS & GUNDLACH
Danville, IN................General Practice

HINKLE & ROPER, P.C.
Oklahoma City, OK................Civil Trial Practice

HINMAN, LOUIS F. III
Philadelphia, PA................Personal Injury; Workers Compensation

HINMAN, HOWARD & KATTELL, LLP
Binghamton, NY................Civil Trial Practice; General Practice; Labor and Employment Law; Municipal Bond/Public Authority Financing; Natural Resources Law; Tax Law

HINMAN, STRAUB, PIGORS & MANNING, P.C.
Albany, NY................Health Care Law

HINSHAW & CULBERTSON
Chicago, IL................General Practice

HINSHAW, WINKLER, DRAA, MARSH & STILL
San Jose, CA................Administrative Law; Civil Trial Practice; Health Care Law; Insurance Defense; Medical Malpractice

HINTON & ALFERT, A PROFESSIONAL CORPORATION
Walnut Creek, CA................Aviation Law; Civil Trial Practice; Commercial Litigation; Personal Injury; Product Liability Law

HINTON, ROBERT, & ASSOCIATES, P.C.
Dallas, TX................Criminal Trial Practice

HIRN DOHENY & HARPER
Louisville, KY................Banking Law; Civil Trial Practice; General Practice

HIRSCH, ARTHUR I.
New York, NY................Family Law

HIRSCH LAW OFFICE, P.C.
Phoenix, AZ................Bankruptcy Law; Family Law

HIRSCH, PARTIN, GROGAN & GROGAN, P.C.
Columbus, GA................Family Law

HIRSCH & WESTHEIMER, P.C.
Houston, TX................Real Estate Law

HIRSCHHORN, AUSTIN, P.C.
Troy, MI..............................Bankruptcy Law; Business Law; Civil Trial Practice; Commercial Law; General Practice; Real Estate Law

HIRSH, DAVIS & PICCARRETA, P.C.
Tucson, AZ ....Criminal Trial Practice

HIRSON WEXLER PERL & STARK, A PROFESSIONAL CORPORATION
Irvine, CA............................Immigration and Naturalization

HIRST & APPLEGATE, A PROFESSIONAL CORPORATION
Cheyenne, WY......................General Practice

HISCOCK & BARCLAY, LLP
Syracuse, NY........................General Practice

HISHON FIRM, THE, LLC
Atlanta, GA ....Business Law; Civil Trial Practice; General Practice; Tax Law

HIXSON, DOWNEY & TRAVELSTED
Bowling Green, KY ....Insurance Defense

HOAGLAND, LONGO, MORAN, DUNST & DOUKAS
New Brunswick, NJ ....Business Law; Civil Trial Practice; Construction Law; Environmental Law; Insurance Defense; Personal Injury; Product Liability Law; Workers Compensation

HOBBS & HAIN, P.C.
Selma, AL..............................General Practice

HOBBS, LARRY F., P.C.
Denver, CO ....Labor and Employment Law

HOBBS, STRAUS, DEAN & WALKER
Washington, DC....................General Practice

HOBSON, CADY & CADY
Hampton, IA..........................Civil Trial Practice; General Practice

HOCHBERG, D. PETER, CO., L.P.A.
Cleveland, OH......................Patent, Trademark, Copyright and Unfair Competition

HOCHMAN, SALKIN AND DEROY, A PROFESSIONAL CORPORATION
Beverly Hills, CA ....Business Law; Criminal Trial Practice; Probate, Trusts and Estate Planning; Tax Law

HODGE, RICHARD E., INC.
Santa Monica, CA..................Business Law; Civil Trial Practice; Real Estate Law

HODGES & DAVIS, P.C.
Merrillville, IN ....Civil Trial Practice; Commercial Law; General Practice; Health Care Law; Real Estate Law
Portage, IN............................Civil Trial Practice; Commercial Law; General Practice; Health Care Law; Real Estate Law

HODGSON, RUSS, ANDREWS, WOODS & GOODYEAR, LLP
Buffalo, NY ....Civil Trial Practice; General Practice; Immigration and Naturalization; Labor and Employment Law; Patent, Trademark, Copyright and Unfair Competition; Tax Law

HODOSH, SPINELLA & ANGELONE
Providence, RI......................Civil Trial Practice; General Practice; Insurance Defense; Personal Injury

HOEPPNER WAGNER AND EVANS
Merrillville, IN ....General Practice; Insurance Defense; Labor and Employment Law; Product Liability Law
Valparaiso, IN......................Employment Benefits Law; General Practice; Insurance Defense; Labor and Employment Law; Product Liability Law; Real Estate Law

HOFF, CURTIS, PACHT, CASSIDY & FRAME, P.C.
Burlington, VT ....General Practice

HOFFERT & ASSOCIATES, P.C.
Southfield, MI ....Tax Law

HOFFINGER FRIEDLAND DOBRISH BERNFELD & STERN, P.C.
New York, NY......................Civil Trial Practice; Commercial Litigation; Criminal Trial Practice; Family Law; Real Estate Law; Tax Law

HOFFMAN, AGGIE R.
Los Angeles, CA ....Immigration and Naturalization

HOFFMAN, JAMES P. LAW OFFICES OF
Keokuk, IA ....Personal Injury; Workers Compensation

HOFFMAN, DIMUZIO & HOFFMAN
Woodbury, NJ......................Personal Injury

HOFFMAN DREWRY HANCOCK & SIMMONS
Indianapolis, IN ....Construction Law

HOFFMAN & HERTZIG, P.A.
Miami, FL ....Civil Trial Practice

HOFFMAN, PAUL S., P.C.
Croton-On-Hudson, NY ....Computer Law

HOFFMAN, WACHTELL, KOSTER, MAIER & MANDEL
White Plains, NY ....Municipal and Zoning Law; Real Estate Law; Workers Compensation

HOFFMANN & BARON
Jericho, NY ....Patent, Trademark, Copyright and Unfair Competition

HOFFMANN, MICHAEL R., P.L.C., LAW OFFICES OF
Des Moines, IA ....Workers Compensation

HOFHEIMER, NUSBAUM, MCPHAUL & SAMUELS, A PROFESSIONAL CORPORATION
Norfolk, VA ....General Practice; Real Estate Law

HOFLER, HAYES, & ASSOCIATES, P.A.
Durham, NC ....Civil Trial Practice; Personal Injury

HOFMANN, SALCITO & STEVENS
Phoenix, AZ ....General Practice

HOGAN, THOMAS R. LAW OFFICES OF
San Jose, CA ....Business Law; Civil Trial Practice; Construction Law; General Practice

HOGAN & HARTSON L.L.P.
Washington, DC......................Banking Law; Communications Law; General Practice; Tax Law

HOGAN & HOGAN
East Providence, RI ....General Practice

HOGAN AND PALACE
Hackensack, NJ......................Civil Trial Practice; Real Estate Law

HOGAN & SARZYNSKI, L.L.P.
Binghamton, NY....................Labor and Employment Law; Municipal and Zoning Law

HOGAN, SMITH & ALSPAUGH, P.C.
Birmingham, AL ....Civil Trial Practice; Environmental Law; Medical Malpractice; Personal Injury; Product Liability Law

HOGUE, HILL, JONES, NASH AND LYNCH
Wilmington, NC......................Civil Trial Practice; General Practice; Insurance Defense

HOHMANN, WERNER & TAUBE, L.L.P.
Austin, TX ....Banking Law; Bankruptcy Law; Civil Trial Practice; Insurance Defense
Houston, TX ....Civil Trial Practice; Insurance Defense

HOLAHAN, MALLOY, MAYBAUGH & MONNICH
Troy, MI................................Civil Trial Practice; Insurance Defense; Medical Malpractice; Personal Injury; Probate, Trusts and Estate Planning

HOLBROOK, HEAVEN & FAY, P.A.
Kansas City, KS......................Civil Trial Practice; General Practice; Insurance Defense

HOLBROOK & PITT
Ashland, KY ....Real Estate Law

HOLCOMB DUNBAR, A PROFESSIONAL ASSOCIATION
Clarksdale, MS......................Bankruptcy Law; Civil Trial Practice; Commercial Law; General Practice; Insurance Defense; Labor and Employment Law; Probate, Trusts and Estate Planning; Workers Compensation
Jackson, MS ....Bankruptcy Law; Civil Trial Practice; Commercial Law; Environmental Law; General Practice; Insurance Defense; Labor and Employment Law; Probate, Trusts and Estate Planning
Oxford, MS ....Bankruptcy Law; Civil Trial Practice; Commercial Law; Environmental Law; General Practice; Insurance Defense; Labor and Employment Law; Probate, Trusts and Estate Planning
Southaven, MS ....Bankruptcy Law; Civil Trial Practice; Commercial Law; General Practice; Insurance Defense; Labor and Employment Law

HOLCOMBE, BOMAR, GUNN AND BRADFORD, P.A.
Spartanburg, SC......................Civil Trial Practice; General Practice; Medical Malpractice; Product Liability Law

HOLDER, FLOYD D. JR., LAW FIRM OF
Lubbock, TX ....Bankruptcy Law; Criminal Trial Practice

HOLLAND & HART LLP
Denver, CO ....General Practice

HOLLAND & HOLLAND
Indianapolis, IN ....Civil Trial Practice; Personal Injury

HOLLAND KAUFMANN & BARTELS, LLC
Greenwich, CT ....Business Law; Family Law; General Practice; Probate, Trusts and Estate Planning; Real Estate Law

HOLLAND & KNIGHT LLP
Washington, DC............General Practice
Fort Lauderdale, FL............General Practice
Jacksonville, FL............General Practice
Lakeland, FL............General Practice
Miami, FL............General Practice
Orlando, FL............General Practice
St. Petersburg, FL............General Practice
Tallahassee, FL............General Practice
Tampa, FL............General Practice
West Palm Beach, FL............General Practice

HOLLAND, RAY & UPCHURCH, P.A.
Tupelo, MS............Banking Law; Commercial Law; Insurance Defense; Labor and Employment Law; Medical Malpractice; Probate, Trusts and Estate Planning; Real Estate Law

HOLLEMAN, BOYCE, A PROFESSIONAL ASSOCIATION
Gulfport, MS............Civil Trial Practice; Criminal Trial Practice; Family Law; General Practice; Personal Injury

HOLLEY, ALBERTSON & POLK, P.C.
Golden, CO............Civil Trial Practice; Construction Law; Land Use Law; Real Estate Law

HOLLEY & GALEN
Los Angeles, CA............Business Law; General Practice; Probate, Trusts and Estate Planning; Tax Law

HOLLIDAY, JAMES S., JR., A PROF. CORP.
Baton Rouge, LA............Business Law; Construction Law

HOLLIER & RINGUET, A PROFESSIONAL LAW CORPORATION
Lafayette, LA............General Practice

HOLLIMAN LANGHOLZ RUNNELS HOLDEN FORSMAN & SELLERS, A PROFESSIONAL CORPORATION
Tulsa, OK............General Practice; Natural Resources Law; Securities Law

HOLLINS, SCHECHTER & FEINSTEIN, A PROFESSIONAL CORPORATION
Orange, CA............Insurance Defense

HOLLINS, WAGSTER & YARBROUGH, P.C.
Nashville, TN............Civil Trial Practice; Criminal Trial Practice; Insurance Defense

HOLLIS AND JOHNSON
Chicago, IL............Bankruptcy Law

HOLLISTER & BRACE, A PROFESSIONAL CORPORATION
Santa Barbara, CA............Civil Trial Practice; General Practice

HOLLOMAN, CHARLES R., P.A.
Ocala, FL............Criminal Trial Practice

HOLLORAN LAW FIRM, THE, P.C.
St. Louis, MO............Medical Malpractice; Personal Injury; Product Liability Law

HOLLOWAY ODEGARD & SWEENEY, P.C.
Phoenix, AZ............Insurance Defense

HOLLOWAY & ROWLEY, P.C.
Houston, TX............Civil Trial Practice

HOLLOWELL & ASSOCIATES, P.A.
Raleigh, NC............Health Care Law

HOLMAN HOGAN DUBOSE & TOWNSEND, L.L.P.
Houston, TX............Appellate Practice

HOLMAN & O'GRADY
San Francisco, CA............Bankruptcy Law; Commercial Litigation

HOLME ROBERTS & OWEN LLP
Boulder, CO............General Practice
Colorado Springs, CO............General Practice
Denver, CO............Banking Law; Business Law; Civil Trial Practice; Environmental Law; General Practice; Health Care Law; International Business Law; Labor and Employment Law; Municipal Bond/Public Authority Financing; Natural Resources Law; Patent, Trademark, Copyright and Unfair Competition; Probate, Trusts and Estate Planning; Real Estate Law; Securities Law; Tax Law
Salt Lake City, UT............General Practice
London, England............General Practice

HOLMES & KLINE, A PROFESSIONAL CORPORATION
Dallas, TX............Real Estate Law

HOLMES & THOMSON, L.L.P.
Charleston, SC............Banking Law; Civil Trial Practice; General Practice; Insurance Defense

HOLMSTROM & KENNEDY, P.C.
Rockford, IL............General Practice

HOLPER, WELSH, MITCHELL & JOANIS, LTD.
Minneapolis, MN............Bankruptcy Law

HOLT, LONGEST, WALL & BLAETZ, P.L.L.C.
Burlington, NC............General Practice

HOLT, NEY, ZATCOFF & WASSERMAN
Atlanta, GA............Business Law; Civil Trial Practice; Commercial Law; Environmental Law; General Practice; Health Care Law; Municipal and Zoning Law; Real Estate Law; Securities Law; Tax Law

HOLT & WATT
Reidsville, NC............General Practice

HOLT & YORK, LLP
Raleigh, NC............Municipal and Zoning Law

HOLTKAMP, LIESE, BECKEMEIER & CHILDRESS, P.C.
St. Louis, MO............Insurance Defense

HOLTON HOWARD & GOODMAN, P.C.
Nashville, TN............Probate, Trusts and Estate Planning; Tax Law

HOLTORF, KOVARIK, ELLISON & MATHIS, P.C.
Gering, NE............General Practice; Insurance Defense

HOLTZMAN, ERIC H.
Hauppauge, NY............Civil Trial Practice; Commercial Law; Environmental Law; General Practice; Product Liability Law

HOMSEY, GARY B. & ASSOCIATES
Oklahoma City, OK............Personal Injury

HOMSEY, MICHAEL S. "MICKEY", & ASSOCIATES, P.C.
Oklahoma City, OK............Criminal Trial Practice; Personal Injury

HONIGMAN MILLER SCHWARTZ AND COHN
Tampa, FL............Civil Trial Practice; Environmental Law; General Practice; Natural Resources Law
West Palm Beach, FL............Environmental Law; General Practice; Natural Resources Law; Real Estate Law
Detroit, MI............Antitrust Law; Bankruptcy Law; Civil Trial Practice; Communications Law; Criminal Trial Practice; Environmental Law; General Practice; Health Care Law; Labor and Employment Law; Municipal Bond/Public Authority Financing; Natural Resources Law; Real Estate Law; Tax Law
Lansing, MI............Civil Trial Practice; Environmental Law; General Practice; Insurance Defense; Natural Resources Law; Real Estate Law; Tax Law; Transportation Law

HONN & SECOF
Los Angeles, CA............Civil Trial Practice; Insurance Defense

HOOD LAW FIRM
Charleston, SC............Civil Trial Practice; General Practice; Insurance Defense; Medical Malpractice; Personal Injury; Product Liability Law

HOOKER, ROBERT THE LAW OFFICE OF
Tucson, AZ............Criminal Trial Practice

HOOPER, HATHAWAY, PRICE, BEUCHE & WALLACE
Ann Arbor, MI............Business Law; Civil Trial Practice; Commercial Litigation; Criminal Trial Practice; Environmental Law; Family Law; General Practice; Labor and Employment Law; Medical Malpractice; Probate, Trusts and Estate Planning; Real Estate Law

HOOPER, LUNDY & BOOKMAN, INC.
Los Angeles, CA............Health Care Law

HOOVER & KOOISTRA
Little Rock, AR............Banking Law; Bankruptcy Law; Civil Trial Practice; Commercial Law; Construction Law; General Practice; Probate, Trusts and Estate Planning; Real Estate Law; Securities Law; Tax Law

HOOVER LEGAL ASSOCIATES, A PROFESSIONAL CORPORATION
Dallas, TX............General Practice

HOOVER, ROBERT D., P.L.C., LAW OFFICES OF
Baton Rouge, LA............Insurance Defense; Personal Injury

HOPE & CAUSEY, P.C.
Conroe, TX............Insurance Defense

HOPKINS & CARLEY, A LAW CORPORATION
San Jose, CA............Commercial Law; Environmental Law; General Practice; Patent, Trademark, Copyright and Unfair Competition; Probate, Trusts and Estate Planning; Real Estate Law; Tax Law

HOPKINS, CRAWLEY, BAGWELL, UPSHAW & PERSONS
Gulfport, MS..........................Environmental Law; Insurance Defense; Product Liability Law; Tax Law; Workers Compensation

HOPKINS LAW FIRM, A PROFESSIONAL ASSOCIATION
Little Rock, AR......................Commercial Law

HOPKINS, RODEN, CROCKETT, HANSEN & HOOPES
Boise, ID..............................General Practice
Idaho Falls, ID......................General Practice

HOPKINS & SUTTER
Chicago, IL.............................General Practice

HOPPEL, MAYER & COLEMAN
Washington, DC......................Admiralty/Maritime Law

HOPPER & GALLIHER, P.C.
Indianapolis, IN.....................Bankruptcy Law; Commercial Law

HOPPER & PLUNK, P.C.
Savannah, TN.........................Civil Trial Practice; General Practice; Insurance Defense; Real Estate Law

HOPPING GREEN SAMS & SMITH, PROFESSIONAL ASSOCIATION
Tallahassee, FL......................Administrative Law; Communications Law; Environmental Law; General Practice; Municipal and Zoning Law; Natural Resources Law

HOPSON AND HABENICHT, LTD.
Chester, VA.............................Civil Trial Practice

HORGER, BARNWELL & REID, L.L.P.
Orangeburg, SC......................General Practice

HORGER, HORGER & LANIER
Orangeburg, SC......................General Practice

HORN, JEROLD I.
Peoria, IL..............................Probate, Trusts and Estate Planning

HORNBERGER, LEE
Cincinnati, OH......................Labor and Employment Law

HORNBERGER & CRISWELL
Los Angeles, CA.....................Business Law; Civil Trial Practice; Construction Law; Environmental Law; Insurance Defense; Labor and Employment Law; Product Liability Law

HORNBUCKLE & CLARK, P.C.
San Antonio, TX.....................Personal Injury

HORNE, FOY S., JR., P.C.
Athens, GA.............................Personal Injury; Workers Compensation

HORNE, HOLLINGSWORTH & PARKER, A PROFESSIONAL ASSOCIATION
Little Rock, AR......................General Practice

HORNE, KAPLAN AND BISTROW, P.C.
Phoenix, AZ...........................Civil Trial Practice; Commercial Litigation; Construction Law; Personal Injury; Trademark, Copyright and Unfair Competition

HORNER, STEPHEN P. & ASSOCIATES
Norwalk, CT...........................Labor and Employment Law

HORNING, JOHNSON, GROVE, MOORE, HULETT & THOMPSON, A PROFESSIONAL CORPORATION
Oklahoma City, OK................Family Law

HORNSBY, WATSON & MEGINNISS
Huntsville, AL.........................Civil Trial Practice; Personal Injury; Product Liability Law; Workers Compensation

HORNTHAL, RILEY, ELLIS & MALAND, L.L.P.
Elizabeth City, NC..................Civil Trial Practice; General Practice

HOROWITZ, DONALD LAW OFFICES OF
Hackensack, NJ......................Civil Trial Practice; Criminal Trial Practice; Environmental Law; General Practice

HOROWITZ, EDWARD J., A PROFESSIONAL CORPORATION
Los Angeles, CA.....................Appellate Practice

HOROWITZ — GUDEMAN, P.C.
Farmington Hills, MI..............Business Law; Probate, Trusts and Estate Planning; Real Estate Law; Securities Law; Tax Law

HORRIGAN & GOEHRS, L.L.P.
Houston, TX...........................Probate, Trusts and Estate Planning

HORTON BARBARO & REILLY
Santa Ana, CA........................Construction Law; Labor and Employment Law; Medical Malpractice; Personal Injury; Product Liability Law

HORTON, KNOX, CARTER & FOOTE
El Centro, CA.........................General Practice

HORTON, SHIELDS & CORMIER, P.C.
Hartford, CT...........................General Practice; Insurance Defense

HORTY, SPRINGER & MATTERN, P.C.
Pittsburgh, PA.......................Health Care Law

HORVITZ & LEVY
Los Angeles, CA.....................Appellate Practice; Health Care Law; Insurance Defense

HORWATT, MICHAEL, & ASSOCIATES P.C.
McLean, VA............................Business Law; Commercial Law; Real Estate Law

HORWITZ & FUSSELL, A PROF. ASSN., LAW OFFICES OF
Orlando, FL............................Criminal Trial Practice

HOSKIN, FARINA, ALDRICH & KAMPF, PROFESSIONAL CORPORATION
Grand Junction, CO................General Practice

HOSTAK, HENZL & BICHLER, S.C.
Racine, WI..............................General Practice

HOSTETLER & KOWALIK, P.C.
Indianapolis, IN.....................Bankruptcy Law; Commercial Law

HOSTETLER & MCNEILL
Raeford, NC............................General Practice

HOTZ & ASSOCIATES, P.C.
Tucker, GA.............................Banking Law; Civil Trial Practice

HOURIGAN, KLUGER, SPOHRER & QUINN, A PROFESSIONAL CORPORATION
Wilkes-Barre, PA....................General Practice; Labor and Employment Law; Medical Malpractice; Personal Injury; Probate, Trusts and Estate Planning; Real Estate Law

HOUSE, STANLEY C.
Augusta, GA...........................Civil Trial Practice; Commercial Litigation; Labor and Employment Law; Personal Injury; Product Liability Law

HOUSE, KINGSMILL, RIESS & SEABOLT, L.L.C.
New Orleans, LA....................Civil Trial Practice

HOUSEMAN, FEIND, GALLO & MALLOY
Grafton, WI............................General Practice

HOUSLEY KANTARIAN & BRONSTEIN, P.C.
Washington, DC......................Banking Law

HOUSTON, DONNELLY & MECK
Pittsburgh, PA.......................General Practice; Probate, Trusts and Estate Planning

HOUSTON AND OSBORN, P.C.
Stillwater, OK.........................General Practice

HOUTCHENS, DANIEL & GREENFIELD, LLC
Greeley, CO............................General Practice

HOVERSTEN, JOHNSON, BECKMANN, WELLMANN & HOVEY, P.L.L.P.
Austin, MN............................Civil Trial Practice; Criminal Trial Practice; General Practice; Insurance Defense; Real Estate Law

HOVEY, KIRBY, THORNTON & HAHN, A PROFESSIONAL CORPORATION
San Diego, CA........................Bankruptcy Law; Business Law; Civil Trial Practice; Commercial Law; Construction Law; Environmental Law; Municipal and Zoning Law; Real Estate Law

HOVEY, WILLIAMS, TIMMONS & COLLINS
Kansas City, MO....................Patent, Trademark, Copyright and Unfair Competition

HOWARD, JOHN H.
Ventura, CA............................Civil Trial Practice

HOWARD, BRAWNER & STONE
Miami, FL...............................General Practice

HOWARD, CARSWELL & BENNETT, P.C.
Jesup, GA...............................General Practice; Insurance Defense

HOWARD & DAVIS, A PROFESSIONAL CORPORATION
Tyler, TX................................Medical Malpractice

HOWARD, FROM, STALLINGS & HUTSON, P.A.
Raleigh, NC............................Bankruptcy Law; Business Law; Civil Trial Practice; Commercial Law; Construction Law; Family Law; Probate, Trusts and Estate Planning; Real Estate Law

HOWARD, GEORGE W., III, P.C. AND ASSOCIATES
Philadelphia, PA....................Civil Trial Practice

HOWARD & GREEN, L.L.P.
Raleigh, NC............................Family Law; General Practice

HOWARD & HOWARD, ATTORNEYS, P.C.
Peoria, IL...............................Banking Law; Business Law; Commercial Litigation; Communications Law; Construction Law; Environmental Law; General Practice; Labor and Employment Law; Municipal Bond/Public Authority Financing; Public Utilities Law

HOWARD & HOWARD ATTORNEYS, P.C.
Bloomfield Hills, MI.................Antitrust Law; Banking Law; Bankruptcy Law; Business Law; Commercial Litigation; Environmental Law; General Practice; Immigration and Naturalization; Labor and Employment Law; Municipal Bond/Public Authority Financing; Patent, Trademark, Copyright and Unfair Competition; Securities Law; Tax Law
Kalamazoo, MI ....Banking Law; Bankruptcy Law; Business Law; Commercial Litigation; Communications Law; Environmental Law; General Practice; Insurance Defense; Labor and Employment Law; Real Estate Law; Securities Law; Tax Law
Lansing, MI............................Banking Law; Business Law; Commercial Litigation; Communications Law; General Practice; Insurance Defense; Labor and Employment Law; Municipal Bond/Public Authority Financing; Real Estate Law; Tax Law

HOWARD, LEGGANS, PIERCY & HOWARD
Mount Vernon, IL ....General Practice

HOWARD, LEWIS & PETERSEN, P.C.
Provo, UT..............................Banking Law; Civil Trial Practice; Commercial Law; Family Law; General Practice; Personal Injury

HOWARD, MACKIE
Calgary, AB, Canada..............General Practice

HOWARD, MOSS, LOVEDER, STRICKROTH & WALKER
Santa Ana, CA ....Insurance Defense

HOWARTH & SMITH
Los Angeles, CA ....Antitrust Law; Appellate Practice; Civil Trial Practice; General Practice

HOWD, LAVIERI & FINCH
Winsted, CT ....General Practice

HOWD & LUDORF
Hartford, CT ....General Practice; Insurance Defense

HOWE, GEDNEY M., III, P.A.
Charleston, SC ....Civil Trial Practice; Criminal Trial Practice

HOWE, WATERS & CARPENTER, P.A.
Hendersonville, NC.................General Practice; Real Estate Law

HOWELL, JOEL W. III
Jackson, MS ....Civil Trial Practice

HOWELL, GATELY, WHITNEY & CARTER, LLP
Towson, MD ....Appellate Practice; Civil Trial Practice; General Practice; Insurance Defense; Product Liability Law; Workers Compensation

HOWELL & HAFERKAMP, L.C.
St. Louis, MO.........................Patent, Trademark, Copyright and Unfair Competition

HOWELL, LEMBHARD G., P.S., LAW OFFICES OF
Seattle, WA ....Personal Injury

HOWETT, KISSINGER & MILES, P.C.
Harrisburg, PA........................Family Law

HOWIE & SWEENEY, L.L.P.
Dallas, TX...............................Aviation Law; Medical Malpractice; Personal Injury; Product Liability Law

HOWREY & SIMON
Washington, DC......................General Practice

HOYLE, MORRIS & KERR
Philadelphia, PA ....Civil Trial Practice; General Practice

HOYLE, WILLIAM V., JR., P.C.
Newport News, VA ....General Practice

HOYT, COLGAN & ANDREU, P.A.
Tampa, FL ....Admiralty/Maritime Law; Civil Trial Practice; Commercial Litigation; Construction Law

HOYT & SALIBA
Morristown, NJ.......................Probate, Trusts and Estate Planning

HUANG & MITCHELL, A PROFESSIONAL LAW CORPORATION
Los Angeles, CA ....Commercial Litigation

HUBBARD, BREEDEN & TERRY
Irvington, VA..........................Business Law; General Practice

HUBBARD, CATES & LONG
Roxboro, NC ....General Practice

HUBBARD & PIERCE, PLLC
Jackson, MS ....Commercial Law; Personal Injury

HUBER, BOOK, CORTESE, HAPPE & BROWN, P.L.C.
Des Moines, IA........................Insurance Defense

HUBER & GOODWIN
Eureka, CA..............................General Practice

HUCKABAY, MUNSON, ROWLETT & TILLEY, P.A.
Little Rock, AR ....Civil Trial Practice; Insurance Defense; Medical Malpractice; Personal Injury; Product Liability Law; Workers Compensation

HUCKABY, FLEMING, FRAILEY, CHAFFIN, CORDELL, GREENWOOD & PERRYMAN
Oklahoma City, OK................Civil Trial Practice; Insurance Defense; Product Liability Law

HUDDLESTON, BOLEN, BEATTY, PORTER & COPEN
Charleston, WV.......................General Practice
Huntington, WV ....General Practice

HUDDLESTON & REED
Bowling Green, KY ....Bankruptcy Law; Civil Trial Practice

HUDGINS CARTER & COLEMAN
Alexandria, VA ....Civil Trial Practice; Health Care Law; Insurance Defense

HUDSON AND MONTGOMERY, P.C.
Athens, GA ....Personal Injury

HUDSON, POTTS & BERNSTEIN
Monroe, LA ....General Practice; Insurance Defense

HUERTA, MARCELINO J., III, P.A.
Tampa, FL ....Criminal Trial Practice

HUFF LAW OFFICES
Harlan, KY ....Insurance Defense; Labor and Employment Law

HUFFAKER, BARNES & CONWAY, A PROFESSIONAL CORPORATION
Albuquerque, NM....................Commercial Litigation; Insurance Defense
Santa Fe, NM..........................Administrative Law; Appellate Practice; Commercial Litigation; Environmental Law; Insurance Defense; Natural Resources Law

HUFFAKER, GREEN & HUFFAKER
Tahoka, TX ....General Practice

HUFFER AND HUFFER CO., L.P.A.
Circleville, OH.........................General Practice; Probate, Trusts and Estate Planning

HUFFORD, HORSTMAN, MCCULLOUGH & MONGINI, P.C.
Flagstaff, AZ ....Labor and Employment Law; Municipal and Zoning Law

HUGGINS & ALLEN, P.C.
Augusta, GA ....Real Estate Law

HUGHES, AMYS
Toronto, ON, Canada..............Insurance Defense

HUGHES & GRANT
Oklahoma City, OK.................Civil Trial Practice; Criminal Trial Practice; General Practice; Personal Injury

HUGHES HUBBARD & REED LLP
Los Angeles, CA ....General Practice
Washington, DC......................General Practice
Miami, FL...............................General Practice
New York, NY.........................General Practice
Paris, France...........................General Practice

HUGHES & LUCE, L.L.P.
Austin, TX ....Administrative Law; General Practice; Sports and Entertainment Law
Dallas, TX...............................Banking Law; Bankruptcy Law; Business Law; Civil Trial Practice; Commercial Law; General Practice; Probate, Trusts and Estate Planning; Real Estate Law; Sports and Entertainment Law; Tax Law
Houston, TX ....General Practice

HUGHES, MATHEWS & DIDIER, P.A.
St. Cloud, MN ....Civil Trial Practice; Commercial Law; Commercial Litigation; Employment Benefits Law; Health Care Law

HUGHES & NUNN
San Diego, CA ....Commercial Litigation

HUGHES, PETER J., A PROFESSIONAL CORPORATION
San Diego, CA ....Criminal Trial Practice

HUGHES AND SALLEE
Indianapolis, IN ....Appellate Practice; Civil Trial Practice; Real Estate Law

HUGHES & STRUMOR, LTD. CO.
Albuquerque, NM....................Municipal Bond/Public Authority Financing; Securities Law

HUGHES, THOREEN, RELPH & HANSON, P.A.
St. Cloud, MN ....Business Law; Employment Benefits Law; Personal Injury; Probate, Trusts and Estate Planning

HUGIE, ELDON R.
Bakersfield, CA ....Business Law; Probate, Trusts and Estate Planning

HUIE, FERNAMBUCQ AND STEWART
Birmingham, AL ....Medical Malpractice

HULL, TOWILL, NORMAN & BARRETT, A PROFESSIONAL CORPORATION
Augusta, GA ....Business Law; Civil Trial Practice; General Practice; Insurance Defense; Real Estate Law; Securities Law; Tax Law

HULLVERSON LAW FIRM, THE
St. Louis, MO.........................Personal Injury

HULL, WEBBER & REIS
Rutland, VT ....General Practice

HULSEY, OLIVER & MAHAR
Gainesville, GA ....General Practice

HULSTRAND ANDERSON LARSON HANSON & SAUNDERS, P.L.L.P.
Willmar, MN............................General Practice

HUMMEL & COAN
Louisville, KY ....Insurance Defense; Personal Injury

HUMPHREYS DUNLAP WELLFORD ACUFF & STANTON, A PROFESSIONAL CORPORATION
Memphis, TN ....General Practice

HUNDLEY & BRUSSLAN
Chicago, IL..............................Civil Trial Practice

HUNEGS, STONE, KOENIG & LENEAVE, P.A.
Minneapolis, MN....................Admiralty/Maritime Law; Aviation Law; Civil Trial Practice; Personal Injury

HUNT, ERNEST L. JR.
Vista, CA................................Business Law; General Practice; Probate, Trusts and Estate Planning; Real Estate Law

HUNT, COLAW & ADAMS, INC.
Santa Ana, CA ....Personal Injury

HUNT, HERMANSEN, MCKIBBEN & ENGLISH, L.L.P.
Corpus Christi, TX ....Appellate Practice; Civil Trial Practice; Insurance Defense

HUNT, RICHARD H., & ASSOCIATES, A PROF. ASSN.
Coral Gables, FL ....General Practice; Probate, Trusts and Estate Planning; Tax Law

HUNT & ROSS, A PROFESSIONAL ASSOCIATION
Clarksdale, MS........................Administrative Law; General Practice; Natural Resources Law; Real Estate Law

HUNT, SUEDHOFF, BORROR & EILBACHER
Fort Wayne, IN.......................Appellate Practice; Civil Trial Practice; Commercial Law; Insurance Defense

HUNTER, MACLEAN, EXLEY & DUNN, P.C.
Savannah, GA ....Business Law; Civil Trial Practice; Environmental Law; General Practice; Labor and Employment Law; Probate, Trusts and Estate Planning; Tax Law

HUNTER RICHEY DI BENEDETTO & BREWER, LLP
Sacramento, CA ....Business Law; Civil Trial Practice; Environmental Law; Health Care Law; Land Use Law; Mergers and Acquisitions; Patent, Trademark, Copyright and Unfair Competition; Real Estate Law; Trademark, Copyright and Unfair Competition

HUNTER, SMITH & DAVIS
Johnson City, TN....................General Practice
Kingsport, TN.........................Banking Law; Civil Trial Practice; Environmental Law; General Practice; Labor and Employment Law; Municipal Bond/Public Authority Financing; Natural Resources Law; Tax Law

HUNTER & SOMMERS
Waukesha, WI ....General Practice

HUNTER, WHARTON & STROUPE, L.L.P.
Raleigh, NC.............................General Practice

HUNTON & WILLIAMS
Richmond, VA.........................General Practice

HUNTSMAN, LAWRENCE D.
Fairfax, VA ....Civil Trial Practice

HUPP, LANUTI, IRION & MARTIN, P.C.
Ottawa, IL...............................General Practice; Insurance Defense

HUPPERT & SWINDLEHURST, P.C.
Livingston, MT ....General Practice

HURBIS & CLINTON
Ann Arbor, MI ....Civil Trial Practice; Construction Law; Insurance Defense; Personal Injury; Product Liability Law; Workers Compensation

HURLEY, FOX, SELIG & KELLEHER
New City, NY ....General Practice
Stony Point, NY......................Civil Trial Practice; Commercial Law; General Practice; Land Use Law; Municipal and Zoning Law; Personal Injury; Product Liability Law

HURLEY, JOSEPH A., P.A.
Wilmington, DE......................Criminal Trial Practice

HURLEY, LYNCH & RE, P.C.
Bend, OR................................General Practice

HURTH, YEAGER & SISK
Boulder, CO ....General Practice

HURWITZ & FINE, P.C.
Buffalo, NY ....Bankruptcy Law; General Practice; Health Care Law; Insurance Defense; Probate, Trusts and Estate Planning; Tax Law

HURWITZ & SAGARIN, P.C.
Milford, CT ....Civil Trial Practice; Commercial Litigation; Land Use Law; Personal Injury

HUSKEY, DOW T.
Dothan, AL..............................Business Law

HUSMAN, LICATA & STEELE, A PROFESSIONAL CORPORATION
Columbia, SC ....Bankruptcy Law; Commercial Litigation

HUTCHESON & GRUNDY, L.L.P.
Houston, TX ....General Practice

HUTCHINS, DOUGHTON & MOORE
Winston-Salem, NC ....General Practice

HUTCHINS, WHEELER & DITTMAR, A PROFESSIONAL CORPORATION
Boston, MA.............................General Practice

HUTTON INGRAM YUZEK GAINEN CARROLL & BERTOLOTTI
New York, NY.........................Appellate Practice; Banking Law; Business Law; Civil Trial Practice; Commercial Law; Construction Law; General Practice; Insurance Defense; International Business Law; Real Estate Law; Securities Law; Tax Law

HUTTON, LAURY, HESSER, LIETZ & WILCOX
Danville, IL ....Civil Trial Practice; General Practice; Insurance Defense

HVASS, WEISMAN & KING, CHARTERED
Minneapolis, MN....................Civil Trial Practice; General Practice; Labor and Employment Law; Medical Malpractice; Personal Injury; Product Liability Law

HYATT & HYATT, P.C.
Decatur, GA............................General Practice; Personal Injury; Workers Compensation

HYDE AND WATERS
San Diego, CA ....Appellate Practice; Business Law; Civil Trial Practice; Real Estate Law

HYMAN AND LIPPITT, P.C.
Birmingham, MI......................Bankruptcy Law; Business Law; Civil Trial Practice; Commercial Litigation; Family Law; General Practice; Mergers and Acquisitions; Probate, Trusts and Estate Planning; Real Estate Law

HYTKEN, FRANKLIN HARRIS, P.C.
Dallas, TX ....Civil Trial Practice; Commercial Law

IBERSHOF & DOLE
San Francisco, CA ....Civil Trial Practice; Probate, Trusts and Estate Planning

ICE MILLER DONADIO & RYAN
Indianapolis, IN ....Antitrust Law; Banking Law; Bankruptcy Law; Civil Trial Practice; Commercial Law; Communications Law; Construction Law; Employment Benefits Law; Environmental Law; General Practice; Health Care Law; Immigration and Naturalization; Insurance Defense; International Trade Law; Labor and Employment Law; Medical Malpractice; Municipal Bond/Public Authority Financing; Natural Resources Law; Personal Injury; Probate, Trusts and Estate Planning; Real Estate Law; Securities Law; Tax Law; Trademark, Copyright and Unfair Competition

IFSHIN & FRIEDMAN, P.L.L.C.
Washington, DC......................Civil Trial Practice

IMAI, TADLOCK & KEENEY
San Francisco, CA ....Insurance Defense

INDIANO, WILLIAMS & WEINSTEIN-BACAL
San Juan, PR ....Bankruptcy Law; Civil Trial Practice; Commercial Law; Construction Law; Personal Injury

INGBER & ARONSON, P.A.
Minneapolis, MN ....Immigration and Naturalization

INGE, TWITTY & DUFFY
Mobile, AL ....Civil Trial Practice; Insurance Defense; Personal Injury; Product Liability Law

INGHAM, SAMUEL D. III
Beverly Hills, CA ....Natural Resources Law; Probate, Trusts and Estate Planning; Real Estate Law; Tax Law

INGLESBY, FALLIGANT, HORNE, COURINGTON & NASH, A PROFESSIONAL CORPORATION
Savannah, GA ....Bankruptcy Law; General Practice; Real Estate Law

INGLIS, LEDBETTER & GOWER
Los Angeles, CA ....Insurance Defense; Mergers and Acquisitions

INGLISH & MONACO, P.C.
Jefferson City, MO ....Civil Trial Practice; General Practice; Insurance Defense

INGRAHAM, FRANK C.
Nashville, TN ....Civil Trial Practice; Probate, Trusts and Estate Planning

INTERNATIONAL LAW FIRM, THE
Riyadh, Saudi Arabia...............General Practice

INZER, STIVENDER, HANEY & JOHNSON, P.A.
Gadsden, AL ....Civil Trial Practice; General Practice

IRELAND, CARROLL & KELLEY, P.C.
Tyler, TX.................................Appellate Practice; Bankruptcy Law; Civil Trial Practice; Insurance Defense

IRELL & MANELLA LLP
Los Angeles, CA ....General Practice

IRSFELD, IRSFELD & YOUNGER LLP
Glendale, CA...........................Business Law; Civil Trial Practice; Commercial Litigation; Construction Law; Probate, Trusts and Estate Planning; Real Estate Law; Tax Law

IRVIN & COSKREY, L.L.P.
Columbia, SC ....Civil Trial Practice

IRVIN, STANFORD & KESSLER
Atlanta, GA ....Labor and Employment Law

IRWIN, SANDRA MCMAHAN
Pasadena, CA ....Business Law

ISAACSON AND ISAACSON
Greensboro, NC.......................Business Law; Commercial Law; General Practice; Municipal and Zoning Law; Real Estate Law

ISAF, LOUIS T., P.C.
Atlanta, GA ....Computer Law; Patent, Trademark, Copyright and Unfair Competition

ISEMAN, CUNNINGHAM, RIESTER & HYDE, L.L.P.
Albany, NY..............................Civil Trial Practice; Construction Law; Health Care Law; Personal Injury; Real Estate Law; Tax Law

ISICOFF & RAGATZ, P.A.
Miami, FL ....Trademark, Copyright and Unfair Competition

ISOM, DAVID K. LAW OFFICES
Salt Lake City, UT..................Commercial Litigation

ISRAELSON, SALSBURY, CLEMENTS & BEKMAN
Baltimore, MD ....Admiralty/Maritime Law; Civil Trial Practice; Medical Malpractice; Personal Injury; Product Liability Law

ISRAEL, WOOD & PUNTIL, P.C.
Pittsburgh, PA ....Insurance Defense

ISSELHARD, TERRELL J., AND ASSOCIATES, LTD., PROF. CORP.
Chicago, IL..............................Business Law; Health Care Law

IVANJACK & LAMBIRTH
Los Angeles, CA ....Banking Law; Commercial Law

IVENER, MARK A., A LAW CORPORATION
Los Angeles, CA ....Immigration and Naturalization

IVERSON, YOAKUM, PAPIANO & HATCH
Los Angeles, CA ....Appellate Practice; Business Law; General Practice; Labor and Employment Law; Product Liability Law

IVESTER, SKINNER & CAMP, P.A.
Little Rock, AR ....Banking Law; Commercial Law; Communications Law; General Practice; Patent, Trademark, Copyright and Unfair Competition; Securities Law

IVEY, BARNUM & O'MARA, LLC
Greenwich, CT ....Banking Law; Civil Trial Practice; Commercial Law; Environmental Law; Family Law; General Practice; Land Use Law; Probate, Trusts and Estate Planning; Real Estate Law; Tax Law

IVEY, IVEY, MCCLELLAN & GATTON, L.L.P.
Greensboro, NC.......................General Practice

IVINS, PHILLIPS & BARKER, CHARTERED
Washington, DC.......................Probate, Trusts and Estate Planning; Tax Law

IVONE, DEVINE & JENSEN
Lake Success, NY ....Civil Trial Practice; Insurance Defense; Medical Malpractice

JABURG & WILK, P.C.
Phoenix, AZ ....Probate, Trusts and Estate Planning; Tax Law

JACK, WELLBORN JR.
Shreveport, LA ....Criminal Trial Practice; Personal Injury

JACKL & KATZEN
Walnut Creek, CA ....Business Law; Civil Trial Practice; Construction Law; Real Estate Law

JACKS, ADAMS & WESTERFIELD, P.A.
Cleveland, MS ....General Practice; Insurance Defense

JACKSON, ROBERT JAMES
Springfield, PA ....General Practice

JACKSON & CAMPBELL, P.C.
Washington, DC.......................General Practice

JACKSON, DEMARCO & PECKENPAUGH, A LAW CORPORATION
Irvine, CA................................Business Law; Real Estate Law

JACKSON & FITZGERALD
Roxboro, NC............................Business Law; Probate, Trusts and Estate Planning; Real Estate Law

JACKSON, HARRIS, BURLINGAME & HUBERT
Danielson, CT ....General Practice

JACKSON & JESSUP, P.C.
Arlington, VA ....Transportation Law

JACKSON & KELLY
Washington, DC.......................General Practice
Lexington, KY ....General Practice
Charleston, WV.......................Administrative Law; Admiralty/Maritime Law; Antitrust Law; Banking Law; Bankruptcy Law; Civil Trial Practice; Commercial Law; Construction Law; Criminal Trial Practice; Employment Benefits Law; Environmental Law; General Practice; Health Care Law; Insurance Defense; Labor and Employment Law; Municipal Bond/Public Authority Financing; Natural Resources Law; Probate, Trusts and Estate Planning; Public Utilities Law; Real Estate Law; Securities Law; Tax Law; Transportation Law; Workers Compensation
Charles Town, WV..................General Practice
Martinsburg, WV ....General Practice
Morgantown, WV ....General Practice
New Martinsville, WV ....General Practice

JACKSON LAW CORPORATION
Tustin, CA...............................Patent, Trademark, Copyright and Unfair Competition

JACKSON, LEWIS, SCHNITZLER & KRUPMAN
White Plains, NY ....General Practice

JACKSON, O'KEEFE AND PHELAN
Hartford, CT ....Appellate Practice; Civil Trial Practice; Family Law; General Practice; Insurance Defense; Medical Malpractice; Personal Injury

JACKSON, SHIELDS, YEISER & CANTRELL
Memphis, TN ....Construction Law; Labor and Employment Law; Workers Compensation

JACKSON TUFTS COLE & BLACK, LLP
San Francisco, CA ....General Practice
San Jose, CA ....General Practice

JACKSON & WALKER, L.L.P.
Austin, TX ....Communications Law; General Practice
Dallas, TX...............................Appellate Practice; Banking Law; Civil Trial Practice; Communications Law; Environmental Law; General Practice; Health Care Law; Insurance Defense; International Business Law; Labor and Employment Law; Patent, Trademark, Copyright and Unfair Competition; Personal Injury; Product Liability Law; Real Estate Law; Securities Law; Tax Law
Fort Worth, TX ....Civil Trial Practice; General Practice; Insurance Defense; Labor and Employment Law

Houston, TX ....Civil Trial Practice; Communications Law; Environmental Law; General Practice; Insurance Defense; International Business Law; Personal Injury; Securities Law

San Antonio, TX...................Civil Trial Practice; General Practice; Health Care Law; Insurance Defense; Labor and Employment Law; Personal Injury

JACKSON, WHITE, GARDNER & DECKER, P.C.
Mesa, AZ...............................Business Law; Commercial Litigation; Real Estate Law

JACOB, ARTHUR LAW OFFICES OF
Hackensack, NJ......................Patent, Trademark, Copyright and Unfair Competition

JACOB & WEINGARTEN
Troy, MI ....Bankruptcy Law; Real Estate Law

JACOBS & BARBONE, P.A., A PROFESSIONAL CORPORATION
Atlantic City, NJ....................Civil Trial Practice; General Practice

JACOBS, DARLEEN M., A PROFESSIONAL LAW CORPORATION
New Orleans, LA ....Admiralty/Maritime Law; Personal Injury

JACOBS, GRUDBERG, BELT & DOW, P.C.
New Haven, CT ....Civil Trial Practice; General Practice

JACOBS & JACOBS
New Haven, CT ....Civil Trial Practice; Medical Malpractice; Personal Injury; Product Liability Law

JACOBSON, SANDRA W.
New York, NY........................Family Law

JACOBSON, BRISTOL, GARRETT & SWARTZ
Waukon, IA ....General Practice

JACOBSON AND GOLDBERG
Garden City, NY ....Health Care Law

JACOBSON, PRICE, HOLMAN & STERN
Washington, DC.....................Patent, Trademark, Copyright and Unfair Competition

JACOBSON, SANDERS & BORDY, LLP
Beverly Hills, CA....................Business Law; Civil Trial Practice; Real Estate Law

JACOBSON & SCHWARTZ
Rockville Centre, NY ....Appellate Practice; Insurance Defense

JACOBUS & MELAMED, L.L.P.
Houston, TX ....Real Estate Law

JAFFE & CLEMENS
Beverly Hills, CA....................Family Law

JAFFE, RAITT, HEUER & WEISS, PROFESSIONAL CORPORATION
Detroit, MI.............................Bankruptcy Law; Business Law; Civil Trial Practice; Employment Benefits Law; Environmental Law; Family Law; General Practice; Health Care Law; Municipal Bond/Public Authority Financing; Municipal and Zoning Law; Probate, Trusts and Estate Planning; Real Estate Law; Securities Law; Tax Law

Monroe, MI............................General Practice; Municipal and Zoning Law

Southfield, MI ....General Practice

JAFFE, RICHARD S., P.C.
Birmingham, AL.....................Criminal Trial Practice; Personal Injury

JAHOS, BROEGE & SHAHEEN
Little Silver, NJ......................Civil Trial Practice; General Practice

JAMES, DENECKE & HARRIS, A PROFESSIONAL CORPORATION
Portland, OR..........................Business Law; Civil Trial Practice; Mergers and Acquisitions; Real Estate Law

JAMES, GOLDMAN & HAUGLAND, A PROFESSIONAL CORPORATION
El Paso, TX............................Banking Law; Bankruptcy Law; General Practice; Insurance Defense

JAMES, GRAY & MCCAFFERTY, P.C.
Great Falls, MT ....Civil Trial Practice

JAMES LAW FIRM, THE, P.C.
Des Moines, IA.......................Medical Malpractice; Personal Injury

JAMES, POTTS AND WULFERS, INC.
Tulsa, OK...............................Business Law; Commercial Law; Probate, Trusts and Estate Planning; Real Estate Law; Tax Law

JAMIESON, MOORE, PESKIN & SPICER, A PROFESSIONAL CORPORATION
Princeton, NJ ....General Practice

JAMIN, EBELL, BOLGER & GENTRY, A PROFESSIONAL CORPORATION
Kodiak, AK ....General Practice

JANECKY, NEWELL, POTTS, WELLS & WILSON, P.C.
Birmingham, AL ....Insurance Defense

Mobile, AL.............................Insurance Defense

Pensacola, FL ....Insurance Defense

JANET, WILLOUGHBY & GERSHON, LLC
Baltimore, MD ....Medical Malpractice; Personal Injury; Product Liability Law

JANIK & DUNN
Cleveland, OH ....Appellate Practice; Civil Trial Practice; Construction Law; Environmental Law; General Practice; Insurance Defense; Labor and Employment Law; Personal Injury; Product Liability Law; Securities Law; Trademark, Copyright and Unfair Competition

JANIS, SCHUELKE & WECHSLER
Washington, DC.....................Criminal Trial Practice

JANSSEN, MALLOY, MARCHI, NEEDHAM & MORRISON
Eureka, CA.............................Bankruptcy Law; Insurance Defense

JANUSZEWSKI, MCQUILLAN AND DENIGRIS
New Britain, CT ....General Practice

JARDINE, LOGAN & O'BRIEN, P.L.L.P.
St. Paul, MN ....Civil Trial Practice; Insurance Defense; Personal Injury

JARDINE & PAGANO, A PROFESSIONAL CORPORATION
Springfield, NJ ....Labor and Employment Law; Probate, Trusts and Estate Planning

JASINSKI AND PARANAC, A PROFESSIONAL CORPORATION
Newark, NJ ....Labor and Employment Law

JAVERBAUM WURGAFT & HICKS, A PROFESSIONAL CORPORATION
Springfield, NJ ....Civil Trial Practice; Commercial Litigation; Personal Injury; Product Liability Law

JEANES, LYLE H., II, P.C.
Paris, TX ....Civil Trial Practice; Insurance Defense

JEANSONNE & REMONDET, L.L.C.
Lafayette, LA ....Insurance Defense

JEFFER, HOPKINSON, VOGEL & PEIFFER
Hawthorne, NJ.......................Business Law; Civil Trial Practice; General Practice; Municipal Bond/Public Authority Financing; Municipal and Zoning Law; Real Estate Law

JEFFERS & BANACK, INCORPORATED
San Antonio, TX....................Appellate Practice; Tax Law

JEFFERS, DANIELSON, SONN & AYLWARD, P.S.
Wenatchee, WA......................General Practice

JEFFRIES, OLSON, FLOM & BULLIS, P.A.
Moorhead, MN ....Civil Trial Practice; General Practice

Fargo, ND..............................Civil Trial Practice; General Practice

JELLIFFE, FERRELL & MORRIS
Harrisburg, IL........................Civil Trial Practice; General Practice; Insurance Defense; Workers Compensation

JENKENS & GILCHRIST, A PROFESSIONAL CORPORATION
Dallas, TX..............................General Practice

JENKINS FENSTERMAKER, P.L.L.C.
Huntington, WV ....Business Law; Civil Trial Practice; Commercial Law; General Practice; Insurance Defense; Labor and Employment Law; Medical Malpractice; Probate, Trusts and Estate Planning; Real Estate Law; Tax Law

JENKINS & JENKINS
Knoxville, TN ....Bankruptcy Law; Criminal Trial Practice

JENKINS & NELSON, P.C.
Cartersville, GA ....General Practice

JENKINS, RICHARD E., A PROFESSIONAL ASSOCIATION
Durham, NC ....Patent, Trademark, Copyright and Unfair Competition

JENKS, SURDYK & COWDREY CO., L.P.A.
Dayton, OH............................Civil Trial Practice; Insurance Defense

JENNER & BLOCK
Chicago, IL.............................General Practice

JENNINGS & HAUG
Phoenix, AZ ....Civil Trial Practice; Construction Law

JENNINGS, JENNINGS & MACDONALD, P.C.
West Branch, MI.....................Insurance Defense

JENNINGS, STROUSS AND SALMON, P.L.C.
Phoenix, AZ ....Banking Law; Bankruptcy Law; Civil Trial Practice; Environmental Law; General Practice; Health Care Law; Insurance Defense; Labor and Employment Law; Medical Malpractice; Municipal Bond/Public Authority Financing; Natural Resources Law; Personal Injury; Probate, Trusts and Estate Planning; Real Estate Law; Securities Law; Tax Law; Trademark, Copyright and Unfair Competition

JENSEN BAIRD GARDNER & HENRY
Biddeford, ME ....General Practice
Portland, ME ....Banking Law; Civil Trial Practice; Environmental Law; General Practice; Probate, Trusts and Estate Planning; Real Estate Law

JENSEN, JACQUELINE M., INC.
Irvine, CA.............................Probate, Trusts and Estate Planning

JEPPSON, H. ROY, A PROFESSIONAL CORPORATION
Camarillo, CA ....Business Law; Commercial Litigation; Labor and Employment Law

JEPPSON & LEE, A PROFESSIONAL CORPORATION
Reno, NV ....General Practice

JEWELL, GATZ, COLLINS, FITZGERALD & DELAY
Norfolk, NE ....General Practice

JIMÉNEZ, GRAFFAM & LAUSELL
San Juan, PR..........................Admiralty/Maritime Law; Civil Trial Practice; Environmental Law; General Practice; Insurance Defense; Labor and Employment Law; Medical Malpractice; Personal Injury; Transportation Law

JIMENEZ, JORGE R., LAW OFFICES
San Juan, PR..........................Antitrust Law; Banking Law; Civil Trial Practice; Commercial Law; General Practice; Real Estate Law

JINKERSON, GUYTON N.
San Jose, CA ....Criminal Trial Practice

JOANNES, JOHN A., A PROFESSIONAL CORPORATION
Los Angeles, CA ....Immigration and Naturalization

JOENS, TIMOTHY L., & ASSOC., A PROF. CORP.
Irvine, CA..............................Appellate Practice; Business Law; Civil Trial Practice

JOHNS & FLAHERTY, S.C.
La Crosse, WI ....General Practice

JOHNSEN, ROGER A.
Philadelphia, PA ....Civil Rights; General Practice; International Business Law

JOHNSON, DAVID CROMWELL
Birmingham, AL ....Criminal Trial Practice; Environmental Law; Family Law; Personal Injury; Product Liability Law

JOHNSON, R. TENNEY
Washington, DC......................Administrative Law

JOHNSON, WILLIAM M.
Frankfort, KY ....Real Estate Law

JOHNSON & ASSOCIATES
Houston, TX ....Personal Injury

JOHNSON, AYERS & MATTHEWS
Roanoke, VA...........................General Practice; Insurance Defense; Personal Injury

JOHNSON & BELL, LTD.
Chicago, IL.............................Civil Trial Practice; Environmental Law; Insurance Defense; Medical Malpractice

JOHNSON, BLAKELY, POPE, BOKOR, RUPPEL & BURNS, P.A.
Clearwater, FL ....General Practice
Tampa, FL ....General Practice

JOHNSON & BOWEN
El Paso, TX.............................General Practice

JOHNSON, BUNCE & NOBLE, P.C.
Peoria, IL...............................General Practice

JOHNSON, C. CLAYTON, CO., A LEGAL PROFESSIONAL ASSOCIATION
Portsmouth, OH......................General Practice; Probate, Trusts and Estate Planning

JOHNSON, CLIFTON, LARSON & CORSON, P.C.
Eugene, OR ....Personal Injury; Product Liability Law

JOHNSON, DON, P.S.C.
Newport, KY ....Personal Injury

JOHNSON, DROZDZIK, VAN DRISKA & ANDROS, LTD. A PROFESSIONAL CORPORATION
Chicago, IL.............................Insurance Defense; Workers Compensation

JOHNSON, EMMETT P., & E. PRESTON JOHNSON, JR., P.C.
Baxley, GA ....Civil Trial Practice

JOHNSON, ERB, BICE, KRAMER, GOOD & MULHOLLAND, P.C.
Fort Dodge, IA ....General Practice

JOHNSON, GARY C., P.S.C.
Pikeville, KY ....Commercial Law; Personal Injury

JOHNSON, GREEN, MILLER & GIBSON, P.A.
Milton, FL...............................General Practice

JOHNSON, GRUSIN, KEE & SURPRISE, P.C.
Memphis, TN ....General Practice; Real Estate Law

JOHNSON, HANSEN, SHAMBEAU, MARONEY & ANDERSON, S.C.
Waupaca, WI ....General Practice

JOHNSON, HEIDEPRIEM, MINER & MARLOW
Yankton, SD ....General Practice

JOHNSON, HESTER, WALTER & HARRISON, L.L.P.
Ottumwa, IA ....General Practice

JOHNSON, HOULIHAN, PAULSON & PRIEBE, S.C.
Rhinelander, WI.......................General Practice

JOHNSON HUFFMAN LAW FIRM, L.L.P.
Rapid City, SD.........................Civil Trial Practice; Commercial Law; Medical Malpractice

JOHNSON & JOHNSON, LAW OFFICES
Las Vegas, NV ....Probate, Trusts and Estate Planning

JOHNSON AND JOHNSON, P.A.
Lillington, NC..........................General Practice

JOHNSON, JOHNSON, BARRIOS & YACOUBIAN, A PROFESSIONAL LAW CORPORATION
New Orleans, LA ....Admiralty/Maritime Law; Insurance Defense

JOHNSON & KENNEDY
Wichita, KS ....Insurance Defense

JOHNSON & LAMBETH
Wilmington, NC.......................Criminal Trial Practice; Insurance Defense

JOHNSON, LAWRENCE E., AND ASSOCIATES, P.C., LAW OFFICES OF
Champaign, IL ....General Practice

JOHNSON & MONTGOMERY
Atlanta, GA ....Business Law; Land Use Law; Municipal and Zoning Law

JOHNSON, PEDDRICK, STANALAND, STAKIAS & RIDENHOUR, P.L.L.C.
Greensboro, NC.......................Business Law; Probate, Trusts and Estate Planning; Tax Law

JOHNSON, POULSON, COONS & SLATER
Los Angeles, CA ....Business Law; Civil Trial Practice; Family Law; Probate, Trusts and Estate Planning

JOHNSON & ROCHE
McLean, VA ....Personal Injury

JOHNSON, RODNEY G., LTD.
Phoenix, AZ ....Labor and Employment Law

JOHNSON, ROSATI, GALICA, LABARGE, ASELTYNE, SUGAMELI & FIELD, P.C.
Farmington Hills, MI ....Insurance Defense; Municipal and Zoning Law

JOHNSON, SCHACHTER & COLLINS, A PROFESSIONAL CORPORATION
Sacramento, CA ....Civil Trial Practice; Insurance Defense; Product Liability Law

JOHNSON, SIMMERMAN & BROUGHTON, L.C.
Clarksburg, WV ....Civil Trial Practice; Construction Law; Environmental Law; General Practice; Medical Malpractice; Personal Injury; Probate, Trusts and Estate Planning; Tax Law

JOHNSON, SMITH, PENCE, DENSBORN, WRIGHT & HEATH
Indianapolis, IN ....Administrative Law; Banking Law; Bankruptcy Law; Civil Trial Practice; Commercial Law; Environmental Law; General Practice; Health Care Law; Insurance Defense; Real Estate Law; Securities Law

JOHNSON, SUDENGA, LATHAM, PEGLOW & O'HARE
Marshalltown, IA.....................General Practice

JOHNSON & SYLVAN, P.C.
Dallas, TX...............................Insurance Defense

JOHNSON & TAYLOR
Pontiac, IL..............................Probate, Trusts and Estate Planning; Real Estate Law

JOHNSON & VALENTINE
Detroit, MI ....Business Law; Civil Trial Practice; Probate, Trusts and Estate Planning

JOHNSON & WARD
Atlanta, GA ....Business Law; Civil Trial Practice; General Practice; Personal Injury; Product Liability Law

JOHNSON, WEBBERT & LAUBENSTEIN
Augusta, ME...........................Civil Trial Practice; Insurance Defense; Labor and Employment Law

JOHNSTON, BARTON, PROCTOR & POWELL
Birmingham, AL ....Antitrust Law; Communications Law; General Practice; Labor and Employment Law; Securities Law; Tax Law

JOHNSTON, DAVID C., JR., P.C., LAW OFFICE
Oklahoma City, OK ....Insurance Defense; Product Liability Law

JOHNSTON, HINESLEY, FLOWERS & CLENNEY, P.C., A PROFESSIONAL CORPORATION
Dothan, AL ....Mergers and Acquisitions; Securities Law; Tax Law

JOHNSTON, HOLROYD & ASSOCIATES
Princeton, WV ....General Practice

JOHNSTON, TAYLOR, ALLISON & HORD, PROFESSIONAL ASSOCIATION
Charlotte, NC ....General Practice

JOHNSTON, WILKINS & DRUHAN
Mobile, AL ....Civil Trial Practice; Municipal Bond/Public Authority Financing

JOHNSTONE, ADAMS, BAILEY, GORDON AND HARRIS, L.L.C.
Mobile, AL ....Admiralty/Maritime Law; Antitrust Law; Banking Law; Bankruptcy Law; Business Law; Civil Trial Practice; Construction Law; Employment Benefits Law; Environmental Law; General Practice; Health Care Law; Insurance Defense; Labor and Employment Law; Natural Resources Law; Probate, Trusts and Estate Planning; Real Estate Law; Tax Law

JOLLEY, URGA, WIRTH & WOODBURY
Las Vegas, NV ....Banking Law; Bankruptcy Law; Business Law; Civil Trial Practice; Commercial Law; Commercial Litigation; Construction Law; Environmental Law; Family Law; General Practice; Labor and Employment Law; Natural Resources Law; Personal Injury; Probate, Trusts and Estate Planning; Real Estate Law

JONAS & LASORTE
West Palm Beach, FL ....Commercial Litigation

JONASSEN, WILLIAM S., P.A.
Largo, FL ....Medical Malpractice; Personal Injury

JONES, O. F. III, LAW OFFICE OF
Victoria, TX ....Civil Trial Practice

JONES, RANDOLPH B.
Nashville, TN ....Business Law

JONES & BAHRET CO., L.P.A.
Toledo, OH ....Civil Trial Practice; Insurance Defense

JONES, BLECHMAN, WOLTZ & KELLY, P.C.
Newport News, VA ....General Practice

JONES, CHARTERED
Pocatello, ID ....General Practice

JONES, CORK & MILLER
Macon, GA ....Civil Trial Practice; General Practice

JONES, DAY, REAVIS & POGUE
Irvine, CA ....Civil Trial Practice; General Practice
Los Angeles, CA ....Antitrust Law; Bankruptcy Law; Civil Trial Practice; General Practice; Insurance Defense; Municipal Bond/Public Authority Financing; Patent, Trademark, Copyright and Unfair Competition; Tax Law; Trademark, Copyright and Unfair Competition
Washington, DC ....Antitrust Law; Civil Trial Practice; Criminal Trial Practice; General Practice; Labor and Employment Law; Municipal Bond/Public Authority Financing; Tax Law
Atlanta, GA ....Antitrust Law; Civil Trial Practice; General Practice; Labor and Employment Law; Municipal Bond/Public Authority Financing; Tax Law
Chicago, IL ....Antitrust Law; Civil Trial Practice; Criminal Trial Practice; General Practice; Labor and Employment Law; Municipal Bond/Public Authority Financing; Tax Law
New York, NY ....Civil Trial Practice; Criminal Trial Practice; General Practice; Insurance Defense; Municipal Bond/Public Authority Financing; Patent, Trademark, Copyright and Unfair Competition; Trademark, Copyright and Unfair Competition
Cleveland, OH ....Antitrust Law; Civil Trial Practice; Criminal Trial Practice; General Practice; Insurance Defense; Labor and Employment Law; Municipal Bond/Public Authority Financing; Patent, Trademark, Copyright and Unfair Competition; Real Estate Law; Tax Law; Trademark, Copyright and Unfair Competition
Columbus, OH ....Civil Trial Practice; General Practice; Labor and Employment Law; Municipal Bond/Public Authority Financing
Pittsburgh, PA ....Civil Trial Practice; General Practice; Insurance Defense; Municipal Bond/Public Authority Financing

Dallas, TX ....Antitrust Law; Civil Trial Practice; General Practice; Municipal Bond/Public Authority Financing; Tax Law
Brussels, Belgium ....General Practice
London, England ....General Practice; Tax Law
Paris, France ....General Practice
Frankfurt/Main, Germany ......General Practice
Hong Kong, Hong Kong ....General Practice
Tokyo, Japan ....General Practice
Geneva, Switzerland ....General Practice
Taipei, Taiwan ....General Practice

JONES, E. STEWART
Troy, NY ....Civil Trial Practice; Criminal Trial Practice; General Practice

JONES, FLYGARE, GALEY, BROWN & WHARTON
Lubbock, TX ....General Practice; Insurance Defense

JONES, FOSTER, JOHNSTON & STUBBS, P.A.
West Palm Beach, FL ....Civil Trial Practice; General Practice; Natural Resources Law; Tax Law

JONES, GALLIGAN, KEY & LOZANO, L.L.P.
Weslaco, TX ....General Practice

JONES, GARY L., CO., L.P.A.
Columbus, OH ....Administrative Law

JONES, GIVENS, GOTCHER & BOGAN, A PROFESSIONAL CORPORATION
Tulsa, OK ....Business Law; General Practice

JONES HALL HILL & WHITE, A PROFESSIONAL LAW CORPORATION
San Francisco, CA ....Municipal Bond/Public Authority Financing

JONES, HEWSON & WOOLARD
Charlotte, NC ....General Practice

JONES, IRIS, & ASSOCIATES, P.C.
Austin, TX ....Civil Trial Practice; Labor and Employment Law; Sports and Entertainment Law

JONES, JACKSON & MOLL, PLC
Fort Smith, AR ....Civil Trial Practice; Insurance Defense

JONES AND JONES
Hackensack, NJ ....Banking Law; Commercial Law; Probate, Trusts and Estate Planning

JONES & JONES
Mineola, NY ....Civil Trial Practice; Probate, Trusts and Estate Planning
Marshall, TX ....Civil Trial Practice; Personal Injury

JONES, JONES & LUSHBAUGH, PLC
Fayetteville, AR ....Insurance Defense

JONES, JONES, VINES & HUNKINS
Wheatland, WY ....General Practice

JONES, KAUFMAN & ACKERMAN LLP
Los Angeles, CA ....Real Estate Law; Tax Law

JONES & KELLER, A PROFESSIONAL CORPORATION
Denver, CO ....Administrative Law; Antitrust Law; Bankruptcy Law; Civil Trial Practice; Energy Law; General Practice; Natural Resources Law; Public Utilities Law; Securities Law; Tax Law; Transportation Law

JONES, KEY, MELVIN & PATTON, P.A.
Franklin, NC ....General Practice

JONES KURTH & TREAT, P.C.
San Antonio, TX ....Civil Trial Practice; Insurance Defense

JONES LAW FIRM, THE, P.C.
Albuquerque, NM ....Business Law; Real Estate Law

JONES, NORPELL, LIST, MILLER & HOWARTH
Newark, OH ....General Practice

JONES, OBENCHAIN, FORD, PANKOW, LEWIS & WOODS
South Bend, IN ....Bankruptcy Law; Civil Trial Practice; Commercial Law; Health Care Law; Insurance Defense; Labor and Employment Law; Real Estate Law

JONES, OSTEEN, JONES & ARNOLD
Hinesville, GA ....General Practice; Personal Injury; Product Liability Law

JONES AND SMITH, P.C.
Metter, GA ....General Practice; Personal Injury

JONES, SNEAD, WERTHEIM, WENTWORTH & JARAMILLO, P.A.
Santa Fe, NM ....Civil Trial Practice; Patent, Trademark, Copyright and Unfair Competition; Transportation Law

JONES, TÊTE, NOLEN, HANCHEY, SWIFT, SPEARS & FONTI, L.L.P.
Lake Charles, LA....................Admiralty/Maritime Law; Bankruptcy Law; Civil Trial Practice; General Practice; Insurance Defense; Labor and Employment Law; Probate, Trusts and Estate Planning

JONES & TROUSDALE
Florence, AL ....Insurance Defense; Medical Malpractice; Personal Injury; Product Liability Law

JONES, TROYAN, PAPPAS & PERKINS, A LEGAL PROFESSIONAL ASSOCIATION
Columbus, OH ....Business Law; Employment Benefits Law; Probate, Trusts and Estate Planning; Real Estate Law; Tax Law

JONES, WALDO, HOLBROOK & MCDONOUGH, A PROFESSIONAL CORPORATION
Washington, DC.....................General Practice
St. George, UT ....General Practice
Salt Lake City, UT...................Antitrust Law; Civil Trial Practice; General Practice; Labor and Employment Law; Natural Resources Law; Patent, Trademark, Copyright and Unfair Competition; Real Estate Law

JONES, WALKER, WAECHTER, POITEVENT, CARRÈRE & DENÈGRE, L.L.P.
New Orleans, LA ....General Practice

JONES, WYATT & ROBERTS
Enid, OK ....Civil Trial Practice; Criminal Trial Practice

JONTOS & LOTTY
Fairfield, CT ....Insurance Defense

JOOS, WILLIAM J., P.A.
Jacksonville, FL ....Probate, Trusts and Estate Planning; Real Estate Law

JORDAN COYNE & SAVITS
Washington, DC.....................Insurance Defense
Baltimore, MD ....Insurance Defense
Rockville, MD.........................Insurance Defense
Fairfax, VA ....Insurance Defense
Leesburg, VA ....Insurance Defense

JORDAN AND HAMBURG
New York, NY........................Patent, Trademark, Copyright and Unfair Competition

JORDAN & O'DONNELL
Brunswick, GA........................Civil Trial Practice; Insurance Defense

JORDAN, PRICE, WALL, GRAY & JONES
Raleigh, NC............................Construction Law; General Practice; Health Care Law

JORDAN, SHAW & HYDEN, P.C.
Corpus Christi, TX ....Bankruptcy Law; Commercial Litigation; Real Estate Law

JORDON, WAYNE A.
Alamogordo, NM ....General Practice

JORGENSON, SIEGEL, MCCLURE & FLEGEL
Menlo Park, CA......................General Practice

JORY, PETERSON, WATKINS & SMITH
Fresno, CA ....Business Law; Civil Trial Practice; Commercial Law; Labor and Employment Law

JOSE, HENRY & BRANTLEY
Fort Worth, TX ....Civil Trial Practice; Personal Injury

JOSEPH, RAYMOND
Lansing, MI............................Civil Trial Practice; Insurance Defense; Product Liability Law

JOSEPH, GREENWALD AND LAAKE, P.A.
Greenbelt, MD ....General Practice

JOSEPH & JOSEPH
Columbus, OH ....Family Law; Real Estate Law

JOSEPHS, BONNIE P.
New York, NY.........................Civil Trial Practice

JOSLYN KEYDEL & WALLACE
Detroit, MI.............................Probate, Trusts and Estate Planning; Tax Law

JOYCE, MEREDITH, FLITCROFT & NORMAND
Oak Ridge, TN.......................General Practice

JOYCE AND POLLARD
Tulsa, OK...............................Banking Law; Business Law; Civil Trial Practice; General Practice; Probate, Trusts and Estate Planning

JUDICE & ADLEY, A PROFESSIONAL LAW CORPORATION
Lafayette, LA ....Insurance Defense

JUGE, NAPOLITANO, LEYVA & GUILBEAU
Metairie, LA ....Insurance Defense; Labor and Employment Law

JULIAN & PERTZ, P.C.
Utica, NY ....Medical Malpractice; Personal Injury

JULIEN & SCHLESINGER, P.C.
New York, NY.........................Civil Trial Practice; Medical Malpractice; Personal Injury; Product Liability Law

JUNEAU FIRM, THE, A PROFESSIONAL LAW CORPORATION
Lafayette, LA ....Insurance Defense

JUNKER & THOMPSON, P.C.
Seattle, WA ....International Business Law

KABALA & GEESEMAN, A PROFESSIONAL CORPORATION
Pittsburgh, PA ....General Practice

KADISH, HINKEL & WEIBEL, A LEGAL PROFESSIONAL ASSOCIATION
Cleveland, OH........................Business Law; Construction Law; Employment Benefits Law; General Practice; Health Care Law; Probate, Trusts and Estate Planning; Real Estate Law; Tax Law

KAFTAN, VAN EGEREN & GILSON, S.C.
Green Bay, WI ....General Practice

KAHN, RONALD H. THE LAW OFFICE OF
San Francisco, CA ....Construction Law

KAHN, DEES, DONOVAN & KAHN
Evansville, IN..........................Admiralty/Maritime Law; Banking Law; Civil Trial Practice; Environmental Law; General Practice; Health Care Law; Insurance Defense; Labor and Employment Law; Real Estate Law; Tax Law

KAHN, GERALD H., P.C.
New Haven, CT ....Family Law

KAHN, KLEINMAN, YANOWITZ & ARNSON CO., L.P.A.
Cleveland, OH........................General Practice

KAHN, SMITH & COLLINS, P.A.
Baltimore, MD ....Administrative Law; Labor and Employment Law; Medical Malpractice; Personal Injury

KAHRS, NELSON, FANNING, HITE & KELLOGG, L.L.P.
Wichita, KS.............................Business Law; Civil Trial Practice; General Practice; Insurance Defense; Natural Resources Law; Product Liability Law; Real Estate Law

KAINEN, STARR, GARFIELD, WRIGHT & ESCALERA, P.C.
Hartford, CT ....Labor and Employment Law

KAISER, JACK I. LAW OFFICES
San Francisco, CA ....Immigration and Naturalization

KAJAN MATHER AND BARISH, A PROFESSIONAL CORPORATION
Beverly Hills, CA ....Tax Law

KALAMAROS, EDWARD N., & ASSOCIATES, PROF. CORP.
South Bend, IN ....Civil Trial Practice; General Practice; Insurance Defense; Personal Injury; Product Liability Law; Workers Compensation

KALCHEIM, SCHATZ & BERGER
Chicago, IL.............................Family Law

KALEEL & KALEEL, P.A.
St. Petersburg, FL....................Civil Trial Practice

KALINA, WILLS, WOODS, GISVOLD & CLARK, P.L.L.P.
Minneapolis, MN ....General Practice

KALINOSKI & RIORDAN, P.A.
Towson, MD ....General Practice

KALISH & GILSTER
St. Louis, MO..........................Patent, Trademark, Copyright and Unfair Competition

KALLAY, THOMAS LAW OFFICES OF
Los Angeles, CA ....Appellate Practice

KAMBERG, BERMAN, P.C.
Springfield, MA.......................Bankruptcy Law; Commercial Law

KAMER & ZUCKER
Las Vegas, NV ....Labor and Employment Law

KAMUF, YEWELL, PACE & CONDON
Owensboro, KY ....Business Law; Civil Trial Practice; Criminal Trial Practice; Family Law; General Practice; Personal Injury; Real Estate Law

KANE, DALSIMER, SULLIVAN, KURUCZ, LEVY, EISELE AND RICHARD, LLP
New York, NY.........................Patent, Trademark, Copyright and Unfair Competition

KANE & DONLEY, P.C.
Colorado Springs, CO.............Civil Trial Practice; General Practice; Insurance Defense

KANE, KANE & KANE
Pawhuska, OK ....General Practice

KANE, NORBY & REDDICK, P.C.
Dubuque, IA ....General Practice

KANE OBBISH PROPES & GARIPPO
Chicago, IL.............................Criminal Trial Practice; Medical Malpractice; Personal Injury

KANE, PUGH, KNOELL & DRISCOLL LLP
Norristown, PA.......................Insurance Defense; Medical Malpractice

KANE, SINGER, PLANCK, DONOGHUE, CLARK & MIXSON, P.A.
Rockledge, FL.........................Insurance Defense

KANIA, LINDNER, LASAK AND FEENEY
Bala Cynwyd, PA....................Business Law; Civil Trial Practice; Commercial Law; Commercial Litigation; Mergers and Acquisitions; Real Estate Law

KANTOR, SAPURSTEIN & BLOCH, P.A.
Miami, FL ....Banking Law

KANTROVITZ, MARTIN LAW OFFICES OF
Boston, MA.............................Personal Injury; Product Liability Law

KANTROW, SPAHT, WEAVER & BLITZER, A PROFESSIONAL LAW CORPORATION
Baton Rouge, LA....................Civil Trial Practice; Commercial Law; General Practice; Probate, Trusts and Estate Planning; Real Estate Law

KAPETAN MEYERS ROSEN LOUIK & RAIZMAN, P.C.
Pittsburgh, PA ....Medical Malpractice; Personal Injury; Product Liability Law

KAPLAN, JEROLD
Phoenix, AZ ....Commercial Law

KAPLAN, JOEL S.
Garden City, NY ....Civil Trial Practice; General Practice

KAPLAN & BEGY
Chicago, IL.............................Construction Law; Insurance Defense; Labor and Employment Law; Product Liability Law; Securities Law

KAPLAN, HOWARD GORDON, LTD.
Chicago, IL.............................Business Law; Employment Benefits Law; Real Estate Law

KAPLAN, STRANGIS AND KAPLAN, P.A.
Minneapolis, MN....................General Practice

KAPNER, LEWIS, P.A.
West Palm Beach, FL ....Civil Trial Practice; Family Law

KAPP LAW OFFICES
Cleveland, OH.........................Family Law

KAPS & BARTO
Hackensack, NJ.......................Business Law; Civil Trial Practice; Commercial Law; Construction Law; Environmental Law; Real Estate Law

KARASZKIEWICZ, KIRK T., & ASSOCIATES, P.C.
Philadelphia, PA ....Criminal Trial Practice

KARFELD, EDWARD J.
St. Louis, MO..........................Bankruptcy Law

KARNS & KARABIAN
Los Angeles, CA ....Administrative Law

KARP, DAVID I.
Van Nuys, CA..........................Civil Trial Practice

KARP, ADRIAN I., A PROFESSIONAL CORPORATION
Morris Plains, NJ....................Civil Trial Practice

KARP, HEURLIN & WEISS, P.L.C.
Tucson, AZ ....Family Law

KARSH AND FULTON, PROFESSIONAL CORPORATION
Denver, CO ....Commercial Law; Real Estate Law

KARSMAN, BROOKS & CALLAWAY, P.C.
Savannah, GA ....Commercial Law; Insurance Defense; Labor and Employment Law; Product Liability Law

KASDAN, SIMONDS, MCINTYRE, EPSTEIN & MARTIN
Irvine, CA...............................Construction Law

KASDIN, PETER D., LTD.
Chicago, IL.............................Medical Malpractice; Personal Injury

KASDORF, LEWIS & SWIETLIK, S.C.
Milwaukee, WI.......................Insurance Defense

KASE & DRUKER
Garden City, NY ....Appellate Practice; Commercial Law; Criminal Trial Practice; General Practice; Tax Law

KASMIR & KRAGE, L.L.P.
Dallas, TX ....Appellate Practice; Civil Trial Practice; Commercial Litigation; Real Estate Law; Securities Law; Tax Law

KASS LAW FIRM
Portsmouth, VA ....Personal Injury

KASSAB ARCHBOLD & O'BRIEN, L.L.P.
Media, PA ....Bankruptcy Law; Civil Trial Practice; Commercial Law; Environmental Law; Family Law; General Practice; Labor and Employment Law; Medical Malpractice; Municipal Bond/Public Authority Financing; Personal Injury; Probate, Trusts and Estate Planning; Product Liability Law; Real Estate Law

KASSEL & KASSEL
San Bernardino, CA.................Criminal Trial Practice; General Practice; Health Care Law; Personal Injury

KATARINCIC & SALMON
Pittsburgh, PA ....Civil Trial Practice; Securities Law

KATSKEE, HENATSCH & SUING
Omaha, NE ....Civil Trial Practice; General Practice; Insurance Defense

KATTEN MUCHIN & ZAVIS
Chicago, IL.............................General Practice

KATZ, BIERER & BRADY, A PROFESSIONAL CORPORATION
Larkspur, CA ....Civil Trial Practice; Personal Injury

KATZ, GREENBERGER & NORTON
Cincinnati, OH ....General Practice

KATZ, HOYT, SEIGEL & KAPOR LLP
Los Angeles, CA ....Bankruptcy Law; Commercial Law; Trademark, Copyright and Unfair Competition

KATZ, KANTOR & PERKINS
Bluefield, WV ....General Practice

KATZ & KLEIN
White Plains, NY ....General Practice

KATZ, KUTTER, HAIGLER, ALDERMAN, MARKS, BRYANT & YON, PROFESSIONAL ASSOCIATION
Tallahassee, FL ....Administrative Law

KATZ, MCHARD, BALCH, LEFSTEIN & FIEWEGER, P.C.
Rock Island, IL.......................Civil Trial Practice; General Practice

KATZ, STEVEN M., P.A.
Rockville, MD.........................Business Law; Probate, Trusts and Estate Planning

KATZ, TELLER, BRANT & HILD, A LEGAL PROFESSIONAL ASSOCIATION
Cincinnati, OH ....Banking Law; Bankruptcy Law; Business Law; Civil Trial Practice; Employment Benefits Law; Environmental Law; Family Law; General Practice; Health Care Law; Labor and Employment Law; Municipal and Zoning Law; Probate, Trusts and Estate Planning; Real Estate Law; Securities Law; Tax Law

KAUFMAN & CANOLES, A PROFESSIONAL CORPORATION
Newport News, VA ....General Practice
Norfolk, VA ....General Practice
Virginia Beach, VA ....General Practice

KAUFMAN, CHAIKEN, RICKERTSEN, KREVOLIN, MILLER & HORST, A PROFESSIONAL CORPORATION
Atlanta, GA ....Business Law; Civil Trial Practice; Family Law; General Practice; Personal Injury; Trademark, Copyright and Unfair Competition

KAUFMAN, COREN, RESS, WEIDMAN & SILVERANG, P.C.
Philadelphia, PA ....Civil Trial Practice; Commercial Litigation; General Practice

KAUFMAN & CUMBERLAND CO., L.P.A.
Cleveland, OH.........................Civil Trial Practice; Environmental Law; General Practice; Insurance Defense; Product Liability Law; Real Estate Law

KAUFMAN & FLORENCE
Lebanon, OH...........................General Practice

KAUFMAN & GREEN, L.L.P.
Wilmington, NC......................Banking Law; Real Estate Law

KAUFMAN MILLER DICKSTEIN & GRUNSPAN, P.A.
Miami, FL ....Civil Trial Practice; Personal Injury

KAUFMAN, NANESS, SCHNEIDER & ROSENSWEIG, P.C.
Jericho, NY ....Labor and Employment Law

KAUFMAN AND PAYTON
Farmington Hills, MI ....Insurance Defense

KAUFMAN & ROTHFEDER, P.C.
Montgomery, AL ....Bankruptcy Law; Real Estate Law; Tax Law

KAUFMAN & YOUNG, A PROFESSIONAL CORPORATION
Beverly Hills, CA ....Family Law

KAVALLER, MILES L., A PROFESSIONAL LAW CORPORATION
Beverly Hills, CA ....Transportation Law

KAVANAGH, SCULLY, SUDOW, WHITE & FREDERICK, P.C.
Galesburg, IL ....General Practice
Peoria, IL...............................Civil Trial Practice; General Practice; Labor and Employment Law

KAY, J. BENJAMIN III
Augusta, GA ....Bankruptcy Law; Business Law; Commercial Law

KAY & ANDERSEN, S.C.
Madison, WI ....Civil Trial Practice; Construction Law; General Practice

KAY, CASTO, CHANEY, LOVE & WISE
Charleston, WV ....Civil Trial Practice; General Practice

KAYE, ALLEN E., P.C.
New York, NY ....Immigration and Naturalization

KAYE, SCHOLER, FIERMAN, HAYS & HANDLER, LLP
Los Angeles, CA ....General Practice
Washington, DC.....................General Practice
New York, NY ....General Practice
Hong Kong, Hong Kong........General Practice

KAZAN, MCCLAIN, EDISES, SIMON & ABRAMS, A PROFESSIONAL LAW CORPORATION
Oakland, CA ....Civil Trial Practice; Personal Injury

KAZEE, KINNER & CHAFIN
Prestonsburg, KY ....General Practice; Insurance Defense; Natural Resources Law

KEAN, MILLER, HAWTHORNE, D'ARMOND, MCCOWAN & JARMAN, L.L.P.
Baton Rouge, LA....................Civil Trial Practice; Commercial Law; Environmental Law; General Practice; Labor and Employment Law; Medical Malpractice; Natural Resources Law; Probate, Trusts and Estate Planning; Public Utilities Law; Real Estate Law; Tax Law

KEANE & BEANE, P.C.
White Plains, NY ....Commercial Law; Environmental Law; General Practice; Labor and Employment Law; Municipal and Zoning Law; Real Estate Law

KEANE & REESE, P.A.
St. Petersburg, FL...................Civil Trial Practice

KEANE, WILLIAM T., P.C.
Phoenix, AZ ....Personal Injury

KEARNEY, GARY W.
Pasadena, CA ....Family Law

KEARNEY & WESTFALL
Fort Worth, TX ....Criminal Trial Practice

KEATING, MUETHING & KLEKAMP
Cincinnati, OH ....Banking Law; Civil Trial Practice; General Practice; Insurance Defense; Medical Malpractice; Real Estate Law; Tax Law

KEATON, TURNER & SPITZER
Hohenwald, TN ....General Practice

KEATS, JOHN A.
Fairfax, VA ....General Practice

KECK, MAHIN & CATE
Washington, DC.....................General Practice
Chicago, IL............................Antitrust Law; General Practice

KEEFE, BRENNAN & BRENNAN
Quincy, IL ....Insurance Defense

KEEFE & DEPAULI, P.C.
Fairview Heights, IL...............Civil Trial Practice; Workers Compensation

KEEFER, O'REILLY, FERRARIO AND LUBBERS
Las Vegas, NV ....Business Law; Civil Trial Practice

KEEFER, WOOD, ALLEN & RAHAL
Harrisburg, PA.......................Civil Trial Practice; General Practice; Health Care Law; Tax Law

KEEGAN, KEEGAN & ASSOCIATES, P.C.
White Plains, NY ....Medical Malpractice; Personal Injury

KEENER DOUCHER CURLEY & PATTERSON, A LEGAL PROFESSIONAL ASSOCIATION
Columbus, OH ....Civil Trial Practice; Insurance Defense; Medical Malpractice; Personal Injury; Product Liability Law

KEENER & KEENER
Centre, AL ....General Practice

KEGAN & KEGAN, LTD.
Chicago, IL............................Computer Law; Patent, Trademark, Copyright and Unfair Competition

KEHART, SHAFTER, HUGHES & WEBBER, P.C.
Decatur, IL.............................General Practice

KEHOE, DENNIS J., A LAW CORPORATION
Aptos, CA ....Civil Trial Practice; Environmental Law; Personal Injury

KEILP, JOE, P.C.
Phoenix, AZ ....Criminal Trial Practice

KEIL & WEINKAUF
Washington, DC.....................Patent, Trademark, Copyright and Unfair Competition

KEISER, JEFFREY M.
Haddonfield, NJ......................Civil Trial Practice

KEITGES, BANGLE & OWENSBY, A PROFESSIONAL LAW CORPORATION
Sacramento, CA ....Insurance Defense

KEITH, DARRELL, P.C., LAW FIRM OF
Fort Worth, TX ....Medical Malpractice

KEITH, MACK, LEWIS, COHEN & LUMPKIN
Miami, FL ....Appellate Practice; Banking Law; Construction Law; Environmental Law; General Practice; Real Estate Law

KEKER & VAN NEST, L.L.P.
San Francisco, CA ....Civil Trial Practice

KELAHER, CONNELL & CONNOR, P.A.
Surfside Beach, SC ....Civil Trial Practice; Personal Injury

KELAHER, GARVEY, BALLOU & VAN DYKE, A PROFESSIONAL CORPORATION
Toms River, NJ......................Civil Trial Practice; General Practice

KELAHER, WIELAND AND HILADO, P.A.
Orlando, FL ....Medical Malpractice; Personal Injury; Workers Compensation

KELEGIAN & THOMAS
Newport Beach, CA ....Civil Trial Practice; Construction Law; Insurance Defense; Personal Injury; Product Liability Law

KELEHER & MCLEOD, P.A.
Albuquerque, NM...................Insurance Defense; Probate, Trusts and Estate Planning; Real Estate Law

KELLAM, W. J. JR.
Charlotte, NC.........................Real Estate Law

KELLER, JENNIFER L. LAW OFFICES OF
Irvine, CA..............................Criminal Trial Practice

KELLER AND CURTIN CO., L.P.A.
Cleveland, OH........................Civil Trial Practice; Environmental Law; General Practice; Insurance Defense; Product Liability Law

KELLER AND PAINE
Florence, AL ....Insurance Defense; Probate, Trusts and Estate Planning; Tax Law

KELLER, REYNOLDS, DRAKE, JOHNSON & GILLESPIE, P.C.
Helena, MT ....Civil Trial Practice; Insurance Defense

KELLER, THOMA, SCHWARZE, SCHWARZE, DUBAY & KATZ, P.C.
Detroit, MI.............................Appellate Practice; Civil Trial Practice; Employment Benefits Law; General Practice; Insurance Defense; Labor and Employment Law; Probate, Trusts and Estate Planning; Workers Compensation

KELLETT & KELLETT, P.A.
Fort Payne, AL.......................General Practice; Insurance Defense

KELLEY, BELCHER & BROWN, A PROFESSIONAL CORPORATION
Bloomington, IN.....................Civil Trial Practice; Insurance Defense; Personal Injury; Product Liability Law

KELLEY DRYE & WARREN LLP
New York, NY........................General Practice

KELLEY, HERMAN & MILLS
Fort Lauderdale, FL ....Probate, Trusts and Estate Planning; Real Estate Law

KELLEY, JASONS, McGUIRE & SPINELLI, L.L.P.
Philadelphia, PA ....Civil Trial Practice; Commercial Law; Environmental Law; Insurance Defense; Personal Injury; Product Liability Law

KELLEY & LOVETT, P.C.
Albany, GA............................Bankruptcy Law

KELLEY, McCANN & LIVINGSTONE
Cleveland, OH........................Appellate Practice; Bankruptcy Law; Business Law; Civil Trial Practice; Environmental Law; Family Law; General Practice; Labor and Employment Law; Municipal and Zoning Law; Real Estate Law; Securities Law

KELLEY & MURPHY
Blue Bell, PA...........................Administrative Law; General Practice

KELLEY, SCRITSMIER & BYRNE, P.C.
North Platte, NE ....General Practice

KELLEY, WEBER, PIETZ & SLATER, S.C.
Wausau, WI............................Civil Trial Practice

KELL & LYNCH, P.C.
Birmingham, MI.....................Civil Trial Practice; Commercial Law; Commercial Litigation; Insurance Defense; Medical Malpractice; Personal Injury; Product Liability Law

KELL, NUELLE & LOIZZO
Woodstock, IL ....General Practice

KELLOGG AND EVANS, L.L.P.
Manteo, NC ....General Practice

KELLUM & JONES, P.A.
New Bern, NC ....Civil Trial Practice; Personal Injury

KELLY AFFLECK GREENE
Toronto, ON, Canada..............Bankruptcy Law; Civil Trial Practice

KELLY, BAUERSFELD, LOWRY & KELLEY
Woodland Hills, CA ....Patent, Trademark, Copyright and Unfair Competition

KELLY, BLACK, BLACK, BYRNE & BEASLEY, PROFESSIONAL ASSOCIATION
Miami, FL ....Civil Trial Practice; General Practice

KELLY, HART & HALLMAN, A PROFESSIONAL CORPORATION
Fort Worth, TX ....General Practice

KELLY, J. MICHAEL, & ASSOCIATES, A PROF. CORP.
Santa Monica, CA....................Family Law

KELLY, PESSOLANO & WITHERS, P.C.
Springfield, MA......................Insurance Defense

KELLY, RODE & KELLY, LLP
Mineola, NY............................Insurance Defense

KELLY & RYBERG, S.C.
Eau Claire, WI ....Civil Trial Practice; Insurance Defense

KELLY, TIMOTHY F., LAW OFFICES OF
Munster, IN ....Civil Trial Practice; General Practice; Insurance Defense; Labor and Employment Law; Medical Malpractice; Personal Injury; Product Liability Law

KELLY & WEAVER, A PROFESSIONAL CORPORATION
Washington, DC......................Environmental Law

KELSCH KELSCH RUFF & KRANDA P.L.L.P.
Mandan, ND ....Environmental Law; General Practice

KEMP, DUCKETT, HOPKINS & SPRADLEY
Little Rock, AR ....General Practice

KEMP AND KEMP
Hopkinsville, KY ....General Practice; Personal Injury

KEMP, SMITH, DUNCAN & HAMMOND, A PROFESSIONAL CORPORATION
Albuquerque, NM....................General Practice
El Paso, TX.............................Antitrust Law; General Practice; Labor and Employment Law; Tax Law

KEMPE, JOSEPH C., PROFESSIONAL ASSOCIATION
Jupiter, FL.............................Probate, Trusts and Estate Planning; Tax Law
Stuart, FL...............................Probate, Trusts and Estate Planning; Tax Law
Vero Beach, FL.......................Probate, Trusts and Estate Planning; Tax Law

KENDALL, HUGH F., ATTORNEY, P.C.
Chattanooga, TN ....Probate, Trusts and Estate Planning; Real Estate Law; Tax Law

KENDRICKS BORDEAU, P.C.
Marquette, MI........................General Practice

KENEFICK, THOMAS A., III, P.C., LAW OFFICES OF
Springfield, MA......................Medical Malpractice; Personal Injury

KENNEDY, JAMES L. JR.
Ketchum, ID ....Environmental Law; Natural Resources Law; Real Estate Law

KENNEDY & CHRISTOPHER, P.C.
Denver, CO ....Civil Trial Practice; Medical Malpractice

KENNEDY, CICCONETTI & RICKETT, L.P.A.
Wooster, OH ....Civil Trial Practice

KENNEDY & COMERFORD
Mineola, NY...........................Commercial Law; General Practice; Insurance Defense; Labor and Employment Law; Real Estate Law

KENNEDY COVINGTON LOBDELL & HICKMAN, L.L.P.
Charlotte, NC.........................General Practice
Raleigh, NC.............................General Practice
Rock Hill, SC..........................General Practice

KENNEDY & KENNEDY
Bloomfield, NJ ....Appellate Practice; Civil Trial Practice; Insurance Defense; Product Liability Law

KENNEDY LILLIS SCHMIDT & ENGLISH
New York, NY........................Admiralty/Maritime Law

KENNEDY & NERVIG
Wadena, MN...........................General Practice

KENNEDY, RICHARD R., A PROFESSIONAL LAW CORPORATION
Lafayette, LA ....Admiralty/Maritime Law; Civil Trial Practice; General Practice; Personal Injury

KENNEY & KEARNEY
Cherry Hill, NJ ....Civil Trial Practice

KENNEY, LACER, SPARLING, DENSFORD AND REYNOLDS, P.A.
Lexington Park, MD...............General Practice

KENNY, BRIMMER, MELLEY & MAHONEY
Hartford, CT ....Environmental Law; General Practice; Insurance Defense; Medical Malpractice; Personal Injury

KENNY NACHWALTER SEYMOUR ARNOLD CRITCHLOW & SPECTOR, PROFESSIONAL ASSOCIATION
Miami, FL ....Antitrust Law; Civil Trial Practice; General Practice; Trademark, Copyright and Unfair Competition

KENNY & STEARNS
Newark, NJ ....Admiralty/Maritime Law; Civil Trial Practice
New York, NY........................Admiralty/Maritime Law; Civil Trial Practice

KENNY, VETTORI & ROBINSON, P.A.
Baltimore, MD ....Civil Trial Practice

KENT, HAZZARD, JAEGER, GREER, WILSON & FAY
White Plains, NY ....General Practice; Probate, Trusts and Estate Planning

KENT, WORSHAM & SMART
Savannah, GA ....Insurance Defense

KENYON & KENYON
Washington, DC......................Patent, Trademark, Copyright and Unfair Competition
New York, NY........................Patent, Trademark, Copyright and Unfair Competition

KEOGH, BURKHART & VETTER
Norwalk, CT ....General Practice

KEPKE, CARLOS E. LAW OFFICE OF
Houston, TX ....International Trade Law

KEPLEY, GILLIGAN & EYRICH, A LEGAL PROFESSIONAL ASSOCIATION
Cincinnati, OH ....Business Law; Civil Trial Practice; Personal Injury; Real Estate Law; Workers Compensation

KERKAM, STOWELL, KONDRACKI & CLARKE, P.C.
Falls Church, VA....................Patent, Trademark, Copyright and Unfair Competition

KERN, LAWRENCE E., A LAW CORPORATION
San Francisco, CA ....Insurance Defense

KERN, ROACH & CARPENTER, P.C.
Boston, MA.............................Civil Trial Practice; Commercial Litigation

KERN, STREETER & GONZALEZ
Los Angeles, CA ....Construction Law; Insurance Defense; Medical Malpractice; Product Liability Law

KERNAN AND KERNAN, P.C.
Utica, NY ....General Practice; Personal Injury

KERR, ANN LOUGHRIDGE
Clearwater, FL ....Family Law

KERR, IRVINE, RHODES & ABLES, A PROFESSIONAL CORPORATION
Oklahoma City, OK.................Administrative Law; Civil Trial Practice; Environmental Law; General Practice; Insurance Defense; Labor and Employment Law

KERR & WARD, L.L.P.
Midland, TX ....Business Law; Civil Trial Practice; General Practice; Health Care Law; Natural Resources Law

KERRICK, GRISE & STIVERS
Bowling Green, KY ....Appellate Practice; Business Law; Civil Trial Practice; Commercial Law; General Practice; Health Care Law; Insurance Defense; Labor and Employment Law; Medical Malpractice; Personal Injury; Probate, Trusts and Estate Planning; Product Liability Law; Real Estate Law

KERRIGAN, ESTESS, RANKIN & MCLEOD
Pensacola, FL........................Civil Trial Practice; Medical Malpractice; Personal Injury

KERSTEN & MCKINNON, S.C.
Milwaukee, WI.......................Antitrust Law; Civil Trial Practice; Commercial Litigation; Personal Injury

KESHEN, NELSON C., P.A.
Miami, FL ....Probate, Trusts and Estate Planning

KESLER & RUST, A PROFESSIONAL CORPORATION
Salt Lake City, UT.................Business Law

KESSLER & COHEN, A PROFESSIONAL CORPORATION
Philadelphia, PA ....Civil Trial Practice; Medical Malpractice; Personal Injury; Product Liability Law

KESSLER, MASSEY, CATRI, HOLTON & KESSLER, P.A.
Fort Lauderdale, FL ....Appellate Practice; Civil Trial Practice; Insurance Defense; Personal Injury; Product Liability Law; Workers Compensation

KESSNER DUCA UMEBAYASHI BAIN & MATSUNAGA, ATTORNEYS AT LAW, A LAW CORPORATION
Honolulu, HI..........................Banking Law; Insurance Defense; Product Liability Law; Workers Compensation

KETCHAM & KETCHAM
Columbus, OH ....Criminal Trial Practice; Probate, Trusts and Estate Planning

KETCHEY HORAN, P.A.
Tampa, FL ....Bankruptcy Law; Commercial Litigation

KEULING-STOUT, P.C.
Big Stone Gap, VA ....Civil Trial Practice; General Practice

KEYES AND DONNELLAN, P.C.
Springfield, MA......................Personal Injury

KEYSER MASON BALL
Mississauga, ON, Canada.......Banking Law
Toronto, ON, Canada.............Banking Law

KEYWELL AND ROSENFELD
Troy, MI................................Business Law; Civil Trial Practice; Labor and Employment Law; Probate, Trusts and Estate Planning

KEZIAH, GATES & SAMET, L.L.P.
High Point, NC.......................General Practice

KIDD & WITCHER
Decatur, GA...........................General Practice

KIERNAN, PLUNKETT & REDIHAN
Providence, RI.......................Civil Trial Practice; Environmental Law; Insurance Defense; Personal Injury

KIESEWETTER WISE KAPLAN SCHWIMMER & PRATHER, PLC
Memphis, TN ....Labor and Employment Law

KIESLER & BERMAN
Chicago, IL.............................Civil Trial Practice; Insurance Defense

KIGER & ALPERN
Pittsburgh, PA ....Civil Trial Practice; General Practice; Insurance Defense; Personal Injury; Product Liability Law

KIGHTLINGER & GRAY
Evansville, IN ....General Practice
Indianapolis, IN ....Civil Trial Practice; General Practice
New Albany, IN ....General Practice

KILBORNE, ROBERT S. IV, LAW OFFICES OF
San Diego, CA ....Business Law; Civil Trial Practice; Insurance Defense; Medical Malpractice; Personal Injury

KILEY, FELDMANN, WHALEN, DEVINE & PATANE, P.C.
Oneida, NY ....Civil Trial Practice

KILEY, KILEY, HARKER, MICHAEL & CERTAIN
Marion, IN ....Appellate Practice; Business Law; Civil Trial Practice; Commercial Litigation; Family Law; General Practice; Insurance Defense; Labor and Employment Law; Personal Injury; Probate, Trusts and Estate Planning; Real Estate Law; Workers Compensation

KILGORE, DONALD C.
Portsmouth, VA ....Commercial Law; General Practice

KILGORE & KILGORE, A PROFESSIONAL CORPORATION
Dallas, TX..............................Civil Trial Practice; General Practice; Natural Resources Law

KILLIAN AND BOYD
Brunswick, GA.......................Bankruptcy Law; Personal Injury

KILLIAN & GEPHART
Harrisburg, PA.......................Administrative Law; Civil Trial Practice; Criminal Trial Practice; Environmental Law; Labor and Employment Law

KILLIAN, NICHOLAS, FISCHER, WIRKEN, COOK & PEW, P.L.C.
Mesa, AZ................................General Practice

KILLWORTH, GOTTMAN, HAGAN & SCHAEFF
Dayton, OH............................Patent, Trademark, Copyright and Unfair Competition

KILPATRICK & CODY
Atlanta, GA ....Antitrust Law; Business Law; Civil Trial Practice; Communications Law; Employment Benefits Law; Environmental Law; General Practice; Health Care Law; Immigration and Naturalization; International Business Law; Labor and Employment Law; Patent, Trademark, Copyright and Unfair Competition; Product Liability Law; Real Estate Law; Securities Law; Tax Law
Augusta, GA ....Civil Trial Practice; General Practice
Washington, DC.....................General Practice

KIMBALL, PARR, WADDOUPS, BROWN & GEE, A PROFESSIONAL CORPORATION
Salt Lake City, UT.................Civil Trial Practice; Environmental Law; General Practice; Insurance Defense; Natural Resources Law; Real Estate Law

KIMBLE, GOTHREAU & NELSON, P.C.
Tucson, AZ ....Civil Trial Practice; General Practice; Insurance Defense; Medical Malpractice; Product Liability Law

KIMBLE, MACMICHAEL & UPTON, A PROFESSIONAL CORPORATION
Fresno, CA ....Banking Law; Bankruptcy Law; Business Law; Civil Trial Practice; Construction Law; Employment Benefits Law; Health Care Law; Patent, Trademark, Copyright and Unfair Competition; Probate, Trusts and Estate Planning; Real Estate Law; Tax Law

KIMERER & LAVELLE, P.L.C.
Phoenix, AZ ....Antitrust Law; Civil Trial Practice; Commercial Litigation; Criminal Trial Practice

KIMMEL, JAMES S.
Littleton, CO ....General Practice

KIMMEL, LANCE JON
Los Angeles, CA ....Business Law

KIMMEL, CARTER & ROMAN, P.A.
Wilmington, DE......................Civil Trial Practice; Personal Injury; Workers Compensation

KINCAID, TAYLOR & GEYER
Zanesville, OH........................General Practice

KINDER, WUERFEL & CHOLAKIAN, A PROFESSIONAL CORPORATION
San Francisco, CA ....Civil Trial Practice; Commercial Litigation; Construction Law; Insurance Defense

KING, A. DUNCAN
Palo Alto, CA ....Natural Resources Law; Real Estate Law; Tax Law

KING, JOHN ROBERT LAW OFFICE OF
McAllen, TX ....Civil Trial Practice; Family Law; Real Estate Law

KING ALLEN & GUTHRIE
Charleston, WV......................Administrative Law; Appellate Practice; Civil Trial Practice; Criminal Trial Practice; Health Care Law; Tax Law

KING & BALLOW
San Diego, CA ....General Practice; Immigration and Naturalization
Nashville, TN.........................Antitrust Law; Civil Trial Practice; Communications Law; General Practice; Labor and Employment Law; Tax Law; Trademark, Copyright and Unfair Competition

KING & BLACKWELL, P.A.
Orlando, FL ....Civil Trial Practice; Commercial Litigation; Personal Injury

KING & CROFT
Atlanta, GA ....Civil Trial Practice

KING, DEEP AND BRANAMAN
Henderson, KY ....Bankruptcy Law; Civil Trial Practice; General Practice; Insurance Defense; Natural Resources Law; Real Estate Law

KING AND KING
Jackson, WY...........................Civil Trial Practice; Personal Injury

KING, MCCARDLE, HERMAN, FREUND & OLEXA
Allentown, PA ....General Practice

KING, PAGANO & HARRISON
Washington, DC.....................Civil Trial Practice
New York, NY.......................Antitrust Law; Civil Trial Practice; Labor and Employment Law

KING ● PETERSON ● BROWN, LLC
Englewood, CO ....Civil Trial Practice; Personal Injury

KING, ROBERTS & BEELER
Oklahoma City, OK................Civil Trial Practice; Insurance Defense; Workers Compensation

KING AND SCHICKLI
Lexington, KY ....Patent, Trademark, Copyright and Unfair Competition

KING & VERNON, P.A.
Columbia, SC ....Civil Trial Practice; Criminal Trial Practice; Family Law; General Practice

KINGCADE, THOMAS E., PROFESSIONAL ASSOCIATION
West Palm Beach, FL ....Civil Trial Practice; Commercial Litigation

KINGERY, DURREE, WAKEMAN & RYAN, ASSOC.
Peoria, IL...............................Civil Trial Practice; General Practice

KINKEAD & COLLIER
Lexington, KY ....Civil Trial Practice; Criminal Trial Practice; Energy Law; General Practice; Insurance Defense

KINKLE, RODIGER AND SPRIGGS, PROFESSIONAL CORPORATION
Santa Barbara, CA ....Civil Trial Practice; Insurance Defense; Personal Injury; Product Liability Law

KINNARD, CLAYTON & BEVERIDGE
Nashville, TN..........................Personal Injury

KINNEY, KEMP, PICKELL, SPONCLER & JOINER
Dalton, GA ....Insurance Defense; Workers Compensation

KIPLE, KIPLE, DENEFE, BEAVER & GARDNER
Ottumwa, IA ....General Practice

KIPP AND CHRISTIAN, P.C.
Salt Lake City, UT..................Banking Law; Civil Trial Practice; General Practice; Insurance Defense; Personal Injury

KIRBY, JACK ARTHUR
Wayne, PA ....Probate, Trusts and Estate Planning

KIRBY, PATRICK M., A PROF. CORP., LAW OFFICES OF
Flint, MI.................................Civil Rights; Civil Trial Practice; Insurance Defense; Labor and Employment Law

KIRCH, DAVID W., P.C.
Aurora, CO ....Probate, Trusts and Estate Planning

KIRKLAND & ELLIS
Los Angeles, CA ....Criminal Trial Practice

KIRKPATRICK & LOCKHART LLP
Pittsburgh, PA ....General Practice

KIRK PINKERTON, A PROFESSIONAL ASSOCIATION
Sarasota, FL ....Administrative Law; Real Estate Law

KIRLIN, CAMPBELL & KEATING
Washington, DC.....................Admiralty/Maritime Law; General Practice; International Business Law
New York, NY.......................Administrative Law; Admiralty/Maritime Law; General Practice; International Business Law

KIRSCHNER, MAIN, GRAHAM, TANNER & DEMONT, PROFESSIONAL ASSOCIATION
Jacksonville, FL ....Bankruptcy Law; Commercial Law; Commercial Litigation; Mergers and Acquisitions; Real Estate Law

KIRSCHNIK, JAMES L., S.C.
Milwaukee, WI ....Construction Law

KIRSHENBAUM LAW ASSOCIATES
Warwick, RI ....Civil Trial Practice; Family Law; Personal Injury

KIRSHMAN, HARRIS & COOPER, A PROFESSIONAL CORPORATION
Las Vegas, NV ....Labor and Employment Law

KIRTON & MCCONKIE, A PROFESSIONAL CORPORATION
Salt Lake City, UT..................Civil Trial Practice; Commercial Law; General Practice; Insurance Defense; Personal Injury; Probate, Trusts and Estate Planning; Real Estate Law

KIRVEN & KIRVEN, P.C.
Buffalo, WY...........................General Practice; Real Estate Law

KIRWAN & BARRETT, P.C.
Bozeman, MT.........................Appellate Practice; Banking Law; Business Law; Civil Trial Practice; Commercial Law; Construction Law; Labor and Employment Law; Municipal and Zoning Law; Personal Injury; Probate, Trusts and Estate Planning; Real Estate Law

KISSOON, CLUGG, LINDER & DITTBERNER, LTD.
Edina, MN ....Family Law

KITCHEN, DEERY & BARNHOUSE CO., L.P.A.
Cleveland, OH ....Civil Trial Practice; Insurance Defense

KITCHENS, BENTON, KITCHENS & WARREN, A PROFESSIONAL LAW CORPORATION
Minden, LA ....General Practice

KITCHIN, NEAL, WEBB & FUTRELL, P.A.
Rockingham, NC ....General Practice

KITRICK, MARK, CO., L.P.A.
Columbus, OH ....Civil Trial Practice; Personal Injury

KITTREDGE, DONLEY, ELSON, FULLEM & EMBICK, LLP
Philadelphia, PA ....Antitrust Law; Civil Trial Practice; Commercial Litigation; Employment Benefits Law; Environmental Law; Insurance Defense; Labor and Employment Law; Personal Injury; Product Liability Law; Tax Law

KIZER AND BLACK
Maryville, TN..........................General Practice

KIZER, HOOD & MORGAN, L.L.P.
Baton Rouge, LA....................Bankruptcy Law; Real Estate Law

KIZER & NEU
Bremen, IN.............................General Practice
Plymouth, IN ....General Practice

KLAINE, WILEY, HOFFMANN & MEURER, A LEGAL PROFESSIONAL ASSOCIATION
Cincinnati, OH ....Business Law; Commercial Law; Employment Benefits Law; General Practice; Labor and Employment Law; Municipal and Zoning Law; Probate, Trusts and Estate Planning; Real Estate Law; Securities Law; Tax Law

KLARQUIST SPARKMAN CAMPBELL LEIGH & WHINSTON, LLP
Portland, OR..........................Patent, Trademark, Copyright and Unfair Competition

KLAUBER & JACKSON
Hackensack, NJ......................Patent, Trademark, Copyright and Unfair Competition; Trademark, Copyright and Unfair Competition

KLECAN, CHILDRESS & HULING
Albuquerque, NM...................Insurance Defense

KLEHR, HARRISON, HARVEY, BRANZBURG & ELLERS
Philadelphia, PA ....Banking Law; Bankruptcy Law; Business Law; Commercial Law; Environmental Law; General Practice; Real Estate Law; Securities Law; Tax Law

KLEIN, HOWARD BRUCE
Philadelphia, PA ....Civil Trial Practice; Criminal Trial Practice; Health Care Law

KLEIN, WEGIS, DENATALE, GOLDNER & MUIR, LLP
Bakersfield, CA ....Bankruptcy Law; Civil Trial Practice; Commercial Law; Construction Law; Environmental Law; General Practice; Labor and Employment Law; Personal Injury; Probate, Trusts and Estate Planning; Real Estate Law; Tax Law

KLEINBARD, BELL & BRECKER
Philadelphia, PA ....Commercial Litigation; General Practice; Labor and Employment Law; Mergers and Acquisitions; Securities Law

KLEINPETER & KLEINPETER
Baton Rouge, LA....................Civil Trial Practice; Insurance Defense

KLENDA, MITCHELL, AUSTERMAN & ZUERCHER, L.L.C.
Wichita, KS ....General Practice

KLIEBENSTEIN, HERONIMUS & SCHMIDT
Grundy Center, IA..................General Practice

KLINE, JOHN R., P.C.
Helena, MT ....Probate, Trusts and Estate Planning; Tax Law

KLINE & SPECTER
Philadelphia, PA ....Civil Trial Practice

KLOS, FLYNN & PAPENFUSS, CHARTERED
La Crosse, WI ....General Practice

KLUGER, PERETZ, KAPLAN & BERLIN, P.A.
Miami, FL ....Civil Trial Practice

KLUTTZ, REAMER, BLANKENSHIP, HAYES & RANDOLPH, L.L.P.
Salisbury, NC ....General Practice; Insurance Defense

KNAPP, MARSH, JONES & DORAN
Los Angeles, CA ....General Practice

KNEE & MASON
Los Angeles, CA ....Labor and Employment Law

KNIGHT, DAHOOD, MCLEAN & EVERETT
Anaconda, MT ....General Practice

KNIGHT, DUDLEY, CLARKE & DOLPH, P.L.C.
Norfolk, VA ....Civil Trial Practice

KNIGHT, FORD, WRIGHT, ATWILL, PARSHALL & BAKER
Columbia, MO ....General Practice

KNIGHT, MANZI, BRENNAN, SHAY AND HAM, A PROFESSIONAL ASSOCIATION
Upper Marlboro, MD.............Administrative Law; Banking Law; Civil Trial Practice; Commercial Law; Criminal Trial Practice; Family Law; General Practice; Municipal Bond/Public Authority Financing; Real Estate Law

KNIGHT, MASAR & POORE, PLLP
Missoula, MT.........................General Practice; Real Estate Law

KNOBBE, MARTENS, OLSON & BEAR, LLP
Newport Beach, CA.................Patent, Trademark, Copyright and Unfair Competition

KNOLLER, GUY DAVID, P.C.
Phoenix, AZ ....Commercial Litigation; Labor and Employment Law

KNOPFLER & ROBERTSON, A PROFESSIONAL LAW CORPORATION
Los Angeles, CA ....Construction Law

KNOTT, JOHN K. JR.
Cheshire, CT............................Municipal and Zoning Law

KNOWLES & ASSOCIATES
Carmel, IN ....Business Law; Civil Trial Practice; Criminal Trial Practice; Probate, Trusts and Estate Planning

KNOX MCLAUGHLIN GORNALL & SENNETT, P.C.
Erie, PA..................................General Practice

KNOX AND SWAN
Thomson, GA ....General Practice

KNOX & TOLLEFSON, P.C.
Irving, TX ....Insurance Defense

KNUDSEN, BERKHEIMER, RICHARDSON, ENDACOTT & ROUTH
Lincoln, NE.............................General Practice; Securities Law

KOBAYASHI, SUGITA & GODA
Honolulu, HI...........................Business Law; Commercial Law; General Practice; Real Estate Law

KOBLENTZ & KOBLENTZ
Cleveland, OH.........................Civil Trial Practice; Criminal Trial Practice; Family Law

KOCH, JONATHAN C., P.A.
Tampa, FL ....Commercial Litigation

KOCHA, STUART E., P.A.
West Palm Beach, FL ....Civil Trial Practice; Medical Malpractice; Personal Injury

KOEPKE, KARL O.
Orlando, FL ....Medical Malpractice; Personal Injury

KOEPPEL MARTONE LEISTMAN & HERMAN, L.L.P.
Mineola, NY............................Real Estate Law

KOFF, WENDOLOWSKI, FERGUSON & MANGAN, P.C.
Wilkes-Barre, PA ....Labor and Employment Law

KOHN, MICHAEL G.
Cincinnati, OH ....Civil Trial Practice

KOHN PARTNERSHIP, THE, L.L.C.
St. Louis, MO.........................Mergers and Acquisitions; Tax Law

KOHN, SHANDS, ELBERT, GIANOULAKIS & GILJUM, LLP
St. Louis, MO.........................Antitrust Law; Labor and Employment Law; Tax Law

KOHNER, MANN & KAILAS, S.C.
Milwaukee, WI ....Banking Law; Bankruptcy Law; Business Law; Civil Trial Practice; Commercial Law; Construction Law

KOHORST LAW FIRM
Harlan, IA ....Insurance Defense; Product Liability Law

KOHRS, FISKE & STEUR
Santa Monica, CA....................Insurance Defense

KOKJER, KIRCHER, BOWMAN & JOHNSON, A PROFESSIONAL CORPORATION
Kansas City, MO ....Patent, Trademark, Copyright and Unfair Competition

KOLB AND HEBAN
Toledo, OH ....Probate, Trusts and Estate Planning

KOLCZYNSKI, PHILLIP J.
Irvine, CA................................Aviation Law

KOLESAR & LEATHAM, CHARTERED
Las Vegas, NV ....Banking Law; Bankruptcy Law; Commercial Litigation; Probate, Trusts and Estate Planning; Real Estate Law

KOLEY, JESSEN, DAUBMAN & RUPIPER, PROFESSIONAL CORPORATION
Omaha, NE ....General Practice

KOLISCH HARTWELL DICKINSON MCCORMACK & HEUSER, A PROFESSIONAL CORPORATION
Palo Alto, CA ....Patent, Trademark, Copyright and Unfair Competition
Portland, OR...........................Patent, Trademark, Copyright and Unfair Competition

KOLLMAN & SHEEHAN, P.A.
Baltimore, MD ....Business Law; Construction Law; Labor and Employment Law

KOLODNY & ANTEAU
Beverly Hills, CA.....................Family Law

KOLTS AND NAWA
Pasadena, CA ....Insurance Defense; Product Liability Law

KOLVOORD, OVERTON AND WILSON
Essex Junction, VT ....General Practice; Personal Injury; Probate, Trusts and Estate Planning

KOMIE AND ASSOCIATES, LAW OFFICES OF
Chicago, IL.............................Civil Trial Practice; Criminal Trial Practice; Family Law

KOMPA, MARK A.
Irvine, CA................................Bankruptcy Law; Real Estate Law

KONCILJA & ASSOCIATES, P.C.
Denver, CO ....Civil Trial Practice; Commercial Litigation

KONIG, RICHARD W.
Stockton, CA...........................Probate, Trusts and Estate Planning

KONOWIECKI & RANK
Los Angeles, CA ....Health Care Law; Mergers and Acquisitions

KOOMAN, RICHARD W. II, LAW OFFICES OF
Clarion, PA ....Commercial Law; General Practice; Insurance Defense

KOONS, JOHN P.
Dallas, TX...............................Banking Law

KOONS, FULLER & VANDEN EYKEL, A PROFESSIONAL CORPORATION
Dallas, TX...............................Family Law

KOONZ, MCKENNEY, JOHNSON, DEPAOLIS & LIGHTFOOT, P.C.
Washington, DC.......................Personal Injury

KOPELMAN AND PAIGE, P.C.
Boston, MA.............................Civil Trial Practice; Environmental Law; General Practice; Insurance Defense; International Business Law; Municipal and Zoning Law

KOPENY & POWELL
Irvine, CA................................Appellate Practice

KOPPLE & KLINGER
Los Angeles, CA ....Tax Law

KOPS, LEE, FUTRELL & PERLES, L.L.P.
New Orleans, LA ....Admiralty/Maritime Law; Civil Trial Practice; Energy Law

KOREN, BERTELL, HOEY & LUTZEL
Buffalo, NY ....Civil Trial Practice; General Practice; Insurance Defense; Personal Injury; Probate, Trusts and Estate Planning

KORN & COHN, PROFESSIONAL CORPORATION
Plymouth Meeting, PA ....Construction Law

KORNEY & HELDT
Bingham Farms, MI ....Banking Law; Bankruptcy Law; Employment Benefits Law; Labor and Employment Law

KORNFIELD, PAUL & BUPP, A PROFESSIONAL CORPORATION
Oakland, CA ....Bankruptcy Law; Commercial Law

KORNIEVSKY, GEORGE M., A PROFESSIONAL CORPORATION
Irvine, CA...............................Family Law

KORNSTEIN VEISZ & WEXLER, LLP
New York, NY.......................Appellate Practice; Commercial Litigation

KORONES, N. DAVID, ATTORNEY AT LAW, P.A.
Clearwater, FL ....Family Law

KORTENHOF & ELY, A PROFESSIONAL CORPORATION
St. Louis, MO..........................Civil Rights; Insurance Defense; Medical Malpractice; Product Liability Law; Workers Compensation

KORTHALS, JOHN L.
Pompano Beach, FL ....General Practice; Probate, Trusts and Estate Planning; Real Estate Law

KOSKOFF, KOSKOFF & BIEDER, P.C.
Bridgeport, CT ....Medical Malpractice

KOSLOV & MEDLEN
Los Angeles, CA ....Civil Trial Practice; Construction Law; Insurance Defense; Product Liability Law; Real Estate Law

KOSTA & ASSOCIATES
St. Louis, MO..........................Civil Trial Practice; Insurance Defense

KOSTELANETZ & FINK, LLP
New York, NY.......................Criminal Trial Practice; Tax Law

KOTTKAMP & O'ROURKE
Pendleton, OR ....General Practice

KOZAK, GAYER & BRODEK, P.A.
Portland, ME ....Health Care Law

KRAEMER, BURNS, MYTELKA & LOVELL, P.A.
Springfield, NJ ....Civil Trial Practice; Commercial Litigation

KRAMER, LYNNE ADAIR LAW OFFICES OF
Commack, NY ....Civil Trial Practice; Family Law

KRAMER, LEVIN, NAFTALIS & FRANKEL
New York, NY.......................Civil Trial Practice; General Practice

KRAMER, PAUL R., P.A.
Baltimore, MD........................Criminal Trial Practice; Personal Injury

KRAMON & GRAHAM, P.A.
Baltimore, MD........................General Practice

KRAMSKY, ELLIOTT N. LAW OFFICES OF
Woodland Hills, CA ....Patent, Trademark, Copyright and Unfair Competition

KRASNOW, SANBERG & COHEN
Chicago, IL.............................Business Law

KRASNY AND DETTMER
Melbourne, FL ....Civil Trial Practice; General Practice; Probate, Trusts and Estate Planning; Real Estate Law

KRATZIG, PAUL G. LAW OFFICES OF
Corpus Christi, TX ....Commercial Litigation; Criminal Trial Practice

KRAUS, SHERRY S.
Rochester, NY.........................Tax Law

KRAUSER & TAUB, P.C.
Landover, MD ....General Practice

KRAVIT, GASS & WEBER, S.C.
Milwaukee, WI........................Insurance Defense

KRAVITZ, SCHNITZER & SLOANE, CHARTERED, A PROFESSIONAL CORPORATION
Las Vegas, NV ....Banking Law; Bankruptcy Law; Insurance Defense; Real Estate Law

KREDER, BROOKS, HAILSTONE & LUDWIG
Scranton, PA ....Civil Trial Practice; General Practice; Personal Injury; Product Liability Law

KREHBIEL, BANNERMAN, HORN & HISEY, P.A.
Albuquerque, NM...................Commercial Litigation; Environmental Law; Natural Resources Law

KREIS, ENDERLE, CALLANDER & HUDGINS, A PROFESSIONAL CORPORATION
Kalamazoo, MI ....Banking Law; Bankruptcy Law; Civil Trial Practice; Commercial Law; Construction Law; Employment Benefits Law; Environmental Law; Family Law; General Practice; Health Care Law; Immigration and Naturalization; Labor and Employment Law; Land Use Law; Municipal and Zoning Law; Probate, Trusts and Estate Planning; Real Estate Law; Tax Law

KREISMAN & RAKICH
Chicago, IL.............................Civil Trial Practice; Personal Injury

KRETSCHMAN, KAREN L.
Austin, TX ....Family Law

KREUSLER-WALSH, JANE
West Palm Beach, FL ....Appellate Practice

KRIEGER, ALBERT J., P.A.
Miami, FL ....Criminal Trial Practice

KRIEGER & KRIEGER
Omaha, NE ....Immigration and Naturalization

KRISLOV & ASSOCIATES, LTD.
Chicago, IL.............................Securities Law

KRIST WELLER NEUMANN
Houston, TX ....Civil Trial Practice; Personal Injury

KRIVCHER, MAGIDS, NEAL, COTTAM & CAMPBELL, P.C.
Memphis, TN ....General Practice; Insurance Defense

KROLL, THOMAS J.
Milwaukee, WI........................Probate, Trusts and Estate Planning

KROLL & TRACT
New York, NY.......................General Practice

KROLOFF, BELCHER, SMART, PERRY & CHRISTOPHERSON
Stockton, CA..........................General Practice

KRONEY • SILVERMAN • MINCEY, INC.
Dallas, TX ....Business Law; Probate, Trusts and Estate Planning

KROOTH & ALTMAN
Washington, DC......................Business Law; Commercial Law; Natural Resources Law

KRUCHKO & FRIES
Towson, MD ....Labor and Employment Law
McLean, VA............................Labor and Employment Law

KRUEGER & CAHILL
Wailuku, HI ....Civil Trial Practice; Medical Malpractice; Personal Injury; Product Liability Law

KRUGLIAK, WILKINS, GRIFFITHS & DOUGHERTY CO., L.P.A.
Canton, OH.............................General Practice

KRUGMAN, CHAPNICK & GRIMSHAW
Saddle Brook, NJ....................Civil Trial Practice

KRUKOWSKI & COSTELLO, S.C.
Milwaukee, WI........................Labor and Employment Law

KRUPNICK CAMPBELL MALONE ROSELLI BUSER SLAMA & HANCOCK, P.A.
Fort Lauderdale, FL ....Admiralty/Maritime Law; Civil Trial Practice; General Practice; Personal Injury

KRUSE, LANDA & MAYCOCK, L.L.C.
Salt Lake City, UT..................Bankruptcy Law

KRYS BOYLE GOLZ FREEDMAN & SCOTT, P.C.
Denver, CO ....Securities Law

KU, FONG, LARSEN & CHEN, LLP
Los Angeles, CA ....Business Law; Civil Trial Practice; Real Estate Law; Trademark, Copyright and Unfair Competition

KUBICKI DRAPER
Fort Lauderdale, FL ....Insurance Defense
Miami, FL ....Insurance Defense
West Palm Beach, FL ....Insurance Defense

KUDER, SMOLLAR & FRIEDMAN, P.C.
Washington, DC......................Family Law; Personal Injury

KUHN AND O'TOOLE
Staten Island, NY ....Probate, Trusts and Estate Planning

KULZER & DIPADOVA, A PROFESSIONAL CORPORATION
Haddonfield, NJ......................Tax Law

KUMMER KAEMPFER BONNER & RENSHAW
Las Vegas, NV ....Commercial Law; Insurance Defense; Securities Law

KUMMER, KNOX, NAUGHTON & HANSBURY, A PROFESSIONAL CORPORATION
Parsippany, NJ.......................Civil Trial Practice; Commercial Law; Environmental Law; Municipal and Zoning Law; Real Estate Law; Securities Law

KUNIHOLM, ELIZABETH F.
Raleigh, NC...........................Medical Malpractice

KUNKEL MILLER & HAMENT
Fort Myers, FL ....Labor and Employment Law
Sarasota, FL ....Labor and Employment Law
Tampa, FL ....Labor and Employment Law

KUPERMAN, ORR, MOUER & ALBERS, A PROFESSIONAL CORPORATION
Austin, TX ....Administrative Law; Antitrust Law; Banking Law; Bankruptcy Law; Business Law; Civil Trial Practice; Commercial Litigation; Construction Law; Employment Benefits Law; Energy Law; Labor and Employment Law; Land Use Law; Probate, Trusts and Estate Planning; Real Estate Law; Securities Law; Tax Law

KUPFER, RICHARD A., P.A.
West Palm Beach, FL ....Appellate Practice

KURRUS, THOMAS W.
Gainesville, FL ....Criminal Trial Practice

KURZMAN & EISENBERG, LLP
White Plains, NY ....Probate, Trusts and Estate Planning

KUSHNER LAW OFFICE
Omaha, NE ....Personal Injury

KUSSMAN & WHITEHILL
Los Angeles, CA ....Medical Malpractice; Personal Injury; Product Liability Law

KUTAK ROCK
Denver, CO ....General Practice
Washington, DC......................General Practice
Atlanta, GA ....General Practice
Omaha, NE ....General Practice

KUTNER, RUBINOFF, BUSH & LERNER
Miami, FL ....Civil Trial Practice; General Practice

KWALL & SHOWERS, P.A.
Clearwater, FL ....Criminal Trial Practice; General Practice

KYNES, MARKMAN & FELMAN, P.A.
Tampa, FL ....Appellate Practice; Criminal Trial Practice

LABARRE & ASSOCIATES, P.C.
Portland, OR...........................Civil Trial Practice; Securities Law

L'ABBATE, BALKAN, COLAVITA & CONTINI, L.L.P.
Garden City, NY ....Civil Trial Practice; General Practice; Insurance Defense; Product Liability Law

LABE, ROBERT B., P.C.
Southfield, MI ....Business Law; Probate, Trusts and Estate Planning; Tax Law

LABORDE & LAFARGUE
Marksville, LA ....General Practice

LABORDE LAW FIRM, THE, L.L.C.
Lafayette, LA ....General Practice

LABORDE & NEUNER
Lafayette, LA ....Insurance Defense

LABRUM AND DOAK
Bethlehem, PA ....General Practice
Philadelphia, PA ....General Practice

LACEY & JONES
Birmingham, MI......................Civil Trial Practice; Insurance Defense; Workers Compensation

LACKENBACH SIEGEL MARZULLO ARONSON & GREENSPAN, P.C.
Scarsdale, NY..........................Patent, Trademark, Copyright and Unfair Competition

LACKEY & LACKEY
Shelby, NC..............................General Practice

LACKEY, NUSBAUM, HARRIS, RENY & TORZEWSKI, A LEGAL PROFESSIONAL ASSOCIATION
Toledo, OH ....Admiralty/Maritime Law; Family Law; Labor and Employment Law; Personal Injury; Product Liability Law

LACKEY, RODGERS, PRICE AND SNEDEKER
Nashville, TN..........................Civil Trial Practice

LACY, KATZEN, RYEN & MITTLEMAN, LLP
Rochester, NY.........................Bankruptcy Law; Family Law; General Practice; Personal Injury; Probate, Trusts and Estate Planning

LADAR & KNAPP
San Francisco, CA ....Criminal Trial Practice

LADNER DOWNS
Vancouver, BC, Canada...........General Practice; Real Estate Law

LADSON, ODOM & DES ROCHES, L.L.P.
New Orleans, LA ....Civil Trial Practice

LAFAYETTE, KUMAGAI & CLARKE
San Francisco, CA ....Civil Trial Practice; Commercial Law; Labor and Employment Law; Product Liability Law

LAFF, WHITESEL, CONTE & SARET, LTD., A PROFESSIONAL CORPORATION
Chicago, IL.............................Patent, Trademark, Copyright and Unfair Competition

LAFLEUR BROWN
Toronto, ON, Canada..............General Practice
Montreal, QU, Canada ....General Practice

LAGERLOF, SENECAL, BRADLEY & SWIFT, LLP
Los Angeles, CA ....Civil Trial Practice; General Practice
Pasadena, CA ....Administrative Law; Bankruptcy Law; Civil Trial Practice; Environmental Law; Municipal and Zoning Law; Natural Resources Law; Probate, Trusts and Estate Planning; Real Estate Law

LA GRANGE, FREDBECK & DEPPE
Franklin, IN ....General Practice

LAGUE, NEWMAN & IRISH, A PROFESSIONAL CORPORATION
Muskegon, MI.........................Business Law; General Practice; Health Care Law; Medical Malpractice

LAHIVE & COCKFIELD
Boston, MA.............................Patent, Trademark, Copyright and Unfair Competition

LAIRD, DALLAS J.
Casper, WY ....Civil Trial Practice

LAKE TINDALL, LLP
Paducah, KY ....Admiralty/Maritime Law
Greenville, MS.........................Admiralty/Maritime Law; General Practice

LAKE, TOBACK & YAVITZ
Chicago, IL.............................Family Law

LAMARCA & LANDRY, P.C.
West Des Moines, IA...............Civil Trial Practice; Commercial Law; Medical Malpractice; Personal Injury

LAMB, MADELINE H.
West Chester, PA ....Family Law

LAMB & LERCH
New York, NY.........................International Trade Law

LAMB, WINDLE & MCERLANE, P.C.
West Chester, PA ....Administrative Law; Banking Law; Business Law; Civil Trial Practice; Commercial Litigation; Criminal Trial Practice; Environmental Law; Family Law; General Practice; Mergers and Acquisitions; Municipal Bond/Public Authority Financing; Municipal and Zoning Law; Personal Injury; Probate, Trusts and Estate Planning; Real Estate Law

LAMBDIN HERLOCKER & SODERBERG, CHARTERED
Wichita, KS.............................Family Law

LAMBERT, JAY
Louisville, KY ....Criminal Trial Practice

LAMBERT, PAUL WATSON
Tallahassee, FL ....Administrative Law

LAMBERT & ROFFMAN
Madison, GA...........................General Practice

LAMBERTH, BONAPFEL, CIFELLI & STOKES, P.A.
Atlanta, GA ....Bankruptcy Law; Business Law

LAMKIN, VAN EMAN, TRIMBLE, BEALS & ROURKE
Columbus, OH ....Civil Trial Practice; Medical Malpractice; Personal Injury; Product Liability Law

LAMMERS, LAMMERS, KLEIBACKER & PARENT
Madison, SD............................General Practice

LAMOTHE & HAMILTON, A PROFESSIONAL LAW CORPORATION
New Orleans, LA ....Antitrust Law; Business Law; Civil Trial Practice; Land Use Law; Municipal and Zoning Law; Securities Law

LANCY, JOHN S., & ASSOCIATES, A PROF. CORP.
Phoenix, AZ ....Business Law; Real Estate Law; Securities Law

LANDAU, JULIE ELLEN LAW OFFICE OF
Baltimore, MD ....Family Law

LAND, CLARK, CARROLL & MENDELSON, P.C.
Alexandria, VA ....General Practice

LANDELS, RIPLEY & DIAMOND, LLP
San Francisco, CA ....General Practice

LANDIS, GRAHAM, FRENCH, HUSFELD, SHERMAN & FORD, P.A.
Daytona Beach, FL.................Criminal Trial Practice; General Practice; Personal Injury; Probate, Trusts and Estate Planning
De Land, FL ....General Practice; Personal Injury; Probate, Trusts and Estate Planning
Deltona, FL.............................General Practice; Probate, Trusts and Estate Planning

LANDOE, BROWN, PLANALP & BRAAKSMA, P.C.
Bozeman, MT ....General Practice

LANDRUM & SHOUSE
Lexington, KY ....Business Law; Civil Trial Practice; Commercial Law; Environmental Law; Family Law; General Practice; Insurance Defense; Labor and Employment Law; Personal Injury; Probate, Trusts and Estate Planning; Real Estate Law; Workers Compensation
Louisville, KY ....Business Law; Family Law; General Practice; Insurance Defense; Personal Injury

LANDRY & WATKINS
New Iberia, LA ....General Practice; Insurance Defense

LANDSMAN, RON M., P.A.
Bethesda, MD ....Probate, Trusts and Estate Planning

LANDWEHR & HOF
New Orleans, LA ....Bankruptcy Law

LANE, AITKEN & MCCANN
Washington, DC......................Patent, Trademark, Copyright and Unfair Competition; Trademark, Copyright and Unfair Competition

LANE & EHRLICH, LTD.
Phoenix, AZ ....Business Law; Probate, Trusts and Estate Planning; Tax Law

LANE, FERTITTA, LANE, JANNEY & THOMAS
Baton Rouge, LA....................Insurance Defense; Medical Malpractice; Personal Injury; Product Liability Law

LANE & LANE
Chicago, IL...............................Medical Malpractice; Personal Injury

LANE, LANE AND KELLY
Braintree, MA ....General Practice

LANE, MARC J., A PROF. CORP., THE LAW OFFICES OF
Chicago, IL...............................Business Law; Tax Law

LANE, MUSE, ARMAN & PULLEN
Hot Springs National Park, AR ....Personal Injury

LANE POWELL SPEARS LUBERSKY LLP
Los Angeles, CA ....Product Liability Law
Portland, OR ....Antitrust Law; General Practice; Labor and Employment Law
Seattle, WA ....Antitrust Law; Bankruptcy Law; Civil Trial Practice; Environmental Law; General Practice; Labor and Employment Law; Real Estate Law; Tax Law

LANE, ROSEN AND STARKEY, P.C.
Willimantic, CT.......................General Practice

LANE, TROHN, CLARKE, BERTRAND, VREELAND & JACOBSEN, P.A.
Bartow, FL...............................Civil Trial Practice; General Practice
Lakeland, FL............................Civil Trial Practice; General Practice

LANE & WATERMAN
Rock Island, IL.......................General Practice
Davenport, IA.........................General Practice

LANER, MUCHIN, DOMBROW, BECKER, LEVIN AND TOMINBERG, LTD.
Chicago, IL...............................Employment Benefits Law; Labor and Employment Law

LANG, HENRY M. Q.C.
Sault Ste. Marie, ON, Canada....................................Civil Trial Practice

LANG MICHENER
Ottawa, ON, Canada ....General Practice
Toronto, ON, Canada.............General Practice

LANG, RICHERT & PATCH, A PROFESSIONAL CORPORATION
Fresno, CA ....Bankruptcy Law; Civil Trial Practice; Construction Law; Environmental Law; General Practice; Labor and Employment Law; Medical Malpractice; Personal Injury; Real Estate Law

LANGAN, DEMPSEY AND BRODIGAN
Boston, MA.............................Civil Trial Practice

LANGBERG, COHN & DROOZ
Los Angeles, CA ....Appellate Practice; Civil Trial Practice; Sports and Entertainment Law; Trademark, Copyright and Unfair Competition

LANGLOIS GAUDREAU
Montreal, QU, Canada ....Admiralty/Maritime Law; General Practice

LANIER FORD SHAVER & PAYNE, P.C.
Huntsville, AL.........................General Practice

LANIER, WILSON, PARKER & SULLIVAN, P.C.
Houston, TX ....Appellate Practice; Commercial Litigation; Medical Malpractice; Personal Injury; Product Liability Law

LANKLER SIFFERT & WOHL
New York, NY.........................Appellate Practice; Civil Trial Practice; Criminal Trial Practice

LANO, NELSON, O'TOOLE & BENGTSON, LTD.
Grand Rapids, MN.................Civil Trial Practice; Insurance Defense

LANTZ, JEFFERY L.
Evansville, IN..........................Criminal Trial Practice

LANZA, GEORGE V., P.A.
Coral Gables, FL ....Medical Malpractice

LAPEYRE, TERRELL & RANDAZZO
New Orleans, LA ....Natural Resources Law

LAPPAS, SPERO T. THE LAW OFFICES OF
Harrisburg, PA........................Criminal Trial Practice; Personal Injury

LARGE, SCAMMELL & DANZIGER, A PROFESSIONAL CORPORATION
Flemington, NJ ....Commercial Law; General Practice; Probate, Trusts and Estate Planning; Real Estate Law

LARKY, SHELDON G.
Bingham Farms, MI ....Family Law

LAROE, WINN, MOERMAN & DONOVAN
Washington, DC......................Transportation Law

LA ROSSA, MITCHELL & ROSS
New York, NY.........................Criminal Trial Practice; General Practice

LARSON & BURNHAM, A PROFESSIONAL CORPORATION
Oakland, CA ....General Practice

LARSON, RONALD F., P.C.
Sun City, AZ............................Probate, Trusts and Estate Planning

LARUE LAW FIRM
Daytona Beach, FL.................Personal Injury

LASATER & KNIGHT
Tyler, TX.................................Natural Resources Law

LASCHER & LASCHER, A PROFESSIONAL CORPORATION
Ventura, CA ....Appellate Practice; International Business Law

LASER, WILSON, BUFFORD & WATTS, P.A.
Little Rock, AR ....Civil Trial Practice; Commercial Law; General Practice; Insurance Defense; Medical Malpractice; Workers Compensation

LASKIN & GRAHAM
Glendale, CA...........................Commercial Law; Municipal and Zoning Law; Real Estate Law

LASKY, HAAS & COHLER, PROFESSIONAL CORPORATION
San Francisco, CA ....Civil Trial Practice

LASPADA, ANTHONY J., P.A.
Tampa, FL ....Criminal Trial Practice; Personal Injury

LASSER, MYRON G., P.C.
Staten Island, NY ....Personal Injury

LASTER, G. A.
San Mateo, CA........................Municipal Bond/Public Authority Financing

LATHAM & WATKINS
Los Angeles, CA ....General Practice

LATHROP & CLARK
Madison, WI ....General Practice; Patent, Trademark, Copyright and Unfair Competition; Trademark, Copyright and Unfair Competition

LATHROP & RUTLEDGE, A PROFESSIONAL CORPORATION
Cheyenne, WY........................Civil Trial Practice; General Practice; Insurance Defense

LAUCHENGCO, JOSÉ Y. JR.
Los Angeles, CA ....Civil Trial Practice; Criminal Trial Practice; Personal Injury

LAUER, E. STEVEN, P.A.
Vero Beach, FL ....Probate, Trusts and Estate Planning; Tax Law

LAUER, PHILIP D., P.C.
Easton, PA ....Criminal Trial Practice

LAUFMAN, ALAN K., J.D., M.D., A PROF. CORP., LAW OFFICES OF
Dallas, TX...............................Medical Malpractice; Personal Injury; Product Liability Law

LAUGHLIN, PETERSON & LANG
Omaha, NE ....Civil Trial Practice; General Practice; Probate, Trusts and Estate Planning; Real Estate Law; Tax Law

LAU, LANE, PIEPER, CONLEY & MCCREADIE, P.A.
Tampa, FL ....Admiralty/Maritime Law; General Practice; Insurance Defense

LAUTSCH, JOHN C., A PROFESSIONAL CORPORATION
Newport Beach, CA................Business Law

LAVERY, DE BILLY
Montreal, QU, Canada ....General Practice
Quebec, QU, Canada ....General Practice

LAVIN, COLEMAN, O'NEIL, RICCI, FINARELLI & GRAY
New York, NY........................Civil Trial Practice; Insurance Defense; Product Liability Law
Philadelphia, PA ....Civil Trial Practice; Insurance Defense; Product Liability Law

LAW, SNAKARD & GAMBILL, A PROFESSIONAL CORPORATION
Fort Worth, TX ....Business Law; Commercial Litigation

LAW, WEATHERS & RICHARDSON, P.C.
Grand Rapids, MI ....Bankruptcy Law; Commercial Law; General Practice; Labor and Employment Law; Municipal and Zoning Law; Real Estate Law; Tax Law

LAWLER, ANDREW M., P.C.
New York, NY........................Criminal Trial Practice

LAWLER, BONHAM & WALSH
Oxnard, CA............................Commercial Litigation; Insurance Defense

LAWRENCE, WILLIAM V.
Craig, CO ....Probate, Trusts and Estate Planning

LAWRENCE, BACA & DONOHUE
Houston, TX ....Bankruptcy Law

LAWRENCE, KAMIN, SAUNDERS & UHLENHOP
Chicago, IL.............................Civil Trial Practice; Construction Law; Securities Law

LAWRENCE AND LAWRENCE
Louisville, KY ....Probate, Trusts and Estate Planning

LAWRENCE, RICHARD D., AND ASSOCIATES CO., L.P.A.
Cincinnati, OH ....Medical Malpractice; Personal Injury

LAWRENCE AND WALSH, P.C.
Hempstead, NY.......................Business Law

LAWRENCE, WERNER, KESSELRING, SWARTOUT & BROWN, LLP
Rochester, NY........................Bankruptcy Law; Commercial Law; Commercial Litigation

LAWS & MURDOCH, P.A.
Russellville, AR ....General Practice

LAWSON, KIPP & FORBES
Fairfax, VA ....Civil Trial Practice

LAWSON LUNDELL LAWSON & MCINTOSH
Vancouver, BC, Canada..........Business Law

LAWTON & CATES, S.C.
Madison, WI ....Civil Trial Practice; Construction Law; Criminal Trial Practice; Labor and Employment Law; Personal Injury

LAYDEN & LAYDEN
Lafayette, IN ....Civil Trial Practice

LAZARUS & ASSOCIATES, A PROFESSIONAL CORPORATION
Phoenix, AZ ....Municipal and Zoning Law

LEA, TYNAN & MCGEHEE, P.L.C.
New Orleans, LA ....Admiralty/Maritime Law; Civil Trial Practice; Commercial Litigation; Insurance Defense; International Business Law

LEACH, MCGREEVY & BAUTISTA
San Francisco, CA ....Construction Law; Environmental Law; Insurance Defense; Product Liability Law; Workers Compensation

LEACH, SULLIVAN, SULLIVAN & WATKINS
Duncan, OK ....General Practice; Probate, Trusts and Estate Planning

LEAHEY & JOHNSON, P.C.
New York, NY........................Civil Trial Practice; Construction Law; Insurance Defense; Medical Malpractice

LEAHY & DENAULT
Claremont, NH ....General Practice

LEAKE & ANDERSSON, L.L.P.
New Orleans, LA ....Civil Trial Practice; Commercial Law; Construction Law; General Practice; Insurance Defense

LEARMAN & MCCULLOCH AND REISING, ETHINGTON, BARNARD & PERRY
Saginaw, MI ....Patent, Trademark, Copyright and Unfair Competition

LEARY, BRIDE, TINKER & MORAN, A PROFESSIONAL CORPORATION
Cedar Knolls, NJ ....Civil Trial Practice

LEATHERMAN, WITZLER, DOMBEY & HART
Perrysburg, OH ....General Practice; Probate, Trusts and Estate Planning

LEATHERWOOD WALKER TODD & MANN, P.C.
Greenville, SC.........................Antitrust Law; Civil Trial Practice; Environmental Law; General Practice; Insurance Defense; Tax Law
Spartanburg, SC......................Civil Trial Practice; General Practice; Insurance Defense

LEAVELL, JEFFREY, S.C.
Racine, WI ....Environmental Law

LEAVY, SCHULTZ, DAVIS & FEARING, P.S.
Kennewick, WA ....General Practice

LEBEAU, CHARLES P. LAW OFFICES OF
San Diego, CA ....International Business Law

LEBLANC & YOUNG
Portland, ME ....Probate, Trusts and Estate Planning; Tax Law

LEBOEUF, LAMB, GREENE & MACRAE, L.L.P.
New York, NY........................General Practice

LEBOVITS & DAVID, A PROFESSIONAL CORPORATION
Los Angeles, CA ....Aviation Law; Civil Trial Practice; Personal Injury; Product Liability Law

LECHOWICZ, ROBERT A.
Telford, PA..............................General Practice

LECKEY, LENK & LUKETINA, L.L.C.
McLean, VA ....Bankruptcy Law; Family Law

LECLAIR RYAN, A PROFESSIONAL CORPORATION
Richmond, VA ....Administrative Law; Appellate Practice; Bankruptcy Law; Business Law; Civil Trial Practice; Health Care Law; Labor and Employment Law; Real Estate Law; Securities Law; Tax Law

LEDFORD, PAUL B., PROFESSIONAL CORPORATION
Vincennes, IN ....Personal Injury

LEDGEWOOD LAW FIRM, A PROFESSIONAL CORPORATION
Philadelphia, PA ....Probate, Trusts and Estate Planning

LEDOUX, WILLIAM J.
Worcester, MA ....Commercial Litigation; General Practice

LEE, RAYMOND JR.
Tuscola, IL ....General Practice

LEE, JOHN PETER, LTD.
Las Vegas, NV ....Bankruptcy Law; Business Law; Civil Trial Practice; General Practice; Probate, Trusts and Estate Planning; Real Estate Law

LEE, KIM, WONG, YEE & LAU, ATTORNEYS AT LAW, A LAW CORPORATION
Honolulu, HI...........................Civil Trial Practice; Medical Malpractice

LEE, MARTIN, GREEN & REITER, INC.
Bellefonte, PA ....General Practice

State College, PA ....General Practice

LEE & MCINISH
Dothan, AL............................Civil Trial Practice; General Practice; Insurance
Defense; Product Liability Law

LEE, SMART, COOK, MARTIN & PATTERSON, P.S., INC.
Seattle, WA ....Insurance Defense; Medical Malpractice; Product
Liability Law

LEE, WILSON & ERTER
Sumter, SC..............................Civil Trial Practice; General Practice; Insurance
Defense

LEESEBERG MALOON SCHULMAN & VALENTINE
Columbus, OH ....Medical Malpractice; Personal Injury; Product
Liability Law

LEESFIELD, LEIGHTON & RUBIO, P.A.
Miami, FL ....Civil Trial Practice; General Practice

LEFEBVRE, FRANCIS, BUREAU
New York, NY........................Business Law; Tax Law

LEFFLER HYLAND HENSHAW & THOMPSON, A PROFESSIONAL CORPORATION
Fairfax, VA ....Civil Trial Practice; Criminal Trial Practice;
Employment Benefits Law; Real Estate Law

LEFKOFF, DUNCAN, MILLER, GRIMES, MILLER & BARWICK, P.C.
Atlanta, GA ....Civil Trial Practice; Probate, Trusts and Estate
Planning; Tax Law

LEFTWICH & DOUGLAS, P.L.L.C.
Washington, DC......................General Practice

LEGAL STRATEGIES GROUP
Emeryville, CA........................Civil Trial Practice; General Practice

LEGROS LAW PARTNERS, P.C.
Berwyn, PA ....Environmental Law

LEHMAN & EILEN
Uniondale, NY ....Business Law; Civil Trial Practice; Securities Law;
Trademark, Copyright and Unfair Competition

LEHMAN & VALENTINO, P.C.
Bloomfield Hills, MI................Commercial Law; Insurance Defense

LEHNER, MITCHELL, RODRIGUES AND SEARS
Portland, OR...........................Insurance Defense

LEHR MIDDLEBROOKS PRICE & PROCTOR, P.C.
Birmingham, AL ....Labor and Employment Law

LEICK, HAMMONS AND BRITTAIN
Corbin, KY ....General Practice

LEITER, WILLIAM
Tulsa, OK................................Probate, Trusts and Estate Planning

LEITMAN, SIEGAL & PAYNE, P.C.
Birmingham, AL ....General Practice

LEITNER, WILLIAMS, DOOLEY & NAPOLITAN, PLLC
Nashville, TN ....General Practice

LEITNER, WILLIAMS, DOOLEY & NAPOLITAN, PLLC
Chattanooga, TN ....General Practice

LELAND, PARACHINI, STEINBERG, FLINN, MATZGER & MELNICK, L.L.P.
San Francisco, CA ....General Practice

LEMON, ARMEY, HEARN & LEININGER
Warsaw, IN ....Civil Trial Practice; Probate, Trusts and Estate
Planning; Product Liability Law

LEMON, SHEARER, EHRLICH, PHILLIPS & GOOD, A PROFESSIONAL CORPORATION
Perryton, TX ....Civil Trial Practice; General Practice; Natural
Resources Law

LENAHAN & DEMPSEY, A PROFESSIONAL CORPORATION
Scranton, PA ....Civil Trial Practice; General Practice; Insurance
Defense; Personal Injury; Securities Law; Workers
Compensation

LENCE LAW FIRM, A PROFESSIONAL CORPORATION
Kalispell, MT ....Tax Law

LENOX, SOCEY, WILGUS, FORMIDONI & CASEY
Trenton, NJ.............................Civil Trial Practice; General Practice; Insurance
Defense; Medical Malpractice; Personal Injury

LENTZ, CANTOR, KILGORE & MASSEY, LTD.
Frazer, PA ....General Practice

LEON, AMBERSON & CARROLL, L.L.P.
San Antonio, TX......................Civil Trial Practice; Criminal Trial Practice

LEONARD FELKER ALTFELD & BATTAILE, P.C.
Tucson, AZ ....Bankruptcy Law; Civil Trial Practice; Real Estate
Law

LEONARD & LYDE
Chico, CA................................General Practice

LEONARD & MORRISON
Fort Lauderdale, FL ....General Practice

LEONARD, RALSTON & STANTON, CHARTERED
Washington, DC.......................Bankruptcy Law; Civil Trial Practice

LEONARD, STREET AND DEINARD, PROFESSIONAL ASSOCIATION
Minneapolis, MN ....General Practice

LEONATTI & BAKER, P.C.
Mexico, MO ....Civil Trial Practice; General Practice; Probate,
Trusts and Estate Planning

LEOPOLD, PETRICH & SMITH, A PROFESSIONAL CORPORATION
Los Angeles, CA ....Civil Trial Practice; Trademark, Copyright and
Unfair Competition

LEPLEY, PATRICK H.
Bellevue, WA ....Personal Injury

LEPRELL, SAMUEL L.
Jacksonville, FL ....Business Law; Real Estate Law

LERNER, DAVID, LITTENBERG, KRUMHOLZ & MENTLIK
Westfield, NJ ....Patent, Trademark, Copyright and Unfair Competition

LERNER, SAMPSON & ROTHFUSS, A LEGAL PROFESSIONAL ASSOCIATION
Cincinnati, OH ....Bankruptcy Law; Commercial Law; Real Estate
Law

LERUM, NORMAN J.
Chicago, IL..............................Appellate Practice; Civil Trial Practice; Commercial
Litigation

LESESNE & CONNETTE
Charlotte, NC...........................Labor and Employment Law

LESH, CASNER & MILLER, A LEGAL PROFESSIONAL ASSOCIATION
Canton, OH ....Civil Trial Practice; Environmental Law; General
Practice; Insurance Defense; Municipal and Zoning
Law; Real Estate Law

LESHER & LESHER, A PROFESSIONAL CORPORATION
Tucson, AZ ....General Practice; Insurance Defense

LESLIE & SMITH, P.C.
El Paso, TX..............................Bankruptcy Law

LESOURD & PATTEN, P.S.
Seattle, WA ....Business Law; Civil Trial Practice; Environmental
Law; Tax Law

LESS, GETZ & LIPMAN
Memphis, TN ....Construction Law

LESSER & KAPLIN, PROFESSIONAL CORPORATION
Blue Bell, PA...........................Banking Law; Bankruptcy Law; Civil Trial Practice;
Commercial Law; Real Estate Law

LETSON, GRIFFITH, WOODALL, LAVELLE & ROSENBERG CO., L.P.A.
Warren, OH.............................Banking Law; General Practice; Labor and
Employment Law; Securities Law

LEVANDER, GILLEN & MILLER, P.A.
South St. Paul, MN ....General Practice

LEVEEN, BARRY G.
Westwood, NJ ....Administrative Law; General Practice; International
Business Law

LEVENE, NEALE & BENDER L.L.P.
Los Angeles, CA ....Bankruptcy Law

LEVENS, WILLIAM P.
Tampa, FL ....Personal Injury

LEVENSTEIN, RICHARD H., P.A., LAW OFFICES OF
Boca Raton, FL ....Business Law; Civil Trial Practice; Securities Law

LEVENTHAL AND BOGUE, P.C.
Denver, CO ....Civil Trial Practice; Medical Malpractice; Personal
Injury

LEVENTHAL & SLADE
New York, NY.........................Civil Trial Practice; Criminal Trial Practice

LEVENTHAL & SLAUGHTER, P.A.
Orlando, FL ....Criminal Trial Practice

LEVENTRITT LEWITTES & BENDER
New York, NY.........................Civil Trial Practice

LEVETT, ROCKWOOD & SANDERS, PROFESSIONAL CORPORATION
Westport, CT.................Business Law; General Practice; Labor and Employment Law; Patent, Trademark, Copyright and Unfair Competition; Tax Law

LEVIN, MARK
Roseland, NJ..........................Probate, Trusts and Estate Planning; Tax Law

LEVIN, FISHBEIN, SEDRAN & BERMAN
Philadelphia, PA ....Admiralty/Maritime Law; Antitrust Law; Civil Trial Practice; Commercial Litigation; Environmental Law; General Practice; Medical Malpractice; Product Liability Law; Securities Law

LEVIN & FULP
Beaufort, SC ....General Practice

LEVIN & GLUCK
Laguna Beach, CA ....Patent, Trademark, Copyright and Unfair Competition

LEVINE, STANLEY A.
Fort Wayne, IN......................Family Law; General Practice; Medical Malpractice; Municipal and Zoning Law; Personal Injury

LEVINE & ASSOCIATES
Los Angeles, CA ....Business Law

LEVINE, CARL S., & ASSOCIATES, P.C.
Roslyn, NY ....Commercial Litigation

LEVINE, HIRSCH & SEGALL, P.A.
Tampa, FL ....Civil Trial Practice; Criminal Trial Practice; Personal Injury

LEVINE, STALLER, SKLAR, CHAN, BRODSKY & DONNELLY, P.A.
Atlantic City, NJ.....................Commercial Law; General Practice; Probate, Trusts and Estate Planning; Real Estate Law; Tax Law

LEVINE, STEINBERG & MILLER
San Diego, CA ....Civil Trial Practice; Personal Injury

LEVINE AND YATES, P.C., LAW OFFICES
Arlington, VA ....Immigration and Naturalization

LEVINGSTON & LEVINGSTON
Cleveland, MS ....General Practice

LEVINSON, MILLER, JACOBS & PHILLIPS, A PROFESSIONAL CORPORATION
Los Angeles, CA ....Civil Trial Practice; Family Law

LEVIT & MANN
Richmond, VA ....Labor and Employment Law

LEVITAN & FRIELAND, P.C.
Livingston, NJ.........................Civil Trial Practice; Commercial Law; General Practice

LEVY, HERBERT MONTE
New York, NY........................Appellate Practice

LEVY, ANGSTREICH, FINNEY, BALDANTE, RUBENSTEIN & COREN, P.C.
Philadelphia, PA ....Civil Trial Practice

LEVY, EHRLICH & KRONENBERG, A PROFESSIONAL CORPORATION
Newark, NJ ....General Practice; Probate, Trusts and Estate Planning; Tax Law

LEVY, JAMES L., PROFESSIONAL CORPORATION
St. Albans, VT ....Immigration and Naturalization

LEVY & PREATE
Scranton, PA ....Commercial Law; General Practice; Real Estate Law

LEVY, ROBERT S., P.A.
West Palm Beach, FL ....General Practice

LEVY, STEVEN B., LTD.
Naperville, IL ....Civil Trial Practice; Personal Injury
Wheaton, IL ....Civil Trial Practice; Personal Injury

LEWALLEN, JO BETSY LAW OFFICES OF
Austin, TX ....Family Law

LEWIN, ROBERT S., A LAW CORPORATION
Laguna Beach, CA ....Business Law; Civil Trial Practice

LEWIS, JOHN B.
Sacramento, CA ....Civil Trial Practice

LEWIS & ALLEN, P.C.
Kalamazoo, MI ....Business Law; Commercial Law; General Practice; Probate, Trusts and Estate Planning; Real Estate Law

LEWIS & ASSOCIATES
Beaumont, TX ....Civil Trial Practice; Insurance Defense

LEWIS, BABCOCK & HAWKINS, L.L.P.
Columbia, SC ....General Practice

LEWIS & BACON, A PROFESSIONAL CORPORATION
Sacramento, CA ....Insurance Defense

LEWIS, CLAY & MUNDAY, A PROFESSIONAL CORPORATION
Washington, DC......................Environmental Law; Municipal Bond/Public Authority Financing; Securities Law
Detroit, MI ....Banking Law; Business Law; Civil Trial Practice; Environmental Law; Health Care Law; Municipal Bond/Public Authority Financing; Real Estate Law; Securities Law; Transportation Law

LEWIS, D'AMATO, BRISBOIS & BISGAARD
Los Angeles, CA ....General Practice

LEWIS & GREER, P.C.
Poughkeepsie, NY ....Construction Law

LEWIS & KAPPES, PROFESSIONAL CORPORATION
Indianapolis, IN ....General Practice

LEWIS LAW FIRM, THE, A PROFESSIONAL CORPORATION
Washington, DC......................Family Law

LEWIS & PRESTON
Elizabethtown, KY ....General Practice

LEWIS, RICE & FINGERSH
St. Louis, MO.........................Admiralty/Maritime Law; Antitrust Law; Civil Trial Practice; General Practice; Labor and Employment Law; Municipal Bond/Public Authority Financing; Tax Law

LEWIS AND ROCA, LLP
Phoenix, AZ ....Antitrust Law; Banking Law; Bankruptcy Law; Business Law; Civil Trial Practice; Commercial Law; Criminal Trial Practice; Environmental Law; General Practice; Health Care Law; Labor and Employment Law; Real Estate Law; Securities Law; Tax Law; Trademark, Copyright and Unfair Competition
Tucson, AZ ....Real Estate Law

LEWIS & ROGERS
Plattsburgh, NY ....General Practice; Municipal and Zoning Law; Probate, Trusts and Estate Planning

LEWIS, TAYLOR & TODD, P.C.
La Grange, GA ....General Practice

LEWIS & TRATTNER
Washington, DC......................Patent, Trademark, Copyright and Unfair Competition

LEWIS, VEGOSEN, ROSENBACH & SILBER, P.A.
West Palm Beach, FL ....Commercial Litigation; Personal Injury; Real Estate Law

LEWIS, WILSON, LEWIS AND JONES, LTD.
Fairfax, VA ....Civil Trial Practice

LEYDIG, VOIT & MAYER, LTD.
Chicago, IL..............................Patent, Trademark, Copyright and Unfair Competition
Rockford, IL ....Patent, Trademark, Copyright and Unfair Competition

LIBERT, VICTOR E., LAW OFFICE OF
Simsbury, CT..........................Patent, Trademark, Copyright and Unfair Competition

LICATA, ARTHUR F., P.C.
Boston, MA............................General Practice

LICCARDO, ROSSI, STURGES & MCNEIL, A PROFESSIONAL LAW CORPORATION
San Jose, CA ....Personal Injury; Probate, Trusts and Estate Planning; Product Liability Law; Real Estate Law

LICHTENAUER, ROBERT A.
Indianapolis, IN ....Probate, Trusts and Estate Planning; Tax Law

LIDDLE & ROBINSON, L.L.P.
New York, NY........................Civil Trial Practice; Family Law; Labor and Employment Law

LIDDY SULLIVAN GALWAY BEGLER & COHEN, P.C.
New York, NY.........................Patent, Trademark, Copyright and Unfair Competition

LIEBER & LIEBER
New York, NY........................Product Liability Law

LIEBER, LIEBER & TARANTINE, P.C.
Pittsburgh, PA ....Business Law; Health Care Law; Probate, Trusts and Estate Planning; Real Estate Law; Tax Law

LIEBERMAN, DODGE, SENDROW & GERDING, LTD.
Phoenix, AZ ....Commercial Litigation; Real Estate Law

LIEBERMAN & NOWAK, LLP
New York, NY.......................Patent, Trademark, Copyright and Unfair Competition

LIEBERMAN & STEIN
Blue Bell, PA...........................Bankruptcy Law; Real Estate Law

LIEBERTHAL, DAVID H.
Tucson, AZ ....Family Law

LIEBMAN, EMMANUEL, CHARTERED, A PROF. CORP.
Cherry Hill, NJ ....Tax Law

LIECHTY, DOUGLAS C.
Newport Beach, CA................Family Law

LIEFF, CABRASER, HEIMANN & BERNSTEIN, LLP
San Francisco, CA ....Antitrust Law; Environmental Law; Labor and Employment Law; Product Liability Law; Securities Law

LIGGIO, JEFFREY M., P.A.
West Palm Beach, FL ....Admiralty/Maritime Law; Personal Injury

LIGHTCAP, ROBERT P.
Latrobe, PA.............................Construction Law

LIGHTFOOT, FRANKLIN & WHITE, L.L.C.
Birmingham, AL ....Antitrust Law; Civil Trial Practice; Environmental Law; Personal Injury; Securities Law

LILES, GAVIN & COSTANTINO
Jacksonville, FL ....Civil Trial Practice; Commercial Litigation; Medical Malpractice; Personal Injury; Product Liability Law

LILLEY, DANIEL G., P.A.
Portland, ME ....Criminal Trial Practice

LILLY, ANDERSON, MORGAN
Toronto, ON, Canada..............Insurance Defense

LILLY & LILLY, P.C.
Kalamazoo, MI ....Civil Trial Practice; Employment Benefits Law; General Practice; Insurance Defense; Labor and Employment Law

LIMANDRI, CHARLES S.
Rancho Santa Fe, CA..............Civil Trial Practice

LIMBACH & LIMBACH, L.L.P.
San Francisco, CA ....Patent, Trademark, Copyright and Unfair Competition

LINDABURY, McCORMICK & ESTABROOK, A PROFESSIONAL CORPORATION
Westfield, NJ ....Banking Law; Civil Trial Practice; Commercial Law; Construction Law; General Practice; Health Care Law; Labor and Employment Law; Municipal Bond/Public Authority Financing; Public Utilities Law; Real Estate Law; Tax Law

LINDER & HOLLOWELL
Indianapolis, IN ....Insurance Defense

LINDHORST & DREIDAME CO., L.P.A.
Cincinnati, OH ....Civil Trial Practice; General Practice; Insurance Defense; Medical Malpractice

LINDLEY, LAZAR & SCALES, A PROFESSIONAL CORPORATION
San Diego, CA ....Banking Law; Bankruptcy Law; Business Law; Civil Trial Practice; Commercial Law; Commercial Litigation; Computer Law; Construction Law; General Practice; Health Care Law; Probate, Trusts and Estate Planning; Real Estate Law; Tax Law

LINDNER & MARSACK, S.C.
Milwaukee, WI ....Labor and Employment Law

LINDSAY, HART, NEIL & WEIGLER, LLP
Portland, OR...........................Admiralty/Maritime Law; General Practice

LINDSEY AND SCHRIMSHER, P.A.
Charlotte, NC..........................Bankruptcy Law; General Practice; Probate, Trusts and Estate Planning

LINES, HINSON AND LINES
Quincy, FL ....General Practice

LINK, FREDERICK H.
Hammond, IN..........................Insurance Defense

LINK & WARHURST
San Francisco, CA ....Commercial Litigation

LINNELL, CHOATE & WEBBER
Auburn, ME.............................General Practice

LINOWES AND BLOCHER LLP
Silver Spring, MD ....General Practice

LINZER & DITSCH, P.C.
Phoenix, AZ ....Business Law; Civil Trial Practice; Real Estate Law

LIONEL SAWYER & COLLINS
Las Vegas, NV ....Bankruptcy Law; Civil Trial Practice; General Practice; Labor and Employment Law; Land Use Law; Real Estate Law
Reno, NV ....General Practice

LIOTTA, DRANITZKE & ENGEL
Washington, DC......................Family Law; Real Estate Law

LIPE, GREEN, PASCHAL & TRUMP, P.C.
Tulsa, OK................................Bankruptcy Law; Civil Trial Practice; Commercial Law; General Practice; Personal Injury

LIPKIN, STANLEY G.
Denver, CO ....Family Law

LIPKIN, MARSHALL, BOHORAD & THORNBURG, A PROFESSIONAL CORPORATION
Pottsville, PA ....General Practice

LIPMAN, ANTONELLI, BATT, DUNLAP, WODLINGER & GILSON, A PROFESSIONAL CORPORATION
Vineland, NJ ....Civil Trial Practice; General Practice

LIPMAN & KATZ, P.A.
Augusta, ME............................Civil Trial Practice; Commercial Litigation; Personal Injury

LIPPE & ASSOCIATES, LAW OFFICES OF
Dallas, TX...............................Appellate Practice; Civil Trial Practice; Insurance Defense

LIPPMAN, MAHFOUZ & MARTIN
Morgan City, LA ....General Practice; Personal Injury

LIPSCOMB, J. RANDOLPH
Columbus, MS..........................Civil Trial Practice

LIPSHULTZ AND HONE, CHARTERED
Silver Spring, MD ....Environmental Law; General Practice; Insurance Defense

LIPSHUTZ, GREENBLATT & KING
Atlanta, GA ....Civil Trial Practice; General Practice; Real Estate Law

LIPSITZ, GREEN, FAHRINGER, ROLL, SALISBURY & CAMBRIA LLP
Buffalo, NY ....Civil Trial Practice; General Practice; Labor and Employment Law

LIPTON & STAPLER
Media, PA ....Patent, Trademark, Copyright and Unfair Competition

LISA & SOUSA, LTD.
Providence, RI.........................Commercial Law; Probate, Trusts and Estate Planning; Real Estate Law

LISKOW & LEWIS, A PROFESSIONAL LAW CORPORATION
Lafayette, LA ....Admiralty/Maritime Law; Banking Law; Bankruptcy Law; Civil Trial Practice; General Practice; Natural Resources Law; Patent, Trademark, Copyright and Unfair Competition
New Orleans, LA.....................Admiralty/Maritime Law; Antitrust Law; Banking Law; Bankruptcy Law; Civil Trial Practice; Environmental Law; General Practice; Natural Resources Law; Patent, Trademark, Copyright and Unfair Competition; Probate, Trusts and Estate Planning; Securities Law; Tax Law

LISLE LAW FIRM, P.C.
Springdale, AR........................Civil Trial Practice; Commercial Law

LISS AND ASSOCIATES, P.C.
Bloomfield Hills, MI................Civil Trial Practice; Commercial Law; Personal Injury

LISTON/LANCASTER
Grenada, MS ....Civil Trial Practice; General Practice
Jackson, MS ....Civil Trial Practice; General Practice
Winona, MS ....Civil Trial Practice; General Practice

LITCHFIELD, C. WAYNE, CORP.
Oklahoma City, OK.................Insurance Defense

LITMAN LAW OFFICES, LTD.
Arlington, VA ....Patent, Trademark, Copyright and Unfair Competition

LITMAN LITMAN HARRIS & BROWN, P.C.
Pittsburgh, PA ....Civil Trial Practice

LITMAN, McMAHON AND BROWN, L.L.C.
Kansas City, MO.....................Patent, Trademark, Copyright and Unfair Competition

LITTEN & SIPE
Harrisonburg, VA ....General Practice

LITTLE & GILMAN, P.A.
Albuquerque, NM..................Family Law

LITTLEJOHN, TALMADGE D.
New Albany, MS ....Civil Trial Practice; Family Law; Personal Injury

LITTLE, LITTLE, LITTLE, WINDEL & COPPEDGE
Madill, OK ....General Practice

LITTLE & MORGAN
Oklahoma City, OK..................Commercial Law; Commercial Litigation

LITTLER, MENDELSON, FASTIFF, TICHY & MATHIASON, A PROFESSIONAL CORPORATION
San Francisco, CA ....General Practice

LITVIN, BLUMBERG, MATUSOW & YOUNG, A PROFESSIONAL ASSOCIATION
Philadelphia, PA ....Civil Trial Practice; Medical Malpractice; Product Liability Law

LITWIN, GERALD H., P.A.
Hackensack, NJ..................Probate, Trusts and Estate Planning; Tax Law

LIVINGSTON, MARKLE, MILLER, RAMOS & ZITO, A PROFESSIONAL CORPORATION
Houston, TX ....Insurance Defense; Medical Malpractice; Personal Injury

LIVINGSTON & MATTESICH, LAW CORPORATION
Sacramento, CA ....Administrative Law; Appellate Practice; Business Law; Civil Trial Practice; Environmental Law; General Practice; Health Care Law; Labor and Employment Law; Real Estate Law; Tax Law

LLOYD, GOSSELINK, FOWLER, BLEVINS & MATHEWS, P.C.
Austin, TX ....Environmental Law

LLOYD, KANE, WIEDER & WILLIS, P.A.
Ellicott City, MD..................General Practice

LLOYD & MCDANIEL, PLC
Louisville, KY ....Bankruptcy Law

LLOYD, SCHREIBER, GRAY AND GAINES, P.C.
Birmingham, AL ....Insurance Defense

LLOYD & WEISSENBERGER
Cincinnati, OH ....Civil Trial Practice

LOBEL & OPERA, PROFESSIONAL CORPORATION
Irvine, CA..................Bankruptcy Law; Commercial Law; General Practice

LOBRANO & KINCAID
Jacksonville, FL ....Commercial Litigation; Real Estate Law

LOCK, CHARLES M.
St. Louis, MO..................Tax Law

LOCKE PURNELL RAIN HARRELL, A PROFESSIONAL CORPORATION
Dallas, TX..................General Practice

LOCKE REYNOLDS BOYD & WEISELL
Indianapolis, IN ....Banking Law; Civil Trial Practice; Construction Law; General Practice; Health Care Law; Insurance Defense; Labor and Employment Law; Medical Malpractice; Patent, Trademark, Copyright and Unfair Competition; Personal Injury; Product Liability Law; Securities Law; Tax Law

LOEB & LOEB LLP
Los Angeles, CA ....Antitrust Law; Appellate Practice; Banking Law; Bankruptcy Law; Civil Trial Practice; Environmental Law; General Practice; Labor and Employment Law; Probate, Trusts and Estate Planning; Real Estate Law; Tax Law; Trademark, Copyright and Unfair Competition
New York, NY..................Antitrust Law; Appellate Practice; Banking Law; Bankruptcy Law; Civil Trial Practice; General Practice; Probate, Trusts and Estate Planning; Real Estate Law; Tax Law; Trademark, Copyright and Unfair Competition
Rome, Italy ....General Practice

LOEWENSTEIN, HAGEN, OEHLERT AND SMITH, P.C.
Springfield, IL ....Administrative Law; General Practice; Labor and Employment Law

LOFTON, LIONEL S.
Charleston, SC ....Criminal Trial Practice

LOGAN, CHARLES E.
San Jose, CA ....Bankruptcy Law

LOGAN, GARY
Las Vegas, NV ....Aviation Law; Medical Malpractice; Personal Injury

LOGAN & LOWRY
Vinita, OK..................General Practice

LOGGANS AND COX
Chicago, IL..................Civil Trial Practice; Medical Malpractice; Personal Injury; Product Liability Law

LOGOTHETIS, PENCE & DOLL
Dayton, OH..................Labor and Employment Law

LOHF, SHAIMAN & JACOBS, P.C.
Denver, CO ....Business Law; Natural Resources Law; Real Estate Law; Tax Law

LOLLIS, JANE D.
Louisville, KY ....Real Estate Law

LOMELL, MUCCIFORI, ADLER, RAVASCHIERE, AMABILE & PEHLIVANIAN, A PROFESSIONAL CORPORATION
Toms River, NJ..................Business Law; Civil Trial Practice; Commercial Litigation; Environmental Law; Insurance Defense; Municipal and Zoning Law; Product Liability Law; Workers Compensation

LOMMEN, NELSON, COLE & STAGEBERG, P.A.
Minneapolis, MN ....Business Law; Civil Trial Practice; Insurance Defense; Real Estate Law

LOMURRO, DAVISON, EASTMAN & MUNOZ, P.A.
Freehold, NJ..................General Practice

LONDON, AMBURN & THOMFORDE, P.C.
Knoxville, TN ....Business Law; Health Care Law; Securities Law

LONDON FISCHER
New York, NY..................Admiralty/Maritime Law; Appellate Practice; Civil Trial Practice; Construction Law; Insurance Defense; Product Liability Law

LONDON & YANCEY
Birmingham, AL ....Appellate Practice; Civil Trial Practice; Construction Law; Employment Benefits Law; Insurance Defense; Medical Malpractice; Product Liability Law

LONG ALDRIDGE & NORMAN, LLP
Atlanta, GA ....Administrative Law; Antitrust Law; Appellate Practice; Banking Law; Bankruptcy Law; Business Law; Civil Trial Practice; Communications Law; Employment Benefits Law; Environmental Law; General Practice; Health Care Law; Immigration and Naturalization; Labor and Employment Law; Municipal Bond/Public Authority Financing; Probate, Trusts and Estate Planning; Public Utilities Law; Real Estate Law; Securities Law; Sports and Entertainment Law; Tax Law

LONG, BURNER, PARKS & SEALY, A PROFESSIONAL CORPORATION
Austin, TX ....Administrative Law; Civil Trial Practice; Commercial Litigation; Insurance Defense; Probate, Trusts and Estate Planning; Workers Compensation

LONG & JAUDON, P.C.
Denver, CO ....Civil Trial Practice; General Practice; Insurance Defense; Labor and Employment Law; Medical Malpractice

LONG & LEVIT LLP
Los Angeles, CA ....General Practice
San Francisco, CA ....General Practice

LONG & LONG
Chapel Hill, NC..................Civil Trial Practice; Criminal Trial Practice; Family Law; Personal Injury

LONG, LUNDMARK & POPPE, P.A.
Phoenix, AZ ....Workers Compensation

LONG, PARKER & WARREN, P.A.
Asheville, NC ....Civil Trial Practice; Criminal Trial Practice

LONG, TUMINELLO, BESSO, SELIGMAN & QUINLAN
Bay Shore, NY ....Civil Trial Practice; Criminal Trial Practice

LONG, WEINBERG, ANSLEY AND WHEELER
Atlanta, GA ....Civil Trial Practice; General Practice

LONG & WILLIAMSON, A PROFESSIONAL CORPORATION
Santa Ana, CA..................Insurance Defense

LOOMIS, EWERT, PARSLEY, DAVIS & GOTTING, P.C.
Lansing, MI..................General Practice

LOONEY & GROSSMAN
Boston, MA..................Bankruptcy Law; Business Law; Civil Trial Practice; General Practice

LOONEY, NICHOLS & JOHNSON
Oklahoma City, OK..................Civil Trial Practice; General Practice

LOPEZ, DAVID T. & ASSOCIATES
Houston, TX ....Labor and Employment Law

LORANCE & THOMPSON, A PROFESSIONAL CORPORATION
Houston, TX ....Civil Trial Practice; Insurance Defense; Medical Malpractice; Personal Injury; Product Liability Law

LORD, BISSELL & BROOK
Los Angeles, CA ....General Practice
Atlanta, GA ....General Practice
Chicago, IL.............................General Practice
Rockford, IL ....General Practice

LOREN, SHIRK & SNELL
Hillsdale, MI ....Insurance Defense

LORENZI, SANCHEZ & ROSTEET, L.L.P.
Lake Charles, LA ....Commercial Litigation; Criminal Trial Practice

LORENZO & KULAKOWSKI, P.C.
Punxsutawney, PA ....Civil Trial Practice; Commercial Litigation; Personal Injury

LORUSSO & LOUD
Boston, MA...........................Patent, Trademark, Copyright and Unfair Competition
Portsmouth, NH ....Patent, Trademark, Copyright and Unfair Competition

LOSCH, ROBERT E., P.C.
Washington, DC.....................Business Law; Construction Law; Natural Resources Law

LOSEY & ASSOCIATES
San Francisco, CA ....Tax Law

LOSKAMP, ALVIN N., A LAW CORPORATION
Burbank, CA ....Business Law; Probate, Trusts and Estate Planning

LOSQUADRO & ZERBO, A PROFESSIONAL CORPORATION
New York, NY.......................Admiralty/Maritime Law; Insurance Defense

LOTT, FRANKLIN, FONDA & FLANAGAN
Greenwood, MS ....General Practice

LOTT & FRIEDLAND, P.A.
Miami, FL ....Patent, Trademark, Copyright and Unfair Competition

LOUNSBERY, FERGUSON, ALTONA & PEAK, LLP
Escondido, CA ....General Practice

LOVE, THORNTON, ARNOLD & THOMASON, P.A.
Greenville, SC.........................Civil Trial Practice; Criminal Trial Practice; Environmental Law; General Practice; Insurance Defense; Medical Malpractice; Product Liability Law; Real Estate Law

LOVELESS & LYONS
Mobile, AL...............................Civil Trial Practice; Commercial Litigation; General Practice

LOVELL & SKIRNICK, LLP
New York, NY.......................Antitrust Law; Civil Trial Practice; Commercial Law; Criminal Trial Practice; Securities Law

LOVETT, THOMAS G.
Minneapolis, MN....................Bankruptcy Law; General Practice; Probate, Trusts and Estate Planning

LOVETT, COOPER & GLASS
Charleston, WV.......................Civil Trial Practice; Family Law; General Practice

LOVITT & HANNAN, INC.
San Francisco, CA ....Civil Trial Practice

LOVITZ AND GOLD, P.C.
Philadelphia, PA ....Civil Trial Practice; Labor and Employment Law

LOW, BALL & LYNCH, A PROFESSIONAL CORPORATION
Redwood City, CA ....Appellate Practice; Civil Trial Practice; Construction Law; Environmental Law; General Practice; Insurance Defense; Medical Malpractice; Personal Injury; Product Liability Law; Real Estate Law

LOWE, WILLIAM J.
Clarendon, TX ....Health Care Law

LOWE, MOBLEY & LOWE
Haleyville, AL ....Insurance Defense

LOWE, SHIRLEY & YEAGER
Knoxville, TN ....Insurance Defense

LOWE, STEIN, HOFFMAN, ALLWEISS & HAUVER, L.L.P.
New Orleans, LA ....General Practice

LOWEN & ABUT, P.A.
Fort Lee, NJ............................Civil Trial Practice; General Practice

LOWENHAUPT & CHASNOFF, L.L.C.
St. Louis, MO.........................General Practice; Tax Law

LOWENSTEIN, SANDLER, KOHL, FISHER & BOYLAN, A PROFESSIONAL CORPORATION
Newark, NJ ....General Practice
Roseland, NJ...........................Banking Law; Civil Trial Practice; Criminal Trial Practice; Environmental Law; General Practice; Tax Law
Somerville, NJ ....Civil Trial Practice; General Practice

LOWERY, J. PAUL, A PROFESSIONAL CORPORATION
Montgomery, AL ....Personal Injury

LOWRY & JOHNSON
Valley Falls, KS ....General Practice

LOWTHORP, RICHARDS, MCMILLAN, MILLER, CONWAY & TEMPLEMAN, A PROFESSIONAL CORPORATION
Oxnard, CA ....General Practice

LOWY, RONALD S. THE LAW OFFICES OF
Miami, FL ....Commercial Litigation

LOZES & CAMBRE
New Orleans, LA ....Insurance Defense

LUBIN, MICHAEL I.
Hackensack, NJ ....Civil Trial Practice; Personal Injury

LUBIN, STANLEY THE LAW OFFICES OF
Phoenix, AZ ....Labor and Employment Law

LUBIN AND GANO, P.A.
West Palm Beach, FL ....Criminal Trial Practice

LUCAS BOWKER & WHITE
Edmonton, AB, Canada ....Civil Trial Practice; Commercial Law; Environmental Law; General Practice

LUCAS, HOLCOMB & MEDREA
Merrillville, IN ....General Practice

LUCAS LAW FIRM, THE
San Francisco, CA ....Civil Trial Practice; Labor and Employment Law

LUCAS & MONAGHAN, P.C.
Miles City, MT........................General Practice

LUCAS, PRENDERGAST, ALBRIGHT, GIBSON & NEWMAN
Columbus, OH ....Real Estate Law

LUCCO BROWN & MUDGE
Edwardsville, IL......................Civil Trial Practice

LUCE, FORWARD, HAMILTON & SCRIPPS LLP
La Jolla, CA ....General Practice; Probate, Trusts and Estate Planning
San Diego, CA ....Banking Law; Bankruptcy Law; Business Law; Environmental Law; Family Law; General Practice; Insurance Defense; Labor and Employment Law; Personal Injury; Product Liability Law; Real Estate Law

LUCE & QUILLINAN
Mountain View, CA.................Business Law; Civil Trial Practice; Probate, Trusts and Estate Planning; Real Estate Law; Securities Law; Tax Law

LUCKETT LAW FIRM, A PROFESSIONAL ASSOCIATION
Clarksdale, MS ....General Practice; Insurance Defense

LUDENS, POTTER & BURCH
Morrison, IL............................General Practice

LUDLUM & LUDLUM
Austin, TX ....Civil Rights; Civil Trial Practice; Communications Law; Insurance Defense; Medical Malpractice; Personal Injury; Product Liability Law; Transportation Law

LUDWIG GOLDBERG & KRENZEL, A PROFESSIONAL CORPORATION
San Francisco, CA ....Employment Benefits Law

LUEDEKA, NEELY & GRAHAM, P.C.
Knoxville, TN ....Patent, Trademark, Copyright and Unfair Competition

LUEDERS, ROBERTSON & KONZEN
Granite City, IL ....General Practice

LUFFEY, JOHN L. JR.
Monroe, LA ....Tax Law

LUNDEEN, DAVID F.
Fergus Falls, MN....................General Practice

LUND LAW CORPORATION
Los Angeles, CA ....Probate, Trusts and Estate Planning

LUNDY & ASSOCIATES, P.C.
Fort Wayne, IN.......................Patent, Trademark, Copyright and Unfair Competition

LUNDY & ASSOCIATES, P.C. — Continued

Indianapolis, IN ....Patent, Trademark, Copyright and Unfair Competition

LUNDY & DAVIS, L.L.P.

Lake Charles, LA ....Admiralty/Maritime Law; Personal Injury

LUPER, SHERIFF & NEIDENTHAL, A LEGAL PROFESSIONAL ASSOCIATION

Columbus, OH ....Bankruptcy Law; Business Law; Medical Malpractice; Personal Injury

LUPO & KOCZKUR, P.C.

Detroit, MI.............................Insurance Defense; Product Liability Law

LUSK & LUSK

Guntersville, AL......................General Practice; Insurance Defense

LUSTBADER, PHILIP M., & DAVID LUSTBADER, A PROFESSIONAL CORPORATION

Livingston, NJ........................Civil Trial Practice; Insurance Defense; Medical Malpractice; Personal Injury; Product Liability Law; Workers Compensation

LUTHER, ANDERSON, PLLP

Chattanooga, TN ....Insurance Defense

LUTTRINGER, WAYNE LAW OFFICES OF

San Francisco, CA ....General Practice; Workers Compensation

LUTY, ROBERT L., A PROFESSIONAL CORPORATION

Los Angeles, CA......................Medical Malpractice; Personal Injury; Product Liability Law

LUTZ, SHAFRANSKI, GORMAN AND MAHONEY, P.A.

New Brunswick, NJ.................Civil Trial Practice; Personal Injury

LUVAAS, COBB, RICHARDS & FRASER, P.C.

Eugene, OR ....General Practice; Insurance Defense

LUXAN & MURFITT

Helena, MT ....General Practice

LUXENBERG, GARBETT, KELLY & SAPIENZA, P.C.

New Castle, PA.......................Insurance Defense

LYLE, JOHN E.

Houston, TX ....Business Law

LYLES, HAMMETT, DARR & CLARK

Spartanburg, SC......................General Practice

LYNBERG & WATKINS, A PROFESSIONAL CORPORATION

Los Angeles, CA......................Civil Trial Practice

LYNCH, J. KENNETH

San Francisco, CA ....Personal Injury; Product Liability Law

LYNCH & ASSOCIATES, P.L.L.C.

Boise, ID................................General Practice; Insurance Defense; Product Liability Law

LYNCH, CHAPPELL & ALSUP, A PROFESSIONAL CORPORATION

Midland, TX ....General Practice; Natural Resources Law; Tax Law

LYNCH, DALLAS, SMITH & HARMAN, P.C.

Cedar Rapids, IA....................Civil Trial Practice; General Practice

LYNCH & FARMER

Honolulu, HI..........................Admiralty/Maritime Law; Bankruptcy Law; Civil Trial Practice; Commercial Law; Family Law; Immigration and Naturalization; Personal Injury; Real Estate Law

LYNCH, GALLAGHER, LYNCH & MARTINEAU, P.L.L.C.

Mount Pleasant, MI.................Environmental Law; General Practice

LYNCH, LYNCH & LYNCH

Winchester, TN ....General Practice

LYNCH, MANN, SMITH & MANN

Beckley, WV...........................Civil Trial Practice; General Practice; Insurance Defense

LYNCH, TRAUB, KEEFE AND ERRANTE, A PROFESSIONAL CORPORATION

New Haven, CT ....Civil Trial Practice; General Practice; Labor and Employment Law; Medical Malpractice; Product Liability Law; Transportation Law

LYNN, FULKERSON AND NICHOLS

Lexington, KY ....Insurance Defense; Medical Malpractice; Workers Compensation

LYNN, JACKSON, SHULTZ & LEBRUN, P.C.

Rapid City, SD........................Civil Trial Practice; Criminal Trial Practice; Employment Benefits Law; General Practice

LYNN LAW OFFICE

Syracuse, NY...........................Personal Injury

LYNN, STODGHILL, MELSHEIMER, TILLOTSON, L.L.P.

Dallas, TX..............................Commercial Law

LYON, P.C.

Bloomfield Hills, MI...............Patent, Trademark, Copyright and Unfair Competition

LYON, FERRITER & FITZPATRICK

Holyoke, MA ....General Practice

LYON & LYON LLP

Los Angeles, CA......................Antitrust Law; Patent, Trademark, Copyright and Unfair Competition

LYON, WEIGAND & GUSTAFSON, P.S.

Yakima, WA............................General Practice

LYONS & BEAUDRY, P.A.

Sarasota, FL............................Probate, Trusts and Estate Planning; Real Estate Law

LYONS, BRANDT, COOK & HIRAMATSU

Honolulu, HI...........................General Practice

LYONS, PIPES & COOK, P.C.

Mobile, AL.............................Admiralty/Maritime Law; Appellate Practice; Banking Law; Bankruptcy Law; Civil Trial Practice; Commercial Law; Environmental Law; General Practice; Labor and Employment Law; Municipal Bond/Public Authority Financing; Natural Resources Law; Probate, Trusts and Estate Planning; Product Liability Law; Real Estate Law; Tax Law

LYTAL, REITER, CLARK, SHARPE, ROCA, FOUNTAIN & WILLIAMS

West Palm Beach, FL..............Medical Malpractice; Personal Injury; Product Liability Law

LYTLE, THOMAS F.

Sacramento, CA ....Civil Trial Practice; Personal Injury

LYTLE SOULÉ & CURLEE

Oklahoma City, OK.................General Practice; Labor and Employment Law; Probate, Trusts and Estate Planning

MABRY, HERBECK & CHILTON, L.L.P.

Texas City, TX........................Civil Trial Practice

MACCABE & MCGUIRE

Chicago, IL.............................Civil Trial Practice; Insurance Defense

MACCARTHY, POJANI & HURLEY

Worcester, MA........................Banking Law; Civil Trial Practice; General Practice; Insurance Defense

MACCARTNEY, MACCARTNEY, KERRIGAN & MACCARTNEY

Nyack, NY ....General Practice; Insurance Defense

MACDONALD, IAIN A. LAW OFFICES OF

San Francisco, CA ....Bankruptcy Law

MACDONALD, FITZGERALD & MACDONALD, P.C.

Flint, MI................................General Practice; Personal Injury; Product Liability Law; Workers Compensation

MACDONALD AND GOREN, P.C.

Birmingham, MI......................Business Law; Civil Trial Practice; Employment Benefits Law; Environmental Law; Labor and Employment Law; Probate, Trusts and Estate Planning; Real Estate Law; Sports and Entertainment Law; Tax Law

MACDONALD, ILLIG, JONES & BRITTON LLP

Erie, PA ....General Practice

MACELREE, HARVEY, GALLAGHER, FEATHERMAN & SEBASTIAN, LTD.

Exton, PA...............................General Practice

Kennett Square, PA ....General Practice

West Chester, PA....................Banking Law; Civil Trial Practice; General Practice; Personal Injury

MACERA & JARZYNA

Ottawa, ON, Canada ....Patent, Trademark, Copyright and Unfair Competition

MACEY, WILENSKY, COHEN, WITTNER & KESSLER, LLP

Atlanta, GA ....Bankruptcy Law; Civil Trial Practice; General Practice; Real Estate Law

MACFARLANE FERGUSON & MCMULLEN

Clearwater, FL ....General Practice

Tampa, FL..............................General Practice

MACIE, JAMES J.

Atlanta, GA ....Family Law

Jonesboro, GA ....Family Law

MACINNIS, DONNER & KOPLOWITZ

San Francisco, CA ....Business Law; Family Law; Probate, Trusts and Estate Planning

MACKALL, MACKALL & GIBB, A PROFESSIONAL CORPORATION
Fairfax, VA ....General Practice; Probate, Trusts and Estate Planning; Real Estate Law

MACKENZIE GERVAIS, S.E.N.C.
Montreal, QU, Canada ....General Practice

MACKENZIE & PEDEN, P.S.C.
Louisville, KY ....Employment Benefits Law; General Practice; Insurance Defense; Probate, Trusts and Estate Planning; Real Estate Law

MACKOFF, KELLOGG, KIRBY & KLOSTER, P.C.
Dickinson, ND ....General Practice

MACLEAN & JACQUES, LTD.
Phoenix, AZ ....Appellate Practice; Commercial Law; Family Law; Probate, Trusts and Estate Planning; Real Estate Law

MACLEAY, LYNCH, GREGG & LYNCH, P.C.
Washington, DC.......................Insurance Defense

MACLEOD, DANIEL B.
San Diego, CA ....Admiralty/Maritime Law; Appellate Practice; Civil Trial Practice

MACPHERSON LAW OFFICES LLC
Rawlins, WY ....General Practice

MACPHERSON LESLIE & TYERMAN
Regina, SK, Canada.................Business Law; Commercial Law; Commercial Litigation; Construction Law; Environmental Law; General Practice; Labor and Employment Law; Natural Resources Law; Securities Law

MACRAE, GERALD C.
Los Angeles, CA ....Civil Trial Practice

MACVEAN, LEWIS, SHERWIN & MCDERMOTT, P.C.
Middletown, NY ....Banking Law; Civil Trial Practice; General Practice; Real Estate Law

MADDEN, FRANK, & ASSOCIATES
Plymouth, MN ....Employment Benefits Law

MADDEN, MADDEN AND DEL DUCA, P.A.
Haddonfield, NJ.......................General Practice

MADDIN, HAUSER, WARTELL, ROTH, HELLER & PESSES, P.C.
Southfield, MI ....Banking Law; Business Law; Employment Benefits Law; Probate, Trusts and Estate Planning; Real Estate Law; Tax Law

MADDIN, MILLER & MCCUNE
Nashville, TN...........................Business Law; Civil Trial Practice; Insurance Defense; Personal Injury; Product Liability Law; Workers Compensation

MADDOX LAW FIRM, PROFESSIONAL CORPORATION
Hobbs, NM ....General Practice

MADDOX, THOMAS E., JR., P.C.
Atlanta, GA ....Civil Rights; Criminal Trial Practice; Medical Malpractice

MADEWELL, JARED & HALFACRE
Cookeville, TN.........................Civil Trial Practice; General Practice; Insurance Defense

MADIGAN & SCOTT, INC.
Springfield, VA.........................Business Law; Civil Trial Practice; Real Estate Law

MADISON, HARBOUR & MROZ, P.A.
Albuquerque, NM.....................Commercial Litigation; Insurance Defense; Medical Malpractice; Product Liability Law

MADORSKY, MARSHA G.
Miami, FL ....Probate, Trusts and Estate Planning

MADORY, ZELL AND PLEISS, A PROFESSIONAL CORPORATION
Tustin, CA................................Medical Malpractice

MAEDER, JEROME A., LAW OFFICES, S.C.
Wausau, WI..............................Medical Malpractice; Personal Injury

MAGAÑA, CATHCART & MCCARTHY
Los Angeles, CA ....Personal Injury

MAGEE, PAGANO & ISHERWOOD
Wall Township, NJ.................Civil Trial Practice; General Practice; Insurance Defense

MAGER, MERCER, SCOTT & ALBER, P.C.
Detroit, MI...............................Banking Law; Civil Trial Practice; Commercial Law; Commercial Litigation; Construction Law; Insurance Defense; Real Estate Law

MAGGIO & KATTAR, P.C.
Washington, DC........................Immigration and Naturalization

MAGILL AND RUMSEY, P.C.
Ann Arbor, MI ....Commercial Litigation; Personal Injury; Tax Law

MAGRUDER & SUMNER
Rome, GA ....Civil Trial Practice

MAGUIRE, SAMUEL F.
Augusta, GA ....Civil Trial Practice; Personal Injury

MAGUIRE & ORBACH, LAW CORPORATION
Los Angeles, CA ....Construction Law

MAGUIRE, VOORHIS & WELLS, P.A.
Orlando, FL ....Immigration and Naturalization; Patent, Trademark, Copyright and Unfair Competition

MAHAN AND ELLIS, CHARTERED
Las Vegas, NV ....Appellate Practice; Commercial Litigation; General Practice; Real Estate Law; Sports and Entertainment Law

MAHASSNI, HASSAN, LAW OFFICE OF
Jeddah, Saudi Arabia ....General Practice

MAHER, GIBSON AND GUILEY, A PROF. ASSN. OF LAWYERS
Orlando, FL ....Medical Malpractice; Personal Injury; Product Liability Law

MAHER, LEE & GODDARD, LLP
Irvine, CA.................................Environmental Law; General Practice

MAHL REHON WALWORTH & ROBERTS, A PROFESSIONAL CORPORATION
San Jose, CA ....Business Law; Commercial Litigation; Construction Law

MAHON & FARLEY, P.A.
Jacksonville, FL ....Family Law

MAHONEY, COPPENRATH, JAFFE & PEARSON LLP
Los Angeles, CA ....Admiralty/Maritime Law; Civil Trial Practice; Commercial Litigation; Probate, Trusts and Estate Planning; Real Estate Law; Tax Law

MAHONEY, DOUGHERTY AND MAHONEY, P.A. PROFESSIONAL ASSOCIATION
Minneapolis, MN ....Civil Trial Practice; Insurance Defense

MAHOWALD, RALPH E., A PROFESSIONAL ASSOCIATION
Scottsdale, AZ..........................Medical Malpractice; Personal Injury; Product Liability Law

MAIDER & SMITH
Gloversville, NY.......................Administrative Law; General Practice

MAIN, JOHN W., P.C.
Phoenix, AZ ....Workers Compensation

MAIN, RONALD, P.C.
Tulsa, OK.................................Business Law; Civil Trial Practice; Family Law; General Practice; Real Estate Law

MAINERO, MARIO W., JR., INC.
Newport Beach, CA.................Civil Trial Practice

MAINS & MAINS, L.C.
Alexandria, VA ....Personal Injury

MAIRE, MANSELL & BEASLEY, A LAW CORPORATION
Redding, CA ....Insurance Defense; Personal Injury

MAIRONE, BIEL, ZLOTNICK & FEINBERG, P.A.
Atlantic City, NJ......................Civil Trial Practice; General Practice

MAJESTIC, PARSONS, SIEBERT & HSUE, A PROFESSIONAL CORPORATION
San Francisco, CA ....Patent, Trademark, Copyright and Unfair Competition

MAKOUL, RICHARD J.
Allentown, PA ....Civil Trial Practice; Criminal Trial Practice; Personal Injury

MALIN, HALEY, DIMAGGIO AND CROSBY, P.A.
Fort Lauderdale, FL................Patent, Trademark, Copyright and Unfair Competition
Miami, FL ....Patent, Trademark, Copyright and Unfair Competition
West Palm Beach, FL..............Patent, Trademark, Copyright and Unfair Competition

MALLIA & JACOBS
Houston, TX ....Medical Malpractice

MALLINCKRODT & MALLINCKRODT
Salt Lake City, UT...................Patent, Trademark, Copyright and Unfair Competition

MALLOY & MALLOY, INC.
Tulsa, OK.................................Bankruptcy Law; Labor and Employment Law

MALNICK, DAVID, A PROFESSIONAL CORPORATION
San Jose, CA ....Civil Trial Practice; Personal Injury; Product Liability Law

MALONE, THOMAS WILLIAM
Atlanta, GA ....Personal Injury

MALONE, THOMAS P., & ASSOCIATES, P.C.
Denver, CO ....Family Law

MALONEY, BARR & HUENNEKENS, A PROFESSIONAL CORPORATION
Richmond, VA ....Bankruptcy Law; Commercial Law; Commercial Litigation; Construction Law; General Practice; Labor and Employment Law; Personal Injury; Securities Law

MALONEY & MALONEY
Aberdeen, SD ....Construction Law; Employment Benefits Law; Labor and Employment Law

MALONEY, MEHLMAN & KATZ
New York, NY ....Business Law; Securities Law

MALONEY & YURACHEK, P.C.
Falls Church, VA ....Probate, Trusts and Estate Planning

MALOON, JERRY L., CO., L.P.A.
Columbus, OH ....Medical Malpractice

MALOVOS & KONEVICH
Los Altos, CA ....Business Law; Civil Trial Practice; Family Law; General Practice; Probate, Trusts and Estate Planning; Real Estate Law

MANAHAN, PIETRYKOWSKI, BAMMAN & DELANEY
Toledo, OH ....Commercial Litigation; Insurance Defense

MANATT, PHELPS & PHILLIPS, LLP
Los Angeles, CA ....General Practice

MANCHESTER, BENNETT, POWERS & ULLMAN, A LEGAL PROFESSIONAL ASSOCIATION
Youngstown, OH ....General Practice

MANCHESTER LAW OFFICES, PROFESSIONAL CORPORATION
Burlington, VT ....Civil Trial Practice; Commercial Law; Environmental Law; Medical Malpractice; Natural Resources Law; Personal Injury

MANCHESTER & PIGNATO, P.C.
Oklahoma City, OK ....Civil Rights; Insurance Defense

MANCHESTER & WILLIAMS
San Jose, CA ....Criminal Trial Practice

MANCINI, ROWLAND & WELCH
Kahului, HI ....General Practice

MANCKE, WAGNER, HERSHEY AND TULLY
Harrisburg, PA ....Civil Trial Practice; Criminal Trial Practice; Family Law; General Practice; Personal Injury; Transportation Law

MANDEL, LIPTON AND STEVENSON LIMITED
Chicago, IL..............................Civil Trial Practice; Family Law; General Practice; Immigration and Naturalization

MANDELSTAMM, JEROME R.
St. Louis, MO..........................Business Law; Probate, Trusts and Estate Planning; Real Estate Law

MANESS, MICHAEL A.
Houston, TX ....General Practice

MANEY, DAMSKER, HARRIS & JONES, P.A.
Tampa, FL ....Appellate Practice; Civil Trial Practice; Commercial Litigation; Criminal Trial Practice; Family Law; Probate, Trusts and Estate Planning; Tax Law

MANEY, RICHARD, & ASSOCIATES, P.A.
Tampa, FL ....Immigration and Naturalization

MANG LAW FIRM, THE, P.A.
Tallahassee, FL ....Insurance Defense; Labor and Employment Law

MANGHAM AND DAVIS
Lafayette, LA ....Administrative Law; Appellate Practice; Civil Trial Practice; Environmental Law; Natural Resources Law

MANGUM, WALL, STOOPS & WARDEN, P.L.L.C.
Flagstaff, AZ ....Civil Trial Practice; General Practice; Insurance Defense; Personal Injury; Probate, Trusts and Estate Planning

MANIER, HEROD, HOLLABAUGH & SMITH, A PROFESSIONAL CORPORATION
Nashville, TN..........................Banking Law; Bankruptcy Law; Business Law; Commercial Law; Construction Law; Environmental Law; General Practice; Health Care Law; Insurance Defense; Labor and Employment Law; Medical Malpractice; Probate, Trusts and Estate Planning; Product Liability Law; Real Estate Law; Tax Law; Workers Compensation

MANION MCDONOUGH & LUCAS, A PROFESSIONAL CORPORATION
Pittsburgh, PA ....Business Law; Commercial Law; General Practice

MANLEY, BURKE, LIPTON & COOK, A LEGAL PROFESSIONAL ASSOCIATION
Cincinnati, OH ....Land Use Law; Municipal and Zoning Law

MANN, HENRY B.
Louisville, KY ....Probate, Trusts and Estate Planning; Real Estate Law

MANN & MITCHELL
Providence, RI........................Civil Rights; Criminal Trial Practice

MANN, TREVINO, HALE & GALLEGO
Laredo, TX..............................General Practice; Natural Resources Law; Probate, Trusts and Estate Planning

MANN, WALTER, WEATHERS, WALTER & BISHOP, L.C.
Springfield, MO......................General Practice

MANNING, THOMAS C.
Raleigh, NC............................Civil Trial Practice; Criminal Trial Practice

MANNING & SIMONE
Toronto, ON, Canada..............Criminal Trial Practice

MANOS, MARTIN, PERGRAM & BROWNING
Delaware, OH ....General Practice

MANSFIELD & TANICK, P.A.
Minneapolis, MN....................Bankruptcy Law; Civil Trial Practice; Labor and Employment Law; Probate, Trusts and Estate Planning

MANSOUR, GAVIN, GERLACK & MANOS CO., L.P.A.
Cleveland, OH........................Civil Trial Practice

MANTA AND WELGE
Philadelphia, PA ....Civil Trial Practice; Environmental Law; Insurance Defense; Product Liability Law

MANWELL & MILTON
San Francisco, CA ....Business Law; Securities Law

MAPOTHER & MAPOTHER
Louisville, KY ....Banking Law; Bankruptcy Law; Real Estate Law

MAPP, HARRY L. JR.
Halifax, VA ....Civil Trial Practice; General Practice

MARAN & MARAN
Newark, NJ ....Appellate Practice; Civil Trial Practice; Medical Malpractice; Personal Injury; Product Liability Law

MARCH & MYATT, P.C.
Fort Collins, CO ....General Practice

MARCO, MARCO & BAILEY
Medina, OH ....Criminal Trial Practice; General Practice; Personal Injury; Product Liability Law

MARCO, WATKINS AND OWSIANY
Grosse Pointe, MI....................Business Law; Probate, Trusts and Estate Planning; Real Estate Law

MARCUS & SHAPIRA, L.L.P.
Pittsburgh, PA ....Antitrust Law; Bankruptcy Law; Civil Trial Practice; Commercial Law; Family Law; General Practice; Insurance Defense; Labor and Employment Law; Personal Injury; Probate, Trusts and Estate Planning; Real Estate Law; Securities Law; Tax Law

MARDEN, DUBORD, BERNIER & STEVENS
Waterville, ME........................General Practice

MAREK & FRANCIS, P.A.
Carlsbad, NM ....Civil Trial Practice; Commercial Litigation; Insurance Defense; Product Liability Law; Real Estate Law

MARGER, JOHNSON, MCCOLLOM & STOLOWITZ, P.C.
Portland, OR..........................Patent, Trademark, Copyright and Unfair Competition

MARGOLIS & CASSIDY
Milwaukee, WI ....Family Law

MARIANI, ROBERT D.
Scranton, PA ....Labor and Employment Law

MARISCAL, WEEKS, MCINTYRE & FRIEDLANDER, P.A.
Phoenix, AZ ....Bankruptcy Law; Commercial Litigation; Family Law; General Practice; Real Estate Law

MARK BOLSON KUNTZ & SEREMBE
San Bernardino, CA ....Workers Compensation

MARKEL, SCHAFER & GOLDMAN, P.C.
Pittsburgh, PA ....Civil Trial Practice; Commercial Law; Commercial Litigation; Health Care Law; Real Estate Law

MARKOW, WALKER, REEVES & ANDERSON, P.A.
Jackson, MS ....Environmental Law; Insurance Defense; Medical Malpractice

MARK & PEARLSTEIN, P.A.
Phoenix, AZ ....Family Law; Insurance Defense; Medical Malpractice; Personal Injury

MARKS, GRAY, CONROY & GIBBS, P.A.
Jacksonville, FL ....Civil Trial Practice; General Practice

MARKS & MADSEN
Sioux City, IA ....General Practice

MARKS & MURASE, L.L.P.
Los Angeles, CA ....General Practice
Washington, DC......................General Practice
New York, NY........................General Practice

MARKS, O'NEILL, REILLY, O'BRIEN & COURTNEY, P.C.
Philadelphia, PA ....Civil Trial Practice; Environmental Law; Insurance Defense; Medical Malpractice; Personal Injury; Product Liability Law; Workers Compensation

MARKS, SHELL, MANESS & MARKS
Clarksville, TN ....General Practice

MARKSON, ALDAN O.
Kenilworth, NJ ....Appellate Practice; General Practice; Real Estate Law

MARKUSON, GLORIA CROWLEY
Scarsdale, NY........................General Practice; Probate, Trusts and Estate Planning

MARKUSSON, GREEN & JARVIS, P.C.
Denver, CO ....Civil Trial Practice; Insurance Defense

MARLER, DAVID F. H. THE LAW OFFICES OF
Montreal, QU, Canada ....Admiralty/Maritime Law

MARLIN & SALTZMAN, A PROFESSIONAL LAW CORPORATION
Orange, CA ....Insurance Defense

MARONEY, CROWLEY, BANKSTON, RICHARDSON & HULL, L.L.P.
Austin, TX ....Civil Trial Practice

MARRINER & CRUMRINE
Washington, PA ....General Practice

MARRONE ROBINSON FREDERICK & FOSTER, PROFESSIONAL CORPORATION
Burbank, CA ....Insurance Defense

MARRS, MICHAEL D., A PROFESSIONAL CORPORATION
St. Joseph, MI ....Personal Injury

MARS, RICHARD D., P.A.
Bartow, FL..............................Criminal Trial Practice

MARSH, DAY & CALHOUN
Bridgeport, CT ....General Practice
Southport, CT ....General Practice

MARSH, SPAEDER, BAUR, SPAEDER & SCHAAF
Erie, PA...................................General Practice; Insurance Defense; Tax Law

MARSHACK & GOE
Santa Ana, CA ....Bankruptcy Law; Commercial Litigation

MARSHALL, THOMAS E. LAW OFFICES OF
Detroit, MI..............................Labor and Employment Law; Municipal and Zoning Law

MARSHALL, DENNEHEY, WARNER, COLEMAN AND GOGGIN
Philadelphia, PA ....Civil Trial Practice; General Practice

MARSHALL, FARRELL, RICCI, SMITH & HADDICK, A PROFESSIONAL CORPORATION
Harrisburg, PA........................Insurance Defense

MARSHALL & GONZALEZ, L.L.P.
Houston, TX ....Insurance Defense
McAllen, TX ....Insurance Defense

MARSHALL, WILLIAMS & GORHAM, L.L.P.
Wilmington, NC......................Admiralty/Maritime Law; Civil Trial Practice; General Practice

MARTIN, CHARLES L.
Decatur, GA............................Administrative Law

MARTIN, ADE, BIRCHFIELD & MICKLER, P.A.
Jacksonville, FL ....General Practice

MARTIN, BACON & MARTIN, P.C.
Mount Clemens, MI................Civil Trial Practice; Medical Malpractice; Personal Injury; Product Liability Law

MARTIN, BROWNE, HULL & HARPER
Springfield, OH ....General Practice

MARTIN, CHAPMAN, SCHILD & LASSAW, CHARTERED
Boise, ID.................................General Practice; Probate, Trusts and Estate Planning
Sun Valley, ID........................Probate, Trusts and Estate Planning
Twin Falls, ID........................Probate, Trusts and Estate Planning

MARTIN, CHURCHILL, OVERMAN, HILL & COLE, CHARTERED
Wichita, KS ....Labor and Employment Law

MARTIN, CLEARWATER & BELL
New York, NY........................Civil Trial Practice; Health Care Law; Insurance Defense; Medical Malpractice; Personal Injury; Product Liability Law

MARTIN, DANIEL N., P.A.
New Port Richey, FL ....Administrative Law; Civil Trial Practice; Real Estate Law

MARTIN, DOUGLAS, A LAW CORPORATION
Indian Wells, CA ....Probate, Trusts and Estate Planning; Real Estate Law

MARTIN, GUNN & MARTIN, A PROFESSIONAL CORPORATION
Westmont, NJ ....Civil Trial Practice

MARTIN, HOPKINS & LEMON, P.C.
Roanoke, VA...........................Business Law; Civil Trial Practice; Probate, Trusts and Estate Planning; Real Estate Law

MARTIN & HUDSON
Pasadena, CA ....Probate, Trusts and Estate Planning; Tax Law

MARTIN, INGLES & INGLES, LTD.
Gloucester, VA........................General Practice

MARTIN, JOHN O., P.C.
Denver, CO ....Civil Trial Practice

MARTIN, JUNGHANS, SNYDER & BERNSTEIN, P.A.
Baltimore, MD ....Criminal Trial Practice; Real Estate Law

MARTIN LAW FIRM, THE, P.C.
Atlanta, GA ....Insurance Defense

MARTIN LAW OFFICE
Oklahoma City, OK................Criminal Trial Practice

MARTIN, LUTZ & BROWER, P.C.
Las Cruces, NM......................Appellate Practice; Civil Trial Practice; Commercial Litigation; Real Estate Law

MARTIN, MAGNUSON, MCCARTHY & KENNEY
Boston, MA.............................General Practice; Insurance Defense

MARTIN & MARTIN, P.A.
Lakeland, FL...........................General Practice

MARTIN, MARTIN & WOODARD, LLP
Syracuse, NY...........................Bankruptcy Law; Civil Trial Practice; Commercial Law; Personal Injury; Probate, Trusts and Estate Planning

MARTIN & MEHAFFY
Boulder, CO ....Civil Trial Practice; Insurance Defense; Real Estate Law

MARTIN, OCKERMAN & BRABANT
Lexington, KY ....Business Law; General Practice; Land Use Law; Real Estate Law

MARTIN & OLIVEIRA
Pittsfield, MA..........................General Practice

MARTIN & PATTERSON, LTD.
Phoenix, AZ ....Real Estate Law

MARTIN, PERGRAM & BROWNING CO., L.P.A.
Columbus, OH ....Civil Trial Practice; Commercial Litigation; Employment Benefits Law; General Practice; Labor and Employment Law; Probate, Trusts and Estate Planning

MARTIN, PICKLESIMER, JUSTICE & VINCENT
Ashland, KY ....Civil Trial Practice; General Practice; Insurance Defense; Personal Injury

MARTIN, PRINGLE, OLIVER, WALLACE & SWARTZ, L.L.P.
Wichita, KS ....General Practice

MARTIN, RONALD T., P.A.
Boca Raton, FL ....Tax Law

MARTIN, SHOWERS, SMITH, MCDONALD & BRYANT, L.L.P.
Hillsboro, TX..........................General Practice

MARTIN, TATE, MORROW & MARSTON, P.C.
Memphis, TN ....General Practice

MARTIN, VAN DE WALLE, DONOHUE, MCGAHAN & CATALANO
Jericho, NY ....Civil Trial Practice; Commercial Law; General
Practice

MARTIN, WILSON, ERICKSON & MACDOWELL, A PROFESSIONAL CORPORATION
Santa Ana, CA.........................Appellate Practice; Civil Trial Practice; Medical
Malpractice; Product Liability Law

MARTINDALE, BRZYTWA & QUICK
Cleveland, OH ....Civil Trial Practice; Insurance Defense; Medical
Malpractice; Product Liability Law

MARTINDELL, SWEARER & SHAFFER
Hutchinson, KS.........................General Practice

MARTINEAU WALKER
Montreal, QU, Canada ....General Practice
Quebec, QU, Canada ....General Practice

MARTINEZ, GEORGE C.
Belvedere-Tiburon, CA ....Civil Trial Practice

MARTINEZ, DALTON, DELLECKER & WILSON, PROFESSIONAL ASSOCIATION
Orlando, FL ....Civil Trial Practice; Medical Malpractice; Personal
Injury; Product Liability Law

MARTÍNEZ ODELL & CALABRIA
San Juan, PR............................Banking Law; Bankruptcy Law; Civil Trial Practice;
Commercial Law; Environmental Law; General
Practice; Labor and Employment Law; Municipal
Bond/Public Authority Financing; Real Estate Law;
Tax Law

MARTSON, DEARDORFF, WILLIAMS & OTTO, A PROFESSIONAL CORPORATION
Carlisle, PA ....General Practice

MARTZELL & BICKFORD
New Orleans, LA ....Personal Injury

MARX & MARX
New York, NY.........................Labor and Employment Law

MARZIK, ROBERT K., P.C., LAW OFFICES OF
Stratford, CT ....Admiralty/Maritime Law

MASCAGNI, FRANK III
Louisville, KY ....Criminal Trial Practice; General Practice

MASERITZ, GUY B.
Columbia, MD ....Business Law

MASKALERIS & ASSOCIATES
Morristown, NJ.........................Civil Trial Practice

MASON, GRIFFIN & PIERSON, A PROFESSIONAL CORPORATION
Princeton, NJ ....Civil Trial Practice; General Practice

MASON, J. CHENEY, P.A.
Orlando, FL ....Criminal Trial Practice; Family Law

MASON, STEINHARDT, JACOBS & PERLMAN, PROFESSIONAL CORPORATION
Southfield, MI ....Commercial Law; Environmental Law; General
Practice; Land Use Law; Municipal and Zoning
Law; Probate, Trusts and Estate Planning; Real
Estate Law; Tax Law

MASON & THOMAS
Sacramento, CA ....Civil Trial Practice; Insurance Defense; Personal
Injury

MASSA, PATRICK C., P.A., LAW OFFICES OF
North Palm Beach, FL ....Civil Trial Practice; Personal Injury

MASSENGILL, CALDWELL, HYDER & BUNN, P.C.
Bristol, TN ....General Practice

MAST, FRANK & ASSOCIATES
Pittsburgh, PA ....Civil Trial Practice; Tax Law

MASTERS & TAYLOR, L.C.
Charleston, WV........................Personal Injury

MASUD, GILBERT & PATTERSON, P.C.
Saginaw, MI ....Labor and Employment Law

MATHENY POIDMORE LINKERT & SEARS
Sacramento, CA ....Civil Trial Practice; Employment Benefits Law;
Insurance Defense; Personal Injury; Real Estate Law

MATHESON, PARR, SCHULER, EWALD & JOLLY, L.L.P.
Troy, MI...................................General Practice; Labor and Employment Law;
Transportation Law

MATHEW & MATHEW
Phoenix, AZ ....Criminal Trial Practice; Tax Law

MATHEWS RAILEY DECUBELLIS & GOODWIN, P.A.
Orlando, FL ....Civil Trial Practice; General Practice

MATHEWS, WOODBRIDGE & COLLINS, A PROFESSIONAL CORPORATION
Princeton, NJ ....Trademark, Copyright and Unfair Competition

MATHIS, MARIFIAN, RICHTER & GRANDY, LTD.
Belleville, IL ....Probate, Trusts and Estate Planning; Tax Law

MATHISON, CARL M. JR.
West Palm Beach, FL ....Personal Injury

MATHISON & MATHISON
Palm Beach Gardens, FL.........Probate, Trusts and Estate Planning; Real Estate
Law

MATKOV, SALZMAN, MADOFF & GUNN
Chicago, IL...............................Employment Benefits Law; Labor and Employment
Law

MATSEN, JEFFREY R. & ASSOCIATES
Santa Ana, CA ....Business Law; Probate, Trusts and Estate Planning

MATTHEWS & BRANSCOMB, A PROFESSIONAL CORPORATION
Corpus Christi, TX ....Civil Trial Practice; General Practice; Natural
Resources Law; Probate, Trusts and Estate
Planning; Real Estate Law; Tax Law
San Antonio, TX......................Antitrust Law; Communications Law; General
Practice; Municipal Bond/Public Authority
Financing; Natural Resources Law; Tax Law; Trans-
portation Law

MATTHEWS, HUTTON & EASTMOORE
Sarasota, FL ....Commercial Law; Medical Malpractice; Personal
Injury

MATTHEWS WHITE & FISCHER, A PROFESSIONAL CORPORATION
Morristown, NJ.........................Banking Law; Commercial Law; Environmental
Law; Insurance Defense; Municipal and Zoning
Law; Product Liability Law

MATTHIAS & BERG LLP
Los Angeles, CA ....Business Law; Commercial Litigation; International
Business Law; Mergers and Acquisitions; Securities
Law; Tax Law

MATTINGLY, RUDOLPH, FINE & PORTER
Evansville, IN...........................Business Law; Commercial Law; Insurance Defense;
Workers Compensation

MATTIONI, MATTIONI & MATTIONI, LTD.
Philadelphia, PA ....Admiralty/Maritime Law; Civil Trial Practice;
Environmental Law; General Practice

MATTOCH, IAN L.
Honolulu, HI.............................Personal Injury; Product Liability Law

MATTOX & MATTOX
New Albany, IN ....General Practice; Medical Malpractice; Personal
Injury; Product Liability Law

MATTSON & MADDEN
Newark, NJ ....Civil Trial Practice; General Practice; Insurance
Defense; Product Liability Law; Transportation Law

MATTSON, RICKETTS, DAVIES, STEWART & CALKINS
Lincoln, NE..............................General Practice

MATZ, JEFFREY A. LAW OFFICES OF
Los Angeles, CA ....Civil Trial Practice

MAUPIN TAYLOR ELLIS & ADAMS, P.A.
Raleigh, NC..............................General Practice; Labor and Employment Law

MAURER, EUGENE J., JR., P.A.
Wilmington, DE........................Criminal Trial Practice; Personal Injury

MAURER LAW FIRM
La Jolla, CA ....Civil Trial Practice

MAUTZ BAUM HOSTETTER & O'HANLON
Pendleton, OR..........................General Practice

MAUZY LAW FIRM
Minneapolis, MN ....Criminal Trial Practice

MAXEY LAW OFFICES, P.S.
Spokane, WA.............................Criminal Trial Practice; Family Law

MAXWELL, MAXWELL, WALSH & LISKO
Waynesboro, PA ....General Practice

MAY, MICHAEL R.
Des Moines, IA ....Public Utilities Law

MAY, ADAM, GERDES & THOMPSON
Pierre, SD ....General Practice

MAY AND MAY, PROFESSIONAL CORPORATION
Detroit, MI...............................Probate, Trusts and Estate Planning

Southfield, MI ....Probate, Trusts and Estate Planning

MAY, OBERFELL & LORBER
South Bend, IN ....Insurance Defense; Trademark, Copyright and Unfair Competition

MAYALL, HURLEY, KNUTSEN, SMITH & GREEN, A PROFESSIONAL CORPORATION
Stockton, CA...........................Business Law; Construction Law; Environmental Law; Insurance Defense; Product Liability Law

MAYER, BROWN & PLATT
Los Angeles, CA ....General Practice
Washington, DC....................General Practice
Chicago, IL ....General Practice
New York, NY ....General Practice
Houston, TX ....General Practice
Brussels, Belgium ....General Practice
London, England ....General Practice
Berlin, Germany.....................General Practice

MAYER, FRIEDLICH, SPIESS, TIERNEY, BROWN & PLATT
Chicago, IL ....General Practice

MAYER & SCANLAN, P.C.
Fairfax, VA ....Bankruptcy Law

MAYER, SMITH & ROBERTS, L.L.P.
Shreveport, LA........................Civil Trial Practice; General Practice; Insurance Defense; Medical Malpractice; Workers Compensation

MAYER, VOGT, SMITH & PALMQUIST
Clarksville, IN ....Civil Trial Practice; General Practice; Personal Injury; Probate, Trusts and Estate Planning; Real Estate Law

MAYFIELD AND BROOKS
Lafayette, IN ....General Practice; Probate, Trusts and Estate Planning

MAYFIELD AND PERRENOT, A PROFESSIONAL CORPORATION
El Paso, TX............................Banking Law; General Practice; Immigration and Naturalization; Insurance Defense; International Trade Law; Probate, Trusts and Estate Planning

MAYNE & MAYNE
Sioux City, IA ....Civil Trial Practice; General Practice; Insurance Defense

MAYNES, BRADFORD, SHIPPS & SHEFTEL
Durango, CO...........................General Practice

MAYOCK, W. MICHAEL
Pasadena, CA ....Criminal Trial Practice

MAYOR, DAY, CALDWELL & KEETON, L.L.P.
Austin, TX ....General Practice
Houston, TX ....General Practice

MAYS, KARBERG & WACHTER
Cleveland, OH.........................Real Estate Law

MAZUR, CARP & RUBIN, P.C.
New York, NY.........................Civil Trial Practice; Construction Law; Probate, Trusts and Estate Planning

MCAFEE & TAFT, A PROFESSIONAL CORPORATION
Oklahoma City, OK.................General Practice; Natural Resources Law; Tax Law

MCALLISTER, MICHAEL L., LTD.
Phoenix, AZ ....Insurance Defense; Product Liability Law

MCALLISTER, WESTMORELAND, VESPER, SCHWARTZ, HYBERG & WHITE, A PROFESSIONAL CORPORATION
Atlantic City, NJ......................Civil Trial Practice; General Practice
West Atlantic City, NJ ....General Practice

MCALOON & FRIEDMAN, P.C.
New York, NY........................Civil Trial Practice; Health Care Law; Medical Malpractice; Personal Injury

MCANANY, VAN CLEAVE & PHILLIPS, P.A.
Kansas City, KS......................Civil Trial Practice; General Practice; Insurance Defense; Personal Injury
Lenexa, KS ....General Practice

MCANDREW, THOMAS J.
Providence, RI........................Labor and Employment Law

MCBRIDE BAKER & COLES
Chicago, IL ....Antitrust Law; Business Law; Employment Benefits Law; General Practice; Labor and Employment Law; Probate, Trusts and Estate Planning; Real Estate Law; Securities Law; Tax Law

MCBRIDE AND MCBRIDE, P.C.
Grove City, PA ....General Practice

MCCABE & COZZENS
Mineola, NY............................Insurance Defense

MCCABE & MACK LLP
Poughkeepsie, NY ....General Practice

MCCABE, O'DONNELL & WRIGHT, A PROFESSIONAL ASSOCIATION
Phoenix, AZ ....Banking Law; Probate, Trusts and Estate Planning; Real Estate Law; Tax Law

MCCAFFREY & TAWWATER
Oklahoma City, OK.................Civil Trial Practice; Labor and Employment Law; Medical Malpractice; Personal Injury; Workers Compensation

MCCAHILL, JOHN A.
Alexandria, VA ....Criminal Trial Practice

MCCAHILL, JOHN A.
Washington, DC......................Criminal Trial Practice

MCCALLAR AND ASSOCIATES
Savannah, GA ....Bankruptcy Law; Civil Trial Practice

MCCALLA, THOMPSON, PYBURN, HYMOWITZ & SHAPIRO
New Orleans, LA ....Labor and Employment Law

MCCAMPBELL & YOUNG, A PROFESSIONAL CORPORATION
Knoxville, TN ....Banking Law; Commercial Law; Communications Law; Natural Resources Law; Real Estate Law; Tax Law

MCCANDLESS & HUNT
Portland, ME ....General Practice; Probate, Trusts and Estate Planning; Tax Law

MCCANDLISH & LILLARD, A PROFESSIONAL CORPORATION
Fairfax, VA ....Business Law; Civil Trial Practice; Commercial Litigation; General Practice; Health Care Law; Medical Malpractice; Probate, Trusts and Estate Planning; Real Estate Law

MCCANN, GARLAND, RIDALL & BURKE
Pittsburgh, PA ....Business Law; Civil Trial Practice; Commercial Law; General Practice; Probate, Trusts and Estate Planning; Real Estate Law

MCCANNA, KONZ, DUDAS & ASSOCIATES, S.C.
Appleton, WI ....Civil Trial Practice; Insurance Defense

MCCARROLL, NUNLEY & HARTZ
Owensboro, KY ....General Practice

MCCARTER & ENGLISH
Wilmington, DE......................General Practice
Cherry Hill, NJ ....Civil Trial Practice; General Practice
Newark, NJ ....Admiralty/Maritime Law; Antitrust Law; Banking Law; Bankruptcy Law; Civil Trial Practice; Commercial Law; Communications Law; Computer Law; Family Law; General Practice; Health Care Law; Insurance Defense; International Business Law; Labor and Employment Law; Municipal Bond/Public Authority Financing; Natural Resources Law; Personal Injury; Probate, Trusts and Estate Planning; Real Estate Law; Securities Law; Tax Law; Trademark, Copyright and Unfair Competition; Transportation Law

MCCARTHY, JOHN C.
Claremont, CA ....Civil Trial Practice; Labor and Employment Law

MCCARTHY & ASSOCIATES, INC.
Oklahoma City, OK.................Patent, Trademark, Copyright and Unfair Competition

MCCARTHY, BACON & COSTELLO, L.L.P.
Lanham, MD............................General Practice; Personal Injury

MCCARTHY, LEBIT, CRYSTAL & HAIMAN CO., L.P.A.
Cleveland, OH.........................Tax Law

MCCARTHY, PALMER, VOLKEMA, BOYD & THOMAS, A LEGAL PROFESSIONAL ASSOCIATION
Columbus, OH ....Civil Trial Practice; Medical Malpractice; Personal Injury; Product Liability Law

MCCARTHY AND SCHATZMAN, P.A.
Princeton, NJ ....Banking Law; Civil Trial Practice; Commercial Law; Family Law; General Practice; Municipal and Zoning Law; Probate, Trusts and Estate Planning; Real Estate Law

MCCARTHY, SUMMERS, BOBKO, MCKEY, WOOD & SAWYER, P.A.
Stuart, FL................................Civil Trial Practice; Commercial Law; Commercial Litigation; Family Law; Land Use Law; Probate, Trusts and Estate Planning; Real Estate Law

MCCARTHY TÉTRAULT
Vancouver, BC, Canada...........General Practice
London, ON, Canada ....General Practice

MCCARTHY TÉTRAULT — *Continued*

    Ottawa, ON, Canada ....General Practice
    Toronto, ON, Canada ....General Practice
    Montreal, QU, Canada ....General Practice
    Quebec, QU, Canada ....General Practice
    London, England ....General Practice

MCCARTHY, WILSON & ETHRIDGE
    Rockville, MD.......................General Practice

MCCAUGHAN, WILLIAM P. LAW OFFICE OF
    Miami, FL.........................General Practice; Real Estate Law

MCCAUGHEY & METOS
    Salt Lake City, UT..................Criminal Trial Practice

MCCAULEY & ASSOCIATES, LLP
    Costa Mesa, CA ....Business Law; Civil Trial Practice

MCCAULEY, MACDONALD & DEVIN, P.C.
    Dallas, TX..............................Appellate Practice; Civil Trial Practice; Commercial Law; Construction Law; Environmental Law; Health Care Law; Insurance Defense; Labor and Employment Law; Medical Malpractice; Municipal and Zoning Law; Patent, Trademark, Copyright and Unfair Competition; Product Liability Law; Real Estate Law; Workers Compensation

MCCAY, JAMES "KEN"
    Baton Rouge, LA....................Real Estate Law

MCCLELLAN & BROWN, A PROFESSIONAL CORPORATION
    San Diego, CA ....Civil Trial Practice; Personal Injury; Product Liability Law

MCCLELLAN, POWERS, EHMLING & DIX, P.C.
    Gallatin, TN...........................Civil Trial Practice; Insurance Defense

MCCLESKEY, HARRIGER, BRAZILL & GRAF, L.L.P.
    Lubbock, TX...........................General Practice

MCCLUNG, PETERS AND SIMON
    Albany, NY.............................Banking Law; Commercial Litigation; Insurance Defense

MCCLURE, DAVID R.
    El Paso, TX.............................Family Law

MCCLURE & MILLER
    Erie, PA...................................General Practice

MCCLURE, RAMSAY & DICKERSON
    Toccoa, GA............................Civil Trial Practice; General Practice; Insurance Defense; Real Estate Law

MCCLUSKEY, HUGH B.
    Parsippany, NJ.......................Civil Trial Practice; Family Law; Probate, Trusts and Estate Planning

MCCONAUGHEY & GOFF
    Decatur, GA...........................Probate, Trusts and Estate Planning

MCCONNAUGHHAY, ROLAND, MAIDA & CHERR, P.A.
    Tallahassee, FL ....Civil Trial Practice

MCCONNELL AND FINNERTY
    North Vernon, IN...................General Practice

MCCONNELL & MENDELSON
    Chicago, IL.............................Antitrust Law; Commercial Litigation; Computer Law; Securities Law

MCCONNELL VALDÉS
    San Juan, PR..........................General Practice

MCCORMACK, COONEY, HILLMAN & ELDER
    Omaha, NE ....General Practice

MCCORMACK & EPSTEIN
    Boston, MA.............................Civil Trial Practice; Insurance Defense; Personal Injury

MCCORMICK AND CHRISTOPH, P.C.
    Boulder, CO ....Criminal Trial Practice; Personal Injury

MCCORMICK, KIDMAN & BEHRENS, LLP
    Costa Mesa, CA ....Environmental Law; General Practice; Natural Resources Law

MCCORMICK LAW FIRM
    Williamsport, PA ....Banking Law; Civil Trial Practice; General Practice; Medical Malpractice; Real Estate Law; Workers Compensation

MCCORMICK & PRIORE
    Philadelphia, PA ....Insurance Defense; Product Liability Law

MCCORRISTON MIHO MILLER MUKAI
    Honolulu, HI...........................Business Law; Civil Trial Practice; General Practice; Insurance Defense; International Business Law; Real Estate Law; Tax Law

MCCOY, EDWIN F.
    Philadelphia, PA ....Civil Trial Practice

MCCOY, BAKER & WEST
    Lexington, KY ....Civil Trial Practice; Criminal Trial Practice

MCCOY, HAWTHORNE, ROBERTS & BEGNAUD, LTD. A LAW CORPORATION
    Natchitoches, LA ....General Practice

MCCOY, WEAVER, WIGGINS, CLEVELAND & RAPER
    Fayetteville, NC ....General Practice

MCCOY, WILKINS, STEPHENS & TIPTON, P.A.
    Jackson, MS ....Insurance Defense

MCCOYD, EDWARD A., P.C.
    Garden City, NY ....Probate, Trusts and Estate Planning

MCCRARY, BARRY N.
    Talladega, AL..........................Civil Trial Practice

MCCUBBIN, DENNIS T.
    Brentwood, MO ....Civil Trial Practice

MCCULLOUGH, SMITH & WRIGHT, P.A.
    St. Paul, MN ....Family Law; Personal Injury

MCCURLEY, KINSER, MCCURLEY & NELSON, L.L.P.
    Dallas, TX...............................Family Law

MCCUTCHEN, BLANTON, RHODES & JOHNSON, L.L.P.
    Columbia, SC ....Appellate Practice; Civil Trial Practice; General Practice; Insurance Defense

MCCUTCHEN, DOYLE, BROWN & ENERSEN
    Los Angeles, CA ....General Practice
    San Francisco, CA ....General Practice
    San Jose, CA ....General Practice
    Walnut Creek, CA ....General Practice
    Washington, DC......................General Practice
    Taipei, Taiwan........................General Practice

MCCUTCHEON, MCCUTCHEON & BAXTER, P.A.
    Conway, SC ....General Practice; Insurance Defense

MCDADE, FOGLER, MAINES & LOHSE, L.L.P.
    Houston, TX ....Civil Trial Practice

MCDANIEL, DUKE A.
    Petersburg, WV ....General Practice

MCDANIEL, HALL & CONERLY, P.C.
    Birmingham, AL ....General Practice

MCDANIEL & MARSH
    Baltimore, MD ....Appellate Practice; Civil Trial Practice; Commercial Litigation; Criminal Trial Practice

MCDAVID, NOBLIN & WEST, PLLC
    Jackson, MS ....Administrative Law; Civil Trial Practice; Natural Resources Law; Probate, Trusts and Estate Planning; Real Estate Law

MCDERMOTT & MCGEE
    Millburn, NJ...........................Appellate Practice; Civil Trial Practice; General Practice; Insurance Defense; Medical Malpractice; Personal Injury

MCDERMOTT, WILL & EMERY
    Los Angeles, CA ....Antitrust Law; Trademark, Copyright and Unfair Competition
    Newport Beach, CA................Labor and Employment Law
    Washington, DC.....................Antitrust Law; Labor and Employment Law; Tax Law; Trademark, Copyright and Unfair Competition
    Miami, FL ....Admiralty/Maritime Law; Antitrust Law; Labor and Employment Law; Trademark, Copyright and Unfair Competition
    Chicago, IL.............................Admiralty/Maritime Law; Antitrust Law; Labor and Employment Law; Tax Law; Trademark, Copyright and Unfair Competition
    Boston, MA.............................Tax Law; Trademark, Copyright and Unfair Competition
    New York, NY ....Antitrust Law; Labor and Employment Law; Tax Law; Trademark, Copyright and Unfair Competition

MCDONALD, DUARD R.
    Marietta, GA...........................Commercial Law; Family Law

MCDONALD, BROWN & FAGEN
    Dallas Center, IA....................General Practice

MCDONALD, C. DOUGLAS, JR. & ASSOCIATES, P.A.
Tampa, FL ....Patent, Trademark, Copyright and Unfair Competition

MCDONALD CARANO WILSON MCCUNE BERGIN FRANKOVICH & HICKS LLP
Las Vegas, NV ....Civil Trial Practice; Commercial Law; General Practice; Municipal and Zoning Law; Probate, Trusts and Estate Planning; Real Estate Law
Reno, NV ....Administrative Law; Civil Trial Practice; Commercial Law; Construction Law; Employment Benefits Law; Environmental Law; General Practice; Labor and Employment Law; Municipal and Zoning Law; Probate, Trusts and Estate Planning; Real Estate Law; Securities Law; Tax Law; Workers Compensation

MCDONALD GROUP, THE, L.L.P.
Erie, PA ....General Practice

MCDONALD & HAYDEN
Toronto, ON, Canada ....Securities Law; Trademark, Copyright and Unfair Competition

MCDONALD, HOPKINS, BURKE & HABER CO., L.P.A.
Cleveland, OH ....General Practice

MCDONALD KUHN
Memphis, TN ....General Practice; Insurance Defense

MCDONALD & MCDONALD
Miami, FL ....Aviation Law

MCDONALD, MCKENZIE, RUBIN, MILLER AND LYBRAND, L.L.P.
Columbia, SC ....General Practice; Insurance Defense

MCDONALD & QUACKENBUSH, A PROFESSIONAL SERVICE CORPORATION
Seattle, WA ....Civil Trial Practice

MCDONALD, SAELTZER, MORRIS, CREEGGAN & WADDOCK
Sacramento, CA ....Civil Trial Practice; Insurance Defense

MCDONALD SANDERS, A PROFESSIONAL CORPORATION
Fort Worth, TX ....General Practice

MCDONALD, WILLIAM H., & ASSOCIATES, P.C.
Springfield, MO ....Civil Trial Practice; Commercial Law; General Practice

MCDONALD, WILLIAM R., P.C.
Denver, CO ....Tax Law

MCDONNELL TRIAL LAWYERS
Naples, FL ....Civil Trial Practice

MCDONOUGH, HOLLAND & ALLEN, A PROFESSIONAL CORPORATION
Sacramento, CA ....General Practice

MCDONOUGH, KORN, EICHHORN & BOYLE, A PROFESSIONAL CORPORATION
Springfield, NJ ....Civil Trial Practice; Criminal Trial Practice; General Practice; Insurance Defense; Medical Malpractice; Personal Injury; Product Liability Law

MCDONOUGH, O'DELL, BEERS, WIELAND, WILLIAMS AND KRAKAR
Orlando, FL ....Insurance Defense; Personal Injury

MCDOUGALL, READY
Regina, SK, Canada ....Banking Law; Civil Trial Practice; Commercial Law; General Practice; Probate, Trusts and Estate Planning; Product Liability Law
Saskatoon, SK, Canada ....General Practice

MCDOWALL, COTTER, DUNN, VALE & BRACCO, A PROFESSIONAL CORPORATION
San Mateo, CA ....Civil Trial Practice; Insurance Defense

MCDOWELL, JOSEPH F., III, P.A.
Manchester, NH ....Personal Injury

MCDOWELL, WICK, DALY, GALLUP, HAUSER AND HARTLE
Bradford, PA ....General Practice

MCDUFF, JOHN, P.C., A PROFESSIONAL CORPORATION
Austin, TX ....Tax Law

MCDUFFEE, PAUL G. II
Tampa, FL ....Personal Injury

MCELDREW & FULLAM, P.C.
Philadelphia, PA ....Labor and Employment Law; Medical Malpractice; Personal Injury; Transportation Law

MCELROY, DEUTSCH AND MULVANEY
Morristown, NJ ....Civil Trial Practice; Commercial Law; Construction Law; Environmental Law; General Practice; Insurance Defense

MCEWEN, SCHMITT & CO.
Vancouver, BC, Canada ....Admiralty/Maritime Law

MCFADDEN & DILLON, A PROFESSIONAL CORPORATION
Chicago, IL ....Banking Law; Civil Trial Practice; Commercial Litigation; General Practice; Labor and Employment Law

MCFALL, SHERWOOD & SHEEHY, A PROFESSIONAL CORPORATION
Houston, TX ....Civil Trial Practice; Insurance Defense; Medical Malpractice; Personal Injury

MCFARLAIN, WILEY, CASSEDY & JONES, PROFESSIONAL ASSOCIATION
Tallahassee, FL ....Administrative Law; Appellate Practice; Civil Trial Practice; Family Law; Health Care Law; Insurance Defense; Personal Injury; Product Liability Law

MCFERRIN (BATES), LINDSAY K.
Kansas City, MO ....Insurance Defense

MCGAHN, FRISS & ISMAN
Atlantic City, NJ ....Civil Trial Practice; General Practice

MCGARITY, J. MICHAEL, P.C.
Lawrenceville, GA ....Personal Injury

MCGARRY & LAUFENBERG
El Segundo, CA ....Insurance Defense; Personal Injury; Product Liability Law

MCGAUGHEY & SPIRITO
Torrance, CA ....Family Law; Probate, Trusts and Estate Planning

MCGEE, LONNIE G.
San Diego, CA ....Probate, Trusts and Estate Planning; Tax Law

MCGEE, TIMOTHY W.
Worcester, MA ....Business Law

MCGEE, GAINEY & HUSKEY, P.A.
Fort Lauderdale, FL ....Commercial Law; Personal Injury

MCGEE & GELMAN
Buffalo, NY ....Civil Trial Practice; General Practice; Patent, Trademark, Copyright and Unfair Competition

MCGEE, HANKLA, BACKES & WHEELER, P.C.
Minot, ND ....Commercial Law; General Practice; Insurance Defense; Probate, Trusts and Estate Planning

MCGEE & POWERS, P.A.
Orlando, FL ....Commercial Litigation; Insurance Defense

MCGILL, GOTSDINER, WORKMAN & LEPP, P.C.
Omaha, NE ....Civil Trial Practice; General Practice; Health Care Law; International Business Law; Labor and Employment Law; Tax Law; Workers Compensation

MCGILLICUDDY, TERRENCE J., P.C.
Phoenix, AZ ....Aviation Law; Personal Injury

MCGILL, R. JACKSON, LAW OFFICES OF
Sarasota, FL ....Personal Injury

MCGIMPSEY & CAFFERTY
Somerset, NJ ....Communications Law; General Practice

MCGINNIS, LOCHRIDGE & KILGORE, L.L.P.
Austin, TX ....Banking Law; Civil Trial Practice; General Practice; Natural Resources Law; Real Estate Law; Tax Law; Transportation Law
Houston, TX ....General Practice

MCGIVERN, SCOTT, GILLIARD, CURTHOYS & ROBINSON, PROFESSIONAL CORPORATION
Tulsa, OK ....Civil Trial Practice; Insurance Defense; Labor and Employment Law; Product Liability Law; Workers Compensation

MCGLINCHEY STAFFORD LANG
New Orleans, LA ....General Practice

MCGLYNN & MCGLYNN
Belleville, IL ....Banking Law; Product Liability Law

MCGLYNN, MCLORG & RITCHIE
San Francisco, CA ....Insurance Defense; Medical Malpractice

MCGOUGAN, WRIGHT, WORLEY AND HARPER
Tabor City, NC ....General Practice

MCGOVERN, CONNELLY & DAVIDSON
New Rochelle, NY ....General Practice; Tax Law

MCGOWAN, EDWARD M.
Maspeth, NY ....General Practice; Probate, Trusts and Estate Planning; Real Estate Law; Tax Law

MCGRATH, J. NICHOLAS, P.C.
Aspen, CO ....Civil Trial Practice; General Practice; Real Estate Law

MCGRATH, NORTH, MULLIN & KRATZ, P.C.
Omaha, NE ....Antitrust Law; Civil Trial Practice; General Practice; Insurance Defense; Labor and Employment Law; Tax Law

MCGREGOR, MALCOLM, INC., A PROF. CORP., LAW OFFICES OF
El Paso, TX ....General Practice; Personal Injury

MCGREGOR & SHEA, P.C.
Boston, MA.............................Environmental Law

MCGUANE, FRANK, & ASSOCIATES, P.C.
Denver, CO ....Family Law

MCGUINESS & WILLIAMS
Washington, DC......................Labor and Employment Law

MCGUIRE, JAMES A.
Edgewater, MD ....Civil Trial Practice

MCGUIRE & MCGUIRE, P.C.
Worcester, MA ....Civil Trial Practice; Criminal Trial Practice; General Practice

MCGUIRE, PRATT, MASIO & FARRANCE, P.A.
Bradenton, FL.........................Commercial Law; Environmental Law; Family Law; Municipal and Zoning Law; Real Estate Law

MCGUIRE, WOOD & BISSETTE, P.A.
Asheville, NC ....Civil Trial Practice; General Practice

MCGUIRE, WOODS, BATTLE & BOOTHE
Jacksonville, FL ....General Practice
Washington, DC......................General Practice
Alexandria, VA ....General Practice
Charlottesville, VA.................General Practice
McLean, VA ....General Practice
Norfolk, VA ....General Practice
Richmond, VA ....Antitrust Law; General Practice; Labor and Employment Law; Municipal Bond/Public Authority Financing; Tax Law

MCHENRY, ROBERT, P.A.
Little Rock, AR ....Medical Malpractice

MCHIE, MYERS, MCHIE & ENSLEN
Hammond, IN.........................Civil Trial Practice; General Practice

MCINERNEY, GARY J., P.C.
Grand Rapids, MI ....Civil Trial Practice; Medical Malpractice; Personal Injury

MCINNES COOPER & ROBERTSON
St. John's, NF, Canada............Administrative Law; Admiralty/Maritime Law; Appellate Practice; Banking Law; Bankruptcy Law; Business Law; Civil Trial Practice; Commercial Law; Construction Law; Employment Benefits Law; Environmental Law; General Practice; Insurance Defense; Labor and Employment Law; Medical Malpractice; Natural Resources Law; Personal Injury; Probate, Trusts and Estate Planning; Product Liability Law; Public Utilities Law; Real Estate Law; Securities Law; Transportation Law
Halifax, NS, Canada ....Administrative Law; Admiralty/Maritime Law; Banking Law; Bankruptcy Law; Business Law; Civil Trial Practice; Commercial Law; Construction Law; Employment Benefits Law; Environmental Law; Family Law; General Practice; Health Care Law; Insurance Defense; Labor and Employment Law; Municipal and Zoning Law; Natural Resources Law; Personal Injury; Probate, Trusts and Estate Planning; Real Estate Law; Tax Law; Transportation Law

MCINTOSH & LEE
Florence, SC ....Insurance Defense

MCINTOSH, SAWRAN & CRAVEN, P.A.
Fort Lauderdale, FL ....Admiralty/Maritime Law; Medical Malpractice

MCINTOSH, SHERARD & SULLIVAN
Anderson, SC ....General Practice

MCKAY, BYRNE & GRAHAM
Los Angeles, CA ....Insurance Defense

MCKAY & GUÉRARD, P.A.
Charleston, SC ....General Practice
Columbia, SC ....General Practice

MCKAY, JOHN J., JR., P.A.
Hilton Head Island, SC ....Civil Trial Practice

MCKAY, MCKAY, HENRY & FOSTER, P.A.
Columbia, SC ....Civil Trial Practice; General Practice; Medical Malpractice; Product Liability Law

MCKEE & BARGE
Atlanta, GA ....Labor and Employment Law

MCKEEVER, STUART A.
Westport, CT...........................Civil Trial Practice; Criminal Trial Practice; General Practice; Probate, Trusts and Estate Planning; Real Estate Law; Tax Law

MCKENDREE, JOHN W., LAW OFFICES OF
Denver, CO ....Labor and Employment Law

MCKENNA & CUNEO, L.L.P.
Washington, DC......................General Practice

MCKENNA, JAMES L., P.C.
Cherry Hill, NJ ....Civil Trial Practice; Environmental Law

MCKENNA & STAHL
Irvine, CA................................Real Estate Law; Securities Law

MCKENNEY, THOMSEN AND BURKE, LLP
Baltimore, MD ....Business Law; Probate, Trusts and Estate Planning; Tax Law

MCKENZIE, GRAVES, MCRAE & VASSER
Hope, AR ....General Practice

MCKEOWN, FITZGERALD, ZOLLNER, BUCK, HUTCHISON & RUTTLE
Joliet, IL..................................Civil Trial Practice; General Practice; Personal Injury; Probate, Trusts and Estate Planning

MCKINNON AND MCKINNON
Holland, MI ....Patent, Trademark, Copyright and Unfair Competition

MCKIRDY AND RISKIN, A PROFESSIONAL CORPORATION
Morristown, NJ.......................Civil Trial Practice; Real Estate Law

MCKISSOCK & HOFFMAN, P.C.
Philadelphia, PA ....Aviation Law; Civil Trial Practice; Commercial Law; Commercial Litigation; Health Care Law; Insurance Defense; Medical Malpractice; Product Liability Law

MCKNIGHT, HUDSON, LEWIS & HENDERSON, PLLC
Memphis, TN ....Labor and Employment Law

MCKOOL SMITH, A PROFESSIONAL CORPORATION
Dallas, TX................................Civil Trial Practice

MCLACHLAN & GOLDMAN, LLC
Durango, CO............................Appellate Practice; Civil Trial Practice; Commercial Litigation; Insurance Defense

MCLAUGHLIN, LESLIE G.
Midland, TX ....Civil Trial Practice; General Practice; Insurance Defense; Personal Injury

MCLAUGHLIN AND FLORINI, LTD.
Sullivan, IL..............................General Practice

MCLAUGHLIN & FOLAN, P.C.
New Bedford, MA ....Civil Trial Practice; Insurance Defense

MCLEAN PETERSON LAW FIRM, CHARTERED
Mankato, MN ....Banking Law; General Practice

MCLENNAN ROSS
Calgary, AB, Canada ....Labor and Employment Law
Edmonton, AB, Canada ....Civil Trial Practice; General Practice; Labor and Employment Law

MCLEOD, ALEXANDER, POWEL & APFFEL, A PROFESSIONAL CORPORATION
Galveston, TX..........................General Practice

MCLEOD, BENTON, BEGNAUD & MARSHALL
Athens, GA ....Civil Trial Practice; General Practice; Health Care Law

MCLEOD, IAN C., P.C.
Okemos, MI ....Patent, Trademark, Copyright and Unfair Competition

MCLEOD VERLANDER
Monroe, LA ....Civil Trial Practice; Family Law; Health Care Law; Medical Malpractice; Personal Injury

MCLURE, PICKELS AND REICHMAN
Alexandria, LA ....Insurance Defense; Product Liability Law

MCMAHON, BERGER, HANNA, LINIHAN, CODY & MCCARTHY, A PROFESSIONAL CORPORATION
St. Louis, MO..........................Labor and Employment Law

MCMAHON & MCCOLLAM
Houma, LA ....Insurance Defense

MCMAHON, TIDWELL, HANSEN, ATKINS & PEACOCK, P.C.
Odessa, TX...............................General Practice

MCMANIMON & SCOTLAND
Newark, NJ ....Banking Law; Commercial Law; Environmental Law; General Practice; Municipal Bond/Public Authority Financing; Real Estate Law; Securities Law; Tax Law

MCMANIS, FAULKNER & MORGAN
San Jose, CA ....Antitrust Law; Appellate Practice; Civil Rights; Civil Trial Practice; Commercial Litigation; Construction Law; Criminal Trial Practice; Environmental Law; Family Law; Labor and Employment Law; Land Use Law; Personal Injury; Trademark, Copyright and Unfair Competition

MCMASTER, CLIFFORD F.
Fort Worth, TX ....Bankruptcy Law

MCMASTER MEIGHEN
Montreal, QU, Canada ....Admiralty/Maritime Law; Banking Law; Bankruptcy Law; Civil Trial Practice; Commercial Law; Construction Law; Environmental Law; General Practice; Insurance Defense; Labor and Employment Law; Municipal Bond/Public Authority Financing; Personal Injury; Probate, Trusts and Estate Planning; Real Estate Law; Tax Law; Transportation Law

MCMATH LAW FIRM, THE, P.A.
Little Rock, AR ....Civil Trial Practice; Medical Malpractice

MCMILLAN BINCH
Toronto, ON, Canada..............General Practice

MCMILLAN, CONSTABILE, MAKER, MURPHY & RAYMOND, LLP
Larchmont, NY........................General Practice

MCMILLEN & REINHART, P.A.
Orlando, FL ....Medical Malpractice

MCNAIR LAW FIRM, P.A.
Columbia, SC ....General Practice

MCNAMAR, FEARNOW & MCSHARAR, P.C.
Indianapolis, IN ....Administrative Law; Health Care Law

MCNAMARA, TODD J., P.C.
Denver, CO ....Labor and Employment Law

MCNAMEE, HOSEA, JERNIGAN & SCOTT, P.A.
Greenbelt, MD ....Business Law

MCNAUL EBEL NAWROT HELGREN & VANCE, P.L.L.C.
Seattle, WA ....Civil Trial Practice; General Practice

MCNEELY, HEFFERON & HEFFERON
Charlotte, NC..........................Personal Injury

MCNEES, WALLACE & NURICK
Harrisburg, PA........................Bankruptcy Law; Civil Trial Practice; Commercial Law; Construction Law; Employment Benefits Law; Environmental Law; General Practice; Health Care Law; Insurance Defense; Labor and Employment Law; Patent, Trademark, Copyright and Unfair Competition; Probate, Trusts and Estate Planning; Real Estate Law; Securities Law; Tax Law; Transportation Law

MCNEESE & ARTHUR, PLLC
Memphis, TN ....Family Law

MCNEIL, SILVEIRA & RICE
San Rafael, CA........................Business Law

MCNEIL AND SUSSON, A PROFESSIONAL CORPORATION
Santa Ana, CA ....Health Care Law; Medical Malpractice

MCNICHOLAS & MCNICHOLAS
Los Angeles, CA ....Civil Trial Practice

MCNULTY, ANTHONY J.
New York, NY.........................General Practice; Insurance Defense; Labor and Employment Law; Medical Malpractice; Personal Injury

MCNULTY, PETER J.
Los Angeles, CA ....Civil Trial Practice; Commercial Litigation; Medical Malpractice; Personal Injury; Product Liability Law

MCPHAIL, IAN D., A PROFESSIONAL CORPORATION
Carmel, CA ....Probate, Trusts and Estate Planning

MCPHARLIN, SPRINKLES & THOMAS, LLP
San Jose, CA ....Commercial Litigation; Labor and Employment Law; Real Estate Law

MCPHEE, CHARLES A. JR.
Walnut Creek, CA ....Business Law; Civil Trial Practice

MCPHERSON, WILLIAM H.
Fairfield, CA ....Family Law

MCPHERSON, WILLIAM V. JR., LAW OFFICE OF
Durham, NC ....Probate, Trusts and Estate Planning

MCQUADES, THE, CO., L.P.A.
Swanton, OH............................General Practice; Personal Injury

MCQUAIDE, BLASKO, SCHWARTZ, FLEMING & FAULKNER, INC.
State College, PA ....General Practice

MCREYNOLDS, GREGG C.
Denver, CO ....Civil Trial Practice

MCREYNOLDS, MARY A., P.C.
Washington, DC......................Civil Trial Practice; Commercial Law

MCSHANE & BOWIE, P.L.C.
Grand Rapids, MI ....General Practice; Probate, Trusts and Estate Planning; Real Estate Law; Securities Law

MCSHANE, BREITFELLER & WITTEN
Columbus, OH ....Antitrust Law; Business Law; Civil Trial Practice

MCSHANE, DAVIS & HANCE, L.L.P.
Dallas, TX...............................Family Law

MCTAGUE LAW FIRM
Windsor, ON, Canada ....Civil Trial Practice; Commercial Law; General Practice; Insurance Defense; Labor and Employment Law; Real Estate Law

MCTIGHE, WEISS, O'ROURKE & MILNER, P.C.
Norristown, PA........................General Practice

MCTURNAN & TURNER
Indianapolis, IN ....Antitrust Law; Appellate Practice; Civil Trial Practice; Labor and Employment Law; Securities Law

MCWHORTER, COBB & JOHNSON, L.L.P.
Lubbock, TX ....Civil Trial Practice; General Practice

MCWILLIAMS AND MINTZER, P.C.
Philadelphia, PA ....Civil Trial Practice; Health Care Law; Insurance Defense; Medical Malpractice

MEAD, HECHT, CONKLIN & GALLAGHER
White Plains, NY ....General Practice

MEAD, MEAD & THOMPSON
Salem, IN ....General Practice

MEADOWS, ICHTER & TRIGG, A PROFESSIONAL CORPORATION
Atlanta, GA ....Civil Trial Practice

MEADOWS, OWENS, COLLIER, REED, COUSINS & BLAU, L.L.P.
Dallas, TX...............................General Practice; Tax Law

MEADOWS, RILEY, KOENENN AND TEEL, L.L.C.
Gulfport, MS...........................Civil Trial Practice; Family Law; General Practice; Probate, Trusts and Estate Planning; Real Estate Law

MEAGHER & GEER, P.L.L.P.
Minneapolis, MN ....General Practice

MEAHER, AUGUSTINE, III, P.C.
Mobile, AL..............................Civil Trial Practice; General Practice

MEARDON, SUEPPEL, DOWNER & HAYES P.L.C.
Iowa City, IA ....Civil Trial Practice; General Practice; Municipal and Zoning Law

MEARS, CHRISTOPHER B., A P.C.
Irvine, CA................................Personal Injury

MEDEIROS KARMEN + SANFORD INC.
Providence, RI.........................Antitrust Law; Civil Trial Practice; General Practice; Labor and Employment Law; Securities Law

MEDLEN & CARROLL, LLP
San Francisco, CA ....Patent, Trademark, Copyright and Unfair Competition

MEDVIN & ELBERG
Newark, NJ ....Civil Trial Practice; Commercial Law; General Practice; Medical Malpractice; Personal Injury

MEEHAN & MEEHAN
Bridgeport, CT ....Criminal Trial Practice; Personal Injury

MEEKISON LAW FIRM
Napoleon, OH ....General Practice

MEENAN, KEVIN
Pasadena, CA ....Civil Trial Practice; Personal Injury; Product Liability Law

MEFFORD AND CARPENTER, A PROFESSIONAL CORPORATION
Auburn, IN ....Appellate Practice; Civil Trial Practice; Municipal and Zoning Law; Probate, Trusts and Estate Planning; Real Estate Law

MEGANCK & COTHORN, P.C.
Detroit, MI..............................Insurance Defense; Medical Malpractice; Product Liability Law

MEHAFFY & WEBER, A PROFESSIONAL CORPORATION
Beaumont, TX..........................Admiralty/Maritime Law; Civil Trial Practice;
Employment Benefits Law; Environmental Law;
General Practice; Insurance Defense; Medical
Malpractice; Personal Injury; Product Liability Law
Houston, TX..........................Civil Trial Practice; Environmental Law; Insurance
Defense; Personal Injury; Product Liability Law
Orange, TX..........................Civil Trial Practice; Environmental Law; Insurance
Defense; Personal Injury

MEHLMAN & GREENBLATT, LLC
Baltimore, MD..........................Bankruptcy Law; Civil Trial Practice; Medical
Malpractice

MEHRENS AND WILEMON, P.A.
Phoenix, AZ..........................Criminal Trial Practice

MEIGHEN DEMERS
Toronto, ON, Canada.............General Practice

MEILS, THOMPSON, DIETZ & CONGLETON
Indianapolis, IN......................Civil Trial Practice; Insurance Defense

MEISNER & ASSOCIATES, P.C.
Bingham Farms, MI..............Business Law; Civil Trial Practice; Real Estate Law

MEISSNER TIERNEY FISHER & NICHOLS, S.C.
Milwaukee, WI......................Business Law; Communications Law; Employment
Benefits Law; Environmental Law; Probate, Trusts
and Estate Planning; Real Estate Law; Securities
Law; Tax Law

MELAT, PRESSMAN, EZELL & HIGBIE
Colorado Springs, CO..............Civil Trial Practice; Personal Injury

MELEDIN, LOUISE Y.
Baltimore, MD......................Tax Law

MELLEY, STEVEN M.
Rhinebeck, NY......................Personal Injury

MELLI, WALKER, PEASE & RUHLY, S.C.
Madison, WI......................General Practice; Labor and Employment Law

MELLON, WEBSTER & MELLON, A PROF. CORP., THE LAW OFFICES OF
Doylestown, PA......................Personal Injury

MELTON, FLOYD M. JR.
Greenwood, MS......................Probate, Trusts and Estate Planning

MELTON, WILLIAM D.
Evergreen, AL......................General Practice

MELTON, ESPY, WILLIAMS & HAYES, P.C.
Montgomery, AL......................Insurance Defense; Medical Malpractice

MELTZER, SANFORD
Syracuse, NY......................Criminal Trial Practice; Family Law; Real Estate
Law

MELVIN & MELVIN
Laurel, MS......................Medical Malpractice; Personal Injury
Syracuse, NY......................General Practice

MENARD, MURPHY & WALSH
Boston, MA......................Business Law; Labor and Employment Law

MENDELSOHN ROSENTZVEIG SHACTER
Montreal, QU, Canada.............Banking Law; Bankruptcy Law; Commercial Law;
Commercial Litigation; Labor and Employment
Law; Patent, Trademark, Copyright and Unfair
Competition; Real Estate Law; Securities Law; Tax
Law

MENDES & MOUNT, L.L.P.
New York, NY......................Insurance Defense

MENES LAW CORPORATION
Los Angeles, CA......................Sports and Entertainment Law

MENG & UREY
Upper Marlboro, MD.............General Practice; Insurance Defense; Personal Injury

MENN, NELSON, SHARRATT, TEETAERT & BEISENSTEIN, LTD.
Appleton, WI......................Business Law; Commercial Law; Commercial
Litigation; Insurance Defense; Personal Injury;
Probate, Trusts and Estate Planning; Real Estate
Law; Workers Compensation

MENTZER & VUILLEMIN
Akron, OH......................Bankruptcy Law; Commercial Law; Commercial
Litigation; Criminal Trial Practice

MERCALDO, RONALD D., LTD.
Tucson, AZ......................Medical Malpractice; Personal Injury

MERCER & MERCER
Pittsburgh, PA......................Personal Injury

MEREDITH, DONNELL & ABERNETHY, A PROFESSIONAL CORPORATION
Corpus Christi, TX................Civil Trial Practice; Real Estate Law

MERKEL & COCKE, A PROFESSIONAL ASSOCIATION
Clarksdale, MS......................Civil Trial Practice; Medical Malpractice; Product
Liability Law; Tax Law

MERLINE & THOMAS, P.A.
Greenville, SC......................Employment Benefits Law; Probate, Trusts and
Estate Planning; Tax Law

MERLO, KANOFSKY & BRINKMEIER, LTD.
Chicago, IL......................Aviation Law; Insurance Defense

MERRILL, ABEL J., P.A.
Annapolis, MD......................Probate, Trusts and Estate Planning

MERRILL & MERRILL, CHARTERED
Pocatello, ID......................Appellate Practice; Business Law; Civil Trial
Practice; General Practice; Health Care Law;
Insurance Defense; Probate, Trusts and Estate
Planning; Public Utilities Law; Real Estate Law

MERRILL & MULLINS, A PROFESSIONAL ASSOCIATION
Memphis, TN......................Commercial Law

MERRILL, PORCH, DILLON & FITE, P.A.
Anniston, AL......................General Practice

MERRILL, STONE & PARKS
Swainsboro, GA......................Civil Trial Practice

MERRIMAN, PATTERSON & ALLISON
Longview, TX......................Insurance Defense

MERRITT, JERALYN E.
Denver, CO......................Criminal Trial Practice

MERRITT & MASON, P.A.
Brooksville, FL......................Family Law

MERVIS, CLARK D.
Miami, FL......................Criminal Trial Practice

MESERVE, MUMPER & HUGHES
Irvine, CA......................General Practice
Los Angeles, CA......................General Practice

MESH, GENE & ASSOCIATES
Cincinnati, OH......................General Practice; Securities Law

MESHBESHER & SPENCE, LTD.
Minneapolis, MN......................Civil Trial Practice; Criminal Trial Practice; General
Practice; Medical Malpractice; Personal Injury

MESIROV GELMAN JAFFE CRAMER & JAMIESON
Philadelphia, PA......................General Practice

MESSER, HOWARD F., P.C.
Pittsburgh, PA......................Civil Trial Practice; Commercial Law; Medical
Malpractice; Personal Injury; Product Liability Law

MESSINA LAW FIRM
Tacoma, WA......................Personal Injury

MESSNER PAVEK & REEVES, LLC
Denver, CO......................Business Law; Commercial Litigation; Real Estate
Law

METNICK, WISE, CHERRY & FRAZIER
Springfield, IL......................Civil Trial Practice; Criminal Trial Practice; Family
Law

METTE, EVANS & WOODSIDE, A PROFESSIONAL CORPORATION
Harrisburg, PA......................Administrative Law; Banking Law; Civil Trial
Practice; Commercial Law; Construction Law;
Environmental Law; General Practice; Municipal
Bond/Public Authority Financing; Real Estate Law;
Tax Law

METTLER, PETER W.
Palm Beach, FL......................Tax Law

METZGER, WICKERSHAM, KNAUSS & ERB
Harrisburg, PA......................Civil Trial Practice; General Practice; Insurance
Defense; Medical Malpractice; Personal Injury;
Probate, Trusts and Estate Planning; Product
Liability Law

MEYER, CAPEL, HIRSCHFELD, MUNCY, JAHN & ALDEEN, P.C.
Champaign, IL......................Business Law; Commercial Litigation; General
Practice

MEYER, FLUEGGE AND TENNEY, P.S.
Yakima, WA......................General Practice

MEYER, JIM, & ASSOCIATES, P.C.
Waco, TX......................Civil Trial Practice; Family Law; Personal Injury

MEYER, KIRK, SNYDER & SAFFORD, PLLC
Bloomfield Hills, MI...............Business Law; Civil Trial Practice; Family Law; General Practice; Probate, Trusts and Estate Planning; Real Estate Law
Detroit, MI.............................Family Law; General Practice

MEYER, MEYER & METLI ESQS., LLP
Smithtown, NY.......................Banking Law; General Practice; Probate, Trusts and Estate Planning

MEYER AND SWATKOSKI ASSOCIATES, A PROFESSIONAL CORPORATION
Wilkes-Barre, PA....................Civil Trial Practice

MEYER, UNKOVIC & SCOTT LLP
Pittsburgh, PA........................General Practice

MEYERS, BIANCHI & MCCONNELL, A PROFESSIONAL CORPORATION
Los Angeles, CA.....................Insurance Defense

MEYERS, BILLINGSLEY, RODBELL & ROSENBAUM, P.A.
Riverdale, MD.......................General Practice; Municipal Bond/Public Authority Financing; Real Estate Law

MEYERS, HENTEMANN, SCHNEIDER & REA CO., L.P.A.
Cleveland, OH.......................Civil Trial Practice; General Practice; Insurance Defense; Product Liability Law

MEYERS LAW FIRM
Phoenix, AZ...........................Antitrust Law; Civil Trial Practice; International Business Law; Municipal Bond/Public Authority Financing; Real Estate Law

MEYERS, O. CHRISTOPHER, INC.
Lawton, OK ....Tax Law

MEYNER AND LANDIS
Newark, NJ............................Banking Law; Civil Trial Practice; Commercial Law; Communications Law; General Practice; Immigration and Naturalization; Labor and Employment Law; Probate, Trusts and Estate Planning; Real Estate Law

MEZEY & MEZEY, A PROFESSIONAL CORPORATION
Princeton, NJ ....Insurance Defense; Land Use Law; Real Estate Law

MEZVINSKY, EDWARD M.
Narberth, PA..........................General Practice; International Business Law; International Trade Law

MEZZULLO & MCCANDLISH, A PROFESSIONAL CORPORATION
Norfolk, VA............................Health Care Law
Richmond, VA........................Health Care Law

MICHAEL, ROBERT J.
Rochester, NY........................Civil Trial Practice; Personal Injury; Product Liability Law

MICHAEL, BEST & FRIEDRICH
Madison, WI..........................General Practice
Milwaukee, WI......................Antitrust Law; General Practice; Labor and Employment Law; Municipal Bond/Public Authority Financing; Natural Resources Law; Patent, Trademark, Copyright and Unfair Competition; Tax Law

MICHAELIS, MONTANARI & JOHNSON, A PROFESSIONAL LAW CORPORATION
Westlake Village, CA.............Insurance Defense

MICHAELS, BELL & SMOLAK, P.C.
Auburn, NY ....Civil Trial Practice

MICHAELS, JONES, MARTIN, PARRIS & TESSENER, LAW OFFICES, P.A.
Raleigh, NC............................Personal Injury; Product Liability Law

MICHAELS, WISHNER & BONNER, P.C.
Washington, DC.....................Health Care Law

MICHAELSON, BENJAMIN, JR., P.A.
Annapolis, MD ....Real Estate Law

MICHAELSON & LEVINE
Los Angeles, CA.....................Criminal Trial Practice

MICHAELSON & MICHAELSON
Providence, RI........................Civil Trial Practice

MICHAUD, BUSCHMANN, FOX, FERRARA & MITTELMARK, P.A.
Boca Raton, FL......................Construction Law; Insurance Defense; Medical Malpractice

MICHELI, BALDWIN, BOPELEY & NORTHRUP
Zanesville, OH.......................Civil Trial Practice; Insurance Defense

MICHENER, LARIMORE, SWINDLE, WHITAKER, FLOWERS, SAWYER, REYNOLDS & CHALK, L.L.P.
Fort Worth, TX ....Business Law; Tax Law

MICHIE, HAMLETT, LOWRY, RASMUSSEN AND TWEEL, P.C.
Charlottesville, VA.................General Practice; Tax Law

MICKEY, WILSON, WEILER & RENZI, P.C.
Aurora, IL..............................General Practice

MIDDENDORF, HENRY S. JR.
New York, NY........................General Practice

MIDDLEBERG, RIDDLE & GIANNA
New Orleans, LA....................Commercial Law; Insurance Defense; Real Estate Law
Dallas, TX..............................Civil Trial Practice; Insurance Defense; Real Estate Law

MIDDLEMAN & MATOUR, A PROFESSIONAL CORPORATION
Philadelphia, PA ....Bankruptcy Law

MIDDLETON & REUTLINGER, P.S.C.
Louisville, KY........................Antitrust Law; Banking Law; Bankruptcy Law; Civil Trial Practice; Environmental Law; General Practice; Insurance Defense; Patent, Trademark, Copyright and Unfair Competition; Personal Injury; Probate, Trusts and Estate Planning; Securities Law; Tax Law

MIDKIFF & HINER, P.C.
Richmond, VA........................Insurance Defense

MIDLEN, JOHN H., JR., CHARTERED
Washington, DC.....................Communications Law; Trademark, Copyright and Unfair Competition

MIEL MIEL & PERRY
Stanton, MI ....General Practice

MIKKELBORG, BROZ, WELLS & FRYER
Seattle, WA ....Admiralty/Maritime Law; General Practice

MIKOS, KENNETH R., P.A.
Fort Lauderdale, FL...............Civil Trial Practice; General Practice

MIKUS LAW ASSOCIATES
Lancaster, PA.........................Personal Injury; Product Liability Law

MILBANK, TWEED, HADLEY & MCCLOY
Los Angeles, CA.....................General Practice
Washington, DC.....................General Practice
New York, NY........................Banking Law; Civil Trial Practice; General Practice
London, England ....General Practice
Hong Kong, Hong Kong........General Practice
Tokyo, Japan..........................General Practice
Moscow, Russia ....General Practice
Singapore, Singapore.............General Practice

MILBERG WEISS BERSHAD HYNES & LERACH, LLP
New York, NY........................Antitrust Law; Civil Trial Practice

MILES AND MILES, A PROFESSIONAL ASSOCIATION
Plymouth, MA ....Family Law

MILES, SEARS & EANNI, A PROFESSIONAL CORPORATION
Fresno, CA.............................Civil Trial Practice; Medical Malpractice; Personal Injury; Product Liability Law

MILIDES, GUS
Easton, PA ....General Practice; Medical Malpractice; Personal Injury; Product Liability Law

MILITELLO, ZANCK & COEN, P.C.
Crystal Lake, IL.....................General Practice

MILLAR & AMBRETTE
Darien, CT.............................General Practice; Probate, Trusts and Estate Planning; Real Estate Law

MILLAR, HODGES & BEMIS
Newport Beach, CA................Civil Trial Practice; Probate, Trusts and Estate Planning; Real Estate Law

MILLARD, PILCHOWSKI, HOLWEGER & CHILD, P.C.
Los Angeles, CA.....................Insurance Defense

MILLBERG & GORDON
Raleigh, NC............................Civil Trial Practice

MILLEDGE IDEN & HELD
Miami, FL..............................Communications Law; Land Use Law; Municipal and Zoning Law; Real Estate Law

MILLEN, WHITE, ZELANO & BRANIGAN, P.C.
Arlington, VA ....Patent, Trademark, Copyright and Unfair Competition
Richmond, VA........................Patent, Trademark, Copyright and Unfair Competition

MILLER, ELEANOR L.
Phoenix, AZ ....Criminal Trial Practice

MILLER, HOWARD B.
El Segundo, CA ....Commercial Litigation; Patent, Trademark, Copyright and Unfair Competition

MILLER, J. JEROME
Destin, FL ....Probate, Trusts and Estate Planning

MILLER, JOHN E.
Palo Alto, CA ....Family Law; Probate, Trusts and Estate Planning

MILLER, L. VERNON JR.
Annapolis, MD ....Civil Trial Practice

MILLER, THOMAS W.
Cincinnati, OH ....Criminal Trial Practice

MILLER, ALFANO & RASPANTI, P.C.
Philadelphia, PA ....Civil Trial Practice

MILLER, CANFIELD, PADDOCK AND STONE, P.L.C.
Washington, DC......................Computer Law
Ann Arbor, MI ....Antitrust Law; Banking Law; Bankruptcy Law; Civil Trial Practice; Environmental Law; Family Law; General Practice; Insurance Defense; International Business Law; Labor and Employment Law; Natural Resources Law; Probate, Trusts and Estate Planning; Real Estate Law; Securities Law; Tax Law; Transportation Law
Birmingham, MI......................General Practice
Bloomfield Hills, MI................General Practice; International Business Law; Securities Law
Detroit, MI..............................Admiralty/Maritime Law; Antitrust Law; Banking Law; Bankruptcy Law; Civil Trial Practice; Communications Law; Computer Law; Construction Law; Environmental Law; Family Law; General Practice; Insurance Defense; International Business Law; Labor and Employment Law; Medical Malpractice; Municipal Bond/Public Authority Financing; Natural Resources Law; Patent, Trademark, Copyright and Unfair Competition; Personal Injury; Probate, Trusts and Estate Planning; Real Estate Law; Securities Law; Tax Law; Transportation Law
Grand Rapids, MI ....Antitrust Law; Banking Law; Bankruptcy Law; Computer Law; General Practice; International Business Law; Personal Injury; Securities Law
Kalamazoo, MI ....Antitrust Law; Banking Law; Bankruptcy Law; Civil Trial Practice; Commercial Law; Construction Law; Environmental Law; Family Law; General Practice; Insurance Defense; International Business Law; Labor and Employment Law; Medical Malpractice; Personal Injury; Probate, Trusts and Estate Planning; Real Estate Law; Securities Law; Tax Law; Transportation Law
Lansing, MI..............................Antitrust Law; Banking Law; Bankruptcy Law; General Practice; Labor and Employment Law; Probate, Trusts and Estate Planning; Real Estate Law
Monroe, MI..............................General Practice; International Business Law; Securities Law

MILLER CARSON BOXBERGER & MURPHY
Bloomington, IN ....Insurance Defense
Fort Wayne, IN........................Banking Law; Business Law; Insurance Defense

MILLER, CASSIDY, LARROCA & LEWIN, L.L.P.
Washington, DC......................Civil Trial Practice; Criminal Trial Practice

MILLER & CHEVALIER, CHARTERED
Washington, DC......................General Practice; Tax Law

MILLER & CHRISTENBURY, P.C.
Philadelphia, PA ....Patent, Trademark, Copyright and Unfair Competition

MILLER, EGGLESTON & CRAMER, LTD.
Burlington, VT........................Antitrust Law; Civil Trial Practice; General Practice; Health Care Law; Tax Law

MILLER & FAIGNANT, A PROFESSIONAL CORPORATION
Rutland, VT ....Appellate Practice; Civil Trial Practice; General Practice; Insurance Defense; Medical Malpractice; Personal Injury; Product Liability Law

MILLER & GALDIERI
Jersey City, NJ ....Civil Trial Practice; General Practice

MILLER, GRIFFIN & MARKS, P.S.C.
Lexington, KY ....Business Law; Civil Trial Practice; Family Law; Probate, Trusts and Estate Planning; Real Estate Law

MILLER AND HARRISON, LLC
Boulder, CO ....Criminal Trial Practice; Personal Injury

MILLER & HERRING ATTORNEYS, P.C.
Amarillo, TX............................Real Estate Law

MILLER, HOWARD B.
Los Angeles, CA ....Commercial Litigation; Patent, Trademark, Copyright and Unfair Competition

MILLER, J. BRUCE, LAW GROUP
Louisville, KY ....Civil Trial Practice; General Practice

MILLER, JOHN WAYNE, & ARLENE S. COHEN, P.C.
Longmont, CO ....Civil Trial Practice

MILLER, KATHLEEN ORTMAN, S.C.
Milwaukee, WI ....Family Law

MILLER, KISTLER, CAMPBELL, MILLER & WILLIAMS, INC.
Bellefonte, PA ....Civil Trial Practice
State College, PA ....Civil Trial Practice

MILLER LAW FIRM, A PROFESSIONAL CORPORATION
Kansas City, MO ....Commercial Litigation; Construction Law

MILLER LAW OFFICES, THE
Studio City, CA ....Immigration and Naturalization

MILLER, MAILLIARD & CULVER, LLP
San Francisco, CA ....Civil Trial Practice; General Practice
Santa Rosa, CA........................Civil Trial Practice; General Practice

MILLER & MARSKE, L.L.C.
Kansas City, MO ....Personal Injury

MILLER & MARTIN
Chattanooga, TN ....General Practice

MILLER, McCARREN & HELMS, P.C.
Denver, CO ....Civil Trial Practice; Commercial Litigation; Medical Malpractice

MILLER, MELVIN B., LTD.
Philadelphia, PA ....Business Law; Real Estate Law

MILLER & MILLER, LTD.
Phoenix, AZ ....Criminal Trial Practice; Personal Injury

MILLER, MILLER & CANBY, CHARTERED
Frederick, MD..........................General Practice
Rockville, MD..........................General Practice

MILLER, MILLER, KEARNEY & GESCHICKTER, L.L.P.
Fairfax, VA ....Personal Injury

MILLER MILOVE & KOB, A.P.C.
San Diego, CA ....Securities Law

MILLER, MORTON, CAILLAT & NEVIS
San Jose, CA ....Bankruptcy Law; Business Law; Civil Trial Practice; Construction Law; General Practice; Mergers and Acquisitions; Probate, Trusts and Estate Planning; Real Estate Law; Tax Law

MILLER MULLER MENDELSON & KENNEDY
Indianapolis, IN ....Business Law; Civil Trial Practice; Medical Malpractice; Personal Injury; Product Liability Law

MILLER, NASH, WIENER, HAGER & CARLSEN L.L.P.
Portland, OR............................Admiralty/Maritime Law; Antitrust Law; General Practice; Labor and Employment Law; Patent, Trademark, Copyright and Unfair Competition

MILLER & OLSEN
Tampa, FL ....Personal Injury

MILLER, PEARSON, GLOE, BURNS, BEATTY & COWIE, P.C.
Decorah, IA..............................General Practice; Insurance Defense; Personal Injury

MILLER, PITT & McANALLY, P.C.
Tucson, AZ ....Civil Trial Practice; General Practice; Personal Injury

MILLER, PORTER & MULLER, P.C.
Princeton, NJ ....General Practice

MILLER, RALSTON & EARLE
Harrisonburg, VA ....General Practice

MILLER, RICHARD F., A PROFESSIONAL CORPORATION
Pasadena, CA ....Probate, Trusts and Estate Planning

MILLER, ROBERT E., INC., A PROFESSIONAL CORPORATION
Menlo Park, CA......................Business Law

MILLER, SCHWARTZ AND MILLER, P.A.
Hollywood, FL........................General Practice

MILLER, SHAKMAN, HAMILTON, KURTZON & SCHLIFKE
Chicago, IL..............................General Practice

MILLER, STEINBERG & HESSLER
Rockville, MD..........................Family Law; General Practice

MILLER, STRATVERT, TORGERSON & SCHLENKER, P.A.
Albuquerque, NM....................Banking Law; Civil Trial Practice; General Practice; Insurance Defense; Natural Resources Law; Probate, Trusts and Estate Planning; Real Estate Law; Tax Law
Las Cruces, NM........................Banking Law; Commercial Law

MILLER THOMSON
Markham, ON, Canada ....General Practice
Toronto, ON, Canada............General Practice

MILLER, TOLBERT, MUEHLHAUSEN, MUEHLHAUSEN & GROFF, P.C.
Logansport, IN ....General Practice; Personal Injury; Probate, Trusts and Estate Planning

MILLER & WRUBEL P.C.
New York, NY........................Civil Trial Practice; Commercial Law

MILLIKEN LAW FIRM
Bowling Green, KY ....Criminal Trial Practice; General Practice; Insurance Defense; Medical Malpractice

MILLING, BENSON, WOODWARD, HILLYER, PIERSON & MILLER, L.L.P.
New Orleans, LA ....Admiralty/Maritime Law; Antitrust Law; General Practice; Natural Resources Law; Tax Law

MILLISOR & NOBIL, A LEGAL PROFESSIONAL ASSOCIATION
Cleveland, OH ....Employment Benefits Law; Labor and Employment Law
Columbus, OH ....Employment Benefits Law; Labor and Employment Law

MILLS & MORAITAKIS
Atlanta, GA ....Civil Trial Practice; Medical Malpractice; Product Liability Law

MILLS, PRESBY & ANDERSON, L.L.P.
Dallas, TX ....Criminal Trial Practice

MILLS, SHIRLEY, ECKEL & BASSETT, L.L.P.
Galveston, TX ....General Practice
Houston, TX ....General Practice

MILLS, TIMMONS & FLOWERS, A PROFESSIONAL LAW CORPORATION
Shreveport, LA........................Bankruptcy Law; Civil Trial Practice; Criminal Trial Practice; Environmental Law; Family Law; Personal Injury; Probate, Trusts and Estate Planning; Workers Compensation

MILLS & WHITTEN, A PROFESSIONAL CORPORATION
Oklahoma City, OK................Civil Rights; Civil Trial Practice; Insurance Defense; Medical Malpractice; Personal Injury; Product Liability Law

MILLSAP, MIKE
Lubbock, TX...........................General Practice

MILLSAP, SINGER & DUNN, P.C.
St. Louis, MO...........................General Practice

MILLSTEIN, DAVID J.
Youngwood, PA.......................Appellate Practice; Business Law; Civil Trial Practice; General Practice; Real Estate Law

MILNER, C. GEORGE, ESQ., A PROF. CORP.
Philadelphia, PA ....Civil Trial Practice; Commercial Litigation; Medical Malpractice; Personal Injury; Probate, Trusts and Estate Planning

MILNER, LOBEL, GORANSON, SORRELS, UDASHEN & WELLS
Dallas, TX...............................Criminal Trial Practice

MILODRAGOVICH, DALE, STEINBRENNER & BINNEY, P.C.
Missoula, MT..........................General Practice

MILTON, LAURENCE & DIXON
Worcester, MA.........................Insurance Defense; Workers Compensation

MINER, BARNHILL & GALLAND, P.C.
Chicago, IL..............................Civil Rights

MINIER, STANLEY, INC., LAW OFFICES OF
Santa Ana, CA ....Bankruptcy Law

MINK & BLAIR
Nashville, TN...........................Civil Trial Practice; Insurance Defense

MINOR, J. FLOYD
Montgomery, AL ....Family Law

MINOR AND ASSOCIATES
Biloxi, MS...............................Admiralty/Maritime Law; Civil Trial Practice; Personal Injury; Product Liability Law

MINOR, BELL & NEAL, P.C.
Dalton, GA ....General Practice

MINSKY, MCCORMICK & HALLAGAN, P.C.
Chicago, IL..............................Immigration and Naturalization

MINTMIRE & ASSOCIATES
Palm Beach, FL.......................Civil Trial Practice; Probate, Trusts and Estate Planning

MINTON, HARVEY S. & ASSOCIATES
Columbus, OH ....Business Law; Probate, Trusts and Estate Planning; Real Estate Law

MINTON, BURTON, FOSTER & COLLINS, A PROFESSIONAL CORPORATION
Austin, TX ....Civil Trial Practice; Criminal Trial Practice

MINTON FIRM, THE
Chicago, IL..............................Family Law

MINTON, MINTON AND RAND LLP
Los Angeles, CA ....Business Law; Probate, Trusts and Estate Planning; Real Estate Law

MINTZ, LEVIN, COHN, FERRIS, GLOVSKY AND POPEO, P.C.
Washington, DC......................General Practice
Boston, MA.............................Antitrust Law; Civil Trial Practice; Communications Law; Criminal Trial Practice; General Practice; Municipal Bond/Public Authority Financing

MIRICK, O'CONNELL, DEMALLIE & LOUGEE
Worcester, MA........................General Practice

MIROFF, CROSS & KLINEMAN
Indianapolis, IN ....Family Law

MIRRIONE, JOSEPH R.
New Haven, CT ....Personal Injury

MISERENDINO, CELNIKER, SEEGERT & ESTOFF, P.C.
Buffalo, NY ....Personal Injury

MITCHELL, LINCOLN A.
Palo Alto, CA ....Family Law

MITCHELL, SHELLEY M.
Fort Lauderdale, FL................Family Law

MITCHELL, BAXTER, O'MEARA & MATHIE, S.C.
Milwaukee, WI ....Insurance Defense

MITCHELL, BRISSO, DELANEY & VRIEZE
Eureka, CA.............................General Practice; Insurance Defense

MITCHELL AND CARTER, PROFESSIONAL ASSOCIATION
Tampa, FL ....Insurance Defense

MITCHELL & DECLERCK, P.C.
Enid, OK ....General Practice

MITCHELL, EDDIE C., P.A.
Winston-Salem, NC ....Criminal Trial Practice

MITCHELL HURST JACOBS & DICK
Indianapolis, IN ....Business Law; Civil Trial Practice; Medical Malpractice; Personal Injury; Product Liability Law; Real Estate Law

MITCHELL, JOINER, HARDESTY & LOWTHER
Madisonville, KY ....General Practice; Workers Compensation

MITCHELL, MCNUTT, THREADGILL, SMITH & SAMS, P.A.
Columbus, MS.........................General Practice
Tupelo, MS..............................General Practice

MITCHELL & MITCHELL
Marion, IL ....General Practice; Insurance Defense
Dalton, GA ....Civil Trial Practice; General Practice

MITCHELL, MITCHELL, GRAY & GALLAGHER, A PROFESSIONAL CORPORATION
Williamsport, PA ....Civil Trial Practice; Insurance Defense; Medical Malpractice; Personal Injury; Product Liability Law; Workers Compensation

MITCHELL, NEUBAUER, SHAW & HANSON, P.C.
Mount Vernon, IL ....Banking Law; General Practice; Real Estate Law

MITCHELL, RALLINGS, SINGER, MCGIRT & TISSUE, PLLC
Charlotte, NC..........................Bankruptcy Law; Civil Trial Practice; Commercial Law

MITCHELL, SAM C., & ASSOCIATES
West Frankfort, IL...................Personal Injury

MITCHELL, SILBERBERG & KNUPP LLP
Los Angeles, CA ....Antitrust Law; Commercial Law; Environmental Law; General Practice; Labor and Employment Law; Probate, Trusts and Estate Planning; Tax Law

MITCHELL, VOGE, BEASLEY AND CORBAN
Tupelo, MS..............................General Practice

MITHOFF & JACKS, L.L.P.
Austin, TX ....Civil Trial Practice; Personal Injury

MITTEN, GOODWIN & RAUP, A PROFESSIONAL CORPORATION
Phoenix, AZ ....Appellate Practice; Civil Trial Practice; Environmental Law; Health Care Law; Insurance Defense; Labor and Employment Law; Medical Malpractice; Personal Injury; Product Liability Law; Workers Compensation

MITZEL, MITZEL & GRAY, P.A.
Tampa, FL ....Personal Injury

MIZE, JAMES M.
Sacramento, CA ....Family Law

MLSNA, TIMOTHY M., & ASSOCIATES, LTD.
Chicago, IL............................Employment Benefits Law

MOBBS, DENNY E.
Cleveland, TN ....Civil Trial Practice; General Practice; Insurance
Defense

MODRALL, SPERLING, ROEHL, HARRIS & SISK, P.A.
Albuquerque, NM...................General Practice
Las Cruces, NM.....................General Practice
Santa Fe, NM........................General Practice

MOEN, BRUCE R.
Seattle, WA ....Probate, Trusts and Estate Planning

MOEN, CAIN & O'BRIEN
Houston, TX ....Criminal Trial Practice

MOEN, SHEEHAN, MEYER, LTD.
La Crosse, WI ....General Practice

MOFFATT, THOMAS, BARRETT, ROCK & FIELDS, CHARTERED
Boise, ID.............................Administrative Law; Antitrust Law; Civil Trial
Practice; Environmental Law; General Practice;
Health Care Law; Labor and Employment Law;
Public Utilities Law; Trademark, Copyright and
Unfair Competition

MOGEL, SPEIDEL, BOBB & KERSHNER, A PROFESSIONAL CORPORATION
Reading, PA ....Banking Law; Bankruptcy Law; Business Law;
Commercial Law; Family Law; General Practice;
Probate, Trusts and Estate Planning; Real Estate
Law; Tax Law

MOGILL, KENNETH M.
Detroit, MI.............................Appellate Practice; Criminal Trial Practice

MOHAN, ALEWELT, PRILLAMAN & ADAMI
Springfield, IL ....Environmental Law; General Practice; Real Estate
Law; Tax Law

MOHER & CANNELLO, P.C.
Sault Ste. Marie, MI ....Civil Trial Practice; General Practice; Personal
Injury

MOHR & ANDERSON, S.C.
Hartford, WI ....Insurance Defense

MOHR, HACKETT, PEDERSON, BLAKLEY, RANDOLPH & HAGA, P.C.
Phoenix, AZ ....General Practice

MOIR & HARDMAN
Washington, DC....................Communications Law

MOLINE & SHOSTAK, L.L.C
St. Louis, MO.........................Business Law; Civil Trial Practice; Criminal Trial
Practice; Securities Law

MOLLER, ARTHUR C., P.A.
Miami, FL ....Insurance Defense

MOLLER, DIPENTIMA, PECK AND O'BRIEN, LLC
Hartford, CT ....General Practice; Insurance Defense

MOLLICA & MURRAY
Pittsburgh, PA ....Business Law; Construction Law; Insurance
Defense; Municipal and Zoning Law; Real Estate
Law

MOLLIGAN, COX & MOYER, A PROFESSIONAL CORPORATION
San Francisco, CA ....Antitrust Law; Civil Trial Practice; Medical
Malpractice; Personal Injury; Product Liability Law

MOMBACH, BOYLE & HARDIN, P.A.
Fort Lauderdale, FL ....Commercial Law

MONAGHAN & GOLD, P.C.
Elkins Park, PA ....Appellate Practice; Civil Trial Practice; Commercial
Law; Insurance Defense; Labor and Employment
Law; Medical Malpractice; Product Liability Law

MONAGHAN, LEAHY, HOCHADEL & LIBBY
Portland, ME ....Banking Law; Insurance Defense

MONAHAN & BIAGI, P.L.L.C.
Seattle, WA ....Civil Trial Practice; Commercial Law; International
Business Law

MONDSCHEIN ASSOCIATES
Allentown, PA ....Family Law

MONE, D'AMBROSE & HANYEN, P.C.
Brockton, MA ....Insurance Defense

MONEYMAKER, RICHARD M., THE LAW FIRM OF
Los Angeles, CA ....Bankruptcy Law; Commercial Litigation

MONK, GOODWIN
Winnipeg, MB, Canada...........:General Practice

MONNET, HAYES, BULLIS, THOMPSON & EDWARDS
Oklahoma City, OK................Civil Trial Practice; General Practice; Natural
Resources Law

MONSEY & ANDREWS
Las Vegas, NV ....Commercial Law; Probate, Trusts and Estate
Planning; Real Estate Law

MONTAGUE, PITTMAN & VARNADO, A PROFESSIONAL ASSOCIATION
Hattiesburg, MS....................Environmental Law; General Practice

MONTANO, SUMMERS, MULLEN, MANUEL, OWENS AND GREGORIO, A PROFESSIONAL CORPORATION
Cherry Hill, NJ ....Civil Trial Practice; General Practice; Insurance
Defense; Personal Injury; Workers Compensation

MONTELEONE & MCCRORY
Los Angeles, CA ....Commercial Litigation; Construction Law; General
Practice

MONTEVERDE, MCALEE, FITZPATRICK, TANKER & HURD, A PROFESSIONAL CORPORATION
Philadelphia, PA ....Banking Law; Civil Trial Practice

MONTFORT, HEALY, MCGUIRE & SALLEY
Garden City, NY ....Civil Trial Practice; Environmental Law; General
Practice

MONTGOMERY, ELTON M. LAW OFFICES OF
Graham, TX..........................Probate, Trusts and Estate Planning

MONTGOMERY & ANDREWS, PROFESSIONAL ASSOCIATION
Santa Fe, NM........................Administrative Law; Civil Rights; Civil Trial
Practice; Environmental Law; General Practice;
Labor and Employment Law; Natural Resources
Law; Tax Law

MONTGOMERY & LARMOYEUX
West Palm Beach, FL ....Civil Trial Practice; Personal Injury

MONTGOMERY LAW OFFICES
Jonesville, VA........................Personal Injury

MONTGOMERY LITTLE & MCGREW, P.C.
Denver, CO ....Civil Trial Practice; Commercial Law; General
Practice

MONTGOMERY, MCCRACKEN, WALKER & RHOADS
Philadelphia, PA ....General Practice

MONTGOMERY, MICHAEL B., A LAW CORPORATION
El Monte, CA........................Civil Trial Practice; Municipal Bond/Public
Authority Financing; Municipal and Zoning Law;
Real Estate Law

MOODIE, MOODIE & WORTMAN
West Point, NE ....General Practice

MOODY & HAYS, L.L.P.
Lubbock, TX..........................General Practice

MOODY, STROPLE & KLOEPPEL, LTD.
Portsmouth, VA ....Civil Trial Practice; Personal Injury

MOON, MOSS, MCGILL & BACHELDER, P.A.
Portland, ME ....Labor and Employment Law

MOONEY, F. BENTLEY, JR., A LAW CORPORATION
North Hollywood, CA.............Business Law; Probate, Trusts and Estate Planning

MOONEY LAW FIRM
Jonesboro, AR ....General Practice

MOORE, GEORGE C. J.
West Palm Beach, FL ....International Business Law

MOORE, JOHN R.
Selinsgrove, PA ....General Practice; Probate, Trusts and Estate
Planning

MOORE, REID JR.
Palm Beach, FL.....................Probate, Trusts and Estate Planning

MOORE, BASKIN & PARKER
Boise, ID.............................General Practice; Insurance Defense; Product
Liability Law

MOORE & BERKOWITZ
Southampton, PA....................Civil Trial Practice

MOORE & BROWNING
San Francisco, CA ....Personal Injury; Product Liability Law

MOORE, CHRISTOPHER M., & ASSOCIATES, A LAW CORPORATION
Torrance, CA.................Family Law; Probate, Trusts and Estate Planning

MOORE, GEORGE E., A PROFESSIONAL LAW CORPORATION
Pasadena, CA.................Medical Malpractice; Personal Injury

MOORE & HANSEN
Minneapolis, MN.................Patent, Trademark, Copyright and Unfair Competition

MOORE, HILL, WESTMORELAND, HOOK & BOLTON, P.A.
Pensacola, FL.................Civil Trial Practice

MOORE INGRAM JOHNSON & STEELE
Marietta, GA.................Civil Trial Practice; Insurance Defense; Real Estate Law

MOORE, MEEGAN, HANSCHU & KASSENBROCK
Sacramento, CA.................Civil Trial Practice; General Practice

MOORE, O'BRIEN & JACQUES
Cheshire, CT.................Aviation Law; Civil Trial Practice; Medical Malpractice

MOORE, RADER, CLIFT AND FITZPATRICK, P.C.
Cookeville, TN.................Civil Trial Practice; General Practice; Insurance Defense

MOORE, RUTTER & EVANS
Long Beach, CA.................Admiralty/Maritime Law; Civil Trial Practice; Criminal Trial Practice; Insurance Defense

MOORE, STOUT, WADDELL & LEDFORD
Kingsport, TN.................Civil Trial Practice; General Practice; Labor and Employment Law; Probate, Trusts and Estate Planning

MOORE, TYNDALL AND CASTELLOW
Moultrie, GA.................General Practice

MOORE & VAN ALLEN, PLLC
Charlotte, NC.................General Practice

MOORE, VIRGADAMO & LYNCH, LTD.
Newport, RI.................General Practice

MOORMAN, TATE, MOORMAN, URQUHART & HALEY, L.L.P.
Brenham, TX.................General Practice

MORA & BAUGH, LTD.
Chicago, IL.................Commercial Litigation; Insurance Defense

MORAN & MORAN
Toledo, OH.................Family Law; General Practice; Probate, Trusts and Estate Planning

MORAN & SHAMS, P.A.
Orlando, FL.................Civil Trial Practice; Commercial Law; Commercial Litigation; Labor and Employment Law; Probate, Trusts and Estate Planning; Real Estate Law; Tax Law

MORCHOWER, MICHAEL
Richmond, VA.................Criminal Trial Practice; Personal Injury

MORGAN, JOSEPH A.
El Paso, TX.................Personal Injury

MORGAN, BROWN & JOY
Boston, MA.................Labor and Employment Law

MORGAN, CARRATT AND O'CONNOR, P.A.
Fort Lauderdale, FL.................General Practice

MORGAN, DAVID JAY, A PROFESSIONAL CORPORATION
San Mateo, CA.................Civil Trial Practice

MORGAN & FINNEGAN, L.L.P.
Washington, DC.................Patent, Trademark, Copyright and Unfair Competition
New York, NY.................Patent, Trademark, Copyright and Unfair Competition

MORGAN AND GOTCHER
Greenville, TX.................Family Law; General Practice; Probate, Trusts and Estate Planning

MORGAN & HANSEN
Salt Lake City, UT.................Civil Trial Practice; General Practice; Insurance Defense; Personal Injury

MORGAN, LEWIS & BOCKIUS LLP
Philadelphia, PA.................General Practice

MORGAN, MELHUISH, MONAGHAN, ARVIDSON, ABRUTYN & LISOWSKI
Livingston, NJ.................Civil Trial Practice; General Practice; Insurance Defense; Personal Injury

MORGAN, MILLER & BLAIR, PROFESSIONAL CORPORATION
Walnut Creek, CA.................Real Estate Law

MORGAN & POTTINGER, P.S.C.
Louisville, KY.................Banking Law; Bankruptcy Law; Commercial Litigation; General Practice; Probate, Trusts and Estate Planning; Real Estate Law

MORGAN, RICHARD M., P.C.
Atlanta, GA.................Probate, Trusts and Estate Planning

MORGANSTERN & QUATELA
Garden City, NY.................General Practice

MORGENSTEIN & JUBELIRER, LLP
San Francisco, CA.................Civil Trial Practice; Commercial Litigation; General Practice; Labor and Employment Law; Product Liability Law

MORGENSTERN, MICHAEL S., & ASSOCIATES, P.C.
Rockville, MD.................Medical Malpractice; Personal Injury

MORGERA, VINCENT D.
Providence, RI.................Admiralty/Maritime Law; Civil Trial Practice; Medical Malpractice; Personal Injury; Product Liability Law

MORIARTY, DONOGHUE & LEJA, P.C.
Springfield, MA.................Insurance Defense; Product Liability Law

MORITT, HOCK & HAMROFF, LLP
Garden City, NY.................Bankruptcy Law; Civil Trial Practice; Commercial Law

MORLEY CASKIN
Washington, DC.................Natural Resources Law; Public Utilities Law

MORMAN LAW FIRM
Sturgis, SD.................General Practice

MORNEAU & MURPHY
Jamestown, RI.................Bankruptcy Law; Civil Trial Practice; General Practice; Real Estate Law

MOROSCO, B. ANTHONY
White Plains, NY.................Appellate Practice; Criminal Trial Practice

MORRILL THOMAS & NOONEY, LLP
Rapid City, SD.................General Practice

MORRIS, JOHN P.
Bridgeton, NJ.................Civil Trial Practice; General Practice

MORRIS, JOHN W.
Philadelphia, PA.................Appellate Practice; Commercial Law; Criminal Trial Practice

MORRIS, CLOUD AND CONCHIN, P.C.
Huntsville, AL.................Civil Trial Practice; Criminal Trial Practice; Personal Injury; Product Liability Law; Workers Compensation

MORRIS & FLOREY, L.L.P.
Austin, TX.................Criminal Trial Practice

MORRIS, HAYNES, INGRAM & HORNSBY
Alexander City, AL.................Civil Trial Practice; Personal Injury; Product Liability Law

MORRIS, J. SCOTT, P.C.
Austin, TX.................Probate, Trusts and Estate Planning; Tax Law

MORRIS, JAMES, HITCHENS & WILLIAMS
Dover, DE.................General Practice
Wilmington, DE.................Civil Trial Practice; General Practice

MORRIS, LAING, EVANS, BROCK & KENNEDY, CHARTERED
Wichita, KS.................Bankruptcy Law; Civil Trial Practice; General Practice; Natural Resources Law

MORRIS LAW FIRM
Tampa, FL.................Commercial Litigation; Construction Law

MORRIS AND MORRIS
Wilmington, DE.................Securities Law
Richmond, VA.................Bankruptcy Law; Civil Trial Practice; General Practice; Insurance Defense; Product Liability Law

MORRIS, NEIL A., ASSOCIATES, P.C.
Philadelphia, PA.................Labor and Employment Law

MORRIS, NICHOLS, ARSHT & TUNNELL
Wilmington, DE.................General Practice; Tax Law

MORRIS, PAUL, PROFESSIONAL ASSOCIATION
Miami, FL.................Appellate Practice

MORRIS, POLICH & PURDY
Los Angeles, CA.................General Practice

MORRIS, ROWLAND, PREKEL, FREDERICK, LEWIS & LEWINSKI, P.L.C.
Troy, MI.................Commercial Law; Tax Law

MORRIS & STELLA
Chicago, IL.............................Product Liability Law

MORRIS, WILLIAM, LAW OFFICES
Hamilton, ON, Canada............Personal Injury

MORRISON COHEN SINGER & WEINSTEIN, LLP
New York, NY.......................General Practice

MORRISON & FOERSTER LLP
San Francisco, CA ....General Practice

MORRISON LAW FIRM
Mount Vernon, NY ....Patent, Trademark, Copyright and Unfair Competition

MORRISON, MORRISON & MILLS, P.A.
Tampa, FL ....Banking Law; Business Law; Civil Trial Practice; Commercial Law; Municipal Bond/Public Authority Financing; Municipal and Zoning Law

MORRISON & SHELTON, A PROFESSIONAL CORPORATION
Wichita Falls, TX...................Civil Trial Practice; General Practice; Personal Injury

MORRISONS, McCARTHY & MOORE
Whitefish, MT ....Civil Trial Practice

MORROW & OTOROWSKI
Bainbridge Island, WA ....Admiralty/Maritime Law; Medical Malpractice; Personal Injury

MORROW, ROMINE & PEARSON, P.C.
Montgomery, AL ....Insurance Defense

MORSE, ALTMAN & BENSON
Boston, MA..........................Patent, Trademark, Copyright and Unfair Competition; Trademark, Copyright and Unfair Competition

MORSE & BRATT
Vancouver, WA......................General Practice

MORSE & MOWBRAY, A PROFESSIONAL CORPORATION
Las Vegas, NV ....Civil Trial Practice; Probate, Trusts and Estate Planning; Real Estate Law

MORSE & SACKS
Northampton, MA...................Probate, Trusts and Estate Planning; Real Estate Law

MORTIMER SOURWINE & SLOANE, LTD.
Reno, NV ....Civil Trial Practice; General Practice

MORVILLO, ABRAMOWITZ, GRAND, IASON & SILBERBERG, P.C.
New York, NY.......................Criminal Trial Practice; General Practice

MOSCATO, SKOPIL & HALLOCK
Portland, OR............................Insurance Defense

MOSELEY & ASSOCIATES, A PROFESSIONAL LAW CORPORATION
New Orleans, LA ....General Practice

MOSELEY, WARREN, PRICHARD & PARRISH, P.A.
Jacksonville, FL ....Admiralty/Maritime Law; General Practice; Insurance Defense; Transportation Law

MOSER AND MARSALEK, P.C.
St. Louis, MO...........................Civil Trial Practice; General Practice

MOSKOWITZ, MANDELL & SALIM, P.A.
Fort Lauderdale, FL ....Commercial Law; Real Estate Law

MOSLEY, CLARE & TOWNES
Louisville, KY ....Civil Trial Practice; Family Law; Immigration and Naturalization

MOSS, HERBERT A.
Santa Ana, CA ....Labor and Employment Law

MOSS & BARNETT, A PROFESSIONAL ASSOCIATION
Minneapolis, MN....................General Practice

MOSS, BENTON & WALLIS, PLLC
Jackson, TN ....Civil Trial Practice; General Practice; Insurance Defense

MOSS AND BLOOMBERG, LTD.
Bolingbrook, IL.......................Banking Law; Insurance Defense; Municipal and Zoning Law; Real Estate Law

MOSS & ENOCHIAN, A LAW CORPORATION
Redding, CA ....General Practice

MOSS, HENDERSON, BLANTON, KOVAL & LANIER, P.A.
Vero Beach, FL.......................Civil Trial Practice; General Practice; Insurance Defense; Medical Malpractice; Probate, Trusts and Estate Planning; Workers Compensation

MOSS, POWERS & POSTERNOCK, A PROFESSIONAL CORPORATION
Moorestown, NJ......................Civil Trial Practice; General Practice

MOSS, STRICKLER & SACHITANO, P.A.
Bethesda, MD ....Family Law

MOSTEN & TUFFIAS
Los Angeles, CA ....Civil Trial Practice; Family Law

MOUKAWSHER & WALSH, LLC
Groton, CT.............................Employment Benefits Law

MOULDER, WILLIAM C. A., P.A.
Jacksonville, FL ....Family Law

MOULTON, BELLINGHAM, LONGO & MATHER, P.C.
Billings, MT ....General Practice

MOUNCE, GREEN, MYERS, SAFI & GALATZAN, A PROFESSIONAL CORPORATION
El Paso, TX............................Antitrust Law; Appellate Practice; Banking Law; General Practice; Insurance Defense; Labor and Employment Law; Medical Malpractice; Product Liability Law

MOUND, COTTON & WOLLAN
New York, NY........................Civil Trial Practice; General Practice; Insurance Defense; International Business Law

MOUNTAIN, DEARBORN & WHITING
Worcester, MA........................Commercial Litigation; General Practice; Labor and Employment Law; Municipal and Zoning Law; Probate, Trusts and Estate Planning; Real Estate Law; Tax Law

MOWER, KOELLER, NEBEKER, CARLSON & HALUCK
Irvine, CA..............................Civil Trial Practice; Insurance Defense
San Diego, CA ....Civil Trial Practice

MOYE, GILES, O'KEEFE, VERMEIRE & GORRELL LLP
Denver, CO ....General Practice

MOYE, O'BRIEN, O'ROURKE, HOGAN & PICKERT
Orlando, FL............................Construction Law

MOYERS, MARTIN, SANTEE, IMEL & TETRICK
Tulsa, OK...............................General Practice

MOYLE, FLANIGAN, KATZ, KOLINS, RAYMOND & SHEEHAN, P.A.
Stuart, FL...............................Civil Trial Practice; General Practice
Tallahassee, FL ....General Practice
West Palm Beach, FL ....Civil Trial Practice; General Practice

MOYLER, MOYLER, RAINEY & COBB, P.L.C.
Franklin, VA...........................General Practice

MOZENTER & MOZENTER
Philadelphia, PA ....General Practice

MOZLEY, FINLAYSON & LOGGINS LLP
Atlanta, GA ....Aviation Law; Business Law; Civil Trial Practice; Insurance Defense; Product Liability Law

MUCHMORE & WALLWORK, A PROFESSIONAL CORPORATION
Phoenix, AZ ....Civil Trial Practice; Commercial Litigation; Environmental Law; Insurance Defense; Personal Injury; Product Liability Law

MUDD, HARRISON & BURCH
Towson, MD ....Insurance Defense

MUDD, JOSEPH E., P.L.C.
Irvine, CA..............................Tax Law

MUDD, MUDD & FITZGERALD, P.A.
La Plata, MD..........................General Practice

MUDIE, F. PATRICIA, A PROFESSIONAL CORPORATION
Los Angeles, CA ....Family Law

MUELLER & GALLIOS, P.C.
Phoenix, AZ ....Family Law

MUELLER AND SMITH, A LEGAL PROFESSIONAL ASSOCIATION
Columbus, OH ....Computer Law; Patent, Trademark, Copyright and Unfair Competition

MUELLER, THOMAS F., A PROFESSIONAL CORPORATION
San Jose, CA ....Criminal Trial Practice

MUETH, JOSEPH E., A LAW CORPORATION
Pasadena, CA ....Patent, Trademark, Copyright and Unfair Competition

MUHLHEIM PALMER ZENNACHÉ & WADE, A PROFESSIONAL CORPORATION
Eugene, OR ....Bankruptcy Law; Commercial Law; Commercial Litigation

MULDOON, MURPHY & FAUCETTE
Washington, DC..................Banking Law; Securities Law

MULHEARN & MULHEARN
Natchez, MS..................Civil Trial Practice; General Practice

MULLEN & HENZELL, L.L.P.
Santa Barbara, CA..................Civil Trial Practice; General Practice; Probate, Trusts and Estate Planning

MULLEN, MACINNES & REDDING
Austin, TX..................Civil Trial Practice; Insurance Defense; Personal Injury

MULLEN & MINELLA
Chicago, IL..................Civil Trial Practice; Personal Injury; Product Liability Law

MULLER, MINTZ, KORNREICH, CALDWELL, CASEY, CROSLAND & BRAMNICK, P.A.
Miami, FL..................Labor and Employment Law
Orlando, FL..................Labor and Employment Law

MULLIN HOARD & BROWN, L.L.P.
Amarillo, TX..................General Practice

MULLINS, THOMASON, HARRIS & JESSEE, A PROFESSIONAL CORPORATION
Norton, VA..................General Practice; Insurance Defense

MULOCK, THOMPSON & LITTLE
Bradenton, FL..................Criminal Trial Practice; Medical Malpractice; Personal Injury

MULVANEY, KAHAN & BARRY, A PROFESSIONAL CORPORATION
San Diego, CA..................Banking Law; Bankruptcy Law; Business Law; Civil Trial Practice

MULVEY, FLANAGAN & CONNELLY, P.C.
Philadelphia, PA..................Personal Injury; Workers Compensation

MUNDAY & NATHAN, THE LAW OFFICES OF
Chicago, IL..................Civil Trial Practice; Medical Malpractice; Personal Injury

MUNDY & GAMMAGE, P.C.
Cedartown, GA..................Civil Trial Practice; General Practice; Personal Injury

MUNDY, ROGERS & FRITH, LLP
Roanoke, VA..................Family Law; Medical Malpractice; Personal Injury

MUNGER AND MUNGER, P.L.C.
Tucson, AZ..................Commercial Law; Probate, Trusts and Estate Planning; Real Estate Law

MUNGER, TOLLES & OLSON
Los Angeles, CA..................General Practice

MUNLEY, MATTISE, KELLY & CARTWRIGHT
Scranton, PA..................Appellate Practice; Civil Trial Practice; Medical Malpractice; Personal Injury; Product Liability Law

MUNZER, STEPHEN I., & ASSOCIATES, P.C.
New York, NY..................Real Estate Law

MURAI, WALD, BIONDO & MORENO, P.A.
Miami, FL..................Civil Trial Practice; General Practice; International Business Law

MURCHIE, CALCUTT & BOYNTON
Beulah, MI..................General Practice
Cadillac, MI..................General Practice
Charlevoix, MI..................General Practice
Leland, MI..................General Practice
Traverse City, MI..................Banking Law; Bankruptcy Law; Civil Trial Practice; Commercial Law; General Practice; Labor and Employment Law; Personal Injury; Real Estate Law

MURCHISON, TAYLOR, KENDRICK, GIBSON & DAVENPORT, L.L.P.
Wilmington, NC..................Civil Trial Practice; Commercial Law; Real Estate Law; Tax Law

MURFREE COPE HUDSON & SCARLETT
Murfreesboro, TN..................General Practice

MURNAGHAN, FERGUSON & MAGUIRE, P.A.
Tampa, FL..................Commercial Litigation; Personal Injury

MURNANE, CONLIN, WHITE & BRANDT, PROFESSIONAL ASSOCIATION
St. Paul, MN..................General Practice

MUROV & WARD, A PROFESSIONAL LAW CORPORATION
New Orleans, LA..................Immigration and Naturalization

MURPHY, MICHAEL M.
Los Angeles, CA..................Real Estate Law

MURPHY, RICHARD V.
Lexington, KY..................Land Use Law; Municipal and Zoning Law

MURPHY, THOMAS D.
Rockville, MD..................General Practice

MURPHY, BARTOL & O'BRIEN, LLP
Mineola, NY..................Civil Trial Practice

MURPHY, BUTTERFIELD & HOLLAND, P.C.
Williamsport, PA..................Civil Trial Practice; Probate, Trusts and Estate Planning; Real Estate Law

MURPHY & DESMOND, S.C.
Madison, WI..................General Practice

MURPHY, GILLICK, WICHT & PRACHTHAUSER
Milwaukee, WI..................Civil Trial Practice; Personal Injury

MURPHY, HUPP, FOOTE, MIELKE AND KINNALLY
Aurora, IL..................Civil Trial Practice; Environmental Law; General Practice; Immigration and Naturalization; Insurance Defense; Personal Injury

MURPHY, LUTEY, SCHMITT & BECK
Kingman, AZ..................Personal Injury
Prescott, AZ..................Civil Trial Practice; Commercial Litigation; General Practice; Personal Injury; Probate, Trusts and Estate Planning
Yuma, AZ..................Personal Injury

MURPHY MORRIS & MITCHELL, P.C.
Alexandria, VA..................Civil Trial Practice

MURPHY AND MURPHY
Hyannis, MA..................General Practice

MURPHY & OLIVER, P.C.
Norristown, PA..................Civil Trial Practice; Insurance Defense; Medical Malpractice; Personal Injury; Product Liability Law

MURPHY, PEARSON, BRADLEY & FEENEY, A PROFESSIONAL CORPORATION
San Francisco, CA..................Appellate Practice; Banking Law; Civil Rights; Civil Trial Practice; Construction Law; General Practice; Insurance Defense; Medical Malpractice; Product Liability Law; Real Estate Law; Tax Law; Trademark, Copyright and Unfair Competition

MURPHY, PEDERSON, WAITE, WILLIAMS & MCWHA
North Platte, NE..................General Practice

MURPHY, REID, PILOTTE, ORD & AUSTIN
Palm Beach, FL..................General Practice; Probate, Trusts and Estate Planning; Real Estate Law; Tax Law

MURPHY, ROGERS & SLOSS, A PROFESSIONAL LAW CORPORATION
New Orleans, LA..................Admiralty/Maritime Law

MURPHY & SHEPARD
Lucedale, MS..................General Practice

MURPHY, SMITH & POLK, A PROFESSIONAL CORPORATION
Chicago, IL..................Construction Law; Employment Benefits Law; Labor and Employment Law; Workers Compensation

MURPHY & WEBER
Washington, DC..................International Business Law

MURPHY, WILLIAM T., LAW OFFICES, INC.
Providence, RI..................Banking Law; Civil Trial Practice; Commercial Law; Criminal Trial Practice; Insurance Defense; Labor and Employment Law

MURRAY, DUNHAM & MURRAY
Seattle, WA..................Insurance Defense

MURRAY, JOHN, & ASSOCIATES, LTD.
St. Paul, MN..................Commercial Litigation; Real Estate Law; Tax Law

MURRAY, JOSEPH E., & ASSOCIATES, P.A.
Berkeley Heights, NJ..................Municipal and Zoning Law; Probate, Trusts and Estate Planning; Real Estate Law

MURRAY LAW FIRM
New Orleans, LA..................Personal Injury

MURRAY AND MURRAY, A PROFESSIONAL CORPORATION
Palo Alto, CA..................Bankruptcy Law

MUSCARELLA, BOCHET, LAHIFF, PECK & EDWARDS, P.C.
Fair Lawn, NJ..................Civil Trial Practice; Insurance Defense

MUSHKIN, MARTIN
New York, NY..................General Practice

MUSSELMAN, ROBERT M. & ASSOCIATES
Charlottesville, VA..................Bankruptcy Law; Probate, Trusts and Estate Planning; Tax Law

MUSTAIN LINDSTROM & HENSON
Galesburg, IL ....Commercial Litigation; General Practice; Insurance Defense; Labor and Employment Law; Personal Injury; Probate, Trusts and Estate Planning; Real Estate Law; Workers Compensation

MYER, SWANSON, ADAMS & WOLF, P.C.
Denver, CO ....Business Law; Civil Trial Practice; Commercial Law; Commercial Litigation; General Practice; Probate, Trusts and Estate Planning

MYERS, FRANK B.
Newport Beach, CA ....Construction Law; International Business Law; Natural Resources Law

MYERS, BRADLEY AND DEVITT, P.C.
Denver, CO ....Environmental Law; Family Law; Medical Malpractice; Municipal and Zoning Law; Personal Injury; Probate, Trusts and Estate Planning

MYERS, BRIER & KELLY, L.L.P.
Scranton, PA ....Civil Rights; Civil Trial Practice; Commercial Litigation; General Practice; Health Care Law; Probate, Trusts and Estate Planning; Tax Law

MYERS, DAUGHERITY, BERRY & O'CONOR, LTD.
Ottawa, IL..........................General Practice; Personal Injury
Streator, IL..........................General Practice

MYERS KRAUSE & STEVENS, CHARTERED
Naples, FL..........................Probate, Trusts and Estate Planning; Real Estate Law

MYERS, OLIVER & PRICE, A PROFESSIONAL CORPORATION
Albuquerque, NM...................Real Estate Law

MYERS, ROBERT J., & ASSOCIATES
San Antonio, TX....................Civil Trial Practice; Tax Law

MYLES AND TYLER, LAW OFFICES OF
Tawas City, MI ....General Practice; Probate, Trusts and Estate Planning

MYLOTTE, DAVID & FITZPATRICK
Philadelphia, PA ....Civil Trial Practice

NACHSHIN & WESTON
Los Angeles, CA ....Family Law

NADELHOFFER, KUHN, MITCHELL, MOSS, SALOGA & LECHOWICZ, P.C.
Naperville, IL.........................General Practice

NAEGELE, TIMOTHY D. & ASSOCIATES
Los Angeles, CA ....Banking Law; General Practice
Washington, DC......................Banking Law; General Practice

NAGELEY, MEREDITH & RAMSEY, INC.
Sacramento, CA ....Construction Law; Insurance Defense; Product Liability Law; Real Estate Law

NAHIN AND NAHIN, LAW CORPORATION
Valencia, CA ....Business Law; Real Estate Law

NAJJAR DENABURG, P.C.
Birmingham, AL ....Banking Law; Bankruptcy Law; Business Law; Family Law; General Practice

NAKAMURA & QUINN
Birmingham, AL......................Labor and Employment Law

NALL, MILLER, OWENS, HOCUTT & HOWARD
Atlanta, GA ....Civil Trial Practice; Medical Malpractice; Product Liability Law

NAMACK, CLARK & KEENEY
Sarasota, FL ....Probate, Trusts and Estate Planning

NAMAN, HOWELL, SMITH & LEE, A PROFESSIONAL CORPORATION
Austin, TX ....General Practice
Waco, TX ....General Practice

NAMEROFF, NEIL M., PROFESSIONAL ASSOCIATION
Miami, FL..........................Criminal Trial Practice

NANCE, CACCIATORE, SISSERSON, DURYEA AND HAMILTON
Melbourne, FL.......................Civil Trial Practice; General Practice; Personal Injury

NAREY, CHOZEN AND SAUNDERS
Spirit Lake, IA ....General Practice

NARRON, O'HALE & WHITTINGTON, P.A.
Smithfield, NC ....General Practice

NARVID, GLICKMAN, SCOTT & FRANGIE, A PROFESSIONAL CORPORATION
Sherman Oaks, CA ....Civil Trial Practice

NASATIR, HIRSCH & PODBERESKY
Santa Monica, CA...................Criminal Trial Practice

NASH, COHENOUR, KELLEY & HUNT
Oklahoma City, OK.................Bankruptcy Law; Commercial Law; Probate, Trusts and Estate Planning

NASH & COMPANY, A PROFESSIONAL CORPORATION
Pittsburgh, PA ....General Practice; Health Care Law

NASH & EDGERTON
Hermosa Beach, CA ....Business Law; Commercial Litigation; Mergers and Acquisitions; Securities Law

NASH, SPINDLER, DEAN & GRIMSTAD
Manitowoc, WI ....Civil Trial Practice; General Practice; Insurance Defense

NASH, WALTER B., III, P.C., LAW OFFICES OF
Tucson, AZ ....Criminal Trial Practice

NASON, GILDAN, YEAGER, GERSON & WHITE, P.A.
West Palm Beach, FL ....Business Law; Civil Trial Practice; Real Estate Law

NASSER LAW OFFICES, P.C.
Sioux Falls, SD......................Insurance Defense; Personal Injury

NATHANSON & GOLDBERG, A PROFESSIONAL CORPORATION
Boston, MA..........................Civil Trial Practice; Construction Law; Personal Injury; Real Estate Law; Securities Law

NATIONS & MUELLER
St. Louis, MO........................General Practice

NATISS, MARVIN, P.C.
Roslyn Heights, NY ....General Practice

NAUFUL, ERNEST J., JR., P.C.
Columbia, SC ....Civil Trial Practice; General Practice; Medical Malpractice; Product Liability Law

NAUMAN, SMITH, SHISSLER & HALL
Harrisburg, PA......................Banking Law; Bankruptcy Law; Civil Trial Practice; Environmental Law; General Practice; Health Care Law; Insurance Defense; Probate, Trusts and Estate Planning; Public Utilities Law; Real Estate Law; Tax Law

NAVRATIL, HARDY & BOURGEOIS
Baton Rouge, LA...................Business Law; Insurance Defense

NEAD, HOFFMAN & KAREY
Baltimore, MD ....Civil Trial Practice; Insurance Defense

NEAL & ASSOCIATES
Oakland, CA ....Bankruptcy Law; Business Law; Probate, Trusts and Estate Planning

NEAL & DAVIS
Shelbyville, KY ....Civil Trial Practice

NEARY, BRIAN J.
Hackensack, NJ......................Appellate Practice; Criminal Trial Practice

NEBLETT, BEARD & ARSENAULT
Alexandria, LA ....Civil Trial Practice

NEEDELL & MCGLONE, A PROFESSIONAL CORPORATION
Trenton, NJ ....Civil Trial Practice; Commercial Law; Construction Law; Environmental Law; General Practice; Insurance Defense; Medical Malpractice; Product Liability Law

NEEDHAM, JOHNSON, LOVELACE & JOHNSON, A PROFESSIONAL CORPORATION
Dallas, TX..............................Medical Malpractice

NEEF, ALLAN
Grosse Pointe Farms, MI ....Business Law; Tax Law

NEEL, HOOPER & KALMANS, P.C.
Houston, TX ....Labor and Employment Law

NEELY & BRIEN
Mayfield, KY ....General Practice

NEIDER & BOUCHER, S.C.
Madison, WI ....Business Law

NEIGHER, ALAN
Westport, CT..........................Sports and Entertainment Law

NEIL, DYMOTT, PERKINS, BROWN & FRANK, A PROFESSIONAL CORPORATION
San Diego, CA ....Civil Trial Practice; Insurance Defense; Medical Malpractice; Product Liability Law

NEILL GRIFFIN JEFFRIES & LLOYD, CHARTERED
Fort Pierce, FL.......................Civil Trial Practice; Personal Injury; Real Estate Law

NEIMAN GINSBURG & MAIRANZ P.C.
New York, NY ....Bankruptcy Law

NEJAME & HYMAN, P.A.
Orlando, FL ....Criminal Trial Practice

NELSON, DRIES & ZIMMERMAN, S.C.
Brookfield, WI........................Civil Trial Practice; Insurance Defense

NELSON ● HESSE
Sarasota, FL ....Civil Trial Practice; Commercial Law; General
Practice; Product Liability Law

NELSON & JORDAN, P.A.
Greenville, SC..........................Civil Trial Practice; Environmental Law; Personal
Injury; Product Liability Law

NELSON & LAFEMINA, P.A.
North Miami Beach, FL..........Probate, Trusts and Estate Planning

NELSON, MCMAHAN, PARKER & NOBLETT
Chattanooga, TN ....Insurance Defense; Municipal and Zoning Law;
Personal Injury

NELSON MULLINS RILEY & SCARBOROUGH L.L.P
Columbia, SC ....General Practice

NELSON & NELSON
Bethesda, MD ....Civil Trial Practice

NELSON OYEN TORVIK
Montevideo, MN......................General Practice

NEMETH, JOHN C. & ASSOCIATES
Columbus, OH ....Civil Trial Practice; Insurance Defense

NEMIER, TOLARI, LANDRY, MAZZEO & JOHNSON, P.C.
Farmington Hills, MI ....Insurance Defense; Medical Malpractice; Product
Liability Law

NEMLAHA, BEATRICE H., P.C.
Los Angeles, CA ....Family Law

NEPPLE, VAN DER KAMP & FLYNN, P.C.
Rock Island, IL........................Probate, Trusts and Estate Planning; Tax Law

NETTLES & NETTLES, P.A.
Florence, SC ....Civil Trial Practice

NETZORG & MCKEEVER, PROFESSIONAL CORPORATION
Denver, CO ....Business Law; Civil Trial Practice; Commercial Law;
Natural Resources Law; Securities Law

NEUBERGER, QUINN, GIELEN, RUBIN & GIBBER, P.A.
Baltimore, MD ....General Practice

NEUMEYER & BOYD, LLP
Los Angeles, CA ....Appellate Practice; Insurance Defense

NEUMILLER & BEARDSLEE, A PROFESSIONAL CORPORATION
Modesto, CA ....General Practice
Stockton, CA............................General Practice

NEVILLE, WILLIAM V. JR.
Eufaula, AL..............................General Practice; Real Estate Law

NEVILLE & KELLEY
Cambridge, MA ....Insurance Defense

NEVILLE, PETERSON & WILLIAMS
New York, NY........................International Trade Law

NEVILLE, RICHARDS, DEFRANCO & WULLER
Belleville, IL ....Civil Trial Practice; Commercial Litigation; General
Practice; Insurance Defense; Real Estate Law

NEVORAL, BERNARD R., AND ASSOCIATES, LTD.
Chicago, IL...............................Civil Trial Practice; Personal Injury; Product
Liability Law

NEWBERRY, HARGROVE & RAMBICURE, P.S.C.
Lexington, KY ....General Practice

NEWBURGH, BALDWIN & GERSHMAN
West Palm Beach, FL..............Aviation Law; Civil Trial Practice; Commercial
Litigation; Criminal Trial Practice; Real Estate Law

NEWBY, LEWIS, KAMINSKI & JONES
La Porte, IN.............................Civil Trial Practice; General Practice; Insurance
Defense; Labor and Employment Law; Product
Liability Law

NEWCOMER, SHAFFER & SPANGLER
Bryan, OH ....General Practice

NEWELL & MARTENS
Denver, CO ....Criminal Trial Practice

NEWLAN, DOUGLAS H.
Redding, CA ....Insurance Defense

NEWMAN, CRAIG
Casper, WY ....Natural Resources Law

NEWMAN FITCH LANE ALTHEIM MYERS, P.C.
New York, NY.........................Civil Trial Practice; Insurance Defense; Medical
Malpractice

NEWMAN & SCHWARTZ
New York, NY.........................Appellate Practice; Criminal Trial Practice

NEWMARK IRVINE, P.A.
Phoenix, AZ ....Tax Law

NEWTON - KIGHT, L.L.P.
Everett, WA ....General Practice

NEXSEN PRUET JACOBS & POLLARD, LLP
Columbia, SC ....General Practice; Workers Compensation

NIBLOCK LAW FIRM
Fayetteville, AR ....Civil Trial Practice

NICHOLAS AND BARRERA, P.C.
San Antonio, TX......................Criminal Trial Practice; General Practice

NICHOLLS, LAWRENCE P., P.C.
Phoenix, AZ ....Workers Compensation

NICHOLS & ANDREWS, A PROFESSIONAL LAW CORPORATION
Irvine, CA.................................Banking Law

NICHOLS, JACKSON, DILLARD, HAGER & SMITH, L.L.P.
Dallas, TX.................................Municipal and Zoning Law

NICHOLSON & GARNER
Maryville, TN...........................Product Liability Law

NICOLETTE & PERKINS, P.A.
Oradell, NJ...............................Administrative Law; Bankruptcy Law; Civil Trial
Practice; Commercial Law; General Practice;
Probate, Trusts and Estate Planning

NICOLETTI HORNIG & SWEENEY
New York, NY.........................Admiralty/Maritime Law; Insurance Defense

NICOLINI & PARADISE
Mineola, NY.............................Civil Trial Practice; Insurance Defense

NIEBLER, PYZYK & WAGNER
Menomonee Falls, WI..............General Practice; Real Estate Law

NIES, KURZ, BERGERT & TAMBURRO
Arlington, VA ....Patent, Trademark, Copyright and Unfair Competition

NIEWALD, WALDECK & BROWN, A PROFESSIONAL CORPORATION
Kansas City, MO ....Civil Trial Practice; General Practice

NILES, BARTON & WILMER
Baltimore, MD ....Admiralty/Maritime Law; Civil Trial Practice;
General Practice

NILLES, HANSEN & DAVIES, LTD.
Fargo, ND.................................Banking Law; Civil Trial Practice; Commercial Law;
General Practice; Insurance Defense; Labor and
Employment Law; Personal Injury; Probate, Trusts
and Estate Planning; Real Estate Law; Tax Law

NIMS, HOWES, COLLISON, HANSEN & LACKERT
New York, NY.........................Trademark, Copyright and Unfair Competition

NIPPARD, LEWIS STRAUGHN, P.A.
Ellicott City, MD....................Civil Trial Practice

NIRO, SCAVONE, HALLER & NIRO
Chicago, IL...............................Patent, Trademark, Copyright and Unfair Competition

NISEN & ELLIOTT
Chicago, IL...............................Business Law; Commercial Litigation; Probate,
Trusts and Estate Planning

NIX, HOLTSFORD & VERCELLI, P.C.
Montgomery, AL.....................Civil Trial Practice; Environmental Law; Insurance
Defense; Workers Compensation

NIXON, HARGRAVE, DEVANS & DOYLE LLP
New York, NY.........................General Practice
Rochester, NY..........................General Practice

NIXON & VANDERHYE, P.C.
Arlington, VA ....Patent, Trademark, Copyright and Unfair Competition

NOBILE, MAGARIAN & DISALVO
Bronxville, NY ....Commercial Litigation

NOBLES, JAMES C. JR.
Atlanta, GA ....International Business Law

NOKES, DAVIS & QUINN, A PROFESSIONAL CORPORATION
Laguna Beach, CA ....Civil Trial Practice

NOLAN, EDWARD J. LAW OFFICES OF
Hackensack, NJ......................Commercial Law

NOLAN & ARMSTRONG
Palo Alto, CA ....Criminal Trial Practice

NOLAN, PLUMHOFF & WILLIAMS, CHARTERED
Towson, MD ....Civil Trial Practice; Criminal Trial Practice; General
Practice; Personal Injury; Probate, Trusts and Estate
Planning

NOLAND, HAMERLY, ETIENNE & HOSS, A PROFESSIONAL CORPORATION
Salinas, CA..............................General Practice

NOONAN & PROKUP
Allentown, PA ....Probate, Trusts and Estate Planning

NORDMAN, CORMANY, HAIR & COMPTON
Oxnard, CA.............................Bankruptcy Law; General Practice

NORMAN, DOWLER, SAWYER, ISRAEL & HANCOCK
Ventura, CA ....General Practice

NORMANDIN, CHENEY & O'NEIL
Laconia, NH.............................Banking Law; Civil Trial Practice; Commercial Law;
General Practice; Personal Injury; Probate, Trusts
and Estate Planning; Product Liability Law; Real
Estate Law

NORMINTON & WIITA
Beverly Hills, CA ....Civil Trial Practice; General Practice

NORRIS, FLOYD H.
Los Angeles, CA ....Civil Trial Practice; Probate, Trusts and Estate
Planning

NORRIS, MCLAUGHLIN & MARCUS, A PROFESSIONAL CORPORATION
Somerville, NJ ....General Practice

NORRIS & NORRIS
Akron, OH ....Personal Injury

NORRIS & ROSSI
San Mateo, CA.........................Family Law

NORTH LAW OFFICE, THE
Nashville, TN ....Civil Trial Practice; Personal Injury

NORTH, STEVEN E., P.C.
New York, NY.........................Medical Malpractice; Personal Injury

NORTHCUTT, CLARK, GARDNER & HRON
Ponca City, OK.......................General Practice

NORTHEN, BLUE, ROOKS, THIBAUT, ANDERSON & WOODS, L.L.P.
Chapel Hill, NC......................Bankruptcy Law; Business Law

NORTON & CHRISTENSEN
Goshen, NY ....Construction Law; Environmental Law; General
Practice

NORTON AND MANCINI
Wheaton, IL ....Civil Trial Practice

NORTON, WASSERMAN, JONES & KELLY
Salina, KS................................Business Law; Probate, Trusts and Estate Planning

NOTARO & MICHALOS P.C.
New York, NY.........................Patent, Trademark, Copyright and Unfair Competition; Trademark, Copyright and Unfair Compe-
tition

NOTO & OSWALD, P.C.
Washington, DC......................Immigration and Naturalization

NOTTAGE AND WARD
Chicago, IL..............................Family Law

NOTTINGHAM, ENGEL, GORDON & KERR
Syracuse, NY...........................Civil Trial Practice; General Practice

NOVACK AND MACEY
Chicago, IL..............................Civil Trial Practice

NOVAK, ROBERT J. & ASSOCIATES
Phoenix, AZ ....Bankruptcy Law; Business Law; Construction Law;
Real Estate Law

NOVAKOV, DAVIDSON & FLYNN, A PROFESSIONAL CORPORATION
Dallas, TX................................Banking Law; Business Law; Civil Trial Practice;
General Practice; Probate, Trusts and Estate
Planning; Real Estate Law; Tax Law

NOVEY, MENDELSON & ADAMSON
Tallahassee, FL ....Family Law; Real Estate Law

NOVINS, YORK & PENTONY, A PROFESSIONAL CORPORATION
Toms River, NJ.......................Civil Trial Practice; Criminal Trial Practice; General
Practice; Insurance Defense

NOVIT, SCARMINACH & WILLIAMS, P.A.
Hilton Head Island, SC ....Real Estate Law

NOVOSELSKY, DAVID A. & ASSOCIATES
Chicago, IL..............................Appellate Practice

NOWELL, GEORGE W. LAW OFFICES OF
San Francisco, CA ....Admiralty/Maritime Law

NOYES & GOSMA, L.L.P.
Davenport, IA.........................Banking Law; Business Law; Commercial Litigation;
General Practice; Probate, Trusts and Estate
Planning; Real Estate Law

NUKES, S. SAMUEL
Akron, OH ....Civil Trial Practice; Personal Injury; Product
Liability Law

NURENBERG, PLEVIN, HELLER & MCCARTHY CO., L.P.A.
Cleveland, OH.........................Aviation Law; Civil Trial Practice; Commercial
Litigation; Medical Malpractice; Personal Injury;
Product Liability Law

NUSBAUM & PARRINO, P.C.
Westport, CT...........................Family Law

NUTTALL BERMAN ATTORNEYS
Fresno, CA ....Criminal Trial Practice

NUTTER, MCCLENNEN & FISH, LLP
Boston, MA ....General Practice

OATES, HUGHES, KNEZEVICH & GARDENSWARTZ, P.C.
Aspen, CO...............................Civil Trial Practice; General Practice; Land Use Law

O'BANNON & O'BANNON, LLC
Florence, AL ....Insurance Defense

OBENSHAIN, WILEY S., III, P.C.
Augusta, GA ....Civil Trial Practice; Insurance Defense; Medical
Malpractice

OBERDANK, LAWRENCE M., CO., L.P.A.
Independence, OH...................Labor and Employment Law

OBERMAN & OBERMAN
Charleston, SC ....Civil Trial Practice; Family Law; Real Estate Law

OBERMAYER, REBMANN, MAXWELL & HIPPEL LLP
Philadelphia, PA ....General Practice

O'BRIEN, WILLIAM M.
Cambridge, MA ....Banking Law; Commercial Law; General Practice;
Real Estate Law

O'BRIEN, ANDERSON, BURGY & GARBOWICZ
Eagle River, WI ....General Practice

O'BRIEN, EHRICK, WOLF, DEANER & MAUS, L.L.P.
Rochester, MN........................Civil Trial Practice; General Practice; Real Estate
Law

O'BRIEN, O'ROURKE & HOGAN
Chicago, IL..............................Civil Trial Practice; Construction Law; Real Estate
Law

O'BRIEN & RYAN
Plymouth Meeting, PA ....Insurance Defense; Medical Malpractice; Workers
Compensation

O'BRIEN, SHAFNER, STUART, KELLY & MORRIS, P.C.
Groton, CT..............................General Practice; Personal Injury
Norwich, CT ....General Practice

O'BRIEN, TANSKI, TANZER & YOUNG
Hartford, CT ....Civil Trial Practice; General Practice; Health Care
Law; Insurance Defense; Medical Malpractice

O'BRYAN, BROWN & TONER
Louisville, KY ....Insurance Defense; Medical Malpractice

OCHOA & SILLAS
Los Angeles, CA ....Administrative Law; Civil Trial Practice;
Construction Law; Immigration and Naturalization;
Insurance Defense; Labor and Employment Law;
Municipal Bond/Public Authority Financing

O'CONNELL AND ARONOWITZ, P.C.
Albany, NY..............................Civil Trial Practice; Criminal Trial Practice; General
Practice; Health Care Law

O'CONNELL, DANIEL H., P.C.
Tucson, AZ ....Business Law; Employment Benefits Law; Probate,
Trusts and Estate Planning; Real Estate Law; Tax
Law

O'CONNELL & MAYHUGH, P.C.
Warrenton, VA...............General Practice

O'CONNOR, CAVANAGH, ANDERSON, KILLINGSWORTH & BESHEARS, A PROFESSIONAL ASSOCIATION
Nogales, AZ............Administrative Law; Civil Trial Practice; Commercial Law; General Practice; International Business Law; Real Estate Law; Tax Law
Phoenix, AZ............Administrative Law; Antitrust Law; Banking Law; Bankruptcy Law; Civil Trial Practice; Commercial Law; Construction Law; Environmental Law; General Practice; Health Care Law; Insurance Defense; International Business Law; Labor and Employment Law; Patent, Trademark, Copyright and Unfair Competition; Product Liability Law; Real Estate Law; Securities Law; Tax Law
Sun City, AZ............Probate, Trusts and Estate Planning

O'CONNOR CAVANAGH MOLLOY JONES, A PROFESSIONAL ASSOCIATION
Tucson, AZ............Bankruptcy Law; Civil Trial Practice; Commercial Law; Construction Law; Environmental Law; General Practice; Insurance Defense; Product Liability Law; Real Estate Law; Securities Law

O'CONNOR, COHN, DILLON & BARR, A LAW CORPORATION
San Francisco, CA............Civil Trial Practice; Medical Malpractice; Product Liability Law

O'CONNOR, DEGRAZIA & TAMM, P.C.
Bloomfield Hills, MI............Medical Malpractice; Municipal and Zoning Law

O'CONNOR, GACIOCH & POPE, L.L.P.
Binghamton, NY............Construction Law; Environmental Law; Insurance Defense; Labor and Employment Law

O'CONNOR & HANNAN
Washington, DC............General Practice; Municipal Bond/Public Authority Financing
Minneapolis, MN............Antitrust Law; General Practice; Municipal Bond/Public Authority Financing; Tax Law

O'CONNOR, McGUINNESS, CONTE, DOYLE, OLESON & COLLINS
White Plains, NY............General Practice; Insurance Defense; Probate, Trusts and Estate Planning

O'CONNOR & RHATICAN, A PROFESSIONAL CORPORATION
Chatham, NJ............Civil Trial Practice; Medical Malpractice; Personal Injury; Product Liability Law

O'CONNOR AND RYAN, P.C.
Fitchburg, MA............Civil Trial Practice; Family Law; Personal Injury

O'CONNOR & THOMAS, P.C.
Dubuque, IA............General Practice

ODELL, JAMES R., P.S.C.
Lexington, KY............General Practice

ODIN, FELDMAN & PITTLEMAN, P.C.
Fairfax, VA............Banking Law; Civil Trial Practice; Commercial Law; Family Law; General Practice; Labor and Employment Law; Real Estate Law; Tax Law; Trademark, Copyright and Unfair Competition

ODOM, ELLIOTT, WINBURN, WATSON, SMITH & ODOM
Fayetteville, AR............Civil Trial Practice; Personal Injury

O'DONNELL, ROBERT G.
White Plains, NY............Commercial Litigation

O'DONNELL, RAMIS, CREW, CORRIGAN & BACHRACH
Portland, OR............Antitrust Law; Business Law; Civil Trial Practice; Environmental Law; Labor and Employment Law; Municipal and Zoning Law; Personal Injury; Real Estate Law

O'DONNELL, SCHWARTZ, GLANSTEIN & ROSEN
New York, NY............General Practice

O'DONOGHUE & O'DONOGHUE
Washington, DC............Labor and Employment Law

O'DONOHUE & O'DONOHUE
Toronto, ON, Canada............General Practice

OFFUTT, HORMAN, BURDETTE & FREY, P.A.
Frederick, MD............General Practice

OGDEN, LEN W. JR.
Paducah, KY............Criminal Trial Practice; Personal Injury

OGGEL, STEPHEN P., A P.C., THE LAW OFFICES OF
San Diego, CA............Antitrust Law; Business Law; Securities Law

OGILVIE, GEORGE F.
Las Vegas, NV............Administrative Law; Municipal and Zoning Law

OGILVIE, DAVID A., P.C.
Denver, CO............Criminal Trial Practice

OGILVY RENAULT
Ottawa, ON, Canada............General Practice
Toronto, ON, Canada............General Practice
Montreal, QU, Canada............General Practice
Quebec, QU, Canada............General Practice
London, England............General Practice

OGLE & MERZON
Morro Bay, CA............General Practice; Probate, Trusts and Estate Planning; Real Estate Law

OGLETREE, DEAKINS, NASH, SMOAK & STEWART, L.L.P.
Atlanta, GA............Labor and Employment Law

OGLETREE, DEAKINS, NASH, SMOAK & STEWART, P.C.
Washington, DC............Labor and Employment Law
Raleigh, NC............Labor and Employment Law
Winston-Salem, NC............Labor and Employment Law
Charleston, SC............Labor and Employment Law
Columbia, SC............Labor and Employment Law
Greenville, SC............Environmental Law; Labor and Employment Law
Houston, TX............Labor and Employment Law

O'HARA, HANLON, KNYCH & POBEDINSKY, LLP
Syracuse, NY............General Practice

O'HARA, PATRICK M., P.A.
West Palm Beach, FL............Commercial Litigation; Personal Injury

O'HARA, RUBERG, TAYLOR, SLOAN AND SERGENT
Covington, KY............Civil Trial Practice; Family Law; General Practice

O'HARE & HEITCZMAN
Bethlehem, PA............Civil Trial Practice; Criminal Trial Practice; General Practice

OHNEGIAN, DONALD C.
Ramsey, NJ............General Practice

OHNSTAD TWICHELL, P.C.
Fargo, ND............Criminal Trial Practice; General Practice; Municipal Bond/Public Authority Financing; Probate, Trusts and Estate Planning

OHRENSTEIN & BROWN, L.L.P.
New York, NY............Civil Trial Practice; Insurance Defense

O'KEEFFE & LINDGREN, LLP
White Plains, NY............Civil Trial Practice; Personal Injury

OLDFATHER & MORRIS
Louisville, KY............Civil Trial Practice; Family Law; General Practice; Medical Malpractice; Personal Injury; Product Liability Law

OLDFIELD & COKER
Oklahoma City, OK............Insurance Defense; Labor and Employment Law; Personal Injury

OLDHAM & DOWLING
Akron, OH............Civil Trial Practice; Insurance Defense; Probate, Trusts and Estate Planning

OLDHAM & OLDHAM CO., L.P.A.
Akron, OH............Patent, Trademark, Copyright and Unfair Competition

O'LEARY, O'LEARY, JACOBS, MATTSON, PERRY & MASON, P.C.
Southfield, MI............Appellate Practice; Civil Trial Practice; Insurance Defense; Medical Malpractice; Transportation Law

OLENDER, JACK H., AND ASSOCIATES, P.C.
Washington, DC............Medical Malpractice; Personal Injury

OLES, MORRISON & RINKER
Seattle, WA............Construction Law; General Practice; Insurance Defense

OLIFF & BERRIDGE
Alexandria, VA............Patent, Trademark, Copyright and Unfair Competition

OLINCY & KARPEL
Los Angeles, CA............Probate, Trusts and Estate Planning; Tax Law

OLINER, MARTIN, P.C.
New York, NY............Bankruptcy Law; International Business Law

OLINGER, LOVALD, ROBBENNOLT & McCAHREN, P.C.
Pierre, SD............General Practice

OLINS, FOERSTER & HAYES
San Diego, CA............Family Law; Labor and Employment Law; Personal Injury

OLIPHANT, HAMMOND & O'HARA
Steamboat Springs, CO............Civil Trial Practice; Personal Injury

OLIVE AND OLIVE, P.A.
Durham, NC ....Patent, Trademark, Copyright and Unfair Competition

OLIVER, FRANK
Austin, TX ....Real Estate Law

OLIVER, DUCKWORTH, SPARGER & WINKLE, P.C.
Jonesboro, GA ....Civil Trial Practice; General Practice

OLIVER, OLIVER & WALTZ, P.C.
Cape Girardeau, MO ....Civil Trial Practice; General Practice; Insurance Defense

OLIVER, VOSE, SANDIFER, MURPHY & LEE, A PROFESSIONAL CORPORATION
Los Angeles, CA ....Environmental Law; Land Use Law; Municipal and Zoning Law; Real Estate Law

OLSEN, M. KENT
Denver, CO ....Probate, Trusts and Estate Planning

OLSEN-SMITH, LTD.
Phoenix, AZ ....Probate, Trusts and Estate Planning; Tax Law

OLSON GIBBONS SARTAIN NICOUD BIRNE SUSSMAN & GUECK, L.L.P.
Dallas, TX ....Bankruptcy Law; Civil Trial Practice; Commercial Law; Commercial Litigation; Energy Law; Mergers and Acquisitions

OLSON, GRABILL & HOFFMAN
Northbrook, IL ....Business Law; Probate, Trusts and Estate Planning; Real Estate Law

OLSON, NOONAN, URSU & RINGSMUTH, P.C.
Traverse City, MI ....Environmental Law

OLTMAN, FLYNN AND KUBLER
Fort Lauderdale, FL ....Patent, Trademark, Copyright and Unfair Competition

OLUP & ASSOCIATES
Minneapolis, MN ....Family Law

O'MALLEY & HARRIS, P.C.
Scranton, PA ....Bankruptcy Law; Civil Trial Practice; General Practice; Insurance Defense; Medical Malpractice; Product Liability Law; Workers Compensation

O'MALLEY LAW FIRM, THE, P.C.
St. Louis, MO..........................Criminal Trial Practice; Insurance Defense

OMAN, GENTRY & YNTEMA, P.A.
Albuquerque, NM....................Personal Injury; Real Estate Law

O'MEARA, ECKERT, POUROS & GONRING
West Bend, WI ....General Practice

O'MELVENY & MYERS LLP
Los Angeles, CA ....Antitrust Law; Appellate Practice; Banking Law; Bankruptcy Law; Business Law; Civil Trial Practice; Commercial Law; Communications Law; Construction Law; Criminal Trial Practice; Employment Benefits Law; Environmental Law; General Practice; Immigration and Naturalization; Insurance Defense; International Business Law; Labor and Employment Law; Municipal and Zoning Law; Natural Resources Law; Patent, Trademark, Copyright and Unfair Competition; Probate, Trusts and Estate Planning; Public Utilities Law; Real Estate Law; Securities Law; Tax Law; Trademark, Copyright and Unfair Competition
Washington, DC......................Communications Law

OMINSKY, MESSA, TANNER, GILES & SHERIDAN, P.C.
Philadelphia, PA ....General Practice

O'NEAL, BROWN & SIZEMORE, A PROFESSIONAL CORPORATION
Macon, GA ....General Practice; Personal Injury

O'NEAL, WALKER & BOEHM
Chattanooga, TN ....Personal Injury

ONEBANE, BERNARD, TORIAN, DIAZ, MCNAMARA & ABELL
Lafayette, LA ....Civil Trial Practice; General Practice; Insurance Defense

O'NEIL, EICHIN, MILLER, SAPORITO & HARRIS, A LAW CORPORATION
New Orleans, LA ....Admiralty/Maritime Law; Insurance Defense

O'NEILL & BORGES
San Juan, PR..........................Bankruptcy Law; Business Law; Civil Trial Practice; Environmental Law; General Practice; Immigration and Naturalization; Labor and Employment Law; Real Estate Law; Tax Law; Trademark, Copyright and Unfair Competition

O'NEILL, CHAPIN, MARKS, LIEBMAN, COOPER & CARR
Orlando, FL ....Civil Trial Practice; Commercial Law; Commercial Litigation; Insurance Defense

O'NEILL CRAWFORD & GREEN, P.C.
Burlington, VT ....Personal Injury

O'NEILL, JOSEPH D., A PROFESSIONAL CORPORATION
Vineland, NJ............................Criminal Trial Practice; Medical Malpractice; Personal Injury

O'NEILL, LYSAGHT & SUN
Santa Monica, CA....................Appellate Practice; Civil Trial Practice; Commercial Law; Criminal Trial Practice

O'NEILL, WALLACE & DOYLE, P.C.
Saginaw, MI ....General Practice; Insurance Defense

O'NEIL, PARKER AND WILLIAMSON
Knoxville, TN ....Civil Trial Practice

OOT LAW OFFICES
East Syracuse, NY ....General Practice

OPPENHEIMER, BLEND, HARRISON & TATE, INC.
San Antonio, TX ....General Practice

OPPENHEIMER POMS SMITH
Irvine, CA..............................Patent, Trademark, Copyright and Unfair Competition
Los Angeles, CA ....Patent, Trademark, Copyright and Unfair Competition

OPPENHEIMER WOLFF & DONNELLY
Minneapolis, MN ....General Practice

OPPENHEIM & PILELSKY, P.A.
Fort Lauderdale, FL ....Commercial Litigation; Family Law; Real Estate Law

ORANS, ELSEN & LUPERT LLP
New York, NY..........................Appellate Practice; Civil Trial Practice; Criminal Trial Practice; Family Law; International Business Law; Securities Law

ORDELL, DAVID J.
Seattle, WA ....Family Law

O'REILLY, ROGER KEVIN LAW OFFICES OF
Wheaton, IL ....Commercial Litigation; Medical Malpractice; Personal Injury

O'REILLY & COLLINS, A PROFESSIONAL CORPORATION
Menlo Park, CA......................Aviation Law; Civil Trial Practice; Medical Malpractice; Personal Injury; Product Liability Law

O'REILLY, NOSEWORTHY
St. John's, NF, Canada............General Practice; Insurance Defense

O'REILLY, RANCILIO, NITZ, ANDREWS & TURNBULL, P.C.
Sterling Heights, MI ....General Practice; Municipal and Zoning Law

ORENDORFF, JAMES M.
Pasadena, CA ....Business Law; Real Estate Law

ORGAIN, BELL & TUCKER, L.L.P.
Beaumont, TX..........................General Practice

ORLOFF, LOWENBACH, STIFELMAN & SIEGEL, A PROFESSIONAL CORPORATION
Roseland, NJ..........................Business Law; Civil Trial Practice; Commercial Law; General Practice; Probate, Trusts and Estate Planning; Securities Law; Tax Law

ORMAN, JAMES M.
Philadelphia, PA ....Probate, Trusts and Estate Planning

O'ROURKE, ALLAN & FONG
Glendale, CA..........................Business Law; Civil Trial Practice; Construction Law; Family Law; Personal Injury; Probate, Trusts and Estate Planning; Real Estate Law; Sports and Entertainment Law

ORR AND EDWARDS, ATTORNEYS AT LAW, P.C.
Decatur, GA............................Medical Malpractice

ORR & RENO, PROFESSIONAL ASSOCIATION
Concord, NH ....Civil Trial Practice; Commercial Law; Environmental Law; General Practice; Health Care Law; Labor and Employment Law; Personal Injury; Probate, Trusts and Estate Planning; Real Estate Law; Tax Law

ORRICK, HERRINGTON & SUTCLIFFE LLP
San Francisco, CA ....General Practice

ORTON, TOOMAN, HALE, MCKOWN AND KIEL, P.C.
Allegan, MI ....General Practice

OSBORN, J. KIRK
Chapel Hill, NC ....Criminal Trial Practice

OSBORN HINER LISHER & ORZESKE, P.C.
Indianapolis, IN ....Civil Trial Practice; Insurance Defense; Personal Injury; Product Liability Law

OSBORN, MALCOLM E., P.A.
Winston-Salem, NC ....Insurance Defense; Tax Law

OSBORN, REED, BURKE & TOBIN, LLP
Rochester, NY ....General Practice

OSBORNE, LOWE, HELMAN & SMITH, L.L.P.
Austin, TX ....Probate, Trusts and Estate Planning; Tax Law

OSBORNE, OSBORNE & DECLAIRE, P.A.
Boca Raton, FL ....General Practice; Probate, Trusts and Estate Planning; Real Estate Law

OSBORNE, WILLIAM G., P.A.
Orlando, FL ....Civil Trial Practice; Personal Injury

O'SHAUGHNESSY, PHILLIPS P., P.A.
Baltimore, MD ....Civil Trial Practice; General Practice

O'SHEA, REYNOLDS & CUMMINGS
Buffalo, NY ....Insurance Defense

OSHINS & ASSOCIATES
Las Vegas, NV ....Business Law; General Practice; Probate, Trusts and Estate Planning; Tax Law

OSLER, HOSKIN & HARCOURT
Calgary, AB, Canada ....General Practice
Ottawa, ON, Canada ....General Practice
Toronto, ON, Canada..............General Practice
London, England ....General Practice
Hong Kong, Hong Kong.........General Practice

OSTERHOUDT, FERGUSON, NATT, AHERON & AGEE, A PROFESSIONAL CORPORATION
Roanoke, VA............................General Practice

OSTROLENK, FABER, GERB & SOFFEN, LLP
New York, NY.........................Patent, Trademark, Copyright and Unfair Competition

OSTROVE, KRANTZ & OSTROVE, A PROFESSIONAL CORPORATION
Los Angeles, CA ....Admiralty/Maritime Law; Commercial Law; General Practice; Insurance Defense; Mergers and Acquisitions; Probate, Trusts and Estate Planning

OSTROW AND TAUB, LLP
Garden City, NY ....Family Law

OSWALD & COTTEY, A PROFESSIONAL CORPORATION
Kirksville, MO ....Civil Trial Practice; General Practice

OTERI, WEINBERG & LAWSON
Boston, MA.............................Criminal Trial Practice

OTHS, HEISER, REGAN AND MILLER
Wellston, OH ....Probate, Trusts and Estate Planning

OTSTOTT, GEORGE A., & ASSOCIATES, A PROF. CORP.
Dallas, TX...............................Medical Malpractice; Personal Injury; Product Liability Law

OTT & HOROWITZ, A PROFESSIONAL CORPORATION
Glendale, CA............................Appellate Practice; Civil Trial Practice; Labor and Employment Law

OTTEN, JOHNSON, ROBINSON, NEFF & RAGONETTI, P.C.
Denver, CO ....Business Law; Commercial Litigation; Construction Law; General Practice; Health Care Law; Labor and Employment Law; Land Use Law; Real Estate Law

OTTERBOURG, STEINDLER, HOUSTON & ROSEN, P.C.
New York, NY.........................Antitrust Law; Appellate Practice; Banking Law; Bankruptcy Law; Business Law; Civil Trial Practice; Commercial Law; Construction Law; Employment Benefits Law; General Practice; International Business Law; Probate, Trusts and Estate Planning; Real Estate Law; Securities Law; Trademark, Copyright and Unfair Competition

OTTERMAN & ALLEN, P.C.
Barre, VT................................Probate, Trusts and Estate Planning

OTTO, PORTERFIELD & POST, LLC
Vail, CO..................................Banking Law; General Practice; Real Estate Law

OTTS, MOORE & JORDAN
Brewton, AL............................Insurance Defense

OUTTEN, BARRETT, BURR & SHARRETT, P.C.
Emporia, VA ....General Practice

OVERCHUCK & LANGA, P.A.
Orlando, FL ....Personal Injury; Product Liability Law

OVERLANDER, LEWIS & RUSSELL
Pasadena, CA ....Civil Rights; Commercial Litigation; Insurance Defense; Labor and Employment Law

OVERSTREET RITCH & THACKER
Kissimmee, FL ....Probate, Trusts and Estate Planning; Real Estate Law

OWEN, WILLIAM L.
Little Rock, AR ....Civil Trial Practice; Real Estate Law

OWEN, LYLE, VOSS & OWEN, P.C.
Plainview, TX...........................General Practice

OWEN & MELBYE, A PROFESSIONAL CORPORATION
Redwood City, CA ....Aviation Law; General Practice; Insurance Defense; Personal Injury; Product Liability Law

OWEN SHOUP TROLSON & KINZIE
Indianapolis, IN ....Labor and Employment Law

OWENS, BENTON & SIMPSON
Bay Minette, AL ....Civil Trial Practice

OWENS & CARVER
Tuscaloosa, AL ....Civil Trial Practice

OWENS, CLARY & AIKEN, L.L.P.
Dallas, TX...............................Civil Trial Practice; Real Estate Law

OWENS DAVIES MACKIE, A PROFESSIONAL SERVICES CORPORATION
Olympia, WA ....General Practice

OWENS & TURNER, A PROFESSIONAL CORPORATION
Anchorage, AK ....Commercial Law; Labor and Employment Law

OWLETT, LEWIS & GINN, P.C.
Wellsboro, PA ....General Practice; Probate, Trusts and Estate Planning; Real Estate Law; Tax Law

OWNBEY, LLOYD C. JR.
Pasadena, CA ....Labor and Employment Law

OXLEY, MALONE, FITZGERALD & HOLLISTER
Findlay, OH ....General Practice; Insurance Defense

OZZARD WHARTON
Somerville, NJ ....Banking Law; Civil Trial Practice; Commercial Law; Environmental Law; Family Law; General Practice; Insurance Defense; Municipal Bond/Public Authority Financing; Municipal and Zoning Law; Personal Injury; Probate, Trusts and Estate Planning; Real Estate Law

PACIFICO, PAUL J. LAW OFFICES OF
Westport, CT...........................Civil Trial Practice; Medical Malpractice; Personal Injury

PACKENHAM, SCHMIDT & FEDERICO, P.C.
Boston, MA.............................Appellate Practice; Family Law; Probate, Trusts and Estate Planning

PADBERG, MCSWEENEY, SLATER, MERZ & GRAHAM, A PROFESSIONAL CORPORATION
St. Louis, MO..........................Civil Trial Practice; Medical Malpractice; Personal Injury; Product Liability Law; Real Estate Law

PAGE & BACEK
Atlanta, GA ....Securities Law

PAGE, MANNINO, PERESICH, DICKINSON & MCDERMOTT
Biloxi, MS...............................General Practice; Insurance Defense; Medical Malpractice; Personal Injury; Product Liability Law
Gulfport, MS...........................General Practice; Insurance Defense; Medical Malpractice; Personal Injury; Product Liability Law

PAGE, POLIN & BUSCH, A PROFESSIONAL CORPORATION
San Diego, CA ....Bankruptcy Law; Business Law; Civil Trial Practice; General Practice; International Business Law; Securities Law; Tax Law

PAIKIN, MICHAEL L., P.C.
New York, NY.........................Commercial Litigation

PAIN AND GARLAND
Anadarko, OK ....General Practice

PAINE EDMONDS
Vancouver, BC, Canada...........General Practice; Insurance Defense

PAINE, MCELREATH & HYDER, P.C.
Augusta, GA ....Commercial Law; Health Care Law; Real Estate Law

PAJCIC & PAJCIC, P.A.
Jacksonville, FL ....Medical Malpractice; Personal Injury; Product Liability Law

PALAZZO, ROBERT P.
Los Angeles, CA ....International Business Law

PALEY, ROTHMAN, GOLDSTEIN, ROSENBERG & COOPER, CHARTERED
Bethesda, MD ....General Practice; Labor and Employment Law; Tax Law

PALKOVITZ, HERBERT
Cleveland, OH..........................Family Law

PALMATIER, SJOQUIST & HELGET, P.A.
Minneapolis, MN....................Patent, Trademark, Copyright and Unfair Competition

PALMER & DODGE LLP
Boston, MA...............................Antitrust Law; Appellate Practice; Banking Law; Bankruptcy Law; Business Law; Civil Trial Practice; Communications Law; Computer Law; Construction Law; Employment Benefits Law; Environmental Law; General Practice; Immigration and Naturalization; Insurance Defense; International Business Law; Labor and Employment Law; Land Use Law; Municipal Bond/Public Authority Financing; Personal Injury; Probate, Trusts and Estate Planning; Product Liability Law; Public Utilities Law; Real Estate Law; Securities Law; Sports and Entertainment Law; Tax Law; Trademark, Copyright and Unfair Competition; Transportation Law

PALMER LAW FIRM
Dyersburg, TN........................Commercial Law; Personal Injury
Hilton Head Island, SC...........Real Estate Law

PALMER & LOWRY
Topeka, KS..............................Medical Malpractice; Personal Injury; Product Liability Law

PALMIERI, TYLER, WIENER, WILHELM & WALDRON, LLP
Irvine, CA................................General Practice

PALMISANO, JAMES ANTHONY, LTD.
Chicago, IL..............................Family Law

PANIELLO, JOSEPH M., P.A., LAW OFFICE OF
Tampa, FL ....Real Estate Law

PANITCH SCHWARZE JACOBS & NADEL, P.C.
Philadelphia, PA ....Patent, Trademark, Copyright and Unfair Competition

PAPA, HERMAN D.
San Francisco, CA ....Civil Trial Practice

PAPERNICK & GEFSKY, A PROFESSIONAL CORPORATION
Pittsburgh, PA ....Real Estate Law

PARCEL, MAURO, HULTIN & SPAANSTRA, P.C.
Denver, CO ....Administrative Law; Civil Trial Practice; Environmental Law; General Practice; Natural Resources Law; Product Liability Law; Real Estate Law

PARDIECK, GILL & VARGO, A PROFESSIONAL CORPORATION
Indianapolis, IN ....Medical Malpractice; Personal Injury; Product Liability Law
Seymour, IN ....Medical Malpractice; Personal Injury; Product Liability Law

PARENTI, FALK & WAAS, P.A.
Coral Gables, FL ....Insurance Defense; Medical Malpractice

PARHAM, HELMS, HARRIS, BLYTHE & MORTON
Charlotte, NC..........................Bankruptcy Law; Real Estate Law

PARHAM & SMITH
Greenville, SC.........................Civil Trial Practice; Medical Malpractice; Personal Injury; Product Liability Law

PARICHAN, RENBERG, CROSSMAN & HARVEY, LAW CORPORATION
Fresno, CA ....Business Law; Civil Trial Practice; Insurance Defense; Probate, Trusts and Estate Planning

PARIS, PHILIP T.
Phoenix, AZ ....Mergers and Acquisitions

PARIS & ASSOCIATES, P.A.
Tampa, FL ....Probate, Trusts and Estate Planning; Real Estate Law

PARIS, BLANK & BROWN, A PROFESSIONAL CORPORATION
Richmond, VA ....General Practice

PARIS AND PARIS
Santa Monica, CA...................Bankruptcy Law; Commercial Litigation

PARISH, WILLIAM W. LAW OFFICES OF
Dallas, TX ....Personal Injury

PARISI, GREGORY LAW OFFICES OF
Mineola, NY.............................Insurance Defense

PARK, MANCE MICHAEL LAW OFFICES OF
Huntsville, TX..........................Civil Trial Practice; Personal Injury

PARKER, JAMES M.
Newport Beach, CA.................Real Estate Law

PARKER CHAPIN FLATTAU & KLIMPL, L.L.P.
New York, NY.........................Antitrust Law; Banking Law; Bankruptcy Law; Civil Trial Practice; Commercial Law; General Practice; Health Care Law; Insurance Defense; Labor and Employment Law; Medical Malpractice; Probate, Trusts and Estate Planning; Product Liability Law; Real Estate Law; Securities Law; Tax Law

PARKER, DAVID YOUNG, P.C.
Nashville, TN ....General Practice

PARKER, HAYES & LOVINGER, P.C.
Hillsdale, MI ....General Practice

PARKER, HUDSON, RAINER & DOBBS
Atlanta, GA ....Antitrust Law; Bankruptcy Law; Business Law; Commercial Law; Health Care Law; Real Estate Law; Securities Law

PARKER, JOHNSON & PARKER, P.S.
Hoquiam, WA ....General Practice

PARKER, LAWRENCE, CANTRELL & DEAN
Nashville, TN ....Civil Trial Practice; General Practice

PARKER, MCCAY & CRISCUOLO, P.A.
Cherry Hill, NJ ....Civil Trial Practice; General Practice
Marlton, NJ..............................Civil Trial Practice; General Practice

PARKER, POE, ADAMS & BERNSTEIN L.L.P.
Charlotte, NC...........................General Practice

PARKER & WAICHMAN
New York, NY.........................Civil Trial Practice

PARKERSON, SHELFER & GROFF
Decatur, GA.............................Insurance Defense; Medical Malpractice; Personal Injury

PARKHURST, WENDEL & BURR, L.L.P.
Alexandria, VA ....Civil Trial Practice; Patent, Trademark, Copyright and Unfair Competition

PARKOWSKI, NOBLE & GUERKE, PROFESSIONAL ASSOCIATION
Dover, DE................................Civil Trial Practice; Environmental Law; General Practice; Real Estate Law

PARLEE MCLAWS
Calgary, AB, Canada ....Administrative Law; Banking Law; Bankruptcy Law; Civil Trial Practice; Commercial Law; Environmental Law; Immigration and Naturalization; Insurance Defense; International Business Law; Natural Resources Law; Personal Injury; Probate, Trusts and Estate Planning; Real Estate Law; Securities Law; Tax Law
Edmonton, AB, Canada ....Administrative Law; Appellate Practice; Banking Law; Bankruptcy Law; Business Law; Civil Trial Practice; Commercial Law; Construction Law; Employment Benefits Law; Environmental Law; Immigration and Naturalization; Insurance Defense; International Business Law; Municipal and Zoning Law; Personal Injury; Probate, Trusts and Estate Planning; Public Utilities Law; Real Estate Law; Securities Law; Tax Law

PARNELL, CRUM & ANDERSON, P.A.
Montgomery, AL ....Bankruptcy Law; Commercial Litigation

PARRA, DEL VALLE, FRAU & LIMERES
Ponce, PR................................General Practice

PARRISH, BAILEY & MORSCH, P.A.
Orlando, FL ....Medical Malpractice; Personal Injury; Product Liability Law

PARRY MURRAY & WARD, A PROFESSIONAL CORPORATION
Salt Lake City, UT..................Civil Trial Practice; Commercial Law; Environmental Law; General Practice; Land Use Law; Securities Law

PARSONS, STEVEN J. LAW OFFICES OF
Las Vegas, NV ....Medical Malpractice; Personal Injury

PARSONS BEHLE & LATIMER, A PROFESSIONAL CORPORATION
Salt Lake City, UT..................Administrative Law; Antitrust Law; Appellate Practice; Banking Law; Bankruptcy Law; Business Law; Civil Trial Practice; Communications Law; Computer Law; Construction Law; Employment Benefits Law; Environmental Law; Health Care Law; Immigration and Naturalization; International Business Law; Labor and Employment Law; Land Use Law; Medical Malpractice; Municipal and Zoning Law; Natural Resources Law; Patent, Trademark, Copyright and Unfair Competition; Personal Injury; Probate, Trusts and Estate Planning; Product Liability Law; Public Utilities Law; Real Estate Law; Securities Law; Tax Law; Transportation Law

PARSONS, DAVIES, KINGHORN & PETERS, P.C.
Salt Lake City, UT..................Bankruptcy Law; Business Law; Commercial Law; Commercial Litigation; Energy Law; Environmental Law; General Practice; Health Care Law; Land Use Law; Municipal and Zoning Law; Natural Resources Law; Probate, Trusts and Estate Planning; Real Estate Law; Tax Law; Trademark, Copyright and Unfair Competition

PARSONS AND DESTIAN
Los Angeles, CA ....Insurance Defense

PARSONS, LEE & JULIANO, P.C.
Birmingham, AL ....General Practice; Health Care Law; Insurance Defense; Municipal and Zoning Law; Product Liability Law

PARTRIDGE & PERKINS
Falls Church, VA ....Probate, Trusts and Estate Planning

PASHMAN STEIN, A PROFESSIONAL CORPORATION
Hackensack, NJ......................Appellate Practice; Bankruptcy Law; Commercial Law

PASQUESI, CENGEL AND PASQUESI, P.C.
Highland Park, IL....................General Practice

PASSEN, STEPHEN M., LTD.
Chicago, IL............................Medical Malpractice; Personal Injury

PATE & DODSON
Beaumont, TX......................Insurance Defense; Product Liability Law

PATERSON, MACDOUGALL
Toronto, ON, Canada..............Insurance Defense

PATLA, STRAUS, ROBINSON & MOORE, P.A.
Asheville, NC ....General Practice

PATRICK, HARPER & DIXON, L.L.P.
Hickory, NC............................General Practice

PATRICK & LACY, P.C.
Birmingham, AL ....Antitrust Law; Appellate Practice; Civil Trial Practice; Securities Law

PATRICK & STOWELL, P.C.
Aspen, CO ....Environmental Law; Natural Resources Law

PATTEN, WORNOM & WATKINS, L.C.
Newport News, VA ....General Practice

PATTERSON, BELKNAP WEBB & TYLER LLP
New York, NY......................Civil Trial Practice; General Practice

PATTERSON, DILTHEY, CLAY & BRYSON, L.L.P.
Raleigh, NC............................Insurance Defense; Personal Injury

PATTERSON & HARMON, P.A.
Deerfield Beach, FL ....General Practice; Probate, Trusts and Estate Planning

PATTERSON, KINNEY & RUGA
Grand Rapids, MI ....Labor and Employment Law

PATTERSON, LORENTZEN, DUFFIELD, TIMMONS, IRISH, BECKER & ORDWAY, L.L.P.
Des Moines, IA ....Civil Trial Practice; General Practice; Insurance Defense; Personal Injury; Product Liability Law; Workers Compensation

PATTERSON PALMER HUNT MURPHY
Saint John, NB, Canada ....Banking Law; Bankruptcy Law; Commercial Law; General Practice; Personal Injury; Real Estate Law

PATTERSON, PHIFER & PHILLIPS, P.C.
Detroit, MI............................Civil Trial Practice; Commercial Law; Insurance Defense; Labor and Employment Law; Personal Injury; Workers Compensation

PATTERSON, RICHARD A., P.C.
Bloomfield Hills, MI................Administrative Law; Insurance Defense

PATTERSON, RICHARDS, HESSERT, WENDORFF & ELLISON
Wausau, WI............................Environmental Law; General Practice

PATTERSON, ROBERT B., LTD., LAW OFFICES OF
Chicago, IL............................Personal Injury

PATTERSON & SWEENY
Miami, FL ....Civil Trial Practice; General Practice; Real Estate Law

PATTIE & DALEY
Christiansted, St. Croix, VI .....General Practice; Insurance Defense

PATTISHALL, MCAULIFFE, NEWBURY, HILLIARD & GERALDSON
Chicago, IL............................International Business Law; Patent, Trademark, Copyright and Unfair Competition; Trademark, Copyright and Unfair Competition

PATTON BOGGS, L.L.P.
Washington, DC......................General Practice

PATTON, DAVID D., & ASSOCIATES, P.C.
Bloomfield Hills, MI................Administrative Law; Business Law; Civil Trial Practice; Health Care Law; Insurance Defense; Labor and Employment Law; Medical Malpractice; Personal Injury; Product Liability Law

PATTON, HALTOM, ROBERTS, MCWILLIAMS & GREER, L.L.P.
Texarkana, TX ....Bankruptcy Law; Civil Trial Practice; General Practice; Insurance Defense; Personal Injury; Probate, Trusts and Estate Planning; Real Estate Law; Tax Law

PATTON, LATHAM, LEGGE & COLE
Athens, AL ....General Practice; Insurance Defense

PATTON, TIDWELL, SANDEFUR & PADDOCK
Texarkana, TX ....Civil Trial Practice; Employment Benefits Law; General Practice; Insurance Defense; Medical Malpractice; Personal Injury; Product Liability Law

PATULA & ASSOCIATES
Chicago, IL............................Patent, Trademark, Copyright and Unfair Competition

PATURIS, E. MICHAEL
Alexandria, VA ....Business Law; Probate, Trusts and Estate Planning; Tax Law

PAUL, JACK
Los Angeles, CA ....Construction Law

PAUL, HASTINGS, JANOFSKY & WALKER LLP
Costa Mesa, CA ....General Practice
Los Angeles, CA ....General Practice
Santa Monica, CA ....General Practice
Stamford, CT..........................General Practice
Washington, DC......................General Practice
Atlanta, GA ....General Practice
New York, NY........................General Practice
Tokyo, Japan ....General Practice

PAULIG AND SINGER
Urbana, OH............................General Practice

PAUL & JANOFSKY
Santa Monica, CA..................Civil Trial Practice

PAUL, JOHNSON, PARK & NILES, ATTORNEYS AT LAW, A LAW CORPORATION
Honolulu, HI..........................General Practice
Wailuku, HI ....General Practice

PAULLING & JAMES
Darlington, SC ....General Practice

PAUL & PAUL
Philadelphia, PA ....Patent, Trademark, Copyright and Unfair Competition; Trademark, Copyright and Unfair Competition

PAULSON, NACE & NORWIND
Washington, DC......................Civil Trial Practice; Medical Malpractice; Personal Injury

PAUL, WEISS, RIFKIND, WHARTON & GARRISON
Washington, DC......................General Practice
New York, NY........................General Practice
Paris, France............................General Practice

PAVALON & GIFFORD
Chicago, IL............................Aviation Law; Civil Trial Practice; Medical Malpractice; Personal Injury; Product Liability Law; Transportation Law

PAXTON, CROW, BRAGG, SMITH & KEYSER, P.A.
Vero Beach, FL ....Civil Trial Practice
West Palm Beach, FL ....Civil Trial Practice

PAYNE & BLANCHARD, L.L.P.
Dallas, TX ....Civil Trial Practice; General Practice

PAYNE, GATES, FARTHING & RADD, P.C.
Norfolk, VA ....Banking Law; Civil Trial Practice; Insurance Defense; Personal Injury

PAYNE & JONES, CHARTERED
Overland Park, KS..................General Practice

PAYNE, LOEB & RAY
Charleston, WV......................Civil Trial Practice; General Practice; Probate, Trusts and Estate Planning; Tax Law

PAYNE, WOOD & LITTLEJOHN
Bridgehampton, NY................Banking Law; General Practice; Real Estate Law
Melville, NY ....Banking Law; General Practice; Real Estate Law

PAYTON, HARRY A., & ASSOCIATES, P.A.
Miami, FL ....Civil Trial Practice

PEABODY & ARNOLD
Boston, MA............................Banking Law; Bankruptcy Law; Business Law; Civil Trial Practice; Commercial Law; Family Law; General Practice; Health Care Law; Insurance Defense; International Business Law; Probate, Trusts and Estate Planning; Real Estate Law; Securities Law

PEACOCK KELLER ECKER & CROTHERS
Washington, PA ....Business Law; Civil Trial Practice; General Practice; Probate, Trusts and Estate Planning

PEAR SPERLING EGGAN & MUSKOVITZ, P.C.
Ann Arbor, MI ....Banking Law; Civil Trial Practice; Family Law; General Practice; Labor and Employment Law; Probate, Trusts and Estate Planning; Real Estate Law
Ypsilanti, MI ....Civil Trial Practice; General Practice; Probate, Trusts and Estate Planning

PEARCE AND DURICK
Bismarck, ND ....Appellate Practice; Civil Trial Practice; Commercial Law; Communications Law; General Practice; Insurance Defense; Labor and Employment Law; Natural Resources Law; Product Liability Law; Real Estate Law; Tax Law; Workers Compensation

PEARLMAN AND CHOSNEK, P.C.
Lafayette, IN ....Commercial Litigation; Family Law; General Practice

PEATROSS, GREER & FRAZIER
Shreveport, LA ....General Practice

PECKAR & ABRAMSON, A PROFESSIONAL CORPORATION
River Edge, NJ ....Construction Law; Labor and Employment Law

PEDDICORD, WHARTON, THUNE AND SPENCER, A PROFESSIONAL CORPORATION
Des Moines, IA ....Aviation Law; Insurance Defense

PEDDIE, COLLYN A., A PROFESSIONAL CORPORATION
Houston, TX ....Appellate Practice

PEDLEY, ZIELKE & GORDINIER
Louisville, KY ....Civil Trial Practice; Insurance Defense; Municipal Bond/Public Authority Financing

PEED & MITNIK, P.A.
Orlando, FL ....Medical Malpractice; Personal Injury

PEEL, BEATTY & WALTERS
Edwardsville, IL ....Civil Trial Practice; Family Law

PEEL LAW FIRM, P.A.
Russellville, AR ....Civil Trial Practice

PELINO & LENTZ, A PROFESSIONAL CORPORATION
Philadelphia, PA ....General Practice

PELLEGRINI & SEELEY, P.C.
Springfield, MA ....Civil Trial Practice; General Practice

PENIX, PENIX, LUSBY AND NIX
Jonesboro, AR ....Civil Trial Practice; General Practice; Insurance Defense

PENNIE & EDMONDS
Washington, DC ....Patent, Trademark, Copyright and Unfair Competition
New York, NY ....Patent, Trademark, Copyright and Unfair Competition; Trademark, Copyright and Unfair Competition

PENNINGTON, CULPEPPER, MOORE, WILKINSON, DUNBAR & DUNLAP, P.A.
Tallahassee, FL ....General Practice

PEOPLES & HALE
St. Louis, MO ....Civil Trial Practice; Patent, Trademark, Copyright and Unfair Competition

PEPER, MARTIN, JENSEN, MAICHEL AND HETLAGE
St. Louis, MO ....Business Law; Civil Trial Practice; Environmental Law; General Practice; Health Care Law; Labor and Employment Law; Real Estate Law; Tax Law

PEPPER & CORAZZINI
Washington, DC ....Communications Law

PEPPER, HAMILTON & SCHEETZ
Wilmington, DE ....General Practice
Washington, DC ....General Practice
Detroit, MI ....General Practice
Harrisburg, PA ....General Practice
Philadelphia, PA ....General Practice

PEPPER, W. ALLEN, JR., P.A.
Cleveland, MS ....Civil Trial Practice

PEQUIGNOT, MARGOT, P.A., LAW OFFICE
Largo, FL ....Family Law

PERANTINIDES & NOLAN CO., L.P.A.
Akron, OH ....Insurance Defense; Medical Malpractice; Personal Injury; Product Liability Law

PERDUE & CLORE, L.L.P.
Houston, TX ....Medical Malpractice; Personal Injury

PEREY, RON LAW OFFICE OF
Seattle, WA ....Medical Malpractice; Personal Injury; Product Liability Law

PERI & STEWART
Maplewood, NJ ....Commercial Law

PERKIN & HOSODA
Honolulu, HI ....Civil Trial Practice; Personal Injury

PERKINS, ROGER A.
Annapolis, MD ....Family Law

PERKINS COIE
Washington, DC ....General Practice
Bellevue, WA ....General Practice
Seattle, WA ....Antitrust Law; General Practice; Labor and Employment Law; Municipal Bond/Public Authority Financing; Tax Law

PERKINS, THOMPSON, HINCKLEY & KEDDY, P.A.
Portland, ME ....Civil Trial Practice; General Practice; International Trade Law

PERLMAN, PETER, LAW OFFICES, P.S.C.
Lexington, KY ....Civil Trial Practice; Personal Injury; Product Liability Law

PERMAN & GREEN, LLP
Fairfield, CT ....Patent, Trademark, Copyright and Unfair Competition; Trademark, Copyright and Unfair Competition

PERONA, LANGER & BECK, A PROFESSIONAL CORPORATION
Long Beach, CA ....Civil Trial Practice; Personal Injury

PERRIN, PERRIN, MANN & PATTERSON
Spartanburg, SC ....Commercial Law; General Practice

PERRY, GREGORY M.
Commerce, GA ....General Practice

PERRY, FIALKOWSKI & PERRY
Philadelphia, PA ....Civil Trial Practice; Health Care Law; Medical Malpractice; Personal Injury; Product Liability Law

PERRY, GENTRY, PERRY & MARSH
Hobart, OK ....General Practice

PERRY, GLENN A., & ASSOCIATES
Longview, TX ....Personal Injury

PERRY, KITTRELL, BLACKBURN & BLACKBURN
Henderson, NC ....General Practice

PERRY, PATRICK, FARMER & MICHAUX, P.A.
Charlotte, NC ....General Practice; Real Estate Law
Raleigh, NC ....General Practice; Real Estate Law

PERRY, PIERSON & SILVER, P.L.C.
Phoenix, AZ ....Bankruptcy Law; Civil Trial Practice; Commercial Litigation; Insurance Defense; Real Estate Law; Trademark, Copyright and Unfair Competition

PERRY & SPANN, A PROFESSIONAL CORPORATION
Las Vegas, NV ....Insurance Defense
Reno, NV ....Insurance Defense

PERRY & WALTERS
Albany, GA ....Banking Law; Insurance Defense; Probate, Trusts and Estate Planning; Workers Compensation

PERSON, WHITWORTH, RAMOS, BORCHERS & MORALES, L.L.P.
Laredo, TX ....General Practice; Natural Resources Law

PESIN, EDWARD, A PROFESSIONAL CORPORATION
North Bergen, NJ ....Probate, Trusts and Estate Planning; Tax Law

PESKIND HYMSON & GOLDSTEIN, P.C.
Scottsdale, AZ ....Bankruptcy Law; Business Law; Civil Trial Practice; Commercial Law; Construction Law; Real Estate Law

PETERS, DONALD, A LAW CORPORATION
Newport Beach, CA ....Civil Trial Practice; Personal Injury

PETERS, FULLER, RUSH, FARNSWORTH & HABIB
Chico, CA ....General Practice

PETERS, JOHN C., P.C.
West Hartford, CT ....General Practice; Securities Law

PETERS LAW FIRM, P.C.
Council Bluffs, IA ....Civil Trial Practice; General Practice

PETERS, ROBERTSON, LAX, PARSONS, WELCHER, MOWERS & PASSARO, P.A.
    Fort Lauderdale, FL ....General Practice
    Fort Myers, FL ....General Practice
    Miami, FL ....General Practice
    West Palm Beach, FL ....General Practice

PETERSEN, G. RUSSELL, P.A.
    Vero Beach, FL ....Family Law

PETERSEN, MOSS, OLSEN, CARR, ESKELSON & HALL
    Idaho Falls, ID......................General Practice

PETERSON & BASHA, P.C.
    Vienna, VA............................Business Law; Civil Trial Practice; Family Law; Probate, Trusts and Estate Planning; Real Estate Law; Tax Law

PETERSON, BERNARD, VANDENBERG, ZEI, GEISLER & MARTIN
    Fort Lauderdale, FL ....Insurance Defense
    West Palm Beach, FL ....Insurance Defense

PETERSON DILLARD YOUNG ASSELIN & POWELL LLP
    Atlanta, GA ....Business Law; Commercial Law; Construction Law; Municipal and Zoning Law; Real Estate Law

PETERSON, HAY AND COMSA, P.C.
    Mount Clemens, MI.................Labor and Employment Law; Municipal and Zoning Law

PETERSON & MYERS, P.A.
    Lakeland, FL..........................Banking Law; Civil Trial Practice; Environmental Law; General Practice; Real Estate Law; Tax Law
    Lake Wales, FL......................Banking Law; Civil Trial Practice; Environmental Law; General Practice; Real Estate Law; Tax Law
    Winter Haven, FL...................Banking Law; Civil Trial Practice; Environmental Law; Family Law; General Practice; Real Estate Law

PETERSON & ROSS
    Chicago, IL............................General Practice

PETILLON & HANSEN
    Torrance, CA..........................Securities Law

PETOCK, MICHAEL F.
    Valley Forge, PA.....................Patent, Trademark, Copyright and Unfair Competition; Trademark, Copyright and Unfair Competition

PETREE STOCKTON, L.L.P.
    Charlotte, NC..........................General Practice
    Raleigh, NC............................General Practice
    Winston-Salem, NC ....General Practice

PETRIKIN, WELLMAN, DAMICO, CARNEY & BROWN, A PROFESSIONAL CORPORATION
    Media, PA ....General Practice

PETRONE & PETRONE, P.C.
    Utica, NY...............................Environmental Law; Insurance Defense

PETRUCCELLI & MARTIN
    Portland, ME ....Appellate Practice; Civil Trial Practice; Commercial Litigation; Communications Law; Construction Law; Environmental Law; Insurance Defense; Labor and Employment Law; Public Utilities Law

PETRY & PETRY, P.C.
    Carrizo Springs, TX ....General Practice

PETTINGELL & REGAN
    Boston, MA.............................Admiralty/Maritime Law; Insurance Defense

PETTY, DAVID K., A PROFESSIONAL CORPORATION
    Guymon, OK ....General Practice

PEYTON, GORDON P., P.C.
    Alexandria, VA ....Bankruptcy Law; Probate, Trusts and Estate Planning

PEZZOLA & REINKE, A PROFESSIONAL CORPORATION
    Oakland, CA ....Business Law; Computer Law; Health Care Law; Patent, Trademark, Copyright and Unfair Competition; Real Estate Law; Securities Law; Tax Law

PFALTZ & WOLLER, P.A. A PROFESSIONAL CORPORATION
    Summit, NJ ....Banking Law; Probate, Trusts and Estate Planning; Real Estate Law

PFAU, PFAU & MARANDO
    Youngstown, OH ....Insurance Defense

PFEIFER, MAXWELL S.
    Bronx, NY..............................Civil Trial Practice; General Practice; Medical Malpractice; Personal Injury; Product Liability Law

PHARES, BANKER
    Port Arthur, TX.......................Labor and Employment Law; Probate, Trusts and Estate Planning

PHEARS & MOLDOVAN
    Norcross, GA ....Health Care Law

PHEBUS, WINKELMANN, WONG & BRAMFELD
    Urbana, IL..............................General Practice

PHELPS, J. MICHAEL
    San Francisco, CA ....Civil Trial Practice

PHELPS DUNBAR, L.L.P.
    Baton Rouge, LA....................Civil Trial Practice; General Practice
    New Orleans, LA ....Admiralty/Maritime Law; Banking Law; Civil Trial Practice; Environmental Law; General Practice; Labor and Employment Law; Natural Resources Law; Tax Law
    Jackson, MS ....Civil Trial Practice; General Practice; Labor and Employment Law
    Tupelo, MS ....Civil Trial Practice; General Practice
    Houston, TX ....Admiralty/Maritime Law; Civil Trial Practice

PHELPS & FARA
    Indianapolis, IN ....Family Law

PHELPS, JENKINS, GIBSON & FOWLER
    Tuscaloosa, AL ....Business Law; Civil Trial Practice; General Practice; Insurance Defense; Tax Law

PHELPS, KASTEN, RUYLE & BURNS
    Carlinville, IL ....Civil Trial Practice; General Practice

PHILIPS, HOPKINS, EAMES & COBB, P.C.
    Denton, TX ....Criminal Trial Practice; Family Law; General Practice; Personal Injury; Probate, Trusts and Estate Planning; Real Estate Law

PHILLIPS, J. HARRISON III
    Ocean City, MD......................General Practice

PHILLIPS, MICHAEL
    Eugene, OR ....Personal Injury

PHILLIPS & AKERS, A PROFESSIONAL CORPORATION
    Houston, TX ....Insurance Defense

PHILLIPS & EZELL
    Phenix City, AL ....Banking Law

PHILLIPS, GARDILL, KAISER & ALTMEYER
    Wheeling, WV ....General Practice

PHILLIPS, GOLDMAN & SPENCE, P.A.
    Wilmington, DE......................Civil Trial Practice; Insurance Defense

PHILLIPS, JAMES J., A PROFESSIONAL CORPORATION
    Pleasanton, CA........................Probate, Trusts and Estate Planning

PHILLIPS, LYTLE, HITCHCOCK, BLAINE & HUBER
    Buffalo, NY ....General Practice; Labor and Employment Law; Tax Law
    Jamestown, NY ....General Practice
    New York, NY........................General Practice
    Rochester, NY.........................General Practice

PHILLIPS MCFALL MCCAFFREY MCVAY & MURRAH, P.C.
    Oklahoma City, OK................General Practice

PHILLIPS & MERICA, P.C.
    Austin, TX ....Bankruptcy Law; Commercial Litigation; Construction Law; General Practice; Real Estate Law

PHILLIPS, MOORE, LEMPIO & FINLEY
    San Francisco, CA ....Patent, Trademark, Copyright and Unfair Competition

PHILLIPS, OLORE & DUNLAVEY, P.A.
    Presque Isle, ME ....General Practice

PHIPPS FIRM, THE
    Tallahassee, FL ....Tax Law

PIAZZA & MELMED
    Stamford, CT..........................Civil Trial Practice; Family Law; Personal Injury

PICADIO MCCALL KANE & NORTON
    Pittsburgh, PA ....Civil Trial Practice

PICCIONE, KEELEY & ASSOCIATES, LTD.
    Wheaton, IL ....General Practice

PICCO HERBERT KENNEDY, A PROFESSIONAL CORPORATION
    Trenton, NJ............................Administrative Law; Civil Trial Practice; Environmental Law

PICHA & SALISBURY
    Rockford, IL ....Insurance Defense; Workers Compensation

PICKENS, BARNES & ABERNATHY
Cedar Rapids, IA....................Civil Trial Practice; Insurance Defense

PICKETT, STANLEY S.
Greenbelt, MD........................Civil Trial Practice; Criminal Trial Practice; Family Law; General Practice; Probate, Trusts and Estate Planning; Real Estate Law

PICKREL, SCHAEFFER & EBELING CO., L.P.A.
Dayton, OH............................Health Care Law; Insurance Defense; Labor and Employment Law; Mergers and Acquisitions

PICO & MITCHELL
Las Vegas, NV........................Business Law; Civil Trial Practice; Commercial Law; Construction Law; General Practice; Health Care Law; Insurance Defense; Labor and Employment Law; Medical Malpractice; Personal Injury; Product Liability Law; Real Estate Law

PIERCE, JOSEPH G.
Tuscaloosa, AL.......................Personal Injury; Product Liability Law

PIERCE ATWOOD
Augusta, ME..........................Administrative Law; Bankruptcy Law; Civil Trial Practice; Criminal Trial Practice; General Practice; Medical Malpractice; Personal Injury; Product Liability Law
Portland, ME.........................Administrative Law; Antitrust Law; Banking Law; Bankruptcy Law; Business Law; Civil Trial Practice; Commercial Law; Criminal Trial Practice; Employment Benefits Law; Environmental Law; General Practice; Immigration and Naturalization; Insurance Defense; Labor and Employment Law; Municipal Bond/Public Authority Financing; Municipal and Zoning Law; Natural Resources Law; Personal Injury; Probate, Trusts and Estate Planning; Public Utilities Law; Real Estate Law; Tax Law

PIERCE COUCH HENDRICKSON BAYSINGER & GREEN
Oklahoma City, OK................General Practice; Insurance Defense; Medical Malpractice; Product Liability Law

PIERCE, LEDYARD, LATTA & WASDEN, P.C.
Mobile, AL.............................Appellate Practice; Civil Trial Practice; Real Estate Law

PIERCE, SAMUEL P., JR., P.C.
Atlanta, GA...........................Medical Malpractice; Product Liability Law

PIERCE & YOUNG
Atlanta, GA...........................Civil Trial Practice; Commercial Law; Health Care Law; Insurance Defense; International Business Law; Medical Malpractice; Personal Injury; Product Liability Law; Sports and Entertainment Law; Workers Compensation

PIERRY & MOORHEAD, LLP
Los Angeles, CA.....................Admiralty/Maritime Law; Medical Malpractice; Personal Injury; Product Liability Law

PIERSON, PIERSON & NOLAN
Baltimore, MD........................Appellate Practice; Civil Trial Practice; General Practice

PIERSON SEMMES AND BEMIS
Washington, DC......................Administrative Law; General Practice; Natural Resources Law

PIETRAGALLO, BOSICK & GORDON
Pittsburgh, PA.......................Civil Trial Practice; General Practice; Insurance Defense; Personal Injury

PIETTE & JACOBSON, S.C.
Milwaukee, WI........................Insurance Defense

PIGG, GAIL P.
Nashville, TN.........................Civil Trial Practice; Commercial Law; Real Estate Law

PIKE & SUMNER, A PROFESSIONAL CORPORATION
San Diego, CA........................Family Law

PILECKAS, PAUL L.
Rome, NY...............................General Practice; Personal Injury

PILIERO GOLDSTEIN JENKINS & HALL, LLP
New York, NY.........................Antitrust Law; Appellate Practice; Business Law; Civil Trial Practice; Commercial Law; Securities Law

PILKINTON, PILKINTON & YOCOM
Hope, AR...............................General Practice

PILLAR • MULROY & FERBER, PROFESSIONAL CORPORATION
Pittsburgh, PA.......................Family Law; Transportation Law

PILLSBURY MADISON & SUTRO LLP
Los Angeles, CA.....................Admiralty/Maritime Law; Antitrust Law; Civil Trial Practice; General Practice; Tax Law
San Diego, CA........................Admiralty/Maritime Law; General Practice

San Francisco, CA.................General Practice
Washington, DC......................General Practice

PINKERTON & FINN, P.C.
Tulsa, OK...............................Civil Trial Practice

PINKERTON AND FRIEDMAN, PROFESSIONAL CORPORATION
Munster, IN...........................Business Law; Employment Benefits Law; Probate, Trusts and Estate Planning; Tax Law

PINTO, COATES & KYRE, L.L.P.
Greensboro, NC......................Insurance Defense

PIPER & MARBURY L.L.P.
Washington, DC......................General Practice
Baltimore, MD........................Antitrust Law; General Practice; Labor and Employment Law; Municipal Bond/Public Authority Financing; Tax Law

PIPER, WELLMAN & BOWERS
Lexington, KY........................Civil Trial Practice; Health Care Law; Insurance Defense; Personal Injury

PIPKIN, KNOTT & CLARK, L.L.P.
Raleigh, NC............................General Practice; Personal Injury

PITLUCK KIDO SATO & STONE
Honolulu, HI..........................Antitrust Law; Business Law; Real Estate Law

PITNEY, HARDIN, KIPP & SZUCH
Morristown, NJ.......................Antitrust Law; Business Law; Civil Trial Practice; Criminal Trial Practice; Environmental Law; General Practice; Labor and Employment Law; Probate, Trusts and Estate Planning; Real Estate Law; Tax Law

PITTMAN, HOOKS, DUTTON & HOLLIS, P.C.
Birmingham, AL......................Admiralty/Maritime Law; Medical Malpractice; Personal Injury; Product Liability Law

PITTMAN AND PITTMAN
Enterprise, AL........................Civil Trial Practice; Personal Injury

PITTS, HAY, HUGENSCHMIDT & DEVEREUX, P.A.
Asheville, NC..........................Bankruptcy Law; Criminal Trial Practice; Family Law

PIVO & HALBREICH
Irvine, CA...............................Civil Trial Practice; Insurance Defense; Medical Malpractice; Probate, Trusts and Estate Planning

PIZER & MICHAELSON INC.
Los Angeles, CA.....................Bankruptcy Law; Commercial Law
Santa Ana, CA........................Commercial Law

PLASSMAN, RUPP, HENSAL & SHORT
Archbold, OH.........................General Practice

PLASTIRAS & FORSBLAD
San Rafael, CA........................Insurance Defense

PLASTIRAS, HYDEN & MIRON
Little Rock, AR.......................Administrative Law; Employment Benefits Law; Probate, Trusts and Estate Planning; Tax Law

PLATTNER, SCHNEIDMAN & SCHNEIDER, P.C.
Phoenix, AZ............................Tax Law

PLATTNER VERDERAME, P.C.
Phoenix, AZ............................Insurance Defense; Personal Injury

PLATZ & THOMPSON, P.A.
Lewiston, ME..........................Commercial Law

PLAUCHÉ SMITH & NIESET, A PROFESSIONAL LAW CORPORATION
Lake Charles, LA....................Admiralty/Maritime Law; Civil Trial Practice; General Practice; Insurance Defense; Personal Injury

PLAUCHÉ, MASELLI & LANDRY
New Orleans, LA.....................Insurance Defense

PLEDGER & ASSOCIATES
McLean, VA............................Civil Trial Practice; General Practice; Insurance Defense; Medical Malpractice

PLETSCH, GREGORY A., & ASSOCIATES, A PROFESSIONAL LAW CORPORATION
Baton Rouge, LA....................Probate, Trusts and Estate Planning; Tax Law

PLEWS SHADLEY RACHER & BRAUN
Indianapolis, IN......................Administrative Law; Appellate Practice; Environmental Law; Natural Resources Law

PLOURDE & LEONARD, LTD.
Providence, RI........................Tax Law

PLOWMAN, SPIEGEL & LEWIS, P.C.
Pittsburgh, PA.......................Banking Law; Bankruptcy Law; Civil Trial Practice; Commercial Law; Construction Law; Environmental Law; General Practice; Insurance Defense; Municipal and Zoning Law; Product Liability Law; Real Estate Law; Securities Law

PLUMMER & FARMER
Houston, TX ....Civil Trial Practice; Family Law

PLUNKETT & GIBSON, INC.
San Antonio, TX ....Civil Trial Practice; General Practice; Insurance Defense

PLUNKETT & JAFFE, P.C.
New York, NY ....Civil Trial Practice; General Practice

PLUNKETT & OEHLSCHLAEGER, P.L.C.
Roanoke, VA...........................Business Law; Probate, Trusts and Estate Planning; Real Estate Law; Tax Law

PLUNKETT & PLUNKETT, P.C.
Augusta, GA ....General Practice

POAGUE, WALL, ESHELMAN & COX
Clinton, MO............................General Practice

POCHÉ, STEPHEN S., P.A.
Shalimar, FL ....Family Law

PODELL & PODELL
Milwaukee, WI ....Family Law

PODELL, RICHARD J., & ASSOCIATES, S.C.
Milwaukee, WI ....Family Law

PODHURST, ORSECK, JOSEFSBERG, EATON, MEADOW, OLIN & PERWIN, P.A.
Miami, FL ....Appellate Practice; Aviation Law; Civil Trial Practice; Commercial Litigation; Criminal Trial Practice; General Practice; Personal Injury

POEHLMANN, THEODORE A. E.
Woodstock, IL ....Civil Trial Practice

POHL & SHORT, P.A.
Kissimmee, FL ....Administrative Law; Antitrust Law; Appellate Practice; Banking Law; Business Law; Civil Trial Practice; Commercial Law; Construction Law; Environmental Law; International Business Law; Labor and Employment Law; Municipal and Zoning Law; Probate, Trusts and Estate Planning; Real Estate Law; Tax Law

Orlando, FL ....Administrative Law; Antitrust Law; Appellate Practice; Banking Law; Business Law; Civil Trial Practice; Commercial Law; Construction Law; Environmental Law; International Business Law; Labor and Employment Law; Municipal and Zoning Law; Probate, Trusts and Estate Planning; Real Estate Law; Tax Law

Winter Park, FL.......................Administrative Law; Antitrust Law; Appellate Practice; Banking Law; Business Law; Civil Trial Practice; Commercial Law; Construction Law; Environmental Law; International Business Law; Labor and Employment Law; Municipal and Zoning Law; Probate, Trusts and Estate Planning; Real Estate Law; Tax Law

POLIDORI, GEROME, FRANKLIN AND JACOBSON, L.L.C.
Lakewood, CO ....Civil Trial Practice; Criminal Trial Practice; Family Law; Personal Injury; Probate, Trusts and Estate Planning

POLING, MCGAW & POLING, P.C.
Troy, MI.................................Business Law; Civil Rights; Civil Trial Practice; Commercial Law; Construction Law; Employment Benefits Law; Environmental Law; Family Law; General Practice; Health Care Law; Insurance Defense; Mergers and Acquisitions; Personal Injury; Product Liability Law; Real Estate Law

POLITO & SMOCK, P.C.
Pittsburgh, PA ....Admiralty/Maritime Law; Labor and Employment Law

POLLACK, GARY LAW OFFICE OF
Farmington Hills, MI ....Probate, Trusts and Estate Planning; Real Estate Law

POLLAK & HOFFMAN LTD.
Chicago, IL..............................Banking Law; Business Law; Probate, Trusts and Estate Planning; Real Estate Law

POLLI, ROBERT P., P.A.
Tampa, FL ....Appellate Practice; Criminal Trial Practice

POLLOCK, MEYERS, EICKSTEADT & WEECH, LTD.
Marengo, IL ....General Practice

POLLOCK, VANDE SANDE & PRIDDY, R.L.L.P.
Washington, DC........................Patent, Trademark, Copyright and Unfair Competition

POLSTER, LIEDER, WOODRUFF & LUCCHESI, L.C.
St. Louis, MO..........................Patent, Trademark, Copyright and Unfair Competition

POMERANZ, DRAYTON & STABNICK
Glastonbury, CT ....General Practice; Workers Compensation

PONZINI, SPENCER & GEIS, L.L.P.
Tarrytown, NY.........................Commercial Litigation

PONZOLI, WASSENBERG & SPERKACZ, P.A.
Miami, FL ....Insurance Defense

POPE & BERGER
San Diego, CA ....Civil Trial Practice

POPE AND HUDGENS, P.A.
Newberry, SC..........................General Practice

POPE, MCGLAMRY, KILPATRICK & MORRISON
Atlanta, GA ....Civil Trial Practice; General Practice; Medical Malpractice; Personal Injury; Product Liability Law

Columbus, GA ....Civil Trial Practice; General Practice; Medical Malpractice; Personal Injury; Product Liability Law

POPE, MCMILLAN, KUTTEH & SIMON, P.A.
Statesville, NC........................General Practice

POPE, POPE AND DRAYER
Clarion, PA ....General Practice

POPE & RODGERS
Columbia, SC ....Business Law; Civil Trial Practice

POPHAM, HAIK, SCHNOBRICH & KAUFMAN, LTD.
Washington, DC.......................General Practice
Minneapolis, MN ....General Practice

POPKOFF & STERN
Los Angeles, CA ....Probate, Trusts and Estate Planning

PORTER, FAIRCHILD, WACHTER & HANEY, P.A.
Topeka, KS.............................General Practice

PORTERFIELD, HARPER & MILLS, P.A.
Birmingham, AL ....Civil Trial Practice; Insurance Defense; Medical Malpractice; Product Liability Law

PORTER, J. CHESTER, & ASSOCIATES
Shepherdsville, KY.................Banking Law

PORTER, JOHN T., P.A., LAW OFFICES OF
Albuquerque, NM...................Banking Law; Commercial Law

PORTER & PORTER
Cincinnati, OH ....Probate, Trusts and Estate Planning; Tax Law

PORTER, SCOTT, WEIBERG & DELEHANT, A PROFESSIONAL CORPORATION
Sacramento, CA ....Civil Trial Practice; Medical Malpractice; Product Liability Law

PORTER & STEEL, PLLC
Research Triangle Park, NC....Business Law

PORTER, WRIGHT, MORRIS & ARTHUR
Washington, DC......................General Practice
Naples, FL..............................General Practice
Cincinnati, OH ....General Practice
Cleveland, OH ....General Practice
Columbus, OH ....Antitrust Law; Banking Law; Bankruptcy Law; Civil Trial Practice; Environmental Law; General Practice; Labor and Employment Law; Municipal Bond/Public Authority Financing; Patent, Trademark, Copyright and Unfair Competition; Tax Law

Dayton, OH............................General Practice

PORTNOY, PIDGEON & ROTH, P.C.
Bloomfield Hills, MI...............Civil Trial Practice; Health Care Law; Insurance Defense; Medical Malpractice; Personal Injury; Product Liability Law

PORZIO, BROMBERG & NEWMAN, A PROFESSIONAL CORPORATION
Morristown, NJ.......................Civil Trial Practice; Commercial Law; Environmental Law; General Practice; Personal Injury

POSNER & ROSEN, P.C.
Los Angeles, CA ....Labor and Employment Law

POST KIRBY NOONAN & SWEAT LLP
San Diego, CA ....Antitrust Law; Business Law; Civil Trial Practice

POST, POLAK, GOODSELL & MACNEILL, P.A.
Roseland, NJ...........................Business Law; Civil Trial Practice; Commercial Law; Family Law; Labor and Employment Law; Medical Malpractice; Real Estate Law

POST & POST
High Point, NC.......................General Practice

POST & SCHELL, P.C.
Philadelphia, PA ....Civil Trial Practice

POSTNER & RUBIN
New York, NY......................Civil Trial Practice; Construction Law

POTHOVEN, BLOMGREN & STRAVERS
Oskaloosa, IA..........................Civil Trial Practice; Insurance Defense; Medical Malpractice

POTTER ANDERSON & CORROON
Wilmington, DE......................Banking Law; Bankruptcy Law; Civil Trial Practice; Employment Benefits Law; Environmental Law; General Practice; Municipal Bond/Public Authority Financing; Patent, Trademark, Copyright and Unfair Competition; Personal Injury; Probate, Trusts and Estate Planning; Tax Law

POTTER, MILLS & BATEMAN, P.A.
Santa Fe, NM..........................Commercial Litigation; Environmental Law; Probate, Trusts and Estate Planning; Real Estate Law

POTTS, DENNIS W., ATTORNEY AT LAW, A LAW CORPORATION
Honolulu, HI..........................Personal Injury

POTTS & YOUNG
Florence, AL ....Civil Trial Practice; General Practice; Personal Injury

POULIOT, MERCURE
Montreal, QU, Canada ....Civil Trial Practice; Commercial Law; Environmental Law; General Practice; Municipal and Zoning Law; Patent, Trademark, Copyright and Unfair Competition

POULSON, JON C.
Accomac, VA ....Employment Benefits Law; Probate, Trusts and Estate Planning; Securities Law

POULSON, ODELL & PETERSON, LLC
Denver, CO ....Natural Resources Law

POUNDERS & ASSOCIATES
Memphis, TN ....Family Law

POWELL, RICHARD L.
Marietta, GA..........................Personal Injury

POWELL & ASSOCIATES
Dallas, TX................................Appellate Practice

POWELL, GOLDSTEIN, FRAZER & MURPHY
Washington, DC.....................General Practice
Atlanta, GA ....General Practice; Immigration and Naturalization; Municipal Bond/Public Authority Financing

POWELL, PEEK & WEAVER
Andalusia, AL..........................Insurance Defense

POWELL & POWELL
Bemidji, MN ....Civil Trial Practice; Insurance Defense

POWELL, STANLEY BRUCE, P.A.
Niceville, FL............................Commercial Litigation; Medical Malpractice; Personal Injury; Product Liability Law

POWER, BOWEN & VALIMONT, LLP
Doylestown, PA ....Civil Trial Practice; General Practice
Sellersville, PA ....Civil Trial Practice

POWER ROGERS & SMITH, P.C.
Chicago, IL..............................Civil Trial Practice; Medical Malpractice; Personal Injury; Product Liability Law

POWERS, CLEGG & WILLARD
Baton Rouge, LA.....................Banking Law; Business Law; Civil Trial Practice; Commercial Litigation; General Practice

POWERS, PYLES, SUTTER & VERVILLE, P.C.
Washington, DC......................Administrative Law; Health Care Law

POWERS & SANTOLA
Albany, NY..............................Medical Malpractice; Personal Injury; Product Liability Law

POYNTER & GEARHART, P.A.
Mountain Home, AR..............General Practice

POZNER & KAPLAN, P.C.
Denver, CO ....Criminal Trial Practice

PRATHER, JOHN G., THE FIRM OF
Somerset, KY ....General Practice

PRAVEL, HEWITT, KIMBALL & KRIEGER, A PROFESSIONAL CORPORATION
Metairie, LA..........................Patent, Trademark, Copyright and Unfair Competition
Houston, TX ....Patent, Trademark, Copyright and Unfair Competition

PRAY, WALKER, JACKMAN, WILLIAMSON & MARLAR, A PROFESSIONAL CORPORATION
Tulsa, OK ....Civil Trial Practice; General Practice

PREIS KRAFT & ROY, A PROFESSIONAL LAW CORPORATION
Lafayette, LA ....Admiralty/Maritime Law; Insurance Defense

PREMINGER, DANIEL M., P.C.
Philadelphia, PA ....Appellate Practice; Criminal Trial Practice; Personal Injury

PRENDERGAST, RICHARD J., LTD.
Chicago, IL..............................Commercial Litigation

PRENOVOST, NORMANDIN, BERGH & DAWE, A PROFESSIONAL CORPORATION
Santa Ana, CA ....Banking Law; Bankruptcy Law; Commercial Law

PRESBERG, ANDREW D., P.C., LAW OFFICES OF
Islandia, NY............................Business Law; Commercial Litigation; Real Estate Law

PRESCOTT, BULLARD & MCLEOD
New Bedford, MA ....General Practice

PRESCOTT & PRESCOTT
Dallas, TX................................Probate, Trusts and Estate Planning

PRESSLY & PRESSLY, P.A.
West Palm Beach, FL..............Probate, Trusts and Estate Planning; Real Estate Law

PRESTHOLT, KLEEGER, FIDONE & VILLASENOR
Los Angeles, CA ....Insurance Defense; Personal Injury

PRESTON GATES & ELLIS
Seattle, WA ....Environmental Law; Municipal and Zoning Law

PRESTON & PRESTON, P.C.
Douglas, GA ....General Practice

PRETI, FLAHERTY, BELIVEAU & PACHIOS
Augusta, ME..........................General Practice
Portland, ME ....Administrative Law; Bankruptcy Law; Business Law; Civil Trial Practice; Commercial Law; Communications Law; Environmental Law; General Practice; Health Care Law; Insurance Defense; Labor and Employment Law; Medical Malpractice; Municipal Bond/Public Authority Financing; Probate, Trusts and Estate Planning; Real Estate Law; Tax Law

PRETTY, SCHROEDER & POPLAWSKI, A PROFESSIONAL CORPORATION
Los Angeles, CA.....................Patent, Trademark, Copyright and Unfair Competition

PREUSS WALKER & SHANAGHER LLP
San Francisco, CA ....Civil Trial Practice; Commercial Litigation; Product Liability Law

PREVATT ENGLAND & TAYLOR
Tampa, FL ....Probate, Trusts and Estate Planning; Tax Law

PREVIANT, GOLDBERG, UELMEN, GRATZ, MILLER & BRUEGGEMAN, S.C.
Milwaukee, WI ....Labor and Employment Law

PREZANT & MOLLATH
Reno, NV ....Land Use Law

PRICE, MARK T. & ASSOCIATES
Houston, TX ....Insurance Defense; Sports and Entertainment Law; Workers Compensation

PRICE & BARKER
Indianapolis, IN ....Civil Trial Practice; Commercial Law; Medical Malpractice; Personal Injury; Product Liability Law

PRICE, HENEVELD, COOPER, DEWITT & LITTON
Grand Rapids, MI ....International Business Law; Patent, Trademark, Copyright and Unfair Competition; Trademark, Copyright and Unfair Competition

PRICE OKAMOTO HIMENO & LUM, ATTORNEYS AT LAW, A LAW CORPORATION
Honolulu, HI...........................Civil Trial Practice; Medical Malpractice; Personal Injury; Real Estate Law

PRICE & VICKERY, P.C.
Austin, TX ....Antitrust Law; Civil Trial Practice

PRICE & ZIRULNIK
Jackson, MS ....Business Law; Civil Trial Practice; Family Law; General Practice; Personal Injury

PRICKETT, JONES, ELLIOTT, KRISTOL & SCHNEE
Dover, DE ....General Practice
Wilmington, DE.....................General Practice; Insurance Defense
Kennett Square, PA ....General Practice

PRIFTI, WILLIAM M.
Lynnfield, MA................Securities Law

PRIMMER & PIPER, PROFESSIONAL CORPORATION
Montpelier, VT................Banking Law; Health Care Law; Public Utilities Law; Securities Law

PRINCE, GLICK & MCFARLANE, P.A., LAW OFFICES
Fort Lauderdale, FL................Civil Trial Practice; Personal Injury

PRINCE, RAYMOND G., P.C.
Nashville, TN................Civil Trial Practice; Insurance Defense

PRINCE, YEATES & GELDZAHLER
Park City, UT................General Practice
Salt Lake City, UT................General Practice; Labor and Employment Law; Real Estate Law; Tax Law

PRINCE, YOUNGBLOOD & MASSAGEE
Hendersonville, NC................General Practice

PRINDLE, MALAND, SELLNER, STENNES AND KNUTSEN, CHARTERED
Montevideo, MN................General Practice

PRINGLE & PRINGLE, A PROFESSIONAL CORPORATION
Oklahoma City, OK................Banking Law; Bankruptcy Law; Commercial Litigation; General Practice; Mergers and Acquisitions

PRITCHARD, CLYDE B.
Farmington Hills, MI................Criminal Trial Practice

PROENZA & ROBERTS, P.A.
Miami, FL................Civil Trial Practice; Medical Malpractice; Personal Injury

PROSKAUER ROSE GOETZ & MENDELSOHN
Paris, France................General Practice
Los Angeles, CA................General Practice
Washington, DC................General Practice
Boca Raton, FL................General Practice
New York, NY................General Practice; Labor and Employment Law

PROVIZER, LICHTENSTEIN & PHILLIPS, P.C.
Southfield, MI................Banking Law; Business Law; Civil Rights; Civil Trial Practice; Commercial Law; Commercial Litigation; Construction Law; Employment Benefits Law; Environmental Law; Insurance Defense; Land Use Law; Medical Malpractice; Mergers and Acquisitions; Personal Injury; Probate, Trusts and Estate Planning; Product Liability Law; Real Estate Law; Workers Compensation

PROVOSTY, SADLER & DELAUNAY
Alexandria, LA................General Practice

PRUITT AND DE BOURBON LAW FIRM
Pikeville, KY................Bankruptcy Law; Civil Trial Practice; Medical Malpractice; Mergers and Acquisitions; Personal Injury; Real Estate Law; Workers Compensation

PRUITT, GUSHEE & BACHTELL
Salt Lake City, UT................Natural Resources Law

PRUITT & PRUITT, P.A.
West Palm Beach, FL................Civil Trial Practice; Family Law; Personal Injury

PRUITT, PRUITT AND WATKINS, P.A.
Livingston, AL................Civil Trial Practice; Environmental Law

PRYOR, FLYNN, PRIEST & HARBER
Knoxville, TN................Civil Trial Practice; Criminal Trial Practice; General Practice; Medical Malpractice; Personal Injury; Product Liability Law

PRYOR & MANDELUP, L.L.P.
Westbury, NY................Bankruptcy Law; Civil Trial Practice

PUCCI, GOLDIN & MEROLLA
Providence, RI................General Practice

PUCCINELLI & PUCCINELLI
Elko, NV................General Practice

PUCKETT, CHARLES H. III
Houston, TX................Business Law; Natural Resources Law

PUGH, IRBY G. LAW OFFICE OF
Orlando, FL................Environmental Law; Personal Injury

PUGH/ASSOCIATES, PATENT & TRADEMARK ATTORNEYS, NATIONAL LAW OFFICES OF
New Orleans, LA................Computer Law; Patent, Trademark, Copyright and Unfair Competition

PULASKI, GIEGER & LABORDE, L.L.C.
New Orleans, LA................Aviation Law; Environmental Law; Insurance Defense; Product Liability Law; Transportation Law

PURDOM LAW OFFICES, P.C.
Lubbock, TX................Family Law

PURDY AND FLYNN, P.A.
Fort Lauderdale, FL................Personal Injury

PURRINGTON, ALFRED L. III
Raleigh, NC................Business Law; Probate, Trusts and Estate Planning

PURVIS, GRAY, SCHUETZE & GORDON
Boulder, CO................Civil Trial Practice; Personal Injury
Denver, CO................Civil Trial Practice; Personal Injury

PYSZKA, DOUBERLEY, BLACKMON, LEVY & SAVOLA, P.A.
Miami, FL................Civil Trial Practice; Insurance Defense

PYTELL, R.H., & ASSOCIATES, P.C.
Detroit, MI................Commercial Litigation; Probate, Trusts and Estate Planning

QUADROS & JOHNSON
San Mateo, CA................Employment Benefits Law; General Practice; Labor and Employment Law

QUALE, FELDBRUEGGE, CALVELLI, THOM & CROKE, S.C.
Milwaukee, WI................Insurance Defense; Product Liability Law

QUALE, HARTMANN, BOHL, REYNOLDS & PULSFUS, S.C.
Baraboo, WI................General Practice

QUANDT, GIFFELS & BUCK CO., L.P.A.
Cleveland, OH................Civil Trial Practice; General Practice; Insurance Defense

QUARLES & BRADY
Phoenix, AZ................Administrative Law; Business Law; Civil Trial Practice; Commercial Law; Commercial Litigation; Environmental Law; General Practice; Health Care Law; International Business Law; Labor and Employment Law; Municipal Bond/Public Authority Financing; Natural Resources Law; Patent, Trademark, Copyright and Unfair Competition; Personal Injury; Product Liability Law; Real Estate Law; Securities Law
Naples, FL................Banking Law; Business Law; Civil Trial Practice; Construction Law; General Practice; Land Use Law; Probate, Trusts and Estate Planning; Real Estate Law
West Palm Beach, FL................Bankruptcy Law; Business Law; Commercial Law; Construction Law; General Practice; Labor and Employment Law; Land Use Law; Patent, Trademark, Copyright and Unfair Competition; Probate, Trusts and Estate Planning; Real Estate Law
Madison, WI................Admiralty/Maritime Law; Antitrust Law; Business Law; Civil Trial Practice; Construction Law; Employment Benefits Law; Environmental Law; General Practice; Health Care Law; Municipal Bond/Public Authority Financing; Patent, Trademark, Copyright and Unfair Competition; Product Liability Law; Securities Law
Milwaukee, WI................Administrative Law; Antitrust Law; Banking Law; Bankruptcy Law; Business Law; Civil Trial Practice; Commercial Law; Construction Law; Employment Benefits Law; Environmental Law; Family Law; General Practice; Health Care Law; Immigration and Naturalization; International Business Law; Labor and Employment Law; Land Use Law; Municipal Bond/Public Authority Financing; Municipal and Zoning Law; Patent, Trademark, Copyright and Unfair Competition; Probate, Trusts and Estate Planning; Product Liability Law; Public Utilities Law; Real Estate Law; Securities Law; Tax Law

QUELLER & FISHER
New York, NY................Civil Trial Practice; Construction Law; Medical Malpractice; Personal Injury; Product Liability Law

QUIGLEY, DILL & QUIGLEY
Valentine, NE................General Practice

QUINN, BUSECK, LEEMHUIS, TOOHEY & KROTO, INC.
Erie, PA................General Practice

QUINN, EIESLAND, DAY & BARKER
Belle Fourche, SD................Civil Trial Practice
Rapid City, SD................Civil Trial Practice

QUINN, JOHNSTON, HENDERSON & PRETORIUS, CHARTERED
Peoria, IL................Civil Trial Practice; General Practice

QUINN, MCGARRY & CAFFERY, P.C.
Buffalo, NY................Insurance Defense

QUINN, PATTERSON & WILLARD
Columbia, SC................Civil Trial Practice; General Practice; Real Estate Law

QUINN, RACUSIN & GAZZOLA, CHARTERED
Washington, DC................Business Law; Probate, Trusts and Estate Planning

QUISUMBING TORRES & EVANGELISTA
Metro Manila, Republic of
The Philippines..........................General Practice

RABBITT, PITZER & SNODGRASS, P.C.
St. Louis, MO..........................Civil Trial Practice

RABE, GEORGE F.
Lexington, KY ....Civil Trial Practice

RABIL, LOUIS
Washington, DC......................General Practice

RABINOVITZ & ASSOCIATES, P.C.
Tucson, AZ ....Civil Trial Practice; Insurance Defense; Medical
Malpractice; Personal Injury; Product Liability Law;
Workers Compensation

RABINOWITZ, RAFAL, SWARTZ, TALIAFERRO & GILBERT, P.C.
Norfolk, VA ....Admiralty/Maritime Law; Civil Trial Practice;
Criminal Trial Practice; General Practice; Personal
Injury

RABON, WOLF & RABON
Hugo, OK...............................General Practice

RACCUGLIA, ANTHONY C. & ASSOCIATES
Peru, IL ....Civil Trial Practice; Medical Malpractice; Personal
Injury; Product Liability Law

RACINE, OLSON, NYE, COOPER & BUDGE, CHARTERED
Pocatello, ID ....General Practice

RACKEMANN, SAWYER & BREWSTER, PROFESSIONAL CORPORATION
Boston, MA............................Business Law; Civil Trial Practice; Environmental
Law; General Practice; Probate, Trusts and Estate
Planning; Real Estate Law; Tax Law

RADCLIFF, FRANDSEN & DONGELL
Los Angeles, CA ....Appellate Practice; Civil Trial Practice; Construction
Law; Environmental Law; Insurance Defense;
International Business Law; Labor and Employment
Law; Product Liability Law; Tax Law

RADER, FISHMAN & GRAUER, PLLC
Bloomfield Hills, MI...............Patent, Trademark, Copyright and Unfair Competition

RADEY McARTHUR & FREHN
Tallahassee, FL ....Administrative Law; Appellate Practice; Commercial
Litigation; Environmental Law; Health Care Law

RAGGHIANTI • FREITAS • MONTOBBIO • WALLACE LLP
San Rafael, CA.......................Business Law; Civil Trial Practice; Commercial
Litigation; Construction Law; Criminal Trial
Practice; Environmental Law; Family Law; Labor
and Employment Law; Land Use Law; Medical
Malpractice; Municipal and Zoning Law; Personal
Injury; Probate, Trusts and Estate Planning;
Product Liability Law; Real Estate Law

RAGGIO, CAPPEL, CHOZEN & BERNIARD
Lake Charles, LA....................Civil Trial Practice; General Practice

RAGSDALE, KIRSCHBAUM & NANNEY, P.A.
Raleigh, NC............................Bankruptcy Law

RAGSDALE, LIGGETT & FOLEY
Raleigh, NC............................Business Law; Civil Trial Practice

RAICHLE, BANNING, WEISS & STEPHENS
Buffalo, NY ....Business Law; Commercial Law; Environmental
Law; General Practice; Labor and Employment Law

RAINES, THOMAS E., P.C.
Norcross, GA ....Probate, Trusts and Estate Planning

RAINEY & BARKSDALE, A PROFESSIONAL CORPORATION
Okmulgee, OK ....General Practice

RAINEY, KIZER, BUTLER, REVIERE & BELL
Jackson, TN ....Banking Law; Bankruptcy Law; Civil Trial Practice;
General Practice; Insurance Defense; Personal Injury

RAINEY, ROSS, RICE & BINNS
Oklahoma City, OK...............Bankruptcy Law; Civil Rights; Civil Trial Practice;
General Practice; Labor and Employment Law;
Probate, Trusts and Estate Planning; Public Utilities
Law

RAINS & POGREBIN, P.C.
Mineola, NY...........................Labor and Employment Law

RAINWATER, HUMBLE & VOWELL
Knoxville, TN ....General Practice

RAISBECK, LARA, RODRIGUEZ & RUEDA
Bogotá, Colombia ....General Practice

RAITT & MORASSE, A PROFESSIONAL CORPORATION
Irvine, CA..............................Civil Trial Practice

RAJKOWSKI HANSMEIER LTD.
St. Cloud, MN ....Environmental Law; Insurance Defense

RAKESTRAW & RAKESTRAW
Findlay, OH ....General Practice

RALSTON, ROBERT W.
Wilmington, DE......................Workers Compensation

RALSTON, EUGENE B., & ASSOCIATES, P.A.
Topeka, KS.............................Civil Trial Practice; Medical Malpractice; Personal
Injury; Product Liability Law

RAMBO, ANDREW C., P.C.
Shelbyville, TN ....General Practice

RAMBOW & AWSUMB, P.A.
Minneapolis, MN....................Personal Injury; Product Liability Law

RAMER AND MOORE
Harbor Springs, MI ....Probate, Trusts and Estate Planning

RAMEY, GEORGE H.
Yukon, OK.............................Civil Trial Practice

RAMEY & FLOCK, A PROFESSIONAL CORPORATION
Tyler, TX................................Appellate Practice; Civil Rights; Civil Trial Practice;
Commercial Law; Health Care Law; Labor and
Employment Law; Medical Malpractice; Product
Liability Law; Workers Compensation

RAMIREZ, LARRY, P.A., LAW OFFICES OF
Las Cruces, NM......................Insurance Defense

RAMMELKAMP, BRADNEY, DAHMAN, KUSTER, KEATON, FRITSCHE & LINDSAY, P.C.
Jacksonville, IL ....General Practice; Insurance Defense

RAMSAY, BRIDGFORTH, HARRELSON & STARLING
Pine Bluff, AR........................Civil Trial Practice; General Practice; Labor and
Employment Law

RAMSAY & CALLOWAY
Atlanta, GA ....Real Estate Law

RAND, ALGEIER, TOSTI & WOODRUFF, A PROFESSIONAL CORPORATION
Morristown, NJ.......................Civil Rights; Commercial Law; Construction Law;
General Practice; Labor and Employment Law;
Personal Injury

RANDOLPH, BOYD, CHERRY AND VAUGHAN
Richmond, VA ....Personal Injury

RANGEL & CHRISS
Corpus Christi, TX ....Civil Trial Practice; Personal Injury

RANKIN, HILL, LEWIS & CLARK
Cleveland, OH.........................Patent, Trademark, Copyright and Unfair Competition

RANKIN, SPROAT, MIRES, TRAPANI & REISER, A PROFESSIONAL CORPORATION
Oakland, CA ....Insurance Defense; Medical Malpractice; Product
Liability Law

RANSMEIER & SPELLMAN, PROFESSIONAL CORPORATION
Concord, NH ....Business Law; Commercial Law; Commercial
Litigation; General Practice; Insurance Defense;
Probate, Trusts and Estate Planning

RANSON, ARTHUR J. III
Orlando, FL ....Civil Trial Practice

RAPPAPORT & FURMAN
Philadelphia, PA ....Real Estate Law

RAPPORT, MEYERS, WHITBECK, SHAW & RODENHAUSEN
Hudson, NY...........................General Practice

RASKIN & RASKIN, P.A.
Miami, FL ....Criminal Trial Practice

RASOR, C. LEWIS JR.
Greenville, SC.........................Probate, Trusts and Estate Planning

RASSIEUR, LONG, YAWITZ & SCHNEIDER
St. Louis, MO.........................Probate, Trusts and Estate Planning

RATH, YOUNG AND PIGNATELLI, P.A.
Concord, NH ....Civil Trial Practice; Environmental Law; General
Practice; Insurance Defense; Medical Malpractice;
Personal Injury; Public Utilities Law; Tax Law
Nashua, NH ....General Practice; Insurance Defense; Medical
Malpractice

RATHJE, WOODWARD, DYER & BURT
Wheaton, IL ....General Practice

RATHMAN, COMBS, SCHAEFER & KAUP
Middletown, OH ....General Practice

RATHMANN & ASSOCIATES
St. Louis, MO...........................Admiralty/Maritime Law; Personal Injury

RATNER & PRESTIA, A PROFESSIONAL CORPORATION
Valley Forge, PA.....................Patent, Trademark, Copyright and Unfair Competition; Trademark, Copyright and Unfair Competition

RATTET HOLLANDER & PASTERNAK, LLP
Harrison, NY ....Bankruptcy Law

RAUSCHER, DAVID J., P.C.
St. Louis, MO..........................Personal Injury

RAVEN, KIRSCHNER & NORELL, P.C.
Tucson, AZ ....Administrative Law; Banking Law; Bankruptcy Law; Business Law; Civil Trial Practice; General Practice; Health Care Law; Labor and Employment Law; Municipal Bond/Public Authority Financing; Real Estate Law

RAVIN, GREENBERG & MARKS, A PROFESSIONAL CORPORATION
Roseland, NJ...........................Bankruptcy Law

RAWLE & HENDERSON
Philadelphia, PA ....Admiralty/Maritime Law; Product Liability Law

RAWLES, O'BYRNE, STANKO & KEPLEY, P.C.
Champaign, IL ....Business Law; General Practice

RAWLINGS, NIELAND, PROBASCO, KILLINGER, ELLWANGER, JACOBS & MOHRHAUSER
Sioux City, IA ....General Practice

RAWLS & DICKINSON, P.A.
Charlotte, NC..........................Criminal Trial Practice; Personal Injury

RAY, CHARLES R.
Nashville, TN ....Criminal Trial Practice

RAY, QUINNEY & NEBEKER, A PROFESSIONAL CORPORATION
Provo, UT................................General Practice
Salt Lake City, UT..................Antitrust Law; Banking Law; Bankruptcy Law; Civil Trial Practice; Commercial Law; General Practice; Insurance Defense; Labor and Employment Law; Municipal Bond/Public Authority Financing; Natural Resources Law; Probate, Trusts and Estate Planning; Real Estate Law; Tax Law

RAY, ROBINSON, CARLE, DAVIES & SNYDER
Chicago, IL.............................Admiralty/Maritime Law
Cleveland, OH........................Admiralty/Maritime Law; Civil Trial Practice; General Practice

RAY, TODARO & ALTON CO., L.P.A.
Columbus, OH ....Civil Trial Practice; Medical Malpractice; Personal Injury; Product Liability Law

RAYBURN, MOON & SMITH, P.A.
Charlotte, NC..........................Business Law; Civil Trial Practice; General Practice; Securities Law

RAYMOND, GREER & SASSAMAN, P.C.
Phoenix, AZ ....Insurance Defense

RAYNES, MCCARTY, BINDER, ROSS & MUNDY
Philadelphia, PA ....Personal Injury

RAZZANO & KINZER
Watseka, IL.............................General Practice

REA, CROSS & AUCHINCLOSS
Washington, DC......................Transportation Law

READY, THOMAS J.
Los Angeles, CA ....Administrative Law; Civil Trial Practice; Commercial Litigation

READY, SULLIVAN & READY, L.L.P.
Monroe, MI.............................General Practice

REAGAN, ADAMS & CADIGAN
Kennebunk, ME......................General Practice; Probate, Trusts and Estate Planning; Real Estate Law

REAGAN, GARY DON, P.A.
Hobbs, NM ....Banking Law; Insurance Defense; Real Estate Law

REAGER & ADLER, P.C.
Camp Hill, PA ....Civil Trial Practice; Construction Law; Real Estate Law

REAM, CHRISTOPHER
Palo Alto, CA ....Business Law; Civil Trial Practice; Securities Law

REAMS, PHILIPS, BROOKS, SCHELL, GASTON & HUDSON, P.C.
Mobile, AL...............................General Practice

REARDON LAW FIRM, THE, P.C.
New London, CT ....Medical Malpractice; Personal Injury; Product Liability Law

REARDON & REARDON
Boston, MA.............................Civil Trial Practice; Criminal Trial Practice; General Practice
Worcester, MA........................Civil Trial Practice; Criminal Trial Practice; General Practice

REASONER, DAVIS & FOX
Washington, DC......................Business Law

REAUD, MORGAN & QUINN
Beaumont, TX.........................Commercial Law; Personal Injury; Product Liability Law

REBACK, ROCHELLE A.
Tampa, FL...............................Criminal Trial Practice

RECKLESS, WALTER W.
Columbus, OH ....Civil Trial Practice

REDDEN, MILLS & CLARK
Birmingham, AL ....Civil Trial Practice; Criminal Trial Practice; Family Law; General Practice; Personal Injury

REDFEARN & BROWN, A PROFESSIONAL CORPORATION
Kansas City, MO ....Medical Malpractice; Personal Injury; Product Liability Law

REDMAN, JAMES E.
Milwaukie, OR ....General Practice

REDMON, BOYKIN & BRASWELL
Alexandria, VA ....General Practice

REDMOND, MARGARET ANN
Pasadena, CA ....Immigration and Naturalization

REDMOND, BURGIN & CRUZ, A PROFESSIONAL ASSOCIATION
Baltimore, MD ....Civil Trial Practice

REDWINE, PHILIP O., P.A.
Raleigh, NC.............................Criminal Trial Practice; Personal Injury; Real Estate Law

REECE & LANG, P.S.C.
London, KY ....General Practice

REED, ARMSTRONG, GORMAN, COFFEY, GILBERT & MUDGE, PROFESSIONAL CORPORATION
Edwardsville, IL.......................Constitutional Law; Insurance Defense

REED, EDERER & MOORE, P.C.
San Antonio, TX.....................Civil Trial Practice; Commercial Law; Criminal Trial Practice; Insurance Defense; Probate, Trusts and Estate Planning; Tax Law

REEDER, SHUMAN & WILEY
Morgantown, WV ....General Practice

REED, LUCE, TOSH, MCGREGOR & WOLFORD, A PROFESSIONAL CORPORATION
Beaver, PA...............................General Practice

REED MCCLURE
Seattle, WA ....General Practice

REED SMITH SHAW & MCCLAY
Washington, DC......................General Practice; Labor and Employment Law
Harrisburg, PA.........................General Practice; Labor and Employment Law
Philadelphia, PA ....General Practice; Labor and Employment Law
Pittsburgh, PA ....General Practice; Labor and Employment Law; Municipal Bond/Public Authority Financing
McLean, VA.............................General Practice; Labor and Employment Law

REES & ASSOCIATES, P.C.
Denver, CO ....Environmental Law

REES, BROOME & DIAZ, P.C.
Vienna, VA...............................Business Law; Probate, Trusts and Estate Planning; Tax Law

REEVES, ALLEN G., P.C.
Denver, CO ....Securities Law

REEVES, CHAVEZ, GREENFIELD & WALKER, P.A.
Las Cruces, NM.......................Banking Law; Civil Trial Practice; Commercial Litigation; Health Care Law; Insurance Defense; Probate, Trusts and Estate Planning; Real Estate Law

REEVES & STEWART, P.C.
Selma, AL................................General Practice

REGAN, RAY R.
Albuquerque, NM...................Patent, Trademark, Copyright and Unfair Competition

REGAN & CANTWELL
Charleston, SC ....Municipal and Zoning Law

REGAN, MICHAEL P., P.C., LAW OFFICES OF
Danville, VA ....Civil Trial Practice; General Practice

REGNIER, TAYLOR, CURRAN & EDDY
Hartford, CT ....Civil Trial Practice; Insurance Defense; Personal Injury

REICH REICH & REICH, P.C.
White Plains, NY ....Bankruptcy Law

REICHELT, NUSSBAUM, LAPLACA & MILLER
Greenbelt, MD ....Business Law; Civil Trial Practice; General Practice

REICHLER, MILTON & MEDEL
Washington, DC......................Administrative Law; Civil Trial Practice; International Business Law

REICHSTEIN, RONALD
West Caldwell, NJ ....Civil Trial Practice; Real Estate Law

REID, BURGE, PREVALLET & COLEMAN
Blytheville, AR.........................Insurance Defense

REID, GARTH O., JR., A PROFESSIONAL LAW CORPORATION
Escondido, CA ....Tax Law

REID & PRIEST LLP
Washington, DC......................General Practice
New York, NY ....General Practice

REID, RICHARDS & MIYAGI
Honolulu, HI...........................Civil Trial Practice; General Practice; Insurance Defense

REID AND RIEGE, P.C.
Hartford, CT ....General Practice

REID, STRICKLAND & GILLETTE, L.L.P.
Baytown, TX ....General Practice

REIFF, MORRISSEY, PRESSMAN & BILY, P.A.
Philadelphia, PA ....Civil Trial Practice

REILLY, THOMAS A.
Laguna Beach, CA ....Personal Injury

REILLY, PETERSEN & HANNAN, P.L.C.
Council Bluffs, IA ....Bankruptcy Law; General Practice; Personal Injury

REILLY, STUART J., P.C.
Phoenix, AZ ....Medical Malpractice; Personal Injury

REIMAN & BAYAZ, P.C.
Denver, CO ....Antitrust Law; Appellate Practice; Civil Trial Practice; Commercial Litigation; Construction Law; Securities Law

REINERT & DUREE, P.C.
St. Louis, MO..........................Commercial Litigation

REINGLASS, MICHELLE A.
Laguna Hills, CA....................Labor and Employment Law

REINHARDT & SCHACHTER, P.C.
Newark, NJ ....Labor and Employment Law

REINHART, BOERNER, VAN DEUREN, NORRIS & RIESELBACH, S.C.
Milwaukee, WI ....General Practice

REINIS & REINIS
Los Angeles, CA ....Business Law

REINWALD, O'CONNOR, MARRACK, HOSKINS & PLAYDON
Honolulu, HI...........................Civil Trial Practice; Probate, Trusts and Estate Planning; Tax Law

REISEMAN & SHARP
Parsippany, NJ.........................Insurance Defense; Medical Malpractice; Personal Injury; Product Liability Law

REISENFELD & STATMAN
Cincinnati, OH ....Banking Law; Bankruptcy Law; Civil Trial Practice; Commercial Law; Family Law; Personal Injury

REISH & LUFTMAN, A PROFESSIONAL CORPORATION
Los Angeles, CA.....................Employment Benefits Law

REISING, ETHINGTON, BARNARD & PERRY, L.L.P. AND LEARMAN & MCCULLOCH
Troy, MI..................................Patent, Trademark, Copyright and Unfair Competition

REMCHO, JOHANSEN AND PURCELL
San Francisco, CA ....Appellate Practice; Civil Trial Practice; Constitutional Law

RENALDO, MYERS, REGAN & PALUMBO, P.C.
Buffalo, NY ....Personal Injury

RENAUD, COOK & DRURY, P.A.
Phoenix, AZ ....Business Law; Civil Trial Practice; Commercial Law; Construction Law; Insurance Defense; Medical Malpractice; Personal Injury; Probate, Trusts and Estate Planning; Product Liability Law; Real Estate Law

RENDIGS, FRY, KIELY & DENNIS
Cincinnati, OH ....Admiralty/Maritime Law; Civil Trial Practice; General Practice; Insurance Defense

RENDLEN, RENDLEN AND BASTIAN, P.C.
Hannibal, MO ....General Practice

RENICK, SINGER AND KAMBER
Lake Worth, FL.......................Family Law

RENNER, KENNER, GREIVE, BOBAK, TAYLOR & WEBER, A LEGAL PROFESSIONAL ASSOCIATION
Akron, OH ....Patent, Trademark, Copyright and Unfair Competition
Canton, OH ....Patent, Trademark, Copyright and Unfair Competition

RENZ, EUGENE E., JR., P.C.
Media, PA ....Patent, Trademark, Copyright and Unfair Competition

REPPETTO, GERALD G.
Los Angeles, CA ....Insurance Defense

RESNICK, STEVEN P.
Annapolis, MD ....Commercial Law

RETHERFORD, MULLEN, JOHNSON & BRUCE, L.L.C.
Colorado Springs, CO.............Civil Trial Practice; General Practice; Insurance Defense; Workers Compensation

RETTIG, OSBORNE, FORGETTE, O'DONNELL, ILLER & ADAMSON, LLP
Kennewick, WA ....General Practice

REUBEN, MARC W. LAW OFFICES OF
Philadelphia, PA ....Personal Injury

REVELLE, BURLESON, LEE & REVELLE
Murfreesboro, NC...................General Practice

REXON, FREEDMAN, KLEPETAR & HAMBLETON, A PROFESSIONAL CORPORATION
Los Angeles, CA ....Labor and Employment Law

REYES, RICHARD R. LAW OFFICES OF
Pasadena, CA ....Personal Injury

REYNOLDS, BEEBY & MAGNUSON, P.C.
Troy, MI..................................Civil Trial Practice; Insurance Defense; Product Liability Law

REYNOLDS, CARONIA & GIANELLI
Hauppauge, NY ....Civil Trial Practice; Criminal Trial Practice

REYNOLDS & CONWAY, P.C.
Springfield, MO.......................General Practice

REYNOLDS, FORKER, BERKLEY, SUTER, ROSE & DOWER
Hutchinson, KS.......................General Practice

REYNOLDS AND MANNING, P.A.
Prince Frederick, MD ....Business Law

REYNOLDS & MCARTHUR
Atlanta, GA ....Civil Trial Practice; Medical Malpractice; Personal Injury; Product Liability Law
Macon, GA ....Civil Trial Practice; Medical Malpractice; Personal Injury; Product Liability Law
Asheville, NC ....Civil Trial Practice; Medical Malpractice; Personal Injury; Product Liability Law

REYNOLDS, SMITH & WINTERS, P.C.
Norfolk, VA ....Insurance Defense

RHEES & HOPKINS
Phoenix, AZ ....Construction Law; Insurance Defense

RHEINGOLD, VALET & RHEINGOLD, P.C.
New York, NY........................Medical Malpractice; Personal Injury; Product Liability Law

RHOADES, RUFUS VON THÜLEN
Los Angeles, CA ....Tax Law

RHOADES, MCKEE, BOER, GOODRICH & TITTA
Grand Rapids, MI ....Business Law; Civil Trial Practice; Probate, Trusts and Estate Planning

RHOADS & SINON LLP
Harrisburg, PA........................Banking Law; Civil Trial Practice; Environmental Law; General Practice; Municipal Bond/Public Authority Financing; Tax Law

RHODA, STOUDT & BRADLEY
Reading, PA ....General Practice

RHODEN, LACY, DOWNEY & COLBERT
Jackson, MS ....Business Law; Insurance Defense; Real Estate Law

RHODES COATS AND BENNETT, L.L.P.
Greensboro, NC......................Patent, Trademark, Copyright and Unfair Competition
Raleigh, NC............................Patent, Trademark, Copyright and Unfair Competition

RHODES, HIERONYMUS, JONES, TUCKER & GABLE
Tulsa, OK..................................Appellate Practice; Aviation Law; Bankruptcy Law; Civil Rights; Civil Trial Practice; Environmental Law; Health Care Law; Insurance Defense; Labor and Employment Law; Medical Malpractice; Personal Injury; Product Liability Law; Real Estate Law; Transportation Law; Workers Compensation

RIBIS, GRAHAM & CURTIN
Morristown, NJ........................General Practice

RICCI, HUBBARD, LEOPOLD & FRANKEL, P.A.
West Palm Beach, FL ....Civil Trial Practice; Personal Injury

RICE DOLAN & KERSHAW
Providence, RI........................General Practice; Insurance Defense; Medical Malpractice

RICE, EVERHART & BABER
Richmond, VA ....Criminal Trial Practice; Personal Injury

RICE & HENDRICKSON
Harlan, KY ....General Practice; Insurance Defense; Labor and Employment Law

RICE, MARTIN ERROL, P.A.
St. Petersburg, FL....................Civil Trial Practice

RICE & ROBINSON, P.A.
Miami, FL ....Bankruptcy Law

RICH & D'AMBROSIO, P.S.C.
Louisville, KY ....Labor and Employment Law

RICH, FUIDGE, MORRIS & IVERSON, INC.
Marysville, CA ....General Practice

RICHARD, DISANTI, GALLAGHER, SCHOENFELD & SURKIN, A PROFESSIONAL CORPORATION
Media, PA ....General Practice; Personal Injury

RICHARD, LEE, COBB & HALL, P.C.
El Paso, TX..............................Commercial Litigation; Personal Injury

RICHARDS AND BRADY, P.C.
Springfield, VT........................General Practice

RICHARDS, BRANDT, MILLER & NELSON, A PROFESSIONAL CORPORATION
Salt Lake City, UT..................Business Law; Insurance Defense; Tax Law

RICHARDS, LAYTON & FINGER, P.A.
Wilmington, DE......................General Practice; Tax Law

RICHARDS AND MEOLA
Warren, OH............................Insurance Defense

RICHARDS, PAUL & RICHARDS
Tulsa, OK..................................Civil Trial Practice; Insurance Defense; Medical Malpractice

RICHARDS, RALPH & SCHWAB, CHTD.
Vernon Hills, IL......................Banking Law; Bankruptcy Law; Business Law; Commercial Litigation; Land Use Law; Real Estate Law

RICHARDSON, GARDNER & BARRICKMAN
Glasgow, KY............................General Practice

RICHARDSON, JAMES AND PLAYER
Sumter, SC..............................General Practice

RICHARDSON, PLOWDEN, CARPENTER & ROBINSON, P.A.
Columbia, SC ....Appellate Practice; Banking Law; Business Law; Civil Trial Practice; Commercial Law; Construction Law; Environmental Law; General Practice; Health Care Law; Insurance Defense; Medical Malpractice; Personal Injury; Probate, Trusts and Estate Planning; Product Liability Law; Real Estate Law

RICHARDSON, WHITMAN, LARGE & BADGER, A PROFESSIONAL CORPORATION
Portland, ME ....Insurance Defense; Personal Injury

RICHESON, J. DAVID, & ASSOCIATES, P.A.
Fort Pierce, FL........................Labor and Employment Law
West Palm Beach, FL ....Labor and Employment Law

RICHEY & DIAZ, P.A.
Miami, FL ....Appellate Practice; Civil Trial Practice; Criminal Trial Practice

RICHILANO, JOHN M., P.C.
Denver, CO ....Civil Trial Practice; Criminal Trial Practice

RICHMAN, GREER, WEIL, BRUMBAUGH, MIRABITO & CHRISTENSEN, P.A.
Miami, FL ....Civil Trial Practice; General Practice

RICHMAN & HENSEN, P.C.
Denver, CO ....Medical Malpractice; Personal Injury

RICKS & ANDERSON, A LAW CORPORATION
Costa Mesa, CA......................Civil Trial Practice; Labor and Employment Law

RIDDLE, LONG, ROWATT & BAUMGARTNER, L.L.P.
Houston, TX ....Personal Injury

RIDEN, EARLE & KIEFNER, P.A.
St. Petersburg, FL..................Civil Trial Practice; Probate, Trusts and Estate Planning; Securities Law; Tax Law; Workers Compensation

RIDENOUR, RIDENOUR & FOX
Clinton, TN ....Personal Injury

RIDENOUR, SWENSON, CLEERE & EVANS, P.C.
Phoenix, AZ ....Banking Law; Civil Trial Practice; Commercial Law; Insurance Defense; Real Estate Law; Tax Law

RIDER, WEINER, FRANKEL & CALHELHA, P.C.
Newburgh, NY........................Business Law; Civil Trial Practice; Probate, Trusts and Estate Planning; Real Estate Law

RIDGE, HOLLEY & MORRIS
Graham, NC............................General Practice

RIDGWAY AND GRIFFIN, CHARTERED
Rockville, MD........................Real Estate Law

RIECKER, VAN DAM, BARKER, BLACK & ZUBER, P.C.
Midland, MI............................Business Law; General Practice; Probate, Trusts and Estate Planning

RIESENBURGER & KIZNER, P.C.
Vineland, NJ............................Appellate Practice; Civil Trial Practice; Environmental Law; Real Estate Law

RIEVES & MAYTON
West Memphis, AR ....Civil Trial Practice; General Practice; Insurance Defense; Product Liability Law

RIFKIN AND WARREN LOLI, P.A.
Miami, FL ....Immigration and Naturalization

RIGBY, THATCHER, ANDRUS, RIGBY, KAM & MOELLER, CHARTERED
Rexburg, ID ....General Practice

RIGGS & NESMITH, P.A.
Montgomery, AL ....Personal Injury

RIGHTHAND, SCOTT D.
San Francisco, CA ....Civil Trial Practice

RIKER, DANZIG, SCHERER, HYLAND & PERRETTI
Morristown, NJ......................General Practice
Trenton, NJ............................General Practice

RIKLI, DONALD C.
Highland, IL............................Probate, Trusts and Estate Planning

RILEY, CARDINAL & FLORES, P.C.
Sierra Vista, AZ......................General Practice

RILEY & HARRIS, L.L.P.
Houston, TX ....Civil Trial Practice; Medical Malpractice; Personal Injury

RILEY, MCNULTY, HEWITT & SWEITZER, A PROFESSIONAL CORPORATION
Pittsburgh, PA ....Civil Trial Practice; Commercial Law; General Practice

RILEY, RAY G., JR., P.C.
Mobile, AL..............................Real Estate Law

RILEY, ROBERT F., P.C.
Dearborn, MI ....Civil Trial Practice

RILEY AND ROUMELL, P.C.
Detroit, MI..............................General Practice; Labor and Employment Law

RILEY, SHOVLIN & JONES, P.C.
Clementon, NJ ....General Practice

RILEY, TOM, LAW FIRM, P.C.
Cedar Rapids, IA....................Personal Injury

RINELLA AND RINELLA, LTD.
Chicago, IL..............................Family Law

RINGSMUTH, PETER D.
Fort Myers, FL.......................Criminal Trial Practice

RION, JOHN H.
Dayton, OH...........................Criminal Trial Practice

RISJORD & JAMES, P.C.
Overland Park, KS.................Civil Trial Practice; Personal Injury; Product Liability Law

RISLEY & ASSOCIATES
Costa Mesa, CA......................Tax Law

RITCHIE, JAMES B., A PROFESSIONAL CORPORATION
Atlanta, GA ....Construction Law

RITCHIE & REDIKER, L.L.C.
Birmingham, AL.....................Securities Law

RITER, MAYER, HOFER, WATTIER & BROWN
Pierre, SD ....General Practice

RITTER EICHNER & NORRIS
Washington, DC.....................Municipal Bond/Public Authority Financing; Tax Law

RITTER AND HANFORD
Bridgeton, NJ..........................Civil Trial Practice; General Practice

RITTER, ROBINSON, MCCREADY & JAMES
Toledo, OH ....Civil Trial Practice; General Practice; Insurance Defense; Municipal and Zoning Law; Personal Injury; Probate, Trusts and Estate Planning; Real Estate Law

RIVKIN, RADLER & KREMER
Uniondale, NY ....Civil Trial Practice; General Practice

ROACH, LOYAL J. III
Tulsa, OK................................General Practice

ROACH, PETER T.
Westbury, NY ....Banking Law

ROACH, BROWN, MCCARTHY, GRUBER & CHIARI, P.C.
Buffalo, NY ....Civil Trial Practice; General Practice; Medical Malpractice; Product Liability Law

ROAN & AUTREY, A PROFESSIONAL CORPORATION
Austin, TX ....Administrative Law; Insurance Defense

ROBB, MESSING, PALMER & DIGNAN, P.C.
Traverse City, MI....................Civil Trial Practice; Product Liability Law

ROBBINS, BERLINER & CARSON
Los Angeles, CA......................Patent, Trademark, Copyright and Unfair Competition

ROBBINS & GREEN, A PROFESSIONAL ASSOCIATION
Phoenix, AZ ....Bankruptcy Law; Civil Trial Practice; Commercial Law; General Practice; Insurance Defense; Personal Injury; Real Estate Law

ROBBINS & LIVINGSTON
Roseville, CA ....Land Use Law

ROBBINS & RHODES, ATTORNEYS AT LAW, A LAW CORPORATION
Honolulu, HI...........................Appellate Practice; Civil Trial Practice; Construction Law; Health Care Law; Insurance Defense; Medical Malpractice; Product Liability Law

ROBBINS, TUNKEY, ROSS, AMSEL, RABEN & WAXMAN, P.A.
Miami, FL ....Appellate Practice; Criminal Trial Practice

ROBENALT & ROBENALT
Lima, OH ....General Practice

ROBERT & MILLER
Louisville, KY ....Patent, Trademark, Copyright and Unfair Competition

ROBERTS, WILLIAM B.
Naples, FL...............................Business Law

ROBERTS, ALLEN P., P.A.
Camden, AR ....Civil Trial Practice; General Practice; Labor and Employment Law

ROBERTS, ASHBY & PARRISH
Fredericksburg, VA..................Civil Trial Practice; Commercial Law; General Practice

ROBERTS, BETZ & BLOSS, P.C.
Grand Rapids, MI ....Civil Trial Practice; Commercial Law; Construction Law; Environmental Law; Insurance Defense; Personal Injury

ROBERTS, GARY, & ASSOCIATES, P.A.
West Palm Beach, FL ....Medical Malpractice

ROBERTS, JAMES V., P.C.
Dallas, TX ....Probate, Trusts and Estate Planning

ROBERTS, MARKEL & FOLGER, L.L.P.
Houston, TX ....Admiralty/Maritime Law; Insurance Defense; Real Estate Law

ROBERTS, PERRYMAN, BOMKAMP & MEIVES, P.C.
St. Louis, MO..........................Civil Trial Practice; Environmental Law; Insurance Defense; Product Liability Law; Workers Compensation

ROBERTS & SALAZAR, L.L.P.
Key Biscayne, FL.....................General Practice

ROBERTS & SMITH
Lexington, KY ....Criminal Trial Practice; General Practice; Insurance Defense; Personal Injury

ROBERTS & SOJKA, P.A.
West Palm Beach, FL ....Personal Injury

ROBERTS, SOJKA & ASSOCIATES, P.A.
New Port Richey, FL ....Insurance Defense; Personal Injury

ROBERTS & STEVENS, P.A.
Asheville, NC ....General Practice

ROBERTSON, W. R. III
Marietta, GA...........................Business Law; Family Law; Probate, Trusts and Estate Planning

ROBERTSON & ASSOCIATES
Charleston, SC ....Construction Law

ROBERTSON, MONAGLE & EASTAUGH, A PROFESSIONAL CORPORATION
Anchorage, AK........................General Practice

ROBERTSON & WILLIAMS, INC.
Oklahoma City, OK................General Practice

ROBERTSON, WILLIAMS & MCDONALD, P.A.
Orlando, FL ....Civil Trial Practice

ROBIE & MATTHAI, A PROFESSIONAL CORPORATION
Los Angeles, CA ....Insurance Defense; Product Liability Law

ROBINETTE, DUGAN & JAKUBOWSKI, P.A.
Baltimore, MD ....Medical Malpractice; Product Liability Law

ROBINS, KAPLAN, MILLER & CIRESI
Minneapolis, MN....................General Practice

ROBINSON, JEFFREY A.
Irvine, CA................................Civil Trial Practice

ROBINSON, MARK P. LAW OFFICES OF
Los Angeles, CA ....Civil Trial Practice

ROBINSON, PETER B.
Lowell, MA ....Business Law

ROBINSON, BLUE, WILSON & SMITH, L.L.P.
Gastonia, NC ....Civil Trial Practice; Real Estate Law

ROBINSON, BRADSHAW & HINSON, P.A.
Charlotte, NC..........................General Practice
Rock Hill, SC..........................General Practice

ROBINSON, DIAMANT, BRILL & KLAUSNER, A PROFESSIONAL CORPORATION
Los Angeles, CA ....Bankruptcy Law

ROBINSON DONOVAN MADDEN & BARRY, P.C.
Springfield, MA.......................Civil Trial Practice; Environmental Law; General Practice; Insurance Defense; Personal Injury; Probate, Trusts and Estate Planning; Workers Compensation

ROBINSON, GAGE & WILLIAMS
Muskogee, OK ....Civil Trial Practice; General Practice

ROBINSON & HARRIS
Dallas, TX ....Real Estate Law

ROBINSON LAW FIRM, THE
Washington, DC.....................Civil Trial Practice; Criminal Trial Practice

ROBINSON MAREADY LAWING & COMERFORD, L.L.P.
Winston-Salem, NC ....Antitrust Law; Business Law; General Practice; Medical Malpractice; Product Liability Law; Trademark, Copyright and Unfair Competition

ROBINSON, MCFADDEN & MOORE, P.C.
Columbia, SC ....Banking Law; Bankruptcy Law; Environmental Law; General Practice; Public Utilities Law; Real Estate Law; Tax Law; Trademark, Copyright and Unfair Competition

ROBINSON, PALMER & LOGAN
Bakersfield, CA ....Civil Trial Practice; General Practice; Insurance Defense

ROBINSON, PHILLIPS & CALCAGNIE, A PROFESSIONAL CORPORATION
Laguna Niguel, CA ....Civil Trial Practice; Personal Injury

ROBINSON SHEPPARD SHAPIRO, G.P.
Montreal, QU, Canada ....General Practice

ROBINSON, SMITH & WELLS
Chattanooga, TN ....Civil Trial Practice; Insurance Defense; Medical Malpractice; Personal Injury; Product Liability Law

ROBINSON & WOOD, INC.
San Jose, CA ....Civil Trial Practice; Commercial Litigation; Insurance Defense; Product Liability Law

ROBISON, BELAUSTEGUI, ROBB AND SHARP, A PROFESSIONAL CORPORATION
Reno, NV ....General Practice

ROBISON & BELSER, P.A.
Montgomery, AL ....Civil Trial Practice

ROBISON & ROBISON
Denton, TX ....Labor and Employment Law; Personal Injury

ROBY & HOOD
Fort Wayne, IN.......................Civil Trial Practice; Personal Injury; Product Liability Law

ROCAP, WITCHGER & THRELKELD
Indianapolis, IN ....Commercial Law; General Practice; Insurance Defense

ROCHE, JOHN J. & ASSOCIATES
Cambridge, MA ....Probate, Trusts and Estate Planning

ROCHE, CARENS & DEGIACOMO, A PROFESSIONAL CORPORATION
Boston, MA..............................General Practice

ROCHE CORRIGAN MCCOY & BUSH
Albany, NY ....Construction Law; General Practice; Insurance Defense; Personal Injury

ROCHE AND MURPHY
Franklin, MA ....Civil Trial Practice; Municipal and Zoning Law; Real Estate Law

ROCKEY, RIFKIN AND RYTHER
Chicago, IL...............................Patent, Trademark, Copyright and Unfair Competition

ROCKHILL, PINNICK, PEQUIGNOT, HELM, LANDIS & RIGDON
Warsaw, IN ....Business Law; Civil Trial Practice; Insurance Defense; Municipal and Zoning Law

ROCKITTER, KEVIN E., P.C.
Melville, NY ....Civil Trial Practice

RODA & NAST, P.C.
Lancaster, PA............................Civil Trial Practice; Commercial Law; Personal Injury; Product Liability Law; Securities Law

RODEY, DICKASON, SLOAN, AKIN & ROBB, P.A.
Albuquerque, NM....................Administrative Law; Antitrust Law; Banking Law; Bankruptcy Law; Business Law; Commercial Law; Construction Law; Criminal Trial Practice; General Practice; Health Care Law; Insurance Defense; International Business Law; Labor and Employment Law; Land Use Law; Medical Malpractice; Natural Resources Law; Personal Injury; Probate, Trusts and Estate Planning; Product Liability Law; Public Utilities Law; Real Estate Law; Securities Law; Tax Law
Santa Fe, NM............................General Practice

RODGERS, JAMES R.
Blackwell, OK ....General Practice; Probate, Trusts and Estate Planning

RODGERS AND CO., L.P.A.
Cleveland, OH...........................Commercial Litigation; Construction Law; Insurance Defense; Product Liability Law; Real Estate Law

RODI, POLLOCK, PETTKER, GALBRAITH & CAHILL, A LAW CORPORATION
Los Angeles, CA.......................Business Law; Civil Trial Practice; Environmental Law; Probate, Trusts and Estate Planning; Real Estate Law; Tax Law

RODMAN, HOLSCHER, FRANCISCO & PECK, P.A.
Washington, NC.......................Civil Trial Practice

RODRIGUEZ, COLVIN & CHANEY, L.L.P.
Brownsville, TX ....Appellate Practice; Civil Trial Practice; Environmental Law; General Practice; Insurance Defense; Personal Injury; Product Liability Law
McAllen, TX..............................Appellate Practice; Civil Trial Practice; Environmental Law; General Practice; Insurance Defense; Personal Injury; Product Liability Law

ROECA, LOUIE & HIRAOKA
Honolulu, HI............................Civil Trial Practice

ROEHL LAW FIRM, P.C.
Albuquerque, NM....................Medical Malpractice; Personal Injury; Product Liability Law

ROETZEL & ANDRESS, A LEGAL PROFESSIONAL ASSOCIATION
Akron, OH................................General Practice

ROGAN GUIDA & ORENSTEIN
White Plains, NY ....Appellate Practice; Business Law; Commercial Litigation; Real Estate Law

ROGERS, BOWERS, DEMPSEY AND PALADINO
West Palm Beach, FL ....Tax Law

ROGERS & GREENBERG
Dayton, OH..............................Business Law; Family Law; General Practice

ROGERS & HARDIN
Atlanta, GA ....General Practice

ROGERS, JOSEPH, O'DONNELL & QUINN, A PROFESSIONAL CORPORATION
San Francisco, CA ....Civil Trial Practice; Construction Law; General Practice; Labor and Employment Law

ROGERS & KILLEEN
Alexandria, VA ....Patent, Trademark, Copyright and Unfair Competition

ROGERS, LAUGHLIN, NUNNALLY, HOOD & CRUM
Greeneville, TN ....Civil Trial Practice; General Practice

ROGERS LAW FIRM, THE
Las Vegas, NV ....Banking Law; Communications Law; Sports and Entertainment Law

ROGERS & MILNE
Toronto, ON, Canada...............Patent, Trademark, Copyright and Unfair Competition

ROGERS TOWNSEND & THOMAS, PC
Columbia, SC ....Family Law; General Practice; Probate, Trusts and Estate Planning; Real Estate Law

ROGERS & WELLS
Los Angeles, CA ....General Practice
Washington, DC.......................General Practice
New York, NY.........................Civil Trial Practice; General Practice
London, England ....General Practice
Paris, France.............................General Practice

ROGIN, NASSAU, CAPLAN, LASSMAN & HIRTLE, LLC
Hartford, CT ....Business Law; Civil Trial Practice; General Practice

ROHDE, DALES, MELZER, TE WINKLE & GASS
Sheboygan, WI ....General Practice

ROHRBACHER, NICHOLSON & LIGHT CO. L.P.A.
Toledo, OH ....Business Law; Civil Trial Practice; Environmental Law; Labor and Employment Law; Probate, Trusts and Estate Planning; Product Liability Law

ROLAND & SCHLEGEL, P.C.
Reading, PA ....General Practice

ROLLESTON, MORETON JR.
Atlanta, GA ....Business Law

ROLLINGS, BORCHERS, STUHLER, CARMICHAEL & GARTNER, P.C.
St. Charles, MO ....Business Law; Probate, Trusts and Estate Planning; Real Estate Law

ROLLINS, SMALKIN, RICHARDS & MACKIE
Baltimore, MD ....Civil Trial Practice; Insurance Defense; Personal Injury; Workers Compensation

ROLLS, JACK M. JR.
Honolulu, HI............................Banking Law; Business Law; Real Estate Law

ROOKS, PITTS AND POUST
Chicago, IL...............................General Practice; Workers Compensation

ROOT, HARRY H. III
Tampa, FL ....Probate, Trusts and Estate Planning

ROOT & SCHINDLER, P.C.
Denver, CO ....Environmental Law; Natural Resources Law

ROPER & QUIGG
Chicago, IL...............................Patent, Trademark, Copyright and Unfair Competition
Arlington, VA ....Patent, Trademark, Copyright and Unfair Competition

ROPERS, MAJESKI, KOHN & BENTLEY, A PROFESSIONAL CORPORATION
Los Angeles, CA.......................General Practice

ROPERS, MAJESKI, KOHN & BENTLEY, A PROFESSIONAL CORPORATION

    Redwood City, CA ....General Practice
    Sacramento, CA ....General Practice
    San Francisco, CA ....General Practice
    San Jose, CA ....General Practice
    Santa Rosa, CA ....General Practice

ROPES & GRAY

    Washington, DC.....................General Practice
    Boston, MA............................Civil Trial Practice; General Practice; Tax Law

ROSE, KOHL & DAVENPORT, LTD.

    Santa Fe, NM........................Civil Trial Practice; Probate, Trusts and Estate Planning; Securities Law; Tax Law

ROSE LAW FIRM, A PROFESSIONAL ASSOCIATION

    Little Rock, AR ....Appellate Practice; Banking Law; Bankruptcy Law; Civil Trial Practice; Commercial Law; Communications Law; Employment Benefits Law; Environmental Law; General Practice; Insurance Defense; International Business Law; Labor and Employment Law; Municipal Bond/Public Authority Financing; Patent, Trademark, Copyright and Unfair Competition; Personal Injury; Probate, Trusts and Estate Planning; Product Liability Law; Public Utilities Law; Real Estate Law; Sports and Entertainment Law; Tax Law; Workers Compensation

ROSE PADDEN & PETTY, L.C.

    Fairmont, WV ....General Practice; Insurance Defense
    Morgantown, WV ....General Practice; Insurance Defense

ROSE, RAND, ORCUTT, CAULEY, BLAKE & ELLIS, P.A.

    Wilson, NC.............................General Practice

ROSE, RAY, WINFREY, O'CONNOR & LESLIE, P.A.

    Fayetteville, NC ....General Practice; Immigration and Naturalization

ROSE & ROSE

    Kenosha, WI ....Criminal Trial Practice; General Practice

ROSE, SCHMIDT, HASLEY & DISALLE, P.C.

    Pittsburgh, PA ....Antitrust Law; Civil Trial Practice; General Practice; Labor and Employment Law

ROSE, SUNDSTROM & BENTLEY

    Tallahassee, FL ....Administrative Law; Environmental Law; Health Care Law; Public Utilities Law; Real Estate Law

ROSEN, AVRUM J. LAW OFFICES OF

    Huntington, NY.....................Bankruptcy Law

ROSEN, CHARLES A.

    Roseland, NJ..........................Commercial Law; General Practice

ROSEN, BIEN & ASARO

    San Francisco, CA ....Antitrust Law; Appellate Practice; Civil Trial Practice; Commercial Law; Labor and Employment Law; Securities Law; Trademark, Copyright and Unfair Competition

ROSEN, DAINOW & JACOBS

    New York, NY........................Patent, Trademark, Copyright and Unfair Competition

ROSEN & DOLAN, P.C.

    New Haven, CT ....Appellate Practice; Civil Rights; Civil Trial Practice; Family Law; General Practice; Labor and Employment Law; Personal Injury

ROSEN & LOVELL, P.C.

    Detroit, MI............................Construction Law; Medical Malpractice; Personal Injury; Product Liability Law

ROSEN & OSBORNE, P.A.

    Tampa, FL ....Workers Compensation

ROSEN, ROSEN & HAGOOD, P.A.

    Charleston, SC ....Administrative Law; Appellate Practice; Bankruptcy Law; Business Law; Construction Law; Family Law; General Practice; Labor and Employment Law; Medical Malpractice; Personal Injury; Probate, Trusts and Estate Planning; Product Liability Law; Tax Law

ROSENBAUM, RICHARD L.

    Fort Lauderdale, FL ....Appellate Practice; Criminal Trial Practice

ROSENBERG LAW FIRM, THE

    Des Moines, IA......................Business Law; Criminal Trial Practice; General Practice; Personal Injury

ROSENBERG, ROBERT MERRILL, P.A.

    Minneapolis, MN ....General Practice; Real Estate Law

ROSENBERG, SEWAK, PIZZI & BELL, P.C.

    Washington, PA.....................Medical Malpractice; Personal Injury

ROSENBLATT, STANLEY M., PROFESSIONAL ASSOCIATION

    Miami, FL...............................Civil Trial Practice

ROSENBLUM & FILAN

    Stamford, CT..........................Civil Trial Practice; Health Care Law; Medical Malpractice
    New York, NY........................Medical Malpractice
    White Plains, NY ....Medical Malpractice

ROSENBLUM, GOLDENHERSH, SILVERSTEIN & ZAFFT, P.C.

    St. Louis, MO.........................Appellate Practice; Civil Trial Practice; Criminal Trial Practice; Family Law; General Practice; Labor and Employment Law; Probate, Trusts and Estate Planning; Real Estate Law; Tax Law

ROSENBLUM AND ROSENBLUM, A PROFESSIONAL CORPORATION

    Alexandria, VA ....General Practice

ROSENBLUM, WOLF & LLOYD, A PROFESSIONAL CORPORATION

    Secaucus, NJ..........................Real Estate Law; Tax Law

ROSENFELD & WOLFF, A PROFESSIONAL CORPORATION

    Los Angeles, CA ....Business Law; Real Estate Law; Securities Law

ROSENFELT, BARLOW, BARBER, BARUDIN & BORG, P.A.

    Albuquerque, NM...................Civil Trial Practice

ROSENMAN & COLIN LLP

    Washington, DC.....................General Practice
    New York, NY........................General Practice

ROSENN, JENKINS & GREENWALD, L.L.P.

    Wilkes-Barre, PA ....Bankruptcy Law; General Practice; Labor and Employment Law; Probate, Trusts and Estate Planning; Real Estate Law; Tax Law

ROSENTHAL & CURRY

    East Meadow, NY ....General Practice

ROSENTHAL AND SCHANFIELD, PROFESSIONAL CORPORATION

    Chicago, IL.............................Civil Trial Practice; General Practice

ROSENTHAL, SIEGEL, MUENKEL & WOLF, LLP

    Amherst, NY..........................Personal Injury
    Buffalo, NY ....Personal Injury

ROSENTHAL AND WEISBERG, P.C.

    Philadelphia, PA ....Criminal Trial Practice; Health Care Law; Medical Malpractice; Personal Injury

ROSENWALD, LAWRENCE S., P.C.

    Philadelphia, PA ....Civil Trial Practice; Commercial Law; Commercial Litigation; Personal Injury; Real Estate Law

ROSENZWEIG, JONES & MACNABB, P.C.

    Newnan, GA ....Civil Trial Practice; General Practice; Real Estate Law

ROSEPINK & ESTES

    Scottsdale, AZ........................Probate, Trusts and Estate Planning; Tax Law

ROSOLIO, SILVERMAN & KOTZ, P.A.

    Towson, MD ....Business Law; Insurance Defense

ROSS, HARRIET

    San Francisco, CA ....Criminal Trial Practice

ROSS, JAMES E. & ASSOCIATES

    Houston, TX ....Admiralty/Maritime Law; General Practice; Insurance Defense

ROSS, BRITTAIN & SCHONBERG CO., L.P.A.

    Cleveland, OH........................Labor and Employment Law

ROSS & COHEN, LLP

    New York, NY........................Construction Law; Real Estate Law

ROSS, DIXON & MASBACK L.L.P.

    Washington, DC.....................Civil Trial Practice

ROSS & HARDIES

    Chicago, IL.............................General Practice
    New York, NY........................General Practice

ROSS & ROSS

    Monticello, AR ....General Practice

ROSS, WILLIAMS & DEAL, P.A.

    Lakeland, FL...........................Real Estate Law; Workers Compensation

ROSSBACHER & ASSOCIATES

    Los Angeles, CA ....Commercial Litigation; Constitutional Law

ROSSI, MURNANE, BALZANO & HUGHES

    Utica, NY ....General Practice

ROSSIE, LUCKETT, PARKER & LAUGHLIN, P.C.

    Memphis, TN ....General Practice

ROSSMAN, BAUMBERGER & REBOSO, A PROFESSIONAL ASSOCIATION
Miami, FL................Civil Trial Practice

ROST & GEIGER
Wailuku, HI...........Personal Injury

ROTH, STEPHEN H.
Hackensack, NJ................Appellate Practice; Civil Trial Practice; Commercial Law; Family Law; Real Estate Law

ROTH AND DUNCAN, P.A.
West Palm Beach, FL.............Criminal Trial Practice

ROTH, VAN AMBERG, GROSS, ROGERS & ORTIZ
Santa Fe, NM................Civil Trial Practice; Commercial Litigation; Construction Law; Personal Injury; Real Estate Law

ROTHBERG & LOGAN
Fort Wayne, IN................Banking Law; Commercial Litigation; Family Law; General Practice

ROTHENBERG, ALLEN L., LAW FIRM OF
Philadelphia, PA................Personal Injury

ROTHMAN GORDON FOREMAN & GROUDINE, P.C.
Pittsburgh, PA................Civil Trial Practice; Communications Law; General Practice; Labor and Employment Law

ROTHSCHILD, EDMUND W.
Cleveland, OH................Business Law; Probate, Trusts and Estate Planning

ROTHSCHILD, BARRY & MYERS
Chicago, IL................Antitrust Law; Aviation Law; General Practice

ROTHSCHILD & MORGAN
Columbus, GA................General Practice; Health Care Law; Insurance Defense; Tax Law

ROTHSCHILD, WISHEK & SANDS
Sacramento, CA................Criminal Trial Practice

ROTHSTEIN, DONATELLI, HUGHES, DAHLSTROM, CRON & SCHOENBURG, LLP
Santa Fe, NM................Civil Trial Practice; Criminal Trial Practice

ROTHWELL, FIGG, ERNST & KURZ, A PROFESSIONAL CORPORATION
Washington, DC................Patent, Trademark, Copyright and Unfair Competition

ROUDA, FEDER & TIETJEN
San Francisco, CA................Personal Injury

ROUNICK, JACK A.
Norristown, PA................Civil Trial Practice; Family Law

ROUNTREE & SEAGLE, L.L.P.
Wilmington, NC................Admiralty/Maritime Law; Civil Trial Practice; General Practice

ROUNTREE & SOUTHER
Brunswick, GA................General Practice

ROUTMAN, MOORE, GOLDSTONE & VALENTINO
New Castle, PA................General Practice
Sharon, PA................General Practice

ROWAN & QUIRK
Rockville, MD................Civil Trial Practice; General Practice

ROWE, GORDON H. JR.
Monte Vista, CO................General Practice

ROWE & HAWKINS
Jasonville, IN................General Practice; Probate, Trusts and Estate Planning

ROWE, ROWE & MAHER
South Bend, IN................Civil Trial Practice; General Practice; Insurance Defense; Medical Malpractice; Personal Injury; Product Liability Law

ROWLEY, FORREST, O'DONNELL, BEAUMONT & PELERSI, P.C.
Albany, NY................Administrative Law; Business Law; Civil Trial Practice; Commercial Law; Employment Benefits Law; Environmental Law; General Practice; Insurance Defense; Labor and Employment Law; Personal Injury

ROWLEY LAW FIRM, P.C.
Clovis, NM................Banking Law; General Practice

ROY, CHRIS J. SR.
Alexandria, LA................Appellate Practice; Civil Trial Practice

ROY, BIVINS, JUDICE & HENKE, A PROFESSIONAL LAW CORPORATION
Lafayette, LA................Admiralty/Maritime Law; General Practice; Medical Malpractice; Product Liability Law; Public Utilities Law

ROY & LAMBERT
Springdale, AR................General Practice; Insurance Defense

ROYALL KOEGEL & WELLS
Washington, DC................General Practice
New York, NY................General Practice

ROYALS, THOMAS E. & ASSOCIATES
Jackson, MS................Criminal Trial Practice

ROYCE, MERLE L. II
Chicago, IL................Appellate Practice; Civil Trial Practice; Commercial Litigation

ROYCE, THOMAS L. JR.
Houston, TX................Criminal Trial Practice

ROYLANCE, ABRAMS, BERDO & GOODMAN, L.L.P.
Washington, DC................Antitrust Law; Patent, Trademark, Copyright and Unfair Competition

ROYSTON, MUELLER, MCLEAN & REID, LLP
Towson, MD................General Practice

ROYSTON, RAYZOR, VICKERY & WILLIAMS, L.L.P.
Brownsville, TX................General Practice
Corpus Christi, TX................General Practice
Galveston, TX................General Practice
Houston, TX................Admiralty/Maritime Law; General Practice

ROZELLE AND CALL
Palm Beach, FL................Civil Trial Practice; General Practice

RUBENSTEIN, SUSAN
San Francisco, CA................Employment Benefits Law

RUBENSTEIN, NOVAK, EINBUND & PAVLIK
Cleveland, OH................Bankruptcy Law; Civil Trial Practice; Medical Malpractice; Personal Injury; Product Liability Law

RUBIN, MICHAEL S.
San Francisco, CA................Transportation Law

RUBIN & ASSOCIATES, P.C.
Paoli, PA................Civil Trial Practice

RUBIN BAUM LEVIN CONSTANT & FRIEDMAN
New York, NY................General Practice

RUBIN & DORNBAUM
Newark, NJ................Immigration and Naturalization

RUBIN, GLICKMAN AND STEINBERG, P.C. A PROFESSIONAL CORPORATION
Lansdale, PA................Civil Trial Practice; Criminal Trial Practice; Family Law; Personal Injury; Probate, Trusts and Estate Planning

RUBIN HAYS & FOLEY
Louisville, KY................Banking Law; Bankruptcy Law; Civil Trial Practice; Family Law; General Practice; Municipal Bond/Public Authority Financing; Personal Injury; Probate, Trusts and Estate Planning; Real Estate Law; Securities Law; Tax Law

RUBIN, KATZ, SALAZAR, ALLEY & ROUSE, A PROFESSIONAL CORPORATION
Santa Fe, NM................Administrative Law; Commercial Law; Commercial Litigation; Probate, Trusts and Estate Planning; Real Estate Law

RUBINSTEIN, KORNIK, BLOOM & MINSKER, A PROFESSIONAL ASSOCIATION
Miami, FL................Commercial Litigation; Family Law; Real Estate Law

RUBY & SCHOFIELD
San Jose, CA................Appellate Practice; Civil Trial Practice; General Practice

RUCCI, BURNHAM, CARTA & EDELBERG
Darien, CT................Business Law; Probate, Trusts and Estate Planning; Real Estate Law

RUDASILL, MICHAEL L., P.A.
Spartanburg, SC................Criminal Trial Practice; Personal Injury

RUDDY, BRADLEY & KOLKHORST, A PROFESSIONAL CORPORATION
Juneau, AK................Civil Trial Practice

RUDEN, MCCLOSKY, SMITH, SCHUSTER & RUSSELL, P.A.
Fort Lauderdale, FL................General Practice

RUDERMAN, ALAN
Chattanooga, TN................Patent, Trademark, Copyright and Unfair Competition

RUDER, WARE & MICHLER, S.C.
Wausau, WI................General Practice

RUDMAN & WINCHELL
Bangor, ME...........................Business Law; Insurance Defense; Labor and Employment Law

RUDNICK & WOLFE
Chicago, IL...........................General Practice

RUDOLF & MAHER, P.A.
Chapel Hill, NC......................Civil Trial Practice; Criminal Trial Practice

RUDOLPH LAW GROUP, THE, A PROFESSIONAL CORPORATION
Costa Mesa, CA.....................Civil Trial Practice; General Practice

RUMBERGER, KIRK & CALDWELL, PROFESSIONAL ASSOCIATION
Miami, FL..............................Civil Trial Practice; General Practice
Orlando, FL...........................Civil Trial Practice; General Practice
Tallahassee, FL.....................Civil Trial Practice; General Practice
Tampa, FL.............................Civil Trial Practice; General Practice

RUMMONDS, WALTZ & MAIR
Aptos, CA..............................Civil Trial Practice; Medical Malpractice; Personal Injury

RUMRELL, COSTABEL & TURK
West Palm Beach, FL..............Civil Trial Practice

RUNFOLA, JOHN M.
San Francisco, CA..................Criminal Trial Practice

RUNNING, WISE, WILSON, FORD AND PHILLIPS, P.L.C.
Traverse City, MI....................Civil Trial Practice; General Practice; Health Care Law; Insurance Defense; Municipal and Zoning Law; Personal Injury; Probate, Trusts and Estate Planning; Real Estate Law

RUNQUIST & ASSOCIATES
Los Angeles, CA.....................Business Law; Health Care Law

RUNYON AND RUNYON
Clarksville, TN.......................Family Law; Personal Injury; Probate, Trusts and Estate Planning

RUS, MILIBAND, WILLIAMS & SMITH
Irvine, CA..............................Bankruptcy Law; Civil Trial Practice; Commercial Litigation

RUSH, HANNULA, HARKINS & KYLER
Tacoma, WA...........................Personal Injury

RUSH MOORE CRAVEN SUTTON MORRY & BEH
Honolulu, HI...........................General Practice

RUSHING & GUICE
Biloxi, MS..............................Admiralty/Maritime Law; Banking Law; Business Law; Civil Trial Practice; Commercial Litigation

RUSS, JAMES M., P.A., LAW OFFICES OF
Orlando, FL...........................Criminal Trial Practice

RUSSELL & BATCHELOR
Grand Rapids, MI...................Probate, Trusts and Estate Planning; Real Estate Law; Tax Law

RUSSELL, BROWN, BICKEL & BRECKENRIDGE
Nevada, MO...........................General Practice

RUSSELL & DUMOULIN
Vancouver, BC, Canada...........General Practice

RUSSELL & HULL, P.A.
Orlando, FL...........................Civil Trial Practice; Commercial Litigation; Construction Law; Real Estate Law

RUSSELL, MCINTYRE, HILLIGOSS & WELKE
Kokomo, IN...........................Medical Malpractice; Personal Injury

RUSSELL & MIRKOVICH
Long Beach, CA.....................Admiralty/Maritime Law; Business Law; Civil Trial Practice; Commercial Law; Environmental Law; General Practice; International Business Law; Personal Injury; Transportation Law

RUSSELL, RICHARD A., A PROFESSIONAL CORPORATION
Ocean City, NJ......................Family Law

RUSSELL, TURNER, LAIRD & JONES, L.L.P.
Fort Worth, TX.......................Civil Trial Practice; Commercial Law; Medical Malpractice; Personal Injury; Product Liability Law

RUSSO, RONALD G.
New York, NY.........................Criminal Trial Practice

RUSSO & CULMO, P.A.
Miami, FL..............................Medical Malpractice; Personal Injury; Product Liability Law

RUSSO & TALISMAN, P.A.
Miami, FL..............................Appellate Practice

RUTAN & TUCKER, LLP
Costa Mesa, CA.....................Antitrust Law; Appellate Practice; Bankruptcy Law; Business Law; Civil Rights; Civil Trial Practice; Commercial Law; Communications Law; Computer Law; Construction Law; Employment Benefits Law; Environmental Law; General Practice; Labor and Employment Law; Land Use Law; Municipal Bond/Public Authority Financing; Municipal and Zoning Law; Probate, Trusts and Estate Planning; Real Estate Law; Securities Law; Tax Law; Trademark, Copyright and Unfair Competition; Workers Compensation

RUTH & MACNEILLE, PROFESSIONAL ASSOCIATION
Hilton Head Island, SC...........Civil Trial Practice; Probate, Trusts and Estate Planning; Tax Law

RUTHRAUFF & ARMBRUST
Philadelphia, PA....................Commercial Litigation; Product Liability Law

RUTKIN AND OLDHAM, L.L.C
Westport, CT..........................Family Law; Personal Injury

RUTLEDGE, MANION, RABAUT, TERRY & THOMAS, P.C.
Detroit, MI.............................Insurance Defense

RUTTER, ROBERT P.
Cleveland, OH........................Personal Injury

RUTTER & DIPIERO
Philadelphia, PA....................Appellate Practice; Civil Trial Practice; Criminal Trial Practice; Personal Injury

RYALS, ROBINSON & SAFFO, P.C.
Wilmington, NC......................General Practice

RYAN, ANDRADA & LIFTER, A PROFESSIONAL CORPORATION
Oakland, CA..........................Civil Trial Practice; Construction Law; Insurance Defense

RYAN AND GANNON
Florham Park, NJ...................Appellate Practice; Civil Trial Practice; Insurance Defense

RYAN, JAMIESON & MORRIS
Kalamazoo, MI.......................Insurance Defense

RYAN, MARTIN, COSTELLO, LEITER, STEIGER & CASS, P.C.
Springfield, MA......................Civil Trial Practice; Employment Benefits Law; General Practice

RYAN, RYAN, JOHNSON, MCCAGHEY & DELUCA, LLP
Stamford, CT.........................Civil Trial Practice; General Practice

RYAN, RYAN & ZIMMERMAN
Aitkin, MN.............................General Practice

RYAN SMITH & CARBINE, LTD.
Rutland, VT............................General Practice

RYCE, DONALD T., P.A.
Miami, FL..............................Labor and Employment Law

RYDBERG & GOLDSTEIN, P.A.
Tampa, FL.............................Bankruptcy Law; Commercial Law; Environmental Law; Municipal and Zoning Law; Real Estate Law

RYMER, WM. W.
Providence, RI.......................Patent, Trademark, Copyright and Unfair Competition

RYWANT, ALVAREZ, JONES & RUSSO, PROFESSIONAL ASSOCIATION
Tampa, FL.............................Civil Trial Practice; Insurance Defense; Medical Malpractice; Product Liability Law

SABBATH, DENNIS M., & ASSOCIATES, CHARTERED, THE LAW FIRM OF
Las Vegas, NV.......................Administrative Law; Civil Trial Practice; Commercial Litigation; Family Law; Labor and Employment Law; Personal Injury

SABLE, MAKOROFF & GUSKY, P.C.
Pittsburgh, PA.......................Bankruptcy Law; Civil Trial Practice

SACCA AND SACCA
Lockport, NY..........................General Practice; Probate, Trusts and Estate Planning

SACHNOFF & WEAVER, LTD.
Chicago, IL............................General Practice

SACHS, MAITLIN, FLEMING, GREENE & WILSON
West Orange, NJ....................Environmental Law; Insurance Defense; Medical Malpractice; Product Liability Law

SACK & ASSOCIATES, P.C.
McLean, VA...........................Tax Law

SACKS MONTGOMERY, P.C.
New York, NY.........................Civil Trial Practice; Construction Law; General Practice

SACKS & SACKS
Norfolk, VA ....Appellate Practice; Civil Trial Practice; Criminal Trial Practice; General Practice; Personal Injury

SACKS TIERNEY P.A.
Phoenix, AZ ....General Practice

SACKS ZWEIG & BURRIS, LLP
Santa Monica, CA...................Business Law; Civil Trial Practice; General Practice; Real Estate Law; Sports and Entertainment Law

SACOPULOS, JOHNSON, CARTER & SACOPULOS
Terre Haute, IN ....Insurance Defense

SADOW, STEVEN H., P.C.
Atlanta, GA ....Criminal Trial Practice

SAEGERT, ANGENEND & AUGUSTINE, P.C.
Austin, TX ....Civil Trial Practice

SAGASER, HANSEN, FRANSON & JAMISON, A PROFESSIONAL CORPORATION
Fresno, CA ....Commercial Litigation; Health Care Law; Labor and Employment Law

SAGER, PAVLICK & WIRTZ, S.C.
Fond du Lac, WI ....General Practice

SAIKLEY, GARRISON & COLOMBO, LTD.
Danville, IL ....Commercial Law

ST. CLAIR, DALLING & MEACHAM
Idaho Falls, ID........................General Practice

ST. JOHN, HOWARD C. AND ASSOCIATES
Kingston, NY..........................General Practice; Probate, Trusts and Estate Planning; Real Estate Law

ST. JOHN & ST. JOHN
Cullman, AL ....Civil Trial Practice; Insurance Defense; Workers Compensation

ST. JOHN & WAYNE
Newark, NJ ....Banking Law; Bankruptcy Law; Civil Trial Practice; Commercial Law; Criminal Trial Practice; Environmental Law; General Practice; Insurance Defense; Municipal Bond/Public Authority Financing; Tax Law

ST. MARTIN & LIRETTE, A PROFESSIONAL LAW CORPORATION
Houma, LA ....Personal Injury

SALEH, JOHN
Lamesa, TX ....Civil Trial Practice

SALEM, ALBERT, AND ASSOCIATES, P.A.
Tampa, FL ....Civil Trial Practice

SALEM, SAXON & NIELSEN, PROFESSIONAL ASSOCIATION
Tampa, FL ....Business Law; Civil Trial Practice; Commercial Litigation

SALERNO, COZZARELLI, MAUTONE, DE SALVO & NUSSBAUM, A PROFESSIONAL CORPORATION
Verona, NJ ....Civil Trial Practice; Commercial Law; General Practice; Municipal and Zoning Law

SALITERMAN & SIEFFERMAN LAW FIRM
Minneapolis, MN....................General Practice; Securities Law

SALLEY & ASSOCIATES
New Orleans, LA ....Admiralty/Maritime Law

SALLY & FITCH
Boston, MA ....Civil Trial Practice

SALMON, GODSMAN & NICHOLSON, PROFESSIONAL CORPORATION
Englewood, CO ....Medical Malpractice; Personal Injury; Product Liability Law

SALOOM & SALOOM
Lafayette, LA ....General Practice

SALVI, PATRICK A., P.C., LAW OFFICES OF
Waukegan, IL...........................Medical Malpractice; Personal Injury

SAMEL, JEFFREY & ASSOCIATES
New York, NY..........................Civil Trial Practice; Insurance Defense; Personal Injury; Product Liability Law

SAMET & GAGE, P.C.
Tucson, AZ ....Personal Injury; Workers Compensation

SAMFORD, DENSON, HORSLEY, PETTEY & MARTIN
Opelika, AL..............................General Practice

SAMMONS & PARKER, A PROFESSIONAL CORPORATION
Tyler, TX ....Insurance Defense; Real Estate Law

SAMNICK, ROBERT L.
Garden City, NY ....Real Estate Law

SAMPSON, WILLIAM A. II & ASSOCIATES
Pacific Palisades, CA ....Civil Trial Practice; Personal Injury

SAMS & MARTIN, P.A.
Miami, FL ....Civil Trial Practice; General Practice; Personal Injury

SAMS AND SAMS
Beaufort, SC ....Civil Trial Practice; General Practice

SAMUEL AND BALLARD, A PROFESSIONAL CORPORATION
Philadelphia, PA ....Civil Rights; Civil Trial Practice; Commercial Law; Constitutional Law; Labor and Employment Law; Medical Malpractice; Personal Injury; Product Liability Law; Workers Compensation

SAMUELS, MILLER, SCHROEDER, JACKSON & SLY
Decatur, IL..............................General Practice

SAMUELSON RIEGER & YOVINO
Garden City, NY ....Family Law

SANCHEZ & DANIELS
Chicago, IL..............................Civil Trial Practice; Insurance Defense; Product Liability Law

SANDBOTE, LOUIS J., P.C.
Dallas, TX ....Insurance Defense

SANDENAW, T. A., LAW OFFICE OF
Las Cruces, NM ....Civil Trial Practice; Insurance Defense; Medical Malpractice

SANDERS, AUSTIN, SWOPE & FLANIGAN
Princeton, WV ....Civil Trial Practice; Personal Injury; Product Liability Law; Workers Compensation

SANDERS, HAUGEN & SEARS, P.C.
Newnan, GA ....General Practice

SANDERS, MCEWAN, MARTINEZ, LUFF & DUKES, P.A.
Orlando, FL ....General Practice; Medical Malpractice

SANDERS, ROBERT E., AND ASSOCIATES, P.S.C.
Covington, KY ....Appellate Practice; Civil Trial Practice; Criminal Trial Practice; Environmental Law; Medical Malpractice; Personal Injury; Product Liability Law

SANDERS, SCHNABEL, BRANDENBURG & ZIMMERMAN, P.C.
Washington, DC.......................Labor and Employment Law

SANDIFER & SANDIFER, P.C.
Indianapolis, IN ....Probate, Trusts and Estate Planning

SANFORD, KUHL & PERKINS
Houston, TX ....Municipal Bond/Public Authority Financing

SANGER, HOWARD L. LAW OFFICES OF
Palm Springs, CA ....Tax Law

SANSONE, CHARLES F.
Tampa, FL ....Civil Trial Practice; Personal Injury; Product Liability Law

SANTOS & DUTTON, P.A.
Tampa, FL ....Insurance Defense

SAPP, DAVID R., P.C., LAW OFFICES OF
Austin, TX ....Administrative Law; Commercial Litigation

SARNOFF & BACCASH
Chicago, IL..............................Tax Law

SARRAIL, LYNCH & HALL
San Francisco, CA ....Insurance Defense; Product Liability Law

SARROUF, TARRICONE & FLEMMING
Boston, MA ....Aviation Law; Civil Trial Practice; Personal Injury

SASSER, DONALD J., P.A.
West Palm Beach, FL ....Family Law; General Practice

SATZ KIRSHON & ROSA, P.C.
Poughkeepsie, NY ....Appellate Practice; Civil Trial Practice; Family Law

SAUCEDO & CORSIGLIA, A LAW CORPORATION
San Jose, CA ....Civil Trial Practice; Medical Malpractice; Personal Injury

SAUL, EWING, REMICK & SAUL
New York, NY.........................General Practice
Berwyn, PA ....General Practice
Philadelphia, PA ....Antitrust Law; General Practice; Municipal Bond/Public Authority Financing

SAUNDERS CARY & PATTERSON
Richmond, VA ....Business Law; Commercial Litigation; Construction Law; Land Use Law

SAUNDERS & MONROE
Chicago, IL..........................Antitrust Law; Civil Trial Practice; Communications Law; Public Utilities Law; Securities Law

SAURBIER, PARADISO & DAVIS, P.L.C.
St. Clair Shores, MI ....Insurance Defense; Medical Malpractice

SAVAGE, GARMER & ELLIOTT, P.S.C.
Lexington, KY ....Civil Trial Practice; Medical Malpractice; Personal Injury

SAVAGE, KRIM & SIMONS, P.A.
Ocala, FL................................General Practice

SAVAGE, ROYALL AND SHEHEEN, L.L.P.
Camden, SC............................Civil Trial Practice; General Practice

SAVAGE & SAVAGE
Charleston, SC........................Criminal Trial Practice; Personal Injury

SAVERI AND SAVERI, A PROFESSIONAL CORPORATION
San Francisco, CA ....Antitrust Law; Securities Law

SAVETT FRUTKIN PODELL & RYAN, P.C.
Philadelphia, PA ....Civil Trial Practice; Commercial Litigation; Securities Law

SAWYER, J. E. JR.
Enterprise, AL........................Civil Trial Practice; General Practice

SAWYER, DAVIS & HALPERN
Garden City, NY ....Civil Trial Practice; Medical Malpractice; Personal Injury

SAYLES, EVANS, BRAYTON, PALMER & TIFFT
Elmira, NY ....Civil Trial Practice

SAYRE LAW OFFICES
Seattle, WA ....General Practice

SAYRE & WITTGRAF
Cherokee, IA ....General Practice

SCADDEN, HAMILTON & RYAN
San Francisco, CA ....Civil Trial Practice; Insurance Defense; Product Liability Law

SCALLEY & READING, A PROFESSIONAL CORPORATION
Salt Lake City, UT..................Environmental Law; Insurance Defense; Real Estate Law

SCANLAN, EDMUND J., LTD., LAW OFFICES OF
Chicago, IL............................Civil Trial Practice; Medical Malpractice; Personal Injury

SCANLAN & ROSEN, P.A.
Baltimore, MD ....Aviation Law; Medical Malpractice; Personal Injury; Product Liability Law

SCANLAN AND SCANLAN, A PROFESSIONAL CORPORATION
Bryn Mawr, PA......................Admiralty/Maritime Law; Labor and Employment Law

SCANLON & GEARINGER CO., L.P.A.
Akron, OH ....Civil Trial Practice; Medical Malpractice; Personal Injury; Product Liability Law

SCANLON & HENRETTA CO., L.P.A.
Akron, OH ....Civil Trial Practice; Personal Injury; Product Liability Law

SCANLON, HOWLEY, SCANLON & DOHERTY
Scranton, PA ....Civil Trial Practice; General Practice; Insurance Defense; Medical Malpractice; Personal Injury; Product Liability Law; Workers Compensation

SCARIANO, KULA, ELLCH AND HIMES, CHARTERED
Chicago, IL............................Civil Trial Practice; Employment Benefits Law; Insurance Defense; Labor and Employment Law; Municipal Bond/Public Authority Financing; Municipal and Zoning Law

SCARPELLO & ALLING, LTD. A PROFESSIONAL CORPORATION
Carson City, NV ....General Practice
Stateline, NV ....General Practice

SCARZAFAVA LAW OFFICE, THE
Oneonta, NY ....Personal Injury; Product Liability Law

SCHAAF & HODGES
Marietta, GA..........................Real Estate Law

SCHACHTER, KRISTOFF, ORENSTEIN & BERKOWITZ, L.L.P.
Sacramento, CA ....Labor and Employment Law
San Francisco, CA ....Labor and Employment Law

SCHACHTER, TROMBADORE, OFFEN, STANTON & PAVICS, A PROFESSIONAL CORPORATION
Somerville, NJ ....Bankruptcy Law; Civil Trial Practice; Commercial Law; Criminal Trial Practice; Family Law; Personal Injury

SCHADEN, KATZMAN & LAMPERT
Broomfield, CO ....Aviation Law; Personal Injury; Product Liability Law
Bloomfield Hills, MI................Aviation Law; Personal Injury; Product Liability Law

SCHAFER, GERALD S.
Greensboro, NC ....Bankruptcy Law

SCHAFER AND WEINER, P.C.
Bloomfield Hills, MI................Bankruptcy Law; Commercial Litigation

SCHAFFER & CABELL, P.C.
Richmond, VA ....Insurance Defense; Product Liability Law

SCHAFFER, LAMBRIGHT, ODOM & SPARKS
Houston, TX ....Criminal Trial Practice

SCHANEVILLE & BARINGER, L.L.C.
Baton Rouge, LA ....Bankruptcy Law; Tax Law

SCHANTZ, STEWART T.
Poughkeepsie, NY ....Family Law

SCHANTZ, SCHATZMAN & AARONSON, P.A.
Miami, FL ....General Practice

SCHAPER, CARLOS E. LAW OFFICE
Broken Bow, NE......................General Practice; Probate, Trusts and Estate Planning; Real Estate Law

SCHECHTER LAW FIRM, THE, P.C.
St. Louis, MO..........................Family Law

SCHEFFLER, WILLIAM L. & ASSOCIATES
Westport, CT..........................Business Law; Immigration and Naturalization; Municipal and Zoning Law; Real Estate Law

SCHEINKMAN, FREDMAN & KOSAN, LLP
White Plains, NY ....Civil Trial Practice; Family Law

SCHELL BRAY AYCOCK ABEL & LIVINGSTON, P.L.L.C.
Greensboro, NC ....Business Law; Real Estate Law; Securities Law; Tax Law

SCHELL & DELAMER, LLP
Los Angeles, CA ....Construction Law; Environmental Law; General Practice; Insurance Defense; Product Liability Law

SCHELLINGER & DOYLE, S.C.
Milwaukee, WI ....Insurance Defense

SCHENCK, PRICE, SMITH & KING
Morristown, NJ......................General Practice

SCHEPER & MCGOWAN
Hamilton, OH ....General Practice; Insurance Defense

SCHERFFIUS, ANDREW M., P.C.
Atlanta, GA ....Aviation Law; Civil Trial Practice; Medical Malpractice; Personal Injury

SCHERMER, COOPER & ASSOCIATES, P.C.
Philadelphia, PA ....Civil Trial Practice; Commercial Litigation; General Practice; Insurance Defense; Probate, Trusts and Estate Planning

SCHERNER & HANSON
Columbus, OH ....Civil Trial Practice; Medical Malpractice; Personal Injury; Product Liability Law

SCHEUER, YOST & PATTERSON, A PROFESSIONAL CORPORATION
Santa Fe, NM..........................Banking Law; Civil Trial Practice; Environmental Law; General Practice; Labor and Employment Law; Probate, Trusts and Estate Planning; Real Estate Law

SCHIER, DENEWETH & PARFITT, P.C.
Troy, MI..................................Construction Law; Insurance Defense; Personal Injury; Real Estate Law

SCHIFF, JOEL P. LAW OFFICES OF
Los Angeles, CA ....Appellate Practice

SCHIFF HARDIN & WAITE
Washington, DC......................General Practice
Chicago, IL..............................General Practice
Peoria, IL................................General Practice
New York, NY........................General Practice

SCHIFFRIN, OLSON & SCHLEMLEIN, P.L.L.C.
Seattle, WA ....Commercial Law; Construction Law

SCHILD, PETER
Boulder, CO ....Criminal Trial Practice; Personal Injury

SCHILLER, MARVIN
Raleigh, NC............................Appellate Practice; Environmental Law; Labor and Employment Law; Securities Law

SCHILLER & ASSOCIATES, P.C.
New York, NY........................Health Care Law

SCHILLER, DU CANTO AND FLECK
Chicago, IL..............................Family Law
Lake Forest, IL ....Family Law

SCHILLER, JAMES J., & ASSOCIATES
Cleveland, OH..........................Business Law; Civil Trial Practice

SCHILLING, JOHN R., A PROFESSIONAL CORPORATION
Newport Beach, CA................Family Law

SCHIMMEL, HILLSHAFER & LOEWENTHAL
Sherman Oaks, CA ....Construction Law

SCHINDLER AND OLSON
Mishawaka, IN........................General Practice; Personal Injury; Probate, Trusts and Estate Planning; Real Estate Law

SCHLAM STONE & DOLAN
New York, NY........................Antitrust Law; Appellate Practice; Bankruptcy Law; Civil Trial Practice; Commercial Law; Criminal Trial Practice; General Practice; Real Estate Law; Securities Law; Tax Law; Trademark, Copyright and Unfair Competition

SCHLANGER, MILLS, MAYER & GROSSBERG, L.L.P.
Houston, TX ....General Practice

SCHLECHT, SHEVLIN & SHOENBERGER, A LAW CORPORATION
Palm Springs, CA ....Business Law; Civil Trial Practice; Family Law; General Practice; Probate, Trusts and Estate Planning; Real Estate Law

SCHLESINGER AND BUCHBINDER
Newton, MA ....Real Estate Law

SCHLESINGER, SHELDON J., P.A.
Fort Lauderdale, FL ....Civil Trial Practice; General Practice; Personal Injury

SCHLICHTER, BOGARD & DENTON
St. Louis, MO..........................Personal Injury

SCHLIFKIN, ROBERT S.
Los Angeles, CA ....Medical Malpractice

SCHLUSSER & REIVER, P.A.
Wilmington, DE......................Probate, Trusts and Estate Planning; Tax Law

SCHMELTZER, APTAKER & SHEPARD, P.C.
Washington, DC......................Admiralty/Maritime Law; Business Law; Civil Trial Practice; Employment Benefits Law; Health Care Law; Labor and Employment Law

SCHMIDT FIRM, THE
Dallas, TX ....Civil Trial Practice; Medical Malpractice; Personal Injury

SCHMIDT & KUEHNE, A PROFESSIONAL LAW CORPORATION
Baton Rouge, LA....................Employment Benefits Law; Tax Law

SCHMIDT & RONCA, P.C.
Harrisburg, PA........................Personal Injury

SCHMIDT, SCHROYER, MORENO & DUPRIS, P.C.
Pierre, SD ....General Practice

SCHMIDT, THOMPSON, JOHNSON & MOODY, P.A.
Willmar, MN............................Civil Trial Practice; General Practice; Insurance Defense

SCHMIEDESKAMP, ROBERTSON, NEU & MITCHELL
Quincy, IL ....Civil Trial Practice; General Practice; Insurance Defense; Mergers and Acquisitions

SCHMITTINGER & RODRIGUEZ, PROFESSIONAL ASSOCIATION
Dover, DE ....General Practice

SCHMITZ & OPHAUG
Northfield, MN ....General Practice

SCHMUKLER, MARTIN L., P.C.
New York, NY........................Criminal Trial Practice

SCHNADER HARRISON SEGAL & LEWIS
Philadelphia, PA ....General Practice

SCHNEIDER, HARRIS & HARRIS
Woodmere, NY ....Health Care Law

SCHNEIDER, KAHN & SIEGEL, P.C.
Memphis, TN ....Probate, Trusts and Estate Planning

SCHNEIDER, KLEINICK, WEITZ, DAMASHEK & SHOOT
New York, NY........................Civil Trial Practice; Insurance Defense; Medical Malpractice; Personal Injury; Product Liability Law

SCHNEIDER LAW FIRM
Willmar, MN............................Civil Trial Practice; Personal Injury; Product Liability Law

SCHNEIDER & MCWILLIAMS, P.C.
George West, TX ....General Practice

SCHNEIDER, REILLY, ZABIN & COSTELLO, P.C.
Boston, MA ....Civil Trial Practice

SCHNEIDLER, JON G.
Seattle, WA ....Business Law; Land Use Law; Real Estate Law

SCHNORF & SCHNORF CO., L.P.A., A PROFESSIONAL CORPORATION
Toledo, OH ....Civil Trial Practice; General Practice; Insurance Defense; Labor and Employment Law; Personal Injury; Probate, Trusts and Estate Planning

SCHOBER & ULATOWSKI, S.C.
Green Bay, WI ....Business Law; Civil Trial Practice; Insurance Defense; Real Estate Law; Transportation Law

SCHOCH & WOODRUFF, L.L.P.
High Point, NC.......................General Practice

SCHOCHOR, FEDERICO AND STATON, P.A.
Baltimore, MD ....Civil Trial Practice; Medical Malpractice; Personal Injury; Product Liability Law

SCHOELLERMAN, JACK L.
Irvine, CA................................Business Law

SCHOEL, OGLE, BENTON AND CENTENO
Birmingham, AL ....Antitrust Law; Bankruptcy Law; Civil Trial Practice; Construction Law; General Practice

SCHOEN, DENNIS T., P.C., LAW OFFICES
Chicago, IL..............................Personal Injury

SCHOENBAUM, CURPHY & SCANLAN, P.C.
San Antonio, TX.....................Business Law; Employment Benefits Law; Probate, Trusts and Estate Planning; Real Estate Law; Tax Law

SCHOLDER, PAUL A., ATTORNEY AT LAW, P.C.
New Haven, CT ....Civil Trial Practice; Insurance Defense; Personal Injury; Product Liability Law

SCHOLZ, LOOS, PALMER, SIEBERS & DUESTERHAUS
Quincy, IL ....General Practice

SCHOTTENSTEIN, ZOX & DUNN, A LEGAL PROFESSIONAL ASSOCIATION
Columbus, OH ....General Practice; Health Care Law; Labor and Employment Law

SCHRADER, BYRD, COMPANION & GURLEY
Wheeling, WV ....Banking Law; Bankruptcy Law; Civil Trial Practice; Commercial Litigation; Criminal Trial Practice; Employment Benefits Law; Family Law; General Practice; Insurance Defense; Labor and Employment Law; Medical Malpractice; Personal Injury; Real Estate Law; Tax Law

SCHRAGGER, LAVINE & NAGY
West Trenton, NJ....................Criminal Trial Practice; General Practice; Probate, Trusts and Estate Planning; Real Estate Law

SCHRAMM & PINES, L.L.C.
St. Louis, MO..........................Business Law; Civil Trial Practice; Commercial Litigation; Family Law; International Business Law; Probate, Trusts and Estate Planning

SCHRECK MORRIS
Las Vegas, NV ....Appellate Practice; Bankruptcy Law; Commercial Law; Labor and Employment Law; Product Liability Law; Real Estate Law

SCHROEDER & HRUBY, LTD.
Wheaton, IL ....Personal Injury

SCHROEDER & LARCHE, P.A.
Boca Raton, FL ....Probate, Trusts and Estate Planning; Real Estate Law

SCHROPP, BUELL & ELLIGETT, PROFESSIONAL ASSOCIATION
Tampa, FL ....Civil Trial Practice

SCHUBERT, BELLWOAR, MALLON & WALHEIM
Philadelphia, PA ....General Practice; Probate, Trusts and Estate Planning

SCHUCHARDT, ROBERT G.
San Francisco, CA ....General Practice

SCHUERING ZIMMERMAN & SCULLY, LLP
Sacramento, CA ....Insurance Defense; Medical Malpractice; Product
Liability Law

SCHULLER & MILLS
Tulsa, OK ....General Practice; Municipal and Zoning Law; Real
Estate Law

SCHULMAN, LEROY AND BENNETT, P.C.
Nashville, TN ....General Practice

SCHULMAN & MCMILLAN, INCORPORATED
Costa Mesa, CA ....Criminal Trial Practice

SCHULTEN, WARD & TURNER
Atlanta, GA ....Business Law; Civil Trial Practice; Insurance
Defense; Labor and Employment Law

SCHULTE ROTH & ZABEL LLP
New York, NY......................Civil Trial Practice; Criminal Trial Practice; General
Practice

SCHULTE, THOMAS J., P.A.
Jupiter, FL..............................Civil Trial Practice; Insurance Defense; Medical
Malpractice; Personal Injury

SCHULTZ, JACK M., P.C.
Southfield, MI ....Employment Benefits Law; Tax Law

SCHUMACHER, STEPHEN J.
Irvine, CA................................Tax Law

SCHUMAN, BUTZ & BABCOCK, P.C.
Toms River, NJ......................Civil Trial Practice; General Practice; Insurance
Defense

SCHUREMAN, FRAKES, GLASS & WULFMEIER
Detroit, MI..............................Civil Trial Practice; Family Law; General Practice;
Insurance Defense; Medical Malpractice; Personal
Injury

**SCHWALB, DONNENFELD, BRAY & SILBERT, A PROFESSIONAL
CORPORATION**
Washington, DC......................Civil Trial Practice; Criminal Trial Practice

SCHWARTZ, THEODORE F.
Clayton, MO ....Commercial Litigation

SCHWARTZ, ARTHUR M., P.C.
Denver, CO ....Civil Rights; Criminal Trial Practice

SCHWARTZ & BLACKMAN
Philadelphia, PA......................Civil Trial Practice

SCHWARTZ, BON, WALKER & STUDER, LLC
Casper, WY ....Business Law; Civil Trial Practice; Personal Injury

SCHWARTZ, CAMPBELL & OATHOUT, L.L.P.
Houston, TX ....Admiralty/Maritime Law; Appellate Practice;
Business Law; Civil Trial Practice; Commercial Law;
Construction Law; Insurance Defense; Labor and
Employment Law

SCHWARTZ AND ELLIS, LTD.
Arlington, VA ....Civil Trial Practice; Family Law; International
Business Law; Medical Malpractice; Personal Injury

SCHWARTZ & JALKANEN, P.C.
Southfield, MI ....Civil Trial Practice; Insurance Defense; Medical
Malpractice; Personal Injury; Product Liability Law

SCHWARTZ, JOHN B., & ASSOCIATES
Chicago, IL..............................Medical Malpractice; Personal Injury

SCHWARTZ, MANES & RUBY, A LEGAL PROFESSIONAL ASSOCIATION
Cincinnati, OH ....Business Law; General Practice; Probate, Trusts and
Estate Planning; Tax Law

SCHWARTZ & SCHWARTZ
Media, PA ....Personal Injury
Hallettsville, TX......................Personal Injury

SCHWARTZ SIMON EDELSTEIN CELSO & KESSLER
Florham Park, NJ ....Civil Trial Practice; Commercial Law; Family Law;
Health Care Law; Labor and Employment Law

SCHWARTZ, STEINSAPIR, DOHRMANN & SOMMERS
Los Angeles, CA ....Civil Trial Practice; Employment Benefits Law;
Labor and Employment Law; Real Estate Law

SCHWARTZ, WISOT & WILSON, LLP
Beverly Hills, CA....................Business Law; Civil Trial Practice; Real Estate Law

SCHWARTZBACH, M. GERALD
Redwood City, CA ....Criminal Trial Practice; Labor and Employment
Law; Personal Injury

SCHWARTZBERG, BARNETT & COHEN
Chicago, IL..............................Appellate Practice; Business Law; Civil Rights;
Commercial Law; Construction Law; Family Law;
General Practice; Health Care Law; Probate, Trusts
and Estate Planning; Real Estate Law

SCHWARTZMAN, JAMES C., & ASSOCIATES, P.C.
Philadelphia, PA ....Civil Trial Practice; Commercial Litigation; Criminal
Trial Practice

SCHWARZ & KAHLE, P.A.
Port Charlotte, FL ....Commercial Litigation; Real Estate Law

SCHWARZSTEIN, RICHARD J.
Newport Beach, CA ....General Practice

**SCOBLIONKO, SCOBLIONKO, MUIR & BARTHOLOMEW, A PROFES-
SIONAL CORPORATION**
Allentown, PA ....General Practice

SCOFIELD, MICHAEL S. LAW OFFICES OF
Charlotte, NC........................Criminal Trial Practice

**SCOFIELD, GERARD, VERON, SINGLETARY & POHORELSKY, A PROFES-
SIONAL LAW CORPORATION**
Lake Charles, LA....................Civil Trial Practice; General Practice

SCOTT & AYLEN
Ottawa, ON, Canada ....Administrative Law; Business Law; Civil Trial
Practice; Commercial Litigation; Labor and
Employment Law; Patent, Trademark, Copyright
and Unfair Competition; Real Estate Law; Securities
Law; Tax Law
Toronto, ON, Canada..............Administrative Law; Civil Trial Practice; Labor and
Employment Law; Patent, Trademark, Copyright
and Unfair Competition

SCOTT, HULSE, MARSHALL, FEUILLE, FINGER & THURMOND, P.C.
El Paso, TX ....General Practice

SCOTT, RICHARD S., P.C.
Pittsburgh, PA ....Probate, Trusts and Estate Planning

**SCOTT, ROYCE, HARRIS, BRYAN, BARRA & JORGENSEN, PROFESSIONAL
ASSOCIATION**
Palm Beach Gardens, FL.........Civil Trial Practice; Environmental Law; General
Practice; Natural Resources Law

SCRUGGS, JORDAN, DODD & DODD, P.A.
Fort Payne, AL ....Banking Law; Civil Trial Practice; General Practice;
Insurance Defense; Personal Injury

SCULLY, SCOTT, MURPHY & PRESSER, A PROFESSIONAL CORPORATION
Garden City, NY ....Patent, Trademark, Copyright and Unfair Competition

SEALE, SMITH, ZUBER & BARNETTE
Baton Rouge, LA....................Civil Trial Practice; Commercial Law; Insurance
Defense; Personal Injury

**SEARCY DENNEY SCAROLA BARNHART & SHIPLEY, PROFESSIONAL
ASSOCIATION**
West Palm Beach, FL..............Civil Trial Practice; Commercial Law; General
Practice; Medical Malpractice; Personal Injury;
Product Liability Law

SEARS, M.H., THE, LAW FIRM
Washington, DC......................Patent, Trademark, Copyright and Unfair Competition

SEBALY, SHILLITO & DYER, A LEGAL PROFESSIONAL ASSOCIATION
Dayton, OH............................Bankruptcy Law; Business Law; Civil Trial Practice;
Environmental Law; Health Care Law; Labor and
Employment Law; Mergers and Acquisitions;
Securities Law

SECOR, CASSIDY & MCPARTLAND, P.C.
Southbury, CT........................Appellate Practice; General Practice
Waterbury, CT ....Appellate Practice; General Practice

SECREST, HILL & FOLLUO
Tulsa, OK................................Insurance Defense; Medical Malpractice; Product
Liability Law

SEDER & CHANDLER
Worcester, MA......................Bankruptcy Law; Business Law; Civil Trial Practice;
Probate, Trusts and Estate Planning; Tax Law

SEDGWICK, DETERT, MORAN & ARNOLD
San Francisco, CA ....General Practice

SEDIVY, BENNETT & WHITE, P.C. PROFESSIONAL CORPORATION
Bozeman, MT..........................General Practice

SEDWICK, EDWIN S. LAW OFFICE OF
Jeffersonville, IN ....Personal Injury

SEED, MACKALL & COLE LLP
Santa Barbara, CA..................Business Law; Commercial Litigation; Probate,
Trusts and Estate Planning; Real Estate Law

SEELEY, SAVIDGE AND AUSSEM, A LEGAL PROFESSIONAL ASSOCIATION
Cleveland, OH........................Civil Trial Practice; Commercial Law; Environ-
mental Law; Family Law; General Practice;
Insurance Defense; Labor and Employment Law;
Municipal and Zoning Law; Probate, Trusts and
Estate Planning; Real Estate Law; Securities Law

SEGAL & MCMAHAN, CHARTERED, A PROF. CORP.
Las Vegas, NV ....Bankruptcy Law; Probate, Trusts and Estate Planning; Tax Law

SEGAL AND SHANKS
Louisville, KY ....Insurance Defense

SEHAM SEHAM MELTZ & PETERSEN
New York, NY ....Labor and Employment Law; Public Utilities Law

SEID, GERALD P.
Skillman, NJ............................General Practice

SEIDEL, GONDA, LAVORGNA & MONACO, P.C.
Philadelphia, PA ....Computer Law; Patent, Trademark, Copyright and Unfair Competition

SEIDEN, MARK, P.A.
Miami, FL ....Criminal Trial Practice

SEIDMAN, SILVERMAN & SEIDMAN, P.C.
New York, NY........................Appellate Practice; Business Law; Civil Trial Practice; Criminal Trial Practice; Tax Law; Trademark, Copyright and Unfair Competition

SEILER, COHN & STEBBINS, L.L.P.
Houston, TX ....Banking Law; Bankruptcy Law; Business Law; Civil Trial Practice; Labor and Employment Law; Natural Resources Law; Real Estate Law

SEILLER & HANDMAKER, LLP
Louisville, KY ....Bankruptcy Law; Business Law; Civil Trial Practice; Criminal Trial Practice; Family Law; General Practice; Labor and Employment Law; Personal Injury; Trademark, Copyright and Unfair Competition; Workers Compensation

SEITELMAN, MARK E. LAW OFFICES
New York, NY ....Personal Injury

SELBY, EARL NICHOLAS
Palo Alto, CA ....Public Utilities Law

SELF, GIDDENS & LEES, INC.
Oklahoma City, OK................Banking Law; Bankruptcy Law; Civil Trial Practice; Commercial Law; Natural Resources Law; Real Estate Law

SELF & SELF
Florence, AL ....Civil Trial Practice; Commercial Law; Personal Injury
Tuscumbia, AL........................Civil Trial Practice; Commercial Law

SELKER & FURBER
Cleveland, OH ....Business Law; Civil Trial Practice; Real Estate Law

SELLAR, RICHARDSON, STUART & CHISHOLM, P.C.
Roseland, NJ............................Appellate Practice; Civil Trial Practice; Insurance Defense; Product Liability Law

SELL & MELTON
Macon, GA ....Banking Law; Bankruptcy Law; Business Law; Civil Trial Practice; General Practice; Health Care Law; Municipal Bond/Public Authority Financing; Personal Injury; Workers Compensation

SELMAN ● BREITMAN
Los Angeles, CA ....Civil Trial Practice; Construction Law; Insurance Defense; Personal Injury

SELTZER CAPLAN WILKINS & MCMAHON, A PROFESSIONAL CORPORATION
San Diego, CA ....Antitrust Law; Civil Trial Practice; Criminal Trial Practice; General Practice; Tax Law

SELTZER LAW GROUP
San Francisco, CA ....Construction Law

SELTZER AND ROSEN, P.C.
Washington, DC......................Construction Law

SEMMES, BOWEN & SEMMES, A PROFESSIONAL CORPORATION
Baltimore, MD ....General Practice

SEMON & MONDSHEIN
Woodbury, NY........................Commercial Litigation

SEMPLE & JACKSON, P.C.
Denver, CO ....Labor and Employment Law

SEMPLINER, THOMAS AND BOAK
Plymouth, MI ....Civil Trial Practice; Real Estate Law

SENN LEWIS VISCIANO & STRAHLE, PROFESSIONAL CORPORATION
Denver, CO ....Appellate Practice; Business Law; Commercial Law; Commercial Litigation; General Practice; Real Estate Law

SEPARK, W. ALLEN
Marietta, GA............................Business Law; Probate, Trusts and Estate Planning; Tax Law

SERCHUK & ZELERMYER, LLP
White Plains, NY ....Banking Law

SERKO & SIMON
New York, NY ....International Business Law; Transportation Law

SERLING, MICHAEL B., P.C.
Birmingham, MI......................Personal Injury

SERVICE, GASSER & KERL
Pocatello, ID ....General Practice

SESSIONS & FISHMAN, L.L.P.
New Orleans, LA ....General Practice

SESSIONS & SESSIONS, L.C.
San Antonio, TX....................Business Law; Civil Trial Practice

SESSUMS & MASON, P.A.
Tampa, FL ....Family Law

SESTRIC LAW FIRM, THE
St. Louis, MO........................Appellate Practice; Civil Trial Practice

SETTLE & POU, P.C.
Dallas, TX..............................Real Estate Law

SEVERS, STADLER & HARRIS, P.A.
Titusville, FL..........................General Practice

SEVERSON & WERSON, A PROFESSIONAL CORPORATION
San Francisco, CA ....General Practice

SEVIER & PHILLIPS, P.C.
Memphis, TN ....Family Law; General Practice; Insurance Defense

SEWARD & KISSEL
Washington, DC......................General Practice
New York, NY ....General Practice

SEWARD, TALLY & PIGGOTT, P.C.
Bay City, MI ....General Practice

SEYFARTH, SHAW, FAIRWEATHER & GERALDSON
Chicago, IL..............................General Practice

SHACKELFORD, HONENBERGER, THOMAS, WILLIS & GREGG, P.L.C.
Orange, VA ....Civil Trial Practice; Criminal Trial Practice; General Practice; Personal Injury; Probate, Trusts and Estate Planning; Real Estate Law

SHACKLEFORD, FARRIOR, STALLINGS & EVANS, PROFESSIONAL ASSOCIATION
Tampa, FL ....General Practice

SHACKLEFORD, PHILLIPS, WINELAND & RATCLIFF, P.A.
El Dorado, AR ....General Practice

SHACKLETON, HAZELTINE AND BISHOP
Ship Bottom, NJ ....Admiralty/Maritime Law; Civil Trial Practice; General Practice; Insurance Defense; Product Liability Law

SHACK & SIEGEL, P.C.
New York, NY........................Business Law; Commercial Law; Labor and Employment Law; Probate, Trusts and Estate Planning; Real Estate Law; Securities Law; Trademark, Copyright and Unfair Competition

SHAFER, DAVIS, ASHLEY, O'LEARY & STOKER, A PROFESSIONAL CORPORATION
Odessa, TX..............................General Practice

SHAFER, SWICK, BAILEY, IRWIN, STACK & MILLIN
Meadville, PA..........................General Practice

SHAFFER & CULBERTSON
Austin, TX ....Patent, Trademark, Copyright and Unfair Competition

SHAFFER AND SHAFFER
Madison, WV ....Civil Trial Practice; General Practice; Insurance Defense; Personal Injury; Real Estate Law

SHAFT, REIS, SHAFT & SOGARD, LTD.
Grand Forks, ND ....General Practice

SHAHEEN, JACOBS & ROSS, P.C.
Detroit, MI..............................Banking Law; Commercial Law; Real Estate Law

SHAIN, SCHAFFER & RAFANELLO, A PROFESSIONAL CORPORATION
Bernardsville, NJ......................Banking Law; General Practice; Real Estate Law

SHAINES & MCEACHERN, PROFESSIONAL ASSOCIATION
Portsmouth, NH ....Business Law; Civil Trial Practice; General Practice

SHALHOUB, ROBERT M.W., P.A., LAW OFFICES OF
West Palm Beach, FL ....Family Law

SHAMBAUGH, KAST, BECK & WILLIAMS
Fort Wayne, IN......................Civil Trial Practice; General Practice; Probate, Trusts and Estate Planning; Tax Law

SHAMBERG, JOHNSON & BERGMAN, CHARTERED
Overland Park, KS..................Civil Trial Practice; Environmental Law; Medical Malpractice; Personal Injury; Product Liability Law

SHAMBERG MARWELL HOCHERMAN DAVIS & HOLLIS, P.C.
Mount Kisco, NY....................General Practice

SHAMBERG, WOLF, MCDERMOTT & DEPUÉ
Grand Island, NE....................General Practice

SHAMEL, C. RICHARD JR.
Deerfield Beach, FL................Probate, Trusts and Estate Planning

SHANE, MICHAEL, P.A., LAW OFFICES OF
Miami, FL..............................Immigration and Naturalization

SHANKLIN & MCDANIEL, L.L.P.
Wilmington, NC.....................Real Estate Law

SHANLEY & FISHER, A PROFESSIONAL CORPORATION
Morristown, NJ......................Banking Law; Bankruptcy Law; Civil Trial Practice; Environmental Law; General Practice; Labor and Employment Law; Real Estate Law; Tax Law

SHANLEY, SWEENEY, REILLY & ALLEN, P.C.
Albany, NY...........................Environmental Law; General Practice; Municipal Bond/Public Authority Financing; Municipal and Zoning Law; Real Estate Law

SHAPIRO, WILLIAM D. LAW OFFICES OF
San Bernardino, CA................Personal Injury

SHAPIRO & ASSOCIATES
Boston, MA............................Insurance Defense; Personal Injury

SHAPIRO, COHEN
Ottawa, ON, Canada ....Patent, Trademark, Copyright and Unfair Competition

SHAPIRO, FUSSELL, WEDGE, SMOTHERMAN & MARTIN
Atlanta, GA ....Commercial Litigation; Construction Law; Labor and Employment Law

SHAPIRO, ROSENFELD & CLOSE, A PROFESSIONAL CORPORATION
Los Angeles, CA.....................Business Law; Patent, Trademark, Copyright and Unfair Competition; Securities Law

SHAPIRO AND SHAPIRO
Arlington, VA ....Patent, Trademark, Copyright and Unfair Competition
Vineland, NJ...........................Civil Trial Practice; Criminal Trial Practice; General Practice

SHARLOCK, REPCHECK & MAHLER
Pittsburgh, PA ....Civil Trial Practice; General Practice

SHARP, CHRISTOPHER G., P.C.
Dallas, TX..............................Administrative Law; Health Care Law; Real Estate Law

SHARP & SMITH, P.A.
Tampa, FL ....International Business Law; Tax Law

SHARP, TERRY, P.C., LAW OFFICE OF
Mount Vernon, IL ....Bankruptcy Law; Commercial Law; Real Estate Law

SHARPE & KRUEGER
Kingsville, TX ....General Practice

SHARPNACK, BIGLEY, DAVID & RUMPLE
Columbus, IN.........................Civil Trial Practice; Family Law; General Practice; Insurance Defense; Probate, Trusts and Estate Planning

SHARRETTS, PALEY, CARTER & BLAUVELT, P.C.
Washington, DC......................International Trade Law
New York, NY........................International Trade Law

SHARTSIS, FRIESE & GINSBURG, LLP
San Francisco, CA ....General Practice

SHATZ, SCHWARTZ AND FENTIN, P.C.
Springfield, MA......................Probate, Trusts and Estate Planning

SHAW & ASSOCIATES, A PROFESSIONAL CORPORATION
Houston, TX ....Real Estate Law

SHAW, BRANSFORD & O'ROURKE, A PROFESSIONAL CORPORATION
Washington, DC......................Labor and Employment Law

SHAW, LEDBETTER, HORNBERGER, COGBILL & ARNOLD
Fort Smith, AR.......................General Practice; Insurance Defense; Medical Malpractice; Product Liability Law; Workers Compensation

SHAW, LICITRA, ESERNIO & SCHWARTZ, P.C.
Garden City, NY ....Appellate Practice; Bankruptcy Law; General Practice

SHAW, MADDOX, GRAHAM, MONK & BOLING
Rome, GA ....Civil Trial Practice; General Practice

SHAW, WEAVER, COLVIN & HENRY, L.L.C.
Homer, LA ....Civil Trial Practice

SHAWE & ROSENTHAL
Baltimore, MD ....Labor and Employment Law

SHAWN, MANN & NIEDERMAYER, L.L.P.
Washington, DC......................Bankruptcy Law; Civil Trial Practice; Commercial Law; International Business Law; Trademark, Copyright and Unfair Competition; Transportation Law

SHAY & SLOCUM
New Haven, CT ....Civil Trial Practice; Insurance Defense

SHAYNE, DACHS, STANISCI, CORKER & SAUER
Mineola, NY...........................Insurance Defense; Medical Malpractice; Personal Injury

SHEA & ASSOCIATES
Cincinnati, OH ....Civil Trial Practice; Medical Malpractice; Personal Injury; Product Liability Law

SHEA & GARDNER
Washington, DC......................General Practice

SHEA AND SHEA
Bryn Mawr, PA ....Probate, Trusts and Estate Planning; Real Estate Law

SHEA & SHEA, A PROFESSIONAL LAW CORPORATION
San Jose, CA ....Civil Trial Practice; Personal Injury; Product Liability Law

SHEAHAN, ROBERT E. & ASSOCIATES
High Point, NC.......................Labor and Employment Law

SHEAR, NEWMAN, HAHN AND ROSENKRANZ, P.A.
Tampa, FL ....Commercial Litigation; General Practice; Health Care Law; Insurance Defense; Real Estate Law

SHEARER, TEMPLER & PINGEL, A PROFESSIONAL CORPORATION
Des Moines, IA ....Commercial Law; Construction Law; General Practice; Labor and Employment Law

SHEARMAN & STERLING
Los Angeles, CA.....................General Practice
San Francisco, CA ....General Practice
Washington, DC......................General Practice
New York, NY........................General Practice
Beijing (Peking), People's Republic of China ....General Practice
London, England ....General Practice
Paris, France...........................General Practice
Düsseldorf, Germany ....General Practice
Frankfurt/Main, Germany ......General Practice
Hong Kong, Hong Kong.........General Practice
Budapest, Hungary ....General Practice
Tokyo, Japan ....General Practice
Singapore, Singapore...............General Practice
Abu Dhabi, United Arab Emirates..................................General Practice

SHEEHAN, BARNETT & HAYS, P.S.C.
Danville, KY ....Insurance Defense; Personal Injury; Real Estate Law

SHEEHAN PHINNEY BASS + GREEN, PROFESSIONAL ASSOCIATION
Manchester, NH......................Commercial Law; Environmental Law; General Practice; Insurance Defense; Labor and Employment Law; Personal Injury; Product Liability Law; Securities Law; Tax Law
Portsmouth, NH ....Labor and Employment Law; Tax Law

SHEEHAN, SHEEHAN & STELZNER, P.A.
Albuquerque, NM...................Civil Trial Practice; Commercial Litigation; Construction Law; Insurance Defense; Personal Injury; Real Estate Law

SHEEHEY BRUE GRAY & FURLONG, PROFESSIONAL CORPORATION
Burlington, VT ....Banking Law; Civil Trial Practice; Environmental Law; General Practice; Health Care Law; Real Estate Law; Securities Law; Tax Law

SHEEHY, LOVELACE & MAYFIELD, P.C. A PROFESSIONAL CORPORATION
Waco, TX ....General Practice

SHEETZ, WILLIAM D.
Dallas, TX..............................Criminal Trial Practice

SHEFFER ● HOFFMAN
Henderson, KY ....General Practice

Owensboro, KY ....General Practice
Paducah, KY..........................General Practice

SHEFFERLY & SILVERMAN
West Bloomfield, MI ....Bankruptcy Law; Commercial Law

SHEFT, GOLUB & KAMLET
New York, NY......................Environmental Law; Insurance Defense; Medical
Malpractice; Product Liability Law

SHEFTE, PINCKNEY & SAWYER, L.L.P.
Charlotte, NC.........................Patent, Trademark, Copyright and Unfair Competition; Trademark, Copyright and Unfair Competition

SHEIMAN, RONALD L.
Westport, CT..........................Business Law; Probate, Trusts and Estate Planning; Tax Law

SHEKETOFF & HOMAN
Boston, MA.............................Criminal Trial Practice

SHELL, BUFORD, BUFKIN, CALLICUTT & PERRY
Jackson, MS ....Civil Trial Practice; Insurance Defense

SHELLER, LUDWIG & BADEY, A PROFESSIONAL CORPORATION
Philadelphia, PA ....Labor and Employment Law; Medical Malpractice; Personal Injury; Product Liability Law

SHELL, FLEMING, DAVIS & MENGE, P.A.
Pensacola, FL ....General Practice

SHELLOW, SHELLOW & GLYNN, S.C.
Milwaukee, WI ....Criminal Trial Practice

SHEPARD, FILBURN & GOODBLATT, P.A.
Orlando, FL ....Civil Trial Practice; Commercial Law; Commercial Litigation; Construction Law; Insurance Defense

SHEPHERD, GARY & MCWHORTER
Swainsboro, GA......................General Practice; Insurance Defense

SHEPPARD, BRETT, STEWART & HERSCH, P.A.
Fort Myers, FL ....General Practice; Probate, Trusts and Estate Planning; Real Estate Law

SHEPPARD, MULLIN, RICHTER & HAMPTON LLP
Los Angeles, CA.....................Antitrust Law; Banking Law; Environmental Law; Labor and Employment Law; Land Use Law; Real Estate Law; Securities Law; Tax Law

SHEPPARD & WHITE, P.A.
Jacksonville, FL ....Criminal Trial Practice

SHERBURNE, POWERS & NEEDHAM, P.C.
Boston, MA.............................Banking Law; Bankruptcy Law; Business Law; Commercial Law; Construction Law; Criminal Trial Practice; Family Law; General Practice; Labor and Employment Law; Municipal and Zoning Law; Patent, Trademark, Copyright and Unfair Competition; Personal Injury; Probate, Trusts and Estate Planning; Real Estate Law; Tax Law

SHERIN AND LODGEN LLP
Boston, MA.............................Business Law; Civil Trial Practice; General Practice; Real Estate Law

SHERMAN, WILLIAM F.
Little Rock, AR ....General Practice

SHERMAN & HOWARD, L.L.C.
Colorado Springs, CO.............General Practice
Denver, CO ....Antitrust Law; Banking Law; Civil Trial Practice; General Practice; Labor and Employment Law; Municipal Bond/Public Authority Financing; Natural Resources Law; Probate, Trusts and Estate Planning; Tax Law

SHERMAN, MEEHAN, CURTIN & AIN, A PROFESSIONAL CORPORATION
Washington, DC......................General Practice

SHERMAN & SHALLOWAY
Alexandria, VA ....Patent, Trademark, Copyright and Unfair Competition

SHERMAN, SILVERSTEIN, KOHL, ROSE & PODOLSKY, A PROFESSIONAL CORPORATION
Pennsauken, NJ......................General Practice

SHERMAN, STEPHEN A., & ASSOCIATES
Oklahoma City, OK................Commercial Law; Real Estate Law

SHERMETA, CHIMKO AND KILPATRICK, P.C.
Rochester, MI ....Bankruptcy Law; Commercial Law

SHERRARD & ROE, PLC
Nashville, TN..........................Commercial Law; Securities Law

SHERRILL, CROSNOE & GOFF, A PROFESSIONAL CORPORATION
Wichita Falls, TX....................General Practice

SHERRILL & ROOF, L.L.P.
Columbia, SC ....Banking Law; Business Law; Probate, Trusts and Estate Planning; Public Utilities Law

SHERWOOD AND HARDGROVE
Los Angeles, CA ....Real Estate Law

SHERWOOD, KLEIN, DUDLEY & ABRAM, P.A.
Phoenix, AZ ....Commercial Litigation; Personal Injury

SHIBLEY RIGHTON
Toronto, ON, Canada..............General Practice

SHIELDS LAW OFFICE, P.A.
St. John, KS ....General Practice

SHIGLEY, KENNETH L.
Atlanta, GA ....Personal Injury; Product Liability Law

SHILOBOD & BALL, P.C.
Pittsburgh, PA ....Construction Law; Public Utilities Law

SHIMKO, TIMOTHY A., & ASSOCIATES, A LEGAL PROF. ASSN.
Cleveland, OH.........................Antitrust Law; Civil Trial Practice; Labor and Employment Law; Medical Malpractice; Personal Injury; Product Liability Law

SHIMMEL, HILL, BISHOP & GRUENDER, P.C.
Phoenix, AZ ....Bankruptcy Law; Commercial Litigation; Employment Benefits Law; Family Law; Insurance Defense; Labor and Employment Law; Real Estate Law; Tax Law

SHINE & MASON LAW OFFICE
Kingsport, TN.........................General Practice; Labor and Employment Law

SHINGLES & CAPPELLI
Plymouth Meeting, PA ....Appellate Practice; Civil Trial Practice; Criminal Trial Practice; Personal Injury

SHINN LAWYERS
Lamar, CO ....General Practice; Probate, Trusts and Estate Planning

SHIOTANI & INOUYE
Los Angeles, CA ....Business Law; Probate, Trusts and Estate Planning; Real Estate Law; Tax Law

SHIPLEY & ASSOCIATES
Fort Wayne, IN.......................Bankruptcy Law; Commercial Law

SHIPLEY & HORNE, P.A.
Largo, MD ....Administrative Law; Civil Trial Practice; Workers Compensation

SHIPLEY, JENNINGS & CHAMPLIN, P.C.
Tulsa, OK................................Civil Trial Practice; Environmental Law

SHIPMAN, DIXON & LIVINGSTON CO., L.P.A.
Troy, OH.................................Civil Trial Practice; General Practice; Insurance Defense

SHIPMAN & GOODWIN LLP
Hartford, CT ....Environmental Law; General Practice; Labor and Employment Law; Probate, Trusts and Estate Planning
Lakeville, CT ....General Practice
Stamford, CT...........................General Practice

SHIRK, WORK, ROBINSON & WORK, A PROFESSIONAL CORPORATION
Oklahoma City, OK................General Practice

SHIVER, FREDERICK H., A PROFESSIONAL CORPORATION
Dallas, TX...............................Civil Trial Practice; Personal Injury; Product Liability Law

SHOCKEY & ZIOBER, A PROFESSIONAL LAW CORPORATION
Baton Rouge, LA....................Bankruptcy Law; Civil Trial Practice; Environmental Law; Insurance Defense; Workers Compensation

SHOECRAFT, JAMES W., P.C., ATTORNEYS' OFFICES OF
Dallas, TX...............................Personal Injury

SHOFI, SMITH, HENNEN & GRAMOVOT, P.A.
Tampa, FL ....Health Care Law; Insurance Defense; Workers Compensation

SHOOK, HARDY & BACON L.L.P
Kansas City, MO ....General Practice

SHOR, FRANK LAW OFFICES OF
Carrollton, TX ....General Practice

SHORR, DAVID I.
Framingham, MA ....Bankruptcy Law; Commercial Litigation; Personal Injury

SHORT, KEVIN J.
Minneapolis, MN ....Criminal Trial Practice

SHORT & BORTH
Overland Park, KS..................Family Law

SHORT, GENTRY & BISHOP, P.A.
Fort Scott, KS........................General Practice

SHORT, GEORGE G., A PROFESSIONAL CORPORATION
Santa Barbara, CA.................Probate, Trusts and Estate Planning; Tax Law

SHORTRIDGE, DOUGLASS R.
Indianapolis, IN......................Personal Injury

SHOSS & ASSOCIATES
Houston, TX ....Mergers and Acquisitions; Securities Law

SHOUN & BACH, P.C.
Fairfax, VA ....Family Law

SHRADER AND KNAPP, A PROFESSIONAL CORPORATION
Westport, CT..........................Civil Trial Practice

SHRAGER, MCDAID, LOFTUS, FLUM & SPIVEY
Philadelphia, PA ....Personal Injury

SHUEY & SMITH
Shreveport, LA........................General Practice

SHUFORD & CADDELL
Salisbury, NC ....General Practice

SHUGHART THOMSON & KILROY, A PROFESSIONAL CORPORATION
Overland Park, KS..................General Practice
Kansas City, MO....................Antitrust Law; Civil Trial Practice; General Practice;
Labor and Employment Law

SHULLAW, WAYNE A.
Lafayette, LA ....Commercial Law

SHULL, COSGROVE, HELLIGE & LUNDBERG
Sioux City, IA ....General Practice; Probate, Trusts and Estate
Planning

SHULMAN, ROGERS, GANDAL, PORDY & ECKER, P.A.
Rockville, MD.........................Civil Trial Practice; Commercial Law; General
Practice

SHULTZ & ROLLINS, LTD.
Tucson, AZ ....Civil Trial Practice; Personal Injury

SHUMAKER, LOOP & KENDRICK LLP
Toledo, OH ....General Practice

SHUMAKER WILLIAMS, A PROFESSIONAL CORPORATION
Harrisburg, PA........................Banking Law

SHUMAN, MARK D.
Boston, MA.............................Civil Trial Practice

SHUMAN, ANNAND & POE
Charleston, WV.......................Appellate Practice; Business Law; Construction
Law; General Practice; Insurance Defense; Medical
Malpractice; Product Liability Law

SHUMARD, THOMAS J.
Phoenix, AZ ....Probate, Trusts and Estate Planning

SHUMATE, FLAHERTY & EUBANKS
Richmond, KY.........................Criminal Trial Practice; General Practice

SHUPE, R. Q., LAW OFFICES OF
Santa Ana, CA ....Insurance Defense

SHUSTERMAN, CARL LAW OFFICES OF
Los Angeles, CA....................Immigration and Naturalization

SHUTTLEWORTH & INGERSOLL, P.C.
Cedar Rapids, IA....................Administrative Law; Banking Law; Civil Trial
Practice; General Practice; Insurance Defense; Labor
and Employment Law; Patent, Trademark,
Copyright and Unfair Competition; Probate, Trusts
and Estate Planning; Real Estate Law; Tax Law

SHUTTLEWORTH RULOFF & GIORDANO, P.C.
Virginia Beach, VA ....Criminal Trial Practice; Medical Malpractice;
Personal Injury; Product Liability Law

SHUTTLEWORTH, SMITH, MCNABB & WILLIAMS, PLLC
Memphis, TN ....Medical Malpractice; Personal Injury; Product
Liability Law

SHUTTS & BOWEN
Miami, FL ....Admiralty/Maritime Law; Antitrust Law; General
Practice; Tax Law
Orlando, FL ....General Practice
West Palm Beach, FL..............General Practice

SIBLEY, THOMAS J., P.C.
Beaumont, TX.........................Commercial Law

SICHOL & HICKS, P.C.
Suffern, NY ....General Practice; Personal Injury

SIDKOFF, PINCUS & GREEN, P.C.
Philadelphia, PA ....Civil Trial Practice

SIDLEY, MICHAEL I.
Los Angeles, CA....................Criminal Trial Practice

SIDLEY & AUSTIN
Los Angeles, CA....................General Practice
Washington, DC.....................General Practice
Chicago, IL.............................General Practice
New York, NY........................General Practice
Dallas, TX...............................General Practice
London, England ....General Practice
Tokyo, Japan...........................General Practice

SIEBEN, GROSE, VON HOLTUM, MCCOY & CAREY, LTD.
Minneapolis, MN....................Medical Malpractice; Personal Injury; Workers
Compensation

SIEBEN, POLK, LAVERDIERE, JONES & HAWN, A PROFESSIONAL ASSOCIATION
Hastings, MN..........................Civil Trial Practice; Personal Injury

SIEGEL, BRILL, GREUPNER & DUFFY, P.A.
Minneapolis, MN....................Antitrust Law; Civil Trial Practice; General Practice;
Land Use Law

SIEGEL, HESTER, STEPHENS, KAHLER & MANION
Utica, NY ....General Practice

SIEGEL, MANDELL & DAVIDSON, P.C.
New York, NY........................Administrative Law; Business Law; International
Trade Law

SIEGEL, MOSES, SCHOENSTADT & WEBSTER, P.C.
Chicago, IL.............................Administrative Law; Commercial Litigation; Constitutional Law; International Business Law

SIEGEL, O'CONNOR, SCHIFF & ZANGARI, P.C.
Hartford, CT ....Labor and Employment Law; Tax Law
New Haven, CT ....Labor and Employment Law; Tax Law

SIEGEL, SOMMERS & SCHWARTZ L.L.P.
New York, NY........................Bankruptcy Law

SIEGFRIED, RIVERA, LERNER DE LA TORRE & SOBEL, P.A.
Miami, FL ....Commercial Law; Construction Law; Real Estate
Law

SIGERMAN & WEGLEY
San Francisco, CA ....Labor and Employment Law

SIGMON, CLARK, MACKIE & HUTTON, P.A.
Hickory, NC............................Civil Trial Practice; General Practice; Real Estate
Law

SIKORA AND PRICE, INCORPORATED
Irvine, CA...............................General Practice

SILBERT, MARC M.
Philadelphia, PA ....Employment Benefits Law

SILK, ADLER & COLVIN, A LAW CORPORATION
San Francisco, CA ....Tax Law

SILLS, NANCY M.
Albany, NY ....Probate, Trusts and Estate Planning; Tax Law

SILLS CUMMIS ZUCKERMAN RADIN TISCHMAN EPSTEIN & GROSS, A PROFESSIONAL CORPORATION
Atlantic City, NJ.....................General Practice
Newark, NJ ....Administrative Law; Antitrust Law; Appellate
Practice; Banking Law; Bankruptcy Law; Business
Law; Civil Rights; Civil Trial Practice; Commercial
Law; Commercial Litigation; Communications Law;
Computer Law; Construction Law; Criminal Trial
Practice; Employment Benefits Law; Energy Law;
Environmental Law; Family Law; General Practice;
Health Care Law; Insurance Defense; International
Business Law; International Trade Law; Labor and
Employment Law; Land Use Law; Medical
Malpractice; Municipal Bond/Public Authority
Financing; Municipal and Zoning Law; Natural
Resources Law; Patent, Trademark, Copyright and
Unfair Competition; Personal Injury; Probate,
Trusts and Estate Planning; Product Liability Law;
Public Utilities Law; Real Estate Law; Securities
Law; Sports and Entertainment Law; Tax Law;
Transportation Law
New York, NY........................General Practice

SILLS, LAW, ESSAD, FIEDLER & CHARBONEAU, P.C.
Bloomfield Hills, MI...............Business Law

SILVER, GOLUB & TEITELL
Stamford, CT...........................Civil Trial Practice; Criminal Trial Practice; Family
Law; Medical Malpractice; Personal Injury; Product
Liability Law

SILVERMAN COOPERSMITH HILLMAN & FRIMMER, A PROFESSIONAL CORPORATION
Philadelphia, PA ....Banking Law; Insurance Defense; Real Estate Law

SILVERMAN & KUDISCH, P.C.
Boston, MA............................Bankruptcy Law; Business Law

SILVERS, SIMPSON & CREASY, P.C.
Savannah, GA ....Health Care Law; Probate, Trusts and Estate Planning; Tax Law

SILVERSTEIN AND MULLENS, P.L.L.C.
Washington, DC....................Tax Law

SILVER & VOIT, P.C.
Mobile, AL.............................Bankruptcy Law

SIM, HUGHES, ASHTON & MCKAY
Toronto, ON, Canada.............Computer Law; Patent, Trademark, Copyright and Unfair Competition

SIMKE CHODOS
Los Angeles, CA ....Civil Trial Practice; Commercial Litigation; Sports and Entertainment Law

SIMMONS, BRUNSON AND SASSER, ATTORNEYS, P.A.
Gadsden, AL............................Civil Trial Practice; Commercial Litigation; Insurance Defense; Product Liability Law

SIMMONS AND DERR
Winnfield, LA ....Banking Law; Civil Trial Practice; General Practice; Probate, Trusts and Estate Planning; Real Estate Law

SIMMONS AND FIELDS, P.A.
Baltimore, MD ....Insurance Defense

SIMMONS, HART & SHEEHE
Miami, FL ....Commercial Litigation; General Practice; International Business Law
Ocala, FL................................Commercial Litigation; General Practice; International Business Law

SIMMONS, OLSEN, EDIGER, SELZER, FERGUSON & CARNEY, P.C.
Scottsbluff, NE........................General Practice

SIMMONS, RITCHIE & SEGAL
Los Angeles, CA ....Probate, Trusts and Estate Planning; Tax Law

SIMMONS, WARREN, SZCZECKO & MCFEE, PROFESSIONAL ASSOCIATION
Decatur, GA............................Business Law; Civil Trial Practice; Family Law; General Practice; Real Estate Law; Tax Law

SIMON, HENRY R.
White Plains, NY ....General Practice

SIMON, J. STEPHEN
Scottsdale, AZ........................Probate, Trusts and Estate Planning

SIMON, FITZGERALD, COOKE, REED & WELCH
Shreveport, LA........................Bankruptcy Law; General Practice

SIMON, MCKINSEY, MILLER, ZOMMICK, SANDOR & DUNDAS, A LAW CORPORATION
Long Beach, CA.......................Probate, Trusts and Estate Planning

SIMON & SCHMIDT
Delray Beach, FL....................General Practice

SIMON AND SIMON
Kansas City, MO ....Criminal Trial Practice

SIMONDS, WINSLOW, WILLIS & ABBOTT, A PROFESSIONAL ASSOCIATION
Boston, MA............................Employment Benefits Law; General Practice; Probate, Trusts and Estate Planning; Real Estate Law

SIMONE, ROBERTS & WEISS, P.A.
Albuquerque, NM...................Insurance Defense

SIMONEAUX & CARLETON
Baton Rouge, LA....................Environmental Law

SIMPSON AYCOCK, P.A.
Morganton, NC........................General Practice

SIMPSON & GIGOUNAS
San Francisco, CA ....Tax Law

SIMPSON, KABLACK & BELL
Indiana, PA ....General Practice

SIMPSON, KEPLER & EDWARDS, L.C.
Cody, WY.................................General Practice; Probate, Trusts and Estate Planning

SIMPSON THACHER & BARTLETT
New York, NY.........................General Practice

Columbus, OH ....General Practice
London, England ....General Practice
Hong Kong, Hong Kong........General Practice
Tokyo, Japan..........................General Practice

SIMS, FLEMING & SPURLIN, P.C.
Tifton, GA...............................General Practice

SINCLAIR, I.B. LAW OFFICES
Media, PA ....Family Law

SINCLAIR, LOUIS, HEATH, NUSSBAUM & ZAVERTNIK, P.A.
Miami, FL ....Civil Trial Practice

SINDEL & SINDEL, P.C.
St. Louis, MO..........................Criminal Trial Practice; Personal Injury

SINGLETON, MURRAY, CRAVEN & INMAN, L.L.P.
Fayetteville, NC ....General Practice

SINGLETON & SINGLETON
Mount Kisco, NY ....General Practice; Municipal and Zoning Law; Real Estate Law

SINGLETON URQUHART SCOTT
Vancouver, BC, Canada..........Construction Law; General Practice; Insurance Defense

SINIARD, LAMAR & MCKINNEY, THE LAW FIRM OF
Huntsville, AL.........................Medical Malpractice; Personal Injury; Workers Compensation

SINKLER & BOYD, P.A.
Charleston, SC ....Admiralty/Maritime Law; Civil Trial Practice; General Practice; Municipal Bond/Public Authority Financing
Columbia, SC ....Admiralty/Maritime Law; Civil Trial Practice; General Practice; Municipal Bond/Public Authority Financing
Greenville, SC..........................Municipal Bond/Public Authority Financing

SINK, POWERS, SINK & POTTER, L.L.P.
Raleigh, NC.............................General Practice

SINOFF, BARRY S., P.A., LAW OFFICE OF
Jacksonville, FL ....Family Law

SIRKIN PINALES MEZIBOV & SCHWARTZ
Cincinnati, OH ....Civil Trial Practice; Criminal Trial Practice; Labor and Employment Law

SIRLIN, JON C., AND ASSOCIATES, A PROF. CORP.
Philadelphia, PA ....Civil Trial Practice

SIROTA & SIROTA
New York, NY.........................Securities Law

SIXBEY, FRIEDMAN, LEEDOM & FERGUSON, P.C.
McLean, VA.............................Patent, Trademark, Copyright and Unfair Competition

SKADDEN, ARPS, SLATE, MEAGHER & FLOM
Wilmington, DE......................General Practice
Washington, DC......................General Practice
New York, NY.........................Bankruptcy Law; Criminal Trial Practice; General Practice; Labor and Employment Law; Municipal Bond/Public Authority Financing

SKARECKY, CALES & HOLDER, A PROFESSIONAL ASSOCIATION
Phoenix, AZ ....Family Law

SKELLEY ROTTNER, P.C.
Hartford, CT ....Insurance Defense

SKELTON, TAINTOR & ABBOTT, A PROFESSIONAL CORPORATION
Auburn, ME............................General Practice

SKEMP, WILLIAM, LAW FIRM, S.C.
La Crosse, WI ....Insurance Defense; Personal Injury

SKIPPER & DAY
St. Petersburg, FL...................Commercial Law; Personal Injury

SKIRBUNT & SKIRBUNT
Cleveland, OH ....Family Law

SKJERVEN, MORRILL, MACPHERSON, FRANKLIN & FRIEL LLP
San Francisco, CA ....General Practice; Patent, Trademark, Copyright and Unfair Competition
San Jose, CA ....General Practice; Patent, Trademark, Copyright and Unfair Competition
Austin, TX ....Patent, Trademark, Copyright and Unfair Competition

SKOLER, ABBOTT & PRESSER, P.C.
Springfield, MA ....Labor and Employment Law
Worcester, MA ....Labor and Employment Law

SKOLOFF & WOLFE, P.C.
Livingston, NJ.........................Civil Trial Practice; Family Law; General Practice; Real Estate Law; Tax Law

SKORNIA LAW FIRM, THE
San Jose, CA ....Business Law

SKOUSEN, SKOUSEN, GULBRANDSEN & PATIENCE, P.C.
Mesa, AZ.................................Personal Injury

SLACK & DAVIS, L.L.P.
Austin, TX ....Aviation Law; Personal Injury; Product Liability Law

SLAFF, MOSK & RUDMAN
Los Angeles, CA ....Appellate Practice; Civil Trial Practice; Sports and Entertainment Law; Trademark, Copyright and Unfair Competition

SLAP, ALBERT J. LAW OFFICES OF
Plymouth Meeting, PA ....Environmental Law

SLATER, MILDRED FLETCHER
Upperville, VA ....Real Estate Law

SLATER LAW FIRM, A PROFESSIONAL CORPORATION
New Orleans, LA ....Antitrust Law; Business Law; Personal Injury; Product Liability Law; Transportation Law

SLATES, RONALD P., A PROFESSIONAL CORPORATION
Los Angeles, CA ....Bankruptcy Law; Business Law; Commercial Law; Real Estate Law

SLATTERY, HAUSMAN & HOEFLE, LTD.
Milwaukee, WI ....Civil Trial Practice; Personal Injury

SLAVET, ARNOLD L.
Boston, MA..............................Probate, Trusts and Estate Planning

SLAWSON & CUNNINGHAM
Palm Beach Gardens, FL.........Civil Trial Practice; Personal Injury

SLENKER, BRANDT, JENNINGS & JOHNSTON
Fairfax, VA ....General Practice

SLEVIN & HART, P.C.
Washington, DC.......................Labor and Employment Law

SLOAN, TODD M. LAW OFFICES OF
Malibu, CA ....Civil Trial Practice

SLOAN, RUBENS & PEEPLES
West Memphis, AR ....Banking Law; Civil Trial Practice; General Practice

SLOMSKI, RAYMOND J., P.C., LAW OFFICES OF
Phoenix, AZ ....Medical Malpractice; Personal Injury

SLOSSER, HUDGINS & STRUSE, P.L.C., LAW OFFICES OF
Tucson, AZ ....Probate, Trusts and Estate Planning; Tax Law

SLOTCHIVER & SLOTCHIVER, L.L.P.
Charleston, SC ....Civil Trial Practice; Tax Law

SLUTZKY, WOLFE AND BAILEY
Atlanta, GA ....Business Law; Real Estate Law

SMALL, DANIEL W.
Nashville, TN..........................Banking Law; Commercial Law; Real Estate Law

SMALL, J. MICHAEL LAW OFFICE OF
Alexandria, LA ....Criminal Trial Practice

SMALLEY, ROBERT H., JR., PROFESSIONAL CORPORATION
Griffin, GA..............................Banking Law; Civil Trial Practice; General Practice

SMALL, HATCH, DOUBEK & PYFER
Helena, MT ....Medical Malpractice

SMALL LARKIN & KIDDÉ
Los Angeles, CA ....Patent, Trademark, Copyright and Unfair Competition

SMALL, TOTH, BALDRIDGE & VAN BELKUM, P.C.
Bingham Farms, MI ....Business Law; Civil Trial Practice; Health Care Law; Insurance Defense; Medical Malpractice

SMALLWOOD-COOK & SCHMIEDER
Warsaw, NY.............................General Practice; Probate, Trusts and Estate Planning; Real Estate Law

SMART & BIGGAR
Ottawa, ON, Canada ....Patent, Trademark, Copyright and Unfair Competition
Toronto, ON, Canada..............Patent, Trademark, Copyright and Unfair Competition
Montreal, QU, Canada ....Patent, Trademark, Copyright and Unfair Competition

SMATHERS & SMATHERS
Washington, DC......................Administrative Law

SMENT, MICHAEL R. LAW OFFICES OF
Ventura, CA ....Bankruptcy Law; Real Estate Law

SMETANA & AVAKIAN
Chicago, IL..............................Labor and Employment Law

SMITH, DANIEL T.
Denver, CO ....Criminal Trial Practice

SMITH, DAVID RANDOLPH & ASSOCIATES
Nashville, TN..........................Medical Malpractice; Personal Injury; Product Liability Law

SMITH, E. ALFRED & ASSOCIATES
Philadelphia, PA ....Civil Trial Practice

SMITH, ROBERT B.
Jesup, GA................................Civil Trial Practice; Personal Injury

SMITH, WALTER LANDRY
Baton Rouge, LA.....................Personal Injury

SMITH, WILBUR C. III
Fort Myers, FL ....Criminal Trial Practice

SMITH, A. RUSSELL
Akron, OH ....Civil Trial Practice; Medical Malpractice

SMITH, BARTLETT, HEEKE, CARPENTER & LEWIS
Jeffersonville, IN ....General Practice

SMITH & BENTLEY
Redwood City, CA ....Criminal Trial Practice

SMITH & BRATCHER, P.C.
Waco, TX ....General Practice

SMITH, BRENDAN P., A PROFESSIONAL CORPORATION
Providence, RI.........................Real Estate Law; Tax Law

SMITH, BRIAN E., LAW FIRM, THE
Yuma, AZ.................................Civil Trial Practice; Personal Injury; Product Liability Law

SMITH & BROOKER, P.C.
Bay City, MI ....General Practice
Flint, MI..................................General Practice
Saginaw, MI ....Civil Trial Practice; General Practice; Labor and Employment Law

SMITH, CARTER, ROSE, FINLEY & GRIFFIS, A PROFESSIONAL CORPORATION
San Angelo, TX ....General Practice

SMITH, CASSIDY, PLATT, HARRIS & RADABAUGH, P.A.
Lakeland, FL............................Personal Injury; Workers Compensation

SMITH, CURRIE & HANCOCK
Atlanta, GA ....Construction Law; Labor and Employment Law

SMITH AND DAVENPORT
Manassas, VA ....General Practice

SMITH DEBNAM HIBBERT & PAHL, L.L.P.
Raleigh, NC.............................Bankruptcy Law; Civil Trial Practice; Commercial Law

SMITH & DEBONIS
Highland, IN............................Civil Trial Practice

SMITH, DUGGAN & JOHNSON
Boston, MA..............................General Practice

SMITH ELLIOTT SMITH & GARMEY, P.A.
Kennebunk, ME......................General Practice
Portland, ME ....General Practice; Medical Malpractice; Personal Injury
Saco, ME ....Civil Trial Practice; Criminal Trial Practice; General Practice; Medical Malpractice; Personal Injury

SMITH, FINKELSTEIN, LUNDBERG, ISLER AND YAKABOSKI
Riverhead, NY ....Civil Trial Practice; General Practice

SMITH, FOLLIN & JAMES
Greensboro, NC......................General Practice

SMITH, GAMBRELL & RUSSELL
Atlanta, GA ....General Practice

SMITH, GENDLER, SHIELL, SHEFF & FORD, P.A.
Minneapolis, MN....................Real Estate Law

SMITH, GILLIAM AND WILLIAMS
Gainesville, GA ....General Practice; Insurance Defense; Real Estate Law; Tax Law

SMITH, GOLDSTEIN & MAGRAM, A PROFESSIONAL CORPORATION
Burlington, NJ..........................Civil Trial Practice; General Practice; Personal Injury

SMITH, GRIMSLEY, BAUMAN, PINKERTON, PETERMANN, SAXER & WELLS
Fort Walton Beach, FL ....General Practice

SMITH & HALE
Columbus, OH ....Municipal Bond/Public Authority Financing; Real Estate Law

SMITH & HARRINGTON
Eastman, GA...........................General Practice

SMITH HAUGHEY RICE & ROEGGE, P.C.
East Lansing, MI ....Civil Trial Practice; General Practice; Insurance Defense; Medical Malpractice
Grand Rapids, MI ....Civil Trial Practice; General Practice; Insurance Defense; Medical Malpractice
Lansing, MI............................Civil Trial Practice; General Practice; Insurance Defense; Medical Malpractice
Traverse City, MI...................Civil Trial Practice; General Practice; Insurance Defense; Medical Malpractice

SMITH HELMS MULLISS & MOORE, L.L.P.
Charlotte, NC..........................General Practice
Greensboro, NC.......................General Practice
Raleigh, NC.............................General Practice

SMITH & HODGES
Elberton, GA...........................General Practice

SMITH, HOWARD & AJAX
Atlanta, GA ....Patent, Trademark, Copyright and Unfair Competition

SMITH HULSEY & BUSEY
Jacksonville, FL ....Business Law; Commercial Litigation; Environmental Law; General Practice; Health Care Law; Medical Malpractice; Probate, Trusts and Estate Planning; Real Estate Law; Tax Law

SMITH & JENSEN, P.C. A PROFESSIONAL CORPORATION
Richmond, VA ....Insurance Defense

SMITH, JOHNSON & BRANDT, ATTORNEYS, P.C.
Traverse City, MI....................Commercial Law; Environmental Law; General Practice

SMITH, JONES & FAWER, L.L.P.
New Orleans, LA ....Civil Trial Practice; Criminal Trial Practice; Environmental Law

SMITH, KATZENSTEIN & FURLOW
Wilmington, DE......................Bankruptcy Law; Business Law; Civil Trial Practice; Commercial Law; General Practice; Insurance Defense; Labor and Employment Law; Medical Malpractice; Personal Injury; Product Liability Law; Securities Law

SMITH, KEN MCFARLANE, P.C.
Arlington, VA ....Probate, Trusts and Estate Planning

SMITH & KOTCHKA, LTD.
Las Vegas, NV ....Employment Benefits Law; Labor and Employment Law; Workers Compensation

SMITH, LANDMEIER & SKAAR, P.C.
Geneva, IL...............................General Practice; Municipal and Zoning Law; Probate, Trusts and Estate Planning; Trademark, Copyright and Unfair Competition

SMITH, LAPARL, MEQUIO & KONING, P.C.
Portage, MI ....Insurance Defense

SMITH, LEWIS, BECKETT, POWELL, ROARK & DURLEY, L.L.P.
Columbia, MO ....General Practice

SMITH LYONS
Toronto, ON, Canada..............General Practice

SMITH, MAJCHER & MUDGE, L.L.P.
Austin, TX ....Administrative Law; Communications Law; Public Utilities Law

SMITH, MARSHALL AND WEAVER
Cleveland, OH.........................Civil Trial Practice; Insurance Defense; Product Liability Law

SMITH MAZURE DIRECTOR WILKINS YOUNG YAGERMAN & TARALLO, P.C.
New York, NY........................Civil Trial Practice; Insurance Defense

SMITH & MCELWAIN
Sioux City, IA ....Labor and Employment Law

SMITH, MERRIFIELD & RICHARDS, L.L.P.
Dallas, TX...............................Real Estate Law

SMITH, MURPHY & SCHOEPPERLE
Buffalo, NY ....Civil Trial Practice; General Practice; Insurance Defense

SMITH, NEVILLE, LAW FIRM OF
Manchester, KY ....General Practice

SMITH AND NOWLIN
Ventura, CA ....Family Law

SMITH PETERSON LAW FIRM
Council Bluffs, IA ....Business Law; Commercial Law; Insurance Defense; Labor and Employment Law; Probate, Trusts and Estate Planning; Real Estate Law; Tax Law

SMITH, RANSCHT, CONNORS, MUTINO, NORDELL & SIRIGNANO, P.C.
White Plains, NY ....General Practice; Probate, Trusts and Estate Planning; Real Estate Law; Tax Law

SMITH, SAUER & DEMARIA
Pensacola, FL ....General Practice

SMITH, SCHODER & BOUCK, P.A.
Daytona Beach, FL..................Insurance Defense; Medical Malpractice; Personal Injury; Workers Compensation

SMITH, SHARP, BENSON, JAHN & FEILMEYER
Ames, IA ....General Practice

SMITH, SMART, HANCOCK, TABLER & SCHWENSEN
Seattle, WA ....Banking Law; Civil Trial Practice; Environmental Law; Municipal and Zoning Law; Natural Resources Law; Real Estate Law

SMITH & SMITH
Vero Beach, FL ....Civil Trial Practice; General Practice; Probate, Trusts and Estate Planning

SMITH AND SMITH
Louisville, KY ....Labor and Employment Law

SMITH, SPIRES & PEDDY
Birmingham, AL ....Civil Trial Practice; Insurance Defense; Product Liability Law; Workers Compensation

SMITH, STRATTON, WISE, HEHER & BRENNAN
Princeton, NJ ....General Practice

SMITH, WALSH, CLARKE & GREGOIRE
Great Falls, MT ....Insurance Defense

SMITH, WELCH, STUDDARD & BRITTAIN
McDonough, GA ....Civil Trial Practice; Family Law; General Practice; Municipal and Zoning Law; Personal Injury; Real Estate Law

SMITH & WILLIAMS
Las Vegas, NV ....Medical Malpractice; Personal Injury

SMITH, WILLIAMS & HUMPHRIES, P.A.
Tampa, FL ....Bankruptcy Law; Civil Trial Practice; Commercial Law; Land Use Law; Real Estate Law

SMITHERMAN, LUNN, CHASTAIN & HILL, L.L.P.
Shreveport, LA........................General Practice

SMOAK, RICHARD
Panama City, FL......................General Practice

SMOOT ADAMS EDWARDS & GREEN, P.A.
Fort Myers, FL ....Appellate Practice; Banking Law; Business Law; Civil Trial Practice; Commercial Law; Commercial Litigation; Construction Law; Employment Benefits Law; General Practice; Insurance Defense; Medical Malpractice; Mergers and Acquisitions; Probate, Trusts and Estate Planning; Product Liability Law; Real Estate Law; Tax Law

SMYTH, JEFFREY A., P.S.
Seattle, WA ....Civil Trial Practice

SNAPKA, KATHRYN
Corpus Christi, TX ....Personal Injury

SNEAD, WILLIAM O. P. III
Fairfax, VA ....Personal Injury

SNEED LANG, P.C.
Tulsa, OK................................Antitrust Law; Banking Law; Bankruptcy Law; Civil Trial Practice; Commercial Law; Commercial Litigation; Criminal Trial Practice; Energy Law; Insurance Defense; Natural Resources Law; Personal Injury; Probate, Trusts and Estate Planning; Real Estate Law; Securities Law; Tax Law

SNELBAKER & BRENNEMAN, A PROFESSIONAL CORPORATION
Mechanicsburg, PA.................General Practice

SNELLGROVE, LASER, LANGLEY, LOVETT & CULPEPPER
Jonesboro, AR ....General Practice; Insurance Defense

SNELLINGS, BREARD, SARTOR, INABNETT & TRASCHER
Monroe, LA ....Civil Trial Practice; General Practice

SNELL & WILMER, L.L.P.
Phoenix, AZ ....Antitrust Law; Banking Law; Bankruptcy Law; Civil Trial Practice; Commercial Law; Commercial Litigation; Construction Law; Employment Benefits Law; Environmental Law; General Practice; Health Care Law; Labor and Employment Law; Municipal Bond/Public Authority Financing; Natural Resources Law; Probate, Trusts and Estate Planning; Product Liability Law; Real Estate Law; Tax Law
Tucson, AZ ....Antitrust Law; Banking Law; Bankruptcy Law; Employment Benefits Law; Environmental Law; Labor and Employment Law; Natural Resources Law; Probate, Trusts and Estate Planning; Real Estate Law; Tax Law
Irvine, CA.............................Environmental Law; General Practice; Labor and Employment Law; Natural Resources Law; Probate, Trusts and Estate Planning; Product Liability Law; Tax Law
Salt Lake City, UT..................Employment Benefits Law; Environmental Law; General Practice; Labor and Employment Law; Natural Resources Law; Probate, Trusts and Estate Planning; Product Liability Law; Tax Law

SNOW, CHRISTENSEN & MARTINEAU, P.C.
Salt Lake City, UT..................General Practice

SNOW, NUFFER, ENGSTROM, DRAKE, WADE & SMART, A PROFESSIONAL CORPORATION
St. George, UT ....General Practice

SNYDER, WILLIAM A.
Davie, FL ....Probate, Trusts and Estate Planning

SOBIESKI, MESSER & ASSOCIATES
Knoxville, TN ....Appellate Practice; Civil Rights; Construction Law

SOCKRIDER, BOLIN & ANGLIN, A PROFESSIONAL LAW CORPORATION
Shreveport, LA ....Civil Trial Practice; Family Law; Personal Injury; Probate, Trusts and Estate Planning

SOKOL, BEHOT AND FIORENZO
Hackensack, NJ.......................Civil Trial Practice; Commercial Law; Environmental Law; General Practice; Real Estate Law

SOKOLOFF, CHARLES S., INCORPORATED
Woonsocket, RI ....Real Estate Law

SOLOMON, STEPHEN E.
Los Angeles, CA ....Tax Law

SOLOMON & BENEDICT, P.A.
Tampa, FL ....Commercial Litigation

SOLOMON, BUDMAN, STRICKER & SCHWARTZ, L.L.P.
Charleston, SC ....Civil Trial Practice; Family Law; Personal Injury; Real Estate Law; Tax Law

SOLOMON PEARL BLUM & QUINN, LLP
Denver, CO ....Bankruptcy Law; Commercial Litigation; International Business Law; Securities Law; Tax Law

SOLOMON WARD SEIDENWURM & SMITH, LLP
San Diego, CA ....Real Estate Law

SOMERS & ASSOCIATES
Tampa, FL ....Medical Malpractice

SOMMER & BARNARD, ATTORNEYS AT LAW, PC
Indianapolis, IN......................Administrative Law; Antitrust Law; Bankruptcy Law; Business Law; Civil Trial Practice; Commercial Law; Computer Law; Environmental Law; General Practice; Labor and Employment Law; Real Estate Law; Securities Law

SOMMER, FOX, UDALL, OTHMER, HARDWICK & WISE, P.A.
Santa Fe, NM.........................Insurance Defense; Real Estate Law

SOMMER & STEELE, L.L.C.
Baltimore, MD ....Construction Law; General Practice; Real Estate Law

SOMMERS, SCHWARTZ, SILVER & SCHWARTZ, P.C.
Southfield, MI ....Appellate Practice; Banking Law; Business Law; Civil Trial Practice; Commercial Law; Criminal Trial Practice; Environmental Law; Family Law; General Practice; Health Care Law; Insurance Defense; Labor and Employment Law; Medical Malpractice; Personal Injury; Probate, Trusts and Estate Planning; Product Liability Law; Real Estate Law; Sports and Entertainment Law; Tax Law

SONDERBY, PETER R., P.C.
Chicago, IL............................Civil Trial Practice; Commercial Litigation; Securities Law

SONNENSCHEIN NATH & ROSENTHAL
Los Angeles, CA ....General Practice

San Francisco, CA ....General Practice
Washington, DC......................General Practice
Chicago, IL............................General Practice
Kansas City, MO.....................General Practice
St. Louis, MO.........................General Practice
New York, NY........................General Practice

SONNETT, NEAL R., P.A.
Miami, FL ....Criminal Trial Practice

SOOHO, SHARYN T.
Newton, MA ....Family Law

SOPKO & FIRTH
South Bend, IN ....Commercial Litigation; Family Law; Personal Injury; Real Estate Law

SORLING, NORTHRUP, HANNA, CULLEN AND COCHRAN, LTD.
Springfield, IL ....General Practice

SOROKIN SOROKIN GROSS HYDE & WILLIAMS, P.C.
Hartford, CT ....Administrative Law; Antitrust Law; Appellate Practice; Business Law; Civil Trial Practice; Commercial Law; Construction Law; Employment Benefits Law; Family Law; General Practice; Insurance Defense; Labor and Employment Law; Probate, Trusts and Estate Planning; Real Estate Law; Securities Law; Tax Law

SOTIROFF ABRAMCZYK & RAUSS, P.C.
Bingham Farms, MI ....Banking Law; Business Law; Civil Trial Practice; Labor and Employment Law; Real Estate Law

SOUTHWELL & O'ROURKE, P.S.
Spokane, WA..........................Bankruptcy Law

SPAIN & GILLON, L.L.C.
Birmingham, AL ....Antitrust Law; Banking Law; Civil Trial Practice; Commercial Law; Environmental Law; General Practice; Insurance Defense; Labor and Employment Law; Municipal Bond/Public Authority Financing; Personal Injury; Probate, Trusts and Estate Planning; Real Estate Law; Tax Law

SPAIN, MERRELL AND MILLER
Poplar Bluff, MO ....Insurance Defense

SPANGENBERG, SHIBLEY & LIBER
Cleveland, OH.........................General Practice

SPANGLER, JENNINGS & DOUGHERTY, P.C.
Merrillville, IN ....Civil Trial Practice; General Practice; Insurance Defense; Personal Injury
Valparaiso, IN.........................General Practice

SPANTON, PARSOFF & SIEGEL, P.C.
Melville, NY...........................Business Law; Probate, Trusts and Estate Planning; Tax Law

SPARBER, FERGUSON, PONDER & RYAN, A PROFESSIONAL LAW CORPORATION
San Diego, CA ....Bankruptcy Law; Civil Trial Practice; Construction Law; Insurance Defense; Land Use Law; Probate, Trusts and Estate Planning; Real Estate Law

SPARKMAN, ROBB, NELSON, MASON & GINSBURG
Miami, FL ....Civil Trial Practice; Insurance Defense

SPARKS, JOHN O., P.C.
Woodward, OK ....General Practice

SPARKS, TEHAN & RYLEY, P.C.
Scottsdale, AZ.........................Commercial Litigation; Environmental Law; Natural Resources Law; Probate, Trusts and Estate Planning; Real Estate Law

SPEAR, WILDERMAN, BORISH, ENDY, SPEAR AND RUNCKEL
Philadelphia, PA ....Employment Benefits Law; Labor and Employment Law

SPEARS, MOORE, REBMAN & WILLIAMS
Chattanooga, TN ....Banking Law; Bankruptcy Law; Civil Rights; Civil Trial Practice; Commercial Law; Construction Law; Criminal Trial Practice; Employment Benefits Law; Environmental Law; General Practice; Insurance Defense; Labor and Employment Law; Probate, Trusts and Estate Planning; Real Estate Law; Tax Law; Workers Compensation

SPEARS & SPEARS
Ironton, OH ....General Practice; Real Estate Law

SPECTOR GADON & ROSEN, P.C.
Philadelphia, PA ....Business Law; Civil Trial Practice; Commercial Litigation

SPECTOR & ROSEMAN, A PROFESSIONAL CORPORATION
Philadelphia, PA ....Antitrust Law; Civil Trial Practice; Commercial Litigation; Securities Law

SPEISER, LAURENCE A., LTD.
Las Vegas, NV ....Business Law

SPELMAN, SAUER & BURDICK, P.C.
St. Joseph, MI ....General Practice

SPENCE, CUSTER, SAYLOR, WOLFE & ROSE
Johnstown, PA ....General Practice

SPENCE, MORIARITY & SCHUSTER
Jackson, WY ....Civil Trial Practice; Criminal Trial Practice; General Practice; Personal Injury

SPENCER, RICHARD C. LAW OFFICES OF
Los Angeles, CA ....Business Law; Civil Trial Practice

SPENCER FANE BRITT & BROWNE
Kansas City, MO ....Civil Trial Practice; Environmental Law; General Practice; Insurance Defense; Labor and Employment Law

SPENCER & FRANK
Washington, DC ....Patent, Trademark, Copyright and Unfair Competition

SPENCER, GLEASON, HEBE & RAGUE
Wellsboro, PA ....Civil Trial Practice; Medical Malpractice; Personal Injury; Probate, Trusts and Estate Planning; Real Estate Law; Workers Compensation

SPENCER AND KLEIN, PROFESSIONAL ASSOCIATION
Miami, FL ....Civil Trial Practice; General Practice; International Business Law; Tax Law

SPENCER & SPENCER, PROFESSIONAL ASSOCIATION
Rock Hill, SC ....General Practice

SPENGLER NATHANSON
Toledo, OH ....Banking Law; Bankruptcy Law; Civil Trial Practice; Commercial Law; General Practice; Insurance Defense; Labor and Employment Law; Municipal Bond/Public Authority Financing; Probate, Trusts and Estate Planning; Real Estate Law; Tax Law

SPERLING & PERGANDE
Santa Ana, CA ....Appellate Practice; Bankruptcy Law; Civil Trial Practice; Commercial Law; General Practice; Real Estate Law

SPERRY, ZODA & KANE
Trenton, NJ ....Patent, Trademark, Copyright and Unfair Competition

SPESIA, AYERS, ARDAUGH & WUNDERLICH
Joliet, IL ....General Practice; Personal Injury

SPIEGEL LIAO & KAGAY
San Francisco, CA ....Antitrust Law; Appellate Practice

SPIETH, BELL, McCURDY & NEWELL CO., L.P.A.
Cleveland, OH ....Civil Trial Practice; General Practice; Labor and Employment Law; Probate, Trusts and Estate Planning; Real Estate Law; Tax Law

SPIKE & MECKLER
Elyria, OH ....Civil Trial Practice; Family Law; General Practice; Medical Malpractice; Personal Injury

SPILE & SIEGAL, LLP
Encino, CA ....Insurance Defense

SPILMAN, THOMAS & BATTLE
Charleston, WV ....General Practice

SPITLER, VOGTSBERGER & HUFFMAN
Bowling Green, OH ....Business Law; General Practice; Personal Injury

SPITZ & CARR
Edmonton, AB, Canada ....Civil Trial Practice

SPIVAK, LIPTON, WATANABE, SPIVAK & MOSS
New York, NY ....Employment Benefits Law; Labor and Employment Law

SPIVEY, GRIGG, KELLY & KNISELY, P.C.
Austin, TX ....Civil Trial Practice; Personal Injury

SPRADLEY & RIESMEYER, A PROFESSIONAL CORPORATION
Kansas City, MO ....Civil Trial Practice; Public Utilities Law

SPRAGUE & LEWIS
Lancaster, PA ....Commercial Litigation; Personal Injury

SPRENGER & LANG
Minneapolis, MN ....Employment Benefits Law

SPRINGER, BUSH & PERRY, A PROFESSIONAL CORPORATION
Pittsburgh, PA ....Antitrust Law; Civil Trial Practice; General Practice; Health Care Law; Labor and Employment Law; Municipal Bond/Public Authority Financing

SPRINGER & STEINBERG, A PROFESSIONAL CORPORATION
Denver, CO ....Criminal Trial Practice; Personal Injury

SPURRIER, RICE, WOOD & HALL
Huntsville, AL ....Civil Trial Practice; Insurance Defense

SQUIRE, SANDERS & DEMPSEY
Phoenix, AZ ....General Practice
Washington, DC ....General Practice
Jacksonville, FL ....General Practice
Miami, FL ....General Practice
New York, NY ....General Practice
Cleveland, OH ....General Practice
Columbus, OH ....General Practice
Brussels, Belgium ....General Practice
Prague, Czech Republic ....General Practice
London, England ....General Practice
Budapest, Hungary ....General Practice
Bratislava, Slovakia ....General Practice

STACK & FILPI, CHARTERED
Chicago, IL ....Administrative Law; Commercial Litigation; Patent, Trademark, Copyright and Unfair Competition

STACKHOUSE, SMITH & NEXSEN
Norfolk, VA ....Banking Law; Bankruptcy Law; Business Law; Civil Trial Practice; General Practice; Insurance Defense

STAHANCYK, GEARING & RACKNER, P.C.
Portland, OR ....Family Law

STAITMAN, SNYDER & TANNENBAUM
Encino, CA ....Civil Trial Practice; Insurance Defense

STALEY, JOBSON & WETHERELL, A PROFESSIONAL CORPORATION
Pleasanton, CA ....Family Law

STAMMER, McKNIGHT, BARNUM & BAILEY
Fresno, CA ....Civil Trial Practice; Health Care Law; Insurance Defense; Product Liability Law

STAMPER & HADLEY
Antlers, OK ....Banking Law; Civil Trial Practice; General Practice; Insurance Defense

STANLEY AND BERTRAM, P.S.C.
Vanceburg, KY ....Insurance Defense; Personal Injury; Probate, Trusts and Estate Planning

STANLEY WINES LAW FIRM, THE, P.A.
Winter Haven, FL ....Personal Injury; Workers Compensation

STANSBURY, JOHN O.
Oakland, CA ....Civil Trial Practice; Commercial Litigation

STANSBURY, RICHARD T., A PROFESSIONAL ASSOCIATION
Baltimore, MD ....Business Law; Probate, Trusts and Estate Planning; Tax Law

STANSELL, LELAND E., JR. P.A.
Miami, FL ....Civil Trial Practice; Insurance Defense; Personal Injury; Product Liability Law

STANTON, WILLIAM E.
Millbrook, NY ....Civil Trial Practice; Criminal Trial Practice; General Practice; Medical Malpractice; Personal Injury; Product Liability Law

STANTON, HUGHES, DIANA & ZUCKER, P.C.
Florham Park, NJ ....Labor and Employment Law

STANWYCK, STEVEN J.
Los Angeles, CA ....Civil Trial Practice; Computer Law

STAPLETON & STAPLETON, A PROFESSIONAL ASSOCIATION
Tustin, CA ....Family Law

STARK DONINGER & SMITH
Indianapolis, IN ....Business Law; Environmental Law; General Practice; Real Estate Law

STARKEY, KELLY, BLANEY & WHITE
Toms River, NJ ....Civil Trial Practice; General Practice; Insurance Defense

STARK & KEENAN, A PROFESSIONAL ASSOCIATION
Bel Air, MD ....Appellate Practice; Business Law; Civil Trial Practice; Municipal and Zoning Law; Personal Injury; Probate, Trusts and Estate Planning; Real Estate Law

STARK & STARK, A PROFESSIONAL CORPORATION
Princeton, NJ ....Business Law; General Practice; Personal Injury

STARN, PETER, A LAW CORPORATION, LAW OFFICES OF
Honolulu, HI ....Commercial Law; Real Estate Law

STARNES & ATCHISON
Birmingham, AL ....Civil Trial Practice; Construction Law; Environmental Law; Insurance Defense; Medical Malpractice; Personal Injury; Product Liability Law

STATHAM, JOHNSON & MCCRAY
Evansville, IN..........................General Practice; Insurance Defense

STATON, PERKINSON, DOSTER, POST, SILVERMAN & ADCOCK, P.A.
Sanford, NC ....General Practice

STAUFFER, MANNIX, ROMMEL, DECKER & DULANY, L.L.C.
McLean, VA............................Banking Law; Civil Trial Practice; Commercial Law; General Practice

STEAGALL & FILMORE, A PROFESSIONAL CORPORATION
Ozark, AL ....Insurance Defense

STEBELTON, ARANDA & SNIDER, A LEGAL PROFESSIONAL ASSOCIATION
Lancaster, OH ....Business Law; Civil Trial Practice; Family Law; Personal Injury

STEEFEL, LEVITT & WEISS, A PROFESSIONAL CORPORATION
San Francisco, CA ....Civil Trial Practice; General Practice

STEEG AND O'CONNOR
New Orleans, LA ....Real Estate Law

STEELE, STEELE, MCSOLEY & MCSOLEY
Bedford, IN ....Banking Law; Civil Trial Practice; General Practice

STEEL HECTOR & DAVIS LLP
Miami, FL ....General Practice

STEELMAN, BARRY L., P.A.
Baltimore, MD ....Civil Trial Practice

STEEL, RUDNICK & RUBEN
Philadelphia, PA ....Immigration and Naturalization

STEEL & STEEL
Nashville, AR..........................General Practice

STEEN REYNOLDS & DALEHITE
Jackson, MS ....Civil Trial Practice; Insurance Defense

STEERS & STEERS, P.S.C.
Franklin, KY............................Civil Trial Practice; Personal Injury

STEIN, RICK M. LAW OFFICES OF
Palm Springs, CA ....Civil Trial Practice

STEIN, ARTHUR, & ASSOCIATES, LAW OFFICES
Forked River, NJ ....Civil Trial Practice; Construction Law; Environmental Law; Land Use Law

STEIN & BATTALIA
Larchmont, NY........................Probate, Trusts and Estate Planning

STEIN, BLIABLIAS, MCGUIRE, PANTAGES & GIGL
Livingston, NJ.........................Civil Trial Practice; General Practice; Tax Law

STEIN, FORD, SCHAAF & TOWZEY, L.L.P.
St. Petersburg, FL....................Civil Trial Practice; Commercial Litigation; Family Law; Real Estate Law

STEIN, HARVEY W., A PROFESSIONAL CORPORATION
Oakland, CA ....General Practice; International Trade Law

STEIN, MOORE & FAY, P.A.
St. Paul, MN ....Bankruptcy Law

STEIN SHOSTAK SHOSTAK & O'HARA, A PROFESSIONAL CORPORATION
Los Angeles, CA ....International Trade Law

STEIN, SPERLING, BENNETT, DE JONG, DRISCOLL, GREENFEIG & METRO, P.A.
Rockville, MD.........................Business Law; Civil Trial Practice; Commercial Law; Construction Law; Criminal Trial Practice; Family Law; General Practice; Labor and Employment Law; Personal Injury; Probate, Trusts and Estate Planning; Real Estate Law; Tax Law

STEIN, STEPHEN, CHARTERED
Las Vegas, NV ....Criminal Trial Practice

STEINBERG BARNESS GLASGOW & FOSTER LLP
Manhattan Beach, CA ....Bankruptcy Law; Business Law; Civil Trial Practice; General Practice; Probate, Trusts and Estate Planning; Real Estate Law
New York, NY.........................Bankruptcy Law; Civil Trial Practice; Commercial Litigation; International Business Law

STEINBERG, NUTTER & BRENT, LAW CORPORATION
Santa Monica, CA....................Bankruptcy Law; Civil Trial Practice; Real Estate Law

STEINBERG, O'CONNOR, PATON & BURNS, P.L.L.C.
Detroit, MI..............................Aviation Law; Construction Law; Labor and Employment Law; Personal Injury

STEINBERG, SLEWETT & YAFFE, P.A.
Miami Beach, FL ....Probate, Trusts and Estate Planning

STEINER, SEGAL & MULLER P.A.
Philadelphia, PA ....Workers Compensation

STEINER AND STEINER
Kittanning, PA ....General Practice

STEINKE, TED
Dallas, TX ....Criminal Trial Practice

STEKETEE, PETER W.
Grand Rapids, MI ....Civil Trial Practice; Environmental Law

STELLATO & SCHWARTZ, LTD.
Chicago, IL..............................Civil Trial Practice; Insurance Defense

STENGER & FINNERTY
Buffalo, NY ....Civil Trial Practice; Commercial Litigation; Constitutional Law; Environmental Law

STENNETT, WILKINSON & PEDEN, A PROFESSIONAL ASSOCIATION
Jackson, MS ....General Practice; Municipal Bond/Public Authority Financing

STENSTROM, MCINTOSH, COLBERT, WHIGHAM & SIMMONS, P.A.
Sanford, FL ....Civil Trial Practice; General Practice; Real Estate Law

STEPANIAN & MUSCATELLO
Butler, PA ....Insurance Defense

STEPEK, DANIEL T.
Mount Clemens, MI................Family Law

STEPHENS, BARONI, REILLY & LEWIS
White Plains, NY ....Criminal Trial Practice; General Practice; Municipal and Zoning Law

STEPHENS, BERG & LASATER, A PROFESSIONAL CORPORATION
Los Angeles, CA ....Antitrust Law; Business Law; Civil Trial Practice; Commercial Litigation; Probate, Trusts and Estate Planning; Real Estate Law; Tax Law

STEPHENS, MILLIRONS, HARRISON & GAMMONS, P.C.
Huntsville, AL.........................Banking Law; Civil Trial Practice; Family Law; Real Estate Law

STEPHENS & STEPHENS, L.L.P.
Houston, TX ....Admiralty/Maritime Law; Personal Injury; Product Liability Law

STEPHENSON DALY MOROW AND KURNIK, P.C.
Indianapolis, IN ....Insurance Defense

STEPHENSON WORLEY GARRATT SCHWARTZ HEIDEL & PRAIRIE
San Diego, CA ....Employment Benefits Law; Land Use Law; Real Estate Law

STEPONOVICH & ASSOCIATES, A PROFESSIONAL LAW CORPORATION
Irvine, CA...............................Civil Trial Practice

STEPTOE & JOHNSON
Charleston, WV ....Civil Trial Practice; General Practice; Insurance Defense; Labor and Employment Law
Charles Town, WV.................General Practice
Clarksburg, WV ....Civil Trial Practice; Environmental Law; General Practice; Health Care Law; Insurance Defense; Labor and Employment Law; Municipal Bond/Public Authority Financing
Martinsburg, WV ....General Practice
Morgantown, WV ....Civil Trial Practice; General Practice
Parkersburg, WV.....................General Practice; Insurance Defense
Phoenix, AZ ....Civil Trial Practice; General Practice
Washington, DC......................Antitrust Law; Civil Trial Practice; Commercial Law; Environmental Law; General Practice; International Business Law; Tax Law; Transportation Law

STERN, DUBROW & MARCUS, A PROFESSIONAL CORPORATION
Maplewood, NJ.......................Bankruptcy Law; Civil Trial Practice; Commercial Law; General Practice; Probate, Trusts and Estate Planning; Tax Law

STERN & EDLIN, P.C.
Atlanta, GA ....Family Law

STERN, KEISER, PANKEN & WOHL
White Plains, NY ....Probate, Trusts and Estate Planning; Tax Law

STERN, NEUBAUER, GREENWALD & PAULY, A PROFESSIONAL CORPORATION
Santa Monica, CA....................Bankruptcy Law; Civil Trial Practice; Commercial Litigation

STERNBERG THOMSON & OKRENT
Seattle, WA ....Bankruptcy Law; Business Law; Personal Injury

STERNS & WEINROTH, A PROFESSIONAL CORPORATION
Atlantic City, NJ.....................General Practice
Trenton, NJ.....................General Practice

STETINA BRUNDA & BUYAN, A PROFESSIONAL CORPORATION
Laguna Hills, CA....................Antitrust Law; Commercial Litigation; Computer Law; Patent, Trademark, Copyright and Unfair Competition

STETTNER, MILLER AND COHN, P.C.
Denver, CO.............................Labor and Employment Law

STEVENS, WILLIAM J.
Chicago, IL..............................Appellate Practice

STEVENS, BAGLEY & STEVENS
Fayetteville, TN.....................General Practice

STEVENS & JOHNSON
Allentown, PA.......................General Practice; Insurance Defense

STEVENS, KRAMER, AVERBUCK & HARRIS, A PROFESSIONAL CORPORATION
Los Angeles, CA.....................Insurance Defense

STEVENS LAW FIRM, P.C.
Loris, SC.....................Civil Trial Practice; Insurance Defense; Labor and Employment Law; Personal Injury; Product Liability Law; Real Estate Law

STEVENS, MCGHEE, MORGAN, LENNON, O'QUINN, TOLL & COLEMAN
Wilmington, NC.....................Commercial Litigation

STEVENSON, RUSIN AND FRIEDMAN, LTD.
Chicago, IL.............................Insurance Defense; Workers Compensation

STEWART, TIMOTHY A.
Agana, GU.............................General Practice

STEWART, COOK, CONSTANCE, STEWART & MINTON, L.L.C.
Independence, MO.................General Practice

STEWART, ESTES & DONNELL
Nashville, TN.....................Insurance Defense; Sports and Entertainment Law

STEWART, HUMPHERYS, BURCHETT, SANDELMAN & MOLIN
Chico, CA.................................Business Law; Personal Injury; Real Estate Law

STEWART, JAMES D., AND ASSOCIATES, INC.
San Antonio, TX.....................Family Law

STEWART MCKELVEY STIRLING SCALES
Moncton, NB, Canada.............General Practice
Saint John, NB, Canada..........General Practice
St. John's, NF, Canada............General Practice
Halifax, NS, Canada...............General Practice
Sydney, NS, Canada................General Practice
Charlottetown, PE, Canada.....General Practice

STEWART, MELVIN & FROST
Gainesville, GA.....................General Practice

STEWART & NALL, P.A.
Vero Beach, FL.......................Health Care Law; Probate, Trusts and Estate Planning; Real Estate Law

STEWART, PLANT & BLUMENTHAL, LLC
Baltimore, MD.......................Probate, Trusts and Estate Planning; Tax Law

STEWART AND STEWART
Washington, DC.....................General Practice; International Business Law

STEWART, STEWART & O'NEIL
Walnut Creek, CA.................Probate, Trusts and Estate Planning

STEWART TILGHMAN FOX & BIANCHI, P.A.
Miami, FL.............................Civil Trial Practice

STICHTER, RIEDEL, BLAIN & PROSSER, P.A.
Tampa, FL.............................Bankruptcy Law

STIKEMAN, ELLIOTT
Vancouver, BC, Canada...........General Practice
Ottawa, ON, Canada...............General Practice
Toronto, ON, Canada..............General Practice
Montreal, QU, Canada............General Practice
London, England....................General Practice
Hong Kong, Hong Kong........General Practice
Taipei, Taiwan.......................General Practice

STIMMEL, STIMMEL & SMITH, A PROFESSIONAL CORPORATION
San Francisco, CA.................Business Law; International Business Law

STINSON, JOSEPH M.
Tylertown, MS.......................General Practice

STINSON, LOUIS, JR., P.A.
Coral Gables, FL....................Admiralty/Maritime Law

STIRBA & HATHAWAY, A PROFESSIONAL CORPORATION
Salt Lake City, UT.................Civil Trial Practice

STIRLING & KLEINTOP
Honolulu, HI.........................Family Law

STITES & HARBISON
Frankfort, KY.......................General Practice
Lexington, KY.......................General Practice; Natural Resources Law
Louisville, KY.......................General Practice; Municipal Bond/Public Authority Financing

STITES, MCELWAIN & FOWLER
Louisville, KY.......................General Practice

STOCK AND LEADER, A PROFESSIONAL CORPORATION
York, PA.............................Civil Trial Practice; General Practice; Labor and Employment Law; Municipal Bond/Public Authority Financing

STOCKTON & HING, P.A.
Scottsdale, AZ.......................Probate, Trusts and Estate Planning; Real Estate Law

STOCKTON & SADLER
Modesto, CA.........................Civil Trial Practice; General Practice

STOCKWELL & COOPERMAN, A LEGAL PROFESSIONAL ASSOCIATION
Toledo, OH.........................Business Law; Probate, Trusts and Estate Planning; Real Estate Law; Tax Law

STOCKWELL, HARRIS, WIDOM & WOOLVERTON, A PROFESSIONAL CORPORATION
Los Angeles, CA.....................Insurance Defense; Labor and Employment Law

STOCKWELL, SIEVERT, VICCELLIO, CLEMENTS & SHADDOCK, L.L.P.
Lake Charles, LA....................General Practice

STOCKWOOD, SPIES & CAMPBELL
Toronto, ON, Canada.............Civil Trial Practice

STOEL RIVES LLP
Portland, OR.........................General Practice

STOGNER, N. CARR
Alexandria, VA.......................Business Law

STOKES, JOHN W. JR.
Decatur, GA.........................Criminal Trial Practice

STOKES & BARTHOLOMEW, P.A.
Nashville, TN.........................General Practice

STOKES, EITELBACH & LAWRENCE, P.S.
Seattle, WA.............................Antitrust Law; Business Law; Civil Trial Practice; Communications Law; Labor and Employment Law; Probate, Trusts and Estate Planning; Trademark, Copyright and Unfair Competition

STOKES LAZARUS & CARMICHAEL
Atlanta, GA.............................Administrative Law; Commercial Law; Labor and Employment Law

STOKES & MURPHY
San Diego, CA.......................Labor and Employment Law
Atlanta, GA.........................Labor and Employment Law

STOLLENWERCK, MOORE & SILVERBERG, P.C.
Dallas, TX.............................Business Law; Probate, Trusts and Estate Planning; Real Estate Law

STOLL, KEENON & PARK, LLP
Frankfort, KY.......................General Practice
Lexington, KY.......................Administrative Law; Antitrust Law; Banking Law; Bankruptcy Law; Business Law; Civil Trial Practice; Commercial Law; Communications Law; Employment Benefits Law; Environmental Law; Family Law; General Practice; Health Care Law; Insurance Defense; Labor and Employment Law; Municipal Bond/Public Authority Financing; Municipal and Zoning Law; Natural Resources Law; Probate, Trusts and Estate Planning; Real Estate Law; Securities Law; Tax Law
Louisville, KY.......................Commercial Law; General Practice

STOLPMAN • KRISSMAN • ELBER • MANDEL & KATZMAN LLP
Long Beach, CA.....................Civil Trial Practice; Personal Injury; Product Liability Law

STOLTZ, MELVIN I.
Milford, CT.............................Patent, Trademark, Copyright and Unfair Competition

STOMPOLY, STROUD, GIDDINGS & GLICKSMAN, P.C.
Tucson, AZ.............................Business Law; Civil Trial Practice; Family Law; General Practice; Medical Malpractice; Personal Injury; Probate, Trusts and Estate Planning; Product Liability Law

STONE, JACK A. AND ASSOCIATES
Evansville, IN............................Probate, Trusts and Estate Planning; Tax Law

STONE, EDWARD H., P.C.
Newport Beach, CA................Probate, Trusts and Estate Planning

STONE, HARRISON, TURK & SHOWALTER, P.C.
Radford, VA ....Criminal Trial Practice; General Practice; Personal
Injury; Tax Law

STONE & HILES
Beverly Hills, CA...................Labor and Employment Law

STONE & HINDS, P.C.
Knoxville, TN ....Business Law; Civil Trial Practice; General Practice;
Probate, Trusts and Estate Planning; Tax Law

STONE JESSUP, P.C.
Tulsa, OK................................Municipal Bond/Public Authority Financing

STONE LAW FIRM, THE, P.C.
Macon, GA ....Family Law

STONE, LEYTON & GERSHMAN, A PROFESSIONAL CORPORATION
St. Louis, MO..........................Bankruptcy Law; Commercial Litigation; Real
Estate Law

STONE, MCGUIRE & BENJAMIN
Chicago, IL..............................Civil Trial Practice; Criminal Trial Practice; Tax
Law

STONE, PIGMAN, WALTHER, WITTMANN & HUTCHINSON, L.L.P.
New Orleans, LA ....General Practice

STONE & ROSENBLATT, A PROFESSIONAL CORPORATION
Encino, CA..............................Insurance Defense

STONE, WILLIAM S., P.C.
Blakely, GA.............................Personal Injury

STONECIPHER, CUNNINGHAM, BEARD & SCHMITT, P.C.
Pittsburgh, PA ....Bankruptcy Law; Civil Trial Practice; General
Practice

STONER & ASSOCIATES
Rochester, NY..........................Computer Law; Tax Law

STOREY ARMSTRONG STEGER & MARTIN, A PROFESSIONAL CORPORATION
Dallas, TX...............................General Practice

STOTT, HOLLOWELL, PALMER & WINDHAM, L.L.P.
Gastonia, NC ....General Practice

STOUFFER & RYAN, P.C.
Philadelphia, PA ....Administrative Law; Civil Rights

STOUT & STOUT
Hobbs, NM..............................General Practice

STOUT AND WINTERBOTTOM
Roswell, NM ....Criminal Trial Practice; Personal Injury

STRADLING, YOCCA, CARLSON & RAUTH, A PROFESSIONAL CORPORATION
Newport Beach, CA................General Practice

STRAMONDO, SALVATORE F.
Lexington, MA ....Aviation Law; Civil Trial Practice

STRANG, FLETCHER, CARRIGER, WALKER, HODGE & SMITH, PLLC
Chattanooga, TN ....General Practice

STRASBURGER & PRICE, L.L.P.
Austin, TX ....General Practice
Dallas, TX...............................General Practice
Houston, TX ....General Practice
Mexico, D.F., Mexico.............General Practice

STRASSER & ASSOCIATES, A PROFESSIONAL CORPORATION
Paramus, NJ............................Civil Trial Practice; Health Care Law

STRASSMAN, HARVEY
Los Angeles, CA ....Family Law

STRATER & STRATER, P.A.
York, ME ....General Practice; Real Estate Law

STRATTON, MAY, HAYS & HOGG, PSC
Pikeville, KY ....Commercial Law; General Practice; Insurance
Defense

STRAUSS & TROY, A LEGAL PROFESSIONAL ASSOCIATION
Covington, KY........................General Practice
Cincinnati, OH........................Business Law; Civil Trial Practice; Employment
Benefits Law; General Practice; Insurance Defense;
Medical Malpractice; Real Estate Law; Securities
Law; Tax Law

STREATER, MURPHY, GERNANDER, FORSYTHE & TELSTAD, P.A.
Winona, MN ....General Practice

STRECKER & KIRKLAND, A PROFESSIONAL CORPORATION
Tulsa, OK................................Civil Trial Practice; Labor and Employment Law

STREET, STREET, STREET, SCOTT & BOWMAN
Grundy, VA ....General Practice

STREIBICH & SEALE
Memphis, TN ....Trademark, Copyright and Unfair Competition

STRICKLAND, JACK V. JR.
Fort Worth, TX ....Criminal Trial Practice

STRICKLAND & HAAPALA
Oakland, CA ....Civil Trial Practice

STRICKLAND & STRICKLAND, P.C.
Tucson, AZ ....Environmental Law; Medical Malpractice; Natural
Resources Law; Personal Injury

STRINGARI, FRITZ, KREGER, AHEARN & CRANDALL, P.C.
Detroit, MI..............................Appellate Practice; Civil Trial Practice; Criminal
Trial Practice; Employment Benefits Law; Labor
and Employment Law

STRINGER, NANETTE SCHULZE
Palo Alto, CA ....Family Law

STRIPLING, MCMICHAEL & STRIPLING, P.A.
Gainesville, FL ....Civil Trial Practice

STRODEL, ROBERT C., LTD.
Peoria, IL................................Civil Trial Practice; General Practice

STROEBEL, EDWARD
Wapakoneta, OH.....................Probate, Trusts and Estate Planning

STROHM, RICHARD L., P.C., LAW OFFICES OF
Phoenix, AZ ....Administrative Law; Appellate Practice; Civil Trial
Practice; Criminal Trial Practice; Insurance Defense;
Medical Malpractice; Personal Injury; Sports and
Entertainment Law

STRONG & HANNI, A PROFESSIONAL CORPORATION
Salt Lake City, UT..................Business Law; General Practice; Insurance Defense;
Labor and Employment Law; Medical Malpractice;
Probate, Trusts and Estate Planning; Product
Liability Law

STRONG, PIPKIN, NELSON & BISSELL, L.L.P.
Beaumont, TX.........................General Practice

STROOCK & STROOCK & LAVAN
Washington, DC......................General Practice
Miami, FL...............................General Practice
Los Angeles, CA ....General Practice
New York, NY.........................Bankruptcy Law; General Practice; Tax Law

STROUD, STROUD, WILLINK, THOMPSON & HOWARD
Madison, WI ....General Practice; Patent, Trademark, Copyright and
Unfair Competition; Probate, Trusts and Estate
Planning

STROUP & TRESIDDER, P.C.
Petoskey, MI ....General Practice; Insurance Defense

STROUT & PAYSON, P.A.
Rockland, ME..........................General Practice; Tax Law

STRUCKMEYER AND WILSON
Phoenix, AZ ....Insurance Defense

STRYKER, TAMS & DILL
Newark, NJ ....General Practice

STUART, CHARLES M. JR.
Greenville, SC.........................Probate, Trusts and Estate Planning

STUART & BRANIGIN
Lafayette, IN...........................Appellate Practice; Banking Law; Bankruptcy Law;
Business Law; Civil Trial Practice; Commercial Law;
Employment Benefits Law; Environmental Law;
General Practice; Health Care Law; Insurance
Defense; Labor and Employment Law; Land Use
Law; Medical Malpractice; Municipal Bond/Public
Authority Financing; Probate, Trusts and Estate
Planning; Real Estate Law; Tax Law; Trademark,
Copyright and Unfair Competition; Transportation
Law

STUART & CLOVER
Shawnee, OK..........................General Practice

STUART, STRICKLAND & CAGLIANONE, P.A.
Tampa, FL ....Civil Trial Practice; Insurance Defense

STUART, TINLEY, PETERS, THORN & HUGHES
Council Bluffs, IA ....General Practice

STUBBS, HITTIG & LEONE, A PROFESSIONAL CORPORATION
San Francisco, CA ....Construction Law; Health Care Law; Insurance Defense; Real Estate Law

STUBBS & STUBBS
San Mateo, CA.................Business Law; Civil Trial Practice; Probate, Trusts and Estate Planning

STUBBS, WILLIAM, FIRM
Lafayette, LA ....Mergers and Acquisitions

STUBENBERG & DURRETT
Honolulu, HI...........................Business Law; International Business Law; Real Estate Law

STUCKERT AND YATES
Newtown, PA ....General Practice

STUDDARD & MELBY, A PROFESSIONAL CORPORATION
El Paso, TX..............................General Practice

STULTS, STULTS, FORSZT & PAWLOWSKI, A PROFESSIONAL ASSOCIATION
Gary, IN.................Civil Trial Practice; General Practice; Insurance Defense

STUMP, T. DOUGLAS AND ASSOCIATES
Oklahoma City, OK................Immigration and Naturalization

STUMP, STOREY & CALLAHAN, P.A.
Orlando, FL ....Civil Trial Practice; Commercial Litigation

STUTMAN, TREISTER & GLATT, PROFESSIONAL CORPORATION
Los Angeles, CA.....................Bankruptcy Law; Commercial Law

SUBIN, ROSENBLUTH, LOSEY, BRENNAN, BITTMAN & MORSE, PROFESSIONAL ASSOCIATION
Orlando, FL ....Civil Trial Practice; Commercial Litigation; Construction Law

SUCHMAN, GALFIN & PASSON, LLP
Irvine, CA.................Business Law; Commercial Litigation

SUGAR, FRIEDBERG & FELSENTHAL
Chicago, IL..............................Business Law; Commercial Litigation; Mergers and Acquisitions; Probate, Trusts and Estate Planning; Real Estate Law; Securities Law; Tax Law

SUGARMAN, WALLACE, MANHEIM & SCHOENWALD
Syracuse, NY...........................Civil Trial Practice; General Practice; Insurance Defense; Personal Injury

SUKLOFF & SCHANZ
Binghamton, NY.....................Family Law

SULLIVAN, BENATOVICH, OLIVERIO & TRIMBOLI
Buffalo, NY ....Civil Trial Practice; Commercial Law; Commercial Litigation

SULLIVAN & CROMWELL
Los Angeles, CA.....................General Practice
Washington, DC.....................General Practice
New York, NY.........................Civil Trial Practice; General Practice
Melbourne, Victoria, Australia.................................General Practice
London, England ....General Practice
Paris, France...........................General Practice
Frankfurt/Main, Germany .....General Practice
Hong Kong, Hong Kong.........General Practice
Tokyo, Japan...........................General Practice

SULLIVAN & DONOVAN, LLP
New York, NY.......................International Business Law; Municipal Bond/Public Authority Financing

SULLIVAN & GOLDEN
Seattle, WA ....Medical Malpractice

SULLIVAN, HAMILTON, SCHULZ, LETZRING, SIMONS, KRETER, TOTH & LEBEUF, P.C.
Battle Creek, MI ....Business Law; Civil Trial Practice; General Practice; Insurance Defense

SULLIVAN LAW CORPORATION
Los Angeles, CA.....................Aviation Law; Business Law; Civil Trial Practice; General Practice

SULLIVAN & LEAVITT, P.C., LAW OFFICES OF
Novi, MI..................................Transportation Law

SULLIVAN, MAHONEY
St. Catharines, ON, Canada ....Business Law; General Practice; Real Estate Law

SULLIVAN AND SULLIVAN
Jackson, MS ....General Practice

SULLIVAN & WARD, P.C.
Des Moines, IA.......................General Practice

SULLIVAN, WARD, BONE, TYLER & ASHER, P.C.
Southfield, MI ....Insurance Defense

SULLIVAN, WORKMAN & DEE
Los Angeles, CA.....................General Practice

SULLOWAY & HOLLIS
Concord, NH ....General Practice

SULMEYER, KUPETZ, BAUMANN & ROTHMAN, A PROFESSIONAL CORPORATION
Los Angeles, CA.....................Bankruptcy Law; Commercial Law

SUMMA & RYAN, P.C.
Waterbury, CT ....Labor and Employment Law

SUMMERS, MCCREA & WYATT, P.C.
Chattanooga, TN ....Civil Trial Practice; Criminal Trial Practice; General Practice; Labor and Employment Law; Medical Malpractice; Personal Injury

SUMNER & ANDERSON
Atlanta, GA ....Antitrust Law; Civil Trial Practice; Construction Law; Health Care Law

SUMNER, ROBERT D., P.A.
Dade City, FL.........................Probate, Trusts and Estate Planning

SUMNER & SCHICK
Dallas, TX ....Civil Trial Practice; Criminal Trial Practice

SUNDAHL, POWERS, KAPP & MARTIN, L.L.C.
Cheyenne, WY.......................Administrative Law; Civil Trial Practice; Insurance Defense

SUNDERLAND, MURPHY, SPENN AND JOHNSON
Watseka, IL.............................General Practice

SUPNIK, PAUL D.
Beverly Hills, CA....................Sports and Entertainment Law; Trademark, Copyright and Unfair Competition

SUPPLEE, ROBERT S., P.C.
West Chester, PA....................Probate, Trusts and Estate Planning

SURRATT, JOHN R., P.A.
Winston-Salem, NC ....Civil Trial Practice; Commercial Law; Commercial Litigation; Real Estate Law

SURRETT & COLEMAN, P.A.
Augusta, GA ....Bankruptcy Law; Family Law; General Practice; Insurance Defense

SUSK, ROBERT A., LAW FIRM OF
San Francisco, CA ....Antitrust Law; Civil Trial Practice; Real Estate Law

SUSMAN, DUFFY & SEGALOFF, P.C.
New Haven, CT ....Business Law; Civil Trial Practice; General Practice; Real Estate Law

SUSMAN, GERALD S., & ASSOCIATES, P.C.
Philadelphia, PA ....Business Law; Probate, Trusts and Estate Planning; Tax Law

SUSMAN GODFREY L.L.P.
Houston, TX ....Civil Trial Practice

SUSSMAN SHANK WAPNICK CAPLAN & STILES, LLP
Portland, OR...........................Bankruptcy Law; Business Law; Commercial Law; Construction Law; Employment Benefits Law; Environmental Law; General Practice; Probate, Trusts and Estate Planning; Real Estate Law; Tax Law

SUSSMAN, WILLIAM C., P.A.
Miami, FL...............................Real Estate Law

SUTHERLAND, RICHARD T.
Wichita Falls, TX....................Family Law

SUTHERLAND, ASBILL & BRENNAN
Atlanta, GA ....Antitrust Law; Banking Law; Bankruptcy Law; Business Law; Civil Trial Practice; Construction Law; Employment Benefits Law; Environmental Law; General Practice; Health Care Law; Municipal Bond/Public Authority Financing; Probate, Trusts and Estate Planning; Real Estate Law; Tax Law; Trademark, Copyright and Unfair Competition

SUTHERLAND & GERBER, A PROFESSIONAL CORPORATION
El Centro, CA ....Business Law

SUTHON, WALTER J. III
New Orleans, LA ....General Practice

SUTKOWSKI & WASHKUHN LTD.
Peoria, IL................................General Practice

SUTLEY, PHILLIP M.
Baltimore, MD ....Criminal Trial Practice

SUTTER & LITTLE
San Diego, CA ....Bankruptcy Law

SWADEN LAW OFFICES
Edina, MN ....Family Law

SWAIM & AHR, P.C.
Albuquerque, NM...................Probate, Trusts and Estate Planning; Tax Law

SWAIN, HARTSHORN & SCOTT
Peoria, IL................................Civil Trial Practice; General Practice

SWAINE, HARRIS, SHEEHAN & MCCLURE, P.A.
Lake Placid, FL......................General Practice
Sebring, FL.............................General Practice

SWANN, HADLEY & ALVAREZ, P.A.
Winter Park, FL......................Civil Trial Practice

SWANSON & DETTMANN
Marquette, MI.........................Civil Trial Practice; Insurance Defense

SWANSON, MARTIN & BELL
Chicago, IL.............................Civil Trial Practice; Insurance Defense; Labor and
Employment Law; Medical Malpractice; Product
Liability Law
Wheaton, IL............................Civil Trial Practice; Insurance Defense

SWANSON, MIDGLEY, GANGWERE, KITCHIN & MCLARNEY, L.L.C.
Kansas City, MO ....Antitrust Law; Bankruptcy Law; Civil Trial
Practice; Commercial Law; Environmental Law;
Family Law; General Practice; Immigration and
Naturalization; Labor and Employment Law;
Natural Resources Law; Probate, Trusts and Estate
Planning; Real Estate Law; Tax Law; Trans-
portation Law

SWANSON, PARR, CORDES, YOUNGLOVE & PEEPLES, P.S.
Olympia, WA ....Labor and Employment Law; Probate, Trusts and
Estate Planning

SWARTZ, CAMPBELL & DETWEILER
Harrisburg, PA.......................General Practice
Media, PA ....General Practice
Philadelphia, PA ....General Practice; Insurance Defense

SWARTZ & REED
Washington, DC......................Medical Malpractice

SWARTZ & SWARTZ
Boston, MA.............................Admiralty/Maritime Law; Civil Trial Practice;
Environmental Law; Medical Malpractice; Personal
Injury; Product Liability Law

SWEARINGEN, JAMES D.
Pensacola, FL.........................Family Law

SWEENEY, DABAGIA, DONOGHUE, THORNE, JANES & PAGOS
Michigan City, IN...................General Practice

SWEENEY, SHEEHAN & SPENCER, A PROFESSIONAL CORPORATION
Philadelphia, PA ....Commercial Litigation; General Practice; Insurance
Defense; Product Liability Law

SWEENY, PETER M., & ASSOCIATES, P.C.
Fairfax, VA ....Personal Injury

SWENDSEID & STERN
Las Vegas, NV ....Municipal Bond/Public Authority Financing
Reno, NV ....Municipal Bond/Public Authority Financing

SWENSEN PERER & JOHNSON
Pittsburgh, PA ....Civil Trial Practice; Criminal Trial Practice; Personal
Injury; Product Liability Law

SWERDLOW, FLORENCE & SANCHEZ, A LAW CORPORATION
Beverly Hills, CA....................Labor and Employment Law

SWERLING, JACK B.
Columbia, SC ....Appellate Practice; Criminal Trial Practice

SWICHKOW, MORTON C., P.C.
McKinney, TX ....Civil Trial Practice

SWIFT & FINLAYSON
Fort Wayne, IN.......................Appellate Practice; Business Law; Commercial Law;
Municipal and Zoning Law; Probate, Trusts and
Estate Planning; Real Estate Law

SWISHER & COHRT, P.L.C.
Waterloo, IA ....Business Law; Civil Trial Practice; Commercial Law;
General Practice; Insurance Defense; Labor and
Employment Law; Real Estate Law

SWOPE, DALE M., P.A.
Tampa, FL ....Personal Injury

SYLVESTER & MALEY, INC.
Burlington, VT ....Civil Trial Practice; Medical Malpractice; Personal
Injury

SYNNESTVEDT & LECHNER
Philadelphia, PA ....Patent, Trademark, Copyright and Unfair Competition

SZAFERMAN, LAKIND, BLUMSTEIN, WATTER & BLADER, P.C.
Lawrenceville, NJ...................Banking Law; Environmental Law; Land Use Law

TABACK, JOSEPH, P.C.
Los Angeles, CA ....Family Law

TABAKIN CARROLL & CURTIN
Pittsburgh, PA ....Family Law; Labor and Employment Law

TABBERT HAHN EARNEST & STARKEY, P.C.
Indianapolis, IN ....Civil Trial Practice; Criminal Trial Practice;
Environmental Law; Medical Malpractice; Natural
Resources Law; Probate, Trusts and Estate Planning

TABNER AND RYAN
Albany, NY ....Business Law; General Practice

TAFARO & FLYNN
New Providence, NJ ....Civil Trial Practice; Medical Malpractice

TAFT & MCSALLY
Cranston, RI ....General Practice; Probate, Trusts and Estate
Planning

TAFT, STETTINIUS & HOLLISTER
Crestview Hills, KY ....General Practice
Cincinnati, OH ....General Practice
Cleveland, OH ....General Practice
Columbus, OH ....General Practice

TAIT, DONALD H. Q.C.
Windsor, ON, Canada ....Criminal Trial Practice

TALBOTT AND GALLAGHER
McLean, VA............................Real Estate Law

TALCOTT, LIGHTFOOT, VANDEVELDE & SADOWSKY
Los Angeles, CA ....Civil Trial Practice; Criminal Trial Practice

TALIAFERRO AND MEHLING
Covington, KY........................Civil Trial Practice; Criminal Trial Practice; Family
Law; Patent, Trademark, Copyright and Unfair
Competition; Personal Injury; Real Estate Law;
Workers Compensation

TALKINGTON & CLARK, L.L.P.
Iola, KS ....General Practice

TALLACKSON, JEFFREY S.
New York, NY.........................Banking Law

TALLEY & SHARP, P.C.
Conyers, GA ....General Practice

TALLMAN, HUDDERS & SORRENTINO, P.C.
Allentown, PA ....Civil Trial Practice; General Practice; Probate,
Trusts and Estate Planning

TALT, ALAN R.
Pasadena, CA ....Business Law; Probate, Trusts and Estate Planning

TAMMELLEO, A. DAVID & ASSOCIATES
Providence, RI........................General Practice; Health Care Law; Medical
Malpractice

TAM, O'CONNOR & HENDERSON, ATTORNEYS AT LAW, A LAW CORPORATION
Honolulu, HI..........................Business Law; Insurance Defense

TANENBAUM, MARK C., P.A.
Charleston, SC ....Civil Trial Practice

TANKARD AND GORDON
Eastville, VA ....General Practice

TANNENBAUM, RICHARD N.
New York, NY.........................Civil Trial Practice; Commercial Law; Family Law;
Personal Injury

TANSEY, ROSEBROUGH, GERDING & STROTHER, P.C.
Farmington, NM.....................Civil Rights; Civil Trial Practice; Health Care Law;
Insurance Defense; Labor and Employment Law

TARASI & ASSOCIATES, P.C.
Pittsburgh, PA ....Civil Trial Practice; General Practice; Medical
Malpractice; Personal Injury

TARASKA, GROWER & KETCHAM, P.A.
Orlando, FL ....Insurance Defense

TARCZA, ROBERT E.
New Orleans, LA ....Civil Trial Practice; Probate, Trusts and Estate
Planning

TARLOW, BARRY, A PROF. CORP., LAW OFFICES OF
Los Angeles, CA ....Criminal Trial Practice

TAROLLI, SUNDHEIM, COVELL, TUMMINO & SZABO
Cleveland, OH........................Patent, Trademark, Copyright and Unfair Competition

TARUTIS & BARRON, INC., P.S.
Seattle, WA ....Health Care Law

TATE, LOWE & ROWLETT, P.C.
Abingdon, VA........................Commercial Litigation; Criminal Trial Practice; General Practice; Labor and Employment Law; Medical Malpractice; Personal Injury; Product Liability Law; Real Estate Law

TATLOW & GUMP
Moberly, MO ....General Practice; Personal Injury; Product Liability Law

TATUM & MCDOWELL
Clovis, NM.............................General Practice; Probate, Trusts and Estate Planning; Tax Law

TAUBMAN, SIMPSON, YOUNG & SULENTOR
Long Beach, CA......................Civil Trial Practice; Environmental Law; General Practice; Real Estate Law; Tax Law

TAUSTINE, POST, SOTSKY, BERMAN, FINEMAN & KOHN
Louisville, KY ....Business Law; Medical Malpractice; Real Estate Law; Tax Law

TAVSS, FLETCHER, EARLEY & KING, P.C.
Norfolk, VA ....Banking Law; Civil Trial Practice; General Practice; Personal Injury; Real Estate Law

TAX, ESTATE, & BUSINESS LAW N.A. LLC
Albuquerque, NM...................Probate, Trusts and Estate Planning; Tax Law

TAYLOR, NELSON W. III
Morehead City, NC ....General Practice

TAYLOR, ROBERTSON B.
Bethlehem, PA ....Civil Trial Practice; Product Liability Law

TAYLOR, BUTTERFIELD, RISEMAN, CLARK, HOWELL AND CHURCHILL, P.C.
Lapeer, MI ....General Practice

TAYLOR & CAWTHORNE, LTD.
Tucson, AZ ....General Practice

TAYLOR & CIRE
Houston, TX ....Civil Trial Practice

TAYLOR, DUANE, BARTON & GILMAN
Boston, MA............................Civil Trial Practice; General Practice; Insurance Defense

TAYLOR & DUNHAM, L.L.P.
Austin, TX ....Commercial Litigation; Insurance Defense; Labor and Employment Law

TAYLOR & FAUST, A PROFESSIONAL CORPORATION
San Francisco, CA ....Tax Law

TAYLOR, HARP & CALLIER
Columbus, GA ....Civil Trial Practice; Personal Injury

TAYLOR, HAZEN & KAUFFMAN, L.C.
Richmond, VA ....Business Law; Commercial Law; Insurance Defense; Tax Law

TAYLOR, HORBALY & BLACK
Jacksonville, NC.....................Criminal Trial Practice

TAYLOR, KELLER & DUNAWAY
London, KY ....Civil Trial Practice; General Practice; Insurance Defense

TAYLOR MCCORD, A LAW CORPORATION
Ventura, CA ....Appellate Practice; Civil Trial Practice; Environmental Law; Family Law; Labor and Employment Law; Personal Injury; Probate, Trusts and Estate Planning

TAYLOR, MILLER, SPROWL, HOFFNAGLE & MERLETTI
Chicago, IL.............................General Practice; Insurance Defense

TAYLOR, PHILBIN, PIGUE, MARCHETTI & BENNETT
Nashville, TN..........................Civil Trial Practice; Insurance Defense; Labor and Employment Law

TAYLOR, PORTER, BROOKS & PHILLIPS
Baton Rouge, LA....................General Practice

TAYLOR & TAYLOR
Philadelphia, PA ....Civil Trial Practice

TAYLOR & WALKER, P.C.
Norfolk, VA ....Business Law; Commercial Law; Insurance Defense

TAYLOR, ZUNKA, MILNOR & CARTER, LTD.
Charlottesville, VA.................General Practice; Insurance Defense

TEAHAN & CONSTANTINO
Poughkeepsie, NY ....Probate, Trusts and Estate Planning; Tax Law

TECHMEIER & VAN GRUNSVEN, S.C.
Milwaukee, WI ....Personal Injury

TEGTMEIER LAW FIRM, THE, P.C.
Colorado Springs, CO.............Criminal Trial Practice; Personal Injury

TEHIN + PARTNERS, A PROFESSIONAL CORPORATION
San Francisco, CA ....Admiralty/Maritime Law; Civil Trial Practice; Medical Malpractice; Personal Injury; Product Liability Law

TEICHBERG, ARTHUR J., A PROFESSIONAL CORPORATION
New York, NY.......................Commercial Law

TEITLER, STANLEY A., P.C.
New York, NY.......................Civil Trial Practice; Criminal Trial Practice

TEKELL, BOOK, MATTHEWS & LIMMER, L.L.P.
Houston, TX ....Civil Trial Practice; Insurance Defense

TELLEEN, BRAENDLE, HORBERG & SMITH, P.C.
Cambridge, IL.........................General Practice

TELLER, MARTIN, CHANEY & HASSELL
Vicksburg, MS........................General Practice

TELPNER, PETERSON, SMITH & RUESCH
Council Bluffs, IA ....General Practice

TEMKIN & ASSOCIATES, LTD.
Providence, RI........................General Practice

TEMPLE, LARRY E.
Austin, TX ....Administrative Law; Banking Law

TEMPLETON, SMITHEE, HAYES & FIELDS
Amarillo, TX...........................Civil Trial Practice

TEPE, THOMAS M.
Cincinnati, OH ....Civil Trial Practice

TEPPER, NANCY BOXLEY, A PROFESSIONAL CORPORATION
Laguna Hills, CA ....Probate, Trusts and Estate Planning

TERRIBERRY, CARROLL & YANCEY, L.L.P.
New Orleans, LA ....Admiralty/Maritime Law; General Practice

TERRY, TERRY AND STAPLETON
Morristown, TN......................Personal Injury

TERRY, VIC, A PROF. CORP., LAW OFFICE OF
Dallas, TX...............................Medical Malpractice; Personal Injury; Product Liability Law

TERWILLIGER, WAKEEN, PIEHLER & CONWAY, S.C.
Wausau, WI............................Civil Trial Practice; General Practice

TESKE, DAVID S. & ASSOCIATES
Seattle, WA ....Admiralty/Maritime Law

TESTA, HURWITZ & THIBEAULT, LLP
Boston, MA............................General Practice

TEW, ALLEN R., P.A.
Clayton, NC ....General Practice

THALER & THALER
Ithaca, NY..............................Civil Trial Practice

THARP, LIOTTA, JANES & YOKUM, LLP
Fairmont, WV ....General Practice

THAYER, BERNSTEIN & BASS, P.C.
Kansas City, MO ....Family Law

THEISEN, LANK, MULFORD & GOLDBERG, P.A.
Wilmington, DE......................Business Law; Civil Trial Practice; General Practice; Insurance Defense; Personal Injury; Real Estate Law

THERIAULT & JOSLIN, P.C.
Montpelier, VT.......................General Practice; Insurance Defense; Medical Malpractice

THERREL BAISDEN & MEYER WEISS
Miami Beach, FL ....General Practice; Tax Law

THIBODEAU, JOSEPH H., P.C., LAW OFFICES OF
Denver, CO ....Tax Law

THIEBLOT, RYAN, MARTIN & MILLER, P.A.
Baltimore, MD ....Admiralty/Maritime Law; Bankruptcy Law;
Business Law; Civil Trial Practice; Commercial Law;
Construction Law; Insurance Defense; Probate,
Trusts and Estate Planning

THINNES, THOMAS A., P.A.
Phoenix, AZ ....Criminal Trial Practice

THIRKELL & CRETAN
San Mateo, CA......................Probate, Trusts and Estate Planning

THISTLE, DANIEL L.
Philadelphia, PA ....Medical Malpractice; Product Liability Law

THOMAN SOULE GAGE
Hamilton, ON, Canada...........Civil Trial Practice; Insurance Defense; Product
Liability Law

THOMAS, CLAYTON H. JR.
Philadelphia, PA ....Environmental Law; Product Liability Law

THOMAS, RICHARD C.
Columbia, MO ....Personal Injury; Product Liability Law

THOMAS, BALLENGER, VOGELMAN AND TURNER, P.C.
Alexandria, VA ....Bankruptcy Law; Commercial Law

THOMAS, BIRDSONG, CLAYTON & BECKER, P.C.
Rolla, MO ....General Practice

THOMAS, BURNS & HOLLIDAY, P.C.
St. Joseph, MO......................General Practice

THOMAS & ELARDO, P.C.
Phoenix, AZ ....Insurance Defense

THOMAS, FELDMAN & WILSHUSEN, L.L.P.
Dallas, TX ....Construction Law

THOMAS, KENNEDY, SAMPSON & PATTERSON
Atlanta, GA ....Civil Trial Practice; Commercial Law; Insurance
Defense; Medical Malpractice; Municipal Bond/
Public Authority Financing; Personal Injury;
Product Liability Law; Real Estate Law; Sports and
Entertainment Law

THOMAS & LIBOWITZ, A PROFESSIONAL ASSOCIATION
Baltimore, MD ....Banking Law; Business Law; Family Law; Securities
Law

THOMAS, MAMER & HAUGHEY
Champaign, IL ....General Practice; Insurance Defense

THOMAS, MEANS & GILLIS, P.C.
Montgomery, AL ....Labor and Employment Law; Personal Injury

THOMAS & NEESE
Dresden, TN...........................General Practice

THOMAS & PRICE
Glendale, CA.........................Civil Trial Practice; Construction Law; General
Practice; Insurance Defense; Medical Malpractice;
Personal Injury; Product Liability Law

THOMAS, SCOTT G., LAW OFFICES OF
Milwaukee, WI ....Insurance Defense

THOMAS & SELF, A PROFESSIONAL CORPORATION
Dallas, TX ....Banking Law; Civil Trial Practice

THOMAS, SHEEHAN & CULP, L.L.P.
Dallas, TX ....Civil Trial Practice

THOMAS, SNELL, JAMISON, RUSSELL AND ASPERGER, A PROFESSIONAL CORPORATION
Fresno, CA ....General Practice

THOMAS, THOMAS & HAFER
Harrisburg, PA.......................Civil Trial Practice; Health Care Law; Insurance
Defense; Labor and Employment Law; Medical
Malpractice; Workers Compensation

THOMASON, HENDRIX, HARVEY, JOHNSON & MITCHELL
Memphis, TN ....Bankruptcy Law; Civil Trial Practice; Environmental
Law; General Practice; Insurance Defense; Personal
Injury; Probate, Trusts and Estate Planning

THOMASSON, GILBERT, COOK, REMLEY & MAGUIRE
Cape Girardeau, MO ....Civil Trial Practice; General Practice

THOMPSON, SARAH M.
Philadelphia, PA ....Civil Trial Practice; Medical Malpractice; Personal
Injury; Product Liability Law

THOMPSON, BETTY A., LTD.
Arlington, VA ....Family Law

THOMPSON & BOWIE
Portland, ME ....Civil Trial Practice; Construction Law; Insurance
Defense; Medical Malpractice; Personal Injury;
Product Liability Law

THOMPSON CALKINS & SUTTER
Pittsburgh, PA ....Insurance Defense; Probate, Trusts and Estate
Planning

THOMPSON COBURN
Washington, DC......................General Practice
Belleville, IL ....Civil Trial Practice; General Practice; Labor and
Employment Law; Tax Law
St. Charles, MO ....General Practice
St. Louis, MO.........................Admiralty/Maritime Law; Antitrust Law; Civil Trial
Practice; Environmental Law; General Practice;
Labor and Employment Law; Municipal Bond/
Public Authority Financing; Probate, Trusts and
Estate Planning; Tax Law

THOMPSON, COE, COUSINS & IRONS, L.L.P.
Dallas, TX..............................Administrative Law; Bankruptcy Law; Business
Law; Civil Trial Practice; General Practice;
Insurance Defense; Labor and Employment Law;
Real Estate Law

THOMPSON, DANIEL R., P.C.
Washington, DC......................Administrative Law; Environmental Law

THOMPSON, E.C., III, P.C.
Warsaw, NC...........................General Practice

THOMPSON, GARRETT & HINES
Brewton, AL...........................General Practice

THOMPSON AND GODWIN, L.L.P.
Dunn, NC...............................Civil Trial Practice

THOMPSON HINE & FLORY LLP
Cleveland, OH........................General Practice

THOMPSON AND HUTSON
Washington, DC......................Labor and Employment Law
Greenville, SC........................Labor and Employment Law

THOMPSON & KNIGHT, A PROFESSIONAL CORPORATION
Austin, TX ....Appellate Practice; Business Law; Civil Trial
Practice; Environmental Law; General Practice;
Health Care Law; Insurance Defense; International
Business Law; Medical Malpractice; Municipal and
Zoning Law; Securities Law; Trademark, Copyright
and Unfair Competition
Dallas, TX..............................Antitrust Law; Appellate Practice; Banking Law;
Bankruptcy Law; Business Law; Civil Trial Practice;
Construction Law; Employment Benefits Law;
Environmental Law; General Practice; Health Care
Law; Insurance Defense; International Business
Law; Labor and Employment Law; Medical
Malpractice; Municipal and Zoning Law; Natural
Resources Law; Patent, Trademark, Copyright and
Unfair Competition; Probate, Trusts and Estate
Planning; Product Liability Law; Real Estate Law;
Securities Law; Tax Law; Trademark, Copyright and
Unfair Competition
Fort Worth, TX ....Business Law; Civil Trial Practice; General Practice;
Health Care Law; Insurance Defense; International
Business Law; Medical Malpractice; Probate, Trusts
and Estate Planning; Real Estate Law; Securities
Law; Tax Law
Houston, TX ....Business Law; Civil Trial Practice; General Practice;
Health Care Law; Insurance Defense; Medical
Malpractice; Natural Resources Law; Securities Law
Monterrey, Nuevo León,
Mexico ....Business Law; General Practice; International
Business Law; Securities Law

THOMPSON LAW FIRM, THE, P.A.
Conway, SC ....Civil Trial Practice; General Practice
Myrtle Beach, SC ....Civil Trial Practice; General Practice

THOMPSON LAW OFFICE, THE
Monterey, CA ....Business Law; Civil Trial Practice; Personal Injury

THOMPSON, MARK E., A PROFESSIONAL CORPORATION
Lancaster, CA ....Probate, Trusts and Estate Planning

THOMPSON & MCMULLAN, A PROFESSIONAL CORPORATION
Richmond, VA ....Business Law; Civil Trial Practice

THOMPSON, MICHAEL, AND ASSOCIATES, L.L.P.
Denison, TX ....Civil Trial Practice; Family Law; Personal Injury

THOMPSON, O'BRIEN, KEMP & NASUTI, P.C.
Norcross, GA ....General Practice

THOMPSON, O'DONNELL, MARKHAM, NORTON & HANNON
Washington, DC......................Civil Trial Practice; Probate, Trusts and Estate
Planning

THOMPSON & O'NEIL, P.C.
Traverse City, MI....................Civil Trial Practice; Medical Malpractice; Personal
Injury; Product Liability Law

THOMPSON, SIZEMORE & GONZALEZ, PROFESSIONAL ASSOCIATION
Tampa, FL ....Labor and Employment Law

THOMPSON & SMITH, P.C.
Augusta, GA ....General Practice; Insurance Defense

THOMPSON, SPARKS, DEAN & MORRIS
Monroe, LA ....Banking Law; Bankruptcy Law; Business Law; Commercial Law; Land Use Law; Probate, Trusts and Estate Planning; Tax Law

THOMPSON & SWEENY, P.C.
Lawrenceville, GA ....General Practice

THOMPSON & THOMPSON
Centreville, MD.....................General Practice

THOMPSON & WALDRON
Alexandria, VA ....Construction Law

THOMS, DAVID M., & ASSOCIATES, P.C.
Bloomfield Hills, MI..............Probate, Trusts and Estate Planning
Detroit, MI...........................Business Law; Probate, Trusts and Estate Planning; Tax Law

THOMSON & BEHR
Edwardsville, IL.....................Civil Trial Practice; Insurance Defense

THOMSON, DOUGLAS W., LTD.
St. Paul, MN ....Criminal Trial Practice

THOMSON MURARO RAZOOK & HART, P.A.
Miami, FL ....Bankruptcy Law; Commercial Litigation; Communications Law; General Practice; Natural Resources Law; Tax Law

THOMSON & NELSON, A PROFESSIONAL LAW CORPORATION
Whittier, CA.........................General Practice

THOMSON, RHODES & COWIE, P.C.
Pittsburgh, PA ....Civil Trial Practice; General Practice

THOMSON, ROGERS
Toronto, ON, Canada.............General Practice

THON, BECK, VANNI, PHILLIPI & NUTT, A PROFESSIONAL CORPORATION
Pasadena, CA ....Personal Injury

THORBURN, SAKOL & THRONE
Boulder, CO ....Family Law

THORN AND GERSHON
Albany, NY............................Civil Trial Practice; Environmental Law; Insurance Defense; Personal Injury

THORNDAL, BACKUS, ARMSTRONG & BALKENBUSH, A PROFESSIONAL CORPORATION
Las Vegas, NV ....Civil Trial Practice; Insurance Defense

THORNTON, DAVIS & MURRAY, P.A.
Miami, FL ....Appellate Practice; Civil Trial Practice; General Practice

THORNTON, HEGG, REIF, JOHNSTON & DOLAN, P.A.
Alexandria, MN ....General Practice

THORNTON, PAYNE, WATSON, KLING & MILLER, P.C.
Bryan, TX...............................Insurance Defense

THORNTON & ROTHMAN, P.A.
Miami, FL ....Criminal Trial Practice

THORNTON, TAYLOR, DOWNS, BECKER, TOLSON & DOHERTY
San Francisco, CA ....Insurance Defense

THORNTON, THORNTON & THOMSEN
Westerly, RI ....Business Law; Probate, Trusts and Estate Planning; Tax Law

THORNTON, TORRENCE & GONZALES, P.A.
Port Richey, FL ....Labor and Employment Law; Probate, Trusts and Estate Planning

THORP AND CLARKE
Fayetteville, NC ....General Practice

THORPE, LAWRENCE W. LAW OFFICES OF
San Francisco, CA ....Family Law

THORPE, NORTH & WESTERN, L.L.P.
Salt Lake City, UT.................Patent, Trademark, Copyright and Unfair Competition

THORSNES, BARTOLOTTA, MCGUIRE & PADILLA
San Diego, CA ....Civil Trial Practice; Commercial Law; General Practice; Product Liability Law

THORSRUD CANE & PAULICH, INC., P.S.
Seattle, WA ....Insurance Defense

THORSTEINSSONS
Vancouver, BC, Canada...........Tax Law

Toronto, ON, Canada..............Tax Law

THRASHER, DOYLE, PELISH & FRANTI, LTD.
Rice Lake, WI ....Insurance Defense

THRASHER, WHITLEY, HAMPTON & MORGAN, A PROFESSIONAL CORPORATION
Atlanta, GA ....Business Law; Probate, Trusts and Estate Planning; Securities Law

THREET AND KING
Albuquerque, NM...................General Practice

THRELKELD & THRELKELD, P.S.C.
Williamstown, KY ....Real Estate Law

THROCKMORTON, BECKSTROM, OAKES & TOMASSIAN LLP
Pasadena, CA ....Civil Trial Practice; General Practice

THUILLEZ, FORD, GOLD & CONOLLY, L.L.P.
Albany, NY ....Civil Trial Practice; General Practice

THURBER, MARY, LAW OFFICES OF
Hackensack, NJ.......................Civil Trial Practice; Construction Law; Labor and Employment Law

THURMAN, HOWALD, WEBER, SENKEL & NORRICK, L.L.C.
Hillsboro, MO.........................Civil Trial Practice; General Practice

TIERNEY & SWIFT
Washington, DC.....................Communications Law

TIERNEY, ZULLO, FLAHERTY & MURPHY, P.C.
Norwalk, CT ....General Practice

TIETZ & RICHARDSON
Decatur, IL..............................Commercial Litigation; Insurance Defense; Mergers and Acquisitions

TIGHE, EVAN, EHRMAN, SCHENCK & PARAS
Pittsburgh, PA ....Insurance Defense

TIGHE, PATTON, TABACKMAN & BABBIN, L.L.P.
Washington, DC.....................Business Law

TILBURY, ROGER
Portland, OR..........................Antitrust Law; Appellate Practice; Civil Trial Practice; General Practice; Personal Injury

TILFORD, DOBBINS, ALEXANDER, BUCKAWAY & BLACK
Louisville, KY ....General Practice; Insurance Defense; Real Estate Law

TILLINGHAST LICHT & SEMONOFF
Providence, RI.......................Civil Trial Practice; General Practice; Tax Law

TILLMAN, MCTIER, COLEMAN, TALLEY, NEWBERN & KURRIE
Valdosta, GA ....Civil Trial Practice; General Practice; Insurance Defense

TIMBANARD & TOLMAN, L.L.P.
Phoenix, AZ ....Personal Injury

TIMBERLAKE, SMITH, THOMAS & MOSES, P.C.
Staunton, VA ....General Practice

TIMMER, JAMO & O'LEARY
Lansing, MI............................Civil Trial Practice; General Practice; Insurance Defense; Medical Malpractice; Personal Injury

TIMMIS & INMAN, L.L.P.
Detroit, MI.............................Antitrust Law; Appellate Practice; Business Law; Civil Trial Practice; Commercial Law; Environmental Law; General Practice; Health Care Law; Insurance Defense; Labor and Employment Law; Mergers and Acquisitions; Probate, Trusts and Estate Planning; Product Liability Law; Real Estate Law; Securities Law; Tax Law

TINDALL & FOSTER, P.C.
Houston, TX ....Immigration and Naturalization

TINLEY, NASTRI, RENEHAN & DOST
Waterbury, CT ....Civil Trial Practice; General Practice

TINSMAN & HOUSER, INC.
San Antonio, TX.....................Civil Trial Practice; Commercial Law; Medical Malpractice; Personal Injury; Product Liability Law

TIPPING, HARRY A., CO., L.P.A., A LEGAL PROF. ASSN.
Akron, OH ....Business Law; Civil Trial Practice; Insurance Defense; Labor and Employment Law

TIPS & GIBSON
Tulsa, OK................................Bankruptcy Law; Business Law; Civil Trial Practice; Commercial Litigation

TISINGER, TISINGER, VANCE & GREER, A PROFESSIONAL CORPORATION
Carrollton, GA ....Business Law; Commercial Law; General Practice; Health Care Law; Insurance Defense; Medical Malpractice; Public Utilities Law; Real Estate Law

TISTAERT, LAWRENCE C.
Los Angeles, CA ....Business Law; Commercial Litigation; Real Estate Law

TITUS, BRUECKNER & BERRY, P.C.
Scottsdale, AZ ....Business Law; Commercial Litigation; Real Estate Law; Securities Law

TOBIN, CRAIG D. & ASSOCIATES
Chicago, IL.............................Civil Trial Practice; Criminal Trial Practice

TOBIN AND DEMPF
Albany, NY...........................General Practice; Health Care Law; Labor and Employment Law

TOCHER, G. NEIL
Redding, CA ....Personal Injury

TODD, VANDERBLOEMEN AND BRADY, P.A.
Lenoir, NC ....General Practice

TOGUT, SEGAL & SEGAL
New York, NY........................Bankruptcy Law

TOKYO AOYAMA LAW OFFICE
Tokyo, Japan.........................General Practice

TOLES & ASSOCIATES, P.C.
Phoenix, AZ ....Criminal Trial Practice; Family Law; Personal Injury

TOLL, EBBY, LANGER & MARVIN, A PROFESSIONAL CORPORATION
Philadelphia, PA ....Bankruptcy Law; Civil Trial Practice; Commercial Litigation; Environmental Law; Real Estate Law

TOLLEY, VANDENBOSCH & WALTON, P.C.
Grand Rapids, MI ....Civil Trial Practice; Construction Law; Insurance Defense; Real Estate Law

TOLLISON LAW FIRM, P.A.
Oxford, MS...........................Civil Trial Practice; Personal Injury

TOMAR, SIMONOFF, ADOURIAN, O'BRIEN, KAPLAN, JACOBY & GRAZIANO, A PROFESSIONAL CORPORATION
Haddonfield, NJ.....................Labor and Employment Law; Natural Resources Law; Personal Injury
Northfield, NJ ....Environmental Law; Labor and Employment Law

TOMAZIN, THOMAS J., P.C.
Englewood, CO ....Civil Trial Practice; Medical Malpractice; Personal Injury

TOMICH, LILLIAN LAW OFFICES OF
San Marino, CA ....Civil Trial Practice

TOMPKINS, CLOUGH, HIRSHON & LANGER, P.A.
Portland, ME ....Admiralty/Maritime Law; Banking Law

TOMPKINS, MCGUIRE & WACHENFELD
Newark, NJ ....Banking Law; Civil Trial Practice; Criminal Trial Practice; General Practice; Insurance Defense

TOMPKINS AND MCMASTER
Columbia, SC ....Business Law; Civil Trial Practice; Criminal Trial Practice; General Practice

TONKIN & MONDL, L.C.
St. Louis, MO.........................Admiralty/Maritime Law; Commercial Litigation; Insurance Defense

TOOMS & HOUSE
London, KY...........................Civil Trial Practice; Criminal Trial Practice; General Practice; Insurance Defense

TORBERT & TORBERT, P.A.
Gadsden, AL...........................Insurance Defense

TORKILDSON, KATZ, FONSECA, JAFFE, MOORE & HETHERINGTON, ATTORNEYS AT LAW, A LAW CORPORATION
Honolulu, HI...........................General Practice; Labor and Employment Law

TORSHEN, SPREYER & GARMISA, LTD.
Chicago, IL.............................Appellate Practice; Commercial Litigation

TORY TORY DESLAURIERS & BINNINGTON
Toronto, ON, Canada..............General Practice
London, England ....General Practice

TOUCHSTONE, BERNAYS, JOHNSTON, BEALL & SMITH, L.L.P.
Dallas, TX..............................Insurance Defense

TOUHEY, T. JOSEPH, P.A.
Glen Burnie, MD....................Civil Trial Practice

TOUSLEY BRAIN, P.L.L.C.
Seattle, WA ....Civil Trial Practice; General Practice; Real Estate Law

TOWNSEND, LAWRENCE G.
San Francisco, CA ....Trademark, Copyright and Unfair Competition

TOWNSEND & BRANNON
Tampa, FL.............................Bankruptcy Law; Commercial Litigation

TOWNSEND, COURTLAND K., JR., CHARTERED
Ocean City, MD.....................Civil Trial Practice; Criminal Trial Practice

TOWNSEND, HOVDE & MONTROSS
Indianapolis, IN ....Aviation Law; Medical Malpractice; Personal Injury; Product Liability Law

TOWNSEND & TOWNSEND
Indianapolis, IN ....Medical Malpractice; Personal Injury

TOWNSEND AND TOWNSEND AND CREW LLP
Palo Alto, CA ....Patent, Trademark, Copyright and Unfair Competition
San Francisco, CA ....Patent, Trademark, Copyright and Unfair Competition

TRABUE, STURDIVANT & DEWITT
Columbia, TN ....General Practice
Nashville, TN ....General Practice

TRACY & MCQUILLAN, THE LEGAL PROF. CORP. OF
Grand Island, NE ....General Practice; Probate, Trusts and Estate Planning; Tax Law

TRAFTON & MATZEN
Auburn, ME............................Real Estate Law

TRAGER, SUSAN M., A PROF. CORP., LAW OFFICES OF
Irvine, CA...............................Environmental Law; Natural Resources Law

TRAGOS, GEORGE E.
Clearwater, FL ....Criminal Trial Practice

TRALINS AND ASSOCIATES, P.A.
Miami, FL ....General Practice

TRASK, BRITT & ROSSA, A PROFESSIONAL CORPORATION
Salt Lake City, UT..................Patent, Trademark, Copyright and Unfair Competition

TRAUB, BONACQUIST & FOX LLP
New York, NY........................Bankruptcy Law; Business Law

TRAVIS, WILLIAM R. LAW OFFICES OF
Austin, TX ....Family Law

TRAVIS & GOOCH
Washington, DC......................Public Utilities Law

TRAYLOR, CHARLES V.
Indianapolis, IN ....Bankruptcy Law

TRAYNOR, RUTTEN & TRAYNOR
Devils Lake, ND ....General Practice

TRECKER & FRITZ
Honolulu, HI...........................Civil Trial Practice; Medical Malpractice; Personal Injury; Product Liability Law

TREDWAY, LUMSDAINE & DOYLE, LLP
Downey, CA............................General Practice

TREECE, ALFREY, MUSAT & BOSWORTH, P.C.
Denver, CO ....Civil Trial Practice; Commercial Litigation; Environmental Law; Medical Malpractice

TREMAYNE, LAY, CARR, BAUER & COLEMAN LLP
Clayton, MO ....General Practice

TREMBLAY, MAURILE C., A PROF. CORP., LAW OFFICES OF
La Jolla, CA............................Civil Trial Practice; Insurance Defense; Real Estate Law

TREMBLAY & SMITH, LLP
Charlottesville, VA..................Civil Trial Practice; General Practice

TREMP, ROBERT P., P.C.
Traverse City, MI....................Insurance Defense; Municipal and Zoning Law

TRENAM, KEMKER, SCHARF, BARKIN, FRYE, O'NEILL & MULLIS, PROFESSIONAL ASSOCIATION
Tampa, FL ....General Practice

TRENCH, ROSSI E WATANABE
Brasília, Brazil ....General Practice
Rio de Janeiro, Brazil ....General Practice
São Paulo, Brazil....................General Practice

TRENTI LAW FIRM
Virginia, MN ....General Practice

TREON, STRICK, LUCIA & AGUIRRE, A PROF. ASSN. OF LAWYERS
Phoenix, AZ ....Personal Injury

TREPEL & CLARK
San Jose, CA ....Business Law; Civil Trial Practice

TREVETT, LENWEAVER & VAN STRYDONCK, P.C.
Rochester, NY..........................Civil Trial Practice; Insurance Defense

TREXLER, BUSHNELL, GIANGIORGI & BLACKSTONE, LTD.
Washington, DC.....................Patent, Trademark, Copyright and Unfair Competition
Chicago, IL.........................Patent, Trademark, Copyright and Unfair Competition

TRIBLER ORPETT PALMER & CRONE, A PROFESSIONAL CORPORATION
Chicago, IL..........................Civil Trial Practice; Commercial Law; Insurance Defense
Schaumburg, IL......................Commercial Law

TRICHILO, BANCROFT, MCGAVIN, HORVATH & JUDKINS, P.C.
Fairfax, VA ....Civil Trial Practice; Insurance Defense

TRIPLETT, WOOLF & GARRETSON, L.L.P.
Wichita, KS ....General Practice

TRIPP, SCOTT, CONKLIN & SMITH
Fort Lauderdale, FL................Environmental Law; Labor and Employment Law; Real Estate Law

TRIPPET AND KEE
Beaver, OK...........................General Practice

TROFF, PETZKE & AMMESON
St. Joseph, MI ....Business Law; Family Law; Labor and Employment Law; Personal Injury; Probate, Trusts and Estate Planning; Real Estate Law

TROPE AND TROPE
Los Angeles, CA......................Family Law

TROTH & VAN TILBURG
Ashland, OH ....General Practice

TROTTER, JAMES R.
Raleigh, NC..........................General Practice

TROUBH, HEISLER & PIAMPIANO, P.C.
Portland, ME ....Banking Law; Business Law; Civil Trial Practice; Commercial Law; Environmental Law; General Practice; Labor and Employment Law; Personal Injury; Real Estate Law; Workers Compensation

TROUT & RICHARDS, P.L.L.C.
Washington, DC.....................Commercial Litigation; Criminal Trial Practice

TROUTMAN, RICHARD B., P.A.
Orlando, FL ....Personal Injury
Winter Park, FL......................Personal Injury

TROUTMAN SANDERS LLP
Atlanta, GA ....General Practice

TROUTMAN, WILLIAMS, IRVIN, GREEN & HELMS, PROFESSIONAL ASSOCIATION
Kissimmee, FL........................Civil Trial Practice; General Practice
Winter Park, FL.....................Civil Trial Practice; General Practice

TROUTT, NAT G.
Senatobia, MS ....Civil Trial Practice

TRUE & SEWELL
Dallas, TX...............................General Practice

TRULY, SMITH, LATHAM & KUEHNLE
Natchez, MS............................Civil Trial Practice; Energy Law

TRUMAN, CRAIG L., P.C.
Denver, CO ....Criminal Trial Practice

TRZUSKOWSKI, KIPP, KELLEHER & PEARCE, P.A.
Wilmington, DE.....................Civil Trial Practice; Family Law; Insurance Defense; Medical Malpractice; Personal Injury

TSCHIDER & SMITH
Bismarck, ND ....Civil Trial Practice; Probate, Trusts and Estate Planning; Tax Law

TUCKER, STEVEN L.
Santa Fe, NM.........................Appellate Practice

TUCKER, HENDRYX, SNYDER & SLADE, P.C.
Houston, TX ....Insurance Defense

TUCKER, KENNETH L., P.C.
Phoenix, AZ ....Medical Malpractice; Personal Injury; Product Liability Law

TUCKER AND TUCKER
Paoli, IN...............................General Practice

TUKE YOPP & SWEENEY
Nashville, TN.........................Commercial Litigation; Mergers and Acquisitions; Trademark, Copyright and Unfair Competition

TULAC, JOHN W.
Claremont, CA ....International Business Law; International Trade Law

TULLOS, TULLOS & TULLOS
Raleigh, MS...........................Personal Injury; Workers Compensation

TUNSTEAD, SCHECHTER & TORRE
Jericho, NY ....Construction Law

TURBIN, RICHARD, A LAW CORPORATION, LAW OFFICES OF
Honolulu, HI.........................Civil Trial Practice; Personal Injury

TURLEY & SWAN, P.C.
Phoenix, AZ ....Civil Trial Practice; Insurance Defense; Medical Malpractice; Personal Injury

TURLEY, WINDLE, P.C., LAW OFFICES OF
Dallas, TX..............................Aviation Law; Personal Injury

TURNAGE & CHAMBERS
Atlanta, GA ....Civil Trial Practice; Family Law

TURNER, BRUCE E.
Dallas, TX..............................Real Estate Law

TURNER, CHARLES B.
South Orange, NJ....................Commercial Law; General Practice

TURNER, PAUL K. LAW OFFICE OF
Hopkinsville, KY ....General Practice

TURNER, SCOTT C.
Pasadena, CA ....Construction Law

TURNER & DAVIS, A PROFESSIONAL CORPORATION
Midland, TX ....Commercial Litigation; Energy Law

TURNER ENOCHS & LLOYD, P.A.
Greensboro, NC......................Banking Law; Commercial Law

TURNER, GERSTENFELD, WILK, AUBERT & YOUNG, LLP
Beverly Hills, CA ....Civil Trial Practice; General Practice; Probate, Trusts and Estate Planning; Real Estate Law

TURNER, GRANZOW & HOLLENKAMP
Dayton, OH............................General Practice

TURNER & GRISCTI, PROFESSIONAL ASSOCIATION
Gainesville, FL ....Criminal Trial Practice

TURNER, JONES & BITTING
Clarinda, IA ....General Practice

TURNER, ONDERDONK, KIMBROUGH & HOWELL, P.A.
Chatom, AL ....Civil Trial Practice; Criminal Trial Practice; Personal Injury; Product Liability Law; Workers Compensation

TURNER, O'NEAL & JORDAN, P.C.
Lubbock, TX..........................Personal Injury

TURNER, PADGET, GRAHAM & LANEY, P.A.
Columbia, SC ....Administrative Law; Antitrust Law; Banking Law; Bankruptcy Law; Business Law; Civil Trial Practice; Commercial Law; Construction Law; Environmental Law; General Practice; Health Care Law; Insurance Defense; Medical Malpractice; Municipal and Zoning Law; Personal Injury; Probate, Trusts and Estate Planning; Product Liability Law; Real Estate Law; Securities Law; Workers Compensation

TURNER, REID, DUNCAN, LOOMER & PATTON, P.C.
Springfield, MO......................Civil Trial Practice

TURNER, SEABERRY & WARFORD
Eastland, TX ....General Practice

TURNER, TURNER & TURNER, P.C.
Atlanta, GA ....Family Law

TURNER, WILSON & SAWYER
Montgomery, AL....................Family Law

TUTTLE & TAYLOR, A LAW CORPORATION
Los Angeles, CA ....General Practice
Sacramento, CA ....General Practice

TUTTLE, TAYLOR & HERON
Washington, DC.....................General Practice

TWIGGS, ABRAMS, STRICKLAND & TREHY, P.A.
Raleigh, NC............................Civil Trial Practice; Commercial Law; Medical Malpractice; Personal Injury; Product Liability Law

TWITCHELL AND RICE
Santa Maria, CA ....General Practice

TWOHIG, RAY, P.C.
Albuquerque, NM....................Constitutional Law; Criminal Trial Practice

TWOMEY, LATHAM, SHEA & KELLEY
Riverhead, NY ....Environmental Law; Real Estate Law

TYAN & ASSOCIES
Beirut, Lebanon........................General Practice

TYDINGS, BRYAN & ADAMS, P.C.
Fairfax, VA ....Banking Law; General Practice

TYE AND TYE
Dayton, OH........................General Practice; Probate, Trusts and Estate
Planning

TYGART AND SCHULER, P.A.
Jacksonville, FL ....Insurance Defense; Personal Injury

TYLER, BARTL, BURKE AND ALBERT, P.L.C.
Alexandria, VA ....Bankruptcy Law

TYLER, CASSELL, JACKSON, PEACE & SILVER, L.L.P.
Columbia, SC ....Commercial Law; Construction Law; Real Estate
Law

TYLER COOPER & ALCORN
Hartford, CT ....General Practice
New Haven, CT......................General Practice
Stamford, CT..........................General Practice

TYNDALL & CAHNERS
San Jose, CA ....Civil Trial Practice; Criminal Trial Practice;
Environmental Law; Medical Malpractice

TYSON, GEORGE H. JR.
Houston, TX ....Criminal Trial Practice

ULMER & BERNE P.L.L.
Cleveland, OH........................Business Law; Civil Trial Practice; General Practice;
Labor and Employment Law; Tax Law

ULRICH, KESSLER & ANGER, P.C.
Phoenix, AZ ....Antitrust Law; Appellate Practice; Health Care
Law; Municipal and Zoning Law

ULRICH AND ULRICH, INC. A PROFESSIONAL CORPORATION
Houston, TX ....Civil Trial Practice

UNDERBERG & KESSLER LLP
Rochester, NY........................Civil Trial Practice; Environmental Law; General
Practice; Insurance Defense

UNDERWOOD, P. JAMES
Annapolis, MD ....Real Estate Law

UNDERWOOD KINSEY WARREN & TUCKER, P.A.
Charlotte, NC..........................General Practice

UNDERWOOD LAW FIRM
Jackson, MS ....Real Estate Law

UNDERWOOD, WILSON, BERRY, STEIN & JOHNSON, P.C.
Amarillo, TX..........................General Practice

UNGERMAN & IOLA
Tulsa, OK................................Family Law; Labor and Employment Law; Personal
Injury

UNGLESBY & KOCH
Baton Rouge, LA......................Criminal Trial Practice; Product Liability Law

UPCHURCH, BAILEY & UPCHURCH, P.A.
St. Augustine, FL....................Civil Trial Practice; General Practice; Land Use
Law; Municipal and Zoning Law; Probate, Trusts
and Estate Planning; Real Estate Law

UPSHAW, WILLIAMS, BIGGERS, BECKHAM & RIDDICK
Greenwood, MS ....Civil Trial Practice; Environmental Law; General
Practice; Insurance Defense; Workers Compensation
Jackson, MS ....Civil Trial Practice; General Practice; Insurance
Defense

URSO, LIGUORI AND URSO
Westerly, RI ....General Practice; Labor and Employment Law;
Probate, Trusts and Estate Planning; Real Estate
Law

USSERY & PARRISH, P.A.
Albuquerque, NM....................Real Estate Law

UTZ, LITVAK, SUMMERS, POWERS & MANRING
St. Joseph, MO........................General Practice

VAAGE, ROBERT F.
San Diego, CA ....Civil Trial Practice

VAALER, WARCUP, WOUTAT, ZIMNEY & FOSTER, CHARTERED
Grand Forks, ND ....General Practice

VACOVEC, MAYOTTE & SINGER
Newton, MA ....International Business Law; Tax Law

VADEN, EICKENROHT & THOMPSON, L.L.P.
Houston, TX ....Patent, Trademark, Copyright and Unfair Competition

VAFIADES, BROUNTAS & KOMINSKY
Bangor, ME............................Civil Trial Practice; Criminal Trial Practice; General
Practice; Insurance Defense; Personal Injury;
Probate, Trusts and Estate Planning; Real Estate
Law

VAGLICA, MEINHOLD & MALDONADO, L.L.C.
Colorado Springs, CO.............Civil Trial Practice

VAIRO, MECHLIN, TOMASI, JOHNSON & MANCHESTER
Houghton, MI ....General Practice; Insurance Defense

VALDER LAW OFFICES, P.C.
Phoenix, AZ ....Medical Malpractice

VALENTINE, ADAMS AND LAMAR, L.L.P.
Nashville, NC..........................General Practice

VALENTINE & ASSOCIATES, P.C.
Troy, MI................................Civil Trial Practice; Labor and Employment Law;
Personal Injury
West Bloomfield, MI...............Business Law; Civil Trial Practice; Labor and
Employment Law; Personal Injury; Real Estate Law

VALLE & CRAIG, P.A.
Miami, FL ....Admiralty/Maritime Law; Civil Trial Practice;
Commercial Law; Insurance Defense

VALORE CHARTERED LAW OFFICES
Atlantic City, NJ....................Civil Trial Practice; General Practice

VANBERG, HAWK
Dallas, TX..............................Civil Trial Practice

VAN BLOIS, KNOWLES, SCHWARTZ & BASKIN
Oakland, CA ....Aviation Law; Civil Trial Practice; Labor and
Employment Law; Medical Malpractice; Personal
Injury; Product Liability Law

VAN CAMP, WEST, HAYES & MEACHAM, A PROFESSIONAL ASSOCIATION
Pinehurst, NC..........................General Practice

VAN COTT, BAGLEY, CORNWALL & MCCARTHY, A PROFESSIONAL CORPORATION
Ogden, UT................................General Practice
Park City, UT ....General Practice
Salt Lake City, UT..................Administrative Law; Antitrust Law; Appellate
Practice; Banking Law; Bankruptcy Law; Business
Law; Civil Trial Practice; Commercial Law;
Communications Law; Computer Law; Construction
Law; Criminal Trial Practice; Employment Benefits
Law; Environmental Law; Family Law; General
Practice; Health Care Law; Insurance Defense;
International Trade Law; Labor and Employment
Law; Land Use Law; Medical Malpractice; Natural
Resources Law; Patent, Trademark, Copyright and
Unfair Competition; Personal Injury; Probate,
Trusts and Estate Planning; Product Liability Law;
Public Utilities Law; Real Estate Law; Securities
Law; Tax Law

VANDEBERG JOHNSON & GANDARA
Tacoma, WA ....General Practice

VANDEMARK, RUTH E. LAW OFFICES OF
Chicago, IL.............................Appellate Practice

VANDEN BOS & CHAPMAN
Portland, OR..........................Bankruptcy Law

VANDEVEER GARZIA, PROFESSIONAL CORPORATION
Detroit, MI.............................Civil Trial Practice; Environmental Law; General
Practice; Insurance Defense; Municipal and Zoning
Law; Personal Injury
Mount Clemens, MI...............General Practice

VANDEVENTER, BLACK, MEREDITH & MARTIN, L.L.P.
Norfolk, VA ....Admiralty/Maritime Law; Bankruptcy Law; Civil
Trial Practice; Environmental Law; General
Practice; Immigration and Naturalization; Labor
and Employment Law; Real Estate Law; Tax Law

VAN DEWATER & VAN DEWATER
Beacon, NY ....General Practice
Poughkeepsie, NY ....Banking Law; Bankruptcy Law; Communications
Law; Family Law; Real Estate Law; Tax Law

VAN HOY, REUTLINGER & TAYLOR
Charlotte, NC..........................Health Care Law; Labor and Employment Law

VAN LANDINGHAM, L. S. JR., LAW OFFICES OF
Arlington, VA ....Patent, Trademark, Copyright and Unfair Competition

VAN LOUCKS & HANLEY
San Jose, CA ....Civil Trial Practice; Commercial Litigation; General
Practice; Insurance Defense

VAN MEER & BELANGER, P.A.
South Portland, ME .... Health Care Law; Tax Law

VANN, FRANK C.
Camilla, GA .... General Practice

VANNAH COSTELLO CANEPA WIESE & RIEDY
Las Vegas, NV .... Insurance Defense; Medical Malpractice; Personal Injury; Product Liability Law

VANNOY, COLVARD, TRIPLETT, MCLEAN & VANNOY
North Wilkesboro, NC .... General Practice

VANNOY & REEVES
West Jefferson, NC .... General Practice

VAN OSDELL, LESTER, HOWE & RICE, P.A.
Myrtle Beach, SC .... Appellate Practice; Civil Trial Practice; Personal Injury

VAN SUILICHEM & BROWN, P.C.
Bloomfield Hills, MI .... Civil Rights; Labor and Employment Law

VAN WERT, RONALD K., A PROFESSIONAL CORPORATION
Newport Beach, CA .... Civil Trial Practice; Tax Law

VAN WINKLE, BUCK, WALL, STARNES AND DAVIS, P.A.
Asheville, NC .... General Practice

VARNADORE, M. DEWAYNE, P.C., LAW OFFICES OF
Tyler, TX .... Natural Resources Law

VARNUM, RIDDERING, SCHMIDT & HOWLETT LLP
Battle Creek, MI .... General Practice
Grand Rapids, MI .... Antitrust Law; Banking Law; Bankruptcy Law; Business Law; Civil Trial Practice; Environmental Law; Family Law; General Practice; Labor and Employment Law; Municipal Bond/Public Authority Financing; Patent, Trademark, Copyright and Unfair Competition; Probate, Trusts and Estate Planning; Real Estate Law; Tax Law; Trademark, Copyright and Unfair Competition
Kalamazoo, MI .... General Practice

VASSALLO, EDDIE, P.C., LAW OFFICES OF
Dallas, TX .... Civil Trial Practice; Personal Injury

VAUGHAN & HULL, LTD., A PROF. CORP., LAW OFFICES
Elko, NV .... General Practice

VAUGHAN & SLAYTON
South Boston, VA .... General Practice

VEATCH, CARLSON, GROGAN & NELSON
Los Angeles, CA .... Insurance Defense; Medical Malpractice

VEDDER, PRICE, KAUFMAN & KAMMHOLZ
Chicago, IL .... Banking Law; General Practice; Labor and Employment Law; Municipal Bond/Public Authority Financing; Tax Law

VEGA, STANLEY, ZELMAN & HANLON, P.A.
Naples, FL .... Civil Trial Practice; Criminal Trial Practice; Family Law; Municipal and Zoning Law; Real Estate Law; Securities Law

VELTMANN & LETO
San Diego, CA .... Family Law

VENA, TRUELOVE & RILEY
Boston, MA .... Construction Law

VENABLE, ATTORNEYS AT LAW, VENABLE, BAETJER, HOWARD & CIVILETTI, LLP
Washington, DC .... Administrative Law; Admiralty/Maritime Law; Antitrust Law; Appellate Practice; Banking Law; Bankruptcy Law; Business Law; Civil Trial Practice; Commercial Law; Communications Law; Construction Law; Criminal Trial Practice; Employment Benefits Law; Environmental Law; General Practice; Health Care Law; Insurance Defense; Labor and Employment Law; Natural Resources Law; Patent, Trademark, Copyright and Unfair Competition; Product Liability Law; Real Estate Law; Securities Law; Trademark, Copyright and Unfair Competition; Transportation Law

VENABLE, ATTORNEYS AT LAW, VENABLE, BAETJER AND HOWARD, LLP
Baltimore, MD .... Administrative Law; Admiralty/Maritime Law; Antitrust Law; Appellate Practice; Banking Law; Bankruptcy Law; Business Law; Civil Trial Practice; Commercial Law; Communications Law; Construction Law; Criminal Trial Practice; Employment Benefits Law; Environmental Law; Family Law; General Practice; Health Care Law; Immigration and Naturalization; Insurance Defense; Labor and Employment Law; Municipal Bond/Public Authority Financing; Municipal and Zoning Law; Natural Resources Law; Patent, Trademark, Copyright and Unfair Competition; Personal Injury; Probate, Trusts and Estate Planning; Product Liability Law; Real Estate Law; Securities Law; Tax Law; Trademark, Copyright and Unfair Competition; Transportation Law

Rockville, MD .... Administrative Law; Appellate Practice; Banking Law; Business Law; Civil Trial Practice; General Practice; Labor and Employment Law
Towson, MD .... Appellate Practice; Banking Law; Business Law; Civil Trial Practice; Commercial Law; Construction Law; General Practice; Insurance Defense; Labor and Employment Law; Municipal Bond/Public Authority Financing; Personal Injury; Probate, Trusts and Estate Planning; Product Liability Law; Real Estate Law
McLean, VA .... Appellate Practice; Banking Law; Civil Trial Practice; Commercial Law; Construction Law; General Practice; Real Estate Law

VERNER, LIIPFERT, BERNHARD, MCPHERSON AND HAND, CHARTERED
Washington, DC .... Commercial Law; Communications Law; Environmental Law; General Practice; Labor and Employment Law; Natural Resources Law; Transportation Law

VERRILL & DANA
Portland, ME .... Administrative Law; General Practice; Health Care Law; Land Use Law

VETTER & WHITE, INCORPORATED
Providence, RI .... Appellate Practice; Civil Trial Practice

VIAL, HAMILTON, KOCH & KNOX, L.L.P.
Dallas, TX .... General Practice

VICKERS, M. COPPLEY, & ASSOCIATES, P.C.
Sevierville, TN .... Real Estate Law

VICKERS, RIIS, MURRAY AND CURRAN, L.L.C.
Mobile, AL .... Admiralty/Maritime Law; Business Law; Environmental Law; General Practice; Tax Law

VICTOR, RAYMOND M., P.C.
Norristown, PA .... Medical Malpractice; Personal Injury; Product Liability Law

VIGIL & HANRATH
Barrington, IL .... Patent, Trademark, Copyright and Unfair Competition

VIMONT & WILLS
Lexington, KY .... Construction Law; Insurance Defense; Labor and Employment Law; Real Estate Law; Workers Compensation

VINAR, BENJAMIN
Garden City, NY .... Appellate Practice; Civil Trial Practice

VINNEDGE, GAFNEY & GLADSON, INC.
Upland, CA .... Probate, Trusts and Estate Planning

VINSON & ELKINS
London, England .... General Practice
Washington, DC .... Civil Trial Practice; General Practice
Austin, TX .... Civil Trial Practice; General Practice
Dallas, TX .... Civil Trial Practice; General Practice
Houston, TX .... Admiralty/Maritime Law; Antitrust Law; Civil Trial Practice; Energy Law; General Practice; Labor and Employment Law; Municipal Bond/Public Authority Financing; Natural Resources Law; Patent, Trademark, Copyright and Unfair Competition; Tax Law

VINYARD & ASSOCIATES
Washington, DC .... Tax Law

VINYARD AND MOISE, ATTORNEYS AT LAW, P.C.
Abingdon, VA .... Civil Trial Practice; Criminal Trial Practice; Family Law

VIRTUE, NAJJAR & BARTELL
Santa Fe, NM .... Administrative Law; Commercial Litigation; Environmental Law; Health Care Law

VITTAL AND STERNBERG
Los Angeles, CA .... Civil Trial Practice

VLADECK, WALDMAN, ELIAS & ENGELHARD, P.C.
New York, NY .... Employment Benefits Law; Labor and Employment Law

VLASSIS & VLASSIS
Phoenix, AZ .... Business Law; Immigration and Naturalization

VLASTOS & DUNCAN
Casper, WY .... Medical Malpractice; Personal Injury; Product Liability Law

VOGELGESANG, HOWES, LINDAMOOD & BRUNN
Canton, OH .... Insurance Defense

VOGEL, KELLY, KNUTSON, WEIR, BYE & HUNKE, LTD.
Fargo, ND .... Banking Law; Bankruptcy Law; Civil Trial Practice; Commercial Law; Criminal Trial Practice; General Practice; Insurance Defense; Labor and Employment Law; Personal Injury; Probate, Trusts and Estate Planning; Real Estate Law; Tax Law

VOGEL, THOMAS & PRUITT
Fort Worth, TX ....Commercial Litigation

VOGL & MEREDITH
San Francisco, CA ....Civil Trial Practice; Environmental Law; Insurance Defense

VOGRIN & RIESTER, P.C.
Pittsburgh, PA ....Criminal Trial Practice

VOLK, HELLERSTEDT & CONNOLLY
Pittsburgh, PA ....Labor and Employment Law

VOLK, MICHAEL D., P.C.
El Paso, TX.............................Medical Malpractice; Personal Injury

VOLLMER, MICHAEL V.
Newport Beach, CA................Probate, Trusts and Estate Planning

VOLLMER RULONG & ASSOCIATES, P.C.
Pittsburgh, PA ....Bankruptcy Law; Civil Trial Practice

VOLPE, EDWARD L., P.C.
Denver, CO ....Civil Trial Practice

VOLZ, PRESTWOOD & HANAN, P.C.
Montgomery, AL ....Administrative Law; Appellate Practice; Banking Law; Business Law; Civil Trial Practice; Commercial Law; General Practice; Labor and Employment Law; Probate, Trusts and Estate Planning; Real Estate Law; Tax Law

VOORHEES & ACCIAVATTI
Morris Plains, NJ....................Civil Trial Practice; Commercial Law

VOORHIES & LABBÉ, A PROFESSIONAL LAW CORPORATION
Lafayette, LA ....Insurance Defense; Personal Injury

VORT, ROBERT A.
Hackensack, NJ.......................Appellate Practice; Family Law

VORYS, SATER, SEYMOUR AND PEASE
Washington, DC......................General Practice
Cincinnati, OH ....General Practice
Cleveland, OH ....General Practice; Labor and Employment Law
Columbus, OH ....Antitrust Law; Banking Law; Bankruptcy Law; General Practice; Labor and Employment Law; Municipal Bond/Public Authority Financing; Natural Resources Law; Real Estate Law; Tax Law

VOUTÉ, LOHRFINK, MAGRO & COLLINS, LLP
White Plains, NY ....General Practice; Insurance Defense; Personal Injury; Product Liability Law

VRANESH AND RAISCH, L.L.C.
Boulder, CO ....Environmental Law; Natural Resources Law

VUONO & GRAY
Pittsburgh, PA ....Civil Trial Practice; Real Estate Law; Tax Law; Transportation Law

WACHTEL, BIEHN & MALM
Lake Havasu City, AZ............General Practice; Personal Injury; Probate, Trusts and Estate Planning

WADDEY & PATTERSON, A PROFESSIONAL CORPORATION
Nashville, TN ....Patent, Trademark, Copyright and Unfair Competition

WADE, WM. KIM
Dallas, TX...............................Criminal Trial Practice

WADE ASH WOODS HILL & FARLEY, P.C.
Denver, CO ....Probate, Trusts and Estate Planning

WADE & CAMPBELL, LLP
Atlanta, GA ....Civil Trial Practice; Commercial Litigation; Insurance Defense; Public Utilities Law

WADLEIGH, STARR, PETERS, DUNN & CHIESA
Manchester, NH......................General Practice

WAGER, DONALD R.
Los Angeles, CA......................Criminal Trial Practice

WAGNER, BAGOT & GLEASON
New Orleans, LA....................Admiralty/Maritime Law; Commercial Law; Environmental Law; Insurance Defense; International Business Law; Labor and Employment Law

WAGNER AND GRUNDY
Tulsa, OK................................Family Law

WAGNER, JOHNSON & MCAFEE, P.A.
West Palm Beach, FL.............Civil Trial Practice; Personal Injury

WAGNER, JOHNSTON, ROSENTHAL & TOBIN, P.C.
Atlanta, GA ....Business Law

WAGNER, MYERS & SANGER, A PROFESSIONAL CORPORATION
Knoxville, TN ....Civil Trial Practice; General Practice; Health Care Law; Natural Resources Law; Public Utilities Law; Securities Law; Tax Law

WAGNER, WATSON & PETTIT
Honolulu, HI..........................Business Law

WAGSTAFF, ALVIS, STUBBEMAN, SEAMSTER & LONGACRE, L.L.P.
Abilene, TX.............................General Practice; Insurance Defense

WAITE, SCHNEIDER, BAYLESS & CHESLEY CO., L.P.A.
Cincinnati, OH ....Antitrust Law; Appellate Practice; Civil Trial Practice; Construction Law; International Business Law; Labor and Employment Law; Medical Malpractice; Personal Injury; Product Liability Law; Public Utilities Law; Securities Law

WALDBAUM, CORN, KOFF, BERGER AND COHEN, P.C.
Denver, CO ....General Practice

WALDER, SONDAK & BROGAN, A PROFESSIONAL CORPORATION
Roseland, NJ...........................Appellate Practice; Business Law; Civil Trial Practice; Commercial Law; Criminal Trial Practice; Environmental Law; Insurance Defense; Tax Law

WALDRON AND FANN
Murfreesboro, TN ....Personal Injury

WALKER, GEORGE R.
Monterey, CA ....Probate, Trusts and Estate Planning

WALKER & BLACK
Little Rock, AR.......................Commercial Law; Probate, Trusts and Estate Planning

WALKER & DURHAM
San Francisco, CA ....Personal Injury

WALKER, GEORGE G., INC.
San Francisco, CA ....Criminal Trial Practice

WALKER, HILL, ADAMS, UMBACH, MEADOWS & WALTON
Opelika, AL ....Banking Law; General Practice; Insurance Defense; Municipal and Zoning Law

WALKER, HULBERT, GRAY & BYRD
Perry, GA................................General Practice

WALKER, JONES, LAWRENCE, DUGGAN & SAVAGE, P.C.
Warrenton, VA........................Real Estate Law

WALKER, KEELING & CARROLL, L.L.P.
Victoria, TX ....Environmental Law; Insurance Defense; Labor and Employment Law

WALKER LAW FIRM, THE, A PROFESSIONAL CORPORATION
Newport Beach, CA................Civil Trial Practice

WALKER, MCKENZIE & WALKER, A PROFESSIONAL CORPORATION
Memphis, TN ....Patent, Trademark, Copyright and Unfair Competition

WALKER, ROBERT D., A PROFESSIONAL CORPORATION
Los Angeles, CA......................Civil Trial Practice; Medical Malpractice; Personal Injury

WALKER & WALKER, P.C.
Knoxville, TN ....Banking Law; Bankruptcy Law; General Practice

WALKER, WATTS, JACKSON & MCFARLAND
Adrian, MI ....Banking Law; General Practice; Real Estate Law

WALKER, WILLIAM G., P.C.
Tucson, AZ ....Civil Trial Practice; Commercial Litigation; Criminal Trial Practice

WALKER & WILLIAMS, PROFESSIONAL CORPORATION
Belleville, IL ....Insurance Defense
Edwardsville, IL......................Insurance Defense

WALKUP, MELODIA, KELLY & ECHEVERRIA, A PROFESSIONAL CORPORATION
San Francisco, CA ....Medical Malpractice; Personal Injury; Product Liability Law

WALLACE & DE MAYO, P.C.
Norcross, GA..........................Bankruptcy Law; Commercial Law; General Practice

WALLACE, MORRIS, BARWICK & ROCHELLE, P.A.
Kinston, NC............................General Practice

WALLACE, SAUNDERS, AUSTIN, BROWN & ENOCHS, CHARTERED
Overland Park, KS..................General Practice

WALLACE & WHEELER, L.L.P.
Corpus Christi, TX ....Tax Law

WALLACK & WALLACK, P.C.
Indianapolis, IN......................Business Law; Real Estate Law

WALLENSTEIN & WAGNER, LTD.
Chicago, IL...................Patent, Trademark, Copyright and Unfair Competition

WALLER LANSDEN DORTCH & DAVIS
Columbia, TN ....General Practice
Nashville, TN.........................Environmental Law; General Practice; Health Care Law; Labor and Employment Law; Trademark, Copyright and Unfair Competition

WALLER AND MARK, P.C.
Denver, CO ....Civil Trial Practice

WALLER, SMITH & PALMER, P.C.
New London, CT....................Banking Law; Bankruptcy Law; Civil Trial Practice; Commercial Law; General Practice; Municipal and Zoning Law; Probate, Trusts and Estate Planning; Real Estate Law
Old Lyme, CT........................General Practice

WALLERSTEIN, MELVIN J., P.A.
West Orange, NJ....................Civil Trial Practice; Probate, Trusts and Estate Planning; Tax Law

WALMSLEY LAW FIRM
Batesville, AR ....General Practice

WALSH, DANIEL R. THE LAW OFFICE OF
Carson City, NV ....Land Use Law

WALSH, MICHAEL R.
Orlando, FL ....Family Law

WALSH, O'NEAL & ASSOCIATES
Baton Rouge, LA....................Insurance Defense

WALSH, ANDERSON, UNDERWOOD, SCHULZE & ALDRIDGE, P.C.
Austin, TX ....Civil Trial Practice; Insurance Defense

WALSH, COLUCCI, STACKHOUSE, EMRICH & LUBELEY, P.C.
Arlington, VA ....Business Law; Civil Trial Practice; Land Use Law; Municipal and Zoning Law; Real Estate Law
Leesburg, VA ....Real Estate Law
Woodbridge, VA.....................Real Estate Law

WALSH & FISHER, A PROFESSIONAL ASSOCIATION
Westminster, MD....................General Practice

WALSH, GERALD R., P.C.
Fairfax, VA ....Civil Trial Practice

WALSH & KEATING, S.C.
Milwaukee, WI........................Probate, Trusts and Estate Planning; Real Estate Law; Tax Law

WALSH, MICHAEL P., P.A.
West Palm Beach, FL ....Family Law; Personal Injury

WALSTON, STABLER, WELLS, ANDERSON & BAINS
Birmingham, AL ....General Practice

WALSWORTH, FRANKLIN, BEVINS & MCCALL
Orange, CA ....Environmental Law

WALTER & HAVERFIELD
Cleveland, OH.........................Communications Law; Employment Benefits Law; Environmental Law; General Practice; Health Care Law; Labor and Employment Law; Municipal and Zoning Law

WALTERS, DAVIS & PUJADAS, P.C.
Ocilla, GA ....Civil Trial Practice; Criminal Trial Practice; General Practice

WALTERS & JOYCE, P.C.
Denver, CO ....Antitrust Law; Civil Trial Practice; General Practice; Real Estate Law

WALTERS & WARD, A PROFESSIONAL CORPORATION
San Diego, CA ....Probate, Trusts and Estate Planning

WALTHER ASSOCIATES
Santa Fe, NM..........................Family Law

WALTHOUR AND GARLAND
Greensburg, PA........................Appellate Practice; Civil Trial Practice; General Practice; Insurance Defense; Probate, Trusts and Estate Planning

WALTON & ASSOCIATES
San Diego, CA ....Admiralty/Maritime Law

WALTON LANTAFF SCHROEDER & CARSON
Coral Gables, FL ....General Practice
Fort Lauderdale, FL.................General Practice
Miami, FL ....General Practice
West Palm Beach, FL ....General Practice

WALTON, SMITH, PHILLIPS & DIXON, P.C.
Traverse City, MI....................Civil Trial Practice; Personal Injury

WALZER, PETER M. LAW OFFICES OF
Los Angeles, CA ....Family Law

WANDERER, HANNA & TALARICO
Danbury, CT ....General Practice

WANSKER & DANIEL
Rockingham, NC ....Personal Injury

WAPNER, NEWMAN & WIGRIZER, A PROFESSIONAL CORPORATION
Philadelphia, PA ....Construction Law; Medical Malpractice

WARBURTON, ADAMI, MCNEILL & PAISLEY, P.C.
Alice, TX.................................General Practice

WARD, CRAIG B., P.A.
Orlando, FL ....General Practice; Probate, Trusts and Estate Planning; Real Estate Law

WARD, KERSHAW & MINTON, A PROFESSIONAL ASSOCIATION
Baltimore, MD ....Admiralty/Maritime Law; Antitrust Law; Civil Trial Practice; Insurance Defense

WARD, MAGUIRE & BYBEE
Pocatello, ID ....General Practice

WARD, NELSON & PELLETERI, L.L.C.
New Orleans, LA ....Insurance Defense

WARDROP & WARDROP, P.C.
Grand Rapids, MI ....General Practice

WARD & WARD
Indianapolis, IN ....Civil Trial Practice; Personal Injury; Product Liability Law

WARD, WARD & WARD, L.L.P.
New Bern, NC ....Civil Trial Practice; General Practice

WARE, DAVID A. M. & ASSOCIATES
Metairie, LA............................Immigration and Naturalization

WARE, BRYSON, WEST & KUMMER
Covington, KY ....Civil Trial Practice; General Practice; Insurance Defense; Workers Compensation

WARHOLA, O'TOOLE, LOUGHMAN, ALDERMAN & STUMPHAUZER
Lorain, OH..............................General Practice

WARING COX, PLC
Memphis, TN ....Civil Trial Practice; General Practice; Insurance Defense; Labor and Employment Law; Municipal Bond/Public Authority Financing; Real Estate Law; Tax Law

WARLICK MILSTED DOTSON & CARTER
Jacksonville, NC......................General Practice

WARLICK, TRITT & STEBBINS
Augusta, GA ....Banking Law; Civil Trial Practice; General Practice

WARNER, CHARLES G. LAW OFFICES OF
Monterey, CA ....Civil Trial Practice

WARNER, MAYOUE & BATES, P.C.
Atlanta, GA ....Family Law

WARNER NORCROSS & JUDD LLP
Grand Rapids, MI ....Antitrust Law; Banking Law; Bankruptcy Law; Civil Trial Practice; Employment Benefits Law; Environmental Law; General Practice; Health Care Law; Immigration and Naturalization; Labor and Employment Law; Natural Resources Law; Patent, Trademark, Copyright and Unfair Competition; Real Estate Law; Securities Law; Tax Law; Transportation Law
Holland, MI ....General Practice
Muskegon, MI.........................General Practice

WARNER, SMITH & HARRIS, PLC
Fort Smith, AR ....Civil Trial Practice; General Practice

WARNER & STACKPOLE LLP
Boston, MA..............................Banking Law; Civil Trial Practice; Environmental Law; General Practice; Insurance Defense; Labor and Employment Law; Land Use Law; Municipal Bond/Public Authority Financing; Probate, Trusts and Estate Planning; Product Liability Law; Real Estate Law; Tax Law

WARNICKE & LITTLER, P.L.C.
Phoenix, AZ ....Bankruptcy Law; Commercial Litigation; Construction Law

WARNOCK & WARNOCK
Greenup, KY ....General Practice

WARREN, PRICE, CAMERON, FAUST & ASCIUTTO, P.C.
Okemos, MI ....Business Law

WARREN & SINKLER, L.L.P.
Charleston, SC ....Business Law; General Practice; Real Estate Law; Securities Law; Tax Law

WARREN AND YOUNG
Ashtabula, OH ....Business Law; General Practice; Insurance Defense; Labor and Employment Law

WARSHAFSKY, ROTTER, TARNOFF, REINHARDT & BLOCH, S.C.
Milwaukee, WI ....Personal Injury

WARTNICK, CHABER, HAROWITZ, SMITH & TIGERMAN, A PROFESSIONAL CORPORATION
San Francisco, CA ....Commercial Litigation; Personal Injury; Product Liability Law

WASKER, DORR, WIMMER & MARCOUILLER, P.C.
Des Moines, IA ....Administrative Law; Civil Trial Practice; General Practice; Personal Injury; Real Estate Law

WASSER, ROSENSON & CARTER
Los Angeles, CA ....Family Law

WASSERMAN, COMDEN & CASSELMAN L.L.P.
Tarzana, CA ....Civil Trial Practice; General Practice; Insurance Defense

WASSERSTROM, DAVID E.
Elkins Park, PA ....Business Law

WATANABE, ING & KAWASHIMA
Honolulu, HI..........................Civil Trial Practice; Commercial Law; General Practice; Insurance Defense

WATERS, HOLT & FIELDS
Pampa, TX ....General Practice

WATERS, MCPHERSON, MCNEILL, P.C.
Secaucus, NJ...........................Civil Trial Practice; General Practice

WATERS, WARNER & HARRIS
Clarksburg, WV ....Civil Trial Practice; General Practice; Insurance Defense; Natural Resources Law; Real Estate Law

WATKINS, JOHN E. JR.
White Plains, NY ....Municipal and Zoning Law; Real Estate Law; Tax Law

WATKINS, BOULWARE, LUCAS, MINER, MURPHY & TAYLOR
St. Joseph, MO.......................General Practice

WATKINS & EAGER
Jackson, MS ....Banking Law; Bankruptcy Law; Civil Trial Practice; Commercial Law; Environmental Law; General Practice; Insurance Defense; Labor and Employment Law; Natural Resources Law; Personal Injury; Tax Law

WATKINS, VANDIVER, KIRVEN, GABLE & GRAY
Anderson, SC ....Civil Trial Practice; General Practice

WATKINSON LAIRD RUBENSTEIN LASHWAY & BALDWIN, P.C.
Eugene, OR ....General Practice

WATKISS DUNNING & WATKISS, A PROFESSIONAL CORPORATION
Salt Lake City, UT..................Antitrust Law; Civil Trial Practice; Construction Law; Criminal Trial Practice; Employment Benefits Law; Product Liability Law

WATROUS & REARDON
Albuquerque, NM....................Bankruptcy Law; Commercial Litigation; Labor and Employment Law; Real Estate Law

WATSON, WILLIAM E. & ASSOCIATES
Wellsburg, WV.......................General Practice

WATSON, BLANCHE, WILSON & POSNER
Baton Rouge, LA....................Commercial Litigation; Health Care Law; Medical Malpractice; Product Liability Law; Tax Law

WATSON & DANA
La Fayette, GA ....General Practice

WATSON, FARLEY & WILLIAMS
New York, NY........................Admiralty/Maritime Law; Banking Law; General Practice; Transportation Law

WATSON, HARRISON & DEGRAFFENRIED
Tuscaloosa, AL ....Business Law; Natural Resources Law

WATSON, HOLLOW & REEVES
Knoxville, TN ....Civil Trial Practice; Communications Law; Insurance Defense; Labor and Employment Law; Medical Malpractice; Product Liability Law

WATT, TIEDER & HOFFAR, L.L.P.
Irvine, CA..............................Civil Trial Practice; Commercial Law; Construction Law; Environmental Law; General Practice; International Business Law; Real Estate Law

Washington, DC......................Civil Trial Practice; Commercial Law; Construction Law; Environmental Law; General Practice; International Business Law; Real Estate Law

McLean, VA...........................Civil Trial Practice; Commercial Law; Construction Law; Environmental Law; General Practice; International Business Law; Real Estate Law

WATTS, SHANNON & MITTS
Meridian, MS ....Civil Trial Practice; General Practice; Insurance Defense

WEARY, DAVIS, HENRY, STRUEBING & TROUP
Junction City, KS....................General Practice

WEATHERLY LAW FIRM, THE
Duluth, GA ....Administrative Law; Civil Trial Practice

WEAVER & ASSOCIATES
Lake Wales, FL.......................Real Estate Law

WEAVER, MOSEBACH, PIOSA, HIXSON & MARLES
Allentown, PA ....General Practice; Municipal and Zoning Law

WEBB, BURNETT, JACKSON, CORNBROOKS, WILBER, VORHIS & DOUSE, LLP
Salisbury, MD ....Business Law; Civil Trial Practice; General Practice

WEBB, CARLOCK, COPELAND, SEMLER & STAIR
Atlanta, GA ....Civil Trial Practice; Insurance Defense; Workers Compensation

WEBB & ELEY, P.C.
Montgomery, AL ....Insurance Defense

WEBB, SANDERS, DEATON, BALDUCCI, SMITH & FAULKS, P.L.L.C.
Tupelo, MS.............................Business Law; Civil Trial Practice; General Practice; Insurance Defense

WEBB, STOKES & SPARKS
San Angelo, TX ....Personal Injury

WEBB, TANNER & POWELL
Lawrenceville, GA ....Banking Law; Business Law; General Practice; Personal Injury

WEBB ZIESENHEIM BRUENING LOGSDON ORKIN & HANSON, P.C.
Pittsburgh, PA ....Patent, Trademark, Copyright and Unfair Competition

WEBBER, CHRISTOPHER A. JR.
Wallingford, VT ....Probate, Trusts and Estate Planning

WEBBER, JOSEPH P. LAW OFFICES OF
Austin, TX ....Civil Trial Practice; Commercial Litigation

WEBBER & THIES, P.C.
Urbana, IL..............................Commercial Litigation; Environmental Law; General Practice; Insurance Defense; Labor and Employment Law; Probate, Trusts and Estate Planning; Tax Law

WEBER, JAMES E., P.A.
West Palm Beach, FL..............Civil Trial Practice; Probate, Trusts and Estate Planning

WEBER, PERRA, MUNZING & MCVITTY, P.C.
Brattleboro, VT ....Civil Trial Practice; Environmental Law; Family Law; General Practice; Probate, Trusts and Estate Planning

WEBER & STERLING
Maumee, OH..........................Probate, Trusts and Estate Planning

WEBER & WEBER
Weston, WV ....Civil Trial Practice; Real Estate Law

WEBSTER, GEOFFREY E.
Columbus, OH ....Health Care Law

WEBSTER, CHAMBERLAIN & BEAN
Washington, DC......................Administrative Law; Tax Law

WEBSTER, MICHAEL T., P.A.
Shalimar, FL ....Family Law

WECHSLER HARWOOD HALEBIAN & FEFFER LLP
New York, NY........................Antitrust Law; Civil Trial Practice; General Practice; Securities Law

WEED, HUBBARD, BERRY & DOUGHTY
Nashville, TN ....Administrative Law

WEEKS & HUTCHINS
Waterville, ME.......................General Practice

WEEMS, WRIGHT, SCHIMPF, HAYTER & CARMOUCHE, A PROFESSIONAL LAW CORPORATION
Shreveport, LA.......................Civil Trial Practice; Construction Law; Real Estate Law

WEGMAN, HESSLER, VANDERBURG & O'TOOLE, A LEGAL PROFESSIONAL ASSOCIATION
Cleveland, OH..........................Business Law; Probate, Trusts and Estate Planning

WEGMANN, GASAWAY, STEWART, SCHNEIDER, DIEFFENBACH, TESREAU, STOLL & SHERMAN, P.C.
Hillsboro, MO..........................General Practice

WEHNER AND PERLMAN
Los Angeles, CA......................Business Law

WEHNER & YORK
Washington, DC......................Civil Trial Practice; Criminal Trial Practice

WEHRLE & SMITH, P.C.
Martinsville, IN........................General Practice

WEICHSEL, JOHN L.
Hackensack, NJ......................Appellate Practice; Civil Trial Practice; Criminal Trial Practice

WEIGHT, MICHAEL A., ATTORNEY AT LAW, A LAW CORPORATION
Honolulu, HI............................Criminal Trial Practice

WEILER, LEONARD D., A PROFESSIONAL CORPORATION
San Ramon, CA ....Family Law

WEIL, GOTSHAL & MANGES LLP
New York, NY..........................General Practice

WEILL & WEILL
Chattanooga, TN ....Civil Trial Practice; Personal Injury

WEIL & PETROCCHI, A PROFESSIONAL CORPORATION
Dallas, TX................................Commercial Litigation

WEIL & WRIGHT
Carlsbad, CA...........................Banking Law; Business Law; Civil Trial Practice; Commercial Law; Real Estate Law

WEINBERG, CAMPBELL, SLONE & SLONE, P.S.C.
Hindman, KY ....Personal Injury; Product Liability Law; Workers Compensation

WEINBERG, HOFFMAN & CASEY
Larkspur, CA ....Business Law; Insurance Defense; Medical Malpractice; Personal Injury; Product Liability Law

WEINBERG, MCCORMICK, CHATZINOFF AND PAUL, A PROFESSIONAL ASSOCIATION
Haddonfield, NJ......................Bankruptcy Law; Family Law

WEINBRENNER, NEIL E., P.A., LAW OFFICES OF
Las Cruces, NM......................Civil Trial Practice; Insurance Defense

WEINER, SAM B.
Columbus, OH ....Criminal Trial Practice

WEINER, ASTRACHAN, GUNST, HILLMAN AND ALLEN, A PROFESSIONAL CORPORATION
Baltimore, MD ....Civil Trial Practice; Criminal Trial Practice; Trademark, Copyright and Unfair Competition

WEINER, JEFFREY S., ATTORNEYS AT LAW, P.A.
Miami, FL ....Commercial Law; Criminal Trial Practice

WEINGARDEN & HAUER, P.C.
Birmingham, MI......................Business Law; Family Law; Probate, Trusts and Estate Planning; Tax Law

WEINGARTEN, SCHURGIN, GAGNEBIN & HAYES
Boston, MA..............................Patent, Trademark, Copyright and Unfair Competition

WEINHAUS AND DOBSON
St. Louis, MO..........................Employment Benefits Law; Labor and Employment Law

WEINSTEIN, JORDAN S. THE LAW OFFICES OF
Alexandria, VA ....Patent, Trademark, Copyright and Unfair Competition

WEINSTEIN, BOLDT, RACINE, HALFHIDE & CAMEL, PROFESSIONAL CORPORATION
Los Angeles, CA ....Tax Law

WEINSTEIN, CHAYT & CHASE, P.C.
Brooklyn, NY...........................General Practice

WEINSTEIN & PENZA, A PROFESSIONAL CORPORATION
Livingston, NJ.........................Family Law

WEINSTEIN, STEPHEN S., A PROFESSIONAL CORPORATION
Morristown, NJ.......................Civil Trial Practice; Criminal Trial Practice; Insurance Defense; Medical Malpractice; Personal Injury; Product Liability Law

WEINSTEIN, WEINER, IGNAL, NAPOLITANO & SHAPIRO, P.C.
Bridgeport, CT ....Commercial Litigation; Criminal Trial Practice

WEINSTOCK, MANION, REISMAN, SHORE & NEUMANN, A LAW CORPORATION
Los Angeles, CA ....Probate, Trusts and Estate Planning; Tax Law

WEINTRAUB, STOCK, BENNETT, ETTINGOFF & GRISHAM, P.C.
Memphis, TN ....General Practice; Labor and Employment Law

WEIR, JAMES A.
Colorado Springs, CO.............Probate, Trusts and Estate Planning; Real Estate Law

WEIR & ALVARADO, P.C.
San Antonio, TX......................Civil Trial Practice; Labor and Employment Law

WEIR & FOULDS
Toronto, ON, Canada..............General Practice

WEIR & PARTNERS
Philadelphia, PA ....Banking Law; Bankruptcy Law; Business Law; Civil Trial Practice; Commercial Law; Commercial Litigation; Real Estate Law

WEIR AND WALLEY
Metairie, LA............................Commercial Law; Probate, Trusts and Estate Planning

WEISER & ASSOCIATES, P.C.
Philadelphia, PA ....Patent, Trademark, Copyright and Unfair Competition

WEISMAN BOWEN & GROSS
Pittsburgh, PA ....Bankruptcy Law; Civil Trial Practice; Commercial Law; Real Estate Law

WEISMAN & LUBELL
Westport, CT...........................Civil Trial Practice; Family Law; General Practice; Municipal Bond/Public Authority Financing; Municipal and Zoning Law

WEISS, DAVID J. LAW OFFICES OF
Santa Monica, CA...................Medical Malpractice

WEISS BERRETT LOYD PETTY, L.C.
Salt Lake City, UT..................Civil Trial Practice; Criminal Trial Practice

WEISS & FREDERICK
Louisville, KY ....Medical Malpractice; Personal Injury; Product Liability Law

WEISS & HANDLER, P.A.
Boca Raton, FL ....Civil Trial Practice; Commercial Law; Commercial Litigation; Family Law; Personal Injury; Real Estate Law

WEISS & HERNANDEZ, P.A.
Miami, FL ....Immigration and Naturalization

WEISS LAW CORPORATION
Los Angeles, CA ....Real Estate Law

WEISSMANN, WOLFF, BERGMAN, COLEMAN & SILVERMAN
Beverly Hills, CA ....Sports and Entertainment Law

WEIST & KEPNER
Fowler, IN................................General Practice; Probate, Trusts and Estate Planning

WEISZ & ASSOCIATES
Atlanta, GA ....Administrative Law; Business Law; Commercial Law; Construction Law

WELBAUM, GUERNSEY, HINGSTON, GREENLEAF & GREGORY, L.L.P.
Miami, FL ....Civil Trial Practice; Construction Law; General Practice

WELBORN SULLIVAN MECK & TOOLEY, P.C.
Denver, CO ....Environmental Law; General Practice; International Business Law; Natural Resources Law

WELCH, MICHAEL
Atlanta, GA ....Construction Law

WELCH, JONES & SMITH
Oklahoma City, OK.................Civil Trial Practice; Environmental Law; Insurance Defense; Labor and Employment Law; Product Liability Law

WELCH, MACALPINE, BAHORSKI, BIEGLECKI & FARRELL, P.C.
Mount Clemens, MI.................Insurance Defense; Municipal and Zoning Law; Product Liability Law

WELCH, OLRICH & MORI, A PROFESSIONAL CORPORATION
San Francisco, CA ....Bankruptcy Law; Construction Law

WELDON, CHARLES R.
Norwalk, CA ....Personal Injury

WELDON, E. DURWARD
Georgetown, KY ....General Practice; Probate, Trusts and Estate Planning; Real Estate Law; Tax Law

WELDON, HUSTON & KEYSER
Mansfield, OH ....General Practice

WELEBIR & MCCUNE, A PROFESSIONAL LAW CORPORATION
Redlands, CA ....Personal Injury; Product Liability Law

WELKER, PAUL
Clarksville, TN ....Personal Injury

WELLBAUM & MCLENNON, P.A.
Englewood, FL ....Probate, Trusts and Estate Planning; Real Estate Law

WELLBORN, HOUSTON, ADKISON, MANN, SADLER & HILL, L.L.P.
Henderson, TX ....Commercial Law; Personal Injury; Product Liability Law

WELLER, GREEN, MCGOWN & TOUPS, L.L.P.
Beaumont, TX ....Insurance Defense; Personal Injury

WELLER, WICKS AND WALLACE, PROFESSIONAL CORPORATION
Pittsburgh, PA ....Natural Resources Law; Probate, Trusts and Estate Planning; Tax Law

WELLES & MCGRATH
Scranton, PA ....Business Law; Civil Trial Practice; General Practice; Probate, Trusts and Estate Planning

WELLS, ANDERSON & RACE, LLC
Denver, CO ....Aviation Law; Civil Trial Practice; Insurance Defense; Product Liability Law

WELLS & BLOSSOM
Wallace, NC ....General Practice

WELLS, FELBER, PURCELL & KRAATZ
Fort Worth, TX ....Personal Injury

WELLS, GALLAGHER, ROEDER & MILLAGE
Bettendorf, IA ....General Practice

WELLS MARBLE & HURST, PLLC
Jackson, MS ....Civil Trial Practice; General Practice; Insurance Defense; Tax Law

WELLS, PEYTON, BEARD, GREENBERG, HUNT & CRAWFORD, L.L.P.
Beaumont, TX ....Admiralty/Maritime Law; General Practice

WELLS PINCKNEY & MCHUGH, A PROFESSIONAL CORPORATION
Austin, TX ....General Practice; Labor and Employment Law

WELLS PINCKNEY & MCHUGH, A PROFESSIONAL CORPORATION
Corpus Christi, TX ....General Practice; Labor and Employment Law
San Antonio, TX ....Antitrust Law; Civil Trial Practice; Communications Law; Criminal Trial Practice; General Practice; Labor and Employment Law; Real Estate Law; Tax Law

WELLS, PORTER, SCHMITT & JONES
Paintsville, KY ....General Practice; Insurance Defense; Workers Compensation

WELLS AND SINGER, P.A.
Bordentown, NJ ....General Practice
Mount Holly, NJ ....General Practice; Probate, Trusts and Estate Planning
Robbinsville, NJ ....General Practice

WELLS WARREN, P.C.
Richmond, VA ....Civil Trial Practice

WELMAN, BEATON, HIVELY & GODLEY
Kennett, MO ....General Practice
Malden, MO ....General Practice

WELTON, CHARLES, A PROFESSIONAL CORPORATION
Denver, CO ....Civil Trial Practice

WELTY, JEAN L.
New Haven, CT ....Family Law

WENDEROTH, LIND & PONACK
Washington, DC ....Patent, Trademark, Copyright and Unfair Competition

WENDT LAW OFFICE, THE, P.C.
Delta, CO ....Family Law

WENTWORTH & PAOLI, P.C.
Newport Beach, CA ....Personal Injury

WERKSMAN, MARK J. LAW OFFICES OF
Los Angeles, CA ....Criminal Trial Practice

WERNLE, RISTINE & AYERS, L.P.C.
Crawfordsville, IN ....General Practice

WESIERSKI & ZUREK
Irvine, CA ....Civil Trial Practice; Insurance Defense

WESNER, KEMPTON, RUSSELL AND DOMINIQUE
Jefferson City, MO ....General Practice
Sedalia, MO ....General Practice

WESSELS & PAUTSCH, P.C.
St. Charles, IL ....Labor and Employment Law

WESSELS, STOJAN & STEPHENS, P.C.
Rock Island, IL ....General Practice

WEST, ROBIN PAGE
Baltimore, MD ....Civil Trial Practice; General Practice; Personal Injury; Product Liability Law

WEST, DAVID WM., P.C., LAW OFFICES OF
Phoenix, AZ ....General Practice

WEST & JONES
Clarksburg, WV ....Civil Trial Practice; Medical Malpractice; Personal Injury; Product Liability Law; Real Estate Law

WEST & ROSE
Kingsport, TN ....Civil Rights; Civil Trial Practice; Insurance Defense; Medical Malpractice

WESTERMAN & ASSOCIATES, P.C.
Ann Arbor, MI ....Probate, Trusts and Estate Planning; Tax Law

WESTERMANN & TRYON
Garden City, NY ....Commercial Litigation

WESTERVELT, JOHNSON, NICOLL & KELLER
Peoria, IL ....General Practice

WESTMAN & LINTZ
Cocoa, FL ....General Practice

WESTON, BURTON S.
Manhasset, NY ....Bankruptcy Law

WESTON HURD FALLON PAISLEY & HOWLEY
Cleveland, OH ....Civil Trial Practice; Environmental Law; General Practice; Insurance Defense; Patent, Trademark, Copyright and Unfair Competition; Tax Law

WHALEY, C. DAVID
Richmond, VA ....Criminal Trial Practice

WHAM & WHAM
Centralia, IL ....Insurance Defense

WHARTON LEVIN EHRMANTRAUT KLEIN & NASH, A PROFESSIONAL ASSOCIATION
Annapolis, MD ....Civil Trial Practice
Baltimore, MD ....Civil Trial Practice
Bethesda, MD ....Civil Trial Practice

WHEAT, JOE F.
Houston, TX ....Real Estate Law

WHEATLY, WHEATLY, NOBLES & WEEKS, P.A.
Beaufort, NC ....Civil Trial Practice; Criminal Trial Practice; General Practice

WHEELER & KORPECK, LLP
Silver Spring, MD ....General Practice

WHEELER, KROMHOLZ & MANION
Milwaukee, WI ....Patent, Trademark, Copyright and Unfair Competition

WHEELER, THOMPSON, PARKER & COUNTS
Easton, MD ....General Practice; Probate, Trusts and Estate Planning

WHEELER UPHAM, A PROFESSIONAL CORPORATION
Grand Rapids, MI ....Administrative Law; Appellate Practice; Business Law; Civil Trial Practice; Commercial Law; Employment Benefits Law; Environmental Law; General Practice; Insurance Defense; Probate, Trusts and Estate Planning; Product Liability Law; Real Estate Law; Transportation Law

WHEELUS, KYLE JR.
Beaumont, TX ....Insurance Defense

WHELCHEL, BROWN, READDICK & BUMGARTNER
Brunswick, GA ....Civil Trial Practice; General Practice; Insurance Defense; Labor and Employment Law

WHELCHEL & DUNLAP
Gainesville, GA ....General Practice

WHELCHEL, WHELCHEL & CARLTON
Moultrie, GA ....General Practice

WHIPPLE AND VIELE, A PROFESSIONAL LAW CORPORATION
Ventura, CA ....Criminal Trial Practice; Family Law; Personal Injury

WHIPPS & WISTNER
Columbus, OH ....Family Law
Dublin, OH ....Family Law

WHITE, DAN E.
Atlanta, GA ....Immigration and Naturalization

WHITE, WILLIAM A. THE LAW OFFICE OF
Austin, TX ....Criminal Trial Practice

WHITE & ADAMS, A PROFESSIONAL CORPORATION
Oklahoma City, OK................Civil Trial Practice; Criminal Trial Practice; Personal Injury

WHITEAKER & WILSON, A PROFESSIONAL CORPORATION
Springfield, MO......................Civil Trial Practice; Insurance Defense; Real Estate Law; Workers Compensation

WHITE, ALLINDER & GRAHAM, L.L.C.
Independence, MO.................Business Law; Commercial Litigation; Labor and Employment Law; Medical Malpractice; Personal Injury

WHITE & CASE
Washington, DC......................General Practice
New York, NY........................Civil Trial Practice; Criminal Trial Practice; General Practice
London, England ....General Practice
Paris, France.........................General Practice
Hong Kong, Hong Kong.........General Practice
Singapore, Singapore..............General Practice
Ankara, Turkey......................General Practice
Istanbul, Turkey....................General Practice
Stockholm, Sweden ....General Practice
Tokyo, Japan..........................General Practice

WHITE, COFFEY, GALT & FITE, P.C.
Oklahoma City, OK................General Practice

WHITE AND CRUMPLER
Winston-Salem, NC ....Criminal Trial Practice; Family Law; Personal Injury

WHITE, DENNIS R., P.A.
Naples, FL..............................Probate, Trusts and Estate Planning

WHITE & FISH, L.P.A., INC.
Columbus, OH ....Bankruptcy Law; Civil Trial Practice; Family Law; Personal Injury

WHITE, FLEISCHNER & FINO
New York, NY........................Civil Trial Practice; Environmental Law; Insurance Defense; Medical Malpractice; Personal Injury; Product Liability Law

WHITEFORD, TAYLOR & PRESTON L.L.P.
Washington, DC......................General Practice
Baltimore, MD........................General Practice; Labor and Employment Law; Municipal Bond/Public Authority Financing
Towson, MD ....General Practice

WHITE, HUSEMAN & PLETCHER
Corpus Christi, TX ....Admiralty/Maritime Law; Civil Trial Practice

WHITE, INKER, ARONSON, P.C.
Boston, MA.............................Family Law; General Practice

WHITE, KOCH, KELLY & MCCARTHY, A PROFESSIONAL ASSOCIATION
Santa Fe, NM..........................Commercial Law; Criminal Trial Practice; Family Law; General Practice; Insurance Defense; Labor and Employment Law; Natural Resources Law; Probate, Trusts and Estate Planning; Real Estate Law

WHITE, PECK, CARRINGTON AND MCDONALD, LLP
Mount Sterling, KY ....General Practice

WHITE, REGEN & GARTON
Dickson, TN............................General Practice

WHITESELL & BICKNESE
Iowa Falls, IA ....General Practice

WHITESIDES & KENNY, L.L.P.
Gastonia, NC ....Civil Trial Practice

WHITE AND STEELE, PROFESSIONAL CORPORATION
Denver, CO.............................Civil Trial Practice; Employment Benefits Law; General Practice; Insurance Defense; Product Liability Law; Public Utilities Law; Sports and Entertainment Law; Workers Compensation

WHITESTONE, BRENT, YOUNG & MERRIL, P.C.
Fairfax, VA ....General Practice

WHITE, WHITE, ASKEW & CRENSHAW
Hopkinsville, KY ....Business Law

WHITFIELD & EDDY, P.L.C.
Des Moines, IA........................Banking Law; Civil Trial Practice; General Practice; Insurance Defense

WHITING, HAGG & HAGG
Rapid City, SD........................General Practice

WHITMAN BREED ABBOTT & MORGAN
Greenwich, CT ....General Practice
New York, NY........................General Practice
London, England ....General Practice

WHITNEY, NEWMAN, MERSCH & OTTO
Aurora, NE ....General Practice

WHITTEN, JAMES M.
Corpus Christi, TX ....Civil Trial Practice; Personal Injury

WHITTEN & YOUNG, P.C.
Abilene, TX............................Commercial Law; Family Law; General Practice

WICKENS, HERZER & PANZA, A LEGAL PROFESSIONAL ASSOCIATION
Lorain, OH.............................General Practice

WICKLIFF & HALL, A PROFESSIONAL CORPORATION
Houston, TX ....Administrative Law; Civil Rights; Civil Trial Practice; Commercial Law; Commercial Litigation; Insurance Defense; Labor and Employment Law; Municipal Bond/Public Authority Financing; Personal Injury; Public Utilities Law; Workers Compensation

WIEDERHOLD, MOSES, BULFIN & RUBIN, P.A.
West Palm Beach, FL.............Civil Trial Practice; Insurance Defense; Personal Injury

WIESNER ASSOCIATES, CHARTERED
Sarasota, FL ....Probate, Trusts and Estate Planning

WIEST, WIEST, SAYLOR & MUOLO
Sunbury, PA ....General Practice

WIGGIN & DANA
Hartford, CT ....General Practice
New Haven, CT ....Antitrust Law; Civil Trial Practice; General Practice; Health Care Law; Labor and Employment Law; Patent, Trademark, Copyright and Unfair Competition

WIGGIN & NOURIE, P.A.
Manchester, NH......................General Practice; Insurance Defense

WIGGINS & MASSON
Ithaca, NY..............................Civil Trial Practice; Criminal Trial Practice; Family Law; General Practice; Medical Malpractice; Personal Injury

WIGMAN, COHEN, LEITNER & MYERS, A PROFESSIONAL CORPORATION
Washington, DC......................International Business Law; Patent, Trademark, Copyright and Unfair Competition

WILBRAHAM, LAWLER & BUBA, A PROFESSIONAL CORPORATION
Haddonfield, NJ......................Appellate Practice; Civil Trial Practice; Criminal Trial Practice; Environmental Law; Insurance Defense; Product Liability Law
Philadelphia, PA ....Appellate Practice; Civil Trial Practice; Criminal Trial Practice; Environmental Law; Insurance Defense; Product Liability Law

WILBURN, MASTERSON & SMILING
Tulsa, OK...............................Insurance Defense; Medical Malpractice

WILCOX, ARTHUR M. JR.
San Diego, CA ....Real Estate Law

WILCOX, WILCOX & ENRIGHT
Eau Claire, WI ....Civil Trial Practice; General Practice; Insurance Defense; Real Estate Law

WILCOXEN, MONTGOMERY & HARBISON
Sacramento, CA ....Medical Malpractice; Personal Injury; Product Liability Law

WILDMAN, HARROLD, ALLEN & DIXON
Chicago, IL.............................Antitrust Law; Appellate Practice; Aviation Law; Civil Trial Practice; Commercial Litigation; Environmental Law; General Practice; Health Care Law; Labor and Employment Law; Patent, Trademark, Copyright and Unfair Competition; Product Liability Law; Real Estate Law

WILDS, JOHN L.
Sioux Falls, SD.......................Probate, Trusts and Estate Planning

WILENCHIK & BARTNESS, A PROFESSIONAL CORPORATION
Phoenix, AZ ....Civil Trial Practice; Real Estate Law

WILENTZ, GOLDMAN & SPITZER, A PROFESSIONAL CORPORATION
Eatontown, NJ ....General Practice
Perth Amboy, NJ....................General Practice

WILENTZ, GOLDMAN & SPITZER, A PROFESSIONAL CORPORATION —

  Woodbridge, NJ ....Banking Law; Civil Trial Practice; Commercial Law; Criminal Trial Practice; Environmental Law; Family Law; General Practice; Health Care Law; Labor and Employment Law; Municipal Bond/Public Authority Financing; Probate, Trusts and Estate Planning; Real Estate Law; Sports and Entertainment Law; Tax Law

WILEY, REIN & FIELDING

  Washington, DC......................General Practice

WILF, MERVIN M., LTD.

  Cambridge, MA ....Employment Benefits Law; Probate, Trusts and Estate Planning; Tax Law

  Philadelphia, PA ....Employment Benefits Law; Probate, Trusts and Estate Planning; Tax Law

WILKES, ARTIS, HEDRICK & LANE, CHARTERED

  Washington, DC......................General Practice; Real Estate Law

WILKINS, FROHLICH, JONES, HEVIA, RUSSELL & SUTTER, P.A.

  Port Charlotte, FL ....General Practice; Personal Injury

WILKINS & SLUSHER

  McAllen, TX ....General Practice; Probate, Trusts and Estate Planning

WILKINSON, CARMODY & GILLIAM

  Shreveport, LA ....Appellate Practice; Civil Trial Practice; Environmental Law; General Practice; Insurance Defense; Labor and Employment Law; Public Utilities Law; Sports and Entertainment Law; Transportation Law

WILKINSON, GOELLER, MODESITT, WILKINSON & DRUMMY

  Terre Haute, IN ....Bankruptcy Law; Civil Trial Practice; General Practice; Health Care Law; Insurance Defense; Probate, Trusts and Estate Planning; Product Liability Law; Tax Law

WILLARD, ROBERT H.

  Columbus, OH ....Insurance Defense

WILLARDSON & LIPSCOMB, L.L.P.

  Wilkesboro, NC......................General Practice

WILLCOX, PIROZZOLO AND MCCARTHY, PROFESSIONAL CORPORATION

  Boston, MA......................Civil Trial Practice; General Practice; Patent, Trademark, Copyright and Unfair Competition

WILLCOX & SAVAGE, P.C.

  Norfolk, VA ....General Practice

WILLETTE & TREVIÑO, L.L.P.

  Brownsville, TX ....Civil Trial Practice; Insurance Defense

WILLEY & CHAMBERLAIN, L.L.P.

  Grand Rapids, MI ....Criminal Trial Practice

WILLIAMS, JOHN R. LAW OFFICES OF

  New Haven, CT ....Appellate Practice; Civil Rights; Civil Trial Practice; Criminal Trial Practice

WILLIAMS & ANDERSON

  Little Rock, AR ....Antitrust Law; Civil Trial Practice; Commercial Law; General Practice; Municipal Bond/Public Authority Financing; Securities Law; Tax Law

WILLIAMS AND BALLAS

  Los Angeles, CA......................Probate, Trusts and Estate Planning; Tax Law

WILLIAMS, BOGER, GRADY, DAVIS & TUTTLE, P.A.

  Concord, NC......................General Practice

WILLIAMS, BOX, FORSHEE & BULLARD, P.C.

  Oklahoma City, OK................Commercial Law; Land Use Law; Municipal Bond/Public Authority Financing; Municipal and Zoning Law; Public Utilities Law; Real Estate Law

WILLIAMS, CALIRI, MILLER & OTLEY, A PROFESSIONAL CORPORATION

  Wayne, NJ......................Banking Law; General Practice; Insurance Defense; Probate, Trusts and Estate Planning; Real Estate Law; Securities Law

WILLIAMS & CONNOLLY

  Washington, DC......................Civil Trial Practice; Criminal Trial Practice; General Practice; Tax Law

WILLIAMS, COONEY & SHEEHY

  Bridgeport, CT ....Civil Trial Practice; General Practice; Insurance Defense; Medical Malpractice; Personal Injury; Product Liability Law

WILLIAMS, EBB H., III, P.C.

  Martinsville, VA......................Personal Injury

WILLIAMS, HAMMOND, MOORE, SHOCKLEY & HARRISON, P.A.

  Ocean City, MD......................Civil Trial Practice; Real Estate Law

WILLIAMS & HENRY

  Atlanta, GA ....Civil Trial Practice; Medical Malpractice; Personal Injury

  Greenville, SC......................Commercial Law; Commercial Litigation; Real Estate Law

WILLIAMS, HERSHMAN & WISLER, P.A.

  Wilmington, DE......................Bankruptcy Law; General Practice; Probate, Trusts and Estate Planning; Real Estate Law; Tax Law

WILLIAMS HEWITT & ROBBINS, LLP

  Greenwood, IN ....Banking Law; Probate, Trusts and Estate Planning; Real Estate Law

WILLIAMS, KASTNER & GIBBS LLP

  Seattle, WA ....Antitrust Law; General Practice; Labor and Employment Law; Tax Law

WILLIAMS, KATHRYN, P.A.

  Greenville, SC......................Workers Compensation

WILLIAMS KELLY & GREER, A PROFESSIONAL CORPORATION

  Norfolk, VA ....Business Law; Civil Trial Practice; General Practice; Health Care Law

WILLIAMS & MCCARTHY, A PROFESSIONAL CORPORATION

  Oregon, IL......................Civil Trial Practice; General Practice

  Rockford, IL......................Civil Trial Practice; General Practice; Tax Law

WILLIAMS AND MONTGOMERY, LTD.

  Chicago, IL......................Civil Trial Practice; General Practice

WILLIAMS, MULLEN, CHRISTIAN & DOBBINS, A PROFESSIONAL CORPORATION

  Richmond, VA ....Administrative Law; Antitrust Law; Banking Law; Bankruptcy Law; Business Law; Civil Trial Practice; Commercial Law; Communications Law; Construction Law; Employment Benefits Law; Environmental Law; General Practice; Health Care Law; Immigration and Naturalization; Insurance Defense; International Business Law; Labor and Employment Law; Municipal Bond/Public Authority Financing; Municipal and Zoning Law; Probate, Trusts and Estate Planning; Real Estate Law; Securities Law; Tax Law; Trademark, Copyright and Unfair Competition

WILLIAMS, PARKER, HARRISON, DIETZ & GETZEN, PROFESSIONAL ASSOCIATION

  Sarasota, FL ....Aviation Law; Banking Law; Civil Trial Practice; Commercial Litigation; General Practice; Health Care Law; International Business Law; Municipal Bond/Public Authority Financing; Probate, Trusts and Estate Planning; Real Estate Law; Tax Law

WILLIAMS, PATTILLO & SQUIRES, L.L.P.

  Waco, TX ....Civil Trial Practice

WILLIAMS, PORTER, DAY & NEVILLE, P.C.

  Casper, WY ....Civil Trial Practice; Environmental Law; General Practice; Insurance Defense

WILLIAMS, REED, WEINSTEIN, SCHIFINO & MANGIONE, P.A.

  Tampa, FL ....Civil Trial Practice; Environmental Law; Real Estate Law; Securities Law

WILLIAMS, ROBINSON, TURLEY, WHITE & RIGLER, A PROFESSIONAL CORPORATION

  Rolla, MO ....General Practice

WILLIAMS, SCHAEFER, RUBY & WILLIAMS, PROFESSIONAL CORPORATION

  Birmingham, MI......................Environmental Law; Family Law; Municipal and Zoning Law; Probate, Trusts and Estate Planning; Real Estate Law

WILLIAMS & SENNETT CO., L.P.A.

  Hudson, OH ....Civil Trial Practice

WILLIAMS, SMITH & SUMMERS, P.A.

  Tavares, FL ....Civil Trial Practice; Family Law

WILLIAMS, STROBEL, MALONE, MASON & RALPH, P.A.

  Dodge City, KS......................General Practice

WILLIAMS & TRINE, P.C.

  Boulder, CO ....Civil Trial Practice; Environmental Law; Medical Malpractice; Personal Injury; Product Liability Law

WILLIAMS & WAGONER

  Louisville, KY ....Insurance Defense; Workers Compensation

WILLIAMS & WILLIAMS

  Buffalo, NY ....Civil Trial Practice; Insurance Defense; Workers Compensation

WILLIAMS, WILLIAMS AND MONTGOMERY, P.A.

  Poplarville, MS......................General Practice

WILLIAMS WOOLLEY COGSWELL NAKAZAWA & RUSSELL

  Long Beach, CA......................Admiralty/Maritime Law; Civil Trial Practice; Commercial Law; Environmental Law; General Practice; International Business Law; Product Liability Law; Transportation Law

WILLIAMS, ZOGRAFOS & PECK, A PROFESSIONAL CORPORATION
Portland, OR............................Labor and Employment Law

WILLIAMSON, STEPHEN T.
Louisville, CO ....Natural Resources Law

WILLIAMSON, DEAN, BROWN, WILLIAMSON & PURCELL, L.L.P.
Laurinburg, NC........................General Practice

WILLIAMSON, DIAMOND & CATON, P.A.
St. Petersburg, FL....................Probate, Trusts and Estate Planning

WILLIAMSON, JIMMY, P.C.
Houston, TX ....Civil Trial Practice; Personal Injury

WILLIAMSON & LAVECCHIA, L.C.
Richmond, VA ....Civil Trial Practice

WILLING, ANDREW RUSSELL
Los Angeles, CA ....Administrative Law; Appellate Practice; Criminal
Trial Practice; Municipal and Zoning Law

WILLIS & SACKETT
Perry, IA.................................General Practice

WILLITS, RICHARD H., P.A.
Lake Worth, FL ....Civil Trial Practice; Personal Injury; Tax Law

WILLKIE FARR & GALLAGHER
Washington, DC.....................General Practice
New York, NY........................Civil Trial Practice; General Practice; Municipal
Bond/Public Authority Financing
London, England ....General Practice
Paris, France..........................General Practice

WILLMAN & ARNOLD, LLP
Pittsburgh, PA ....Environmental Law; Insurance Defense

WILLONER, CALABRESE & ROSEN, P.A.
College Park, MD ....General Practice

WILLOUGHBY & HOEFER, P.A.
Columbia, SC ....Communications Law

WILLS, JOHN B.
Denver, CO ....Securities Law

WILLS LAW FIRM, THE
Colorado Springs, CO..............Civil Trial Practice; Personal Injury

WILLSEY LAW OFFICES, OWNED BY A PROF. CORP.
Pasadena, CA ....Bankruptcy Law; Family Law; Natural Resources
Law; Real Estate Law; Tax Law

WILMER, CHARLES M., P.C.
Phoenix, AZ ....Workers Compensation

WILMER, CUTLER & PICKERING
Washington, DC.....................Antitrust Law; Banking Law; Bankruptcy Law;
Business Law; Civil Trial Practice; Communications
Law; Criminal Trial Practice; Environmental Law;
General Practice; Insurance Defense; International
Business Law; Securities Law; Tax Law; Trans-
portation Law
Brussels, Belgium ....General Practice
London, England ....General Practice
Berlin, Germany.....................General Practice

WILMER & GREATHOUSE
Middletown, OH.....................General Practice

WILMETH LAW FIRM
Hartsville, SC ....General Practice

WILNER, KLEIN & SIEGEL, A PROFESSIONAL CORPORATION
Beverly Hills, CA....................Insurance Defense; Real Estate Law

WILSHIRE SCOTT & DYER, A PROFESSIONAL CORPORATION
Houston, TX ....Appellate Practice; Banking Law; Civil Trial
Practice; Environmental Law

WILSMAN & SCHOONOVER
Cleveland, OH.........................Family Law

WILSON, BRUCE H.
Akron, OH ....Civil Trial Practice; Patent, Trademark, Copyright
and Unfair Competition

WILSON, CRAIG R.
North Palm Beach, FL ....Criminal Trial Practice

WILSON, GREGORY F.
Reno, NV ....Civil Trial Practice

WILSON & ASSOCIATES, P.C.
Roanoke, VA............................Construction Law

WILSON AND BARROWS, LTD.
Elko, NV ....General Practice; Probate, Trusts and Estate
Planning; Real Estate Law

WILSON, BAVE, CONBOY, COZZA & COUZENS, P.C.
White Plains, NY ....General Practice; Insurance Defense; Personal Injury

WILSON, BORROR, DUNN & DAVIS
San Bernardino, CA.................Appellate Practice; Civil Trial Practice; General
Practice; Insurance Defense; Probate, Trusts and
Estate Planning

WILSON & BOWLING
New Orleans, LA ....Civil Trial Practice

WILSON, BROCK & IRBY, L.L.C.
Atlanta, GA ....Appellate Practice; Bankruptcy Law; Civil Trial
Practice; Commercial Law; Land Use Law;
Municipal Bond/Public Authority Financing

WILSON & CAIN
Oklahoma City, OK................Civil Trial Practice; Product Liability Law

WILSON & CRAIG, PROFESSIONAL CORPORATION
Eldora, IA ....General Practice

WILSON, DECAMP & TALBOTT, P.S.C.
Lexington, KY ....General Practice

WILSON, ELSER, MOSKOWITZ, EDELMAN & DICKER
New York, NY........................Civil Trial Practice; Insurance Defense

WILSON, ENGSTROM, CORUM & COULTER
Little Rock, AR ....Civil Trial Practice; Criminal Trial Practice

WILSON, JOHNSON & PRESSER
Owensboro, KY ....Insurance Defense

WILSON, KEHOE & WININGHAM
Indianapolis, IN ....Aviation Law; Medical Malpractice; Personal
Injury; Product Liability Law

WILSON, LEAVITT & SMALL, P.A.
Orlando, FL ....Civil Trial Practice; Environmental Law; Real Estate
Law

WILSON & MCILVAINE
Chicago, IL..............................Business Law; Civil Trial Practice; General Practice;
Probate, Trusts and Estate Planning; Real Estate
Law

WILSON, MCRAE, IVY, MCTYIER AND STRAIN
Memphis, TN ....General Practice; Insurance Defense

WILSON AND PRYOR, P.C.
Albuquerque, NM...................Civil Rights; Civil Trial Practice; Construction Law;
Labor and Employment Law; Real Estate Law

WILSON, SONSINI, GOODRICH & ROSATI, PROFESSIONAL
CORPORATION
Palo Alto, CA ....General Practice

WILSON, STRICKLAND & BENSON, P.C.
Atlanta, GA ....Bankruptcy Law; Business Law; Civil Trial Practice;
Family Law; General Practice; Insurance Defense;
Probate, Trusts and Estate Planning; Securities Law;
Tax Law; Workers Compensation

WILSON, WORLEY & GAMBLE, P.C.
Kingsport, TN.........................Civil Trial Practice; General Practice; Health Care
Law; Labor and Employment Law; Probate, Trusts
and Estate Planning; Real Estate Law; Tax Law

WIMER LAW OFFICES, P.C.
Pittsburgh, PA ....Civil Trial Practice; Personal Injury

WINDELS, MARX, DAVIES & IVES
New York, NY........................General Practice

WINDERWEEDLE, HAINES, WARD & WOODMAN, P.A.
Orlando, FL ....General Practice; Probate, Trusts and Estate
Planning; Real Estate Law
Winter Park, FL......................General Practice; Probate, Trusts and Estate
Planning; Real Estate Law

WINETSKY AND WINETSKY
Linden, NJ...............................General Practice

WINGERT, GREBING, ANELLO & BRUBAKER
San Diego, CA ....Civil Trial Practice; Insurance Defense; Probate,
Trusts and Estate Planning

WINGET & KANE
Peoria, IL.................................Civil Trial Practice; Family Law

WINIKATES & WINIKATES
Frisco, TX ....Banking Law; Civil Trial Practice; Probate, Trusts
and Estate Planning

WINSTEAD SECHREST & MINICK P.C.
Austin, TX ....General Practice
Dallas, TX ....General Practice
Houston, TX ....General Practice

WINSTEIN, KAVENSKY & WALLACE
Rock Island, IL.......................Civil Trial Practice

WINSTON, BARRY T.
Chapel Hill, NC......................Civil Trial Practice; Criminal Trial Practice

WINSTON & BYRNE, LAWYERS, A PROFESSIONAL CORPORATION
Mason City, IA........................Civil Trial Practice; General Practice; Probate, Trusts and Estate Planning

WINSTON & CASHATT, LAWYERS, A PROFESSIONAL SERVICE CORPORATION
Spokane, WA............................Construction Law; General Practice

WINSTON & STRAWN
Washington, DC.....................General Practice
Chicago, IL.............................Antitrust Law; General Practice
New York, NY........................General Practice

WINTER & RHODEN
Gaffney, SC ....General Practice

WINTERS, BREWSTER, CROSBY & PATCHETT
Marion, IL.................................General Practice

WINTERS & FORTE
Cheshire, CT............................Business Law; Commercial Law; Probate, Trusts and Estate Planning; Tax Law

WINTERS, KRUG & DELBON
Burlingame, CA........................Insurance Defense

WINTERS & MERKLE
Columbus, OH ....Criminal Trial Practice

WINTHROP COUCHOT PROFESSIONAL CORPORATION
Newport Beach, CA.................Bankruptcy Law

WINTHROP, STIMSON, PUTNAM & ROBERTS
Stamford, CT............................General Practice
Washington, DC.....................General Practice
Palm Beach, FL........................General Practice
New York, NY........................Antitrust Law; Banking Law; Bankruptcy Law; Civil Trial Practice; General Practice; Tax Law
Brussels, Belgium ....General Practice
London, England ....General Practice
Hong Kong, Hong Kong.........General Practice
Tokyo, Japan ....General Practice

WINTHROP & WEINSTINE, A PROFESSIONAL ASSOCIATION
St. Paul, MN ....General Practice

WISE, PRATT-THOMAS, PEARCE, EPTING & WALKER, P.A.
Charleston, SC ....Bankruptcy Law

WISE & SHEPARD, LLP
Palo Alto, CA ....General Practice

WISE, WIEZOREK, TIMMONS & WISE, A PROFESSIONAL CORPORATION
Long Beach, CA.......................Civil Trial Practice; General Practice; Insurance Defense

WISEHART & KOCH
New York, NY........................Bankruptcy Law; Labor and Employment Law

WISOTSKY, ALAN E. LAW OFFICES OF
Oxnard, CA ....Insurance Defense

WISTI & WISTI, P.C.
Hancock, MI ....Civil Trial Practice; Construction Law; Criminal Trial Practice; Personal Injury

WITHERS, BRANT, IGOE & MULLENNIX, P.C.
Liberty, MO ....General Practice

WITHERSPOON, JOHN F.
Washington, DC.....................Patent, Trademark, Copyright and Unfair Competition

WITHERSPOON, KELLEY, DAVENPORT & TOOLE, P.S.
Spokane, WA...........................Communications Law; General Practice

WITMER, KARP, WARNER & THUOTTE
Boston, MA..............................Civil Trial Practice; Family Law

WITT, GAITHER & WHITAKER, P.C.
Chattanooga, TN ....Civil Trial Practice; Employment Benefits Law; Environmental Law; General Practice; Labor and Employment Law; Probate, Trusts and Estate Planning; Securities Law

WITT, NOLAN & BINDEMAN
Washington, DC.....................Family Law

WITTENBERG, JOSEPH L., A LEGAL PROFESSIONAL ASSOCIATION
Toledo, OH ....Probate, Trusts and Estate Planning

WITTER AND HARPOLE
Pasadena, CA ....General Practice; Probate, Trusts and Estate Planning; Real Estate Law; Tax Law

WITWER, OLDENBURG, BARRY & BEDINGFIELD, LLP
Greeley, CO.............................General Practice

WITWER, POLTROCK & GIAMPIETRO
Chicago, IL..............................Labor and Employment Law

WITZEL, KEARNS, KENNEY & DIMMITT
St. Louis, MO...........................Business Law

WOBBROCK, D. LAWRENCE
Portland, OR ....Medical Malpractice; Personal Injury; Product Liability Law

WOBENSMITH, ZACHARY T. III
Valley Forge, PA....................Patent, Trademark, Copyright and Unfair Competition; Trademark, Copyright and Unfair Competition

WOFFORD, FAILS, ZOBAL & MANTOOTH
Fort Worth, TX ....Patent, Trademark, Copyright and Unfair Competition

WOFSEY, ROSEN, KWESKIN & KURIANSKY
Stamford, CT............................Banking Law; Civil Trial Practice; Commercial Law; Family Law; Personal Injury; Probate, Trusts and Estate Planning; Tax Law

WOLCOTT, RIVERS, WHEARY, BASNIGHT & KELLY, P.C.
Virginia Beach, VA ....Banking Law; Bankruptcy Law; Family Law; General Practice; Personal Injury; Real Estate Law

WOLF, ROBERT W.
Forest City, NC ....General Practice

WOLF AND AKERS, A LEGAL PROFESSIONAL ASSOCIATION
Cleveland, OH.........................Family Law

WOLF, BLOCK, SCHORR AND SOLIS-COHEN
Philadelphia, PA ....Antitrust Law; General Practice; Labor and Employment Law; Municipal Bond/Public Authority Financing; Tax Law

WOLF & PFEIFER, A LAW CORPORATION
Newport Beach, CA.................Banking Law; Bankruptcy Law; Real Estate Law

WOLF, RIFKIN & SHAPIRO, LLP
Los Angeles, CA ....Civil Trial Practice; Product Liability Law; Real Estate Law; Sports and Entertainment Law

WOLF & TIEDEKEN
Cheyenne, WY.........................Criminal Trial Practice; Personal Injury

WOLFF, DONALD L.
Clayton, MO ....Criminal Trial Practice

WOLFF & SAMSON, P.A.
Roseland, NJ............................Civil Trial Practice; Environmental Law; General Practice; Insurance Defense; Municipal Bond/Public Authority Financing; Tax Law

WOLFSDORF, BERNARD P., A PROFESSIONAL CORPORATION
Los Angeles, CA ....Immigration and Naturalization

WOLSKE & BLUE, A LEGAL PROFESSIONAL ASSOCIATION
Columbus, OH ....Appellate Practice; Medical Malpractice; Personal Injury

WOMACK, LANDIS, PHELPS, MCNEILL & MCDANIEL, A PROFESSIONAL ASSOCIATION
Jonesboro, AR ....General Practice; Insurance Defense

WOMACK LAW FIRM, THE
La Fayette, GA ....General Practice

WOMACK & MCCLISH, P.C.
Austin, TX ....Civil Trial Practice; Real Estate Law

WOMBLE CARLYLE SANDRIDGE & RICE
Charlotte, NC..........................Appellate Practice; Banking Law; Business Law; Civil Trial Practice; Commercial Law; Construction Law; Employment Benefits Law; Environmental Law; General Practice; Insurance Defense; International Business Law; Labor and Employment Law; Municipal Bond/Public Authority Financing; Natural Resources Law; Real Estate Law; Securities Law; Tax Law
Raleigh, NC.............................Administrative Law; Antitrust Law; Appellate Practice; Banking Law; Business Law; Civil Trial Practice; Commercial Law; Computer Law; Construction Law; Employment Benefits Law; Environmental Law; General Practice; Health Care Law; Insurance Defense; International Business Law; Labor and Employment Law; Municipal Bond/Public Authority Financing; Natural Resources Law; Patent, Trademark, Copyright and Unfair Competition; Product Liability Law; Real Estate Law; Securities Law; Tax Law

Winston-Salem, NC ....Administrative Law; Antitrust Law; Appellate Practice; Banking Law; Bankruptcy Law; Business Law; Civil Rights; Civil Trial Practice; Commercial Law; Communications Law; Computer Law; Construction Law; Employment Benefits Law; Environmental Law; Family Law; General Practice; Health Care Law; Insurance Defense; International Business Law; Labor and Employment Law; Medical Malpractice; Municipal Bond/Public Authority Financing; Municipal and Zoning Law; Natural Resources Law; Patent, Trademark, Copyright and Unfair Competition; Probate, Trusts and Estate Planning; Product Liability Law; Real Estate Law; Securities Law; Tax Law

WONG, MARGARET W. & ASSOCIATES
Cleveland, OH ....Immigration and Naturalization

WONG, MICHAEL J. Y.
Honolulu, HI ....Civil Trial Practice; Family Law; General Practice; Personal Injury

WONG & LEOW
Singapore, Singapore ....General Practice

WOODALL AND MACKENZIE, P.C.
Savannah, GA ....Civil Trial Practice; Commercial Litigation; Insurance Defense

WOODARD, EMHARDT, NAUGHTON, MORIARTY & MCNETT
Indianapolis, IN ....Patent, Trademark, Copyright and Unfair Competition

WOODARD, HALL & PRIMM, A PROFESSIONAL CORPORATION
Houston, TX ....General Practice

WOODBRIDGE & REAMY
Fredericksburg, VA ....Civil Trial Practice; Criminal Trial Practice

WOODBURN AND WEDGE
Las Vegas, NV ....Business Law; Civil Trial Practice; Commercial Law; Natural Resources Law; Probate, Trusts and Estate Planning; Real Estate Law
Reno, NV ....Business Law; Civil Trial Practice; Commercial Law; Natural Resources Law; Probate, Trusts and Estate Planning; Real Estate Law

WOODBURY, J. WAYNE
Silver City, NM ....General Practice

WOODCOCK WASHBURN KURTZ MACKIEWICZ & NORRIS
Philadelphia, PA ....Patent, Trademark, Copyright and Unfair Competition

WOOD, CRIST & VALENTI, P.A.
Tampa, FL ....Insurance Defense

WOODEN & MCLAUGHLIN
Indianapolis, IN ....General Practice

WOOD, HERRON & EVANS, P.L.L.
Cincinnati, OH ....Computer Law; Patent, Trademark, Copyright and Unfair Competition

WOOD & LOCKHART, A PROFESSIONAL ASSOCIATION
Little Rock, AR ....General Practice

WOOD & MURPHY
West Palm Beach, FL ....Probate, Trusts and Estate Planning; Real Estate Law

WOOD, ODOM AND EDGE, P.A.
Newnan, GA ....General Practice

WOODROW & ROUSHAR
Montrose, CO ....General Practice

WOODRUFF, O'HAIR & POSNER, INC. A LAW CORPORATION
Sacramento, CA ....Family Law

WOODS, RONALD G.
Houston, TX ....Criminal Trial Practice

WOODS & BATES
Lincoln, IL ....General Practice

WOODS & PARTNERS
Montreal, QU, Canada ....General Practice

WOODS ROSENBAUM & LUCKEROTH
San Juan, PR ....General Practice

WOODSON, DANNY LAW OFFICES OF
Mount Pleasant, TX ....Family Law; Personal Injury

WOODSON, FORD, SAYERS, LAWTHER, SHORT, PARROTT & HUDSON, LLP
Salisbury, NC ....General Practice

WOOD TATUM SANDERS & MURPHY
Portland, OR ....Admiralty/Maritime Law; General Practice; Insurance Defense

WOOD, THACKER & WEATHERLY, P.C.
Denton, TX ....Appellate Practice; Civil Trial Practice; Personal Injury

WOODWARD COTHRAN & HERNDON, L.L.P.
Columbia, SC ....Banking Law; Business Law; Civil Trial Practice; Personal Injury; Real Estate Law

WOODWARD & EPLEY
Magnolia, AR ....General Practice

WOODWARD, HOBSON & FULTON
Louisville, KY ....Antitrust Law; Civil Trial Practice; Environmental Law; General Practice; Health Care Law; Insurance Defense; Labor and Employment Law; Product Liability Law; Sports and Entertainment Law

WOODWARD, M. KENNETH, JR.
Austin, TX ....International Business Law

WOOD AND WOOD, P.C.
Richmond, VA ....Civil Trial Practice

WOOLSEY & SCHMIDT, L.L.P.
Corpus Christi, TX ....Civil Trial Practice; General Practice

WOOTEN & HART, A PROFESSIONAL CORPORATION
Roanoke, VA ....Banking Law; Business Law; Civil Trial Practice; Commercial Litigation; Health Care Law; Insurance Defense; Medical Malpractice; Product Liability Law; Workers Compensation

WOOTTON, RICHARD H., P.A.
Hot Springs National Park, AR ....General Practice

WORDEN, THANE & HAINES, P.C.
Missoula, MT ....General Practice

WORDES, WILSHIN, GOREN & CONNER
Aliso Viejo, CA ....Business Law; Real Estate Law

WORKMAN, NYDEGGER & SEELEY, A PROFESSIONAL CORPORATION
Salt Lake City, UT ....Patent, Trademark, Copyright and Unfair Competition

WORREL & WORREL
Fresno, CA ....Patent, Trademark, Copyright and Unfair Competition

WOSKA HASBROOK DOWD UNDERWOOD & HELMS, A PROFESSIONAL CORPORATION
Oklahoma City, OK ....Bankruptcy Law; Business Law; Commercial Litigation

WOTITZKY, WOTITZKY, MIZELL & ROSS, P.A.
Punta Gorda, FL ....General Practice; Probate, Trusts and Estate Planning; Real Estate Law

WRAY, JAMES C.
McLean, VA ....Patent, Trademark, Copyright and Unfair Competition

WRAY & KRACHT, L.L.P.
Baton Rouge, LA ....Construction Law

WRIGHT, CHANEY, BERRY & DANIEL, P.A.
Arkadelphia, AR ....General Practice

WRIGHT, CONSTABLE & SKEEN
Baltimore, MD ....Admiralty/Maritime Law; General Practice
Elkton, MD ....General Practice

WRIGHT, COON & CUNNINGHAM, P.A.
Portland, ME ....Environmental Law; Insurance Defense; Labor and Employment Law; Product Liability Law

WRIGHT, DALE & JETT
Guymon, OK ....General Practice

WRIGHT, EVANS AND DALY
Evansville, IN ....Civil Trial Practice; Commercial Law; General Practice; Insurance Defense; Probate, Trusts and Estate Planning; Real Estate Law

WRIGHT, HENSON, SOMERS, SEBELIUS, CLARK & BAKER, LLP
Topeka, KS ....Administrative Law; Banking Law; Bankruptcy Law; Civil Trial Practice; Commercial Law; Family Law; General Practice; Insurance Defense; Labor and Employment Law; Medical Malpractice; Patent, Trademark, Copyright and Unfair Competition; Personal Injury

WRIGHT, JUDD & WINCKLER
Las Vegas, NV ....Appellate Practice; Civil Trial Practice; Criminal Trial Practice; Health Care Law

WRIGHT, LENNON C., P.L.L.C.
Houston, TX ....Product Liability Law

WRIGHT, LINDSEY & JENNINGS
Little Rock, AR ....Bankruptcy Law; Commercial Litigation; Labor and Employment Law; Municipal Bond/Public Authority Financing; Securities Law

WRIGHT, MAX E., A PROFESSIONAL CORPORATION
Midland, TX ....Medical Malpractice

WRIGHT & MILLS, P.A.
Skowhegan, ME ....Civil Trial Practice; Criminal Trial Practice; General Practice; Personal Injury

WRIGHT PENNING
Farmington Hills, MI ....Commercial Law; Commercial Litigation; Probate, Trusts and Estate Planning

WRIGHT, STOUT & FITE
Muskogee, OK ....General Practice

WRIGHT, TOLLIVER AND GUTHALS, A PROFESSIONAL SERVICE CORPORATION
Billings, MT ....Bankruptcy Law; Commercial Law

WRIGHT AND WRIGHT, A PROFESSIONAL CORPORATION
Guntersville, AL......................General Practice; Real Estate Law

WUNSCH, KATHRYN S. AND ASSOCIATED COUNSEL
Palo Alto, CA ....Business Law

WUNSCH, JOHN C., P.C.
Chicago, IL............................Medical Malpractice; Personal Injury; Product Liability Law

WUSINICH AND BROGAN
Downingtown, PA ....Civil Trial Practice; Commercial Litigation; Environmental Law; Medical Malpractice; Municipal and Zoning Law; Personal Injury; Product Liability Law; Workers Compensation

WYATT, JAMES F. III, LAW OFFICES OF
Charlotte, NC.........................Civil Trial Practice; Criminal Trial Practice

WYATT, EARLY, HARRIS & WHEELER, L.L.P.
High Point, NC.......................Civil Trial Practice; General Practice

WYATT, GERBER, BURKE & BADIE, LLP
New York, NY........................Patent, Trademark, Copyright and Unfair Competition

WYATT, TARRANT & COMBS
New Albany, IN ....General Practice
Frankfort, KY.........................General Practice
Lexington, KY ....General Practice
Louisville, KY.........................Banking Law; Civil Trial Practice; Communications Law; General Practice
Nashville, TN..........................Communications Law; General Practice; Trademark, Copyright and Unfair Competition

WYCHE, BURGESS, FREEMAN & PARHAM, PROFESSIONAL ASSOCIATION
Greenville, SC.........................Antitrust Law; Banking Law; Bankruptcy Law; Civil Trial Practice; Communications Law; Employment Benefits Law; Environmental Law; General Practice; Health Care Law; Insurance Defense; Labor and Employment Law; Municipal Bond/Public Authority Financing; Probate, Trusts and Estate Planning; Real Estate Law; Securities Law; Tax Law

WYLIE, PAUL R., A PROFESSIONAL CORPORATION
Bozeman, MT..........................Patent, Trademark, Copyright and Unfair Competition

WYNNE SPIEGEL ITKIN, A LAW CORPORATION
Los Angeles, CA ....Bankruptcy Law

WYRSCH HOBBS MIRAKIAN & LEE, P.C.
Kansas City, MO ....Civil Trial Practice; Criminal Trial Practice; General Practice

YAMAMOTO, TOSH G., A PROFESSIONAL CORPORATION
Sacramento, CA ....Probate, Trusts and Estate Planning

YANITY, JOSEPH BLAIR
Athens, OH ....General Practice

YANNI, PALMA R.
Washington, DC......................Immigration and Naturalization

YARLING, ROBINSON, HAMMEL & LAMB
Indianapolis, IN ....Bankruptcy Law; Civil Trial Practice; Commercial Law; Insurance Defense; Personal Injury; Probate, Trusts and Estate Planning; Product Liability Law

YAROSKY, DAVIAULT, LA HAYE, STOBER & ISAACS
Montreal, QU, Canada ....Antitrust Law; Appellate Practice; Criminal Trial Practice

YATES, MCLAMB & WEYHER, L.L.P.
Raleigh, NC.............................Civil Trial Practice; Insurance Defense; Medical Malpractice; Product Liability Law; Workers Compensation

YEARY & ASSOCIATES, P.C.
Abingdon, VA.........................Criminal Trial Practice; General Practice; Medical Malpractice; Personal Injury; Product Liability Law; Real Estate Law

YENGICH, RICH & XAIZ
Salt Lake City, UT..................Criminal Trial Practice

YERRID, KNOPIK & MUDANO, P.A.
Tampa, FL ....Admiralty/Maritime Law; Commercial Litigation; Personal Injury; Product Liability Law

YODER, AINLAY, ULMER & BUCKINGHAM
Goshen, IN..............................General Practice

YORK, MCRAE & YORK
Cedartown, GA ....General Practice

YOSHA LADENDORF KRAHULIK & WEDDLE
Indianapolis, IN ....Civil Trial Practice; Medical Malpractice; Personal Injury; Product Liability Law

YOSHIDA, GERALD T.
Santa Monica, CA...................Business Law; Construction Law; Real Estate Law

YOUNG & ALEXANDER CO., L.P.A.
Dayton, OH............................Civil Trial Practice; Environmental Law; General Practice; Insurance Defense; Medical Malpractice; Real Estate Law; Tax Law

YOUNG & AMUNDSEN
Newport Beach, CA.................Commercial Litigation; Construction Law; Employment Benefits Law; International Business Law; Real Estate Law

YOUNG & ASSOCIATES, P.C.
Southfield, MI ....Antitrust Law; Civil Trial Practice; Commercial Litigation

YOUNG, B. RICHARD, P.A.
Pensacola, FL..........................Civil Trial Practice; Construction Law; Insurance Defense; Product Liability Law

YOUNG, BERMAN & KARPF, PROFESSIONAL ASSOCIATION
North Miami Beach, FL..........Family Law

YOUNG, BOGLE, MCCAUSLAND, WELLS & CLARK, P.A.
Wichita, KS ....Civil Trial Practice; Commercial Law; Criminal Trial Practice; Environmental Law; General Practice; Insurance Defense; Natural Resources Law; Personal Injury; Probate, Trusts and Estate Planning; Product Liability Law; Real Estate Law

YOUNG, CONAWAY, STARGATT & TAYLOR
Georgetown, DE......................General Practice
Wilmington, DE......................General Practice

YOUNG, GOLDMAN & VAN BEEK, A PROFESSIONAL CORPORATION
Alexandria, VA ....Business Law

YOUNG & HAMPTON, L.L.P.
Houston, TX ....Civil Trial Practice; Commercial Law; Medical Malpractice; Personal Injury; Product Liability Law

YOUNG, HASKINS, MANN & GREGORY, A PROFESSIONAL CORPORATION
Martinsville, VA.....................General Practice

YOUNG AND HUBBELL
Lebanon, OH ....General Practice; Probate, Trusts and Estate Planning; Real Estate Law

YOUNG, KESTERSON & PICKETT
Texarkana, TX ....Criminal Trial Practice; Personal Injury

YOUNG MOORE AND HENDERSON, P.A.
Raleigh, NC.............................Civil Trial Practice; General Practice

YOUNG, RICHARD W., A PROF. CORP., LAW OFFICES OF
Reno, NV ....Criminal Trial Practice; Family Law

YOUNG & RILEY
Indianapolis, IN ....Personal Injury

YOUNG, THAGARD, HOFFMAN, SCOTT & SMITH
Valdosta, GA ....Insurance Defense

YOUNG & THOMPSON
Arlington, VA ....Patent, Trademark, Copyright and Unfair Competition

YOUNG & VALKENET, L.L.C.
Baltimore, MD ....Insurance Defense

YOUNG WOOLDRIDGE, LAW OFFICES OF
Bakersfield, CA ....Civil Trial Practice; General Practice; Personal Injury

YOUNGS, JOHN C., P.C.
Arlington, VA ....Civil Trial Practice

YOUNKIN, JACK C.
Danville, PA............General Practice
Shamokin, PA............Civil Trial Practice; General Practice

YUDES, JAMES P., A PROFESSIONAL CORPORATION
Springfield, NJ............Family Law

YUDITSKI AND ZACKRISON, P.C.
Bridgeport, CT............Personal Injury

YUEN, RENEE M. L., ATTORNEY AT LAW, A LAW CORPORATION
Honolulu, HI............Appellate Practice; Criminal Trial Practice

YUKEVICH, BLUME, MARCHETTI & ZANGRILLI, P.C.
Pittsburgh, PA............Banking Law; Business Law; Civil Trial Practice; Securities Law

YURKO & OWENS, P.A.
Charlotte, NC............Civil Trial Practice

ZABEL, JUDITH L., P.A.
Albuquerque, NM............Probate, Trusts and Estate Planning; Tax Law

ZACK, SPARBER, KOSNITZKY, SPRATT & BROOKS, P.A.
Miami, FL............Business Law; Civil Trial Practice; Commercial Law; General Practice; Health Care Law; Probate, Trusts and Estate Planning; Real Estate Law; Securities Law; Tax Law

ZAGRANS LAW FIRM
Elyria, OH............Antitrust Law; Appellate Practice; Civil Trial Practice; Medical Malpractice; Product Liability Law; Securities Law

ZAHND, ROSS & THOMSON
Maryville, MO............General Practice

ZALKIND, RODRIGUEZ, LUNT & DUNCAN
Boston, MA............Criminal Trial Practice

ZALTAS, MEDOFF & RAIDER
Natick, MA............Probate, Trusts and Estate Planning

ZALUTSKY & KLARQUIST, P.C.
Portland, OR............Employment Benefits Law; Probate, Trusts and Estate Planning; Tax Law

ZAMANSKY PROFESSIONAL ASSOCIATION
Minneapolis, MN............Business Law; Real Estate Law

ZAMECK, HARVEY J.
Southfield, MI............Commercial Litigation

ZAMPLAS, JOHNSON, SOPT & CAVANAGH, P.C.
Bloomfield Hills, MI............Civil Trial Practice

ZAPRUDER & ODELL
Washington, DC............Tax Law

ZARIN, IRA J. LAW OFFICES OF
Newark, NJ............Appellate Practice; Civil Trial Practice; Medical Malpractice; Personal Injury; Product Liability Law

ZARLEY, MCKEE, THOMTE, VOORHEES & SEASE
Des Moines, IA............Patent, Trademark, Copyright and Unfair Competition

ZARWIN, BAUM, DEVITO, KAPLAN & O'DONNELL, P.C.
Philadelphia, PA............Civil Trial Practice; Insurance Defense

ZAVARELLO, A. WILLIAM, CO., L.P.A.
Akron, OH............Civil Trial Practice; Medical Malpractice

ZAZZALI, ZAZZALI, FAGELLA & NOWAK, A PROFESSIONAL CORPORATION
Newark, NJ............Appellate Practice; Civil Trial Practice; General Practice; Labor and Employment Law; Real Estate Law

ZDARSKY, SAWICKI & AGOSTINELLI
Buffalo, NY............Civil Trial Practice; Commercial Litigation; Construction Law

ZEANAH, HUST, SUMMERFORD, DAVIS & JONES, L.L.C.
Tuscaloosa, AL............Civil Trial Practice; General Practice; Insurance Defense; Real Estate Law

ZEFF AND ZEFF, P.C.
Detroit, MI............Civil Trial Practice; Personal Injury; Product Liability Law

ZEGAS, ALAN L.
West Orange, NJ............Appellate Practice; Civil Trial Practice; Criminal Trial Practice; General Practice

ZEIHER, WILLIAM A., P.A.
Fort Lauderdale, FL............Probate, Trusts and Estate Planning; Real Estate Law

ZEITLIN & ZEITLIN, P.C.
Phoenix, AZ............Bankruptcy Law; Land Use Law; Real Estate Law

ZELDES, NEEDLE & COOPER, A PROFESSIONAL CORPORATION
Bridgeport, CT............General Practice

ZELLE & LARSON
Minneapolis, MN............Civil Trial Practice; General Practice

ZELLER & STRULOWITZ
Roseland, NJ............Probate, Trusts and Estate Planning; Tax Law

ZEMAN, WILLIAM S.
Hartford, CT............Labor and Employment Law

ZERRENNER & ROANE
Grand Rapids, MI............Family Law

ZEVNIK HORTON GUIBORD & MCGOVERN, P.C.
Washington, DC............Civil Trial Practice; Environmental Law; Sports and Entertainment Law

ZIDE & O'BIECUNAS
Los Angeles, CA............Commercial Law

ZIEGLER, METZGER & MILLER
Cleveland, OH............Bankruptcy Law; Business Law; Civil Trial Practice; Commercial Law; Insurance Defense; Probate, Trusts and Estate Planning; Real Estate Law; Tax Law

ZIEMAN, SPEEGLE, OLDWEILER & JACKSON, L.L.C.
Mobile, AL............Business Law; Mergers and Acquisitions

ZIEMER, STAYMAN, WEITZEL & SHOULDERS
Evansville, IN............Banking Law; Bankruptcy Law; Business Law; Commercial Law; Construction Law; Health Care Law; Labor and Employment Law

ZIERCHER & HOCKER, P.C.
St. Louis, MO............General Practice

ZIFFREN, BRITTENHAM, BRANCA & FISCHER
Los Angeles, CA............Sports and Entertainment Law

ZIMET, HAINES, FRIEDMAN & KAPLAN
New York, NY............Business Law; Probate, Trusts and Estate Planning; Securities Law; Tax Law

ZIMMER KUNZ, PROFESSIONAL CORPORATION
Pittsburgh, PA............Civil Trial Practice; General Practice; Insurance Defense

ZIMMER AND ZIMMER, L.L.P.
Wilmington, NC............Criminal Trial Practice; Personal Injury

ZIMMERMAN, ROBERT H.
Philadelphia, PA............Business Law; Real Estate Law

ZIMMERMAN, LIEBERMAN & DERENZO
Pottsville, PA............General Practice

ZIMMERMAN, PFANNEBECKER & NUFFORT
Lancaster, PA............General Practice

ZIMMERMAN, SHUFFIELD, KISER & SUTCLIFFE, P.A.
Orlando, FL............Civil Trial Practice; General Practice; Workers Compensation

ZIMRING, STUART D.
Los Angeles, CA............Probate, Trusts and Estate Planning; Real Estate Law

ZINOBER & MCCREA, P.A.
Tampa, FL............General Practice; Labor and Employment Law

ZINSER AND PATTERSON
Nashville, TN............Labor and Employment Law

ZION, TARLETON & SISKIN, P.C.
Tucker, GA............Real Estate Law

ZISMAN AND INGRAHAM, P.C.
Denver, CO............Probate, Trusts and Estate Planning; Tax Law

ZOLLA AND MEYER
Los Angeles, CA............Family Law

ZUCKER, FACHER AND ZUCKER, A PROFESSIONAL CORPORATION
West Orange, NJ............Banking Law; Civil Trial Practice; Insurance Defense; Personal Injury

ZUGER KIRMIS & SMITH
Bismarck, ND............Civil Trial Practice; General Practice

ZUKOWSKI, ROGERS, FLOOD & MCARDLE
Crystal Lake, IL............Family Law; General Practice; Municipal and Zoning Law

ZUMBRUNN, LYNN E., A LAW CORPORATION
Victorville, CA ....Civil Trial Practice; Family Law

ZWEIG, DAVID S., LAW FIRM OF
San Diego, CA ....Tax Law

PRACTICE AREAS SECTION

Volume I

Alabama—Michigan

ADMINISTRATIVE LAW

ALABAMA

BIRMINGHAM, Jefferson Co.

BAXLEY, DILLARD, DAUPHIN & McKNIGHT (AV)

2000 Sixteenth Avenue South, 35205
Telephone: 205-939-0995
Telecopier: 205-939-5025

MEMBERS OF FIRM

William J. Baxley	Charles A. Dauphin
Joel E. Dillard	Stewart D. McKnight, III

ASSOCIATES

Donald R. James, Jr	Paul R. Ellis
Mary Margaret Bailey	

For full biographical listings, see the Martindale-Hubbell Law Directory

---

MOBILE, Mobile Co.

ARMBRECHT, JACKSON, DeMOUY, CROWE, HOLMES & REEVES, L.L.C. (AV)

1300 AmSouth Center, P.O. Box 290, 36601
Telephone: 334-405-1300
Facsimile: 334-432-6843; 433-3821

MEMBERS OF FIRM

Rae M. Crowe	Grover E. Asmus II
E. B. Peebles III	David A. Bagwell
William B. Harvey	Douglas L. Brown
Kirk C. Shaw	Christopher I. Gruenewald
Conrad P. Armbrecht	James Donald Hughes
Edward G. Hawkins	David E. Hudgens
Broox G. Holmes	

Representative Clients: AmSouth Bank of Alabama (Regional Counsel); Burlington Northern Railroad Co. (District Counsel); Loyal American Life Insurance Co.; Scott Paper Co.; Travelers Insurance Co.; WKRG TV, Inc.; Mobile Gas Service Corp.; State Pilotage Commission.

For Complete List of Firm Personnel, See General Section

For full biographical listings, see the Martindale-Hubbell Law Directory

---

MONTGOMERY, Montgomery Co.

VOLZ, PRESTWOOD & HANAN, P.C. (AV)

350 Adams Avenue, P.O. Box 1910, 36102-1910
Telephone: 334-264-6401
Fax: 334-834-4954

Charles H. Volz, Jr.	Charles H. Volz, III
Alvin T. Prestwood	Clinton Chadwell Carter
Ellis D. Hanan	Daniel Lewis Feinstein

LEGAL SUPPORT PERSONNEL
Mark A.W. Turpen

For full biographical listings, see the Martindale-Hubbell Law Directory

---

ARIZONA

NOGALES, Santa Cruz Co.

O'CONNOR, CAVANAGH, ANDERSON, KILLINGSWORTH & BESHEARS, A PROFESSIONAL ASSOCIATION (AV)

1891 North Mastick Way, 85621
Telephone: 520-761-4215
FAX: 520-761-3505
Email: firminfo@arizlaw.com
Phoenix, Arizona Office: One East Camelback Road, Suite 1100, 85012.
Telephone: 602-263-2400.
FAX: 602-263-2900.
Tucson, Arizona Office: O'Connor Cavanagh Molloy Jones, 33 N. Stone, Suite 2100, 85701, P.O. Box 2268, 85702.
Telephone: 520-622-3531.
FAX: 520-624-2816.
Sun City, Arizona Office: 13250 North Del Webb Boulevard, Suite B, 85351.
Telephone: 602-263-2808.
FAX: 602-933-3100.

Hector G. Arana	Kimberly A. Howard Arana

(See Next Column)

Brian G. Larson

Representative Clients: Omega Produce Co.; Frank's Distributing, Inc.; City of Nogales; Collectron of Ariz., Inc.; James K. Wilson Produce Co.; Agricola Bon, S. de R.L. de C.V.; Angel Demerutis E.; Rene Carrillo C.; Arturo Lomeli; Theojary Crisantes E.

For Complete List of Firm Personnel, See General Section

For full biographical listings, see the Martindale-Hubbell Law Directory

---

PHOENIX, Maricopa Co.

CARMICHAEL & POWELL, PROFESSIONAL CORPORATION (AV)

7301 North 16th Street, 85020-5224
Telephone: 602-861-0777
Facsimile: 602-870-0296

Ronald W. Carmichael

Stephen Manes

Representative Clients: Home Builders Association of Central Arizona.

For full biographical listings, see the Martindale-Hubbell Law Directory

---

FENNEMORE CRAIG, A PROFESSIONAL CORPORATION (AV)

Two North Central, Suite 2200, 85004
Telephone: 602-257-8700
Fax: 602-257-8527
Scottsdale, Arizona Office: 6263 North Scottsdale Road, Suite 290, 85250.
Telephone: 602-257-5400.
Fax: 602-257-5409.
Tucson, Arizona Office: One South Church Avenue, Suite 1030, 85701.
Telephone: 520-791-6800.
Fax: 520-791-6820.

C. Webb Crockett	Timothy Berg
Michael Preston Green	Andrew M. Federhar
Robert D. Anderson	

For Complete List of Firm Personnel, See General Section

For full biographical listings, see the Martindale-Hubbell Law Directory

---

O'CONNOR, CAVANAGH, ANDERSON, KILLINGSWORTH & BESHEARS, A PROFESSIONAL ASSOCIATION (AV)

One East Camelback Road, Suite 1100, 85012-1656
Telephone: 602-263-2400
FAX: 602-263-2900
Email: firminfo@arizlaw.com
Sun City, Arizona Office: 13250 North Del Webb Boulevard, Suite B, 85351.
Telephone: 602-263-2808.
FAX: 602-933-3100.
Tucson, Arizona Office: O'Connor Cavanagh Molloy Jones, 33 N. Stone, Suite 2100, 85701, P.O. Box 2268, 85702.
Telephone: 520-622-3531.
FAX: 520-624-2816.
Nogales, Arizona Office: 1891 North Mastick Way, 85621.
Telephone: 520-761-4215.
FAX: 520-761-3505.

Harding B. Cure	Paul J. Giancola
Peter C. Guild	Lucas J. Narducci

Mark J. DePasquale	Troy B. Froderman

Carla A. Wortley
OF COUNSEL
Shoshana B. Tancer

Representative Clients: Bashas', Inc.; Arizona Payphone Assn.; Nevada Payphone Assn.; Phoenix Children's Hospital; Happy Trails Golf Resort; Charles Schwab & Co., Inc.; Norcross Securities, Inc.

For Complete List of Firm Personnel, See General Section

For full biographical listings, see the Martindale-Hubbell Law Directory

---

QUARLES & BRADY (AV)

One Camelback Building, One East Camelback Road, Suite 400, 85012-1649
Telephone: 602-230-5500
Fax: 602-230-5598
Milwaukee, Wisconsin Office: 411 East Wisconsin Avenue.
Telephone: 414-277-5000.
Fax: 414-271-3552.
Madison, Wisconsin Office: First Wisconsin Plaza, One South Pinckney Street, P.O. Box 2113.
Telephone: 608-251-5000.
Fax: 608-251-9166.

(See Next Column)

QUARLES & BRADY, *Phoenix—Continued*

West Palm Beach, Florida Office: 222 Lakeview Ave., 4th Floor.
Telephone: 407-653-5000.
Fax: 407-653-5333.
Naples, Florida Office: Barnett Center, 4501 Tamiami Trail North, Suite 300.
Telephone: 813-262-5959.
Fax: 813-434-4999.

MEMBER OF THE FIRM
P. Robert Fannin

For Complete List of Firm Personnel, See General Section

For full biographical listings, see the Martindale-Hubbell Law Directory

LAW OFFICES OF RICHARD L. STROHM, P.C. (AV)

1136 East Campbell, 85014
Telephone: 602-279-6316
Mobile: 602-616-7094
Facsimile: 602-279-7102
Email: 102442.1444@compuserve.com

Richard L. Strohm
OF COUNSEL

Brad K. Keogh	Nedra J. Bates

LEGAL SUPPORT PERSONNEL

Mindy L. Raymond	Barbara A. Shore
(Legal Assistant)	(Nurse Paralegal)
Richard M. Knaeble	
(Licensed Private Investigator)	

For full biographical listings, see the Martindale-Hubbell Law Directory

TUCSON, Pima Co.

RAVEN, KIRSCHNER & NORELL, P.C. (AV)

Suite 1600, One South Church Avenue, 85701-1612
Telephone: 520-628-8700
Telefax: 520-798-5200

Dennis J. Clancy	Mark B. Raven
Susan M. Freund	S. Leonard Scheff

Representative Clients: Continental Medical Systems, Inc.; El Paso Natural Gas Co.; Norwest Bank Arizona; El Rio-Santa Cruz Neighborhood Health Center, Inc.; Resolution Trust Corp.; Sierra Vista Community Hospital; Southern Arizona Rehabilitation Hospital; Northern Cochise Community Hospital.

For Complete List of Firm Personnel, See General Section

For full biographical listings, see the Martindale-Hubbell Law Directory

ARKANSAS

LITTLE ROCK, Pulaski Co.

GARY EUBANKS & ASSOCIATES, P.A. (AV)

708 West Second Street, 72201
Telephone: 501-372-0266

Gary L. Eubanks	Hugh F. Spinks

William Gary Holt	Jack D. Files
James G. Schulze	Jason Files
Herman W. Eubanks	Matthew Hartness

For full biographical listings, see the Martindale-Hubbell Law Directory

PLASTIRAS, HYDEN & MIRON (AV)

A Partnership of Professional Associations
200 Louisiana, 72201
Telephone: 501-376-8222
Fax: 501-376-7047
1-800-467-8297
Hot Springs Village, Arkansas Office: Village Square, Suite "G", 4501 North Highway 7.
Telephone: 501-984-6366.
Fax: 501-984-6366. 1-800-467-8297.
Pine Bluff, Arkansas Office: 620 South Laurel.
Telephone: 501-536-8222. 1-800-467-8297.

MEMBERS OF FIRM

George N. Plastiras (P.A.)	James W. Hyden (P.A.)
	Philip Miron (P.A.)

OF COUNSEL
James F. Goodhart

(See Next Column)

ASSOCIATES

Lyle D. Foster	Anthony A. Hilliard

For full biographical listings, see the Martindale-Hubbell Law Directory

CALIFORNIA

LOS ANGELES, Los Angeles Co.

BECK, DE CORSO, DALY, BARRERA & OH, A PROFESSIONAL LAW CORPORATION (AV)

601 West Fifth Street, 12th Floor, 90071-2025
Telephone: 213-688-1198
Fax: 213-489-7532
Email: beckdecorso@earthlink.net *URL:*
http://www.earthlink.net/~beckdecorso

Mark E. Beck	Bryan D. Daly
Anthony A. De Corso	Teresa R. Barrera
	Angela E. Oh

Peter J. Diedrich	Joan M. Steinmann
	Evan Scheffel

OF COUNSEL
Godfrey Isaac

For full biographical listings, see the Martindale-Hubbell Law Directory

DEMETRIOU, DEL GUERCIO, SPRINGER & MOYER, LLP (AV)

801 South Grand Avenue, 10th Floor, 90017
Telephone: 213-624-8407
Telecopy: 213-624-0174
Email: ddsm@juno.com *URL:* http://www.ddsm.com

MEMBERS OF FIRM

Chris G. Demetriou (1915-1989)	Laurie E. Davis
Jeffrey Z. B. Springer	Gregory D. Trimarche
Craig A. Moyer	Karen McLaurin Chang
Angela Shanahan	Leslie M. Smario
Stephen A. Del Guercio	Andrew J. Bracker
Michael A. Francis	Kimberly E. Lewand
Regina Liudzius Cobb	Jennifer T. Taggart
	Robert P. Silverstein

OF COUNSEL

Ronald J. Del Guercio	Richard A. Del Guercio
	James P. Del Guercio

Reference: Bank of America, L.A. Main Office, Los Angeles, Calif.

For full biographical listings, see the Martindale-Hubbell Law Directory

KARNS & KARABIAN (AV)

Suite 530 Omni Centre, 900 Wilshire Boulevard, 90017
Telephone: 213-680-9522
FAX: 213-627-3602

MEMBERS OF FIRM

John Karns	Walter J. Karabian

ASSOCIATES

Jeff C. Marderosian	David E. Kenney
	Jeff A. Harrison

For full biographical listings, see the Martindale-Hubbell Law Directory

OCHOA & SILLAS (AV)

444 South, Flower Street, 18th Floor, 90071
Telephone: 213-362-1400
Fax: 213-622-0162
Sacramento, California Office: Wells Fargo Center, 400 Capitol Mall, Suite 1850.
Telephone: 916-447-3383.
FAX: 916-447-3495.
Mexico City, Mexico Office: Bosques de Duraznos, No. 65-507-B, Bosques de Las Lomas, 11700 Mexico, D.F.
Telephone: 905-596-68-48.

MEMBERS OF FIRM

Ralph M. Ochoa	Jesse M. Jauregui
Herman Sillas	Jacqueline Rich Moore

ASSOCIATES

Jack T. Molodanof	Joyce E. Earl
Tomás R. Lopez	Christopher Eric Ochoa
Rita A. Reyes	Christopher Gonzalez
Carlos Hilario	Evan F. Hadnot
	Mario Cordero

OF COUNSEL
Cochran & Lotkin, Washington, D.C.

(See Next Column)

OCHOA & SILLAS—*Continued*

LEGAL SUPPORT PERSONNEL
Manuel Tejeda (Paralegal)   Jeanette M. Palma (Paralegal)
Lori Lee Marino (Paralegal)

For full biographical listings, see the Martindale-Hubbell Law Directory

THOMAS J. READY (AV)

333 South Grand Avenue, 33rd Floor, 90071-1504
Telephone: 213-229-9009
Facsimile: 213-229-9010
Email: TJRLA@AOL.com

For full biographical listings, see the Martindale-Hubbell Law Directory

ANDREW RUSSELL WILLING (AV)

Promenade West, 880 West First Street Suite 302, 90012
Telephone: 213-626-6600
Facsimile: 213-626-0488

Reference: Wells Fargo Bank (Pasadena Main Office).

For full biographical listings, see the Martindale-Hubbell Law Directory

---

PASADENA, Los Angeles Co.

LAGERLOF, SENECAL, BRADLEY & SWIFT, LLP (AV)

301 North Lake Avenue, 10th Floor, 91101-4108
Telephone: 818-793-9400
FAX: 818-793-5900

MEMBERS OF FIRM
Joseph J. Burris (1913-1980)   John F. Bradley
Stanley C. Lagerlof (Retired)   Timothy J. Gosney
H. Melvin Swift, Jr.   William F. Kruse
H. Jess Senecal   Thomas S. Bunn, III
Jack T. Swafford   Andrew D. Turner
Rebecca J. Thyne

ASSOCIATES
James D. Ciampa   Robert W. Renken

Representative Clients: Anchor Glass Container Corp.; Bethlehem Steel Corp.; Orthopaedic Hospital; Palmdale Water District; Public Water Agencies Group; Ventura Port District; Walnut Valley Water District; Metric Construction Co., Inc.

For full biographical listings, see the Martindale-Hubbell Law Directory

---

SACRAMENTO, * Sacramento Co.

HARMATA LAW OFFICES (AV)

2201 Q Street, 95816
Telephone: 916-442-2842
Fax: 916-442-2015

Donald D. Harmata

LEGAL SUPPORT PERSONNEL
PARALEGAL
Debra D. Morrow

Representative Clients: Control Data Corp.; Deloitte & Touche; General Electric Co.; Myers Electric, Inc.; Syblon-Reid Co.; Systemhouse Inc.; TRW, Inc.

For full biographical listings, see the Martindale-Hubbell Law Directory

---

LIVINGSTON & MATTESICH, LAW CORPORATION (AV)

1201 K Street, Suite 1100, 95814
Telephone: 916-442-1111
Fax: 916-448-1709
Email: liv-matt@gvn.net

Gene Livingston   Carol Livingston
James M. Mattesich   Rebecca M. Ceniceros

Steven P. Belzer   Trisha M. McAlmond

Reference: Bank of California.

For full biographical listings, see the Martindale-Hubbell Law Directory

---

SAN JOSE, * Santa Clara Co.

HINSHAW, WINKLER, DRAA, MARSH & STILL (AV)

152 North Third Street, Suite 300, P.O. Box 15030, 95115-0030
Telephone: 408-293-5959
Fax: 408-280-0966
Email: hinshaw-law.com

MEMBERS OF FIRM
Edward A. Hinshaw   Gerhard O. Winkler
Tyler G. Draa   Barry C. Marsh
Thomas E. Still

(See Next Column)

ASSOCIATES
Lynne Thaxter Brown   Jennifer H. Still
Bradford J. Hinshaw   Megan A. Smith

For full biographical listings, see the Martindale-Hubbell Law Directory

---

COLORADO

DENVER, * Denver Co.

ALEXANDER & CRABTREE, P.C. (AV)

216 16th Street, Suite 1300, 80202-5127
Telephone: 303-825-7307
Fax: 303-825-3202
Email: halexand@alexcrab.com *URL:* http://www.alexcrab.com

Hugh Alexander   C. Scott Crabtree

Stephen Fitzsimmons

For full biographical listings, see the Martindale-Hubbell Law Directory

BROWNSTEIN HYATT FARBER & STRICKLAND, P.C. (AV)

Twenty-Second Floor, 410 Seventeenth Street, 80202-4437
Telephone: 303-534-6335
Telecopier: 303-623-1956
Washington, D.C. Office: 601 Pennsylvania Avenue, N.W., Suite 900.
Telephone: 202-434-8377.
Telecopier: 202-393-7864.

Norman Brownstein   Gary M. Reiff
Steven W. Farber   Wayne F. Forman
Thomas L. Strickland   Bruce A. James
Andrew W. Loewi   Cole Finegan

OF COUNSEL
William T. Brack (Resident, Washington, D.C. Office)

Mark J. Mathews   Joshua J. Widoff
Beth Doherty Quinn

Representative Clients: Columbia/HCA Healthcare Corporation; The Denver Broncos; The Hertz Corporation; McDonald's Corporation; Morrison Knudsen Corporation; Pfizer, Inc.; Siemens Transportation Systems; Union Pacific Railroad; United Airlines, Inc.; Tele-Communications, Inc.

For Complete List of Firm Personnel, See General Section

For full biographical listings, see the Martindale-Hubbell Law Directory

JONES & KELLER, A PROFESSIONAL CORPORATION (AV)

Suite 1600, 1625 Broadway, 80202
Telephone: 303-573-1600
Fax: 303-893-6506

Marion F. Jones (1898-1978)   Thomas J. Burke, Jr.
Alec J. Keller (1913-1995)   Samuel E. Wing
Alvin J. Meiklejohn, Jr.   Reid A. Godbolt
Leslie R. Kehl   Rodney D. Knutson
Edward T. Lyons, Jr.   Kevin L. Brown
David E. Driggers   Barry L. Wilkie

Howard R. Hertzberg   Brent Nicholls
David A. Thayer   Michael Brian Cavanaugh
Nathan D. Simmons

Reference: Colorado State Bank; Union Bank & Trust.

For full biographical listings, see the Martindale-Hubbell Law Directory

PARCEL, MAURO, HULTIN & SPAANSTRA, P.C. (AV)

Suite 3600, 1801 California Street, 80202
Telephone: 303-292-6400
Telecopier: 303-295-3040

Dean R. Massey   James R. Spaanstra
Kenneth L. Salazar   Christopher J. Sutton

OF COUNSEL
Peggy E. Montaño

Reference: 1st Interstate, Denver, Colorado.

For Complete List of Firm Personnel, See General Section

For full biographical listings, see the Martindale-Hubbell Law Directory

CONNECTICUT

HARTFORD,* Hartford Co.

SOROKIN SOROKIN GROSS HYDE & WILLIAMS P.C. (AV)

One Corporate Center, 06103
Telephone: 860-525-6645
Fax: 860-522-1781
Simsbury, Connecticut Office: 730 Hopmeadow Street.
Telephone: 860-651-9348.
Rocky Hill, Connecticut Office: 2360 Main Street.
Telephone: 860-563-9305.
Fax: 860-529-6931.

| Clifford J. Grandjean | Lewis Rabinovitz |

OF COUNSEL
Ethel Silver Sorokin

For Complete List of Firm Personnel, See General Section

For full biographical listings, see the Martindale-Hubbell Law Directory

---

DISTRICT OF COLUMBIA

WASHINGTON, D.C. Co.

* indicates certain Bar Register subscribers, in cities of comparable size and importance, who maintain an additional office in Washington, D.C. and who have arranged for representation as a part of the Washington, D.C. listings that follow

ADDUCI, MASTRIANI & SCHAUMBERG, L.L.P. (AV)

1140 Connecticut Avenue, N.W., Suite 250, 20036
Telephone: 202-467-6300
Telefax: 202-466-2006
Email: adduci.com

MEMBERS OF FIRM

V. James Adduci, II	James C. Lydon
Louis S. Mastriani	(Not admitted in DC)
Tom M. Schaumberg	David A. Guth
Ronald J. Kubovcik	Katherine S. Nucci
Barbara A. Murphy	Larry L. Shatzer, II
Timothy Sullivan	Marcela B. Stras

Anri Suzuki	Peter B. Martine
Gregory C. Anthes	Michael L. Doane
	Martin R. Fischer

A list of Representative Clients and References will be furnished upon request.

For full biographical listings, see the Martindale-Hubbell Law Directory

ALEXANDER, BEARDEN, HAIRSTON & MARKS, LLP (AV)

Limited Liability Partnership
2021 L Street, N.W., Suite 300, 20036
Telephone: 202-293-3700
Fax: 202-293-7359
Silver Spring, Maryland Office: Lee Plaza, Suite 805, 8601 Georgia Avenue, 20910.
Telephone: 301-589-2222.
Facsimile: 301-539-2523.
New York, New York Office: 330 Madison Avenue, 36th Floor.
Telephone: 212-808-0008.
Fax: 212-599-1028.

| Koteles Alexander | Michelle C. Clay |

Susan C. Lee

Reference: Riggs National Bank of Washington, D.C.

For full biographical listings, see the Martindale-Hubbell Law Directory

* BAKER & BOTTS, L.L.P. (AV)

A Registered Limited Liability Partnership
The Warner, 1299 Pennsylvania Avenue, N.W., 20004-2400
Telephone: 202-639-7700
Fax: 202-639-7832
Email: postmaster@bakerbotts.com
Houston, Texas Office: One Shell Plaza, 910 Louisiana.
Telephone: 713-229-1234.
Austin, Texas Office: 1600 San Jacinto Center, 98 San Jacinto Boulevard.
Telephone: 512-322-2500.
Dallas, Texas Office: 2001 Ross Avenue.
Telephone: 214-953-6500.

(See Next Column)

New York, New York Office: 599 Lexington Avenue.
Telephone: 212-705-5000.
Moscow, Russian Federation Office: 10 ul. Bolshaya Dmitrovka (formerly Pushkinskaya), 103031.
Telephone: 7095/921-5300 (Local); 7501/929-7070 (International).

MEMBERS OF FIRM

Charles M. Darling, IV	William D. Kramer
Thomas J. Eastment	John B. McDaniel
Steven R. Hunsicker	Randolph Quaile McManus
Bruce F. Kiely	B. Donovan Picard

ASSOCIATES

Debra Raggio Bolton	Paul T. Luther
Jennifer S. Leete	Martin T. Lutz
Mark K. Lewis	Michael X. Marinelli
	Jeffrey A. Stonerock

For Complete List of Firm Personnel, See General Section

For full biographical listings, see the Martindale-Hubbell Law Directory

BAKER & HOSTETLER (AV)

Washington Square, Suite 1100, 1050 Connecticut Avenue, N.W., 20036-5304
Telephone: 202-861-1500
In Cleveland, Ohio: 3200 National City Center, 1900 East Ninth Street.
Telephone: 216-621-0200.
In Columbus, Ohio: Capitol Square, Suite 2100, 65 East State Street.
Telephone: 614-228-1541.
In Denver, Colorado: 303 East 17th Avenue, Suite 1100.
Telephone: 303-861-0600.
In Houston, Texas: 1000 Louisiana, Suite 2000.
Telephone: 713-751-1600.
In Long Beach, California: 300 Oceangate, Suite 620.
Telephone: 310-432-2827.
In Los Angeles, California: 600 Wilshire Boulevard.
Telephone: 213-624-2400.
In Orlando, Florida: SunBank Center, Suite 2300, 200 South Orange Avenue.
Telephone: 305-841-1111.
In College Park, Maryland: 9658 Baltimore Boulevard, Suite 206.
Telephone: 301-441-2781.
In Alexandria, Virginia: 437 North Lee Street.
Telephone: 703-549-1294.
In San Francisco, California: One Sansome Street, Suite 2000.
Telephone: 415-951-4705.

PARTNERS

| Frederick H. Graefe | Richard A. Hauser |

OF COUNSEL
E. Mark Braden

For Complete List of Firm Personnel, See General Section

For full biographical listings, see the Martindale-Hubbell Law Directory

BRAUDE & MARGULIES, P.C. (AV)

The Brawner Building, 888 Seventeenth Street, N.W., Suite 500, 20006
Telephone: 202-293-2993
Fax: 202-331-7916
Email: Braudemarg@aol.com
Riyadh, Saudi Arabia Office: Mohammed A. Al-Abdullah, P.O. Box 59446, Nuzha Building, Sixth Floor, 11525.
Telephone: 966-1-405-1291.
Fax: 966-1-405-1291.
Abu Dhabi, United Arab Emirates Office: P.O. Box 43908.
Telephone: (971-2) 787222.
Fax: (971-2) 784001.

Herman M. Braude

Samuel M. Morrison, Jr.	Conrad Christopher Ledoux
Robert D. Windus	Stuart H. Sakwa
John P. McGowan, Jr. (Not admitted in DC; Resident, Abu Dhabi, U.A.E. Office)	(Not admitted in DC)
	James D. Finn, Jr.

OF COUNSEL
J. Richard Margulies

For full biographical listings, see the Martindale-Hubbell Law Directory

BRICKFIELD, BURCHETTE & RITTS, P.C. (AV)

8th Floor, West Tower, 1025 Thomas Jefferson Street, N.W., 20007-0805
Telephone: 202-342-0800
Fax: 202-342-0807
Austin, Texas Office: Suite 1050, 1005 Congress Avenue.
Telephone: 512-472-1081.

(See Next Column)

BRICKFIELD, BURCHETTE & RITTS P.C.—*Continued*

Peter J. P. Brickfield
William H. Burchette
Mark C. Davis (Not admitted in DC; Resident, Austin, Texas Office)
Michael E. Kaufmann
Peter J. Mattheis

Michael N. McCarty
Frederick H. Ritts
Fernando Rodriguez (Not admitted in DC; Resident, Austin, Texas Office)
Christine C. Ryan
Garrett A. Stone

COUNSEL

James W. Brew
(Not admitted in DC)

Robert L. McCarty
A. Hewitt Rose

Dean S. Brockbank
(Not admitted in DC)
Elizabeth Grieco Cunningham
(Resident, Austin, Texas Office)
Vincent P. Duane

Julie B. Greenisen
Stephen J. Karina
(Not admitted in DC)
Christopher C. O'Hara
Sonnet C. Schmidt
Damon E. Xenopoulos

For full biographical listings, see the Martindale-Hubbell Law Directory

BRUDER, GENTILE & MARCOUX, L.L.P. (AV)

1100 New York Avenue, N.W., Suite 510 East, 20005-3934
Telephone: 202-783-1350
Telecopiers: 202-737-9117; 347-2644
Email: brugen@ix.netcom.com

MEMBERS OF FIRM

George F. Bruder
Carmen L. Gentile
Albert R. Simonds, Jr.
J. Michel Marcoux

David E. Goroff
Gary E. Guy
James H. McGrew
Thomas L. Blackburn

Arlene Pianko Groner

ASSOCIATE

Cheryl Lynn Belkowitz

For full biographical listings, see the Martindale-Hubbell Law Directory

COHN AND MARKS (AV)

Suite 600, 1333 New Hampshire Avenue, N.W., 20036
Telephone: 202-293-3860
Fax: 202-293-4827
URL: http://www.cohnmarks.com

MEMBERS OF FIRM

Joel H. Levy
Robert B. Jacobi
Roy R. Russo
Ronald A. Siegel
Lawrence N. Cohn

Richard A. Helmick
Wayne Coy, Jr.
Mark L. Pelesh
J. Brian De Boice
Edward N. Leavy

ASSOCIATES

Susan Valerie Sachs
John R. Przypszny
A. Sheba Chacko

Kevin M. Goldberg
Michael A. McVicker
(Not admitted in DC)

OF COUNSEL

Marcus Cohn
Leonard H. Marks

Stanley S. Neustadt
Stanley B. Cohen

Richard M. Schmidt, Jr.

LEGAL SUPPORT PERSONNEL
SPECIALIST (NON-LAWYER)

Sharon H. Bob (Higher Education Specialist on Policy and Regulation)

For full biographical listings, see the Martindale-Hubbell Law Directory

DUNAWAY & CROSS, A PROFESSIONAL CORPORATION (AV)

Suite 400, 1146 19th Street, N.W., 20036
Telephone: 202-862-9700
Fax: 202-862-9710

Mac S. Dunaway
Gary E. Cross

George C. Courtot
Michael P. Bentzen

Stanley J. Green

Matthew F. Hall
Christopher E. Anders

Raymond B. Grochowski
Cary W. Mergele

COUNSEL

Raymond P. Shafer (Not admitted in DC)

For full biographical listings, see the Martindale-Hubbell Law Directory

THE FALK LAW FIRM (AV)

A Professional Limited Company
Suite 260 One Westin Center, 2445 M Street, N.W., 20037
Telephone: 202-833-8700
Telecopier: 202-872-1725
Email: FalkLaw@erols.com

(See Next Column)

James H. Falk, Sr.
James H. Falk, Jr.

John M. Falk
Robert K. Tompkins

OF COUNSEL

Pierre E. Murphy

Elizabeth C. Collins

For full biographical listings, see the Martindale-Hubbell Law Directory

FRANK W. FRISK, JR., P.C. (AV)

Suite 125, Canal Square, 1054 Thirty-First Street, N.W., 20007
Telephone: 202-333-8433
Fax: 202-333-8431

Frank W. Frisk, Jr.

For full biographical listings, see the Martindale-Hubbell Law Directory

R. TENNEY JOHNSON (AV)

Suite 600, 2300 N Street, N.W., 20037-1122
Telephone: 202-663-9030
Fax: 202-663-9040

For full biographical listings, see the Martindale-Hubbell Law Directory

PIERSON SEMMES AND BEMIS (AV)

Canal Square, 1054 31st Street, N.W., 20007
Telephone: 202-333-4000
Telex: 248528 PSF UR;
Telecopier: 202-965-0100

MEMBERS OF FIRM

W. DeVier Pierson
David H. Semmes
Douglas Knox Bemis, Jr.
Peter J. Levin
Mark E. Greenwold

William C. Lieblich
David J. Hill
David F. B. Smith
Paul Ryberg, Jr.
Thomas S. Warrick

Gerard A. Clark

ASSOCIATES

Clinton E. Cameron

Tamara R. Gelboin

For Complete List of Firm Personnel, See General Section

For full biographical listings, see the Martindale-Hubbell Law Directory

POWERS, PYLES, SUTTER & VERVILLE, P.C. (AV)

Third Floor, 1275 Pennsylvania Avenue, N.W., 20004
Telephone: 202-466-6550; 296-9243
Fax: 202-785-1756
Email: ppsv@ppsv.com *URL:* http://www.ppsv.com

Galen D. Powers
James C. Pyles
Ronald N. Sutter
Richard E. Verville
Mary Susan Philp

Mark R. Fitzgerald
Thomas K. Hyatt
Robert J. Saner, II
Stanley A. Freeman
Barbara E. Straub

David C. Beck

Peter W. Thomas
Christopher L. Keough
Joel M. Rudnick
(Not admitted in DC)

Suzanne Seftel
Deena M. Umbarger
(Not admitted in DC)
Daniel H. Orenstein
(Not admitted in DC)

OF COUNSEL

Jenny Ann Brody
Rebecca L. Burke

Donald W. Aaronson
Joe R. G. Fulcher

Douglas Benson Tesdahl

LEGAL SUPPORT PERSONNEL

Marina Weiss

For full biographical listings, see the Martindale-Hubbell Law Directory

REICHLER, MILTON & MEDEL (AV)

Suite 1200, 1747 Pennsylvania Avenue, N.W., 20006-4604
Telephone: 202-223-1200
Fax: 202-785-6687

Paul S. Reichler
Kathleen M. Milton

Arthur V. Medel
Janis H. Brennan

ASSOCIATES

Padideh Ala'i
Melissa E. Crow
(Not admitted in DC)

Alima Joned
Daniel M. Malabonga
(Not admitted in DC)

OF COUNSEL

T. Jay Barrymore

Traci Duvall Humes

For full biographical listings, see the Martindale-Hubbell Law Directory

Washington—Continued

SMATHERS & SMATHERS (AV)

Suite 222 Washington Square, 1050 Connecticut Avenue, N.W., 20036
Telephone: 202-862-5510
Cable Address: "Smathers"
Fax: 202-296-4439
Jacksonville, Florida Office: 1 Independent Drive, Suite 2201.
Telephone: 904-358-2201.

MEMBERS OF FIRM

George A. Smathers
Bruce A. Smathers (Not
admitted in DC; Resident,
Jacksonville, Florida Office)

OF COUNSEL

John T. Hoang (Not admitted in DC)

For full biographical listings, see the Martindale-Hubbell Law Directory

DANIEL R. THOMPSON, P.C. (AV)

Suite 925, 1620 I Street, N.W., 20006
Telephone: 202-293-5800
Facsimile: 202-463-8998

Daniel R. Thompson	Gregory E. Thompson
John B. Hallagan	

Reference: NationsBank, Washington, D.C.

For full biographical listings, see the Martindale-Hubbell Law Directory

* VENABLE ATTORNEYS AT LAW VENABLE, BAETJER, HOWARD & CIVILETTI, LLP (AV)

A Partnership including Professional Corporations
Suite 1000, 1201 New York Avenue, N.W., 20005
Telephone: 202-962-4800
Fax: 202-962-8300
Baltimore, Maryland Office: Venable, Baetjer and Howard LLP, 1800 Mercantile Bank & Trust Building, 2 Hopkins Plaza.
Telephone: 410-244-7400.
McLean, Virginia Office: Venable, Baetjer and Howard LLP, Suite 400, 2010 Corporate Ridge.
Telephone: 703-760-1600.
Rockville, Maryland Office: Venable, Baetjer and Howard LLP, Suite 500, One Church Street, P. O. Box 1906.
Telephone: 301-217-5600.
Towson, Maryland Office: Venable, Baetjer and Howard LLP, 210 Allegheny Avenue, P. O. Box 5517.
Telephone: 410-494-6200.

MEMBERS OF FIRM

Thomas J. Madden	John F. Cooney
Ronald R. Glancz	N. Frank Wiggins
Michael Schatzow (Also at	Jeffrey D. Knowles
Baltimore, Maryland Office)	John J. Pavlick, Jr.
Gary M. Hnath	

OF COUNSEL

Richard H. Mays (Not admitted in DC; Also at McLean, Virginia Office)

ASSOCIATE

James Nicholas Czaban (Not admitted in DC)

For Complete List of Firm Personnel, See General Section

For full biographical listings, see the Martindale-Hubbell Law Directory

WEBSTER, CHAMBERLAIN & BEAN (AV)

Suite 1000, 1747 Pennsylvania Avenue, N.W., 20006
Telephone: 202-785-9500

MEMBERS OF FIRM

Arthur L. Herold	Burkett Van Kirk
Alan P. Dye	Frank M. Northam
Edward D. Coleman	John W. Hazard, Jr.
Kent Masterson Brown	Hugh K. Webster
(Not admitted in DC)	

OF COUNSEL

Charles E. Chamberlain	J. Coleman Bean

ASSOCIATES

Charles M. Watkins	Brenley Locke Elias
David P. Goch	David L. Finch
	(Not admitted in DC)

For full biographical listings, see the Martindale-Hubbell Law Directory

FLORIDA

FORT LAUDERDALE, * Broward Co.

LAW PRACTICE OF J.B. GROSSMAN, P.A. (AV)

2300 East Las Olas Boulevard Fourth Floor, 33301
Telephone: 954-767-3345
Fax: 954-767-3347

J.B. Grossman	Kenneth J. Dunn
Gary Arnold Feder	Blaine H. Hibberd

LEGAL SUPPORT PERSONNEL

Scott L. Lampert

For full biographical listings, see the Martindale-Hubbell Law Directory

FORT MYERS, * Lee Co.

ALLEN, KNUDSEN & DeBOEST, P.A. (AV)

1415 Hendry Street, P.O. Box 1480, 33902
Telephone: 941-334-1381
Telecopier: 941-334-0266
Naples, Florida Office: Park North Center, 5121 Castello Drive, Suite 1.
Telephone: 941-263-5040.
Fax: 941-263-6944.

George E. Allen (1916-1993)	Terrence F. Lenick
Arthur K. Knudsen, Jr.	William E. Stockman
Richard D. DeBoest	Tamela Eady Wiseman
Christopher N. Davies	Brenda A. Bayly
Robert H. Duckwall	Lori Westhrin Clifford
Richard D. DeBoest II	Dana M. Gallup
C. Michael Jackson	Thaddeus Dennis Kirkpatrick
P. Michael Villalobos	

LEGAL SUPPORT PERSONNEL

Carolyn Fox Lambert (Paralegal)

Representative Clients: Lennar Homes, Inc.; Pulte Home Corp.; Cobb Theatres, Inc.; International Paper; Saxon Properties, Inc.; Scott's Hospitality, Inc.; WCN Communities, L.P.; Evelyn Jackman and Sons, Inc.; Pacificorp; Nite-Bright Sign Co.

For full biographical listings, see the Martindale-Hubbell Law Directory

KISSIMMEE, * Osceola Co.

POHL & SHORT, P.A.

(See Winter Park)

MIAMI, * Dade Co.

NEIL FLAXMAN PROFESSIONAL ASSOCIATION (AV)

550 Biltmore Way (Coral Gables), 33134
Telephone: 305-445-1388
Fax: 305-443-0279

Neil Flaxman

Maria E. Cespedes

For full biographical listings, see the Martindale-Hubbell Law Directory

NEW PORT RICHEY, Pasco Co.

DANIEL N. MARTIN, P.A. (AV)

Suite B-1, 8406 Massachusetts Avenue, P.O. Box 786, 34653
Telephone: 813-842-8439

Daniel N. Martin

Representative Clients: Regency Communities, Inc., formerly Minieri Communities of Florida, Inc.; Greene Builders, Inc.; Barnett Bank of Pasco County; Hospital Corporation of America.
Approved Attorneys for: Attorneys' Title Insurance Fund; First American Title Insurance Co.; Commonwealth Land Title Insurance Company.
Reference: Barnett Bank of Pasco County.

ORLANDO, * Orange Co.

POHL & SHORT, P.A.

(See Winter Park)

SARASOTA, * Sarasota Co.

KIRK PINKERTON, A PROFESSIONAL ASSOCIATION (AV)

720 South Orange Avenue, P.O. Box 3798, 34230
Telephone: 941-364-2400
Fax: 941-364-2490
Venice, Florida Office: 245 North Tamiami Trail, Suite A, 34285.
Telephone: 941-488-7811.
Fax: 941-488-2544.

(See Next Column)

KIRK PINKERTON A PROFESSIONAL ASSOCIATION—*Continued*

Robert J. Carr	L. Norman Vaughan-Birch
William C. Strode	Timothy S. Shaw
L. Howard Payne	William E. Robertson, Jr.
Phillip A. Wolff	Michael A. Ortiz
David M. Silberstein	

Daniel A. Bechtold	David W. Payne
Anita J. Hanna	Michael E. Garlington

For full biographical listings, see the Martindale-Hubbell Law Directory

---

TALLAHASSEE,* Leon Co.

ERVIN, VARN, JACOBS AND ERVIN (AV)

305 South Gadsden Street, P.O. Drawer 1170, 32302
Telephone: 904-224-9135
Telecopier: 904-222-9164
Email: EVJE@NETTALLY.COM

MEMBERS OF FIRM

Thomas M. Ervin, Jr.	Melissa Fletcher Allaman
C. Everett Boyd, Jr.	Robert M. Ervin Jr.
J. Stanley Chapman	

ASSOCIATE
David R. Westcott

COUNSEL CONSULTANT
Robert M. Ervin

OF COUNSEL

Wilfred C. Varn	Richard W. Ervin
Joseph C. Jacobs	Marilyn K. Morris
Pamela K. Frazier	

Representative Clients: Florida Association of Broadcasters; E. I. duPont de Nemours & Co., Inc.; Florida Credit Union League; Atlantic Richfield Co.; Wells Fargo Ag Credit Corp.; American Acceptance Corp.; Coastal Petroleum Co.; General Motors Corp.; Goodyear Tire and Rubber Co.; The Grand Union Co.

For full biographical listings, see the Martindale-Hubbell Law Directory

---

GATLIN, WOODS & CARLSON (AV)

A Partnership including a Professional Corporation
The Mahan Station, 1709-D Mahan Drive, 32308
Telephone: 904-877-7191
Telecopier: 904-877-9031

MEMBERS OF FIRM

B. Kenneth Gatlin (P.A.)	Thomas F. Woods
John D. Carlson	

ASSOCIATE
Wayne L. Schiefelbein

For full biographical listings, see the Martindale-Hubbell Law Directory

---

HOPPING GREEN SAMS & SMITH, PROFESSIONAL ASSOCIATION (AV)

123 South Calhoun Street, P.O. Box 6526, 32314
Telephone: 904-222-7500
Fax: 904-224-8551

James S. Alves	Wade L. Hopping
Brian H. Bibeau	Frank E. Matthews
Kathleen L. Blizzard	Richard D. Melson
Elizabeth C. Bowman	David L. Powell
Richard S. Brightman	William D. Preston
Peter C. Cunningham	Carolyn S. Raepple
Ralph A. DeMeo	Douglas S. Roberts
Thomas M. DeRose	Gary P. Sams
William H. Green	Robert P. Smith
Cheryl G. Stuart	

Gary K. Hunter, Jr.	Karen Peterson
Jonathan T. Johnson	Michael P. Petrovich
Robert A. Manning	R. Scott Ruth
Angela R. Morrison	W. Steve Sykes
Gary V. Perko	T. Kent Wetherell, II

OF COUNSEL
W. Robert Fokes

Representative Clients: Atlantic Gulf Communities; Dunes and Viera East Community Development Districts; Florida Electric Power Coordinating Group; Florida Power & Light Co.; MCI Telecommunications; Seminole Electric Co.; Sugar Cane Growers Cooperative of Florida; UPS; Waste Management, Inc.; Wheelabrator.

For full biographical listings, see the Martindale-Hubbell Law Directory

---

KATZ, KUTTER, HAIGLER, ALDERMAN, MARKS, BRYANT & YON, PROFESSIONAL ASSOCIATION (AV)

106 East College Avenue, 12th Floor, P.O. Box 1877, 32301
Telephone: 904-224-9634
Telecopier: 904-224-0781; 222-0103
Orlando, Florida Office: SunTrust Center, Suite 1428, 200 South Orange Avenue, 32801.
Telephone: 407-423-8480.
Fax: 407-843-0553.

Silvia Morell Alderman	Richard P. Lee
Daniel C. Brown	John C. Lovett
Bill L. Bryant, Jr.	John R. Marks, III
J. Riley Davis	Brian M. Nugent
Martin R. Dix	Arthur L. Stern, III
Paul R. Ezatoff, Jr.	Harry O. Thomas
William M. Furlow	Gary P. Timin
Mitchell B. Haigler	J. Larry Williams
Allan J. Katz	David A. Yon
Edward L. Kutter	Paul A. Zeigler

Alan Harrison Brents	Kenneth W. Donnelly
Nancy Mason Burke	David P. Healy
Jonathan Brennan Butler	Mark E. Kaplan
Richard E. Coates	Christopher B. Lunny
Bert L. Combs	Travis L. Miller
Jose A. Diez-Arguelles	Bruce D. Platt
Lisa D. Stream	

OF COUNSEL

Edward S. Jaffry	Patrick F. Maroney
Craig A. Meyer	

LEGAL SUPPORT PERSONNEL

Gerald C. Wester	Pat Griffith O'Connell
(Governmental Consultant)	(Governmental Consultant)
E. Clinton Smawley	J. Andrew Keller, III
(Governmental Consultant)	(Executive Director)

For full biographical listings, see the Martindale-Hubbell Law Directory

---

PAUL WATSON LAMBERT (AV)

1114 East Park Avenue, 32301-2651
Telephone: 904-224-9393
Fax: 904-224-9396

For full biographical listings, see the Martindale-Hubbell Law Directory

---

McFARLAIN, WILEY, CASSEDY & JONES, PROFESSIONAL ASSOCIATION (AV)

215 South Monroe Street, Suite 600, P.O. Box 2174, 32316-2174
Telephone: 904-222-2107
Telecopier: 904-222-8475

Richard C. McFarlain	Charles A. Stampelos
William B. Wiley	Linda McMullen
Marshall R. Cassedy	H. Darrell White, Jr.
Douglas P. Jones	Christopher Barkas

Harold R. Mardenborough, Jr.	Rogelio J. Fontela
Robert A. McNeely	Patrick John McGinley

For full biographical listings, see the Martindale-Hubbell Law Directory

---

RADEY McARTHUR & FREHN (AV)

101 South Monroe Street, 32301
Telephone: 904-681-7766
Fax: 904-681-0160
Email: Radeylaw@aol.com

John Radey	Elizabeth Waas McArthur
Jeffrey L. Frehn	

Representative Clients: Electronic Data Systems Corp.; Lee County Mosquito Control District; AIB Financial Group, Inc.; Agrifos; Ringling Bros. Barnum-Bailey Combined Shows; Tampa General Hospital; Columbia/HCA Healthcare Corp.; Columbia Tallahassee Community Hospital; Columbia Lawnwood Regional Medical Center; Columbia Center-Sanford.

For full biographical listings, see the Martindale-Hubbell Law Directory

---

ROSE, SUNDSTROM & BENTLEY (AV)

A Partnership including Professional Associations
2548 Blairstone Pines Drive, P.O. Box 1567, 32302-1567
Telephone: 904-877-6555
Telecopier: 904-656-4029

MEMBERS OF FIRM

Chris H. Bentley (P.A.)	Robert M. C. Rose
F. Marshall Deterding	William E. Sundstrom (P.A.)
Martin S. Friedman (P.A.)	Diane D. Tremor (P.A.)
John R. Jenkins (P.A.)	John L. Wharton

(See Next Column)

ROSE, SUNDSTROM & BENTLEY, *Tallahassee—Continued*

Representative Clients: Aloha Utilities, Inc.; Arbor Health Care Co.; Bonita Springs Water System, Inc.; East Central Florida Services, Inc.; Florida Waterworks Assn.; Hydratech Utilities, Inc.; National Premium Budget Plan Corp.; Utility Board of the City of Key West.
Reference: Barnett Bank, Tallahassee.

For full biographical listings, see the Martindale-Hubbell Law Directory

---

WINTER PARK, Orange Co.

POHL & SHORT, P.A. (AV)

280 West Canton Avenue, Suite 410, P.O. Box 3208, 32790
Telephone: 407-647-7645; 407-647-POHL
Telefax: 407-647-2314

Frank L. Pohl	C. Teresa de Arrigoitia
Houston E. Short	George A. Golder
Dwight I. Cool	Norma Stanley
James Everett Shepherd V	Mark W. Garrett
John R. Simpson, Jr.	

Representative Clients: American Pioneer Title Insurance Company; Institute of Internal Auditors, Inc.; Thompson Steel, Inc.; SunTrust, N.A.; The Bank of Winter Park; Bekins Moving and Storage Co., Inc.; Champion Boats, Inc.; KeyCom Telephone Systems, Inc.

For full biographical listings, see the Martindale-Hubbell Law Directory

---

GEORGIA

ATLANTA,* Fulton Co.

CHILIVIS, COCHRAN, LARKINS & BEVER (AV)

3127 Maple Drive, N.E., 30305
Telephone: 404-233-4171
Facsimile: 404-261-2842

Nickolas P. Chilivis	Daniel P. Griffin
Anthony L. Cochran	John D. Dalbey
John K. Larkins, Jr.	Merrilee Aynes Gober
Thomas D. Bever	James D. Durham

For full biographical listings, see the Martindale-Hubbell Law Directory

CHOREY, TAYLOR & FEIL, A PROFESSIONAL CORPORATION (AV)

Suite 1700, The Lenox Building, 3399 Peachtree Road, N.E., 30326
Telephone: 404-841-3200
Facsimile: 404-841-3221

Thomas V. Chorey, Jr.	John L. Taylor, Jr.

For Complete List of Firm Personnel, See General Section

For full biographical listings, see the Martindale-Hubbell Law Directory

HARKLEROAD & HERMANCE, A PROFESSIONAL CORPORATION (AV)

2500 Cain Tower-Peachtree Center, 229 Peachtree Street, N.E., 30303
Telephone: 404-588-9211
Telex II: 810-751-3228
Telecopier: 404-659-0860

Donald R. Harkleroad	James P. Hermance

For full biographical listings, see the Martindale-Hubbell Law Directory

LONG ALDRIDGE & NORMAN, LLP (AV)

A Limited Liability Partnership including Professional Corporations
One Peachtree Center, Suite 5300, 303 Peachtree Street, 30308
Telephone: 404-527-4000
Telecopier: 404-527-4198
Washington, D.C. Office: Suite 600, 701 Pennsylvania Avenue, N.W., 20004.
Telephone: 202-624-1200.
FAX: 202-624-1298.

MEMBERS OF FIRM

Douglas L. Beresford (Resident, Washington, D.C. Office)	Albert G. Norman, Jr.
George (Buddy) Darden	Jacolyn A. Simmons (Resident, Washington, D.C. Office)
L. Craig Dowdy	John T. Stough, Jr. (Resident, Washington, D.C. Office)
Gordon D. Giffin	Jack H. Watson, Jr. (Resident, Washington, D.C. Office)
John E. Holtzinger, Jr. (Resident, Washington, D.C. Office)	Robert I. White (Resident, Washington, D.C. Office)

(See Next Column)

ASSOCIATES

Kevin M. Downey (Resident, Washington, D.C. Office)	Kyle Michel (Resident, Washington, D.C. Office)
George F. Hobday, Jr. (Resident, Washington, D.C. Office)	Thadd A. Prisco (Resident, Washington, D.C. Office)
	William E. Rice

OF COUNSEL

Matthew A. Towery	Nancy A. White (Resident, Washington, D.C. Office)

For Complete List of Firm Personnel, See General Section

For full biographical listings, see the Martindale-Hubbell Law Directory

STOKES LAZARUS & CARMICHAEL (AV)

80 Peachtree Park Drive, N.E., 30309-1320
Telephone: 404-352-1465
Fax: 404-352-8463

MEMBERS OF FIRM

Marion B. Stokes	William K. Carmichael
Wayne H. Lazarus	Michael J. Ernst

ASSOCIATES

Richard J. Joseph	Gregory Mark Simpson
Douglas L. Brooks	Kevin R. Wolff

For full biographical listings, see the Martindale-Hubbell Law Directory

WEISZ & ASSOCIATES (AV)

Suite 900 Live Oak Center, 3475 Lenox Road, N.E., 30326-1232
Telephone: 404-233-7888
Facsimile: 404-261-1925

Peter R. Weisz

ASSOCIATE

Cathy Rae Nash

LEGAL SUPPORT PERSONNEL

PARALEGALS

Jo Anne Gunn

Representative Clients: Marion & Cass Street Corp.; H.K. Brewing Co.; Deerfield Construction Co.; Cee Klein Accessories, LTD; Atlanta Valet, Inc.; Central Bank of Tampa; Aloha Leasing div. of Bennett Funding Group, Inc.
Reference: First Union National Bank.

For full biographical listings, see the Martindale-Hubbell Law Directory

---

DECATUR,* De Kalb Co.

CHARLES L. MARTIN (AV)

123 North McDonough Street, 30030
Telephone: 404-373-3116
FAX: 404-373-4110
Email: CLMARTIN@MINDSPRING.COM

For full biographical listings, see the Martindale-Hubbell Law Directory

---

DULUTH, Gwinnett Co.

THE WEATHERLY LAW FIRM (AV)

Gwinnett Commerce Center, 3700 Crestwood Parkway, N.W. Suite 140, 30136
Telephone: 770-564-9400
Fax: 770-564-9401

Charles L. Weatherly	Julie J. Weatherly

For full biographical listings, see the Martindale-Hubbell Law Directory

---

HAWAII

HONOLULU,* Honolulu Co.

DWYER IMANAKA SCHRAFF KUDO MEYER & FUJIMOTO ATTORNEYS AT LAW, A LAW CORPORATION (AV)

1800 Pioneer Plaza, 900 Fort Street Mall, 96813
Telephone: 808-524-8000
Telecopier: 808-526-1419
Mailing Address: P.O. Box 2727, 96803
Email: hawaiilaw@dwyer-imanaka.com *URL:* http://www.dwyer-imanaka.com

John R. Dwyer, Jr.	William G. Meyer, III
Mitchell A. Imanaka	Wesley M. Fujimoto
Paul A. Schraff	Ronald Van Grant
Benjamin A. Kudo (Atty. at Law, A Law Corp.)	Jon M. H. Pang
	Blake W. Bushnell
Adelbert Green	

(See Next Column)

DWYER IMANAKA SCHRAFF KUDO MEYER & FUJIMOTO ATTORNEYS AT LAW, A LAW CORPORATION—Continued

Richard T. Asato, Jr.	Jeffery S. Werbelow
Scott W. Settle	Lori Ann K. Koseki
Darcie S. Yoshinaga	Troy T. Fukuhara
Lawrence I. Kawasaki	Katy Y. Chen
Stacy E. Uehara	Naomi S. Uyeno
Kris N. Nakagawa	Roger B. McKeague

OF COUNSEL

Randall Y. Iwase	R. Brian Tsujimura

For full biographical listings, see the Martindale-Hubbell Law Directory

IDAHO

BOISE,* Ada Co.

MOFFATT, THOMAS, BARRETT, ROCK & FIELDS, CHARTERED (AV)

101 South Capitol Boulevard, P.O. Box 829, 83702
Telephone: 208-345-2000
FAX: 208-385-5384
Email: info@moffatt.com
Idaho Falls Office: 525 Park Avenue, Suite 2D, P.O. Box 1367, 83403.
Telephone: 208-522-6700.
FAX: 208-522-5111.
Pocatello, Idaho Office: 845 West Center, Suite C, P.O. Box 4941, 83201.
Telephone: 208-233-2001.

Morgan W. Richards, Jr.

Representative Clients: BMC West Corporation; Chevron, U.S.A.; First Security Bank of Idaho, N.A.; General Motors Corp.; Idaho Potato Commission; Intermountain Gas Co.; John Alden Life Insurance Co.; Micron Technology, Inc.; Royal Insurance Cos.; St. Luke's Regional Medical Center & Mountain States Tumor Institute.

For Complete List of Firm Personnel, See General Section

For full biographical listings, see the Martindale-Hubbell Law Directory

ILLINOIS

CHICAGO,* Cook Co.

SIEGEL, MOSES, SCHOENSTADT & WEBSTER, P.C. (AV)

111 East Wacker Drive Suite 2800, 60601-4801
Telephone: 312-658-2000
Fax: 312-658-2022

Morton Siegel	Richard G. Schoenstadt
Michael A. Moses	James L. Webster
	Jennifer G. Hoff

For full biographical listings, see the Martindale-Hubbell Law Directory

STACK & FILPI, CHARTERED (AV)

Suite 411, 140 South Dearborn Street, 60603-5298
Telephone: 312-782-0690; 236-5032
Telecopier: 312-782-0936

Paul F. Stack	Robert A. Filpi

Christine R. Norgle-Loewer

OF COUNSEL

John H. Shurtleff	James A. McGurk

For full biographical listings, see the Martindale-Hubbell Law Directory

SPRINGFIELD,* Sangamon Co.

LOEWENSTEIN, HAGEN, OEHLERT AND SMITH, P.C. (AV)

1204 South Fourth Street, 62703
Telephone: 217-525-1199
Telecopier: 217-522-6047

Ralph H. Loewenstein	Allen J. Oehlert
Henry C. Hagen	Gary L. Smith

For full biographical listings, see the Martindale-Hubbell Law Directory

INDIANA

INDIANAPOLIS,* Marion Co.

DANN PECAR NEWMAN & KLEIMAN, PROFESSIONAL CORPORATION (AV)

Suite 2300, One American Square Box 82008, 46282
Telephone: 317-632-3232; Indiana: 800-622-4799
Telecopy: 317-632-2962

Theodore R. Dann (1907-1993)	Walter E. Wolf, Jr.
Joel Yonover (1932-1995)	Barry E. Beldin
Philip D. Pecar	Robert D. Swhier, Jr.
Norman R. Newman	James P. Moloy
David H. Kleiman	Robert J. Schuckit
Jon B. Abels	Andrew A. Kleiman
Melvin R. Daniel	Michael J. Gabovitch
Lawrence F. Dorocke	Steven M. Pecar
Jeffrey A. Abrams	Benjamin A. Pecar
James H. Schwarz	Richard O. Kissel, II
Robert A. Rose	Joseph D. Calderon

OF COUNSEL

Linda E. Cantor	Anthony J. Rose

Ellen C. Siakotos	Angela L. Mansfield
Stacy L. Hill	Martha M. K. Baird
	Karin L. Veatch

Attorneys for: Indianapolis Machinery Co., Inc.; Melvin Simon & Associates, Inc.; Pacers Basketball Corp.; Universal Fire & Casualty Co., Inc.; Bank One, Indianapolis, NA; INB National Bank; Nachi Technology, Inc.; Pharmaceutical Corporation of America; Logo 7, Inc.

For full biographical listings, see the Martindale-Hubbell Law Directory

HACKMAN McCLARNON HULETT & CRACRAFT (AV)

2400 One Indiana Square, 46204
Telephone: 317-636-5401
Facsimile: 317-686-3288
Email: hmhc@indy.net

MEMBERS OF FIRM

Marvin L. Hackman	Timothy K. Ryan
Robert S. Hulett	Philip B. McKiernan
Michael B. Cracraft	Vicki L. Anderson

ASSOCIATES

Thomas A. Dickey	Marci A. Reddick

OF COUNSEL

James R. McClarnon	John D. Cochran, Jr.
	Mark S. Alderfer

Representative Clients: Ameritech Indiana; AT&T Technologies, Inc.; Citizens Gas & Coke Utility; Texas Eastern Products Pipeline Co.; Indiana Municipal Power Agency; Indiana Municipal Electric Assn.

For full biographical listings, see the Martindale-Hubbell Law Directory

JOHNSON, SMITH, PENCE, DENSBORN, WRIGHT & HEATH (AV)

One Indiana Square Suite 1800, 46204
Telephone: 317-634-9777
Telecopier: 317-636-9061

MEMBERS OF FIRM

David G. Blachly	Robert B. Hebert
John R. Hammond, III	Mark A. Palmer

ASSOCIATE

David A. Tucker

For Complete List of Firm Personnel, See General Section

For full biographical listings, see the Martindale-Hubbell Law Directory

McNAMAR, FEARNOW & McSHARAR, P.C. (AV)

Bank One Center Tower, 111 Monument Circle, Suite 4500, 46204-5145
Telephone: 317-630-4500
Fax: 317-630-4501
Email: dmcnamara40@aol.com

David F. McNamar	Alastair J. Warr
Randall R. Fearnow	John H. Sharpe
Janet A. McSharar	Paul (Rick) Rauch, III

For full biographical listings, see the Martindale-Hubbell Law Directory

PLEWS SHADLEY RACHER & BRAUN (AV)

1346 North Delaware Street, 46202-2415
Telephone: 317-637-0700
Telecopier: 317-637-0710

(See Next Column)

PLEWS SHADLEY RACHER & BRAUN, *Indianapolis—Continued*

MEMBERS OF FIRM

George M. Plews	Peter M. Racher
Sue A. Shadley	Christopher J. Braun
	Jeffrey D. Claflin

ASSOCIATES

Harinder Kaur	Jeffrey D. Featherstun
Leonardo D. Robinson	Donna C. Marron
Frederick D. Emhardt	Michael A. Myers
S. Curtis DeVoe	Julie E. Polizzotto

OF COUNSEL

Christine C. H. Plews	Timothy J. Paris

For full biographical listings, see the Martindale-Hubbell Law Directory

SOMMER & BARNARD, ATTORNEYS AT LAW, PC (AV)

4000 Bank One Tower, 111 Monument Circle, 46204-5140
Telephone: 317-630-4000
FAX: 317-236-9802
North Office: 8900 Keystone Crossing, Suite 1046, Indianapolis, Indiana, 46240-2134.
Telephone: 317-630-4000.
FAX: 317-844-4780.

Edward W. Harris, III	Frederick M. King

Representative Clients: Comerica Bank; Excel Industries; Federal Express; Kimball International; Monsanto; Renault Automation; TRW, Inc.

For Complete List of Firm Personnel, See General Section

For full biographical listings, see the Martindale-Hubbell Law Directory

IOWA

CEDAR RAPIDS,* Linn Co.

SHUTTLEWORTH & INGERSOLL, P.C. (AV)

500 Firstar Bank Building, P.O. Box 2107, 52406-2107
Telephone: 319-365-9461
Fax: 319-365-8443
Email: si-law@inav.net

Thomas M. Collins	Steven J. Pace
James C. Nemmers	Glenn L. Johnson
Michael O. McDermott	Thomas P. Peffer
Richard S. Fry	Kevin H. Collins
Richard C. Garberson	William P. Prowell
Gary J. Streit	Diane Kutzko
Carroll J. Reasoner	Mark L. Zaiger
	William S. Hochstetler

William H. Courter

COUNSEL

Joan Lipsky

Representative Clients: Amana Society; Archer-Daniels-Midland Co.; Cargill, Inc.; Firstar Bank Cedar Rapids, N.A.; General Mills, Inc.; IES Industries; MCI; McLeod Telecommunications, Inc.; PMX Industries, Inc.

For Complete List of Firm Personnel, See General Section

For full biographical listings, see the Martindale-Hubbell Law Directory

DES MOINES,* Polk Co.

WASKER, DORR, WIMMER & MARCOUILLER, P.C. (AV)

801 Grand Avenue, Suite 3100, 50309-8036
Telephone: 515-283-1801
Facsimile: 515-283-1802

Charles F. Wasker	William J. Wimmer
Fred L. Dorr	D. Mark Marcouiller
	Robert A. Sims

Matthew D. Kern

For Complete List of Firm Personnel, See General Section

For full biographical listings, see the Martindale-Hubbell Law Directory

KANSAS

TOPEKA,* Shawnee Co.

BENNETT & DILLON, L.L.P. (AV)

1605 Southwest 37th Street, 66611
Telephone: 913-267-5063
Fax: 913-267-2652

MEMBERS OF FIRM

Mark L. Bennett, Jr.	Wilburn Dillon, Jr.
	Ann L. Hoover

Jeffrey D. Jackson

References: Commerce Bank and Trust; Columbian National Bank and Trust; Silver Lake State Bank.

For full biographical listings, see the Martindale-Hubbell Law Directory

FOULSTON & SIEFKIN L.L.P. (AV)

1515 Bank IV Tower, 534 Kansas Avenue, 66603
Telephone: 913-233-3600
Fax: 913-233-1610
Wichita, Kansas Office: 100 North Broadway, 700 Fourth Financial Center, 67202.
Telephone: 316-267-6371.
Fax: 316-267-6345.
Dodge City, Kansas Office: 810 Frontview, P.O. Box 1147, 67801.
Telephone: 316-227-8126.
Fax: 316-227-8451.
Member: Lex Mundi, A Global Association of 126 Independent Firms.

SPECIAL COUNSEL

James L. Grimes, Jr.

For full biographical listings, see the Martindale-Hubbell Law Directory

WRIGHT, HENSON, SOMERS, SEBELIUS, CLARK & BAKER, LLP (AV)

Commerce Bank Building, 100 Southeast Ninth Street, 2nd Floor, P.O. Box 3555, 66601-3555
Telephone: 913-232-2200
FAX: 913-232-3344

MEMBERS OF FIRM

Thomas E. Wright	K. Gary Sebelius
Charles N. Henson	Anne Lamborn Baker
	Evelyn Zabel Wilson

For Complete List of Firm Personnel, See General Section

For full biographical listings, see the Martindale-Hubbell Law Directory

WICHITA,* Sedgwick Co.

FOULSTON & SIEFKIN L.L.P. (AV)

700 Fourth Financial Center, 67202
Telephone: 316-267-6371
Facsimile: 316-267-6345
Topeka, Kansas Office: 1515 Bank IV Tower, 534 Kansas Avenue, 66603.
Telephone: 913-233-3600.
Fax: 913-233-1610.
Dodge City, Kansas Office: 810 Frontview, P.O. Box 1147, 67801.
Telephone: 316-227-8126.
Fax: 316-227-8451.
Member: Lex Mundi, A Global Association of 126 Independent Firms.

MEMBERS OF FIRM

Mary Kathleen Babcock	Gloria G. Farha Flentje
	Douglas L. Stanley

SPECIAL COUNSEL

James L. Grimes, Jr. (Resident, Topeka Office)

For Complete List of Firm Personnel, See General Section

For full biographical listings, see the Martindale-Hubbell Law Directory

HERSHBERGER, PATTERSON, JONES & ROTH, L.C. (AV)

600 Hardage Center, 100 South Main, 67202-3779
Telephone: 316-263-7583
Fax: 316-263-7595

A. W. Hershberger (1897-1976)	J. Michael Kennalley
J. B. Patterson (1895-1957)	John A. Vetter
Richard Jones (1914-1988)	Edward L. Keeley
Jerome E. Jones	Bryce A. Abbott
Robert J. Roth	David J. Morgan
William R. Smith	Ken W. Dannenberg
	Tracy A. Applegate

T. Lynn Ward	Gary K. Albin

(See Next Column)

HERSHBERGER, PATTERSON, JONES & ROTH L.C.—*Continued*
OF COUNSEL
H. E. Jones   John L. Kratzer, Jr.

Counsel for: First National Bank in Wichita; Anadarko Petroleum Corporation; Chinese Industries; Mobil Oil Corp.; CNA Insurance; Royal Exchange Group; Central National Insurance Group; Transamerica Insurance Group; Northwestern National Insurance Group.

For full biographical listings, see the Martindale-Hubbell Law Directory

---

KENTUCKY

*FRANKFORT,** Franklin Co.

HAZELRIGG AND COX (AV)

415 West Main Street, First Floor, P.O. Box 676, 40602-0676
Telephone: 502-227-2271
Facsimile: 502-875-7158

MEMBERS OF FIRM
William P. Curlin, Jr.   Robert C. Moore
John B. Baughman   Richard S. Taylor
ASSOCIATE
Holland B. Spade

Representative Clients: A-K Steel, Inc.; BellSouth Cellular; Independent Insurance Agents of Kentucky; Motorola, Inc.; Atmos Energy Corporation.

For full biographical listings, see the Martindale-Hubbell Law Directory

*LEXINGTON,** Fayette Co.

STOLL, KEENON & PARK, LLP (AV)

201 E. Main Street, Suite 1000, 40507-1380
Telephone: 606-231-3000
Telecopier: 606-253-1093; 606-253-1027
Frankfort, Kentucky Office: 307 Washington Street, 40601.
Telephone: 502-875-6220.
Telecopier: 502-875-6235.
Louisville, Kentucky Office: 400 West Market Street, Suite 2650, 40202-3377.
Telephone: 502-568-9100.
Telecopier: 502-568-5700.

MEMBERS OF FIRM
Lindsey W. Ingram, Jr.   Herbert A. Miller, Jr.
Robert M. Watt, III   Lizbeth Ann Tully
ASSOCIATES
R. Douglas Martin   John Browning Park

Representative Clients: Delta Natural Gas Co.; Independent Telephone Group; Kentucky American Water Co.

For Complete List of Firm Personnel, See General Section

For full biographical listings, see the Martindale-Hubbell Law Directory

---

LOUISIANA

*LAFAYETTE,** Lafayette Parish

MANGHAM AND DAVIS (AV)

Suite 1400 First National Bank Towers, 600 Jefferson Street, P.O. Box 93110, 70509-3110
Telephone: 318-233-6200
Fax: 318-233-6521

Michael R. Mangham   Louis R. Davis
ASSOCIATES
Dawn Mayeux Fuqua   Claire A. Fisher
SPECIAL COUNSEL
Michael J. O'Shee

Reference: Hibernia National Bank, Lafayette, Louisiana.

For full biographical listings, see the Martindale-Hubbell Law Directory

*SHREVEPORT,** Caddo Parish

BARLOW AND HARDTNER L.C. (AV)

Tenth Floor, Louisiana Tower, 401 Edwards Street, 71101-3289
Telephone: 318-227-1131
Telecopier: 318-227-1141
Mailing Address: P.O. Box 8, Shreveport, Louisiana, 71161-0008

(See Next Column)

Malcolm S. Murchison   Clair F. White
David R. Taggart   Philip E. Downer, III
Michael B. Donald

Representative Clients: Anderson Oil & Gas, Inc.; Energy Management Corporation; Central Louisiana Electric Co., Inc.; Central and South West; Franks Petroleum Inc.; Louisiana Intrastate Gas Corp.; NorAm Energy Corp. (formerly Arkla, Inc.); Panhandle Eastern Corp.; Southwestern Electric Power Company; TE Products Pipeline Company.

For Complete List of Firm Personnel, See General Section

For full biographical listings, see the Martindale-Hubbell Law Directory

---

MAINE

*AUGUSTA,** Kennebec Co.

* indicates certain Bar Register subscribers whose principal office is located elsewhere in the state and who have arranged for representation as a part of the state capital listings that follow

* PIERCE ATWOOD (AV)

77 Winthrop Street, 04330
Telephone: 207-622-6311
Fax: 207-623-9367
Email: info@PierceAtwood.com
Portland, Maine Office: One Monument Square.
Telephone: 207-791-1100.
Fax: 207-791-1350.
Newburyport, Massachusetts Office: 6 Harris Street.
Telephone: 508-465-9599.
Fax: 508-465-9945.

MEMBERS OF FIRM
Warren E. Winslow, Jr.   Michael D. Seitzinger
Malcolm L. Lyons   John C. Nivison
ASSOCIATE
Daniel J. Stevens

For full biographical listings, see the Martindale-Hubbell Law Directory

---

*PORTLAND,** Cumberland Co.

PIERCE ATWOOD (AV)

One Monument Square, 04101
Telephone: 207-791-1100
Fax: 207-791-1350
Email: info@PierceAtwood.com
Augusta, Maine Office: 77 Winthrop Street.
Telephone: 207-622-6311.
Fax: 207-623-9367.
Newburyport, Massachusetts Office: 6 Harris Street.
Telephone: 508-465-9599.
Fax: 508-465-9945.

MEMBERS OF FIRM
Daniel E. Boxer   Philip F. W. Ahrens, III
John D. Delahanty   Kenneth Fairbanks Gray
Thomas R. Doyle   William E. Taylor
Dixon P. Pike
ASSOCIATES
Kate L. Geoffroy   David P. Littell
Matthew D. Manahan   Abigail M. Holman
Adam H. Steinman   Helen L. Edmonds
                             (Not admitted in ME)

For Complete List of Firm Personnel, See General Section

For full biographical listings, see the Martindale-Hubbell Law Directory

PRETI, FLAHERTY, BELIVEAU & PACHIOS (AV)

A Limited Liability Company
443 Congress Street, P.O. Box 11410, 04104-7410
Telephone: 207-791-3000
Telecopier: 207-791-3111
Email: admin@pfbpnet.com
Augusta, Maine Office: 45 Memorial Circle, P.O. Box 1058, 04332-1058.
Telephone: 207-623-5300.
Telecopier: 207-623-2914.

MEMBERS OF FIRM
Severin M. Beliveau   Virginia E. Davis
(Augusta Office)   (Augusta Office)
Harold C. Pachios   Estelle A. Lavoie
Bruce C. Gerrity   Joseph G. Donahue
(Augusta Office)   (Augusta Office)
Anthony W. Buxton   David B. Van Slyke
(Augusta Office)   Ann R. Robinson
                             (Augusta Office)

(See Next Column)

PRETI, FLAHERTY, BELIVEAU & PACHIOS, Portland—Continued
OF COUNSEL
Charles F. Dingman
(Augusta Office)

Mark B. LeDuc (Augusta Office)
Jeanne T. Cohn-Connor

ASSOCIATE
Deirdre M. O'Callaghan (Augusta Office)

Representative Clients: American Insurance Assn.; New England Cable Television Assn.; Industrial Energy Consumer Group; Canadian Pacific Railroad; Bangor Hydroelectric Co.; Maine Oil Dealers Assn.; American Express; The Hampton Group; Maine Auto Dealers Assn.; Medco Containment Services.

For Complete List of Firm Personnel, See General Section

For full biographical listings, see the Martindale-Hubbell Law Directory

VERRILL & DANA (AV)
One Portland Square, P.O. Box 586, 04112-0586
Telephone: 207-774-4000
Fax: 207-774-7499
Email: advice@verdan.com *URL:* http://www.verdan.com
Augusta, Maine Office: 45 Memorial Circle, P.O. Box 957.
Telephone: 207-623-3889.
Fax: 207-622-3117.
Kennebunk, Maine Office: Lafayette Center, P.O. Box 266.
Telephone: 207-985-7193.
Fax: 207-985-3957.
Washington, D.C. Office: 400 North Capitol Street, Suite 585.
Telephone: 202-624-9733.
Fax: 202-393-5218.

MEMBERS OF FIRM
Andrew M. Horton

William S. Harwood
Beth Dobson

For Complete List of Firm Personnel, See General Section

For full biographical listings, see the Martindale-Hubbell Law Directory

MARYLAND

BALTIMORE,* (Independent City)

FUNK & BOLTON, A PROFESSIONAL ASSOCIATION (AV)
USF&G Tower Building, Suite 900, 100 Light Street, 21202
Telephone: 410-659-7700
Facsimile: 410-659-7773
Email: FBLAW.COM

David M. Funk
Bryan D. Bolton
Timothy E. Dixon

Lindsey A. Rader
Steven Jared Troy
Derek B. Yarmis

OF COUNSEL
J. Frank Nayden

Bryson F. Popham
Deborah R. Rivkin

For full biographical listings, see the Martindale-Hubbell Law Directory

KAHN, SMITH & COLLINS, P.A. (AV)
110 Saint Paul Street, 6th Floor, 21202
Telephone: 410-244-1010
Fax: 410-244-8001
Email: incourt@ari.net *URL:* http://www.interbit.com/ksc

Andrew H. Kahn
Joel A. Smith

Francis J. Collins
David V. Diggs
Christyne L. Neff

Sarah Pazourek Harlan

Leslie A. Pladna

For full biographical listings, see the Martindale-Hubbell Law Directory

VENABLE ATTORNEYS AT LAW VENABLE, BAETJER AND HOWARD, LLP (AV)
A Partnership including Professional Corporations
1800 Mercantile Bank & Trust Building, 2 Hopkins Plaza, 21201
Telephone: 410-244-7400
Email: INFO@Venable.win.net
Washington, D.C. Office: Venable, Baetjer, Howard & Civiletti LLP. Suite 1000, 1201 New York Avenue, N.W.
Telephone: 202-962-4800.
McLean, Virginia Office: Suite 400, 2010 Corporate Ridge.
Telephone: 703-760-1600.
Rockville, Maryland Office: Suite 500, One Church Street, P. O. Box 1906.
Telephone: 301-217-5600.
Towson, Maryland Office: 210 Allegheny Avenue, P. O. Box 5517.
Telephone: 410-494-6200.

(See Next Column)

MEMBERS OF FIRM
Thomas P. Perkins, III (P.C.)
Roger W. Titus (Resident, Rockville, Maryland Office)
Thomas J. Madden (Not admitted in MD; Resident, Washington, D.C. Office)
William L. Walsh, Jr. (P.C.) (Not admitted in MD; Resident, McLean, Virginia Office)
Ronald R. Glancz (Not admitted in MD; Resident, Washington, D.C. Office)
Kenneth C. Bass, III (Not admitted in MD; Washington, D.C. and McLean, Virginia Offices)
Paul F. Strain (P.C.)
Paul T. Glasgow (Resident, Rockville, Maryland Office)

Sondra Harans Block (Resident, Rockville, Maryland Office)
Michael Schatzow (Also at Washington, D.C. Office)
John F. Cooney (Not admitted in MD; Resident, Washington, D.C. Office)
L. Paige Marvel
N. Frank Wiggins (Not admitted in MD; Resident, Washington, D.C. Office)
Jeffrey D. Knowles (Not admitted in MD; Resident, Washington, D.C. Office)
John J. Pavlick, Jr. (Not admitted in MD; Resident, Washington, D. C. Office)
M. King Hill, III (Resident, Towson, Maryland Office)
Gary M. Hnath (Resident, Washington, D.C. Office)

OF COUNSEL
Richard H. Mays (Not admitted in MD; Washington, D.C. and McLean, Virginia Offices)

Emried D. Cole, Jr.
Judith A. Armold

ASSOCIATES
Paul D. Barker, Jr.
Kevin B. Collins (Also at Rockville, Maryland Office)
Christine J. Warren

James Nicholas Czaban (Not admitted in MD; Resident, Washington, D.C. Office)

For Complete List of Firm Personnel, See General Section

For full biographical listings, see the Martindale-Hubbell Law Directory

LARGO, Prince Georges Co.

SHIPLEY & HORNE, P.A. (AV)
1101 Mercantile Lane, Suite 240, 20774
Telephone: 301-925-1800
Fax: 301-925-1803

Russell W. Shipley

Arthur J. Horne, Jr.

For full biographical listings, see the Martindale-Hubbell Law Directory

ROCKVILLE,* Montgomery Co.

VENABLE ATTORNEYS AT LAW VENABLE, BAETJER AND HOWARD, LLP (AV)
A Partnership including Professional Corporations
Suite 500, One Church Street, P.O. Box 1906, 20850-4129
Telephone: 301-217-5600
FAX: 301-217-5617
Baltimore, Maryland Office: 1800 Mercantile Bank & Trust Building, 2 Hopkins Plaza.
Telephone: 410-244-7400.
Washington, D.C. Office: Venable, Baetjer, Howard & Civiletti LLP, Suite 1000, 1201 New York Avenue, N.W.
Telephone: 202-962-4800.
McLean, Virginia Office: Suite 400, 2010 Corporate Ridge.
Telephone: 703-760-1600.
Towson, Maryland, Office: 210 Allegheny Avenue, P. O. Box 5517.
Telephone: 410-494-6200.

MEMBERS OF FIRM
Roger W. Titus

Paul T. Glasgow
Sondra Harans Block

ASSOCIATE
Kevin B. Collins (Also at Baltimore, Maryland Office)

For Complete List of Firm Personnel, See General Section

For full biographical listings, see the Martindale-Hubbell Law Directory

UPPER MARLBORO,* Prince Georges Co.

KNIGHT, MANZI, BRENNAN, SHAY AND HAM, A PROFESSIONAL ASSOCIATION (AV)
14440 Old Mill Road, 20772
Telephone: 301-952-0100
Annapolis/Baltimore 410-792-3786
Fax: 301-952-0221
Crofton, Maryland Office: 2411 Crofton Lane, # 26.
Telephone: 301-261-0808.
Fax: 301-261-6945.
Mitchellville, Maryland Office: 12164 Central Avenue, Suite 228.
Telephone: 301-390-0577.
Fax: 301-390-8464.

(See Next Column)

KNIGHT, MANZI, BRENNAN, SHAY AND HAM A PROFESSIONAL
ASSOCIATION—*Continued*

William E. Knight	John F. Shay, Jr.
Robert A. Manzi	Richard J. Ham
William C. Brennan, Jr.	Martin J. Shuham

Monica M. Haley-Pierson	Norman D. Rivera
Daniel F. Lynch III	Robert L. Lombardo

OF COUNSEL

Stuart R. Hammett

For full biographical listings, see the Martindale-Hubbell Law Directory

---

MASSACHUSETTS

*BOSTON,** Suffolk Co.

FINNEGAN, UNDERWOOD, RYAN & TIERNEY (AV)

20 Custom House Street Suite 550, 02110
Telephone: 617-345-0020
Fax: 617-345-0150

MEMBERS OF FIRM

David I. Finnegan	John G. Ryan
Richard J. Underwood	Philip T. Tierney

ASSOCIATES

Peter J. McCue	Kim Beringhause Peacock
Susan E. Ireland	Susan Underwood
Stimpson B. Hubbard	Susan Schramm

For full biographical listings, see the Martindale-Hubbell Law Directory

---

MICHIGAN

BLOOMFIELD HILLS, Oakland Co.

RICHARD A. PATTERSON, P.C. (AV)

6905 Telegraph Road Suite 215, 48301
Telephone: 810-647-6950
Facsimile: 810-645-0917

Richard A. Patterson

For full biographical listings, see the Martindale-Hubbell Law Directory

---

DAVID D. PATTON & ASSOCIATES, P.C. (AV)

100 Bloomfield Hills Parkway, Suite 110, 48304
Telephone: 810-258-6020
Fax: 810-258-6052
Email: Litigation@Aol.Com

David D. Patton

Ellen Bartman Jannette	Patricia C. White
David H. Patton (1912-1993)	

For full biographical listings, see the Martindale-Hubbell Law Directory

---

*DETROIT,** Wayne Co.

BODMAN, LONGLEY & DAHLING LLP (AV)

34th Floor 100 Renaissance Center, 48243
Telephone: 313-259-7777
Fax: 313-393-7579
Email: 2080194@mcimail.com
Troy, Michigan Office: Suite 2020, 755 West Big Beaver Road.
Telephone: 810-362-2110.
Fax: 810-244-0780.
Ann Arbor, Michigan Office: 110 Miller, Suite 300.
Telephone: 313-761-3780.
Fax: 313-930-2494.
Northern Michigan Office: 229 Court Street, P.O. Box 405, Cheboygan.
Telephone: 616-627-4351.
Fax: 616-627-2802.

MEMBERS OF FIRM

Richard D. Rohr	Randolph S. Perry
Thomas A. Roach	James J. Walsh
(Ann Arbor Office)	Charles N. Raimi
James A. Smith	F. Thomas Lewand

For Representative Client List, See General Section.

For Complete List of Firm Personnel, See General Section

For full biographical listings, see the Martindale-Hubbell Law Directory

---

BRADY HATHAWAY, PROFESSIONAL CORPORATION (AV)

1330 Buhl Building, 48226-3602
Telephone: 313-965-3700
Telecopier: 313-965-2830

John F. Brady	Daniel J. Bretz
Thomas M. J. Hathaway	Liliana A. Ciccodicola
Thomas P. Brady	Connie M. Cessante

Representative Clients: Beam Stream, Inc.; Bundy Tubing Company; Energy Conversion Devices, Inc.; Schering Corporation; Warner-Lambert; Wolverine Technologies; ABB Environmental Services; GMIS, Inc.; Marriott Corp.

For Complete List of Firm Personnel, See General Section

For full biographical listings, see the Martindale-Hubbell Law Directory

---

BUTZEL LONG, A PROFESSIONAL CORPORATION (AV)

Suite 900, 150 West Jefferson, 48226
Telephone: 313-225-7000
Telecopier: 313-225-7080
Email: melnick@butzel.com *URL:* http://www.butzel.com
Birmingham, Michigan Office: Suite 200, 32270 Telegraph Road.
Telephone: 810-258-1616.
Telecopier: 810-258-1439.
Lansing, Michigan Office: 118 West Ottawa Street.
Telephone: 517-372-6622.
Telecopier: 517-372-6672.
Ann Arbor, Michigan Office: Suite 300, 350 South Main Street.
Telephone: 313-995-3110.
Telecopier: 313-995-1777.
Grosse Pointe Farms, Michigan Office: Suite 260, 21 Kercheval.
Telephone: 313-886-5446.
Telecopier: 313-886-2114.

Robert J. Battista	James C. Bruno
William R. Ralls (Lansing)	Carl Rashid, Jr.
John P. Hancock, Jr.	Steven D. Weyhing (Lansing)
Leonard F. Charla	Robert A. Boonin

Representative Clients: Bridgestone/Firestone, Inc.; Detroit Diesel Corp.; The Detroit News, Inc.; Kelly Services; Kelsey Hayes Co.; Merrill Lynch Pierce Fenner & Smith, Inc.; Stroh Brewery Co.; Takata Corp.; United Parcel Services of America, Inc.; The University of Michigan.

For Complete List of Firm Personnel, See General Section

For full biographical listings, see the Martindale-Hubbell Law Directory

---

CLARK HILL P.L.C. (AV)

500 Woodward Avenue, Suite 3500, 48226
Telephone: 313-965-8300
Facsimile: 313-962-4348
Oakland County, Michigan Office: Third Floor, 255 South Woodward Avenue, Birmingham.
Telephone: 810-642-9692.
Facsimile: 810-642-2174.
Lansing, Michigan Office: Suite 600, 200 North Capitol Avenue.
Telephone: 517-484-4481.
Facsimile: 517-484-1246.
Minneapolis, Minnesota Office: Suite 1000, One Financial Plaza, 120 South Sixth Street.
Telephone: 612-332-0102.
Facsimile: 612-332-3225.
Kansas City, Missouri Office: Suite 1400, Bryant Building, 1102 Grand Avenue.
Telephone: 816-221-5578.
Facsimile: 816-221-0303.

Douglas H. West	Robert A. W. Strong
Richard C. Marsh	Louis J. Porter
Roderick S. Coy	(Resident, Lansing Office)
(Resident, Lansing Office)	

Stewart A. Binke	Stephen J. Videto
(Resident, Lansing Office)	(Resident, Lansing Office)

Representative Clients: Booth Communications, Inc.; LCI International Telecom Corp.; Chrysler Corp.; Ford Motor Co.; General Motors Corp.; National Steel Corp.

For Complete List of Firm Personnel, See General Section

For full biographical listings, see the Martindale-Hubbell Law Directory

---

EAMES WILCOX (AV)

1400 Buhl Building, 48226-3602
Telephone: 313-963-3750
Facsimile: 313-963-8485

MEMBERS OF FIRM

Leonard A. Wilcox, Jr.	Jerry R. Swift
Ronald J. Mastej	Neill T. Riddell
John W. Bryant	Kevin N. Summers
Robert E. Gesell	Keith M. Aretha

(See Next Column)

EAMES WILCOX, *Detroit—Continued*

OF COUNSEL

Rex Eames   William B. McIntyre, Jr.

David R. Ritter

Representative Clients: ABF Freight System, Inc.; Chrysler Credit Corp.; City Transfer Co.; Engineered Heat Treat, Inc.; Fetz Engineering Co.; I E & E Industries, Inc.; Schneider Transport; Tank Carrier Employers Association of Michigan; TNT Transport Group, Inc.; Waste Management of Michigan.

For full biographical listings, see the Martindale-Hubbell Law Directory

GRAND RAPIDS,* Kent Co.

WHEELER UPHAM, A PROFESSIONAL CORPORATION (AV)

Second Floor, Trust Building, 40 Pearl Street, N.W., 49503-3001
Telephone: 616-459-7100
Fax: 616-459-6366

Gordon B. Wheeler (1904-1986)	William H. Heritage, Jr.
Buford A. Upham (Retired)	Kenneth E. Tiews
Robert H. Gillette	Jack L. Hoffman
Geoffrey L. Gillis	Janet C. Baxter
John M. Roels	Peter Kladder, III
Gary A. Maximiuk	James M. Shade
Timothy J. Orlebeke	Thomas A. Kuiper

Counsel For: Prudential Ins. Co.; Metropolitan Life Ins. Co.; Travelers Ins. Co.; Farmers Ins. Group; Auto-Owners Ins. Co.; Independent Cooperative Milk Producers Assn.; Medtronic, Inc.; Navistar; Westdale Better Homes and Gardens; Gospel Films, Inc.

For full biographical listings, see the Martindale-Hubbell Law Directory

LANSING, Ingham Co.

DUNNINGS & FRAWLEY, P.C. (AV)

Duncan Building, 530 South Pine Street, 48933-2299
Telephone: 517-487-8222
Fax: 517-487-2026
Email: conrights@voyager.net

Stuart J. Dunnings, Jr.   John J. Frawley

Stuart J. Dunnings, III   Steven D. Dunnings

Shauna L. Dunnings

Representative Clients: Lansing Board of Education; Lansing Housing Commission; Ford Motor Co.
References: First of America; Michigan National Bank.

For full biographical listings, see the Martindale-Hubbell Law Directory

SOUTHFIELD, Oakland Co.

FRIMET & ROGALSKI, P.C. (AV)

2000 Town Center, Suite 2700, 48075-1108
Telephone: 810-358-0080
Telecopier: 810-358-0449

Gilbert M. Frimet   Alan T. Rogalski

John A. Michalsen (1955-1994)

OF COUNSEL

Bruce C. Blanton   Rubenstein Plotkin, Professional
Edward B. Meth   Corporation, , Southfield,
                                   Michigan

Representative Clients: Westland Convalescent Center; Northwood, Inc.; Basha Diagnostics, P.C.; Binson's Hospital Supplies, Inc.; Beaumont Physicians Group; Providence Medical Group; Macomb Anesthesia, P.C.; Family Home Care; Camelids of Delaware, Inc.; Downriver Mental Health Clinic, P.C.

For full biographical listings, see the Martindale-Hubbell Law Directory

ADMIRALTY/MARITIME LAW

ALABAMA

BIRMINGHAM,* Jefferson Co.

CABANISS, JOHNSTON, GARDNER, DUMAS & O'NEAL (AV)

Park Place Tower, 2001 Park Place North, Suite 700, P.O. Box 830612, 35283-0612
Telephone: 205-716-5200
Telecopier: 205-716-5200
Email: CabJohnston@aol.com
Mobile, Alabama Office: 700 AmSouth Center, P.O. Box 2906.
Telephone: 334-433-6961.
Telecopier: 334-433-1060.

MEMBERS OF FIRM

Crawford S. McGivaren, Jr.	R. Boyd Miller
Patrick H. Sims	(Resident, Mobile Office)
(Resident, Mobile Office)	

Counsel for: Alabaster Industries, Inc.; Schuler Industries, Inc.; Carraway Methodist Hospitals of Alabama; Doster Construction Co., Inc.; Liberty Mutual Insurance Co.; John Alden Life Insurance Co.; MacMillan Bloedel Packaging, Inc.; Norfolk Southern Corp.; O'Neal Steel, Inc.

For Complete List of Firm Personnel, See General Section

For full biographical listings, see the Martindale-Hubbell Law Directory

PITTMAN, HOOKS, DUTTON & HOLLIS, P.C. (AV)

1100 Park Place Tower, 35203
Telephone: 205-322-8880
Telecopier: 205-328-2711

W. Lee Pittman	L. Andrew Hollis, Jr.
Kenneth W. Hooks	Jeffrey C. Kirby
Tom Dutton	Ralph Bohanan, Jr.
	Nat Bryan

Chris T. Hellums	Emily H. Nelson
Adam P. Morel	John Robert Potter

OF COUNSEL

James H. Davis	Myra B. Staggs
(Not admitted in AL)	

For full biographical listings, see the Martindale-Hubbell Law Directory

MOBILE,* Mobile Co.

ARMBRECHT, JACKSON, DEMOUY, CROWE, HOLMES & REEVES, L.L.C. (AV)

1300 AmSouth Center, P.O. Box 290, 36601
Telephone: 334-405-1300
Facsimile: 334-432-6843; 433-3821

MEMBERS OF FIRM

Rae M. Crowe	Douglas L. Brown
Broox G. Holmes, Jr.	Donald C. Radcliff
W. Boyd Reeves	Christopher I. Gruenewald
E. B. Peebles III	M. Kathleen Miller
Grover E. Asmus II	Ray Morgan Thompson
	Scott G. Brown

Representative Clients: Cove Shipping Co.; Warrior & Gulf Navigation Co.; Cooper/T. Smith Co., Inc.; Strachan Shipping Co.; Mobile River Terminal; National Marine, Inc.; ProMar Insurance Co.; Cooper T. Smith Company, Inc.

For Complete List of Firm Personnel, See General Section

For full biographical listings, see the Martindale-Hubbell Law Directory

CUNNINGHAM, BOUNDS, YANCE, CROWDER & BROWN (AV)

1601 Dauphin Street, P.O. Box 66705, 36660
Telephone: 334-471-6191
Fax: 334-479-1031

Richard Bounds	Joseph M. Brown, Jr.
James A. Yance	Gregory B. Breedlove
John T. Crowder, Jr.	Andrew T. Citrin
Robert T. Cunningham, Jr.	Michael A. Worel

David G. Wirtes, Jr.	Mitchell K. Shelly
Toby D. Brown	Kelli Denise Taylor

OF COUNSEL

Robert T. Cunningham	Valentino D. B. Mazzia

References: First Alabama Bank; AmSouth Bank, N.A.

For full biographical listings, see the Martindale-Hubbell Law Directory

DIAMOND, HASSER & FROST (AV)

1325 Dauphin Street, P.O. Drawer 40600, 36640
Telephone: 334-432-3362
Fax: 334-432-3367

MEMBERS OF FIRM

Ross Diamond, Jr. (1919-1978)	James E. Hasser, Jr.
Ross M. Diamond, III	James H. Frost

References: First Alabama Bank, Mobile; AM South Bank, Mobile.

For full biographical listings, see the Martindale-Hubbell Law Directory

JOHNSTONE, ADAMS, BAILEY, GORDON AND HARRIS, L.L.C. (AV)

Royal St. Francis Building, 104 St. Francis Street, P.O. Box 1988, 36633
Telephone: 334-432-7682
Facsimile: 334-432-2800
Telex: 782040

MEMBERS OF FIRM

Joseph M. Allen, Jr.	Alan C. Christian
Thomas S. Rue	Gregory C. Buffalow

ASSOCIATE

E. Erich Bergdolt

Representative Clients: The West of England Ship Owners Mutual Protection and Indemnity Assn. (Luxembourg); The Standard Steamship Owners Protection and Indemnity Assn. (Bermuda) Ltd.; Waterman Steamship Corp.; Lykes Bros. Steamship Co., Inc.; The Shipowners' Mutual Protection and Indemnity Assn. (Luxemburg); Sea-Land Service, Inc.; Great Lakes Dredge & Dock Co.; Maritime Overseas Corp.

For Complete List of Firm Personnel, See General Section

For full biographical listings, see the Martindale-Hubbell Law Directory

LYONS, PIPES & COOK, P.C. (AV)

2 North Royal Street, P.O. Box 2727, 36652-2727
Telephone: 334-432-4481
Cable Address: "Lysea"
Telecopier: 334-433-1820

Wesley Pipes	Walter M. Cook, Jr.
Marion A. Quina, Jr.	Allen E. Graham

General Counsel: Alabama State Docks Department (an agency of the State of Alabama); Southern Steamship Agency, Inc.
Counsel: McKenzie Tank Lines, Inc.; SCNO Barge Lines, Inc.; Scott Paper Co.; Shell Oil Corp.
Trial Counsel: Aetna Life and Casualty Co.; Chubb Group of Insurance Companies.

For Complete List of Firm Personnel, See General Section

For full biographical listings, see the Martindale-Hubbell Law Directory

VICKERS, RIIS, MURRAY AND CURRAN, L.L.C. (AV)

8th Floor, First Alabama Bank Building, 106 Saint Francis Street, P.O. Box 2568, 36652
Telephone: 334-432-9772
Fax: 334-432-9781

MEMBERS OF FIRM

J. Manson Murray	Thomas E. Sharp, III
J. W. Goodloe, Jr.	J. Marshall Gardner

Representative Clients: Midstream Fuel Services; McPhillips Manufacturing Co.; Spring Hill College; Steiner Shipyard, Inc.; Homeowners Marketing Services, Inc.; Marine Office of America Corp.; Cummins Alabama, Inc.; Ben M. Radcliff Contractor, Inc.; Marine Office of America Corp.; Murray Stevedoring Co., Inc.

For Complete List of Firm Personnel, See General Section

For full biographical listings, see the Martindale-Hubbell Law Directory

CALIFORNIA

IRVINE, Orange Co.

ANDRADE & MUZI (AV)

Marine National Bank Building, 18401 Von Karman, Suite 350, 92715
Telephone: 714-553-1951
Telecopier: 714-553-0655
San Diego, California Office: Tokia Bank Building, 3111 Camino Del Rio North, Suite 1100.
Telephone: 619-291-2481.

MEMBERS OF FIRM

Richard B. Andrade	Abilio Tavares, Jr.
Andrew C. Muzi	Samuel G. Broyles, Jr.
Ronald G. Holbert	Frank A. Satalino

(See Next Column)

ANDRADE & MUZI, *Irvine—Continued*

OF COUNSEL
Kurt Kupferman

Representative Clients: American International Cos.; American Home Assurance; Lloyds of London; Veco International; Veco Drilling, Inc.; Shell Oil Co.; Unocal.

For full biographical listings, see the Martindale-Hubbell Law Directory

---

LONG BEACH, Los Angeles Co.

LAW OFFICES OF JAMES H. ACKERMAN (AV)

Suite 1440, One World Trade Center, 90831-1440
Telephone: 310-436-9911
Cable Address: "Jimack"
Telecopier: 310-436-1897

References: Farmers and Merchants Bank (Long Beach Main Office); Sumitomo Bank of California (Long Beach Main Office).

For full biographical listings, see the Martindale-Hubbell Law Directory

---

BAKER & HOSTETLER (AV)

300 Oceangate, Suite 620, 90802-6807
Telephone: 310-432-2827
FAX: 310-432-6698
In Cleveland, Ohio: 3200 National City Center, 1900 East Ninth Street.
Telephone: 216-621-0200.
In Columbus, Ohio: Capitol Square, Suite 2100, 65 East State Street.
Telephone: 614-228-1541.
In Denver, Colorado: 303 East 17th Avenue, Suite 1100.
Telephone: 303-861-0600.
In Houston, Texas: 1000 Louisiana, Suite 2000.
Telephone: 713-236-0020.
In Los Angeles, California: 600 Wilshire Boulevard.
Telephone: 213-624-2400.
In Orlando, Florida: SunBank Center, Suite 2300, 200 South Orange Avenue.
Telephone: 407-649-4000.
In Washington, D. C.: Washington Square, Suite 1100, 1050 Connecticut Avenue, N. W.
Telephone: 202-861-1500.
In College Park, Maryland: 9658 Baltimore Boulevard, Suite 206.
Telephone: 301-441-2781.
In Alexandria, Virginia: 437 North Lee Street.
Telephone: 703-549-1294.
In San Francisco, California: One Sansome Street, Suite 2000.
Telephone: 415-951-4705.

PARTNERS

Robert E. Coppola   David A. Kettel
(Partner in Charge)   Christina L. Owen

For Complete List of Firm Personnel, See General Section

For full biographical listings, see the Martindale-Hubbell Law Directory

---

FISHER & PORTER, A LAW CORPORATION (AV)

110 Pine Avenue, 11th Floor, P.O. Box 22686, 90801-5686
Telephone: 310-435-5626
Telex: 284549 FPKLAW UR
Fax: 310-432-5399

Gerald M. Fisher   Therese G. Groff
David S. Porter   Michael W. Lodwick
         George P. Hassapis

OF COUNSEL

Stephen C. Klausen   Stephen Chace Bass
       Anthony P. Lombardo

Vicki L. Hassman   Michael J. McLaughlin
Linda A. Mancini   Sandra L. Gryder
       Kenneth F. Mattfeld

For full biographical listings, see the Martindale-Hubbell Law Directory

---

FLYNN, DELICH & WISE (AV)

One World Trade Center, Suite 1800, 90831-1800
Telephone: 310-435-2626
Fax: 310-437-7555
San Francisco, California Office: Suite 1750, 580 California Street.
Telephone: 415-693-5566.
Fax: 415-693-0410.

Erich P. Wise   Nicholas S. Politis

Thomas C. Jorgensen

Representative Clients: American Hawaii Cruises; Holland America Line; Through Transport Mutual Insurance Association, Ltd.; The Britannia Steam Ship Insurance Association Limited; The Steamship Mutual Underwriting Association (Bermuda) Ltd.; General Steamship Corp., Ltd.; Com-

(See Next Column)

---

modore Cruise Line, Ltd.; Interocean Steamship Corporation; Sea-Land Service, Inc.; Hatteras Yachts.

For full biographical listings, see the Martindale-Hubbell Law Directory

---

MOORE, RUTTER & EVANS (AV)

A Partnership including a Professional Corporation
555 East Ocean Boulevard, Suite 500, 90802-5090
Telephone: 310-494-6667; 435-4499
Facsimile: 310-495-4229
Huntington Beach, California Office: 2100 Main Street, Suite 280, 92648.
Telephone: 714-374-3333.

RESIDENT PARTNERS

Neal Moore   Mark D. Rutter
      William D. Evans (P.C.)

OF COUNSEL
Michael J. Emling

For full biographical listings, see the Martindale-Hubbell Law Directory

---

RUSSELL & MIRKOVICH (AV)

One World Trade Center, Suite 1450, 90831-1450
Telephone: 310-436-9911
FAX: 310-436-1897

Carlton E. Russell   Joseph N. Mirkovich

For full biographical listings, see the Martindale-Hubbell Law Directory

---

WILLIAMS WOOLLEY COGSWELL NAKAZAWA & RUSSELL (AV)

111 West Ocean Boulevard, Suite 2000, 90802-4614
Telephone: 310-495-6000
Telecopier: 310-435-1359; 310-435-6812
Telex: ITT: 4933872; WU: 984929
Email: wwlaw@msn.com
Rancho Santa Fe, California Office: P.O. Box 9120, 16236 San Dieguito Road, Building 3, Suite 3-15, 92067.
Telephone: 619-497-0284.
Fax: 619-759-9938.
Port Hueneme, California Office: 237 E. Hueneme Road, Suite A, 93041.
Telephone: 805-488-8560.
Fax: 805-488-7896.

MEMBERS OF FIRM

Reed M. Williams   Alan Nakazawa
David E. R. Woolley   Blake W. Larkin
Forrest R. Cogswell   Thomas A. Russell

ASSOCIATES

Todd A. Valdes   Thomas G. Walsh
      Richard J. Nikas

For full biographical listings, see the Martindale-Hubbell Law Directory

---

LOS ANGELES,* Los Angeles Co.

BAKER & HOSTETLER (AV)

600 Wilshire Boulevard, 90017-3212
Telephone: 213-624-2400
FAX: 213-975-1740
In Cleveland, Ohio: 3200 National City Center, 1900 East Ninth Street.
Telephone: 216-621-0200.
In Columbus, Ohio: Capitol Square, Suite 2100, 65 East State Street.
Telephone: 614-228-1541.
In Denver, Colorado: 303 East 17th Avenue, Suite 1100.
Telephone: 303-861-0600.
In Houston, Texas: 1000 Louisiana, Suite 2000.
Telephone: 713-236-0020.
In Long Beach, California: 300 Oceangate, Suite 620.
Telephone: 310-432-2827.
In Orlando, Florida: SunBank Center, Suite 2300, 200 South Orange Avenue.
Telephone: 407-649-4000.
In Washington, D. C.: Washington Square, Suite 1100, 1050 Connecticut Avenue, N. W.
Telephone: 202-861-1500.
In College Park, Maryland: 9658 Baltimore Boulevard, Suite 206.
Telephone: 301-441-2781.
In Alexandria, Virginia: 437 North Lee Street.
Telephone: 703-549-1294.
In San Francisco, California: One Sansome Street, Suite 2000.
Telephone: 415-951-4705.

MEMBERS OF FIRM IN LOS ANGELES, CALIFORNIA

Sheldon A. Gebb (Managing
Partner-Los Angeles, Long
Beach, California and
Houston, Texas Offices)

PARTNER
William P. Barry

(See Next Column)

BAKER & HOSTETLER—*Continued*

ASSOCIATE

Kathleen E. Bailey

For Complete List of Firm Personnel, See General Section

For full biographical listings, see the Martindale-Hubbell Law Directory

MAHONEY, COPPENRATH, JAFFE & PEARSON LLP (AV)

A Partnership including Professional Corporations
2049 Century Park East, Suite 2480, 90067-3283
Telephone: 310-557-1919
Telecopier: 310-277-6536

MEMBERS OF FIRM

James E. Mahoney (P.C.)	Ronald C. Pearson
Walter G. Coppenrath, Jr.,	Daryl G. Parker
(P.C.)	Charles L. Grotts
Howard M. Jaffe (P.C.)	Arthur L. Martin

OF COUNSEL

Gerald Lee Tahajian

Reference: First Professional Bank, Santa Monica, California.

For full biographical listings, see the Martindale-Hubbell Law Directory

OSTROVE, KRANTZ & OSTROVE, A PROFESSIONAL CORPORATION (AV)

(Successor To: Ostrove and Lancer, A Professional Corporation; David Ostrove, A Professional Corporation)
5757 Wilshire Boulevard, Suite 535, 90036-3600
Telephone: 213-939-3400
Fax: 213-939-3500
Email: OSTROVE@AOL.COM

David Ostrove	David S. Krantz
	Kenneth E. Ostrove

Reference: First Business Bank.

For full biographical listings, see the Martindale-Hubbell Law Directory

PIERRY & MOORHEAD, LLP (AV)

A Partnership including a Professional Corporation
301 North Avalon Boulevard, 90744-5888
Telephone: 310-834-2691, 213-775-8348, 714-636-2970
FAX: 310-518-5814

MEMBERS OF FIRM

Thomas J. Pierry, Sr.	Michael D. Moorhead (P.C.)

James M. McAdams	F. Javier Trujillo
F. Joseph Ford, Jr.	Thomas J. Pierry, III
Robert W. Ford	Joseph P. Pierry

For full biographical listings, see the Martindale-Hubbell Law Directory

PILLSBURY MADISON & SUTRO LLP (AV)

Citicorp Plaza, 725 South Figueroa Street, Suite 1200, 90017-2513
Telephone: 213-488-7100
Fax: 213-629-1033
Costa Mesa, California Office: Plaza Tower, Suite 1100, 600 Anton Boulevard, 92626.
Telephone: 714-436-6800.
Fax: 714-662-6999.
Silicon Valley Office: 2700 San Hill Road, Menlo Park, 94025.
Telephone: 415-233-4500.
Fax: 415-233-4545.
Sacramento, California Office: 400 Capitol Mall, Suite 1700, 95814.
Telephone: 916-329-4700.
Fax: 916-441-3583.
San Diego, California Office: 101 West Broadway, Suite 1800, 92101.
Telephone: 619-234-5000.
Fax: 619-236-1995.
San Francisco, California Office: 235 Montgomery Street, 94104.
Telephone: 415-983-1000.
Fax: 415-983-1200.
Washington, D.C. Office: 1100 New York Avenue, N.W., Ninth Floor, 20005.
Telephone: 202-861-3000.
Fax: 202-822-0944.
New York, New York Office: 520 Madison Avenue, 40th Floor, 10022.
Telephone: 212-328-4810.
Fax: 212-328-4824. One Liberty Plaza, 165 Broadway, 51st Floor.
Telephone: 212-374-1890.
Fax: 212-374-1852.
Hong Kong Office: 6/F Asia Pacific Finance Tower, Citibank Plaza, 3 Garden Road, Central.
Telephone: 011-852-2509-7100.
Fax: 011-852-2509-7188.

(See Next Column)

Tokyo, Japan Office: Pillsbury Madison & Sutro, Gaikokuho Jimu Bengoshi Jimusho, 5th Floor, Samon Eleven Building, 3-1, Samon-cho, Shinjuku-ku, Tokyo 160 Japan.
Telephone: 800-729-9830; 011-813-3354-3531.
Fax: 011-813-3354-3534.

MEMBER OF FIRM

Lawrence D. Bradley, Jr.

For Complete List of Firm Personnel, See General Section

For full biographical listings, see the Martindale-Hubbell Law Directory

---

SAN DIEGO, * San Diego Co.

BROWN, McDONNELL & ROMAKER, A PROFESSIONAL LAW CORPORATION (AV)

2390 Shelter Island Drive, Suite 210, 92106
Telephone: 619-221-9181
Fax: 619-221-9181

Sampson A. Brown	Michael B. McDonnell
	John L. Romaker

Representative Clients: A to Z Marine Service; Knight & Carver Custom Yachts, Inc.; Lester & Lester Marine Survey, Inc.

For full biographical listings, see the Martindale-Hubbell Law Directory

DOUGHERTY & HILDRE (AV)

2550 Fifth Avenue, Suite 600, 92103-5624
Telephone: 619-232-9131
Telefax: 619-232-7317

William O. Dougherty	Fred M. Dudek
Donald F. Hildre	Mona H. Freedman

For full biographical listings, see the Martindale-Hubbell Law Directory

LAW OFFICES OF ROBERT G. DYER (AV)

600 West Broadway, Suite 1400, 92101-3302
Telephone: 619-544-9300
Fax: 619-544-9598

For full biographical listings, see the Martindale-Hubbell Law Directory

DANIEL B. MacLEOD (AV)

McClintock Plaza, 1202 Kettner Boulvard, Suite 4400, 92101
Telephone: 619-234-7000
Telefax: 619-234-9973
San Francisco, California Affiliated Office: King & MacLeod 101 California Street, Suite 4050 94111.
Telephone: 415-352-0675.

For full biographical listings, see the Martindale-Hubbell Law Directory

PILLSBURY MADISON & SUTRO LLP (AV)

101 West Broadway, Suite 1800, 92101
Telephone: 619-234-5000
FAX: 619-236-1995
Costa Mesa, California Office: Plaza Tower, 600 Anton Boulevard, Suite 1100, 92626.
Telephone: 714-436-6800.
Fax: 714-662-6999.
Los Angeles, California Office: Citicorp Plaza, 725 South Figueroa, Suite 1200, 90017.
Telephone: 213-488-7100.
Fax: 213-629-1033.
New York, New York Office: 520 Madison Avenue, 40th Floor, 10022.
Telephone: 212-328-4810.
Fax: 212-328-4824.
Silicon Valley Office: 2700 Sand Hill Road, Menlo Park, 94025.
Telephone: 415-233-4500.
Fax: 415-233-4545.
Sacramento, California Office: 400 Capitol Mall, Suite 1700, 95814.
Telephone: 916-329-4700.
Fax: 916-441-3583.
San Francisco, California Office: 235 Montgomery Street, 94104.
Telephone: 415-983-1000.
Fax: 415-983-1200.
Washington, D.C. Office: 1100 New York Avenue, N.W., Ninth Floor, 20005.
Telephone: 202-861-3000.
Fax: 202-822-0944.
Hong Kong Office: 6/F Asia Pacific Finance Tower, Citibank Plaza, 3 Garden Road, Central.
Telephone: 011-852-2509-7100.
Fax: 011-852-2509-7188.
Tokyo, Japan Office: Pillsbury Madison & Sutro, Gaikokuho Jimu Bengoshi Jimusho, 5th Floor, Samon Eleven Building, 3-1, Samon-cho, Shinjuku-ku, Tokyo 160 Japan.
Telephone: 800-729-9830; 011-813-3354-3531.
Fax: 011-813-3354-3534.

(See Next Column)

PILLSBURY MADISON & SUTRO LLP, *San Diego—Continued*
MEMBER OF FIRM
Daniel C. Minteer

For Complete List of Firm Personnel, See General Section

For full biographical listings, see the Martindale-Hubbell Law Directory

WALTON & ASSOCIATES (AV)

402 West Broadway, Suite 1210, 92101
Telephone: 619-234-7422
Fax: 619-234-4144
Email: ecwalton@aol.com

Edward C. Walton
ASSOCIATE
Lisa M. Goeden

Reference: San Diego National Bank, San Diego, CA.

For full biographical listings, see the Martindale-Hubbell Law Directory

SAN FRANCISCO,* San Francisco Co.

BOUGHEY, GARVIE & BUSHNER (AV)

One Post Street, Suite 2400, 94104-5228
Telephone: 415-398-4500
Fax: 415-398-2455
Email: 73410.1133@compuserve.com
Honolulu, Hawaii Office: Seven Waterfront Plaza, 500 Alla Moana
Boulevard, Suite 400, 96813.
Telephone: 808-599-8856.
Fax: 800-585-9332. Fax out of U.S.A.: 510-472-6569.
MEMBERS OF FIRM

James D. Boughey	Ronald S. Bushner
Robert C. Garvie	Eileen R. Ridley

Donald A. Velez, Jr.	George H. Keller
Ginger M. English	Larry E. Wollert, II

For full biographical listings, see the Martindale-Hubbell Law Directory

PHILIP A. FANT (AV⊤)

88 Kearny Street, Suite 1100, 94108-5530
Telephone: 415-982-2006
FAX: 415-393-8087

For full biographical listings, see the Martindale-Hubbell Law Directory

FLYNN, DELICH & WISE (AV)

Suite 1750, 580 California Street, 94104
Telephone: 415-693-5566
Fax: 415-693-0410
Long Beach, California Office: 1 World Trade Center, Suite 1800.
Telephone: 310-435-2626.
Fax: 310-437-7555.

John Allen Flynn	Sam D. Delich
James B. Nebel	

Faye Lee

Representative Clients: American Hawaii Cruises; Holland America Line; Through Transport Mutual Insurance Association, Ltd.; The Britannia Steam Ship Insurance Association Limited; The Steamship Mutual Underwriting Association (Bermuda) Ltd.; General Steamship Corp., Ltd.; Commodore Cruise Line, Ltd.; Interocean Steamship Corporation; Sea-Land Service, Inc.; Hatteras Yachts.

For full biographical listings, see the Martindale-Hubbell Law Directory

GRAHAM & JAMES LLP (AV)

One Maritime Plaza, Suite 300, 94111
Telephone: 415-954-0200
Cable Address: "Chalgray"
Telex: WU 340143; WUI 67565
Telecopier: 415-391-2493
Email: mlevin@gj.com *URL:* http://www.gj.com
Other offices located in: Los Angeles, Orange County, Palo Alto, Sacramento and Fresno, California; Seattle, Washington; Washington, D.C.; New York, New York; Milan, Italy; Beijing, China; Tokyo, Japan; London, England; Dusseldorf, Germany.
Associated Offices: Deacons Graham & James, Hong Kong, Sydney, Melbourne, Brisbane, Perth and Canberra, Australia.
Affiliated Offices: Deacons Graham & James, Hanoi and Ho Chi Minh City, Vietnam; Taipei, Taiwan and Bangkok, Thailand; In association with Dewi Soeharto & Rekan, Jakarta, Indonesia; Graham & James in affiliation with Taylor Joynson Garrett, London, England, Bucharest, Romania and Brussels, Belgium; Mishare M. Al-Ghazali & Partners, Safat, Kuwait; Law Firm of Salah Al-Hejailan, Jeddah and Riyadh, Saudi Arabia.

(See Next Column)

Eric M. Danoff	Andrew I. Port

For Complete List of Firm Personnel, See General Section

For full biographical listings, see the Martindale-Hubbell Law Directory

LAW OFFICES OF GEORGE W. NOWELL (AV)

120 Montgomery Street Suite 1900, 94104-4322
Telephone: 415-362-1333
Fax: 415-362-1344

Paul B. Arenas
OF COUNSEL
Keith L. Barker

For full biographical listings, see the Martindale-Hubbell Law Directory

TEHIN + PARTNERS, A PROFESSIONAL CORPORATION (AV)

Bank of America Center, 555 California Street, 33rd Floor, 94104-1609
Telephone: 415-951-8800
Fax: 415-951-8808

Nikolai Tehin (Professional Corporation)	Reilly Atkinson, IV
	Michael E. Brown
Pamela J. Stevens	Marcia A. Pollioni

For full biographical listings, see the Martindale-Hubbell Law Directory

CONNECTICUT

STAMFORD, Fairfield Co.

HEALY & BAILLIE, LLP (AV⊤)

Stamford Harbor Park, 333 Ludlow Street, 06902-6987
Telephone: 203-961-7250
Telecopier: 203-357-7909
Email: RECEPTION@HEALY.COM
New York, N.Y. Office: 29 Broadway, 10006-3293.
Telephone: 212-943-3980.
Telecopier: 212-425-0131. INTERNET E-MAIL: RECEPTION@HEALY.COM.
Hong Kong Office: Healy & Baillie, Luk Hoi Tong Building, Suite 1301, 31 Queen's Road Central.
Telephone: 852-2537-8628.
Telecopier: 852-2521-9072. INTERNET E-MAIL: 6412689@MCIMAIL.COM.
RESIDENT PARTNER
John W. Wall

For full biographical listings, see the Martindale-Hubbell Law Directory

STRATFORD, Fairfield Co.

LAW OFFICES OF ROBERT K. MARZIK, P.C. (AV)

1512 Main Street, 06497
Telephone: 203-375-4803
Telecopier: 203-386-0136
New York, New York Office: 120 East 41st Street.
Telephone: 212-683-2805.

Robert K. Marzik

For full biographical listings, see the Martindale-Hubbell Law Directory

DISTRICT OF COLUMBIA

WASHINGTON, D.C. Co.

* indicates certain Bar Register subscribers, in cities of comparable size and importance, who maintain an additional office in Washington, D.C. and who have arranged for representation as a part of the Washington, D.C. listings that follow

H. CLAYTON COOK, JR. (AV)

1133 21st Street, N.W., Suite 500, 20036
Telephone: 202-338-8088
Facsimile: 202-338-1843
McLean, Virginia Office: 1011 Langley Hill Drive. 22101.
Telephone: 703-821-2468.
Facsimile: 703-821-2469.

For full biographical listings, see the Martindale-Hubbell Law Directory

Washington—Continued

HOPPEL, MAYER & COLEMAN (AV)

1000 Connecticut Avenue, N.W., Suite 400, 20036
Telephone: 202-296-5460
Telecopier: 202-296-5463
Email: hmc1@ix.netcom.com

MEMBERS OF FIRM

Neal Michael Mayer   Paul D. Coleman

For full biographical listings, see the Martindale-Hubbell Law Directory

* KIRLIN, CAMPBELL & KEATING (AV)

2nd Floor, 1 Farragut Square South, 888 Sixteenth Street, N.W., 20006
Telephone: 202-639-8000
Telecopier: 202-835-8238
Other Offices Located in: New York, N.Y., Long Beach, California, Stamford, Connecticut, Caldwell, New Jersey and Ft. Lauderdale, Fl.

RESIDENT OF COUNSEL

Gerald A. Malia   Russell T. Weil

For full biographical listings, see the Martindale-Hubbell Law Directory

SCHMELTZER, APTAKER & SHEPARD, P.C. (AV)

The Watergate, Suite 1000, 2600 Virginia Avenue, N.W., 20037-1905
Telephone: 202-333-8800
Cable Address: "Ship"
Telex: 440517
Facsimile: 202-342-3434
Email: sas@saslaw.com *URL:* http://www.saspc.com
Los Angeles, California Office: 1999 Avenue of the Stars, Twenty-Seventh Floor, 90067-4095.
Telephone: 310-557-2966.
FAX: 310-286-6610.

Edward Schmeltzer   J. Thomas Esslinger

Deana Frances Dudley

For full biographical listings, see the Martindale-Hubbell Law Directory

* VENABLE ATTORNEYS AT LAW VENABLE, BAETJER, HOWARD & CIVILETTI, LLP (AV)

A Partnership including Professional Corporations
Suite 1000, 1201 New York Avenue, N.W., 20005
Telephone: 202-962-4800
Fax: 202-962-8300
Baltimore, Maryland Office: Venable, Baetjer and Howard LLP, 1800 Mercantile Bank & Trust Building, 2 Hopkins Plaza.
Telephone: 410-244-7400.
McLean, Virginia Office: Venable, Baetjer and Howard LLP, Suite 400, 2010 Corporate Ridge.
Telephone: 703-760-1600.
Rockville, Maryland Office: Venable, Baetjer and Howard LLP, Suite 500, One Church Street, P. O. Box 1906.
Telephone: 301-217-5600.
Towson, Maryland Office: Venable, Baetjer and Howard LLP, 210 Allegheny Avenue, P. O. Box 5517.
Telephone: 410-494-6200.

MEMBER OF FIRM

Douglas D. Connah, Jr. (P.C.) (Also at Baltimore, Maryland Office)

For Complete List of Firm Personnel, See General Section

For full biographical listings, see the Martindale-Hubbell Law Directory

FLORIDA

CORAL GABLES, Dade Co.

LOUIS STINSON, JR., P.A. (AV)

4675 Ponce de Leon Boulevard, Suite 305, 33146-2113
Telephone: 305-667-7571
Fax: 305-667-0206

Louis Stinson, Jr.
OF COUNSEL
Robert J. Schaffer

For full biographical listings, see the Martindale-Hubbell Law Directory

**FORT LAUDERDALE,* Broward Co.

KRUPNICK CAMPBELL MALONE ROSELLI BUSER SLAMA & HANCOCK, P.A. (AV)

700 Southeast 3rd Avenue, 33316
Telephone: 954-763-8181
Fax: 954-763-8292

Jon E. Krupnick	Thomas E. Buser
Walter G. Campbell, Jr.	Joseph J. Slama
Kevin A. Malone	Kelly D. Hancock
Richard J. Roselli	Lisa A. McNelis

Louis R. Battista	Carol J. Healy
Ivan F. Cabrera	Elaine P. Krupnick
Robert D. Erben	Scott S. Liberman
Kelley Badger Gelb	Cinthia M. Manzano

Robert J. McKee
OF COUNSEL

Ben J. Weaver   Dianne Jay Weaver

Reference: Nations Bank.

For full biographical listings, see the Martindale-Hubbell Law Directory

MCINTOSH, SAWRAN & CRAVEN, P.A. (AV)

Broward Financial Centre, Suite 1800, 500 East Broward Boulevard, P.O. Box 029008, 33302-9008
Telephone: 954-765-1001
Facsimile: 954-765-1005
Email: MCDEFENLAW@AOL.COM
West Palm Beach, Florida Office: Northridge Centre, 515 North Flagler Drive , Third Floor Pavillion, 33401.
Telephone: 561-802-4110.

Douglas M. McIntosh	Robert A. Craven
James C. Sawran	Carmen Y. Cartaya

Karina P. Gonzalez	Michael A. Petruccelli

Jacqueline J. Porth

For full biographical listings, see the Martindale-Hubbell Law Directory

**JACKSONVILLE,* Duval Co.

GABEL & HAIR (AV)

76 South Laura Street, Suite 1600, 32202-3421
Telephone: 904-353-7329
Fax: 904-358-1637
Email: lawoffcs@gabelhair.com

MEMBERS OF FIRM

George D. Gabel, Jr.	Sheldon Boney Forte
Mattox S. Hair	Timothy J. Conner
Joel B. Toomey	Suzanne Meyer Judas
Robert M. Dees	Karen Harris Williams

ASSOCIATES

Michael L. Berry, Jr.	Karl B. Hanson, III
Robert Blaine Birthisel	Brooks Charles Rathet

Scott M. Loftin (1878-1953)   Harold B. Wahl (1907-1993)

Representative Clients: The Japan Ship Owners Mutual Protection & Indemnity Association; Liverpool & London Steamship Protection & Indemnity Association; The Standard Steamship Owners Protection & Indemnity Association, Ltd.; The Steamship Mutual Underwriting Association, Ltd.; A. B. Indemnitas; Trampfahrt P&I, Hamburg; Scandinavian Marine Claims Office, Inc.; Exxon Corp.; Marine Office of America Corp.; Water Quality Insurance Syndicate.

For full biographical listings, see the Martindale-Hubbell Law Directory

MOSELEY, WARREN, PRICHARD & PARRISH, P.A. (AV)

501 West Bay Street, 32202
Telephone: 904-356-1306
Cable Address: "Ragland"
Telex: 5-6374
Telecopier: 904-354-0194

Reuben Ragland (1882-1954)	Joseph W. Prichard, Jr.
Louis Kurz (1891-1965)	Robert B. Parrish
E. Dale Joyner (1943-1993)	Andrew J. Knight II
James F. Moseley	Richard K. Jones
Robert E. Warren	James F. Moseley, Jr.

Phillip A. Buhler	Stanley M. Weston
Melanie E. Shepherd	Kimberly Held Israel
Victor J. Zambetti	Tracy A. Chesser
Mathew G. Nasrallah	Ivan A. Colao

(See Next Column)

MOSELEY, WARREN, PRICHARD & PARRISH P.A., *Jacksonville—Continued*

OF COUNSEL

James E. Williams   Neil C. Taylor

Counsel for: CSX Transportation; Britannia Steam Ship Insurance Assn., Ltd.; The West of England Protection & Indemnity Assn. (Luxembourg); Crowley American Transport Services, Inc.; Howard Johnson Co.; United Kingdom Mutual Steamship Assurance Assn., Ltd. (Bermuda); General Food Corp.; The London Steam-Ship Owners' Mutual Insurance Assn., Ltd.

For full biographical listings, see the Martindale-Hubbell Law Directory

---

MIAMI,* Dade Co.

ARÁN CORREA & GUARCH, P.A. (AV)

710 South Dixie Highway (Coral Gables), 33146
Telephone: 305-665-3400
Fax: 305-665-2250
Email: d013508C@ycfreenet.seflin.lilo.fl.us

Fernando S. Arán   Danny Correa
Jorge M. Guarch, Jr.

Richard Duarte   Silva M. Rodriguez
Joseph A. Miles

OF COUNSEL

Christian D. Keedy

For full biographical listings, see the Martindale-Hubbell Law Directory

---

ARMSTRONG & MEJER, P.A. (AV)

Suite 1111 Douglas Centre, 2600 Douglas Road (Coral Gables), 33134
Telephone: 305-444-3355
Fax: 305-442-4300

Timothy J. Armstrong   Alvaro L. Mejer

M. Emelina Mejer-Kondla

Reference: First Union National Bank.

For full biographical listings, see the Martindale-Hubbell Law Directory

---

CLARKE SILVERGLATE WILLIAMS & MONTGOMERY (AV)

A Partnership of Professional Corporations
100 North Biscayne Boulevard Suite 2401, 33132
Telephone: 305-377-0700
Facsimile: 305-377-3001
Chicago, Illinois Office: Williams & Montgomery, Ltd., 20 North Wacker Drive, Suite 2100.
Telephone: 312-443-3200.
Telex: 206598.
Facsimile: 312-443-1323.
Waukegan, Illinois Office: Williams & Montgomery, Ltd., 33 North County Street.
Telephone: 847-360-1220.
Wheaton, Illinois Office: Williams & Montgomery, Ltd., 310 S. County Farm Road.
Telephone: 708-690-3200.
Joliet, Illinois Office: Williams & Montgomery, Ltd., 81 North Chicago Avenue.
Telephone: 815-727-2653.

Mercer K. Clarke   Spencer H. Silverglate

OF COUNSEL

Henry H. Bolz, III

ASSOCIATES

Kelly Anne Luther   Eric L. Lundt
William C. Abruzzo   Carol A. Grant

For full biographical listings, see the Martindale-Hubbell Law Directory

---

HAYDEN AND MILLIKEN, P.A. (AV)

Suite 63, 5915 Ponce de Leon Boulevard, 33146-2477
Telephone: 305-662-1523
Fax: 305-663-1358
Tampa, Florida Office: 615 De Leon Street 33606-2719.
Telephone: 813-251-1770.
Fax: 813-254-5436.

Reginald M. Hayden, Jr.   Timothy P. Shusta (Resident,
William Barry Milliken   Tampa, Florida Office)
William R. Boeringer   Michael J. Cappucio
Thomas W. Snook

(See Next Column)

Matthew J. Valcourt   Patricia R. Spivey
(Resident, Tampa Office)

Representative Clients: Regency Cruise Lines; Seaboard Marine, Ltd.; Tropical Shipping and Construction Co., Ltd.; Great American Insurance Co.; Marine Office of America Corp.; St. Paul Fire and Marine Insurance Co.; Britannia P & I; Newcastle P & I; Steamship Mutual; The Swedish Club.

For full biographical listings, see the Martindale-Hubbell Law Directory

---

McDERMOTT, WILL & EMERY (AV)

A Partnership including Professional Corporations
201 South Biscayne Boulevard, 33131-4336
Telephone: 305-358-3500
Facsimile: 305-347-6500
URL: http://www.mwe.com
Chicago, Illinois Office: 227 West Monroe Street.
Telephone: 312-372-2000.
Facsimile: 312-984-7700.
Boston, Massachusetts Office: 75 State Street, Suite 1700.
Telephone: 617-345-5000.
Facsimile: 617-345-5077.
Washington, D.C. Office: 1850 K Street, N.W.
Telephone: 202-887-8000.
Facsimile: 202-778-8087.
Los Angeles, California Office: 2049 Century Park East.
Telephone: 310-277-4110.
Facsimile: 310-277-4730.
Newport Beach, California Office: 1301 Dove Street, Suite 500.
Telephone: 714-851-0633.
Facsimile: 714-851-9348.
New York, N.Y. Office: 50 Rockefeller Plaza.
Telephone: 212-547-5508.
Facsimile: 212-547-5444.
St. Petersburg, Russia Office: AOZT McDermott, Will & Emery, Griboyedova Canal 36, 191023 St. Petersburg, Russia.
Telephone: (7) (812) 310-52-44; 310-55-44; 310-59-44; 850-20-45.
Facsimile: (7) (812) 310-54-46; 325-84-50.
Vilnius, Lithuania Office: Smetonos 6, 2600 Vilnius, Lithuania.
Telephone: 370 2 61-43-08.
Facsimile: 370 2 22-79-55.

MEMBER OF FIRM

James E. McDonald *

*Denotes a lawyer employed by a Professional Corporation which is a member of the Firm.

For full biographical listings, see the Martindale-Hubbell Law Directory

---

SHUTTS & BOWEN (AV)

A Partnership including Professional Associations
1500 Miami Center, 201 South Biscayne Boulevard, 33131
Telephone: 305-358-6300
Telefax: 305-381-9982
URL: HTTP://WWW.LAWWORLD.COM/SHUTTS/
Orlando, Florida Office: 20 North Orange Avenue, Suite 1000.
Telephone: 407-423-3200.
Fax: 407-425-8316.
West Palm Beach, Florida Office: One Clearlake Centre, 250 Australian Avenue, Suite 500.
Telephone: 561-835-8500.
Fax: 561-650-8530.
Amsterdam, The Netherlands Office: Shutts & Bowen, B.V., Europa Boulevard 59, 1083 AD, Amsterdam.
Telephone: (31 20) 661-0969.
Fax: (31 20) 642-1475.
London, England Office: 43 Grosvenor Street, London W1X 9PG.
Telephone: 441-71-493-4840.
Telefax: 441-71-493-4299.

MEMBER OF FIRM

Richard M. Leslie (P.A.)

Representative Clients: Paquet Cruises, Inc.; Ulysses Cruises Inc.; Dolphin Cruises Inc.; Holland America Cruises; West of England P and I Club; Lykes Bros. Steamship; United Kingdom P and I Club.

For Complete List of Firm Personnel, See General Section

For full biographical listings, see the Martindale-Hubbell Law Directory

---

VALLE & CRAIG, P.A. (AV)

Suite 2520 World Trade Center, 80 Southwest Eighth Street, P.O. Box 113009, 33111-3009
Telephone: 305-373-2888; 1800-609-6151
Facsimile: 305-373-2889

Laurence F. Valle   Lawrance B. Craig, III
Timothy Maze Hartley

Frank J. Sioli, Jr.   Nicole F. Ehart
Michael J. Lynott

For full biographical listings, see the Martindale-Hubbell Law Directory

ST. PETERSBURG, Pinellas Co.

CHAMBERS, SALZMAN & BANNON, PROFESSIONAL ASSOCIATION (AV)

520 Fourth Street North, 33701
Telephone: 813-896-2167
Fax: 813-822-8981

Joseph H. Chambers   Rick G. Bannon

Reference: NationsBank.

For full biographical listings, see the Martindale-Hubbell Law Directory

*TAMPA,** Hillsborough Co.

HAYDEN AND MILLIKEN, P.A. (AV)

615 de Leon Street, 33606-2719
Telephone: 813-251-1770
Fax: 813-254-5436
Miami, Florida Office: Suite 63, 5915 Ponce de Leon Boulevard.
Telephone: 305-662-1523.
Fax: 305-663-1358.

Reginald M. Hayden, Jr.   William Barry Milliken
Timothy P. Shusta (Resident)

Matthew J. Valcourt

Representative Clients: Regency Cruise Lines; Seaboard Marine, Ltd.; Tropical Shipping and Construction Co., Ltd.; Great American Insurance Co.; Marine Office of America Corp.; St. Paul Fire and Marine Insurance Co.; Britannia P & I; Newcastle P & I; Steamship Mutual.
Reference: Dadeland Bank.

For full biographical listings, see the Martindale-Hubbell Law Directory

HOYT, COLGAN & ANDREU, P.A. (AV)

3000 Barnett Plaza, 101 East Kennedy Boulevard, 33602
Telephone: 813-229-6688
Facsimile: 813-229-3331

Brooks P. Hoyt   Michael B. Colgan
Timothy A. Andreu

Brian K. French
OF COUNSEL
Louis J. Beltrami

For full biographical listings, see the Martindale-Hubbell Law Directory

LAU, LANE, PIEPER, CONLEY & MCCREADIE, P.A. (AV)

Suite 1700, 100 South Ashley, P.O. Box 838, 33601
Telephone: 813-229-2121
Telecopier: 813-228-7710
Port Canaveral, Florida Office: 405 Atlantis Road, Suite F.
Telephone: 407-799-3400.
Telecopier: 407-868-1025.

James V. Lau   Timothy C. Conley
Charles C. Lane   David W. McCreadie
Nathaniel G. W. Pieper   Annette Horan
Mary A. Lau   David F. Pope

For Complete List of Firm Personnel, See General Section

For full biographical listings, see the Martindale-Hubbell Law Directory

YERRID, KNOPIK & MUDANO, P.A. (AV)

Barnett Plaza, Suite 2160, 101 East Kennedy Boulevard, 33602
Telephone: 813-222-8222
Fax: 813-222-8224

C. Steven Yerrid   Christopher S. Knopik
Matthew S. Mudano

Ralph L. Gonzalez   Adam M. Wolfe

For full biographical listings, see the Martindale-Hubbell Law Directory

*WEST PALM BEACH,** Palm Beach Co.

JEFFREY M. LIGGIO, P.A. (AV)

213 Southern Boulevard, 33405
Telephone: 407-833-6604
Fax: 407-833-0870

Jeffrey M. Liggio
LEGAL SUPPORT PERSONNEL
Yara B. Vega (Paralegal)

For full biographical listings, see the Martindale-Hubbell Law Directory

GEORGIA

*SAVANNAH,** Chatham Co.

CHAMLEE, DUBUS & SIPPLE (AV)

Suite 301 Cluskey Building, 127 Abercorn Street, P.O. Box 9523, 31412
Telephone: 912-232-3311
Cable Address: "Floodtide"
Telecopier: 912-232-3253

MEMBERS OF FIRM
George H. Chamlee   Gustave R. Dubus, III
David F. Sipple

For full biographical listings, see the Martindale-Hubbell Law Directory

HAWAII

*HONOLULU,** Honolulu Co.

ALCANTARA & FRAME ATTORNEYS AT LAW, A LAW CORPORATION (AV)

Suite 1100 Pioneer Plaza, 900 Fort Street Mall, 96813
Telephone: 808-536-6922
Fax: 808-521-8898
Telex: 650-225-8816
WUI: 101-650 225-8816
MCI ID: 225-8816
San Diego, California: 402 West Broadway, Suite 400.
Telephone: 619-595-3175.
Fax: 619-595-3176.

Leonard F. Alcantara   Robert G. Frame
Bryan Y. Y. Ho

Joy Lee Cauble   Michael D. Formby
John O'Kane, Jr.   Eldon M. Ching
Evelyn J. Black   James W. Alcantara (Resident, San Diego, California)

Reference: City Bank, Honolulu.

For full biographical listings, see the Martindale-Hubbell Law Directory

GEORGE W. ASHFORD, JR. (AV)

2910 Pacific Tower, 1001 Bishop Street, 96813
Telephone: 808-528-0444
Telecopier: (808) 533-0761
Cable Address: Justlaw

Representative Clients: Lloyds of London; Baker Industries, Inc.; Burns International Security Services; Clark Equipment Co.; Great Lakes Chemical Corporation; California Union Insurance Co.; Great American Insurance Companies; Guaranty National Companies; Horace Mann Insurance Company; Marine Office of America Corp.

For full biographical listings, see the Martindale-Hubbell Law Directory

LAW OFFICES OF STUART M. COWAN (AV)

Ocean View Center, 707 Richards Street, Suite 728, 96813
Telephone: 808-533-1767
Fax: 808-533-0549
Kaneohe, Hawaii Office: Suite 202, 47-653 Kamehameha Highway.
Telephone: 808-533-1767.
Fax: 808-239-9175.
(Also Of Counsel, Price, Okamoto Himeno & Lum)

Reference: 1st Hawaiian Bank.

For full biographical listings, see the Martindale-Hubbell Law Directory

CRONIN, FRIED, SEKIYA, KEKINA & FAIRBANKS ATTORNEYS AT LAW, A LAW CORPORATION (AV)

1900 Davies Pacific Center, 841 Bishop Street, 96813
Telephone: 808-524-1433
Fax: 808-536-2073

Paul F. Cronin   John D. Thomas, Jr.
L. Richard Fried, Jr.   Stuart A. Kaneko
Gerald Y. Sekiya   Bert S. Sakuda
Wayne K. Kekina   Allen K. Williams
David L. Fairbanks   Keith K. H. Young

Patrick W. Border   Clarence S.K. Kekina
Gregory L. Lui-Kwan   Sylvia E.J. Luke
Patrick F. McTernan   Geoffrey K.S. Komeya

For full biographical listings, see the Martindale-Hubbell Law Directory

Honolulu—Continued

LYNCH & FARMER (AV)

Suite 2500, Mauka Tower Grosvenor Center, 737 Bishop Street, 96813
Telephone: 808-528-0100
Facsimile: 808-528-4997

Steven J. Kim   Paul A. Lynch
OF COUNSEL
Jerilynn Ono Hall   David W. Proudfoot
LEGAL SUPPORT PERSONNEL
Sylvia M. Lee

For full biographical listings, see the Martindale-Hubbell Law Directory

---

ILLINOIS

BELLEVILLE,* St. Clair Co.

BROWN & GAVIN (AV)

23 Public Square, Suite 410, 62220
Telephone: 618-236-2886
Missouri: 314-231-0953
MEMBERS OF FIRM
Terry N. Brown   William P. Gavin
ASSOCIATES
Gregg N. Johnson   P.K. Johnson, V

For full biographical listings, see the Martindale-Hubbell Law Directory

---

CHICAGO,* Cook Co.

BELGRADE AND O'DONNELL, A PROFESSIONAL CORPORATION (AV)

311 South Wacker Drive, Suite 2770, 60606
Telephone: 312-360-9500
Facsimile: 312-360-9550

Steven B. Belgrade   Kim Richard Kardas
John A. O'Donnell   Rachel A. Tindel
George M. Velcich   Daniel Donohue

For full biographical listings, see the Martindale-Hubbell Law Directory

McDERMOTT, WILL & EMERY (AV)

A Partnership including Professional Corporations
227 West Monroe Street, 60606-5096
Telephone: 312-372-2000
Facsimile: 312-984-7700
Boston, Massachusetts Office: 75 State Street, Suite 1700.
Telephone: 617-345-5000.
Facsimile: 617-345-5077.
Miami, Florida Office: 201 South Biscayne Boulevard.
Telephone: 305-358-3500.
Facsimile: 305-347-6500.
Washington, D.C. Office: 1850 K Street, N.W.
Telephone: 202-887-8000.
Facsimile: 202-778-8087.
Los Angeles, California Office: 2049 Century Park East.
Telephone: 310-277-4110.
Facsimile: 310-277-4730.
Newport Beach, California Office: 1301 Dove Street, Suite 500.
Telephone: 714-851-0633.
Facsimile: 714-851-9348.
New York, N.Y. Office: 1211 Avenue of the Americas.
Telephone: 212-768-5400.
Facsimile: 212-768-5444.
St. Petersburg, Russia Office: AOZT McDermott, Will & Emery, Griboyedova Canal 36, 191023 St. Petersburg, Russia.
Telephone: (7) (812) 310-52-44; 310-55-44; 310-59-44; 850-20-45.
Facsimile: (7) (812) 310-54-46; 325-84-50.
Vilnius, Lithuania Office: Smetonos 6, 2600 Vilnius, Lithuania.
Telephone: 370 2 61-43-08.
Facsimile: 370 2 22-79-55.

MEMBERS OF FIRM
Paul J. Kozacky   Douglas M. Reimer *
Jeffrey E. Stone

*Denotes a lawyer employed by a Professional Corporation which is a member of the Firm.

For full biographical listings, see the Martindale-Hubbell Law Directory

---

RAY, ROBINSON, CARLE, DAVIES & SNYDER (AV)

A Partnership including a Professional Corporation
850 West Jackson Boulevard, Suite 310, 60607-3011
Telephone: 312-421-3110
Telex: 25200 BRADMIR CGO
Cable Address: Lakelaw-Chicago
Facsimile: 312-421-2808
Cleveland, Ohio Office: 1650 The East Ohio Building, 1717 East 9th Street.
Telephone: 216-861-4533.
Telex: 810-421-8402.
Cable Address: Lakelaw-Cleveland.
Facsimile: 216-861-4568.

Michael A. Snyder, Ltd.

William P. Ryan   Shanshan Zhou
OF COUNSEL
Theodore C. Robinson

For full biographical listings, see the Martindale-Hubbell Law Directory

---

EAST ST. LOUIS, St. Clair Co.

CARR, KOREIN, TILLERY, KUNIN, MONTROY & GLASS (AV)

412 Missouri Avenue, 62201
Telephone: 618-274-0434
Telecopier: 618-274-8369
St. Louis, Missouri Office: 701 Market Street, Suite 300.
Telephone: 314-241-4844.
Telecopier: 314-241-3525.
Belleville, Illinois Office: 5520 West Main.
Telephone: 618-277-1180.
MEMBER OF FIRM
Sandor Korein
Rivers Counsel for: National Maritime Union of America.

For Complete List of Firm Personnel, See General Section

For full biographical listings, see the Martindale-Hubbell Law Directory

---

INDIANA

EVANSVILLE,* Vanderburgh Co.

KAHN, DEES, DONOVAN & KAHN (AV)

P.O. Box 3646, 47735-3646
Telephone: 812-423-3183
Fax: 812-423-3841
Email: evvlaw@k2d2.com
MEMBER OF FIRM
Jeffrey W. Ahlers
ASSOCIATE
Richard O. Hawley, Jr.
Representative Clients: Neare Gibbs Maritime Insurance; United States Fidelity & Guarantee; Ohio Valley Marine Service; Mulzer Crushed Stone; Mt. Vernon Barge Service.

For Complete List of Firm Personnel, See General Section

For full biographical listings, see the Martindale-Hubbell Law Directory

---

KENTUCKY

PADUCAH,* McCracken Co.

LAKE TINDALL, LLP (AV⊤)

Formerly Firm of Wynn, Hafter, Lake & Tindall
One Executive Boulevard Suite 318, P.O. Box 30, 42002
Telephone: 502-442-1900
Facsimile: 502-442-8247
Greenville, Mississippi Office: 127 South Poplar Street, P.O. Box 918.
Telephone: 601-378-2121.
Facsimile: 601-378-2183.
Jackson, Mississippi Office: One Jackson Place, 188 East Capitol Street, Suite 450, P.O. Box 1789.
Telephone: 601-948-2121.
Facsimile: 601-948-0603.

Edwin Spivey Gault (Resident)   Carl J. Marshall (Resident)
Bobby R. Miller, Jr. (Resident)

For full biographical listings, see the Martindale-Hubbell Law Directory

LOUISIANA

BATON ROUGE,* East Baton Rouge Parish

GEORGE AND GEORGE, LTD., A PROFESSIONAL LAW CORPORATION (AV)

8110 Summa Avenue, 70809
Telephone: 504-769-3064
Fax: 504-766-9974
Toll Free Numbers: 1-800-654-2335
Nationwide: 1-800-843-5702

James A. George

Reference: Hibernia National Bank of Baton Rouge.

For full biographical listings, see the Martindale-Hubbell Law Directory

---

LAFAYETTE,* Lafayette Parish

DOMENGEAUX WRIGHT MOROUX & ROY A PROFESSIONAL LAW CORPORATION (AV)

556 Jefferson Street, Suite 500, P.O. Box 3668, 70502-3668
Telephone: 318-233-3033; 1-800-375-3106
Fax: 318-232-8213

James Domengeaux (1907-1988)	Frank Edwards
Anthony D. Moroux (1948-1993)	James H. Domengeaux
Bob F. Wright (A Professional Law Corporation)	Gilbert Hennigan Dozier (A Professional Law Corporation)
James Parkerson Roy (A Professional Law Corporation)	Carla Marie Perron
	Vivian Veron Neumann
Thomas R. Edwards (A Professional Law Corporation)	Michael D. Goss

OF COUNSEL

Jerome E. Domengeaux

Reference: Mid-South National Bank; Advocate Financial, L.L.C.

For full biographical listings, see the Martindale-Hubbell Law Directory

---

HILL & BEYER, A PROFESSIONAL LAW CORPORATION (AV)

101 LaRue France, Suite 502, P.O. Box 53006, 70505-3006
Telephone: 318-232-9733
Fax: 1-318-237-2566

John K. Hill, Jr.	Eugene P. Matherne (1962-1996)
Bret C. Beyer	Robert B. Purser
David R. Rabalais	Erin J. Sherburne
Marianna Broussard	

For full biographical listings, see the Martindale-Hubbell Law Directory

---

RICHARD R. KENNEDY A PROFESSIONAL LAW CORPORATION (AV)

309 Polk Street, P.O. Box 3243, 70502-3243
Telephone: 318-232-1934
Fax: 318-232-9720
Email: kennedy@net-connect.net

Richard R. Kennedy

For full biographical listings, see the Martindale-Hubbell Law Directory

---

LISKOW & LEWIS, A PROFESSIONAL LAW CORPORATION (AV)

822 Harding Street, P.O. Box 52008, 70505
Telephone: 318-232-7424
Telecopier: 318-267-2399
New Orleans, Louisiana Office: 50th Floor, One Shell Square.
Telephone: 504-581-7979.
Telecopier: 504-592-5108; 504-592-5109.

RESIDENT PERSONNEL

George H. Robinson, Jr.	Mark A. Lowe
George Arceneaux III	

Matt Jones

Representative Clients: Amoco Corporation; Anadarko Petroleum Corp.; BP America Inc.; Caltex Petroleum Corp.; Forest Oil Corp.; Freeport McMoRan Inc.; Ingram Industries Inc.; Mobil Oil Corp.; Pennzoil Company; Sea Mar Inc.; Texaco Inc.; Todd Shipyards Corp.; Unocal Corp.

For Complete List of Firm Personnel, See General Section

For full biographical listings, see the Martindale-Hubbell Law Directory

---

PREIS KRAFT & ROY, A PROFESSIONAL LAW CORPORATION (AV)

Suite 400, Versailles Centré, 102 Versailles Boulevard, P.O. Drawer 94-C, 70509
Telephone: 318-237-6062
Fax: 318-237-9129
New Orleans, Louisiana Office: Pan American Life Center, 601 Poydras Street, Suite 2582.
Telephone: 504-581-6062.
Fax: 504-581-4862.

Edwin G. Preis, Jr.	Charles A. Mouton
Ralph E. Kraft	Kay A. Theunissen
L. Lane Roy	Jennifer E. Beyer
Ward Lafleur	George D. Ernest, III
F. Douglas Gatz, Jr.	Richard J. Hymel

Christopher Shannon Hardy	Timothy W. Basden
Wesley Elmer	Earl F. Sundmaker, III
Marc C. Greco	Jennifer Smith Lee
G. Edward Williams, Jr.	Anita L. Wolverton
Macy M. Hamm	

Approved Counsel for: American Gulf Group; American International Group; American Oilfield Divers, Inc.; American P & I Club; American United Life Insurance Company; Association of Diving Contractors, Inc.; Assuranceforeningen Gard; Assuranceforeningen Skuld, Automation Communication Engineering Corporation; Cal Dive International, Inc.; CBI Industries, Inc.

For full biographical listings, see the Martindale-Hubbell Law Directory

---

ROY, BIVINS, JUDICE & HENKE, A PROFESSIONAL LAW CORPORATION (AV)

600 Jefferson Street, Suite 800, P.O. Drawer Z, 70502
Telephone: 318-233-7430
Telecopier: 318-233-8403

Harmon F. Roy	Kenneth M. Henke
John A. Bivins	W. Alan Lilley
Ronald J. Judice	Philip E. Roberts
Patrick M. Wartelle	

Representative Clients: Employers Insurance of Wausau; C.N.A.; Aetna Casualty & Surety; Zurich Ins. Co.; St Paul Fire & Marine Ins. Co.; First Financial Insurance Company; Great Lakes Chemical; Cardinal Services, Inc.; C.S.I. Hydro Static Testers, Inc.

For full biographical listings, see the Martindale-Hubbell Law Directory

---

LAKE CHARLES,* Calcasieu Parish

BERGSTEDT & MOUNT (AV)

Second Floor, Magnolia Life Building, P.O. Drawer 3004, 70602-3004
Telephone: 318-433-3004
Facsimile: 318-433-8080

MEMBERS OF FIRM

Thomas M. Bergstedt	Benjamin W. Mount

ASSOCIATES

Van C. Seneca	Gregory P. Marceaux
Billy E. Loftin, Jr.	

OF COUNSEL

Charles S. Ware

Representative Clients: Armstrong World Industries; Ashland Oil Co.; CIGNA Property & Casualty Companies; Homequity; Lake Area Medical Center; Leach Company; Olin Corporation; Terra Corporation; Town of Iowa; R. D. Werner Company.

For full biographical listings, see the Martindale-Hubbell Law Directory

---

JONES, TÊTE, NOLEN, HANCHEY, SWIFT, SPEARS & FONTI, L.L.P. (AV)

First Federal Building, P.O. Box 910, 70602
Telephone: 318-439-8315
Telefax: 436-5606; 433-5536

MEMBERS OF FIRM

Sam H. Jones (1897-1978)	Kenneth R. Spears
William R. Tête	Edward J. Fonti
William M. Nolen	Charles N. Harper
James C. Hanchey	Gregory W. Belfour
Carl H. Hanchey	Robert J. Tête
William B. Swift	Yul D. Lorio

OF COUNSEL

John A. Patin	Edward D. Myrick

ASSOCIATE

Lilynn A. Cutrer

General Counsel for: First Federal Savings & Loan Association of Lake Charles; Beauregard Electric Cooperative, Inc.

(See Next Column)

JONES, TÊTE, NOLEN, HANCHEY, SWIFT, SPEARS & FONTI L.L.P., *Lake Charles—Continued*

Representative Clients: Atlantic Richfield Company; CITGO Petroleum Corp.; Conoco Inc.; MONTELL U.S.A., Inc.; ITT Hartford; Olin Corporation; OXY USA Inc.; Premier Bank, National Association; W.R. Grace & Co.

For full biographical listings, see the Martindale-Hubbell Law Directory

LUNDY & DAVIS, L.L.P. (AV)

Calcasieu Marine Tower, One Lakeshore Drive, Suite 1600, P.O. Box 3010, 70602
Telephone: 318-439-0707
FAX: 318-439-1029
Jackson, Mississippi Office: 111 East Capitol Street, Suite 250.
Telephone: 601-948-3010.
Facsimile: 601-948-2143.
Houston, Texas Office: 1201 Louisiana, Suite 3179.
Telephone: 713-650-1204.
Facsimile: 713-650-1070.
Biloxi, Mississippi Office: 999 Howard Avenue.
Telephone: 601-435-7733.
Facsimile: 601-435-7737.

MEMBERS OF FIRM

Hunter W. Lundy	Jerry A. Johnson
Clayton A. L. Davis	David A. Bowers (Resident,
Matthew E. Lundy (Resident,	Jackson, Mississippi Office)
Houston, Texas Office)	

ASSOCIATES

Jackey W. South	Jody Brian Martin (Resident,
DeAnn Gibson	Jackson, Mississippi Office)
Samuel B. Gabb	Michael D. Carleton
James D. Cain, Jr.	Thomas P. LeBlanc

OF COUNSEL

Walter L. Nixon, Jr.

For full biographical listings, see the Martindale-Hubbell Law Directory

PLAUCHÉ SMITH & NIESET, A PROFESSIONAL LAW CORPORATION (AV)

1123 Pithon Street, P.O. Drawer 1705, 70602
Telephone: 318-436-0522
Facsimile: 318-436-9637

S. W. Plauché (1889-1952)	Jeffrey M. Cole
S. W. Plauché, Jr. (1915-1966)	Andrew R. Johnson, IV
A. Lane Plauché	Charles V. Musso, Jr.
Allen L. Smith, Jr.	Christopher P. Ieyoub
James R. Nieset	H. David Vaughan, II
Frank M. Walker, Jr.	Joseph R. Pousson, Jr.
Michael J. McNulty, III	Rebecca S. Young

Representative Clients: CIGNA; CNA Insurance Cos.; Commercial Union Insurance Cos.; Crum & Forster; General Motors Corp.; Reliance Insurance Cos.; Royal Insurance Group; State Farm; U.S. Insurance Group.

For full biographical listings, see the Martindale-Hubbell Law Directory

MANDEVILLE, St. Tammany Parish

BAILEY & DWYER (AV)

600 Mariner's Plaza, Suite 607, 70448
Telephone: 504-674-1105
Fax: 504-674-1966
Metairie Area Telephone: 504-833-8241
Fax: 504-837-4534

MEMBERS OF FIRM

B. Ralph Bailey	Frederick H. N. Dwyer
	Scott O. Gaspard

For full biographical listings, see the Martindale-Hubbell Law Directory

METAIRIE, Jefferson Parish

HAILEY, McNAMARA, HALL, LARMANN & PAPALE, L.L.P. (AV)

A Partnership including Law Corporations
Suite 1400, One Galleria Boulevard, P.O. Box 8288, 70011
Telephone: 504-836-6500
Fax: 504-836-6565

MEMBERS OF FIRM

James W. Hailey, Jr., (P.L.C.)	Michael J. Vondenstein
Henry D. McNamara, Jr.,	David K. Persons
(P.L.C.)	Dominic J. Ovella
W. Marvin Hall (P.L.C.)	C. Kelly Lightfoot
Antonio E. Papale, Jr., (P.L.C.)	John T. Culotta (P.L.C.)
Laurence E. Larmann (P.L.C.)	John E. Unsworth, Jr.
Michael P. Mentz	Julie DiFulco Robles
Richard T. Simmons, Jr.,(P.L.C.)	Claude A. Greco

(See Next Column)

ASSOCIATES

William R. Seay, Jr.	Barbara E. Bourdonnay
Cyril B. Burck, Jr.	Kathryn T. Wiedorn
Valerie T. Schexnayder	Joseph L. Spilman, III
W. Evan Plauche	Caroline D. Ibos
Kurt D. Engelhardt	Robert D. Ford
W. Glenn Burns	David C. Fawley
James W. Hailey, III	Sharon Yarasavich Piper
Ivan A. Orihuela	Lynnette Hall-Lewis
Frederic Theodore Le Clercq	
(Not admitted in LA)	

Representative Clients: Certain Underwriters at Lloyds of London; Diamond Offshore Drilling Inc.; First American Title Insurance Company; The Flintkote Co.; Litton Industries; Lockheed Martin Corporation; Rheem Manufacturing Co.; State Farm Fire & Casualty Co.; Textron, Inc; Travelers Companies.

For full biographical listings, see the Martindale-Hubbell Law Directory

NEW ORLEANS,* Orleans Parish

BEST KOEPPEL, A PROFESSIONAL LAW CORPORATION (AV)

LL & E Tower, 909 Poydras Street Suite 2200, 70112
Telephone: 504-593-2400
Telecopier: 504-593-2401
Houston, Texas Office: Weslayan Tower, 24 Greenway Plaza, Suite 925, 77046.
Telephone: 713-622-9761.
Telecopier: 713-622-0448.

Laurence E. Best	André C. Gaudin
Peter S. Koeppel	R. Jeffrey Bridger
Steven K. Best (Resident,	Steven D. Naumann (Resident,
Houston, Texas Office)	Houston, Texas Office)
	Don Paul Landry

LEGAL SUPPORT PERSONNEL

PARALEGAL

Rhonda A. Usey

Representative Clients: Lexington Insurance Co.; Hanover Insurance Co.; Rowan Companies, Inc.

For full biographical listings, see the Martindale-Hubbell Law Directory

CAPITELLI & WICKER (AV)

2950 Energy Centre, 1100 Poydras Street, 70163-2950
Telephone: 504-582-2425
FAX: 504-582-2422

Ralph Capitelli	T. Carey Wicker, III
	Paul Michael Elvir, Jr.

OF COUNSEL

Terry Q. Alarcon

For full biographical listings, see the Martindale-Hubbell Law Directory

CHAFFE, McCALL, PHILLIPS, TOLER & SARPY, L.L.P. (AV)

A Partnership including a Professional Law Corporation
2300 Energy Centre, 1100 Poydras Street, 70163-2300
Telephone: 504-585-7000
Telecopier: 504-585-7075
Cable Address: "Denegre"
Telex: (AT&T) 460122 CMPTS
Email: cmptsno%2049698@mcimail.com *URL:* http://www.chaffe.com/
Baton Rouge, Louisiana Office: 202 Two United Plaza, 8550 United Plaza Boulevard.
Telephone: 504-922-4300.
Fax: 504-922-4304.
Miami, Florida Office: 2600 Brickell Bay Office Tower, 1001 South Bayshore Drive, 33131.
Telephone: 305-377-3770.
Fax: 305-377-0080.
Caracas, Venezuela Office: Edificio Exa, Piso 10, Oficina PH-10, Avenida Venezuela entre Calles EL Retiro y Alameda, El Rosal.
Telephone: 011-582-953-4136.
Fax: 011-582-953-6518.

MEMBERS OF FIRM

Leon Sarpy	Daniel L. Daboval
Donald A. Lindquist	Thomas D. Forbes
Robert B. Deane	John H. Clegg
J. Dwight LeBlanc, Jr.	Mark L. Gundlach
Robert B. Fisher, Jr.	Daphne P. McNutt
Derek Anthony Walker	Scott A. Soule

ASSOCIATES

Eric J. Simonson	Frederick W. Veters

Representative Clients: Liverpool and London Steamship Protection and Indemnity Association, Ltd.; The West of England Ship Owners Mutual Insurance Association (Luxembourg); The United Kingdom Mutual Steamship Assurance Association (Bermuda) Ltd.; The Sunderland Steamship Protecting & Indemnity Association; The Standard Steamship Owners' Protection and Indemnity Association (Bermuda) Ltd.; The Britannia Steam Ship Insur-

(See Next Column)

CHAFFE, McCALL, PHILLIPS, TOLER & SARPY, L.L.P.—Continued

ance Association Ltd.; The Japan Ship Owners' Mutual Protection and Indemnity Association; The North of England Protecting and Indemnity Association Ltd.; Newcastle Protection and Indemnity Association; Nedlloyd Bulk B.V.

For Complete List of Firm Personnel, See General Section

For full biographical listings, see the Martindale-Hubbell Law Directory

CHRISTOVICH AND KEARNEY, L.L.P. (AV)

Suite 2300 Pan American Life Center, 601 Poydras Street, 70130-6078
Telephone: 504-561-5700
Fax: 504-561-5743
Houston, Texas Office: 700 Louisiana, Suite 4550, 77002.
Telephone: 713-225-2255.
Fax: 713-225-1112.

MEMBERS OF FIRM

Alvin R. Christovich, Jr.	E. Phelps Gay
William K. Christovich	Thomas C. Cowan
J. Walter Ward, Jr.	Geoffrey P. Snodgrass
Lawrence J. Ernst	J. Warren Gardner, Jr.
James F. Holmes	Kevin R. Tully
Robert E. Peyton	Lance R. Rydberg
C. Edgar Cloutier	Elizabeth S. Cordes
Charles W. Schmidt, III	John K. Leach
Richard K. Christovich	Fred T. Hinrichs
Terry Christovich Gay	Daniel A. Rees
Paul G. Preston	Charles M. Lanier, Jr.
Michael M. Christovich	Lyon H. Garrison

Philip J. Borne

ASSOCIATES

Bennett A. Midlo	Robert D. Peyton
(Not admitted in LA)	Kenan S. Rand, Jr.
J. Roslyn Lemmon	Joseph E. Cullens, Jr.
James A. Holmes	Todd A. Riddle
Scott P. Yount	(Not admitted in LA)
Patricia Broussard Judice	Steve C. Dollinger
Ellen B. Woody	(Not admitted in LA)
Patrick W. Drouilhet	D. Scott Slawson

Representative Clients: AMOCO; Atlantic Richfield Co.; Brown & Root, Inc.; Dual Drilling Co.; Freeport-McMoran; Grace Offshore Co.; Oceaneering International; Texas Eastern; Union Oil of California; Western Oceanic, Inc.

For full biographical listings, see the Martindale-Hubbell Law Directory

DEUTSCH, KERRIGAN & STILES, L.L.P. (AV)

A Partnership including Professional Law Corporations
755 Magazine Street, 70130-3672
Telephone: 504-581-5141
Cable Address: "Dekest"
Telex: 584358
Telecopier: 504-566-1201
Email: dks@dksno.com *URL:* http://www.dksno.com
St. Tammany Parish Office: 550 Pontchartrain Drive, Suite 200, Slidell, LA. 70458.
Telephone: 504-639-0555.
Fax: 504-639-0550.

MEMBERS OF FIRM

Bertrand M. Cass, Jr.	A. Wendel Stout, III
Francis J. Barry, Jr.	Howard L. Murphy
Allen F. Campbell	Gary B. Roth
G. Alex Weller	Gene R. Smith

OF COUNSEL

Brunswick G. Deutsch (P.L.C.)

For Complete List of Firm Personnel, See General Section

For full biographical listings, see the Martindale-Hubbell Law Directory

EMMETT, COBB, WAITS & KESSENICH, A PROFESSIONAL LAW CORPORATION (AV)

Suite 1950, 1515 Poydras Street, 70112
Telephone: 504-581-1301
Telex: 58-4430
Telecopier: 504-581-6020

Francis Emmett	John F. Emmett
Randolph J. Waits	Susan E. Henning
J. Fredrick Kessenich	Michael G. Helm
James A. Cobb, Jr.	Jack C. Benjamin, Jr.

Eugene W. Policastri

Reference: First National Bank of Commerce, New Orleans.

For full biographical listings, see the Martindale-Hubbell Law Directory

FRANSEN & HARDIN, A P.L.C. (AV)

814 Howard Avenue, P.O. Box 52676, 70152-2676
Telephone: 504-522-1188
Telecopier: 504-524-8317

A. Remy Fransen, Jr.	Allain F. Hardin

P. Chris Christofferson

Christopher J. Fransen

For full biographical listings, see the Martindale-Hubbell Law Directory

GAINSBURGH, BENJAMIN, DAVID, MEUNIER, NORIEA & WARSHAUER (AV)

2800 Energy Centre, 1100 Poydras, 70163-2800
Telephone: 504-522-2304
Telecopier: 504-528-9973
Email: GAINSBEN@IAMERICA.NET

OF COUNSEL

Jack C. Benjamin (P.L.C.)

MEMBERS OF FIRM

Robert J. David	Irving J. Warshauer
Gerald E. Meunier	Stevan C. Dittman
Nick F. Noriea, Jr.	Madeleine M. Landrieu

Darryl M. Phillips

ASSOCIATES

Michael G. Calogero	Jeffrey A. Mitchell

For full biographical listings, see the Martindale-Hubbell Law Directory

HEBERT, MOULEDOUX & BLAND, A PROFESSIONAL LAW CORPORATION (AV)

Pan-American Life Center, Suite 1650, 601 Poydras Street, 70130
Telephone: 504-525-3333
Cable Address: "HMBL"
Telex: 588-092;
Fax: 504-523-4224

Maurice C. Hebert, Jr.	Alan Guy Brackett
André J. Mouledoux	David M. Flotte
Wilton E. Bland, III	C. William Emory
Georges M. Legrand	C. Michael Parks
Roch P. Poelman	Daniel J. Hoerner

John H. Musser, V

Representative Clients: Archer-Daniels Midland Company; Bisso Marine Company, Inc.; Carline Geismar Fleet, Inc.; Cooper/T. Smith Stevedoring Company, Inc.; Delta Queen Steamboat Co.; Diamond Offshore Drilling, Inc.; LOOP INC.; Marine Equipment Management Corporation; McDermott Incorporated; Olympic Marine Company.

For full biographical listings, see the Martindale-Hubbell Law Directory

DARLEEN M. JACOBS A PROFESSIONAL LAW CORPORATION (AV)

823 St. Louis Street, 70112
Telephone: 504-522-3287; 522-0155
Cable Address: "Darjac."

Darleen M. Jacobs	Honorable S. Sanford Levy
	(1902-1989)

For full biographical listings, see the Martindale-Hubbell Law Directory

JOHNSON, JOHNSON, BARRIOS & YACOUBIAN, A PROFESSIONAL LAW CORPORATION (AV)

4900 One Shell Square, 70139-4901
Telephone: 504-528-3001
Facsimile: 504-528-3030

Ronald A. Johnson	Bettye A. Barrios
Edward S. Johnson	Alan J. Yacoubian

Salvador J. Pusateri	Cindy T. Matherne
Rene S. Paysse, Jr.	William K. Hawkins

Representative Clients: Adams & Porter International, Inc.; Alexander & Alexander, Inc.; Alliance Steel, Inc.; Amoco Corporation; Burnett & Company; Charter Group, Inc.; Community Associates, Inc.; Concord General Corporation; Continental Underwriters, Ltd.; Riscorp Risk Management Services LLC.

For full biographical listings, see the Martindale-Hubbell Law Directory

KOPS, LEE, FUTRELL & PERLES, L.L.P. (AV)

Suite 2409 Place St. Charles 201 St. Charles Avenue, 70170
Telephone: 504-569-1725
Fax: 504-569-1726
Email: 103622.1066@compuserve.com

(See Next Column)

KOPS, LEE, FUTRELL & PERLES L.L.P., *New Orleans—Continued*

John Michael Kops	John Maurice Futrell
Gary A. Lee	Richard M. Perles

Representative Clients: Certain Underwriters at Lloyd's, London; Institute of London Underwriters Companies.

For full biographical listings, see the Martindale-Hubbell Law Directory

LEA, TYNAN & McGEHEE, P.L.C. (AV)

Southern Marine and Aviation Building, 610 Poydras Street Suite 500, 70130
Telephone: 504-523-4500
Fax: 504-525-7208

Arden J. Lea   Joseph P. Tynan
W. Clay McGehee
MEXICAN LEGAL ADVISOR
Ricardo Lan (Not admitted in the United States)

For full biographical listings, see the Martindale-Hubbell Law Directory

LISKOW & LEWIS, A PROFESSIONAL LAW CORPORATION (AV)

50th Floor, One Shell Square, 70139
Telephone: 504-581-7979
Telecopier: 504-556-4108; 504-556-4109
Lafayette, Louisiana Office: 822 Harding Street, P.O. Box 52008.
Telephone: 318-232-7424.
Telecopier: 318-267-2399.

Donald R. Abaunza	Don K. Haycraft
S. Gene Fendler	R. Keith Jarrett
William W. Pugh	Thomas P. Diaz
David W. Leefe	Mark D. Latham

Carol Welborn Reisman   David L. Reisman
Harold J. Flanagan
RESIDENT PERSONNEL AT LAFAYETTE OFFICE
George H. Robinson, Jr.   Mark A. Lowe
George Arceneaux III

Matt Jones

Representative Clients: Amoco Production Company; Anadarko Petroleum Corp.; BP America Inc.; Caltex Petroleum Corp.; Forest Oil Corporation; Freeport-McMoRan, Inc.; Ingram Industries, Inc.; Mobil Oil Corporation; Pennzoil Company; Sea Mar, Inc.; Texaco Inc.; Todd Shipyards Corporation; Unocal Corp.

For Complete List of Firm Personnel, See General Section

For full biographical listings, see the Martindale-Hubbell Law Directory

MILLING, BENSON, WOODWARD, HILLYER, PIERSON & MILLER, L.L.P. (AV)

A Partnership including Professional Law Corporations
Suite Twenty-Three Hundred, 909 Poydras Street, 70112-1017
Telephone: 504-569-7000
Cable Address: "Milling"
Telex: 58-4211
Telecopier: 504-569-7001
ABA net: 15656
MCI Mail: "Milling"
Lafayette, Louisiana Office: 101 La Rue France, Suite 200.
Telephone: 318-232-3929.
Telecopier: 318-233-4957.

MEMBERS OF FIRM
Neal D. Hobson (P.C.)   Bruce R. Hoefer, Jr. (P.C.)
SPECIAL COUNSEL
Timothy T. Roniger
ASSOCIATE
Benjamin O. Schupp

See General Section for list of Representative Clients.

For Complete List of Firm Personnel, See General Section

For full biographical listings, see the Martindale-Hubbell Law Directory

MURPHY, ROGERS & SLOSS, A PROFESSIONAL LAW CORPORATION (AV)

One Shell Square, Suite 400, 701 Poydras Street, 70139
Telephone: 504-523-0400
Facsimile: 504-523-5574

Robert H. Murphy	Gary J. Gambel
E. Carroll Rogers	James M. Jacobs
Peter B. Sloss	Molly B. Halloran
Charles L. Whited, Jr.	Scott E. Oliphant

(See Next Column)

Representative Clients: American Overseas Marine Corporation; The Britannia Steam Ship Insurance Association Limited; Clarendon National Insurance Company; CSX Corporation; G&B Marine, Inc.; Great Lakes Dredge & Dock Company, Inc.; Harris Transport, Inc.; Liverpool and London Steamship Protection and Indemnity Limited; National-Oilwell.

For full biographical listings, see the Martindale-Hubbell Law Directory

O'NEIL, EICHIN, MILLER, SAPORITO & HARRIS, A LAW CORPORATION (AV)

639 Loyola Avenue, Suite 2200, 70113
Telephone: 504-525-3200
Cable Address: ONEMILL NLN
Telex: ITT 460125
Answer Back: ONEMILL NLN
Facsimile: 504-529-7389 (Groups 1, 2 & 3)

William E. O'Neil	John F. Fay, Jr.
Earl S. Eichin, Jr.	Alfred J. Rufty
Machale A. Miller	Michael D. Sledge
Jerry L. Saporito	Brandt K. Enos
Rufus C. Harris, III	Gregory G. Barnett
I. Matthew Williamson	Iliaura Hands
Lindsay A. Larson, III	Spiro J. Verras

OF COUNSEL
Terry A. McCall

For full biographical listings, see the Martindale-Hubbell Law Directory

PHELPS DUNBAR, L.L.P. (AV)

Texaco Center, 400 Poydras Street, 70130-3245
Telephone: 504-566-1311
Telecopier: 504-568-9130, 504-568-9007
Cable Address: "Howspencer"
Telex: 584125 WU
Telex: 6821155 WUI
Email: info@phelps.com
Baton Rouge, Louisiana Office: Suite 701, City National Bank Building, P.O. Box 4412.
Telephone: 504-346-0285.
Telecopier: 504-381-9197.
Jackson, Mississippi Office: Suite 500, Mtel Centré, 200 South Lamar Street, P.O. Box 23066.
Telephone: 601-352-2300.
Telecopier: 601-360-9777.
Tupelo, Mississippi Office: Seventh Floor, One Mississippi Plaza, P.O. Box 1220.
Telephone: 601-842-7907.
Telecopier: 601-842-3873.
Houston, Texas Office: Suite 900, 3040 Post Oak Boulevard.
Telephone: 713-626-1386.
Telecopier: 713-626-1388.
London, England Office: Suite 731, Level 7, Lloyd's, 1 Lime Street, London EC3M 7DQ England.
Telephone: 011-44-171-929-4765.
Telecopier: 011-44-171-929-0046.
Telex: 987321.

OF COUNSEL
John W. Sims   J. Barbee Winston
George W. Healy, III
MEMBERS OF FIRM

James Bradley Kemp, Jr.	Robert C. Clotworthy
James H. Roussel	George M. Gilly
Charles M. Steen	Christopher O. Davis
Walker W. (Bill) Jones, III (Not admitted in LA; Houston, Texas, Jackson, Mississippi and London, England Offices)	Robert P. McCleskey, Jr.
	Julia Marie Adams (Not admitted in LA; Resident, Houston, Texas Office)
Kent E. Westmoreland (Not admitted in LA)	Brian D. Wallace
Claude LeRoy Stuart, III (Not admitted in LA; Resident, Houston, Texas Office)	Mark C. Dodart

COUNSEL
Edwin K. Legnon
Matthew R. Muth (Not admitted in LA; Resident, Houston, Texas Office)

ASSOCIATES

David A. Abramson	Malinda York Crouch (Not admitted in LA; Resident, Houston, Texas Office)
Sheryl Bey (Resident, Jackson, Mississippi Office)	
Maurice E. Bostick	John C. Cunningham (Not admitted in LA; Resident, Houston, Texas Office)
Evan T. Caffrey (Not admitted in LA; Resident, Houston, Texas Office)	
	Stephanie G. McShane
Laura C. Capshaw (Not admitted in LA; Resident, Houston, Texas Office)	Karen Klaas Milhollin (Not admitted in LA; Resident, Houston, Texas Office)
Rebecca Y. Cooper	

(See Next Column)

PHELPS DUNBAR L.L.P.—*Continued*

ASSOCIATES (Continued)

Stanley T. Proctor (Not
admitted in LA; Resident,
Houston, Texas Office)
William J. Riviere

Daniel C. Rodgers
John L. Schouest (Resident,
Houston, Texas Office)
Stacy Singleton

Dawei Zhang

Representative Clients: Bludworth Bond Shipyard; The Britannia Steamship Insurance Assn., Ltd.; Edison Chouest Offshore, Inc.; Fairfield Industries, Inc.; John E. Chance & Associates, Inc.; McDonough Marine Service, A Division of MARMAC Corp.; Standard Steamship Owners P&I Association; The Steamship Mutual Underwriting Association, Ltd.; Underwriters at Lloyd's, London.

For Complete List of Firm Personnel, See General Section

For full biographical listings, see the Martindale-Hubbell Law Directory

---

SALLEY & ASSOCIATES (AV)

Causeway Plaza, 3510 North Causeway Boulevard, Suite 601, P.O. Box 50700, 70150-0700
Telephone: 504-524-2627; 504-846-4260
Fax: 504-846-4265
Covington, Louisiana Office: 77378 Stafford Road.
Telephone: 504-867-9761.

Fred E. Salley   Lee Morgan Peacocke

For full biographical listings, see the Martindale-Hubbell Law Directory

---

TERRIBERRY, CARROLL & YANCEY, L.L.P. (AV)

3100 Energy Centre, 1100 Poydras Street, 70163-3100
Telephone: 504-523-6451
Cable Address: "Terrib"
Telex: 6821224 (WUI)
Fax: 504-524-3257

MEMBERS OF FIRM

Benjamin W. Yancey
(1906-1991).
Walter Carroll, Jr. (Retired)
Maurie D. Yager
G. Edward Merritt
James L. Schupp, Jr.
John A. Bolles
Charles F. Lozes
Robert J. Barbier

Hugh Ramsay Straub
David B. Lawton
Roger D. Allen
Janet Wessler Marshall
D. Kirk Boswell
Gary A. Hemphill
Laurence R. De Buys, IV
Kevin J. LaVie
Stephen E. Mattesky

COUNSEL

Andrew T. Martinez   Cynthia Anne Wegmann

ASSOCIATES

Gerald M. Baca   Michael M. Butterworth
John A. Scialdone

Representative Clients: Assuranceforeningen Gard; Assuranceforeningen Skuld; Certain Underwriters at Lloyd's; The London Steam-Ship Owners' Mutual Insurance Assn. Ltd.; Lykes Bros. Steamship Co., Inc.; New Orleans Steamship Assn.; Nordisk Skibsrederforening (Northern Shipowners Defence Club); Scandinavian Marine Claims Office, Inc.; Steamship Mutual Underwriting Assn. Ltd.; United Kingdom Mutual Steam Ship Assurance Assn. Ltd.

For full biographical listings, see the Martindale-Hubbell Law Directory

---

WAGNER, BAGOT & GLEASON (AV)

Suite 2660, Poydras Center, 650 Poydras Street, 70130-6105
Telephone: 504-525-2141
Telecopier: 504-523-1587
TWX: 5106017673
ELN: 62928850
"INCISIVE"

Thomas J. Wagner
Michael H. Bagot, Jr.

Harvey G. Gleason
Whitney L. Cole
Eric D. Suben

For full biographical listings, see the Martindale-Hubbell Law Directory

---

MAINE

*PORTLAND,** Cumberland Co.

TOMPKINS, CLOUGH, HIRSHON & LANGER, P.A. (AV)

Three Canal Plaza, P.O. Box 15060, 04101
Telephone: 207-874-6700
FAX: 207-874-6705

(See Next Column)

Bruce M. Tompkins
Lawrence R. Clough

David M. Hirshon
Leonard W. Langer
Marshall J. Tinkle

For full biographical listings, see the Martindale-Hubbell Law Directory

---

MARYLAND

*BALTIMORE,** (Independent City)

FERGUSON, SCHETELICH, HEFFERNAN & MURDOCK, P.A. (AV)

1300 NationsBank Center 1, 100 South Charles Street, 21201
Telephone: 410-837-2200
Fax: 410-837-1188
Email: fshm@ix.netcom

Robert L. Ferguson, Jr.
Thomas J. Schetelich

Christopher J. Heffernan
M. Brooke Murdock

Michael N. Russo, Jr.
Jodi K. Ebersole

Peter Joseph Basile
Ann D. Ware

For full biographical listings, see the Martindale-Hubbell Law Directory

---

ISRAELSON, SALSBURY, CLEMENTS & BEKMAN (AV)

300 West Pratt Street Suite 450, 21201
Telephone: 410-539-6633
FAX: 410-625-9554

MEMBERS OF FIRM

Stuart Marshall Salsbury
Paul D. Bekman

Daniel M. Clements
Matthew Zimmerman
Laurence A. Marder

Scott R. Scherr
Carol J. Glover

Lauren R. Calia
Andrew David Alpert

COUNSEL TO THE FIRM

Max R. Israelson

OF COUNSEL

Samuel Omar Jackson, Jr. (Semi-Retired)

For full biographical listings, see the Martindale-Hubbell Law Directory

---

NILES, BARTON & WILMER (AV)

1400 Legg Mason Tower, 111 South Calvert Street, 21202-6185
Telephone: 410-783-6300
Cable Address: "Nilwo"
Telecopier: 410-783-6363

MEMBERS OF FIRM

Paul B. Lang   Robert P. O'Brien
Steven E. Leder

For Complete List of Firm Personnel, See General Section

For full biographical listings, see the Martindale-Hubbell Law Directory

---

THIEBLOT, RYAN, MARTIN & MILLER, P.A. (AV)

4th Floor, The World Trade Center, 21202-3091
Telephone: 410-837-1140
Washington, D.C. Line: 202-628-8223
Fax: 410-837-3282
Towson, Maryland Office: Atlantic Federal Building. Suite 400. 100 West Road. 21204.
Telephone: 410-828-5900.

Robert J. Thieblot
Anthony W. Ryan
J. Edward Martin, Jr.
Bruce R. Miller

Robert D. Harwick, Jr.
Anne M. Hrehorovich
Donna Marie Raffaele
Hamilton Fisk Tyler
Samuel S. Field III

Representative Clients: Allianz Underwriters Insurance Co.; Nautilus Insurance Co.; Scottsdale Insurance Co.; USF&G Company.

For full biographical listings, see the Martindale-Hubbell Law Directory

---

VENABLE ATTORNEYS AT LAW VENABLE, BAETJER AND HOWARD, LLP (AV)

A Partnership including Professional Corporations
1800 Mercantile Bank & Trust Building, 2 Hopkins Plaza, 21201
Telephone: 410-244-7400
Email: INFO@Venable.win.net
Washington, D.C. Office: Venable, Baetjer, Howard & Civiletti LLP. Suite 1000, 1201 New York Avenue, N.W.
Telephone: 202-962-4800.
McLean, Virginia Office: Suite 400, 2010 Corporate Ridge.
Telephone: 703-760-1600.

(See Next Column)

VENABLE ATTORNEYS AT LAW VENABLE, BAETJER AND HOWARD, LLP, *Baltimore—Continued*

Rockville, Maryland Office: Suite 500, One Church Street, P. O. Box 1906.
Telephone: 301-217-5600.
Towson, Maryland Office: 210 Allegheny Avenue, P. O. Box 5517.
Telephone: 410-494-6200.

MEMBERS OF FIRM

Douglas D. Connah, Jr. (P.C.) (Also at Washington, D.C. Office)　　Lars E. Anderson (Not admitted in MD; Resident, McLean, Virginia Office)

For Complete List of Firm Personnel, See General Section

For full biographical listings, see the Martindale-Hubbell Law Directory

---

WARD, KERSHAW & MINTON, A PROFESSIONAL ASSOCIATION (AV)

113 West Monument Street, 21201
Telephone: 410-685-6700
Fax: 410-685-6704
Email: wkmfirm@aol.com

John T. Ward　　　　　　Robert B. Kershaw
Thomas J. Minton
OF COUNSEL
Richard V. Falcon

For full biographical listings, see the Martindale-Hubbell Law Directory

---

WRIGHT, CONSTABLE & SKEEN (AV)

250 West Pratt Street, 13th Floor, 21201-2423
Telephone: 410-539-5541
Telex: 710 234-2383 CALDAS
Fax: 301-659-1350
Elkton, Maryland Office: 138 East Main Street.
Telephone: 301-398-1844.

MEMBERS OF FIRM

James W. Constable　　　　　James D. Skeen
Stephen F. White

Representative Clients: General Ship Repair Corp.; Egan Marine Contracting Co., Inc.; Atlantic Mutual Insurance Co.; Marine Office of America Corp.; Recovery Services International; Toplis & Harding, Inc.; Firemen's Fund; Royal Insurance Co.; Gradman & Holler, Gmbh; Arkwright-Boston Insurance.

For Complete List of Firm Personnel, See General Section

For full biographical listings, see the Martindale-Hubbell Law Directory

---

MASSACHUSETTS

*BOSTON,** Suffolk Co.

PETTINGELL & REGAN (AV)

85 Devonshire Street, 02109
Telephone: 617-723-0901
Fax: 617-723-0977

Richard H. Pettingell　　　　Joseph A. Regan
ASSOCIATES
Robert E. Kiely　　　　　　Paige L. Tobin
Brian J. Gunning　　　　　Malcolm Patrick Galvin, III

For full biographical listings, see the Martindale-Hubbell Law Directory

SWARTZ & SWARTZ (AV)

10 Marshall Street, 02108
Telephone: 617-742-1900
Fax: 617-367-7193

Edward M. Swartz　　　　Joan E. Swartz
Alan L. Cantor　　　　　James A. Swartz
Joseph A. Swartz　　　　Harold David Levine
Victor A. Denaro　　　　David P. Angueira
OF COUNSEL
Fredric A. Swartz

For full biographical listings, see the Martindale-Hubbell Law Directory

CHATHAM, Barnstable Co.

CONNORS & FARRELL (AV)

Routes 28 and 137 (Cape Cod), 02659-0186
Telephone: 508-432-2121
Fax: 508-432-2334
Mailing Address: P.O. Box 186, South Chatham, Massachusetts, 02659
Email: sealaw@virtualcapecod.com *URL:* http://www.virtualcapecod.com/market/connorsandfarr

(See Next Column)

MEMBERS OF FIRM

Rose Connors　　　　　　David Farrell, Jr.
ASSOCIATE
John Hilary Sweeney

For full biographical listings, see the Martindale-Hubbell Law Directory

---

MICHIGAN

*DETROIT,** Wayne Co.

BRADY HATHAWAY, PROFESSIONAL CORPORATION (AV)

1330 Buhl Building, 48226-3602
Telephone: 313-965-3700
Telecopier: 313-965-2830

Thomas M. J. Hathaway

Representative Client: Kinsman Lines.

For Complete List of Firm Personnel, See General Section

For full biographical listings, see the Martindale-Hubbell Law Directory

---

FOSTER, MEADOWS & BALLARD, P.C. (AV)

3200 Penobscot Building, 48226
Telephone: 313-961-3234
Cable Address: "Foster"
Telex: 23-5823
Facsimile: 313-961-6184

Sparkman D. Foster (1897-1967)　　Richard A. Dietz
Charles R. Hrdlicka　　　　　　　Robert H. Fortunate
Paul D. Galea　　　　　　　　　Robert G. Lahiff
　　　　　Camille A. Raffa-Dietz

Michael J. Liddane　　　　　　Paul A. Kettunen
OF COUNSEL
John L. Foster　　　　　　　　John F. Langs
　　　　　John A. Mundell, Jr.

Counsel For: Ashland Petroleum Co.; Cleveland Tankers 1991, Inc.; Marine Office of America; St. Paul Companies; United Kingdom Mutual Steamship Owners Protection and Indemnity Association.

For full biographical listings, see the Martindale-Hubbell Law Directory

---

MILLER, CANFIELD, PADDOCK AND STONE, P.L.C. (AV)

A Professional Limited Liability Company
Founded in 1852 by Sidney Davy Miller
150 West Jefferson, Suite 2500, 48226-4415
Telephone: 313-963-6420
Fax: 313-496-7500
Cable Address: "Stem Detroit"
Detroit, Michigan Office: 150 West Jefferson, Suite 2500, 48226-4415.
Telephone: 313-963-6420.
Fax: 313-496-7500.
Cable Address: "Stem Detroit."
Ann Arbor, Michigan Office: 101 North Main Street, 7th Floor, 48104-1400.
Telephone: 313-663-2445.
Fax: 313-747-7147.
Bloomfield Hills, Michigan Office: Suite 100, Pinehurst Office Center, 1400 North Woodward, 48303-2014.
Telephone: 313-645-5000.
Fax: 313-645-1917.
Grand Rapids, Michigan Office: 1200 Campau Square Plaza, 99 Monroe, N.W., 49503-2639.
Telephone: 616-454-8656.
Fax: 616-776-6322.
Howell, Michigan Office: 121 South Barnard Street, Suite 4, 48843-2305.
Telephone: 517-546-7600.
Telecopier: 517-546-6974.
Kalamazoo, Michigan Office: 444 West Michigan Avenue, 49007-3752.
Telephone: 616-381-7030.
Fax: 616-382-0244.
Lansing, Michigan Office: One Michigan Avenue, Suite 900, 48933-1609.
Telephone: 517-487-2070.
Fax: 517-374-6304.
Monroe, Michigan Office: The Executive Centre, 214 East Elm Avenue, 48161-2682.
Telephone: 313-243-2000.
Fax: 313-243-0901.
Washington, D.C. Office: 1225 Nineteenth Street, N.W., Suite 400. 20036.
Telephone: 202-429-5575; 785-0600.
Fax: 202-331-1118; 785-1234.
Pensacola, Florida Office: 25 West Cedar, 32501.
Telephone: 904-469-1088.
Fax: 904-432-0677.

(See Next Column)

MILLER, CANFIELD, PADDOCK AND STONE P.L.C.—Continued

St. Petersburg, Florida Office: 100 Second Avenue S., Suite 7045, 33701.
Telephone: 813-982-6000.
Fax: 813-892-6002.
New York, New York Office: Eleventh Floor, 135 East 57th Street, 10022-2087.
Telephone: 212-754-5400.
Fax: 212-754-5401.
Gdansk, Poland Office: Suite 322, Dom Technika Building, UI. Rajska 6, 80-850.
Telephone: 011-485-831-2808.
Fax: 011-485-831-4719.
Warsaw, Poland Office: UI. Marszalkowska 82, Suite 561, 00-517.
Telephone: 011-482-623-6457 and 6458.
Fax: 011-482-623-6459.

PRINCIPALS OF FIRM

Lawrence A. King (P.C.)
   (Bloomfield Hills Office)
Robert E. Hammell
John W. Gelder
   (Bloomfield Hills Office)
George E. Parker, III
Stevan Uzelac (P.C.)
Gilbert E. Gove
Robert S. Ketchum
Samuel J. McKim, III, (P.C.)
Rocque E. Lipford (P.C.)
   (Monroe Office)
Joel L. Piell
Robert E. Gilbert
   (Ann Arbor Office)
Eric V. Brown, Jr.
   (Kalamazoo Office)
Bruce D. Birgbauer
John A. Thurber (P.C.)
   (Bloomfield Hills Office)
Orin D. Brustad
Carl H. von Ende
Erik H. Serr (Ann Arbor Office)
Allyn D. Kantor
   (Ann Arbor Office)
Charles E. Ritter
   (Kalamazoo Office)
Thomas G. Parachini
John A. Campbell
   (Kalamazoo Office)
David D. Joswick (P.C.)
Charles L. Burleigh, Jr.
John A. Marxer (P.C.)
   (Bloomfield Hills Office)
Gregory L. Curtner
   (New York, N.Y. Office)
Dennis R. Neiman
Kenneth E. Konop
   (Bloomfield Hills Office)
Leonard D. Givens
W. Mack Faison
Joseph F. Galvin
Ronald H. Riback
   (Bloomfield Hills Office)
James W. Williams
   (Bloomfield Hills Office)
Thomas P. Hustoles
   (Kalamazoo Office)
William J. Danhof
   (Lansing Office)
Clarence L. Pozza, Jr.
Jerry T. Rupley
Michael W. Hartmann
Kent E. Shafer
James C. Foresman
John J. Collins, Jr.
   (Bloomfield Hills Office)
John R. Cook
   (Kalamazoo Office)
Thomas W. Linn
Stephen G. Palms
   (Bloomfield Hills Office)
Jerome R. Watson
Frank L. Andrews (Detroit and
   Bloomfield Hills Offices)
Donna J. Donati
Donald W. Keim
Larry J. Saylor
Mark E. Putney (Grand Rapids
   Office Resident Director)
James G. Vantine, Jr.
   (Kalamazoo Office)
Richard J. Seryak
Michael R. Atkins
   (Lansing Office)
Leland D. Barringer

Timothy D. Sochocki
   (Ann Arbor Office)
Thomas C. Phillips
   (Lansing Office)
Christopher J. Dembowski
   (Lansing Office)
Marjory G. Basile
Terrence M. Crawford
Michael J. Hodge
   (Lansing Office)
J. Kevin Trimmer
   (Bloomfield Hills Office)
Richard A. Gaffin
   (Grand Rapids Office)
Kevin M. McCarthy
   (Kalamazoo Office)
Ronald E. Baylor
   (Kalamazoo Office)
Beverly Hall Burns
Charles S. Mishkind (Grand
   Rapids, Lansing and
   Kalamazoo Offices)
Stephen J. Ott
Amanda Van Dusen
Peter W. Waldmeir
Thomas G. Appleman
   (Bloomfield Hills Office)
Thomas H. Van Dis
   (Kalamazoo Office)
Walter Briggs Connolly, Jr.
Michael P. Coakley
Cynthia B. Faulhaber
   (Lansing Office)
Jeffrey M. McHugh
Robert F. Rhoades
James E. Spurr
   (Kalamazoo Office)
Gregory V. Di Censo
   (Bloomfield Hills Office)
Brad B. Arbuckle
   (Bloomfield Hills Office)
Mark T. Boonstra
Harold W. Bulger, Jr.
Michael G. Campbell
   (Grand Rapids Office)
David A. French
   (Ann Arbor Office)
Michael A. Limauro
Karen Ann McCoy
Kevin J. Moody (Lansing Office)
Steven M. Stankewicz
   (Kalamazoo Office)
Robert E. Lee Wright
Michael A. Indenbaum
Alison B. Marshall
   (Washington, D.C. Office)
J. David Reck (Ann Arbor and
   Howell Offices)
Michael H. Traison
Jonathan S. Green
Le Roy L. Asher, Jr.
Vernon Bennett III (Grand
   Rapids and Kalamazoo
   Offices)
Douglas W. Crim
   (Grand Rapids Office)
Pamela Chapman Enslen
   (Kalamazoo Office)
Michael P. McGee
David N. Parsigian
   (Ann Arbor Office)
Jay B. Rising (Lansing Office)
Deborah W. Thompson
Richard T. Urbis
Richard F. X. Urisko
Steven A. Roach

(See Next Column)

PRINCIPALS OF FIRM (Continued)

Richard A. Walawender
Brian J. Doren
Irene Bruce Hathaway
Michael A. Luberto, Jr.
Megan P. Norris
Lawrence M. Dudek
Charles A. Duerr, Jr.
   (Ann Arbor Office)
Ronald E. Hodess
   (Bloomfield Hills Office)

Donald J. Hutchinson
Marta A. Manildi
   (Ann Arbor Office)
Kathryn L. Ossian
Don M. Schmidt
   (Kalamazoo Office)
Kurt N. Sherwood
   (Kalamazoo Office)

OF COUNSEL

William G. Butler
Eric V. Brown, Sr.
   (Kalamazoo Office)
Edmond F. DeVine
   (Ann Arbor Office)
James E. Tobin
John B. DeVine
   (Ann Arbor Office)
Stratton S. Brown
Richard B. Gushée
Peter P. Thurber
Joseph F. Maycock, Jr.
Allen Schwartz
Richard A. Jones (P.C.)
David E. Hathaway
   (Grand Rapids Office)
Gerard Thomas
   (Kalamazoo Office)
George E. Bushnell, Jr.
Henry R. Nolte, Jr.
   (Bloomfield Hills Office)
Lawrence D. Owen
   (Lansing Office)
Anne H. Hiemstra

Richard I. Lott
   (Pensacola, Florida Office)
Nicholas P. Miller
   (Washington, D.C. Office)
Joseph Van Eaton
   (Washington, D.C. Office)
Tillman L. Lay
   (Washington, D.C. Office)
William R. Malone
   (Washington, D.C. Office)
David K. McLeod
David L. Kaser (Principal)
Edward F. Langs
Steven E. Chester
   (Resident, Lansing Office)
Raphael A. Monsanto
   (Not admitted in MI)
Benita J. Rohm
   (Not admitted in MI)
Geoffrey M. Chinn
   (New York Office)
Richard I. Loebl
William R. Kotila
   (Ann Arbor Office)

SENIOR ATTORNEYS

Leo P. Goddeyne
   (Kalamazoo Office)
Ronald D. Gardner
   (Ann Arbor Office)
Elise S. Levasseur
William B. Beach
Robert J. Sandler
Sherry Katz-Crank
   (Lansing Office)
David J. Hasper
   (Grand Rapids Office)
Susan E. Juroe
   (Washington, D.C. Office)
Michael A. Alaimo
David A. Gatchell
   (St. Petersburg Office)

John G. VanSlambrouck
   (Kalamazoo Office)
Roselyn R. Parmenter
George D. Mesritz
Steven C. Kahn
   (Washington, D.C. Office)
Frederick E. Ellrod III
   (Washington, D.C. Office)
Douglas M. Kilbourne
   (Ann Arbor Office)
Walter A. Payne, III
Stephen L. Elkins
   (Grand Rapids Office)
Clifford T. Flood
   (Lansing Office)

ASSOCIATES

Patricia D. Lott
   (Pensacola Office)
Matthew C. Ames
   (Washington, D.C. Office)
Ballard Jay Yelton III
   (Kalamazoo Office)
Thomas R. Cox
Lori L. Purkey
   (Kalamazoo Office)
Joanne B. Faycurry
Dawn M. Schluter
   (Bloomfield Hills Office)
Robert J. Haddad
John H. Willems
James R. Lancaster, Jr.
   (Lansing Office)
John O. Renken (Ann Arbor
   and Washington, D.C. Offices)
J. Darrell Peterson
   (Washington, D.C. Office)
Frederick A. Acomb
Joseph G. Sullivan
John C. Arndts
Brian S. Westenberg
Amy S. Davis
A. Michael Palizzi
Sally A. Hamby
   (Bloomfield Hills Office)
Patrick F. McGow
Paul G. Machesky
Robert R. Lech
Lisa D. Pick
   (Bloomfield Hills Office)
Michael C. Fayz
Anna M. Maiuri
   (Bloomfield Hills Office)
Thomas D. Colis

Dean M. Altobelli
   (Lansing Office)
Derek T. Montgomery
Diane Benedict Cabbell
   (Ann Arbor Office)
Mark K. Schrupp
Terence A. Thomas
Kristin M. Neun
   (Washington, D.C. Office)
Bradley C. White
   (Grand Rapids Office)
Jeffrey D. Adelman
Loyal A. Eldridge, III
   (Kalamazoo Office)
Kurt P. McCamman
   (Kalamazoo Office)
Daniel H. Roberts
   (Grand Rapids Office)
Scott R. Sikkenga
   (Kalamazoo Office)
Erin Quinn Gery
   (Washington, D.C. Office)
Karl N. Gellert
Julie S. Silberg
James B. Thelen
   (Kalamazoo Office)
Yvonne R. Haddad
Anthony J. Mavrinac
John T. Stecco
   (Grand Rapids Office)
Clara G. Dequick
Michael V. Camarota
   (Grand Rapids Office)
Robbi L. Sackville
Alice Censoplano
   (Ann Arbor Office)
Thomas A. Norton

(See Next Column)

MILLER, CANFIELD, PADDOCK AND STONE P.L.C., *Detroit—Continued*

ASSOCIATES (Continued)

Louis B. Reinwasser   Karen M. Hassevoort
(Lansing Office)   (Kalamazoo Office)
Suzanne L. DeVine   Susan I. Robbins
(Ann Arbor Office)   (New York Office)

Representative Firm Clients: Chrysler Corporation; Comerica, Incorporated; City of Detroit, Michigan; Detroit Tigers, Inc.; First of Michigan; Ford Motor Company; Ford Motor Credit Company; Great Lakes Bancorp; Henry Ford Hospital; INVETECH Company.

For full biographical listings, see the Martindale-Hubbell Law Directory

ANTITRUST LAW

ALABAMA

BIRMINGHAM,* Jefferson Co.

BERKOWITZ, LEFKOVITS, ISOM & KUSHNER, A PROFESSIONAL CORPORATION (AV)

1600 SouthTrust Tower, 420 North Twentieth Street, 35203
Telephone: 205-328-0480
Telecopier: 205-322-8007

B. G. Minisman, Jr.   Susan S. Wagner

Representative Clients: AlaTenn Resources, Inc.; B.A.S.S., Inc.; Hanna Steel Co., Inc.; Liberty Trouser Co., Inc.; McDonald's Corp.; Parisian, Inc.; Southern Pipe & Supply Co., Inc.

For Complete List of Firm Personnel, See General Section

For full biographical listings, see the Martindale-Hubbell Law Directory

BRADLEY, ARANT, ROSE & WHITE (AV)

2001 Park Place, Suite 1400, P.O. Box 830709, 35283-0709
Telephone: 205-521-8000
Facsimile: 205-252-0264
Facsimile (SouthTrust Tower Office): 205-251-9915
URL: http://www.BARW.COM
Huntsville, Alabama Office: 200 Clinton Avenue West, Suite 900, 35801.
Telephone: 205-517-5100.
Facsimile: 205-533-5069.

MEMBERS OF FIRM

John James Coleman, Jr.   Joseph B. Mays, Jr.
Hobart A. McWhorter, Jr.   Sid J. Trant
Thad Gladden Long   Philip J. Carroll III
James Patrick Alexander   James S. Christie, Jr.
Linda A. Friedman   John E. Goodman
                  Susan Donovan Josey

ASSOCIATES

Michael S. Denniston   Fred M. Haston, III

Counsel for: SouthTrust Bank of Alabama, National Association; Stockham Valves & Fittings, Inc.; Wolverine Tube, Inc.; Blount, Inc.; Coca-Cola Bottling Company United, Inc.; Russell Corp.; Walter Industries, Inc.

For Complete List of Firm Personnel, See General Section

For full biographical listings, see the Martindale-Hubbell Law Directory

BURR & FORMAN (AV)

3100 SouthTrust Tower, 420 North 20th Street, 35203
Telephone: 205-251-3000
Telecopier: 205-458-5100
Huntsville, Alabama Office: Suite 204, Regency Center, 400 Meridian Street.
Telephone: 205-551-0010.
Atlanta, Georgia Office: Suite 1800, One Georgia Center, 600 West Peachtree Street, 30308.
Telephone: 404-817-3536.
Facsimile: 404-817-3244.

MEMBERS OF FIRM

John D. Clements   J. Patrick Logan
James Ross Forman, III   Gary M. London
                  J. Hunter Phillips, III

OF COUNSEL

A. Jackson Noble, Jr.

ASSOCIATE

Darin W. Collier

For Complete List of Firm Personnel, See General Section

For full biographical listings, see the Martindale-Hubbell Law Directory

HASKELL SLAUGHTER & YOUNG, L.L.C. (AV)

1200 AmSouth/Harbert Plaza, 1901 Sixth Avenue North, 35203
Telephone: 205-251-1000
Facsimile: 205-324-1133
Montgomery, Alabama Office: 305 South Lawrence Street, P.O. Box 4660.
36103-4660.
Telephone: 334-265-8573.
Facsimile: 334-264-7945.

James C. Huckaby, Jr.   Michael K. K. Choy

Representative Clients: The Equitable Life Assurance Society of the United States; Exxon Corporation; NationsBank Corporation; Rhone-Poulenc Rorer Pharmaceuticals, Inc.; Sandoz Pharmaceuticals Corporation.

(See Next Column)

For Complete List of Firm Personnel, See General Section

For full biographical listings, see the Martindale-Hubbell Law Directory

JOHNSTON, BARTON, PROCTOR & POWELL (AV)

2900 AmSouth/Harbert Plaza, 1901 Sixth Avenue North, 35203-2618
Telephone: 205-458-9400
Telecopier: 205-458-9500

MEMBERS OF FIRM

Harvey Deramus (1904-1970)   James C. Barton, Jr.
Alfred M. Naff (1923-1993)   Thomas E. Walker
Gilbert E. Johnston (1916-1994)   Anne P. Wheeler
G. Burns Proctor, Jr.   Barry V. Frederick
Sydney L. Lavender   Hollinger F. Barnard
Charles A. Powell, III   William D. Jones III
Jerome K. Lanning   David W. Proctor
Don B. Long, Jr.   Oscar M. Price III
Charles L. Robinson   W. Hill Sewell
J. William Rose, Jr.   Robert S. Vance, Jr.
Gilbert E. Johnston, Jr.   Richard J. Brockman
Ralph H. Smith II   Anthony A. Joseph
              William G. Somerville, III

COUNSEL

Josh Mullins, Jr.   Paul E. Toppins
              R. Marcus Givhan

OF COUNSEL

James C. Barton   Alfred Swedlaw
              Alan W. Heldman

ASSOCIATES

William K. Hancock   Helen Kathryn Downs
James P. Pewitt   Jennifer Fox Swain
Scott Wells Ford   Spencer A. Kinderman
David M. Hunt   Scott R. McLaughlin
Lee M. Pope   Bradley C. Mayhew
John W. Sheffield   W. Jonathan Daniel
Haskins W. Jones   J. Vincent Edge
Russell L. Irby, III   Allison Powell

General Counsel for: Allied Products Co.; Anderson News Co.; The Birmingham News Co. (Publishers of The Birmingham News and owner of The Huntsville Times Co.).
Counsel for: General Motors Corp.; General Electric Credit Corp.

For full biographical listings, see the Martindale-Hubbell Law Directory

LIGHTFOOT, FRANKLIN & WHITE, L.L.C. (AV)

300 Financial Center, 505 20th Street North, 35203-2706
Telephone: 205-581-0700
Facsimile: 205-581-0799

Warren B. Lightfoot   John M. Johnson
Samuel H. Franklin   E. Glenn Waldrop, Jr.

Sarah Bruce Jackson   Wynn M. Shuford

Counsel for: AT&T; Ford Motor Co.; Emerson Electric Co.; Monsanto Co.; Chrysler Corp.; Unocal Corp.; The Upjohn Co.; Bristol-Myers Squibb Co.; The Goodyear Tire & Rubber Co.; Mitsubishi Motor Sales of America, Inc.

For full biographical listings, see the Martindale-Hubbell Law Directory

PATRICK & LACY, P.C. (AV)

1201 Financial Center, 35203
Telephone: 205-323-5665
Telecopier: 205-324-6221

J. Vernon Patrick, Jr.   William M. Acker, III
Alex S. Lacy   Elizabeth N. Pitman

For full biographical listings, see the Martindale-Hubbell Law Directory

SCHOEL, OGLE, BENTON AND CENTENO (AV)

600 Financial Center, 505 North 20th Street, P.O. Box 1865, 35201-1865
Telephone: 205-521-7000
Telecopier: 205-521-7007

MEMBERS OF FIRM

Jerry W. Schoel   Douglas J. Centeno
Richard F. Ogle   Melinda Murphy Dionne
Lee R. Benton   Gilbert M. Sullivan, Jr.
Paul A. Liles   David O. Upshaw

Reference: National Bank of Commerce; First Alabama Bank.

For full biographical listings, see the Martindale-Hubbell Law Directory

SPAIN & GILLON, L.L.C. (AV)

The Zinszer Building, 2117 2nd Avenue North, 35203
Telephone: 205-328-4100
Telecopier: 205-324-8866

(See Next Column)

SPAIN & GILLON L.L.C., *Birmingham—Continued*
MEMBERS OF FIRM
Ollie L. Blan, Jr.   Alton B. Parker, Jr.

General Counsel for: Liberty National Life Insurance Co.; Piggly Wiggly Alabama Distributing Co.; AmSouth Mortgage Co., Inc.; Alabama Insurance Guaranty Association; Alabama Life and Disability Insurance Guaranty Association; Alabama Insurance Underwriters Association.
Counsel for: Government Employees Insurance Co.; Massachusetts Mutual Life Insurance Co.

For Complete List of Firm Personnel, See General Section

For full biographical listings, see the Martindale-Hubbell Law Directory

---

MOBILE, * Mobile Co.

ARMBRECHT, JACKSON, DEMOUY, CROWE, HOLMES & REEVES, L.L.C. (AV)
1300 AmSouth Center, P.O. Box 290, 36601
Telephone: 334-405-1300
Facsimile: 334-432-6843; 433-3821
MEMBERS OF FIRM
Wm. H. Armbrecht, III   E. B. Peebles III
David A. Bagwell

Representative Clients: AmSouth Bank of Alabama (Regional Counsel); Loyal American Life Insurance Co.; Mobile Gas Service Corp.; Mobile Steamship Ass'n -- International Longshoremen's Pension, Welfare & Vacation Plans; Smith's Bakery, Inc.; Southern Pine Inspection Bureau; United Bank; WKRG-TV, Inc.

For Complete List of Firm Personnel, See General Section

For full biographical listings, see the Martindale-Hubbell Law Directory

---

JOHNSTONE, ADAMS, BAILEY, GORDON AND HARRIS, L.L.C. (AV)
Royal St. Francis Building, 104 St. Francis Street, P.O. Box 1988, 36633
Telephone: 334-432-7682
Facsimile: 334-432-2800
Telex: 782040
MEMBERS OF FIRM
William H. Hardie, Jr.   Celia J. Collins
For a list of Representative Clients, see General Section.

For Complete List of Firm Personnel, See General Section

For full biographical listings, see the Martindale-Hubbell Law Directory

---

ARIZONA

PHOENIX, * Maricopa Co.

ALLEN & PRICE, P.L.C. (AV)
2850 East Camelback Road, Suite 170, 85016-4380
Telephone: 602-381-0500
Fax: 602-381-8899
Email: price@aplaw.com
Email: allen@aplaw.com

Robert E. B. Allen   Charles S. Price

For full biographical listings, see the Martindale-Hubbell Law Directory

BROWN & BAIN, A PROFESSIONAL ASSOCIATION (AV)
2901 North Central Avenue, P.O. Box 400, 85001-0400
Telephone: 602-351-8000
Telecopier: 602-351-8516
Palo Alto, California Affiliated Office: Brown & Bain, 1755 Embarcadero Road, Suite 200.
Telephone: 415-856-9411.
Telecopier: 415-856-6061.
Tucson, Arizona Affiliated Office: Brown & Bain, A Professional Association. One South Church Avenue, Nineteenth Floor, P.O. Box 2265.
Telephone: 602-798-7900.
Telecopier: 602-798-7945.

Lois W. Abraham (Resident at Palo Alto Office)	Terry E. Fenzl
C. Randall Bain	Douglas Gerlach
Charles A. Blanchard	Philip R. Higdon (Resident at Tucson Office)
Alan H. Blankenheimer	Jonathan M. James
Jack E. Brown	Joseph E. Mais
John A. Buttrick	Anthony L. Marks
Howard Ross Cabot	Joel W. Nomkin
H. Michael Clyde	Kelly A. O'Connor
Paul F. Eckstein	Michael W. Patten

(See Next Column)

John W. Rogers   Craig W. Soland
Lawrence G. D. Scarborough   Antonio T. Viera
Kim E. Williamson

Susan D. Berney-Key   Timothy A. Nelson
(Resident at Palo Alto Office)

For Complete List of Firm Personnel, See General Section

For full biographical listings, see the Martindale-Hubbell Law Directory

COPPERSMITH & GORDON P.L.C. (AV)
2633 East Indian School Road, Suite 300, 85016-6759
Telephone: 602-224-0999
Fax: 602-224-6020
Email: SAMnANDY@aol.com

Andrew S. Gordon
OF COUNSEL
M. Joyce Geyser   James J. Belanger

Reference: Norwest Bank Arizona, N.A.

For full biographical listings, see the Martindale-Hubbell Law Directory

FENNEMORE CRAIG, A PROFESSIONAL CORPORATION (AV)
Two North Central, Suite 2200, 85004
Telephone: 602-257-8700
Fax: 602-257-8527
Scottsdale, Arizona Office: 6263 North Scottsdale Road, Suite 290, 85250.
Telephone: 602-257-5400.
Fax: 602-257-5409.
Tucson, Arizona Office: One South Church Avenue, Suite 1030, 85701.
Telephone: 520-791-6800.
Fax: 520-791-6820.

Timothy J. Burke   C. Owen Paepke

For Complete List of Firm Personnel, See General Section

For full biographical listings, see the Martindale-Hubbell Law Directory

GALBUT & CONANT, A PROFESSIONAL CORPORATION (AV)
Camelback Esplanade, Suite 1020, 2425 East Camelback Road, 85016
Telephone: 602-955-1455
Fax: 602-955-1585

Martin R. Galbut   Paul A. Conant

John R. Augustine, Jr.

For full biographical listings, see the Martindale-Hubbell Law Directory

KIMERER & LAVELLE, P.L.C. (AV)
100 W. Clarendon Suite 2100, 85013
Telephone: 602-279-5900; 800-220-6817
FAX: 602-264-5566
Email: kimlav@msn.com

Michael J. LaVelle

For full biographical listings, see the Martindale-Hubbell Law Directory

LEWIS AND ROCA, LLP (AV)
A Limited Liability Partnership including a Professional Corporation
40 North Central Avenue, 85004-4429
Telephone: 602-262-5311
Fax: 602-262-5747
Email: mlp@lrlaw.com
Tucson, Arizona Office: One South Church Avenue, Suite 700, 86701-1620.
Telephone: 520-622-2090.
Fax: 520-622-3088. E-Mail: mlp@lrlaw.com.
MEMBERS OF FIRM
John P. Frank   George L. Paul
Karen Carter Owens

Representative Clients: Arizona Hospital Assn.; The Heil Co.; Rockford Corp.; Samaritan Health System.

For Complete List of Firm Personnel, See General Section

For full biographical listings, see the Martindale-Hubbell Law Directory

MEYERS LAW FIRM (AV)
Suite 900, 2398 East Camelback Road, 85016
Telephone: 602-468-8900
Telecopier: 602-468-8910

Donald D. Meyers

(See Next Column)

MEYERS LAW FIRM—*Continued*

Charles W. Lotzar   James F. Wees
Donald L. Meyers   Jason A. Donkersley

Reference: Bank of America, Arizona.

For full biographical listings, see the Martindale-Hubbell Law Directory

O'CONNOR, CAVANAGH, ANDERSON, KILLINGSWORTH & BESHEARS, A PROFESSIONAL ASSOCIATION (AV)

One East Camelback Road, Suite 1100, 85012-1656
Telephone: 602-263-2400
FAX: 602-263-2900
Email: firminfo@arizlaw.com
Sun City, Arizona Office: 13250 North Del Webb Boulevard, Suite B, 85351.
Telephone: 602-263-2808.
FAX: 602-933-3100.
Tucson, Arizona Office: O'Connor Cavanagh Molloy Jones, 33 N. Stone, Suite 2100, 85701, P.O. Box 2268, 85702.
Telephone: 520-622-3531.
FAX: 520-624-2816.
Nogales, Arizona Office: 1891 North Mastick Way, 85621.
Telephone: 520-761-4215.
FAX: 520-761-3505.

Harry J. Cavanagh   Stephen E. Richman
David A. Van Engelhoven

Representative Clients: Karsten Manufacturing Corp.; Arizona Physicians, IPA; Samaritan Health Systems.

For Complete List of Firm Personnel, See General Section

For full biographical listings, see the Martindale-Hubbell Law Directory

SNELL & WILMER, L.L.P. (AV)

One Arizona Center, 85004-0001
Telephone: 602-382-6000
Fax: 602-382-6070
Tucson, Arizona Office: 1500 Norwest Tower, One South Church Avenue 85701-1612.
Telephone: 520-882-1200.
Fax: 520-884-1294.
Orange County Office: 1920 Main Street, Suite 1200, P.O. Box 57062, Irvine, California, 92619-7062.
Telephone: 714-253-2700.
Fax: 714-955-2507.
Salt Lake City, Utah Office: Broadway Centre, 111 East Broadway, Suite 900, 84111-1004.
Telephone: 801-237-1900.
Fax: 801-237-1950.

MEMBERS OF FIRM
John J. Bouma   Daniel J. McAuliffe
Arthur P. Greenfield
SENIOR ATTORNEY
Bruce P. White

Representative Clients: Arizona Public Service; Arvin Industries; Baptist Hospitals and Health Systems; Coca-Cola Bottling Co. of Phoenix; Good Samaritan Hospital Medical Staff; Holsum Bakery; Lincoln Health Systems; Maricopa Foundation for Medical Care; Phoenix Board of Realtors; The Tanner Companies.

For Complete List of Firm Personnel, See General Section

For full biographical listings, see the Martindale-Hubbell Law Directory

ULRICH, KESSLER & ANGER, P.C. (AV)

Suite 1000, 3030 North Central Avenue, 85012-2717
Telephone: 602-248-9465
Fax: 602-248-0165
Email: ukapc@aol.com

Paul G. Ulrich   Donn G. Kessler
William H. Anger

For full biographical listings, see the Martindale-Hubbell Law Directory

---

TUCSON, * Pima Co.

SNELL & WILMER, L.L.P. (AV)

1500 Norwest Tower, One South Church Avenue, 85701-1612
Telephone: 520-882-1200
Fax: 520-884-1294
Phoenix, Arizona Office: One Arizona Center, 85004-0001.
Telephone: 602-382-6000.
Fax: 602-382-6070.
Orange County Office: 1920 Main Street, Suite 1200, P.O. Box 57062, Irvine, California, 92619-7062.
Telephone: 714-253-2700.
Fax: 714-955-2507.

(See Next Column)

Salt Lake City, Utah Office: Broadway Centre, 111 East Broadway, Suite 900, 84111- 1004.
Telephone: 801-237-1900.
Fax: 801-237-1950.

MEMBER OF FIRM
Sandra S. Froman

Representative Clients: Arizona Public Service Company; Arvin Industries; Baptist Hospitals and Health Systems; Coca Cola Bottling Co. of Phoenix; Good Samaritan Hospital Medical Staff; Holsum Bakery; Lincoln Health Systems; Maricopa Foundation for Medical Care; Phoenix Board of Realtors; The Tanner Companies.

For full biographical listings, see the Martindale-Hubbell Law Directory

---

ARKANSAS

LITTLE ROCK, * Pulaski Co.

FRIDAY, ELDREDGE & CLARK (AV)

A Partnership including Professional Associations
Formerly, Smith, Williams, Friday, Eldredge & Clark
2000 First Commercial Building, 400 West Capitol Avenue, 72201-3493
Telephone: 501-376-2011
Telecopier: 501-376-2147; 376-6369
Email: fecmh@fec.sprint.com

MEMBER OF FIRM
James M. Simpson, Jr., (P.A.)
ASSOCIATE
Tony L. Wilcox

Counsel for: Union Pacific System; St. Paul Insurance Co.; Liberty Mutual Insurance Co.; Cigna Property & Casualty Co.; Arkansas Power & Light Co.; Dillard Department Stores, Inc.; First Commercial Corp.; Browning Arms Co.; Phillips Petroleum Co.; Aetna Casualty & Surety Co.

For Complete List of Firm Personnel, See General Section

For full biographical listings, see the Martindale-Hubbell Law Directory

WILLIAMS & ANDERSON (AV)

Twenty-Second Floor, 111 Center Street, 72201
Telephone: 501-372-0800
FAX: 501-372-6453

MEMBERS OF FIRM
Philip S. Anderson   Peter G. Kumpe
J. Leon Holmes

Jeanne L. Seewald

Representative Clients: Arkansas Development Finance Authority; Dean Witter Reynolds Inc.; Entergy Power, Inc.; Little Rock Newspapers, Inc. d/b/a/ Arkansas Democrat-Gazette; Potlatch Corporation; Texaco, Inc.; Wal-Mart Stores, Inc.

For Complete List of Firm Personnel, See General Section

For full biographical listings, see the Martindale-Hubbell Law Directory

---

CALIFORNIA

COSTA MESA, Orange Co.

RUTAN & TUCKER, LLP (AV)

A Partnership including Professional Corporations
611 Anton Boulevard, Suite 1400, P.O. Box 1950, 92626
Telephone: 714-641-5100; 213-625-7586
Telecopier: 714-546-9035
Email: rutan&tucker@mcimail.com *URL:* http://www.rutan.com

MEMBERS OF FIRM
Edward D. Sybesma, Jr., (P.C.)   Michael T. Hornak

For Complete List of Firm Personnel, See General Section

For full biographical listings, see the Martindale-Hubbell Law Directory

---

IRVINE, Orange Co.

GAUNTLETT & ASSOCIATES (AV)

18400 Von Karman, Suite 300, 92612
Telephone: 714-553-1010
Fax: 714-553-2050
Email: ugauntlett@aol.com

David A. Gauntlett

(See Next Column)

GAUNTLETT & ASSOCIATES, *Irvine*—Continued

David A. Stall	Elizabeth A. Gillis
Leo E. Lundberg, Jr.	(Not admitted in CA)
Michael Danton Richardson	Mark H. Plager
William P. Warden	(Not admitted in CA)
Stanley H. Shure	Jeffrey S. Allison

OF COUNSEL

Gary L. Hinman   Jose Zorrilla, Jr.

For full biographical listings, see the Martindale-Hubbell Law Directory

LAGUNA HILLS, Orange Co.

STETINA BRUNDA & BUYAN, A PROFESSIONAL CORPORATION (AV)

Suite 401, 24221 Calle De La Louisa, 92653
Telephone: 714-855-1246
Telex: 704355
Facsimile: 714-855-6371
Email: 104052.1330@compuserve.com

Kit M. Stetina (Mr.)   Bruce B. Brunda
Robert Dean Buyan

Mark B. Garred	Thomas C. Naber
William J. Brucker	(Not admitted in CA)
Matthew A. Newboles	Darren S. Rimer

LEGAL SUPPORT PERSONNEL

Norman E. Carte   Kristy Kay Moore

For full biographical listings, see the Martindale-Hubbell Law Directory

LOS ANGELES,* Los Angeles Co.

BLECHER & COLLINS, A PROFESSIONAL CORPORATION (AV)

611 West Sixth Street, 20th Floor, 90017
Telephone: 213-622-4222
Telecopier: 213-622-1656

Maxwell M. Blecher	Ralph C. Hofer
Harold R. Collins, Jr.	William C. Hsu
John E. Andrews	James Robert Noblin
Florence F. Cameron	Donald R. Pepperman
	Alicia G. Rosenberg

For full biographical listings, see the Martindale-Hubbell Law Directory

BRIGHT & LORIG, A PROFESSIONAL CORPORATION (AV)

633 West Fifth Street, Suite 3330, 90071
Telephone: 213-627-7774
Telecopier: 213-627-8508

Frederick A. Lorig   Patrick F. Bright

Lois A. Stone	Edward C. Schewe
Sidford Lewis Brown	Bruce R. Zisser

Reference: Manufacturers Bank (Headquarters Office).

For full biographical listings, see the Martindale-Hubbell Law Directory

CORINBLIT & SELTZER, A PROFESSIONAL CORPORATION (AV)

Suite 820 Wilshire Park Place, 3700 Wilshire Boulevard, 90010-3085
Telephone: 213-380-4200
Telecopier: 213-385-7503; 385-4560
Email: mseltzer@AOL.com

Marc M. Seltzer   Christina A. Snyder

OF COUNSEL

Jack Corinblit, A Law Corporation	Earl P. Willens

Gretchen M. Nelson	George A. Shohet
	Moses Garcia

For full biographical listings, see the Martindale-Hubbell Law Directory

LAW OFFICES OF RICHARD I. FINE & ASSOCIATES A PROFESSIONAL CORPORATION (AV)

Suite 1000, 10100 Santa Monica Boulevard (Century City), 90067-4090
Telephone: 310-277-5833
Rapifax: 310-277-1543

Richard I. Fine

Sunny S. Huo	Genalin Y. Sulat

LEGAL SUPPORT PERSONNEL

Mary Benson (Senior Paralegal)

For full biographical listings, see the Martindale-Hubbell Law Directory

HENNIGAN, MERCER & BENNETT (AV)

601 South Figueroa Street, Suite 3300, 90017
Telephone: 213-694-1200
Fax: 213-694-1234
Email: Silverm@hmb.com

J. Michael Hennigan	Laura Lindgren
James W. Mercer	Bruce R. MacLeod
Bruce Bennett	Elizabeth D. Mann
John L. Amsden	Robert L. Palmer
C. Dana Hobart	Lauren A. Smith
Jeanne E. Irving	Peter J. Most
Pamala J. King	Lee W. Potts

ASSOCIATES

Nichole M. Auden	Linda A. Kontos
Jacqueline Bendy	Jennifer Sulla
Mary H. Chu	Michael Swartz
A. Ann Hered	Shawna L. Ballard
Gregory K. Jones	Claudia Schweikert
Ellen M. Keane	David H. Martin

OF COUNSEL

Anthony Castanares

For full biographical listings, see the Martindale-Hubbell Law Directory

HOWARTH & SMITH (AV)

Suite 2900, 700 South Flower Street, 90017
Telephone: 213-955-9400
Fax: 213-622-0791

MEMBERS OF FIRM

Don Howarth	David K. Ringwood
Suzelle M. Smith	Kenneth S. Tune
	Brian D. Bubb

Marcus J. Berger	Katy Jacobs
Patricia Lee-Gulley	Sheila M. Bradley
Thomas F. Vandenburg	Julia S. Swanson
Gregory S. Tamkin	Kimberly L. Honus
	Randall Boese

For full biographical listings, see the Martindale-Hubbell Law Directory

JONES, DAY, REAVIS & POGUE (AV)

555 West Fifth Street Suite 4600, 90013-1025
Telephone: 213-489-3939
Telex: 181439 UD
Telecopier: 213-243-2539
In Irvine, California: 2603 Main Street, Suite 900.
Telephone: 714-851-3939.
Telex: 194911 Lawyers LSA.
Telecopier: 714-553-7539.
In Atlanta, Georgia: 3500 One Peachtree Center, 303 Peachtree Street, N.E.
Telephone: 404-521-3939.
Cable Address: "Attorneys Atlanta".
Telex: 54-2711.
Telecopier: 404-581-8330.
In Brussels, Belgium: Avenue Louise 480, 7th Floor, B-1050 Brussels.
Telephone: 32-2-645-14-11.
Telecopier: 32-2-645-14-45.
In Chicago, Illinois: 77 West Wacker.
Telephone: 312-782-3939.
Telecopier: 312-782-8585.
In Cleveland, Ohio: North Point, 901 Lakeside Avenue.
Telephone: 216-586-3939.
Cable Address: "Attorneys Cleveland."
Telex: 980389.
Telecopier: 216-579-0212.
In Columbus, Ohio: 1900 Huntington Center.
Telephone: 614-469-3939.
Cable Address: "Attorneys Columbus."
Telecopier: 614-461-4198.
In Dallas, Texas: 2300 Trammell Crow Center, 2001 Ross Avenue.
Telephone: 214-220-3939.
Cable Address: "Attorneys Dallas."
Telex: 730852.
Telecopier: 214-969-5100.
In Frankfurt, Germany: Triton Haus, Bockenheimer Landstrasse 42, 60323 Frankfurt am Main.
Telephone: 49-69-9726-3939.
Telecopier: 49-69-9726-3993.
In Geneva, Switzerland: 20, rue de Candolle.
Telephone: 41-22-320-2339.
Telecopier: 41-22-320-1232.
In Hong Kong: 29th Floor, Entertainment Building, 30 Queen's Road Central.
Telephone: 852-2526-6895.
Telecopier: 852-2868-5871.

(See Next Column)

JONES, DAY, REAVIS & POGUE—*Continued*

In London England: Bucklersbury House, 3 Queen Victoria Street.
Telephone: 44-171-236-3939.
Telecopier: 44-171-236-1113.
In New Delhi, India: Pathak & Associates, 13th Floor, Dr. Gopal Das Bhaven, 28 Barakhamba Road.
Telephone: 91-11-373-8793.
Telecopier: 91-11-335-3761.
In New York, New York: 599 Lexington Avenue.
Telephone: 212-326-3939.
Cable Address: "JONESDAY NEWYORK."
Telex: 237013 JDRP UR.
Telecopier: 212-755-7306.
In Paris, France: 62, rue du Faubourg Saint-Honore.
Telephone: 33-1-44-71-3939.
Telex: 290156 Surgoe.
Telecopier: 33-1-49-24-0471.
In Pittsburgh, Pennsylvania: 500 Grant Street, 31st Floor.
Telephone: 412-391-3939.
Cable Address: "Attorneys Pittsburgh".
Telecopier: 412-394-7959.
In Riyadh, Saudi Arabia: The International Law Firm, Sulaymaniyah Center, Tahlia Street, P.O. Box 22166.
Telephone: (966-1) 462-8866.
Telecopier: (966-1) 462-9001.
In Taipei, Taiwan: 8th Floor, 2 Tun Hwa South Road, Section 2.
Telephone: (886-2) 704-6808.
Telecopier: (886-2) 704-6791.
In Tokyo, Japan: Toranomon MT Building, 4th Floor, 10-3, Toranomon 3-Chome, Minato-ku, Tokyo 105, Japan.
Telephone: 81-3-3433-3939.
Telecopier: 81-3-5401-2725.
In Washington, D.C.: Metropolitan Square, 1450 G Street, N.W.
Telephone: 202-879-3939.
Cable Address: "Attorneys Washington."
Telex: 89-2410 ATTORNEYS WASH.
Telecopier: 202-737-2832.

MEMBERS OF FIRM IN LOS ANGELES

Gerald W. Palmer   Frederick L. McKnight
Jeffrey A. LeVee

For Complete List of Firm Personnel, See General Section

For full biographical listings, see the Martindale-Hubbell Law Directory

LOEB & LOEB LLP (AV)

A Limited Liability Partnership including Professional Corporations
Suite 1800, 1000 Wilshire Boulevard, 90017-2475
Telephone: 213-688-3400
Facsimile: 213-688-3460; 688-3461; 688-3462
Century City, California Office: Suite 2200, 10100 Santa Monica Boulevard, Los Angeles, 90067-4164.
Telephone: 310-282-2000.
Facsimile: 310-282-2191; 282-2192.
New York, N.Y. Office: 345 Park Avenue, 10154-0037.
Telephone: 212-407-4000.
Facsimile: 212-407-4990.
Washington, D.C. Office: Suite 601, 2100 M Street N.W., 20037-1207.
Telephone: 202-223-5700.
Facsimile: 202-223-5704.
Nashville, Tennessee Office: 45 Music Square West, 37203-3205.
Telephone: 615-749-8300;
Facsimile: 615-749-8308.
Rome, Italy Office: Piazza Digione 1, 00197.
Telephone: 011-396-808-8456.
Facsimile: 011-396-808-8288.

MEMBERS OF FIRM

Phillip E. Adler (A P.C.)   David B. Shontz
Robert A. Meyer   (New York City Office)
Charles H. Miller
   (New York City Office)

OF COUNSEL

Harry First   Howard I. Friedman (A P.C.)
(New York City Office)   Robert A. Holtzman (A P.C.)
      Alfred I. Rothman (A P.C.)

For Complete List of Firm Personnel, See General Section

For full biographical listings, see the Martindale-Hubbell Law Directory

LYON & LYON LLP (AV)

A Limited Liability Partnership including Professional Corporations
First Interstate World Center, 47th Floor, 633 West Fifth
   Street, 90071-2066
Telephone: 213-489-1600
Fax: 213-955-0440
Email: lyon@lyonlyon.com *URL:* http://www.lyonlyon.com
Costa Mesa, California Office: Suite 1200, 3200 Park Center Drive.
Telephone: 714-751-6606.
Fax: 714-751-8209.

(See Next Column)

San Jose, California Office: Suite 1150, 303 Almaden Boulevard.
Telephone: 408-993-1555.
Fax: 408-287-2664.
La Jolla, California Office: Suite 660, 4250 Executive Square.
Telephone: 619-552-8400.
Fax: 619-552-0159.

MEMBERS OF FIRM

Roland N. Smoot
Conrad R. Solum, Jr.
James W. Geriak (A Professional Corporation) (Costa Mesa Office)
Robert M. Taylor, Jr. (Costa Mesa Office)
Samuel B. Stone (A Professional Corporation) (Costa Mesa Office)
Douglas E. Olson (A Professional Corporation) (La Jolla Office)
Robert E. Lyon (A Professional Corporation)
Robert C. Weiss (A Professional Corporation)
Richard E. Lyon, Jr., (A Professional Corporation)
John D. McConaghy (A Professional Corporation)
William C. Steffin (A Professional Corporation)
Coe A. Bloomberg (A Professional Corporation)
J. Donald McCarthy (A Professional Corporation)

Arnold Sklar
John M. Benassi (La Jolla Office)
James H. Shalek
Allan W. Jansen (Costa Mesa Office)
Robert W. Dickerson
Roy L. Anderson
David B. Murphy (Costa Mesa Office)
James C. Brooks
Jeffrey M. Olson
Steven D. Hemminger (San Jose Office)
Jerrold B. Reilly
Paul H. Meier
John A. Rafter, Jr.
Kenneth H. Ohriner
Mary S. Consalvi (La Jolla Office)
Lois M. Kwasigroch
Lawrence R. LaPorte
Robert C. Laurenson (La Jolla Office)
Carol A. Schneider

ASSOCIATES

Hope E. Melville
Michael J. Wise
Kurt T. Mulville (Costa Mesa Office)
Theodore S. Maceiko
Richard Warburg (La Jolla Office)
James P. Brogan (Costa Mesa Office)
Jeffrey D. Tekanic
Corrine M. Freeman (Costa Mesa Office)
David A. Randall
Christopher A. Vanderlaan
Bruce G. Chapman
David T. Burse (San Jose Office)
Charles R. Balgenorth
Wayne B. Brown (La Jolla Office)
Jeffrey A. Miller (San Jose Office)
Armand F. Ayazi
Jessica R. Wolff (La Jolla Office)
Mark J. Carlozzi (Costa Mesa Office)
Sheldon O. Heber (La Jolla Office)
Jeffrey William Guise (La Jolla Office)
Charles S. Berkman (La Jolla Office)
Sheryl Rubinstein Silverstein (La Jolla Office)
David E. Wang
Anthony C. Chen (La Jolla Office)
Kenneth S. Roberts (Costa Mesa Office)
Brent D. Sokol
Clarke W. Neumann, Jr. (La Jolla Office)

John C. Kappos (Costa Mesa Office)
Thomas J. Brindisi
Richard C. Hsu
Catherine Joyce
Charles Calvin Fowler (Costa Mesa Office)
Lisa Ward Karmelich
Vicki Gee Norton (La Jolla Office)
Jonathan T. Losk
Timothy J. Lithgow (La Jolla Office)
Michael A. Tomasulo
Thomas R. Rouse
Edward M. Jordan
Charles A. Kertell
James K. Sakaguchi (Costa Mesa Office)
Gary H. Silverstein (La Jolla Office)
Amy Stark Hellenkamp (La Jolla Office)
Richard H. Pagliery
William J. Kolegraff (La Jolla Office)
Andrei Iancu
Jonathan Hallman (La Jolla Office)
Lynn Y. McKernan (San Jose Office)
Michael Bolan (San Jose Office)
Farshad Farjami
Dmitry Milikovsy (San Jose Office)
Gregory R. Stephenson
Howard N. Wisnia (La Jolla Office)
Mary Agnes Tuck
Arlyn Alonzo
Neal Matthew Cohen (Costa Mesa Office)

OF COUNSEL

Bradford J. Duft (La Jolla Office)
Suzanne L. Biggs (La Jolla Office)

F.T. Alexandra Mahaney (La Jolla Office)
Stephen S. Korniczky (La Jolla Office)

Representative Clients: Cedars-Sinai Medical Center; Genentech; Honda; Mag Instrument, Inc.; Mitsubishi; Panavision; Quantum Corporation; Spectra-Physics, Inc

For full biographical listings, see the Martindale-Hubbell Law Directory

Los Angeles—Continued

McDERMOTT, WILL & EMERY (AV)

A Partnership including Professional Corporations
2049 Century Park East, 90067-3208
Telephone: 310-277-4110
Facsimile: 310-277-4730
URL: http://www.mwe.com
Chicago, Illinois Office: 227 West Monroe Street.
Telephone: 312-372-2000.
Facsimile: 312-984-7700.
Boston, Massachusetts Office: 75 State Street, Suite 1700.
Telephone: 617-345-5000.
Facsimile: 617-345-5077.
Miami, Florida Office: 201 South Biscayne Boulevard.
Telephone: 305-358-3500.
Facsimile: 305-347-6500.
Washington, D.C. Office: 1850 K Street, N.W.
Telephone: 202-887-8000.
Facsimile: 202-778-8087.
Newport Beach, California Office: 1301 Dove Street, Suite 500.
Telephone: 714-851-0633.
Facsimile: 714-851-9348.
New York, N.Y. Office: 50 Rockefeller Plaza.
Telephone: 212-547-5508.
Facsimile: 212-547-5444.
St. Petersburg, Russia Office: AOZT McDermott, Will & Emery, Griboyedova Canal 36, 191023, St. Petersburg, Russia.
Telephone: (7) (812) 310-52-44; 310-55-44; 310-59-44; 850-20-45.
Facsimile: (7) (812) 310-54-46; 325-84-50.
Vilnius, Lithuania Office: Smetonos 6, 2600 Vilnius, Lithuania.
Telephone: 370 2 61-43-08.
Facsimile: 370 2 22-79-55.

MEMBERS OF FIRM

Lee L. Blackman   Robert P. Mallory
         Allan L. Schare

For full biographical listings, see the Martindale-Hubbell Law Directory

MITCHELL, SILBERBERG & KNUPP LLP (AV)

A Partnership including Professional Corporations
11377 West Olympic Boulevard, 90064
Telephone: 310-312-2000
Fax: 310-312-3100

MEMBERS OF FIRM

Edward M. Medvene (A   Roy L. Shults (A Professional
Professional Corporation)   Corporation)
Thomas P. Lambert (A
Professional Corporation)

References: Wells Fargo Bank, N.A.; Merrill, Lynch.

For Complete List of Firm Personnel, See General Section

For full biographical listings, see the Martindale-Hubbell Law Directory

O'MELVENY & MYERS LLP (AV)

400 South Hope Street, 90071-2899
Telephone: 213-669-6000
Cable Address: "Moms"
Facsimile: 213-669-6407
Email: omminfo@omm.com
Century City, California Office: 1999 Avenue of the Stars, 90067-6035.
Telephone: 310-553-6700.
Facsimile: 310-246-6779.
Newport Beach, California Office: 610 Newport Center Drive, 92660-6429.
Telephone: 714-760-9600.
Cable Address: "Moms".
Facsimile: 714-669-6994.
San Francisco, California Office: Embarcadero Center West Tower, 275 Battery Street, 94111-3305.
Telephone: 415-984-8700.
Facsimile: 415-984-8701.
New York, New York Office: Citicorp Center, 153 East 53rd Street, 10022-4611.
Telephone: 212-326-2000.
Facsimile: 212-326-2061.
Washington, D.C. Office: 555 13th Street, N.W., 20004-1109.
Telephone: 202-383-5300.
Cable Address: "Moms".
Facsimile: 202-383-5414.
London, England Office: 10 Finsbury Square, London, EC2A 1LA.
Telephone: 0171-256-8451.
Facsimile: 0171-638-8205.
Tokyo, Japan Office: Sanbancho KB-6 Building, 6 Sanbancho, Chiyoda-ku, Tokyo 102, Japan.
Telephone: 03-3239-2900.
Facsimile: 03-3239-2432.
Hong Kong Office: Suite 1905, Peregrine Tower, Lippo Centre, 89 Queensway, Central, Hong Kong.
Telephone: 852-2523-8266.
Facsimile: 852-2522-1760.

(See Next Column)

Shanghai, Peoples Republic of China Office: Shanghai International Trade Centre, Suite 2011, 2200 Yan An Road West, Shanghai, 200335, PRC.
Telephone: 86-21-6219-5363.
Facsimile: 86-21-6275-4949.

PARTNER

Henry C. Thumann

For Complete List of Firm Personnel, See General Section

For full biographical listings, see the Martindale-Hubbell Law Directory

PILLSBURY MADISON & SUTRO LLP (AV)

Citicorp Plaza, 725 South Figueroa Street, Suite 1200, 90017-2513
Telephone: 213-488-7100
Fax: 213-629-1033
Costa Mesa, California Office: Plaza Tower, Suite 1100, 600 Anton Boulevard, 92626.
Telephone: 714-436-6800.
Fax: 714-662-6999.
Silicon Valley Office: 2700 San Hill Road, Menlo Park, 94025.
Telephone: 415-233-4500.
Fax: 415-233-4545.
Sacramento, California Office: 400 Capitol Mall, Suite 1700, 95814.
Telephone: 916-329-4700.
Fax: 916-441-3583.
San Diego, California Office: 101 West Broadway, Suite 1800, 92101.
Telephone: 619-234-5000.
Fax: 619-236-1995.
San Francisco, California Office: 235 Montgomery Street, 94104.
Telephone: 415-983-1000.
Fax: 415-983-1200.
Washington, D.C. Office: 1100 New York Avenue, N.W., Ninth Floor, 20005.
Telephone: 202-861-3000.
Fax: 202-822-0944.
New York, New York Office: 520 Madison Avenue, 40th Floor, 10022.
Telephone: 212-328-4810.
Fax: 212-328-4824. One Liberty Plaza, 165 Broadway, 51st Floor.
Telephone: 212-374-1890.
Fax: 212-374-1852.
Hong Kong Office: 6/F Asia Pacific Finance Tower, Citibank Plaza, 3 Garden Road, Central.
Telephone: 011-852-2509-7100.
Fax: 011-852-2509-7188.
Tokyo, Japan Office: Pillsbury Madison & Sutro, Gaikokuho Jimu Bengoshi Jimusho, 5th Floor, Samon Eleven Building, 3-1, Samon-cho, Shinjuku-ku, Tokyo 160 Japan.
Telephone: 800-729-9830; 011-813-3354-3531.
Fax: 011-813-3354-3534.

MEMBERS OF FIRM

Kenneth R. Chiate   Michael J. Finnegan
Amy D. Hogue   Sidney K. Kanazawa
Jennie L. La Prade   Charles E. Patterson
Patrick G. Rogan   Matthew R. Rogers
         William E. Stoner

ASSOCIATE

William T. Gillespie

For Complete List of Firm Personnel, See General Section

For full biographical listings, see the Martindale-Hubbell Law Directory

SHEPPARD, MULLIN, RICHTER & HAMPTON LLP (AV)

A Limited Liability Partnership including Professional Corporations
Forty-Eighth Floor, 333 South Hope Street, 90071-1448
Telephone: 213-620-1780
Telecopier: 213-620-1398
Cable Address: "Sheplaw"
Email: info@smrh.com *URL:* http://www.smrh.com
Orange County, California Office: 650 Town Center Drive, 4th Floor, Costa Mesa.
Telephone: 714-513-5100.
Telecopier: 714-513-5130. Home Page Address: http://www.smrh.com.
San Francisco, California Office: Seventeenth Floor, Four Embarcadero Center.
Telephone: 415-434-9100.
Telecopier: 415-434-3947. Home Page Address: http://www.smrh.com.
San Diego, California Office: Nineteenth Floor, 501 West Broadway.
Telephone: 619-338-6500.
Telecopier: 619-234-3815. Home Page Address: http://www.smrh.com.

MEMBERS OF FIRM

Robert S. Beall   Robert B. Flaig
(Orange County Office)   Gerald N. Gordon
James R. Brueggemann   Gordon A. Greenberg
James J. Carroll, III *   Andrew J. Guilford
Joseph F. Coyne, Jr.   (Orange County Office)
André J. Cronthall   Gary L. Halling
Joseph A. Darrell   (San Francisco Office)
(San Francisco Office)   Harold E. Hamersmith
Phillip A. Davis   Don T. Hibner, Jr.
Polly Towill Dennis   Gregory A. Long *
Frank Falzetta

(See Next Column)

SHEPPARD, MULLIN, RICHTER & HAMPTON LLP—*Continued*
MEMBERS OF FIRM (Continued)

Charles H. MacNab, Jr.	James L. Sanders
(San Francisco Office)	Pierce T. Selwood *
Paul S. Malingagio	Richard L. Stone
M. Elizabeth McDaniel	Finley L. Taylor
James F. McShane	* (Orange County Office)
James J. Mittermiller	Stephen C. Taylor *
(San Diego Office)	Timothy B. Taylor
Kathyleen A. O'Brien	(San Diego Office)
Stephen J. O'Neil	Carlton A. Varner *
John R. Pennington	Perry Joseph Viscounty
Fred R. Puglisi	(Orange County Office)
Kent R. Raygor	Edward D. Vogel
Paul M. Reitler *	(San Diego Office)
Mark Riera	Michael J. Weaver *
Scott F. Roybal	Darryl M. Woo
John F. Runkel, Jr.	(San Francisco Office)
(San Francisco Office)	Roy G. Wuchitech
Theodore A. Russell	John A. Yacovelle
	(San Diego Office)

SPECIAL COUNSEL

Fredric I. Albert	David A. Pursley
(Orange County Office)	(San Francisco Office)
Thomas M. Brown	Paul F. Rafferty
Frederick V. Geisler	(Orange County Office)

*Professional Corporation

For full biographical listings, see the Martindale-Hubbell Law Directory

---

STEPHENS, BERG & LASATER, A PROFESSIONAL CORPORATION (AV)

1055 West Seventh Street, Twenty-Ninth Floor, 90017
Telephone: 213-629-3111
Telecopy: 213-629-2302; 213-624-4734

Lawrence M. Berg (1947-1995)	Frederick A. Clark
R. Wicks Stephens II	Joel A. Goldman
Richard W. Lasater II	C. Stephen Davis
Mark G. Ancel	Kenneth A. Feinfield
Dudley M. Lang	Jean-Paul Menard
Joseph F. Butler	Michael J. Kaminsky
	John A. Dragonette

OF COUNSEL

Louis R. Baker	J. Lane Tilson

For full biographical listings, see the Martindale-Hubbell Law Directory

---

PALO ALTO, Santa Clara Co.

FTHENAKIS & COLVIN (AV)

540 University Avenue, Suite 300, 94301
Telephone: 415-326-1397
Telecopier: 415-326-3203

MEMBERS OF FIRM

Basil P. Fthenakis	Oliver P. Colvin

For full biographical listings, see the Martindale-Hubbell Law Directory

---

SAN DIEGO, * San Diego Co.

FERRIS & BRITTON, A PROFESSIONAL CORPORATION (AV)

1600 First National Bank Center, 401 West A Street, 92101
Telephone: 619-233-3131
Fax: 619-232-9316

Christopher Q. Britton	Michael R. Weinstein

Representative Clients: Agouron Pharmaceuticals, Inc.; Allstate Insurance Co.; Cox Communications, Inc.; Enterprise Rent-a-Car; Exxon; Invitrogen Corporation; Peninsula Bank; Structural Bioinformatics, Inc.; Teleport Communications Group; Southwest Airlines.

For Complete List of Firm Personnel, See General Section

For full biographical listings, see the Martindale-Hubbell Law Directory

---

THE LAW OFFICES OF STEPHEN P. OGGEL, A P.C. (AV)

111 Elm Street, Suite 400, 92101
Telephone: 619-696-7500
Fax: 619-232-1065

Stephen P. Oggel

Brian J. McCormack

For full biographical listings, see the Martindale-Hubbell Law Directory

---

POST KIRBY NOONAN & SWEAT LLP (AV)

A Partnership including Professional Corporations
America Plaza 600 West Broadway 11th Floor, 92101
Telephone: 619-231-8666
FAX: 619-231-9593;
619-231-4360
Email: PKNS@cert.net

MEMBERS OF FIRM

Gregory A. Post	Stephanie Sontag
Michael L. Kirby (A P.C.)	David B. Oberholtzer
David J. Noonan	Charles T. Hoge
Richard W. Sweat	Natalie C. Venezia
R. Bruce Wayne (A P.C.)	Dickran A. Semerdjian
Thomas W. Bettles	Jeffrey A. Haile
Sandra L. Lackey	James R. Lance
Ross J. Schwartz	Steven W. Sanchez
Lise N. Wilson	Theresa M. Brehl
	Jeffrey P. Lendrum

OF COUNSEL

Paul R. Kennerson

Steven B. Duke	Kristen T. Bruesehoff
Martha O. Anderson	Jonathan A. Boynton
Mary L. Waltari	Ethan T. Boyer
M. E. Stephens	Matthew C. McGrath
Jeffrey A. Unger	Monique Ballard Candor
Kelli A. Hokanson	Jodie M. Hardmeyer
	James R. Ballard

LEGAL SUPPORT PERSONNEL

Laurel E. Scott	Susan O'Keefe Head
Maureen A. McCarthy	(Litigation Paralegal)
Jean D. Billings (Paralegal)	Ruth S. Friis (Paralegal)
Katherine G. Hicks (Paralegal)	Nicole Abrahamson (Paralegal)
	Gail E. Bayley (Paralegal)

For full biographical listings, see the Martindale-Hubbell Law Directory

---

SELTZER CAPLAN WILKINS & McMAHON, A PROFESSIONAL CORPORATION (AV)

2100 Symphony Towers, 750 B Street, 92101
Telephone: 619-685-3003
Fax: 619-685-3100

Gerald L. McMahon	Dennis J. Wickham
Reginald A. Vitek	Michael H. Riney
	David P. Chiappetta

Representative Clients: Chicago Title; Girard Savings Bank; Goodyear Tire & Rubber Co.; W.R. Grace & Co--Conn.; McDonnell-Douglas Corp.; McMillin Communities; Philip Morris Incorporated; Western Financial Savings Bank.

For Complete List of Firm Personnel, See General Section

For full biographical listings, see the Martindale-Hubbell Law Directory

---

SAN FRANCISCO, * San Francisco Co.

LIEFF, CABRASER, HEIMANN & BERNSTEIN, LLP (AV)

Embarcadero Center West, 30th Floor, 275 Battery Street, 94111
Telephone: 415-956-1000
Telecopier: 415-956-1008
Email: mail@lchb.com

Robert L. Lieff	Michael F. Ram
Elizabeth J. Cabraser	Joseph R. Saveri
Richard M. Heimann	Donald C. Arbitblit
William Bernstein	Robert J. Nelson
William B. Hirsch	Jacqueline E. Mottek
James M. Finberg	Morris A. Ratner
Karen E. Karpen	Melanie M. Piech

Richard L. Akel	Anthony K. Lee
Christine J. Anderson	Fabrice V. Nijhof
Kelly M. Dermody	Trina N. Parker
Eric B. Fastiff	Jonathan D. Selbin
Richard M. Franco	Mark N. Todzo
	Heather A. Woodard

For full biographical listings, see the Martindale-Hubbell Law Directory

---

MOLLIGAN, COX & MOYER, A PROFESSIONAL CORPORATION (AV)

703 Market Street, Suite 1800, 94103
Telephone: 415-543-9464
Fax: 415-777-1828
Email: mocoxmoy@aol.com

Ingemar E. Hoberg (1903-1971)	Peter N. Molligan
John H. Finger (1913-1991)	Stephen T. Cox
Phillip E. Brown (Retired)	David W. Moyer

(See Next Column)

MOLLIGAN, COX & MOYER A PROFESSIONAL CORPORATION, *San Francisco—Continued*

John C. Hentschel
OF COUNSEL

Kenneth W. Rosenthal   Barbara A. Zuras

For full biographical listings, see the Martindale-Hubbell Law Directory

ROSEN, BIEN & ASARO (AV)

Eighth Floor, 155 Montgomery Street, 94104
Telephone: 415-433-6830
Fax: 415-433-7104
Email: rba@rbalaw.com

Sanford Jay Rosen   Michael W. Bien
Andrea G. Asaro

Thomas Nolan   William H.D. Fernholz
Donna Petrine   Doris Y. Ng
M.J. Tony Paikeday   A. Marie Villafaña

For full biographical listings, see the Martindale-Hubbell Law Directory

SAVERI AND SAVERI, A PROFESSIONAL CORPORATION (AV)

41st Floor, Spear Street Tower, One Market Plaza, 94105-1001
Telephone: 415-243-4005
Fax: 415-243-4009

Richard Saveri   Guido Saveri

R. Alexander Saveri
OF COUNSEL
John A. Kithas

For full biographical listings, see the Martindale-Hubbell Law Directory

SPIEGEL LIAO & KAGAY (AV)

88 Kearny Street, Suite 1310, 94108-5530
Telephone: 415-956-5959
Telecopier: 415-362-1431

Michael I. Spiegel   Charles M. Kagay
OF COUNSEL
Bartholomew Lee   Wayne M. Liao

For full biographical listings, see the Martindale-Hubbell Law Directory

LAW FIRM OF ROBERT A. SUSK (AV)

333 Bush Street, 26th Floor, 94104
Telephone: 415-982-3950
Fax: 415-982-6143

Robert A. Susk   Leslie J. Mann
ASSOCIATE
Jeffrey A. Glick

For full biographical listings, see the Martindale-Hubbell Law Directory

*SAN JOSE,** Santa Clara Co.

BERGESON, ELIOPOULOS, GRADY & GRAY (AV)

Ten Almaden Boulevard, Suite 200, 95113
Telephone: 408-291-6200
Fax: 408-297-6000
Email: BEGG215958@AOL.Com

Daniel J. Bergeson   Richard J. Gray
William T. Eliopoulos   Mary Anne Rodgers
Michael F. Grady   John L. Antracoli
ASSOCIATES
Donald P. Gagliardi   Siobhán Lawlor
Mark E. Waite   John P. Shinn

For full biographical listings, see the Martindale-Hubbell Law Directory

McMANIS, FAULKNER & MORGAN (AV)

160 West Santa Clara Street, 10th Floor, 95113
Telephone: 408-279-8700
Fax: 408-279-3244; 408-279-0494
Email: mfm@mfmlaw.com
MEMBERS OF FIRM
James McManis   William Faulkner
Donelle Morgan

(See Next Column)

ASSOCIATES
Nora Rousso   Michael Reedy
Lisa Herrick   Douglas Watanabe
Kelly McHaffie

For full biographical listings, see the Martindale-Hubbell Law Directory

COLORADO

*DENVER,** Denver Co.

DUFFORD & BROWN, P.C. (AV)

1700 Broadway, Suite 1700, 80290-1701
Telephone: 303-861-8013
Facsimile: 303-832-3804
Affiliated Office: Solomon, Pearl, Blum & Quinn, L.L.P., New York, NY and Denver, Colorado.

Thomas G. Brown   David W. Furgason
Edward D. White

Representative Clients: CF&I Steel, L.P.; The Colorado and Wyoming Railway Co.

For Complete List of Firm Personnel, See General Section

For full biographical listings, see the Martindale-Hubbell Law Directory

JONES & KELLER, A PROFESSIONAL CORPORATION (AV)

Suite 1600, 1625 Broadway, 80202
Telephone: 303-573-1600
Fax: 303-893-6506

Marion F. Jones (1898-1978)   Thomas J. Burke, Jr.
Alec J. Keller (1913-1995)   Samuel E. Wing
Alvin J. Meiklejohn, Jr.   Reid A. Godbolt
Leslie R. Kehl   Rodney D. Knutson
Edward T. Lyons, Jr.   Kevin L. Brown
David E. Driggers   Barry L. Wilkie

Howard R. Hertzberg   Brent Nicholls
David A. Thayer   Michael Brian Cavanaugh
Nathan D. Simmons

Reference: Colorado State Bank; Union Bank & Trust.

For full biographical listings, see the Martindale-Hubbell Law Directory

REIMAN & BAYAZ, P.C. (AV)

1600 Broadway, Suite 1640, 80202
Telephone: 303-860-1500
Fax: 303-839-4380

Jeff Reiman   Marcie K. Bayaz

Darren E. Temkin-Nadel   Eric B. Liebman

For full biographical listings, see the Martindale-Hubbell Law Directory

SHERMAN & HOWARD L.L.C. (AV)

Attorneys and Counselors at Law
633 Seventeenth Street, Suite 3000, 80202
Telephone: 303-297-2900
Telecopier: 303-298-0940
Colorado Springs, Colorado Office: Suite 1500, 90 South Cascade Avenue, 80903.
Telephone: 719-475-2440.
Las Vegas, Nevada Office: Swendseid & Stern a member in Sherman & Howard L.L.C., 317 Sixth Street, 89101.
Telephone: 702-387-6073.
Reno, Nevada Office: Swendseid & Stern, a member in Sherman & Howard L.L.C., 50 West Liberty Street, Suite 660, 89501.
Telephone: 702-323-1980.

James E. Hautzinger   Paul Curtis Daw

Representative Clients: AT&T Corp.; Newmont Gold Corp.; Keystone Resort; Tele-Communications, Inc.; VICORP Restaurants, Inc.

For Complete List of Firm Personnel, See General Section

For full biographical listings, see the Martindale-Hubbell Law Directory

WALTERS & JOYCE, P.C. (AV)

2015 York Street, 80205
Telephone: 303-322-1404
FAX: 303-377-5668

William E. Walters, III
Reference: Norwest Bank of Buckingham Square.

(See Next Column)

WALTERS & JOYCE P.C.—*Continued*

For Complete List of Firm Personnel, See General Section

For full biographical listings, see the Martindale-Hubbell Law Directory

CONNECTICUT

HARTFORD, * Hartford Co.

SOROKIN SOROKIN GROSS HYDE & WILLIAMS P.C. (AV)

One Corporate Center, 06103
Telephone: 860-525-6645
Fax: 860-522-1781
Simsbury, Connecticut Office: 730 Hopmeadow Street.
Telephone: 860-651-9348.
Rocky Hill, Connecticut Office: 2360 Main Street.
Telephone: 860-563-9305.
Fax: 860-529-6931.

Clifford J. Grandjean   Richard C. Robinson

For Complete List of Firm Personnel, See General Section

For full biographical listings, see the Martindale-Hubbell Law Directory

NEW HAVEN, * New Haven Co.

WIGGIN & DANA (AV)

One Century Tower, 06508-1832
Telephone: 203-498-4400
Telefax: 203-782-2889
Hartford, Connecticut Office: One CityPlace.
Telephone: 203-297-3700.
FAX: 203-525-9380.
Stamford, Connecticut Office: Three Stamford Plaza, 301 Tresser
Boulevard.
Telephone: 203-363-7600.
Telefax: 203-363-7676.

MEMBERS OF FIRM

Shaun S. Sullivan   Patrick J. Monahan, II
Mark R. Kravitz   (Resident at Hartford)
Edward Wood Dunham   Robert M. Langer
William G. Millman, Jr.   (Resident at Hartford)

ASSOCIATES

Michelle Wilcox DeBarge   Thomas J. Witt
Merton G. Gollaher   (Resident at Hartford)
Lynn F. Guelzow
  (Resident at Hartford)

For Complete List of Firm Personnel, See General Section

For full biographical listings, see the Martindale-Hubbell Law Directory

DISTRICT OF COLUMBIA

WASHINGTON, D.C. Co.

* indicates certain Bar Register subscribers, in cities of comparable size and importance, who maintain an additional office in Washington, D.C. and who have arranged for representation as a part of the Washington, D.C. listings that follow

BAKER & HOSTETLER (AV)

Washington Square, Suite 1100, 1050 Connecticut Avenue,
  N.W., 20036-5304
Telephone: 202-861-1500
In Cleveland, Ohio: 3200 National City Center, 1900 East Ninth Street.
Telephone: 216-621-0200.
In Columbus, Ohio: Capitol Square, Suite 2100, 65 East State Street.
Telephone: 614-228-1541.
In Denver, Colorado: 303 East 17th Avenue, Suite 1100.
Telephone: 303-861-0600.
In Houston, Texas: 1000 Louisiana, Suite 2000.
Telephone: 713-751-1600.
In Long Beach, California: 300 Oceangate, Suite 620.
Telephone: 310-432-2827.
In Los Angeles, California: 600 Wilshire Boulevard.
Telephone: 213-624-2400.
In Orlando, Florida: SunBank Center, Suite 2300, 200 South Orange
Avenue.
Telephone: 305-841-1111.
In College Park, Maryland: 9658 Baltimore Boulevard, Suite 206.
Telephone: 301-441-2781.
In Alexandria, Virginia: 437 North Lee Street.
Telephone: 703-549-1294.

(See Next Column)

In San Francisco, California: One Sansome Street, Suite 2000.
Telephone: 415-951-4705.

PARTNERS

Gerald A. Connell   Lee H. Simowitz
Louis R. Sernoff   Alan S. Ward

ASSOCIATE

Jenifer M. Brown

For Complete List of Firm Personnel, See General Section

For full biographical listings, see the Martindale-Hubbell Law Directory

* BELL, BOYD & LLOYD (AV)

1615 L Street, N.W., 20036
Telephone: 202-466-6300
FAX: 202-463-0678
Chicago, Illinois Office: Three First National Plaza, Suite 3300, 70 West
Madison Street.
Telephone: 312-372-1121.
FAX: 312-372-2098.

RESIDENT PARTNER

Charles A. Zielinski (Not admitted in DC)

OF COUNSEL

Andrew I. Gavil

RESIDENT ASSOCIATES

Anthony M. Black   Ross A. Buntrock
                                  (Not admitted in DC)

For Complete List of Firm Personnel, See General Section

For full biographical listings, see the Martindale-Hubbell Law Directory

COHEN, MILSTEIN, HAUSFELD & TOLL, P.L.L.C. (AV)

West Tower, Suite 500, 1100 New York Avenue, N.W., 20005-3964
Telephone: 202-408-4600
Facsimile: 202-408-4699

MEMBERS OF FIRM

Jerry S. Cohen (1925-1995)   Lisa M. Mezzetti
Herbert E. Milstein   Andrew N. Friedman
Michael D. Hausfeld   Richard S. Lewis
Steven J. Toll   Daniel S. Sommers
Ann C. Yahner   Daniel A. Small
                                  (Not admitted in DC)

ASSOCIATES

Gary E. Mason   Michael J. Flannery
Cyrus Mehri   Paul T. Gallagher
Sharon A. Snyder   Alexander E. Barnett
Mark S. Willis   Angeline G. Chen
  (Not admitted in DC)   Victoria C. Arthaud
Lillian S. Hagen   (Not admitted in DC)

OF COUNSEL

Anthony Z. Roisman

For full biographical listings, see the Martindale-Hubbell Law Directory

DOW, LOHNES & ALBERTSON, PLLC (AV)

1200 New Hampshire Avenue, N.W. Suite 800, 20036-6802
Telephone: 202-776-2000
Facsimile: 202-776-2222
Email: postmaster@dla.com *URL:* http://www.dlalaw.com
Atlanta, Georgia Office: One Ravinia Drive, Suite 1600.
Telephone: 770-901-8800.
Telecopier: 770-901-8874.

MEMBERS OF THE FIRM

Jonathan D. Hart   James A. Treanor, III

For Complete List of Firm Personnel, See General Section

For full biographical listings, see the Martindale-Hubbell Law Directory

DUNAWAY & CROSS, A PROFESSIONAL CORPORATION (AV)

Suite 400, 1146 19th Street, N.W., 20036
Telephone: 202-862-9700
Fax: 202-862-9710

Mac S. Dunaway   George C. Courtot
Gary E. Cross   Michael P. Bentzen
                  Stanley J. Green

Matthew F. Hall   Raymond B. Grochowski
Christopher E. Anders   Cary W. Mergele

COUNSEL

Raymond P. Shafer (Not admitted in DC)

For full biographical listings, see the Martindale-Hubbell Law Directory

Washington—Continued

* JONES, DAY, REAVIS & POGUE (AV)

Metropolitan Square, 1450 G Street, N.W., 20005-2088
Telephone: 202-879-3939
Cable Address: "Attorneys Washington"
Telex: W.U. (Domestic) 89-2410 ATTORNEYS WASH (International)
64363 ATTORNEYS WASH
Telecopier: 202-737-2832
In Atlanta, Georgia: 3500 One Peachtree Center, 303 Peachtree Street, N.E
.
Telephone: 404-521-3939.
Cable Address: "Attorneys Atlanta".
Telex: 54-2711.
Telecopier: 404-581-8330.
In Brussels, Belgium: Avenue Louise 480, 7th Floor, B-1050 Brussels.
Telephone: 32-2-645-14-11.
Telecopier: 32-2-645-14-45.
In Chicago, Illinois: 77 West Wacker.
Telephone: 312-782-3939.
Telecopier: 312-782-8585.
In Cleveland, Ohio: North Point, 901 Lakeside Avenue.
Telephone: 216-586-3939.
Cable Address: "Attorneys Cleveland."
Telex: 980389.
Telecopier: 216-579-0212.
In Columbus, Ohio: 1900 Huntington Center.
Telephone: 614-469-3939.
Cable Address: "Attorneys Columbus."
Telecopier: 614-461-4198.
In Dallas, Texas: 2300 Trammell Crow Center, 2001 Ross Avenue.
Telephone: 214-220-3939.
Cable Address: "Attorneys Dallas."
Telex: 730852.
Telecopier: 214-969-5100.
In Frankfurt, Germany: Triton Haus, Bockenheimer Landstrasse 42, 60323 Frankfurt am Main.
Telephone: 49-69-9726-3939.
Telecopier: 49-69-9726-3993.
In Geneva, Switzerland: 20, rue de Candolle.
Telephone: 41-22-320-2339.
Telecopier: 41-22-320-1232.
In Hong Kong: 29th Floor, Entertainment Building, 30 Queen's Road Central.
Telephone: 852-2526-6895.
Telecopier: 852-2868-5871.
In Irvine, California: 2603 Main Street, Suite 900 .
Telephone: 714-851-3939.
Telex: 194911 Lawyers LSA.
Telecopier: 714-553-7539.
In London, England: One Mount Street.
Telephone: 44-71-493-9361.
Cable Address: "Surgoe London WI."
Telecopier: 44-71-493-9666.
In Los Angeles, California: 555 West Fifth Street, Suite 4600.
Telephone: 213-489-3939.
Telex: 181439 UD.
Telecopier: 213-243-2539.
In New Delhi, India: Pathak & Associates, 13th Floor, Dr. Gopal Das Bhaven, 28 Barakhamba Road.
Telephone: 91-11-373-8793.
Telecopier: 91-11-335-3761.
In New York, New York: 599 Lexington Avenue.
Telephone: 212-326-3939.
Cable Address: "JONESDAY NEWYORK."
Telex: 237013 JDRP UR.
Telecopier: 212-755-7306.
In Paris, France: 62, rue du Faubourg Saint-Honore.
Telephone: 33-1-44-71-3939.
Cable Address: "Surgoe Paris."
Telex: 290156 Surgoe.
Telecopier: 33-1-49-24-0471.
In Pittsburgh, Pennsylvania: 500 Grant Street, 31st Floor.
Telephone: 412-391-3939.
Cable Address: "Attorneys Pittsburgh".
Telecopier: 412-394-7959.
In Riyadh, Saudi Arabia: Law Offices of Saud M.A. Shawwaf, P.O. Box 22166.
Telephone: (966-1) 462-8866.
Telex: 401831 SAUCON SJ.
Telecopier: (966-1) 462-9001.
In Taipai, Taiwan: 8th Floor, 2 Tun Hwa South Road, Section 2.
Telephone: (886-2) 704-6808.
Telecopier: (886-2) 704-6791.
In Tokyo, Japan: Toranomon MT Building, 4th Floor, 10-3, Toranomon 3-Chome, Minato-Ku, Tokyo 105, Japan.
Telephone: 81-3-3433-3939.
Telecopier: 81-3-5401-2725.

(See Next Column)

MEMBERS OF FIRM IN WASHINGTON, D.C.

Joe Sims	Toby G. Singer
Tom D. Smith	Kathryn M. Fenton
Phillip A. Proger	Kevin D. McDonald
Thomas F. Cullen, Jr.	Charles A. James
George T. Manning	William V. O'Reilly

OF COUNSEL
William E. Swope

SENIOR ATTORNEY
Robert C. Jones

ASSOCIATES

James E. Anklam	Gregory G. Katsas
Darryl R. Marsch	Peter J. Love

For Complete List of Firm Personnel, See General Section

For full biographical listings, see the Martindale-Hubbell Law Directory

---

* McDERMOTT, WILL & EMERY (AV)

A Partnership including Professional Corporations
1850 K Street, N.W., 20006-2296
Telephone: 202-887-8000
Facsimile: 202-778-8087
URL: http://www.mwe.com
Chicago, Illinois Office: 227 West Monroe Street.
Telephone: 312-372-2000.
Facsimile: 312-984-7700.
Boston, Massachusetts Office: 75 State Street, Suite 1700.
Telephone: 617-345-5000.
Facsimile: 617-345-5077.
Miami, Florida Office: 201 South Biscayne Boulevard.
Telephone: 305-358-3500.
Facsimile: 305-347-6500.
Los Angeles, California Office: 2049 Century Park East.
Telephone: 310-277-4110.
Facsimile: 310-277-4730.
Newport Beach, California Office: 1301 Dove Street, Suite 500.
Telephone: 714-851-0633.
Facsimile: 714-851-9348.
New York, N.Y. Office: 50 Rockefeller Plaza.
Telephone: 212-547-5508.
Facsimile: 212-547-5444.
St. Petersburg, Russia Office: AOZT McDermott, Will & Emery, Griboyedova Canal 36, 191023, St. Petersburg, Russia.
Telephone: (7) (812) 310-52-44; 310-55-44; 310-59-44; 850-20-45.
Facsimile: (7) (812) 310-54-46; 325-84-50.
Vilnius, Lithuania Office: Smetonos 6, 2600 Vilnius, Lithuania.
Telephone: 370 2 61-43-08.
Facsimile: 370 2 22-79-55.

MEMBERS OF FIRM

William H. Barrett	Robert S. Schwartz
Jeanne A. Carpenter	Carl W. Schwarz
Seth D. Greenstein	James H. Sneed
Amy E. Hancock	Timothy J. Waters
Paul J. Pantano, Jr.	John P. Wintrol

COUNSEL
Ronald A. Bloch

For full biographical listings, see the Martindale-Hubbell Law Directory

---

ROYLANCE, ABRAMS, BERDO & GOODMAN, L.L.P. (AV)

1225 Connecticut Avenue, N.W., 20036-2680
Telephone: 202-659-9076
Cable Address: "Roypat"
Telex: 64416
Facsimile: 202-659-9344
Email: RABG@roylance.com

D. C. Roylance (1920-1995)	David L. Tarnoff
David S. Abrams	Michael T. Murphy
Robert H. Berdo	Garrett V. Davis
Alfred N. Goodman	Stacey J. Longanecker
Mark S. Bicks	(Not admitted in DC)
Richard A. Flynt	Thomas P. Hilliard
John E. Holmes	(Not admitted in DC)

SENIOR OF COUNSEL
Frank E. Robbins

OF COUNSEL
Susan Neuberger Weller

For full biographical listings, see the Martindale-Hubbell Law Directory

Washington—Continued

STEPTOE & JOHNSON LLP (AV)

1330 Connecticut Avenue, N.W., 20036
Telephone: 202-429-3000
Cable Address: "Stepjohn"
Telex: 89-2503
Telecopier: 202-429-3902
Email: wbatterton@steptoe.com *URL:* http://www.steptoe.com
Phoenix, Arizona Office: Two Renaissance Square, 40 N. Central Avenue,
Suite 2400, 85004.
Telephone: 602-257-5200.
Moscow, Russia Office: Steptoe & Johnson International AOZT. 25
Tsvetnoy Boulevard, Building 3 Moscow, Russia 103051.
Telephone: 011-7-501-258-5250.
Fax: 011-7-501-258-5251.
Almaty, Kazakhstan Office: Steptoe & Johnson Company Almaty. 84
Gogol Street, Suite 213, 480083.
Telephones: (3272) 50-11-25, (3272) 32-25-39.

MEMBERS

Betty Jo Christian	Robert W. Fleishman
Robert E. Jordan III	Mark F. Horning
Richard O. Cunningham	Ellen M. McNamara
David L. Roll	Timothy M. Walsh
Richard H. Porter	Stephen A. Fennell
Daniel J. Plaine	Samuel M. Sipe, Jr.
John R. Labovitz	Philip L. Malet
F. Michael Kail	Edward J. Krauland

John D. Graubert

OF COUNSEL

Richard A. Whiting	Richard Diamond

For Complete List of Firm Personnel, See General Section

For full biographical listings, see the Martindale-Hubbell Law Directory

* VENABLE ATTORNEYS AT LAW VENABLE, BAETJER, HOWARD & CIVILETTI, LLP (AV)

A Partnership including Professional Corporations
Suite 1000, 1201 New York Avenue, N.W., 20005
Telephone: 202-962-4800
Fax: 202-962-8300
Baltimore, Maryland Office: Venable, Baetjer and Howard LLP, 1800
Mercantile Bank & Trust Building, 2 Hopkins Plaza.
Telephone: 410-244-7400.
McLean, Virginia Office: Venable, Baetjer and Howard LLP, Suite 400,
2010 Corporate Ridge.
Telephone: 703-760-1600.
Rockville, Maryland Office: Venable, Baetjer and Howard LLP, Suite 500,
One Church Street, P. O. Box 1906.
Telephone: 301-217-5600.
Towson, Maryland Office: Venable, Baetjer and Howard LLP, 210
Allegheny Avenue, P. O. Box 5517.
Telephone: 410-494-6200.

MEMBERS OF FIRM

Benjamin R. Civiletti (P.C.) (Also at Baltimore and Towson, Maryland Offices)	James K. Archibald (Also at Baltimore, Maryland Office)
Douglas D. Connah, Jr. (P.C.) (Also at Baltimore, Maryland Office)	James R. Myers
	Jeffrey D. Knowles
	William D. Coston
Kenneth C. Bass, III (Also at McLean, Virginia Office)	Maurice Baskin
	Amy Berman Jackson
Edward F. Glynn, Jr.	William D. Quarles (Also at Towson, Maryland Office)
Michael Schatzow (Also at Baltimore, Maryland Office)	

ASSOCIATE

David W. Goewey

For Complete List of Firm Personnel, See General Section

For full biographical listings, see the Martindale-Hubbell Law Directory

WILMER, CUTLER & PICKERING (AV)

2445 M Street, N.W., 20037-1420
Telephone: 202-663-6000
Fax: 202-663-6363
Email: Law@Wilmer.Com
Baltimore, Maryland Office: 100 Light Street, 21202.
Telephone: 410-986-2800.
Fax: 410-986-2828.
European Offices:
4 Carlton Gardens, London, SW1Y 5AA, England. *Telephone:* +44 (171)
872-1000.
Fax: +44 (171) 839-3537.
Rue de la Loi 15Wetstraat, B-1040 Brussels, Belgium. *Telephone:* +32 (2)
285-4900.
Fax: +32 (2) 285-4949.
Friedrichstrasse 95, D-10117 Berlin, Germany. *Telephone:* +49 (30)
2022-6400.
Fax: +49 (30)2022-6500.

(See Next Column)

MEMBERS OF FIRM

Daniel K. Mayers	John Rounsaville, Jr.
James S. Campbell	James S. Venit (Not admitted in DC; Resident, European Office, Brussels, Belgium)
Ronald J. Greene	
Gary D. Wilson	
C. Loring Jetton, Jr.	
William J. Kolasky, Jr.	Dr. Andreas Weitbrecht (Resident, European Office, Brussels, Belgium)

COUNSEL

John J. Kallaugher (Resident, European Office, London, England)

OF COUNSEL

Robert A. Hammond, III

For Complete List of Firm Personnel, See General Section

For full biographical listings, see the Martindale-Hubbell Law Directory

---

FLORIDA

FORT LAUDERDALE, * Broward Co.

LAW PRACTICE OF J.B. GROSSMAN, P.A. (AV)

2300 East Las Olas Boulevard Fourth Floor, 33301
Telephone: 954-767-3345
Fax: 954-767-3347

J.B. Grossman	Kenneth J. Dunn
Gary Arnold Feder	Blaine H. Hibberd

LEGAL SUPPORT PERSONNEL

Scott L. Lampert

For full biographical listings, see the Martindale-Hubbell Law Directory

---

KISSIMMEE, * Osceola Co.

POHL & SHORT, P.A.

(See Winter Park)

MIAMI, * Dade Co.

KENNY NACHWALTER SEYMOUR ARNOLD CRITCHLOW & SPECTOR, PROFESSIONAL ASSOCIATION (AV)

1100 Miami Center, 201 South Biscayne Boulevard, 33131-4327
Telephone: 305-373-1000
Facsimile: 305-372-1861
ABA/net: 18338
Email: 7502552@MCIMAIL.COM
Rogersville, Tennessee Office: 107 East Main Street, Suite 301, 37857-3347.
Telephone: 423-272-5300.
Facsimile: 423-272-4961.

James J. Kenny	Kevin J. Murray
Michael Nachwalter	William J. Blechman
Richard Alan Arnold	Harry R. Schafer
Brian F. Spector	David H. Lichter

Scott E. Perwin

Representative Clients: Albertson's, Inc.; American Stores; A&P, Inc.; Cartier, Inc.; GTE Directories; The Kroger Co.; Nestle Food Co.; Safeway, Inc.; GTE Florida.

For Complete List of Firm Personnel, See General Section

For full biographical listings, see the Martindale-Hubbell Law Directory

McDERMOTT, WILL & EMERY (AV)

A Partnership including Professional Corporations
201 South Biscayne Boulevard, 33131-4336
Telephone: 305-358-3500
Facsimile: 305-347-6500
URL: http://www.mwe.com
Chicago, Illinois Office: 227 West Monroe Street.
Telephone: 312-372-2000.
Facsimile: 312-984-7700.
Boston, Massachusetts Office: 75 State Street, Suite 1700.
Telephone: 617-345-5000.
Facsimile: 617-345-5077.
Washington, D.C. Office: 1850 K Street, N.W.
Telephone: 202-887-8000.
Facsimile: 202-778-8087.
Los Angeles, California Office: 2049 Century Park East.
Telephone: 310-277-4110.
Facsimile: 310-277-4730.
Newport Beach, California Office: 1301 Dove Street, Suite 500.
Telephone: 714-851-0633.
Facsimile: 714-851-9348.
New York, N.Y. Office: 50 Rockefeller Plaza.
Telephone: 212-547-5508.
Facsimile: 212-547-5444.

(See Next Column)

McDermott, Will & Emery, *Miami—Continued*

St. Petersburg, Russia Office: AOZT McDermott, Will & Emery, Griboyedova Canal 36, 191023 St. Petersburg, Russia.
Telephone: (7) (812) 310-52-44; 310-55-44; 310-59-44; 850-20-45.
Facsimile: (7) (812) 310-54-46; 325-84-50.
Vilnius, Lithuania Office: Smetonos 6, 2600 Vilnius, Lithuania.
Telephone: 370 2 61-43-08.
Facsimile: 370 2 22-79-55.

MEMBER OF FIRM
Steven E. Siff *

*Denotes a lawyer employed by a Professional Corporation which is a member of the Firm.

For full biographical listings, see the Martindale-Hubbell Law Directory

SHUTTS & BOWEN (AV)

A Partnership including Professional Associations
1500 Miami Center, 201 South Biscayne Boulevard, 33131
Telephone: 305-358-6300
Telefax: 305-381-9982
URL: HTTP://WWW.LAWWORLD.COM/SHUTTS/
Orlando, Florida Office: 20 North Orange Avenue, Suite 1000.
Telephone: 407-423-3200.
Fax: 407-425-8316.
West Palm Beach, Florida Office: One Clearlake Centre, 250 Australian Avenue, Suite 500.
Telephone: 561-835-8500.
Fax: 561-650-8530.
Amsterdam, The Netherlands Office: Shutts & Bowen, B.V., Europa Boulevard 59, 1083 AD, Amsterdam.
Telephone: (31 20) 661-0969.
Fax: (31 20) 642-1475.
London, England Office: 43 Grosvenor Street, London W1X 9PG.
Telephone: 441-71-493-4840.
Telefax: 441-71-493-4299.

MEMBERS OF FIRM

Frank B. Shutts (1870-1947)
Crate D. Bowen (1871-1959)
Gary M. Bagliebter
Arnold L. Berman (Resident at West Palm Beach Office)
Joseph D. Bolton
Bowman Brown (P.A.)
Andrew M. Brumby (Resident at Orlando Office)
Judith A. Burke
Sheila M. Cesarano
Gary J. Cohen
Jonathan Cohen
Kevin D. Cowan
Luis A. de Armas
Jean-Charles Dibbs
James F. Durham, II
James A. Farrell (Resident at West Palm Beach Office)
Charles Robinson Fawsett (P.A.)
Robert G. Fracasso, Jr.
Robert A. Freyer (Resident at Orlando Office)
Roger Friedbauer
David A. Gart (Resident at West Palm Beach Office)
Andrew L. Gordon
Michael L. Gore (Resident at Orlando Office)
Michael J. Grindstaff (P.A.) (Resident at Orlando Office)
Robert E. Gunn (P.A.) (Resident at West Palm Beach Office)
Edmund T. Henry, III
Mary Ruth Houston (Resident at Orlando Office)
William N. Jacobs
Rod Jones (Resident at Orlando Office)
John Thomas Kolinski

Richard M. Leslie (P.A.)
Maxine Master Long
Don A. Lynn (P.A.)
Lee D. Mackson
Antonio Martinez, Jr., (P.A.)
David B. McCrea (P.A.)
Joseph F. McSorley (Resident at West Palm Beach Office)
John E. Meagher
Arthur J. Menor (Resident at West Palm Beach Office)
C. Richard Morgan
Timothy J. Murphy
Phillip G. Newcomm (P.A.)
Louis Nostro
Harold E. Patricoff Jr.
Geoffrey Randall
Margaret A. Rolando
Allan M. Rubin
Raul J. Salas
Robert A. Savill (Resident at Orlando Office)
John C. Shawde
Alfred G. Smith, II
William F. Smith
Robert C. Sommerville (P.A.) (Resident; West Palm Beach Office)
Xavier L. Suarez
Robert A. Wainger
Joseph Donald Wasil
Robert Wexler (Resident at West Palm Beach Office)
John B. White (P.A.)
James G. Willard (Resident at Orlando Office)
Scott G. Williams (Resident at West Palm Beach Office)
Kenneth W. Wright (Resident at Orlando Office)
Robert T. Wright, Jr.

ASSOCIATES

Suzanne M. Amaducci (Resident at Orlando Office)
Maria J. Beguiristain
Christopher W. Boyett
Thomas P. Callan (Resident at Orlando Office)
Gregory L. Denes
Terry B. Fein
Emilio Fernandez
Jonathan D. Gerber (Resident at West Palm Beach Office)
Robert B. Goldman (Resident at West Palm Beach Office)
David S. Goldstein
Joseph M. Goldstein

René J. González-Llorens
Bradley S. Gould
Meredith A. Harper (Resident at Orlando Office)
Marc J. Jason (Resident at Orlando Office)
Brian M. Jones (Resident, Orlando Office)
Jeffrey M. Landau
Lourdes B. Martinez-Esquivel
William G. Mc Cullough
Patrick M. Muldowney (Resident at Orlando Office)
Michelle R. North (Resident at West Palm Beach Office)

(See Next Column)

ASSOCIATES (Continued)

Aileen Ortega
Dario A. Perez
Bryan S. Wells
Joey Schlosberg
Geoffrey L. Travis

OF COUNSEL

Jordan Bittel (P.A.)
John S. Chowning (P.A.)
John R. Day (P.A.)
Stephen J. Gray (Resident, London, England Office)
Marshall J. Langer (P.A.) (Resident, London, England Office)
Alexander Penelas
Stephen L. Perrone (P.A.)
Preston L. Prevatt
Rosemarie N. Sanderson Schade (P.A.) (Resident at Amsterdam, The Netherlands)

CONSULTING ATTORNEY
Patrick L. Murray (Not admitted in the United States)

Representative Clients: Southern Bell Telephone Co.; BellSouth Advertising & Publishing Co.; General Electric Co.; Equitable Life Assurance Society of the U.S.; New England Mutual Life Insurance Co.; New York Life Insurance Co.; Dadeland Bank.

For full biographical listings, see the Martindale-Hubbell Law Directory

ORLANDO,* Orange Co.

POHL & SHORT, P.A.

(See Winter Park)

TAMPA,* Hillsborough Co.

MICHAEL C. ADDISON (AV)

Suite 2175, 100 North Tampa Street, 33602-5145
Telephone: 813-223-2000
Facsimile: 813-228-6000
Mailing Address: P.O. Box 2175, Tampa, Florida, 33601-2175
Email: 72100.337@compuserve.com

For full biographical listings, see the Martindale-Hubbell Law Directory

WEST PALM BEACH,* Palm Beach Co.

BURT & PUCILLO (AV)

Esperanté, Suite 300 East, 222 Lakeview Avenue, 33401
Telephone: 407-835-9400
Telecopier: 407-835-0322

MEMBERS OF FIRM

C. Oliver Burt, III
Michael J. Pucillo
Wendy Hope Zoberman

ASSOCIATE
Leo W. Desmond

OF COUNSEL

Carol McLean Brewer
Lauren S. Dadario

For full biographical listings, see the Martindale-Hubbell Law Directory

WINTER PARK, Orange Co.

DEMPSEY & ASSOCIATES, P.A. (AV)

Suite 200, 1031 West Morse Boulevard, 32789
Telephone: 407-740-7778
Telecopier: 407-740-0911

Bernard H. Dempsey, Jr.
Michael C. Sasso

Frederick C. Barnes
Daniel N. Brodersen
Peter Francis Carr, Jr.

For full biographical listings, see the Martindale-Hubbell Law Directory

POHL & SHORT, P.A. (AV)

280 West Canton Avenue, Suite 410, P.O. Box 3208, 32790
Telephone: 407-647-7645; 407-647-POHL
Telefax: 407-647-2314

Frank L. Pohl
Houston E. Short
Dwight I. Cool
James Everett Shepherd V
John R. Simpson, Jr.
C. Teresa de Arrigoitia
George A. Golder
Norma Stanley
Mark W. Garrett

Representative Clients: American Pioneer Title Insurance Company; Institute of Internal Auditors, Inc.; Thompson Steel, Inc.; SunTrust, N.A.; The Bank of Winter Park; Bekins Moving and Storage Co., Inc.; Champion Boats, Inc.; KeyCom Telephone Systems, Inc.

For full biographical listings, see the Martindale-Hubbell Law Directory

GEORGIA

---

*ATLANTA,** Fulton Co.

ALSTON & BIRD (AV)

A Partnership including Professional Corporations
One Atlantic Center, 1201 West Peachtree Street, 30309-3424
Telephone: 404-881-7000
Telecopier: 404-881-7777
Cable Address: AMGRAM GA
Telex: 54-2996
Easylink: 62985848
Washington, D.C. Office: 601 Pennsylvania Ave., N.W., North Building, Suite 250 20004.
Telephone: 202-508-3300.
Telecopier: 202-508-3333.

MEMBERS OF FIRM

Michael A. Doyle	H. Stephen Harris, Jr.
John K. Train III	Michael P. Kenny
Peter Kontio	Randall L. Allen
Kevin E. Grady	William R. Mitchelson Jr.
Frank G. Smith III	James J. Wolfson
Martin J. Elgison	Beth K. Toberman

ASSOCIATES

Julia L. Bassett	Philip R. Stein
John P. Fry	David J. Stewart
Elise Kirban	Teresa D. Thebaut
(Not admitted in GA)	M. Russell Wofford, Jr.
Jason Klitenic	(Not admitted in GA)
H. Suzanne Smith	Susan L. Wright

COUNSEL
J. Kennard Neal

Representative Clients: American Airlines, Inc.; Boral Industries; Borden, Inc.; CIGNA Corporation; Citibank, FSB; Genuine Parts Company; Goodyear Tire & Rubber Co.; GTE Personal Communications Services; Mohawk Industries.

For Complete List of Firm Personnel, See General Section

For full biographical listings, see the Martindale-Hubbell Law Directory

---

BONDURANT, MIXSON & ELMORE, LLP (AV)

1201 W. Peachtree Street Suite 3900, 30309
Telephone: 404-881-4100
FAX: 404-881-4111

MEMBERS OF FIRM

Emmet J. Bondurant II	Dirk G. Christensen
H. Lamar Mixson	Jane E. Fahey
M. Jerome Elmore	John E. Floyd
Edward B. Krugman	Michael A. Sullivan
Jeffrey O. Bramlett	Michael B. Terry

Representative Clients: The Aetna Casualty and Surety Company; Blue Circle of America; Circle K; Conoco, Inc.; Delta Air Lines, Inc.; Queen Carpets, Inc.; Sanifill, Inc.; Ticketmaster; Trammell Crow Co.; Wylie Laboratories.

For full biographical listings, see the Martindale-Hubbell Law Directory

---

JONES, DAY, REAVIS & POGUE (AV)

3500 One Peachtree Center, 303 Peachtree Street, N.E., 30308-3242
Telephone: 404-521-3939
Cable Address: "Attorneys Atlanta"
Telex: 54-2711
Telecopier: 404-581-8330
In Brussels, Belgium: Avenue Louise 480, 7th Floor, B-1050 Brussels.
Telephone: 32-2-645-14-11.
Telecopier: 32-2-645-14-45.
In Chicago, Illinois: 77 West Wacker.
Telephone: 312-782-3939.
Telecopier: 312-782-8585.
In Cleveland, Ohio: North Point. 901 Lakeside Avenue.
Telephone: 216-586-3939.
Cable Address: "Attorneys Cleveland".
Telex: 980389.
Telecopier: 216-579-0212.
In Columbus, Ohio: 1900 Huntington Center.
Telephone: 614-469-3939.
Cable Address: "Attorneys Columbus".
Telecopier: 614-461-4198.
In Dallas, Texas: 2300 Trammell Crow Center, 2001 Ross Avenue.
Telephone: 214-220-3939.
Cable Address: "Attorneys Dallas."
Telex: 730852.
Telecopier: 214-969-5100.
In Frankfurt, Germany: Triton Haus, Bockenheimer Landstrasse 42, 60323 Frankfurt am Main.
Telephone: 49-69-9726-3939.
Telecopier: 49-69-9726-3993.

(See Next Column)

In Geneva, Switzerland: 20, rue de Candolle.
Telephone: 41-22-320-2339.
Telecopier: 41-22-320-1232.
In Hong Kong: 29th Floor, Entertainment Building, 30 Queen's Road Central.
Telephone: 852-2526-6895.
Telecopier: 852-2868-5871 or 852-2868-5699.
In Irvine, California: 2603 Main Street, Suite 900.
Telephone: 714-851-3939.
Telex: 194911 Lawyers LSA.
Telecopier: 714-553-7539.
In London, England: One Mount Street.
Telephone: 44-71-493-9361.
Cable Address: "Surgoe London WI."
Telecopier: 44-71-493-9666.
In Los Angeles, California: 555 West Fifth Street, Suite 4600.
Telephone: 213-489-3939.
Telex: 181439 UD.
Telecopier: 213-243-2539.
In New Delhi, India: Pathak & Associates, 9th Floor, Dr. Gopal Das Bhaven, 28 Barakhamba Road.
Telephone: 91-11-331-9719.
Telecopier: 91-11-331-7802.
In New York, New York: 599 Lexington Avenue.
Telephone: 212-326-3939.
Cable Address: "JONESDAY NEWYORK."
Telex: 237013 JDRP UR.
Telecopier: 212-755-7306.
In Paris, France: 62, rue du Faubourg Saint-Honore.
Telephone: 33-1-44-71-3939.
Cable Address: "Surgoe Paris."
Telex: 290156 Surgoe.
Telecopier: 33-1-49-24-0471.
In Pittsburgh, Pennsylvania: 500 Grant Street, 31st Floor.
Telephone: 412-391-3939.
Cable Address: "Attorneys Pittsburgh".
Telecopier: 412-394-7959.
In Riyadh, Saudi Arabia: Law Offices of Saud M.A. Shawwaf, P.O. Box 22166.
Telephone: (966-1) 462-8866.
Telex: 401831 SAUCON SJ.
Telecopier: (966-1) 462-9001.
In Taipei, Taiwan: 8th Floor, 2 Tun Hwa South Road, Section 2.
Telephone: (886-2) 704-6808.
Telecopier: (886-2) 704-6791.
In Tokyo, Japan: Toranomon MT Building, 4th Floor, 10-3, Toranomon 3-Chome, Minato-ku, Tokyo 105, Japan.
Telephone: 81-3-3433-3939.
Telecopier: 81-3-5401-2725.
In Washington, D.C.: Metropolitan Square, 1450 G Street, N.W.
Telephone: 202-879-3939.
Cable Address: "Attorneys Washington."
Telex: 89-2410 ATTORNEYS WASH.
Telecopier: 202-737-2832.

MEMBERS OF FIRM IN ATLANTA
Girard E. Boudreau, Jr.   William B. B. Smith

SENIOR ATTORNEY
L. Trammell Newton, Jr.

For Complete List of Firm Personnel, See General Section

For full biographical listings, see the Martindale-Hubbell Law Directory

---

KILPATRICK & CODY LLP (AV)

Suite 2800, 1100 Peachtree Street, 30309-4530
Telephone: 404-815-6500
Telephone Copier: 404-815-6555
Telex: 54-2307
Washington, D.C. Office: Suite 800, 700 13th Street, N.W., 20005.
Telephone: 202-508-5800. Telephone Copier: 202-508-5858.
Brussels, Belgium Office: Avenue Louise 65, BTE 3, 1050 Brussels.
Telephone: (32) (2) 533-03-00.
Telecopier: (32) (2) 534-86-38.
London, England Office: 68 Pall Mall, London, SW1Y 5ES, England.
Telephone: (44) (71) 321 0477.
Telecopier: (44) (71) 930 9733.
Augusta, Georgia Office: Suite 1400 First Union Bank Building, P.O. Box 2043, 30903. Telephone (706) 724-2622. Telecopier (706) 722-0219.

MEMBERS OF FIRM

Miles J. Alexander	Kent E. Mast
Susan A. Cahoon	Jerre B. Swann
A. Stephens Clay	Virginia S. Taylor
Frederick H. von Unwerth	

For Complete List of Firm Personnel, See General Section

For full biographical listings, see the Martindale-Hubbell Law Directory

Atlanta—Continued

LONG ALDRIDGE & NORMAN, LLP (AV)

A Limited Liability Partnership including Professional Corporations
One Peachtree Center, Suite 5300, 303 Peachtree Street, 30308
Telephone: 404-527-4000
Telecopier: 404-527-4198
Washington, D.C. Office: Suite 600, 701 Pennsylvania Avenue, N.W., 20004.
Telephone: 202-624-1200.
FAX: 202-624-1298.

MEMBERS OF FIRM

J. James Johnson	J. Allen Maines
Carl W. Mullis, III	

ASSOCIATES

Sharon M. Glenn	J. Michael Wiggins

For Complete List of Firm Personnel, See General Section

For full biographical listings, see the Martindale-Hubbell Law Directory

PARKER, HUDSON, RAINER & DOBBS (AV)

1500 Marquis Two Tower, 285 Peachtree Center Avenue, N.E., 30303
Telephone: 404-523-5300
FAX: 404-522-8409
Tallahassee, Florida Office: The Perkins House, 118 North Gadsden Street, 32301.
Telephone: 904-681-0191.
FAX: 904-681-9493.

MEMBER OF FIRM

J. Marbury Rainer

For full biographical listings, see the Martindale-Hubbell Law Directory

SUMNER & ANDERSON (AV)

A Limited Liability Company
Suite 700, The Hurt Building, 50 Hurt Plaza, 30303
Telephone: 404-588-9000
Fax: 404-525-1116
Orlando, Florida Office: 940 Highland Avenue, 32802.
Telephone: 407-841-3000.
Fax: 407-841-0022.
Beaufort, South Carolina Office: 1001 Bay Street, Suite 102, 29902.
Telephone: 803-986-1000.
Fax: 803-986-1002.

MEMBERS OF FIRM

William E. Sumner	Steven E. Harbour
Stephen J. Anderson	David A. Webster

ASSOCIATES

Gerald Kirk Domescik	Anne S. Douds (Resident, Beaufort, South Carolina)
Kathleen M. Fischer	
Everrette V. Snotherly, III	Elizabeth A. Green (Resident, Orlando, Florida Office)
Jerry P. Doyle	

For full biographical listings, see the Martindale-Hubbell Law Directory

SUTHERLAND, ASBILL & BRENNAN, L.L.P. (AV)

999 Peachtree Street, N.E., 30309-3996
Telephone: 404-853-8000
Facsimile: 404-853-8806
Email: postmaster@sablaw.com
Washington, D.C. Office: 1275 Pennsylvania Avenue, N.W., 20004-2404.
Telephone: 202-383-0100.
New York, N.Y. Office: 600 Madison Avenue, 11th Floor, 10022-1615.
Telephone: 212-605-6400.
Austin, Texas Office: 111 Congress Avenue, 23rd Floor, 78701-4079.
Telephone: 512-469-3350.

Carey P. DeDeyn	Charles T. Lester, Jr.
William M. Hames	James R. McGibbon

For Complete List of Firm Personnel, See General Section

For full biographical listings, see the Martindale-Hubbell Law Directory

HAWAII

*HONOLULU,** Honolulu Co.

PITLUCK KIDO SATO & STONE (AV)

701 Bishop Street, 96813
Telephone: 808-523-5030
Telecopier: 808-545-4015
Email: reilly@aloha.net

MEMBERS OF FIRM

Wayne Marshall Pitluck	Dana Kiyomi Nalani Sato
Alan Takashi Kido	James Mauliola Keaka Stone, Jr.

(See Next Column)

OF COUNSEL

John W. Reilly

Reference: Bank of Hawaii.

For full biographical listings, see the Martindale-Hubbell Law Directory

IDAHO

*BOISE,** Ada Co.

EBERLE, BERLIN, KADING, TURNBOW & McKLVEEN, CHARTERED (AV)

Capitol Park Plaza, 300 North Sixth Street, P.O. Box 1368, 83701
Telephone: 208-344-8535
Facsimile: 208-344-8542

R.M. Turnbow	William A. Fuhrman

Representative Clients: TJ International; Key Bank of Idaho; Agri Beef Co.

For Complete List of Firm Personnel, See General Section

For full biographical listings, see the Martindale-Hubbell Law Directory

ELAM & BURKE, A PROFESSIONAL ASSOCIATION (AV)

Key Financial Center, 702 West Idaho Street, P.O. Box 1539, 83701
Telephone: 208-343-5454
Telecopier: 208-384-5844
Email: eblaw@elamburke.com

William G. Dryden	William J. Batt

Representative Clients: Morrison-Knudsen, Inc.; Texas Instruments, Inc.; Pechiney Corp.; U.S. West Communications; Sinclair Oil Company d/b/a Sun Valley Co.; Farmers Insurance Group; Caremark, Inc.; Healthtrust-The Hospital Co.

For Complete List of Firm Personnel, See General Section

For full biographical listings, see the Martindale-Hubbell Law Directory

MOFFATT, THOMAS, BARRETT, ROCK & FIELDS, CHARTERED (AV)

101 South Capitol Boulevard, P.O. Box 829, 83702
Telephone: 208-345-2000
FAX: 208-385-5384
Email: info@moffatt.com
Idaho Falls Office: 525 Park Avenue, Suite 2D, P.O. Box 1367, 83403.
Telephone: 208-522-6700.
FAX: 208-522-5111.
Pocatello, Idaho Office: 845 West Center, Suite C, P.O. Box 4941, 83201.
Telephone: 208-233-2001.

R. B. Rock	Michael E. Thomas

Representative Clients: BMC West Corporation; Chevron, U.S.A.; First Security Bank of Idaho, N.A.; General Motors Corp.; Idaho Potato Commission; Intermountain Gas Co.; John Alden Life Insurance Co.; Micron Technology, Inc.; Royal Insurance Cos.; St. Luke's Regional Medical Center & Mountain States Tumor Institute.

For Complete List of Firm Personnel, See General Section

For full biographical listings, see the Martindale-Hubbell Law Directory

ILLINOIS

*CHICAGO,** Cook Co.

BELL, BOYD & LLOYD (AV)

Three First National Plaza Suite 3300, 70 West Madison Street, 60602
Telephone: 312-372-1121
FAX: 312-372-2098
Email: bbl@bbl.com
Washington, D.C. Office: 1615 L Street, N.W.
Telephone: 202-466-6300.
FAX: 202-463-0678.

MEMBERS OF FIRM

Jeffrey B. Aaronson	Robert T. Johnson, Jr.
Michael J. Abernathy	Scott M. Mendel
William F. Dolan	Rebecca C. Meriwether
Joseph V. Giffin	John R. Myers
Victor E. Grimm	Michael Sennett

OF COUNSEL

John T. Loughlin

(See Next Column)

BELL, BOYD & LLOYD—*Continued*

ASSOCIATES

Mark D. Bauer   Carolyn S. Palk
Kathryn D. Ingraham   Matthew A. Phillips
                   Stephen H. Wenc

For Complete List of Firm Personnel, See General Section

For full biographical listings, see the Martindale-Hubbell Law Directory

---

CHERRY & FLYNN (AV)

30 North La Salle Street, Suite 2300, 60602
Telephone: 312-372-2100
Telecopier: 312-853-0279

Myron M. Cherry   William R. Coulson
Peter Flynn   David D. Merritt
                   Adam J. Levitt

For full biographical listings, see the Martindale-Hubbell Law Directory

---

DAVIS, MANNIX & McGRATH (AV)

125 South Wacker Drive, Suite 1700, 60606
Telephone: 312-332-3033
Fax: 312-332-6376

David C. Bogan (1946-1995)   Julia D. Mannix
Champ W. Davis, Jr.   Gini S. Marziani
Marsha K. Hoover   William T. McGrath

John B. Alsterda   J. Thomas Warlick, IV
Richard R. Danis, Jr.   (Not admitted in IL)

OF COUNSEL

Celeste Ebers Kralovec   Margaret F. Woulfe

For full biographical listings, see the Martindale-Hubbell Law Directory

---

FREEMAN, FREEMAN & SALZMAN, P.C. (AV)

401 North Michigan Avenue, Suite 3200, 60611-4207
Telephone: 312-222-5100
Facsimile: 312-822-0870
Email: freeman@wwa.com

Lee A. Freeman (1909-1995)   James T. Malysiak
Lee A. Freeman, Jr.   Glynna W. Freeman
Jerrold E. Salzman   Phillip L. Stern
John F. Kinney   Albert F. Ettinger
                   Chris C. Gair

Christopher M. Kelly   Michelle Reese Andrew
Derek J. Meyer   Kevin P. Kappock

For full biographical listings, see the Martindale-Hubbell Law Directory

---

HALFPENNY, HAHN, ROCHE & MARCHESE (AV)

Suite 3330, 20 North Wacker Drive, 60606-2806
Telephone: 312-782-1829
FAX: 312-782-4868

MEMBERS OF FIRM

Thomas F. Roche   Neil J. Kuenn
Louis R. Marchese   George W. Keeley
                   Michael T. Reid

ASSOCIATES

Thomas E. Roche   Robert W. Baker

For full biographical listings, see the Martindale-Hubbell Law Directory

---

ARAM A. HARTUNIAN AND ASSOCIATES A PROFESSIONAL CORPORATION (AV)

122 South Michigan Avenue, Suite 1850, 60603
Telephone: 312-427-3600
FAX: 312-427-1850

Aram A. Hartunian

For full biographical listings, see the Martindale-Hubbell Law Directory

---

JONES, DAY, REAVIS & POGUE (AV)

77 West Wacker, 60601-1692
Telephone: 312-782-3939
Telecopier: 312-782-8585
In Atlanta, Georgia: 3500 One Peachtree Center, 303 Peachtree Street, N.E.
Telephone: 404-521-3939.
Cable Address: "Attorneys Atlanta".
Telex: 54-2711.
Telecopier: 404-581-8330.
In Brussels, Belgium: Avenue Louise 480, 7th Floor, B-1050 Brussels.
Telephone: 32-2-645-14-11.
Telecopier: 32-2-645-14-45.

(See Next Column)

In Cleveland, Ohio: North Point, 901 Lakeside Avenue.
Telephone: 216-586-3939.
Cable Address: "Attorneys Cleveland."
Telex: 980389.
Telecopier: 216-579-0212.
In Columbus, Ohio: 1900 Huntington Center.
Telephone: 614-469-3939.
Cable Address: "Attorneys Columbus."
Telecopier: 614-461-4198.
In Dallas, Texas: 2300 Trammell Crow Center, 2001 Ross Avenue.
Telephone: 214-220-3939.
Cable Address: "Attorneys Dallas."
Telex: 730852.
Telecopier: 214-969-5100.
In Frankfurt, Germany: Triton Haus, Bockenheimer Landstrasse 42, 60323 Frankfurt am Main.
Telephone: 49-69-9726-3939.
Telecopier: 49-69-9726-3993.
In Geneva, Switzerland: 20, rue de Candolle.
Telephone: 41-22-320-2339.
Telecopier: 41-22-320-1232.
In Hong Kong: 29th Floor, Entertainment Building, 30 Queen's Road Central.
Telephone: 852-2526-6895.
Telecopier: 852-2868-5871 or 852-2868-5699.
In Irvine, California: 2603 Main Street, Suite 900.
Telephone: 714-851-3939.
Telex: 194911 Lawyers LSA.
Telecopier: 714-553-7539.
In London, England: One Mount Street.
Telephone: 44-71-493-9361.
Cable Address: "Surgoe London WI."
Telecopier: 44-71-493-9666.
In Los Angeles, California: 555 West Fifth Street, Suite 4600.
Telephone: 213-489-3939.
Telex: 181439 UD.
Telecopier: 213-243-2539.
In New Delhi, India: Pathak & Associates, 9th Floor, Dr. Gopal Das Bhaven, 28 Barakhamba Road.
Telephone: 91-11-331-9719.
Telecopier: 91-11-331-7802.
In New York, New York: 599 Lexington Avenue.
Telephone: 212-326-3939.
Cable Address: "JONESDAY NEWYORK."
Telex: 237013 JDRP UR.
Telecopier: 212-755-7306.
In Paris, France: 62, rue du Faubourg Saint-Honore.
Telephone: 33-1-44-71-3939.
Cable Address: "Surgoe Paris."
Telex: 290156 Surgoe.
Telecopier: 33-1-49-24-0471.
In Pittsburgh, Pennsylvania: 500 Grant Street, 31st Floor.
Telephone: 412-391-3939.
Cable Address: "Attorneys Pittsburgh."
Telecopier: 412-394-7959.
In Riyadh, Saudi Arabia: Law Offices of Saud M.A. Shawwaf, P.O. Box 22166.
Telephone: (966-1) 462-8866.
Telex: 401831 SAUCON SJ.
Telecopier: (966-1) 462-9001.
In Taipei, Taiwan: 8th Floor, 2 Tun Hwa South Road, Section 2.
Telephone: (886-2) 704-6808.
Telecopier: (886-2) 704-6791.
In Tokyo, Japan: Toranomon MT Building, 4th Floor, 10-3, Toranomon 3-Chome, Minato-ku, Tokyo 105, Japan.
Telephone: 81-3-3433-3939.
Telecopier: 81-3-5401-2725.
In Washington, D.C.: Metropolitan Square, 1450 G Street, N.W.
Telephone: 202-879-3939.
Cable Address: "Attorneys Washington."
Telex: 89-2410 ATTORNEYS WASH.
Telecopier: 202-737-2832.

MEMBER OF FIRM IN CHICAGO

Thomas F. Gardner

For Complete List of Firm Personnel, See General Section

For full biographical listings, see the Martindale-Hubbell Law Directory

---

KECK, MAHIN & CATE (AV)

A Partnership including Professional Corporations
77 West Wacker Drive Suite 4900, 60601-1693
Telephone: 312-634-7700
Cable Address: "Hamscott"
Telex: 25-3411
Fax: 312-634-5000
Washington, D.C. Office: 555 12th St., N.W., 6th Floor.
Telephone: 202-637-3601.
Telecopier: 202-347-0140.
Peoria, Illinois Office: 401 Main Street, Suite 1600.
Telephone: 309-673-1681.
Telecopier: 309-673-1690.

(See Next Column)

KECK, MAHIN & CATE, *Chicago—Continued*

New York, N.Y. Office: 100 Maiden Lane, Suite 1600.
Telephone: 212-504-5630.
Telecopier: 212-504-5631.

MEMBERS OF FIRM AND ASSOCIATES

William C. Ives (P.C.)	Robert W. Pratt
Sheldon Karon (P.C.)	Richard L. Reinish (P.C.)
Robin R. Lunn (P.C.)	
Philip L. O'Neill (P.C.)	
(Resident, Washington, D.C. Office)	

OF COUNSEL
Thomas W. Johnston

For Complete List of Firm Personnel, See General Section

For full biographical listings, see the Martindale-Hubbell Law Directory

McBRIDE BAKER & COLES (AV)

500 West Madison Street 40th Floor, 60661
Telephone: 312-715-5700
Cable Address: "Chilaw"
Telex: 270258
Telecopier: 312-993-9350
Email: lastname@mbc.com *URL:* http://www.mbc.com
Oakbrook Terrace, Illinois Office: Suite 1000, One Mid America Plaza, 60181-4710.
Telephone: 630-954-2100.
Telecopier: 630-954-2112.

MEMBERS OF FIRM

Henry S. Allen, Jr.	Robert C. Schnitz
Malcolm H. Brooks	Steven B. Varick
Clifton A. Lake	Richard R. Winter

ASSOCIATE
George Michael Sanders

For Complete List of Firm Personnel, See General Section

For full biographical listings, see the Martindale-Hubbell Law Directory

McCONNELL & MENDELSON (AV)

140 South Dearborn Street, 9th Floor, 60603
Telephone: 312-263-1212
Telecopier: 312-263-0402

Francis J. McConnell	Peter S. Lubin

Reference: The Northern Trust Co., Chicago, Illinois.

For full biographical listings, see the Martindale-Hubbell Law Directory

McDERMOTT, WILL & EMERY (AV)

A Partnership including Professional Corporations
227 West Monroe Street, 60606-5096
Telephone: 312-372-2000
Facsimile: 312-984-7700
Boston, Massachusetts Office: 75 State Street, Suite 1700.
Telephone: 617-345-5000.
Facsimile: 617-345-5077.
Miami, Florida Office: 201 South Biscayne Boulevard.
Telephone: 305-358-3500.
Facsimile: 305-347-6500.
Washington, D.C. Office: 1850 K Street, N.W.
Telephone: 202-887-8000.
Facsimile: 202-778-8087.
Los Angeles, California Office: 2049 Century Park East.
Telephone: 310-277-4110.
Facsimile: 310-277-4730.
Newport Beach, California Office: 1301 Dove Street, Suite 500.
Telephone: 714-851-0633.
Facsimile: 714-851-9348.
New York, N.Y. Office: 1211 Avenue of the Americas.
Telephone: 212-768-5400.
Facsimile: 212-768-5444.
St. Petersburg, Russia Office: AOZT McDermott, Will & Emery, Griboyedova Canal 36, 191023 St. Petersburg, Russia.
Telephone: (7) (812) 310-52-44; 310-55-44; 310-59-44; 850-20-45.
Facsimile: (7) (812) 310-54-46; 325-84-50.
Vilnius, Lithuania Office: Smetonos 6, 2600 Vilnius, Lithuania.
Telephone: 370 2 61-43-08.
Facsimile: 370 2 22-79-55.

MEMBERS OF FIRM

Robert E. Bouma *	David Marx, Jr.
Byron L. Gregory *	Anne R. Pramaggiore
Steven P. Handler *	N. Rosie Rosenbaum *
Mercedes A. Laing	William P. Schuman
	Mark L. Yeager

*Denotes a lawyer employed by a Professional Corporation which is a member of the Firm.

For full biographical listings, see the Martindale-Hubbell Law Directory

ROTHSCHILD, BARRY & MYERS (AV)

A Partnership including Professional Corporations
Suite 3900, 55 West Monroe Street, 60603-5012
Telephone: 312-372-2345
FAX: 312-372-2350

MEMBERS OF FIRM

Edward I. Rothschild (P.C.)	John J. Coffey, III
William G. Myers (P.C.)	Joseph P. Della Maria, Jr.
Melvin I. Mishkin	Christopher G. Walsh, Jr.
Kenneth P. Taube	

For Complete List of Firm Personnel, See General Section

For full biographical listings, see the Martindale-Hubbell Law Directory

SAUNDERS & MONROE (AV)

Suite 4201, 205 North Michigan Avenue, 60601
Telephone: 312-946-9000
Facsimile: 312-946-0528

MEMBERS OF FIRM

George L. Saunders, Jr.	Thomas F. Bush, Jr.
Lee A. Monroe	Matthew E. Van Tine
Thomas A. Doyle	

Gwen A. Niedbalski

OF COUNSEL

Kenneth K. Howell	Victoria S. Kaplan

For full biographical listings, see the Martindale-Hubbell Law Directory

WILDMAN, HARROLD, ALLEN & DIXON (AV)

225 West Wacker Drive, 30th Floor, 60606-1229
Telephone: 312-201-2000
Cable Address: "Whad"
Fax: 312-201-2555
URL: http://www.whad.com
Aurora, Illinois Office: 1851 W. Galena Boulevard, Suite 210.
Telephone: 630-892-7021.
Fax: 630-892-7158.
Waukegan, Illinois Office: 404 West Water, P. O. Box 890.
Telephone: 847-623-0700.
Fax: 847-244-5273.
Lisle, Illinois Office: 4300 Commerce Court.
Telephone: 630-955-0555.
New York, New York Office: Wildman, Harrold, Allen, Dixon & Smith. The International Building, 45 Rockefeller Plaza, Suite 353.
Telephone: 212-632-3850.
Fax: 212-632-3858.
Toronto, Ontario affiliated Office: Keel Cottrelle. 36 Toronto Street, Ninth Floor, Suite 920.
Telephone: 416-367-2900.
Telefax: 416-367-2791.
Telex: 062-18660.
Mississauga, Ontario affiliated Office: Keel Cottrelle. 100 Matatson Avenue East, Suite 104.
Telephone: 416-890-7700.
Fax: 416-890-8006.

MEMBERS OF FIRM

Michael R. Blankshain	Bernard Harrold
Douglas R. Carlson	Michael L. McCluggage
Stewart S. Dixon	Timothy G. Nickels
Michael Dockterman	Fred E. Schulz
Jerald P. Esrick	Lisa S. Simmons
Donald Flayton	R. John Street

Eric P. Berlin	David M. Simon
Scott Z. Hochfelder	Andrew E. Skopp
Jeannine Y. Sano	Robin L. Wolkoff

For Complete List of Firm Personnel, See General Section

For full biographical listings, see the Martindale-Hubbell Law Directory

WINSTON & STRAWN (AV)

35 West Wacker Drive, 60601
Telephone: 312-558-5600
Cable Address: "Winston Chicago"
Facsimile: 312-558-5700
Email: postmaster@winston.com *URL:*
http://www.lcp.com/The-Legal-List/LawFirms/7.260.html
Washington, D.C. Office: 1400 L Street, N.W., 20005-3502.
Telephone: 202-371-5700.
Telecopier: 202-371-5950.
Telex: 440574 INTLAW UI.
New York, N.Y. Office: 200 Park Avenue, 10166-4193.
Telephone: 212-294-6700.
Telecopier: 212-294-4700.

(See Next Column)

WINSTON & STRAWN—*Continued*

Cable Address: "Coledeitz, NYK".
Telex: (RCA) 232459.
Geneva, Switzerland Office: 43 Rue du Rhone, 1204.
Telephone: (4122) 7810506.
Fax: (4122) 7810361.
Paris, France Office: 6, rue du Cirque, 75008.
Telephone: (3314) 225-1055.
Fax: (3314) 225-0921.

MEMBERS OF FIRM

Edward L. Foote	Duane M. Kelley
John W. Stack	R. Mark McCareins

Representative Clients: Windmere Corp.; Tropicana Products; Illinois Bell Telephone Co.; Amertech; Marmon Group.

For Complete List of Firm Personnel, See General Section

For full biographical listings, see the Martindale-Hubbell Law Directory

INDIANA

INDIANAPOLIS,* Marion Co.

BOSE MCKINNEY & EVANS (AV)

2700 First Indiana Plaza, 135 North Pennsylvania Street, 46204
Telephone: 317-684-5000
Facsimile: 317-684-5173
Indianapolis North Office: Suite 1201, 8888 Keystone Crossing, 46240.
Telephone: 317-574-3700.
Facsimile: 317-574-3716.

MEMBERS OF FIRM

Kendall C. Crook	Stephen E. Arthur
Ronald E. Elberger	Gary L. Chapman

ASSOCIATE
J. Scott Enright

Representative Clients: Agmax, Inc.; Ameritech Publishing; Erbrich Products Co., Inc.; First Indiana Bank; Indiana Supply Corp.; Kenra Laboratories Inc.; Lawyers Title Insurance Corp.; Muncie Power Products, Inc.; Indianapolis Life Insurance Co.; BMW Constructors, Inc.; Indiana Academy of Ophthalmology, Inc.

For Complete List of Firm Personnel, See General Section

For full biographical listings, see the Martindale-Hubbell Law Directory

ICE MILLER DONADIO & RYAN (AV)

One American Square Box 82001, 46282-0002
Telephone: 317-236-2100
Fax: 317-236-2219
Email: leel@imdr.com *URL:* http://www.imdr.com
South Bend, Indiana Office: 211 West Washington Street, Suite 2420.
Telephone: 219-234-7933.
Fax: 219-234-7965. Internet E-mail: leel@imdr.com. Web Site Address: http://www.imdr.com.

MEMBERS OF FIRM

Jay G. Taylor	Fred R. Biesecker
Philip A. Whistler	John R. Thornburgh
Gregory L. Pemberton	

OF COUNSEL

Karen Ann P. Lloyd	Susan B. Rivas

ASSOCIATES

Curtis W. McCauley	Melissa R. Garrard
Angela R. Lang	

Counsel for: Indianapolis Motor Speedway; Community Hospitals of Indiana; Avesta Sheffield, Inc.; Haynes International, Inc.; Reilly Industries, Inc.; Indiana Bankers Assn.; Biomet, Inc.; Coca Cola Company; RJR Nabisco; Indiana Association of Cities and Towns.

For Complete List of Firm Personnel, See General Section

For full biographical listings, see the Martindale-Hubbell Law Directory

MCTURNAN & TURNER (AV)

2400 Market Tower, 10 West Market Street, 46204
Telephone: 317-464-8181
Telecopier: 317-464-8131

Lee B. McTurnan	Jacqueline Bowman Ponder
Wayne C. Turner	Steven M. Badger
Judy L. Woods	Matthew W. Foster
Matthew J. Salzman	

For full biographical listings, see the Martindale-Hubbell Law Directory

SOMMER & BARNARD, ATTORNEYS AT LAW, PC (AV)

4000 Bank One Tower, 111 Monument Circle, 46204-5140
Telephone: 317-630-4000
FAX: 317-236-9802
North Office: 8900 Keystone Crossing, Suite 1046, Indianapolis, Indiana, 46240-2134.
Telephone: 317-630-4000.
FAX: 317-844-4780.

William C. Barnard	Edward W. Harris, III
James E. Hughes	Gordon L. Pittenger
Gayle A. Reindl	

Representative Clients: Excel Industries, Inc.; Monsanto Co.; Comerica Bank; Federal Express; Renault Automation; Kimball International; TRW, Inc.

For Complete List of Firm Personnel, See General Section

For full biographical listings, see the Martindale-Hubbell Law Directory

KANSAS

WICHITA,* Sedgwick Co.

FOULSTON & SIEFKIN L.L.P. (AV)

700 Fourth Financial Center, 67202
Telephone: 316-267-6371
Facsimile: 316-267-6345
Topeka, Kansas Office: 1515 Bank IV Tower, 534 Kansas Avenue, 66603.
Telephone: 913-233-3600.
Fax: 913-233-1610.
Dodge City, Kansas Office: 810 Frontview, P.O. Box 1147, 67801.
Telephone: 316-227-8126.
Fax: 316-227-8451.
Member: Lex Mundi, A Global Association of 126 Independent Firms.

MEMBERS OF FIRM

Robert L. Howard	James D. Oliver
Jim H. Goering	

For Complete List of Firm Personnel, See General Section

For full biographical listings, see the Martindale-Hubbell Law Directory

KENTUCKY

LEXINGTON,* Fayette Co.

GESS MATTINGLY & ATCHISON, P.S.C. (AV)

201 West Short Street, 40507-1269
Telephone: 606-252-9000
Facsimile: 606-233-4269

William B. Gess (1906-1985)	Walter R. Morris, Jr.
John G. Atchison, Jr.	Robert E. Maclin, III
Charles G. Wylie	Linda W. Christian
Natalie S. Wilson	Jeffrey R. Walker
Carl Timothy Cone	Elizabeth S. Hughes
Joseph H. Miller	Christel Schrader Nash
William W. Allen	Stephen P. Stoltz
Guy M. Graves	Stephen W. Atwood

OF COUNSEL

Jack F. Mattingly	Leslie G. Phillips
William R. Hilliard, Jr.	

Representative Clients: National City Bank; WLEX-TV, Inc.; Prudential Insurance Company of America; Central Kentucky Agricultural Credit Assn.; B.F. Saul Real Estate Investment Trust; American Hardware Mutual Insurance Co.; The Procter & Gamble Co.; University of Kentucky Federal Credit Union; Prudential Securities, Inc.; Thomas & King, Inc.

For full biographical listings, see the Martindale-Hubbell Law Directory

STOLL, KEENON & PARK, LLP (AV)

201 E. Main Street, Suite 1000, 40507-1380
Telephone: 606-231-3000
Telecopier: 606-253-1093; 606-253-1027
Frankfort, Kentucky Office: 307 Washington Street, 40601.
Telephone: 502-875-6220.
Telecopier: 502-875-6235.
Louisville, Kentucky Office: 400 West Market Street, Suite 2650, 40202-3377.
Telephone: 502-568-9100.
Telecopier: 502-568-5700.

(See Next Column)

STOLL, KEENON & PARK LLP, *Lexington—Continued*

MEMBERS OF FIRM

Samuel D. Hinkle IV   Donald P. Wagner

Representative Clients: Bank One, Lexington, NA; C. Lee Cook; Farmers Capital Bank Corp.; Link Belt Construction Equipment Co.; General Motors Corp.; International Business Machines Corp.; Square D Co.; Jim Walter Homes, Inc.

For Complete List of Firm Personnel, See General Section

For full biographical listings, see the Martindale-Hubbell Law Directory

LOUISVILLE,* Jefferson Co.

MIDDLETON & REUTLINGER, P.S.C. (AV)

2500 Brown and Williamson Tower, 40202-3410
Telephone: 502-584-1135
Fax: 502-561-0442
New Albany, Indiana Office: 2623 Charlestown Road, 47150.
Telephone: 812-944-7215.

Charles G. Middleton, III   C. Kent Hatfield
William Jay Hunter, Jr.

Counsel For: Louisville Gas & Electric Co.; Logan Aluminum, Inc.; The Kroger Co.; MCI Telecommunications Corp.; EnTrade Corp.; Stevens Contractors, Inc.; Associated General Contractors of Kentucky; Builders Exchange of Louisville, Inc.

For Complete List of Firm Personnel, See General Section

For full biographical listings, see the Martindale-Hubbell Law Directory

WOODWARD, HOBSON & FULTON (AV)

2500 National City Tower, 101 South Fifth Street, 40202
Telephone: 502-581-8000
Fax: 502-581-8111
Lexington, Kentucky Office: PNC Bank Plaza, 200 West Vine Street, Suite 500.
Telephone: 606-244-7100.
Telecopier: 606-244-7111.
New Albany, Indiana Office: 611 East Spring Street, P.O. Box 288.
Telephone: 812-941-1800.
Telecopier: 812-941-1855.

MEMBER OF FIRM

Kenneth L. Anderson

Representative Clients: International Minerals & Chemical Corp.; Ralston Purina Co.; Sears, Roebuck & Co.; Prairie Farms Dairy, Inc.; Mid-America Dairymen, Inc.

For Complete List of Firm Personnel, See General Section

For full biographical listings, see the Martindale-Hubbell Law Directory

LOUISIANA

BATON ROUGE,* East Baton Rouge Parish

BREAZEALE, SACHSE & WILSON, L.L.P. (AV)

Twenty-Third Floor, One American Place, P.O. Box 3197, 70821-3197
Telephone: 504-387-4000
Fax: 504-387-5397
New Orleans, Louisiana Office: LL&E Tower, Suite 2400, 909 Poydras Street.
Telephone: 504-582-1170.
Fax: 504-584-5452.

MEMBERS OF FIRM

Gordon A. Pugh
Claude F. Reynaud, Jr.
Emile C. Rolfs, III
John F. Whitney (Resident, New Orleans Office)

Joseph E. Friend (Resident, New Orleans Office)
Jude C. Bursavich
James R. Chastain, Jr.

ASSOCIATES

Linda Perez Clark   Luis A. Leitzelar
Jeanne C. Comeaux

Counsel for: Hibernia National Bank; South Central Bell Telephone Co.; Allied-Signal Corp.; Reynolds Metal Co.; Illinois Central Railroad Co.; The Continental Insurance Cos.; Fireman's Fund American Group; Chicago Bridge & Iron Co.; Montgomery Ward & Co.

For Complete List of Firm Personnel, See General Section

For full biographical listings, see the Martindale-Hubbell Law Directory

NEW ORLEANS,* Orleans Parish

DEUTSCH, KERRIGAN & STILES, L.L.P. (AV)

A Partnership including Professional Law Corporations
755 Magazine Street, 70130-3672
Telephone: 504-581-5141
Cable Address: "Dekest"
Telex: 584358
Telecopier: 504-566-1201
Email: dks@dksno.com *URL:* http://www.dksno.com
St. Tammany Parish Office: 550 Pontchartrain Drive, Suite 200, Slidell, LA. 70458.
Telephone: 504-639-0555.
Fax: 504-639-0550

MEMBERS OF FIRM

William E. Wright, Jr.   Ellis B. Murov (P.L.C.)
Duris L. Holmes

OF COUNSEL

Charles K. Reasonover (P.L.C.)

ASSOCIATES

W. Christopher Beary   Charles F. Seemann III

For Complete List of Firm Personnel, See General Section

For full biographical listings, see the Martindale-Hubbell Law Directory

LAMOTHE & HAMILTON, A PROFESSIONAL LAW CORPORATION (AV)

Pan American Life Center, 601 Poydras Street, Suite 2750, 70130
Telephone: 504-566-1805
Telecopier: 504-566-1569
MCI Mail: 382-4472
Email: lhplc@neosoft.com

Frank E. Lamothe, III
Charles E. Hamilton, III
Karen Edginton Milner

Galen S. Brown
M. Lizabeth Talbott
Thomas J. Cortazzo

Reference: Jefferson Guaranty Bank, New Orleans, Louisiana.

For full biographical listings, see the Martindale-Hubbell Law Directory

LISKOW & LEWIS, A PROFESSIONAL LAW CORPORATION (AV)

50th Floor, One Shell Square, 70139
Telephone: 504-581-7979
Telecopier: 504-556-4108; 504-556-4109
Lafayette, Louisiana Office: 822 Harding Street, P.O. Box 52008.
Telephone: 318-232-7424.
Telecopier: 318-267-2399.

Gene W. Lafitte   George Denegre, Jr.
Marie Breaux

Karen Daniel Ancelet

Representative Clients: Atlantic Richfield Co.; BASF Corp.; Federal Deposit Insurance Corporation; First National Bank of Commerce; Hibernia National Bank; Legg Mason Wood Walker; Mobil Oil Corporation; Pennzoil Company; Prudential Securities Inc.; Texaco, Inc.

For Complete List of Firm Personnel, See General Section

For full biographical listings, see the Martindale-Hubbell Law Directory

MILLING, BENSON, WOODWARD, HILLYER, PIERSON & MILLER, L.L.P. (AV)

A Partnership including Professional Law Corporations
Suite Twenty-Three Hundred, 909 Poydras Street, 70112-1017
Telephone: 504-569-7000
Cable Address: "Milling"
Telex: 58-4211
Telecopier: 504-569-7001
ABA net: 15656
MCI Mail: "Milling"
Lafayette, Louisiana Office: 101 La Rue France, Suite 200.
Telephone: 318-232-3929.
Telecopier: 318-233-4957.

MEMBERS OF FIRM

James K. Irvin (P.C.)   Katherine Goldman (P.C.)
See General Section for list of Representative Clients.

For Complete List of Firm Personnel, See General Section

For full biographical listings, see the Martindale-Hubbell Law Directory

SLATER LAW FIRM, A PROFESSIONAL CORPORATION (AV)

650 Poydras Street Suite 2600, 70130-6101
Telephone: 504-523-7333
Fax: 504-528-1080

(See Next Column)

SLATER LAW FIRM A PROFESSIONAL CORPORATION—*Continued*

Benjamin R. Slater, Jr.	Kevin M. Wheeler
Benjamin R. Slater, III	Anne Elise Brown
Mark E. Van Horn	Donald J. Miester, Jr.

Cory Rabin Cahn	James L. Bradford, III

SPECIAL COUNSEL

W. Malcolm Stevenson	Robert B. Acomb, III
Michael O. Waguespack	

Representative Clients: Norfolk Southern Corporation; New Orleans Steamship Association; The Quaker Oats Company; Anheuser-Busch, Incorporated; Primerica Financial Services, Inc.; Primerica Life Insurance Company; Electric Mutual Liability Insurance Company; Patterson Pump Company; Diversified Foods and Seasonings, Inc.

For full biographical listings, see the Martindale-Hubbell Law Directory

MAINE

BANGOR, * Penobscot Co.

EATON, PEABODY, BRADFORD & VEAGUE, P.A. (AV)

Fleet Center-Exchange Street, P.O. Box 1210, 04402-1210
Telephone: 207-947-0111
Telecopier: 207-942-3040
Email: epbv@aol.com
Augusta, Maine Office: 2 Central Plaza.
Telephone: 207-622-3747.
Telecopier: 207-622-9732.
Blue Hill, Maine Office: One East Blue Hill Road.
Telephone: 207-374-2812.
Telecopier: 207-374-2548.
Brunswick, Maine Office: 167 Park Row.
Telephone: 207-729-1144.
Telecopier: 207-729-1140.
Camden, Maine Office: 7-9 Washington Street.
Telephone: 207-236-3325.
Telecopier: 207-236-8611.
Dover-Foxcroft, Maine Office: 30 East Main Street.
Telephone: 207-564-8378.
Telecopier: 207-564-7059.

Daniel G. McKay	Thad B. Zmistowski
Gordon H. S. Scott	
(Resident, Augusta Office)	

A List of Representative Clients available upon request.

For Complete List of Firm Personnel, See General Section

For full biographical listings, see the Martindale-Hubbell Law Directory

PORTLAND, * Cumberland Co.

PIERCE ATWOOD (AV)

One Monument Square, 04101
Telephone: 207-791-1100
Fax: 207-791-1350
Email: info@PierceAtwood.com
Augusta, Maine Office: 77 Winthrop Street.
Telephone: 207-622-6311.
Fax: 207-623-9367.
Newburyport, Massachusetts Office: 6 Harris Street.
Telephone: 508-465-9599.
Fax: 508-465-9945.

MEMBER OF FIRM
Jeffrey M. White

ASSOCIATE
William L. Worden

For Complete List of Firm Personnel, See General Section

For full biographical listings, see the Martindale-Hubbell Law Directory

MARYLAND

BALTIMORE, * (Independent City)

PIPER & MARBURY L.L.P. (AV)

Charles Center South, 36 South Charles Street, 21201-3018
Telephone: 410-539-2530
FAX: 410-539-0489
Email: lawfirm@pipermar.com
Washington, D.C. Office: 1200 Nineteenth Street, N.W., 20036-2430.
Telephone: 202-861-3900.
FAX: 202-223-2085.
Easton, Maryland Office: 117 Bay Street, 21601-2703.
Telephone: 410-820-4460.
FAX: 410-820-4463.
New York, N.Y. Office: 1251 Avenue of the Americas, 10020-1104.
Telephone: 212-835-6000.
FAX: 212-835-6001.
Philadelphia, Pennsylvania Office: 3400 Two Logan Square, 18th & Arch Streets, 19103-2762.
Telephone: 215-656-3300.
FAX: 215-656-3301.

MEMBERS OF FIRM

Lewis A. Noonberg (Resident, Washington, D.C. Office)	Jeffrey F. Liss (Resident, Washington, D.C. Office)
Jeffrey D. Herschman	Michael F. Brockmeyer

ASSOCIATES

H. Mark Stichel	Leonard L. Gordon (Resident, Washington, D.C. Office)

For Complete List of Firm Personnel, See General Section

For full biographical listings, see the Martindale-Hubbell Law Directory

VENABLE ATTORNEYS AT LAW VENABLE, BAETJER AND HOWARD, LLP (AV)

A Partnership including Professional Corporations
1800 Mercantile Bank & Trust Building, 2 Hopkins Plaza, 21201
Telephone: 410-244-7400
Email: INFO@Venable.win.net
Washington, D.C. Office: Venable, Baetjer, Howard & Civiletti LLP. Suite 1000, 1201 New York Avenue, N.W.
Telephone: 202-962-4800.
McLean, Virginia Office: Suite 400, 2010 Corporate Ridge.
Telephone: 703-760-1600.
Rockville, Maryland Office: Suite 500, One Church Street, P. O. Box 1906.
Telephone: 301-217-5600.
Towson, Maryland Office: 210 Allegheny Avenue, P. O. Box 5517.
Telephone: 410-494-6200.

MEMBERS OF FIRM

Benjamin R. Civiletti (P.C.) (Also at Washington, D.C. and Towson, Maryland Offices)	James R. Myers (Not admitted in MD; Resident, Washington, D.C. Office)
John Henry Lewin, Jr. (P.C.)	Jeffrey D. Knowles (Not admitted in MD; Resident, Washington, D.C. Office)
Douglas D. Connah, Jr. (P.C.) (Also at Washington, D.C. Office)	William D. Coston (Not admitted in MD; Resident, Washington, D.C. Office)
Kenneth C. Bass, III (Not admitted in MD; Washington, D.C. and McLean, Virginia Offices)	Maurice Baskin (Resident, Washington, D.C. Office)
Edward F. Glynn, Jr. (Resident, Washington, D.C. Office)	Amy Berman Jackson (Not admitted in MD; Resident, Washington, D.C. Office)
Michael Schatzow (Also at Washington, D.C. Office)	William D. Quarles (Also at Washington, D.C. and Towson, Maryland Offices)
G. Stewart Webb, Jr.	Christopher R. Mellott
James K. Archibald (Also at Washington, D.C. Office)	James A. Dunbar (Also at Washington, D.C. Office)

OF COUNSEL
Emried D. Cole, Jr.

ASSOCIATES

David W. Goewey (Not admitted in MD; Resident, Washington, D.C. Office)	Melissa Landau Steinman (Resident, Washington, D.C. Office)
Vicki Margolis (Also at Washington, D.C. Office)	

For Complete List of Firm Personnel, See General Section

For full biographical listings, see the Martindale-Hubbell Law Directory

WARD, KERSHAW & MINTON, A PROFESSIONAL ASSOCIATION (AV)

113 West Monument Street, 21201
Telephone: 410-685-6700
Fax: 410-685-6704
Email: wkmfirm@aol.com

(See Next Column)

WARD, KERSHAW & MINTON A PROFESSIONAL ASSOCIATION, *Baltimore*—
Continued

John T. Ward	Robert B. Kershaw

Thomas J. Minton

OF COUNSEL

Richard V. Falcon

For full biographical listings, see the Martindale-Hubbell Law Directory

---

MASSACHUSETTS

---

*BOSTON,** Suffolk Co.

BROWN & STADFELD (AV)

66 Long Wharf, 02110
Telephone: 617-720-4200
Fax: 617-720-0240
Email: brownsta@world.std.com

Harold Brown	L. Seth Stadfeld

L. Michael Hankes	Linda J. Keogh

Catherine M. Keenan

For Complete List of Firm Personnel, See General Section

For full biographical listings, see the Martindale-Hubbell Law Directory

CESARI AND MCKENNA (AV)

30 Rowes Wharf, 02110
Telephone: 617-951-2500
Fax: 617-951-3927

Robert A. Cesari	Joseph H. Born
John F. McKenna	Patricia A. Sheehan
Martin J. O'Donnell	Michael E. Attaya
Thomas C. O'Konski	Steven J. Frank

Charles J. Barbas

Patrick J. O'Shea	George J. Jakobsche
Michael R. Reinemann	William A. Loginov

Rita M. Rooney

LEGAL SUPPORT PERSONNEL

Dora V. Dodin	Heather B. Shapiro
(Patent Engineer)	(Technical Specialist)

For full biographical listings, see the Martindale-Hubbell Law Directory

HANIFY & KING, PROFESSIONAL CORPORATION (AV)

One Federal Street, 02110-2007
Telephone: 617-423-0400
Telefax: 617-423-0498

James Coyne King	Daniel J. Lyne
John D. Hanify	Donald F. Farrell, Jr.
Harold B. Murphy	Barbara Wegener Pfirrman
David Lee Evans	Gerard P. Richer

Timothy P. O'Neill

Jean A. Musiker	Joseph F. Cortellini
Ann M. Chiacchieri	Eddirland Duncan
Melissa J. Cassedy	Andrew G. Lizotte
Jeffrey J. Upton	Karen A. Whitley
Michael R. Perry	Christopher K. Barry-Smith
Charles A. Dale, III	William T. Harrington
Kathleen E. Cross	Matthew McCue
David M. Wright	Robyn J. Bartlett

Owen P. Kane

For full biographical listings, see the Martindale-Hubbell Law Directory

MINTZ, LEVIN, COHN, FERRIS, GLOVSKY AND POPEO, P.C. (AV)

One Financial Center, 02111
Telephone: 617-542-6000
FAX: 617-542-2241
Internet: Each Attorney's Internet Address takes the following form: first
initial last name @mintz.com (e.g., rmintz@mintz.com)
Washington, D.C. Office: 701 Pennsylvania Avenue, N.W. Suite 900.
Telephone: 202-434-7300.
Fax: 202-434-7400.

Jerome Gotkin	Charles Alan Samuels (Resident,
R. Robert Popeo	Washington, D.C. Office)
Bruce D. Sokler (Resident,	Bruce F. Metge
Washington, D.C. Office)	

(See Next Column)

Christopher J. Harvie (Resident, Washington, D.C. Office)

For Complete List of Firm Personnel, See General Section

For full biographical listings, see the Martindale-Hubbell Law Directory

PALMER & DODGE LLP (AV)

One Beacon Street, 02108
Telephone: 617-573-0100
Facsimile: 617-227-4420

MEMBERS OF FIRM

Michael T. Gass	Thane D. Scott

For Complete List of Firm Personnel, See General Section

For full biographical listings, see the Martindale-Hubbell Law Directory

---

MICHIGAN

---

*ANN ARBOR,** Washtenaw Co.

MILLER, CANFIELD, PADDOCK AND STONE, P.L.C. (AV)

A Professional Limited Liability Company
Founded in 1852 by Sidney Davy Miller
101 North Main Street, Seventh Floor, 48104-1400
Telephone: 313-663-2445
Fax: 313-747-7147
Detroit, Michigan Office: 150 West Jefferson, Suite 2500, 48226-4415.
Telephone: 313-963-6420.
Fax: 313-496-7500.
Cable Address: "Stem Detroit."
Bloomfield Hills, Michigan Office: Suite 100, Pinehurst Office Center, 1400
North Woodward, 48303-2014.
Telephone: 313-645-5000.
Fax: 313-645-1917.
Grand Rapids, Michigan Office: 1200 Campau Square Plaza, 99 Monroe,
N.W., 49503-2639.
Telephone: 616-454-8656.
Fax: 616-776-6322.
Howell, Michigan Office: 121 South Barnard Street, Suite 4, 48843-2305.
Telephone: 517-546-7600.
Telecopier: 517-546-6974.
Kalamazoo, Michigan Office: 444 West Michigan Avenue, 49007-3752.
Telephone: 616-381-7030.
Fax: 616-382-0244.
Lansing, Michigan Office: One Michigan Avenue, Suite 900, 48933-1609.
Telephone: 517-487-2070.
Fax: 517-374-6304.
Monroe, Michigan Office: The Executive Centre, 214 East Elm Avenue,
48161-2682.
Telephone: 313-243-2000.
Fax: 313-243-0901.
Washington, D.C. Office: 1225 Nineteenth Street, N.W., Suite 400. 20036.
Telephone: 202-429-5575; 785-0600.
Fax: 202-331-1118; 785-1234.
Pensacola, Florida Office: 25 West Cedar, 32501.
Telephone: 904-469-1088.
Fax: 904-432-0677.
St. Petersburg, Florida Office: 100 Second Avenue S., Suite 7045, 33701.
Telephone: 813-982-6000.
Fax: 813-892-6002.
New York, New York Office: Eleventh Floor, 135 East 57th Street,
10022-2087.
Telephone: 212-754-5400.
Fax: 212-754-5401.
Gdansk, Poland Office: Suite 322, Dom Technika Building, UI. Rajska 6,
80-850.
Telephone: 011-485-831-2808.
Fax: 011-485-831-4719.
Warsaw, Poland Office: UI. Marszalkowska 82, Suite 561, 00-517.
Telephone: 011-482-623-6457 and 6458.
Fax: 011-482-623-6459.

RESIDENT PRINCIPALS

Robert E. Gilbert

OF COUNSEL

Edmond F. DeVine

Representative Firm Clients: Chrysler Corporation; Comerica, Incorporated;
City of Detroit, Michigan; Detroit Tigers, Inc.; First of Michigan; Ford Motor Company; Ford Motor Credit Company; Great Lakes Bancorp; Henry
Ford Hospital; INVETECH Company.

For Complete List of Firm Personnel, See General Section

For full biographical listings, see the Martindale-Hubbell Law Directory

BLOOMFIELD HILLS, Oakland Co.

HOWARD & HOWARD ATTORNEYS, P.C. (AV)

The Pinehurst Office Center, Suite 101, 1400 North Woodward
  Avenue, 48304-2856
Telephone: 810-645-1483
Telecopier: 810-645-1568
Kalamazoo, Michigan Office: The Kalamazoo Building, Suite 400, 107
West Michigan Avenue.
Telephone: 616-382-1483.
Telecopier: 616-382-1568.
Lansing, Michigan Office: The Phoenix Building, Suite 500, 222
Washington Square, North.
Telephone: 517-485-1483.
Telecopier: 517-485-1568.
Peoria, Illinois Office: The Creve Coeur Building, Suite 200, 321 Liberty
Street.
Telephone: 309-672-1483.
Telecopier: 309-672-1568.
Tampa, Florida Office: First of America Plaza, Suite 2000, 201 East
Kennedy Boulevard.
Telephone: 813-229-1483.
Telecopier: 813-229-1568.

Thomas R. Curran, Jr.	Thomas J. Tallerico
Sally Lee Foley	John E. Young

Representative Clients: For Representative Client list, see General Practice,
Bloomfield Hills, MI.

For Complete List of Firm Personnel, See General Section

For full biographical listings, see the Martindale-Hubbell Law Directory

DETROIT,* Wayne Co.

BODMAN, LONGLEY & DAHLING LLP (AV)

34th Floor 100 Renaissance Center, 48243
Telephone: 313-259-7777
Fax: 313-393-7579
Email: 2080194@mcimail.com
Troy, Michigan Office: Suite 2020, 755 West Big Beaver Road.
Telephone: 810-362-2110.
Fax: 810-244-0780.
Ann Arbor, Michigan Office: 110 Miller, Suite 300.
Telephone: 313-761-3780.
Fax: 313-930-2494.
Northern Michigan Office: 229 Court Street, P.O. Box 405, Cheboygan.
Telephone: 616-627-4351.
Fax: 616-627-2802.

MEMBERS OF FIRM

Richard D. Rohr	Michael B. Lewiston
Theodore Souris	Herold McC. Deason
David G. Chardavoyne	

COUNSEL

Robert A. Nitschke

For Representative Client List, See General Section.

For Complete List of Firm Personnel, See General Section

For full biographical listings, see the Martindale-Hubbell Law Directory

BUTZEL LONG, A PROFESSIONAL CORPORATION (AV)

Suite 900, 150 West Jefferson, 48226
Telephone: 313-225-7000
Telecopier: 313-225-7080
Email: melnick@butzel.com *URL:* http://www.butzel.com
Birmingham, Michigan Office: Suite 200, 32270 Telegraph Road.
Telephone: 810-258-1616.
Telecopier: 810-258-1439.
Lansing, Michigan Office: 118 West Ottawa Street.
Telephone: 517-372-6622.
Telecopier: 517-372-6672.
Ann Arbor, Michigan Office: Suite 300, 350 South Main Street.
Telephone: 313-995-3110.
Telecopier: 313-995-1777.
Grosse Pointe Farms, Michigan Office: Suite 260, 21 Kercheval.
Telephone: 313-886-5446.
Telecopier: 313-886-2114.

Richard E. Rassel	Leonard M. Niehoff
Edward M. Kronk	(Ann Arbor)
Philip J. Kessler	Sheldon H. Klein

Representative Clients: Bridgestone/Firestone, Inc.; The Detroit News, Inc.;
Kelly Services; Kelsey Hayes Co.; Merrill Lynch Pierce Fenner & Smith,
Inc.; Stroh Brewery Co.; Takata Corp.; United Parcel Services of America,
Inc.; The University of Michigan.

For Complete List of Firm Personnel, See General Section

For full biographical listings, see the Martindale-Hubbell Law Directory

CLARK HILL P.L.C. (AV)

500 Woodward Avenue, Suite 3500, 48226
Telephone: 313-965-8300
Facsimile: 313-962-4348
Oakland County, Michigan Office: Third Floor, 255 South Woodward
Avenue, Birmingham.
Telephone: 810-642-9692.
Facsimile: 810-642-2174.
Lansing, Michigan Office: Suite 600, 200 North Capitol Avenue.
Telephone: 517-484-4481.
Facsimile: 517-484-1246.
Minneapolis, Minnesota Office: Suite 1000, One Financial Plaza, 120 South
Sixth Street.
Telephone: 612-332-0102.
Facsimile: 612-332-3225.
Kansas City, Missouri Office: Suite 1400, Bryant Building, 1102 Grand
Avenue.
Telephone: 816-221-5578.
Facsimile: 816-221-0303.

D. Kerry Crenshaw	David E. Nims, III
David M. Hayes	John J. Hern, Jr.
Robert L. Weyhing, III	John E. Berg

Patrice Asimakis	John P. Hensien
Georgette Borrego Dulworth	Margery Siegel Klausner

For Complete List of Firm Personnel, See General Section

For full biographical listings, see the Martindale-Hubbell Law Directory

DYKEMA GOSSETT PLLC (AV)

400 Renaissance Center, 48243-1668
Telephone: 313-568-6800
Cable Address: "Dyke-Detroit"
Telex: 23-0121
Fax: 313-568-6594
Email: 2084153@mcimail.com
Ann Arbor, Michigan Office: 315 East Eisenhower Parkway, Suite 100,
48108-3306.
Telephone: 313-747-7660.
Fax: 313-747-7696.
Bloomfield Hills, Michigan Office: 1577 North Woodward Avenue, Suite
300, 48304-2820.
Telephone: 810-540-0700.
Fax: 810-540-0763.
Chicago, Illinois Office: 55 East Monroe Street, Suite 3250, 60603-5709.
Telephone: 312-551-4900.
Fax: 312-551-4919.
Grand Rapids, Michigan Office: 200 Oldtown Riverfront Building, 248
Louis Campau Promenade, N.W., 49503-2668.
Telephone: 616-776-7500.
Fax: 616-776-7573.
Lansing, Michigan Office: 800 Michigan National Tower, 48933-1707.
Telephone: 517-374-9100.
Fax: 517-374-9191.
Washington, D.C. Office: Franklin Square, Suite 300 West, 1300 I Street,
N.W., 20005-3306.
Telephone: 202-522-8600.
Fax: 202-522-8669.

MEMBERS OF FIRM

Barbara L. Goldman (Resident at Bloomfield Hills Office)	Howard E. O'Leary, Jr. (Resident at Washington, D.C. Office)
Edward A. Groobert (Not admitted in MI; Resident at Washington, D.C. Office)	Thomas W. B. Porter
	Roger K. Timm
Dennis M. Haffey (Member in Charge of Bloomfield Hills Office)	Fred L. Woodworth (Member in Charge of Washington, D.C. Office)
D. Biard MacGuineas (Not admitted in MI; Resident at Washington, D.C. Office)	

ASSOCIATES

Judy Parker Jenkins (Not admitted in MI; Resident at Washington, D.C. Office)	Ava K. Ortner

For Complete List of Firm Personnel, See General Section

For full biographical listings, see the Martindale-Hubbell Law Directory

HONIGMAN MILLER SCHWARTZ AND COHN (AV)

A Partnership including Professional Corporations
2290 First National Building, 48226
Telephone: 313-256-7800
Telecopier: 313-962-0176
Telex: 235705
URL: http://law.honigman.com
Lansing, Michigan Office: Phoenix Building, 222 North Washington
Square, Suite 400, 48933-1800.
Telephone: 517-484-8282.

(See Next Column)

HONIGMAN MILLER SCHWARTZ AND COHN, *Detroit—Continued*

West Palm Beach, Florida Office: Suite 800 Esperante Building, 222 Lakeview Avenue, 33401-6112.
Telephone: 561-838-4500.
Tampa, Florida Office: 2700 SunTrust Financial Centre, 401 E. Jackson Street, 33602-5226.
Telephone: 813-221-6600.

MEMBERS OF FIRM

Stanford P. Berenbaum	Gerald S. Cook
Maurice S. Binkow	David A. Ettinger
	Howard B. Iwrey

RESIDENT IN TAMPA, FLORIDA OFFICE

MEMBER

Harry Christopher Goplerud (P.A.)

Representative Clients: American Speedy Printing Company, Inc.; Bronson Healthcare Group, Inc; Citicorp; Compuware; Handleman Co.; J.P. Industries, Inc.; Intergraph Corporation; Mercy Health Services; Prime Computer, Inc.; T & N, Inc.

For Complete List of Firm Personnel, See General Section

For full biographical listings, see the Martindale-Hubbell Law Directory

MILLER, CANFIELD, PADDOCK AND STONE, P.L.C. (AV)

A Professional Limited Liability Company
Founded in 1852 by Sidney Davy Miller
150 West Jefferson, Suite 2500, 48226-4415.
Telephone: 313-963-6420.
Fax: 313-496-7500.
Cable Address: "Stem Detroit"
Detroit, Michigan Office: 150 West Jefferson, Suite 2500, 48226-4415.
Telephone: 313-963-6420.
Fax: 313-496-7500.
Cable Address: "Stem Detroit."
Ann Arbor, Michigan Office: 101 North Main Street, 7th Floor, 48104-1400.
Telephone: 313-663-2445.
Fax: 313-747-7147.
Bloomfield Hills, Michigan Office: Suite 100, Pinehurst Office Center, 1400 North Woodward, 48303-2014.
Telephone: 313-645-5000.
Fax: 313-645-1917.
Grand Rapids, Michigan Office: 1200 Campau Square Plaza, 99 Monroe, N.W., 49503-2639.
Telephone: 616-454-8656.
Fax: 616-776-6322.
Howell, Michigan Office: 121 South Barnard Street, Suite 4, 48843-2305.
Telephone: 517-546-7600.
Telecopier: 517-546-6974.
Kalamazoo, Michigan Office: 444 West Michigan Avenue, 49007-3752.
Telephone: 616-381-7030.
Fax: 616-382-0244.
Lansing, Michigan Office: One Michigan Avenue, Suite 900, 48933-1609.
Telephone: 517-487-2070.
Fax: 517-374-6304.
Monroe, Michigan Office: The Executive Centre, 214 East Elm Avenue, 48161-2682.
Telephone: 313-243-2000.
Fax: 313-243-0901.
Washington, D.C. Office: 1225 Nineteenth Street, N.W., Suite 400. 20036.
Telephone: 202-429-5575; 785-0600.
Fax: 202-331-1118; 785-1234.
Pensacola, Florida Office: 25 West Cedar, 32501.
Telephone: 904-469-1088.
Fax: 904-432-0677.
St. Petersburg, Florida Office: 100 Second Avenue S., Suite 7045, 33701.
Telephone: 813-982-6000.
Fax: 813-892-6002.
New York, New York Office: Eleventh Floor, 135 East 57th Street, 10022-2087.
Telephone: 212-754-5400.
Fax: 212-754-5401.
Gdansk, Poland Office: Suite 322, Dom Technika Building, UI. Rajska 6, 80-850.
Telephone: 011-485-831-2808.
Fax: 011-485-831-4719.
Warsaw, Poland Office: UI. Marszalkowska 82, Suite 561, 00-517.
Telephone: 011-482-623-6457 and 6458.
Fax: 011-482-623-6459.

PRINCIPALS OF FIRM

George E. Parker, III	Gregory L. Curtner
Rocque E. Lipford (P.C.)	(New York, N.Y. Office)
(Monroe Office)	Larry J. Saylor
David D. Joswick (P.C.)	Mark T. Boonstra

(See Next Column)

OF COUNSEL

Edmond F. DeVine	Richard B. Gushée
(Ann Arbor Office)	

Representative Firm Clients: Chrysler Corporation; Comerica, Incorporated; City of Detroit, Michigan; Detroit Tigers, Inc.; First of Michigan; Ford Motor Company; Ford Motor Credit Company; Great Lakes Bancorp; Henry Ford Hospital; INVETECH Company.

For Complete List of Firm Personnel, See General Section

For full biographical listings, see the Martindale-Hubbell Law Directory

TIMMIS & INMAN, L.L.P. (AV)

300 Talon Centre, 48207
Telephone: 313-396-4200
Telecopier: 313-396-4228

Charles W. Royer	Richard M. Miettinen
Henry J. Brennan, III	Lisa R. Gorman
	Bradley J. Knickerbocker

OF COUNSEL

Wayne C. Inman

For Complete List of Firm Personnel, See General Section

For full biographical listings, see the Martindale-Hubbell Law Directory

---

GRAND RAPIDS, * Kent Co.

MILLER, CANFIELD, PADDOCK AND STONE, P.L.C. (AV)

A Professional Limited Liability Company
Founded in 1852 by Sidney Davy Miller
1200 Campau Square Plaza, 99 Monroe, N.W., P.O. Box 329, 49503-2639
Telephone: 616-454-8656
Fax: 616-776-6322
Detroit, Michigan Office: 150 West Jefferson, Suite 2500, 48226-4415.
Telephone: 313-963-6420.
Fax: 313-496-7500.
Cable Address: "Stem Detroit."
Ann Arbor, Michigan Office: 101 North Main Street, 7th Floor, 48104-1400.
Telephone: 313-663-2445.
Fax: 313-747-7147.
Bloomfield Hills, Michigan Office: Suite 100, Pinehurst Office Center, 1400 North Woodward, 48303-2014.
Telephone: 313-645-5000.
Fax: 313-645-1917.
Howell, Michigan Office: 121 South Barnard Street, Suite 4, 48843-2305.
Telephone: 517-546-7600.
Telecopier: 517-546-6974.
Kalamazoo, Michigan Office: 444 West Michigan Avenue, 49007-3752.
Telephone: 616-381-7030.
Fax: 616-382-0244.
Lansing, Michigan Office: One Michigan Avenue, Suite 900, 48933-1609.
Telephone: 517-487-2070.
Fax: 517-374-6304.
Monroe, Michigan Office: The Executive Centre, 214 East Elm Avenue, 48161-2682.
Telephone: 313-243-2000.
Fax: 313-243-0901.
Washington, D.C. Office: 1225 Nineteenth Street, N.W., Suite 400. 20036.
Telephone: 202-429-5575; 785-0600.
Fax: 202-331-1118; 785-1234.
Pensacola, Florida Office: 25 West Cedar 32501.
Telephone: 904-469-1088.
Fax: 904-432-0677.
St. Petersburg Florida Office: 100 Second Avenue S., Suite 7045, 33701.
Telephone: 813-982-6000.
Fax: 813-892-6002.
New York, New York Office: Eleventh Floor, 135 East 57th Street, 10022-2087.
Telephone: 212-754-5400.
Fax: 212-754-5401.
Gdansk, Poland Office: Suite 322, Dom Technika Building, UI. Rajska 6, 80-850.
Telephone: 011-485-831-2808.
Fax: 011-485-831-4719.
Warsaw, Poland Office: UI. Marszalkowska 82, Suite 561, 00-517.
Telephone: 011-482-623-6457 and 6458.
Fax: 011-482-623-6459.

PRINCIPALS OF FIRM

Mark E. Putney (Resident Director, Grand Rapids Office)	Michael G. Campbell
	Robert E. Lee Wright
	Vernon Bennett III
Richard A. Gaffin	Douglas W. Crim
Charles S. Mishkind (Detroit, Lansing and Kalamazoo Offices)	

OF COUNSEL

David E. Hathaway

(See Next Column)

MILLER, CANFIELD, PADDOCK AND STONE P.L.C.—*Continued*

SENIOR ATTORNEYS

David J. Hasper   Stephen L. Elkins

ASSOCIATES

John C. Arndts   Daniel H. Roberts
Bradley C. White   John T. Stecco
                    Michael V. Camarota

Representative Firm Clients: Chrysler Corporation; Comerica, Incorporated; City of Detroit, Michigan; Detroit Tigers, Inc.; First of Michigan; Ford Motor Company; Ford Motor Credit Company; Great Lakes Bancorp; Henry Ford Hospital; INVETECH Company.

For full biographical listings, see the Martindale-Hubbell Law Directory

---

VARNUM, RIDDERING, SCHMIDT & HOWLETT LLP (AV)

A Limited Liability Partnership including Professional Corporations
Bridgewater Place, P.O. Box 352, 49501-0352
Telephone: 616-336-6000
800-262-0011
Facsimile: 616-336-7000
Telex: 1561593 VARN
Email: varnum@vrsh.com
Lansing, Michigan Office: The Victor Center, Suite 810, 210 North Washington Square, 48933.
Telephone: 517-482-6237.
Facsimile: 517-482-6937.
Kalamazoo, Michigan Office: 350 East Michigan Avenue, 49007.
Telephone: 616-382-2300.
Facsimile: 616-382-2382.
Grand Haven, Michigan Office: 321 Washington Street, P.O. Box 288, 49417.
Telephone: 616-846-7100.
Facsimile: 616-846-7101.
Battle Creek, Michigan Office: 4950 West Dickman Road, Suite B-1, 49015.
Telephone: 616-962-7144.
Bingham Farms, Michigan Office: 31600 Telegraph Road, Suite 230, 48025.
Telephone: 810-594-7330.
Facsimile: 810-594- 7331.

MEMBERS OF FIRM

J. Terry Moran   Jeffrey W. Beswick (Resident at
Robert L. Diamond   Grand Haven Office)
William J. Lawrence III   Kathleen P. Fochtman

ASSOCIATES

Steven J. Morren   Jon M. Bylsma

Counsel for: Donnelly Corporation; First Michigan Bank Corporation; Gainey Corporation; Gentex Corporation; Grand Rapids Association of Realtors; Herman Miller, Inc.; Holland Hitch Co.; X-Rite Incorporated; Tiara Yachts; Universal Forest Products, Inc.

For Complete List of Firm Personnel, See General Section

For full biographical listings, see the Martindale-Hubbell Law Directory

---

WARNER NORCROSS & JUDD LLP (AV)

900 Old Kent Building, 111 Lyon Street, N.W., 49503-2489
Telephone: 616-752-2000
Fax: 616-752-2500
Muskegon, Michigan Office: 400 Terrace Plaza, P.O. Box 900.
Telephone: 616-727-2600.
Fax: 616-727-2699.
Holland, Michigan Office: Curtis Center, Suite 300, 170 College Avenue.
Telephone: 616-396-9800.
Fax: 616-396-3656.

MEMBERS OF FIRM

R. Malcolm Cumming   Stephen C. Waterbury
William K. Holmes   Tracy T. Larsen
J. A. Cragwall, Jr.   Richard L. Bouma

General Counsel for: Bissell Inc.; Blodgett Memorial Medical Center; Guardsman Products, Inc.; Haworth, Inc.; Kysor Industrial Corp.; Michigan Bankers Assn.; Old Kent Financial Corp.; Steelcase Inc.; Wolverine World Wide Inc.

For Complete List of Firm Personnel, See General Section

For full biographical listings, see the Martindale-Hubbell Law Directory

---

KALAMAZOO, * Kalamazoo Co.

MILLER, CANFIELD, PADDOCK AND STONE, P.L.C. (AV)

A Professional Limited Liability Company
Founded in 1852 by Sidney Davy Miller
444 West Michigan Avenue, 49007-3752
Telephone: 616-381-7030
Fax: 616-382-0244
Detroit, Michigan Office: 150 West Jefferson, Suite 2500, 48226-4415.
Telephone: 313-963-6420.
Fax: 313-496-7500.
Cable Address: "Stem Detroit."
Ann Arbor, Michigan Office: 101 North Main Street, 7th Floor, 48104-1400.
Telephone: 313-663-2445.
Fax: 313-747-7147.
Bloomfield Hills, Michigan Office: Suite 100, Pinehurst Office Center, 1400 North Woodward, 48303-2014.
Telephone: 313-645-5000.
Fax: 313-645-1917.
Grand Rapids, Michigan Office: 1200 Campau Square Plaza, 99 Monroe, N.W., 49503-2639.
Telephone: 616-454-8656.
Fax: 616-776-6322.
Howell, Michigan Office: 121 South Barnard Street, Suite 4, 48843-2305.
Telephone: 517-546-7600.
Telecopier: 517-546-6974.
Lansing, Michigan Office: One Michigan Avenue, Suite 900, 48933-1609.
Telephone: 517-487-2070.
Fax: 517-374-6304.
Monroe, Michigan Office: The Executive Centre, 214 East Elm Avenue, 48161-2682.
Telephone: 313-243-2000.
Fax: 313-243-0901.
Washington, D.C. Office: 1225 Nineteenth Street, N.W., Suite 400. 20036.
Telephone: 202-429-5575; 785-0600.
Fax: 202-331-1118; 785-1234.
Pensacola, Florida Office: 25 West Cedar, 32501.
Telephone: 904-469-1088.
Fax: 904-432-0677.
St. Petersburg, Florida Office: 100 Second Avenue S., Suite 7045, 33701.
Telephone: 813-982-6000.
Fax: 813-892-6002.
New York, New York Office: Eleventh Floor, 135 East 57th Street, 10022-2087.
Telephone: 212-754-5400.
Fax: 212-754-5401.
Gdansk, Poland Office: Suite 322, Dom Technika Building, UI. Rajska 6, 80-850.
Telephone: 011-485-831-2808.
Fax: 011-485-831-4719.
Warsaw, Poland Office: UI. Marszalkowska 82, Suite 561, 00-517.
Telephone: 011-482-623-6457 and 6458.
Fax: 011-482-623-6459.

PRINCIPALS OF FIRM

Eric V. Brown, Jr.   John R. Cook
                James G. Vantine, Jr.

Representative Firm Clients: Chrysler Corporation; Comerica, Incorporated; City of Detroit, Michigan; Detroit Tigers, Inc.; First of Michigan; Ford Motor Company; Ford Motor Credit Company; Great Lakes Bancorp; Henry Ford Hospital; INVETECH Company.

For Complete List of Firm Personnel, See General Section

For full biographical listings, see the Martindale-Hubbell Law Directory

---

LANSING, Ingham Co.

MILLER, CANFIELD, PADDOCK AND STONE, P.L.C. (AV)

A Professional Limited Liability Company
Founded in 1852 by Sidney Davy Miller
Suite 900, One Michigan Avenue, 48933-1609
Telephone: 517-487-2070
Fax: 517-374-6304
Detroit, Michigan Office: 150 West Jefferson, Suite 2500, 48226-4415.
Telephone: 313-963-6420.
Fax: 313-496-7500.
Cable Address: "Stem Detroit."
Ann Arbor, Michigan Office: 101 North Main Street, 7th Floor, 48104-1400.
Telephone: 313-663-2445.
Fax: 313-747-7147.
Bloomfield Hills, Michigan Office: Suite 100, Pinehurst Office Center, 1400 North Woodward, 48303-2014.
Telephone: 313-645-5000.
Fax: 313-645-1917.
Grand Rapids, Michigan Office: 1200 Campau Square Plaza, 99 Monroe, N.W., 49503-2639.
Telephone: 616-454-8656.
Fax: 616-776-6322.

(See Next Column)

MILLER, CANFIELD, PADDOCK AND STONE P.L.C., *Lansing—Continued*

Howell, Michigan Office: 121 South Barnard Street, Suite 4, 48843-2305.
Telephone: 517-546-7600.
Telecopier: 517-546-6974.
Kalamazoo, Michigan Office: 444 West Michigan Avenue, 49007-3752.
Telephone: 616-381-7030.
Fax: 616-382-0244.
Monroe, Michigan Office: The Executive Centre, 214 East Elm Avenue, 48161-2682.
Telephone: 313-243-2000.
Fax: 313-243-0901.
Washington, D.C. Office: 1225 Nineteenth Street, N.W., Suite 400. 20036.
Telephone: 202-429-5575; 785-0600.
Fax: 202-331-1118; 785-1234.
Pensacola, Florida Office: 25 West Cedar, 32501.
Telephone: 904-469-1088.
Fax: 904-432-0677.
St. Petersburg Office: 100 Second Avenue S., Suite 7045, 33701.
Telephone: 813-982-6000.
Fax: 813-892-6002.
New York, New York Office: Eleventh Floor, 135 East 57th Street, 10022-2087.
Telephone: 212-754-5400.
Fax: 212-754-5401.
Gdansk, Poland Office: Suite 322, Dom Technika Building, UI. Rajska 6, 80-850.
Telephone: 011-485-831-2808.
Fax: 011-485-831-4719.
Warsaw, Poland Office: UI. Marszalkowska 82, Suite 561, 00-517.
Telephone: 011-482-623-6457 and 6458.
Fax: 011-482-623-6459.

PRINCIPALS OF FIRM
William J. Danhof (Resident)

Representative Firm Clients: Chrysler Corporation; Comerica, Incorporated; City of Detroit, Michigan; Detroit Tigers, Inc.; First of Michigan; Ford Motor Company; Ford Motor Credit Company; Great Lakes Bancorp; Henry Ford Hospital; INVETECH Company.

For Complete List of Firm Personnel, See General Section

For full biographical listings, see the Martindale-Hubbell Law Directory

---

SOUTHFIELD, Oakland Co.

YOUNG & ASSOCIATES, P.C. (AV)

Suite 305 Westview Office Center, 26200 American Drive, 48034
Telephone: 810-353-8620
Telecopier: 810-353-6559
Email: youngp@aol.com

Rodger D. Young

Anthony Cho   Steven Susser
Michael J. Fergestrom   Thomas A. Pinch

For full biographical listings, see the Martindale-Hubbell Law Directory

---

TROY, Oakland Co.

HACKETT, MAXWELL & PHILLIPS, P.L.L.C. (AV)

City Center Building, Suite 1470, 888 West Big Beaver Road, 48084
Telephone: 810-362-2600
Fax: 810-362-3610
Email: hackmax@michbar.org

Patrick E. Hackett   Phillip B. Maxwell
Dawn L. Phillips

Mark T. Butler   Lisa Rycus Mikalonis
Jill Tilton Silverman   Jason W. Johnson

For full biographical listings, see the Martindale-Hubbell Law Directory

APPELLATE PRACTICE

ALABAMA

*BIRMINGHAM,** Jefferson Co.

BRADLEY, ARANT, ROSE & WHITE (AV)

2001 Park Place, Suite 1400, P.O. Box 830709, 35283-0709
Telephone: 205-521-8000
Facsimile: 205-252-0264
Facsimile (SouthTrust Tower Office): 205-251-9915
URL: http://www.BARW.COM
Huntsville, Alabama Office: 200 Clinton Avenue West, Suite 900, 35801.
Telephone: 205-517-5100.
Facsimile: 205-533-5069.

MEMBERS OF FIRM

Hobart A. McWhorter, Jr.
Gary C. Huckaby
(Resident, Huntsville Office)
E. Cutter Hughes, Jr.
(Resident, Huntsville Office)

Sid J. Trant
Philip J. Carroll III
James S. Christie, Jr.
Susan Donovan Josey

COUNSEL

Scott M. Phelps

ASSOCIATES

Kimberly A. Bessiere
(Resident, Huntsville Office)

David M. Lawson

For Complete List of Firm Personnel, See General Section

For full biographical listings, see the Martindale-Hubbell Law Directory

LONDON & YANCEY (AV)

1000 Park Place Tower, 2001 Park Place, 35203
Telephone: 205-251-2531
FAX: 205-251-8929

MEMBERS OF FIRM

Alex T. London (1847-1908)
John London (1848-1935)
George W. Yancey (1883-1962)

Thomas R. Elliott, Jr.
Bert S. Nettles
Richard W. Lewis

ASSOCIATES

Allen R. Trippeer, Jr.
Mark David Hess
Lisa Wright Borden
A. David Fawal

Laura Ellison Proctor
Paige Elliott-Pinson
F. Daniel Wood, Jr.
C. Dennis Hughes

Michael J. Velezis

OF COUNSEL

Robert W. Norris

Representative Clients: State of Alabama; Cincinnati Ins. Co.; Lloyd's of London; Blue Cross/Blue Shield; Attorney's Mutual of Alabama; State Farm; CIGNA; Royal Ins. Co. of America; Paul Revere Ins. Co.; Chubb Group.

For full biographical listings, see the Martindale-Hubbell Law Directory

PATRICK & LACY, P.C. (AV)

1201 Financial Center, 35203
Telephone: 205-323-5665
Telecopier: 205-324-6221

J. Vernon Patrick, Jr.
Alex S. Lacy

William M. Acker, III
Elizabeth N. Pitman

For full biographical listings, see the Martindale-Hubbell Law Directory

*HUNTSVILLE,** Madison Co.

BERRY, ABLES, TATUM, BAXTER, PARKER & HALL, P.C. (AV)

Legal Building, 315 Franklin Street, S.E., P.O. Box 165, 35804-0165
Telephone: 205-533-3740
Facsimile: 205-533-3751
Email: BAXTERJ@ATTMAIL.COM

William H. Blanton (1889-1973)
Joe M. Berry
L. Bruce Ables

James T. Tatum, Jr.
James T. Baxter, III
Thomas E. Parker, Jr.

Bill G. Hall

James K. Brabston

Mark Rogers Hunter

Representative Clients: AmSouth Bank; First Alabama Bank; General Shale Products Co.; The Hertz Corp.; Litton Industries, Inc.; Farmers Tractor Co.; Colonial Bank; Farm Credit Bank of Texas; SouthBank; Regions Mortgage.
Reference: First Alabama Bank.

For full biographical listings, see the Martindale-Hubbell Law Directory

*MOBILE,** Mobile Co.

LYONS, PIPES & COOK, P.C. (AV)

2 North Royal Street, P.O. Box 2727, 36652-2727
Telephone: 334-432-4481
Cable Address: "Lysea"
Telecopier: 334-433-1820

Joseph H. Lyons (1874-1957)
Sam W. Pipes, III (1916-1982)
Walter M. Cook (1915-1988)
Wesley Pipes
Norton W. Brooker, Jr.
Cooper C. Thurber
Marion A. Quina, Jr.
Thomas F. Garth
Claude D. Boone
Walter M. Cook, Jr.
John Patrick Courtney, III
W. David Johnson, Jr.
Joseph J. Minus, Jr.

Caroline C. McCarthy
William E. Shreve, Jr.
R. Mark Kirkpatrick
Kenneth A. Nixon
Daniel S. Cushing
Allen E. Graham
Michael C. Niemeyer
John C. Bell
M. Warren Butler
Christopher Lee George
M. Lauren Lemmon
J. Murphy McMillan, III
S. Wesley Pipes, V

General Counsel: Inchcape Shipping Services.
Counsel: The Hertz Corp.; McKenzie Tank Lines, Inc.; SCNO Barge Lines, Inc.; Scott Paper Co.; Shell Oil Corp.
Trial Counsel: Aetna Life & Casualty Co.; Chubb Group of Insurance Companies.

For full biographical listings, see the Martindale-Hubbell Law Directory

PIERCE, LEDYARD, LATTA & WASDEN, P.C. (AV)

Suite 900 Montlimar Place Office Building, 1110 Montlimar Drive, P.O. Box 16046, 36616
Telephone: 334-344-5151
Facsimile: 334-344-9696

Donald F. Pierce

Forrest S. Latta

John Chas. S. Pierce

W. Pemble DeLashmet

Representative Clients: Blue Cross and Blue Shield; Alabama Power Company; Auto Owners Insurance Company; The Business Council of Alabama; Sears, Roebuck & Co.; USF&G.

For full biographical listings, see the Martindale-Hubbell Law Directory

*MONTGOMERY,** Montgomery Co.

VOLZ, PRESTWOOD & HANAN, P.C. (AV)

350 Adams Avenue, P.O. Box 1910, 36102-1910
Telephone: 334-264-6401
Fax: 334-834-4954

Charles H. Volz, Jr.
Alvin T. Prestwood
Ellis D. Hanan

Charles H. Volz, III
Clinton Chadwell Carter
Daniel Lewis Feinstein

LEGAL SUPPORT PERSONNEL

Mark A.W. Turpen

For full biographical listings, see the Martindale-Hubbell Law Directory

ARIZONA

*PHOENIX,** Maricopa Co.

BONN, LUSCHER, PADDEN & WILKINS, CHARTERED (AV)

805 North Second Street, 85004
Telephone: 602-254-5557
Fax: 602-254-0656

Paul V. Bonn
Brian A. Luscher
Jeff C. Padden
Randall D. Wilkins

John H. Cassidy
D. Michael Hall
Samuel C. Wisotzkey
Ronald A. Rice

OF COUNSEL

Marvin Kantor

Ruth Sproull

For full biographical listings, see the Martindale-Hubbell Law Directory

BROWN & BAIN, A PROFESSIONAL ASSOCIATION (AV)

2901 North Central Avenue, P.O. Box 400, 85001-0400
Telephone: 602-351-8000
Telecopier: 602-351-8516
Palo Alto, California Affiliated Office: Brown & Bain, 1755 Embarcadero Road, Suite 200.
Telephone: 415-856-9411.
Telecopier: 415-856-6061.

(See Next Column)

BROWN & BAIN A PROFESSIONAL ASSOCIATION, *Phoenix—Continued*

Tucson, Arizona Affiliated Office: Brown & Bain, A Professional Association. One South Church Avenue, Nineteenth Floor, P.O. Box 2265.
Telephone: 602-798-7900
Telecopier: 602-798-7945.

C. Randall Bain	Jodi Knobel Feuerhelm
Alan H. Blankenheimer	Joel W. Nomkin
Paul F. Eckstein	Lawrence G. D. Scarborough

Dan L. Bagatell

For Complete List of Firm Personnel, See General Section

For full biographical listings, see the Martindale-Hubbell Law Directory

BURCH & CRACCHIOLO, P.A. (AV)

702 East Osborn Road, Suite 200, 85014
Telephone: 602-274-7611
Fax: 602-234-0341
Mailing Address: P.O. Box 16882, Phoenix, AZ, 85011

Daniel Cracchiolo	Daryl Manhart
Jack D. Klausner	Daniel R. Malinski

J. Brent Welker

Representative Clients: Bashas' Inc.; Farmers Insurance Group; U-Haul International, Inc.

For Complete List of Firm Personnel, See General Section

For full biographical listings, see the Martindale-Hubbell Law Directory

COPPLE, CHAMBERLIN & BOEHM, P.C. (AV)

Suite 300 The Brookstone, 2025 North Third Street, 85004
Telephone: 602-528-4700
Fax: 602-253-4909

Steven D. Copple	Scott E. Boehm
Thomas J. Chamberlin	Robert S. Murphy

OF COUNSEL
Frederick O. Robertshaw

Representative Clients: Aetna Casualty & Surety Co.; Verco Manufacturing Co.

For full biographical listings, see the Martindale-Hubbell Law Directory

FOGEL AND LAMBER, PROFESSIONAL ASSOCIATION (AV)

One Windsor Professional Building, 2627 North Third Street, 85004-1197
Telephone: 602-264-3330
Fax: 602-274-5117

Sherman D. Fogel	Dennis M. Lamber
	Rex P. Bronnenkant

Reference: Chase Bank of Arizona.

For full biographical listings, see the Martindale-Hubbell Law Directory

GOLDSTEIN & McGRODER, LTD. A PROFESSIONAL CORPORATION (AV)

2200 East Camelback Road, Suite 221, 85016-3456
Telephone: 602-957-1500
Fax: 602-956-9294

Philip T. Goldstein	Patrick J. McGroder, III
	Suzanne P. Clarke

Jane E. Evans	Serena C. Montague

LEGAL SUPPORT PERSONNEL
Kevan S. DeWitt (Paralegal)

For full biographical listings, see the Martindale-Hubbell Law Directory

MacLEAN & JACQUES, LTD. (AV)

Suite 202, 40 East Virginia, 85004
Telephone: 602-263-5771
FAX: 602-279-5569

John H. MacLean (1932-1992)	Raoul T. Jacques

Cary T. Inabinet	Macre S. Inabinet

LEGAL SUPPORT PERSONNEL
Sharon Petterson

For full biographical listings, see the Martindale-Hubbell Law Directory

MITTEN, GOODWIN & RAUP, A PROFESSIONAL CORPORATION (AV)

One Columbus Plaza, 3636 North Central, Suite 1200, 85012
Telephone: 602-650-2000
Fax: 602-264-7033
Email: mgr@starlink.com

Roger C. Mitten

Steven P. Kramer
OF COUNSEL

Donald F. Froeb	Richard M. Davis

For full biographical listings, see the Martindale-Hubbell Law Directory

LAW OFFICES OF RICHARD L. STROHM, P.C. (AV)

1136 East Campbell, 85014
Telephone: 602-279-6316
Mobile: 602-616-7094
Facsimile: 602-279-7102
Email: 102442.1444@compuserve.com

Richard L. Strohm
OF COUNSEL

Brad K. Keogh	Nedra J. Bates

LEGAL SUPPORT PERSONNEL

Mindy L. Raymond	Barbara A. Shore
(Legal Assistant)	(Nurse Paralegal)
Richard M. Knaeble	
(Licensed Private Investigator)	

For full biographical listings, see the Martindale-Hubbell Law Directory

ULRICH, KESSLER & ANGER, P.C. (AV)

Suite 1000, 3030 North Central Avenue, 85012-2717
Telephone: 602-248-9465
Fax: 602-248-0165
Email: ukapc@aol.com

Paul G. Ulrich	Donn G. Kessler
	William H. Anger

For full biographical listings, see the Martindale-Hubbell Law Directory

PRESCOTT, * Yavapai Co.

FAVOUR, MOORE & WILHELMSEN, A PROFESSIONAL ASSOCIATION (AV)

1580 Plaza West Drive, P.O. Box 1391, 86302
Telephone: 520-445-2444
Fax: 520-771-0450

John M. Favour

Representative Client: Yavapai Title Co.
Reference: Bank of America.

For Complete List of Firm Personnel, See General Section

For full biographical listings, see the Martindale-Hubbell Law Directory

ARKANSAS

LITTLE ROCK, * Pulaski Co.

ROSE LAW FIRM, A PROFESSIONAL ASSOCIATION (AV)

120 East Fourth Street, 72201
Telephone: 501-375-9131
Telecopy: 501-375-1309

Tim Boe	James Hunter Birch
Jerry C. Jones	Richard T. Donovan
Thomas P. Thrash	James H. Druff
	Amy Lee Stewart

COUNSEL
Phillip Carroll

Mark Alan Peoples	Kathryn Bennett Perkins
David P. Martin	Michael N. Shannon

Counsel for: ALLTEL Corporation; Aluminum Company of America; Bridgestone/Firestone, Inc.; The Equitable Life Assurance Society of The United States; General Motors Corp.; The Prudential Insurance Company of America; Stephens Group Inc.; Tyson Foods, Inc.

For Complete List of Firm Personnel, See General Section

For full biographical listings, see the Martindale-Hubbell Law Directory

CALIFORNIA

BEVERLY HILLS, Los Angeles Co.

GREINES, MARTIN, STEIN & RICHLAND (AV)

Suite 544, 9601 Wilshire Boulevard, 90210
Telephone: 310-859-7811
Telecopier: 310-276-5261

MEMBERS OF FIRM

Alan G. Martin (1948-1990)	Robin Meadow
Irving H. Greines	Timothy T. Coates
Martin Stein	Feris M. Greenberger (Ms.)
Kent L. Richland	Barbara W. Ravitz
Marc J. Poster	Robert A. Olson

ASSOCIATES

Carolyn Oill	Barry M. Wolf
Sheila S. Kato	Brian J. Wright
Alison M. Turner	Jennifer L. King
Randel L. Ledesma	Edward Laucks Xanders

OF COUNSEL
Barbara S. Perry

Reference: City National Bank (Beverly Hills Branch).

For full biographical listings, see the Martindale-Hubbell Law Directory

COSTA MESA, Orange Co.

COULOMBE & KOTTKE, A PROFESSIONAL CORPORATION (AV)

Comerica Bank Tower, 611 Anton Boulevard, Suite 1260, 92626
Telephone: 714-540-1234
Fax: 714-754-0808; 714-754-0707
Email: c-k@coulombe.com

Ronald B. Coulombe	Jon S. Kottke

COUNSEL
Roy B. Woolsey

LEGAL SUPPORT PERSONNEL
PARALEGALS

Vicky M. Pearson	Abeer F. Rider

LEGAL ADMINISTRATOR
Yvonne Mendoza

For full biographical listings, see the Martindale-Hubbell Law Directory

RUTAN & TUCKER, LLP (AV)

A Partnership including Professional Corporations
611 Anton Boulevard, Suite 1400, P.O. Box 1950, 92626
Telephone: 714-641-5100; 213-625-7586
Telecopier: 714-546-9035
Email: rutan&tucker@mcimail.com *URL:* http://www.rutan.com

MEMBERS OF FIRM

David C. Larsen (P.C.)	M. Katherine Jenson
William W. Wynder	Duke Wahlquist
Matthew K. Ross	

For Complete List of Firm Personnel, See General Section

For full biographical listings, see the Martindale-Hubbell Law Directory

GLENDALE, Los Angeles Co.

OTT & HOROWITZ, A PROFESSIONAL CORPORATION (AV)

700 North Central Avenue, 8th Floor, Suite 850, 91203
Telephone: 818-242-3100
Fax: 818-242-3102
Email: ohlaw@aol.com

Thomas H. Ott	Craig A. Horowitz
Wayne D. Clayton	

Steven H. Taylor	Janine R. Menhennet
Patrick Carey	

For full biographical listings, see the Martindale-Hubbell Law Directory

IRVINE, Orange Co.

BORCHARD & WILLOUGHBY, A PROFESSIONAL CORPORATION (AV)

18881 Von Karman Avenue, Suite 1400, 92612
Telephone: 714-644-6161
Fax: 714-263-1913

Michael D. Borchard	Michael L. Willoughby
Mark A. Rodriguez	

(See Next Column)

Stephanie A. Pittaluga

For full biographical listings, see the Martindale-Hubbell Law Directory

GAUNTLETT & ASSOCIATES (AV)

18400 Von Karman, Suite 300, 92612
Telephone: 714-553-1010
Fax: 714-553-2050
Email: ugauntlett@aol.com

David A. Gauntlett

David A. Stall	Elizabeth A. Gillis
Leo E. Lundberg, Jr.	(Not admitted in CA)
Michael Danton Richardson	Mark H. Plager
William P. Warden	(Not admitted in CA)
Stanley H. Shure	Jeffrey S. Allison

OF COUNSEL

Gary L. Hinman	Jose Zorrilla, Jr.

For full biographical listings, see the Martindale-Hubbell Law Directory

TIMOTHY L. JOENS & ASSOCIATES A PROFESSIONAL CORPORATION (AV)

Jamboree Center, Five Park Plaza, Suite 1480, 92714
Telephone: 714-553-1950
Fax: 714-553-8835

Timothy L. Joens

Representative Clients: Century 21 of the Pacific, Inc.; Century 21 Region V, Inc.; Century 21 Real Estate Corp.

For full biographical listings, see the Martindale-Hubbell Law Directory

KOPENY & POWELL (AV)

8001 Irvine Center Drive, Suite 1170, 92618
Telephone: 714-453-2243
Facsimile: 714-453-1916
Email: KPATKP@AOL.COM

William J. Kopeny	John W. Powell

For full biographical listings, see the Martindale-Hubbell Law Directory

LONG BEACH, Los Angeles Co.

EDWARD P. GEORGE, JR., INC. A PROFESSIONAL CORPORATION (AV)

Suite 430, 5000 East Spring Street, 90815
Telephone: 310-497-2900
Facsimile: 310-497-2904

Edward P. George, Jr.	Timothy L. O'Reilly

OF COUNSEL
Albert C. S. Ramsey

Reference: Harbor Bank, Long Beach.

For full biographical listings, see the Martindale-Hubbell Law Directory

LOS ANGELES,* Los Angeles Co.

BERMAN, BLANCHARD, MAUSNER & RESSER, A LAW CORPORATION (AV)

4727 Wilshire Boulevard, Suite 500, 90010
Telephone: 213-965-1200
Telecopier: 213-965-1919
Email: BBMR@ix.netcom.com

Laurence M. Berman	Jeffrey N. Mausner
Lonnie C. Blanchard, III	Bernard M. Resser

Paul A. Hoffman	Cary P. Ocon
Eric Levinrad	Lisé Hamilton

For full biographical listings, see the Martindale-Hubbell Law Directory

BLACK COMPEAN HALL & LENNEMAN (AV)

One Wilshire, Suite 1000 624 South Grand Avenue, 90017
Telephone: 213-629-9500
FAX: 213-629-4868
Email: bchl@earthlink.net

MEMBERS OF FIRM

Robert H. Black	Frederick G. Hall
Michael D. Compean	Annette J. Lenneman

ASSOCIATES

William J. Light	Margie Castillo
Vicente Valencia, Jr.	Lara Michelle Brya
Meredith A. Czapla	

(See Next Column)

BLACK COMPEAN HALL & LENNEMAN, *Los Angeles—Continued*

Reference: Sterling Bank.

For full biographical listings, see the Martindale-Hubbell Law Directory

BLECHER & COLLINS, A PROFESSIONAL CORPORATION (AV)

611 West Sixth Street, 20th Floor, 90017
Telephone: 213-622-4222
Telecopier: 213-622-1656

Maxwell M. Blecher	Ralph C. Hofer
Harold R. Collins, Jr.	William C. Hsu
John E. Andrews	James Robert Noblin
Florence F. Cameron	Donald R. Pepperman

Alicia G. Rosenberg

For full biographical listings, see the Martindale-Hubbell Law Directory

BOTTUM & FELITON, A PROFESSIONAL CORPORATION (AV)

Suite 1500, South Tower, 3200 Wilshire Boulevard, 90010
Telephone: 213-487-0402
Fax: 213-386-9803
San Diego, California Office: Suite 400 Emerald Plaza, 402 West
Broadway.
Telephone: 619-595-4857.
Fax: 619-595-4863.

John R. Feliton, Jr.	Steve Johnson
Robert A. Wooten, Jr.	Mark A. Oertel

Alexander F. Giovanniello

Kenneth C. Feldman	Scott A. Hampton
Jerry Garcia	Julie A. Covell

For full biographical listings, see the Martindale-Hubbell Law Directory

DANIELS, BARATTA & FINE (AV)

A Partnership including a Professional Corporation
1801 Century Park East, 9th Floor, 90067
Telephone: 310-556-7900
Telecopier: 310-556-2807
Bakersfield, California Office: 5201 California Avenue, Suite 400.
Telephone: 805-335-7788.
Telecopier: 805-324-3660.

MEMBERS OF FIRM

John P. Daniels (Inc.)	Mary Hulett
James M. Baratta	Michael B. Geibel
Paul R. Fine	James I. Montgomery, Jr.
Nathan B. Hoffman	Lance D. Orloff

Mark R. Israel

ASSOCIATES

Ilene Wendy Kurtzman	Spencer A. Schneider
Janet Sacks	Angelo A. Du Plantier, III
Michael N. Schonbuch	Leslie E. Wright, III.
Scott M. Leavitt	Erin B. Hallissy
Michelle R. Press	Kena B. Chin
Scott Ashford Brooks	Dean Bengston
Craig A. Laidig	Peter Anders Nyquist
Robin A. Webb	Jeannie Masse
Craig S. Momita	Lori Chotiner

Maureen M. Michail

OF COUNSEL

Timothy J. Hughes	Drew T. Hanker

Mark A. Vega

For full biographical listings, see the Martindale-Hubbell Law Directory

DIDAK & JACK (AV)

11755 Wilshire Boulevard, 15th Floor, 90025
Telephone: 310-473-7173
Fax: 310-312-1077

MEMBERS OF FIRM

Mark F. Didak	Travis R. Jack

For full biographical listings, see the Martindale-Hubbell Law Directory

HILL, FARRER & BURRILL LLP (AV)

A Limited Liability Partnership including Professional Corporations
35th Floor, Union Bank Square, 445 South Figueroa Street, 90071
Telephone: 213-620-0460
Fax: 213-624-4840

MEMBERS OF FIRM

Stanley E. Tobin (P.C.)	Ronald W. Novotny (P.C.)
Jack R. White (P.C.)	Dean E. Dennis
James G. Johnson (P.C.)	Jennifer L. Pancake

For Complete List of Firm Personnel, See General Section

For full biographical listings, see the Martindale-Hubbell Law Directory

EDWARD J. HOROWITZ A PROFESSIONAL CORPORATION (AV)

Suite 1015, 11661 San Vicente Boulevard, 90049
Telephone: 310-826-6619
Fax: 310-826-8242
Email: Horowitz@appellatelaw.com

Edward J. Horowitz

Reference: Union Bank (Brentwood Branch).

For full biographical listings, see the Martindale-Hubbell Law Directory

HORVITZ & LEVY (AV)

A Partnership including Professional Corporations
18th Floor, 15760 Ventura Boulevard (Encino), 91436
Telephone: 818-995-0800; 213-872-0802
FAX: 818-995-3157

Ellis J. Horvitz (A P.C.)	Daniel J. Gonzalez
Barry R. Levy (A P.C.)	Mitchell C. Tilner
Peter Abrahams	Christina J. Imre
David M. Axelrad	Lisa Perrochet
Frederic D. Cohen	Stephen E. Norris
S. Thomas Todd	Sandra J. Smith
David S. Ettinger	John A. Taylor, Jr.

Mary F. Dant	Andrea M. Gauthier
Ari R. Kleiman	Elizabeth Skorcz Anthony
Lisa R. Jaskol	Christine A. Pagac
Julie L. Woods	Judith E. Gordon
Holly R. Paul	Patricia Lofton
H. Thomas Watson	L. Rachel Lerman Helyar
	(Not admitted in CA)

OF COUNSEL

Jon B. Eisenberg

Reference: Bank of California (Pasadena, California Office).

For full biographical listings, see the Martindale-Hubbell Law Directory

HOWARTH & SMITH (AV)

Suite 2900, 700 South Flower Street, 90017
Telephone: 213-955-9400
Fax: 213-622-0791

MEMBERS OF FIRM

Don Howarth	David K. Ringwood
Suzelle M. Smith	Kenneth S. Tune

Brian D. Bubb

Marcus J. Berger	Katy Jacobs
Patricia Lee-Gulley	Sheila M. Bradley
Thomas F. Vandenburg	Julia S. Swanson
Gregory S. Tamkin	Kimberly L. Honus

Randall Boese

For full biographical listings, see the Martindale-Hubbell Law Directory

IVERSON, YOAKUM, PAPIANO & HATCH (AV)

One Wilshire Building, 27th Floor 624 South Grand Avenue, 90017
Telephone: 213-624-7444
Telecopier: 213 629-4563

MEMBERS OF FIRM

Neil Papiano	Arnold D. Larson
Patrick M. Mc Adam	John M. Garrick

ASSOCIATES

Douglas C. Pease	Melissa A. Immel
Andrew K. Doty	Mary P. Lightfoot

OF COUNSEL

R. Noel Hatch

Representative Clients: Lockheed Corp.; International Paper; Bridgestone/-Firestone, Inc.
Reference: Security Pacific National Bank (Los Angeles Head Office).

For Complete List of Firm Personnel, See General Section

For full biographical listings, see the Martindale-Hubbell Law Directory

LAW OFFICES OF THOMAS KALLAY (AV)

445 South Figueroa Street 27th Floor, 90071-1603
Telephone: 213-612-7717
Facsimile: 213-426-2181

For full biographical listings, see the Martindale-Hubbell Law Directory

LANGBERG, COHN & DROOZ (AV)

A Partnership including a Professional Corporation
12100 Wilshire Boulevard Suite 1650, 90025
Telephone: 310-979-3200
Telecopier: 310-979-3220

(See Next Column)

LANGBERG, COHN & DROOZ—*Continued*

Barry B. Langberg (A Professional Corporation)	Beth F. Dumas
Eileen M. Cohn	Mitchell J. Langberg
Deborah Drooz	Mary L. Muir
	Brian A. Murphy

OF COUNSEL

Peter C. Richards (A Professional Corporation)	Gilbert Gaynor
	Polin Cohanne
Milton Segal	

LEGAL SUPPORT PERSONNEL

PARALEGALS

Patricia Ann Essig	Jeanne A. Logé

For full biographical listings, see the Martindale-Hubbell Law Directory

LOEB & LOEB LLP (AV)

A Limited Liability Partnership including Professional Corporations
Suite 1800, 1000 Wilshire Boulevard, 90017-2475
Telephone: 213-688-3400
Facsimile: 213-688-3460; 688-3461; 688-3462
Century City, California Office: Suite 2200, 10100 Santa Monica
Boulevard, Los Angeles, 90067-4164.
Telephone: 310-282-2000.
Facsimile: 310-282-2191; 282-2192.
New York, N.Y. Office: 345 Park Avenue, 10154-0037.
Telephone: 212-407-4000.
Facsimile: 212-407-4990.
Washington, D.C. Office: Suite 601, 2100 M Street N.W., 20037-1207.
Telephone: 202-223-5700.
Facsimile: 202-223-5704.
Nashville, Tennessee Office: 45 Music Square West, 37203-3205.
Telephone: 615-749-8300;
Facsimile: 615-749-8308.
Rome, Italy Office: Piazza Digione 1, 00197.
Telephone: 011-396-808-8456.
Facsimile: 011-396-808-8288.

MEMBERS OF FIRM

Andrew S. Garb (A P.C.)	Douglas E. Mirell
Jeffrey M. Loeb	Anthony Murray

OF COUNSEL

Howard I. Friedman (A P.C.)

For Complete List of Firm Personnel, See General Section

For full biographical listings, see the Martindale-Hubbell Law Directory

NEUMEYER & BOYD, LLP (AV)

2029 Century Park East, Suite 1100, 90067
Telephone: 310-553-9393
Fax: 310-553-8437

MEMBERS OF FIRM

Richard A. Neumeyer	Lydia E. Hachmeister
Carol Boyd	Steven A. Freeman

ASSOCIATES

Katherine Tatikian	Daniel F. Sanchez
Susie J. Kater	Stuart L. Brody
Reid L. Denham	

For full biographical listings, see the Martindale-Hubbell Law Directory

O'MELVENY & MYERS LLP (AV)

400 South Hope Street, 90071-2899
Telephone: 213-669-6000
Cable Address: "Moms"
Facsimile: 213-669-6407
Email: omminfo@omm.com
Century City, California Office: 1999 Avenue of the Stars, 90067-6035.
Telephone: 310-553-6700.
Facsimile: 310-246-6779.
Newport Beach, California Office: 610 Newport Center Drive, 92660-6429.
Telephone: 714-760-9600.
Cable Address: "Moms".
Facsimile: 714-669-6994.
San Francisco, California Office: Embarcadero Center West Tower, 275
Battery Street, 94111-3305.
Telephone: 415-984-8700.
Facsimile: 415-984-8701.
New York, New York Office: Citicorp Center, 153 East 53rd Street,
10022-4611.
Telephone: 212-326-2000.
Facsimile: 212-326-2061.
Washington, D.C. Office: 555 13th Street, N.W., 20004-1109.
Telephone: 202-383-5300.
Cable Address: "Moms".
Facsimile: 202-383-5414.
London, England Office: 10 Finsbury Square, London, EC2A 1LA.
Telephone: 0171-256-8451.
Facsimile: 0171-638-8205.

(See Next Column)

Tokyo, Japan Office: Sanbancho KB-6 Building, 6 Sanbancho, Chiyoda-ku,
Tokyo 102, Japan.
Telephone: 03-3239-2900.
Facsimile: 03-3239-2432.
Hong Kong Office: Suite 1905, Peregrine Tower, Lippo Centre, 89
Queensway, Central, Hong Kong.
Telephone: 852-2523-8266.
Facsimile: 852-2522-1760.
Shanghai, Peoples Republic of China Office: Shanghai International Trade
Centre, Suite 2011, 2200 Yan An Road West, Shanghai, 200335, PRC.
Telephone: 86-21-6219-5363.
Facsimile: 86-21-6275-4949.

PARTNER

Charles C. Lifland

For Complete List of Firm Personnel, See General Section

For full biographical listings, see the Martindale-Hubbell Law Directory

RADCLIFF, FRANDSEN & DONGELL (AV)

40th Floor, 777 South Figueroa Street, 90017
Telephone: 213-614-1990
Facsimile: 213-489-9263
San Francisco, California Office: 88 Kearny Street, Suite 1475.
Telephone: 415-399-8393.
Facsimile: 415-989-5465.
Rome, Italy Office: Via Tacito, 7.
Telephone: (39) 06-323-5588.
Facsimile: (39) 06-324-3392.

MEMBERS OF FIRM

Jules G. Radcliff, Jr.	Russell Mackay Frandsen
Richard A. Dongell	

OF COUNSEL

Tal Clifton Finney

ASSOCIATES

Francis P. Aspessi	Jeffrey C. Mayes
Ruben A. Castellon	Marisa A. Moret
William W. Funderburk, Jr.	Daniel E. Park
Jeffrey A. Gagliardi	Scott D. Pinsky
David K. Lee	Eric H. Saiki
Maria Anna Mancini	Steve R. Segura
Glenn M. White	

For full biographical listings, see the Martindale-Hubbell Law Directory

LAW OFFICES OF JOEL P. SCHIFF (AV)

1801 Century Park East Twenty Third Floor, 90067
Telephone: 310-201-2550
Fax: 310-201-2551

For full biographical listings, see the Martindale-Hubbell Law Directory

SLAFF, MOSK & RUDMAN (AV)

Suite 825, 9200 Sunset Boulevard, 90069
Telephone: 310-275-5351
Telecopier: 310-273-8706

George Slaff (1906-1989)	Edward Mosk (1916-1989)

MEMBERS OF FIRM

Norman G. Rudman	Marc R. Stein
Valerie V. Flugge	

Reference: City National Bank.

For full biographical listings, see the Martindale-Hubbell Law Directory

ANDREW RUSSELL WILLING (AV)

Promenade West, 880 West First Street Suite 302, 90012
Telephone: 213-626-6600
Facsimile: 213-626-0488

Reference: Wells Fargo Bank (Pasadena Main Office).

For full biographical listings, see the Martindale-Hubbell Law Directory

MONTEREY, Monterey Co.

HARRAY, MASUDA & LINKER (AV)

80 Garden Court, Suite 260, 93940
Telephone: 408-373-3101
Fax: 408-373-6712

Richard K. Harray	Michael P. Masuda
Stan L. Linker	

For full biographical listings, see the Martindale-Hubbell Law Directory

NEWPORT BEACH, Orange Co.

CALLAHAN & ASSOCIATES (AV)

5120 Campus Drive, 92660
Telephone: 714-476-2898
Facsimile: 714-752-8770

(See Next Column)

CALLAHAN & ASSOCIATES, *Newport Beach—Continued*

Rebecca Callahan
ASSOCIATE
Katherine T. Corrigan
LEGAL SUPPORT PERSONNEL
Sandra A. Thompson (Paralegal)

For full biographical listings, see the Martindale-Hubbell Law Directory

PASADENA, Los Angeles Co.

BURNS, AMMIRATO, PALUMBO, MILAM & BARONIAN, A PROFESSIONAL LAW CORPORATION (AV)

65 North Raymond Avenue, 2nd Floor, 91103-3919
Telephone: 818-796-5053; 213-258-8282
Fax: 818-792-3078
Long Beach, California Office: One World Trade Center, Suite 1200.
Telephone: 310-436-8338; 714-952-1047.
Fax: 310-432-6049.

Michael A. Burns	Bruce Palumbo
Vincent A. Ammirato,	Jeffrey L. Milam
Resident, Long Bch	Robert H. Baronian

Normand A. Ayotte	Michael P. Vicencia,
Colleen Clark	Resident, LOng Bch
Valerie Julien-Peto	Michael E. Wenzel,
Susan E. Luhring	Resident, Long Bch
Grace C. Mori,	
Resident, Long Bch	

Reference: First Los Angeles Bank.

For full biographical listings, see the Martindale-Hubbell Law Directory

BURTON & NORRIS (AV)

35 South Raymond Avenue, Fourth Floor, 91105
Telephone: 818-449-8300
Fax: 818-449-4417

John C. Burton	Donald G. Norris
	Victoria E. King

Reference: Bank of America (Pasadena).

For full biographical listings, see the Martindale-Hubbell Law Directory

FRANSCELL, STRICKLAND, ROBERTS & LAWRENCE, A PROFESSIONAL CORPORATION (AV)

Penthouse, 225 South Lake Avenue, 91101-3005
Telephone: 818-304-7830; 213-684-7830
Fax: 818-795-7460
Santa Ana, California Office: Suite 800, 401 Civic Center Drive West.
Telephone: 714-543-6511.
Fax: 714-543-6711.
Riverside, California Office: Suite 670, 3801 University Avenue.
Telephone: 909-686-1000.
Fax: 909-686-2565.

George J. Franscell	Donald C. McFarlane
Tracy Strickland	(Resident, Santa Ana Office)
(Resident, Santa Ana Office)	Libby Wong
Barbara E. Roberts	Cindy S. Lee
(Resident, Riverside Office)	Martin J. De Vries
David D. Lawrence	(Resident, Riverside Office)
Carol Ann Rohr	Ann Marie Sanders
Scott D. MacLatchie	Priscilla F. Slocum
S. Frank Harrell	Garth Matthew Drozin
(Resident, Santa Ana Office)	

For full biographical listings, see the Martindale-Hubbell Law Directory

REDWOOD CITY,* San Mateo Co.

LOW, BALL & LYNCH, A PROFESSIONAL CORPORATION (AV)

10 Twin Dolphin, Suite B-500, 94065
Telephone: 415-591-8822
Fax: 415-591-8884
San Francisco, California Office: 601 California Street, Suite 2100, 94108.
Telephone: 415-981-6630.
Monterey, California Office: 10 Ragsdale Drive, Suite 175, 93940.
Telephone: 408-655-8822.

Raymond Coates	David L. Blinn
Chester G. Moore, III	Janet Kulig
James D. Miller	Thomas E. Mulvihill
William H. Holsinger	Jennifer Elizabeth Acheson

John R. Baumann	Joseph M. Fenech
	Michael E. Sandgren

For full biographical listings, see the Martindale-Hubbell Law Directory

SACRAMENTO,* Sacramento Co.

EISEN & JOHNSTON (AV)

980 Ninth Street, Suite 1400, P.O. Box 111, 95812-0111
Telephone: 916-444-6171
Fax: 916-441-5810

MEMBERS OF FIRM

Jay-Allen Eisen	Marian M. Johnston

For full biographical listings, see the Martindale-Hubbell Law Directory

HANSEN, BOYD, CULHANE & WATSON (AV)

A Partnership including Professional Corporations
Central City Centre, 1331 Twenty-First Street, 95814
Telephone: 916-444-2550
Telecopier: 916-444-2358

Hartley T. Hansen (Inc.)	Lawrence R. Watson
Kevin R. Culhane (Inc.)	John J. Rueda
David E. Boyd	James J. Banks
	Lorraine M. Pavlovich

OF COUNSEL
Betsy S. Kimball

Thomas L. Riordan	Pamela B. Hooley
James O. Moses	Roger R. Billings

For full biographical listings, see the Martindale-Hubbell Law Directory

LIVINGSTON & MATTESICH, LAW CORPORATION (AV)

1201 K Street, Suite 1100, 95814
Telephone: 916-442-1111
Fax: 916-448-1709
Email: liv-matt@gvn.net

Gene Livingston	Carol Livingston
James M. Mattesich	Rebecca M. Ceniceros

Steven P. Belzer	Trisha M. McAlmond

Reference: Bank of California.

For full biographical listings, see the Martindale-Hubbell Law Directory

SAN BERNARDINO,* San Bernardino Co.

WILSON, BORROR, DUNN & DAVIS (AV)

Suite 307, The Bank of California Building, 255 North D Street, 92401
Telephone: 909-884-8855
Fax: 909-884-5161

MEMBERS OF FIRM

Fred A. Wilson (1886-1973)	James R. Dunn
Wm. H. Wilson (1915-1981)	Thomas M. Davis
	Keith D. Davis

ASSOCIATES

Timothy P. Prince	Sarah L. Overton

OF COUNSEL
Caywood J. Borror

Representative Clients: Travelers Insurance Co.; Rockwell International; Westinghouse Air Brake Co.; Goodyear Tire and Rubber Co.; Home Insurance Co.; Cities of: Redlands, Chino, Colton, San Bernardino and Upland; The Canadian Insurance Co.

For full biographical listings, see the Martindale-Hubbell Law Directory

SAN DIEGO,* San Diego Co.

HYDE AND WATERS (AV)

401 West "A" Street, Suite 1200, 92101
Telephone: 619-696-6911
Telecopier: 619-696-6919

MEMBERS OF FIRM

Laurel Lee Hyde	Timothy Doyle Waters

Representative Clients: Cardio Theatre, Inc.; C.W. Clark, Inc.; Foster Investment Corporation; Home Capital Corporation; Kmart Corporation; Midland Loan Services, L.P.; New World Communications Co.; The Regents of the University of California; San Diego Gas and Electric Company; Standard Process of Southern California.

For full biographical listings, see the Martindale-Hubbell Law Directory

DANIEL B. MacLEOD (AV)

McClintock Plaza, 1202 Kettner Boulevard, Suite 4400, 92101
Telephone: 619-234-7000
Telefax: 619-234-9973
San Francisco, California Affiliated Office: King & MacLeod 101 California Street, Suite 4050 94111.
Telephone: 415-352-0675.

(See Next Column)

DANIEL B. MACLEOD—*Continued*

For full biographical listings, see the Martindale-Hubbell Law Directory

SAN FRANCISCO,* San Francisco Co.

BIEN & SUMMERS (AV)

Mills Building, 220 Montgomery Street Tower Suite 1210, 94104
Telephone: 415-291-0300; 510-531-3106
Fax: 415-291-0409

Elliot L. Bien   E. Elizabeth Summers

For full biographical listings, see the Martindale-Hubbell Law Directory

MURPHY, PEARSON, BRADLEY & FEENEY, A PROFESSIONAL CORPORATION (AV)

88 Kearny Street, 11th Floor, 94108
Telephone: 415-788-1900
Telecopier: 415-393-8087
Sacramento, California Office: Suite 200, 3600 American River Drive, 95864.
Telephone: 916-483-6074.
Telecopier: 916-483-6088.

John H. Feeney   Mark Ellis
                                  (Resident, Sacramento Office)

For Complete List of Firm Personnel, See General Section

For full biographical listings, see the Martindale-Hubbell Law Directory

REMCHO, JOHANSEN AND PURCELL (AV)

Suite 800, 220 Montgomery Street, 94104
Telephone: 415-398-6230
Fax: 415-398-7256
Email: Info@RJP.com
Sacramento, California Office: Suite 625, 555 Capitol Mall.
Telephone: 916-264-1818.
Fax: 916-264-1824.

MEMBERS OF FIRM
Joseph Remcho   Robin B. Johansen
            Kathleen J. Purcell

Janet Sommer   Deborah L. Breiner
LEGAL SUPPORT PERSONNEL
Douglas Denton (Paralegal)   Ruth Fridhandler
                                 (Legal Administrator)

For full biographical listings, see the Martindale-Hubbell Law Directory

ROSEN, BIEN & ASARO (AV)

Eighth Floor, 155 Montgomery Street, 94104
Telephone: 415-433-6830
Fax: 415-433-7104
Email: rba@rbalaw.com

Sanford Jay Rosen   Michael W. Bien
            Andrea G. Asaro

Thomas Nolan   William H.D. Fernholz
Donna Petrine   Doris Y. Ng
M.J. Tony Paikeday   A. Marie Villafaña

For full biographical listings, see the Martindale-Hubbell Law Directory

SPIEGEL LIAO & KAGAY (AV)

88 Kearny Street, Suite 1310, 94108-5530
Telephone: 415-956-5959
Telecopier: 415-362-1431

Michael I. Spiegel   Charles M. Kagay
            OF COUNSEL
Bartholomew Lee   Wayne M. Liao

For full biographical listings, see the Martindale-Hubbell Law Directory

SAN JOSE,* Santa Clara Co.

CRAIG M. BROWN, INC. (AV)

333 West Santa Clara Street, Suite 618, 95113
Telephone: 408-286-8844
Fax: 408-286-6699
Email: cmbtrialaw@aol.com

Craig M. Brown

For full biographical listings, see the Martindale-Hubbell Law Directory

McMANIS, FAULKNER & MORGAN (AV)

160 West Santa Clara Street, 10th Floor, 95113
Telephone: 408-279-8700
Fax: 408-279-3244; 408-279-0494
Email: mfm@mfmlaw.com

MEMBERS OF FIRM
James McManis   William Faulkner
            Donelle Morgan
            ASSOCIATES
Nora Rousso   Michael Reedy
Lisa Herrick   Douglas Watanabe
            Kelly McHaffie

For full biographical listings, see the Martindale-Hubbell Law Directory

RUBY & SCHOFIELD (AV)

A Partnership of Law Corporations
60 South Market Street, Suite 1500, 95113-2379
Telephone: 408-998-8500
Fax: 408-998-8503

Allen Ruby (L.C.)   Glen W. Schofield (L.C.)

For full biographical listings, see the Martindale-Hubbell Law Directory

SANTA ANA,* Orange Co.

MARTIN, WILSON, ERICKSON & MacDOWELL, A PROFESSIONAL CORPORATION (AV)

6 Hutton Centre, Suite 500, 92707
Telephone: 714-972-1200
Facsimile: 714-972-1283

Scott A. Martin   Mary Fingal Erickson
Thomas L. Wilson   John R. MacDowell

Douglas M. Carasso   Wendy A. Weber
            Kevin F. Cahill

For full biographical listings, see the Martindale-Hubbell Law Directory

SPERLING & PERGANDE (AV)

3 Hutton Centre, Suite 670, 92707
Telephone: 714-540-8500
Facsimile: 714-540-2599

MEMBERS OF FIRM
Dean P. Sperling   K. William Pergande

For full biographical listings, see the Martindale-Hubbell Law Directory

SANTA BARBARA,* Santa Barbara Co.

ANGLE, CARLSON, GOLDRICK & ROBERTS (AV)

A Partnership including a Professional Corporation
200 East Carrillo Street, Suite 310, 93101
Telephone: 805-963-7400
Fax: 805-963-7610

Robert O. Angle   Miles T. Goldrick
Arthur W. Carlson (A P.C.)   Paul A. Roberts
            OF COUNSEL
            Georgia C. McDermott

For full biographical listings, see the Martindale-Hubbell Law Directory

SANTA MONICA, Los Angeles Co.

O'NEILL, LYSAGHT & SUN (AV)

100 Wilshire Boulevard, Suite 700, 90401
Telephone: 310-451-5700
Telecopier: 310-399-7201

Brian O'Neill   Yolanda Orozco
Brian C. Lysaght   John M. Moscarino
Frederick D. Friedman   Harriet Beegun Leva
Brian A. Sun   Edward A. Klein
            Robert L. Meylan

David E. Rosen   Paul D. Murphy
Ellyn S. Garofalo   Brian D. Hershman
            OF COUNSEL
            J. Joseph Connolly
Reference: Wells Fargo Bank, Santa Monica.

For full biographical listings, see the Martindale-Hubbell Law Directory

VENTURA, Ventura Co.

LASCHER & LASCHER, A PROFESSIONAL CORPORATION (AV)

605 Poli Street, P.O. Box 25540, 93002
Telephone: 805-648-3228
Fax: 805-643-7692
Email: lascher@isle.net

Edward L. Lascher (1928-1991)   Wendy Cole Lascher

Gabriele Mezger-Lashly

Reference: First National Bank of Ventura.

For full biographical listings, see the Martindale-Hubbell Law Directory

TAYLOR MCCORD, A LAW CORPORATION (AV)

721 East Main Street, P.O. Box 1477, 93002
Telephone: 805-648-4700
Fax: 805-653-6124

Richard L. Taylor   Robert L. McCord, Jr.
David L. Praver

Patrick Cherry   Susan D. Siple
Rebbecca F. Calderwood

LEGAL SUPPORT PERSONNEL
PARALEGALS
Stephanie Gibson   Adele Rubino
Diane Lovato

For full biographical listings, see the Martindale-Hubbell Law Directory

COLORADO

ASPEN, Pitkin Co.

AUSTIN, PEIRCE & SMITH, P.C. (AV)

Suite 205, 600 East Hopkins Avenue, 81611
Telephone: 970-925-2600
FAX: 970-925-4720
Email: apspc@rof.net

Ronald D. Austin   Frederick F. Peirce
Thomas Fenton Smith

Michael P. Fossenier

Counsel for: Chase Manhattan of Colorado, Inc.; Clark's Market; Cootes, Reid & Waldron Property Management, Inc.; Crystal Palace Corp.; Snowmass Shopping Center; Coldwell Banker The Aspen Brokers, Ltd.; William Poss & Assoc., Architects; Snowmass Resort Association; Aspen/Pitkin County Housing Authority; Nations Title Insurance, Inc.

For full biographical listings, see the Martindale-Hubbell Law Directory

DENVER, Denver Co.

REIMAN & BAYAZ, P.C. (AV)

1600 Broadway, Suite 1640, 80202
Telephone: 303-860-1500
Fax: 303-839-4380

Jeff Reiman   Marcie K. Bayaz

Darren E. Temkin-Nadel   Eric B. Liebman

For full biographical listings, see the Martindale-Hubbell Law Directory

SENN LEWIS VISCIANO & STRAHLE, PROFESSIONAL CORPORATION (AV)

Suite 4300, 1801 California Street, 80202
Telephone: 303-298-1122
Telecopier: 303-296-9101

Frank W. Visciano

Brian J. Reichel   Luis A. Toro

For Complete List of Firm Personnel, See General Section

For full biographical listings, see the Martindale-Hubbell Law Directory

DURANGO, La Plata Co.

MCLACHLAN & GOLDMAN, LLC (AV)

850 1/2 Main Avenue, P.O. Box 2270, 81302-2270
Telephone: 970-259-8747
Facsimile: 970-259-8790
Email: LAWMCGLD@FRONTIER.NET

Michael E. McLachlan   Michael A. Goldman

Jeffery P. Robbins

For full biographical listings, see the Martindale-Hubbell Law Directory

CONNECTICUT

HARTFORD, Hartford Co.

JACKSON, O'KEEFE AND PHELAN (AV)

36 Russ Street, 06106-1571
Telephone: 860-278-4040
Fax: 860-527-2500
West Hartford, Connecticut Office: 62 LaSalle Road.
Telephone: 860-521-7500.
Fax: 860-561-5399.
Bethlehem, Connecticut Office: 423 Munger Lane. Telephone/
Fax: 203-266-5255.

MEMBERS OF FIRM
Jay W. Jackson   Michael E. Riley
Andrew J. O'Keefe   Peter K. O'Keefe
Denise Martino Phelan   Philip R. Dunn, Jr.
Matthew J. O'Keefe   Kathryn M. Cunningham
Joseph M. Busher, Jr.

Representative Clients: Travelers Aetna Property Casualty Co.; ITT Hartford; Liberty Mutual Insurance Co.; Connecticut Medical Insurance Co.

For full biographical listings, see the Martindale-Hubbell Law Directory

SOROKIN SOROKIN GROSS HYDE & WILLIAMS P.C. (AV)

One Corporate Center, 06103
Telephone: 860-525-6645
Fax: 860-522-1781
Simsbury, Connecticut Office: 730 Hopmeadow Street.
Telephone: 860-651-9348.
Rocky Hill, Connecticut Office: 2360 Main Street.
Telephone: 860-563-9305.
Fax: 860-529-6931.

Clifford J. Grandjean   Lewis Rabinovitz
Lisa A. Magliochetti   Richard C. Robinson

For Complete List of Firm Personnel, See General Section

For full biographical listings, see the Martindale-Hubbell Law Directory

NEW HAVEN, New Haven Co.

GALLAGHER GALLAGHER & CALISTRO (AV)

1377 Boulevard, P.O. Box 1925, 06509
Telephone: 203-624-4165
Fax: 203-865-5598

William F. Gallagher   Cynthia C. Bott
Elizabeth A. Gallagher   Barbara L. Cox
Roger B. Calistro   Kurt D. Koehler
Thomas J. Airone

Approved Attorneys for: Chicago Title Insurance Co.; Centerbank; Dime Savings Bank of Wallingford; New Haven Savings Bank; Bank of Boston Connecticut; Fleet Bank; People's Bank; Bank of New Haven.
References: Bank of New Haven; Prime Bank.

NEW HAVEN, New Haven Co.

ROSEN & DOLAN, P.C. (AV)

400 Orange Street, 06511
Telephone: 203-787-3513
Fax: 203-789-1605
Email: davidrosen@counsel.com
Email: spincus@counsel.com

David N. Rosen

Stephen M. Pincus

Reference: Peoples Bank.

For Complete List of Firm Personnel, See General Section

For full biographical listings, see the Martindale-Hubbell Law Directory

New Haven—Continued

LAW OFFICES OF JOHN R. WILLIAMS (AV)

51 Elm Street, 06510
Telephone: 203-562-9931
Fax: 203-776-9494

ASSOCIATES

Diane Polan	Norman A. Pattis
Katrena Engstrom	William S. Palmieri

References: Webster Bank; Bank of New Haven.

For full biographical listings, see the Martindale-Hubbell Law Directory

---

SOUTHBURY, New Haven Co.

SECOR, CASSIDY & McPARTLAND, P.C. (AV)

Successors to Bronson, Lewis, Upson & Secor; Lewis, Hart, Upson & Secor; Upson, Secor, Greene & Cassidy and Upson, Secor, Cassidy & McPartland, P.C.
900 Main Street South, 06488
Telephone: 203-264-8223
Fax: 203-264-6730
Waterbury, Connecticut Office: 41 Church Street, P.O. Box 2818.
Telephone: 203-757-9261.
Fax: 203-756-5762.

James R. Healey

Attorneys for: The Mattatuck Museum; American Republican, Inc.; Hubbard-Hall, Inc.; The Siemon Co.; Engineered Sinterings and Plastics, Inc.; Boutin Industries; County Line Buick-Nissan, Inc.

For full biographical listings, see the Martindale-Hubbell Law Directory

---

WATERBURY, New Haven Co.

SECOR, CASSIDY & McPARTLAND, P.C. (AV)

Successors to Bronson, Lewis, Upson & Secor; Lewis, Hart, Upson & Secor; Upson, Secor, Greene & Cassidy and Upson, Secor, Cassidy & McPartland, P.C.
41 Church Street, P.O. Box 2818, 06723-2818
Telephone: 203-757-9261
Fax: 203-756-5762
Southbury, Connecticut Office: 900 Main Street South.
Telephone: 203-264-8223.
Fax: 203-264-6730.

Nath'l R. Bronson (1860-1949)	Gail E. McTaggart
Lawrence L. Lewis (1881-1965)	Thomas G. Parisot
Charles E. Hart (1884-1972)	Elizabeth A. Bozzuto
J. Warren Upson (1903-1992)	Patrick W. Finn
John H. Cassidy, Jr.	Eric R. Brown
Donald McPartland	David J. Bozzuto
W. Fielding Secor	Victor E. Gatti
James R. Healey	
(Resident, Southbury Office)	

SPECIAL TAX COUNSEL
Bruce C. Johnson

COUNSEL

William J. Secor, Jr.	Milton A. Seymour

Attorneys for: The Mattatuck Museum; American Republican, Inc.; Hubbard-Hall, Inc.; The Siemon Co.; Engineered Sinterings and Plastics, Inc.; Boutin Industries; County Line Buick-Nissan, Inc.

For full biographical listings, see the Martindale-Hubbell Law Directory

---

WESTPORT, Fairfield Co.

ANDREW B. BOWMAN (AV)

1804 Post Road East, 06880
Telephone: 203-259-0599
Fax: 203-255-2570

Reference: Peoples Bank.

For full biographical listings, see the Martindale-Hubbell Law Directory

DISTRICT OF COLUMBIA

WASHINGTON, D.C. Co.

* indicates certain Bar Register subscribers, in cities of comparable size and importance, who maintain an additional office in Washington, D.C. and who have arranged for representation as a part of the Washington, D.C. listings that follow

* VENABLE ATTORNEYS AT LAW VENABLE, BAETJER, HOWARD & CIVILETTI, LLP (AV)

A Partnership including Professional Corporations
Suite 1000, 1201 New York Avenue, N.W., 20005
Telephone: 202-962-4800
Fax: 202-962-8300
Baltimore, Maryland Office: Venable, Baetjer and Howard LLP, 1800 Mercantile Bank & Trust Building, 2 Hopkins Plaza.
Telephone: 410-244-7400.
McLean, Virginia Office: Venable, Baetjer and Howard LLP, Suite 400, 2010 Corporate Ridge.
Telephone: 703-760-1600.
Rockville, Maryland Office: Venable, Baetjer and Howard LLP, Suite 500, One Church Street, P. O. Box 1906.
Telephone: 301-217-5600.
Towson, Maryland Office: Venable, Baetjer and Howard LLP, 210 Allegheny Avenue, P. O. Box 5517.
Telephone: 410-494-6200.

MEMBERS OF FIRM

Benjamin R. Civiletti (P.C.) (Also at Baltimore and Towson, Maryland Offices	James R. Myers
	Jeffrey A. Dunn (Also at Baltimore, Maryland Office)
Thomas J. Madden	George F. Pappas (Also at Baltimore, Maryland Office)
Ronald R. Glancz	
David J. Levenson	William D. Coston
Douglas D. Connah, Jr. (P.C.) (Also at Baltimore, Maryland Office)	James L. Shea (Not admitted in DC; also at Baltimore, Maryland Office)
Kenneth C. Bass, III (Also at McLean, Virginia Office)	Maurice Baskin
	Amy Berman Jackson
Edward F. Glynn, Jr.	William D. Quarles (Also at Towson, Maryland Office)
Robert G. Ames (Also at Baltimore, Maryland Office)	James A. Dunbar (Also at Baltimore, Maryland Office)
Michael Schatzow (Also at Baltimore, Maryland Office)	Thomas J. Kelly, Jr.
John F. Cooney	Patrick J. Stewart (Also at Baltimore, Maryland Office)
N. Frank Wiggins	
James K. Archibald (Also at Baltimore, Maryland Office)	Gary M. Hnath
Judson W. Starr (Also at Baltimore and Towson, Maryland Offices)	Geoffrey R. Garinther (Not admitted in DC; Also at Baltimore, Maryland Office)

ASSOCIATES

Carla Draluck Craft	Edward Brendan Magrab
David W. Goewey	Lawrence C. Renbaum
Melissa Landau Steinman	

For Complete List of Firm Personnel, See General Section

For full biographical listings, see the Martindale-Hubbell Law Directory

---

FLORIDA

---

*FORT LAUDERDALE,** Broward Co.

HALICZER, PETTIS & WHITE, P.A. (AV)

101 Northeast Third Avenue, Sixth Floor, 33301
Telephone: 954-523-9922
Fax: 954-522-2512
Orlando, Florida Office: NationsBank Building. Suite 1275. 111 North Orange Avenue. 32801.
Telephone: 407-841-9866.
Fax: 407-841-9915.

James S. Haliczer	Kenneth E. White
Eugene K. Pettis	Lorna E. Brown-Burton

Amy B. Talisman	Margaret A. Benenati
Dean A. Robertson	Gina E. Caruso

For full biographical listings, see the Martindale-Hubbell Law Directory

---

KESSLER, MASSEY, CATRI, HOLTON & KESSLER, P.A. (AV)

110 Tower, Twentieth Floor, 110 Southeast Sixth Street, 33301
Telephone: 954-463-8593
Fax: 954-462-1303

(See Next Column)

KESSLER, MASSEY, CATRI, HOLTON & KESSLER P.A., *Fort Lauderdale—Continued*

Charles T. Kessler	Paula C. Kessler
Albert P. Massey, III	Gregory G. Coican
Wesley L. Catri	Andrea L. Kessler
Raymond O. Holton, Jr.	Edward D. Schuster

Gerard A. Tuzzio	Edwina V. Kessler

For full biographical listings, see the Martindale-Hubbell Law Directory

RICHARD L. ROSENBAUM (AV)

Suite 1500 - Barnett Bank Plaza, One East Broward Boulevard, 33301
Telephone: 954-522-7000
Facsimile: 954-522-7003
Email: rlrappeal@aol.com

For full biographical listings, see the Martindale-Hubbell Law Directory

FORT MYERS,* Lee Co.

SMOOT ADAMS EDWARDS & GREEN, P.A. (AV)

One University Park Suite 600, 12800 University Drive, P.O. Box 60259, 33906-6259
Telephone: 941-489-1776
(800) 226-1777 (in Florida)
Fax: 941-489-2444
Email: 71600.2745@compuserve.com

J. Tom Smoot, Jr.	Bruce D. Green
Hal Adams	Steven I. Winer
Franklyn A. (Chip) Johnson (1947-1991)	Mark R. Komray
	Clayton W. Crevasse
Charles B. Edwards	M. Brian Cheffer

Robert S. Forman	C. Berk Edwards, Jr.
Kathleen W. McBride	Melville G. Brinson, III
Lowell Schoenfeld	Samuel J. Hagan, IV.

For full biographical listings, see the Martindale-Hubbell Law Directory

KISSIMMEE,* Osceola Co.

POHL & SHORT, P.A.

(See Winter Park)

MIAMI,* Dade Co.

BERGER & CHAFETZ (AV)

NationsBank Building, 9350 South Dixie Highway, Penthouse One, 33156
Telephone: 305-670-3404
Fax: 305-670-3412

MEMBERS OF FIRM

Steven R. Berger	Amy Berger Chafetz

For full biographical listings, see the Martindale-Hubbell Law Directory

BIERMAN, SHOHAT, LOEWY, PERRY & KLEIN, PROFESSIONAL ASSOCIATION (AV)

Penthouse Two, 800 Brickell Avenue, 33131-2944
Telephone: 305-358-7000
Facsimile: 305-358-4010
Email: BSLPK@AOL.COM

Donald I. Bierman	Pamela I. Perry
Edward R. Shohat	Theodore Klein
Ira N. Loewy	Maria Beguiristain Shohat

Reference: United National Bank of Miami.

For full biographical listings, see the Martindale-Hubbell Law Directory

WILLIAM P. CAGNEY, III, P.A. (AV)

Suite 3400 First Union Financial Center, 200 South Biscayne Boulevard, 33131-2393
Telephone: 305-371-1411
Fax: 305-371-3810
Chicago, Illinois Office: Suite 1800, 100 West Monroe Street.

William P. Cagney, III

For full biographical listings, see the Martindale-Hubbell Law Directory

HICKS, ANDERSON & BLUM, P.A. (AV)

Twenty Fourth Floor, 100 North Biscayne Boulevard, 33132
Telephone: 305-374-8171
Fax: 305-372-8038

Mark Hicks	Bambi G. Blum
Ralph O. Anderson	Jean Kneale

(See Next Column)

Gary A. Magnarini	Cindy L. Ebenfeld
Alyssa M. Campbell	Ila J. Klion
	Dinah S. Stein

OF COUNSEL

James E. Tribble	Roger L. Blackburn

For full biographical listings, see the Martindale-Hubbell Law Directory

KEITH, MACK, LEWIS, COHEN & LUMPKIN (AV)

First Union Financial Center, Twentieth Floor, 200 South Biscayne Boulevard, 33131-2310
Telephone: 305-358-7605
Fax: 305-358-4755
Email: PREVAIL@KEITHMACK.COM

MEMBERS OF FIRM

Edgar Lewis	Jan Carson Cheezem
Robert A. Cohen	Loren S. Granoff
R. Hugh Lumpkin	Jack S. Lewis
Gregg S. Ahrens	Alan Rosenthal
	Norman S. Segall

ASSOCIATES

Michael J. Hogsten	Michele S. Primeau
Felix M. Lasarte	Cynthia Ramos
Dawn Marshall	Jack R. Reiter
Mercedes Padin	Karl J. Schumer
	Jeffrey P. Shapiro

OF COUNSEL

Seymour D. Keith	James L. Mack

Representative Clients: CitiBank, F.S.B.; Attorneys Title Insurance Fund, Inc.; Barnett Bank, N.A.
Approved Counsel: First American Title Insurance Co.; Attorneys Title Insurance Fund, Inc.; Commonwealth Title Insurance Co.
Reference: CitiBank, F.S.B.

For full biographical listings, see the Martindale-Hubbell Law Directory

PAUL MORRIS PROFESSIONAL ASSOCIATION (AV)

Suite 550, 999 Ponce de Leon Boulevard (Coral Gables), 33134
Telephone: 305-446-2020
Fax: 305-442-4371

Paul Morris

For full biographical listings, see the Martindale-Hubbell Law Directory

PODHURST, ORSECK, JOSEFSBERG, EATON, MEADOW, OLIN & PERWIN, P.A. (AV)

Suite 800 City National Bank Building, 25 West Flagler Street, 33130-1780
Telephone: 305-358-2800; Fort Lauderdale: 954-463-4346
Fax: 305-358-2382
Email: 76666.2340@COMPUSERVE.COM *URL:* http://www.turbosales.com/"sfbj/podhurst.html

Joel D. Eaton	Joel S. Perwin

References: City National Bank of Miami; United National Bank of Miami.

For Complete List of Firm Personnel, See General Section

For full biographical listings, see the Martindale-Hubbell Law Directory

RICHEY & DIAZ, P.A. (AV)

3100 First Union Financial Center, 200 South Biscayne Boulevard, 33131-2327
Telephone: 305-372-8808
Telefax: 305-372-3669; 374-4652
Email: richdiaz@netrunner.net

William L. Richey	Michael Diaz, Jr.

OF COUNSEL

Kirk W. Munroe

For full biographical listings, see the Martindale-Hubbell Law Directory

ROBBINS, TUNKEY, ROSS, AMSEL, RABEN & WAXMAN, P.A. (AV)

2250 Southwest Third Avenue, Fourth Floor, 33129
Telephone: Dade County 305-858-9550; Broward County 954-522-6244
(All Telephones Open 24 Hours); 1-800-226-9550
Fax: 305-858-7491

Frederick S. Robbins	Robert G. Amsel
William R. Tunkey	David Raben
Alan S. Ross	Benjamin S. Waxman

(See Next Column)

ROBBINS, TUNKEY, ROSS, AMSEL, RABEN & WAXMAN P.A.—*Continued*

Alan L. Quiles   Mark R. Eiglarsh
Marco A. Vazquez (1968-1995)

Reference: United National Bank, Miami, Florida.

For full biographical listings, see the Martindale-Hubbell Law Directory

RUSSO & TALISMAN, P.A. (AV)

Suite 2001, Terremark Centre, 2601 South Bayshore Drive (Coconut Grove), 33133
Telephone: 305-859-8100
Fax: 305-856-8823

Elizabeth Koebel Russo   Patrice A. Talisman

Kimberly L. Boldt   Laura P. Denault

For full biographical listings, see the Martindale-Hubbell Law Directory

THORNTON, DAVIS & MURRAY, P.A. (AV)

World Trade Center, 80 Southwest Eighth Street Suite 2900, 33130
Telephone: 305-446-2646
Fax: 305-441-2374
Email: tdm@gate.net

John M. Murray	Frederick J. Fein
Barry L. Davis	Ana Maria Marin
J. Thompson Thornton	David P. Herman

Holly S. Harvey   Kathleen M. O'Connor

For Complete List of Firm Personnel, See General Section

For full biographical listings, see the Martindale-Hubbell Law Directory

NORTH MIAMI BEACH, Dade Co.

BECKHAM & BECKHAM, P.A. (AV)

17071 West Dixie Highway, Suite B, 33160
Telephone: 305-945-1851
Fax: 305-940-8706
Email: Beckham-Beckham@worldnet.att.net

Pamela Beckham   Eugene G. Beckham
Robert J. Beckham, Jr.

For full biographical listings, see the Martindale-Hubbell Law Directory

ORLANDO,* Orange Co.

POHL & SHORT, P.A.

(See Winter Park)

PALM BEACH GARDENS, Palm Beach Co.

MARJORIE GADARIAN GRAHAM, P.A. (AV)

Suite D 129, 11211 Prosperity Farms Road, 33410
Telephone: 407-775-1204

Marjorie Gadarian Graham

For full biographical listings, see the Martindale-Hubbell Law Directory

TALLAHASSEE,* Leon Co.

McFARLAIN, WILEY, CASSEDY & JONES, PROFESSIONAL ASSOCIATION (AV)

215 South Monroe Street, Suite 600, P.O. Box 2174, 32316-2174
Telephone: 904-222-2107
Telecopier: 904-222-8475

Richard C. McFarlain	Charles A. Stampelos
William B. Wiley	Linda McMullen
Marshall R. Cassedy	H. Darrell White, Jr.
Douglas P. Jones	Christopher Barkas

Harold R. Mardenborough, Jr.	Rogelio J. Fontela
Robert A. McNeely	Patrick John McGinley

For full biographical listings, see the Martindale-Hubbell Law Directory

RADEY McARTHUR & FREHN (AV)

101 South Monroe Street, 32301
Telephone: 904-681-7766
Fax: 904-681-0160
Email: Radeylaw@aol.com

(See Next Column)

John Radey   Elizabeth Waas McArthur
Jeffrey L. Frehn

Representative Clients: Electronic Data Systems Corp.; Columbia Tallahassee Community Hospital; Tampa General Hospital; Columbia/HCA Healthcare Corp.; Columbia Lawnwood Regional Medical Center.

For full biographical listings, see the Martindale-Hubbell Law Directory

TAMPA,* Hillsborough Co.

KYNES, MARKMAN & FELMAN, P.A. (AV)

P.O. Box 3396, 33601
Telephone: 813-229-1118
Facsimile: 813-221-6750

James H. Kynes (1953-1993)	James E. Felman
Stuart C. Markman	Susan H. Freemon

For full biographical listings, see the Martindale-Hubbell Law Directory

MANEY, DAMSKER, HARRIS & JONES, P.A. (AV)

606 Madison Street, P.O. Box 172009, 33672-0009
Telephone: 813-228-7371
Fax: 813-223-4846

Lee S. Damsker   David A. Maney

Patricia F. Kuhlman

For full biographical listings, see the Martindale-Hubbell Law Directory

ROBERT P. POLLI, P.A. (AV)

Barnett Bank Plaza, 101 East Kennedy Boulevard, Suite 3130, 33602
Telephone: 813-222-8350
Fax: Available Upon Request

Robert P. Polli

For full biographical listings, see the Martindale-Hubbell Law Directory

WEST PALM BEACH,* Palm Beach Co.

CARUSO, BURLINGTON, BOHN & COMPIANI, P.A. (AV)

Suite 3A Barristers Building, 1615 Forum Place, 33401
Telephone: 561-686-8010
Fax: 561-686-8663

Edna L. Caruso	Russell S. Bohn
Philip M. Burlington	Barbara J. Compiani

For full biographical listings, see the Martindale-Hubbell Law Directory

JANE KREUSLER-WALSH (AV)

Suite 503 Flagler Center, 501 South Flagler Drive, 33401
Telephone: 407-659-5455
Fax: 407-820-8762

For full biographical listings, see the Martindale-Hubbell Law Directory

RICHARD A. KUPFER, P.A. (AV)

The Forum, Tower C, Suite 810, 1655 Palm Beach Lakes Boulevard, 33401
Telephone: 561-684-8600
FAX: 561-684-1508

Richard A. Kupfer
LEGAL SUPPORT PERSONNEL
Jan M. Setchell

For full biographical listings, see the Martindale-Hubbell Law Directory

WINTER PARK, Orange Co.

POHL & SHORT, P.A. (AV)

280 West Canton Avenue, Suite 410, P.O. Box 3208, 32790
Telephone: 407-647-7645; 407-647-POHL
Telefax: 407-647-2314

Frank L. Pohl	C. Teresa de Arrigoitia
Houston E. Short	George A. Golder
Dwight I. Cool	Norma Stanley
James Everett Shepherd V	Mark W. Garrett
John R. Simpson, Jr.	

Representative Clients: American Pioneer Title Insurance Company; Institute of Internal Auditors, Inc.; Thompson Steel, Inc.; SunTrust, N.A.; The Bank of Winter Park; Bekins Moving and Storage Co., Inc.; Champion Boats, Inc.; KeyCom Telephone Systems, Inc.

For full biographical listings, see the Martindale-Hubbell Law Directory

GEORGIA

ATLANTA, Fulton Co.

C. MICHAEL ABBOTT, P.C. (AV)

One Atlantic Center, Suite 3410, 1201 West Peachtree Street, 30309-3400
Telephone: 404-885-1994
Fax: 404-885-1677

Michael Abbott

For full biographical listings, see the Martindale-Hubbell Law Directory

JAKE ARBES (AV)

2300 Harris Tower, 233 Peachtree Street, N.E., 30303
Telephone: 404-522-1980
FAX: 404-588-0648

For full biographical listings, see the Martindale-Hubbell Law Directory

BONDURANT, MIXSON & ELMORE, LLP (AV)

1201 W. Peachtree Street Suite 3900, 30309
Telephone: 404-881-4100
FAX: 404-881-4111

MEMBERS OF FIRM

Emmet J. Bondurant II	Dirk G. Christensen
H. Lamar Mixson	Jane E. Fahey
M. Jerome Elmore	John E. Floyd
Edward B. Krugman	Michael A. Sullivan
Jeffrey O. Bramlett	Michael B. Terry

Representative Clients: The Aetna Casualty and Surety Company; Blue Circle of America; Circle K; Conoco, Inc.; Delta Air Lines, Inc.; Queen Carpets, Inc.; Sanifill, Inc.; Ticketmaster; Trammell Crow Co.; Wylie Laboratories.

For full biographical listings, see the Martindale-Hubbell Law Directory

GARLAND, SAMUEL & LOEB, P.C. (AV)

3151 Maple Drive, N.E., 30305
Telephone: 404-262-2225
Fax: 404-365-5041
Email: TrialLaw@aol.com

Edward T. M. Garland	Donald F. Samuel
	Robin N. Loeb

For full biographical listings, see the Martindale-Hubbell Law Directory

LONG ALDRIDGE & NORMAN, LLP (AV)

A Limited Liability Partnership including Professional Corporations
One Peachtree Center, Suite 5300, 303 Peachtree Street, 30308
Telephone: 404-527-4000
Telecopier: 404-527-4198
Washington, D.C. Office: Suite 600, 701 Pennsylvania Avenue, N.W., 20004.
Telephone: 202-624-1200.
FAX: 202-624-1298.

MEMBERS OF FIRM

John L. Watkins	Robert I. White (Resident,
Jack H. Watson, Jr. (Resident,	Washington, D.C. Office)
Washington, D.C. Office)	

SENIOR COUNSEL
F. T. Davis, Jr., (P.C.)

For Complete List of Firm Personnel, See General Section

For full biographical listings, see the Martindale-Hubbell Law Directory

WILSON, BROCK & IRBY, L.L.C. (AV)

999 Peachtree Street, N.E., Suite 2000, 30309
Telephone: 404-853-5050
Fax: 404-853-1812

MEMBERS OF FIRM

Richard W. Wilson, Jr.	Lethco H. Brock, Jr.
Frank L. Wilson, III	John H. Irby

ASSOCIATES

Jerry D. Gerald	James Stuart Teague, Jr.
	Paul Schillawski

OF COUNSEL
L. Robert Lovett

For full biographical listings, see the Martindale-Hubbell Law Directory

AUGUSTA, Richmond Co.

GARRETT & GILLIARD (AV)

SunTrust Bank Building, 801 Broad Street, Suite 1001, 30901
Telephone: 706-724-1896
Fax: 706-724-0047

(See Next Column)

MEMBERS OF FIRM

Michael C. Garrett	Kirk Emerson Gilliard

ASSOCIATE
Melissa S. Padgett

For full biographical listings, see the Martindale-Hubbell Law Directory

HAWAII

HONOLULU, Honolulu Co.

ROBBINS & RHODES ATTORNEYS AT LAW, A LAW CORPORATION (AV)

Suite 2200 Davies Pacific Center, 841 Bishop Street, 96813
Telephone: 808-524-2355
Fax: 808-526-0290

Kenneth S. Robbins	Shinken Naitoh

Representative Clients: Argonaut Insurance Co.; City and County of Honolulu; County of Maui; Employers Reinsurance Co.; General Reinsurance Co.; Guaranty National Insurance Co.; Transamerica Insurance Co.; Truck Insurance Group; Westchester Insurance Co.

For full biographical listings, see the Martindale-Hubbell Law Directory

RENEE M. L. YUEN ATTORNEY AT LAW, A LAW CORPORATION (AV)

Haseko Center, 820 Mililani Street, Suite 702A, 96813-2937
Telephone: 808-523-0125
Facsimile: 808-523-0127

Renee M. L. Yuen

For full biographical listings, see the Martindale-Hubbell Law Directory

IDAHO

POCATELLO, Bannock Co.

MERRILL & MERRILL, CHARTERED (AV)

Key Bank Building, P.O. Box 991, 83204
Telephone: 208-232-2286
Fax: 208-232-2499

Wesley F. Merrill	D. Russell Wight
Stephen S. Dunn	David C. Nye

Representative Clients: Farm Bureau Mutual Insurance Co. of Idaho; J.R. Simplot Co.; Fibreboard Corporation; Owens-Illinois, Inc.; Pittsburgh Corning Corporation; Travelers Insurance Co.; E.I. DuPont.

For Complete List of Firm Personnel, See General Section

For full biographical listings, see the Martindale-Hubbell Law Directory

ILLINOIS

CHICAGO, Cook Co.

ALLAN A. ACKERMAN, P.C. (AV)

2000 North Clifton Avenue, 60614
Telephone: 312-332-2891; 332-2863
Fax: 312-871-3304

Allan A. Ackerman

For full biographical listings, see the Martindale-Hubbell Law Directory

BRYDGES RISEBOROUGH PETERSON FRANKE AND MORRIS (AV)

A Partnership including Professional Corporations
28th Floor, 150 North Michigan Avenue, 60601
Telephone: 312-782-5042
FAX: 312-704-9107
Waukegan, Illinois Office: 110 North West Street.
Telephone: 847-249-0300.
FAX: 847-249-4755.
Phoenix, Arizona Office: 3030 North Central Avenue, Suite 408.
Telephone: 602-631-4400.
FAX: 602-631-4404.

(See Next Column)

BRYDGES RISEBOROUGH PETERSON FRANKE AND MORRIS—*Continued*

MEMBERS OF FIRM

Louis W. Brydges, Sr.	Scott E. Nemanich
Allyn J. Franke	Reid S. Jacobson
George E. Riseborough (A	Donald M. Lonchar, Jr.
Professional Corporation)	Peter J. Nordigian
J. V. Schaffenegger (1914-1986)	Robert L. Snook
Ralph Miller (1922-1988)	Stacey L. Seneczko
Donald G. Peterson	Rebecca Sarah Larson
Thomas A. Morris, Jr., (A	Neal T. Goldstein
Professional Corporation)	Monica J. Conrad
Donald L. Sime	Gioconda (Jackie) V. Iannicelli
John H. Krackenberger	Jennifer M. Lundy
Jay Scott Nelson	Eleanor P. Cabreré
Michael A. Strom	Linda A. White
Louis W. Brydges, Jr.	William G. Berg
Leslie A. Peterson	John W. Dixon
Thomas K. Gerling	Thomas A. Kiepura

OF COUNSEL

Harry D. Strouse	Thomas J. Moran (1920-1995)
	Jack L. Watson

For full biographical listings, see the Martindale-Hubbell Law Directory

---

DOWD & DOWD, LTD. (AV)

Suite 1000, 55 West Wacker Drive, 60601
Telephone: 312-704-4400
Telecopier: 312-704-4500

Joseph V. Dowd	Robert C. Yelton III
Michael E. Dowd	Patrick C. Dowd
Kenneth Gurber	Robert J. Golden
	Karen W. Worsek

S. Robert Depke	John M. McAndrews
Ryan J. Harrington	Edward W. McNabola
Jeffrey Edward Kehl	Martha A. Niles
Sarah A. Kennedy	Michael G. Patrizio
Richard B. Korn	Patrick J. Ruberry
Joseph J. Leonard	Anthony R. Rutkowski
Ronald J. Lukes	Jeffrey Scott Wrage

LEGAL SUPPORT PERSONNEL

Carol Barnes	Jill A. Weiseman

OF COUNSEL

Guenther Ahlf	John A. Garrity, III
	Joel S. Ostrow

Reference: American National Bank in Chicago.

For full biographical listings, see the Martindale-Hubbell Law Directory

---

NORMAN J. LERUM (AV)

Suite 2100, 100 West Monroe Street, 60603
Telephone: 312-782-1087
Facsimile: 312-332-6020

For full biographical listings, see the Martindale-Hubbell Law Directory

---

DAVID A. NOVOSELSKY & ASSOCIATES (AV)

120 North La Salle Street, Suite 1400, 60602-2401
Telephone: 312-346-8930
Fax: 312-346-9453

Linda A Bryceland	Margarita T. Kulys
Kevin S. Besetzny	Eduard Adam Glavinskas

For full biographical listings, see the Martindale-Hubbell Law Directory

---

MERLE L. ROYCE, II (AV)

111 West Washington Street Suite 1710, 60606
Telephone: 312-553-1233
Fax: 312-372-4700

ASSOCIATE

Marshall J. Burt

OF COUNSEL

James J. Macchitelli	Khurram Hussain

For full biographical listings, see the Martindale-Hubbell Law Directory

---

SCHWARTZBERG, BARNETT & COHEN (AV)

55 West Monroe Street, 2400 Xerox Centre, 60603-5040
Telephone: 312-726-3555
Fax: 312-726-6299
Cable Address: "Justice"
Email: sb&c@twty.chi.il.us

MEMBERS OF FIRM

Ralph M. Schwartzberg	Mark T. Barnett (1939-1970)
(1939-1975)	Hugh J. Schwartzberg
	Benjamin H. Cohen

(See Next Column)

OF COUNSEL

Eugene P. Thomas Jr.

For full biographical listings, see the Martindale-Hubbell Law Directory

---

WILLIAM J. STEVENS (AV)

135 South La Salle Street, Suite 3600, 60603
Telephone: 312-845-2903
Fax: 312-641-0727

For full biographical listings, see the Martindale-Hubbell Law Directory

---

TORSHEN, SPREYER & GARMISA, LTD. (AV)

105 West Adams Street, Suite 3200, 60603
Telephone: 312-372-9282
Fax: 312-372-7914

Jerome H. Torshen	Steven P. Garmisa
Abigail Kay Spreyer	Robert J. Slobig
James K. Genden	Eric James Rietz
Zoran Dragutinovich	Thomas J. Ramsdell

For full biographical listings, see the Martindale-Hubbell Law Directory

---

LAW OFFICES OF RUTH E. VANDEMARK (AV)

Suite 2200, 225 West Washington Street, 60606
Telephone: 312-419-7162
Fax: 312-419-7285

ASSOCIATE

Ralph N. Glader

For full biographical listings, see the Martindale-Hubbell Law Directory

---

WILDMAN, HARROLD, ALLEN & DIXON (AV)

225 West Wacker Drive, 30th Floor, 60606-1229
Telephone: 312-201-2000
Cable Address: "Whad"
Fax: 312-201-2555
URL: http://www.whad.com
Aurora, Illinois Office: 1851 W. Galena Boulevard, Suite 210.
Telephone: 630-892-7021.
Fax: 630-892-7158.
Waukegan, Illinois Office: 404 West Water, P. O. Box 890.
Telephone: 847-623-0700.
Fax: 847-244-5273.
Lisle, Illinois Office: 4300 Commerce Court.
Telephone: 630-955-0555.
New York, New York Office: Wildman, Harrold, Allen, Dixon & Smith. The International Building, 45 Rockefeller Plaza, Suite 353.
Telephone: 212-632-3850.
Fax: 212-632-3858.
Toronto, Ontario affiliated Office: Keel Cottrelle. 36 Toronto Street, Ninth Floor, Suite 920.
Telephone: 416-367-2900.
Telefax: 416-367-2791.
Telex: 062-18660.
Mississauga, Ontario affiliated Office: Keel Cottrelle. 100 Matatson Avenue East, Suite 104.
Telephone: 416-890-7700.
Fax: 416-890-8006.

MEMBERS OF FIRM

Thomas D. Allen	James T. Nyeste
Anthony G. Hopp	David F. Pardys
Robert E. Kehoe, Jr.	(Waukegan Office)
Thomas M. Lynch	Lisa S. Simmons
Mark P. Miller	Linda E. Spring
Richard D. Murphy Jr.	(Waukegan Office)

Jody A. Ballmer	Michael J. Lotus
John T. Benz	Jeffrey A. McIntyre
Eric P. Berlin	Stephanie B. Miller
David J. Chroust (Lisle Office)	Vania Montero
Leo P. Dombrowski	Barbara M. Prohaska
Lawrence W. Falbe	(Lisle Office)
Wendy L. Fink	Kevin B. Reid
Adam J. Glazer	John A. Roberts
James C. James, III	Elizabeth A. Sanders
(Aurora Office)	Jeannine Y. Sano
Elizabeth Keiley	Paul A. Slager
	Joleen S. Willis

For Complete List of Firm Personnel, See General Section

For full biographical listings, see the Martindale-Hubbell Law Directory

INDIANA

AUBURN,* De Kalb Co.

MEFFORD AND CARPENTER, A PROFESSIONAL CORPORATION (AV)

130 East Seventh Street, P.O. Box 667, 46706-0667
Telephone: 219-925-2300
Facsimile: 219-925-2610
URL: http://www.lawmc.com

Donald T. Mefford   Kirk D. Carpenter
J. Bryan Nugen

For full biographical listings, see the Martindale-Hubbell Law Directory

EVANSVILLE,* Vanderburgh Co.

BOWERS, HARRISON, KENT & MILLER, LLP (AV)

25 N.W. Riverside Drive, P.O. Box 1287, 47706-1287
Telephone: 812-426-1231
Fax: 812-464-3676

MEMBERS OF FIRM

F. Wesley Bowers   David E. Gray
David V. Miller   James P. Casey
George C. Barnett, Jr.   Joseph H. Harrison, Jr.

Division Counsel in Indiana for: Southern Railway Co.
Representative Clients: Permanent Federal Savings Bank; Citizens Realty & Insurance, Inc.

For Complete List of Firm Personnel, See General Section

For full biographical listings, see the Martindale-Hubbell Law Directory

FINE & HATFIELD (AV)

520 N.W. Second Street, P.O. Box 779, 47705-0779
Telephone: 812-425-3592
Telecopier: 812-421-4269
Email: Fine@Fine-Hatfield.com *URL:* http://www.Fine-Hatfield.com

MEMBERS OF FIRM

Thomas H. Bryan   Danny E. Glass
Patricia Kay Woodring

ASSOCIATE
Todd I. Glass

A List of Representative Clients Furnished Upon Request.

For full biographical listings, see the Martindale-Hubbell Law Directory

FORT WAYNE,* Allen Co.

HUNT, SUEDHOFF, BORROR & EILBACHER (AV)

900 Courtside, 803 South Calhoun Street, P.O. Box 11489, 46858-1489
Telephone: 219-423-1311
Telecopier: 219-424-5396

RETIRED
Carl J. Suedhoff, Jr.

MEMBERS OF FIRM

Leigh L. Hunt (1899-1975)   Thomas W. Belleperche
William E. Borror (1932-1989)   Mark W. Baeverstad
Leonard E. Eilbacher   Michael D. Mustard
Robert E. Kabisch   Branch R. Lew
Arthur G. Surguine, Jr.   Carla J. Baird
Thomas C. Ewing   James J. Shea
Carolyn White Spengler   Scott L. Bunnell
Dane L. Tubergen

ASSOCIATES

Charles H. Bassford, IV   Daniel J. Palmer
Carolyn M. Trier   Brian L. England
Kathleen A. Kilar   Craig J. Bobay
W. Douglas Lemon

For full biographical listings, see the Martindale-Hubbell Law Directory

SWIFT & FINLAYSON (AV)

803 South Calhoun Street Suite 500, 46802-2480
Telephone: 219-423-4422
Fax: 219-423-4427
Affiliated Law Firm: Leeuw, Plopper & Beeman-Poland, First Indiana Plaza, Suite 2000, 135 North Pennsylvania Street, Indianapolis, Indiana, 46204-2456.

MEMBERS OF FIRM
Frank A. Higgins (1925-1976)   William D. Swift
Craig R. Finlayson

ASSOCIATE
Charles D. Bash

(See Next Column)

OF COUNSEL
Gene R. Leeuw   Craig D. Doyle
Joseph W. Murphy   Charleyne L. Gabriel
John Michael Mead

For full biographical listings, see the Martindale-Hubbell Law Directory

INDIANAPOLIS,* Marion Co.

HUGHES AND SALLEE (AV)

(Not a Partnership)
Two Meridian Plaza, Suite 202, 10401 North Meridian Street, 46290
Telephone: 317-573-2255
Telecopier: 317-573-2266

David B. Hughes   Gary D. Sallee

For full biographical listings, see the Martindale-Hubbell Law Directory

McTURNAN & TURNER (AV)

2400 Market Tower, 10 West Market Street, 46204
Telephone: 317-464-8181
Telecopier: 317-464-8131

Lee B. McTurnan   Jacqueline Bowman Ponder
Wayne C. Turner   Steven M. Badger
Judy L. Woods   Matthew W. Foster
Matthew J. Salzman

For full biographical listings, see the Martindale-Hubbell Law Directory

PLEWS SHADLEY RACHER & BRAUN (AV)

1346 North Delaware Street, 46202-2415
Telephone: 317-637-0700
Telecopier: 317-637-0710

MEMBERS OF FIRM

George M. Plews   Peter M. Racher
Sue A. Shadley   Christopher J. Braun
Jeffrey D. Claflin

ASSOCIATES

Harinder Kaur   Jeffrey D. Featherstun
Leonardo D. Robinson   Donna C. Marron
Frederick D. Emhardt   Michael A. Myers
S. Curtis DeVoe   Julie E. Polizzotto

OF COUNSEL
Christine C. H. Plews   Timothy J. Paris

For full biographical listings, see the Martindale-Hubbell Law Directory

LAFAYETTE,* Tippecanoe Co.

BALL, EGGLESTON, BUMBLEBURG & McBRIDE (AV)

810 Bank One Building, P.O. Box 1535, 47902
Telephone: 317-742-9046
Fax: 317-742-1966

Cable G. Ball (1904-1981)   Warren N. Eggleston
Owen Crook (1908-1977)   (1923-1991)

MEMBERS OF FIRM

Joseph T. Bumbleburg   Jeffrey J. Newell
John K. McBride   James T. Hodson
Jack L. Walkey   Brian Wade Walker
Michael J. Stapleton   Cheryl M. Knodle
Randy J. Williams

General Counsel for: The Lafayette Union Railway Co.; Bank One, Lafayette, N.A.
Representative Clients: Farmers Insurance Group; General Accident Fire & Life Assurance Corp.; City of Lafayette Board of Parks and Recreation; West Lafayette Community School Corp.; Travelers Insurance Co.; Trustees, West Lafayette Public Library.

For full biographical listings, see the Martindale-Hubbell Law Directory

STUART & BRANIGIN (AV)

The Life Building, 300 Main Street, Suite 800, 47902
Telephone: 317-423-1561
Telecopier: 317-742-8175

MEMBERS OF FIRM

Allison Ellsworth Stuart   Stephen R. Pennell
(1886-1950)   Anthony S. Benton
Roger D. Branigin (1902-1975)   Erik D. Spykman
Russell H. Hart   William E. Emerick
Roger D. Branigin, Jr.   John C. Duffey
Thomas L. Ryan   Mark E. DeYoung
James V. McGlone   Thomas B. Parent
Carl W. Kloepfer   Laura L. Bowker
Thomas R. McCully   Kevin D. Nicoson
Larry R. Fisher   Susan K. Roberts
Nina B. Kirkpatrick   John M. Stuckey
Mark Lillianfeld   Deborah B. Trice

(See Next Column)

STUART & BRANIGIN—*Continued*

COUNSEL

John F. Bodle

ASSOCIATES

Brent W. Huber   David A. Starkweather
William P. Kealey   Geoffrey Blazi

A. James Chareq

General Counsel for: The Lafayette Life Insurance Co.; INB National Bank, N.W.; Lafayette Home Hospital, Inc.
State Counsel for: Norfolk & Western Railway Co.
Mr. Ryan is Counsel to: The Trustees of Purdue University.
Representative Clients: Aluminum Company of America; Liberty Mutual Insurance Group.

For full biographical listings, see the Martindale-Hubbell Law Directory

---

*MARION,** Grant Co.

KILEY, KILEY, HARKER, MICHAEL & CERTAIN (AV)

300 West Third Street, P.O. Box 899, 46952-0899
Telephone: 317-664-9041
Fax: 317-664-8119

MEMBERS OF FIRM

Robert Ralph Batton   David L. Kiley, Sr.
  (1890-1963)   Michael J. Kiley
Albert L. Harker (1904-1965)   Albert C. Harker
Albert Bonner Brown   Thomas W. Michael
  (1911-1981)   Harry J. Certain

ASSOCIATE

Therese McCullough Pryor

Counsel for: Bank One, Marion, N.A.; Liniger Co., Inc.; Atlas Foundry Co.
Local Counsel for: GenCorp.; CPC Group; General Motors; Indiana Michigan Power Co./AEP; Indiana Bell Telephone Co.; Foster-Forbes, Division of American National Can Corp.

For full biographical listings, see the Martindale-Hubbell Law Directory

---

IOWA

*DES MOINES,** Polk Co.

FINLEY, ALT, SMITH, SCHARNBERG, MAY & CRAIG, P.C. (AV)

604 Locust Street, Fourth Floor Equitable Building, 50309
Telephone: 515-288-0145
Telecopier: 515-288-2724

Lorraine J. May   V. Glenn Goodwin, Jr.

Dawn R. Siebert

Representative Clients: Aetna Casualty & Surety Co.; Aetna Life Insurance Co.; ALAS; American Society of Composers, Authors and Publishers; Equitable Life Assurance Society of the U.S.; Federated Insurance Co.; Meredith Corp.
Iowa Attorneys for: Midwest Medical Insurance Co.
District Attorneys for: Norfolk & Southern Railroad; Soo Line Railroad Company.

For Complete List of Firm Personnel, See General Section

For full biographical listings, see the Martindale-Hubbell Law Directory

---

KANSAS

*TOPEKA,** Shawnee Co.

FISHER, PATTERSON, SAYLER & SMITH, L.L.P. (AV)

534 South Kansas Avenue, Suite 400, P.O. Box 949, 66601
Telephone: 913-232-7761
Fax: 913-232-6604
Overland Park, Kansas Office: 11050 Roe Avenue, Suite 210, 66211.
Telephone: 913-339-6757.
Fax: 913-339-6187.

MEMBERS OF FIRM

Donald Patterson   Steve R. Fabert
Edwin Dudley Smith (Resident,   Ronald J. Laskowski
  Overland Park Office)   Michael K. Seck (Resident,
Larry G. Pepperdine   Overland Park Office)
James P. Nordstrom   David P. Madden (Resident,
Justice B. King   Overland Park Office)
J. Steven Pigg   Steven K. Johnson

ASSOCIATES

Kristine A. Larscheid   Billy E. Newman
Patrick G. Reavey (Resident,   David R. Cooper
  Overland Park Office)

(See Next Column)

OF COUNSEL

David H. Fisher

RETIRED

Charles Keith Sayler (Retired)

Representative Clients: Gage Shopping Center, Inc.; Fireman's Fund-American Insurance Cos.; United States Fidelity and Guaranty Co.; The Procter & Gamble Company; American Cyanamid Company; Commercial Union Insurance Companies; National Casualty/Scottsdale Insurance Co.; The Hartford; Berkshire Hathaway Companies.

For full biographical listings, see the Martindale-Hubbell Law Directory

---

*WICHITA,** Sedgwick Co.

HERSHBERGER, PATTERSON, JONES & ROTH, L.C. (AV)

600 Hardage Center, 100 South Main, 67202-3779
Telephone: 316-263-7583
Fax: 316-263-7595

Robert J. Roth   William R. Smith

Tracy A. Applegate

Counsel for: First National Bank in Wichita; Anadarko Petroleum Corporation; Chinese Industries; Mobil Oil Corp.; CNA Insurance; Royal Exchange Group; Central National Insurance Group; Transamerica Insurance Group; Northwestern National Insurance Group.

For Complete List of Firm Personnel, See General Section

For full biographical listings, see the Martindale-Hubbell Law Directory

---

KENTUCKY

*BOWLING GREEN,** Warren Co.

HARLIN & PARKER, P.S.C. (AV)

519 East Tenth Street, P.O. Box 390, 42102-0390
Telephone: 502-842-5611
Telefax: 502-842-2607

William Jerry Parker   James David Bryant

Insurance Clients: Allstate Insurance Co.; CNA Insurance Company.
Railroad and Utilities Clients: District Attorneys for BellSouth Telecommunications, Inc.; CSX Transportation, Inc.
Local Counsel for: General Motors Corp.; News Publishing Co.

For Complete List of Firm Personnel, See General Section

For full biographical listings, see the Martindale-Hubbell Law Directory

---

KERRICK, GRISE & STIVERS (AV)

1025 State Street, P.O. Box 9547, 42102-9547
Telephone: 502-782-8160
Fax: 502-782-5856
Elizabethtown, Kentucky Office: 2935 Dolphin Drive, Suite 102.
Telephone: 502-769-5788.
Fax: 502-737-9285.

MEMBERS OF FIRM

Thomas N. Kerrick   Gregory N. Stivers
John R. Grise   H. Brent Brennenstuhl

ASSOCIATES

Lanna Martin Kilgore   Shawn Rosso Alcott
Laura M. Hagan (Resident,   Jason B. Bell
  Elizabethtown Office)

Representative Clients: Dollar General Corp.; Columbia Greenview Regional Hospital; Hospital Corporation of America; Hardin Memorial Hospital; Monarch Environmental, Inc.; Mid-South Management Group, Inc.; Trans Financial Bank; TKR Cable.

For full biographical listings, see the Martindale-Hubbell Law Directory

---

COVINGTON, Kenton Co.

ROBERT E. SANDERS AND ASSOCIATES, P.S.C. (AV)

The Charles H. Fisk House, 1017 Russell Street, 41011
Telephone: 606-491-3000
Fax: 606-655-4642
Email: 74762.3055@compuserve.com

Robert E. Sanders

Julie Lippert Duncan   Peggy A. Murphy

Lisa Pruitt Thorner

LEGAL SUPPORT PERSONNEL

Shirley L. Sanders   Sandra A. Head

Sheila D. Rachal

For full biographical listings, see the Martindale-Hubbell Law Directory

DANVILLE, * Boyle Co.

LAW OFFICES OF KENT MASTERSON BROWN (AV)

304 West Main Street, Suite 201, 40422
Telephone: 606-238-7383
Fax: 606-238-7442

ASSOCIATE
Christopher J. Shaughnessy

For full biographical listings, see the Martindale-Hubbell Law Directory

LOUISIANA

ALEXANDRIA, * Rapides Parish

CHRIS J. ROY, SR. (AV)

1100 Tenth Street, 71301
Telephone: 318-487-9537
Fax: 381-482-1353

For full biographical listings, see the Martindale-Hubbell Law Directory

LAFAYETTE, * Lafayette Parish

MANGHAM AND DAVIS (AV)

Suite 1400 First National Bank Towers, 600 Jefferson Street, P.O. Box
93110, 70509-3110
Telephone: 318-233-6200
Fax: 318-233-6521

Michael R. Mangham	Louis R. Davis

ASSOCIATES

Dawn Mayeux Fuqua	Claire A. Fisher

SPECIAL COUNSEL
Michael J. O'Shee

Reference: Hibernia National Bank, Lafayette, Louisiana.

For full biographical listings, see the Martindale-Hubbell Law Directory

NEW ORLEANS, * Orleans Parish

BARHAM & ARCENEAUX, A PROFESSIONAL LAW CORPORATION (AV)

Suite 2700, Poydras Center, 650 Poydras Street, 70130-6101
Telephone: 504-525-4400
Fax: 504-525-6378

Mack E. Barham	Julia C. Symon
Robert E. Arceneaux	Travis Louis Bourgeois
Gail N. Wise	Hansel A. Harlen
Jerry Barfield Jordan	Robert Markle

OF COUNSEL
James A. Comiskey

For full biographical listings, see the Martindale-Hubbell Law Directory

SHREVEPORT, * Caddo Parish

BARLOW AND HARDTNER L.C. (AV)

Tenth Floor, Louisiana Tower, 401 Edwards Street, 71101-3289
Telephone: 318-227-1131
Telecopier: 318-227-1141
Mailing Address: P.O. Box 8, Shreveport, Louisiana, 71161-0008

Malcolm S. Murchison	Philip E. Downer, III
Joseph L. Shea, Jr.	Michael B. Donald
David R. Taggart	Jay A. Greenleaf

Representative Clients: Central and South West Corporation; Kelley Oil Corporation; Louisiana Intrastate Gas Corp.; NorAm Energy Corp. (formerly Arkla, Inc.); Southwestern Electric Power Company; Wagner & Brown; Central and South West; Panhandle Eastern Corp.; Pennzoil Producing Co.

For Complete List of Firm Personnel, See General Section

For full biographical listings, see the Martindale-Hubbell Law Directory

WILKINSON, CARMODY & GILLIAM (AV)

1700 Beck Building, 400 Travis Street, P.O. Box 1707, 71166
Telephone: 318-221-4196
Telecopier: 318-221-3705

MEMBERS OF FIRM

John D. Wilkinson (1867-1929)	Bobby S. Gilliam
William Scott Wilkinson (1895-1985)	Mark E. Gilliam
	Penny D. Sellers
Arthur R. Carmody, Jr.	Patrick F. Robinson
Michael J. Ryan	

(See Next Column)

Representative Clients: Farmers Insurance Group; Home Federal Savings & Loan Association of Shreveport; The Kansas City Southern Railway Co.; KTAL-TV; Lincoln National Life Insurance Co.; Mobil Oil Co.; Schumpert Medical Center; Sears, Roebuck & Co.; Southern Pacific Transportation Co.; Southwestern Electric Power Co.

For full biographical listings, see the Martindale-Hubbell Law Directory

MAINE

PORTLAND, * Cumberland Co.

PETRUCCELLI & MARTIN (AV)

50 Monument Square, P.O. Box 9733, 04104-5033
Telephone: 207-775-0200
Telecopier: 207-775-2360

MEMBERS OF FIRM

Gerald F. Petruccelli	Joel C. Martin
James B. Haddow	

Representative Clients: Associated Aviation Underwriters; Bangor Hydro-Electric Co.; Chicago Title Insurance Co.; Chubb Insurance Co.; Cumberland Farms; Maine Medical Center; Town of Jay, Maine; Union Mutual Fire Insurance Co.

For full biographical listings, see the Martindale-Hubbell Law Directory

MARYLAND

BALTIMORE, * (Independent City)

FUNK & BOLTON, A PROFESSIONAL ASSOCIATION (AV)

USF&G Tower Building, Suite 900, 100 Light Street, 21202
Telephone: 410-659-7700
Facsimile: 410-659-7773
Email: FBLAW.COM

David M. Funk	Lindsey A. Rader
Bryan D. Bolton	Steven Jared Troy
Timothy E. Dixon	Derek B. Yarmis

OF COUNSEL

J. Frank Nayden	Bryson F. Popham
Deborah R. Rivkin	

For full biographical listings, see the Martindale-Hubbell Law Directory

McDANIEL & MARSH (AV)

118 West Mulberry Street, 21201-3600
Telephone: 410-685-3810
Telecopier: 410-685-0203

William Alden McDaniel, Jr.	Jo Bennett Marsh

ASSOCIATE
Laura M. L. Maroldy

For full biographical listings, see the Martindale-Hubbell Law Directory

PIERSON, PIERSON & NOLAN (AV)

Suite 1600 Redwood Tower, 217 East Redwood Street, 21202
Telephone: 410-727-7733
FAX: 410-625-0253

MEMBERS OF FIRM

W. Michel Pierson	James J. Nolan, Jr.
	Robert L. Pierson

OF COUNSEL
David S. Sykes

For Complete List of Firm Personnel, See General Section

For full biographical listings, see the Martindale-Hubbell Law Directory

VENABLE ATTORNEYS AT LAW VENABLE, BAETJER AND HOWARD, LLP (AV)

A Partnership including Professional Corporations
1800 Mercantile Bank & Trust Building, 2 Hopkins Plaza, 21201
Telephone: 410-244-7400
Email: INFO@Venable.win.net
Washington, D.C. Office: Venable, Baetjer, Howard & Civiletti LLP. Suite 1000, 1201 New York Avenue, N.W.
Telephone: 202-962-4800.
McLean, Virginia Office: Suite 400, 2010 Corporate Ridge.
Telephone: 703-760-1600.
Rockville, Maryland Office: Suite 500, One Church Street, P. O. Box 1906.
Telephone: 301-217-5600.

(See Next Column)

VENABLE ATTORNEYS AT LAW VENABLE, BAETJER AND HOWARD, LLP—
Continued

Towson, Maryland Office: 210 Allegheny Avenue, P. O. Box 5517.
Telephone: 410-494-6200.

MEMBERS OF FIRM

Benjamin R. Civiletti (P.C.)
  (Also at Washington, D.C.
  and Towson, Maryland
  Offices)
George Cochran Doub (P.C.)
John Henry Lewin, Jr. (P.C.)
Stanley Mazaroff (P.C.)
Roger W. Titus (Resident,
  Rockville, Maryland Office)
Thomas J. Madden (Not
  admitted in MD; Resident,
  Washington, D.C. Office)
Ronald R. Glancz (Not
  admitted in MD; Resident,
  Washington, D.C. Office)
David J. Levenson (Not
  admitted in MD; Resident,
  Washington, D.C. Office)
Douglas D. Connah, Jr. (P.C.)
  (Also at Washington, D.C.
  Office)
Kenneth C. Bass, III (Not
  admitted in MD; Washington,
  D.C. and McLean, Virginia
  Offices)
John H. Zink, III (Resident,
  Towson, Maryland Office)
Bruce E. Titus (Resident,
  McLean, Virginia Office)
Paul F. Strain (P.C.)
William D. Dolan, III (P.C.)
  (Not admitted in MD;
  Resident, McLean, Virginia
  Office)
Paul T. Glasgow (Resident,
  Rockville, Maryland Office)
Joseph C. Wich, Jr. (Resident,
  Towson, Maryland Office)
Sondra Harans Block (Resident,
  Rockville, Maryland Office)
Edward F. Glynn, Jr. (Resident,
  Washington, D.C. Office)
Craig E. Smith
Robert G. Ames (Also at
  Washington, D.C. Office)
Michael Schatzow (Also at
  Washington, D.C. Office)
Nell B. Strachan
David G. Lane (Resident,
  McLean, Virginia Office)
L. Paige Marvel
N. Frank Wiggins (Not admitted
  in MD; Resident, Washington,
  D.C. Office)
G. Stewart Webb, Jr.
James K. Archibald (Also at
  Washington, D.C. Office)
George W. Johnston (P.C.)

Judson W. Starr (Not admitted
  in MD; Also at Washington,
  D.C. and Towson, Maryland
  Offices)
James R. Myers (Not admitted
  in MD; Resident, Washington,
  D.C. Office)
Jana Howard Carey (P.C.)
Jeffrey A. Dunn (also at
  Washington, D.C. Office)
George F. Pappas (Also at
  Washington, D.C. Office)
William D. Coston (Not
  admitted in MD; Resident,
  Washington, D.C. Office)
James L. Shea (Also at
  Washington, D.C. Office)
Jeffrey P. Ayres (P.C.)
Elizabeth C. Honeywell
Maurice Baskin (Resident,
  Washington, D.C. Office)
Amy Berman Jackson (Not
  admitted in MD; Resident,
  Washington, D.C. Office)
William D. Quarles (Also at
  Washington, D.C. and
  Towson, Maryland Offices)
C. Carey Deeley, Jr. (Also at
  Towson, Maryland Office)
Kathleen Gallogly Cox
  (Resident, Towson, Maryland
  Office)
Christopher R. Mellott
Cynthia M. Hahn (Resident,
  Towson, Maryland Office)
M. King Hill, III (Resident,
  Towson, Maryland Office)
James A. Dunbar (Also at
  Washington, D.C. Office)
Ronald W. Taylor
Thomas J. Kelly, Jr. (Not
  admitted in MD; Resident,
  Washington, D. C. Office)
David J. Heubeck
Herbert G. Smith, II (Not
  admitted in MD; Resident,
  Washington, D.C. Office)
Patrick J. Stewart (Also at
  Washington, D.C. Office)
Gary M. Hnath (Resident,
  Washington, D.C. Office)
Mitchell Y. Mirviss
Geoffrey R. Garinther (Also at
  Washington, D.C. Office)
Terri L. Turner
Michael W. Robinson (Resident,
  McLean, Virginia Office)
Elizabeth Marzo Borinsky

OF COUNSEL

A. Samuel Cook (P.C.)
  (Resident, Towson, Maryland
  Office)

Todd K. Snyder
Mary T. Flynn (Not admitted in
  MD; Resident, McLean,
  Virginia Office)

ASSOCIATES

Paul D. Barker, Jr.
Daniel William China
Patricia Gillis Cousins (Resident,
  Rockville, Maryland Office)
Carla Draluck Craft (Resident,
  Washington, D.C. Office)
Gregory A. Cross
Marina Lolley Dame (Resident,
  Towson, Maryland Office)
David W. Goewey (Not
  admitted in MD; Resident,
  Washington, D.C. Office)
E. Anne Hamel
David R. Hodnett (Not
  admitted in MD; Resident,
  McLean, Virginia Office)
J. Scott Hommer, III (Not
  admitted in MD; Resident,
  McLean, Virginia Office)
Todd J. Horn
Maria F. Howell

Mary-Dulany James (Resident,
  Towson, Maryland Office)
Gregory L. Laubach (Resident,
  Rockville, Maryland Office)
Edward Brendan Magrab
  (Resident, Washington, D.C.
  Office)
Patricia A. Malone (Resident,
  Towson, Maryland Office)
Vicki Margolis (Also at
  Washington, D.C. Office)
Christine M. McAnney (Not
  admitted in MD; Resident,
  McLean, Virginia Office)
John A. McCauley
Traci H. Mundy (Not admitted
  in MD; Resident, McLean,
  Virginia Office)
John T. Prisbe

(See Next Column)

ASSOCIATES (Continued)

Lawrence C. Renbaum
  (Resident, Washington, D.C.
  Office)
John Peter Sarbanes
Melissa Landau Steinman
  (Resident, Washington, D.C.
  Office)

Paul N. Wengert (Not admitted
  in MD; Resident, McLean,
  Virginia Office)

For Complete List of Firm Personnel, See General Section

For full biographical listings, see the Martindale-Hubbell Law Directory

---

BEL AIR,* Harford Co.

STARK & KEENAN, A PROFESSIONAL ASSOCIATION (AV)

30 Office Street, 21014
Telephone: 410-838-5522
Baltimore: 410-879-2222
Fax: 410-879-0688

Elwood V. Stark, Jr.
Charles B. Keenan, Jr.
Edwin G. Carson

Judith Cline-Silverstein
Gregory A. Szoka
Robert S. Lynch

Claire Prin Blomquist
Kimberly Kahoe Muenter

Paul W. Ishak
Lawrence F. Kreis, Jr.

For full biographical listings, see the Martindale-Hubbell Law Directory

---

ROCKVILLE,* Montgomery Co.

VENABLE ATTORNEYS AT LAW VENABLE, BAETJER AND HOWARD, LLP (AV)

A Partnership including Professional Corporations
Suite 500, One Church Street, P.O. Box 1906, 20850-4129
Telephone: 301-217-5600
FAX: 301-217-5617
Baltimore, Maryland Office: 1800 Mercantile Bank & Trust Building, 2
Hopkins Plaza.
Telephone: 410-244-7400.
Washington, D.C. Office: Venable, Baetjer, Howard & Civiletti LLP, Suite
1000, 1201 New York Avenue, N.W.
Telephone: 202-962-4800.
McLean, Virginia Office: Suite 400, 2010 Corporate Ridge.
Telephone: 703-760-1600.
Towson, Maryland, Office: 210 Allegheny Avenue, P. O. Box 5517.
Telephone: 410-494-6200.

MEMBERS OF FIRM

Roger W. Titus
Sondra Harans Block

Paul T. Glasgow

ASSOCIATES

Patricia Gillis Cousins

Gregory L. Laubach

For Complete List of Firm Personnel, See General Section

For full biographical listings, see the Martindale-Hubbell Law Directory

---

TOWSON,* Baltimore Co.

HOWELL, GATELY, WHITNEY & CARTER, LLP (AV)

401 Washington Avenue, Twelfth Floor, 21204
Telephone: 410-583-8000
Fax: 410-583-8031

MEMBERS OF FIRM

H. Thomas Howell
William F. Gately
Benjamin R. Goertemiller

Daniel W. Whitney
David A. Carter
William R. Levasseur

ASSOCIATES

Una M. Perez
George D. Bogris

Kathleen D. Leslie
Gerard Wm. Wittstadt, Jr.

Laura A. Gregory

For full biographical listings, see the Martindale-Hubbell Law Directory

---

VENABLE ATTORNEYS AT LAW VENABLE, BAETJER AND HOWARD, LLP (AV)

A Partnership including Professional Corporations
210 Allegheny Avenue, P.O. Box 5517, 21204
Telephone: 410-494-6200
FAX: 410-821-0147
Baltimore, Maryland Office: 1800 Mercantile Bank & Trust Building, 2
Hopkins Plaza.
Telephone: 410-244-7400.
Washington, D.C. Office: Venable, Baetjer, Howard & Civiletti LLP, Suite
1000, 1201 New York Avenue, N.W.
Telephone: 202-962-4800.
McLean, Virginia Office: Suite 400, 2010 Corporate Ridge.
Telephone: 703-760-1600.
Rockville, Maryland Office: Suite 500, One Church Street, P. O. Box 1906.
Telephone: 301-217-5600.

(See Next Column)

VENABLE ATTORNEYS AT LAW VENABLE, BAETJER AND HOWARD, LLP, Towson—*Continued*

PARTNERS

Benjamin R. Civiletti (P.C.) (Also at Washington, D.C. and Baltimore, Maryland Offices)
John H. Zink, III
Joseph C. Wich, Jr.

William D. Quarles (Also at Washington, D.C. Office)
C. Carey Deeley, Jr. (Also at Baltimore, Maryland Office)
Kathleen Gallogly Cox
Cynthia M. Hahn

M. King Hill, III

ASSOCIATES

Marina Lolley Dame
Patricia A. Malone
Mary-Dulany James

For Complete List of Firm Personnel, See General Section

For full biographical listings, see the Martindale-Hubbell Law Directory

MASSACHUSETTS

*BOSTON,** Suffolk Co.

PACKENHAM, SCHMIDT & FEDERICO, P.C. (AV)

Four Longfellow Place, 35th Floor, 02114-2832
Telephone: 617-742-6565
Fax: 617-742-0292

Richard D. Packenham
Mary H. Schmidt
Phyllis E. Federico

David A. Schwartz

For full biographical listings, see the Martindale-Hubbell Law Directory

PALMER & DODGE LLP (AV)

One Beacon Street, 02108
Telephone: 617-573-0100
Facsimile: 617-227-4420

MEMBER OF FIRM
Jeffrey Swope

For Complete List of Firm Personnel, See General Section

For full biographical listings, see the Martindale-Hubbell Law Directory

MICHIGAN

*DETROIT,** Wayne Co.

BENDURE & THOMAS (AV)

577 East Larned, Suite 210, 48226-4392
Telephone: 313-961-1525
Fax: 313-961-1553

MEMBERS OF FIRM
Mark R. Bendure
Marc E. Thomas

ASSOCIATES
J. Christopher Caldwell
Victor S. Valenti
Kevin P. Kavanagh

OF COUNSEL
John A. Lydick
Thomas R. Present

For full biographical listings, see the Martindale-Hubbell Law Directory

BODMAN, LONGLEY & DAHLING LLP (AV)

34th Floor 100 Renaissance Center, 48243
Telephone: 313-259-7777
Fax: 313-393-7579
Email: 2080194@mcimail.com
Troy, Michigan Office: Suite 2020, 755 West Big Beaver Road.
Telephone: 810-362-2110.
Fax: 810-244-0780.
Ann Arbor, Michigan Office: 110 Miller, Suite 300.
Telephone: 313-761-3780.
Fax: 313-930-2494.
Northern Michigan Office: 229 Court Street, P.O. Box 405, Cheboygan.
Telephone: 616-627-4351.
Fax: 616-627-2802.

MEMBERS OF FIRM
Richard D. Rohr
Theodore Souris
Carson C. Grunewald
Michael B. Lewiston
Thomas A. Roach (Ann Arbor Office)
James A. Smith
George G. Kemsley

(See Next Column)

MEMBERS OF FIRM (Continued)

James J. Walsh
David G. Chardavoyne
Robert G. Brower
Charles N. Raimi
Thomas Van Dusen (Troy Office)
John C. Cashen (Troy Office)
Lloyd C. Fell (Northern Michigan Office)

Martha Bedsole Goodloe (Troy Office)
Harvey W. Berman (Ann Arbor Office)
Lawrence P. Hanson (Northern Michigan Office)
Jerold Lax (Ann Arbor Office)
Diane L. Akers
Dennis J. Levasseur

For Representative Client List, See General Section

For Complete List of Firm Personnel, See General Section

For full biographical listings, see the Martindale-Hubbell Law Directory

BUTZEL LONG, A PROFESSIONAL CORPORATION (AV)

Suite 900, 150 West Jefferson, 48226
Telephone: 313-225-7000
Telecopier: 313-225-7080
Email: melnick@butzel.com *URL:* http://www.butzel.com
Birmingham, Michigan Office: Suite 200, 32270 Telegraph Road.
Telephone: 810-258-1616.
Telecopier: 810-258-1439.
Lansing, Michigan Office: 118 West Ottawa Street.
Telephone: 517-372-6622.
Telecopier: 517-372-6672.
Ann Arbor, Michigan Office: Suite 300, 350 South Main Street.
Telephone: 313-995-3110.
Telecopier: 313-995-1777.
Grosse Pointe Farms, Michigan Office: Suite 260, 21 Kercheval.
Telephone: 313-886-5446.
Telecopier: 313-886-2114.

William M. Saxton
William R. Ralls (Lansing)
John H. Dudley, Jr.
Richard E. Rassel
Edward M. Kronk
Philip J. Kessler
Donald B. Miller
John P. Hancock, Jr.

Mark T. Nelson
Keefe A. Brooks
Richard P. Saslow
Lynne E. Deitch
Leonard M. Niehoff (Ann Arbor)
David H. Oermann (Birmingham)

Sheldon H. Klein

Representative Clients: Blue Cross/Blue Shield of Michigan; The Detroit News, Inc.; Indian Head Industries, Inc; Jackson National Life Insurance Co.; Kelly Services; Michigan Road Builders Assn.; Stroh Brewery Co.; Takata Corp.; The University of Michigan.

For Complete List of Firm Personnel, See General Section

For full biographical listings, see the Martindale-Hubbell Law Directory

DAVID F. DUMOUCHEL, P.C. (AV)

150 West Jefferson, Suite 900, 48226-4430
Telephone: 313-225-7004

David F. DuMouchel

For full biographical listings, see the Martindale-Hubbell Law Directory

KELLER, THOMA, SCHWARZE, SCHWARZE, DUBAY & KATZ, P.C. (AV)

440 East Congress, 5th Floor, 48226
Telephone: 313-965-7610
Bloomfield Hills, Michigan Office: Suite 122, 100 West Long Lake Road.
Telephone: 810-642-5218.

OF COUNSEL
Charles E. Keller

Counsel for: Livonia Public Schools; Ludington News Co., Inc.
Representative Clients: Borg-Warner Corp.; E & L Transport Co.; The Kroger Co.; Holnam, Inc.
Public Employer Clients: City of Farmington Hills; City of Flint; City of Grosse Pointe Woods; Saginaw Public Schools.

For Complete List of Firm Personnel, See General Section

For full biographical listings, see the Martindale-Hubbell Law Directory

KENNETH M. MOGILL (AV)

One Kennedy Square Building, Suite 1930, 719 Griswold, 48226
Telephone: 313-962-7210
Fax: 313-961-7799
(Also Member Mogill, Posner & Cohen)

For full biographical listings, see the Martindale-Hubbell Law Directory

STRINGARI, FRITZ, KREGER, AHEARN & CRANDALL, P.C. (AV)

510 First National Building, 48226-3538
Telephone: 313-961-6474
Fax: 313-961-5688

(See Next Column)

STRINGARI, FRITZ, KREGER, AHEARN & CRANDALL P.C.—*Continued*

Arthur M. Stringari (Retired)
Richard J. Fritz
Conrad W. Kreger

Brian S. Ahearn
Martin E. Crandall
Kenneth S. Wilson

Dallas G. Moon

John C. Dickinson
OF COUNSEL

Karl R. Bennett, Jr.

Matt W. Zeigler

For full biographical listings, see the Martindale-Hubbell Law Directory

---

TIMMIS & INMAN, L.L.P. (AV)

300 Talon Centre, 48207
Telephone: 313-396-4200
Telecopier: 313-396-4228

Michael T. Timmis
Robert E. Graziani
George A. Peck
Charles W. Royer
Richard L. Levin

Henry J. Brennan, III
Mark W. Peyser
Richard M. Miettinen
Bradley J. Knickerbocker
George M. Malis

Michael F. Wais

Erich J. D'Andrea
OF COUNSEL
Wayne C. Inman

Representative Clients: Stylecraft Printing Co.; Stylerite Label Corp.; Retail Resources, Inc.; Deneb Robotics, Inc.; Applied Process, Inc.; Insilco Corp.; Variety Foods, Inc.; Certain Underwriters at Lloyds of London; Eastpointe Radiologists, P.C.; Talon Automotive Group L.L.C.

For Complete List of Firm Personnel, See General Section

For full biographical listings, see the Martindale-Hubbell Law Directory

---

EAST LANSING, Ingham Co.

FARHAT, STORY & KRAUS, P.C. (AV)

Beacon Place, 4572 South Hagadorn Road, Suite 3, 48823
Telephone: 517-351-3700
Fax: 517-332-4122
Email: rkraus@sojourn.com

Leo A. Farhat
James E. Burns (1925-1979)
Monte R. Story
Richard C. Kraus
Max R. Hoffman Jr.

Chris A. Bergstrom
Kitty L. Groh
Charles R. Toy
David M. Platt
Thomas L. Sparks

Lawrence P. Schweitzer
Debra A. Geroux

Daniel B. Morgan
Mary K. Robbins-Kralapp

Representative Clients: Big L. Corp.; Michigan Automotive Wholesalers Association.; Hartman-Fabco, Inc.; Lansing Electric Motors, Inc.; Mike Miller Lincoln Mercury; Edward Rose Realty, Inc.; GTE Directory Services Corp.
Reference: City Bank, St. Johns; Old Kent Bank & Trust, Lansing.

For full biographical listings, see the Martindale-Hubbell Law Directory

---

GRAND RAPIDS,* Kent Co.

WHEELER UPHAM, A PROFESSIONAL CORPORATION (AV)

Second Floor, Trust Building, 40 Pearl Street, N.W., 49503-3001
Telephone: 616-459-7100
Fax: 616-459-6366

Gordon B. Wheeler (1904-1986)
Buford A. Upham (Retired)
Robert H. Gillette
Geoffrey L. Gillis
John M. Roels
Gary A. Maximiuk
Timothy J. Orlebeke

William H. Heritage, Jr.
Kenneth E. Tiews
Jack L. Hoffman
Janet C. Baxter
Peter Kladder, III
James M. Shade
Thomas A. Kuiper

Counsel For: Prudential Ins. Co.; Metropolitan Life Ins. Co.; Travelers Ins. Co.; Farmers Ins. Group; Auto-Owners Ins. Co.; Farm Bureau Ins. Co.; Countrywide Services; American Premier Underwriters, Inc.; Medtronic, Inc.; Global Claims Services.

For full biographical listings, see the Martindale-Hubbell Law Directory

---

SOUTHFIELD, Oakland Co.

COLLINS, EINHORN, FARRELL & ULANOFF, A PROFESSIONAL CORPORATION (AV)

4000 Town Center, Suite 909, 48075-1473
Telephone: 810-355-4141
Facsimile: 810-355-2277

Morton H. Collins
Brian D. Einhorn
Clayton F. Farrell
Stuart A. Ulanoff

Dale J. McLellan
Kenneth C. Merritt
Noreen L. Slank
Michael J. Sullivan

Janice G. Hildenbrand

Gerald A. Pawlak
Neil W. MacCallum
Timothy Orlando
Theresa M. Asoklis
Karen C. Liddle
Lisa L. Fadler

Deborah A. Lujan
Barbara H. Goldman
Shannon M. Kos
Kevin P. Moloughney
Susan P. Saltzman
Laura A. Ruckle

For full biographical listings, see the Martindale-Hubbell Law Directory

---

HIGHLAND & ZANETTI (AV)

Suite 205, 24445 Northwestern Highway, 48075
Telephone: 810-352-9580

John N. Highland

J. R. Zanetti, Jr.
R. Michael John

Duncan Hall Brown

Ronald D. Holton

For full biographical listings, see the Martindale-Hubbell Law Directory

---

O'LEARY, O'LEARY, JACOBS, MATTSON, PERRY & MASON, P.C. (AV)

26777 Central Park Boulevard, Suite 275, 48076
Telephone: 810-948-1000
Fax: 810-799-8265
Email: olearyjacobs@michbar.org

John P. Jacobs

Kevin P. Hanbury

For full biographical listings, see the Martindale-Hubbell Law Directory

---

SOMMERS, SCHWARTZ, SILVER & SCHWARTZ, P.C. (AV)

2000 Town Center, Suite 900, 48075
Telephone: 810-355-0300
Telecopier: 810-746-4001
Plymouth, Michigan Office: 747 South Main Street.
Telephone: 313-455-4250.

Richard D. Toth

Patrick Burkett
Carl B. Downing

General Counsel for: City of Taylor; Foodland Distributors; C.A. Muer Corporation; Vlasic & Company; Nederlander Corporation; Midwest Health Centers, P.C.
Representative Clients: Crum & Forster Insurance Company; City of Pontiac; Michigan National Bank.

For Complete List of Firm Personnel, See General Section

For full biographical listings, see the Martindale-Hubbell Law Directory

AVIATION LAW

ARIZONA

PHOENIX,* Maricopa Co.

TERRENCE J. McGILLICUDDY, P.C. (AV)

5080 North 40th Street, Suite 335, 85018
Telephone: 602-957-1960
800-957-1960
Fax: 602-957-7015

Terrence J. McGillicuddy

For full biographical listings, see the Martindale-Hubbell Law Directory

CALIFORNIA

CARLSBAD, San Diego Co.

GATZKE, MISPAGEL & DILLON (AV)

A Partnership including a Professional Law Corporation
Suite 200, 1921 Palomar Oaks Way, P.O. Box 1636, 92009
Telephone: 619-431-9501
Fax: 619-431-9512

MEMBERS OF FIRM

Michael Scott Gatzke	Mark J. Dillon
Mark F. Mispagel	Lori D. Ballance

ASSOCIATES

David P. Hubbard	Stephen F. Tee
Kristin Beth White	Tom Deak

For full biographical listings, see the Martindale-Hubbell Law Directory

IRVINE, Orange Co.

LAWRENCE J. GALARDI (AV)

Wells Fargo Tower, 2030 Main Street Suite 1050, 92714
Telephone: 714-852-1100
Telecopier: 714-252-7780

For full biographical listings, see the Martindale-Hubbell Law Directory

PHILLIP J. KOLCZYNSKI (AV)

Lakeshore Towers, 18101 Von Karman Avenue, Suite 1800, 92715
Telephone: 714-833-8999
Fax: 714-833-7878
Email: Klawcorp@aol.com

For full biographical listings, see the Martindale-Hubbell Law Directory

LOS ANGELES,* Los Angeles Co.

BELCHER, HENZIE & BIEGENZAHN, A PROFESSIONAL CORPORATION (AV)

333 South Hope Street, Suite 3650, 90071-1479
Telephone: 213-624-8293
Telecopier: 213-895-6082

Frank B. Belcher (1891-1979)	E. Lee Horton
David Bernard (1931-1978)	William T. DelHagen
John S. Curtis	Julia Azrael

Jeffrey L. Horwith	James C. Hildebrand
Georgette Renata Herget	Robert S. Cooper
David L. Bonar	Wun-ee Chelsea Chen
Raymond E. Hane, III	John Erin McOsker
	Mary E. Gram

OF COUNSEL

George M. Henzie	Leo J. Biegenzahn
	James M. Derr

Reference: Bank of America (Los Angeles Main Office).

For full biographical listings, see the Martindale-Hubbell Law Directory

HARNEY LAW OFFICES A LEGAL CORPORATION (AV)

Suite 1300 Figueroa Plaza, 201 North Figueroa Street, 90012-2636
Telephone: 213-482-0881
Fax: 213-250-4042

(See Next Column)

David M. Harney	Andrew J. Nocas
David T. Harney	Vincent McGowan
Julie A. Harney	Thomas A. Schultz

Reference: Bank of America.

For full biographical listings, see the Martindale-Hubbell Law Directory

LEBOVITS & DAVID, A PROFESSIONAL CORPORATION (AV)

Suite 3100, Two Century Plaza, 2049 Century Park East, 90067
Telephone: 310-277-0200
Fax: 310-552-1028

Moses Lebovits	Deborah A. David

OF COUNSEL

Joseph J. M. Lange

Reference: Imperial Bank (Main Office - Beverly Hills).

For full biographical listings, see the Martindale-Hubbell Law Directory

SULLIVAN LAW CORPORATION (AV)

545 South Figueroa Street, Suite 1216, 90071-1599
Telephone: 213-488-9200
Telecopier: 213-488-9664

Michael R. Sullivan

Douglas G. Carroll

For full biographical listings, see the Martindale-Hubbell Law Directory

MENLO PARK, San Mateo Co.

O'REILLY & COLLINS, A PROFESSIONAL CORPORATION (AV)

2500 Sand Hill Road, Suite 201, 94025
Telephone: 415-854-7700
Fax: 415-854-8350

Terry O'Reilly	James P. Collins
James P. Tessier	Michael Danko

For full biographical listings, see the Martindale-Hubbell Law Directory

OAKLAND,* Alameda Co.

VAN BLOIS, KNOWLES, SCHWARTZ & BASKIN (AV)

Suite 2245 Ordway Building, One Kaiser Plaza, 94612
Telephone: 510-444-1906
Contra Costa County 510-947-1055
Fax: 510-444-1294

MEMBERS OF FIRM

R. Lewis Van Blois	Ellen R. Schwartz
Thomas C. Knowles	Richard J. Baskin

OF COUNSEL

Charles E. Farnsworth

For full biographical listings, see the Martindale-Hubbell Law Directory

REDDING,* Shasta Co.

DUGAN BARR & ASSOCIATES (AV)

1824 Court Street, P.O. Box 994390, 96099-1648
Telephone: 916-243-8008
Fax: 916-243-1648
URL: http://www.CA-Lawyer.com/

Dugan Barr

ASSOCIATES

David L. Case	Douglas Mudford

Representative Clients: City of Redding; Mid Valley Bank; Scott Valley Bank; 3M; Enloe Hospital.

For full biographical listings, see the Martindale-Hubbell Law Directory

REDWOOD CITY,* San Mateo Co.

OWEN & MELBYE, A PROFESSIONAL CORPORATION (AV)

700 Jefferson Street, 94063
Telephone: 415-364-6500
Fax: 415-365-7036
Tahoe City, California Office: P.O. Box 1524.
Telephone: 916-546-2473.

William H. Owen	Edmund M. Scott
Richard B. Melbye	Pamela J. Helmer
Norman J. Roger	John S. Posthauer
	Paul R. Mangiantini

(See Next Column)

OWEN & MELBYE A PROFESSIONAL CORPORATION, *Redwood City—Continued*

Albert P. Blake, Jr.	Conor A. Meyers
Dawn M. Patterson	Mary P. Derner

Representative Clients: Aetna Cravens Dargan Co.; Avco Lycoming; Beech Aircraft Corp.; California Casualty Indemnity Exchange; K & K Claims Service; Kemper Insurance Cos.; Mutual Service Insurance Co.; State Farm Mutual Insurance Cos.; Underwriters at Lloyds; United States Aviation Insurance Group.

For full biographical listings, see the Martindale-Hubbell Law Directory

---

SAN MATEO, San Mateo Co.

MICHAEL L. DWORKIN (AV)

155 Bovet Road, Suite 455, 94402
Telephone: 415-577-1321
Fax: 415-372-1077
Email: law@avialex.com *URL:* http://www.avialex.com

For full biographical listings, see the Martindale-Hubbell Law Directory

---

WALNUT CREEK, Contra Costa Co.

HINTON & ALFERT, A PROFESSIONAL CORPORATION (AV)

Suite 600, 1646 North California Boulevard, 94596-4113
Telephone: 510-932-6006
Fax: 510-932-3412

Peter J. Hinton	Peter W. Alfert
	Michael P. Clark

Scott H. Z. Sumner	Nancy A. Beninati

For full biographical listings, see the Martindale-Hubbell Law Directory

COLORADO

BROOMFIELD, Boulder Co.

SCHADEN, KATZMAN & LAMPERT (AV)

11870 Airport Way, 80021
Telephone: 303-465-3663
Facsimile: 303-465-3884
Bloomfield Hills, Michigan Office: Schaden, Katzman & Lampert, 33 Bloomfield Hills Parkway, Suite 145, 48304.
Telephone: 810-258-4800.
Fax: 810-258-9212.
Ft. Lauderdale, Florida Office: 1700 E. Las Olas Boulevard, Suite 7, 33301-2408.
Telephone: 954-522-5154.
Facsimile: 954-522-5184.

Richard F. Schaden
ASSOCIATE
Kathleen M. Schaden

For full biographical listings, see the Martindale-Hubbell Law Directory

---

DENVER, * Denver Co.

DIXON AND SNOW, P.C. (AV)

425 South Cherry Street, Suite 1000, 80222
Telephone: 303-394-2200
FAX: 303-394-2340

Jerre W. Dixon	Rod W. Snow
	Steven Janiszewski

For full biographical listings, see the Martindale-Hubbell Law Directory

GRUND & BRESLAU, P.C. (AV)

303 East Seventeenth Avenue, Suite 1030, 80203-1260
Telephone: 303-830-7770
Facsimile: 303-830-2313

John W. Grund	Della S. Nelson
Brad W. Breslau	Phillip Jeffrey Frazee

Representative Clients: Avco Corp.; Delta Air Lines, Inc.; United States Aviation Underwriters, Inc.

For full biographical listings, see the Martindale-Hubbell Law Directory

WELLS, ANDERSON & RACE, LLC (AV)

1700 Broadway, Suite 1850, 80290
Telephone: 303-830-1212
Fax: 303-830-0898

(See Next Column)

Mary A. Wells	Sheryl L. Anderson
Geoffrey S. Race	

Gregory E. Sopkin

Representative Clients: Raytheon Aircraft Company; The Cessna Aircraft Company; Associated Aviation Underwriters; American Eagle Group.

For full biographical listings, see the Martindale-Hubbell Law Directory

CONNECTICUT

CHESHIRE, New Haven Co.

MOORE, O'BRIEN & JACQUES (AV)

700 West Johnson Avenue Suite 207, 06410
Telephone: 203-272-5881
Fax: 203-272-9273

MEMBERS OF FIRM

Garrett M. Moore	Stephen L. Jacques
Gregory E. O'Brien	Lisa Marie Ferraro

For full biographical listings, see the Martindale-Hubbell Law Directory

---

WESTPORT, Fairfield Co.

KEITH D. DUNNIGAN (AV)

River's Ford, 25 Ford Road, 06880
Telephone: 203-227-0567
Fax: 203-227-9097

ASSOCIATE
Joanne B. Galante

For full biographical listings, see the Martindale-Hubbell Law Directory

DISTRICT OF COLUMBIA

WASHINGTON, D.C. Co.

COALE & VAN SUSTEREN, A PROFESSIONAL CORPORATION (AV)

Chevy Chase Pavilion, 5335 Wisconsin Avenue N.W., Suite 720, 20015
Telephone: 202-686-6500
Facsimile: 202-686-9739

John P. Coale (A Professional Corporation)	Greta C. Van Susteren (Currently on leave)

Diane E. Cooley	Julia Wernett McInerny
David K. Lietz	Charlsa (Sandy) Broadus

For full biographical listings, see the Martindale-Hubbell Law Directory

CUTLER & STANFIELD, L.L.P. (AV)

700 Fourteenth Street, N.W., 20005-2010
Telephone: 202-624-8400
Fax: 202-624-8410
Denver, Colorado Office: 1675 Broadway, 80202.
Telephone: 303-825-7000.
FAX: 303-825-7005.

MEMBERS OF FIRM

Eliot R. Cutler	Peter J. Kirsch
Jeffrey L. Stanfield	Barry Conaty
Sheila D. Jones	Stephen H. Kaplan
Perry M. Rosen	(Not admitted in DC)

OF COUNSEL

Byron Keith Huffman, Jr.	Sarah M. Rockwell
	(Not admitted in DC)

ASSOCIATES

Katherine Boonin Andrus	Dana C. Nifosi
Françoise M. Carrier	Barbara Paley
Christopher M. Kamper	W. Eric Pilsk
(Not admitted in DC)	Timothy A. Pohle
William G. Malley	Thomas D. Roth

For full biographical listings, see the Martindale-Hubbell Law Directory

Washington—Continued

GILMAN & PANGIA (AV)

Suite 600 Federal Bar Building, 1815 H Street, N.W., 20006
Telephone: 202-466-5100
Facsimile: 202-331-8986
McLean, Virginia Office: Suite 1070, 8180 Greensboro Drive.
Telephone: 703-356-5070.
Fax: 703-356-5085.

MEMBERS OF FIRM

Nicholas Gilman	Barry C. Hansen
Michael J. Pangia	John J. Carlino (1946-1987)

Karla E. Saguil (Not admitted in DC)

OF COUNSEL

William J. Olson

For full biographical listings, see the Martindale-Hubbell Law Directory

FLORIDA

MIAMI,* Dade Co.

McDONALD & McDONALD (AV)

Suite 200, 1393 S.W. First Street, 33135
Telephone: 305-643-5313
TWX: 8108485179 McDonaldco Mia
Fax: 305-643-4990

MEMBERS OF FIRM

David C. McDonald (1897-1971)	David McDonald

ASSOCIATES

H. C. Palmer, III	David M. McDonald

For full biographical listings, see the Martindale-Hubbell Law Directory

---

PODHURST, ORSECK, JOSEFSBERG, EATON, MEADOW, OLIN & PERWIN, P.A. (AV)

Suite 800 City National Bank Building, 25 West Flagler
Street, 33130-1780
Telephone: 305-358-2800; Fort Lauderdale: 954-463-4346
Fax: 305-358-2382
Email: 76666.2340@COMPUSERVE.COM *URL:*
http://www.turbosales.com/"sfbj/podhurst.html

Aaron Podhurst	Michael S. Olin
Robert Orseck (1934-1978)	Joel S. Perwin
Robert C. Josefsberg	Steven C. Marks
Joel D. Eaton	Victor M. Diaz, Jr.
Barry L. Meadow	Katherine W. Ezell

Karen Podhurst Dern	Xavier Martínez

OF COUNSEL

Walter H. Beckham, Jr.

References: City National Bank of Miami; United National Bank of Miami.

For full biographical listings, see the Martindale-Hubbell Law Directory

---

ORLANDO,* Orange Co.

LAW OFFICES OF DURIE & LAWSON, P.A. (AV)

1000 East Robinson Street, 32801
Telephone: 407-841-6000; 1-800-940-0442
Fax: 407-841-2425

Jack F. (Jay) Durie, Jr.	C. Alan Lawson

For full biographical listings, see the Martindale-Hubbell Law Directory

---

SARASOTA,* Sarasota Co.

WILLIAMS, PARKER, HARRISON, DIETZ & GETZEN, PROFESSIONAL ASSOCIATION (AV)

200 South Orange Avenue, 34236-6749
Telephone: 941-366-4800
Telecopier: 941-366-5109
Mailing Address: P.O. Box 3258, Sarasota, Florida, 34230-3258
Email: wphdg.law@netsrg.com *URL:*
http://www.sarasota-online.com/williamspa-w

J.J. Williams, Jr. (1886-1968)	John T. Berteau
W. Davis Parker (1920-1982)	John V. Cannon, III
William T. Harrison, Jr.	Charles D. Bailey, Jr.
George A. Dietz	J. Michael Hartenstine
Monte K. Marshall	Michele Boardman Grimes
James L. Ritchey	James L. Turner
William G. Lambrecht	William M. Seider

(See Next Column)

Elizabeth C. Marshall	John L. Moore
Robert W. Benjamin	Morgan R. Bentley
Frank Strelec	Susan A. Barrett
Terri Salt Costa	Carol Ann Kalish
David A. Wallace	Linda R. Getzen
Mark A. Schwartz	Kimberly J. Page
Ric Gregoria	Phillip D. Eck
Elvin W. Phillips	J. Hugh Middlebrooks
Jeffrey A. Grebe	Robert A. Warram

OF COUNSEL

William E. Getzen	Frazer F. Hilder

Hugh McPheeters, Jr.

LEGAL SUPPORT PERSONNEL

Mark Loveridge (Land Planner)

General Counsel for: Sarasota County Public Hospital Board; Sarasota-Manatee Airport Authority; Taylor Woodrow Homes Ltd.; FCCI Mutual Insurance Co.
Local Counsel for: NationsBank of Florida; Barnett Bank of Southwest Florida; Northern Trust Bank of Florida; SunTrust Bank, Gulfcoast.

For full biographical listings, see the Martindale-Hubbell Law Directory

---

WEST PALM BEACH,* Palm Beach Co.

NEWBURGH, BALDWIN & GERSHMAN (AV)

1675 Palm Beach Lakes Boulevard, Suite 700, 33401
Telephone: 561-684-8898; 561-471-0470
Fax: 561-684-8820; 561-471-4222

MEMBERS OF FIRM

Steven S. Newburgh	Fletcher N. Baldwin, III

Robert Scott Gershman

OF COUNSEL

Barry L. Clayton

For full biographical listings, see the Martindale-Hubbell Law Directory

GEORGIA

ATLANTA,* Fulton Co.

MOZLEY, FINLAYSON & LOGGINS LLP (AV)

A Limited Liability Partnership
One Premier Plaza Suite 900, 5605 Glenridge Drive, 30342
Telephone: 404-256-0700
Telecopier: 404-250-9355

MEMBERS OF FIRM

J. Arthur Mozley	Sewell K. Loggins
Robert M. Finlayson II	Eric D. Griffin, Jr.

ASSOCIATE

J. Marcus Howard

For full biographical listings, see the Martindale-Hubbell Law Directory

---

ANDREW M. SCHERFFIUS, P.C. (AV)

3166 Mathieson Drive, P.O. Box 53299, 30355
Telephone: 404-261-3562; 1-800-521-2867
Fax: 404-841-0861

Andrew M. Scherffius

Tamara McDowell Ayres

For full biographical listings, see the Martindale-Hubbell Law Directory

ILLINOIS

CHICAGO,* Cook Co.

CONNELLY & SCHROEDER (AV)

One North Franklin Street, Suite 1200, 60606
Telephone: 312-251-9600
FAX: 312-251-9601
Geneva, Illinois Office: 1250 Executive Place, Suite 201.
Telephone: 708-232-6440.
FAX: 708-232-6450

MEMBERS OF FIRM

Michael P. Connelly	Charles H. Cole
John L. Schroeder	Daniel F. Konicek
(Resident, Geneva Office)	(Resident, Geneva Office)
Thomas F. Tobin	Eugene S. Kraus
Raymond E. Stachnik	Patrick G. Donnelly

(See Next Column)

CONNELLY & SCHROEDER, *Chicago—Continued*
OF COUNSEL
John W. Hough
ASSOCIATES

Michelle L. Adams	Colleen Konicek
(Resident, Geneva Office)	Charina de los Reyes
Matthew Patrick Connelly	Abbey Fishman Romanek
Thomas W. Dillon	Martha Swatek
(Resident, Geneva Office)	(Resident, Geneva Office)
Mary Lisa Kamins	Carla A. Summers
John Michael Kelly	(Resident, Geneva Office)

For full biographical listings, see the Martindale-Hubbell Law Directory

JEFFREY M. GOLDBERG & ASSOCIATES, LTD. (AV)

20 North Clark Street, Suite 3100, 60602
Telephone: 312-236-4146
Fax: 312-236-5913

Jeffrey M. Goldberg

Mark N. Pera	Suzanne Bonds
Lawrence R. Kream	Mark T. Solmor
Geoffrey Johnson	Barry I. Mortge

For full biographical listings, see the Martindale-Hubbell Law Directory

MERLO, KANOFSKY & BRINKMEIER, LTD. (AV)

208 South La Salle Street, Suite 950, 60604
Telephone: 312-553-5500
Facsimile: 312-553-1586

Michael J. Merlo	Alan J. Brinkmeier
Martin A. Kanofsky	Michael R. Gregg

Steven R. Apel	Anne M. O'Brien
Michael J. Gilmartin	Joseph R. Ramos
Donald G. Machalinski	Linda J. Schneider
Suzanne J. Massel	Perry M. Shorris
Mary K. McGahey	William M. Sweetnam

Sandra J. Weber

For full biographical listings, see the Martindale-Hubbell Law Directory

PAVALON & GIFFORD (AV)

Two North La Salle Street, Suite 1600, 60602
Telephone: 312-419-7400
Fax: 312-419-7408
Rockford, Illinois Office: 501 Seventh Street, Suite 501, 61104.
Telephone: 815-968-5100.
MEMBERS OF FIRM

Eugene I. Pavalon	Gary K. Laatsch
Geoffrey L. Gifford	Frank C. Marino

Henry Phillip Gruss

Kathleen A. Russell	Christine Walsh Donnelly

Christopher B. Meister

For full biographical listings, see the Martindale-Hubbell Law Directory

ROTHSCHILD, BARRY & MYERS (AV)

A Partnership including Professional Corporations
Suite 3900, 55 West Monroe Street, 60603-5012
Telephone: 312-372-2345
FAX: 312-372-2350
MEMBERS OF FIRM

Norman J. Barry (P.C.)	Daniel Cummings
Roger J. Guerin	Alan S. Madans

ASSOCIATE
Mary T. Meegan

For Complete List of Firm Personnel, See General Section

For full biographical listings, see the Martindale-Hubbell Law Directory

WILDMAN, HARROLD, ALLEN & DIXON (AV)

225 West Wacker Drive, 30th Floor, 60606-1229
Telephone: 312-201-2000
Cable Address: "Whad"
Fax: 312-201-2555
URL: http://www.whad.com
Aurora, Illinois Office: 1851 W. Galena Boulevard, Suite 210.
Telephone: 630-892-7021.
Fax: 630-892-7158.
Waukegan, Illinois Office: 404 West Water, P. O. Box 890.
Telephone: 847-623-0700.
Fax: 847-244-5273.
Lisle, Illinois Office: 4300 Commerce Court.
Telephone: 630-955-0555.

(See Next Column)

New York, New York Office: Wildman, Harrold, Allen, Dixon & Smith.
The International Building, 45 Rockefeller Plaza, Suite 353.
Telephone: 212-632-3850.
Fax: 212-632-3858.
Toronto, Ontario affiliated Office: Keel Cottrelle. 36 Toronto Street, Ninth Floor, Suite 920.
Telephone: 416-367-2900.
Telefax: 416-367-2791.
Telex: 062-18660.
Mississauga, Ontario affiliated Office: Keel Cottrelle. 100 Matatson Avenue East, Suite 104.
Telephone: 416-890-7700.
Fax: 416-890-8006.

MEMBERS OF FIRM

Thomas D. Allen	Robert E. Haley
	Richard C. Palmer

Adam J. Glazer	Lauren S. Tashma
Stephanie B. Miller	Jeanne Walker

For Complete List of Firm Personnel, See General Section

For full biographical listings, see the Martindale-Hubbell Law Directory

INDIANA

INDIANAPOLIS,* Marion Co.

TOWNSEND, HOVDE & MONTROSS (AV)

230 East Ohio Street, 46204
Telephone: 317-264-4444
FAX: 317-264-2080

F. Boyd Hovde	W. Scott Montross
John F. Townsend, Jr.	Frederick R. Hovde

OF COUNSEL
John F. Townsend

Reference: N.B.D. Bank, N.A.

For full biographical listings, see the Martindale-Hubbell Law Directory

WILSON, KEHOE & WININGHAM (AV)

2859 North Meridian, 46208
Telephone: 317-920-6400
Fax: 317-920-6405
Richmond, Indiana Office: 42 South 9th Street, 47374.
Telephone: 317-962-9113.
Connersville, Indiana Office: 118 West 30th Street, 47331.
Telephone: 317-827-1100.
Muncie, Indiana Office: 3310 West Fox Ridge Lane, 47304.
Telephone: 317-284-2474.
MEMBERS OF FIRM

Harry A. Wilson, Jr.	D. Bruce Kehoe
	William E. Winingham, Jr.

ASSOCIATES

Ralph E. Dowling	Gerald A. Griffin, M.D.

Reference: The Indiana National Bank.

For full biographical listings, see the Martindale-Hubbell Law Directory

IOWA

DES MOINES,* Polk Co.

PEDDICORD, WHARTON, THUNE AND SPENCER, A PROFESSIONAL CORPORATION (AV)

700 Des Moines Building, 405 Sixth Avenue, P.O. Box 9130, 50306-9130
Telephone: 515-243-2100
Fax: 515-243-2132
1-800-383-2100

Roland D. Peddicord	Stephen W. Spencer
John M. Wharton	Lee P. Hook
Paul C. Thune	Fred L. Morris

Joseph M. Barron	Michael S. Roling
Timothy W. Wegman	Steven T. Durick

For full biographical listings, see the Martindale-Hubbell Law Directory

LOUISIANA

LAFAYETTE,* Lafayette Parish

DAVIDSON, MEAUX, SONNIER, MCELLIGOTT & SWIFT (AV)

810 South Buchanan Street, P.O. Drawer 2908, 70502
Telephone: 318-237-1660
Fax: 318-237-3676

MEMBERS OF FIRM

James J. Davidson, Jr.   John E. McElligott, Jr.
  (1904-1990)   John G. Swift
V. Farley Sonnier (1942-1988)   Jeffrey A. Rhoades
Richard C. Meaux, Sr.   Philip A. Fontenot
James J. Davidson, III   Kyle L. Gideon
                Theodore G. Edwards, IV

ASSOCIATES

Jhan C. Boudreaux Beaullieu   Mark C. Andrus

OF COUNSEL

Jan Whitehead Swift

General Counsel: Southwest Louisiana Electric Membership Corp., Inc.;
Macro Oil Co., Inc.; Dwight W. Andrus Insurance Agency; Lafayette Airport Commission.
Local Counsel: Southern Pacific Transportation Co.
Representative Clients: Highlands Insurance Co.; Wal-Mart Stores, Inc.;
USAA.

For full biographical listings, see the Martindale-Hubbell Law Directory

NEW ORLEANS,* Orleans Parish

PULASKI, GIEGER & LABORDE, L.L.C. (AV)

Suite 4800, One Shell Square, 701 Poydras Street, 70139
Telephone: 504-561-0400
Telecopier: 504-561-1011

Michael T. Pulaski (P.C.)   Leo R. McAloon, III
Ernest P. Gieger, Jr., (P.C.)   John P. Gonzalez
Kenneth H. Laborde (P.C.)   J. Jeffery Raborn
Robert W. Maxwell (P.C.)   Lance Blake Williams
Keith W. McDaniel (P.C.)   James E. Swinnen
Sharon D. Smith (P.C.)   Gina S. Montgomery
Gary G. Hebert   Mary Beth Meyer
                Julianne T. Echols

For full biographical listings, see the Martindale-Hubbell Law Directory

MARYLAND

BALTIMORE,* (Independent City)

SCANLAN & ROSEN, P.A. (AV)

26 South Street, 21202-3399
Telephone: 410-244-1155
FAX: 410-244-1157

Alfred L. Scanlan, Jr.   Marc Seldin Rosen

Michael Stuart Warshaw   Colleen A. Cavanaugh

OF COUNSEL

James Lee Katz

For full biographical listings, see the Martindale-Hubbell Law Directory

MASSACHUSETTS

BOSTON,* Suffolk Co.

SARROUF, TARRICONE & FLEMMING (AV)

95 Commercial Wharf, 02110
Telephone: 617-227-5800
Fax: 617-227-5470

Camille Francis Sarrouf   Daniel J. Gibson
Anthony Tarricone   Sheryl M. Bourbeau
John B. Flemming   Camille F. Sarrouf, Jr.
George J. Leary, Jr.   Donald J. Savery

For full biographical listings, see the Martindale-Hubbell Law Directory

LEXINGTON, Middlesex Co.

SALVATORE F. STRAMONDO (AV)

3 Ballard Terrace, 02173
Telephone: 617-862-6422

For full biographical listings, see the Martindale-Hubbell Law Directory

MICHIGAN

BLOOMFIELD HILLS, Oakland Co.

SCHADEN, KATZMAN & LAMPERT (AV)

33 Bloomfield Hills Parkway, Suite 145, 48304
Telephone: 810-258-4800
Fax: 810-258-9212
Broomfield, Colorado Office: Schaden, Katzman & Lampert, 11870
Airport Way.
Telephone: 303-465-3663.
Facsimile: 303-465-3884.
Ft. Lauderdale, Florida Office: 1700 E. Las Olas Boulevard, Suite 7,
33301-2408.
Telephone: 954-522-5154.
Facsimile: 954-522-5184.

MEMBERS OF FIRM

Richard F. Schaden   David I. Katzman
                Bruce A. Lampert
ASSOCIATES

Kathleen M. Schaden   John D. McClune
OF COUNSEL

Bruce O. Wilson

For full biographical listings, see the Martindale-Hubbell Law Directory

DETROIT,* Wayne Co.

HAYDUK, ANDREWS & HYPNAR, P.C. (AV)

1700 Buhl Building, 535 Griswold, 48226
Telephone: 313-962-4500
Fax: 313-964-6577

Mark S. Hayduk   Robin K. Andrews
                Mark A. Hypnar

Sean Angus McPhillips   Lynn E. Radke

Representative Clients: Farmers Insurance Group; GameTime, Inc.; Admiral
Insurance Co.; Heritage Ins. Alexis; Meijer, Inc.; Condon & Forsyth; Pinkerton's Inc.; Vik Brothers Ins.; Investors Ins. Group; Scibal Ins. Co.

For full biographical listings, see the Martindale-Hubbell Law Directory

STEINBERG, O'CONNOR, PATON & BURNS, P.L.L.C. (AV)

1724 Ford Building, 615 Griswold Street, 48226-3901
Telephone: 313-962-3738
Telefax: 313-962-3779

Richard L. Steinberg   Alison L. Paton
Doyle O'Connor   Janice L. Burns

For full biographical listings, see the Martindale-Hubbell Law Directory

BANKING LAW

ALABAMA

ALBERTVILLE, Marshall Co.

GULLAHORN & HARE, P.C. (AV)

310 West Main Street, P.O. Box 1669, 35950
Telephone: 205-878-1891
Fax: 205-878-1965

Charles R. Hare, Jr.   John C. Gullahorn

Jeffrey B. Carr

Representative Clients: First Bank of Boaz; The Home Bank; Peoples Independent Bank of Boaz; AmSouth Bank; Compass Bank; Albertville Industrial Development Board; Boaz Industrial Development Board; Marshall-Dekalb Electric Cooperative; Olympia Construction, Inc.

For full biographical listings, see the Martindale-Hubbell Law Directory

*BIRMINGHAM,** Jefferson Co.

BRADLEY, ARANT, ROSE & WHITE (AV)

2001 Park Place, Suite 1400, P.O. Box 830709, 35283-0709
Telephone: 205-521-8000
Facsimile: 205-252-0264
Facsimile (SouthTrust Tower Office): 205-251-9915
URL: http://www.BARW.COM
Huntsville, Alabama Office: 200 Clinton Avenue West, Suite 900, 35801.
Telephone: 205-517-5100.
Facsimile: 205-533-5069.

MEMBERS OF FIRM

Edward M. Selfe	J. David Dresher
John P. Adams	John E. Hagefstration, Jr.
Charles Larimore Whitaker	Paul S. Ware
P. Nicholas Greenwood	Kenneth T. Wyatt
Laurence Duncan Vinson, Jr.	J. Paul Compton, Jr.
Carleta Roberts Hawley	L. Susan Doss

COUNSEL

J. Reese Murray   J. Robert Fleenor

ASSOCIATES

Paige Maddox Davis   Helena F. Tozzi
Lauren E. Wagner

For Complete List of Firm Personnel, See General Section

For full biographical listings, see the Martindale-Hubbell Law Directory

BURR & FORMAN (AV)

3100 SouthTrust Tower, 420 North 20th Street, 35203
Telephone: 205-251-3000
Telecopier: 205-458-5100
Huntsville, Alabama Office: Suite 204, Regency Center, 400 Meridian Street.
Telephone: 205-551-0010.
Atlanta, Georgia Office: Suite 1800, One Georgia Center, 600 West Peachtree Street, 30308.
Telephone: 404-817-3536.
Facsimile: 404-817-3244.

MEMBERS OF FIRM

J. Fred Powell	Bruce A. Rawls
Joseph G. Stewart	Dwight L. Mixson, Jr.
A. Brand Walton	Gene T. Price
Eric L. Carlton	Deborah P. Fisher
George M. Taylor, III	Gail Livingston Mills
Jeffrey T. Baker	

For Complete List of Firm Personnel, See General Section

For full biographical listings, see the Martindale-Hubbell Law Directory

GORDON, SILBERMAN, WIGGINS & CHILDS, A PROFESSIONAL CORPORATION (AV)

1400 SouthTrust Tower, 420 North 20th Street, 35203
Telephone: 205-328-0640
Telecopier: 205-254-1500

Bruce L. Gordon   Ray D. Gibbons

Timothy D. Davis

For Complete List of Firm Personnel, See General Section

For full biographical listings, see the Martindale-Hubbell Law Directory

HASKELL SLAUGHTER & YOUNG, L.L.C. (AV)

1200 AmSouth/Harbert Plaza, 1901 Sixth Avenue North, 35203
Telephone: 205-251-1000
Facsimile: 205-324-1133
Montgomery, Alabama Office: 305 South Lawrence Street, P.O. Box 4660. 36103-4660.
Telephone: 334-265-8573.
Facsimile: 334-264-7945.

Benjamin B. Spratling III   James C. Huckaby, Jr.
E. Alston Ray   Gwen L. Windle

Counsel For: NationsBank Corporation; Banker's Trust; BancOne; Key Bank; Bank Leumi; Federal Deposit Insurance Corporation; The Equitable Life Assurance Society of the United States (Real Estate); First National Bank of Chicago.

For Complete List of Firm Personnel, See General Section

For full biographical listings, see the Martindale-Hubbell Law Directory

NAJJAR DENABURG, P.C. (AV)

2125 Morris Avenue, 35203
Telephone: 205-250-8400
Telecopier: 205-326-3837

Charles L. Denaburg	Gary S. Schiff
Edward P. Meyerson	Robert H. Adams
Ben L. Zarzaur	Marvin E. Franklin
Douglas L. McWhorter	Marvin L. Stewart, Jr.
	Jesse P. Evans III

General Counsel: Acousti Engineering of Alabama, Inc.
Representative Client: Compass Bank.
Approved Attorneys for: Mississippi Valley Title Insurance Co.
Reference: Compass Bank.

For Complete List of Firm Personnel, See General Section

For full biographical listings, see the Martindale-Hubbell Law Directory

SPAIN & GILLON, L.L.C. (AV)

The Zinszer Building, 2117 2nd Avenue North, 35203
Telephone: 205-328-4100
Telecopier: 205-324-8866

MEMBERS OF FIRM

Samuel H. Frazier   Glenn E. Estess, Jr.
Alton B. Parker, Jr.   Harold H. Goings

General Counsel for: Liberty National Life Insurance Co.; Piggly Wiggly Alabama Distributing Co.; Alabama Insurance Guaranty Association; Alabama Life and Disability Insurance Guaranty Association; Alabama Insurance Underwriters Association.
Counsel for: The Minnesota Mutual Insurance Company of America; Compass Bank; Southtrust Bank; AmSouth Bank; America's First Federal Credit Union.

For Complete List of Firm Personnel, See General Section

For full biographical listings, see the Martindale-Hubbell Law Directory

*FORT PAYNE,** De Kalb Co.

SCRUGGS, JORDAN, DODD & DODD, P.A. (AV)

207 Alabama Avenue, South, P.O. Box 1109, 35967
Telephone: 205-845-5932
Fax: 205-845-4325

William D. Scruggs, Jr.   David Dodd
Robert K. Jordan   E. Allen Dodd, Jr.

Representative Clients: Compass Bank of the South; Bank of Powell; First Federal Savings and Loan Association of De Kalb County; The Farmers Home Administration; Federal Land Bank; Nucor, Inc.; "ALABAMA" Bank; State Farm Insurance Company; Allstate Insurance Co., Inc.; USF&G Insurance Co.

For full biographical listings, see the Martindale-Hubbell Law Directory

*HUNTSVILLE,** Madison Co.

BURR & FORMAN (AV)

Suite 204, Regency Center, 400 Meridian Street, 35801
Telephone: 205-551-0010
Birmingham, Alabama Office: 3100 SouthTrust Tower, 420 North 20th Street.
Telephone: 205-251-3000.
Telecopier: 205-458-5100.
Atlanta, Georgia Office: Suite 1800, One Georgia Center, 600 West Peachtree Street, 30308.
Telephone: 404-817-3536.
Facsimile: 404-817-3244.

RESIDENT PARTNER

S. Dagnal Rowe

For full biographical listings, see the Martindale-Hubbell Law Directory

Huntsville—Continued

STEPHENS, MILLIRONS, HARRISON & GAMMONS, P.C. (AV)

333 Franklin Street, P.O. Box 307, 35801
Telephone: 205-533-7711
Telecopier: 205-536-9388

Arthur M. Stephens	James G. Harrison
Paul L. Millirons	Robert C. Gammons

Attorneys for: Lomas Mortgage USA, Inc.; AmSouth Mortgage Co., Inc.; SouthTrust Bank of Alabama, N.A.

For full biographical listings, see the Martindale-Hubbell Law Directory

---

MOBILE,* Mobile Co.

ARMBRECHT, JACKSON, DeMOUY, CROWE, HOLMES & REEVES, L.L.C. (AV)

1300 AmSouth Center, P.O. Box 290, 36601
Telephone: 334-405-1300
Facsimile: 334-432-6843; 433-3821

MEMBERS OF FIRM

Marshall J. DeMouy	Christopher I. Gruenewald
E. B. Peebles III	Edward A. Dean
David A. Bagwell	David E. Hudgens
	James Dale Smith

Representative Clients: AmSouth Bank of Alabama (Regional Counsel); United Bank; United Bancorporation of Alabama, Inc.

For Complete List of Firm Personnel, See General Section

For full biographical listings, see the Martindale-Hubbell Law Directory

---

JOHNSTONE, ADAMS, BAILEY, GORDON AND HARRIS, L.L.C. (AV)

Royal St. Francis Building, 104 St. Francis Street, P.O. Box 1988, 36633
Telephone: 334-432-7682
Facsimile: 334-432-2800
Telex: 782040

MEMBERS OF FIRM

Charles B. Bailey, Jr.	I. David Cherniak
Brock B. Gordon	R. Gregory Watts
William H. Hardie, Jr.	William Alexander Gray, Jr.

General Counsel for: First Alabama Bank, Mobile; Infirmary Health System/Mobile Infirmary Medical Center/Rotary Rehabilitation Hospital (Multi-Hospital System).
Counsel for: Oil and Gas: Exxon Corp. Business and Corporate: Bell South Telecommunications, Inc.; Aluminum Co. of America; Michelin North America, Inc.; Metropolitan Life Insurance Co.; The Travelers Insurance Cos. Marine: The West of England Ship Owners Mutual Protection and Indemnity Association (Luxembourg); The Standard Steamship Owners' Protection and Indemnity Association (Bermuda) Ltd.

For Complete List of Firm Personnel, See General Section

For full biographical listings, see the Martindale-Hubbell Law Directory

---

LYONS, PIPES & COOK, P.C. (AV)

2 North Royal Street, P.O. Box 2727, 36652-2727
Telephone: 334-432-4481
Cable Address: "Lysea"
Telecopier: 334-433-1820

Wesley Pipes	John Patrick Courtney, III
	W. David Johnson, Jr.

Representative Clients: Chemical Bank; First National Bank of Atmore; SouthTrust Bank of Mobile.

For Complete List of Firm Personnel, See General Section

For full biographical listings, see the Martindale-Hubbell Law Directory

---

MONTGOMERY,* Montgomery Co.

BENKWITH AND HEARD, A PROFESSIONAL CORPORATION (AV)

172 Commerce Street, P.O. Box 5198, 36104
Telephone: 334-263-9782
Fax: 334-263-6010

Karl B. Benkwith, Jr.	J. Cliff Heard

Reference: AmSouth Bank, N.A., Montgomery.

For full biographical listings, see the Martindale-Hubbell Law Directory

---

VOLZ, PRESTWOOD & HANAN, P.C. (AV)

350 Adams Avenue, P.O. Box 1910, 36102-1910
Telephone: 334-264-6401
Fax: 334-834-4954

(See Next Column)

Charles H. Volz, Jr.	Charles H. Volz, III
Alvin T. Prestwood	Clinton Chadwell Carter
Ellis D. Hanan	Daniel Lewis Feinstein

LEGAL SUPPORT PERSONNEL
Mark A.W. Turpen

For full biographical listings, see the Martindale-Hubbell Law Directory

---

OPELIKA,* Lee Co.

WALKER, HILL, ADAMS, UMBACH, MEADOWS & WALTON (AV)

Walker Building, 205 South 9th Street, P.O. Box 2069, 36803
Telephone: 334-745-6466
Fax: 334-749-2800

MEMBERS OF FIRM

Jacob A. Walker (1889-1973)	Robert T. Meadows, III
Phillip E. Adams, Jr.	Will O. (Trip) Walton, III
Arnold W. Umbach, Jr.	Jacob A. Walker, III

ASSOCIATES

Russell K. Bush	Robbie A. Hyde

OF COUNSEL

Jacob Walker	Hoyt W. Hill

For full biographical listings, see the Martindale-Hubbell Law Directory

---

PHENIX CITY,* Russell Co.

PHILLIPS & EZELL (AV)

703 13th Street, P.O. Box 2500, 36868-2500
Telephone: 334-297-2400
Telecopier: 334-297-3842

MEMBERS OF FIRM

Roy H. Phillips	Jeffrey C. Ezell

For full biographical listings, see the Martindale-Hubbell Law Directory

---

ARIZONA

PHOENIX,* Maricopa Co.

BEUS, GILBERT & MORRILL, P.L.L.C. (AV)

Suite 1000, Great American Tower 3200 North Central Avenue, 85012-2417
Telephone: 602-274-8229
Fax: 602-234-5893

Leo R. Beus	John V. Berry
Paul E. Gilbert	Michael R. Devitt
K. Layne Morrill	Laurie B. Craig
J. Tyrrell Taber	Anthony H. Misseldine
Martin A. Aronson	Scott D. Larmore
	Jeffrey D. Gross

Joseph M. Leal, III	Quinn C. Wheeler
Christine R. Taradash	Robert A. Miller
Maria Crimi Speth	William D. Cleaveland
Dalon J. Morgan	H. Paul Honsinger
Tony J. Rudman	Richard R. Thomas
Keith A. Call	Michael E. Gottfried
Kelly W. Lewis	Nicholas J. DiCarlo
Brian K. Moll	Michelle C. Lombino
Carol Woods Frazier	Jason Barclay Morris

For full biographical listings, see the Martindale-Hubbell Law Directory

---

BROWN & BAIN, A PROFESSIONAL ASSOCIATION (AV)

2901 North Central Avenue, P.O. Box 400, 85001-0400
Telephone: 602-351-8000
Telecopier: 602-351-8516
Palo Alto, California Affiliated Office: Brown & Bain, 1755 Embarcadero Road, Suite 200.
Telephone: 415-856-9411.
Telecopier: 415-856-6061.
Tucson, Arizona Affiliated Office: Brown & Bain, A Professional Association. One South Church Avenue, Nineteenth Floor, P.O. Box 2265.
Telephone: 602-798-7900
Telecopier: 602-798-7945.

Richard Calvin Cooledge	Kyle B. Hettinger
	Ronald E. Lowe

COUNSEL
Michael C. Jones

For Complete List of Firm Personnel, See General Section

For full biographical listings, see the Martindale-Hubbell Law Directory

Phoenix—Continued

CRUSE, FIRETAG & BOCK, P.C. (AV)

5611 North 16th Street, 85016
Telephone: 602-279-9411
Facsimile: 602-241-1260

Robert J. Cruse   Jules I. Firetag
                  Daniel A. Bock
_____

John L. Stoss
OF COUNSEL
Stephen T. Meadow (P.C.)

Reference: Bank One (Sun City/Lakeview Office).

For full biographical listings, see the Martindale-Hubbell Law Directory

FENNEMORE CRAIG, A PROFESSIONAL CORPORATION (AV)

Two North Central, Suite 2200, 85004
Telephone: 602-257-8700
Fax: 602-257-8527
Scottsdale, Arizona Office: 6263 North Scottsdale Road, Suite 290, 85250.
Telephone: 602-257-5400.
Fax: 602-257-5409.
Tucson, Arizona Office: One South Church Avenue, Suite 1030, 85701.
Telephone: 520-791-6800.
Fax: 520-791-6820.

Robert P. Robinson   Cathy L. Reece
Robert J. Hackett   Jay S. Kramer

For Complete List of Firm Personnel, See General Section

For full biographical listings, see the Martindale-Hubbell Law Directory

JENNINGS, STROUSS AND SALMON, P.L.C. (AV)

A Professional Limited Liability Company
One Renaissance Square, Two North Central, 85004-2393
Telephone: 602-262-5911
Fax: 602-253-3255

Lee E. Esch   I. Douglas Dunipace
              Anne L. Kleindienst

For Complete List of Firm Personnel, See General Section

For full biographical listings, see the Martindale-Hubbell Law Directory

LEWIS AND ROCA, LLP (AV)

A Limited Liability Partnership including a Professional Corporation
40 North Central Avenue, 85004-4429
Telephone: 602-262-5311
Fax: 602-262-5747
Email: mlp@lrlaw.com
Tucson, Arizona Office: One South Church Avenue, Suite 700, 86701-1620.
Telephone: 520-622-2090.
Fax: 520-622-3088. E-Mail: mlp@lrlaw.com.

MEMBERS OF FIRM

Gerald K. Smith   Peter D. Baird
Richard N. Goldsmith   David E. Manch
Patricia K. Norris   Thomas H. Campbell
David M. Bixby   Newman R. Porter
Scott DeWald   Brent C. Gardner
Kenneth Van Winkle, Jr.   Robert H. McKirgan

Representative Clients: Bank One, Arizona, NA; Citibank; Northern Trust Bank of Arizona, N.A.; Arizona Bank Wells Fargo.

For Complete List of Firm Personnel, See General Section

For full biographical listings, see the Martindale-Hubbell Law Directory

McCABE, O'DONNELL & WRIGHT, A PROFESSIONAL ASSOCIATION (AV)

3101 North Central Avenue Suite 700, 85012
Telephone: 602-264-0800
Facsimile: 602-274-0146
Email: mowphx@aol.com
Email: mowphx@mowphx.com

Joseph I. McCabe

A List of Representative Clients will be Furnished upon Request.

For full biographical listings, see the Martindale-Hubbell Law Directory

O'CONNOR, CAVANAGH, ANDERSON, KILLINGSWORTH & BESHEARS, A PROFESSIONAL ASSOCIATION (AV)

One East Camelback Road, Suite 1100, 85012-1656
Telephone: 602-263-2400
FAX: 602-263-2900
Email: firminfo@arizlaw.com
Sun City, Arizona Office: 13250 North Del Webb Boulevard, Suite B, 85351.
Telephone: 602-263-2808.
FAX: 602-933-3100.
Tucson, Arizona Office: O'Connor Cavanagh Molloy Jones, 33 N. Stone, Suite 2100, 85701, P.O. Box 2268, 85702.
Telephone: 520-622-3531.
FAX: 520-624-2816.
Nogales, Arizona Office: 1891 North Mastick Way, 85621.
Telephone: 520-761-4215.
FAX: 520-761-3505.

Jeffrey H. Verbin   Gilbert L. Rudolph
_____

Karl A. Freeburg   Mark W. Daliere
_____

Becky L. Brooks

Representative Clients: Bank of America; Chase Manhattan Bank; First Interstate Bank of Arizona, N.A.; M & I Thunderbird Bank; Northern Trust Bank; Sears National Bank; Countrywide Credit Industries; GE Capital Mortgage Services, Inc.; Merrill Lynch Credit Corp.

For Complete List of Firm Personnel, See General Section

For full biographical listings, see the Martindale-Hubbell Law Directory

RIDENOUR, SWENSON, CLEERE & EVANS, P.C. (AV)

40 North Central Avenue, Suite 1400, 85004
Telephone: 602-254-2143
Fax: 602-254-8670

William G. Ridenour   William D. Fearnow
Gerard R. Cleere   Natalie P. Garth
                  Kurt A. Peterson

For full biographical listings, see the Martindale-Hubbell Law Directory

SNELL & WILMER, L.L.P. (AV)

One Arizona Center, 85004-0001
Telephone: 602-382-6000
Fax: 602-382-6070
Tucson, Arizona Office: 1500 Norwest Tower, One South Church Avenue 85701-1612.
Telephone: 520-882-1200.
Fax: 520-884-1294.
Orange County Office: 1920 Main Street, Suite 1200, P.O. Box 57062, Irvine, California, 92619-7062.
Telephone: 714-253-2700.
Fax: 714-955-2507.
Salt Lake City, Utah Office: Broadway Centre, 111 East Broadway, Suite 900, 84111-1004.
Telephone: 801-237-1900.
Fax: 801-237-1950.

MEMBERS OF FIRM

Jon S. Cohen   David A. Sprentall
Craig K. Williams   Timothy W. Moser
                  Nicholas J. Wood

Representative Clients: Bank One, Arizona N A; Bank of America Arizona; First Interstate Bank of Arizona, N.A.; First Securities Bank of Utah; Wells Fargo Bank, N.A.; National Bank of Arizona.

For Complete List of Firm Personnel, See General Section

For full biographical listings, see the Martindale-Hubbell Law Directory

_____

TUCSON,* Pima Co.
_____

RAVEN, KIRSCHNER & NORELL, P.C. (AV)

Suite 1600, One South Church Avenue, 85701-1612
Telephone: 520-628-8700
Telefax: 520-798-5200

Dennis J. Clancy   Lane D. Oden
L. Anthony Fines   Mark B. Raven
Barry Kirschner   S. Leonard Scheff
Andrew Oldland Norell   Stephen A. Thomas

Representative Clients: Continental Medical Systems, Inc.; El Paso Natural Gas Co.; Norwest Bank Arizona; El Rio-Santa Cruz Neighborhood Health Center, Inc.; Resolution Trust Corp.; Sierra Vista Community Hospital; Southern Arizona Rehabilitation Hospital; Northern Cochise Community Hospital.

For Complete List of Firm Personnel, See General Section

For full biographical listings, see the Martindale-Hubbell Law Directory

Tucson—Continued

SNELL & WILMER, L.L.P. (AV)

1500 Norwest Tower, One South Church Avenue, 85701-1612
Telephone: 520-882-1200
Fax: 520-884-1294
Phoenix, Arizona Office: One Arizona Center, 85004-0001.
Telephone: 602-382-6000.
Fax: 602-382-6070.
Orange County Office: 1920 Main Street, Suite 1200, P.O. Box 57062, Irvine, California, 92619-7062.
Telephone: 714-253-2700
Fax: 714-955-2507.
Salt Lake City, Utah Office: Broadway Centre, 111 East Broadway, Suite 900, 84111- 1004.
Telephone: 801-237-1900.
Fax: 801-237-1950.

MEMBERS OF FIRM

Michael S. Milroy   Curt D. Reimann

Representative Clients: Transit Management, Inc.; Tucson Airport Authority; Allstate Insurance Co.; Bank One, Arizona, NA; Southern Pacific Railroad Co.; Ford Motor Co.; Chrysler Motors Corp.; Toyota Motor Sales, U.S.A., Inc.; BHP Copper, Inc.; Pinnacle West Capital Corp.; Safeway Inc.; Honeywell, Inc.; Wells Fargo Bank, N.A.

For full biographical listings, see the Martindale-Hubbell Law Directory

---

ARKANSAS

LITTLE ROCK, * Pulaski Co.

ALLEN LAW FIRM, A PROFESSIONAL CORPORATION (AV)

950 Centre Place, 212 Center Street, 72201
Telephone: 501-374-7100
Telecopier: 501-374-1611
Email: hwallen@cei.net

H. William Allen

Sandra E. Jackson

Representative Clients: Boatmen's National Bank of Arkansas; National Bank of Commerce.

For full biographical listings, see the Martindale-Hubbell Law Directory

---

ARNOLD, GROBMYER & HALEY, A PROFESSIONAL ASSOCIATION (AV)

875 Union National Plaza, 124 West Capitol Avenue, P.O. Box 70, 72203
Telephone: 501-376-1171
Fax: 501-375-3548

Benjamin F. Arnold   Charles D. McDaniel
Mark W. Grobmyer   Joe A. Polk
       Richard L. Ramsay

For Complete List of Firm Personnel, See General Section

For full biographical listings, see the Martindale-Hubbell Law Directory

---

FRIDAY, ELDREDGE & CLARK (AV)

A Partnership including Professional Associations
Formerly, Smith, Williams, Friday, Eldredge & Clark
2000 First Commercial Building, 400 West Capitol Avenue, 72201-3493
Telephone: 501-376-2011
Telecopier: 501-376-2147; 376-6369
Email: fecmh@fec.sprint.com

MEMBERS OF FIRM

Paul B. Benham, III, (P.A.)   Thomas N. Rose (P.A.)
Richard D. Taylor (P.A.)   Harry A. Light (P.A.)
     John Clayton Randolph (P.A.)

ASSOCIATE

Allison Graves

Representative Clients: Arkansas Power & Light Co.; First Commercial Bank; First National Bank of Fort Smith; First National Bank of Marianna; First National Bank of Berryville; Arvest Trust Co., N.A.; Farmers Bank & Trust Co. of Magnolia; Dillard Department Stores, Inc.; Union Pacific Railroad.

For Complete List of Firm Personnel, See General Section

For full biographical listings, see the Martindale-Hubbell Law Directory

---

HOOVER & KOOISTRA (AV)

111 Center Street, 11th Floor, 72201-4445
Telephone: 501-376-8500
Facsimile: 501-372-3255

(See Next Column)

MEMBERS OF FIRM

Paul W. Hoover, Jr.   John Kooistra, III
     Max C. Mehlburger

For full biographical listings, see the Martindale-Hubbell Law Directory

---

IVESTER, SKINNER & CAMP, P.A. (AV)

Suite 1200, 111 Center Street, 72201
Telephone: 501-376-7788
FAX: 501-376-8536

Hermann Ivester   Charles R. Camp
H. Edward Skinner   Randal B. Frazier
     Laura G. Wiltshire

For Complete List of Firm Personnel, See General Section

For full biographical listings, see the Martindale-Hubbell Law Directory

---

ROSE LAW FIRM, A PROFESSIONAL ASSOCIATION (AV)

120 East Fourth Street, 72201
Telephone: 501-375-9131
Telecopy: 501-375-1309

George E. Campbell   Kevin R. Burns
Herbert C. Rule, III   Richard N. Massey
Allen W. Bird, II   John T. Hardin
Garland J. Garrett   Stephen N. Joiner
Thomas P. Thrash   Brian Rosenthal
Charles W. Baker   J. Scott Schallhorn
     Jeffrey J. Gearhart

Representative Clients: Arkansas Association of Bank Holding Cos.; CoreStates Bank, N.A.; Mercantile Bank of Central Arkansas; Mid-South Bancshares, Inc.; Stephens Group Inc.; Tyson Foods, Inc.

For Complete List of Firm Personnel, See General Section

For full biographical listings, see the Martindale-Hubbell Law Directory

---

WEST MEMPHIS, Crittenden Co.

SLOAN, RUBENS & PEEPLES (AV)

600 North Missouri Street, P.O. Box 768, 72303
Telephone: 501-735-5500
Telecopy: 501-735-2624

MEMBERS OF FIRM

Edward J. Rubens (1913-1977)   Kent J. Rubens
     David C. Peeples

ASSOCIATES

J. Michael Stephenson   James A. Davis

OF COUNSEL

Ralph W. Sloan   Edward B. Johnson
       (Not admitted in AR)

General Counsel for: Bank of West Memphis; Crittenden Publishing Co., Inc.; West Memphis School District; Razorback Concrete; Flash Markets, Inc.
Representative Clients: Earle School District; Crawfordsville School District; Citizens Bank Marion; Marion School District; AgriBank, FCB.

For full biographical listings, see the Martindale-Hubbell Law Directory

---

CALIFORNIA

CARLSBAD, San Diego Co.

WEIL & WRIGHT (AV)

1921 Palomar Oaks Way, Suite 301, 92008
Telephone: 619-438-1214
Telefax: 619-438-2666

Paul M. Weil   David A. Ebersole
Archie T. Wright III   John F. Hilbert

For full biographical listings, see the Martindale-Hubbell Law Directory

---

FRESNO, * Fresno Co.

KIMBLE, MacMICHAEL & UPTON, A PROFESSIONAL CORPORATION (AV)

Fig Garden Financial Center, 5260 North Palm Avenue, Suite 221, P.O. Box 9489, 93792-9489
Telephone: 209-435-5500
Telecopier: 209-435-1500
Email: kmu@primenet.com

(See Next Column)

KIMBLE, MACMICHAEL & UPTON A PROFESSIONAL CORPORATION—*Continued*

Joseph C. Kimble (1910-1972)
Thomas A. MacMichael
(1920-1990)
Jon Wallace Upton
Robert E. Bergin
Jeffrey G. Boswell
Steven D. McGee
Robert E. Ward
John P. Eleazarian

Robert H. Scribner
Michael E. Moss
Mark D. Miller
Michael F. Tatham
W. Richard Lee
D. Tyler Tharpe
Sylvia Halkousis Coyle
S. Brett Sutton
Michael J. Jurkovich

Douglas V. Thornton
Robert William Branch
Donald J. Pool

Susan King Hatmaker
Lawrence J. Salisbury
Daniel R. Foster

Meredith E. Allen

OF COUNSEL

Mary Ann Bluhm

For full biographical listings, see the Martindale-Hubbell Law Directory

---

IRVINE, Orange Co.

ALDRICH & BONNEFIN, P.L.C. (AV)

18200 Von Karman Avenue, Suite 730, P.O. Box 19686, 92623
Telephone: 714-474-1944
Telecopier: 714-474-0617
Email: 103132.2601@compuserve.com

Mark E. Aldrich
Janet M. Bonnefin

Mark Alan Moore
David Bustamante

Eric G. Baron
Keith R. Forrester

Anne M. McEachran
Kristen Welles Lanham

Robert K. Olsen

Representative Clients: Bankers' Compliance Group; Bank Leumi Le Israel, B.M.; California Commerce Bank; California Korea Bank; Fallbrook National Bank; State Bank of India (California); Valley Independent Bank; Valliwide Bank.
References: S. Suresh Kumar, President, Brentwood Bank of California; Curtis Reis, President, Alliance Bank.

For full biographical listings, see the Martindale-Hubbell Law Directory

---

NICHOLS & ANDREWS, A PROFESSIONAL LAW CORPORATION (AV)

5 Park Plaza, Suite 800, 92614-6501
Telephone: 714-475-4477
Fax: 714-475-4475

Robert F. Nichols, Jr.

Camilla N. Andrews

For full biographical listings, see the Martindale-Hubbell Law Directory

---

LONG BEACH, Los Angeles Co.

CAYER, KILSTOFTE & CRATON, A PROFESSIONAL LAW CORPORATION (AV)

Suite 700, 444 West Ocean Boulevard, 90802
Telephone: 310-435-6008
Fax: 310-435-3704
Email: CKCCRC@AOL.COM

John J. Cayer

Stephen R. Kilstofte

Curt R. Craton

Cortlen R. Hauge

For full biographical listings, see the Martindale-Hubbell Law Directory

---

LOS ANGELES,* Los Angeles Co.

ANGEL AND NEISTAT, A PROFESSIONAL CORPORATION (AV)

28th Floor 555 South Flower Street, 90017-2205
Telephone: 213-689-4500
Fax: 213-689-4651

Michael A. Angel
Douglas M. Neistat
Alan Holmberg
Steven L. Crane

Steven A. Schwaber
Alan J. Stomel
Gary R. Wallace
Daniel H. Reiss

For full biographical listings, see the Martindale-Hubbell Law Directory

---

BARTON, KLUGMAN & OETTING (AV)

A Partnership including Professional Corporations
37th Floor, 333 South Grand Avenue, 90071-1599
Telephone: 213-621-4000
Telecopier: 213-625-1832
Newport Beach Office: Suite 700, 4400 MacArthur Boulevard, P.O. Box 2350, 92660.
Telephone: 714-752-7551.
Telecopier: 714-752-0288.

COUNSEL TO FIRM

Robert M. Barton *

Robert H. Klugman *

Richard F. Oetting *

MEMBERS OF FIRM

David F. Morgan *
William D. Herz *
Charles J. Schufreider *
Robert Louis Fisher *
Gilbert D. Jensen *

David J. Cartano *
Martin J. Spear
Tod V. Beebe *
Ronald R. St. John
Mark A. Newton *

Margot I. McLeay

ASSOCIATES

Barbara W. G. Crowley

Reiko L. Furuta

Jaleen Nelson

References: The Bank of California (Southern California Headquarters); Wells Fargo Bank, N.A. (Wells Fargo Center, Los Angeles).
*Denotes a lawyer whose Professional Corporation is a member of the partnership or is Counsel to the Firm

For full biographical listings, see the Martindale-Hubbell Law Directory

---

LAW OFFICES OF DAVID B. BLOOM A PROFESSIONAL CORPORATION (AV)

3325 Wilshire Boulevard, Ninth Floor, 90010
Telephone: 213-938-5248; 384-4088
Telecopier: 213-385-2009

David B. Bloom

Stephen S. Monroe (A
Professional Corporation)
Raphael A. Rosemblat
James E. Adler
Bonni S. Mantovani
Roy A. Levun
Cherie S. Raidy
Jonathan Udell

Susan Carole Jay
Edward Idell
Sandra Kamenir
Steven Wayne Lazarus
Andrew Edward Briseno
Harold C. Klaskin
Shelley M. Gould
Peter O. Israel

For full biographical listings, see the Martindale-Hubbell Law Directory

---

CLARK & TREVITHICK, A PROFESSIONAL CORPORATION (AV)

800 Wilshire Boulevard, 12th Floor, 90017
Telephone: 213-629-5700
Telecopier: 213-624-9441
San Francisco, California Office: 456 Montgomery Street, 20th Floor.
Telephone: 415-288-6520.
Fax: 415-398-2820.

Philip W. Bartenetti

John A. Lapinski

Leslie R. Horowitz

OF COUNSEL

Judith Ilene Bloom

References: Wells Fargo Bank (Los Angeles Main Office); National Bank of California.

For Complete List of Firm Personnel, See General Section

For full biographical listings, see the Martindale-Hubbell Law Directory

---

FRIED, BIRD & CRUMPACKER, A PROFESSIONAL CORPORATION (AV)

10100 Santa Monica Boulevard, Suite 300, 90067-6031
Telephone: 310-551-7400
Facsimile: 310-556-4487

Jack Fried
Brian James Bird

David W. Crumpacker, Jr.
Nikki Wolontis

David M. Schachter

David K. Johnson

For full biographical listings, see the Martindale-Hubbell Law Directory

---

LAW OFFICES OF RICHARD H. GIBSON A PROFESSIONAL CORPORATION (AV)

Wells Fargo Center, 333 South Grand Avenue, Suite 1860, 90071
Telephone: 213-617-1185
Facsimile: 213-617-1902

Richard H. Gibson

For full biographical listings, see the Martindale-Hubbell Law Directory

Los Angeles—Continued

IVANJACK & LAMBIRTH (AV)

A Partnership including Professional Corporations
12301 Wilshire Boulevard, Suite 600, 90025-1000
Telephone: 310-820-7211
Telecopier: 310-820-0687
Email: ivanjack@AOL.com
Irvine, California Office: 5 Park Plaza, Suite 800. 92614.
Telephone: 714-475-4477.
Telecopier: 714-475-4475.

Larry G. Ivanjack (P.C.)	Thomas E. Shuck (P.C.)
Timothy A. Lambirth (P.C.)	Kathryn B. Milstead

Joseph H. Lowther	Gary Tokumori
Elise A. Ross	Mary G. Lee

OF COUNSEL

Robert F. Nichols, Jr.	Camilla N. Andrews

Representative Clients: Bank of America; Citibank N.A.; Union Bank of California, N.A.; Sanwa Bank California; Great Western Bank; Imperial Bank; First Republic Thrift and Loan; General Electric Capital Corp.; Fleet Credit Corp.; Western Bank.

For full biographical listings, see the Martindale-Hubbell Law Directory

LOEB & LOEB LLP (AV)

A Limited Liability Partnership including Professional Corporations
Suite 1800, 1000 Wilshire Boulevard, 90017-2475
Telephone: 213-688-3400
Facsimile: 213-688-3460; 688-3461; 688-3462
Century City, California Office: Suite 2200, 10100 Santa Monica Boulevard, Los Angeles, 90067-4164.
Telephone: 310-282-2000.
Facsimile: 310-282-2191; 282-2192.
New York, N.Y. Office: 345 Park Avenue, 10154-0037.
Telephone: 212-407-4000.
Facsimile: 212-407-4990.
Washington, D.C. Office: Suite 601, 2100 M Street N.W., 20037-1207.
Telephone: 202-223-5700.
Facsimile: 202-223-5704.
Nashville, Tennessee Office: 45 Music Square West, 37203-3205.
Telephone: 615-749-8300;
Facsimile: 615-749-8308.
Rome, Italy Office: Piazza Digione 1, 00197.
Telephone: 011-396-808-8456.
Facsimile: 011-396-808-8288.

MEMBERS OF FIRM

Christopher K. Aidun (New York City Office)	Joseph P. Heffernan (A P.C.)
Robert S. Barry, Jr.	Robert A. Meyer
Harold A. Barza	Charles H. Miller (New York City Office)
Maribeth A. Borthwick (Century City Office)	Susan V. Noonoo
David B. Eizenman (New York City Office)	David S. Schaefer (New York City Office)
Frank E. Feder (A P.C.) (Century City and New York Offices)	Richard P. Streicher (New York City Office)
	Susan A. Wolf

For Complete List of Firm Personnel, See General Section

For full biographical listings, see the Martindale-Hubbell Law Directory

TIMOTHY D. NAEGELE & ASSOCIATES (AV⊤)

Suite 2430, 1900 Avenue of the Stars, 90067
Telephone: 310-557-2300
Facsimile: 310-457-4014
Email: naegelewdc@aol.com *URL:* http://www.naegele.com
Washington, D.C. Office: Suite 300, 1250 24th Street, N.W., 20037.
Telephone: 202-466-7500.
Facsimile: 202-466-3079 or 466-2888. Internet Web Site: http://www.naegele.com. Internet E-mail: naegelewdc@aol.com.

For full biographical listings, see the Martindale-Hubbell Law Directory

O'MELVENY & MYERS LLP (AV)

400 South Hope Street, 90071-2899
Telephone: 213-669-6000
Cable Address: "Moms"
Facsimile: 213-669-6407
Email: omminfo@omm.com
Century City, California Office: 1999 Avenue of the Stars, 90067-6035.
Telephone: 310-553-6700.
Facsimile: 310-246-6779.
Newport Beach, California Office: 610 Newport Center Drive, 92660-6429.
Telephone: 714-760-9600.
Cable Address: "Moms".
Facsimile: 714-669-6994.

(See Next Column)

San Francisco, California Office: Embarcadero Center West Tower, 275 Battery Street, 94111-3305.
Telephone: 415-984-8700.
Facsimile: 415-984-8701.
New York, New York Office: Citicorp Center, 153 East 53rd Street, 10022-4611.
Telephone: 212-326-2000.
Facsimile: 212-326-2061.
Washington, D.C. Office: 555 13th Street, N.W., 20004-1109.
Telephone: 202-383-5300.
Cable Address: "Moms".
Facsimile: 202-383-5414.
London, England Office: 10 Finsbury Square, London, EC2A 1LA.
Telephone: 0171-256-8451.
Facsimile: 0171-638-8205.
Tokyo, Japan Office: Sanbancho KB-6 Building, 6 Sanbancho, Chiyoda-ku, Tokyo 102, Japan.
Telephone: 03-3239-2900.
Facsimile: 03-3239-2432.
Hong Kong Office: Suite 1905, Peregrine Tower, Lippo Centre, 89 Queensway, Central, Hong Kong.
Telephone: 852-2523-8266.
Facsimile: 852-2522-1760.
Shanghai, Peoples Republic of China Office: Shanghai International Trade Centre, Suite 2011, 2200 Yan An Road West, Shanghai, 200335, PRC.
Telephone: 86-21-6219-5363.
Facsimile: 86-21-6275-4949.

PARTNER

Matthew T. Kirby (Los Angeles, California and New York, N.Y. Offices)

For Complete List of Firm Personnel, See General Section

For full biographical listings, see the Martindale-Hubbell Law Directory

SHEPPARD, MULLIN, RICHTER & HAMPTON LLP (AV)

A Limited Liability Partnership including Professional Corporations
Forty-Eighth Floor, 333 South Hope Street, 90071-1448
Telephone: 213-620-1780
Telecopier: 213-620-1398
Cable Address: "Sheplaw"
Email: info@smrh.com *URL:* http://www.smrh.com
Orange County, California Office: 650 Town Center Drive, 4th Floor, Costa Mesa.
Telephone: 714-513-5100.
Telecopier: 714-513-5130. Home Page Address: http://www.smrh.com.
San Francisco, California Office: Seventeenth Floor, Four Embarcadero Center.
Telephone: 415-434-9100.
Telecopier: 415-434-3947. Home Page Address: http://www.smrh.com.
San Diego, California Office: Nineteenth Floor, 501 West Broadway.
Telephone: 619-338-6500.
Telecopier: 619-234-3815. Home Page Address: http://www.smrh.com.

COUNSEL

George R. Richter, Jr. (Retired)

MEMBERS OF FIRM

John D. Berchild, Jr.	Prentice L. O'Leary *
Richard W. Brunette, Jr.	Joel R. Ohlgren
Steven W. Cardoza (Orange County Office)	Sara Pfrommer
Dean A. Demetre (Orange County Office)	Nancy Baldwin Reimann
	D. Ronald Ryland (San Francisco Office)
Juliette M. Ebert (San Francisco Office)	William M. Scott IV
Merrill R. Francis *	Mark K. Slater (San Francisco Office)
Geraldine A. Freeman (San Francisco Office)	Richard L. Sommers
Marsha D. Galinsky	Mark A. Spitzer
Alan H. Martin (Orange County Office)	Laura S. Taylor (San Diego Office)
David J. McCarty	Victor A. Vilaplana (San Diego Office)
Charles E. McCormick	William R. Wyatt (San Francisco Office)

*Professional Corporation

For full biographical listings, see the Martindale-Hubbell Law Directory

---

NEWPORT BEACH, Orange Co.

THEODORE M. HANKIN (AV)

Suite 900, One Newport Place, 92660
Telephone: 714-752-8840
FAX: 714-851-1732

For full biographical listings, see the Martindale-Hubbell Law Directory

WOLF & PFEIFER, A LAW CORPORATION (AV)

500 Newport Center Drive Suite 800, 92660
Telephone: 714-720-9200
Fax: 714-720-9250
URL: http://www.wolfpfeifer.com

(See Next Column)

WOLF & PFEIFER A LAW CORPORATION—*Continued*

Alan S. Wolf
Michael R. Pfeifer
Melissa L. Richards
Janice L. Celotti
Donald R. Davidson, III

Roland P. Reynolds
Donna L. La Porte
C. Robert Simpson
Diane Weifenbach
James F. Lewin

OF COUNSEL

Kay Virginia Gustafson

LEGAL SUPPORT PERSONNEL

Dona M. Harman

For full biographical listings, see the Martindale-Hubbell Law Directory

ORANGE, Orange Co.

FABOZZI, THIERBACH & CALEY (AV)

3111 North Tustin Avenue, Suite 200, 92665
Telephone: 714-637-3385
FAX: 714-637-3489

Dennis F. Fabozzi
Marlene L. Thierbach
Rebecca A. Caley

ASSOCIATES

Jima Ikegawa
Bruce T. Bauer

For full biographical listings, see the Martindale-Hubbell Law Directory

PASADENA, Los Angeles Co.

CAIRNS, DOYLE, LANS, NICHOLAS & SONI, A LAW CORPORATION (AV)

Ninth Floor, 225 South Lake Avenue, 91101
Telephone: 818-683-3111
Telecopier: 818-683-4999

John D. Cairns
John C. Doyle
Stephen M. Lans
Francisco J. Nicholas
Rohini Soni (1956-1994)

Representative Clients: Allstate Insurance Companies; Burger King Corp.; California Insurance Guarantee Assn.; California United Bank; CIGNA Insurance Companies; City of Pasadena; Cumis Insurance Society, Inc.; Employer's Mutual Insurance Companies; State Farm Insurance Companies; Tokio Marine Insurance.

For full biographical listings, see the Martindale-Hubbell Law Directory

SAN DIEGO,* San Diego Co.

FERRIS & BRITTON, A PROFESSIONAL CORPORATION (AV)

1600 First National Bank Center, 401 West A Street, 92101
Telephone: 619-233-3131
Fax: 619-232-9316

Alfred G. Ferris
Steven J. Pynes
Michael R. Weinstein

OF COUNSEL

James J. Granby

Representative Clients: Central Carolina Bank; Peninsula Bank; Valley Independent Bank.

For Complete List of Firm Personnel, See General Section

For full biographical listings, see the Martindale-Hubbell Law Directory

HIGGS, FLETCHER & MACK LLP (AV)

2000 First National Bank Building, 401 West "A" Street, 92101
Telephone: 619-236-1551
Telecopier: 619-696-1410
Email: info@higgslaw.com

MEMBERS OF FIRM

Franklin T. Lloyd
Kurt L. Kicklighter

Representative Clients: Frazee Industries; Kawasaki Motors Corp.; Rohr Industries; Allstate Insurance Co.; Associated Aviation Underwriters; Physicians & Surgeons Insurance Exchange.

For Complete List of Firm Personnel, See General Section

For full biographical listings, see the Martindale-Hubbell Law Directory

LINDLEY, LAZAR & SCALES, A PROFESSIONAL CORPORATION (AV)

One America Plaza, 600 West Broadway, Suite 1400, 92101-3302
Telephone: 619-234-9181
Fax: 619-234-8475
Email: 104413.1175@compuserve.com

(See Next Column)

Luke R. Corbett
John M. Seitman
Michael H. Wexler
George C. Lazar
James Henry Fox
Kenneth C. Jones

Representative Clients: Bank of Commerce; Palomar Savings & Loan.

For Complete List of Firm Personnel, See General Section

For full biographical listings, see the Martindale-Hubbell Law Directory

LUCE, FORWARD, HAMILTON & SCRIPPS LLP (AV)

A Partnership including Professional Corporations
600 West Broadway, Suite 2600, 92101
Telephone: 619-236-1414
Fax: 619-232-8311
URL: http://www.luce.com
La Jolla, California Office: 4275 Executive Square, Suite 800, 92037.
Telephone: 619-535-2639.
Fax: 619-453-2812.
Los Angeles, California Office: 777 South Figueroa, Suite 3600, 90017.
Telephone: 213-892-4992.
Fax: 213-892-7731.
San Francisco, California Office: 100 Bush Street, 20th Floor, 94104.
Telephone: 415-395-7900.
Fax: 415-395-7949.
New York, N.Y. Office: Citicorp Center, 153 East 53rd Street, 26th Floor, 10022.
Telephone: 212-754-1414.
Fax: 212-644-9727.
Chicago, Illinois Office: 180 North La Salle Street, Suite 1125, 60601.
Telephone: 312-641-0580.
Fax: 312-641-0380.

MEMBERS OF FIRM

John B. McNeece III
Mikel R. Bistrow
Margaret M. Mann
Christopher Celentino

OF COUNSEL

Michael T. Andrew
Stephen R. Brown

ASSOCIATES

Teryl Murabayashi
(Resident, Los Angeles Office)
Kathryn M. S. Catherwood
Helen T. Chao

For Complete List of Firm Personnel, See General Section

For full biographical listings, see the Martindale-Hubbell Law Directory

MULVANEY, KAHAN & BARRY, A PROFESSIONAL CORPORATION (AV)

Seventeenth Floor, First National Bank Center, 401 West "A" Street, 92101-7994
Telephone: 619-238-1010
Fax: 619-238-1981
Email: mkb@mkblaw.com
Los Angeles, California Office: Union Bank Plaza, 445 South Figueroa Street, Suite 2600.
Telephone: 213-612-7765.
La Jolla, California Office: Glendale Federal Building, 7911 Herschel, Suite 300, P.O Box 1885.
Telephone: 619-454-0142.
Fax: 619-454-7858.
Orange, California Office: The Koll Center, 500 North State College Boulevard, Suite 440.
Telephone: 714-634-7069.
Fax: 714-939-8000.

James F. Mulvaney
Lawrence Kahan
Everett G. Barry, Jr.
Donald G. Johnson, Jr.
Robert A. Linn
Maureen E. Markey
Paula Rotenberg
Melissa A. Blackburn
Julie A. Jones
Maureen F. Hallahan
Mark R. Raftery
Charles F. Bethel
Diane M. Racicot
John A. Mayers
Steven W. Pite
Patricia A. Sieveke (Resident, Los Angeles and Orange Offices)
Linda C. Schumacher
John D. Duncan

OF COUNSEL

Rex B. Beatty
Robert K. Edmunds
James P. McGowan, Jr.
(Resident, La Jolla Office)
Derrick W. Samuelson
(Not admitted in CA)

Representative Clients: Union Bank; Wells Fargo Bank; NationsBank; San Diego National Bank; Fallbrook National Bank; Rancho Santa Fe National Bank.

For full biographical listings, see the Martindale-Hubbell Law Directory

SAN FRANCISCO, San Francisco Co.

MURPHY, PEARSON, BRADLEY & FEENEY, A PROFESSIONAL CORPORATION (AV)

88 Kearny Street, 11th Floor, 94108
Telephone: 415-788-1900
Telecopier: 415-393-8087
Sacramento, California Office: Suite 200, 3600 American River Drive, 95864.
Telephone: 916-483-6074.
Telecopier: 916-483-6088.

James A. Murphy

Mark Ellis
(Resident, Sacramento Office)

For Complete List of Firm Personnel, See General Section

For full biographical listings, see the Martindale-Hubbell Law Directory

SANTA ANA, Orange Co.

PRENOVOST, NORMANDIN, BERGH & DAWE, A PROFESSIONAL CORPORATION (AV)

2020 East First Street, Suite 500, 92705
Telephone: 714-547-2444
Fax: 714-835-2889
Email: PNBD@worldnet.att.net

Thomas J. Prenovost, Jr.	Steven L. Bergh
Tom Roddy Normandin	Michael G. Dawe

Doris Andree Faust	Paula M. Harrelson
Eric P. Francisconi	Daniel H. McLinden
James Andrew Fraser	Nancy R. Tragarz

Reference: Marine National Bank.

For full biographical listings, see the Martindale-Hubbell Law Directory

SANTA MONICA, Los Angeles Co.

HAIGHT, BROWN & BONESTEEL (AV)

A Partnership including Professional Corporations
1620 26th Street, Suite 4000 North, P.O. Box 680, 90404
Telephone: 310-449-6000
Telecopier: 310-829-5117
Telex: 705837
Santa Ana, California Office: Suite 900, 5 Hutton Centre Drive.
Telephone: 714-754-1100.
Telecopier: 714-754-0826.
Riverside, California Office: 3750 University Avenue, Suite 650.
Telephone: 909-341-8300.
Fax: 909-341-8309.
San Francisco, California Office: 201 Sansome Street, Suite 300.
Telephone: 415-986-7700.
Fax: 415-986-6954.

MEMBERS OF FIRM

Morton Rosen	William E. Ireland

OF COUNSEL
R. Roy Finkle

For Complete List of Firm Personnel, See General Section

For full biographical listings, see the Martindale-Hubbell Law Directory

SANTA ROSA, Sonoma Co.

BELDEN, ABBEY, WEITZENBERG & KELLY, A PROFESSIONAL CORPORATION (AV)

1105 North Dutton Avenue, P.O. Box 1566, 95402
Telephone: 707-542-5050
Telecopier: 707-542-2589

Richard W. Abbey

Representative Clients: Exchange Bank of Santa Rosa; Westamerica Bank; North Bay Title Co.; Northwestern Title Security Co.; Geyser Peak Winery; Santa Rosa City School District; Sonoma National Bank; Arrowood Vineyards & Winery; Arthur & DeVincenzi Concrete; Friedman Bros. Hardware, Inc.

For Complete List of Firm Personnel, See General Section

For full biographical listings, see the Martindale-Hubbell Law Directory

COLORADO

COLORADO SPRINGS, El Paso Co.

FLYNN MCKENNA WRIGHT & KARSH (AV)

limited liability company
Plaza of the Rockies 111 South Tejon, Suite 202, 80903
Telephone: 719-578-8444
Fax: 719-578-8836

James T. Flynn	Randolph M. Karsh
R. Tim McKenna	Brian T. Murphy
Bruce M. Wright	Michael C. Potarf

Representative Clients: Western National Bank of Colorado; Colorado Springs Savings and Loan Association; Chase Manhattan Mortgage Corp.; First National Bank of Canon City; Colorado Bank and Trust Company of La Junta; Merrill Lynch Credit Corporation; Bank of the Rockies, N.A.

For full biographical listings, see the Martindale-Hubbell Law Directory

DENVER, Denver Co.

BENJAMIN & ASSOCIATES, P.C. (AV)

5555 DTC Parkway Suite 4000-A (Englewood) 80111, P.O. Box 370509, 80237-0509
Telephone: 303-290-6600
Facsimile: 303-290-8323

James G. Benjamin

David M. Suhr

For full biographical listings, see the Martindale-Hubbell Law Directory

BERENBAUM, WEINSHIENK & EASON, P.C. (AV)

Suite 2600 Republic Plaza, 370 17th Street, 80202
Telephone: 303-825-0800
Facsimile: 303-629-7610
Durango, Colorado Office: 2815 Main.
Telephone: 303-247-1333.

Mandel Berenbaum (1914-1993)	Kenneth S. Kramer
Hubert T. Weinshienk	James L. Kurtz-Phelan
(1931-1983)	Charles P. Leder
Joseph Berenbaum	A. Elizabeth Meyers
Charles A. Bewley	H. Michael Miller
Joseph S. Borus	Neil B. Oberfeld
Martin D. Buckley	Dean G. Panos
M. Frances Cetrulo	Edwin G. Perlmutter
Daniel S. Duggan	Barry M. Permut
David R. Eason	Keith M. Pockross
Richard L. Eason	Dan A. Sciullo
Steven C. Hoth	Edward L. Sperry
James A. Jacobson	Eugene M. Sprague
I. H. Kaiser	Robert G. Wilson, Jr.
Ronald I. Zall	

J. Hunter Banbury	Amy L. Durfee
Patricia Bellac	Heather Scheel Hagemann
Stephen K. Schutte	

SPECIAL COUNSEL
John E. Bush

Representative Clients: Stanley Works; Columbine Venture Funds; The Home Depot; Karman, Inc.; Lomas Mortgage; Southwest State Bank; The Bank of Boulder; Teamsters; Trinity Ventures; The David Johnson Group.

For full biographical listings, see the Martindale-Hubbell Law Directory

IVAN D. FUGATE (AV)

North Valley Bank Building, 9001 North Washington Street, P.O. Box 29429, 80229
Telephone: 303-741-2484

For full biographical listings, see the Martindale-Hubbell Law Directory

HOLME ROBERTS & OWEN LLP (AV)

Suite 4100, 1700 Lincoln, 80203
Telephone: 303-861-7000
Telecopier: 303-866-0200
Email: hro@hro.com *URL:* http://www.hro.com
Boulder, Colorado Office: Suite 400, 1401 Pearl Street.
Telephone: 303-444-5955.
Telecopier: 303-444-1063.
Colorado Springs, Colorado Office: Suite 1300, 90 South Cascade Avenue.
Telephone: 719-473-3800.
Telecopier: 719-633-1518.
Salt Lake City, Utah Office: Suite 1100, 111 East Broadway.
Telephone: 801-521-5800.
Telecopier: 801-521-9639.

(See Next Column)

HOLME ROBERTS & OWEN LLP—*Continued*

London, England Office: Mellier House, 26a Albemarle Street.
Telephone: 44-171-499-8776.
Telecopier: 44-171-499-7769.
Moscow, Russia Office: Kosmodamianskaya Nab. #52/1, Suite 9100, 113054.
Telephone: 7095-961-3000.
Telecopier: 7095-961-3001.
Kiev, Ukraine Office: Terestchenkovskaya #19, Suite 2, 252004.
Telephone: 380-44-224-1348.
Telecopier: 380-44-224-4986.

PARTNERS OF FIRM

James C. Owen Jr.	Phillip R. Clark
Bruce R. Kohler (Co-Resident Managing Partner, London, England Office)	Martha Traudt Collins Lynn Parker Hendrix David Harold Little
William R. Roberts (Managing Partner, Boulder Office)	(Salt Lake City Office) Robert H. Bach

ASSOCIATES

Edward E. Abels, Jr.	Rebecca Hall (Boulder Office)
Daron J. Arnold	Peter O. Hansen
(Not admitted in CO)	Lisa Anne Hawkins

For Complete List of Firm Personnel, See General Section

For full biographical listings, see the Martindale-Hubbell Law Directory

---

SHERMAN & HOWARD L.L.C. (AV)

Attorneys and Counselors at Law
633 Seventeenth Street, Suite 3000, 80202
Telephone: 303-297-2900
Telecopier: 303-298-0940
Colorado Springs, Colorado Office: Suite 1500, 90 South Cascade Avenue, 80903.
Telephone: 719-475-2440.
Las Vegas, Nevada Office: Swendseid & Stern a member in Sherman & Howard L.L.C., 317 Sixth Street, 89101.
Telephone: 702-387-6073.
Reno, Nevada Office: Swendseid & Stern, a member in Sherman & Howard L.L.C., 50 West Liberty Street, Suite 660, 89501.
Telephone: 702-323-1980.

James L. Cunningham	Kenneth B. Siegel
Andrew L. Blair, Jr.	Cynthia C. Benson
Mark L. Fulford	Joseph J. Bronesky
James F. Wood	Robert L. Brown
Ronald M. Eddy	

COUNSEL

John W. Low	Garth C. Grissom
Stephen S. Halasz	

Representative Clients: The Colorado State Bank of Denver; Rocky Mountain Automated Clearing House Assoc., Denver; Denver Clearing House Association; The Bank N.A.(Breckenridge); Community Bank of Parker; Mountain Parks Bank; Platte Valley Bank (Brighton); Frontier Bank of Denver.

For Complete List of Firm Personnel, See General Section

For full biographical listings, see the Martindale-Hubbell Law Directory

---

VAIL, Eagle Co.

OTTO, PORTERFIELD & POST, LLC (AV)

51 Eagle Road, P.O. Box 3149, 81658-3149
Telephone: 970-949-5380
Fax: 970-845-9135

Frederick S. Otto	Wendell B. Porterfield, Jr.
William J. Post	

References: 1st Bank of Vail; WestStar Bank.

For full biographical listings, see the Martindale-Hubbell Law Directory

---

CONNECTICUT

GREENWICH, Fairfield Co.

IVEY, BARNUM & O'MARA, LLC (AV)

Meridian Building, 170 Mason Street, P.O. Box 1689, 06830
Telephone: 203-661-6000
Telecopier: 203-661-9462

MEMBERS OF FIRM

Michael J. Allen	Donat C. Marchand
Robert C. Barnum, Jr.	Miles F. McDonald, Jr.
Edward C. Cosden, Jr.	Edwin J. O'Mara, Jr.
Wilmot L. Harris, Jr.	Remy A. Rodas
William I. Haslun II	Gregory A. Saum
Michael J. Jones	Lorraine Slavin
Edward T. Krumeich, Jr.	Steven B. Steinmetz

(See Next Column)

ASSOCIATES

Paul G. Amicucci	Melissa Townsend Klauberg
Stephan B. Grozinger	Cristin L. Rothfuss
Juerg A. Heim	Alan S. Rubenstein
Jennifer B. Kallenbach	Sheryl L. Sensale
	(Not admitted in CT)

OF COUNSEL

James W. Cuminale	Jennifer D. Port
Philip R. McKnight	(Not admitted in CT)

For full biographical listings, see the Martindale-Hubbell Law Directory

---

*HARTFORD,** Hartford Co.

GORDON, MUIR AND FOLEY (AV)

Hartford Square North, Ten Columbus Boulevard, 06106-5123
Telephone: 860-525-5361
Telecopier: 860-525-4849

MEMBERS OF FIRM

William S. Gordon, Jr. (1946-1956)	William J. Gallitto
George Muir (1939-1976)	Gerald R. Swirsky
Edward J. Foley (1955-1983)	Robert J. O'Brien
Peter C. Schwartz	Philip J. O'Connor
John J. Reid	Kenneth G. Williams
John H. Goodrich, Jr.	Chester J. Bukowski
R. Bradley Wolfe	Mary Ann Santacroce
Jon Stephen Berk	J. Lawrence Price
	Mary Anne Alicia Charron
James G. Kelly	

ASSOCIATES

Kevin F. Morin	Andrew J. Hern
Claudia A. Baio	Eileen McCarthy Geel
Patrick T. Treacy	Christopher L. Slack
Renee W. Dwyer	

OF COUNSEL

Stephen M. Riley

Reference: Fleet Bank.

For full biographical listings, see the Martindale-Hubbell Law Directory

---

NEW LONDON, New London Co.

WALLER, SMITH & PALMER, P.C. (AV)

52 Eugene O'Neill Drive, P.O. Box 88, 06320
Telephone: 860-442-0367
Telecopier: 860-447-9915
Old Lyme, Connecticut Office: 103-A Halls Road.
Telephone: 860-434-8063.
Telecopier: 860-434-9452.

Tracy Waller (1862-1947)	Robert W. Marrion
J. Rodney Smith (1906-1979)	Hughes Griffis
Birdsey G. Palmer (Retired)	Edward B. O'Connell
William W. Miner	Frederick B. Gahagan
Robert P. Anderson, Jr.	Mary E. Driscoll

Tracy M. Collins	Valerie Ann Votto
Edward B. Potter	Charles C. Anderson
David P. Condon	Ames B. Shea

General Counsel For: Town of East Lyme; Town of Lebanon.
Counsel For: Citizens Savings Bank; Sonoco/Northeastern, Inc.; The Nature Conservancy; Fleet Bank.
Local Counsel For: McCue Mortgage Co.; Citicorp Mortgage; U.S. Department of Housing and Urban Development.

For full biographical listings, see the Martindale-Hubbell Law Directory

---

STAMFORD, Fairfield Co.

WOFSEY, ROSEN, KWESKIN & KURIANSKY (AV)

600 Summer Street, 06901
Telephone: 203-327-2300
Fax: 203-967-9273

MEMBERS OF FIRM

Abraham Wofsey (1915-1944)	Edward M. Kweskin
Michael Wofsey (1927-1951)	David M. Cohen
David M. Rosen (1926-1967)	Marshall Goldberg
Julius B. Kuriansky (1910-1992)	Stephen A. Finn
Monroe Silverman	Judith Rosenberg
Emanuel Margolis	Mark H. Henderson
Howard C. Kaplan	Steven D. Grushkin
Anthony R. Lorenzo	Matthew J. Forstadt

OF COUNSEL

Saul Kwartin	Sydney C. Kweskin (Retired)

ASSOCIATES

Joseph Brachfeld	Eric M. Higgins
John J.L. Chobor	Valerie E. Maze
Steven M. Frederick	Randall M. Skigen
Joy A. Katz	Peter J. Schaffer
Galit Kierkut	Robert W. Finke

(See Next Column)

WOFSEY, ROSEN, KWESKIN & KURIANSKY, *Stamford—Continued*

Representative Clients: Banque Paribas; Benenson Realty; Cellular Information Systems, Inc.; The Chase Manhattan Bank; First County Bank; Hartford Provision Co.; Louis Dreyfus Corp.; Norwalk Federation of Teachers; People's Bank; Ridgeway Shopping Center.

For full biographical listings, see the Martindale-Hubbell Law Directory

DELAWARE

WILMINGTON,* New Castle Co.

POTTER ANDERSON & CORROON (AV)

350 Delaware Trust Building, P.O. Box 951, 19899-0951
Telephone: 302-984-6000
FAX: 302-658-1192
URL: http://www.ATTYS.PACDELAWARE.COM

MEMBERS OF FIRM

Leonard S. Togman	David B. Brown
Charles S. McDowell	Harold I. Salmons, III

COUNSEL

W. Laird Stabler, Jr.

OF COUNSEL

Blaine T. Phillips	Richard L. McMahon

Representative Clients: Chase Manhattan Bank (U.S.A.) N.A.; Delaware Trust Capital Management, Inc.; First National Bank of Maryland; Mellon Bank (East); Mercantile Bankshares; Midatlantic Bank; Second National Federal Savings Bank; Signet Bank; Wilmington Trust Company.

For Complete List of Firm Personnel, See General Section

For full biographical listings, see the Martindale-Hubbell Law Directory

DISTRICT OF COLUMBIA

WASHINGTON, D.C. Co.

* indicates certain Bar Register subscribers, in cities of comparable size and importance, who maintain an additional office in Washington, D.C. and who have arranged for representation as a part of the Washington, D.C. listings that follow

BAKER & HOSTETLER (AV)

Washington Square, Suite 1100, 1050 Connecticut Avenue, N.W., 20036-5304
Telephone: 202-861-1500
In Cleveland, Ohio: 3200 National City Center, 1900 East Ninth Street.
Telephone: 216-621-0200.
In Columbus, Ohio: Capitol Square, Suite 2100, 65 East State Street.
Telephone: 614-228-1541.
In Denver, Colorado: 303 East 17th Avenue, Suite 1100.
Telephone: 303-861-0600.
In Houston, Texas: 1000 Louisiana, Suite 2000.
Telephone: 713-751-1600.
In Long Beach, California: 300 Oceangate, Suite 620.
Telephone: 310-432-2827.
In Los Angeles, California: 600 Wilshire Boulevard.
Telephone: 213-624-2400.
In Orlando, Florida: SunBank Center, Suite 2300, 200 South Orange Avenue.
Telephone: 305-841-1111.
In College Park, Maryland: 9658 Baltimore Boulevard, Suite 206.
Telephone: 301-441-2781.
In Alexandria, Virginia: 437 North Lee Street.
Telephone: 703-549-1294.
In San Francisco, California: One Sansome Street, Suite 2000.
Telephone: 415-951-4705.

PARTNERS

William J. Conti	Mario V. Mirabelli

For Complete List of Firm Personnel, See General Section

For full biographical listings, see the Martindale-Hubbell Law Directory

∗ BELL, BOYD & LLOYD (AV)

1615 L Street, N.W., 20036
Telephone: 202-466-6300
FAX: 202-463-0678
Chicago, Illinois Office: Three First National Plaza, Suite 3300, 70 West Madison Street.
Telephone: 312-372-1121.
FAX: 312-372-2098.

(See Next Column)

RESIDENT PARTNER

Henry M. Polmer

For Complete List of Firm Personnel, See General Section

For full biographical listings, see the Martindale-Hubbell Law Directory

CAMERON & HORNBOSTEL, L.L.P. (AV)

Suite 700, 818 Connecticut Avenue, N.W., 20006
Telephone: 202-293-4690
Cable Address: "Continent"
Telecopier: 202-293-1877
Email: camhorn@ix.netcom.com
New York, N.Y. Office: 230 Park Avenue.
Telephone: 212-682-4902.
Cable Address: "Continents, New York".
Telecopier: 212-697-0946.

MEMBERS OF FIRM

Duncan H. Cameron	Alexander W. Sierck
Bertrand J. Delanney (Resident, New York, N.Y. Office)	Frederick Simpich
Peter A. Hornbostel	Larry W. Thomas
William K. Ince	Howard L. Vickery (Resident, New York, N.Y. Office)
Dennis James, Jr.	Bruce Zagaris

ASSOCIATES

Zoe J. Bercovitch (Resident, New York, N.Y. Office)	Theodore R. Lazo
	Michele C. Sherman
David M. Schwartz	

OF COUNSEL

Carolyn W. Davenport (Resident, New York, N.Y. Office)	Richard C. Katz (Not admitted in DC)
	Geoffrey H. Ward (Resident, New York, N.Y. Office)
Stephen M. Wallenstein	

For full biographical listings, see the Martindale-Hubbell Law Directory

FRIEDLANDER, MISLER, FRIEDLANDER, SLOAN & HERZ (AV)

Suite 700, 1101 Seventeenth Street, N.W., 20036
Telephone: 202-872-0800
Cable Address: "FMSHLAW"
Telex: 64273
URL: http://www.dclawfirm.com

MEMBERS OF FIRM

Stephen H. Friedlander	Morris Kletzkin
Leonard A. Sloan	Jeffrey W. Ochsman
Gerald Herz	Jerome Ostrov
Jana Kay Guggenheim	

ASSOCIATES

Philippa T. Gasnier	Mark D. Crawford
Robert J. Strayhorne	Glenn W. D. Golding
Alan Dean Sundburg	Roberto L. Veloso
Todd S. Sapiro	

OF COUNSEL

Robert E. Greenberg

SPECIAL COUNSEL

Judith A. Hoggan

RETIRED

Jack L. Friedlander	Albert D. Misler

For full biographical listings, see the Martindale-Hubbell Law Directory

HOGAN & HARTSON L.L.P. (AV)

Columbia Square, 555 13th Street, N.W., 20004-1109
Telephone: 202-637-5600
Telex: 89-2757
Cable Address: "Hogander Washington"
Fax: 202-637-5910
Email: HHINFO@DC4.HHLAW.COM
Brussels, Belgium Office: Avenue des Arts 41, 1040.
Telephone: (32.2) 505.09.11.
Fax: (32.2) 505.09.96.
Budapest, Hungary Office: Bank Center, Granite Tower, 9th Floor, 1944 Budapest, Hungary.
Telephone: (36-1) 302-9050.
Fax: (36-1) 302-9060.
London, England Office: 21 Garlick Hill, EC4V 2AU.
Telephone: (44 171) 815 1200.
Fax: (44 171) 329 0299.
Moscow, Russia Office: 33/2 Usacheva Street, Building 3, 119048.
Telephone: (7095) 245-5190. Int'l
Telephone: (7501-907-0451).
Fax: (7095) 245-5192.
Fax: (7501) 907-0462 (International).
Paris, France (Affiliated Office): Cariddi, Mee, Rué, Avocats Associés à la Cour de Paris, 12, rue de la Paix, 75002.
Telephone: (33-1) 42.61.57.71.
Fax: (33-1) 42.61.79.21.

(See Next Column)

HOGAN & HARTSON L.L.P.—*Continued*

Prague, Czech Republic Office: Opletalova 37, 110 00.
Telephone: (42-2) 2422-9009.
Fax: (42-2) 2421-5105.
Warsaw, Poland Office: Marszalkowska 6/6, 00-590.
Telephone: (48 22) 628 0201; Int'l (48) 3912 1413.
Fax: (48 22) 628 7787; Int'l (48) 3912 1511.
Baltimore, Maryland Office: 111 South Calvert Street, 16th Floor.
Telephone: 410-659-2700.
Fax: 410-539-6981.
Bethesda, Maryland Office: Two Democracy Center, Suite 720, 6903 Rockledge Drive.
Telephone: 301-564-5000.
Fax: 301-493-5169.
Colorado Springs, Colorado Office: Two North Cascade Avenue, Suite 1300.
Telephone: 719-448-5900.
Fax: 719-448-5922.
Denver, Colorado Office: One Tabor Center, Suite 1500, 1200 Seventeenth Street.
Telephone: 303-899-7300.
Fax: 303-899-7333.
McLean, Virginia Office: 8300 Greensboro Drive.
Telephone: 703-848-2600.
Fax: 703-448-7650.

MEMBERS OF FIRM

Michael D. Colglazier (Resident, Baltimore, Maryland Office)	David P. King (Resident, Baltimore, Maryland Office)
Edward C. Dolan	Duncan S. Klinedinst (Resident, McLean, Virginia Office)
Robert J. Elliott	Kathleen M. Miko
Kevin G. Gralley (Resident, Baltimore, Maryland Office)	Craig H. Ulman
Benton R. Hammond	Pamela G. Winthrop
J. Clinton Kelly (Resident, Baltimore, Maryland Office)	

COUNSEL
Susan E. Joseph

ASSOCIATE
Helen P. McClure

For Complete List of Firm Personnel, See General Section

For full biographical listings, see the Martindale-Hubbell Law Directory

---

HOUSLEY KANTARIAN & BRONSTEIN, P.C. (AV)

Suite 700, 1220 19th Street, N.W., 20036
Telephone: 202-822-9611
Facsimile: 202-822-0140
URL: http://www.hkb.com

Allan D. Housley (Not admitted in DC)	Howard S. Parris
Harry K. Kantarian	James C. Stewart
Leonard S. Volin	Joseph Mark Poerio (Not admitted in DC)
Gary R. Bronstein	K. Scott Fife

Cynthia Rebecca Cross

Joel E. Rappoport	Kathleen K. H. Kim
Joan S. Guilfoyle (Not admitted in DC)	Julie D. Keegan (Not admitted in DC)
Daniel Lee Hogans (Not admitted in DC)	Evan M. Seigel

For full biographical listings, see the Martindale-Hubbell Law Directory

---

MULDOON, MURPHY & FAUCETTE (AV)

5101 Wisconsin Avenue, N.W., 20016
Telephone: 202-362-0840
Telecopier: 202-966-9409; 202-363-5068

MEMBERS OF FIRM

Joseph A. Muldoon, Jr.	Richard V. Fitzgerald
George W. Murphy, Jr.	Joseph G. Passaic, Jr.
Douglas P. Faucette	Joseph P. Daly
John R. Hall	Mary M. Jackley Sjoquist
Thomas J. Haggerty (Not admitted in DC)	Lori M. Beresford
	Christina M. Gattuso

ASSOCIATES

Leslie Murphy	Kent M. Krudys
Ann E. Cox	Philip G. Feigen
Cynthia M. Krus (Not admitted in DC)	Marc Paul Levy
William E. Donnelly	Gwen Mulberry Morris
Lawrence M. F. Spaccasi (Not admitted in DC)	Geoffrey W. Ryan (Not admitted in DC)
Patricia A. Murphy (Not admitted in DC)	Thomas W. France (Not admitted in DC)

OF COUNSEL
Mary V. Harcar

For full biographical listings, see the Martindale-Hubbell Law Directory

---

TIMOTHY D. NAEGELE & ASSOCIATES (AV)

Suite 300, 1250 24th Street, N.W., 20037
Telephone: 202-466-7500
Facsimile: 202-466-3079 or 466-2888
Email: naegelewdc@aol.com *URL:* http://www.naegele.com
Los Angeles, California Office: Suite 2430, 1900 Avenue of the Stars, 90067.
Telephone: 310-557-2300.
Facsimile: 310-457-4014. Internet Web Site: http://www.naegele.com.
Internet E-mail: naegelewdc@aol.com.

ASSOCIATE
Ashley Gauthier (Not admitted in DC)

LEGAL SUPPORT PERSONNEL

LAW CLERKS

Robert C. Kersey (Not admitted in DC)	Kurt D. Naegele
	Darren H. Lubetzky

For full biographical listings, see the Martindale-Hubbell Law Directory

---

* VENABLE ATTORNEYS AT LAW VENABLE, BAETJER, HOWARD & CIVILETTI, LLP (AV)

A Partnership including Professional Corporations
Suite 1000, 1201 New York Avenue, N.W., 20005
Telephone: 202-962-4800
Fax: 202-962-8300
Baltimore, Maryland Office: Venable, Baetjer and Howard LLP, 1800 Mercantile Bank & Trust Building, 2 Hopkins Plaza.
Telephone: 410-244-7400.
McLean, Virginia Office: Venable, Baetjer and Howard LLP, Suite 400, 2010 Corporate Ridge.
Telephone: 703-760-1600.
Rockville, Maryland Office: Venable, Baetjer and Howard LLP, Suite 500, One Church Street, P. O. Box 1906.
Telephone: 301-217-5600.
Towson, Maryland Office: Venable, Baetjer and Howard LLP, 210 Allegheny Avenue, P. O. Box 5517.
Telephone: 410-494-6200.

MEMBERS OF FIRM

Benjamin R. Civiletti (P.C.) (Also at Baltimore and Towson, Maryland Offices)	Jeffrey A. Dunn (Also at Baltimore, Maryland Office)
Ronald R. Glancz	George F. Pappas (Also at Baltimore, Maryland Office)
David J. Levenson	James L. Shea (Not admitted in DC; also at Baltimore, Maryland Office)
Joe A. Shull	
Kenneth C. Bass, III (Also at McLean, Virginia Office)	William D. Quarles (Also at Towson, Maryland Office)
Edward F. Glynn, Jr.	James A. Dunbar (Also at Baltimore, Maryland Office)
Thomas B. Hudson (Also at Baltimore, Maryland Office)	Bruce H. Jurist (Also at Baltimore, Maryland Office)
James R. Myers	

ASSOCIATES

David S. Darland	Andrew R. Herrup

For Complete List of Firm Personnel, See General Section

For full biographical listings, see the Martindale-Hubbell Law Directory

---

WILMER, CUTLER & PICKERING (AV)

2445 M Street, N.W., 20037-1420
Telephone: 202-663-6000
Fax: 202-663-6363
Email: Law@Wilmer.Com
Baltimore, Maryland Office: 100 Light Street, 21202.
Telephone: 410-986-2800.
Fax: 410-986-2828.
European Offices:
4 Carlton Gardens, London, SW1Y 5AA, England. Telephone: +44 (171) 872-1000.
Fax: +44 (171) 839-3537.
Rue de la Loi 15Wetstraat, B-1040 Brussels, Belgium. Telephone: +32 (2) 285-4900.
Fax: +32 (2) 285-4949.
Friedrichstrasse 95, D-10117 Berlin, Germany. Telephone: +49 (30) 2022-6400.
Fax: +49 (30)2022-6500.

MEMBERS OF FIRM

Ronald J. Greene	Christopher R. Lipsett
Michael S. Helfer	Russell J. Bruemmer

COUNSEL

Marc R. Cohen	Murray A. Indick
	Thomas J. Delaney

For Complete List of Firm Personnel, See General Section

For full biographical listings, see the Martindale-Hubbell Law Directory

FLORIDA

FORT MYERS,* Lee Co.

SMOOT ADAMS EDWARDS & GREEN, P.A. (AV)

One University Park Suite 600, 12800 University Drive, P.O. Box 60259, 33906-6259
Telephone: 941-489-1776
(800) 226-1777 (in Florida)
Fax: 941-489-2444
Email: 71600.2745@compuserve.com

J. Tom Smoot, Jr.	Bruce D. Green
Hal Adams	Steven I. Winer
Franklyn A. (Chip) Johnson	Mark R. Komray
(1947-1991)	Clayton W. Crevasse
Charles B. Edwards	M. Brian Cheffer

Robert S. Forman	C. Berk Edwards, Jr.
Kathleen W. McBride	Melville G. Brinson, III
Lowell Schoenfeld	Samuel J. Hagan, IV.

For full biographical listings, see the Martindale-Hubbell Law Directory

KISSIMMEE,* Osceola Co.

POHL & SHORT, P.A.

(See Winter Park)

LAKELAND, Polk Co.

PETERSON & MYERS, P.A. (AV)

100 East Main Street, P.O. Box 24628, 33802-4628
Telephone: 941-683-6511; 676-6934
Telecopier: 941-682-8031
Lake Wales, Florida Office: 130 East Central Avenue, P.O. Box 1079.
Telephones: 941-676-7611; 683-8942.
Winter Haven, Florida Office: Suite 300, 141 5th Street, N.W., P.O. Drawer 7608.
Telephone: 941-294-3360.

Philip O. Allen	Peter J. Munson
Jack P. Brandon	Corneal B. Myers
Beach A Brooks, Jr.	Cornelius B. Myers, III
Kristen Marie Buzzanca	E. Blake Paul
J. Davis Connor	Robert E. Puterbaugh
Michael S. Craig	Abel A. Putnam
Roy A. Craig, Jr.	Thomas B. Putnam, Jr.
Jacob C. Dykxhoorn	Deborah A. Ruster
Dennis P. Johnson	Stephen R. Senn
Kevin C. Knowlton	Andrea Teves Smith
Douglas A. Lockwood, III	Keith H. Wadsworth
M. Craig Massey	Kerry M. Wilson

General Counsel for: Barnett Bank of Polk County.
Representative Clients: Mutual Wholesale Co.; Barnett Banks, Inc.; Ben Hill Griffin, Inc.; Alcoma Association, Inc.
Approved Attorneys for: Equitable Life Assurance Society of the United States; Federal Land Bank, Columbia, South Carolina; Attorneys' Title Insurance Fund.

For full biographical listings, see the Martindale-Hubbell Law Directory

LAKE WALES, Polk Co.

PETERSON & MYERS, P.A. (AV)

130 East Central Avenue, P.O. Box 1079, 33853
Telephone: 941-676-7611; 683-8942
Telecopier: 941-676-0643
Lakeland, Florida Office: 100 East Main Street, P.O. Box 24628.
Telephones: 941-683-6511; 676-6934.
Winter Haven, Florida Office: Suite 300, 141 5th Street, N.W., P.O. Drawer 7608.
Telephone: 941-294-3360.

Philip O. Allen	Peter J. Munson
Jack P. Brandon	Corneal B. Myers
Beach A Brooks, Jr.	Cornelius B. Myers, III
Kristen Marie Buzzanca	E. Blake Paul
J. Davis Connor	Robert E. Puterbaugh
Michael S. Craig	Abel A. Putnam
Roy A. Craig, Jr.	Thomas B. Putnam, Jr.
Jacob C. Dykxhoorn	Deborah A. Ruster
Dennis P. Johnson	Stephen R. Senn
Kevin C. Knowlton	Andrea Teves Smith
Douglas A. Lockwood, III	Keith H. Wadsworth
M. Craig Massey	Kerry M. Wilson

General Counsel for: Barnett Bank of Polk County.
Representative Clients: Mutual Wholesale Co.; Barnett Banks, Inc.; Ben Hill Griffin, Inc.; Alcoma Association, Inc.
Approved Attorneys for: Equitable Life Assurance Society of the United States; Federal Land Bank, Columbia, South Carolina; Attorneys' Title Insurance Fund.

(See Next Column)

For full biographical listings, see the Martindale-Hubbell Law Directory

MIAMI,* Dade Co.

KANTOR, SAPURSTEIN & BLOCH, P.A. (AV)

Suite 1000, 9700 South Dixie Highway, 33156
Telephone: 305-670-9500
Telecopier: 305-670-6900

Charles Kantor	Bertram A. Sapurstein
	Bruce E. Bloch

For full biographical listings, see the Martindale-Hubbell Law Directory

KEITH, MACK, LEWIS, COHEN & LUMPKIN (AV)

First Union Financial Center, Twentieth Floor, 200 South Biscayne Boulevard, 33131-2310
Telephone: 305-358-7605
Fax: 305-358-4755
Email: PREVAIL@KEITHMACK.COM

MEMBERS OF FIRM

Edgar Lewis	Jan Carson Cheezem
Robert A. Cohen	Loren S. Granoff
R. Hugh Lumpkin	Jack S. Lewis
Gregg S. Ahrens	Alan Rosenthal
	Norman S. Segall

ASSOCIATES

Michael J. Hogsten	Michele S. Primeau
Felix M. Lasarte	Cynthia Ramos
Dawn Marshall	Jack R. Reiter
Mercedes Padin	Karl J. Schumer
	Jeffrey P. Shapiro

OF COUNSEL

Seymour D. Keith	James L. Mack

Representative Clients: CitiBank, F.S.B.; Attorneys Title Insurance Fund, Inc.; Barnett Bank, N.A.
Approved Counsel: First American Title Insurance Co.; Attorneys Title Insurance Fund, Inc.; Commonwealth Title Insurance Co.
Reference: CitiBank, F.S.B.

For full biographical listings, see the Martindale-Hubbell Law Directory

NAPLES,* Collier Co.

QUARLES & BRADY (AV)

Barnett Center, 4501 Tamiami Trail North Suite 300, 33940-3060
Telephone: 941-262-5959
Fax: 941-434-4999
Milwaukee, Wisconsin Office: 411 East Wisconsin Avenue, 53202-4497.
Telephone: 414-277-5000.
Fax: 414-271-3552.
Madison, Wisconsin Office: Firstar Plaza, One South Pinckney Street, P.O. Box 2113, 53701-2113.
Telephone: 608-251-5000.
Fax: 608-251-9166.
West Palm Beach, Florida Office: 222 Lakeview Avenue, 4th Floor, 33401.
Telephone: 561-653-5000.
Fax: 561-653-5333.
Phoenix, Arizona Office: One Camelback Building, One East Camelback Road, Suite 400, 85012-1649.
Telephone: 602-230-5500.
Fax: 602-230-5598.

PARTNERS

F. Joseph McMackin, III	Timothy G. Hains

ASSOCIATE

John D. Humphreville

For Complete List of Firm Personnel, See General Section

For full biographical listings, see the Martindale-Hubbell Law Directory

ORLANDO,* Orange Co.

POHL & SHORT, P.A.

(See Winter Park)

SARASOTA,* Sarasota Co.

WILLIAMS, PARKER, HARRISON, DIETZ & GETZEN, PROFESSIONAL ASSOCIATION (AV)

200 South Orange Avenue, 34236-6749
Telephone: 941-366-4800
Telecopier: 941-366-5109
Mailing Address: P.O. Box 3258, Sarasota, Florida, 34230-3258
Email: wphdg.law@netsrg.com *URL:*
http://www.sarasota-online.com/williamspa-w

(See Next Column)

WILLIAMS, PARKER, HARRISON, DIETZ & GETZEN PROFESSIONAL
ASSOCIATION—*Continued*

J.J. Williams, Jr. (1886-1968)	Frank Strelec
W. Davis Parker (1920-1982)	Terri Salt Costa
William T. Harrison, Jr.	David A. Wallace
George A. Dietz	Mark A. Schwartz
Monte K. Marshall	Ric Gregoria
James L. Ritchey	Elvin W. Phillips
William G. Lambrecht	Jeffrey A. Grebe
John T. Berteau	John L. Moore
John V. Cannon, III	Morgan R. Bentley
Charles D. Bailey, Jr.	Susan A. Barrett
J. Michael Hartenstine	Carol Ann Kalish
Michele Boardman Grimes	Linda R. Getzen
James L. Turner	Kimberly J. Page
William M. Seider	Phillip D. Eck
Elizabeth C. Marshall	J. Hugh Middlebrooks
Robert W. Benjamin	Robert A. Warram

OF COUNSEL

William E. Getzen	Frazer F. Hilder

Hugh McPheeters, Jr.

LEGAL SUPPORT PERSONNEL

Mark Loveridge (Land Planner)

General Counsel for: Sarasota County Public Hospital Board; Sarasota-Manatee Airport Authority; Taylor Woodrow Homes Ltd.; FCCI Mutual Insurance Co.
Local Counsel for: NationsBank of Florida; Barnett Bank of Southwest Florida; Northern Trust Bank of Florida; SunTrust Bank, Gulfcoast.

For full biographical listings, see the Martindale-Hubbell Law Directory

---

TALLAHASSEE,* Leon Co.

DAVIS & TAFF (AV)

210 East College Avenue, Suite 200, P.O. Box 37190, 32315-7190
Telephone: 904-222-6026
Telecopier: 904-224-1039

MEMBERS OF FIRM

Ken Davis	Angus Broward Taff, Jr.

For full biographical listings, see the Martindale-Hubbell Law Directory

---

TAMPA,* Hillsborough Co.

MORRISON, MORRISON & MILLS, P.A. (AV)

1200 West Platt Street Suite 100, 33606
Telephone: 813-258-3311
Telecopier: 813-258-3209

Thomas K. Morrison	Frederick J. Mills
Susan B. Morrison	James E. Holmes, Jr.

Representative Clients: SouthTrust Bank of West Florida; SouthTrust Bank of Alabama, National Association; NationsBank of Florida, N.A.; Mercantile Bank; Barnett Banks, Inc.; Southern Commerce Bank; Sun Bank of Pasco County; Hillsborough County Industrial Development Authority; Automation Packaging, Inc.; Medical Data Management, Inc.

For full biographical listings, see the Martindale-Hubbell Law Directory

---

WINTER HAVEN, Polk Co.

PETERSON & MYERS, P.A. (AV)

Suite 300, 141 5th Street N.W., P.O. Drawer 7608, 33883-7608
Telephone: 941-294-3360
Lake Wales, Florida Office: 130 East Central Avenue, P.O. Box 1079.
Telephones: 941-676-7611; 683-8942.
Lakeland, Florida Office: 100 East Main Street, P.O. Box 24628.
Telephones: 941-683-6511; 676-6934.

Philip O. Allen	Peter J. Munson
Jack P. Brandon	Corneal B. Myers
Beach A Brooks, Jr.	Cornelius B. Myers, III
Kristen Marie Buzzanca	E. Blake Paul
J. Davis Connor	Robert E. Puterbaugh
Michael S. Craig	Abel A. Putnam
Roy A. Craig, Jr.	Thomas B. Putnam, Jr.
Jacob C. Dykxhoorn	Deborah A. Ruster
Dennis P. Johnson	Stephen R. Senn
Kevin C. Knowlton	Andrea Teves Smith
Douglas A. Lockwood, III	Keith H. Wadsworth
M. Craig Massey	Kerry M. Wilson

General Counsel for: Barnett Bank of Polk County.
Representative Clients: Mutual Wholesale Co.; Barnett Banks, Inc.; Ben Hill Griffin, Inc.; Alcoma Association, Inc.
Approved Attorneys for: Attorneys' Title Insurance Fund; Federal Land Bank, Columbia, South Carolina; Equitable Life Assurance Society of the United States.

For full biographical listings, see the Martindale-Hubbell Law Directory

---

WINTER PARK, Orange Co.

POHL & SHORT, P.A. (AV)

280 West Canton Avenue, Suite 410, P.O. Box 3208, 32790
Telephone: 407-647-7645; 407-647-POHL
Telefax: 407-647-2314

Frank L. Pohl	C. Teresa de Arrigoitia
Houston E. Short	George A. Golder
Dwight I. Cool	Norma Stanley
James Everett Shepherd V	Mark W. Garrett

John R. Simpson, Jr.

Representative Clients: American Pioneer Title Insurance Company; Institute of Internal Auditors, Inc.; Thompson Steel, Inc.; SunTrust, N.A.; The Bank of Winter Park; Bekins Moving and Storage Co., Inc.; Champion Boats, Inc.; KeyCom Telephone Systems, Inc.

For full biographical listings, see the Martindale-Hubbell Law Directory

---

GEORGIA

ALBANY,* Dougherty Co.

PERRY & WALTERS (AV)

409-411 North Jackson Street, P.O. Box 469, 31702-0469
Telephone: 912-432-7438; 432-7481
Telecopier: 912-436-1417
Other Albany, Georgia Office: 503 North Jackson Street, P.O. Box 445, 31702-0445.
Telephone: 912-432-9960.

MEMBERS OF FIRM

R. Edgar Campbell	Samuel Brown Lippitt, Jr.
Keith T. Dorough	R. Kelly Raulerson
Richard W. Fields	James E. Reynolds, Jr.

Edgar B. Wilkin, Jr.

OF COUNSEL

H. H. Perry, Jr.	Jesse W. Walters

Division Counsel for: Seaboard Coast Line Railroad Co.
General Counsel for: First State Bank & Trust Co.; Carlton Co.; Bob's Candies, Inc.; Alcon Associates, Inc.; Albany-Dougherty County Hospital Authority.
Representative Clients: Merck & Co., Inc.; CNA Insurance; Chrysler Credit Corp.

For full biographical listings, see the Martindale-Hubbell Law Directory

---

ATLANTA,* Fulton Co.

ALSTON & BIRD (AV)

A Partnership including Professional Corporations
One Atlantic Center, 1201 West Peachtree Street, 30309-3424
Telephone: 404-881-7000
Telecopier: 404-881-7777
Cable Address: AMGRAM GA
Telex: 54-2996
Easylink: 62985848
Washington, D.C. Office: 601 Pennsylvania Ave., N.W., North Building, Suite 250 20004.
Telephone: 202-508-3300.
Telecopier: 202-508-3333.

MEMBERS OF FIRM

B. Harvey Hill, Jr.	Laura Glover Thatcher
F. Dean Copeland	Frank M. Conner III
John L. Douglas	Ira H. Parker
Ralph F. MacDonald III	David E. Brown, Jr.
John A. Buchman (Not admitted in GA)	

ASSOCIATES

W. Thomas Carter III	Michael L. Stevens
Kathryn M. Cole (Not admitted in GA)	Jonathan H. Talcott (Not admitted in GA)
Randolph A. Moore III	Susan J. Wilson

Robert Y. Wood III

Representative Clients: AFLAC, Inc.; Bear, Stearns & Co., Inc.; Centura Banks, Inc.; Citibank Corporation; First Union Corporation; Fortis, Inc.; Provident Life & Accident Insurance Company; Raymond James & Associates; Regions Financial Corporation; Robinson-Humphrey Company, Inc.; Wheat First Securities, Inc.

For Complete List of Firm Personnel, See General Section

For full biographical listings, see the Martindale-Hubbell Law Directory

Atlanta—Continued

LONG ALDRIDGE & NORMAN, LLP (AV)

A Limited Liability Partnership including Professional Corporations
One Peachtree Center, Suite 5300, 303 Peachtree Street, 30308
Telephone: 404-527-4000
Telecopier: 404-527-4198
Washington, D.C. Office: Suite 600, 701 Pennsylvania Avenue, N.W., 20004.
Telephone: 202-624-1200.
FAX: 202-624-1298.

MEMBERS OF FIRM

John G. Aldridge	C. Edward Kuntz
Thomas D. Hall	Patrick M. McGeehan

ASSOCIATES

Charles D. Weiss	John F. Woodham

OF COUNSEL

James W. Culbreth	Gerald D. Walling

For Complete List of Firm Personnel, See General Section

For full biographical listings, see the Martindale-Hubbell Law Directory

SUTHERLAND, ASBILL & BRENNAN, L.L.P. (AV)

999 Peachtree Street, N.E., 30309-3996
Telephone: 404-853-8000
Facsimile: 404-853-8806
Email: postmaster@sablaw.com
Washington, D.C. Office: 1275 Pennsylvania Avenue, N.W., 20004-2404.
Telephone: 202-383-0100.
New York, N.Y. Office: 600 Madison Avenue, 11th Floor, 10022-1615.
Telephone: 212-605-6400.
Austin, Texas Office: 111 Congress Avenue, 23rd Floor, 78701-4079.
Telephone: 512-469-3350.

Peter H. Dean	Edward W. Kallal, Jr.
B. Knox Dobbins	Mark D. Kaufman
Peter A. Fozzard	Richard G. Murphy, Jr.
Thomas B. Hyman, Jr.	Haynes R. Roberts

For Complete List of Firm Personnel, See General Section

For full biographical listings, see the Martindale-Hubbell Law Directory

---

AUGUSTA,* Richmond Co.

CAPERS, DUNBAR, SANDERS & BRUCKNER (AV)

Fifteenth Floor, First Union Bank Building, 30901-1454
Telephone: 706-722-7542
Telecopier: 706-724-7776

MEMBERS OF FIRM

John D. Capers	E. Frederick Sanders
Paul H. Dunbar, III	Ziva P. Bruckner

ASSOCIATE

Carl P. Dowling

For full biographical listings, see the Martindale-Hubbell Law Directory

WARLICK, TRITT & STEBBINS (AV)

15th Floor, First Union Bank Building, 30901
Telephone: 706-722-7543
Fax: 706-722-1822
Columbia County Office: 119 Davis Road, Martinez, Georgia 30907.
Telephone: 706-860-7595.
Fax: 706-860-7597.

MEMBERS OF FIRM

William Byrd Warlick	Charles C. Stebbins, III
Roy D. Tritt	E. L. Clark Speese
(Resident, Martinez Office)	

ASSOCIATES

D. Scott Broyles	C. Gregory Bryan
Robert C. Threlkeld	

OF COUNSEL

Richard E. Miley

For full biographical listings, see the Martindale-Hubbell Law Directory

---

COLUMBUS,* Muscogee Co.

DAVIDSON, CALHOUN, MILLER & BUEHLER, P.C. (AV)

The Joseph House, 828 Broadway, P.O. Box 2828, 31902-2828
Telephone: 706-327-2552
Telecopier: 706-323-5838

J. Quentin Davidson, Jr.	Charles W. Miller
H. Owen Lee	

For Complete List of Firm Personnel, See General Section

For full biographical listings, see the Martindale-Hubbell Law Directory

---

HATCHER, STUBBS, LAND, HOLLIS & ROTHSCHILD (AV)

A Limited Liability Partnership
Suite 500 The Corporate Center, 233 12th Street, P.O. Box 2707, 31902-2707
Telephone: 706-324-0201
Telecopier: 706-322-7747

MEMBERS OF FIRM

Albert W. Stubbs	George W. Mize, Jr.
William B. Hardegree	John M. Tanzine, III
J. Barrington Vaught	Alan F. Rothschild, Jr.
Mote W. Andrews III	

General Counsel for: SunTrust Bank, West Georgia, N.A.; TOM'S Foods Inc.; Muscogee County Board of Education; Kinnett Dairies, Inc.; St. Francis Hospital, Inc.
Local Counsel for: First Union National Bank of Georgia.

For Complete List of Firm Personnel, See General Section

For full biographical listings, see the Martindale-Hubbell Law Directory

---

GRIFFIN,* Spalding Co.

ROBERT H. SMALLEY, JR. PROFESSIONAL CORPORATION (AV)

115 North Sixth Street, P.O. Box 907, 30224
Telephone: 770-228-2125
Telecopier: 770-228-5018

Robert H. Smalley, Jr.	Thomas E. Baynham, III

Representative Clients: The Bank Holding Company; The Bank of Spalding County; First Community Bank of Henry County; Griffin Spalding County Development Authority; Masada Communications, Ltd. (CATV); Union Camp Corp. (Local Counsel).

For full biographical listings, see the Martindale-Hubbell Law Directory

---

LAWRENCEVILLE,* Gwinnett Co.

ANDERSEN, DAVIDSON & TATE, P.C. (AV)

324 West Pike Street, Suite 200, P.O. Box 2000, 30246-2000
Telephone: 770-822-0900
Telecopier: 770-822-9680

Thomas J. Andersen	Jeffrey R. Mahaffey

References: Sun Trust Bank; The Bank of Gwinnett County; Embry National Bank; Chicago Title Insurance Co.; Title Insurance Company of Minnesota; Lawyers Title Insurance Co.

For Complete List of Firm Personnel, See General Section

For full biographical listings, see the Martindale-Hubbell Law Directory

---

WEBB, TANNER & POWELL (AV)

Suite 300 Gwinnett Federal Building, 750 South Perry Street, P.O. Box 27, 30246
Telephone: 770-962-8545; 963-3423
Fax: 770-963-3424

MEMBERS OF FIRM

Jones Webb	Anthony O. L. Powell
William G. Tanner	Ralph L. Taylor, III
Andrew R. Mertz	

Attorneys for: Brand Banking Co.; City of Lawrenceville, Ga.; Water and Sewer Authority of Gwinnett County; Federal Land Bank of Columbia; Georgia Power Co.; Lawyers Title Insurance Corp.; Young Harris College, Young Harris, Georgia; Chicago Title Insurance Co.; Federal Home Loan Mortgage Corp.; International Safety Instruments.

For Complete List of Firm Personnel, See General Section

For full biographical listings, see the Martindale-Hubbell Law Directory

---

MACON,* Bibb Co.

HALL, BLOCH, GARLAND & MEYER (AV)

1500 Charter Medical Building, P.O. Box 5088, 31213-3199
Telephone: 912-745-1625
Telecopier: 912-741-8822

MEMBERS OF FIRM

J. E. Hall (1876-1945)	Benjamin M. Garland
Charles J. Bloch (1893-1974)	J. Patrick Meyer, Jr.
Ellsworth Hall, Jr. (1908-1984)	J. Steven Stewart
J. René Hawkins (1924-1971)	J. Burton Wilkerson, Jr.
Ellsworth Hall, III	Duncan D. Walker, III
F. Kennedy Hall	Mark E. Toth

ASSOCIATES

John Flanders Kennedy	Todd C. Brooks

F. Kennedy Hall, Division Counsel (Georgia): Norfolk Southern Railway Company.
Counsel for: Wachovia Bank of Georgia, N.A.; Helena Chemical Corp.; Fickling & Walker Asset and Property Management, Inc.; Navistar International Corporation.

(See Next Column)

HALL, BLOCH, GARLAND & MEYER—*Continued*

For Complete List of Firm Personnel, See General Section

For full biographical listings, see the Martindale-Hubbell Law Directory

---

SELL & MELTON (AV)

A Partnership including a Professional Corporation
14th Floor, Charter Medical Building, P.O. Box 229, 31297-2899
Telephone: 912-746-8521
Telecopier: 912-745-6426

Andrew W. McKenna	Joseph W. Popper, Jr.
(1918-1981)	Doye E. Green
E. S. Sell, Jr.	Edward S. Sell, III
John D. Comer	John A. Draughon
Buckner F. Melton	R. (Chix) Miller
Mitchel P. House, Jr.	Russell M. Boston (P.C.)

Brian J. Passante
ASSOCIATE
Jeffrey B. Hanson

General Counsel for: Macon Telegraph Publishing Co. (The Macon Telegraph); Macon-Bibb County Hospital Authority; County of Bibb; County of Twiggs; Smith & Sons Foods, Inc. (S & S Cafeterias); Macon Bibb County Industrial Authority; Burgess Pigment Co.

For Complete List of Firm Personnel, See General Section

For full biographical listings, see the Martindale-Hubbell Law Directory

---

MARIETTA, * Cobb Co.

BARNES, BROWNING, TANKSLEY & CASURELLA (AV)

Suite 225, 166 Anderson Street, 30060
Telephone: 770-424-1500
Fax: 770-424-1740

MEMBERS OF FIRM

Roy E. Barnes	Jerry A. Landers, Jr.
Thomas J. Browning	Jeffrey G. Casurella

OF COUNSEL

George T. Smith	Howard D. Rothbloom

For full biographical listings, see the Martindale-Hubbell Law Directory

---

TUCKER, De Kalb Co.

HOTZ & ASSOCIATES, P.C. (AV)

Suite 200, 1979 Lakeside Parkway, 30084
Telephone: 770-939-4861
Fax: 770-270-9749

Richard F. Taylor (1921-1993)	J. Tyler Tippett
Walter H. Hotz	James H. Baskin

Representative Clients: Regional Counsel for GE Supply, a Division of General Electric Company; Atlanta Postal Credit Union; CDC Federal Credit Union; Federal Employees Credit Union; Georgia Federal Credit Union; Peachtree Federal Credit Union; Deutsche Steinindustrie A.G.; Destag of North America, Inc.; General Trailer Services, Inc.; The Network Connection, Inc.

For full biographical listings, see the Martindale-Hubbell Law Directory

HAWAII

HONOLULU, * Honolulu Co.

CADES SCHUTTE FLEMING & WRIGHT (AV)

Formerly Smith, Wild, Beebe & Cades
1000 Bishop Street, P.O. Box 939, 96808
Telephone: 808-521-9200
Telecopier: 808-531-8738
Email: cades@cades.com
Affiliated Law Firm: Udom-Prok Associates Law Offices, 105/36 Tharinee Mansion, Borom Raj Chananee Road Bangkoknoi, Bangkok, Thailand, 10700.
Telephone: 011 662 435-4146.
Kailua-Kona, Hawaii Office: Hualalai Center, Suite B-303, 75-170 Hualalai Road.
Telephone: 808-329-5811.
Telecopier: 808-326-1175.

MEMBERS OF FIRM

Robert B. Bunn	Philip J. Leas
E. Gunner Schull	Larry T. Takumi
Donald E. Scearce	Nelson N. S. Chun
Richard A. Hicks	Darryl H. W. Johnston
Bernice Littman	Cary S. Matsushige
Nicholas C. Dreher	Gino L. Gabrio
Mark A. Hazlett	Martin E. Hsia

(See Next Column)

MEMBERS OF FIRM (Continued)

Gail M. Tamashiro	Donna Y. L. Leong
Grace Nihei Kido	David F.E. Banks

ASSOCIATES

Jeffrey D. Watts	Carlito P. Caliboso
Laurie A. Kuribayashi	Daniel H. Devaney IV
Michele M. Sunahara	Karen Wong
Cynthia M. Johiro	Dean T. Yamamoto

Marc E. Rousseau
OF COUNSEL
Harold S. Wright

Counsel for: First Hawaiian Bank; The Bank of Tokyo, Ltd.; American Savings Bank, F.S.B.; The Industrial Bank of Japan, Ltd.

For Complete List of Firm Personnel, See General Section

For full biographical listings, see the Martindale-Hubbell Law Directory

---

CHING, YUEN & MORIKAWA (AV)

Pacific Tower, Suite 2700, 1001 Bishop Street, 96813
Telephone: 808-524-8880
Telecopier: 808-524-7664

MEMBERS OF FIRM

Russell L. Ching	William W. L. Yuen

Randall I. Morikawa
ASSOCIATE
Joyce T. Tamanaha

Representative Clients: Finance Enterprises, Ltd.; Finance Factors, Ltd.; Finance Realty, Ltd.; Gentry Pacific, Ltd.; Goldman, Sachs & Co.; The Hertz Corporation; Kamehamela Schools Bernice Pauahi Bishop Estate; Merrill Lynch & Co.; The Sakura Bank, Ltd.; Sen Plex Corp.

For full biographical listings, see the Martindale-Hubbell Law Directory

---

DWYER IMANAKA SCHRAFF KUDO MEYER & FUJIMOTO ATTORNEYS AT LAW, A LAW CORPORATION (AV)

1800 Pioneer Plaza, 900 Fort Street Mall, 96813
Telephone: 808-524-8000
Telecopier: 808-526-1419
Mailing Address: P.O. Box 2727, 96803
Email: hawaiilaw@dwyer-imanaka.com *URL:*
http://www.dwyer-imanaka.com

John R. Dwyer, Jr.	William G. Meyer, III
Mitchell A. Imanaka	Wesley M. Fujimoto
Paul A. Schraff	Ronald Van Grant
Benjamin A. Kudo (Atty. at	Jon M. H. Pang
Law, A Law Corp.)	Blake W. Bushnell

Adelbert Green

Richard T. Asato, Jr.	Jeffery S. Werbelow
Scott W. Settle	Lori Ann K. Koseki
Darcie S. Yoshinaga	Troy T. Fukuhara
Lawrence I. Kawasaki	Katy Y. Chen
Stacy E. Uehara	Naomi S. Uyeno
Kris N. Nakagawa	Roger B. McKeague

OF COUNSEL

Randall Y. Iwase	R. Brian Tsujimura

For full biographical listings, see the Martindale-Hubbell Law Directory

---

KESSNER DUCA UMEBAYASHI BAIN & MATSUNAGA ATTORNEYS AT LAW, A LAW CORPORATION (AV)

19th Floor, Central Pacific Plaza, 220 South King Street, 96813
Telephone: 808-536-1900
Telecopier: 808-529-7177
Telex: 723 8616 OPAC IIR

Robert C. Kessner	Elton John Bain
James N. Duca	Emma S. Matsunaga
Clyde S. Umebayashi	Muriel M. Taira

Beverly S. K. Tom	Melanie S. Ono
Jacqueline W.S. Amai	Darin P. Wright
Dawn Jordan	Cori Ann C. Yokota

For full biographical listings, see the Martindale-Hubbell Law Directory

IDAHO

BOISE,* Ada Co.

ELAM & BURKE, A PROFESSIONAL ASSOCIATION (AV)

Key Financial Center, 702 West Idaho Street, P.O. Box 1539, 83701
Telephone: 208-343-5454
Telecopier: 208-384-5844
Email: eblaw@elamburke.com

Randall A. Peterman   William J. Batt

Representative Clients: West One Bank; U.S. Bancorp; Wells Fargo Bank; Citizen's Community Bank.

For Complete List of Firm Personnel, See General Section

For full biographical listings, see the Martindale-Hubbell Law Directory

ILLINOIS

BELLEVILLE,* St. Clair Co.

McGLYNN & McGLYNN (AV)

65 South 65th Street, 62223
Telephone: 618-398-5112; 314-381-5112
Telecopier: 618-398-5189

MEMBERS OF FIRM
Robert E. McGlynn   James McGlynn
Joseph B. McGlynn, Jr.

ASSOCIATES
Michael L. McGlynn   Stephen P. McGlynn
Maureen A. McGlynn

LEGAL SUPPORT PERSONNEL
Lawrence L. McGlynn

For full biographical listings, see the Martindale-Hubbell Law Directory

BOLINGBROOK, Will Co.

MOSS AND BLOOMBERG, LTD. (AV)

305 West Briarcliff Road, Suite 201, P.O. Box 1158, 60440-0858
Telephone: 630-759-0800
Telecopier: 630-759-8504

Barry L. Moss   Steven P. Bloomberg
George A. Marchetti

David J. Freeman   Daniel C Shapiro
Norma J. Guess   Judson L. Strain

For full biographical listings, see the Martindale-Hubbell Law Directory

CHICAGO,* Cook Co.

ARONBERG GOLDGEHN DAVIS & GARMISA (AV)

Suite 3000 One IBM Plaza, 60611
Telephone: 312-828-9600
Telecopier: 312-828-9635

MEMBERS OF FIRM
Ronald J. Aronberg   Marc W. O'Brien
Melvin A. Blum   Ned S. Robertson
Young Kim   David H. Sachs
Nathan H. Lichtenstein   Robert N. Sodikoff
Andrew S. Williams

ASSOCIATE
Susan H. Mendelsohn

For Complete List of Firm Personnel, See General Section

For full biographical listings, see the Martindale-Hubbell Law Directory

BELL, BOYD & LLOYD (AV)

Three First National Plaza Suite 3300, 70 West Madison Street, 60602
Telephone: 312-372-1121
FAX: 312-372-2098
Email: bbl@bbl.com
Washington, D.C. Office: 1615 L Street, N.W.
Telephone: 202-466-6300.
FAX: 202-463-0678.

MEMBERS OF FIRM
Brian A. Bates   James P. Hemmer
Steven E. Ducommun   Patrick J. Maloney
Richard L. Sevcik

For Complete List of Firm Personnel, See General Section

For full biographical listings, see the Martindale-Hubbell Law Directory

BERMAN & YOTIS, A PROFESSIONAL ASSOCIATION (AV)

(A Professional Association comprised of Professional Corporations)
Suite 2215, 100 North La Salle Street, 60602
Telephone: 312-726-0531
Fax: 312-726-4928

Michael H. Berman (P.C.)   William W. Yotis, III, (P.C.)

Joy C. Airaudi   Dean J. Papadakis
Eric D. Kaplan   Dean Gournis

OF COUNSEL
Karen C. Yotis

For full biographical listings, see the Martindale-Hubbell Law Directory

BOEHM, PEARLSTEIN & BRIGHT, LTD. (AV)

33 North La Salle Street Suite 3500, 60602
Telephone: 312-782-7474
Fax: 312-782-0380

Robert I. Boehm   Gary I. Blackman
Mark D. Pearlstein   Roy D. Kessel
Steven Bright   Donna Richman
Konstantinos Armiros   Bryan I. Schwartz
William Scott Schwartz

Representative Clients: First Bank; Cole Taylor Bank; LaSalle National Bank; LaSalle Bank N.I.; The Northern Trust Company; Firstar Bank of Illinois; First Union National Bank of North Carolina; CB Commerical; Merrill Lynch Business Financial Services, Inc.

For full biographical listings, see the Martindale-Hubbell Law Directory

FAGEL & HABER (AV)

140 South Dearborn Street 14th Floor, 60603
Telephone: 312-346-7500
FAX: 312-580-2201
Telex No: 754542
Cable: "NOFLAWLAW"
URL: HTTP://WWW.FANDH.COM.

MEMBERS OF FIRM
Allen J. Fagel   Howard M. Berrington
Gina Marie Gentili

ASSOCIATES
Victor A. Des Laurier   Carole A. Morey

For full biographical listings, see the Martindale-Hubbell Law Directory

FIELD GOLAN & SWIGER (AV)

Three First National Plaza Twenty-First Floor, 60602-4206
Telephone: 312-263-2300
Fax: 312-263-0939

MEMBERS OF FIRM
Robert E. Field   Cynthia G. Swiger
Stephen L. Golan   Margaret A. Christie

ASSOCIATES
William J. Arendt   Margaret A. Gisch
Peter C. Quigley   Matthew J. Cozzi

OF COUNSEL
Leonard W. Golan   Stephen Edward Smith
Donna F. Hartl   Frank J. Dolan

For full biographical listings, see the Martindale-Hubbell Law Directory

McFADDEN & DILLON, A PROFESSIONAL CORPORATION (AV)

135 South La Salle Street, Suite 2110, 60603
Telephone: 312-201-8300
Facsimile: 312-201-0535

Roger J. McFadden   Thomas J. Dillon

Tyrrel J. Penn

For full biographical listings, see the Martindale-Hubbell Law Directory

POLLAK & HOFFMAN LTD. (AV)

Suite 1100, 150 North Wacker Drive, 60606
Telephone: 312-726-0001
FAX: 312-726-1098
Northbrook, Illinois Office: 1200 Shermer Road.
Telephone: 847-564-0130.
FAX: 847-564-0160.

Bertram L. Pollak   Michael E. Pollak
Jay M. Pollak   Bruce F. Hoffman
Lee J. Lewin

For full biographical listings, see the Martindale-Hubbell Law Directory

Chicago—Continued

VEDDER, PRICE, KAUFMAN & KAMMHOLZ (AV)

A Partnership including Vedder, Price, Kaufman & Kammholz, P.C.
222 North La Salle Street, 60601-1003
Telephone: 312-609-7500
Fax: 312-609-5005
New York, New York Office: Vedder, Price, Kaufman, Kammholz & Day, 805 Third Avenue.
Telephone: 212-407-7700.

MEMBERS OF FIRM

Robert J. Stucker	Dalius F. Vasys
Daniel O'Rourke	Thomas P. Desmond
John T. McEnroe	Douglas M. Hambleton
James M. Kane	Daniel C. McKay, II
Cathy G. O'Kelly	Dean N. Gerber
Michael A. Nemeroff	

ASSOCIATES

Lynne A. Gochanour	Dana Simaitis Armagno
Catherine A. Lemmer	Melissa J. Krasnow
Jeffrey C. Davis	Dahlia M. Ronen
Lane R. Moyer	Matthew T. O'Connor
William J. Bettman	Patrick J. Bruks

OF COUNSEL IN CHICAGO

William L. Conaghan

PARTNERS AT NEW YORK CITY

Donald A. Wassall	Ronald Scheinberg
Denise L. Blau	Alfrado D. Donelson

For Complete List of Firm Personnel, See General Section

For full biographical listings, see the Martindale-Hubbell Law Directory

---

MATTOON, Coles Co.

CRAIG & CRAIG (AV)

1807 Broadway, P.O. Box 689, 61938-0689
Telephone: 217-234-6481
Telecopier: 217-234-6486
Mount Vernon, Illinois Office: 227 1/2 South 9th Street.
Telephone: 618-244-7511.

MEMBERS OF FIRM

Craig Van Meter (1895-1981)	Stephen L. Corn
Fred H. Kelly (1894-1971)	Richard Charles Hayden
Robert M. Werden (1908-1969)	Robert G. Grierson
George N. Gilkerson	Gregory C. Ray
(1911-1985)	Paul R. Lynch (Resident, Mount
John H. Armstrong	Vernon Office)
John P. Ewart	Kenneth F. Werts (Resident,
Richard F. Record, Jr.	Mount Vernon Office)
John L. Barger	

ASSOCIATES

Joshua N. Rosen (Resident,	Theresa M. Thomson
Mount Vernon Office)	Kristine M. Tuttle
Kathleen M. Stockwell	Henry P. Villani (Resident,
	Mount Vernon Office)

OF COUNSEL

Jack E. Horsley

Counsel for: Monterey Coal Co., a Division of Exxon Coal USA, Inc.; Marathon Oil Co.; Illinois Central R.R. Co.; Okaw Building & Loan Assn., Mattoon, Illinois; The Medical Protective Insurance Co.; Consolidated Communications, Inc.; Lloyds Underwriters at London; Hartford Insurance Co.; Coles Together, a Not-For-Profit Corp.; Coles Building Corporation.

For full biographical listings, see the Martindale-Hubbell Law Directory

---

MOUNT VERNON,* Jefferson Co.

MITCHELL, NEUBAUER, SHAW & HANSON, P.C. (AV)

123 South 10th Street, Mercantile Bank Building, 6th Floor, P.O. Box 1088, 62864
Telephone: 618-242-0705
Telecopier: 618-242-4820

A. Ben Mitchell	Robert E. Shaw
Timothy R. Neubauer	Leslie James Hanson

Curtis W. Martin	T. David Purcell
Michael D. McHaney	David K. Overstreet

Attorneys For: Mercantile Bank of Mt. Vernon; Mt. Vernon Grade School District #80; Stewart Brothers Oil Producers; Illinois Super Foods, Inc.; Mt. Vernon Airport Authority; Henne Excavating & Construction.; J. M. Behimer Enterprises; Crossroads Community Hospital; Marion Ford-Mercury, Inc.

For full biographical listings, see the Martindale-Hubbell Law Directory

---

PEORIA,* Peoria Co.

HOWARD & HOWARD ATTORNEYS, P.C. (AV)

The Creve Coeur Building, Suite 200, 321 Liberty Street, 61602-1403
Telephone: 309-672-1483
Telecopier: 309-672-1568
Kalamazoo, Michigan Office: The Kalamazoo Building, Suite 400, 107 West Michigan Avenue.
Telephone: 616-382-1483.
Telecopier: 616-382-1568.
Bloomfield Hills, Michigan Office: The Pinehurst Office Center, Suite 101, 1400 North Woodward Avenue.
Telephone: 810-645-1483.
Telecopier: 810-645-1568.
Lansing, Michigan Office: Suite 500, The Phoenix Building, 222 Washington Square, North.
Telephone: 517-485-1483.
Telecopier: 517-485-1568.
Tampa, Florida Office: First of America Plaza, Suite 2000, 201 East Kennedy Boulevard.
Telephone: 813-229-1483.
Telecopier: 813-229-1568.

Stephen C. Ferlmann	Timothy J. Howard
Frederick G. Hoffman	Jeffrey G. Sorenson
	Sandra M. Traicoff

Representative Clients: For Representative Client list, see General Practice, Peoria, IL.

For Complete List of Firm Personnel, See General Section

For full biographical listings, see the Martindale-Hubbell Law Directory

---

VERNON HILLS, Lake Co.

RICHARDS, RALPH & SCHWAB, CHTD. (AV)

Suite 345, One Hawthorn Place, 175 East Hawthorn Parkway, 60061
Telephone: 708-367-9699
FAX: 708-367-9621

Michael L. Ralph	Alan E. Richards
	David J. Schwab

For full biographical listings, see the Martindale-Hubbell Law Directory

---

INDIANA

BEDFORD,* Lawrence Co.

STEELE, STEELE, McSOLEY & McSOLEY (AV)

Bank One Building, Suite One, 1602 I Street, 47421
Telephone: 812-279-3513
Fax: 812-275-3504

MEMBERS OF FIRM

Byron W. Steele	Brent E. Steele

Representative Clients: Bank One, Bloomington, NA, Bedford Branch; The First National Bank of Mitchell; The Times Mail (newspaper); Ralph Rogers & Co., Inc.; Indiana Bell Telephone Co.; Texas Gas Transmission Corporation; U.S. Gypsum Company.

For Complete List of Firm Personnel, See General Section

For full biographical listings, see the Martindale-Hubbell Law Directory

---

BLOOMINGTON,* Monroe Co.

BUNGER & ROBERTSON (AV)

226 South College Square, P.O. Box 910, 47402-0910
Telephone: 812-332-9295
Fax: 812-331-8808

MEMBER OF FIRM

Don M. Robertson

Representative Clients: Aetna Insurance Companies; Bloomington Hospital; Commercial Union Group; Indiana Insurance Co.; Liberty Mutual Insurance; Medical Protective Co.; Monroe County Community School Corp.; Professional Golf Car, Inc.; Prudential Insurance Company of America; State Farm Automobile Insurance Co.

For Complete List of Firm Personnel, See General Section

For full biographical listings, see the Martindale-Hubbell Law Directory

---

EVANSVILLE,* Vanderburgh Co.

BAMBERGER, FOREMAN, OSWALD AND HAHN (AV)

7th Floor Hulman Building, P.O. Box 657, 47704-0657
Telephone: 812-425-1591
Fax: 812-421-4936

(See Next Column)

BAMBERGER, FOREMAN, OSWALD AND HAHN, *Evansville—Continued*

OF COUNSEL

William P. Foreman

MEMBER OF FIRM

Terry G. Farmer

ASSOCIATES

Marjorie A. Meeks   Jason Lueking

Lori A. Yarbor

Representative Clients: Citizens Bank of Central Indiana; Citizens Bank of Henderson County; CNB Bancshares, Inc.; CNB Bank of Kentucky; Dubois County Bank; Jasper State Bank; Peoples Bank & Trust Co.; The Citizens National Bank of Evansville; Valley Bank F.S.B.

For Complete List of Firm Personnel, See General Section

For full biographical listings, see the Martindale-Hubbell Law Directory

---

BOWERS, HARRISON, KENT & MILLER, LLP (AV)

25 N.W. Riverside Drive, P.O. Box 1287, 47706-1287
Telephone: 812-426-1231
Fax: 812-464-3676

MEMBERS OF FIRM

Joseph H. Harrison   Paul E. Black

Gary R. Case

OF COUNSEL

K. Wayne Kent

Representative Clients: Permanent Federal Savings Bank; The Citizens National Bank of Evansville; First Indiana Bank; Citizens National Bank of Tell City.

For Complete List of Firm Personnel, See General Section

For full biographical listings, see the Martindale-Hubbell Law Directory

---

KAHN, DEES, DONOVAN & KAHN (AV)

P.O. Box 3646, 47735-3646
Telephone: 812-423-3183
Fax: 812-423-3841
Email: evvlaw@k2d2.com

MEMBERS OF FIRM

Alan N. Shovers   G. Michael Schopmeyer
Brian P. Williams   Jeffrey K. Helfrich

ASSOCIATE

Marjorie J. Scharpf

OF COUNSEL

Marilyn R. Ratliff

Representative Clients: Citizens National Bank of Evansville; Old National Bancorp; Waterfield Mortgage Co.; American General Finance; German American Bank; Jasper State Bank; Terre Haute First National Bank.

For Complete List of Firm Personnel, See General Section

For full biographical listings, see the Martindale-Hubbell Law Directory

---

ZIEMER, STAYMAN, WEITZEL & SHOULDERS (AV)

(Formerly Early, Arnold & Ziemer)
One Riverfront Place, 20 N.W. First Street 9th Floor, P.O. Box 916, 47706-0916
Telephone: 812-424-7575
Telecopier: 812-421-5089

MEMBERS OF FIRM

Robert F. Stayman   Marco L. DeLucio
Stephan E. Weitzel   Gregory G. Meyer

Reference: Old National Bank in Evansville.

For full biographical listings, see the Martindale-Hubbell Law Directory

---

FORT WAYNE,* Allen Co.

BARRETT & McNAGNY (AV)

215 East Berry Street, P.O. Box 2263, 46801-2263
Telephone: 219-423-9551
Telecopier: 219-423-8924

MEMBERS OF FIRM

Howard L. Chapman   Dennis C. Becker
Patrick G. Michaels   Ronald J. Ehinger
Richard E. Fox   Stephen L. Chapman

Michael P. O'Hara

ASSOCIATE

Anne E. Simerman

Counsel for: Fort Wayne National Corp.; Fort Wayne National Bank; Lincoln National Corp.; N.B.D. Bank, N.A.; Union Federal Savings Bank of Indianapolis; Waterfield Mortgage Company, Incorporated.

(See Next Column)

For Complete List of Firm Personnel, See General Section

For full biographical listings, see the Martindale-Hubbell Law Directory

---

BEERS, MALLERS, BACKS & SALIN (AV)

110 West Berry Street, Suite 1100, 46802
Telephone: 219-426-9706
Fax: 219-420-1314
LaGrange, Indiana Office: 108 West Michigan Street.
Telephone: 219-463-4949.
FAX: 219-463-2789.

MEMBERS OF FIRM

Vincent J. Backs   G. William Fishering

Peter G. Mallers

Representative Client: Farmers Mutual Insurance Company of Noble Co.

For Complete List of Firm Personnel, See General Section

For full biographical listings, see the Martindale-Hubbell Law Directory

---

MILLER CARSON BOXBERGER & MURPHY (AV)

1400 One Summit Square, 46802-3137
Telephone: 219-423-9411
Telecopier: 219-423-4329
Bloomington, Indiana Office: 3100 John Hinkle Place, Suite 106.
Telephone: 812-333-1225.
Fax: 812-333-1925.

MEMBERS OF FIRM

Milford M. Miller, Jr.   Richard P. Samek
Philip L. Carson   Phillip A. Renz
Bruce O. Boxberger   Edward J. Liptak (Resident,
Edward L. Murphy, Jr.   Bloomington, Indiana Office)
Thomas W. Yoder   Robert T. Keen, Jr.
Charles R. Cogdell   Larry L. Barnard
John J. Wernet   Arthur E. Mandelbaum

ASSOCIATES

Diana Carol Bauer   Douglas A. Hoffman
James P. Buchholz   Karl J. Veracco
Timothy A. Manges   Timothy M. Pape
(Not admitted in IN)

Representative Clients: NBD Bank; Norwest Bank of Fort Wayne; Fort Wayne National Bank.

For full biographical listings, see the Martindale-Hubbell Law Directory

---

ROTHBERG & LOGAN (AV)

(Formerly, Rothberg, Gallmeyer, Fruechtenicht & Logan)
2100 Fort Wayne National Bank Building, 110 West Berry Street, P.O. Box 11647, 46859-1647
Telephone: 219-422-9454
Telefax: 219-422-1622

MEMBERS OF FIRM

Thomas D. Logan   David R. Smelko
F. L. Dennis Logan   Dennis F. Dykhuizen
Scott T. Niemann   Gregory Martin Cole

Michael T. Deam

ASSOCIATES

James A. Butz   J. Rickard Donovan

Counsel for: Parkview Memorial Hospital; Cameron Memorial Community Hospital; Norwest Bank Indiana, N.A.; NBD Bank, N.A.; Parkview Health System; Azar's, Incorporated; Fort Wayne-Allen County Airport Authority; Fort Wayne Public Transportation Corporation; Avis Industrial Corp.; Farm Credit Services of Mid-America, ASA; Slater Fort Wayne Federal Credit Union.

For Complete List of Firm Personnel, See General Section

For full biographical listings, see the Martindale-Hubbell Law Directory

---

GREENWOOD, Johnson Co.

WILLIAMS HEWITT & ROBBINS, LLP (AV)

Suite 400, National City Bank Building, 300 South Madison Avenue, P.O. Box 405, 46142
Telephone: 317-888-1121
Facsimile: 317-887-4069

PARTNERS

Jon E. Williams   Brian C. Hewitt

J. Lee Robbins

ASSOCIATES

John M. White   Mark E. Need

John P. Wilkowski

For full biographical listings, see the Martindale-Hubbell Law Directory

HAMMOND, Lake Co.

GALVIN, GALVIN & LEENEY (AV)

5231 Hohman Avenue, 46320
Telephone: 219-933-0380
Fax: 219-933-0471

MEMBERS OF FIRM

Edmond J. Leeney (1897-1978)	Carl N. Carpenter
Timothy P. Galvin, Sr.	John E. Chevigny
(1894-1993)	Timothy P. Galvin, Jr.
Francis J. Galvin, Sr.	Patrick J. Galvin
(1902-1995)	W. Patrick Downes

William G. Crabtree II	Julie A. Rosenwinkel
John H. Lloyd, IV	Amy Galvin Grogan

Representative Clients: Mercantile National Bank of Indiana, N.A.; Citizens Financial Services, FSB; First Federal Savings and Loan of Hammond; Security Federal Bank, FSB; First National Bank of Illinois; Home State Bank, N.A. (Crystal Lake, IL).

For full biographical listings, see the Martindale-Hubbell Law Directory

INDIANAPOLIS,* Marion Co.

BOSE MCKINNEY & EVANS (AV)

2700 First Indiana Plaza, 135 North Pennsylvania Street, 46204
Telephone: 317-684-5000
Facsimile: 317-684-5173
Indianapolis North Office: Suite 1201, 8888 Keystone Crossing, 46240.
Telephone: 317-574-3700.
Facsimile: 317-574-3716.

MEMBERS OF FIRM

David A. Butcher	R. J. McConnell
Theodore J. Nowacki	Michael A. Trentadue
Alan W. Becker	Dwight L. Miller

ASSOCIATE

J. Scott Enright

Representative Clients: First Indiana Bank; Francisco State Bank; National City Bank; Old National Bancorp; Citizens Banking Co.; Eli Lilly Federal Credit Union; Monroe County Bank; State Bank of Oxford; Star Financial Bank; Huntington National Bank of Indiana.

For Complete List of Firm Personnel, See General Section

For full biographical listings, see the Martindale-Hubbell Law Directory

DANN PECAR NEWMAN & KLEIMAN, PROFESSIONAL CORPORATION (AV)

Suite 2300, One American Square Box 82008, 46282
Telephone: 317-632-3232; Indiana: 800-622-4799
Telecopy: 317-632-2962

Theodore R. Dann (1907-1993)	Walter E. Wolf, Jr.
Joel Yonover (1932-1995)	Barry E. Beldin
Philip D. Pecar	Robert D. Swhier, Jr.
Norman R. Newman	James P. Moloy
David H. Kleiman	Robert J. Schuckit
Jon B. Abels	Andrew A. Kleiman
Melvin R. Daniel	Michael J. Gabovitch
Lawrence F. Dorocke	Steven M. Pecar
Jeffrey A. Abrams	Benjamin A. Pecar
James H. Schwarz	Richard O. Kissel, II
Robert A. Rose	Joseph D. Calderon

OF COUNSEL

Linda E. Cantor	Anthony J. Rose

Ellen C. Siakotos	Angela L. Mansfield
Stacy L. Hill	Martha M. K. Baird

Karin L. Veatch

Attorneys for: Indianapolis Machinery Co., Inc.; Melvin Simon & Associates, Inc.; Pacers Basketball Corp.; Universal Fire & Casualty Co., Inc.; Bank One, Indianapolis, NA; INB National Bank; Nachi Technology, Inc.; Pharmaceutical Corporation of America; Logo 7, Inc.

For full biographical listings, see the Martindale-Hubbell Law Directory

ICE MILLER DONADIO & RYAN (AV)

One American Square Box 82001, 46282-0002
Telephone: 317-236-2100
Fax: 317-236-2219
Email: leel@imdr.com *URL:* http://www.imdr.com
South Bend, Indiana Office: 211 West Washington Street, Suite 2420.
Telephone: 219-234-7933.
Fax: 219-234-7965. Internet E-mail: leel@imdr.com. Web Site Address: http://www.imdr.com.

(See Next Column)

MEMBERS OF FIRM

Evan E. Steger	Fred R. Biesecker
Berkley W. Duck	Richard J. Thrapp
Harry L. Gonso	Zeff A. Weiss
Thomas H. Ristine	Stephen J. Hackman
Philip A. Whistler	Michael A. Wukmer
Marcus B. Chandler	Michael J. Lewinski

Henry A. Efroymson

OF COUNSEL

Peggy J. Naile

RETIRED PARTNER

John A. Grayson

ASSOCIATES

Dominic F. Polizzotto	Michael E. Schrader
John M. Hakes	

Counsel for: Federal Deposit Insurance Corp.; Indiana Bankers Assn.; Irwin Union Bank & Trust Co.; NBD, Indiana, Inc.; Union County National Bank of Liberty; Kentland Bank; Farmers & Merchants Bank of Rochester; Fifth Third Bank of Central Indiana; KeyBank National Assn.; La Salle National Bank.

For Complete List of Firm Personnel, See General Section

For full biographical listings, see the Martindale-Hubbell Law Directory

JOHNSON, SMITH, PENCE, DENSBORN, WRIGHT & HEATH (AV)

One Indiana Square Suite 1800, 46204
Telephone: 317-634-9777
Telecopier: 317-636-9061

MEMBERS OF FIRM

David R. Day	Richard L. Johnson
Donald K. Densborn	Michael J. Kaye
Thomas N. Eckerle	John R. Kirkwood
Dennis A. Johnson	David E. Wright

ASSOCIATES

Carolyn H. Andretti	Patricia L. Marshall

For Complete List of Firm Personnel, See General Section

For full biographical listings, see the Martindale-Hubbell Law Directory

LOCKE REYNOLDS BOYD & WEISELL (AV)

1000 Capital Center South, 201 North Illinois Street, 46204
Telephone: 317-237-3800
Telecopier: 317-237-3900

Stephen J. Dutton	Jeffrey B. Bailey
Michael D. Moriarty	Paul G. Reis
Michael J. Schneider	Howard R. Cohen

Curt W. Hidde

Representative Clients: American Express Financial Services; Bank One Indianapolis, N.A.; The Huntington National Bank of Indiana; Indiana Corporate Federal Credit Union; NBD Bank, N.A.

For Complete List of Firm Personnel, See General Section

For full biographical listings, see the Martindale-Hubbell Law Directory

LAFAYETTE,* Tippecanoe Co.

STUART & BRANIGIN (AV)

The Life Building, 300 Main Street, Suite 800, 47902
Telephone: 317-423-1561
Telecopier: 317-742-8175

MEMBERS OF FIRM

Allison Ellsworth Stuart	Stephen R. Pennell
(1886-1950)	Anthony S. Benton
Roger D. Branigin (1902-1975)	Erik D. Spykman
Russell H. Hart	William E. Emerick
Roger D. Branigin, Jr.	John C. Duffey
Thomas L. Ryan	Mark E. DeYoung
James V. McGlone	Thomas B. Parent
Carl W. Kloepfer	Laura L. Bowker
Thomas R. McCully	Kevin D. Nicoson
Larry R. Fisher	Susan K. Roberts
Nina B. Kirkpatrick	John M. Stuckey
Mark Lillianfeld	Deborah B. Trice

COUNSEL

John F. Bodle

ASSOCIATES

Brent W. Huber	David A. Starkweather
William P. Kealey	Geoffrey Blazi
A. James Chareq	

General Counsel for: The Lafayette Life Insurance Co.; INB National Bank, N.W.; Lafayette Home Hospital, Inc.

(See Next Column)

STUART & BRANIGIN, *Lafayette—Continued*

State Counsel for: Norfolk & Western Railway Co.
Mr. Ryan is Counsel to: The Trustees of Purdue University.
Representative Clients: Aluminum Company of America; Liberty Mutual Insurance Group.

For full biographical listings, see the Martindale-Hubbell Law Directory

RICHMOND,* Wayne Co.

HARRINGTON, MALEY, GARDNER & SAYRE (AV)

Third Floor, Harrington Bank Building, Two North Eighth, 47374-3090
Telephone: 317-966-6643
FAX: 317-966-6799

MEMBERS OF FIRM

Alonzo M. Gardner (1886-1941)	Robert J. Maley
Wilfred Jessup (1900-1944)	Gayle W. Gardner
Frank K. Chambers (1938-1955)	John M. Sayre, III
Floyd W. Gardner (1933-1965)	Kirk A. Weikart
Clifford M. Haworth (1923-1967)	

OF COUNSEL

John R. Harrington

General Counsel for: Harrington Bank, FSB.
Local Counsel for: Belden Manufacturing Co.; CIGNA.

For full biographical listings, see the Martindale-Hubbell Law Directory

TERRE HAUTE,* Vigo Co.

COX, ZWERNER, GAMBILL & SULLIVAN (AV)

511 Wabash Avenue, P.O. Box 1625, 47808-1625
Telephone: 812-232-6003
Fax: 812-232-6567

MEMBERS OF FIRM

Ernest J. Zwerner (1918-1980)	David W. Sullivan
Benjamin G. Cox (1915-1988)	Robert L. Gowdy
Gilbert W. Gambill, Jr.	Louis F. Britton
James E. Sullivan	Carroll D. Smeltzer
Benjamin G. Cox, Jr.	Jeffry A. Lind

ASSOCIATE

Ronald E. Jumps

OF COUNSEL

Robert D. Hepburn

Counsel for: Terre Haute First National Bank; Farmers Insurance Group; Indiana-American Water Co.; Indiana State University; Merchants National Bank of Terre Haute; Rose-Hulman Institute of Technology; Tribune-Star Publishing Co., Inc.; Weston Paper & Manufacturing Co.

For full biographical listings, see the Martindale-Hubbell Law Directory

IOWA

CEDAR RAPIDS,* Linn Co.

SHUTTLEWORTH & INGERSOLL, P.C. (AV)

500 Firstar Bank Building, P.O. Box 2107, 52406-2107
Telephone: 319-365-9461
Fax: 319-365-8443
Email: si-law@inav.net

Thomas M. Collins	Thomas P. Peffer
Richard S. Fry	Kevin H. Collins
Gary J. Streit	William P. Prowell
Carroll J. Reasoner	William S. Hochstetler
Steven J. Pace	LeeAnn M. Ferry

Dean D. Carrington

COUNSEL

Joan Lipsky

Representative Clients: Firstar Bank Cedar Rapids, N.A.; First National Bank of Cedar Rapids; Hills Bank and Trust Company.

For Complete List of Firm Personnel, See General Section

For full biographical listings, see the Martindale-Hubbell Law Directory

DAVENPORT,* Scott Co.

NOYES & GOSMA, L.L.P. (AV)

400 North Main Street, Suite 106, 52801
Telephone: 319-322-8223
Fax: 319-322-8234

MEMBERS OF FIRM

Michael L. Noyes	John S. Gosma

(See Next Column)

ASSOCIATE

Marie R. Rolling-Tarbox

OF COUNSEL

Clay LeGrand	Charles G. Rehling

Reference: Quad City Bank and Trust Company.

For full biographical listings, see the Martindale-Hubbell Law Directory

DES MOINES,* Polk Co.

DICKINSON, MACKAMAN, TYLER & HAGEN, P.C. (AV)

Suite 1600 Hub Tower, 699 Walnut Street, 50309-3986
Telephone: 515-244-2600
Telecopier: 515-246-4550

Howard O. Hagen	Jeffrey T. Ramsey
Richard A. Malm	Jon P. Sullivan
James W. O'Brien	Paul R. Tyler
Arthur F. Owens	J. Marc Ward

Representative Clients: First Citizens National Bank; Hills Bank and Trust Co.; Merchants Bank, Des Moines; Norwest Bank Iowa, N.A.; United Bank of Iowa; Waukee State Bank.

For Complete List of Firm Personnel, See General Section

For full biographical listings, see the Martindale-Hubbell Law Directory

FINLEY, ALT, SMITH, SCHARNBERG, MAY & CRAIG, P.C. (AV)

604 Locust Street, Fourth Floor Equitable Building, 50309
Telephone: 515-288-0145
Telecopier: 515-288-2724

Glenn L. Smith	David C. Craig

Representative Clients: Aetna Casualty & Surety Co.; Aetna Life Insurance Co.; ALAS; American Society of Composers, Authors and Publishers; Equitable Life Assurance Society of the U.S.; Federated Insurance Co.; Meredith Corp.
Iowa Attorneys for: Midwest Medical Insurance Co.
District Attorneys for: Norfolk & Southern Railroad; Soo Line Railroad Company.

For Complete List of Firm Personnel, See General Section

For full biographical listings, see the Martindale-Hubbell Law Directory

WHITFIELD & EDDY, P.L.C. (AV)

317 6th Avenue, Suite 1200 Locust at 6th, 50309-4110
Telephone: 515-288-6041
Fax: 515-246-1474

Rod Kubat	Wendy L. Carlson
William L. Fairbank	Gary A. Norton
Robert G. Bridges	Mark V. Hanson
Thomas H. Burke	Jeffrey William Courter
George H. Frampton	August B. Landis

OF COUNSEL

John C. Eddy	Harley A. Whitfield

Representative Clients: Brenton National Bank of Perry; Brenton State Bank of Jefferson; Brenton National Bank, N.A.; Farm Credit Banks of Omaha; Production Credit Association of the Midlands; Citizen States Bank; Decatur County State Bank; Iowa Trust & Savings Bank.

For Complete List of Firm Personnel, See General Section

For full biographical listings, see the Martindale-Hubbell Law Directory

KANSAS

TOPEKA,* Shawnee Co.

WRIGHT, HENSON, SOMERS, SEBELIUS, CLARK & BAKER, LLP (AV)

Commerce Bank Building, 100 Southeast Ninth Street, 2nd Floor, P.O. Box 3555, 66601-3555
Telephone: 913-232-2200
FAX: 913-232-3344

MEMBERS OF FIRM

Charles N. Henson	Dale L. Somers
Anne Lamborn Baker	

Representative Clients: Kaw Valley State Bank & Trust Co.; Kansas Bankers Association; Peoples State Bank of Topeka.

For Complete List of Firm Personnel, See General Section

For full biographical listings, see the Martindale-Hubbell Law Directory

WICHITA, * Sedgwick Co.

FOULSTON & SIEFKIN L.L.P. (AV)

700 Fourth Financial Center, 67202
Telephone: 316-267-6371
Facsimile: 316-267-6345
Topeka, Kansas Office: 1515 Bank IV Tower, 534 Kansas Avenue, 66603.
Telephone: 913-233-3600.
Fax: 913-233-1610.
Dodge City, Kansas Office: 810 Frontview, P.O. Box 1147, 67801.
Telephone: 316-227-8126.
Fax: 316-227-8451.
Member: Lex Mundi, A Global Association of 126 Independent Firms.

MEMBERS OF FIRM

Benjamin C. Langel   William R. Wood, II

For Complete List of Firm Personnel, See General Section

For full biographical listings, see the Martindale-Hubbell Law Directory

---

KENTUCKY

BOWLING GREEN, * Warren Co.

BELL, ORR, AYERS & MOORE, P.S.C. (AV)

1010 College Street, P.O. Box 738, 42102-0738
Telephone: 502-781-8111
Telecopier: 502-781-9027

Ray B. Buckberry, Jr.   Kevin C. Brooks

General Counsel for: First American National Bank of Kentucky; Houchens Industries, Inc. (Food Markets and Shopping Centers); Warren County Board of Education; Bowling Green Municipal Utilities.
Representative Clients: Chicago Title Insurance Co.; Commonwealth Land Title Insurance Co.; Kentucky Farm Bureau Mutual Insurance Co.; Martin Automotive Group; Home Insurance Group; Farm Credit Services of Mid-America, ACA.

For Complete List of Firm Personnel, See General Section

For full biographical listings, see the Martindale-Hubbell Law Directory

---

COLE, MOORE & BAKER (AV)

921 College Street-Phoenix Place, P.O. Box 10240, 42102-7240
Telephone: 502-782-6666
FAX: 502-782-8666

MEMBERS OF FIRM

John David Cole   Frank Hampton Moore, Jr.
                 Matthew J. Baker

ASSOCIATES

Dov Moore   John David Cole, Jr.
C. Terrell Miller   Stefan R. Hughes

OF COUNSEL

Frank R. Goad

Counsel for: Western Kentucky Cola-Cola Bottling Co.; Clark Distributing Co., Inc.; Scotty's Contracting & Stone Co.
Local Counsel for: General Electric Co.; Bucyrus-Erie Company; Wal-Mart Stores, Inc.; Kroger/Country Oven.
Representative Insurance Clients: Liberty Mutual Insurance Co.; Travelers Insurance Co.; Wausau Insurance Co.

For full biographical listings, see the Martindale-Hubbell Law Directory

---

ENGLISH, LUCAS, PRIEST & OWSLEY (AV)

1101 College Street, P.O. Box 770, 42102-0770
Telephone: 502-781-6500
Telecopier: 502-782-7782
Email: inquiry@elpo.com

MEMBERS OF FIRM

Charles E. English   Whayne C. Priest, Jr.
                 Keith M. Carwell

ASSOCIATE

Marc Allen Lovell

General Counsel for: Medical Center at Bowling Green; Warren Rural Electric Cooperative Corporation; Trans Financial Bank, N.A.; Southern Sanitation, Inc.
Representative Clients: Commercial Union Insurance Cos.; Kemper Insurance Group; St. Paul Insurance Co.; Desa International; Kentucky Finance Co.; Sumitomo Electric Wiring Systems, Inc.

For Complete List of Firm Personnel, See General Section

For full biographical listings, see the Martindale-Hubbell Law Directory

---

HARLIN & PARKER, P.S.C. (AV)

519 East Tenth Street, P.O. Box 390, 42102-0390
Telephone: 502-842-5611
Telefax: 502-842-2607

William Jerry Parker   Jerry A. Burns
                 Scott Charles Marks

Insurance Clients: American Hardware Mutual Insurance Co.; CNA Insurance Companies; Government Employees Insurance Co.; American International Group.
Railroad and Utilities Clients: District Attorneys for BellSouth Telecommunications, Inc.; CSX Transportation, Inc.
Local Counsel for: General Motors Corp.; Ford Motor Co.; Chrysler Corp.

For Complete List of Firm Personnel, See General Section

For full biographical listings, see the Martindale-Hubbell Law Directory

---

LEXINGTON, * Fayette Co.

STOLL, KEENON & PARK, LLP (AV)

201 E. Main Street, Suite 1000, 40507-1380
Telephone: 606-231-3000
Telecopier: 606-253-1093; 606-253-1027
Frankfort, Kentucky Office: 307 Washington Street, 40601.
Telephone: 502-875-6220.
Telecopier: 502-875-6235.
Louisville, Kentucky Office: 400 West Market Street, Suite 2650, 40202-3377.
Telephone: 502-568-9100.
Telecopier: 502-568-5700.

MEMBERS OF FIRM

William L. Montague   Harvie B. Wilkinson
Joseph M. Scott, Jr.   J. David Smith, Jr.
R. David Lester   Dan M. Rose
Herbert A. Miller, Jr.   Gregory D. Pavey

ASSOCIATES

R. Douglas Martin   William L. Montague, Jr.

Representative Clients: Farmers Capital Bank Corp.; Bank One, Lexington, NA; Whitaker Bank Corporation; Fifth Third Bank of Kentucky.

For Complete List of Firm Personnel, See General Section

For full biographical listings, see the Martindale-Hubbell Law Directory

---

LOUISVILLE, * Jefferson Co.

HIRN DOHENY & HARPER (AV)

A Partnership including a Professional Service Corporation
2000 Meidinger Tower, 40202
Telephone: 502-585-2450
Telecopiers: 502-585-2207; 585-2529

MEMBERS OF FIRM

Marvin J. Hirn   David W. Harper
                 Scott W. Brinkman

Representative Clients: Bank of Louisville; Indiana United Bancorp; Bourbon Bancshares, Inc.; Hazard Bancorp, Inc.; Marie R. Turner Holding Co.; First Midwest Bancshares; National City Bank Kentucky; PNC Bank; River City Bank.

For Complete List of Firm Personnel, See General Section

For full biographical listings, see the Martindale-Hubbell Law Directory

---

MAPOTHER & MAPOTHER (AV)

801 West Jefferson Street, 40202
Telephone: 502-587-5400
Fax: 502-587-5444
Email: 103210.1130@compuserve.com
Lexington, Kentucky Office: 177 North Upper Street.
Telephone: 606-253-0003.
Fax: 606-255-3961.
Jeffersonville, Indiana Office: 505 East Seventh Street.
Telephone: 812-288-5059.
Fax: 502-587-5444.
Cincinnati, Ohio Office: Kroger Building, Suite 2220, 1014 Vine Street.
Telephone: 513-381-4888.
Fax: 513-381-3117.
Huntington, West Virginia Office: Morris Building, Suite 701, 845 Fourth Avenue.
Telephone: 304-525-1185.
Fax: 304-529-3764.
Evansville, Indiana Office: 329 Main Street.
Telephone: 812-421-9108.
Fax: 812-421-9109.

MEMBERS OF FIRM

Thomas Cruise Mapother, Jr.   William R. Mapother
 (1907-1986)   Thomas L. Canary, Jr.
                 Charles M. Friedman

(See Next Column)

MAPOTHER & MAPOTHER, *Louisville—Continued*

Brian P. Conaty (Resident, Huntington, West Virginia Office)	Lee W. Grace
	Roy Fugitt (Resident, Lexington Office)
Andrea Fried Neichter	Susan E. Morton-Smith (Resident, Huntington, West Virginia Office)
Kathryn Pry Coryell (Resident, Jeffersonville, Indiana Office)	
Roberta S. Dunlap (Resident, Evansville, Indiana Office)	Brian E. Chapman (Resident, Cincinnati, Ohio Office)
Dean A. Langdon (Resident, Lexington Office)	T. Lawson McSwain, II
	Lisa A. Herndon

Representative Clients: Bank One; PNC Bank; NBD Bank; Fifth Third Bank; General Electric Capital Corp.; Ford Motor Credit Co.; General Motors Acceptance Corp.; Associates Commercial Corp.; Cuna Mutual Insurance Society.

For full biographical listings, see the Martindale-Hubbell Law Directory

MIDDLETON & REUTLINGER, P.S.C. (AV)

2500 Brown and Williamson Tower, 40202-3410
Telephone: 502-584-1135
Fax: 502-561-0442
New Albany, Indiana Office: 2623 Charlestown Road, 47150.
Telephone: 812-944-7215.

Charles G. Middleton, III	G. Kennedy Hall, Jr.
Charles D. Greenwell	David J. Kellerman

Margaret E. Thorp

Counsel for: Chevron USA; Logan Aluminum, Inc.; Louisville Gas & Electric Co.; MCI Telecommunications Corp.; Metropolitan Life Insurance Co.; Kosmos Cement Co.; Porcelain Metal Corp.; The Home Insurance Co.; The Kroger Co.; Demars Haka Development, Inc.

For Complete List of Firm Personnel, See General Section

For full biographical listings, see the Martindale-Hubbell Law Directory

MORGAN & POTTINGER, P.S.C. (AV)

601 West Main Street, 40202
Telephone: 502-589-2780
Telecopier: 502-585-3498
Lexington, Kentucky Office: 133 West Short Street.
Telephone: 606-253-1900.
Telecopier: 606-255-2038.
New Albany, Indiana Office: 400 Pearl Street, Suite 100.
Telephone: 812-948-0008.
Telecopier: 812-944-6215.

Patrick E. Morgan	Mark J. Sandlin
John T. McGarvey	Scott T. Rickman (Resident, Lexington Office)
Douglas Gene Sharp	
John A. Majors	M. Thurman Senn

COUNSEL TO FIRM
Thomas C. Fenton

For Complete List of Firm Personnel, See General Section

For full biographical listings, see the Martindale-Hubbell Law Directory

RUBIN HAYS & FOLEY (AV)

First Trust Centre 200 South Fifth Street, 40202
Telephone: 502-569-7550
Telecopier: 502-569-7555

MEMBERS OF FIRM

Wm. Carl Fust	Lisa Koch Bryant
Harry Lee Meyer	Sharon C. Hardy
David W. Gray	Charles S. Musson
Irvin D. Foley	W. Randall Jones
Joseph R. Gathright, Jr.	K. Gail Russell

ASSOCIATES

Christian L. Juckett	Courtney Lynn McCall

OF COUNSEL

James E. Fahey	Newman T. Guthrie

Representative Clients: J.C. Bradford & Co., Inc.; J.J.B. Hilliard, W.L. Lyons, Inc.; Huntington National Bank; Liberty National Bank and Trust Company; National City Bank; PNC Bank; Prudential Bache & Co., Inc.; Prudential Securities, Inc.; Society Bank; Stock Yards Bank and Trust Co.

For full biographical listings, see the Martindale-Hubbell Law Directory

WYATT, TARRANT & COMBS (AV)

Citizens Plaza, 40202
Telephone: 502-589-5235
Telecopier: 502-589-0309
URL: http://www.wyattfirm.com
Lexington, Kentucky Office: 1700 Lexington Financial Center.
Telephone: 606-233-2012.
Telecopier: 606-259-0649.

(See Next Column)

Frankfort, Kentucky Office: The Taylor-Scott Building, 311 West Main Street.
Telephone: 502-223-2104.
Telecopier: 502-227-7681.
New Albany, Indiana Office: The Elsby Building, 117 East Spring Street,
Telephone: 812-945-3561.
Telecopier: 812-949-2524.
Memphis, Tennessee Office: Crescent Center, Suite 650, 6075 Poplar Avenue.
Telephone: 901-537-1000.
Telecopier: 901-537-1010.
Nashville, Tennessee Office: 1500 Nashville City Center, 511 Union Street.
Telephone: 615-244-0020.
Telecopier: 615-256-1726.
Music Row, Nashville Office: 29 Music Square East.
Telephone: 615-255-6161.
Telecopier: 615-254-4490.
Hendersonville, Tennessee Office: 313 E. Main Street, Suite 1.
Telephone: 615-822-8822.
Telecopier: 615-824-4684.

MEMBER OF FIRM
Stewart E. Conner

Representative Clients: Bank One, Kentucky, NA (formerly Liberty National Bank & Trust Co.); CBT Corp.; Cardinal Bancshares, Inc.; Citizens Bank & Trust Company and its affiliates; First Kentucky Trust Co.; PNC Bank, Kentucky, Inc.; Republic Bank and Trust Co.; Trans Financial, Inc.; Vine Street Trust Co.

For Complete List of Firm Personnel, See General Section

For full biographical listings, see the Martindale-Hubbell Law Directory

MOREHEAD,* Rowan Co.

DEHNER & ELLIS (AV)

206 East Main Street, 40351
Telephone: 606-783-1504
FAX: 606-784-2744

Truman L. Dehner	John J. Ellis

For full biographical listings, see the Martindale-Hubbell Law Directory

SHEPHERDSVILLE,* Bullitt Co.

J. CHESTER PORTER & ASSOCIATES (AV)

318 South Buckman Street, P.O. Box 767, 40165
Telephone: 502-543-2296; 955-6034
FAX: 502-543-2694
Taylorsville, Kentucky Office: 312 Main Street, P.O. Box 509.
Telephone: 502-477-6412.
FAX: 502-477-2169.

J. Chester Porter

Joseph J. Wantland	Phillip K. Wicker
Linda S. Bouvette (Resident, Taylorsville Office)	Jennifer Elizabeth Porter

For full biographical listings, see the Martindale-Hubbell Law Directory

SOMERSET,* Pulaski Co.

ADAMS & ADAMS (AV)

35 Public Square, P.O. Box 35, 42502-0035
Telephone: 606-679-6741; 678-4916
Fax: 606-679-3691

MEMBERS OF FIRM

Charles C. Adams	Norma B. Adams

ASSOCIATE
Jane Adams Venters

Counsel for: First and Farmers Bank of Somerset, Inc.; Aluminum Wheel Technology, Inc.
Representative Clients: Community Trust Bank, FSB; Aluminum Wheel Technology, Inc.; Food Fair Cos.; Kentucky Farm Bureau Mutual Insurance Cos.; Cumberland Valley Communications; Shamrock Coal Co.; Railum, Inc.; Hartco Flooring Co.

For full biographical listings, see the Martindale-Hubbell Law Directory

LOUISIANA

BATON ROUGE,* East Baton Rouge Parish

GUGLIELMO, MARKS, SCHUTTE, TERHOEVE & LOVE (AV)

(A Registered Limited Liability Partnership)
320 Somerulos Street, P.O. Box 3177, 70821-3177
Telephone: 504-387-6966
Fax: 504-387-8338

(See Next Column)

GUGLIELMO, MARKS, SCHUTTE, TERHOEVE & LOVE—*Continued*

Carey J. Guglielmo	Glen Scott Love
Paul Marks, Jr.	Dawn T. Trabeau-Mire
Charles A. Schutte, Jr.	Joseph W. Mengis
Henry G. Terhoeve	Kevin P. Landreneau

Representative Clients: City National Bank; Greyhound Corp.; The Travelers Insurance Co.; Chrysler Corp.; State Farm Insurance Co's.; Travelers/Aetna Insurance Group; Aetna Life & Casualty Co.

For full biographical listings, see the Martindale-Hubbell Law Directory

POWERS, CLEGG & WILLARD (AV)

7967 Office Park Boulevard, P.O. Box 15948, 70895
Telephone: 504-928-1951
Telecopier: 504-929-9834

MEMBERS OF FIRM

John Dale Powers	Michael V. Clegg
William E. Willard	

ASSOCIATES

Neil H. Mixon	Robert J. Daigre
Mary A. Cazes	Nicholas Soileau

General Counsel for: Audubon Insurance Co.
Louisiana Counsel for: Hancock Bank & Trust Co.; Hertz Corp.; Ciba-Geigy Corp.; Utica Mutual Insurance Co.

For full biographical listings, see the Martindale-Hubbell Law Directory

LAFAYETTE,* Lafayette Parish

LISKOW & LEWIS, A PROFESSIONAL LAW CORPORATION (AV)

822 Harding Street, P.O. Box 52008, 70505
Telephone: 318-232-7424
Telecopier: 318-267-2399
New Orleans, Louisiana Office: 50th Floor, One Shell Square.
Telephone: 504-581-7979.
Telecopier: 504-592-5108; 504-592-5109.

RESIDENT PERSONNEL

Joseph C. Giglio, Jr.	Billy J. Domingue
Joseph P. Hebert	

Representative Clients: Amerada Hess Corp.; Amoco Corporation; Bank One; BP America Inc.; Hibernia National Bank; Hunt Oil Company; Louisiana Public Service Commission; Mobil Oil Corp.; OXY U.S.A. Inc.; Union Oil Company of California; Union Pacific Resources Company.

For Complete List of Firm Personnel, See General Section

For full biographical listings, see the Martindale-Hubbell Law Directory

LAKE CHARLES,* Calcasieu Parish

BERGSTEDT & MOUNT (AV)

Second Floor, Magnolia Life Building, P.O. Drawer 3004, 70602-3004
Telephone: 318-433-3004
Facsimile: 318-433-8080

MEMBERS OF FIRM

Thomas M. Bergstedt	Benjamin W. Mount

ASSOCIATES

Van C. Seneca	Gregory P. Marceaux
Billy E. Loftin, Jr.	

OF COUNSEL

Charles S. Ware

Representative Clients: Armstrong World Industries; Ashland Oil Co.; CIGNA Property & Casualty Companies; Homequity; Lake Area Medical Center; Leach Company; Olin Corporation; Terra Corporation; Town of Iowa; R. D. Werner Company.

For full biographical listings, see the Martindale-Hubbell Law Directory

MONROE,* Ouachita Parish

THOMPSON, SPARKS, DEAN & MORRIS (AV)

A Partnership including a Professional Corporation
1401 Royal Street, P.O. Box 2867, 71207
Telephone: 318-388-1440
Fax: 318-322-0887

MEMBERS OF FIRM

M. C. Thompson (1885-1970)	George B. Dean, Jr., (P.C.)
James D. Sparks (1910-1987)	Wood T. Sparks
John C. Morris, III	

Representative Clients: South Central Bell Telephone Co.; Greater Ouachita Water Company; PHH Homequity Corp.; Commonwealth Relocation Services, Inc.; Remax, Monroe; Bell South Advertising & Publishing Corp.; Premier Mortgage Corp.; Countrywide Funding Corp.
Approved Attorneys for: Central Bank; Federal Land Bank.

For full biographical listings, see the Martindale-Hubbell Law Directory

NEW ORLEANS,* Orleans Parish

LISKOW & LEWIS, A PROFESSIONAL LAW CORPORATION (AV)

50th Floor, One Shell Square, 70139
Telephone: 504-581-7979
Telecopier: 504-556-4108; 504-556-4109
Lafayette, Louisiana Office: 822 Harding Street, P.O. Box 52008.
Telephone: 318-232-7424.
Telecopier: 318-267-2399.

Leon J. Reymond, Jr.	Marguerite A. Noonan
Marilyn C. Maloney	Wm. Blake Bennett

RESIDENT PERSONNEL AT LAFAYETTE OFFICE

Joseph C. Giglio, Jr.	Billy J. Domingue
Joseph P. Hebert	

Representative Clients: Hibernia National Bank; First National Bank of Commerce.

For Complete List of Firm Personnel, See General Section

For full biographical listings, see the Martindale-Hubbell Law Directory

PHELPS DUNBAR, L.L.P. (AV)

Texaco Center, 400 Poydras Street, 70130-3245
Telephone: 504-566-1311
Telecopier: 504-568-9130, 504-568-9007
Cable Address: "Howspencer"
Telex: 584125 WU
Telex: 6821155 WUI
Email: info@phelps.com
Baton Rouge, Louisiana Office: Suite 701, City National Bank Building, P.O. Box 4412.
Telephone: 504-346-0285.
Telecopier: 504-381-9197.
Jackson, Mississippi Office: Suite 500, Mtel Centré, 200 South Lamar Street, P.O. Box 23066.
Telephone: 601-352-2300.
Telecopier: 601-360-9777.
Tupelo, Mississippi Office: Seventh Floor, One Mississippi Plaza, P.O. Box 1220.
Telephone: 601-842-7907.
Telecopier: 601-842-3873.
Houston, Texas Office: Suite 900, 3040 Post Oak Boulevard.
Telephone: 713-626-1386.
Telecopier: 713-626-1388.
London, England Office: Suite 731, Level 7, Lloyd's, 1 Lime Street, London EC3M 7DQ England.
Telephone: 011-44-171-929-4765.
Telecopier: 011-44-171-929-0046.
Telex: 987321.

MEMBERS OF FIRM

James H. Roussel	Virginia Boulet
Philip deV. Claverie	Richard E. Matheny (Resident, Baton Rouge, Louisiana Office)
Robert U. Soniat	
F. M. Bush, III (Not admitted in LA; Jackson and Tupelo, Mississippi Offices)	Dana E. Kelly (Not admitted in LA; Resident, Jackson, Mississippi Office)
Harvey D. Wagar, III	
E. Clifton Hodge, Jr. (Not admitted in LA; Also at Jackson and Tupelo, Mississippi Offices)	Randy P. Roussel (Resident, Baton Rouge, Louisiana Office)
Shaun B. Rafferty	Charles D. Porter (Not admitted in LA; Resident, Jackson, Mississippi Office)
Jean Magee Hogan (Not admitted in LA; Jackson and Tupelo, Mississippi Offices)	Jonathan C. Benda (Resident, Baton Rouge, Louisiana Office)
James A. Stuckey	
Stephen H. Leech, Jr. (Not admitted in LA; Resident, Jackson, Mississippi Office)	David P. Steiner

COUNSEL

J. Michael Cutshaw (Resident, Baton Rouge, Louisiana Office)	Gary Meringer

ASSOCIATES

Lee R. Adler	Daniel E. Davillier
Stratton Bull (Not admitted in LA; Resident, Jackson, Mississippi Office)	Daniel T. Pancamo

Representative Clients: Bank of Mississippi; Citicorp Real Estate, Inc.; City National Bank of Baton Rouge; Deposit Guaranty National Bank; First National Bank of Commerce; Hibernia National Bank; Morgan Guaranty Trust Company of New York; NationsBank; Trustmark National Bank; Whitney National Bank.

For Complete List of Firm Personnel, See General Section

For full biographical listings, see the Martindale-Hubbell Law Directory

*WINNFIELD,** Winn Parish

SIMMONS AND DERR (AV)

Simmons Building, Church Street, P.O. Box 525, 71483
Telephone: 318-628-3951

MEMBERS OF FIRM

Kermit M. Simmons
Jacque D. Derr

Reference: Bank of Winnfield & Trust Co.

For full biographical listings, see the Martindale-Hubbell Law Directory

MAINE

*BANGOR,** Penobscot Co.

EATON, PEABODY, BRADFORD & VEAGUE, P.A. (AV)

Fleet Center-Exchange Street, P.O. Box 1210, 04402-1210
Telephone: 207-947-0111
Telecopier: 207-942-3040
Email: epbv@aol.com
Augusta, Maine Office: 2 Central Plaza.
Telephone: 207-622-3747.
Telecopier: 207-622-9732.
Blue Hill, Maine Office: One East Blue Hill Road.
Telephone: 207-374-2812.
Telecopier: 207-374-2548.
Brunswick, Maine Office: 167 Park Row.
Telephone: 207-729-1144.
Telecopier: 207-729-1140.
Camden, Maine Office: 7-9 Washington Street.
Telephone: 207-236-3325.
Telecopier: 207-236-8611.
Dover-Foxcroft, Maine Office: 30 East Main Street.
Telephone: 207-564-8378.
Telecopier: 207-564-7059.

Edward D. Leonard, III
Douglas M. Smith (Dover-Foxcroft and Augusta Offices)
Daniel G. McKay
John A. Cunningham (Resident, Brunswick Office)
Jonathan B. Huntington (Resident, Dover-Foxcroft Office)

Lorena R. Rush

A List of Representative Clients available upon request.

For Complete List of Firm Personnel, See General Section

For full biographical listings, see the Martindale-Hubbell Law Directory

GROSS, MINSKY, MOGUL & SINGAL, P.A. (AV)

Key Plaza, 23 Water Street, P.O. Box 917, 04402-0917
Telephone: 207-942-4644
Telecopier: 207-942-3699
Email: gmm&s-law@atlsysnet.com *URL:* http://www.atlsysnet.com/gmms

Edward I. Gross (Retired)
Jules L. Mogul (1930-1994)
Norman Minsky
George Z. Singal
Louis H. Kornreich
George C. Schelling
Edward W. Gould
Steven J. Mogul
James R. Wholly
Daniel A. Pileggi
Philip K. Clarke

Wayne P. Libhart (Retired)
Sandra L. Rothera
James S. Nixon
F. Todd Lowell

Representative Clients: Merrill Merchants Bank; Union Trust Company of Ellsworth.

For full biographical listings, see the Martindale-Hubbell Law Directory

*PORTLAND,** Cumberland Co.

JENSEN BAIRD GARDNER & HENRY (AV)

Ten Free Street, P.O. Box 4510, 04112
Telephone: 207-775-7271
Telecopier: 207-775-7935
York County Office: 419 Alfred Street, Biddeford, Maine.
Telephone: 207-282-5107.
Telecopier: 207-282-6301.

OF COUNSEL

Merton G. Henry
John D. Bradford (Resident, York County Office)

(See Next Column)

MEMBERS OF FIRM

Ronald A. Epstein
Peter W. Greenleaf
F. Bruce Sleeper

Representative Clients: General Motors Acceptance Corp.; York Insurance Co.; Key Bank; Owens Corning Fiberglass; Peoples Heritage Bank; Atlantic Bank.

For Complete List of Firm Personnel, See General Section

For full biographical listings, see the Martindale-Hubbell Law Directory

MONAGHAN, LEAHY, HOCHADEL & LIBBY (AV)

95 Exchange Street, P.O. Box 7046, 04112-7046
Telephone: 207-774-3906
Facsimile: 207-774-3965

MEMBERS OF FIRM

Thomas G. Leahy
Michael H. Hill

OF COUNSEL

William E. Saufley

Representative Client: Oxford Bank & Trust.
Reference: Maine National Bank.

For full biographical listings, see the Martindale-Hubbell Law Directory

PIERCE ATWOOD (AV)

One Monument Square, 04101
Telephone: 207-791-1100
Fax: 207-791-1350
Email: info@PierceAtwood.com
Augusta, Maine Office: 77 Winthrop Street.
Telephone: 207-622-6311.
Fax: 207-623-9367.
Newburyport, Massachusetts Office: 6 Harris Street.
Telephone: 508-465-9599.
Fax: 508-465-9945.

MEMBERS OF FIRM

James B. Zimpritch
Richard P. Hackett
David J. Champoux

ASSOCIATE

Foster A. Stewart, Jr

For Complete List of Firm Personnel, See General Section

For full biographical listings, see the Martindale-Hubbell Law Directory

TOMPKINS, CLOUGH, HIRSHON & LANGER, P.A. (AV)

Three Canal Plaza, P.O. Box 15060, 04101
Telephone: 207-874-6700
FAX: 207-874-6705

Bruce M. Tompkins
Lawrence R. Clough
David M. Hirshon
Leonard W. Langer
Marshall J. Tinkle

For full biographical listings, see the Martindale-Hubbell Law Directory

TROUBH, HEISLER & PIAMPIANO, P.C. (AV)

511 Congress Street, P.O. Box 9711, 04104-5011
Telephone: 207-780-6789
Fax: 207-774-2339

William B. Troubh
Edwin A. Heisler
Robert J. Piampiano
Kevin M. Gillis
Michael P. Boyd
Thomas E. Getchell
Michael Richards
William K. McKinley
Daniel F. Gilligan
Paul S. Bulger

John G. Richardson
Linda L. Sears
Daniel R. Felkel

For full biographical listings, see the Martindale-Hubbell Law Directory

MARYLAND

*BALTIMORE,** (Independent City)

BALLARD SPAHR ANDREWS & INGERSOLL (AV)

300 East Lombard Street, 19th Floor, 21202-3268
Telephone: 410-528-5600
Fax: 410-528-5650
Philadelphia, Pennsylvania Office: 1735 Market Street, 51st Floor.
Telephone: 215-665-8500.
Fax: 215-864-8999.
Harrisburg, Pennsylvania Office: 105 North Front Street.
Telephone: 717-236-3333.
Fax: 717-236-3884.

(See Next Column)

BALLARD SPAHR ANDREWS & INGERSOLL—*Continued*

Denver, Colorado Office: Seventeenth Street Plaza Building, Suite 2300, 1225 17th Street.
Telephone: 303-292-2400.
Fax: 303-296-3956.
Salt Lake City, Utah Office: One Utah Center, 201 South Main Street, Suite 1200.
Telephone: 801-531-3000.
Fax: 801-531-3001.
Washington, D.C. Office: Suite 900 East, 555 13th Street, N.W.
Telephone: 202-383-8800.
Fax: 202-383-8877; 383-8893.
Camden, New Jersey Office: 800 Hudson Square, 5th Floor.
Telephone: 609-541-5577.
Fax: 609-541-8272.

Sophie D. Goetz   S. Nelson Weeks

OF COUNSEL
Joseph W. Janssens, Jr.

For full biographical listings, see the Martindale-Hubbell Law Directory

THOMAS & LIBOWITZ, A PROFESSIONAL ASSOCIATION (AV)

USF&G Tower, Suite 1100, 100 Light Street, 21202-1053
Telephone: 410-752-2468
Telecopier: 410-752-2046

Steven Anargyros Thomas   John R. Wise
C. Wayne Davis

For full biographical listings, see the Martindale-Hubbell Law Directory

VENABLE ATTORNEYS AT LAW VENABLE, BAETJER AND HOWARD, LLP (AV)

A Partnership including Professional Corporations
1800 Mercantile Bank & Trust Building, 2 Hopkins Plaza, 21201
Telephone: 410-244-7400.
Email: INFO@Venable.win.net
Washington, D.C. Office: Venable, Baetjer, Howard & Civiletti LLP. Suite 1000, 1201 New York Avenue, N.W.
Telephone: 202-962-4800.
McLean, Virginia Office: Suite 400, 2010 Corporate Ridge.
Telephone: 703-760-1600.
Rockville, Maryland Office: Suite 500, One Church Street, P. O. Box 1906.
Telephone: 301-217-5600.
Towson, Maryland Office: 210 Allegheny Avenue, P. O. Box 5517.
Telephone: 410-494-6200.

MEMBERS OF FIRM

William J. McCarthy (P.C.)
Russell Ronald Reno, Jr. (P.C.)
James A. Cole
Benjamin R. Civiletti (P.C.)
  (Also at Washington, D.C. and Towson, Maryland Offices)
John Henry Lewin, Jr. (P.C.)
Lee M. Miller (P.C.)
Robert A. Shelton
Roger W. Titus (Resident, Rockville, Maryland Office)
Daniel O'C. Tracy, Jr. (Also at Rockville, Maryland Office)
Thomas W. W. Haines (P.C.)
Ronald R. Glancz (Not admitted in MD; Resident, Washington, D.C. Office)
David J. Levenson (Not admitted in MD; Resident, Washington, D.C. Office)
Joe A. Shull (Resident, Washington, D.C. Office)
Kenneth C. Bass, III (Not admitted in MD; Washington, D.C. and McLean, Virginia Offices)
John H. Zink, III (Resident, Towson, Maryland Office)
Lars E. Anderson (Not admitted in MD; Resident, McLean, Virginia Office)
William D. Dolan, III (P.C.) (Not admitted in MD; Resident, McLean, Virginia Office)
Joseph C. Wich, Jr. (Resident, Towson, Maryland Office)
Mitchell Y. Mirviss

Edward F. Glynn, Jr. (Resident, Washington, D.C. Office)
Thomas B. Hudson (Also at Washington, D.C. Office)
Nell B. Strachan
James R. Myers (Not admitted in MD; Resident, Washington, D.C. Office)
Edward L. Wender (P.C.)
David M. Fleishman
Jeffrey A. Dunn (also at Washington, D.C. Office)
Mitchell Kolkin
George F. Pappas (Also at Washington, D.C. Office)
James L. Shea (Also at Washington, D.C. Office)
Ellen F. Dyke (Not admitted in MD; Resident, McLean, Virginia Office)
William D. Quarles (Also at Washington, D.C. and Towson, Maryland Offices)
Donald R. Hartman (Not admitted in MD; Resident, Washington, D.C. Office)
Christopher R. Mellott
James A. Dunbar (Also at Washington, D.C. Office)
Elizabeth R. Hughes
Robert A. Cook
Aline C. Ryan
David J. Heubeck
J. Michael Brennan (Resident, Towson, Maryland Office)
Bruce H. Jurist (Also at Washington, D.C. Office)
Ariel Vannier

(See Next Column)

OF COUNSEL

David D. Downes (Resident, Towson, Maryland Office)
Thomas J. Cooper (Not admitted in MD; Resident, Washington, D. C. Office)
Mary T. Flynn (Not admitted in MD; Resident, McLean, Virginia Office)

ASSOCIATES

David S. Darland (Not admitted in MD; Resident, Washington, D.C. Office)
Andrew R. Herrup (Resident, Washington, D.C. Office)
Frederick M. Hopkins
Mary-Dulany James (Resident, Towson, Maryland Office)
Michael S. Kosmas
Gregory L. Laubach (Resident, Rockville, Maryland Office)
Wingrove S. Lynton
Vicki Margolis (Also at Washington, D.C. Office)
John A. McCauley
Joseph C. Schmelter

For Complete List of Firm Personnel, See General Section

For full biographical listings, see the Martindale-Hubbell Law Directory

ROCKVILLE,* Montgomery Co.

VENABLE ATTORNEYS AT LAW VENABLE, BAETJER AND HOWARD, LLP (AV)

A Partnership including Professional Corporations
Suite 500, One Church Street, P.O. Box 1906, 20850-4129
Telephone: 301-217-5600
FAX: 301-217-5617
Baltimore, Maryland Office: 1800 Mercantile Bank & Trust Building, 2 Hopkins Plaza.
Telephone: 410-244-7400.
Washington, D.C. Office: Venable, Baetjer, Howard & Civiletti LLP, Suite 1000, 1201 New York Avenue, N.W.
Telephone: 202-962-4800.
McLean, Virginia Office: Suite 400, 2010 Corporate Ridge.
Telephone: 703-760-1600.
Towson, Maryland, Office: 210 Allegheny Avenue, P. O. Box 5517.
Telephone: 410-494-6200.

MEMBERS OF FIRM

Daniel O'C. Tracy, Jr. (Also at Baltimore, Maryland Office)
Paul T. Glasgow
John A. Roberts (Also at Baltimore, Maryland Office)

ASSOCIATE
Gregory L. Laubach

For Complete List of Firm Personnel, See General Section

For full biographical listings, see the Martindale-Hubbell Law Directory

TOWSON,* Baltimore Co.

VENABLE ATTORNEYS AT LAW VENABLE, BAETJER AND HOWARD, LLP (AV)

A Partnership including Professional Corporations
210 Allegheny Avenue, P.O. Box 5517, 21204
Telephone: 410-494-6200
FAX: 410-821-0147
Baltimore, Maryland Office: 1800 Mercantile Bank & Trust Building, 2 Hopkins Plaza.
Telephone: 410-244-7400.
Washington, D.C. Office: Venable, Baetjer, Howard & Civiletti LLP, Suite 1000, 1201 New York Avenue, N.W.
Telephone: 202-962-4800.
McLean, Virginia Office: Suite 400, 2010 Corporate Ridge.
Telephone: 703-760-1600.
Rockville, Maryland Office: Suite 500, One Church Street, P. O. Box 1906.
Telephone: 301-217-5600.

PARTNERS

Benjamin R. Civiletti (P.C.) (Also at Washington, D.C. and Baltimore, Maryland Offices)
John H. Zink, III
Joseph C. Wich, Jr.
J. Michael Brennan

OF COUNSEL
David D. Downes

ASSOCIATE
Mary-Dulany James

For Complete List of Firm Personnel, See General Section

For full biographical listings, see the Martindale-Hubbell Law Directory

UPPER MARLBORO, Prince Georges Co.

KNIGHT, MANZI, BRENNAN, SHAY AND HAM, A PROFESSIONAL ASSOCIATION (AV)

14440 Old Mill Road, 20772
Telephone: 301-952-0100
Annapolis/Baltimore: 410-792-3786
Fax: 301-952-0221
Crofton, Maryland Office: 2411 Crofton Lane, # 26.
Telephone: 301-261-0808.
Fax: 301-261-6945.
Mitchellville, Maryland Office: 12164 Central Avenue, Suite 228.
Telephone: 301-390-0577.
Fax: 301-390-8464.

William E. Knight	John F. Shay, Jr.
Robert A. Manzi	Richard J. Ham
William C. Brennan, Jr.	Martin J. Shuham

Monica M. Haley-Pierson	Norman D. Rivera
Daniel F. Lynch III	Robert L. Lombardo

OF COUNSEL
Stuart R. Hammett

For full biographical listings, see the Martindale-Hubbell Law Directory

MASSACHUSETTS

BOSTON, Suffolk Co.

BARRON & STADFELD, P.C. (AV)

Two Center Plaza, 02108
Telephone: 617-723-9800
Telecopier: 617-523-8359
Email: PUBLIC@BARRONSTAD.COM *URL:*
HTTP://WWW.BARRONSTAD.COM
Hyannis, Massachusetts Office: 258 Winter Street.
Telephone: 617-778-6622.

Thomas V. Bennett	Kevin F. Moloney
Julie Taylor Moran	

Alison L. Berman
OF COUNSEL
Hertz N. Henkoff

For Complete List of Firm Personnel, See General Section

For full biographical listings, see the Martindale-Hubbell Law Directory

CRAIG AND MACAULEY, PROFESSIONAL CORPORATION (AV)

Federal Reserve Plaza, 600 Atlantic Avenue, 02210
Telephone: 617-367-9500
Telecopier: 617-742-1788; 617-248-0886
Email: cmpc@ultranet.com

John C. Craig	David F. Hannon
William F. Macauley	Mary P. Brody
John G. Snyder	

Mark A. Dorff

For Complete List of Firm Personnel, See General Section

For full biographical listings, see the Martindale-Hubbell Law Directory

PALMER & DODGE LLP (AV)

One Beacon Street, 02108
Telephone: 617-573-0100
Facsimile: 617-227-4420

MEMBERS OF FIRM

Matthew C. Dallett	Jerry V. Klima
John L. Whitlock	

For Complete List of Firm Personnel, See General Section

For full biographical listings, see the Martindale-Hubbell Law Directory

PEABODY & ARNOLD (AV)

A Partnership including Professional Corporations
50 Rowes Wharf, 02110-3342
Telephone: 617-951-2100
Telecopier: 617-951-2125
Providence, Rhode Island Office: One Citizens Plaza, Suite 840.
Telephone: 401-831-8330.
Fax: 401-831-8359.

(See Next Column)

MEMBERS OF FIRM

Paul J. Ayoub	David F. Hendren
Jonathan Bangs	James A. P. Homans
Michael F. Burke	John A. Kessler, Jr.
Philip H. Cahalin	Anil Khosla
Robert J. Coughlin	Andrew R. Menard
Amanda D. Darwin	Frank N. Ray (Resident,
John K. Dineen	Providence, Rhode Island
John R. Gowell, Jr. (Resident,	Office)
Providence, Rhode Island	Douglas C. Reynolds
Office)	Suanne C. St. Charles
Ripley E. Hastings	Donald E. Vaughan

ASSOCIATES

Frank S. Hamblett	Robert Payne Fox, Jr.
Amelia M. Charamba	John P. Dougherty
Jane E. Kirk	

For Complete List of Firm Personnel, See General Section

For full biographical listings, see the Martindale-Hubbell Law Directory

SHERBURNE, POWERS & NEEDHAM, P.C. (AV)

One Beacon Street, 02108
Telephone: 617-523-2700
Fax: 617-523-6850
Email: @SHERBURNE.COM

William D. Weeks	Benjamin Volinski
John T. Collins	Mark Schonfeld
Allan J. Landau	James D. Smeallie
Stephen A. Hopkins	Paul Killeen
Alan I. Falk	Gordon P. Katz
C. Thomas Swaim	Joseph B. Darby, III
James Pollock	Richard M Yanofsky
William V. Tripp III	James E. McDermott
Stephen S. Young	Kenneth P. Brier
William F. Machen	Robert V. Lizza
W. Robert Allison	Miriam Goldstein Altman
Philip J. Notopoulos	John J. Monaghan
Richard J. Hindlian	Margaret J. Palladino
Paul E. Troy	Mark C. Michalowski
Harold W. Potter, Jr.	David Scott Sloan
Philip S. Lapatin	M. Chrysa Long
Pamela A. Duckworth	Lawrence D. Bradley
Miriam J. McKendall	

Cynthia A. Brown	Amy J. Mastrobattista
Cynthia M. Hern	Leslie A. Sprinkle
Meredeth A. Beers	Douglas W. Clapp
Dianne R. Phillips	Jeffrey A. Huebschmann
Paul M. James	Tamara E. Goulston
Theodore F. Hanselman	Paul G. Lannon, Jr.
Joshua C. Krumholz	Nicholas J. Psyhogeos
Ieuan G. Mahony	Edward J. Naughton
Jeffrey J. Nix	Kathaleen Kelly Cutone
(Not admitted in MA)	Laurie A. Tribble
Kenneth L. Harvey	Neil C. Higgins
Christopher J. Trombetta	Deborah Paige Stone
Elise N. Zoli	Brian R. Popiel

COUNSEL

Haig Der Manuelian	Karl J. Hirshman
Mason M. Taber, Jr.	Dale R. Johnson

For full biographical listings, see the Martindale-Hubbell Law Directory

WARNER & STACKPOLE LLP (AV)

75 State Street, 02109
Telephone: 617-951-9000
Telecopier: 617-951-9151
Email: w&s@warstack.com

MEMBERS OF FIRM

Paul C. Bauer	Stephen E. Moore
John C. Hutchins	Christopher E. Nolin
John J. McCarthy	Stanley V. Ragalevsky

ASSOCIATE
David J. Powers

For Complete List of Firm Personnel, See General Section

For full biographical listings, see the Martindale-Hubbell Law Directory

CAMBRIDGE, Middlesex Co.

WILLIAM M. O'BRIEN (AV)

Suite 216, 186 Alewife Brook Parkway, 02138
Telephone: 617-661-2600
Fax: 617-864-0654

For full biographical listings, see the Martindale-Hubbell Law Directory

SPRINGFIELD, * Hampden Co.

HENDEL, COLLINS & NEWTON, P.C. (AV)

101 State Street, 01103
Telephone: 413-734-6411
Fax: 413-734-8069

Philip J. Hendel	Joseph H. Reinhardt
Joseph B. Collins	Jonathan R. Goldsmith
Carla W. Newton	Henry E. Geberth, Jr.

George I. Roumeliotis

Representative Clients: Springfield Institution for Savings; United Cooperative Bank.
Approved Attorneys for: First American Title Insurance Co.; Commonwealth Land Title Ins. Co.
Reference: Shawmut Bank, N.A.

For full biographical listings, see the Martindale-Hubbell Law Directory

WORCESTER, * Worcester Co.

MacCarthy, Pojani & Hurley (AV)

Worcester Plaza, 446 Main Street, 01608
Telephone: 508-798-2480
Fax: 508-797-9561

Dennis Pojani	John F. Hurley, Jr.

John Macuga, Jr.

Representative Clients: Fleet Bank of Massachusetts, N.A.; Melville Corp.; Travelers Insurance Co.; Liberty Mutual Co.; Commerce Insurance Co.; Worcester Mutual Insurance Co.; Health Plans, Inc.; Marane Oil Corp.

For Complete List of Firm Personnel, See General Section

For full biographical listings, see the Martindale-Hubbell Law Directory

MICHIGAN

ADRIAN, * Lenawee Co.

WALKER, WATTS, JACKSON & McFARLAND (AV)

160 North Winter Street, 49221
Telephone: 517-265-8138
Fax: 517-265-8286

MEMBERS OF FIRM

William H. Walker	Mark A. Jackson
Prosser M. Watts, Jr.	Michael McFarland

Attorneys for: Bank of Lenawee.

For full biographical listings, see the Martindale-Hubbell Law Directory

ANN ARBOR, * Washtenaw Co.

BRAUN KENDRICK FINKBEINER PLC (AV)

700 First National Building, 48104
Telephone: 313-995-4100
Telecopier: 313-995-4798
URL: http://www.bkf-law.com
Bay City, Michigan Office: 201 Phoenix Building, P.O. Box 2039.
Telephone: 517-895-8505.
Telecopier: 517-895-8437.
Saginaw, Michigan Office: 101 N. Washington, Suite 812.
Telephone: 517-753-3461.
Telecopier: 517-753-3951.

Barry M. Levine

Representative Clients: The Dow Chemical Co.; General Motors Corp.; Lobdell Emery Manufacturing Co.; Merrill, Lynch, Inc.; Saginaw General Hospital; Saginaw News; The Wickes Foundation.

For full biographical listings, see the Martindale-Hubbell Law Directory

CONLIN, McKENNEY & PHILBRICK, P.C. (AV)

350 South Main Street Suite 400, 48104-2131
Telephone: 313-761-9000
Fax: 313-761-9001

Edward F. Conlin (1902-1953)	Robert M. Brimacombe
John W. Conlin (1904-1972)	James A. Schriemer
Albert J. Parker (1901-1970)	William M. Sweet
Chris L. McKenney	Elizabeth M. Petoskey
Karl R. Frankena	Bradley J. MeLampy
Allen J. Philbrick	Joseph W. Phillips
Phillip J. Bowen	Lori A. Buiteweg
Michael D. Highfield	Douglas G. McClure
Bruce N. Elliott	Thomas B. Bourque
Neil J. Juliar	Marjorie M. Dixon

Kenneth L. Spencer

(See Next Column)

OF COUNSEL
John W. Conlin

Representative Clients: Fingerle Lumber Co.; Ann Arbor Area Board of Realtors; Borders, Inc.; Auto-Owners Insurance Co.; Key Bank.
Approved Attorneys for: Nations Title Insurance Co.; Ticor Title Insurance Co.

For full biographical listings, see the Martindale-Hubbell Law Directory

MILLER, CANFIELD, PADDOCK AND STONE, P.L.C. (AV)

A Professional Limited Liability Company
Founded in 1852 by Sidney Davy Miller
101 North Main Street, Seventh Floor, 48104-1400
Telephone: 313-663-2445
Fax: 313-747-7147
Detroit, Michigan Office: 150 West Jefferson, Suite 2500, 48226-4415.
Telephone: 313-963-6420.
Fax: 313-496-7500.
Cable Address: "Stem Detroit."
Bloomfield Hills, Michigan Office: Suite 100, Pinehurst Office Center, 1400 North Woodward, 48303-2014.
Telephone: 313-645-5000.
Fax: 313-645-1917.
Grand Rapids, Michigan Office: 1200 Campau Square Plaza, 99 Monroe, N.W., 49503-2639.
Telephone: 616-454-8656.
Fax: 616-776-6322.
Howell, Michigan Office: 121 South Barnard Street, Suite 4, 48843-2305.
Telephone: 517-546-7600.
Telecopier: 517-546-6974.
Kalamazoo, Michigan Office: 444 West Michigan Avenue, 49007-3752.
Telephone: 616-381-7030.
Fax: 616-382-0244.
Lansing, Michigan Office: One Michigan Avenue, Suite 900, 48933-1609.
Telephone: 517-487-2070.
Fax: 517-374-6304.
Monroe, Michigan Office: The Executive Centre, 214 East Elm Avenue, 48161-2682.
Telephone: 313-243-2000.
Fax: 313-243-0901.
Washington, D.C. Office: 1225 Nineteenth Street, N.W., Suite 400. 20036.
Telephone: 202-429-5575; 785-0600.
Fax: 202-331-1118; 785-1234.
Pensacola, Florida Office: 25 West Cedar, 32501.
Telephone: 904-469-1088.
Fax: 904-432-0677.
St. Petersburg, Florida Office: 100 Second Avenue S., Suite 7045, 33701.
Telephone: 813-982-6000.
Fax: 813-892-6002.
New York, New York Office: Eleventh Floor, 135 East 57th Street, 10022-2087.
Telephone: 212-754-5400.
Fax: 212-754-5401.
Gdansk, Poland Office: Suite 322, Dom Technika Building, UI. Rajska 6, 80-850.
Telephone: 011-485-831-2808.
Fax: 011-485-831-4719.
Warsaw, Poland Office: UI. Marszalkowska 82, Suite 561, 00-517.
Telephone: 011-482-623-6457 and 6458.
Fax: 011-482-623-6459.

RESIDENT PRINCIPALS
Robert E. Gilbert

Representative Firm Clients: Chrysler Corporation; Comerica, Incorporated; City of Detroit, Michigan; Detroit Tigers, Inc.; First of Michigan; Ford Motor Company; Ford Motor Credit Company; Great Lakes Bancorp; Henry Ford Hospital; INVETECH Company.

For Complete List of Firm Personnel, See General Section

For full biographical listings, see the Martindale-Hubbell Law Directory

PEAR SPERLING EGGAN & MUSKOVITZ, P.C. (AV)

Domino's Farms, 24 Frank Lloyd Wright Drive, 48105
Telephone: 313-665-4441
Fax: 313-665-8788
Ypsilanti, Michigan Offices: 5 South Washington Street.
Telephone: 313-483-3626 and 2164 Bellevue at Washtenaw.
Telephone: 313-483-7177.

Edwin L. Pear	Joel F. Graziani
Andrew M. Eggan	Helen Conklin Vick

Counsel For: Domino's Pizza, Inc.; Citizens Banking Corporation; The Credit Bureau of Ypsilanti.

For Complete List of Firm Personnel, See General Section

For full biographical listings, see the Martindale-Hubbell Law Directory

BAY CITY,* Bay Co.

BRAUN KENDRICK FINKBEINER PLC (AV)

201 Phoenix Building, P.O. Box 2039, 48708
Telephone: 517-895-8505
Telecopier: 517-895-8437
URL: http://www.bkf-law.com
Saginaw, Michigan Office: 101 N. Washington, Suite 812. 8th Floor
Second National Bank Building.
Telephone: 517-753-3461.
Telecopier: 517-753-3951.
Ann Arbor, Michigan Office: 700 First National Building.
Telephone: 313-995-4100.
Telecopier: 313-995-4798.

Ralph J. Isackson	Gregory E. Meter
George F. Gronewold, Jr.	Daniel S. Opperman
Frank M. Quinn	Gregory T. Demers

OF COUNSEL
Patrick D. Neering

Representative Clients: APV Chemical Machinery, Inc.; Bay Health Systems; Catholic Federal Credit Union; City of Saginaw; City of Vassar; City of Milwaukee; Corporate Service; Cox Cable.

For Complete List of Firm Personnel, See General Section

For full biographical listings, see the Martindale-Hubbell Law Directory

BINGHAM FARMS, Oakland Co.

KORNEY & HELDT (AV)

30700 Telegraph Road, Suite 1551, 48025
Telephone: 810-646-1050
Fax: 810-646-1054

J. Douglas Korney	Jeffrey A. Heldt

For full biographical listings, see the Martindale-Hubbell Law Directory

SOTIROFF ABRAMCZYK & RAUSS, P.C. (AV)

30400 Telegraph Road, Suite 444, 48025-4541
Telephone: 810-642-6000
Facsimile: 810-642-9001

Philip Sotiroff	Lawrence A. Tower
Lawrence R. Abramczyk	Robert B. Goldi
Dennis M. Rauss	Keith A. Sotiroff

For full biographical listings, see the Martindale-Hubbell Law Directory

BLOOMFIELD HILLS, Oakland Co.

ADKISON NEED (AV)

1533 North Woodward Avenue, Suite 210, 48304
Telephone: 810-540-7400
Fax: 810-540-7401
Email: AdkisNeed@aol.com

MEMBERS OF FIRM

Phillip G. Adkison	Paul Green
Gregory K. Need	Kelly A. Allen
Deborah M. Schneider	

ASSOCIATES

Richard D. Kuhn, Jr.	Ann D. Christ
Kathryn N. Nichols	Laura B. Andoni

For full biographical listings, see the Martindale-Hubbell Law Directory

HOWARD & HOWARD ATTORNEYS, P.C. (AV)

The Pinehurst Office Center, Suite 101, 1400 North Woodward Avenue, 48304-2856
Telephone: 810-645-1483
Telecopier: 810-645-1568
Kalamazoo, Michigan Office: The Kalamazoo Building, Suite 400, 107 West Michigan Avenue.
Telephone: 616-382-1483.
Telecopier: 616-382-1568.
Lansing, Michigan Office: The Phoenix Building, Suite 500, 222 Washington Square, North.
Telephone: 517-485-1483.
Telecopier: 517-485-1568.
Peoria, Illinois Office: The Creve Coeur Building, Suite 200, 321 Liberty Street.
Telephone: 309-672-1483.
Telecopier: 309-672-1568.
Tampa, Florida Office: First of America Plaza, Suite 2000, 201 East Kennedy Boulevard.
Telephone: 813-229-1483.
Telecopier: 813-229-1568.

(See Next Column)

Gustaf R. Andreasen	Robert D. Mollhagen
Philip T. Carter	Roshunda L. Price-Harper
Michael G. Cruse	Robert C. Rosselot
J. Michael Kemp	(Not admitted in MI)
Timothy E. Kraepel	Robert L. Schwartz
Howard A. Lax	Melanie Mayo West
John E. Young	

Representative Clients: For Representative Client list, see General Practice, Bloomfield Hills, MI.

For Complete List of Firm Personnel, See General Section

For full biographical listings, see the Martindale-Hubbell Law Directory

CHEBOYGAN,* Cheboygan Co.

BODMAN, LONGLEY & DAHLING LLP (AV)

229 Court Street, P.O. Box 405, 49721
Telephone: 616-627-4351
Fax: 616-627-2802
Email: 2080194@mcimail.com
Detroit, Michigan Office: 34th Floor, 100 Renaissance Center.
Telephone: 313-259-7777.
Fax: 313-393-7579.
Troy, Michigan Office: Suite 2020, 755 West Big Beaver Road.
Telephone: 810-362-2110.
Fax: 810-244-0780.
Ann Arbor, Michigan Office: 110 Miller, Suite 300.
Telephone: 313-761-3780.
Fax: 313-930-2494.

RESIDENT PARTNERS

James C. Conboy, Jr.	Kathleen A. Lieder
Lloyd C. Fell	Lawrence P. Hanson
Michael A. Stack	Linda J. Throne
David W. Barton	

RESIDENT ASSOCIATES

W. Allen De Young	Amy J. Durant

LEGAL SUPPORT PERSONNEL

REGULATORY CONSULTANT
Becky D. Kelly

For full biographical listings, see the Martindale-Hubbell Law Directory

DETROIT,* Wayne Co.

BODMAN, LONGLEY & DAHLING LLP (AV)

34th Floor 100 Renaissance Center, 48243
Telephone: 313-259-7777
Fax: 313-393-7579
Email: 2080194@mcimail.com
Troy, Michigan Office: Suite 2020, 755 West Big Beaver Road.
Telephone: 810-362-2110.
Fax: 810-244-0780.
Ann Arbor, Michigan Office: 110 Miller, Suite 300.
Telephone: 313-761-3780.
Fax: 313-930-2494.
Northern Michigan Office: 229 Court Street, P.O. Box 405, Cheboygan.
Telephone: 616-627-4351.
Fax: 616-627-2802.

MEMBERS OF FIRM

Richard D. Rohr	Robert J. Diehl, Jr.
Joseph A. Sullivan	James C. Conboy, Jr.
Thomas A. Roach	(Northern Michigan Office)
(Ann Arbor Office)	Lloyd C. Fell
James T. Heimbuch	(Northern Michigan Office)
Herold McC. Deason	Michael A. Stack
Joseph J. Kochanek	(Northern Michigan Office)
Randolph S. Perry	Lawrence P. Hanson
David G. Chardavoyne	(Northern Michigan Office)
Larry R. Shulman	Christopher J. Dine
Thomas Van Dusen	(Troy Office)
(Troy Office)	Kathleen O'C. Hickey

For Representative Client List, See General Section

For Complete List of Firm Personnel, See General Section

For full biographical listings, see the Martindale-Hubbell Law Directory

FEIKENS, VANDER MALE, STEVENS, BELLAMY & GILCHRIST, P.C. (AV)

One Detroit Center Suite 3400, 500 Woodward Avenue, 48226-3406
Telephone: 313-962-5909
Fax: 313-962-3125
Email: FEIKENS@COUNSEL.COM

(See Next Column)

FEIKENS, VANDER MALE, STEVENS, BELLAMY & GILCHRIST P.C.—*Continued*

Robert E. Dice (1922-1983)	Lee A. Stevens
Jon Feikens	William C. Hurley
Jack E. Vander Male	Linda M. Galbraith
Frederick B. Bellamy	Michael S. Cafferty
Alan Gordon Gilchrist	Robert H. Feikens
L. Neal Kennedy	Gerald W. Van Wyke
Bruce A. VandeVusse	Roger L. Wolcott
	Sharon McPhail

Richard G. Koefod	Keith J. Soltis
Joseph E. Kozely, Jr.	Michael B. Barey
Jeffrey Feikens	Renee T. VanderHagen
	Michael P. Citrin

OF COUNSEL

Sam W. Thomas (P.C.)　　　　Walter Vincent Bernard III

LEGAL SUPPORT PERSONNEL

PARALEGALS

Robert Westveer　　　　　　　Linda Barthlow

For full biographical listings, see the Martindale-Hubbell Law Directory

LEWIS, CLAY & MUNDAY, A PROFESSIONAL CORPORATION (AV)

(Formerly Lewis, White & Clay, P.C.)
1300 First National Building, 660 Woodward Avenue, 48226-3531
Telephone: 313-961-2550
Troy, Michigan Office: Liberty Center, Suite 200. 100 West Big Beaver Road. 48084.
Telephone: 810-680-6702.
Fax: 810-680-6703.
Washington, D.C. Office: 1000 16th Street, N.W., Suite 401. 20036.
Telephone: 202-835-0616.
Fax: 202-833-3316.
Boston, Massachusetts Office: 10 Post Office Square.
Telephone: 617-422-8646.
Fax: 617-338-5693.

David Baker Lewis	Frank E. Barbee
Eric Lee Clay	Camille Stearns Miller
Reuben A. Munday	Michael T. Raymond
Ulysses Whittaker Boykin	Jacqueline H. Sellers
Carl F. Stafford	David N. Zacks
Helen Francine Strong	Thomas J. Guyer
	Blair A. Person

Karen Kendrick Brown	Hans J. Massaquoi, Jr.
(Resident, Washington, D.C. Office)	Nancy C. Borland
	Tammy L. Terry
J. Taylor Teasdale	Lynn Westfall Gross
Wade Harper McCree	Suzanne P. Pope
Tyrone A. Powell	Matthew R. Halpin
Susan D. Hoffman	Donica Thomas Varner
John J. Walsh	Damon L. White
Andrea L. Powell	(Not admitted in MI)
Althea Lynn Foster	Kathleen L. Royal

COUNSEL

Otis M. Smith (1922-1994)	G. Allen Bass (Resident, Boston,
Herbert O. Reid, Sr. (1915-1991)	Massachusetts Office)

Representative Clients: Omnicare Health Plan; Aetna Life & Casualty Co.; Chrysler Motors Corp.; Chrysler Financial Corp.; MCI Communications Corp.; City of Detroit; City of Detroit Building Authority; City of Detroit Downtown Development Authority; Consolidated Rail Corp. (Conrail); Equitable Life Assurance Society of the United States.

For full biographical listings, see the Martindale-Hubbell Law Directory

MAGER, MERCER, SCOTT & ALBER, P.C. (AV)

500 Woodward Avenue Suite 3400, 48226
Telephone: 313-962-8212
Facsimile: 313-962-5413
Oakland County Office: Top of Troy Building, 755 West Big Beaver, Suite 1700, Troy, Michigan.
Telephone: 810-362-8212.
Facsimile: 810-362-6944.
Macomb County Office: 18285 Ten Mile Road, Suite 100, Roseville, Michigan.
Telephone: 810-771-1100.
Facsimile: 810-775-5170.

George J. Mager, Jr.

Representative Clients: ABB Flakt, Inc.; American States Insurance Co.; CEI Industries; Central Venture Corp.; CIGNA; Construction Management, Inc.

For full biographical listings, see the Martindale-Hubbell Law Directory

MILLER, CANFIELD, PADDOCK AND STONE, P.L.C. (AV)

A Professional Limited Liability Company
Founded in 1852 by Sidney Davy Miller
150 West Jefferson, Suite 2500, 48226-4415
Telephone: 313-963-6420
Fax: 313-496-7500
Cable Address: "Stem Detroit"
Detroit, Michigan Office: 150 West Jefferson, Suite 2500, 48226-4415.
Telephone: 313-963-6420.
Fax: 313-496-7500.
Cable Address: "Stem Detroit."
Ann Arbor, Michigan Office: 101 North Main Street, 7th Floor, 48104-1400.
Telephone: 313-663-2445.
Fax: 313-747-7147.
Bloomfield Hills, Michigan Office: Suite 100, Pinehurst Office Center, 1400 North Woodward, 48303-2014.
Telephone: 313-645-5000.
Fax: 313-645-1917.
Grand Rapids, Michigan Office: 1200 Campau Square Plaza, 99 Monroe, N.W., 49503-2639.
Telephone: 616-454-8656.
Fax: 616-776-6322.
Howell, Michigan Office: 121 South Barnard Street, Suite 4, 48843-2305.
Telephone: 517-546-7600.
Telecopier: 517-546-6974.
Kalamazoo, Michigan Office: 444 West Michigan Avenue, 49007-3752.
Telephone: 616-381-7030.
Fax: 616-382-0244.
Lansing, Michigan Office: One Michigan Avenue, Suite 900, 48933-1609.
Telephone: 517-487-2070.
Fax: 517-374-6304.
Monroe, Michigan Office: The Executive Centre, 214 East Elm Avenue, 48161-2682.
Telephone: 313-243-2000.
Fax: 313-243-0901.
Washington, D.C. Office: 1225 Nineteenth Street, N.W., Suite 400. 20036.
Telephone: 202-429-5575; 785-0600.
Fax: 202-331-1118; 785-1234.
Pensacola, Florida Office: 25 West Cedar, 32501.
Telephone: 904-469-1088.
Fax: 904-432-0677.
St. Petersburg, Florida Office: 100 Second Avenue S., Suite 7045, 33701.
Telephone: 813-982-6000.
Fax: 813-892-6002.
New York, New York Office: Eleventh Floor, 135 East 57th Street, 10022-2087.
Telephone: 212-754-5400.
Fax: 212-754-5401.
Gdansk, Poland Office: Suite 322, Dom Technika Building, UI. Rajska 6, 80-850.
Telephone: 011-485-831-2808.
Fax: 011-485-831-4719.
Warsaw, Poland Office: UI. Marszalkowska 82, Suite 561, 00-517.
Telephone: 011-482-623-6457 and 6458.
Fax: 011-482-623-6459.

PRINCIPALS OF FIRM

George E. Parker, III	Thomas W. Linn
Rocque E. Lipford (P.C.)	Terrence M. Crawford
(Monroe Office)	J. Kevin Trimmer
David D. Joswick (P.C.)	(Bloomfield Hills Office)
John A. Marxer (P.C.)	Brad B. Arbuckle
(Bloomfield Hills Office)	(Bloomfield Hills Office)
Ronald H. Riback	Karen Ann McCoy
(Bloomfield Hills Office)	Ronald E. Hodess
	(Bloomfield Hills Office)

OF COUNSEL

Richard B. Gushée	Henry R. Nolte, Jr.
Richard A. Jones (P.C.)	(Bloomfield Hills Office)

SENIOR ATTORNEYS

Elise S. Levasseur	Susan E. Juroe
	(Washington, D.C. Office)

ASSOCIATE

Sally A. Hamby　(Bloomfield Hills Office)

Representative Firm Clients: Chrysler Corporation; Comerica, Incorporated; City of Detroit, Michigan; Detroit Tigers, Inc.; First of Michigan; Ford Motor Company; Ford Motor Credit Company; Great Lakes Bancorp; Henry Ford Hospital; INVETECH Company.

For Complete List of Firm Personnel, See General Section

For full biographical listings, see the Martindale-Hubbell Law Directory

SHAHEEN, JACOBS & ROSS, P.C. (AV)

585 East Larned, Suite 200, 48226-4316
Telephone: 313-963-1301
Telecopier: 313-963-7123
Email: LAWSJR@AOL.COM

(See Next Column)

SHAHEEN, JACOBS & ROSS P.C., Detroit—Continued

Joseph Shaheen (1920-1984) Steven P. Ross
Michael A. Jacobs (1949-1992) Michael J. Thomas
Thomas J. Wall, Jr.

For full biographical listings, see the Martindale-Hubbell Law Directory

GRAND RAPIDS,* Kent Co.

BORRE, PETERSON, FOWLER & REENS, P.C. (AV)

The Philo C. Fuller House, 44 Lafayette, N.E., P.O. Box
1767, 49501-1767
Telephone: 616-459-1971
Fax: 616-459-2393

Mark D. Sevald Harold E. Nelson
William R. Vander Sluis

References: NBD Bank; FMB-First Michigan Bank - Grand Rapids.

For Complete List of Firm Personnel, See General Section

For full biographical listings, see the Martindale-Hubbell Law Directory

MILLER, CANFIELD, PADDOCK AND STONE, P.L.C. (AV)

A Professional Limited Liability Company
Founded in 1852 by Sidney Davy Miller
1200 Campau Square Plaza, 99 Monroe, N.W., P.O. Box 329, 49503-2639
Telephone: 616-454-8656
Fax: 616-776-6322
Detroit, Michigan Office: 150 West Jefferson, Suite 2500, 48226-4415.
Telephone: 313-963-6420.
Fax: 313-496-7500.
Cable Address: "Stem Detroit."
Ann Arbor, Michigan Office: 101 North Main Street, 7th Floor, 48104-1400.
Telephone: 313-663-2445.
Fax: 313-747-7147.
Bloomfield Hills, Michigan Office: Suite 100, Pinehurst Office Center, 1400 North Woodward, 48303-2014.
Telephone: 313-645-5000.
Fax: 313-645-1917.
Howell, Michigan Office: 121 South Barnard Street, Suite 4, 48843-2305.
Telephone: 517-546-7600.
Telecopier: 517-546-6974.
Kalamazoo, Michigan Office: 444 West Michigan Avenue, 49007-3752.
Telephone: 616-381-7030.
Fax: 616-382-0244.
Lansing, Michigan Office: One Michigan Avenue, Suite 900, 48933-1609.
Telephone: 517-487-2070.
Fax: 517-374-6304.
Monroe, Michigan Office: The Executive Centre, 214 East Elm Avenue, 48161-2682.
Telephone: 313-243-2000.
Fax: 313-243-0901.
Washington, D.C. Office: 1225 Nineteenth Street, N.W., Suite 400. 20036.
Telephone: 202-429-5575; 785-0600.
Fax: 202-331-1118; 785-1234.
Pensacola, Florida Office: 25 West Cedar 32501.
Telephone: 904-469-1088.
Fax: 904-432-0677.
St. Petersburg Florida Office: 100 Second Avenue S., Suite 7045, 33701.
Telephone: 813-982-6000.
Fax: 813-892-6002.
New York, New York Office: Eleventh Floor, 135 East 57th Street, 10022-2087.
Telephone: 212-754-5400.
Fax: 212-754-5401.
Gdansk, Poland Office: Suite 322, Dom Technika Building, UI. Rajska 6, 80-850.
Telephone: 011-485-831-2808.
Fax: 011-485-831-4719.
Warsaw, Poland Office: UI. Marszalkowska 82, Suite 561, 00-517.
Telephone: 011-482-623-6457 and 6458.
Fax: 011-482-623-6459.

PRINCIPALS OF FIRM

Mark E. Putney (Resident Director, Grand Rapids Office) Michael G. Campbell
Robert E. Lee Wright
Vernon Bennett III
Richard A. Gaffin Douglas W. Crim
Charles S. Mishkind (Detroit, Lansing and Kalamazoo Offices)

OF COUNSEL

David E. Hathaway

SENIOR ATTORNEYS

David J. Hasper Stephen L. Elkins

ASSOCIATES

John C. Arndts Daniel H. Roberts
Bradley C. White John T. Stecco
Michael V. Camarota

(See Next Column)

Representative Firm Clients: Chrysler Corporation; Comerica, Incorporated; City of Detroit, Michigan; Detroit Tigers, Inc.; First of Michigan; Ford Motor Company; Ford Motor Credit Company; Great Lakes Bancorp; Henry Ford Hospital; INVETECH Company.

For full biographical listings, see the Martindale-Hubbell Law Directory

VARNUM, RIDDERING, SCHMIDT & HOWLETT LLP (AV)

A Limited Liability Partnership including Professional Corporations
Bridgewater Place, P.O. Box 352, 49501-0352
Telephone: 616-336-6000
800-262-0011
Facsimile: 616-336-7000
Telex: 1561593 VARN
Email: varnum@vrsh.com
Lansing, Michigan Office: The Victor Center, Suite 810, 210 North Washington Square, 48933.
Telephone: 517-482-6237.
Facsimile: 517-482-6937.
Kalamazoo, Michigan Office: 350 East Michigan Avenue, 49007.
Telephone: 616-382-2300.
Facsimile: 616-382-2382.
Grand Haven, Michigan Office: 321 Washington Street, P.O. Box 288, 49417.
Telephone: 616-846-7100.
Facsimile: 616-846-7101.
Battle Creek, Michigan Office: 4950 West Dickman Road, Suite B-1, 49015.
Telephone: 616-962-7144.
Bingham Farms, Michigan Office: 31600 Telegraph Road, Suite 230, 48025.
Telephone: 810-594-7330.
Facsimile: 810-594- 7331.

MEMBERS OF FIRM

Donald L. Johnson Jeffrey R. Hughes
Timothy J. Curtin Michael G. Wooldridge
Jeffrey L. Schad Joan E. Schleef
Thomas G. Demling Maureen Potter

Counsel for: Eastern Michigan Financial Corp.; First Manistique Corporation; First Michigan Bank Corp.; FNBH Bancorp Inc.; Independent Bank Corp.; Lenawee Bancorp Inc.; West Shore Bank Corp.
Special Counsel for: Comerica Bank, N.A.; Grand Bank; Michigan National Bank NA.

For Complete List of Firm Personnel, See General Section

For full biographical listings, see the Martindale-Hubbell Law Directory

WARNER NORCROSS & JUDD LLP (AV)

900 Old Kent Building, 111 Lyon Street, N.W., 49503-2489
Telephone: 616-752-2000
Fax: 616-752-2500
Muskegon, Michigan Office: 400 Terrace Plaza, P.O. Box 900.
Telephone: 616-727-2600.
Fax: 616-727-2699.
Holland, Michigan Office: Curtis Center, Suite 300, 170 College Avenue.
Telephone: 616-396-9800.
Fax: 616-396-3656.

MEMBERS OF FIRM

James H. Breay Thomas H. Thornhill
Ernest M. Sharpe (Resident at Muskegon Office)
Rodney D. Martin

ASSOCIATES

Jeffrey A. Ott Timothy L. Horner

Representative Clients: Michigan Bankers Assn.; Old Kent Financial Corp.; Shoreline Financial Corp.

For Complete List of Firm Personnel, See General Section

For full biographical listings, see the Martindale-Hubbell Law Directory

HOLLAND, Ottawa Co.

CUNNINGHAM DALMAN, P.C. (AV)

321 Settlers Road, P.O. Box 1767, 49422-1767
Telephone: 616-392-1821
Fax: 616-392-4769

Gordon H. Cunningham Kenneth B. Breese
Ronald L. Dalman Jeffrey K. Helder
Max R. Murphy Ronald J. Vander Veen
James A. Bidol David M. Zessin
Andrew J. Mulder Mark H. Zietlow
Joel G. Bouwens James W. Bouwens
Randall S. Schipper

Susan E. Vroegop Melinda M. Abney

(See Next Column)

CUNNINGHAM DALMAN P.C.—*Continued*
OF COUNSEL
Vernon D. Ten Cate   Kenneth B. Peirce, Jr.

Representative Clients: FMB-First Michigan Bank; First of America Bank-Holland, N.A.; Ottawa Savings Bank; City of Holland; The Title Office; Donnelly Corp.; Waste Management of Michigan.

For full biographical listings, see the Martindale-Hubbell Law Directory

---

KALAMAZOO,* Kalamazoo Co.

HOWARD & HOWARD ATTORNEYS, P.C. (AV)

The Kalamazoo Building, Suite 400, 107 West Michigan
  Avenue, 49007-3956
Telephone: 616-382-1483
Telecopier: 616-382-1568
Bloomfield Hills, Michigan Office: The Pinehurst Office Center, Suite 101,
1400 North Woodward Avenue.
Telephone: 810-645-1483.
Telecopier: 810-645-1568.
Lansing, Michigan Office: The Phoenix Building, Suite 500, 222
Washington Square North.
Telephone: 517-485-1483.
Telecopier: 517-485-1568.
Peoria, Illinois Office: The Creve Coeur Building, Suite 200, 321 Liberty
Street.
Telephone: 309-672-1483.
Telecopier: 309-672-1568.
Tampa, Florida Office: First of America Plaza, Suite 2000, 201 East
Kennedy Boulevard.
Telephone: 813-229-1483.
Telecopier: 813-229-1568.

John W. Allen	James H. Geary
Stephen D. Bigelow	Bruce R. Grubb
Jeffrey P. Chalmers	Joseph B. Hemker
William A. Dornbos	David E. Riggs

Representative Clients: For Representative Client list, see General Practice, Kalamazoo, MI.

For Complete List of Firm Personnel, See General Section

For full biographical listings, see the Martindale-Hubbell Law Directory

---

KREIS, ENDERLE, CALLANDER & HUDGINS, A PROFESSIONAL CORPORATION (AV)

One Moorsbridge, P.O. Box 4010, 49003-4010
Telephone: 616-324-3000
Telecopier: 616-324-3010
Email: kech@sapien.net *URL:* http://www.kech.com

Russell A. Kreis	C. Reid Hudgins III
Alan G. Enderle	Thomas G. King

For Complete List of Firm Personnel, See General Section

For full biographical listings, see the Martindale-Hubbell Law Directory

---

MILLER, CANFIELD, PADDOCK AND STONE, P.L.C. (AV)

A Professional Limited Liability Company
Founded in 1852 by Sidney Davy Miller
444 West Michigan Avenue, 49007-3752
Telephone: 616-381-7030
Fax: 616-382-0244
Detroit, Michigan Office: 150 West Jefferson, Suite 2500, 48226-4415.
Telephone: 313-963-6420.
Fax: 313-496-7500.
Cable Address: "Stem Detroit."
Ann Arbor, Michigan Office: 101 North Main Street, 7th Floor,
48104-1400.
Telephone: 313-663-2445.
Fax: 313-747-7147.
Bloomfield Hills, Michigan Office: Suite 100, Pinehurst Office Center, 1400
North Woodward, 48303-2014.
Telephone: 313-645-5000.
Fax: 313-645-1917.
Grand Rapids, Michigan Office: 1200 Campau Square Plaza, 99 Monroe,
N.W., 49503-2639.
Telephone: 616-454-8656.
Fax: 616-776-6322.
Howell, Michigan Office: 121 South Barnard Street, Suite 4, 48843-2305.
Telephone: 517-546-7600.
Telecopier: 517-546-6974.
Lansing, Michigan Office: One Michigan Avenue, Suite 900, 48933-1609.
Telephone: 517-487-2070.
Fax: 517-374-6304.
Monroe, Michigan Office: The Executive Centre, 214 East Elm Avenue,
48161-2682.
Telephone: 313-243-2000.
Fax: 313-243-0901.

(See Next Column)

Washington, D.C. Office: 1225 Nineteenth Street, N.W., Suite 400. 20036.
Telephone: 202-429-5575; 785-0600.
Fax: 202-331-1118; 785-1234.
Pensacola, Florida Office: 25 West Cedar, 32501.
Telephone: 904-469-1088.
Fax: 904-432-0677.
St. Petersburg, Florida Office: 100 Second Avenue S., Suite 7045, 33701.
Telephone: 813-982-6000.
Fax: 813-892-6002.
New York, New York Office: Eleventh Floor, 135 East 57th Street,
10022-2087.
Telephone: 212-754-5400.
Fax: 212-754-5401.
Gdansk, Poland Office: Suite 322, Dom Technika Building, UI. Rajska 6,
80-850.
Telephone: 011-485-831-2808.
Fax: 011-485-831-4719.
Warsaw, Poland Office: UI. Marszalkowska 82, Suite 561, 00-517.
Telephone: 011-482-623-6457 and 6458.
Fax: 011-482-623-6459.

PRINCIPALS OF FIRM
Eric V. Brown, Jr.	James G. Vantine, Jr.
John R. Cook	Thomas H. Van Dis

Representative Firm Clients: Chrysler Corporation; Comerica, Incorporated; City of Detroit, Michigan; Detroit Tigers, Inc.; First of Michigan; Ford Motor Company; Ford Motor Credit Company; Great Lakes Bancorp; Henry Ford Hospital; INVETECH Company.

For Complete List of Firm Personnel, See General Section

For full biographical listings, see the Martindale-Hubbell Law Directory

---

LANSING, Ingham Co.

FOSTER, SWIFT, COLLINS & SMITH, P.C. (AV)

313 South Washington Square, 48933-2193
Telephone: 517-371-8100
Telecopier: 517-371-8200
URL: http://www.fosterswift.com
Farmington Hills, Michigan Office: 32300 Northwestern Highway, Suite
230.
Telephone: 810-539-9900.
Fax: 810-851-7504.

Richard B. Foster	Steven L. Owen
Robert J. McCullen	Brent A. Titus
James B. Jensen, Jr.	Deanna Swisher
James B. Croom	Michael W. Puerner
Mark J. Burzych	

LEGAL SUPPORT PERSONNEL
LEGAL ASSISTANTS
Jeanne M. Phillips   Janice S. Underwood

Representative Clients: First of America Bank; M.S.U. Federal Credit Union, Community First Bank.

For Complete List of Firm Personnel, See General Section

For full biographical listings, see the Martindale-Hubbell Law Directory

---

FRASER TREBILCOCK DAVIS & FOSTER, P.C. (AV)

1000 Michigan National Tower, 48933
Telephone: 517-482-5800
Fax: 517-482-0887

Ronald R. Pentecost

Counsel for: Pioneer Bank; Northern Michigan Savings Bank; Bank One-East Lansing; Old Kent Bank; First National Bank of Michigan.

For Complete List of Firm Personnel, See General Section

For full biographical listings, see the Martindale-Hubbell Law Directory

---

HOWARD & HOWARD ATTORNEYS, P.C. (AV)

The Phoenix Building, Suite 500, 222 Washington Square,
  North, 48933-1817
Telephone: 517-485-1483
Telecopier: 517-485-1568
Kalamazoo, Michigan Office: The Kalamazoo Building, Suite 400, 107
West Michigan Avenue.
Telephone: 616-382-1483.
Telecopier: 616-382-1568.
Bloomfield Hills, Michigan Office: The Pinehurst Office Center, Suite 101,
1400 North Woodward Avenue.
Telephone: 810-645-1483.
Telecopier: 810-645-1568.
Peoria, Illinois Office: The Creve Coeur Building, Suite 200, 321 Liberty
Street.
Telephone: 309-672-1483.
Telecopier: 309-672-1568.
Tampa, Florida Office: First of America Plaza, Suite 2000, 201 East
Kennedy Boulevard.
Telephone: 813-229-1483.
Telecopier: 813-229-1568.

(See Next Column)

HOWARD & HOWARD ATTORNEYS P.C., *Lansing—Continued*

Todd D. Chamberlain	James E. Lozier
Kim D. Crooks	C. Douglas Moran
	Brad S. Rutledge

Representative Clients: For Representative Client list, see General Practice, Lansing, MI.

For Complete List of Firm Personnel, See General Section

For full biographical listings, see the Martindale-Hubbell Law Directory

MILLER, CANFIELD, PADDOCK AND STONE, P.L.C. (AV)

A Professional Limited Liability Company
Founded in 1852 by Sidney Davy Miller
Suite 900, One Michigan Avenue, 48933-1609
Telephone: 517-487-2070
Fax: 517-374-6304
Detroit, Michigan Office: 150 West Jefferson, Suite 2500, 48226-4415.
Telephone: 313-963-6420.
Fax: 313-496-7500.
Cable Address: "Stem Detroit."
Ann Arbor, Michigan Office: 101 North Main Street, 7th Floor, 48104-1400.
Telephone: 313-663-2445.
Fax: 313-747-7147.
Bloomfield Hills, Michigan Office: Suite 100, Pinehurst Office Center, 1400 North Woodward, 48303-2014.
Telephone: 313-645-5000.
Fax: 313-645-1917.
Grand Rapids, Michigan Office: 1200 Campau Square Plaza, 99 Monroe, N.W., 49503-2639.
Telephone: 616-454-8656.
Fax: 616-776-6322.
Howell, Michigan Office: 121 South Barnard Street, Suite 4, 48843-2305.
Telephone: 517-546-7600.
Telecopier: 517-546-6974.
Kalamazoo, Michigan Office: 444 West Michigan Avenue, 49007-3752.
Telephone: 616-381-7030.
Fax: 616-382-0244.
Monroe, Michigan Office: The Executive Centre, 214 East Elm Avenue, 48161-2682.
Telephone: 313-243-2000.
Fax: 313-243-0901.
Washington, D.C. Office: 1225 Nineteenth Street, N.W., Suite 400. 20036.
Telephone: 202-429-5575; 785-0600.
Fax: 202-331-1118; 785-1234.
Pensacola, Florida Office: 25 West Cedar, 32501.
Telephone: 904-469-1088.
Fax: 904-432-0677.
St. Petersburg Office: 100 Second Avenue S., Suite 7045, 33701.
Telephone: 813-982-6000.
Fax: 813-892-6002.
New York, New York Office: Eleventh Floor, 135 East 57th Street, 10022-2087.
Telephone: 212-754-5400.
Fax: 212-754-5401.
Gdansk, Poland Office: Suite 322, Dom Technika Building, UI. Rajska 6, 80-850.
Telephone: 011-485-831-2808.
Fax: 011-485-831-4719.
Warsaw, Poland Office: UI. Marszalkowska 82, Suite 561, 00-517.
Telephone: 011-482-623-6457 and 6458.
Fax: 011-482-623-6459.

PRINCIPALS OF FIRM
William J. Danhof (Resident)

Representative Firm Clients: Chrysler Corporation; Comerica, Incorporated; City of Detroit, Michigan; Detroit Tigers, Inc.; First of Michigan; Ford Motor Company; Ford Motor Credit Company; Great Lakes Bancorp; Henry Ford Hospital; INVETECH Company.

For Complete List of Firm Personnel, See General Section

For full biographical listings, see the Martindale-Hubbell Law Directory

---

SAGINAW,* Saginaw Co.

BRAUN KENDRICK FINKBEINER PLC (AV)

101 N. Washington Suite 812, 48607-1297
Telephone: 517-753-3461
Telecopier: 517-753-3951
URL: http://www.bkf-law.com
Bay City, Michigan Office: 201 Phoenix Building, P.O. Box 2039.
Telephone: 517-895-8505.
Telecopier: 517-895-8437.
Ann Arbor, Michigan Office: 700 First National Building.
Telephone: 313-995-4100.
Telecopier: 313-995-4798.

Hugo E. Braun, Jr.	Michael J. Sauer

OF COUNSEL
Morton E. Weldy

Representative Clients: The Dow Chemical Co.; General Motors Corp.; Lobdell Emery Manufacturing Co.; Merrill, Lynch, Inc.; Saginaw General Hospital; Saginaw News; The Wickes Foundation.

For Complete List of Firm Personnel, See General Section

For full biographical listings, see the Martindale-Hubbell Law Directory

---

SOUTHFIELD, Oakland Co.

MADDIN, HAUSER, WARTELL, ROTH, HELLER & PESSES, P.C. (AV)

Third Floor Essex Center, 28400 Northwestern Highway, P.O. Box 215, 48037
Telephone: 810-354-4030, 355-5200
Telefax: 810-354-1422

Milton M. Maddin (1902-1984)	Robert D. Kaplow
Michael W. Maddin	William E. Sigler
Mark R. Hauser	Stewart C. W. Weiner
C. Robert Wartell	Charles M. Lax
Richard J. Maddin	Stuart M. Bordman
Richard F. Roth	Steven D. Sallen
Harvey R. Heller	Joseph M. Fazio
Ian D. Pesses	Gregory J. Gamalski
Michael S. Leib	Julie Chenot Mayer

Nathaniel H. Simpson	Lowell D. Salesin
Ronald A. Sollish	Marc J. Mendelson
Mark H. Fink	Joseph W. Girardot
Steven M. Wolock	Lori E. Talsky

OF COUNSEL
Joel D. Kellman

Reference: Comerica Bank.

For full biographical listings, see the Martindale-Hubbell Law Directory

PROVIZER, LICHTENSTEIN & PHILLIPS, P.C. (AV)

4000 Town Center, Suite 1800, 48075
Telephone: 810-352-9080
Facsimile: 810-352-1491

Harold M. Provizer	David S. Lichtenstein
	Robert I. Brown

Representative Clients: Investuid Corporation; Mortgage Institute of Michigan.

For full biographical listings, see the Martindale-Hubbell Law Directory

SOMMERS, SCHWARTZ, SILVER & SCHWARTZ, P.C. (AV)

2000 Town Center, Suite 900, 48075
Telephone: 810-355-0300
Telecopier: 810-746-4001
Plymouth, Michigan Office: 747 South Main Street.
Telephone: 313-455-4250.

Steven J. Schwartz	Victor A. Coen
Gary A. Taback	David M. Black
	Joseph H. Bourgon

OF COUNSEL

Norman Samuel Sommers	Paul Groffsky

General Counsel for: City of Taylor; Foodland Distributors; C.A. Muer Corporation; Vlasic & Company; Midwest Health Centers, P.C.
Representative Clients: Michigan National Bank; Bank Hapoalim, B.M.; Beal Bank, S.A.

For Complete List of Firm Personnel, See General Section

For full biographical listings, see the Martindale-Hubbell Law Directory

---

TRAVERSE CITY,* Grand Traverse Co.

MURCHIE, CALCUTT & BOYNTON (AV)

109 East Front Street, Suite 300, 49684
Telephone: 616-947-7190
Fax: 616-947-4341

Robert B. Murchie (1894-1975)	William B. Calcutt
Harry Calcutt	Mark A. Burnheimer
Jack E. Boynton	Dawn M. Rogers

ASSOCIATE
Ralph J. Dilley (Not admitted in MI)

General Counsel for: Old Kent Bank-Grand Traverse; Northwestern Savings Bank & Trust; Central-State Bancorp; Traverse City Record Eagle; WPNB-7 & WTOM-4; Emergency Consultants, Inc.; National Guardian Risk Retention Group, Inc.; Farmers Mutual Insurance Co.; Environmental Solutions, Inc.
Local Counsel for: Consumers Power Co.

For full biographical listings, see the Martindale-Hubbell Law Directory

BANKRUPTCY LAW

ALABAMA

BIRMINGHAM, * Jefferson Co.

BRADLEY, ARANT, ROSE & WHITE (AV)

2001 Park Place, Suite 1400, P.O. Box 830709, 35283-0709
Telephone: 205-521-8000
Facsimile: 205-252-0264
Facsimile (SouthTrust Tower Office): 205-251-9915
URL: http://www.BARW.COM
Huntsville, Alabama Office: 200 Clinton Avenue West, Suite 900, 35801.
Telephone: 205-517-5100.
Facsimile: 205-533-5069.

MEMBERS OF FIRM

John P. Whittington　　　　　　　　Sherri Tucker Freeman

ASSOCIATES

J. Patrick Darby　　　　　　　　　Helena F. Tozzi
Jay R. Bender　　　　　　　　　　Lauren E. Wagner

For Complete List of Firm Personnel, See General Section

For full biographical listings, see the Martindale-Hubbell Law Directory

---

CORLEY, MONCUS & WARD, P.C. (AV)

400 Shades Creek Parkway, Suite 100, P.O. Box 59807, 35259
Telephone: 205-879-5959
Telecopier: 205-871-4411

Ezra B. Perry, Jr.

For Complete List of Firm Personnel, See General Section

For full biographical listings, see the Martindale-Hubbell Law Directory

---

GORDON, SILBERMAN, WIGGINS & CHILDS, A PROFESSIONAL CORPORATION (AV)

1400 SouthTrust Tower, 420 North 20th Street, 35203
Telephone: 205-328-0640
Telecopier: 205-254-1500

Wilbur G. Silberman　　　　　　　Harvey L. Wachsman

Mark P. Williams

For Complete List of Firm Personnel, See General Section

For full biographical listings, see the Martindale-Hubbell Law Directory

---

NAJJAR DENABURG, P.C. (AV)

2125 Morris Avenue, 35203
Telephone: 205-250-8400
Telecopier: 205-326-3837

Charles L. Denaburg　　　　　　　Robert H. Adams
David A. (Chip) Schwartz　　　　　Marvin E. Franklin

Walter F. McArdle

General Counsel: Acousti Engineering of Alabama, Inc.
Representative Client: Compass Bank.
Approved Attorneys for: Mississippi Valley Title Insurance Co.
Reference: Compass Bank.

For Complete List of Firm Personnel, See General Section

For full biographical listings, see the Martindale-Hubbell Law Directory

---

SCHOEL, OGLE, BENTON AND CENTENO (AV)

600 Financial Center, 505 North 20th Street, P.O. Box 1865, 35201-1865
Telephone: 205-521-7000
Telecopier: 205-521-7007

MEMBERS OF FIRM

Jerry W. Schoel　　　　　　　　　Lee R. Benton
Melinda Murphy Dionne

Reference: National Bank of Commerce; First Alabama Bank.

For Complete List of Firm Personnel, See General Section

For full biographical listings, see the Martindale-Hubbell Law Directory

---

HUNTSVILLE, * Madison Co.

BERRY, ABLES, TATUM, BAXTER, PARKER & HALL, P.C. (AV)

Legal Building, 315 Franklin Street, S.E., P.O. Box 165, 35804-0165
Telephone: 205-533-3740
Facsimile: 205-533-3751
Email: BAXTERJ@ATTMAIL.COM

William H. Blanton (1889-1973)　　James T. Tatum, Jr.
Joe M. Berry　　　　　　　　　　James T. Baxter, III
L. Bruce Ables　　　　　　　　　Thomas E. Parker, Jr.
　　　　　　　Bill G. Hall

James K. Brabston　　　　　　　　Mark Rogers Hunter

Representative Clients: AmSouth Bank; First Alabama Bank; General Shale Products Co.; The Hertz Corp.; Litton Industries, Inc.; Farmers Tractor Co.; Colonial Bank; Farm Credit Bank of Texas; Regions Mortgage.
Reference: First Alabama Bank.

For full biographical listings, see the Martindale-Hubbell Law Directory

---

MOBILE, * Mobile Co.

FINKBOHNER AND LAWLER, L.L.C. (AV)

169 Dauphin Street Suite 300, P.O. Box 3085, 36652
Telephone: 334-438-5871
Fax: 334-432-8052

MEMBERS OF FIRM

George W. Finkbohner, Jr.　　　　George W. Finkbohner, III
John L. Lawler　　　　　　　　　Royce A. Ray, III

For full biographical listings, see the Martindale-Hubbell Law Directory

---

JOHNSTONE, ADAMS, BAILEY, GORDON AND HARRIS, L.L.C. (AV)

Royal St. Francis Building, 104 St. Francis Street, P.O. Box 1988, 36633
Telephone: 334-432-7682
Facsimile: 334-432-2800
Telex: 782040

MEMBERS OF FIRM

I. David Cherniak　　　　　　　　William Alexander Gray, Jr.

General Counsel for: First Alabama Bank, Mobile; Infirmary Health System/Mobile Infirmary Medical Center/Rotary Rehabilitation Hospital (Multi-Hospital System).
Counsel for: Oil and Gas: Exxon Corp. Business and Corporate: Bell South Telecommunications, Inc.; Aluminum Co. of America; Michelin North America, Inc.; Metropolitan Life Insurance Co.; The Travelers Insurance Cos. Marine: The West of England Ship Owners Mutual Protection and Indemnity Association (Luxembourg); The Standard Steamship Owners' Protection and Indemnity Association (Bermuda) Ltd.

For Complete List of Firm Personnel, See General Section

For full biographical listings, see the Martindale-Hubbell Law Directory

---

LYONS, PIPES & COOK, P.C. (AV)

2 North Royal Street, P.O. Box 2727, 36652-2727
Telephone: 334-432-4481
Cable Address: "Lysea"
Telecopier: 334-433-1820

Wesley Pipes　　　　　　　　　　W. David Johnson, Jr.
　　　　　　　John C. Bell

Representative Clients: Chrysler Credit Corporation; SouthTrust Bank of Mobile.

For Complete List of Firm Personnel, See General Section

For full biographical listings, see the Martindale-Hubbell Law Directory

---

SILVER & VOIT, P.C. (AV)

4317 Midmost Drive, 36609-5589
Telephone: 334-343-0800
Fax: 334-343-0862
Email: IRVSILV@AOL.COM

Irving Silver　　　　　　　　　　Lawrence B. Voit
　　　　　　　Barry L. Thompson

Thomas G. F. Landry

For full biographical listings, see the Martindale-Hubbell Law Directory

---

MONTGOMERY, * Montgomery Co.

KAUFMAN & ROTHFEDER, P.C. (AV)

2740 Zelda Road Post Office Drawer 4540, 36103-4540
Telephone: 334-244-1111
Fax: 334-244-1969

(See Next Column)

KAUFMAN & ROTHFEDER P.C., *Montgomery—Continued*

Samuel Kaufman	George W. Thomas
Alan E. Rothfeder	John Ward Weiss
Jo Karen Parr	Robert M. Ritchey
Thomas R. DeBray	Simeon F. Penton
Richardson B. McKenzie, III	William B. Sellers
Robert E. L. Gilpin	J. Scott Pierce

Carla R. Cole

OF COUNSEL

William T. Carlson, Jr.

Counsel for: Russell Corp.; Sanders Lead Co., Inc.; Waste Management of North America, Inc.

For full biographical listings, see the Martindale-Hubbell Law Directory

PARNELL, CRUM & ANDERSON, P.A. (AV)

641 South Lawrence Street, P.O. Box 2189, 36102
Telephone: 334-832-4202
Telecopier: 334-832-4703

Charles N. Parnell, III	Charles L. Anderson
G. Barton Crum	Bernard B. Carr

Robert J. Russell, Jr.	Rita L. Hullett
Jennifer M. Chambliss	Kyle Dennis Massingale
Betty B. Byrne	James McCauley Smith

Reference: Colonial Bank of Montgomery.

For full biographical listings, see the Martindale-Hubbell Law Directory

ARIZONA

PHOENIX,* Maricopa Co.

BURCH & CRACCHIOLO, P.A. (AV)

702 East Osborn Road, Suite 200, 85014
Telephone: 602-274-7611
Fax: 602-234-0341
Mailing Address: P.O. Box 16882, Phoenix, AZ, 85011

Thomas A. Longfellow

OF COUNSEL

Howard C. Meyers

Representative Clients: Bashas' Inc.; Farmers Insurance Group; U-Haul International, Inc.

For Complete List of Firm Personnel, See General Section

For full biographical listings, see the Martindale-Hubbell Law Directory

CARMICHAEL & POWELL, PROFESSIONAL CORPORATION (AV)

7301 North 16th Street, 85020-5224
Telephone: 602-861-0777
Facsimile: 602-870-0296

Donald W. Powell	Sid A. Horwitz

Representative Clients: Kawasaki Motors Corp; Wendy's International, Inc.; Firstar Metropolitan Bank & Trust.

For full biographical listings, see the Martindale-Hubbell Law Directory

DAVIS & LOWE, P.C. (AV)

Suite 722, Security Building, 234 North Central Avenue, 85004
Telephone: 602-253-2882
Fax: 602-253-3088

Edward E. Davis	Virginia S. Matte
Charles W. Lowe	Don A. Beskrone
Ilene J. Lashinsky	Alisa C. Lacey

Representative Clients: Citgo Petroleum Corporation; Republic Companies; Tilden Financial Corp.; Douglas Allred Company; all Arizona Chapter 13 Trustees; Fresh Quest Produce, Inc. .
Reference: Firstar Metropolitan Bank.

For full biographical listings, see the Martindale-Hubbell Law Directory

DILLINGHAM CROSS, P.L.C. (AV)

5080 North 40th Street Suite 335, 85018
Telephone: 602-468-1811
Fax: 602-468-0442

John L. Dillingham	James E. Cross

James W. Reynolds

(See Next Column)

Thomas H. Allen

Representative Clients: Bank of New York; Textron Financial Corporation; Triad Financial Systems Corp.; General Financial Services, Inc.; LDI Corporation; Typetronics Business Systems, Inc.; Colliers Macaulay Nicolls (AZ); Lothar Goernitz, Bankruptcy Trustee; Superstition Crushing Co.; Superior Steel Building, Inc.

For full biographical listings, see the Martindale-Hubbell Law Directory

FENNEMORE CRAIG, A PROFESSIONAL CORPORATION (AV)

Two North Central, Suite 2200, 85004
Telephone: 602-257-8700
Fax: 602-257-8527
Scottsdale, Arizona Office: 6263 North Scottsdale Road, Suite 290, 85250.
Telephone: 602-257-5400.
Fax: 602-257-5409.
Tucson, Arizona Office: One South Church Avenue, Suite 1030, 85701.
Telephone: 520-791-6800.
Fax: 520-791-6820.

C. Webb Crockett	David A. Weatherwax
Leland M. Jones	Cathy L. Reece

Bryan A. Albue

Dewain D. Fox

For Complete List of Firm Personnel, See General Section

For full biographical listings, see the Martindale-Hubbell Law Directory

GAMMAGE & BURNHAM, P.L.C. (AV)

One Renaissance Square, Two North Central Avenue, Suite 1800, 85004
Telephone: 602-256-0566
Fax: 602-256-4475

MEMBERS OF FIRM

F. William Sheppard	Mary B. Artigue
Michael R. King	Ellen Harris Hoff

Representative Clients: Resolution Trust Corp.; Canadian Imperial Bank of Commerce; American Bantrust Mortgage; Bank of America.

For Complete List of Firm Personnel, See General Section

For full biographical listings, see the Martindale-Hubbell Law Directory

HIRSCH LAW OFFICE, P.C. (AV)

4614 E. Shea Boulevard Suite D250, 85028
Telephone: 602-996-9544
Fax: 602-494-0815

Lawrence D. Hirsch	Iva S. Hirsch

For full biographical listings, see the Martindale-Hubbell Law Directory

JENNINGS, STROUSS AND SALMON, P.L.C. (AV)

A Professional Limited Liability Company
One Renaissance Square, Two North Central, 85004-2393
Telephone: 602-262-5911
Fax: 602-253-3255

Gary G. Keltner	Wendy D. Woodrow

Brian N. Spector

Margaret A. Gillespie

For Complete List of Firm Personnel, See General Section

For full biographical listings, see the Martindale-Hubbell Law Directory

LEWIS AND ROCA, LLP (AV)

A Limited Liability Partnership including a Professional Corporation
40 North Central Avenue, 85004-4429
Telephone: 602-262-5311
Fax: 602-262-5747
Email: mlp@lrlaw.com
Tucson, Arizona Office: One South Church Avenue, Suite 700, 86701-1620.
Telephone: 520-622-2090.
Fax: 520-622-3088. E-Mail: mlp@lrlaw.com.

MEMBERS OF FIRM

Gerald K. Smith	Susan M. Freeman
Randolph J. Haines	Brent C. Gardner
Cathy M. Holt	Bret A. Maidman

For Complete List of Firm Personnel, See General Section

For full biographical listings, see the Martindale-Hubbell Law Directory

MARISCAL, WEEKS, McINTYRE & FRIEDLANDER, P.A. (AV)

2901 North Central Avenue Suite 200, 85012-2705
Telephone: 602-285-5000
Fax: 602-285-5100

(See Next Column)

MARISCAL, WEEKS, MCINTYRE & FRIEDLANDER P.A.—*Continued*

William L. Novotny   Franklin D. Dodge

References: Northern Trust Bank of Arizona; National Bank of Arizona.

For Complete List of Firm Personnel, See General Section

For full biographical listings, see the Martindale-Hubbell Law Directory

ROBERT J. NOVAK & ASSOCIATES (AV)

1440 E. Washington Street Suite 100, 85034
Telephone: 602-253-8000
Fax: 602-271-4733

ASSOCIATE
Herbert T. Swafford

Representative Clients: SouthTrust Mortgage, BancBoston; L.V. Associates, Ltd.; AEI Real Estate Fund Limited Partnership; Heron North American Property Trust; Tippmann Construction, Inc.; Sun World Corporation; G.B. Mannisto, Inc.; Phoenix Computer Systems, Inc.; Pasternack Architect, Inc.; Phoenix Plastics, Inc.

For full biographical listings, see the Martindale-Hubbell Law Directory

O'CONNOR, CAVANAGH, ANDERSON, KILLINGSWORTH & BESHEARS, A PROFESSIONAL ASSOCIATION (AV)

One East Camelback Road, Suite 1100, 85012-1656
Telephone: 602-263-2400
FAX: 602-263-2900
Email: firminfo@arizlaw.com
Sun City, Arizona Office: 13250 North Del Webb Boulevard, Suite B, 85351.
Telephone: 602-263-2808.
FAX: 602-933-3100.
Tucson, Arizona Office: O'Connor Cavanagh Molloy Jones, 33 N. Stone, Suite 2100, 85701, P.O. Box 2268, 85702.
Telephone: 520-622-3531.
FAX: 520-624-2816.
Nogales, Arizona Office: 1891 North Mastick Way, 85621.
Telephone: 520-761-4215.
FAX: 520-761-3505.

Henry L. Timmerman   Richard M. Lorenzen
Philip G. Mitchell

Craig J. Bolton

For Complete List of Firm Personnel, See General Section

For full biographical listings, see the Martindale-Hubbell Law Directory

PERRY, PIERSON & SILVER, P.L.C. (AV)

2901 North Central Avenue Suite 300, 85012
Telephone: 602-285-5165
Facsimile: 602-285-5100

Allan R. Perry   Timothy L. Pierson
Leon B. Silver

For full biographical listings, see the Martindale-Hubbell Law Directory

ROBBINS & GREEN, A PROFESSIONAL ASSOCIATION (AV)

1800 Norwest Tower, 3300 North Central Avenue, 85012-9826
Telephone: 602-248-7600
Fax: 602-266-5369

Wayne A. Smith   Bradley J. Stevens
Jeffrey P. Boshes   Peter W. Sorensen

For Complete List of Firm Personnel, See General Section

For full biographical listings, see the Martindale-Hubbell Law Directory

SHIMMEL, HILL, BISHOP & GRUENDER, P.C. (AV)

3700 North 24th Street, 85016
Telephone: 602-224-9500
Telecopier: 602-955-6176

Daniel F. Gruender   Joseph Wm. Kruchek
James H. Hazlewood

Representative Clients: Talley Industries; Farmers Insurance Cos.; Hein Werner Corp.; Norwest Equipment Finance; Arizona State Carpenters Pension Trust Funds; Operating Engineers Local 428 Pension Trust Funds; Arizona Laborers, Teamsters, Cement Masons Local 395 Pension Trust Funds.

For full biographical listings, see the Martindale-Hubbell Law Directory

SNELL & WILMER, L.L.P. (AV)

One Arizona Center, 85004-0001
Telephone: 602-382-6000
Fax: 602-382-6070
Tucson, Arizona Office: 1500 Norwest Tower, One South Church Avenue 85701-1612.
Telephone: 520-882-1200.
Fax: 520-884-1294.
Orange County Office: 1920 Main Street, Suite 1200, P.O. Box 57062, Irvine, California, 92619-7062.
Telephone: 714-253-2700.
Fax: 714-955-2507.
Salt Lake City, Utah Office: Broadway Centre, 111 East Broadway, Suite 900, 84111-1004.
Telephone: 801-237-1900.
Fax: 801-237-1950.

MEMBERS OF FIRM
Peter J. Rathwell   Donald L. Gaffney
Patrick E. Hoog   Christopher H. Bayley
Robert R. Kinas

ASSOCIATE
Eugene F. O'Connor II

Representative Clients: Arizona Public Service Company; Ford Motor Credit Corp.; Executive Claimants as Member Official Unsecured Creditors Committee in MCorp; Graybar Electronic; Heron Financial Corporation; Mutual Life Insurance of New York; Official Unsecured Creditors Committee of American Continental Corp.; Travelers Insurance; Bank One, Arizona, NA.

For Complete List of Firm Personnel, See General Section

For full biographical listings, see the Martindale-Hubbell Law Directory

WARNICKE & LITTLER, P.L.C. (AV)

2020 North Central Avenue, Fifth Floor, 85004-4506
Telephone: 602-256-0400
FAX: 602-256-0345

Ronald E. Warnicke   Ellen B. Davis
Thomas E. Littler   Mark J. Giunta

LEGAL SUPPORT PERSONNEL
Cheryl A. Menefee (Certified Paralegal)

For full biographical listings, see the Martindale-Hubbell Law Directory

ZEITLIN & ZEITLIN, P.C. (AV)

A Partnership including a Professional Corporation
Camel Headquarters, 3900 East Camelback Road Suite 406, 85018
Telephone: 602-234-8905
Fax: 602-285-5589
Annapolis, Maryland Office: 2007 Tidewater Colony Drive, Suite 2B, 21401-8686.
Telephone: 410-266-9500.
Facsimile: 410-266-9522.

Dale S. Zeitlin   Dawn Stoll Zeitlin (P.C.)

For full biographical listings, see the Martindale-Hubbell Law Directory

SCOTTSDALE, Maricopa Co.

PESKIND HYMSON & GOLDSTEIN, P.C. (AV)

14595 North Scottsdale Road, Suite 14, 85254
Telephone: 602-991-9077
Fax: 602-443-8854

David B. Goldstein

For full biographical listings, see the Martindale-Hubbell Law Directory

TUCSON,* Pima Co.

LEONARD FELKER ALTFELD & BATTAILE, P.C. (AV)

250 North Meyer Avenue, P.O. Box 191, 85702-0191
Telephone: 520-622-7733
Fax: 520-622-7967

David J. Leonard   Judith B. Leonard
Sidney L. Felker   Donna M. Aversa
Clifford B. Altfeld   Lynne M. Schwartz
John F. Battaile III   Edward O. Comitz
Russell E. Krone

For full biographical listings, see the Martindale-Hubbell Law Directory

Tucson—Continued

O'CONNOR CAVANAGH MOLLOY JONES, A PROFESSIONAL ASSOCIATION (AV)

Suite 2100 33 N. Stone, P.O. Box 2268, 85702
Telephone: 520-622-3531
FAX: 520-624-2816
Email: firminfo@arizlaw.com
Phoenix, Arizona Office: O'Connor, Cavanagh, Anderson, Killingsworth & Beshears, One East Camelback Road, Suite 1100, 85012.
Telephone: 602-263-2400.
FAX: 602-263-2900.
Sun City, Arizona Office: O'Connor, Cavanagh, Anderson, Killingsworth & Beshears, 13250 North Del Webb Boulevard, Suite B, 85351.
Telephone: 602-263-2808.
FAX: 602-933-3100.
Nogales, Arizona Office: O'Connor, Cavanagh, Anderson, Killingsworth & Beshears, 1891 North Mastick Way, 85621.
Telephone: 520-761-4215.
FAX: 520-761-3505.

Scott D. Gibson

Chris B. Nakamura

Representative Clients: Three-Five Systems; Main Street & Main; ITT Cannon; Bank of America; The Dial Corp; The Hartford; Dow Corning Corp.; Charles Schwab & Co., Inc.

For Complete List of Firm Personnel, See General Section

For full biographical listings, see the Martindale-Hubbell Law Directory

RAVEN, KIRSCHNER & NORELL, P.C. (AV)

Suite 1600, One South Church Avenue, 85701-1612
Telephone: 520-628-8700
Telefax: 520-798-5200

Dennis J. Clancy   Lane D. Oden
Stephen A. Thomas

Representative Clients: Continental Medical Systems, Inc.; El Paso Natural Gas Co.; Norwest Bank Arizona; El Rio-Santa Cruz Neighborhood Health Center, Inc.; Resolution Trust Corp.; Sierra Vista Community Hospital; Southern Arizona Rehabilitation Hospital; Northern Cochise Community Hospital.

For Complete List of Firm Personnel, See General Section

For full biographical listings, see the Martindale-Hubbell Law Directory

SNELL & WILMER, L.L.P. (AV)

1500 Norwest Tower, One South Church Avenue, 85701-1612
Telephone: 520-882-1200
Fax: 520-884-1294
Phoenix, Arizona Office: One Arizona Center, 85004-0001.
Telephone: 602-382-6000.
Fax: 602-382-6070.
Orange County Office: 1920 Main Street, Suite 1200, P.O. Box 57062, Irvine, California, 92619-7062.
Telephone: 714-253-2700.
Fax: 714-955-2507.
Salt Lake City, Utah Office: Broadway Centre, 111 East Broadway, Suite 900, 84111-1004.
Telephone: 801-237-1900.
Fax: 801-237-1950.

OF COUNSEL
Clague A. Van Slyke

ASSOCIATE
Todd V. Jones

Representative Clients: Arizona Public Service Company; Graybar Electronic; Heron Financial Corporation; Mutual Life Insurance of New York; Official Unsecured Creditors Committee of American Continental Corp.; Travelers Insurance; Bank One, Arizona, NA.

For full biographical listings, see the Martindale-Hubbell Law Directory

YUMA,* Yuma Co.

ROBERT M. COOK (AV)

201 West Second Street, 85364
Telephone: 520-539-0959
Fax: 520-539-0960
1-800 ROBERT M

For full biographical listings, see the Martindale-Hubbell Law Directory

ARKANSAS

*LITTLE ROCK,** Pulaski Co.

ARNOLD, GROBMYER & HALEY, A PROFESSIONAL ASSOCIATION (AV)

875 Union National Plaza, 124 West Capitol Avenue, P.O. Box 70, 72203
Telephone: 501-376-1171
Fax: 501-375-3548

Benjamin F. Arnold   Richard L. Ramsay
James F. Dowden   Robert R. Ross

For Complete List of Firm Personnel, See General Section

For full biographical listings, see the Martindale-Hubbell Law Directory

HOOVER & KOOISTRA (AV)

111 Center Street, 11th Floor, 72201-4445
Telephone: 501-376-8500
Facsimile: 501-372-3255

MEMBERS OF FIRM
Paul W. Hoover, Jr.   John Kooistra, III
Max C. Mehlburger

For full biographical listings, see the Martindale-Hubbell Law Directory

ROSE LAW FIRM, A PROFESSIONAL ASSOCIATION (AV)

120 East Fourth Street, 72201
Telephone: 501-375-9131
Telecopy: 501-375-1309

Herbert C. Rule, III   Charles W. Baker
Allen W. Bird, II   John T. Hardin
Garland J. Garrett   Stephen N. Joiner
Thomas P. Thrash   Brian Rosenthal
J. Scott Schallhorn

Representative Clients: Acxiom Corp.; Arkansas Freightways Corp.; The Equitable Life Assurance Society of the United States; Fairfield Communities, Inc.; General Electric Co.; General Motors Corp.; Mercantile Bank of Central Arkansas; The Prudential Insurance Company of America; Stephens Inc.; J.A. Riggs Tractor Co.

For Complete List of Firm Personnel, See General Section

For full biographical listings, see the Martindale-Hubbell Law Directory

WRIGHT, LINDSEY & JENNINGS (AV)

200 West Capitol Avenue, Suite 2200, 72201
Telephone: 501-371-0808
Fax: 501-376-9442
Email: tgraves@wlj.com *URL:* http://www.wlj.com/
Fayetteville, Arkansas Office: 101 West Mountain Street, Suite 206, 72701.
Telephone: 501-575-0808.
Fax: 501-575-0999.
Russellville, Arkansas Office: Suite E, 1110 West B Street.
Telephone: 501-968-7995.

Isaac A. Scott, Jr.   Judy Simmons Henry
Charles T. Coleman   Kimberly Wood Tucker
James J. Glover   Ainsley H. Lang

Representative Clients: Boatmen's National Bank of Arkansas; Associates Commercial Corporation.

For full biographical listings, see the Martindale-Hubbell Law Directory

CALIFORNIA

*BAKERSFIELD,** Kern Co.

KLEIN, WEGIS, DeNATALE, GOLDNER & MUIR, LLP (AV)

A Partnership including Professional Corporations
(Formerly Di Giorgio, Davis, Klein, Wegis, Duggan & Friedman)
ARCO Tower, 4550 California Avenue, Second Floor, P.O. Box 11172, 93389-1172
Telephone: 805-395-1000
Telecopier: 805-326-0418
Email: kwdgm@kwdgm.com

MEMBERS OF FIRM
Anthony J. Klein (Inc.)   Claude P. Kimball
ASSOCIATE
Michael S. Abril

Representative Clients: Bank of America; Great Western Bank; Mojave Pipeline Co.; Transamerican Title Insurance Co.; Dean Whittier Reynolds, Inc.; California Republic Bank; San Joaquin Bank; Nahama & Weagant Energy Co.; Freymiller Trucking, Inc.; Westinghouse Electric Co.

(See Next Column)

KLEIN, WEGIS, DeNATALE, GOLDNER & MUIR LLP—*Continued*

For Complete List of Firm Personnel, See General Section

For full biographical listings, see the Martindale-Hubbell Law Directory

---

COSTA MESA, Orange Co.

ALBERT, WEILAND & GOLDEN (AV)

Center Tower, 650 Town Center Drive, Suite 1350, 92626
Telephone: 714-966-10000
FAX: 714-966-1002
Email: awglawyers@aol.com

Theodor C. Albert	Jennifer Ann Golison
Michael J. Weiland	Evan D. Smiley
Jeffrey I. Golden	Lei Lei Wang Ekvall
	Philip E. Strok

For full biographical listings, see the Martindale-Hubbell Law Directory

RUTAN & TUCKER, LLP (AV)

A Partnership including Professional Corporations
611 Anton Boulevard, Suite 1400, P.O. Box 1950, 92626
Telephone: 714-641-5100; 213-625-7586
Telecopier: 714-546-9035
Email: rutan&tucker@mcimail.com *URL:* http://www.rutan.com

MEMBER OF FIRM
Lori Sarner Smith

ASSOCIATES

Michael K. Slattery	Paul J. Sievers

For Complete List of Firm Personnel, See General Section

For full biographical listings, see the Martindale-Hubbell Law Directory

---

EUREKA,* Humboldt Co.

JANSSEN, MALLOY, MARCHI, NEEDHAM & MORRISON (AV)

730 Fifth Street, P.O. Drawer 1288, 95501
Telephone: 707-445-2071
Fax: 707-445-8305

MEMBERS OF FIRM

Clayton R. Janssen	Michael F. Malloy
Nicholas R. Marchi	Michael W. Morrison
W. Timothy Needham	

ASSOCIATE
Catherine M. Koshkin

Counsel for: Clinic Mutual Insurance Co.; TRW, Inc.; U.S. Bank; The Travelers Insurance Co.; General Hospital; Pacific Bell; Reichhold Chemicals, Inc.; Safeco Insurance Companies of America; Lawyers Mutual Insurance Co.

For full biographical listings, see the Martindale-Hubbell Law Directory

---

FRESNO,* Fresno Co.

KIMBLE, MacMICHAEL & UPTON, A PROFESSIONAL CORPORATION (AV)

Fig Garden Financial Center, 5260 North Palm Avenue, Suite 221, P.O. Box 9489, 93792-9489
Telephone: 209-435-5500
Telecopier: 209-435-1500
Email: kmu@primenet.com

Joseph C. Kimble (1910-1972)	Robert H. Scribner
Thomas A. MacMichael (1920-1990)	Michael E. Moss
	Mark D. Miller
Jon Wallace Upton	Michael F. Tatham
Robert E. Bergin	W. Richard Lee
Jeffrey G. Boswell	D. Tyler Tharpe
Steven D. McGee	Sylvia Halkousis Coyle
Robert E. Ward	S. Brett Sutton
John P. Eleazarian	Michael J. Jurkovich

Douglas V. Thornton	Susan King Hatmaker
Robert William Branch	Lawrence J. Salisbury
Donald J. Pool	Daniel R. Foster
	Meredith E. Allen

OF COUNSEL
Mary Ann Bluhm

For full biographical listings, see the Martindale-Hubbell Law Directory

LANG, RICHERT & PATCH, A PROFESSIONAL CORPORATION (AV)

Fig Garden Financial Center, 5200 North Palm Avenue, 4th Floor, P.O. Box 40012, 93755
Telephone: 209-228-6700
Fax: 209-228-6727

(See Next Column)

Frank H. Lang	Victoria J. Salisch
William T. Richert (1937-1993)	Bradley A. Silva
Robert L. Patch, II	Charles Trudrung Taylor
Val W. Saldaña	Mark L. Creede
Douglas E. Noll	Peter N. Zeitler
Michael T. Hertz	Charles L. Doerksen

Laurie L. Quigley	Nabil E. Zumout
Douglas E. Griffin	Shawn H. Alikian
	Thomas E. Gauthier

References: Wells Fargo Bank (Fresno Main Office).

For full biographical listings, see the Martindale-Hubbell Law Directory

---

IRVINE, Orange Co.

BARNETT & RUBIN, A PROFESSIONAL CORPORATION (AV)

2 Park Plaza, Suite 980, 92614
Telephone: 714-261-9700
Facsimile: 714-261-9799
Email: Lawyers@Pacbell.net

Richard L. Barnett	Jeffrey D. Rubin
	Kathryn B. Salmond

For full biographical listings, see the Martindale-Hubbell Law Directory

MARK A. KOMPA (AV)

2603 Main Street, Suite 1170, 92714
Telephone: 714-250-9500
Facsimile: 714-250-9515

For full biographical listings, see the Martindale-Hubbell Law Directory

LOBEL & OPERA, PROFESSIONAL CORPORATION (AV)

Suite 1100, 19800 MacArthur Boulevard, P.O. Box 19588, 92713
Telephone: 714-476-7400
Fax: 714-476-7444

William N. Lobel	Tavi Claire Stanley
Robert E. Opera	Metiner G. Kimel
Alan J. Friedman	Edward P. Christian
Pamela Z. Karger	Robert J. Mrofka
Cheryl A. Skigin	Hamid R. Rafatjoo

For full biographical listings, see the Martindale-Hubbell Law Directory

RUS, MILIBAND, WILLIAMS & SMITH (AV)

Suite 700, 2600 Michelson Drive, 92612
Telephone: 714-752-7100
Fax: 714-252-1514

Ronald Rus	J. Scott Williams
Joel S. Miliband	Randall A. Smith
	Laurel Zaeske

M. Peter Crinella	David Edward Hays
Jeffrey H. Sussman	Steven Joseph Kraemer
Cathrine M. Castaldi	Leo J. Presiado

For full biographical listings, see the Martindale-Hubbell Law Directory

---

LOS ANGELES,* Los Angeles Co.

ANGEL AND NEISTAT, A PROFESSIONAL CORPORATION (AV)

28th Floor 555 South Flower Street, 90017-2205
Telephone: 213-689-4500
Fax: 213-689-4651

Michael A. Angel	Steven A. Schwaber
Douglas M. Neistat	Alan J. Stomel
Alan Holmberg	Gary R. Wallace
Steven L. Crane	Daniel H. Reiss

For full biographical listings, see the Martindale-Hubbell Law Directory

BAKER & HOSTETLER (AV)

600 Wilshire Boulevard, 90017-3212
Telephone: 213-624-2400
FAX: 213-975-1740
In Cleveland, Ohio: 3200 National City Center, 1900 East Ninth Street. *Telephone:* 216-621-0200.
In Columbus, Ohio: Capitol Square, Suite 2100, 65 East State Street. *Telephone:* 614-228-1541.
In Denver, Colorado: 303 East 17th Avenue, Suite 1100. *Telephone:* 303-861-0600.
In Houston, Texas: 1000 Louisiana, Suite 2000. *Telephone:* 713-236-0020.
In Long Beach, California: 300 Oceangate, Suite 620. *Telephone:* 310-432-2827.

(See Next Column)

BAKER & HOSTETLER, *Los Angeles—Continued*

In Orlando, Florida: SunBank Center, Suite 2300, 200 South Orange Avenue.
Telephone: 407-649-4000.
In Washington, D. C.: Washington Square, Suite 1100, 1050 Connecticut Avenue, N. W.
Telephone: 202-861-1500.
In College Park, Maryland: 9658 Baltimore Boulevard, Suite 206.
Telephone: 301-441-2781.
In Alexandria, Virginia: 437 North Lee Street.
Telephone: 703-549-1294.
In San Francisco, California: One Sansome Street, Suite 2000.
Telephone: 415-951-4705.

PARTNER
Dean G. Rallis Jr.

For Complete List of Firm Personnel, See General Section

For full biographical listings, see the Martindale-Hubbell Law Directory

---

BAKER AND JACOBSON, A PROFESSIONAL CORPORATION (AV)

Suite 500, 11377 West Olympic Boulevard, 90064-1683
Telephone: 310-914-7990
Fax: 310-914-7913

Robert P. Baker　　　　　　Lawrence M. Jacobson

For full biographical listings, see the Martindale-Hubbell Law Directory

---

LAW OFFICES OF DAVID B. BLOOM A PROFESSIONAL CORPORATION (AV)

3325 Wilshire Boulevard, Ninth Floor, 90010
Telephone: 213-938-5248; 384-4088
Telecopier: 213-385-2009

David B. Bloom

Stephen S. Monroe (A　　　　Susan Carole Jay
　Professional Corporation)　Edward Idell
Raphael A. Rosemblat　　　　Sandra Kamenir
James E. Adler　　　　　　　Steven Wayne Lazarus
Bonni S. Mantovani　　　　　Andrew Edward Briseno
Roy A. Levun　　　　　　　　Harold C. Klaskin
Cherie S. Raidy　　　　　　　Shelley M. Gould
Jonathan Udell　　　　　　　Peter O. Israel

For full biographical listings, see the Martindale-Hubbell Law Directory

---

LAW OFFICES OF EDYTHE L. BRONSTON (AV)

11377 West Olympic Boulevard, Suite 900, 90064-1683
Telephone: 310-914-7972
Fax: 310-914-7973

For full biographical listings, see the Martindale-Hubbell Law Directory

---

BUCHALTER, NEMER, FIELDS & YOUNGER, A PROFESSIONAL CORPORATION (AV)

24th Floor, 601 South Figueroa Street, 90017
Telephone: 213-891-0700
Fax: 213-896-0400
Email: buchalter@earthlink.net URL: http://www.buchalter.com
New York, New York Office: 15th Floor, 605 Third Avenue.
Telephone: 212-490-8600.
Fax: 212-490-6022.
San Francisco, California Office: 29th Floor, 333 Market Street.
Telephone: 415-227-0900.
Fax: 415-227-0770.
Newport Beach, California Office: Suite 1450, 620 Newport Center Drive.
Telephone: 714-760-1121.
Fax: 714-720-0182.

Richard Jay Goldstein　　　Pamela Kohlman Webster
Randye B. Soref　　　　　　Bernard D. Bollinger, Jr.
OF COUNSEL
Ronald E. Gordon　　　　　Scott O. Smith

Julie A. Goren　　　　　　　William S. Brody
Paul S. Arrow　　　　　　　William P. Fong
　　　　　Brett Michael Broderick

References: City National Bank; Wells Fargo Bank; Metrobank.

For Complete List of Firm Personnel, See General Section

For full biographical listings, see the Martindale-Hubbell Law Directory

---

J. T. CAIRNS & ASSOCIATES (AV)

200 North Larchmont Boulevard, 90004
Telephone: 213-962-5588
Telecopier: 213-463-4412

(See Next Column)

ASSOCIATE
Deann Hampton

For full biographical listings, see the Martindale-Hubbell Law Directory

---

CLARK & TREVITHICK, A PROFESSIONAL CORPORATION (AV)

800 Wilshire Boulevard, 12th Floor, 90017
Telephone: 213-629-5700
Telecopier: 213-624-9441
San Francisco, California Office: 456 Montgomery Street, 20th Floor.
Telephone: 415-288-6520.
Fax: 415-398-2820.

John A. Lapinski　　　　　　Leslie R. Horowitz
OF COUNSEL
Judith Ilene Bloom

References: Wells Fargo Bank (Los Angeles Main Office); National Bank of California.

For Complete List of Firm Personnel, See General Section

For full biographical listings, see the Martindale-Hubbell Law Directory

---

DANNING, GILL, DIAMOND & KOLLITZ, LLP (AV)

A Limited Liability Partnership Composed of Professional Corporations
2029 Century Park East, Suite 1900, 90067-3005
Telephone: 310-277-0077
Fax: 310-277-5735
Email: dgdk@dgdk.com

MEMBERS OF FIRM
David A. Gill (A Professional　　Steven E. Smith (A Professional
　Corporation)　　　　　　　　　Corporation)
Richard K. Diamond (A　　　　　Eric P. Israel (A Professional
　Professional Corporation)　　　　Corporation)
Howard Kollitz (A Professional　David M. Poitras (A
　Corporation)　　　　　　　　　　Professional Corporation)
John J. Bingham, Jr., (A　　　　George E. Schulman (A
　Professional Corporation)　　　　Professional Corporation)

ASSOCIATES
Robert A. Hessling　　　　　Daniel H. Gill
Kevin L. Hing　　　　　　　Glenn C. Kelble
Barry Lurie　　　　　　　　Sarah E. Petty
Kathy Bazoian Phelps　　　　Elan R. Schwartz

OF COUNSEL
Curtis B. Danning (A　　　　James J. Joseph (A Professional
　Professional Corporation)　　Corporation)

For full biographical listings, see the Martindale-Hubbell Law Directory

---

FEDER & MILLS, A PROFESSIONAL CORPORATION (AV)

1901 Avenue of the Stars, Seventh Floor, 90067
Telephone: 310-201-2075
Facsimile: 310-284-6020; 310-284-6018

James J. Feder　　　　　　　John W. Mills, III

For full biographical listings, see the Martindale-Hubbell Law Directory

---

LAW OFFICES OF RICHARD H. GIBSON A PROFESSIONAL CORPORATION (AV)

Wells Fargo Center, 333 South Grand Avenue, Suite 1860, 90071
Telephone: 213-617-1185
Facsimile: 213-617-1902

Richard H. Gibson

For full biographical listings, see the Martindale-Hubbell Law Directory

---

GOLDMAN & GORDON, L.L.P. (AV)

Suite 1920, 1801 Century Park East, 90067
Telephone: 310-277-7171
FAX: 310-277-1547

MEMBERS OF FIRM
A. S. Goldman (1895-1966)　　Leonard A. Goldman
　　　　Robert P. Gordon
ASSOCIATE
Melody G. Anderson

References: Bank of America, Fourth and Spring Branch, Los Angeles; Bank of America, Wilshire-San Vincente Branch, Beverly Hills.

For full biographical listings, see the Martindale-Hubbell Law Directory

---

HENNIGAN, MERCER & BENNETT (AV)

601 South Figueroa Street, Suite 3300, 90017
Telephone: 213-694-1200
Fax: 213-694-1234
Email: Silverm@hmb.com

(See Next Column)

HENNIGAN, MERCER & BENNETT—*Continued*

J. Michael Hennigan	Laura Lindgren
James W. Mercer	Bruce R. MacLeod
Bruce Bennett	Elizabeth D. Mann
John L. Amsden	Robert L. Palmer
C. Dana Hobart	Lauren A. Smith
Jeanne E. Irving	Peter J. Most
Pamala J. King	Lee W. Potts

ASSOCIATES

Nichole M. Auden	Linda A. Kontos
Jacqueline Bendy	Jennifer Sulla
Mary H. Chu	Michael Swartz
A. Ann Hered	Shawna L. Ballard
Gregory K. Jones	Claudia Schweikert
Ellen M. Keane	David H. Martin

OF COUNSEL

Anthony Castanares

For full biographical listings, see the Martindale-Hubbell Law Directory

---

JONES, DAY, REAVIS & POGUE (AV)

555 West Fifth Street Suite 4600, 90013-1025
Telephone: 213-489-3939
Telex: 181439 UD
Telecopier: 213-243-2539
In Irvine, California: 2603 Main Street, Suite 900.
Telephone: 714-851-3939.
Telex: 194911 Lawyers LSA.
Telecopier: 714-553-7539.
In Atlanta, Georgia: 3500 One Peachtree Center, 303 Peachtree Street, N.E.
Telephone: 404-521-3939.
Cable Address: "Attorneys Atlanta".
Telex: 54-2711.
Telecopier: 404-581-8330.
In Brussels, Belgium: Avenue Louise 480, 7th Floor, B-1050 Brussels.
Telephone: 32-2-645-14-11.
Telecopier: 32-2-645-14-45.
In Chicago, Illinois: 77 West Wacker.
Telephone: 312-782-3939.
Telecopier: 312-782-8585.
In Cleveland, Ohio: North Point, 901 Lakeside Avenue.
Telephone: 216-586-3939.
Cable Address: "Attorneys Cleveland."
Telex: 980389.
Telecopier: 216-579-0212.
In Columbus, Ohio: 1900 Huntington Center.
Telephone: 614-469-3939.
Cable Address: "Attorneys Columbus."
Telecopier: 614-461-4198.
In Dallas, Texas: 2300 Trammell Crow Center, 2001 Ross Avenue.
Telephone: 214-220-3939.
Cable Address: "Attorneys Dallas."
Telex: 730852.
Telecopier: 214-969-5100.
In Frankfurt, Germany: Triton Haus, Bockenheimer Landstrasse 42, 60323 Frankfurt am Main.
Telephone: 49-69-9726-3939.
Telecopier: 49-69-9726-3993.
In Geneva, Switzerland: 20, rue de Candolle.
Telephone: 41-22-320-2339.
Telecopier: 41-22-320-1232.
In Hong Kong: 29th Floor, Entertainment Building, 30 Queen's Road Central.
Telephone: 852-2526-6895.
Telecopier: 852-2868-5871.
In London England: Bucklersbury House, 3 Queen Victoria Street.
Telephone: 44-171-236-3939.
Telecopier: 44-171-236-1113.
In New Delhi, India: Pathak & Associates, 13th Floor, Dr. Gopal Das Bhaven, 28 Barakhamba Road.
Telephone: 91-11-373-8793.
Telecopier: 91-11-335-3761.
In New York, New York: 599 Lexington Avenue.
Telephone: 212-326-3939.
Cable Address: "JONESDAY NEWYORK."
Telex: 237013 JDRP UR.
Telecopier: 212-755-7306.
In Paris, France: 62, rue du Faubourg Saint-Honore.
Telephone: 33-1-44-71-3939.
Telex: 290156 Surgoe.
Telecopier: 33-1-49-24-0471.
In Pittsburgh, Pennsylvania: 500 Grant Street, 31st Floor.
Telephone: 412-391-3939.
Cable Address: "Attorneys Pittsburgh".
Telecopier: 412-394-7959.
In Riyadh, Saudi Arabia: The International Law Firm, Sulaymaniyah Center, Tahlia Street, P.O. Box 22166.
Telephone: (966-1) 462-8866.
Telecopier: (966-1) 462-9001.

(See Next Column)

In Taipei, Taiwan: 8th Floor, 2 Tun Hwa South Road, Section 2.
Telephone: (886-2) 704-6808.
Telecopier: (886-2) 704-6791.
In Tokyo, Japan: Toranomon MT Building, 4th Floor, 10-3, Toranomon 3-Chome, Minato-ku, Tokyo 105, Japan.
Telephone: 81-3-3433-3939.
Telecopier: 81-3-5401-2725.
In Washington, D.C.: Metropolitan Square, 1450 G Street, N.W.
Telephone: 202-879-3939.
Cable Address: "Attorneys Washington."
Telex: 89-2410 ATTORNEYS WASH.
Telecopier: 202-737-2832.

MEMBER OF FIRM IN LOS ANGELES

William G. Wilson

ASSOCIATE

Thomas Botz

For Complete List of Firm Personnel, See General Section

For full biographical listings, see the Martindale-Hubbell Law Directory

---

KATZ, HOYT, SEIGEL & KAPOR LLP (AV)

A Partnership including a Professional Corporation
Suite 820, 11111 Santa Monica Boulevard, 90025-3342
Telephone: 310-473-1300
Telecopier: 310-473-7138

MEMBERS OF FIRM

Charles J. Katz (1905-1983)	William Schoenholz
Louis C. Hoyt (1905-1994)	Jack R. Lenack
Benjamin S. Seigel (P.C.)	Russell L. Allyn
Jeffrey H. Kapor	Douglas M. Lipstone
Scott H. Jacobs	Moira Doherty
Alan Jay Cohen	Marla Milner

For full biographical listings, see the Martindale-Hubbell Law Directory

---

LEVENE, NEALE & BENDER L.L.P. (AV)

1801 Avenue of the Stars, Suite 1120, 90067
Telephone: 310-229-1234
Fax: 310-229-1244
Email: (attorneys initials)@LNBLAW.COM

David W. Levene	David L. Neale
	Ron Bender

ASSOCIATE

Craig M. Rankin	Nellwyn Voorhies
	Monica Y. Kim

Reference: 1st Business Bank.

For full biographical listings, see the Martindale-Hubbell Law Directory

---

LOEB & LOEB LLP (AV)

A Limited Liability Partnership including Professional Corporations
Suite 1800, 1000 Wilshire Boulevard, 90017-2475
Telephone: 213-688-3400
Facsimile: 213-688-3460; 688-3461; 688-3462
Century City, California Office: Suite 2200, 10100 Santa Monica Boulevard, Los Angeles, 90067-4164.
Telephone: 310-282-2000.
Facsimile: 310-282-2191; 282-2192.
New York, N.Y. Office: 345 Park Avenue, 10154-0037.
Telephone: 212-407-4000.
Facsimile: 212-407-4990.
Washington, D.C. Office: Suite 601, 2100 M Street N.W., 20037-1207.
Telephone: 202-223-5700.
Facsimile: 202-223-5704.
Nashville, Tennessee Office: 45 Music Square West, 37203-3205.
Telephone: 615-749-8300;
Facsimile: 615-749-8308.
Rome, Italy Office: Piazza Digione 1, 00197.
Telephone: 011-396-808-8456.
Facsimile: 011-396-808-8288.

MEMBERS OF FIRM

Andrew S. Clare (A P.C.)	David M. Satnick
David B. Eizenman	(New York City Office)
(New York City Office)	P. Gregory Schwed
Lawrence B. Gutcho	(New York City Office)
Lance N. Jurich	Michael F. Sitzer
Mary D. Lane	Ronald Weinstein (A P.C.)

ASSOCIATES

Paula K. Colbath	Karen Nielsen Higgins
(New York City Office)	John W. Kittleson
Helen Gavaris	Gerald J. Strenio
(New York City Office)	

For Complete List of Firm Personnel, See General Section

For full biographical listings, see the Martindale-Hubbell Law Directory

Los Angeles—Continued

THE LAW FIRM OF RICHARD M. MONEYMAKER (AV)

Suite 2102 Broadway Plaza, 700 Flower Street, 90017
Telephone: 213-622-1088
Telecopier: 213-622-7002

Richard M. Moneymaker
ASSOCIATES

Vincent B. Moneymaker   Sheri R. Handel
OF COUNSEL
Frank W. Molloy

Reference: Bank of America (Los Angeles Main Office).

For full biographical listings, see the Martindale-Hubbell Law Directory

O'MELVENY & MYERS LLP (AV)

400 South Hope Street, 90071-2899
Telephone: 213-669-6000
Cable Address: "Moms"
Facsimile: 213-669-6407
Email: omminfo@omm.com
Century City, California Office: 1999 Avenue of the Stars, 90067-6035.
Telephone: 310-553-6700.
Facsimile: 310-246-6779.
Newport Beach, California Office: 610 Newport Center Drive, 92660-6429.
Telephone: 714-760-9600.
Cable Address: "Moms".
Facsimile: 714-669-6994.
San Francisco, California Office: Embarcadero Center West Tower, 275 Battery Street, 94111-3305.
Telephone: 415-984-8700.
Facsimile: 415-984-8701.
New York, New York Office: Citicorp Center, 153 East 53rd Street, 10022-4611.
Telephone: 212-326-2000.
Facsimile: 212-326-2061.
Washington, D.C. Office: 555 13th Street, N.W., 20004-1109.
Telephone: 202-383-5300.
Cable Address: "Moms".
Facsimile: 202-383-5414.
London, England Office: 10 Finsbury Square, London, EC2A 1LA.
Telephone: 0171-256-8451.
Facsimile: 0171-638-8205.
Tokyo, Japan Office: Sanbancho KB-6 Building, 6 Sanbancho, Chiyoda-ku, Tokyo 102, Japan.
Telephone: 03-3239-2900.
Facsimile: 03-3239-2432.
Hong Kong Office: Suite 1905, Peregrine Tower, Lippo Centre, 89 Queensway, Central, Hong Kong.
Telephone: 852-2523-8266.
Facsimile: 852-2522-1760.
Shanghai, Peoples Republic of China Office: Shanghai International Trade Centre, Suite 2011, 2200 Yan An Road West, Shanghai, 200335, PRC.
Telephone: 86-21-6219-5363.
Facsimile: 86-21-6275-4949.

PARTNER
Robert J. White

For Complete List of Firm Personnel, See General Section

For full biographical listings, see the Martindale-Hubbell Law Directory

PIZER & MICHAELSON INC. (AV)

2029 Century Park East, Suite 600, 90067
Telephone: 310-843-9729
Fax: 310-843-9619
Santa Ana, California Office: 2122 North Broadway, Suite 100, 92706.
Telephone: 714-558-0535.
Telecopier: 714-550-0841.

Bradley J. Pizer

For full biographical listings, see the Martindale-Hubbell Law Directory

ROBINSON, DIAMANT, BRILL & KLAUSNER, A PROFESSIONAL CORPORATION (AV)

Suite 1500, 1888 Century Park East (Century City), 90067
Telephone: 310-277-7400
Telecopier: 310-277-7584

Gilbert Robinson (1927-1991)	Douglas D. Kappler
Elliott Lisnek (1939-1992)	Philip A. Gasteier
Lawrence A. Diamant	Karl E. Block
Martin J. Brill	Leslie A. Cohen
Edward M. Wolkowitz	Gregg D. Lundberg
Gary E. Klausner	Sandford L. Frey
Irving M. Gross	Jeffrey A. Resler

(See Next Column)

Judith E. Miller	Nicole D. Lance
Sandro F. Piedrahita	Robyn B. Sokol
Christopher E. Jones	Jeffrey W. Dulberg
	Seth D. Garland

References: Fidelity & Deposit Co.; Home Savings of America (Century City Office); Metrobank (Los Angeles Regional Office); Wells Fargo Bank (Century City Office).

For full biographical listings, see the Martindale-Hubbell Law Directory

RONALD P. SLATES A PROFESSIONAL CORPORATION (AV)

548 South Spring Street, Suite 1012, 90013-2309
Telephone: 213-624-1515; 213-654-1461
Fax: 213-624-7536; 213-654-1463

Ronald P. Slates

G. Michael Jackson

For full biographical listings, see the Martindale-Hubbell Law Directory

STUTMAN, TREISTER & GLATT, PROFESSIONAL CORPORATION (AV)

3699 Wilshire Boulevard, Suite 900, 90010
Telephone: 213-251-5100
FAX: 213-251-5288

Jack Stutman (Retired Founder)	Michael H. Goldstein
George M. Treister	Lee R. Bogdanoff
Herman L. Glatt	Frank A. Merola
Richard M. Neiter	K. John Shaffer
Robert A. Greenfield	Mareta C. Hamre
Charles D. Axelrod	Michael L. Tuchin
Theodore B. Stolman	Jeffrey H. Davidson
Isaac M. Pachulski	Ronald L. Fein
Kenneth N. Klee	Mark S. Wallace
Alan Pedlar	Eric D. Goldberg
George C. Webster, II	Eve H. Karasik
Stephan M. Ray	Thomas R. Kreller
Michael A. Morris	Martin R. Barash
Jeffrey C. Krause	James O. Johnston Jr.
	Michael C. Standlee

For full biographical listings, see the Martindale-Hubbell Law Directory

SULMEYER, KUPETZ, BAUMANN & ROTHMAN, A PROFESSIONAL CORPORATION (AV)

300 South Grand Avenue, 14th Floor, 90071
Telephone: 213-626-2311
Fax: 213-629-4520

Irving Sulmeyer	Israel Saperstein
Arnold L. Kupetz	Victor A. Sahn
Richard G. Baumann	Steven R. Wainess
Don Rothman	David S. Kupetz
Alan G. Tippie	Howard M. Ehrenberg
	Kathryn Kerfes

Nathan H. Harris	Mark S. Horoupian
Susan Frances Moley	Stephen C. Seto
Matthew Rothman	Howard N. Madris
Wesley Avery	Tanya M. Vince
OF COUNSEL	
Marilyn S. Scheer	Suzanne L. Weakley
Frank Vram Zerunyan	Elissa D. Miller

Representative Clients: General Electric Capital Corp.; Continental Insurance Co.; Litton Industries; North American Phillips Corp.; Ventura Port District; Northwest Financial; Heller Financial Inc.; Transamerica Occidental Life Insurance Co.; Transamerica Realty Services, Inc.; Body Glove International.

For full biographical listings, see the Martindale-Hubbell Law Directory

WYNNE SPIEGEL ITKIN, A LAW CORPORATION (AV)

1901 Avenue of the Stars, Suite 1600, 90067-6080
Telephone: 310-551-1015
Fax: 310-551-3059

Richard L. Wynne	Christopher W. Combs
Bennett L. Spiegel	Stuart J. Wald
Robbin L. Itkin	Hayley E. Ramer
Eve Jaffe	Jacqueline H. Sloan

For full biographical listings, see the Martindale-Hubbell Law Directory

MANHATTAN BEACH, Los Angeles Co.

STEINBERG BARNESS GLASGOW & FOSTER LLP (AV)

1334 Park View Avenue, Suite 100, 90266
Telephone: 310-546-5838
Telecopier: 310-546-5630
Email: SGBF@ix.netcom.com

MEMBERS OF FIRM

Alex Steinberg	Jordan G. Barness
Daniel I. Barness	Paul J. Laurin
Donna Glasgow	Shannon M. Foley
(Not admitted in CA)	Richard L. Weiner
Douglas B. Foster	William R. (Randy) Kirkpatrick

Jeffrey Michael Lee

OF COUNSEL

Roanld D. Harari (Not admitted in CA)

References: Home Bank; Imperial Bank; Citizens Commerical Trust & Savings Bank; Bank of America.

For full biographical listings, see the Martindale-Hubbell Law Directory

MISSION VIEJO, Orange Co.

THE BUCKLEY FIRM, P.C. (AV)

Suite 200, 26522 La Alameda, 92691
Telephone: 714-348-8300
Facsimile: 714-348-8310
Email: TBF__law@ix.netcom.com
Email: 73321.331@compuserve.com

Lawrence J. Buckley	John W. Klein
John Thomas Callan	Paula Scotland
Jeffrey W. Griffith	Edgar C. Smith, III
Stephen J. Kane	Adam H. Springel

OF COUNSEL

Timothy D. Carlyle	Jonathan C. Cavett

Reference: Bank of California.

For full biographical listings, see the Martindale-Hubbell Law Directory

NEWPORT BEACH, Orange Co.

BROKER & O'KEEFE, PROFESSIONAL CORPORATION (AV)

4695 MacArthur Court Suite 1200, 92660
Telephone: 714-222-2000
Fax: 714-222-2022
Email: chpter11@aol.com *URL:* http://wwwbroker-okeefe.com

Jeffrey W. Broker	Sean A. O'Keefe

Lauren B. Lessler	David D. Piper

For full biographical listings, see the Martindale-Hubbell Law Directory

CALLAHAN & ASSOCIATES (AV)

5120 Campus Drive, 92660
Telephone: 714-476-2898
Facsimile: 714-752-8770

Rebecca Callahan

ASSOCIATE

Katherine T. Corrigan

LEGAL SUPPORT PERSONNEL

Sandra A. Thompson (Paralegal)

For full biographical listings, see the Martindale-Hubbell Law Directory

WINTHROP COUCHOT PROFESSIONAL CORPORATION (AV)

3 Civic Plaza, Suite 280, 92660
Telephone: 714-720-4100
Fax: 714-720-4111

Marc J. Winthrop	Paul J. Couchot
	Robert W. Pitts

Richard H. Golubow	Dorit Goossens
	Peter Lianides

For full biographical listings, see the Martindale-Hubbell Law Directory

WOLF & PFEIFER, A LAW CORPORATION (AV)

500 Newport Center Drive Suite 800, 92660
Telephone: 714-720-9200
Fax: 714-720-9250
URL: http://www.wolfpfeifer.com

Alan S. Wolf	Melissa L. Richards
Michael R. Pfeifer	Janice L. Celotti
	Donald R. Davidson, III

(See Next Column)

Roland P. Reynolds	C. Robert Simpson
Donna L. La Porte	Diane Weifenbach
	James F. Lewin

OF COUNSEL

Kay Virginia Gustafson

LEGAL SUPPORT PERSONNEL

Dona M. Harman

For full biographical listings, see the Martindale-Hubbell Law Directory

OAKLAND,* Alameda Co.

KORNFIELD, PAUL & BUPP, A PROFESSIONAL CORPORATION (AV)

Suite 800, Lake Merritt Plaza, 1999 Harrison Street, 94612
Telephone: 510-763-1000
Fax: 510-273-8669

Irving J. Kornfield	C. Randall Bupp
Aaron Paul	Merridith A. Schneider
	Eric A. Nyberg

Charles D. Novack	Chris D. Kuhner
	Gareth M. Chow

For full biographical listings, see the Martindale-Hubbell Law Directory

NEAL & ASSOCIATES (AV)

Montclair Village, 6200 Antioch Street, Suite 202, P.O. Box 13314, 500, 94661-0314
Telephone: 510-339-0233
FAX: 510-339-6672
URL: http://seamless.com/hdn/hdn.html

Howard D. Neal

Frank J. Gilbert	Steven S. Miyake

For full biographical listings, see the Martindale-Hubbell Law Directory

ORANGE, Orange Co.

FABOZZI, THIERBACH & CALEY (AV)

3111 North Tustin Avenue, Suite 200, 92665
Telephone: 714-637-3385
FAX: 714-637-3489

Dennis F. Fabozzi	Marlene L. Thierbach
	Rebecca A. Caley

ASSOCIATES

Jima Ikegawa	Bruce T. Bauer

For full biographical listings, see the Martindale-Hubbell Law Directory

OXNARD, Ventura Co.

NORDMAN, CORMANY, HAIR & COMPTON (AV)

1000 Town Center Drive, Sixth Floor, P.O. Box 9100, 93031-9100
Telephone: 805-485-1000
Ventura: 805-656-3304
Telecopier: 805-988-8387
805-988-7790
Westlake Village, California Office: 920 Hampshire Road, Suite A-17, 91361.
Telephone: 805-497-2795.

MEMBERS OF FIRM

Ronald H. Gill	William E. Winfield
	Gerald M. Etchingham

Representative Clients: Berry Petroleum Co.; Real Estate Investment Trust of California; Amgen; Kmart Corp.; Saticoy Lemon Assn.; The Procter & Gamble Paper Products Co.; Halliburton Services; Schlumberger; The Prudential Insurance Company of America; Laguna Pacific Development.

For Complete List of Firm Personnel, See General Section

For full biographical listings, see the Martindale-Hubbell Law Directory

PALM DESERT, Riverside Co.

CRISTE, PIPPIN & GOLDS (AV)

Suite 200, 73-550 Alessandro Drive, 92260
Telephone: 619-862-1111
Fax: 619-776-4197
Email: cpgca@aol.com

MEMBERS OF FIRM

Michael A. Criste	Robert L. Pippin
	Irwin L. Golds

(See Next Column)

CRISTE, PIPPIN & GOLDS, *Palm Desert—Continued*

ASSOCIATE
Marie A. Bochnewich

For full biographical listings, see the Martindale-Hubbell Law Directory

---

PALO ALTO, Santa Clara Co.

MURRAY AND MURRAY, A PROFESSIONAL CORPORATION (AV)

Suite 200, 3030 Hansen Way, 94304
Telephone: 415-852-9000
Telecopier: 415-852-9244

David S. Murray	Janice M. Murray
John Walshe Murray	Kenneth T. Law
Craig M. Prim	Patrick M. Costello

Stephen T. O'Neill	David S. Levin
Robert A. Franklin	Gaye Nell Heck
Maureen Colligan Harrison	Bradley N. Raderman

For full biographical listings, see the Martindale-Hubbell Law Directory

---

PASADENA, Los Angeles Co.

CAIRNS, DOYLE, LANS, NICHOLAS & SONI, A LAW CORPORATION (AV)

Ninth Floor, 225 South Lake Avenue, 91101
Telephone: 818-683-3111
Telecopier: 818-683-4999

John D. Cairns	Stephen M. Lans
John C. Doyle	Francisco J. Nicholas

Rohini Soni (1956-1994)

Representative Clients: Allstate Insurance Companies; Burger King Corp.; California Insurance Guarantee Assn.; California United Bank; CIGNA Insurance Companies; City of Pasadena; Cumis Insurance Society, Inc.; Employer's Mutual Insurance Companies; State Farm Insurance Companies; Tokio Marine Insurance.

For full biographical listings, see the Martindale-Hubbell Law Directory

LAGERLOF, SENECAL, BRADLEY & SWIFT, LLP (AV)

301 North Lake Avenue, 10th Floor, 91101-4108
Telephone: 818-793-9400
FAX: 818-793-5900

MEMBERS OF FIRM

Joseph J. Burris (1913-1980)	John F. Bradley
Stanley C. Lagerlof (Retired)	Timothy J. Gosney
H. Melvin Swift, Jr.	William F. Kruse
H. Jess Senecal	Thomas S. Bunn, III
Jack T. Swafford	Andrew D. Turner

Rebecca J. Thyne

ASSOCIATES

James D. Ciampa	Robert W. Renken

Representative Clients: Anchor Glass Container Corp.; Bethlehem Steel Corp.; Orthopaedic Hospital; Palmdale Water District; Public Water Agencies Group; Ventura Port District; Walnut Valley Water District; Metric Construction Co., Inc.

For full biographical listings, see the Martindale-Hubbell Law Directory

WILLSEY LAW OFFICES OWNED BY A PROFESSIONAL CORPORATION (AV)

553 S. Marengo Avenue, 91101
Telephone: 818-577-1086
Fax: 818-304-2959

Burke W. Willsey	Daniel P. Willsey (A Professional Corporation)

Reference: Sanwa Bank.

For full biographical listings, see the Martindale-Hubbell Law Directory

---

REDDING,* Shasta Co.

DENNIS K. COWAN (AV)

280 Hemsted Drive, Suite B, P.O. Box 992090, 96099-2090
Telephone: 916-221-7300
Fax: 916-221-7389
Email: dennisk@snowcrest.net

For full biographical listings, see the Martindale-Hubbell Law Directory

---

SACRAMENTO,* Sacramento Co.

JOHN D. BESSEY (AV)

1025 Ninth Street, Suite 222, 95814
Telephone: 916-443-7354
Fax: 916-443-7077

For full biographical listings, see the Martindale-Hubbell Law Directory

---

HARDY ERICH BROWN & WILSON, A PROFESSIONAL CORPORATION (AV)

1000 G Street, 95814
Telephone: 916-449-3800
Fax: 916-449-3888
Mailing Address: P.O. Box 13530, Sacramento, California, 95853-4530

David L. Perrault	Glenda N. Reager
L. Kent Wyatt	John C. Miller, Jr.
	Michael J. Nelson

Linda Wilson Bloom

Representative Clients: Little Caesar Enterprises, Inc.

For full biographical listings, see the Martindale-Hubbell Law Directory

---

SAN BERNARDINO,* San Bernardino Co.

HANOVER & SCHNITZER (AV)

665 North Arrowhead Avenue, 92401
Telephone: 909-884-2147
Fax: 909-889-1828

MEMBERS OF FIRM

Norman L. Hanover	Mark C. Schnitzer

ASSOCIATES

Marc Andrews	Paul R. Shankman

For full biographical listings, see the Martindale-Hubbell Law Directory

---

SAN DIEGO,* San Diego Co.

ESTES & HOYT, A PROFESSIONAL CORPORATION (AV)

Suite 1300, 1010 Second Avenue, 92101
Telephone: 619-234-2111
Fax: 619-234-1509

Joel C. Estes	Kevin J. Hoyt
	Bernard M. Hansen

Melvin E. Morris	Richard C. Norton

For full biographical listings, see the Martindale-Hubbell Law Directory

RADMILA A. FULTON (AV)

1545 Hotel Circle South, Suite 190, 92108-3413
Telephone: 619-293-7737
Fax: 619-293-3463

For full biographical listings, see the Martindale-Hubbell Law Directory

HOVEY, KIRBY, THORNTON & HAHN, A PROFESSIONAL CORPORATION (AV)

101 West Broadway, Suite 1100, 92101-8297
Telephone: 619-685-4000
Fax: 619-685-4004
Email: 74754.3143@compuserve.com

Dean T. Kirby, Jr.	Geraldine A. Valdez

For full biographical listings, see the Martindale-Hubbell Law Directory

LINDLEY, LAZAR & SCALES, A PROFESSIONAL CORPORATION (AV)

One America Plaza, 600 West Broadway, Suite 1400, 92101-3302
Telephone: 619-234-9181
Fax: 619-234-8475
Email: 104413.1175@compuserve.com

John M. Seitman	Michael H. Wexler
	George C. Lazar

For Complete List of Firm Personnel, See General Section

For full biographical listings, see the Martindale-Hubbell Law Directory

LUCE, FORWARD, HAMILTON & SCRIPPS LLP (AV)

A Partnership including Professional Corporations
600 West Broadway, Suite 2600, 92101
Telephone: 619-236-1414
Fax: 619-232-8311
URL: http://www.luce.com
La Jolla, California Office: 4275 Executive Square, Suite 800, 92037.
Telephone: 619-535-2639.
Fax: 619-453-2812.
Los Angeles, California Office: 777 South Figueroa, Suite 3600, 90017.
Telephone: 213-892-4992.
Fax: 213-892-7731.
San Francisco, California Office: 100 Bush Street, 20th Floor, 94104.
Telephone: 415-395-7900.
Fax: 415-395-7949.

(See Next Column)

LUCE, FORWARD, HAMILTON & SCRIPPS LLP—*Continued*

New York, N.Y. Office: Citicorp Center, 153 East 53rd Street, 26th Floor, 10022.
Telephone: 212-754-1414.
Fax: 212-644-9727.
Chicago, Illinois Office: 180 North La Salle Street, Suite 1125, 60601.
Telephone: 312-641-0580.
Fax: 312-641-0380.

MEMBERS OF FIRM

Mikel R. Bistrow	Margaret M. Mann

Christopher Celentino

OF COUNSEL

Michael T. Andrew	Stephen R. Brown

ASSOCIATES

Teryl Murabayashi	Kathryn M. S. Catherwood
(Resident, Los Angeles Office)	Helen T. Chao

For Complete List of Firm Personnel, See General Section

For full biographical listings, see the Martindale-Hubbell Law Directory

---

MULVANEY, KAHAN & BARRY, A PROFESSIONAL CORPORATION (AV)

Seventeenth Floor, First National Bank Center, 401 West "A" Street, 92101-7994
Telephone: 619-238-1010
Fax: 619-238-1981
Email: mkb@mkblaw.com
Los Angeles, California Office: Union Bank Plaza, 445 South Figueroa Street, Suite 2600.
Telephone: 213-612-7765.
La Jolla, California Office: Glendale Federal Building, 7911 Herschel, Suite 300, P.O Box 1885.
Telephone: 619-454-0142.
Fax: 619-454-7858.
Orange, California Office: The Koll Center, 500 North State College Boulevard, Suite 440.
Telephone: 714-634-7069.
Fax: 714-939-8000.

James F. Mulvaney	Mark R. Raftery
Lawrence Kahan	Charles F. Bethel
Everett G. Barry, Jr.	Diane M. Racicot
Donald G. Johnson, Jr.	John A. Mayers
Robert A. Linn	Steven W. Pite
Maureen E. Markey	Patricia A. Sieveke (Resident,
Paula Rotenberg	Los Angeles and Orange
Melissa A. Blackburn	Offices)
Julie A. Jones	Linda C. Schumacher
Maureen F. Hallahan	John D. Duncan

OF COUNSEL

Rex B. Beatty	Derrick W. Samuelson
Robert K. Edmunds	(Not admitted in CA)
James P. McGowan, Jr.	
(Resident, La Jolla Office)	

Representative Clients: Union Bank; Wells Fargo Bank; Visa USA, Inc.

For full biographical listings, see the Martindale-Hubbell Law Directory

---

PAGE, POLIN & BUSCH, A PROFESSIONAL CORPORATION (AV)

350 West Ash Street, Suite 900, 92101-3436
Telephone: 619-231-1822
Fax: 619-231-1877
Fax: 619-231-1875
Email: pagepolin@pagepolin.com

Michael E. Busch	Richard W. Page
Kathleen A. Cashman-Kramer	Kenneth D. Polin
Richard L. Moskitis	Steven G. Rowles

Rod S. Fiori	Michael G. Rowles
Dorothy A. Johnson	(Not admitted in CA)
Jolene L. Parker	Barry M. Taira

For full biographical listings, see the Martindale-Hubbell Law Directory

---

SPARBER, FERGUSON, PONDER & RYAN, A PROFESSIONAL LAW CORPORATION (AV)

Imperial Bank Building, 701 "B" Street, Tenth Floor, 92101-8103
Telephone: 619-239-3600
Facsimile: 619-239-5601

Richard E. Sparber	Greg J. Ryan
James P. Ferguson	Richard J. Annen
John E. Ponder	Daniel F. Morrin

Gary B. Rudolph

Todd R. Gabriel	William P. Fennell
Carol R. McGinnis	James E. Highsmith

(See Next Column)

OF COUNSEL
Mark P. Mandell
LEGAL SUPPORT PERSONNEL
LEGAL ADMINISTRATOR
Beverly K. Driscoll

For full biographical listings, see the Martindale-Hubbell Law Directory

---

SUTTER & LITTLE (AV)

185 West "F" Street, Suite 430, 92101-6025
Telephone: 619-232-2330
Fax: 619-232-4916

Joe R. Sutter	Russel T. Little

For full biographical listings, see the Martindale-Hubbell Law Directory

---

SAN FRANCISCO, * San Francisco Co.

BECKER LAW OFFICE (AV)

220 Montgomery Street, Suite 388, P.O. Box 192991, 94119-2991
Telephone: 415-434-8000
Telex: 6731234 BECKER SFO
Telecopier: 415-362-7411
WUW Cable: BECKER, CALIF

Stephen C. Becker

For full biographical listings, see the Martindale-Hubbell Law Directory

---

FELDMAN, WALDMAN & KLINE, A PROFESSIONAL CORPORATION (AV)

3 Embarcadero Center, Suite 2800, 94111
Telephone: 415-981-1300
Fax: 415-981-1350
Email: info@fwk.com
Stockton, California Office: Sperry Building, 146-148 West Weber Avenue.
Telephone: 209-943-2004.
Fax: 209-943-0905.

Murry J. Waldman	Martha Jeanne Shaver
Leland R. Selna, Jr.	(Resident, Stockton Office)
Michael L. Korbholz	Robert Cedric Goodman
Howard M. Wexler	Laura Grad
Patricia S. Mar	William F. Adams
Kenneth W. Jones	Elizabeth A. Thompson
Paul J. Dion	Julie A. Jones
Vern S. Bothwell	David L. Kanel
L.J. Chris Martiniak	Abram S. Feuerstein

Linda Sorensen

Laura J. Dawson	Dana A. Suntag
Joanne M. Lafreniere	(Resident, Stockton Office)
Paul A. Weiss	Danielle Ochs-Tillotson

OF COUNSEL

Richard L. Jaeger	Gerald A. Sherwin
	(Resident, Stockton Office)

For full biographical listings, see the Martindale-Hubbell Law Directory

---

GOLDBERG, STINNETT, MEYERS & DAVIS, A PROFESSIONAL CORPORATION (AV)

Suite 2900, 44 Montgomery Street, 94104
Telephone: 415-362-5045
Fax: 415-362-2392

Lawrence Goldberg	Dennis D. Davis
Terrance L. Stinnett	Daniel M. Linchey
Merle C. Meyers	Katherine D. Ray

Joseph K. Falzon	Albert Flor, Jr.

Kenneth G. DeJarnette

Representative Clients: Alps Electric (USA) Inc.; Fremont Bank; K-Mart Corp.; Mitsubishi International Corp.; Hexcel Corp.; Finova Capital Corp.; Hambrecht & Quist; Supercuts.

For full biographical listings, see the Martindale-Hubbell Law Directory

---

HOLMAN & O'GRADY (AV)

345 California Street, Suite 1770, 94104-2622
Telephone: 415-352-0500
Facsimile: 415-352-0505
Email: HandOSF@aol.com

Thomas C. Holman	Sharon L. O'Grady

JUNIOR SHAREHOLDER
Kathryn E. McQueen

For full biographical listings, see the Martindale-Hubbell Law Directory

San Francisco—Continued

LAW OFFICES OF IAIN A. MACDONALD (AV)

Two Embarcadero Center Suite 1670, 94111
Telephone: 415-362-0449
Fax: 415-394-6446

ASSOCIATE
Lawrence J. Fallon

For full biographical listings, see the Martindale-Hubbell Law Directory

WELCH, OLRICH & MORI, A PROFESSIONAL CORPORATION (AV)

Four Embarcadero Center, 37th Floor, 94111
Telephone: 415-397-4100
Telecopier: 415-986-0245
Santa Rosa, California Office: 50 Courthouse Square, Suite 602.
Telephone: 707-577-0220.

Vernon D. Stokes (Retired)   Denise L. Olrich
Craig K. Welch   James S. Mori

Jan C. Nielsen

For full biographical listings, see the Martindale-Hubbell Law Directory

SAN JOSE,* Santa Clara Co.

CAMPEAU & THOMAS, A LAW CORPORATION (AV)

Market Post Tower, 55 South Market Street, Suite 1660, 95113
Telephone: 408-295-9555
Fax: 408-295-6606

Kenneth J. Campeau   Wayne H. Thomas
                Scott L. Goodsell

Marcie E. Schaap   Kathryn J. Diemer

For full biographical listings, see the Martindale-Hubbell Law Directory

CHARLES E. LOGAN (AV)

95 South Market Street, Suite 570, 95113
Telephone: 408-995-0256
Fax: 408-995-0256; 408-283-1440

ASSOCIATES
Susan B. Luce   Mark A. Heyl

For full biographical listings, see the Martindale-Hubbell Law Directory

MILLER, MORTON, CAILLAT & NEVIS (AV)

50 West San Fernando Street, Suite 1300, 95113-2413
Telephone: 408-292-1765
Telecopier: 408-292-4484

Richard W. Morton (1916-1975)   Charles V. Caillat (1920-1990)
        Harvey C. Miller (1906-1993)
MEMBERS OF FIRM
David L. Nevis   Joseph A. Scanlan, Jr.
Francis J. Hughes   Carolyn Tobiason Stuart
Peter A. Kline   William K. Hurley
Stevan C. Adelman   Peter V. Dessau
            Eric Mogensen
OF COUNSEL
Nancy F. Symons   Susan L. Sutton
        Pamela J. Silberstein
ASSOCIATES
Kathryn E. Barrett   David I. Kornbluh
Katherine S. Pak   Kimberly Holtz MacMillan

Representative Clients: Trammell Crow Residential Services; Joe Kerley Lincoln Mercury Co.; Milligan News Co.; Joseph George Distributors; The Frozen Food Employees Pension Trust; Santa Clara Dental Society; New West Foods; Bay Apartment Communities; Guy F. Atkinson Company; A. Hathaway Co.

For full biographical listings, see the Martindale-Hubbell Law Directory

SAN LUIS OBISPO,* San Luis Obispo Co.

FARMER & READY, A LAW CORPORATION (AV)

1254 Marsh Street, P.O. Box 1443, 93406
Telephone: 805-541-1626
Fax: 805-541-0769

David Y. Farmer   Paul F. Ready
        Sandra K. Fahey

Representative Clients: Ticor Title Insurance & Trust Co.; State Farm Mutual Automobile Insurance Co.; Chubb Pacific Indemnity; Reliance Insurance Co.

For full biographical listings, see the Martindale-Hubbell Law Directory

SANTA ANA,* Orange Co.

BURD & NAYLOR (AV)

201 East Sandpointe, Suite 460, 92707
Telephone: 714-708-3900

Karen Sue Naylor   William M. Burd

For full biographical listings, see the Martindale-Hubbell Law Directory

MARSHACK & GOE (AV)

Six Hutton Centre Drive, Suite 900, 92707
Telephone: 714-540-5400
Facsimile: 714-540-4330
Email: marshack@mglaw.com URL: http://www.mglaw.com
PARTNERS
Richard A. Marshack   Robert P. Goe
        Leonard M. Shulman
PRINCIPALS
Thomas H. Casey   Thomas J. Polis
        Ronald S. Hodges
ASSOCIATES
Vicki L. Schennum   Judith E. Marshack
Leslie Anne Hawes   James Charles Bastian, Jr.
        Stacey D. Sarowatz
TAX COUNSEL
A. Lavar Taylor
LITIGATION COUNSEL
Robert M. Ruben

For full biographical listings, see the Martindale-Hubbell Law Directory

LAW OFFICES OF STANLEY MINIER, INC. (AV)

2677 North Main Street, Suite 870, 92705-6631
Telephone: 714-558-0181
Fax: 714-558-7435

Stanley W. Minier

Reference: Bank of America.

For full biographical listings, see the Martindale-Hubbell Law Directory

PRENOVOST, NORMANDIN, BERGH & DAWE, A PROFESSIONAL CORPORATION (AV)

2020 East First Street, Suite 500, 92705
Telephone: 714-547-2444
Fax: 714-835-2889
Email: PNBD@worldnet.att.net

Thomas J. Prenovost, Jr.   Steven L. Bergh
Tom Roddy Normandin   Michael G. Dawe

Doris Andree Faust   Paula M. Harrelson
Eric P. Francisconi   Daniel H. McLinden
James Andrew Fraser   Nancy R. Tragarz

Reference: Marine National Bank.

For full biographical listings, see the Martindale-Hubbell Law Directory

SPERLING & PERGANDE (AV)

3 Hutton Centre, Suite 670, 92707
Telephone: 714-540-8500
Facsimile: 714-540-2599

MEMBERS OF FIRM
Dean P. Sperling   K. William Pergande

For full biographical listings, see the Martindale-Hubbell Law Directory

SANTA BARBARA,* Santa Barbara Co.

ANGLE, CARLSON, GOLDRICK & ROBERTS (AV)

A Partnership including a Professional Corporation
200 East Carrillo Street, Suite 310, 93101
Telephone: 805-963-7400
Fax: 805-963-7610

Robert O. Angle   Miles T. Goldrick
Arthur W. Carlson (A P.C.) Paul A. Roberts
OF COUNSEL
Georgia C. McDermott

For full biographical listings, see the Martindale-Hubbell Law Directory

SANTA MONICA, Los Angeles Co.

PARIS AND PARIS (AV)

Paris Law Building, 424 Pico Boulevard, 90405-1197
Telephone: 310-392-8722
Telecopier: 310-392-1768
Email: PandP424@aol.com
San Rafael, California Office: 4286 Redwood Highway, Suite, 391. 94903.

Reynold F. Paris	Jeffrey A. Paris
Bette S. Paris	Karen M. Paris
Murray A. Zeffren	Richard E. Paris

J. Robert Force

For full biographical listings, see the Martindale-Hubbell Law Directory

STEINBERG, NUTTER & BRENT, LAW CORPORATION (AV)

501 Colorado Avenue, Suite 300, 90401
Telephone: 310-451-9714
Telecopier: 310-451-0929
Woodland Hills, California Office: 21031 Ventura Boulevard, Suite 419.
Telephone: 818-703-6204.

Peter T. Steinberg   Guy B. Nutter
Paul M. Brent

James M. Buck

Reference: Santa Monica Bank.

For full biographical listings, see the Martindale-Hubbell Law Directory

STERN, NEUBAUER, GREENWALD & PAULY, A PROFESSIONAL CORPORATION (AV)

1299 Ocean Avenue, Tenth Floor, 90401-1007
Telephone: 310-451-8001
Telecopier: 310-395-5961

David M. Stern	Joshua D. Wayser
Mark A. Neubauer	Richard L. Miller
Dennis L. Greenwald	M. Tracy McGeagh
Andrew S. Pauly	Kirsten Shirley Ellis
Russell F. Wolpert	Owen Scott Solomon
Randall S. Rothschild	Wendy Angela Loo
Richard M. Foster	Nena W. Wong
David C. Smith	Michael F. Donner

Christine Millee Henricks
LEGAL SUPPORT PERSONNEL
Carol Leemom

For full biographical listings, see the Martindale-Hubbell Law Directory

SANTA ROSA, * Sonoma Co.

BELDEN, ABBEY, WEITZENBERG & KELLY, A PROFESSIONAL CORPORATION (AV)

1105 North Dutton Avenue, P.O. Box 1566, 95402
Telephone: 707-542-5050
Telecopier: 707-542-2589

Thomas P. Kelly, Jr.   Candace H. Shirley
Richard W. Abbey   Timothy W. Hoffman

Representative Clients: Exchange Bank of Santa Rosa; Westamerica Bank; North Bay Title Co.; Northwestern Title Security Co.; Geyser Peak Winery; Santa Rosa City School District; Sonoma National Bank; Arrowood Vineyards & Winery; Arthur & DeVincenzi Concrete; Friedman Bros. Hardware, Inc.

For Complete List of Firm Personnel, See General Section

For full biographical listings, see the Martindale-Hubbell Law Directory

SIGNAL HILL, Los Angeles Co.

RICHARD R. CLEMENTS A PROFESSIONAL CORPORATION (AV)

2201 East Willow Street, P.O. Box D177, 90806-2142
Telephone: 310-424-7919
Voice Mail: 213-228-1300

Richard R. Clements

Gail W. Richardson   Samuel T. Casazza

For full biographical listings, see the Martindale-Hubbell Law Directory

TORRANCE, Los Angeles Co.

FINER, KIM & STEARNS (AV)

An Association of Professional Corporations
City National Bank Building, 3424 Carson Street, Suite 500, 90503
Telephone: 310-214-1477
Telecopier: 310-214-0764

(See Next Column)

Robert B. Parsons
OF COUNSEL
Bennett A. Rheingold   Ryan E. Stearns

For Complete List of Firm Personnel, See General Section

For full biographical listings, see the Martindale-Hubbell Law Directory

VENTURA, * Ventura Co.

LAW OFFICES OF MICHAEL R. SMENT (AV)

674 County Square Drive, Suite 108, 93003-5402
Telephone: 805-654-0311
Telecopier: 805-984-2399
Email: rockjr@aol.com
Los Angeles, California Office: 1800 Avenue of the Stars, Suite 1000.
Telephone: 310-277-6361; 277-6362.
Fax: 310-277-6517.

For full biographical listings, see the Martindale-Hubbell Law Directory

COLORADO

DENVER, * Denver Co.

JON B. CLARKE, P.C. (AV)

Two DTC, Suite 150, 5290 DTC Parkway (Englewood), 80111-2721
Telephone: 303-779-0600
Fax: 303-850-7115
Email: jbclarke102421.2703@compuserve.com

Jon B. Clarke

For full biographical listings, see the Martindale-Hubbell Law Directory

DUFFORD & BROWN, P.C. (AV)

1700 Broadway, Suite 1700, 80290-1701
Telephone: 303-861-8013
Facsimile: 303-832-3804
Affiliated Office: Solomon, Pearl, Blum & Quinn, L.L.P., New York, NY and Denver, Colorado.

David W. Furgason   Randall J. Feuerstein
Scott J. Mikulecky

Terry Jo Epstein   Thomas E. J. Hazard
OF COUNSEL
Morris B. Hecox, Jr.

Representative Clients: Bondholders' Committee-Wheeler Realty Company; Reorganized CF&I Steel Corporation; Amdura Corporation; United Steelworkers of America; Air Line Pilots Association; Graphics Information, Inc.; IDS Life Insurance Company; Hall & Hall Mortgage Corporation; Magic Chef; Unsecured Creditor's Committee-Sargent, Inc.

For Complete List of Firm Personnel, See General Section

For full biographical listings, see the Martindale-Hubbell Law Directory

JONES & KELLER, A PROFESSIONAL CORPORATION (AV)

Suite 1600, 1625 Broadway, 80202
Telephone: 303-573-1600
Fax: 303-893-6506

Marion F. Jones (1898-1978)	Thomas J. Burke, Jr.
Alec J. Keller (1913-1995)	Samuel E. Wing
Alvin J. Meiklejohn, Jr.	Reid A. Godbolt
Leslie R. Kehl	Rodney D. Knutson
Edward T. Lyons, Jr.	Kevin L. Brown
David E. Driggers	Barry L. Wilkie

Howard R. Hertzberg	Brent Nicholls
David A. Thayer	Michael Brian Cavanaugh

Nathan D. Simmons

Reference: Colorado State Bank; Union Bank & Trust.

For full biographical listings, see the Martindale-Hubbell Law Directory

SOLOMON PEARL BLUM & QUINN LLP (AV)

1700 Broadway, Suite 1820, 80290
Telephone: 303-832-6686
Fax: 303-832-6653
Email: SolPearl@aol.com
New York, New York Office: Woolworth Building, 37th Floor, 233 Broadway, 10007.
Charlotte Amalie, St. Thomas, Virgin Islands Affiliated Office: Grunet Stout & Bruch, 24-25 Kongens Gade, P.O. Box 1030, 00804.
Telephone: 809-774-1320.
Fax: 809-774-7839.

(See Next Column)

SOLOMON PEARL BLUM & QUINN LLP, Denver—Continued

Denver, Colorado Affiliated Office: Dufford & Brown, P.C., 1700 Broadway, Suite 1700, 80290.
Telephone: 303-861-8013.
Facsimile: 303-832-3804.

Robert A. Solomon	William L. Blum
Clifford R. Pearl	(Not admitted in CO)
	Thomas F. Quinn

For full biographical listings, see the Martindale-Hubbell Law Directory

---

CONNECTICUT

HARTFORD,* Hartford Co.

HEBB & GITLIN, A PROFESSIONAL CORPORATION (AV)

One State Street, 06103-3178
Telephone: 860-240-2700
Telecopier: 860-278-8968
Email: 5111037@MCIMail.com
London, England Office: York House, 199 Westminster Bridge Road, London SE1 7UT, U.K.
Telephone: 011-44-171-395-9400.
Telecopier: 011-44-171-395-9409.

MEMBERS OF FIRM

G. Eric Brunstad, Jr.	William E. Kelly
David M. Cain	Jeffery S. Kuperstock
Richard F. Casher	Thomas J. Love, Jr.
John B. D'Agostino	George A. McKeon
Chester L. Fisher III	(Of Counsel)
Douglas E. Fiske	M. Bree Nesbitt
Evan D. Flaschen	Peter M. Nolin
John J. Gillies, Jr.	Gregory W. Nye
Richard A. Gitlin	Michael J. Reilly
James Greenfield	Barry G. Russell (Resident
Gary S. Hammersmith	Member, London Office)
Edwin Gordon Hebb, Jr.	R. Jeffrey Smith
Harold S. Horwich	Lorraine Murphy Weil
Eric W. Johnson	Jeffrey L. Williams

COUNSEL

Thomas H. Day	Deborah Samuels Freeman
Garrett J. Delehanty, Jr.	John D. Inwood
Timothy B. DeSieno	James P. Maher
Scott A. Falk	Joyce M. Resnick

ASSOCIATES

Claude M. Brouillard	Michael B. Nadolski
Mark E. Chavey	Thomas F. O'Connor
Laura Gonzalez Ciabarra	Thomas J. O'Shea
Jane M. Domboski	Brenda J. Page
William H. Erickson	Peter C.L. Roth
Judith H. Friedman	Joseph L. Scibilia
(Not admitted in CT)	Patricia Ann Shackelford
Brad Christian Gustafson	David Silber
Jonathan A. Harris	Ronald J. Silverman
James P. Juliano	J. Dormer Stephen
Gregory W. Kulak	Oscar Urizar
R. Michael Meo, Jr.	Brian N. Watkins
Theodore C. Morris	William J. Yoo

For full biographical listings, see the Martindale-Hubbell Law Directory

---

MILFORD, New Haven Co.

HARLOW, ADAMS & FRIEDMAN, P.C. (AV)

300 Bic Drive, 06460-3508
Telephone: 203-878-0661
Fax: 203-878-9568
Email: attorney@quidproquo.com

William D. Harlow (1921-1988)	Michael P. A. Williams
George W. Adams, III	Eric R. Gaynor
Dana Eric Friedman	Joseph A. Kubic
Theodore H. Shumaker	Elizabeth Stuckal
Stephen P. Wright	James M. Nugent

For full biographical listings, see the Martindale-Hubbell Law Directory

---

NEW HAVEN,* New Haven Co.

BERGMAN, HOROWITZ & REYNOLDS, P.C. (AV)

157 Church Street, 19th Floor, P.O. Box 426, 06502
Telephone: 203-789-1320
Fax: 203-785-8127
Email: mailbox@taxlawyers.com *URL:* http://www.taxlawyers.com
New York, N.Y. Office: 499 Park Avenue, 26th Floor.
Telephone: 212-688-4150.

Melvin Ditman	Jeremy A. Mellitz

(See Next Column)

Richard M. Porter	Paul J. Stankewich

For full biographical listings, see the Martindale-Hubbell Law Directory

---

NEW LONDON, New London Co.

WALLER, SMITH & PALMER, P.C. (AV)

52 Eugene O'Neill Drive, P.O. Box 88, 06320
Telephone: 860-442-0367
Telecopier: 860-447-9915
Old Lyme, Connecticut Office: 103-A Halls Road.
Telephone: 860-434-8063.
Telecopier: 860-434-9452.

William W. Miner	Hughes Griffis
Robert P. Anderson, Jr.	Edward B. O'Connell
Robert W. Marrion	Frederick B. Gahagan
	Mary E. Driscoll

Tracy M. Collins

General Counsel For: Town of East Lyme; Town of Lebanon.
Counsel For: Citizens Savings Bank; Sonoco/Northeastern, Inc.; The Nature Conservancy; Fleet Bank.
Local Counsel For: McCue Mortgage Co.; Citicorp Mortgage; U.S. Department of Housing and Urban Development.

For Complete List of Firm Personnel, See General Section

For full biographical listings, see the Martindale-Hubbell Law Directory

---

WETHERSFIELD, Hartford Co.

CHORCHES & NOVAK, P.C. (AV)

1260 Silas Deane Highway, 06109-4331
Telephone: 860-257-1980
Telecopier: 860-257-1988

Martin Chorches	Anthony S. Novak
	Honor S. Heath

Edward C. Taiman, Jr.	Ronald I. Chorches
	Theresa A. Caldarone

For full biographical listings, see the Martindale-Hubbell Law Directory

---

DELAWARE

WILMINGTON,* New Castle Co.

POTTER ANDERSON & CORROON (AV)

350 Delaware Trust Building, P.O. Box 951, 19899-0951
Telephone: 302-984-6000
FAX: 302-658-1192
URL: HTTP://ATTYS.PACDELAWARE.COM

MEMBERS OF FIRM

Laurie Selber Silverstein	William R. Denny

ASSOCIATE

Joanne Ceballos

Representative Clients: Meridian Oil Production, Inc.; Consolidated Rail Corporation; Travellers International; A.G.; ConAgra, Inc.; Swift Eckrich, Inc.; Beatrice Cheese, Inc.; Midlantic National Bank; Delaware Trust Capital Management, Inc.; DR Holdings Inc. of Delaware.

For Complete List of Firm Personnel, See General Section

For full biographical listings, see the Martindale-Hubbell Law Directory

SMITH, KATZENSTEIN & FURLOW (AV)

The Corporate Plaza, 800 Delaware Avenue, P.O. Box 410, 19899
Telephone: 302-652-8400
Fax: 302-652-8405

MEMBERS OF FIRM

Craig B. Smith	Anne E. Bookout
	Stephen M. Miller

Joanne M. Shalk

For Complete List of Firm Personnel, See General Section

For full biographical listings, see the Martindale-Hubbell Law Directory

WILLIAMS, HERSHMAN & WISLER, P.A. (AV)

Suite 600, One Commerce Center, Twelfth and Orange Streets, P.O. Box 511, 19899-0511
Telephone: 302-575-0873
Telecopier: 302-575-1642

(See Next Column)

WILLIAMS, HERSHMAN & WISLER P.A.—_Continued_

David Nicol Williams
Douglas M. Hershman

Jeffrey C. Wisler
Barbara Snapp Danberg

References: Wilmington Trust Co.; PNC Bank.

For full biographical listings, see the Martindale-Hubbell Law Directory

DISTRICT OF COLUMBIA

WASHINGTON, D.C. Co.

* indicates certain Bar Register subscribers, in cities of comparable size and importance, who maintain an additional office in Washington, D.C. and who have arranged for representation as a part of the Washington, D.C. listings that follow

GEORGE FRANCIS BASON, JR. (AV)

4910 Massachusetts Avenue, N.W., Suite 18, 20016
Telephone: 202-537-0219
Telefax: 301-654-7917
Chevy Chase, Maryland Office: 4601 North Park Avenue, No. 110.
(Also Of Counsel to Michael J. Goergen)

For full biographical listings, see the Martindale-Hubbell Law Directory

DECKELBAUM OGENS & FISCHER, CHARTERED (AV)

1140 Connecticut Avenue, N.W., 20036
Telephone: 202-223-1474
Fax: 202-293-1471
Bethesda, Maryland Office: 6701 Democracy Boulevard.
Telephone: 301-564-5100.

Nelson Deckelbaum
Ronald L. Ogens
Lawrence H. Fischer

Deborah E. Reiser
Charles A. Moster
Andrew J. Shedlock, III

Ronald G. Scheraga
Bryn Hope Sherman
Thomas Peter Mann
(Not admitted in DC)

Phyllis Lea Bean
Darryl Alan Feldman
(Not admitted in DC)

Representative Clients: The Charles E. Smith Companies; The Trammell Crow Co.
References: Franklin National Bank; Century National Bank.

For full biographical listings, see the Martindale-Hubbell Law Directory

LEONARD, RALSTON & STANTON, CHARTERED (AV)

1000 Thomas Jefferson Street, N.W. Suite 609, 20007
Telephone: 202-342-3342
Fax: 202-298-7810
Fairfax, Virginia Office: Leonard, Ralston & Stanton, Chartered, Sherwood Plaza, Suite 150, 9990 Lee Highway, 22030.
Telephone: 703-591-6200.
Fax: 703-591-6556.

Jerris Leonard
David T. Ralston, Jr.
Thomas J. Stanton
(Not admitted in DC)

Mary Gayle Holden
(Not admitted in DC)
Daniel F. Rinzel

Roderick B. Williams
Rachel Danish Campbell
Karen M. Grane
Theodore Charles Curtin

Douglas J. Hoffman
(Not admitted in DC)
Walter C. Hazlitt, Jr.
(Not admitted in DC)

OF COUNSEL
John D. Brosnan

LOBBYING/ADMINISTRATIVE
Kathleen A. Leonard

REGULATORY AFFAIRS
Russell Wapensky

For full biographical listings, see the Martindale-Hubbell Law Directory

SHAWN, MANN & NIEDERMAYER, L.L.P. (AV)

1850 M Street, N.W., Suite 280, 20036-5803
Telephone: 202-331-7900
Fax: 202-331-0726
Washington, D.C., Government Affairs Office: 499 S. Capitol Street, S.W., Suite 420.
Telephone: 202-842-3000.
Fax: 202-547-7161.
Los Angeles, California Office: 2029 Century Park East, Suite 1690.
Telephone: 310-553-8065.
Fax: 310-557-0729.

(See Next Column)

San Diego, California Office: 401 West "A" Street, Suite 1850.
Telephone: 619-236-0303.
Fax: 619-238-8181.
San Francisco, California Office: The Fox Plaza, 1390 Market Street, Suite 1204.
Telephone: 415-982-0150.
Fax: 415-522-0513.
Bloomington, Minnesota Office: 2090 West 98th Street.
Telephone: 612-881-6577.
Fax: 612-881-6894.

MEMBER OF FIRM
Joseph L. Steinfeld, Jr.

For full biographical listings, see the Martindale-Hubbell Law Directory

* VENABLE ATTORNEYS AT LAW VENABLE, BAETJER, HOWARD & CIVILETTI, LLP (AV)

A Partnership including Professional Corporations
Suite 1000, 1201 New York Avenue, N.W., 20005
Telephone: 202-962-4800
Fax: 202-962-8300
Baltimore, Maryland Office: Venable, Baetjer and Howard LLP, 1800 Mercantile Bank & Trust Building, 2 Hopkins Plaza.
Telephone: 410-244-7400.
McLean, Virginia Office: Venable, Baetjer and Howard LLP, Suite 400, 2010 Corporate Ridge.
Telephone: 703-760-1600.
Rockville, Maryland Office: Venable, Baetjer and Howard LLP, Suite 500, One Church Street, P. O. Box 1906.
Telephone: 301-217-5600.
Towson, Maryland Office: Venable, Baetjer and Howard LLP, 210 Allegheny Avenue, P. O. Box 5517.
Telephone: 410-494-6200.

MEMBERS OF FIRM
Joe A. Shull
Kenneth C. Bass, III (Also at McLean, Virginia Office)

George F. Pappas (Also at Baltimore, Maryland Office)

For Complete List of Firm Personnel, See General Section

For full biographical listings, see the Martindale-Hubbell Law Directory

WILMER, CUTLER & PICKERING (AV)

2445 M Street, N.W., 20037-1420
Telephone: 202-663-6000
Fax: 202-663-6363
Email: Law@Wilmer.Com
Baltimore, Maryland Office: 100 Light Street, 21202.
Telephone: 410-986-2800.
Fax: 410-986-2828.
European Offices:
4 Carlton Gardens, London, SW1Y 5AA, England. Telephone: +44 (171) 872-1000.
Fax: +44 (171) 839-3537.
Rue de la Loi 15Wetstraat, B-1040 Brussels, Belgium. Telephone: +32 (2) 285-4900.
Fax: +32 (2) 285-4949.
Friedrichstrasse 95, D-10117 Berlin, Germany. Telephone: +49 (30) 2022-6400.
Fax: +49 (30)2022-6500.

MEMBERS OF FIRM
Louis R. Cohen
F. David Lake, Jr.
Stephen F. Black
Dr. Manfred Balz (Not admitted in the United States; Resident, European Office, Berlin, Germany)
Mary Carolyn Cox

William J. Perlstein
Russell J. Bruemmer
William J. Wilkins
Thomas W. White
Duane D. Morse
Philip D. Anker
Bryan Slone (Resident, Baltimore, Maryland Office)

For Complete List of Firm Personnel, See General Section

For full biographical listings, see the Martindale-Hubbell Law Directory

FLORIDA

AVENTURA, Dade Co.

BUCHANAN INGERSOLL, PROFESSIONAL CORPORATION (AVⓉ)

One Turnberry Place, 19495 Biscayne Boulevard, Suite 606, 33180
Telephone: 305-933-5600
Telecopier: 305-933-2350
URL: http://www.bipc.com
Pittsburgh, Pennsylvania Office: One Oxford Centre, 301 Grant Street, 20th Floor.
Telephone: 412-562-8800.
Philadelphia, Pennsylvania Office: Two Logan Square, Twelfth Floor, 18th & Arch Streets.
Telephone: 215-665-8700.

(See Next Column)

BUCHANAN INGERSOLL PROFESSIONAL CORPORATION, *Aventura—Continued*

Harrisburg, Pennsylvania Office: 30 North Third Street.
Telephone: 717-237-4800.
Miami, Florida Office: NationsBank Tower, 100 S.E. Second Street.
Telephone: 305-347-4080.
Tampa, Florida Office: Suite 2500, 401 East Jackson Street.
Telephone: 813-222-8180.
Princeton, New Jersey Office: Buchanan Ingersoll, A Partnership, College Centre, 500 College Road East.
Telephone: 609-987-6800.
Lexington, Kentucky Office: Suite 600, PNC Bank Plaza, 200 West Vine Street.
Telephone: 606-225-5333.
Buffalo, New York Office: 1100 Main Place Tower, 350 Main Street.
Telephone: 716-854-4100.
Fax: 816-854-4227.

Richard N. Schermer

For Complete List of Firm Personnel, See General Section

For full biographical listings, see the Martindale-Hubbell Law Directory

---

BOCA RATON, Palm Beach Co.

FURR AND COHEN, P.A. (AV)

Suite 412, 1499 W. Palmetto Park Road, 33486
Telephone: 407-395-0500
Broward: 954-421-0300 0
Fax: 407-338-7532

Robert C. Furr	Charles I. Cohen

Leslie Scott Osborne	Jordi Guso
Lisa Judith Chaiklin	Brendan A. Barry

OF COUNSEL
C. William Berger

For full biographical listings, see the Martindale-Hubbell Law Directory

---

HOLLYWOOD, Broward Co.

JAY M. GAMBERG, P.A. (AV)

4000 Hollywood Boulevard, Suite 350 North, 33021
Telephone: Broward: 954-981-4411
Dade: 305-670-8600
Fax: 954-966-6259
Miami, Florida Office: 9700 South Dixie Highway, Suite 1030. 33156.
Telephone: 305-670-8600.
Fax: 305-966-6259.

Jay M. Gamberg
OF COUNSEL
Jerome H. Shevin

Representative Clients: Metromedia Long Distance; RICOH Corp.; McArthur Dairy.

For full biographical listings, see the Martindale-Hubbell Law Directory

---

JACKSONVILLE,* Duval Co.

COHEN & THURSTON, P.A. (AV)

1723 Blanding Boulevard Suite 102, 32210
Telephone: 904-388-6500
FAX: 904-387-4192
Email: 70303553@compuserve.com

Lance P. Cohen	Janet Hall Thurston

For full biographical listings, see the Martindale-Hubbell Law Directory

---

FISCHETTE, OWEN & HELD (AV)

1301 Riverplace Boulevard Suite 1916, 32207
Telephone: 904-398-7036
Fax: 904-398-4283

MEMBERS OF FIRM

James A. Fischette	Edwin W. Held, Jr.
Philip C. Owen	Charles W. McBurney, Jr.

ASSOCIATES

Dale R. Campion	R. Joseph Dill
	Robert J. Perry, Jr.

References: First Union National Bank of Florida; Enterprise National Bank of Jacksonville.

For full biographical listings, see the Martindale-Hubbell Law Directory

---

KIRSCHNER, MAIN, GRAHAM, TANNER & DEMONT, PROFESSIONAL ASSOCIATION (AV)

One Independent Drive, Suite 2000, P.O. Box 1559, 32201-1559
Telephone: 904-354-4141
Telecopier: 904-358-2199

Barry C. Averitt	Kenneth M. Kirschner
Babette L. Fletcher	James L. Main
T. Malcolm Graham	John T. Rogerson, III
Lee Stathis Haramis	Michael G. Tanner

Howard L. Alford	Judy Ossi Marko
Robin C. Barco	Charles S. McCall
John F. Germany, Jr.	Beth E. Weitzman
Eric S. Kolar	(Not admitted in FL)

OF COUNSEL

Michael E. Demont	Wyman R. Duggan
G. Stephen Manning	Reese J. Henderson, Jr.

Representative Clients: The Maryland Insurance Group; NationsBank; The Suddath Cos.; Wickes Lumber Co.; BFI, Inc.

For full biographical listings, see the Martindale-Hubbell Law Directory

---

MIAMI,* Dade Co.

JOEL M. ARESTY, P.A. (AV)

Atrium Court, 11077 Biscayne Boulevard, Penthouse, 33161
Telephone: 305-899-9876
Telecopy: 305-899-9889
Email: 102717.664@Compuserve.com

Joel M. Aresty

For full biographical listings, see the Martindale-Hubbell Law Directory

---

RICE & ROBINSON, P.A. (AV)

848 Brickell Avenue, Suite 1100, 33131
Telephone: 305-379-3121
Fax: 305-379-4119
Email: AHRPA@AOL.COM

Arthur Halsey Rice	Kenneth B. Robinson

Lisa M. Schiller

For full biographical listings, see the Martindale-Hubbell Law Directory

---

THOMSON MURARO RAZOOK & HART, P.A. (AV)

17th Floor, One Southeast Third Avenue, 33131
Telephone: 305-350-7200
Telecopier: 305-374-1005

Dennis M. Campbell	Timothy J. Norris

Gregg H. Metzger

Representative Clients: The Chase Manhattan Bank; Mercedes Benz Credit Corp.; Transamerica Commercial; Stewart Title Guaranty Co.; Wells Fargo Bank, N.A.; TCF Banking & Savings; Citibank, F.S.B.; First Union National Bank; Lennar Corp.

For Complete List of Firm Personnel, See General Section

For full biographical listings, see the Martindale-Hubbell Law Directory

---

ORLANDO,* Orange Co.

A. CLIFTON BLACK (AV)

126 East Jefferson Street, 32801
Telephone: 407-843-4310
800-433-8149 (Florida Only)
Fax: 407-649-3038

Representative Clients: American Polymers, Inc.; Banc One Leasing Corp.; Maury L. Carter & Associates, Inc.; Douglass Fertilizer & Chemical, Inc.

For full biographical listings, see the Martindale-Hubbell Law Directory

---

JULES S. COHEN, P.A. (AV)

810 North Mills Avenue, 32803
Telephone: 407-896-4493

Jules S. Cohen

Miriam G. Suarez

Representative Clients: The American Bank of the South; First Federal Savings & Loan Association of Osceola County; Peoples State Bank; Aetna Bank; Swiss Bank Corporation; John Hancock Mutual Life Insurance Co.; Sony Corp.; Great American Insurance Co.
Reference: Sun Bank.

For full biographical listings, see the Martindale-Hubbell Law Directory

TAMPA,* Hillsborough Co.

KETCHEY HORAN, P.A. (AV)

100 North Tampa Street, Suite 1900, P.O. Box 500, 33601-0500
Telephone: 813-223-9395
Fax: 813-221-1348
Sun City Center, Florida Office: 1647 Sun City Center Plaza, Suite 200.
Telephone: 813-633-1200.

Michael P. Horan　　　　　　　Alfred A. Colby

For full biographical listings, see the Martindale-Hubbell Law Directory

RYDBERG & GOLDSTEIN, P.A. (AV)

Suite 200, 500 East Kennedy Boulevard, 33602
Telephone: 813-229-3900
Telecopier: 813-229-6101

Marsha Griffin Rydberg　　　　　Bruce S. Goldstein

Peter Baker　　　　　　　　　Tammy N. Giroux
Brian T. FitzGerald　　　　　　Cynthia L. Bulan
　　　　　　　Susan Greco Tuttle

For full biographical listings, see the Martindale-Hubbell Law Directory

SMITH, WILLIAMS & HUMPHRIES, P.A. (AV)

Old Hyde Park, 712 South Oregon Avenue, 33606
Telephone: 813-253-5400
Fax: 813-254-3459
Orlando, Florida Office: Southeast Bank Building, Suite 701, 201 East Pine Street.
Telephone: 407-849-5151.
Fax: 407-843-4076.

David Lisle Smith　　　　　　Robert L. Harding
Gregory L. Williams　　　　　　(Resident, Orlando Office)
J. Gregory Humphries　　　　　Gregory E. Mierzwinski
　(Resident, Orlando Office)　　Carole Taylor Kirkwood
　　　　　Daniel William King

For full biographical listings, see the Martindale-Hubbell Law Directory

STICHTER, RIEDEL, BLAIN & PROSSER, P.A. (AV)

110 East Madison Street, Suite 200, 33602-4700
Telephone: 813-229-0144
Fax: 813-229-1811

Don M. Stichter　　　　　　　Scott A. Stichter
Harley E. Riedel, II　　　　　　Wanda Hagan Anthony
Russell M. Blain　　　　　　　Alberto F. Gomez, Jr.
Richard C. Prosser　　　　　　W. Gregory Golson
Charles A. Postler　　　　　　Stephen R. Leslie
　　　　　Monika L. Schilcher

For full biographical listings, see the Martindale-Hubbell Law Directory

TOWNSEND & BRANNON (AV)

608 West Horatio Street, 33606-2228
Telephone: 813-254-0088
Telecopier: 813-254-0093

MEMBERS OF FIRM
David A. Townsend　　　　　　Anita C. Brannon

For full biographical listings, see the Martindale-Hubbell Law Directory

WEST PALM BEACH,* Palm Beach Co.

QUARLES & BRADY (AV)

222 Lakeview Avenue, 4th Floor, 33401
Telephone: 561-653-5000
Fax: 561-653-5333
Milwaukee, Wisconsin Office: 411 East Wisconsin Avenue, 53202-4497.
Telephone: 414-277-5000.
Fax: 414-271-3552.
Madison, Wisconsin Office: Firstar Plaza, One South Pinckney Street, P.O. Box 2113, 53701-2113.
Telephone: 608-251-5000.
Fax: 608-251-9166.
Naples, Florida Office: Barnett Center, 4501 Tamiami Trail North, Suite 300, 33940-3060.
Telephone: 941-262-5959.
Fax: 941-434-4999.
Phoenix, Arizona Office: One Camelback Building, One East Camelback Road, Suite 400, 85012-1649.
Telephone: 602-230-5500.
Fax: 602-230-5598.

PARTNER
Ned R. Nashban

(See Next Column)

ASSOCIATE
Nancy Berz Colman

For Complete List of Firm Personnel, See General Section

For full biographical listings, see the Martindale-Hubbell Law Directory

GEORGIA

ALBANY,* Dougherty Co.

KELLEY & LOVETT, P.C. (AV)

2539 Lafayette Plaza Drive, 31707
Telephone: 912-888-9128
Fax: 912-888-0966

Walter W. Kelley　　　　　　Thomas D. Lovett

David P. Ward　　　　　　　Allen P. Turnage

Reference: 1st State Bank, Albany, Georgia

AMERICUS,* Sumter Co.

ELLIS, EASTERLIN, PEAGLER, GATEWOOD, HARPER & SKIPPER, P.C., A PROFESSIONAL CORPORATION (AV)

410 West Lamar Street, P.O. Box 488, 31709
Telephone: 912-924-9316
Fax: 912-924-6248

George R. Ellis, Sr. (1905-1988)　　James C. Gatewood
George R. Ellis, Jr.　　　　　　　John V. Harper
Benjamin F. Easterlin, IV　　　　James M. Skipper, Jr.
George M. Peagler, Jr.　　　　　Russ F. Barnes
　　　　　William H. Dudley

For full biographical listings, see the Martindale-Hubbell Law Directory

ATLANTA,* Fulton Co.

DAVID G. CROCKETT, P.C. (AV)

1950 Equitable Building, 100 Peachtree Street, N.W., 30303
Telephone: 404-522-4280
Telecopier: 404-589-9891

David G. Crockett

Tait O. Norton

Approved Attorney for: Chicago Title Insurance Co.
Reference: NationsBank, N.A.

For full biographical listings, see the Martindale-Hubbell Law Directory

GEORGE M. GEESLIN (AV)

1819 Peachtree Road, N.E., Suite 604, 30309
Telephone: 404-351-4785
FAX: 404-351-1165

For full biographical listings, see the Martindale-Hubbell Law Directory

HICKS, MALOOF & CAMPBELL, A PROFESSIONAL CORPORATION (AV)

Suite 2200 Marquis Two Tower, 285 Peachtree Center
　Avenue, 30303-1234
Telephone: 404-588-1100
Telecopy: 404-420-7474

Charles E. Campbell　　　　　J. Michael Levengood
Robert A. Bartlett　　　　　　Henry F. Sewell, Jr.

Jeffery W. Cavender

For full biographical listings, see the Martindale-Hubbell Law Directory

LAMBERTH, BONAPFEL, CIFELLI & STOKES, P.A. (AV)

Atlanta Financial Center, 3343 Peachtree Road, N.E. East Tower, Suite 550, 30326
Telephone: 404-262-7373

J. Michael Lamberth　　　　　James Craig Cifelli
　　　　　Paul W. Bonapfel

G. Frank Nason, IV　　　　　　Donahue S. Silvis
Stuart F. Clayton, Jr.　　　　　A. Alexander Teel
Gregory D. Ellis　　　　　　　Laura E. Woodson

(See Next Column)

LAMBERTH, BONAPFEL, CIFELLI & STOKES P.A., *Atlanta—Continued*
OF COUNSEL
William H. Willson, Jr.

Reference: The Riverside Bank.

For full biographical listings, see the Martindale-Hubbell Law Directory

LONG ALDRIDGE & NORMAN, LLP (AV)

A Limited Liability Partnership including Professional Corporations
One Peachtree Center, Suite 5300, 303 Peachtree Street, 30308
Telephone: 404-527-4000
Telecopier: 404-527-4198
Washington, D.C. Office: Suite 600, 701 Pennsylvania Avenue, N.W.,
20004.
Telephone: 202-624-1200.
FAX: 202-624-1298.

MEMBERS OF FIRM

Evan Appel	Gary W. Marsh
Mark S. Kaufman	Laura Fink Nix
	Russell A. Tolley

ASSOCIATES

Charles D. Weiss	Angelyn M. Wright

For Complete List of Firm Personnel, See General Section

For full biographical listings, see the Martindale-Hubbell Law Directory

MACEY, WILENSKY, COHEN, WITTNER & KESSLER, LLP (AV)

285 Peachtree Center Avenue, Suite 600, 30303-1229
Telephone: 404-584-1200
Telecopier: 404-681-4355
Other Atlanta, Georgia Office: 5784 Lake Forrest Drive, Suite 214, 30328.

MEMBERS OF FIRM

Morris W. Macey	Neil C. Gordon
Frank B. Wilensky	James R. Sacca
	David B. Kurzweil

ASSOCIATES

Shayna M. (Salomon) Steinfeld	Barbara Ellis-Monro

For Complete List of Firm Personnel, See General Section

For full biographical listings, see the Martindale-Hubbell Law Directory

PARKER, HUDSON, RAINER & DOBBS (AV)

1500 Marquis Two Tower, 285 Peachtree Center Avenue, N.E., 30303
Telephone: 404-523-5300
FAX: 404-522-8409
Tallahassee, Florida Office: The Perkins House, 118 North Gadsden
Street, 32301.
Telephone: 904-681-0191.
FAX: 904-681-9493.

MEMBERS OF FIRM

C. Edward Dobbs	Rufus Thomas Dorsey, IV

For full biographical listings, see the Martindale-Hubbell Law Directory

SUTHERLAND, ASBILL & BRENNAN, L.L.P. (AV)

999 Peachtree Street, N.E., 30309-3996
Telephone: 404-853-8000
Facsimile: 404-853-8806
Email: postmaster@sablaw.com
Washington, D.C. Office: 1275 Pennsylvania Avenue, N.W., 20004-2404.
Telephone: 202-383-0100.
New York, N.Y. Office: 600 Madison Avenue, 11th Floor, 10022-1615.
Telephone: 212-605-6400.
Austin, Texas Office: 111 Congress Avenue, 23rd Floor, 78701-4079.
Telephone: 512-469-3350.

Alfred G. Adams, Jr.	James Bruce Jordan
Thomas M. Byrne	Richard G. Murphy, Jr.
H. Edward Hales, Jr.	James R. Paulk, Jr.
	Haynes R. Roberts

For Complete List of Firm Personnel, See General Section

For full biographical listings, see the Martindale-Hubbell Law Directory

WILSON, BROCK & IRBY, L.L.C. (AV)

999 Peachtree Street, N.E., Suite 2000, 30309
Telephone: 404-853-5050
Fax: 404-853-1812

MEMBERS OF FIRM

Richard W. Wilson, Jr.	Lethco H. Brock, Jr.
Frank L. Wilson, III	John H. Irby

ASSOCIATES

Jerry D. Gerald	James Stuart Teague, Jr.
	Paul Schillawski

(See Next Column)

OF COUNSEL
L. Robert Lovett

For full biographical listings, see the Martindale-Hubbell Law Directory

WILSON, STRICKLAND & BENSON, P.C. (AV)

1100 One Midtown Plaza, 1360 Peachtree Street, N.E., 30309
Telephone: 404-870-1800
Telecopier: 404-870-1808

L. Lou Allen
OF COUNSEL
John C. Pennington

For Complete List of Firm Personnel, See General Section

For full biographical listings, see the Martindale-Hubbell Law Directory

AUGUSTA,* Richmond Co.

J. BENJAMIN KAY, III (AV)

808 First Union Bank Building, 30901
Telephone: 706-722-2008

Approved Attorney for: Lawyers Title Insurance Corp.
Reference: First Union National Bank of Georgia.
Representative Clients: American National Bank & Trust Company; Biotech Park, Inc.; Caterpillar Financial Services, Inc.; Davis-McGraw, Inc.; Ford Leasing Development Company; Ford Motor Credit Company; Gary Concrete Products, Inc.; Globe Life Insurance Company.

For full biographical listings, see the Martindale-Hubbell Law Directory

SURRETT & COLEMAN, P.A. (AV)

901 Suntrust Bank Building, P.O. Box 1497, 30903
Telephone: 706-722-3301
Telecopier: 706-722-3318

Carl J. Surrett	Edward J. Coleman, III

Representative Clients: Sears, Roebuck & Co.; American Home Assurance Co.; Great Southwest Fire Insurance Co.; Duke Buick, Inc.; American Southern Insurance Co.; Scottsdale Insurance Co.; Providence Washington Insurance Co.; Nautilus Insurance Co.

For full biographical listings, see the Martindale-Hubbell Law Directory

BRUNSWICK,* Glynn Co.

KILLIAN AND BOYD (AV)

506 Monk Street, P.O. Box 1795, 31521
Telephone: 912-265-5063; 1-800-339-5063 (S.E. Georgia only)
Fax: 912-265-1209

MEMBERS OF FIRM

Robert P. Killian	Roy J. Boyd, Jr.

ASSOCIATE
Nathan P. Carter

For full biographical listings, see the Martindale-Hubbell Law Directory

MACON,* Bibb Co.

SELL & MELTON (AV)

A Partnership including a Professional Corporation
14th Floor, Charter Medical Building, P.O. Box 229, 31297-2899
Telephone: 912-746-8521
Telecopier: 912-745-6426

Edward S. Sell, III	Brian J. Passante

General Counsel for: Macon Telegraph Publishing Co. (The Macon Telegraph); Macon-Bibb County Hospital Authority; County of Bibb; County of Twiggs; Smith & Sons Foods, Inc. (S & S Cafeterias); Macon Bibb County Industrial Authority; Burgess Pigment Co.

For Complete List of Firm Personnel, See General Section

For full biographical listings, see the Martindale-Hubbell Law Directory

NEWNAN,* Coweta Co.

GLOVER & DAVIS, P.A. (AV)

10 Brown Street, P.O. Box 1038, 30264
Telephone: 770-253-4330
Fax: 770-251-7152
Peachtree City, Georgia Office: Suite 130, 200 Westpark Drive.
Telephone: 770-487-5834.
Fax: 770-487-3492.

(See Next Column)

GLOVER & DAVIS P.A.—*Continued*

J. Littleton Glover	W. Robert Hancock, Jr.
Welborn B. Davis, Jr.	(Resident, Peachtree Office)
(1922-1974)	Asa M. Powell, Jr.
J. Littleton Glover, Jr.	Jerry Ann Conner
Alan W. Jackson	Mark E. Dacy (Resident,
Randy E. Connell	Peachtree City Office)

Representative Clients: Newnan Savings Bank; Pike Transfer Co.; Batson-Cook Company, General Corporate and Construction Divisions; Coweta County, Georgia; Heard County, Georgia; Putnam-Greene Financial Corporation.

Local Counsel for: International Latex Corp.; First Union National Bank of Georgia; Wear Georgia; Farm Credit, ACA.

For full biographical listings, see the Martindale-Hubbell Law Directory

---

NORCROSS, Gwinnett Co.

WALLACE & DE MAYO, P.C. (AV)

6356 Corley Road, 30071-1704
Telephone: 707-446-9996
Fax: 707-368-8331

Richard T. De Mayo	Douglas W. Wallace

Paul J. Gallo

For full biographical listings, see the Martindale-Hubbell Law Directory

---

*SAVANNAH,** Chatham Co.

INGLESBY, FALLIGANT, HORNE, COURINGTON & NASH, A PROFESSIONAL CORPORATION (AV)

17 West McDonough Street, P.O. Box 1368, 31402-1368
Telephone: 912-232-7000
Telecopier: 912-232-7300

Kathleen Horne	Dolly Chisholm

Representative Clients: Ford Motor Credit Co.; NationsBank of Georgia, N.A.; Chemical Financial Management Corp.; Resolution Trust Corp.; Federal Home Loan Mortgage Corp.

For Complete List of Firm Personnel, See General Section

For full biographical listings, see the Martindale-Hubbell Law Directory

---

McCALLAR AND ASSOCIATES (AV)

115 Oglethorpe Avenue West, P.O. Box 9026, 31412
Telephone: 912-234-1215
Telecopier: 912-236-7549

C. James McCallar, Jr.

Mark Bulovic	Todd E. Schwartz

For full biographical listings, see the Martindale-Hubbell Law Directory

---

HAWAII

*HONOLULU,** Honolulu Co.

THE LAW OFFICES OF JOHN A. CHANIN (AV)

The Executive Centre, 1088 Bishop Street, Suite 511, 96813
Telephone: 808-538-1637
Fax: 808-531-5055

For full biographical listings, see the Martindale-Hubbell Law Directory

---

DWYER IMANAKA SCHRAFF KUDO MEYER & FUJIMOTO ATTORNEYS AT LAW, A LAW CORPORATION (AV)

1800 Pioneer Plaza, 900 Fort Street Mall, 96813
Telephone: 808-524-8000
Telecopier: 808-526-1419
Mailing Address: P.O. Box 2727, 96803
Email: hawaiilaw@dwyer-imanaka.com *URL:*
http://www.dwyer-imanaka.com

John R. Dwyer, Jr.	William G. Meyer, III
Mitchell A. Imanaka	Wesley M. Fujimoto
Paul A. Schraff	Ronald Van Grant
Benjamin A. Kudo (Atty. at	Jon M. H. Pang
Law, A Law Corp.)	Blake W. Bushnell
	Adelbert Green

(See Next Column)

Richard T. Asato, Jr.	Jeffery S. Werbelow
Scott W. Settle	Lori Ann K. Koseki
Darcie S. Yoshinaga	Troy T. Fukuhara
Lawrence I. Kawasaki	Katy Y. Chen
Stacy E. Uehara	Naomi S. Uyeno
Kris N. Nakagawa	Roger B. McKeague

OF COUNSEL

Randall Y. Iwase	R. Brian Tsujimura

For full biographical listings, see the Martindale-Hubbell Law Directory

---

LYNCH & FARMER (AV)

Suite 2500, Mauka Tower Grosvenor Center, 737 Bishop Street, 96813
Telephone: 808-528-0100
Facsimile: 808-528-4997

David C. Farmer	Paul A. Lynch

ASSOCIATE

Timothy J. Hogan

LEGAL SUPPORT PERSONNEL

Doreen C. Watanabe

For full biographical listings, see the Martindale-Hubbell Law Directory

---

IDAHO

*BOISE,** Ada Co.

ELAM & BURKE, A PROFESSIONAL ASSOCIATION (AV)

Key Financial Center, 702 West Idaho Street, P.O. Box 1539, 83701
Telephone: 208-343-5454
Telecopier: 208-384-5844
Email: eblaw@elamburke.com

Randall A. Peterman	Jeffery J. Ventrella

Representative Clients: West One Bank; U.S. Bancorp; Gulf USA Corporation; Pintlaw Corporation; Morrison-Knudsen.

For Complete List of Firm Personnel, See General Section

For full biographical listings, see the Martindale-Hubbell Law Directory

---

ILLINOIS

*CHICAGO,** Cook Co.

ADELMAN, GETTLEMAN, MERENS, BERISH & CARTER, LTD. (AV)

Suite 1050, 53 West Jackson Boulevard, 60604
Telephone: 312-435-1050
Fax: 312-435-1059

Howard L. Adelman	Henry B. Merens
Chad H. Gettleman	Brad A. Berish
	Mark A. Carter

Kimberly L. Krawczyk	Kimberly J. Robinson
	Michelle G. Novick

OF COUNSEL

Harry Adelman

For full biographical listings, see the Martindale-Hubbell Law Directory

---

FAGEL & HABER (AV)

140 South Dearborn Street 14th Floor, 60603
Telephone: 312-346-7500
FAX: 312-580-2201
Telex No: 754542
Cable: "NOFLAWLAW"
URL: HTTP://WWW.FANDH.COM.

MEMBERS OF FIRM

Floyd Babbitt	Dennis E. Quaid

ASSOCIATES

John S. Delnero	Victor A. Des Laurier

For full biographical listings, see the Martindale-Hubbell Law Directory

---

HOLLIS AND JOHNSON (AV)

One Quincy Court, Suite 1204, 60604
Telephone: 312-427-0700
Fax: 312-427-8407

(See Next Column)

HOLLIS AND JOHNSON, *Chicago—Continued*

Pamela S. Hollis   Donald E. Johnson

ASSOCIATES

Kimberly Centella Roach   Michael J. Barron, Jr.

For full biographical listings, see the Martindale-Hubbell Law Directory

MOUNT VERNON,* Jefferson Co.

LAW OFFICE OF TERRY SHARP, P.C. (AV)

1115 Harrison Street, P.O. Box 906, 62864
Telephone: 618-242-0246
Fax: 618-242-1170
Benton, Illinois Office: 105 North Main Street.
Telephone: 618-435-5109.
FAX: 618-242-1170.

Terrell Lee Sharp

Brian Thomas McGovern

For full biographical listings, see the Martindale-Hubbell Law Directory

VERNON HILLS, Lake Co.

RICHARDS, RALPH & SCHWAB, CHTD. (AV)

Suite 345, One Hawthorn Place, 175 East Hawthorn Parkway, 60061
Telephone: 708-367-9699
FAX: 708-367-9621

Michael L. Ralph   Alan E. Richards
David J. Schwab

For full biographical listings, see the Martindale-Hubbell Law Directory

INDIANA

ELKHART, Elkhart Co.

CHESTER, PFAFF & BROTHERSON (AV)

317 West Franklin Street, P.O. Box 507, 46515-0507
Telephone: 219-294-5421
Fax: 219-522-1476

MEMBERS OF FIRM

Robert A. Pfaff   Glenn E. Killoren

For Complete List of Firm Personnel, See General Section

For full biographical listings, see the Martindale-Hubbell Law Directory

EVANSVILLE,* Vanderburgh Co.

BAMBERGER, FOREMAN, OSWALD AND HAHN (AV)

7th Floor Hulman Building, P.O. Box 657, 47704-0657
Telephone: 812-425-1591
Fax: 812-421-4936

OF COUNSEL

William P. Foreman

MEMBER OF FIRM

Terry G. Farmer

ASSOCIATES

Marjorie A. Meeks   Lori A. Yarbor

Representative Clients: Citizens Bank of Central Indiana; Citizens Bank of Henderson County; CNB Bancshares, Inc.; CNB Bank of Kentucky; Dubois County Bank; Jasper State Bank; Peoples Bank & Trust Co.; Southern Indiana Gas and Electric Co.; The Citizens National Bank of Evansville; Valley Bank.

For Complete List of Firm Personnel, See General Section

For full biographical listings, see the Martindale-Hubbell Law Directory

BOWERS, HARRISON, KENT & MILLER, LLP (AV)

25 N.W. Riverside Drive, P.O. Box 1287, 47706-1287
Telephone: 812-426-1231
Fax: 812-464-3676

MEMBERS OF FIRM

Joseph H. Harrison   Gary R. Case
Paul E. Black   Paul J. Wallace

Representative Clients: Vantage Healthcare Corporation; International Steel Company; Mellon Bank N.A.; Champion Homes, Inc.

For Complete List of Firm Personnel, See General Section

For full biographical listings, see the Martindale-Hubbell Law Directory

FINE & HATFIELD (AV)

520 N.W. Second Street, P.O. Box 779, 47705-0779
Telephone: 812-425-3592
Telecopier: 812-421-4269
Email: Fine@Fine-Hatfield.com *URL:* http://www.Fine-Hatfield.com

MEMBERS OF FIRM

James E. Marchand   Thomas H. Bryan
Danny E. Glass

A List of Representative Clients Furnished Upon Request.

For full biographical listings, see the Martindale-Hubbell Law Directory

ZIEMER, STAYMAN, WEITZEL & SHOULDERS (AV)

(Formerly Early, Arnold & Ziemer)
One Riverfront Place, 20 N.W. First Street 9th Floor, P.O. Box 916, 47706-0916
Telephone: 812-424-7575
Telecopier: 812-421-5089

MEMBERS OF FIRM

Robert F. Stayman   Marco L. DeLucio
Gregory G. Meyer

Reference: Old National Bank in Evansville.

For full biographical listings, see the Martindale-Hubbell Law Directory

FORT WAYNE,* Allen Co.

BARRETT & McNAGNY (AV)

215 East Berry Street, P.O. Box 2263, 46801-2263
Telephone: 219-423-9551
Telecopier: 219-423-8924

MEMBERS OF FIRM

Thomas P. Yoder   Stephen L. Chapman
Michael P. O'Hara

ASSOCIATE

Anne E. Simerman

Counsel for: Fort Wayne National Bank; N.B.D. Bank, N.A.; Union Federal Savings Bank of Indianapolis; Waterfield Mortgage Company, Incorporated.

For Complete List of Firm Personnel, See General Section

For full biographical listings, see the Martindale-Hubbell Law Directory

BECKMAN, LAWSON, SANDLER, SNYDER & FEDEROFF (AV)

800 Standard Federal Plaza, 46802
Telephone: 219-422-0800
Facsimile: 219-420-1013
Syracuse, Indiana Office: 200 West Main Street.
Telephone: 219-457-5727.
Facsimile: 219-457-2056.

MEMBERS OF FIRM

Jack W. Lawson   William L. Sweet, Jr.
Frank J. Gray   John H. Brandt
Howard B. Sandler   Jeffrey L. Gage
Stephen R. Snyder   Thomas J. Goeglein
James A. Federoff   Jon A. Bragalone
Brian J. T'Kindt

ASSOCIATES

Douglas R. Adelsperger   David D. Cornwell
Travis S. Friend   Craig R. Patterson
Jack C. Birch   Edward J. Ormsby
Robert L. Nicholson   Daniel B. Starr
W. Randall Kammeyer   Laurie A. Singh

OF COUNSEL

Frederick A. Beckman   Neil F. Sandler
Douglas E. Miller

Reference: NBD, N.A.

For full biographical listings, see the Martindale-Hubbell Law Directory

SHIPLEY & ASSOCIATES (AV)

130 West Main Street, Suite 25, 46802
Telephone: 219-424-2505
Fax: 219-424-2960

Grant F. Shipley

For full biographical listings, see the Martindale-Hubbell Law Directory

GREENFIELD,* Hancock Co.

BRAND & ALLEN (AV)

Five Courthouse Plaza, P.O. Box 455, 46140
Telephone: 317-462-3455
Fax: 317-467-6109

Waldo C. Ging (1892-1971)   James L. Brand (1938-1996)

(See Next Column)

BRAND & ALLEN—*Continued*

MEMBERS OF FIRM

Eric N. Allen	Dawn E. Wellman
James W. McNew	

ASSOCIATES

Gregory A. Brand	Nicole A. Zelin
Mary G. Willis	Jeffrey W. Eakins

For full biographical listings, see the Martindale-Hubbell Law Directory

---

INDIANAPOLIS,* Marion Co.

ANCEL & DUNLAP (AV)

Suite 1770 Market Square Center, 46204-2503
Telephone: 317-634-9052
Fax: 317-263-3871

MEMBERS OF FIRM

Steven H. Ancel	Timothy L. Black
David L. Dunlap	Paul T. Deignan
Sorelle J. Ancel	Mark C. Bainbridge
F. Jonathan Zusy	Paula F. Cardoza

Reference: National Bank of Indianapolis.

For full biographical listings, see the Martindale-Hubbell Law Directory

---

BAKER & DANIELS (AV)

300 North Meridian Street, 46204
Telephone: 317-237-0300
FAX: 317-237-1000
Fort Wayne, Indiana Office: 111 East Wayne Street, Suite 800.
Telephone: 219-424-8000.
South Bend, Indiana Office: First Bank Building, 205 West Jefferson Boulevard.
Telephone: 219-234-4149.
Elkhart, Indiana Office: 301 B South Main Street, Suite 307,
Telephone: 219-296-6000.
Washington, D.C. Office: 1701 K Street, N.W., Suite 400.
Telephone: 202-785-1565.

MEMBERS OF FIRM

Stephen A. Claffey	Rebecca A. Richardson
James M. Carr	Jay Jaffe
Robert S. Wynne	

ASSOCIATES

Wendy Wright Ponader	Gregory J. Seketa
Stephen L. Foutty	

Representative Clients: Anthem Insurance Companies, Inc.; AT&T Corp.; Bank One, Indianapolis, N.A.; Borg-Warner Corp.; City of Indianapolis; Cummins Engine Co.; Eli Lilly and Co.; General Motors Corp.; Indianapolis Public Schools; United Airlines.

For Complete List of Firm Personnel, See General Section

For full biographical listings, see the Martindale-Hubbell Law Directory

---

BAMBERGER & FEIBLEMAN (AV)

54 Monument Circle Suite 600, 46204-2947
Telephone: 317-639-5151
FAX: 317-269-2030

MEMBERS OF FIRM

A. Thomas Cobb	Edward B. Hopper, II

Representative Clients: C.I.T. Corp.; FFI Corporation; Kipp Brothers, Inc.; BancPlus Mortgage Corp.; Hiway Parts, Inc.; NBD, Indiana; Tube Processing Corp.; Indiana Mortgage Corp.

For full biographical listings, see the Martindale-Hubbell Law Directory

---

BOSE MCKINNEY & EVANS (AV)

2700 First Indiana Plaza, 135 North Pennsylvania Street, 46204
Telephone: 317-684-5000
Facsimile: 317-684-5173
Indianapolis North Office: Suite 1201, 8888 Keystone Crossing, 46240.
Telephone: 317-574-3700.
Facsimile: 317-574-3716.

MEMBERS OF FIRM

Wayne C. Ponader	V. Samuel Laurin III
Michael A. Trentadue	James E. Carlberg

ASSOCIATE

Alan S. Townsend

Representative Clients: Aetna Life Insurance Co.; First Indiana Bank; Indiana League of Savings Institutions, Inc.; Prudential Life Insurance Co.; Metropolitan Insurance Co.; NBD Bank, N.A.; Farm Credit Services; Fannie Mae; Connecticut General Life Insurance Co.

For Complete List of Firm Personnel, See General Section

For full biographical listings, see the Martindale-Hubbell Law Directory

---

BUSCHMANN, CARR & SHANKS, PROFESSIONAL CORPORATION (AV)

1020 Market Tower, 10 West Market Street, 46204-2963
Telephone: 317-636-5511
Fax: 317-636-3661
Email: bcs@indy.net *URL:* http://www.buschmann.com/bcs/

John R. Carr, Jr.	Bret S. Clement
John R. Carr, III	Gary L. Dilk
Lisa T. Hamilton	

Representative Clients: Archer-Daniels Midland Co.; Ball Corp.; Industrial Valley Title Insurance; Creative Risk Management, Inc.; Deflecto Corporation; Glenfed Mortgage Corp.; Gates McDonald; Merchants National Bank & Trust Company of Muncie; Monumental Life Insurance Co.; National Council on Compensation Insurance.

For full biographical listings, see the Martindale-Hubbell Law Directory

---

DANN PECAR NEWMAN & KLEIMAN, PROFESSIONAL CORPORATION (AV)

Suite 2300, One American Square Box 82008, 46282
Telephone: 317-632-3232; Indiana: 800-622-4799
Telecopy: 317-632-2962

Theodore R. Dann (1907-1993)	Walter E. Wolf, Jr.
Joel Yonover (1932-1995)	Barry E. Beldin
Philip D. Pecar	Robert D. Swhier, Jr.
Norman R. Newman	James P. Moloy
David H. Kleiman	Robert J. Schuckit
Jon B. Abels	Andrew A. Kleiman
Melvin R. Daniel	Michael J. Gabovitch
Lawrence F. Dorocke	Steven M. Pecar
Jeffrey A. Abrams	Benjamin A. Pecar
James H. Schwarz	Richard O. Kissel, II
Robert A. Rose	Joseph D. Calderon

OF COUNSEL

Linda E. Cantor	Anthony J. Rose

Ellen C. Siakotos	Angela L. Mansfield
Stacy L. Hill	Martha M. K. Baird
Karin L. Veatch	

Attorneys for: Indianapolis Machinery Co., Inc.; Melvin Simon & Associates, Inc.; Pacers Basketball Corp.; Universal Fire & Casualty Co., Inc.; Bank One, Indianapolis, NA; INB National Bank; Nachi Technology, Inc.; Pharmaceutical Corporation of America; Logo 7, Inc.

For full biographical listings, see the Martindale-Hubbell Law Directory

---

FEIWELL & HANNOY, PROFESSIONAL CORPORATION (AV)

251 North Illinois Street, Suite 1700, P.O. Box 44141, 46244-0141
Telephone: 317-237-2727
Facsimile: 317-237-2722

Murray J. Feiwell	Douglas J. Hannoy

John P. Sieger	Michael J. Feiwell

Representative Clients: Fifth Third Bank; Temple Inland Mortgage Corp.; United Companies Lending Corp.; Ford Consumer Finance Company, Inc.; GMAC Mortgage Corp.; Associates Financial Services; First National Bank; NationsBanc Mortgage Corp.; Norwest Mortgage, Inc.

For full biographical listings, see the Martindale-Hubbell Law Directory

---

HOPPER & GALLIHER, P.C. (AV)

Bank One Center/Circle, 111 Monument Circle, Suite 452, 46204-5170
Telephone: 317-635-5005
Facsimile: 317-634-2501

George W. Hopper	Jeffrey E. Ramsey
Mark R. Galliher	David G. Pardo

Representative Clients: Bank One, Indianapolis, N.A.; National City Bank, Indiana; Mutual Guaranty Corporation; I.T.T. Financial Services, Commercial Division; ABC Supply Co., Inc.; Sholodge, Inc.

For full biographical listings, see the Martindale-Hubbell Law Directory

---

HOSTETLER & KOWALIK, P.C. (AV)

101 West Ohio Street Suite 2100, 46204
Telephone: 317-262-1001
Fax: 317-262-1010

Gary Lynn Hostetler	David R. Krebs
James S. Kowalik	J. Bradley Schooley

For full biographical listings, see the Martindale-Hubbell Law Directory

Indianapolis—Continued

ICE MILLER DONADIO & RYAN (AV)

One American Square Box 82001, 46282-0002
Telephone: 317-236-2100
Fax: 317-236-2219
Email: leel@imdr.com *URL:* http://www.imdr.com
South Bend, Indiana Office: 211 West Washington Street, Suite 2420.
Telephone: 219-234-7933.
Fax: 219-234-7965. Internet E-mail: leel@imdr.com. Web Site Address:
http://www.imdr.com.

MEMBERS OF FIRM

John R. Thornburgh   Richard J. Thrapp
          Henry A. Efroymson

OF COUNSEL

Peggy J. Naile

ASSOCIATES

Dominic F. Polizzotto   John M. Hakes
Michael E. Schrader   Ponce D. Tidwell, Jr.

Representative Clients: NBD Bank (Trust); National City Bank (Trust); Bank One, Indianapolis (Trust); Union County National Bank; Rockwell International; Eastman Kodak Co.; Perry Manufacturing Co.; Hewlett Packard Corp.; Phoenix Home Life Insurance; Providian Capital Services, Inc.

For Complete List of Firm Personnel, See General Section

For full biographical listings, see the Martindale-Hubbell Law Directory

JOHNSON, SMITH, PENCE, DENSBORN, WRIGHT & HEATH (AV)

One Indiana Square Suite 1800, 46204
Telephone: 317-634-9777
Telecopier: 317-636-9061

MEMBER OF FIRM

Thomas N. Eckerle

ASSOCIATES

Patricia L. Marshall   Bradley C. Morris

For Complete List of Firm Personnel, See General Section

For full biographical listings, see the Martindale-Hubbell Law Directory

SOMMER & BARNARD, ATTORNEYS AT LAW, PC (AV)

4000 Bank One Tower, 111 Monument Circle, 46204-5140
Telephone: 317-630-4000
FAX: 317-236-9802
North Office: 8900 Keystone Crossing, Suite 1046, Indianapolis, Indiana, 46240-2134.
Telephone: 317-630-4000.
FAX: 317-844-4780.

Jerald I. Ancel   Marlene Reich
          Richard C. Richmond, III

Secured Creditor Representation: Bank One Bloomington, N.A.; Comerica Bank; Northwestern National Life Insurance Co.; PNC Realty Holding Corp;

Debtor Representation: Early-Daniel Company; Early-Daniel Industries; Indiana Grocery Company; Integrated Plastic Technology, Inc; Preston Safeway Foods.

For Complete List of Firm Personnel, See General Section

For full biographical listings, see the Martindale-Hubbell Law Directory

CHARLES V. TRAYLOR (AV)

1715 Market Square Center, 151 North Delaware Street, 46204
Telephone: 317-630-9404
Fax: 317-630-9417

For full biographical listings, see the Martindale-Hubbell Law Directory

YARLING, ROBINSON, HAMMEL & LAMB (AV)

151 North Delaware, Suite 1535, P.O. Box 44128, 46204
Telephone: 317-262-8800
Fax: 317-262-3046

MEMBERS OF FIRM

Richard W. Yarling   Edgar H. Lamb
Charles F. Robinson, Jr.   Douglas E. Rogers
John W. Hammel   Mark S. Gray
Linda Y. Hammel   Matthew C. Robinson

Representative Clients: Allstate Insurance Co.; American Family Mutual Insurance Company; Chrysler Credit Corporation; Fleet Financenter; General Motors Acceptance Corporation; Household Finance Corporation; Monroe Guaranty Insurance Company; Northbrook Property & Casualty Company; Pafco General Insurance Company; Security Pacific Finance Corporation.

For full biographical listings, see the Martindale-Hubbell Law Directory

LAFAYETTE,* Tippecanoe Co.

STUART & BRANIGIN (AV)

The Life Building, 300 Main Street, Suite 800, 47902
Telephone: 317-423-1561
Telecopier: 317-742-8175

MEMBERS OF FIRM

Allison Ellsworth Stuart   Stephen R. Pennell
  (1886-1950)   Anthony S. Benton
Roger D. Branigin (1902-1975) Erik D. Spykman
Russell H. Hart   William E. Emerick
Roger D. Branigin, Jr.   John C. Duffey
Thomas L. Ryan   Mark E. DeYoung
James V. McGlone   Thomas B. Parent
Carl W. Kloepfer   Laura L. Bowker
Thomas R. McCully   Kevin D. Nicoson
Larry R. Fisher   Susan K. Roberts
Nina B. Kirkpatrick   John M. Stuckey
Mark Lillianfeld   Deborah B. Trice

COUNSEL

John F. Bodle

ASSOCIATES

Brent W. Huber   David A. Starkweather
William P. Kealey   Geoffrey Blazi
          A. James Chareq

General Counsel for: The Lafayette Life Insurance Co.; INB National Bank, N.W.; Lafayette Home Hospital, Inc.
State Counsel for: Norfolk & Western Railway Co.
Mr. Ryan is Counsel to: The Trustees of Purdue University.
Representative Clients: Aluminum Company of America; Liberty Mutual Insurance Group.

For full biographical listings, see the Martindale-Hubbell Law Directory

MERRILLVILLE, Lake Co.

BURKE, MURPHY, COSTANZA & CUPPY (AV)

Suite 600 8585 Broadway, 46410-7064
Telephone: 219-769-1313
Telecopier: 219-769-6806
East Chicago, Indiana Office: First National Bank Building. 720 West Chicago Avenue.
Telephone: 219-397-2401.
Telecopier: 219-397-0508.
Valparaiso, Indiana Office: 15 North Franklin Street, Suite 200.
Telephone: 219-531-0134.
Telecopier: 219-531-0507.
Palm Harbor, Florida Office: Suite 280, 33920 U.S. Highway 19 North.
Telephone: 813-787-7799.
Telecopier: 813-787-7237.

MEMBERS OF FIRM

Andrew J. Kopko   Lambert C. Genetos
          David K. Ranich

ASSOCIATES

Stacia L. Yoon   Kevin E. Steele

Representative Clients: Federal National Mortgage Association; Waterfield Mortgage Co.; NBD Bank, N.A.; Centier Bank; Pinnacle Bank.

For Complete List of Firm Personnel, See General Section

For full biographical listings, see the Martindale-Hubbell Law Directory

SOUTH BEND,* St. Joseph Co.

JONES, OBENCHAIN, FORD, PANKOW, LEWIS & WOODS (AV)

1800 Valley American Bank Building, P.O. Box 4577, 46634
Telephone: 219-233-1194
Fax: 233-8957; 233-9675

Vitus G. Jones (1879-1951)   Roland Obenchain (Retired)
Roland Obenchain (1890-1961)   Milton A. Johnson (Retired)
Francis Jones (1907-1988)   James H. Pankow (Retired)

MEMBERS OF FIRM

Thomas F. Lewis, Jr.   Robert M. Edwards, Jr.
Timothy W. Woods   John B. Ford
John R. Obenchain   Mark J. Phillipoff
Robert W. Mysliwiec   John W. Van Laere

ASSOCIATES

Edward P. Benchik   Robert S. Sanderson
          Thomas F. Lewis, III

OF COUNSEL

G. Burt Ford

Representative Clients: South Bend Lathe, Inc.; Mallard Coach Co., Inc.; Uniroyal, Inc.; State Exchange Finance Co.; Commodore Corp.

For full biographical listings, see the Martindale-Hubbell Law Directory

TERRE HAUTE,* Vigo Co.

WILKINSON, GOELLER, MODESITT, WILKINSON & DRUMMY (AV)

333 Ohio Street, P.O. Box 800, 47808-0800
Telephone: 812-232-4311
Fax: 812-235-5107

MEMBERS OF FIRM

Kelvin L. Roots   William M. Olah

ASSOCIATE

Anthony R. Jost

Representative Corporate Clients: Merchants National Bank; American General Finance; Transamerica Financial Services; Farm Credit Services of Mid-America, ACA.

For Complete List of Firm Personnel, See General Section

For full biographical listings, see the Martindale-Hubbell Law Directory

IOWA

COUNCIL BLUFFS,* Pottawattamie Co.

REILLY, PETERSEN & HANNAN, P.L.C. (AV)

215 South Main Street, P.O. Box 1016, 51502-1016
Telephone: 712-328-1575
Fax: 712-328-1562

C. R. Hannan   Michael G. Reilly
Deborah L. Petersen

References: FirsTier; Firstar Bank of Council Bluffs.

For full biographical listings, see the Martindale-Hubbell Law Directory

SIOUX CITY,* Woodbury Co.

GILES AND GILES (AV)

322 Frances Building, 505 Fifth Street, 51101
Telephone: 712-252-4458
FAX: 712-252-3400
Crofton, Nebraska Office: P. O. Box 88.
Telephone: 402-388-4215.

MEMBER OF FIRM

W. Jefferson Giles, III

Representative Clients: Security National Bank, Firstar Bank, Boatmen's Bank, all in Sioux City, Iowa; Live Stock State Bank, Yankton, SD.

For Complete List of Firm Personnel, See General Section

For full biographical listings, see the Martindale-Hubbell Law Directory

KANSAS

LENEXA, Johnson Co.

EVANS & MULLINIX, P.A. (AV)

15301 W. 87th Street, Suite 220, 66219
Telephone: 913-541-1200
Facsimile: 913-541-1010
Kansas City, Kansas Office: 1314 North 38th Street, 66102.
Telephone: 913-621-1200.
Telecopier: 913-621-1263.

Timothy J. Evans   Joanne B. Stutz
Thomas M. Mullinix, III   John E. Larson
Richard C. Wallace   Kristen F. Heidenreich

OF COUNSEL

Vito C. Barbieri

For full biographical listings, see the Martindale-Hubbell Law Directory

TOPEKA,* Shawnee Co.

WRIGHT, HENSON, SOMERS, SEBELIUS, CLARK & BAKER, LLP (AV)

Commerce Bank Building, 100 Southeast Ninth Street, 2nd Floor, P.O. Box 3555, 66601-3555
Telephone: 913-232-2200
FAX: 913-232-3344

MEMBERS OF FIRM

Dale L. Somers   Bruce J. Clark
Anne Lamborn Baker

(See Next Column)

ASSOCIATE

Theron L. Sims

For Complete List of Firm Personnel, See General Section

For full biographical listings, see the Martindale-Hubbell Law Directory

WICHITA,* Sedgwick Co.

FOULSTON & SIEFKIN L.L.P. (AV)

700 Fourth Financial Center, 67202
Telephone: 316-267-6371
Facsimile: 316-267-6345
Topeka, Kansas Office: 1515 Bank IV Tower, 534 Kansas Avenue, 66603.
Telephone: 913-233-3600.
Fax: 913-233-1610.
Dodge City, Kansas Office: 810 Frontview, P.O. Box 1147, 67801.
Telephone: 316-227-8126.
Fax: 316-227-8451.
Member: Lex Mundi, A Global Association of 126 Independent Firms.

MEMBERS OF FIRM

Terry C. Cupps   William R. Wood, II

For Complete List of Firm Personnel, See General Section

For full biographical listings, see the Martindale-Hubbell Law Directory

MORRIS, LAING, EVANS, BROCK & KENNEDY, CHARTERED (AV)

Fourth Floor, 200 West Douglas, 67202-3084
Telephone: 316-262-2671
Fax: 316-262-6226; 262-5991
Topeka, Kansas Office: 800 S.W. Jackson, Suite 914, 66612-2214.
Telephone: 913-232-2662.
Fax: 913-232-9983.

David C. Adams   Karl R. Swartz
William B. Sorensen, Jr.   Richard F. Hayse
Robert E. Nugent   (Resident, Topeka Office)

References: The Emprise Banks of Kansas; Mercantile Bank of Topeka; Southwest National Bank; Twin Lakes National Bank.

For Complete List of Firm Personnel, See General Section

For full biographical listings, see the Martindale-Hubbell Law Directory

KENTUCKY

BOWLING GREEN,* Warren Co.

ENGLISH, LUCAS, PRIEST & OWSLEY (AV)

1101 College Street, P.O. Box 770, 42102-0770
Telephone: 502-781-6500
Telecopier: 502-782-7782
Email: inquiry@elpo.com

MEMBER OF FIRM

Keith M. Carwell

ASSOCIATE

Marc Allen Lovell

General Counsel for: Medical Center at Bowling Green; Bowling Green Independent School District; Warren Rural Electric Cooperative Corporation; Trans Financial Bank, N.A.
Representative Clients: Commercial Union Insurance Cos.; Kemper Insurance Group; St. Paul Insurance Co.; Desa International; Kentucky Finance Co.; Sumitomo Electric Wiring Systems, Inc.

For Complete List of Firm Personnel, See General Section

For full biographical listings, see the Martindale-Hubbell Law Directory

HARLIN & PARKER, P.S.C. (AV)

519 East Tenth Street, P.O. Box 390, 42102-0390
Telephone: 502-842-5611
Telefax: 502-842-2607

William Jerry Parker   Jerry A. Burns
Scott Charles Marks

Representative Clients: Jim Walter Corp.; Deere & Co.; Federal Deposit Insurance Corp.; Equitable Life Assurance Society of the United States.

For Complete List of Firm Personnel, See General Section

For full biographical listings, see the Martindale-Hubbell Law Directory

Bowling Green—Continued

HUDDLESTON & REED (AV)

1032 College Street, P.O. Box 2130, 42102-2130
Telephone: 502-781-9870
Fax: 502-842-1659
Cave City, Kentucky: 210 Broadway, P.O. 810, 42127.
Telephone: 502-773-5511.
Fax: 502-773-5510.

MEMBERS OF FIRM

Philip I. Huddleston   Lee Huddleston
          Jeffrey A. Reed

Representative Clients: Dow Corning Corp.; Borg Warner Corp.; HFC Commercial Realty, Inc.; Transamerica Financial Services; South Central Banks; Autotruck Federal Credit Union.

For full biographical listings, see the Martindale-Hubbell Law Directory

---

GLASGOW,* Barren Co.

GARMON & GOODMAN (AV)

139 North Public Square, P.O. Box 663, 42142-0663
Telephone: 502-651-8812
Telecopier: 502-651-8846

MEMBER OF FIRM

Charles A. Goodman III

Representative Clients: The New Farmers National Bank of Glasgow; United Farm Tools, Inc.; Dufour Petroleum, Inc.; Chrysler Credit Corp.
References: Trans Financial Bank, N.A., Glasgow, Ky.; South Central Bank of Barren County, Inc., Glasgow, Ky.; Farm Credit Services of Mid-America, ACA.

For Complete List of Firm Personnel, See General Section

For full biographical listings, see the Martindale-Hubbell Law Directory

---

HENDERSON,* Henderson Co.

KING, DEEP AND BRANAMAN (AV)

127 North Main Street, P.O. Box 43, 42420
Telephone: 502-827-1852
FAX: 502-826-7729

MEMBERS OF FIRM

Leo King (1893-1982)   Harry L. Mathison, Jr.
William M. Deep (1920-1990)   W. Mitchell Deep, Jr.
William Branaman   H. Randall Redding
          Dorin E. Luck

ASSOCIATES

Leslie M. Newman   Greg L. Gager

Counsel for: Ohio Valley National Bank of Henderson; Fireman's Fund; Reynolds Metals Co.; Medical Protective Co.; Allstate Insurance Co.; Able Energy Co.; Western Casualty & Surety Co.; Commercial Casualty Insurance Co.; First Indiana Bank; Farm Credit Services.

For full biographical listings, see the Martindale-Hubbell Law Directory

---

LEXINGTON,* Fayette Co.

BUNCH & BROCK (AV)

271 West Short Street, Suite 805, P.O. Box 2086, 40594
Telephone: 606-254-5522
Fax: 606-233-1434

MEMBERS OF FIRM

W. Thomas Bunch   W. Thomas Bunch II
Dan D. Brock, Jr.   Matthew B. Bunch
Gail M. Bunch   Caryn L. Belobraidich

For full biographical listings, see the Martindale-Hubbell Law Directory

---

FOWLER, MEASLE & BELL, L.L.P. (AV)

Kincaid Towers, 300 West Vine Street, Suite 650, 40507-1660
Telephone: 606-252-6700
Fax: 606-255-3735

MEMBERS OF FIRM

Taft A. McKinstry   Robert S. Ryan
John E. Hinkel, Jr.   Michael W. Troutman

Representative Clients: Bank One, Lexington, N.A.; PNC Bank, Kentucky, Inc.; Citizens Union Bank of Shelbyville; National City Bank & Trust Co.; Fifth Third Bank; Fifth Third Leasing; Union Bank, CA.

For Complete List of Firm Personnel, See General Section

For full biographical listings, see the Martindale-Hubbell Law Directory

---

STOLL, KEENON & PARK, LLP (AV)

201 E. Main Street, Suite 1000, 40507-1380
Telephone: 606-231-3000
Telecopier: 606-253-1093; 606-253-1027
Frankfort, Kentucky Office: 307 Washington Street, 40601.
Telephone: 502-875-6220.
Telecopier: 502-875-6235.
Louisville, Kentucky Office: 400 West Market Street, Suite 2650, 40202-3377.
Telephone: 502-568-9100.
Telecopier: 502-568-5700.

MEMBERS OF FIRM

Joseph M. Scott, Jr.   Robert W. Kellerman
Harvie B. Wilkinson   Gregory D. Pavey
          Lea Pauley Goff

ASSOCIATES

Laura Day DelCotto   William L. Montague, Jr.

Representative Clients: Bank One, Lexington, NA; Bank One, Kentucky, NA; Fifth Third Bank; Whitaker Bank Corporation of Kentucky.

For Complete List of Firm Personnel, See General Section

For full biographical listings, see the Martindale-Hubbell Law Directory

---

LOUISVILLE,* Jefferson Co.

GOLDBERG & SIMPSON, P.S.C. (AV)

3000 National City Tower, 40202
Telephone: 502-589-4440
Telefax: 502-581-1344
Washington, D.C. Office: 1200 G Street, N.W. - Suite 800, 20005.
Telephone: 202-434-8968.
Telefax: 202-737-5822.

Fred M. Goldberg   William J. Hust, III
David B. Ratterman   (Not admitted in KY)
Jonathan D. Goldberg   Mary Alice Maple
James S. Goldberg   Emily L. Lawrence
Mitchell A. Charney   Douglas S. Haynes
Steven A. Goodman   Jan M. West
Edward L. Schoenbaechler Charles H. Cassis
Cathy S. Pike   Robin Sylvester Craddock
Stephen E. Smith   John Joseph McLaughlin
Cynthia Buss Maddox   Leslie E. Huber
          Anthony J Elpers

OF COUNSEL

Ronald V. Simpson   Kenneth G. Lee (Not admitted
David A. Brill   in KY; Resident, Washington,
                           D.C. Office)

Representative Clients: National City Bank; Liberty Mutual Insurance Co.; Jewish Hospital Healthcare Services, Inc.; Louisville & Jefferson County Board of Health; Providian Corp.

For full biographical listings, see the Martindale-Hubbell Law Directory

---

LLOYD & MCDANIEL, PLC (AV)

1700 Meidinger Tower, 462 South Fourth Avenue, 40202-3450
Telephone: 502-585-1880
Fax: 502-585-3054
Email: 76221.3655@compuserve.com
Jeffersonville, Indiana Office: 220 East Court Avenue, P.O. Box 934. 47131.
Telephone: 812-282-4380.

Jeremiah A. Lloyd   James M. Lloyd
          Michael V. Brodarick

Anthony H. Ambrose   James M. McDonough
Jervis C. Mobley   Amy Elam-Krizan

References: Bank One, Kentucky, N.A.; PNC Bank, Kentucky, Inc.; United Mercantile Agencies; National Association of Credit Management (NACM).

For full biographical listings, see the Martindale-Hubbell Law Directory

---

MAPOTHER & MAPOTHER (AV)

801 West Jefferson Street, 40202
Telephone: 502-587-5400
Fax: 502-587-5444
Email: 103210.1130@compuserve.com
Lexington, Kentucky Office: 177 North Upper Street.
Telephone: 606-253-0003.
Fax: 606-255-3961.
Jeffersonville, Indiana Office: 505 East Seventh Street.
Telephone: 812-288-5059.
Fax: 502-587-5444.
Cincinnati, Ohio Office: Kroger Building, Suite 2220, 1014 Vine Street.
Telephone: 513-381-4888.
Fax: 513-381-3117.

(See Next Column)

MAPOTHER & MAPOTHER—*Continued*

Huntington, West Virginia Office: Morris Building, Suite 701, 845 Fourth Avenue.
Telephone: 304-525-1185.
Fax: 304-529-3764.
Evansville, Indiana Office: 329 Main Street.
Telephone: 812-421-9108.
Fax: 812-421-9109.

MEMBERS OF FIRM

Thomas Cruise Mapother, Jr. (1907-1986)	William R. Mapother
	Thomas L. Canary, Jr.
Charles M. Friedman	

Brian P. Conaty (Resident, Huntington, West Virginia Office)	Lee W. Grace
	Roy Fugitt (Resident, Lexington Office)
Andrea Fried Neichter	Susan E. Morton-Smith (Resident, Huntington, West Virginia Office)
Kathryn Pry Coryell (Resident, Jeffersonville, Indiana Office)	
Roberta S. Dunlap (Resident, Evansville, Indiana Office)	Brian E. Chapman (Resident, Cincinnati, Ohio Office)
Dean A. Langdon (Resident, Lexington Office)	T. Lawson McSwain, II
	Lisa A. Herndon

Representative Clients: Ford Motor Credit Co.; General Motors Acceptance Corp.; Associates Commercial Corp.; Bank One; PNC Bank; The CIT Group/Sales Financing; NBD Bank; Fifth Third Bank; Nissan Motor Acceptance Corp.; First Merchants Acceptance Corp.

For full biographical listings, see the Martindale-Hubbell Law Directory

MIDDLETON & REUTLINGER, P.S.C. (AV)

2500 Brown and Williamson Tower, 40202-3410
Telephone: 502-584-1135
Fax: 502-561-0442
New Albany, Indiana Office: 2623 Charlestown Road, 47150.
Telephone: 812-944-7215.

Charles G. Middleton, III	James R. Higgins, Jr.
Thomas W. Frentz	

Margaret E. Thorp

Counsel for: Chevron USA; Logan Aluminum, Inc.; Louisville Gas & Electric Co.; MCI Telecommunications Corp.; Metropolitan Life Insurance Co.; Kosmos Cement Co.; Porcelain Metal Corp.; The Home Insurance Co.; The Kroger Co.; Demars Haka Development, Inc.

For Complete List of Firm Personnel, See General Section

For full biographical listings, see the Martindale-Hubbell Law Directory

MORGAN & POTTINGER, P.S.C. (AV)

601 West Main Street, 40202
Telephone: 502-589-2780
Telecopier: 502-585-3498
Lexington, Kentucky Office: 133 West Short Street.
Telephone: 606-253-1900.
Telecopier: 606-255-2038.
New Albany, Indiana Office: 400 Pearl Street, Suite 100.
Telephone: 812-948-0008.
Telecopier: 812-944-6215.

Patrick E. Morgan	Scott T. Rickman (Resident, Lexington Office)
John T. McGarvey	
John A. Majors	Garret B. Hannegan (Resident, New Albany, Indiana Office)
Mark J. Sandlin	
Hal D. Friedman	

SENIOR COUNSEL

David C. Pottinger

For Complete List of Firm Personnel, See General Section

For full biographical listings, see the Martindale-Hubbell Law Directory

RUBIN HAYS & FOLEY (AV)

First Trust Centre 200 South Fifth Street, 40202
Telephone: 502-569-7550
Telecopier: 502-569-7555

MEMBERS OF FIRM

Wm. Carl Fust	Lisa Koch Bryant
Harry Lee Meyer	Sharon C. Hardy
David W. Gray	Charles S. Musson
Irvin D. Foley	W. Randall Jones
Joseph R. Gathright, Jr.	K. Gail Russell

ASSOCIATES

Christian L. Juckett	Courtney Lynn McCall

(See Next Column)

OF COUNSEL

James E. Fahey	Newman T. Guthrie

Representative Clients: J.C. Bradford & Co., Inc.; J.J.B. Hilliard, W.L. Lyons, Inc.; Huntington National Bank; Liberty National Bank and Trust Company; National City Bank; PNC Bank; Prudential Bache & Co., Inc.; Prudential Securities, Inc.; Society Bank; Stock Yards Bank and Trust Co.

For full biographical listings, see the Martindale-Hubbell Law Directory

SEILLER & HANDMAKER, LLP (AV)

2200 Meidinger Tower, 40202
Telephone: 502-584-7400
Telecopier: 502-583-2100
Paris, Kentucky Office: Seiller, Handmaker & Blevins, P.S.C., 1431 South Main Street.
Telephone: 606-987-3980.
Telecopier: 606-987-3982.
Cynthiana, Kentucky Office: Seiller, Handmaker & Blevins, P.S.C., 9 South Walnut.
Telephone: 606-234-2880.
New Albany, Indiana Office: 202 Pearl Street.
Telephone: 812-948-8307.
Telecopier: 812-948-8383.

Edward F. Seiller (1897-1990)

MEMBERS OF FIRM

Stuart Allen Handmaker	Maury D. Kommor
Bill V. Seiller	Cynthia Compton Stone
David M. Cantor	Glenn A. Cohen
Neil C. Bordy	Tomi Anne Blevins Pulliam (Paris and Cynthiana Offices)
Kyle Anne Citrynell	

ASSOCIATES

Pamela M. Greenwell	Donna F. Townsend
Michael C. Bratcher	Gregory A. Lindsey
John E. Brengle	Vicki L. Buba
Patrick R. Holland, II	Allen C. Platt III (Resident, New Albany, Indiana Office)
Edwin Jon Wolfe	

OF COUNSEL

Robert S. Frey

For full biographical listings, see the Martindale-Hubbell Law Directory

OWENSBORO,* Daviess Co.

BAMBERGER & ABSHIER (AV)

111 West 2nd Street, 42303-4113
Telephone: 502-926-4545
Fax: 502-684-0064

MEMBERS OF FIRM

Ronald J. Bamberger	Phillip G. Abshier

ASSOCIATE

Angela L. Wathen

For full biographical listings, see the Martindale-Hubbell Law Directory

PIKEVILLE,* Pike Co.

PRUITT AND DE BOURBON LAW FIRM (AV)

The Call Building, Second Street, P.O. Box 339, 41502
Telephone: 606-437-7366; 437-7367; 237-1280
Fax: 606-432-2367

MEMBERS OF FIRM

James P. Pruitt, Jr.	P. Michael de Bourbon

Reference: The Citizen's Bank of Pikeville.

For full biographical listings, see the Martindale-Hubbell Law Directory

LOUISIANA

BATON ROUGE,* East Baton Rouge Parish

KIZER, HOOD & MORGAN, L.L.P. (AV)

A Partnership including a Professional Corporation
748 Main Street, 70802-5526
Telephone: 504-387-3121
Fax: 504-387-5611
Email: KHMLLP@AOL.COM

Roland C. Kizer (1899-1988)	Ralph E. Hood
Roland C. Kizer, Jr., (Ltd., A Law Corporation)	J. Donald Morgan
	Walter N. O'Roark, III
Stacy G. Butler	

Representative Clients: Hibernia National Bank; Bank One, Louisiana, N.A.; The Dime Savings Bank of New York, FSB; G.E. Capital Asset Management Corp.; Bankers Systems, Inc.; United Companies Lending Corporation;

(See Next Column)

KIZER, HOOD & MORGAN L.L.P., *Baton Rouge*—Continued

Rabenhorst Life Insurance Co.; General Equipment, Inc. d/b/a Scott General; Old South Builders, Inc.; P.P.R., Inc.

For full biographical listings, see the Martindale-Hubbell Law Directory

SCHANEVILLE & BARINGER, L.L.C. (AV)

918 Government Street Second Floor, 70802
Telephone: 504-383-9953
Fax: 504-387-3198

Dan D. Schaneville　　　　　　Dale R. Baringer
Donald Meltzer

John C. Hopewell, III
OF COUNSEL
David O. Mooney

For full biographical listings, see the Martindale-Hubbell Law Directory

SHOCKEY & ZIOBER, A PROFESSIONAL LAW CORPORATION (AV)

Suite 3-A, 5551 Corporate Boulevard, P.O. Box 80286, 70898-0286
Telephone: 504-929-8929
Telecopier: 504-928-7694

John David Ziober　　　　　　William C. Shockey

Emily Phillips Ziober　　　　　Jennifer R. Treadway Morris
Douglas J. Cochran　　　　　　James E. Moore, Jr.

For full biographical listings, see the Martindale-Hubbell Law Directory

LAFAYETTE,* Lafayette Parish

LISKOW & LEWIS, A PROFESSIONAL LAW CORPORATION (AV)

822 Harding Street, P.O. Box 52008, 70505
Telephone: 318-232-7424
Telecopier: 318-267-2399
New Orleans, Louisiana Office: 50th Floor, One Shell Square.
Telephone: 504-581-7979
Telecopier: 504-592-5108; 504-592-5109.

RESIDENT PERSONNEL
Joseph C. Giglio, Jr.　　　　　Joseph P. Hebert

Representative Clients: Amerada Hess Corp.; Amoco Corporation; Bank One; BP America Inc.; Hibernia National Bank; Hunt Oil Company; Louisiana Public Service Commission; Mobil Oil Corp.; OXY U.S.A. Inc.; Union Oil Company of California; Union Pacific Resources Company.

For Complete List of Firm Personnel, See General Section

For full biographical listings, see the Martindale-Hubbell Law Directory

LAKE CHARLES,* Calcasieu Parish

JONES, TÊTE, NOLEN, HANCHEY, SWIFT, SPEARS & FONTI, L.L.P. (AV)

First Federal Building, P.O. Box 910, 70602
Telephone: 318-439-8315
Telefax: 436-5606; 433-5536

MEMBERS OF FIRM
Sam H. Jones (1897-1978)　　　Kenneth R. Spears
William R. Tête　　　　　　　Edward J. Fonti
William M. Nolen　　　　　　Charles N. Harper
James C. Hanchey　　　　　　Gregory W. Belfour
Carl H. Hanchey　　　　　　　Robert J. Tête
William B. Swift　　　　　　　Yul D. Lorio
OF COUNSEL
John A. Patin　　　　　　　　Edward D. Myrick
ASSOCIATE
Lilynn A. Cutrer

General Counsel for: First Federal Savings & Loan Association of Lake Charles; Beauregard Electric Cooperative, Inc.
Representative Clients: Atlantic Richfield Company; CITGO Petroleum Corp.; Conoco Inc.; MONTELL U.S.A., Inc.; ITT Hartford; Olin Corporation; OXY USA Inc.; Premier Bank, National Association; W.R. Grace & Co.

For full biographical listings, see the Martindale-Hubbell Law Directory

MONROE,* Ouachita Parish

THOMPSON, SPARKS, DEAN & MORRIS (AV)

A Partnership including a Professional Corporation
1401 Royal Street, P.O. Box 2867, 71207
Telephone: 318-388-1440
Fax: 318-322-0887

(See Next Column)

MEMBERS OF FIRM
M. C. Thompson (1885-1970)　　George B. Dean, Jr., (P.C.)
James D. Sparks (1910-1987)　　Wood T. Sparks
John C. Morris, III

Representative Clients: South Central Bell Telephone Co.; Greater Ouachita Water Company; PHH Homequity Corp.; Commonwealth Relocation Services, Inc.; Remax, Monroe; Bell South Advertising & Publishing Corp.; Premier Mortgage Corp.; Countrywide Funding Corp.
Approved Attorneys for: Central Bank; Federal Land Bank.

For full biographical listings, see the Martindale-Hubbell Law Directory

NEW ORLEANS,* Orleans Parish

BRONFIN & HELLER, L.L.C. (AV)

2500 Poydras Center, 650 Poydras Street, 70130-6103
Telephone: 504-568-1888
Fax: 504-522-0949

Isaac S. Heller (1893-1967)
OF COUNSEL
Fred Bronfin

Edward M. Heller　　　　　　Jan Marie Hayden
Sylvan J. Steinberg　　　　　Warren Horn
Bernard H. Berins　　　　　　Robyn Jeana Spalter

Tristan E. Manthey

For full biographical listings, see the Martindale-Hubbell Law Directory

LANDWEHR & HOF (AV)

Suite 1100, Commerce Building, 821 Gravier Street, 70112
Telephone: 504-561-8086

MEMBERS OF FIRM
Merrill T. Landwehr　　　　　Ronald J. Hof
Darryl T. Landwehr

Reference: Bank of Louisiana, New Orleans, La.

For full biographical listings, see the Martindale-Hubbell Law Directory

LISKOW & LEWIS, A PROFESSIONAL LAW CORPORATION (AV)

50th Floor, One Shell Square, 70139
Telephone: 504-581-7979
Telecopier: 504-556-4108; 504-556-4109
Lafayette, Louisiana Office: 822 Harding Street, P.O. Box 52008.
Telephone: 318-232-7424.
Telecopier: 318-267-2399.

Philip K. Jones, Jr.　　　　　Dena L. Olivier

Michael D. Rubenstein
RESIDENT PERSONNEL AT LAFAYETTE OFFICE
Joseph C. Giglio, Jr.　　　　　Joseph P. Hebert

Representative Clients: First National Bank of Commerce; International Nederland Credit Corp.; Mirage Resorts Inc.; Mobil Oil Corp; Northrop Grumman Corp.; Prudential Insurance Co. of America; Texaco, Inc.

For Complete List of Firm Personnel, See General Section

For full biographical listings, see the Martindale-Hubbell Law Directory

SHREVEPORT,* Caddo Parish

MILLS, TIMMONS & FLOWERS, A PROFESSIONAL LAW CORPORATION (AV)

300 Law Center, 331 Milam Street, P.O. Box 1784, 71166-1784
Telephone: 318-222-0337
Fax: 318-222-5400

George H. Mills, Jr.　　　　　David C. Turansky
Wayne Timmons　　　　　　　J. Broocks Greer III
Peter R. Flowers　　　　　　　Sandra Lynn Walker
OF COUNSEL
William T. Allison

Reference: Hibernia National Bank.

For full biographical listings, see the Martindale-Hubbell Law Directory

SIMON, FITZGERALD, COOKE, REED & WELCH (AV)

Suite 200, 4700 Line Avenue, 71106
Telephone: 318-868-2600
Telecopier: 318-868-8966

MEMBERS OF FIRM
Fred Simon (1904-1993)　　　　Paul M. Cooke
Archie M. Simon　　　　　　　Chatham H. Reed
Thomas P. Fitzgerald　　　　　Keith M. Welch
(1914-1993)　　　　　　　　　Kevin R. Molloy

(See Next Column)

SIMON, FITZGERALD, COOKE, REED & WELCH—*Continued*

A list of Representative Clients will be furnished upon request.

For full biographical listings, see the Martindale-Hubbell Law Directory

---

MAINE

---

*AUGUSTA,** Kennebec Co.

* indicates certain Bar Register subscribers whose principal office is located elsewhere in the state and who have arranged for representation as a part of the state capital listings that follow

*** PIERCE ATWOOD** (AV)

77 Winthrop Street, 04330
Telephone: 207-622-6311
Fax: 207-623-9367
Email: info@PierceAtwood.com
Portland, Maine Office: One Monument Square.
Telephone: 207-791-1100.
Fax: 207-791-1350.
Newburyport, Massachusetts Office: 6 Harris Street.
Telephone: 508-465-9599.
Fax: 508-465-9945.

MEMBER OF FIRM
Warren E. Winslow, Jr.

For Complete List of Firm Personnel, See General Section

For full biographical listings, see the Martindale-Hubbell Law Directory

---

*BANGOR,** Penobscot Co.

GROSS, MINSKY, MOGUL & SINGAL, P.A. (AV)

Key Plaza, 23 Water Street, P.O. Box 917, 04402-0917
Telephone: 207-942-4644
Telecopier: 207-942-3699
Email: gmm&s-law@atlsysnet.com *URL:*
http://www.atlsysnet.com/gmms

Edward I. Gross (Retired)	George C. Schelling
Jules L. Mogul (1930-1994)	Edward W. Gould
Norman Minsky	Steven J. Mogul
George Z. Singal	James R. Wholly
Louis H. Kornreich	Daniel A. Pileggi

Philip K. Clarke

Wayne P. Libhart (Retired)	James S. Nixon
Sandra L. Rothera	F. Todd Lowell

Representative Client: Dahl Chase Pathology Associates.
Local Counsel for: The St. Paul Insurance Cos.; Aetna Life & Casualty Co.; Imperial Casualty & Indemnity Co.

For full biographical listings, see the Martindale-Hubbell Law Directory

---

*PORTLAND,** Cumberland Co.

PIERCE ATWOOD (AV)

One Monument Square, 04101
Telephone: 207-791-1100
Fax: 207-791-1350
Email: info@PierceAtwood.com
Augusta, Maine Office: 77 Winthrop Street.
Telephone: 207-622-6311.
Fax: 207-623-9367.
Newburyport, Massachusetts Office: 6 Harris Street.
Telephone: 508-465-9599.
Fax: 508-465-9945.

MEMBER OF FIRM
Jacob A. Manheimer
ASSOCIATES

Richard P. Olson	Keith J. Cunningham
	(Not admitted in ME)

For Complete List of Firm Personnel, See General Section

For full biographical listings, see the Martindale-Hubbell Law Directory

PRETI, FLAHERTY, BELIVEAU & PACHIOS (AV)

A Limited Liability Company
443 Congress Street, P.O. Box 11410, 04104-7410
Telephone: 207-791-3000
Telecopier: 207-791-3111
Email: admin@pfbpnet.com
Augusta, Maine Office: 45 Memorial Circle, P.O. Box 1058, 04332-1058.
Telephone: 207-623-5300.
Telecopier: 207-623-2914.

(See Next Column)

MEMBERS OF FIRM

Harold C. Pachios	Estelle A. Lavoie
Leonard M. Gulino	Michael Kaplan

John P. McVeigh
ASSOCIATE
Scott T. Rodgers

Representative Clients: Key Bank of Maine, Inc.; Peoples Heritage Savings Bank; RECOLL Management, Corp.; Meadowledge Associates; Southern Maine Medical Center; Colonial Supply Corp.; Fleet Bank of Maine.

For Complete List of Firm Personnel, See General Section

For full biographical listings, see the Martindale-Hubbell Law Directory

---

MARYLAND

---

*BALTIMORE,** (Independent City)

BALLARD SPAHR ANDREWS & INGERSOLL (AV)

300 East Lombard Street, 19th Floor, 21202-3268
Telephone: 410-528-5600
Fax: 410-528-5650
Philadelphia, Pennsylvania Office: 1735 Market Street, 51st Floor.
Telephone: 215-665-8500.
Fax: 215-864-8999.
Harrisburg, Pennsylvania Office: 105 North Front Street.
Telephone: 717-236-3333.
Fax: 717-236-3884.
Denver, Colorado Office: Seventeenth Street Plaza Building, Suite 2300, 1225 17th Street.
Telephone: 303-292-2400.
Fax: 303-296-3956.
Salt Lake City, Utah Office: One Utah Center, 201 South Main Street, Suite 1200.
Telephone: 801-531-3000.
Fax: 801-531-3001.
Washington, D.C. Office: Suite 900 East, 555 13th Street, N.W.
Telephone: 202-383-8800.
Fax: 202-383-8877; 383-8893.
Camden, New Jersey Office: 800 Hudson Square, 5th Floor.
Telephone: 609-541-5577.
Fax: 609-541-8272.

Nancy V. Alquist

Thomas A. Hauser	Robert A. Weber

For full biographical listings, see the Martindale-Hubbell Law Directory

GOLDMAN & VETTER, P.A. (AV)

Twenty-Fourth Floor, 36 South Charles Street, 21201-3110
Telephone: 410-547-1400
Toll Free: 800-736-0102
Telecopier: 410-547-8818

Brian A. Goldman	Gerard R. Vetter

Lori Schultz Simpson
OF COUNSEL
Neil S. Kurlander

Reference: NationsBank of Maryland, Baltimore, Md.

For full biographical listings, see the Martindale-Hubbell Law Directory

ROBERT N. GROSSBART, P.A. (AV)

Suite 1902, Blaustein Building, One North Charles Street, 21201
Telephone: 410-837-0590; In MD: 1-800-286-0730
FAX: 410-837-0085

Robert Neil Grossbart

Christopher M. Fascetta
LEGAL SUPPORT PERSONNEL
Sheila A. White

For full biographical listings, see the Martindale-Hubbell Law Directory

MEHLMAN & GREENBLATT, LLC (AV)

4 Reservoir Circle, Suite 100, 21208
Telephone: 410-486-4790
Fax: 410-486-4360

Gerson B. Mehlman	Frank W. Spector
Gary R. Greenblatt	Francis X. Leary
Wendy Lozinsky Shiff	Constance M. Hare

(See Next Column)

MEHLMAN & GREENBLATT LLC, *Baltimore—Continued*
LEGAL SUPPORT PERSONNEL
Stephanie A. Ristvey (Paralegal)   Ruth P. Stein

For full biographical listings, see the Martindale-Hubbell Law Directory

THIEBLOT, RYAN, MARTIN & MILLER, P.A. (AV)

4th Floor, The World Trade Center, 21202-3091
Telephone: 410-837-1140
Washington, D.C. Line: 202-628-8223
Fax: 410-837-3282
Towson, Maryland Office: Atlantic Federal Building. Suite 400. 100 West Road. 21204.
Telephone: 410-828-5900.

Robert J. Thieblot	Robert D. Harwick, Jr.
Anthony W. Ryan	Anne M. Hrehorovich
J. Edward Martin, Jr.	Donna Marie Raffaele
Bruce R. Miller	Hamilton Fisk Tyler
Samuel S. Field III	

Representative Clients: Ford Motor Credit Co.; Ford Consumer Finance Co., Inc.; MBNA America, N.A.; Nissan Motor Acceptance Corp.

For full biographical listings, see the Martindale-Hubbell Law Directory

VENABLE ATTORNEYS AT LAW VENABLE, BAETJER AND HOWARD, LLP (AV)

A Partnership including Professional Corporations
1800 Mercantile Bank & Trust Building, 2 Hopkins Plaza, 21201
Telephone: 410-244-7400
Email: INFO@Venable.win.net
Washington, D.C. Office: Venable, Baetjer, Howard & Civiletti LLP. Suite 1000, 1201 New York Avenue, N.W.
Telephone: 202-962-4800.
McLean, Virginia Office: Suite 400, 2010 Corporate Ridge.
Telephone: 703-760-1600.
Rockville, Maryland Office: Suite 500, One Church Street, P. O. Box 1906.
Telephone: 301-217-5600.
Towson, Maryland Office: 210 Allegheny Avenue, P. O. Box 5517.
Telephone: 410-494-6200.

MEMBERS OF FIRM

Daniel O'C. Tracy, Jr. (Also at Rockville, Maryland Office)	Joseph C. Wich, Jr. (Resident, Towson, Maryland Office)
Joe A. Shull (Resident, Washington, D.C. Office)	Richard L. Wasserman (P.C.)
Kenneth C. Bass, III (Not admitted in MD; Washington, D.C. and McLean, Virginia Offices)	George F. Pappas (Also at Washington, D.C. Office)
	Christopher R. Mellott
	David Eugene Rice
Paul T. Glasgow (Resident, Rockville, Maryland Office)	John A. Roberts (Also at Rockville, Maryland Office)

OF COUNSEL
Mary T. Flynn (Not admitted in MD; Resident, McLean, Virginia Office)

ASSOCIATES

Gregory A. Cross	Myriam Judith Schmell
Rochelle Block Fowler	Brian R. Trumbauer
Gregory L. Laubach (Resident, Rockville, Maryland Office)	

For Complete List of Firm Personnel, See General Section

For full biographical listings, see the Martindale-Hubbell Law Directory

BETHESDA, Montgomery Co.

DECKELBAUM OGENS & FISCHER, CHARTERED (AV)

6701 Democracy Boulevard, 20817
Telephone: 301-564-5100
Washington D.C. Office: 1140 Connecticut Avenue, N.W.
Telephone: 202-223-1474.

Nelson Deckelbaum	Ronald L. Ogens
Lawrence H. Fischer	

Ronald G. Scheraga	Bryn Hope Sherman
Darryl Alan Feldman	

LEGAL SUPPORT PERSONNEL
Shirley Mostow

Representative Clients: The Charles E. Smith Companies; The Trammell Crow Company.
References: Franklin National Bank; Century National Bank.

For full biographical listings, see the Martindale-Hubbell Law Directory

EASTON,* Talbot Co.

ALEXANDER GORDON, IV (AV)

8615 Commerce Drive, Unit 1, 21601-7421
Telephone: 410-822-3702
Fax: 410-822-9356
References: Nations Bank, Easton Branch, Easton, Maryland.

For full biographical listings, see the Martindale-Hubbell Law Directory

GAITHERSBURG, Montgomery Co.

TERENCE BRIAN GARVEY (AV)

839C Quince Orchard Boulevard, 20878
Telephone: 301-948-1227
FAX: 301-840-2265
Reference: Potomac Valley Bank.

For full biographical listings, see the Martindale-Hubbell Law Directory

MASSACHUSETTS

BOSTON,* Suffolk Co.

CRAIG AND MACAULEY, PROFESSIONAL CORPORATION (AV)

Federal Reserve Plaza, 600 Atlantic Avenue, 02210
Telephone: 617-367-9500
Telecopier: 617-742-1788; 617-248-0886
Email: cmpc@ultranet.com

William F. Macauley	William R. Moorman, Jr.
Stephen Wald	Martin P. Desmery

For Complete List of Firm Personnel, See General Section

For full biographical listings, see the Martindale-Hubbell Law Directory

HANIFY & KING, PROFESSIONAL CORPORATION (AV)

One Federal Street, 02110-2007
Telephone: 617-423-0400
Telefax: 617-423-0498

James Coyne King	Daniel J. Lyne
John D. Hanify	Donald F. Farrell, Jr.
Harold B. Murphy	Barbara Wegener Pfirrman
David Lee Evans	Gerard P. Richer
Timothy P. O'Neill	

Jean A. Musiker	Joseph F. Cortellini
Ann M. Chiacchieri	Eddirland Duncan
Melissa J. Cassedy	Andrew G. Lizotte
Jeffrey J. Upton	Karen A. Whitley
Michael R. Perry	Christopher K. Barry-Smith
Charles A. Dale, III	William T. Harrington
Kathleen E. Cross	Matthew McCue
David M. Wright	Robyn J. Bartlett
Owen P. Kane	

For full biographical listings, see the Martindale-Hubbell Law Directory

LOONEY & GROSSMAN (AV)

A Partnership including Professional Corporations
101 Arch Street, 02110-1112
Telephone: 617-951-2800
Fax: 617-951-2819

Stewart F. Grossman (P.C.)	Bradley W. Snyder
Richard J. Grahn	Wesley S. Chused
Bertram E. Snyder	Melvin S. Hoffman (P.C.)
Robert Cushman Barber	Joseph H. Matzkin

SENIOR COUNSEL
William F. Looney, Jr.

OF COUNSEL

Paul D. McCarthy	Sherman H. Starr, Jr.

ASSOCIATES

Seth H. Salinger	Lisa Sternschuss
Erin M. Gilligan	Keir J. Beadling
Maria Galvagna	Lauren K. Heggestad Dillon
Adam J. Ruttenberg	

For full biographical listings, see the Martindale-Hubbell Law Directory

PALMER & DODGE LLP (AV)

One Beacon Street, 02108
Telephone: 617-573-0100
Facsimile: 617-227-4420

(See Next Column)

PALMER & DODGE LLP—*Continued*

MEMBERS OF FIRM

Jeanne P. Darcey	Richard S. Rosenstein
Richard Hiersteiner	Thomas G. Schnorr
Raymond M. Murphy	Thomas M. Spera
John E. Rattigan, Jr.	George Ticknor

John L. Whitlock

For Complete List of Firm Personnel, See General Section

For full biographical listings, see the Martindale-Hubbell Law Directory

PEABODY & ARNOLD (AV)

A Partnership including Professional Corporations
50 Rowes Wharf, 02110-3342
Telephone: 617-951-2100
Telecopier: 617-951-2125
Providence, Rhode Island Office: One Citizens Plaza, Suite 840.
Telephone: 401-831-8330.
Fax: 401-831-8359.

MEMBERS OF FIRM

Amanda D. Darwin	Deborah S. Griffin

Douglas C. Reynolds

ASSOCIATE

Robert Payne Fox, Jr.

For Complete List of Firm Personnel, See General Section

For full biographical listings, see the Martindale-Hubbell Law Directory

SHERBURNE, POWERS & NEEDHAM, P.C. (AV)

One Beacon Street, 02108
Telephone: 617-523-2700
Fax: 617-523-6850
Email: @SHERBURNE.COM

William D. Weeks	Benjamin Volinski
John T. Collins	Mark Schonfeld
Allan J. Landau	James D. Smeallie
Stephen A. Hopkins	Paul Killeen
Alan I. Falk	Gordon P. Katz
C. Thomas Swaim	Joseph B. Darby, III
James Pollock	Richard M Yanofsky
William V. Tripp III	James E. McDermott
Stephen S. Young	Kenneth P. Brier
William F. Machen	Robert V. Lizza
W. Robert Allison	Miriam Goldstein Altman
Philip J. Notopoulos	John J. Monaghan
Richard J. Hindlian	Margaret J. Palladino
Paul E. Troy	Mark C. Michalowski
Harold W. Potter, Jr.	David Scott Sloan
Philip S. Lapatin	M. Chrysa Long
Pamela A. Duckworth	Lawrence D. Bradley

Miriam J. McKendall

Cynthia A. Brown	Amy J. Mastrobattista
Cynthia M. Hern	Leslie A. Sprinkle
Meredeth A. Beers	Douglas W. Clapp
Dianne R. Phillips	Jeffrey A. Huebschmann
Paul M. James	Tamara E. Goulston
Theodore F. Hanselman	Paul G. Lannon, Jr.
Joshua C. Krumholz	Nicholas J. Psyhogeos
Ieuan G. Mahony	Edward J. Naughton
Jeffrey J. Nix	Kathaleen Kelly Cutone
(Not admitted in MA)	Laurie A. Tribble
Kenneth L. Harvey	Neil C. Higgins
Christopher J. Trombetta	Deborah Paige Stone
Elise N. Zoli	Brian R. Popiel

COUNSEL

Haig Der Manuelian	Karl J. Hirshman
Mason M. Taber, Jr.	Dale R. Johnson

For full biographical listings, see the Martindale-Hubbell Law Directory

SILVERMAN & KUDISCH, P.C. (AV)

Successor to Silverman & Kudisch.
One Longfellow Place, Suite 3608, 02114-2434
Telephone: 617-523-1711
Fax: 617-523-6037

Sumner Darman	Peter L. Zimmerman

Richard L. Blumenthal

For full biographical listings, see the Martindale-Hubbell Law Directory

FRAMINGHAM, Middlesex Co.

DAVID I. SHORR (AV)

24 Union Avenue, 01701
Telephone: 508-879-4412
Fax: 508-872-2888

(See Next Column)

Marlene Kerble

References: Shawmut Bank; Framingham Savings Bank.

For full biographical listings, see the Martindale-Hubbell Law Directory

SPRINGFIELD,* Hampden Co.

HENDEL, COLLINS & NEWTON, P.C. (AV)

101 State Street, 01103
Telephone: 413-734-6411
Fax: 413-734-8069

Philip J. Hendel	Joseph H. Reinhardt
Joseph B. Collins	Jonathan R. Goldsmith
Carla W. Newton	Henry E. Geberth, Jr.

George I. Roumeliotis

Representative Clients: Springfield Institution for Savings; United Cooperative Bank.
Reference: Shawmut Bank, N.A.

For full biographical listings, see the Martindale-Hubbell Law Directory

KAMBERG, BERMAN, P.C. (AV)

One Financial Plaza, 1350 Main Street, 01103-1628
Telephone: 413-781-1300
Facsimile: 413-732-0860
ABA/net: KAMBERGB

Abraham Kamberg (1895-1981)	Eugene B. Berman

Kerry David Strayer

References: Fleet Bank of Massachusetts, N.A.; Baybank; Shawmut Bank, N.A.

For full biographical listings, see the Martindale-Hubbell Law Directory

WORCESTER,* Worcester Co.

SEDER & CHANDLER (AV)

A Partnership including a Professional Corporation
Established 1918
Burnside Building, 339 Main Street, 01608
Telephone: 508-757-7721
Telecopiers: 508-798-1863; 508-831-0955

MEMBERS OF FIRM

Samuel Seder (1918-1964)	Marvin S. Silver, P.C.
Harold Seder (1934-1988)	John L. Pfeffer, Jr.
Burton Chandler	Robert S. Adler
J. Robert Seder	Dawn E. Caccavaro
Darragh K. Kasakoff	Kevin C. McGee

Kurt L. Binder

ASSOCIATES

Paul J. O'Riordan	Jeffrey P. Greenberg

Denise M. Tremblay

OF COUNSEL

Saul A. Seder	Gerald E. Norman

Philip C. Lombardo, Jr.

Reference: First National Bank of Boston; Safety Fund National Bank; Fleet National Bank.

For full biographical listings, see the Martindale-Hubbell Law Directory

MICHIGAN

ANN ARBOR,* Washtenaw Co.

CONLIN, McKENNEY & PHILBRICK, P.C. (AV)

350 South Main Street Suite 400, 48104-2131
Telephone: 313-761-9000
Fax: 313-761-9001

Edward F. Conlin (1902-1953)	Robert M. Brimacombe
John W. Conlin (1904-1972)	James A. Schriemer
Albert J. Parker (1901-1970)	William M. Sweet
Chris L. McKenney	Elizabeth M. Petoskey
Karl R. Frankena	Bradley J. MeLampy
Allen J. Philbrick	Joseph W. Phillips
Phillip J. Bowen	Lori A. Buiteweg
Michael D. Highfield	Douglas G. McClure
Bruce N. Elliott	Thomas B. Bourque
Neil J. Juliar	Marjorie M. Dixon

Kenneth L. Spencer

OF COUNSEL

John W. Conlin

Representative Clients: Fingerle Lumber Co.; Ann Arbor Area Board of Realtors; Borders, Inc.; Auto-Owners Insurance Co.; Key Bank.

(See Next Column)

CONLIN, MCKENNEY & PHILBRICK P.C., *Ann Arbor—Continued*

Approved Attorneys for: Nations Title Insurance Co.; Ticor Title Insurance Co.

For full biographical listings, see the Martindale-Hubbell Law Directory

ELLMANN & ELLMANN, P.C. (AV)

106 South Fifth, Suite 200, 48104
Telephone: 313-668-4800
Facsimile: 313-662-3893
Email: ELLMANN@AOL.COM
Farmington Hills, Michigan Office: 28000 Weymouth.
Telephone: 313-851-0737.
Fax: 313-851-0738.

James I. Ellmann (1887-1969)   Douglas S. Ellmann
Claudia Roberts Ellmann
OF COUNSEL
William M. Ellmann   Robert L. Ellmann
(Not admitted in MI)

For full biographical listings, see the Martindale-Hubbell Law Directory

MILLER, CANFIELD, PADDOCK AND STONE, P.L.C. (AV)

A Professional Limited Liability Company
Founded in 1852 by Sidney Davy Miller
101 North Main Street, Seventh Floor, 48104-1400
Telephone: 313-663-2445
Fax: 313-747-7147
Detroit, Michigan Office: 150 West Jefferson, Suite 2500, 48226-4415.
Telephone: 313-963-6420.
Fax: 313-496-7500.
Cable Address: "Stem Detroit."
Bloomfield Hills, Michigan Office: Suite 100, Pinehurst Office Center, 1400 North Woodward, 48303-2014.
Telephone: 313-645-5000.
Fax: 313-645-1917.
Grand Rapids, Michigan Office: 1200 Campau Square Plaza, 99 Monroe, N.W., 49503-2639.
Telephone: 616-454-8656.
Fax: 616-776-6322.
Howell, Michigan Office: 121 South Barnard Street, Suite 4, 48843-2305.
Telephone: 517-546-7600.
Telecopier: 517-546-6974.
Kalamazoo, Michigan Office: 444 West Michigan Avenue, 49007-3752.
Telephone: 616-381-7030.
Fax: 616-382-0244.
Lansing, Michigan Office: One Michigan Avenue, Suite 900, 48933-1609.
Telephone: 517-487-2070.
Fax: 517-374-6304.
Monroe, Michigan Office: The Executive Centre, 214 East Elm Avenue, 48161-2682.
Telephone: 313-243-2000.
Fax: 313-243-0901.
Washington, D.C. Office: 1225 Nineteenth Street, N.W., Suite 400. 20036.
Telephone: 202-429-5575; 785-0600.
Fax: 202-331-1118; 785-1234.
Pensacola, Florida Office: 25 West Cedar, 32501.
Telephone: 904-469-1088.
Fax: 904-432-0677.
St. Petersburg, Florida Office: 100 Second Avenue S., Suite 7045, 33701.
Telephone: 813-982-6000.
Fax: 813-892-6002.
New York, New York Office: Eleventh Floor, 135 East 57th Street, 10022-2087.
Telephone: 212-754-5400.
Fax: 212-754-5401.
Gdansk, Poland Office: Suite 322, Dom Technika Building, UI. Rajska 6, 80-850.
Telephone: 011-485-831-2808.
Fax: 011-485-831-4719.
Warsaw, Poland Office: UI. Marszalkowska 82, Suite 561, 00-517.
Telephone: 011-482-623-6457 and 6458.
Fax: 011-482-623-6459.

RESIDENT PRINCIPALS
Robert E. Gilbert

Representative Firm Clients: Chrysler Corporation; Comerica, Incorporated; City of Detroit, Michigan; Detroit Tigers, Inc.; First of Michigan; Ford Motor Company; Ford Motor Credit Company; Great Lakes Bancorp; Henry Ford Hospital; INVETECH Company.

For Complete List of Firm Personnel, See General Section

For full biographical listings, see the Martindale-Hubbell Law Directory

---

BAY CITY, * Bay Co.

BRAUN KENDRICK FINKBEINER PLC (AV)

201 Phoenix Building, P.O. Box 2039, 48708
Telephone: 517-895-8505
Telecopier: 517-895-8437
URL: http://www.bkf-law.com
Saginaw, Michigan Office: 101 N. Washington, Suite 812. 8th Floor Second National Bank Building.
Telephone: 517-753-3461.
Telecopier: 517-753-3951.
Ann Arbor, Michigan Office: 700 First National Building.
Telephone: 313-995-4100.
Telecopier: 313-995-4798.

Ralph J. Isackson   Daniel S. Opperman
George F. Gronewold, Jr.   Gregory T. Demers
OF COUNSEL
Patrick D. Neering

Representative Clients: APV Chemical Machinery, Inc.; Bay Health Systems; Catholic Federal Credit Union; City of Saginaw; City of Vassar; City of Milwaukee; Corporate Service; Cox Cable.

For Complete List of Firm Personnel, See General Section

For full biographical listings, see the Martindale-Hubbell Law Directory

---

BINGHAM FARMS, Oakland Co.

KORNEY & HELDT (AV)

30700 Telegraph Road, Suite 1551, 48025
Telephone: 810-646-1050
Fax: 810-646-1054

J. Douglas Korney   Jeffrey A. Heldt

For full biographical listings, see the Martindale-Hubbell Law Directory

---

BIRMINGHAM, Oakland Co.

CARSON FISCHER, P.L.C. (AV)

Third Floor, 300 East Maple Road, 48009-6317
Telephone: 810-644-4840
Facsimile: 810-644-1832

Joseph M. Fischer   Lawrence A. Lichtman
Robert A. Weisberg   James E. Owings

For full biographical listings, see the Martindale-Hubbell Law Directory

HYMAN AND LIPPITT, P.C. (AV)

185 Oakland Avenue, Suite 300, P.O. Box 1750, 48009
Telephone: 810-646-8292
Facsimile: 810-646-8375

J. Leonard Hyman   Kenneth F. Neuman
Norman L. Lippitt   Terry S. Givens
Douglas A. Hyman   Paul J. Fischer
Brian D. O'Keefe   John A. Sellers
H. Joel Newman   Robert H. Lippitt
Nazli G. Sater   Roger L. Myers
David N. Morrell, Jr.

For full biographical listings, see the Martindale-Hubbell Law Directory

---

BLOOMFIELD HILLS, Oakland Co.

HOWARD & HOWARD ATTORNEYS, P.C. (AV)

The Pinehurst Office Center, Suite 101, 1400 North Woodward Avenue, 48304-2856
Telephone: 810-645-1483
Telecopier: 810-645-1568
Kalamazoo, Michigan Office: The Kalamazoo Building, Suite 400, 107 West Michigan Avenue.
Telephone: 616-382-1483.
Telecopier: 616-382-1568.
Lansing, Michigan Office: The Phoenix Building, Suite 500, 222 Washington Square, North.
Telephone: 517-485-1483.
Telecopier: 517-485-1568.
Peoria, Illinois Office: The Creve Coeur Building, Suite 200, 321 Liberty Street.
Telephone: 309-672-1483.
Telecopier: 309-672-1568.
Tampa, Florida Office: First of America Plaza, Suite 2000, 201 East Kennedy Boulevard.
Telephone: 813-229-1483.
Telecopier: 813-229-1568.

Philip T. Carter   Michael G. Cruse
Kevin M. Chudler   Roger M. Groves
Robert D. Mollhagen

Representative Clients: For Representative Client list, see General Practice, Bloomfield Hills, MI.

(See Next Column)

HOWARD & HOWARD ATTORNEYS P.C.—*Continued*

For Complete List of Firm Personnel, See General Section

For full biographical listings, see the Martindale-Hubbell Law Directory

---

SCHAFER AND WEINER, P.C. (AV)

2050 North Woodward Avenue Suite 100, 48304
Telephone: 810-540-3340
Facsimile: 810-642-2127

Arnold Schafer	Daniel J. Weiner
	Michael E. Baum

Elaine Temesan	Max J. Newman
Robert S. McWhorter	James C. Lamb

For full biographical listings, see the Martindale-Hubbell Law Directory

---

DETROIT,* Wayne Co.

ALLARD & FISH, A PROFESSIONAL CORPORATION (AV)

2600 Buhl Building, 535 Griswold Avenue, 48226
Telephone: 313-961-6141
Facsimile: 313-961-6142
Email: afish@michbar.org

David W. Allard	Ralph R. McKee
Deborah L. Fish	Elias Themistocles Majoros

Rodney M. Glusac

For full biographical listings, see the Martindale-Hubbell Law Directory

---

BODMAN, LONGLEY & DAHLING LLP (AV)

34th Floor 100 Renaissance Center, 48243
Telephone: 313-259-7777
Fax: 313-393-7579
Email: 2080194@mcimail.com
Troy, Michigan Office: Suite 2020, 755 West Big Beaver Road.
Telephone: 810-362-2110.
Fax: 810-244-0780.
Ann Arbor, Michigan Office: 110 Miller, Suite 300.
Telephone: 313-761-3780.
Fax: 313-930-2494.
Northern Michigan Office: 229 Court Street, P.O. Box 405, Cheboygan.
Telephone: 616-627-4351.
Fax: 616-627-2802.

MEMBERS OF FIRM

David G. Chardavoyne	Lawrence P. Hanson
Robert J. Diehl, Jr.	(Northern Michigan Office)
	Ralph E. McDowell

ASSOCIATE
Marc M. Bakst

For Representative Client List, See General Section

For Complete List of Firm Personnel, See General Section

For full biographical listings, see the Martindale-Hubbell Law Directory

---

CLARK HILL P.L.C. (AV)

500 Woodward Avenue, Suite 3500, 48226
Telephone: 313-965-8300
Facsimile: 313-962-4348
Oakland County, Michigan Office: Third Floor, 255 South Woodward Avenue, Birmingham.
Telephone: 810-642-9692.
Facsimile: 810-642-2174.
Lansing, Michigan Office: Suite 600, 200 North Capitol Avenue.
Telephone: 517-484-4481.
Facsimile: 517-484-1246.
Minneapolis, Minnesota Office: Suite 1000, One Financial Plaza, 120 South Sixth Street.
Telephone: 612-332-0102.
Facsimile: 612-332-3225.
Kansas City, Missouri Office: Suite 1400, Bryant Building, 1102 Grand Avenue.
Telephone: 816-221-5578.
Facsimile: 816-221-0303.

Michael S. Khoury	Peter A. Jackson
	Judith Greenstone Miller

John M. Ketcham	Michael I. Conlon
	Bernard T. Lourim

For Complete List of Firm Personnel, See General Section

For full biographical listings, see the Martindale-Hubbell Law Directory

---

EAMES WILCOX (AV)

1400 Buhl Building, 48226-3602
Telephone: 313-963-3750
Facsimile: 313-963-8485

MEMBERS OF FIRM

Leonard A. Wilcox, Jr.	Jerry R. Swift
Ronald J. Mastej	Neill T. Riddell
John W. Bryant	Kevin N. Summers
Robert E. Gesell	Keith M. Aretha

OF COUNSEL

Rex Eames	William B. McIntyre, Jr.
	David R. Ritter

Representative Clients: Chrysler Credit Corp.

For full biographical listings, see the Martindale-Hubbell Law Directory

---

HONIGMAN MILLER SCHWARTZ AND COHN (AV)

A Partnership including Professional Corporations
2290 First National Building, 48226
Telephone: 313-256-7800
Telecopier: 313-962-0176
Telex: 235705
URL: http://law.honigman.com
Lansing, Michigan Office: Phoenix Building, 222 North Washington Square, Suite 400, 48933-1800.
Telephone: 517-484-8282.
West Palm Beach, Florida Office: Suite 800 Esperante Building, 222 Lakeview Avenue, 33401-6112.
Telephone: 561-838-4500.
Tampa, Florida Office: 2700 SunTrust Financial Centre, 401 E. Jackson Street, 33602-5226.
Telephone: 813-221-6600.

MEMBERS OF FIRM

Donald F. Baty, Jr.	Theodore B. Sylwestrzak
Judy B. Calton	Sheryl L. Toby
Steven G. Howell	Sheldon S. Toll
	Robert B. Weiss

ASSOCIATES

Gail A. Eynon	Michelle Epstein Taigman
	Eugene V. Wade, Jr.

OF COUNSEL

Asher Rabinowitz

Representative Clients: AT&T Commercial Finance Corp.; Barclays Business Credit, Inc.; First Wisconsin National Bank of Milwaukee; General Motors Corporation Legal Staff (General Motors Acceptance Corporation, General Motors Corporation); Hibernia National Bank; Hughes Aircraft Company Legal Staff; NBD Bank, N.A.; Security Pacific Automotive Financial Services Corp.; The Travelers Insurance Company and World Omni Leasing, Inc.

For Complete List of Firm Personnel, See General Section

For full biographical listings, see the Martindale-Hubbell Law Directory

---

JAFFE, RAITT, HEUER & WEISS, PROFESSIONAL CORPORATION (AV)

One Woodward Avenue, Suite 2400, 48226
Telephone: 313-961-8380
Telecopier: 313-961-8358
Cable Address: "Jafsni"
Southfield, Michigan Office: Travelers Tower, Suite 1520.
Telephone: 313-961-8380.
Monroe, Michigan Office: 214 East Elm Avenue, Suite 208,
Telephone: 313-241-6470.
Telefacsimile: 313-241-3849.

Thomas E. Coughlin	Daniella Saltz
Victor F. Ptasznik	Linda C. Scheuerman
Louis P. Rochkind	Jay L. Welford

Stephen S. Laplante	Jon A. Sherk
Jane Derse Quasarano	Wendy L Zabriskie

For Complete List of Firm Personnel, See General Section

For full biographical listings, see the Martindale-Hubbell Law Directory

---

MILLER, CANFIELD, PADDOCK AND STONE, P.L.C. (AV)

A Professional Limited Liability Company
Founded in 1852 by Sidney Davy Miller
150 West Jefferson, Suite 2500, 48226-4415
Telephone: 313-963-6420
Fax: 313-496-7500
Cable Address: "Stem Detroit"
Detroit, Michigan Office: 150 West Jefferson, Suite 2500, 48226-4415.
Telephone: 313-963-6420.
Fax: 313-496-7500.
Cable Address: "Stem Detroit."

(See Next Column)

MILLER, CANFIELD, PADDOCK AND STONE P.L.C., *Detroit—Continued*

Ann Arbor, Michigan Office: 101 North Main Street, 7th Floor, 48104-1400.
Telephone: 313-663-2445.
Fax: 313-747-7147.
Bloomfield Hills, Michigan Office: Suite 100, Pinehurst Office Center, 1400 North Woodward, 48303-2014.
Telephone: 313-645-5000.
Fax: 313-645-1917.
Grand Rapids, Michigan Office: 1200 Campau Square Plaza, 99 Monroe, N.W., 49503-2639.
Telephone: 616-454-8656.
Fax: 616-776-6322.
Howell, Michigan Office: 121 South Barnard Street, Suite 4, 48843-2305.
Telephone: 517-546-7600.
Telecopier: 517-546-6974.
Kalamazoo, Michigan Office: 444 West Michigan Avenue, 49007-3752.
Telephone: 616-381-7030.
Fax: 616-382-0244.
Lansing, Michigan Office: One Michigan Avenue, Suite 900, 48933-1609.
Telephone: 517-487-2070.
Fax: 517-374-6304.
Monroe, Michigan Office: The Executive Centre, 214 East Elm Avenue, 48161-2682.
Telephone: 313-243-2000.
Fax: 313-243-0901.
Washington, D.C. Office: 1225 Nineteenth Street, N.W., Suite 400. 20036.
Telephone: 202-429-5575; 785-0600.
Fax: 202-331-1118; 785-1234.
Pensacola, Florida Office: 25 West Cedar, 32501.
Telephone: 904-469-1088.
Fax: 904-432-0677.
St. Petersburg, Florida Office: 100 Second Avenue S., Suite 7045, 33701.
Telephone: 813-982-6000.
Fax: 813-892-6002.
New York, New York Office: Eleventh Floor, 135 East 57th Street, 10022-2087.
Telephone: 212-754-5400.
Fax: 212-754-5401.
Gdansk, Poland Office: Suite 322, Dom Technika Building, UI. Rajska 6, 80-850.
Telephone: 011-485-831-2808.
Fax: 011-485-831-4719.
Warsaw, Poland Office: UI. Marszalkowska 82, Suite 561, 00-517.
Telephone: 011-482-623-6457 and 6458.
Fax: 011-482-623-6459.

PRINCIPALS OF FIRM

Terrence M. Crawford	Michael H. Traison
Robert E. Lee Wright	Jonathan S. Green
Donald J. Hutchinson	

ASSOCIATE
Lori L. Purkey (Kalamazoo Office)

Representative Firm Clients: Chrysler Corporation; Comerica, Incorporated; City of Detroit, Michigan; Detroit Tigers, Inc.; First of Michigan; Ford Motor Company; Ford Motor Credit Company; Great Lakes Bancorp; Henry Ford Hospital; INVETECH Company.

For Complete List of Firm Personnel, See General Section

For full biographical listings, see the Martindale-Hubbell Law Directory

---

FARMINGTON HILLS, Oakland Co.

COUZENS, LANSKY, FEALK, ELLIS, ROEDER & LAZAR, P.C. (AV)

33533 West Twelve Mile Road, Suite 150, P.O. Box 9057, 48333-9057
Telephone: 810-489-8600
Telecopier: 810-489-4156

Sheldon A. Fealk	Lisa J. Walters
Jack S. Couzens, II	Stephen Scapelliti
Jerry M. Ellis	Donald A. Wagner
Donald M. Lansky	Michael P. Witzke
Bruce J. Lazar	Cyrus Raamin Kashef
Alan C. Roeder	Gregg A. Nathanson
Renard J. Kolasa	Mark S. Frankel
Kathryn Gilson Sussman	Lynette M. Sheldon
Jeffrey A. Levine	Roger E. Winkelman
Phillip L. Sternberg	David B. Deutsch
Marc L. Prey	Monica Demko Moons

Representative Clients: Provided upon request.
Reference: Comerica Bank-Southfield.

For full biographical listings, see the Martindale-Hubbell Law Directory

---

GRAND RAPIDS,* Kent Co.

BORRE, PETERSON, FOWLER & REENS, P.C. (AV)

The Philo C. Fuller House, 44 Lafayette, N.E., P.O. Box 1767, 49501-1767
Telephone: 616-459-1971
Fax: 616-459-2393

(See Next Column)

William C. Reens	Mark D. Sevald
Frank H. Johnson	Harold E. Nelson

References: NBD Bank; FMB-First Michigan Bank - Grand Rapids.

For Complete List of Firm Personnel, See General Section

For full biographical listings, see the Martindale-Hubbell Law Directory

---

DAY & SAWDEY, A PROFESSIONAL CORPORATION (AV)

200 Monroe Avenue, Suite 500, 49503-2217
Telephone: 616-774-8121
Telefax: 616-774-0168

George B. Kingston (1889-1965)	James B. Frakie
John R. Porter (1915-1975)	Larry A. Ver Merris
Charles E. Day, Jr.	John Boyko, Jr.
Robert W. Sawdey	Jonathan F. Thoits
C. Mark Stoppels	John T. Piggins
Thomas A. DeMeester	

Representative Clients: American National Bank & Trust Company of Chicago; Bank One Dayton, N.A.; Barclays Business Credit, Inc.; Chemical Bank, N.A.; Comerica Bank, N.A.; First of America Bank - West Michigan; Heller Financial, Inc.; Michigan National Bank; National Westminster Bank U.S.A.; Old Kent Bank and Trust Co.

For full biographical listings, see the Martindale-Hubbell Law Directory

---

DE GROOT, KELLER & VINCENT (AV)

300 Michigan Trust Building, 49503
Telephone: 616-459-6251
Fax: 616-459-6352

MEMBERS OF FIRM

Murray B. De Groot	Brian D. Vincent
James M. Keller	

For full biographical listings, see the Martindale-Hubbell Law Directory

---

LAW, WEATHERS & RICHARDSON, P.C. (AV)

Bridgewater Place, Suite 800, 333 Bridge Street, N.W., 49504
Telephone: 616-459-1171
Facsimile: 616-732-1740

OF COUNSEL
John R. Nichols

Alan C. Bennett	Henry G. Swain
	Ingrid A. Jensen

David W. Centner

Representative Clients: First Federal of Michigan; Kent City State Bank; Chase Manhattan Leasing Co.; Mercedes-Benz Credit Corporation; Federal Deposit Insurance Corporation; PACCAR Financial Corp.; Sears Consumer Financial Corp.; Mack Financial Corp.; General Motors Corporation.

For Complete List of Firm Personnel, See General Section

For full biographical listings, see the Martindale-Hubbell Law Directory

---

MILLER, CANFIELD, PADDOCK AND STONE, P.L.C. (AV)

A Professional Limited Liability Company
Founded in 1852 by Sidney Davy Miller
1200 Campau Square Plaza, 99 Monroe, N.W., P.O. Box 329, 49503-2639
Telephone: 616-454-8656
Fax: 616-776-6322
Detroit, Michigan Office: 150 West Jefferson, Suite 2500, 48226-4415.
Telephone: 313-963-6420.
Fax: 313-496-7500.
Cable Address: "Stem Detroit."
Ann Arbor, Michigan Office: 101 North Main Street, 7th Floor, 48104-1400.
Telephone: 313-663-2445.
Fax: 313-747-7147.
Bloomfield Hills, Michigan Office: Suite 100, Pinehurst Office Center, 1400 North Woodward, 48303-2014.
Telephone: 313-645-5000.
Fax: 313-645-1917.
Howell, Michigan Office: 121 South Barnard Street, Suite 4, 48843-2305.
Telephone: 517-546-7600.
Telecopier: 517-546-6974.
Kalamazoo, Michigan Office: 444 West Michigan Avenue, 49007-3752.
Telephone: 616-381-7030.
Fax: 616-382-0244.
Lansing, Michigan Office: One Michigan Avenue, Suite 900, 48933-1609.
Telephone: 517-487-2070.
Fax: 517-374-6304.
Monroe, Michigan Office: The Executive Centre, 214 East Elm Avenue, 48161-2682.
Telephone: 313-243-2000.
Fax: 313-243-0901.

(See Next Column)

MILLER, CANFIELD, PADDOCK AND STONE P.L.C.—_Continued_

Washington, D.C. Office: 1225 Nineteenth Street, N.W., Suite 400. 20036.
Telephone: 202-429-5575; 785-0600.
Fax: 202-331-1118; 785-1234.
Pensacola, Florida Office: 25 West Cedar 32501.
Telephone: 904-469-1088.
Fax: 904-432-0677.
St. Petersburg Florida Office: 100 Second Avenue S., Suite 7045, 33701.
Telephone: 813-982-6000.
Fax: 813-892-6002.
New York, New York Office: Eleventh Floor, 135 East 57th Street, 10022-2087.
Telephone: 212-754-5400.
Fax: 212-754-5401.
Gdansk, Poland Office: Suite 322, Dom Technika Building, UI. Rajska 6, 80-850.
Telephone: 011-485-831-2808.
Fax: 011-485-831-4719.
Warsaw, Poland Office: UI. Marszalkowska 82, Suite 561, 00-517.
Telephone: 011-482-623-6457 and 6458.
Fax: 011-482-623-6459.

PRINCIPALS OF FIRM

Mark E. Putney (Resident
  Director, Grand Rapids
  Office)
Richard A. Gaffin
Charles S. Mishkind (Detroit,
  Lansing and Kalamazoo
  Offices)

Michael G. Campbell
Robert E. Lee Wright
Vernon Bennett III
Douglas W. Crim

OF COUNSEL
David E. Hathaway
SENIOR ATTORNEYS

David J. Hasper

Stephen L. Elkins

ASSOCIATES

John C. Arndts
Bradley C. White

Daniel H. Roberts
John T. Stecco

Michael V. Camarota

Representative Firm Clients: Chrysler Corporation; Comerica, Incorporated; City of Detroit, Michigan; Detroit Tigers, Inc.; First of Michigan; Ford Motor Company; Ford Motor Credit Company; Great Lakes Bancorp; Henry Ford Hospital; INVETECH Company.

For full biographical listings, see the Martindale-Hubbell Law Directory

VARNUM, RIDDERING, SCHMIDT & HOWLETT LLP (AV)

A Limited Liability Partnership including Professional Corporations
Bridgewater Place, P.O. Box 352, 49501-0352
Telephone: 616-336-6000
800-262-0011
Facsimile: 616-336-7000
Telex: 1561593 VARN
Email: varnum@vrsh.com
Lansing, Michigan Office: The Victor Center, Suite 810, 210 North Washington Square, 48933.
Telephone: 517-482-6237.
Facsimile: 517-482-6937.
Kalamazoo, Michigan Office: 350 East Michigan Avenue, 49007.
Telephone: 616-382-2300.
Facsimile: 616-382-2382.
Grand Haven, Michigan Office: 321 Washington Street, P.O. Box 288, 49417.
Telephone: 616-846-7100.
Facsimile: 616-846-7101.
Battle Creek, Michigan Office: 4950 West Dickman Road, Suite B-1, 49015.
Telephone: 616-962-7144.
Bingham Farms, Michigan Office: 31600 Telegraph Road, Suite 230, 48025.
Telephone: 810-594-7330.
Facsimile: 810-594- 7331.

MEMBERS OF FIRM

Timothy J. Curtin
Thomas G. Demling
Jeffrey R. Hughes
Jeffrey D. Smith (Resident at
  Kalamazoo Office)

Michael S. McElwee (Resident
  at Kalamazoo Office)
Joan E. Schleef
Scott A. Huizenga
Maureen Potter

Counsel for: First Michigan Bank Corp.; Independent Bank Corp.
Special Counsel for: Comerica Bank, NA.; Michigan National Bank, N.A.; Great Lakes Bank Corp.; Old Kent Bank.

For Complete List of Firm Personnel, See General Section

For full biographical listings, see the Martindale-Hubbell Law Directory

WARNER NORCROSS & JUDD LLP (AV)

900 Old Kent Building, 111 Lyon Street, N.W., 49503-2489
Telephone: 616-752-2000
Fax: 616-752-2500
Muskegon, Michigan Office: 400 Terrace Plaza, P.O. Box 900.
Telephone: 616-727-2600.
Fax: 616-727-2699.
Holland, Michigan Office: Curtis Center, Suite 300, 170 College Avenue.
Telephone: 616-396-9800.
Fax: 616-396-3656.

MEMBERS OF FIRM

Charles E. McCallum
Timothy Hillegonds

Kathleen M. Hanenburg
Stephen B. Grow

ASSOCIATE
Jeffrey S. Battershall

Representative Clients: Steelcase, Inc.; Bissell, Inc.; Old Kent Bank Financial Corporation; Haworth, Inc.; Country Fresh, Inc.; Challenge Machinery Company; Morbark Industries; Whirlpool Corporation; The Zondervan Corporation; Union Pump Company.

For Complete List of Firm Personnel, See General Section

For full biographical listings, see the Martindale-Hubbell Law Directory

KALAMAZOO,* Kalamazoo Co.

PAUL F. DAVIDOFF A PROFESSIONAL CORPORATION (AV)

405 West Michigan Avenue, Suite 130, P.O. Box 51066, 49005
Telephone: 616-388-2100
Fax: 616-388-5454

Paul F. Davidoff

Reference: First of America Bank-Michigan N.A.

For full biographical listings, see the Martindale-Hubbell Law Directory

HOWARD & HOWARD ATTORNEYS, P.C. (AV)

The Kalamazoo Building, Suite 400, 107 West Michigan
  Avenue, 49007-3956
Telephone: 616-382-1483
Telecopier: 616-382-1568
Bloomfield Hills, Michigan Office: The Pinehurst Office Center, Suite 101, 1400 North Woodward Avenue.
Telephone: 810-645-1483.
Telecopier: 810-645-1568.
Lansing, Michigan Office: The Phoenix Building, Suite 500, 222 Washington Square North.
Telephone: 517-485-1483.
Telecopier: 517-485-1568.
Peoria, Illinois Office: The Creve Coeur Building, Suite 200, 321 Liberty Street.
Telephone. 309-672-1483.
Telecopier: 309-672-1568.
Tampa, Florida Office: First of America Plaza, Suite 2000, 201 East Kennedy Boulevard.
Telephone: 813-229-1483.
Telecopier: 813-229-1568.

Jeffrey P. Chalmers
        Bruce R. Grubb

William A. Dornbos

Representative Clients: For Representative Client list, see General Practice, Kalamazoo, MI.

For Complete List of Firm Personnel, See General Section

For full biographical listings, see the Martindale-Hubbell Law Directory

KREIS, ENDERLE, CALLANDER & HUDGINS, A PROFESSIONAL CORPORATION (AV)

One Moorsbridge, P.O. Box 4010, 49003-4010
Telephone: 616-324-3000
Telecopier: 616-324-3010
Email: kech@sapien.net _URL:_ http://www.kech.com

Russell A. Kreis
Robert B. Borsos

Thomas G. King
Daniel P. McGlinn

For Complete List of Firm Personnel, See General Section

For full biographical listings, see the Martindale-Hubbell Law Directory

MILLER, CANFIELD, PADDOCK AND STONE, P.L.C. (AV)

A Professional Limited Liability Company
Founded in 1852 by Sidney Davy Miller
444 West Michigan Avenue, 49007-3752
Telephone: 616-381-7030
Fax: 616-382-0244
Detroit, Michigan Office: 150 West Jefferson, Suite 2500, 48226-4415.
Telephone: 313-963-6420.
Fax: 313-496-7500.
Cable Address: "Stem Detroit."

(See Next Column)

MILLER, CANFIELD, PADDOCK AND STONE P.L.C., *Kalamazoo—Continued*

Ann Arbor, Michigan Office: 101 North Main Street, 7th Floor, 48104-1400.
Telephone: 313-663-2445.
Fax: 313-747-7147.
Bloomfield Hills, Michigan Office: Suite 100, Pinehurst Office Center, 1400 North Woodward, 48303-2014.
Telephone: 313-645-5000.
Fax: 313-645-1917.
Grand Rapids, Michigan Office: 1200 Campau Square Plaza, 99 Monroe, N.W., 49503-2639.
Telephone: 616-454-8656.
Fax: 616-776-6322.
Howell, Michigan Office: 121 South Barnard Street, Suite 4, 48843-2305.
Telephone: 517-546-7600.
Telecopier: 517-546-6974.
Lansing, Michigan Office: One Michigan Avenue, Suite 900, 48933-1609.
Telephone: 517-487-2070.
Fax: 517-374-6304.
Monroe, Michigan Office: The Executive Centre, 214 East Elm Avenue, 48161-2682.
Telephone: 313-243-2000.
Fax: 313-243-0901.
Washington, D.C. Office: 1225 Nineteenth Street, N.W., Suite 400. 20036.
Telephone: 202-429-5575; 785-0600.
Fax: 202-331-1118; 785-1234.
Pensacola, Florida Office: 25 West Cedar, 32501.
Telephone: 904-469-1088.
Fax: 904-432-0677.
St. Petersburg, Florida Office: 100 Second Avenue S., Suite 7045, 33701.
Telephone: 813-982-6000.
Fax: 813-892-6002.
New York, New York Office: Eleventh Floor, 135 East 57th Street, 10022-2087.
Telephone: 212-754-5400.
Fax: 212-754-5401.
Gdansk, Poland Office: Suite 322, Dom Technika Building, UI. Rajska 6, 80-850.
Telephone: 011-485-831-2808.
Fax: 011-485-831-4719.
Warsaw, Poland Office: UI. Marszalkowska 82, Suite 561, 00-517.
Telephone: 011-482-623-6457 and 6458.
Fax: 011-482-623-6459.

PRINCIPALS OF FIRM
James G. Vantine, Jr.

ASSOCIATE
Lori L. Purkey

Representative Firm Clients: Chrysler Corporation; Comerica, Incorporated; City of Detroit, Michigan; Detroit Tigers, Inc.; First of Michigan; Ford Motor Company; Ford Motor Credit Company; Great Lakes Bancorp; Henry Ford Hospital; INVETECH Company.

For Complete List of Firm Personnel, See General Section

For full biographical listings, see the Martindale-Hubbell Law Directory

---

LANSING, Ingham Co.

MILLER, CANFIELD, PADDOCK AND STONE, P.L.C. (AV)

A Professional Limited Liability Company
Founded in 1852 by Sidney Davy Miller
Suite 900, One Michigan Avenue, 48933-1609
Telephone: 517-487-2070
Fax: 517-374-6304
Detroit, Michigan Office: 150 West Jefferson, Suite 2500, 48226-4415.
Telephone: 313-963-6420.
Fax: 313-496-7500.
Cable Address: "Stem Detroit."
Ann Arbor, Michigan Office: 101 North Main Street, 7th Floor, 48104-1400.
Telephone: 313-663-2445.
Fax: 313-747-7147.
Bloomfield Hills, Michigan Office: Suite 100, Pinehurst Office Center, 1400 North Woodward, 48303-2014.
Telephone: 313-645-5000.
Fax: 313-645-1917.
Grand Rapids, Michigan Office: 1200 Campau Square Plaza, 99 Monroe, N.W., 49503-2639.
Telephone: 616-454-8656.
Fax: 616-776-6322.
Howell, Michigan Office: 121 South Barnard Street, Suite 4, 48843-2305.
Telephone: 517-546-7600.
Telecopier: 517-546-6974.
Kalamazoo, Michigan Office: 444 West Michigan Avenue, 49007-3752.
Telephone: 616-381-7030.
Fax: 616-382-0244.
Monroe, Michigan Office: The Executive Centre, 214 East Elm Avenue, 48161-2682.
Telephone: 313-243-2000.
Fax: 313-243-0901.

(See Next Column)

Washington, D.C. Office: 1225 Nineteenth Street, N.W., Suite 400. 20036.
Telephone: 202-429-5575; 785-0600.
Fax: 202-331-1118; 785-1234.
Pensacola, Florida Office: 25 West Cedar, 32501.
Telephone: 904-469-1088.
Fax: 904-432-0677.
St. Petersburg Office: 100 Second Avenue S., Suite 7045, 33701.
Telephone: 813-982-6000.
Fax: 813-892-6002.
New York, New York Office: Eleventh Floor, 135 East 57th Street, 10022-2087.
Telephone: 212-754-5400.
Fax: 212-754-5401.
Gdansk, Poland Office: Suite 322, Dom Technika Building, UI. Rajska 6, 80-850.
Telephone: 011-485-831-2808.
Fax: 011-485-831-4719.
Warsaw, Poland Office: UI. Marszalkowska 82, Suite 561, 00-517.
Telephone: 011-482-623-6457 and 6458.
Fax: 011-482-623-6459.

PRINCIPALS OF FIRM
William J. Danhof (Resident)

Representative Firm Clients: Chrysler Corporation; Comerica, Incorporated; City of Detroit, Michigan; Detroit Tigers, Inc.; First of Michigan; Ford Motor Company; Ford Motor Credit Company; Great Lakes Bancorp; Henry Ford Hospital; INVETECH Company.

For Complete List of Firm Personnel, See General Section

For full biographical listings, see the Martindale-Hubbell Law Directory

---

PONTIAC,* Oakland Co.

BOOTH PATTERSON, P.C. (AV)

1090 West Huron Street, 48328
Telephone: 810-681-1200
Fax: 810-681-1754

Douglas W. Booth (1918-1992)	David J. Lee
Calvin E. Patterson (1913-1987)	Allan T. Motzny
Parvin C. Lee, Jr.	Michael J. Hughes
J. Timothy Patterson	Michael D. Bishop
Eric S. Meier	

For full biographical listings, see the Martindale-Hubbell Law Directory

---

ROCHESTER, Oakland Co.

SHERMETA, CHIMKO AND KILPATRICK, P.C. (AV)

445 South Livernois, Suite 221, P.O. Box 5016, 48308
Telephone: 810-652-8200
Fax: 810-652-1292
Detroit, Michigan Office: Ford Building, 48226.
Telephone: 313-961-4848.
Fax: 313-961-4365.
Grand Rapids, Michigan Office: 169 Louis Campau Prom., Suite 2B.
Telephone: 616-531-6980.
Fax: 616-531-7475.
Sacramento, California Office: 555 Capital Mall, Suite 530.
Telephone: 916-448-5039.
Facsimile: 916-448-7461.
San Leandro, California Office: 777 Davis Street, Suite 100.
Telephone: 510-614-0800.
Facsimile: 510-614-0670.

Douglass H. Shermeta	Barbara L. Adams
Darryl J. Chimko	Karen E. Evangelista
Richardo I. Kilpatrick	Henry J. Mittelstaedt III

Mariana J. Richmond	Julie M. Carroll
Robert D. Dzialo	Mark A. Wolff (Resident, Sacramento, California Office)
Kelly L. Scola	
Karen Lamoreaux Rice	Richard A. Morton (Resident, San Leandro, California Office)
Christopher E. Mcneely	
David R. Shook	
Patrick (Casey) Coston	Mitchell L. Wong (Resident, San Leandro, California Office)
Krispen S. Carroll	
Sheryl S. Zamplas	Kathryn E. Walters (Resident, San Leandro, California Office)
Lisa E. Gocha	

For full biographical listings, see the Martindale-Hubbell Law Directory

---

SAGINAW,* Saginaw Co.

BRAUN KENDRICK FINKBEINER PLC (AV)

101 N. Washington Suite 812, 48607-1297
Telephone: 517-753-3461
Telecopier: 517-753-3951
URL: http://www.bkf-law.com
Bay City, Michigan Office: 201 Phoenix Building, P.O. Box 2039.
Telephone: 517-895-8505.
Telecopier: 517-895-8437.

(See Next Column)

BRAUN KENDRICK FINKBEINER PLC—*Continued*

Ann Arbor, Michigan Office: 700 First National Building.
Telephone: 313-995-4100.
Telecopier: 313-995-4798.

Kenneth W. Kable	Timothy L Curtiss
	Francis J. Keating

Representative Clients: The Dow Chemical Co.; General Motors Corp.; Lobdell Emery Manufacturing Co.; Merrill, Lynch, Inc.; Saginaw General Hospital; Saginaw News; The Wickes Foundation.

For Complete List of Firm Personnel, See General Section

For full biographical listings, see the Martindale-Hubbell Law Directory

---

SOUTHFIELD, Oakland Co.

ERMAN, TEICHER, MILLER, ZUCKER & FREEDMAN, A PROFESSIONAL CORPORATION (AV)

100 Galleria Officentre, Suite 333, 48034
Telephone: 810-827-4100
Telecopier: 810-827-4106

Earle I. Erman	Craig E. Zucker
Julie Beth Teicher	David H. Freedman
David M. Miller	Robert D. Gordon

For full biographical listings, see the Martindale-Hubbell Law Directory

---

*TRAVERSE CITY,** Grand Traverse Co.

MURCHIE, CALCUTT & BOYNTON (AV)

109 East Front Street, Suite 300, 49684
Telephone: 616-947-7190
Fax: 616-947-4341

Robert B. Murchie (1894-1975)	William B. Calcutt
Harry Calcutt	Mark A. Burnheimer
Jack E. Boynton	Dawn M. Rogers

ASSOCIATE
Ralph J. Dilley (Not admitted in MI)

General Counsel for: Old Kent Bank-Grand Traverse; Northwestern Savings Bank & Trust; Central-State Bancorp; Traverse City Record Eagle; WPNB-7 & WTOM-4; Emergency Consultants, Inc.; National Guardian Risk Retention Group, Inc.; Farmers Mutual Insurance Co.; Environmental Solutions, Inc.
Local Counsel for: Consumers Power Co.

For full biographical listings, see the Martindale-Hubbell Law Directory

---

TROY, Oakland Co.

AUSTIN HIRSCHHORN, P.C. (AV)

Suite 710 Columbia Center, 201 West Big Beaver Road, 48084-4152
Telephone: 810-680-1660
Fax: 810-680-1671

Austin Hirschhorn

For full biographical listings, see the Martindale-Hubbell Law Directory

---

JACOB & WEINGARTEN (AV)

2301 West Big Beaver Road, Suite 777, 48084
Telephone: 810-649-1900
Facsimile: 810-649-2920
West Palm Beach, Florida Office: 1555 Palm Beach Lake Boulevard, Suite 1510, 33401.
Telephone: 561-640-5600.
Facsimile: 561-683-0799.

Peter A. Nathan (Resident, West Palm Beach, Florida Office)	Howard S. Sher
	Phillip J. Neuman
Steven P. Schubiner	Robert K. Siegel

Representative Clients: Afco Credit Corporation; IBM Credit Corp.; Michigan National Bank; Various Trustees; Zahn Associates, Inc.

For full biographical listings, see the Martindale-Hubbell Law Directory

---

WEST BLOOMFIELD, Oakland Co.

SHEFFERLY & SILVERMAN (AV)

7115 Orchard Lake Road, Suite 500, 48322
Telephone: 810-539-1330
Fax: 810-539-1355

MEMBERS OF FIRM

Phillip J. Shefferly	Geoffrey L. Silverman
	Thomas R. Morris

ASSOCIATES

Karin F. Barto	Kathryn R.S. Spray

Representative Clients: Textron Financial Corp.; Townsend Hotel Corp.; Continental Ins. Co.; Country Home Bakers; D.N.T.; Mr. Bulky Treats & Gifts; Medsker Electric, Inc.; Spartan Finance Company; Neal R. Sutherland, trustee.

For full biographical listings, see the Martindale-Hubbell Law Directory

BUSINESS LAW

ALABAMA

BIRMINGHAM,* Jefferson Co.

BAINBRIDGE, MIMS, ROGERS & SMITH (AV)

The Luckie Building, Suite 415, 600 Luckie Drive, P.O. Box 530886, 35253
Telephone: 205-879-1100
Fax: 205-879-4300

MEMBERS OF FIRM

Frank Bainbridge (1895-1980)	Frank M. Bainbridge
Walter L. Mims (1910-1993)	Bruce F. Rogers
Alfred F. Smith, Jr.	

For full biographical listings, see the Martindale-Hubbell Law Directory

BERKOWITZ, LEFKOVITS, ISOM & KUSHNER, A PROFESSIONAL CORPORATION (AV)

1600 SouthTrust Tower, 420 North Twentieth Street, 35203
Telephone: 205-328-0480
Telecopier: 205-322-8007

Arnold K. Lefkovits	W. Clark Goodwin
Harold B. Kushner	Denise W. Killebrew
B. G. Minisman, Jr.	Thomas O. Kolb
David A. Larsen	Thomas J. Mahoney, Jr.
A. Lee Martin, Jr.	Richard A. Pizitz, Jr.
Barry S. Marks	Andrew J. Potts
D. J. Simonetti	Walton E. Williams III

Judy P. Hamer

Representative Clients: AlaTenn Resources, Inc.; AlaTenn Natural Gas Co.; B.A.S.S., Inc.; Hanna Steel Co., Inc.; Liberty Trouser Co. Inc.; McDonald's Corp.; Parisian, Inc.; Southern Pipe & Supply Co., Inc.; Supreme Beverage, Inc.

For Complete List of Firm Personnel, See General Section

For full biographical listings, see the Martindale-Hubbell Law Directory

BRADLEY, ARANT, ROSE & WHITE (AV)

2001 Park Place, Suite 1400, P.O. Box 830709, 35283-0709
Telephone: 205-521-8000
Facsimile: 205-252-0264
Facsimile (SouthTrust Tower Office): 205-251-9915
URL: http://www.BARW.COM
Huntsville, Alabama Office: 200 Clinton Avenue West, Suite 900, 35801.
Telephone: 205-517-5100.
Facsimile: 205-533-5069.

MEMBERS OF FIRM

Edward M. Selfe	M. Williams Goodwyn, Jr.
Thomas Neely Carruthers, Jr.	John B. Grenier
William L. Hinds, Jr.	J. David Dresher
Charles Larimore Whitaker	Scott E. Ludwig
John G. Harrell	(Resident, Huntsville Office)
Charles R. Smith, Jr.	John E. Hagefstration, Jr.
(Resident, Huntsville Office)	Stuart Joseph Frentz
P. Nicholas Greenwood	Paul S. Ware
James E. Rotch	Virginia Calvert Patterson
John K. Molen	Denson Nauls Franklin III
Lant B. Davis	J. Paul Compton, Jr.
Carleta Roberts Hawley	L. Susan Doss
George Bryan Harris	

COUNSEL

Wm. Bew White, Jr. (Retired)	Walter H. Monroe, III
Robert R. Reid, Jr.	Joan Crowder Ragsdale
John N. Wrinkle	K. Wood Herren

ASSOCIATES

Kevin J. Henderson	Dorothy C. Daigle
Hall B, Bryant III	Helena F. Tozzi
(Resident, Huntsville Office)	Joseph E. Smith
Paul D. Gilbert	Hugh Chester Boston, III
Jennifer Byers McLeod	Steven Austin King

For Complete List of Firm Personnel, See General Section

For full biographical listings, see the Martindale-Hubbell Law Directory

BURR & FORMAN (AV)

3100 SouthTrust Tower, 420 North 20th Street, 35203
Telephone: 205-251-3000
Telecopier: 205-458-5100
Huntsville, Alabama Office: Suite 204, Regency Center, 400 Meridian Street.
Telephone: 205-551-0010.
Atlanta, Georgia Office: Suite 1800, One Georgia Center, 600 West Peachtree Street, 30308.
Telephone: 404-817-3536.
Facsimile: 404-817-3244.

MEMBERS OF FIRM

J. Fred Powell	Bruce A. Rawls
Samuel W. Oliver, Jr.	Dwight L. Mixson, Jr.
Louis H. Anders, Jr.	Gene T. Price
Joseph G. Stewart	Henry Graham Beene
A. Brand Walton	Deborah P. Fisher
Jack P. Stephenson, Jr.	Gail Livingston Mills
Eric L. Carlton	Marvin Glenn Perry, Jr.
George M. Taylor, III	Jeffrey T. Baker
Jill Verdeyen Deer	

For Complete List of Firm Personnel, See General Section

For full biographical listings, see the Martindale-Hubbell Law Directory

GORDON, SILBERMAN, WIGGINS & CHILDS, A PROFESSIONAL CORPORATION (AV)

1400 SouthTrust Tower, 420 North 20th Street, 35203
Telephone: 205-328-0640
Telecopier: 205-254-1500

Bruce L. Gordon	Ray D. Gibbons
Timothy D. Davis	Joseph H. Calvin, III
Linda J. Peacock	

For Complete List of Firm Personnel, See General Section

For full biographical listings, see the Martindale-Hubbell Law Directory

HASKELL SLAUGHTER & YOUNG, L.L.C. (AV)

1200 AmSouth/Harbert Plaza, 1901 Sixth Avenue North, 35203
Telephone: 205-251-1000
Facsimile: 205-324-1133
Montgomery, Alabama Office: 305 South Lawrence Street, P.O. Box 4660. 36103-4660.
Telephone: 334-265-8573.
Facsimile: 334-264-7945.

Mark Edward Ezell	Ross N. Cohen
Gwen L. Windle	

Representative Clients: The Bradford Group, Inc.; HEALTHSOUTH Corporation/HEALTHSOUTH Medical Centers; Manpower Temporary Services (Alabama); Marshall Durbin Companies; MedPartners, Inc.; Revere, Inc.; Ridout's-Brown-Service Inc.; United Leisure Corp.; United Restaurants, Inc.

For Complete List of Firm Personnel, See General Section

For full biographical listings, see the Martindale-Hubbell Law Directory

NAJJAR DENABURG, P.C. (AV)

2125 Morris Avenue, 35203
Telephone: 205-250-8400
Telecopier: 205-326-3837

Charles L. Denaburg	Robert H. Adams
Edward P. Meyerson	Marvin E. Franklin
Ben L. Zarzaur	Marvin L. Stewart, Jr.
David A. (Chip) Schwartz	Jesse P. Evans III
Douglas L. McWhorter	Hub Harrington
Gary S. Schiff	Richard W. Theibert

Rachel Jackson Moore

General Counsel: Acousti Engineering of Alabama, Inc.
Representative Client: Compass Bank.
Approved Attorneys for: Mississippi Valley Title Insurance Co.
Reference: Compass Bank.

For Complete List of Firm Personnel, See General Section

For full biographical listings, see the Martindale-Hubbell Law Directory

DOTHAN,* Houston Co.

DOW T. HUSKEY (AV)

112 West Adams Street, P.O. Box 1501, 36302
Telephone: 334-794-3366
Telecopier: 334-794-7292

Representative Clients: Troy State University; Northside Mall; CNA Insurance Cos.; Employers Reinsurance; Tudor Insurance Co.; Rail Management; Wilmington Terminal Railway; Atlantic & Western Railway; Sony Federal Credit Union; S & S Imports.

(See Next Column)

Dow T. Huskey, *Dothan—Continued*

For full biographical listings, see the Martindale-Hubbell Law Directory

---

HUNTSVILLE,* Madison Co.

BERRY, ABLES, TATUM, BAXTER, PARKER & HALL, P.C. (AV)

Legal Building, 315 Franklin Street, S.E., P.O. Box 165, 35804-0165
Telephone: 205-533-3740
Facsimile: 205-533-3751
Email: BAXTERJ@ATTMAIL.COM

William H. Blanton (1889-1973)	James T. Tatum, Jr.
Joe M. Berry	James T. Baxter, III
L. Bruce Ables	Thomas E. Parker, Jr.
	Bill G. Hall

James K. Brabston	Mark Rogers Hunter

Representative Clients: AmSouth Bank; First Alabama Bank; General Shale Products Co.; The Hertz Corp.; Litton Industries, Inc.; Farmers Tractor Co.; Colonial Bank; Farm Credit Bank of Texas; SouthBank; Regions Mortgage.
Reference: First Alabama Bank.

For full biographical listings, see the Martindale-Hubbell Law Directory

BURR & FORMAN (AV)

Suite 204, Regency Center, 400 Meridian Street, 35801
Telephone: 205-551-0010
Birmingham, Alabama Office: 3100 SouthTrust Tower, 420 North 20th Street.
Telephone: 205-251-3000.
Telecopier: 205-458-5100.
Atlanta, Georgia Office: Suite 1800, One Georgia Center, 600 West Peachtree Street, 30308.
Telephone: 404-817-3536.
Facsimile: 404-817-3244.

RESIDENT PARTNER
S. Dagnal Rowe

For full biographical listings, see the Martindale-Hubbell Law Directory

---

MOBILE,* Mobile Co.

ARMBRECHT, JACKSON, DeMOUY, CROWE, HOLMES & REEVES, L.L.C. (AV)

1300 AmSouth Center, P.O. Box 290, 36601
Telephone: 334-405-1300
Facsimile: 334-432-6843; 433-3821

MEMBERS OF FIRM

Marshall J. DeMouy	David A. Bagwell
E. B. Peebles III	Christopher I. Gruenewald
Edward G. Hawkins	David E. Hudgens
	James Dale Smith

ASSOCIATE
James F. Watkins

Representative Clients: AmSouth Bank of Alabama (Regional Counsel); Dean Witter Reynolds, Inc.; General Electric Credit Corp.; Loyal American Life Insurance Co.; Mobile Gas Service Corp.; Southern Pine Inspection Bureau; United Bank; WKRG-TV, Inc.

For Complete List of Firm Personnel, See General Section

For full biographical listings, see the Martindale-Hubbell Law Directory

JOHNSTONE, ADAMS, BAILEY, GORDON AND HARRIS, L.L.C. (AV)

Royal St. Francis Building, 104 St. Francis Street, P.O. Box 1988, 36633
Telephone: 334-432-7682
Facsimile: 334-432-2800
Telex: 782040

MEMBERS OF FIRM

Charles B. Bailey, Jr.	Joseph M. Allen, Jr.
Ben H. Harris, Jr.	I. David Cherniak
William H. Hardie, Jr.	Wade B. Perry, Jr.
	R. Gregory Watts

General Counsel for: First Alabama Bank, Mobile; Infirmary Health System/Mobile Infirmary Medical Center/Rotary Rehabilitation Hospital (Multi-Hospital System).
Counsel for: Oil and Gas: Exxon Corp. Business and Corporate: Bell South Telecommunications, Inc.; Aluminum Co. of America; Michelin North America, Inc.; Metropolitan Life Insurance Co.; The Travelers Insurance Cos. Marine: The West of England Ship Owners Mutual Protection and Indemnity Association (Luxembourg); The Standard Steamship Owners' Protection and Indemnity Association (Bermuda) Ltd.

For Complete List of Firm Personnel, See General Section

For full biographical listings, see the Martindale-Hubbell Law Directory

---

VICKERS, RIIS, MURRAY AND CURRAN, L.L.C. (AV)

8th Floor, First Alabama Bank Building, 106 Saint Francis Street, P.O. Box 2568, 36652
Telephone: 334-432-9772
Fax: 334-432-9781

MEMBERS OF FIRM

J. Manson Murray	Zebulon M. P. Inge, Jr.
Edwin J. Curran, Jr.	Ronald P. Davis

Representative Clients: Mobile Forest Products, Inc.; Azalea Aviation, Inc.; Midstream Fuel Services; McPhillips Manufacturing Co.; Spring Hill College; Steiner Shipyard, Inc.; Homeowners Marketing Services, Inc.; Marine Office of America Corp.; Cummins Alabama, Inc.; Ben M. Radcliff Contractor, Inc.

For Complete List of Firm Personnel, See General Section

For full biographical listings, see the Martindale-Hubbell Law Directory

ZIEMAN, SPEEGLE, OLDWEILER & JACKSON, L.L.C. (AV)

Suite 3200, First National Bank Building, P.O. Box 11, 36601
Telephone: 334-694-1700
Facsimile: 334-694-1998

MEMBERS OF THE FIRM

Thomas Troy Zieman, Jr.	Thomas P. Oldweiler
Jerome E. Speegle	Robert G. Jackson, Jr.

ASSOCIATE
Anthony Michael Hoffman

For full biographical listings, see the Martindale-Hubbell Law Directory

---

MONTGOMERY,* Montgomery Co.

VOLZ, PRESTWOOD & HANAN, P.C. (AV)

350 Adams Avenue, P.O. Box 1910, 36102-1910
Telephone: 334-264-6401
Fax: 334-834-4954

Charles H. Volz, Jr.	Charles H. Volz, III
Alvin T. Prestwood	Clinton Chadwell Carter
Ellis D. Hanan	Daniel Lewis Feinstein

LEGAL SUPPORT PERSONNEL
Mark A.W. Turpen

For full biographical listings, see the Martindale-Hubbell Law Directory

---

TUSCALOOSA,* Tuscaloosa Co.

PHELPS, JENKINS, GIBSON & FOWLER (AV)

1201 Greensboro Avenue, P.O. Box 020848, 35402-0848
Telephone: 205-345-5100
Fax: 205-758-4394
Fax: 205-391-6658

MEMBERS OF FIRM

Sam M. Phelps	Randolph M. Fowler
James J. Jenkins	Michael S. Burroughs
Johnson Russell Gibson, III	C. Barton Adcox
	Farley A. Poellnitz

ASSOCIATES

Karen C. Welborn	Stephen E. Snow
Sandra C. Guin	Thomas W. Davis
Lisa Paul Hodges	M. Kristi Wallace

LEGAL SUPPORT PERSONNEL

Alicia Suzanne Wilson	Ashley D. Sparks
Cathey Raye Hartline	Kimberly Susan Wright

Attorneys for: Aetna Insurance Co.; Allstate Insurance Co.; Carolina Casualty Insurance Co.; Continental Insurance Cos.; Fireman's Fund-American Insurance Cos.; Great American Insurance Co.; Hanover Insurance Co.

For full biographical listings, see the Martindale-Hubbell Law Directory

WATSON, HARRISON & DeGRAFFENRIED (AV)

1651 McFarland Boulevard North, 35406-2212
Telephone: 205-345-1577
Fax: 205-345-1583

William T. Watson	Steven F. Harrison
	Thomas W. Holley

OF COUNSEL
Ryan DeGraffenried, Jr.

Michael C. Cornwell	Ricky J. McKinney

Representative Clients: BTA Oil Producers; Black Warrior Methane Corp.; Chevron U.S.A. Inc.; Cobra Oil & Gas Corp.; CXY Energy, Inc.; Exxon Co., USA; Fina Oil & Chemical Co.; Legacy Resources; Meridian Oil Inc.; Mitchell Energy Corp.

For full biographical listings, see the Martindale-Hubbell Law Directory

ALASKA

BONN, LUSCHER, PADDEN & WILKINS, CHARTERED (AV)

805 North Second Street, 85004
Telephone: 602-254-5557
Fax: 602-254-0656

Paul V. Bonn	John H. Cassidy
Brian A. Luscher	D. Michael Hall
Jeff C. Padden	Samuel C. Wisotzkey
Randall D. Wilkins	Ronald A. Rice

OF COUNSEL

Marvin Kantor   Ruth Sproull

For full biographical listings, see the Martindale-Hubbell Law Directory

ANCHORAGE, Third Judicial District

DELISIO MORAN GERAGHTY & ZOBEL, P.C. (AV)

943 West Sixth Avenue, 99501-2033
Telephone: 907-279-9574
Facsimile: 907-276-4231
Email: 74151,2533@compuserve.com

Joseph M. Moran	Gregory L. Youngmun
Patricia L. Zobel	David D. Floerchinger

Jeffrey L. Leclerc

Representative Clients: Artic Slope Regional Corporation; National Bank of Alaska.

For full biographical listings, see the Martindale-Hubbell Law Directory

COPPERSMITH & GORDON P.L.C. (AV)

2633 East Indian School Road, Suite 300, 85016-6759
Telephone: 602-224-0999
Fax: 602-224-6020
Email: SAMnANDY@aol.com

Samuel G. Coppersmith   Andrew S. Gordon

OF COUNSEL

M. Joyce Geyser   James J. Belanger

Reference: Norwest Bank Arizona, N.A.

For full biographical listings, see the Martindale-Hubbell Law Directory

ARIZONA

FLAGSTAFF, Coconino Co.

ASPEY, WATKINS & DIESEL, P.L.L.C. (AV)

123 North San Francisco, 3rd Floor, 86001
Telephone: 520-774-1478
Facsimile: 520-774-8404
Sedona, Arizona Office: 120 Soldier Pass Road.
Telephone: 520-282-5955.
Facsimile: 520-282-5962.
Page, Arizona Office: 904 North Navajo.
Telephone: 520-645-9694.
Cottonwood, Arizona Office: 2400 E. Highway 89A, Suite C.
Telephone: 520-639-1881.
Facsimile: 520-639-0272.

MEMBERS OF FIRM

Frederick M. Fritz Aspey	Donald H. Bayles, Jr.
Harold L. Watkins	Kaign N. Christy
Louis M. Diesel	John J. Dempsey
Bruce S. Griffen	Zachary J. Markham

James E. Ledbetter	Roger M. Baeurle
Whitney Cunningham	Amy E. Mabius
Pernell Whynn McGuire	Stephen A. Thompson
Joel E. Sannes	

LEGAL SUPPORT PERSONNEL

Karla H. Falls, CLAS (Legal Assistant)	Dominic M. Marino, Jr, (Paralegal Assistant)
Rocky C. Nissen (Paralegal Assistant, Sedona, Arizona Office)	Carrie R. Flynn (Litigation Paralegal, Cottonwood, Arizona Office)
Deborah D. Roberts, CLA (Legal Assistant)	

Representative Clients: Farmer's Insurance Company of Arizona; Pepsi-Cola Bottling Company of Northern Arizona; Bill Luke's Chrysler-Plymouth, Inc.; First American Title Insurance Company; Transnation Title Insurance Co.; Page Electric Utility; Comprehensive Access Health Plan, Inc.; Northern Arizona Healthcare Corporation.
Reference: First Interstate Bank-Arizona, N.A., Flagstaff, Arizona.

For full biographical listings, see the Martindale-Hubbell Law Directory

FENNEMORE CRAIG, A PROFESSIONAL CORPORATION (AV)

Two North Central, Suite 2200, 85004
Telephone: 602-257-8700
Fax: 602-257-8527
Scottsdale, Arizona Office: 6263 North Scottsdale Road, Suite 290, 85250.
Telephone: 602-257-5400.
Fax: 602-257-5409
Tucson, Arizona Office: One South Church Avenue, Suite 1030, 85701.
Telephone: 520-791-6800.
Fax: 520-791-6820.

C. Webb Crockett	David A. Weatherwax
Robert P. Robinson	Cathy L. Reece
Ronald L. Ballard	Karen Ciupak McConnell
Stephen M. Savage	J. Barry Shelley

W. T. Eggleston, Jr.

For Complete List of Firm Personnel, See General Section

For full biographical listings, see the Martindale-Hubbell Law Directory

FOGEL AND LAMBER, PROFESSIONAL ASSOCIATION (AV)

One Windsor Professional Building, 2627 North Third Street, 85004-1197
Telephone: 602-264-3330
Fax: 602-274-5117

Sherman D. Fogel	Dennis M. Lamber
	Rex P. Bronnenkant

Reference: Chase Bank of Arizona.

For full biographical listings, see the Martindale-Hubbell Law Directory

MESA, Maricopa Co.

JACKSON, WHITE, GARDNER & DECKER, P.C. (AV)

Suite 12000, 1201 S. Alma School Road, 85210
Telephone: 602-464-1111
Fax: 602-464-5692 *Statewide:* 800-243-1160
Email: JWGD@JWGDLAW.COM
Payson, Arizona Office: 260 Building C. Suite E, 108 E. Highway.
Telephone: 520-472-8878.

Roger C. Decker	Michael R. Pruitt
Wayne L. Gardner	Bradley D. Weech
Eric M. Jackson	David L. Weed
J. Grant Walker	Richard A. White
	Roger R. Foote

William G. Rood	Hank E. Pearson
Eric K. MacDonald	Christine A. Wigton
	Kelly G. Black

For full biographical listings, see the Martindale-Hubbell Law Directory

GOODSON, MANLEY & DURFEE, P.L.C. (AV)

The Brookstone Building, 2025 North 3rd Street, Suite 200, 85004-1471
Telephone: 602-252-5110
Fax: 602-257-1883

John F. Goodson	Colleen C. Manley
	Richard E. Durfee, Jr.

Lawrence F. Scaringelli	Bryan C. Moody

A list of Representative Clients will be furnished upon request.
Reference: First National Bank of Arizona.

For full biographical listings, see the Martindale-Hubbell Law Directory

JOHN S. LANCY & ASSOCIATES A PROFESSIONAL CORPORATION (AV)

Suite 390, 2425 East Camelback Road, 85016
Telephone: 602-381-6555
Fax: 602-381-6550

John S. Lancy

Steven W. Bienstock	Nina A. Ortega

For full biographical listings, see the Martindale-Hubbell Law Directory

Phoenix—Continued

LANE & EHRLICH, LTD. (AV)

Fairmount Place, Suite 400, 4001 North Third Street, 85012
Telephone: 602-264-4442
Telecopier: 602-264-5006

Robert L. Lane   Gerald F. Ehrlich

References: Bank One Arizona; Harris Trust & Savings Bank; The Northern Trust Bank Arizona.

For full biographical listings, see the Martindale-Hubbell Law Directory

LEWIS AND ROCA, LLP (AV)

A Limited Liability Partnership including a Professional Corporation
40 North Central Avenue, 85004-4429
Telephone: 602-262-5311
Fax: 602-262-5747
Email: mlp@lrlaw.com
Tucson, Arizona Office: One South Church Avenue, Suite 700, 86701-1620.
Telephone: 520-622-2090.
Fax: 520-622-3088. E-Mail: mlp@lrlaw.com.

MEMBERS OF FIRM

Gerald K. Smith	Douglas R. Chandler
Richard N. Goldsmith	Susan M. Freeman
David E. Manch	Randolph J. Haines
Patrick Derdenger	Beth J. Schermer
Kevin L. Olson	David M. Bixby
Amy R. Porter	Scott DeWald
Rosemarie Christofolo	Bryant D. Barber
Kenneth Van Winkle, Jr.	Hope Leibsohn
J. Tyler Haahr	

ASSOCIATES

Barbara Anstey Hoerner	Kevin G. Hunter
Anthony J. Blackwell	Julie M. Arvo MacKenzie
Julie Mathis Nelson	Glenn D. Forcucci
	(Not admitted in AZ)

OF COUNSEL
Lance J. Rose

Representative Clients: Arizona Hospital Assn.; Blood Systems, Inc.; The Dial Corp; The Industrial Development Authority of the City of Phoenix; MarkAir; Phoenix Memorial Hospital; Rockford Corp.; Samaritan Health System; Skymall, Inc.

For Complete List of Firm Personnel, See General Section

For full biographical listings, see the Martindale-Hubbell Law Directory

LINZER & DITSCH, P.C. (AV)

3242 North Sixteenth Street, 85016
Telephone: 602-956-2525
Fax: 602-241-9885

Stephen P. Linzer

Terry D. Warren

For full biographical listings, see the Martindale-Hubbell Law Directory

ROBERT J. NOVAK & ASSOCIATES (AV)

1440 E. Washington Street Suite 100, 85034
Telephone: 602-253-8000
Fax: 602-271-4733

ASSOCIATE
Herbert T. Swafford

Representative Clients: SouthTrust Mortgage, BancBoston; L.V. Associates, Ltd.; AEI Real Estate Fund Limited Partnership; Heron North American Property Trust; Tippmann Construction, Inc.; Sun World Corporation; G.B. Mannisto, Inc.; Phoenix Computer Systems, Inc.; Pasternack Architect, Inc.; Phoenix Plastics, Inc.

For full biographical listings, see the Martindale-Hubbell Law Directory

QUARLES & BRADY (AV)

One Camelback Building, One East Camelback Road, Suite 400, 85012-1649
Telephone: 602-230-5500
Fax: 602-230-5598
Milwaukee, Wisconsin Office: 411 East Wisconsin Avenue.
Telephone: 414-277-5000.
Fax: 414-271-3552.
Madison, Wisconsin Office: First Wisconsin Plaza, One South Pinckney Street, P.O. Box 2113.
Telephone: 608-251-5000.
Fax: 608-251-9166.
West Palm Beach, Florida Office: 222 Lakeview Ave., 4th Floor.
Telephone: 407-653-5000.
Fax: 407-653-5333.

(See Next Column)

Naples, Florida Office: Barnett Center, 4501 Tamiami Trail North, Suite 300.
Telephone: 813-262-5959.
Fax: 813-434-4999.

MEMBERS OF THE FIRM

P. Robert Moya	Daniel L. Muchow
Robert C. Houser, Jr.	Paul M. Gales
Peter A. Terry	Steven P. Emerick

ASSOCIATES

Robert S. Bornhoft	Mark N. Rogers
Colleen A. Scherkenbach	Mark K. Briggs

For Complete List of Firm Personnel, See General Section

For full biographical listings, see the Martindale-Hubbell Law Directory

RENAUD, COOK & DRURY, P.A. (AV)

617 North 2nd Avenue, 85003
Telephone: 602-253-5101
Fax: 602-254-1448
Email: rcdlaw@rcdlaw.com
Scottsdale, Arizona Office: 6991 East Camelback Road, #D-103, 85251.
Telephone: 602-874-9000.
Fax: 602-874-9866.

J. Gordon Cook	Cathey L. Joseph
William W. Drury, Jr.	Mark W. Roth

Cynthia L. Fulton

For full biographical listings, see the Martindale-Hubbell Law Directory

VLASSIS & VLASSIS (AV)

1545 West Thomas Road, 85015
Telephone: 602-248-8811
Fax: 602-274-8983

George P. Vlassis   Elizabeth D. Vlassis

References: Bank One; Citibank.

For full biographical listings, see the Martindale-Hubbell Law Directory

PRESCOTT,* Yavapai Co.

FAVOUR, MOORE & WILHELMSEN, A PROFESSIONAL ASSOCIATION (AV)

1580 Plaza West Drive, P.O. Box 1391, 86302
Telephone: 520-445-2444
Fax: 520-771-0450

John M. Favour	Mark M. Moore
	David K. Wilhelmsen

Representative Client: Yavapai Title Co.
Reference: Bank of America.

For full biographical listings, see the Martindale-Hubbell Law Directory

SCOTTSDALE, Maricopa Co.

PESKIND HYMSON & GOLDSTEIN, P.C. (AV)

14595 North Scottsdale Road, Suite 14, 85254
Telephone: 602-991-9077
Fax: 602-443-8854

Irving Hymson	Marilee Miller Clarke
	Jeffrey A. Leyton

Eddie A. Pantiliat

For full biographical listings, see the Martindale-Hubbell Law Directory

TITUS, BRUECKNER & BERRY, P.C. (AV)

Scottsdale Centre Suite B-252, 7373 North Scottsdale Road, 85253-3527
Telephone: 602-483-9600
Fax: 602-483-3215
Email: TBandB@aol.com

Jon A. Titus	Charles R. Berry
Kurt M. Brueckner	Alex B. Vakula
	Garry S. O'Rafferty

David R. Jordan	K. Scott Reynolds
Scott K. Risley	Michael F. Patterson

LEGAL SUPPORT PERSONNEL

Janice L. Innocenzi	Belle Taylor

Representative Clients: Arizona Department of Insurance; Dickinson & Co. Hancock Homes; McCallum Hill; Heritage Mint, Ltd.; Baukol Construction, Inc.; Office of Special Deputy Receiver, Illinois Department of Insurance; Peacock, Hislop, Staley & Given, Inc.; H.E.R.C. Products., Incorporated; Stewart Title and Trust of Phoenix, Inc.; Beazer Homes.

For full biographical listings, see the Martindale-Hubbell Law Directory

TUCSON,* Pima Co.

ERNEST ALLEN COHEN (AV)

6426 Calle de Los Seris, P.O. Box 37273, 85740
Telephone: 520-297-4100
Fax: 520-297-4105

Representative Clients: International Organization of Masters, Mates & Pilots, ILA, AFL-CIO; Lawyers Mediation Service Corp.; Coast Guard Legal Aid Counsel; Masters, Mates & Pilots Health & Benefit Plan; Co-Counsel, Officers Union of International Seamen.

For full biographical listings, see the Martindale-Hubbell Law Directory

DANIEL H. O'CONNELL, P.C. (AV)

Suite 510, 6245 East Broadway, 85711
Telephone: 520-790-2535
Telefax: 520-571-8148

Daniel H. O'Connell

Benjamin J. Burnside
OF COUNSEL
Rosanne F. Lapan

Representative Clients: Empire West Cos.; Southwest Energy, Inc.; Alban Medical Associates; Industrial Motor & Control, Inc.; Allergy Asthma Associates, P.C.
Reference: Bank of America.

For full biographical listings, see the Martindale-Hubbell Law Directory

RAVEN, KIRSCHNER & NORELL, P.C. (AV)

Suite 1600, One South Church Avenue, 85701-1612
Telephone: 520-628-8700
Telefax: 520-798-5200

Susan M. Freund	Mark B. Raven
Andrew Oldland Norell	S. Leonard Scheff
Lane D. Oden	Stephen A. Thomas

Representative Clients: Continental Medical Systems, Inc.; El Paso Natural Gas Co.; Norwest Bank Arizona; El Rio-Santa Cruz Neighborhood Health Center, Inc.; Resolution Trust Corp.; Sierra Vista Community Hospital; Southern Arizona Rehabilitation Hospital; Northern Cochise Community Hospital.

For Complete List of Firm Personnel, See General Section

For full biographical listings, see the Martindale-Hubbell Law Directory

STOMPOLY, STROUD, GIDDINGS & GLICKSMAN, P.C. (AV)

1820 Citibank Tower, One South Church Avenue, 85702
Telephone: 520-628-8300
Telefax: 520-628-9948
Mailing Address: P.O. Box 190, Tucson, AZ, 85702-0190

John G. Stompoly	James L. Stroud
	Charles E. Giddings

For Complete List of Firm Personnel, See General Section

For full biographical listings, see the Martindale-Hubbell Law Directory

ARKANSAS

FORT SMITH,* Sebastian Co.

HARPER, YOUNG, SMITH & MAURRAS, PLC (AV)

510 North Greenwood Avenue, P.O. Box 10205, 72917
Telephone: 501-782-1001
Telefax: 501-782-1279

Thomas Harper (1908-1989)	Tom Harper, Jr.
R. A. Young, Jr. (1908-1973)	S. Walton Maurras
Don A. Smith	Robert Y. Cohen, II
	Michael K. Redd

Counsel for: Arkansas Best Corp.; ABF Freight System, Inc.; Riverside Furniture Corp.; The City National Bank of Fort Smith; O.K. Industries, Inc.
Insurance Clients: Zurich Insurance Co.; Wausau Insurance Companies.

For full biographical listings, see the Martindale-Hubbell Law Directory

LITTLE ROCK,* Pulaski Co.

RICHARD C. DOWNING, P.A. (AV)

Lafayette Building, Suite 750, 523 South Louisiana, 72201
Telephone: 501-372-2066
FAX: 501-376-6420
Email: RCDown@aol.com

(See Next Column)

Richard C. Downing

For full biographical listings, see the Martindale-Hubbell Law Directory

GILL LAW FIRM, A PROFESSIONAL ASSOCIATION (AV)

3801 TCBY Tower, Capitol and Broadway, 72201
Telephone: 501-376-3800
Fax: 501-372-3359

John P. Gill	Heartsill Ragon III, (P.A.)
Charles C. Owen (P.A.)	Joseph D. Calhoun III
W. W. Elrod, II	W. Bradford Sherman
Victor A. Fleming	Glenn E. Kelley

C. Tad Bohannon	Robert B. Holitik

OF COUNSEL
John A. Fogleman

For Complete List of Firm Personnel, See General Section

For full biographical listings, see the Martindale-Hubbell Law Directory

CALIFORNIA

ALISO VIEJO, Orange Co.

WORDES, WILSHIN, GOREN & CONNER (AV)

31 Journey Street, Suite 120, 92656-3334
Telephone: 714-643-1000
Telecopier: 714-643-2000
Email: firm@wwgc.com *URL:* http://www.wwgc.com

MEMBERS OF FIRM

Richard S. Wordes	Michael E. Goren
David B. Wilshin	Frank A. Conner

For full biographical listings, see the Martindale-Hubbell Law Directory

BAKERSFIELD,* Kern Co.

ELDON R. HUGIE (AV)

841 Mohawk Street, Suite 140, 93309
Telephone: 805-328-0200
Fax: 805-328-0204

Representative Clients: Tri-Fanucchi Farms, Inc.; Aquaculture Enterprises; Kern College Land Co.; Lake Boulevard Shopping Center.
References: Valliwide Bank (Bakersfield Main Branch).

For full biographical listings, see the Martindale-Hubbell Law Directory

BEVERLY HILLS, Los Angeles Co.

HERZOG, FISHER & GRAYSON, A LAW CORPORATION (AV)

9460 Wilshire Boulevard Fifth Floor, 90212
Telephone: 310-278-4300
Fax: 310-278-5430

James P. Herzog	David R. Fisher
	Michael A. Grayson

Pamela M. Rosenthal	Eric M. Rosin

OF COUNSEL
Todd I. Grayson

For full biographical listings, see the Martindale-Hubbell Law Directory

HOCHMAN, SALKIN AND DEROY, A PROFESSIONAL CORPORATION (AV)

9150 Wilshire Boulevard Suite 300, 90212-3414
Telephone: 310-281-3200; 273-1181
Fax: 310-859-1430

Bruce I. Hochman	Charles P. Rettig
Avram Salkin	Dennis Perez
	Steven R. Toscher

OF COUNSEL
George DeRoy

Stuart A. Simon	Michael W. Popoff
	Frederic J. Adam

Reference: Union Bank of California.

For full biographical listings, see the Martindale-Hubbell Law Directory

Beverly Hills—Continued

JACOBSON, SANDERS & BORDY, LLP (AV)

A Partnership including a Professional Corporation
9777 Wilshire Boulevard, Suite 718, 90212-1907
Telephone: 310-777-7488

MEMBERS OF FIRM

Lawrence H. Jacobson (A P.C.)   Michael J. Bordy
Michael R. E. Sanders

OF COUNSEL

David S. White   Patricia B. Kolber

For full biographical listings, see the Martindale-Hubbell Law Directory

SCHWARTZ, WISOT & WILSON, LLP (AV)

Suite 315, 315 South Beverly Drive, 90212
Telephone: 310-277-2323
Fax: 310-556-2308

Bruce Edward Schwartz   John D. Wilson
Valerie Wisot   Kathleen A. Calaway

OF COUNSEL

Paula Reddish Zinnemann

Reference: Great Western Bank (Century City Office, Los Angeles, California)

For full biographical listings, see the Martindale-Hubbell Law Directory

BURBANK, Los Angeles Co.

ALVIN N. LOSKAMP A LAW CORPORATION (AV)

290 East Verdugo Avenue, Suite 103, 91502
Telephone: 818-846-9000
Fax: 818-843-1441

Alvin N. Loskamp

References: Wells Fargo Bank, Glenoaks Branch, Burbank; Highland Savings & Loan, Burbank.

For full biographical listings, see the Martindale-Hubbell Law Directory

CAMARILLO, Ventura Co.

H. ROY JEPPSON A PROFESSIONAL CORPORATION (AV)

1100 Paseo Camarillo, 93010
Telephone: 805-482-3322
FAX: 805-482-6672
Email: roy@vcol.net

H. Roy Jeppson

Robyn F. Stalk

For full biographical listings, see the Martindale-Hubbell Law Directory

CARLSBAD, San Diego Co.

WEIL & WRIGHT (AV)

1921 Palomar Oaks Way, Suite 301, 92008
Telephone: 619-438-1214
Telefax: 619-438-2666

Paul M. Weil   David A. Ebersole
Archie T. Wright III   John F. Hilbert

For full biographical listings, see the Martindale-Hubbell Law Directory

CHICO, Butte Co.

CRAIG AND SHEPHERD (AV)

Suite 1, 1367 East Lassen Avenue, P.O. Box 658, 95927-0658
Telephone: 916-893-3700
Fax: 916-893-1579

MEMBERS OF FIRM

Maynard C. Craig   Michael T. Shepherd

ASSOCIATES

Bruce S. Alpert   Richard L. Crabtree

For full biographical listings, see the Martindale-Hubbell Law Directory

STEWART, HUMPHERYS, BURCHETT, SANDELMAN & MOLIN (AV)

Suite 6, 3120 Cohasset Road, P.O. Box 720, 95927
Telephone: 916-891-6111
Telecopier: 916-894-2103
Email: shbsm@sunset.net

MEMBERS OF FIRM

Ronald E. Stewart   Raymond L. Sandelman
Keith S. Humpherys   Richard J. Molin
Alan E. Burchett   Carol J. Tener
Stephen P. Trover

(See Next Column)

Representative Clients: North State National Bank; Northern California Federal Land Bank; Lassen Tractor Company; Northern California Production Credit Assn.; Drake Homes, Avag, Inc.; Meeks Building Center.

For full biographical listings, see the Martindale-Hubbell Law Directory

CLAREMONT, Los Angeles Co.

C. ROBERT FERGUSON (AV)

237 West Fourth Street, 91711
Telephone: 909-482-0782; 818-795-4181
Fax: 909-624-7291

CORONA, Riverside Co.

CLAYSON, MANN & YAEGER, A PROFESSIONAL LAW CORPORATION (AV)

Clayson Law Building, 601 South Main Street, P.O. Box 1447, 91718-1447
Telephone: 909-737-1910
Riverside: 909-689-7241
Fax: 909-737-4384

Walter S. Clayson (1887-1972)   Gary K. Rosenzweig
E. Spurgeon Rothrock   Elisabeth Sichel
   (1918-1979)   Kent A. Hansen
Roy H. Mann   Roland C. Bainer
Derrill E. Yaeger   David R. Saunders

Sallie Barnett

Scott Carleton Brenner

Counsel for: Citizens Business Bank; Lee Lake Municipal Water District; Palo Verde Irrigation District; Loma Linda University.
Local Counsel: Minnesota Mining & Manufacturing Co.; Western Waste Industries.

For full biographical listings, see the Martindale-Hubbell Law Directory

COSTA MESA, Orange Co.

COULOMBE & KOTTKE, A PROFESSIONAL CORPORATION (AV)

Comerica Bank Tower, 611 Anton Boulevard, Suite 1260, 92626
Telephone: 714-540-1234
Fax: 714-754-0808; 714-754-0707
Email: c-k@coulombe.com

Ronald B. Coulombe   Jon S. Kottke

COUNSEL

Roy B. Woolsey

LEGAL SUPPORT PERSONNEL

PARALEGALS

Vicky M. Pearson   Abeer F. Rider

LEGAL ADMINISTRATOR

Yvonne Mendoza

For full biographical listings, see the Martindale-Hubbell Law Directory

McCAULEY & ASSOCIATES, LLP (AV)

611 Anton Boulevard, Suite 1260, 92626
Telephone: 714-438-9108
Fax: 714-957-3718

MEMBER OF FIRM

John J. McCauley

Mark S. Flynn

For full biographical listings, see the Martindale-Hubbell Law Directory

RUTAN & TUCKER, LLP (AV)

A Partnership including Professional Corporations
611 Anton Boulevard, Suite 1400, P.O. Box 1950, 92626
Telephone: 714-641-5100; 213-625-7586
Telecopier: 714-546-9035
Email: rutan&tucker@mcimail.com *URL:* http://www.rutan.com

MEMBERS OF FIRM

Edward D. Sybesma, Jr., (P.C.)   Thomas G. Brockington
Joseph D. Carruth   Evridiki (Vicki) Dallas
Marcia A. Forsyth   Thomas J. Crane
Steven A. Nichols   Kim D. Thompson

ASSOCIATES

Debra Dunn Steel   Kraig C. Kilger
David H. Hochner   Scott R. Santagata
James S. Weisz   Steven John Goon

Sue Lee Collins

For Complete List of Firm Personnel, See General Section

For full biographical listings, see the Martindale-Hubbell Law Directory

EL CENTRO,* Imperial Co.

SUTHERLAND & GERBER, A PROFESSIONAL CORPORATION (AV)

Suite 7 The Imperial Building, 300 South Imperial Avenue, 92243
Telephone: 619-353-4444
Telefax: 619-352-2533

Lowell F. Sutherland   Neil Gerber
Ravinder Samra

For full biographical listings, see the Martindale-Hubbell Law Directory

ENCINO, Los Angeles Co.

ALPERT, BARR AND GROSS, A PROFESSIONAL LAW CORPORATION (AV)

Encino Office Park I, Suite 300, 6345 Balboa Boulevard, 91316-1523
Telephone: 818-881-5000
Fax: 818-881-1150

Lee Kanon Alpert   Mark S. Blackman
Gary L. Barr   Michael N. Balikian
Lisa W. Glazener   Judith R. Simon
Mark P. Gross   Jack S. Mack

OF COUNSEL

Charles M. Hughes   Leonard S. Levy (A Professional
                                  Corporation)

For full biographical listings, see the Martindale-Hubbell Law Directory

FRESNO,* Fresno Co.

DOWLING, AARON & KEELER, INCORPORATED (AV)

Suite 200, 6051 North Fresno Street, 93710
Telephone: 209-432-4500
Fax: 209-432-4590
Email: dowling-law.com

Michael D. Dowling   Philip David Kopp
Richard M. Aaron   Christopher A. Brown

Reference: Wells Fargo Bank (Main).

For Complete List of Firm Personnel, See General Section

For full biographical listings, see the Martindale-Hubbell Law Directory

JORY, PETERSON, WATKINS & SMITH (AV)

555 West Shaw, Suite C-1, P.O. Box 5394, 93755
Telephone: 209-225-6700
Telecopier: 209-225-3416

MEMBERS OF FIRM

Jay V. Jory   Michael Jens F. Smith
John E. Peterson   Marcia A. Ross
Cal B. Watkins, Jr.   William M. Woolman

ASSOCIATES

John J. Stander   Carla M. McCormack
Jeff W. Reisig   Matthew D. Ruyak

Reference: Valliwide Bank.

For full biographical listings, see the Martindale-Hubbell Law Directory

KIMBLE, MACMICHAEL & UPTON, A PROFESSIONAL CORPORATION (AV)

Fig Garden Financial Center, 5260 North Palm Avenue, Suite 221, P.O.
Box 9489, 93792-9489
Telephone: 209-435-5500
Telecopier: 209-435-1500
Email: kmu@primenet.com

Joseph C. Kimble (1910-1972)   Robert H. Scribner
Thomas A. MacMichael   Michael E. Moss
   (1920-1990)   Mark D. Miller
Jon Wallace Upton   Michael F. Tatham
Robert E. Bergin   W. Richard Lee
Jeffrey G. Boswell   D. Tyler Tharpe
Steven D. McGee   Sylvia Halkousis Coyle
Robert E. Ward   S. Brett Sutton
John P. Eleazarian   Michael J. Jurkovich

Douglas V. Thornton   Susan King Hatmaker
Robert William Branch   Lawrence J. Salisbury
Donald J. Pool   Daniel R. Foster
            Meredith E. Allen
            OF COUNSEL
            Mary Ann Bluhm

For full biographical listings, see the Martindale-Hubbell Law Directory

PARICHAN, RENBERG, CROSSMAN & HARVEY, LAW CORPORATION (AV)

Suite 130, 2350 West Shaw Avenue, P.O. Box 9950, 93794-0950
Telephone: 209-431-6300
Fax: 209-432-1018

Harold A. Parichan   Stephen T. Knudsen
Charles L. Renberg   Larry C. Gollmer
Richard C. Crossman   Robert G. Eliason
Ima Jean Harvey   Steven M. McQuillan

Deborah A. Coe   Karen L. Lynch
Maureen P. Holford   Michael L. Renberg

Reference: Bank of America, Commercial Banking Office, Fresno, California.

For full biographical listings, see the Martindale-Hubbell Law Directory

GLENDALE, Los Angeles Co.

BRIGHT AND BROWN (AV)

550 North Brand Boulevard, Suite 2100, 91203
Telephone: 818-243-2121; 213-489-1414
Facsimile: 818-243-3225

James S. Bright   Maureen J. Bright
Gregory C. Brown   John Quirk
            Brian L. Becker
            ASSOCIATES
Anthony S. Brill   Doris A. Mendenhall

For full biographical listings, see the Martindale-Hubbell Law Directory

GILL AND BALDWIN (AV)

130 North Brand Boulevard Fourth Floor, 91203
Telephone: 818-500-7755; 213-245-3131
Fax: 818-242-4305

MEMBERS OF FIRM

Samuel S. Gill (1912-1965)   Joseph C. Malpasuto
John M. Carmack   Kirk S. MacDonald

OF COUNSEL

Ernest R. Baldwin

Representative Clients: Kasler Corp.; Bireley Foundation.
Reference: American West Bank.

For full biographical listings, see the Martindale-Hubbell Law Directory

GREENWALD, HOFFMAN & MEYER (AV)

500 North Brand Boulevard, Suite 920, 91203-1904
Telephone: 818-507-8100; 213-381-1131
Fax: 818-507-8484

MEMBERS OF FIRM

Guy Preston Greenwald, Jr.   Donald M. Hoffman
   (1914-1984)   Lawrence F. Meyer
            Raul M. Montes
            ASSOCIATE
        Jeanne Burns-Haindel

References: Bank of America (Los Angeles and Pasadena Trust Offices); Northern Trust of California (Headquarters Office); Bank of America (Glendale Main Branch).

For full biographical listings, see the Martindale-Hubbell Law Directory

IRSFELD, IRSFELD & YOUNGER LLP (AV)

A Partnership including Professional Corporations
Suite 900, 100 West Broadway, 91210-1296
Telephone: 818-242-6859
Fax: 818-240-7728
Email: 104736.1745@compuserver.com

MEMBERS OF FIRM

James B. Irsfeld (1880-1966)   Peter J. Irsfeld (P.C.)
Kenneth C. Younger   James J. Waldorf (P.C.)
   (1922-1996)   C. Phillip Jackson (P.C.)
John H. Brink (P.C.)   Norman H. Green (P.C.)
         Kathryn E. Van Houten
            ASSOCIATES
Peter C. Wright   Diane L. Walker
            RETIRED
         James B. Irsfeld, Jr.

Representative Clients: Lear Sieglar, Inc.; Chrysler Credit Corp.
References: First Interstate Bank (Glendale Main Office); Bank of Hollywood.

For full biographical listings, see the Martindale-Hubbell Law Directory

Glendale—Continued

O'ROURKE, ALLAN & FONG (AV)

3rd Floor, 104 North Belmont, P.O. Box 10220, 91209-3220
Telephone: 818-247-4303
Fax: 818-247-1451

MEMBERS OF FIRM

Denis M. O'Rourke   Joan H. Allan
Roderick D. Fong

ASSOCIATE

Denise Michelle O'Rourke

References: Verdugo Banking Co. (Glendale, California); Community Bank (Glendale, California).

For full biographical listings, see the Martindale-Hubbell Law Directory

---

HERMOSA BEACH, Los Angeles Co.

NASH & EDGERTON (AV)

A Limited Liability Partnership
2615 Pacific Coast Highway, Suite 322, 90254
Telephone: 310-937-2066
Fax: 310-937-2063
Torrance, California Office: 3625 Del Amo Boulevard, suite 360.
Telephone: 310-370-8272.
Fax: 310-214-9677.

Savery L. Nash   Shelley Nash
Samuel Y. Edgerton, III   David Maurer
Damon Rubin

For full biographical listings, see the Martindale-Hubbell Law Directory

---

IRVINE, Orange Co.

CALLAHAN & BLAINE, A PROFESSIONAL LAW CORPORATION (AV)

Suite 800, 18500 Von Karman, 92612
Telephone: 714-553-1155
Fax: 714-553-0784
Email: info@callahan-law.com

Daniel J. Callahan (A   Stephen E. Blaine
Professional Corporation)

Kathleen L. Dunham   Andrew A. Smits
Jim P. Mahacek   Gary S. Spitzer
Michael J. Sachs   Edward Susolik
Graig R. Woodburn

OF COUNSEL

Shelley M. Liberto   Walt D. Mahaffa

For full biographical listings, see the Martindale-Hubbell Law Directory

---

CONNOR, CULVER, BLAKE & GRIFFIN LLP (AV)

2600 Michelson Drive, Suite 1450, 92612
Telephone: 714-622-2600
Fax: 714-622-2626

Edmond M. Connor   Laura Lee Blake
Marilyn Martin Culver   Craig L. Griffin

Roma R. Hanlon   David J. Hasseltime

For full biographical listings, see the Martindale-Hubbell Law Directory

---

GAUNTLETT & ASSOCIATES (AV)

18400 Von Karman, Suite 300, 92612
Telephone: 714-553-1010
Fax: 714-553-2050
Email: ugauntlett@aol.com

David A. Gauntlett

David A. Stall   Elizabeth A. Gillis
Leo E. Lundberg, Jr.   (Not admitted in CA)
Michael Danton Richardson   Mark H. Plager
William P. Warden   (Not admitted in CA)
Stanley H. Shure   Jeffrey S. Allison

OF COUNSEL

Gary L. Hinman   Jose Zorrilla, Jr.

For full biographical listings, see the Martindale-Hubbell Law Directory

---

GRECO, MOLLIS & O'HARA, A PROFESSIONAL CORPORATION (AV)

18400 Von Karman, Suite 500, 92612-1514
Telephone: 714-263-0600
Fax: 714-263-1513

(See Next Column)

Thomas A. Greco   Kevin O'Hara
Ronald A. Mollis   Charles A. Mollis

For full biographical listings, see the Martindale-Hubbell Law Directory

---

JACKSON, DEMARCO & PECKENPAUGH, A LAW CORPORATION (AV)

4 Park Plaza, 16th Floor, P.O. Box 19704, 92714
Telephone: 714-752-8585
Fax: 714-752-0597

Lance A. Adair   Roger A. Grad
Marc D. Alexander   William Michael Hensley
Thomas D. Arnold   Darren L. Hereford
Diane P. Carey   Joan M. Huckabone
Brian W. Casserly   F. Scott Jackson
John W. Cochrane   Andrew V. Leitch
John C. Condas   Thomas D. Peckenpaugh
James R. DeMarco   John Petrasich
Steven J. Dzida   Andrew C. Schutz
Roger M. Franks   David C. Smith
Helene Z. Fransz   Douglas P. Smith
Edward A. Galloway   Jay R. Steinman
Michael L. Tidus

LEGAL SUPPORT PERSONNEL

Lavon DeGraw

For full biographical listings, see the Martindale-Hubbell Law Directory

---

TIMOTHY L. JOENS & ASSOCIATES A PROFESSIONAL CORPORATION (AV)

Jamboree Center, Five Park Plaza, Suite 1480, 92714
Telephone: 714-553-1950
Fax: 714-553-8835

Timothy L. Joens

Representative Clients: Century 21 of the Pacific, Inc.; Century 21 Region V, Inc.; Century 21 Real Estate Corp.

For full biographical listings, see the Martindale-Hubbell Law Directory

---

JACK L. SCHOELLERMAN (AV)

2030 Main Street, Suite 1600, 92614
Telephone: 714-660-7000
Fax: 714-660-6096

For full biographical listings, see the Martindale-Hubbell Law Directory

---

SUCHMAN, GALFIN & PASSON, LLP (AV)

18101 Von Karman Avenue, Suite 1400, 92612-1043
Telephone: 714-752-2444
Facsimile: 714-833-8256
Email: sgplaw1@aol.com
Santa Ana, California Office: 2122 North Broadway, Suite 100.
Telephone: 714-752-2444.

MEMBERS OF FIRM

Stewart R. Suchman   Michael R. Adams
Ted A. Galfin   William E. Alsnauer, Jr.
Kenneth D. Passon   Marcelle Suzanne Strauss
Lorraine Kay Smyth   Adam M. Greely

For full biographical listings, see the Martindale-Hubbell Law Directory

---

LAGUNA BEACH, Orange Co.

ROBERT S. LEWIN A LAW CORPORATION (AV)

105 Crescent Bay Drive, Suite F, 92651
Telephone: 714-497-8897
FAX: 714-497-1714

Robert S. Lewin

LEGAL SUPPORT PERSONNEL

Diane E. Fedden

For full biographical listings, see the Martindale-Hubbell Law Directory

---

LAGUNA NIGUEL, Orange Co.

ASHWORTH & MORAN (AV)

28202 Cabot Road, Suite 300, 92677-1249
Telephone: 714-365-5776
Fax: 714-365-5720
Newport Beach, California Office: 18 Corporate Plaza, Suite 114.
Telephone: 714-720-1477.
Fax: 714-720-1478.

Bernard L. Moran   Eric K. Billings

For full biographical listings, see the Martindale-Hubbell Law Directory

LARKSPUR, Marin Co.

WEINBERG, HOFFMAN & CASEY (AV)

A Partnership including a Professional Corporation
900 Larkspur Landing Circle, Suite 155, 94939
Telephone: 415-461-9666
Fax: 415-461-9681

Ivan Weinberg   Joseph Hoffman
A. Michael Casey
OF COUNSEL
Mark Ropers

For full biographical listings, see the Martindale-Hubbell Law Directory

---

LONG BEACH, Los Angeles Co.

RUSSELL & MIRKOVICH (AV)

One World Trade Center, Suite 1450, 90831-1450
Telephone: 310-436-9911
FAX: 310-436-1897

Carlton E. Russell   Joseph N. Mirkovich

For full biographical listings, see the Martindale-Hubbell Law Directory

---

LOS ALTOS, Santa Clara Co.

MALOVOS & KONEVICH (AV)

Los Altos Plaza, 5150 El Camino Real, Suite A-22, 94022
Telephone: 415-988-9700
Facsimile: 415-988-9639

Marian Malovos Konevich   Robert W. Konevich
RETIRED FOUNDING PARTNER
Kenneth R. Malovos

For full biographical listings, see the Martindale-Hubbell Law Directory

---

*LOS ANGELES,** Los Angeles Co.

ANGEL AND NEISTAT, A PROFESSIONAL CORPORATION (AV)

28th Floor 555 South Flower Street, 90017-2205
Telephone: 213-689-4500
Fax: 213-689-4651

Michael A. Angel   Steven A. Schwaber
Douglas M. Neistat   Alan J. Stomel
Alan Holmberg   Gary R. Wallace
Steven L. Crane   Daniel H. Reiss

For full biographical listings, see the Martindale-Hubbell Law Directory

BACON & MILLS, LLP (AV)

800 Wilshire Boulevard, Suite 950, 90017
Telephone: 213-486-6500
Fax: 213-486-6552
West Covina, California Office: 100 North Barranca Street, 11th Floor.
Telephone: 818-915-6555.
Fax: 818-915-8855.

Robert Parker Mills   James W. Colfer
Robert L. Bacon   Carl Andrew Botterud
Theodore E. Bacon (Resident at   Adam J. Gerard
   West Covina Office)   Howard S. Hou

For full biographical listings, see the Martindale-Hubbell Law Directory

BARTON, KLUGMAN & OETTING (AV)

A Partnership including Professional Corporations
37th Floor, 333 South Grand Avenue, 90071-1599
Telephone: 213-621-4000
Telecopier: 213-625-1832
Newport Beach Office: Suite 700, 4400 MacArthur Boulevard, P.O. Box 2350, 92660.
Telephone: 714-752-7551.
Telecopier: 714-752-0288.

COUNSEL TO FIRM
Robert M. Barton *   Robert H. Klugman *
Richard F. Oetting *
MEMBERS OF FIRM
David F. Morgan *   David J. Cartano *
William D. Herz *   Martin J. Spear
Charles J. Schufreider *   Tod V. Beebe *
Robert Louis Fisher *   Ronald R. St. John
Gilbert D. Jensen *   Mark A. Newton *
Margot I. McLeay

(See Next Column)

ASSOCIATES
Barbara W. G. Crowley   Reiko L. Furuta
Jaleen Nelson

References: The Bank of California (Southern California Headquarters); Wells Fargo Bank, N.A. (Wells Fargo Center, Los Angeles).
*Denotes a lawyer whose Professional Corporation is a member of the partnership or is Counsel to the Firm

For full biographical listings, see the Martindale-Hubbell Law Directory

BECK, DE CORSO, DALY, BARRERA & OH, A PROFESSIONAL LAW CORPORATION (AV)

601 West Fifth Street, 12th Floor, 90071-2025
Telephone: 213-688-1198
Fax: 213-489-7532
Email: beckdecorso@earthlink.net *URL:*
http://www.earthlink.net/~beckdecorso

Mark E. Beck   Bryan D. Daly
Anthony A. De Corso   Teresa R. Barrera
Angela E. Oh

Peter J. Diedrich   Joan M. Steinmann
Evan Scheffel
OF COUNSEL
Godfrey Isaac

For full biographical listings, see the Martindale-Hubbell Law Directory

BELIN RAWLINGS & BADAL (AV)

11601 Wilshire Boulevard, Suite 2200, 90025-1758
Telephone: 310-575-5300
Fax: 310-445-0884

MEMBERS OF FIRM
Daniel N. Belin   Robert G. Badal
Douglas M. Rawlings   Paul N. Sorrell
Burton Falk
ASSOCIATES
Stephanie Blackman   John A. Schlaff
OF COUNSEL
Martin S. Schwartz   James Edward Doroshow

For full biographical listings, see the Martindale-Hubbell Law Directory

BERGMAN & WEDNER, INC. (AV)

Suite 900, 10880 Wilshire Boulevard, 90024
Telephone: 310-470-6110
Fax: Available on Request

Gregory M. Bergman   Robert M. Mason III
Gregory A. Wedner   Kristi Anne Sjoholm-Sierchio
Mark E. Fingerman   Keith A. Robinson
Alan Harvey Mittelman   John P. Dacey

John V. Tamborelli   Lisa S. Shukiar
Blithe Ann Smith   Daphne M. Humphreys
Suzanne Z. Shbaro
OF COUNSEL
Lloyd A. Bergman (1923-1994)   Jacob A. Wedner
SPECIAL COUNSEL
Richard V. Godino

For full biographical listings, see the Martindale-Hubbell Law Directory

BLECHER & COLLINS, A PROFESSIONAL CORPORATION (AV)

611 West Sixth Street, 20th Floor, 90017
Telephone: 213-622-4222
Telecopier: 213-622-1656

Maxwell M. Blecher   Ralph C. Hofer
Harold R. Collins, Jr.   William C. Hsu
John E. Andrews   James Robert Noblin
Florence F. Cameron   Donald R. Pepperman
Alicia G. Rosenberg

For full biographical listings, see the Martindale-Hubbell Law Directory

LAW OFFICES OF DAVID B. BLOOM A PROFESSIONAL CORPORATION (AV)

3325 Wilshire Boulevard, Ninth Floor, 90010
Telephone: 213-938-5248; 384-4088
Telecopier: 213-385-2009

David B. Bloom

(See Next Column)

LAW OFFICES OF DAVID B. BLOOM A PROFESSIONAL CORPORATION, *Los Angeles—Continued*

Stephen S. Monroe (A Professional Corporation)	Susan Carole Jay
Raphael A. Rosemblat	Edward Idell
James E. Adler	Sandra Kamenir
Bonni S. Mantovani	Steven Wayne Lazarus
Roy A. Levun	Andrew Edward Briseno
Cherie S. Raidy	Harold C. Klaskin
Jonathan Udell	Shelley M. Gould
	Peter O. Israel

For full biographical listings, see the Martindale-Hubbell Law Directory

CLARK & TREVITHICK, A PROFESSIONAL CORPORATION (AV)

800 Wilshire Boulevard, 12th Floor, 90017
Telephone: 213-629-5700
Telecopier: 213-624-9441
San Francisco, California Office: 456 Montgomery Street, 20th Floor.
Telephone: 415-288-6520.
Fax: 415-398-2820.

Donald P. Clark	Dean I. Friedman
Alexander C. McGilvray, Jr.	Michael K. Wofford
Kevin P. Fiore	Brent A. Reinke
James S. Arico	

References: Wells Fargo Bank (Los Angeles Main Office); National Bank of California.

For Complete List of Firm Personnel, See General Section

For full biographical listings, see the Martindale-Hubbell Law Directory

CORINBLIT & SELTZER, A PROFESSIONAL CORPORATION (AV)

Suite 820 Wilshire Park Place, 3700 Wilshire Boulevard, 90010-3085
Telephone: 213-380-4200
Telecopier: 213-385-7503; 385-4560
Email: mseltzer@AOL.com

Marc M. Seltzer	Christina A. Snyder
OF COUNSEL	
Jack Corinblit, A Law Corporation	Earl P. Willens
Gretchen M. Nelson	George A. Shohet
Moses Garcia	

For full biographical listings, see the Martindale-Hubbell Law Directory

PAUL N. CRANE (AV)

Suite 900, Two Century Plaza, 2049 Century Park East, 90067-3111
Telephone: 310-282-8118
FAX: 310-282-8077

For full biographical listings, see the Martindale-Hubbell Law Directory

DARLING, HALL & RAE (AV)

777 South Figueroa, 37th Floor, 90017
Telephone: 213-627-8104
Fax: 213-627-7795
Email: 71555.1466@Compuserve.com

MEMBERS OF FIRM

Hugh W. Darling (1901-1986)	Donald Keith Hall (1918-1984)
Edward S. Shattuck (1901-1965)	Matthew S. Rae, Jr.
George Gaylord Gute (1922-1981)	Richard L. Stack
	Edwin Freston
OF COUNSEL	
John L. Flowers	

Reference: City National Bank (Pershing Square Office, Los Angeles, California).

For full biographical listings, see the Martindale-Hubbell Law Directory

DAVIS & FOX (AV)

1901 Avenue of the Stars, Suite 400, 90067
Telephone: 310-286-2915
Fax: 310-286-2916

MEMBERS OF FIRM

Calvin E. Davis	Steven A. Fox
ASSOCIATES	
Brian Aronson	Amy L. Freisleben
Susan R. Peck	
OF COUNSEL	
Herbert D. Meyers	

For full biographical listings, see the Martindale-Hubbell Law Directory

DEMETRIOU, DEL GUERCIO, SPRINGER & MOYER, LLP (AV)

801 South Grand Avenue, 10th Floor, 90017
Telephone: 213-624-8407
Telecopy: 213-624-0174
Email: ddsm@juno.com *URL:* http://www.ddsm.com

MEMBERS OF FIRM

Angela Shanahan	Stephen A. Del Guercio
Laurie E. Davis	
OF COUNSEL	
Ronald J. Del Guercio	

Reference: Bank of America, L.A. Main Office, Los Angeles, Calif.

For full biographical listings, see the Martindale-Hubbell Law Directory

HOLLEY & GALEN (AV)

800 South Figueroa, Suite 1100, 90017
Telephone: 213-629-1880
Fax: 213-895-0363

MEMBERS OF FIRM

Clyde E. Holley (1891-1980)	W. Michael Johnson
Albert J. Galen (Retired)	A. Steven Brown
ASSOCIATES	
Debra Burchard Coffeen	Charles A. Jordan

For full biographical listings, see the Martindale-Hubbell Law Directory

HORNBERGER & CRISWELL (AV)

444 South Flower, 31st Floor, 90071
Telephone: 213-488-1655
Facsimile: 213-488-1255
Email: kbranch0@counsel.com

MEMBERS OF FIRM

Nicholas W. Hornberger	Ann M. Ghazarians
Leslie E. Criswell	Michael A. Brewer
Scott Alan Freedman	
ASSOCIATES	
Marlin E. Howes	James M. Slominski
Christopher T. Olsen	Michael C. Denlinger
Scott B. Cloud	Gayle L. Eskridge
OF COUNSEL	
David E. Bower	William P. Driscoll

For full biographical listings, see the Martindale-Hubbell Law Directory

IVERSON, YOAKUM, PAPIANO & HATCH (AV)

One Wilshire Building, 27th Floor 624 South Grand Avenue, 90017
Telephone: 213-624-7444
Telecopier: 213 629-4563

Paul E. Iverson (1907-1975)	Frank B. Yoakum, Jr. (1906-1991)

MEMBERS OF FIRM

Neil Papiano	Patrick M. Mc Adam
Dennis A. Page	Arnold D. Larson
John M. Garrick	
ASSOCIATES	
Douglas C. Pease	Barbara Lee Berkowitz
Andrew K. Doty	Mark Pearson
Melissa A. Immel	Frederick Brevard Hayes
Mary P. Lightfoot	Gioia M. Fasi
Denise Renee Byrnes	
OF COUNSEL	
R. Noel Hatch	

Representative Clients: Lockheed Corp.; International Paper; Bridgestone/-Firestone, Inc.
Reference: Security Pacific National Bank (Los Angeles Head Office).

For full biographical listings, see the Martindale-Hubbell Law Directory

JOHNSON, POULSON, COONS & SLATER (AV)

10880 Wilshire Boulevard, Suite 1800, 90024
Telephone: 310-475-0611
Telecopier: 310-475-0143

MEMBERS OF FIRM

Jonathan E. Johnson	Lynn O. Poulson (Mr.)
Michael H. Coons	
OF COUNSEL	
Martin R. Slater	

For full biographical listings, see the Martindale-Hubbell Law Directory

Los Angeles—Continued

LANCE JON KIMMEL (AV)

Suite 1400, 10940 Wilshire Boulevard, 90024
Telephone: 310-208-0775
Telecopier: 310-208-8582
(Also Of Counsel to Goodson and Wachtel, A Professional Corporation)
Reference: Bank of America.

For full biographical listings, see the Martindale-Hubbell Law Directory

KU, FONG, LARSEN & CHEN, LLP (AV)

523 West Sixth Street, Suite 528, 90014
Telephone: 213-488-1400
Telecopier: 213-236-9235

MEMBERS OF FIRM

H. G. Robert Fong   Paul A. Larsen
          Frank W. Chen
          OF COUNSEL
          Edward Y. Ku
          ASSOCIATES

Jack S. Yeh   Victor S. Sze

For full biographical listings, see the Martindale-Hubbell Law Directory

LEVINE & ASSOCIATES (AV)

Suite 710, 2049 Century Park East, 90067
Telephone: 310-553-8400
Fax: 310-553-8455
Seattle, Washington Office: 999 Third Avenue, Suite 3210, 98104.
Telephone: 206-626-5310.
Fax: 206-626-5313.

Jerome L. Levine
ASSOCIATES

Mary L. Prevost (Resident,   Erin M. Copeland
Seattle, Washington Office)   Frank R. Lawrence
          OF COUNSEL
          Allan Albala

For full biographical listings, see the Martindale-Hubbell Law Directory

MATTHIAS & BERG LLP (AV)

Seventh Floor, 515 South Flower Street, 90071
Telephone: 213-895-4200
Telecopier: 213-895-4058

Michael R. Matthias   Stuart R. Singer
Jeffrey P. Berg   Kenneth M. H. Hoff
          Michael D. Berger

Representative Clients: Synagro Technologies, Inc.; Mexalit, S.A.; Maxitile, Inc.; Allstar Inns; Chatsworth Products, Inc.; International Meta Systems, Inc.; Residential Resources, Inc.; AVIC Group International, Inc.; AutoBitter Group, Inc. National Quality Care, Inc.; Greater China Corp.; HBO Ole.
Reference: First Professional Bank.

For full biographical listings, see the Martindale-Hubbell Law Directory

MINTON, MINTON AND RAND LLP (AV)

510 West Sixth Street, 90014
Telephone: 213-624-9394
Fax: 213-624-9323
MEMBERS OF FIRM

Carl W. Minton (1902-1974)   Carl Minton
          David E. Rand

Reference: Bank of America National Trust & Savings Assn. (Seventh & Flower Office, Los Angeles, Calif.).

For full biographical listings, see the Martindale-Hubbell Law Directory

O'MELVENY & MYERS LLP (AV)

400 South Hope Street, 90071-2899
Telephone: 213-669-6000
Cable Address: "Moms"
Facsimile: 213-669-6407
Email: omminfo@omm.com
Century City, California Office: 1999 Avenue of the Stars, 90067-6035.
Telephone: 310-553-6700.
Facsimile: 310-246-6779.
Newport Beach, California Office: 610 Newport Center Drive, 92660-6429.
Telephone: 714-760-9600.
Cable Address: "Moms".
Facsimile: 714-669-6994.
San Francisco, California Office: Embarcadero Center West Tower, 275 Battery Street, 94111-3305.
Telephone: 415-984-8700.
Facsimile: 415-984-8701.

(See Next Column)

New York, New York Office: Citicorp Center, 153 East 53rd Street, 10022-4611.
Telephone: 212-326-2000.
Facsimile: 212-326-2061.
Washington, D.C. Office: 555 13th Street, N.W., 20004-1109.
Telephone: 202-383-5300.
Cable Address: "Moms".
Facsimile: 202-383-5414.
London, England Office: 10 Finsbury Square, London, EC2A 1LA.
Telephone: 0171-256-8451.
Facsimile: 0171-638-8205.
Tokyo, Japan Office: Sanbancho KB-6 Building, 6 Sanbancho, Chiyoda-ku, Tokyo 102, Japan.
Telephone: 03-3239-2900.
Facsimile: 03-3239-2432.
Hong Kong Office: Suite 1905, Peregrine Tower, Lippo Centre, 89 Queensway, Central, Hong Kong.
Telephone: 852-2523-8266.
Facsimile: 852-2522-1760.
Shanghai, Peoples Republic of China Office: Shanghai International Trade Centre, Suite 2011, 2200 Yan An Road West, Shanghai, 200335, PRC.
Telephone: 86-21-6219-5363.
Facsimile: 86-21-6275-4949.

PARTNER
Frederick B. McLane

For Complete List of Firm Personnel, See General Section

For full biographical listings, see the Martindale-Hubbell Law Directory

REINIS & REINIS (AV)

550 South Hope Street, 20th Floor, 90071
Telephone: 213-624-4246
Facsimile: 213-624-4709

MEMBERS OF FIRM

Mitchell N. Reinis   Richard G. Reinis
          ASSOCIATES

Laura P. Worsinger   Steven M. Harrison
          Gregory N. Weisman
          OF COUNSEL
          L. Douglas Brown

For full biographical listings, see the Martindale-Hubbell Law Directory

RODI, POLLOCK, PETTKER, GALBRAITH & CAHILL, A LAW CORPORATION (AV)

Suite 400 801 South Grand Avenue, 90017
Telephone: 213-895-4900; 680-0823
Telecopiers: 213-895-4921; 895-4922; 895-4750

Karl B. Rodi (1908-1982)   Elizabeth B. Blakely
John D. Cahill   Robert C. Norton
John D. Pettker   John F. Cermak, Jr.
Daniel C. Bond (1942-1977)   Tim G. Ceperley
William R. Christian   Coralie Kupfer
Henry P. Pramov, Jr.   Cris K. O'Neall
Robert A. Yahiro   John S. Cha
          Scott E. Adamson

Sonja A. Inglin   Richard Nessary
Thomas J. Yoo   Mark McCleary
          OF COUNSEL
John P. Pollock   Margaret Rosenthal

For full biographical listings, see the Martindale-Hubbell Law Directory

ROSENFELD & WOLFF, A PROFESSIONAL CORPORATION (AV)

2049 Century Park East, Suite 600, 90067
Telephone: 310-556-1221
Fax: 310-556-0401

Morton M. Rosenfeld   Steven G. Wolff
          Alan D. Aronson

For full biographical listings, see the Martindale-Hubbell Law Directory

RUNQUIST & ASSOCIATES (AV)

10821 Huston Street (North Hollywood), 91601-4613
Telephone: 818-760-8986
Fax: 818-760-8314
Email: RUNQUIST@silicon.net

Lisa A. Runquist

Ingrid P. Mittermaier
OF COUNSEL
J. Diane Parrish

For full biographical listings, see the Martindale-Hubbell Law Directory

Los Angeles—Continued

SHAPIRO, ROSENFELD & CLOSE, A PROFESSIONAL CORPORATION (AV)

Suite 2600, One Century Plaza, 2029 Century Park East, 90067
Telephone: 310-277-1818
Telecopier: 310-201-4776
Email: src__law@ix.netcom.com

Mitchell S. Shapiro	Jonathan J. Panzer
Edward M. Rosenfeld	Cathryn S. Gawne
Richard H. Close	Lisa K. Skaist
Helmut F. Furth	Rhonda H. Mehlman
Rochelle Buchsbaum Spandorf	Marna F. Miller
Douglas L. Carden	Jennifer A. DeMarrais

OF COUNSEL

Alan D. Jacobson　　　　Alan G. Dowling

Barry Kurtz

For full biographical listings, see the Martindale-Hubbell Law Directory

SHIOTANI & INOUYE (AV)

11100 Santa Monica Boulevard, Suite 1820, 90025
Telephone: 310-575-3688
Telecopier: 310-575-4095

MEMBERS OF FIRM

Barney B. Shiotani　　　　Lawrence G. Inouye

ASSOCIATE

Nicole Grattan Pearson

LEGAL SUPPORT PERSONNEL

Gabriela Velasquez (Paralegal)

References: First Los Angeles Bank (Airport Office); Bank of California.

For full biographical listings, see the Martindale-Hubbell Law Directory

RONALD P. SLATES A PROFESSIONAL CORPORATION (AV)

548 South Spring Street, Suite 1012, 90013-2309
Telephone: 213-624-1515; 213-654-1461
Fax: 213-624-7536; 213-654-1463

Ronald P. Slates

G. Michael Jackson

For full biographical listings, see the Martindale-Hubbell Law Directory

LAW OFFICES OF RICHARD C. SPENCER (AV)

One Wilshire Boulevard, Suite 2100, 90017
Telephone: 213-629-7900
Fax: 213-629-7990

For full biographical listings, see the Martindale-Hubbell Law Directory

STEPHENS, BERG & LASATER, A PROFESSIONAL CORPORATION (AV)

1055 West Seventh Street, Twenty-Ninth Floor, 90017
Telephone: 213-629-3111
Telecopy: 213-629-2302; 213-624-4734

Lawrence M. Berg (1947-1995)	Frederick A. Clark
R. Wicks Stephens II	Joel A. Goldman
Richard W. Lasater II	C. Stephen Davis
Mark G. Ancel	Kenneth A. Feinfield
Dudley M. Lang	Jean-Paul Menard
Joseph F. Butler	Michael J. Kaminsky

John A. Dragonette

OF COUNSEL

Louis R. Baker　　　　J. Lane Tilson

For full biographical listings, see the Martindale-Hubbell Law Directory

SULLIVAN LAW CORPORATION (AV)

545 South Figueroa Street, Suite 1216, 90071-1599
Telephone: 213-488-9200
Telecopier: 213-488-9664

Michael R. Sullivan

Douglas G. Carroll

For full biographical listings, see the Martindale-Hubbell Law Directory

LAWRENCE C. TISTAERT (AV)

11766 Wilshire Boulevard, Suite 1580, 90025-6537
Telephone: 310-312-0874
Fax: 310-312-1034
Email: lctist@ix.netcom.com

Representative Clients: Bell Foundry Co.; Brendan Tours; Franklin Telecommunications Corp.; Munro Properties; United States Tour Operators Association.
Reference: Bank of America.

For full biographical listings, see the Martindale-Hubbell Law Directory

WEHNER AND PERLMAN (AV)

A Partnership of Professional Corporations
11100 Santa Monica Boulevard, Suite 800, 90025-3384
Telephone: 310-478-3131
Facsimile: 310-312-0078

MEMBERS OF FIRM

Charles C. Wehner (P.C.)　　　　Rodney M. Perlman (P.C.)

ASSOCIATES

Steven M. Cohen	David Eum
Steven A. Berliner	Stephen T. Hodge

John C. Steele

For full biographical listings, see the Martindale-Hubbell Law Directory

MANHATTAN BEACH, Los Angeles Co.

STEINBERG BARNESS GLASGOW & FOSTER LLP (AV)

1334 Park View Avenue, Suite 100, 90266
Telephone: 310-546-5838
Telecopier: 310-546-5630
Email: SGBF@ix.netcom.com

MEMBERS OF FIRM

Alex Steinberg	Jordan G. Barness
Daniel I. Barness	Paul J. Laurin
Donna Glasgow	Shannon M. Foley
(Not admitted in CA)	Richard L. Weiner
Douglas B. Foster	William R. (Randy) Kirkpatrick

Jeffrey Michael Lee

OF COUNSEL

Roanld D. Harari (Not admitted in CA)

References: Home Bank; Imperial Bank; Citizens Commerical Trust & Savings Bank; Bank of America.

For full biographical listings, see the Martindale-Hubbell Law Directory

MENLO PARK, San Mateo Co.

ENTERPRISE LAW GROUP, INC. (AV)

Menlo Oaks Corporate Center, 4400 Bohannon Drive, Suite 280, 94025-1041
Telephone: 415-462-4700
Facsimile: 415-462-4747
Email: info@enterpriselaw.com

Sherwood M. Sullivan

For full biographical listings, see the Martindale-Hubbell Law Directory

ROBERT E. MILLER, INC. A PROFESSIONAL CORPORATION (AV)

1550 El Camino Real, Suite 220, 94025-4111
Telephone: 415-326-6135
Fax: 415-324-1031
Email: 73532.77@compuserve.com

Robert E. Miller

Representative Clients: Aeroground, Inc.; Hussmann Corp.; International Scientific Products, Inc.; Space Power, Inc.; Tiburon Systems, Inc.; Walt & Company Communications, Inc.; Western Multiplex Corp.; Z-Tech Sales, Inc.

For full biographical listings, see the Martindale-Hubbell Law Directory

MODESTO,* Stanislaus Co.

RICHARD DOUGLAS BREW A PROFESSIONAL LAW CORPORATION (AV)

Suite 350 / Judge Frank C. Damrell Building, 1601 I Street, 95354-1110
Telephone: 209-572-3157
Telefax: 209-572-4641
Email: interleg.com

Richard Douglas Brew

For full biographical listings, see the Martindale-Hubbell Law Directory

MONTEREY, Monterey Co.

THE THOMPSON LAW FIRM (AV)

580 Calle Principal, First Floor, 93940-2818
Telephone: 408-646-1224
Fax: 408-646-1225

Ralph W. Thompson, III

For full biographical listings, see the Martindale-Hubbell Law Directory

MOUNTAIN VIEW, Santa Clara Co.

LUCE & QUILLINAN (AV)

444 Castro Street, Suite 900, 94041-2073
Telephone: 415-969-4000
FAX: 415-969-6953

MEMBERS OF FIRM

James G. Luce	James V. Quillinan
Melissa C. Johnson	

ASSOCIATE

Sally F. Berry

For full biographical listings, see the Martindale-Hubbell Law Directory

*NAPA,** Napa Co.

DICKENSON, PEATMAN & FOGARTY, A PROFESSIONAL LAW CORPORATION (AV)

809 Coombs Street, 94559-2977
Telephone: 707-252-7122
Telecopier: 707-255-6876

C. Richard Lemon	Joseph M. Keebler
David B. Gilbreth	James W. Terry
Stanley D. Blyth	

For Complete List of Firm Personnel, See General Section

For full biographical listings, see the Martindale-Hubbell Law Directory

NEWPORT BEACH, Orange Co.

KRISTIN M. CANO (AV)

One Corporate Plaza, 92660
Telephone: 714-759-1505
FAX: 714-640-9535
Email: KristinCanoLawOffice@internetMCI.com

For full biographical listings, see the Martindale-Hubbell Law Directory

CAPRETZ & RADCLIFFE (AV)

5000 Birch Street, West Tower Suite 2500, 92660-2139
Telephone: 714-724-3000
Fax: 714-757-2635
Email: CRLAWYERS@AOL.CON *URL:* http://www.CAPRETZ.com

James T. Capretz	Richard J. Radcliffe

ASSOCIATE

Peter A. Martin

OF COUNSEL

William B. Lawless (Not admitted in CA)

LEGAL SUPPORT PERSONNEL

Rosanna S. Bertheola

For full biographical listings, see the Martindale-Hubbell Law Directory

DAVIS, PUNELLI, KEATHLEY & WILLARD (AV)

610 Newport Center Drive, Suite 1000, P.O. Box 7920, 92658-7920
Telephone: 714-640-0700
Telecopier: 714-640-0714
San Diego, California Office: 501 West Broadway, Suite 900, 92101.
Telephone: 619-558-2581.

MEMBERS OF FIRM

Robert E. Willard	H. James Keathley
S. Eric Davis	Eric G. Anderson
Frank Punelli, Jr.	Katherine D. Keathley

OF COUNSEL

Lewis K. Uhler

For full biographical listings, see the Martindale-Hubbell Law Directory

EADINGTON, MERHAB & EADINGTON, A PROFESSIONAL CORPORATION (AV)

Suite 600, South Tower, 3501 Jamboree Road, P.O. Box 9408, 92658-9408
Telephone: 714-854-5000
Telecopier: 714-854-5138

(See Next Column)

George Eadington	Marla Merhab Robinson
	Debra L. Klevatt

References: Orange National Bank.

For full biographical listings, see the Martindale-Hubbell Law Directory

THEODORE M. HANKIN (AV)

Suite 900, One Newport Place, 92660
Telephone: 714-752-8840
FAX: 714-851-1732

For full biographical listings, see the Martindale-Hubbell Law Directory

JOHN C. LAUTSCH A PROFESSIONAL CORPORATION (AV)

1200 Quail Street, Suite 140, 92660
Telephone: 714-955-9095
Telefax: 714-955-2978

John C. Lautsch

For full biographical listings, see the Martindale-Hubbell Law Directory

NORTH HOLLYWOOD, Los Angeles Co.

F. BENTLEY MOONEY, JR. A LAW CORPORATION (AV)

4605 Lankershim Boulevard, Suite 718, 91602
Telephone: 818-769-4221
213-877-3902
FAX: 818-769-5002

F. Bentley Mooney, Jr.

For full biographical listings, see the Martindale-Hubbell Law Directory

*OAKLAND,** Alameda Co.

AIKEN, KRAMER & CUMMINGS, INCORPORATED (AV)

Suite 550 Ordway Building, One Kaiser Plaza, 94612
Telephone: 510-834-6800
Fax: 510-834-9017
Email: aikenkrame@aol.com

Benj. R. Aiken (1879-1955)	John A. Harkavy
Bauer E. Kramer (Retired)	Elizabeth M. Engh
Benj. R. Aiken, Jr. (Retired)	Matthew F. Graham
Fred V. Cummings (Retired)	Steven J. Cramer
	Richard A. Sipos

OF COUNSEL

Russell L. Barlow	Bruce G. Herold
	Michael A. Coan

Ellen Suzanne Wyatt	Michael S. Treppa

Reference: Union Bank of California, Oakland, California.

For full biographical listings, see the Martindale-Hubbell Law Directory

GENERAL COUNSEL SERVICES, A PROFESSIONAL LAW CORPORATION (AV)

725 Washington Street, 2nd Floor, 94607
Telephone: 510-891-0620
Fax: 510-836-3331
Email: dhicks@astsoft.com *URL:* http://www.genlaw.com
Beverly Hills, California Office: 9606 Santa Monica Boulevard, Third Floor, 90210.

David Hicks

ASSOCIATE COUNSEL

Daniel E. Behrendt, Esq.

OF COUNSEL

Christopher P. Valle-Riestra, Esq.

For full biographical listings, see the Martindale-Hubbell Law Directory

NEAL & ASSOCIATES (AV)

Montclair Village, 6200 Antioch Street, Suite 202, P.O. Box 13314, 500, 94661-0314
Telephone: 510-339-0233
FAX: 510-339-6672
URL: http://seamless.com/hdn/hdn.html

Howard D. Neal

Frank J. Gilbert	Steven S. Miyake

For full biographical listings, see the Martindale-Hubbell Law Directory

Oakland—Continued

PEZZOLA & REINKE, A PROFESSIONAL CORPORATION (AV)

Suite 1300, Lake Merritt Plaza, 1999 Harrison Street, 94612
Telephone: 510-273-8750
Telecopier: 510-834-7440
San Francisco, California Office: 650 California Street, 32nd Floor, 94111.
Telephone: 415-989-9710.
Menlo Park, California Office: 3000 Sand Hill Road, Building 4, Suite 160, 94025.
Telephone: 415-854-8797.

Stephen P. Pezzola	Bruce D. Whitley
Donald C. Reinke	Bruce P. Johnson
Thomas A. Maier	Gizelle A. Barany
Thomas C. Armstrong	Jeremy E. Wenokur

OF COUNSEL
Robert E. Krebs

LEGAL SUPPORT PERSONNEL

Loretta H. Hintz	Mary A. Fitzpatrick
Gayle F. Detillion	

For full biographical listings, see the Martindale-Hubbell Law Directory

---

PALM DESERT, Riverside Co.

CRISTE, PIPPIN & GOLDS (AV)

Suite 200, 73-550 Alessandro Drive, 92260
Telephone: 619-862-1111
Fax: 619-776-4197
Email: cpgca@aol.com

MEMBERS OF FIRM

Michael A. Criste	Robert L. Pippin
Irwin L. Golds	

ASSOCIATE
Marie A. Bochnewich

For full biographical listings, see the Martindale-Hubbell Law Directory

---

PALM SPRINGS, Riverside Co.

SCHLECHT, SHEVLIN & SHOENBERGER, A LAW CORPORATION (AV)

Suite 100, 801 East Tahquitz Canyon Way, P.O. Box 2744, 92263-2744
Telephone: 619-320-7161
Facsimile: 619-323-1758; 619-325-4623

James M. Schlecht	Jon A. Shoenberger
John C. Shevlin	Daniel T. Johnson

David Darrin	Elizabeth A. Dreier

OF COUNSEL

Donald B. McNelley	Allen O. Perrier (Retired)

Representative Clients: Outdoor Resorts of America; The Escrow Connection; Wells Fargo Bank; Canyon Country Club; Waste Management Co.

For full biographical listings, see the Martindale-Hubbell Law Directory

---

PALO ALTO, Santa Clara Co.

FLICKER & KERIN (AV)

Suite 460, 285 Hamilton, P.O. Box 840, 94302
Telephone: 415-321-0947
Fax: 415-326-9722

MEMBERS OF FIRM

Michael R. Flicker	Anthony J. Kerin, III

ASSOCIATES

Rhesa C. Rubin	Cheri A. Bell

For full biographical listings, see the Martindale-Hubbell Law Directory

---

CHRISTOPHER REAM (AV)

1717 Embarcadero Road, 94303
Telephone: 415-424-0821
Facsimile: 415-857-1288

For full biographical listings, see the Martindale-Hubbell Law Directory

---

KATHRYN S. WUNSCH AND ASSOCIATED COUNSEL (AV)

Law Chambers, 701 Welch Road, Suite 3320, 94304
Telephone: 415-833-1880
Fax: 415-833-1888

For full biographical listings, see the Martindale-Hubbell Law Directory

---

PASADENA, Los Angeles Co.

SANDRA McMAHAN IRWIN (AV)

Penthouse Suite 930, 150 South Los Robles Avenue, 91101-2437
Telephone: 818-577-1065
Telecopier: 818-577-5219

For full biographical listings, see the Martindale-Hubbell Law Directory

---

JAMES M. ORENDORFF (AV)

25 East Union Street, 91103
Telephone: 818-449-8200
FAX: 818-449-8370

For full biographical listings, see the Martindale-Hubbell Law Directory

---

ALAN R. TALT (AV)

Suite 710, 790 East Colorado Boulevard, 91101
Telephone: 818-356-0853
Telecopier: 818-356-0731
Reference: U.S. Trust Company California.

For full biographical listings, see the Martindale-Hubbell Law Directory

---

SACRAMENTO,* Sacramento Co.

DIEPENBROCK, WULFF, PLANT & HANNEGAN, LLP (AV)

Suite 1700, 300 Capitol Mall, P.O. Box 3034, 95812-3034
Telephone: 916-444-3910
Telecopier: 916-446-1696
URL: http://www.dwph.com

MEMBERS OF FIRM

Forrest A. Plant	Suzanne E. Hennessy
James T. Freeman	Donald E. Brodeur
Steven H. Felderstein	Jeffrey W. Curcio
Cary M. Adams	Charles S. Farman
Patricia J. Hartman	Harold J. Marcus

ASSOCIATE
William C. Belanger

Representative Clients: California Public Employees Retirement System; Catholic Healthcare West; Bank of California; Fibreboard Corp.

For full biographical listings, see the Martindale-Hubbell Law Directory

---

HANSEN, BOYD, CULHANE & WATSON (AV)

A Partnership including Professional Corporations
Central City Centre, 1331 Twenty-First Street, 95814
Telephone: 916-444-2550
Telecopier: 916-444-2358

Hartley T. Hansen (Inc.)	Lawrence R. Watson
Kevin R. Culhane (Inc.)	John J. Rueda
David E. Boyd	James J. Banks
Lorraine M. Pavlovich	

OF COUNSEL
Betsy S. Kimball

Thomas L. Riordan	Pamela B. Hooley
James O. Moses	Roger R. Billings

For full biographical listings, see the Martindale-Hubbell Law Directory

---

HUNTER RICHEY DI BENEDETTO & BREWER, LLP (AV)

A Limited Liability Partnership
Renaissance Tower, 801 K Street, 23rd Floor, 95814-3525
Telephone: 916-491-3000
Facsimile: 916-491-3080
Email: hrdb@hrdb.com *URL:* http://www.hrdb.com

MEMBERS OF FIRM

William S. Hunter	James F. Geary
Win R. Richey	Janet C. Eisenbeis
Florence L. Di Benedetto	Jeffery D. Harris
Roy E. Brewer	Stephen C. Ruehmann
Anne E. Ferguson	Ralph T. Ferguson
Judith J. Citko	Sharon K. Sandeen
Kathryn T. Papalia	

LEGAL SUPPORT PERSONNEL

Lori J. Kelly (Paralegal)	Michele L. Nickell
Deborah M. Romero (Paralegal)	(Legal Assistant)
Linda Jane Hall	Dawn Krein (Legal Assistant)
(Legal Assistant)	Stephanie L. Neumann
Jennifer E. Mueller	(Legal Assistant)
(Legal Assistant)	

For full biographical listings, see the Martindale-Hubbell Law Directory

Sacramento—Continued

LIVINGSTON & MATTESICH, LAW CORPORATION (AV)

1201 K Street, Suite 1100, 95814
Telephone: 916-442-1111
Fax: 916-448-1709
Email: liv-matt@gvn.net

Gene Livingston   Carol Livingston
James M. Mattesich   Rebecca M. Ceniceros

Steven P. Belzer   Trisha M. McAlmond

Reference: Bank of California.

For full biographical listings, see the Martindale-Hubbell Law Directory

SAN DIEGO,* San Diego Co.

BARNHORST, SCHREINER & GOONAN, A PROFESSIONAL CORPORATION (AV)

550 West C Street, Suite 1350, 92101-3532
Telephone: 619-544-0900
Fax: 619-544-0703
Email: BSG@CTS.COM

Howard J. Barnhorst, II   Gregory P. Goonan
Stephen L. Schreiner   Niles Rice Sharif
                  Brian W. DeWitt
                  OF COUNSEL
                  David L. Dick

Representative Clients: Century 21 All Service Realtors; Continental Lawyers Title Co.; Guthy-Renker, Corp.; Heritage Surgical Corp.; Inacom Corp.; James Hardle Industries (USA), Inc.; OASE Pumps, Inc.; Pioneer Liquidating Corp.; Premier Food Services, Inc.; Seaquest, Inc.; USLIFE Corp.

For full biographical listings, see the Martindale-Hubbell Law Directory

CHAPIN, FLEMING & WINET, A PROFESSIONAL CORPORATION (AV)

Library, 501 West Broadway, 15th Floor, 92101
Telephone: 619-232-4261
Telefax: 619-232-4840
Email: cfwlaw@adnc.com *URL:* http://www.sandiego-online.com/cfwlaw
Vista, California Office: 410 South Melrose Drive, Suite 101.
Telephone: 619-758-4261.
Telefax: 619-758-6420.
Los Angeles, California Office: 12121 Wilshire Boulevard, Suite 401.
Telephone: 310-826-0133.
Telefax: 310-207-4236.
Palm Springs, California Office: 225 North El Cielo Road, Suite 470.
Telephone: 619-416-1400.
Telefax: 619-416-1405.

Victor M. Barr, Jr.
Craig H. Bell
  (Resident, Los Angeles Office)
Darryn L. Berner
Kelli Jean Brooks
Michael S. Burke
David H. Bushnell
  (Resident, Los Angeles Office)
Richard D. Carter
  (Resident, Los Angeles Office)
Dean G. Chandler
  (Resident, Vista Office)
Edward D. Chapin
Victoria Chen
George Chuang
  (Resident, Los Angeles Office)
Amber L. Eck
Robert Ehrenreich
  (Resident, Los Angeles Office)
Scott K. Endsley
George E. Fleming
Antonio Gastelum (Not
  admitted in United States)
Shirley A. Gauvin
Katherine M. Green
Terence L. Greene
Gregory Kevin Hansen
Howard L. Hoffenberg
  (Resident, Los Angeles Office)
Patrick M. Howe
Aaron H. Katz
Elizabeth J. Koumas
Traci Lynn Kuchta
Dana Marie Lawson
  (Resident, Los Angeles Office)
Jeffrey J. Leist
  (Resident, Los Angeles Office)
Tonya L. Morgan
  (Resident, Los Angeles Office)
David A. Myers
  (Resident, Los Angeles Office)
Brenda J. Pannell
  (Resident, Los Angeles Office)
Kennett L. Patrick
  (Resident, Vista Office)
Thomas V. Perea
  (Resident, Los Angeles Office)
Roger L. Popeney
Maria C. Roberts
Lawrence W. Shea, II
Douglas J. Simpson
Spencer C. Skeen
  (Resident, Los Angeles Office)
Howard Smith
  (Resident, Los Angeles Office)
Patricia L. Sullivan
Gregory S. Tavill
Frank L. Tobin
Grace I. Wang
  (Resident, Los Angeles Office)
Peter C. Ward
Jeffrey A. Weaver (Resident,
  Palm Springs Office)
Randall L. Winet
  (Resident, Vista Office)

(See Next Column)

OF COUNSEL

George F. Braun   Irwin Waldman (A P.C.)
Arthur D. Rutledge   (Resident, Los Angeles Office)
  (Resident, Los Angeles Office)   James Michael Zimmerman
Jeffrey C. Stodel
  (Resident, Los Angeles Office)

For full biographical listings, see the Martindale-Hubbell Law Directory

DOSTART CLAPP STERRETT & COVENEY, LLP (AV)

4370 La Jolla Village Drive, Suite 970, 92122
Telephone: 619-623-4200
Facsimile: 619-623-4299
Email: (f)(last)@sdlaw.com *URL:* http://www.sdlaw.com
                  PARTNERS
Paul J. Dostart   James K. Sterrett
James F. Clapp   Kenneth G. Coveney
                  ASSOCIATES
Olivia Olsen   Scott Johnson

For full biographical listings, see the Martindale-Hubbell Law Directory

FERRIS & BRITTON, A PROFESSIONAL CORPORATION (AV)

1600 First National Bank Center, 401 West A Street, 92101
Telephone: 619-233-3131
Fax: 619-232-9316

Alfred G. Ferris   Tamara K. Fogg
                  Gary T. Moyer
                  OF COUNSEL
                  William M. Winter

Representative Clients: Agouron Pharmaceuticals, Inc.; Allstate Insurance Co.; Cox Communications, Inc.; Enterprise Rent-a-Car; Exxon; Immuno Pharmaceutics, Inc.; Invitrogen Corporation; Peninsula Bank; Teleport Communications Group; Southwest Airlines.

For Complete List of Firm Personnel, See General Section

For full biographical listings, see the Martindale-Hubbell Law Directory

HOVEY, KIRBY, THORNTON & HAHN, A PROFESSIONAL CORPORATION (AV)

101 West Broadway, Suite 1100, 92101-8297
Telephone: 619-685-4000
Fax: 619-685-4004
Email: 74754.3143@compuserve.com

Gregg B. Hovey   Patrick R. Kitchin
Dean T. Kirby, Jr.   Geraldine A. Valdez

For full biographical listings, see the Martindale-Hubbell Law Directory

HYDE AND WATERS (AV)

401 West "A" Street, Suite 1200, 92101
Telephone: 619-696-6911
Telecopier: 619-696-6919

                  MEMBERS OF FIRM
Laurel Lee Hyde   Timothy Doyle Waters

Representative Clients: Cardio Theatre, Inc.; C.W. Clark, Inc.; Foster Investment Corporation; Home Capital Corporation; Kmart Corporation; Midland Loan Services, L.P.; New World Communications Co.; The Regents of the University of California; San Diego Gas and Electric Company; Standard Process of Southern California.

For full biographical listings, see the Martindale-Hubbell Law Directory

LAW OFFICES OF ROBERT S. KILBORNE IV (AV)

First National Bank Building, 401 West "A' Street, Suite 1850, 92101
Telephone: 619-237-1047
Fax: 619-237-1096

                  ASSOCIATE
                  David Arbogast
                  OF COUNSEL
                  Russell B. Wagner

For full biographical listings, see the Martindale-Hubbell Law Directory

LINDLEY, LAZAR & SCALES, A PROFESSIONAL CORPORATION (AV)

One America Plaza, 600 West Broadway, Suite 1400, 92101-3302
Telephone: 619-234-9181
Fax: 619-234-8475
Email: 104413.1175@compuserve.com

(See Next Column)

LINDLEY, LAZAR & SCALES A PROFESSIONAL CORPORATION, *San Diego—Continued*

Luke R. Corbett	Michael H. Wexler
John M. Seitman	Richard J. Pekin, Jr.
Robert M. McLeod	George C. Lazar
William E. Johns	Raymond L. Heidemann
Stephen F. Treadgold	James Henry Fox
	Kenneth C. Jones

Representative Clients: McGraw-Hill Broadcasting Co.; City Chevrolet; Metro Imports; Shapell Industries, Inc.; Dura Pharmaceuticals; Driscoll, Inc.; Pointe Builders; Morrison Homes, Inc.

For Complete List of Firm Personnel, See General Section

For full biographical listings, see the Martindale-Hubbell Law Directory

---

LUCE, FORWARD, HAMILTON & SCRIPPS LLP (AV)

A Partnership including Professional Corporations
600 West Broadway, Suite 2600, 92101
Telephone: 619-236-1414
Fax: 619-232-8311
URL: http://www.luce.com
La Jolla, California Office: 4275 Executive Square, Suite 800, 92037.
Telephone: 619-535-2639.
Fax: 619-453-2812.
Los Angeles, California Office: 777 South Figueroa, Suite 3600, 90017.
Telephone: 213-892-4992.
Fax: 213-892-7731.
San Francisco, California Office: 100 Bush Street, 20th Floor, 94104.
Telephone: 415-395-7900.
Fax: 415-395-7949.
New York, N.Y. Office: Citicorp Center, 153 East 53rd Street, 26th Floor, 10022.
Telephone: 212-754-1414.
Fax: 212-644-9727.
Chicago, Illinois Office: 180 North La Salle Street, Suite 1125, 60601.
Telephone: 312-641-0580.
Fax: 312-641-0380.

MEMBERS OF FIRM

Robert G. Steiner	Dennis J. Doucette
John W. Brooks	Terrence L. Bingman
Charles A. Bird	Otto E. Sorensen
G. Edward Arledge	Robert H. Roe
Mark L. Mann	Phillip L. Jelsma
John B. McNeece III	Robert G. Copeland
Darryl Steinhause	Cary W. Miller
Richard R. Spirra	Charles A. Danaher
R. William Bowen	Peter K. Hahn

SPECIAL COUNSEL

Richard T. Forsyth

ASSOCIATES

John P. Cooley	Jana Ford-Harder
Michael G. Fraunces	Robert L. Young
Nancy Fuller-Jacobs	Russell A. Gold
James A. Mercer III	William G. Peterson
John T. Brooks	(Not admitted in CA)
Richard C. Turner	Steven J. Davis

For Complete List of Firm Personnel, See General Section

For full biographical listings, see the Martindale-Hubbell Law Directory

---

MULVANEY, KAHAN & BARRY, A PROFESSIONAL CORPORATION (AV)

Seventeenth Floor, First National Bank Center, 401 West "A" Street, 92101-7994
Telephone: 619-238-1010
Fax: 619-238-1981
Email: mkb@mkblaw.com
Los Angeles, California Office: Union Bank Plaza, 445 South Figueroa Street, Suite 2600.
Telephone: 213-612-7765.
La Jolla, California Office: Glendale Federal Building, 7911 Herschel, Suite 300, P.O Box 1885.
Telephone: 619-454-0142.
Fax: 619-454-7858.
Orange, California Office: The Koll Center, 500 North State College Boulevard, Suite 440.
Telephone: 714-634-7069.
Fax: 714-939-8000.

James F. Mulvaney	Julie A. Jones
Lawrence Kahan	Maureen F. Hallahan
Everett G. Barry, Jr.	Mark R. Raftery
Donald G. Johnson, Jr.	Charles F. Bethel
Robert A. Linn	Diane M. Racicot
Maureen E. Markey	John A. Mayers
Paula Rotenberg	Steven W. Pite
Melissa A. Blackburn	

(See Next Column)

Patricia A. Sieveke (Resident, Los Angeles and Orange Offices) — Linda C. Schumacher / John D. Duncan

OF COUNSEL

Rex B. Beatty	Derrick W. Samuelson
Robert K. Edmunds	(Not admitted in CA)
James P. McGowan, Jr.	
(Resident, La Jolla Office)	

Representative Clients: Aoki Construction (CA) Co., Ltd.; ITT Corp.; National Car Rental System, Inc.; Capital Growth Properties; Sentra Securities; Unilab Corp.

For full biographical listings, see the Martindale-Hubbell Law Directory

---

THE LAW OFFICES OF STEPHEN P. OGGEL, A P.C. (AV)

111 Elm Street, Suite 400, 92101
Telephone: 619-696-7500
Fax: 619-232-1065

Stephen P. Oggel

Brian J. McCormack

For full biographical listings, see the Martindale-Hubbell Law Directory

---

PAGE, POLIN & BUSCH, A PROFESSIONAL CORPORATION (AV)

350 West Ash Street, Suite 900, 92101-3436
Telephone: 619-231-1822
Fax: 619-231-1877
Fax: 619-231-1875
Email: pagepolin@pagepolin.com

Michael E. Busch	Richard W. Page
Kathleen A. Cashman-Kramer	Kenneth D. Polin
Richard L. Moskitis	Steven G. Rowles

Rod S. Fiori	Michael G. Rowles
Dorothy A. Johnson	(Not admitted in CA)
Jolene L. Parker	Barry M. Taira

For full biographical listings, see the Martindale-Hubbell Law Directory

---

POST KIRBY NOONAN & SWEAT LLP (AV)

A Partnership including Professional Corporations
America Plaza 600 West Broadway 11th Floor, 92101
Telephone: 619-231-8666
FAX: 619-231-9593;
619-231-4360
Email: PKNS@cert.net

MEMBERS OF FIRM

Gregory A. Post	Stephanie Sontag
Michael L. Kirby (A P.C.)	David B. Oberholtzer
David J. Noonan	Charles T. Hoge
Richard W. Sweat	Natalie C. Venezia
R. Bruce Wayne (A P.C.)	Dickran A. Semerdjian
Thomas W. Bettles	Jeffrey A. Haile
Sandra L. Lackey	James R. Lance
Ross J. Schwartz	Steven W. Sanchez
Lise N. Wilson	Theresa M. Brehl
	Jeffrey P. Lendrum

OF COUNSEL

Paul R. Kennerson

Steven B. Duke	Kristen T. Bruesehoff
Martha O. Anderson	Jonathan A. Boynton
Mary L. Waltari	Ethan T. Boyer
M. E. Stephens	Matthew C. McGrath
Jeffrey A. Unger	Monique Ballard Candor
Kelli A. Hokanson	Jodie M. Hardmeyer
	James R. Ballard

LEGAL SUPPORT PERSONNEL

Laurel E. Scott	Susan O'Keefe Head
Maureen A. McCarthy	(Litigation Paralegal)
Jean D. Billings (Paralegal)	Ruth S. Friis (Paralegal)
Katherine G. Hicks (Paralegal)	Nicole Abrahamson (Paralegal)
	Gail E. Bayley (Paralegal)

For full biographical listings, see the Martindale-Hubbell Law Directory

---

SAN FRANCISCO,* San Francisco Co.

LAW OFFICES OF RAYMOND N. STELLA ERLACH (AV)

4 Embarcadero Center, Seventeenth Floor, 94111
Telephone: 415-788-3322
FAX: 415-788-8613

Raymond N. Erlach

(See Next Column)

LAW OFFICES OF RAYMOND N. STELLA ERLACH—*Continued*

OF COUNSEL

Gregory J. Erlach   Stephen Peter U. Erlach

For full biographical listings, see the Martindale-Hubbell Law Directory

---

FELDMAN, WALDMAN & KLINE, A PROFESSIONAL CORPORATION (AV)

3 Embarcadero Center, Suite 2800, 94111
Telephone: 415-981-1300
Fax: 415-981-1350
Email: info@fwk.com
Stockton, California Office: Sperry Building, 146-148 West Weber Avenue.
Telephone: 209-943-2004.
Fax: 209-943-0905.

Murry J. Waldman	Martha Jeanne Shaver
Leland R. Selna, Jr.	(Resident, Stockton Office)
Michael L. Korbholz	Robert Cedric Goodman
Howard M. Wexler	Laura Grad
Patricia S. Mar	William F. Adams
Kenneth W. Jones	Elizabeth A. Thompson
Paul J. Dion	Julie A. Jones
Vern S. Bothwell	David L. Kanel
L.J. Chris Martiniak	Abram S. Feuerstein
	Linda Sorensen

Laura J. Dawson	Dana A. Suntag
Joanne M. Lafreniere	(Resident, Stockton Office)
Paul A. Weiss	Danielle Ochs-Tillotson

OF COUNSEL

Richard L. Jaeger   Gerald A. Sherwin
                                     (Resident, Stockton Office)

For full biographical listings, see the Martindale-Hubbell Law Directory

---

LAW OFFICES OF KEVIN W. FINCK (AV)

Two Embarcadero Center, Suite 1670, 94111
Telephone: 415-296-9100
Facsimile: 415-394-6446

Michael L. Dobrov

OF COUNSEL

Marla Raucher Osborn

For full biographical listings, see the Martindale-Hubbell Law Directory

---

FLEISCHMANN & FLEISCHMANN, L.L.P. (AV)

650 California Street, Suite 2550, 94108-2606
Telephone: 415-981-0140
FAX: 415-788-6234
Email: ROGFL@CCNET.COM

MEMBERS OF FIRM

Hartly Fleischmann   Roger Justice Fleischmann

For full biographical listings, see the Martindale-Hubbell Law Directory

---

MacINNIS, DONNER & KOPLOWITZ (AV)

Suite 222, 465 California Street, 94104
Telephone: 415-434-2400
FAX: 415-433-1917

MEMBERS OF FIRM

James Martin MacInnis   Conrad Donner
(1914-1979)   Edward A. Koplowitz

For full biographical listings, see the Martindale-Hubbell Law Directory

---

MANWELL & MILTON (AV)

20 California Street, Third Floor, 94111
Telephone: 415-362-2375
Telecopier: 415-362-1010
URL: HTTP://WWW.MM.LAWOFFICES.COM

Edmund R. Manwell   Denise B. Milton

ASSOCIATES

Mari C. Siebold   Ian R. Schwartz
                Katayoon M. Cotto

For full biographical listings, see the Martindale-Hubbell Law Directory

---

STIMMEL, STIMMEL & SMITH, A PROFESSIONAL CORPORATION (AV)

100 Bush Street, Suite 850, 94104
Telephone: 415-392-2018
Fax: 415-392-2018

(See Next Column)

Norman S. Stimmel (1914-1991)   Lee D. Stimmel
        Andrine K. Smith

OF COUNSEL

Linda S. Votaw   Jeffrey S. Rosen

For full biographical listings, see the Martindale-Hubbell Law Directory

---

SAN JOSE, * Santa Clara Co.

THE ALEXANDER LAW FIRM (AV)

55 South Market Street, Suite 1080, 95113
Telephone: 408-289-1776
Fax: 408-287-1776
Email: access@alexanderlaw.com *URL:* http://www.alexanderlaw.com/
Cincinnati, Ohio Office: The Alexander Law Firm, 1300 Mercantile Library Building, 414 Walnut Street.
Telephone: 513-723-1776.
Fax: 513-421-1776.

Richard Alexander

ASSOCIATES

Michael T. Alexander (Resident,	Michael McShane
Cincinnati, Ohio Office)	Amanda Hawes
Jonathan D. Pendleton	Ann Saponara
	Tyler A. Shaw

OF COUNSEL

William M. Audet

For full biographical listings, see the Martindale-Hubbell Law Directory

---

THE BOCCARDO LAW FIRM (AV)

Eleventh Floor, 111 West St. John Street, 95115-0001
Telephone: 408-298-5678
Fax: 408-298-7503

MEMBERS OF FIRM

James F. Boccardo	John C. Stein
John W. McDonald	Richard L. Bowers
Brian N. Lawther	Russell L. Moore, Jr.

ASSOCIATES

Stephen Foster	Victor F. Stefan
David P. Moyles	Robert W. Thayer
Byron C. Foster	Richard Gregg

For full biographical listings, see the Martindale-Hubbell Law Directory

---

CRAIG M. BROWN, INC. (AV)

333 West Santa Clara Street, Suite 618, 95113
Telephone: 408-286-8844
Fax: 408-286-6699
Email: cmbtrialaw@aol.com

Craig M. Brown

For full biographical listings, see the Martindale-Hubbell Law Directory

---

LAW OFFICES OF THOMAS R. HOGAN (AV)

60 South Market Street, Suite 1125, 95113-2332
Telephone: 408-292-7600
Facsimile: 408-292-7611

ASSOCIATE

Kelly W. Bhirdo

PARALEGAL

Leslie Holmes

For full biographical listings, see the Martindale-Hubbell Law Directory

---

MAHL REHON WALWORTH & ROBERTS, A PROFESSIONAL CORPORATION (AV)

Ten Almaden Boulevard, Suite 1440, 95113
Telephone: 408-494-0900
Fax: 408-494-0909

Susan J. Mahl	Janet R. Walworth
Peter M. Rehon	Lisa C. Roberts
	Michael T. Parsons

For full biographical listings, see the Martindale-Hubbell Law Directory

---

MILLER, MORTON, CAILLAT & NEVIS (AV)

50 West San Fernando Street, Suite 1300, 95113-2413
Telephone: 408-292-1765
Telecopier: 408-292-4484

Richard W. Morton (1916-1975)   Charles V. Caillat (1920-1990)
        Harvey C. Miller (1906-1993)

(See Next Column)

MILLER, MORTON, CAILLAT & NEVIS, *San Jose—Continued*

MEMBERS OF FIRM

David L. Nevis
Francis J. Hughes
Peter A. Kline
Stevan C. Adelman
Eric Mogensen
Joseph A. Scanlan, Jr.
Carolyn Tobiason Stuart
William K. Hurley
Peter V. Dessau

OF COUNSEL

Nancy F. Symons
Susan L. Sutton
Pamela J. Silberstein

ASSOCIATES

Kathryn E. Barrett
Katherine S. Pak
David I. Kornbluh
Kimberly Holtz MacMillan

Representative Clients: Trammell Crow Residential Services; Joe Kerley Lincoln Mercury Co.; Milligan News Co.; Joseph George Distributors; The Frozen Food Employees Pension Trust; Santa Clara Dental Society; New West Foods; Bay Apartment Communities; Guy F. Atkinson Company; A. Hathaway Co.

For full biographical listings, see the Martindale-Hubbell Law Directory

THE SKORNIA LAW FIRM (AV)

160 West Santa Clara Street, Suite 1500, 95113
Telephone: 408-280-2820
Fax: 408-280-2801
Email: 4799261@mcimail.com *URL:*
http://www.internet-is.com/skornia/index.html

Thomas A. Skornia

ASSOCIATE

Ronald S. Kramer

LEGAL SUPPORT PERSONNEL

Sharii E. Rey
Paula K. Gray

For full biographical listings, see the Martindale-Hubbell Law Directory

TREPEL & CLARK (AV)

50 West San Fernando Street, 13th Floor, 95113
Telephone: 408-275-0501
Fax: 408-293-3369

Anthony J. Trepel
Daniel Clark

ASSOCIATE

Sandra R. McIntosh

For full biographical listings, see the Martindale-Hubbell Law Directory

SAN LUIS OBISPO,* San Luis Obispo Co.

GEORGE, GALLO & SULLIVAN, A LAW CORPORATION (AV)

694 Santa Rosa, P.O. Box 12710, 93406
Telephone: 805-544-3351
Facsimile: 805-528-5598
Email: jgeorgeggs@aol.com
Los Osos, California Office: 2238 Bayview Heights Drive, P.O. Box 6129.
Telephone: 805-528-3351.
Telecopier: 805-528-5598.

J. K. George
Ray A. Gallo
Shaunna L. Sullivan

Anne C. Cyr
Claire M. Corcoran

Reference: Mid State Bank, Los Osos, California.

For full biographical listings, see the Martindale-Hubbell Law Directory

SAN MATEO, San Mateo Co.

STUBBS & STUBBS (AV)

Borel Estate Building, Suite 505, 1700 South El Camino Real, 94402-3051
Telephone: 415-345-4350
Telecopier: 415-345-6748
Email: stubbs__stubbs@msn.com

MEMBERS OF FIRM

Barry Stubbs
Brian P. Stubbs

Reference: Wells Fargo Bank.

For full biographical listings, see the Martindale-Hubbell Law Directory

SAN RAFAEL,* Marin Co.

McNEIL, SILVEIRA & RICE (AV)

A Partnership including Professional Corporations
55 Professional Center Parkway, Suite A, 94903
Telephone: 415-472-3434
FAX Telecopier: 415-472-1298

(See Next Column)

Patrick J. McNeil (A Professional Corporation)
Ronald A. Silveira (A Professional Corporation)
Mark J. Rice

For full biographical listings, see the Martindale-Hubbell Law Directory

RAGGHIANTI • FREITAS • MONTOBBIO • WALLACE LLP (AV)

874 Fourth Street, Suite D, 94901
Telephone: 415-453-9433
Fax: 415-453-8269

Gary T. Ragghianti
David P. Freitas
J. Mark Montobbio
J. Randolph Wallace
Patrick M. Macias
Robert F. Epstein
John Ralph Thomas

For full biographical listings, see the Martindale-Hubbell Law Directory

SANTA ANA,* Orange Co.

JOHN G. BRADSHAW A PROFESSIONAL LAW CORPORATION (AV)

3 Imperial Promenade, Suite 800, 92707
Telephone: 714-641-1690
Fax: 714-641-1780

John G. Bradshaw

For full biographical listings, see the Martindale-Hubbell Law Directory

FERRUZZO & FERRUZZO (AV)

A Partnership of Professional Corporations
2114 North Broadway, 92706
Telephone: 714-834-9322
Telecopier: 714-834-9358

MEMBERS OF FIRM

Thomas G. Ferruzzo (A Professional Corporation)
James J. Ferruzzo (A Professional Corporation)
James K. Leese (A Professional Corporation)

ASSOCIATES

John R. Pelle
Dirk E. Petchul
Gregory J. Ferruzzo
Maria Ann Newkirk
Paul A. Madruga
Lisa L. Schultz

OF COUNSEL

M. Susan Watson

For full biographical listings, see the Martindale-Hubbell Law Directory

JEFFREY R. MATSEN & ASSOCIATES (AV)

3 Imperial Promenade, Suite 445, 92707-5908
Telephone: 714-433-7850
Telecopier: 719-433-7815

Arlin P. Neser

For full biographical listings, see the Martindale-Hubbell Law Directory

SANTA BARBARA,* Santa Barbara Co.

SEED, MACKALL & COLE LLP (AV)

1332 Anacapa Street, Suite 200, 93101
Telephone: 805-963-0669
Fax: 805-962-1404

MEMBERS OF FIRM

John R. Mackall
Joseph L. Cole
Gregory Canova-Parker
Thomas N. Harding
Peter A. Umoff
Barton E. Clemens, Jr.
Christopher E. Hahn
Sandra Hitchens Thoits
David E. Reese
K. Andrew Kent
Alan D. Condren
Nicholas J. Schneider

Representative Clients: City Commerce Bank; Montecito Bank & Trust; Santa Barbara Bank & Trust; Digital Instruments, Inc.; G & H Technology Inc.; Mission Research Corporation; Bermant Development Company; The Investec Real Estate Companies; STAR Telecommunications, Inc.; TELNET Communications Group.

For full biographical listings, see the Martindale-Hubbell Law Directory

SANTA MONICA, Los Angeles Co.

LAW OFFICES OF GARY FREEDMAN (AV)

725 Arizona Avenue, Suite 100, 90401
Telephone: 310-576-2444
Telecopier: 310-576-2440

MEMBER OF FIRM

Gary A. Freedman

Emily Bresler

(See Next Column)

LAW OFFICES OF GARY FREEDMAN—*Continued*
OF COUNSEL
Paul H. Samuels

For full biographical listings, see the Martindale-Hubbell Law Directory

GILCHRIST & RUTTER, PROFESSIONAL CORPORATION (AV)

Wilshire Palisades Building, 1299 Ocean Avenue, Suite 900, 90401
Telephone: 310-393-4000
Facsimile: 310-394-4700
Los Angeles, California Office: 355 South Grand Avenue, Suite 4100.
Telephone: 213-617-8000.
Facsimile: 213-346-7973.

Frank Gooch, III	Susan Fowler McNally
Jonathan S. Gross	Thomas E. Stindt
Paul S. Rutter	Donald C. Nanney
James R. Andrews	Diana P. Scott

Michael E. Hagan	Sean T. Prosser

OF COUNSEL

Richard I. Gilchrist	Herbert Katz
Christine A. Page	

For full biographical listings, see the Martindale-Hubbell Law Directory

RICHARD E. HODGE, INC. (AV)

The Water Garden East Tower, Suite 600, 2425 West Olympic
Boulevard, 90404-4043
Telephone: 310-453-5344
Fax: 310-315-0051

Richard E. Hodge	Gary G. Kuist
Jefferson W. Gross	

For full biographical listings, see the Martindale-Hubbell Law Directory

SACKS ZWEIG & BURRIS, LLP (AV)

100 Wilshire Building, Suite 1300, 100 Wilshire Boulevard, 90401
Telephone: 310-451-3113
Facsimile: 310-451-0089
San Francisco, California Office: 100 Pine Street, 21st Floor.
Telephone: 415-788-6794.
Facsimile: 415-788-7009.

MEMBERS

Donald S. Burris	Lee Sacks
Michael K. Zweig	

ASSOCIATES

Les Bradford Hairrell	Filomena E. Meyer

OF COUNSEL

Dennis Holahan	Barton S. Selden

For full biographical listings, see the Martindale-Hubbell Law Directory

GERALD T. YOSHIDA (AV)

100 Wilshire Boulevard, Suite 1000, 90401
Telephone: 310-393-9212
Telecopier: 310-395-2132

Representative Clients: Vido Artukovich & Sons Construction; McKean Construction; Spiess Construction; Gierlich-Mitchell, Inc.; Ullibarri Construction; Hill Crane Service, Inc.; ACI General Engineering Contractors; A.A. Portanova & Sons, Inc.; Rough Terraih, Inc.; Altfillisch Construction.

For full biographical listings, see the Martindale-Hubbell Law Directory

SANTA ROSA,* Sonoma Co.

BELDEN, ABBEY, WEITZENBERG & KELLY, A PROFESSIONAL CORPORATION (AV)

1105 North Dutton Avenue, P.O. Box 1566, 95402
Telephone: 707-542-5050
Telecopier: 707-542-2589

Thomas P. Kelly, Jr.	Richard W. Abbey
Lewis R. Warren	

Representative Clients: Exchange Bank of Santa Rosa; Westamerica Bank; North Bay Title Co.; Northwestern Title Security Co.; Geyser Peak Winery; Santa Rosa City School District; Sonoma National Bank; Arrowood Vineyards & Winery; Arthur & DeVincenzi Concrete; Friedman Bros. Hardware, Inc.

For Complete List of Firm Personnel, See General Section

For full biographical listings, see the Martindale-Hubbell Law Directory

STOCKTON,* San Joaquin Co.

MAYALL, HURLEY, KNUTSEN, SMITH & GREEN, A PROFESSIONAL CORPORATION (AV)

2453 Grand Canal Boulevard, Second Floor, 95207-8253
Telephone: 209-477-3833
Fax: 209-473-4818

Edwin Mayall (1907-1980)	William W. Hale
John J. Hurley (Retired)	Mark Stephen Adams
Clarence D. Knutsen	J. Anthony Abbott
Alan E. Smith	Peter J. Whipple
Dennis J. Green	Kristen M. Hegge
Vladimir F. Kozina	

William L. Anderson	William J. Gorham, III
Donald W. West	Matthew Christopher Felix
Robert E. Laubengayer	Joseph A. Salazar, Jr.
Mark E. Berry	Steven A. Malcoun
Lesley Solomon	

Representative Clients: Allstate Insurance Co.; California State Automobile Assn.; Fireman's Fund Insurance Co.; General Motors Corp.; Texaco, Inc; State Farm Mutual Insurance Cos.; Beck Development, Inc; HD Arnaiz, Ltd; Vito Transporation; The Alpine Group.

For full biographical listings, see the Martindale-Hubbell Law Directory

TORRANCE, Los Angeles Co.

FINER, KIM & STEARNS (AV)

An Association of Professional Corporations
City National Bank Building, 3424 Carson Street, Suite 500, 90503
Telephone: 310-214-1477
Telecopier: 310-214-0764

Harry J. Kim (A Professional Corporation)	Robert David Ciaccio
	Robert B. Parsons
W. A. Finer (A Professional Corporation)	

OF COUNSEL

Bennett A. Rheingold	Ryan E. Stearns

LEGAL SUPPORT PERSONNEL
Marcia E. Talbert

For Complete List of Firm Personnel, See General Section

For full biographical listings, see the Martindale-Hubbell Law Directory

UPLAND, San Bernardino Co.

ALTHOUSE & McDONOUGH (AV)

Second Floor, Metro Commerce Bank Building, 188 North Euclid
Avenue, P.O. Box 698, 91785
Telephone: 909-985-9828
Telecopier: 909-985-3282

Charles S. Althouse	Elizabeth A. McDonough

References: Security Pacific National Bank, Upland Branch; First National Bank & Trust Company, Upland Branch.

For Complete List of Firm Personnel, See General Section

For full biographical listings, see the Martindale-Hubbell Law Directory

VALENCIA, Los Angeles Co.

NAHIN AND NAHIN, LAW CORPORATION (AV)

23929 West Valencia Boulevard, Suite 411, 91355
Telephone: 805-287-3610
Fax: 805-287-3612
Email: nahin@aol.com
Los Angeles, California Office: 6500 Wilshire Boulevard, Suite 550.
Telephone: 213-651-0170.
Telecopier: 213-651-0158.

Bruce A. Nahin

For full biographical listings, see the Martindale-Hubbell Law Directory

VENTURA,* Ventura Co.

LAW OFFICES OF FREDERICK H. BYSSHE, JR. (AV)

10 South California Street, 93001
Telephone: 805-648-3224
Fax: 805-653-0267

Terence Geoghegan

For full biographical listings, see the Martindale-Hubbell Law Directory

Ventura—Continued

FAIRFIELD, STRAUSS, URITZ & KINIGSTEIN, A PROFESSIONAL CORPORATION (AV)

290 Maple Court, Suite 200, 93003
Telephone: 805-644-7458
Fax: 805-644-4325
Email: mail@venturalaw.com *URL:* http://www.venturalaw.com

William D. Fairfield	Curt W. Uritz
Anthony R. Strauss	Terry Kinigstein

Wilfred J. Freeman   Bruce P. Crary

For full biographical listings, see the Martindale-Hubbell Law Directory

VISTA, San Diego Co.

ERNEST L. HUNT, JR. (AV)

630 Alta Vista Drive, Suite 103, P.O. Box 640, 92085-0640
Telephone: 619-726-3839
Fax: 619-726-5491

For full biographical listings, see the Martindale-Hubbell Law Directory

WALNUT CREEK, Contra Costa Co.

JACKL & KATZEN (AV)

2033 North Main Street, Suite 700, 94596
Telephone: 510-932-8500
Fax: 510-932-1961
Email: jklawfirm@aol.com

MEMBERS OF FIRM
V. James Jackl   Linda R. Katzen

Andrew N. Contopoulos

For full biographical listings, see the Martindale-Hubbell Law Directory

CHARLES A. McPHEE, JR. (AV)

1981 North Broadway, Suite 345, 94596
Telephone: 510-975-5990
Fax: 510-975-5999

For full biographical listings, see the Martindale-Hubbell Law Directory

COLORADO

BOULDER, * Boulder Co.

DOTY & SHAPIRO, P.C. (AV)

1720 Fourteenth Street, Suite 100, 80302-6353
Telephone: 303-443-3234
Telecopier: 303-443-3438

H. McGregor Doty, II   Mark R. Shapiro

For full biographical listings, see the Martindale-Hubbell Law Directory

COLORADO SPRINGS, * El Paso Co.

BELTZ, EDWARDS & SABO, L.L.P. (AV)

729 South Cascade, 80903
Telephone: 719-473-4444; 719-634-6620
Fax: 719-444-0186

W. Thomas Beltz   Daniel P. Edwards
John W. Sabo, III

Daniel A. West

Representative Clients: AMI Industries, Inc.; Analytical Surveys, Inc.; A.C. Israel Enterprises, Inc.; Boddington Lumber Co., Inc.; Cardiovascular Surgeons of Colorado Springs, P.C.; Colorado Springs Radiologists, P.C.; Digital, Inc.; Music Semiconductors, Inc.; Schlage Lock Co.; Texas Instruments.

For full biographical listings, see the Martindale-Hubbell Law Directory

DENVER, * Denver Co.

ALEXANDER & CRABTREE, P.C. (AV)

216 16th Street, Suite 1300, 80202-5127
Telephone: 303-825-7307
Fax: 303-825-3202
Email: halexand@alexcrab.com *URL:* http://www.alexcrab.com

Hugh Alexander   C. Scott Crabtree

Stephen Fitzsimmons

For full biographical listings, see the Martindale-Hubbell Law Directory

BRENMAN KEY & BROMBERG, P.C. (AV)

Mellon Financial Center Suite 1001, 1775 Sherman Street, 80203
Telephone: 303-894-0234
Fax: 303-839-1633

Albert Brenman	Donna A. Key
Thomas R. Bromberg	Steven W. McDonald

Theresa M. Mehringer   George D. Kreye
OF COUNSEL
Heather H. S. Sander   A. Thomas Tenenbaum
D. Elizabeth Wills   Edmund L. Epstein (Inactive)

For full biographical listings, see the Martindale-Hubbell Law Directory

BROWNSTEIN HYATT FARBER & STRICKLAND, P.C. (AV)

Twenty-Second Floor, 410 Seventeenth Street, 80202-4437
Telephone: 303-534-6335
Telecopier: 303-623-1956
Washington, D.C. Office: 601 Pennsylvania Avenue, N.W., Suite 900.
Telephone: 202-434-8377.
Telecopier: 202-393-7864.

Norman Brownstein	Michael J. Sternick
Steven W. Farber	Gary M. Reiff
Edward N. Barad	Michael R. McGinnis
John R. Call	Bruce A. James
Steven M. Sommers	Thomas J. Mancuso
Ronald B. Merrill	Jeffrey M. Knetsch
Lynda A. McNeive	Hubert A. Farbes, Jr.
Laura Jean Christman	John R. Garrett
Wayne H. Hykan	Steven S. Siegel

John L. Ruppert
OF COUNSEL
Jack N. Hyatt   Ann B. Riley
Steven C. Demby

Robert Kaufmann	Jill E. Murray
Brent T. Slosky	Gregory W. Berger
Jay F. Kamlet	Howard J. Pollack
Ana Lazo Tenzer	Ellen O. Kauffmann
David M. Brown	Joshua J. Widoff

Lea Ann T. Groesser

Representative Clients: Alfalfa's, Inc.; Boston Chicken, Inc.; Brothers Gourmet Coffees, Inc.; Capital Associates, Inc.; Corporate Express; Donaldson Lufkin & Jenrette Securities Corp.; Kohlberg & Co.; The Prudential Insurance Company of America; Renaissance Cosmetics, Inc.; SunAmerica Inc.

For Complete List of Firm Personnel, See General Section

For full biographical listings, see the Martindale-Hubbell Law Directory

BURNS WALL SMITH AND MUELLER, A PROFESSIONAL CORPORATION (AV)

303 East Seventeenth Avenue Suite 800, 80203-1260
Telephone: 303-830-7000
Telecopier: 303-830-6708
Email: BWSM@MCIMAIL.COM

Peter J. Wall	James E. Bosik
Gregory J. Smith	Steven F. Mueller
George W. Mueller	Robert T. Cosgrove

Gretchen L. Aultman   Donald D. Farlow
OF COUNSEL
Thomas M. Burns   Darrell C. Miller
Frank H. Houck   Anthony van Westrum
SPECIAL COUNSEL
John D. Amen   Robert Neece
Jack M. Merritts

Representative Clients: IBM Credit Corporation; Coopers & Lybrand; Colorado Chapter of the American Physical Therapy Association; QC Data Inc.; Ford Motor Company; Meadowbrook Rehabilitation Group, Inc.; Landmark Graphics Corporation; In-Situ, Inc.

For full biographical listings, see the Martindale-Hubbell Law Directory

DUFFORD & BROWN, P.C. (AV)

1700 Broadway, Suite 1700, 80290-1701
Telephone: 303-861-8013
Facsimile: 303-832-3804
Affiliated Office: Solomon, Pearl, Blum & Quinn, L.L.P., New York, NY and Denver, Colorado.

Thomas G. Brown   Randall J. Feuerstein
Edward D. White

Representative Clients: CF&I Steel, L.P.; Colorado Permanente Medical Group, Inc.; Equilease Corporation; General Electric Company; Hall and Hall Mortgage Corporation; Metallurgy International Inc.; Hewlett-

(See Next Column)

DUFFORD & BROWN P.C.—Continued

Packard; Hong Kong & Shanghai Banking Corporation; The Lincoln National Life Insurance Company; G.T. Colorado, Inc.

For Complete List of Firm Personnel, See General Section

For full biographical listings, see the Martindale-Hubbell Law Directory

ELROD, KATZ, PREEO, LOOK, MOISON & SILVERMAN, PROFESSIONAL CORPORATION (AV)

Suite 1100, 1120 Lincoln Street, 80203
Telephone: 303-832-1900
Fax: 303-863-0412

Richard B. Elrod	Harley K. Look, Jr.
Michael M. Katz	Peter R. Moison
Robert L. Preeo	Eldon E. Silverman

Jersey M. Green	Kathryn A. Reeves
Richard M. Hess, Jr.	Gilbert R. Egle
Martin J. Green	Timothy Kyle Jordan
Marilyn McWilliams	Brian E. Onorato

OF COUNSEL
Richard P. Rosen

For full biographical listings, see the Martindale-Hubbell Law Directory

FRIEDLOB SANDERSON RASKIN PAULSON & TOURTILLOTT, LLC (AV)

1400 Glenarm Place, 80202-5099
Telephone: 303-571-1400
Fax: 303-595-3159; 303-595-3970; 303-615-5472
Email: 72731.505@Compuserve.Com
Englewood, Colorado Office: 8400 East Prentice Avenue, 80111-2918.
Telephone: 303-571-1400.

Raymond L. Friedlob	Christopher R. Paulson
James W. Sanderson	Herrick K. Lidstone, Jr.
Gerald Raskin	Mary M. Maikoetter

John W. Kellogg
OF COUNSEL
Jack D. Feuer

For full biographical listings, see the Martindale-Hubbell Law Directory

HAMILTON AND FAATZ, A PROFESSIONAL CORPORATION (AV)

Suite 500 Colorado State Bank Building, 1600 Broadway, 80202-4988
Telephone: 303-830-0500
Facsimile: 303-860-7855

Pierpont Fuller (1906-1983)	John T. Willson
John M. Evans (1911-1984)	Michael E. Gurley
Dwight Alan Hamilton	James H. Marlow
Clyde A. Faatz, Jr.	Jan E. Montgomery
Gregory W. Smith	

Robert L. Bartholic	Christopher J.W. Forrest
Meghan Welch Martinez	

OF COUNSEL
Kenneth W. Caughey

Representative Clients: PPG Industries, Inc.; Public Employees Retirement Association of Colorado; Masonic Temple Association of Denver; Lockton Silversmith, Inc.; Muller, Sirhall and Associates, Inc.; South Denver Cardiology Associates, P.C.; Landmark Reclamation, Inc.; Stone's Farm Supply, Inc.; Heather Gardens Association; DCX, Inc.

For full biographical listings, see the Martindale-Hubbell Law Directory

HOLME ROBERTS & OWEN LLP (AV)

Suite 4100, 1700 Lincoln, 80203
Telephone: 303-861-7000
Telecopier: 303-866-0200
Email: hro@hro.com *URL:* http://www.hro.com
Boulder, Colorado Office: Suite 400, 1401 Pearl Street.
Telephone: 303-444-5955.
Telecopier: 303-444-1063.
Colorado Springs, Colorado Office: Suite 1300, 90 South Cascade Avenue.
Telephone: 719-473-3800.
Telecopier: 719-633-1518.
Salt Lake City, Utah Office: Suite 1100, 111 East Broadway.
Telephone: 801-521-5800.
Telecopier: 801-521-9639.
London, England Office: Mellier House, 26a Albemarle Street.
Telephone: 44-171-499-8776.
Telecopier: 44-171-499-7769.
Moscow, Russia Office: Kosmodamianskaya Nab. #52/1, Suite 9100, 113054.
Telephone: 7095-961-3000.
Telecopier: 7095-961-3001.

(See Next Column)

Kiev, Ukraine Office: Terestchenkovskaya #19, Suite 2, 252004.
Telephone: 380-44-224-1348.
Telecopier: 380-44-224-4986.

PARTNERS OF FIRM

James C. Owen Jr.	Mary L. Groves
Richard G. Wohlgenant	Manuel L. Martinez
Joseph W. Morrisey, Jr.	Marla J. Williams
G. Kevin Conwick	Steven B. Richardson
Paul D. Holleman	Thomas M. James
W. Dean Salter	(Colorado Springs Office)
Frank Erisman	McKay Marsden
Thomas A. Richardson	(Salt Lake City Office)
William D. Watson	Martha Dugan Rehm
Charles A. Ramunno	John F. Knoeckel
Bruce R. Kohler (Co-Resident	Jill K. Rood (Boulder Office)
Managing Partner, London,	David Harold Little
England Office)	(Salt Lake City Office)
Bruce L. Likoff	Robert H. Bach
William R. Roberts (Managing	Garth B. Jensen
Partner, Boulder Office)	Paul V. Timmins
Phillip R. Clark	Margaret B. McLean (Resident
Martha Traudt Collins	Managing Partner, Moscow,
David K. Detton	Russia Office and Co-Resident
(Salt Lake City Office)	Managing Partner, London,
Thomas F. Cope	England Office)
Francis R. Wheeler	James F. Cress
Lynn Parker Hendrix	Paul G. Thompson
Nick Nimmo	Patrick K. Perrin
Jan N. Steiert	(Boulder Office)
P. Christian Anderson	
(Salt Lake City Office)	

OF COUNSEL

Harold S. Bloomenthal	Kay M. Small (Boulder Office)
	John P. Babb

SPECIAL COUNSEL

Diane S. Barrett	John B. Wood (Boulder Office)

SENIOR COUNSEL

Kathryn P. Beller	Kathryn Stoker Worford

ASSOCIATES

Daron J. Arnold	Peter-Christian Olivo
(Not admitted in CO)	(Boulder Office)
Blaine J. Benard	Sandra Orihuela
(Salt Lake City Office)	Timothy G. Pfeifer
Valery Fedichin (Kiev Office)	(Colorado Springs Office)
Mary C. Gordon	Alan Romero
(Salt Lake City Office)	(Salt Lake City Office)
Lisa Anne Hawkins	Rashid Sharipov (Resident,
Brent P. Karasiuk	Moscow, Russia Office)
(Colorado Springs Office)	J. Alison Shelton
Elena Kuryatnikova	Steven B. Smith
(Moscow, Russia Office)	(Colorado Springs Office)
William C. Letzsch, III	Alexander Udovenko
Maria Mashenka Lundberg	(Moscow, Russia Office)
Neil F. O'Donnell	Maria V. Woods
(Moscow Office)	

For Complete List of Firm Personnel, See General Section

For full biographical listings, see the Martindale-Hubbell Law Directory

LOHF, SHAIMAN & JACOBS, P.C. (AV)

950 South Cherry Street, Suite 900, 80222
Telephone: 303-753-9000
Telecopier: 303-753-9997

Neil E. Ayervais	Moshe Luber
Charles H. Jacobs	Robert Shaiman

Reference: Professional Bank.

For full biographical listings, see the Martindale-Hubbell Law Directory

MESSNER PAVEK & REEVES, LLC (AV)

600 Seventeenth Street, Suite 2800-South, 80202
Telephone: 303-623-1800
Facsimile: 303-623-0552
Evergreen, Colorado Office: 1202 Bergen Parkway, Suite 300.
Telephone: 303-670-1800.
Facsimile: 303-670-2606.

Bryant S. Messner	Ronald K. Reeves
David D. Pavek	(Resident, Evergreen Office)

SPECIAL COUNSEL
Robert W. Berry (Not admitted in CO)

OF COUNSEL
James R. Everson

(See Next Column)

MESSNER PAVEK & REEVES LLC, *Denver—Continued*

John K. Shunk	Mary Jo Dougherty
David A. Reeves	Julia Griffith McVey
Heather Anne Hawker	Montgomery F. Moran

For full biographical listings, see the Martindale-Hubbell Law Directory

MYER, SWANSON, ADAMS & WOLF, P.C. (AV)

The Colorado State Bank Building, 1600 Broadway, Suite 1480, 80202-4915
Telephone: 303-866-9800
Facsimile: 303-866-9818

Rendle Myer	Robert K. Swanson
Allan B. Adams	Thomas J. Wolf

Philip T. Masterson
OF COUNSEL

Robert Swanson	Fred E. Neef (1910-1986)

Representative Clients: The Oppenheimer Funds; Daily Cash Accumulation Fund; The Centennial Trusts; Mile High Chapter of American Red Cross; Master Lease; Heartland Management Co.; Kan-Build of Colorado, Inc. *Reference:* The Colorado State Bank of Denver.

For full biographical listings, see the Martindale-Hubbell Law Directory

NETZORG & McKEEVER, PROFESSIONAL CORPORATION (AV)

Republic Plaza, 370 Seventeenth Street, Suite 3590, 80202
Telephone: 303-892-7100
Fax: 303-446-0506

Gordon W. Netzorg	Peter G. Koclanes
Cecil E. Morris, Jr.	Joan M. Collopy

OF COUNSEL
J. Nicholas McKeever, Jr.

For full biographical listings, see the Martindale-Hubbell Law Directory

OTTEN, JOHNSON, ROBINSON, NEFF & RAGONETTI, P.C. (AV)

950 Seventeenth Street, 16th Floor, 80202
Telephone: 303-825-8400
Telecopier: 303-825-6525

Arthur E. Otten, Jr.	Henry I. Lowe
A. Bruce Campbell	David W. Fell
William R. Neff	Karen L. Barsch
Neil M. Goff	Michael C. Villano
Blair L. Lockwood	James D. Leonard
Kevin A. Gliwa	Lisa A. Osman

OF COUNSEL
Kenneth M. Robins

Representative Clients: Aetna Life Insurance Co.; The Broe Companies; Inc.; Colorado National Bank; Connecticut General Life Insurance Co.; First Nationwide Bank; Homart Development Co.; Land Title Guarantee Co.; Trizec Corporation Ltd.; U.S. West Communications, Inc.; The Western Sugar Co.

For Complete List of Firm Personnel, See General Section

For full biographical listings, see the Martindale-Hubbell Law Directory

SENN LEWIS VISCIANO & STRAHLE, PROFESSIONAL CORPORATION (AV)

Suite 4300, 1801 California Street, 80202
Telephone: 303-298-1122
Telecopier: 303-296-9101

Mark A. Senn	Wynn E. Strahle
Fredric J. Lewis	Stephen W. Arent

David C. Camp	Margie J. Titus

Laura B. Redstone
OF COUNSEL
Lawrence A. Atler (P.C.)
SPECIAL COUNSEL
Ellen Kirschenbaum

For Complete List of Firm Personnel, See General Section

For full biographical listings, see the Martindale-Hubbell Law Directory

GREELEY, Weld Co.

BREGA & WINTERS, P.C. (AV)

1100 Tenth Street, Suite 402, 80631
Telephone: 970-352-4805
Fax: 970-352-6547
Denver, Colorado Office: One United Bank Center. 1700 Lincoln Street, Suite 2222 Street.
Telephone: 303-866-9400.
FAX: 303-861-9109.

Jerry D. Winters	Pamela A. Shaddock

Bradley D. Laue

For full biographical listings, see the Martindale-Hubbell Law Directory

CONNECTICUT

BRIDGEPORT, Fairfield Co.

ELSTEIN AND ELSTEIN, P.C. (AV)

Suite 400 1087 Broad Street, 06604-4231
Telephone: 203-367-4421
Telecopier: 203-366-8615

Henry Elstein	Bruce L. Elstein

For full biographical listings, see the Martindale-Hubbell Law Directory

CHESHIRE, New Haven Co.

WINTERS & FORTE (AV)

Waverly Professional Park, 315 Highland Avenue, Suite 102, P.O. Box 844, 06410
Telephone: 203-272-2927
Fax: 203-271-1222

MEMBERS OF FIRM

David Wayne Winters	Michael C. Forte

A List of Representative Clients will be furnished upon request.
References: Bank of Boston, Connecticut; Centerbank; LaFayette American Bank & Trust Co.

For full biographical listings, see the Martindale-Hubbell Law Directory

DARIEN, Fairfield Co.

RUCCI, BURNHAM, CARTA & EDELBERG (AV)

800 Post Road, P.O. Box 1107, 06820
Telephone: 203-655-7695
Facsimile: 203-655-4302
Email: rbce@netaxis.com

MEMBERS OF FIRM

Joseph J. Rucci, Jr.	Mark R. Carta
Paul H. Burnham	Paul B. Edelberg

Kevin C. Beuttenmuller
ASSOCIATES

Thomas C. Healey	Karen K. Linder
William M. Carello	John E. Seelert
Colette C. Symon	(Not admitted in CT)

OF COUNSEL

Ian R. Crawford	James C. Dempsey

George A. Reilly

For full biographical listings, see the Martindale-Hubbell Law Directory

GREENWICH, Fairfield Co.

HOLLAND KAUFMANN & BARTELS, LLC (AV)

289 Greenwich Avenue, 06830-6595
Telephone: 203-869-5600
Fax: 203-869-4648

Alexander J. Holland	Amy K. Wilfert
Charles B. Kaufmann, III	Harold R. Burke
Philip H. Bartels	Jean Mills Aranha
Beth K. Hansson	Lori E. Romano

John C. Fusco

For full biographical listings, see the Martindale-Hubbell Law Directory

HARTFORD, Hartford Co.

GOULD, KILLIAN & WYNNE (AV)

One Commercial Plaza, 25th Floor, 06103-3595
Telephone: 860-278-1270
Telecopier: 860-244-9290

(See Next Column)

GOULD, KILLIAN & WYNNE—*Continued*

MEMBERS OF FIRM

Samuel Gould (1905-1994)	Mark W. Baronas
Robert K. Killian	William F. Healey
Francis J. Wynne	Nancy E. Gould
Martin A. Gould	Robert O. Wynne

For full biographical listings, see the Martindale-Hubbell Law Directory

ROGIN, NASSAU, CAPLAN, LASSMAN & HIRTLE, LLC (AV)

CityPlace I, 22nd Floor, 185 Asylum Street, 06103-3460
Telephone: 860-278-7480
Fax: 860-278-2179

MEMBERS OF FIRM

Jerome E. Caplan	David J. Heinlein
Edwin A. Lassman	Lewis K. Wise
Robert L. Hirtle	Joan G. Engel
William R. Breetz	Mark A. Rosenblum
Steven D. Bartelstone	Barry S. Feigenbaum
David M. Call	Donald G. Gaudreau
Paul B. Zolan	Peter S. Sorokin

Iris June Brown

ASSOCIATES

Jeffrey W. Stein	Brendan T. Flynn
Mark J. Lassman	Elizabeth R. Houde
Benjamin Engel	Jonathan M. Starble

OF COUNSEL

Arthur M. Nassau

RETIRED

Edward S. Rogin (Retired)	Louis E. Nassau (Retired)

For full biographical listings, see the Martindale-Hubbell Law Directory

SOROKIN SOROKIN GROSS HYDE & WILLIAMS P.C. (AV)

One Corporate Center, 06103
Telephone: 860-525-6645
Fax: 860-522-1781
Simsbury, Connecticut Office: 730 Hopmeadow Street.
Telephone: 860-651-9348.
Rocky Hill, Connecticut Office: 2360 Main Street.
Telephone: 860-563-9305.
Fax: 860-529-6931.

Morris W. Banks	Barry D. Greene
Andrew C. Glassman	Charles R. Moore, Jr.

Sharon Kowal Freilich

For Complete List of Firm Personnel, See General Section

For full biographical listings, see the Martindale-Hubbell Law Directory

NEW HAVEN,* New Haven Co.

BERGMAN, HOROWITZ & REYNOLDS, P.C. (AV)

157 Church Street, 19th Floor, P.O. Box 426, 06502
Telephone: 203-789-1320
Fax: 203-785-8127
Email: mailbox@taxlawyers.com *URL:* http://www.taxlawyers.com
New York, N.Y. Office: 499 Park Avenue, 26th Floor.
Telephone: 212-688-4150.

Stanley N. Bergman	James Russell Brockway
Robert H. Horowitz	Bruce I. Judelson
David L. Reynolds	David A. Ringold
Melvin Ditman	Kathryn Harner Smith
Paul L. Behling	Donald S. Hendel
Kenneth N. Musen	Joy M. Miyasaki
William C. G. Swift, Jr.	Paul M. Roy
Richard J. Klein	Jeremy A. Mellitz

Louis R. Piscatelli	Paul J. Stankewich
James G. Dattaro	Christopher J. Galuppo
Edward A. Renn	Jay H. Rubinstein
Richard M. Porter	(Not admitted in CT)
Tina E. Albright	David M. Hryck
Jay F. Krause	Margaret M. Murphy

For full biographical listings, see the Martindale-Hubbell Law Directory

GORMAN & ENRIGHT P.C. (AV)

59 Elm Street, P.O. Box 1961, 06509
Telephone: 203-865-1382
Telecopier: 203-776-7250

John R. Gorman	Brian G. Enright

(See Next Column)

OF COUNSEL

Patricia King	Earle Giovanniello

References: Bank of New Haven; AT&T Capital Corp.; McGladrey & Pullen.

For full biographical listings, see the Martindale-Hubbell Law Directory

SUSMAN, DUFFY & SEGALOFF, P.C. (AV)

55 Whitney Avenue, 06510-1300
Telephone: 203-624-9830
Telecopier: 203-562-8430
Mailing Address: P.O. Box 1684, New Haven, Connecticut, 06507-1684

Allen H. Duffy (1931-1986)	Susan W. Wolfson
Michael Susman	Laura M. Sklaver
James H. Segaloff	Andrew R. Lubin
David A. Reif	James J. Perito
Joseph E. Faughnan	Matthew C. Susman
Thomas E. Katon	

Jennifer L. Schancupp	Peter G. Kruzynski
Donna Decker Morris	Joshua W. Cohen
Vincent J. Candelora	

OF COUNSEL

Diana C. Ballard	David P. Hambleton

For full biographical listings, see the Martindale-Hubbell Law Directory

SOUTHPORT, Fairfield Co.

BRODY AND OBER, P.C. (AV)

135 Rennell Drive, P.O. Box 572, 06490-0572
Telephone: 203-259-7405
Fax: 203-255-8572

Charles S. Brody (1894-1976)	S. Giles Payne
Seth O. L. Brody	William J. Britt
Stanley B. Garrell	Barbara S. Miller
Frank F. Ober	Ronald B. Noren

Diane F. Martucci	Seth L. Cooper
Douglas R. Brown	

OF COUNSEL

James M. Thorburn	John F. Merchant

For full biographical listings, see the Martindale-Hubbell Law Directory

WESTPORT, Fairfield Co.

LEVETT, ROCKWOOD & SANDERS, PROFESSIONAL CORPORATION (AV)

33 Riverside Avenue, P.O. Box 5116, 06881
Telephone: 203-222-0885
Telecopier: 203-226-8025

David R. Levett	Sharon M. Schweitzer
John Sanders	Barbara A. Young
B. Lance Sauerteig	Steven M. Siegelaub
Madeleine F. Grossman	Marc J. Kurzman
James M. Barton	Suzanne B. Albani
Judy A. Rabkin	Peter H. Struzzi
Dorit Schutzengel Heimer	Edward B. Chansky
Cheryl L. Johnson	

OF COUNSEL

William O. Rockwood, Jr.

Robin K. Higgins	Ernest C. Mysogland
Patricia D. Weitzman	

Representative Clients: Bankers Trust Company; Cannondale Corp.; Caradon, Inc.; Electrolux Corporation; Exxon Chemical Corporation; HealthSouth Corp.; Heyman Properties; Hospital of Saint Raphael; Marketing Corporation of America; St. Vincent's Medical Center.

For full biographical listings, see the Martindale-Hubbell Law Directory

WILLIAM L. SCHEFFLER & ASSOCIATES (AVⓉ)

P.O. Box 2773, 06880-0773
Telephone: 203-226-6600; 1-800-429-4480
Telecopier: 203-227-1873

For full biographical listings, see the Martindale-Hubbell Law Directory

RONALD L. SHEIMAN (AV)

1804 Post Road East, 06880
Telephone: 203-259-0599
Telecopier: 203-255-2570

For full biographical listings, see the Martindale-Hubbell Law Directory

DELAWARE

WILMINGTON,* New Castle Co.

CONNOLLY, BOVE, LODGE & HUTZ (AV)

1220 Market Street, P.O. Box 2207, 19899-2207
Telephone: 302-658-9141
Telecopier: 302-658-5614
URL: http://WWW.CBLHLAW.COM

James M. Mulligan, Jr.	Charles J. Durante
Arthur G. Connolly, Jr.	F. L. Peter Stone
Henry E. Gallagher, Jr.	John C. Kairis
Richard David Levin	Arthur G. Connolly, III
Jeffrey B. Bove	James D. Heisman
Collins J. Seitz, Jr.	Anne Love Barnett

For Complete List of Firm Personnel, See General Section

For full biographical listings, see the Martindale-Hubbell Law Directory

SMITH, KATZENSTEIN & FURLOW (AV)

The Corporate Plaza, 800 Delaware Avenue, P.O. Box 410, 19899
Telephone: 302-652-8400
Fax: 302-652-8405

MEMBERS OF FIRM

Craig B. Smith	Anne E. Bookout
David A. Jenkins	Brett D. Fallon
Stephen M. Miller	

Joanne M. Shalk
COUNSEL
Charles E. Butler
OF COUNSEL
Clark W. Furlow

For Complete List of Firm Personnel, See General Section

For full biographical listings, see the Martindale-Hubbell Law Directory

THEISEN, LANK, MULFORD & GOLDBERG, P.A. (AV)

Ninth Floor, One Commerce Center, P.O. Box 1470, 19899
Telephone: 302-656-7712
Fax: 302-655-0923
Email: Theisen@delcorp.com *URL:* http://www.delcorp.theisen.com

Aubrey B. Lank	Steven D. Goldberg
John G. Mulford	Michael J. Goodrick
David S. Lank	

Richard L. Abbott
OF COUNSEL
Vincent A. Theisen (Retired)

References: Wilmington Trust Co.; PNC Bank.

For full biographical listings, see the Martindale-Hubbell Law Directory

DISTRICT OF COLUMBIA

WASHINGTON, D.C. Co.

* indicates certain Bar Register subscribers, in cities of comparable size and importance, who maintain an additional office in Washington, D.C. and who have arranged for representation as a part of the Washington, D.C. listings that follow

* BAKER & BOTTS, L.L.P. (AV)

A Registered Limited Liability Partnership
The Warner, 1299 Pennsylvania Avenue, N.W., 20004-2400
Telephone: 202-639-7700
Fax: 202-639-7832
Email: postmaster@bakerbotts.com
Houston, Texas Office: One Shell Plaza, 910 Louisiana.
Telephone: 713-229-1234.
Austin, Texas Office: 1600 San Jacinto Center, 98 San Jacinto Boulevard.
Telephone: 512-322-2500.
Dallas, Texas Office: 2001 Ross Avenue.
Telephone: 214-953-6500.
New York, New York Office: 599 Lexington Avenue.
Telephone: 212-705-5000.
Moscow, Russian Federation Office: 10 ul. Bolshaya Dmitrovka (formerly Pushkinskaya), 103031.
Telephone: 7095/921-5300 (Local); 7501/929-7070 (International).

(See Next Column)

MEMBERS OF FIRM

James R. Doty	David N. Powers
	Hugh Tucker

ASSOCIATES

Kevin B. Dent	Tamar C. Snyder
Michael A. Gold	Jennifer J. Yi
Estee S. Levine	(Not admitted in DC)

For Complete List of Firm Personnel, See General Section

For full biographical listings, see the Martindale-Hubbell Law Directory

BERLINER, CORCORAN & ROWE, L.L.P. (AV)

A Partnership including a Professional Corporation
1101 Seventeenth Street, N.W., 20036-4798
Telephone: 202-293-5555
FAX: 202-293-9035

MEMBERS OF FIRM

Thomas G. Corcoran, Jr.	Michael W. Beasley
Neal E. Krucoff	Clemens Kochinke
Henry M. Lloyd (P.C.)	John A. Ordway, Jr.
Wayne H. Rusch	John L. Simson

COUNSEL

Henry A. Berliner, Jr.	Peter Heidenberger
Rufus King	Lothar Griessbach

ASSOCIATES

Kathleen S. Rice	Jay A. Rosenthal

For full biographical listings, see the Martindale-Hubbell Law Directory

JOSEPH A. BOSCO (AV)

Suite 900 1150 Connecticut Avenue, N.W., 20036
Telephone: 202-293-1922
Telecopier: 202-293-9202

For full biographical listings, see the Martindale-Hubbell Law Directory

CAPLIN & DRYSDALE, CHARTERED (AV)

One Thomas Circle, N.W., 20005
Telephone: 202-862-5000
Cable Address: "Capdale"
Telex: 904001 CAPL UR WSH
Fax: 202-429-3301
New York, N.Y. Office: 399 Park Avenue.
Telephone: 212-319-7125.
Fax: 212-644-6755.

Mortimer M. Caplin	Douglas D. Drysdale
Robert A. Klayman	Thomas A. Troyer
Ralph A. Muoio	David N. Webster
Elihu Inselbuch	H. David Rosenbloom
(Resident, New York Office)	Peter Van N. Lockwood
Ronald B. Lewis	Cono R. Namorato
Richard W. Skillman	Daniel B. Rosenbaum
Patricia G. Lewis	Richard E. Timbie
Bernard S. Bailor	Graeme W. Bush
Stafford Smiley	Albert G. Lauber, Jr.
Sally A. Regal	Scott D. Michel
Julie W. Davis	Kent A. Mason
Carl S. Kravitz	Trevor W. Swett III
Robert A. Boisture	Robert E. Culbertson
James Sottile, IV	Charles T. Plambeck
Harry J. Hicks, III	James E. Salles
Milton Cerny	Craig A. Sharon
Paul G. Cellupica	Matthew W. Frank
Michael T. Doran	Christian R. Pastore
Nathan D. Finch	(Not admitted in DC)
Jessica L. Goldstein	Elizabeth M. Sellers
Laura J. Kerrigan	Douglas N. Varley
	(Not admitted in DC)

OF COUNSEL

Robert H. Elliott, Jr.	Myron C. Baum
Vivian L. Cavalieri	C. Sanders McNew
Ann C. McMillan	(Resident, New York Office)
Janne G. Gallagher	

For full biographical listings, see the Martindale-Hubbell Law Directory

DAVID, HAGNER, KUNEY & KRUPIN, P.C. (AV)

1120 Nineteenth Street, N.W., 20036
Telephone: 202-467-6900
Telecopier: 202-467-6910

Richard G. David	Paul A. Kaplan
John D. Hagner	Kenneth W. Logwood
David R. Kuney	Desmond D. Connall, Jr.
Dennis A. Davison	Stuart A. Kruger
Jay P. Krupin	Howard N. Solodky
Stanley J. Wrobel	Pamela V. Rothenberg

(See Next Column)

DAVID, HAGNER, KUNEY & KRUPIN P.C.—*Continued*

Christine M. Carstens	Jonathan W. Greenbaum
Janet M. Meiburger	Elizabeth C. Lee
Jeffrey L. Tarkenton	Robert P. Goodridge
Janis B. Schiff	James J. O'Brien
Cameron Cohick	Erik D. Bolog

Caryn G. Pass	John G. Nahajzer
Timothy R. Epp	Jeffrey A. Liesemer
Tara A. Scanlon	Alison J. Hurewitz
Carolyn D. Chabrow	Jennifer L. Kocher
Jeffrey A. Spector	(Not admitted in DC)

For full biographical listings, see the Martindale-Hubbell Law Directory

DE MARTINO FINKELSTEIN ROSEN & VIRGA (AV)

A Partnership including Professional Corporations
Suite 400, 1818 N Street, N.W., 20036
Telephone: 202-659-0494
Telecopier: 202-659-1290
Email: DFRV90Brd@aol.com *URL:* http://www.dfrv.com
New York, N.Y. Office: Suite 1700, 90 Broad Street.
Telephone: 212-363-2500.
Telecopier: 212-363-2723.

MEMBERS OF FIRM

Kathleen L. Cerveny (Resident)	Jeffrey S. Rosen (Resident)
Ralph V. De Martino (Resident)	Gerard A. Virga (Not admitted
Steven R. Finkelstein (Not	in DC; Resident, New York,
admitted in DC; Resident,	N.Y. Office)
New York, N.Y. Office)	

Keith H. Peterson (Not	Victoria A. Baylin (Not
admitted in DC; Resident,	admitted in DC; Resident)
New York, N.Y. Office)	

LEGAL SUPPORT PERSONNEL

J. Keoni Robinson (Paralegal)	Patricia A. Lamm (Paralegal)
Peter S. Cruttenden (Paralegal)	

For full biographical listings, see the Martindale-Hubbell Law Directory

KENNETH R. FEINBERG & ASSOCIATES (AV)

1120 20th Street, N.W. Suite 740 South, 20036
Telephone: 202-371-1110
Fax: 202-962-9290
New York, N.Y. Office: 780 3rd Avenue, Suite 2202.
Telephone: 212-527-9600.
Fax: 212-527-9611.

ASSOCIATES

Deborah E. Greenspan	Peter H. Woodin
Michael K. Rozen	(Not admitted in DC)
(Not admitted in DC)	M. Catherine Faint

OF COUNSEL

Jacqueline E. Zins

For full biographical listings, see the Martindale-Hubbell Law Directory

KROOTH & ALTMAN (AV)

Suite 400, 1850 M Street, N.W., 20036-5803
Telephone: 202-293-8200
Telecopier: 202-872-0145, 202-775-5872
Columbia, Maryland Office: 5401 Twin Knolls Road, Suite 7, 21045.
Telephone: 301-596-1140.
Sterling, Virginia Office: 45591 Shepard Drive, Suite 101J, 20164.
Telephone: 703-450-2755.

MEMBERS OF FIRM

David L. Krooth (1907-1978)	Daniel Randolph Cole, Jr.
Norman S. Altman (Retired)	Patrick J. Clancy
William S. Tennant	James F. Perna
William J. Delany	Harrison C. Smith
Donald F. Libretta	Mario Greszes
E. Joseph Knoll	David A. Barsky
Michael E. Mazer	John E. Vihstadt
Bonnie Hochman Rothell	

OF COUNSEL

Victor A. Altman	Michael J. Milton
J. Stephen Britt	Robert J. Siciliano

ASSOCIATES

Jon I. Opert	Stephen J. Krooth
Felicia M. Groner	(Not admitted in DC)

For full biographical listings, see the Martindale-Hubbell Law Directory

ROBERT E. LOSCH, P.C. (AV)

1716 New Hampshire Avenue, N.W., 20009
Telephone: 202-296-4222

Robert E. Losch

QUINN, RACUSIN & GAZZOLA, CHARTERED (AV)

1401 H Street, N.W. Suite 510, 20005-2178
Telephone: 202-842-9300
Facsimile: 202-682-0148

John H. Quinn, Jr.	Joseph DiStefano
Robert A. Gazzola	Susan Yoder Torres
	Eric John Edwardson

RETIRED

Aaron J. Racusin (Retired)

LEGAL SUPPORT PERSONNEL

Mary G. Wheeler

For full biographical listings, see the Martindale-Hubbell Law Directory

REASONER, DAVIS & FOX (AV)

Suite 800, 888 17th Street, N.W., 20006
Telephone: 202-463-8282
Fax: 202-659-8285

MEMBERS OF FIRM

Michael A. Dymersky	C. Dean Reasoner
Stephen W. Nealon	E. Tillman Stirling
	Philip J. Sweeney, III

SPECIAL COUNSEL

Thomas D. Quinn, Jr.	South Trimble, III

ASSOCIATE

Justin Bayly Smith

For full biographical listings, see the Martindale-Hubbell Law Directory

SCHMELTZER, APTAKER & SHEPARD, P.C. (AV)

The Watergate, Suite 1000, 2600 Virginia Avenue, N.W., 20037-1905
Telephone: 202-333-8800
Cable Address: "Ship"
Telex: 440517
Facsimile: 202-342-3434
Email: sas@saslaw.com *URL:* http://www.saspc.com
Los Angeles, California Office: 1999 Avenue of the Stars, Twenty-Seventh Floor, 90067-4095.
Telephone: 310-557-2966.
FAX: 310-286-6610.

J. Thomas Esslinger	J. Anthony Smith
Mark I. Gruhin	(Not admitted in DC)

For full biographical listings, see the Martindale-Hubbell Law Directory

TIGHE, PATTON, TABACKMAN & BABBIN, L.L.P. (AV)

A Limited Liability Partnership
1750 Pennsylvania Avenue, N.W. Suite 1201, 20006
Telephone: 202-347-5065
Telecopier: 202-393-0363
Email: TPATTON290@AOL.COM

MEMBERS

Kevin P. Tighe (P.C.)	Jed L. Babbin
Thomas Earl Patton	Paul N. Murphy
Steven C. Tabackman	Walter G. Birkel
	Brent S. Franzel

ASSOCIATE

Babak Pooya

OF COUNSEL

Alan H. Kent

For full biographical listings, see the Martindale-Hubbell Law Directory

* VENABLE ATTORNEYS AT LAW VENABLE, BAETJER, HOWARD & CIVILETTI, LLP (AV)

A Partnership including Professional Corporations
Suite 1000, 1201 New York Avenue, N.W., 20005
Telephone: 202-962-4800
Fax: 202-962-8300
Baltimore, Maryland Office: Venable, Baetjer and Howard LLP, 1800 Mercantile Bank & Trust Building, 2 Hopkins Plaza.
Telephone: 410-244-7400.
McLean, Virginia Office: Venable, Baetjer and Howard LLP, Suite 400, 2010 Corporate Ridge.
Telephone: 703-760-1600.
Rockville, Maryland Office: Venable, Baetjer and Howard LLP, Suite 500, One Church Street, P. O. Box 1906.
Telephone: 301-217-5600.
Towson, Maryland Office: Venable, Baetjer and Howard LLP, 210 Allegheny Avenue, P. O. Box 5517.
Telephone: 410-494-6200.

(See Next Column)

VENABLE ATTORNEYS AT LAW VENABLE, BAETJER, HOWARD & CIVILETTI, LLP, *Washington—Continued*

MEMBERS OF FIRM

Benjamin R. Civiletti (P.C.) (Also at Baltimore and Towson, Maryland Offices)	Kenneth C. Bass, III (Also at McLean, Virginia Office)
Anthony M. Carey (Not admitted in DC; Also at Baltimore, Maryland Office)	Joseph G. Block
	Bryson L. Cook (P.C.) (Not admitted in DC; Also at Baltimore, Maryland Office)
Neal D. Borden (Not admitted in DC; Also at Baltimore, Maryland Office)	Jeffrey D. Knowles
	William D. Coston
	Maurice Baskin
Jan K. Guben (Not admitted in DC; Also at Baltimore, Maryland Office)	Robert J. Bolger, Jr. (Not admitted in DC; Also at Baltimore, Maryland Office)
David J. Levenson	Bruce H. Jurist (Also at Baltimore, Maryland Office)
Joe A. Shull	

John M. Gurley

ASSOCIATES

Donald P. Creston　　　　　　Fernand A. Lavallee

For Complete List of Firm Personnel, See General Section

For full biographical listings, see the Martindale-Hubbell Law Directory

WILMER, CUTLER & PICKERING (AV)

2445 M Street, N.W., 20037-1420
Telephone: 202-663-6000
Fax: 202-663-6363
Email: Law@Wilmer.Com
Baltimore, Maryland Office: 100 Light Street, 21202.
Telephone: 410-986-2800.
Fax: 410-986-2828.
European Offices:
4 Carlton Gardens, London, SW1Y 5AA, England. Telephone: +44 (171) 872-1000.
Fax: +44 (171) 839-3537.
Rue de la Loi 15 Wetstraat, B-1040 Brussels, Belgium. Telephone: +32 (2) 285-4900.
Fax: +32 (2) 285-4949.
Friedrichstrasse 95, D-10117 Berlin, Germany. Telephone: +49 (30) 2022-6400.
Fax: +49 (30)2022-6500.

MEMBERS OF FIRM

Louis R. Cohen	Russell J. Bruemmer
Michael R. Klein	Thomas W. White
Richard W. Cass	John B. Watkins V (Resident, Baltimore, Maryland Office)
Stephen P. Doyle	
George P. Stamas (Resident, Baltimore, Maryland Office)	

COUNSEL

Roger J. Patterson (Resident, Baltimore, Maryland Office)

For Complete List of Firm Personnel, See General Section

For full biographical listings, see the Martindale-Hubbell Law Directory

FLORIDA

BOCA RATON, Palm Beach Co.

LAW OFFICES OF RICHARD H. LEVENSTEIN, P.A. (AV)

2101 Northwest 2nd Avenue Suite 2, 33431
Telephone: 561-392-7887
Fax: 561-392-3348
Stuart, Florida Office: 312 West Ocean Boulevard, 34994.
Telephone: 561-221-0521.
Fax: 561-221-0290.

Richard H. Levenstein

For full biographical listings, see the Martindale-Hubbell Law Directory

*FORT LAUDERDALE,** Broward Co.

BERGER & DAVIS, P.A. (AV)

Suite 400, 100 N.E. 3rd Avenue, 33301
Telephone: 954-525-9900
Fax: 954-523-2872
Tallahassee, Florida Office: 215 South Monroe Street, Suite 804, 32301.
Telephone: 904-561-3010.
FAX: 904-561-3013.

(See Next Column)

Thomas L. Abrams	Manuel Kushner
James L. Berger	John D. C. Newton, II (Resident, Tallahassee Office)
Mitchell W. Berger	
Franklin H. Caplan	Leonard K. Samuels
James B. Davis	Laz L. Schneider
Nick Jovanovich	Daniel H. Thompson (Resident, Tallahassee Office)
Robert B. Judd	

Vincent J. Altino	Lisa D. MacClugage
Christine A. Butler	Dawn M. Meyers
Lawrence C. Callaway, III	Scott L. Pestcoe
Janice L. Griffin	Holiday Hunt Russell

Jeffrey Scott Wertman

OF COUNSEL

Henry H. (Bucky) Fox

For full biographical listings, see the Martindale-Hubbell Law Directory

*FORT MYERS,** Lee Co.

SMOOT ADAMS EDWARDS & GREEN, P.A. (AV)

One University Park Suite 600, 12800 University Drive, P.O. Box 60259, 33906-6259
Telephone: 941-489-1776
(800) 226-1777 (in Florida)
Fax: 941-489-2444
Email: 71600.2745@compuserve.com

J. Tom Smoot, Jr.	Bruce D. Green
Hal Adams	Steven I. Winer
Franklyn A. (Chip) Johnson (1947-1991)	Mark R. Komray
	Clayton W. Crevasse
Charles B. Edwards	M. Brian Cheffer

Robert S. Forman	C. Berk Edwards, Jr.
Kathleen W. McBride	Melville G. Brinson, III
Lowell Schoenfeld	Samuel J. Hagan, IV.

For full biographical listings, see the Martindale-Hubbell Law Directory

*JACKSONVILLE,** Duval Co.

ALLEN, BRINTON & SIMMONS, P.A. (AV)

One Independent Drive, Suite 3200, 32202
Telephone: 904-353-8800
Fax: 904-353-8770

A. Graham Allen	Sidney S. Simmons, II
William D. Brinton	Edward McCarthy, III

Joelle Jackson Dillard	Christopher M. Hodge

Representative Clients: Amoco Oil Co.; Anheuser-Busch Companies, Inc.; Avis Rent A Car System, Inc.; Bridgestone/Firestone, Inc.; Coggin-O'Steen Investment Corp. (and related automobile dealerships); Digital Design, Inc.; The Dow Chemical Co.; The Haskell Co.; Johnson & Johnson; Masthead Industries, Inc.

For full biographical listings, see the Martindale-Hubbell Law Directory

SAMUEL L. LePRELL (AV)

901 Blackstone Building, 233 East Bay Street, 32202
Telephone: 904-353-3877
Fax: 904-359-9717

For full biographical listings, see the Martindale-Hubbell Law Directory

SMITH HULSEY & BUSEY (AV)

1800 First Union National Bank Tower, 225 Water Street, P.O. Box 53315, 32201-3315
Telephone: 904-359-7700
Facsimile: 904-359-7708; 353-9908

Lloyd Smith (1915-1987)

MEMBERS OF FIRM

Dennis L. Blackburn	E. Owen McCuller, Jr.
Stephen D. Busey	James H. Post
Douglas D. Chunn	Bryan L. Putnal
Earl E. Googe, Jr.	E. Lanny Russell
Jeanne E. Helton	Joel Settembrini, Jr.
Cynthia C. Jackson	Tim E. Sleeth
G. Preston Keyes	John R. Smith, Jr.
William E. Kuntz	James J. Taylor, Jr.
M. Richard Lewis, Jr.	Timothy W. Volpe
John F. MacLennan	Waddell A. Wallace, III
Raymond R. Magley	Harry M. Wilson, III

Michael M. Bajalia	Michael R. Freed
James A. Bolling, Jr.	Lee G. Kellison
E. Lanier Drew	Lauren P. Langham
Diana Salama Farhat	Marjorie Conner Makar
Martin A. Fitzpatrick	Bradley R. Markey

(See Next Column)

SMITH HULSEY & BUSEY—*Continued*

R. Leanne McKnight	Steven G. Spears
Mary E. McManus	Melissa Smith Turra
Jeanne M. Miller	Herschel T. Vinyard, Jr
Stephen D. Moore, Jr.	Leslie A. Wickes
Howard J. Smith	Karl A. Zillgitt

OF COUNSEL

Mark Hulsey	John E. Thrasher

Representative Clients: Baptist/St. Vincent's Health System, Inc.; Browning-Ferris Industries, Inc.; Champion Realty Corp. (Florida); First Union National Bank of Florida; Florida Rock Industries, Inc.; PGA Tour, Inc.; KPMG Peat Marwick; The Regency Group, Inc.; The Ritz-Carlton Hotel Co.; University of Florida.

For full biographical listings, see the Martindale-Hubbell Law Directory

KISSIMMEE,* Osceola Co.

POHL & SHORT, P.A.

(See Winter Park)

MIAMI,* Dade Co.

ZACK, SPARBER, KOSNITZKY, SPRATT & BROOKS, P.A. (AV)

International Place, 100 Southeast Second Street, Suite 2800, 33131-2144
Telephone: 305-539-8400
Facsimile: 305-539-1307

Stephen N. Zack	Jorge A. Gonzalez
Byron L. Sparber	Debra Weiss Goodstone
Michael Kosnitzky	Deborah R. Mayo
Marc H. Auerbach	Thomas O. Wells

For Complete List of Firm Personnel, See General Section

For full biographical listings, see the Martindale-Hubbell Law Directory

NAPLES,* Collier Co.

QUARLES & BRADY (AV)

Barnett Center, 4501 Tamiami Trail North Suite 300, 33940-3060
Telephone: 941-262-5959
Fax: 941-434-4999
Milwaukee, Wisconsin Office: 411 East Wisconsin Avenue, 53202-4497.
Telephone: 414-277-5000.
Fax: 414-271-3552.
Madison, Wisconsin Office: Firstar Plaza, One South Pinckney Street, P.O. Box 2113, 53701-2113.
Telephone: 608-251-5000.
Fax: 608-251-9166.
West Palm Beach, Florida Office: 222 Lakeview Avenue, 4th Floor, 33401.
Telephone: 561-653-5000.
Fax: 561-653-5333.
Phoenix, Arizona Office: One Camelback Building, One East Camelback Road, Suite 400, 85012-1649.
Telephone: 602-230-5500.
Fax: 602-230-5598.

PARTNERS

Timothy G. Hains	Kimberly Leach Johnson

For Complete List of Firm Personnel, See General Section

For full biographical listings, see the Martindale-Hubbell Law Directory

WILLIAM B. ROBERTS (AV)

4532 Tamiami Trail, East Suite 303, 34112-6783
Telephone: 941-774-6778
Fax: 941-774-6286
Email: Billr33962@aol.com

For full biographical listings, see the Martindale-Hubbell Law Directory

ORLANDO,* Orange Co.

BROWN & VAN LEUVEN, P.A. (AV)

111 North Orange Avenue, Suite 875, P.O. Box 2873, 32802-2873
Telephone: 407-425-9566
Fax: 407-425-9596
Kissimmee, Florida Office: 201 East Ruby Avenue, Suite A, 34741.
Telephone: 407-870-9998.
Fax: 407-870-5510.

Usher L. Brown	Mary B. Van Leuven

Suzanne D'Agresta	Sandra J. Pomerantz
	Mark A. Tittle

For full biographical listings, see the Martindale-Hubbell Law Directory

HADDOCK PROFESSIONAL ASSOCIATION

(See Winter Park)
Email: edhaddock@aol.com

Approved Attorneys For: American Pioneer Title Insurance Co.
Reference: Southern Bank of Central Florida.

POHL & SHORT, P.A.

(See Winter Park)

TALLAHASSEE,* Leon Co.

ERVIN, VARN, JACOBS AND ERVIN (AV)

305 South Gadsden Street, P.O. Drawer 1170, 32302
Telephone: 904-224-9135
Telecopier: 904-222-9164
Email: EVJE@NETTALLY.COM

MEMBERS OF FIRM

Thomas M. Ervin, Jr.	Melissa Fletcher Allaman
C. Everett Boyd, Jr.	Robert M. Ervin Jr.
J. Stanley Chapman	

ASSOCIATE

David R. Westcott

COUNSEL CONSULTANT

Robert M. Ervin

OF COUNSEL

Wilfred C. Varn	Richard W. Ervin
Joseph C. Jacobs	Marilyn K. Morris
	Pamela K. Frazier

Representative Clients: Florida Association of Broadcasters; E. I. duPont de Nemours & Co., Inc.; Florida Credit Union League; Atlantic Richfield Co.; Wells Fargo Ag Credit Corp.; American Acceptance Corp.; Coastal Petroleum Co.; General Motors Corp.; Goodyear Tire and Rubber Co.; The Grand Union Co.

For full biographical listings, see the Martindale-Hubbell Law Directory

TAMPA,* Hillsborough Co.

MORRISON, MORRISON & MILLS, P.A. (AV)

1200 West Platt Street Suite 100, 33606
Telephone: 813-258-3311
Telecopier: 813-258-3209

Thomas K. Morrison	Frederick J. Mills
Susan B. Morrison	James E. Holmes, Jr.

Representative Clients: SouthTrust Bank of West Florida; SouthTrust Bank of Alabama, National Association; NationsBank of Florida, N.A.; Mercantile Bank; Barnett Banks, Inc.; Southern Commerce Bank; Sun Bank of Pasco County; Hillsborough County Industrial Development Authority; Automation Packaging, Inc.; Medical Data Management, Inc.

For full biographical listings, see the Martindale-Hubbell Law Directory

SALEM, SAXON & NIELSEN, PROFESSIONAL ASSOCIATION (AV)

Suite 3200, One Barnett Plaza, 101 East Kennedy Boulevard, P.O. Box 3399, 33601
Telephone: 813-224-9000
Telecopier: 813-221-8811

Richard J. Salem	Lisa M. Castellano
Bernice S. Saxon	Beth M. Coleman
Richard A. Nielsen	Roy J. Ford, Jr.
David J. Tong	Marilyn Mullen Healy
Marian B. Rush	Troy M. Lovell
Ricardo L. Gilmore	Evin L. Netzer
Steven M. Berman	Lynn Van Hyning Ramey
C. Graham Carothers, Jr.	Susan K. S. Scarcelli
J. Frazier Carraway	Jacqueline M. Spoto

OF COUNSEL

John Crider

Reference: The Bank of Tampa.

For full biographical listings, see the Martindale-Hubbell Law Directory

WEST PALM BEACH,* Palm Beach Co.

NASON, GILDAN, YEAGER, GERSON & WHITE, P.A. (AV)

Penthouse Suite United National Bank Tower, 1645 Palm Beach Lakes Boulevard, 33401
Telephone: 561-686-3307
Fax: 561-686-5442

Herbert L. Gildan	Susan Fleischner Kornspan
Thomas J. Yeager	Alan I. Armour, II
Gary N. Gerson	Mark A. Pachman
John White, II	Elaine Johnson James
Phillip C. Gildan	Nathan E. Nason
Domenick R. Lioce	Gregory L. Scott

(See Next Column)

NASON, GILDAN, YEAGER, GERSON & WHITE P.A., *West Palm Beach—Continued*

John M. McDivitt	Jeffrey B. Kahn
Craig S. Barnett	

LEGAL SUPPORT PERSONNEL

Sandra R. Gronek	Constance Schiraldi
(Office Administrator)	(Real Estate Paralegal)
Kathy Pelly	Georgina J. Popham
(Litigation Paralegal)	(Corporate/Securities
Elsie T. Pollak	Paralegal)
(Litigation Paralegal)	

For full biographical listings, see the Martindale-Hubbell Law Directory

QUARLES & BRADY (AV)

222 Lakeview Avenue, 4th Floor, 33401
Telephone: 561-653-5000
Fax: 561-653-5333
Milwaukee, Wisconsin Office: 411 East Wisconsin Avenue, 53202-4497.
Telephone: 414-277-5000.
Fax: 414-271-3552.
Madison, Wisconsin Office: Firstar Plaza, One South Pinckney Street, P.O. Box 2113, 53701-2113.
Telephone: 608-251-5000.
Fax: 608-251-9166.
Naples, Florida Office: Barnett Center, 4501 Tamiami Trail North, Suite 300, 33940-3060.
Telephone: 941-262-5959.
Fax: 941-434-4999.
Phoenix, Arizona Office: One Camelback Building, One East Camelback Road, Suite 400, 85012-1649.
Telephone: 602-230-5500.
Fax: 602-230-5598.

PARTNERS

John S. Sammond	David L. Petersen
Ned R. Nashban	

ASSOCIATE

Nancy Berz Colman

For Complete List of Firm Personnel, See General Section

For full biographical listings, see the Martindale-Hubbell Law Directory

WINTER PARK, Orange Co.

HADDOCK PROFESSIONAL ASSOCIATION (AV)

3260 University Boulevard, Suite 210, 32792
Telephone: 407-679-6171
FAX: 407-679-8810
Mailing Address: P.O. Box 5148, Winter Park, FL, 32793-5148
Email: edhaddock@aol.com

Edward E. Haddock, Jr.

Approved Attorneys For: American Pioneer Title Insurance Co.
Reference: Southern Bank of Central Florida.

For full biographical listings, see the Martindale-Hubbell Law Directory

POHL & SHORT, P.A. (AV)

280 West Canton Avenue, Suite 410, P.O. Box 3208, 32790
Telephone: 407-647-7645; 407-647-POHL
Telefax: 407-647-2314

Frank L. Pohl	C. Teresa de Arrigoitia
Houston E. Short	George A. Golder
Dwight I. Cool	Norma Stanley
James Everett Shepherd V	Mark W. Garrett
John R. Simpson, Jr.	

Representative Clients: American Pioneer Title Insurance Company; Institute of Internal Auditors, Inc.; Thompson Steel, Inc.; SunTrust, N.A.; The Bank of Winter Park; Bekins Moving and Storage Co., Inc.; Champion Boats, Inc.; KeyCom Telephone Systems, Inc.

For full biographical listings, see the Martindale-Hubbell Law Directory

GEORGIA

ATLANTA,* Fulton Co.

ALEMBIK, FINE & CALLNER, P.A. (AV)

Marquis One Tower, Fourth Floor, 245 Peachtree Center Avenue, N.E., 30303
Telephone: 404-688-8800
Telecopier: 404-420-7191

(See Next Column)

Michael D. Alembik (1936-1993)	Ronald T. Gold
Lowell S. Fine	G. Michael Banick
Bruce W. Callner	Mark E. Bergeson
Kathy L. Portnoy	Russell P. Love

Z. Ileana Martinez	Janet Lichiello Franchi
Susan M. Lieppe	Heidi Koch Martin
Bruce R. Steinfeld	Janet Caroline Moja
John H. Zwald	

For full biographical listings, see the Martindale-Hubbell Law Directory

FRANCIS M. BIRD, JR. (AV)

100 Galleria Parkway, N.W. Suite 1540, 30339
Telephone: 770-951-4720
Fax: 770-951-4723

For full biographical listings, see the Martindale-Hubbell Law Directory

BIVENS, HOFFMAN & FOWLER (AV)

A Partnership of Professional Corporations
5040 Roswell Road, N.E., 30342
Telephone: 404-256-6464
FAX: 404-256-1422

MEMBERS OF FIRM

Clifford G. Hoffman (P.C.)	Michael C. Fowler (P.C.)

For full biographical listings, see the Martindale-Hubbell Law Directory

BODKER, RAMSEY & ANDREWS, A PROFESSIONAL CORPORATION (AV)

Suite 615 1800 Peachtree Street, N.W., 30309-2507
Telephone: 404-351-1615
Telecopier: 404-352-1285

Brian D. Bodker	Timothy J. Ramsey
Jon G. Blaustein	

For full biographical listings, see the Martindale-Hubbell Law Directory

BOVIS, KYLE & BURCH (AV)

A Partnership including Professional Corporations
Third Floor, 53 Perimeter Center East, 30346
Telephone: 770-391-9100
Telecopier: 770-668-0878

MEMBERS OF FIRM

John M. Bovis (P.C.)	C. Sam Thomas (P.C.)
J. Wesley Skinner	

ASSOCIATES

Claude P. Czaja	Gregory K. Gale

For full biographical listings, see the Martindale-Hubbell Law Directory

CARTER & ANSLEY (AV)

Suite 1000 One Ninety One Peachtree Tower, 191 Peachtree Street, 30303-1747
Telephone: 404-658-9220
Fax: 404-658-9726
Email: firm@carteransley.com

MEMBERS OF FIRM

Shepard Bryan (1871-1970)	Robert A. Barnaby, II
W. Colquitt Carter (1904-1988)	Thomas E. Magill
Ben Kingree, III	Robert O. McCloud, Jr.
Tommy T. Holland	Christopher N. Shuman
H. Sanders Carter, Jr.	Elizabeth J. Bondurant
A. T. Sorrells	Michael A. Coval

OF COUNSEL

Bonneau Ansley

ASSOCIATES

Rebecca J. Schmidt	Kenton J. Coppage
Keith L. Lindsay	Allison Mary Burns
Burke B. Johnson	Mary K. Pickard
Patrick C. DiCarlo	

For full biographical listings, see the Martindale-Hubbell Law Directory

GLASS, McCULLOUGH, SHERRILL & HARROLD (AV)

1409 Peachtree Street, N.E., 30309
Telephone: 404-885-1500
Telecopier: 404-892-1801
Buckhead Office: Monarch Plaza, 3414 Peachtree Road, N.E., Suite 450, Atlanta, Georgia, 30326-1162.
Telephone: 404-885-1500.
Telecopier: 404-231-1978.
Washington, D.C. Office: 1150 17th Street, N.W., Suite 605. Washington, D.C., 20036.
Telephone: 202-785-8118.
Telecopier: 202-785-0128.

(See Next Column)

GLASS, McCULLOUGH, SHERRILL & HARROLD—*Continued*

Knoxville, Tennessee Office: 606 West Main Avenue, Suite 205, P.O. Box 2543. Knoxville, Tennessee, 37901-2543.
Telephone: 423-971-5418.
Telecopier: 423-971-1706.

MEMBERS OF FIRM

Thomas J. Harrold, Jr.	Ross P. Kendall
Gregory Bartko	James W. King
Mark A. Block	R. Phillip Shinall, III
T. Kennerly Carroll, Jr.	W. Clayton Sparrow, Jr.
Ugo F. Ippolito	John M. Stuckey, Jr.

Bradley E. Wahl

OF COUNSEL

S. Andrew McKay

TAX COUNSEL

William M. Joseph

ASSOCIATES

L. Neill Edwards	Betsy Birns McCall
D. Lynn Holliday	Christina Sungyoon Pak

For Complete List of Firm Personnel, See General Section

For full biographical listings, see the Martindale-Hubbell Law Directory

---

HARKLEROAD & HERMANCE, A PROFESSIONAL CORPORATION (AV)

2500 Cain Tower-Peachtree Center, 229 Peachtree Street, N.E., 30303
Telephone: 404-588-9211
Telex II: 810-751-3228
Telecopier: 404-659-0860

Donald R. Harkleroad	James P. Hermance

For full biographical listings, see the Martindale-Hubbell Law Directory

---

HARMAN, OWEN, SAUNDERS & SWEENEY, A PROFESSIONAL CORPORATION (AV)

1900 Peachtree Center Tower, 230 Peachtree Street, N.W., 30303
Telephone: 404-688-2600
Telecopier: 404-525-4347

H. Andrew Owen	Timothy J. Sweeney
Frederick F. Saunders, Jr.	Perry A. Phillips

David C. Will

For full biographical listings, see the Martindale-Hubbell Law Directory

---

HICKS, MALOOF & CAMPBELL, A PROFESSIONAL CORPORATION (AV)

Suite 2200 Marquis Two Tower, 285 Peachtree Center
Avenue, 30303-1234
Telephone: 404-588-1100
Telecopy: 404-420-7474

Robert E. Hicks	J. David Dantzler, Jr.
Maurice Ted Maloof	Steven K. Bender
Charles E. Campbell	Michael S. Bradley
Robert A. Bartlett	Lisa W. Wannamaker
Charles E. Wilson, III	Henry F. Sewell, Jr.
Robert E. Tritt	James E. Meadows
J. Michael Levengood	Edward D. Hirsch

Karl J. Forrest	Terri Annette Herron

For full biographical listings, see the Martindale-Hubbell Law Directory

---

THE HISHON FIRM, LLC (AV)

999 Peachtree Street N.E. Suite 1900, 30309
Telephone: 404-817-7791
Fax: 404-817-2486

Robert H. Hishon

Nancy R. Daspit

For full biographical listings, see the Martindale-Hubbell Law Directory

---

HOLT, NEY, ZATCOFF & WASSERMAN (AV)

A Partnership including Professional Corporations
100 Galleria Parkway, Suite 600, 30339
Telephone: 770-956-9600
Facsimile Number: 770-956-1490

MEMBERS OF FIRM

Robert G. Holt (P.C.)	Sanford H. Zatcoff (P.C.)
James M. Ney (P.C.)	Michael G. Wasserman (P.C.)

Charles D. Vaughn

Representative Clients: Champion Healthcare Corporation; Cummins South, Inc.; Gables Residential Trust; The University Financing Foundation, Inc.; Hen Co., Inc. (Georgia); Trammell Crow Residential; Citicorp Real Estate,

(See Next Column)

Inc.; Cobb County Chamber of Commerce, Inc.; Roberts Realty Investors, Inc.; Sterling Trust.

For Complete List of Firm Personnel, See General Section

For full biographical listings, see the Martindale-Hubbell Law Directory

---

JOHNSON & MONTGOMERY (AV)

One Buckhead Plaza, 3060 Peachtree Road, N.W., Suite 400, 30305
Telephone: 404-262-1000
Telecopier: 404-262-1222

MEMBERS OF FIRM

Thomas E. Jones, Jr.	William D. Montgomery

C. Talbot Nunnally, III

ASSOCIATE

Andrew Parks Kaiser

For full biographical listings, see the Martindale-Hubbell Law Directory

---

JOHNSON & WARD (AV)

2100 The Equitable Building, 100 Peachtree Street N.W., 30303-1962
Telephone: 404-524-5626
Facsimile: 404-524-1769

MEMBERS OF FIRM

John C. Dabney, Jr.	Baxter P. Jones

William D. deGolian

For Complete List of Firm Personnel, See General Section

For full biographical listings, see the Martindale-Hubbell Law Directory

---

KAUFMAN, CHAIKEN, RICKERTSEN, KREVOLIN, MILLER & HORST, A PROFESSIONAL CORPORATION (AV)

400 Perimeter Center Terrace, N.E., Suite 720, 30346-1234
Telephone: 770-390-9200
Facsimile: 770-395-6720
Email: rkaufm03@counsel.com

Robert J. Kaufman	Fredric Chaiken

References: Gulf States Mortgage Co., Inc.; Dyer & Dyer Volvo, Inc.; Trust Company Bank; Wachovia Bank of Georgia.

For Complete List of Firm Personnel, See General Section

For full biographical listings, see the Martindale-Hubbell Law Directory

---

KILPATRICK & CODY LLP (AV)

Suite 2800, 1100 Peachtree Street, 30309-4530
Telephone: 404-815-6500
Telephone Copier: 404-815-6555
Telex: 54-2307
Washington, D.C. Office: Suite 800, 700 13th Street, N.W., 20005.
Telephone: 202-508-5800. Telephone Copier: 202-508-5858.
Brussels, Belgium Office: Avenue Louise 65, BTE 3, 1050 Brussels.
Telephone: (32) (2) 533-03-00.
Telecopier: (32) (2) 534-86-38.
London, England Office: 68 Pall Mall, London, SW1Y 5ES, England.
Telephone: (44) (71) 321 0477.
Telecopier: (44) (71) 930 9733.
Augusta, Georgia Office: Suite 1400 First Union Bank Building, P.O. Box 2043, 30903. Telephone (706) 724-2622. Telecopier (706) 722-0219.

MEMBERS OF FIRM

Harold E. Abrams	Melinda A. Marbes
Luis A. Aguilar	Dennis S. Meir
Rupert M. Barkoff	John M. Mitnick
W. Stanley Blackburn	C. Ray Mullins
William A. Burnham	Keith T. Ott (Resident, London,
Richard R. Cheatham	England Office)
Gregory K. Cinnamon	Reinaldo Pascual
Evelyn H. Coats	Barry Phillips
Jerome F. Connell, Jr.	Joel B. Piassick
A. Kimbrough Davis	Marc K. Ritzmann
W. Randy Eaddy	Duncan A. Roush
James L. Ewing, IV	Dean W. Russell
Candace L. Fowler	Gary K. Saidman
F. Sheffield Hale	Brian Leonard Schleicher
Frederick K. Heller, Jr.	David A. Stockton
(Resident, Brussels, Belgium	Earle R. Taylor, III
Office)	G. Kimbrough Taylor, Jr.
Hilary P. Jordan	Michael H. Trotter
Wyck A. Knox, Jr.	Timothy N. Tucker
(Augusta Office)	J. William Veatch, III
Colvin T. Leonard, III	Dennis L. Zakas
Alfred S. Lurey	Deborah B. Zink

COUNSEL

Jan Meadows Davidson

(See Next Column)

KILPATRICK & CODY, *Atlanta—Continued*

ASSOCIATES

William B. Barkley	Michael Dean Langford
Richard Cicchillo, Jr.	Stephanie K. Maffett
Cecil L. Davis, Jr.	Kevin M. McMahon
Donald C. Evans, Jr.	Todd C. Meyers
J. Griffin Foster	Jeffrey T. Skinner
William H. Fussell	W. Craig Smith
Nancy G. Gilreath	(Augusta, Georgia Office)
Ralph H. Harrison, III	James D. Steinberg
Wei Hu	Whit F. Stolz

For Complete List of Firm Personnel, See General Section

For full biographical listings, see the Martindale-Hubbell Law Directory

---

LAMBERTH, BONAPFEL, CIFELLI & STOKES, P.A. (AV)

Atlanta Financial Center, 3343 Peachtree Road, N.E. East Tower, Suite 550, 30326
Telephone: 404-262-7373

J. Michael Lamberth	Paul W. Bonapfel
James Craig Cifelli	Gary D. Stokes
	Carter L. Stout

G. Frank Nason, IV	Donahue S. Silvis
Stuart F. Clayton, Jr.	A. Alexander Teel
Gregory D. Ellis	Laura E. Woodson

OF COUNSEL

William H. Willson, Jr.

Reference: The Riverside Bank.

For full biographical listings, see the Martindale-Hubbell Law Directory

---

LONG ALDRIDGE & NORMAN, LLP (AV)

A Limited Liability Partnership including Professional Corporations
One Peachtree Center, Suite 5300, 303 Peachtree Street, 30308
Telephone: 404-527-4000
Telecopier: 404-527-4198
Washington, D.C. Office: Suite 600, 701 Pennsylvania Avenue, N.W., 20004.
Telephone: 202-624-1200.
FAX: 202-624-1298.

MEMBERS OF FIRM

Stephen L. Camp	David M. Ivey
Jeffrey K. Haidet	Clay C. Long
	Jesse J. Spikes

SENIOR COUNSEL

F. T. Davis, Jr., (P.C.)	W. Stell Huie

ASSOCIATES

Claire Alison Addlestone	H. Franklin Layson
(Not admitted in GA)	Ann-Marie M. McGaughey
Sheila Shuster Baye	Johnathan H. Short
Wayne N. Bradley	Briggs L. Tobin
Robert J. LaPorta	Richard R. Willis

OF COUNSEL

William J. Carney

For Complete List of Firm Personnel, See General Section

For full biographical listings, see the Martindale-Hubbell Law Directory

---

MOZLEY, FINLAYSON & LOGGINS LLP (AV)

A Limited Liability Partnership
One Premier Plaza Suite 900, 5605 Glenridge Drive, 30342
Telephone: 404-256-0700
Telecopier: 404-250-9355

MEMBERS OF FIRM

Robert M. Finlayson II	R. Ann Grier
Sewell K. Loggins	Scott D. Calhoun

For full biographical listings, see the Martindale-Hubbell Law Directory

---

PARKER, HUDSON, RAINER & DOBBS (AV)

1500 Marquis Two Tower, 285 Peachtree Center Avenue, N.E., 30303
Telephone: 404-523-5300
FAX: 404-522-8409
Tallahassee, Florida Office: The Perkins House, 118 North Gadsden Street, 32301.
Telephone: 904-681-0191.
FAX: 904-681-9493.

MEMBERS OF FIRM

Paul L. Hudson, Jr.	Mitchell M. Purvis

For full biographical listings, see the Martindale-Hubbell Law Directory

---

PETERSON DILLARD YOUNG ASSELIN & POWELL LLP (AV)

Suite 1100, 230 Peachtree Street, N.W., 30303
Telephone: 404-523-3300
Telecopier: 404-522-6000

MEMBERS OF FIRM

Jerry G. Peterson	Thomas O. Powell
	Thomas M. Duffy

For full biographical listings, see the Martindale-Hubbell Law Directory

---

MORETON ROLLESTON, JR. (AV)

Suite 1870, Riverwood 100, 3350 Cumberland Circle, N.W., 30339
Telephone: 770-850-1816

Reference: Wachovia Bank of Georgia, Private Banking Department.

SCHULTEN, WARD & TURNER (AV)

Suite 1100 The Hurt Building, 50 Hurt Plaza, 30303
Telephone: 404-688-6800
Fax: 404-688-6840

MEMBERS OF FIRM

Wm. Scott Schulten	Kevin L. Ward
	David L. Turner

ASSOCIATES

Lou Litchfield	Clay Morris Westbrook
Susan Kastan Murphey	Julie H. McGhee

OF COUNSEL

Donald W. Osborne

Reference: NationsBank of Georgia, N.A.

For full biographical listings, see the Martindale-Hubbell Law Directory

---

SLUTZKY, WOLFE AND BAILEY (AV)

2255 Cumberland Parkway, Building 1300, 30339
Telephone: 770-438-8000
Telecopier: 770-438-9657

MEMBERS OF FIRM

Stanley K. Slutzky	Bernard R. Wolfe
	Danny C. Bailey

ASSOCIATES

Ray S. Smith III	Barry M. Wolfe
William J. Lieberbaum	Brad M. Wolfe

For full biographical listings, see the Martindale-Hubbell Law Directory

---

SUTHERLAND, ASBILL & BRENNAN, L.L.P. (AV)

999 Peachtree Street, N.E., 30309-3996
Telephone: 404-853-8000
Facsimile: 404-853-8806
Email: postmaster@sablaw.com
Washington, D.C. Office: 1275 Pennsylvania Avenue, N.W., 20004-2404.
Telephone: 202-383-0100.
New York, N.Y. Office: 600 Madison Avenue, 11th Floor, 10022-1615.
Telephone: 212-605-6400.
Austin, Texas Office: 111 Congress Avenue, 23rd Floor, 78701-4079.
Telephone: 512-469-3350.

F. Louise Adams	Thomas B. Hyman, Jr.
Reginald J. Clark	Edward W. Kallal, Jr.
George L. Cohen	Mark D. Kaufman
N. Jerold Cohen	Bennett Lexon Kight
Peter H. Dean	Cada T. Kilgore, III
B. Knox Dobbins	James R. Paulk, Jr.
Peter A. Fozzard	Herbert J. Short, Jr.
Barrett K. Hawks	C. Christopher Trower
Thomas C. Herman	James H. Wilson, Jr.

COUNSEL OF THE FIRM IN ATLANTA, GEORGIA

Charles M. Flickinger

For Complete List of Firm Personnel, See General Section

For full biographical listings, see the Martindale-Hubbell Law Directory

---

THRASHER, WHITLEY, HAMPTON & MORGAN, A PROFESSIONAL CORPORATION (AV)

Suite 2150, Five Concourse Parkway, 30328
Telephone: 770-804-8000
Telecopier: 770-804-5555

H. Grady Thrasher, III	Robert E. Whitley
	Robert T. Morgan

Representative Clients: First Southern Securities Group, Inc.; Georgia Dental Assn.; Kearney National, Inc.; Middle Bay Oil Company, Inc.; Perry & Co.; Smallwood, Reynolds, Stewart, Stewart & Assoc., Inc.; Sunchase Holdings, Ltd.; Touch Industries, Inc.

For full biographical listings, see the Martindale-Hubbell Law Directory

Atlanta—Continued

WAGNER, JOHNSTON, ROSENTHAL & TOBIN, P.C. (AV)

Suite 800, East Tower Atlanta Financial Center, 3343 Peachtree Road, N.E., 30326-1044
Telephone: 404-261-0500
Facsimile: 404-261-6779

Craig A. Wagner	R. Scott Tobin
C. David Johnston	John R. Thornburgh
Michael S. Rosenthal	Ralph A. Jordan

OF COUNSEL

Melvin E. Weinstein (P.C.)	Roger A. Kirschenbaum
Stuart M. Neiman	M. Debra Gold

For full biographical listings, see the Martindale-Hubbell Law Directory

WEISZ & ASSOCIATES (AV)

Suite 900 Live Oak Center, 3475 Lenox Road, N.E., 30326-1232
Telephone: 404-233-7888
Facsimile: 404-261-1925

Peter R. Weisz

ASSOCIATE

Cathy Rae Nash

LEGAL SUPPORT PERSONNEL

PARALEGALS

Jo Anne Gunn

Representative Clients: Marion & Cass Street Corp.; H.K. Brewing Co.; Deerfield Construction Co.; Cee Klein Accessories, LTD; Atlanta Valet, Inc.; Central Bank of Tampa; Aloha Leasing div. of Bennett Funding Group, Inc.
Reference: First Union National Bank.

For full biographical listings, see the Martindale-Hubbell Law Directory

WILSON, STRICKLAND & BENSON, P.C. (AV)

1100 One Midtown Plaza, 1360 Peachtree Street, N.E., 30309
Telephone: 404-870-1800
Telecopier: 404-870-1808

Frank B. Strickland	R. Milton Crouch

Daniel I. MacIntyre

For Complete List of Firm Personnel, See General Section

For full biographical listings, see the Martindale-Hubbell Law Directory

AUGUSTA,* Richmond Co.

FULCHER, HAGLER, REED, HANKS & HARPER (AV)

A Partnership including Professional Corporations
520 Greene Street, P.O. Box 1477, 30903-1477
Telephone: 706-724-0171
Telecopier: 706-724-4573

MEMBERS OF FIRM

William M. Fulcher (1902-1993)	Michael B. Hagler (P.C.)
Gould B. Hagler (Retired)	James W. Purcell (P.C.)
William C. Reed (Retired)	J. Arthur Davison (P.C.)
David H. Hanks (P.C.)	Mark C. Wilby (P.C.)
John I. Harper (P.C.)	Ronald C. Griffeth
Robert C. Hagler (P.C.)	N. Staten Bitting, Jr. (P.C.)

David P. Dekle (P.C.)

ASSOCIATES

Scott W. Kelly	Elizabeth A. McLeod
Cynthia A. Gray	Barry A. Fleming

General Counsel for: GIW Industries, Inc.
Division Counsel for: CSX Transportation; Textron, Inc. (E-Z Go Car Division).
Counsel for: NationsBank; Georgia Natural Gas Co. (a division of Atlanta Gas Light Co.); Champion International Corp.; Aetna Life and Casualty; Liberty Mutual Insurance Company; St. Paul Fire & Marine Insurance Co.; Kimberly Clark Corporation.

For full biographical listings, see the Martindale-Hubbell Law Directory

HULL, TOWILL, NORMAN & BARRETT, A PROFESSIONAL CORPORATION (AV)

Seventh Floor, Trust Company Bank Building, P.O. Box 1564, 30903-1564
Telephone: 706-722-4481
Fax: 706-722-9779

James M. Hull (1885-1975)	Lawton Jordan, Jr.
George B. Barrett (1894-1942)	Patrick J. Rice
Julian S. Willingham (1887-1963)	Douglas D. Batchelor, Jr.
John Bell Towill (1907-1991)	David E. Hudson
Robert C. Norman	Neal W. Dickert
(Retired, 1991)	John W. Gibson
W. Hale Barrett	William F. Hammond

(See Next Column)

Mark S. Burgreen	James B. Ellington
George R. Hall	F. Michael Taylor

Robert A. Mullins	Michael S. Carlson
William J. Keogh, III	Ralph Emerson Hanna, III
Edward J. Tarver	Susan D. Barrett
J. Noel Schweers, III	Timothy E. Moses

Counsel for: Sun Trust Bank Augusta, N.A.; Georgia Federal Bank, FSB, Augusta Division; Southeastern Newspapers Corp.; Georgia Power Co.; Southern Bell Telephone & Telegraph Co.; St. Joseph Hospital, Augusta, Georgia, Inc.; Norfolk Southern Corp.; Merry Land & Investment Co., Inc.; Housing Authority of the City of Augusta; Georgia Press Association.

For full biographical listings, see the Martindale-Hubbell Law Directory

J. BENJAMIN KAY, III (AV)

808 First Union Bank Building, 30901
Telephone: 706-722-2008

Approved Attorney for: Lawyers Title Insurance Corp.
Reference: First Union National Bank of Georgia.
Representative Clients: American National Bank & Trust Company; Biotech Park, Inc.; Caterpillar Financial Services, Inc.; Davis-McGraw, Inc.; Ford Leasing Development Company; Ford Motor Credit Company; Gary Concrete Products, Inc.; Globe Life Insurance Company.

For full biographical listings, see the Martindale-Hubbell Law Directory

CARROLLTON,* Carroll Co.

TISINGER, TISINGER, VANCE & GREER, A PROFESSIONAL CORPORATION (AV)

100 Wagon Yard Plaza, P.O. Box 2069, 30117
Telephone: 770-834-4467
Fax: 770-834-5426

Richard G. Tisinger, Sr.	G. Gregory Shadrix
J. Thomas Vance	Stacey L. Blackmon
C. David Mecklin, Jr.	Steven T. Minor

Edith Freeman Rooks

Representative Clients: Carrollton Federal Bank-FSB; Richards Homes, Inc.; Southwire Company; Tanner Medical Center, Inc.

For Complete List of Firm Personnel, See General Section

For full biographical listings, see the Martindale-Hubbell Law Directory

DECATUR,* De Kalb Co.

SIMMONS, WARREN, SZCZECKO & McFEE, PROFESSIONAL ASSOCIATION (AV)

315 West Ponce de Leon Avenue, Suite 850, 30030
Telephone: 404-378-1711
Fax: 404-377-6101

Wesley B. Warren, Jr.	William C. McFee, Jr.

Representative Clients: David Hocker & Associates (Shopping Center Development); Julian LeCraw & Company (Real Estate); Intown Suites, Inc.; Preferred Lodging Systems, Inc.; Royal Oldsmobile,; Cotter & Co.; Atlanta Neurosurgical Associates, P.A.; Troncalli Motors, Inc.

For Complete List of Firm Personnel, See General Section

For full biographical listings, see the Martindale-Hubbell Law Directory

GRIFFIN,* Spalding Co.

JOHN M. COGBURN, JR. (AV)

115 North Sixth Street, P.O. Box 907, 30224
Telephone: 770-228-2148
Telecopier: 770-228-5018

ASSOCIATE

Michael S. Evans

Representative Clients: Griffin-Spalding County Hospital Authority; Allstar Knitwear Co., Inc. (Textiles); Atlanta Tees, Inc. (Sportswear Distribution); Industrial Refrigeration Enterprises, Inc. (Refrigeration Engineers and Contractors).

For full biographical listings, see the Martindale-Hubbell Law Directory

LAWRENCEVILLE,* Gwinnett Co.

ANDERSEN, DAVIDSON & TATE, P.C. (AV)

324 West Pike Street, Suite 200, P.O. Box 2000, 30246-2000
Telephone: 770-822-0900
Telecopier: 770-822-9680

Thomas J. Andersen	Jeffrey R. Mahaffey
Thomas T. Tate	William M. Ray, II

References: Sun Trust Bank; The Bank of Gwinnett County; Chicago Title Insurance Co.; Title Insurance Company of Minnesota.

(See Next Column)

ANDERSEN, DAVIDSON & TATE P.C., *Lawrenceville—Continued*

For Complete List of Firm Personnel, See General Section

For full biographical listings, see the Martindale-Hubbell Law Directory

WEBB, TANNER & POWELL (AV)

Suite 300 Gwinnett Federal Building, 750 South Perry Street, P.O. Box 27, 30246
Telephone: 770-962-8545; 963-3423
Fax: 770-963-3424

MEMBERS OF FIRM

Jones Webb	Anthony O. L. Powell
William G. Tanner	Ralph L. Taylor, III
Andrew R. Mertz	

Attorneys for: Brand Banking Co.; City of Lawrenceville, Ga.; Water and Sewer Authority of Gwinnett County; Federal Land Bank of Columbia; Georgia Power Co.; Lawyers Title Insurance Corp.; Young Harris College, Young Harris, Georgia; Chicago Title Insurance Co.; International Safety Instruments.

For Complete List of Firm Personnel, See General Section

For full biographical listings, see the Martindale-Hubbell Law Directory

LOUISVILLE,* Jefferson Co.

ABBOT, MURPHY AND HARVEY, P.C. (AV)

190 East 7th Street, P.O. Box 31, 30434
Telephone: 912-625-7281
Facsimile: 912-625-8200

W. Wright Abbot (1892-1969)	John R. Murphy, III
James C. Abbot	Fred K. Harvey, Jr.

B. Michael Arrington

First National Bank & Trust Co., Louisville, Georgia; City of Louisville; J.M. Huber Corp.; Jefferson E.M.C.; Town of Bartow; Bank of Wadley; Forstmann and Company, Inc.; Fulghum Industries, Inc.; Hospital Authority of Jefferson County; Allied Business Systems.

For full biographical listings, see the Martindale-Hubbell Law Directory

MACON,* Bibb Co.

CHAMBLESS, HIGDON & CARSON (AV)

Suite 200 Ambrose Baber Building, 577 Walnut Street, P.O. Box 246, 31298-5399
Telephone: 912-745-1181
Telecopier: 912-746-9479

MEMBERS OF FIRM

Joseph H. Davis	Thomas F. Richardson
Joseph H. Chambless	Mary Mendel Katz
David B. Higdon	Emmitte H. Griggs
James F. Carson, Jr.	Marc T. Treadwell

ASSOCIATES

Kim H. Stroup	Jon Christopher Wolfe
James D. Tolliver	

LEGAL SUPPORT PERSONNEL

Angie Horton	Erie Reed

Local Counsel for: Atlanta Gas Light Co.; First Union National Bank of Georgia; Security National Bank.

For full biographical listings, see the Martindale-Hubbell Law Directory

HALL, BLOCH, GARLAND & MEYER (AV)

1500 Charter Medical Building, P.O. Box 5088, 31213-3199
Telephone: 912-745-1625
Telecopier: 912-741-8822

MEMBERS OF FIRM

Benjamin M. Garland	Duncan D. Walker, III
J. Steven Stewart	Mark E. Toth

ASSOCIATES

John Flanders Kennedy	Kimberly Cofer Harris

Counsel for: Wachovia Bank of Georgia, N.A.; BellSouth Mobility, Inc.; Helena Chemical Corp.; Fickling & Walker Asset and Property Management, Inc.; Navistar International Corporation.

For Complete List of Firm Personnel, See General Section

For full biographical listings, see the Martindale-Hubbell Law Directory

SELL & MELTON (AV)

A Partnership including a Professional Corporation
14th Floor, Charter Medical Building, P.O. Box 229, 31297-2899
Telephone: 912-746-8521
Telecopier: 912-745-6426

(See Next Column)

E. S. Sell, Jr.	Joseph W. Popper, Jr.
Buckner F. Melton	Brian J. Passante

General Counsel for: Macon Telegraph Publishing Co. (The Macon Telegraph); Macon-Bibb County Hospital Authority; County of Bibb; County of Twiggs; Smith & Sons Foods, Inc. (S & S Cafeterias); Macon Bibb County Industrial Authority; Burgess Pigment Co.

For Complete List of Firm Personnel, See General Section

For full biographical listings, see the Martindale-Hubbell Law Directory

MARIETTA,* Cobb Co.

W. R. ROBERTSON, III (AV)

244 Roswell Street, Suite 600, 30060-2000
Telephone: 770-422-0200
Fax: 770-424-1322
Email: wrobert244@aol.com

For full biographical listings, see the Martindale-Hubbell Law Directory

W. ALLEN SEPARK (AV)

250 Church Street, Second Floor, P.O. Box 3475, 30061
Telephone: 770-422-3200
Fax: 770-514-1148

Reference: First Union National Bank, formerly Georgia State Bank.

For full biographical listings, see the Martindale-Hubbell Law Directory

NEWNAN,* Coweta Co.

GLOVER & DAVIS, P.A. (AV)

10 Brown Street, P.O. Box 1038, 30264
Telephone: 770-253-4330
Fax: 770-251-7152
Peachtree City, Georgia Office: Suite 130, 200 Westpark Drive.
Telephone: 770-487-5834.
Fax: 770-487-3492.

J. Littleton Glover, Jr.	Alan W. Jackson

Representative Clients: Newnan Savings Bank; Pike Transfer Co.; Batson-Cook Company, General Corporate and Construction Divisions; Coweta County, Georgia; Book Warehouse of Georgia, Inc.; Bailey & Associates; J. Smith Lanier & Co.
Local Counsel for: International Latex Corp.; First Union National Bank of Georgia.

For Complete List of Firm Personnel, See General Section

For full biographical listings, see the Martindale-Hubbell Law Directory

ROME,* Floyd Co.

BRINSON, ASKEW, BERRY, SEIGLER, RICHARDSON & DAVIS (AV)

A Partnership including Professional Corporations
Omberg House, 615 West First Street, P.O. Box 5513, 30162-5513
Telephone: 706-291-8853;
Atlanta: 404-521-0908
Telecopier: 706-234-3574

MEMBERS OF FIRM

Robert M. Brinson (P.C.)	Hendrick L. Cromartie, III
C. King Askew (P.C.)	Wright W. Smith
Robert L. Berry	Mark M. J. Webb
Joseph M. Seigler, Jr.	Joseph B. Atkins
Thomas D. Richardson	I. Stewart Duggan, Jr.
J. Anderson Davis	James Daniel Blitch

Representative Clients: City of Rome; Georgia Power Co.; General Electric Company; News Publishing Company (Rome News Tribune); Redmond Regional Medical Center; Oglethorpe Power Corp.; Suhner Manufacturing, Inc.; The Federal Land Bank of Columbia; AmSouth Bank of Georgia; United States Fidelity & Guaranty Co.

For full biographical listings, see the Martindale-Hubbell Law Directory

SAVANNAH,* Chatham Co.

HUNTER, MACLEAN, EXLEY & DUNN, P.C. (AV)

200 East St. Julian Street, P.O. Box 9848, 31412
Telephone: 912-236-0261
Cable Address: "Ancan"
Telecopier: 912-236-4936
Telex: 54-6483
Atlanta, Georgia Office: The Peachtree, 1355 Peachtree Street, N.E., Suite 1050.
Telephone: 404-876-3611.
Fax: 404-870-2025.

Henry M. Dunn, Jr.	Don L. Waters
John M. Tatum	J. Reid Williamson, III
John M. Hewson, III	Michael Jonas Thomerson

(See Next Column)

HUNTER, MACLEAN, EXLEY & DUNN P.C.—*Continued*

Representative Clients: Savannah Foods & Industries, Inc.; SunTrust Bank, Savannah, N.A.; Great Dane Trailers, Inc.; Atlantic Wood Industries, Inc.; Carson Products Co.; Brasseler, U.S.A., Inc.; Prudential Insurance Company of America; Historic Savannah Foundation, Inc.; John Hancock Mutual Life Insurance Co.; Norfolk Southern Corp.

For Complete List of Firm Personnel, See General Section

For full biographical listings, see the Martindale-Hubbell Law Directory

HAWAII

HONOLULU,* Honolulu Co.

GEORGE W. ASHFORD, JR. (AV)

2910 Pacific Tower, 1001 Bishop Street, 96813
Telephone: 808-528-0444
Telecopier: (808) 533-0761
Cable Address: Justlaw

Representative Clients: Lloyds of London; Baker Industries, Inc.; Burns International Security Services; Clark Equipment Co.; Great Lakes Chemical Corporation; California Union Insurance Co.; Great American Insurance Companies; Guaranty National Companies; Horace Mann Insurance Company; Marine Office of America Corp.

For full biographical listings, see the Martindale-Hubbell Law Directory

CHAR SAKAMOTO ISHII & LUM (AV)

Suite 850, 841 Bishop Street, 96813
Telephone: 808-522-5133
Facsimile: 808-522-5144

MEMBERS OF FIRM

Vernon F. L. Char	David M. K. Lum
Steven Ching	Charles E. McKay
Elizabeth Ann Ishii	Ronald R. Sakamoto

OF COUNSEL

Michael K. Tanigawa

Lana Proctor Banbury	Jacqueline H. Furuta
Earl M. Ching	Carolyn E. Hayashi
Carolyn M. Oshiro	

For full biographical listings, see the Martindale-Hubbell Law Directory

LAW OFFICES OF DAVID F. DAY (AV)

Grosvenor Center Mauka Tower Suite 1788, 737 Bishop Street, 96813
Telephone: 808-531-8020
Fax: 808-521-0962
Email: ddayofc@lava.net

For full biographical listings, see the Martindale-Hubbell Law Directory

DWYER IMANAKA SCHRAFF KUDO MEYER & FUJIMOTO ATTORNEYS AT LAW, A LAW CORPORATION (AV)

1800 Pioneer Plaza, 900 Fort Street Mall, 96813
Telephone: 808-524-8000
Telecopier: 808-526-1419
Mailing Address: P.O. Box 2727, 96803
Email: hawaiilaw@dwyer-imanaka.com *URL:*
http://www.dwyer-imanaka.com

John R. Dwyer, Jr.	William G. Meyer, III
Mitchell A. Imanaka	Wesley M. Fujimoto
Paul A. Schraff	Ronald Van Grant
Benjamin A. Kudo (Atty. at Law, A Law Corp.)	Jon M. H. Pang
	Blake W. Bushnell
Adelbert Green	

Richard T. Asato, Jr.	Jeffery S. Werbelow
Scott W. Settle	Lori Ann K. Koseki
Darcie S. Yoshinaga	Troy T. Fukuhara
Lawrence I. Kawasaki	Katy Y. Chen
Stacy E. Uehara	Naomi S. Uyeno
Kris N. Nakagawa	Roger B. McKeague

OF COUNSEL

Randall Y. Iwase	R. Brian Tsujimura

For full biographical listings, see the Martindale-Hubbell Law Directory

GELBER, GELBER, INGERSOLL, KLEVANSKY & FARIS, A LAW CORPORATION (AV)

Suite 1400 Hawaii Building, 745 Fort Street, 96813
Telephone: 808-524-0155
Telecopier: 808-531-6963
Email: lawfirm@aloha.net

(See Next Column)

Don Jeffrey Gelber	Richard K. Ingersoll
Stephen M. Gelber	Simon Klevansky
Robert J. Faris	

Thomas D. Morell

For full biographical listings, see the Martindale-Hubbell Law Directory

KOBAYASHI, SUGITA & GODA (AV)

A Partnership including Professional Corporations
8th Floor, Hawaii Tower, 745 Fort Street, 96813
Telephone: 808-539-8700
Telecopier: 808-539-8799
Telex: 6502396585 MCI
MCI Mail: 23 96585
ABA/Net: ABA2281

OF COUNSEL

Bert T. Kobayashi, Sr.

Reference: First Hawaiian Bank.

For Complete List of Firm Personnel, See General Section

For full biographical listings, see the Martindale-Hubbell Law Directory

McCORRISTON MIHO MILLER MUKAI (AV)

Five Waterfront Plaza, 4th Floor, 500 Ala Moana Boulevard, 96813
Telephone: 808-529-7300
Facsimile: 808-524-8293
Cable: Attorneys, Honolulu
Mailing Address: P.O. Box 2800, Honolulu, Hawaii, 96803-2800
Hilo, Hawaii Office: 56 Waianuenue Avenue, Suite 217, 96720.
Telephone: 808-935-6537.
Facsimile: 808-935-3398.

PARTNERS

Jon T. Miho	David N. Kuriyama
Clifford J. Miller	Michael J. O'Malley
Franklin K. Mukai	Eric T. Kawatani
Stanley Y. Mukai	Keith K. Suzuka
D. Scott MacKinnon	Michael Rosenthal
Kenneth B. Marcus	Sharon H. Nishi
Kenneth G. K. Hoo	Randall F. Sakumoto
Patrick K. Lau	Andrew W. Char
Alexander R. Jampel	

OF COUNSEL

Robert E. Warner

COUNSEL

Brian T. Hirai	Charles E. Pear, Jr.

ASSOCIATES

Peter J. Hamasaki	Joel D. Kam
Darren Patrick Conley	Shulammite Kim

Representative Clients: The Neiman Marcus Group; Seven-Eleven Hawaii, Inc.; Toshiba Hawaii, Inc.; Daewoo Hawaii Corporation; Hawaii Dental Service; Pacific Basin Economic Council; Gallo Winery; Oahu Gas Service; New Oji Paper Co., Ltd.; Marubeni Corporation.

For Complete List of Firm Personnel, See General Section

For full biographical listings, see the Martindale-Hubbell Law Directory

PITLUCK KIDO SATO & STONE (AV)

701 Bishop Street, 96813
Telephone: 808-523-5030
Telecopier: 808-545-4015
Email: reilly@aloha.net

MEMBERS OF FIRM

Wayne Marshall Pitluck	Dana Kiyomi Nalani Sato
Alan Takashi Kido	James Mauliola Keaka Stone, Jr.

OF COUNSEL

John W. Reilly

Reference: Bank of Hawaii.

For full biographical listings, see the Martindale-Hubbell Law Directory

STUBENBERG & DURRETT (AV)

1400 Pauahi Tower, 1001 Bishop Street, 96813
Telephone: 808-526-0892
Fax: 808-533-4399

James A. Stubenberg	Jonathan S. Durrett

(See Next Column)

STUBENBERG & DURRETT, *Honolulu—Continued*

Richard A. Kersenbrock, Jr.	Joseph L. Dwight, IV
Valerie J. Lam	Vivien Mia Weber

OF COUNSEL

Lorrie L. Stone	Russell W. Lousich
James P. Clarke	

For full biographical listings, see the Martindale-Hubbell Law Directory

TAM, O'CONNOR & HENDERSON ATTORNEYS AT LAW, A LAW CORPORATION (AV)

20th Floor, Central Pacific Plaza, 220 South King Street, 96813
Telephone: 808-545-3030
Fax: 808-523-8051
Fax: 808-537-6782

James K. Tam	Wayne K. T. Mau
Michael F. O'Connor	Lissa H. Andrews
Harvey E. Henderson, Jr.	Robert M. Yamauchi
William J. Nagle, III	Darryl M. Taira
Ashley K. Ikeda	

Christopher Shea Goodwin	Stuart M. Kodish
Lisa Anne Gruebner	John S. Nitao
Wesley H. Ikeda	Nathan M. Osada

Representative Clients: Bank of Hawaii; Chubb/Pacific Indemnity Group; Alexander & Baldwin, Inc.; GECC Financial Corp.; Castle Medical Center; International Savings & Loan; Bank of America; First Federal Savings & Loan; Territorial Savings & Loan Assn.; United States Services Automobile Assn.

For full biographical listings, see the Martindale-Hubbell Law Directory

WAGNER, WATSON & PETTIT (AV)

Suite 2480 Mauka Tower, 737 Bishop Street, 96813
Telephone: 808-533-1872
Telecopier: 808-521-6117
Email: pettit@alohalaw.com

James A. Wagner	James H. Watson
Ted N. Pettit	

ASSOCIATES

James F. Evers	Susan M. Ireland
John D. Zalewski	James J.S. Chang
Chuck C. Choi	J. Christian Bangerter, Jr.

LEGAL SUPPORT PERSONNEL

Terry Imai	Charles Demeree
Connie M. Gardner	

For full biographical listings, see the Martindale-Hubbell Law Directory

IDAHO

BOISE, * Ada Co.

ELAM & BURKE, A PROFESSIONAL ASSOCIATION (AV)

Key Financial Center, 702 West Idaho Street, P.O. Box 1539, 83701
Telephone: 208-343-5454
Telecopier: 208-384-5844
Email: eblaw@elamburke.com

Carl P. Burke	David B. Lincoln
William J. Batt	

Bradlee R. Frazer	
Jeffrey W. Pusch	Sandra L. Clapp
	Victoria C. Yu

Representative Clients: Morrison-Knudsen; J.R. Simplot Co.; West One Bank; U.S. Bankcorp; Sinclair Oil d/b/a Sun Valley Co.; U.S. West; Boise WestCoast Hotel and Bank of America Centre; Micron Construction, Inc.; United Heritage Life Insurance Co.; Idaho Life and Health Guaranty Association.

For Complete List of Firm Personnel, See General Section

For full biographical listings, see the Martindale-Hubbell Law Directory

POCATELLO, * Bannock Co.

MERRILL & MERRILL, CHARTERED (AV)

Key Bank Building, P.O. Box 991, 83204
Telephone: 208-232-2286
Fax: 208-232-2499

(See Next Column)

Wesley F. Merrill	D. Russell Wight
Dave R. Gallafent	Kent L. Hawkins

Representative Clients: West One Bank of Idaho; J.R. Simplot Co.; School District #25, Bannock County, Idaho; First American Title Insurance Co.; Pocatello Dental Group, P.L.L.C.; Jackson State Bank; Eastern Idaho Development Corp.

For Complete List of Firm Personnel, See General Section

For full biographical listings, see the Martindale-Hubbell Law Directory

ILLINOIS

*BLOOMINGTON,** McLean Co.

HARTWEG, MUELLER, TURNER, DRAZEWSKI & WOOD, P.C. (AV)

207 West Jefferson Street, Suite 400, P.O. Box 397, 61701-0397
Telephone: 309-827-0044
Telecopier: 309-829-0328

Darrell L. Hartweg	Ralph T. Turner
William A. Mueller, Jr.	Scott D. Drazewski
George C Wood	

Michael J. Robak
OF COUNSEL
John R. Luedtke

Reference: Magna Bank of McLean County.

For full biographical listings, see the Martindale-Hubbell Law Directory

CHAMPAIGN, Champaign Co.

MEYER, CAPEL, HIRSCHFELD, MUNCY, JAHN & ALDEEN, P.C. (AV)

306 West Church Street, P.O. Box 6750, 61826-6750
Telephone: 217-352-1800
Telecopier: 217-352-1083
Email: attorneys@meyercapel.com *URL:* http://www.meyercapel.com
Urbana, Illinois Office: 300 West Main Street.
Telephone: 217-328-5520.

James L. Capel, Jr. (1933-1991)	Tracy J. Nugent
John C. Hirschfeld	Richard T. West
Dennis K. Muncy	Rusty W. Freeland
Francis J. Jahn	Lorna K. Geiler
Donald R. Aldeen	Patrick T. Fitzgerald
John H. Elder	Todd J. Black
David B. Sholem	Mark P. Miller
Mark D. Lipton	Joseph Dwyer Murphy

Neil R. Rafferty	Patricia L. Gruber
James M. Mullady	William B. Moore
Adam B. Hirschfeld	Rochelle A. Funderburg
Evan D. Coobs	

OF COUNSEL

August C. Meyer, Jr.	Richard J. Winkel, Jr.

Representative Clients: Bank of Illinois in Champaign; Bell Foods, Inc.; Champaign News-Gazette; Christie Clinic; Federal Deposit Insurance Corp.; Illini Cablevision, Inc.; Kuck & Associates, Inc.; Midwest Television, Inc.; Parkland College.

For full biographical listings, see the Martindale-Hubbell Law Directory

RAWLES, O'BYRNE, STANKO & KEPLEY, P.C. (AV)

501 West Church Street, P.O. Box 800, 61824-0800
Telephone: 217-352-7661
Telecopier: 217-352-2169

Donald M. Reno (1906-1987)	Edward H. Rawles
J. Michael O'Byrne	Stephen M. O'Byrne
Vance I. Kepley (Retired)	Glenn A. Stanko
Brett A. Kepley	

Timothy S. Jefferson
LEGAL SUPPORT PERSONNEL

Rose M. Lanter (Legal Assistant)	Karen B. Judd (Legal Assistant)

Local Counsel for: Bank One of Champaign, Urbana; Covenant Medical Center; Gibson Community Hospital; Frances Nelson Health Center; University of Illinois; Pekin Insurance Company; Union Insurance Group; New Hampshire Insurance Group; Construction Industry Welfare Fund of Central Illinois; Terra International Inc.

For full biographical listings, see the Martindale-Hubbell Law Directory

CHICAGO, * Cook Co.

ALBERT, BATES, WHITEHEAD & McGAUGH, P.C. (AV)

One South Wacker Drive, Suite 1990, 60606
Telephone: 312-357-6300
Fax: 312-357-6219

Jorge C. Albala	Laurie D. Jaffe
Charles G. Albert	Robert Kinchen
Peter H. Barrow	Raymond S. McGaugh
Fredrick H. Bates	Rory Dean Smith
Jerry D. Brown	Laura D. Ryan
Kathie M. Contois	Gregory C. Whitehead
	Allison L. Wood

For full biographical listings, see the Martindale-Hubbell Law Directory

BERMAN & YOTIS, A PROFESSIONAL ASSOCIATION (AV)

(A Professional Association comprised of Professional Corporations)
Suite 2215, 100 North La Salle Street, 60602
Telephone: 312-726-0531
Fax: 312-726-4928

Michael H. Berman (P.C.)	William W. Yotis, III, (P.C.)
Joy C. Airaudi	Dean J. Papadakis
Eric D. Kaplan	Dean Gournis

OF COUNSEL
Karen C. Yotis

For full biographical listings, see the Martindale-Hubbell Law Directory

CARNEY & BROTHERS, LTD. (AV)

30 North La Salle Street, Suite 3100, 60602
Telephone: 312-372-2909
Fax: 312-704-6693

Demetrius E. Carney	Ellen E. Douglass
Alan W. Brothers	Lori A. Owens
Hubert O. Thompson	James L. Bebley

Cheryl J Colston	Andre Gamble
Trasha A. Embry	Angela M. Williams
	Oswald G. Lewis

OF COUNSEL

Joyce A. Hughes	Henry I. Thomas

Representative Clients: Allstate Life Insurance Co.; Amoco Oil Co.; Commonwealth Edison Co.; First National Bank of Chicago; General Motors Corp.; McDonald's Corp.; New York Life Insurance Co.; Pathway Financial; Seaway National Bank.

For full biographical listings, see the Martindale-Hubbell Law Directory

CHERRY & FLYNN (AV)

30 North La Salle Street, Suite 2300, 60602
Telephone: 312-372-2100
Telecopier: 312-853-0279

Myron M. Cherry	William R. Coulson
Peter Flynn	David D. Merritt
	Adam J. Levitt

For full biographical listings, see the Martindale-Hubbell Law Directory

THE ELDEN LAW FIRM (AV)

150 North Michigan Avenue, 30th Floor, 60601-7567
Telephone: 312-781-3600
Fax: 312-781-3601

Douglas L. Elden	Robbin C. Elden

OF COUNSEL

Charles M. Jacobs	Susan Weagly

For full biographical listings, see the Martindale-Hubbell Law Directory

FIELD GOLAN & SWIGER (AV)

Three First National Plaza Twenty-First Floor, 60602-4206
Telephone: 312-263-2300
Fax: 312-263-0939

MEMBERS OF FIRM

Robert E. Field	Cynthia G. Swiger
Stephen L. Golan	Margaret A. Christie

ASSOCIATES

William J. Arendt	Margaret A. Gisch
Peter C. Quigley	Matthew J. Cozzi

(See Next Column)

OF COUNSEL

Leonard W. Golan	Stephen Edward Smith
Donna F. Hartl	Frank J. Dolan

For full biographical listings, see the Martindale-Hubbell Law Directory

GORDON & EINSTEIN, LTD. (AV)

224 East Ontario, 60611
Telephone: 312-280-7766
Telecopier: 312-280-9599

Raymond P. Gordon	Jean M. Einstein

LEGAL SUPPORT PERSONNEL
Laura A. Kozicki

For full biographical listings, see the Martindale-Hubbell Law Directory

ARAM A. HARTUNIAN AND ASSOCIATES A PROFESSIONAL CORPORATION (AV)

122 South Michigan Avenue, Suite 1850, 60603
Telephone: 312-427-3600
FAX: 312-427-1850

Aram A. Hartunian

For full biographical listings, see the Martindale-Hubbell Law Directory

TERRELL J. ISSELHARD AND ASSOCIATES, LTD. PROFESSIONAL CORPORATION (AV)

Suite 3000, Thirtieth Floor, 200 North La Salle Street, 60601-1083
Telephone: 312-372-5225
Fax: 312-704-4959

Terrell J. Isselhard

David T. Pence

For full biographical listings, see the Martindale-Hubbell Law Directory

HOWARD GORDON KAPLAN, LTD. (AV)

180 North La Salle Street, 28th Floor, 60601
Telephone: 312-641-2555
Facsimile No.: 312-641-6265
Email: howie641@aol.com

Howard Gordon Kaplan

Leonard J. Brenner	Rhonda D. Kaplan-Katz

For full biographical listings, see the Martindale-Hubbell Law Directory

KRASNOW, SANBERG & COHEN (AV)

444 North Michigan Avenue, 60611
Telephone: 312-755-5700
Fax: 312-755-5720
Email: KSC@interaccess.com

MEMBERS OF FIRM

Henry C. Krasnow	Glen R. Cornblath
Lora K. Sanberg	Jeremy W. Hobbs
Steven H. Cohen	Colby M. Green
	William K. Blanchard, Jr.

OF COUNSEL
Mark T. Neil

For full biographical listings, see the Martindale-Hubbell Law Directory

THE LAW OFFICES OF MARC J. LANE A PROFESSIONAL CORPORATION (AV)

Suite 2100 180 North La Salle Street, 60601-2701
Telephone: 312-372-1040
800-372-1040
Fax: 312-346-1040
Email: success@marcjlane.com *URL:* http://www.marcjlane.com

Marc J. Lane

Gregory A. Papiernik

For full biographical listings, see the Martindale-Hubbell Law Directory

Chicago—Continued

McBRIDE BAKER & COLES (AV)

500 West Madison Street 40th Floor, 60661
Telephone: 312-715-5700
Cable Address: "Chilaw"
Telex: 270258
Telecopier: 312-993-9350
Email: lastname@mbc.com *URL:* http://www.mbc.com
Oakbrook Terrace, Illinois Office: Suite 1000, One Mid America Plaza, 60181-4710.
Telephone: 630-954-2100.
Telecopier: 630-954-2112.

MEMBERS OF FIRM

David Ackerman	Evan M. Kjellenberg
Michael J. Boland	David S. Mann
Martin J. Campanella	G. Gale Roberson, Jr.
William J. Cooney	Anne Hamblin Schiave
Lola Miranda Hale	Robert I. Schwimmer
Kenneth A. Jenero	Thomas J. Smedinghoff
Thomas J. Kinasz	Michael L. Weissman
	Larry M. Zanger

SENIOR COUNSEL

Lawrence A. Coles, Jr.

OF COUNSEL

Robert O. Case

ASSOCIATES

Adam E. Berman	Jerald Holisky
Ruth Hill Bro	Laura Newton
Edward J. Hannon	Thomas R. Stilp
	Douglas C. Taylor

For Complete List of Firm Personnel, See General Section

For full biographical listings, see the Martindale-Hubbell Law Directory

NISEN & ELLIOTT (AV)

200 West Adams Street, Suite 2500, 60606
Telephone: 312-346-7800
Telecopier: 312-346-9316

MEMBERS OF FIRM

Paul F. Gerbosi	John Foster Lesch
Edward B. Mueller	John K. Kneafsey
Anthony Packard	Michael H. Moirano
Donald C. Shine	Robert O. Middleton
Mark F. Zaenger	William G. Daluga, Jr.
Michael J. Daley	Kenneth J. Rojc
	Thomas V. McCauley

Robert Christie	Michael J. Pavlicek
Daniel P. Dawson	Brian D. Proctor
Donald F. Froehlke	Jeffrey S. Torosian
Helen M. Jensen	William A. Walker
Thomas K. Juffernbruch	Gregory C. Ward
Adam O. Kirwan	Eric R. Wilen
(Not admitted in IL)	

OF COUNSEL

Charles M. Nisen

For full biographical listings, see the Martindale-Hubbell Law Directory

POLLAK & HOFFMAN LTD. (AV)

Suite 1100, 150 North Wacker Drive, 60606
Telephone: 312-726-0001
FAX: 312-726-1098
Northbrook, Illinois Office: 1200 Shermer Road.
Telephone: 847-564-0130.
FAX: 847-564-0160.

Bertram L. Pollak	Michael E. Pollak
Jay M. Pollak	Bruce F. Hoffman
	Lee J. Lewin

For full biographical listings, see the Martindale-Hubbell Law Directory

SCHWARTZBERG, BARNETT & COHEN (AV)

55 West Monroe Street, 2400 Xerox Centre, 60603-5040
Telephone: 312-726-3555
Fax: 312-726-6299
Cable Address: "Justice"
Email: sb&c@twty.chi.il.us

MEMBERS OF FIRM

Ralph M. Schwartzberg	Mark T. Barnett (1939-1970)
(1939-1975)	Hugh J. Schwartzberg
	Benjamin H. Cohen

OF COUNSEL

Eugene P. Thomas Jr.

For full biographical listings, see the Martindale-Hubbell Law Directory

SUGAR, FRIEDBERG & FELSENTHAL (AV)

30 North La Salle Street, Suite 2600, 60602
Telephone: 312-704-9400
Telecopier: 312-372-7951
Cable: "SUGARFREE"

MEMBERS OF FIRM

Richard A. Sugar	Ira S. Neiman
Michael R. Friedberg	Jonathan L. Mills
Steven A. Felsenthal	Etahn M. Cohen
Andrew B. David	Howard M. Helsinger
Leslie J. Weiss	Robert F. Simon
	Martin M. Weinstein

ASSOCIATES

Kathryn A. Erickson	Jay R. Hoffman
Norman J. Ginsparg	Sophia Stergianis
	Jonathan W. Michael

For full biographical listings, see the Martindale-Hubbell Law Directory

WILSON & McILVAINE (AV)

500 West Madison, Suite 3700, 60661-2511
Telephone: 312-715-5000
Telecopier: 312-715-5155

PARTNERS

Richard P. Blessen	Douglas R. Hoffman
Michael F. Csar	Daniel C. McKay
Marie K. Eitrheim	Kendall R. Meyer
James J. Gatziolis	Janice E. Rodgers
	John P. Vail

ASSOCIATES

Charles A. Lande	Alison L. Paul
	Mark A. Trager

For Complete List of Firm Personnel, See General Section

For full biographical listings, see the Martindale-Hubbell Law Directory

---

MATTOON, Coles Co.

CRAIG & CRAIG (AV)

1807 Broadway, P.O. Box 689, 61938-0689
Telephone: 217-234-6481
Telecopier: 217-234-6486
Mount Vernon, Illinois Office: 227 1/2 South 9th Street.
Telephone: 618-244-7511.

MEMBERS OF FIRM

Craig Van Meter (1895-1981)	Stephen L. Corn
Fred H. Kelly (1894-1971)	Richard Charles Hayden
Robert M. Werden (1908-1969)	Robert G. Grierson
George N. Gilkerson	Gregory C. Ray
(1911-1985)	Paul R. Lynch (Resident, Mount
John H. Armstrong	Vernon Office)
John P. Ewart	Kenneth F. Werts (Resident,
Richard F. Record, Jr.	Mount Vernon Office)
	John L. Barger

ASSOCIATES

Joshua N. Rosen (Resident,	Theresa M. Thomson
Mount Vernon Office)	Kristine M. Tuttle
Kathleen M. Stockwell	Henry P. Villani (Resident,
	Mount Vernon Office)

OF COUNSEL

Jack E. Horsley

Counsel for: Monterey Coal Co., a Division of Exxon Coal USA, Inc.; Marathon Oil Co.; Illinois Central R.R. Co.; Okaw Building & Loan Assn., Mattoon, Illinois; The Medical Protective Insurance Co.; Consolidated Communications, Inc.; Lloyds Underwriters at London; Hartford Insurance Co.; Coles Together, a Not-For-Profit Corp.; Coles Building Corporation.

For full biographical listings, see the Martindale-Hubbell Law Directory

---

NORTHBROOK, Cook Co.

OLSON, GRABILL & HOFFMAN (AV)

Suite 420, 707 Skokie Boulevard, 60062
Telephone: 847-564-8880; 564-9110
FAX: 847-564-8886
Chicago, Illinois Office: Olson, Grabill, Hoffman & Louis, 300 South Wacker Drive, Suite 2400.
Telephone: 312-332-6823.

MEMBERS OF FIRM

Norman L. Olson, Jr.	Fred Louis III
Edward M. Grabill, Jr.	Gregg A. Flitcraft
Thomas G. Hoffman	Kent J. Donewald

OF COUNSEL

G. Kent Yowell

For full biographical listings, see the Martindale-Hubbell Law Directory

OAKBROOK TERRACE, Du Page Co.

GALLAGHER & JOSLYN (AV)

One Lincoln Centre, Suite 300, 60181
Telephone: 630-916-2600
FAX: 630-916-2606

MEMBERS OF FIRM

Gerard B. Gallagher
David L. Joslyn
L. Judson Todhunter

Barry E. Garley
Susan B. Shelton
Ira E. Sussman

OF COUNSEL

Peter A. Bauer
Leonard S. DeFranco

Laurie A. Silvestri
Daniel G. McNamara

For full biographical listings, see the Martindale-Hubbell Law Directory

OAK PARK, Cook Co.

GOEDERT & HUNTINGTON (AV)

6525 West North Avenue, 60302
Telephone: 708-848-6066
FAX: 708-848-6067

MEMBERS OF FIRM

John P. Goedert
Robert A. Huntington
Michael J. DeBoer

For full biographical listings, see the Martindale-Hubbell Law Directory

*PEORIA,** Peoria Co.

BEHRENDS & GENTRY (AV)

700 Jefferson Building, 331 Fulton Street, 61602
Telephone: 309-676-0475
Telecopier: 309-676-0126

F. Louis Behrends

Richard N. Gentry, Jr.

Frank A. Hess

Ambrose V. McCall

For full biographical listings, see the Martindale-Hubbell Law Directory

HOWARD & HOWARD ATTORNEYS, P.C. (AV)

The Creve Coeur Building, Suite 200, 321 Liberty Street, 61602-1403
Telephone: 309-672-1483
Telecopier: 309-672-1568
Kalamazoo, Michigan Office: The Kalamazoo Building, Suite 400, 107 West Michigan Avenue.
Telephone: 616-382-1483.
Telecopier: 616-382-1568.
Bloomfield Hills, Michigan Office: The Pinehurst Office Center, Suite 101, 1400 North Woodward Avenue.
Telephone: 810-645-1483.
Telecopier: 810-645-1568.
Lansing, Michigan Office: Suite 500, The Phoenix Building, 222 Washington Square, North.
Telephone: 517-485-1483.
Telecopier: 517-485-1568.
Tampa, Florida Office: First of America Plaza, Suite 2000, 201 East Kennedy Boulevard.
Telephone: 813-229-1483.
Telecopier: 813-229-1568.

Frederick G. Hoffman

Timothy J. Howard

Representative Clients: For Representative Client list, see General Practice, Peoria, IL.

For Complete List of Firm Personnel, See General Section

For full biographical listings, see the Martindale-Hubbell Law Directory

*SPRINGFIELD,** Sangamon Co.

BROWN, HAY & STEPHENS (AV)

700 First National Bank Building, P.O. Box 2459, 62701-1489
Telephone: 217-544-8491
Fax: 217-544-9609

MEMBERS OF FIRM

Harvey B. Stephens
Edward J. Cunningham
Robert M. Magill
Norman P. Jones
Robert A. Stuart, Jr.
J. Patrick Joyce, Jr.
Eric L. Grenzebach
Jeffery M. Wilday

William F. Trapp
Paul Bown
Almon A. Manson, Jr.
Dwight H. O'Keefe, III
Donald R. Tracy
Emmet A. Fairfield
Denise M. Druhot
Harvey M. Stephens

COUNSEL

Ben L. DeBoice

Simon L. Friedman

(See Next Column)

ASSOCIATES

Elizabeth W. Anderson
Andrew T. Pribe
John Edward Childress

James W. Bruner
Lorilea Burkette
Frank I. Choi

Representative Clients: Athens Community Unit School District; Ball Chatham Community Unit School District; Lincoln Land Community College; Springfield School District #186; Fred Davey Scholarship Trust; Littler Trust Estate; Scully Trusts; Capitol Machinery Co., Inc.; Capital Supply Co.; Excel Corp.

For full biographical listings, see the Martindale-Hubbell Law Directory

VERNON HILLS, Lake Co.

RICHARDS, RALPH & SCHWAB, CHTD. (AV)

Suite 345, One Hawthorn Place, 175 East Hawthorn Parkway, 60061
Telephone: 708-367-9699
FAX: 708-367-9621

Michael L. Ralph

Alan E. Richards

David J. Schwab

For full biographical listings, see the Martindale-Hubbell Law Directory

INDIANA

*BLOOMINGTON,** Monroe Co.

BUNGER & ROBERTSON (AV)

226 South College Square, P.O. Box 910, 47402-0910
Telephone: 812-332-9295
Fax: 812-331-8808

MEMBERS OF FIRM

Don M. Robertson

James L. Whitlatch

Representative Clients: Aetna Insurance Companies; Bloomington Hospital; Commercial Union Group; Indiana Insurance Co.; Liberty Mutual Insurance; Medical Protective Co.; Monroe County Community School Corp.; Professional Golf Car, Inc.; Prudential Insurance Company of America; State Farm Automobile Insurance Co.

For Complete List of Firm Personnel, See General Section

For full biographical listings, see the Martindale-Hubbell Law Directory

CARMEL, Hamilton Co.

KNOWLES & ASSOCIATES (AV)

811 South Range Line Road, 46032
Telephone: 317-848-4360
Telecopier: 317-848-4363
URL: http://www.courts9@1x.netcom.com

William W. Knowles

D. Brandon Johnston

Tracy J. Follstad

For full biographical listings, see the Martindale-Hubbell Law Directory

ELKHART, Elkhart Co.

CHESTER, PFAFF & BROTHERSON (AV)

317 West Franklin Street, P.O. Box 507, 46515-0507
Telephone: 219-294-5421
Fax: 219-522-1476

MEMBERS OF FIRM

Robert A. Pfaff
Edward J. Chester
Glenn E. Killoren

OF COUNSEL

James R. Brotherson

ASSOCIATES

Robert C. Whippo

Craig A. Carpenter

LEGAL SUPPORT PERSONNEL

Wanda S. Wyrick (Paralegal)

For Complete List of Firm Personnel, See General Section

For full biographical listings, see the Martindale-Hubbell Law Directory

*EVANSVILLE,** Vanderburgh Co.

BOWERS, HARRISON, KENT & MILLER, LLP (AV)

25 N.W. Riverside Drive, P.O. Box 1287, 47706-1287
Telephone: 812-426-1231
Fax: 812-464-3676

(See Next Column)

BOWERS, HARRISON, KENT & MILLER LLP, *Evansville—Continued*

MEMBERS OF FIRM

David V. Miller   George C. Barnett, Jr.

Division Counsel in Indiana for: Southern Railway Co.
Representative Clients: Permanent Federal Savings Bank; Citizens Realty & Insurance, Inc.

For Complete List of Firm Personnel, See General Section

For full biographical listings, see the Martindale-Hubbell Law Directory

---

BUTHOD & BUTHOD (AV)

4962 Lincoln Avenue, P.O. Box 2298, 47728-0298
Telephone: 812-473-8500
Fax: 812-473-8505

MEMBERS OF FIRM

James M. Buthod   John J. Buthod

Representative Clients: Custom Engineering, Inc.; Schlumberger Technology Corp.; Watco Transit, Inc.

For full biographical listings, see the Martindale-Hubbell Law Directory

---

LAW OFFICES OF RANDALL K. CRAIG (AV)

5000 East Virginia, Suite 1, 47715
Telephone: 812-477-3337
Telefax: 812-477-3658

For full biographical listings, see the Martindale-Hubbell Law Directory

---

FINE & HATFIELD (AV)

520 N.W. Second Street, P.O. Box 779, 47705-0779
Telephone: 812-425-3592
Telecopier: 812-421-4269
Email: Fine@Fine-Hatfield.com *URL:* http://www.Fine-Hatfield.com

MEMBERS OF FIRM

James E. Marchand   Thomas R. Fitzsimmons

ASSOCIATE

Todd I. Glass

A List of Representative Clients Furnished Upon Request.

For full biographical listings, see the Martindale-Hubbell Law Directory

---

MATTINGLY, RUDOLPH, FINE & PORTER (AV)

221 N.W. Fifth Street, Second Floor, P.O. Box 1507, 47706
Telephone: 812-422-9444
Fax: 812-421-7459
Email: mrfp@evansville.net

MEMBERS OF FIRM

Ross E. Rudolph   L. Montgomery Porter
Marc D. Fine   James D. Johnson

ASSOCIATES

Krista L. Bonewitz   Scott S. Stone
Keith A. Sermersheim

Reference: National City Bank of Evansville.

For full biographical listings, see the Martindale-Hubbell Law Directory

---

ZIEMER, STAYMAN, WEITZEL & SHOULDERS (AV)

(Formerly Early, Arnold & Ziemer)
One Riverfront Place, 20 N.W. First Street 9th Floor, P.O. Box 916, 47706-0916
Telephone: 812-424-7575
Telecopier: 812-421-5089

MEMBERS OF FIRM

Stephan E. Weitzel   Marco L. DeLucio

Reference: Old National Bank in Evansville.

For full biographical listings, see the Martindale-Hubbell Law Directory

---

FORT WAYNE,* Allen Co.

BONAHOOM & BONAHOOM (AV)

110 W. Berry Street, Suite 1700, 46802
Telephone: 219-420-4055
Fax: 219-424-5311

Otto M. Bonahoom   Joseph G. Bonahoom

For full biographical listings, see the Martindale-Hubbell Law Directory

---

MILLER CARSON BOXBERGER & MURPHY (AV)

1400 One Summit Square, 46802-3137
Telephone: 219-423-9411
Telecopier: 219-423-4329
Bloomington, Indiana Office: 3100 John Hinkle Place, Suite 106.
Telephone: 812-333-1225.
Fax: 812-333-1925.

(See Next Column)

MEMBERS OF FIRM

Milford M. Miller, Jr.   Richard P. Samek
Philip L. Carson   Phillip A. Renz
Bruce O. Boxberger   Edward J. Liptak (Resident,
Edward L. Murphy, Jr.   Bloomington, Indiana Office)
Thomas W. Yoder   Robert T. Keen, Jr.
Charles R. Cogdell   Larry L. Barnard
John J. Wernet   Arthur E. Mandelbaum

ASSOCIATES

Diana Carol Bauer   Douglas A. Hoffman
James P. Buchholz   Karl J. Veracco
Timothy A. Manges   Timothy M. Pape
(Not admitted in IN)

Representative Corporate and Financial Clients: Advanced Machine & Tool Corporation; Ford Motor Credit Company; NBD Bank, N.A.; Wal-Mart Inc.
Representative Insurance Clients: Bliss-McKnight Group; Employer's Mutual Company; Employers Mutual of Wausau; General Accident Fire & Life Assurance Corp., LTD.

For full biographical listings, see the Martindale-Hubbell Law Directory

---

SWIFT & FINLAYSON (AV)

803 South Calhoun Street Suite 500, 46802-2480
Telephone: 219-423-4422
Fax: 219-423-4427
Affiliated Law Firm: Leeuw, Plopper & Beeman-Poland, First Indiana Plaza, Suite 2000, 135 North Pennsylvania Street, Indianapolis, Indiana, 46204-2456.

MEMBERS OF FIRM

Frank A. Higgins (1925-1976)   William D. Swift
Craig R. Finlayson

ASSOCIATE

Charles D. Bash

OF COUNSEL

Gene R. Leeuw   Craig D. Doyle
Joseph W. Murphy   Charleyne L. Gabriel
John Michael Mead

For full biographical listings, see the Martindale-Hubbell Law Directory

---

INDIANAPOLIS,* Marion Co.

BOBERSCHMIDT, MILLER, O'BRYAN & TURNER, A PROFESSIONAL ASSOCIATION (AV)

Bank One Center/Circle, 111 Monument Circle, Suite 302, 46204-5169
Telephone: 317-632-5892
Telecopier: 317-686-3423

Philip F. Boberschmidt   Berton W. O'Bryan
L. Craig Turner

A List of Representative Clients will be furnished upon request.

For full biographical listings, see the Martindale-Hubbell Law Directory

---

DANN PECAR NEWMAN & KLEIMAN, PROFESSIONAL CORPORATION (AV)

Suite 2300, One American Square Box 82008, 46282
Telephone: 317-632-3232; Indiana: 800-622-4799
Telecopy: 317-632-2962

Theodore R. Dann (1907-1993)   Walter E. Wolf, Jr.
Joel Yonover (1932-1995)   Barry E. Beldin
Philip D. Pecar   Robert D. Swhier, Jr.
Norman R. Newman   James P. Moloy
David H. Kleiman   Robert J. Schuckit
Jon B. Abels   Andrew A. Kleiman
Melvin R. Daniel   Michael J. Gabovitch
Lawrence F. Dorocke   Steven M. Pecar
Jeffrey A. Abrams   Benjamin A. Pecar
James H. Schwarz   Richard O. Kissel, II
Robert A. Rose   Joseph D. Calderon

OF COUNSEL

Linda E. Cantor   Anthony J. Rose

Ellen C. Siakotos   Angela L. Mansfield
Stacy L. Hill   Martha M. K. Baird
Karin L. Veatch

Attorneys for: Indianapolis Machinery Co., Inc.; Melvin Simon & Associates, Inc.; Pacers Basketball Corp.; Universal Fire & Casualty Co., Inc.; Bank One, Indianapolis, NA; INB National Bank; Nachi Technology, Inc.; Pharmaceutical Corporation of America; Logo 7, Inc.

For full biographical listings, see the Martindale-Hubbell Law Directory

Indianapolis—Continued

MILLER MULLER MENDELSON & KENNEDY (AV)

8900 Keystone Crossing Suite 1250, 46240
Telephone: 317-574-4500
1-800-394-3094
Fax: 317-574-4501

MEMBERS OF FIRM

Michael S. Miller	Tilden Mendelson
John Muller	Timothy J. Kennedy

ASSOCIATE

Catherine A. Kling

For full biographical listings, see the Martindale-Hubbell Law Directory

MITCHELL HURST JACOBS & DICK (AV)

152 East Washington Street, 46204
Telephone: 317-636-0808
1-800-636-0808
Fax: 317-633-7680

MEMBERS OF FIRM

Marvin H. Mitchell	Richard J. Dick
	Steven K. Huffer

ASSOCIATE

Michael T. McNelis

General Counsel For: Dr. Tavel's Vision Center; Calderon Bros. Vending Machines, Inc.; Grocers Supply Co., Inc.; Power Train Services, Inc.; Frank E. Irish, Inc.; Bedding Liquidators; Galyan's Trading Co.; Harcourt Management Co., Inc.; Kosene & Kosene Mgt. & Dev. Co., Inc.; Hasten Bankcorp.

For full biographical listings, see the Martindale-Hubbell Law Directory

SOMMER & BARNARD, ATTORNEYS AT LAW, PC (AV)

4000 Bank One Tower, 111 Monument Circle, 46204-5140
Telephone: 317-630-4000
FAX: 317-236-9802
North Office: 8900 Keystone Crossing, Suite 1046, Indianapolis, Indiana, 46240-2134.
Telephone: 317-630-4000.
FAX: 317-844-4780.

James K. Sommer	James A. Strain
Jerald I. Ancel	Eric R. Johnson
	Julianne S. Lis-Milam

OF COUNSEL

Philip L. McCool	Charles E. Valliere

Representative Clients: Comerica Bank; Excel Industries; Federal Express; Kimball International; Monsanto; Renault Automation; TRW, Inc.

For Complete List of Firm Personnel, See General Section

For full biographical listings, see the Martindale-Hubbell Law Directory

STARK DONINGER & SMITH (AV)

Suite 700, 50 South Meridian Street, 46204
Telephone: 317-638-2400
Fax: 317-633-6618; 633-6619

MEMBERS OF FIRM

John C. Stark	Patricia Seasor Bailey
Bruce E. Smith	Brian J. Tuohy
John W. Van Buskirk	Mark A. Bailey
Richard W. Dyar	Lewis E. Willis, Jr.

ASSOCIATES

Thomas A. Brodnik	Richard B. Kaufman
Neil E. Lucas	Patrick J. Dietrick

COUNSEL

Clarence H. Doninger	Robert D. Maas
Gregory S. Fehribach	William K. Byrum

Reference: Huntington National Bank of Indiana; National Bank of Indianapolis.

For full biographical listings, see the Martindale-Hubbell Law Directory

WALLACK & WALLACK, P.C. (AV)

One Indiana Square, Suite 2230, 46204
Telephone: 317-231-9000
FAX: 317-231-9900

Barry Z. Wallack	Michael S. Wallack

For full biographical listings, see the Martindale-Hubbell Law Directory

LAFAYETTE,* Tippecanoe Co.

STUART & BRANIGIN (AV)

The Life Building, 300 Main Street, Suite 800, 47902
Telephone: 317-423-1561
Telecopier: 317-742-8175

(See Next Column)

MEMBERS OF FIRM

Allison Ellsworth Stuart (1886-1950)	Stephen R. Pennell
Roger D. Branigin (1902-1975)	Anthony S. Benton
Russell H. Hart	Erik D. Spykman
Roger D. Branigin, Jr.	William E. Emerick
Thomas L. Ryan	John C. Duffey
James V. McGlone	Mark E. DeYoung
Carl W. Kloepfer	Thomas B. Parent
Thomas R. McCully	Laura L. Bowker
Larry R. Fisher	Kevin D. Nicoson
Nina B. Kirkpatrick	Susan K. Roberts
Mark Lillianfeld	John M. Stuckey
	Deborah B. Trice

COUNSEL

John F. Bodle

ASSOCIATES

Brent W. Huber	David A. Starkweather
William P. Kealey	Geoffrey Blazi
	A. James Chareq

General Counsel for: The Lafayette Life Insurance Co.; INB National Bank, N.W.; Lafayette Home Hospital, Inc.
State Counsel for: Norfolk & Western Railway Co.
Mr. Ryan is Counsel to: The Trustees of Purdue University.
Representative Clients: Aluminum Company of America; Liberty Mutual Insurance Group.

For full biographical listings, see the Martindale-Hubbell Law Directory

MARION,* Grant Co.

KILEY, KILEY, HARKER, MICHAEL & CERTAIN (AV)

300 West Third Street, P.O. Box 899, 46952-0899
Telephone: 317-664-9041
Fax: 317-664-8119

MEMBERS OF FIRM

Robert Ralph Batton (1890-1963)	David L. Kiley, Sr.
Albert L. Harker (1904-1965)	Michael J. Kiley
Albert Bonner Brown (1911-1981)	Albert C. Harker
	Thomas W. Michael
	Harry J. Certain

ASSOCIATE

Therese McCullough Pryor

Counsel for: Bank One, Marion, N.A.; Liniger Co., Inc.; Atlas Foundry Co.
Local Counsel for: GenCorp.; CPC Group; General Motors; Indiana Michigan Power Co./AEP; Indiana Bell Telephone Co.; Foster-Forbes, Division of American National Can Corp.

For full biographical listings, see the Martindale-Hubbell Law Directory

MUNSTER, Lake Co.

PINKERTON AND FRIEDMAN, PROFESSIONAL CORPORATION (AV)

The Fairmont, 9245 Calumet Avenue Suite 201, 46321
Telephone: 219-836-3050
Fax: 219-836-2955

Milton Roth (1925-1996)	Jeffrey F. Gunning
Kirk A. Pinkerton	Gail Oosterhof
Stuart J. Friedman	Richard N. Shapiro

For full biographical listings, see the Martindale-Hubbell Law Directory

WARSAW,* Kosciusko Co.

ROCKHILL, PINNICK, PEQUIGNOT, HELM, LANDIS & RIGDON (AV)

105 East Main Street, 46580-2742
Telephone: 219-267-6116
Telecopier: 219-269-9264

MEMBERS OF FIRM

Brooks C. Pinnick	Vern K. Landis
Stanley E. Pequignot	Jay A. Rigdon
Richard K. Helm	Jamelyn E. Freeman

OF COUNSEL

Alvin T. Rockhill

Representative Clients: First National Bank of Warsaw, Warsaw, Indiana; Warsaw Times-Union Newspaper and WRSW Radio and Broadcast Station; State Farm Insurance Cos.; Warsaw Chemical Co., Inc.; Little Crow Milling Co., Inc.; Farmers State Bank; C & D Foods, Inc.; Maple Leaf Farms, Inc.; United Farm Bureau Mutual Insurance Co.

For full biographical listings, see the Martindale-Hubbell Law Directory

IOWA

COUNCIL BLUFFS,* Pottawattamie Co.

SMITH PETERSON LAW FIRM (AV)

35 Main Place, Suite 300, P.O. Box 249, 51502
Telephone: 712-328-1833
Fax: 712-328-8320
Omaha, Nebraska Office: 9290 West Dodge Road, Suite 205.
Telephone: 402-397-8500.
Fax: 402-397-5519.

MEMBERS OF FIRM

Raymond A. Smith (1892-1977)	Lawrence J. Beckman
John LeRoy Peterson (1895-1969)	Gregory G. Barntsen
	W. Curtis Hewett
Harold T. Beckman	Steven H. Krohn
Robert J. Laubenthal	Randy R. Ewing
Richard A. Heininger	Joseph D. Thornton

ASSOCIATES

T. J. Pattermann	Paul M. Shotkoski
Daniel Fretheim	(Not admitted in IA)

Representative Clients: Redland Insurance Group; Iowa Western Community College; Farm Credit Bank of Omaha; Demma Fruit Co.; Peoples National Bank; Council Bluffs Board of Water Works Trustee.

For full biographical listings, see the Martindale-Hubbell Law Directory

DAVENPORT,* Scott Co.

NOYES & GOSMA, L.L.P. (AV)

400 North Main Street, Suite 106, 52801
Telephone: 319-322-8223
Fax: 319-322-8234

MEMBERS OF FIRM

Michael L. Noyes	John S. Gosma

ASSOCIATE

Marie R. Rolling-Tarbox

OF COUNSEL

Clay LeGrand	Charles G. Rehling

Reference: Quad City Bank and Trust Company.

For full biographical listings, see the Martindale-Hubbell Law Directory

DES MOINES,* Polk Co.

FINLEY, ALT, SMITH, SCHARNBERG, MAY & CRAIG, P.C. (AV)

604 Locust Street, Fourth Floor Equitable Building, 50309
Telephone: 515-288-0145
Telecopier: 515-288-2724

Glenn L. Smith	David C. Craig

Representative Clients: Aetna Casualty & Surety Co.; Aetna Life Insurance Co.; ALAS; American Society of Composers, Authors and Publishers; Equitable Life Assurance Society of the U.S.; Federated Insurance Co.; Meredith Corp.
Iowa Attorneys for: Midwest Medical Insurance Co.
District Attorneys for: Norfolk & Southern Railroad; Soo Line Railroad Company.

For Complete List of Firm Personnel, See General Section

For full biographical listings, see the Martindale-Hubbell Law Directory

THE ROSENBERG LAW FIRM (AV)

1010 Insurance Exchange Building, 505 Fifth Avenue, 50309
Telephone: 515-243-7600

MEMBERS OF FIRM

Raymond Rosenberg	Brent D. Rosenberg
Dean A. Stowers	Carole L. Hunt

Reference: Firstar Bank, Des Moines, Iowa.

For full biographical listings, see the Martindale-Hubbell Law Directory

WATERLOO,* Black Hawk Co.

SWISHER & COHRT, P.L.C. (AV)

528 West Fourth Street, P.O. Box 1200, 50704
Telephone: 319-232-6555
FAX: 319-232-4835

Benjamin F. Swisher (1878-1959)	J. Douglas Oberman
L. J. Cohrt (1898-1974)	Stephen J. Powell
Charles F. Swisher (1919-1986)	Jim D. DeKoster
Jeffrey J. Greenwood (1953-1995)	Samuel C. Anderson
	Robert C. Griffin
Eldon R. McCann	Kevin R. Rogers
Steven A. Weidner	Beth E. Hansen
Larry J. Cohrt	Mark F. Conway

(See Next Column)

Natalie Williams Burris

Firm is Counsel for: Koehring Corp.; Clay Equipment; Chamberlain Manufacturing Co.; Waterloo Courier.
Local Counsel for: Allied Group; John Deere Insurance; Liberty Mutual Insurance Co.

For full biographical listings, see the Martindale-Hubbell Law Directory

KANSAS

DODGE CITY,* Ford Co.

FOULSTON & SIEFKIN L.L.P. (AV)

810 Frontview, P.O. Box 1147, 67801
Telephone: 316-227-8126
Fax: 316-227-8451
Wichita, Kansas Office: 100 North Broadway, 700 Fourth Financial Center, 67202.
Telephone: 316-267-6371.
FAX: 316-267-6345.
Topeka, Kansas Office: 1515 Bank IV Tower, 534 Kansas Avenue, 66603.
Telephone: 913-233-3600.
FAX: 913-233-1610.
Member: Lex Mundi, A Global Association of 126 Independent Firms.

MEMBERS OF FIRM

William P. Trenkle, Jr.	David J. Rebein

For Complete List of Firm Personnel, See General Section

For full biographical listings, see the Martindale-Hubbell Law Directory

SALINA,* Saline Co.

NORTON, WASSERMAN, JONES & KELLY (AV)

215 South Santa Fe, P.O. Box 2388, 67402-2388
Telephone: 913-827-3646
Fax: 913-827-0538

MEMBERS OF FIRM

Frank C. Norton	Robert S. Jones
Kenneth W. Wasserman	Norman R. Kelly

ASSOCIATE

Robert A. Martin

Reference: Gypsum Valley Bank.

For full biographical listings, see the Martindale-Hubbell Law Directory

TOPEKA,* Shawnee Co.

FOULSTON & SIEFKIN L.L.P. (AV)

1515 Bank IV Tower, 534 Kansas Avenue, 66603
Telephone: 913-233-3600
Fax: 913-233-1610
Wichita, Kansas Office: 100 North Broadway, 700 Fourth Financial Center, 67202.
Telephone: 316-267-6371.
Fax: 316-267-6345.
Dodge City, Kansas Office: 810 Frontview, P.O. Box 1147, 67801.
Telephone: 316-227-8126.
Fax: 316-227-8451.
Member: Lex Mundi, A Global Association of 126 Independent Firms.

MEMBER OF FIRM

James P. Rankin

SPECIAL COUNSEL

James L. Grimes, Jr.

For full biographical listings, see the Martindale-Hubbell Law Directory

WICHITA,* Sedgwick Co.

FOULSTON & SIEFKIN L.L.P. (AV)

700 Fourth Financial Center, 67202
Telephone: 316-267-6371
Facsimile: 316-267-6345
Topeka, Kansas Office: 1515 Bank IV Tower, 534 Kansas Avenue, 66603.
Telephone: 913-233-3600.
Fax: 913-233-1610.
Dodge City, Kansas Office: 810 Frontview, P.O. Box 1147, 67801.
Telephone: 316-227-8126.
Fax: 316-227-8451.
Member: Lex Mundi, A Global Association of 126 Independent Firms.

MEMBERS OF FIRM

Benjamin C. Langel	Harvey R. Sorensen
Stanley G. Andeel	James D. Oliver
William R. Wood, II	

(See Next Column)

FOULSTON & SIEFKIN L.L.P.—*Continued*

For Complete List of Firm Personnel, See General Section

For full biographical listings, see the Martindale-Hubbell Law Directory

KAHRS, NELSON, FANNING, HITE & KELLOGG, L.L.P. (AV)

Suite 630, 200 West Douglas Street, 67202-3089
Telephone: 316-265-7761
Telecopier: 316-267-7803

MEMBERS OF FIRM

William A. Kahrs (1904-1989)	Arthur S. Chalmers
Robert H. Nelson (1904-1977)	Marc A. Powell
Darrell D. Kellogg (1931-1992)	Kim R. Martens
Richard C. Hite	Linda S. Parks
Richard L. Honeyman	Forrest James Robinson, Jr.
Larry A. Withers	Don D. Gribble, II
Gary A. Winfrey	John G. Pike
Clark R. Nelson	Vince P. Wheeler
Steven D. Gough	Alan R. Pfaff
Scott J. Gunderson	Dennis V. Lacey
Randy Troutt	Donald N. Peterson, II

ASSOCIATES

Todd M. Connell	Jeffrey R. Emerson
J. Scott Pohl	Lisa Adrian McPherson
	Mary E. Giovanni

OF COUNSEL

H. W. Fanning	Robert Hall

Representative Clients: Advance Chemical Dist., Inc.; Amoco Production Co.; Business Systems, Inc.; Central Detroit Diesel Allison, Inc.; Coastal Oil & Gas Corp.; Professional Engineering Consultants, P.A.; Ruffin Hotel Corp.; Vornado Air Circulation Systems, Inc.

For full biographical listings, see the Martindale-Hubbell Law Directory

KENTUCKY

*BOWLING GREEN,** Warren Co.

KERRICK, GRISE & STIVERS (AV)

1025 State Street, P.O. Box 9547, 42102-9547
Telephone: 502-782-8160
Fax: 502-782-5856
Elizabethtown, Kentucky Office: 2935 Dolphin Drive, Suite 102.
Telephone: 502-769-5788.
Fax: 502-737-9285.

MEMBERS OF FIRM

Thomas N. Kerrick	Gregory N. Stivers
John R. Grise	H. Brent Brennenstuhl

ASSOCIATES

Lanna Martin Kilgore	Shawn Rosso Alcott
Laura M. Hagan (Resident, Elizabethtown Office)	Jason B. Bell

Representative Clients: Dollar General Corp.; Columbia Greenview Regional Hospital; Hospital Corporation of America; Hardin Memorial Hospital; Monarch Environmental, Inc.; Mid-South Management Group, Inc.; Trans Financial Bank; TKR Cable.

For full biographical listings, see the Martindale-Hubbell Law Directory

*HOPKINSVILLE,** Christian Co.

WHITE, WHITE, ASKEW & CRENSHAW (AV)

707 South Main Street, P.O. Box 2, 42241
Telephone: 502-885-5377
Fax: 502-885-5383

MEMBERS OF FIRM

Pollard White	Logan B. Askew
Lee T. White	Julia T. Crenshaw

ASSOCIATE

Scott P. Kasierski

Counsel for: First City Bank & Trust Co.; Jennie Stuart Medical Center; Hopkinsville Milling Co., Inc.; White Hydraulics, Inc.; Plymouth Tube Co.; Pennyrile Collection, Inc.
Representative Clients: Farm Credit Services; The Equitable Life Assurance Society; Government Employees Insurance Co.; NationsBank of Kentucky, Inc.

For full biographical listings, see the Martindale-Hubbell Law Directory

*LEXINGTON,** Fayette Co.

LANDRUM & SHOUSE (AV)

106 West Vine Street, P.O. Box 951, 40588-0951
Telephone: 606-255-2424
Facsimile: 606-233-0308
Louisville, Kentucky Office: 400 West Market Street, Suite 1550, 40202.
Telephone: 502-589-7616.
Facsimile: 502-589-2119.

MEMBERS OF FIRM

John H. Burrus	Mark L. Moseley
William C. Shouse	Jack E. Toliver

ASSOCIATE

Charles E. Christian

District Attorneys: CSX Transportation, Inc.
Special Trial Counsel: Ford Motor Co. and Affiliates (Eastern Kentucky); Clark Equipment Co.
Representative Clients: The Continental Insurance Cos.; U.S. Insurance Group; U.S. Fidelity & Guaranty Co.; Ohio Casualty Insurance Co.; CIGNA; Royal Insurance Cos.

For Complete List of Firm Personnel, See General Section

For full biographical listings, see the Martindale-Hubbell Law Directory

MARTIN, OCKERMAN & BRABANT (AV)

200 North Upper Street, 40507
Telephone: 606-254-4401
Fax: 606-231-7367
Email: ockerman@counsel.com

MEMBERS OF FIRM

Hogan Yancey (1881-1960)	Thomas C. Brabant
William B. Martin (1895-1975)	Foster Ockerman, Jr.
	Madeleine T. Baugh

OF COUNSEL

Foster Ockerman

Counsel for: Lexington Federal Savings Bank; Good Samaritan Foundation, Inc.; Equity Property and Development Co.; Park Communications of KY (WTVQ); AAA Blue Grass/Kentucky; Turfland Mall.
Reference: Bank One, Lexington, N.A.

For full biographical listings, see the Martindale-Hubbell Law Directory

MILLER, GRIFFIN & MARKS, P.S.C. (AV)

Suite 700 Security Trust Building, 271 West Short Street, 40507-1292
Telephone: 606-255-6676
Telecopier: 606-259-1562
URL: http://www.mis.net/mgm/

Harry B. Miller, Jr.	Michael D. Meuser
James M. Marks (1928-1963)	Thomas C. Marks
Robert S. Miller	Theodore E. Cowen
Thomas W. Miller	Judith K. Jones
Catesby Woodford	Stephen G. Amato
Donald R. Rose	Carroll M. Redford, III
Frank T. Becker	Helen M. Marks

Representative Clients: Paul Miller Ford, Inc.; Chrisman, Miller, Woodford, Inc.; Shoppers Village Liquors, Inc.; C.V. Whitney Farm; G.F. Vaughan Tabacco Co.; R.R. Dawson Bridge Co.; Three Chimneys Farm; Lexington Trots Breeders Association, Inc. d/b/a The Red Mile; WDKY-TV; WKYT-TV.
Reference: Bank One Lexington, N.A.

For full biographical listings, see the Martindale-Hubbell Law Directory

STOLL, KEENON & PARK, LLP (AV)

201 E. Main Street, Suite 1000, 40507-1380
Telephone: 606-231-3000
Telecopier: 606-253-1093; 606-253-1027
Frankfort, Kentucky Office: 307 Washington Street, 40601.
Telephone: 502-875-6220.
Telecopier: 502-875-6235.
Louisville, Kentucky Office: 400 West Market Street, Suite 2650, 40202-3377.
Telephone: 502-568-9100.
Telecopier: 502-568-5700.

MEMBERS OF FIRM

William L. Montague	Herbert A. Miller, Jr.
Robert M. Watt, III	Robert W. Kellerman
Samuel D. Hinkle IV	J. David Smith, Jr.
R. David Lester	Dan M. Rose
Gary L. Stage	John W. Walters, Jr.

ASSOCIATES

Mary Beth Griffith	Richard A. Nunnelley
Culver V. Halliday	William L. Montague, Jr.
R. Douglas Martin	T. Christopher Daniel

(See Next Column)

STOLL, KEENON & PARK LLP, Lexington—Continued

Representative Clients: Bank One, Lexington, NA; Delta Natural Gas Co.; Farmers Capital Bank Corp.; Keeneland Association, Inc.; Kentucky American Water Co.; Kentucky Utilities Co.; Link Belt Construction Equipment Co.; General Motors Corp.; International Business Machines Corp.; Lexmark International, Inc.

For Complete List of Firm Personnel, See General Section

For full biographical listings, see the Martindale-Hubbell Law Directory

LOUISVILLE,* Jefferson Co.

LANDRUM & SHOUSE (AV)

400 West Market Street Suite 1550, 40202
Telephone: 502-589-7616
Facsimile: 502-589-2119
Lexington, Kentucky Office: 106 West Vine Street, P.O. Box 951.
Telephone: 606-255-2424.
Facsimile: 606-233-0308.

RESIDENT MEMBERS OF THE FIRM

John R. Martin, Jr.	R. Kent Westberry
Delores Hill Pregliasco	J. Denis Ogburn

RESIDENT ASSOCIATES

Dave Whalin	Courtney T. Baxter

For Complete List of Firm Personnel, See General Section

For full biographical listings, see the Martindale-Hubbell Law Directory

SEILLER & HANDMAKER, LLP (AV)

2200 Meidinger Tower, 40202
Telephone: 502-584-7400
Telecopier: 502-583-2100
Paris, Kentucky Office: Seiller, Handmaker & Blevins, P.S.C., 1431 South Main Street.
Telephone: 606-987-3980.
Telecopier: 606-987-3982.
Cynthiana, Kentucky Office: Seiller, Handmaker & Blevins, P.S.C., 9 South Walnut.
Telephone: 606-234-2880.
New Albany, Indiana Office: 202 Pearl Street.
Telephone: 812-948-8307.
Telecopier: 812-948-8383.

Edward F. Seiller (1897-1990)

MEMBERS OF FIRM

Stuart Allen Handmaker	Maury D. Kommor
Bill V. Seiller	Cynthia Compton Stone
David M. Cantor	Glenn A. Cohen
Neil C. Bordy	Tomi Anne Blevins Pulliam
Kyle Anne Citrynell	(Paris and Cynthiana Offices)

ASSOCIATES

Pamela M. Greenwell	Donna F. Townsend
Michael C. Bratcher	Gregory A. Lindsey
John E. Brengle	Vicki L. Buba
Patrick R. Holland, II	Allen C. Platt III (Resident,
Edwin Jon Wolfe	New Albany, Indiana Office)

OF COUNSEL
Robert S. Frey

For full biographical listings, see the Martindale-Hubbell Law Directory

TAUSTINE, POST, SOTSKY, BERMAN, FINEMAN & KOHN (AV)

8th Floor Marion E. Taylor Building, 40202
Telephone: 502-589-5760
FAX: 502-584-5927
Email: 73344.624@compuserve.com

MEMBERS OF FIRM

Marvin M. Sotsky	Robert A. Kohn
Jerome D. Berman	Alex Berman
Joseph E. Fineman	Stanley W. Whetzel, Jr.
Maria A. Fernandez	

ASSOCIATE
Sandra Sotsky Harrison
OF COUNSEL

David A. Friedman	Craig I. Lustig

For full biographical listings, see the Martindale-Hubbell Law Directory

OWENSBORO,* Daviess Co.

KAMUF, YEWELL, PACE & CONDON (AV)

Great Financial Federal Building, 322 Frederica Street, 42301
Telephone: 502-685-3901
Fax: 502-926-2005

MEMBERS OF FIRM

Charles J. Kamuf	Patrick D. Pace
David L. Yewell	David C. Condon

(See Next Column)

ASSOCIATE
John M. Mischel

Representative Clients: Owensboro Municipal Utilities Commission; Lincoln Service Corp.; Hancock County Planning Commission; Daviess County Board of Education; Barmet Aluminum Corp.; Owensboro Sewer Commission; TICOR Title Insurance Co.; Chicago Title Insurance Co.; Owensboro Riverport Authority; Housing Authority of Owensboro.

For full biographical listings, see the Martindale-Hubbell Law Directory

LOUISIANA

ALEXANDRIA,* Rapides Parish

CROWELL & OWENS, L.L.C. (AV)

Hibernia National Bank Building Sixth Floor, P.O. Box 330, 71309-0330
Telephone: 318-445-1488
Fax: 318-445-9098

MEMBERS OF FIRM

Richard L. Crowell (1916-1994)	William B. Owens
Richard B. Crowell	W. Brent Pearson

ASSOCIATE
W. Alan Pesnell

Counsel For: Empire Construction Company; Hixson Brothers Funeral Home; L.H. Bossier, Inc.; Louisiana College; Provine School Pictures; Southern Chevrolet-Geo; Ratcliff Construction Company.
References: Rapides Bank and Trust Company, Alexandria, La.; Whitney National Bank, New Orleans, La.; Hibernia National Bank, Alexandria, La.

For full biographical listings, see the Martindale-Hubbell Law Directory

BATON ROUGE,* East Baton Rouge Parish

GUGLIELMO, MARKS, SCHUTTE, TERHOEVE & LOVE (AV)

(A Registered Limited Liability Partnership)
320 Somerulos Street, P.O. Box 3177, 70821-3177
Telephone: 504-387-6966
Fax: 504-387-8338

Carey J. Guglielmo	Glen Scott Love
Paul Marks, Jr.	Dawn T. Trabeau-Mire
Charles A. Schutte, Jr.	Joseph W. Mengis
Henry G. Terhoeve	Kevin P. Landreneau

Representative Clients: City National Bank; Greyhound Corp.; The Travelers Insurance Co.; Chrysler Corp.; State Farm Insurance Co's.; Travelers/Aetna Insurance Group; Aetna Life & Casualty Co.

For full biographical listings, see the Martindale-Hubbell Law Directory

JAMES S. HOLLIDAY, JR. A PROFESSIONAL CORPORATION (AV)

3538 Cole Drive, P.O. Box 65203, 70896
Telephone: 504-344-2100
Fax: 504-344-4005
Email: shobli03@counsel.com *URL:* http://www.hollidaylaw.com

James S. Holliday, Jr.

Susan Wall Griffin	Stephen J. Holliday

For full biographical listings, see the Martindale-Hubbell Law Directory

NAVRATIL, HARDY & BOURGEOIS (AV)

445 North Boulevard, Suite 800, P.O. Box 3551, 70821-3551
Telephone: 504-379-7300
Fax: 504-379-7316

MEMBERS OF FIRM

Boris F. Navratil	David H. Hardy
	André G. Bourgeois

ASSOCIATE
Alan P. McGlynn
OF COUNSEL

Robert L. Boese	Johnnie L. Matthews
	George Sheram King

For full biographical listings, see the Martindale-Hubbell Law Directory

POWERS, CLEGG & WILLARD (AV)

7967 Office Park Boulevard, P.O. Box 15948, 70895
Telephone: 504-928-1951
Telecopier: 504-929-9834

MEMBERS OF FIRM

John Dale Powers	Michael V. Clegg
	William E. Willard

(See Next Column)

POWERS, CLEGG & WILLARD—*Continued*

ASSOCIATES

Neil H. Mixon	Robert J. Daigre
Mary A. Cazes	Nicholas Soileau

General Counsel for: Audubon Insurance Co.
Louisiana Counsel for: Hancock Bank & Trust Co.; Hertz Corp.; Ciba-Geigy Corp.; Utica Mutual Insurance Co.

For full biographical listings, see the Martindale-Hubbell Law Directory

*LAFAYETTE,** Lafayette Parish

DAVIDSON, MEAUX, SONNIER, McELLIGOTT & SWIFT (AV)

810 South Buchanan Street, P.O. Drawer 2908, 70502
Telephone: 318-237-1660
Fax: 318-237-3676

MEMBERS OF FIRM

James J. Davidson, Jr.	John E. McElligott, Jr.
(1904-1990)	John G. Swift
V. Farley Sonnier (1942-1988)	Jeffrey A. Rhoades
Richard C. Meaux, Sr.	Philip A. Fontenot
James J. Davidson, III	Kyle L. Gideon
Theodore G. Edwards, IV	

ASSOCIATES

Jhan C. Boudreaux Beaullieu	Mark C. Andrus

General Counsel: Southwest Louisiana Electric Membership Corp., Inc.; Macro Oil Co., Inc.; Dwight W. Andrus Insurance Agency; Lafayette Airport Commission.
Local Counsel: Southern Pacific Transportation Co.
Representative Clients: Highlands Insurance Co.; Wal-Mart Stores, Inc.; USAA.

For Complete List of Firm Personnel, See General Section

For full biographical listings, see the Martindale-Hubbell Law Directory

HILL & BEYER, A PROFESSIONAL LAW CORPORATION (AV)

101 LaRue France, Suite 502, P.O. Box 53006, 70505-3006
Telephone: 318-232-9733
Fax: 1-318-237-2566

John K. Hill, Jr.	Eugene P. Matherne (1962-1996)
Bret C. Beyer	Robert B. Purser
David R. Rabalais	Erin J. Sherburne
Marianna Broussard	

For full biographical listings, see the Martindale-Hubbell Law Directory

*MONROE,** Ouachita Parish

THOMPSON, SPARKS, DEAN & MORRIS (AV)

A Partnership including a Professional Corporation
1401 Royal Street, P.O. Box 2867, 71207
Telephone: 318-388-1440
Fax: 318-322-0887

MEMBERS OF FIRM

M. C. Thompson (1885-1970)	George B. Dean, Jr., (P.C.)
James D. Sparks (1910-1987)	Wood T. Sparks
John C. Morris, III	

Representative Clients: South Central Bell Telephone Co.; Greater Ouachita Water Company; PHH Homequity Corp.; Commonwealth Relocation Services, Inc.; Remax, Monroe; Bell South Advertising & Publishing Corp.; Premier Mortgage Corp.; Countrywide Funding Corp.
Approved Attorneys for: Central Bank; Federal Land Bank.

For full biographical listings, see the Martindale-Hubbell Law Directory

*NEW ORLEANS,** Orleans Parish

BARRIOS, KINGSDORF & CASTEIX, L.L.P. (AV)

36th Floor, One Shell Square, 701 Poydras Street, 70139
Telephone: 504-524-3300
Fax: 504-524-3313

Dawn M. Barrios	Bruce S. Kingsdorf
Barbara Treuting Casteix	

For full biographical listings, see the Martindale-Hubbell Law Directory

BROOK, PIZZA & VAN LOON, L.L.P. (AV)

400 Poydras Street, Suite 2500, 70130
Telephone: 504-566-0600
Telecopier: 504-595-8715
Email: lawfirm@bpvl.com
Slidell, Louisiana Office: 1400 A Gause Boulevard.
Telephone: 504-641-9468.
Telecopier: 504-643-7631.
Baton Rouge, Louisiana Office: 9100 Bluebonnet Centre Boulevard, Suite 402.
Telephone: 504-291-7300.
Telecopier: 504-291-4524.

(See Next Column)

Jack Pierce Brook	Normand F. Pizza
Ernest N. Morial (1929-1989)	Jan T. Van Loon
Richard Ernest Santora	

David M. Latham	Christopher J. Shenfield
David Shaw	Douglas R. Kinler
Stephanie B. LaBorde (Resident, Baton Rouge Office)	

SPECIAL COUNSEL

Betty Jean George Ray (Resident, Baton Rouge Office)	Mark D. Hudak

OF COUNSEL

Nyda Brook Zelenka	Carlina Davila L. Shenfield (not admitted in the United States)
Herschel C. Adcock	

For full biographical listings, see the Martindale-Hubbell Law Directory

MICHAEL L. ECKSTEIN ATTORNEY AT LAW A PROFESSIONAL CORPORATION (AV)

1515 Poydras Street, Suite 2195, 70112
Telephone: 504-527-0701
Telecopier: 504-566-0040
VMX: 504-889-8876

Michael L. Eckstein	David Coleman Raphael, Jr.

Representative Clients: Anserphone of New Orleans, Inc.; Dixie Web Graphic Corporation; Kencoil, Inc.; Life Point Systems, Inc.; Meeks Petroleum Company; Int-Oil Ventures, Ltd.; Dan-Gulf Shipping, Inc.; Axonn Corporation; Action Ink, Inc.; TCB Industries, Inc.

For full biographical listings, see the Martindale-Hubbell Law Directory

LAMOTHE & HAMILTON, A PROFESSIONAL LAW CORPORATION (AV)

Pan American Life Center, 601 Poydras Street, Suite 2750, 70130
Telephone: 504-566-1805
Telecopier: 504-566-1569
MCI Mail: 382-4472
Email: lhplc@neosoft.com

Frank E. Lamothe, III	Galen S. Brown
Charles E. Hamilton, III	M. Lizabeth Talbott
Karen Edginton Milner	Thomas J. Cortazzo

Reference: Jefferson Guaranty Bank, New Orleans, Louisiana.

For full biographical listings, see the Martindale-Hubbell Law Directory

SLATER LAW FIRM, A PROFESSIONAL CORPORATION (AV)

650 Poydras Street Suite 2600, 70130-6101
Telephone: 504-523-7333
Fax: 504-528-1080

Benjamin R. Slater, Jr.	Kevin M. Wheeler
Benjamin R. Slater, III	Anne Elise Brown
Mark E. Van Horn	Donald J. Miester, Jr.

Cory Rabin Cahn	James L. Bradford, III

SPECIAL COUNSEL

W. Malcolm Stevenson	Robert B. Acomb, III
Michael O. Waguespack	

Representative Clients: Norfolk Southern Corporation; New Orleans Steamship Association; Anheuser-Busch, Incorporated; The Quaker Oats Company; Primerica Financial Services, Inc.; Primerica Life Insurance Company; Electric Mutual Liability Insurance Company; Diversified Foods and Seasonings.

For full biographical listings, see the Martindale-Hubbell Law Directory

*SHREVEPORT,** Caddo Parish

BARLOW AND HARDTNER L.C. (AV)

Tenth Floor, Louisiana Tower, 401 Edwards Street, 71101-3289
Telephone: 318-227-1131
Telecopier: 318-227-1141
Mailing Address: P.O. Box 8, Shreveport, Louisiana, 71161-0008

Quintin T. Hardtner, III	Clair F. White
Malcolm S. Murchison	Philip E. Downer, III
Joseph L. Shea, Jr.	Michael B. Donald
David R. Taggart	Jay A. Greenleaf

OF COUNSEL

Cecil E. Ramey, Jr.

Representative Clients: Kelley Oil Corporation; NorAm Energy Corp. (formerly Arkla, Inc.); Central and South West Corporation; Panhandle Eastern Corp.; Pennzoil Producing Co.; Johnson Controls, Inc.; Ashland Oil, Inc.; Southwestern Electric Power Company; The Centex Construction Group; The Brinkmann Corporation.

(See Next Column)

BARLOW AND HARDTNER L.C., *Shreveport—Continued*

For Complete List of Firm Personnel, See General Section

For full biographical listings, see the Martindale-Hubbell Law Directory

ROBERT U. GOODMAN, P.L.C. (AV)

Mid South Towers, 416 Travis Street, Suite 1105, 71101-5514
Telephone: 318-221-1601
Fax: 318-221-1749

Robert U. Goodman

Representative Clients: Trans-World Life Insurance Co.; Aeropres Corp.; Dealers Truck & Equipment Co.; Pioneer Bank & Trust Co.; Steel Erectors, Inc.; Powell Buick, Inc.; Housing Authority of the City of Shreveport; Specht Newspapers, Inc.; Graham Brothers Entertainment, Inc.; Integrated Exploration, Inc.

For full biographical listings, see the Martindale-Hubbell Law Directory

MAINE

BANGOR,* Penobscot Co.

EATON, PEABODY, BRADFORD & VEAGUE, P.A. (AV)

Fleet Center-Exchange Street, P.O. Box 1210, 04402-1210
Telephone: 207-947-0111
Telecopier: 207-942-3040
Email: epbv@aol.com
Augusta, Maine Office: 2 Central Plaza.
Telephone: 207-622-3747.
Telecopier: 207-622-9732.
Blue Hill, Maine Office: One East Blue Hill Road.
Telephone: 207-374-2812.
Telecopier: 207-374-2548.
Brunswick, Maine Office: 167 Park Row.
Telephone: 207-729-1144.
Telecopier: 207-729-1140.
Camden, Maine Office: 7-9 Washington Street.
Telephone: 207-236-3325.
Telecopier: 207-236-8611.
Dover-Foxcroft, Maine Office: 30 East Main Street.
Telephone: 207-564-8378.
Telecopier: 207-564-7059.

Malcolm E. Morrell, Jr.	Michael B. Trainor
Daniel G. McKay	Judy A.S. Metcalf
	(Resident, Brunswick Office)

Allison C. Lucy

A List of Representative Clients available upon request.

For Complete List of Firm Personnel, See General Section

For full biographical listings, see the Martindale-Hubbell Law Directory

RUDMAN & WINCHELL (AV)

84 Harlow Street, P.O. Box 1401, 04402-1401
Telephone: 207-947-4501
Telecopy: 207-941-9715

MEMBERS OF FIRM

Abraham M. Rudman	Frank T. McGuire
(1896-1970)	Bruce C. Mallonee
Albert H. Winchell, Jr.	Paul H. Sighinolfi
(1924-1992)	William H. Hanson
Gerald E. Rudman	George Franklin Eaton, II
Phillip D. Buckley	Edith A. Richardson
Michael P. Friedman	Michael M. McAleer
Winfred A. Stevens	Brett D. Baber
Robert E. Sutcliffe	Barbara A. Cardone
Paul W. Chaiken	Robert E. Murray, Jr.
David C. King	Edmond J. Bearor
John W. McCarthy	Curtis E. Kimball

ASSOCIATES

Jane E. Skelton	Karen D. Kemble
Brent A. Singer	Leigh Stephens McCarthy

Counsel for: Penobscot Shoe Co.; Sherman Lumber Co.; Webber Oil Co.; Fleet Bank of Maine; Key Bank of Maine; McCain Foods, Inc.
Local Counsel for: Commercial Union Assurance Cos.; Hanover Insurance Company; Kemper Insurance Group; Liberty Mutual Insurance Co.

For full biographical listings, see the Martindale-Hubbell Law Directory

PORTLAND,* Cumberland Co.

PIERCE ATWOOD (AV)

One Monument Square, 04101
Telephone: 207-791-1100
Fax: 207-791-1350
Email: info@PierceAtwood.com
Augusta, Maine Office: 77 Winthrop Street.
Telephone: 207-622-6311.
Fax: 207-623-9367.
Newburyport, Massachusetts Office: 6 Harris Street.
Telephone: 508-465-9599.
Fax: 508-465-9945.

MEMBERS OF FIRM

Bruce A. Coggeshall	Christopher E. Howard
James B. Zimprich	David J. Champoux
Richard P. Hackett	Gloria A. Pinza

OF COUNSEL

Jeremiah D. Newbury

ASSOCIATES

James M. Saffian	Foster A. Stewart, Jr
Marcia A. Metcalf	

For Complete List of Firm Personnel, See General Section

For full biographical listings, see the Martindale-Hubbell Law Directory

PRETI, FLAHERTY, BELIVEAU & PACHIOS (AV)

A Limited Liability Company
443 Congress Street, P.O. Box 11410, 04104-7410
Telephone: 207-791-3000
Telecopier: 207-791-3111
Email: admin@pfbpnet.com
Augusta, Maine Office: 45 Memorial Circle, P.O. Box 1058, 04332-1058.
Telephone: 207-623-5300.
Telecopier: 207-623-2914.

MEMBERS OF FIRM

Harold C. Pachios	Leonard M. Gulino
Michael J. Gentile	Dennis C. Sbrega
(Augusta Office)	Estelle A. Lavoie
Eric P. Stauffer	Susan E. LoGiudice
Jonathan S. Piper	Michael Kaplan
Randall B. Weill	Michael L. Sheehan
James C. Pitney, Jr.	John P. McVeigh
(Augusta Office)	

OF COUNSEL

Jeanne T. Cohn-Connor

ASSOCIATES

James E. Phipps	Scott T. Rodgers

Representative Clients: Key Bank of Maine; Guy Gannett Publishing Co.; Peoples Heritage Savings Bank; Liberty Group, Inc.; RECOLL Management Cor;.; NRG Barriers, Inc.; Hussey Corp.; Northeast Air Group; The Woodlands Club; P.H. Chadbourne and Co.

For Complete List of Firm Personnel, See General Section

For full biographical listings, see the Martindale-Hubbell Law Directory

TROUBH, HEISLER & PIAMPIANO, P.C. (AV)

511 Congress Street, P.O. Box 9711, 04104-5011
Telephone: 207-780-6789
Fax: 207-774-2339

William B. Troubh	Thomas E. Getchell
Edwin A. Heisler	Michael Richards
Robert J. Piampiano	William K. McKinley
Kevin M. Gillis	Daniel F. Gilligan
Michael P. Boyd	Paul S. Bulger

John G. Richardson	Linda L. Sears
Daniel R. Felkel	

For full biographical listings, see the Martindale-Hubbell Law Directory

MARYLAND

BALTIMORE,* (Independent City)

ABRAMOFF, NEUBERGER AND LINDER, LLP (AV)

Suite 800, 250 West Pratt Street, 21201
Telephone: 410-539-8300
Fax: 410-539-8304

(See Next Column)

ABRAMOFF, NEUBERGER AND LINDER LLP—*Continued*

MEMBERS OF FIRM

David B. Abramoff   Rita A. Linder
Anilkumar J. Hoffberg   Richard S. Lehmann
Yaakov S. Neuberger   Steven M. Rosen

Nancy Haas

OF COUNSEL

Stephen F. Bisbee

For full biographical listings, see the Martindale-Hubbell Law Directory

DAVID RODMAN COHAN & ASSOCIATES, P.C. (AV)

The B & O Building, 2 North Charles Street, Suite 820, 21201-3217
Telephone: 410-332-1400
Facsimile: 410-332-4079

David Rodman Cohan

Sandon L. Cohen   Rayanne T. Beers

LEGAL SUPPORT PERSONNEL

H. Rosita Hill (Legal Secretary)   Brandy Thurman
                 (Legal Secretary)

For full biographical listings, see the Martindale-Hubbell Law Directory

GOLDMAN & VETTER, P.A. (AV)

Twenty-Fourth Floor, 36 South Charles Street, 21201-3110
Telephone: 410-547-1400
Toll Free: 800-736-0102
Telecopier: 410-547-8818

Brian A. Goldman   Gerard R. Vetter

Lori Schultz Simpson

OF COUNSEL

Neil S. Kurlander

Reference: NationsBank of Maryland, Baltimore, Md.

For full biographical listings, see the Martindale-Hubbell Law Directory

KOLLMAN & SHEEHAN, P.A. (AV)

Sun Life Building, 20 South Charles Street, 21201
Telephone: 410-727-4300
Telecopier: 410-727-4391

Frank L. Kollman   Peter S. Saucier
David M. Sheehan   Francis R. Laws
Darrell R. VanDeusen

Bruce M. Luchansky   Jonathan J. Biedron
Clifford B. Geiger   Randi A. Klein
Charles J. Kresslein

For full biographical listings, see the Martindale-Hubbell Law Directory

MCKENNEY, THOMSEN AND BURKE, LLP (AV)

Suite 400, One North Charles Street, 21201
Telephone: 410-539-2595
FAX: 410-783-0710
Washington, D.C. Office: Suite 500, 1225 Eye Street, N.W.
Telephone: 202-682-4741.
FAX: 202-547-3713.

OF COUNSEL

W. Gibbs McKenney

MEMBERS OF FIRM

George E. Thomsen   Paul E. Burke, Jr.
Roszel C. Thomsen, II

ASSOCIATES

Hedley A. Clark   Robin McDaniel Hough

References: NationsBank; Mercantile-Safe Deposit & Trust Co.; Carroll County Bank and Trust Co.

For full biographical listings, see the Martindale-Hubbell Law Directory

RICHARD T. STANSBURY A PROFESSIONAL ASSOCIATION (AV)

Suite 920, The B & O Building, Two North Charles Street, 21201-3754
Telephone: 410-727-6200
Facsimile: 410-385-2939
Annapolis, Maryland Office: 5th Floor, The Conte Building, 116 Defense Highway.
Telephone: 410-974-6007.
Facsimile: 410-974-6019.

Richard T. Stansbury

For full biographical listings, see the Martindale-Hubbell Law Directory

THIEBLOT, RYAN, MARTIN & MILLER, P.A. (AV)

4th Floor, The World Trade Center, 21202-3091
Telephone: 410-837-1140
Washington, D.C. Line: 202-628-8223
Fax: 410-837-3282
Towson, Maryland Office: Atlantic Federal Building. Suite 400. 100 West Road. 21204.
Telephone: 410-828-5900.

Robert J. Thieblot   Robert D. Harwick, Jr.
Anthony W. Ryan   Anne M. Hrehorovich
J. Edward Martin, Jr.   Donna Marie Raffaele
Bruce R. Miller   Hamilton Fisk Tyler
Samuel S. Field III

Representative Clients: Al Packer Ford, Inc.; Brundage Bone Concrete Pumping, Inc.; Cornerstone Management & Development, Inc.; Dynasplint Systems, Inc.; Baltimore & Annapolis R.R. Co.; Fidelity Engineering Co.; Musselman's Dodge, Inc.; Norris Ford, Inc.; The North Charles St. Design Organization; Water Street Limited Partnership.

For full biographical listings, see the Martindale-Hubbell Law Directory

THOMAS & LIBOWITZ, A PROFESSIONAL ASSOCIATION (AV)

USF&G Tower, Suite 1100, 100 Light Street, 21202-1053
Telephone: 410-752-2468
Telecopier: 410-752-2046

Steven Anargyros Thomas   Clinton R. Black, IV

For full biographical listings, see the Martindale-Hubbell Law Directory

VENABLE ATTORNEYS AT LAW VENABLE, BAETJER AND HOWARD, LLP (AV)

A Partnership including Professional Corporations
1800 Mercantile Bank & Trust Building, 2 Hopkins Plaza, 21201
Telephone: 410-244-7400
Email: INFO@Venable.win.net
Washington, D.C. Office: Venable, Baetjer, Howard & Civiletti LLP. Suite 1000, 1201 New York Avenue, N.W.
Telephone: 202-962-4800.
McLean, Virginia Office: Suite 400, 2010 Corporate Ridge.
Telephone: 703-760-1600.
Rockville, Maryland Office: Suite 500, One Church Street, P. O. Box 1906.
Telephone: 301-217-5600.
Towson, Maryland Office: 210 Allegheny Avenue, P. O. Box 5517.
Telephone: 410-494-6200.

MEMBERS OF FIRM

Jacques T. Schlenger (P.C.)   Sondra Harans Block (Resident, Rockville, Maryland Office)
William J. McCarthy (P.C.)
Thomas P. Perkins, III (P.C.)   Bryson L. Cook (P.C.) (Also at Washington, D.C. Office)
Benjamin R. Civiletti (P.C.) (Also at Washington, D.C. and Towson, Maryland Offices)   David M. Fleishman
     Jana Howard Carey (P.C.)
     Jeffrey D. Knowles (Not admitted in MD; Resident, Washington, D.C. Office)
John B. Howard (Resident, Towson, Maryland Office)
Anthony M. Carey (Also at Washington, D.C. Office)   William D. Coston (Not admitted in MD; Resident, Washington, D.C. Office)
Lee M. Miller (P.C.)
Neal D. Borden (Also at Washington, D.C. Office)   Maurice Baskin (Resident, Washington, D.C. Office)
Robert A. Shelton   W. Robert Zinkham
Roger W. Titus (Resident, Rockville, Maryland Office)   Elizabeth R. Hughes
     Robert J. Bolger, Jr. (Also at Washington, D.C. Office)
Daniel O'C. Tracy, Jr. (Also at Rockville, Maryland Office)   J. Michael Brennan (Resident, Towson, Maryland Office)
Jan K. Guben (Also at Washington, D. C Office)   Bruce H. Jurist (Also at Washington, D.C. Office)
David J. Levenson (Not admitted in MD; Resident, Washington, D.C. Office)   Ariel Vannier
     John M. Gurley (Not admitted in MD; Resident, Washington, D.C. Office)
Joe A. Shull (Resident, Washington, D.C. Office)
Kenneth C. Bass, III (Not admitted in MD; Washington, D.C. and McLean, Virginia Offices)   Newton B. Fowler, III
     Michael J. Baader
     Davis V. R. Sherman
     Jeffrey K. Gonya
John H. Zink, III (Resident, Towson, Maryland Office)   Francis X. Gallagher, Jr. (Not admitted in MD)
Paul T. Glasgow (Resident, Rockville, Maryland Office)   Robert H. Geis, Jr.
Joseph G. Block (Not admitted in MD; Resident, Washington, D.C. Office)

OF COUNSEL

Arthur W. Machen, Jr. (P.C.)   Emried D. Cole, Jr.
Herbert R. O'Conor, Jr. (Resident, Towson, Maryland Office)   Todd K. Snyder

(See Next Column)

VENABLE ATTORNEYS AT LAW VENABLE, BAETJER AND HOWARD, LLP,
Baltimore—Continued

ASSOCIATES

Wallace E. Christner (Also at Washington, D.C. Office)	Fernand A. Lavallee (Not admitted in MD; Resident, Washington, D. C. Office)
Kevin B. Collins (Also at Rockville, Maryland Office)	Wingrove S. Lynton
Michael W. Conron	John A. McCauley
Donald P. Creston (Not admitted in MD; Resident, Washington, D.C. Office)	Traci H. Mundy (Not admitted in MD; Resident, McLean, Virginia Office)
John P. Edgar	Joseph C. Schmelter
Mary-Dulany James (Resident, Towson, Maryland Office)	Neal H. Strum
	Linda Marotta Thomas
Gregory L. Laubach (Resident, Rockville, Maryland Office)	Brian R. Trumbauer
	Christine J. Warren

Robin L. Zimelman

For Complete List of Firm Personnel, See General Section

For full biographical listings, see the Martindale-Hubbell Law Directory

BEL AIR,* Harford Co.

STARK & KEENAN, A PROFESSIONAL ASSOCIATION (AV)

30 Office Street, 21014
Telephone: 410-838-5522
Baltimore: 410-879-2222
Fax: 410-879-0688

Elwood V. Stark, Jr.	Judith Cline-Silverstein
Charles K. Keenan, Jr.	Gregory A. Szoka
Edwin G. Carson	Robert S. Lynch
Claire Prin Blomquist	Paul W. Ishak
Kimberly Kahoe Muenter	Lawrence F. Kreis, Jr.

For full biographical listings, see the Martindale-Hubbell Law Directory

BETHESDA, Montgomery Co.

HADLEY & HOUSE, P.C. (AV)

4824 Montgomery Lane, 20814
Telephone: 301-654-1181
Facsimile: 301-654-6779

Donald H. Hadley	Arthur G. House
Richard D. Mirsky	James C. Brennan
Marilyn E. Nelson	Fredric D. Firestone

Reference: Citizens Bank of Maryland.

For full biographical listings, see the Martindale-Hubbell Law Directory

COLUMBIA, Howard Co.

GUY B. MASERITZ (AV)

Hobbit's Glen, 5040 Rushlight Path, 21044
Telephone: 410-997-9400
Fax: 410-997-3116

Reference: First National Bank of Maryland.

GREENBELT, Prince Georges Co.

McNAMEE, HOSEA, JERNIGAN & SCOTT, P.A. (AV)

Capital Office Park, Suite 200, 6411 Ivy Lane, 20770
Telephone: 301-441-2420
FAX: 301-982-9450
Annapolis, Maryland Office: 69 Franklin Street.
Telephone: 410-263-1107.
Middleburg, Virginia Office: 7 South Liberty Street, P.O. Box 903.
Telephone: 703-687-3902.

David A. McNamee	Milton D. Jernigan, II
Stephen C. Hosea	Richard L. Whelton, Jr.
Randall L. Scott	Jeffrey A. Weber
Robert J. Kim	John P. Lynch
N. Nelson Phelps	Paul A. D'Amico, Jr.
Paula Maria Elbich	Diane K. Kuwamura

G Arthur Robbins

OF COUNSEL

Edward MacMahon (Resident, Middleburg, Virginia Office)

For full biographical listings, see the Martindale-Hubbell Law Directory

REICHELT, NUSSBAUM, LaPLACA & MILLER (AV)

The Maryland Trade Center, Suite 1000, 7500 Greenway Center Drive,
  P.O. Box 627, 20768-0627
Telephone: 301-474-9000
Fax: 301-345-0565

MEMBERS OF FIRM

Herbert W. Reichelt (1908-1993)	Sheldon L. Gnatt
Ronald M. Miller	Raymond G. LaPlaca
T. Summers Gwynn, III	Daniel A. LaPlaca
Gary Greenwald	Gail Borjeson Viens
Andrew W. Nussbaum	Roger C. Thomas

(See Next Column)

ASSOCIATE

Wanda G. Caporaletti

OF COUNSEL

Paul M. Nussbaum	Toni Evon Clarke

Representative Clients: Tower Federal Credit Union; Suburban Bank of Maryland.
Reference: NationsBank of Maryland, N.A.

For full biographical listings, see the Martindale-Hubbell Law Directory

PRINCE FREDERICK,* Calvert Co.

REYNOLDS AND MANNING, P.A. (AV⊤)

260 Merrimac Court, P.O. Box 2809, 20678
Telephone: 410-535-9220; 301-855-1932
Fax: 410-535-9171

Christopher J. Reynolds	Michael K. Manning

OF COUNSEL

Warren F. Sengstack

For full biographical listings, see the Martindale-Hubbell Law Directory

ROCKVILLE,* Montgomery Co.

BRAULT, GRAHAM, SCOTT & BRAULT (AV)

101 South Washington Street, 20850
Telephone: 301-424-1060
Fax: 301-424-7991
Washington, D.C. Office: 1906 Sunderland Place, N.W.
Telephone: 202-785-1200.
FAX: 202-785-4301.
Arlington, Virginia Office: Suite 1201, 2300 North Clarendon Boulevard,
Courthouse Plaza.
Telephone: 703-358-9200.

OF COUNSEL

Laurence T. Scott	Janet S. Zigler (Resident)

MEMBERS OF FIRM

Denver H. Graham (1922-1987)	Daniel L. Shea (Resident)
Albert E. Brault (Retired)	M. Kathleen Parker (Resident)
Albert D. Brault (Resident)	David G. Mulquin (Resident)
Leo A. Roth, Jr.	James M. Brault (Resident)
James S. Wilson (Resident)	Regina Ann Casey (Resident)
Ronald G. Guziak	Sanford A. Friedman

ASSOCIATES

Holly D. Shupert (Resident)	Joan F. Brault (Resident)
Rhonda Ann Hurwitz (Resident)	Joseph P. Morra (Resident)

Michael A. Carlo

Representative Clients: American Oil Co.; Crum & Forster Group; Fireman's Fund American Insurance Cos.; Kemper Group; Reliance Insurance Cos.; Safeco Group; Government Employees Insurance Co.; Medical Mutual Insurance Society of Maryland; Legal Mutual Liability Insurance Society of Maryland.

For full biographical listings, see the Martindale-Hubbell Law Directory

STEVEN M. KATZ, P.A. (AV)

Suite 208 401 East Jefferson Street, 20850
Telephone: 301-738-8441
Fax: 301-251-8888

Steven M. Katz

For full biographical listings, see the Martindale-Hubbell Law Directory

STEIN, SPERLING, BENNETT, DE JONG, DRISCOLL, GREENFEIG & METRO, P.A. (AV)

25 West Middle Lane, 20850
Telephone: 301-340-2020; 800-435-5230
Telecopier: 301-340-8217

Millard S. Bennett	Ann G. Jakabcin
David S. De Jong	A. Howard Metro
Jack A. Garson	Donald N. Sperling

For Complete List of Firm Personnel, See General Section

For full biographical listings, see the Martindale-Hubbell Law Directory

VENABLE ATTORNEYS AT LAW VENABLE, BAETJER AND HOWARD, LLP (AV)

A Partnership including Professional Corporations
Suite 500, One Church Street, P.O. Box 1906, 20850-4129
Telephone: 301-217-5600
FAX: 301-217-5617
Baltimore, Maryland Office: 1800 Mercantile Bank & Trust Building, 2
Hopkins Plaza.
Telephone: 410-244-7400.
Washington, D.C. Office: Venable, Baetjer, Howard & Civiletti LLP, Suite
1000, 1201 New York Avenue, N.W.
Telephone: 202-962-4800.
McLean, Virginia Office: Suite 400, 2010 Corporate Ridge.
Telephone: 703-760-1600.

(See Next Column)

VENABLE ATTORNEYS AT LAW VENABLE, BAETJER AND HOWARD, LLP—
Continued

Towson, Maryland, Office: 210 Allegheny Avenue, P. O. Box 5517.
Telephone: 410-494-6200.

MEMBERS OF FIRM

Roger W. Titus   Paul T. Glasgow
Daniel O'C. Tracy, Jr. (Also at
  Baltimore, Maryland Office)

ASSOCIATE
Gregory L. Laubach

For Complete List of Firm Personnel, See General Section

For full biographical listings, see the Martindale-Hubbell Law Directory

---

SALISBURY,* Wicomico Co.

WEBB, BURNETT, JACKSON, CORNBROOKS, WILBER, VORHIS & DOUSE, LLP (AV)

115 Broad Street, P.O. Box 910, 21801
Telephone: 410-742-3176
Fax: 410-742-0438
Email: webnett@shore.intercom.net

MEMBERS OF FIRM

Frederick W. C. Webb   W. Newton Jackson, 3rd
  (1889-1956)   Ernest I. Cornbrooks, III
John W. T. Webb (1918-1990)   Paul D. Wilber
K. King Burnett   David A. Vorhis
              David B. Douse

ASSOCIATE
Chris Schiller Mason

Counsel for: First National Bank of Maryland (Salisbury branch); K & L Microwave, Inc.; Peninsula General Hospital Medical Center.
Local Attorneys for: State Farm Insurance Cos.; Nationwide Insurance Cos.; Travelers Insurance Co.; United States Fidelity & Guaranty Co.; Aetna Casualty & Surety Co.; Insurance Company of North America.

For full biographical listings, see the Martindale-Hubbell Law Directory

---

TOWSON,* Baltimore Co.

ROSOLIO, SILVERMAN & KOTZ, P.A. (AV)

Suite 220 Nottingham Centre, 502 Washington Avenue, 21204
Telephone: 410-339-7100
Fax: 410-339-7107

Charles E. Rosolio   Jeffrey M. Kotz
Steven D. Silverman   Deborah C. Dopkin
              Douglas S. Curtis

OF COUNSEL
Stephen M. Ehudin

For full biographical listings, see the Martindale-Hubbell Law Directory

---

VENABLE ATTORNEYS AT LAW VENABLE, BAETJER AND HOWARD, LLP (AV)

A Partnership including Professional Corporations
210 Allegheny Avenue, P.O. Box 5517, 21204
Telephone: 410-494-6200
FAX: 410-821-0147
Baltimore, Maryland Office: 1800 Mercantile Bank & Trust Building, 2 Hopkins Plaza.
Telephone: 410-244-7400.
Washington, D.C. Office: Venable, Baetjer, Howard & Civiletti LLP, Suite 1000, 1201 New York Avenue, N.W.
Telephone: 202-962-4800.
McLean, Virginia Office: Suite 400, 2010 Corporate Ridge.
Telephone: 703-760-1600.
Rockville, Maryland Office: Suite 500, One Church Street, P. O. Box 1906.
Telephone: 301-217-5600.

PARTNERS

Benjamin R. Civiletti (P.C.)   John B. Howard
  (Also at Washington, D.C.   John H. Zink, III
  and Baltimore, Maryland   J. Michael Brennan
  Offices)

OF COUNSEL
Herbert R. O'Conor, Jr.

ASSOCIATE
Mary-Dulany James

For Complete List of Firm Personnel, See General Section

For full biographical listings, see the Martindale-Hubbell Law Directory

---

MASSACHUSETTS

AMESBURY, Essex Co.

HAMEL, DESHAIES & GAGLIARDI (AV)

Five Market Square, P.O. Box 198, 01913-0398
Telephone: 508-388-3558
Telecopier: 508-388-0441

MEMBER OF FIRM
Richard P. Hamel

ASSOCIATE
Peter R. Ayer, Jr.

Representative Clients: Essex County Gas Co., Amesbury, MA; First and Ocean National Bank, Newburyport, MA.
Approved Attorneys for: Chicago Title Insurance; Old Republic Title Insurance Co.

For Complete List of Firm Personnel, See General Section

For full biographical listings, see the Martindale-Hubbell Law Directory

---

BOSTON,* Suffolk Co.

BERNKOPF, GOODMAN & BASEMAN LLP (AV)

125 Summer Street, 02110-1621
Telephone: 617-790-3000
Telecopier: 617-790-3300

MEMBERS OF FIRM

Abraham K. Cohen (1891-1957)   James B. Fox
Max E. Bernkopf (1919-1967)   Peter B. McGlynn
Sylvan A. Goodman (1935-1981)   Sheryl C. Starr
Harris I. Baseman   Richard B. Michaud
Kenneth M. Goldberg   Lydia G. Chesnick
Alan J. Grace   Martin C. Pomeroy
Marvin N. Geller   Eric R. Allon
Neil R. Markson   David L. Doyle
Gary P. Lilienthal   Barry S. Fischer

ASSOCIATES

John B. Harkavy   James M. Godec
James D. Friedman   Edward W. Wayland
Gwen P. Weisberg   Sharona Eliahou
Bruce D. Levin   Francis C. Morrissey
Richard P. Bennett   Todd D. Goldberg

For full biographical listings, see the Martindale-Hubbell Law Directory

---

BROMBERG & SUNSTEIN (AV)

125 Summer Street, 11th Floor, 02110
Telephone: 617-443-9292
Fax: 617-443-0004
Email: IPLAW@BROMSUN.COM

MEMBERS OF FIRM

Bruce D. Sunstein   Lee Carl Bromberg
              Kerry L. Timbers

ASSOCIATES

Joel R. Leeman   Julia Huston

For full biographical listings, see the Martindale-Hubbell Law Directory

---

CASNER & EDWARDS, LLP (AV)

1 Federal Street, 27th Floor, 02110-2003
Telephone: 617-426-5900
Telecopier: 617-426-8810

MEMBERS OF FIRM

Thomas D. Edwards (1931-1987)   Terrance J. Hamilton
Andrew J. Casner, Jr.   Robert S. Kutner
Walter H. Mayo, III   David J. Chavolla
Martin E. Greenblatt   Robert L. Ciociola
Charles M. Hamann   Stephen M. Perry
Robert A. Murphy   Gary L. Hoff
Robert E. Cowden, III   Anita W. Robboy
John H. Ashby   Robert M. Mendillo
Douglas K. Mansfield   Peter A. Caro
Andrew M. Higgins   Joan M. Griffin

ASSOCIATES

Gaynor D. Casner   Matthew T. Murphy
Donna Brewer MacKenna   Thomas J. Walsh
Gary L. Kemp   Cristina V. Coletta

For full biographical listings, see the Martindale-Hubbell Law Directory

---

CHERWIN, GLICKMAN & THEISE, LLP (AV)

A Limited Liability Partnership including Professional Corporations
One International Place, 02110-2622
Telephone: 617-330-1625
Fax: 617-330-1642

(See Next Column)

CHERWIN, GLICKMAN & THEISE LLP, Boston—Continued

Stanley A. Glickman (1937-1994)	Douglas L. Jones (P.C.)
Joel I. Cherwin (P.C.)	David K. Wanger
Jay F. Theise	William O. Rizzo
Marshall D. Stein	Stanley B. Kay
	Lisa Lee Foster

For full biographical listings, see the Martindale-Hubbell Law Directory

CRAIG AND MACAULEY, PROFESSIONAL CORPORATION (AV)

Federal Reserve Plaza, 600 Atlantic Avenue, 02210
Telephone: 617-367-9500
Telecopier: 617-742-1788; 617-248-0886
Email: cmpc@ultranet.com

John C. Craig	Mary P. Brody
David F. Hannon	A. Van C. Lanckton
	John G. Snyder

Christopher J. Panos	Christopher S. Dalton

For Complete List of Firm Personnel, See General Section

For full biographical listings, see the Martindale-Hubbell Law Directory

CUDDY BIXBY (AV)

One Financial Center, 02111
Telephone: 617-348-3600
Telecopier: 617-348-3643
Wellesley, Massachusetts Office: 60 Walnut Street.
Telephone: 617-235-1034.

Anthony M. Ambriano	Steven J. Marullo

For Complete List of Firm Personnel, See General Section

For full biographical listings, see the Martindale-Hubbell Law Directory

GLOVSKY, TARLOW & MILBERG (AV)

Suite 810, 31 Milk Street, 02109-5104
Telephone: 617-423-7100
Telecopier: 617-482-8034
Washington, D.C. Office: 1090 Vermont Avenue, N.W.
Telephone: 202-659-1971.

Richard D. Glovsky	Melinda Milberg
	Daniel S. Tarlow

ASSOCIATES

Peter M. Kelley	John F. Tocci
	Debra L. Feldstein

OF COUNSEL

Harry M. Carey, Jr.	Lynne K. Zusman (Not
Paul S. Davis	admitted in MA; Resident,
Barry H. Field	Washington, D.C. Office)

For full biographical listings, see the Martindale-Hubbell Law Directory

HEMENWAY & BARNES (AV)

60 State Street, 02109
Telephone: 617-227-7940
Fax: 617-227-0781

MEMBERS OF FIRM

Alfred Hemenway (1863-1927)	Michael J. Puzo
Charles B. Barnes (1893-1956)	Thomas L. Guidi
George H. Kidder	Edward Notis-McConarty
David H. Morse	Diane C. Tillotson
Roy A. Hammer	Stephen W. Kidder
Lawrence T. Perera	Susan Hughes Banning
John J. Madden	Frederic J. Marx
George T. Shaw	Deborah J. Hall
Timothy F. Fidgeon	Kurt F. Somerville
Ruth R. Budd	Teresa A. Belmonte
Michael B. Elefante	Brian C. Broderick

COUNSEL

Michael L. Leshin

ASSOCIATES

Ellen Cope-Flanagan	Charles Fayerweather
Andrea H. Maislen	Miranda Pickells Gooding
Barbara Zicht Richmond	James P. Warner
Marsha K. Zierk	Alan H. Roth
	Brendan P. Doherty

OF COUNSEL

Guido R. Perera

For Complete List of Firm Personnel, See General Section

For full biographical listings, see the Martindale-Hubbell Law Directory

LOONEY & GROSSMAN (AV)

A Partnership including Professional Corporations
101 Arch Street, 02110-1112
Telephone: 617-951-2800
Fax: 617-951-2819

Stewart F. Grossman (P.C.)	Bradley W. Snyder
Richard J. Grahn	Wesley S. Chused
Bertram E. Snyder	Melvin S. Hoffman (P.C.)
Robert Cushman Barber	Joseph H. Matzkin

SENIOR COUNSEL

William F. Looney, Jr.

OF COUNSEL

Paul D. McCarthy	Sherman H. Starr, Jr.

ASSOCIATES

Seth H. Salinger	Lisa Sternschuss
Erin M. Gilligan	Keir J. Beadling
Maria Galvagna	Lauren K. Heggestad Dillon
	Adam J. Ruttenberg

For full biographical listings, see the Martindale-Hubbell Law Directory

MENARD, MURPHY & WALSH (AV)

One Financial Center, 02111
Telephone: 617-832-2500
Telecopier: 617-832-2550

Arthur P. Menard	John E. Coyne
Paul J. Murphy	John S. Leonard
Joseph H. Walsh	Theodore E. Daiber
	Kevin G. Mahoney

For full biographical listings, see the Martindale-Hubbell Law Directory

PALMER & DODGE LLP (AV)

One Beacon Street, 02108
Telephone: 617-573-0100
Facsimile: 617-227-4420

MEMBERS OF FIRM

F. Andrew Anderson	Jerry V. Klima
F. Kingston Berlew	Michael Lytton
Matthew C. Dallett	Maureen P. Manning
Jeanne P. Darcey	David R. Pokross, Jr.
Robert Duggan	Richard S. Rosenstein
Lynnette C. Fallon	James L. Terry
Steven N. Farber	George Ticknor
Nathaniel S. Gardiner	William T. Whelan
Leon J. Glazerman	John L. Whitlock
Richard Hiersteiner	John Taylor Williams
Stanley Keller	William Williams II
Ronald H. Kessel	Peter Wirth

COUNSEL

David J. Corrsin	Zick Rubin

For Complete List of Firm Personnel, See General Section

For full biographical listings, see the Martindale-Hubbell Law Directory

PEABODY & ARNOLD (AV)

A Partnership including Professional Corporations
50 Rowes Wharf, 02110-3342
Telephone: 617-951-2100
Telecopier: 617-951-2125
Providence, Rhode Island Office: One Citizens Plaza, Suite 840.
Telephone: 401-831-8330.
Fax: 401-831-8359.

MEMBERS OF FIRM

Paul J. Ayoub	James A. P. Homans
Jonathan Bangs	William E. Kelly
James H. Belanger	John A. Kessler, Jr.
Michael F. Burke	Anil Khosla
Donald S. Burnham	Andrew R. Menard
Philip H. Cahalin	Frank N. Ray (Resident,
Jason M. Cotton	Providence, Rhode Island
Robert J. Coughlin	Office)
Amanda D. Darwin	Douglas C. Reynolds
John K. Dineen	Suanne C. St. Charles
John R. Gowell, Jr. (Resident,	Peter B. Seamans
Providence, Rhode Island	Donald E. Vaughan
Office)	Robert A. Vigoda
Ripley E. Hastings	Gregory L. White
David F. Hendren	Thomas A. Wooters
Joseph D. S. Hinkley	Stephen Ziobrowski

OF COUNSEL

Dale A. Coggins

(See Next Column)

PEABODY & ARNOLD—*Continued*

ASSOCIATES

Frank S. Hamblett	John P. Dougherty
Amelia M. Charamba	Scott D. Karchmer
Robert Payne Fox, Jr.	Ingrid Sorensen
Sandra P. Criss	Timothy J. Culver
Anna M. Magliocco-Chagnon	Laurie Golding Bazarian
Mark W. McCarthy	Jane E. Kirk

For Complete List of Firm Personnel, See General Section

For full biographical listings, see the Martindale-Hubbell Law Directory

RACKEMANN, SAWYER & BREWSTER, PROFESSIONAL CORPORATION (AV)

One Financial Center, 02111
Telephone: 617-542-2300
Telecopier: 617-542-7437

William B. Tyler	Janet M. Smith
Henry H. Thayer	Peter Friedenberg
Stephen Carr Anderson	Richard S. Novak
Albert M. Fortier, Jr.	J. David Leslie
Michael F. O'Connell	Sanford M. Matathia
Stuart T. Freeland	Richard J. Gallogly
Alan B. Rubenstein	James A. Wachta
James R. Shea, Jr.	Hanson S. Reynolds
Brian M. Hurley	Donald R. Pinto, Jr.

COUNSEL

Ronald S. Duby	Gordon M. Orloff
Lucy West Behymer	Eric A. Smith

OF COUNSEL

Albert B. Wolfe	George V. Anastas
August R. Meyer	Edward M. Condit
Richard H. Lovell	Alexander H. Spaulding

Margaret L. Hayes	Peter A. Alpert
Daniel J. Ossoff	Ellen M. Harrington
Melissa Langer Ellis	Lauren D. Armstrong
Daniel J. Bailey, III	Robert B. Foster
Michael S. Giaimo	Andrew H. Butler
Maura E. Murphy	Gayle E. Parlee
Mary L. Gallant	Elizabeth A. Gibbons
	Melissa Fang

For full biographical listings, see the Martindale-Hubbell Law Directory

SHERBURNE, POWERS & NEEDHAM, P.C. (AV)

One Beacon Street, 02108
Telephone: 617-523-2700
Fax: 617-523-6850
Email: @SHERBURNE.COM

William D. Weeks	Benjamin Volinski
John T. Collins	Mark Schonfeld
Allan J. Landau	James D. Smeallie
Stephen A. Hopkins	Paul Killeen
Alan I. Falk	Gordon P. Katz
C. Thomas Swaim	Joseph B. Darby, III
James Pollock	Richard M Yanofsky
William V. Tripp III	James E. McDermott
Stephen S. Young	Kenneth P. Brier
William F. Machen	Robert V. Lizza
W. Robert Allison	Miriam Goldstein Altman
Philip J. Notopoulos	John J. Monaghan
Richard J. Hindlian	Margaret J. Palladino
Paul E. Troy	Mark C. Michalowski
Harold W. Potter, Jr.	David Scott Sloan
Philip S. Lapatin	M. Chrysa Long
Pamela A. Duckworth	Lawrence D. Bradley
	Miriam J. McKendall

Cynthia A. Brown	Amy J. Mastrobattista
Cynthia M. Hern	Leslie A. Sprinkle
Meredeth A. Beers	Douglas W. Clapp
Dianne R. Phillips	Jeffrey A. Huebschmann
Paul M. James	Tamara E. Goulston
Theodore F. Hanselman	Paul G. Lannon, Jr.
Joshua C. Krumholz	Nicholas J. Psyhogeos
Ieuan G. Mahony	Edward J. Naughton
Jeffrey J. Nix	Kathaleen Kelly Cutone
(Not admitted in MA)	Laurie A. Tribble
Kenneth L. Harvey	Neil C. Higgins
Christopher J. Trombetta	Deborah Paige Stone
Elise N. Zoli	Brian R. Popiel

COUNSEL

Haig Der Manuelian	Karl J. Hirshman
Mason M. Taber, Jr.	Dale R. Johnson

For full biographical listings, see the Martindale-Hubbell Law Directory

SHERIN AND LODGEN LLP (AV)

100 Summer Street, 02110
Telephone: 617-426-5720
Fax: 617-542-5186
Email: lawyers@sherin.com
Los Angeles, California Office: 11300 W. Olympic Boulevard, Suite 700.
Telephone: 310-914-7891.
Fax: 310-552-5327.

MEMBERS OF FIRM

Arthur L. Sherin (1946-1964)	Mark A. Nowak
George E. Lodgen (1946-1971)	Ronald W. Ruth
Morton B. Brown	Steven D. Eimert
George Waldstein	Barbara A. O'Donnell
John M. Reed	A. Neil Hartzell
Robert J. Muldoon, Jr.	Kenneth J. Mickiewicz
Alette E. Reed	Craig M. Brown
Edward M. Bloom	Andrew Royce
Thomas J. Raftery	Daniel O. Gaquin
Joshua M. Alper	Thomas A. Hippler
Gary M. Markoff	Rhonda B. Parker
Bryan G. Killian	John J. Slater III
David A. Guberman	Philip G. Boyle
Kenneth R. Berman	Nereyda Garcia
Frank J. Bailey	John C. La Liberte
Thomas P. Gorman	Christopher A. Kenney
Dorothy Nelson Stookey	C. Forbes Sargent III

ASSOCIATES

Karen Elise Berman	Michael S. Bloom
Margaret H. Leeson	Carolyn M. Barker
Robert M. Carney	Karen O'Malley
Mary Ellen McDonough	Susanne M. Walsh
Caroline Woodward	Susan S. Sampson
	Anne Marie Dowd

OF COUNSEL

Michael S. Strauss	David M. Franek

LEGAL SUPPORT PERSONNEL
Marilyn J. Stewart (Executive Director)

For full biographical listings, see the Martindale-Hubbell Law Directory

SILVERMAN & KUDISCH, P.C. (AV)

Successor to Silverman & Kudisch.
One Longfellow Place, Suite 3608, 02114-2434
Telephone: 617-523-1711
Fax: 617-523-6037

Sumner Darman	Richard L. Blumenthal
Peter L. Zimmerman	Lisa B. Darman

For full biographical listings, see the Martindale-Hubbell Law Directory

FRAMINGHAM, Middlesex Co.

HARGRAVES, KARB, WILCOX & GALVANI (AV)

The Corporate Center, 550 Cochituate Road, P.O. Box 966, 01701
Telephone: 508-620-0140
Fax: 508-875-7728

MEMBERS OF FIRM

Paul V. Galvani	Mark R. Haranas
William H. Mayer	Robert P. Jachowicz
Dana L. Mason	Evans J. Carter
William M. Pezzoni	Jack Merrill, Jr.

OF COUNSEL

Francis P. Wilcox, Jr.	Arthur M. Mason
Victor H. Galvani	Brenda S. Steinberg
Edward J. Mahan	Arthur M. Pearlman

Counsel for: Framingham Cooperative Bank; Lind-Farquhar Co.; Strathmore Machine Toole Co.; Framingham Housing Authority.
Local Counsel for: General Motors Corp. (Framingham, Mass.); Bose Corp.; Consolidated Rail Corp.; Kens Foods, Inc.; Framingham Ford.

For full biographical listings, see the Martindale-Hubbell Law Directory

LOWELL, Middlesex Co.

DONAHUE & DONAHUE ATTORNEYS, P.C. (AV)

21 George Street, 01852
Telephone: 508-458-6887
Fax: 508-458-3424

Daniel J. Donahue (1860-1939)	Peter V. Lawlor
Joseph P. Donahue (1889-1973)	Bradford P. Fortin
Charles A. Donahue (1891-1964)	Richard K. Donahue, Jr.
Richard K. Donahue	Andrea S. Barisano
Joseph P. Donahue, Jr.	Matthew C. Donahue
Joseph D. Regan	Richard E. Cavanaugh
Michael W. Gallagher	Kelly R. Spencer
	Alicia A. Donahue

(See Next Column)

DONAHUE & DONAHUE ATTORNEYS, P.C., *Lowell—Continued*

Representative Clients: The Travelers Insurance Co.; L'Energia Cogeneration, Inc.; Black & Decker; Jim Witt Automotive Group; Demoulas Super Markets, Inc.

For full biographical listings, see the Martindale-Hubbell Law Directory

GOLDMAN & CURTIS (AV)

Lowell Place, 144 Merrimack Street, 01852
Telephone: 508-454-8804, 729-2625

MEMBERS OF FIRM

Frank Goldman (1890-1965)	James T. Curtis
Robert H. Goldman (1918-1991)	Cornelia C. Adams

Gregory T. Curtis	Carolyn L. Greenberg

OF COUNSEL

Efthemios J. Bentas	James T. Curtis, Jr.
Matthew P. Demaras	

For full biographical listings, see the Martindale-Hubbell Law Directory

PETER B. ROBINSON (AV)

Nine Central Street, 01852-1927
Telephone: 508-452-5130
Telecopier: 508-452-4136

For full biographical listings, see the Martindale-Hubbell Law Directory

WORCESTER,* Worcester Co.

TIMOTHY W. McGEE (AV)

446 Main Street, Suite 1525, 01608
Telephone: 508-754-8100
Fax: 508-754-8170

ASSOCIATE

Barbara A. Ahalt

OF COUNSEL

Thomas A. Manning

For full biographical listings, see the Martindale-Hubbell Law Directory

SEDER & CHANDLER (AV)

A Partnership including a Professional Corporation
Established 1918
Burnside Building, 339 Main Street, 01608
Telephone: 508-757-7721
Telecopiers: 508-798-1863; 508-831-0955

MEMBERS OF FIRM

Samuel Seder (1918-1964)	Marvin S. Silver, P.C.
Harold Seder (1934-1988)	John L. Pfeffer, Jr.
Burton Chandler	Robert S. Adler
J. Robert Seder	Dawn E. Caccavaro
Darragh K. Kasakoff	Kevin C. McGee
	Kurt L. Binder

ASSOCIATES

Paul J. O'Riordan	Jeffrey P. Greenberg
	Denise M. Tremblay

OF COUNSEL

Saul A. Seder	Gerald E. Norman
	Philip C. Lombardo, Jr.

Reference: First National Bank of Boston; Safety Fund National Bank; Fleet National Bank.

For full biographical listings, see the Martindale-Hubbell Law Directory

MICHIGAN

ANN ARBOR,* Washtenaw Co.

HOOPER, HATHAWAY, PRICE, BEUCHE & WALLACE (AV)

126 South Main Street, 48104
Telephone: 313-662-4426
Fax: 313-662-9559

James R. Beuche	Charles W. Borgsdorf
	Bruce C. Conybeare, Jr.

Representative Clients: Chem-Trend, Inc.; Dundee Cement Co.; Ervin Industries, Inc.; First Martin Corp.; Group 243 Design, Inc.; Honeywell; Microwave Sensors, Inc.; Shearson Lehman Hutton; O'Neal Construction Co.; Pittsfield Products, Inc.

For Complete List of Firm Personnel, See General Section

For full biographical listings, see the Martindale-Hubbell Law Directory

BATTLE CREEK, Calhoun Co.

SULLIVAN, HAMILTON, SCHULZ, LETZRING, SIMONS, KRETER, TOTH & LEBEUF, P.C. (AV)

One West Michigan Avenue, 49017
Telephone: 616-965-3216
Fax: 616-965-2919

Maxwell B. Allen (1884-1942)	Bert W. Schulz
John M. Allen (1914-1985)	Kurt F. Letzring
Ronald H. Ryan (1901-1988)	Stephen L. Simons
Raymond R. Allen (1919-1996)	Mark E. Kreter
James M. Sullivan	Michael J. Toth
	Ronald A. Lebeuf

OF COUNSEL

Robert P. Hamilton

General Counsel for: Michigan Woodwork and Specialties.
Local Counsel for: The Medical Protective Co.; Gannett, Inc.; Automobile Club of Michigan Insurance Group and Insurance Assn. (AAA); Michigan Physicians Mutual Liability Co.; State Farm Mutual Insurance Co.; Auto Owners Insurance Co.; Cincinnati Insurance Co.; Nationwide Insurance Co.

For full biographical listings, see the Martindale-Hubbell Law Directory

BINGHAM FARMS, Oakland Co.

MEISNER & ASSOCIATES, P.C. (AV)

Suite 467, 30200 Telegraph Road, 48025-4506
Telephone: 810-644-4433

Robert M. Meisner

Robert R. Maxwell

For full biographical listings, see the Martindale-Hubbell Law Directory

SMALL, TOTH, BALDRIDGE & VAN BELKUM, P.C. (AV)

30100 Telegraph Road Suite 250, 48025-4516
Telephone: 810-647-9595
Facsimile: 810-647-9599

Richard L. Small	David M. Baldridge
John M. Toth	Thomas G. Van Belkum
	Keith P. Felty

Representative Clients: Michigan Society of Oral and Maxillofacial Surgeons; Michigan Association of Orthodontists; Michigan Association of Endodontists; Illinois Society of Oral and Maxillofacial Surgeons; California Association of Oral and Maxillofacial Surgeons; New York Society of Oral and Maxillofacial Surgeons.

For full biographical listings, see the Martindale-Hubbell Law Directory

SOTIROFF ABRAMCZYK & RAUSS, P.C. (AV)

30400 Telegraph Road, Suite 444, 48025-4541
Telephone: 810-642-6000
Facsimile: 810-642-9001

Philip Sotiroff	Lawrence A. Tower
Lawrence R. Abramczyk	Robert B. Goldi
Dennis M. Rauss	Keith A. Sotiroff

For full biographical listings, see the Martindale-Hubbell Law Directory

BIRMINGHAM, Oakland Co.

LOUIS J. BURNETT, P.C. (AV)

255 East Brown, Suite 210, 48009-6782
Telephone: 810-642-4345
Fax: 810-642-2005

Louis J. Burnett

Reference: Comerica, Detroit, Michigan.

For full biographical listings, see the Martindale-Hubbell Law Directory

CARSON FISCHER, P.L.C. (AV)

Third Floor, 300 East Maple Road, 48009-6317
Telephone: 810-644-4840
Facsimile: 810-644-1832

Robert M. Carson	Peter L. Wanger
Joseph M. Fischer	William C. Edmunds
	Todd M. Fink

For full biographical listings, see the Martindale-Hubbell Law Directory

HYMAN AND LIPPITT, P.C. (AV)

185 Oakland Avenue, Suite 300, P.O. Box 1750, 48009
Telephone: 810-646-8292
Facsimile: 810-646-8375

(See Next Column)

HYMAN AND LIPPITT P.C.—*Continued*

J. Leonard Hyman	Kenneth F. Neuman
Norman L. Lippitt	Terry S. Givens
Douglas A. Hyman	Paul J. Fischer
Brian D. O'Keefe	John A. Sellers
H. Joel Newman	Robert H. Lippitt
Nazli G. Sater	Roger L. Myers

David N. Morrell, Jr.

For full biographical listings, see the Martindale-Hubbell Law Directory

MacDONALD AND GOREN, P.C. (AV)

Suite 200, 260 East Brown Street, 48009
Telephone: 810-645-5940
Fax: 810-645-2490

Harold C. MacDonald	Kalman G. Goren

Cindy Rhodes Victor

Amy L. Glenn	Lawrence C. Atorthy
David D. Marsh	Miriam Blanks-Smart
Glenn G. Ross	John T. Klees

Rose Marie Karadsheh

OF COUNSEL

Robert L. Biederman

Representative Clients: Beaudin, Gallanis; Beaudin, Incorporated; Orlandi Gear Co., Inc.; Bing Steel, Inc.; Superb Manufacturing, Inc.; Spring Engineering, Inc.; Adrian Steel Co.; Southfield Radiology Associates, P.C.; HDS Services, Inc.; TGI Friday's Inc.; Quality Gold of Cincinnati, Inc.

For full biographical listings, see the Martindale-Hubbell Law Directory

WEINGARDEN & HAUER, P.C. (AV)

30100 Telegraph Road, Suite 221, 48025
Telephone: 810-258-0800
Telecopier: 810-258-2750

Larry A. Weingarden

Reference: Security Bank & Trust.

For full biographical listings, see the Martindale-Hubbell Law Directory

BLOOMFIELD HILLS, Oakland Co.

ADKISON NEED (AV)

1533 North Woodward Avenue, Suite 210, 48304
Telephone: 810-540-7400
Fax: 810-540-7401
Email: AdkisNeed@aol.com

MEMBERS OF FIRM

Phillip G. Adkison	Paul Green
Gregory K. Need	Kelly A. Allen

Deborah M. Schneider

ASSOCIATES

Richard D. Kuhn, Jr.	Ann D. Christ
Kathryn N. Nichols	Laura B. Andoni

For full biographical listings, see the Martindale-Hubbell Law Directory

DAWDA, MANN, MULCAHY & SADLER, P.L.C. (AV)

1533 North Woodward Avenue Suite 200, 48304
Telephone: 810-642-3700
Fax: 810-642-7791
Email: EMail@DMMS.Com

Michael D. Mulcahy	Curtis J. Mann
Edward C. Dawda	William L. Rosin

Todd A. Schafer	Tara E. Barr

Daniel M. Halprin

Representative Clients: AEGON USA Realty Advisors, Inc.; BASF Corporation; Cardell Corporation; Cargill, Inc.; City Management; Ford Motor Company; Ladbroke Racing Corporation; La-Z-Boy, Inc.; The Sherwin-Williams Company; Walker Wire & Steel Corp.

For full biographical listings, see the Martindale-Hubbell Law Directory

HARDIG PARSONS & PEDERSEN (AV)

74 West Long Lake Road, Suite 203, 48304
Telephone: 810-642-3500
Facsimile: 810-645-1128
Charlevoix, Michigan Office: 212 Bridge Street.
Telephone: 616-547-1200.
Facsimile: 616-547-1026.
Pawley's Island, South Carolina Office: 216 Highway 17, P.O. Box 1607, 29585.
Telephone: 803-237-9219.
Facsimile: 803-237-9530.

(See Next Column)

West Palm Beach, Florida Office: Suite 1450, 515 North Flagler.
Telephone: 407-833-1622.
Facsimile: 407-833-6933.

MEMBERS OF FIRM

Joseph L. Hardig, Jr.	Joseph L. Hardig, III
Donald H. Parsons	Edward C. Pedersen

Bradley S. Stout

ASSOCIATE

Capri L. Pelshaw

OF COUNSEL

Edward K. Pedersen, Jr.

MEMBER IN SOUTH CAROLINA

John C. Benso

For full biographical listings, see the Martindale-Hubbell Law Directory

HOWARD & HOWARD ATTORNEYS, P.C. (AV)

The Pinehurst Office Center, Suite 101, 1400 North Woodward Avenue, 48304-2856
Telephone: 810-645-1483
Telecopier: 810-645-1568
Kalamazoo, Michigan Office: The Kalamazoo Building, Suite 400, 107 West Michigan Avenue.
Telephone: 616-382-1483.
Telecopier: 616-382-1568.
Lansing, Michigan Office: The Phoenix Building, Suite 500, 222 Washington Square, North.
Telephone: 517-485-1483.
Telecopier: 517-485-1568.
Peoria, Illinois Office: The Creve Coeur Building, Suite 200, 321 Liberty Street.
Telephone: 309-672-1483.
Telecopier: 309-672-1568.
Tampa, Florida Office: First of America Plaza, Suite 2000, 201 East Kennedy Boulevard.
Telephone: 813-229-1483.
Telecopier: 813-229-1568.

Gustaf R. Andreasen	D. Craig Martin
Thomas R. Curran, Jr.	Roshunda L. Price-Harper
J. Michael Kemp	Melanie Mayo West
Timothy E. Kraepel	James C. Wickens

John E. Young

Representative Clients: For Representative Client list, see General Practice, Bloomfield Hills, MI.

For Complete List of Firm Personnel, See General Section

For full biographical listings, see the Martindale-Hubbell Law Directory

MEYER, KIRK, SNYDER & SAFFORD, PLLC (AV)

Suite 100, 100 West Long Lake Road, 48304
Telephone: 810-647-5111
Telecopier: 810-647-6079
Detroit, Michigan Office: 2500 Penobscot Building.
Telephone: 313-961-1261.

George H. Meyer	John M. Kirk

Donald H. Baker, Jr.

Representative Clients: Available Upon Request.

For Complete List of Firm Personnel, See General Section

For full biographical listings, see the Martindale-Hubbell Law Directory

DAVID D. PATTON & ASSOCIATES, P.C. (AV)

100 Bloomfield Hills Parkway, Suite 110, 48304
Telephone: 810-258-6020
Fax: 810-258-6052
Email: Litigation@Aol.Com

David D. Patton

Ellen Bartman Jannette	Patricia C. White

David H. Patton (1912-1993)

For full biographical listings, see the Martindale-Hubbell Law Directory

SILLS, LAW, ESSAD, FIEDLER & CHARBONEAU, P.C. (AV)

1550 Woodward Avenue, Suite 200, 48304
Telephone: 810-644-3600
Fax: 810-901-4842
Lansing, Michigan Office: 3900 Collins Road, Suite 1021.
Telephone: 517-372-1717.
Fax: 517-372-0209.
Traverse City, Michigan Office: 900 East Front Street, Suite 125.
Telephone: 616-941-2218.
Fax: 616-941-8958.

(See Next Column)

SILLS, LAW, ESSAD, FIEDLER & CHARBONEAU P.C., *Bloomfield Hills—Continued*

John D. Sills	Thomas R. Charboneau, Jr.
Robert C. Law	Victor A. Zambardi
Ernest J. Essad, Jr.	David W. Geiss
Charles Arthur Fiedler	Christopher L. Buday

T. David Law

OF COUNSEL

Paul E. Stern (Not admitted in MI; Lansing Office)

For full biographical listings, see the Martindale-Hubbell Law Directory

---

BRIGHTON, Livingston Co.

BURCHFIELD, PARK & HEDDON, P.C. (AV)

225 East Grand River, Suite 203, 48116
Telephone: 810-227-3100
Facsimile: 810-227-2996

Kenneth E. Burchfield	David L. Park
	Shari L. Heddon

Mack T. Spickard

LEGAL SUPPORT PERSONNEL

Janet M. Schillinger

For full biographical listings, see the Martindale-Hubbell Law Directory

---

DETROIT,* Wayne Co.

ABBOTT, NICHOLSON, QUILTER, ESSHAKI & YOUNGBLOOD, P.C. (AV)

19th Floor, One Woodward Avenue, 48226
Telephone: 313-963-2500
Telecopier: 313-963-7882

C. Richard Abbott	Carl F. Jarboe
John R. Nicholson	Jay A. Kennedy
Thomas R. Quilter III	Timothy A. Stoepker
Gene J. Esshaki	Timothy J. Kramer
John F. Youngblood	Norbert T. Madison, Jr.
James B. Perry	William D. Gilbride, Jr.

Mary P. Nelson	Kathryn L. Ritchie
Michael R. Blum	Jill A. Bankey
Thomas F. Hatch	Dawn M. Macaddino
Anne Warren Bagno	Casimir J. Swastek
Eric J. Girdler	Daniel G. Kielczewski

George M. Mesrey

OF COUNSEL

Thomas C. Shumaker	Karen Smith Kienbaum

For full biographical listings, see the Martindale-Hubbell Law Directory

---

BODMAN, LONGLEY & DAHLING LLP (AV)

34th Floor 100 Renaissance Center, 48243
Telephone: 313-259-7777
Fax: 313-393-7579
Email: 2080194@mcimail.com
Troy, Michigan Office: Suite 2020, 755 West Big Beaver Road.
Telephone: 810-362-2110.
Fax: 810-244-0780.
Ann Arbor, Michigan Office: 110 Miller, Suite 300.
Telephone: 313-761-3780.
Fax: 313-930-2494.
Northern Michigan Office: 229 Court Street, P.O. Box 405, Cheboygan.
Telephone: 616-627-4351.
Fax: 616-627-2802.

MEMBERS OF FIRM

Richard D. Rohr	James R. Buschmann
Theodore Souris	Joseph J. Kochanek
Joseph A. Sullivan	David G. Chardavoyne
Walter O. Koch (Troy Office)	Terrence B. Larkin (Troy Office)
Michael B. Lewiston	Robert J. Diehl, Jr.
George D. Miller, Jr.	Martha Bedsole Goodloe (Troy Office)
Mark W. Griffin (Ann Arbor Office)	Harvey W. Berman (Ann Arbor Office)
Thomas A. Roach (Ann Arbor Office)	Barbara Bowman Bluford
Kenneth R. Lango (Troy Office)	Christopher J. Dine (Troy Office)
James T. Heimbuch	Sandra L. Sorini (Ann Arbor Office)
Herold McC. Deason	

COUNSEL

Lewis A. Rockwell

For Representative Client List, See General Section.

For Complete List of Firm Personnel, See General Section

For full biographical listings, see the Martindale-Hubbell Law Directory

---

BUTZEL LONG, A PROFESSIONAL CORPORATION (AV)

Suite 900, 150 West Jefferson, 48226
Telephone: 313-225-7000
Telecopier: 313-225-7080
Email: melnick@butzel.com *URL:* http://www.butzel.com
Birmingham, Michigan Office: Suite 200, 32270 Telegraph Road.
Telephone: 810-258-1616.
Telecopier: 810-258-1439.
Lansing, Michigan Office: 118 West Ottawa Street.
Telephone: 517-372-6622.
Telecopier: 517-372-6672.
Ann Arbor, Michigan Office: Suite 300, 350 South Main Street.
Telephone: 313-995-3110.
Telecopier: 313-995-1777.
Grosse Pointe Farms, Michigan Office: Suite 260, 21 Kercheval.
Telephone: 313-886-5446.
Telecopier: 313-886-2114.

Harold A. Ruemenapp	Carl Rashid, Jr.
Morris Milmet (Birmingham)	Justin G. Klimko
Frank B. Vecchio (Birmingham)	Michael F. Golab (Birmingham)
William R. Ralls (Lansing)	James L. Hughes
C. Peter Theut	Arthur Dudley II
Robert B. Foster (Ann Arbor)	Gordon W. Didier (Birmingham)
Paul L. Triemstra (Birmingham)	Terry O. Lang
Thomas E. Sizemore	James Y. Stewart (Birmingham)
James C. Bruno	Melvin J. Hollowell, Jr.

COUNSEL

Oscar H. Feldman (Birmingham)

OF COUNSEL

Erwin S. Simon

Lois Elizabeth Bingham	Laurie Callahan Endsley

Representative Clients: American Tape Co.; The Detroit News; Dunham's Athleisure, Inc.; Harvard Industries; Jackson National Life Insurance Co.; New Venture Gear; Ricardo Companies; Stroh Brewery Co.; Takata, Inc.; William Beaumont Hospital.

For Complete List of Firm Personnel, See General Section

For full biographical listings, see the Martindale-Hubbell Law Directory

---

CLARK HILL P.L.C. (AV)

500 Woodward Avenue, Suite 3500, 48226
Telephone: 313-965-8300
Facsimile: 313-962-4348
Oakland County, Michigan Office: Third Floor, 255 South Woodward Avenue, Birmingham.
Telephone: 810-642-9692.
Facsimile: 810-642-2174.
Lansing, Michigan Office: Suite 600, 200 North Capitol Avenue.
Telephone: 517-484-4481.
Facsimile: 517-484-1246.
Minneapolis, Minnesota Office: Suite 1000, One Financial Plaza, 120 South Sixth Street.
Telephone: 612-332-0102.
Facsimile: 612-332-3225.
Kansas City, Missouri Office: Suite 1400, Bryant Building, 1102 Grand Avenue.
Telephone: 816-221-5578.
Facsimile: 816-221-0303.

George N. Bashara, Jr.	Duane L. Tarnacki
D. Kerry Crenshaw	Michael S. Khoury
Timothy W. Mast (Resident, Oakland County Office)	Daniel H. Minkus (Resident, Oakland County Office)
John F. Burns	Kevin M. Bernys (Resident, Oakland County Office)
James E. Brenner	
Robert L. Weyhing, III	John J. Hern, Jr.
David E. Nims, III	Andrea M. Kanski

COUNSEL

Charles M. Bayer

OF COUNSEL

Martin C. Oetting	Lee B. Durham, Jr. (Resident, Oakland County Office)

Michael I. Conlon	John P. Hensien
Patrice Asimakis	Christopher A. McMican
Georgette Borrego Dulworth	Margery Siegel Klausner

Representative Clients: R. P. Scherer Corporation; The Budd Co.; Code-Alarm, Inc.; Detrex Corporation; Booth Communications, Inc.; Rouge Steel Company; City of Detroit General Retirement System; Horizon Heath Systems, Inc.; Michigan Manufacturers Association; Council of Michigan Foundations.

For Complete List of Firm Personnel, See General Section

For full biographical listings, see the Martindale-Hubbell Law Directory

Detroit—Continued

EGGENBERGER, EGGENBERGER, McKINNEY, WEBER & HOFMEISTER, P.C. (AV)

42nd Floor Penobscot Building, 48226
Telephone: 313-961-9722

William J. Eggenberger (1900-1984)	John P. McKinney
William D. Eggenberger	Stephen L. Weber
Robert E. Eggenberger	Paul D. Hofmeister
	Thomas R. Paxton

Mary T. Humbert	James B. Eggenberger

Representative Clients: Amoco Oil Co.; Central National Insurance Group of Omaha; City of Wayne, Michigan; Clark Oil & Refining Corp.; Country Mutual Casualty Co.; Auto Club Insurance Assn.; General Accident Assurance Co., Ltd.; Great Central Insurance Co.; Inland Mutual Insurance Co.; Midwest Mutual Insurance Co.

For full biographical listings, see the Martindale-Hubbell Law Directory

FEIKENS, VANDER MALE, STEVENS, BELLAMY & GILCHRIST, P.C. (AV)

One Detroit Center Suite 3400, 500 Woodward Avenue, 48226-3406
Telephone: 313-962-5909
Fax: 313-962-3125
Email: FEIKENS@COUNSEL.COM

Robert E. Dice (1922-1983)	Lee A. Stevens
Jon Feikens	William C. Hurley
Jack E. Vander Male	Linda M. Galbraith
Frederick B. Bellamy	Michael S. Cafferty
Alan Gordon Gilchrist	Robert H. Feikens
L. Neal Kennedy	Gerald W. Van Wyke
Bruce A. VandeVusse	Roger L. Wolcott
	Sharon McPhail

Richard G. Koefod	Keith J. Soltis
Joseph E. Kozely, Jr.	Michael B. Barey
Jeffrey Feikens	Renee T. VanderHagen
	Michael P. Citrin

OF COUNSEL

Sam W. Thomas (P.C.)	Walter Vincent Bernard III

LEGAL SUPPORT PERSONNEL
PARALEGALS

Robert Westveer	Linda Barthlow

For full biographical listings, see the Martindale-Hubbell Law Directory

JAFFE, RAITT, HEUER & WEISS, PROFESSIONAL CORPORATION (AV)

One Woodward Avenue, Suite 2400, 48226
Telephone: 313-961-8380
Telecopier: 313-961-8358
Cable Address: "Jafsni"
Southfield, Michigan Office: Travelers Tower, Suite 1520.
Telephone: 313-961-8380
Monroe, Michigan Office: 214 East Elm Avenue, Suite 208,
Telephone: 313-241-6470.
Telefacsimile: 313-241-3849.

Judith Lowitz Adler	Mark P. Krysinski
Penny L. Carolan	Joel J. Morris
Wallace H. Glendening	Gerald F. Reinhart
Robert J. Gordon	Stephen G. Schafer
Jeffrey G. Heuer	Elliot A. Spoon
Blair B. Hysni	David D. Warner
Ira J. Jaffe	Arthur A. Weiss
Robin H. Krueger	Richard A. Zussman

Derek S. Adolf	Carla M. Mecoli Kamp
Lesley A. Gaber	Jeffrey M. Weiss

Representative Clients: Durr Industries; Edgemere Enterprises; McClain Industries, Inc.; New England Mutual Life Insurance Co.

For Complete List of Firm Personnel, See General Section

For full biographical listings, see the Martindale-Hubbell Law Directory

JOHNSON & VALENTINE (AV)

4372 Penobscot Building, 48226
Telephone: 313-961-4700

MEMBERS OF FIRM

Edward C. Johnson	Glenn L. Valentine

ASSOCIATE
Dale T. McPherson

(See Next Column)

OF COUNSEL
Jarvis J. Schmidt

Representative Clients: Huntington Banks of Michigan; The Huntington Mortgage Co.; First of America Bank, Michigan; Sun Bank-Miami, N.A., Coral Gables, Tr. Dpt.; Fifth Third Bank of Toledo, N.A.; Cozadd Rotary Foundation Trust; Colonial Hockey League; National Transportation Counsellors.
References: First of America Bank; Southeast Michigan, N.A.

For full biographical listings, see the Martindale-Hubbell Law Directory

LEWIS, CLAY & MUNDAY, A PROFESSIONAL CORPORATION (AV)

(Formerly Lewis, White & Clay, P.C.)
1300 First National Building, 660 Woodward Avenue, 48226-3531
Telephone: 313-961-2550
Troy, Michigan Office: Liberty Center, Suite 200. 100 West Big Beaver Road. 48084.
Telephone: 810-680-6702.
Fax: 810-680-6703.
Washington, D.C. Office: 1000 16th Street, N.W., Suite 401. 20036.
Telephone: 202-835-0616.
Fax: 202-833-3316.
Boston, Massachusetts Office: 10 Post Office Square.
Telephone: 617-422-8646.
Fax: 617-338-5693.

David Baker Lewis	Frank E. Barbee
Eric Lee Clay	Camille Stearns Miller
Reuben A. Munday	Michael T. Raymond
Ulysses Whittaker Boykin	Jacqueline H. Sellers
Carl F. Stafford	David N. Zacks
Helen Francine Strong	Thomas J. Guyer
	Blair A. Person

Karen Kendrick Brown (Resident, Washington, D.C. Office)	Hans J. Massaquoi, Jr.
	Nancy C. Borland
J. Taylor Teasdale	Tammy L. Terry
Wade Harper McCree	Lynn Westfall Gross
Tyrone A. Powell	Suzanne P. Pope
Susan D. Hoffman	Matthew H. Halpin
John J. Walsh	Donica Thomas Varner
Andrea L. Powell	Damon L. White
Althea Lynn Foster	(Not admitted in MI)
	Kathleen L. Royal

COUNSEL

Otis M. Smith (1922-1994)	G. Allen Bass (Resident, Boston, Massachusetts Office)
Herbert O. Reid, Sr. (1915-1991)	

Representative Clients: Omnicare Health Plan; Aetna Life & Casualty Co.; Chrysler Motors Corp.; Chrysler Financial Corp.; MCI Communications Corp.; City of Detroit; City of Detroit Building Authority; City of Detroit Downtown Development Authority; Consolidated Rail Corp. (Conrail); Equitable Life Assurance Society of the United States.

For full biographical listings, see the Martindale-Hubbell Law Directory

DAVID M. THOMS & ASSOCIATES, P.C. (AV)

400 Renaissance Center, Suite 950, 48243
Telephone: 313-259-6333
Facsimile: 313-259-7037
Bloomfield Hills, Michigan Office: 1500 Woodward Avenue, Suite 100.
Telephone: 313-259-6333.
Fax: 313-259-7037.

David M. Thoms

Audrey R. Holley	Duane B. Brown

OF COUNSEL

Allan G. Meganck	Thomas V. Trainer

Representative Clients: Avion Concepts, Inc.; Fowler Agency Corp.; Gibbs World Wide Wines, Inc.; deBary Travel, Inc.; North Management, Inc.; R.G. & G.R. Harris Funeral Home, Inc.; St. Jude Children's Research Hospital; The Salvation Army.
References: Comerica Bank-Detroit; National Bank of Detroit.

For full biographical listings, see the Martindale-Hubbell Law Directory

TIMMIS & INMAN, L.L.P. (AV)

300 Talon Centre, 48207
Telephone: 313-396-4200
Telecopier: 313-396-4228

Michael T. Timmis	Henry J. Brennan, III
Robert E. Graziani	Mark W. Peyser
George A. Peck	Richard M. Miettinen
Charles W. Royer	Lisa R. Gorman
Richard L. Levin	Bradley J. Knickerbocker
	George M. Malis

(See Next Column)

TIMMIS & INMAN L.L.P., *Detroit—Continued*

Michael F. Wais	Patrick B. Carey
John P. Kanan	Erich J. D'Andrea

OF COUNSEL

Wayne C. Inman	William B. Fitzgerald

W. Clark Durant, III

Representative Clients: Deneb Robotics; Combine International; Chateau Properties, Inc.; Eastpointe Radiologists, P.C.; Talon Automotive Group L.L.C.; Reflectolite Products Co.; North American Die Casting Corp.; Atlas Holding Company; Universal Image Productions, Inc.

For Complete List of Firm Personnel, See General Section

For full biographical listings, see the Martindale-Hubbell Law Directory

---

EAST LANSING, Ingham Co.

FARHAT, STORY & KRAUS, P.C. (AV)

Beacon Place, 4572 South Hagadorn Road, Suite 3, 48823
Telephone: 517-351-3700
Fax: 517-332-4122
Email: rkraus@sojourn.com

Leo A. Farhat	Chris A. Bergstrom
James E. Burns (1925-1979)	Kitty L. Groh
Monte R. Story	Charles R. Toy
Richard C. Kraus	David M. Platt
Max R. Hoffman Jr.	Thomas L. Sparks

Lawrence P. Schweitzer	Daniel B. Morgan
Debra A. Geroux	Mary K. Robbins-Kralapp

Representative Clients: Big L. Corp.; Michigan Automotive Wholesalers Association; Hartman-Fabco, Inc.; Lansing Electric Motors, Inc.; Mike Miller Lincoln Mercury; GTE Directories Service Corp.; American Medical Malpractice, Inc.; Jackson National Life Ins. Co.; State Farm Life Insurance Co.; Lansing School District.

For full biographical listings, see the Martindale-Hubbell Law Directory

---

FARMINGTON HILLS, Oakland Co.

COUZENS, LANSKY, FEALK, ELLIS, ROEDER & LAZAR, P.C. (AV)

33533 West Twelve Mile Road, Suite 150, P.O. Box 9057, 48333-9057
Telephone: 810-489-8600
Telecopier: 810-489-4156

Sheldon A. Fealk	Lisa J. Walters
Jack S. Couzens, II	Stephen Scapelliti
Jerry M. Ellis	Donald A. Wagner
Donald M. Lansky	Michael P. Witzke
Bruce J. Lazar	Cyrus Raamin Kashef
Alan C. Roeder	Gregg A. Nathanson
Renard J. Kolasa	Mark S. Frankel
Kathryn Gilson Sussman	Lynette M. Sheldon
Jeffrey A. Levine	Roger E. Winkelman
Phillip L. Sternberg	David B. Deutsch
Marc L. Prey	Monica Demko Moons

Representative Clients: Provided upon request.
Reference: Comerica Bank-Southfield.

For full biographical listings, see the Martindale-Hubbell Law Directory

---

HALIW, SICILIANO AND MYCHALOWYCH (AV)

37000 Grand River, Suite 350, 48335
Telephone: 810-442-0510
Fax: 810-442-0518

MEMBERS OF FIRM

Andrew J. Haliw III	Nanette Lynn Korpi
Joseph A. Siciliano	Raymond L. Feul
Andrew W. Mychalowych	Frank E. Henke

For full biographical listings, see the Martindale-Hubbell Law Directory

---

HOROWITZ — GUDEMAN, P.C. (AV)

31700 Middlebelt, Suite 140, 48334
Telephone: 810-855-6020
Facsimile: 810-855-6025

Marvin I. Horowitz	Edward J. Gudeman

Stuart L. Sherman

Leslie I. Kollin

LEGAL SUPPORT PERSONNEL

Robin E. Cornell (Paralegal)

For full biographical listings, see the Martindale-Hubbell Law Directory

---

FLINT,* Genesee Co.

GAULT DAVISON A PROFESSIONAL SERVICE CORPORATION (AV)

Tenth Floor, Northbank Center, 432 North Saginaw Street, 48502-2032
Telephone: 810-234-3633
Fax: 810-233-3387
Email: GLTDAV@tir.com

Russell E. Bowers	Bernard L. McAra

Christine A. Scherba

Representative Clients: Al Serra Automobile Cos.; Milburn Peat Co.; Eldon L. Auker Associates; NBD Bancorp, Inc.; NBD Bank; Citizens Commercial & Savings Bank; Howard Delivery Service, Inc.

For full biographical listings, see the Martindale-Hubbell Law Directory

---

GRAND RAPIDS,* Kent Co.

BORRE, PETERSON, FOWLER & REENS, P.C. (AV)

The Philo C. Fuller House, 44 Lafayette, N.E., P.O. Box 1767, 49501-1767
Telephone: 616-459-1971
Fax: 616-459-2393

Glen V. Borre	Frank H. Johnson
James B. Peterson	Mark D. Sevald
Ben A. Fowler	William R. Vander Sluis
William C. Reens	William G. Krupar

References: Old Kent Bank; NBD Bank; FMB-First Michigan Bank - Grand Rapids.

For Complete List of Firm Personnel, See General Section

For full biographical listings, see the Martindale-Hubbell Law Directory

---

DAMON & DAMON (AV)

220 Lyon Street, N.W., Suite 525, 49503-2210
Telephone: 616-459-8357
Facsimile: 616-459-3462

MEMBERS OF FIRM

John E. Damon	Charles E. Damon

ASSOCIATE

Shawn M. Gotch

RHOADES, MCKEE, BOER, GOODRICH & TITTA (AV)

161 Ottawa N.W., Suite 600, 49503-2793
Telephone: 616-235-3500
Fax: 616-459-5102
Email: grlaw@grlaw.com *URL:* http://www.grlaw.com

Edward B. Goodrich	Mary Ann Cartwright
Peter A. Titta	James L. Schipper
Arthur C. Spalding	Stephen A. Hilger
Robert J. Dugan	Gregory G. Timmer
Terrence L. Groesser	Mary Lynette Williams
Thomas P. Hogan	Scott J. Steiner
James M. Flaggert	Robert C. Shaver

Jeff A. Moyer	Kenneth M. Horjus
Todd Allen Hendricks	Randy J. Kolar

Reference: First Michigan Bank.

For full biographical listings, see the Martindale-Hubbell Law Directory

---

VARNUM, RIDDERING, SCHMIDT & HOWLETT LLP (AV)

A Limited Liability Partnership including Professional Corporations
Bridgewater Place, P.O. Box 352, 49501-0352
Telephone: 616-336-6000
800-262-0011
Facsimile: 616-336-7000
Telex: 1561593 VARN
Email: varnum@vrsh.com
Lansing, Michigan Office: The Victor Center, Suite 810, 210 North Washington Square, 48933.
Telephone: 517-482-6237.
Facsimile: 517-482-6937.
Kalamazoo, Michigan Office: 350 East Michigan Avenue, 49007.
Telephone: 616-382-2300.
Facsimile: 616-382-2382.
Grand Haven, Michigan Office: 321 Washington Street, P.O. Box 288, 49417.
Telephone: 616-846-7100.
Facsimile: 616-846-7101.
Battle Creek, Michigan Office: 4950 West Dickman Road, Suite B-1, 49015.
Telephone: 616-962-7144.

(See Next Column)

Varnum, Riddering, Schmidt & Howlett LLP—Continued

Bingham Farms, Michigan Office: 31600 Telegraph Road, Suite 230, 48025.
Telephone: 810-594-7330.
Facsimile: 810-594-7331.

MEMBERS OF FIRM

James N. DeBoer, Jr.	Frank G. Dunten, P.C.
Hilary F. Snell	Robert L. Diamond
John C. Carlyle (Resident at Grand Haven Office)	Lawrence P. Burns
	Carl Oosterhouse, P.C.
Donald L. Johnson	William J. Lawrence III
Daniel C. Molhoek	Kaplin S. Jones, P.C.
Thomas T. Huff (Resident at Kalamazoo Office)	Michael G. Wooldridge
	Jeffrey W. Beswick (Resident at Grand Haven Office)
J. Terry Moran	
Robert D. Kullgren	Scott A. Huizenga
Robert P. Cooper	Kathleen P. Fochtman

COUNSEL

William J. Halliday, Jr.	H. Raymond Andrews, Jr.
Fred M. Woodruff, Jr. (Resident at Bingham Farms Office)	

ASSOCIATES

Patrick A. Miles, Jr.	Joseph B. Levan
Steven J. Morren	Dale R. Rietberg
Alfred L. Schubkegel, Jr. (Resident at Kalamazoo Office)	

Counsel For: Donnelly Corporation; First Michigan Bank Corporation; Gainey Corporation; Gentex Corporation; Herman Miller, Inc.; Blodgett Memorial Medical Center; Bradford-White Corp.; X-Rite Incorporated; Universal Forest Products, Inc.; Ameriwood Industries International Corporation.

For Complete List of Firm Personnel, See General Section

For full biographical listings, see the Martindale-Hubbell Law Directory

---

WHEELER UPHAM, A PROFESSIONAL CORPORATION (AV)

Second Floor, Trust Building, 40 Pearl Street, N.W., 49503-3001
Telephone: 616-459-7100
Fax: 616-459-6366

Gordon B. Wheeler (1904-1986)	William H. Heritage, Jr.
Buford A. Upham (Retired)	Kenneth E. Tiews
Robert H. Gillette	Jack L. Hoffman
Geoffrey L. Gillis	Janet C. Baxter
John M. Roels	Peter Kladder, III
Gary A. Maximiuk	James M. Shade
Timothy J. Orlebeke	Thomas A. Kuiper

Counsel For: Independent Cooperative Milk Producers Assn.; National Food Processors Assn.; Monsanto Co.; Medtronic, Inc.; Navistar; Westdale Better Homes and Gardens; Gospel Films, Inc.; Michigan Credit Union League.

For full biographical listings, see the Martindale-Hubbell Law Directory

---

GROSSE POINTE, Wayne Co.

MARCO, WATKINS AND OWSIANY (AV)

20180 Mack Avenue, 48236
Telephone: 313-882-8800
Fax: 313-882-6211

MEMBERS OF FIRM

Paul Marco	Robert D. Watkins
Michael J. Owsiany	

OF COUNSEL

William E. Kennedy

For full biographical listings, see the Martindale-Hubbell Law Directory

---

GROSSE POINTE FARMS, Wayne Co.

ALLAN NEEF (AV)

18580 Mack Avenue, 48236
Telephone: 313-343-9200
Fax: 313-343-0207

For full biographical listings, see the Martindale-Hubbell Law Directory

---

HOLLAND, Ottawa Co.

CUNNINGHAM DALMAN, P.C. (AV)

321 Settlers Road, P.O. Box 1767, 49422-1767
Telephone: 616-392-1821
Fax: 616-392-4769

(See Next Column)

Gordon H. Cunningham	Kenneth B. Breese
Ronald L. Dalman	Jeffrey K. Helder
Max R. Murphy	Ronald J. Vander Veen
James A. Bidol	David M. Zessin
Andrew J. Mulder	Mark H. Zietlow
Joel G. Bouwens	James W. Bouwens
	Randall S. Schipper

Susan E. Vroegop	Melinda M. Abney

OF COUNSEL

Vernon D. Ten Cate	Kenneth B. Peirce, Jr.

Representative Clients: FMB-First Michigan Bank; First of America Bank-Holland, N.A.; Ottawa Savings Bank; City of Holland; Auto Club Insurance Assn. (AAA); American States Insurance Co.; Holland Economic Development Corp.; Hope College; Western Theological Seminary.
Reference: FMB-First Michigan Bank.

For full biographical listings, see the Martindale-Hubbell Law Directory

---

KALAMAZOO,* Kalamazoo Co.

DIETRICH, ZODY, HOWARD & VANDERROEST, P.C. (AV)

834 King Highway, Suite 110, 49001
Telephone: 616-344-9236
Fax: 616-344-0412

G. Philip Dietrich	James W. Smith
Richard J. Howard	James E. VanderRoest
	Philip W. Dietrich

OF COUNSEL

Brenda Wheeler Zody

For full biographical listings, see the Martindale-Hubbell Law Directory

---

EARLY, LENNON, PETERS & CROCKER, P.C. (AV)

900 Comerica Building, 49007-4752
Telephone: 616-381-8844
Fax: 616-349-8525

George H. Lennon, III	Gordon C. Miller
Lawrence M. Brenton	Robert M. Taylor
	Andrew J. Vorbrich

Attorneys for: General Motors Corp.; Wal-Mart Stores; Borgess Medical Center; Aetna Insurance: Kemper Group; Medical Protective Co.; Zurich Insurance; AAA; Liberty Mutual; Home Insurance.

For Complete List of Firm Personnel, See General Section

For full biographical listings, see the Martindale-Hubbell Law Directory

---

HOWARD & HOWARD ATTORNEYS, P.C. (AV)

The Kalamazoo Building, Suite 400, 107 West Michigan Avenue, 49007-3956
Telephone: 616-382-1483
Telecopier: 616-382-1568
Bloomfield Hills, Michigan Office: The Pinehurst Office Center, Suite 101, 1400 North Woodward Avenue.
Telephone: 810-645-1483.
Telecopier: 810-645-1568.
Lansing, Michigan Office: The Phoenix Building, Suite 500, 222 Washington Square North.
Telephone: 517-485-1483.
Telecopier: 517-485-1568.
Peoria, Illinois Office: The Creve Coeur Building, Suite 200, 321 Liberty Street.
Telephone: 309-672-1483.
Telecopier: 309-672-1568.
Tampa, Florida Office: First of America Plaza, Suite 2000, 201 East Kennedy Boulevard.
Telephone: 813-229-1483.
Telecopier: 813-229-1568.

Stephen D. Bigelow	Peter J. Livingston
Jeffrey P. Chalmers	D. Craig Martin
John C. Howard	Shamra M. Van Wagoner

Representative Clients: For Representative Client list, see General Practice, Kalamazoo, MI.

For Complete List of Firm Personnel, See General Section

For full biographical listings, see the Martindale-Hubbell Law Directory

---

LEWIS & ALLEN, P.C. (AV)

Old Kent Bank Building, Suite 800, 136 East Michigan Avenue, 49007-3946
Telephone: 616-388-7600
Fax: 616-349-3831

(See Next Column)

LEWIS & ALLEN P.C., *Kalamazoo—Continued*

Dean S. Lewis
W. Fred Allen, Jr.
Winfield J. Hollander
Bruce W. Martin
Daniel L. Conklin

William A. Redmond
Stephen M. Denenfeld
Gregory G. St. Arnauld
Anne McGregor Fries
Thomas P. Lewis

Christopher T. Haenicke

LEGAL SUPPORT PERSONNEL

Dorothy B. Kelly

For full biographical listings, see the Martindale-Hubbell Law Directory

LANSING, Ingham Co.

HOWARD & HOWARD ATTORNEYS, P.C. (AV)

The Phoenix Building, Suite 500, 222 Washington Square,
North, 48933-1817
Telephone: 517-485-1483
Telecopier: 517-485-1568
Kalamazoo, Michigan Office: The Kalamazoo Building, Suite 400, 107
West Michigan Avenue.
Telephone: 616-382-1483.
Telecopier: 616-382-1568.
Bloomfield Hills, Michigan Office: The Pinehurst Office Center, Suite 101,
1400 North Woodward Avenue.
Telephone: 810-645-1483.
Telecopier: 810-645-1568.
Peoria, Illinois Office: The Creve Coeur Building, Suite 200, 321 Liberty
Street.
Telephone: 309-672-1483.
Telecopier: 309-672-1568.
Tampa, Florida Office: First of America Plaza, Suite 2000, 201 East
Kennedy Boulevard.
Telephone: 813-229-1483.
Telecopier: 813-229-1568.

Todd D. Chamberlain
Christopher C. Cinnamon

Kim D. Crooks
D. Craig Martin

Gina M. Torielli

Representative Clients: For Representative Client list, see General Practice,
Lansing, MI.

For Complete List of Firm Personnel, See General Section

For full biographical listings, see the Martindale-Hubbell Law Directory

MIDLAND,* Midland Co.

RIECKER, VAN DAM, BARKER, BLACK & ZUBER, P.C. (AV)

414 Townsend Street, P.O. Box 632, 48640
Telephone: 517-631-1025
Facsimile: 517-631-9880

Philip Van Dam

Richard William Barker

R. Drummond Black

General Counsel for: Herbert H. and Grace A. Dow Foundation; Harry A.
and Margaret D. Towsley Foundation; Midland Center for the Arts; Dow-
Howell-Gilmore Associates, Inc.
Counsel for: Comerica Bank N.A.; Mid Michigan Regional Health System;
Wolverine Bank, F.B.S.; Northern Star Companies; Midland County Growth
and Economic Development Corp.; Bresnan Communications, Inc.

For Complete List of Firm Personnel, See General Section

For full biographical listings, see the Martindale-Hubbell Law Directory

MUSKEGON,* Muskegon Co.

LAGUE, NEWMAN & IRISH, A PROFESSIONAL CORPORATION (AV)

600 Terrace Plaza, P.O. Box 389, 49443
Telephone: 616-725-8148
Telecopier: 616-726-3404
Email: firm@lnilaw.com

Richard C. Lague
Chris Ann McGuigan

William M. Newman
J. Scott Timmer

Alvin D. Treado

General Counsel: Hackley Hospital & Medical Center; Kaydon Corp.; Cole's
Quality Foods; Kurdziel Industries.
Local Counsel: SPX Corp.; Booth Newspapers Inc.; First of America Bank-
West Michigan; Spring Manufacturers Institute, Inc.

For Complete List of Firm Personnel, See General Section

For full biographical listings, see the Martindale-Hubbell Law Directory

OKEMOS, Ingham Co.

WARREN, PRICE, CAMERON, FAUST & ASCIUTTO, P.C. (AV)

2161 Commons Parkway, 48864
Telephone: 517-349-8600
Fax: 517-349-3311
Mailing Address: P.O. Box 26067, Lansing, Michigan, 48909

(See Next Column)

J. Michael Warren
Kathaleen Rae Price

Josephine L. Cameron
Owen J. Faust

Linda R. Asciutto

LEGAL SUPPORT PERSONNEL

Gloria J. Odlum (Paralegal)

For full biographical listings, see the Martindale-Hubbell Law Directory

PONTIAC,* Oakland Co.

BOOTH PATTERSON, P.C. (AV)

1090 West Huron Street, 48328
Telephone: 810-681-1200
Fax: 810-681-1754

Douglas W. Booth (1918-1992)
Calvin E. Patterson (1913-1987)
Parvin C. Lee, Jr.
J. Timothy Patterson

David J. Lee
Allan T. Motzny
Michael J. Hughes
Michael D. Bishop

Eric S. Meier

For full biographical listings, see the Martindale-Hubbell Law Directory

ST. JOSEPH,* Berrien Co.

FISHER LAW OFFICE (AV)

Law & Title Building, 811 Ship Street, P.O. Box 83, 49085-0083
Telephone: 616-983-5511
Telecopier: 616-893-5571

Vance A. Fisher

For full biographical listings, see the Martindale-Hubbell Law Directory

TROFF, PETZKE & AMMESON (AV)

Law and Title Building, 811 Ship Street, P.O. Box 67, 49085
Telephone: 616-983-0161
Facsimile: 616-983-0166

MEMBERS OF FIRM

Theodore E. Troff

Roger A. Petzke

Charles F. Ammeson

ASSOCIATES

Bennett S. Schwartz

Daniel G. Lambrecht

Deborah L. Berecz

For full biographical listings, see the Martindale-Hubbell Law Directory

SOUTHFIELD, Oakland Co.

DE VINE & KOHN (AV)

29800 Telegraph Road, 48034
Telephone: 810-353-6500
Fax: 810-353-2514

Clifford J. De Vine

Sheldon B. Kohn

For full biographical listings, see the Martindale-Hubbell Law Directory

ROBERT B. LABE, P.C. (AV)

2000 Town Center, Suite 1780, 48075
Telephone: 810-354-3100
Telecopier: 810-354-3926

Robert B. Labe

Heather Andrews Healy

Reference: Comerica Bank, N.A.; Dean Witter.

For full biographical listings, see the Martindale-Hubbell Law Directory

MADDIN, HAUSER, WARTELL, ROTH, HELLER & PESSES, P.C. (AV)

Third Floor Essex Center, 28400 Northwestern Highway, P.O. Box
215, 48037
Telephone: 810-354-4030, 355-5200
Telefax: 810-354-1422

Milton M. Maddin (1902-1984)
Michael W. Maddin
Mark R. Hauser
C. Robert Wartell
Richard J. Maddin
Richard F. Roth
Harvey R. Heller
Ian D. Pesses
Michael S. Leib

Robert D. Kaplow
William E. Sigler
Stewart C. W. Weiner
Charles M. Lax
Stuart M. Bordman
Steven D. Sallen
Joseph M. Fazio
Gregory J. Gamalski
Julie Chenot Mayer

Nathaniel H. Simpson
Ronald A. Sollish
Mark H. Fink
Steven M. Wolock

Lowell D. Salesin
Marc J. Mendelson
Joseph W. Girardot
Lori E. Talsky

(See Next Column)

MADDIN, HAUSER, WARTELL, ROTH, HELLER & PESSES P.C.—*Continued*
OF COUNSEL
Joel D. Kellman

Reference: Comerica Bank.

For full biographical listings, see the Martindale-Hubbell Law Directory

---

PROVIZER, LICHTENSTEIN & PHILLIPS, P.C. (AV)

4000 Town Center, Suite 1800, 48075
Telephone: 810-352-9080
Facsimile: 810-352-1491

Harold M. Provizer	Constance S. Hall
David S. Lichtenstein	Noel F. Beck
Randall E. Phillips	William J. Selinsky
Marilyn A. Madorsky	Robert I. Brown
Deborah Molitz	Todd B. Denenberg

Jason Milstone

Representative Clients: Investaid Corp.; Leo, Frank & Sims; Mortgage Institute of Michigan; Norm's Jewelry & Loan.

For full biographical listings, see the Martindale-Hubbell Law Directory

---

SOMMERS, SCHWARTZ, SILVER & SCHWARTZ, P.C. (AV)

2000 Town Center, Suite 900, 48075
Telephone: 810-355-0300
Telecopier: 810-746-4001
Plymouth, Michigan Office: 747 South Main Street.
Telephone: 313-455-4250.

Steven J. Schwartz	Gary A. Taback
Patrick B. McCauley	James J. Vlasic

Joseph H. Bourgon
OF COUNSEL

Paul Groffsky	Donald R. Epstein

General Counsel For: City of Taylor; Foodland Distributors; C.A. Muer Corporation; Vlasic & Company; Nederlander Corporation; Midwest Health Centers, P.C.
Representative Clients: City of Pontiac; Michigan National Bank; Perry Drugs.

For Complete List of Firm Personnel, See General Section

For full biographical listings, see the Martindale-Hubbell Law Directory

---

TRAVERSE CITY,* Grand Traverse Co.

BISHOP & HEINTZ, P.C. (AV)

440 W. Front at Oak Street, P.O. Box 707, 49685
Telephone: 616-946-4100
Fax: 616-946-8543

Douglas S. Bishop	Patrick E. Heintz

David A. Cvengros
OF COUNSEL
Arthur R. Curtis

Representative Clients: Old Kent Bank-Grand Traverse; Old Kent Bank & Trust Co.; NBD Bank, N.A.; Ball Aircraft, Inc.; Power Play International Inc.; National Cherry Festival; PDM Industries, Inc.; Bolthouse Machine Corp.; Corrections Management, Inc.; Buck Wilder, Inc.

For full biographical listings, see the Martindale-Hubbell Law Directory

---

TROY, Oakland Co.

BARLOW & LANGE, P.C. (AV)

3290 West Big Beaver Road Suite 310, 48084
Telephone: 810-649-3150
Facsimile: 810-649-3175

Thomas W. H. Barlow	Craig S. Schwartz
Craig W. Lange	Matthew S. Derby
Paul W. Coughenour	Gary S. Fealk

LEGAL SUPPORT PERSONNEL
Laura L. Russell

For full biographical listings, see the Martindale-Hubbell Law Directory

---

CAMPBELL, O'BRIEN & MISTELE, P.C. (AV)

850 Stephenson Highway Suite 410, 48083-1163
Telephone: 810-588-5800
Fax: 810-588-6669

Edwin G. O'Brien (1907-1983)	Arthur R. Spears, Jr.
Dale C. Campbell	Paul W. Loock
Henry E. Mistele	Robert J. Figa

Curtis H. Mistele

References: First of America; Comerica Bank.

For full biographical listings, see the Martindale-Hubbell Law Directory

---

DRIGGERS, SCHULTZ & HERBST, A PROFESSIONAL CORPORATION (AV)

2600 West Big Beaver Road, Suite 550, 48084
Telephone: 810-649-6000
Telecopier: 810-649-6442

Nathan B. Driggers (1929-1996)	Richard B. Tomlinson
Laurence S. Schultz	Daniel R. Boynton
Jay A. Herbst	Joseph W. Thomas

Raymond J. Sterling

Edward S. Toth
OF COUNSEL
Dennis W. Krakow

Representative Clients: Applied Dynamics International, Inc.; Automotive Industries, Inc.; Autotek Sealants; Peter A. Basile Sons, Inc.; Chrysler Corp.; C & I Mechanical Contractors; Dunn Blue Print Co.;
Reference: National Bank of Detroit.

For full biographical listings, see the Martindale-Hubbell Law Directory

---

GRASSI & TOERING, P.L.C. (AV)

888 West Big Beaver, Suite 750, 48084
Telephone: 810-269-2020
Fax: 810-269-2025

Sebastian V. Grassi, Jr.	Douglas L. Toering

For full biographical listings, see the Martindale-Hubbell Law Directory

---

HAINER, DEMOREST & BERMAN, P.C. (AV)

888 West Big Beaver, Suite 1400, 48084
Telephone: 810-244-8424
Fax: 810-244-8455

Michael J. Hainer	Mark S. Demorest

Leonard K. Berman

James D. Zazakis	Paul S. Miller

Rae Ann LaFrance
OF COUNSEL

John P. Charters	Michael A. Kus
Michael A. Heck	Douglas W. Mires

Representative Clients: American Empire Surplus Lines Insurance Co.; Central Distributors of Beer, Inc.; City Management Corp.; Clarklift of Detroit, Inc.; Federal Reserve Bank of Chicago; Hotel Investment Services, Inc.; Michigan Pumping Service; Mid-West Instrument, Inc.; Rockwell International Corp.; Zurich Insurance Co.

For full biographical listings, see the Martindale-Hubbell Law Directory

---

AUSTIN HIRSCHHORN, P.C. (AV)

Suite 710 Columbia Center, 201 West Big Beaver Road, 48084-4152
Telephone: 810-680-1660
Fax: 810-680-1671

Austin Hirschhorn

For full biographical listings, see the Martindale-Hubbell Law Directory

---

KEYWELL AND ROSENFELD (AV)

Suite 600, 2301 West Big Beaver Road, 48084
Telephone: 810-649-3200
Fax: 810-649-0454

MEMBERS OF FIRM

Frederic I. Keywell	Norman E. Greenfield
Gary A. Goldberg	Lucy R. Benham
Jimm F. White	Kelly M. Hayes

Jeffrey B. Levine
ASSOCIATES

Robert A. Gross	David M. Elkin

Reference: National Bank of Detroit.

For full biographical listings, see the Martindale-Hubbell Law Directory

---

POLING, McGAW & POLING, P.C. (AV)

Suite 275, 5435 Corporate Drive, 48098
Telephone: 810-641-0500
Telecopier: 810-641-0506

Benson T. Buck (1926-1989)	Richard B. Poling, Jr.
Richard B. Poling	Gregory C. Hamilton
D. Douglas McGaw	Veronica B. O'Haro

James R. Parker

(See Next Column)

POLING, MCGAW & POLING P.C., *Troy—Continued*

OF COUNSEL
Ralph S. Moore

Representative Clients: County of Oakland; City of Troy; United States Fidelity & Guaranty Co.; Sentry Insurance Co.; Admiral Insurance; DeMaria Construction Co.; Leo Corporation; Aetna Casualty and Surety Co.; Concord Design; Pneumo-Abex.

For full biographical listings, see the Martindale-Hubbell Law Directory

---

WEST BLOOMFIELD, Oakland Co.

VALENTINE & ASSOCIATES, P.C. (AV)

5767 West Maple Road, Suite 400, 48322
Telephone: 810-851-3010

Stephen K. Valentine, Jr.

OF COUNSEL
Philip G. Meyer

For full biographical listings, see the Martindale-Hubbell Law Directory

CIVIL RIGHTS

ALABAMA

BIRMINGHAM, Jefferson Co.

BRADLEY, ARANT, ROSE & WHITE (AV)

2001 Park Place, Suite 1400, P.O. Box 830709, 35283-0709
Telephone: 205-521-8000
Facsimile: 205-252-0264
Facsimile (SouthTrust Tower Office): 205-251-9915
URL: http://www.BARW.COM
Huntsville, Alabama Office: 200 Clinton Avenue West, Suite 900, 35801.
Telephone: 205-517-5100.
Facsimile: 205-533-5069.

ASSOCIATES

Arnold W. Umbach, III   T. Matthew Miller
Abdul K. Kallon

For Complete List of Firm Personnel, See General Section

For full biographical listings, see the Martindale-Hubbell Law Directory

GORDON, SILBERMAN, WIGGINS & CHILDS, A PROFESSIONAL CORPORATION (AV)

1400 SouthTrust Tower, 420 North 20th Street, 35203
Telephone: 205-328-0640
Telecopier: 205-254-1500

Bruce L. Gordon   James Mendelsohn
Ann K. Wiggins

Elizabeth Evans Courtney   Gregory O. Wiggins
Rocco Calamusa, Jr.

For Complete List of Firm Personnel, See General Section

For full biographical listings, see the Martindale-Hubbell Law Directory

CALIFORNIA

COSTA MESA, Orange Co.

RUTAN & TUCKER, LLP (AV)

A Partnership including Professional Corporations
611 Anton Boulevard, Suite 1400, P.O. Box 1950, 92626
Telephone: 714-641-5100; 213-625-7586
Telecopier: 714-546-9035
Email: rutan&tucker@mcimail.com   *URL:* http://www.rutan.com

MEMBERS OF FIRM

David C. Larsen (P.C.)   M. Katherine Jenson
Robert S. Bower   Hans Van Ligten
Philip D. Kohn   Jeffrey Wertheimer
William W. Wynder   Jeffrey A. Goldfarb

For Complete List of Firm Personnel, See General Section

For full biographical listings, see the Martindale-Hubbell Law Directory

PASADENA, Los Angeles Co.

BURTON & NORRIS (AV)

35 South Raymond Avenue, Fourth Floor, 91105
Telephone: 818-449-8300
Fax: 818-449-4417

John C. Burton   Donald G. Norris
Victoria E. King

Reference: Bank of America (Pasadena).

For full biographical listings, see the Martindale-Hubbell Law Directory

FRANSCELL, STRICKLAND, ROBERTS & LAWRENCE, A PROFESSIONAL CORPORATION (AV)

Penthouse, 225 South Lake Avenue, 91101-3005
Telephone: 818-304-7830; 213-684-7830
Fax: 818-795-7460
Santa Ana, California Office: Suite 800, 401 Civic Center Drive West.
Telephone: 714-543-6511.
Fax: 714-543-6711.
Riverside, California Office: Suite 670, 3801 University Avenue.
Telephone: 909-686-1000.
Fax: 909-686-2565.

(See Next Column)

George J. Franscell
Tracy Strickland
    (Resident, Santa Ana Office)
Barbara E. Roberts
    (Resident, Riverside Office)
David D. Lawrence
Carol Ann Rohr
Scott D. MacLatchie
S. Frank Harrell
    (Resident, Santa Ana Office)

Donald C. McFarlane
    (Resident, Santa Ana Office)
Libby Wong
Cindy S. Lee
Martin J. De Vries
    (Resident, Riverside Office)
Ann Marie Sanders
Priscilla F. Slocum
Garth Matthew Drozin

For full biographical listings, see the Martindale-Hubbell Law Directory

OVERLANDER, LEWIS & RUSSELL (AV)

65 North Raymond Avenue, Suite 210, 91103
Telephone: 818-304-0500
Fax: 818-304-9750

Thomas F. Overlander   Edwin A. Lewis
Richard L. Russell, Jr.

Craig J. Miller   Sherri Lynette Woods

For full biographical listings, see the Martindale-Hubbell Law Directory

SAN FRANCISCO, San Francisco Co.

MURPHY, PEARSON, BRADLEY & FEENEY, A PROFESSIONAL CORPORATION (AV)

88 Kearny Street, 11th Floor, 94108
Telephone: 415-788-1900
Telecopier: 415-393-8087
Sacramento, California Office: Suite 200, 3600 American River Drive, 95864.
Telephone: 916-483-6074.
Telecopier: 916-483-6088.

John H. Feeney

For Complete List of Firm Personnel, See General Section

For full biographical listings, see the Martindale-Hubbell Law Directory

SAN JOSE, Santa Clara Co.

McMANIS, FAULKNER & MORGAN (AV)

160 West Santa Clara Street, 10th Floor, 95113
Telephone: 408-279-8700
Fax: 408-279-3244; 408-279-0494
Email: mfm@mfmlaw.com

MEMBERS OF FIRM

James McManis   William Faulkner
Donelle Morgan

ASSOCIATES

Nora Rousso   Michael Reedy
Lisa Herrick   Douglas Watanabe
Kelly McHaffie

For full biographical listings, see the Martindale-Hubbell Law Directory

COLORADO

DENVER, Denver Co.

ARTHUR M. SCHWARTZ, P.C. (AV)

Dominion Plaza, Suite 2250 South Tower 600 Seventeenth Street, 80202
Telephone: 303-893-2500
Fax: 303-893-3349

Arthur M. Schwartz

Michael W. Gross   Cindy D. Schwartz
Gary M. Kramer

Reference: First Interstate Bank of Denver.

For full biographical listings, see the Martindale-Hubbell Law Directory

CONNECTICUT

*NEW HAVEN,** New Haven Co.

Rosen & Dolan, P.C. (AV)

400 Orange Street, 06511
Telephone: 203-787-3513
Fax: 203-789-1605
Email: davidrosen@counsel.com
Email: spincus@counsel.com

David N. Rosen

Stephen M. Pincus

Reference: Peoples Bank.

For Complete List of Firm Personnel, See General Section

For full biographical listings, see the Martindale-Hubbell Law Directory

Law Offices of John R. Williams (AV)

51 Elm Street, 06510
Telephone: 203-562-9931
Fax: 203-776-9494

ASSOCIATES

Diane Polan
Katrena Engstrom

Norman A. Pattis
William S. Palmieri

References: Webster Bank; Bank of New Haven.

For full biographical listings, see the Martindale-Hubbell Law Directory

DISTRICT OF COLUMBIA

WASHINGTON, D.C. Co.

Cohen, Milstein, Hausfeld & Toll, P.L.L.C. (AV)

West Tower, Suite 500, 1100 New York Avenue, N.W., 20005-3964
Telephone: 202-408-4600
Facsimile: 202-408-4699

MEMBERS OF FIRM

Jerry S. Cohen (1925-1995)
Herbert E. Milstein
Michael D. Hausfeld
Steven J. Toll
Ann C. Yahner

Lisa M. Mezzetti
Andrew N. Friedman
Richard S. Lewis
Daniel S. Sommers
Daniel A. Small
   (Not admitted in DC)

ASSOCIATES

Gary E. Mason
Cyrus Mehri
Sharon A. Snyder
Mark S. Willis
   (Not admitted in DC)
Lillian S. Hagen

Michael J. Flannery
Paul T. Gallagher
Alexander E. Barnett
Angeline G. Chen
Victoria C. Arthaud
   (Not admitted in DC)

OF COUNSEL

Anthony Z. Roisman

For full biographical listings, see the Martindale-Hubbell Law Directory

FLORIDA

*FORT MYERS,** Lee Co.

Patrick E. Geraghty A Professional Association (AV)

The Courtney Building, Suite 100, 2069 First Street, P.O. Box
  1605, 33902-1605
Telephone: 941-334-9500
Fax: 941-334-8930

Patrick E. Geraghty

Thomas M. Dougherty

For full biographical listings, see the Martindale-Hubbell Law Directory

*TAMPA,** Hillsborough Co.

Anthony F. Gonzalez (AV)

701 North Franklin Street Mall, Franklin and Zack Streets, 33602
Telephone: 813-224-0431

For full biographical listings, see the Martindale-Hubbell Law Directory

GEORGIA

*ATLANTA,** Fulton Co.

Drew Eckl & Farnham (AV)

880 West Peachtree Street, P.O. Box 7600, 30357
Telephone: 404-885-1400
Facsimile: 404-876-0992
Email: drew@igc.apc.org

MEMBERS OF FIRM

Theodore Freeman
B. Holland Pritchard

Benton J. Mathis, Jr.
Stephen W. Mooney

ASSOCIATES

William T. Mitchell
Philip Wade Savrin
April Rich
Maureen M. Middleton

Bruce A. Taylor, Jr.
Nancy F. Rigby
Mary Anne Ackourey
Jennifer E. Moore

OF COUNSEL

Christopher E. Parker

Representative Clients: SAFECO Select Markets; Scottsdale Insurance Company; Titan Indemnity Company; Zurich American Insurance Companies; Dekalb County, Georgia; Douglas County, Georgia; Clayton County, Georgia; Pike County, Georgia; Clayton County School District; Coregis Group.

For Complete List of Firm Personnel, See General Section

For full biographical listings, see the Martindale-Hubbell Law Directory

Hawkins & Parnell (AV)

4000 SunTrust Plaza, 303 Peachtree Street, N.E., 30308-3243
Telephone: 404-614-7400
Fax: 404-614-7500
Email: 73541.1626@compuserve.com

MEMBERS OF FIRM

Michael J. Goldman
H. Lane Young, II
Frank C. Bedinger, III

T. Ryan Mock, Jr.
Robert U. Wright
Kimberly Houston Ridley

ASSOCIATES

Charles R. Beans
Cullen Christie Wilkerson, Jr.
Allen W. Nelson

Stephen M. Brooks
Allen L. Broughton
Kristen K. Duggan

Debra L. Dewar

Representative Clients: ACCG-IRMA; GIRMA; Willis Corroon Corporation of Georgia; Titan Insurance Co.; American International Group; Gallagher Bassett Services, Inc.

For Complete List of Firm Personnel, See General Section

For full biographical listings, see the Martindale-Hubbell Law Directory

Thomas E. Maddox, Jr., P.C. (AV)

3521 Habersham at Northlake (Tucker), 30084-4001
Telephone: 770-414-8055
Telecopier: 770-414-8755

Thomas E. Maddox, Jr.

LEGAL SUPPORT PERSONNEL

Matthew K. Johnson, Jr.

For full biographical listings, see the Martindale-Hubbell Law Directory

*ROME,** Floyd Co.

Brinson, Askew, Berry, Seigler, Richardson & Davis (AV)

A Partnership including Professional Corporations
Omberg House, 615 West First Street, P.O. Box 5513, 30162-5513
Telephone: 706-291-8853;
Atlanta: 404-521-0908
Telecopier: 706-234-3574

MEMBERS OF FIRM

Robert M. Brinson (P.C.)
C. King Askew (P.C.)
Robert L. Berry
Joseph M. Seigler, Jr.
Thomas D. Richardson
J. Anderson Davis

Hendrick L. Cromartie, III
Wright W. Smith
Mark M. J. Webb
Joseph B. Atkins
I. Stewart Duggan, Jr.
James Daniel Blitch

Representative Clients: City of Rome; Georgia Power Co.; General Electric Company; News Publishing Company (Rome News Tribune); Redmond Regional Medical Center; Oglethorpe Power Corp.; Suhner Manufacturing, Inc.; The Federal Land Bank of Columbia; AmSouth Bank of Georgia; United States Fidelity & Guaranty Co.

For full biographical listings, see the Martindale-Hubbell Law Directory

ILLINOIS

CHICAGO, * Cook Co.

MINER, BARNHILL & GALLAND, P.C. (AV)

14 West Erie Street, 60610
Telephone: 312-751-1170
Telecopier: 312-751-0438
Madison, Wisconsin Office: Suite 803, 44 East Mifflin Street.
Telephone: 608-255-5200.
Telecopier: 608-255-5380.
Visalia, California Office: Suite A, 1612 West Mineral King Avenue.
Telephone: 209-738-9905.
Telecopier: 209-738-9912.

Charles Barnhill, Jr. (Resident, Madison, Wisconsin Office)	William A. Miceli
John F. Belcaster	Judson H. Miner
Jeffrey I. Cummings	Valeriano Saucedo (Resident, Visalia, California Office)
William P. Dixon (Resident, Madison, Wisconsin Office)	Sarah E. Siskind (Resident, Madison, Wisconsin Office)
George F. Galland, Jr.	Paul L. Strauss

Laura E. Tilly
OF COUNSEL

Allison S. Davis   Barack H. Obama

For full biographical listings, see the Martindale-Hubbell Law Directory

SCHWARTZBERG, BARNETT & COHEN (AV)

55 West Monroe Street, 2400 Xerox Centre, 60603-5040
Telephone: 312-726-3555
Fax: 312-726-6299
Cable Address: "Justice"
Email: sb&c@twty.chi.il.us

MEMBERS OF FIRM

Ralph M. Schwartzberg   Mark T. Barnett (1939-1970)
(1939-1975)   Hugh J. Schwartzberg
Benjamin H. Cohen

OF COUNSEL

Eugene P. Thomas Jr.

For full biographical listings, see the Martindale-Hubbell Law Directory

INDIANA

EVANSVILLE, * Vanderburgh Co.

FINE & HATFIELD (AV)

520 N.W. Second Street, P.O. Box 779, 47705-0779
Telephone: 812-425-3592
Telecopier: 812-421-4269
Email: Fine@Fine-Hatfield.com *URL:* http://www.Fine-Hatfield.com

MEMBERS OF FIRM

Ronald R. Allen   Danny E. Glass
Thomas H. Bryan   Patricia Kay Woodring
William H. Mullis

ASSOCIATE

Debra S. McGowan

A List of Representative Clients Furnished Upon Request.

For full biographical listings, see the Martindale-Hubbell Law Directory

FORT WAYNE, * Allen Co.

GALLUCCI, HOPKINS & THEISEN, P.C. (AV)

229 West Berry Street, Suite 400, P.O. Box 12663, 46864-2663
Telephone: 219-424-3800
Telecopier: 219-420-1260
Email: gallucci@ghtlaw.com

William T. Hopkins, Jr.	Mark S. Kittaka
John C. Theisen	Tonya S. Shea
John T. Menzie	Eric H. J. Stahlhut
M. Scott Hall	Jeffrey S. Schafer
Michael A. Scheer	Holly A. Brady
Thomas N. O'Malley	Karen A. Festa

For full biographical listings, see the Martindale-Hubbell Law Directory

KANSAS

OVERLAND PARK, Johnson Co.

FISHER, PATTERSON, SAYLER & SMITH, L.L.P. (AV)

11050 Roe Avenue, Suite 210, 66211
Telephone: 913-339-6757
FAX: 913-339-6187
Topeka, Kansas Office: 534 South Kansas Avenue, Suite 400, P.O. Box 949, 66601.
Telephone: 913-232-7761.
Fax: 913-232-6604.

MEMBERS OF FIRM

Edwin Dudley Smith (Resident)   Michael K. Seck (Resident)
David P. Madden (Resident)

ASSOCIATE

Patrick G. Reavey (Resident)

For full biographical listings, see the Martindale-Hubbell Law Directory

TOPEKA, * Shawnee Co.

FISHER, PATTERSON, SAYLER & SMITH, L.L.P. (AV)

534 South Kansas Avenue, Suite 400, P.O. Box 949, 66601
Telephone: 913-232-7761
Fax: 913-232-6604
Overland Park, Kansas Office: 11050 Roe Avenue, Suite 210, 66211.
Telephone: 913-339-6757.
Fax: 913-339-6187.

MEMBERS OF FIRM

Donald Patterson	Steve R. Fabert
Edwin Dudley Smith (Resident, Overland Park Office)	Ronald J. Laskowski
Larry G. Pepperdine	Michael K. Seck (Resident, Overland Park Office)
James P. Nordstrom	David P. Madden (Resident, Overland Park Office)
Justice B. King	
J. Steven Pigg	Steven K. Johnson

ASSOCIATES

Kristine A. Larscheid	Billy E. Newman
Patrick G. Reavey (Resident, Overland Park Office)	David R. Cooper

OF COUNSEL

David H. Fisher

RETIRED

Charles Keith Sayler (Retired)

Representative Clients: Gage Shopping Center, Inc.; Fireman's Fund-American Insurance Cos.; United States Fidelity and Guaranty Co.; The Procter & Gamble Company; American Cyanamid Company; Commercial Union Insurance Companies; National Casualty/Scottsdale Insurance Co.; The Hartford; Berkshire Hathaway Companies.

For full biographical listings, see the Martindale-Hubbell Law Directory

MARYLAND

BALTIMORE, * (Independent City)

ALLEN, JOHNSON, ALEXANDER & KARP, P.A. (AV)

Suite 1540, 100 East Pratt Street, 21202
Telephone: 410-727-5000
Fax: 410-727-0861
Washington, D.C. Office: 1707 L Street, N.W., Suite 1050.
Telephone: 202-828-4141.

Daniel Karp

Representative Clients: Scottsdale Insurance Co.; Nautilus Insurance Co.; Jefferson Insurance Co.; Liberty Mutual Insurance Co.; Avis Rent-A-Car; Otis Elevator Co.; Montgomery Elevator Co.; Admiral Insurance Co.; Local Government Insurance Trust; Lancer Insurance Co.

For Complete List of Firm Personnel, See General Section

For full biographical listings, see the Martindale-Hubbell Law Directory

MICHIGAN

BLOOMFIELD HILLS, Oakland Co.

VAN SUILICHEM & BROWN, P.C. (AV)

525 North Woodward Avenue, Suite 1000, 48304
Telephone: 810-642-0900
Fax: 810-642-7123

(See Next Column)

VAN SUILICHEM & BROWN P.C., *Bloomfield Hills—Continued*

Donald A. Van Suilichem | Malcolm D. Brown

Robert C. Tice
Valerie L. MacFarlane
Christina M. Brookshire
Scott T. Patterson
Gary C. Ankers
Jeffrey T. Harrison

For full biographical listings, see the Martindale-Hubbell Law Directory

FLINT,* Genesee Co.

LAW OFFICES OF PATRICK M. KIRBY A PROFESSIONAL CORPORATION (AV)

G1335 South Linden Road, Suite G, 48532
Telephone: 810-230-0833
Fax: 810-230-8222

Patrick M. Kirby

Todd O. Pope

For full biographical listings, see the Martindale-Hubbell Law Directory

SOUTHFIELD, Oakland Co.

PROVIZER, LICHTENSTEIN & PHILLIPS, P.C. (AV)

4000 Town Center, Suite 1800, 48075
Telephone: 810-352-9080
Facsimile: 810-352-1491

Randall E. Phillips
Marilyn A. Madorsky
William J. Selinsky
Jason Milstone

Representative Clients: Jefferson Ins. Co.; Protective National Ins. Co.; City of Inkster.

For full biographical listings, see the Martindale-Hubbell Law Directory

TROY, Oakland Co.

POLING, McGAW & POLING, P.C. (AV)

Suite 275, 5435 Corporate Drive, 48098
Telephone: 810-641-0500
Telecopier: 810-641-0506

Benson T. Buck (1926-1989)
Richard B. Poling
D. Douglas McGaw
Richard B. Poling, Jr.
Gregory C. Hamilton
Veronica B. O'Haro

James R. Parker
OF COUNSEL
Ralph S. Moore

Representative Clients: County of Oakland; City of Troy; United States Fidelity & Guaranty Co.; Sentry Insurance Co.; Admiral Insurance; DeMaria Construction Co.; Leo Corporation; Aetna Casualty and Surety Co.; Concord Design; Pneumo-Abex.

For full biographical listings, see the Martindale-Hubbell Law Directory

CIVIL TRIAL PRACTICE

ALABAMA

ALBERTVILLE, Marshall Co.

GULLAHORN & HARE, P.C. (AV)

310 West Main Street, P.O. Box 1669, 35950
Telephone: 205-878-1891
Fax: 205-878-1965

Charles R. Hare, Jr.   John C. Gullahorn

Jeffrey B. Carr

Representative Clients: First Bank of Boaz; The Home Bank; Peoples Independent Bank of Boaz; AmSouth Bank; Compass Bank; Albertville Industrial Development Board; Boaz Industrial Development Board; Marshall-Dekalb Electric Cooperative; Olympia Construction, Inc.

For full biographical listings, see the Martindale-Hubbell Law Directory

ALEXANDER CITY, Tallapoosa Co.

MORRIS, HAYNES, INGRAM & HORNSBY (AV)

131 Main Street, P.O. Box 1660, 35011-1660
Telephone: 205-329-2000
Fax: 205-329-2015

Larry W. Morris   Kenneth F. Ingram, Jr.
Randall Stark Haynes   Clay Hornsby

OF COUNSEL

John F. Dillon, IV   Jennie Lee Kelley

Representative Clients: First National Bank; City of Alexander City; Town of Wadley; Russell Corp.
Approved Attorneys for: Lawyers Title Insurance Corp.; Mississippi Valley Title Insurance Co.

For full biographical listings, see the Martindale-Hubbell Law Directory

ANNISTON,* Calhoun Co.

BURNHAM & KLINEFELTER, P.C. (AV)

South Trust Bank Building, Suite 401, P.O. Box 1618, 36202
Telephone: 205-237-8515
Fax: 205-236-5150

H. R. Burnham   Patrick S. Burnham
J. L. Klinefelter   Thomas M. Sowa
       Polly D. Enger

Representative Clients: Alfa Insurance Cos.; United Services Auto Assn.; Motors Insurance Corp.; Fireman's Fund; SouthTrust Bank of Calhoun County, N.A.; America's First Credit Union; First South Production Credit; Calhoun County Board of Education; Calhoun County Commission; Coca-Cola Enterprises, Inc.

For Complete List of Firm Personnel, See General Section

For full biographical listings, see the Martindale-Hubbell Law Directory

BAY MINETTE,* Baldwin Co.

OWENS, BENTON & SIMPSON (AV)

Dahlberg Building, 104 Hand Avenue, P.O. Box 729, 36507
Telephone: 334-937-9473
Fairhope, Alabama Office: 200 Fairhope Avenue.
Telephone: 334-928-0282.

MEMBERS OF FIRM

J. Connor Owens, Jr.   Charles C. Simpson, III
Daniel A. Benton
  (Resident, Fairhope Office)

OF COUNSEL

Robert D. Johnston, Jr.

Counsel For: Allstate Insurance Co.; AmSouth Bank, N.A.; Citizens' Bank; Exxon Corp.; First Alabama Bank; First American Insurance Cos.; First Bank of Baldwin County; Malbis Plantation; Prudential Property & Casualty Insurance Co.; St. Paul Insurance Cos.

For full biographical listings, see the Martindale-Hubbell Law Directory

BIRMINGHAM,* Jefferson Co.

BAINBRIDGE, MIMS, ROGERS & SMITH (AV)

The Luckie Building, Suite 415, 600 Luckie Drive, P.O. Box 530886, 35253
Telephone: 205-879-1100
Fax: 205-879-4300

(See Next Column)

MEMBERS OF FIRM

Frank Bainbridge (1895-1980)   Frank M. Bainbridge
Walter L. Mims (1910-1993)   Bruce F. Rogers
       Alfred F. Smith, Jr.

For full biographical listings, see the Martindale-Hubbell Law Directory

BARNETT, HANES, O'NEAL, DUFFEE & GARFIELD, LLC (AV)

850 Park Place Tower, 2001 Park Place North, 35203
Telephone: 205-322-0471; 205-322-0484

MEMBERS OF FIRM

Robert C. Barnett   Cecil G. Duffee
Thomas B. Hanes   Frederick Mott Garfield, Jr.
James P. O'Neal   Janice G. Formato

OF COUNSEL

Arthur J. Hanes

Counsel for: City of Gardendale; State of Alabama Highway Department.
Approved Attorneys for: Alabama Title Co., Inc.

For full biographical listings, see the Martindale-Hubbell Law Directory

BERKOWITZ, LEFKOVITS, ISOM & KUSHNER, A PROFESSIONAL CORPORATION (AV)

1600 SouthTrust Tower, 420 North Twentieth Street, 35203
Telephone: 205-328-0480
Telecopier: 205-322-8007

Henry I. Frohsin   Frank S. James III
Susan S. Wagner   Patricia Clotfelter
       Wesley C. Redmond

Michael R. Silberman   N. Andrew Rotenstreich

Representative Clients: AlaTenn Resources, Inc.; AlaTenn Natural Gas Co.; B.A.S.S., Inc.; Hanna Steel Co., Inc.; Liberty Trouser Co., Inc.; McDonald's Corp.; Parisian, Inc.; Southern Pipe & Supply Co., Inc.

For Complete List of Firm Personnel, See General Section

For full biographical listings, see the Martindale-Hubbell Law Directory

BRADLEY, ARANT, ROSE & WHITE (AV)

2001 Park Place, Suite 1400, P.O. Box 830709, 35283-0709
Telephone: 205-521-8000
Facsimile: 205-252-0264
Facsimile (SouthTrust Tower Office): 205-251-9915
URL: http://www.BARW.COM
Huntsville, Alabama Office: 200 Clinton Avenue West, Suite 900, 35801.
Telephone: 205-517-5100.
Facsimile: 205-533-5069.

MEMBERS OF FIRM

John H. Morrow   John D. Watson, III
Hobart A. McWhorter, Jr.   Jay D. St. Clair
Macbeth Wagnon, Jr.   G. Edward Cassady, III
Thad Gladden Long   Michael R. Pennington
A. H. Gaede, Jr.   Michael D. McKibben
Gary C. Huckaby   David Glenn Hymer
  (Resident, Huntsville Office)   G. Rick Hall
James W. Gewin   (Resident, Huntsville Office)
Brittin Turner Coleman   Sid J. Trant
Patrick H. Graves, Jr.   Stewart M. Cox
  (Resident, Huntsville Office)   Forrest K. Covington
E. Mabry Rogers   Philip J. Carroll III
Andrew J. Noble, III   James S. Christie, Jr.
Walter J. Sears, III   John E. Goodman
Robert K. Spotswood   T. Michael Brown
Joseph B. Mays, Jr.   George Bryan Harris
Norman Jetmundsen, Jr.   Warne S. Heath
Joseph S. Bird, III   (Resident, Huntsville Office)
       Susan Donovan Josey

COUNSEL

Stanley D. Bynum   Scott M. Phelps

ASSOCIATES

J. Patrick Darby   Justin T. McDonald
Denise Avery Dodson   Carolyn Reed Douglas
Matthew H. Lembke   (Resident, Huntsville Office)
Richard H. Monk III   Douglas E. Eckert
Amy K. Myers   Kenneth M. Perry
John W. Smith T   Fred M. Haston, III
James W. Davis   T. Matthew Miller
James Tassin   Charles K. Hamilton
  (Resident, Huntsville Office)   Julie Scharfenberg Elmer
James F. Archibald, III   David M. Lawson

Representative Clients: Ford Motor Co.; Volkswagen of America; Chrysler Corp.; The Firestone Tire & Rubber Co.; The Goodyear Tire & Rubber Co.; Torchmark Corp.; Lincoln National Life Insurance Co.; J. I. Case Co.; Monsanto Co.; A. H. Robins Co.

For Complete List of Firm Personnel, See General Section

For full biographical listings, see the Martindale-Hubbell Law Directory

Birmingham—Continued

BURR & FORMAN (AV)

3100 SouthTrust Tower, 420 North 20th Street, 35203
Telephone: 205-251-3000
Telecopier: 205-458-5100
Huntsville, Alabama Office: Suite 204, Regency Center, 400 Meridian Street.
Telephone: 205-551-0010.
Atlanta, Georgia Office: Suite 1800, One Georgia Center, 600 West Peachtree Street, 30308.
Telephone: 404-817-3536.
Facsimile: 404-817-3244.

MEMBERS OF FIRM

C. V. Stelzenmuller	F. A. Flowers, III
Robert G. Tate	Michael L. Lucas
J. Fredric Ingram	J. Hunter Phillips, III
William C. Knight, Jr.	Carol H. Stewart
John D. Clements	Robert H. Rutherford, Jr.
John F. DeBuys, Jr.	Henry Graham Beene
James Ross Forman, III	John C. Morrow
D. Frank Davis	Victor L. Hayslip
William F. Murray, Jr.	E. Clayton Lowe, Jr.
James J. Robinson	Robert S. W. Given
Joseph W. Letzer	Mark McCarroll Lawson
T. Thomas Cottingham, III	Dent M. Morton
J. Patrick Logan	Paul P. Bolus
Gary M. London	David A. Elliott

Harri J. Haikala

OF COUNSEL

A. Jackson Noble, Jr.

ASSOCIATES

Jennifer M. Busby   Gerald P. Gillespy
Timothy M. Lupinacci

For Complete List of Firm Personnel, See General Section

For full biographical listings, see the Martindale-Hubbell Law Directory

CABANISS, JOHNSTON, GARDNER, DUMAS & O'NEAL (AV)

Park Place Tower, 2001 Park Place North, Suite 700, P.O. Box 830612, 35283-0612
Telephone: 205-716-5200
Telecopier: 205-716-5200
Email: CabJohnston@aol.com
Mobile, Alabama Office: 700 AmSouth Center, P.O. Box 2906.
Telephone: 334-433-6961.
Telecopier: 334-433-1060.

MEMBERS OF FIRM

William F. Gardner	R. Carlton Smyly
Crawford S. McGivaren, Jr.	Steve A. Tucker
Sydney F. Frazier, Jr.	Sandy G. Robinson
William K. Thomas	(Resident, Mobile Office)

R. Taylor Abbot, Jr.

COUNSEL

L. Murray Alley

Counsel for: Alabaster Industries, Inc.; Schuler Industries, Inc.; Carraway Methodist Hospitals of Alabama; Doster Construction Co., Inc.; Liberty Mutual Insurance Co.; John Alden Life Insurance Co.; MacMillan Bloedel Packaging, Inc.; Norfolk Southern Corp.; O'Neal Steel, Inc.

For Complete List of Firm Personnel, See General Section

For full biographical listings, see the Martindale-Hubbell Law Directory

COOPER, MITCH, CRAWFORD, KUYKENDALL & WHATLEY, L.L.C. (AV)

1100 Financial Center, 505 20th Street North, 35203-2605
Telephone: 205-328-9576
Telecopier: 205-328-9669

MEMBERS OF FIRM

Jerome A. Cooper	Frederick T. Kuykendall, III
William E. Mitch	Joe R. Whatley, Jr.
Thomas N. Crawford, Jr.	Glen M. Connor

Patricia Guthrie Fraley

ASSOCIATES

Candis A. McGowan	Maureen Kane Berg
Andrew C. Allen	Gerald B. Taylor, Jr.
William Z. Cullen	Peter H. Burke
Samuel H. Heldman	Charlene Cullen
Hilary E. Ball-Walker	William Todd Harvey

Richard Paul Rouco

OF COUNSEL

W. Braxton Schell, Jr.   Russell Jackson Drake

Counsel for: United Steelworkers of America, AFL-CIO; Birmingham Plumbers & Steamfitters Local Union No. 91 Pension Fund.

(See Next Column)

Reference: AMSouth Bank of Birmingham.

For full biographical listings, see the Martindale-Hubbell Law Directory

DOMINICK, FLETCHER, YEILDING, WOOD & LLOYD, P.A. (AV)

2121 Highland Avenue, 35205
Telephone: 205-939-0033

J. Fred Wood, Jr.	B. Boozer Downs, Jr.
Harold L. Ferguson, Jr.	J. Mitchell Frost, Jr.

John W. Dodson	L. Hunter Compton, Jr.

Peter McKeever Wright

Counsel for: Citizens Federal Savings Bank; St. Vincent's Hospital; Birmingham-Southern College; Castle Mortgage Corporation; Methodist Homes for the Aging.

For Complete List of Firm Personnel, See General Section

For full biographical listings, see the Martindale-Hubbell Law Directory

GORDON, SILBERMAN, WIGGINS & CHILDS, A PROFESSIONAL CORPORATION (AV)

1400 SouthTrust Tower, 420 North 20th Street, 35203
Telephone: 205-328-0640
Telecopier: 205-254-1500

Bruce L. Gordon	James Mendelsohn
Robert L. Wiggins, Jr.	Richard J. Ebbinghouse
Robert F. Childs, Jr.	Samuel Fisher
Dennis George Pantazis	Ann C. Robertson

Mark P. Williams	Jon E. Lewis
Timothy C. Gann	Rocco Calamusa, Jr.
Joseph H. Calvin, III	Brian M. Clark

For Complete List of Firm Personnel, See General Section

For full biographical listings, see the Martindale-Hubbell Law Directory

HARE, WYNN, NEWELL AND NEWTON (AV)

A Partnership including Professional Corporations
Suite 800 Massey Building, 290 21st Street North, 35203
Telephone: 205-328-5330
FAX: 205-324-2165

MEMBERS OF FIRM

Francis H. Hare (1904-1983)	John W. Haley (P.C.)
Carlton T. Wynn	D. Leon Ashford (P.C.)
Neal C. Newell	Scott A. Powell
Alex W. Newton	James R. Pratt, III
Terrell Wynn, Jr.	S. Shay Samples
James J. Thompson, Jr.	Bruce J. McKee
Alva C. Caine	Michael D. Ermert
Ray O. Noojin, Jr., (P.C.)	Robert R. Riley, Jr.

Nolan Edward Awbrey

COUNSEL

Francis H. Hare, Jr., (P.C.)	James O. Haley

James K. Baker

References: AmSouth Bank of Birmingham; First Commercial Bank of Birmingham.

For full biographical listings, see the Martindale-Hubbell Law Directory

HARRIS, CLECKLER, BERG & ROGERS, P.C. (AV)

Historic 2007 Building, 2007 Third Avenue North, 35203-2366
Telephone: 205-328-2366
Telecopier: 205-328-0013
Email: hcbr@bham.mindspring.com

Lyman H. Harris	Lonette Lamb Berg
Michael H. Cleckler	Susan Rogers

Matthew J. Dougherty	Jeffrey K. Hollis

Brock G. Murphy

For full biographical listings, see the Martindale-Hubbell Law Directory

HASKELL SLAUGHTER & YOUNG, L.L.C. (AV)

1200 AmSouth/Harbert Plaza, 1901 Sixth Avenue North, 35203
Telephone: 205-251-1000
Facsimile: 205-324-1133
Montgomery, Alabama Office: 305 South Lawrence Street, P.O. Box 4660. 36103-4660.
Telephone: 334-265-8573.
Facsimile: 334-264-7945.

(See Next Column)

HASKELL SLAUGHTER & YOUNG L.L.C.—Continued

William M. Slaughter	Stephen L. Poer
Frank M. Young, III	Beverly P. Baker
Thomas T. Gallion, III	Richard H. Walston
(Resident, Montgomery Office)	Constance A. Caldwell (Resident, Montgomery Office)
James C. Huckaby, Jr.	

Michael K. K. Choy

Carter H. Dukes	Barry D. Woodham
Paula B. Carroll	Georgia S. Roberson
John W. Scott	Susan E. Kennedy

Rebecca Higgins Hunt

Representative Clients: The Equitable Life Assurance Society of the United States; Exxon Corporation; Federal Deposit Insurance Corporation; Fireman's Fund Insurance Companies; Marshall Durbin Companies; Montgomery County, Alabama; NationsBank Corporation; Raytheon Aircraft Company; Rhone-Poulenc Rorer Pharmaceuticals, Inc.; Ridout's-Brown-Service, Inc.; Sandoz Pharmaceuticals Corporation.

For Complete List of Firm Personnel, See General Section

For full biographical listings, see the Martindale-Hubbell Law Directory

HOGAN, SMITH & ALSPAUGH, P.C. (AV)

2323 Second Avenue, North, 35203
Telephone: 205-324-5635
Telecopier: 205-324-5637

William W. Smith	Ronald R. Crook
M. Clay Alspaugh	Richard D. Stratton
R. Benjamin Hogan, III	Pamela D. Beard
David R. Donaldson	Jack Lee Roberts, Jr.
David J. Guin	Benjamin E. Baker, Jr.

Reference: First Alabama Bank.

For full biographical listings, see the Martindale-Hubbell Law Directory

LIGHTFOOT, FRANKLIN & WHITE, L.L.C. (AV)

300 Financial Center, 505 20th Street North, 35203-2706
Telephone: 205-581-0700
Facsimile: 205-581-0799

Warren B. Lightfoot	E. Glenn Waldrop, Jr.
Samuel H. Franklin	Adam K. Peck
Jere F. White, Jr.	Harlan I. Prater, IV
Mac M. Moorer	Michael L. Bell
John M. Johnson	William S. Cox, III
M. Christian King	William H. King, III

OF COUNSEL
Sara Anne Ford

Sarah Bruce Jackson	Wynn M. Shuford
William H. Brooks	Julia S. McIntyre
J. Banks Sewell, III	Stephanie Keller Womack
Lee M. Hollis	James R. Sturdivant
Jackson R. Sharman, III (Not admitted in AL)	Melody L. Hurdle
Sabrina A. Simon	Robin Hansen Graves
Madeline H. Haikala	Robert Jeffery Kelsey
	Charles L. Rice, Jr.

Counsel for: AT&T; Ford Motor Co.; Emerson Electric Co.; Monsanto Co.; Chrysler Corp.; Unocal Corp.; The Upjohn Co.; Bristol-Myers Squibb Co.; The Goodyear Tire & Rubber Co.; Mitsubishi Motor Sales of America, Inc.

For full biographical listings, see the Martindale-Hubbell Law Directory

LONDON & YANCEY (AV)

1000 Park Place Tower, 2001 Park Place, 35203
Telephone: 205-251-2531
FAX: 205-251-8929

MEMBERS OF FIRM

Alex T. London (1847-1908)	Thomas R. Elliott, Jr.
John London (1848-1935)	Bert S. Nettles
George W. Yancey (1883-1962)	Richard W. Lewis

ASSOCIATES

Allen R. Trippeer, Jr.	Laura Ellison Proctor
Mark David Hess	Paige Elliott-Pinson
Lisa Wright Borden	F. Daniel Wood, Jr.
A. David Fawal	C. Dennis Hughes

Michael J. Velezis

OF COUNSEL
Robert W. Norris

Representative Clients: State of Alabama; Cincinnati Ins. Co.; Lloyd's of London; Blue Cross/Blue Shield; Attorney's Mutual of Alabama; State Farm; CIGNA; Royal Ins. Co. of America; Paul Revere Ins. Co.; Chubb Group.

For full biographical listings, see the Martindale-Hubbell Law Directory

PATRICK & LACY, P.C. (AV)

1201 Financial Center, 35203
Telephone: 205-323-5665
Telecopier: 205-324-6221

J. Vernon Patrick, Jr.	William M. Acker, III
Alex S. Lacy	Elizabeth N. Pitman

For full biographical listings, see the Martindale-Hubbell Law Directory

PORTERFIELD, HARPER & MILLS, P.A. (AV)

22 Inverness Center Parkway, Suite 600, P.O. Box 530790, 35253-0790
Telephone: 205-980-5000
Fax: 205-980-5001

Jack B. Porterfield, Jr.	Philip F. Hutcheson
Larry W. Harper	H. C. "Trey" Ireland, III
William T. Mills, II	Keith J. Pflaum
William Dudley Motlow, Jr.	Michael L. Haggard

Representative Clients: CIGNA; St. Paul Insurance Co.; The Travelers; Figge International; White Consolidated Industries; Terex Corp.; Wausau Insurance; Baptist Health Systems, Inc.; Bruno's, Inc.; Harley Davidson, Inc.

For full biographical listings, see the Martindale-Hubbell Law Directory

REDDEN, MILLS & CLARK (AV)

940 First Alabama Bank Building, 417 North 20th Street, 35203
Telephone: 205-322-0457
Fax: 205-322-8481

MEMBERS OF FIRM

L. Drew Redden	William N. Clark
William H. Mills	Gerald L. Miller

Stephen W. Shaw

ASSOCIATE
Maxwell H. Pulliam, Jr.

References: SouthTrust Bank; First Alabama Bank.

For full biographical listings, see the Martindale-Hubbell Law Directory

SCHOEL, OGLE, BENTON AND CENTENO (AV)

600 Financial Center, 505 North 20th Street, P.O. Box 1865, 35201-1865
Telephone: 205-521-7000
Telecopier: 205-521-7007

MEMBERS OF FIRM

Jerry W. Schoel	Douglas J. Centeno
Richard F. Ogle	Melinda Murphy Dionne
Lee R. Benton	Gilbert M. Sullivan, Jr.
Paul A. Liles	David O. Upshaw

Reference: National Bank of Commerce; First Alabama Bank.

For full biographical listings, see the Martindale-Hubbell Law Directory

SMITH, SPIRES & PEDDY (AV)

650 Financial Center, 505 North Twentieth Street, 35203-2662
Telephone: 205-251-5885

Paul G. Smith	Michael B. Walls
Thomas S. Spires	Todd Hamilton
A. Joe Peddy	Scott M. Roberts

ASSOCIATES

Thomas Coleman, Jr.	Alan B. Lasseter
D. Gregory Dunagan	Reed R. Bates

David A. Hughes

Representative Clients: Banker's & Shippers Insurance Co.; Alfa Insurance Co.; United States Fidelity & Guaranty Insurance Co.; R & D Trucking, Inc.; Racetrac Petroleum, Inc.; Transport South Inc.; Old Dominion Freight Line, Inc.; American States Insurance Co.; Trinity Industries, Inc.; Penn General.

For full biographical listings, see the Martindale-Hubbell Law Directory

SPAIN & GILLON, L.L.C. (AV)

The Zinszer Building, 2117 2nd Avenue North, 35203
Telephone: 205-328-4100
Telecopier: 205-324-8866

MEMBERS OF FIRM

H. Hobart Grooms, Jr.	Alton B. Parker, Jr.
Ollie L. Blan, Jr.	Charles D. Stewart
Eugene P. Stutts	Elizabeth Ann McMahan

Thomas M. Eden, III

General Counsel for: Liberty National Life Insurance Co.; Piggly Wiggly Alabama Distributing Co.; Alabama Insurance Guaranty Association; Alabama Life and Disability Insurance Guaranty Association; Alabama Insurance Underwriters Association.
Counsel for: The Minnesota Mutual Insurance Company of America; Government Employees Insurance Co.; Massachusetts Mutual Life Insurance Co.

(See Next Column)

SPAIN & GILLON L.L.C., *Birmingham—Continued*

For Complete List of Firm Personnel, See General Section

For full biographical listings, see the Martindale-Hubbell Law Directory

STARNES & ATCHISON (AV)

100 Brookwood Place, P.O. Box 598512, 35259-8512
Telephone: 205-868-6000
Telecopier: 205-868-6099

MEMBERS OF FIRM

Stancil R. Starnes (1922-1983)	J. Bentley Owens, III
W. Stancil Starnes	Walter William Bates
W. Michael Atchison	Michael K. Wright
William Anthony Davis, III	Michael K. Beard
Michael A. Florie	Robert P. Mackenzie, III
L. Graves Stiff, III	Allan R. Wheeler
Carol A. Smith	Jeffrey E. Friedman
Randal H. Sellers	Laura Howard Peck
E. Martin Bloom	Thomas Lawson Selden

Mark Christopher Eagan

ASSOCIATES

Sybil Vogtle Abbot	J. David Michaels
Steven T. McMeekin	Arthur Clair Brunson, III
Sharon A. Woodard	P. Thomas Dazzio, Jr.
Joe L. Leak	Kenneth Davis Graves
Joseph S. Miller	Elizabeth S. Webb
Scott M. Salter	Rik S. Tozzi
Jeannie Bugg Walston	Brenen Gene Ely
Ashley E. Watkins	Christopher John Zulanas

Representative Clients: Mutual Assurance, Inc.; USF&G; CNA Insurance Co.; Travelers Insurance Co.; Drummond Co.; Honda Motor Co.; Harbert International; Brookwood Hospital; Associated Aviation Underwriters; Kawasaki Motors Corp.; Mercedez Benz of North America, Inc.; GTE Mobilnet; Glaxo Wellcome, Inc.; Protective, Inc.

For full biographical listings, see the Martindale-Hubbell Law Directory

---

CHATOM,* Washington Co.

TURNER, ONDERDONK, KIMBROUGH & HOWELL, P.A. (AV)

100 Central Avenue, P.O. Drawer 1389, 36518
Telephone: 334-847-2237
Fax: 334-847-3115
Mobile, Alabama Office: 1359 Dauphin Street.
Telephone: 334-432-2855.
Fax: 334-432-2863.

Edward P. Turner, Jr.	Gordon K. Howell
A. Michael Onderdonk	Marc E. Bradley
William A. Kimbrough, Jr.	(Resident, Mobile Office)
(Resident, Mobile Office)	

Halron W. Turner	David M. Huggins
Frank Woodson	(Resident, Mobile Office)
(Resident, Mobile Office)	E. Tatum Turner

For full biographical listings, see the Martindale-Hubbell Law Directory

---

CULLMAN,* Cullman Co.

ST. JOHN & ST. JOHN (AV)

108 Third Street South East, P.O. Drawer K, 35055
Telephone: 205-734-3542
Fax: 205-734-3544

MEMBERS OF FIRM

F. E. St. John (1874-1943)	Juliet G. St. John
Finis E. St. John (1909-1984)	Finis E. St. John, IV
Finis E. St. John, III	Gaynor L. St. John
(1933-1984)	Wells Rutland Turner, III

Attorneys for: U.S. Fidelity & Guaranty Co.; Golden-Rod Broilers, Inc.; Travelers Insurance Cos.; Liberty Mutual Insurance Cos.; ALFA Mutual Insurance Cos.; First Federal Savings & Loan; The Atlanta Casualty Companies; Auto-Owners Insurance Co.

For full biographical listings, see the Martindale-Hubbell Law Directory

---

DECATUR,* Morgan Co.

HARRIS, CADDELL & SHANKS, P.C. (AV)

214 Johnston Street, S.E., P.O. Box 2688, 35602-2688
Telephone: 205-340-8000
Telecopier: 205-340-8040

Julian Harris (1904-1994)	Robert H. Harris
Norman W. Harris (P.C.)	Jon H. Moores
(Retired)	Thomas A. Caddell
Philip T. Shanks (Retired)	William E. Shinn, Jr.
Charles L. Murphree (Retired)	Gary A. Phillips
John A. Caddell (P.A.)	Dow M. Perry, Jr.

(See Next Column)

Barnes F. Lovelace, Jr.	J. Noel King
Arthur W. Orr	Jeffrey S. Brown

Attorneys for: First American Bank, Decatur, Alabama; SouthTrust Bank of Morgan County; Morgan County Commission; The Industrial Development Board of the City of Decatur, Alabama; Amoco Chemical Co.; South Central Bell Telephone Co.; Auto-Owners Insurance Co.; ALFA Insurance Cos.; American General Life & Accident Insurance Co.; U.S.F. & G. Co.

For full biographical listings, see the Martindale-Hubbell Law Directory

---

DOTHAN,* Houston Co.

COBB & SHEALY, P.A. (AV)

206 North Lena Street, P.O. Box 6346, 36302
Telephone: 334-794-8526
Fax: 334-677-0030

Herman W. Cobb	Richard Elder Crum
Steadman S. Shealy, Jr.	James H. Pike
Raymond Todd Derrick	Joseph A. Morris

A. Gary Jones

OF COUNSEL

Joey Hornsby

Representative Clients: Travelers Insurance; Nationwide Insurance; Auto-Owners Insurance; Employers Casualty of Texas; Safeco Insurance; Federated Insurance; Universal Underwriters; National Security Insurance; Great Central Insurance.
Approved Title Attorneys for: Lawyers Title Insurance Corp.

For full biographical listings, see the Martindale-Hubbell Law Directory

---

HARDWICK, HAUSE & SEGREST (AV)

212 North Lena Street, P.O. Box 1469, 36302
Telephone: 334-794-4144
Fax: 334-671-9330

W. G. Hardwick (1910-1993)   William G. Hause (Retired)

MEMBERS OF FIRM

Jere C. Segrest	Kevin Walding
	Tina Whitehead Stamps

ASSOCIATE

G. Ward Beeson, III

Counsel for: Dothan City Board of Education; American General; Alabama Power Co.; General Motors Acceptance Corp.; Liberty National Life Ins. Co.

For full biographical listings, see the Martindale-Hubbell Law Directory

---

LEE & McINISH (AV)

238 West Main Street, P.O. Box 1665, 36302
Telephone: 334-792-4156
Facsimile: 334-794-8342

MEMBERS OF FIRM

W. L. Lee (1873-1944)	William C. Carn, III
Alto V. Lee, III (1915-1987)	Peter A. McInish
William L. Lee, III	Jerry M. White
Alan C. Livingston	William L. Lee, IV

OF COUNSEL

H. Dwight McInish

Counsel for: Seaboard Coast Line Railroad Co.; Atlanta & St. Andrews Bay Railroad Co.; ALFA; U. S. F. & G. Co.; Maryland Casualty Co.; Continental Insurance Cos.; Royal-Globe Group; Slocomb National Bank; The Federal Land Bank of Jackson; GTE South.

For full biographical listings, see the Martindale-Hubbell Law Directory

---

ENTERPRISE, Coffee Co.

CASSADY, FULLER & MARSH (AV)

203 East Lee Avenue, P.O. Box 780, 36331
Telephone: 334-347-2626
Telecopier: 334-393-1396

MEMBERS OF FIRM

Joe C. Cassady	M. Dale Marsh
Kenneth T. Fuller	Joe C. Cassady, Jr.

Mark E. Fuller

ASSOCIATES

R. Rainer Cotter, III   J.P. Sawyer

Representative Clients: First Alabama Bank; Enterprise Hospital Board; Sessions Co., Inc.; Allstate; State Farm Mutual Insurance Co.; Community Bank & Trust Co.; Conagra, Inc.
Approved Attorneys for: First American Title Insurance Co.

For full biographical listings, see the Martindale-Hubbell Law Directory

---

PITTMAN AND PITTMAN (AV)

304 South Edwards Street, P.O. Drawer 1180, 36330
Telephone: 334-347-2655
Fax: 334-347-2657

(See Next Column)

PITTMAN AND PITTMAN—Continued

MEMBERS OF FIRM

Joe S. Pittman   Joseph Stafford Pittman, Jr.

Representative Clients: City of Enterprise; Industrial Development Board of City of Enterprise; Enco Engineering Corp.; E. L. Gibson Foundation.
Approved Attorneys for: Mississippi Valley Title Insurance Co.

For full biographical listings, see the Martindale-Hubbell Law Directory

J. E. SAWYER, JR. (AV)

203 South Edwards Street, P.O. Box 720, 36331-0720
Telephone: 334-347-6447
Fax: 334-347-8217

For full biographical listings, see the Martindale-Hubbell Law Directory

---

FLORENCE,* Lauderdale Co.

POTTS & YOUNG (AV)

107 East College Street, 35630
Telephone: 205-764-7142
Fax: 205-764-7717

OF COUNSEL

Doyle R. Young (Retired)   Robert L. Potts

MEMBERS OF FIRM

Frank V. Potts   Frank B. Potts

ASSOCIATES

Robert W. Beasley   Debra H. Coble

Representative Clients: E. A. Nelson Co., Inc.; Nelco, Inc.; American Abrasive Air & Service Co., Inc.; Diversified Products, Inc.; Big Deli Stores, Inc.; Spry Funeral Homes of Russellville, Sheffield & Florence; Americans United for the Separation of Church & State; Colbert County Community Economic Development Corp.
Reference: Bank Independent.

For full biographical listings, see the Martindale-Hubbell Law Directory

SELF & SELF (AV)

408 West Dr. Hicks Boulevard, P.O. Box 1062, 35631
Telephone: 205-767-2570; 1-800-336-2574
Fax: 205 767-2632

MEMBERS OF FIRM

Henry (Hank) H. Self, Jr.   Gilbert P. Self

Reference: Bank Independent; AmSouth Bank; Compass Bank.

For full biographical listings, see the Martindale-Hubbell Law Directory

---

FORT PAYNE,* De Kalb Co.

SCRUGGS, JORDAN, DODD & DODD, P.A. (AV)

207 Alabama Avenue, South, P.O. Box 1109, 35967
Telephone: 205-845-5932
Fax: 205-845-4325

William D. Scruggs, Jr.   David Dodd
Robert K. Jordan   E. Allen Dodd, Jr.

Representative Clients: State Farm Insurance Company; Allstate Insurance Co., Inc.; USF&G Insurance Co.; Nucor, Inc.; Ladd Engineering, Inc.; ALABAMA Band; First Federal Savings & Loan Association of Dekalb County; Fritz Structural Steel, Inc.; Williamson Oil Co., Inc.

For full biographical listings, see the Martindale-Hubbell Law Directory

---

GADSDEN,* Etowah Co.

FLOYD, KEENER, CUSIMANO & ROBERTS, P.C. (AV)

816 Chestnut Street, P.O. Box 49, 35902
Telephone: 205-547-6328
Fax: 205-546-8173

Jack Floyd   Gregory S. Cusimano
Larry H. Keener   Michael L. Roberts
     David A. Kimberley

John D. Floyd

For Complete List of Firm Personnel, See General Section

For full biographical listings, see the Martindale-Hubbell Law Directory

FORD AND ASSOCIATES, P.C. (AV)

The Lancaster Building, 645 Walnut Street, Suite 5, P.O. Box 388, 35902
Telephone: 205-546-5432
Fax: 205-546-5435

George P. Ford

(See Next Column)

Richard M. Blythe

Reference: AmSouth Bank, N.A.

For Complete List of Firm Personnel, See General Section

For full biographical listings, see the Martindale-Hubbell Law Directory

INZER, STIVENDER, HANEY & JOHNSON, P.A. (AV)

(Inzer, Suttle, Swann & Stivender)
Second Floor, Compass Bank Building, 601 Broad Street, P.O. Drawer 287, 35999-0287
Telephone: 205-546-1656
Telecopier: 205-546-1093

W. Roscoe Johnson, III   F. Michael Haney
James C. Inzer, III   Robert D. McWhorter, Jr.

James W. McGlaughn   Elizabeth Golson McGlaughn

Assistant Division Counsel for: Southern Railway System.
Attorneys for: L & N Railroad; General Motors Corp.; Goodyear Tire & Rubber Corp.; Alabama Power Co.; Insurance Company of North America; Allstate Insurance Co.; Travelers Insurance Co.; Liberty Mutual Insurance Co.; Home Insurance Co.

For Complete List of Firm Personnel, See General Section

For full biographical listings, see the Martindale-Hubbell Law Directory

SIMMONS, BRUNSON AND SASSER, ATTORNEYS, P.A. (AV)

1411 Rainbow Drive, P.O. Box 1189, 35902
Telephone: 205-546-9206
Telecopier: 205-546-8091

Clarence Simmons, Jr.   Steve P. Brunson
     James T. Sasser

Rebecca A. Walker   Jeff George Underwood
Jeffrey A. Brown   Scott C. Lloyd
     (Not admitted in AL)

Attorneys for: Preferred Risk Mutual Insurance Co.; ALFA Mutual Insurance Co.; Royal Insurance Cos.
Approved Attorneys for: Lawyers Title Insurance Corp.; Mississippi Valley Title Insurance Co.

For full biographical listings, see the Martindale-Hubbell Law Directory

---

HUNTSVILLE,* Madison Co.

BERRY, ABLES, TATUM, BAXTER, PARKER & HALL, P.C. (AV)

Legal Building, 315 Franklin Street, S.E., P.O. Box 165, 35804-0165
Telephone: 205-533-3740
Facsimile: 205-533-3751
Email: BAXTERJ@ATTMAIL.COM

William H. Blanton (1889-1973)   James T. Tatum, Jr.
Joe M. Berry   James T. Baxter, III
L. Bruce Ables   Thomas E. Parker, Jr.
     Bill G. Hall

James K. Brabston   Mark Rogers Hunter

Representative Clients: AmSouth Bank; First Alabama Bank; General Shale Products Co.; The Hertz Corp.; Litton Industries, Inc.; Farmers Tractor Co.; Colonial Bank; Farm Credit Bank of Texas; SouthBank; Regions Mortgage.
Reference: First Alabama Bank.

For full biographical listings, see the Martindale-Hubbell Law Directory

BRADLEY, ARANT, ROSE & WHITE (AV)

200 Clinton Avenue West, Suite 900, 35801
Telephone: 205-517-5100
Facsimile: 205-533-5069
URL: http://www.BARW.COM
Birmingham, Alabama Office: 2001 Park Place, Suite 1400, P.O. Box 830709.
Telephone: 205-521-8000.
Facsimile: 205-251-8611, 251-8665, 252-0264. Facsimile (SouthTrust Tower Office): 205-251-9915.

RESIDENT PARTNERS

Gary C. Huckaby   Patrick H. Graves, Jr.
E. Cutter Hughes, Jr.   G. Rick Hall
     Warne S. Heath

RESIDENT ASSOCIATES

James Tassin   Carolyn Reed Douglas
     Kimberly A. Bessiere

For Complete List of Firm Personnel, See General Section

For full biographical listings, see the Martindale-Hubbell Law Directory

Huntsville—Continued

HORNSBY, WATSON & MEGINNISS (AV)

1110 Gleneagles Drive, 35801
Telephone: 205-650-5500
Fax: 205-650-5504

Ralph W. Hornsby	David H. Meginniss
S. A. "Bud" Watson, Jr.	Ralph W. Hornsby, Jr.

For full biographical listings, see the Martindale-Hubbell Law Directory

MORRIS, CLOUD AND CONCHIN, P.C. (AV)

521 Madison Street, P.O. Box 248, 35804
Telephone: 205-534-0065
Fax: 205-539-0741

Harvey B. Morris (P.C.)	Joseph M. Cloud
Gary V. Conchin	

Maureen "Mike" K. Cooper	Daniel B. Banks, Jr.

For full biographical listings, see the Martindale-Hubbell Law Directory

SPURRIER, RICE, WOOD & HALL (AV)

3226 Bob Wallace Avenue, 35805
Telephone: 205-533-5015
Fax: 205-536-0105

MEMBERS OF FIRM

Donald N. Spurrier	Robert V. Wood, Jr.
Benjamin R. Rice	Ruth Ann Hall

ASSOCIATES

Earl Thomas Forbes	Deborah S. Hensley
G. Douglas Benson	Jonathan B. Medlock

Representative Clients: Alabama Hospital Association Trust Fund; Alfa Insurance Co.; Allstate Insurance Co.; Atlanta Casualty; Auto-Owners Insurance Co.; Balboa Property & Casualty Co.; Bruno's; Casualty Indemnity Exchange; Chubb Group of Insurance Cos.; CIGNA Insurance Cos.

For full biographical listings, see the Martindale-Hubbell Law Directory

STEPHENS, MILLIRONS, HARRISON & GAMMONS, P.C. (AV)

333 Franklin Street, P.O. Box 307, 35801
Telephone: 205-533-7711
Telecopier: 205-536-9388

Arthur M. Stephens	James G. Harrison
Paul L. Millirons	Robert C. Gammons

Attorneys for: Lomas Mortgage USA, Inc.; AmSouth Mortgage Co., Inc.

For full biographical listings, see the Martindale-Hubbell Law Directory

*LIVINGSTON,** Sumter Co.

PRUITT, PRUITT AND WATKINS, P.A. (AV)

105 Washington Street, P.O. Box 1037, 35470
Telephone: 205-652-9627
Fax: 205-652-9620

Ira D. Pruitt (1904-1984)	Ira D. Pruitt, Jr.
Nathan G. Watkins, Jr.	

OF COUNSEL

Nathan G. Watkins

Representative Clients Banks: First Alabama Bank; Alabama Power Co. Corporations: Waste Management, Inc.; McGregor Printing Corp.; Liv Lite Corp., A division of Big River Industries. Insurance: Hartford Insurance Co.; St. Paul Insurance Co.; Standard Guaranty Insurance Co.

For full biographical listings, see the Martindale-Hubbell Law Directory

*MOBILE,** Mobile Co.

ARMBRECHT, JACKSON, DeMOUY, CROWE, HOLMES & REEVES, L.L.C. (AV)

1300 AmSouth Center, P.O. Box 290, 36601
Telephone: 334-405-1300
Facsimile: 334-432-6843; 433-3821

MEMBERS OF FIRM

Rae M. Crowe	Edward A. Dean
Broox G. Holmes, Jr.	Reggie Copeland, Jr.
W. Boyd Reeves	David E. Hudgens
Kirk C. Shaw	Ray Morgan Thompson
Norman E. Waldrop, Jr.	Robert J. Mullican
Conrad P. Armbrecht	Wm. Steele Holman II
Edward G. Hawkins	Coleman F. Meador
Grover E. Asmus II	Broox G. Holmes
David A. Bagwell	James E. Robertson, Jr.
Douglas L. Brown	Scott G. Brown
Donald C. Radcliff	Clifford C. Brady
M. Kathleen Miller	Richard W. Franklin

(See Next Column)

ASSOCIATES

Stephen Russell Copeland	Rodney R. Cate

Representative Clients: American Surety Group (Regional Counsel); AmSouth Bank of Alabama (Regional Counsel); Burlington Northern Railroad Co. (District Counsel); Loyal American Life Insurance Co.; Kimberly Clark Corporation; Travelers Insurance Co.

For Complete List of Firm Personnel, See General Section

For full biographical listings, see the Martindale-Hubbell Law Directory

BRISKMAN & BINION, P.C. (AV)

205 Church Street, P.O. Box 43, 36601
Telephone: 334-433-7600
Fax: 334-433-4485

Donald M. Briskman	Christ N. Coumanis
Mack B. Binion	Walter G. (Stoney) Chavers

A List of Representative Clients will be furnished upon request.
References: First Alabama Bank; AmSouth Bank, N.A.; Southtrust Bank of Mobile.

For full biographical listings, see the Martindale-Hubbell Law Directory

BURNS, CUNNINGHAM & MACKEY, P.C. (AV)

50 St. Emanuel Street, P.O. Box 1583, 36633
Telephone: 334-432-0612

Peter F. Burns	Peter S. Mackey
William M. Cunningham, Jr.	Gary W. Fillingim

For full biographical listings, see the Martindale-Hubbell Law Directory

CABANISS, JOHNSTON, GARDNER, DUMAS & O'NEAL (AV)

700 AmSouth Center, P.O. Box 2906, 36652
Telephone: 334-433-6961
Telecopier: 334-433-1060
Birmingham, Alabama Office: Park Place Tower. 2001 Park Place North, Suite 700. P.O. Box 830612.
Telephone: 205-716-5200.
Telecopier: 205-716-5389.

MEMBERS OF FIRM

Benjamen T. Rowe (Resident)	William K. Thomas
William A. Robinson (Resident)	David L. Kane (Resident)
Patrick H. Sims (Resident)	R. Boyd Miller (Resident)
Donald J. Stewart (Resident)	Sandy G. Robinson (Resident)

Representative Clients: American Marine Underwriters, Inc.; Liberty Mutual Insurance Co.; Union Carbide Corp.; Rohr, Inc.

For full biographical listings, see the Martindale-Hubbell Law Directory

CUNNINGHAM, BOUNDS, YANCE, CROWDER & BROWN (AV)

1601 Dauphin Street, P.O. Box 66705, 36660
Telephone: 334-471-6191
Fax: 334-479-1031

Richard Bounds	Joseph M. Brown, Jr.
James A. Yance	Gregory B. Breedlove
John T. Crowder, Jr.	Andrew T. Citrin
Robert T. Cunningham, Jr.	Michael A. Worel

David G. Wirtes, Jr.	Mitchell K. Shelly
Toby D. Brown	Kelli Denise Taylor

OF COUNSEL

Robert T. Cunningham	Valentino D. B. Mazzia

References: First Alabama Bank; AmSouth Bank, N.A.

For full biographical listings, see the Martindale-Hubbell Law Directory

FINKBOHNER AND LAWLER, L.L.C. (AV)

169 Dauphin Street Suite 300, P.O. Box 3085, 36652
Telephone: 334-438-5871
Fax: 334-432-8052

MEMBERS OF FIRM

George W. Finkbohner, Jr.	George W. Finkbohner, III
John L. Lawler	Royce A. Ray, III

For full biographical listings, see the Martindale-Hubbell Law Directory

HELMSING, LYONS, SIMS & LEACH, P.C. (AV)

The Laclede Building, 150 Government Street, P.O. Box 2767, 36652
Telephone: 334-432-5521
Telecopy: 334-432-0633

(See Next Column)

HELMSING, LYONS, SIMS & LEACH P.C.—Continued

Larry U. Sims	Robert H. Rouse
Champ Lyons, Jr.	Charles H. Dodson, Jr.
Frederick G. Helmsing	Richard E. Davis
John N. Leach, Jr.	Joseph P. H. Babington
Warren C. Herlong, Jr.	John J. Crowley, Jr.
James B. Newman	Joseph D. Steadman

Todd S. Strohmeyer	John Townsend Dukes
William R. Lancaster	P. Bradley Murray
Robin Kilpatrick Fincher	Leslie T. Fields

For full biographical listings, see the Martindale-Hubbell Law Directory

INGE, TWITTY & DUFFY (AV)

1410 First Alabama Bank Building, 56 St. Joseph Street, P.O. Box 1109, 36633
Telephone: 334-433-3200
Facsimile: 334-433-3444

MEMBERS OF FIRM

James J. Duffy, Jr.	James J. Duffy, III

Francis H. Inge (1902-1959)	Thos. E. Twitty (1901-1975)
	Richard H. Inge (1912-1980)

For full biographical listings, see the Martindale-Hubbell Law Directory

JOHNSTON, WILKINS & DRUHAN (AV)

Hannah Houses, 157-159 North Conception Street, P.O. Box 154, 36601
Telephone: 334-432-0738
Telecopier: 334-432-4874

MEMBERS OF FIRM

Samuel M. Johnston, Jr.	J. Michael Druhan, Jr.
(1919-1993)	James C. Johnston
Robert B. Wilkins (1922-1992)	Joseph S. Johnston

ASSOCIATE
Robert B. Stewart

Representative Clients: International Paper Co.; Morrison's, Inc.; SouthTrust Bank of Mobile; Employers Casualty Insurance Co.; Fidelity & Deposit Company of Maryland; General Accident Insurance Co.

For full biographical listings, see the Martindale-Hubbell Law Directory

JOHNSTONE, ADAMS, BAILEY, GORDON AND HARRIS, L.L.C. (AV)

Royal St. Francis Building, 104 St. Francis Street, P.O. Box 1988, 36633
Telephone: 334-432-7682
Facsimile: 334-432-2800
Telex: 782040

MEMBERS OF FIRM

Brock B. Gordon	David C. Hannan
Ben H. Harris, Jr.	Wade B. Perry, Jr.
William H. Hardie, Jr.	Thomas S. Rue
Joseph M. Allen, Jr.	Alan C. Christian
I. David Cherniak	Gregory C. Buffalow
	Celia J. Collins

ASSOCIATES

Tracy P. Turner	E. Russell March, III
E. Erich Bergdolt	Scott Alton Browning

General Counsel for: First Alabama Bank, Mobile; Infirmary Health System/Mobile Infirmary Medical Center/Rotary Rehabilitation Hospital (Multi-Hospital System).
Counsel for: Oil and Gas: Exxon Corp. Business and Corporate: Bell South Telecommunications, Inc.; Aluminum Co. of America; Michelin North America, Inc.; Metropolitan Life Insurance Co.; The Travelers Insurance Cos. Marine: The West of England Ship Owners Mutual Protection and Indemnity Association (Luxembourg); The Standard Steamship Owners' Protection and Indemnity Association (Bermuda) Ltd.

For Complete List of Firm Personnel, See General Section

For full biographical listings, see the Martindale-Hubbell Law Directory

LOVELESS & LYONS (AV)

28 North Florida Street, 36607
Telephone: 334-476-7857
Fax: 334-476-8510

MEMBER OF FIRM
Ralph P. Loveless

For Complete List of Firm Personnel, See General Section

For full biographical listings, see the Martindale-Hubbell Law Directory

LYONS, PIPES & COOK, P.C. (AV)

2 North Royal Street, P.O. Box 2727, 36652-2727
Telephone: 334-432-4481
Cable Address: "Lysea"
Telecopier: 334-433-1820

Wesley Pipes	Joseph J. Minus, Jr.
Norton W. Brooker, Jr.	William E. Shreve, Jr.
Cooper C. Thurber	Daniel S. Cushing
Marion A. Quina, Jr.	Allen E. Graham
Walter M. Cook, Jr.	M. Warren Butler
John Patrick Courtney, III	Christopher Lee George

General Counsel: Alabama State Docks Department (an agency of the State of Alabama).
Counsel: McKenzie Tank Lines, Inc.; SCNO Barge Lines, Inc.; Scott Paper Co.; Shell Oil Corp.
Trial Counsel: Aetna Life & Casualty Co.; Chubb Group of Insurance Companies.

For Complete List of Firm Personnel, See General Section

For full biographical listings, see the Martindale-Hubbell Law Directory

AUGUSTINE MEAHER, III, P.C. (AV)

Suite 2118, First National Bank Building, 36602
Telephone: 334-432-9971
FAX: 334-432-9978

Augustine Meaher, III

References: Bank of Mobile, Mobile, Alabama; AmSouth Bank, Mobile, Alabama.

For full biographical listings, see the Martindale-Hubbell Law Directory

PIERCE, LEDYARD, LATTA & WASDEN, P.C. (AV)

Suite 900 Montlimar Place Office Building, 1110 Montlimar Drive, P.O. Box 16046, 36616
Telephone: 334-344-5151
Facsimile: 334-344-9696

Donald F. Pierce	Forrest S. Latta
Goodman G. Ledyard	H. William Wasden

OF COUNSEL
Caroline Wells Hinds

John Chas. S. Pierce	W. Pemble DeLashmet
	C. William Daniels, Jr.

Representative Clients: Grove Worldwide; Beloit Corp.; Koehring Cranes & Excavators; Winnebago; Toyota Motor Sales Corp.; Blue Cross and Blue Shield; Connecticut Mutual Life Insurance Co.; Harnischfeger Industries; Terex Corporation.

For full biographical listings, see the Martindale-Hubbell Law Directory

MONTGOMERY,* Montgomery Co.

BALL, BALL, MATTHEWS & NOVAK, P.A. (AV)

Suite 1100, 60 Commerce Street, P.O. Box 2148, 36102-2148
Telephone: 334-834-7680
Fax: 334-265-3222

Fred S. Ball (1866-1942)	C. Winston Sheehan, Jr.
Charles A. Ball (1904-1969)	William H. Brittain II
Fred S. Ball, Jr. (1896-1974)	Joana S. Ellis
Richard A. Ball (1906-1983)	E. Hamilton Wilson, Jr.
John R. Matthews, Jr.	Richard E. Broughton
Richard A. Ball, Jr.	T. Cowin Knowles
Tabor R. Novak, Jr.	Gerald C. Swann, Jr.
Clyde C. Owen, Jr.	Mark T. Davis
	James A. Rives

Fred B. Matthews	Allison L. Alford

Counsel for: Beech Aircraft Corporation; Bell Helicopter Co.; John Deere Co.; Government Employees Insurance Co.; Chubb & Son; Cigna Co.; Chrysler Corp.; Associated Aviation Underwriters.

For full biographical listings, see the Martindale-Hubbell Law Directory

BEERS, ANDERSON, JACKSON & SMITH, P.C. (AV)

250 Commerce Street, P.O. Box 1988, 36102
Telephone: 334-834-5311
Fax: 334-834-5362
Birmingham, Alabama Office: 2101 6th Avenue North, Suite 701, 35203.
Telephone: 205-254-1958.
Fax: 205-224-3802.

Michael B. Beers	Jeffrey W. Smith
James H. Anderson	Christopher J. Hughes
Micheal S. Jackson	David B. Chancellor
	William F. Patty

(See Next Column)

BEERS, ANDERSON, JACKSON & SMITH P.C., Montgomery—Continued

OF COUNSEL
D. Patrick Harris

For full biographical listings, see the Martindale-Hubbell Law Directory

HASKELL SLAUGHTER & YOUNG, L.L.C. (AV)

305 South Lawrence Street, P.O. Box 4660, 36103-4660
Telephone: 334-265-8573
Facsimile: 334-264-7945
Birmingham, Alabama Office: 1200 AmSouth/Harbert Plaza, 1901 Sixth
Avenue North. 35203
Telephone: 205-251-1000.
Facsimile: 205-324-1133.

Thomas T. Gallion, III	Constance A. Caldwell
Barry D. Woodham	Susan E. Kennedy

Representative Clients: The Equitable Life Assurance Society of the United
States; Exxon Corporation; Federal Deposit Insurance Corporation; Fireman's Fund Insurance Companies; Marshall Durbin Companies; Montgomery County, Alabama; Raytheon Aircraft Company; Ridout's-Brown-Service
Inc.

For full biographical listings, see the Martindale-Hubbell Law Directory

HILL, HILL, CARTER, FRANCO, COLE & BLACK, P.C. (AV)

425 South Perry Street, P.O. Box 116, 36101-0116
Telephone: 334-834-7600
Fax: 334-263-5969

Thomas B. Hill, Jr. (1903-1984)	John M. Milling, Jr.
Wm. Inge Hill (1911-1995)	William Inge Hill, Jr.
James T. Stovall (1905-1972)	Gerald W. Hartley
James J. Carter (1913-1985)	Randall Morgan
William A. Oldacre (1932-1973)	Robert W. Bradford, Jr.
Ralph A. Franco	David E. Allred
T. Bowen Hill, III	Laura L. Crum
Harry Cole	Mark A. Franco
Robert C. Black, Sr.	Terry A. Sides
William I. Hill, II	John R. Bradwell
William C. McGowin	
Robert C. Black, Jr.	Pamela Pelekis Swan

Representative Clients: The Aetna Group; The State Farm Group; ALFA;
General Electric Co.; General Motors Corp; Blue Cross and Blue Shield of
Alabama; Allstate Insurance Co.; Winn-Dixie Stores, Inc.; Scottsdale Insur-
ance Co.; National Casualty Co.

For Complete List of Firm Personnel, See General Section

For full biographical listings, see the Martindale-Hubbell Law Directory

NIX, HOLTSFORD & VERCELLI, P.C. (AV)

300 A Water Street, Suite 300, P.O. Box 4128, 36103
Telephone: 334-262-2006
Fax: 334-834-3616

H. E. Nix, Jr.	Charles E. Vercelli, Jr.
Alex L. Holtsford, Jr.	Floyd R. Gilliland
T. Randall Lyons	
Marianne T. Cosse	Phil Collins
Steven A. Higgins	G. Gregory Locklier
David M. Anderson	David P. Stevens

For full biographical listings, see the Martindale-Hubbell Law Directory

ROBISON & BELSER, P.A. (AV)

210 Commerce Street, P.O. Drawer 1470, 36102
Telephone: 334-834-7000
Telecopier: 334-834-7011

Vaughan H. Robison (States) (1918-1995)	John M. Bolton, III
	Charles B. Paterson
Richard C. Belser (1927-1991)	Justice D. Smyth, III
Philip H. Butler	Robert F. Northcutt
David B. Byrne, Jr.	J. Elizabeth Kellum
James R. Seale	Martha Ann Miller

General Counsel for: Montgomery County Board of Education.
Representative Clients: Union Bank & Trust Co.; Liberty National Life Insurance Co.; State Farm Mutual Fire & Casualty Co.
Approved Attorneys for: Lawyers Title Insurance Corp.; Louisville Title Insurance Co.; Federal Land Bank; Liberty National Life Insurance Co.

For full biographical listings, see the Martindale-Hubbell Law Directory

VOLZ, PRESTWOOD & HANAN, P.C. (AV)

350 Adams Avenue, P.O. Box 1910, 36102-1910
Telephone: 334-264-6401
Fax: 334-834-4954

(See Next Column)

Charles H. Volz, Jr.	Charles H. Volz, III
Alvin T. Prestwood	Clinton Chadwell Carter
Ellis D. Hanan	Daniel Lewis Feinstein

LEGAL SUPPORT PERSONNEL
Mark A.W. Turpen

For full biographical listings, see the Martindale-Hubbell Law Directory

---

PELL CITY, St. Clair Co.

BLAIR, HOLLADAY AND PARSONS (AV)

St. Clair Land Title Building, 1711 Cogswell Avenue, 35125
Telephone: 205-884-3440
Fax: 205-884-3442

MEMBERS OF FIRM

A. Dwight Blair	Hugh E. Holladay
Elizabeth S. Parsons	

Representative Clients: Colonial Bank; Metro Bank; Am South Bank; St.
Clair Federal Savings Bank; State Farm Mutual Insurance Cos; ALFA Mu-
tual Insurance Co.; Allstate Insurance Co.; St. Paul Insurance Cos.; Auto
Owners Insurance Co.; Reliance Insurance Cos.

For full biographical listings, see the Martindale-Hubbell Law Directory

---

TALLADEGA,* Talladega Co.

BARRY N. McCRARY (AV)

223 West North Street, 35160
Telephone: 205-362-2190
Telecopier: 205-362-8280
Mailing Address: P.O. Drawer 56,

References: First National Bank of Talladega; Talladega Federal Savings and
Loan Assn.

For full biographical listings, see the Martindale-Hubbell Law Directory

---

TROY,* Pike Co.

CALHOUN, FAULK, WATKINS & CLOWER, L.L.C. (AV)

78 South Court Square, P.O. Box 489, 36081
Telephone: 334-566-7200
Fax: 334-566-7584

Richard F. Calhoun	William Keith Watkins
Joseph E. Faulk	James G. Clower (Retired)
Robert Curry Faircloth	

General Counsel for: City of Troy; City of Brundidge; First Alabama Bank,
Troy; First National Bank of Brundidge; Troy City Board of Education; Pike
County Board of Education; South Alabama Electric Cooperative, Inc.; B &
D Plastics, Inc.; Battery Marketing Corporation.

For full biographical listings, see the Martindale-Hubbell Law Directory

---

TUSCALOOSA,* Tuscaloosa Co.

DAVIDSON, WIGGINS & CROWDER, P.C. (AV)

2625 Eighth Street, P.O. Box 1939, 35403
Telephone: 205-759-5771
Fax: 205-752-8259

M. McCoy Davidson	A. Courtney Crowder
G. Stephen Wiggins	David Ryan

OF COUNSEL
Hugh W. Roberts, Jr.

Brett Ross

Attorneys for: Canal Insurance Co.; Government Employees Insurance Co.;
The Travelers Group; Auto-Owners Insurance Co.; Continental National
American Group; Federated Insurance; Lynn Insurance Group; The Trinity
Cos.; The PMA Group; Nationwide Ins. Co.; Colonial Ins. Co. of California.

For full biographical listings, see the Martindale-Hubbell Law Directory

OWENS & CARVER (AV)

2720 6th Street, Suite 3, P.O. Box 2487, 35403-2487
Telephone: 205-750-0750
Facsimile: 205-750-0355

John A. Owens	Susie Taylor Carver

ASSOCIATES

M. Bradley Almond	Apsilah G. Owens

For full biographical listings, see the Martindale-Hubbell Law Directory

PHELPS, JENKINS, GIBSON & FOWLER (AV)

1201 Greensboro Avenue, P.O. Box 020848, 35402-0848
Telephone: 205-345-5100
Fax: 205-758-4394
Fax: 205-391-6658

(See Next Column)

PHELPS, JENKINS, GIBSON & FOWLER—*Continued*

MEMBERS OF FIRM

Sam M. Phelps	Randolph M. Fowler
James J. Jenkins	Michael S. Burroughs
Johnson Russell Gibson, III	C. Barton Adcox
Farley A. Poellnitz	

ASSOCIATES

Karen C. Welborn	Stephen E. Snow
Sandra C. Guin	Thomas W. Davis
Lisa Paul Hodges	M. Kristi Wallace

LEGAL SUPPORT PERSONNEL

Alicia Suzanne Wilson	Ashley D. Sparks
Cathey Raye Hartline	Kimberly Susan Wright

Attorneys for: Aetna Insurance Co.; Allstate Insurance Co.; Carolina Casualty Insurance Co.; Continental Insurance Cos.; Fireman's Fund-American Insurance Cos.; Great American Insurance Co.; Hanover Insurance Co.

For full biographical listings, see the Martindale-Hubbell Law Directory

ZEANAH, HUST, SUMMERFORD, DAVIS & JONES, L.L.C. (AV)

Seventh Floor, AmSouth Bank Building, P.O. Box 1310, 35403
Telephone: 205-349-1383
Fax: 205-391-1319

MEMBERS OF FIRM

Olin W. Zeanah (1922-1987)	Kenneth D. Davis
Wilbor J. Hust, Jr.	Christopher H. Jones
E. Clark Summerford	Beverly A. Smith

OF COUNSEL

Marvin T. Ormond

Representative Clients: Alfa Insurance Cos.; Hartford Insurance Group; Home Insurance Co.; Nationwide Insurance Co.; Alabama Power Co.; Liberty Mutual Insurance Co.; The Uniroyal Goodrich Tire Co.

For full biographical listings, see the Martindale-Hubbell Law Directory

---

TUSCUMBIA, * Colbert Co.

SELF & SELF

(See Florence)

ALASKA

ANCHORAGE, * Third Judicial District

ASHBURN & MASON, A PROFESSIONAL CORPORATION (AV)

1130 West 6th Avenue, Suite 100, 99501
Telephone: 907-276-4331
Telecopier: 907-277-8235

Mark E. Ashburn	Donald W. McClintock, III
Julian L. Mason, III	A. William Saupe
John C. McCarron	Kirsten A. Tinglum

William S. Cummings	Roseann Marie Rotandaro

LEGAL SUPPORT PERSONNEL

Karen M. Procter

Reference: First National Bank of Anchorage.

For full biographical listings, see the Martindale-Hubbell Law Directory

DeLISIO MORAN GERAGHTY & ZOBEL, P.C. (AV)

943 West Sixth Avenue, 99501-2033
Telephone: 907-279-9574
Facsimile: 907-276-4231
Email: 74151,2533@compuserve.com

Michael C. Geraghty	Gregory L. Youngmun
Patricia L. Zobel	David D. Floerchinger
Deirdre D. Ford	

Tracey L. Knutson	Harland H. McElhany
Sarah Diemer Moyer	

For full biographical listings, see the Martindale-Hubbell Law Directory

---

JUNEAU, * First Judicial District

RUDDY, BRADLEY & KOLKHORST, A PROFESSIONAL CORPORATION (AV)

Jordan Creek Center, 8800 Glacier Highway, Suite 223, P.O. Box 34338, 99801
Telephone: 907-789-0047
FAX: 907-789-0783

(See Next Column)

William G. Ruddy	J. B. Bradley
Kathryn Kolkhorst	

For full biographical listings, see the Martindale-Hubbell Law Directory

---

ARIZONA

FLAGSTAFF, * Coconino Co.

ASPEY, WATKINS & DIESEL, P.L.L.C. (AV)

123 North San Francisco, 3rd Floor, 86001
Telephone: 520-774-1478
Facsimile: 520-774-8404
Sedona, Arizona Office: 120 Soldier Pass Road.
Telephone: 520-282-5955.
Facsimile: 520-282-5962.
Page, Arizona Office: 904 North Navajo.
Telephone: 520-645-9694.
Cottonwood, Arizona Office: 2400 E. Highway 89A, Suite C.
Telephone: 520-639-1881.
Facsimile: 520-639-0272.

MEMBERS OF FIRM

Frederick M. Fritz Aspey	Donald H. Bayles, Jr.
Harold L. Watkins	Kaign N. Christy
Louis M. Diesel	John J. Dempsey
Bruce S. Griffen	Zachary J. Markham

James E. Ledbetter	Roger M. Baeurle
Whitney Cunningham	Amy E. Mabius
Pernell Whynn McGuire	Stephen A. Thompson
Joel E. Sannes	

LEGAL SUPPORT PERSONNEL

Karla H. Falls, CLAS (Legal Assistant)	Dominic M. Marino, Jr, (Paralegal Assistant)
Rocky C. Nissen (Paralegal Assistant, Sedona, Arizona Office)	Carrie R. Flynn (Litigation Paralegal, Cottonwood, Arizona Office)
Deborah D. Roberts, CLA (Legal Assistant)	

Representative Clients: Farmer's Insurance Company of Arizona; Pepsi-Cola Bottling Company of Northern Arizona; Bill Luke's Chrysler-Plymouth, Inc.; First American Title Insurance Company; Transnation Title Insurance Co.; Page Electric Utility; Comprehensive Access Health Plan, Inc.; Northern Arizona Healthcare Corporation.
Reference: First Interstate Bank-Arizona, N.A., Flagstaff, Arizona.

For full biographical listings, see the Martindale-Hubbell Law Directory

---

ANN RAE HEITLAND (AV(T))

Bank of America Building, 121 East Birch Avenue, Suite 408, 86001
Telephone: 520-556-8698
Fax: 520-556-8747
Email: arhatty@aol.com

For full biographical listings, see the Martindale-Hubbell Law Directory

---

MANGUM, WALL, STOOPS & WARDEN, P.L.L.C. (AV)

222 East Birch Avenue, P.O. Box 10, 86002
Telephone: 520-779-6951
Fax: 520-773-1312

OF COUNSEL

Douglas J. Wall	Robert W. Warden

MEMBERS OF FIRM

Daniel J. Stoops	Melinda L. Garrahan

ASSOCIATES

Deborah M. Fine	David L. Anderson
Michael H. Hinson	

Representative Clients: United States Automobile Assn.; Federated Insurance; Hartford Insurance Co.; State Farm Fire & Casualty Insurance Co.; Cincinnati Insurance Co.; Canal Insurance Co.; Economy Fire & Casualty Co.; Guaranty National Insurance Co.; Progressive Insurance Co.; Transamerica Insurance Co.

For Complete List of Firm Personnel, See General Section

For full biographical listings, see the Martindale-Hubbell Law Directory

GREEN VALLEY, Pima Co.

DUFFIELD, MILLER, YOUNG, ADAMSON & ALFRED, P.C. (AV)

101-65 South La Canada, Green Valley Mall, 85614
Telephone: 520-625-4404
FAX: 520-625-4453
Tucson, Arizona Office: Suite 711, Transamerica Building, 177 North Church Avenue.
Telephone: 520-792-1181.
Fax: 520-792-2859.
La Paloma Office: La Paloma Corporate Center, 3573 East Sunrise Drive, Suite 115, Tucson, Arizona.
Telephone: 520-577-1135.
Fax: 520-577-1079.

Richard Duffield	Larry R. Adamson
Michael C. Young	K. Alexander Hobson
Eugene C. Gieseler	

Representative Clients: San Xavier Rock & Materials, Inc.; Mobat-Adamson Tire Co.
Insurance Company Clientele: State Farm Mutual Insurance Cos.; Automobile Club Insurance Co.; Colonial Penn Insurance Co.; Crum & Forster Group.

For full biographical listings, see the Martindale-Hubbell Law Directory

NOGALES,* Santa Cruz Co.

O'CONNOR, CAVANAGH, ANDERSON, KILLINGSWORTH & BESHEARS, A PROFESSIONAL ASSOCIATION (AV)

1891 North Mastick Way, 85621
Telephone: 520-761-4215
FAX: 520-761-3505
Email: firminfo@arizlaw.com
Phoenix, Arizona Office: One East Camelback Road, Suite 1100, 85012.
Telephone: 602-263-2400.
FAX: 602-263-2900.
Tucson, Arizona Office: O'Connor Cavanagh Molloy Jones, 33 N. Stone, Suite 2100, 85701, P.O. Box 2268, 85702.
Telephone: 520-622-3531.
FAX: 520-624-2816.
Sun City, Arizona Office: 13250 North Del Webb Boulevard, Suite B, 85351.
Telephone: 602-263-2808.
FAX: 602-933-3100.

Kimberly A. Howard Arana

Representative Clients: Omega Produce Co.; Frank's Distributing, Inc.; City of Nogales; Collectron of Ariz., Inc.; James K. Wilson Produce Co.; Agricola Bon, S. de R.L. de C.V.; Angel Demerutis E.; Rene Carrillo C.; Arturo Lomeli; Theojary Crisantes E.

For Complete List of Firm Personnel, See General Section

For full biographical listings, see the Martindale-Hubbell Law Directory

PHOENIX,* Maricopa Co.

ALLEN & PRICE, P.L.C. (AV)

2850 East Camelback Road, Suite 170, 85016-4380
Telephone: 602-381-0500
Fax: 602-381-8899
Email: price@aplaw.com
Email: allen@aplaw.com

Robert E. B. Allen	Charles S. Price

For full biographical listings, see the Martindale-Hubbell Law Directory

APKER, APKER, HAGGARD & KURTZ, P.C. (AV)

2111 East Highland Avenue, Suite 230, 85016
Telephone: 602-381-0085
Telecopier: 602-956-3457

Burton M. Apker	David B. Apker
Jerry L. Haggard	Gerrie Apker Kurtz

Kevin M. Moran

Representative Clients: ASARCO Incorporated; Douglas Land Corp.; Frito-Lay, Inc.; Nevada Power Company; The North West Life Assurance Co.; Phelps Dodge Corporation; Santa Fe Pacific Gold Corporation; Santa Fe Pacific Industrials; Western Federal Savings & Loan Assn.

For full biographical listings, see the Martindale-Hubbell Law Directory

BEGAM, LEWIS, MARKS & WOLFE A PROFESSIONAL ASSOCIATION OF LAWYERS (AV)

111 West Monroe Street, Suite 1400, 85003-1787
Telephone: 602-254-6071
Fax: 602-252-0042

(See Next Column)

Robert G. Begam	Daniel J. Adelman
Frank Lewis	Lisa Kurtz
Stanley J. Marks	Dena Rosen Epstein
Elliot G. Wolfe	Steven M. Friedman
Kelly J. McDonald	Richard P. Traulsen

Reference: National Bank of Arizona.

For full biographical listings, see the Martindale-Hubbell Law Directory

BESS & DYSART, P.C. (AV)

7210 North 16th Street, 82020-5201
Telephone: 602-331-4600
Telecopier: 602-331-8600

Leon D. Bess	Timothy R. Hyland
Robert L. Dysart	William M. Demlong
Donald R. Kunz	Matthew D. Kleifield

Stephanie L. Chilton	Donald J. Sapala

For full biographical listings, see the Martindale-Hubbell Law Directory

BONN, LUSCHER, PADDEN & WILKINS, CHARTERED (AV)

805 North Second Street, 85004
Telephone: 602-254-5557
Fax: 602-254-0656

Paul V. Bonn	Randall D. Wilkins
Brian A. Luscher	John H. Cassidy
	D. Michael Hall

OF COUNSEL

Ruth Sproull

For full biographical listings, see the Martindale-Hubbell Law Directory

BONNETT, FAIRBOURN, FRIEDMAN & BALINT, P.C. (AV)

4041 North Central Avenue Suite 1100, 85012
Telephone: 602-274-1100
Fax: 602-274-1199

Jerry C. Bonnett	Elaine A. Ryan
William G. Fairbourn	Tara L. Jackson
Andrew S. Friedman	Wendy J. Harrison
Francis J. Balint, Jr.	Scott A. Erickson
H. Sullivan Bunch	Thomas B. Dixon
Michael N. Widener	Martin E. Latz
Robert J. Spurlock	Robert D. Ryan
C. Kevin Dykstra	Guy P. Roll

For full biographical listings, see the Martindale-Hubbell Law Directory

CHARLES M. BREWER, LTD. (AV)

Brewer Building, 5500 North 24th Street, P.O. Box 10720, 85064
Telephone: 602-381-8787
Fax: 602-381-1152

Charles M. Brewer

Mark S. O'Connor	Luis Pedro Guerra
Dane London Wood	

For full biographical listings, see the Martindale-Hubbell Law Directory

BROWN & BAIN, A PROFESSIONAL ASSOCIATION (AV)

2901 North Central Avenue, P.O. Box 400, 85001-0400
Telephone: 602-351-8000
Telecopier: 602-351-8516
Palo Alto, California Affiliated Office: Brown & Bain, 1755 Embarcadero Road, Suite 200.
Telephone: 415-856-9411.
Telecopier: 415-856-6061.
Tucson, Arizona Affiliated Office: Brown & Bain, A Professional Association. One South Church Avenue, Nineteenth Floor, P.O. Box 2265.
Telephone: 602-798-7900
Telecopier: 602-798-7945.

Lynne Christensen Adams	Terry E. Fenzl
C. Randall Bain	Jodi Knobel Feuerhelm
Eddward P. Ballinger, Jr.	Douglas Gerlach
Daniel C. Barr	Amy J. Gittler
Michael P. Berman	Philip R. Higdon
Charles A. Blanchard	(Resident at Tucson Office)
Alan H. Blankenheimer	Jonathan M. James
David P. Brooks	Jeanean Kirk
Jack E. Brown	Joseph E. Mais
John A. Buttrick	Anthony L. Marks
Howard Ross Cabot	Joel W. Nomkin
H. Michael Clyde	Kelly A. O'Connor
Richard Calvin Cooledge	Michael W. Patten
Paul F. Eckstein	John W. Rogers

(See Next Column)

BROWN & BAIN A PROFESSIONAL ASSOCIATION—*Continued*

Lawrence G. D. Scarborough	Craig W. Soland
Lex J. Smith	Antonio T. Viera
Kim E. Williamson	

Timothy J. Franks	C. Mark Kittredge
Shirley Ann Kaufman	Deborah Henscheid Lyon
Todd R. Kerr	Timothy A. Nelson

For Complete List of Firm Personnel, See General Section

For full biographical listings, see the Martindale-Hubbell Law Directory

BURCH & CRACCHIOLO, P.A. (AV)

702 East Osborn Road, Suite 200, 85014
Telephone: 602-274-7611
Fax: 602-234-0341
Mailing Address: P.O. Box 16882, Phoenix, AZ, 85011

Daniel Cracchiolo	Donald W. Lindholm
Stephen E. Silver	F. Michael Carroll
Brian Kaven	Daniel R. Malinski
Daryl Manhart	Edwin D. Fleming
Ian Neale	Ralph D. Harris
David G. Derickson	Stephen M. Hart
Andrew Abraham	David M. Villadolid

Paul F. Dowdell	Thomas A. Longfellow
Theodore (Todd) Julian	Steven M. Serrano
J. Brent Welker	

Representative Clients: Bashas' Inc.; Farmers Insurance Group; U-Haul International, Inc.

For Complete List of Firm Personnel, See General Section

For full biographical listings, see the Martindale-Hubbell Law Directory

COHEN AND COTTON, P.C. A PROFESSIONAL CORPORATION (AV)

One Arizona Center, Suite 400, 400 East Van Buren Street, 85004
Telephone: 602-252-8400
FAX: 602-252-5339
Las Vegas, Nevada Office: 1001 First Interstate Bank Building, 302 East Carson Avenue, 89101.
Telephone: 702-387-7870.
Fax: 702-385-3331.

Ronald Jay Cohen	Joshua R. Woodard
John H. Cotton	Robert N. Mann
Laura H. Kennedy	John Maston O'Neal
Daniel G. Dowd	Jennifer Lynn Chutick
David W. Smith	Ed F. Hendricks, Jr.
Scott L. Long	Michael J. Ryan
	(Not admitted in AZ)

SPECIAL COUNSEL

Stacy J. Crouch	Paula M. DeMore

Representative Clients: American Continental/Amex Life Assurance Co.; Coopers & Lybrand; Del Webb Corp.; Fireman's Fund; Grubb & Ellis Realty Co.; MMI Companies; Talley Industries, Inc.; The Doctor's Company; United States Fidelity and Guaranty Co.

For full biographical listings, see the Martindale-Hubbell Law Directory

DUSHOFF & McCALL, A PROFESSIONAL CORPORATION (AV)

Two Renaissance Square, Suite 1000, 40 North Central, 85004
Telephone: 602-254-3800
Fax: 602-258-2551
URL: http://www.dushoff@neta.com

Jay Dushoff	Robert H. Kreutzer
Jack E. McCall (1942-1995)	Michael Riikola
Denise J. Henslee	

LEGAL SUPPORT PERSONNEL

Thomas M. Flynn	Roger L. Dunlap
Brad D. Larson	(Certified Legal Assistant)

For full biographical listings, see the Martindale-Hubbell Law Directory

FENNEMORE CRAIG, A PROFESSIONAL CORPORATION (AV)

Two North Central, Suite 2200, 85004
Telephone: 602-257-8700
Fax: 602-257-8527
Scottsdale, Arizona Office: 6263 North Scottsdale Road, Suite 290, 85250.
Telephone: 602-257-5400.
Fax: 602-257-5409.
Tucson, Arizona Office: One South Church Avenue, Suite 1030, 85701.
Telephone: 520-791-6800.
Fax: 520-791-6820.

(See Next Column)

Calvin H. Udall	David A. Weatherwax
James Powers	Graeme E. M. Hancock
Kenneth J. Sherk	Kaye L. McCarthy
John D. Everroad	Scott M. Finical
F. Pendleton Gaines, III	William T. Burghart
Donald R. Gilbert	Andrew M. Federhar
Roger T. Hargrove	Christopher L. Callahan
David T. Maddox	Loral Deatherage
John G. Ryan	Christopher P. Staring
Leland M. Jones	Janet W. Lord
William L. Thorpe	James J. Trimble

Mark H. Brain	Marc H. Lamber
Keith L. Hendricks	Richard A. Kasper

For Complete List of Firm Personnel, See General Section

For full biographical listings, see the Martindale-Hubbell Law Directory

FOGEL AND LAMBER, PROFESSIONAL ASSOCIATION (AV)

One Windsor Professional Building, 2627 North Third Street, 85004-1197
Telephone: 602-264-3330
Fax: 602-274-5117

Sherman D. Fogel	Dennis M. Lamber
Rex P. Bronnenkant	

Reference: Chase Bank of Arizona.

For full biographical listings, see the Martindale-Hubbell Law Directory

GALBUT & CONANT, A PROFESSIONAL CORPORATION (AV)

Camelback Esplanade, Suite 1020, 2425 East Camelback Road, 85016
Telephone: 602-955-1455
Fax: 602-955-1585

Martin R. Galbut	Paul A. Conant
John R. Augustine, Jr.	

For full biographical listings, see the Martindale-Hubbell Law Directory

GOLDSTEIN & McGRODER, LTD. A PROFESSIONAL CORPORATION (AV)

2200 East Camelback Road, Suite 221, 85016-3456
Telephone: 602-957-1500
Fax: 602-956-9294

Philip T. Goldstein	Patrick J. McGroder, III
Suzanne P. Clarke	

Jane E. Evans	Serena C. Montague

LEGAL SUPPORT PERSONNEL
Kevan S. DeWitt (Paralegal)

For full biographical listings, see the Martindale-Hubbell Law Directory

DAVID F. GOMEZ A PROFESSIONAL CORPORATION (AV)

2525 East Camelback Road Suite 860, 85016
Telephone: 602-957-8686
Telecopier: 602-956-9854
Email: DFGPC@aol.com

David F. Gomez

Michael J. Petitti, Jr.

For full biographical listings, see the Martindale-Hubbell Law Directory

RICHARD J. HERTZBERG (AV)

16 Luhrs Arcade 11 West Jefferson, 85003
Telephone: 602-253-1781
Fax: 602-253-0928

For full biographical listings, see the Martindale-Hubbell Law Directory

HORNE, KAPLAN AND BISTROW, P.C. (AV)

Renaissance Two, 40 North Central, Suite 2800, 85004
Telephone: 602-253-9700
Fax: 602-258-4805

Thomas C. Horne	Eric J. Bistrow
Martha Bachner Kaplan	Michael S. Dulberg
Kimball J. Corson	

For full biographical listings, see the Martindale-Hubbell Law Directory

Phoenix—Continued

JENNINGS & HAUG (AV)

2800 North Central Avenue Suite Eighteen Hundred, 85004-1019
Telephone: 602-234-7800
Fax: 602-277-5595
Email: jhlaw@syspac.com
Irvine, California Office: 1920 Main Street, Suite Eight-Thirty, 92714.
Telephone: 714-250-7800.
Fax: 714-250-4913.

MEMBERS OF FIRM

Curtis A. Jennings	Chad L. Schexnayder
William F. Haug	Mark E. Barker
Robert A. Scheffing	John G. Sinodis
Robert O. Dyer	James L. Csontos
Jack R. Cunningham	Robert J. Berens
Jay M. Mann	Jeff R. Wilhelm
Carolyn M. Kaluzniacki	Edward Rubacha
Dean Kim Lough	Larry J. Crown

Christopher C. Wooten

ASSOCIATES

Paul D. Kramer (Resident, Irvine, California Office)	Laurence R. Sharlot
	Lori A. Metcalf
Paul S. Ruderman	Stacey A. Dowdell

Neal H. Bookspan

OF COUNSEL

James W. Washington (Not admitted in AZ)

For full biographical listings, see the Martindale-Hubbell Law Directory

JENNINGS, STROUSS AND SALMON, P.L.C. (AV)

A Professional Limited Liability Company
One Renaissance Square, Two North Central, 85004-2393
Telephone: 602-262-5911
Fax: 602-253-3255

Gary G. Keltner	Michael R. Palumbo
T. Patrick Flood	David W. Kash
W. Michael Flood	Glenn J. Carter
Gary L. Stuart	H. Christian Bode
Douglas G. Zimmerman	James M. Ackerman
Gerald W. Alston	Ernest Calderon
John G. Sestak, Jr.	Jon D. Schneider
Kenneth C. Sundlof, Jr.	Wendy D. Woodrow
Rita A. Meiser	Brian N. Spector
Gary L. Lassen	Michael J. O'Connor
Richard N. Morrison	Katherine M. Cooper
Barry E. Lewin	John J. Egbert
Jay A. Fradkin	Charles D. Onofry

Robert D. Haws

Michael J. Farrell	David B. Earl
Jennifer M. Bligh	Lisa A. Frey
Kim D. Steinmetz	Gordon Lewis
Cody M. Hall	Stephanie McRae

For Complete List of Firm Personnel, See General Section

For full biographical listings, see the Martindale-Hubbell Law Directory

KIMERER & LAVELLE, P.L.C. (AV)

100 W. Clarendon Suite 2100, 85013
Telephone: 602-279-5900; 800-220-6817
FAX: 602-264-5566
Email: kimlav@msn.com

Michael J. LaVelle   Merrick B. Firestone

Representative Clients: The National Basketball Association; Aetna Insurance Co.; Kaibab Industries; Centric Jones Constructors; B & B Masonry; Western Block.

For full biographical listings, see the Martindale-Hubbell Law Directory

LEWIS AND ROCA, LLP (AV)

A Limited Liability Partnership including a Professional Corporation
40 North Central Avenue, 85004-4429
Telephone: 602-262-5311
Fax: 602-262-5747
Email: mlp@lrlaw.com
Tucson, Arizona Office: One South Church Avenue, Suite 700, 86701-1620.
Telephone: 520-622-2090.
Fax: 520-622-3088. E-Mail: mlp@lrlaw.com.

MEMBERS OF FIRM

John P. Frank	Joseph E. McGarry
Peter D. Baird	Douglas L. Irish
Merton E. Marks (P.C.)	Tom Galbraith
Marty Harper	R. Kent Klein
Richard S. Cohen	Barry Fish
Judith E. Sirkis	Patricia K. Norris
José A. Cárdenas	Dale A. Danneman
Foster Robberson	Thomas H. Campbell

(See Next Column)

MEMBERS OF FIRM (Continued)

Michael J. Holden	David J. Cantelme
Newman R. Porter	Sheila Carmody
George L. Paul	Thomas G. Ryan
Betfy L. Hum	Stephen M. Bressler
Thomas Klinkel	Barbara J. Muller
Allen R. Clarke	Jesse B. Simpson
James K. Kloss	Robert F. Roos
Mary Ellen Simonson	James T. Acuff, Jr.
Steven J. Hulsman	Carl F. Mariano
Christopher J. Brelje	Robert H. McKirgan
Steven J. Burr	Pamela B. Petersen
L. Keith Beauchamp	Jane E. Reddin
Kim C. Stanger	Greg S. Como
Richard A. Halloran	Deanna Salazar

ASSOCIATES

Barbara Anstey Hoerner	Stephen R. Winkelman
R. Neil Taylor, III	Margaret R. Russell
Dawn M. Bergin	Jeff A. Shumway
Janell M. Adams-Vogl	Todd A. Rigby

Randy Papetti

OF COUNSEL

Jeremy E. Butler	James L. Hohnbaum
	Deborah A. Nye

Representative Clients: Blood Systems, Inc.; Bristol-Myers Squibb Co.; Del Webb Corp.; The Dial Corp; E.I. du Pont de Nemours and Co.; MCI Communications Corp.; The Prudential Insurance Company of America; Southwest Risk Services; Target Stores; Zurich Insurance Co.

For Complete List of Firm Personnel, See General Section

For full biographical listings, see the Martindale-Hubbell Law Directory

LINZER & DITSCH, P.C. (AV)

3242 North Sixteenth Street, 85016
Telephone: 602-956-2525
Fax: 602-241-9885

Stephen P. Linzer   Brian E. Ditsch

For full biographical listings, see the Martindale-Hubbell Law Directory

MEYERS LAW FIRM (AV)

Suite 900, 2398 East Camelback Road, 85016
Telephone: 602-468-8900
Telecopier: 602-468-8910

Donald D. Meyers

Charles W. Lotzar	James F. Wees
Donald L. Meyers	Jason A. Donkersley

Reference: Bank of America, Arizona.

For full biographical listings, see the Martindale-Hubbell Law Directory

MITTEN, GOODWIN & RAUP, A PROFESSIONAL CORPORATION (AV)

One Columbus Plaza, 3636 North Central, Suite 1200, 85012
Telephone: 602-650-2000
Fax: 602-264-7033
Email: mgr@starlink.com

Roger C. Mitten	Edward R. Glady, Jr.
Brian M. Goodwin	Stephen C. Yost
Calvin L. Raup	Martin P. Clare

Scott J. Hergenroether

Steven P. Kramer	Gary Beren
Sharon Elizabeth Ravenscroft	Jeffrey J. Campbell
Jeffery S. Slater	Lori V. Berke

For full biographical listings, see the Martindale-Hubbell Law Directory

MUCHMORE & WALLWORK, A PROFESSIONAL CORPORATION (AV)

2700 North Central Avenue, Suite 1225, 85004-1165
Telephone: 602-240-6699
Data: 602-240-6698
Facsimile: 602-240-6697
Email: muchwork@mmww.com *URL:* http://www.mmww.com

Charles J. Muchmore   Nicholas J. Wallwork

COUNSEL

Margaret M. Dean	Fredric D. Bellamy
	Kathy E. Shimpock

Bridget S. Bade (Senior Associate)	Carolina L. Carver
	Margaret Benny Hurst

(See Next Column)

MUCHMORE & WALLWORK A PROFESSIONAL CORPORATION—*Continued*
LEGAL SUPPORT PERSONNEL

Gloria A. Torres (Administrator
and Senior Paralegal)
John A. Bennett
(Litigation Support Manager)

Gale James (Finance Manager
and Paralegal)

Representative Clients: AgrEvo USA Company; BHP Copper Inc.; City of Scottsdale; Cyprus Amax Minerals Company; General Electric Co.; Homes by Dave Brown, Inc.; National Indemnity Insurance Company; Standard Insurance Company; Washington Mills Electro Minerals Company.
Reference: M & I Thunderbird Bank.

For full biographical listings, see the Martindale-Hubbell Law Directory

---

O'CONNOR, CAVANAGH, ANDERSON, KILLINGSWORTH & BESHEARS, A PROFESSIONAL ASSOCIATION (AV)

One East Camelback Road, Suite 1100, 85012-1656
Telephone: 602-263-2400
FAX: 602-263-2900
Email: firminfo@arizlaw.com
Sun City, Arizona Office: 13250 North Del Webb Boulevard, Suite B, 85351.
Telephone: 602-263-2808.
FAX: 602-933-3100.
Tucson, Arizona Office: O'Connor Cavanagh Molloy Jones, 33 N. Stone, Suite 2100, 85701, P.O. Box 2268, 85702.
Telephone: 520-622-3531.
FAX: 520-624-2816.
Nogales, Arizona Office: 1891 North Mastick Way, 85621.
Telephone: 520-761-4215.
FAX: 520-761-3505.

Harry J. Cavanagh	Carol N. Cure
Robert G. Beshears	Scott A. Salmon
Ralph E. Hunsaker	David L. Kurtz
George H. Mitchell	Stephen E. Richman
Richard J. Woods	David A. Van Engelhoven
Jeffrey B. Smith	Paul J. Giancola
Jolyon Grant	Pamela M. Overton
Harding B. Cure	Frank M. Fox
Steven D. Smith	Christina S. Hamilton
Henry L. Timmerman	Lisa M. Sommer
Philip C. Gerard	Lucas J. Narducci

Robert L. Ehmann	Timothy F. Bolden
R. Corey Hill	Mark J. DePasquale
Troy B. Froderman	

Ashley D. Adams	Mark D. Dillon
Carla A. Wortley	Frank W. Moskowitz
Carl O. Wortley, III	Steven J. German
Eric A. Mark	

Representative Clients: Coldwell Banker Real Estate; Karsten Manufacturing Co.; The Dial Corp; M&I Thunderbird Bank; State Farm Mutual Automobile Insurance Co.; The Hartford.

For Complete List of Firm Personnel, See General Section

For full biographical listings, see the Martindale-Hubbell Law Directory

---

PERRY, PIERSON & SILVER, P.L.C. (AV)

2901 North Central Avenue Suite 300, 85012
Telephone: 602-285-5165
Facsimile: 602-285-5100

Allan R. Perry	Timothy L. Pierson
Leon B. Silver	

For full biographical listings, see the Martindale-Hubbell Law Directory

---

QUARLES & BRADY (AV)

One Camelback Building, One East Camelback Road, Suite 400, 85012-1649
Telephone: 602-230-5500
Fax: 602-230-5598
Milwaukee, Wisconsin Office: 411 East Wisconsin Avenue.
Telephone: 414-277-5000.
Fax: 414-271-3552.
Madison, Wisconsin Office: First Wisconsin Plaza, One South Pinckney Street, P.O. Box 2113.
Telephone: 608-251-5000.
Fax: 608-251-9166.
West Palm Beach, Florida Office: 222 Lakeview Ave., 4th Floor.
Telephone: 407-653-5000.
Fax: 407-653-5333.
Naples, Florida Office: Barnett Center, 4501 Tamiami Trail North, Suite 300.
Telephone: 813-262-5959.
Fax: 813-434-4999.

(See Next Column)

MEMBERS OF THE FIRM

Charles W. Herf	William M. Shattuck
Daniel L. Muchow	

ASSOCIATES

Benjamin R. Norris	Jose L. Martinez
Colleen A. Scherkenbach	Amy O'Melia-Endres

For Complete List of Firm Personnel, See General Section

For full biographical listings, see the Martindale-Hubbell Law Directory

---

RENAUD, COOK & DRURY, P.A. (AV)

617 North 2nd Avenue, 85003
Telephone: 602-253-5101
Fax: 602-254-1448
Email: rcdlaw@rcdlaw.com
Scottsdale, Arizona Office: 6991 East Camelback Road, #D-103, 85251.
Telephone: 602-874-9000.
Fax: 602-874-9866.

J. Gordon Cook	Steven G. Mesaros
William W. Drury, Jr.	Mark W. Roth
James L. Blair	Charles A. Struble

W. Lloyd Benner	Cynthia L. Fulton
Diana L. Clarke	Charles S. Hover, III
Richard N. Crenshaw	Diane Mihalsky
Tamara D. Nydell	

For full biographical listings, see the Martindale-Hubbell Law Directory

---

RIDENOUR, SWENSON, CLEERE & EVANS, P.C. (AV)

40 North Central Avenue, Suite 1400, 85004
Telephone: 602-254-2143
Fax: 602-254-8670

Harold H. Swenson	John W. Storer, III
James W. Evans	Tamalyn E. Lewis
Robert R. Beltz	Joseph A. Kendhammer
Lloyd J. Andrews	Peter S. Spaw
Michael J. Frazelle	Alan R. Costello
Timothy H. Barnes	

OF COUNSEL
Ronald A. Schlosser

David M. Reaves	Gregory P. Gillis
Jeffrey A. Bernick	Roger W. Riviere
Scott A. Holden	Lee P. Blake

Representative Clients: State Farm Insurance Co.; Travelers Insurance Co.; Allstate Insurance Co.; TIG Insurance Co.; St. Paul Fire & Marine Insurance Co.; Grain Dealers Mutual Insurance Co.; Omaha Property and Casualty Insurance Co.; Vesta Insurance Group; Performance Claims Service; Progressive Insurance Cos.

For full biographical listings, see the Martindale-Hubbell Law Directory

---

ROBBINS & GREEN, A PROFESSIONAL ASSOCIATION (AV)

1800 Norwest Tower, 3300 North Central Avenue, 85012-9826
Telephone: 602-248-7600
Fax: 602-266-5369

Philip A. Robbins	Janet B. Hutchison
Richard W. Abbuhl	Ronald G. Wilson
Wayne A. Smith	Bradley J. Stevens
Edmund F. Richardson	Dwayne Ross
William H. Sandweg III	Alfred W. Ricciardi
Jack N. Rudel	Sarah McGiffert
Jeffrey P. Boshes	Peter W. Sorensen
Brian Imbornoni	Daniel L. Brown
Robert D. Peak	

For full biographical listings, see the Martindale-Hubbell Law Directory

---

SNELL & WILMER, L.L.P. (AV)

One Arizona Center, 85004-0001
Telephone: 602-382-6000
Fax: 602-382-6070
Tucson, Arizona Office: 1500 Norwest Tower, One South Church Avenue 85701-1612.
Telephone: 520-882-1200.
Fax: 520-884-1294.
Orange County Office: 1920 Main Street, Suite 1200, P.O. Box 57062, Irvine, California, 92619-7062.
Telephone: 714-253-2700.
Fax: 714-955-2507.
Salt Lake City, Utah Office: Broadway Centre, 111 East Broadway, Suite 900, 84111-1004.
Telephone: 801-237-1900.
Fax: 801-237-1950.

(See Next Column)

SNELL & WILMER L.L.P., Phoenix—Continued

MEMBERS OF FIRM

John J. Bouma	Warren E. Platt
George H. Lyons	Peter J. Rathwell
Daniel J. McAuliffe	Donald D. Colburn
Douglas W. Seitz	Robert B. Hoffman
Barry D. Halpern	Joel P. Hoxie
James R. Condo	Lonnie J. Williams, Jr.
Vaughn A. Crawford	Arthur P. Greenfield
Suzanne McCann	Donald L. Gaffney
Arthur T. Anderson	Patrick E. Hoog
Richard W. Shapiro	Timothy G. O'Neill
Heidi L. McNeil	Martha E. Gibbs
Katherine M. Harmeyer	James J. Sienicki
E. Jeffrey Walsh	George J. Coleman, III
Janet E. Barton	Kevin J. Parker
Donald H. Smith	Peter M. Wittekind
Steven S. Guy	Christopher H. Bayley
Robert R. Kinas	Charles P. Keller
Thea Foglietta Silverstein	Patrick X. Fowler
Barbara J. Dawson	Brian J. Foster
Bob J. McCullough	Patrick G. Byrne
Prithviraj S. Sivananthan	Patricia Lee Refo

SENIOR ATTORNEYS

Bruce P. White	Lisa M. Coulter

ASSOCIATES

Brian J. Campbell	Timothy J. Casey
Jeffrey Webb Crockett	Joseph C. Kreamer
Eugene F. O'Connor II	GinaMarie Rossano
Scott D. Sherman	

Representative Clients: Arizona Public Service Company; Cigna Healthplan of Arizona; Del Webb Corporation; Emerson Electric Co.; Ford Motor Co.; Honeywell; Mardian Construction; McCarthy Western; Price-Waterhouse; Bank One, Arizona, NA.

For Complete List of Firm Personnel, See General Section

For full biographical listings, see the Martindale-Hubbell Law Directory

STEPTOE & JOHNSON LLP (AV)

Two Renaissance Square, 40 N. Central, Suite 2400, 85004
Telephone: 602-257-5200
Telecopier: 602-257-5299
Washington, D.C. Office: 1330 Connecticut Avenue, N.W.
Telephone: 202-429-3000.
Cable Address: "Stepjohn".
Telex: 89-2503.
Telecopier: 202-429-9204.
Moscow, Russia Office: Steptoe & Johnson International Affiliate in Moscow. 25 Tsvetnoy Boulevard, Building 3 Moscow Russia.
Telephone: 011-7-501-258-5250.
Fax: 011-7-501-258-5251.
Almaty, Kazakhstan Office: Steptoe & Johnson Company Almaty, 84 Gogol Street, Suite 213, 480083.
Telephones: (3272) 50-11-25, (3272) 32-25-39.

PARTNERS

Lawrence A. Katz	David J. Bodney
Francis J. Burke, Jr.	Floyd P. Bienstock
Barry J. Dale	David A. Selden

For Complete List of Firm Personnel, See General Section

For full biographical listings, see the Martindale-Hubbell Law Directory

LAW OFFICES OF RICHARD L. STROHM, P.C. (AV)

1136 East Campbell, 85014
Telephone: 602-279-6316
Mobile: 602-616-7094
Facsimile: 602-279-7102
Email: 102442.1444@compuserve.com

Richard L. Strohm

OF COUNSEL

Brad K. Keogh	Nedra J. Bates

LEGAL SUPPORT PERSONNEL

Mindy L. Raymond (Legal Assistant)	Barbara A. Shore (Nurse Paralegal)
Richard M. Knaeble (Licensed Private Investigator)	

For full biographical listings, see the Martindale-Hubbell Law Directory

TURLEY & SWAN, P.C. (AV)

The Brookstone Office Complex, 2025 North Third Street, Suite 350, 85004-1471
Telephone: 602-254-1444
Fax: 602-229-1936

(See Next Column)

Albert R. Vermeire (1947-1988)	Christopher J. Bork
Kent E. Turley	Christopher M. O'Donnell
Joseph B. Swan, Jr.	Elizabeth Savoini Fitch
Thomas J. Howard	

For full biographical listings, see the Martindale-Hubbell Law Directory

WILENCHIK & BARTNESS, A PROFESSIONAL CORPORATION (AV)

2828 North Central Avenue, Thirteenth Floor, 85004
Telephone: 602-274-2828
Facsimile: 602-274-2822

Dennis I. Wilenchik	George H. Foster, Jr.
Becky Ann Bartness	Charles A. Grube
Craig T. Irish	Linda DuMars Bach
Ann A. Scott Timmer	

David N. Farren

OF COUNSEL

Allen D. Harnisch

Representative Clients: Alexander & Alexander, Inc.; The Chase Manhattan Bank, N.A.; Founders Bank of Arizona; Republic National Bank of Arizona; Richmond American Homes; Saddleback Homes; Geoffrey Edmunds & Associates; Home Depot U.S.A.; Scottsdale Racquet Club; International Surfacing, Inc.

For full biographical listings, see the Martindale-Hubbell Law Directory

PRESCOTT,* Yavapai Co.

FAVOUR, MOORE & WILHELMSEN, A PROFESSIONAL ASSOCIATION (AV)

1580 Plaza West Drive, P.O. Box 1391, 86302
Telephone: 520-445-2444
Fax: 520-771-0450

John M. Favour	Mark M. Moore
David K. Wilhelmsen	

Representative Clients: Yavapai Regional Medical Center; Yavapai Title Co.; Father Wasson's Orphans; Hidden Valley Ranch; Bank of America; Employers Mutual Co.; Lawyers Title Insurance Co.; Farmers Insurance Group; Inter-Cal Corp.; Arroyo Seco Development.

For full biographical listings, see the Martindale-Hubbell Law Directory

MURPHY, LUTEY, SCHMITT & BECK (AV)

Elks Building, 117 East Gurley Street, 86301
Telephone: 520-445-6860
Fax: 520-445-6488
Yuma, Arizona Office: Valley Professional Plaza, 1763 West Twenty-Fourth Street, Suite 200.
Telephone: 520-726-0314.
Fax: 520-341-1079.
Kingman, Arizona Office: 2601 Stockton Hill Road, Suite H8.
Telephone: 520-718-0888; 1-800-281-0822.

MEMBERS OF FIRM

Thelton D. Beck	Selmer D. Lutey
Michael R. Murphy	Robert E. Schmitt

ASSOCIATES

Dan A. Wilson	Bruce E. Rosenberg

OF COUNSEL

Keith F. Quail

Counsel for: State Farm Mutual Automobile Insurance Co.; Allstate Insurance Co.; Farmers Insurance; Western Agricultural Insurance Co.
Local Counsel for: Bank One Arizona, NA; The Stockmen's Bank.
Representative Clients: Prescott College; Galpin Ford, Inc.; Sedona-Oak Creek Airport Authority; Yavapai County Fair Association (Prescott Downs).

For full biographical listings, see the Martindale-Hubbell Law Directory

SCOTTSDALE, Maricopa Co.

PESKIND HYMSON & GOLDSTEIN, P.C. (AV)

14595 North Scottsdale Road, Suite 14, 85254
Telephone: 602-991-9077
Fax: 602-443-8854

E. J. Peskind	Marilee Miller Clarke
David B. Goldstein	Jeffrey A. Leyton

For full biographical listings, see the Martindale-Hubbell Law Directory

TUCSON,* Pima Co.

CHANDLER, TULLAR, UDALL & REDHAIR (AV)

1700 Bank of America Plaza, 33 North Stone Avenue, 85701
Telephone: 520-623-4353
Telefax: 520-792-3426

(See Next Column)

CHANDLER, TULLAR, UDALL & REDHAIR—*Continued*

MEMBERS OF FIRM

Thomas Chandler	Dwight M. Whitley, Jr.
D. B. Udall	E. Hardy Smith
Jack Redhair	John J. Brady
Joe F. Tarver, Jr.	Christopher J. Smith
Steven Weatherspoon	Charles V. Harrington
Edwin M. Gaines, Jr.	Bruce G. MacDonald

Christopher C. Browning

ASSOCIATES

Joel T. Ireland	Kurt Kroese
Mark Fredenberg	Sean C. Chapman
Mariann T. Shinoskie	Anne M. Fulton

Representative Clients: Arizona Electric Power Cooperative, Inc.; Atlantic & Richfield Co.; Northwestern Mutual Life Insurance Co.; Rex Broadcasting Co.; Citizen Auto Stage Company; Grayline Tours.

For full biographical listings, see the Martindale-Hubbell Law Directory

---

DUFFIELD, MILLER, YOUNG, ADAMSON & ALFRED, P.C. (AV)

Suite 711, Transamerica Building, 177 North Church Avenue, 85701
Telephone: 520-792-1181
FAX: 520-792-2859
Green Valley, Arizona Office: 101-65 South La Canada, Green Valley Mall.
Telephone: 520-625-4404.
Fax: 520-625-4453.
La Paloma Office: La Paloma Corporate Center, 3573 East Sunrise Drive, Suite 115, Tucson, Arizona.
Telephone: 520-577-1135.
Fax: 520-577-1079.

Philip Hawley Smith	Thomas R. Althaus
Arthur H. Miller (1935-1995)	Richard Duffield
Larry R. Adamson	Eugene C. Gieseler
Samuel D. Alfred	K. Alexander Hobson

Michael C. Young

LEGAL SUPPORT PERSONNEL

Cynthia Sargent Althaus	Joan Shelton, CLA
Mary Jane Arnesen	Christine M. Smith
Katrina Hillman	Barbara L. Steimle
Elizabeth Kohl-Sturgeon	Elaine Webb

Representative Clients: San Xavier Rock & Materials; Community Water Company of Green Valley.
Insurance Company Clientele: State Farm Mutual Insurance Cos.; Automobile Club Insurance Co.; Colonial Penn Insurance Co.; Metropolitan Property & Liability Insurance Co.; National Indemnity Ins. Co.

For full biographical listings, see the Martindale-Hubbell Law Directory

---

GABROY, ROLLMAN & BOSSÉ, P.C. (AV)

Suite 201, 2195 East River Road, 85718
Telephone: 520-577-1300
Telefax: 520-577-0717

Richard M. Rollman	Ronald M. Lehman
John Gabroy	Lyle D. Aldridge

Ronna L. Fickbohm

Richard A. Brown

For Complete List of Firm Personnel, See General Section

For full biographical listings, see the Martindale-Hubbell Law Directory

---

GOERING, ROBERTS, BERKMAN, RUBIN & BROGNA, P.C. (AV)

Suite 302, 1840 East River Road, 85718
Telephone: 520-577-9300
Fax: 520-577-0848

Scott Goering	David L. Berkman
Howard T. Roberts, Jr.	William L. Rubin

Carmine A. Brogna

Christopher L. Enos

Representative Clients: Fireman's Fund Insurance; Safeco Insurance; Royal Insurance; Sentry Insurance; American International Group; Farmers Insurance Co.; USAA; Country Companies; Cigna.
Reference: Bank One.

For full biographical listings, see the Martindale-Hubbell Law Directory

---

HARALSON, KINERK & MOREY (AV)

82 South Stone Avenue, 85701
Telephone: 520-792-4330
Fax: 520-623-9568

Burton J. Kinerk

Reference: The National Bank of Arizona.

For full biographical listings, see the Martindale-Hubbell Law Directory

---

KIMBLE, GOTHREAU & NELSON, P.C. (AV)

5285 East Williams Circle, Suite 3500, 85711-7411
Telephone: 520-748-2440
Fax: 520-748-2469

Michael J. Gothreau (1943-1990)	David F. Toone
Darwin J. Nelson	Michelle T. Lopez
Daryl A. Audilett	Negatu Molla
Lawrence McDonough	Michael E. Medina

Andrew J. Petersen

OF COUNSEL

William Kimble

Representative Clients: State of Arizona; General Motors Corp.; Procter & Gamble Co.; St. Paul Fire and Marine Insurance Co.; City of Tucson; Tucson Electric Power Co.; United States Fidelity & Guaranty Co.; Coriegis Co.; Allstate Insurance Co.

For full biographical listings, see the Martindale-Hubbell Law Directory

---

LEONARD FELKER ALTFELD & BATTAILE, P.C. (AV)

250 North Meyer Avenue, P.O. Box 191, 85702-0191
Telephone: 520-622-7733
Fax: 520-622-7967

David J. Leonard	Judith B. Leonard
Sidney L. Felker	Donna M. Aversa
Clifford B. Altfeld	Lynne M. Schwartz
John F. Battaile III	Edward O. Comitz

Russell E. Krone

For full biographical listings, see the Martindale-Hubbell Law Directory

---

MILLER, PITT & MCANALLY, P.C. (AV)

111 South Church Avenue, 85701-1680
Telephone: 520-792-3836
Telecopier: 520-624-5080
Nogales, Arizona Office: 272 West View Point, 85621.
Telephone: 520-281-1361.
Correspondent Office: Lizarraga, Robles, Savinon & Tapia, S.C. Boulevard Hidalgo 64, Colonia Centenario. CP 83000 Hermosillo, Sonora, Mexico.
Telephone: (62) 17-27-28, 12-79-89, 13-47-10, 12-79-18, 13-33-25, 12-77-70.

Barry N. Akin (1939-1988)	Grace McIlvain
G. Eugene Isaak	Thomas G. Cotter
Gerald Maltz	Lindsay E. Brew
Janice A. Wezelman	Armando Rivera
Philip J. Hall	Gus Aragón, Jr.

Carole A. Summers

OF COUNSEL

Richard L. McAnally

Representative Clients: Bell Atlantic Metro Mobile; Evergreen International Aviation; Farmers Investment Co.; Forest City Enterprises; Vince Granatelli Racing; KVOA Channel 4 TV; Newmont Mining Corp.; S.L. Industries, Inc.; Tucson Unified School District; University of Arizona Foundation.

For Complete List of Firm Personnel, See General Section

For full biographical listings, see the Martindale-Hubbell Law Directory

---

O'CONNOR CAVANAGH MOLLOY JONES, A PROFESSIONAL ASSOCIATION (AV)

Suite 2100 33 N. Stone, P.O. Box 2268, 85702
Telephone: 520-622-3531
FAX: 520-624-2816
Email: firminfo@arizlaw.com
Phoenix, Arizona Office: O'Connor, Cavanagh, Anderson, Killingsworth & Beshears, One East Camelback Road, Suite 1100, 85012.
Telephone: 602-263-2400.
FAX: 602-263-2900.
Sun City, Arizona Office: O'Connor, Cavanagh, Anderson, Killingsworth & Beshears, 13250 North Del Webb Boulevard, Suite B, 85351.
Telephone: 602-263-2808.
FAX: 602-933-3100.
Nogales, Arizona Office: O'Connor, Cavanagh, Anderson, Killingsworth & Beshears, 1891 North Mastick Way, 85621.
Telephone: 520-761-4215.
FAX: 520-761-3505.

Peter Akmajian	Drue A. Morgan-Birch

Amy M. Samberg	James D. Campbell

Representative Clients: Three-Five Systems; Main Street & Main; ITT Cannon; Bank of America; The Dial Corp; The Hartford; Dow Corning Corp.; Charles Schwab & Co., Inc.

For Complete List of Firm Personnel, See General Section

For full biographical listings, see the Martindale-Hubbell Law Directory

Tucson—Continued

RABINOVITZ & ASSOCIATES, P.C. (AV)

721 North 4th Avenue, P.O. Box 41600, 85717
Telephone: 520-624-5526
Toll Free: 1-800-365-0821
Fax: 520-622-3776

Bernard I. Rabinovitz

John D. Ellis
OF COUNSEL
Clark J. Sloan (Not admitted in AZ)
LEGAL SUPPORT PERSONNEL
Michael Nelson (Paralegal)   Lisa Busciglio (Paralegal)
Ruth Polizz

Representative Client: Firemans Fund Insurance Co.

For full biographical listings, see the Martindale-Hubbell Law Directory

RAVEN, KIRSCHNER & NORELL, P.C. (AV)

Suite 1600, One South Church Avenue, 85701-1612
Telephone: 520-628-8700
Telefax: 520-798-5200

Donald T. Awerkamp	L. Anthony Fines
Dennis J. Clancy	Barry Kirschner
	Lane D. Oden

Representative Clients: Continental Medical Systems, Inc.; El Paso Natural Gas Co.; Norwest Bank Arizona; El Rio-Santa Cruz Neighborhood Health Center, Inc.; Resolution Trust Corp.; Sierra Vista Community Hospital; Southern Arizona Rehabilitation Hospital; Northern Cochise Community Hospital.

For Complete List of Firm Personnel, See General Section

For full biographical listings, see the Martindale-Hubbell Law Directory

SHULTZ & ROLLINS, LTD. (AV)

St. Philip's Plaza, 4280 North Campbell Avenue, Suite 214, 85718-6580
Telephone: 520-577-7777

Silas H. Shultz   Michael F. Rollins

Dora Fitzpatrick

For full biographical listings, see the Martindale-Hubbell Law Directory

STOMPOLY, STROUD, GIDDINGS & GLICKSMAN, P.C. (AV)

1820 Citibank Tower, One South Church Avenue, 85702
Telephone: 520-628-8300
Telefax: 520-628-9948
Mailing Address: P.O. Box 190, Tucson, AZ, 85702-0190

John G. Stompoly	Charles E. Giddings
James L. Stroud	Elliot A. Glicksman
	George Erickson

For full biographical listings, see the Martindale-Hubbell Law Directory

WILLIAM G. WALKER, P.C. (AV)

145 South Sixth Avenue, 85701
Telephone: 520-622-3330
Fax: 520-622-0521

William G. Walker

For full biographical listings, see the Martindale-Hubbell Law Directory

*YUMA,** Yuma Co.

ROBERT M. COOK (AV)

201 West Second Street, 85364
Telephone: 520-539-0959
Fax: 520-539-0960
1-800 ROBERT M

For full biographical listings, see the Martindale-Hubbell Law Directory

THE BRIAN E. SMITH LAW FIRM (AV)

The Brian Smith Building, 301 South 2nd Avenue, 85364
Telephone: 520-783-8811

Brian E. Smith	Frank A. Fila
William J. Kerekes	Thomas W. Anderson

LEGAL SUPPORT PERSONNEL
Bridget M. Hughes
Reference: Bank of America.

For full biographical listings, see the Martindale-Hubbell Law Directory

ARKANSAS

*BENTON,** Saline Co.

ELLIS LAW FIRM (AV)

126 North Main Street, P.O. Box 1259, 72015
Telephone: 501-776-3916; Little Rock: 375-5210
Fax: 501-776-2278
Email: ellislaw@aol.com
Email: 76403.507@compuserve.com
MEMBER OF FIRM
George D. Ellis
LEGAL SUPPORT PERSONNEL
Rhonda Beck Malone (Paralegal)
References: The Union Bank of Benton; Benton State Bank.

For full biographical listings, see the Martindale-Hubbell Law Directory

*CAMDEN,** Ouachita Co.

ALLEN P. ROBERTS, P.A. (AV)

119 Van Buren Street, NW, P.O. Box 280, 71701
Telephone: 501-836-5310
FAX: 501-836-9662

Allen P. Roberts

Representative Clients: International Paper Co.; Camden Fairview School District; The City of Camden; Byars Oil Co.; American Fuel Cell & Coated Fabrics Co.; Star City School District; Highland Resources, Inc.; Circle B Logging Co.; First National Bank, Magnolia, Arkansas.

For full biographical listings, see the Martindale-Hubbell Law Directory

*FAYETTEVILLE,** Washington Co.

BASSETT LAW FIRM (AV)

221 North College Avenue, P.O. Box 3618, 72702-3618
Telephone: 501-521-9996
Fax: 501-521-9600

MEMBERS OF FIRM

Woodson W. Bassett, Jr.	Angela M. Doss
Woodson W. Bassett, III	Gary V. Weeks
Tod C. Bassett	J. David Wall
Wm. Robert Still, Jr.	Shawn David Twing
Walker Dale Garrett	Vincent O. Chadick
Curtis L. Nebben	Michael W. Langley
Earl Buddy Chadick, Jr.	James M. Graves
	Patricia A. Hines

Representative Clients: The Home Insurance Co.; Hartford Insurance Group; Tyson Foods, Inc.; CIGNA; Scottsdale Insurance Co.; St. Paul Fire and Marine Insurance Co.; AIG Aviation Ins. Co.; WAUSAU; USAA.

For full biographical listings, see the Martindale-Hubbell Law Directory

DAVIS, COX & WRIGHT, PLC (AV)

19 East Mountain Street, P.O. Drawer 1688, 72702-1688
Telephone: 501-521-7600
Fax: 501-521-7661

Sidney P. Davis, Jr.	William Jackson Butt, II
Walter B. Cox	Kelly P. Carithers
Tilden P. Wright, III	Tim E. Howell
Constance G. Clark	Don A. Taylor
	Paul H. Taylor

John G. Trice	Mark W. Dossett
Laura J. Andress	David L. McCune

Representative Clients: Arkansas Farm Bureau Insurance Cos.; Fireman's Fund Insurance Group; United States Fidelity and Guaranty Co.; St. Paul Insurance Cos; Chrysler Motors Corp.; Kemper Insurance Group; Kawasaki Motors Corp.; CIGNA.

For full biographical listings, see the Martindale-Hubbell Law Directory

NIBLOCK LAW FIRM (AV)

20 East Mountain Street, P.O. Drawer 818, 72701
Telephone: 501-521-5510
1-800-446-3314 Toll Free (Ark. only)
Fax: 501-444-7608

MEMBERS OF FIRM
Walter R. Niblock   George H. Niblock
Raymond L. Niblock

For full biographical listings, see the Martindale-Hubbell Law Directory

Fayetteville—Continued

ODOM, ELLIOTT, WINBURN, WATSON, SMITH & ODOM (AV)

No. 1 East Mountain Street, P.O. Drawer 1868, 72702
Telephone: 501-442-7575
FAX: 501-442-9008

MEMBERS OF FIRM

Bobby Lee Odom   Jason L. Watson
Don R. Elliott, Jr.   J. Timothy Smith
Russell B. Winburn   Conrad T. Odom

Timothy J. Myers

Reference: Bank of Fayetteville, Fayetteville, Arkansas.

For full biographical listings, see the Martindale-Hubbell Law Directory

FORREST CITY,* St. Francis Co.

BUTLER, HICKY & LONG (AV)

2216 North Washington Street, P.O. Box 989, 72335
Telephone: 501-633-4611
FAX: 501-633-6848

MEMBERS OF FIRM

Philip Hicky   Fletcher Long, Jr.

ASSOCIATES

Gary J. Mitchusson   Rita Reed Harris

Representative Clients: First National Bank of Eastern Arkansas; Southern Farm Bureau Insurance Cos.; United States Aviation Underwriters Group; National Aviation Underwriters; Hartford Accident and Indemnity Co.; Peoples Implement Co.

For full biographical listings, see the Martindale-Hubbell Law Directory

FORT SMITH,* Sebastian Co.

BETHELL, CALLAWAY, ROBERTSON, BEASLEY & COWAN (AV)

615 North "B" Street, P.O. Box 23, 72902
Telephone: 501-782-7911
Fax: 501-782-7964
Waldron, Arkansas Office: 80 West Second Street, 72958.
Telephone: 501-637-1197.
Fax: 501-782-7964.

MEMBERS OF FIRM

Donald P. Callaway (1935-1984)   John R. Beasley
Thomas E. Robertson, Jr.   Kenneth W. Cowan
J. Michael Fitzhugh

ASSOCIATE

Matthew J. Ketcham

OF COUNSEL

Edgar E. Bethell

Representative Clients: The Aetna Casualty & Surety Co.; James River - Dixie Cup; Arkansas-Oklahoma Gas Corp.; Beverage Products Corp. (Pepsi-Cola); The Prudential Insurance Company of America; Sentry - Dairyland Insurance Co; General Tire and Rubber; Quanex Corp.; The Fort Smith Municipal Airport Commission; Southern Steel & Wire Co.

For full biographical listings, see the Martindale-Hubbell Law Directory

DAILY, WEST, CORE, COFFMAN & CANFIELD (AV)

Stephens Office Building, 623 Garrison Avenue, P.O. Box 1446, 72902
Telephone: 501-782-0361
Fax: 501-782-6160

MEMBERS OF FIRM

Ben Core   Wyman R. Wade, Jr.
Eldon F. Coffman   Stanley A. Leasure
Jerry L. Canfield   Douglas M. Carson
Thomas A. Daily   Robert W. Bishop

OF COUNSEL

James E. West

Counsel for: Claims Management, Inc. (Wal-Mart); Arkla, Inc.; City of Fort Smith; Commercial Union Insurance Cos.; Pennzoil Exploration and Production Co.; Silvey Cos., Inc.; Metropolitan Life Insurance Co.; Chevron U.S.A., Inc.

For full biographical listings, see the Martindale-Hubbell Law Directory

JONES, JACKSON & MOLL, PLC (AV)

401 North Seventh Street, P.O. Box 2023, 72902
Telephone: 501-782-7203
Fax: 501-782-9460
Email: jjmlaw@aol.com

MEMBERS OF FIRM

Robert L. Jones, Jr.   Kendall B. Jones
Randolph C. Jackson   Mark A. Moll
J. Scott Hardin

(See Next Column)

Insurance Counsel for: Farmers Insurance Group; State Farm Insurance Cos.; Maryland Insurance Cos.; Shelter Insurance Cos.; Travelers Insurance Co.; CNA Insurance Co.; Automobile Club Insurance Cos.
Counsel for: Merchants National Bank, Fort Smith, Arkansas; Beverly Enterprises, Inc.; Austin Powder Co.

For full biographical listings, see the Martindale-Hubbell Law Directory

WARNER, SMITH & HARRIS, PLC (AV)

214 North Sixth Street, P.O. Box 1626, 72901
Telephone: 501-782-6041
Fax: 501-782-0841

Harry Preston Warner (1885-1969)   Lillard Cody Hayes
Cecil Randolph Warner (1890-1955)   G. Alan Wooten
James Melvin Dunn
Thomas G. Graves (1939-1971)   John Alan Lewis
Douglas O. Smith, Jr.   Joel D. Johnson
C. Wayne Harris   Gary W. Udouj
Gerald L. DeLung   J. Randall McGinnis
Patrick Neill Moore   Kathryn Stocks Campbell
R. Gregory Aclin

OF COUNSEL

C. R. Warner, Jr.

District Attorneys for: Burlington Northern Railroad Co.
Counsel for: Fairfield Communities, Inc.
Local Counsel for: Planters Division, Nabisco Brands, Inc.; Gerber Products Co.; United States Fidelity & Guaranty Co.; Aetna Group; Fireman's Fund-American Insurance Cos.; Hiram Walker & Sons, Inc.; Continental National American Group.

For full biographical listings, see the Martindale-Hubbell Law Directory

JONESBORO,* Craighead Co.

BARRETT & DEACON (AV)

Union Planters Bank Building, 300 South Church Street, P.O. Box 1700, 72403
Telephone: 501-931-1700
FAX: 501-931-1800

MEMBERS OF FIRM

Joe C. Barrett (1897-1980)   David W. Cahoon
John C. Deacon   Ralph W. Waddell
J. Barry Deacon   Paul D. Waddell
D. Price Marshall, Jr.

ASSOCIATES

James D. Bradbury   Kevin W. Cole
Anita S. Perkins

For full biographical listings, see the Martindale-Hubbell Law Directory

PENIX, PENIX, LUSBY AND NIX (AV)

401 South Main Street, P.O. Box 1306, 72403-1306
Telephone: 501-932-7449
Fax: 501-933-7281

MEMBERS OF FIRM

Roy Penix (1891-1978)   Bill Penix
Marian F. Penix (1924-1991)   Richard A. Lusby
J. Robin Nix, II

Representative Clients: American Policyholders Ins. Co.; CIGNA Cos.; K-Mart Corp.; Liberty Mutual Insurance Co.; Sentry and Dairyland Insurance; Southwestern Bell Telephone Co.; The Jonesboro Sun.

For full biographical listings, see the Martindale-Hubbell Law Directory

LITTLE ROCK,* Pulaski Co.

ALLEN LAW FIRM, A PROFESSIONAL CORPORATION (AV)

950 Centre Place, 212 Center Street, 72201
Telephone: 501-374-7100
Telecopier: 501-374-1611
Email: hwallen@cei.net

H. William Allen

Sandra E. Jackson

Representative Clients: Boatmen's National Bank of Arkansas; Colonia Insurance Co.; Shoney's Inc.; Garlock, Inc.; National Bank of Commerce.

For full biographical listings, see the Martindale-Hubbell Law Directory

ARNOLD, GROBMYER & HALEY, A PROFESSIONAL ASSOCIATION (AV)

875 Union National Plaza, 124 West Capitol Avenue, P.O. Box 70, 72203
Telephone: 501-376-1171
Fax: 501-375-3548

Benjamin F. Arnold   Richard L. Ramsay
James F. Dowden   Robert R. Ross

(See Next Column)

ARNOLD, GROBMYER & HALEY A PROFESSIONAL ASSOCIATION, *Little Rock—Continued*

OF COUNSEL
John H. Haley

For Complete List of Firm Personnel, See General Section

For full biographical listings, see the Martindale-Hubbell Law Directory

CEARLEY LAW FIRM (AV)

Centre Place, Second Floor, 212 Center Street, 72201
Telephone: 501-375-9451
Fax: 501-374-3463
Email: 102574.227@compuserve.com

Robert M. Cearley, Jr.

Counsel for: Arkansas Bankers Association; Greyhound Lines, Inc.

For full biographical listings, see the Martindale-Hubbell Law Directory

DUNCAN & RAINWATER TRIAL LAWYERS A PROFESSIONAL ASSOCIATION (AV)

Suite 500 Three Financial Centre, 900 South Shackleford, P.O. Box 25938, 72221-5938
Telephone: 501-228-7600
FAX: 501-228-7664

Phillip J. Duncan (P.A.)	Robert A. Russell, Jr.
Michael R. Rainwater (P.A.)	Neil Ray Chamberlin
Michelle Banks Odum	

For full biographical listings, see the Martindale-Hubbell Law Directory

FRIDAY, ELDREDGE & CLARK (AV)

A Partnership including Professional Associations
Formerly, Smith, Williams, Friday, Eldredge & Clark
2000 First Commercial Building, 400 West Capitol Avenue, 72201-3493
Telephone: 501-376-2011
Telecopier: 501-376-2147; 376-6369
Email: fecmh@fec.sprint.com

MEMBERS OF FIRM

William H. Sutton (P.A.)	Elizabeth Robben Murray (P.A.)
John Dewey Watson (P.A.)	Kevin A. Crass (P.A.)
Paul B. Benham, III, (P.A.)	William A. Waddell, Jr., (P.A.)
Larry W. Burks (P.A.)	Tonia P. Jones (P.A.)
James M. Simpson, Jr., (P.A.)	David D. Wilson (P.A.)
Jeffrey H. Moore (P.A.)	

ASSOCIATES

Jonann C. Roosevelt	Tony L. Wilcox

Counsel for: Union Pacific System; St. Paul Insurance Co.; Liberty Mutual Insurance Co.; Cigna Property & Casualty Co.; Arkansas Power & Light Co.; Dillard Department Stores, Inc.; First Commercial Corp.; Browning Arms Co.; Phillips Petroleum Co.; Aetna Casualty & Surety Co.

For Complete List of Firm Personnel, See General Section

For full biographical listings, see the Martindale-Hubbell Law Directory

HILBURN, CALHOON, HARPER, PRUNISKI & CALHOUN, LTD. (AV)

P.O. Box 1256, 72203-1256
Telephone: 501-372-0110
Fax: 501-372-2029
North Little Rock, Arkansas Office: Eighth Floor, Mercantile Bank Building, One Riverfront Place, P.O. Box 5551, 72119.
Telephone: 501-372-0110.
Fax: 501-372-2029.

Sam Hilburn	Phil Campbell
John E. Pruniski, III	J. Maurice Rogers
John C. Calhoun, Jr.	Scott E. Daniel
David M. Fuqua	Scott Thomas Vaughn
James M. McHaney, Jr.	James D. Lawson

Dorcy Kyle Corbin	Graham F. Sloan
Pamela A. Moseley	

Representative Clients: Mercantile Bank of Central Arkansas; Merrill Lynch Pierce Fenner & Smith, Inc.; Allstate Insurance Company; Central Arkansas Risk Management Association; Smith Barney, Inc.; Deere & Co.; Case Corp.

For Complete List of Firm Personnel, See General Section

For full biographical listings, see the Martindale-Hubbell Law Directory

HOOVER & KOOISTRA (AV)

111 Center Street, 11th Floor, 72201-4445
Telephone: 501-376-8500
Facsimile: 501-372-3255

(See Next Column)

MEMBERS OF FIRM

Paul W. Hoover, Jr.	John Kooistra, III
Max C. Mehlburger	

For full biographical listings, see the Martindale-Hubbell Law Directory

HUCKABAY, MUNSON, ROWLETT & TILLEY, P.A. (AV)

First Commercial Building, Suite 1900, 400 West Capitol, 72201
Telephone: 501-374-6535
Fax: 501-374-5906

Mike Huckabay	John E. Moore
Bruce E. Munson	Tim Boone
Beverly A. Rowlett	Rick Runnells
James W. Tilley	Sarah Ann Presson
Edward T. Oglesby	

D. Michael Huckabay, Jr.	Elizabeth Fletcher Rogers
Carol Lockard Worley	Julia L. Busfield
Mark S. Breeding	Jane M. Yocum
Terry D. Dugger	

Representative Clients: Allstate Insurance Company; American International Group; Farmers Insurance Group; General Electric Company; Nationwide Insurance Company; Safeco Insurance Company; State Farm Mutual Automobile Insurance Company; State Farm Fire and Casualty Company; Tenet Healthcare Corp.; United States Fidelity and Guaranty Company.

For full biographical listings, see the Martindale-Hubbell Law Directory

LASER, WILSON, BUFFORD & WATTS, P.A. (AV)

101 S. Spring Street, Suite 300, 72201-2488
Telephone: 501-376-2981
Telecopier: 501-376-2417

Sam Laser	David M. Donovan
Dan F. Bufford	Walter A. Kendel, Jr.
Richard N. Watts	Brian A. Brown
J. Kendal "Ken" Cook	Karen J. Hughes
Kevin J. Staten	Gena Gregory
Alfred F. Angulo, Jr.	Keith Martin McPherson
Thomas J. Diaz	

Representative Clients: Allstate Insurance Co.; American International Insurance Group; Continental Insurance Cos.; Farm Bureau Insurance Cos. (Casualty & Fire); Farmers Insurance Group; GAB Business Services, Inc.; St. Paul Insurance Cos.; Scottsdale Insurance Co.; State Farm Auto (Fire) Insurance Cos.

For Complete List of Firm Personnel, See General Section

For full biographical listings, see the Martindale-Hubbell Law Directory

THE MCMATH LAW FIRM, P.A. (AV)

711 West Third Street, P.O. Box 3457, 72203
Telephone: 501-376-3021
Fax: 501-374-5118

Sidney S. McMath	James Bruce McMath
Leland F. Leatherman	Mart Vehik
Sandy S. McMath	Winslow Drummond
Phillip H. McMath	Paul E. Harrison
Sandra L. Sanders	

For full biographical listings, see the Martindale-Hubbell Law Directory

WILLIAM L. OWEN (AV)

The Fones House, 902 West Second, P.O. Box 989, 72203
Telephone: 501-372-1655
Fax: 501-372-7884

For full biographical listings, see the Martindale-Hubbell Law Directory

ROSE LAW FIRM, A PROFESSIONAL ASSOCIATION (AV)

120 East Fourth Street, 72201
Telephone: 501-375-9131
Telecopy: 501-375-1309

Jerry C. Jones	Richard T. Donovan
David L. Williams	James H. Druff
Amy Lee Stewart	

COUNSEL

Phillip Carroll

David P. Martin	Kathryn Bennett Perkins
Michael N. Shannon	

Representative Clients: Acxiom Corporation; Aluminum Company of America; The Equitable Life Assurance Society of the United States; Bridgestone/Firestone, Inc.; CIGNA Companies; General Motors Corp.; Kemper Insurance Group; New York Life Insurance Co.; The Prudential Insurance Company of America.

(See Next Column)

ROSE LAW FIRM A PROFESSIONAL ASSOCIATION—*Continued*

For Complete List of Firm Personnel, See General Section

For full biographical listings, see the Martindale-Hubbell Law Directory

WILLIAMS & ANDERSON (AV)

Twenty-Second Floor, 111 Center Street, 72201
Telephone: 501-372-0800
FAX: 501-372-6453

MEMBERS OF FIRM

W. Jackson Williams	James E. Hathaway III
Philip S. Anderson	John E. Tull, III
Peter G. Kumpe	Rush B. Deacon
David F. Menz	J. Leon Holmes
Steven W. Quattlebaum	Thomas G. Williams

Jeanne L. Seewald	Edie R. Ervin
Katharine R. Cloud	Stephen B. Niswanger

Representative Clients: Arkansas Development Finance Authority; Coca-Cola Enterprises, Inc.; Dean Witter Reynolds Inc.; Entergy Power, Inc.; Little Rock Newspapers, Inc. d/b/a/ Arkansas Democrat-Gazette; Potlatch Corporation; Texaco, Inc.; Wal-Mart Stores, Inc.

For Complete List of Firm Personnel, See General Section

For full biographical listings, see the Martindale-Hubbell Law Directory

WILSON, ENGSTROM, CORUM & COULTER (AV)

809 West Third Street, P.O. Box 71, 72203
Telephone: 501-375-6453
FAX: 501-375-5914

MEMBERS OF FIRM

Roxanne Wilson (1947-1992)	Gary D. Corum
Stephen Engstrom	Nate Coulter

For full biographical listings, see the Martindale-Hubbell Law Directory

PINE BLUFF,* Jefferson Co.

RAMSAY, BRIDGFORTH, HARRELSON & STARLING (AV)

11th Floor, Simmons First National Building, P.O. Drawer 8509, 71611
Telephone: 501-535-9000
FAX: 501-535-8544

MEMBERS OF FIRM

William Franklin Coleman (1870-1956)	F. Daniel Harrelson
	Spencer F. Robinson
Nicholas J. Gantt, Jr. (1879-1975)	Phillip A. Raley
	Patrick A. Burrow
Marion J. Starling, Jr. (1941-1990)	Rosalind M. Mouser
	William M. Bridgforth
William C. Bridgforth	David R. Bridgforth

ASSOCIATES

William Jay Harrelson	John Thomas Starling

OF COUNSEL

Louis L. Ramsay, Jr.

Representative Clients: Simmons First National Bank; Pine Bluff Sand & Gravel Co.; Stant, Inc.; McGeorge Contracting Co., Inc.; Television Station KATV.

For full biographical listings, see the Martindale-Hubbell Law Directory

RUSSELLVILLE,* Pope Co.

PEEL LAW FIRM, P.A. (AV)

120 South Glenwood, P.O. Box 986, 72811
Telephone: 501-968-4000
Fax: 501-968-4388

Richard L. Peel

John R. Peel	Scott M. Simmons

Representative Clients: First Bank Arkansas; Valley Motors Inc.; Russellville School District; City of Russellville, Arkansas.
Agents for: Fidelity Title Insurance Co.
Reference: First Bank of Arkansas, Russellville, Arkansas.

For full biographical listings, see the Martindale-Hubbell Law Directory

SPRINGDALE, Washington Co.

LISLE LAW FIRM, P.C. (AV)

P.O. Box 6877, 72766-6877
Telephone: 501-750-4444
Fax: 501-751-6792

John Lisle

(See Next Column)

Joe B. Reed	Donnie W. Rutledge, II
Christopher James Lisle	Stephen A. Lisle

For full biographical listings, see the Martindale-Hubbell Law Directory

TEXARKANA,* Miller Co.

DUNN, NUTTER, MORGAN & SHAW (AV)

State Line Plaza, Box 8030, 71854-5945
Telephone: 501-773-5651
Telecopier: 501-772-2037
Email: law@clover.cleaf.com

MEMBERS OF FIRM

Winford L. Dunn, Jr.	Nelson V. Shaw
R. Gary Nutter	R. David Freeze
	W. David Carter

ASSOCIATES

Mark A. Daniels	Christie G. Adams
Jeff M. Addison	(Not admitted in AR)

OF COUNSEL

Hayes C. McClerkin

LEGAL SUPPORT PERSONNEL
LEGAL ASSISTANTS

Myra Conaway Wells	Sonja L. Oliver

Representative Clients: The State First National Bank of Texarkana; CNA Insurance Cos.; First Federal Savings & Loan Assn.; St. Michael Hospital; Shelter Insurance Cos.; CIGNA Insurance Cos.; Sentry Insurance; State Auto Insurance Co.; Kemper Insurance Co.; Georgia-Pacific Corp.

For Complete List of Firm Personnel, See General Section

For full biographical listings, see the Martindale-Hubbell Law Directory

WEST MEMPHIS, Crittenden Co.

RIEVES & MAYTON (AV)

304 East Broadway, P.O. Box 1359, 72303
Telephone: 501-735-3420
Telecopier: 501-735-4678

MEMBERS OF FIRM

Elton A. Rieves, Jr. (1909-1984)	Michael R. Mayton
Elton A. Rieves, III	Elton A. Rieves, IV
	Martin W. Bowen

ASSOCIATES

William Terrell Smith, Jr.	David S. Wilson, III

For full biographical listings, see the Martindale-Hubbell Law Directory

SLOAN, RUBENS & PEEPLES (AV)

600 North Missouri Street, P.O. Box 768, 72303
Telephone: 501-735-5500
Telecopy: 501-735-2624

MEMBERS OF FIRM

Edward J. Rubens (1913-1977)	Kent J. Rubens
	David C. Peeples

ASSOCIATES

J. Michael Stephenson	James A. Davis

OF COUNSEL

Ralph W. Sloan	Edward B. Johnson
	(Not admitted in AR)

General Counsel for: Bank of West Memphis; Crittenden Publishing Co., Inc.; West Memphis School District; Razorback Concrete; Flash Markets, Inc.
Representative Clients: Earle School District; Crawfordsville School District; Citizens Bank Marion; Marion School District; AgriBank, FCB.

For full biographical listings, see the Martindale-Hubbell Law Directory

CALIFORNIA

APTOS, Santa Cruz Co.

DENNIS J. KEHOE A LAW CORPORATION (AV)

311 Bonita Drive, 95003
Telephone: 408-662-8444
Fax: 408-662-0227

Dennis J. Kehoe

For full biographical listings, see the Martindale-Hubbell Law Directory

Aptos—Continued

RUMMONDS, WALTZ & MAIR (AV)

311 Bonita Drive, P.O. Box 1870, 95001
Telephone: 408-688-2911
Sacramento, California Office: 6991 Garden Highway. 95837.
Telephone: 916-927-4610.

MEMBERS OF FIRM

James S. Rummonds   Peter K. Mair
Patrick J. Waltz
  (Resident, Sacramento Office)

For full biographical listings, see the Martindale-Hubbell Law Directory

BAKERSFIELD,* Kern Co.

KLEIN, WEGIS, DeNATALE, GOLDNER & MUIR, LLP (AV)

A Partnership including Professional Corporations
(Formerly Di Giorgio, Davis, Klein, Wegis, Duggan & Friedman)
ARCO Tower, 4550 California Avenue, Second Floor, P.O. Box
  11172, 93389-1172
Telephone: 805-395-1000
Telecopier: 805-326-0418
Email: kwdgm@kwdgm.com

MEMBERS OF FIRM

Anthony J. Klein (Inc.)   Gregory A. Muir
Ralph B. Wegis (Inc.)   Barry L. Goldner
Thomas V. DeNatale, Jr.   Jay L. Rosenlieb
        David J. Cooper

Representative Clients: Bank of America; Great Western Bank; Mojave Pipeline Co.; Transamerican Title Insurance Co.; Dean Whittier Reynolds, Inc.; California Republic Bank; San Joaquin Bank; Nahama & Weagant Energy Co.; Freymiller Trucking, Inc.; Westinghouse Electric Co.

For Complete List of Firm Personnel, See General Section

For full biographical listings, see the Martindale-Hubbell Law Directory

ROBINSON, PALMER & LOGAN (AV)

Suite 150, 3434 Truxtun Avenue, 93301
Telephone: 805-323-8277
Fax: 805-323-4205

MEMBERS OF FIRM

Oliver U. Robinson   William D. Palmer
       Gary L. Logan

For Complete List of Firm Personnel, See General Section

For full biographical listings, see the Martindale-Hubbell Law Directory

LAW OFFICES OF YOUNG WOOLDRIDGE (AV)

1800 30th Street, Fourth Floor, 93301
Telephone: 805-327-9661
Facsimile: 805-327-1087

MEMBERS OF FIRM

G. Neil Farr   Larry R. Cox
Steve W. Nichols   Scott K. Kuney

ASSOCIATE

Russell B. Hicks

Representative Clients: Arvin-Edison Water Storage District; Motor City Truck Sales and Service.
References: Wells Fargo Bank; First Interstate Bank; California Republic Bank.

For Complete List of Firm Personnel, See General Section

For full biographical listings, see the Martindale-Hubbell Law Directory

BELVEDERE-TIBURON, Marin Co.

GEORGE C. MARTINEZ (AV)

1610 Tiburon Boulevard, 94920
Telephone: 415-789-5086
FAX: 415-789-5088
Email: GCMartinez@aol.com

For full biographical listings, see the Martindale-Hubbell Law Directory

BEVERLY HILLS, Los Angeles Co.

DAPEER, ROSENBLIT & LITVAK, LLP (AV)

9460 Wilshire Boulevard, Fifth Floor, 90212
Telephone: 310-203-8200; 310-777-6676
Fax: 310-203-8213; 310-777-6675
Metropolitan Cities Office: 2770 East Slauson Avenue, P.O. Box 2067, Huntington Park, 90255.
Telephone: 213-587-5221.
Fax: 213-587-4190.

(See Next Column)

William Litvak   Steven H. Rosenblit
     Kenneth B. Dapeer

For full biographical listings, see the Martindale-Hubbell Law Directory

JACOBSON, SANDERS & BORDY, LLP (AV)

A Partnership including a Professional Corporation
9777 Wilshire Boulevard, Suite 718, 90212-1907
Telephone: 310-777-7488

MEMBERS OF FIRM

Lawrence H. Jacobson (A P.C.)   Michael J. Bordy
Michael R. E. Sanders

OF COUNSEL

David S. White   Patricia B. Kolber

For full biographical listings, see the Martindale-Hubbell Law Directory

NORMINTON & WIITA (AV)

A Partnership of Professional Corporations
433 North Camden Drive Twelfth Floor, 90210
Telephone: 310-288-5900
Facsimile: 310-288-5901
Email: norminton@aol.com

Thomas M. Norminton (P.C.)   Kathleen Dority Fuster (P.C.).
Douglas P. Wiita (P.C.)   A. Rick Atwood, Jr.

For full biographical listings, see the Martindale-Hubbell Law Directory

SCHWARTZ, WISOT & WILSON, LLP (AV)

Suite 315, 315 South Beverly Drive, 90212
Telephone: 310-277-2323
Fax: 310-556-2308

Bruce Edward Schwartz   John D. Wilson
Valerie Wisot   Kathleen A. Calaway

OF COUNSEL

Paula Reddish Zinnemann

Reference: Great Western Bank (Century City Office, Los Angeles, California)

For full biographical listings, see the Martindale-Hubbell Law Directory

TURNER, GERSTENFELD, WILK, AUBERT & YOUNG, LLP (AV)

Formerly Turner, Gerstenfeld, Wilk & Tigerman
Suite 510, 8383 Wilshire Boulevard, 90211
Telephone: 213-653-3900
Facsimile: 213-653-3021

MEMBERS OF FIRM

Steven E. Young   Edward Friedman
     Linda Wight Mazur

ASSOCIATES

Dortha Larene Pyles   Steven A. Morris

OF COUNSEL

Bert Z. Tigerman

For Complete List of Firm Personnel, See General Section

For full biographical listings, see the Martindale-Hubbell Law Directory

CARLSBAD, San Diego Co.

GATZKE, MISPAGEL & DILLON (AV)

A Partnership including a Professional Law Corporation
Suite 200, 1921 Palomar Oaks Way, P.O. Box 1636, 92009
Telephone: 619-431-9501
Fax: 619-431-9512

MEMBERS OF FIRM

Michael Scott Gatzke   Mark J. Dillon
Mark F. Mispagel   Lori D. Ballance

ASSOCIATES

David P. Hubbard   Kristin Beth White

For full biographical listings, see the Martindale-Hubbell Law Directory

WEIL & WRIGHT (AV)

1921 Palomar Oaks Way, Suite 301, 92008
Telephone: 619-438-1214
Telefax: 619-438-2666

Paul M. Weil   David A. Ebersole

For full biographical listings, see the Martindale-Hubbell Law Directory

CLAREMONT, Los Angeles Co.

C. ROBERT FERGUSON (AV)

237 West Fourth Street, 91711
Telephone: 909-482-0782; 818-795-4181
Fax: 909-624-7291

JOHN C. MCCARTHY (AV)

401 Harvard Avenue, 91711
Telephone: 909-621-4984
Telecopier: 909-621-5757
(Also Member, Morrisons, McCarthy & Moore, in Whitefish, Montana)

For full biographical listings, see the Martindale-Hubbell Law Directory

COSTA MESA, Orange Co.

COULOMBE & KOTTKE, A PROFESSIONAL CORPORATION (AV)

Comerica Bank Tower, 611 Anton Boulevard, Suite 1260, 92626
Telephone: 714-540-1234
Fax: 714-754-0808; 714-754-0707
Email: c-k@coulombe.com

Ronald B. Coulombe   Jon S. Kottke
COUNSEL
Roy B. Woolsey
LEGAL SUPPORT PERSONNEL
PARALEGALS
Vicky M. Pearson   Abeer F. Rider
LEGAL ADMINISTRATOR
Yvonne Mendoza

For full biographical listings, see the Martindale-Hubbell Law Directory

ELY, FRITZ & HOGAN (AV)

3100 Bristol Street #200, 92626
Telephone: 714-556-1480
Telecopier: 714-556-2863

MEMBERS OF FIRM
Thomas W. Ely   Michael G. Hogan
James H. Fritz   Jerome D. Rybarczyk

Charles A. Correia   Ronald F. Templer
Allen D. MacNeil
OF COUNSEL
Gerald W. Mouzis

For full biographical listings, see the Martindale-Hubbell Law Directory

MCCAULEY & ASSOCIATES, LLP (AV)

611 Anton Boulevard, Suite 1260, 92626
Telephone: 714-438-9108
Fax: 714-957-3718

MEMBER OF FIRM
John J. McCauley

Mark S. Flynn

For full biographical listings, see the Martindale-Hubbell Law Directory

RICKS & ANDERSON, A LAW CORPORATION (AV)

3200 Park Center Drive, Suite 1155, 92626-4413
Telephone: 714-966-9190

Cecil E. Ricks, Jr.   Annette L. Anderson

For full biographical listings, see the Martindale-Hubbell Law Directory

THE RUDOLPH LAW GROUP A PROFESSIONAL CORPORATION (AV)

3200 Park Center Drive, Suite 1370, 92626
Telephone: 714-545-7272; 714-757-7272
Fax: 714-545-7273

George C. Rudolph

For full biographical listings, see the Martindale-Hubbell Law Directory

RUTAN & TUCKER, LLP (AV)

A Partnership including Professional Corporations
611 Anton Boulevard, Suite 1400, P.O. Box 1950, 92626
Telephone: 714-641-5100; 213-625-7586
Telecopier: 714-546-9035
Email: rutan&tucker@mcimail.com *URL:* http://www.rutan.com

(See Next Column)

MEMBERS OF FIRM
Leonard A. Hampel, Jr.   Robert S. Bower
John B. Hurlbut, Jr.   William M. Marticorena
Milford W. Dahl, Jr.   William J. Caplan
Theodore I. Wallace, Jr., (P.C.)   Michael T. Hornak
Robert C. Braun   Joel D. Kuperberg
Edward D. Sybesma, Jr., (P.C.)   William W. Wynder
Thomas S. Salinger (P.C.)   Duke Wahlquist
Clifford E. Frieden   Jayne Taylor Kacer
Michael D. Rubin   Stephen A. Ellis
Ira G. Rivin (P.C.)   Matthew K. Ross
Layne H. Melzer
ASSOCIATES
David H. Hochner   Allen C. Ostergar III
Richard K. Howell   Jennifer White-Sperling
A. Patrick Muñoz   Robert Elliot Adel II
Paul J. Sievers   Steven M. Coleman
S. Daniel Harbottle   Steven John Goon
Steven M. Muldowney

For Complete List of Firm Personnel, See General Section

For full biographical listings, see the Martindale-Hubbell Law Directory

EL MONTE, Los Angeles Co.

MICHAEL B. MONTGOMERY A LAW CORPORATION (AV)

10501 Valley Boulevard, Suite 121, 91731
Telephone: 818-452-1222
Fax: 818-452-8323
Ft. Lauderdale, Florida Office: Justice Building, 524 S. Andrews Avenue, Suite 320 N.
Telephone: 954-522-9441.
Fax: 954-522-2076.

Michael B. Montgomery
Reference: Bank of America (San Marino Branch).

For full biographical listings, see the Martindale-Hubbell Law Directory

EMERYVILLE, Alameda Co.

LEGAL STRATEGIES GROUP (AV)

5905 Christie Avenue, 94608
Telephone: 510-450-9600
Fax: 510-450-9601
URL: http://www.legalstrategies.com/lsgdemoindex3.html

Timothy R. Cahn   Peter H. Goldsmith
Joshua R. Floum   Vincent L. Johnson
Karen S. Frank   Leigh A. Kirmssé
Gregory S. Gilchrist   Louise E. Ma
Heather A. Young
OF COUNSEL
Robert J. Vizas

For full biographical listings, see the Martindale-Hubbell Law Directory

ENCINO, Los Angeles Co.

STAITMAN, SNYDER & TANNENBAUM (AV)

Suite 1401, 16633 Ventura Boulevard, 91436-1840
Telephone: 818-981-5300; 213-872-3530
FAX: 818-981-7104

Jack M. Staitman   Jack J. Tannenbaum
Bradley A. Snyder   David K. Dorenfeld

Rodger S. Greiner   Gerald P. Peters
Deborah K. Galer

For full biographical listings, see the Martindale-Hubbell Law Directory

*FRESNO,** Fresno Co.

DOWLING, AARON & KEELER, INCORPORATED (AV)

Suite 200, 6051 North Fresno Street, 93710
Telephone: 209-432-4500
Fax: 209-432-4590
Email: dowling-law.com

Adolfo M. Corona   Philip David Kopp
Francine Marie Kanne

Richard E. Heatter   James C. Sherwood
Reference: Wells Fargo Bank (Main).

For Complete List of Firm Personnel, See General Section

For full biographical listings, see the Martindale-Hubbell Law Directory

Fresno—Continued

JORY, PETERSON, WATKINS & SMITH (AV)

555 West Shaw, Suite C-1, P.O. Box 5394, 93755
Telephone: 209-225-6700
Telecopier: 209-225-3416

MEMBERS OF FIRM

Jay V. Jory	Michael Jens F. Smith
John E. Peterson	Marcia A. Ross
Cal B. Watkins, Jr.	William M. Woolman

ASSOCIATES

John J. Stander	Carla M. McCormack
Jeff W. Reisig	Matthew D. Ruyak

Reference: Valliwide Bank.

For full biographical listings, see the Martindale-Hubbell Law Directory

KIMBLE, MacMICHAEL & UPTON, A PROFESSIONAL CORPORATION (AV)

Fig Garden Financial Center, 5260 North Palm Avenue, Suite 221, P.O. Box 9489, 93792-9489
Telephone: 209-435-5500
Telecopier: 209-435-1500
Email: kmu@primenet.com

Joseph C. Kimble (1910-1972)	Robert H. Scribner
Thomas A. MacMichael (1920-1990)	Michael E. Moss
	Mark D. Miller
Jon Wallace Upton	Michael F. Tatham
Robert E. Bergin	W. Richard Lee
Jeffrey G. Boswell	D. Tyler Tharpe
Steven D. McGee	Sylvia Halkousis Coyle
Robert E. Ward	S. Brett Sutton
John P. Eleazarian	Michael J. Jurkovich

Douglas V. Thornton	Susan King Hatmaker
Robert William Branch	Lawrence J. Salisbury
Donald J. Pool	Daniel R. Foster
Meredith E. Allen	

OF COUNSEL

Mary Ann Bluhm

For full biographical listings, see the Martindale-Hubbell Law Directory

LANG, RICHERT & PATCH, A PROFESSIONAL CORPORATION (AV)

Fig Garden Financial Center, 5200 North Palm Avenue, 4th Floor, P.O. Box 40012, 93755
Telephone: 209-228-6700
Fax: 209-228-6727

Frank H. Lang	Victoria J. Salisch
William T. Richert (1937-1993)	Bradley A. Silva
Robert L. Patch, II	Charles Trudrung Taylor
Val W. Saldaña	Mark L. Creede
Douglas E. Noll	Peter N. Zeitler
Michael T. Hertz	Charles L. Doerksen

Laurie L. Quigley	Nabil E. Zumout
Douglas E. Griffin	Shawn H. Alikian
Thomas E. Gauthier	

References: Wells Fargo Bank (Fresno Main Office).

For full biographical listings, see the Martindale-Hubbell Law Directory

MILES, SEARS & EANNI, A PROFESSIONAL CORPORATION (AV)

2844 Fresno Street, P.O. Box 1432, 93716
Telephone: 209-486-5200
Fax: 209-486-5240

Wm. M. Miles (1909-1991)	Richard C. Watters
Robert E. Sears (1918-1992)	Gerald J. Maglio
Carmen A. Eanni	William J. Seiler
Douglas L. Gordon	

For full biographical listings, see the Martindale-Hubbell Law Directory

PARICHAN, RENBERG, CROSSMAN & HARVEY, LAW CORPORATION (AV)

Suite 130, 2350 West Shaw Avenue, P.O. Box 9950, 93794-0950
Telephone: 209-431-6300
Fax: 209-432-1018

Harold A. Parichan	Stephen T. Knudsen
Charles L. Renberg	Larry C. Gollmer
Richard C. Crossman	Robert G. Eliason
Ima Jean Harvey	Steven M. McQuillan

(See Next Column)

Deborah A. Coe	Karen L. Lynch
Maureen P. Holford	Michael L. Renberg

Reference: Bank of America, Commercial Banking Office, Fresno, California.

For full biographical listings, see the Martindale-Hubbell Law Directory

STAMMER, McKNIGHT, BARNUM & BAILEY (AV)

2540 West Shaw Lane, Suite 110, P.O. Box 9789, 93794-9789
Telephone: 209-449-0571
Fax: 209-432-2619

W. H. Stammer (1891-1969)	Frank D. Maul
James K. Barnum (1918-1987)	Craig M. Mortensen
Dean A. Bailey (1924-1995)	Jerry D. Jones
Galen McKnight (1904-1991)	Michael P. Mallery
James N. Hays	M. Bruce Smith
Carey H. Johnson	Thomas J. Georgouses

ASSOCIATES

Steven R. Stoker	Bruce J. Berger
M. Jaqueline Yates	Celene M.E. Boggs

Representative Clients: Pacific Bell; Chevron, U.S.A.; Fresno Irrigation District; The Travelers Insurance Group; State Farm Insurance Cos.;
Reference: Bank of America National Trust & Savings Assn. (Fresno Main Office).

For full biographical listings, see the Martindale-Hubbell Law Directory

FULLERTON, Orange Co.

ELENBAAS & SCHOEMAN (AV)

Suite 235, 1370 N. Brea Boulevard, 92635
Telephone: 714-871-7100
Fax: 714-871-7142

Thomas E. Elenbaas	Cara Hagan Schoeman

For full biographical listings, see the Martindale-Hubbell Law Directory

GLENDALE, Los Angeles Co.

BAKER, OLSON, LeCROY & DANIELIAN, A LAW CORPORATION (AV)

144 North Brand Boulevard, P.O. Box 29062, 91209-9062
Telephone: 818-502-5600
Facsimile: 818-241-2653

Sheldon S. Baker	Charles L. LeCroy, III
Eric Olson	Arsen Danielian

Michael S. Simon

OF COUNSEL

John J. Jacobson

For full biographical listings, see the Martindale-Hubbell Law Directory

GILL AND BALDWIN (AV)

130 North Brand Boulevard Fourth Floor, 91203
Telephone: 818-500-7755; 213-245-3131
Fax: 818-242-4305

MEMBERS OF FIRM

Samuel S. Gill (1912-1965)	Joseph C. Malpasuto
John M. Carmack	Kirk S. MacDonald

OF COUNSEL

Ernest R. Baldwin

Representative Clients: Kasler Corp.; Bireley Foundation.
Reference: American West Bank.

For full biographical listings, see the Martindale-Hubbell Law Directory

IRSFELD, IRSFELD & YOUNGER LLP (AV)

A Partnership including Professional Corporations
Suite 900, 100 West Broadway, 91210-1296
Telephone: 818-242-6859
Fax: 818-240-7728
Email: 104736.1745@compuserver.com

MEMBERS OF FIRM

James B. Irsfeld (1880-1966)	Peter J. Irsfeld (P.C.)
Kenneth C. Younger (1922-1996)	James J. Waldorf (P.C.)
	C. Phillip Jackson (P.C.)
John H. Brink (P.C.)	Norman H. Green (P.C.)
Kathryn E. Van Houten	

ASSOCIATES

Peter C. Wright	Diane L. Walker

(See Next Column)

IRSFELD, IRSFELD & YOUNGER LLP—Continued
RETIRED
James B. Irsfeld, Jr.

Representative Clients: Lear Sieglar, Inc.; Chrysler Credit Corp.
References: First Interstate Bank (Glendale Main Office); Bank of Hollywood.

For full biographical listings, see the Martindale-Hubbell Law Directory

O'ROURKE, ALLAN & FONG (AV)

3rd Floor, 104 North Belmont, P.O. Box 10220, 91209-3220
Telephone: 818-247-4303
Fax: 818-247-1451

MEMBERS OF FIRM
Denis M. O'Rourke   Joan H. Allan
Roderick D. Fong
ASSOCIATE
Denise Michelle O'Rourke

References: Verdugo Banking Co. (Glendale, California); Community Bank (Glendale, California).

For full biographical listings, see the Martindale-Hubbell Law Directory

OTT & HOROWITZ, A PROFESSIONAL CORPORATION (AV)

700 North Central Avenue, 8th Floor, Suite 850, 91203
Telephone: 818-242-3100
Fax: 818-242-3102
Email: ohlaw@aol.com

Thomas H. Ott   Craig A. Horowitz
Wayne D. Clayton

Steven H. Taylor   Janine R. Menhennet
Patrick Carey

Representative Clients: Alhambra Unified School District; Calif. Credit Union League; Cuna Mutual Ins. Group; Hughes Aircraft Corp.; Lockheed Federal Credit Union.

For full biographical listings, see the Martindale-Hubbell Law Directory

THOMAS & PRICE (AV)

535 North Brand Boulevard, 7th Floor, 91203
Telephone: 213-387-4800; 818-500-4800
FAX: 818-500-4822
Ventura, California Office: 1655 Mesa Verde Avenue, Suite 230.
Telephone: 805-642-6255.
Fax: 805-642-4580.

MEMBERS OF FIRM
Michael Thomas   Craig R. Donahue
Bonnie R. Louis   Maureen F. Thomas
ASSOCIATES
John P. DeGomez   Christian E. Sanne
Timothy A. Hodge   Benjimin M. Brees
Linda B. Hurevitz   Janet L. Keuper
Kevin M. McCormick
OF COUNSEL
Lawrence E. Price

For full biographical listings, see the Martindale-Hubbell Law Directory

HAYWARD, Alameda Co.

HALEY, PURCHIO, SAKAI & SMITH (AV)

P.O. Box 450, 22320 Foothill Boulevard, Suite 620, 94543
Telephone: 510-538-6400
Oakland: 510-351-1932

MEMBERS OF FIRM
J. Kenneth Birchfield   John K. Smith
(1920-1978)   Robert Sakai
Cynthia K. Smith
OF COUNSEL
John J. Purchio   Donald A. Pearce (1898-1982)
Marlin W. Haley (1910-1993)

Representative Clients: City Center Commercial (Shopping Center); Oak Hills, Walnut Hills, Creekwood (Apartment Complexes); R. Zaballos & Sons (General Contractors); Hospital Associates; Wolf Investment Co.; Chicago Title Company of Alameda County; Sunnyside Nurseries, Inc.; Mission Valley Rock Co. (quarry); LaVista Quarry.

For full biographical listings, see the Martindale-Hubbell Law Directory

INDIAN WELLS, Riverside Co.

JOSEPH A. GIBBS (AV)

74-900 Highway 111, Suite 211, 92210
Telephone: 619-779-1790
Fax: 619-779-1780
Palm Springs California Office: 901 E. Tahquitz Canyon Way, Suite C-203.
Telephone: 619-320-7111.
Fax: 619-320-6392.

ASSOCIATE
Gregory R. Oleson

For full biographical listings, see the Martindale-Hubbell Law Directory

IRVINE, Orange Co.

BARNETT & RUBIN, A PROFESSIONAL CORPORATION (AV)

2 Park Plaza, Suite 980, 92614
Telephone: 714-261-9700
Facsimile: 714-261-9799
Email: Lawyers@Pacbell.net

Richard L. Barnett   Jeffrey D. Rubin

Kathryn B. Salmond

For full biographical listings, see the Martindale-Hubbell Law Directory

LAWRENCE J. GALARDI (AV)

Wells Fargo Tower, 2030 Main Street Suite 1050, 92714
Telephone: 714-852-1100
Telecopier: 714-252-7780

For full biographical listings, see the Martindale-Hubbell Law Directory

GEORGE & SHIELDS, LLP (AV)

30 Corporate Park, Suite 300, 92714-5133
Telephone: 714-263-1085
Fax: 714-263-0585

MEMBERS OF FIRM
Robert K. George   Timothy F. Shields
David W. Sparks

For full biographical listings, see the Martindale-Hubbell Law Directory

HALL & BAILEY (AV)

5 Park Plaza Suite 1440, 92714
Telephone: 714-553-8663
Facsimile: 714-476-8640
Riverside, California Office: 6761 Brockton Avenue, 92506.
Telephone: 909-682-7334.

Donald R. Hall   John L. Bailey
(Resident, Riverside Office)

TIMOTHY L. JOENS & ASSOCIATES A PROFESSIONAL CORPORATION (AV)

Jamboree Center, Five Park Plaza, Suite 1480, 92714
Telephone: 714-553-1950
Fax: 714-553-8835

Timothy L. Joens

Representative Clients: Century 21 of the Pacific, Inc.; Century 21 Region V, Inc.; Century 21 Real Estate Corp.

For full biographical listings, see the Martindale-Hubbell Law Directory

JONES, DAY, REAVIS & POGUE (AV)

2603 Main Street, Suite 900, 92714-6232
Telephone: 714-851-3939
Telex: 194911 Lawyers LSA
Telecopier: 714-553-7539
In Los Angeles, California: 555 West Fifth Street, Suite 4600.
Telephone: 213-489-3939.
Telex: 181439 UD.
Telecopier: 213-243-2539.
In Atlanta, Georgia: 3500 One Peachtree Center, 303 Peachtree Street, N.E.
Telephone: 404-521-3939.
Cable Address: "Attorneys Atlanta".
Telex: 54-2711.
Telecopier: 404-581-8330.
In Brussels, Belgium: Avenue Louise 480, 7th Floor, B-1050 Brussels.
Telephone: 32-2-645-14-11.
Telecopier: 32-2-645-14-45.
In Chicago, Illinois: 77 West Wacker.
Telephone: 312-782-3939.
Telecopier: 312-782-8585.

(See Next Column)

JONES, DAY, REAVIS & POGUE, *Irvine—Continued*

In Cleveland, Ohio: North Point, 901 Lakeside Avenue.
Telephone: 216-586-3939.
Cable Address: "Attorneys Cleveland."
Telex: 980389.
Telecopier: 216-579-0212.
In Columbus, Ohio: 1900 Huntington Center.
Telephone: 614-469-3939.
Cable Address: "Attorneys Columbus."
Telecopier: 614-461-4198.
In Dallas, Texas: 2300 Trammell Crow Center, 2001 Ross Avenue.
Telephone: 214-220-3939.
Cable Address: "Attorneys Dallas."
Telex: 730852.
Telecopier: 214-969-5100.
In Frankfurt, Germany: Triton Haus, Bockenheimer Landstrasse 42, 60323 Frankfurt am Main.
Telephone: 49-69-9726-3939.
Telecopier: 49-69-9726-3993.
In Geneva, Switzerland: 20, rue de Candolle.
Telephone: 41-22-320-2339.
Telecopier: 41-22-320-1232.
In Hong Kong: 29th Floor, Entertainment Building, 30 Queen's Road Central.
Telephone: 852-2526-6895.
Telecopier: 852-2868-5871.
In London, England: Bucklersbury House, 3 Queen Victoria Street.
Telephone: 44-171-236-3939.
Telecopier: 44-171-236-1113.
In New Delhi, India: Pathak & Associates, 13th Floor, Dr. Gopal Das Bhavan, 28 Barakhamba Road.
Telephone: 91-11-373-8793.
Telecopy: 91-11-335-3761.
In New York, New York: 599 Lexington Avenue.
Telephone: 212-326-3939.
Cable Address: "JONESDAY NEWYORK."
Telex: 237013 JDRP UR.
Telecopier: 212-755-7306.
In Paris, France: 62, rue du Faubourg Saint-Honore.
Telephone: 33-1-44-71-3939.
Telex: 290156 Surgoe.
Telecopier: 33-1-49-24-0471.
In Pittsburgh, Pennsylvania: 500 Grant Street, 31st Floor.
Telephone: 412-391-3939.
Cable Address: "Attorneys Pittsburgh."
Telecopier: 412-394-7959.
In Riyadh, Saudi Arabia: The International Law Firm, Sulaymaniyah Center, Tahlia Street, P.O. Box 22166.
Telephone: (966-1) 462-8866.
Telecopier: (966-1) 462-9001.
In Taipei, Taiwan: 8th Floor, 2 Tun Hwa South Road, Section 2.
Telephone: (886-2) 704-6808.
Telecopier: (886-2) 704-6791.
In Tokyo, Japan: Toranomon MT Building, 4th Floor, 10-3, Toranomon 3-Chome, Minato-ku, Tokyo 105, Japan.
Telephone: 81-3-3433-3939.
Telecopier: 81-3-5401-2725.
In Washington, D.C.: Metropolitan Square, 1450 G Street, N.W.
Telephone: 202-879-3939.
Cable Address: "Attorneys Washington."
Telex: 89-2410 ATTORNEYS WASH.
Telecopier: 202-737-2832.

MEMBER OF FIRM IN IRVINE
Thomas R. Malcolm

For Complete List of Firm Personnel, See General Section

For full biographical listings, see the Martindale-Hubbell Law Directory

MOWER, KOELLER, NEBEKER, CARLSON & HALUCK (AV)

108 Pacifica, P.O. Box 19799, 92713-9799
Telephone: 714-753-1229
Fax: 714-753-1413
San Bernardino, California Office: 412 West Hospitality Lane, Suite 300, 92408.
Telephone: 909-381-3334.
Fax: 909-889-2007.
San Diego, California Office: 225 Broadway, 21st Floor.
Telephone: 619-233-1600.
Fax: 619-236-0527.
Yuma, Arizona Office: 212 South 2nd Avenue, P.O. Bin 11791.
Telephone: 520-782-2531.
Fax: 520-782-5319.

MEMBERS OF FIRM

Jon R. Mower	Patrick A. Carreon
Keith D. Koeller	Lynn M. Bouslog
William L. Haluck	Edward W. Schmitt
Joseph J. Cullen	Ellen E. Hunter

(See Next Column)

Nancy J. Altman	Ferdinand M. Trampe
Mark D. Newcomb	James A. Burton
Terrence J. Giannone	Eric W. Smith
Steven G. Holett	

For full biographical listings, see the Martindale-Hubbell Law Directory

PIVO & HALBREICH (AV)

1920 Main Street, Suite 800, 92714
Telephone: 714-253-2000

Kenneth R. Pivo	Douglas A. Amo
Eva S. Halbreich	Richard O. Schwartz
Mona Z. Hanna	

ASSOCIATES

Charles A. Palmer	Michael A. Brodie
William J. Mall, III	Lance Gordon Greene
Kathleen E. Wilcox	Annie Glass Henshel
Timothy J. Lippert	Jennifer Batliner

Representative Clients: Physicians and Surgeons Underwriters Corp.; Fremont Indemnity; American Continental Insurance Co.; AKROS Medico Enterprises; Kaiser Foundation Healthplan, Inc.; Caronia Corp.; The Doctor's Co.; Harbor Regional Center; Developmental Disabilities Regional Center; South Central Los Angeles Regional Center.

For full biographical listings, see the Martindale-Hubbell Law Directory

RAITT & MORASSE, A PROFESSIONAL CORPORATION (AV)

17320 Redhill Avenue, Suite 370, 92614-5644
Telephone: 714-261-1700
Fax: 714-261-2073

G. Emmett Raitt, Jr.	Steven R. Morasse

Desmond J. Collins

For full biographical listings, see the Martindale-Hubbell Law Directory

JEFFREY A. ROBINSON (AV)

2301 Dupont Drive, Suite 410, 92612
Telephone: 714-752-7007
Fax: 714-752-7023

For full biographical listings, see the Martindale-Hubbell Law Directory

RUS, MILIBAND, WILLIAMS & SMITH (AV)

Suite 700, 2600 Michelson Drive, 92612
Telephone: 714-752-7100
Fax: 714-252-1514

Ronald Rus	J. Scott Williams
Joel S. Miliband	Randall A. Smith
Laurel Zaeske	

M. Peter Crinella	David Edward Hays
Jeffrey H. Sussman	Steven Joseph Kraemer
Cathrine M. Castaldi	Leo J. Presiado

For full biographical listings, see the Martindale-Hubbell Law Directory

STEPONOVICH & ASSOCIATES, A PROFESSIONAL LAW CORPORATION (AV)

Koll Center Irvine - Transamerica Tower, 18201 Von Karman Avenue, Suite 650, 92612-1005
Telephone: 714-852-1073
Fax: 714-852-1276
Email: STEPOLAW@aol.com

Michael J. Steponovich, Jr.

For full biographical listings, see the Martindale-Hubbell Law Directory

WATT, TIEDER & HOFFAR, L.L.P. (AV(T))

3 Park Plaza, Suite 1530, 92714
Telephone: 714-852-6700
Telecopier: 714-261-0771
McLean Virginia Office: 7929 Westpark Drive, Suite 400,
Telephone: 703-749-1000.
Telecopier: 703-893-8029.
Washington, D.C. Office: 601 Pennsylvania Avenue, N.W. Suite 900,
Telephone: 202-462-4697.

MEMBERS OF FIRM

John B. Tieder, Jr.	Michael G. Long
(Not admitted in CA)	Christopher P. Pappas
Robert M. Fitzgerald	
(Not admitted in CA)	

ASSOCIATE
Gregory John Dukellis

For full biographical listings, see the Martindale-Hubbell Law Directory

Irvine—Continued

WESIERSKI & ZUREK (AV)

Suite 1500, 5 Park Plaza, 92714
Telephone: 714-975-1000
Telecopier: 714-756-0517
Glendale, California Office: 800 North Brand Boulevard, Suite 250.
Telephone: 818-543-6100.
Telecopier: 818-543-6101.

PARTNERS

Christopher P. Wesierski	Terence P. Carney
Ronald Zurek	Thomas G. Wianecki
(Resident, Glendale Office)	Stephen M. Ziemann
Daniel J. Ford, Jr.	Mark E. Brubaker

ASSOCIATES

Christopher M. Fisher	Steven D. Turner
Mark J. Giannamore	Robert M. Binam
Paul J. Lipman	Diane E. Jacobs
David F. Mastan	Bruce V. Rorty

For full biographical listings, see the Martindale-Hubbell Law Directory

---

LAGUNA BEACH, Orange Co.

ROBERT S. LEWIN A LAW CORPORATION (AV)

105 Crescent Bay Drive, Suite F, 92651
Telephone: 714-497-8897
FAX: 714-497-1714

Robert S. Lewin
LEGAL SUPPORT PERSONNEL
Diane E. Fedden

For full biographical listings, see the Martindale-Hubbell Law Directory

---

NOKES, DAVIS & QUINN, A PROFESSIONAL CORPORATION (AV)

450 Ocean Avenue, 92651
Telephone: 714-376-3055
FAX: 714-376-3070

Laurence P. Nokes	Thomas P. Davis
	Thomas P. Quinn, Jr.

For full biographical listings, see the Martindale-Hubbell Law Directory

---

LAGUNA NIGUEL, Orange Co.

ROBINSON, PHILLIPS & CALCAGNIE, A PROFESSIONAL CORPORATION (AV)

Incorporated 1986
28202 Cabot Road Suite 200, 92677
Telephone: 714-347-8855
Fax: 714-347-8774
Email: rpc@robinson-pilaw.com
San Diego, California Office: 110 Laurel Street.
Telephone: 619-338-4060.
Fax: 619-338-0423.

Mark P. Robinson, Jr.	Gordon G. Phillips, Jr.
	Kevin F. Calcagnie

Allan F. Davis	Susan Lee Guinn
	Jeoffrey L. Robinson

LEGAL SUPPORT PERSONNEL

Lin Moen	Darleen Perkins
Donna Hosea	Francine Teer
	Linda Audeoud

For full biographical listings, see the Martindale-Hubbell Law Directory

---

LA JOLLA, San Diego Co.

MAURER LAW FIRM (AV)

7825 Fay Avenue, Suite 200, 92037
Telephone: 619-456-5570
Fax: 619-551-8919

Charles D. Maurer, Jr.

For full biographical listings, see the Martindale-Hubbell Law Directory

---

LAW OFFICES OF MAURILE C. TREMBLAY A PROFESSIONAL CORPORATION (AV)

4180 La Jolla Village Drive, Suite 210, 92037
Telephone: 619-558-3030
FAX: 619-558-2502

Maurile C. Tremblay	Mark D. Estle

For full biographical listings, see the Martindale-Hubbell Law Directory

---

LARKSPUR, Marin Co.

KATZ, BIERER & BRADY, A PROFESSIONAL CORPORATION (AV)

101 Larkspur Landing Circle, Suite 223, 94939
Telephone: 415-925-1600
FAX: 415-925-0940

Richard L. Katz	Joel D. Bierer
	Steven J. Brady

OF COUNSEL

Alvin J. Schifrin

For full biographical listings, see the Martindale-Hubbell Law Directory

---

LONG BEACH, Los Angeles Co.

BENNETT & KISTNER (AV)

115 Pine Avenue, Suite 600, 90802-4446
Telephone: 310-435-6675
Fax: 310-437-8375

Charles J. Bennett	Wayne T. Kistner
	Richard R. Bradbury

ASSOCIATE

Charles H. Smith

OF COUNSEL

Christopher Johns

Representative Clients: The Hertz Corp.; Mattel, Inc.; Di Salvo Trucking Co.; Long Beach Community Medical Center; Los Angeles County Metropolitan Transportation Authority; Long Beach Memorial Medical Center; Saddleback Memorial Medical Center; Utah Home Fire Insurance; P.C.H. Enterprise, Inc.
Reference: Ken Walker of Farmers & Merchants Bank, Long Beach, California.

CAMERON, MADDEN, PEARLSON, GALE & SELLARS (AV)

One World Trade Center Suite 1600, 90831-1600
Telephone: 310-436-3888
Telecopier: 310-437-1967

MEMBERS OF THE FIRM

Timothy C. Cameron	Patrick T. Madden
Charles M. Gale	Paul R. Pearlson
	James D. Sellars

ASSOCIATE

Lillian D. Salinger

For full biographical listings, see the Martindale-Hubbell Law Directory

---

CAYER, KILSTOFTE & CRATON, A PROFESSIONAL LAW CORPORATION (AV)

Suite 700, 444 West Ocean Boulevard, 90802
Telephone: 310-435-6008
Fax: 310-435-3704
Email: CKCCRC@AOL.COM

John J. Cayer	Stephen R. Kilstofte
	Curt R. Craton

Cortlen R. Hauge

For full biographical listings, see the Martindale-Hubbell Law Directory

---

FLYNN, DELICH & WISE (AV)

One World Trade Center, Suite 1800, 90831-1800
Telephone: 310-435-2626
Fax: 310-437-7555
San Francisco, California Office: Suite 1750, 580 California Street.
Telephone: 415-693-5566.
Fax: 415-693-0410.

Erich P. Wise	Nicholas S. Politis

Representative Clients: American Hawaii Cruises; Holland America Line; Through Transport Mutual Insurance Association, Ltd.; The Britannia Steam Ship Insurance Association Limited; The Steamship Mutual Underwriting Association (Bermuda) Ltd.; General Steamship Corp., Ltd.; Commodore Cruise Line, Ltd.; Interocean Steamship Corporation; Sea-Land Service, Inc.; Hatteras Yachts.

For full biographical listings, see the Martindale-Hubbell Law Directory

---

FORD, WALKER, HAGGERTY & BEHAR, PROFESSIONAL LAW CORPORATION (AV)

One World Trade Center, Twenty Seventh Floor, 90831
Telephone: 310-983-2500
Telecopier: 310-983-2555

(See Next Column)

FORD, WALKER, HAGGERTY & BEHAR PROFESSIONAL LAW CORPORATION, *Long Beach—Continued*

G. Richard Ford	Donna Rogers Kirby
Timothy L. Walker	Tina Ivankovic Mangarpan
William C. Haggerty	Susan D. Berger
Jeffrey S. Behar	Joseph A. Heath
Mark Steven Hennings	Robert J. Chavez

J. Michael McClure

Arthur W. Schultz	Theodore A. Clapp
Jon T. Moseley	Stanley L. Scarlett
Maxine J. Lebowitz	Scott A. Ritsema
Timothy P. McDonald	Michael Guy Martin
K. Michele Williams	Colleen A. Strong
Stephen Ward Moore	Thomas L. Gourde
James D. Savage	Patrick J. Stark
Todd D. Pearl	Shayne L. Wulterin
Patrick J. Gibbs	Charles D. Jarrell
James O. Miller	Charles J. Schmitt
David Huchel	Kyle A. Ostergrad
Robert Reisinger	Todd L. Kessler

OF COUNSEL
Theodore P. Shield, P.L.C.

For full biographical listings, see the Martindale-Hubbell Law Directory

---

EDWARD P. GEORGE, JR., INC. A PROFESSIONAL CORPORATION (AV)

Suite 430, 5000 East Spring Street, 90815
Telephone: 310-497-2900
Facsimile: 310-497-2904

Edward P. George, Jr.	Timothy L. O'Reilly

OF COUNSEL
Albert C. S. Ramsey

Reference: Harbor Bank, Long Beach.

For full biographical listings, see the Martindale-Hubbell Law Directory

---

MOORE, RUTTER & EVANS (AV)

A Partnership including a Professional Corporation
555 East Ocean Boulevard, Suite 500, 90802-5090
Telephone: 310-494-6667; 435-4499
Facsimile: 310-495-4229
Huntington Beach, California Office: 2100 Main Street, Suite 280, 92648.
Telephone: 714-374-3333.

RESIDENT PARTNERS

Neal Moore	Mark D. Rutter

William D. Evans (P.C.)

OF COUNSEL
Michael J. Emling

For full biographical listings, see the Martindale-Hubbell Law Directory

---

PERONA, LANGER & BECK, A PROFESSIONAL CORPORATION (AV)

300 East San Antonio, 90807
Telephone: 310-426-6155
Facsimile: 310-490-9823
Los Angeles, California Office: 9255 Sunset Boulevard, Suite 920.
Telephone: 800-435-7542.

James T. Perona	Wayne M. Robertshaw
Major A. Langer	John C. Thornton
Ronald Beck	M. Lawrence Lallande

Ellen R. Serbin

Nelson L. Cohen	Edward T. Trumper
R. Paul Katrinak	Richard L. Stuhlbarg
Susan Graham	Rhonda Ann Visniski

For full biographical listings, see the Martindale-Hubbell Law Directory

---

RUSSELL & MIRKOVICH (AV)

One World Trade Center, Suite 1450, 90831-1450
Telephone: 310-436-9911
FAX: 310-436-1897

Carlton E. Russell	Joseph N. Mirkovich

For full biographical listings, see the Martindale-Hubbell Law Directory

---

STOLPMAN • KRISSMAN • ELBER • MANDEL & KATZMAN LLP (AV)

A Partnership including Professional Corporations
Nineteenth Floor, 111 West Ocean Boulevard, 90802-4649
Telephone: 310-435-8300
Telecopier: 310-435-8304
Los Angeles (Westwood) Office: Suite 1800, 10880 Wilshire Boulevard.

MEMBERS OF FIRM

Thomas G. Stolpman (Inc.)	Joel Krissman
Leonard H. Mandel	Mary Nielsen Abbott
Bernard Katzman (Inc.)	Donna Silver

Dennis M. Elber

ASSOCIATES

Edwin Silver	Lynne Rasmussen

Elaine Mandel

For full biographical listings, see the Martindale-Hubbell Law Directory

---

TAUBMAN, SIMPSON, YOUNG & SULENTOR (AV)

249 East Ocean Boulevard, Suite 700, P.O. Box 22670, 90801-5670
Telephone: 310-436-9201
FAX: 310-590-9695

E. C. Denio (1864-1952)	Richard G. Wilson (1928-1993)
Geo. A. Hart (1881-1967)	Roger W. Young
Geo. P. Taubman, Jr. (1897-1970)	William J. Sulentor
Matthew C. Simpson (1900-1988)	Peter M. Williams
	Scott R. Magee
	Maria M. Rohaidy

Stuart C. Talley

Attorneys for: Bixby Land Co.; Renick Cadillac, Inc.; Oil Operators Inc.
Local Counsel: Crown Cork & Seal Co., Inc.

For full biographical listings, see the Martindale-Hubbell Law Directory

---

WILLIAMS WOOLLEY COGSWELL NAKAZAWA & RUSSELL (AV)

111 West Ocean Boulevard, Suite 2000, 90802-4614
Telephone: 310-495-6000
Telecopier: 310-435-1359; 310-435-6812
Telex: ITT: 4933872; WU: 984929
Email: wwlaw@msn.com
Rancho Santa Fe, California Office: P.O. Box 9120, 16236 San Dieguito Road, Building 3, Suite 3-15, 92067.
Telephone: 619-497-0284.
Fax: 619-759-9938.
Port Hueneme, California Office: 237 E. Hueneme Road, Suite A, 93041.
Telephone: 805-488-8560.
Fax: 805-488-7896.

MEMBERS OF FIRM

Reed M. Williams	Alan Nakazawa
David E. R. Woolley	Blake W. Larkin
Forrest R. Cogswell	Thomas A. Russell

ASSOCIATES

Todd A. Valdes	Thomas G. Walsh

Richard J. Nikas

For full biographical listings, see the Martindale-Hubbell Law Directory

---

WISE, WIEZOREK, TIMMONS & WISE, A PROFESSIONAL CORPORATION (AV)

3700 Santa Fe Avenue, Suite 300, P.O. Box 2190, 90810
Telephone: 310-834-5028
Fax: 310-834-8018
Redding, California Office: 443 Redcliff Drive, Suite 230.
Telephone: 916-221-7632.
Fax: 916-221-8832.

George E. Wise	Richard P. Dieffenbach
Duane H. Timmons	Steven C. Rice
Anthony F. Wiezorek	Stephen M. Smith
Susan E. Anderson Wise	Thomas J. Yocis
Albert F. Padley, III	James M. Cox
Michael J. Pearce	Mathew J. Vande Wydeven
Mark C. Allen, III	Tae J. Im

For full biographical listings, see the Martindale-Hubbell Law Directory

---

LOS ALTOS, Santa Clara Co.

MALOVOS & KONEVICH (AV)

Los Altos Plaza, 5150 El Camino Real, Suite A-22, 94022
Telephone: 415-988-9700
Facsimile: 415-988-9639

Marian Malovos Konevich	Robert W. Konevich

RETIRED FOUNDING PARTNER
Kenneth R. Malovos

For full biographical listings, see the Martindale-Hubbell Law Directory

LOS ANGELES, * Los Angeles Co.

AGAPAY, LEVYN & HALLING, A PROFESSIONAL CORPORATION (AV)

Fourth Floor, 10801 National Boulevard, 90064
Telephone: 310-470-1700
Fax: 310-470-2602
Orange, California Office: One City Boulevard West, Suite 835, 92668.
Telephone: 714-634-1744.
Fax: 714-634-0417.

Joe M. Agapay, Jr.	Thomas S. Levyn
Chris W. Halling	

Glen R. Segal (Resident Member, Orange Office)	Tracey P. Hom
	Richard D. Coats
Peter J. Krupinsky	Steven A. Sokol
Laurie J. Bergren	Pamela J. Paluga

OF COUNSEL

Alan B. Grass	Glen Dresser
Nanci E. Murdock	

For full biographical listings, see the Martindale-Hubbell Law Directory

AGNEW & BRUSAVICH

(See Torrance)

ANGEL AND NEISTAT, A PROFESSIONAL CORPORATION (AV)

28th Floor 555 South Flower Street, 90017-2205
Telephone: 213-689-4500
Fax: 213-689-4651

Michael A. Angel	Steven A. Schwaber
Douglas M. Neistat	Alan J. Stomel
Alan Holmberg	Gary R. Wallace
Steven L. Crane	Daniel H. Reiss

For full biographical listings, see the Martindale-Hubbell Law Directory

BAKER & HOSTETLER (AV)

600 Wilshire Boulevard, 90017-3212
Telephone: 213-624-2400
FAX: 213-975-1740
In Cleveland, Ohio: 3200 National City Center, 1900 East Ninth Street.
Telephone: 216-621-0200.
In Columbus, Ohio: Capitol Square, Suite 2100, 65 East State Street.
Telephone: 614-228-1541.
In Denver, Colorado: 303 East 17th Avenue, Suite 1100.
Telephone: 303-861-0600.
In Houston, Texas: 1000 Louisiana, Suite 2000.
Telephone: 713-236-0020.
In Long Beach, California: 300 Oceangate, Suite 620.
Telephone: 310-432-2827.
In Orlando, Florida: SunBank Center, Suite 2300, 200 South Orange Avenue.
Telephone: 407-649-4000.
In Washington, D. C.: Washington Square, Suite 1100, 1050 Connecticut Avenue, N. W.
Telephone: 202-861-1500.
In College Park, Maryland: 9658 Baltimore Boulevard, Suite 206.
Telephone: 301-441-2781.
In Alexandria, Virginia: 437 North Lee Street.
Telephone: 703-549-1294.
In San Francisco, California: One Sansome Street, Suite 2000.
Telephone: 415-951-4705.

PARTNERS

Angela C. Agrusa	Patrick J. Cain
Penny M. Costa	Richard A. Deeb
David A. Destino	Jack D. Fudge
Richard A. Goette	Emil W. Herich
Peter W. James	Lynn S. Loeb
Larry W. McFarland	Bill E. Schroeder
Diane C. Stanfield	Ralph Zarefsky

ASSOCIATES

Marcia T. Law	Gregg A. Rapoport
Dennis L. Wilson	

For Complete List of Firm Personnel, See General Section

For full biographical listings, see the Martindale-Hubbell Law Directory

BAKER AND JACOBSON, A PROFESSIONAL CORPORATION (AV)

Suite 500, 11377 West Olympic Boulevard, 90064-1683
Telephone: 310-914-7990
Fax: 310-914-7913

Robert P. Baker	Lawrence M. Jacobson

For full biographical listings, see the Martindale-Hubbell Law Directory

BARTON, KLUGMAN & OETTING (AV)

A Partnership including Professional Corporations
37th Floor, 333 South Grand Avenue, 90071-1599
Telephone: 213-621-4000
Telecopier: 213-625-1832
Newport Beach Office: Suite 700, 4400 MacArthur Boulevard, P.O. Box 2350, 92660.
Telephone: 714-752-7551.
Telecopier: 714-752-0288.

COUNSEL TO FIRM

Robert M. Barton *	Robert H. Klugman *
	Richard F. Oetting *

MEMBERS OF FIRM

David F. Morgan *	David J. Cartano *
William D. Herz *	Martin J. Spear *
Charles J. Schufreider *	Tod V. Beebe *
Robert Louis Fisher *	Ronald R. St. John
Gilbert D. Jensen *	Mark A. Newton *
	Margot I. McLeay

ASSOCIATES

Barbara W. G. Crowley	Reiko L. Furuta
	Jaleen Nelson

References: The Bank of California (Southern California Headquarters); Wells Fargo Bank, N.A. (Wells Fargo Center, Los Angeles).
*Denotes a lawyer whose Professional Corporation is a member of the partnership or is Counsel to the Firm

For full biographical listings, see the Martindale-Hubbell Law Directory

BAUM, HEDLUND, ARISTEI, GUILFORD & DOWNEY, A PROFESSIONAL CORPORATION (AV)

Suite 950, 12100 Wilshire Boulevard, 90025
Telephone: 310-207-3233; 800-827-0087
Facsimile: 310-820-7444
Email: bhagd@bhagd.com *URL:* http://www.bhagd.com/attorneys/
Washington, D.C. Office: 1250 24th Street, N.W., Suite 300.
Telephone: 202-466-0513; 800-827-0097.
Facsimile: 202-466-0527.

Michael L. Baum	J. Clark Aristei
Paul J. Hedlund	Robert E. Guilford
	William J. Downey III

John A. Greaves	Robert F. Foss
Cara L. Belle	Karen A. Barth
(Not admitted in CA)	V. Neil Forn, II

Reference: Union Bank.

For full biographical listings, see the Martindale-Hubbell Law Directory

BERGMAN & WEDNER, INC. (AV)

Suite 900, 10880 Wilshire Boulevard, 90024
Telephone: 310-470-6110
Fax: Available on Request

Gregory M. Bergman	Robert M. Mason III
Gregory A. Wedner	Kristi Anne Sjoholm-Sierchio
Mark E. Fingerman	Keith A. Robinson
Alan Harvey Mittelman	John P. Dacey

John V. Tamborelli	Lisa S. Shukiar
Blithe Ann Smith	Daphne M. Humphreys
	Suzanne Z. Shbaro

OF COUNSEL

Lloyd A. Bergman (1923-1994)	Jacob A. Wedner

SPECIAL COUNSEL

Richard V. Godino

For full biographical listings, see the Martindale-Hubbell Law Directory

BERMAN, BLANCHARD, MAUSNER & RESSER, A LAW CORPORATION (AV)

4727 Wilshire Boulevard, Suite 500, 90010
Telephone: 213-965-1200
Telecopier: 213-965-1919
Email: BBMR@ix.netcom.com

Laurence M. Berman	Jeffrey N. Mausner
Lonnie C. Blanchard, III	Bernard M. Resser

Paul A. Hoffman	Cary P. Ocon
Eric Levinrad	Lisé Hamilton

For full biographical listings, see the Martindale-Hubbell Law Directory

Los Angeles—Continued

BLACK COMPEAN HALL & LENNEMAN (AV)

One Wilshire, Suite 1000 624 South Grand Avenue, 90017
Telephone: 213-629-9500
FAX: 213-629-4868
Email: bchl@earthlink.net

MEMBERS OF FIRM

Robert H. Black	Frederick G. Hall
Michael D. Compean	Annette J. Lenneman

ASSOCIATES

William J. Light	Margie Castillo
Vicente Valencia, Jr.	Lara Michelle Brya
Meredith A. Czapla	

Reference: Sterling Bank.

For full biographical listings, see the Martindale-Hubbell Law Directory

BLECHER & COLLINS, A PROFESSIONAL CORPORATION (AV)

611 West Sixth Street, 20th Floor, 90017
Telephone: 213-622-4222
Telecopier: 213-622-1656

Maxwell M. Blecher	Ralph C. Hofer
Harold R. Collins, Jr.	William C. Hsu
John E. Andrews	James Robert Noblin
Florence F. Cameron	Donald R. Pepperman
Alicia G. Rosenberg	

For full biographical listings, see the Martindale-Hubbell Law Directory

LAW OFFICES OF DAVID B. BLOOM A PROFESSIONAL CORPORATION (AV)

3325 Wilshire Boulevard, Ninth Floor, 90010
Telephone: 213-938-5248; 384-4088
Telecopier: 213-385-2009

David B. Bloom

Stephen S. Monroe (A Professional Corporation)	Susan Carole Jay
Raphael A. Rosemblat	Edward Idell
James E. Adler	Sandra Kamenir
Bonni S. Mantovani	Steven Wayne Lazarus
Roy A. Levun	Andrew Edward Briseno
Cherie S. Raidy	Harold C. Klaskin
Jonathan Udell	Shelley M. Gould
	Peter O. Israel

For full biographical listings, see the Martindale-Hubbell Law Directory

BOTTUM & FELITON, A PROFESSIONAL CORPORATION (AV)

Suite 1500, South Tower, 3200 Wilshire Boulevard, 90010
Telephone: 213-487-0402
Fax: 213-386-9803
San Diego, California Office: Suite 400 Emerald Plaza, 402 West Broadway.
Telephone: 619-595-4857.
Fax: 619-595-4863.

John R. Feliton, Jr.	Steve Johnson
Robert A. Wooten, Jr.	Mark A. Oertel
Alexander F. Giovanniello	

Kenneth C. Feldman	Julie A. Covell
Jerry Garcia	Karl R. Loureiro
Paul K. Schrieffer	Sean T. Hamada
Scott A. Hampton	Gary F. Werner
Gregg S. Garfinkel	Victor I. King
Brian E. Cooper	Andrea J. Lang
Linwood Warren, Jr.	

For full biographical listings, see the Martindale-Hubbell Law Directory

BRONSON, BRONSON & McKINNON LLP (AV)

A Partnership including Professional Corporations
444 South Flower Street, 24th Floor, 90071
Telephone: 213-627-2000
Fax: 213-627-2277
San Francisco, California Office: 505 Montgomery Street.
Telephone: 415-986-4200.
San Jose, California Office: 10 Almaden Boulevard, Suite 600.
Telephone: 408-293-0599.

RESIDENT PARTNERS

Eric A. Amador	Edwin W. Green
Donna P. Arlow	Claudia L. Greenspoon
Stephen L. Backus	Ralph S. LaMontagne, Jr.
Charles N. Bland, Jr.	Richard C. Macias
John D. Boyle	Dani H. Rogers
Thomas T. Carpenter	Manuel Saldaña
Elizabeth A. Erskine	David M. Walsh
Sheldon J. Warren	

(See Next Column)

RESIDENT ASSOCIATES

Janet Andrea	Charles E. Koro
Raymon B. Bilbeaux, III	Kathleen R. O'Laughlin
Laurie S. Julien	Hayley L. Sneiderman
John F. Stephens	

For Complete List of Firm Personnel, See General Section

For full biographical listings, see the Martindale-Hubbell Law Directory

BUCHALTER, NEMER, FIELDS & YOUNGER, A PROFESSIONAL CORPORATION (AV)

24th Floor, 601 South Figueroa Street, 90017
Telephone: 213-891-0700
Fax: 213-896-0400
Email: buchalter@earthlink.net *URL:* http://www.buchalter.com
New York, New York Office: 15th Floor, 605 Third Avenue.
Telephone: 212-490-8600.
Fax: 212-490-6022.
San Francisco, California Office: 29th Floor, 333 Market Street.
Telephone: 415-227-0900.
Fax: 415-227-0770.
Newport Beach, California Office: Suite 1450, 620 Newport Center Drive.
Telephone: 714-760-1121.
Fax: 714-720-0182.

Murray M. Fields	Michael J. Cereseto
Jay R. Ziegler	Bernard E. Le Sage

References: City National Bank; Wells Fargo Bank; Metrobank.

For Complete List of Firm Personnel, See General Section

For full biographical listings, see the Martindale-Hubbell Law Directory

DEBORAH CHODOS (AV)

12400 Wilshire Boulevard, Suite 400, 90025-1023
Telephone: 310-207-0569
Fax: 310-207-5313

For full biographical listings, see the Martindale-Hubbell Law Directory

CLARK & TREVITHICK, A PROFESSIONAL CORPORATION (AV)

800 Wilshire Boulevard, 12th Floor, 90017
Telephone: 213-629-5700
Telecopier: 213-624-9441
San Francisco, California Office: 456 Montgomery Street, 20th Floor.
Telephone: 415-288-6520.
Fax: 415-398-2820.

Philip W. Bartenetti	Leonard Brazil
Dolores Cordell	Leslie R. Horowitz
Vincent Tricarico	Arturo Santana Jr.
Kerry T. Ryan	

OF COUNSEL

Judith Ilene Bloom

References: Wells Fargo Bank (Los Angeles Main Office); National Bank of California.

For Complete List of Firm Personnel, See General Section

For full biographical listings, see the Martindale-Hubbell Law Directory

COLEMAN & RICHARDS, A PROFESSIONAL CORPORATION (AV)

Suite 810, 1801 Avenue of the Stars (Century City), 90067
Telephone: 310-277-2700

Richard M. Coleman	Laurie J. Richards

For full biographical listings, see the Martindale-Hubbell Law Directory

CORINBLIT & SELTZER, A PROFESSIONAL CORPORATION (AV)

Suite 820 Wilshire Park Place, 3700 Wilshire Boulevard, 90010-3085
Telephone: 213-380-4200
Telecopier: 213-385-7503; 385-4560
Email: mseltzer@AOL.com

Marc M. Seltzer	Christina A. Snyder

OF COUNSEL

Jack Corinblit, A Law Corporation	Earl P. Willens

Gretchen M. Nelson	George A. Shohet
Moses Garcia	

For full biographical listings, see the Martindale-Hubbell Law Directory

CRAWFORD & REIMANN LLP (AV)

15th Floor, 11755 Wilshire Boulevard, 90025
Telephone: 310-478-7442
Fax: 310-575-4575

(See Next Column)

CRAWFORD & REIMANN LLP—*Continued*
MEMBERS OF FIRM
Thomas W. Crawford   David W. Reimann
ASSOCIATES
Robert C. Cartwright   Glenn D. Hamovitz

Reference: Santa Monica Bank, Brentwood Office.

For full biographical listings, see the Martindale-Hubbell Law Directory

DANIELS, BARATTA & FINE (AV)

A Partnership including a Professional Corporation
1801 Century Park East, 9th Floor, 90067
Telephone: 310-556-7900
Telecopier: 310-556-2807
Bakersfield, California Office: 5201 California Avenue, Suite 400.
Telephone: 805-335-7788.
Telecopier: 805-324-3660.
MEMBERS OF FIRM
John P. Daniels (Inc.)   Mary Hulett
James M. Baratta   Michael B. Geibel
Paul R. Fine   James I. Montgomery, Jr.
Nathan B. Hoffman   Lance D. Orloff
Mark R. Israel
ASSOCIATES
Ilene Wendy Kurtzman   Spencer A. Schneider
Janet Sacks   Angelo A. Du Plantier, III
Michael N. Schonbuch   Leslie E. Wright, III.
Scott M. Leavitt   Erin B. Hallissy
Michelle R. Press   Kena B. Chin
Scott Ashford Brooks   Dean Bengston
Craig A. Laidig   Peter Anders Nyquist
Robin A. Webb   Jeannie Masse
Craig S. Momita   Lori Chotiner
Maureen M. Michail
OF COUNSEL
Timothy J. Hughes   Drew T. Hanker
Mark A. Vega

For full biographical listings, see the Martindale-Hubbell Law Directory

DARLING, HALL & RAE (AV)

777 South Figueroa, 37th Floor, 90017
Telephone: 213-627-8104
Fax: 213-627-7795
Email: 71555.1466@Compuserve.com
MEMBERS OF FIRM
Hugh W. Darling (1901-1986)   Donald Keith Hall (1918-1984)
Edward S. Shattuck (1901-1965)   Matthew S. Rae, Jr.
George Gaylord Gute   Richard L. Stack
(1922-1981)   Edwin Freston
OF COUNSEL
John L. Flowers

Reference: City National Bank (Pershing Square Office, Los Angeles, California).

For full biographical listings, see the Martindale-Hubbell Law Directory

DAVIS & FOX (AV)

1901 Avenue of the Stars, Suite 400, 90067
Telephone: 310-286-2915
Fax: 310-286-2916
MEMBERS OF FIRM
Calvin E. Davis   Steven A. Fox
ASSOCIATES
Brian Aronson   Amy L. Freisleben
Susan R. Peck
OF COUNSEL
Herbert D. Meyers

For full biographical listings, see the Martindale-Hubbell Law Directory

DEMETRIOU, DEL GUERCIO, SPRINGER & MOYER, LLP (AV)

801 South Grand Avenue, 10th Floor, 90017
Telephone: 213-624-8407
Telecopy: 213-624-0174
Email: ddsm@juno.com *URL:* http://www.ddsm.com
MEMBERS OF FIRM
Jeffrey Z. B. Springer   Leslie M. Smario
Regina Liudzius Cobb   Andrew J. Bracker
Gregory D. Trimarche   Kimberly E. Lewand
Karen McLaurin Chang   Jennifer T. Taggart
Robert P. Silverstein

Reference: Bank of America, L.A. Main Office, Los Angeles, Calif.

For full biographical listings, see the Martindale-Hubbell Law Directory

RICK EDWARDS, INC. (AV)

20th Floor, 1925 Century Park East, 90067
Telephone: 310-277-6464
Telecopier: 310-286-9501

Rick Edwards

Anthony C. Edwards   Ken Yuwiler
OF COUNSEL
William R. Bishin

Reference: Union Bank, 445 South Figueroa Street, Los Angeles, California 90071.

For full biographical listings, see the Martindale-Hubbell Law Directory

LAW OFFICES OF ROBERT W. EISFELDER, P.C. (AV)

Suite 400, 11726 San Vicente Boulevard, 90049-5047
Telephone: 310-820-4500

Robert W. Eisfelder

For full biographical listings, see the Martindale-Hubbell Law Directory

ENGSTROM, LIPSCOMB & LACK, A PROFESSIONAL CORPORATION (AV)

16th Floor, 10100 Santa Monica Boulevard, 90067
Telephone: 310-552-3800
Telecopier: 310-552-9434
URL: http://www.elllaw.com

Paul W. Engstrom   Brian D. Depew
Lee G. Lipscomb   Jeffrey T. Bolson
Walter J. Lack   Alan B. Nishimura
Jerry A. Ramsey   Gary A. Praglin
Steven C. Shuman   William T. Clemons III
Elizabeth Lane Crooke   Matthew J. Saunders
Robert J. Wolfe

Daniel G. Whalen   Joy L. Robertson
Brian J. Heffernan   Jill P. McDonell
Eric Berg   Laura M. Watkins
Karen-Denise Lee   Mark Evans Millard
Adam D. Miller   Stuart R. Fraenkel
Jill L. Feinberg   Tracy Michelle Tuso
Dawn M. Flores-Oster   David M. Robinson
Paul A. Traina   Karen L. Hindin
Cynthia Jane Emry   Troy H. Slome
Brian J. Leinbach   Daniel J. Padova

Reference: Comerica Bank.

For full biographical listings, see the Martindale-Hubbell Law Directory

FREDERICKSON & YOUNG (AV)

Suite 481, 5757 Wilshire Boulevard, 90036-3664
Telephone: 213-964-7373
Fax: 213-964-7377
Email: FNYMAN@AOL.com
MEMBERS OF FIRM
David H. Frederickson   Robert E. Young
ASSOCIATE
Brian M. Plessala

Representative Clients: Information International, Inc.; Nordoff Investments, Inc.; International Broadcasting, Inc.; Patrick Media Group; Palm Plaza Development; Cobe Laboratories, Inc.; Amusements International; Oxford Group of Companies.

For full biographical listings, see the Martindale-Hubbell Law Directory

GALTON & HELM (AV)

500 South Grand Avenue, Suite 1200, 90071
Telephone: 213-629-8800
Telecopier: 213-629-0037
Palm Desert, California Office: 73-290 El Paseo, Suite 377.
Telephone: 619-776-5600.
Fax: 619-776-5602.
MEMBERS OF FIRM
Stephen H. Galton   Daniel W. Maguire
Hugh H. Helm   (Resident at Palm Desert)
Michael F. Bell   David A. Lingenbrink
ASSOCIATES
Chris D. Olsen   Joanna M. Eoff
Melissa M. Cowan   Michael B. Bernacchi
Edith Sanchez Shea   Mark A. Riekhof
       (Resident, Glendale Office)

(See Next Column)

GALTON & HELM, *Los Angeles—Continued*

LEGAL SUPPORT PERSONNEL

Lana Banks (Paralegal)   Stephanie M. McCarthy
(Paralegal)

For full biographical listings, see the Martindale-Hubbell Law Directory

---

GIRARDI AND KEESE (AV)

1126 Wilshire Boulevard, 90017-1904
Telephone: 213-977-0211
FAX: 213-481-1554
San Bernardino, California Office: 596 North Arrowhead.
Telephone: 714-381-1551.
FAX: 714-381-2566.

MEMBERS OF FIRM

Thomas V. Girardi	V. Andre Rekte (Resident, San
Robert M. Keese	Bernardino Office)
John A. Girardi	John K. Courtney
James B. Kropff	Amy Fisch Solomon
Robert W. Finnerty	Thomas C. Morgan
James G. O'Callahan	David N. Bigelow
	Carrie J. Rognlien

References: Wells Fargo Bank (Los Angeles Head Office); Bank of Industry.

For full biographical listings, see the Martindale-Hubbell Law Directory

---

GOLDMAN & GORDON, L.L.P. (AV)

Suite 1920, 1801 Century Park East, 90067
Telephone: 310-277-7171
FAX: 310-277-1547

MEMBERS OF FIRM

A. S. Goldman (1895-1966)   Leonard A. Goldman
Robert P. Gordon

ASSOCIATE

Melody G. Anderson

References: Bank of America, Fourth and Spring Branch, Los Angeles; Bank of America, Wilshire-San Vincente Branch, Beverly Hills.

For full biographical listings, see the Martindale-Hubbell Law Directory

---

GRAY, YORK, DUFFY & RATTET (AV)

15760 Ventura Boulevard, 16th Floor (Encino), 91436
Telephone: 818-907-4000; 310-553-0445
FAX: 818-783-4551

MEMBERS OF FIRM

Gary S. Gray	Arlene A. Colman
James R. York	Barry D. Brown
John J. Duffy	William F. Flahavan
Gary S. Rattet	Jeffrey S. Stern

ASSOCIATES

Amalia L. Taylor	John L. Barber
Kenneth A. Hearn	Miloslav Khadilkar
Gabriel H. Wainfeld	Michael S. Eisenbaum
	Frank J. Ozello, Jr.

Reference: Marathon National Bank, Los Angeles, California.

For full biographical listings, see the Martindale-Hubbell Law Directory

---

HANNA AND MORTON (AV)

A Partnership including Professional Corporations
Seventeenth Floor, Wilshire-Grand Building, 600 Wilshire
Boulevard, 90017
Telephone: 213-628-7131
Facsimile: 213-623-3379

MEMBERS OF FIRM

Edward S. Renwick (A	Robert M. Newell, Jr.
Professional Corporation)	James P. Modisette
James P. Lower	David A. Ossentjuk
	John A. Belcher

OF COUNSEL

Milo V. Olson   David A. Thomas

ASSOCIATES

Thomas N. Campbell	Michael P. Wippler
Robert J. Roche	Daniel Y. Zohar

For Complete List of Firm Personnel, See General Section

For full biographical listings, see the Martindale-Hubbell Law Directory

---

HARNEY LAW OFFICES A LEGAL CORPORATION (AV)

Suite 1300 Figueroa Plaza, 201 North Figueroa Street, 90012-2636
Telephone: 213-482-0881
Fax: 213-250-4042

(See Next Column)

David M. Harney	Andrew J. Nocas
David T. Harney	Vincent McGowan
Julie A. Harney	Thomas A. Schultz

Reference: Bank of America.

For full biographical listings, see the Martindale-Hubbell Law Directory

---

HAWKINS, SCHNABEL, LINDAHL & BECK (AV)

660 South Figueroa Street, Suite 1500, 90017
Telephone: 213-488-3900
Telecopier: 213-486-9883
Email: 102175.3573@compuserve.com

MEMBERS OF FIRM

Roger E. Hawkins	Jon P. Kardassakis
Laurence H. Schnabel	William E. Keitel
George M. Lindahl	Timothy A. Gonzales
Kelley K. Beck	R. Timothy Stone
	Richard C. Weston

For full biographical listings, see the Martindale-Hubbell Law Directory

---

HENNIGAN, MERCER & BENNETT (AV)

601 South Figueroa Street, Suite 3300, 90017
Telephone: 213-694-1200
Fax: 213-694-1234
Email: Silverm@hmb.com

J. Michael Hennigan	Laura Lindgren
James W. Mercer	Bruce R. MacLeod
Bruce Bennett	Elizabeth D. Mann
John L. Amsden	Robert L. Palmer
C. Dana Hobart	Lauren A. Smith
Jeanne E. Irving	Peter J. Most
Pamala J. King	Lee W. Potts

ASSOCIATES

Nichole M. Auden	Linda A. Kontos
Jacqueline Bendy	Jennifer Sulla
Mary H. Chu	Michael Swartz
A. Ann Hered	Shawna L. Ballard
Gregory K. Jones	Claudia Schweikert
Ellen M. Keane	David H. Martin

OF COUNSEL

Anthony Castanares

For full biographical listings, see the Martindale-Hubbell Law Directory

---

HILL, FARRER & BURRILL LLP (AV)

A Limited Liability Partnership including Professional Corporations
35th Floor, Union Bank Square, 445 South Figueroa Street, 90071
Telephone: 213-620-0460
Fax: 213-624-4840

MEMBERS OF FIRM

Stanley E. Tobin (P.C.)	Kevin H. Brogan
William M. Bitting (P.C.)	Ronald W. Novotny (P.C.)
James G. Johnson (P.C.)	Michael S. Turner
	Jennifer L. Pancake

ASSOCIATES

Ian M. Green   Arnold D. Woo
Karen S. Seigel

For Complete List of Firm Personnel, See General Section

For full biographical listings, see the Martindale-Hubbell Law Directory

---

HONN & SECOF (AV)

510 West Sixth Street, Suite 910, 90014-1310
Telephone: 213-629-3900
Telecopier: 213-624-5362

Richard A. Honn   Howard S. Secof

ASSOCIATE

Wayne T. Kasai

Reference: Wells Fargo Bank.

For full biographical listings, see the Martindale-Hubbell Law Directory

---

HORNBERGER & CRISWELL (AV)

444 South Flower, 31st Floor, 90071
Telephone: 213-488-1655
Facsimile: 213-488-1255
Email: kbranch0@counsel.com

MEMBERS OF FIRM

Nicholas W. Hornberger	Ann M. Ghazarians
Leslie E. Criswell	Michael A. Brewer
	Scott Alan Freedman

(See Next Column)

HORNBERGER & CRISWELL—Continued

ASSOCIATES

Marlin E. Howes	James M. Slominski
Christopher T. Olsen	Michael C. Denlinger
Scott B. Cloud	Gayle L. Eskridge

OF COUNSEL

David E. Bower	William P. Driscoll

For full biographical listings, see the Martindale-Hubbell Law Directory

---

HOWARTH & SMITH (AV)

Suite 2900, 700 South Flower Street, 90017
Telephone: 213-955-9400
Fax: 213-622-0791

MEMBERS OF FIRM

Don Howarth	David K. Ringwood
Suzelle M. Smith	Kenneth S. Tune
	Brian D. Bubb

Marcus J. Berger	Katy Jacobs
Patricia Lee-Gulley	Sheila M. Bradley
Thomas F. Vandenburg	Julia S. Swanson
Gregory S. Tamkin	Kimberly L. Honus
	Randall Boese

For full biographical listings, see the Martindale-Hubbell Law Directory

---

JOHNSON, POULSON, COONS & SLATER (AV)

10880 Wilshire Boulevard, Suite 1800, 90024
Telephone: 310-475-0611
Telecopier: 310-475-0143

MEMBERS OF FIRM

Jonathan E. Johnson	Lynn O. Poulson (Mr.)
	Michael H. Coons

OF COUNSEL

Martin R. Slater

For full biographical listings, see the Martindale-Hubbell Law Directory

---

JONES, DAY, REAVIS & POGUE (AV)

555 West Fifth Street Suite 4600, 90013-1025
Telephone: 213-489-3939
Telex: 181439 UD
Telecopier: 213-243-2539
In Irvine, California: 2603 Main Street, Suite 900.
Telephone: 714-851-3939.
Telex: 194911 Lawyers LSA.
Telecopier: 714-553-7539.
In Atlanta, Georgia: 3500 One Peachtree Center, 303 Peachtree Street, N.E.
Telephone: 404-521-3939.
Cable Address: "Attorneys Atlanta".
Telex: 54-2711.
Telecopier: 404-581-8330.
In Brussels, Belgium: Avenue Louise 480, 7th Floor, B-1050 Brussels.
Telephone: 32-2-645-14-11.
Telecopier: 32-2-645-14-45.
In Chicago, Illinois: 77 West Wacker.
Telephone: 312-782-3939.
Telecopier: 312-782-8585.
In Cleveland, Ohio: North Point, 901 Lakeside Avenue.
Telephone: 216-586-3939.
Cable Address: "Attorneys Cleveland."
Telex: 980389.
Telecopier: 216-579-0212.
In Columbus, Ohio: 1900 Huntington Center.
Telephone: 614-469-3939.
Cable Address: "Attorneys Columbus."
Telecopier: 614-461-4198.
In Dallas, Texas: 2300 Trammell Crow Center, 2001 Ross Avenue.
Telephone: 214-220-3939.
Cable Address: "Attorneys Dallas."
Telex: 730852.
Telecopier: 214-969-5100.
In Frankfurt, Germany: Triton Haus, Bockenheimer Landstrasse 42, 60323 Frankfurt am Main.
Telephone: 49-69-9726-3939.
Telecopier: 49-69-9726-3993.
In Geneva, Switzerland: 20, rue de Candolle.
Telephone: 41-22-320-2339.
Telecopier: 41-22-320-1232.
In Hong Kong: 29th Floor, Entertainment Building, 30 Queen's Road Central.
Telephone: 852-2526-6895.
Telecopier: 852-2868-5871.
In London England: Bucklersbury House, 3 Queen Victoria Street.
Telephone: 44-171-236-3939.
Telecopier: 44-171-236-1113.

(See Next Column)

In New Delhi, India: Pathak & Associates, 13th Floor, Dr. Gopal Das Bhaven, 28 Barakhamba Road.
Telephone: 91-11-373-8793.
Telecopier: 91-11-335-3761.
In New York, New York: 599 Lexington Avenue.
Telephone: 212-326-3939.
Cable Address: "JONESDAY NEWYORK."
Telex: 237013 JDRP UR.
Telecopier: 212-755-7306.
In Paris, France: 62, rue du Faubourg Saint-Honore.
Telephone: 33-1-44-71-3939.
Telex: 290156 Surgoe.
Telecopier: 33-1-49-24-0471.
In Pittsburgh, Pennsylvania: 500 Grant Street, 31st Floor.
Telephone: 412-391-3939.
Cable Address: "Attorneys Pittsburgh".
Telecopier: 412-394-7959.
In Riyadh, Saudi Arabia: The International Law Firm, Sulaymaniyah Center, Tahlia Street, P.O. Box 22166.
Telephone: (966-1) 462-8866.
Telecopier: (966-1) 462-9001.
In Taipei, Taiwan: 8th Floor, 2 Tun Hwa South Road, Section 2.
Telephone: (886-2) 704-6808.
Telecopier: (886-2) 704-6791.
In Tokyo, Japan: Toranomon MT Building, 4th Floor, 10-3, Toranomon 3-Chome, Minato-ku, Tokyo 105, Japan.
Telephone: 81-3-3433-3939.
Telecopier: 81-3-5401-2725.
In Washington, D.C.: Metropolitan Square, 1450 G Street, N.W.
Telephone: 202-879-3939.
Cable Address: "Attorneys Washington."
Telex: 89-2410 ATTORNEYS WASH.
Telecopier: 202-737-2832.

MEMBERS OF FIRM IN LOS ANGELES

Gerald W. Palmer	Elwood Lui
	Frederick L. McKnight

For Complete List of Firm Personnel, See General Section

For full biographical listings, see the Martindale-Hubbell Law Directory

---

KOSLOV & MEDLEN (AV)

30141 Agoura Road, Suite 200, 91301-4334
Telephone: 818-597-9996
FAX: 818-597-8848

MEMBERS OF FIRM

John Koslov	William P. Medlen

ASSOCIATE

Sabrina Simmons-Brill

For full biographical listings, see the Martindale-Hubbell Law Directory

---

KU, FONG, LARSEN & CHEN, LLP (AV)

523 West Sixth Street, Suite 528, 90014
Telephone: 213-488-1400
Telecopier: 213-236-9235

MEMBERS OF FIRM

H. G. Robert Fong	Paul A. Larsen
	Frank W. Chen

OF COUNSEL

Edward Y. Ku

ASSOCIATES

Jack S. Yeh	Victor S. Sze

For full biographical listings, see the Martindale-Hubbell Law Directory

---

LAGERLOF, SENECAL, BRADLEY & SWIFT, LLP

(See Pasadena)

LANGBERG, COHN & DROOZ (AV)

A Partnership including a Professional Corporation
12100 Wilshire Boulevard Suite 1650, 90025
Telephone: 310-979-3200
Telecopier: 310-979-3220

Barry B. Langberg (A Professional Corporation)	Beth F. Dumas
	Mitchell J. Langberg
Eileen M. Cohn	Mary L. Muir
Deborah Drooz	Brian A. Murphy

OF COUNSEL

Peter C. Richards (A Professional Corporation)	Gilbert Gaynor
	Polin Cohanne
	Milton Segal

LEGAL SUPPORT PERSONNEL

PARALEGALS

Patricia Ann Essig	Jeanne A. Logé

For full biographical listings, see the Martindale-Hubbell Law Directory

Los Angeles—Continued

José Y. Lauchengco, Jr. (AV)

3545 Wilshire Boulevard, Suite 247, 90010
Telephone: 213-380-9897

OF COUNSEL
Paul J. Estuar

For full biographical listings, see the Martindale-Hubbell Law Directory

Lebovits & David, A Professional Corporation (AV)

Suite 3100, Two Century Plaza, 2049 Century Park East, 90067
Telephone: 310-277-0200
Fax: 310-552-1028

Moses Lebovits
Deborah A. David

OF COUNSEL
Joseph J. M. Lange

Reference: Imperial Bank (Main Office - Beverly Hills).

For full biographical listings, see the Martindale-Hubbell Law Directory

Leopold, Petrich & Smith, A Professional Corporation (AV)

(Formerly Youngman, Hungate & Leopold)
Suite 3110, 2049 Century Park East (Century City), 90067
Telephone: 310-277-3333
Telecopier: 310-277-7444

Gordon E. Youngman (1903-1983)
A. Fredric Leopold
Louis P. Petrich
Joel McCabe Smith
Edward A. Ruttenberg
Vincent Cox
Donald R. Gordon
Walter R. Sadler
Daniel M. Mayeda

OF COUNSEL
Richard Hungate

Paul M. Krekorian
David Aronoff
Gary M. Grossenbacher
Robert S. Gutierrez

For full biographical listings, see the Martindale-Hubbell Law Directory

Levinson, Miller, Jacobs & Phillips, A Professional Corporation (AV)

Suite 2000, 1875 Century Park East, 90067-2534
Telephone: 310-557-2455
Cable Address: "Levrom"
Facsimile: 310-282-0472

Paul Levinson
Gary S. Jacobs
Stanton Lee Phillips
Samuel M. Robin

Sharon Jill Sandler
J. Bennett Friedman
Fern S. Nisen
Erin L. Prouty

OF COUNSEL
Milton Louis Miller
Stephen I. Halper

References: First Charter Bank; Wells Fargo Trust (Trust Dept., Southern California Headquarters).

For full biographical listings, see the Martindale-Hubbell Law Directory

Loeb & Loeb LLP (AV)

A Limited Liability Partnership including Professional Corporations
Suite 1800, 1000 Wilshire Boulevard, 90017-2475
Telephone: 213-688-3400
Facsimile: 213-688-3460; 688-3461; 688-3462
Century City, California Office: Suite 2200, 10100 Santa Monica
Boulevard, Los Angeles, 90067-4164.
Telephone: 310-282-2000.
Facsimile: 310-282-2191; 282-2192.
New York, N.Y. Office: 345 Park Avenue, 10154-0037.
Telephone: 212-407-4000.
Facsimile: 212-407-4990.
Washington, D.C. Office: Suite 601, 2100 M Street N.W., 20037-1207.
Telephone: 202-223-5700.
Facsimile: 202-223-5704.
Nashville, Tennessee Office: 45 Music Square West, 37203-3205.
Telephone: 615-749-8300;
Facsimile: 615-749-8308.
Rome, Italy Office: Piazza Digione 1, 00197.
Telephone: 011-396-808-8456.
Facsimile: 011-396-808-8288.

MEMBERS OF FIRM

Harold A. Barza
Carol Laurene Belfield
David B. Eizenman
(New York City Office)
John F. Lang
(New York City Office)
Robert A. Meyer
Stephen R. Mick
Charles H. Miller
(New York City Office)
Douglas E. Mirell
Daniel G. Murphy

(See Next Column)

MEMBERS OF FIRM (Continued)

Anthony Murray
Martin R. Pollner
(New York City Office)
Victor A. Rodgers
David M. Satnick
(New York City Office)
P. Gregory Schwed
(New York City Office)
Peter S. Selvin
David B. Shontz
(New York City Office)
Robert N. Treiman
Rebecca E. White
(New York City Office)
Alan W. Wilken
Michael P. Zweig
(New York City Office)

OF COUNSEL
Harry First
(New York City Office)
Howard I. Friedman (A P.C.)
Robert A. Holtzman (A P.C.)
Alfred I. Rothman (A P.C.)

ASSOCIATES
Elana C. Bloom
(New York City Office)
Matthew Clark Bures
Paula K. Colbath
(New York City Office)
Brant H. Dveirin
David A. Fleissig
(New York City Office)
Daniel J. Friedman
Helen Gavaris
(New York City Office)
Kurtiss Lee Grossman
Sharon S. Mequet
Beth R. Meyers
(New York City Office)
Glen A. Rothstein
Roni Schneider
(New York City Office)
Rachel Schwartz
(New York City Office)
Brian R. Socolow
(New York City Office)
Adam F. Streisand
Maria L. Zanfini
(New York City Office)

For Complete List of Firm Personnel, See General Section

For full biographical listings, see the Martindale-Hubbell Law Directory

Lynberg & Watkins, A Professional Corporation (AV)

Sixteenth Floor International Tower Plaza, 888 South Figueroa
Street, 90017-2516
Telephone: 213-624-8700
Fax: 213-892-2763
Santa Ana, California Office: Suite 101, 2020 E. 1st Street.
Telephone: 714-973-1220.
Fax: 714-973-1002.

Charles A. Lynberg
Judith Gold
Norman J. Watkins
R. Jeff Carlisle
Dana J. McCune
Michael J. Larin
Randall J. Peters
Ric C. Ottaiano **
Dana A. Fox
Stephen M. Harber
Ruth Segal
Catherine L. Ferro
Heller-Ann C. Hancock
Louis E. Marino, Jr.

Douglas G. MacKay

Christine H. Gosney
William F. Bernard **
Michael A. Cartelli
Pamela H. Roth
Claudia H. Hanzlick
Thomas G. Oesterreich
Peggy Kolkey
Wendy E. Schultz
Jason M. Booth
Jerome P. Doctors
Guy N. Webster
Jamie L. Vels
David K. Morrison
Timothy F. Rivers
Barry L. Bookbinder
Todd J. Wenzel
Mark F. Gamboa
Nicholas R. Andrea
Dina M. De Laurentis
Antonia M. Chan
Charles C. McKenna
Brian C. Plante
Mary E. Lynch **
Denah H. Yoshiyama
Michael T. Taurek
Kathy M. Gandara
Mark A. Hooper
Michael J. Pepek
Heather C. Jelensky
Lisa M. Baker
Alan Aghabegian
Kara J. Petreccia
Todd Harrison Stitt
Alex H. Cherin

OF COUNSEL
Martin D. Kaplan

Representative Clients: The American International Group of Companies (AIG); Universal Underwriters; National Home Life Insurance Co.; Gallagher-Bassett, Keenan & Associates (Third Party Administrators).
**Santa Ana Office

For full biographical listings, see the Martindale-Hubbell Law Directory

Gerald C. MacRae (AV)

1840 Century Park East, Suite 800, 90067-2109
Telephone: 310-553-6370
Fax: 310-553-4432

For full biographical listings, see the Martindale-Hubbell Law Directory

Mahoney, Coppenrath, Jaffe & Pearson LLP (AV)

A Partnership including Professional Corporations
2049 Century Park East, Suite 2480, 90067-3283
Telephone: 310-557-1919
Telecopier: 310-277-6536

(See Next Column)

MAHONEY, COPPENRATH, JAFFE & PEARSON LLP—*Continued*

MEMBERS OF FIRM

James E. Mahoney (P.C.)
Walter G. Coppenrath, Jr., (P.C.)
Howard M. Jaffe (P.C.)

Ronald C. Pearson
Daryl G. Parker
Charles L. Grotts
Arthur L. Martin

OF COUNSEL

Gerald Lee Tahajian

Reference: First Professional Bank, Santa Monica, California.

For full biographical listings, see the Martindale-Hubbell Law Directory

---

LAW OFFICES OF JEFFREY A. MATZ (AV)

23822 Valencia Boulevard Suite 210, 91355
Telephone: 805-222-9131
Scottsdale, Arizona Office: 6711 East Camelback Road, Suite 8.
Telephone: 602-955-0900.
Fax: 602-970-3172.

For full biographical listings, see the Martindale-Hubbell Law Directory

---

McNICHOLAS & McNICHOLAS (AV)

10866 Wilshire Boulevard, 90024
Telephone: 310-474-1582
FAX: 310-475-7871

MEMBERS OF FIRM

John P. McNicholas
David M. Ring

Patrick McNicholas

ASSOCIATES

Mark K. Flores

Eric A. Gowey

For full biographical listings, see the Martindale-Hubbell Law Directory

---

PETER J. McNULTY (AV)

827 Moraga Drive (Bel Air), 90049
Telephone: 310-471-2707
Fax: 310-472-7014
Gilroy, California Office: Suite F-2, 8352 Church Street.
Telephone: 408-848-5900.
Fax: 408-848-1391.
Aurora, Illinois Office: 8 East Galena Street.
(Also of Counsel to Carl A. McMahan)

ASSOCIATE

Michael L. Oran (A Professional Corporation)

OF COUNSEL

John A. Alvarez
(Resident, Gilroy Office)
Robert M. Foote
(Not admitted in CA)

Robert P. Friedman
Carl A. McMahan

Reference: City National Bank (Beverly Hills, California).

For full biographical listings, see the Martindale-Hubbell Law Directory

---

MOSTEN & TUFFIAS (AV)

10990 Wilshire Boulevard, Suite 940, 90024
Telephone: 310-473-7611
Facsimile: 310-473-7422
Email: FMostenn@counsel.com

MEMBERS OF FIRM

Forrest S. Mosten

Heidi S. Tuffias

For full biographical listings, see the Martindale-Hubbell Law Directory

---

FLOYD H. NORRIS (AV)

Suite 405 Norris Building, 714 South Hill Street, 90014
Telephone: 213-624-4088
FAX: 213-624-4080

References: Bank of America; Wells Fargo.

For full biographical listings, see the Martindale-Hubbell Law Directory

---

OCHOA & SILLAS (AV)

444 South, Flower Street, 18th Floor, 90071
Telephone: 213-362-1400
Fax: 213-622-0162
Sacramento, California Office: Wells Fargo Center, 400 Capitol Mall, Suite 1850.
Telephone: 916-447-3383.
FAX: 916-447-3495.
Mexico City, Mexico Office: Bosques de Duraznos, No. 65-507-B, Bosques de Las Lomas, 11700 Mexico, D.F.
Telephone: 905-596-68-48.

MEMBERS OF FIRM

Herman Sillas
Jacqueline Rich Moore

Jesse M. Jauregui

(See Next Column)

ASSOCIATES

Jack T. Molodanof
Tomás R. Lopez
Rita A. Reyes
Joyce E. Earl

Christopher Gonzalez
Evan F. Hadnot
Thomas J. Joy
Mario Cordero

OF COUNSEL

Cochran & Lotkin, , Washington, D.C.

LEGAL SUPPORT PERSONNEL

Manuel Tejeda (Paralegal)
Lori Lee Marino (Paralegal)

Jeanette M. Palma (Paralegal)

For full biographical listings, see the Martindale-Hubbell Law Directory

---

O'MELVENY & MYERS LLP (AV)

400 South Hope Street, 90071-2899
Telephone: 213-669-6000
Cable Address: "Moms"
Facsimile: 213-669-6407
Email: omminfo@omm.com
Century City, California Office: 1999 Avenue of the Stars, 90067-6035.
Telephone: 310-553-6700.
Facsimile: 310-246-6779.
Newport Beach, California Office: 610 Newport Center Drive, 92660-6429.
Telephone: 714-760-9600.
Cable Address: "Moms".
Facsimile: 714-669-6994.
San Francisco, California Office: Embarcadero Center West Tower, 275 Battery Street, 94111-3305.
Telephone: 415-984-8700.
Facsimile: 415-984-8701.
New York, New York Office: Citicorp Center, 153 East 53rd Street, 10022-4611.
Telephone: 212-326-2000.
Facsimile: 212-326-2061.
Washington, D.C. Office: 555 13th Street, N.W., 20004-1109.
Telephone: 202-383-5300.
Cable Address: "Moms".
Facsimile: 202-383-5414.
London, England Office: 10 Finsbury Square, London, EC2A 1LA.
Telephone: 0171-256-8451.
Facsimile: 0171-638-8205.
Tokyo, Japan Office: Sanbancho KB-6 Building, 6 Sanbancho, Chiyoda-ku, Tokyo 102, Japan.
Telephone: 03-3239-2900.
Facsimile: 03-3239-2432.
Hong Kong Office: Suite 1905, Peregrine Tower, Lippo Centre, 89 Queensway, Central, Hong Kong.
Telephone: 852-2523-8266.
Facsimile: 852-2522-1760.
Shanghai, Peoples Republic of China Office: Shanghai International Trade Centre, Suite 2011, 2200 Yan An Road West, Shanghai, 200335, PRC.
Telephone: 86-21-6219-5363.
Facsimile: 86-21-6275-4949.

PARTNER

Henry C. Thumann

For Complete List of Firm Personnel, See General Section

For full biographical listings, see the Martindale-Hubbell Law Directory

---

PILLSBURY MADISON & SUTRO LLP (AV)

Citicorp Plaza, 725 South Figueroa Street, Suite 1200, 90017-2513
Telephone: 213-488-7100
Fax: 213-629-1033
Costa Mesa, California Office: Plaza Tower, Suite 1100, 600 Anton Boulevard, 92626.
Telephone: 714-436-6800.
Fax: 714-662-6999.
Silicon Valley Office: 2700 San Hill Road, Menlo Park, 94025.
Telephone: 415-233-4500.
Fax: 415-233-4545.
Sacramento, California Office: 400 Capitol Mall, Suite 1700, 95814.
Telephone: 916-329-4700.
Fax: 916-441-3583.
San Diego, California Office: 101 West Broadway, Suite 1800, 92101.
Telephone: 619-234-5000.
Fax: 619-236-1995.
San Francisco, California Office: 235 Montgomery Street, 94104.
Telephone: 415-983-1000.
Fax: 415-983-1200.
Washington, D.C. Office: 1100 New York Avenue, N.W., Ninth Floor, 20005.
Telephone: 202-861-3000.
Fax: 202-822-0944.
New York, New York Office: 520 Madison Avenue, 40th Floor, 10022.
Telephone: 212-328-4810.
Fax: 212-328-4824. One Liberty Plaza, 165 Broadway, 51st Floor.
Telephone: 212-374-1890.
Fax: 212-374-1852.

(See Next Column)

PILLSBURY MADISON & SUTRO LLP, *Los Angeles—Continued*

Hong Kong Office: 6/F Asia Pacific Finance Tower, Citibank Plaza, 3 Garden Road, Central.
Telephone: 011-852-2509-7100.
Fax: 011-852-2509-7188.
Tokyo, Japan Office: Pillsbury Madison & Sutro, Gaikokuho Jimu Bengoshi Jimusho, 5th Floor, Samon Eleven Building, 3-1, Samon-cho, Shinjuku-ku, Tokyo 160 Japan.
Telephone: 800-729-9830; 011-813-3354-3531.
Fax: 011-813-3354-3534.

MEMBERS OF FIRM

Lawrence D. Bradley, Jr.	John R. Cadarette, Jr.
Kenneth R. Chiate	Kent B. Goss
Amy D. Hogue	Sidney K. Kanazawa
Ralph D. Kirwan	John Y. Liu
Catherine D. Meyer	Faisal Shah

William E. Stoner

ASSOCIATE

Jeffrey A. Rich

For Complete List of Firm Personnel, See General Section

For full biographical listings, see the Martindale-Hubbell Law Directory

RADCLIFF, FRANDSEN & DONGELL (AV)

40th Floor, 777 South Figueroa Street, 90017
Telephone: 213-614-1990
Facsimile: 213-489-9263
San Francisco, California Office: 88 Kearny Street, Suite 1475.
Telephone: 415-399-8393.
Facsimile: 415-989-5465.
Rome, Italy Office: Via Tacito, 7.
Telephone: (39) 06-323-5588.
Facsimile: (39) 06-324-3392.

MEMBERS OF FIRM

Jules G. Radcliff, Jr.	Russell Mackay Frandsen
	Richard A. Dongell

OF COUNSEL

Tal Clifton Finney

ASSOCIATES

Francis P. Aspessi	Jeffrey C. Mayes
Ruben A. Castellon	Marisa A. Moret
William W. Funderburk, Jr.	Daniel E. Park
Jeffrey A. Gagliardi	Scott D. Pinsky
David K. Lee	Eric H. Saiki
Maria Anna Mancini	Steve R. Segura

Glenn M. White

For full biographical listings, see the Martindale-Hubbell Law Directory

THOMAS J. READY (AV)

333 South Grand Avenue, 33rd Floor, 90071-1504
Telephone: 213-229-9009
Facsimile: 213-229-9010
Email: TJRLA @AOL.com

For full biographical listings, see the Martindale-Hubbell Law Directory

LAW OFFICES OF MARK P. ROBINSON (AV)

One Wilshire Boulevard, 22nd Floor, 90017-3383
Telephone: 213-485-1798
FAX: 213-236-0791

For full biographical listings, see the Martindale-Hubbell Law Directory

RODI, POLLOCK, PETTKER, GALBRAITH & CAHILL, A LAW CORPORATION (AV)

Suite 400 801 South Grand Avenue, 90017
Telephone: 213-895-4900; 680-0823
Telecopiers: 213-895-4921; 895-4922; 895-4750

Karl B. Rodi (1908-1982)	Elizabeth B. Blakely
John D. Cahill	Robert C. Norton
John D. Pettker	John F. Cermak, Jr.
Daniel C. Bond (1942-1977)	Tim G. Ceperley
William R. Christian	Coralie Kupfer
Henry P. Pramov, Jr.	Cris K. O'Neall
Robert A. Yahiro	John S. Cha

Scott E. Adamson

Sonja A. Inglin	Richard Nessary
Thomas J. Yoo	Mark McCleary

OF COUNSEL

John P. Pollock	Margaret Rosenthal

For full biographical listings, see the Martindale-Hubbell Law Directory

SCHWARTZ, STEINSAPIR, DOHRMANN & SOMMERS (AV)

6300 Wilshire Boulevard, Suite 2000, 90048
Telephone: 213-655-4700
Fax: 213-655-4488
Pittsburgh, Pennsylvania Office: 3600 One Oxford Centre.
Telephone: 412-456-2008.
Fax: 412-456-2020.

MEMBERS OF FIRM

Laurence D. Steinsapir	Margo A. Feinberg
Robert M. Dohrmann	Henry M. Willis
Richard D. Sommers	Dennis J. Murphy
Stuart Libicki	D. William Heine, Jr.
Michael R. Feinberg	Claude Cazzulino
Michael D. Four	Dolly M. Gee

ASSOCIATES

Brenda E. Sutton	Erika A. Zucker

For full biographical listings, see the Martindale-Hubbell Law Directory

SELMAN ● BREITMAN (AV)

11766 Wilshire Boulevard, Sixth Floor, 90025-6538
Telephone: 310-445-0800
Fax: 310-473-2525
San Diego, California Office: Emerald Plaza, 402 W. Broadway, Suite 400.
Telephone: 619-595-4880.
Facsimile: 619-595-4890.
San Francisco, California Office: Citicorp Center, One Sansome Street, Suite 1900.
Telephone: 415-951-4646.
Fax: 415-951-4676.

MEMBERS OF FIRM

Neil H. Selman	Elaine K. Fresch
Craig R. Breitman	Nicholas Banko
Robert A. Steller (Partner, San Diego Office)	Brad D. Bleichner
	David L. Jones
Alan B. Yuter	Mark L. Jubelt
Nancy W. Shokohi	Monica Cruz Thornton
Jeffrey C. Segal	David T. Bamberger
A. Scott Goldberg	Sterling Tao (Partner, San Francisco Office)

Lynette Klawon	James B. Kamanski
Ramon Z. Bacerdo (Resident, San Francisco Office)	Michael L. Mengoli
	Rita H. Issagholian
John S. Knowlton	Sarah F. Burke (Resident, San Diego Office)
Murray M. Sinclair	
Jeffrey A. Simmons	Darcy D. Jorgensen
Mark S. Gruskin	Linda S. Wendell (Resident, San Francisco Office)
Anthony L. Cione	
Christopher J. Harrington	Jeffrey S. Bolender
Sheryl W. Leichenger	Jeffrey T. Briggs
Theresa Ann Loss	Marcie A. Keenan
Jerry C. Popovich	Lisa M. Dyson (Resident, San Francisco Office)
Lisa Hannah Kahn	
David H. Oken	Aimee Y. Wong
Katy A. Nelson	Grace Horoupian
Jan Long Pocaterra	Kathleen T. Deeley
Kim Karelis	Christopher A. Petrovic
Asim K. Desai	Kimberly D. Allario (Resident, San Diego Office)
Pauline A. New	
Dianne M. Costales	Wendy Wen Yun Chang
Eldon S. Edson	Jack M. Zakariaie

OF COUNSEL

Thomas A. Leary (Of Counsel, San Diego Office)

Reference: City National Bank (Beverly Hills Branch).

For full biographical listings, see the Martindale-Hubbell Law Directory

SIMKE CHODOS (AV)

A Partnership of Professional Corporation
Suite 1511, 1880 Century Park East, 90067
Telephone: 310-203-3888
Fax: 310-203-3866

Stuart A. Simke	David M. Chodos

Richard A. Fond	Ellen Resinski Rosen
	James Robertson Martin

OF COUNSEL

James L. Keane

Reference: City National Bank (Wilshire-La Cienega Branch).

For full biographical listings, see the Martindale-Hubbell Law Directory

SLAFF, MOSK & RUDMAN (AV)

Suite 825, 9200 Sunset Boulevard, 90069
Telephone: 310-275-5351
Telecopier: 310-273-8706

(See Next Column)

SLAFF, MOSK & RUDMAN—*Continued*

George Slaff (1906-1989)   Edward Mosk (1916-1989)

MEMBERS OF FIRM

Norman G. Rudman   Marc R. Stein

Valerie V. Flugge

Reference: City National Bank.

For full biographical listings, see the Martindale-Hubbell Law Directory

LAW OFFICES OF RICHARD C. SPENCER (AV)

One Wilshire Boulevard, Suite 2100, 90017
Telephone: 213-629-7900
Fax: 213-629-7990

For full biographical listings, see the Martindale-Hubbell Law Directory

STEVEN J. STANWYCK (AV)

1900 Avenue of the Stars, Suite 1700, 90067-4403
Telephone: 310-557-8390
Telecopier: 310-557-8391

For full biographical listings, see the Martindale-Hubbell Law Directory

STEPHENS, BERG & LASATER, A PROFESSIONAL CORPORATION (AV)

1055 West Seventh Street, Twenty-Ninth Floor, 90017
Telephone: 213-629-3111
Telecopy: 213-629-2302; 213-624-4734

Lawrence M. Berg (1947-1995)   Frederick A. Clark
R. Wicks Stephens II   Joel A. Goldman
Richard W. Lasater II   C. Stephen Davis
Mark G. Ancel   Kenneth A. Feinfield
Dudley M. Lang   Jean-Paul Menard
Joseph F. Butler   Michael J. Kaminsky

John A. Dragonette

OF COUNSEL

Louis R. Baker   J. Lane Tilson

For full biographical listings, see the Martindale-Hubbell Law Directory

SULLIVAN LAW CORPORATION (AV)

545 South Figueroa Street, Suite 1216, 90071-1599
Telephone: 213-488-9200
Telecopier: 213-488-9664

Michael R. Sullivan

Douglas G. Carroll

For full biographical listings, see the Martindale-Hubbell Law Directory

TALCOTT, LIGHTFOOT, VANDEVELDE & SADOWSKY (AV)

Thirteenth Floor 655 South Hope Street, 90017
Telephone: 213-622-4750
Fax: 213-622-2690

MEMBERS OF FIRM

Robert M. Talcott   Stephen B. Sadowsky
Michael J. Lightfoot   John S. Crouchley
John D. Vandevelde   John P. Martin

Melissa N. Widdifield

ASSOCIATE

James H. Locklin

Reference: Sterling Bank, Los Angeles, California.

For full biographical listings, see the Martindale-Hubbell Law Directory

VITTAL AND STERNBERG (AV)

2121 Avenue of the Stars, 22nd Floor, 90067-5010
Telephone: 310-551-0900
Facsimile: 310-551-2710
Email: javittal@ix.netcom.com
Woodland Hills, California Office: 21700 Oxnard Street. Suite 1640.
91367-7326.
Telephone: 818-710-7801.
Facsimile: 818-593-6192.

J. Anthony Vittal (Resident)   Terence M. Sternberg (Resident, Woodland Hills Office)

For full biographical listings, see the Martindale-Hubbell Law Directory

ROBERT D. WALKER A PROFESSIONAL CORPORATION (AV)

Suite 1208, One Park Plaza, 3250 Wilshire Boulevard, 90010-1606
Telephone: 213-382-8010
Fax: 213-388-1033

Robert D. Walker

(See Next Column)

Delia Flores

Reference: Bank of America (Los Angeles Main Office)

For full biographical listings, see the Martindale-Hubbell Law Directory

WOLF, RIFKIN & SHAPIRO, LLP (AV)

A Partnership including a Professional Corporation
11400 West Olympic Boulevard Ninth Floor, 90064-1565
Telephone: 310-478-4100
FAX: 310-479-1422

MEMBERS OF FIRM

Michael Wolf (A Professional   Allan M. Rosenthal
Corporation)   Mindy Sheps
Daniel C. Shapiro   Norman S. Wisnicki
Roy G. Rifkin   Barry T. Mitidiere
Michael T. Schulman   Marc E. Rohatiner
Leslie Steven Marks   Charles H. Baren

Michael W. Rabkin

ASSOCIATES

Andrew S. Gelb   Richard S. Grant
Matthew L. Grode   Karin E. Freeman
Matthew Fladell   Lori A. Van Oosterhout
Steven A. Silver   Paul W. Windust
Mark J. Rosenbaum   Daniel Ng
Kelly Marie Allegra   Laura S. Blint

OF COUNSEL

Gerald Lloyd Friedman   Jeffrey R. Liebster

Denise M. Parga

For full biographical listings, see the Martindale-Hubbell Law Directory

MALIBU, *Los Angeles Co.*

LAW OFFICES OF TODD M. SLOAN (AV)

22601 Pacific Coast Highway, Suite 240, 90265
Telephone: 310-456-7900
Facsimile: 310-317-6266

ASSOCIATE

Julia L. Birkel

For full biographical listings, see the Martindale-Hubbell Law Directory

MANHATTAN BEACH, *Los Angeles Co.*

STEINBERG BARNESS GLASGOW & FOSTER LLP (AV)

1334 Park View Avenue, Suite 100, 90266
Telephone: 310-546-5838
Telecopier: 310-546-5630
Email: SGBF@ix.netcom.com

MEMBERS OF FIRM

Alex Steinberg   Jordan G. Barness
Daniel I. Barness   Paul J. Laurin
Donna Glasgow   Shannon M. Foley
  (Not admitted in CA)   Richard L. Weiner
Douglas B. Foster   William R. (Randy) Kirkpatrick

Jeffrey Michael Lee

OF COUNSEL

Roanld D. Harari (Not admitted in CA)

References: Home Bank; Imperial Bank; Citizens Commerical Trust & Savings Bank; Bank of America.

For full biographical listings, see the Martindale-Hubbell Law Directory

MENLO PARK, *San Mateo Co.*

DYER & WHITE (AV)

Suite 200, 800 Oak Grove Avenue, 94025
Telephone: 415-325-7000
Fax: 415-325-3116

MEMBERS OF FIRM

Charles A. Dyer   Rand N. White

For full biographical listings, see the Martindale-Hubbell Law Directory

ENTERPRISE LAW GROUP, INC. (AV)

Menlo Oaks Corporate Center, 4400 Bohannon Drive, Suite 280, 94025-1041
Telephone: 415-462-4700
Facsimile: 415-462-4747
Email: info@enterpriselaw.com

Sherwood M. Sullivan

For full biographical listings, see the Martindale-Hubbell Law Directory

Menlo Park—Continued

O'REILLY & COLLINS, A PROFESSIONAL CORPORATION (AV)

2500 Sand Hill Road, Suite 201, 94025
Telephone: 415-854-7700
Fax: 415-854-8350

Terry O'Reilly   James P. Collins

James P. Tessier   Michael Danko

For full biographical listings, see the Martindale-Hubbell Law Directory

---

MERCED, * Merced Co.

ALLEN, POLGAR, PROIETTI & FAGALDE (AV)

A Partnership including a Professional Corporation
1640 "N" Street, Suite 200, P.O. Box 2184, 95344
Telephone: 209-723-4372
Fax: 209-723-7397
Mariposa, California Office: 5079 Highway 140. P.O. Box 1907.
Telephone: 209-966-3007.
Fax: 209-742-6353.

MEMBERS OF FIRM

Terry L. Allen (P.C.)   Jeffrey S. Kaufman
Gary B. Polgar   F. Dana Walton
Donald J. Proietti   (Resident, Mariposa Office)
Michael A. Fagalde   Brian L. McCabe
                    Paul C. Lo

For full biographical listings, see the Martindale-Hubbell Law Directory

---

MISSION VIEJO, Orange Co.

THE BUCKLEY FIRM, P.C. (AV)

Suite 200, 26522 La Alameda, 92691
Telephone: 714-348-8300
Facsimile: 714-348-8310
Email: TBF__law@ix.netcom.com
Email: 73321.331@compuserve.com

Lawrence J. Buckley   John W. Klein
John Thomas Callan   Paula Scotland
Jeffrey W. Griffith   Edgar C. Smith, III
Stephen J. Kane   Adam H. Springel
                OF COUNSEL
Timothy D. Carlyle   Jonathan C. Cavett

Reference: Bank of California.

For full biographical listings, see the Martindale-Hubbell Law Directory

---

MODESTO, * Stanislaus Co.

BRUNN & FLYNN, A PROFESSIONAL CORPORATION (AV)

928 12th Street, P.O. Box 3366, 95353
Telephone: 209-521-2133
Fax: 209-521-7584
Email: brunnfly@ix.netcom.com

Charles K. Brunn   Gerald E. Brunn
Timothy T. Flynn   Roger S. Matzkind

Michael G. Donovan   Andrew N. Eshoo

Representative Clients: ACWA-Joint Powers Insurance Authority; Basic Resources, Inc.; Boudreau Corp.; Donco Carriers, Inc.; Duarte Nurseries, Inc.; George Reed, Inc.; Independent Tractor Rental; International Paper Co.; Kmart Corp.; May Company Department Stores, Inc.

For full biographical listings, see the Martindale-Hubbell Law Directory

---

DAMRELL, NELSON, SCHRIMP, PALLIOS & LADINE, A PROFESSIONAL CORPORATION (AV)

1601 I Street, Fifth Floor, 95354
Telephone: 209-526-3500
Fax: 209-526-3534
Email: dnsp1@ix.netcom.com
Sacramento, California Office: Suite 200, 1100 K Street.
Telephone: 916-447-2909.
Fax: 916-447-0552.
Oakdale, California Office: 703 West "F" Street, P.O. Drawer C.
Telephone: 209-848-3500.
Fax: 209-848-3400.

Frank C. Damrell (1898-1988)   Steven G. Pallios
Frank C. Damrell, Jr.   Wray F. Ladine
Duane L. Nelson   Matthew O. Pacher
Roger M. Schrimp   Fred A. Silva

(See Next Column)

Craig W. Hunter   Wendelin Z. Warwick
John K. Peltier   Lisa L. Gillispie
Brian J. Bartow   Amy E. Elliott
Jefferey A. Wooten   Kristine L. Burks
C. Kelley Evans   Michelle Luisa Christian
                OF COUNSEL
Surendra J. Sood, M.D.   Cressey H. Nakagawa

Representative Clients: American Honda Motor Co., Inc.; Bronco Wine Co.; E. & J. Gallo Winery; Gallo Glass Co.; The Luckey Co.; Norfolk Southern Corp.; Pep Boys of California, Inc.; W. R. Grace & Co.; National Medical Enterprises, Inc.; Ogden Corp.

For full biographical listings, see the Martindale-Hubbell Law Directory

---

STOCKTON & SADLER (AV)

1034 Twelfth Street, P.O. Box 3153, 95353
Telephone: 209-523-6416
Fax: 209-523-2315

MEMBERS OF FIRM

Cleveland J. Stockton   James L. Sadler
                ASSOCIATE
            Karen Tall Sadler

Representative Clients: Dan Mellis Liquors; American Lumber Co.; Paul's Rexall Drug Stores; American Distributing Co.; Tro-Pic-Kal Mfg. Co.; Pete Pappas Broadcasting Co.; Pete Pappas Broadcasting, Inc.; Sanders Construction Co.; Goldrush Broadcasting, Inc.; Paul M. Zagaris Realtor, Inc.

For full biographical listings, see the Martindale-Hubbell Law Directory

---

MONTEREY, Monterey Co.

HARRAY, MASUDA & LINKER (AV)

80 Garden Court, Suite 260, 93940
Telephone: 408-373-3101
Fax: 408-373-6712

Richard K. Harray   Michael P. Masuda
                Stan L. Linker

Representative Clients: Travelers/Aetna; The Doctors' Company/CHIC; Program Beta; CNA; DPIC; Sequoia Insurance Co.; Midstate Ins. Co.; County of Monterey; Cities of Monterey, Pacific Grove & Seaside.

For full biographical listings, see the Martindale-Hubbell Law Directory

---

THE THOMPSON LAW FIRM (AV)

580 Calle Principal, First Floor, 93940-2818
Telephone: 408-646-1224
Fax: 408-646-1225

Ralph W. Thompson, III

For full biographical listings, see the Martindale-Hubbell Law Directory

---

LAW OFFICES OF CHARLES G. WARNER (AV)

2340 Garden Road, Suite 208, 93940
Telephone: 408-375-0203
Facsimile: 408-375-4159

For full biographical listings, see the Martindale-Hubbell Law Directory

---

MOUNTAIN VIEW, Santa Clara Co.

LUCE & QUILLINAN (AV)

444 Castro Street, Suite 900, 94041-2073
Telephone: 415-969-4000
FAX: 415-969-6953

MEMBERS OF FIRM

James G. Luce   James V. Quillinan
            Melissa C. Johnson
                ASSOCIATE
            Sally F. Berry

For full biographical listings, see the Martindale-Hubbell Law Directory

---

NEVADA CITY, * Nevada Co.

BERLINER LAW OFFICES (AV)

224 Main Street, 95959
Telephone: 916-265-5585
Fax: 916-478-0303
Email: berlinlw@nccn.net

Harold A. Berliner   Eric L. Berliner
                ASSOCIATE
            Lawrence D. Sanders

For full biographical listings, see the Martindale-Hubbell Law Directory

NEWPORT BEACH, Orange Co.

BUCHALTER, NEMER, FIELDS & YOUNGER, A PROFESSIONAL CORPORATION (AV)

Suite 1450, 620 Newport Center Drive, 92660
Telephone: 714-760-1121
Fax: 714-720-0182
Email: buchalter@earthlink.net *URL:* http://www.buchalter.com
Los Angeles, California Office: 24th Floor, 601 South Figueroa Street.
Telephone: 213-891-0700.
Fax: 213-896-0400.
New York, New York Office: 15th Floor, 605 Third Avenue.
Telephone: 212-490-8600.
Fax: 212-490-6022.
San Francisco, California Office: 29th Floor, 333 Market Street.
Telephone: 415-227-0900.
Fax: 415-227-0770.

Clifford John Meyer   Debra Solle Healy
Kirk S. Rense

Lori S. Ross   Mark M. Scott
References: City National Bank; Wells Fargo Bank; Metrobank.

For full biographical listings, see the Martindale-Hubbell Law Directory

CALLAHAN & ASSOCIATES (AV)

5120 Campus Drive, 92660
Telephone: 714-476-2898
Facsimile: 714-752-8770

Rebecca Callahan
ASSOCIATE
Katherine T. Corrigan
LEGAL SUPPORT PERSONNEL
Sandra A. Thompson (Paralegal)

For full biographical listings, see the Martindale-Hubbell Law Directory

CAPRETZ & RADCLIFFE (AV)

5000 Birch Street, West Tower Suite 2500, 92660-2139
Telephone: 714-724-3000
Fax: 714-757-2635
Email: CRLAWYERS@AOL.CON *URL:* http://www.CAPRETZ.com

James T. Capretz   Richard J. Radcliffe
ASSOCIATE
Peter A. Martin
OF COUNSEL
William B. Lawless (Not admitted in CA)
LEGAL SUPPORT PERSONNEL
Rosanna S. Bertheola

For full biographical listings, see the Martindale-Hubbell Law Directory

DAVIS, PUNELLI, KEATHLEY & WILLARD (AV)

610 Newport Center Drive, Suite 1000, P.O. Box 7920, 92658-7920
Telephone: 714-640-0700
Telecopier: 714-640-0714
San Diego, California Office: 501 West Broadway, Suite 900, 92101.
Telephone: 619-558-2581.

MEMBERS OF FIRM
Robert E. Willard   H. James Keathley
S. Eric Davis   Eric G. Anderson
Frank Punelli, Jr.   Katherine D. Keathley
OF COUNSEL
Lewis K. Uhler

For full biographical listings, see the Martindale-Hubbell Law Directory

KELEGIAN & THOMAS (AV)

4685 MacArthur Court, Suite 400, 92660
Telephone: 714-553-1200
Fax: 714-553-1013
Email: KelThomLaw@aol.com

Mark A. Kelegian   James P. Habel
Michael Paul Thomas   Jeri E. Tabback
Joseph P. Gallo   Dean H. McVay
Bruce A. Thomason   Erik R. Musurlian
Steven M. Hepps   William N. Villard

For full biographical listings, see the Martindale-Hubbell Law Directory

MARIO W. MAINERO, JR., INC. (AV)

Suite 201, 5160 Birch Street, 92660
Telephone: 714-851-7763
FAX: 714-851-8188 (7765)
Email: mwmlaw@aol.com

Mario W. Mainero, Jr.   Jan A. Zemanek
Reference: Bank of Newport.

For full biographical listings, see the Martindale-Hubbell Law Directory

MILLAR, HODGES & BEMIS (AV)

One Newport Place, Suite 900, 1301 Dove Street, 92660-2448
Telephone: 714-752-7722
FAX: 714-752-6131
MEMBERS OF FIRM
Richard W. Millar, Jr.   Kenneth R. Hodges
Larry R. Bemis
ASSOCIATE
David A. St. Clair
Reference: Manufacturers Bank, Newport Beach, California.

For full biographical listings, see the Martindale-Hubbell Law Directory

DONALD PETERS A LAW CORPORATION (AV)

1300 Dove Street, Suite 200, 92660
Telephone: 714-955-3818
Fax: 714-955-1341

Donald Peters

For full biographical listings, see the Martindale-Hubbell Law Directory

RONALD K. VAN WERT A PROFESSIONAL CORPORATION (AV)

One Newport Place, Suite 900, 1301 Dove Street, 92660
Telephone: 714-752-7964

Ronald K. Van Wert

For full biographical listings, see the Martindale-Hubbell Law Directory

THE WALKER LAW FIRM A PROFESSIONAL CORPORATION (AV)

Suite 450, 1301 Dove Street, 92660-2464
Telephone: 714-752-2522
Telecopier: 714-752-0439
Email: JWALKER208@AOL.COM

Joseph A. Walker
OF COUNSEL
Duff S. McEvers   David T. Sanford
Karyn S. Neue
Reference: Marine National Bank.

For full biographical listings, see the Martindale-Hubbell Law Directory

OAKLAND,* Alameda Co.

ANTHONY & CARLSON (AV)

1999 Harrison Street, Suite 1750, 94612
Telephone: 510-835-8400
Fax: 510-835-5566
MEMBERS OF FIRM
Steven R. Anthony   Richard H. Carlson
ASSOCIATE
Barbara L. Vankoll
OF COUNSEL
Jane L. Trigero

For full biographical listings, see the Martindale-Hubbell Law Directory

BENNETT, SAMUELSEN, REYNOLDS AND ALLARD, A PROFESSIONAL CORPORATION (AV)

1951 Webster Street, Suite 200, 94612
Telephone: 510-444-7688; 510-987-8001
Fax: 510-444-5849

Bryant M. Bennett (Retired)   Richard L. Reynolds
David J. Samuelsen   Anthony J. Allard
John G. Cowperthwaite

Roger Blake Hohnsbeen   Frederick W. Gatt
Don Henry Schaefer   Rodney Ian Headington
Thomas S. Gelini   Candace Smith-Dabney
Representative Clients: Allstate Insurance Co.; California State Automobile Assn.; The Continental Insurance Cos.; County of Alameda.

For full biographical listings, see the Martindale-Hubbell Law Directory

Oakland—Continued

HAIMS, JOHNSON, MACGOWAN & MCINERNEY (AV)

490 Grand Avenue, 94610
Telephone: 510-835-0500
Facsimile: 510-835-2833

MEMBERS OF FIRM

Arnold B. Haims	Randy M. Marmor
Gary R. Johnson	John K. Kirby
Clyde L. MacGowan	Robert J. Frassetto
Thomas McInerney	Caroline N. Valentino
Lawrence A. Baker	Dianne D. Peebles

ASSOCIATES

Joseph Y. Ahn	Anne M. Michaels
Edward D. Baldwin	Michelle Diane Perry
Marc P. Bouret	Edward C. Schroeder, Jr.

For full biographical listings, see the Martindale-Hubbell Law Directory

HARDIN, COOK, LOPER, ENGEL & BERGEZ (AV)

1999 Harrison Street, 18th Floor, 94612-3541
Telephone: 510-444-3131
Telecopier: 510-839-7940

MEMBERS OF FIRM

J. Marcus Hardin (1905-1993)	Stephen McKae
L. S. Fletcher (1905-1964)	Bruce P. Loper
Herman Cook (1914-1982)	Bruce E. McLeod
John C. Loper	Eugene Brown, Jr.
(Partner Emeritus)	Linda C. Roodhouse
Barrie Engel	Matthew S. Conant
Raymond J. Bergez	Chris P. Lavdiotis
George S. Peyton, Jr.	Robert D. Eassa
Ralph A. Lombardi	Peter O. Glaessner
Sandra F. Wagner	Nicholas D. Kayhan
Willard L. Alloway	John A. De Pasquale
Gennaro A. Filice, III	Peter A. Strotz

Amber L. Kelly	Amee A. Mikacich
Elsa M. Baldwin	Timothy J. McCaffery
Marshall A. Johnson	Stephen J. Valen
Diane R. Stanton	Troy D. McMahan
Jennifer M. Walker	GayLynn Renee Kirn
Margaret L. Kotzebue	Richard V. Normington III

OF COUNSEL

Ronald A. Wagner	Rachel K. Angress

Representative Clients: Firemans Fund Insurance Cos.; City of Piedmont; The Dow Chemical Co.; Nissan Motor Corp.; Subaru of America; Weyerhauser Co.; Bay Area Rapid Transit District; Diamond Shamrock; Home Indemnity Co.; Rhone-Poulenc.

For Complete List of Firm Personnel, See General Section

For full biographical listings, see the Martindale-Hubbell Law Directory

KAZAN, MCCLAIN, EDISES, SIMON & ABRAMS, A PROFESSIONAL LAW CORPORATION (AV)

171 Twelfth Street, Suite 300, 94607
Telephone: 510-465-7728; 893-7211
TDD: (510) 763-8808
Fax: 510-835-4913
Email: postmaster@kmes.com

Steven Kazan	Aaron H. Simon
David M. McClain	Denise Abrams

Francis E. Fernandez	Frances C. Schreiberg
Anne Michelle Burr	Simona A. Farrise
Dianna J. Lyons	Ronald J. Shingler

LEGAL SUPPORT PERSONNEL

Elizabeth C. Johnson (Director of Administration and Finance)

Reference: Union Bank (Oakland Main Branch).

For full biographical listings, see the Martindale-Hubbell Law Directory

RYAN, ANDRADA & LIFTER, A PROFESSIONAL CORPORATION (AV)

Tenth Floor, Kaiser Center Building, 300 Lakeside Drive, Suite 1045, 94612-3536
Telephone: 510-763-6510
Fax: 510-763-3921

Joseph D. Ryan, Jr.	Charles E. Kallgren
J. Randall Andrada	Rhonda D. Shelton
Jill J. Lifter	Lora Vail French
Jolie Krakauer	Vikki L. Barron
Glenn Gould	Bruce A. McIntosh
Michael J. Daley	Michael J. Thomas
	Laura E. Ozak

(See Next Column)

Representative Clients: Alameda Contra Costa County Transit District; CNA Insurance Companies; Truck Insurance Exchange; Liberty Mutual Insurance Group; Safeway Stores, Inc.

For full biographical listings, see the Martindale-Hubbell Law Directory

JOHN O. STANSBURY (AV)

5th Floor, 2030 Franklin Street, 94612
Telephone: 510-444-4022
Fax: 510-444-3667

For full biographical listings, see the Martindale-Hubbell Law Directory

STRICKLAND & HAAPALA (AV)

Suite 800, Park Plaza Building, 1939 Harrison Street, 94612
Telephone: 510-763-2324
Fax: 510-273-8534

PARTNERS OF FIRM

William R. Strickland	Charles J. Maguire, Jr.
John E. Haapala	Clyde A. Thompson
Christopher M. Harnett, Jr.	Judith B. Altura

Representative Clients: Allstate Insurance Co.; California State Automobile Association; County of Alameda; The Farmers Insurance Group of Cos.; Sisters of Providence Hospital.

For full biographical listings, see the Martindale-Hubbell Law Directory

VAN BLOIS, KNOWLES, SCHWARTZ & BASKIN (AV)

Suite 2245 Ordway Building, One Kaiser Plaza, 94612
Telephone: 510-444-1906
Contra Costa County 510-947-1055
Fax: 510-444-1294

MEMBERS OF FIRM

R. Lewis Van Blois	Ellen R. Schwartz
Thomas C. Knowles	Richard J. Baskin

OF COUNSEL

Charles E. Farnsworth

For full biographical listings, see the Martindale-Hubbell Law Directory

ONTARIO, San Bernardino Co.

COVINGTON & CROWE (AV)

1131 West Sixth Street, P.O. Box 1515, 91762
Telephone: 909-983-9393
Fax: 909-391-6762
Email: covcrowe@ix.netcom.com

MEMBERS OF FIRM

Harold A. Bailin (1930-1988)	Stephen R. Wade
Samuel P. Crowe	Jette R. Anderson
George W. Porter	Audrey A. Perri
Robert E. Dougherty	Tracy L. Tibbals
Donald G. Haslam	Melanie Fisch
Robert F. Schauer	Robert H. Reeder
Edward A. Hopson	R. Doug Donesky
	Tammy S. Jager

ASSOCIATES

Howard S. Borenstein	Richard R. Muir
Denise Matthey	Kimberly A. Rohn
Katrina West	J. Michael Kaler
	Eric S. Vail

For full biographical listings, see the Martindale-Hubbell Law Directory

ORINDA, Contra Costa Co.

GILLIN, JACOBSON, ELLIS, LARSEN & DOYLE (AV)

2 Theatre Square Suite 230, 94563
Telephone: 510-258-0800
Fax: 510-848-0266
Email: lawfirm@gjeld.com
San Francisco Office: One Sutter Street, 10th Floor.
Telephone: 415-986-4777.

Andrew R. Gillin	Richard P. Doyle, Jr.
Ralph L. Jacobson	Susan Hunt
Luke Ellis	Mitchell S. Rosenfeld
James Paul Larsen	Catherine T. Doyle

For full biographical listings, see the Martindale-Hubbell Law Directory

OROVILLE,* Butte Co.

HENDREN LAW OFFICES (AV)

19 Nelson Avenue, P.O. Box 1822, 95965
Telephone: 916-533-0661
Fax: 916-533-3956

(See Next Column)

HENDREN LAW OFFICES—*Continued*

Ed W. Hendren

Reference: Butte Community Bank.

For full biographical listings, see the Martindale-Hubbell Law Directory

---

PACIFIC PALISADES, Los Angeles Co.

WILLIAM A. SAMPSON II & ASSOCIATES (AV)

15332 Antioch Street, Suite 525, 90272
Telephone: 310-472-1839
Fax: 310-472-8670

For full biographical listings, see the Martindale-Hubbell Law Directory

---

PALM DESERT, Riverside Co.

CRISTE, PIPPIN & GOLDS (AV)

Suite 200, 73-550 Alessandro Drive, 92260
Telephone: 619-862-1111
Fax: 619-776-4197
Email: cpgca@aol.com

MEMBERS OF FIRM

Michael A. Criste   Robert L. Pippin
Irwin L. Golds

ASSOCIATE

Marie A. Bochnewich

For full biographical listings, see the Martindale-Hubbell Law Directory

---

PALM SPRINGS, Riverside Co.

SCHLECHT, SHEVLIN & SHOENBERGER, A LAW CORPORATION (AV)

Suite 100, 801 East Tahquitz Canyon Way, P.O. Box 2744, 92263-2744
Telephone: 619-320-7161
Facsimile: 619-323-1758; 619-325-4623

James M. Schlecht   Jon A. Shoenberger
John C. Shevlin   Daniel T. Johnson

David Darrin   Elizabeth A. Dreier

OF COUNSEL

Donald B. McNelley   Allen O. Perrier (Retired)

Representative Clients: Outdoor Resorts of America; The Escrow Connection; Wells Fargo Bank; Canyon Country Club; Waste Management Co.

For full biographical listings, see the Martindale-Hubbell Law Directory

LAW OFFICES OF RICK M. STEIN (AV)

400 South Farrell Drive Suite B-203, 92262
Telephone: 619-325-5990
Facsimile: 619-325-6265

For full biographical listings, see the Martindale-Hubbell Law Directory

---

PALO ALTO, Santa Clara Co.

FTHENAKIS & COLVIN (AV)

540 University Avenue, Suite 300, 94301
Telephone: 415-326-1397
Telecopier: 415-326-3203

MEMBERS OF FIRM

Basil P. Fthenakis   Oliver P. Colvin

For full biographical listings, see the Martindale-Hubbell Law Directory

CHRISTOPHER REAM (AV)

1717 Embarcadero Road, 94303
Telephone: 415-424-0821
Facsimile: 415-857-1288

For full biographical listings, see the Martindale-Hubbell Law Directory

---

PASADENA, Los Angeles Co.

BARKER & ROMNEY, A PROFESSIONAL CORPORATION (AV)

301 East Colorado Boulevard Suite 200, 91101-1977
Telephone: 818-578-1970; 213-617-3112
Facsimile: 818-578-0768

Lee Barker (1943-1996)   Timothy M. Howett
David T. Romney   Blaine Jay Wanke
Cheryl A. Orr

Reference: City National Bank.

For full biographical listings, see the Martindale-Hubbell Law Directory

---

BURNS, AMMIRATO, PALUMBO, MILAM & BARONIAN, A PROFESSIONAL LAW CORPORATION (AV)

65 North Raymond Avenue, 2nd Floor, 91103-3919
Telephone: 818-796-5053; 213-258-8282
Fax: 818-792-3078
Long Beach, California Office: One World Trade Center, Suite 1200.
Telephone: 310-436-8338; 714-952-1047.
Fax: 310-432-6049.

Michael A. Burns   Bruce Palumbo
Vincent A. Ammirato,   Jeffrey L. Milam
  Resident, Long Bch   Robert H. Baronian

Normand A. Ayotte   Michael P. Vicencia,
Colleen Clark   Resident, LOng Bch
Valerie Julien-Peto   Michael E. Wenzel,
Susan E. Luhring   Resident, Long Bch
Grace C. Mori,
  Resident, Long Bch

Reference: First Los Angeles Bank.

For full biographical listings, see the Martindale-Hubbell Law Directory

---

BURTON & NORRIS (AV)

35 South Raymond Avenue, Fourth Floor, 91105
Telephone: 818-449-8300
Fax: 818-449-4417

John C. Burton   Donald G. Norris
              Victoria E. King

Reference: Bank of America (Pasadena).

For full biographical listings, see the Martindale-Hubbell Law Directory

---

CAIRNS, DOYLE, LANS, NICHOLAS & SONI, A LAW CORPORATION (AV)

Ninth Floor, 225 South Lake Avenue, 91101
Telephone: 818-683-3111
Telecopier: 818-683-4999

John D. Cairns   Stephen M. Lans
John C. Doyle   Francisco J. Nicholas
              Rohini Soni (1956-1994)

Representative Clients: Allstate Insurance Companies; Burger King Corp.; California Insurance Guarantee Assn.; California United Bank; CIGNA Insurance Companies; City of Pasadena; Cumis Insurance Society, Inc.; Employer's Mutual Insurance Companies; State Farm Insurance Companies; Tokio Marine Insurance.

For full biographical listings, see the Martindale-Hubbell Law Directory

---

COLLINS, COLLINS, MUIR & TRAVER (AV)

Successor to Collins & Collins
Suite 300, 265 North Euclid, 91101
Telephone: 818-793-1163
FAX: 818-793-5982
Newport Beach, California Office: 333 Bayside Drive, 92660.
Telephone: 714-723-6284.
Fax: 714-723-7701.

MEMBERS OF FIRM

James E. Collins (1910-1987)   Robert J. Traver
John J. Collins   Frank J. D'Oro
Samuel J. Muir   Brian K. Stewart

ASSOCIATES

Paul L. Rupard   Christine E. Drage
Robert H. Stellwagen, Jr.   Peter L. Stacy
Tomas A. Guterres   Stephen W. Olson

For full biographical listings, see the Martindale-Hubbell Law Directory

---

FRANSCELL, STRICKLAND, ROBERTS & LAWRENCE, A PROFESSIONAL CORPORATION (AV)

Penthouse, 225 South Lake Avenue, 91101-3005
Telephone: 818-304-7830; 213-684-7830
Fax: 818-795-7460
Santa Ana, California Office: Suite 800, 401 Civic Center Drive West.
Telephone: 714-543-6511.
Fax: 714-543-6711.
Riverside, California Office: Suite 670, 3801 University Avenue.
Telephone: 909-686-1000.
Fax: 909-686-2565.

George J. Franscell   David D. Lawrence
Tracy Strickland   Carol Ann Rohr
  (Resident, Santa Ana Office) Scott D. MacLatchie
Barbara E. Roberts   S. Frank Harrell
  (Resident, Riverside Office)   (Resident, Santa Ana Office)

(See Next Column)

FRANSCELL, STRICKLAND, ROBERTS & LAWRENCE A PROFESSIONAL CORPORATION, *Pasadena—Continued*

Donald C. McFarlane (Resident, Santa Ana Office)	Martin J. De Vries (Resident, Riverside Office)
Libby Wong	Ann Marie Sanders
Cindy S. Lee	Priscilla F. Slocum
Garth Matthew Drozin	

For full biographical listings, see the Martindale-Hubbell Law Directory

---

FREEBURG, JUDY & NETTELS (AV)

600 South Lake Avenue, 91106
Telephone: 818-585-4150
FAX: 818-585-0718
Santa Ana, California Office: Xerox Centre. 1851 East First Street, Suite 120. 92705-4017.
Telephone: 714-569-0950.
Facsimile: 714-569-0955.

Steven J. Freeburg	J. Lawrence Judy
Charles F. Nettels	

ASSOCIATES

Ingall W. Bull, Jr.	Holly A. McNulty
Richard B. Castle	Karen S. Freeburg
Cynthia B. Schaldenbrand (Resident, Santa Ana Office)	Jennifer D. Helsel
	William R. Francis
Robert S. Brody	Fred W. Brandt
Carla Crochet	

For full biographical listings, see the Martindale-Hubbell Law Directory

---

HAMMOND, ZUETEL & CAHILL (AV)

Suite 540, 180 South Lake Avenue, 91101
Telephone: 818-449-5144; 213-684-2898
FAX: 213-684-1275

MEMBERS OF FIRM

Kenneth R. Zuetel, Jr.	Richard F. Cahill

ASSOCIATES

Cynthia L.K. Steele	Victoria K. Torigian

OF COUNSEL

John C. Cushman	P. Theodore Hammond

For full biographical listings, see the Martindale-Hubbell Law Directory

---

LAGERLOF, SENECAL, BRADLEY & SWIFT, LLP (AV)

301 North Lake Avenue, 10th Floor, 91101-4108
Telephone: 818-793-9400
FAX: 818-793-5900

MEMBERS OF FIRM

Joseph J. Burris (1913-1980)	John F. Bradley
Stanley C. Lagerlof (Retired)	Timothy J. Gosney
H. Melvin Swift, Jr.	William F. Kruse
H. Jess Senecal	Thomas S. Bunn, III
Jack T. Swafford	Andrew D. Turner
Rebecca J. Thyne	

ASSOCIATES

James D. Ciampa	Robert W. Renken

Representative Clients: Anchor Glass Container Corp.; Bethlehem Steel Corp.; Orthopaedic Hospital; Palmdale Water District; Public Water Agencies Group; Ventura Port District; Walnut Valley Water District; Metric Construction Co., Inc.

For full biographical listings, see the Martindale-Hubbell Law Directory

---

KEVIN MEENAN (AV)

790 East Colorado Boulevard Ninth Floor Penthouse, 91101-2105
Telephone: 818-398-0000
FAX: 818-585-0999
Email: 73313.1624@compuserve.com

For full biographical listings, see the Martindale-Hubbell Law Directory

---

THROCKMORTON, BECKSTROM, OAKES & TOMASSIAN LLP (AV)

Corporate Center Pasadena, 225 South Lake Avenue, Suite 500, 91101-3005
Telephone: 818-568-2500; 213-681-2321
Fax: 818-405-0786
Irvine, California Office: Suite 350, 19800 MacArthur Boulevard 92715.
Telephone: 714-955-2280.
Fax: 714-467-8081.

MEMBERS OF FIRM

A. Robert Throckmorton (Resident, Irvine Office)	Serge Tomassian (Resident, Irvine Office)
Spencer S. Beckstrom	David Alan Huffaker
George A. Oakes	Robert S. Throckmorton

References Available Upon Request.

For full biographical listings, see the Martindale-Hubbell Law Directory

---

RANCHO SANTA FE, San Diego Co.

CHARLES S. LiMANDRI (AV)

Building 3, 16236 San Dieguito Road, Suite 3-15, P.O. Box 9120, 92067
Telephone: 619-759-9930
Fax: 619-759-9938

ASSOCIATES

Hugh K. Swift	Lawrence G. Campitiello

Representative Clients: The Standard Steamship Owners Protection and Indemnity Association, Ltd. (London); Caribbean Marine Service Co., Inc. (San Diego); Century National Insurance.
Reference: Wells Fargo Bank.

For full biographical listings, see the Martindale-Hubbell Law Directory

---

REDDING, Shasta Co.

DUGAN BARR & ASSOCIATES (AV)

1824 Court Street, P.O. Box 994390, 96099-1648
Telephone: 916-243-8008
Fax: 916-243-1648
URL: http://www.CA-Lawyer.com/

Dugan Barr

ASSOCIATES

David L. Case	Douglas Mudford

Representative Clients: City of Redding; Mid Valley Bank; Scott Valley Bank; 3M; Enloe Hospital.
References: Scott Valley Bank, Redding Branch; Mid Valley Bank, Redding Branch.

For full biographical listings, see the Martindale-Hubbell Law Directory

---

CARR, KENNEDY, PETERSON & FROST, A LAW CORPORATION (AV)

420 Redcliff Drive, P.O. Box 492396, 96049
Telephone: 916-222-2100
Fax: 916-222-0504

Francis Carr (1875-1944)	Daniel S. Frost
Lawrence J. Kennedy, Sr. (1883-1975)	Robert M. Harding
	Evan L. Delgado
Laurence J. Kennedy, Jr. (1918-1986)	Stephen H. Baker
	Michael P. Ashby
Laurence W. Carr (1912-1991)	Randall C. Nelson
R. Russ Peterson	Robert A. West

Representative Clients: Chicago Title Insurance Co.; CH2M Hill California, Inc.; Fruit Growers Supply Co.; ITT Rayonier, Inc.; Louisiana-Pacific Corp.; Minnesota Mining & Manufacturing; Northbrook Insurance Co.; Roseburg Lumber Co.; Security Union Title Insurance Co.; Stewart Title Insurance Co.

For full biographical listings, see the Martindale-Hubbell Law Directory

---

REDWOOD CITY, San Mateo Co.

CODDINGTON, HICKS & DANFORTH, A PROFESSIONAL CORPORATION (AV)

Suite 300, 555 Twin Dolphin Drive, Paragon Center, Redwood Shores, 94065
Telephone: 415-592-5400
Facsimile: 415-592-5027

Clinton H. Coddington	Lee J. Danforth
Randolph S. Hicks	David M. King
Richard G. Grotch	

Edward A. Heinlein	Pamela Ann Smith
David W. Wessel	Peter L. Candy
R. Wardell Loveland	David K. Levine

OF COUNSEL

William G. Tucker	Arnold I Bennigson

For full biographical listings, see the Martindale-Hubbell Law Directory

---

LOW, BALL & LYNCH, A PROFESSIONAL CORPORATION (AV)

10 Twin Dolphin, Suite B-500, 94065
Telephone: 415-591-8822
Fax: 415-591-8884
San Francisco, California Office: 601 California Street, Suite 2100, 94108.
Telephone: 415-981-6630.
Monterey, California Office: 10 Ragsdale Drive, Suite 175, 93940.
Telephone: 408-655-8822.

Raymond Coates	David L. Blinn
Chester G. Moore, III	Janet Kulig
James D. Miller	Thomas E. Mulvihill
William H. Holsinger	Jennifer Elizabeth Acheson

(See Next Column)

LOW, BALL & LYNCH A PROFESSIONAL CORPORATION—*Continued*

John R. Baumann	Joseph M. Fenech
Michael E. Sandgren	

For full biographical listings, see the Martindale-Hubbell Law Directory

RIVERSIDE,* Riverside Co.

LAW OFFICES OF TERRY BRIDGES (AV)

Mission Square Plaza, 3750 University Avenue, Suite 240, 92501-3313
Telephone: 909-682-2760
Facsimile: 909-682-8626

ASSOCIATE
Alan J. Leahy
LEGAL SUPPORT PERSONNEL
PARAPROFESSIONAL
Mechelle Winsor

For full biographical listings, see the Martindale-Hubbell Law Directory

SACRAMENTO,* Sacramento Co.

THE BLEIER LAW FIRM (AV)

2100 21st Street, 95818-1708
Telephone: 916-454-2100
Fax: 916-454-2121
Email: tblf@bleier.com *URL:* http://www.bleier.com

Brenton A. Bleier
ASSOCIATES

Alan C. Campbell	Robert W. Hunt
Peter H. Mixon	Bradford A. Bleier

For full biographical listings, see the Martindale-Hubbell Law Directory

BOLLING, WALTER & GAWTHROP, A PROFESSIONAL CORPORATION (AV)

8880 Cal Center Drive, Suite 400, P.O. Box 255200, 95826
Telephone: 916-369-0777
Telecopier: 916-369-2698

Laurence L. Angelo	Bruce A. Kilday
Theodore D. Bolling, Jr.	Carolee Kilduff
John P. Coleman	Marjorie E. Manning
Michael J. Conlan	Bruno D. Marraccini
Alfred Gawthrop, Jr.	J. Brian Powers
Glenn M. Holley	Thomas A. Tweedy
Michael F. Keddy	Donald S. Walter
John A. Whitesides	

Glenn V. Lawson	Peter M. Williams
William Lucas Marder	J. Scott Smith
Christine Green Sanfilippo	David R. Feniger
C. Scott Tocher	Gary A. Wood
Erica R. Williams	Jeffrey S. Stone
Kevin W. Higgins	

OF COUNSEL

Gerald K. Petersen	Marion H. Pothoven

LEGAL SUPPORT PERSONNEL

Susan M. Jarboe	Candace D. Morgan
(Paralegal-Law Librarian)	David Buffington

Representative Clients: Aetna Casualty & Surety; Cal-Farm Insurance; California State Auto Assn.; Fireman's Fund American Co.; Gallagher Bassett Insurance Services; General Adjustment Bureau; Industrial Indemnity Co.; Nationwide Insurance Co.; Royal Insurance Co.
Reference: River City Bank.

For full biographical listings, see the Martindale-Hubbell Law Directory

CALLAHAN & DEACON (AV)

A Partnership including a Corporation
77 Cadillac Drive, Suite 240, 95825
Telephone: 916-929-1999
Fax: 916-929-1090
Email: gbc8esd@calweb.com

Gary B. Callahan (Inc.)	Edward S. Deacon

ASSOCIATE
Judith Clark Martin

For full biographical listings, see the Martindale-Hubbell Law Directory

DIEPENBROCK, WULFF, PLANT & HANNEGAN, LLP (AV)

Suite 1700, 300 Capitol Mall, P.O. Box 3034, 95812-3034
Telephone: 916-444-3910
Telecopier: 916-446-1696
URL: http://www.dwph.com

(See Next Column)

MEMBERS OF FIRM

John S. Gilmore	Forrest A. Plant, Jr.
David A. Riegels	Jeffery Owensby
Dennis M. Campos	William J. Coyne
Jack V. Lovell	Frank P. Fedor
John E. Fischer	David L. Ditora
Charity Kenyon	P. John Swanson
Francis M. Goldsberry, II	V. Blair Shahbazian
Raymond M. Cadei	Melinda Guzman Moore

ASSOCIATES

Sean O. Sheridan	Jason M. Heath
Richard K. Voss	Rhonda Canby
Holly B. Armstrong	Andrea J. McNeil
James F. Curran	Samuel T. McAdam
Christine Cusick Nesbit	Elias Hayek
Craig S. Meyers	

Representative Clients: Southern Pacific Transportation Co.; Chevron Corp.; Metropolitan Life Insurance Co.; Aerojet-General Corp.; Farmers Insurance Group; Sears, Roebuck and Co.

For full biographical listings, see the Martindale-Hubbell Law Directory

GAY, HALL & DITORE (AV)

300 Capitol Mall Suite 1550, 95814
Telephone: 916-444-3495
FAX: 916-444-8030

Stephen J. Gay	Gary L. Hall
Deborah D. Ditore	

ASSOCIATES

Stephanie Ann Allen	Kevin M. Erwin

For full biographical listings, see the Martindale-Hubbell Law Directory

HANSEN, BOYD, CULHANE & WATSON (AV)

A Partnership including Professional Corporations
Central City Centre, 1331 Twenty-First Street, 95814
Telephone: 916-444-2550
Telecopier: 916-444-2358

Hartley T. Hansen (Inc.)	Lawrence R. Watson
Kevin R. Culhane (Inc.)	John J. Rueda
David E. Boyd	James J. Banks
Lorraine M. Pavlovich	

OF COUNSEL
Betsy S. Kimball

Thomas L. Riordan	Pamela B. Hooley
James O. Moses	Roger R. Billings

For full biographical listings, see the Martindale-Hubbell Law Directory

HARDY ERICH BROWN & WILSON, A PROFESSIONAL CORPORATION (AV)

1000 G Street, 95814
Telephone: 916-449-3800
Fax: 916-449-3888
Mailing Address: P.O. Box 13530, Sacramento, California, 95853-4530

John Quincy Brown, Jr.	Bruce E. Salenko
Anthony D. Osmundson	Daniel J. Coyle
Thomas C. Richards	Brian H. Charter
L. Thomas Wagner	Larry Caldwell
David L. Perrault	Richard L. Alley
John Quincy Brown, III	Glenda N. Reager
David S. Worthington	Whitney A. Davis
L. Kent Wyatt	John C. Miller, Jr.
Michael J. Nelson	

OF COUNSEL

Cavan Hardy	William A. Wilson
Norwood R. Erich	Richard M. Cunha

Linda Wilson Bloom	Jay A. Resendez
Sara A. Clark	Kelly F. Watson
Kristine E. Balough	

Representative Clients: Crain Industries, Inc.; The Dial Corporation; General Motors Corporation; Goodyear Tire & Rubber Company; Kmart Corporation; Redman Industries, Inc.; Swift Transportation; Synnex Information Technologies, Inc.; United Way Sacramento Area; VIAD Corporation.

For full biographical listings, see the Martindale-Hubbell Law Directory

HUNTER RICHEY DI BENEDETTO & BREWER, LLP (AV)

A Limited Liability Partnership
Renaissance Tower, 801 K Street, 23rd Floor, 95814-3525
Telephone: 916-491-3000
Facsimile: 916-491-3080
Email: hrdb@hrdb.com *URL:* http://www.hrdb.com

(See Next Column)

HUNTER RICHEY DI BENEDETTO & BREWER LLP, *Sacramento—Continued*

MEMBERS OF FIRM

William S. Hunter	James F. Geary
Win R. Richey	Janet C. Eisenbeis
Florence L. Di Benedetto	Jeffery D. Harris
Roy E. Brewer	Stephen C. Ruehmann
Anne E. Ferguson	Ralph T. Ferguson
Judith J. Citko	Sharon K. Sandeen

Kathryn T. Papalia

LEGAL SUPPORT PERSONNEL

Lori J. Kelly (Paralegal)	Michele L. Nickell (Legal Assistant)
Deborah M. Romero (Paralegal)	
Linda Jane Hall (Legal Assistant)	Dawn Krein (Legal Assistant)
Jennifer E. Mueller (Legal Assistant)	Stephanie L. Neumann (Legal Assistant)

For full biographical listings, see the Martindale-Hubbell Law Directory

JOHNSON, SCHACHTER & COLLINS, A PROFESSIONAL CORPORATION (AV)

701 University Avenue, Suite 150, 95825
Telephone: 916-921-5800
Telecopier: 916-921-0247
Email: 102514.3714@COMPUSERVE.COM

Robert H. Johnson	Alesa M. Schachter
	Kim H. Collins

George W. Holt	Carrie G. Pratt
Timothy P. Dailey	R. James Miller

OF COUNSEL

Ford R. Smith	Carolyn M. Wood
	Susanne M. Shelley

Representative Clients: Fireman's Fund Insurance Cos.; GAB Business Services; Jonsson Communications Corp.; McClatchy Newspapers and Broadcasting; State Farm Fire & Casualty Co.; State Farm Mutual Automobile Insurance Co.
Reference: Business & Professional Bank, Sacramento.

For full biographical listings, see the Martindale-Hubbell Law Directory

JOHN B. LEWIS (AV)

1006 Fourth Street, 10th Floor, 95814
Telephone: 916-443-2051
Fax: 916-443-2651

For full biographical listings, see the Martindale-Hubbell Law Directory

LIVINGSTON & MATTESICH, LAW CORPORATION (AV)

1201 K Street, Suite 1100, 95814
Telephone: 916-442-1111
Fax: 916-448-1709
Email: liv-matt@gvn.net

Gene Livingston	Carol Livingston
James M. Mattesich	Rebecca M. Ceniceros

Steven P. Belzer	Trisha M. McAlmond

Reference: Bank of California.

For full biographical listings, see the Martindale-Hubbell Law Directory

THOMAS F. LYTLE (AV)

Court Plaza Building, 901 H Street, Suite 609, 95814-1809
Telephone: 916-442-0701
Fax: 916-442-0780

For full biographical listings, see the Martindale-Hubbell Law Directory

MASON & THOMAS (AV)

2151 River Plaza Drive, Suite 100, P.O. Box 868, 95812-0868
Telephone: 916-567-8211
Fax: 916-567-8212

MEMBERS OF FIRM

Stephen A. Mason	Bradley S. Thomas

ASSOCIATES

Douglas W. Brown	Kevin L. Elder
Robert G. Kruse	Michele Raley
David S. Yost	David T. Ludington
Patrick J. Hehir	Timothy T. Wright

Anastasia Baskerville

For full biographical listings, see the Martindale-Hubbell Law Directory

MATHENY POIDMORE LINKERT & SEARS (AV)

3638 American River Drive, P.O. Box 13711, 95853-4711
Telephone: 916-978-3434
Fax: 916-978-3430
Email: mpls1@netcom.com

MEMBERS OF FIRM

Henry G. Matheny (1933-1984)	James C. Damir
Anthony J. Poidmore	Michael A. Bishop
Douglas A. Sears	Ernest A. Long
Richard S. Linkert	Joann Georgallis

Kent M. Luckey

ASSOCIATES

Matthew C. Jaime	Cathy A. Reynolds
Robert B. Berrigan	Eric R. Wiesel
Stephen J. Nardine	Reed R. Johnson
Ronald E. Enabnit	Danielle M. Guard

Andrea M. Croak

LEGAL SUPPORT PERSONNEL
PARALEGALS

Karen D. Fisher	Lynell Rae Steed
Fran Studer	Jennifer Bachman

Debbie Sue Miller

For full biographical listings, see the Martindale-Hubbell Law Directory

McDONALD, SAELTZER, MORRIS, CREEGGAN & WADDOCK (AV)

555 Capitol Mall, Suite 700, 95814
Telephone: 916-444-5706
Fax: 916-444-8529

MEMBERS OF FIRM

Eugene W. Saeltzer	Richard C. Creeggan
William O. Morris	Thomas P. Waddock

Gregory R. Madsen

ASSOCIATES

Hank G. Greenblatt	Andrea Rae Austin
Jon S. Allin	S. Maylee Singer
Scott W. DePeel	Jay Steven Linden
Denise C. Standridge	Kenneth M. Goulart

Matthew P. Maniscalco

OF COUNSEL

Douglas B. McDonald

Reference: Wells Fargo Bank.

For full biographical listings, see the Martindale-Hubbell Law Directory

MOORE, MEEGAN, HANSCHU & KASSENBROCK (AV)

1545 River Park Drive, Suite 550, 95815
Telephone: 916-925-1800

MEMBERS OF FIRM

John M. Moore	James L. Hanschu
David M. Meegan	Mark R. Kassenbrock

Roberta Lindsey-Scott	Peter J. Pullen
Mary Clarke Ver Hoef	Wendy S. Dezzani

For full biographical listings, see the Martindale-Hubbell Law Directory

PORTER, SCOTT, WEIBERG & DELEHANT, A PROFESSIONAL CORPORATION (AV)

350 University Avenue, Suite 200, 95825
Telephone: 916-929-1481
Fax: 916-927-3706

Russell G. Porter	Terence J. Cassidy
A. Irving Scott, Jr.	Tom H. Bailey
Edwin T. Weiberg	Carl J. Calnero
John W. Delehant	Russ J. Wunderli
Anthony S. Warburg	Nancy J. Sheehan
Ned P. Telford	Norman V. Prior
James K. Mirabell	Timothy M. Blaine
Craig A. Caldwell	Stephen E. Horan

Amanda R. Lowe	Alysa Erdman Meyer
Clay A. Jackson	Richard Joseph Corbo, Jr.
Elisa Ungerman	Bruce A. Monfross
John Carl Padrick	Marcos Kropf
Erik Z. Revai	Valerie Mercier
Karen Beth Ebel	Jennifer E. Duggan
Carl L. Fessenden	Vanessa W. Whang
Grant Collins Woodruff	Dennis C. Huie
James W. Walter, Jr.	Stephanie A. Sahakian
Michael J. Baytosh	Kristin M. Engstom
David A. Melton	Jeffrey S. Kravitz

For full biographical listings, see the Martindale-Hubbell Law Directory

SAN BERNARDINO, San Bernardino Co.

WILSON, BORROR, DUNN & DAVIS (AV)

Suite 307, The Bank of California Building, 255 North D Street, 92401
Telephone: 909-884-8855
Fax: 909-884-5161

MEMBERS OF FIRM

Fred A. Wilson (1886-1973) James R. Dunn
Wm. H. Wilson (1915-1981) Thomas M. Davis
Keith D. Davis

ASSOCIATES

Timothy P. Prince Sarah L. Overton

OF COUNSEL

Caywood J. Borror

Representative Clients: Travelers Insurance Co.; Rockwell International; Westinghouse Air Brake Co.; Goodyear Tire and Rubber Co.; Home Insurance Co.; Cities of: Redlands, Chino, Colton, San Bernardino and Upland; The Canadian Insurance Co.

For full biographical listings, see the Martindale-Hubbell Law Directory

SAN DIEGO, San Diego Co.

JOSEPH J. BARR, JR. A PROFESSIONAL CORPORATION (AV)

501 West Broadway, Suite 2080, 92101
Telephone: 619-235-0444
Facsimile: 619-235-0650

Joseph J. Barr, Jr. Gary L. Ritchie
Dennis S. O'Neill

For full biographical listings, see the Martindale-Hubbell Law Directory

BROWN, MCDONNELL & ROMAKER, A PROFESSIONAL LAW CORPORATION (AV)

2390 Shelter Island Drive, Suite 210, 92106
Telephone: 619-221-9181
Fax: 619-221-9181

Sampson A. Brown Michael B. McDonnell
John L. Romaker

Representative Clients: A to Z Marine Service; Knight & Carver Custom Yachts, Inc.; Lester & Lester Marine Survey, Inc.

For full biographical listings, see the Martindale-Hubbell Law Directory

BUTZ, LUCAS & DUNN, A PROFESSIONAL CORPORATION (AV)

101 West Broadway, Suite 1700, 92101-8289
Telephone: 619-233-4777
Fax: 619-231-0341
Email: BLD@BLD.COM
Orange County, California Office: 1 Park Plaza, Suite 1250, Irvine, 92614-8509.
Telephone: 714-261-7733.
Fax: 714-261-7892.

Douglas M. Butz Richard L. Boyer
Stephen D. Lucas Kevin V. DeSantis
K. Elizabeth Dunn Albert E. Haverkamp
Linda Hunt Mullany

Roger P. Bingham Louis R. Chao
Pamela J. Rand James P. Souza
Robert Kevin Jassoy Kevin F. Greer

OF COUNSEL

J. Lawrence Irving

For full biographical listings, see the Martindale-Hubbell Law Directory

CASEY, GERRY, REED & SCHENK (AV)

110 Laurel Street, 92101
Telephone: 619-238-1811
Fax: 619-544-9232
Email: cglaw@cglaw.com

OF COUNSEL

David S. Casey Richard F. Gerry

MEMBERS OF FIRM

David S. Casey, Jr. T. Michael Reed
Frederick Schenk

ASSOCIATES

Robert J. Francavilla Michael P. Montgomery
Gayle Meryl Blatt Suzanne C. Etpison
Thomas D. Penfield Bonnie E. Kane

Reference: San Diego National Bank.

For full biographical listings, see the Martindale-Hubbell Law Directory

CHAPIN, FLEMING & WINET, A PROFESSIONAL CORPORATION (AV)

Library, 501 West Broadway, 15th Floor, 92101
Telephone: 619-232-4261
Telefax: 619-232-4840
Email: cfwlaw@adnc.com *URL:* http://www.sandiego-online.com/cfwlaw
Vista, California Office: 410 South Melrose Drive, Suite 101.
Telephone: 619-758-4261.
Telefax: 619-758-6420.
Los Angeles, California Office: 12121 Wilshire Boulevard, Suite 401.
Telephone: 310-826-0133.
Telefax: 310-207-4236.
Palm Springs, California Office: 225 North El Cielo Road, Suite 470.
Telephone: 619-416-1400.
Telefax: 619-416-1405.

Victor M. Barr, Jr. Traci Lynn Kuchta
Craig H. Bell Dana Marie Lawson
  (Resident, Los Angeles Office)   (Resident, Los Angeles Office)
Darryn L. Berner Jeffrey J. Leist
Kelli Jean Brooks   (Resident, Los Angeles Office)
Michael S. Burke Tonya L. Morgan
David H. Bushnell   (Resident, Los Angeles Office)
  (Resident, Los Angeles Office) David A. Myers
Richard D. Carter   (Resident, Los Angeles Office)
  (Resident, Los Angeles Office) Brenda J. Pannell
Dean G. Chandler   (Resident, Los Angeles Office)
  (Resident, Vista Office) Kennett L. Patrick
Edward D. Chapin   (Resident, Vista Office)
Victoria Chen Thomas V. Perea
George Chuang   (Resident, Los Angeles Office)
  (Resident, Los Angeles Office) Roger L. Popeney
Amber L. Eck Maria C. Roberts
Robert Ehrenreich Lawrence W. Shea, II
  (Resident, Los Angeles Office) Douglas J. Simpson
Scott K. Endsley Spencer C. Skeen
George E. Fleming   (Resident, Los Angeles Office)
Antonio Gastelum (Not Howard Smith
  admitted in United States)   (Resident, Los Angeles Office)
Shirley A. Gauvin Patricia L. Sullivan
Katherine M. Green Gregory S. Tavill
Terence L. Greene Frank L. Tobin
Gregory Kevin Hansen Grace I. Wang
Howard L. Hoffenberg   (Resident, Los Angeles Office)
  (Resident, Los Angeles Office) Peter C. Ward
Patrick M. Howe Jeffrey A. Weaver (Resident,
Aaron H. Katz   Palm Springs Office)
Elizabeth J. Koumas Randall L. Winet
    (Resident, Vista Office)

OF COUNSEL

George F. Braun Irwin Waldman (A P.C.)
Arthur D. Rutledge   (Resident, Los Angeles Office)
  (Resident, Los Angeles Office) James Michael Zimmerman
Jeffrey C. Stodel
  (Resident, Los Angeles Office)

For full biographical listings, see the Martindale-Hubbell Law Directory

COUGHLAN, SEMMER & LIPMAN (AV)

501 West Broadway, Suite 400, 92101
Telephone: 619-232-0800
Fax: 619-232-0107

MEMBERS OF FIRM

R. J. (Jerry) Coughlan, Jr. Robert F. Semmer
Michael L. Lipman

ASSOCIATES

Cathleen Gilliland Fitch Barbara Howe Murray
Duane Tyler Katherine Koransky Pothier
Angela L. Baxter Daniel A. Kaplan

OF COUNSEL

Alexandra M. Kwoka

Representative Clients: Ernst & Young; U.S. Air; Wells Fargo Bank; Lawyers Mutual Insurance Co.; Prudential-Bache Securities, Inc.; CAMICO; Shell Oil; IBP, Inc.; UST Inc.; San Diego National Bank.

For full biographical listings, see the Martindale-Hubbell Law Directory

DOUGHERTY & HILDRE (AV)

2550 Fifth Avenue, Suite 600, 92103-5624
Telephone: 619-232-9131
Telefax: 619-232-7317

William O. Dougherty Fred M. Dudek
Donald F. Hildre Mona H. Freedman

For full biographical listings, see the Martindale-Hubbell Law Directory

San Diego—Continued

DUCKOR SPRADLING & METZGER, A LAW CORPORATION (AV)

401 West A Street, Suite 2400, 92101-7909
Telephone: 619-231-3666
Telecopier: 619-231-6629
Email: dsm@dsmlaw.wanet.com

Michael J. Duckor	K. Michael Garrett
Gary J. Spradling	Patrick L. Prindle
Scott L. Metzger	Li-An C. Leonard
John C. Wynne	Stephen A. Bond
John W. Cutchin	R. Anthony Mahavier
Robert D. Rochelle	Robin Assaf Wofford
Robert L. Kenny	Leslie S. Akins
Laurie J. Orange	Jill Osmars Wolcott

Thomas R. Darton

Brian A. Barnhorst	Jamie M. Ryan
Catriona M. Cahill	Douglas A. Dube
Robert J. Solis	Gregory P. Olson
John J. Freni	Susan B. Hansen
Jessica M. Amgwerd	Julie D. Wiley

Laura B. Riesenberg

Representative Clients: E & J Gallo Wineries; McMillen Communities; National Dispatch Center; Sedgwick James International; Siemens Credit Corp.; Transamerica Financial Services; Van Camp Seafood Co.; Western Energy Management; Watt Industries.

For full biographical listings, see the Martindale-Hubbell Law Directory

LAW OFFICES OF ROBERT G. DYER (AV)

600 West Broadway, Suite 1400, 92101-3302
Telephone: 619-544-9300
Fax: 619-544-9598

For full biographical listings, see the Martindale-Hubbell Law Directory

EDWARDS, SOOY & BYRON, A PROFESSIONAL CORPORATION (AV)

101 West Broadway, Ninth Floor, 92101
Telephone: 619-231-1500
Fax: 619-231-1588
URL: http://sdclaw.com/ews
Orange County Office: 660 Newport Center Drive, Suite 465, Newport Beach, California, 92660.
Telephone: 714-717-5000.
Fax: 714-717-5001.

Michael M. Edwards	John A. Simpson
Richard R. Sooy	William P. Harris, III
Charles R. Bongard	John D. Marino
Thomas W. Byron	Scott L. Ghormley (Resident,
Glen M. Rasmussen	Newport Beach Office)
Karen Anderson Holmes	Robyn S. McClain

Paul J. Delmore

Lisa G. Shemonsky	Kenneth R. Wright
Erich J. Lidl	Michael M. Edwards, Jr.
Michael J. Orzel	Patrick J. Mendes
John J. Philpott	Ted M. Lee
Grant R. Mullen	Gary D. Anderson
Arthur D. Hodge	Steve Bergen
Daniel L. Rodriguez	Michele Marie Macosky
Whitney B. Wilds	Napoleon L.D. Taylor

OF COUNSEL
Stanley J. Wezelman

For full biographical listings, see the Martindale-Hubbell Law Directory

ESTES & HOYT, A PROFESSIONAL CORPORATION (AV)

Suite 1300, 1010 Second Avenue, 92101
Telephone: 619-234-2111
Fax: 619-234-1509

Joel C. Estes	Kevin J. Hoyt

Bernard M. Hansen

Melvin E. Morris	Richard C. Norton

For full biographical listings, see the Martindale-Hubbell Law Directory

FERRIS & BRITTON, A PROFESSIONAL CORPORATION (AV)

1600 First National Bank Center, 401 West A Street, 92101
Telephone: 619-233-3131
Fax: 619-232-9316

(See Next Column)

Christopher Q. Britton	Steven J. Pynes

Michael R. Weinstein

Representative Clients: Agouron Pharmaceuticals, Inc.; Allstate Insurance Co.; Cox Communications, Inc.; Enterprise Rent-a-Car; Exxon; Immuno Pharmaceutics, Inc.; Invitrogen Corporation; Peninsula Bank; Teleport Communications Group; Southwest Airlines.

For Complete List of Firm Personnel, See General Section

For full biographical listings, see the Martindale-Hubbell Law Directory

LOUIS E. GOEBEL (AV)

The Historic "Britt-Scripps" House, 406 Maple Street, 92103
Telephone: 619-239-2611
Fax: 619-239-4269
Email: goebellaw@aol.com

For full biographical listings, see the Martindale-Hubbell Law Directory

LAW OFFICES OF STEVEN R. HAASIS (AV)

First National Bank Building, 401 West "A" Street, 14th Floor, 92101-3509
Telephone: 619-236-9933
Fax: 619-236-8961

ASSOCIATE
Nelson J. Goodin

For full biographical listings, see the Martindale-Hubbell Law Directory

HIGGS, FLETCHER & MACK LLP (AV)

2000 First National Bank Building, 401 West "A" Street, 92101
Telephone: 619-236-1551
Telecopier: 619-696-1410
Email: info@higgslaw.com

MEMBERS OF FIRM

Henry Pitts Mack (1909-1974)	Steven H. Kruis
John W. Netterblad	David R. Clark
Joe N. Turner	Jeanne S. Gallagher
Craig D. Higgs	M. Cory Brown
Harry L. Carter	Patricia P. Hollenbeck
Michael F. Boyle	Thomas P. Sayer, Jr.
Steven B. Davis	James M. Peterson
John Morris	Greg A. McAtee
John L. Morrell	Susan Moriarty Hack

OF COUNSEL
Ferdinand T. Fletcher
SPECIAL COUNSEL
Andrew S. Albert (P.C.)
ASSOCIATES

Phillip C. Samouris	Debra G. Kaufman
Dolores E. Gonzales	Michael T. Quinn
Daniel C. Herbert	James E. Fox
Liong Lie Gan Penfield	Scott D. Kumpf
Jeff G. Harmeyer	Lauren F. Weidner

Representative Clients: Frazee Industries; Kawasaki Motors Corp.; Rohr Industries; Allstate Insurance Co.; Associated Aviation Underwriters; Physicians & Surgeons Insurance Exchange.

For Complete List of Firm Personnel, See General Section

For full biographical listings, see the Martindale-Hubbell Law Directory

HOVEY, KIRBY, THORNTON & HAHN, A PROFESSIONAL CORPORATION (AV)

101 West Broadway, Suite 1100, 92101-8297
Telephone: 619-685-4000
Fax: 619-685-4004
Email: 74754.3143@compuserve.com

Gregg B. Hovey	Jane Hahn
Dean T. Kirby, Jr.	Patrick R. Kitchin
Cynthia K. Thornton	Geraldine A. Valdez

For full biographical listings, see the Martindale-Hubbell Law Directory

HYDE AND WATERS (AV)

401 West "A" Street, Suite 1200, 92101
Telephone: 619-696-6911
Telecopier: 619-696-6919

MEMBERS OF FIRM

Laurel Lee Hyde	Timothy Doyle Waters

Representative Clients: Cardio Theatre, Inc.; C.W. Clark, Inc.; Foster Investment Corporation; Home Capital Corporation; Kmart Corporation; Midland Loan Services, L.P.; New World Communications Co.; The Regents of the University of California; San Diego Gas and Electric Company; Standard Process of Southern California.

For full biographical listings, see the Martindale-Hubbell Law Directory

San Diego—Continued

LAW OFFICES OF ROBERT S. KILBORNE IV (AV)

First National Bank Building, 401 West "A' Street, Suite 1850, 92101
Telephone: 619-237-1047
Fax: 619-237-1096

ASSOCIATE
David Arbogast
OF COUNSEL
Russell B. Wagner

For full biographical listings, see the Martindale-Hubbell Law Directory

LEVINE, STEINBERG & MILLER (AV)

550 West C Street, Suite 1810, 92101-8596
Telephone: 619-231-9449
Telecopier: 619-231-8638

MEMBERS OF FIRM

Harvey R. Levine	Craig A. Miller
Harris I. Steinberg	Jordan M. Cohen
	Richard A. Huver

For full biographical listings, see the Martindale-Hubbell Law Directory

LINDLEY, LAZAR & SCALES, A PROFESSIONAL CORPORATION (AV)

One America Plaza, 600 West Broadway, Suite 1400, 92101-3302
Telephone: 619-234-9181
Fax: 619-234-8475
Email: 104413.1175@compuserve.com

Luke R. Corbett	Michael H. Wexler
John M. Seitman	Richard J. Pekin, Jr.
Robert M. McLeod	George C. Lazar
R. Gordon Huckins	

Marc A. Geffen

Representative Clients: Commonwealth Land Title Insurance Company; Bank of Commerce; Palomar Savings & Loan Association; FDIC; Southern California Soil & Testing, Inc.; Chicago Title Insurance Company.

For Complete List of Firm Personnel, See General Section

For full biographical listings, see the Martindale-Hubbell Law Directory

DANIEL B. MacLEOD (AV)

McClintock Plaza, 1202 Kettner Boulvard, Suite 4400, 92101
Telephone: 619-234-7000
Telefax: 619-234-9973
San Francisco, California Affiliated Office: King & MacLeod 101 California Street, Suite 4050 94111.
Telephone: 415-352-0675.

For full biographical listings, see the Martindale-Hubbell Law Directory

McCLELLAN & BROWN, A PROFESSIONAL CORPORATION (AV)

1144 State Street, 92101
Telephone: 619-231-0505
Fax: 619-544-0540

Craig R. McClellan	LaMar B. Brown

For full biographical listings, see the Martindale-Hubbell Law Directory

MOWER, KOELLER, NEBEKER, CARLSON & HALUCK (AV)

225 Broadway, 21st Floor, 92101
Telephone: 619-233-1600
Fax: 619-236-0527
Irvine, California Office: 108 Pacifica, P.O. Box 19799.
Telephone: 714-753-1229.
Fax: 714-753-1413.
San Bernardino, California Office: 412 West Hospitality Lane, Suite 300, 92408.
Telephone: 909-381-3334.
Fax: 909-889-2007.
Yuma, Arizona Office: 212 South 2nd Avenue, P.O. Bin 11791.
Telephone: 520-782-2531.
Fax: 520-782-5319.

MEMBERS OF FIRM

William A. Nebeker	Christopher J. Hallman
Robert C. Carlson (Resident)	Scott P. Cranny

Megan K. Dorsey	Martha J. Dorsey
Michael J. Kielty	Laura Ellen Barton
Robert N. Clark	Laurence Frederick Haines
Anna Tomalino Amundson	Todd L. Burnight

For full biographical listings, see the Martindale-Hubbell Law Directory

MULVANEY, KAHAN & BARRY, A PROFESSIONAL CORPORATION (AV)

Seventeenth Floor, First National Bank Center, 401 West "A" Street, 92101-7994
Telephone: 619-238-1010
Fax: 619-238-1981
Email: mkb@mkblaw.com
Los Angeles, California Office: Union Bank Plaza, 445 South Figueroa Street, Suite 2600.
Telephone: 213-612-7765.
La Jolla, California Office: Glendale Federal Building, 7911 Herschel, Suite 300, P.O Box 1885.
Telephone: 619-454-0142.
Fax: 619-454-7858.
Orange, California Office: The Koll Center, 500 North State College Boulevard, Suite 440.
Telephone: 714-634-7069.
Fax: 714-939-8000.

James F. Mulvaney	Mark R. Raftery
Lawrence Kahan	Charles F. Bethel
Everett G. Barry, Jr.	Diane M. Racicot
Donald G. Johnson, Jr.	John A. Mayers
Robert A. Linn	Steven W. Pite
Maureen E. Markey	Patricia A. Sieveke (Resident,
Paula Rotenberg	Los Angeles and Orange
Melissa A. Blackburn	Offices)
Julie A. Jones	Linda C. Schumacher
Maureen F. Hallahan	John D. Duncan

OF COUNSEL

Rex B. Beatty	Derrick W. Samuelson
Robert K. Edmunds	(Not admitted in CA)
James P. McGowan, Jr.	
(Resident, La Jolla Office)	

Representative Clients: Air Products & Chemicals, Inc.; Aoki Construction (CA) Co., Ltd.; AT&T Capital Corp.; BellSouth Communications Systems, Inc.; ITT Corp.; NationsBank; Phoenix Home Life Mutual Insurance Co.; Textron, Inc.; Union Bank; Wells Fargo Bank.

For full biographical listings, see the Martindale-Hubbell Law Directory

NEIL, DYMOTT, PERKINS, BROWN & FRANK, A PROFESSIONAL CORPORATION (AV)

1010 Second Avenue, Suite 2500, 92101-4959
Telephone: 619-238-1712
Fax: 619-238-1562

Michael I. Neil	Thomas H. Knudsen
Thomas M. Dymott	Kyle A. Cruse
Roger G. Perkins	Nicole R. Hough
David G. Brown	Catherine A. Zingale
Robert W. Frank	Michael E. Rogaski
Gina L. Lacagnina	Craig T. Mann
Robert W. Harrison	Bradley R. Roppé
James A. McFall	Scott R. Omohundro
Sheila S. Trexler	Claire M. Stockmeyer
Constantine D. Buzunis	Scott B. Hilberg
Hugh A. McCabe	John Alessio
Michael S. Dea	Todd C. Smith
Jaye E. Okamoto	Margaret A. Dewey
Clark R. Hudson	Brian C. Dawson
Kris P. Thompson	Idan A. Ravin
Carolyn Taylor	Robyn Dimino
James D. Boley	Stephen Thatcher Sigler
Lewis M. Wolensky	Ben Cole Casey

Reference: Scripps Bank.

For full biographical listings, see the Martindale-Hubbell Law Directory

PAGE, POLIN & BUSCH, A PROFESSIONAL CORPORATION (AV)

350 West Ash Street, Suite 900, 92101-3436
Telephone: 619-231-1822
Fax: 619-231-1877
Fax: 619-231-1875
Email: pagepolin@pagepolin.com

Michael E. Busch	Richard W. Page
Kathleen A. Cashman-Kramer	Kenneth D. Polin
Richard L. Moskitis	Steven G. Rowles

Rod S. Fiori	Michael G. Rowles
Dorothy A. Johnson	(Not admitted in CA)
Jolene L. Parker	Barry M. Taira

For full biographical listings, see the Martindale-Hubbell Law Directory

POPE & BERGER (AV)

550 West "C" Street, Seventeenth Floor, 92101
Telephone: 619-595-1366
Facsimile: 619-595-1313

(See Next Column)

POPE & BERGER, San Diego—Continued

A. Mark Pope   Harvey C. Berger

ASSOCIATE

Pamela A. McKay

For full biographical listings, see the Martindale-Hubbell Law Directory

POST KIRBY NOONAN & SWEAT LLP (AV)

A Partnership including Professional Corporations
America Plaza 600 West Broadway 11th Floor, 92101
Telephone: 619-231-8666
FAX: 619-231-9593;
619-231-4360
Email: PKNS@cert.net

MEMBERS OF FIRM

Gregory A. Post	Stephanie Sontag
Michael L. Kirby (A P.C.)	David B. Oberholtzer
David J. Noonan	Charles T. Hoge
Richard W. Sweat	Natalie C. Venezia
R. Bruce Wayne (A P.C.)	Dickran A. Semerdjian
Thomas W. Bettles	Jeffrey A. Haile
Sandra L. Lackey	James R. Lance
Ross J. Schwartz	Steven W. Sanchez
Lise N. Wilson	Theresa M. Brehl

Jeffrey P. Lendrum

OF COUNSEL

Paul R. Kennerson

Steven B. Duke	Kristen T. Bruesehoff
Martha O. Anderson	Jonathan A. Boynton
Mary L. Waltari	Ethan T. Boyer
M. E. Stephens	Matthew C. McGrath
Jeffrey A. Unger	Monique Ballard Candor
Kelli A. Hokanson	Jodie M. Hardmeyer

James R. Ballard

LEGAL SUPPORT PERSONNEL

Laurel E. Scott	Susan O'Keefe Head
Maureen A. McCarthy	(Litigation Paralegal)
Jean D. Billings (Paralegal)	Ruth S. Friis (Paralegal)
Katherine G. Hicks (Paralegal)	Nicole Abrahamson (Paralegal)
Gail E. Bayley (Paralegal)	

For full biographical listings, see the Martindale-Hubbell Law Directory

SELTZER CAPLAN WILKINS & McMAHON, A PROFESSIONAL CORPORATION (AV)

2100 Symphony Towers, 750 B Street, 92101
Telephone: 619-685-3003
Fax: 619-685-3100

Gerald L. McMahon	Julie Genthner Simon
Reginald A. Vitek	Daniel A. Andrist
James B. Franklin	J. Scott Scheper
Julie P. Dubick	David J. Zubkoff
Joyce A. McCoy	Elisa A. Brandes
Dennis J. Wickham	Virginia C. Pearson
Michael H. Riney	Patricia Garcia
James P. Delphey	Gregory E. Flynn
Craig E. Courter	Tamara L. Reed
Michael G. Nardi	Kelly Rae Waggonner
Neal P. Panish	Lee E. Hejmanowski
Janice Patrice Brown	Christine M. Dabrowski
Vera P. Pardee	David P. Chiappetta
Michael R. Seyle	Daniel W. Negroni
David S. Minton	Michael A. Leone

OF COUNSEL

Elizabeth C. Eldridge   John D. Hershberger

Representative Clients: Chicago Title; Girard Savings Bank; Goodyear Tire & Rubber Co.; W.R. Grace & Co--Conn.; McDonnell-Douglas Corp.; McMillin Communities; Philip Morris Incorporated; Western Financial Savings Bank.

For Complete List of Firm Personnel, See General Section

For full biographical listings, see the Martindale-Hubbell Law Directory

SPARBER, FERGUSON, PONDER & RYAN, A PROFESSIONAL LAW CORPORATION (AV)

Imperial Bank Building, 701 "B" Street, Tenth Floor, 92101-8103
Telephone: 619-239-3600
Facsimile: 619-239-5601

Richard E. Sparber	Greg J. Ryan
James P. Ferguson	Richard J. Annen
John E. Ponder	Daniel F. Morrin
	Gary B. Rudolph

(See Next Column)

Todd R. Gabriel	William P. Fennell
Carol R. McGinnis	James E. Highsmith

OF COUNSEL

Mark P. Mandell

LEGAL SUPPORT PERSONNEL

LEGAL ADMINISTRATOR

Beverly K. Driscoll

For full biographical listings, see the Martindale-Hubbell Law Directory

THORSNES, BARTOLOTTA, McGUIRE & PADILLA (AV)

A Partnership including Professional Corporations
Fifth Avenue Financial Center, 11th Floor, 2550 Fifth Avenue, 92103
Telephone: 619-236-9363
Fax: 619-236-9653
Email: TBMP@lawinfo.com *URL:* http://www.tbmp.com

Michael T. Thorsnes (P.C.)	Mitchell S. Golub (P.C.)
Vincent J. Bartolotta, Jr., (P.C.)	Frederic L. Gordon (P.C.)
John F. McGuire (P.C.)	Palma Cesar Hooper (P.C.)
Michael D. Padilla (P.C.)	Neal H. Rockwood (P.C.)
Kevin F. Quinn (P.C.)	Daral B. Mazzarella (P.C.)
C. Brant Noziska (P.C.)	R. Christian Hulburt (P.C.)

ASSOCIATES

Jeffrey F. LaFave	John J. Rice
Stephen D. Lipkin	Robert E. Bright
Rhonda J. Thompson	Douglas J. Billings
Scott A. Kennedy	James T. Atkins

Charles L. Stott

OF COUNSEL

Robert S. Kennedy

For full biographical listings, see the Martindale-Hubbell Law Directory

ROBERT F. VAAGE (AV)

110 West "C" Street, Suite 2105, 92101
Telephone: 619-338-0505
Fax: 619-338-0588

For full biographical listings, see the Martindale-Hubbell Law Directory

WINGERT, GREBING, ANELLO & BRUBAKER (AV)

A Partnership including Professional Corporations
One America Plaza, Seventh Floor, 600 West Broadway, 92101-3370
Telephone: 619-232-8151
Facsimile: 619-232-4665
Email: wgab@wgab.com
Las Vegas, Nevada Office: Ryan, Marks and Johnson, 317 South Sixth Street, 89101.
Telephone: 702-471-7270.
Facsimile: 702-471-1245.

MEMBERS OF FIRM

John R. Wingert (A Professional Corporation)	James Goodwin
Charles R. Grebing (A Professional Corporation)	Shawn D. Morris
	Robert M. Caietti
Michael M. Anello (A Professional Corporation)	Eileen Mulligan Marks (Resident, Las Vegas, Nevada Office)
Alan K. Brubaker (A Professional Corporation)	Christopher W. Todd
Norman A. Ryan (Resident, Las Vegas, Nevada Office)	Robert L. Johnson (Resident, Las Vegas, Nevada Office)
	Robert M. Juskie

John S. Addams

ASSOCIATES

Julie E. Saake	James J. Brown, Jr.
Michael Sullivan	Craig Gross
Carolyn P. Gallinghouse	Stephen C. Grebing
Kimberly I. Cary	Brian P. Worthington
Terie M. Theis	Melanie A. Jubelirer
James P. Broder (Resident, Las Vegas, Nevada Office)	Kimberly A. Davis
	Michael W. Vivoli

OF COUNSEL

William L. Todd, Jr.

Representative Clients: California Casualty Insurance Co.; Farmers Insurance Group; The Ohio Casualty Group; United Services Automobile Assn.; United States Fidelity & Guaranty Co.

For full biographical listings, see the Martindale-Hubbell Law Directory

SAN FRANCISCO,* San Francisco Co.

ALDEN ARONOVSKY & SAX (AV)

235 Montgomery Street, 28th Floor, 94104-2902
Telephone: 415-732-5820
Facsimile: 415-732-5840
Email: law@aaslaw.com

(See Next Column)

ALDEN ARONOVSKY & SAX—*Continued*

MEMBERS OF FIRM

David W. Alden   Ronald G. Aronovsky

Brian M. Sax

ASSOCIATES

Jeffrey S. Koppelmaa   Sherry A. Glassman

For full biographical listings, see the Martindale-Hubbell Law Directory

LAW OFFICE OF GEORGE G. BENETATOS (AV)

100 California Street, Suite 640, 94111
Telephone: 415-398-2296
Facsimile: 415-398-2290
Corresponding Office, Athens, Greece: Kefaleas & Moussas.

For full biographical listings, see the Martindale-Hubbell Law Directory

BERG, ZIEGLER, ANDERSON & PARKER, LLP (AV)

4 Embarcadero Center, Suite 1400, 94111
Telephone: 415-397-6000
Telecopier: 415-397-9449

MEMBERS OF FIRM

James M. Berg   Robert Ted Parker
William J. Ziegler   David B. Franklin
Robert L. Anderson   David L. Monetta

F. Gale Connor

Douglas A. Applegate   Jennifer M. Malloy
Jeffrey B. Kirschenbaum   Patrick J. O'Brien

PARALEGALS

David A. Dunbar   Diane E. Gresham

Sharon L. Gostlin

For full biographical listings, see the Martindale-Hubbell Law Directory

LAW OFFICES OF PHILIP BOROWSKY A PROFESSIONAL CORPORATION (AV)

88 Kearny Street, Suite 1750, 94108
Telephone: 415-391-9675
Fax: 415-391-9679

Philip Borowsky

Dennis Kruszynski

For full biographical listings, see the Martindale-Hubbell Law Directory

BUCHALTER, NEMER, FIELDS & YOUNGER, A PROFESSIONAL CORPORATION (AV)

29th Floor, 333 Market Street, 94105
Telephone: 415-227-0900
Fax: 415-227-0770
Email: buchalter@earthlink.net *URL:* http://www.buchalter.com
Los Angeles, California Office: 24th Floor, 601 South Figueroa Street.
Telephone: 213-891-0700.
Fax: 213-896-0400.
New York, New York Office: 15th Floor, 605 Third Avenue.
Telephone: 212-490-8600.
Fax: 212-490-6022.
Newport Beach, California Office: Suite 1450, 620 Newport Center Drive.
Telephone: 714-760-1121.
Fax: 714-720-0182.

Elizabeth A. Fox

References: City National Bank; Wells Fargo Bank; Metrobank.

For Complete List of Firm Personnel, See General Section

For full biographical listings, see the Martindale-Hubbell Law Directory

CHICKERING & GREGORY, A PROFESSIONAL CORPORATION (AV)

615 Battery Street, 94104
Telephone: 415-393-9000
FAX: 415-788-0596
Washington, D.C. Office: 1815 H Street, N.W., Suite 650.
Telephone: 202-463-7456.
Fax: 202-835-0663.

Donald M. Gregory (1897-1991)   Donald L. Field, Jr.
Sherman Chickering (1911-1993)   Putnam Livermore
C. Hayden Ames   Elvis J. Stahr, Jr.
                                (Not admitted in CA)

For full biographical listings, see the Martindale-Hubbell Law Directory

CYRIL & CROWLEY (AV)

17th Floor, 456 Montgomery Street, 94104
Telephone: 415-989-1100
Facsimile: 415-421-6651
Email: candc@ix.netcom.com

MEMBERS OF FIRM

John W. Crowley   Michael W. Field
Robert B. Stringer   Carol P. Rohwer
David W. Gordon   Wendy J. Hannum

OF COUNSEL

Paul H. Cyril (A Professional Corporation)

ASSOCIATES

Elizabeth L. Dolter   Mark D. Fenske
Mark D. Skilling   Shannon M. Finnegan

For full biographical listings, see the Martindale-Hubbell Law Directory

LAW OFFICES OF RAYMOND N. STELLA ERLACH (AV)

4 Embarcadero Center, Seventeenth Floor, 94111
Telephone: 415-788-3322
FAX: 415-788-8613

Raymond N. Erlach

OF COUNSEL

Gregory J. Erlach   Stephen Peter U. Erlach

For full biographical listings, see the Martindale-Hubbell Law Directory

FELDMAN, WALDMAN & KLINE, A PROFESSIONAL CORPORATION (AV)

3 Embarcadero Center, Suite 2800, 94111
Telephone: 415-981-1300
Fax: 415-981-1350
Email: info@fwk.com
Stockton, California Office: Sperry Building, 146-148 West Weber Avenue.
Telephone: 209-943-2004.
Fax: 209-943-0905.

Murry J. Waldman   Martha Jeanne Shaver
Leland R. Selna, Jr.   (Resident, Stockton Office)
Michael L. Korbholz   Robert Cedric Goodman
Howard M. Wexler   Laura Grad
Patricia S. Mar   William F. Adams
Kenneth W. Jones   Elizabeth A. Thompson
Paul J. Dion   Julie A. Jones
Vern S. Bothwell   David L. Kanel
L.J. Chris Martiniak   Abram S. Feuerstein

Linda Sorensen

Laura J. Dawson   Dana A. Suntag
Joanne M. Lafreniere   (Resident, Stockton Office)
Paul A. Weiss   Danielle Ochs-Tillotson

OF COUNSEL

Richard L. Jaeger   Gerald A. Sherwin
                         (Resident, Stockton Office)

For full biographical listings, see the Martindale-Hubbell Law Directory

FLYNN, DELICH & WISE (AV)

Suite 1750, 580 California Street, 94104
Telephone: 415-693-5566
Fax: 415-693-0410
Long Beach, California Office: 1 World Trade Center, Suite 1800.
Telephone: 310-435-2626.
Fax: 310-437-7555.

John Allen Flynn   Sam D. Delich
James B. Nebel

Representative Clients: American Hawaii Cruises; Holland America Line; Through Transport Mutual Insurance Association, Ltd.; The Britannia Steam Ship Insurance Association Limited; The Steamship Mutual Underwriting Association (Bermuda) Ltd.; General Steamship Corp., Ltd.; Commodore Cruise Line, Ltd.; Interocean Steamship Corporation; Sea-Land Service, Inc.; Hatteras Yachts.

For full biographical listings, see the Martindale-Hubbell Law Directory

FRIEDMAN, ROSS & HERSH, A PROFESSIONAL CORPORATION (AV)

One Maritime Plaza, Suite 1040, 94111
Telephone: 415-788-2200
Telecopier: 415-394-0222

Jeffrey S. Ross   Jill Hersh

Michael J. Kass   Brigeda D. Bank
Ellen L. Winick   Paul E. Jahn

(See Next Column)

FRIEDMAN, ROSS & HERSH A PROFESSIONAL CORPORATION, *San Francisco—Continued*

OF COUNSEL
Gale A. Mondry

For full biographical listings, see the Martindale-Hubbell Law Directory

GOLDSTEIN & PHILLIPS, A PROFESSIONAL CORPORATION (AV)

One Embarcadero Center, Eighth Floor, 94111
Telephone: 415-981-8855
Telecopier: 415-981-0196

Alvin H. Goldstein, Jr.	R. Scott Erlewine
David C. Phillips	Mark L. Musto

Gary A. Berticevich	David M. Given
Tracey A. Gross	Kelly J. Snowden

OF COUNSEL
Robert D. Carrow

For full biographical listings, see the Martindale-Hubbell Law Directory

LAW OFFICES OF JOHN E. HILL (AV)

30 Hotaling Place, First Floor, 94111
Telephone: 415-398-2434
Facsimile: 415-392-2809
Oakland, California Office: 8105 Edgewater Drive, Suite 100.
Telephone: 510-729-6330.
Facsimile: 510-729-6333.

Daniel A. Stenson	Michael P. Guta
LeRoy F. Vadney	Thomas J. Kaster
Barbara J. Coffey	Mary-Lou Williams
James E. Keller	Ian M. Cooper
Dylan R. Lawrence	

For full biographical listings, see the Martindale-Hubbell Law Directory

IBERSHOF & DOLE (AV)

180 Montgomery Street Suite 1250, 94104
Telephone: 415-421-1144
FAX: 415-989-7359
Email: ibershof@aol.com

MEMBERS OF FIRM
William C. Ibershof	Stuart R. Dole

For full biographical listings, see the Martindale-Hubbell Law Directory

KEKER & VAN NEST, L.L.P. (AV)

710 Sansome Street, 94111-1704
Telephone: 415-391-5400
Fax: 415-397-7188

MEMBERS OF FIRM
John W. Keker	Karin Kramer
Robert A. Van Nest	Christopher C. Kearney
Jeffrey R. Chanin	Elliot R. Peters
Henry C. Bunsow	Stuart L. Gasner
Gary M. Cohen	James M. Emery
Susan J. Harriman	Loretta Lynch
Jan Nielsen Little	Jon S. Tigar

ASSOCIATES
Michael J. Proctor	Orly Degani
Daralyn Jeannine Durie	Mary Jane Mona
Wendy J. Thurm	(Not admitted in CA)
Steven A. Hirsch	Jonathan Gentin
Denise M. DeMory	(Not admitted in CA)
Ragesh K. Tangri	Kara M. Andersen
Elizabeth A. Egan	Christa M. Anderson
Michael H. Page	Leo L. Lam
Michael M. Edson	Karen P. Scarr
Brian L. Ferrall	David J. Silbert
E. Stewart Moritz	

For full biographical listings, see the Martindale-Hubbell Law Directory

KINDER, WUERFEL & CHOLAKIAN, A PROFESSIONAL CORPORATION (AV)

555 Montgomery Street, Ninth Floor, 94111
Telephone: 415-398-1551; 800-992-5990
FAX: 415-398-3301
URL: www.kwcapc.com
Santa Rosa, California Office: 2300 Northpoint Parkway.
Telephones: 707-522-8020; 800-992-5990.
FAX: 707-522-8022.
Costa Mesa, California Office: Avenue of the Arts.
Telephone: 714-825-3590; 800-992-5990.

(See Next Column)

H. Stuart Kinder	Kevin K. Cholakian
Mark D. Wuerfel	Julian J. Pardini
	(Resident, Santa Rosa Office)

SPECIAL COUNSEL
Mark A. Koop	Nan R. Hooven
	Paul B. Justi

Robert E. Belshaw	Peter R. Harris
David H. Bennett	(Resident, Santa Rosa Office)
Dean C. Burnick	Kathleen M. Hurly
Cheryl Castrogiovanni	Timothy S. Kirk
Douglas M. Chapman	Bryan A. McBurney
Christopher J. Connell	Steven J. Plas
(Resident, Santa Rosa Office)	Anthony O. Ricucci
Michael J. Estep	Charlene P. Rosack
James M. Gentile	Scott A. Slomiak
Garth A. Gersten	Michael A. Topp
Victor G. Greene	Harold A. Weston

LEGAL SUPPORT PERSONNEL
Gary T. Hall, Legal Administrator

For full biographical listings, see the Martindale-Hubbell Law Directory

LAFAYETTE, KUMAGAI & CLARKE (AV)

100 Spear Street, Suite 400, 94105
Telephone: 415-357-4600
Facsimile: 415-357-4605

MEMBERS OF FIRM
Gary T. Lafayette	Kevin M. Clarke
	Susan T. Kumagai

ASSOCIATES
Valerie A. Andersen	Forrest E. Fang
	Lupe C. Garcia

For full biographical listings, see the Martindale-Hubbell Law Directory

LASKY, HAAS & COHLER, PROFESSIONAL CORPORATION (AV)

Two Transamerica Center, 505 Sansome Street, 12th Floor, 94111-3183
Telephone: 415-788-2700
Facsimile: 415-981-4025

Moses Lasky	William A. Logan, Jr.
Charles B. Cohler	Kevin C. McCann
	David M. Rosenberg-Wohl

Jeffrey F. Silverman	Christopher S. Yates
Deborah E. Beck	Stacey M. Sklar
	Anthony D. Giles

For full biographical listings, see the Martindale-Hubbell Law Directory

LOVITT & HANNAN, INC. (AV)

900 Front Street, Suite 300, 94111
Telephone: 415-362-8769
Facsimile: 415-362-7528

Ronald Lovitt	J. Thomas Hannan

OF COUNSEL
Henry I. Bornstein

For full biographical listings, see the Martindale-Hubbell Law Directory

THE LUCAS LAW FIRM (AV)

Embarcadero West, Suite 1450, 275 Battery Street, 94111
Telephone: 415-434-3100
FAX: 415-434-0300

Kathleen M. Lucas

ASSOCIATE
Thomas E. Duckworth

For full biographical listings, see the Martindale-Hubbell Law Directory

MILLER, MAILLIARD & CULVER, LLP (AV)

A Partnership including Professional Corporations
155 Montgomery Street, Suite 1212, 94104
Telephone: 415-391-4291
Fax: 415-391-4292
Email: mmc@sirius.com
Santa Rosa, California Office: 100 B Street, Suite 200. P.O. Box 5257.
Telephone: 707-571-8112.
Fax: 707-575-9116. *Email:* milmaicul@aol.com.

(See Next Column)

MILLER, MAILLIARD & CULVER LLP—*Continued*

Christopher R. Miller (P.C.)   Kevin F. Barrett
William S. Mailliard, Jr.   William D. Evers
David C. Culver   Jay P. Hendrickson
R. W. Achor (P.C.) (Retired)   Paul E. Manasian
Phyllis E. Andelin   Philip J. Nicholsen, P.C.
Chigusa Saotome

OF COUNSEL

Stephen T. Kong

Representative Clients: BioZone Laboratories; California Dept. of Insurance; Dover Elevator Co.; Pacific Coast Apparel; Red Rose Collections; Sanwa Bank; Schug Carneros Estate Winery; TransMotive Technologies; Veriflo Corporation; Wyse Technology, Inc.

For full biographical listings, see the Martindale-Hubbell Law Directory

---

MOLLIGAN, COX & MOYER, A PROFESSIONAL CORPORATION (AV)

703 Market Street, Suite 1800, 94103
Telephone: 415-543-9464
Fax: 415-777-1828
Email: mocoxmoy@aol.com

Ingemar E. Hoberg (1903-1971)   Peter N. Molligan
John H. Finger (1913-1991)   Stephen T. Cox
Phillip E. Brown (Retired)   David W. Moyer

John C. Hentschel

OF COUNSEL

Kenneth W. Rosenthal   Barbara A. Zuras

For full biographical listings, see the Martindale-Hubbell Law Directory

---

MORGENSTEIN & JUBELIRER, LLP (AV)

A Partnership including a Professional Corporation
One Market Plaza, Spear Street Tower, 32nd Floor, 94105
Telephone: 415-896-0666
Fax: 415-896-5592
Email: jubelirer@aol.com

MEMBERS OF FIRM

Marvin D. Morgenstein (P.C.)   Rocky N. Unruh
Eliot S. Jubelirer   James L. McGinnis
Lee Ann Huntington   Charles W. LaGrave
Jean L. Bertrand   Wendi J. Berkowitz
Jeffrey R. Williams   John S. Worden
James R. Balich   Robert B. Mullen

OF COUNSEL

Laurie K. Anger

Lewis D. Barr   Natasha L. Golding
David H. Bromfield   Stephen M. Hankins
Michael "Cael" S. Davis   Simon E. Kisch
Roberta Nicol Dempster   John J. Petry
Bruce A. Wagman

For full biographical listings, see the Martindale-Hubbell Law Directory

---

MURPHY, PEARSON, BRADLEY & FEENEY, A PROFESSIONAL CORPORATION (AV)

88 Kearny Street, 11th Floor, 94108
Telephone: 415-788-1900
Telecopier: 415-393-8087
Sacramento, California Office: Suite 200, 3600 American River Drive, 95864.
Telephone: 916-483-6074.
Telecopier: 916-483-6088.

James A. Murphy   Michael P. Bradley

For Complete List of Firm Personnel, See General Section

For full biographical listings, see the Martindale-Hubbell Law Directory

---

O'CONNOR, COHN, DILLON & BARR, A LAW CORPORATION (AV)

The Folger Coffee Building, 101 Howard Street, Fifth Floor, 94105-1619
Telephone: 415-281-8888
Fax: 415-281-8890
Email: ocdb@slip.net

Joseph T. O'Connor   Janet L. Grove
  (Deceased, 1959)   Mark Oium
Harold H. Cohn (1910-1992)   Lisa T. Ungerer
James L. Dillon   Joel C. Lamp
Duncan Barr   Michael J. FitzSimons
Dexter B. Louie

(See Next Column)

Thomas G. Manning   Karen K. Smith
Susan Reifel Goins   Daniel J. Herp
Deborah L. Panter   James A. Beltzer
Marirose Piciucco   (Not admitted in CA)
Keith Reyen   M. Elizabeth Bootle

For full biographical listings, see the Martindale-Hubbell Law Directory

---

HERMAN D. PAPA (AV)

Suite 333, 22 Battery Street, 94111
Telephone: 415-391-4903
Fax: 415-392-3729

For full biographical listings, see the Martindale-Hubbell Law Directory

---

J. MICHAEL PHELPS (AV)

One Maritime Plaza, Suite 1600, 94111
Telephone: 415-433-3733
Voicemail: 415-433-3739
Fax: 415-781-1034
Email: jmphelps@ix.netcom.com

Representative Clients: Heinz, U.S.A.; Continental Insurance Cos.; Farmers Insurance Group; Travelers Insurance Co.

For full biographical listings, see the Martindale-Hubbell Law Directory

---

PREUSS WALKER & SHANAGHER LLP (AV)

595 Market Street, 16th Floor, 94105
Telephone: 415-978-2600
Facsimile: 415-978-2613
Email: pws@pwsllp.com

MEMBERS OF FIRM

Charles F. Preuss   Donald F. Zimmer, Jr.
Gary T. Walker   Sheila Doyle Kelley
Denis F. Shanagher   Thomas W. Pulliam, Jr.
Vernon I. Zvoleff   Alan J. Lazarus
         Michael J. Stortz

John J. Powers   Constance D. Burton
Cynthia C. Roenisch   Paul S. Lecky
Kenneth P. Conour   Catherine M. Leon
Paula R. Lee   Elizabeth L. W. Ewert
         Mel M. Negussie

Representative Clients: Envision Claims Management Corp.; Federal Deposit Insurance Corp. (FDIC); Honda North America, Inc.; Johnson & Johnson; Merck & Co., Inc.; Minnesota Mining & Manufacturing Co. (3M); Nissan Motor Corporation of USA; Resolution Trust Corporation (RTC); Plough Incorporated; Toyota Motor Sales, USA.

For full biographical listings, see the Martindale-Hubbell Law Directory

---

REMCHO, JOHANSEN AND PURCELL (AV)

Suite 800, 220 Montgomery Street, 94104
Telephone: 415-398-6230
Fax: 415-398-7256
Email: Info@RJP.com
Sacramento, California Office: Suite 625, 555 Capitol Mall.
Telephone: 916-264-1818.
Fax: 916-264-1824.

MEMBERS OF FIRM

Joseph Remcho   Robin B. Johansen
         Kathleen J. Purcell

Janet Sommer   Deborah L. Breiner

LEGAL SUPPORT PERSONNEL

Douglas Denton (Paralegal)   Ruth Fridhandler
         (Legal Administrator)

For full biographical listings, see the Martindale-Hubbell Law Directory

---

SCOTT D. RIGHTHAND (AV)

755 Sansome Street, Suite 350, 94111
Telephone: 415-544-0115
Fax: 415-399-1552

For full biographical listings, see the Martindale-Hubbell Law Directory

---

ROGERS, JOSEPH, O'DONNELL & QUINN, A PROFESSIONAL CORPORATION (AV)

311 California Street, 94104
Telephone: 415-956-2828
Fax: 415-956-6457

(See Next Column)

ROGERS, JOSEPH, O'DONNELL & QUINN A PROFESSIONAL CORPORATION, San Francisco—Continued

Allan J. Joseph	Anna M. Rossi
Martin Quinn	Connie M. Teevan
Neil H. O'Donnell	Allen Samelson
Margot Wenger	Suzanne M. Mellard
Pamela Phillips	Neil H. Weinstein
Renée D. Wasserman	Patricia A. Meagher

Merri A. Baldwin

OF COUNSEL

Joseph W. Rogers	William Bennett Turner

Kyra A. Subbotin

David F. Innis	Ian K. Sweedler
Jennifer M. Kawamura	Matthew D. Levett
Sean M. SeLegue	E. Sean McLoughlin

Aaron P. Silberman

SPECIAL COUNSEL

Valerie Ackerman

For full biographical listings, see the Martindale-Hubbell Law Directory

---

ROSEN, BIEN & ASARO (AV)

Eighth Floor, 155 Montgomery Street, 94104
Telephone: 415-433-6830
Fax: 415-433-7104
Email: rba@rbalaw.com

Sanford Jay Rosen	Michael W. Bien

Andrea G. Asaro

Thomas Nolan	William H.D. Fernholz
Donna Petrine	Doris Y. Ng
M.J. Tony Paikeday	A. Marie Villafaña

For full biographical listings, see the Martindale-Hubbell Law Directory

---

SCADDEN, HAMILTON & RYAN (AV)

580 California Street, Suite 1400, 94104
Telephone: 415-362-5116
Facsimile: 415-362-4214

James G. Scadden	Robert J. Ryan
Robert P. Hamilton	James P. Cunningham

James F. Hetherington	Eileen Santana Wright
Charles O. Thompson	Vincent C. Milani

LEGAL SUPPORT PERSONNEL

Laurie C. Meyer

For full biographical listings, see the Martindale-Hubbell Law Directory

---

STEEFEL, LEVITT & WEISS, A PROFESSIONAL CORPORATION (AV)

30th Floor, One Embarcadero Center, 94111
Telephone: 415-788-0900
Fax: 415-788-2019
Email: slw@steefel.com

Lenard G. Weiss	Michael D. Early
Richard A. Kramer	Marc A. Lackner
Michael J. Lawson	Barry W. Lee
Leonard R. Stein	Daryl S. Landy

For Complete List of Firm Personnel, See General Section

For full biographical listings, see the Martindale-Hubbell Law Directory

---

LAW FIRM OF ROBERT A. SUSK (AV)

333 Bush Street, 26th Floor, 94104
Telephone: 415-982-3950
Fax: 415-982-6143

Robert A. Susk	Leslie J. Mann

ASSOCIATE

Jeffrey A. Glick

For full biographical listings, see the Martindale-Hubbell Law Directory

---

TEHIN + PARTNERS, A PROFESSIONAL CORPORATION (AV)

Bank of America Center, 555 California Street, 33rd Floor, 94104-1609
Telephone: 415-951-8800
Fax: 415-951-8808

Nikolai Tehin (Professional Corporation)	Reilly Atkinson, IV
	Michael E. Brown
Pamela J. Stevens	Marcia A. Pollioni

For full biographical listings, see the Martindale-Hubbell Law Directory

---

VOGL & MEREDITH (AV)

456 Montgomery Street, 20th Floor, 94104
Telephone: 415-398-0200
Facsimile: 415-398-2820

Samuel E. Meredith	Jean N. Yeh
David R. Vogl	Janet Brayer
John P. Walovich	Thomas S. Clifton

Jill M. Thayer	Mark Ginalski

Nicole L. Meredith

For full biographical listings, see the Martindale-Hubbell Law Directory

---

SAN JOSE, * Santa Clara Co.

THE ALEXANDER LAW FIRM (AV)

55 South Market Street, Suite 1080, 95113
Telephone: 408-289-1776
Fax: 408-287-1776
Email: access@alexanderlaw.com *URL:* http://www.alexanderlaw.com/
Cincinnati, Ohio Office: The Alexander Law Firm, 1300 Mercantile Library Building, 414 Walnut Street.
Telephone: 513-723-1776.
Fax: 513-421-1776.

Richard Alexander

ASSOCIATES

Michael T. Alexander (Resident, Cincinnati, Ohio Office)	Michael McShane
	Amanda Hawes
Jonathan D. Pendleton	Ann Saponara

Tyler A. Shaw

OF COUNSEL

William M. Audet

For full biographical listings, see the Martindale-Hubbell Law Directory

---

BERGESON, ELIOPOULOS, GRADY & GRAY (AV)

Ten Almaden Boulevard, Suite 200, 95113
Telephone: 408-291-6200
Fax: 408-297-6000
Email: BEGG215958@AOL.Com

Daniel J. Bergeson	Richard J. Gray
William T. Eliopoulos	Mary Anne Rodgers
Michael F. Grady	John L. Antracoli

ASSOCIATES

Donald P. Gagliardi	Siobhán Lawlor
Mark E. Waite	John P. Shinn

For full biographical listings, see the Martindale-Hubbell Law Directory

---

THE BOCCARDO LAW FIRM (AV)

Eleventh Floor, 111 West St. John Street, 95115-0001
Telephone: 408-298-5678
Fax: 408-298-7503

MEMBERS OF FIRM

James F. Boccardo	John C. Stein
John W. McDonald	Richard L. Bowers
Brian N. Lawther	Russell L. Moore, Jr.

ASSOCIATES

Stephen Foster	Victor F. Stefan
David P. Moyles	Robert W. Thayer
Byron C. Foster	Richard Gregg

For full biographical listings, see the Martindale-Hubbell Law Directory

---

CRAIG M. BROWN, INC. (AV)

333 West Santa Clara Street, Suite 618, 95113
Telephone: 408-286-8844
Fax: 408-286-6699
Email: cmbtrialaw@aol.com

Craig M. Brown

For full biographical listings, see the Martindale-Hubbell Law Directory

---

CAMPBELL, WARBURTON, FITZSIMMONS, SMITH, MENDELL & PASTORE, A PROFESSIONAL CORPORATION (AV)

111 West St. John Street, Suite 440, P.O. Box 1867, 95113
Telephone: 408-295-7701
Fax: 408-295-1423

John R. Fitzsimmons, Jr.	Ralph E. Mendell
C. Michael Smith	Nicholas Pastore

J. Michael Fitzsimmons

William R. Colucci	Carolyn M. Rose

Representative Corporate Clients: Helene Curtis, Inc.; Viking Freight System, Inc.

(See Next Column)

CAMPBELL, WARBURTON, FITZSIMMONS, SMITH, MENDELL & PASTORE A
PROFESSIONAL CORPORATION—*Continued*

Representative Insurance Clients: California State Automobile Assn.; Farmers
Insurance Group; Travelers Insurance Co.; Westfield Insurance Cos.; Michelin Tire Corp. (Self Insured).

For Complete List of Firm Personnel, See General Section

For full biographical listings, see the Martindale-Hubbell Law Directory

CAMPEAU & THOMAS, A LAW CORPORATION (AV)

Market Post Tower, 55 South Market Street, Suite 1660, 95113
Telephone: 408-295-9555
Fax: 408-295-6606

Kenneth J. Campeau	Wayne H. Thomas
	Scott L. Goodsell

Marcie E. Schaap	Kathryn J. Diemer

For full biographical listings, see the Martindale-Hubbell Law Directory

JAN CHAMPION (AV)

Ten Almaden Boulevard, Tenth Floor, 95113-2233
Telephone: 408-286-5550
Fax: 408-270-6777

For full biographical listings, see the Martindale-Hubbell Law Directory

HAWKINS, BLICK & FITZPATRICK (AV)

96 North Third Street, Suite 300, 95112
Telephone: 408-280-7111
Fax: 408-292-7868
Palo Alto, California Office: 418 Florence Street.
Telephone: 415-321-5656.
Fax: 415-326-9636.

MEMBERS OF FIRM

Charles F. Hawkins	Stephen L. Blick
	Michael J. Fitzpatrick

ASSOCIATE
Mark F. Bernal

For full biographical listings, see the Martindale-Hubbell Law Directory

HINSHAW, WINKLER, DRAA, MARSH & STILL (AV)

152 North Third Street, Suite 300, P.O. Box 15030, 95115-0030
Telephone: 408-293-5959
Fax: 408-280-0966
Email: hinshaw-law.com

MEMBERS OF FIRM

Edward A. Hinshaw	Gerhard O. Winkler
Tyler G. Draa	Barry C. Marsh
	Thomas E. Still

ASSOCIATES

Lynne Thaxter Brown	Jennifer H. Still
Bradford J. Hinshaw	Megan A. Smith

For full biographical listings, see the Martindale-Hubbell Law Directory

LAW OFFICES OF THOMAS R. HOGAN (AV)

60 South Market Street, Suite 1125, 95113-2332
Telephone: 408-292-7600
Facsimile: 408-292-7611

ASSOCIATE
Kelly W. Bhirdo
PARALEGAL
Leslie Holmes

For full biographical listings, see the Martindale-Hubbell Law Directory

DAVID MALNICK A PROFESSIONAL CORPORATION (AV)

10 Almaden Boulevard Tenth Floor, 95113-2233
Telephone: 408-292-5900
Fax: 408-292-5995

David E. Malnick

For full biographical listings, see the Martindale-Hubbell Law Directory

McMANIS, FAULKNER & MORGAN (AV)

160 West Santa Clara Street, 10th Floor, 95113
Telephone: 408-279-8700
Fax: 408-279-3244; 408-279-0494
Email: mfm@mfmlaw.com
MEMBERS OF FIRM

James McManis	William Faulkner
	Donelle Morgan

(See Next Column)

ASSOCIATES

Nora Rousso	Michael Reedy
Lisa Herrick	Douglas Watanabe
	Kelly McHaffie

For full biographical listings, see the Martindale-Hubbell Law Directory

MILLER, MORTON, CAILLAT & NEVIS (AV)

50 West San Fernando Street, Suite 1300, 95113-2413
Telephone: 408-292-1765
Telecopier: 408-292-4484

Richard W. Morton (1916-1975)   Charles V. Caillat (1920-1990)
Harvey C. Miller (1906-1993)
MEMBERS OF FIRM

David L. Nevis	Joseph A. Scanlan, Jr.
Francis J. Hughes	Carolyn Tobiason Stuart
Peter A. Kline	William K. Hurley
Stevan C. Adelman	Peter V. Dessau
	Eric Mogensen

OF COUNSEL

Nancy F. Symons	Susan L. Sutton
	Pamela J. Silberstein

ASSOCIATES

Kathryn E. Earrett	David I. Kornbluh
Katherine S. Pak	Kimberly Holtz MacMillan

Representative Clients: Trammell Crow Residential Services; Joe Kerley Lincoln Mercury Co.; Milligan News Co.; Joseph George Distributors; The Frozen Food Employees Pension Trust; Santa Clara Dental Society; New West Foods; Bay Apartment Communities; Guy F. Atkinson Company; A. Hathaway Co.

For full biographical listings, see the Martindale-Hubbell Law Directory

ROBINSON & WOOD, INC. (AV)

227 North First Street, 95113
Telephone: 408-298-7120
Fax: 408-298-0477
Email: rw@r-winc.com

Archie S. Robinson	Jonathan L. Lee
Weldon S. Wood	Jon B. Zimmerman
Thomas R. Fellows	Mark B. Schellerup
David S. Henningsen	Andrew W. Olsson
Hugh F. Lennon	Erica R. Yew
Jesse F. Ruiz	Arthur J. Casey
Christian B. Nielsen	Joseph C. Balestrieri

John L. Winchester, III	Wendy Woolpert
Chadney C. Ankele	Ann A. Nguyen
Robert A. Nakamae	Kenneth I. Schumaker
Rebecca L. Moon	Anne C. Bailey
Wendy E. Flockhart	Stephen D. Bays

For full biographical listings, see the Martindale-Hubbell Law Directory

RUBY & SCHOFIELD (AV)

A Partnership of Law Corporations
60 South Market Street, Suite 1500, 95113-2379
Telephone: 408-998-8500
Fax: 408-998-8503

Allen Ruby (L.C.)	Glen W. Schofield (L.C.)

For full biographical listings, see the Martindale-Hubbell Law Directory

SAUCEDO & CORSIGLIA, A LAW CORPORATION (AV)

50 West San Fernando Street, Suite 425, 95113
Telephone: 408-289-1417
Fax: 408-289-8127

Norman W. Saucedo	Bradley M. Corsiglia

For full biographical listings, see the Martindale-Hubbell Law Directory

SHEA & SHEA, A PROFESSIONAL LAW CORPORATION (AV)

The James Square Building, 255 North Market Street, Suite 190, 95110
Telephone: 408-292-2434
Fax: 408-292-1264

Michael M. Shea	Michael M. Shea, Jr.

Beth C. Watkins

For full biographical listings, see the Martindale-Hubbell Law Directory

TREPEL & CLARK (AV)

50 West San Fernando Street, 13th Floor, 95113
Telephone: 408-275-0501
Fax: 408-293-3369

(See Next Column)

TREPEL & CLARK, *San Jose—Continued*

Anthony J. Trepel　　　　　　Daniel Clark

ASSOCIATE

Sandra R. McIntosh

For full biographical listings, see the Martindale-Hubbell Law Directory

TYNDALL & CAHNERS (AV)

An Association of Attorneys including a Professional Corporation
96 North Third Street, Suite 580, 95112
Telephone: 408-297-3700
Fax: 408-297-3721

John G. Tyndall III (P.C.)　　　　John D. Cahners

Michael Francis Brown

For full biographical listings, see the Martindale-Hubbell Law Directory

VAN LOUCKS & HANLEY (AV)

160 West Santa Clara Street, Suite 1050, 95113
Telephone: 408-494-0400
Fax: 408-494-0404

Geoffrey Van Loucks　　　　　Anthony L. Hanley

Michael K. Budra

Reference: San Jose National Bank.

For full biographical listings, see the Martindale-Hubbell Law Directory

SAN MARINO, Los Angeles Co.

LAW OFFICES OF LILLIAN TOMICH (AV)

2460 Huntington Drive, 91108-2657
Telephone: 818-287-1248
Fax: 818-287-7111

References: Home Savings & Loan, San Marino, California; Bank of America, San Marino, California; First Interstate Bank, San Gabriel, California.

SAN MATEO, San Mateo Co.

McDOWALL, COTTER, DUNN, VALE & BRACCO, A PROFESSIONAL CORPORATION (AV)

2070 Pioneer Court, P.O. Box 937, 94403
Telephone: 415-572-7933
Fax: 415-572-0834
Palo Alto, California Office: 425 Sherman Avenue, Suite 100.
Telephone: 408-244-8755; *Other Areas:* 415-326-8410.
Fax: 415-326-3911.

William D. McDowall　　　　Robert D. Vale
Bernard T. Cotter　　　　　　Michael A. Bracco
Thomas G. Dunn　　　　　　David S Rosenbaum
　　　　　　Richard M. Kelly

Representative Clients: State Farm Mutual Automobile Insurance Co.; State Farm Fire & Casualty Co.; California State Automobile Assn.; Insurance Company of the West; Allegiance Insurance Co.; Argonaut Insurance Cos.

For full biographical listings, see the Martindale-Hubbell Law Directory

DAVID JAY MORGAN A PROFESSIONAL CORPORATION (AV)

1900 O'Farrell Street, Suite 190, 94403
Telephone: 415-286-1212
Fax: 415-286-1216

David Jay Morgan

David R. Lira　　　　　　Dominic J. Baldini

For full biographical listings, see the Martindale-Hubbell Law Directory

STUBBS & STUBBS (AV)

Borel Estate Building, Suite 505, 1700 South El Camino Real, 94402-3051
Telephone: 415-345-4350
Telecopier: 415-345-6748
Email: stubbs__stubbs@msn.com

MEMBERS OF FIRM

Barry Stubbs　　　　　　Brian P. Stubbs

Reference: Wells Fargo Bank.

For full biographical listings, see the Martindale-Hubbell Law Directory

SAN RAFAEL,* Marin Co.

RAGGHIANTI • FREITAS • MONTOBBIO • WALLACE LLP (AV)

874 Fourth Street, Suite D, 94901
Telephone: 415-453-9433
Fax: 415-453-8269

(See Next Column)

Gary T. Ragghianti　　　　J. Randolph Wallace
David P. Freitas　　　　　　Patrick M. Macias
J. Mark Montobbio　　　　Robert F. Epstein
　　　　　John Ralph Thomas

For full biographical listings, see the Martindale-Hubbell Law Directory

SANTA ANA,* Orange Co.

THOMAS A. CULBERTSON (AV)

1851 East First Street, Suite 1100, 92705-4017
Telephone: 714-541-4454; 310-379-7298
Fax: 714-558-0967: 310-379-7298

For full biographical listings, see the Martindale-Hubbell Law Directory

HAIGHT, BROWN & BONESTEEL (AV)

A Partnership including Professional Corporations
Suite 900, 5 Hutton Centre Drive, 92707
Telephone: 714-754-1100
Telecopier: 714-754-0826
Santa Monica, California Office: 1620 26th Street, Suite 4000 North, P.O. Box 680.
Telephone: 310-449-6000.
Telecopier: 310-829-5117.
Telex: 705837.
Riverside, California Office: 3750 University Avenue, Suite 650.
Telephone: 909-341-8300.
Fax: 909-341-8309.
San Francisco, California Office: 20 Sansome Street, Suite 300.
Telephone: 415-986-7700.
Fax: 415-986-6954.

RESIDENT MEMBERS

Bruce L. Cleeland　　　　　Jay T. Thompson

ASSOCIATES

Laura M. Knox (Resident)　　Jeffrey S. Gerardo (Resident)

Counsel for: Orange County: Aetna Casualty and Surety Co.; Zurich-American Insurance Cos.; Industrial Indemnity Co.; Professional Liability Claims Managers; Maryland Casualty Insurance Co.; Royal Insurance Company of America.

For Complete List of Firm Personnel, See General Section

For full biographical listings, see the Martindale-Hubbell Law Directory

MARTIN, WILSON, ERICKSON & MacDOWELL, A PROFESSIONAL CORPORATION (AV)

6 Hutton Centre, Suite 500, 92707
Telephone: 714-972-1200
Facsimile: 714-972-1283

Scott A. Martin　　　　　　Mary Fingal Erickson
Thomas L. Wilson　　　　　John R. MacDowell

Douglas M. Carasso　　　　Wendy A. Weber
　　　　　Kevin F. Cahill

For full biographical listings, see the Martindale-Hubbell Law Directory

SPERLING & PERGANDE (AV)

3 Hutton Centre, Suite 670, 92707
Telephone: 714-540-8500
Facsimile: 714-540-2599

MEMBERS OF FIRM

Dean P. Sperling　　　　　K. William Pergande

For full biographical listings, see the Martindale-Hubbell Law Directory

SANTA BARBARA,* Santa Barbara Co.

ARCHBALD & SPRAY (AV)

505 Bath Street, 93101
Telephone: 805-564-2070
Telecopier: 805-564-2081
Email: arch@silcom.com

MEMBERS OF FIRM

Malcolm Archbald (Retired)　　Karen T. Burgett
Joseph L. Spray (1927-1985)　　Edwin K. Loskamp
Kenneth L. Moes　　　　　　Wm. Brennan Lynch
J. William McLafferty　　　　Michael A. Colton
Douglas B. Large　　　　　　Ann Gormican Anderson

SENIOR ATTORNEYS

Peri Maziarz　　　　　　Katherine H. Bower

ASSOCIATE

Cheryl A. Shaw

(See Next Column)

ARCHBALD & SPRAY—*Continued*

OF COUNSEL

John W. Warnock

Representative Clients: Browning-Ferris Industries, Inc.; Design Professional Insurance Companies; EnviroSource, Inc.; Ingersoll-Rand; Laidlaw Transportation; Lawyers' Mutual Insurance Company; National Chiropractic Mutual Insurance Company; Nestlé, USA, Inc.; State Farm Insurance; Superior National Insurance.

For full biographical listings, see the Martindale-Hubbell Law Directory

---

HOLLISTER & BRACE, A PROFESSIONAL CORPORATION (AV)

1126 Santa Barbara Street, P.O. Box 630, 93101
Telephone: 805-963-6711
Fax: 805-965-0329

William A. Brace (Retired)	Bradford F. Ginder
J. James Hollister, III (Retired)	John G. Busby
John S. Poucher	Susan H. McCollum
Richard C. Monk	Richard G. Kravetz
George A. Rempe, III	Robert L. Brace
Steven Evans Kirby	Marcus Scott Bird
David Frank Hubbard	

OF COUNSEL

Julie A. Turner

Attorneys for: First American Title Insurance Co.; Celite Corp.; Chevron, U.S.A., Inc.; Mission Industries; Gaviota Marine Terminal Co.; Hyatt Hotels; Occidental Petroleum Corp.; Great Universal Capital Corp; Mobil Oil Corp.; Texaco Inc.

For full biographical listings, see the Martindale-Hubbell Law Directory

---

KINKLE, RODIGER AND SPRIGGS, PROFESSIONAL CORPORATION (AV)

125 East De La Guerra Street, 93101-2239
Telephone: 805-966-4700
Fax: 805-966-4120
Los Angeles, California Office: 600 North Grand Avenue.
Telephone: 213-629-1261.
Fax: 213-629-8382.
Santa Ana, California Office: 837 North Ross Street.
Telephone: 714-835-9011.
Fax: 714-667-7806.
Riverside, California Office: 3333 14th Street.
Telephone: 909-683-2410; 800-235-2039.
Fax: 909-683-7759.
San Diego, California Office: Suite 900 Driver Insurance Center, 1620 Fifth Avenue, P.O. Box 127900.
Telephone: 619-233-4566.
Fax: 619-233-8554.

John V. Hager	Joy L. Lim
(Managing Attorney)	Jeffery D. Lim
Edwin C. Mann	Chad M. Slack
Donna D. Geck	

For full biographical listings, see the Martindale-Hubbell Law Directory

---

MULLEN & HENZELL, L.L.P. (AV)

A California registered limited liability partnership
112 East Victoria Street, Post Office Drawer 789, 93102-0789
Telephone: 805-966-1501
FAX: 805-966-9204

MEMBERS OF FIRM

Thomas M. Mullen (1915-1991)	Robert A. Zeavin
Arthur A. Henzell (Retired)	Joseph F. Green
J. Robert Andrews	Gary W. Robinson
James W. Brown	Lawrence T. Sorensen
Dennis W. Reilly	Gregory F. Faulkner
Jeffrey C. Nelson	Richard G. Battles
Charles S. Bargiel	Edward C. Thoits
Jay L. Beckerman	William E. Degen
Michael E. Cage	

OF COUNSEL

Kim A. Harley Seefeld

ASSOCIATES

Andrew M. Polinsky	Paul K. Wilcox
Catherine Perlman	Thomas Y. Chen
Richard E. Fogg	

Representative Clients: Goleta Sanitary District; Interinsurance Exchange of the Automobile Club of Southern California; State Farm Fire & Casualty Co.; State Farm Mutual Automobile Insurance Co.

For full biographical listings, see the Martindale-Hubbell Law Directory

---

SANTA MONICA, Los Angeles Co.

BIENSTOCK & CLARK (AV)

A Partnership of Professional Corporations
3340 Ocean Park Boulevard, Suite 3075, 90405
Telephone: 310-314-8660
Telecopier: 310-314-8662
Miami, Florida Office: First Union Financial Center. 200 South Biscayne Boulevard, Suite 3160.
Telephone: 305-373-1100.
Telecopier: 305-358-1226.

Terry S. Bienstock (P.A.)	Roger W. Clark
(Not admitted in CA)	

Robert D. Goldberg	Christopher L. Mass

For full biographical listings, see the Martindale-Hubbell Law Directory

---

FOGEL, FELDMAN, OSTROV, RINGLER & KLEVENS, A LAW CORPORATION (AV)

1620 26th Street, Suite 100 South, 90404-4040
Telephone: 310-453-6711
Fax: 310-828-2191

Daniel Fogel (1923-1991)	Joel N. Klevens
Lester G. Ostrov	Robert M. Turner
Larry R. Feldman	Jerome L. Ringler
Richard L. Rosett	

Stephen D. Rothschild	Toni Martinson
Leighanne Lake	David Bricker
Thomas H. Peters	Mark S. Eisenberg

OF COUNSEL

Carol S. May

Reference: Republic Bank of California, Beverly Hills, California.

For full biographical listings, see the Martindale-Hubbell Law Directory

---

LAW OFFICES OF GARY FREEDMAN (AV)

725 Arizona Avenue, Suite 100, 90401
Telephone: 310-576-2444
Telecopier: 310-576-2440

MEMBER OF FIRM

Gary A. Freedman

Emily Bresler

OF COUNSEL

Paul H. Samuels

For full biographical listings, see the Martindale-Hubbell Law Directory

---

HAIGHT, BROWN & BONESTEEL (AV)

A Partnership including Professional Corporations
1620 26th Street, Suite 4000 North, P.O. Box 680, 90404
Telephone: 310-449-6000
Telecopier: 310-829-5117
Telex: 705837
Santa Ana, California Office: Suite 900, 5 Hutton Centre Drive.
Telephone: 714-754-1100.
Telecopier: 714-754-0826.
Riverside, California Office: 3750 University Avenue, Suite 650.
Telephone: 909-341-8300.
Fax: 909-341-8309.
San Francisco, California Office: 201 Sansome Street, Suite 300.
Telephone: 415-986-7700.
Fax: 415-986-6954.

MEMBERS OF FIRM

Fulton Haight (A Professional Corporation) (Retired)	Bruce A. Armstrong (A Professional Corporation)
Harold Hansen Brown (A Professional Corporation)	Morton Rosen
	Peter A. Dubrawski
Michael J. Bonesteel (A Professional Corporation)	Michael J. Leahy
Gary C. Ottoson (A Professional Corporation)	Lori R. Behar
	Robert L. Kaufman
Roy G. Weatherup	William J. Sayers
Peter Q. Ezzell (A Professional Corporation)	Michael McCarthy
	Barry Z. Brodsky
Dennis K. Wheeler (A Professional Corporation)	Gary A. Bague
	J. R. Seashore
Steven L. Hoch (A Professional Corporation)	Kevin R. Crisp
	Lee Marshall
John W. Sheller (A Professional Corporation)	George Christensen
	Steven E. Moyer
William G. Baumgaertner (A Professional Corporation)	Denis J. Moriarty
	Desmond J. Hinds, Jr.
	Jules Solomon Zeman

(See Next Column)

HAIGHT, BROWN & BONESTEEL, *Santa Monica—Continued*

MEMBERS OF FIRM (Continued)

Thomas N. Charchut	Jennifer K. Saunders
Neil G. McNiece	Timothy B. Bradford
Thomas M. Moore	Amor A. Esteban
Rita (Sucharita) Gunasekaran	William E. Ireland
Kenneth G. Anderson	Valerie A. Moore
Victor Anderson III	David C. McGovern
William O. Martin, Jr.	Jeffrey B. Margulies
Theresa M. Marchlewski	Tamara Equals Holmes

ASSOCIATES

Kelly C. McSpadden	Holly M. Teel
Cynthia A. Robins	S. Christian Stouder
Marsha L. Kempson	Michael J. Sipos
Jon M. Kasimov	Cary D. Glassner
Alicia E. Taylor	Caroline E. Chan
Dorothy B. Ceccon	Caroline Craddock Raggio
Margaret Johnson Wiley	Michael H. Gottschlich
Jodi L. Girten	Caroline Kelley Hunt

Farah Sohaili Nicol

OF COUNSEL

William M. Fitzhugh	R. Roy Finkle
Ira E. Bilson	Donald S. Ralphs
Richard F. Runkle	Kathryn M. Forgie

For Complete List of Firm Personnel, See General Section

For full biographical listings, see the Martindale-Hubbell Law Directory

RICHARD E. HODGE, INC. (AV)

The Water Garden East Tower, Suite 600, 2425 West Olympic
  Boulevard, 90404-4043
Telephone: 310-453-5344
Fax: 310-315-0051

Richard E. Hodge	Gary G. Kuist

Jefferson W. Gross

For full biographical listings, see the Martindale-Hubbell Law Directory

O'NEILL, LYSAGHT & SUN (AV)

100 Wilshire Boulevard, Suite 700, 90401
Telephone: 310-451-5700
Telecopier: 310-399-7201

Brian O'Neill	Yolanda Orozco
Brian C. Lysaght	John M. Moscarino
Frederick D. Friedman	Harriet Beegun Leva
Brian A. Sun	Edward A. Klein

Robert L. Meylan

David E. Rosen	Paul D. Murphy
Ellyn S. Garofalo	Brian D. Hershman

OF COUNSEL

J. Joseph Connolly

Reference: Wells Fargo Bank, Santa Monica.

For full biographical listings, see the Martindale-Hubbell Law Directory

PAUL & JANOFSKY (AV)

1401 Ocean Avenue, Suite 200, 90401-1701
Telephone: 310-458-4584
Facsimile: 310-458-6823

MEMBERS OF FIRM

Gary M. Paul	John S. Janofsky

William A. Daniels

ASSOCIATE

Michael B. Gurien

OF COUNSEL

Michael L. Goldberg

For full biographical listings, see the Martindale-Hubbell Law Directory

SACKS ZWEIG & BURRIS, LLP (AV)

100 Wilshire Building, Suite 1300, 100 Wilshire Boulevard, 90401
Telephone: 310-451-3113
Facsimile: 310-451-0089
San Francisco, California Office: 100 Pine Street, 21st Floor.
Telephone: 415-788-6794.
Facsimile: 415-788-7009.

MEMBERS

Donald S. Burris	Lee Sacks

Michael K. Zweig

ASSOCIATES

Les Bradford Hairrell	Filomena E. Meyer

(See Next Column)

OF COUNSEL

Dennis Holahan	Barton S. Selden

For full biographical listings, see the Martindale-Hubbell Law Directory

STEINBERG, NUTTER & BRENT, LAW CORPORATION (AV)

501 Colorado Avenue, Suite 300, 90401
Telephone: 310-451-9714
Telecopier: 310-451-0929
Woodland Hills, California Office: 21031 Ventura Boulevard, Suite 419.
Telephone: 818-703-6204.

Peter T. Steinberg	Guy B. Nutter

Paul M. Brent

James M. Buck

Reference: Santa Monica Bank.

For full biographical listings, see the Martindale-Hubbell Law Directory

STERN, NEUBAUER, GREENWALD & PAULY, A PROFESSIONAL CORPORATION (AV)

1299 Ocean Avenue, Tenth Floor, 90401-1007
Telephone: 310-451-8001
Telecopier: 310-395-5961

David M. Stern	Joshua D. Wayser
Mark A. Neubauer	Richard L. Miller
Dennis L. Greenwald	M. Tracy McGeagh
Andrew S. Pauly	Kirsten Shirley Ellis
Russell F. Wolpert	Owen Scott Solomon
Randall S. Rothschild	Wendy Angela Loo
Richard M. Foster	Nena W. Wong
David C. Smith	Michael F. Donner

Christine Millee Henricks

LEGAL SUPPORT PERSONNEL

Carol Leemom

For full biographical listings, see the Martindale-Hubbell Law Directory

---

SANTA ROSA, * Sonoma Co.

BELDEN, ABBEY, WEITZENBERG & KELLY, A PROFESSIONAL CORPORATION (AV)

1105 North Dutton Avenue, P.O. Box 1566, 95402
Telephone: 707-542-5050
Telecopier: 707-542-2589

Thomas P. Kelly, Jr.	Candace H. Shirley
W. Barton Weitzenberg	Wayne R. Wolski

Lewis R. Warren

Representative Clients: Exchange Bank of Santa Rosa; Westamerica Bank; North Bay Title Co.; Northwestern Title Security Co.; Geyser Peak Winery; Santa Rosa City School District; Sonoma National Bank; Arrowood Vineyards & Winery; Arthur & DeVincenzi Concrete; Friedman Bros. Hardware, Inc.

For Complete List of Firm Personnel, See General Section

For full biographical listings, see the Martindale-Hubbell Law Directory

MILLER, MAILLIARD & CULVER, LLP (AV)

A Partnership including Professional Corporations
100 B Street, Suite 200, P.O. Box 5257, 95402
Telephone: 707-571-8112
Fax: 707-575-9116
Email: milmaicul@aol.com
San Francisco, California Office: 155 Montgomery Street, Suite 1212.
Telephone: 415-391-4291.
Fax: 415-391-4292. Email: mmc@sirius.com.

Christopher R. Miller (P.C.)	Kevin F. Barrett
William S. Mailliard, Jr.	William D. Evers
David C. Culver	Jay P. Hendrickson
R. W. Achor (P.C.) (Retired)	Paul E. Manasian
Phyllis E. Andelin	Philip J. Nicholsen, P.C.

Chigusa Saotome

OF COUNSEL

Stephen T. Kong

Representative Clients: BioZone Laboratories; California Dept. of Insurance; Dover Elevator Co.; Pacific Coast Apparel; Red Rose Collections; Sanwa Bank; Schug Carneros Estate Winery; TransMotive Technologies; Veriflo Corporation; Wyse Technology, Inc.

For full biographical listings, see the Martindale-Hubbell Law Directory

SHERMAN OAKS, Los Angeles Co.

NARVID, GLICKMAN, SCOTT & FRANGIE, A PROFESSIONAL CORPORATION (AV)

15060 Ventura Boulevard, Suite 490, 91403
Telephone: 818-907-8986
Fax: 818-907-9896

Michael J. Narvid	Michael B. Scott
Roy S. Glickman	J. M. Frangie

Leslie J. Garber	Linda B. Takahashi
Valerie Mattson	Linda Thornton

Reference: Union Bank - Encino Branch.

For full biographical listings, see the Martindale-Hubbell Law Directory

*STOCKTON,** San Joaquin Co.

DIEHL, STEINHEIMER, RIGGIO, HAYDEL & MORDAUNT, A PROFESSIONAL LAW CORPORATION (AV)

400 East Main Street, Suite 600, 95290-0600
Telephone: 209-464-8732
Fax: 209-464-9165
Email: 104714.654@compuserve.com
Sonora, California Office: 38 North Washington Street, Suite A.
Telephone: 209-532-1424.
Fax: 209-532-4233.
Affiliated Office: Law Offices of M. Max Steinheimer and P. Gary Cassel, 301 Flint Street, Reno, Nevada 89505-3295.
Telephone: 702-322-2240.

M. Max Steinheimer	Joseph H. Fagundes
Donald M. Riggio	William D. Johnson
Douglas A. Haydel	Frank J. Enright
Michael R. Mordaunt	Kate Powell Segerstrom
Peter J. Kelly	(Resident, Sonora Office)
P. Gary Cassel	Kevin M. Seibert
Scott Malm	Scott A. Ginns
Mark F. Ornellas	Tamara M. Polley

Elizabeth R. Bogart	Corinne K. Reynolds
Darin T. Judd	Edward P. Murphy
Frank R. Perrott	Bruce J. Boehm
Rachelle C. Sanchez	Maria E. Gutierrez

OF COUNSEL
Joseph W. Diehl

Counsel for: Pacific Gas and Electric Co.; Kleinfelder Inc.; Turlock Irrigation District.
Insurance Clients: Allied Insurance Group; Design Professional Insurance Co.; The Doctors Co.; Kemper Insurance Co.; Norcal Mutual Insurance Co.; The Travelers.

For full biographical listings, see the Martindale-Hubbell Law Directory

TARZANA, Los Angeles Co.

WASSERMAN, COMDEN & CASSELMAN L.L.P. (AV)

5567 Reseda Boulevard, Suite 330, P.O. Box 7033, 91357-7033
Telephone: 818-705-6800; 213-872-0995
Fax: 818-345-0162; 996-8266

MEMBERS OF FIRM

Steve K. Wasserman	Jay N. Rosenwald
Leonard J. Comden	Daniel E. Lewis
David B. Casselman	Crystal A. Zarpas
Clifford H. Pearson	Gary S. Soter
Rebecca J. Schroer	Catherine Stevenson Garcia
Glenn A. Brown, Jr.	

ASSOCIATES

Joel Fischman	Richard A. Brownstein
Jeffrey K. Jayson	Albert G. Turner, Jr.
Lloyd S. Mann	Kenneth M. Jones
J. Christopher Bennington	Sharon Zemel
Norman L. Pearl	L. Stephen Albright
Todd A. Chamberlain	John A. Raymond
Howard S. Blum	Michael E. Garner
Marina N. Vitek	

OF COUNSEL
Cecilia S. Wu

Representative Clients: Toplis & Harding; Appalachian Insurance; Lumbermens Mutual Insurance Co.; State Farm Fire and Casualty Co.; Factory Mutual Engineering; Cravens, Dargan & Co.; Lloyd's of London.

For full biographical listings, see the Martindale-Hubbell Law Directory

TORRANCE, Los Angeles Co.

AGNEW & BRUSAVICH (AV)

20355 Hawthorne Boulevard, 90503
Telephone: 310-793-1400
Facsimile: 310-793-1499
Email: agnewbru@ix.netcom.com

Gerald E. Agnew, Jr.	Bruce M. Brusavich

ASSOCIATES

Susan E. Hargrove	Christopher A. Kall
Mark J. Peacock	

For full biographical listings, see the Martindale-Hubbell Law Directory

FINER, KIM & STEARNS (AV)

An Association of Professional Corporations
City National Bank Building, 3424 Carson Street, Suite 500, 90503
Telephone: 310-214-1477
Telecopier: 310-214-0764

Harry J. Kim (A Professional Corporation)	Robert David Ciaccio
	Robert B. Parsons
W. A. Finer (A Professional Corporation)	

OF COUNSEL

Bennett A. Rheingold	Ryan E. Stearns

LEGAL SUPPORT PERSONNEL
Marcia E. Talbert

For Complete List of Firm Personnel, See General Section

For full biographical listings, see the Martindale-Hubbell Law Directory

UPLAND, San Bernardino Co.

ALTHOUSE & McDONOUGH (AV)

Second Floor, Metro Commerce Bank Building, 188 North Euclid Avenue, P.O. Box 698, 91785
Telephone: 909-985-9828
Telecopier: 909-985-3282

Charles S. Althouse	Elizabeth A. McDonough

References: Security Pacific National Bank, Upland Branch; First National Bank & Trust Company, Upland Branch.

For Complete List of Firm Personnel, See General Section

For full biographical listings, see the Martindale-Hubbell Law Directory

VAN NUYS, Los Angeles Co.

DAVID I. KARP (AV)

13818 Cumpston Street, 91401
Telephone: 818-781-1458
Fax: 818-781-7733
URL: http://home.aol.com/DavidIKarp
(Also Of Counsel to Krivis, Spile & Siegel, Encino)

For full biographical listings, see the Martindale-Hubbell Law Directory

*VENTURA,** Ventura Co.

BENTON, ORR, DUVAL & BUCKINGHAM, A PROFESSIONAL CORPORATION (AV)

39 North California Street, P.O. Box 1178, 93002
Telephone: 805-648-5111; 656-1166
Fax: 805-648-7218
Email: BentonOrr@usa.net

James T. Sherren	Thomas E. Olson
Ronald L. Colton	Dean W. Hazard
Robert A. Davidson	Brenda L. DeHart
Mark S. Borrell	

Counsel for: American Commercial Bank; Petoseed Co., Inc.
Trial Counsel for: Southern California Edison Co.; Shell Oil Co.; Automobile Club of Southern California; Southern California Physicians Insurance Exchange.

For full biographical listings, see the Martindale-Hubbell Law Directory

LAW OFFICES OF FREDERICK H. BYSSHE, JR. (AV)

10 South California Street, 93001
Telephone: 805-648-3224
Fax: 805-653-0267

Terence Geoghegan

For full biographical listings, see the Martindale-Hubbell Law Directory

Ventura—Continued

FAIRFIELD, STRAUSS, URITZ & KINIGSTEIN, A PROFESSIONAL CORPORATION (AV)

290 Maple Court, Suite 200, 93003
Telephone: 805-644-7458
Fax: 805-644-4325
Email: mail@venturalaw.com *URL:* http://www.venturalaw.com

William D. Fairfield	Curt W. Uritz
Anthony R. Strauss	Terry Kinigstein

Wilfred J. Freeman	Bruce P. Crary

For full biographical listings, see the Martindale-Hubbell Law Directory

FERGUSON, CASE, ORR, PATERSON & CUNNINGHAM (AV)

1050 South Kimball Road, 93004
Telephone: 805-659-6800
Telecopier: 805-659-6818
Email: info@fcopc.com

Thomas R. Ferguson	Joseph L. Strohman, Jr.
Michael W. Case	Robert L. Gallaway
John C. Orr	Sandra M. Robertson
William E. Paterson	William B. Smith
David L. Cunningham	Gisele Goetz
Lou Carpiac	Ramon L. Guizar
	Gregory W. Herring

Douglas E. Kulper
OF COUNSEL
Allen F. Camp

Representative Clients: First American Title Insurance Company; Wells Fargo Bank; The Hahn Company (Oaks Regional Shopping Center); Area Housing Authority of the County of Ventura; Buenaventura Medical Clinic, Inc.; Southern Pacific Milling Company; USA Petroleum Corporation; Cellular One.

For full biographical listings, see the Martindale-Hubbell Law Directory

JOHN H. HOWARD (AV)

3585 Maple Street, Suite 220, 93003
Telephone: 805-644-5894; 656-2300
Fax: 805-644-6482
Email: 1111SOoakland@msn.com

ASSOCIATE
James Edward Doles

For full biographical listings, see the Martindale-Hubbell Law Directory

TAYLOR MCCORD, A LAW CORPORATION (AV)

721 East Main Street, P.O. Box 1477, 93002
Telephone: 805-648-4700
Fax: 805-653-6124

Richard L. Taylor	Robert L. McCord, Jr.
	David L. Praver

Patrick Cherry	Susan D. Siple
	Rebbecca F. Calderwood

LEGAL SUPPORT PERSONNEL
PARALEGALS

Stephanie Gibson	Adele Rubino
	Diane Lovato

For full biographical listings, see the Martindale-Hubbell Law Directory

VICTORVILLE, San Bernardino Co.

LYNN E. ZUMBRUNN A LAW CORPORATION (AV)

14335 Park Avenue, Suite A, 92392-2365
Telephone: 619-245-5333
Fax: 619-245-2000

Lynn Edward Zumbrunn

James Bruce Minton	Gregory L. Zumbrunn

Representative Clients: H.D. Medical Home Care Supply, Inc.; Progressive Suspension, Inc.; Rammar Painting, Inc.; Sunland Ford, Inc.; T.L. Timmerman Construction, Inc.

For full biographical listings, see the Martindale-Hubbell Law Directory

WALNUT CREEK, Contra Costa Co.

ANDERSON, GALLOWAY & LUCCHESE, A PROFESSIONAL CORPORATION (AV)

1676 North California Boulevard, Suite 500, 94596-4183
Telephone: 510-943-6383
Facsimile: 510-943-7542

Robert L. Anderson	Stephen J. Brooks
George Patrick Galloway	Joseph S. Picchi
David R. Lucchese	Coleen L. Welch
Martin J. Everson	Deborah C. Moritz-Farr
Thomas J. Donnelly	Marc G. Cowden
Ralph J. Smith	Erin Ruddy Sabey
James M. Nelson	Lea K. McMahan
Scott E. Murray	Michael E. Brewer
David A. Depolo	Sonja M. Dahl
Karen A. Sparks	Thomas J. Tarkoff

For full biographical listings, see the Martindale-Hubbell Law Directory

HINTON & ALFERT, A PROFESSIONAL CORPORATION (AV)

Suite 600, 1646 North California Boulevard, 94596-4113
Telephone: 510-932-6006
Fax: 510-932-3412

Peter J. Hinton	Peter W. Alfert
	Michael P. Clark

Scott H. Z. Sumner	Nancy A. Beninati

For full biographical listings, see the Martindale-Hubbell Law Directory

JACKL & KATZEN (AV)

2033 North Main Street, Suite 700, 94596
Telephone: 510-932-8500
Fax: 510-932-1961
Email: jklawfirm@aol.com

MEMBERS OF FIRM

V. James Jackl	Linda R. Katzen

Andrew N. Contopoulos

For full biographical listings, see the Martindale-Hubbell Law Directory

CHARLES A. MCPHEE, JR. (AV)

1981 North Broadway, Suite 345, 94596
Telephone: 510-975-5990
Fax: 510-975-5999

For full biographical listings, see the Martindale-Hubbell Law Directory

WHITTIER, Los Angeles Co.

BEWLEY, LASSLEBEN & MILLER (AV)

13215 East Penn Street, Suite 510, 90602-1797
Telephone: 310-698-9771
Fax: 310-696-6357

MEMBERS OF FIRM

Thomas W. Bewley (1903-1986)	Ernie Zachary Park
William M. Lassleben, Jr. (Retired)	Robert H. Dewberry
	Richard L. Dewberry
Edward L. Miller	Jeffrey S. Baird
J. Terrence Mooschekian	Kevin P. Duthoy
	Joseph A. Vinatieri

ASSOCIATES

Jason C. Demille	John P. Godsil
Suzanne R. Kramer	Peter B. Fan

Representative Clients: Quaker City Federal Savings & Loan Assn.; Whittier College; Presbyterian Intercommunity Hospital; Bank of Whittier; Circuit Systems, Inc.; Lockhart Industries, Inc.; Subdivided Land, Inc.; United Ad-Label Co., Inc.
References: Bank of America National Trust & Savings Assn. (Whittier Main Office); Southern California Bank.

For full biographical listings, see the Martindale-Hubbell Law Directory

COLORADO

ASPEN,* Pitkin Co.

AUSTIN, PEIRCE & SMITH, P.C. (AV)

Suite 205, 600 East Hopkins Avenue, 81611
Telephone: 970-925-2600
FAX: 970-925-4720
Email: apspc@rof.net

(See Next Column)

AUSTIN, PEIRCE & SMITH P.C.—*Continued*

Ronald D. Austin   Frederick F. Peirce
Thomas Fenton Smith

Michael P. Fossenier

Counsel for: Chase Manhattan of Colorado, Inc.; Clark's Market; Cootes, Reid & Waldron Property Management, Inc.; Crystal Palace Corp.; Snowmass Shopping Center; Coldwell Banker The Aspen Brokers, Ltd.; William Poss & Assoc., Architects; Snowmass Resort Association; Aspen/Pitkin County Housing Authority; Nations Title Insurance, Inc.

For full biographical listings, see the Martindale-Hubbell Law Directory

J. NICHOLAS MCGRATH, P.C. (AV)

Suite 203, 600 East Hopkins Avenue, 81611
Telephone: 970-925-2612
Telecopier: 970-925-4402
Email: nicklaw@csn.net *URL:* http://www.aspenlink.com/nicklaw

J. Nicholas McGrath

Susan W. Laatsch

Representative Clients: Aspen Center for Physics; Aspen Chamber Resort Association.; The Gant Condominium Association; Aspen Alps Condominium Assn.; Gerald D. Hines Interests; Steak Pit, Inc.; Hotel Jerome Associates, Ltd. Partners; Redstone Investments, Inc. (Cleveholm Castle).

For Complete List of Firm Personnel, See General Section

For full biographical listings, see the Martindale-Hubbell Law Directory

OATES, HUGHES, KNEZEVICH & GARDENSWARTZ, P.C. (AV)

Aspen Plaza Building, 3rd Floor, 533 East Hopkins Avenue, 81611
Telephone: 970-920-1700
Telecopier: 970-920-1121
Email: ohkg@rof.net

Leonard M. Oates   Richard A. Knezevich
Ted D. Gardenswartz

David B. Kelly   Rich Orman
OF COUNSEL
Robert W. Hughes   John Thomas Kelly

Counsel for: Stapleton Insurance Agency; Pitkin County Title, Inc.

For full biographical listings, see the Martindale-Hubbell Law Directory

BOULDER,* Boulder Co.

HOWARD BITTMAN (AV)

1406 Pearl Street, Suite 200, 80302
Telephone: 303-443-2281
Fax: 303-443-2862

For full biographical listings, see the Martindale-Hubbell Law Directory

COOK & LEE, P.C. (AV)

5390 Manhattan Circle, 2nd Floor, 80303
Telephone: 303-543-1000
Fax: 303-543-8582

Stephen H. Cook   Larry D. Lee

Deborah R. Kirschman

For full biographical listings, see the Martindale-Hubbell Law Directory

LAW OFFICES OF MICHAEL R. ENWALL (AV)

720 Pearl Street, 80302
Telephone: 303-449-3891
FAX: 303-449-3992
Email: Enwall@nilenet.com

ASSOCIATE
Barbara K. Grant

For full biographical listings, see the Martindale-Hubbell Law Directory

FRENCH & STONE, P.C. (AV)

720 Pearl Street, 80302
Telephone: 303-449-3891
Fax: 303-449-3992

Joseph C. French   David M. Haynes
Robert W. Stone   Mark M. Haynes

References: Bank One of Boulder; Boulder; Bank of Boulder.

For full biographical listings, see the Martindale-Hubbell Law Directory

MARTIN & MEHAFFY (AV)

1655 Walnut Street, P.O. Box 1260, 80302
Telephone: 303-442-3375
Fax: 303-444-8398
Email: mmllc@aol.com *URL:* http://www.planetnetwork.com/law/
MEMBERS OF FIRM
James G. Martin (Retired)   Joel C. Maguire
John R. Mehaffy   Jeffrey L. Skovron
Lawrence C. Rider   Matthew S. Humphrey
Donald James Humphrey   Jonathan L. Miller
OF COUNSEL
Richard A. Tharp

Approved Attorneys for: Attorneys Title Guaranty Fund, Inc.

For full biographical listings, see the Martindale-Hubbell Law Directory

PURVIS, GRAY, SCHUETZE & GORDON (AV)

The Exeter Building, Suite 501, 1050 Walnut Street, 80302
Telephone: 303-442-3366
Fax: 303-440-3688
Denver, Colorado Office: 303 East 17th Avenue, Suite 700.
Telephone: 303-860-1888.
MEMBERS OF FIRM
William R. Gray   Robert A. Schuetze
John A. Purvis   Glen F. Gordon

For full biographical listings, see the Martindale-Hubbell Law Directory

WILLIAMS & TRINE, P.C. (AV)

1435 Arapahoe Avenue, 80302-6390
Telephone: 303-442-0173
Fax: 303-443-7677

William A. Trine   J. Conard Metcalf
Joel H. Greenstein (1933-1984)   Mari C. Bush
Michael A. Patrick
OF COUNSEL
Charles E. Williams

Reference: Norwest Bank of Boulder.

For full biographical listings, see the Martindale-Hubbell Law Directory

COLORADO SPRINGS,* El Paso Co.

BELTZ, EDWARDS & SABO, L.L.P. (AV)

729 South Cascade, 80903
Telephone: 719-473-4444; 719-634-6620
Fax: 719-444-0186

W. Thomas Beltz   Daniel P. Edwards
John W. Sabo, III

Daniel A. West

Representative Clients: A.M.I. Industries, Inc.; Analytical Surveys, Inc.; A.C. Israel Enterprises, Inc.; Boddington Lumber Co., Inc.; Cardiovascular Surgeons of Colorado Springs, P.C.; Colorado Springs Radiologists, P.C.; Digital, Inc.; Music Semi-Conductors, Inc.; Schlage Lock Co.; Texas Instruments.

For full biographical listings, see the Martindale-Hubbell Law Directory

GADDIS, KIN & HERD, P.C. (AV)

118 South Wahsatch, Suite 100, 80903
Telephone: 719-471-3848
Fax: 719-471-0317

Larry R. Gaddis   Thomas J. Herd
James W. Kin   David L. Quicksall (1950-1991)
OF COUNSEL
James B. Turner

Reference: Norwest Bank of Colorado Springs.

For full biographical listings, see the Martindale-Hubbell Law Directory

HANES & SCHUTZ, P.C. (AV)

7222 Commerce Center Drive Suite 243, 80919
Telephone: 719-260-7900
Denver Line: 303-740-9694
Fax: 719-260-7904
Email: hands@rmii.com

Richard W. Hanes   Tim Schutz

Mark D. Francis (Not admitted in CO)

Representative Clients: Colorado State University Research Foundation; Dieterich Standard; Beech Aircraft Corp.; Surevoid Products, Inc.; Pikes Peak National Bank; Western Filter Co.; Pacer Industries; El Paso County Medical Society; Dynamic Materials Corporation; Injection Research Specialists, Inc.

(See Next Column)

HANES & SCHUTZ P.C., *Colorado Springs—Continued*

For full biographical listings, see the Martindale-Hubbell Law Directory

KANE & DONLEY, P.C. (AV)

90 South Cascade Avenue, Suite 830, 80903
Telephone: 719-471-1650
Fax: 719-471-1663
Mailing Address: P.O. Box 1119, Colorado Springs, CO, 80901

Jerry A. Donley

Mark H. Kane

Jack E. Donley

William A. Palmer

Hayden W. Kane, II

OF COUNSEL

Hayden W. Kane

Representative Clients: American International Companies; Shelter Insurance Co.; Metropolitan Insurance Co.
Reference: Norwest Bank of Colorado Springs.

For full biographical listings, see the Martindale-Hubbell Law Directory

MELAT, PRESSMAN, EZELL & HIGBIE (AV)

711 South Tejon Street, 80903-4041
Telephone: 719-475-0304
Fax: 719-475-0242

MEMBERS OF FIRM

Justin R. Melat

E. Steven Ezell

Glenn S. Pressman

Alanson Higbie

ASSOCIATE

Rebecca A. Lorenz

OF COUNSEL

Bernard R. Baker

References: Colorado Springs National Bank; Colorado Bank-Exchange.

For full biographical listings, see the Martindale-Hubbell Law Directory

RETHERFORD, MULLEN, JOHNSON & BRUCE, L.L.C. (AV)

415 South Sahwatch, P.O. Box 1580, 80901
Telephone: 719-475-2014
Fax: 719-630-1267

MEMBERS OF FIRM

Jerry A. Retherford

Neil C. Bruce

J. Stephen Mullen

Patrick R. Salt

Anthony A. Johnson

J. Ronald Voss

Lori M. Moore

ASSOCIATES

Amelia L. Klemme

Debra A. Long

M. James Zendejas

Patricia Richardson

OF COUNSEL

E. William Shaffer, Jr.

Carla M. Albers

Representative Clients: Albertson's, Inc.; Boulder Community Hospital (Boulder); City of Colorado Springs Memorial Hospital; Parkview Episcopal Hospital (Pueblo); Rhone-Poulenc Agricultural Company; South West Memorial Hospital (Boulder).

For full biographical listings, see the Martindale-Hubbell Law Directory

VAGLICA, MEINHOLD & MALDONADO, L.L.C. (AV)

105 East Moreno, Suite 100, 80903
Telephone: 719-634-5724
Telefax: 719-634-8592
Denver, Colorado Office: 600 Seventeenth Street, Suite 2710 S.
Telephone: 303-620-0995.
Fax: 303-534-4536.
Affiliated Offices in Salt Lake City, Utah and Albuquerque, New Mexico.

Phillip A. Vaglica

Don H. Meinhold

Elizabeth A. Maldonado

William Strohmeyer

Alice Norman

For full biographical listings, see the Martindale-Hubbell Law Directory

THE WILLS LAW FIRM (AV)

Holly Sugar Building, 2 North Cascade Avenue, Suite 1000, 80903-1651
Telephone: 719-633-8500
Telecopier: 719-471-7750

MEMBERS OF FIRM

Lee R. Wills

Wm. Andrew Wills, II

For full biographical listings, see the Martindale-Hubbell Law Directory

DENVER, Denver Co.

ALEXANDER & CRABTREE, P.C. (AV)

216 16th Street, Suite 1300, 80202-5127
Telephone: 303-825-7307
Fax: 303-825-3202
Email: halexand@alexcrab.com *URL:* http://www.alexcrab.com

C. Scott Crabtree

Stephen Fitzsimmons

For full biographical listings, see the Martindale-Hubbell Law Directory

ANKELE, ICENOGLE, NORTON, WHITE & SETER, A PROFESSIONAL CORPORATION (AV)

5690 DTC Boulevard (Greenwood Village) Suite 300, 80111
Telephone: 303-773-1666
Fax: 303-773-1883

T. Edward Icenogle

Kim J. Seter

Charles E. Norton

Tamara K. Gilida

For full biographical listings, see the Martindale-Hubbell Law Directory

BADER & VILLANUEVA, P.C. (AV)

Suite 1100, 1660 Wynkoop Street, 80202
Telephone: 303-534-1700
Telecopier: 303-534-0725
Avon, Colorado Office: P.O. Box 3379, 48 E. Beavercreek Boulevard, Suite 102, 81620-3379.
Telephone: 970-949-6203.
Telecopier: 970-949-6215.

Gerald L. Bader, Jr.

Randolph S. Dement

Jeffrey M. Villanueva

Steven M. Feder

Renée Beth Taylor (Resident, Avon, Colorado Office)

Kelly Lynn Shafer

LEGAL SUPPORT PERSONNEL

Colette Poeppel (Paralegal)

Reference: The Bank of Denver.

For full biographical listings, see the Martindale-Hubbell Law Directory

BAKER & HOSTETLER (AV)

303 East 17th Avenue, Suite 1100, 80203-1264
Telephone: 303-861-0600
FAX: 303-861-7805
In Cleveland, Ohio: 3200 National City Center, 1900 East Ninth Street.
Telephone: 216-621-0200.
In Columbus, Ohio: Capitol Square, Suite 2100, 65 East State Street.
Telephone: 614-228-1541.
In Houston, Texas: 1000 Louisiana, Suite 2000.
Telephone: 713-751-1600.
In Long Beach, California: 300 Oceangate, Suite 620.
Telephone: 310-432-2827.
In Los Angeles, California: 600 Wilshire Boulevard. Telephone 213-624-2400.
In Orlando, Florida: SunBank Center, Suite 2300, 200 South Orange Avenue.
Telephone: 305-841-1111.
In Washington, D. C.: Washington Square, Suite 1100, 1050 Connecticut Avenue, N.W.
Telephone: 202-861-1500.
In College Park, Maryland: 9658 Baltimore Boulevard, Suite 206.
Telephone: 301-441-2781.
In Alexandria, Virginia: 437 North Lee Street.
Telephone: 703-549-1294.
In San Francisco, California: One Sansome Street, Suite 2000.
Telephone: 415-951-4705.

PARTNERS

Timothy R. Beyer

Marc D. Flink

Mary Price Birk

Todd L. Lundy

James A. Clark (Managing Partner-Denver Office)

Michael G. Martin

John B. Moorhead

Kathryn A. Elzi

Marjorie N. Sloan

ASSOCIATES

Peter J. Korneffel, Jr.

Michael J. Roche

OF COUNSEL

Winchester Cooley, III (Not admitted in CO)

For Complete List of Firm Personnel, See General Section

For full biographical listings, see the Martindale-Hubbell Law Directory

Denver—Continued

BALLARD SPAHR ANDREWS & INGERSOLL (AV)

Seventeenth Street Plaza Building, Suite 2300, 1225 17th
Street, 80202-5596
Telephone: 303-292-2400
Fax: 303-296-3956
Philadelphia, Pennsylvania Office: 1735 Market Street, 51st Floor.
Telephone: 215-665-8500.
Fax: 215-864-8999.
Harrisburg, Pennsylvania Office: 105 North Front Street.
Telephone: 717-236-3333.
Fax: 717-236-3884.
Salt Lake City, Utah Office: One Utah Center, 201 South Main Street,
Suite 1200.
Telephone: 801-531-3000.
Fax: 801-531-3001.
Washington, D.C. Office: Suite 900 East, 555 13th Street, N.W.
Telephone: 202-383-8800.
Fax: 202-383-8877; 383-8893.
Baltimore, Maryland Office: 300 East Lombard Street, 19th Floor.
Telephone: 410-528-5600.
Fax: 410-528-5650.
Camden, New Jersey Office: 800 Hudson Square, 5th Floor.
Telephone: 609-541-5577.
Fax: 609-541-8272.

Leslie A. Eaton	Roger P. Thomasch
Kevin Michael Shea	Mark Wielga

Erika Zimmer Enger	Nathan M. Longenecker
Barbara A. Grandjean	Judith I. Meyka
William T. Slamkowski	

For Complete List of Firm Personnel, See General Section

For full biographical listings, see the Martindale-Hubbell Law Directory

BREGA & WINTERS, P.C. (AV)

One Norwest Center, 1700 Lincoln Street, Suite 2222, 80203
Telephone: 303-866-9400
Fax: 303-861-9109
Email: bwpc@indra.com
Greeley, Colorado Office: 1100 Tenth Street, Suite 402, 80631.
Telephone: 303-352-4805.
Fax: 303-352-6547.

James W. Bain	Brian A. Magoon
Stuart N. Bennett	Loren L. Mall
Charles F. Brega	Pamela A. Shaddock
Robert R. Dormer	(Resident, Greeley Office)
Robert C. Kaufman	Jay John Schnell
Ronald S. Loser	Jerry D. Winters
	(Resident, Greeley Office)

Peter A. Gergely	Bradley D. Laue
Wesley B. Howard, Jr.	(Resident, Greeley Office)
Yvonne Marie Kreye	Jack R. Luellen
S. Scott Lasher	(Not admitted in CO)

OF COUNSEL

Carolyn Jane Hariton	Mark Spitalnik

COUNSEL

Jay W. Enyart

For full biographical listings, see the Martindale-Hubbell Law Directory

BRENMAN KEY & BROMBERG, P.C. (AV)

Mellon Financial Center Suite 1001, 1775 Sherman Street, 80203
Telephone: 303-894-0234
Fax: 303-839-1633

Albert Brenman	Donna A. Key
Thomas R. Bromberg	Steven W. McDonald

Theresa M. Mehringer	George D. Kreye

OF COUNSEL

Heather H. S. Sander	A. Thomas Tenenbaum
D. Elizabeth Wills	Edmund L. Epstein (Inactive)

For full biographical listings, see the Martindale-Hubbell Law Directory

BROWN, HARMON & ECKSTEIN, P.C. (AV)

Suite 3000 1700 Lincoln Street, 80203
Telephone: 303-293-3636
Fax: 303-830-2653
Email: eckstein@csn.org
Email: BHE@Lawyernet.com *URL:* http://eckstein.net/ecksteinlaw

David S. Harmon

For full biographical listings, see the Martindale-Hubbell Law Directory

BROWNSTEIN HYATT FARBER & STRICKLAND, P.C. (AV)

Twenty-Second Floor, 410 Seventeenth Street, 80202-4437
Telephone: 303-534-6335
Telecopier: 303-623-1956
Washington, D.C. Office: 601 Pennsylvania Avenue, N.W., Suite 900.
Telephone: 202-434-8377.
Telecopier: 202-393-7864.

Mark F. Leonard	Lisa Hogan
Andrew W. Loewi	Wayne F. Forman
Stanley L. Garnett	Hubert A. Farbes, Jr.
	Terence C. Gill

Anne M. Murphy	Peter Q. Murphy
Robert C. Troyer	Stephen D. Gurr
Patrick F Carrigan	Joshua J. Widoff
Mark J. Mathews	Beth Doherty Quinn
	David S. Chipman

Representative Clients: Air Line Pilots Association; Amrion, Inc.; Citicorp
North America, Inc.; Columbia/HCA Healthcare Corporation; Franklin
Haney Company; Med-Alliance, Inc.; Metro Taxi, Inc.; Ticketmaster Colo-
rado, Inc.; Trammell Crow Company; United Airlines, Inc.

For Complete List of Firm Personnel, See General Section

For full biographical listings, see the Martindale-Hubbell Law Directory

BURG & ELDREDGE, P.C. (AV)

P.O. Box 370385, 80237
Telephone: 303-779-5595
Fax: 303-779-0527
Albuquerque, New Mexico Office: 201 Third Street N.W., Suite 1500.
Telephone: 505-242-7020.
Fax: 505-242-7247.

Michael S. Burg	R. Hunter Ellington
Peter W. Burg	Thomas W. Henderson
Scott J. Eldredge	Janet R. Spies
David P. Hersh	Tom Van Buskirk
David M. Houliston	Matthew R. Giacomini
	Kerry N. Jardine

Kieth Van Doren	Rosemary Orsini
Brendan O'Rourke Powers	Robb A. Nelson
Jack D. Robinson	Matthew David Bailis
Kirstin G. Lindberg	Christina C. Vigil (Resident,
Bradley W. Howard (Resident,	Albuquerque, New Mexico)
Albuquerque, New Mexico	Holly S. Baer
Office)	James R. Brewster (Resident,
Matthew S. McElhiney	Albuquerque, New Mexico
Christian C. Doherty (Resident,	Office)
Albuquerque, New Mexico	Jonathon P. Brody
Office)	Brett Myer Perry

OF COUNSEL

Dale J. Coplan

Reference: Norwest Colorado, Inc.

For full biographical listings, see the Martindale-Hubbell Law Directory

CANGES, IWASHKO & BETHKE, A PROFESSIONAL CORPORATION (AV)

303 East 17th Avenue Suite 400, 80203-1261
Telephone: 303-860-1900
Fax: 303-860-1665

E. Michael Canges	Nina A. Iwashko
	Erich L. Bethke

Stephen R. Fatzinger	James S. Bailey

Reference: Norwest Bank Denver.

For full biographical listings, see the Martindale-Hubbell Law Directory

DUFFORD & BROWN, P.C. (AV)

1700 Broadway, Suite 1700, 80290-1701
Telephone: 303-861-8013
Facsimile: 303-832-3804
Affiliated Office: Solomon, Pearl, Blum & Quinn, L.L.P., New York, NY
and Denver, Colorado.

Philip G. Dufford	S. Kirk Ingebretsen
David W. Furgason	Peggy J. Anderson
Phillip D. Barber	Craig B. Shaffer
	Scott J. Mikulecky

Terry Jo Epstein	Thomas E. J. Hazard

Representative Clients: CF&I Steel, L.P.; The Colorado and Wyoming Railway Co.; Echo Bay-Sunnyside Gold; Federal Deposit Insurance Corporation;
Hewlett-Packard Co.; Ingersoll Rand Financial Co.; Peabody Holding Company, Inc.; Reorganized CF&I Steel Corporation; Stewart & Stevenson Services, Inc.; Tenneco Oil Co.

(See Next Column)

DUFFORD & BROWN P.C., *Denver—Continued*

For Complete List of Firm Personnel, See General Section

For full biographical listings, see the Martindale-Hubbell Law Directory

ELROD, KATZ, PREEO, LOOK, MOISON & SILVERMAN, PROFESSIONAL CORPORATION (AV)

Suite 1100, 1120 Lincoln Street, 80203
Telephone: 303-832-1900
Fax: 303-863-0412

Richard B. Elrod	Harley K. Look, Jr.
Michael M. Katz	Peter R. Moison
Robert L. Preeo	Eldon E. Silverman

Jersey M. Green	Kathryn A. Reeves
Richard M. Hess, Jr.	Gilbert R. Egle
Martin J. Green	Timothy Kyle Jordan
Marilyn McWilliams	Brian E. Onorato

OF COUNSEL
Richard P. Rosen

For full biographical listings, see the Martindale-Hubbell Law Directory

FAIRFIELD AND WOODS, P.C. (AV)

One Norwest Center, Suite 2400, 1700 Lincoln Street, 80203-4524
Telephone: 303-830-2400
Telecopier: 303-830-1033
Email: sseifert@fwlaw.com *URL:* http://www.fwlaw.com/

Peter F. Breitenstein	John J. Silver
Charlton H. Carpenter	Thomas P. Kearns
Howard Holme	Rocco A. Dodson
Robert S. Slosky	Mary E. Moser
James L. Stone	Brent T. Johnson
Michael M. McKinstry	Stephen H. Leonhardt
Robert L. Loeb, Jr.	Caroline C. Fuller
Daniel R. Frost	Gregory C. Smith
Stephen W. Seifert	John M. Tanner
Mary Jo Gross	Neil T. Duggan
Robert A. Holmes	Douglas J. Becker

SPECIAL COUNSEL
John S. Pfeiffer

Thomas M. Pierce	Jacalyn W. Peter
Suzanne R. Kalutkiewicz	David L. Joeris
Philip J. Roselli	Christine E. Payne
	Sean D. Baker

Representative Clients: Deutsche Financial Services Corporation; IBM Credit Corp.; Morrison Knudson Corporation; Olivetti Office U.S.A., Inc.; Pacific Gas and Electric Company; PaineWebber, Incorporated.

For full biographical listings, see the Martindale-Hubbell Law Directory

FRIEDLOB SANDERSON RASKIN PAULSON & TOURTILLOTT, LLC (AV)

1400 Glenarm Place, 80202-5099
Telephone: 303-571-1400
Fax: 303-595-3159; 303-595-3970; 303-615-5472
Email: 72731.505@Compuserve.Com
Englewood, Colorado Office: 8400 East Prentice Avenue, 80111-2918.
Telephone: 303-571-1400.

Richard H. Goldberg	Michael J. Norton

For full biographical listings, see the Martindale-Hubbell Law Directory

HALABY CROSS LIECHTY & SCHLUTER (AV)

Suite 1400, 1873 South Bellaire Street, 80222
Telephone: 303-691-5300
Fax: 303-691-5307

Theodore S. Halaby	Robert M. Liechty
Jonathan A. Cross	Leslie L. Schluter

ASSOCIATES

Jon A. Halaby	R. Craig Hess
	Heidi A. Harpowiski

For full biographical listings, see the Martindale-Hubbell Law Directory

HAMILTON AND FAATZ, A PROFESSIONAL CORPORATION (AV)

Suite 500 Colorado State Bank Building, 1600 Broadway, 80202-4988
Telephone: 303-830-0500
Facsimile: 303-860-7855

(See Next Column)

Pierpont Fuller (1906-1983)	John T. Willson
John M. Evans (1911-1984)	Michael E. Gurley
Dwight Alan Hamilton	James H. Marlow
Clyde A. Faatz, Jr.	Jan E. Montgomery
Gregory W. Smith	

Robert L. Bartholic	Christopher J.W. Forrest
Meghan Welch Martinez	

OF COUNSEL
Kenneth W. Caughey

Representative Clients: PPG Industries, Inc.; Public Employees Retirement Association of Colorado; Masonic Temple Association of Denver; Lockton Silversmith, Inc.; Muller, Sirhall and Associates, Inc.; South Denver Cardiology Associates, P.C.; Landmark Reclamation, Inc.; Stone's Farm Supply, Inc.; Heather Gardens Association; DCX, Inc.

For full biographical listings, see the Martindale-Hubbell Law Directory

HOLME ROBERTS & OWEN LLP (AV)

Suite 4100, 1700 Lincoln, 80203
Telephone: 303-861-7000
Telecopier: 303-866-0200
Email: hro@hro.com *URL:* http://www.hro.com
Boulder, Colorado Office: Suite 400, 1401 Pearl Street.
Telephone: 303-444-5955.
Telecopier: 303-444-1063.
Colorado Springs, Colorado Office: Suite 1300, 90 South Cascade Avenue.
Telephone: 719-473-3800.
Telecopier: 719-633-1518.
Salt Lake City, Utah Office: Suite 1100, 111 East Broadway.
Telephone: 801-521-5800.
Telecopier: 801-521-9639.
London, England Office: Mellier House, 26a Albemarle Street.
Telephone: 44-171-499-8776.
Telecopier: 44-171-499-7769.
Moscow, Russia Office: Kosmodamianskaya Nab. #52/1, Suite 9100, 113054.
Telephone: 7095-961-3000.
Telecopier: 7095-961-3001.
Kiev, Ukraine Office: Terestchenkovskaya #19, Suite 2, 252004.
Telephone: 380-44-224-1348.
Telecopier: 380-44-224-4986.

PARTNERS OF FIRM

Donald K. Bain	Daniel J. Dunn
Lawrence L. Levin	Linnea Brown
Edward J. McGrath	Boyd N. Boland
David T. Mitzner	Robert Tuchman
William S. Huff	Anne Stark Walker
Richard R. Young (Managing Partner, Colorado Springs Office)	Katherine Jean Peck
	Brent E. Rychener (Colorado Springs Office)
John R. Webb	Susan E. Duffey Campbell (Colorado Springs Office)
Spencer T. Denison	Stephanie M. Tuthill
Henry W. Ipsen	David B. Wilson
Brent V. Manning (Salt Lake City Office)	James R. Ghiselli (Boulder Office)
Richard L. Nagl (Colorado Springs Office)	Alan C. Bradshaw (Salt Lake City Office)
Carolyn E. Daniels	John D. McCarthy
John Leonard Watson	Eric E. Johnson
Charlotte Louise Neitzel	Duncan E. Barber
David S. Steefel	Richard L. Gabriel
Nancy J. Gegenheimer	Mary Hurley Stuart
Bruce F. Black	Colin G. Harris
LeGrand R. Curtis, Jr. (Managing Partner, Salt Lake City Office)	Kenneth W. Lund
	George G. Matava
Patricia C. Tisdale	Edwin P. Aro
Dennis L. Arfmann	Steven C. Bednar (Salt Lake City Office)

OF COUNSEL

A. Edgar Benton	Richard L. Schrepferman

SPECIAL COUNSEL

David H. Goldberg	Laurence B. James

SENIOR COUNSEL

Kathryn P. Beller	Michael W. Bruzga
	Lawrence M. Zavadil

ASSOCIATES

Blaine J. Benard (Salt Lake City Office)	Cody Winchester Field (Salt Lake City Office)
Charles B. Bruce, Jr.	Elizabeth M. Flores
Loretta (Laurie) A. Cahill	Harriet M. Hageman
Kelly M. Condon	Sherri A. Heckel
Denise M. DeForest	Martin D. Litt
Susan B. Dussault (Not admitted in CO)	Daniel P. Maguire
	Deborah S. Menkins (Colorado Springs Office)
G. Leland Dutcher, Jr. (Colorado Springs Office)	Adrian Miller

(See Next Column)

HOLME ROBERTS & OWEN LLP—*Continued*
ASSOCIATES (Continued)

Cynthia A. Mitchell   Dominic Jude Ricotta
(Boulder Office)   (Colorado Springs Office)
Felicity A. O'Herron   Matthew J. Rita
Timothy G. Pfeifer   Alan Romero
(Colorado Springs Office)   (Salt Lake City Office)
Edward E. Stevenson

For Complete List of Firm Personnel, See General Section

For full biographical listings, see the Martindale-Hubbell Law Directory

---

JONES & KELLER, A PROFESSIONAL CORPORATION (AV)

Suite 1600, 1625 Broadway, 80202
Telephone: 303-573-1600
Fax: 303-893-6506

Marion F. Jones (1898-1978)   Thomas J. Burke, Jr.
Alec J. Keller (1913-1995)   Samuel E. Wing
Alvin J. Meiklejohn, Jr.   Reid A. Godbolt
Leslie R. Kehl   Rodney D. Knutson
Edward T. Lyons, Jr.   Kevin L. Brown
David E. Driggers   Barry L. Wilkie

Howard R. Hertzberg   Brent Nicholls
David A. Thayer   Michael Brian Cavanaugh
Nathan D. Simmons

Reference: Colorado State Bank; Union Bank & Trust.

For full biographical listings, see the Martindale-Hubbell Law Directory

---

KENNEDY & CHRISTOPHER, P.C. (AV)

1660 Wynkoop Street, Suite 900, 80202
Telephone: 303-825-2700
Fax: 303-825-0434

Frank R. Kennedy   Lisa B. Heintz
Daniel R. Christopher   Ronald H. Nemirow
Kim B. Childs   Barbara H. Glogiewicz
Elizabeth A. Starrs   Dawn E. Mitzner
Richard B. Caschette   John R. Mann
Mark A. Fogg   Daniel R. McCune
Michael T. Mihm   Dean A. McConnell
Charles R. Ledbetter   Edward D. Bronfin

OF COUNSEL
Paul E. Scott

Matthew S. Feigenbaum   Christopher K. Miller
Catherine O'Brien-Crum   Carolyn Sprinthall Knaut
Steven J. Picardi   David B. Gelman
Theresa A. Dettling   Gary W. Flanagan

Representative Clients: AETNA Casualty and Surety Co.; American Medical International; Blue Cross/Blue Shield of Colorado; COPIC; The Doctors Co.; Hartford Insurance Co.; Home Insurance Co.; St. Paul Fire and Marine Insurance Co.; PRMS, Colorado Insurance Guaranty Association.

For full biographical listings, see the Martindale-Hubbell Law Directory

---

KONCILJA & ASSOCIATES, P.C. (AV)

Suite 2050, 1700 Broadway, 80290
Telephone: 303-832-2110
Facsimile: 303-832-2623
Email: koncilja@ix.netcom.com

Frances A. Koncilja

Peter C. Forbes   Elizabeth A. Woodcock
Dorothy Huysman Dean   Michael A. Vellone
Julie Leamon Rosen

For full biographical listings, see the Martindale-Hubbell Law Directory

---

LEVENTHAL AND BOGUE, P.C. (AV)

950 South Cherry Street, Suite 600, 80222
Telephone: 303-759-9945
Fax: 303-759-9692
Email: LEVENBOG@AOL.COM

Jim Leventhal   Natalie Brown
Jeffrey A. Bogue   Victoria J. Koury
Bruce J. Kaye   Kelly P. Roberts
Grant Marylander

Reference: Southwest State Bank.

For full biographical listings, see the Martindale-Hubbell Law Directory

---

LONG & JAUDON, P.C. (AV)

The Bailey Mansion, 1600 Ogden Street, 80218-1414
Telephone: 303-832-1122
FAX: 303-832-1348

(See Next Column)

Lawrence A. Long (1908-1992)   Alan D. Avery
Joseph C. Jaudon, Jr.   Cecelia A. Fleischner
David B. Higgins   Walter N. Houghtaling
Frederick W. Long   Ellen Rubright Ivy
Gary B. Blum   Christine Anne Craigmile
Michael T. McConnell   Carla M. LaRosa
Stephen P. Hopkins   Sheri Lyn Hood
Robert M. Baldwin   Thomas C. Kearns, Jr.
Dennis Woodfin Brown   Margaret J. Walton
David H. Yun

Representative Clients: St. Joseph Hospital, Inc.; King Soopers, Inc.; Aetna Casualty & Surety Co.; COPIC; The Doctors Co.; Home Insurance Company; Montgomery Wards.

For Complete List of Firm Personnel, See General Section

For full biographical listings, see the Martindale-Hubbell Law Directory

---

MARKUSSON, GREEN & JARVIS, P.C. (AV)

Suite 2300, 1050 Seventeenth Street, 80265
Telephone: 303-572-4200
Fax: 303-595-3780

James K. Green   H. Keith Jarvis
Dennis H. Markusson

Thomas E. Napp   Jason L. Romero
Kimberly J. Kernan
(Not admitted in CO)

Representative Clients: Club Mediterranean; Commercial Union Insurance Cos.; Owens Corning Fiberglass Corp.; Sherwin-Williams; Travelers Insurance Cos.; Reliance Insurance Co.; Republic Insurance; Electric Mutual Insurance; Ohio Casualty Insurance Co.; Dow Chemical Co.

For full biographical listings, see the Martindale-Hubbell Law Directory

---

JOHN O. MARTIN, P.C. (AV)

1660 17th Street, Suite 100, 80202
Telephone: 303-892-8988
Fax: 303-820-3531

John O. Martin   Kathleen M. Shea

For full biographical listings, see the Martindale-Hubbell Law Directory

---

GREGG C. McREYNOLDS (AV)

Quebec Centre II, Suite 300 7400 East Caley Avenue
(Englewood), 80111-6714
Telephone: 303-694-1800
Fax: 303-694-9370

For full biographical listings, see the Martindale-Hubbell Law Directory

---

MILLER, McCARREN & HELMS, P.C. (AV)

410 Seventeenth Street, Suite 1200, 80202
Telephone: 303-436-1163
Telecopier: 303-436-1143

William J. McCarren   J. Kent Miller
Thomas J. Helms

For full biographical listings, see the Martindale-Hubbell Law Directory

---

MONTGOMERY LITTLE & McGREW, P.C. (AV)

The Quadrant, 5445 DTC Parkway, Suite 800 (Englewood), 80111
Telephone: 303-773-8100
Telecopier: 303-220-0412

Roy E. Montgomery   William H. ReMine, III
(1907-1986)   William H. Knapp
Robert R. Montgomery   Daniel P. Murphy
David C. Little   Thomas C. Deline
Dan McGrew   Karen B. Best
James J. Soran, III   John R. Riley
Richard L. Murray, Jr.   Rebecca B. Givens
Kevin J. Kuhn   Christopher B. Little
David A. Burlage   Melinda L. Sanders
Robert J. Beattie   Timothy M. Schulte
Brian K. Stutheit   Carole Salamaha
Michael H. Smith   Patrick T. O'Rourke
Joel A. Mayo
OF COUNSEL
J. Bayard Young

Representative Clients: Amoco Oil Co.; Bristol-Myers Squibb; Colorado Medical Society; Chrysler Corp.; Cyprus Minerals; Dillon Cos., Inc., d/b/a King Soopers; The St. Paul Insurance Cos.; University of Colorado Health Sciences Center.

For Complete List of Firm Personnel, See General Section

For full biographical listings, see the Martindale-Hubbell Law Directory

Denver—Continued

MYER, SWANSON, ADAMS & WOLF, P.C. (AV)

The Colorado State Bank Building, 1600 Broadway, Suite
1480, 80202-4915
Telephone: 303-866-9800
Facsimile: 303-866-9818

Rendle Myer	Robert K. Swanson
Allan B. Adams	Thomas J. Wolf

Philip T. Masterson
OF COUNSEL

Robert Swanson	Fred E. Neef (1910-1986)

Representative Clients: The Oppenheimer Funds; Daily Cash Accumulation
Fund; The Centennial Trusts; Mile High Chapter of American Red Cross;
Master Lease; Heartland Management Co.; Kan-Build of Colorado, Inc.
Reference: The Colorado State Bank of Denver.

For full biographical listings, see the Martindale-Hubbell Law Directory

NETZORG & McKEEVER, PROFESSIONAL CORPORATION (AV)

Republic Plaza, 370 Seventeenth Street, Suite 3590, 80202
Telephone: 303-892-7100
Fax: 303-446-0506

Gordon W. Netzorg	Peter G. Koclanes
Cecil E. Morris, Jr.	Joan M. Collopy

OF COUNSEL
J. Nicholas McKeever, Jr.

For full biographical listings, see the Martindale-Hubbell Law Directory

PARCEL, MAURO, HULTIN & SPAANSTRA, P.C. (AV)

Suite 3600, 1801 California Street, 80202
Telephone: 303-292-6400
Telecopier: 303-295-3040

David A. Bailey	Lori L. Roberts
James D. Butler	Marcus L. Squarrell
William A. Hillhouse II	Edward W. Stern
Paul F. Hultin	John R. Trigg
Robert B. Hunter	Joseph B. Valentine
Mark F. Kennedy	(Not admitted in CO)
William R. Marsh	Gary Wagner
Christopher J. Meyer	Malcolm E. Wheeler
Michael L. O'Donnell	Gwen Jarahian Young

OF COUNSEL

Richard P. Barkley	Peggy E. Montaño

Angella K. Bond	Lee A. Mickus
Cheryl Burnside	Andrew J. Mihalick
Jodi S. Coviello	(Not admitted in CO)
Michelle J. Hirth	Geoffrey H. Simon
Susan J. Keller	Edward C. Stewart
Laurie L. Korneffel	Kimberly Ann Tempel

Reference: 1st Interstate, Denver, Colorado.

For Complete List of Firm Personnel, See General Section

For full biographical listings, see the Martindale-Hubbell Law Directory

PURVIS, GRAY, SCHUETZE & GORDON (AV)

303 East 17th Avenue, Suite 700, 80203
Telephone: 303-860-1888
Boulder, Colorado Office: The Exeter Building, Suite 501, 1050 Walnut
Street.
Telephone: 303-442-3366.
Fax: 303-440-3688.

MEMBERS OF FIRM

William R. Gray	Robert A. Schuetze
John A. Purvis	Glen F. Gordon

For full biographical listings, see the Martindale-Hubbell Law Directory

REIMAN & BAYAZ, P.C. (AV)

1600 Broadway, Suite 1640, 80202
Telephone: 303-860-1500
Fax: 303-839-4380

Jeff Reiman	Marcie K. Bayaz

Darren E. Temkin-Nadel	Eric B. Liebman

For full biographical listings, see the Martindale-Hubbell Law Directory

JOHN M. RICHILANO P.C. (AV)

1660 Wynkoop Suite 1160, 80202
Telephone: 303-893-8000
Telecopier: 303-893-8055

(See Next Column)

John M. Richilano

For full biographical listings, see the Martindale-Hubbell Law Directory

SHERMAN & HOWARD L.L.C. (AV)

Attorneys and Counselors at Law
633 Seventeenth Street, Suite 3000, 80202
Telephone: 303-297-2900
Telecopier: 303-298-0940
Colorado Springs, Colorado Office: Suite 1500, 90 South Cascade Avenue,
80903.
Telephone: 719-475-2440.
Las Vegas, Nevada Office: Swendseid & Stern a member in Sherman &
Howard L.L.C., 317 Sixth Street, 89101.
Telephone: 702-387-6073.
Reno, Nevada Office: Swendseid & Stern, a member in Sherman &
Howard L.L.C., 50 West Liberty Street, Suite 660, 89501.
Telephone: 702-323-1980.

Christopher Lane	Joseph J. Bronesky
Hugh J. McClearn	Richard N. Baer
Mark L. Fulford	Leanne B. DeVos
Kenneth B. Siegel	Cynthia P. Delaney

Stefan D. Stein

Milton L. "Skip" Smith, III	Christopher R. Mosley
(Colorado Springs Office)	John J. Cyran
John W. Mill	Maria L. Sepúlveda

Representative Clients: AT&T Corp.; Hathaway Corp.; Newmont Gold
Corp.; Tele-Communications, Inc.

For Complete List of Firm Personnel, See General Section

For full biographical listings, see the Martindale-Hubbell Law Directory

TREECE, ALFREY, MUSAT & BOSWORTH, P.C. (AV)

Denver Place, 999 18th Street, Suite 1600, 80202
Telephone: 303-292-2700
Facsimile: 303-295-0414
Email: 73507.2446@compuserve.com

Robert S. Treece	Arthur H. Bosworth, II
L. Richard Musat	Timothy J. Judson

Paul E. Collins

June Baker Laird	David C. von Gunten
Michael L. Hutchinson	Victor M. Morales

R. Bruce Phillips

For full biographical listings, see the Martindale-Hubbell Law Directory

EDWARD L. VOLPE, P.C. (AV)

Suite 780 Seventeenth and Grant Building, 303 East 17th
Avenue, 80203-1261
Telephone: 303-861-7800
Fax: 303-860-9364

Edward L. Volpe

For full biographical listings, see the Martindale-Hubbell Law Directory

WALLER AND MARK, P.C. (AV)

Denver Corporate Center, Tower II, 7800 East Union Avenue, Suite
210, 80237
Telephone: 303-741-4741
Fax: 303-741-4765

William C. Waller, Jr.	Denis H. Mark

For full biographical listings, see the Martindale-Hubbell Law Directory

WALTERS & JOYCE, P.C. (AV)

2015 York Street, 80205
Telephone: 303-322-1404
FAX: 303-377-5668

Craig D. Joyce

Anne Baudino Holton
OF COUNSEL
Julia T. Waggener

Reference: Norwest Bank of Buckingham Square; Mountain States Bank.

For Complete List of Firm Personnel, See General Section

For full biographical listings, see the Martindale-Hubbell Law Directory

WELLS, ANDERSON & RACE, LLC (AV)

1700 Broadway, Suite 1850, 80290
Telephone: 303-830-1212
Fax: 303-830-0898

(See Next Column)

WELLS, ANDERSON & RACE LLC—*Continued*

Mary A. Wells	Geoffrey S. Race
Sheryl L. Anderson	Suanne M. Dell

Gregory E. Sopkin

Representative Clients: Associated Aviation Underwriters; Baxter Healthcare Corporation; The Cessna Aircraft Co.; Raytheon Aircraft Company; State Farm Mutual Auto. Ins. Co.; State Farm Fire & Casualty Co.; American Eagle Group Inc.; Royal Insurance Co.; Great American Insurance Cos.; United Fire and Casualty Co.

For full biographical listings, see the Martindale-Hubbell Law Directory

CHARLES WELTON A PROFESSIONAL CORPORATION (AV)

The Old Smith Mansion, 1751 Gilpin Street, 80218
Telephone: 303-333-8447
Fax: 303-322-9546

Charles E. Welton

Reference: Mountain States Bank, Denver, Colorado.

For full biographical listings, see the Martindale-Hubbell Law Directory

WHITE AND STEELE, PROFESSIONAL CORPORATION (AV)

1225 17th Street, Suite 2800, 80202
Telephone: 303-296-2828
Telecopier: 303-296-3131
Email: law@wsteele.com
Cheyenne, Wyoming Office: 1912 Capital Avenue, Suite 416, 82003.
Telephone: 307-778-4160.
Telecopier: 307-778-7041.

Lowell White (1897-1983)	Sandra L. Spencer
Walter A. Steele	John M. Palmeri
R. Eric Peterson	Frederick W. Klann
Stephen K. Gerdes	Richard M. Kaudy
Michael W. Anderson	Peter W. Rietz
James M. Dieterich	Thomas B. Quinn
Glendon L. Laird	Michael J. Daugherty
John Lebsack	Ted A. Krumreich
Stephen G. Sparr	William F. Campbell, Jr.
John P. Craver	Kurt A. Horton
David J. Nowak	Stewart J. Rourke
	Robert R. Carlson

Christopher P. Kenney	Kimberly A. Viergever
Robert H. Coate	J. Barton Maxwell
Michelle R. Magruder	Sherri L. Sweers
Monty L. Barnett	Shanise M. Black
Joseph R. King	Matthew W. Tills
Frank D. Sledge	Claire Diaz
Kristi Blumhardt	Charles W. Yett
Keith R. Olivera	Laura E. David Fuller

OF COUNSEL

Fred L. Witsell	Kevin W. Hecht

Colorado Tort Counsel for: Goodyear Tire and Rubber Co.; The Dow Chemical Co.; Celotex.
Insurance Clients: Allied Insurance Co.; CNA; Kemper Insurance Group; Massachusetts Mutual Life Insurance Co.; U.S.A.A.; Underwriters at Lloyds; Farmers Insurance Group.

For Complete List of Firm Personnel, See General Section

For full biographical listings, see the Martindale-Hubbell Law Directory

---

DURANGO,* La Plata Co.

McLACHLAN & GOLDMAN, LLC (AV)

850 1/2 Main Avenue, P.O. Box 2270, 81302-2270
Telephone: 970-259-8747
Facsimile: 970-259-8790
Email: LAWMCGLD@FRONTIER.NET

Michael E. McLachlan	Michael A. Goldman

Jeffery P. Robbins

For full biographical listings, see the Martindale-Hubbell Law Directory

---

ENGLEWOOD, Arapahoe Co.

BANTA, HOYT, EVERALL & FARRINGTON, L.L.C. (AV)

Suite 240E, 5690 DTC Boulevard, 80111
Telephone: 303-220-8000
Fax: 303-220-0153

Richard J. Banta	Stephen G. Everall

(See Next Column)

OF COUNSEL

Richard D. Greene	Craig E. Wagner

Representative Clients: American Institute of Timber Construction; Cherry Creek School District No. 5; City of Greenwood Village; Colorado School District Self Insurance Pool; Intermountain Rural Electric Association; Kiewit Western Co.; Littleton Public Schools; National Union Fire Insurance Co. (local); Southgate Sanitation and Water Districts.

For Complete List of Firm Personnel, See General Section

For full biographical listings, see the Martindale-Hubbell Law Directory

KING ● PETERSON ● BROWN, LLC (AV)

Suite 1040 8400 East Prentice Avenue, P.O. Box 256, 80111
Telephone: 303-793-3400
Facsimile: 303-793-3678
Email: CEK5473@aol.com
Morrison, Colorado Office: 19423 North Turkey Creek Road, Suite G, 80465.
Telephone: 303-697-0575.
Facsimile: 303-697-5259.

Charles E. King	Richard G. Peterson
	James L. Brown

Michael W. Reagor	Jeffrey N. Cole

For full biographical listings, see the Martindale-Hubbell Law Directory

THOMAS J. TOMAZIN, P.C. (AV)

Suite 200, 5655 South Yosemite, 80111
Telephone: 303-771-1900
FAX: 303-793-0923

Thomas J. Tomazin

Representative Clients: Sheridan, Inc. (Leasing Division); Sovran Leasing; The Leasing Group; Contract Design Services, Inc.; American Natural Gas Corp.; Sonex Enterprises, Inc.; Am West Energy, Inc.; Mountain States Asphalt Paving, Inc.
Reference: Key Bank.

For full biographical listings, see the Martindale-Hubbell Law Directory

---

FORT COLLINS,* Larimer Co.

BAILEY, PICKERING & STOCK (AV⊤)

Nineteen Old Town Square, Suite 238, 80524
Telephone: 970-482-1977
Fax: 970-416-9540
Cheyenne, Wyoming Office: 221 East 21st Street, P.O. Box 1557, 82001.
Telephone: 307-638-7745.
Fax: 307-638-7749.

MEMBER OF FIRM
Robert G. Pickering

For full biographical listings, see the Martindale-Hubbell Law Directory

---

GOLDEN,* Jefferson Co.

BRADLEY, CAMPBELL, CARNEY & MADSEN, PROFESSIONAL CORPORATION (AV)

1717 Washington Avenue, 80401-1994
Telephone: 303-278-3300
Fax: 303-278-3379
Email: firm@bccm.com

Leo N. Bradley	Thomas A. Nolan

Counsel for: Coors Brewing Co.; Coors Ceramics Co.; Evergreen National Bank, Evergreen, Colorado; Clear Creek National Bank, Georgetown, Colorado; ASARCO, Inc.; Morrison-Knudsen; Westinghouse Electric Corp.
Local Counsel for: Public Service Company of Colorado.
Reference: Colorado National Bank, Denver, Colorado.

For Complete List of Firm Personnel, See General Section

For full biographical listings, see the Martindale-Hubbell Law Directory

HOLLEY, ALBERTSON & POLK, P.C. (AV)

Suite 100, 1667 Cole Boulevard, 80401
Telephone: 303-233-7838
Fax: 303-233-2860

George Alan Holley	Scott D. Albertson
	Dennis B. Polk

Eric E. Torgersen	Thomas A. Walsh
	Howard R. Stone

Reference: First Bank of Wheat Ridge.

For full biographical listings, see the Martindale-Hubbell Law Directory

GREELEY, Weld Co.

BREGA & WINTERS, P.C. (AV)

1100 Tenth Street, Suite 402, 80631
Telephone: 970-352-4805
Fax: 970-352-6547
Denver, Colorado Office: One United Bank Center. 1700 Lincoln Street,
Suite 2222 Street.
Telephone: 303-866-9400.
FAX: 303-861-9109.

Jerry D. Winters　　　　　　　Pamela A. Shaddock

Bradley D. Laue

For full biographical listings, see the Martindale-Hubbell Law Directory

LAKEWOOD, Jefferson Co.

POLIDORI, GEROME, FRANKLIN AND JACOBSON, L.L.C. (AV)

Suite 300, 550 South Wadsworth Boulevard, 80226
Telephone: 303-936-3300
Fax: 303-936-0125

Gary L. Polidori　　　　　　Dennis J. Jacobson
R. Jerold Gerome　　　　　　Peter L. Franklin

Lesleigh W. Monahan　　　　　Barry J. Seidenfeld

Representative Clients: Lakewood City Center; Treeforms, Inc.; Lakewood
Chrysler-Plymouth, Inc.; Western Fasteners U.S.A., Inc.; Horizon Glass and
Glazing Co., Inc.; Grif-Fab Corp.; Commercial Architectural Products, Inc.;
Voyaguers International, Inc.; 1st Bank, Villa Italia.

For full biographical listings, see the Martindale-Hubbell Law Directory

LAMAR, Prowers Co.

JOHN GEHLHAUSEN, P.C. (AV)

200 South Fifth Street, Drawer 1079, 81052
Telephone: 719-336-9071
Fax: Available Upon Request

John Gehlhausen

Darla Scranton Specht

For full biographical listings, see the Martindale-Hubbell Law Directory

LONGMONT, Boulder Co.

JOHN WAYNE MILLER & ARLENE S. COHEN, P.C. (AV)

344 Main Street, P.O. Box 1259, 80502-1259
Telephone: 303-772-0165
Metro Denver: 303-666-4158
Nationally: 800-606-0165
Fax: 303-772-6450

John Wayne Miller　　　　　　Arlene S. Cohen

Kathy Hix

For full biographical listings, see the Martindale-Hubbell Law Directory

MONTROSE, Montrose Co.

EDWARD D. DURHAM (AV)

524 South First Street, P.O. Box 1721, 81402
Telephone: 970-249-2274
Fax: 970-249-6482

Reference: Norwest Bank of Montrose.

For full biographical listings, see the Martindale-Hubbell Law Directory

STEAMBOAT SPRINGS, Routt Co.

OLIPHANT, HAMMOND & O'HARA (AV)

A Law Partnership of Professional Corporations
919 Oak Street, P.O. Box 774425, 80477
Telephone: 970-879-6060
Fax: 970-879-5199

MEMBERS OF FIRM

James B. F. Oliphant, P.C.　　　Kristopher L. Hammond, P.C.
　　　　Michael A. O'Hara, III, P.C.

ASSOCIATE

Christopher D. Atwell (Not admitted in CO)

For full biographical listings, see the Martindale-Hubbell Law Directory

VAIL, Eagle Co.

DUNN, ABPLANALP & CHRISTENSEN, P.C. (AV)

Suite 300 Vail Bank Building, 108 South Frontage Road
West, 81657-5087
Telephone: 970-476-0300
Telecopier: 970-476-4765

John W. Dunn　　　　　　Allen C. Christensen
　　　　　　Diane L. Herman
　　　　　SPECIAL COUNSEL
　　　　　Jerry W. Hannah

Representative Clients: Towns of Avon, Minturn and Red Cliff, Colorado.

For Complete List of Firm Personnel, See General Section

For full biographical listings, see the Martindale-Hubbell Law Directory

CONNECTICUT

BRIDGEPORT, Fairfield Co.

BAI, POLLOCK AND COYNE, P.C. (AV)

Park City Plaza, 10 Middle Street, P.O. Box 1978, 06604
Telephone: 203-366-7991
Fax: 203-366-4723
Email: bpc@snet.net

Arnold J. Bai (1931-1992)　　　Garie J. Mulcahey
Paul E. Pollock　　　　　　　Raymond J. Plouffe, Jr.
James E. Coyne　　　　　　　Philip F. von Kuhn
Jeffrey A. Blueweiss　　　　　Madonna A. Sacco
　　　　　　Michael S. Lynch

David J. Robertson　　　　　Colleen D. Fries
Edward P. Brady III　　　　　Neal P. Rogan
Andrew S. Turret　　　　　　Jacquelyn Conlon
Gaileen A. Kaufman　　　　　Janine M. Savarese
Kevin S. Coyne　　　　　　　Louis A. Annecchino
　　　　　Kristin Beth Comstock

For full biographical listings, see the Martindale-Hubbell Law Directory

WILLIAMS, COONEY & SHEEHY (AV)

One Lafayette Circle, 06604
Telephone: 203-331-0888
Telecopier: 203-331-0896

MEMBERS OF FIRM

Ronald D. Williams　　　　　Peter J. Dauk
Robert J. Cooney　　　　　　Dion W. Moore
Edward Maum Sheehy　　　　Ronald D. Williams, Jr.
Peter D. Clark　　　　　　　Francis A. Smith, Jr.
　　　　　　　　　　　　(1951-1989)

Michael P. Bowler　　　　　Paul Sean Curtin
Michael Cuff Deakin　　　　Suzannah Kim Nigro

Representative Clients: Aetna Life & Casualty Co.; Nationwide Insurance
Co.; Connecticut Medical Insurance Co.; Zimmer Manufacturing Co.; Textron-Lycoming; The Stop & Shop Companies, Inc.; Shawmut Bank Connecticut, N.A.; Podiatry Insurance Company of America; Town of Easton, Conn.

For full biographical listings, see the Martindale-Hubbell Law Directory

CHESHIRE, New Haven Co.

MOORE, O'BRIEN & JACQUES (AV)

700 West Johnson Avenue Suite 207, 06410
Telephone: 203-272-5881
Fax: 203-272-9273

MEMBERS OF FIRM

Garrett M. Moore　　　　　Stephen L. Jacques
Gregory E. O'Brien　　　　Lisa Marie Ferraro

For full biographical listings, see the Martindale-Hubbell Law Directory

GREENWICH, Fairfield Co.

ALBERT, WARD & JOHNSON, P.C. (AV)

125 Mason Street, P.O. Box 1668, 06836
Telephone: 203-661-8600
Telecopier: 203-661-8051

OF COUNSEL

David Albert　　　　　　C. Robton Perelli-Minetti

(See Next Column)

ALBERT, WARD & JOHNSON P.C.—*Continued*

Tom S. Ward, Jr.	Howard R. Wolfe
Scott R. Johnson	Christopher A. Kristoff
Jane D. Hogeman	Vicki K. Comberiati

For full biographical listings, see the Martindale-Hubbell Law Directory

BENTLEY, MOSHER, BABSON & LAMBERT, P.C. (AV)

20 Dayton Avenue, P.O. Box 788, 06836-0788
Telephone: 203-629-2424
Telecopier: 203-629-2545

John F. Lambert

For full biographical listings, see the Martindale-Hubbell Law Directory

IVEY, BARNUM & O'MARA, LLC (AV)

Meridian Building, 170 Mason Street, P.O. Box 1689, 06830
Telephone: 203-661-6000
Telecopier: 203-661-9462

MEMBERS OF FIRM

Michael J. Allen	Donat C. Marchand
Robert C. Barnum, Jr.	Miles F. McDonald, Jr.
Edward D. Cosden, Jr.	Edwin J. O'Mara, Jr.
Wilmot L. Harris, Jr.	Remy A. Rodas
William I. Haslun II	Gregory A. Saum
Michael J. Jones	Lorraine Slavin
Edward T. Krumeich, Jr.	Steven B. Steinmetz

ASSOCIATES

Paul G. Amicucci	Melissa Townsend Klauberg
Stephan B. Grozinger	Cristin L. Rothfuss
Juerg A. Heim	Alan S. Rubenstein
Jennifer B. Kallenbach	Sheryl L. Sensale
	(Not admitted in CT)

OF COUNSEL

James W. Cuminale	Jennifer D. Port
Philip R. McKnight	(Not admitted in CT)

For full biographical listings, see the Martindale-Hubbell Law Directory

---

HARTFORD,* Hartford Co.

GORDON, MUIR AND FOLEY (AV)

Hartford Square North, Ten Columbus Boulevard, 06106-5123
Telephone: 860-525-5361
Telecopier: 860-525-4849

MEMBERS OF FIRM

William S. Gordon, Jr.	William J. Gallitto
(1946-1956)	Gerald R. Swirsky
George Muir (1939-1976)	Robert J. O'Brien
Edward J. Foley (1955-1983)	Philip J. O'Connor
Peter C. Schwartz	Kenneth G. Williams
John J. Reid	Chester J. Bukowski
John H. Goodrich, Jr.	Mary Ann Santacroce
R. Bradley Wolfe	J. Lawrence Price
Jon Stephen Berk	Mary Anne Alicia Charron
	James G. Kelly

ASSOCIATES

Kevin F. Morin	Andrew J. Hern
Claudia A. Baio	Eileen McCarthy Geel
Patrick T. Treacy	Christopher L. Slack
	Renee W. Dwyer

OF COUNSEL

Stephen M. Riley

Reference: Fleet Bank.

For full biographical listings, see the Martindale-Hubbell Law Directory

LAW OFFICES OF R. BARTLEY HALLORAN, P.C. (AV)

One Lewis Street, 06103
Telephone: 860-493-1923
Facsimile: 860-493-1924

R. Bartley Halloran	Henry K. Snyder

Representative Clients: Kentucky Fried Chicken, Hartford Franchise; Connecticut Criminal Defense Lawyers Association; Colonial Realty Limited Partners Class Action; Victims of Collapse of L'Ambiance Plaza (Bridgeport, Connecticut).

For full biographical listings, see the Martindale-Hubbell Law Directory

THOMAS P. HESLIN (AV)

40 Russ Street, 06106
Telephone: 860-549-3750
Fax: 860-244-9826

JACKSON, O'KEEFE AND PHELAN (AV)

36 Russ Street, 06106-1571
Telephone: 860-278-4040
Fax: 860-527-2500
West Hartford, Connecticut Office: 62 LaSalle Road.
Telephone: 860-521-7500.
Fax: 860-561-5399.
Bethlehem, Connecticut Office: 423 Munger Lane. Telephone/ Fax: 203-266-5255.

MEMBERS OF FIRM

Jay W. Jackson	Michael E. Riley
Andrew J. O'Keefe	Peter K. O'Keefe
Denise Martino Phelan	Philip R. Dunn, Jr.
Matthew J. O'Keefe	Kathryn M. Cunningham
	Joseph M. Busher, Jr.

Representative Clients: Travelers Aetna Property Casualty Co.; ITT Hartford; Liberty Mutual Insurance Co.; Connecticut Medical Insurance Co.

For full biographical listings, see the Martindale-Hubbell Law Directory

O'BRIEN, TANSKI, TANZER & YOUNG (AV)

CityPlace II, 06103
Telephone: 860-525-2700
Telefax: 860-247-7861

MEMBERS OF FIRM

Donald W. O'Brien	Roland F. Young, III
James M. Tanski	Robert E. Kiley
Lois B. Tanzer	Thomas O. Anderson
	Nancy Phillips Maxwell

OF COUNSEL

Hilary Fisher Nelson	Donna R. Zito

ASSOCIATES

Caroline Schnog	P. Jo Anne Burgh
Robert D. Silva	Jennifer L. Cox
Albert G. Danker, Jr.	Tanya Feliciano

References: Shawmut National Bank; New England Bank.

For full biographical listings, see the Martindale-Hubbell Law Directory

REGNIER, TAYLOR, CURRAN & EDDY (AV)

CityPlace, 06103-4402
Telephone: 860-249-9121
FAX: 860-527-4343

MEMBERS OF FIRM

J. Ronald Regnier (1906-1987)	Ralph G. Eddy
Robert F. Taylor (1930-1994)	Jack D. Miller
Edmund T. Curran	Lawrence L. Connelli

ASSOCIATES

A. Patrick Alcarez	Frederick M. O'Brien
Robert B. McLaughlin	Keith Mccabe
A. Alan Sheffy	Beth D. Griffin
Robert A. Byers	Douglas E. Gilmore
Jay F. Huntington	Peter J. Casey
	Andrew W. Bray

Representative Clients: Atlantic Mutual Insurance Co.; Government Employees Insurance Co.; Hartford Accident & Indemnity Co.; Hartford Fire Insurance Co.; Pioneer Co-operative Fire; United Services Automobile Assn.; Vermont Mutual Insurance Co.

For full biographical listings, see the Martindale-Hubbell Law Directory

ROGIN, NASSAU, CAPLAN, LASSMAN & HIRTLE, LLC (AV)

CityPlace I, 22nd Floor, 185 Asylum Street, 06103-3460
Telephone: 860-278-7480
Fax: 860-278-2179

MEMBERS OF FIRM

Jerome E. Caplan	David J. Heinlein
Edwin A. Lassman	Lewis K. Wise
Robert L. Hirtle	Joan G. Engel
William R. Breetz	Mark A. Rosenblum
Steven D. Bartelstone	Barry S. Feigenbaum
David M. Call	Donald G. Gaudreau
Paul B. Zolan	Peter S. Sorokin
	Iris June Brown

ASSOCIATES

Jeffrey W. Stein	Brendan T. Flynn
Mark J. Lassman	Elizabeth R. Houde
Benjamin Engel	Jonathan M. Starble

OF COUNSEL

Arthur M. Nassau

RETIRED

Edward S. Rogin (Retired)	Louis E. Nassau (Retired)

For full biographical listings, see the Martindale-Hubbell Law Directory

Hartford—Continued

SOROKIN SOROKIN GROSS HYDE & WILLIAMS P.C. (AV)

One Corporate Center, 06103
Telephone: 860-525-6645
Fax: 860-522-1781
Simsbury, Connecticut Office: 730 Hopmeadow Street.
Telephone: 860-651-9348.
Rocky Hill, Connecticut Office: 2360 Main Street.
Telephone: 860-563-9305.
Fax: 860-529-6931.

John J. Bracken III	Jeffrey R. Martin
Clifford J. Grandjean	Lewis Rabinovitz
Lisa A. Magliochetti	Richard C. Robinson

Jeffery P. Apuzzo

For Complete List of Firm Personnel, See General Section

For full biographical listings, see the Martindale-Hubbell Law Directory

---

MILFORD, New Haven Co.

HURWITZ & SAGARIN, P.C. (AV)

147 North Broad Street, P.O. Box 112, 06460
Telephone: 203-877-8000
Fax: 203-878-9800

J. Daniel Sagarin	Elias A. Alexiades
David A. Slossberg	

For full biographical listings, see the Martindale-Hubbell Law Directory

---

NEW HAVEN, * New Haven Co.

WILLIAM H. CLENDENEN, JR. A PROFESSIONAL CORPORATION (AV)

400 Orange Street, P.O. Box 301, 06502-0301
Telephone: 203-787-1183
Fax: 203-787-2847

William H. Clendenen, Jr.

James E. Clifford	Nancy L. Walker
Thomas C. Pellegrino	

For full biographical listings, see the Martindale-Hubbell Law Directory

DEL SOLE & DEL SOLE (AV)

Suite 410, 900 Chapel Street, P.O. Box 405, 06502-0405
Telephone: 203-785-8500
Fax: 203-777-4485

MEMBERS OF FIRM

Dominic P. Del Sole	Michael P. Del Sole
Stephen P. Del Sole	Janine W. Hodgson
Denise Del Sole-Kennedy	

ASSOCIATES

Edward F. Piazza	Thomas P. Chapman
Laureen J. Vitale	Anthony J. Pantuso

For full biographical listings, see the Martindale-Hubbell Law Directory

JONATHAN J. EINHORN (AV)

412 Orange Street, 06511
Telephone: 203-777-3777
Telecopier: 203-782-1721

LEGAL SUPPORT PERSONNEL
PARALEGALS

Gina R. Sack	Gail A. Berg

For full biographical listings, see the Martindale-Hubbell Law Directory

GALLAGHER GALLAGHER & CALISTRO (AV)

1377 Boulevard, P.O. Box 1925, 06509
Telephone: 203-624-4165
Fax: 203-865-5598

William F. Gallagher	Cynthia C. Bott
Elizabeth A. Gallagher	Barbara L. Cox
Roger B. Calistro	Kurt D. Koehler
Thomas J. Airone	

Approved Attorneys For: Chicago Title Insurance Co.; Security Title and Guaranty Co.; American Title Insurance Co.; Connecticut Savings Bank; Dime Savings Bank of Wallingford; New Haven Savings Bank; Essex Savings Bank; Branford Savings Bank; First Federal Savings & Loan of Madison; First Constitution Bank.

For full biographical listings, see the Martindale-Hubbell Law Directory

GREENFIELD AND MURPHY (AV)

234 Church Street, P.O. Box 1103, 06504-1103
Telephone: 203-787-6711
Telecopier: 203-777-6442

MEMBERS OF FIRM

James R. Greenfield	Helen D. Murphy
Maureen M. Murphy	

Reference: First Fidelity Bank.

For full biographical listings, see the Martindale-Hubbell Law Directory

---

JACOBS, GRUDBERG, BELT & DOW, P.C. (AV)

350 Orange Street, P.O. Box 606, 06503
Telephone: 203-772-3100
Fax: 203-772-1691
Email: jacobslaw@jacobslaw.com *URL:* http://www.jacobslaw.com

Israel J. Jacobs (1918-1963)	Alice S. Miskimin
Howard A. Jacobs	Charles B. Price, Jr.
Ira B. Grudberg	F. Herbert Gruendel
David L. Belt	William M. Bloss
William F. Dow, III	Shirley V. Hoogstra
Jonathan Katz	Mark R. Soboslai
Susan H. Bartholomew	David T. Grudberg

Steven J. DeFrank	Alinor C. Sterling
David A. Leff	Phillip A. Escoriaza
Marybeth C. Gauthier	

For full biographical listings, see the Martindale-Hubbell Law Directory

---

JACOBS & JACOBS (AV)

700 State Street, 3rd Floor, 06511
Telephone: 203-777-2300
Fax: 203-787-5628

MEMBERS OF FIRM

Israel J. Jacobs (1918-1963)	Bruce D. Jacobs
Stanley A. Jacobs	Carol Wolven
Irene Prosky Jacobs	

Reference: Center Bank/First Union.

For full biographical listings, see the Martindale-Hubbell Law Directory

---

LYNCH, TRAUB, KEEFE AND ERRANTE, A PROFESSIONAL CORPORATION (AV)

52 Trumbull Street, P.O. Box 1612, 06506
Telephone: 203-787-0275
Fax: 203-782-0278
Email: ltke@snet.com *URL:* http://www.ltke.com

Stephen I. Traub	Donn A. Swift
Hugh F. Keefe	Charles E. Tiernan, III
Steven J. Errante	Robert W. Lynch
John J. Keefe, Jr.	Richard W. Lynch
John M. Walsh, Jr.	

Suzanne L. McAlpine	Lee Kennedy Tiernan
Christopher M. Licari	William F. Clark
Eric P. Smith	James A. Mongillo

OF COUNSEL
William C. Lynch

Local Counsel for: Transport Insurance Co., Dallas, Texas; American Trucking Associations; Roadway Express, Inc., Akron, Ohio; A.R.A. Philadelphia, Penn.; Consolidated Freightways, Menlo Park, California; Ogden Corp.; The Hauler Work.
Labor Counsel: Coca-Cola, U.S.A., Atlanta, Georgia (Private Truck Operation); The Dow Chemical Co.; Cincinnati Milacron.

For full biographical listings, see the Martindale-Hubbell Law Directory

---

ROSEN & DOLAN, P.C. (AV)

400 Orange Street, 06511
Telephone: 203-787-3513
Fax: 203-789-1605
Email: davidrosen@counsel.com
Email: spincus@counsel.com

David N. Rosen

Stephen M. Pincus

Reference: Peoples Bank.

For Complete List of Firm Personnel, See General Section

For full biographical listings, see the Martindale-Hubbell Law Directory

New Haven—Continued

PAUL A. SCHOLDER ATTORNEY AT LAW, P.C. (AV)

2 Whitney Avenue, P.O. Box 1722, 06507
Telephone: 203-777-7218
Fax: 203-772-2672
Email: PaulA.Scholder,P.C.102261.2673@CompuServe.com

Paul A. Scholder

John J. Morgan

References: Peoples Bank; Lafayette American Bank.

For full biographical listings, see the Martindale-Hubbell Law Directory

SHAY & SLOCUM (AV)

234 Church Street, P.O. Box 1921, 06509
Telephone: 203-772-3600
Fax: 203-787-4581

MEMBERS OF FIRM

Edward N. Shay   Shaun M. Slocum

Representative Clients: Hartford Accident and Indemnity Co.; United Services Automobile Association; Commercial Union Insurance Co.; Atlantic Mutual Insurance Co.; Northbrook Insurance Co.; Safeco Insurance Co.; Andover Insurance Co.; National Interstate Transportation Insurance Specialists; First Financial Insurance Co.; Burlington Insurance Group.

For full biographical listings, see the Martindale-Hubbell Law Directory

SUSMAN, DUFFY & SEGALOFF, P.C. (AV)

55 Whitney Avenue, 06510-1300
Telephone: 203-624-9830
Telecopier: 203-562-8430
Mailing Address: P.O. Box 1684, New Haven, Connecticut, 06507-1684

Allen H. Duffy (1931-1986)	Susan W. Wolfson
Michael Susman	Laura M. Sklaver
James H. Segaloff	Andrew R. Lubin
David A. Reif	James J. Perito
Joseph E. Faughnan	Matthew C. Susman
Thomas E. Katon	

Jennifer L. Schancupp	Peter G. Kruzynski
Donna Decker Morris	Joshua W. Cohen
Vincent J. Candelora	

OF COUNSEL

Diana C. Ballard   David P. Hambleton

For full biographical listings, see the Martindale-Hubbell Law Directory

WIGGIN & DANA (AV)

One Century Tower, 06508-1832
Telephone: 203-498-4400
Telefax: 203-782-2889
Hartford, Connecticut Office: One CityPlace.
Telephone: 203-297-3700.
FAX: 203-525-9380.
Stamford, Connecticut Office: Three Stamford Plaza, 301 Tresser Boulevard.
Telephone: 203-363-7600.
Telefax: 203-363-7676.

MEMBERS OF FIRM

William J. Doyle	Alan G. Schwartz
Shaun S. Sullivan	Penny Quinn Seaman
Jeremy G. Zimmermann	Patrick J. Monahan, II
William H. Prout, Jr.	(Resident at Hartford)
Mark R. Kravitz	Robert M. Langer
Edward Wood Dunham	(Resident at Hartford)
John F. Conway	

SENIOR COUNSEL

S. Robert Jelley

ASSOCIATES

Jeffrey R. Babbin	Kevin M. Kennedy
Penelope I. Bellamy	Daniel J. Klau
Ian E. Bjorkman	Richard F. Nace, Jr.
Joaquina L. Borges	Eric P. Neff
Thomas L. Casagrande	(Resident at Hartford)
Isabel E. Chenoweth	Susan M. Neilson
Patrick J. Corcoran	Phyllis M. Pari
Michelle Wilcox DeBarge	Bonnie Lynne Patten
Eleanor Stuart Devane	Charles P. Reed
Elise R. Epner	Thomas J. Witt
Lisa Page Heslin	(Resident at Hartford)
Marcella Ann Hourihane	
(Resident at Hartford)	

For Complete List of Firm Personnel, See General Section

For full biographical listings, see the Martindale-Hubbell Law Directory

LAW OFFICES OF JOHN R. WILLIAMS (AV)

51 Elm Street, 06510
Telephone: 203-562-9931
Fax: 203-776-9494

ASSOCIATES

Diane Polan	Norman A. Pattis
Katrena Engstrom	William S. Palmieri

References: Webster Bank; Bank of New Haven.

For full biographical listings, see the Martindale-Hubbell Law Directory

---

NEW LONDON, New London Co.

WALLER, SMITH & PALMER, P.C. (AV)

52 Eugene O'Neill Drive, P.O. Box 88, 06320
Telephone: 860-442-0367
Telecopier: 860-447-9915
Old Lyme, Connecticut Office: 103-A Halls Road.
Telephone: 860-434-8063.
Telecopier: 860-434-9452.

Edward B. O'Connell

Tracy M. Collins

General Counsel For: Town of East Lyme; Town of Lebanon.
Counsel For: Citizens Savings Bank; Sonoco/Northeastern, Inc.; The Nature Conservancy; Fleet Bank.
Local Counsel For: McCue Mortgage Co.; Citicorp Mortgage; U.S. Department of Housing and Urban Development.

For Complete List of Firm Personnel, See General Section

For full biographical listings, see the Martindale-Hubbell Law Directory

---

SOUTHPORT, Fairfield Co.

BRODY AND OBER, P.C. (AV)

135 Rennell Drive, P.O. Box 572, 06490-0572
Telephone: 203-259-7405
Fax: 203-255-8572

Charles S. Brody (1894-1976)	S. Giles Payne
Seth O. L. Brody	William J. Britt
Stanley B. Garrell	Barbara S. Miller
Frank F. Ober	Ronald B. Noren

Diane F. Martucci	Seth L. Cooper
Douglas R. Brown	

OF COUNSEL

James M. Thorburn   John F. Merchant

For full biographical listings, see the Martindale-Hubbell Law Directory

---

STAMFORD, Fairfield Co.

CACACE, TUSCH & SANTAGATA (AV)

777 Summer Street, P.O. Box 15859, 06901-0859
Telephone: 203-327-2000
Telecopier: 203-353-3392

MEMBERS OF FIRM

Michael J. Cacace	Mark P. Santagata
	Paul T. Tusch

ASSOCIATES

Edward F. Nemchek	Ronald E. Kowalski, II
Alice Ann Fitzpatrick	Pierrette A. Newman
Russell A. Green	

For full biographical listings, see the Martindale-Hubbell Law Directory

PIAZZA & MELMED (AV)

112 Prospect Street, P.O. Box 15390, 06901
Telephone: 203-348-2465
Fax: 203-964-9509

MEMBERS OF FIRM

Anthony A. Piazza   Julian K. Melmed

Alan Scott Pickel	Angela M. Trombly
Tara C. F. Ryan	

For full biographical listings, see the Martindale-Hubbell Law Directory

ROSENBLUM & FILAN (AV ⓣ)

One Landmark Square, 06901
Telephone: 203-358-9200
Fax: 203-969-6140
Email: JBR@counsel.com
White Plains, New York Office: 50 Main Street. 10606.
Telephone: 914-686-6100.
Fax: 914-686-6140.

(See Next Column)

ROSENBLUM & FILAN, *Stamford—Continued*

New York, New York Office: 400 Madison Avenue. 10017.
Telephone: 212-888-8001.
Fax: 212-888-3331.

MEMBERS OF FIRM

Patrick J. Filan   James B. Rosenblum

James S. Newfield
Michelle L. Youtz
Brian M. Rosen

Theodore J. Greene
Christina M. Casagrande
JoAnn Provetto

For full biographical listings, see the Martindale-Hubbell Law Directory

RYAN, RYAN, JOHNSON, MCCAGHEY & DELUCA, LLP (AV)

80 Fourth Street, P.O. Box 3057, 06905
Telephone: 203-357-9200
FAX: 203-357-7915
Email: cdelucoo@counsel.com
New York, New York Office: Park Avenue Atrium, 237 Park Avenue.
Telephone: 212-949-0722.

MEMBERS OF FIRM

Daniel E. Ryan, Jr.
W. Patrick Ryan
J. Paul Johnson
Charles A. Deluca
Daniel E. Ryan, III

Michael T. Ryan
Charles M. McCaghey
John W. Mullin
Elizabeth W. Carter
Holly K. Dustin

ASSOCIATES

Beverly J. Hunt
Richard P. Colbert
John F. Leydon, Jr.
Barbara J. Pulaski
Thomas J. O'Neill

Robert C.E. Laney
Catherine S. Nietzel
Darren P. Renner
Kieran M. Ryan
Joseph P. Sargent

For full biographical listings, see the Martindale-Hubbell Law Directory

SILVER, GOLUB & TEITELL (AV)

184 Atlantic Street, P.O. Box 389, 06904
Telephone: 203-325-4491
Fax: 203-325-3769

MEMBERS OF FIRM

Richard A. Silver
David S. Golub
Ernest F. Teitell

Patricia M. Haugh (1942-1988)
Elaine T. Silver
John D. Josel

Mario DiNatale
Jonathan M. Levine
Marilyn J. Ramos

Jonathan L. Mannina
Jennifer Cohen Goldstein
J. Michael Lewis

For full biographical listings, see the Martindale-Hubbell Law Directory

WOFSEY, ROSEN, KWESKIN & KURIANSKY (AV)

600 Summer Street, 06901
Telephone: 203-327-2300
Fax: 203-967-9273

MEMBERS OF FIRM

Abraham Wofsey (1915-1944)
Michael Wofsey (1927-1951)
David M. Rosen (1926-1967)
Julius B. Kuriansky (1910-1992)
Monroe Silverman
Emanuel Margolis
Howard C. Kaplan
Anthony R. Lorenzo

Edward M. Kweskin
David M. Cohen
Marshall Goldberg
Stephen A. Finn
Judith Rosenberg
Mark H. Henderson
Steven D. Grushkin
Matthew J. Forstadt

OF COUNSEL

Saul Kwartin   Sydney C. Kweskin (Retired)

ASSOCIATES

Joseph Brachfeld
John J.L. Chobor
Steven M. Frederick
Joy A. Katz
Galit Kierkut

Eric M. Higgins
Valerie E. Maze
Randall M. Skigen
Peter J. Schaffer
Robert W. Finke

Representative Clients: Banque Paribas; Benenson Realty; Cellular Information Systems, Inc.; The Chase Manhattan Bank; First County Bank; Hartford Provision Co.; Louis Dreyfus Corp.; Norwalk Federation of Teachers; People's Bank; Ridgeway Shopping Center.

For full biographical listings, see the Martindale-Hubbell Law Directory

VERNON,* Tolland Co.

FLAHERTY, MEISLER & COURTNEY (AV)

30 Lafayette Square, P.O. Box 508, 06066
Telephone: 860-872-7200
Fax: 860-875-6594
Email: FMACATTY@aol.com

(See Next Column)

MEMBERS OF FIRM

Leo B. Flaherty Jr.
Joseph D. Courtney

Arthur P. Meisler

ASSOCIATE

Elizabeth C. Foran

Reference: Savings Bank of Rockville.

For full biographical listings, see the Martindale-Hubbell Law Directory

WALLINGFORD, New Haven Co.

DELANEY, ZEMETIS, DONAHUE, DURHAM & NOONAN, P.C. (AV)

111 South Main Street, P.O. Box 747, 06492
Telephone: 203-269-1441
Fax: 203-284-9428

Joseph M. Delaney
Terence A. Zemetis

Timothy W. Donahue
Michael G. Durham

Patrick M. Noonan

Edward W. Mayer, Jr.
Thomas J. Flanagan

Edward T. Falsey, III
Mark Popolizio

For full biographical listings, see the Martindale-Hubbell Law Directory

FARRELL & LESLIE (AV)

375 Center Street, P.O. Box 369, 06492
Telephone: 203-269-7756
Fax: 203-269-1927

MEMBERS OF FIRM

Gerald E. Farrell
Gerald E. Farrell, Jr.

Ann Farrell Leslie
Brian J. Leslie

References: Dime Savings Bank of Wallingford; Shawmut Bank (Wallingford Office).

For full biographical listings, see the Martindale-Hubbell Law Directory

WATERBURY, New Haven Co.

TINLEY, NASTRI, RENEHAN & DOST (AV)

161 North Main Street, 06702
Telephone: 203-596-9030
Fax: 203-596-9036

Jeffrey J. Tinley
Robert Nastri, Jr.

Richard P. Renehan
Mark W. Dost

William T. Blake, Jr.

ASSOCIATE

Barbara W. Reynolds

Representative Clients: Center Capital Corp.; Gar-San Corp.; General Electric Capital Commercial Automotive Finance, Inc.; Mobil Oil Corp.; Teikyo Post University; The May Department Stores Company; Watertown Construction Company, Inc.

For full biographical listings, see the Martindale-Hubbell Law Directory

WESTPORT, Fairfield Co.

LESLIE BYELAS (AV)

1804 Post Road East, 06880
Telephone: 203-259-0599
Fax: 203-255-2570

For full biographical listings, see the Martindale-Hubbell Law Directory

STUART A. MCKEEVER (AV)

155 Post Road, East, 06880
Telephone: 203-227-4756
Fax: 203-454-2031

Reference: Fleet Bank.

For full biographical listings, see the Martindale-Hubbell Law Directory

LAW OFFICES OF PAUL J. PACIFICO (AV)

25 Ford Road, Suite 2, 06880
Telephone: 203-221-8066
Fax: 203-222-4833

For full biographical listings, see the Martindale-Hubbell Law Directory

SHRADER AND KNAPP, A PROFESSIONAL CORPORATION (AV)

25 Ford Road, 06880
Telephone: 203-227-6628
Fax: 203-227-6922

(See Next Column)

SHRADER AND KNAPP A PROFESSIONAL CORPORATION—*Continued*

L. Douglas Shrader   Beverly Stauffer Knapp

For full biographical listings, see the Martindale-Hubbell Law Directory

WEISMAN & LUBELL (AV)

5 Sylvan Road South, P.O. Box 3184, 06880
Telephone: 203-226-8307
Telecopier: 203-221-7279

MEMBERS OF FIRM

Lawrence P. Weisman   Ellen B. Lubell

Debra B. Wolfert-Marino

For full biographical listings, see the Martindale-Hubbell Law Directory

DELAWARE

DOVER, * Kent Co.

PARKOWSKI, NOBLE & GUERKE, PROFESSIONAL ASSOCIATION (AV)

116 West Water Street, P.O. Box 598, 19903
Telephone: 302-678-3262
Telecopier: 302-678-9415

F. Michael Parkowski	Jeremy W. Homer
John W. Noble	John C. Andrade
I. Barry Guerke	Jonathan Eisenberg
Clay T. Jester	Dana J. Schaefer

Mark F. Dunkle

OF COUNSEL

George F. Gardner, III

Representative Clients: Delaware Solid Waste Authority; Cabe Associates (Consulting Engineers).
Approved Attorneys for: Ticor Title Insurance Co.
Reference: First National Bank of Wyoming.

For full biographical listings, see the Martindale-Hubbell Law Directory

WILMINGTON, * New Castle Co.

ASHBY & GEDDES (AV)

One Rodney Square, P.O. Box 1150, 19899
Telephone: 302-654-1888
Fax: 302-654-2067

MEMBERS OF FIRM

Lawrence C. Ashby	Randall E. Robbins
James McC. Geddes	Steven J. Balick
Stephen E. Jenkins	Regina A. Iorii

William P. Bowden

ASSOCIATES

Richard D. Heins	Steven T. Margolin
Philip Trainer, Jr.	Christopher S. Sontchi
Amy Arnott Quinlan	John S. Grimm

For full biographical listings, see the Martindale-Hubbell Law Directory

BIGGS AND BATTAGLIA (AV)

1800 Mellon Bank Center, P.O. Box 1489, 19899-1489
Telephone: 302-655-9677

MEMBERS OF FIRM

Victor F. Battaglia	Jeffrey S. Marlin
Alan W. Behringer	Charles Slanina
Francis S. Babiarz	Philip B. Bartoshesky
Robert D. Goldberg	Victor F. Battaglia, Jr.
Robert K. Beste, Jr.	Christopher J. Battaglia

Linda F. Shopland

OF COUNSEL

John Biggs, III	Gerard P. Kavanaugh, Sr.

S. Bernard Ableman

For full biographical listings, see the Martindale-Hubbell Law Directory

CASARINO, CHRISTMAN & SHALK (AV)

Suite 1220, 222 Delaware Avenue, P.O. Box 1276, 19899
Telephone: 302-594-4500
Telecopier: 302-594-4509

MEMBERS OF FIRM

Stephen P. Casarino	Beth H. Christman
Colin M. Shalk	Donald M. Ransom

Patricia L. Peterson

(See Next Column)

Kenneth M. Doss	Diane M. Willette
Patricia Bartley Schwartz	Stacey L. Cummings

For full biographical listings, see the Martindale-Hubbell Law Directory

KIMMEL, CARTER & ROMAN, P.A. (AV)

12th Floor, 913 Market Street, P.O. Box 272, 19899-0272
Telephone: 302-571-0800

Morton Richard Kimmel	Edward B. Carter, Jr.

Thomas J. Roman

William R. Peltz	Michael D. Bednash

Matthew M. Bartkowski

References: Wilmington Trust Co.; Delaware Trust Co.

For full biographical listings, see the Martindale-Hubbell Law Directory

MORRIS, JAMES, HITCHENS & WILLIAMS (AV)

222 Delaware Avenue, P.O. Box 2306, 19899-2306
Telephone: 302-888-6800
Telecopier: 302-571-1750
URL: http://www.morrisjames.com
Dover, Delaware Office: Suite 202, 32 West Loockerman Street, 19904.
Telephone: 302-678-8815.
Telecopier: 302-678-9063.

MEMBERS OF FIRM

Henry N. Herndon, Jr.	Richard Galperin
George C. Hering, III	Steven R. Director
Grover C. Brown	Richard D. Kirk
Arden B. Engebretsen	Lewis H. Lazarus
William R. Hitchens, Jr.	Michael M. Ledyard
Richard P. Beck	Francis J. Jones, Jr.
Glenn E. Hitchens	Daniel P. McCollom
(Resident at Dover)	Barbara MacDonald
Edward M. McNally	Kent A. Jordan
Norris P. Wright	Robert L. Symonds, Jr.
James W. Semple	John D. Demmy
David H. Williams	Mary M. Culley
P. Clarkson Collins, Jr.	Joseph R. Slights, III

ASSOCIATES

Sherry C. McReynolds	Joseph C. Schoell
Michael J. Maimone	Eric D. Schwartz
(Not admitted in DE)	John T. Meli, Jr.
Neal C. Belgam	Matthew J. O'Toole
Norman M. Powell	Paul P. Rooney
Eileen K. Andersen	Michael A. Weidinger
Gretchen S. Knight	Mary L. Sutherland
Peter A. Pietra	(Resident at Dover)
Lewis C. Ledyard, III	Nancy Shane Rappaport

OF COUNSEL

Howard L. Williams	William F. Lynch, II

Alfred M. Isaacs

For full biographical listings, see the Martindale-Hubbell Law Directory

PHILLIPS, GOLDMAN & SPENCE, P.A. (AV)

1200 North Broom Street, 19806
Telephone: 302-655-4200
Telecopier: 302-655-4210

John C. Phillips, Jr.	Robert S. Goldman

Stephen W. Spence

Robert F. Phillips	Steven K. Kortanek
Lisa Cresci McLaughlin	James P. Hall

For full biographical listings, see the Martindale-Hubbell Law Directory

POTTER ANDERSON & CORROON (AV)

350 Delaware Trust Building, P.O. Box 951, 19899-0951
Telephone: 302-984-6000
FAX: 302-658-1192
URL: HTTP://ATTYS.PACDELAWARE.COM

MEMBERS OF FIRM

Charles S. Crompton, Jr.	David J. Baldwin
Robert K. Payson	John E. James
Richard E. Poole	W. Harding Drane, Jr.
Michael D. Goldman	Richard L. Horwitz
James F. Burnett	William J. Marsden, Jr.
Daniel F. Wolcott, Jr.	Kathleen Furey McDonough
David B. Brown	Laurie Selber Silverstein
Somers S. Price, Jr.	Peter J. Walsh
Donald J. Wolfe, Jr.	Stephen C. Norman
Gregory A. Inskip	Arthur L. Dent

William R. Denny

COUNSEL

David L. Baumberger

(See Next Column)

POTTER ANDERSON & CORROON, *Wilmington—Continued*

ASSOCIATES

Peter L. Tracey	Joanne Ceballos
Jennifer Gimler Brady	Wendy K. Voss

Representative Clients: Monsanto Company; Philips North America Corporation; KAO Corporation; Delmarva Power & Light Company; General Motors Corporation; Chrysler Corporation; Delaware Trust Capital Management, Inc.; University of Delaware; Conrail; Hercules, Incorporated.

For Complete List of Firm Personnel, See General Section

For full biographical listings, see the Martindale-Hubbell Law Directory

SMITH, KATZENSTEIN & FURLOW (AV)

The Corporate Plaza, 800 Delaware Avenue, P.O. Box 410, 19899
Telephone: 302-652-8400
Fax: 302-652-8405

MEMBERS OF FIRM

Craig B. Smith	Susan L. Parker
Robert J. Katzenstein	Laurence V. Cronin
David A. Jenkins	Brett D. Fallon
Anne E. Bookout	Stephen M. Miller

Joanne M. Shalk	Kathleen M. Miller

COUNSEL
Charles E. Butler
OF COUNSEL
Clark W. Furlow

For full biographical listings, see the Martindale-Hubbell Law Directory

THEISEN, LANK, MULFORD & GOLDBERG, P.A. (AV)

Ninth Floor, One Commerce Center, P.O. Box 1470, 19899
Telephone: 302-656-7712
Fax: 302-655-0923
Email: Theisen@delcorp.com *URL:* http://www.delcorp.theisen.com

Aubrey B. Lank	Steven D. Goldberg
John G. Mulford	Michael J. Goodrick
	David S. Lank

Richard L. Abbott
OF COUNSEL
Vincent A. Theisen (Retired)

References: Wilmington Trust Co.; PNC Bank.

For full biographical listings, see the Martindale-Hubbell Law Directory

TRZUSKOWSKI, KIPP, KELLEHER & PEARCE, P.A. (AV)

1020 North Bancroft Parkway, P.O. Box 429, 19899-0429
Telephone: 302-571-1782
Fax: 302-571-1638

Francis J. Trzuskowski	Robert K. Pearce
James F. Kipp	Edward F. Kafader
Daniel F. Kelleher	Francis J. Schanne

For full biographical listings, see the Martindale-Hubbell Law Directory

DISTRICT OF COLUMBIA

WASHINGTON, D.C. Co.

* indicates certain Bar Register subscribers, in cities of comparable size and importance, who maintain an additional office in Washington, D.C. and who have arranged for representation as a part of the Washington, D.C. listings that follow

ALLEN, JOHNSON, ALEXANDER & KARP, P.A. (AV)

1707 L Street, N.W., Suite 1050, 20036
Telephone: 202-828-4141
Fax: 202-429-8798
Baltimore, Maryland Office: Suite 1540, 100 East Pratt Street.
Telephone: 410-727-5000.

D'Ana E. Johnson

Representative Clients: Scottsdale Insurance Co.; Nautilus Insurance Co.; Jefferson Insurance Co.; Liberty Mutual Insurance Co.; Avis Rent-A-Car; Otis Elevator Co.; Montgomery Elevator Co.; Admiral Insurance Co.; Local Government Insurance Trust; Lancer Insurance Co.

For Complete List of Firm Personnel, See General Section

For full biographical listings, see the Martindale-Hubbell Law Directory

* ANDERSON KILL & OLICK, L.L.P. (AV)

2000 Pennsylvania Avenue, N.W. Suite 7500, 20006
Telephone: 202-728-3100
Telecopier: 202-728-3199
Email: akodc@andersonkill.com *URL:* http://www.andersonkill.com
New York, N.Y. Office: Anderson Kill & Olick, P.C., 1251 Avenue of the Americas.
Telephone: 212-278-1000.
Fax: 212-278-1733 and 212-953-7249.
Philadelphia, Pennsylvania Office: Anderson Kill & Olick, P.C., 1600 Market Street.
Telephone: 215-568-4202.
Fax: 215-568-4573.
Newark, New Jersey Office: Anderson Kill & Olick. One Gateway Center, Suite 901.
Telephone: 201-642-5858.
Fax: 201-621-6361.
San Francisco, California Office: Anderson Kill & Olick. One Sansome Street, Suite 1610.
Telephone: 415-677-1450.
Fax: 415-677-1475.
Phoenix, Arizona Office: Anderson Kill & Olick. One Renaissance Square, Two North Central, Suite 1910.
Telephone: 602-252-0002.
Fax: 602-252-0003.
Tucson, Arizona Office: Anderson Kill & Olick. Bank of America Plaza, 33 North Stone Avenue, Suite 1825.
Telephone: 520-822-8299.
Fax: 520-882-9299.

Rhonda D. Orin	Lorelie S. Masters

For Complete List of Firm Personnel, See General Section

For full biographical listings, see the Martindale-Hubbell Law Directory

ASBILL, JUNKIN & MOFFITT, CHTD. (AV)

1615 New Hampshire Avenue, N.W., 20009
Telephone: 202-234-9000
Facsimile: 202-332-6480

Henry W. Asbill	William B. Moffitt
Timothy deForest Junkin	(Not admitted in DC)

OF COUNSEL

Oscar I. Dodek, Jr.	Matthew L. Myers

For full biographical listings, see the Martindale-Hubbell Law Directory

* BAKER & BOTTS, L.L.P. (AV)

A Registered Limited Liability Partnership
The Warner, 1299 Pennsylvania Avenue, N.W., 20004-2400
Telephone: 202-639-7700
Fax: 202-639-7832
Email: postmaster@bakerbotts.com
Houston, Texas Office: One Shell Plaza, 910 Louisiana.
Telephone: 713-229-1234.
Austin, Texas Office: 1600 San Jacinto Center, 98 San Jacinto Boulevard.
Telephone: 512-322-2500.
Dallas, Texas Office: 2001 Ross Avenue.
Telephone: 214-953-6500.
New York, New York Office: 599 Lexington Avenue.
Telephone: 212-705-5000.
Moscow, Russian Federation Office: 10 ul. Bolshaya Dmitrovka (formerly Pushkinskaya), 103031.
Telephone: 7095/921-5300 (Local); 7501/929-7070 (International).

MEMBERS OF FIRM

Charles M. Darling, IV	Bruce F. Kiely
Thomas J. Eastment	Randolph Quaile McManus
Steven R. Hunsicker	Kirk K. Van Tine

ASSOCIATES

Wendy L. Cox	Mark K. Lewis
Kelly Riley Donovan	Martin Schaefermeier
Jennifer S. Leete	David A. Super

For Complete List of Firm Personnel, See General Section

For full biographical listings, see the Martindale-Hubbell Law Directory

BAKER & HOSTETLER (AV)

Washington Square, Suite 1100, 1050 Connecticut Avenue, N.W., 20036-5304
Telephone: 202-861-1500
In Cleveland, Ohio: 3200 National City Center, 1900 East Ninth Street.
Telephone: 216-621-0200.
In Columbus, Ohio: Capitol Square, Suite 2100, 65 East State Street.
Telephone: 614-228-1541.
In Denver, Colorado: 303 East 17th Avenue, Suite 1100.
Telephone: 303-861-0600.
In Houston, Texas: 1000 Louisiana, Suite 2000.
Telephone: 713-751-1600.
In Long Beach, California: 300 Oceangate, Suite 620.
Telephone: 310-432-2827.

(See Next Column)

BAKER & HOSTETLER—*Continued*

In Los Angeles, California: 600 Wilshire Boulevard.
Telephone: 213-624-2400.
In Orlando, Florida: SunBank Center, Suite 2300, 200 South Orange Avenue.
Telephone: 305-841-1111.
In College Park, Maryland: 9658 Baltimore Boulevard, Suite 206.
Telephone: 301-441-2781.
In Alexandria, Virginia: 437 North Lee Street.
Telephone: 703-549-1294.
In San Francisco, California: One Sansome Street, Suite 2000.
Telephone: 415-951-4705.

MEMBER OF FIRM IN WASHINGTON, D.C.

William H. Schweitzer (Managing Partner, Washington, D.C. Office)

PARTNERS

Ralph G. Blasey, III
Frederick W. Chockley, III
Mark A. Cymrot
Lee T. Ellis, Jr.
Leonard C. Greenebaum
Thomas Hylden
Richard J. Leon
Bruce W. Sanford

Belinda Jayne Scrimenti

ASSOCIATES

Margaret E. Goss
Robert D. Lystad
Kent W. McAllister
(Not admitted in DC)

For Complete List of Firm Personnel, See General Section

For full biographical listings, see the Martindale-Hubbell Law Directory

BAUM, HEDLUND, ARISTEI, GUILFORD & DOWNEY A PROFESSIONAL CORPORATION (AV)

1250 24th Street, N.W., Suite 300, 20037
Telephone: 202-466-0513; 800-827-0097
Fax: 202-466-0527
Email: bhagd@bhagd.com *URL:* http://www.bhagd.com/attorneys/
Los Angeles, California Office: Suite 950, 12100 Wilshire Boulevard.
Telephones: 310-207-3233; 800-827-0087.
Facsimile: 310-820-7444.

Cara L. Belle

For full biographical listings, see the Martindale-Hubbell Law Directory

* BELL, BOYD & LLOYD (AV)

1615 L Street, N.W., 20036
Telephone: 202-466-6300
FAX: 202-463-0678
Chicago, Illinois Office: Three First National Plaza, Suite 3300, 70 West Madison Street.
Telephone: 312-372-1121.
FAX: 312-372-2098.

RESIDENT PARTNERS

Raymond C. Fay
Thomas R. Gibbon
Charles A. Zielinski
(Not admitted in DC)

For Complete List of Firm Personnel, See General Section

For full biographical listings, see the Martindale-Hubbell Law Directory

BOOTHBY & YINGST (AV)

4545 42nd Street, N.W., 20016
Telephone: 202-363-1773
Fax: 202-363-0304
Berrien Springs, Michigan Office: 9047-4 US 31 North. P.O. Box 268.
Telephone: 616-471-7787.
Fax: 616-471-7400.

MEMBERS OF FIRM

Lee Boothby
Robert A. Yingst
(Not admitted in DC)

For full biographical listings, see the Martindale-Hubbell Law Directory

BRAUDE & MARGULIES, P.C. (AV)

The Brawner Building, 888 Seventeenth Street, N.W., Suite 500, 20006
Telephone: 202-293-2993
Fax: 202-331-7916
Email: Braudemarg@aol.com
Riyadh, Saudi Arabia Office: Mohammed A. Al-Abdullah, P.O. Box 59446, Nuzha Building, Sixth Floor, 11525.
Telephone: 966-1-405-1291.
Fax: 966-1-405-1291.
Abu Dhabi, United Arab Emirates Office: P.O. Box 43908.
Telephone: (971-2) 787222.
Fax: (971-2) 784001.

Herman M. Braude

(See Next Column)

Samuel M. Morrison, Jr.
Robert D. Windus
John P. McGowan, Jr. (Not admitted in DC; Resident, Abu Dhabi, U.A.E. Office)
Conrad Christopher Ledoux
Stuart H. Sakwa
(Not admitted in DC)
James D. Finn, Jr.

OF COUNSEL

J. Richard Margulies

For full biographical listings, see the Martindale-Hubbell Law Directory

CAPLIN & DRYSDALE, CHARTERED (AV)

One Thomas Circle, N.W., 20005
Telephone: 202-862-5000
Cable Address: "Capdale"
Telex: 904001 CAPL UR WSH
Fax: 202-429-3301
New York, N.Y. Office: 399 Park Avenue.
Telephone: 212-319-7125.
Fax: 212-644-6755.

Mortimer M. Caplin
Robert A. Klayman
Ralph A. Muoio
Elihu Inselbuch
(Resident, New York Office)
Ronald B. Lewis
Richard W. Skillman
Patricia G. Lewis
Bernard S. Bailor
Stafford Smiley
Sally A. Regal
Julie W. Davis
Carl S. Kravitz
Robert A. Boisture
James Sottile, IV
Harry J. Hicks, III
Milton Cerny
Paul G. Cellupica
Michael T. Doran
Nathan D. Finch
Jessica L. Goldstein
Laura J. Kerrigan
Douglas D. Drysdale
Thomas A. Troyer
David N. Webster
H. David Rosenbloom
Peter Van N. Lockwood
Cono R. Namorato
Daniel B. Rosenbaum
Richard E. Timbie
Graeme W. Bush
Albert G. Lauber, Jr.
Scott D. Michel
Kent A. Mason
Trevor W. Swett III
Robert E. Culbertson
Charles T. Plambeck
James E. Salles
Craig A. Sharon
Matthew W. Frank
Christian R. Pastore
(Not admitted in DC)
Elizabeth M. Sellers
Douglas N. Varley
(Not admitted in DC)

OF COUNSEL

Robert H. Elliott, Jr.
Vivian L. Cavalieri
Ann C. McMillan
Myron C. Baum
C. Sanders McNew
(Resident, New York Office)

Janne G. Gallagher

For full biographical listings, see the Martindale-Hubbell Law Directory

COALE & VAN SUSTEREN, A PROFESSIONAL CORPORATION (AV)

Chevy Chase Pavilion, 5335 Wisconsin Avenue N.W., Suite 720, 20015
Telephone: 202-686-6500
Facsimile: 202-686-9739

John P. Coale (A Professional Corporation)
Greta C. Van Susteren
(Currently on leave)

Diane E. Cooley
David K. Lietz
Julia Wernett McInerny
Charlsa (Sandy) Broadus

For full biographical listings, see the Martindale-Hubbell Law Directory

COHEN & LEGON, P.C. (AV)

(Formerly Mark A. Cohen & Associates, P.C.)
1501 M Street, N.W. Suite 1150, 20005-1702
Telephone: 202-835-3800
Fax: 202-331-9253
Email: macassoc@markcohen.com *URL:*
http://www.markcohen.com/~macassoc
Miami, Florida Office: Cohen & Legon, P.A., 1221 Brickell Avenue, Suite 1780, 33131.
Telephone: 305-375-9292.
Facsimile: 305-381-6799.

Mark A. Cohen
Todd R. Legon
(Not admitted in DC)
David J. Federbush

OF COUNSEL

Stephen M. Koslow

Fred Goldberg
(Not admitted in DC)
Neil L. Potash
(Not admitted in DC)
Darin S. Engelhardt
(Not admitted in DC)
Karen G. Morton
(Not admitted in DC)

(See Next Column)

COHEN & LEGON P.C., *Washington—Continued*

Andrea M. Wong	David M. Knasel
Janet B. Salzman	(Not admitted in DC)
(Not admitted in DC)	William H. White, Jr.
Michael J. Prame	(Not admitted in DC)
Henrietta "Locky" Bright	Marc J. Leipzig
(Not admitted in DC)	(Not admitted in DC)
Kevin B. Bedell	Kenyetta R. Coner
Scott M. Behren	(Not admitted in DC)
(Not admitted in DC)	

For full biographical listings, see the Martindale-Hubbell Law Directory

DECKELBAUM OGENS & FISCHER, CHARTERED (AV)

1140 Connecticut Avenue, N.W., 20036
Telephone: 202-223-1474
Fax: 202-293-1471
Bethesda, Maryland Office: 6701 Democracy Boulevard.
Telephone: 301-564-5100.

Nelson Deckelbaum	Deborah E. Reiser
Ronald L. Ogens	Charles A. Moster
Lawrence H. Fischer	Andrew J. Shedlock, III

Ronald G. Scheraga	Phyllis Lea Bean
Bryn Hope Sherman	Darryl Alan Feldman
Thomas Peter Mann	(Not admitted in DC)
(Not admitted in DC)	

Representative Clients: The Charles E. Smith Companies; The Trammell Crow Co.
References: Franklin National Bank; Century National Bank.

For full biographical listings, see the Martindale-Hubbell Law Directory

THE FALK LAW FIRM (AV)

A Professional Limited Company
Suite 260 One Westin Center, 2445 M Street, N.W., 20037
Telephone: 202-833-8700
Telecopier: 202-872-1725
Email: FalkLaw@erols.com

James H. Falk, Sr.	John M. Falk
James H. Falk, Jr.	Robert K. Tompkins

OF COUNSEL

Pierre E. Murphy	Elizabeth C. Collins

For full biographical listings, see the Martindale-Hubbell Law Directory

KENNETH R. FEINBERG & ASSOCIATES (AV)

1120 20th Street, N.W. Suite 740 South, 20036
Telephone: 202-371-1110
Fax: 202-962-9290
New York, N.Y. Office: 780 3rd Avenue, Suite 2202.
Telephone: 212-527-9600.
Fax: 212-527-9611.

ASSOCIATES

Deborah E. Greenspan	Peter H. Woodin
Michael K. Rozen	(Not admitted in DC)
(Not admitted in DC)	M. Catherine Faint

OF COUNSEL
Jacqueline E. Zins

For full biographical listings, see the Martindale-Hubbell Law Directory

IFSHIN & FRIEDMAN, P.L.L.C. (AV)

888 16th Street N.W., Suite 400, 20006
Telephone: 202-293-4175
Fax: 202-296-8791

MEMBERS OF FIRM

David M. Ifshin (1948-1996)	Philip S. Friedman

For full biographical listings, see the Martindale-Hubbell Law Directory

* JONES, DAY, REAVIS & POGUE (AV)

Metropolitan Square, 1450 G Street, N.W., 20005-2088
Telephone: 202-879-3939
Cable Address: "Attorneys Washington"
Telex: W.U. (Domestic) 89-2410 ATTORNEYS WASH (International)
64363 ATTORNEYS WASH
Telecopier: 202-737-2832
In Atlanta, Georgia: 3500 One Peachtree Center, 303 Peachtree Street, N.E
.
Telephone: 404-521-3939.
Cable Address: "Attorneys Atlanta".
Telex: 54-2711.
Telecopier: 404-581-8330.
In Brussels, Belgium: Avenue Louise 480, 7th Floor, B-1050 Brussels.
Telephone: 32-2-645-14-11.
Telecopier: 32-2-645-14-45.

(See Next Column)

In Chicago, Illinois: 77 West Wacker.
Telephone: 312-782-3939.
Telecopier: 312-782-8585.
In Cleveland, Ohio: North Point, 901 Lakeside Avenue.
Telephone: 216-586-3939.
Cable Address: "Attorneys Cleveland."
Telex: 980389.
Telecopier: 216-579-0212.
In Columbus, Ohio: 1900 Huntington Center.
Telephone: 614-469-3939.
Cable Address: "Attorneys Columbus."
Telecopier: 614-461-4198.
In Dallas, Texas: 2300 Trammell Crow Center, 2001 Ross Avenue.
Telephone: 214-220-3939.
Cable Address: "Attorneys Dallas."
Telex: 730852.
Telecopier: 214-969-5100.
In Frankfurt, Germany: Triton Haus, Bockenheimer Landstrasse 42, 60323 Frankfurt am Main.
Telephone: 49-69-9726-3939.
Telecopier: 49-69-9726-3993.
In Geneva, Switzerland: 20, rue de Candolle.
Telephone: 41-22-320-2339.
Telecopier: 41-22-320-1232.
In Hong Kong: 29th Floor, Entertainment Building, 30 Queen's Road Central.
Telephone: 852-2526-6895.
Telecopier: 852-2868-5871.
In Irvine, California: 2603 Main Street, Suite 900 .
Telephone: 714-851-3939.
Telex: 194911 Lawyers LSA.
Telecopier: 714-553-7539.
In London, England: One Mount Street.
Telephone: 44-71-493-9361.
Cable Address: "Surgoe London WI."
Telecopier: 44-71-493-9666.
In Los Angeles, California: 555 West Fifth Street, Suite 4600.
Telephone: 213-489-3939.
Telex: 181439 UD.
Telecopier: 213-243-2539.
In New Delhi, India: Pathak & Associates, 13th Floor, Dr. Gopal Das Bhaven, 28 Barakhamba Road.
Telephone: 91-11-373-8793.
Telecopier: 91-11-335-3761.
In New York, New York: 599 Lexington Avenue.
Telephone: 212-326-3939.
Cable Address: "JONESDAY NEWYORK."
Telex: 237013 JDRP UR.
Telecopier: 212-755-7306.
In Paris, France: 62, rue du Faubourg Saint-Honore.
Telephone: 33-1-44-71-3939.
Cable Address: "Surgoe Paris."
Telex: 290156 Surgoe.
Telecopier: 33-1-49-24-0471.
In Pittsburgh, Pennsylvania: 500 Grant Street, 31st Floor.
Telephone: 412-391-3939.
Cable Address: "Attorneys Pittsburgh".
Telecopier: 412-394-7959.
In Riyadh, Saudi Arabia: Law Offices of Saud M.A. Shawwaf, P.O. Box 22166.
Telephone: (966-1) 462-8866.
Telex: 401831 SAUCON SJ.
Telecopier: (966-1) 462-9001.
In Taipai, Taiwan: 8th Floor, 2 Tun Hwa South Road, Section 2.
Telephone: (886-2) 704-6808.
Telecopier: (886-2) 704-6791.
In Tokyo, Japan: Toranomon MT Building, 4th Floor, 10-3, Toranomon 3-Chome, Minato-Ku, Tokyo 105, Japan.
Telephone: 81-3-3433-3939.
Telecopier: 81-3-5401-2725.

MEMBERS OF FIRM IN WASHINGTON, D.C.

Timothy B. Dyk	Thomas F. Cullen, Jr.
	Stephen J. Brogan

For Complete List of Firm Personnel, See General Section

For full biographical listings, see the Martindale-Hubbell Law Directory

KING, PAGANO & HARRISON (AV)

901 Fifteenth Street, N.W., 20005
Telephone: 202-371-6550
Fax: 202-371-6770
New York, New York Office: 425 Park Avenue.
Telephone: 212-233-4000.
FAX: 212-223-4134.

MEMBERS OF FIRM

Jeffrey W. King	James E. Kellett
Jeffrey W. Pagano	(Not admitted in DC)
Keith J. Harrison	Steven Schaars (Resident)

ASSOCIATES

Jeffrey L. Poston	Christopher Flynn

(See Next Column)

KING, PAGANO & HARRISON—*Continued*

OF COUNSEL
Erling Hansen

Representative Clients: Brink's Inc.; Burlington Air Express; The Pittston Co.; The Union Corp.; Philadelphia National Bank; Kaiser Permanente; Del Laboratories; E-Systems; Group Health Association of America; Capital Credit Corp.

For full biographical listings, see the Martindale-Hubbell Law Directory

LEONARD, RALSTON & STANTON, CHARTERED (AV)

1000 Thomas Jefferson Street, N.W. Suite 609, 20007
Telephone: 202-342-3342
Fax: 202-298-7810
Fairfax, Virginia Office: Leonard, Ralston & Stanton, Chartered, Sherwood Plaza, Suite 150, 9990 Lee Highway, 22030.
Telephone: 703-591-6200.
Fax: 703-591-6556.

Jerris Leonard	Mary Gayle Holden
David T. Ralston, Jr.	(Not admitted in DC)
Thomas J. Stanton	Daniel F. Rinzel
(Not admitted in DC)	

Roderick B. Williams	Douglas J. Hoffman
Rachel Danish Campbell	(Not admitted in DC)
Karen M. Grane	Walter C. Hazlitt, Jr.
Theodore Charles Curtin	(Not admitted in DC)

OF COUNSEL
John D. Brosnan
LOBBYING/ADMINISTRATIVE
Kathleen A. Leonard
REGULATORY AFFAIRS
Russell Wapensky

For full biographical listings, see the Martindale-Hubbell Law Directory

MARY A. McREYNOLDS, P.C. (AV)

Suite 400, 888 Sixteenth Street, N.W., 20006
Telephone: 202-835-7455
Telecopier: 202-296-8791

Mary A. McReynolds

For full biographical listings, see the Martindale-Hubbell Law Directory

MILLER, CASSIDY, LARROCA & LEWIN, L.L.P. (AV)

2555 M Street, N.W., 20037
Telephone: 202-293-6400
Telecopier: 202-293-1827

MEMBERS OF FIRM

Herbert J. Miller, Jr.	Scott L. Nelson
John Joseph Cassidy	Julia E. Guttman
Raymond G. Larroca	Niki Kuckes
Nathan Lewin	Jay L. Alexander
Martin D. Minsker	Cynthia Thomas Calvert
William H. Jeffress, Jr.	Paul F. Enzinna
R. Stan Mortenson	Douglas F. Curtis
Thomas B. Carr	Michael J. Barta
James E. Rocap, III	Bradford M. Berry
Randall J. Turk	Stuart A. Levey
Stephen L. Braga	David S. Cohen
Joe R. Caldwell, Jr.	David R. Fontaine
J. Bradley Bennett	

ASSOCIATES

Ellen Fels Berkman	Katherine L. Pringle
Hugh P. Quinn	Robert J. McGahan
Barry J. Pollack	Daniel J. Cloherty
James R. Heavner, Jr.	Jody A. Manier
Mathew S. Nosanchuk	(Not admitted in DC)
Alison E. Grossman	Timothy J. Preso
Kirsten D. Levingston	(Not admitted in DC)

OF COUNSEL
Courtney A. Evans

For full biographical listings, see the Martindale-Hubbell Law Directory

PAULSON, NACE & NORWIND (AV)

1814 N Street, N.W., 20036
Telephone: 202-463-1999
Fax: 202-223-6824
Email: pnn@lawtort.com

MEMBERS OF FIRM
Richard S. Paulson (1928-1986)   Barry J. Nace
Edward L. Norwind

ASSOCIATES
Gloria A. Worch   James A. Ferguson

(See Next Column)

OF COUNSEL
Irving R. M. Panzer

For full biographical listings, see the Martindale-Hubbell Law Directory

REICHLER, MILTON & MEDEL (AV)

Suite 1200, 1747 Pennsylvania Avenue, N.W., 20006-4604
Telephone: 202-223-1200
Fax: 202-785-6687

Paul S. Reichler	Arthur V. Medel
Kathleen M. Milton	Janis H. Brennan

ASSOCIATES

Padideh Ala'i	Alima Joned
Melissa E. Crow	Daniel M. Malabonga
(Not admitted in DC)	(Not admitted in DC)

OF COUNSEL

T. Jay Barrymore	Traci Duvall Humes

For full biographical listings, see the Martindale-Hubbell Law Directory

THE ROBINSON LAW FIRM (AV)

Market Square, 717 D Street, N.W., 4th Floor, 20004
Telephone: 202-347-6100
Fax: 202-347-0081
Email: RLAW@aol.com

MEMBERS OF FIRM
Kenneth Michael Robinson   Nicholas H. Hantzes

ASSOCIATES

Randall W. Roy	Stacey Papa
	(Not admitted in DC)

OF COUNSEL
Daniel E. Ellenbogen   Dennis M. Hart

For full biographical listings, see the Martindale-Hubbell Law Directory

ROSS, DIXON & MASBACK L.L.P. (AV)

601 Pennsylvania Avenue, N.W., North Building, 20004-2688
Telephone: 202-662-2000
Irvine, California Office: 5 Park Plaza, Suite 1200, 92714.
Telephone: 714-622-2700.
Fax: 714-622-2739.

MEMBERS OF FIRM

Stuart Philip Ross	William H. Briggs, Jr.
Gary V. Dixon	James E. Grossberg
Wallace A. Christensen	(Resident, Irvine, California)
John R. Gerstein	Charles I. Hadden
Curtis Emery von Kann	William E. O'Brian, Jr.
Cathy Ann Simon	Lona Triplett Perry
David M. Gische	Andrew L. Shapiro
Richard A. Simpson	Celeste Phillips (Not admitted in
Lee Levine	DC; Resident, Irvine,
Sean M. Hanifin	California)
Peter G. Thompson	Elizabeth C. Koch
Elizabeth Sarah Gere	Merril Jay Hirsh
Barbara E. Etkind	Daniel J. Standish
Rebecca L. Ross	Martin G. Hacala
Robert M. Pozin	Joel Scott Townsend
(Resident, Irvine, California)	William D. Hopkins
Michael D. Sullivan	David R. Dwares
Lewis K. Loss	Leslie S. Ahari
	David L. Perry

Seth D. Berlin	Farhana Y. Khera
Charles T. Blair	(Not admitted in DC)
Jay Ward Brown	Thomas T. Locke
Lisa A. Burns	(Not admitted in DC)
Jodi L. Cleesattle	Michele L. Lynch
(Not admitted in DC)	(Resident, Irvine, California)
Alys I. Cohen	Wendy G. Macy
(Not admitted in DC)	(Resident, Irvine, California)
R. Darryl Cooper	Cynthia Ruth Mather
Pascal W. Di Fronzo	(Not admitted in DC)
(Resident, Irvine, California)	Stacey L. McGraw
John W. Duchelle	Terrence R. McInnis
(Not admitted in DC)	Liza M. Murphy
Jeffrey H. Dygert	(Not admitted in DC)
(Not admitted in DC)	Richard J. Pratt
Elizabeth Fitch	Michael D. Rothberg
John R. Griffiths	(Not admitted in DC)
Garrick P. Grobler	Erik Jorma Salovaara
Eric M. Jaffe	Roland G. Schroeder
(Not admitted in DC)	Richard C. Seavey
Thomas J. Judge	(Not admitted in DC)
(Not admitted in DC)	

(See Next Column)

ROSS, DIXON & MASBACK L.L.P., *Washington—Continued*

OF COUNSEL

Harold E. Masback, III   Dee Lord
Alec M. Barinholtz
  (Resident, Irvine, California)

For full biographical listings, see the Martindale-Hubbell Law Directory

---

SCHMELTZER, APTAKER & SHEPARD, P.C. (AV)

The Watergate, Suite 1000, 2600 Virginia Avenue, N.W., 20037-1905
Telephone: 202-333-8800
Cable Address: "Ship"
Telex: 440517
Facsimile: 202-342-3434
Email: sas@saslaw.com *URL:* http://www.saspc.com
Los Angeles, California Office: 1999 Avenue of the Stars, Twenty-Seventh Floor, 90067-4095.
Telephone: 310-557-2966.
FAX: 310-286-6610.

J. Thomas Esslinger	Ralph H. Johnson
Stephen Horn	Robert L. Zisk
	Leon B. Taranto

Lynn K. McKay	Adrienne T. Vadell
Wayne T. Ault	(Not admitted in DC)
Jeremy M. Griffin	Steven A. Browne
	(Not admitted in DC)

COUNSEL

C. Robert Manor

For full biographical listings, see the Martindale-Hubbell Law Directory

---

SCHWALB, DONNENFELD, BRAY & SILBERT, A PROFESSIONAL CORPORATION (AV)

1025 Thomas Jefferson Street, N.W. Suite 300 East, 20007
Telephone: 202-965-7910
Telecopier: 202-337-0676

Burton A. Schwalb	Lucinda J. Bach
John M. Bray	Cary M. Feldman
Earl J. Silbert	Joseph M. Jones
David J. Curtin	Adam S. Hoffinger
Charles B. Wayne	Kevin M. Dinan
Steven Sarfatti	Patricia L. Maher

SENIOR COUNSEL

Charles R. Donnenfeld

OF COUNSEL

Debra Ornstein

Robert A. Salerno	James T. Phalen
Carmen R. Kelley	Robert J. McAuliffe
Richard J. Oparil	Jeffrey D. Clark

For full biographical listings, see the Martindale-Hubbell Law Directory

---

SHAWN, MANN & NIEDERMAYER, L.L.P. (AV)

1850 M Street, N.W., Suite 280, 20036-5803
Telephone: 202-331-7900
Fax: 202-331-0726
Washington, D.C., Government Affairs Office: 499 S. Capitol Street, S.W., Suite 420.
Telephone: 202-842-3000.
Fax: 202-547-7161.
Los Angeles, California Office: 2029 Century Park East, Suite 1690.
Telephone: 310-553-8065.
Fax: 310-557-0729.
San Diego, California Office: 401 West "A" Street, Suite 1850.
Telephone: 619-236-0303.
Fax: 619-238-8181.
San Francisco, California Office: The Fox Plaza, 1390 Market Street, Suite 1204.
Telephone: 415-982-0150.
Fax: 415-522-0513.
Bloomington, Minnesota Office: 2090 West 98th Street.
Telephone: 612-881-6577.
Fax: 612-881-6894.

MEMBERS OF FIRM

William H. Shawn	James E. King
Roy I. Niedermayer	Gregory S. Abrams
	James O'Neil Attridge

For full biographical listings, see the Martindale-Hubbell Law Directory

---

STEPTOE & JOHNSON LLP (AV)

1330 Connecticut Avenue, N.W., 20036
Telephone: 202-429-3000
Cable Address: "Stepjohn"
Telex: 89-2503
Telecopier: 202-429-3902
Email: wbatterton@steptoe.com *URL:* http://www.steptoe.com
Phoenix, Arizona Office: Two Renaissance Square, 40 N. Central Avenue, Suite 2400, 85004.
Telephone: 602-257-5200.
Moscow, Russia Office: Steptoe & Johnson International AOZT. 25 Tsvetnoy Boulevard, Building 3 Moscow, Russia 103051.
Telephone: 011-7-501-258-5250.
Fax: 011-7-501-258-5251.
Almaty, Kazakhstan Office: Steptoe & Johnson Company Almaty. 84 Gogol Street, Suite 213, 480083.
Telephones: (3272) 50-11-25, (3272) 32-25-39.

MEMBERS

John E. Nolan	Peter L. Wellington
Robert D. Wallick	Stephen A. Fennell
Richard H. Porter	J. William Koegel, Jr.
Kenneth I. Jonson	Daniel C. Sauls
Ronald S. Cooper	Philip L. Malet
Roger E. Warin	Antonia B. Ianniello
Morgan D. Hodgson	Jerald S. Howe Jr.
Christopher T. Lutz	Virginia L. White-Mahaffey
Richard K. Willard	Alfred M. Mamlet
Reid H. Weingarten	Steven K. Davidson
Charles G. Cole	Harry Lee
Thomas P. Barletta	Thomas M. Barba

OF COUNSEL

Anita G. Fox

For Complete List of Firm Personnel, See General Section

For full biographical listings, see the Martindale-Hubbell Law Directory

---

THOMPSON, O'DONNELL, MARKHAM, NORTON & HANNON (AV)

The Southern Building, 805 Fifteenth Street, N.W., Suite 705, 20005
Telephone: 202-289-1133
Facsimile: 202-289-0275

John Jude O'Donnell	Randell Hunt Norton
Julian E. Markham, Jr.	J. Michael Hannon

ASSOCIATES

Kenneth G. Stallard	Brooke A. Pinkerton
	Matthew W Carlson

OF COUNSEL

J. Roy Thompson, Jr.	Henry F. Harding

Representative Clients: C. J. Langenfelder & Sons, Inc., Baltimore, Maryland; Bernard F. Locraft, Civil Engineers, Washington, D. C.; Security Trust, N.A. *References:* American Security Bank, N.A.; Franklin National Bank.

For full biographical listings, see the Martindale-Hubbell Law Directory

---

* VENABLE ATTORNEYS AT LAW VENABLE, BAETJER, HOWARD & CIVILETTI, LLP (AV)

A Partnership including Professional Corporations
Suite 1000, 1201 New York Avenue, N.W., 20005
Telephone: 202-962-4800
Fax: 202-962-8300
Baltimore, Maryland Office: Venable, Baetjer and Howard LLP, 1800 Mercantile Bank & Trust Building, 2 Hopkins Plaza.
Telephone: 410-244-7400.
McLean, Virginia Office: Venable, Baetjer and Howard LLP, Suite 400, 2010 Corporate Ridge.
Telephone: 703-760-1600.
Rockville, Maryland Office: Venable, Baetjer and Howard LLP, Suite 500, One Church Street, P. O. Box 1906.
Telephone: 301-217-5600.
Towson, Maryland Office: Venable, Baetjer and Howard LLP, 210 Allegheny Avenue, P. O. Box 5517.
Telephone: 410-494-6200.

MEMBERS OF FIRM

Benjamin R. Civiletti (P.C.) (Also at Baltimore and Towson, Maryland Offices)	Michael Schatzow (Also at Baltimore, Maryland Office)
Thomas J. Madden	N. Frank Wiggins
Ronald R. Glancz	James K. Archibald (Also at Baltimore, Maryland Office)
David J. Levenson	Judson W. Starr (Also at Baltimore and Towson, Maryland Offices)
Douglas D. Connah, Jr. (P.C.) (Also at Baltimore, Maryland Office)	James R. Myers
Kenneth C. Bass, III (Also at McLean, Virginia Office)	Jeffrey A. Dunn (Also at Baltimore, Maryland Office)
Edward F. Glynn, Jr.	George F. Pappas (Also at Baltimore, Maryland Office)
Robert G. Ames (Also at Baltimore, Maryland Office)	William D. Coston

(See Next Column)

VENABLE ATTORNEYS AT LAW VENABLE, BAETJER, HOWARD & CIVILETTI, LLP—*Continued*

MEMBERS OF FIRM (Continued)

James L. Shea (Not admitted in DC; also at Baltimore, Maryland Office)

Maurice Baskin

Amy Berman Jackson

William D. Quarles (Also at Towson, Maryland Office)

James A. Dunbar (Also at Baltimore, Maryland Office)

Thomas J. Kelly, Jr.

Patrick J. Stewart (Also at Baltimore, Maryland Office)

Gary M. Hnath

Geoffrey R. Garinther (Not admitted in DC; Also at Baltimore, Maryland Office)

ASSOCIATES

Carla Draluck Craft

David W. Goewey

Edward Brendan Magrab

Lawrence C. Renbaum

Melissa Landau Steinman

For Complete List of Firm Personnel, See General Section

For full biographical listings, see the Martindale-Hubbell Law Directory

* VINSON & ELKINS L.L.P. (AV)

A Registered Limited Liability Partnership
The Willard Office Building, 1455 Pennsylvania Avenue, N.W., 20004-1008
Telephone: 202-639-6500
Fax: 202-639-6604
Houston, Texas Office: 2300 First City Tower, 1001 Fannin.
Telephone: 713-758-2222.
Fax: 713-758-2346.
Austin, Texas Office: One American Center, Suite 2700, 600 Congress Avenue.
Telephone: 512-495-8400.
Fax: 512-495-8612.
Dallas, Texas Office: 3700 Trammell Crow Center, 2001 Ross Avenue.
Telephone: 214-220-7700.
Fax: 214-220-7716.
London Office: 47 Charles Street, Berkeley Square, London, W1X 7PB, England.
Telephone: (441-171) 491-7236.
Fax: (44-171) 499-5320.
Moscow, Russia Office: 16 Ulitsa Spiridonovka, Second Floor, 103001 Moscow, Russia.
Telephone: (70-95) 956-1995.
Telecopy: (70-95) 956-1996.
Singapore Office: 16 Collyer Quay, #33-01 Hitachi Tower, 049318.
Telephone: (65) 536-8300.
Fax: (65) 536-8311.

RESIDENT PARTNERS

Alden L. Atkins

C. Michael Buxton

Ky P. Ewing, Jr.

Michael J. Henke

Neil W. Imus

Cathy A. Lewis

John D. Taurman

Charles D. Tetrault

Mark H. Tuohey, III

RESIDENT OF COUNSEL

Dennis A. Klejna

William E. Lawler, III

Paul L. Yde

RESIDENT ASSOCIATES

Robert H. Cox

John M. Faust

Glenn S. Greene

Joseph E. Hunsader (Not admitted in DC)

Tara Isa Koslov

Craig D. Margolis (Not admitted in DC)

Philip A. Nickles (Not admitted in DC)

For Complete List of Firm Personnel, See General Section

For full biographical listings, see the Martindale-Hubbell Law Directory

WATT, TIEDER & HOFFAR, L.L.P. (AV)

601 Pennsylvania Avenue, N.W., Suite 900, 20004
Telephone: 202-462-4697
Telecopier: 703-893-8029
McLean Virginia Office: 7929 Westpark Drive, Suite 400,
Telephone: 703-749-1000.
Telecopier: 703-893-8029.
Irvine California Office: 3 Park Plaza, Suite 1530.
Telephone: 714-852-6700.

MEMBERS OF FIRM

John B. Tieder, Jr.

Robert K. Cox

David C. Romm

For full biographical listings, see the Martindale-Hubbell Law Directory

WEHNER & YORK (AV)

513 Capitol Court, N.E. Suite 200, 20002
Telephone: 202-543-2700
Facsimile: 202-543-2023
Email: litigation@wehner-york-law.com
Philadelphia, Pennsylvania Office: 2650 Provident Mutual, 1600 Market Street.
Telephone: 215-569-8777.
Facsimile: 215-569-8884. E-Mail: litigation@wehner-york-law.com.
Bridgeport, West Virginia Office: Grande Meadows, Saltwell Road and Route 73, Suite 230.
Telephone: 304-592-3400. E-Mail: litigation@wehner-york-law.com.

MEMBERS OF FIRM

Stephen V. Wehner

Michael M. York

Kay Millicent Brown

LEGAL SUPPORT PERSONNEL

Lela Rao (Paralegal)

For full biographical listings, see the Martindale-Hubbell Law Directory

WILLIAMS & CONNOLLY (AV)

725 Twelfth Street, N.W., 20005
Telephone: 202-434-5000

MEMBERS OF FIRM

Vincent J. Fuller

Raymond W. Bergan

Jeremiah C. Collins

David Povich

Steven M. Umin

John W. Vardaman

Paul Martin Wolff

J. Alan Galbraith

John G. Kester

William E. McDaniels

Brendan V. Sullivan, Jr.

Aubrey M. Daniel, III

Richard M. Cooper

Gerald A. Feffer

Robert P. Watkins

Jerry L. Shulman

Lawrence Lucchino

Lewis H. Ferguson, III

Robert B. Barnett

David E. Kendall

Gregory B. Craig

John J. Buckley, Jr.

Douglas R. Marvin

John K. Villa

Barry S. Simon

Kevin T. Baine

Stephen L. Urbanczyk

Philip J. Ward

Peter J. Kahn

Lon S. Babby

Michael S. Sundermeyer

James T. Fuller, III

David D. Aufhauser

Bruce R. Genderson

Carolyn H. Williams

Frank Lane Heard III

Steven R. Kuney

Gerson A. Zweifach

Paul Mogin

Howard W. Gutman

Nancy F. Lesser

Richard S. Hoffman

Steven A. Steinbach

Mark S. Levinstein

Mary Greer Clark

Daniel F. Katz

Nicole K. Seligman

Robert M. Krasne

Kathleen L. Beggs

William R. Murray, Jr.

Eva Petko Esber

Stephen D. Raber

David C. Kiernan

Lon E. Musslewhite

Robin E. Jacobsohn

Charles A. Sweet

Glenn J. Pfadenhauer

George A. Borden

Robert J. Shaughnessy

Jonathan P. Graham

Allen P. Waxman

Eric M. Braun

David S. Blatt

Ari S. Zymelman

Joseph D. Piorkowski, Jr.

Dane H. Butswinkas

Laurie S. Fulton

OF COUNSEL

Lyman G. Friedman

For Complete List of Firm Personnel, See General Section

For full biographical listings, see the Martindale-Hubbell Law Directory

WILMER, CUTLER & PICKERING (AV)

2445 M Street, N.W., 20037-1420
Telephone: 202-663-6000
Fax: 202-663-6363
Email: Law@Wilmer.Com
Baltimore, Maryland Office: 100 Light Street, 21202.
Telephone: 410-986-2800.
Fax: 410-986-2828.
European Offices:
4 Carlton Gardens, London, SW1Y 5AA, England. Telephone: +44 (171) 872-1000.
Fax: +44 (171) 839-3537.
Rue de la Loi 15Wetstraat, B-1040 Brussels, Belgium. Telephone: +32 (2) 285-4900.
Fax: +32 (2) 285-4949.
Friedrichstrasse 95, D-10117 Berlin, Germany. Telephone: +49 (30) 2022-6400.
Fax: +49 (30)2022-6500.

MEMBERS OF FIRM

Daniel K. Mayers

Stephen H. Sachs

Arthur F. Mathews

Dennis M. Flannery

Louis R. Cohen

Michael R. Klein

Paul J. Mode, Jr.

Stephen F. Black

Gary D. Wilson

James A. Rogers

(See Next Column)

285A

WILMER, CUTLER & PICKERING, *Washington—Continued*

MEMBERS OF FIRM (Continued)

Michael L. Burack
Robert B. McCaw
William J. Kolasky, Jr.
Arthur L. Marriott (Resident, European Office, London, England)
A. Stephen Hut, Jr.
John Rounsaville, Jr.
Roger M. Witten
David M. Becker
Christopher R. Lipsett
William J. Perlstein
Andrew B. Weissman
Lynn Bregman
Juanita A. Crowley

John Payton
Bruce M. Berman
Thomas F. Connell
Charles E. Davidow
Gary B. Born (Resident, European Office, London, England)
Philip D. Anker
Joseph K. Brenner
Carol Clayton
Thomas P. Olson
Patrick J. Carome
David P. Donovan
Stephen M. Cutler
Roger W. Yoerges

Mark D. Cahn

COUNSEL

Joseph E. Killory, Jr.

OF COUNSEL

Howard P. Willens   Max O. Truitt, Jr.

For Complete List of Firm Personnel, See General Section

For full biographical listings, see the Martindale-Hubbell Law Directory

ZEVNIK HORTON GUIBORD & McGOVERN, P.C. (AV)

Ninth Floor, 1299 Pennsylvania Avenue, N.W., 20004
Telephone: 202-824-0950
FAX: 202-824-0955
Chicago, Illinois Office: Suite 3300, 77 West Wacker Drive.
Telephone: 312-977-2500.
Telefax: 312-977-2560.
Los Angeles, California Office: 333 South Grand Avenue, Twenty First Floor.
Telephone: 213-437-5200.
Telefax: 213-437-5222.
New York, N.Y. Office: 745 Fifth Avenue, Twenty-Fifth Floor.
Telephone: 212-935-2735.
Telefax: 212-935-0614.
Palo Alto, California Office: 5 Palo Alto Square, 3000 El Camino Real.
Telephone: 415-842-5900.
Facsimile: 415-855-9226.
London, England Office: 4 Kings Bench Walk, Temple, London EC4Y 7DL.
Telephone: 071-353-0478.
Facsimile: 071-583-3549.
Norfolk, Virginia Office: Main Street Tower, 300 East Main Street, 13th Floor.
Telephone: 757-624-3480.
Fax: 757-624-3479.

Paul Anton Zevnik
Michel Yves Horton
Barbara B. Guibord
(Not admitted in DC)
Patrick Michael McGovern
(Not admitted in DC)

Joseph G. Homsy
(Not admitted in DC)
John W. Roberts
(Not admitted in DC)
John K. Crossman
(Not admitted in DC)

Jonathan L. Osborne

Yolanda C. Griffin
(Not admitted in DC)

Michael J. Wilson

For full biographical listings, see the Martindale-Hubbell Law Directory

FLORIDA

ALTAMONTE SPRINGS, Seminole Co.

FISHER AND MATTHEWS, P.A. (AV)

813 Douglas Avenue, 32714
Telephone: 407-682-2727; 1-800-545-2863
Fax: 407-682-4025

James C. Fisher   J. Michael Matthews

For full biographical listings, see the Martindale-Hubbell Law Directory

AVENTURA, Dade Co.

BUCHANAN INGERSOLL, PROFESSIONAL CORPORATION (AV⊤)

One Turnberry Place, 19495 Biscayne Boulevard, Suite 606, 33180
Telephone: 305-933-5600
Telecopier: 305-933-2350
URL: http://www.bipc.com
Pittsburgh, Pennsylvania Office: One Oxford Centre, 301 Grant Street, 20th Floor.
Telephone: 412-562-8800.

(See Next Column)

Philadelphia, Pennsylvania Office: Two Logan Square, Twelfth Floor, 18th & Arch Streets.
Telephone: 215-665-8700.
Harrisburg, Pennsylvania Office: 30 North Third Street.
Telephone: 717-237-4800.
Miami, Florida Office: NationsBank Tower, 100 S.E. Second Street.
Telephone: 305-347-4080.
Tampa, Florida Office: Suite 2500, 401 East Jackson Street.
Telephone: 813-222-8180.
Princeton, New Jersey Office: Buchanan Ingersoll, A Partnership, College Centre, 500 College Road East.
Telephone: 609-987-6800.
Lexington, Kentucky Office: Suite 600, PNC Bank Plaza, 200 West Vine Street.
Telephone: 606-225-5333.
Buffalo, New York Office: 1100 Main Place Tower, 350 Main Street.
Telephone: 716-854-4100.
Fax: 816-854-4227.

Joshua L. Dubin   Mark J. Neuberger

SENIOR ATTORNEY

Ralph B. Bekkevold

Todd A. Bancroft
Kevin Carmichael
Jeffrey M. Goodz

Randi S. Rothfield
Richard N. Schermer
Rebecca S. Trinkler

For full biographical listings, see the Martindale-Hubbell Law Directory

BARTOW, * Polk Co.

FROST, O'TOOLE & SAUNDERS, P.A. (AV)

395 South Central Avenue, P.O. Box 2188, 33830
Telephone: 941-533-0314; 800-533-0967
Telecopier: 941-533-8985

John W. Frost, II
Neal L. O'Toole
Thomas C. Saunders
Richard E. "Rick" Dantzler

Robert A. Carr
Robert H. Van Hart
John Marc Tamayo
Mark A. Sessums

Robert J. Aranda

Reference: Community National Bank, Bartow.

For full biographical listings, see the Martindale-Hubbell Law Directory

LANE, TROHN, CLARKE, BERTRAND, VREELAND & JACOBSEN, P.A. (AV)

150 East Davidson Street, P.O. Box 1578, 33830-1578
Telephone: 941-533-0866
Telecopier: 941-533-7255
Lakeland, Florida Office: One Lake Morton Drive. 38802.
Telephone: 941-284-2200.
Fax: 941-688-0310.

C. A. Boswell
Wofford Hampton Stidham
Dabney L. Conner

Donald H. Wilson, Jr.
Jonathan Stidham
Steven L. Selph

For full biographical listings, see the Martindale-Hubbell Law Directory

BOCA RATON, Palm Beach Co.

CARTER, CARLILE, NEALE & FRIEDMAN, P.A. (AV)

Suite 312, 1200 North Federal Highway, 33432
Telephone: 561-368-9900

John E. Carter
Robert T. Carlile

Thomas E. Neale
Annette Friedman

For full biographical listings, see the Martindale-Hubbell Law Directory

LAW OFFICES OF RICHARD H. LEVENSTEIN, P.A. (AV)

2101 Northwest 2nd Avenue Suite 2, 33431
Telephone: 561-392-7887
Fax: 561-392-3348
Stuart, Florida Office: 312 West Ocean Boulevard, 34994.
Telephone: 561-221-0521.
Fax: 561-221-0290.

Richard H. Levenstein

For full biographical listings, see the Martindale-Hubbell Law Directory

WEISS & HANDLER, P.A. (AV)

Suite 218A, One Boca Place, 2255 Glades Road, 33431-7313
Telephone: 407-997-9995
Broward: 954-421-5101
Palm Beach: 407-734-8008
Telecopier: 407-997-5280

Howard I. Weiss   Henry B. Handler

(See Next Column)

WEISS & HANDLER P.A.—*Continued*

Donald Feldman
David K. Friedman
Carol A. Kartagener

Marissa I. Laakso
Mark R. Osherow
Howard M. Rudolph (Resident, West Palm Beach Office)

OF COUNSEL

Malcolm L. Stein
(Not admitted in FL)
Raoul Lionel Felder
(Not admitted in FL)

Stanley E. Preiser
(Not admitted in FL)

For full biographical listings, see the Martindale-Hubbell Law Directory

BRADENTON,* Manatee Co.

GRIMES GOEBEL GRIMES HAWKINS & GLADFELTER, P.A. (AV)

The Professional Building, 1023 Manatee Avenue West, P.O. Box 1550, 34206
Telephone: 941-748-0151
Fax: 941-748-0158

William C. Grimes
Caleb J. Grimes

John D. Hawkins
William S. Galvano

Douglas A. Peebles

For Complete List of Firm Personnel, See General Section

For full biographical listings, see the Martindale-Hubbell Law Directory

CRYSTAL RIVER, Citrus Co.

BEST & ANDERSON, P.A. (AV)

7655 West Gulf to Lake Highway, Suite 6, 34429
Telephone: 352-795-1107
Orlando, Florida Office: 20 North Orange Avenue, Suite 505.
Telephone: 407-425-2985.
Melbourne, Florida Office: Marina Towers, 709 South Harbor City Boulevard, Suite 220, 32901.
Telephone: 407-727-9923.

David R. Best
George H. "Dutch" Anderson, III

Lawrence I. Hauser

G. Clay Morris

Angela O'Neil

Natt O. Reifler

For full biographical listings, see the Martindale-Hubbell Law Directory

DAYTONA BEACH, Volusia Co.

DUNN, ABRAHAM & SWAIN (AV)

A Partnership of Professional Associations
347 South Ridgewood Avenue, P.O. Drawer 2600, 32115-2600
Telephone: 904-258-1222
Fax: 904-255-8521
Email: 71722.3430@compuserve.com

MEMBERS OF FIRM

Edgar M. Dunn, Jr., (P.A.)
Catherine G. Swain (P.A.)

Robert Abraham (P.A.)

ASSOCIATE

Suzanne A. Novak

For full biographical listings, see the Martindale-Hubbell Law Directory

FINK & SWEET (AV)

149 East International Speedway Boulevard, P.O. Box 265386, 32126
Telephone: 904-252-7653
Fax: 904-238-3604

Wesley A. Fink

Jeffrey C. Sweet

Representative Clients: SunTrust Bank of East Central Florida.
Approved Attorneys for: Attorneys' Title Insurance Fund; Commonwealth Land Title Insurance Co.; Chicago Title Insurance Co.
Reference: SunTrust Bank of East Central Florida.

For full biographical listings, see the Martindale-Hubbell Law Directory

FORT LAUDERDALE,* Broward Co.

BERGER & DAVIS, P.A. (AV)

Suite 400, 100 N.E. 3rd Avenue, 33301
Telephone: 954-525-9900
Fax: 954-523-2872
Tallahassee, Florida Office: 215 South Monroe Street, Suite 804, 32301.
Telephone: 904-561-3010.
FAX: 904-561-3013.

(See Next Column)

Thomas L. Abrams
James L. Berger
Mitchell W. Berger
Franklin H. Caplan
James B. Davis
Nick Jovanovich
Robert B. Judd

Manuel Kushner
John D. C. Newton, II
(Resident, Tallahassee Office)
Leonard K. Samuels
Laz L. Schneider
Daniel H. Thompson
(Resident, Tallahassee Office)

Vincent J. Altino
Christine A. Butler
Lawrence C. Callaway, III
Janice L. Griffin

Lisa D. MacClugage
Dawn M. Meyers
Scott L. Pestcoe
Holiday Hunt Russell

Jeffrey Scott Wertman

OF COUNSEL

Henry H. (Bucky) Fox

For full biographical listings, see the Martindale-Hubbell Law Directory

CONRAD, SCHERER & JENNE (AV)

A Partnership of Professional Associations
Eighth Floor, 633 South Federal Highway, P.O. Box 14723, 33302
Telephone: 954-462-5500
Facsimile: 954-463-9244
Miami, Florida Office: International Place. 100 Southeast 2nd Street. Suite 2800. 33131.
Telephone: 305-856-9920.
Facsimile: 305-374-4408.

MEMBERS OF FIRM

William R. Scherer, Jr., (P.A.)
Kenneth C. Jenne, II (P.A.)

Gary S. Genovese (P.A.)
William V. Carcioppolo (P.A.)

Lynn Futch Cooney (P.A.)

OF COUNSEL

Rex Conrad

ASSOCIATES

Linda Rae Spaulding
Kimberly A. Kisslan

Reid A. Cocalis
Albert L. Frevola, Jr.

Local Counsel for: American Home Assurance Group; Caterpillar Tractor Co.; Division of Risk Management, State of Florida; Florida East Coast Railway; Fort Motor Co.; Liberty Mutual Insurance Co.; Ryder Truck Lines; Unigard Insurance Group.
Approved Attorneys for: Attorneys' Title Insurance Fund.
Reference: Barnett Bank of Fort Lauderdale.

For Complete List of Firm Personnel, See General Section

For full biographical listings, see the Martindale-Hubbell Law Directory

ESLER, PETRIE & LINDIE, P.A. (AV)

Suite 300 The Advocate Building, 315 S.E. Seventh Street, 33301
Telephone: 954-764-5400
FAX: 954-764-5408

Gary A. Esler

C. Daniel Petrie, Jr.

Beth G. Lindie

Representative Clients: The Chubb Group of Insurance Cos.; Fireman's Fund Insurance Co.; State of Florida-Department of Risk Management; Marriott Corp.; Gregson Furniture Industries, Inc.; Winsloew, Inc.; Richfield Hotel Management, Inc.; Mobile America Insurance Group, Inc.; Colonial Penn Insurance Co.
Reference: Capital Bank.

For full biographical listings, see the Martindale-Hubbell Law Directory

GILLESPIE & GOLDMAN (AV)

Port Royale Financial Center, 6550 North Federal Highway, 33308
Telephone: 954-761-8600
Facsimile: 954-525-2134

MEMBERS OF FIRM

John R. Gillespie, Jr.

Peter R. Goldman

For full biographical listings, see the Martindale-Hubbell Law Directory

LAW PRACTICE OF J.B. GROSSMAN, P.A. (AV)

2300 East Las Olas Boulevard Fourth Floor, 33301
Telephone: 954-767-3345
Fax: 954-767-3347

J.B. Grossman
Gary Arnold Feder

Kenneth J. Dunn
Blaine H. Hibberd

LEGAL SUPPORT PERSONNEL

Scott L. Lampert

For full biographical listings, see the Martindale-Hubbell Law Directory

Fort Lauderdale—Continued

HALICZER, PETTIS & WHITE, P.A. (AV)

101 Northeast Third Avenue, Sixth Floor, 33301
Telephone: 954-523-9922
Fax: 954-522-2512
Orlando, Florida Office: NationsBank Building. Suite 1275. 111 North
Orange Avenue. 32801.
Telephone: 407-841-9866.
Fax: 407-841-9915.

James S. Haliczer	Kenneth E. White
Eugene K. Pettis	Lorna E. Brown-Burton

Amy B. Talisman	Margaret A. Benenati
Dean A. Robertson	Gina E. Caruso

For full biographical listings, see the Martindale-Hubbell Law Directory

HEINRICH GORDON HARGROVE WEIHE & JAMES, P.A. (AV)

500 East Broward Boulevard, Suite 1000, 33394-3092
Telephone: 954-527-2800
Facsimile: 954-524-9481
Email: heinrich-gordon.com
Palm Beach, Florida Office: 140 Royal Palm Way, Suite 206.
Telephone: 561-832-7600.
Facsimile: 561-833-0805.

Mark R. Boyd	Eugene L. Heinrich
William Kent Brown	Jeffrey A. O'Keefe
Richard G. Gordon	Gilbert E. Theissen
John R. Hargrove	Kenneth W. Waterway
	Bruce A. Weihe

Representative Clients: Aetna Life Insurance Company; Allstate Insurance Company; Amerisure Companies; The BellSouth Companies; Blackfin Yacht Corporation, Inc.; First Union National Bank of Florida; First Westinghouse Equities Corporation; Schindler Elevator Corporation; Sears, Roebuck and Co.; Westinghouse Electric Corporation.

For Complete List of Firm Personnel, See General Section

For full biographical listings, see the Martindale-Hubbell Law Directory

KESSLER, MASSEY, CATRI, HOLTON & KESSLER, P.A. (AV)

110 Tower, Twentieth Floor, 110 Southeast Sixth Street, 33301
Telephone: 954-463-8593
Fax: 954-462-1303

Charles T. Kessler	Paula C. Kessler
Albert P. Massey, III	Gregory G. Coican
Wesley L. Catri	Andrea L. Kessler
Raymond O. Holton, Jr.	Edward D. Schuster

Gerard A. Tuzzio	Edwina V. Kessler

For full biographical listings, see the Martindale-Hubbell Law Directory

KRUPNICK CAMPBELL MALONE ROSELLI BUSER SLAMA & HANCOCK, P.A. (AV)

700 Southeast 3rd Avenue, 33316
Telephone: 954-763-8181
Fax: 954-763-8292

Jon E. Krupnick	Thomas E. Buser
Walter G. Campbell, Jr.	Joseph J. Slama
Kevin A. Malone	Kelly D. Hancock
Richard J. Roselli	Lisa A. McNelis

Louis R. Battista	Carol J. Healy
Ivan F. Cabrera	Elaine P. Krupnick
Robert D. Erben	Scott S. Liberman
Kelley Badger Gelb	Cinthia M. Manzano
	Robert J. McKee

OF COUNSEL

Ben J. Weaver	Dianne Jay Weaver

Reference: Nations Bank.

For full biographical listings, see the Martindale-Hubbell Law Directory

KENNETH R. MIKOS, P.A. (AV)

2780 East Oakland Park Boulevard, 33306
Telephone: 954-566-7200
Facsimile: 954-566-1568

Kenneth R. Mikos

Special Counsel to: Fort Lauderdale Civil Service Board.

For Complete List of Firm Personnel, See General Section

For full biographical listings, see the Martindale-Hubbell Law Directory

LAW OFFICES PRINCE, GLICK & McFARLANE, P.A. (AV)

1112 Southeast 3rd Avenue, 33316
Telephone: Broward: 954-525-1112
Dade: 305-940-6414
Fax: 954-462-1243

Charles M. Prince	Joseph Glick
	William J. McFarlane, III

For full biographical listings, see the Martindale-Hubbell Law Directory

SHELDON J. SCHLESINGER, P.A. (AV)

1212 Southeast Third Avenue, 33335
Telephone: 954-467-8800

Sheldon J. Schlesinger	Robert W. Kelley
Scott P. Schlesinger	Sara C. Lindsey

For full biographical listings, see the Martindale-Hubbell Law Directory

FORT MYERS,* Lee Co.

ALLEN, KNUDSEN & DeBOEST, P.A. (AV)

1415 Hendry Street, P.O. Box 1480, 33902
Telephone: 941-334-1381
Telecopier: 941-334-0266
Naples, Florida Office: Park North Center, 5121 Castello Drive, Suite 1.
Telephone: 941-263-5040.
Fax: 941-263-6944.

George E. Allen (1916-1993)	Terrence F. Lenick
Arthur K. Knudsen, Jr.	William E. Stockman
Richard D. DeBoest	Tamela Eady Wiseman
Christopher N. Davies	Brenda A. Bayly
Robert H. Duckwall	Lori Westhrin Clifford
Richard D. DeBoest II	Dana M. Gallup
C. Michael Jackson	Thaddeus Dennis Kirkpatrick
	P. Michael Villalobos

LEGAL SUPPORT PERSONNEL

Carolyn Fox Lambert (Paralegal)

Representative Clients: Lennar Homes, Inc.; Pulte Home Corp.; Cobb Theatres, Inc.; International Paper; Saxon Properties, Inc.; Scott's Hospitality, Inc.; WCN Communities, L.P.; Evelyn Jackman and Sons, Inc.; Pacificorp; Nite-Bright Sign Co.

For full biographical listings, see the Martindale-Hubbell Law Directory

PATRICK E. GERAGHTY A PROFESSIONAL ASSOCIATION (AV)

The Courtney Building, Suite 100, 2069 First Street, P.O. Box
1605, 33902-1605
Telephone: 941-334-9500
Fax: 941-334-8930

Patrick E. Geraghty	Thomas M. Dougherty

For full biographical listings, see the Martindale-Hubbell Law Directory

HENDERSON, FRANKLIN, STARNES & HOLT, PROFESSIONAL ASSOCIATION (AV)

1715 Monroe Street, P.O. Box 280, 33902-0280
Telephone: 941-334-4121
Telecopier: 941-332-4494

Stephen L. Helgemo	Harold N. Hume, Jr.
John A. Noland	Bruce M. Stanley
Gerald W. Pierce	Daniel W. Sheppard
J. Terrence Porter	Steven G. Koeppel
Michael J. Corso	Douglas B. Szabo
Vicki L. Sproat	Robert C. Shearman
John W. Lewis	Andrew L. Ringers, Jr.
Craig Ferrante	John F. Potanovic, Jr.
James L. Nulman	Jeffrey D. Kottkamp

Representative Clients: Aetna Property & Casualty Group; CIGNA Group; CSX Transportation, Inc.; Fireman's Fund Insurance Cos.; Barnett Bank of Lee County, N.A.; Northern Trust Bank of Florida, N.A.; The Hartford Insurance Group; Travelers Group; United Telephone Company of Florida.

For Complete List of Firm Personnel, See General Section

For full biographical listings, see the Martindale-Hubbell Law Directory

SMOOT ADAMS EDWARDS & GREEN, P.A. (AV)

One University Park Suite 600, 12800 University Drive, P.O. Box
60259, 33906-6259
Telephone: 941-489-1776
(800) 226-1777 (in Florida)
Fax: 941-489-2444
Email: 71600.2745@compuserve.com

(See Next Column)

SMOOT ADAMS EDWARDS & GREEN P.A.—*Continued*

J. Tom Smoot, Jr.	Bruce D. Green
Hal Adams	Steven I. Winer
Franklyn A. (Chip) Johnson	Mark R. Komray
(1947-1991)	Clayton W. Crevasse
Charles B. Edwards	M. Brian Cheffer

Robert S. Forman	C. Berk Edwards, Jr.
Kathleen W. McBride	Melville G. Brinson, III
Lowell Schoenfeld	Samuel J. Hagan, IV.

For full biographical listings, see the Martindale-Hubbell Law Directory

FORT PIERCE,* St. Lucie Co.

BRENNAN, HAYSKAR, JEFFERSON, WALKER & SCHWERER, PROFESSIONAL ASSOCIATION (AV)

515-519 South Indian River Drive, P.O. Box 3779, 34948-3779
Telephone: 561-461-2310
Fax: 561-468-6580

John T. Brennan	Bradford L. Jefferson
Thad H. Carlton (1906-1965)	Robert V. Schwerer
Stephen G. Hayskar	James T. Walker

Garrison M. Dundas	Steven R. McCain

Representative Clients: Allstate Insurance Co.; Auto Owners Insurance Co.; Canal Insurance Co.; Florida Farm Bureau Insurance Group; Kemper Insurance Group; First Union National Bank of Fla.; Scottsdale Insurance Group; USF&G; Gallagher Bassett.

For Complete List of Firm Personnel, See General Section

For full biographical listings, see the Martindale-Hubbell Law Directory

NEILL GRIFFIN JEFFRIES & LLOYD, CHARTERED (AV)

311 South Second Street, P.O. Box 1270, 34954
Telephone: 561-464-8200
Fax: 561-464-2566

Richard V. Neill	J. Stephen Tierney, III
Michael Jeffries	Richard V. Neill, Jr.

Local Counsel for: Sun Trust Bank Treasure Coast, N.A., (Commercial and Trust Departments); St. Paul Fire and Marine Insurance Co.; Chubb Group of Insurances Cos.
Approved Attorneys for: Attorneys' Title Insurance Fund; Commonwealth Land Title Insurance Co.
Reference: Sun Bank Treasure Coast, N.A., Fort Pierce, Florida (Commercial and Trust Departments).

For full biographical listings, see the Martindale-Hubbell Law Directory

GAINESVILLE,* Alachua Co.

STRIPLING, MCMICHAEL & STRIPLING, P.A. (AV)

102 N.W. Second Avenue, P.O. Box 1287, 32602
Telephone: 352-376-8888
Fax: 352-376-4645

Robert O. Stripling, Jr.	Alan E. McMichael
Sylvia A. K. Stripling	

For full biographical listings, see the Martindale-Hubbell Law Directory

HOLLYWOOD, Broward Co.

ELLIS, SPENCER AND BUTLER (AV)

Emerald Hills Executive Plaza I, 4601 Sheridan Street, Suite 505, 33021
Telephone: Broward: 954-986-2291
Dade Line: 305-947-0620
Facsimile: 954-986-2778
Email: esb@esblaw.com

MEMBERS OF FIRM

Robert B. Butler	Robert Paul Keeley
W. Tinsley Ellis	Jonathan E. Brody
William S. Spencer	Chapman L. Smith, Jr.
Mark F. Butler	Charles S. Kyriazos
	John C. Primeau

OF COUNSEL

Sherwood Spencer (Retired)

General Counsel for: American Bank of Hollywood.
Representative Clients: American Bank of Hollywood; Bank of North America; Banaszak Concrete Corp.; Peakload, Inc. of America; Doby Building Supply, Inc.; Michael Swerdlow Companies; Construction Management Services, Inc.

For full biographical listings, see the Martindale-Hubbell Law Directory

JACKSONVILLE,* Duval Co.

ALLEN, BRINTON & SIMMONS, P.A. (AV)

One Independent Drive, Suite 3200, 32202
Telephone: 904-353-8800
Fax: 904-353-8770

A. Graham Allen	Sidney S. Simmons, II
William D. Brinton	Edward McCarthy, III

Joelle Jackson Dillard	Christopher M. Hodge

Representative Clients: Amoco Oil Co.; Anheuser-Busch Companies, Inc.; Avis Rent A Car System, Inc.; Bridgestone/Firestone, Inc.; Coggin-O'Steen Investment Corp. (and related automobile dealerships); Digital Design, Inc.; The Dow Chemical Co.; The Haskell Co.; Johnson & Johnson; Masthead Industries, Inc.

For full biographical listings, see the Martindale-Hubbell Law Directory

GLENN K. ALLEN A PROFESSIONAL ASSOCIATION (AV)

The Plaza Building, 353 East Forsyth Street, 32202
Telephone: 904-355-7506
Facsimile: 904-353-8814

Glenn K. Allen

For full biographical listings, see the Martindale-Hubbell Law Directory

BLEDSOE, SCHMIDT & LIPPES, P.A. (AV)

1301 Riverplace Boulevard, Suite 1818, 32202
Telephone: 904-398-1818
Fax: 904-398-7073

James A. Bledsoe, Jr.	Harold S. Lippes
Terrance E. Schmidt	Stephen K. Moonly
	Cheryl A. Roberson

For full biographical listings, see the Martindale-Hubbell Law Directory

BOYER, TANZLER & BOYER (AV)

200 East Forsyth Street, 32202
Telephone: 904-358-3030
Fax: 904-634-0036

MEMBERS OF FIRM

Tyrie A. Boyer	Tyrie W. Boyer
	Herbert T. Sussman

ASSOCIATE

Richard C. Watson

Reference: American National Bank of Jacksonville.

For full biographical listings, see the Martindale-Hubbell Law Directory

JOHN F. CALLENDER (AV)

1301 River Place Boulevard Suite 2105, 32207
Telephone: 904-398-8833
Fax: 904-396-4457

Reference: First Union National Bank.

For full biographical listings, see the Martindale-Hubbell Law Directory

FANNIN, TYLER & HAMILTON, P.A. (AV)

Park Pointe, Suite D, 4741 Atlantic Boulevard, 32207-2127
Telephone: 904-398-9999
Facsimile: 904-398-0806

John F. Fannin	H. Tyrone Tyler
	J. Clark Hamilton, Jr.

Laura Fannin Jacqmein

For full biographical listings, see the Martindale-Hubbell Law Directory

GABEL & HAIR (AV)

76 South Laura Street, Suite 1600, 32202-3421
Telephone: 904-353-7329
Fax: 904-358-1637
Email: lawoffcs@gabelhair.com

MEMBERS OF FIRM

George D. Gabel, Jr.	Sheldon Boney Forte
Mattox S. Hair	Timothy J. Conner
Joel B. Toomey	Suzanne Meyer Judas
Robert M. Dees	Karen Harris Williams

ASSOCIATES

Michael L. Berry, Jr.	Karl B. Hanson, III
Robert Blaine Birthisel	Brooks Charles Rathet

(See Next Column)

GABEL & HAIR, *Jacksonville—Continued*

Scott M. Loftin (1878-1953)   Harold B. Wahl (1907-1993)

Representative Clients: Florida Publishing Co.; Southern Bell Telephone & Telegraph Co.; Florida East Coast Railway Co.; Florida Hotel-Motel Self Insurers Fund; The Steamship Mutual Underwriting Association, Ltd.; The Standard Steamship Owners Protection & Indemnity Association, Ltd.; The Japan Ship Owners Mutual Protection & Indemnity Association; Liverpool & London Steamship Protection & Indemnity Association; Exxon Corp.; Sea-Land Services, Inc.

For full biographical listings, see the Martindale-Hubbell Law Directory

---

HEDRICK, DEWBERRY & REGAN, P.A. (AV)

50 North Laura Street, Suite 2225, 32202
Telephone: 904-356-1300
Fax: 904-356-8050

Michael J. Dewberry   Alexandra Krueger Hedrick
Jeffrey C. Regan

Clinton Allen Wright, III   Evan G. Frayman

For full biographical listings, see the Martindale-Hubbell Law Directory

---

LILES, GAVIN & COSTANTINO (AV)

One Enterprise Center, Suite 1500, 225 Water Street, 32202
Telephone: 904-634-1100
Fax: 904-634-1234

Rutledge R. Liles   R. Kyle Gavin
R. Scott Costantino
ASSOCIATE
Niels P. Murphy

For full biographical listings, see the Martindale-Hubbell Law Directory

---

MARKS, GRAY, CONROY & GIBBS, P.A. (AV)

Suite 800, 1200 Riverplace Boulevard, 32207
Telephone: 904-398-0900
Telecopier: 904-399-8440
Mailing Address: P.O. Box 447, 32201
Email: marksgra@gate.net

Richard P. Marks (1876-1942)	William M. Corley
Francis Michael Holt (1884-1946)	Jeptha F. Barbour
	Linda Cobb Ingham
James A. Yates (1885-1960)	Susan Smith Erdelyi
Sam R. Marks (1885-1973)	Robert E. Broach
Harry T. Gray (1890-1975)	Alan K. Ragan
Francis P. Conroy (1912-1991)	Daniel A. Nicholas
Delbridge L. Gibbs (1917-1992)	Stephen B. Gallagher
James C. Rinaman, Jr.	Milo Scott Thomas
H. Franklin Perritt, Jr.	Gregory A. Lawrence
Victor M. Halbach, Jr.	Edward Keenan Cottrell
Gerald W. Weedon	Leigh A. Studdard
Nicholas V. Pulignano, Jr.	James A. Hoener

OF COUNSEL
Randal C. Fairbanks

Representative Clients: Alamo Rent-A-Car, Inc.; American International Group; American President Lines, Ltd.; American Savings of Florida; Amerisure Insurance Group; Anesthesiologists' Professional Assurance Trust; Associated Aviation Underwriters; Barnett Bank, Inc.; Baxter Healthcare Corp.; Clorox Company.

For full biographical listings, see the Martindale-Hubbell Law Directory

---

JUPITER, Palm Beach Co.

THOMAS J. SCHULTE, P.A. (AV)

Suite 500, 1001 North U.S. Highway One, 33477
Telephone: 561-746-8600
Fax: 561-744-0670

Thomas J. Schulte

Representative Clients: Firemens' Fund Insurance Co.; Liberty Mutual Insurance, Co.; CIGNA; Professional Risk Management Services, Inc.; Florida Out-Patient Self Insurance Co.; Florida Physicians Insurance Trust; Investors Insurance Group; Catholic Diocese of Palm Beach; Gallagher & Bassett Services, Inc.; Anesthesiologists Professional Assurance Co.

For full biographical listings, see the Martindale-Hubbell Law Directory

---

*KISSIMMEE,** Osceola Co.

POHL & SHORT, P.A.

(See Winter Park)

TROUTMAN, WILLIAMS, IRVIN, GREEN & HELMS, PROFESSIONAL ASSOCIATION (AV)

Suite 206, 120 Broadway, 34741
Telephone: 407-933-8834
Telefax: 407-933-8253
Toll Free: 1-800-486-5149
Winter Park, Florida Office: 311 West Fairbanks Avenue, 32789.
Telephone: 407-647-2277.
Telefax: 407-628-2986.

Russell Troutman   Jack E. Bowen

LAKELAND, Polk Co.

LANE, TROHN, CLARKE, BERTRAND, VREELAND & JACOBSEN, P.A. (AV)

One Lake Morton Drive, P.O. Box 3, 33802-0003
Telephone: 941-284-2200
Telecopier: 941-688-0310
Bartow, Florida Office: 150 East Davidson Street. 33803.
Telephone: 941-533-0866.

A. H. Lane (Retired)	John A. Attaway, Jr.
Robert L. Trohn	Hank B. Campbell
Thomas L. Clarke, Jr.	Judith J. Flanders
Robert J. Bertrand	Patrick J. Murphy
John K. Vreeland	Mitchell D. Franks
Donald G. Jacobsen	Janet M. Stuart
Christopher M. Fear	Robert G. Stokes
Gary S. Rabin	Mark N. Miller
Robert M. Brush	Jonathan B. Trohn
Kingswood Sprott, Jr.	Edwin A. Scales, III

Christine M. Casingal   Stephen B. French

Counsel for: Ewell Industries, Inc.
Local Counsel for: Auto Owners Insurance Co.; Liberty Mutual Insurance Co.; St. Paul Fire & Marine Insurance Cos.; U.S. Fidelity & Guaranty Co.; State Farm Insurance Cos.
Approved Attorneys for: Attorneys' Title Insurance Fund; Chicago Title Insurance Co.

For full biographical listings, see the Martindale-Hubbell Law Directory

---

PETERSON & MYERS, P.A. (AV)

100 East Main Street, P.O. Box 24628, 33802-4628
Telephone: 941-683-6511; 676-6934
Telecopier: 941-682-8031
Lake Wales, Florida Office: 130 East Central Avenue, P.O. Box 1079.
Telephones: 941-676-7611; 683-8942.
Winter Haven, Florida Office: Suite 300, 141 5th Street, N.W., P.O. Drawer 7608.
Telephone: 941-294-3360.

Philip O. Allen	Peter J. Munson
Jack P. Brandon	Corneal B. Myers
Beach A Brooks, Jr.	Cornelius B. Myers, III
Kristen Marie Buzzanca	E. Blake Paul
J. Davis Connor	Robert E. Puterbaugh
Michael S. Craig	Abel A. Putnam
Roy A. Craig, Jr.	Thomas B. Putnam, Jr.
Jacob C. Dykxhoorn	Deborah A. Ruster
Dennis P. Johnson	Stephen R. Senn
Kevin C. Knowlton	Andrea Teves Smith
Douglas A. Lockwood, III	Keith H. Wadsworth
M. Craig Massey	Kerry M. Wilson

General Counsel for: Barnett Bank of Polk County.
Representative Clients: Mutual Wholesale Co.; Barnett Banks, Inc.; Ben Hill Griffin, Inc.; Alcoma Association, Inc.
Approved Attorneys for: Equitable Life Assurance Society of the United States; Federal Land Bank, Columbia, South Carolina; Attorneys' Title Insurance Fund.

For full biographical listings, see the Martindale-Hubbell Law Directory

---

LAKE WALES, Polk Co.

PETERSON & MYERS, P.A. (AV)

130 East Central Avenue, P.O. Box 1079, 33853
Telephone: 941-676-7611; 683-8942
Telecopier: 941-676-0643
Lakeland, Florida Office: 100 East Main Street, P.O. Box 24628.
Telephones: 941-683-6511; 676-6934.
Winter Haven, Florida Office: Suite 300, 141 5th Street, N.W., P.O. Drawer 7608.
Telephone: 941-294-3360.

Philip O. Allen	Roy A. Craig, Jr.
Jack P. Brandon	Jacob C. Dykxhoorn
Beach A Brooks, Jr.	Dennis P. Johnson
Kristen Marie Buzzanca	Kevin C. Knowlton
J. Davis Connor	Douglas A. Lockwood, III
Michael S. Craig	M. Craig Massey

(See Next Column)

PETERSON & MYERS P.A.—Continued

Peter J. Munson	Thomas B. Putnam, Jr.
Corneal B. Myers	Deborah A. Ruster
Cornelius B. Myers, III	Stephen R. Senn
E. Blake Paul	Andrea Teves Smith
Robert E. Puterbaugh	Keith H. Wadsworth
Abel A. Putnam	Kerry M. Wilson

General Counsel for: Barnett Bank of Polk County.
Representative Clients: Mutual Wholesale Co.; Barnett Banks, Inc.; Ben Hill Griffin, Inc.; Alcoma Association, Inc.
Approved Attorneys for: Equitable Life Assurance Society of the United States; Federal Land Bank, Columbia, South Carolina; Attorneys' Title Insurance Fund.

For full biographical listings, see the Martindale-Hubbell Law Directory

---

LAKE WORTH, Palm Beach Co.

RICHARD H. WILLITS, P.A. (AV)

2290 10th Avenue, North Suite 404, 33461
Telephone: 1-800-870-0573
561-582-7600
Fax: 407-588-8819

Richard H. Willits, P.A.

For full biographical listings, see the Martindale-Hubbell Law Directory

---

LEESBURG, Lake Co.

AUSTIN & PEPPERMAN (AV)

Suite C 1321 West Citizens Boulevard, P.O. Drawer 490200, 34749-0200
Telephone: 352-728-1020
Fax: 352-728-0595

Robert E. Austin, Jr.	Carla R. Pepperman

Representative Clients: Allstate Insurance Co.; American Excess Insurance Co.; American Re-Insurance Co.; Florida Rock Industries, Inc.; Goodyear Tire & Rubber Co.; Great American Insurance Co.

For full biographical listings, see the Martindale-Hubbell Law Directory

---

LONGWOOD, Seminole Co.

JAMES B. BYRNE, JR., P.A. (AV)

Crown Oak Centre, 370 Crown Oak Centre Drive, 32750
Telephone: 407-831-0450
Fax: 407-339-0542

James B. Byrne, Jr.

For full biographical listings, see the Martindale-Hubbell Law Directory

---

MELBOURNE, Brevard Co.

BEST & ANDERSON, P.A. (AV)

Marina Towers, 709 South Harbor City Boulevard, Suite 220, 32901
Telephone: 407-727-9923
Orlando, Florida Office: 20 North Orange Avenue, Suite 505, 32801.
Telephone: 407-425-2985.
Crystal River, Florida Office: 7655 West Gulf to Lake Highway, Suite 6.
Telephone: 352-795-1107.

David R. Best	Lawrence I. Hauser
George H. "Dutch" Anderson, III	

G. Clay Morris	Angela O'Neil
Natt O. Reifler	

For full biographical listings, see the Martindale-Hubbell Law Directory

---

KRASNY AND DETTMER (AV)

A Partnership of Professional Associations
780 South Apollo Boulevard, P.O. Box 428, 32902-0428
Telephone: 407-723-5646
Telecopier: 407-768-1147

Myron S. (Mike) Krasny (P.A.)	Dale A. Dettmer (P.A.)

Scott Krasny

Representative Clients: Security National Bank; The Coy A. Clark Co.

For full biographical listings, see the Martindale-Hubbell Law Directory

---

NANCE, CACCIATORE, SISSERSON, DURYEA AND HAMILTON (AV)

525 North Harbor City Boulevard, 32935
Telephone: 407-254-8416
Fax: 407-259-8243

(See Next Column)

MEMBERS OF FIRM

James H. Nance	John N. Hamilton
Sammy Cacciatore	Charles G. Barger, Jr.
Ronald G. Duryea	James N. Nance

OF COUNSEL
James A. Sisserson

Reference: First Union Bank.

For full biographical listings, see the Martindale-Hubbell Law Directory

---

*MIAMI,** Dade Co.

ADAMS & ADAMS (AV)

5th Floor, Concord Building, 66 West Flagler Street, 33130
Telephone: 305-371-3333
Broward: 954-728-8770
Telecopier: 305-372-3987

Richard B. Adams (1926-1983)	Richard B. Adams, Jr.
R. Wade Adams	

ASSOCIATES

Mai-Ling E. Castillo	Anthony P. Strasius
Bryant Esquenazi	

For full biographical listings, see the Martindale-Hubbell Law Directory

---

ANGONES, HUNTER, McCLURE, LYNCH & WILLIAMS, P.A. (AV)

Ninth Floor-Concord Building, 66 West Flagler Street, 33130
Telephone: 305-371-5000
Fort Lauderdale: 954-728-9112
FAX: 305-371-3948

Frank R. Angones	Christopher J. Lynch
Steven Kent Hunter	Stewart D. Williams
John McClure	B. Scott Hunter
Leopoldo Garcia, Jr.	

Thomas W. Paradise	Lourdes Alfonsin Ruiz
Donna Joy Hunter	Kara D. Phinney
C. David Durkee	

Insurance Clients: Allstate Insurance Co.; Prudential Property & Casualty Insurance Co.; Travelers Insurance Co.; Rollins Hudig Hall Healthcare Risk, Inc.

For Complete List of Firm Personnel, See General Section

For full biographical listings, see the Martindale-Hubbell Law Directory

---

ARAGON, BURLINGTON, WEIL & CROCKETT, P.A. (AV)

Office in the Grove - Penthouse, 2699 South Bayshore Drive, 33133
Telephone: 305-858-2900
Telefax: 305-858-5261

Rudolph F. Aragon	Kevin C. Kaplan
Robert K. Burlington	Ava Borrasso
Jeffrey B. Crockett	Dianne O. Fischer
Ronald P. Weil	Daniel F. Blonsky
Paul J. Schwiep	Lawrence D. Goodman
Mark A. Salzberg	

For full biographical listings, see the Martindale-Hubbell Law Directory

---

ARMSTRONG & MEJER, P.A. (AV)

Suite 1111 Douglas Centre, 2600 Douglas Road (Coral Gables), 33134
Telephone: 305-444-3355
Fax: 305-442-4300

Timothy J. Armstrong	Alvaro L. Mejer

M. Emelina Mejer-Kondla

Reference: First Union National Bank.

For full biographical listings, see the Martindale-Hubbell Law Directory

---

BIENSTOCK & CLARK (AV)

A Partnership of Professional Corporations
Suite 3160 First Union Financial Center, 200 South Biscayne Boulevard, 33131-2367
Telephone: 305-373-1100
Telecopier: 305-358-1226
Santa Monica, California Office: 3340 Ocean Park Boulevard, Suite 3075.
Telephone: 310-314-8660.
Telecopier: 310-314-8662.

Terry S. Bienstock (P.A.)	Michael C. Cesarano
Roger W. Clark	Philip J. Kantor

Jaime A. Bianchi	Hector R. Rivera
Kimberly A. Levine	Andrew I. Rosenberg
John A. Thornton	

(See Next Column)

BIENSTOCK & CLARK, *Miami—Continued*

Reference: Great Western Bank.

For full biographical listings, see the Martindale-Hubbell Law Directory

---

WILLIAM P. CAGNEY, III, P.A. (AV)

Suite 3400 First Union Financial Center, 200 South Biscayne
　Boulevard, 33131-2393
Telephone: 305-371-1411
Fax: 305-371-3810
Chicago, Illinois Office: Suite 1800, 100 West Monroe Street.

William P. Cagney, III

For full biographical listings, see the Martindale-Hubbell Law Directory

---

COHEN & LEGON, P.A. (AV)

(Formerly Mark A. Cohen & Associates, P.A.)
1221 Brickell Avenue, Suite 1780, 33131-3260
Telephone: 305-375-9292
Facsimile: 305-381-6799
Email: lawfirm@conen-legon.com *URL:* http://www.cohen-legon.com
Washington, D.C. Office: Cohen & Legon, P.C., 1501 M Street, N.W.,
　Suite 1150, 20005-1702.
Telephone: 202-835-3800.
Fax: 202-331-9253.

Mark A. Cohen　　　　　　　　　Todd R. Legon
　　　　　　　David J. Federbush
OF COUNSEL
Stephen M. Koslow (Not admitted in FL)

Fred Goldberg	Kevin B. Bedell
Neil L. Potash	(Not admitted in FL)
Darin S. Engelhardt	Scott M. Behren
Karen G. Morton	David M. Knasel
Andrea M. Wong	(Not admitted in FL)
(Not admitted in FL)	William H. White, Jr.
Janet B. Salzman	Marc J. Leipzig
Michael J. Prame	(Not admitted in FL)
(Not admitted in FL)	Kenyetta R. Coner
Henrietta "Locky" Bright	(Not admitted in FL)

For full biographical listings, see the Martindale-Hubbell Law Directory

---

LAW OFFICES OF DAVID L. DEEHL (AV)

Suite 1575 Courthouse Tower, 44 West Flagler Street, 33130
Telephone: 305-358-9700
Telecopier: 305-358-4036
Email: DAVID@DEEHL.COM

ASSOCIATES
Susan Stanfill Carlson　　　　　Susan Guller
OF COUNSEL
Michele K. Feinzig

For full biographical listings, see the Martindale-Hubbell Law Directory

---

DEUTSCH & BLUMBERG, P.A. (AV)

Suite 2802 New World Tower, 100 North Biscayne Boulevard, 33132
Telephone: 305-358-6329
Fax: 305-358-9304

Steven K. Deutsch　　　　　　　James C. Blecke
Edward R. Blumberg　　　　　　Louis Thaler

For full biographical listings, see the Martindale-Hubbell Law Directory

---

DUNN, LODISH & WIDOM, P.A. (AV)

24th Floor One Biscayne Tower, Two South Biscayne Boulevard, 33131
Telephone: 305-374-4401
Fax: 305-374-6401
Email: Dunn@Shadow.net

Richard M. Dunn	Scott D. Kravetz
Alvin D. Lodish	Sherril M. Colombo
Mitchell E. Widom	Lynn S. Waterman
Sean R. Santini	

For full biographical listings, see the Martindale-Hubbell Law Directory

---

FERRELL & FERTEL, P.A. (AV)

Suite 1920 Miami Center, 201 South Biscayne Boulevard, 33131-2305
Telephone: 305-371-8585
Telecopier: 305-371-5732

Milton M. Ferrell, Jr.　　　　　Alan K. Fertel

Reference: City National Bank of Florida.

For full biographical listings, see the Martindale-Hubbell Law Directory

---

HADDAD, JOSEPHS, JACK, GAEBE & MARKARIAN (AV)

1493 Sunset Drive (Coral Gables), P.O. Box 345118, 33114
Telephone: Dade County: 305-666-6006
Telecopier: 305-662-9931
URL: http://www.haddadjosephs.com
MEMBERS OF FIRM
Gil Haddad　　　　　　　　　　Lewis N. Jack, Jr.
Michael R. Josephs　　　　　　John S. Gaebe
　　　　　　　David K. Markarian
ASSOCIATES
Elisabeth M. Allen　　　　　　Lauren M. Ilvento
Helen Leen Miranda　　　　　Clifford A. Wolff
　　　　　　　John William Gautier

Representative Clients: U-Haul Corporation; ITT Sheraton; Zurich-American Insurance Company; Republic Claims Service Company; Southern Fire Insurance Adjusters.

For full biographical listings, see the Martindale-Hubbell Law Directory

---

ANDREW HALL AND ASSOCIATES, P.A. (AV)

Penthouse, 1428 Brickell Avenue, 33131
Telephone: 305-374-5030
Fax: 305-374-5033

Andrew C. Hall

Christopher M. David　　　　　William H. Strop
Christopher J. Dawes　　　　　Allan A. Joseph
　　　　　　　Douglas M. Horn

For full biographical listings, see the Martindale-Hubbell Law Directory

---

HARDY & BISSETT, P.A. (AV)

501 Northeast First Avenue, 33132
Telephone: 305-358-6200
Broward: 954-462-6377
Fax: 305-577-8230
Email: 102132.403@compuserve.com
Boca Raton, Florida Office: 2201 Corporate Boulevard, N.W., Suite 205.
Telephone: 407-998-9202.
Telecopier: 407-998-9693.

G. Jack Hardy　　　　　　　　G. William Bissett

Howard K. Cherna　　　　　　H. Dane Mottlau
Lee Philip Teichner　　　　　Jana Marie Yaw

Representative Clients: International Paper Co.; Masonite Corp.; Bridgestone/Firestone Inc.; American International Underwriters; American International Group, Inc.; Crown Equipment Corp.; The Coleman Co., Inc.; Brown & Williamson; Black & Decker (U.S.), Inc.; S-B Power Tool Company.

For full biographical listings, see the Martindale-Hubbell Law Directory

---

HOFFMAN & HERTZIG, P.A. (AV)

Suite 900, 241 Sevilla Avenue (Coral Gables), 33134
Telephone: 305-445-3100
Fax: 305-444-5656
Email: CHOFFM04@COUNSEL.COM

Carl H. Hoffman　　　　　　　David Hertzig

References: City National Bank of Miami; Barnett Bank, Coral Gables.

For full biographical listings, see the Martindale-Hubbell Law Directory

---

KAUFMAN MILLER DICKSTEIN & GRUNSPAN, P.A. (AV)

Suite 4650 First Union Financial Center, 200 South Biscayne
　Boulevard, 33131
Telephone: 305-372-5200
Telecopy: 305-374-3200

Jeffrey W. Dickstein　　　　　Edward A. Kaufman
Alan M. Grunspan　　　　　　Raymond V. Miller, Jr.

David James Smith　　　　　　Niall T. McLachlan

For full biographical listings, see the Martindale-Hubbell Law Directory

---

KELLY, BLACK, BLACK, BYRNE & BEASLEY, PROFESSIONAL ASSOCIATION (AV)

1400 Alfred I. du Pont Building, 169 East Flagler Street, 33131
Telephone: 305-358-5700
Fax: 305-358-7269

Hugo L. Black, Jr.　　　　　　Joseph W. Beasley
Robert Carleton Byrne　　　　Bonnie J. Losak-Jimenez
　　　　　　　Nancy Hagan Henry

(See Next Column)

KELLY, BLACK, BLACK, BYRNE & BEASLEY PROFESSIONAL ASSOCIATION—
Continued

Representative Clients: Credit Suisse; Multi-Media Entertainment, Inc.; Japan
Development Company; Israel Discount Bank; Bacardi Imports, Inc.; Peoples Telephone Co.; City of Miami Beach Employees Retirement Trust;
Pueblo International Inc.; Gumenick Properties Inc.
Reference: United National Bank.

For full biographical listings, see the Martindale-Hubbell Law Directory

KENNY NACHWALTER SEYMOUR ARNOLD CRITCHLOW & SPECTOR, PROFESSIONAL ASSOCIATION (AV)

1100 Miami Center, 201 South Biscayne Boulevard, 33131-4327
Telephone: 305-373-1000
Facsimile: 305-372-1861
ABA/net: 18338
Email: 7502552@MCIMAIL.COM
Rogersville, Tennessee Office: 107 East Main Street, Suite 301, 37857-3347.
Telephone: 423-272-5300.
Facsimile: 423-272-4961.

James J. Kenny	Kevin J. Murray
Michael Nachwalter	William J. Blechman
Thomas H. Seymour	Harry R. Schafer
Richard Alan Arnold	Deborah Sampieri Corbishley
Richard H. Critchlow	David H. Lichter
Brian F. Spector	Scott E. Perwin

Jeffrey T. Foreman	Amanda M. McGovern
Lauren C. Ravkind	Paul C. Huck, Jr.
Katherine Clark Silverglate	Tara Mary Higgins
Miriam Lefkowitz	

Representative Clients: Albertson's, Inc.; American Bankers Insurance
Group; Cartier, Inc.; Ethan Allen, Inc.; Federated Department Stores, Inc.;
The Florida Bar; GTE Directories Corp.; Siemens Credit Corp.; Providence
Journal Company; GTE Florida; Columbia HCA.

For Complete List of Firm Personnel, See General Section

For full biographical listings, see the Martindale-Hubbell Law Directory

KLUGER, PERETZ, KAPLAN & BERLIN, P.A. (AV)

1970 Miami Center, 201 South Biscayne Boulevard, 33131
Telephone: Dade: 305-379-9000
Broward: 954-728-8100
Fax: 305-379-3428

Alan J. Kluger	Bruce A. Katzen
Abbey L. Kaplan	Andrew P. Gold
Steven I. Peretz	Jon C. Chassen
Howard J. Berlin	Paul L. Orshan
Steve I. Silverman	Michael B. Chesal
Donna E. Miller	

Michael D. Ehrenstein	Todd A. Levine
Kimberly D. Kolback	Deborah Berlin Talenfeld
Craig T. Galle	Michael S. Perse
Ronny J. Halperin	Jason S. Oletsky

OF COUNSEL

James R. Longacre   Richard A. Sharpstein
(Not admitted in FL)

LEGAL SUPPORT PERSONNEL
PARALEGALS

Vernia Contreras	Kristine H. Kadlac
Maria DeDonatis	Diane M. Payne
Maria A. Tucci	

For full biographical listings, see the Martindale-Hubbell Law Directory

KUTNER, RUBINOFF, BUSH & LERNER (AV)

501 N.E. 1st Avenue, 33132
Telephone: 305-358-6200; Broward: 954-462-6377
Fax: 305-577-8230

MEMBERS OF FIRM

Arno Kutner	Kenneth J. Bush
Edward G. Rubinoff	Susan Scrivani Lerner

For full biographical listings, see the Martindale-Hubbell Law Directory

LEESFIELD, LEIGHTON & RUBIO, P.A. (AV)

2350 South Dixie Highway, 33133
Telephone: 305-854-4900/1-800-836-6400 (toll free)
Fax: 305-854-8266
Email: LEESFIELD@AOL.COM
Key West, Florida Office: 615 1/2 Whitehead Street.
Telephone: 305-296-1342.
Fax: 305-294-1793.

(See Next Column)

Ira H. Leesfield	John Elliott Leighton
Maria L. Rubio	
George G. Mahfood	Steven R. Kozlowski

For full biographical listings, see the Martindale-Hubbell Law Directory

MURAI, WALD, BIONDO & MORENO, P.A. (AV)

9th Floor Ingraham Building, 25 Southeast 2nd Avenue, 33131
Telephone: 305-358-5900
Fax: 305-358-9490

Rene V. Murai	Gerald J. Biondo
Gerald B. Wald	M. Cristina Moreno
William E. Davis	

Cristina Echarte Brochin	Lynette Ebeoglu McGuinness
Mary Leslie Smith	

Reference: Republic National Bank of Miami.

For full biographical listings, see the Martindale-Hubbell Law Directory

PATTERSON & SWEENY (AV)

A Partnership of Professional Associations
Suite 2450, Courthouse Tower, 44 West Flagler Street, 33130
Telephone: 305-350-9000
Fax: 305-372-3940

John H. Patterson (P.A.)   John H. Patterson, Jr. (P.A.)
James H. Sweeny, III (P.A.)
OF COUNSEL
Cynthia Byrne Hall   Mark V. Silverio

For full biographical listings, see the Martindale-Hubbell Law Directory

HARRY A. PAYTON & ASSOCIATES, P.A. (AV)

One Biscayne Tower, Suite 3270, 2 South Biscayne Boulevard, 33131
Telephone: 305-577-4997
Fax: 305-577-4895
Email: H100LAW@AOL.COM

Harry A. Payton

Maria C. Montenegro

For full biographical listings, see the Martindale-Hubbell Law Directory

PODHURST, ORSECK, JOSEFSBERG, EATON, MEADOW, OLIN & PERWIN, P.A. (AV)

Suite 800 City National Bank Building, 25 West Flagler
Street, 33130-1780
Telephone: 305-358-2800; Fort Lauderdale: 954-463-4346
Fax: 305-358-2382
Email: 76666.2340@COMPUSERVE.COM *URL:*
http://www.turbosales.com/"sfbj/podhurst.html

Aaron Podhurst	Michael S. Olin
Robert Orseck (1934-1978)	Joel S. Perwin
Robert C. Josefsberg	Steven C. Marks
Joel D. Eaton	Victor M. Diaz, Jr.
Barry L. Meadow	Katherine W. Ezell

Karen Podhurst Dern	Xavier Martínez

OF COUNSEL
Walter H. Beckham, Jr.

Representative Clients: Burger King Corp.; Ryder System, Inc.; Ernst &
Young; Lennar Corporation; The Continental Companies.
Reference: United National Bank of Miami; City National Bank of Miami.

For full biographical listings, see the Martindale-Hubbell Law Directory

PROENZA & ROBERTS, P.A. (AV)

Grove Plaza, 2900 Middle Street, 33133
Telephone: 305-442-1700
Telecopier: 305-442-2559

Morris C. Proenza (1940-1995)   H. Clay Roberts

Michael A. Vazquez
OF COUNSEL
Thomas L. Hurst

For full biographical listings, see the Martindale-Hubbell Law Directory

PYSZKA, DOUBERLEY, BLACKMON, LEVY & SAVOLA, P.A. (AV)

Fifth Floor, Grand Bay Plaza, 2665 South Bayshore Drive, 33133
Telephone: 305-858-6614

(See Next Column)

PYSZKA, DOUBERLEY, BLACKMON, LEVY & SAVOLA P.A., *Miami—Continued*

| Gerard E. Pyszka | Phillip D. Blackmon, Jr. |
| William M. Douberley | Benjamin D. Levy |

L.H. Steven Savola

For full biographical listings, see the Martindale-Hubbell Law Directory

RICHEY & DIAZ, P.A. (AV)

3100 First Union Financial Center, 200 South Biscayne
Boulevard, 33131-2327
Telephone: 305-372-8808
Telefax: 305-372-3669; 374-4652
Email: richdiaz@netrunner.net

William L. Richey   Michael Diaz, Jr.
OF COUNSEL
Kirk W. Munroe

For full biographical listings, see the Martindale-Hubbell Law Directory

RICHMAN, GREER, WEIL, BRUMBAUGH, MIRABITO & CHRISTENSEN, P.A. (AV)

Miami Center, Tenth Floor, 201 South Biscayne Boulevard, 33131
Telephone: 305-373-4000
Fax: 305-373-4099
West Palm Beach, Florida Office: Phillips Point East. Suite 1100. 777
South Flagler Drive. 33401.
Telephone: 407-803-3500.
Fax: 407-820-1608.

Gerald F. Richman	Gary S. Betensky
Alan G. Greer	Diane Wagner Katzen
Kenneth J. Weil	Manuel A. Garcia-Linares
John M. Brumbaugh	Carroll J. Kelly
Andrew J. Mirabito	Mark Anthony Romance
Bruce A. Christensen	Steven M. Brady
Charles H. Johnson	Lawrence Hugh Kunin
	M. Margaret Haley

Kenneth L. Dobkin   Christine R. Roberts
OF COUNSEL
Robert L. Floyd   Ray H. Pearson
Jeffrey D. Fisher

Representative Clients: Shriners Hospitals for Crippled Children; Motorola, Inc.; Minnesota Mining and Manufacturing Co.; South Florida Hotel and Motel Assn.; The Lubrizol Corp.; Republic of Panama; Hallmark.

For full biographical listings, see the Martindale-Hubbell Law Directory

STANLEY M. ROSENBLATT PROFESSIONAL ASSOCIATION (AV)

12th Floor, Concord Building, 66 West Flagler Street, 33130
Telephone: 305-374-6131
Fax: 305-381-8818

Stanley M. Rosenblatt

Susan Rosenblatt   Mary Margaret Schneider
David C. Rash

For full biographical listings, see the Martindale-Hubbell Law Directory

ROSSMAN, BAUMBERGER & REBOSO, A PROFESSIONAL ASSOCIATION (AV)

23rd Floor, Courthouse Tower, 44 West Flagler Street, 33130
Telephone: 305-373-0708
Fax: 305-577-4370

Charles H. Baumberger   Stephen F. Rossman
Manuel A. Reboso

Reference: United National Bank of Miami.

For full biographical listings, see the Martindale-Hubbell Law Directory

RUMBERGER, KIRK & CALDWELL, PROFESSIONAL ASSOCIATION (AV)

One Biscayne Tower, 2 South Biscayne Boulevard, Suite 3100, 33131
Telephone: 305-358-5577
Fax: 305-371-7580
URL: http://www.rumberger.com
Orlando, Florida Office: Signature Plaza, Suite 300, 201 South Orange
Avenue, (32801), P.O. Box 1873, 32802.
Telephone: 407-872-7300.
Fax: 407-841-2133.
Tallahassee, Florida Office: 106 East College Avenue, Suite 700, (32301),
P.O. Box 10507, 32302.
Telephone: 904-222-6550.
Fax: 940-222-8783.

(See Next Column)

Tampa, Florida Office: 100 North Tampa Street, Suite 2000, (33602), P.O.
Box 3390, 33601.
Telephone: 813-223-4253.
Fax: 813-221-4752.

M. Stephen Smith	Holly Kelly Ennis
John Bond Atkinson	Joshua D. Lerner
Robert J. Rudock	Douglas E. Ede
Scott M. Sarason	Henry Salas
	Lori Anne Brown

Donald E. Fucik	Gustavo D. Lage
Mark E. Grimes	Daniel T. Doyle
Stuart L. Cohen	Lee S. Miller
Anthony J. Petrillo	Joseph M. Maus

Representative Clients: Automotive and other Manufacturers: General Motors Corp.; Nissan Motor Corporation in U.S.A.; Toyota Motor Sales, U.S.A., Inc. Insurance: Royal Insurance Co. Products Liability: Bombardier, Inc.; Outboard Marine Corp.

For full biographical listings, see the Martindale-Hubbell Law Directory

SAMS & MARTIN, P.A. (AV)

The Atrium, Suite 200, 1500 San Remo Avenue (Coral Gables), 33146
Telephone: 305-666-3181
Fax: 305-666-5867
Miami Lakes, Florida Office: Sams, Spier & Hollon, 7975 Northwest
154th Street, 33016.
Telephone: 305-362-6222.
Fax: 305-362-0111.

Murray Sams, Jr.   Timothy M. Martin

Joseph I. Lipsky   Arthur B. Stark, P.A.
Lisa Fialkow Levine

For full biographical listings, see the Martindale-Hubbell Law Directory

SINCLAIR, LOUIS, HEATH, NUSSBAUM & ZAVERTNIK, P.A. (AV)

11th Floor Alfred I. Du Pont Building, 33131
Telephone: 305-374-0544
FAX: 305-381-6869

Henry M. Sinclair (1908-1977)	Bayard E. Heath (Retired)
Paul A. Louis	Frank Nussbaum
	John L. Zavertnik

OF COUNSEL
Leonard H. Rubin   Steven I. Weissman

For full biographical listings, see the Martindale-Hubbell Law Directory

SPARKMAN, ROBB, NELSON, MASON & GINSBURG (AV)

Suite 1003 Biscayne Building, 19 West Flagler Street, 33130
Telephone: 305-374-0033
Broward: 954-522-0045
Fax: 305-539-0767
Fort Lauderdale, Florida Office: Suite 1210, 110 Tower, 110 S.E. Sixth
Street.
Telephones: 305-463-3590; Dade: 305-945-4461.
West Palm Beach, Florida Office: 324 Datura Street, Suite 303. Telephone
407-659-6933.
Fax: 407-659-4328.

MEMBERS OF FIRM
James T. Sparkman	Donald Edward Mason
Michael A. Robb	Paul S. Ginsburg
Richard M. Nelson	Dan Kaufman
	Valerie Kiffin Lewis

ASSOCIATE
John W. Reis

For full biographical listings, see the Martindale-Hubbell Law Directory

SPENCER AND KLEIN, PROFESSIONAL ASSOCIATION (AV)

Suite 1901, 801 Brickell Avenue, 33131
Telephone: 305-374-7700
Telecopier: 305-374-4890

Thomas R. Spencer, Jr.

Paul D. Breitner   David M. Tarlow

Representative Clients: Aerocar Aviation, Inc.; America Publishing Group; American Association of Physicians and Surgeons; Coldwell Banker; Editorial Televisa; Grupo Anaya, S.A.; Independent Living Care, Inc.; Managed Care of America, Inc.; New Times, Inc.; Winn-Dixie Stores.

For Complete List of Firm Personnel, See General Section

For full biographical listings, see the Martindale-Hubbell Law Directory

Miami—Continued

LELAND E. STANSELL, JR., P.A. (AV)

903 Biscayne Building, 19 West Flagler Street, 33130
Telephone: 305-374-5911
Fax: 305-374-5337

Leland E. Stansell, Jr.

Roberto M. Ureta

For full biographical listings, see the Martindale-Hubbell Law Directory

STEWART TILGHMAN FOX & BIANCHI, P.A. (AV)

One Southeast Third Avenue Suite 3000, 33131
Telephone: 305-358-6644
Fax: 305-358-4707

Larry S. Stewart	Gary D. Fox
James B. Tilghman, Jr.	David W. Bianchi

Stuart N. Ratzan

For full biographical listings, see the Martindale-Hubbell Law Directory

THORNTON, DAVIS & MURRAY, P.A. (AV)

World Trade Center, 80 Southwest Eighth Street Suite 2900, 33130
Telephone: 305-446-2646
Fax: 305-441-2374
Email: tdm@gate.net

John M. Murray	Frederick J. Fein
Barry L. Davis	Ana Maria Marin
J. Thompson Thornton	David P. Herman
Jeffrey F. D. Bogert	Harold E. Rambo, Jr.
Mark D. Bohm	Scott D. Rembold
Ury Fischer	Mario M. Ruiz
Holly S. Harvey	Steven E. Wallach
Kathleen M. O'Connor	Rebecca B. Watford

For full biographical listings, see the Martindale-Hubbell Law Directory

VALLE & CRAIG, P.A. (AV)

Suite 2520 World Trade Center, 80 Southwest Eighth Street, P.O. Box 113009, 33111-3009
Telephone: 305-373-2888; 1800-609-6151
Facsimile: 305-373-2889

Laurence F. Valle	Lawrance B. Craig, III
Timothy Maze Hartley	
Frank J. Sioli, Jr.	Nicole F. Ehart
Michael J. Lynott	

For full biographical listings, see the Martindale-Hubbell Law Directory

WELBAUM, GUERNSEY, HINGSTON, GREENLEAF & GREGORY, L.L.P. (AV)

Penthouse Suite, 901 Ponce de Leon Boulevard (Coral Gables), 33134-3009
Telephone: 305-441-8900
Fax: 305-441-2255

MEMBERS OF FIRM

R. Earl Welbaum	Robert A. Hingston
Dan B. Guernsey	W. Frank Greenleaf
John H. Gregory	

ASSOCIATES

Michael Yates	Mark D. Greenwell

OF COUNSEL

Alice E. Warwick	René Sacasas

For full biographical listings, see the Martindale-Hubbell Law Directory

ZACK, SPARBER, KOSNITZKY, SPRATT & BROOKS, P.A. (AV)

International Place, 100 Southeast Second Street, Suite 2800, 33131-2144
Telephone: 305-539-8400
Facsimile: 305-539-1307

Stephen N. Zack	Alan G. Geffin
Gary S. Brooks	Bertha Claire Lee
Jennifer G. Altman	Mitchell W. Mandler
Orion Gray Callison, III	H. Stephen Rash
William Henry Stafford	

OF COUNSEL

Kimarie R. Stratos

For Complete List of Firm Personnel, See General Section

For full biographical listings, see the Martindale-Hubbell Law Directory

NAPLES, * Collier Co.

HARDT LAW OFFICES, P.A. (AV)

Suite 705 SunTrust Building, 801 Laurel Oak Drive, 34108
Telephone: 941-598-2900
Fax: 941-598-3785

Frederick R. Hardt

References: Northern Trust Bank of Florida/Naples, N.A.; U.S. Trust Company of Florida; Sun Bank/Naples, N.A.

For full biographical listings, see the Martindale-Hubbell Law Directory

McDONNELL TRIAL LAWYERS (AV)

1165 Eighth Street South, 33940
Telephone: 941-434-7711; Fort Myers: 860-873-8060
Fax: 941-434-5629
Email: MLO@fortmyers.com

Michael McDonnell

Eric J. Vasquez

For full biographical listings, see the Martindale-Hubbell Law Directory

QUARLES & BRADY (AV)

Barnett Center, 4501 Tamiami Trail North Suite 300, 33940-3060
Telephone: 941-262-5959
Fax: 941-434-4999
Milwaukee, Wisconsin Office: 411 East Wisconsin Avenue, 53202-4497.
Telephone: 414-277-5000.
Fax: 414-271-3552.
Madison, Wisconsin Office: Firstar Plaza, One South Pinckney Street, P.O. Box 2113, 53701-2113.
Telephone: 608-251-5000.
Fax: 608-251-9166.
West Palm Beach, Florida Office: 222 Lakeview Avenue, 4th Floor, 33401.
Telephone: 561-653-5000.
Fax: 561-653-5333.
Phoenix, Arizona Office: One Camelback Building, One East Camelback Road, Suite 400, 85012-1649.
Telephone: 602-230-5500.
Fax: 602-230-5598.

PARTNER
Robert E. Doyle, Jr.
ASSOCIATES

Louis D. D'Agostino	Mark Hubert Muller
Kevin A. Denti	James T. Demarest

For Complete List of Firm Personnel, See General Section

For full biographical listings, see the Martindale-Hubbell Law Directory

VEGA, STANLEY, ZELMAN & HANLON, P.A. (AV)

2660 Airport Road South, 34112
Telephone: 941-774-3333
Fax: 941-776-6420

George Vega, Jr.	Theodore W. Zelman
John F. Stanley	Sharon M. Hanlon
Thomas J. Wood	Paula J. Rhoads
	John G. Vega

OF COUNSEL
Thomas R. Brown

General Counsel for: Lely Estates; Naples Community Hospital.
Local Counsel: Quail Creek Developments.

For full biographical listings, see the Martindale-Hubbell Law Directory

NEW PORT RICHEY, Pasco Co.

DANIEL N. MARTIN, P.A. (AV)

Suite B-1, 8406 Massachusetts Avenue, P.O. Box 786, 34653
Telephone: 813-842-8439

Daniel N. Martin

Representative Clients: Regency Communities, Inc., formerly Minieri Communities of Florida, Inc.; Greene Builders, Inc.; Barnett Bank of Pasco County; Hospital Corporation of America.
Approved Attorneys for: Attorneys' Title Insurance Fund; First American Title Insurance Co.; Commonwealth Land Title Insurance Company.
Reference: Barnett Bank of Pasco County.

NORTH PALM BEACH, Palm Beach Co.

LAW OFFICES OF PATRICK C. MASSA, P.A. (AV)

11891 U.S. Highway One, Suite 110, 33408-2864
Telephone: 407-694-1800
Facsimile: 407-694-1833

(See Next Column)

LAW OFFICES OF PATRICK C. MASSA, P.A., *North Palm Beach—Continued*

Patrick C. Massa

For full biographical listings, see the Martindale-Hubbell Law Directory

ORLANDO,* Orange Co.

ADAMS, HILL, REIS, ADAMS, HALL & SCHIEFFELIN (AV)

1417 East Concord Street, 32803
Telephone: 407-896-0425
Fax: 407-896-9236

MEMBERS OF FIRM

George E. Adams	Janet W. Adams
G. Bruce Hill	Larry D. Hall
Gregory F. Reis	Thomas L. Schieffelin, Jr.

ASSOCIATES

William W. Large	William H. Olney
Matthew P. Bartolomei	Richard Coaxum, Jr
Christopher E. Butler	

Representative Clients: Everglades Regional Medical Center; The Florida Hospital Trust Fund; The Florida Hospital Excess Trust Fund; Florida Hospital Workers Compensation/Self Insurance Trust Fund; Bartow Memorial Hospital; Bay Medical Center; Brooksville Regional Hospital; Cape Canaveral Hospital; Cape Coral Hospital; Desoto Memorial Hospital.

For full biographical listings, see the Martindale-Hubbell Law Directory

ADAMS & SPEARS, P.A. (AV)

940 Highland Avenue, P.O. Box 3627, 32802
Telephone: 407-422-8116
Fax: 407-648-1044
Email: 74767.2745@compuserve.com

Richard H. Adams, Jr.	Richard D. Connor, Jr.
Douglas C. Spears	Deborah B. Ansbro

Peter C. Vilmos	Elizabeth A. Baker
Joyce R. Adams	

OF COUNSEL

Ley H. Smith

General Counsel for: Lochaven Federal Savings & Loan; Independence Mortgage Corporation of America.
Representative Clients: Ensign Property Group, Inc.; Deere Credit Services.

For full biographical listings, see the Martindale-Hubbell Law Directory

ARNOLD, MATHENY & EAGAN, P.A. (AV)

801 North Magnolia Avenue, Suite 201, P.O. Box 2967, 32802
Telephone: 407-841-1550
Facsimile: 407-841-8746

William W. Arnold	Alexander J. Ombres
William L. Eagan	Arthur R. Louv
Lehn E. Abrams	R. Craig Cooley
Barbara Anne Eagan	

Representative Clients: Center Lake Properties, Ltd.; Chase Manhattan of Florida; Combustion Tec. Inc.; Commonwealth Land Title Insurance Com.; Contemporary Services; Dillard's Inc. of Florida; Doctor's Home Health Agency, Inc.; Electro-Science Invest Group, Ltd.; First Union National Bank; Forbes-Hamilton Management Co.

For full biographical listings, see the Martindale-Hubbell Law Directory

BAKER & HOSTETLER (AV)

SunBank Center, Suite 2300, 200 South Orange Avenue, 32802-3432
Telephone: 407-649-4000
In Cleveland, Ohio: 3200 National City Center, 1900 East Ninth Street.
Telephone: 216-621-0200.
In Columbus, Ohio: Capitol Square, Suite 2100, 65 East State Street.
Telephone: 614-228-1541.
In Denver, Colorado: 303 East 17th Avenue, Suite 1100.
Telephone: 303-861-0600.
In Houston, Texas: 1000 Louisiana, Suite 2000.
Telephone: 713-751-1600.
In Long Beach, California: 300 Oceangate, Suite 620.
Telephone: 310-432-2827.
In Los Angeles, California: 600 Wilshire Boulevard.
Telephone: 213-624-2400.
In Washington, D.C.: Washington Square, Suite 1100, 1050 Connecticut Avenue, N.W., Suite 1100.
Telephone: 202-861-1500.
In College Park, Maryland: 9658 Baltimore Boulevard, Suite 206.
Telephone: 301-441-2781.
In Alexandria, Virginia: 437 North Lee Street.
Telephone: 703-549-1294.
In San Francisco, California: One Sansome Street, Suite 2000.
Telephone: 415-951-4705.

(See Next Column)

PARTNERS

John W. Foster, Sr.	Jerry R. Linscott

For Complete List of Firm Personnel, See General Section

For full biographical listings, see the Martindale-Hubbell Law Directory

BEST & ANDERSON, P.A. (AV)

20 North Orange Avenue, Suite 505, 32801
Telephone: 407-425-2985
Crystal River, Florida Office: 7655 West Gulf to Lake Highway, Suite 6.
Telephone: 352-795-1107.
Melbourne, Florida Office: Marina Towers, 709 South Harbor City Boulevard, Suite 220, 32901.
Telephone: 407-727-9923.

David R. Best	Lawrence I. Hauser
George H. "Dutch" Anderson, III	

G. Clay Morris	Angela O'Neil
	Natt O. Reifler

For full biographical listings, see the Martindale-Hubbell Law Directory

CABANISS & BURKE, P.A. (AV)

One Orlando Centre, Suite 1800, 800 North Magnolia Avenue, P.O. Box 2513, 32802-2513
Telephone: 407-246-1800
Fax: 407-246-1895
Tallahassee, Florida Office: 909 East Park Avenue, 32301.
Telephone: 904-561-6212.
Fax: 904-561-6214.

Ronald E. Cabaniss	Francis M. McDonald, Jr.
Thomas M. Burke	Larry D. Smith
Dean Bunch	Chris N. Kolos
(Resident Tallahassee Office)	J. Hood Roberts
Michael J. Wiggins	

Scott E. Damon	Michelle M. Perez-Sotolongo
Sarah A. Long	Winifred H. Quinlan
F. Rand Wallis	

For full biographical listings, see the Martindale-Hubbell Law Directory

CAMERON, MARRIOTT, WALSH, HODGES & COLEMAN, P.A. (AV)

15 West Church Street, 32801
Telephone: 407-841-5030
Fax: 407-843-1727
Daytona Beach, Florida Office: 432 South Beach Street.
Telephone: 904-257-1755.
Fax: 904-252-5601.
Ocala, Florida Office: 18 Northeast First Ave.
Telephone: 904-351-1119.
Fax: 904-351-0151.

A. Craig Cameron	E. Peyton Hodges
Frank Marriott, Jr.	Christopher C. Coleman
J. David Walsh (Resident, Daytona Beach Office)	

James A. Chereskin (Resident, Daytona Beach Office)	Douglas J. LaPointe
Patrick M. DeLong	Sheryl Simonetta Zust (Resident, Daytona Beach Office)
Kevin K. Chase	Louis D. Kaye

Representative Clients: Albertson's; AIG; All-State; Auto Owners; American Family Insurance Group; American Fire and Casualty Insurance Co.; AT&T; Automobile Club Insurance Co.; Avis; Black & Decker.

For full biographical listings, see the Martindale-Hubbell Law Directory

DeWOLF, WARD, O'DONNELL & GLATT, P.A. (AV)

Suite 1750, 111 North Orange Avenue, 32801-2399
Telephone: 407-841-7000
Telecopy: 407-843-6035

Thomas B. DeWolf	John H. Ward
James E. Glatt, Jr.	

Representative Clients: Walt Disney World Co.; The Walt Disney Co.; Fleetwood Enterprises, Inc.; Roadway Express; Massachusetts Mutual Life Insurance Co.; Employers Insurance of Wausau; World Transportation, Inc.; Marriott Corp; World Transportation, Inc.; Utah Home Fire Ins. Co.

For full biographical listings, see the Martindale-Hubbell Law Directory

LAW OFFICES OF DURIE & LAWSON, P.A. (AV)

1000 East Robinson Street, 32801
Telephone: 407-841-6000; 1-800-940-0442
Fax: 407-841-2425

(See Next Column)

LAW OFFICES OF DURIE & LAWSON, P.A.—*Continued*

Jack F. (Jay) Durie, Jr.   C. Alan Lawson

For full biographical listings, see the Martindale-Hubbell Law Directory

FISHER AND MATTHEWS, P.A.

(See Altamonte Springs)

GURNEY & HANDLEY, P.A. (AV)

225 East Robinson Street, Suite 450, 32801
Telephone: 407-843-9500
Facsimile: 407-649-4941
Email: 74011.2161@compuserve.com

Leon H. Handley   Robert S. Green
Richard W. Lassiter   W. Marvin Hardy, III
John L. Sewell   Ronald L. Harrop
David W. Roquemore, Jr.   Francis E. Pierce, III
                Peter N. Smith

David Brian Falstad   Michael V. Barszcz
J. Brian Baird   Steven H. Preston
                Paul D. Rang

Representative Clients: Atlanta Casualty Company; Beneficial Mortgage Corp.; California Federal Bank, FSB; Government Employees Insurance Co.; Huntington National Bank of Florida; John Hancock Mutual Life Insurance Co.; Meritor Credit Corp.; Orlando Utilities Commission; Phoenix Home Life Mutual Insurance Co.; University of Florida.

For full biographical listings, see the Martindale-Hubbell Law Directory

HARTLEY & WALL (AV)

200 South Orange Avenue, Suite 2810, P.O. Box 2168, 32802
Telephone: 407-422-7992
Fax: 407-425-2182

MEMBERS OF FIRM
Carl W. Hartley, Jr.   Richard F. Wall
ASSOCIATE
Todd K. Norman

Reference: Sun Bank, N.A.

For full biographical listings, see the Martindale-Hubbell Law Directory

HILL AND PONTON, PROFESSIONAL ASSOCIATION (AV)

Suite 500, 605 East Robinson Street, P.O. Box 2673, 32801
Telephone: 407-422-4665

Brian D. Hill   Carol J. Ponton

Rebecca Jean Alexander   Shea A. Fugate
Maria T. Fabré   Karen M. Marcell
Maria D. Santana
    (Not admitted in FL)

For full biographical listings, see the Martindale-Hubbell Law Directory

KING & BLACKWELL, P.A. (AV)

25 East Pine Street, P.O. Box 1631, 32802-1631
Telephone: 407-422-2472
Fax: 407-648-0161
Email: kbfirm@aol.com

David B. King   Bruce B. Blackwell
                Mayanne Downs

John F. Tannian   Thomas A. Zehnder

For full biographical listings, see the Martindale-Hubbell Law Directory

MARTINEZ, DALTON, DELLECKER & WILSON, PROFESSIONAL ASSOCIATION (AV)

719 Vassar Street, 32804
Telephone: 407-425-0712
Fax: 407-425-1856
URL: http://www.pixelstorm.com/mddw

Mel R. Martinez   Robert H. Dellecker
Roy B. Dalton, Jr.   Brian T. Wilson

Leticia Marques

For full biographical listings, see the Martindale-Hubbell Law Directory

MATHEWS RAILEY DECUBELLIS & GOODWIN, P.A. (AV)

Suite 801 Citrus Center, 255 South Orange Avenue, P.O. Box 4976, 32802-4976
Telephone: 407-872-2200
Telecopier: 407-423-1038

(See Next Column)

Lawrence G. Mathews, Jr.   Frank M. Bedell
David C. Goodwin   Mary M. Wills
Lilburn R. Railey, III   Jennifer S. Eden
Daniel L. DeCubellis   Mark L. Van Valkenburgh
            OF COUNSEL
            Lynn Walker Wright
        LEGAL SUPPORT PERSONNEL
Carol D. Methven   Georgette Freid
W. Rogers Turner, Jr.   (Firm Administrator)

Representative Clients: Centex-Great Southwest Corp.; Design Professional Insurance Corp.; Florida Lawyers Mutual Insurance Corp.; International Game Technology, Inc.; Jennings Environmental Services, Inc.; Mader Southeast, Inc.; McDonald's Corporation; Orange County; PGA Tour, Inc.; SunTrust Bank, Inc.

For full biographical listings, see the Martindale-Hubbell Law Directory

MORAN & SHAMS, P.A. (AV)

111 North Orange Avenue, Suite 1200, P.O. Box 472, 32802-0472
Telephone: 407-841-4141
Fax: 407-841-4148
Email: moran-shams@moran-shams.com

Kelly T. Blystone   Robert W. Rasch
Brian J. Moran   Christopher C. Skambis
            Sidney H. Shams

Representative Clients: Adventist Health System Sunbelt Healthcare Corporation; All Florida Resorts Management; Dayron, Inc.; Gencor Industries Inc.; H.J. Heinz Co.; Insurance Office of Florida, Inc.; Kvaerner Trafalgar House Construction Co.; Photo Chemical Systems of Florida, Inc.; U.S. Foodservice, Inc.; Vermont American Corporation.

For full biographical listings, see the Martindale-Hubbell Law Directory

O'NEILL, CHAPIN, MARKS, LIEBMAN, COOPER & CARR (AV)

A Partnership including Professional Associations
865 Eola Park Center, 200 East Robinson Street, 32801
Telephone: 407-425-2751
Telex: 407-423-1192

Bernard C. O'Neill, Jr. (P.A.)   John B. Liebman (P.A.)
Bruce E. Chapin (P.A.)   Mark O. Cooper (P.A.)
Robert O. Marks (P.A.)   George E. Carr (P.A.)
            ASSOCIATE
            Rod C. Lundy

Reference: First Union National Bank.

For full biographical listings, see the Martindale-Hubbell Law Directory

WILLIAM G. OSBORNE, P.A. (AV)

538 East Washington Street, 32801-1996
Telephone: 407-422-5385
Fax: 407-422-5381

William G. Osborne
        LEGAL SUPPORT PERSONNEL
Janet C. Pelletier (CLA)   Elizabeth I. Dunnigan
                                    (Office Manager)

For full biographical listings, see the Martindale-Hubbell Law Directory

POHL & SHORT, P.A.

(See Winter Park)

ARTHUR J. RANSON, III (AV)

201 East Pine Street, 32801
Telephone: 407-649-4886

For full biographical listings, see the Martindale-Hubbell Law Directory

ROBERTSON, WILLIAMS & McDONALD, P.A. (AV)

538 East Washington Street, 32801
Telephone: 407-425-1606
Fax: 407-425-6195
Other Orlando Office: 20 North Eola Drive.

John M. Robertson   Hubert W. Williams (1937-1986)
            J. Stephen McDonald

            Beth S. Schick
Reference: First Union Bank.

For full biographical listings, see the Martindale-Hubbell Law Directory

Orlando—Continued

RUMBERGER, KIRK & CALDWELL, PROFESSIONAL ASSOCIATION (AV)

Signature Plaza, Suite 300, 201 South Orange Avenue (32801), P.O. Box 1873, 32802
Telephone: 407-872-7300
Fax: 407-841-2133; 407-841-7710
URL: http://www.rumberger.com
Miami, Florida Office: One Biscayne Tower. 2 South Biscayne Boulevard, Suite 3100, 33131.
Telephone: 305-358-5577.
Fax: 305-371-7580.
Tallahassee, Florida Office: 106 East College Avenue, Suite 700, (32301), P.O. Box 10507, 32302.
Telephone: 904-222-6550.
Fax: 904-222-8783.
Tampa, Florida Office: 100 North Tampa Street, Suite 2000, (33602), P.O. Box 3390, 33601.
Telephone: 813-223-4253.
Fax: 813-221-4752.

E. Thom Rumberger	Francis H. Sheppard
William L. Kirk, Jr.	Douglas B. Brown
Lori Jean Caldwell	David C. Schwartz
J. Scott Kirk	Ernest H. Eubanks, Jr.
Michael R. Levin	Darryl L. Gavin
Clifford L. Adams	David B. Shelton
Wendy Vomacka	Daniel J. Gerber
Craig P. Niedenthal	Jeffrey S. Weiss

G. Mark Thompson	John W. Dill
Charles P. Mitchell	Richard A. Keller
Suzanne M. Barto Hill	Hayden R. Dempsey
Christopher T. Hill	Frank T. Allen
Lori M. M. Huckabee	Michael D. Crosbie
Sharon J. Duncan	Henry N. Didier, Jr.

Christa M. Cowart

Representative Clients: Automotive and other Manufacturers: General Motors Corp.; Mazda Motor of America Inc.; Nissan Motor Corp. in U.S.A.; Toyota Motor Sales, U.S.A., Inc. General: Allstate Insurance Co.; Royal Insurance Co. Aviation: AIG Aviation, Inc. Professional Liability: American International Group.

For full biographical listings, see the Martindale-Hubbell Law Directory

RUSSELL & HULL, P.A. (AV)

537 North Magnolia Avenue, P.O. Box 2751, 32802
Telephone: 407-422-1234
Telecopier: 407-423-2842

Rodney Laird Russell	Norman L. Hull

Reference: First Union National Bank, N.A.

For full biographical listings, see the Martindale-Hubbell Law Directory

SHEPARD, FILBURN & GOODBLATT, P.A. (AV)

First Union Tower, Suite 1107, 20 North Orange Avenue, 32801
Telephone: 407-481-2020
Fax: 407-481-0208
Email: sf2law@aol.com

Clifford B. Shepard, III	Jenna R. Rinehart
Mark C. Filburn	Michael J. Kirwin
Amy E. Goodblatt	(Not admitted in FL)

Representative Clients: Sovereign Bank; Cintas Corporation; Intercargo Insurance Company; Trade Insurance Services, Inc.; Integon General Insurance Company; Danella Construction Company; Adventist Health Systems, Inc.; Hersh National Painting & Roofing Company; Team America, Inc.; Sysco Food Services, Inc.

For full biographical listings, see the Martindale-Hubbell Law Directory

STUMP, STOREY & CALLAHAN, P.A. (AV)

28 East Washington Street, P.O. Box 3388, 32802-3388
Telephone: 407-425-2571
Telecopier: 407-425-0827

John R. Stump	Philip D. Storey

W. Scott Callahan

Donald Paul Dietrich II	Robin L. Hoyle

Representative Clients: Amresco Management, Inc.; Chase Manhattan Service Corp.; Federal Deposit Insurance Corp.; The Huntington National Bank; Jackson Management Group, Inc.; Mobile Home Park Associates, L.P.; NationsBank, N.A.; Orange County, Florida; Seminole Finance Corp.

For full biographical listings, see the Martindale-Hubbell Law Directory

SUBIN, ROSENBLUTH, LOSEY, BRENNAN, BITTMAN & MORSE, PROFESSIONAL ASSOCIATION (AV)

Suite 900, 111 North Orange Avenue, P.O. Box 4950, 32802-4950
Telephone: 407-841-7100
Facsimile: 407-648-0660
Email: lawyer@orlando.com

Eli H. Subin	Ralph C. Losey
Emery H. Rosenbluth, Jr.	John M. Brennan
Stacey R. Littler	Sandra A. Kenny

Representative Clients: Connecticut General Life Insurance Co.; Gilbane Building Company; Subaru of America; Dania JuiAla (Division of the Aragon Group, Inc.); Brice Building Company, Inc.; Trammel Crow Company; Principal Mutual Life Insurance Company; Reynolds Metals Company; SouthTrust Bank of Florida, N.A.; U.S. Foodservice, Inc.

For full biographical listings, see the Martindale-Hubbell Law Directory

WILSON, LEAVITT & SMALL, P.A. (AV)

Nations Bank Tower, 111 North Orange Avenue, Suite 1575, 32801
Telephone: 407-843-4321
Fax: 407-423-1505

J. Christy Wilson, III	Jay W. Small
Mark R. Leavitt	Lauren B. Shapiro

Representative Clients: Circle K; Cumberland Farms; Hardee's Food Systems; Mobil Oil; Public Storage; Southland Corp.; NationsBank, N.A.; U.S.F.& G.; Oerther Foods; Seventh Day Adventists.

For full biographical listings, see the Martindale-Hubbell Law Directory

ZIMMERMAN, SHUFFIELD, KISER & SUTCLIFFE, P.A. (AV)

Landmark Center One, Suite 600, 315 East Robinson Street, P.O. Box 3000, 32802
Telephone: 407-425-7010
Telecopier: 407-425-2747

Bernard J. Zimmerman	Robert L. Dietz
W. Charles Shuffield	Stephen B. Hatcher
Wendell J. Kiser	Robert W. Peacock, Jr.
Roland A. Sutcliffe Jr.	Clement L. Hyland
Robert E. Mansbach, Jr.	J. Timothy Schulte

Pamela Lynn Foels
OF COUNSEL
Gerard J. Turner

Melissa Dubina Kaplan	Kevin G. Malchow
Eric P. Gibbs	Thomas Warren Sculco
Joseph C. L. Wettach	Kevin L. Lienard
Edward C. Duncan, III	Daniel R. Murphy
Charles H. Leo	Michael C. Tyson
Vivian M. Reeves	Lori A. Walsingham Smith
Kraig N. Johnson	Scot G. Nimmo
Gene E. Crick, Jr.	Lynne R. Wilson
Charles B. Costar III	Lori A. Newsome

Joanne Marie Toner
LEGAL SUPPORT PERSONNEL
PARALEGALS

Jeanne Ann Roper	Shannon E. Brooks

L. Darlene Riley

For full biographical listings, see the Martindale-Hubbell Law Directory

PALM BEACH, Palm Beach Co.

MINTMIRE & ASSOCIATES (AV)

265 Sunrise Avenue, Suite 204, 33480
Telephone: 561-832-5696
Fax: 561-659-5371

Donald F. Mintmire	Jeffrey A. Shaffer
Paul Safran, Jr.	Timothy D. Friedman

For full biographical listings, see the Martindale-Hubbell Law Directory

ROZELLE AND CALL (AV)

223 Sunset Avenue, Suite 200, P.O. Box 229, 33480
Telephone: 407-655-8585
Fax: 407-655-8663

MEMBERS OF FIRM

Douglas D. Rozelle, Jr.	John S. Call, Jr.

ASSOCIATE
Marc P. Barmat

Representative Clients: Wal-Mart Stores, Inc.; Motors Insurance Corp.; American Contractors Insurance Group, Inc.; Continental Loss Adjusting Co.; The Equitable Life Assurance Society; Connecticut General Life Insurance Co.; Safeco Insurance Co.; Phar-Mor of Florida, Inc.; World Wide Insurance Group; Chrysler Insurance Co.; United Service Automobile Association.

(See Next Column)

ROZELLE AND CALL—*Continued*

For full biographical listings, see the Martindale-Hubbell Law Directory

PALM BEACH GARDENS, Palm Beach Co.

SCOTT, ROYCE, HARRIS, BRYAN, BARRA & JORGENSEN, PROFESSIONAL ASSOCIATION (AV)

4400 PGA Boulevard, Suite 800, 33410
Telephone: 561-624-3900
Fax: 561-624-3533

John L. Bryan, Jr.   John M. Jorgensen
Donna A. Nadeau

Representative Clients: First Union National Bank of Florida, N.A.; Barnett Banks, Inc.; The Realtors Association of the Palm Beaches, Inc.; Lost Tree Village; Art Moran Pontiac, Inc.; Admiralty Bank; Enterprise National Bank of Palm Beach, N.A.; Alandco, Inc.; Northern Trust Bank of Florida, N.A.; Chicago Title Insurance Co.

For Complete List of Firm Personnel, See General Section

For full biographical listings, see the Martindale-Hubbell Law Directory

SLAWSON & CUNNINGHAM (AV)

Harbour Financial Center, 2401 PGA Boulevard, Suite 140, 33410
Telephone: 407-625-6260
Facsimile: 407-625-6269

Richard W. Slawson (P.A.)   Fred A. Cunningham
Jeanmarie Whalen

For full biographical listings, see the Martindale-Hubbell Law Directory

PENSACOLA,* Escambia Co.

FULLER, JOHNSON & FARRELL, P.A. (AV)

Quayside Quarters, 700 South Palafox, Suite 170, P.O. Box 12219, 32581
Telephone: 904-434-8845
Fax: 904-432-6667
Tallahassee, Florida Office: 111 North Calhoun Street, P.O. Box 1739, 32302-1739.
Telephone: 904-224-4663.
Fax: 904-561-8839.

Belinda Barnes deKozan   Alan R. Horky
Michael W. Kehoe   Christopher R. Johnson

Representative Clients: Aetna Life & Casualty; Amoco Oil Co.; Anesthesiologists' Professional Assurance Trust; CIGNA; Crum & Forster Insurance Cos.; Fireman's Fund; Florida Physicians Insurance Reciprocal; GEICO; Toyota Motor Corp.

For full biographical listings, see the Martindale-Hubbell Law Directory

KERRIGAN, ESTESS, RANKIN & McLEOD (AV)

400 East Government Street, 32501
Telephone: 904-444-4444
Watts No.: 1-800-444-4404
FAX: 904-444-4495
Email: kerrigan@olis.com *URL:* http://www.kerrigan.com
Fort Walton Beach, Florida Office: 212 SE Eglin Parkway, Suite C.
Telephone: 904-244-1111.
Century, Florida Courtesy Office: 8210 North Century Boulevard.
Telephone: 800-256-1120.
Gulf Breeze, Florida Courtesy Office: 50 Fort Pickens Road.
Telephone: 800-433-7777.
Panama City, Florida Office: 836 Jenks Avenue.
Telephone: 904-871-5000.
FAX: 904-872-2148.
Tallahassee, Florida Courtesy Office: 217 South Adams Street, First Floor.
Telephone: 904-671-5000.

MEMBERS OF FIRM

Robert G. Kerrigan   T. Michael McLeod
George W. Estess   Randle D. Thompson
William Rankin   Marcus J. Michles II
Kristin L. Stewart

LEGAL SUPPORT PERSONNEL

Sam R. Peebles   James Michael Kerrigan, Ph.D.
Renée J. Miller

Reference: 1st American Bank of Pensacola.

For full biographical listings, see the Martindale-Hubbell Law Directory

MOORE, HILL, WESTMORELAND, HOOK & BOLTON, P.A. (AV)

9th Floor, Sun Bank Tower, 220 West Garden Street, P.O. Box 1792, 32598-1792
Telephone: 904-434-3541
Telefax: 904-435-7899

(See Next Column)

H. Edward Moore, Jr.   Michael D. Hook
J. Lofton Westmoreland   Stephen F. Bolton
Larry Hill   Yancey F. Langston

William R. Mitchell   Brian H. Kirkland
Charles F. Beall, Jr.

For full biographical listings, see the Martindale-Hubbell Law Directory

B. RICHARD YOUNG, P.A. (AV)

309B South Palafox Place, 32501
Telephone: 904-432-2222
Fax: 904-432-1444

B. Richard Young

Penny L. Hendrix   Michael T. Bill

For full biographical listings, see the Martindale-Hubbell Law Directory

PLANTATION, Broward Co.

FENSTER AND FAERBER, PROFESSIONAL ASSOCIATION (AV)

Suite 307, The Gulfstream Building, 8751 West Broward Boulevard, 33324
Telephone: 954-473-1500; Miami: 305-949-9998
Mailing Address: P.O. Box 16688, 33318

Jeffrey M. Fenster   Stacie L. Cohen
Jesse S. Faerber   Jene P. Williams
OF COUNSEL
Betty Anne Beavers

For full biographical listings, see the Martindale-Hubbell Law Directory

ST. AUGUSTINE,* St. Johns Co.

UPCHURCH, BAILEY & UPCHURCH, P.A. (AV)

780 North Ponce de Leon Boulevard, P.O. Drawer 3007, 32085-3007
Telephone: 904-829-9066
Facsimile: 904-825-4862

Frank D. Upchurch, III   Katherine Gaertner Jones
OF COUNSEL
Hamilton D. Upchurch

Representative Clients: Aero Sport, Inc.; American Culinary Federation, Inc.; Barnett Bank, N.A. Penney Retirement Community, Inc.; St. Augustine Alligator Farm, Inc.; St. Augustine-St. Johns County Board of Realtors, Inc. *General Counsel:* Flagler College; Flagler Hospital, Inc.; Prosperity Bank of St. Augustine; St. Johns County School Board.

For Complete List of Firm Personnel, See General Section

For full biographical listings, see the Martindale-Hubbell Law Directory

ST. PETERSBURG, Pinellas Co.

JAMES D. ECKERT (AV)

401 Fourth Street North, 33701
Telephone: 813-895-6505
Fax: 813-822-7686

For full biographical listings, see the Martindale-Hubbell Law Directory

KALEEL & KALEEL, P.A. (AV)

3819 Central Avenue, P.O. Box 15697, 33733-5697
Telephone: 813-321-0744

Wm. C. Kaleel, Sr. (1903-1976)   H. Shelton Philips
William C. Kaleel, Jr.   Robert L. Kaleel

Representative Clients: State Farm Mutual Automobile Insurance Co.; Auto Owners Insurance Co.
Reference: First Union National Bank of Florida.

For full biographical listings, see the Martindale-Hubbell Law Directory

KEANE & REESE, P.A. (AV)

North Trust Bank Building, 100 Second Avenue, South Suite 1201, P.O. Box 57, 33731-0057
Telephone: 813-823-5000
Fax: 813-894-1023
Palm Harbor, Florida Office: 36426 U.S. 19 North, 34684.
Telephone: 813-787-1355.
Fax: 813-789-0821.

Michael J. Keane   Michael K. Reese

Shirin Mohammadbhoy Vesely   Richard Scott Maselli
OF COUNSEL
Charles M. Waygood

For full biographical listings, see the Martindale-Hubbell Law Directory

St. Petersburg—Continued

MARTIN ERROL RICE, P.A. (AV)

696 First Avenue North, Suite 400, P.O. Box 205, 33731
Telephone: 813-821-4884
Fax: 813-821-7961

Martin Errol Rice

For full biographical listings, see the Martindale-Hubbell Law Directory

RIDEN, EARLE & KIEFNER, P.A. (AV)

City Center, North Tower, 100 Second Avenue South, Suite
400, 33701-4336
Telephone: 813-822-6000
Telecopier: 813-821-3721

Thomas K. Riden	Christopher C. Ferguson
James T. Earle, Jr.	Timothy A. Miller
John R. Kiefner, Jr.	Gary E. Frazier
Paul Castagliola	James C. Rowe
Robert H. Crawford	Christopher B. Young
Neil G. Kiefer	Clifford J. Hunt
D. Jay Snyder	Benjamin Felder

M. Deanna Harris	Camille J. Iurillo
	Michael Francis Bremer

For full biographical listings, see the Martindale-Hubbell Law Directory

STEIN, FORD, SCHAAF & TOWZEY, L.L.P. (AV)

501 First Avenue North, Suite 1000, 33701
Telephone: 813-894-4333
Fax: 813-894-0175; 813-822-7222

Henry A. Stein	Gary M. Schaaf
Harvey A. Ford	Phyllis J. Towzey
Paul A. Nelson	Sarah E. Williams

For full biographical listings, see the Martindale-Hubbell Law Directory

---

SANFORD, * Seminole Co.

STENSTROM, MCINTOSH, COLBERT, WHIGHAM & SIMMONS, P.A. (AV)

Suite 22 Sun Bank-Downtown, P.O. Box 4848, 32772-4848
Telephone: 407-322-2171
Fax: 407-330-2379
Email: stenstrom.com

Thomas E. Whigham (1952-1988)	Franklin C. Whigham
Douglas Stenstrom (Retired)	Clayton D. Simmons
William L. Colbert	Robert K. McIntosh
	Donna L. Surratt-McIntosh
William E. Reischmann, Jr.	

Catherine D. Reischmann	James J. Partlow
	Edgar J. Hedrick, III

OF COUNSEL

Kenneth W. McIntosh	S. Kirby Moncrief

Representative Clients: City of Sanford; City of Oviedo; City of Casselberry; Seminole Community College; City of Lake Mary; Sanford Housing Authority; City of DeBary; Seminole Soccer Club, Inc.; Tuskawilla Homeowners' Association; South Seminole-North Orange Wastewater Transmission Authority.

For full biographical listings, see the Martindale-Hubbell Law Directory

---

SARASOTA, * Sarasota Co.

DICKINSON & GIBBONS, P.A. (AV)

1750 Ringling Boulevard, P.O. Box 3979, 34230
Telephone: 941-366-4680
FAX: 941-953-3136

G. Hunter Gibbons	Burwell J. Jones
Ward E. Dahlgren	Richard R. Garland
Lewis F. Collins, Jr.	Stephen G. Brannan
Gary H. Larsen	Deborah J. Blue
Camden T. French	Jeffrey D. Peairs
Ralph L. Marchbank, Jr.	Douglas R. Wight
A. James Rolfes	Stephen R. Kanzer
	David S. Preston

OF COUNSEL

Patrick H. Dickinson

Representative Clients: Allstate Insurance Co.; Liberty Mutual; Nationwide Insurance Co.; St. Paul Fire & Marine Insurance Co.; Cincinnati Insurance Co.; Ohio Casualty Insurance Co.; Florida Physicians Insurance Co.; Travelers Insurance Co.; Prudential Insurance Co.; State Farm Insurance Company.

(See Next Column)

For Complete List of Firm Personnel, See General Section

For full biographical listings, see the Martindale-Hubbell Law Directory

NELSON ● HESSE (AV)

2070 Ringling Boulevard, P.O. Box 2524, 34230
Telephone: 941-366-7550
Fax: 941-955-3708

MEMBERS OF FIRM

Richard E. Nelson	Omer S. Causey
Ronald Alexander Cyril (1938-1988)	William A. Dooley
Richard L. Smith	Michael S. Drews
F. Steven Herb	Frederick J. Elbrecht
	Gary W. Peal

ASSOCIATES

Philip Sypula	J. Neal Mobley
	Stephen M. Walker

General Counsel for: Enterprise National Bank; Dooley Mack Construction Co.;
Representative Clients: Wellcraft Marine; Attorneys Title Insurance Fund; Travelers Insurance; SMH Radiology, Inc.; The Carlton Ranch, Inc.
References: Southtrust Bank; Enterprise National Bank.

For full biographical listings, see the Martindale-Hubbell Law Directory

---

WILLIAMS, PARKER, HARRISON, DIETZ & GETZEN, PROFESSIONAL ASSOCIATION (AV)

200 South Orange Avenue, 34236-6749
Telephone: 941-366-4800
Telecopier: 941-366-5109
Mailing Address: P.O. Box 3258, Sarasota, Florida, 34230-3258
Email: wphdg.law@netsrg.com *URL:*
http://www.sarasota-online.com/williamspa-w

J.J. Williams, Jr. (1886-1968)	Frank Strelec
W. Davis Parker (1920-1982)	Terri Salt Costa
William T. Harrison, Jr.	David A. Wallace
George A. Dietz	Mark A. Schwartz
Monte K. Marshall	Ric Gregoria
James L. Ritchey	Elvin W. Phillips
William G. Lambrecht	Jeffrey A. Grebe
John T. Berteau	John L. Moore
John V. Cannon, III	Morgan R. Bentley
Charles D. Bailey, Jr.	Susan A. Barrett
J. Michael Hartenstine	Carol Ann Kalish
Michele Boardman Grimes	Linda R. Getzen
James L. Turner	Kimberly J. Page
William M. Seider	Phillip D. Eck
Elizabeth C. Marshall	J. Hugh Middlebrooks
Robert W. Benjamin	Robert A. Warram

OF COUNSEL

William E. Getzen	Frazer F. Hilder
	Hugh McPheeters, Jr.

LEGAL SUPPORT PERSONNEL

Mark Loveridge (Land Planner)

General Counsel for: Sarasota County Public Hospital Board; Sarasota-Manatee Airport Authority; Taylor Woodrow Homes Ltd.; FCCI Mutual Insurance Co.
Local Counsel for: NationsBank of Florida; Barnett Bank of Southwest Florida; Northern Trust Bank of Florida; SunTrust Bank, Gulfcoast.

For full biographical listings, see the Martindale-Hubbell Law Directory

---

STUART, * Martin Co.

MCCARTHY, SUMMERS, BOBKO, MCKEY, WOOD & SAWYER, P.A. (AV)

2081 East Ocean Boulevard, Suite 2-A, 34996
Telephone: 561-286-1700
Fax: 561-283-1803
Email: mcsumm@gate.net *URL:* http://www.gate.net/~mcsumm/

Terence P. McCarthy	John D. McKey, Jr.
Robert P. Summers	Steven J. Wood
Noel A. Bobko	Thomas R. Sawyer

Representative Clients: American Bank of Martin County; First National Bank and Trust Company of the Treasure Coast; Great Western Bank; Hydratech Utilities; Lost Lake at Hobe Sound; Taylor Creek Marina, Inc.; GBS Excavating, Inc.; Seaboard Savings Bank; Gary Player Design Group.

For full biographical listings, see the Martindale-Hubbell Law Directory

Stuart—Continued

MOYLE, FLANIGAN, KATZ, KOLINS, RAYMOND & SHEEHAN, P.A. (AV)

900 South Federal Highway, 1st Floor, P.O. Box 658, 34995
Telephone: 561-288-1144
Facsimile: 561-288-1499
Palm Beach Gardens, Florida Office: 2401 P.G.A. Boulevard, Building C - Suite 120.
Telephone: 561-625-6480.
Facsimile: 561-625-5979.
Tallahassee, Florida Office: 210 South Monroe Street.
Telephone: 904-681-3828.
Facsimile: 904-681-8788.
West Palm Beach, Florida Office: 625 North Flagler Drive, 9th Floor.
Telephone: 561-659-7500.
Facsimile: 561-659-1789.

Linda R. McCann

For full biographical listings, see the Martindale-Hubbell Law Directory

---

TALLAHASSEE,* Leon Co.

* indicates certain Bar Register subscribers whose principal office is located elsewhere in the state and who have arranged for representation as a part of the state capital listings that follow

---

COOPER, COPPINS & MONROE, P.A. (AV)

1319 Thomaswood Drive P.O. Drawer 14447, 32317-4447
Telephone: 904-422-2420
Facsimile: 904-422-2730

John C. Cooper	Michael F. Coppins
D. Lloyd Monroe, IV	

Gwendolyn P. Adkins	James E. Messer, Jr.
Floy M. Busby	David B. Switalski
Cassandra K. Jackson	

Reference: Barnett Bank of Tallahassee.

For full biographical listings, see the Martindale-Hubbell Law Directory

---

FULLER, JOHNSON & FARRELL, P.A. (AV)

111 North Calhoun Street, P.O. Box 1739, 32302-1739
Telephone: 904-224-4663
Fax: 904-561-8839
Pensacola, Florida Office: Quayside Quarters, 700 South Palafox, Suite 170, P.O. Box 12219, 32581.
Telephone: 904-434-8845.
FAX: 904-432-6667.

Ben A. Andrews	Kathryn L. Johnson
Jeannette M. Andrews	Michael W. Kehoe
Wm. Stephen Black, II	(Resident, Pensacola Office)
Marjorie M. Cain	J. Craig Knox
Robert C. Crabtree	Belinda Barnes deKozan
Patrick J. Farrell, Jr.	(Resident, Pensacola Office)
S. William Fuller, Jr.	William R. Mabile, III
Alan R. Horky	P. Scott Mitchell
(Resident, Pensacola Office)	Steven Michael Puritz
Christopher R. Johnson	Paul A. Shapiro
(Resident, Pensacola Office)	Cynthia D. Simmons
Fred M. Johnson	Beverly H. Smith
Michael J. Thomas	

Representative Clients: Aetna Life & Casualty; CIGNA Companies; Cotton States Insurance; Crum & Forster Insurance Companies; Ford Motor Company; Gallagher Bassett Services, Inc.; MMI Companies; The St. Paul Insurance Companies, Inc.; Toyota Motor Sales, U.S.A., Inc.

For full biographical listings, see the Martindale-Hubbell Law Directory

---

HENRY, BUCHANAN, HUDSON, SUBER & WILLIAMS, P.A. (AV)

117 South Gadsden Street P.O. Drawer 1049, 32302
Telephone: 904-222-2920
Telecopier: 904-224-0034

Bryan W. Henry (1925-1986)	Jesse F. Suber
John D. Buchanan, Jr.	Harriet W. Williams
Edwin R. Hudson	J. Steven Carter
Laura Beth Faragasso	

GOVERNMENTAL CONSULTANT
Curt Blair

Reference: Barnett Bank of Tallahassee, Inc.

For full biographical listings, see the Martindale-Hubbell Law Directory

---

McCONNAUGHHAY, ROLAND, MAIDA & CHERR, P.A. (AV)

Suite 900, 101 North Monroe Street, P.O. Drawer 229, 32302-0229
Telephone: 904-222-8121
Telecopier: 904-222-4359
Pensacola, Florida Office: 316 South Baylen Street, Suite 500.
Telephone: 904-434-7122.
Telecopier: 904-435-0924.
Panama City, Florida Office: 825 Jenks Avenue.
Telephone: 904-784-2599.
Telecopier: 904-769-5461.
Jacksonville, Florida Office: 8381 Dix Ellis Trail, Suite 100.
Telephone: 904-363-1950.
Telecopier: 904-363-1510.
Sarasota, Florida Office: 1800 Second Street, Suite 954.
Telephone: 941-955-6141.
Telecopier: 941-955-6244.

James N. McConnaughhay	R. Stephen Coonrod
R. William Roland	Patrick E. Weaver
Thomas J. Maida	(Resident at Panama City)
Gordon D. Cherr	Robert D. Pope
Christopher John DuBois	(Resident at Jacksonville)
Brian S. Duffy	

Michael J. Rudicell	Sarah M. Stokes
(Resident at Pensacola Office)	Clyde W. (Billy) Galloway, Jr.
Mary Lalley Wakeman	Austin B. Neal
Cecil L. Davis, Jr.	Tracey J. Hyde (Resident at
Mary Ellen Ingley	Panama City Office)
Joe G. Durrett	Michael E. Ingram
Michael C. Crumpler (Resident	Laurie T. Dodson
at Jacksonville Office)	Mark H. Gelman
M. Kemmerly Thomas	(Resident at Jacksonville)
Robert C. Palmer, III	Jacquelyn Lewis
(Resident at Pensacola Office)	Jessica Enciso Varn
E. Louis Stern	Peter S. Roumbos
(Resident at Sarasota Office)	(Resident at Pensacola)
Mary E. Cruickshank	Jacqueline L. Blanton
Elizabeth L. Campo (Resident at	(Resident at Sarasota)
Jacksonville Office)	Susan L. Fara
Jana M. Black	(Resident at Sarasota)

OF COUNSEL
Roderic G. Magie (Resident at Pensacola Office)

For full biographical listings, see the Martindale-Hubbell Law Directory

---

McFARLAIN, WILEY, CASSEDY & JONES, PROFESSIONAL ASSOCIATION (AV)

215 South Monroe Street, Suite 600, P.O. Box 2174, 32316-2174
Telephone: 904-222-2107
Telecopier: 904-222-8475

Richard C. McFarlain	Charles A. Stampelos
William B. Wiley	Linda McMullen
Marshall R. Cassedy	H. Darrell White, Jr.
Douglas P. Jones	Christopher Barkas

Harold R. Mardenborough, Jr.	Rogelio J. Fontela
Robert A. McNeely	Patrick John McGinley

For full biographical listings, see the Martindale-Hubbell Law Directory

---

* RUMBERGER, KIRK & CALDWELL, PROFESSIONAL ASSOCIATION (AV)

106 East College Avenue, Suite 700 (32301), P.O. Box 10507, 32302
Telephone: 904-222-6550
Fax: 904-222-8783
URL: http://www.rumberger.com
Orlando, Florida Office: Signature Plaza, Suite 300, 201 South Orange Avenue, (32801), P.O. Box 1873, 32802.
Telephone: 407-872-7300.
Fax: 407-841-2133.
Miami, Florida Office: One Biscayne Tower. 2 South Biscayne Boulevard, Suite 3100, 33131.
Telephone: 305-358-5577.
Fax: 305-371-7580.
Tampa, Florida Office: 100 North Tampa Street, Suite 2000, (33602), P.O. Box 3390, 33601.
Telephone: 813-223-4253.
Fax: 813-221-4752.

George N. Meros, Jr.	Robert L. Hessman

Michael E. Riley	Mary W. Chaisson
Lisa M. Appelo	William L. Sundberg

Representative Clients: Aviation: Aviation Underwriting Specialists. Automotive: General Motors Corp.; Mazda Motor of America, Inc.; Nissan Motor Corp. in U.S.A.; Toyota Motor Sales, U.S.A. Commercial: Metropolitan Life Insurance Co. General: Allstate Insurance Co.; Royal Insurance Co. Professional Liability: American International Group; COREGIS.

For full biographical listings, see the Martindale-Hubbell Law Directory

TAMPA, * Hillsborough Co.

MICHAEL C. ADDISON (AV)

Suite 2175, 100 North Tampa Street, 33602-5145
Telephone: 813-223-2000
Facsimile: 813-228-6000
Mailing Address: P.O. Box 2175, Tampa, Florida, 33601-2175
Email: 72100.337@compuserve.com

For full biographical listings, see the Martindale-Hubbell Law Directory

ALLEN, DELL, FRANK & TRINKLE, P.A. (AV)

1240 Barnett Plaza, 101 East Kennedy Boulevard, P.O. Box 2111, 33601
Telephone: 813-223-5351
Telecopier: 813-229-6682

Ralph C. Dell	Robert A. Mora
Stewart C. Eggert	Benjamin G. Morris
Gary M. Witters	A. Christopher Kasten, II
Joseph G. Heyck, Jr.	Richard A. Harrison
Michael N. Brown	James S. Eggert
Marian P. McCulloch	Steven F. Thompson

Representative Clients: Tampa International Airport; Bank of Tampa; Florida Citrus Processors Assn.; The Coca Cola Co., Foods Division; Montgomery Elevator Co.; Seminole Electric Cooperative Inc.; Hillsborough County Hospital Authority; Tampa General Healthcare; Tampa Greyhound Track.

For Complete List of Firm Personnel, See General Section

For full biographical listings, see the Martindale-Hubbell Law Directory

ALLEY AND ALLEY/FORD & HARRISON (AV)

205 Brush Street, P.O. Box 1427, 33601
Telephone: 813-229-6481
Fax: 813-223-7029
Atlanta, Georgia Office: Ford & Harrison, 600 Peachtree at the Circle Building, 1275 Peachtree Street, N.E., 30309.
Telephone: 404-888-3800.
Fax: 404-888-3863.
Los Angeles, California Office: Ford & Harrison, 333 South Grand Avenue, Suite 3680, 90071.
Telephone: 213-680-3410.
Fax: 213-680-4161.
Miami, Florida Office: 516 Ingraham Building, 25 S.E. 2nd Avenue, 33131.
Telephone: 305-379-3811.
Fax: 305-358-5933.
Washington, D.C. Office: Ford & Harrison, 1920 N Street, N.W., Suite 200, 20036.
Telephone: 202-463-6633.
Fax: 202-466-5705.

Granville M. Alley, Jr.	Robert D. Hall, Jr.
(1929-1976)	James M. Craig
John-Edward Alley	David S. Shankman
Joseph Z. Fleming	Edmund J. McKenna
(Resident, Miami Office)	

ASSOCIATES

Pedro P. Forment	Tracey Karen Jaensch
Collins Guyton	Amy Wright Littrell
	John A. Rine

Representative Clients: TCI Cablevision; K-Mart Corp.; Pasco County School Board; Pinellas County, Florida; Publix Super Markets, Inc.; Southern Bakeries, Inc.; Sysco Corp.; The Wackenhut Corp. and subsidiaries; TJX Cos. (T.J. Maxx).

For full biographical listings, see the Martindale-Hubbell Law Directory

ALPERT, BARKER & CALCUTT, P.A. (AV)

First Union Center, Suite 2000, 100 South Ashley Drive (33602), P.O. Box 3270, 33601-3270
Telephone: 813-223-4131
Fax: 813-228-9612

Jonathan L. Alpert	Chris A. Barker
	Patrick B. Calcutt

R. Christopher Rodems	William J. Cook
Gregory Joseph Blackburn	Emma Sleeth Hemness
David D. Ferrentino	Scott J. Flint
	David A. Kessler

Representative Clients: AABCO Mortgage & Investments, Inc.; Alexander & Alexander, Inc.; AMI Memorial Hospital; Georgia-Pacific Corp.; Hospital Underwriting Group; American International Group; National Reinsurance Corp.; Professional Service Industries; RLI Insurance Co.

For full biographical listings, see the Martindale-Hubbell Law Directory

TIMOTHY G. ANDERSON, P.A. (AV)

213 South Brevard Avenue, 33606
Telephone: 813-251-0072

(See Next Column)

Timothy G. Anderson

Leslie L. Harley	Scott T. McCullough

For full biographical listings, see the Martindale-Hubbell Law Directory

BARR, MURMAN, TONELLI, HERZFELD & RUBIN (AV)

Enterprise Plaza, Suite 901, 201 East Kennedy Boulevard, P.O. Box 172669, 33672-0669
Telephone: 813-223-3951
Fax: 813-229-2254

James A. Murman	Ellen H. Lorenzen
Michael A. Tonelli	John R. Dixon
Daniel H. Sleet	Michael A. Connolly
	Ashley J. McCorvey

OF COUNSEL

Billy R. Barr

Representative Client: CIGNA Insurance Co.

For full biographical listings, see the Martindale-Hubbell Law Directory

BUCHANAN INGERSOLL, PROFESSIONAL CORPORATION (AV(T))

Suite 2500, 401 East Jackson Street, 33602
Telephone: 813-222-8180
Telecopier: 813-222-8189
URL: http://www.bipc.com
Pittsburgh, Pennsylvania Office: One Oxford Centre, 301 Grant Street, 20th Floor.
Telephone: 412-562-8800.
Philadelphia, Pennsylvania Office: Two Logan Square, Twelfth Floor, 18th & Arch Streets.
Telephone: 215-665-8700.
Harrisburg, Pennsylvania Office: 30 North Third Street.
Telephone: 717-237-4800.
Aventura, Florida Office: 19495 Biscayne Boulevard, Suite 606.
Telephone: 305-933-5600.
Miami, Florida Office: NationsBank Tower, 100 S.E. Second Street.
Telephone: 305-347-4080.
Princeton, New Jersey Office: Buchanan Ingersoll, A Partnership, College Centre, 500 College Road East.
Telephone: 609-987-6800.
Lexington, Kentucky Office: Suite 600, PNC Bank Plaza, 200 West Vine Street.
Telephone: 606-225-5333.
Buffalo, New York Office: 1100 Main Place Tower, 350 Main Street.
Telephone: 716-854-4100.
Fax: 716-854-4227.

James J. Kennedy III

For Complete List of Firm Personnel, See General Section

For full biographical listings, see the Martindale-Hubbell Law Directory

RAY CALAFELL, JR., P.A. (AV)

105 South Armenia Avenue, 33609
Telephone: 813-871-3890
Fax: Available upon Request

Ray Calafell

For full biographical listings, see the Martindale-Hubbell Law Directory

CLARK, CHARLTON & MARTINO, A PROFESSIONAL ASSOCIATION (AV)

Westshore Center, Suite 700, 1715 North Westshore Boulevard, P.O. Box 24268, 33623-4268
Telephone: 813-289-0700
Fax: 813-289-5498

Scott T. Borders	James W. Clark
Scott Charlton	Anthony T. Martino

Reference: Southtrust Bank of Tampa.

For full biographical listings, see the Martindale-Hubbell Law Directory

THE LAW FIRM OF COHEN, JAYSON & FOSTER, P.A. (AV)

First of America Plaza, Suite 1700, 201 East Kennedy Boulevard, P.O. Box 172538, 33672
Telephone: 813-225-1655
Fax: 813-225-1921

Barry A. Cohen	Christopher P. Jayson
Todd Foster	Mark H. Wright
	Michelle Lee Pickett

E. Patrick Buntz

For full biographical listings, see the Martindale-Hubbell Law Directory

Tampa—Continued

CUNNINGHAM LAW GROUP, P.A. (AV)

100 Ashley Drive, South, Suite 100, 33602
Telephone: 813-228-0505
Telefax: 813-229-7982

Anthony W. Cunningham   James D. Clark
Donald G. Greiwe   Dana Solin Kanfer

For full biographical listings, see the Martindale-Hubbell Law Directory

PATRICK H. DEKLE, P.A. (AV)

808 Landmark Building, 412 Madison Street, 33602-4640
Telephone: 813-223-2300

Patrick H. Dekle

For full biographical listings, see the Martindale-Hubbell Law Directory

GARDNER, WILKES, SHAHEEN & CANDELORA (AV)

2650 SunTrust Financial Centre, 401 East Jackson Street, 33602
Telephone: 813-221-8000
Telefax: 813-229-1597
Mailing Address: P.O. Box 1810, Tampa, FL, 33601-1810

Richard Candelora   L. Joseph Shaheen, Jr.
Merritt A. Gardner   Ted R. Tamargo
Anthony Thomas Leon   Kevin J. Wilcox
Michael A. Peters   Richard Benjamin Wilkes

For full biographical listings, see the Martindale-Hubbell Law Directory

HONIGMAN MILLER SCHWARTZ AND COHN (AV)

A Partnership including Professional Associations
2700 SunTrust Financial Centre, 401 E. Jackson Street, 33602-5226
Telephone: 813-221-6600
Telecopier: 813-223-4410
URL: http://law.honigman.com
West Palm Beach, Florida Office: Suite 800 Esperante Building, 222 Lakeview Avenue, 33401-6112.
Telephone: 561-838-4500.
Detroit, Michigan Office: 2290 First National Building, 48226.
Telephone: 313-256-7800.
Lansing, Michigan Office: 222 North Washington Square, Suite 400, 48933-1800.
Telephone: 517-484-8282.

MEMBERS
Robert W. Boos (P.A.)   Gregory G. Jones (P.A.)
Harry Christopher Goplerud (P.A.)

ASSOCIATES
Kevin M. Gilhool   Donald A. Mihokovich
Susan M. Salvatore

Representative Clients: Commonwealth Land Title Insurance Co.; First American Title Insurance Co.; General Host Corp.; Pulte Home Corp.; The Sembler Company; Wilma South Corp.

For Complete List of Firm Personnel, See General Section

For full biographical listings, see the Martindale-Hubbell Law Directory

HOYT, COLGAN & ANDREU, P.A. (AV)

3000 Barnett Plaza, 101 East Kennedy Boulevard, 33602
Telephone: 813-229-6688
Facsimile: 813-229-3331

Brooks P. Hoyt   Michael B. Colgan
Timothy A. Andreu

Brian K. French
OF COUNSEL
Louis J. Beltrami

For full biographical listings, see the Martindale-Hubbell Law Directory

LEVINE, HIRSCH & SEGALL, P.A. (AV)

First Union Center, 100 South Ashley Drive, Suite 1600, P.O. Box 3429, 33601-3429
Telephone: 813-229-6585
Telecopier: 813-229-7210

Arnold D. Levine   Richard A. Hirsch
Stephen L. Segall

Edward M. Brennan

For full biographical listings, see the Martindale-Hubbell Law Directory

MANEY, DAMSKER, HARRIS & JONES, P.A. (AV)

606 Madison Street, P.O. Box 172009, 33672-0009
Telephone: 813-228-7371
Fax: 813-223-4846

Lee S. Damsker   David A. Maney

Lorena L. Kiely

For full biographical listings, see the Martindale-Hubbell Law Directory

MORRISON, MORRISON & MILLS, P.A. (AV)

1200 West Platt Street Suite 100, 33606
Telephone: 813-258-3311
Telecopier: 813-258-3209

Thomas K. Morrison   Frederick J. Mills
Susan B. Morrison   James E. Holmes, Jr.

Representative Clients: SouthTrust Bank of West Florida; SouthTrust Bank of Alabama, National Association; NationsBank of Florida, N.A.; Mercantile Bank; Barnett Banks, Inc.; Southern Commerce Bank; Sun Bank of Pasco County; Hillsborough County Industrial Development Authority; Automation Packaging, Inc.; Medical Data Management, Inc.

For full biographical listings, see the Martindale-Hubbell Law Directory

RUMBERGER, KIRK & CALDWELL, PROFESSIONAL ASSOCIATION (AV)

100 North Tampa Street, Suite 2000 (33602), P.O. Box 3390, 33601
Telephone: 813-223-4253
Fax: 813-221-4752
URL: http://www.rumberger.com
Miami, Florida Office: One Biscayne Tower, 2 South Biscayne Boulevard, Suite 3100, 33131.
Telephone: 305-358-5577.
Fax: 305-371-7580.
Orlando, Florida Office: Signature Plaza, Suite 300, 201 South Orange Avenue, (32801), P.O. Box 1873, 32802.
Telephone: 407-872-7300.
Fax: 407-841-2133.
Tallahassee, Florida Office: 106 East College Avenue, Suite 700, (32301), P.O. Box 10507, 32302.
Telephone: 904-222-6550.
Fax: 904-222-8783.

J. Richard Caldwell, Jr.   Susan Droppleman Duff

Ronald D. Darrigo   Bradley A. Kustin
Robert L. Blank   Kari A. Metzger
Angelina M. Grimes

Representative Clients: Automotive and other Manufacturers: General Motors Corp.; Mazda Motors of America, Inc.; Nissan Motor Corp. in U.S.A.; Toyota Motor Sales, U.S.A., Inc. General: Allstate Insurance Co.; Royal Insurance Co. Professional Liability: American International Group.

For full biographical listings, see the Martindale-Hubbell Law Directory

RYWANT, ALVAREZ, JONES & RUSSO, PROFESSIONAL ASSOCIATION (AV)

Suite 500 Perry Paint & Glass Building, 109 North Brush Street, P.O. Box 3283, 33601
Telephone: 813-229-7007
Fax: 813-223-6544
Ocala, Florida Office: 3300 S.W. 34th Avenue, Suite 124C, 32674.
Telephone: 904-237-8810.
FAX: 904-237-2022.

Manuel J. Alvarez   Steven D. Lehner
Jill Diziel Emerson   Burke G. Lopez
Darrell D. Dirks   Kerry C. McGuinn, Jr.
Matthew D. Emerson   Andrew F. Russo
John A.C. Guyton, III   Michael S. Rywant
Gregory D. Jones   James R. Wilson

LEGAL SUPPORT PERSONNEL
Bradley Hugh Holt

Representative Clients: Peerless Insurance Co.; Gulf Insurance Group; Employers Casualty Co.; Landmark Insurance Co.

For full biographical listings, see the Martindale-Hubbell Law Directory

ALBERT SALEM AND ASSOCIATES, P.A. (AV)

Suite 100 Salem Building, 4600 West Kennedy Boulevard, P.O. Box 18607, 33679-8607
Telephone: 813-286-3000
Telecopier: 813-287-0517
Email: AMS0403@AOL.COM

Albert M. Salem, Jr.

(See Next Column)

ALBERT SALEM AND ASSOCIATES, P.A., *Tampa—Continued*

Diana K. Wallace   Albert M. Salem, III
Barbara C. Peddicord

Reference: First Commercial Bank; SunTrust.

For full biographical listings, see the Martindale-Hubbell Law Directory

SALEM, SAXON & NIELSEN, PROFESSIONAL ASSOCIATION (AV)

Suite 3200, One Barnett Plaza, 101 East Kennedy Boulevard, P.O. Box 3399, 33601
Telephone: 813-224-9000
Telecopier: 813-221-8811

Richard J. Salem	Lisa M. Castellano
Bernice S. Saxon	Beth M. Coleman
Richard A. Nielsen	Roy J. Ford, Jr.
David J. Tong	Marilyn Mullen Healy
Marian B. Rush	Troy M. Lovell
Ricardo L. Gilmore	Evin L. Netzer
Steven M. Berman	Lynn Van Hyning Ramey
C. Graham Carothers, Jr.	Susan K. S. Scarcelli
J. Frazier Carraway	Jacqueline M. Spoto

OF COUNSEL
John Crider

Reference: The Bank of Tampa.

For full biographical listings, see the Martindale-Hubbell Law Directory

CHARLES F. SANSONE (AV)

Suite 200, 701 North Franklin Street, 33602
Telephone: 813-223-9282
FAX: 813-229-0595

For full biographical listings, see the Martindale-Hubbell Law Directory

SCHROPP, BUELL & ELLIGETT, PROFESSIONAL ASSOCIATION (AV)

401 East Jackson Street, Suite 2600, 33602-5226
Telephone: 813-221-2600
FAX: 813-221-1760

Charles P. Schropp   Mark P. Buell
Raymond T. Elligett, Jr.

William R. Daniel	Amy S. Farrior
Shirley Thompson Faircloth	Donna S. Koch

For full biographical listings, see the Martindale-Hubbell Law Directory

SMITH, WILLIAMS & HUMPHRIES, P.A. (AV)

Old Hyde Park, 712 South Oregon Avenue, 33606
Telephone: 813-253-5400
Fax: 813-254-3459
Orlando, Florida Office: Southeast Bank Building, Suite 701, 201 East Pine Street.
Telephone: 407-849-5151.
Fax: 407-843-4076.

David Lisle Smith	Robert L. Harding
Gregory L. Williams	(Resident, Orlando Office)
J. Gregory Humphries	Gregory E. Mierzwinski
(Resident, Orlando Office)	Carole Taylor Kirkwood
Daniel William King	

For full biographical listings, see the Martindale-Hubbell Law Directory

STUART, STRICKLAND & CAGLIANONE, P.A. (AV)

605 South Boulevard, 33606
Telephone: 813-251-8081
Fax: 813-254-2459
Brooksville, Florida Office: 217 Howell Avenue.
Telephone: 904-796-6733.
Fax: 904-799-7506.

Stephen K. Stuart   Steven A. Strickland
Jeffrey A. Caglianone

Francis Anthony Miller

Reference: City Bank of Tampa.

For full biographical listings, see the Martindale-Hubbell Law Directory

WILLIAMS, REED, WEINSTEIN, SCHIFINO & MANGIONE, P.A. (AV)

One Tampa City Center, 201 North Franklin Street, Suite 2600, P.O. Box 380, 33601
Telephone: 813-221-2626
Telefax: 813-221-7335

(See Next Column)

Robert V. Williams	Ralph P. Mangione
James M. Reed	Scott I. Steady
David B. Weinstein	R. Marshall Rainey
William J. Schifino, Jr.	David S. Jennis
Russell S. Thomas	

Kenneth G. Turkel	Robert R. Hearn
Aminie Mohip	John A. Schifino
Ricardo A. Roig	Jennifer A. Powers
V. Stephen Cohen	Elizabeth S. Hoskins

FIRM ADMINISTRATOR
Joseph C. Simmons

For full biographical listings, see the Martindale-Hubbell Law Directory

TAVARES,* Lake Co.

WILLIAMS, SMITH & SUMMERS, P.A. (AV)

380 West Alfred Street, 32778
Telephone: 352-343-6655
Fax: 352-343-4267

Robert Q. Williams   Christopher J. Smith
Gary L. Summers

Approved Attorneys for: Attorneys' Title Insurance Fund.
Reference: Sun Bank, N.A.

For full biographical listings, see the Martindale-Hubbell Law Directory

VERO BEACH,* Indian River Co.

CLEM, POLACKWICH, VOCELLE & TAYLOR (AV)

A Partnership including Professional Associations
Univest Building-Suite 501, 2770 North Indian River Boulevard, 32960
Telephone: 561-562-8111
Fax: 561-562-2870

MEMBERS OF FIRM

Chester Clem (P.A.)	Louis B. Vocelle, Jr., (P.A.)
Alan S. Polackwich, Sr. (P.A.)	James A. Taylor, III

ASSOCIATE
Paul Richard Berg

OF COUNSEL
Robert Golden

References: Barnett Bank of The Treasure Coast; Northern Trust Bank of Vero Beach; Indian River National Bank; Riverside National Bank of Florida.

For full biographical listings, see the Martindale-Hubbell Law Directory

COLLINS, BROWN, CALDWELL, BARKETT, ROSSWAY, GARAVAGLIA & MOORE, CHARTERED (AV)

756 Beachland Boulevard, P.O. Box 3686, 32964
Telephone: 561-231-4343
FAX: 561-234-5213

George G. Collins, Jr.	Bradley W. Rossway
Calvin B. Brown	Michael J. Garavaglia
William W. Caldwell	John E. Moore, III
Bruce D. Barkett	Lisa N. Thompson

Reference: First Union Bank of Indian River County, Vero Beach, Florida.

For full biographical listings, see the Martindale-Hubbell Law Directory

GOULD, COOKSEY, FENNELL, O'NEILL & MARINE, PROFESSIONAL ASSOCIATION (AV)

979 Beachland Boulevard, 32963
Telephone: 561-231-1100
Fax: 561-231-2020

John R. Gould (1921-1988)	Darrell Fennell
Byron T. Cooksey	Eugene J. O'Neill
Christopher H. Marine	

David M. Carter   Todd W. Fennell

Counsel for: Barnett Bank of Indian River County; Indian River National Bank; Citrus Bank, N.A.
Approved Attorneys for: Attorneys' Title Insurance Fund; Commonwealth Land Title Insurance Company; Lawyers Title Insurance Corp.; Federal Land Bank of Columbia.
Local Counsel for: Los Angeles Dodgers, Inc.

For full biographical listings, see the Martindale-Hubbell Law Directory

MOSS, HENDERSON, BLANTON, KOVAL & LANIER, P.A. (AV)

817 Beachland Boulevard, P.O. Box 3406, 32964-3406
Telephone: 561-231-1900
Fax: 561-231-4387

(See Next Column)

MOSS, HENDERSON, BLANTON, KOVAL & LANIER P.A.—*Continued*

George H. Moss, II
Steve L. Henderson
Robin A. Blanton
Lisa D. Harpring
Thomas A. Koval
Clinton W. Lanier
Fred L. Kretschmer, Jr.

Lewis W. Murphy, Jr.
Judith Goodman Hill
Kelly Cambron
Lawrence Y. Leonard
David F. Mancini

OF COUNSEL

Charles E. Garris
Ford J. Fegert
Everett J. Van Gaasbeck

Representative Clients: Aetna Life & Casualty; Alcoa Florida, Inc.; Florida Power & Light Co.; Insurance Company of North America; Liberty Mutual Insurance Co.; Sears, Roebuck & Co.; Sugar Cane Growers Cooperative of Florida.

For full biographical listings, see the Martindale-Hubbell Law Directory

PAXTON, CROW, BRAGG, SMITH & KEYSER, P.A. (AV)

1717 Indian River Boulevard Suite 202C, 32960
Telephone: 561-778-1755
FAX: 561-778-2433
West Palm Beach, Florida Office: Barristers Building, Suite 500, 1615 Forum Place.
Telephone: 561-684-2121.
FAX: 561-684-6855.

Morgan S. Bragg
Julia Luyster

For full biographical listings, see the Martindale-Hubbell Law Directory

SMITH & SMITH (AV)

Citrus Financial Center, Suite 301, 1717 Indian River Boulevard, 32960
Telephone: 561-567-4351
Fax: 561-567-4298

MEMBERS OF FIRM

Sherman N. Smith, Jr.
Sherman N. Smith, III

ASSOCIATE

Anthony T. Golden

References: Citrus Bank, N.A.; Northern Trust Bank of Vero Beach.

For full biographical listings, see the Martindale-Hubbell Law Directory

WEST PALM BEACH,* Palm Beach Co.

ADAMS, COOGLER, WATSON & MERKEL, P.A. (AV)

Suite 1600, 1555 Palm Beach Lakes Boulevard, P.O. Box 2069, 33402
Telephone: 561-478-4500
Fax: 561-684-7346

Samuel H. Adams (1913-1981)
Roy R. Watson
Robert G. Merkel
Keith R. Pallo
James C. Barry
Reed W. Kellner
Catherine Lynn Kasten
Louis P. Pfeffer

Jeanne Cleary Brady
J. Rod Cameron
Faith L. Connor
Peter A. Cooke
Paul L. Harwood
Carlos J. Hernandez
Thomas Hodas
Patricia A. Judge
Stephanie Karp
Jeffrey L. Marks
Andrea D. McMillan
James C. Paine, Jr.
Kathryn L. Tignor
Karen J. Valente
Scott S. Warburton
Maura A. Ziska

OF COUNSEL

Monroe A. Coogler, Jr.
Shala J. Espina
L. C. Shepard, Jr.

Representative Client: Auto-Owners Insurance.

For full biographical listings, see the Martindale-Hubbell Law Directory

CHRISTIANSEN & JACKNIN (AV)

Suite 1010, NationsBank Tower, 1555 Palm Beach Lakes Boulevard, P.O. Box 3346, 33402
Telephone: 561-689-1888
Fax: 561-689-0586

MEMBERS OF FIRM

John T. Christiansen
Jay R. Jacknin
Neil B. Jagolinzer
Eric Ash

Clients and References Furnished by Request.

For full biographical listings, see the Martindale-Hubbell Law Directory

DAMSEL & GELSTON, P.A. (AV)

601B North Dixie Highway Post Office Drawer 4507, 33402-4507
Telephone: 407-832-6455
FAX: 407-832-5773

(See Next Column)

Charles H. Damsel, Jr.
Fred H. Gelston

Stuart M. Silverman

For full biographical listings, see the Martindale-Hubbell Law Directory

DAVIS, GORDON, DONER & CHANDLER, P.A. (AV)

515 North Flagler Drive, 7th Floor, 33401
Telephone: 561-659-7337
Facsimile: 561-659-0143
URL: http://www.dgdc.com

Zell Davis, Jr.
Robert E. Gordon
Adam S. Doner
Lawrence U. L. Chandler

Lawrence L. Klayman
Deirdre E. Brett

OF COUNSEL

Charles J. Oswald
Mikel D. Jones
(Not admitted in FL)

For full biographical listings, see the Martindale-Hubbell Law Directory

FARISH, FARISH & ROMANI (AV)

316 Banyan Boulevard, P.O. Box 4118, 33402
Telephone: 561-659-3500
1-800-401-4LAW
Fax: 561-655-3158

MEMBERS OF FIRM

Joseph D. Farish (1892-1977)
Joseph D. Farish, Jr.
Robert V. Romani

References: 1st Union Bank; Clewiston National Bank; Barnett Bank of Palm Beach County.

For full biographical listings, see the Martindale-Hubbell Law Directory

GAMOT & FREEMAN (AV)

315 Fifth Street, 33401-3709
Telephone: 561-655-6025
Fax: 561-655-5759
Palatka, Florida Office: 415 St. Johns Avenue.
Telephone: 904-325-6239.
Fax: 904-329-9626.

Melinda Penney Gamot
Terry N. Freeman
Albert J. Gamot, Jr.

For full biographical listings, see the Martindale-Hubbell Law Directory

JONES, FOSTER, JOHNSTON & STUBBS, P.A. (AV)

Flagler Center Tower, 505 South Flagler Drive, Suite 1100, P.O. Box 3475, 33402-3475
Telephone: 561-659-3000
Fax: 561-832-1454

Sidney A. Stubbs
John Blair McCracken
John C. Randolph
Herbert Adams Weaver, Jr.
Larry B. Alexander
Thornton M. Henry
Margaret L. Cooper
D. Culver Smith, III
Allen R. Tomlinson
Peter S. Holton
Peter A. Sachs
Michael T. Kranz
John S. Trimper
Mark B. Kleinfeld
Scott Gardner Hawkins
Steven J. Rothman
Rebecca G. Doane
Carl Angeloff (P.A.)
H. Michael Easley
Joyce A. Conway

Christopher S. Duke
Scott L. McMullen
M. Tracey Biagiotti
Clay C. Brooker
Edward Diaz
David Pratt
Brian K. Waxman
David E. Dreyer
(Not admitted in FL)

Counsel for: U.S. Trust Co.; NationsBank of Florida, N.A.; Island National Bank; Bankers Trust Company of Florida; Sun Bank/South Florida, N.A.; General Motors Acceptance Corp.

For full biographical listings, see the Martindale-Hubbell Law Directory

LEWIS KAPNER, P.A. (AV)

Suite 1402, One Clearlake Centre, 250 Australian Avenue South, P.O. Box 1428, 33402
Telephone: 561-655-3000
Delray/Ft. Lauderdale: 305-930-9191
Fax: 561-655-8899
Email: KAPNER1@AOL.COM
Boca Raton, Florida Office: 621 Northwest 53rd Street.
Telephone: 305-930-9191.

(See Next Column)

LEWIS KAPNER, P.A., *West Palm Beach—Continued*

Lewis Kapner   Victoria A. Calebrese
Michael C. Spain

For full biographical listings, see the Martindale-Hubbell Law Directory

THOMAS E. KINGCADE PROFESSIONAL ASSOCIATION (AV)

209 South Olive Avenue, 33401
Telephone: 407-659-7300
FAX: 407-655-1593

Thomas E. Kingcade

William W. Booth

For full biographical listings, see the Martindale-Hubbell Law Directory

STUART E. KOCHA, P.A. (AV)

118 Clematis Street, P.O. Box 1427, 33402
Telephone: 561-659-5611
Fax: 561-659-5636

Stuart E. Kocha
LEGAL SUPPORT PERSONNEL
David L. Halderman (Chief Investigator)
References: Admiralty Bank.

For full biographical listings, see the Martindale-Hubbell Law Directory

MONTGOMERY & LARMOYEUX (AV)

1016 Clearwater Place, Drawer 3086, 33402-3086
Telephone: 561-832-2880
Fax: 561-832-0887

MEMBERS OF FIRM
Robert M. Montgomery, Jr.   Christopher M. Larmoyeux
ASSOCIATES
Charles C. Powers   John B. Moores
Sharon Johnson Calix

For full biographical listings, see the Martindale-Hubbell Law Directory

MOYLE, FLANIGAN, KATZ, KOLINS, RAYMOND & SHEEHAN, P.A. (AV)

625 North Flagler Drive 9th Floor, P.O. Box 3888, 33402
Telephone: 561-659-7500
Facsimile: 561-659-1789
Palm Beach Gardens, Florida Office: 2401 P.G.A. Boulevard, Building C - Suite 120.
Telephone: 561-625-6480.
Facsimile: 561-625-5979.
Stuart, Florida Office: 900 South Federal Highway, 1st Floor.
Telephone: 561-288-1144.
Facsimile: 561-288-1499.
Tallahassee, Florida Office: 210 South Monroe Street.
Telephone: 904-681-3828.
Facsimile: 904-681-8788.

Peter L. Breton   Jon C. Moyle
John R. Eubanks   Jon C. Moyle, Jr.
John F. Flanigan   (Resident, Tallahassee Office)
Myra Gendel   Mark E. Raymond
Martin V. Katz   Thomas A. Sheehan, III
Ronald K. Kolins   Marta M. Suarez-Murias
Paul Andrew Krasker   Wilton L. White
Linda R. McCann
(Resident, Stuart Office)

OF COUNSEL
William J. Payne

For full biographical listings, see the Martindale-Hubbell Law Directory

NASON, GILDAN, YEAGER, GERSON & WHITE, P.A. (AV)

Penthouse Suite United National Bank Tower, 1645 Palm Beach Lakes Boulevard, 33401
Telephone: 561-686-3307
Fax: 561-686-5442

Herbert L. Gildan   Susan Fleischner Kornspan
Thomas J. Yeager   Alan I. Armour, II
Gary N. Gerson   Mark A. Pachman
John White, II   Elaine Johnson James
Phillip C. Gildan   Nathan E. Nason
Domenick R. Lioce   Gregory L. Scott

John M. McDivitt   Jeffrey B. Kahn
Craig S. Barnett

(See Next Column)

LEGAL SUPPORT PERSONNEL
Sandra R. Gronek   Constance Schiraldi
(Office Administrator)   (Real Estate Paralegal)
Kathy Pelly   Georgina J. Popham
(Litigation Paralegal)   (Corporate/Securities
Elsie T. Pollak   Paralegal)
(Litigation Paralegal)

For full biographical listings, see the Martindale-Hubbell Law Directory

NEWBURGH, BALDWIN & GERSHMAN (AV)

1675 Palm Beach Lakes Boulevard, Suite 700, 33401
Telephone: 561-684-8898; 561-471-0470
Fax: 561-684-8820; 561-471-4222

MEMBERS OF FIRM
Steven S. Newburgh   Fletcher N. Baldwin, III
Robert Scott Gershman
OF COUNSEL
Barry L. Clayton

For full biographical listings, see the Martindale-Hubbell Law Directory

PAXTON, CROW, BRAGG, SMITH & KEYSER, P.A. (AV)

Barristers Building, Suite 500, 1615 Forum Place, 33401
Telephone: 561-684-2121
Fax: 561-684-6855
Vero Beach, Florida Office: 1717 Indian River Boulevard, Suite 202C, 32960.
Telephone: 561-778-1755.
FAX: 561-778-2433.

Ralph B. Paxton (Retired)   Clark W. Smith
David F. Crow   Gregory M. Keyser
Morgan S. Bragg   Michele I. Nelson

John E. Peterson   Sandra Bosso-Pardo
Thomas Brown Miller   Anthony V. Falzon (not
Michael B. Davis   admitted in the United States)
Julia Luyster   M. Alisandra Deyoung
OF COUNSEL
Stephen C. McAliley
LEGAL SUPPORT PERSONNEL
Nicole Hickman (Paralegal)   James E. Marcum (Paralegal)
Richard J. Smith (Paralegal)

For full biographical listings, see the Martindale-Hubbell Law Directory

PRUITT & PRUITT, P.A. (AV)

Suite 400 Flagler Tower, 505 South Flagler Drive, 33401
Telephone: 407-655-8080
Fax: 407-655-4134

William H. Pruitt   William E. Pruitt
Reference: Flagler National Bank.

For full biographical listings, see the Martindale-Hubbell Law Directory

RICCI, HUBBARD, LEOPOLD & FRANKEL, P.A. (AV)

United National Bank Building, Suite 250, 1645 Palm Beach Lakes Boulevard, P.O. Box 2946, 33402
Telephone: 561-684-6500
Fax: 651-697-2383
URL: http://www.PBOL.COM/RICCI

Edward M. Ricci   Theodore J. Leopold
James R. Hubbard   Lois J. Frankel
Scott C. Murray

For full biographical listings, see the Martindale-Hubbell Law Directory

RUMRELL, COSTABEL & TURK (AV)

A Partnership of Professional Associations
One Clearlake Centre, Suite 1504, 250 South Australian Avenue, 33401
Telephone: 561-820-8813
Facsimile: 561-832-0302
URL: http://www.rctlaw.com
Jacksonville, Florida Office: One Hundred Building, Suite 250. 10151 Deerwood Park Boulevard.
Telephone: 904-996-1100.
Facsimile: 904-996-1120.
Miami, Florida Office: 80 South West Eighth Street, Suite 2014.
Telephone: 305-371-2618.
Facsimile: 305-371-4643.

PRINCIPALS
Richard G. Rumrell (P.A.)   Attilio M. Costabel (P.A.)
(Practicing in Jacksonville   (Practicing in Miami and
Office)   Jacksonville Offices)
Paul A. Turk, Jr., (P.A.)

(See Next Column)

RUMRELL, COSTABEL & TURK—*Continued*

Lindsey C. Brock III   William David Vaughn
Ross Logan Bilbrey   Kimberly A. Wilson
Charles T. Moore

Representative Clients: American Centennial Insurance Company; American Surety & Casualty Company; Anglo American Insurance Company; Commercial Union Assurance Company; Crum and Forster Insurance; The Dickerson Group; Excess Insurance Company; Florida Insurance Guaranty Association; GRE Group of Companies; Great American Insurance Company.

For full biographical listings, see the Martindale-Hubbell Law Directory

---

SEARCY DENNEY SCAROLA BARNHART & SHIPLEY, PROFESSIONAL ASSOCIATION (AV)

2139 Palm Beach Lakes Boulevard, P.O. Drawer 3626, 33402-3626
Telephone: 407-686-6300
800-780-8607
800-220-7006 (Spanish)
Fax: 407-478-0754

Christian D. Searcy, Sr.   Lawrence J. Block, Jr.
Earl L. Denney, Jr.   C. Calvin Warriner, III
John Scarola   William A. Norton
F. Gregory Barnhart   David J. Sales
John A. Shipley   Christopher K. Speed
David K. Kelley, Jr.   William B. King

Karen E. Terry   T. Michael Kennedy
Katherine Ann Martinez   Todd S. Stewart
Laurie J. Briggs

LEGAL SUPPORT PERSONNEL

Deane L. Cady   J. Peter Love
(Paralegal/Investigator)   (Paralegal/Investigator)
James E. Cook   Marjorie A. Morgan (Paralegal)
(Paralegal/Investigator)   William H. Seabold
Emilio Diamantis   (Paralegal/Investigator)
(Paralegal/Investigator)   Kathleen Simon (Paralegal)
David W. Gilmore   Steve M. Smith
(Paralegal/Investigator)   (Paralegal/Investigator)
Thaddeus E. Kulesa   Judson Whitehorn
(Paralegal/Investigator)   (Paralegal/Investigator)

For full biographical listings, see the Martindale-Hubbell Law Directory

---

WAGNER, JOHNSON & McAFEE, P.A. (AV)

Commerce Pointe, Suite 450, 1818 South Australian Avenue, P.O. Box 3466, 33402
Telephone: 561-686-5200; 1-800-899-5200
Fax: 561-686-6710
Email: macwjm@icanect.net

Ward Wagner, Jr.   Helen Wagner McAfee
Robert R. Johnson   William J. McAfee

Michael G. Bodik   Stacy D. Strolla

References: SunTrust Bank, South Florida, N.A.; Fidelity Federal Savings & Loan Association of West Palm Beach.

For full biographical listings, see the Martindale-Hubbell Law Directory

---

JAMES E. WEBER, P.A. (AV)

Suite 502 The Flagler Center, 501 South Flagler Drive, 33401
Telephone: 407-832-2266
Fax: 407-833-3816

James E. Weber

For full biographical listings, see the Martindale-Hubbell Law Directory

---

WIEDERHOLD, MOSES, BULFIN & RUBIN, P.A. (AV)

Northbridge Centre, Suite 800, 515 North Flagler Drive, P.O. Box 3918, 33401
Telephone: 407-659-2296;
Broward: 954-763-5630
FAX: 407-659-2865

John P. Wiederhold   John J. Bulfin
Robert D. Moses   Kenneth M. Rubin

Lawrence I. Bass   Kay Seeber Hoff
Bruce R. Katzell

LEGAL SUPPORT PERSONNEL
Thomas M. Blinstrub

Reference: Barnett Bank of Palm Beach County.

For full biographical listings, see the Martindale-Hubbell Law Directory

---

WINTER HAVEN, Polk Co.

PETERSON & MYERS, P.A. (AV)

Suite 300, 141 5th Street N.W., P.O. Drawer 7608, 33883-7608
Telephone: 941-294-3360
Lake Wales, Florida Office: 130 East Central Avenue, P.O. Box 1079.
Telephones: 941-676-7611; 683-8942.
Lakeland, Florida Office: 100 East Main Street, P.O. Box 24628.
Telephones: 941-683-6511; 676-6934.

Philip O. Allen   Peter J. Munson
Jack P. Brandon   Corneal B. Myers
Beach A Brooks, Jr.   Cornelius B. Myers, III
Kristen Marie Buzzanca   E. Blake Paul
J. Davis Connor   Robert E. Puterbaugh
Michael S. Craig   Abel A. Putnam
Roy A. Craig, Jr.   Thomas B. Putnam, Jr.
Jacob C. Dykxhoorn   Deborah A. Ruster
Dennis P. Johnson   Stephen R. Senn
Kevin C. Knowlton   Andrea Teves Smith
Douglas A. Lockwood, III   Keith H. Wadsworth
M. Craig Massey   Kerry M. Wilson

General Counsel for: Barnett Bank of Polk County.
Representative Clients: Mutual Wholesale Co.; Barnett Banks, Inc.; Ben Hill Griffin, Inc.; Alcoma Association, Inc.
Approved Attorneys for: Attorneys' Title Insurance Fund; Federal Land Bank, Columbia, South Carolina; Equitable Life Assurance Society of the United States.

For full biographical listings, see the Martindale-Hubbell Law Directory

---

WINTER PARK, Orange Co.

WENDY L. AIKIN, P.A. (AV)

288 Park Avenue North, 32789
Telephone: 407-644-4040
Fax: 407-644-4414

Wendy L. Aikin

For full biographical listings, see the Martindale-Hubbell Law Directory

---

KENNETH E. BROOTEN, JR. CHARTERED (AV)

631 West Fairbanks Avenue, 32789
Telephone: 407-645-4447
Fax: 407-628-2220

Kenneth E. Brooten, Jr.

For full biographical listings, see the Martindale-Hubbell Law Directory

---

DEMPSEY & ASSOCIATES, P.A. (AV)

Suite 200, 1031 West Morse Boulevard, 32789
Telephone: 407-740-7778
Telecopier: 407-740-0911

Bernard H. Dempsey, Jr.   Michael C. Sasso

Frederick C. Barnes   Daniel N. Brodersen
Peter Francis Carr, Jr.

For full biographical listings, see the Martindale-Hubbell Law Directory

---

GRAHAM, CLARK, JONES, BUILDER, PRATT & MARKS (AV)

Third Floor, NationsBank Building, 369 North New York Avenue, P.O. Drawer 1690, 32790
Telephone: 407-647-4455
Telefax: 407-740-7063

MEMBERS OF FIRM

Jesse E. Graham   Howard S. Marks
Scott D. Clark   Geoffrey D. Withers
Frederick W. Jones   Mary W. Christian
J. Lindsay Builder, Jr.   Jesse E. Graham, Jr.
James R. Pratt   Samuel M. Nelson
Jessica K. Hew

Approved Attorneys for: Chicago Title Insurance Co.
Reference: NationsBank of Florida.

For full biographical listings, see the Martindale-Hubbell Law Directory

---

POHL & SHORT, P.A. (AV)

280 West Canton Avenue, Suite 410, P.O. Box 3208, 32790
Telephone: 407-647-7645; 407-647-POHL
Telefax: 407-647-2314

Frank L. Pohl   C. Teresa de Arrigoitia
Houston E. Short   George A. Golder
Dwight I. Cool   Norma Stanley
James Everett Shepherd V   Mark W. Garrett
John R. Simpson, Jr.

(See Next Column)

Pohl & Short P.A., *Winter Park—Continued*

Representative Clients: American Pioneer Title Insurance Company; Institute of Internal Auditors, Inc.; Thompson Steel, Inc.; SunTrust, N.A.; The Bank of Winter Park; Bekins Moving and Storage Co., Inc.; Champion Boats, Inc.; KeyCom Telephone Systems, Inc.

For full biographical listings, see the Martindale-Hubbell Law Directory

Swann, Hadley & Alvarez, P.A. (AV)

1031 West Morse Boulevard, Suite 270, 32789
Telephone: 407-647-2777
Fax: 407-647-2157

Richard R. Swann	Ralph V. Hadley, III
	P. Raúl Alvarez, Jr.
Jeffrey P. Milhausen	Stuart P. Buchanan

For full biographical listings, see the Martindale-Hubbell Law Directory

Troutman, Williams, Irvin, Green & Helms, Professional Association (AV)

311 West Fairbanks Avenue, 32789
Telephone: 407-647-2277
Telefax: 407-628-2986
Toll Free: 1-800-486-5149
Kissimmee, Florida Office: Suite 206, 120 Broadway, 34741.
Telephone: 407-933-8834.
FAX: 407-933-8253.

Russell Troutman	Roger D. Helms
Joseph H. Williams	Jack E. Bowen
Paul B. Irvin	Joseph J. Polich, Jr.
Robert F. Green	Kim Michael Cullen
	Joseph C. Perzan

For full biographical listings, see the Martindale-Hubbell Law Directory

GEORGIA

*ALBANY,** Dougherty Co.

Cannon & Meyer Von Bremen, LLP (AV)

2417 Westgate Drive, P.O. Box 70909, 31708-0909
Telephone: 912-435-1470
Telefax: 912-888-2156

MEMBERS OF FIRM

William E. Cannon, Jr.	Michael S. Meyer von Bremen

ASSOCIATES

Toysha M. Flowers	William H. Gregory, II

OF COUNSEL

Timothy O. Davis

For full biographical listings, see the Martindale-Hubbell Law Directory

*ATHENS,** Clarke Co.

Blasingame, Burch, Garrard, Bryant & Ashley, P.C. (AV)

440 College Avenue North, P.O. Box 832, 30603
Telephone: 706-354-4000
Telecopier: 706-353-0673
Greensboro, Georgia Office: 122 N. Main Street, P.O. Box 67, 30642.
Telephone: 706-453-7139.
Fax: 706-453-7842.

J. Ralph Beaird	Andrew J. Hill, III
Gary B. Blasingame	Michael A. Morris
E. Davison Burch	Thomas H. Rogers, Jr.
Henry G. Garrard, III	William D. Harvard
Everett Clay Bryant	Rikard L. Bridges
W. Seaborn Ashley, Jr.	Ivan A. Gustafson
M. Steven Heath	David S. Thomson

Richard W. Schmidt	Christopher G. Conley
Milton F. Eisenberg	Lloyd N. Bell
Stephen E.B. Smith	Kim T. Stephens
J. Branson Parker	Amy Lou Reynolds
J. David Felt, Jr.	C. Kathryn Hackney
	Kathleen M. Timmons

Representative Clients: NationsBank of Georgia, N.A.; Georgia Power Co.; Georgia Natural Gas Co.; Pittsburgh Corning Corp.; Downtown Athens Development Authority; Georgia National Bank; Fowler Products Co., Inc.; St. Paul Fire & Marine Insurance Co.; Athens Newspapers, Inc.; First Commerce Bancorp, Inc.

For full biographical listings, see the Martindale-Hubbell Law Directory

McLeod, Benton, Begnaud & Marshall (AV)

8th Floor, NationsBank Building, P.O. Box 8108, 30603
Telephone: 706-549-9400
Fax: 706-549-9406

MEMBERS OF FIRM

Larry V. McLeod	Malcolm C. McArthur
Terrell W. Benton, Jr.	William C. Berryman, Jr.
Jeanette S. Scott	Daniel C. Haygood
Darrel Begnaud	Hilary N. Shuford
Andrew H. Marshall	Richard L. Brittain
Michael C. Pruett	

OF COUNSEL

Robert E. Gibson

Counsel for: NationsBank; Athens First Bank & Trust Company; Georgia Power Company; CSX Transportation, Inc.; St. Mary's Hospital; Benson's Inc.

For full biographical listings, see the Martindale-Hubbell Law Directory

*ATLANTA,** Fulton Co.

Alembik, Fine & Callner, P.A. (AV)

Marquis One Tower, Fourth Floor, 245 Peachtree Center Avenue, N.E., 30303
Telephone: 404-688-8800
Telecopier: 404-420-7191

Michael D. Alembik (1936-1993)	Ronald T. Gold
Lowell S. Fine	G. Michael Banick
Bruce W. Callner	Mark E. Bergeson
Kathy L. Portnoy	Russell P. Love

Z. Ileana Martinez	Janet Lichiello Franchi
Susan M. Lieppe	Heidi Koch Martin
Bruce R. Steinfeld	Janet Caroline Moja
	John H. Zwald

For full biographical listings, see the Martindale-Hubbell Law Directory

Alston & Bird (AV)

A Partnership including Professional Corporations
One Atlantic Center, 1201 West Peachtree Street, 30309-3424
Telephone: 404-881-7000
Telecopier: 404-881-7777
Cable Address: AMGRAM GA
Telex: 54-2996
Easylink: 62985848
Washington, D.C. Office: 601 Pennsylvania Ave., N.W., North Building, Suite 250 20004.
Telephone: 202-508-3300.
Telecopier: 202-508-3333.

MEMBERS OF FIRM

G. Conley Ingram	R. Wayne Thorpe
Michael A. Doyle	John I. Spangler III
Ronald L. Reid	Grant T. Stein
C. David Butler	Theodore E. G. Pound
R. Neal Batson	Bernard Taylor
Oscar N. Persons	Richard T. Fulton
Benjamin F. Johnson III	Mary C. Gill
William C. Humphreys, Jr.	William H. Hughes, Jr.
James S. Stokes	Donna Potts Bergeson
Dow N. Kirkpatrick II	Gerald L. Mize, Jr.
W. Terence Walsh	Robert P. Riordan
Robert D. McCallum, Jr.	John E. Stephenson, Jr.
Jack H. Senterfitt	Rebecca McLemore Lamberth
Peter Q. Bassett	Laura Lewis Owens
Judson Graves	Dennis J. Connolly
Peter M. Degnan	Todd R. David
Lee A. DeHihns III	Elizabeth A. Gilley
Jay D. Bennett	Richard R. Hays
J. William Boone	H. Douglas Hinson
Steven M. Collins	Jennifer Brown Moore
John C. Weitnauer	Robert L. Crewdson
Nill V. Toulme	Susan B. Devitt
	Robert D. Mowrey

OF COUNSEL

Sidney O. Smith, Jr.

ASSOCIATES

Lori G. Baer	W. Hunter Holliday
Lonnie T. Brown, Jr.	Lori P. Hughes
Alston D. Correll III	Susan E. Hurd
Cynthia L. Counts	Clifton M. Iler
Kristen K. Darnell	John A. Jordak, Jr.
Jo C. Dearing	Daniel A. Kent
A. McCampbell Gibson	Matthew W. Levin
James C. Grant	David M. Maxwell
Ernest LaMont Greer	Scott A. McLaren
James W. Hagan	Daniel L. Rikard

(See Next Column)

ALSTON & BIRD—*Continued*

ASSOCIATES (Continued)

Candace N. Smith   K. David Steele
Robyn Ice Sosebee   Jeffrey W. Stump
Paul F. Wellborn III

COUNSEL

Lawrie E. Demorest

Representative Clients: Bristol-Myers Co.; Chrysler Corp.; CSX Transportation, Inc.; E.I. du Pont de Nemours and Company; Exxon Corporation; NationsBank Corporation; Prudential Insurance Company of America; Sears, Roebuck and Co.

For Complete List of Firm Personnel, See General Section

For full biographical listings, see the Martindale-Hubbell Law Directory

---

E. ALAN ARMSTRONG (AV)

Building 5, 2900 Chamblee-Tucker Road, 30341
Telephone: 770-451-0313
Fax: 770-451-0317
(Also Of Counsel, Kellogg & Saccoccia)

OF COUNSEL

Edward H. Kellogg, Jr., P.C.

LEGAL SUPPORT PERSONNEL

Jane Maxwell

Representative Clients: Brock Candy Company; Airline Transport Professionals, Inc.
References: NationsBank; Aircraft Owners and Pilots Association.

For full biographical listings, see the Martindale-Hubbell Law Directory

---

BAUER & DEITCH, P.C. (AV)

Building D, 6111 Peachtree-Dunwoody Road, N.E., 30328
Telephone: 770-394-9004
Telecopier: 770-394-8840

Henry R. Bauer, Jr.   Gilbert H. Deitch

For full biographical listings, see the Martindale-Hubbell Law Directory

---

BIRD, BALLARD & STILL (AV)

14 Seventeenth Street, Suite 5, P.O. Box 7009, 30357
Telephone: 404-873-4696
Fax: 404-872-3745

William Q. Bird   William L. Ballard
Edward R. Still   John G. Mabrey
John   Karin L. Allen

For full biographical listings, see the Martindale-Hubbell Law Directory

---

BIVENS, HOFFMAN & FOWLER (AV)

A Partnership of Professional Corporations
5040 Roswell Road, N.E., 30342
Telephone: 404-256-6464
FAX: 404-256-1422

MEMBER OF FIRM

L. Brown Bivens (P.C.)

For full biographical listings, see the Martindale-Hubbell Law Directory

---

BLACKWOOD, MATTHEWS & STEEL (AV)

2695 Buford Highway Suite 100, 30324-3239
Telephone: 404-636-9797
Fax: 404-320-9790

MEMBERS OF FIRM

James B. Matthews, III   John B. Briggs
John D. Steel   H. Craig Stafford

For full biographical listings, see the Martindale-Hubbell Law Directory

---

BODKER, RAMSEY & ANDREWS, A PROFESSIONAL CORPORATION (AV)

Suite 615 1800 Peachtree Street, N.W., 30309-2507
Telephone: 404-351-1615
Telecopier: 404-352-1285

Harry J. Winograd

David J. Maslia

For full biographical listings, see the Martindale-Hubbell Law Directory

---

BONDURANT, MIXSON & ELMORE, LLP (AV)

1201 W. Peachtree Street Suite 3900, 30309
Telephone: 404-881-4100
FAX: 404-881-4111

(See Next Column)

MEMBERS OF FIRM

Emmet J. Bondurant II   Dirk G. Christensen
H. Lamar Mixson   Jane E. Fahey
M. Jerome Elmore   John E. Floyd
Edward B. Krugman   Michael A. Sullivan
Jeffrey O. Bramlett   Michael B. Terry

Representative Clients: The Aetna Casualty and Surety Company; Blue Circle of America; Circle K; Conoco, Inc.; Delta Air Lines, Inc.; Queen Carpets, Inc.; Sanifill, Inc.; Ticketmaster; Trammell Crow Co.; Wyle Laboratories.

For full biographical listings, see the Martindale-Hubbell Law Directory

---

DAVID WM. BOONE, P.C. (AV)

3155 Roswell Road Suite 100, The Cotton Exchange, 30305
Telephone: 404-239-0305
FAX: 404-239-0520

David William Boone

For full biographical listings, see the Martindale-Hubbell Law Directory

---

BOVIS, KYLE & BURCH (AV)

A Partnership including Professional Corporations
Third Floor, 53 Perimeter Center East, 30346
Telephone: 770-391-9100
Telecopier: 770-668-0878

MEMBERS OF FIRM

John M. Bovis (P.C.)   W. Bruce Barrickman
Steven J. Kyle (P.C.)   Gregory R. Veal
John V. Burch (P.C.)   Charles M. McDaniel, Jr.
James E. Singer   Timothy J. Burson
William S. Allred

ASSOCIATES

Charles M. Medlin   Claude P. Czaja
J.S. Scott Busby   John H. Peavy Jr.

For full biographical listings, see the Martindale-Hubbell Law Directory

---

BUTLER, WOOTEN, OVERBY, CHEELEY, PEARSON & FRYHOFER (AV)

2719 Buford Highway, 30324
Telephone: 404-321-1700
WATS 1-800-242-2962
Fax: 404-321-1713
Columbus, Georgia Office: 1500 Second Avenue, P.O. Box 2766.
Telephone: 706-322-1990; National Wats: 1-800-233-4086.
Fax: 706-323-2962.

MEMBERS OF FIRM

James E. Butler, Jr.   Albert M. Pearson, III
Joel O. Wooten, Jr.   George W. Fryhofer III
C. Frederick Overby   Peter J. Daughtery
Robert D. Cheeley   J. Frank Myers, III
Lee Tarte Wallace

ASSOCIATES

Jason L. Crawford   Joshua Sacks
Keith A. Pittman   Teresa Thomas Abell
Cale H. Conley

Reference: Columbus Bank and Trust, Columbus, Ga.

For full biographical listings, see the Martindale-Hubbell Law Directory

---

CARR, TABB & POPE (AV)

1355 Peachtree Street, N.E. Suite 2000, 30309
Telephone: 404-876-7790
Fax: 404-873-4683
URL: http://www.net.sales.com/carrtabbandpope
URL: http://www.carr@america.net

MEMBERS OF FIRM

W. Pitts Carr   David H. Pope
Judy N. Tabb   J. Reneé Kastanakis

ASSOCIATES

Render Crayton Freeman   Richard M. Bayus, II.

OF COUNSEL

Noah J. Stone

For full biographical listings, see the Martindale-Hubbell Law Directory

---

CARTER & ANSLEY (AV)

Suite 1000 One Ninety One Peachtree Tower, 191 Peachtree Street, 30303-1747
Telephone: 404-658-9220
Fax: 404-658-9726
Email: firm@carteransley.com

(See Next Column)

CARTER & ANSLEY, *Atlanta—Continued*

MEMBERS OF FIRM

Shepard Bryan (1871-1970)	Robert A. Barnaby, II
W. Colquitt Carter (1904-1988)	Thomas E. Magill
Ben Kingree, III	Robert O. McCloud, Jr.
Tommy T. Holland	Christopher N. Shuman
H. Sanders Carter, Jr.	Elizabeth J. Bondurant
A. T. Sorrells	Michael A. Coval

OF COUNSEL

Bonneau Ansley

ASSOCIATES

Rebecca J. Schmidt	Kenton J. Coppage
Keith L. Lindsay	Allison Mary Burns
Burke B. Johnson	Mary K. Pickard

Patrick C. DiCarlo

For full biographical listings, see the Martindale-Hubbell Law Directory

CHOREY, TAYLOR & FEIL, A PROFESSIONAL CORPORATION (AV)

Suite 1700, The Lenox Building, 3399 Peachtree Road, N.E., 30326
Telephone: 404-841-3200
Facsimile: 404-841-3221

Thomas V. Chorey, Jr.	Otto F. Feil III
John L. Taylor, Jr.	Celeste McCollough

Matthew L. Hess

For Complete List of Firm Personnel, See General Section

For full biographical listings, see the Martindale-Hubbell Law Directory

COOPER, HEWITT & KATZ (AV)

Resurgens Plaza Suite 1700, 945 East Paces Ferry Road, 30326
Telephone: 404-814-0000
Fax: 404-816-8900

MEMBERS OF FIRM

Lawrence A. Cooper	A. Kenneth Hewitt, III

Robert Neal Katz

ASSOCIATE

Julie Ann Hauge

For full biographical listings, see the Martindale-Hubbell Law Directory

CRIM & BASSLER (AV)

100 Galleria Parkway, Suite 1510, 30339
Telephone: 770-956-1813
Fax: 770-955-5976

MEMBERS OF FIRM

Candler Crim, Jr.	Nikolai Makarenko, Jr.
Harry W. Bassler	Kimberly Leigh Schwartz
Thomas S. Bechtel	Mitchel S. Evans
Joseph M. Murphey	Terence D. Williams

ASSOCIATES

Kelly Amanda Lee	Michael O. Sheridan

OF COUNSEL

William W. Horton

References: The Bank of the South; First Georgia Bank; Trust Company of Georgia.

For full biographical listings, see the Martindale-Hubbell Law Directory

DAVID G. CROCKETT, P.C. (AV)

1950 Equitable Building, 100 Peachtree Street, N.W., 30303
Telephone: 404-522-4280
Telecopier: 404-589-9891

David G. Crockett

Tait O. Norton

Approved Attorney for: Chicago Title Insurance Co.
Reference: NationsBank, N.A.

For full biographical listings, see the Martindale-Hubbell Law Directory

DAVIS, MATTHEWS & QUIGLEY, P.C. (AV)

Fourteenth Floor, Lenox Towers II, 3400 Peachtree Road, 30326
Telephone: 404-261-3900
Telecopier: 404-261-0159
Email: dmq@interserv.com

Baxter L. Davis	Richard W. Schiffman, Jr.
Ron L. Quigley	Frank A. DeVincent

Elizabeth Green Lindsey

Sylvia A. Martin	Ted Matthew Scartz

Approved Attorneys for: Lawyers Title Insurance Corp.

(See Next Column)

For Complete List of Firm Personnel, See General Section

For full biographical listings, see the Martindale-Hubbell Law Directory

DENNIS, CORRY, PORTER & GRAY (AV)

3300 One Atlanta Plaza, 950 East Paces Ferry Road, P.O. Box 18640, 30326
Telephone: 404-816-2800
Wats: 800-735-0838
Fax: 404-816-5656

MEMBERS OF FIRM

Robert E. Corry, Jr.	James S. Strawinski
R. Clay Porter	Grant B. Smith
William E. Gray, II	Frederick D. Evans, III

OF COUNSEL

Douglas Dennis

ASSOCIATES

Robert G. Ballard	Brian DeVoe Rogers
Matthew J. Jewell	Julia J. Yoffee
Pamela Jean Gray	Scott W. McMickle
J. Steven Fisher	Susan E. Cartwright
Thomas D. Trask	Christopher D. Pixley
Robert David Schoen	Raymond J. Kurey
Alison Roberts Solomon	Amber B. Shushan

Representative Clients: Schneider National, Inc.; Roadway Express, Inc.; Caliber System, Inc.

For full biographical listings, see the Martindale-Hubbell Law Directory

DOFFERMYRE, SHIELDS, CANFIELD, KNOWLES & DEVINE (AV)

Suite 1600, 1355 Peachtree Street, 30309
Telephone: 404-881-8900

Robert E. Shields	Kenneth S. Canfield
Everette L. Doffermyre	Ralph I. Knowles, Jr.

ASSOCIATES

Leslie J. Bryan	Robert Hutton Brown, III
Georgiana Rizk	Laura M. Shamp

Samuel W. Wethern

For full biographical listings, see the Martindale-Hubbell Law Directory

DREW ECKL & FARNHAM (AV)

880 West Peachtree Street, P.O. Box 7600, 30357
Telephone: 404-885-1400
Facsimile: 404-876-0992
Email: drew@igc.apc.org

MEMBERS OF FIRM

W. Wray Eckl	T. Bart Gary
Clayton H. Farnham	Kenneth A. Hindman
Arthur H. Glaser	Paul W. Burke
James M. Poe	Daniel C. Kniffen
John A. Ferguson, Jr.	John C. Bruffey, Jr.
Theodore Freeman	Benton J. Mathis, Jr.
John P. Reale	John G. Blackmon, Jr.
Stevan A. Miller	Gary R. Hurst
H. Michael Bagley	Dennis M. Hall
Hall F. McKinley III	J. William Haley
G. Randall Moody	Ann Bishop Byars
B. Holland Pritchard	Stephen W. Mooney

ASSOCIATES

Nicole D. Tifverman	Patricia R. Stevens
L. Lee Bennett, Jr.	C. Lawrence Meyer
Katherine D. Dixon	Philip G. Pompilio
William T. Mitchell	Robert J. Moye III
J. Robb Cruser	Sean W. Conley
Philip Wade Savrin	Mary Anne Ackourey
Lucian Gillis, Jr.	Beverly Powell Sisk
Peter H. Schmidt, II	Marion M. Handley
April Rich	Stuart B. Bagley
Maureen M. Middleton	Thomas L. Walker
Robert L. Welch	James P. Anderson
Suzanne VonHarten Sanders	Kathryn Blythe Offer
Leigh Lawson Reeves	Donald M. McManus, Jr.
Bruce A. Taylor, Jr.	Peter B. Barlow
Douglas M. Baker	Nancy L. Pasterz
David R. Bergquist	Gregory G. Schultz
Charles L. Norton, Jr.	Christopher R. Stovall
Nancy F. Rigby	Charles E. Symington, Jr.
Douglas G. Smith, Jr.	Kristian Knochel
Terrence T. Rock	(Not admitted in GA)
Phillip Comer Griffeth	Lewis P. Perling
Marian S. Singer	Scott P. Archer
Steven D. Prelutsky	(Not admitted in GA)
Julianne L. Swilley	Fred L. Hubbs Jr.
B. Greg Cline	W. Gregory Pope

Jennifer E. Moore

SENIOR ATTORNEY

Richard Metzger

(See Next Column)

DREW ECKL & FARNHAM—*Continued*

OF COUNSEL

Charles L. Drew   Anne M. Landrum
            Christopher E. Parker

Representative Clients: American International Group; Argonaut Insurance Co.; Atlantic Steel Company; Carolina Freight Carriers Corp.; Crown Central Petroleum Corp.; Denman Tire Corporation; Federated Department Stores; Chicago Title & Trust Co.; Rock-Tenn Company.

For full biographical listings, see the Martindale-Hubbell Law Directory

EIDSON & ASSOCIATES, P.C. (AV)

Suite 201, 600 South Central Avenue (Hapeville), 30354
Telephone: 404-763-3401
FAX: 404-763-3404

James A. Eidson

Timothy R. Brennan   Penni A. Dudley
            William Gowan Moïse
Reference: First Bank of Georgia.

For full biographical listings, see the Martindale-Hubbell Law Directory

ENGLAND & McKNIGHT (AV)

Suite 410 River Ridge, 9040 Roswell Road, 30350
Telephone: 770-641-6010
FAX: 770-641-6003

MEMBERS OF FIRM

J. Melvin England   Robert H. McKnight, Jr.
Reference: Nations Bank N.A.

For full biographical listings, see the Martindale-Hubbell Law Directory

FAIN, MAJOR & WILEY, P.C. (AV)

The Hurt Building, 50 Hurt Plaza, Suite 300, 30303
Telephone: 404-688-6633
Telecopier: 404-420-1544

Gene A. Major   Thomas E. Brennan
Charles A. Wiley, Jr.   John K. Miles, Jr.
            Darryl G. Haynes

Brian Alligood   Robert G. Mikell
Derek A. Mendicino   C. Todd Van Dyke
Kim Monroe Jackson   Debra C. Chew
            Tracy M. Culver
OF COUNSEL
Donald M. Fain

Representative Clients: Allstate Insurance Co.; Budget Rent-A-Car; Arkansas Best Corp.; Chrysler Insurance Co.; Georgia Farm Bureau Mutual Insurance Co.; Hertz Corp.; Universal Underwriters Insurance Co.; Westfield Insurance co.; Winn-Dixie Stores, Inc.

For full biographical listings, see the Martindale-Hubbell Law Directory

GAMBRELL & STOLZ, L.L.P. (AV)

Suite 4300, One Peachtree Center, 303 Peachtree Street, 30308
Telephone: 404-577-6000
FAX: 404-221-6501
Email: lawfirm@gambrell.com
Northpark Office: Suite 1230, Northpark 400 Tower, 1000 Abernathy Road, N.E., Atlanta, 30328.
Telephone: 404-577-6000.
FAX: 404-589-3400.

David H. Gambrell   William C. Tinsley, II
Irwin W. Stolz, Jr.   Henry B. Levi
Bryan M. Cavan   Leo J. Fogarty
Jon Lee Andersen   Linda A. Klein
James R. McGuone   Gary A. Barnes
Nedom A. Haley   Nancy E. Gordon
Robert G. Brazier   Michael M. Smith
Tobin N. Watt   Andrew H. Prussack
George M. Bobo   Verley J. Spivey
            Alvin T. Wong
ASSOCIATES
Seaton D. Purdom   Sophia L. Herbert-Peterson
Charles N. Bowen   Ronald C. Melcher
James A. Nystrom   Vipanj B. Patel
Anna Marie Bacon-Tinsley Che   Michelle Kenyon

For full biographical listings, see the Martindale-Hubbell Law Directory

GARLAND, SAMUEL & LOEB, P.C. (AV)

3151 Maple Drive, N.E., 30305
Telephone: 404-262-2225
Fax: 404-365-5041
Email: TrialLaw@aol.com

(See Next Column)

Edward T. M. Garland   Donald F. Samuel
            Robin N. Loeb

For full biographical listings, see the Martindale-Hubbell Law Directory

GLASS, McCULLOUGH, SHERRILL & HARROLD (AV)

1409 Peachtree Street, N.E., 30309
Telephone: 404-885-1500
Telecopier: 404-892-1801
Buckhead Office: Monarch Plaza, 3414 Peachtree Road, N.E., Suite 450, Atlanta, Georgia, 30326-1162.
Telephone: 404-885-1500.
Telecopier: 404-231-1978.
Washington, D.C. Office: 1150 17th Street, N.W., Suite 605. Washington, D.C., 20036.
Telephone: 202-785-8118.
Telecopier: 202-785-0128.
Knoxville, Tennessee Office: 606 West Main Avenue, Suite 205, P.O. Box 2543. Knoxville, Tennessee, 37901-2543.
Telephone: 423-971-5418.
Telecopier: 423-971-1706.

MEMBERS OF FIRM

John A. Sherrill   George L. Murphy, Jr.
Jeffrey C. Baxter   Lori Ann Olejniczak
Geoffrey H. Cederholm   R. Phillip Shinall, III
William F. Clark   Elizabeth S. Tonkin (Resident,
Gardner G. Courson   Knoxville, Tennessee Office)
William A. DuPre, IV   Laura H. Walter (Not admitted
Allen W. Groves   in GA; Resident, Washington,
C. Walker Ingraham   D.C. Office)
            Robert E. Wilson
ASSOCIATES
Michael David Crisp   Vincent J. Miraglia (Resident,
Bryan A. Downs   Washington, D.C. Office)
Jana L. Evans   Donna J. Nance
Keven K. Kenison   Robert T. Quackenboss
Jamie G. Miller   (Not admitted in GA)
            Richard D. Sanders

For Complete List of Firm Personnel, See General Section

For full biographical listings, see the Martindale-Hubbell Law Directory

GOLDNER, SOMMERS, SCRUDDER & BASS (AV)

900 Circle 75 Parkway Suite 850, 30339
Telephone: 770-612-9200
Facsimile: 770-612-9201

Stephen L. Goldner   Henry E. Scrudder, Jr.
Susan V. Sommers   Glenn S. Bass
            C. G. Jester, Jr.

For Complete List of Firm Personnel, See General Section

For full biographical listings, see the Martindale-Hubbell Law Directory

GOODMAN, McGUFFEY, AUST & LINDSEY (AV)

2100 Tower Place, 3340 Peachtree Road, N.E., 30326-1084
Telephone: 404-264-1500
Fax: 404-264-1737

MEMBERS OF FIRM

William S. Goodman   Edward H. Lindsey, Jr.
C. Wade McGuffey, Jr.   Joe David Jackson
Judy Farrington Aust   William P. Claxton

ASSOCIATES

Leslie Stewart Sullivan   Kimberly Cronkright Raley
Kathryn A. Cater   James Bradley McClung
            J. Matthew Maguire, Jr.

For full biographical listings, see the Martindale-Hubbell Law Directory

HARMON, SMITH, BRIDGES & WILBANKS (AV)

1795 Peachtree Street, N.E., 30309
Telephone: 404-881-1200
Fax: 404-881-8523

MEMBERS OF FIRM

Archer D. Smith, III   Tyrone M. Bridges
            Marlan B. Wilbanks
ASSOCIATES
Fred Paul Anthony, Jr.   Cathy Carpenter
OF COUNSEL
Nolan B. (Joe) Harmon

For full biographical listings, see the Martindale-Hubbell Law Directory

Atlanta—Continued

HAWKINS & PARNELL (AV)

4000 SunTrust Plaza, 303 Peachtree Street, N.E., 30308-3243
Telephone: 404-614-7400
Fax: 404-614-7500
Email: 73541.1626@compuserve.com

MEMBERS OF FIRM

Paul M. Hawkins	William H. Major, III
J. Bruce Welch	Edward M. Newsom
Albert H. Parnell	T. Ryan Mock, Jr.
A. Timothy Jones	Lawrence J. Myers
Alan F. Herman	Jack N. Sibley
Howell Hollis, III	Warner S. Fox
Michael J. Goldman	Robert U. Wright
H. Lane Young, II	Thomas F. Wamsley, Jr.
Joseph R. Cullens	Michael E. Hutchins
Frank C. Bedinger, III	Ollie M. Harton
Julia Bennett Jagger	Kimberly Houston Ridley
Stephen M. Lore	Barry S. Noeltner

Kenan G. Loomis

ASSOCIATES

Kevin J. Bahr	Peter R. York
Edwin L. Hall, Jr.	Cullen Christie Wilkerson, Jr.
Roger M. Goode	Allen W. Nelson
Robert Rache Elarbee	Stephen M. Brooks
Charles R. Beans	Thomas G. Tidwell
Dennis J. Manganiello	Jennifer A. Grandoff

Jeb T. Branham

Representative Clients: The Coca-Cola Company; Ashland Oil Company; Eli Lilly and Co.; American International Group; Chrysler Corporation; Tenneco Oil Co.; Goodyear Tire & Rubber Co.; Georgia-Pacific Corp.; Monsanto Corporation; American Suzuki Motor Corp.

For Complete List of Firm Personnel, See General Section

For full biographical listings, see the Martindale-Hubbell Law Directory

THE HISHON FIRM, LLC (AV)

999 Peachtree Street N.E. Suite 1900, 30309
Telephone: 404-817-7791
Fax: 404-817-2486

Robert H. Hishon

Nancy R. Daspit

For full biographical listings, see the Martindale-Hubbell Law Directory

HOLT, NEY, ZATCOFF & WASSERMAN (AV)

A Partnership including Professional Corporations
100 Galleria Parkway, Suite 600, 30339
Telephone: 770-956-9600
Facsimile Number: 770-956-1490

MEMBERS OF FIRM

J. Scott Jacobson   Stephen C. Greenberg
David S. O'Quinn

ASSOCIATE

Jay Frank Castle

Representative Clients: Cummins South, Inc.; First American Title Insurance Co.; Gables Residential Trust; Lincoln Property Co.; Old Republic National Title Insurance Co.; Safety-Kleen Corp.; Trammell Crow Residential Cos.; John Wieland Homes, Inc.; Childress Klein Properties.

For Complete List of Firm Personnel, See General Section

For full biographical listings, see the Martindale-Hubbell Law Directory

JOHNSON & WARD (AV)

2100 The Equitable Building, 100 Peachtree Street N.W., 30303-1962
Telephone: 404-524-5626
Facsimile: 404-524-1769

OF COUNSEL

D. Lake Rumsey, Jr.

MEMBERS OF FIRM

William C. Lanham	Baxter P. Jones
Clark H. McGehee	William D. deGolian
John C. Dabney, Jr.	Bruce A. Maxwell

For Complete List of Firm Personnel, See General Section

For full biographical listings, see the Martindale-Hubbell Law Directory

JONES, DAY, REAVIS & POGUE (AV)

3500 One Peachtree Center, 303 Peachtree Street, N.E., 30308-3242
Telephone: 404-521-3939
Cable Address: "Attorneys Atlanta"
Telex: 54-2711
Telecopier: 404-581-8330
In Brussels, Belgium: Avenue Louise 480, 7th Floor, B-1050 Brussels.
Telephone: 32-2-645-14-11.
Telecopier: 32-2-645-14-45.
In Chicago, Illinois: 77 West Wacker.
Telephone: 312-782-3939.
Telecopier: 312-782-8585.
In Cleveland, Ohio: North Point. 901 Lakeside Avenue.
Telephone: 216-586-3939.
Cable Address: "Attorneys Cleveland".
Telex: 980389.
Telecopier: 216-579-0212.
In Columbus, Ohio: 1900 Huntington Center.
Telephone: 614-469-3939.
Cable Address: "Attorneys Columbus".
Telecopier: 614-461-4198.
In Dallas, Texas: 2300 Trammell Crow Center, 2001 Ross Avenue.
Telephone: 214-220-3939.
Cable Address: "Attorneys Dallas."
Telex: 730852.
Telecopier: 214-969-5100.
In Frankfurt, Germany: Triton Haus, Bockenheimer Landstrasse 42, 60323 Frankfurt am Main.
Telephone: 49-69-9726-3939.
Telecopier: 49-69-9726-3993.
In Geneva, Switzerland: 20, rue de Candolle.
Telephone: 41-22-320-2339.
Telecopier: 41-22-320-1232.
In Hong Kong: 29th Floor, Entertainment Building, 30 Queen's Road Central.
Telephone: 852-2526-6895.
Telecopier: 852-2868-5871 or 852-2868-5699.
In Irvine, California: 2603 Main Street, Suite 900.
Telephone: 714-851-3939.
Telex: 194911 Lawyers LSA.
Telecopier: 714-553-7539.
In London, England: One Mount Street.
Telephone: 44-71-493-9361.
Cable Address: "Surgoe London WI."
Telecopier: 44-71-493-9666.
In Los Angeles, California: 555 West Fifth Street, Suite 4600.
Telephone: 213-489-3939.
Telex: 181439 UD.
Telecopier: 213-243-2539.
In New Delhi, India: Pathak & Associates, 9th Floor, Dr. Gopal Das Bhaven, 28 Barakhamba Road.
Telephone: 91-11-331-9719.
Telecopier: 91-11-331-7802.
In New York, New York: 599 Lexington Avenue.
Telephone: 212-326-3939.
Cable Address: "JONESDAY NEWYORK."
Telex: 237013 JDRP UR.
Telecopier: 212-755-7306.
In Paris, France: 62, rue du Faubourg Saint-Honore.
Telephone: 33-1-44-71-3939.
Cable Address: "Surgoe Paris."
Telex: 290156 Surgoe.
Telecopier: 33-1-49-24-0471.
In Pittsburgh, Pennsylvania: 500 Grant Street, 31st Floor.
Telephone: 412-391-3939.
Cable Address: "Attorneys Pittsburgh".
Telecopier: 412-394-7959.
In Riyadh, Saudi Arabia: Law Offices of Saud M.A. Shawwaf, P.O. Box 22166.
Telephone: (966-1) 462-8866.
Telex: 401831 SAUCON SJ.
Telecopier: (966-1) 462-9001.
In Taipei, Taiwan: 8th Floor, 2 Tun Hwa South Road, Section 2.
Telephone: (886-2) 704-6808.
Telecopier: (886-2) 704-6791.
In Tokyo, Japan: Toranomon MT Building, 4th Floor, 10-3, Toranomon 3-Chome, Minato-ku, Tokyo 105, Japan.
Telephone: 81-3-3433-3939.
Telecopier: 81-3-5401-2725.
In Washington, D.C.: Metropolitan Square, 1450 G Street, N.W.
Telephone: 202-879-3939.
Cable Address: "Attorneys Washington."
Telex: 89-2410 ATTORNEYS WASH.
Telecopier: 202-737-2832.

MEMBERS OF FIRM IN ATLANTA

Girard E. Boudreau, Jr.   Dorothy Yates Kirkley

For Complete List of Firm Personnel, See General Section

For full biographical listings, see the Martindale-Hubbell Law Directory

Atlanta—Continued

KAUFMAN, CHAIKEN, RICKERTSEN, KREVOLIN, MILLER & HORST, A PROFESSIONAL CORPORATION (AV)

400 Perimeter Center Terrace, N.E., Suite 720, 30346-1234
Telephone: 770-390-9200
Facsimile: 770-395-6720
Email: rkaufm03@counsel.com

Robert J. Kaufman

References: Gulf States Mortgage Co., Inc.; Dyer & Dyer Volvo, Inc.; Trust Company Bank; Wachovia Bank of Georgia.

For Complete List of Firm Personnel, See General Section

For full biographical listings, see the Martindale-Hubbell Law Directory

KILPATRICK & CODY LLP (AV)

Suite 2800, 1100 Peachtree Street, 30309-4530
Telephone: 404-815-6500
Telephone Copier: 404-815-6555
Telex: 54-2307
Washington, D.C. Office: Suite 800, 700 13th Street, N.W., 20005.
Telephone: 202-508-5800. Telephone Copier: 202-508-5858.
Brussels, Belgium Office: Avenue Louise 65, BTE 3, 1050 Brussels.
Telephone: (32) (2) 533-03-00.
Telecopier: (32) (2) 534-86-38.
London, England Office: 68 Pall Mall, London, SW1Y 5ES, England.
Telephone: (44) (71) 321 0477.
Telecopier: (44) (71) 930 9733.
Augusta, Georgia Office: Suite 1400 First Union Bank Building, P.O. Box 2043, 30903. Telephone (706) 724-2622. Telecopier (706) 722-0219.

MEMBERS OF FIRM

G. William Austin, III	Neil I. Levy
Neal S. Berinhout	(Washington, D.C. Office)
William H. Boice	Kent E. Mast
Susan A. Cahoon	Gregg E. McDougal
Raymond G. Chadwick, Jr.	(Augusta Office)
(Augusta Office)	Mara McRae
Ted H. Clarkson	Matthew H. Patton
(Augusta Office)	Alan R. Perry, Jr.
A. Stephens Clay	Judith A. Powell
Roderick C. Dennehy, Jr.	Caroline W. Spangenberg
Thomas C. Harney	R. Scott Tewes
Stephen E. Hudson	Michael W. Tyler

Frederick H. von Unwerth

ASSOCIATES

Craig E. Bertschi	William F. Long
James F. Bogan, III	Christopher B. Lyman
Michael E. Brooks	David G. Michell
S. Kendall Butterworth	W. Craig Smith
Joseph H. Huff	(Augusta, Georgia Office)
(Augusta, Georgia Office)	Trent B. Speckhals

Jeffrey J. Toney

For Complete List of Firm Personnel, See General Section

For full biographical listings, see the Martindale-Hubbell Law Directory

KING & CROFT (AV)

191 Peachtree Street, N.E. 20th Floor, 30303-1741
Telephone: 404-577-8400
Facsimile: 404-577-8401

MEMBERS OF FIRM

Terrence Lee Croft	F. Carlton King, Jr.
Thomas A. Croft	Charlotte H. Beltrami

For full biographical listings, see the Martindale-Hubbell Law Directory

LEFKOFF, DUNCAN, MILLER, GRIMES, MILLER & BARWICK, P.C. (AV)

Suite 806, Eleven Piedmont Center, 3495 Piedmont Road, N.E., 30305
Telephone: 404-262-2000
Fax: 404-262-2897
Email: lawfirm@lefkoff-duncan.com

Joseph Lefkoff	Joseph C. Miller
Douglas W. Duncan	John R. Grimes
Kimberly A. Richardson	

For full biographical listings, see the Martindale-Hubbell Law Directory

LIPSHUTZ, GREENBLATT & KING (AV)

2300 Harris Tower-Peachtree Center, 233 Peachtree Street, N.E., 30303
Telephone: 404-688-2300
Fax: 404-588-0648

MEMBERS OF FIRM

Robert J. Lipshutz	Edward L. Greenblatt
Randall M. Lipshutz	

(See Next Column)

OF COUNSEL

William R. King	Tito Mazzetta
James V. Zito	

ASSOCIATES

Paula B. Smith	Timothy L. S. Sitz

For full biographical listings, see the Martindale-Hubbell Law Directory

LONG ALDRIDGE & NORMAN, LLP (AV)

A Limited Liability Partnership including Professional Corporations
One Peachtree Center, Suite 5300, 303 Peachtree Street, 30308
Telephone: 404-527-4000
Telecopier: 404-527-4198
Washington, D.C. Office: Suite 600, 701 Pennsylvania Avenue, N.W., 20004.
Telephone: 202-624-1200.
FAX: 202-624-1298.

MEMBERS OF FIRM

David L. Balser	Barbara A. McIntyre
Phillip A. Bradley	Carl W. Mullis, III
Bruce P. Brown	James J. Thomas II
Deborah S. Ebel	John L. Watkins
J. James Johnson	Jack H. Watson, Jr. (Resident,
J. Allen Maines	Washington, D.C. Office)

Terry R. Weiss

ASSOCIATES

Barry J. Armstrong	Melinda McNally
Susan Rappa Bain	Paula Rafferty Miller
R. Daniel Beale	Russell J. Rogers
Sharon M. Glenn	Lawrence A. Slovensky
Sherri L. Kimmell	Steven Paul Smith
Eric Charles Lang	Charles D. Weiss

J. Michael Wiggins

OF COUNSEL

J. Michell Philpott

For Complete List of Firm Personnel, See General Section

For full biographical listings, see the Martindale-Hubbell Law Directory

LONG, WEINBERG, ANSLEY AND WHEELER (AV)

A Partnership including Professional Corporations
999 Peachtree Street, N.E. Suite 2700, 30309
Telephone: 404-876-2700
Facsimile: 404-875-9433
Email: firm@lwaw.org

MEMBERS OF FIRM

Thomas J. Long (1898-1965)	Alan L. Newman
Palmer H. Ansley (1927-1991)	Marvin A. Devlin
Ben L. Weinberg, Jr., (P.C.)	Earl W. Gunn
Sidney F. Wheeler	C. Bradford Marsh
J. Kenneth Moorman	Arnold E. Gardner
John M. Hudgins, IV, (P.C.)	Lance D. Lourie
Robert G. Tanner	Milton B. Satcher, III
Joseph W. Watkins	David A. Sapp
James H. Fisher, II	Stephen H. Sparwath
M. Diane Owens	Kathryn S. Whitlock
Robert D. Roll	Mark E. Robinson
Kenneth Marc Barré, Jr.	Frederick N. Sager, Jr.

Patricia M. Peters

ASSOCIATES

Quinton S. Seay	Dennis J. Webb, Jr.
Charles K. Reed	George A. Koenig
Sharon B. Austin	Griffith J. Winthrop, III
Carol P. Michel	Anandhi S. Rajan
John K. Train, IV	Christopher J. Graddock
Johnathan T. Krawcheck	Alan M. Maxwell
John C. Bonnie	Bonny H. Richardson
Emily J. Brantley	Stephen R. Chance
Paul L. Weisbecker	Pamela C. Corley
J. Calhoun Harris, Jr.	F. Faison Middleton, IV
Michele L. Davis	Kari A. Mercer

OF COUNSEL

Meade Burns

Representative Clients: Aetna Casualty & Surety Corp.; Chrysler Motors Corp.; Emory University; Dow Corning Corp.; Ford Motor Co.; Freuhauf Trailer Corp.; Merck; Otis Elevator Co.; St. Paul Fire & Marine Insurance Co.; Toyota Motor Sales U.S.A., Inc.

For Complete List of Firm Personnel, See General Section

For full biographical listings, see the Martindale-Hubbell Law Directory

MACEY, WILENSKY, COHEN, WITTNER & KESSLER, LLP (AV)

285 Peachtree Center Avenue, Suite 600, 30303-1229
Telephone: 404-584-1200
Telecopier: 404-681-4355
Other Atlanta, Georgia Office: 5784 Lake Forrest Drive, Suite 214, 30328.

(See Next Column)

MACEY, WILENSKY, COHEN, WITTNER & KESSLER LLP, *Atlanta—Continued*

MEMBERS OF FIRM

Morris W. Macey	Neil C. Gordon
Frank B. Wilensky	Susan L. Howick
H. William Cohen	M. Todd Westfall
Richard P. Kessler, Jr.	James R. Sacca
David B. Kurzweil	

ASSOCIATES

Shayna M. (Salomon) Steinfeld	Rachel Anderson Snider
Robert A. Winter	Barbara Ellis-Monro
Pamela Gronauer Hill	Ronald Alan Weiner
Richard C. Litwin	

For Complete List of Firm Personnel, See General Section

For full biographical listings, see the Martindale-Hubbell Law Directory

MEADOWS, ICHTER & TRIGG, A PROFESSIONAL CORPORATION (AV)

Eight Piedmont Center, Suite 300, 3525 Piedmont Road, N.E., 30305
Telephone: 404-261-6020
Telecopier: 404-261-3656
Email: dartmead@mindspring.com

James Dartlin (Dart) Meadows	Mark G. Trigg
Cary Ichter	Lauren Slepin Antonino

Celia P. Quillian	Steven M. Kushner
Karen Reed Cashion	Margie M. Eget
Rhett Wade Marionneaux, Jr.	Amy C. Nerenberg

OF COUNSEL

Craig M. Frankel

Representative Clients: American Insurance Group; Bank South; Baskin-Robbins; BMW of North America, Inc.; Delta Air Lines, Inc.; Dunkin Donuts, Inc.; SCMI Corporation.
Reference: SunTrust Bank.

For full biographical listings, see the Martindale-Hubbell Law Directory

MILLS & MORAITAKIS (AV)

Resurgens Plaza, Suite 2515 945 East Paces Ferry Road, Northeast, 30326
Telephone: 404-261-0016
Facsimile: 404-261-0024

Roger Mills	Nicholas C. Moraitakis
Glenn E. Kushel	

For full biographical listings, see the Martindale-Hubbell Law Directory

MOZLEY, FINLAYSON & LOGGINS LLP (AV)

A Limited Liability Partnership
One Premier Plaza Suite 900, 5605 Glenridge Drive, 30342
Telephone: 404-256-0700
Telecopier: 404-250-9355

MEMBERS OF FIRM

J. Arthur Mozley	C. David Hailey
Robert M. Finlayson II	Richard D. Hall
Sewell K. Loggins	R. Ann Grier
William D. Harrison	Wayne D. Taylor
Eric D. Griffin, Jr.	Lawrence B. Domenico

ASSOCIATES

Edward C. Bresee, Jr.	J. Marcus Howard

For full biographical listings, see the Martindale-Hubbell Law Directory

NALL, MILLER, OWENS, HOCUTT & HOWARD (AV)

Suite 200 Peachtree & Broad Building, 66 Luckie Street, 30303
Telephone: 404-522-2200
Fax: 404-522-2208

MEMBERS OF FIRM

A. Walton Nall (1908-1984)	James R. Howard
James W. Dorsey (1914-1978)	George Robert Neuhauser
Edward S. White (1913-1992)	Robert L. Goldstucker
James S. Owens, Jr.	Kenneth P. McDuffie
Robert B. Hocutt	Kelly Eulenfeld Malone
Michael D. Hostetter	

COUNSEL

Samuel A. Miller

ASSOCIATES

Charles Richard Carson	Paul Jay Pontrelli
Mary Anne Palma	

(See Next Column)

LEGAL SUPPORT PERSONNEL

W. Gary Bush (Registered Nurse, Legal Assistant)	Michelle McGhee (Paralegal)
	Sheri L. Jordan (Paralegal)

Approved Attorneys for: Lawyers Title Insurance Corp.; Commonwealth Land Title Insurance Co.

For full biographical listings, see the Martindale-Hubbell Law Directory

PIERCE & YOUNG (AV)

Building 1700, 2255 Cumberland Parkway Northwest, 30339-4575
Telephone: 770-435-0500
Telecopier: 770-435-0362

MEMBERS OF FIRM

J. Wayne Pierce	Richard M. Young

ASSOCIATE

Christy A. Dunkelberger

For full biographical listings, see the Martindale-Hubbell Law Directory

POPE, McGLAMRY, KILPATRICK & MORRISON (AV)

A Partnership including Professional Corporations
83 Walton Street, N.W., P.O. Box 1733, 30303
Telephone: 404-523-7706;
Phenix City, Alabama: 334-298-7354
Columbus, Georgia Office: 318 11th Street, 2nd Floor, P.O. Box 2128, 31902-2128.
Telephone: 706-324-0050.

MEMBERS OF FIRM

C. Neal Pope (P.C.)	R. Timothy Morrison
Max R. McGlamry (P.C.) (Resident, Columbus, Georgia Office)	Michael L. McGlamry
	Earle F. Lasseter
	William Usher Norwood, III
Paul V. Kilpatrick, Jr. (Resident, Columbus, Georgia Office)	William J. Cornwell
	Jay F. Hirsch
Wade H. Tomlinson, III	

RESIDENT ASSOCIATE

C. Elizabeth Pope

Reference: Columbus Bank & Trust Co.

For full biographical listings, see the Martindale-Hubbell Law Directory

REYNOLDS & McARTHUR (AV)

A Partnership including a Professional Corporation
Suite 1080, One Buckhead Plaza, 3060 Peachtree Road, N.W., 30305
Telephone: 404-240-0265
Fax: 404-262-3557
Macon, Georgia Office: 850 Walnut Street.
Telephone: 912-741-6000.
Fax: 912-742-0750.
Asheville, North Carolina Office: The Jackson Building, 22 South Pack Square, Suite 1200.
Telephone: 704-254-8523.
Fax: 704-254-3038.

MEMBERS OF FIRM

W. Carl Reynolds (P.C.)	O. Wendell Horne, III
Katherine L. McArthur	Bradley J. Survant
Charles M. Cork, III	Steve Ray Warren (Not admitted in GA)

For full biographical listings, see the Martindale-Hubbell Law Directory

ANDREW M. SCHERFFIUS, P.C. (AV)

3166 Mathieson Drive, P.O. Box 53299, 30355
Telephone: 404-261-3562; 1-800-521-2867
Fax: 404-841-0861

Andrew M. Scherffius

Tamara McDowell Ayres

For full biographical listings, see the Martindale-Hubbell Law Directory

SCHULTEN, WARD & TURNER (AV)

Suite 1100 The Hurt Building, 50 Hurt Plaza, 30303
Telephone: 404-688-6800
Fax: 404-688-6840

MEMBERS OF FIRM

Wm. Scott Schulten	Kevin L. Ward
David L. Turner	

ASSOCIATES

Lou Litchfield	Clay Morris Westbrook
Susan Kastan Murphey	Julie H. McGhee

OF COUNSEL

Donald W. Osborne

Reference: NationsBank of Georgia, N.A.

For full biographical listings, see the Martindale-Hubbell Law Directory

Atlanta—Continued

SUMNER & ANDERSON (AV)

A Limited Liability Company
Suite 700, The Hurt Building, 50 Hurt Plaza, 30303
Telephone: 404-588-9000
Fax: 404-525-1116
Orlando, Florida Office: 940 Highland Avenue, 32802.
Telephone: 407-841-3000.
Fax: 407-841-0022.
Beaufort, South Carolina Office: 1001 Bay Street, Suite 102, 29902.
Telephone: 803-986-1000.
Fax: 803-986-1002.

MEMBERS OF FIRM

William E. Sumner	Steven E. Harbour
Stephen J. Anderson	David A. Webster

ASSOCIATES

Gerald Kirk Domescik	Anne S. Douds (Resident,
Kathleen M. Fischer	Beaufort, South Carolina)
Everrette V. Snotherly, III	Elizabeth A. Green (Resident,
Jerry P. Doyle	Orlando, Florida Office)

For full biographical listings, see the Martindale-Hubbell Law Directory

SUTHERLAND, ASBILL & BRENNAN, L.L.P. (AV)

999 Peachtree Street, N.E., 30309-3996
Telephone: 404-853-8000
Facsimile: 404-853-8806
Email: postmaster@sablaw.com
Washington, D.C. Office: 1275 Pennsylvania Avenue, N.W., 20004-2404.
Telephone: 202-383-0100.
New York, N.Y. Office: 600 Madison Avenue, 11th Floor, 10022-1615.
Telephone: 212-605-6400.
Austin, Texas Office: 111 Congress Avenue, 23rd Floor, 78701-4079.
Telephone: 512-469-3350.

Peter J. Anderson	C. Christopher Hagy
William D. Barwick	Charles T. Lester, Jr.
John W. Bonds, Jr.	Alfred A. Lindseth
Thomas M. Byrne	James R. McGibbon
John A. Chandler	Richard G. Murphy, Jr.
Thomas A. Cox	Judith A. O'Brien
Patricia Bayer Cunningham	James A. Orr
Carey P. DeDeyn	Richard L. Robbins
J. D. Fleming, Jr.	Teresa Wynn Roseborough
John H. Fleming	George Anthony Smith
James P. Groton	Elizabeth Vranicar Tanis

COUNSEL OF THE FIRM
IN ATLANTA, GEORGIA

Elizabeth W. Boswell	Patricia Anne Gorham
Edmund B. Burke	S. Lawrence Polk
Louise B. Duffy	William R. Wildman

For Complete List of Firm Personnel, See General Section

For full biographical listings, see the Martindale-Hubbell Law Directory

THOMAS, KENNEDY, SAMPSON & PATTERSON (AV)

55 Marietta Street, N.W., Suite 1600, 30303
Telephone: 404-688-4503
Telecopier: 404-681-2950

MEMBERS OF FIRM

John Loren Kennedy	P. Andrew Patterson
(1942-1994)	Myra H. Dixon
Thomas G. Sampson	Jeffrey E. Tompkins

ASSOCIATES

Rosalind T. Drakeford	Adam L. Smith
Melynee C. Leftridge	Thomas G. Sampson, II
La'Sean M. Zilton	Ceasar C. Mitchell, II.

R. E. Thomas, Jr. (1911-1996)

LEGAL SUPPORT PERSONNEL

Gwendolyn C.H. Dixon	Yvonne Torrence
Elbetha (Beth) Martin	Priscilla Yolanda Kelly
Nancy Allen-Haskell	Lureece D. Lewis (Paralegal)

For full biographical listings, see the Martindale-Hubbell Law Directory

TURNAGE & CHAMBERS (AV)

999 Peachtree Street, N.E., Suite 1750, 30309
Telephone: 404-872-0000
Fax: 404-873-2748

Kirby L. Turnage	Eugene P. Chambers, III

OF COUNSEL

Carol A. Paulk

For full biographical listings, see the Martindale-Hubbell Law Directory

WADE & CAMPBELL, LLP (AV)

Cumberland Center II, 3100 Cumberland Circle, Suite 1500, 30339
Telephone: 770-850-5000
FAX: 770-850-5075
Email: wadecamp@mindspring.com

MEMBERS OF FIRM

Allison Wade	Douglas N. Campbell
	Michael S. Thwaites

ASSOCIATES

Nancy P. Parson	Steven W. Hardy
Edward H. Nicholson, Jr.	Steven H. Jackman
	Walter Hamberg, III

Representative Clients: Allstate Insurance Company; Beneficial Management Corporation of America, Inc.; MBNA American Bank, N.A.; The Murray Manufacturing Company; NSA Inc.; Primerica Life Insurance Company; Sears Roebuck & Company; Southwire Co.; United Companies Lending Corporation; Western Auto Supply Company.

For full biographical listings, see the Martindale-Hubbell Law Directory

WEBB, CARLOCK, COPELAND, SEMLER & STAIR (AV)

A Partnership including Professional Corporations
2600 Marquis Two Tower, 285 Peachtree Center Avenue, P.O. Box 56887, 30343-0887
Telephone: 404-522-8220
Fax: 404-523-2345

MEMBERS OF FIRM

Dennis J. Webb (P.C.)	Wayne D. McGrew, III
Thomas S. Carlock (P.C.)	Douglas A. Wilde
Robert C. Semler (P.C.)	Frederick M. Valz, III
Wade K. Copeland (P.C.)	E. Alan Miller
Kent T. Stair (P.C.)	Johannes S. Kingma
Douglas W. Smith	Dennis G. Lovell, Jr.
David F. Root	Brian R. Neary
William E. Zschunke	Marvin D. Dikeman

ASSOCIATES

Robert W. Browning	Mary Katherine Smith
Philip P. Taylor	Leslie B. Zacks
David D. Cookson	Andrette Watson
Todd M. Yates	Gregg A. Landau
Adam L. Appel	James R. Doyle, II
R. Michael Ethridge	Lynn B. Olmert
Daniel J. Huff	Alissa H. Codel
Scott D. Huray	Kimberly L. Kilpatrick
Gregory H. Wheeler	Colleen P. O'Neill
Christopher A. Whitlock	Martin Enrique Valbuena
John W. Sandifer	Melissa C. Duffey
Craig A. Brookes	Matthew L. Hilt
	Michael J. Azzariti

For full biographical listings, see the Martindale-Hubbell Law Directory

WILLIAMS & HENRY (AV)

Suite 2020, 1100 Peachtree Street, N.E., 30309-4520
Telephone: 404-873-3000
Fax: 404-873-4508

MEMBERS OF FIRM

Benjamin S. Williams	Philip C. Henry
	Harvey R. Spiegel

ASSOCIATE

Joseph A. Fried

OF COUNSEL

Robert L. Callahan, III

Reference: Trust Company Bank.

For full biographical listings, see the Martindale-Hubbell Law Directory

WILSON, BROCK & IRBY, L.L.C. (AV)

999 Peachtree Street, N.E., Suite 2000, 30309
Telephone: 404-853-5050
Fax: 404-853-1812

MEMBERS OF FIRM

Richard W. Wilson, Jr.	Lethco H. Brock, Jr.
Frank L. Wilson, III	John H. Irby

ASSOCIATES

Jerry D. Gerald	James Stuart Teague, Jr.
	Paul Schillawski

OF COUNSEL

L. Robert Lovett

For full biographical listings, see the Martindale-Hubbell Law Directory

WILSON, STRICKLAND & BENSON, P.C. (AV)

1100 One Midtown Plaza, 1360 Peachtree Street, N.E., 30309
Telephone: 404-870-1800
Telecopier: 404-870-1808

(See Next Column)

WILSON, STRICKLAND & BENSON P.C., *Atlanta—Continued*

Warner R. Wilson, Jr.   Mary M. Brockington

OF COUNSEL
John C. Pennington

COUNSEL
Craig N. Goodrich

Anne W. Lewis   F. Robert Slotkin, Jr.
Samuel T. Brannan   Sara L. Doyle

For Complete List of Firm Personnel, See General Section

For full biographical listings, see the Martindale-Hubbell Law Directory

AUGUSTA,* Richmond Co.

RICHARD E. ALLEN (AV)

440 Greene Street, 30901
Telephone: 706-724-4466

For full biographical listings, see the Martindale-Hubbell Law Directory

BURNSIDE, WALL, DANIEL, ELLISON & REVELL (AV)

A Partnership including Professional Corporations
454 Greene Street, P.O. Box 2125, 30903
Telephone: 706-722-0768
Fax: 706-722-5984

MEMBERS OF FIRM
Robert C. Daniel, Jr.   James B. Wall (P.C.)
(1943-1993)   James W. Ellison
Thomas R. Burnside, Jr. (P.C.) Harry D. Revell
Thomas R. Burnside, III

ASSOCIATE
Lori S. D'Alessio

Representative Clients: Augusta-Richmond County Commission-Council; National Science Center Foundation, Inc.; CSRA Regional Development Center; City of Harlem, Georgia; Liquid Carbonic Corp.; Southern Machine & Tool Co.; Jefferson EMC; Southeastern Equipment Co.; SECO Aviation, Inc.; SECO Parts & Equipment, Inc.

For full biographical listings, see the Martindale-Hubbell Law Directory

CAPERS, DUNBAR, SANDERS & BRUCKNER (AV)

Fifteenth Floor, First Union Bank Building, 30901-1454
Telephone: 706-722-7542
Telecopier: 706-724-7776

MEMBERS OF FIRM
John D. Capers   E. Frederick Sanders
Paul H. Dunbar, III   Ziva P. Bruckner

ASSOCIATE
Carl P. Dowling

For full biographical listings, see the Martindale-Hubbell Law Directory

DYE, TUCKER, EVERITT, WHEALE & LONG, A PROFESSIONAL ASSOCIATION (AV)

453 Greene Street, P.O. Box 2426, 30903
Telephone: 706-722-0771
Fax: 706-722-7028

A. Rowland Dye   Duncan D. Wheale
Thomas W. Tucker   John B. Long
A. Zachry Everitt   Benjamin H. Brewton
Troy A. Lanier

OF COUNSEL
A. Montague Miller

Representative Clients: State Farm Insurance Cos.; The Travelers Insurance Co.; Georgia Power Co.; Wachovia National Bank (Augusta Division); Chubb Group; Montgomery Ward; Augusta Board of Realtors; Ryder Truck Rental, Inc.; Canal Insurance Company; St. Paul Fire and Marine Insurance Company.

For full biographical listings, see the Martindale-Hubbell Law Directory

FULCHER, HAGLER, REED, HANKS & HARPER (AV)

A Partnership including Professional Corporations
520 Greene Street, P.O. Box 1477, 30903-1477
Telephone: 706-724-0171
Telecopier: 706-724-4573

(See Next Column)

MEMBERS OF FIRM
William M. Fulcher (1902-1993)   Michael B. Hagler (P.C.)
Gould B. Hagler (Retired)   James W. Purcell (P.C.)
William C. Reed (Retired)   J. Arthur Davison (P.C.)
David H. Hanks (P.C.)   Mark C. Wilby (P.C.)
John I. Harper (P.C.)   Ronald C. Griffeth
Robert C. Hagler (P.C.)   N. Staten Bitting, Jr. (P.C.)
David P. Dekle (P.C.)

ASSOCIATES
Elizabeth A. McLeod   Barry A. Fleming

General Counsel for: GIW Industries, Inc.
Division Counsel for: CSX Transportation; Textron, Inc. (E-Z Go Car Division).
Counsel for: NationsBank; Georgia Natural Gas Co. (a division of Atlanta Gas Light Co.); Champion International Corp.; Aetna Life and Casualty; Liberty Mutual Insurance Company; St. Paul Fire & Marine Insurance Co.; Kimberly Clark Corporation.

For Complete List of Firm Personnel, See General Section

For full biographical listings, see the Martindale-Hubbell Law Directory

STANLEY C. HOUSE (AV)

Suite 506 The Lamar Building, 753 Broad Street, P.O. Box 915, 30903-0915
Telephone: 706-722-3341
Fax: 706-722-0471
Email: schouse@counsel.com

Approved Attorney for: Lawyers Title Insurance Corp.
References: First Union Bank & Trust (Augusta); NationsBank (Augusta).

For full biographical listings, see the Martindale-Hubbell Law Directory

HULL, TOWILL, NORMAN & BARRETT, A PROFESSIONAL CORPORATION (AV)

Seventh Floor, Trust Company Bank Building, P.O. Box 1564, 30903-1564
Telephone: 706-722-4481
Fax: 706-722-9779

James M. Hull (1885-1975)   Douglas D. Batchelor, Jr.
George B. Barrett (1894-1942)   David E. Hudson
Julian J. Willingham (1887-1963) Neal W. Dickert
John Bell Towill (1907-1991)   John W. Gibson
Robert C. Norman   William F. Hammond
(Retired, 1991)   Mark S. Burgreen
W. Hale Barrett   George R. Hall
Lawton Jordan, Jr.   James B. Ellington
Patrick J. Rice   F. Michael Taylor

Robert A. Mullins   Michael S. Carlson
William J. Keogh, III   Ralph Emerson Hanna, III
Edward J. Tarver   Susan D. Barrett
J. Noel Schweers, III   Timothy E. Moses

Counsel for: Sun Trust Bank Augusta, N.A.; Georgia Federal Bank, FSB, Augusta Division; Southeastern Newspapers Corp.; Georgia Power Co.; Southern Bell Telephone & Telegraph Co.; St. Joseph Hospital, Augusta, Georgia, Inc.; Norfolk Southern Corp.; Merry Land & Investment Co., Inc.; Housing Authority of the City of Augusta; Georgia Press Association.

For full biographical listings, see the Martindale-Hubbell Law Directory

KILPATRICK & CODY LLP (AV)

Suite 1400, First Union Bank Building, P.O. Box 2043, 30903
Telephone: 706-724-2622
Telephone Copier: 706-722-0219
Atlanta, Georgia Office: Suite 2800, 1100 Peachtree Street.
Telephone: 404-815-6500.
Telecopier: 404-815-6555.
Washington, D.C. Office: Suite 800, 700 13th Street, N.W., 20005.
Telephone: 202-508-5800. *Telephone Copier:* 202-508-5858.
Brussels, Belgium Office: Avenue Louise 65, BTE 3, 1050 Brussels.
Telephone: (32) (2) 533-03-00.
Telecopier: (32) (2) 534-86-38.
London, England Office: 68 Pall Mall, London, SW1Y 5ES, England.
Telephone: (44) (71) 321 0477.
Telecopier: (44) (71) 930 9733.

MEMBERS OF FIRM
Raymond G. Chadwick, Jr.   Wyck A. Knox, Jr.
Ted H. Clarkson   Gregg E. McDougal

ASSOCIATES
Jackson E. Cox, II   Joseph H. Huff
Daniel W. Hamilton   R. Perry Sentell, III
W. Craig Smith

Representative Clients: University Health Services, Inc.; National Cardiovascular Network, Inc.; Atlanta Cardiology, P.C.; First Union National Bank of Georgia; A.A. Friedman Co.; Blanchard & Calhoun Real Estate Co., Inc.; Boardman Petroleum, Inc.; Castleberry's Food Co., Inc.; DSM Chemicals North America, Inc.; Westinghouse Savannah River Company.

(See Next Column)

KILPATRICK & CODY—*Continued*

For full biographical listings, see the Martindale-Hubbell Law Directory

SAMUEL F. MAGUIRE (AV)

448 Telfair Street, 30901
Telephone: 706-722-4341
Fax: 706-724-8300
(Also Of Counsel to Samuel F. Maguire, Jr., Atlanta)

Representative Clients: Utilities of Augusta; Electrical Equipment Co.; Bil-bub, Inc.; Hospital Authority of the City of Augusta; Residential Care Facilities for the Elderly Authority.
Approved Attorney For: First American Title Insurance Co.

For full biographical listings, see the Martindale-Hubbell Law Directory

WILEY S. OBENSHAIN, III, P.C. (AV)

511 Courthouse Lane, 30901
Telephone: 706-722-1789
Fax: 706-722-3934

Wiley S. Obenshain, III

For full biographical listings, see the Martindale-Hubbell Law Directory

WARLICK, TRITT & STEBBINS (AV)

15th Floor, First Union Bank Building, 30901
Telephone: 706-722-7543
Fax: 706-722-1822
Columbia County Office: 119 Davis Road, Martinez, Georgia 30907.
Telephone: 706-860-7595.
Fax: 706-860-7597.

MEMBERS OF FIRM

William Byrd Warlick	Charles C. Stebbins, III
Roy D. Tritt	E. L. Clark Speese
(Resident, Martinez Office)	

ASSOCIATES

D. Scott Broyles	C. Gregory Bryan
Robert C. Threlkeld	

OF COUNSEL

Richard E. Miley

For full biographical listings, see the Martindale-Hubbell Law Directory

---

BAXLEY, * Appling Co.

EMMETT P. JOHNSON & E. PRESTON JOHNSON, JR., P.C. (AV)

410 North Boulevard, US I North, P.O. Box 304, 31513
Telephone: 912-367-2476; 367-2477
Fax: 912-367-4650

Emmett P. Johnson   E. Preston Johnson, Jr.

Representative Clients: Lawyers Title Insurance Corp.; Ticor Title Insurance Co.; Chicago Title Insurance Co.; Georgia Development Authority; Farmers Home Administration; Federal Land Bank of Columbia, South Carolina; Fidelity National Title Insurance Company of Tennessee f/k/a/ Southern Title Insurance Co. (Binding Agents); Southeastern Mortgage Corp.

For full biographical listings, see the Martindale-Hubbell Law Directory

---

BRUNSWICK, * Glynn Co.

FENDIG, McLEMORE, TAYLOR, WHITWORTH & DURHAM, P.C. (AV)

Suite 200 Suntrust Bank Building, P.O. Box 1996, 31521
Telephone: 912-264-4126
Telecopier: 912-264-0591

Albert Fendig, Jr.	Philip R. Taylor
Gilbert C. McLemore, Jr.	David T. Whitworth
James B. Durham	

Donna L. Crossland	Beth M. Duncan

Counsel for: Suntrust Bank of S.E. Georgia, N.A.; First Federal Savings Bank; Sea Island Property Owners Assn.; Calsilite Manufacturing Co.; Continental Insurance Cos.; Crum & Forster; MIM Insurance Companies, Inc.; The Hertz Corp.; Insurance Company of North America; United States Fidelity & Guaranty Co.

For full biographical listings, see the Martindale-Hubbell Law Directory

GILBERT, HARRELL, GILBERT, SUMERFORD & MARTIN, P.C. (AV)

Suite 200 First Federal Plaza, 31521
Telephone: 912-265-6700
Fax: 912-264-3917

(See Next Column)

Wallace E. Harrell	Jameson L. Gregg
James B. Gilbert, Jr.	Wallace E. Harrell, III
Rees M. Sumerford	Charles G. Spalding
M. Fleming Martin, III	Lisa Godbey
Monroe Lynn Frey, III	Mark D. Johnson

OF COUNSEL

James B. Gilbert	Joseph A. Whittle
H. Hall Ware, III	

Attorneys for: Sea Island Co.; American National Bank; Georgia-Pacific Corp.; Atlanta Gas Light Co.; Sea Harvest Packing Co.; Zurich General Accident & Liability Insurance Co.; Lumbermens Mutual Casualty Co.; BMW of North America.
Assistant Division Counsel for: Southern Railway Co.
Counsel for: Hercules Inc.

For Complete List of Firm Personnel, See General Section

For full biographical listings, see the Martindale-Hubbell Law Directory

JORDAN & O'DONNELL (AV)

1528 Ellis Street, P.O. Box 2115, 31521
Telephone: 912-262-9200
Fax: 912-262-0277

Randall A. Jordan	Rita C. Spalding
Christopher J. O'Donnell	Steven P. Bristol

For full biographical listings, see the Martindale-Hubbell Law Directory

WHELCHEL, BROWN, READDICK & BUMGARTNER (AV)

5 Glynn Avenue, P.O. Box 220, 31521-0220
Telephone: 912-264-8544
Telecopier: 912-264-9667

MEMBERS OF FIRM

J. Thomas Whelchel	Terry L. Readdick
Richard A. Brown, Jr.	John E. Bumgartner
B. Kaye Katz	

ASSOCIATES

G. Todd Carter	Raleigh W. Rollins, Jr.
Richard K. Strickland	Bradley J. Watkins

Representative Clients: Georgia Power Co.; Sears, Roebuck & Co.; Allstate Insurance Co.; Commercial Union Insurance Co.; Georgia Farm Bureau Mutual Insurance Co.; Government Employees Insurance Co.; Nationwide Insurance Co.; State Farm Insurance Cos.; Wausau Insurance Cos.

For full biographical listings, see the Martindale-Hubbell Law Directory

---

CEDARTOWN, * Polk Co.

MUNDY & GAMMAGE, P.C. (AV)

216 Main Street, P.O. Box 930, 30125-0930
Telephone: 706-748-3870
Fax: 706-748-2489
Rome, Georgia Office: The Carnegie Building, 607 Broad Street.
Telephone: 706-290-5180.

Emil Lamar Gammage, Jr.	George E. Mundy
William D. Sparks	Miles L. Gammage
(Mrs.) Gerry E. Holmes	John S. Husser
B. Jean Crane	

For Complete List of Firm Personnel, See General Section

For full biographical listings, see the Martindale-Hubbell Law Directory

---

COLUMBUS, * Muscogee Co.

BUTLER, WOOTEN, OVERBY, CHEELEY, PEARSON & FRYHOFER (AV)

1500 Second Avenue, P.O. Box 2766, 31902
Telephone: 706-322-1990;
National Wats: 1-800-233-4086
Fax: 706-323-2962
Atlanta, Georgia Office: 2719 Buford Highway, 30324.
Telephone: 404-321-1700.
Fax: 404-321-1713. Wats Line: 1-800-242-2962.

MEMBERS OF FIRM

James E. Butler, Jr.	Albert M. Pearson, III
Joel O. Wooten, Jr.	George W. Fryhofer III
C. Frederick Overby	Peter J. Daughtery
Robert D. Cheeley	J. Frank Myers, III
Lee Tarte Wallace	

ASSOCIATES

Jason L. Crawford	Joshua Sacks
Keith A. Pittman	Teresa Thomas Abell
Cale H. Conley	

For full biographical listings, see the Martindale-Hubbell Law Directory

Columbus—Continued

HARP & JOHNSON, P.C. (AV)

936 Second Avenue, P.O. Box 1172, 31902
Telephone: 706-323-2761
Fax: 706-323-0182

Beverly R. Keil (1924-1983) B. Seth Harp, Jr.
Gary L. Johnson

Reference: Trust Company Bank of Columbus.

For full biographical listings, see the Martindale-Hubbell Law Directory

POPE, McGLAMRY, KILPATRICK & MORRISON (AV)

A Partnership including Professional Corporations
318 11th Street, 2nd Floor, P.O. Box 2128, 31902-2128
Telephone: 706-324-0050;
Phenix City, Alabama: 334-298-7354
Atlanta, Georgia Office: 83 Walton Street, N.W., P.O. Box 1733, 30303.
Telephone: 404-523-7706.

MEMBERS OF FIRM

C. Neal Pope (P.C.) Michael L. McGlamry
Max R. McGlamry (P.C.) Earle F. Lasseter
(Resident) William Usher Norwood, III
Paul V. Kilpatrick, Jr. (Resident, Atlanta Office)
(Resident) William J. Cornwell
R. Timothy Morrison Jay F. Hirsch
Wade H. Tomlinson, III

RESIDENT ASSOCIATES

Joan S. Redmond Teresa Pike Majors
Matthew N. Pope

Reference: Columbus Bank & Trust Co.

For full biographical listings, see the Martindale-Hubbell Law Directory

TAYLOR, HARP & CALLIER (AV)

Suite 900 The Corporate Center, P.O. Box 2645, 31902-2645
Telephone: 706-323-7711
National WATS: 1-800-422-3352
Fax: 706-323-7544

MEMBERS OF FIRM

J. Sherrod Taylor J. Anderson Harp
Jefferson C. Callier

For full biographical listings, see the Martindale-Hubbell Law Directory

CORNELIA, Habersham Co.

CATHEY & STRAIN (AV)

6 Irvin Street, P.O. Box 689, 30531
Telephone: 706-778-2601
Fax: 706-776-2899

MEMBERS OF FIRM

Dennis T. Cathey Edward E. Strain, III
ASSOCIATES
J. Edward Staples David A. Sleppy

For full biographical listings, see the Martindale-Hubbell Law Directory

DALTON,* Whitfield Co.

MITCHELL & MITCHELL, P.C. (AV)

101 North Thornton Avenue, 30720
Telephone: 706-278-2040
Fax: 706-278-3040

D. Wright Mitchell (1895-1970) James H. Bisson, III
Douglas W. Mitchell Terry L. Miller
(1921-1984) Susan Williams Bisson
Erwin Mitchell William J. Kimsey
Neil Wester G. Gargandi Vaughn

Counsel for: The City of Dalton, Georgia; Conquest Carpet Mills, Inc.
Local Counsel for: Bituminous Casualty Corp.; CSX Corp.; NationsBank of Dalton, Georgia.
Reference: Nations Bank of Dalton, Georgia.

For full biographical listings, see the Martindale-Hubbell Law Directory

DECATUR,* De Kalb Co.

DAVIS & DAVIS (AV)

921 Wachovia Bank Building, 30030
Telephone: 404-373-2531

Jefferson James Davis Patricia Kunze Davis

Reference: Wachovia Bank of Atlanta.

For full biographical listings, see the Martindale-Hubbell Law Directory

SIMMONS, WARREN, SZCZECKO & McFEE, PROFESSIONAL ASSOCIATION (AV)

315 West Ponce de Leon Avenue, Suite 850, 30030
Telephone: 404-378-1711
Fax: 404-377-6101

M. T. Simmons, Jr. Joseph Szczecko
Wesley B. Warren, Jr. William C. McFee, Jr.

Representative Clients: David Hocker & Associates (Shopping Center Development); Julian LeCraw & Company (Real Estate); Intown Suites, Inc.; Preferred Lodging Systems, Inc.; Royal Oldsmobile,; Cotter & Co.; Atlanta Neurosurgical Associates, P.A.; Troncalli Motors, Inc.

For full biographical listings, see the Martindale-Hubbell Law Directory

DULUTH, Gwinnett Co.

THE WEATHERLY LAW FIRM (AV)

Gwinnett Commerce Center, 3700 Crestwood Parkway, N.W. Suite 140, 30136
Telephone: 770-564-9400
Fax: 770-564-9401

Charles L. Weatherly Julie J. Weatherly

For full biographical listings, see the Martindale-Hubbell Law Directory

GRIFFIN,* Spalding Co.

ROBERT H. SMALLEY, JR. PROFESSIONAL CORPORATION (AV)

115 North Sixth Street, P.O. Box 907, 30224
Telephone: 770-228-2125
Telecopier: 770-228-5018

Robert H. Smalley, Jr. Thomas E. Baynham, III

Representative Clients: The Bank Holding Company; The Bank of Spalding County; First Community Bank of Henry County; Griffin Spalding County Development Authority; Masada Communications, Ltd. (CATV); Union Camp Corp. (Local Counsel).

For full biographical listings, see the Martindale-Hubbell Law Directory

HARTWELL,* Hart Co.

GORDON LAW FIRM (AV)

Gordon Building, P.O. Box 870, 30643
Telephone: 706-376-5418
FAX: 706-376-5416
Email: wgordon@counsel.com

Walter James Gordon

Eleanor Patat Cotton Kimberly A. Wilkerson
LEGAL SUPPORT PERSONNEL
Flo W. Brown

References: NationsBank of Georgia, N.A.; The Bank of Hartwell; Athens First Bank & Trust Company.

For full biographical listings, see the Martindale-Hubbell Law Directory

JESUP,* Wayne Co.

ROBERT B. SMITH (AV)

356 East Cherry Street, P.O. Box 285, 31598
Telephone: 912-427-4779; 427-4629
FAX: 912-427-9203

References: Trust Company Bank of Southeast Georgia; Wayne National Bank.

For full biographical listings, see the Martindale-Hubbell Law Directory

JONESBORO,* Clayton Co.

DRIEBE & DRIEBE, P.C. (AV)

6 Courthouse Way, P.O. Box 975, 30237
Telephone: 770-478-8894
Fax: 770-478-9606
Atlanta, Georgia Office: 152 Nassau Street, N.W.
Telephone: 404-524-0606.

Charles J. Driebe Charles J. Driebe, Jr.

Approved Attorneys for: First American Title Insurance Co.; Attorney's Title Guaranty Fund.
Representative Clients: Henry County Airport, Inc.; Clayton News/Daily; Atlanta Beach Sports & Entertainment Park, Inc.; Los Toribios Mexican Restaurants, Inc.

For full biographical listings, see the Martindale-Hubbell Law Directory

OLIVER, DUCKWORTH, SPARGER & WINKLE, P.C. (AV)

146 McDonough Street, P.O. Box 37, 30236
Telephone: 770-478-8883
Fax: 770-473-0872

(See Next Column)

OLIVER, DUCKWORTH, SPARGER & WINKLE P.C.—Continued

G. Robert Oliver   Kevin W. Sparger
David P. Winkle

Kathy Brown Valencia
OF COUNSEL
William H. Duckworth, Jr.

Local Counsel for: Department of Transportation, State of Georgia.
Representative Clients: Clayton County Hospital Authority; Clayton County Water Authority; Clayton State College Foundation, Inc.; Clayton County Development Authority; Low Temp Industries, Inc.; Medical Association of Georgia Mutual Insurance Co.

For full biographical listings, see the Martindale-Hubbell Law Directory

---

LAWRENCEVILLE, * Gwinnett Co.

ANDERSEN, DAVIDSON & TATE, P.C. (AV)

324 West Pike Street, Suite 200, P.O. Box 2000, 30246-2000
Telephone: 770-822-0900
Telecopier: 770-822-9680

Gerald Davidson, Jr.   Thomas T. Tate
William M. Ray, II

Jonathan D. Crumly

References: Sun Trust Bank; The Bank of Gwinnett County; Commercial Bank of Georgia; Madison Ventures, Ltd.; Gwinnett Hospital System, Inc.; AT&T Wireless.

For Complete List of Firm Personnel, See General Section

For full biographical listings, see the Martindale-Hubbell Law Directory

---

MACON, * Bibb Co.

HALL, BLOCH, GARLAND & MEYER (AV)

1500 Charter Medical Building, P.O. Box 5088, 31213-3199
Telephone: 912-745-1625
Telecopier: 912-741-8822

MEMBERS OF FIRM

J. E. Hall (1876-1945)	Benjamin M. Garland
Charles J. Bloch (1893-1974)	J. Patrick Meyer, Jr.
Ellsworth Hall, Jr. (1908-1984)	J. Steven Stewart
J. René Hawkins (1924-1971)	J. Burton Wilkerson, Jr.
Ellsworth Hall, III	Duncan D. Walker, III
F. Kennedy Hall	Mark E. Toth

ASSOCIATES

John Flanders Kennedy   Todd C. Brooks
Kimberly Cofer Harris

F. Kennedy Hall, Division Counsel (Georgia): Norfolk Southern Railway Company.
Counsel for: Wachovia Bank of Georgia, N.A.; BellSouth Mobility, Inc.; United States Fidelity and Guaranty Company; Fina Oil and Chemical Company; Helena Chemical Corporation; Ear, Nose & Throat Medical Group, P.A.; Fickling & Walker Asset and Property Management, Inc.

For full biographical listings, see the Martindale-Hubbell Law Directory

---

JONES, CORK & MILLER (AV)

435 Second Street, Fifth Floor, P.O. Box 6437, 31201-2724
Telephone: 912-745-2821
Telecopier: 912-743-9609
Email: lawyer@jonescork.com

MEMBERS OF FIRM

C. Baxter Jones (1895-1968)	Thomas C. Alexander
Charles M. Cork (1908-1982)	C. Ashley Royal
Charles M. Cork, Jr.	Robert C. Norman, Jr.
Carr G. Dodson	Jerry A. Lumley
Timothy K. Adams	John T. Mitchell, Jr.
John C. Cork	W. Carter Bates III
H. Jerome Strickland	Timothy Harden, III
Hubert C. Lovein, Jr.	Howard J. Strickland, Jr.
W. Warren Plowden, Jr.	Cater C. Thompson
Rufus D. Sams, III	Thomas W. Joyce
Thomas C. James, III	Brandon A. Oren
Steve L. Wilson	W. Kerry Howell

ASSOCIATES

David A. Pope	Scott W. Spivey
William T. Prescott	Sharon Hurt Reeves
Alan G. Snipes	

OF COUNSEL

Wallace Miller, Jr.   John W. Smith

General Counsel for: The Bibb Co.; Sun Trust Bank Middle Georgia, N.A.; First Liberty Bank; Wesleyan College; Bibb County Board of Education.
Division Counsel for: Georgia Power Co.
Represent Locally: Southern Bell Telephone & Telegraph Co.; Allstate Insurance Co.; The City of Macon; St. Paul Fire & Marine Insurance Co.

(See Next Column)

For full biographical listings, see the Martindale-Hubbell Law Directory

REYNOLDS & McARTHUR (AV)

A Partnership including a Professional Corporation
850 Walnut Street, 31201
Telephone: 912-741-6000
Fax: 912-742-0750
Atlanta, Georgia Office: Suite 1080, One Buckhead Plaza, 3060 Peachtree Road, N.W.
Telephone: 404-240-0265.
Fax: 404-262-3557.
Asheville, North Carolina Office: The Jackson Building, 22 South Pack Square, Suite 1200.
Telephone: 704-254-8523.
Fax: 704-254-3038.

MEMBERS OF FIRM

W. Carl Reynolds (P.C.)	O. Wendell Horne, III
Katherine L. McArthur	Bradley J. Survant
Charles M. Cork, III	Steve Ray Warren
	(Not admitted in GA)

For full biographical listings, see the Martindale-Hubbell Law Directory

SELL & MELTON (AV)

A Partnership including a Professional Corporation
14th Floor, Charter Medical Building, P.O. Box 229, 31297-2899
Telephone: 912-746-8521
Telecopier: 912-745-6426

Andrew W. McKenna	Joseph W. Popper, Jr.
(1918-1981)	Doye E. Green
E. S. Sell, Jr.	Edward S. Sell, III
John D. Comer	John A. Draughon
Buckner F. Melton	R. (Chix) Miller
Mitchel P. House, Jr.	Russell M. Boston (P.C.)
	Brian J. Passante

ASSOCIATES

Jeffrey B. Hanson	David M. Cusson
Robert D. McCullers	John E. Payne
Michelle W. Johnson	W. Baxley Chew

General Counsel for: Macon Telegraph Publishing Co. (The Macon Telegraph); Macon-Bibb County Hospital Authority; County of Bibb; County of Twiggs; Smith & Sons Foods, Inc. (S & S Cafeterias); Macon Bibb County Industrial Authority; Burgess Pigment Co.

For Complete List of Firm Personnel, See General Section

For full biographical listings, see the Martindale-Hubbell Law Directory

---

MARIETTA, * Cobb Co.

AWTREY AND PARKER, P.C. (AV)

211 Roswell Street, P.O. Box 997, 30061
Telephone: 770-424-8000
Fax: 770-424-1594

L. M. Awtrey, Jr. (1915-1986)	Donald A. Mangerie (1924-1988)
George L. Dozier, Jr.	Barbara H. Martin
Harvey D. Harkness	A. Sidney Parker
Mike Harrison	Robert B. Silliman

General Counsel for: Kennesaw Finance Co.; Cobb Electric Membership Corporation; Development Authority of Cobb County.
Local Counsel for: Coats & Clark; Bell South Mobility; Lockheed-Georgia Corp.; Post Properties, Inc.; CSX Transportation, Inc.; Southern Bell; Cobb County Department of Transportation.

For full biographical listings, see the Martindale-Hubbell Law Directory

---

DOWNEY & CLEVELAND (AV)

288 Washington Avenue, 30060
Telephone: 770-422-3233
Fax: 770-423-4199

OF COUNSEL
Lynn A. Downey

MEMBERS OF FIRM

Robert H. Cleveland	Y. Kevin Williams
(1940-1989)	Russell B. Davis
Joseph C. Parker	G. Lee Welborn
	Rodney S. Shockley

ASSOCIATES

W. Curtis Anderson	Todd E. Hatcher
Scott D. Clay	Richard A. Griggs
	Tara M. Waller

Representative Clients: Allstate Insurance Co.; St. Paul Insurance Cos.; Georgia Farm Bureau Mutual Insurance Co.; State Farm Insurance Cos.; Cotton States Mutual Insurance Co.; Colonial Insurance Co. of California; Progressive Insurance Company; Auto Owners Insurance Company; Deep South Surplus, Inc.; Ed Voyles Oldsmobile, Honda and Chrysler-Plymouth.

For full biographical listings, see the Martindale-Hubbell Law Directory

Marietta—Continued

MOORE INGRAM JOHNSON & STEELE (AV)

A Limited Liability Company
192 Anderson Street, P.O. Box 3305, 30060
Telephone: 770-429-1499
Telecopier: 770-429-8631

MEMBERS OF FIRM

John H. Moore	Robert D. Ingram
Stephen C. Steele	G. Phillip Beggs
William R. Johnson	Eldon L. Basham

ASSOCIATES

Diane Matassino Busch	Kevin J. McGrath
David Ian Matthews	Kevin B. Carlock
Jere C. Smith	Alexander T. Galloway, III
Jeffrey A. Watkins	G. Andy Adamek
Robert E. Jones	J. Kevin Moore
Kenneth T. Israel	Scott Gregory Wagner

Representative Client: C.W. Matthews Contracting Co., Inc.
Approved Attorneys for: Chicago Title Insurance Co.
References: Charter Bank and Trust Co.; First Alliance Bank.

For full biographical listings, see the Martindale-Hubbell Law Directory

---

MCDONOUGH,* Henry Co.

SMITH, WELCH, STUDDARD & BRITTAIN (AV)

200 The Commerce Building, 235 Keys Ferry Street, P.O. Box 31, 30253
Telephone: 770-957-3937
Fax: 770-957-9165
Stockbridge, Georgia Office: 1231-A Eagle's Landing Parkway.
Telephone: 770-389-4864.
Fax: 770-389-5157.

MEMBERS OF FIRM

Ernest M. Smith (1911-1992)	Ben W. Studdard, III
A. J. Welch, Jr.	J. Mark Brittain
	(Resident, Stockbridge Office)

ASSOCIATES

Patrick D. Jaugstetter	Shawn Marie Story
E. Gilmore Maxwell	Arthur Scully Barbee

Representative Clients: Alliance Corp.; Atlanta Motor Speedway, Inc.; Bellamy-Strickland Chevrolet, Inc.; Ceramic and Metal Coatings Corp.; City of Hampton; City of Locust Grove; City of Stockbridge.

For full biographical listings, see the Martindale-Hubbell Law Directory

---

NEWNAN,* Coweta Co.

GLOVER & DAVIS, P.A. (AV)

10 Brown Street, P.O. Box 1038, 30264
Telephone: 770-253-4330
Fax: 770-251-7152
Peachtree City, Georgia Office: Suite 130, 200 Westpark Drive.
Telephone: 770-487-5834.
Fax: 770-487-3492.

J. Littleton Glover, Jr.	Asa M. Powell, Jr.

Representative Clients: Newnan Savings Bank; Pike Transfer Co.; Batson-Cook Company, General Corporate and Construction Divisions; Coweta County, Georgia; Heard County, Georgia; Bailey & Associates; Book Warehouse of Georgia, Inc.; West Georgia Farm Credit, ACA.
Local Counsel for: International Latex Corp.; First Union National Bank of Georgia.

For Complete List of Firm Personnel, See General Section

For full biographical listings, see the Martindale-Hubbell Law Directory

---

ROSENZWEIG, JONES & MACNABB, P.C. (AV)

32 South Court Square, P.O. Box 220, 30264
Telephone: 770-253-3282
Fax: 770-251-7262

George C. Rosenzweig	Sidney Pope Jones, Jr.
Joseph P. MacNabb	

Douglas L. Dreyer

Approved Attorneys for: Lawyers Title Insurance Corp.; Chicago Title Insurance Co.

For Complete List of Firm Personnel, See General Section

For full biographical listings, see the Martindale-Hubbell Law Directory

---

OCILLA,* Irwin Co.

WALTERS, DAVIS & PUJADAS, P.C. (AV)

South Cherry Street, P.O. Box 247, 31774
Telephone: 912-468-7472; 468-9433
Fax: 912-468-9022

(See Next Column)

W. Emory Walters	Thomas E. Pujadas
J. Harvey Davis	C. Vinson Walters, II

Attorneys for: Irwin County Board of Education; First State Bank of Ocilla; Irwin County; Wilcox County.
Local Counsel for: Georgia Farm Bureau Mutual Insurance Co.
Approved Attorneys for: Kaiser Aluminum & Chemical Sales, Inc.; Lawyers Title Insurance Corp.; Ticor Title Insurance Co.; Farmers Home Administration; Federal Land Bank of Columbia.

For Complete List of Firm Personnel, See General Section

For full biographical listings, see the Martindale-Hubbell Law Directory

---

ROME,* Floyd Co.

BRINSON, ASKEW, BERRY, SEIGLER, RICHARDSON & DAVIS (AV)

A Partnership including Professional Corporations
Omberg House, 615 West First Street, P.O. Box 5513, 30162-5513
Telephone: 706-291-8853;
Atlanta: 404-521-0908
Telecopier: 706-234-3574

MEMBERS OF FIRM

Robert M. Brinson (P.C.)	Hendrick L. Cromartie, III
C. King Askew (P.C.)	Wright W. Smith
Robert L. Berry	Mark M. J. Webb
Joseph M. Seigler, Jr.	Joseph B. Atkins
Thomas D. Richardson	I. Stewart Duggan, Jr.
J. Anderson Davis	James Daniel Blitch

Representative Clients: City of Rome; Georgia Power Co.; General Electric Company; News Publishing Company (Rome News Tribune); Redmond Regional Medical Center; Oglethorpe Power Corp.; Suhner Manufacturing, Inc.; The Federal Land Bank of Columbia; AmSouth Bank of Georgia; United States Fidelity & Guaranty Co.

For full biographical listings, see the Martindale-Hubbell Law Directory

---

MAGRUDER & SUMNER (AV)

701 Broad Street, P.O. Drawer 5187, 30162-5187
Telephone: 706-291-7050
Telefax: 706-291-9881

MEMBERS OF FIRM

J. Clinton Sumner, Jr.	Karl M. Kothe

ASSOCIATES

Clay M. White	Kay Ann Atha
Edward A. Johnson, II	

OF COUNSEL

Dudley B. Magruder, Jr.	Jack Rogers (Retired)
(1914-1995)	Wade C. Hoyt, Jr. (Retired)

Counsel for: State Farm Insurance Cos.; Atlanta Gas Light Co.; Best Manufacturing Co.; Georgia Power Co.; West Point-Stevens. Inc.; BellSouth Telecommunications, Inc.; Liberty Mutual Insurance Co.

For full biographical listings, see the Martindale-Hubbell Law Directory

---

SHAW, MADDOX, GRAHAM, MONK & BOLING (AV)

SunTrust Company Bank Building, P.O. Box 29, 30162-0029
Telephone: 706-291-6223
Telecopier: 706-291-7429

MEMBERS OF FIRM

Charles C. Shaw	David F. Guldenschuh
James D. Maddox	Daniel M. Roper
John M. Graham, III	Jule W. Peek, Jr.
C. Wade Monk	Virginia B. Harman
William H. Boling, Jr.	Scott M. Smith
Jo H. Stegall, III	Thomas H. Manning

ASSOCIATES

D. David Tomlin	Mather D. Graham

OF COUNSEL

Oscar M. Smith

Representative Clients: SunTrust Bank of Northwest Georgia; Inland-Rome Inc.; Norfolk Southern Railway Co.; Aetna Casualty & Surety Co.; American Mutual Liability Insurance; Commercial Union Insurance Cos.; Hartford Accident & Indemnity Co.; St. Paul Insurance Cos.; Zurich-American Insurance Co.

For full biographical listings, see the Martindale-Hubbell Law Directory

---

SAVANNAH,* Chatham Co.

BRANNEN, SEARCY & SMITH (AV)

22 East Thirty-Fourth Street, P.O. Box 8002, 31412
Telephone: 912-234-8875
Fax: 912-232-1792

(See Next Column)

BRANNEN, SEARCY & SMITH—*Continued*

Perry Brannen (1903-1984)	David R. Smith
Frank P. Brannen	Daniel C. Cohen
William N. Searcy	Wayne L. Durden

OF COUNSEL

William T. Daniel, Jr.

ASSOCIATES

Robert L. Jenkins	Margaret G. Culclasure
Bernard F. Kistler, Jr.	(Not admitted in GA)

Counsel for: Continental Insurance Co.

For full biographical listings, see the Martindale-Hubbell Law Directory

---

HUNTER, MACLEAN, EXLEY & DUNN, P.C. (AV)

200 East St. Julian Street, P.O. Box 9848, 31412
Telephone: 912-236-0261
Cable Address: "Ancan"
Telecopier: 912-236-4936
Telex: 54-6483
Atlanta, Georgia Office: The Peachtree, 1355 Peachtree Street, N.E., Suite 1050.
Telephone: 404-876-3611.
Fax: 404-870-2025.

Malcolm R. Maclean	J. Reid Williamson, III
John B. Miller	William E. Dillard, III
John M. Tatum	R. Jason D'Cruz
Arnold C. Young	Christopher Weis Phillips
Robert S. Glenn, Jr.	Robert Alvin Lewallen, Jr.
Wade W. Herring, II	Darrin L. McCullough

Representative Clients: Savannah Foods & Industries, Inc.; SunTrust Bank, Savannah, N.A.; Memorial Medical Center, Inc.; Prudential Insurance Company of America; Historic Savannah Foundation, Inc.; John Hancock Mutual Life Insurance Co.; Norfolk Southern Corp.

For Complete List of Firm Personnel, See General Section

For full biographical listings, see the Martindale-Hubbell Law Directory

---

McCALLAR AND ASSOCIATES (AV)

115 Oglethorpe Avenue West, P.O. Box 9026, 31412
Telephone: 912-234-1215
Telecopier: 912-236-7549

C. James McCallar, Jr.

Mark Bulovic	Todd E. Schwartz

For full biographical listings, see the Martindale-Hubbell Law Directory

---

WOODALL AND MACKENZIE, P.C. (AV)

327 Tattnall Street, P.O. Box 10166, 31412
Telephone: 912-238-9999

John T. Woodall	Malcolm Mackenzie, III

Peter A. Giusti

Reference: Trust Company Bank.

For full biographical listings, see the Martindale-Hubbell Law Directory

---

STATESBORO, * Bulloch Co.

EDENFIELD & COX, P.C. (AV)

201 South Main Street, P.O. Box 1700, 30459
Telephone: 912-764-8600
FAX: 912-764-8862

Gerald M. Edenfield	Susan W. Cox

Claude M. Kicklighter, Jr.	Tiffany T. Stanton

For full biographical listings, see the Martindale-Hubbell Law Directory

---

SUMMERVILLE, * Chattooga Co.

COOK & CONNELLY (AV)

128 South Commerce Street, P.O. Box 370, 30747
Telephone: 706-857-3421
Fax: 706-857-1520

MEMBERS OF FIRM

Bobby Lee Cook	L. Branch S. Connelly
A. Cecil Palmour (1913-1980)	Todd Johnson
Bobby Lee Cook, Jr. (1950-1995)	

For full biographical listings, see the Martindale-Hubbell Law Directory

---

SWAINSBORO, * Emanuel Co.

MERRILL, STONE & PARKS (AV)

2nd Floor, 101 South Main Street, P.O. Box 129, 30401
Telephone: 912-237-7029
Fax: 912-237-9211
Augusta, Georgia Office: 411 Telfair Street, 30901.
Telephone: 800-557-7029.
Statesboro, Georgia Office: 201 South Zetterower, 30458.
Telephone: 912-764-3897.

MEMBER OF FIRM

Chas. Brett Merrill, Jr.

References: First Liberty Bank; The Spivey State Bank.

For full biographical listings, see the Martindale-Hubbell Law Directory

---

TOCCOA, * Stephens Co.

McCLURE, RAMSAY & DICKERSON (AV)

400 Falls Road, P.O. Drawer 1408, 30577
Telephone: 706-886-3178
Fax: 706-886-1150

MEMBERS OF FIRM

Clyde M. McClure (1892-1976)	John A. Dickerson
George B. Ramsay, Jr.	Allan R. Ramsay
Marlin R. Escoe	

ASSOCIATES

Alice D. Hayes	Elizabeth Felton Moore
Luther H. Beck, Jr.	

OF COUNSEL

Knox Bynum

Counsel for: Coats and Clark, Inc.; Stephens Federal Savings & Loan Assn.; St. Paul Insurance Cos.; State Farm Insurance Cos.; Cotton States Insurance Cos.; City of Toccoa; Citizens Bank; Habersham Plantation Corp.; Patterson Pump Co; Georgia Farm Bureau Insurance Companies.

For full biographical listings, see the Martindale-Hubbell Law Directory

---

TUCKER, De Kalb Co.

HOTZ & ASSOCIATES, P.C. (AV)

Suite 200, 1979 Lakeside Parkway, 30084
Telephone: 770-939-4861
Fax: 770-270-9749

Richard F. Taylor (1921-1993)	J. Tyler Tippett
Walter H. Hotz	James H. Baskin

Representative Clients: Regional Counsel for GE Supply, a Division of General Electric Company; Atlanta Postal Credit Union; CDC Federal Credit Union; Federal Employees Credit Union; Georgia Federal Credit Union; Peachtree Federal Credit Union; Deutsche Steinindustrie A.G.; Destag of North America, Inc.; General Trailer Services, Inc.; The Network Connection, Inc.

For full biographical listings, see the Martindale-Hubbell Law Directory

---

VALDOSTA, * Lowndes Co.

BARHAM, DOVER, BENNETT, MILLER, SHERWOOD & STONE (AV)

701 North Patterson Street, P.O. Box 729, 31603-0729
Telephone: 912-242-0314
Fax: 912-242-6495

Edwin G. Barham (1935-1992)	Willis L. Miller, III
John R. Bennett	J. Carol Sherwood, Jr.
J. Michael Dover	Wilton E. Stone, Jr.

Patricia McCorvey Karras	William W. Broadfoot, III

Representative Clients: First State Bank & Trust Co.; Liberty Savings Bank; Borg-Warner Acceptance Corp.; National Mortgage Co.; Lacoga Federal Credit Union; Valdosta Teachers Federal Credit Union; W WSHF Radio; South Georgia Medical Center; Bell South.

For full biographical listings, see the Martindale-Hubbell Law Directory

---

DODD AND DENNIS, P.C. (AV)

613 N. Patterson Street, P.O. Box 1066, 31603-1066
Telephone: 912-242-4470
Telefax: 912-245-7731
Email: doddlaw@mail.datasys.net *URL:* http://www.doddlaw.com

Roger J. Dodd	Sam D. Dennis

References: First Union Bank; First State Bank and Trust Co.; Park Avenue Bank.

For full biographical listings, see the Martindale-Hubbell Law Directory

Valdosta—Continued

ELLIOTT & BLACKBURN (AV)

First Liberty Bank Building, 509 North Patterson Street Suite 201, P.O. Box 579, 31603-0579
Telephone: 912-247-0800
912-242-3333
Telecopier: 912-242-0696

W. Gus Elliott	Walter G. Elliott, II
Oris D. Blackburn, Jr.	James L. Elliott

Representative Clients: Hospital Authority of Valdosta and Lowndes County d/b/a South Georgia Medical Center; Lowndes County; The Valdosta Daily Times; Bell South Telecommunications, Inc.; Sears, Roebuck & Company; Levi Strauss & Co.; John Deere & Co.; E. I. DuPont de Nemours & Company; BP Exploration & Oil, Inc.; National Indemnity Company.

For full biographical listings, see the Martindale-Hubbell Law Directory

TILLMAN, McTIER, COLEMAN, TALLEY, NEWBERN & KURRIE (AV)

910 North Patterson Street, P.O. Box 5437, 31603-5437
Telephone: 912-242-7562
Fax: 912-333-0885

MEMBERS OF FIRM

John T. McTier	Richard L. Coleman
Wade H. Coleman	Edward F. Preston
George T. Talley	William E. Holland
C. George Newbern	R. Clay Powell
Thompson Kurrie, Jr.	Gregory T. Talley

Attorneys for: NationsBank; Georgia Power Company; Atlanta Gas Company; Griffin Agricultural Chemicals Group; SAFT America Inc.; Sears; The Park Avenue Bank; Liberty Mutual Insurance Company; USF&G Company; MAG Mutual Insurance Company.

For Complete List of Firm Personnel, See General Section

For full biographical listings, see the Martindale-Hubbell Law Directory

WAYCROSS,* Ware Co.

DILLARD, BOWER AND EAST (AV)

209 Tebeau Street, P.O. Box 898, 31501
Telephone: 912-285-2915
Fax: 912-285-2249

MEMBERS OF FIRM

Terry A. Dillard	Bryant H. Bower, Jr.
	Joseph E. East

ASSOCIATES

Scott C. Crowley	Rebecca R. Crowley

Attorneys For: American International Adjustment Co.; Auto-Owners Insurance Co.; Chrysler Corp.; Farmers Insurance Group; Georgia Farm Bureau Mutual Insurance Co.; G.M.A.C.; Grange Mutual Insurance Co.; Guaranty National Insurance Co.; Hoffman La Roche.

For full biographical listings, see the Martindale-Hubbell Law Directory

HAWAII

HONOLULU,* Honolulu Co.

ALSTON, HUNT, FLOYD & ING ATTORNEYS AT LAW, A LAW CORPORATION (AV)

18th Floor Pacific Tower, 1001 Bishop Street, P.O. Box 2281, 96804
Telephone: 808-524-1800
Telecopier: 808-524-4591

Paul D. Alston	Bruce S. Noborikawa
William S. Hunt	Sharon A. Merkle
Shelby Anne Floyd	Everett S. Kaneshige
Louise K. Y. Ing	David A. Nakashima
Ellen Godbey Carson	Neil F. Hulbert

Mei Nakamoto	Marilyn Chung Ushijima
Peter C. Hsieh	Susan Jameson
Mary Martin	Joseph P. Viola
Jade Lynne Holck	Richard A. Yanagi
	Bradford L. Tannen

OF COUNSEL

Bruce H. Wakuzawa	Robert A. Marks

Representative Clients: Kaiser Aluminum and Chemical Co.; Federal Deposit Insurance Corp.; Kaiser Foundation Health Plan, Inc.; Chicago Title Insurance Co.; Amfac, Inc.

For full biographical listings, see the Martindale-Hubbell Law Directory

GEORGE W. ASHFORD, JR. (AV)

2910 Pacific Tower, 1001 Bishop Street, 96813
Telephone: 808-528-0444
Telecopier: (808) 533-0761
Cable Address: Justlaw

Representative Clients: Lloyds of London; Baker Industries, Inc.; Burns International Security Services; Clark Equipment Co.; Great Lakes Chemical Corporation; California Union Insurance Co.; Great American Insurance Companies; Guaranty National Companies; Horace Mann Insurance Company; Marine Office of America Corp.

For full biographical listings, see the Martindale-Hubbell Law Directory

AYABE, CHONG, NISHIMOTO, SIA & NAKAMURA (AV)

A Partnership including a Professional Corporation
Pauahi Tower, Suite 2500, 1001 Bishop Street, 96813
Telephone: 808-537-6119
Telecopier: 808-526-3491

MEMBERS OF FIRM

Sidney K. Ayabe (P.C.)	Calvin E. Young
Robert A. Chong	Diane W. Wong
John S. Nishimoto	Rodney S. Nishida
Richard F. Nakamura	Patricia T. Fujii
Jeffrey H. K. Sia	Rhonda A. Nishimura
Kenneth T. Goya	Gail M. Kang
Francis M. Nakamoto	Ann H. Aratani

Philip S. Uesato	Virgil B. Prieto
Ronald M. Shigekane	J. Thomas Weber
Robin R. Horner	Robert Y. Nakamoto
Stephen G. Dyer	Robert A. Mash
Steven L. Goto	Gary S. Miyamoto

Representative Clients: Travelers Insurance Co.; St. Paul Fire and Marine Insurance Co.; The Employers Group of Insurance Companies; TIG Insurance Co.; Pacific Insurance Co.; Hartford Accident and Indemnity Co.; Continental Casualty Co.; CNA Insurance Co.; Montgomery Kone; Wausau Insurance Co.

For full biographical listings, see the Martindale-Hubbell Law Directory

LAW OFFICE OF SHERRY P. BRODER A LAW CORPORATION (AV)

PRI Tower, Suite 1800, 733 Bishop Street, 96813
Telephone: 808-531-1411
Facsimile: 808-531-8411

Sherry P. Broder

Reference: Bank of Honolulu.

For full biographical listings, see the Martindale-Hubbell Law Directory

CADES SCHUTTE FLEMING & WRIGHT (AV)

Formerly Smith, Wild, Beebe & Cades
1000 Bishop Street, P.O. Box 939, 96808
Telephone: 808-521-9200
Telecopier: 808-531-8738
Email: cades@cades.com
Affiliated Law Firm: Udom-Prok Associates Law Offices, 105/36 Tharinee Mansion, Borom Raj Chananee Road Bangkoknoi, Bangkok, Thailand, 10700.
Telephone: 011 662 435-4146.
Kailua-Kona, Hawaii Office: Hualalai Center, Suite B-303, 75-170 Hualalai Road.
Telephone: 808-329-5811.
Telecopier: 808-326-1175.

MEMBERS OF FIRM

Jeffrey S. Portnoy	David Schulmeister
Philip J. Leas	Milton M. Yasunaga
William A. Cardwell	Susan Oki Mollway
C. Michael Hare	Colin O. Miwa
Richard R. Clifton	Peter W. Olson
Roy A. Vitousek, III	Patricia J. McHenry
(Resident, Kona Office)	K. James Steiner, Jr.

ASSOCIATES

James H. Ashford	Alexander Woody
Dennis W. Chong Kee	Christopher I.L. Parsons
Catherine A. Carey	Kenneth C. May
Alan K. Hyde	Sarah O. Wang
Kelly G. LaPorte	Kimberly O'Neill Jackson
Maria B. Mazzeo	(Resident, Kona Office)

Counsel for: First Hawaiian Bank; Alexander & Baldwin, Inc.; Theo. H. Davies & Co., Ltd.; C. Brewer & Company, Ltd.; Bank of America, FSB; The Bank of Tokyo, Ltd.; Haseko (Hawaii), Inc.; The Industrial Bank of Japan, Ltd.

For Complete List of Firm Personnel, See General Section

For full biographical listings, see the Martindale-Hubbell Law Directory

Honolulu—Continued

BENJAMIN B. CASSIDAY, III (AV)

2440 Mauka Tower, Grosvenor Center, 737 Bishop Street, 96813-3215
Telephone: 808-523-9007
Fax: 808-531-8898

For full biographical listings, see the Martindale-Hubbell Law Directory

THE LAW OFFICES OF JOHN A. CHANIN (AV)

The Executive Centre, 1088 Bishop Street, Suite 511, 96813
Telephone: 808-538-1637
Fax: 808-531-5055

For full biographical listings, see the Martindale-Hubbell Law Directory

LAW OFFICES OF STUART M. COWAN (AV)

Ocean View Center, 707 Richards Street, Suite 728, 96813
Telephone: 808-533-1767
Fax: 808-533-0549
Kaneohe, Hawaii Office: Suite 202, 47-653 Kamehameha Highway.
Telephone: 808-533-1767.
Fax: 808-239-9175.
Reference: 1st Hawaiian Bank.

For full biographical listings, see the Martindale-Hubbell Law Directory

CRONIN, FRIED, SEKIYA, KEKINA & FAIRBANKS ATTORNEYS AT LAW, A LAW CORPORATION (AV)

1900 Davies Pacific Center, 841 Bishop Street, 96813
Telephone: 808-524-1433
Fax: 808-536-2073

Paul F. Cronin	John D. Thomas, Jr.
L. Richard Fried, Jr.	Stuart A. Kaneko
Gerald Y. Sekiya	Bert S. Sakuda
Wayne K. Kekina	Allen K. Williams
David L. Fairbanks	Keith K. H. Young

Patrick W. Border	Clarence S.K. Kekina
Gregory L. Lui-Kwan	Sylvia E.J. Luke
Patrick F. McTernan	Geoffrey K.S. Komeya

For full biographical listings, see the Martindale-Hubbell Law Directory

DWYER IMANAKA SCHRAFF KUDO MEYER & FUJIMOTO ATTORNEYS AT LAW, A LAW CORPORATION (AV)

1800 Pioneer Plaza, 900 Fort Street Mall, 96813
Telephone: 808-524-8000
Telecopier: 808-526-1419
Mailing Address: P.O. Box 2727, 96803
Email: hawaiilaw@dwyer-imanaka.com *URL:*
http://www.dwyer-imanaka.com

John R. Dwyer, Jr.	William G. Meyer, III
Mitchell A. Imanaka	Wesley M. Fujimoto
Paul A. Schraff	Ronald Van Grant
Benjamin A. Kudo (Atty. at Law, A Law Corp.)	Jon M. H. Pang
	Blake W. Bushnell
Adelbert Green	

Richard T. Asato, Jr.	Jeffery S. Werbelow
Scott W. Settle	Lori Ann K. Koseki
Darcie S. Yoshinaga	Troy T. Fukuhara
Lawrence I. Kawasaki	Katy Y. Chen
Stacy E. Uehara	Naomi S. Uyeno
Kris N. Nakagawa	Roger B. McKeague

OF COUNSEL

Randall Y. Iwase	R. Brian Tsujimura

For full biographical listings, see the Martindale-Hubbell Law Directory

FUJIYAMA, DUFFY & FUJIYAMA ATTORNEYS AT LAW, A LAW CORPORATION (AV)

2700 Pauahi Tower, Bishop Square, 1001 Bishop Street, 96813
Telephone: 808-536-0802
Telecopier: 808-536-5117

Wallace S. Fujiyama (1925-1994)	Rodney M. Fujiyama
James E. Duffy, Jr.	Archie T. Ikehara
Leslie E. Kobayashi	

Ward F. N. Fujimoto	Lee T. Nakamura
Gregg M. Ushiroda	Lisa-Ann L. Kimura
Reese R. Nakamura	Rew K. Ikazaki
Danielle Noel Degele-Mathews (Not admitted in HI)	

Representative Clients: Hartford Accident & Indemnity Co.; Maryland Casualty Co.; New England Mutual Life Insurance Co.; Duty Free Shoppers, Ltd.; West Beach Estates (Ko Olina Resort).

(See Next Column)

For full biographical listings, see the Martindale-Hubbell Law Directory

FUKUNAGA MATAYOSHI HERSHEY & CHING (AV)

A Partnership including a Law Corporation
City Center, Third Floor, 810 Richards Street, 96813
Telephone: 808-533-4300
Fax: 808-531-7585

PARTNERS

Kenneth K. Fukunaga	James H. Hershey
Jerold T. Matayoshi (A Law Corporation)	Wesley W. H. Ching
	Patricia Kehau Wall

ASSOCIATES

Lois H. Yamaguchi	Robert R. Sadaoka
Lindai M. Dang	

OF COUNSEL

Leighton K. Chong

For full biographical listings, see the Martindale-Hubbell Law Directory

GREELEY WALKER & KOWEN (AV)

A Partnership including a Law Corporation
Suite 1300 Pauahi Tower, 1001 Bishop Street, 96813
Telephone: 808-526-2211
Telecopier: 808-528-4690

MEMBERS OF FIRM

Burnham H. Greeley (A Law Corporation)	Susan P. Walker
	Richard J. Kowen
Janice T. Futa	

ASSOCIATES

Frank P. Richardson	Kimberly Ann Greeley
Andrew D. Smith	

For full biographical listings, see the Martindale-Hubbell Law Directory

DAVID W. HALL ATTORNEY AT LAW, A LAW CORPORATION (AV)

Dillingham Transportation Building, Suite 237, 735 Bishop Street, 96813
Telephone: 808-526-0402
Fax: 808-526-0404

David W. Hall

For full biographical listings, see the Martindale-Hubbell Law Directory

LEE, KIM, WONG, YEE & LAU ATTORNEYS AT LAW, A LAW CORPORATION (AV)

Suite 700 Media Five Plaza, 345 Queen Street, 96813
Telephone: 808-536-4421
Telecopier: 808-521-3566

Douglas T. Y. Lee	Edmund K. U. Yee
Wayson W. S. Wong	Eric T. W. Kim
Gene K. Lau	

Arthur H. Kuwahara	Kendall J. Moser

OF COUNSEL

Steven H. Lee

For full biographical listings, see the Martindale-Hubbell Law Directory

LYNCH & FARMER (AV)

Suite 2500, Mauka Tower Grosvenor Center, 737 Bishop Street, 96813
Telephone: 808-528-0100
Facsimile: 808-528-4997

LEGAL SUPPORT PERSONNEL

Sylvia M. Lee	Linda L. Tauotaba

For full biographical listings, see the Martindale-Hubbell Law Directory

McCORRISTON MIHO MILLER MUKAI (AV)

Five Waterfront Plaza, 4th Floor, 500 Ala Moana Boulevard, 96813
Telephone: 808-529-7300
Facsimile: 808-524-8293
Cable: Attorneys, Honolulu
Mailing Address: P.O. Box 2800, Honolulu, Hawaii, 96803-2800
Hilo, Hawaii Office: 56 Waianuenue Avenue, Suite 217, 96720.
Telephone: 808-935-6537.
Facsimile: 808-935-3398.

PARTNERS

William C. McCorriston	John Y. Yamano
Mark J. Bennett	R. John Seibert
Nadine Y. Ando	Thomas E. Bush
Richard B. Miller	David J. Minkin
Randall K. Schmitt	Lisa M. Ginoza

(See Next Column)

McCORRISTON MIHO MILLER MUKAI, *Honolulu—Continued*

ASSOCIATES

Kimberly Rae McCorkle
Carrie K. Okinaga
Christopher J. Cole

Douglas K. Ushijima
David R. Harada-Stone
Dean J. Myatt

Stacey M. Robinson

Representative Clients: Deloitte & Touche; City & County of Hawaii; County of Kauai; Hawaii County and Shared Medical Systems Corporation.

For Complete List of Firm Personnel, See General Section

For full biographical listings, see the Martindale-Hubbell Law Directory

---

PERKIN & HOSODA (AV)

2440 Mauka Tower, Grosvenor Center, 737 Bishop Street, 96813
Telephone: 808-523-2300
Fax: 808-531-8898

MEMBERS OF FIRM

John Francis Perkin

Lyle S. Hosoda

For full biographical listings, see the Martindale-Hubbell Law Directory

---

PRICE OKAMOTO HIMENO & LUM ATTORNEYS AT LAW, A LAW CORPORATION (AV)

Suite 728, Ocean View Center, 707 Richards Street, 96813
Telephone: 808-538-1113
Fax: 808-533-0549

Warren Price, III
Kenneth T. Okamoto

Sharon R. Himeno
Bettina W. J. Lum

Terence S. Yamamoto

Robert Kohn

OF COUNSEL

Stuart M. Cowan

Lawrence R. Cohen

Michael K. Kaneshiro

For full biographical listings, see the Martindale-Hubbell Law Directory

---

REID, RICHARDS & MIYAGI (AV)

A Partnership including Professional Corporations
Pauahi Tower, Suite 1200, 1001 Bishop Street, 96813-3498
Telephone: 808-524-2466
Fax: 808-524-2556

MEMBERS OF FIRM

Carleton B. Reid (A Law
  Corporation)
Robert P. Richards (A Law
  Corporation)

Melvyn M. Miyagi (A Law
  Corporation)
Ralph J. O'Neill
Katharine M. Nohr

James V. Myhre
Roy F. Epstein
Michele-Lynn E. Luke
L. Darlene Mitchell
Marie A. Sheldon
Michael H. Tsuchida

Tamara M. Gerrard
John E. Drotz
Deborah Chen
Jennifer Ellen Reid
Celia A. Urion
Irene C. Sun

Duane R. Miyashiro

For full biographical listings, see the Martindale-Hubbell Law Directory

---

REINWALD, O'CONNOR, MARRACK, HOSKINS & PLAYDON (AV)

(Formerly Anthony, Hoddick, Reinwald & O'Connor)
2400 PRI Tower, Grosvenor Center, P.O. Box 3199, 96801-3199
Telephone: 808-524-8350
Cable Address: "Hermes" Honolulu
Telecopier: 808-531-8628

MEMBERS OF FIRM

Dennis E. W. O'Connor
John A. Hoskins
George W. Playdon, Jr.

W. Thomas Fagan
Michael J. McGuigan
Cid H. Inouye

Kelvin H. Kaneshiro

For full biographical listings, see the Martindale-Hubbell Law Directory

---

ROBBINS & RHODES ATTORNEYS AT LAW, A LAW CORPORATION (AV)

Suite 2200 Davies Pacific Center, 841 Bishop Street, 96813
Telephone: 808-524-2355
Fax: 808-526-0290

Kenneth S. Robbins

Vincent A. Rhodes

Shinken Naitoh

Representative Clients: City and County of Honolulu; CNA Insurance Co.; Coldwell Banker Pacific Properties; County of Maui; Farmers Insurance Group; Guaranty National Insurance Co.; Kapiolani Health Care Systems, Inc.; State of Hawaii; Textron, Inc.; Westin Hotel Company, Inc.

For full biographical listings, see the Martindale-Hubbell Law Directory

---

ROECA, LOUIE & HIRAOKA (AV)

900 Davies Pacific Center, 841 Bishop Street, 96813
Telephone: 808-538-7500
Facsimile: 808-521-9648

MEMBERS OF FIRM

Arthur F. Roeca
David M. Louie

Keith K. Hiraoka
Kari A. Wilhelm

Ryan M. Akamine

OF COUNSEL

H. William Goebert, Jr.

ASSOCIATES

Daniel T. Kim
Jodie D. Roeca
Robert B. Frija

April Luria
Kelley G.A. Nakano
James S. Kawashima

LEGAL SUPPORT PERSONNEL

LEGAL ASSISTANTS

Patrick J. Saxton
Andrea J. Playdon

Elinor H. Tomita
Gayle A. Bullington

For full biographical listings, see the Martindale-Hubbell Law Directory

---

TRECKER & FRITZ (AV)

820 Mililani Street, Suite 701, 96813
Telephone: 808-528-3900
Fax: 808-533-3684

MEMBERS OF FIRM

Steven J. Trecker
Collin (Marty) Fritz

Magali V. Sunderland
Hilary Benson Gangnes

For full biographical listings, see the Martindale-Hubbell Law Directory

---

LAW OFFICES OF RICHARD TURBIN A LAW CORPORATION (AV)

Suite 1850 Mauka Tower, Grosvenor Center, 737 Bishop Street, 96813
Telephone: 808-528-4000
FAX: 808-599-1984

Richard Turbin

Rai Saint Chu

Thomas M. Pico, Jr.

For full biographical listings, see the Martindale-Hubbell Law Directory

---

WATANABE, ING & KAWASHIMA (AV)

A Partnership including Professional Corporations
Hawaii Tower, 5th & 6th Floors, 745 Fort Street, 96813
Telephone: 808-544-8300
Facsimile: 808-544-8399

MEMBERS OF FIRM

Jeffrey N. Watanabe (Atty. at
  Law, A Law Corp.)
James Kawashima (Atty. at
  Law, A Law Corp.)
J. Douglas Ing (Atty. at Law, A
  Law Corp.)
Wray H. Kondo (Atty. at Law,
  A Law Corp.)
John T. Komeiji (Atty. at Law,
  A Law Corp.)
Ronald Y. K. Leong (Atty. at
  Law, A Law Corp.)
Robert T. Takamatsu (Atty. at
  Law, A Law Corp.)
Cynthia Winegar (Atty. at Law,
  A Law Corp.)

Randall Y. Yamamoto (Atty. at
  Law, A Law Corp.)
Lyle Y. Harada (Atty. at Law,
  A Law Corp.)
Michael A. Lorusso (Atty. at
  Law, A Law Corp.)
Pamela J. Larson (Atty. At
  Law, A Law Corp.)
William H. Gilardy, Jr. (Atty.
  At Law, A Law Corp.)
John R. Aube (Atty. at Law, A
  Law Corp.)
Jan M.L.Y. Amii (Atty. at Law,
  A Law Corp.)
Seth M. Reiss
Curtis C. Kim

ASSOCIATES

Donna Y. Kanemaru
George B. Apter
Marcus B. Sierra
Lani Narikiyo
Peter L. Fritz
LLoyd S. Yoshioka
Beth K. Fujimoto

Patsy H. Kirio
Kevin H. Oda
Michael C. Bird
Brian Y. Hiyane
Dennis J. Hwang
Teri Y. Kondo
Jeff N. Miyashiro

OF COUNSEL

George R. Ariyoshi

ASIA PACIFIC CONSULTANT

Victor Hao Li (Not admitted in HI)

LEGAL SUPPORT PERSONNEL

GOVERNMENT AFFAIRS ADVISOR

Millicent M. Y. H. Kim

References: First Hawaiian Bank; American Savings Bank.

For Complete List of Firm Personnel, See General Section

For full biographical listings, see the Martindale-Hubbell Law Directory

Honolulu—Continued

MICHAEL J. Y. WONG (AV)

2222 Central Pacific Plaza, 220 South King Street, 96813
Telephone: 808-536-1855
Fax: 808-536-1857

ASSOCIATE
R. Malia Taum

For full biographical listings, see the Martindale-Hubbell Law Directory

KAILUA-KONA, Hawaii Co.

CADES SCHUTTE FLEMING & WRIGHT (AV)

Hualalai Center, Suite B-303, 75-170 Hualalai Road, 96740
Telephone: 808-329-5811
Telecopier: 808-326-1175
Email: cades@cades.com
Honolulu, Hawaii Office: 1000 Bishop Street, P. O. Box 939.
Telephone: 808-521-9200.
Affiliated Law Firm: Udom-Prok Associates Law Offices, 105/36 Tharinee Mansion, Bormo Raj Chananee Road Bangkoknoi, Bangkok, Thailand, 10700.
Telephone: 011 662 435-4146.

RESIDENT PARTNER
Roy A. Vitousek, III
RESIDENT ASSOCIATE
Kimberly O'Neill Jackson

For Complete List of Firm Personnel, See General Section

For full biographical listings, see the Martindale-Hubbell Law Directory

WAILUKU,* Maui Co.

KRUEGER & CAHILL (AV)

2065 Main Street, 96793
Telephone: 808-244-7444; Honolulu: 536-7474
Facsimile: 808-244-4177
Email: maulaw@maui.net

MEMBERS OF FIRM
James Krueger   Peter T. Cahill
          John M. O'Neill
LEGAL SUPPORT PERSONNEL
LEGAL ASSISTANTS
Sharon O'Shaughnessy   Theresa N. Coletti

A List of Representative Clients and References will be furnished upon request.

For full biographical listings, see the Martindale-Hubbell Law Directory

IDAHO

BOISE,* Ada Co.

EBERLE, BERLIN, KADING, TURNBOW & McKLVEEN, CHARTERED (AV)

Capitol Park Plaza, 300 North Sixth Street, P.O. Box 1368, 83701
Telephone: 208-344-8535
Facsimile: 208-344-8542

R.B. Kading, Jr.   Scott D. Hess
Warren Eugene Jones   Bradley G. Andrews
Mark S. Geston   William A. Fuhrman

General Counsel: Key Bank of Idaho; Key Trust Company of The West; Key Mortgage Funding; Diamond Sports.
Representative Clients: Key Bank of Idaho; U.S. West Communications; Cessna Aircraft Co.

For Complete List of Firm Personnel, See General Section

For full biographical listings, see the Martindale-Hubbell Law Directory

ELAM & BURKE, A PROFESSIONAL ASSOCIATION (AV)

Key Financial Center, 702 West Idaho Street, P.O. Box 1539, 83701
Telephone: 208-343-5454
Telecopier: 208-384-5844
Email: eblaw@elamburke.com

Carl P. Burke   John Magel
M. Allyn Dingel, Jr.   James D. LaRue

Representative Clients: Morrison-Knudsen, Inc.; Texas Instruments, Inc.; Prudential Securities, Inc.; Pechiney Corp.; Dow Corning Corporation; U.S. West Communications; State Farm Insurance Cos.; Sinclair Oil Co. d/b/a Sun Valley Co.; Farmers Insurance Group.

(See Next Column)

For Complete List of Firm Personnel, See General Section

For full biographical listings, see the Martindale-Hubbell Law Directory

ELLIS, BROWN & SHEILS, CHARTERED (AV)

707 North 8th, P.O. Box 388, 83701
Telephone: 208-345-7832
Fax: 208-345-9564

Allen B. Ellis   Stephen C. Brown
          Max M. Sheils, Jr.

Representative Clients: Farm Credit Services Northwest, A.C.A.; Wausau Insurance Cos.; State Insurance Fund; Crawford & Company; Idaho Power Co.; Ada Planning Assn.; Consolidated Supply Co.; Finch-Brown Co.
References: West One Bank; First Interstate Bank.

For full biographical listings, see the Martindale-Hubbell Law Directory

MOFFATT, THOMAS, BARRETT, ROCK & FIELDS, CHARTERED (AV)

101 South Capitol Boulevard, P.O. Box 829, 83702
Telephone: 208-345-2000
FAX: 208-385-5384
Email: info@moffatt.com
Idaho Falls Office: 525 Park Avenue, Suite 2D, P.O. Box 1367, 83403.
Telephone: 208-522-6700.
FAX: 208-522-5111.
Pocatello, Idaho Office: 845 West Center, Suite C, P.O. Box 4941, 83201.
Telephone: 208-233-2001.

R. B. Rock   Larry C. Hunter
          Stephen R. Thomas

Representative Clients: BMC West Corporation; Chevron, U.S.A.; First Security Bank of Idaho, N.A.; General Motors Corp.; Idaho Potato Commission; Intermountain Gas Co.; John Alden Life Insurance Co.; Micron Technology, Inc.; Royal Insurance Cos.; St. Luke's Regional Medical Center & Mountain States Tumor Institute.

For Complete List of Firm Personnel, See General Section

For full biographical listings, see the Martindale-Hubbell Law Directory

POCATELLO,* Bannock Co.

MERRILL & MERRILL, CHARTERED (AV)

Key Bank Building, P.O. Box 991, 83204
Telephone: 208-232-2286
Fax: 208-232-2499

Dave R. Gallafent   Thomas W. Clark
Stephen S. Dunn   David C. Nye
D. Russell Wight   Kent L. Hawkins

Representative Clients: Western States Equipment Co.; J. R. Simplot Co.

For Complete List of Firm Personnel, See General Section

For full biographical listings, see the Martindale-Hubbell Law Directory

ILLINOIS

AURORA, Kane Co.

MURPHY, HUPP, FOOTE, MIELKE AND KINNALLY (AV)

North Island Center, P.O. Box 5030, 60507
Telephone: 708-844-0056
FAX: 708-844-1905

MEMBERS OF FIRM
William C. Murphy   Patrick M. Kinnally
Robert B. Hupp   Paul G. Krentz
Robert M. Foote   Joseph C. Loran
Craig S. Mielke   Gerald K. Hodge

Timothy D. O'Neil
OF COUNSEL
Robert T. Olson

Representative Clients: American Telephone & Telegraph Co.; Fox Valley Park District; Lyon Metal Products; Kane County Forest Preserve District; Hollywood Casino; Employers Mutual Insurance Co.; Forty-Eight Insulations, Inc.; UNR Asbestos Disease Trust; Richards-Wilcox Co.; National Bank & Trust Company of Syracuse.

For full biographical listings, see the Martindale-Hubbell Law Directory

BELLEVILLE,* St. Clair Co.

DONOVAN, ROSE, NESTER, SZEWCZYK & JOLEY, P.C. (AV)

8 East Washington Street, 62220
Telephone: 618-235-2020
Telecopier: 618-235-9632

(See Next Column)

DONOVAN, ROSE, NESTER, SZEWCZYK & JOLEY P.C., *Belleville—Continued*

Dennis E. Rose	Edward J. Szewczyk
Michael J. Nester	Charles L. Joley

Kenneth M. Nussbaumer   Georgiann Oliver

Representative Clients: State Farm Mutual Auto & Life Co.; Travelers Insurance Co.; Liberty Mutual Insurance Co.; Government Employees Insurance Co.; Great American Insurance Co.; Aetna Casualty & Surety Co.; Royal Globe Insurance Co.; Illinois Founders Insurance Co.; INA (Insurance Company of North America).

For Complete List of Firm Personnel, See General Section

For full biographical listings, see the Martindale-Hubbell Law Directory

NEVILLE, RICHARDS, DeFRANCO & WULLER (AV)

5 Park Place, 62221
Telephone: 618-277-0900
Facsimile: 618-277-0970

MEMBERS OF FIRM

James E. Neville	James E. DeFranco
Timothy S. Richards	Robert G. Wuller, Jr.

ASSOCIATES

Shari M. Brunton	Ellen M. Edmonds
Richard Thomas Roustio	

For full biographical listings, see the Martindale-Hubbell Law Directory

THOMPSON COBURN (AV)

525 West Main Street, 62220
Telephone: 618-277-4700; 314-271-1800
Telecopier: 618-236-3434
St. Louis, Missouri Office: One Mercantile Center.
Telephone: 314-552-6000.
Telecopier: 314-552-7000.
St. Charles, Missouri Office: 200 North Third Street.
Telephone: 314-946-7717.
Telecopier: 314-946-4938.
Washington, D.C. Office: 700 14th Street, N.W., Suite 900.
Telephone: 202-508-1000.
Telecopier: 202-508-1010.
Houston, Texas Office: 2400 NationsBank Center, 700 Louisiana.
Telephone: 713-225-3800.
Telecopier: 713-225-3828.

MEMBERS OF FIRM

W. Thomas Coghill, Jr.	Dan H. Ball
Michael D. O'Keefe	William R. Bay
Thomas W. Alvey, Jr.	Mark Sableman
Karl D. Dexheimer	Edward S. Bott, Jr.
Raymond L. Massey	Bradley A. Winters
Gary Mayes	Edward A. Cohen
Thomas F. Hennessy, III	Nicholas J. Lamb
William A. Schmitt	Kurt E. Reitz
Robert H. Brownlee	David A. Stratmann
Thomas R. Jayne	Roman P. Wuller
Mary M. Bonacorsi	Mark S. Schuver
Allen D. Allred	Conny Davinroy Beatty

ASSOCIATES

D. Kimberly Brown	Crystal M. Kennedy
David S. Corwin	Cherie K. Harpole Macdonald
Mary Sue Juen	Melissa L. Mitchell

Representative Clients: General Motors Corp.; Illinois Central Railroad Co.; S. C. Johnson & Sons, Inc.; Joy Technologies Inc.; Memorial Hospital of Belleville; Nissan Motor Corporation in U.S.A.; Norfolk Southern Corp. & affiliates; Peabody Coal Company; U-Haul International Inc.; Union Electric Co.

For Complete List of Firm Personnel, See General Section

For full biographical listings, see the Martindale-Hubbell Law Directory

BENTON,* Franklin Co.

HART AND HART (AV)

602 West Public Square, P.O. Box 937, 62812-0937
Telephone: 618-435-8123
Telecopier: 618-435-2962

Richard O. Hart	A. Courtney Cox
Murphy C. Hart	Pamela Sue Lacey

Representative Clients: Boatmen's Bank; State Bank of Whittington; Magna Bank of Southern Illinois; Benton Park District; Benton Public Library District; HHL Financial Services; St. Mary's Hospital (Centralia); Credit Bureau Systems, Inc.

For Complete List of Firm Personnel, See General Section

For full biographical listings, see the Martindale-Hubbell Law Directory

CARLINVILLE,* Macoupin Co.

PHELPS, KASTEN, RUYLE & BURNS (AV)

130 East Main Street, 62626
Telephone: 217-854-3283
FAX: 217-854-9527
Email: pkrb@cnmnet.com

MEMBERS OF FIRM

Carl E. Kasten	Nancy L. Ruyle
Thomas P. Burns	

ASSOCIATE

Byron J. Sims

Representative Clients: Carlinville National Bank; Blackburn University; Area Diesel Service, Inc.; Farmers and Merchants Bank; H & H Construction Services, Inc.

For Complete List of Firm Personnel, See General Section

For full biographical listings, see the Martindale-Hubbell Law Directory

CHICAGO,* Cook Co.

ABRAMSON & FOX (AV)

One East Wacker Drive, 60601
Telephone: 312-644-8500
FAX: 644-0798
Evergreen, Colorado Office: 1202 Highway 74.
Telephone: 303-674-1328.
FAX: 303-674-0437.

MEMBERS OF FIRM

Floyd H. Abramson	John K. Eggers (1936-1991)
Thomas Brejcha	Joseph C. Grayson
William D. Brejcha	Richard S. Hartford
Donald P. Colleton	Anthony P. Janik
	Peter J. Karabas

Steven P. Pherson

OF COUNSEL

John J. Alioto	Jacob N. Gross (Ltd.)
Robert J. Amedeo (Resident, Evergreen, Colorado Office)	Richard Hirschtritt
	Anthony R. Hofeld
Renato L. Amponin	Malcolm S. Kamin
Michael P. Cannon	Juris Kins
James L. Fox	Marc R. Kromelow
	Carol A. Seelig

For full biographical listings, see the Martindale-Hubbell Law Directory

ALBERT, BATES, WHITEHEAD & McGAUGH, P.C. (AV)

One South Wacker Drive, Suite 1990, 60606
Telephone: 312-357-6300
Fax: 312-357-6219

Jorge C. Albala	Laurie D. Jaffe
Charles G. Albert	Robert Kinchen
Peter H. Barrow	Raymond S. McGaugh
Fredrick H. Bates	Rory Dean Smith
Jerry D. Brown	Laura D. Ryan
Kathie M. Contois	Gregory C. Whitehead
	Allison L. Wood

For full biographical listings, see the Martindale-Hubbell Law Directory

ANESI, OZMON & RODIN, LTD. (AV)

161 North Clark Street, 21st Floor, 60601
Telephone: 312-372-3822
Fax: 312-372-3833

Nat P. Ozmon	Scott H. Rudin
Charles E. Anesi (1912-1995)	John A. Salzeider
Richard A. Lewin (1925-1985)	David Figlioli
Curt N. Rodin	Martin J. Lucas
Mark Novak	Daniel V. O'Connor
Bruce M. Kohen	Paul W. Pasche
Richard A. Kimnach	John M. Popelka
Joseph J. Miroballi	Telly C. Nakos
Douglas A. Colby	Michelle Dekalb
David J. Comeau	Mark Murnane
James J. Morici, Jr.	Richard B. Vaughn
Alain Leval	Darius Bozorgi
Stephen S. Phalen	R. Andrew Hahn
Marc A. Taxman	Ilonka E. Ulrich
	Marc J. Cairo

OF COUNSEL

Noel C. Lindenmuth	Irving D. Fasman

For full biographical listings, see the Martindale-Hubbell Law Directory

Chicago—Continued

ARONBERG GOLDGEHN DAVIS & GARMISA (AV)

Suite 3000 One IBM Plaza, 60611
Telephone: 312-828-9600
Telecopier: 312-828-9635

MEMBERS OF FIRM

Christopher J. Bannon	Gene H. Hansen
Deborah G. Cole	Nathan H. Lichtenstein
Mitchell S. Goldgehn	James A. Smith

ASSOCIATES

Lisa J. Brodsky	John M. Riccione
John A. DiSalvo	William J. Serritella, Jr.
Howard J. Fishman	William C. Wilder
James J. Hickey	Dawn C. Wrona

For Complete List of Firm Personnel, See General Section

For full biographical listings, see the Martindale-Hubbell Law Directory

BATES MECKLER BULGER & TILSON (AV)

8200 Sears Tower, 233 South Wacker, 60606
Telephone: 312-474-7900
Facsimile: 312-474-7898
URL: http://www.bmbt.com

MEMBERS OF FIRM

Robert J. Bates, Jr.	Maryann C. Hayes
Brian W. Bulger	Kathleen H. Jensen
Scott L. Carey	Mari Henry Leigh
Janet R. Davis	Mary F. Licari
Maria G. Enriquez	Michael M. Marick
Patrick J. Foley	Bruce R. Meckler
J. Stuart Garbutt	Steven D. Pearson
Paul R. Garry	Scott M. Seaman
Francis X. Grossi, Jr.	Joseph E. Tilson

ASSOCIATES

Anne L. Blume	Christopher E. Kentra
Dina L. Brantman	Charlene Kittredge
Catherine M. Crisham	Michael I. Leonard
Joseph E. Cwik	Lisa A. Miller
John K. Daly	Felicia Lynn Gerber Perlman
(Not admitted in IL)	John R. Rapasky
Robin Edelstein	Brett G. Rawitz
Josh M. Friedman	John E. Rodewald
Mary E. Gootjes	Mark G. Sheridan
Robert C. Heist	Frederick W. Stein
Darlene M. Jarzyna-Price	Monica T. Sullivan
James H. Kallianis, Jr.	Timothy A. Wolfe

OF COUNSEL

Stanley V. Figura	Matthew M. Murphy
Joseph Frontino	Thomas J. O'Brien
Philip R. King	Brian J. Williams

For full biographical listings, see the Martindale-Hubbell Law Directory

BECKER ASSOCIATES (AV)

19 South La Salle Street Suite 1500, 60603
Telephone: 312-621-9500
Fax: 312-621-9011
Email: Firm@becker-law.com *URL:* http://www.becker-law.com

Theodore M. Becker	Daniel Steven Kaplan
Michael Jeffrey Boxerman	

OF COUNSEL

Ira J. Marcus	Anthony C. Campanale
Lee Scott Perres	Steven J. Gross
John P. Connell	

For full biographical listings, see the Martindale-Hubbell Law Directory

BELL, BOYD & LLOYD (AV)

Three First National Plaza Suite 3300, 70 West Madison Street, 60602
Telephone: 312-372-1121
FAX: 312-372-2098
Email: bbl@bbl.com
Washington, D.C. Office: 1615 L Street, N.W.
Telephone: 202-466-6300.
FAX: 202-463-0678.

MEMBERS OF FIRM

Michael J. Abernathy	Frank K. Heap
D. Daniel Barr	Francis J. Higgins
William L. Barr, Jr.	Maureen Ward Kirby
Paul M. Bauch	Daniel Lawler
William R. Carney	Brian E. Martin
David D. Cleary	Brigid M. McGrath
James W. Collins	Rebecca C. Meriwether
Randy J. Curato	David M. Novak
Nicholas J. Etten	Stephen J. O'Neil
Lawrence M. Gavin	Kenneth E. Rechtoris
Carol A. Genis	James A. Romanyak

(See Next Column)

John W. Rotunno	Robert V. Shannon
Peter G. Rush	Stuart A. Shanus
John P. Scotellaro	Edwin C. Thomas, III
Larry L. Thompson	

OF COUNSEL

Richard L. Curry

ASSOCIATES

Douglas M. Chalmers	Ari J. Rosenthal
Kathleen M. Meyers-Grabemann	James P. Tutaj

For Complete List of Firm Personnel, See General Section

For full biographical listings, see the Martindale-Hubbell Law Directory

BERMAN & YOTIS, A PROFESSIONAL ASSOCIATION (AV)

(A Professional Association comprised of Professional Corporations)
Suite 2215, 100 North La Salle Street, 60602
Telephone: 312-726-0531
Fax: 312-726-4928

Michael H. Berman (P.C.)	William W. Yotis, III, (P.C.)

Joy C. Airaudi	Dean J. Papadakis
Eric D. Kaplan	Dean Gournis

OF COUNSEL

Karen C. Yotis

For full biographical listings, see the Martindale-Hubbell Law Directory

BRYDGES RISEBOROUGH PETERSON FRANKE AND MORRIS (AV)

A Partnership including Professional Corporations
28th Floor, 150 North Michigan Avenue, 60601
Telephone: 312-782-5042
FAX: 312-704-9107
Waukegan, Illinois Office: 110 North West Street.
Telephone: 847-249-0300.
FAX: 847-249-4755.
Phoenix, Arizona Office: 3030 North Central Avenue, Suite 408.
Telephone: 602-631-4400.
FAX: 602-631-4404.

MEMBERS OF FIRM

Louis W. Brydges, Sr.	Scott E. Nemanich
Allyn J. Franke	Reid S. Jacobson
George E. Riseborough (A Professional Corporation)	Donald M. Lonchar, Jr.
	Peter J. Nordigian
J. V. Schaffenegger (1914-1986)	Robert L. Snook
Ralph Miller (1922-1988)	Stacey L. Seneczko
Donald G. Peterson	Rebecca Sarah Larson
Thomas A. Morris, Jr., (A Professional Corporation)	Neal T. Goldstein
	Monica J. Conrad
Donald L. Sime	Gioconda (Jackie) V. Iannicelli
John H. Krackenberger	Jennifer M. Lundy
Jay Scott Nelson	Eleanor P. Cabreré
Michael A. Strom	Linda A. White
Louis W. Brydges, Jr.	William G. Berg
Leslie A. Peterson	John W. Dixon
Thomas K. Gerling	Thomas A. Kiepura

OF COUNSEL

Harry D. Strouse	Thomas J. Moran (1920-1995)
Jack L. Watson	

For full biographical listings, see the Martindale-Hubbell Law Directory

CARNEY & BROTHERS, LTD. (AV)

30 North La Salle Street, Suite 3100, 60602
Telephone: 312-372-2909
Fax: 312-704-6693

Demetrius E. Carney	Ellen E. Douglass
Alan W. Brothers	Lori A. Owens
Hubert O. Thompson	James L. Bebley

Cheryl J Colston	Andre Gamble
Trasha A. Embry	Angela M. Williams
Oswald G. Lewis	

OF COUNSEL

Joyce A. Hughes	Henry I. Thomas

Representative Clients: Allstate Life Insurance Co.; Amoco Oil Co.; Commonwealth Edison Co.; First National Bank of Chicago; General Motors Corp.; McDonald's Corp.; New York Life Insurance Co.; Pathway Financial; Seaway National Bank.

For full biographical listings, see the Martindale-Hubbell Law Directory

CARPONELLI & KRUG, P.C. (AV)

Suite 2350, 55 West Monroe Street, 60603
Telephone: 312-372-2707
Fax: 312-641-6174

(See Next Column)

CARPONELLI & KRUG P.C., Chicago—*Continued*

Stephen P. Carponelli   Robert F. Krug, Jr.

Albert M. T. Finch, III

For full biographical listings, see the Martindale-Hubbell Law Directory

CHERRY & FLYNN (AV)

30 North La Salle Street, Suite 2300, 60602
Telephone: 312-372-2100
Telecopier: 312-853-0279

Myron M. Cherry   William R. Coulson
Peter Flynn   David D. Merritt
          Adam J. Levitt

For full biographical listings, see the Martindale-Hubbell Law Directory

CLIFFORD LAW OFFICES, P.C. (AV)

120 North La Salle Street, 31st Floor, 60602
Telephone: 312-899-9090
1-800-899-0410
Fax: 312-251-1160
Email: 102554.2453@compuserve.com

Robert A. Clifford   Keith A. Hebeisen
          Kevin P. Durkin

Robert P. Walsh, Jr.   Richard L. Pullano
Susan A. Capra   Patricia C. Durkin
Jeffrey J. Kroll   Matthew I. Baker
Thomas K. Prindable   Timothy P. Rhatigan
Richard F. Burke, Jr.   Isobel S. Thomas

OF COUNSEL
Robert P. Sheridan

For full biographical listings, see the Martindale-Hubbell Law Directory

CORBOY & DEMETRIO, P.C. (AV)

33 North Dearborn Street 21st Floor, 60602
Telephone: 312-346-3191
FAX: 312-346-5562
TDD: 312-236-3191
Email: phcorboy@aol.com

Philip H. Corboy   Thomas A. Demetrio
          Philip Harnett Corboy, Jr.

Robert J. Bingle   Susan J. Schwartz
Francis Patrick Murphy   Michael K. Demetrio
          Kevin G. Burke

Renee Blahuta   Daniel M. Kotin
Thomas F. Boleky   Kenneth T. Lumb
Timothy J. Cavanagh   Michael G. Mahoney
Barry R. Chafetz   Michael K. Muldoon
G. Grant Dixon III   Mindy J. Nam
Mary E. Doherty   Margaret M. Power
Shawn S. Kasserman   Edward G. Willer
          David C. Wise

Reference: The American National Bank & Trust Company, Chicago, Illinois.

For full biographical listings, see the Martindale-Hubbell Law Directory

DEUTSCH, LEVY & ENGEL, CHARTERED (AV)

Suite 1700, 225 West Washington Street, 60606
Telephone: 312-346-1460
Wheaton, Illinois Office: Suite B2, 620 West Roosevelt Road.
Telephone: 708-665-9112.

Paul M. Levy   LaDonna M. Loitz
Michael J. Devine   Phillip J. Zisook
Stuart Berks   Steven C. Weiss

Stephen A. Viz   Phillip Michael Schreiber
Thomas W. Goedert   Brian D. Saucier

For full biographical listings, see the Martindale-Hubbell Law Directory

DOWD & DOWD, LTD. (AV)

Suite 1000, 55 West Wacker Drive, 60601
Telephone: 312-704-4400
Telecopier: 312-704-4500

Joseph V. Dowd   Robert C. Yelton III
Michael E. Dowd   Patrick C. Dowd
Kenneth Gurber   Robert J. Golden
          Karen W. Worsek

(See Next Column)

S. Robert Depke   John M. McAndrews
Ryan J. Harrington   Edward W. McNabola
Jeffrey Edward Kehl   Martha A. Niles
Sarah A. Kennedy   Michael G. Patrizio
Richard B. Korn   Patrick J. Ruberry
Joseph J. Leonard   Anthony R. Rutkowski
Ronald J. Lukes   Jeffrey Scott Wrage

LEGAL SUPPORT PERSONNEL
Carol Barnes   Jill A. Weiseman

OF COUNSEL
Guenther Ahlf   John A. Garrity, III
          Joel S. Ostrow

For full biographical listings, see the Martindale-Hubbell Law Directory

THE LAW OFFICES OF EDNA SELAN EPSTEIN (AV)

321 South Plymouth Court Suite 800, 60603
Telephone: 312-408-2750
FAX: 312-408-2760

Edna Selan Epstein

For full biographical listings, see the Martindale-Hubbell Law Directory

FORAN & SCHULTZ (AV)

Suite 3000, 30 North La Salle Street, 60602
Telephone: 312-368-8330
Fax: 312-580-2600

MEMBERS OF FIRM
Thomas A. Foran   Jack J. Carriglio
Richard G. Schultz   Steven H. Gistenson
James R. Figliulo   Brooke R. Whitted
Stephen A. Gorman   Jeffrey C. Blumenthal
Jeff D. Harris   Carl A. Gigante
          Carmen D. Caruso

ASSOCIATES
Teresa F. Frisbie   Brian P. Liston
Peter A. Silverman   Paul A. Henmueller
Marla B. Wilneff   James J. Sipchen, Jr.
Daniel D. Kasten   Mitchell S. Chaban
Patrick R. Gabrione   Dana L. Romaniuk
          Jessica Dickstein

OF COUNSEL
Harry G. Comerford

References: American National Bank and Trust Co. of Chicago; Amalgamated Trust and Savings Bank.

For full biographical listings, see the Martindale-Hubbell Law Directory

FOX & GROVE, CHARTERED (AV)

311 South Wacker Drive Suite 6200, 60606
Telephone: 312-876-0500
Telecopier: 312-362-0700
St. Petersburg, Florida Office: Fox, Grove, Abbey, Adams, Byelick & Kiernan, Eleventh Floor, 360 Central Avenue.
Telephone: 813-821-2080.
Tampa, Florida Office: Fox, Grove, Abbey, Adams, Byelick & Kiernan, 500 East Kennedy Boulevard, Suite 200.
Telephone: 813-223-7800.
San Francisco, California Office: 240 Stockton Street, Suite 900.
Telephone: 415-956-1360.

Shayle P. Fox   Marty Denis
Kalvin M. Grove   Steven L. Gillman
Lawrence M. Cohen   William Henry Barrett
S. Richard Pincus   Allison C. Blakley
Russell M. Kofoed   Jeffrey E. Beeson
Jeffrey S. Goldman   Robert M. Mintz
          Joel W. Rice

Mark T. Dabertin   Elisabeth E. Snyder
Tamra S. Domeyer   (Not admitted in IL)
Davi L. Hirsch   Todd D. Steenson
Joshua D. Holleb   Michael L. Sullivan
Daniel A. Kazlauski   Lynn Urkov Thorpe
Daniel R. Madock   Douglas M. Werman
Michael Paull   David Zatuchni

Labor Counsel for: National Association of Independent Insurers; Alliance of American Insurers; Great American Insurance Co.; CNA Financial Corp.; California Casualty Management.
Representative Labor Clients: Liberty Mutual Insurance Co.; Certified Grocers Midwest; Sears Logistics Services; National Wrecking Co.; GAB Business Services, Inc.

For full biographical listings, see the Martindale-Hubbell Law Directory

Chicago—Continued

GESSLER, HUGHES & SOCOL, LTD. (AV)

Three First National Plaza, Suite 2200, 60602
Telephone: 312-580-0100
Telecopy: 312-580-1994

Mark S. Dym	Terence J. Moran
George W. Gessler	Mark D. Olson
John K. Hughes	Matthew J. Piers
William P. Jones	David J. Pritchard
Peter M. Katsaros	Kalman D. Resnick
Mark A. LaRose	Frederick S. Rhine
Kimberley Marsh	Jonathan A. Rothstein

Donna Kaner Socol

Benjamin P. Beringer	Alex W. Miller
Darilyn W. Bock	Belkis Cervantes Muldoon
Gary Chodorow	Jonathan D. Rosenblum
Anjali Dayal	Marci S. Sperling
Ruth M. Dunning	Dana H. Sukenik
Adam D. Ingber	J. Eric Vander Arend
Michael J. Klein	Maria L. Vertuno
Laura C. Liu	Mark B. Weiner

Charles H. Wintersteen

OF COUNSEL

James T. Derico, Jr.	Darius S. Francescatti, M.D.

Susan R. Gzesh

For full biographical listings, see the Martindale-Hubbell Law Directory

MICHAEL T. HANNAFAN & ASSOCIATES, LTD. (AV)

Three First National Plaza, Suite 4040, 60602
Telephone: 312-782-7490
FAX: 312-782-9440

Michael T. Hannafan

Cory A. Johnson	Gregory M. Jordan

LEGAL SUPPORT PERSONNEL

Tracy D. Hannafan

Reference: The Northern Trust Co.

For full biographical listings, see the Martindale-Hubbell Law Directory

HARRINGTON, THOMPSON, ACKER & HARRINGTON, LTD. (AV)

310 South Michigan Avenue Suite 2000, 60604
Telephone: 312-922-8833

Robert E. Harrington, Jr.	Kenneth J. Sophie, Jr.
Robert B. Thompson	Robert W. Coster
Laurence C. Acker	Stephen A. Murphy
Patrick J. Harrington	Monica A. Coscia

Christy L. LeVan

Reference: American National Bank and Trust Co., Chicago, Illinois.

For full biographical listings, see the Martindale-Hubbell Law Directory

WILLIAM J. HARTE, LTD. (AV)

Suite 1100, 111 West Washington Street, 60602
Telephone: 312-726-5015
Fax: 312-641-1288

William J. Harte

Sylvia A. Sotiras	Stephen L. Garcia
Erik D. Gruber	Joan M. Mannix

Cynthia E. Cervini

OF COUNSEL

Daniel K. Schlorf	P. A. Sorrentino
David J. Walker	Irving R. Norman

Robert L. Tucker

For full biographical listings, see the Martindale-Hubbell Law Directory

JOHN PATRICK HEALY (AV)

29 South La Salle - Suite 640, 60603
Telephone: 312-332-7950
Fax: 312-782-4502

ASSOCIATE

Sheryl E. Healy

For full biographical listings, see the Martindale-Hubbell Law Directory

HUNDLEY & BRUSSLAN (AV)

Suite 1320, 14 East Jackson Boulevard, 60604
Telephone: 312-427-3777
Fax: 312-427-7236
Email: envnlaw@ripco.com

(See Next Column)

MEMBERS OF FIRM

John T. Hundley	James D. Brusslan

Representative Clients: Commonwealth Edison Co.; Gottlieb Memorial Hospital; In-Home Health, Inc.; The Koll Company (Investment Management Division); National Advertising Co.; North Dakota Mill & Elevator Ass'n; RB&W (A Park-Ohio Company); USAA Realty Company.

For full biographical listings, see the Martindale-Hubbell Law Directory

JOHNSON & BELL, LTD. (AV)

Suite 2200, 222 North La Salle Street, 60601
Telephone: 312-372-0770
Facsimile: 312-372-9818
Wheaton, Illinois Office: Suite 1640, 2100 Manchester Road.
Telephone: 630-510-0880.
Facsimile: 630-510-0939.

William V. Johnson	Edward D. D'Arcy, Jr.
John W. Bell	Michael P. Siavelis
Jack T. Riley, Jr.	William A. Geiser
Brian C. Fetzer	Thomas J. Koch
Thomas H. Fegan	Kevin G. Owens
Thomas W. Murphy	Dennis C. Cusack
Thomas J. Andrews	Emilio E. Machado
William G. Beatty	Charles P. Rantis
John A. Childers	Dean M. Athans
Robert L. Nora	Robert J. Comfort
Margaret A. Unger	Alan Jay Goldstein
Timothy J. McKay	Susan Marzec Hannigan
Howard Patrick Morris	Daniel C. Murray
Scott W. Hoyne	Thomas F. Poelking
James S. Stickles, Jr.	William S. Allen
Frederick S. Mueller	William K. McVisk
Joseph R. Marconi	Gary A. Grasso
Robert M. Burke	Glenn F. Fencl
Kurt C. Meihofer	Frances J. Skinner-Lewis
Debra A. DiMaggio	Joseph F. Spitzzeri
Cornelius J. Harrington, III	Joseph B. Carini, III
Michael B. Gunzburg	Kathryn K. Loft
Charles W. Planek	Paul A. Tanzillo

William J. Anaya	Brian T. Levin
Susan Choi Brennan	Bruce M. Lichtcsien
Jean Harris Brown	Steven E. Lieb
Frank S. Capuani	Richard P. Long
Gregory D. Conforti	Michael J. Lynch
Christopher M. Daddino	David M. Macksey
Maria S. Doughty	Robert R. McNamara
Patrick T. Garvey	Joseph J. McNerney
Laura B. Glaser	Peter A. Nicholson
Kevin J. Greenwood	Frank P. Nowicki
Sean J. Hardy	Richard C. Perna
Guy Halpern	Brendan S. Power
William O. Ivy, Jr.	Lynne M. Reardon
Mark D. Johnson	Marilyn McCabe Reidy
Matthew L. Johnson	Zachary S. Rudman
Robert Johnson	Joseph D. Ryan
Janet A. Kachoyeanos	Ann M. Smith
Mindy L. Kallus	Robert Spitkovsky, Jr.
Mary Kenney	Terry Takash
Andrea H. Kott	Kelly N. Warnick
Genevie F. Labuda	Steven F. Wittman
Elizabeth Olen Lazzara	Robert W. York

References available upon request.

For full biographical listings, see the Martindale-Hubbell Law Directory

JONES, DAY, REAVIS & POGUE (AV)

77 West Wacker, 60601-1692
Telephone: 312-782-3939
Telecopier: 312-782-8585
In Atlanta, Georgia: 3500 One Peachtree Center, 303 Peachtree Street, N.E.
Telephone: 404-521-3939.
Cable Address: "Attorneys Atlanta".
Telex: 54-2711.
Telecopier: 404-581-8330.
In Brussels, Belgium: Avenue Louise 480, 7th Floor, B-1050 Brussels.
Telephone: 32-2-645-14-11.
Telecopier: 32-2-645-14-45.
In Cleveland, Ohio: North Point, 901 Lakeside Avenue.
Telephone: 216-586-3939.
Cable Address: "Attorneys Cleveland."
Telex: 980389.
Telecopier: 216-579-0212.
In Columbus, Ohio: 1900 Huntington Center.
Telephone: 614-469-3939.
Cable Address: "Attorneys Columbus."
Telecopier: 614-461-4198.

(See Next Column)

JONES, DAY, REAVIS & POGUE, Chicago—Continued

In Dallas, Texas: 2300 Trammell Crow Center, 2001 Ross Avenue.
Telephone: 214-220-3939.
Cable Address: "Attorneys Dallas."
Telex: 730852.
Telecopier: 214-969-5100.
In Frankfurt, Germany: Triton Haus, Bockenheimer Landstrasse 42, 60323 Frankfurt am Main.
Telephone: 49-69-9726-3939.
Telecopier: 49-69-9726-3993.
In Geneva, Switzerland: 20, rue de Candolle.
Telephone: 41-22-320-2339.
Telecopier: 41-22-320-1232.
In Hong Kong: 29th Floor, Entertainment Building, 30 Queen's Road Central.
Telephone: 852-2526-6895.
Telecopier: 852-2868-5871 or 852-2868-5699.
In Irvine, California: 2603 Main Street, Suite 900.
Telephone: 714-851-3939.
Telex: 194911 Lawyers LSA.
Telecopier: 714-553-7539.
In London, England: One Mount Street.
Telephone: 44-71-493-9361.
Cable Address: "Surgoe London WI."
Telecopier: 44-71-493-9666.
In Los Angeles, California: 555 West Fifth Street, Suite 4600.
Telephone: 213-489-3939.
Telex: 181439 UD.
Telecopier: 213-243-2539.
In New Delhi, India: Pathak & Associates, 9th Floor, Dr. Gopal Das Bhaven, 28 Barakhamba Road.
Telephone: 91-11-331-9719.
Telecopier: 91-11-331-7802.
In New York, New York: 599 Lexington Avenue.
Telephone: 212-326-3939.
Cable Address: "JONESDAY NEWYORK."
Telex: 237013 JDRP UR.
Telecopier: 212-755-7306.
In Paris, France: 62, rue du Faubourg Saint-Honore.
Telephone: 33-1-44-71-3939.
Cable Address: "Surgoe Paris."
Telex: 290156 Surgoe.
Telecopier: 33-1-49-24-0471.
In Pittsburgh, Pennsylvania: 500 Grant Street, 31st Floor.
Telephone: 412-391-3939.
Cable Address: "Attorneys Pittsburgh."
Telecopier: 412-394-7959.
In Riyadh, Saudi Arabia: Law Offices of Saud M.A. Shawwaf, P.O. Box 22166.
Telephone: (966-1) 462-8866.
Telex: 401831 SAUCON SJ.
Telecopier: (966-1) 462-9001.
In Taipei, Taiwan: 8th Floor, 2 Tun Hwa South Road, Section 2.
Telephone: (886-2) 704-6808.
Telecopier: (886-2) 704-6791.
In Tokyo, Japan: Toranomon MT Building, 4th Floor, 10-3, Toranomon 3-Chome, Minato-ku, Tokyo 105, Japan.
Telephone: 81-3-3433-3939.
Telecopier: 81-3-5401-2725.
In Washington, D.C.: Metropolitan Square, 1450 G Street, N.W.
Telephone: 202-879-3939.
Cable Address: "Attorneys Washington."
Telex: 89-2410 ATTORNEYS WASH.
Telecopier: 202-737-2832.

MEMBERS OF FIRM IN CHICAGO

Thomas F. Gardner	David L. Carden

For Complete List of Firm Personnel, See General Section

For full biographical listings, see the Martindale-Hubbell Law Directory

KIESLER & BERMAN (AV)

Suite 1300, 188 West Randolph Street, 60601
Telephone: 312-332-2840
FAX: 312-332-4547
Email: info@thekillerbees.com
Wheaton Office: 2100 Manchester, Suite 504.
Telephone: 630-752-8247.
Fax: 630-752-9587.
Joliet Office: 57 West Jefferson Street.
Telephone: 815-723-2755.
Fax: 815-723-2763.
Waukegan Office: 216 Madison Street.
Telephone: 847-244-5805.
Fax: 847-244-3996.

(See Next Column)

MEMBERS OF FIRM

Marvin D. Berman	Dale L. Schlafer
Robert L. Kiesler	Edward L. Cooper
Clinton J. Feil	Lyle F. Koester
Alan P. Miller	Mark S. Vilimek
John R. Garofalo	Rory D. Cassidy
Stephen B. Frew	Patti Olson Deuel
	David J. Kiesler

ASSOCIATES

Bradley D. Alexander	Cynthia A. Meister
Robert A. Barba	Peter R. Mennella
Donna D. Ciancio	Shannon Francis O'Shea
James V. Creen	Jeffrey S. Pavlovich
Daniel E. Falb	John J. Piegore
Mary E. Haeger	Paul N. Reidy
Shari J. Kalik	Michael G. Ryan
Hector Ledesma	Daniel J. Softcheck
Bryan W. Luce	Lisa A. Weiss
William P. McElligott	Jeanne M. Zeiger

SENIOR COUNSEL

Eugene S. Goldenson	Frank N. Rago

For full biographical listings, see the Martindale-Hubbell Law Directory

LAW OFFICES OF KOMIE AND ASSOCIATES (AV)

Suite 3500 Avondale Centre, 20 North Clark Street, 60602-5002
Telephone: 312-263-4383
Fax: 312-263-2803

Stephen M. Komie

ASSOCIATES

Julia A. McConnahy	Terrance McWhorter
	Mark A. Walwyn

OF COUNSEL

Douglas W. Godfrey	Marc D. Wolfe

LEGAL SUPPORT PERSONNEL

Paul J. Ciolino

For full biographical listings, see the Martindale-Hubbell Law Directory

KREISMAN & RAKICH (AV)

An Association of Attorneys
33 North Dearborn Street Suite 2220, 60602-3109
Telephone: 312-346-0045
Fax: 312-346-2380
Email: RobertK233@AOL.COM
Matteson, Illinois Office: 21141 Governors Highway, Suite 200, 60443.
Telephone: 708-747-6700.
Fax: 708-481-6770.

Robert D. Kreisman (P.C.)	Steven D. Rakich

Edward L. Morrison, Jr.	James A. Haiser

For full biographical listings, see the Martindale-Hubbell Law Directory

LAWRENCE, KAMIN, SAUNDERS & UHLENHOP (AV)

208 South La Salle Street, Suite 1750, 60604
Telephone: 312-372-1947
Telecopier: 312-372-2389

MEMBERS OF FIRM

Howard P. Kamin	Kenneth S. Perlman
Raymond E. Saunders	David E. Muschler
Paul B. Uhlenhop	Charles J. Risch
Kent Lawrence	Lawrence A. Rosen
Robert J. Lawrence	Michael Wise
	Randall B. Gold

OF COUNSEL

Patricia Brosterhous

ASSOCIATE

David L. Reich

For full biographical listings, see the Martindale-Hubbell Law Directory

NORMAN J. LERUM (AV)

Suite 2100, 100 West Monroe Street, 60603
Telephone: 312-782-1087
Facsimile: 312-332-6020

For full biographical listings, see the Martindale-Hubbell Law Directory

LOGGANS AND COX (AV)

Suite 2850, 200 West Madison Street, 60606
Telephone: 312-201-8600
Telecopier: 312-201-1180
Email: loggans@aol.com

(See Next Column)

LOGGANS AND COX—*Continued*

Susan E. Loggans Michael J. Cox

Miles M. Dore Ian Robert Alexander

For full biographical listings, see the Martindale-Hubbell Law Directory

MacCabe & McGuire (AV)

Suite 3333, 77 West Wacker Drive, 60601
Telephone: 312-357-2600
Fax: 312-357-0317
Email: MacMcLaw77@aol.com

MEMBERS OF FIRM
Edward H. MacCabe Maureen A. McGuire

ASSOCIATES
Timothy J. Murphy Margaret T. Conway
Diedre S. Dunn John C. Hurley
Lori G. Gabriel

OF COUNSEL
Brian J. Mulhern

For full biographical listings, see the Martindale-Hubbell Law Directory

Mandel, Lipton and Stevenson Limited (AV)

Suite 2900, 120 North La Salle Street, 60602
Telephone: 312-236-7080
Facsimile: 312-236-0781

Richard L. Mandel Richard A. Lifshitz
Alfred R. Lipton Terry Yale Feiertag
Leonard M. Malkin Kathleen Hogan Morrison
R. Peter Carey Uve R. Jerzy
Henry A. Waller Carolyn E. Winter
Kathleen Roseborough Audrey L. Gaynor

Andrés J. Gallegos Megan Kennedy Riordan
  (Not admitted in IL)

OF COUNSEL
Nicholas Stevenson Mark R. Ordower

LEGAL SUPPORT PERSONNEL
Jacqueline Steffens (Paralegal)

References: Northern Trust Co.; American National Bank of Chicago.

For full biographical listings, see the Martindale-Hubbell Law Directory

McFadden & Dillon, A Professional Corporation (AV)

135 South La Salle Street, Suite 2110, 60603
Telephone: 312-201-8300
Facsimile: 312-201-0535

Roger J. McFadden Thomas J. Dillon

Tyrrel J. Penn

For full biographical listings, see the Martindale-Hubbell Law Directory

Mullen & Minella (AV)

A Partnership including Professional Corporations
Three First National Plaza, Suite 2700, 60602
Telephone: 312-346-2998
Fax: 312-346-6024

MEMBERS OF FIRM
John C. Mullen (Ltd.) Mary R. Minella
Christopher Mullen (P.C.) Michael T. Mullen

For full biographical listings, see the Martindale-Hubbell Law Directory

The Law Offices of Munday & Nathan (AV)

33 North Dearborn Street, Suite 2220, 60602
Telephone: 312-346-5678
Fax: 312-346-8394

John J. Munday Thomas J. Nathan

James A. Tobin Lisa Pach

For full biographical listings, see the Martindale-Hubbell Law Directory

Bernard R. Nevoral and Associates Ltd. (AV)

150 North Wacker Drive, Suite 2450, 60606
Telephone: 312 263-7058
FAX: 312-263-4566

Bernard R. Nevoral

(See Next Column)

Maurice E. Dusky Douglas C. Dorn

For full biographical listings, see the Martindale-Hubbell Law Directory

Novack and Macey (AV)

303 West Madison Street, Suite 1500, 60606
Telephone: 312-419-6900
Fax: 312-419-6928

MEMBERS OF FIRM
Bruce E. Braverman Mitchell L. Marinello
P. Andrew Fleming Timothy J. Miller
Karen Levine Stephen Novack
Eric N. Macey Donald A. Tarkington
Michael A. Weinberg

ASSOCIATES
Timothy G. Compall Heather Ross
Jennifer Friedes Joel Schreier
Pauline Levy Stephen J. Siegel

For full biographical listings, see the Martindale-Hubbell Law Directory

O'Brien, O'Rourke & Hogan (AV)

135 South La Salle Street Suite 830, 60603
Telephone: 312-372-1462
Fax: 312-372-8029
Orlando, Florida Office: Moye, O'Brien, O'Rourke, Hogan & Pickert, 201 East Pine Street, Suite 710.
Telephone: 407-843-3341.
Fax: 407-843-3048.
Atlanta, Georgia Office: Moye, O'Brien, O'Rourke, Hogan & Pickert, 999 Peachtree Street, Northeast, Suite 2020.
Telephone: 404-875-6300.

MEMBERS OF FIRM
William J. Cotter James Elton Moye (Resident at
William T. Dwyer, Jr. Orlando, Florida Office)
W. Craig Fowler Donald V. O'Brien
Michael A. Gilman John C. O'Rourke, Jr.
Frederic G. Hogan Stephen W. Pickert (Resident at
  Orlando, Florida Office)

For full biographical listings, see the Martindale-Hubbell Law Directory

Pavalon & Gifford (AV)

Two North La Salle Street, Suite 1600, 60602
Telephone: 312-419-7400
Fax: 312-419-7408
Rockford, Illinois Office: 501 Seventh Street, Suite 501, 61104.
Telephone: 815-968-5100.

MEMBERS OF FIRM
Eugene I. Pavalon Gary K. Laatsch
Geoffrey L. Gifford Frank C. Marino
  Henry Phillip Gruss

Kathleen A. Russell Christine Walsh Donnelly
  Christopher B. Meister

For full biographical listings, see the Martindale-Hubbell Law Directory

Power Rogers & Smith, P.C. (AV)

35 West Wacker Drive, Suite 3700, 60601
Telephone: 312-236-9381
Fax: 312-236-0920

Joseph A. Power, Jr. Thomas G. Siracusa
Larry R. Rogers Paul L. Salzetta
Todd A. Smith Thomas M. Power

Larry R. Rogers, Jr. Ruth M. Degnan
Devon C. Bruce

For full biographical listings, see the Martindale-Hubbell Law Directory

Rosenthal and Schanfield, Professional Corporation (AV)

46th Floor, 55 East Monroe Street, 60603
Telephone: 312-236-5622
Telecopier: 312-236-7274

James M. Dash Mark S. Lieberman
Jay Russell Goldberg Howard L. Mocerf
David A. Golin Gerald B. Mullin
David E. Gordon Joseph R. Podlewski, Jr.
William H. Kelly, Jr. Mark L. Shapiro
Stephen P. Kikoler Ronald K. Szopa
Richard F. Lee David L. Weinstein
Ira M. Levin Edward J. Wong, III

(See Next Column)

ROSENTHAL AND SCHANFIELD PROFESSIONAL CORPORATION, *Chicago—*
Continued

For Complete List of Firm Personnel, See General Section

For full biographical listings, see the Martindale-Hubbell Law Directory

MERLE L. ROYCE, II (AV)

111 West Washington Street Suite 1710, 60606
Telephone: 312-553-1233
Fax: 312-372-4700

ASSOCIATE
Marshall J. Burt
OF COUNSEL
James J. Macchitelli   Khurram Hussain

For full biographical listings, see the Martindale-Hubbell Law Directory

SANCHEZ & DANIELS (AV)

Suite 500, 333 West Wacker Drive, 60606
Telephone: 312-641-1555
Fax: 312-641-3004
Wheaton, Illinois Office: 2100 Manchester Road, Suite 101.
Telephone: 708-871-6161.
Fax: 708-871-9771.
Boston, Massachusetts Office: Sanchez, Daniels & Fitch, 101 Federal Street,
Suite 1934.
Telephone: 617-478-0547.
Fax: 617-478-0544.

MEMBERS OF FIRM

Manuel "Manny" Sanchez	Timothy V. Hoffman
John D. Daniels	Robert T. Varney
Lori S. Yokoyama	Franklin U. Valderrama

George L. Acosta

John J. Skawski	Vanessa L. Vargas
Lela D. Johnson	Marcelle R. Kott
Rebecca Morrissey	Yvette Rivas Diamond
Hugh C. O'Donnell	Stacey Sherr Michelon
Jane Solmor-Mordini	Julie F. Furer
Francine Stulac	Darryl Tom
Edward N. Robles	Susan K. Chae
Joseph P. Bonaccorsi	Edward M. Ordonez
Mark I. Fishbein	Paige Donaldson
Deborah L. Nico	Lesley A. Corey

For full biographical listings, see the Martindale-Hubbell Law Directory

SAUNDERS & MONROE (AV)

Suite 4201, 205 North Michigan Avenue, 60601
Telephone: 312-946-9000
Facsimile: 312-946-0528

MEMBERS OF FIRM

George L. Saunders, Jr.	Thomas F. Bush, Jr.
Lee A. Monroe	Matthew E. Van Tine

Thomas A. Doyle

Gwen A. Niedbalski
OF COUNSEL
Kenneth K. Howell   Victoria S. Kaplan

For full biographical listings, see the Martindale-Hubbell Law Directory

LAW OFFICES OF EDMUND J. SCANLAN, LTD. (AV)

134 North La Salle-Suite 220, 60602
Telephone: 312-372-0020
Fax: 312-372-1211

Edmund J. Scanlan   Richard C. Gleason

For full biographical listings, see the Martindale-Hubbell Law Directory

SCARIANO, KULA, ELLCH AND HIMES, CHARTERED (AV)

Two Prudential Plaza 180 North Stetson Suite 3100, 60601-6224
Telephone: 312-565-3100
Facsimile: 312-565-0000
Chicago Heights, Illinois Office: 1450 Aberdeen.
Telephone: 708-755-1900.
Facsimile: 708-755-0000.

Anthony G. Scariano	Kathleen Field Orr
David P. Kula	John M. Izzo
Robert H. Ellch	Raymond A. Hauser
Alan T. Sraga	Kathleen Roche Hirsman
A. Lynn Himes	Joanne W. Schochat
Justino D. Petrarca	Anthony Ficarelli
Lawrence Jay Weiner	G. Robb Cooper

Daniel M. Boyle
OF COUNSEL
Max A. Bailey   John B. Kralovec

(See Next Column)

Patrick J. Broncato	Kelly A. Hayden
Rosanne Ciambrone	Todd K. Hayden
Jon G. Crawford	David A. Hemenway
Joel R. DeTella	Sarah E. Joyce
Teri E. Engler	Christopher L. Petrarca
Andrew C. Eulass	Shelia C. Riley

Janet L. Schwieters

For full biographical listings, see the Martindale-Hubbell Law Directory

PETER R. SONDERBY, P.C. (AV)

135 South La Salle Street Suite 1424, 60603
Telephone: 312-201-0999
Fax: 312-201-0749;
Fax: 312-641-1930

Peter R. Sonderby

For full biographical listings, see the Martindale-Hubbell Law Directory

STELLATO & SCHWARTZ, LTD. (AV)

120 North La Salle Street, 34th Floor, 60602
Telephone: 312-419-1011
Telecopier: 312-419-1012

Donald E. Stellato	Robert A. Muhr
Esther Joy Schwartz	James Bartlett

John W. Gilligan III

Steven Blair Borkan	Paul R. Walker-Bright
James Scott McMahon	Derek M. Barker
Nicholas J. Scarpelli	Joseph D. Gergeni
Ann Killian Perry	Thomas Krieger
Jennifer M. Ellin	John H. Silvestri
Michael P. Bregenzer	Cheryl L. Sepulveda

Elaine S. Vorberg

Representative Clients: American Drug Stores Company; Automobile Club of
Michigan; Budget Rent A Car Corp.; The Fireman's Fund Insurance; First
Mercury Syndicate; First Nonprofit Companies; Jewel Companies, Inc.;
Kmart Corporation; Northland Insurance Co.; United Services Automobile
Association.

For full biographical listings, see the Martindale-Hubbell Law Directory

STONE, McGUIRE & BENJAMIN (AV)

Suite 3230, 55 East Monroe Street, 60603
Telephone: 312-372-4100
Fax: 312-372-9461
Northbrook, Illinois Office: 801 Skokie Boulevard.
Telephone: 847-205-9700.
FAX: 847-205-9492.

MEMBERS OF FIRM

Howard L. Stone	Lee E. Gussin
David A. McGuire	(Resident, Northbrook Office)
Marc A. Benjamin	Michael L. Siegel
(Resident, Northbrook Office)	Edward C. Richard

ASSOCIATES

Carl E. Poli	Michael A. Harsch
	(Resident, Northbrook Office)

For full biographical listings, see the Martindale-Hubbell Law Directory

SWANSON, MARTIN & BELL (AV)

One IBM Plaza, Suite 2900, 60611
Telephone: 312-321-9100
Fax: 312-321-0990
Wheaton, Illinois Office: 2100 Manchester Road, C-1420.
Telephone: 708-653-2266.
Fax: 708-653-2292.

MEMBERS OF FIRM

Lenard C. Swanson	Lawrence Helms
Kevin T. Martin	Joseph P. Switzer
Brian W. Bell	George F. Fitzpatrick, Jr.
Stanley V. Boychuck	David E. Kawala
Kay L. Schichtel	Bruce S. Terlep
David J. Cahill	(Resident, Wheaton Office)
(Resident, Wheaton Office)	Robert J. Meyer

ASSOCIATES

Kevin V. Boyle	A. Jay Koehler, III
Michael J. Hossack	Sheryl A. Pethers
Matthew D. Jacobson	Barbara N. Petrungaro
(Resident, Wheaton Office)	Aaron T. Shepley
Joseph P. Kincaid	André Martin Thapedi
Patricia S. Kocour	William Blake Weiler

OF COUNSEL

Edward T. Butt, Jr.	John C. Church

For full biographical listings, see the Martindale-Hubbell Law Directory

Chicago—Continued

CRAIG D. TOBIN & ASSOCIATES (AV)

Three First National Plaza, Suite 535, 60602
Telephone: 312-641-1321
FAX: 312-641-5220

OF COUNSEL
Robert J. Collins

Tomas Petkus	Thomas C. Crooks

For full biographical listings, see the Martindale-Hubbell Law Directory

TRIBLER ORPETT PALMER & CRONE, A PROFESSIONAL CORPORATION (AV)

30 North La Salle Street, Suite 2200, 60602
Telephone: 312-201-6400
Fax: 312-201-6401
Schaumburg, Illinois Office: Suite 1260, 1450 East American Lane.
Telephone: 847-517-8400.
Fax: 847-517-8401.

Douglas C. Crone	H. Wesley Sunu
Steven R. McMannon	Willis R. Tribler
Michael J. Meyer	William J. Wall
Mitchell A. Orpett	(Not admitted in IL)
Thomas R. Palmer	
(Resident, Schaumburg Office)	

John W. Carver	Lisa O'Malley
Molly A. Griffin	Christopher J. Ondrula
David P. Hahn	Matthew B. Parker
Kyle J. Kirkham	Stanley D. Sterna
(Resident, Schaumburg Office)	Panos T. Topalis

OF COUNSEL

Daniel D. Drew	John W. Wardell
	(Resident, Schaumburg Office)

For full biographical listings, see the Martindale-Hubbell Law Directory

WILDMAN, HARROLD, ALLEN & DIXON (AV)

225 West Wacker Drive, 30th Floor, 60606-1229
Telephone: 312-201-2000
Cable Address: "Whad"
Fax: 312-201-2555
URL: http://www.whad.com
Aurora, Illinois Office: 1851 W. Galena Boulevard, Suite 210.
Telephone: 630-892-7021.
Fax: 630-892-7158.
Waukegan, Illinois Office: 404 West Water, P. O. Box 890.
Telephone: 847-623-0700.
Fax: 847-244-5273.
Lisle, Illinois Office: 4300 Commerce Court.
Telephone: 630-955-0555.
New York, New York Office: Wildman, Harrold, Allen, Dixon & Smith. The International Building, 45 Rockefeller Plaza, Suite 353.
Telephone: 212-632-3850.
Fax: 212-632-3858.
Toronto, Ontario affiliated Office: Keel Cottrelle. 36 Toronto Street, Ninth Floor, Suite 920.
Telephone: 416-367-2900.
Telefax: 416-367-2791.
Telex: 062-18660.
Mississauga, Ontario affiliated Office: Keel Cottrelle. 100 Matatson Avenue East, Suite 104.
Telephone: 416-890-7700.
Fax: 416-890-8006.

MEMBERS OF FIRM

Thomas D. Allen	Mark P. Miller
Richard C. Bartelt	Kathryn A. Mrkonich
Cal R. Burnton	Richard D. Murphy Jr.
James A. Christman	Timothy G. Nickels
Steven E. Danekas	Sarah L. Olson
James P. Dorr	Richard C. Palmer
Kathy Pinkstaff Fox	David F. Pardys
Robert E. Haley	(Waukegan Office)
Helaine Wachs Heydemann	Douglas L. Prochnow
Anthony G. Hopp	Robert L. Shuftan
David A. Kanter	Robert A. Strelecky
Steven L. Larson	(Lisle Office)
(Waukegan Office)	Peter A. Tomaras
Donald R. McGarrah	James B. Vogts
	Dale G. Wills

John T. Benz	Adam J. Glazer
Eric P. Berlin	Scott Z. Hochfelder
Lawrence W. Falbe	Michael J. Lotus
Wendy L. Fink	Jeffrey A. McIntyre
Shanthi V. Gaur	Stephanie B. Miller

(See Next Column)

Vania Montero	John A. Roberts
Martha D. Owens	Paul A. Slager
Barbara M. Prohaska	John A. Terselic
(Lisle Office)	(Waukegan Office)
Kevin B. Reid	Jeanne Walker

For Complete List of Firm Personnel, See General Section

For full biographical listings, see the Martindale-Hubbell Law Directory

WILLIAMS AND MONTGOMERY, LTD. (AV)

20 North Wacker Drive Suite 2100, 60606
Telephone: 312-443-3200
Facsimile: 312-443-1323
Email: WILLMONT@ATTMAIL.COM
Waukegan, Illinois Office: 33 North County Street.
Telephone: 847-360-1220.
Wheaton, Illinois Office: 310 S. County Farm Road.
Telephone: 708-690-3200.
Joliet, Illinois Office: 81 North Chicago Avenue.
Telephone: 815-727-2653.
Miami, Florida Office: Clarke, Silverglate, Williams and Montgomery, 100 North Biscayne Boulevard.
Telephone: 305-377-0700.
Facsimile: 305-377-3001.

Lloyd E. Williams, Jr.	Kevin Campbell
C. Barry Montgomery	David P. Boyd
Barry L. Kroll	Rodney E. VanAusdal
Thomas H. Neuckranz	Lori E. Iwan
Anthony P. Katauskas	Lawrence K. Rynning
David E. Morgans	Jeffrey H. Lipe
Craig A. Tomassi	Bruce W. Lyon
Nunzio C. Radogno	Thomas F. Cameli
Anthony J. Kiselis	Michael D. Huber
Edward J. Murphy	Lawrence A. Szymanski
Alton C. Haynes	Gregory J. Bird
James K. Horstman	Perry W. Hoag
Patrick F. Klunder	Hall Adams, III
David E. Stevenson	Mary Anne Sliwinski
Michael R. La Barge	Thomas J. Pontikis
	Mark R. Misiorowski

OF COUNSEL
Manya A. Pastalan Grant

Brigid E. Kennedy	Shimon B. Kahan
Peter J. Szatkowski	Mark E. Winters
Douglas A. Miller	Brian J. Hunt
Stephen W. Heil	Bradley C. Nahrstadt
Edward R. Moor	Karen M. Talty
J. Calvin Downing, III	Edward O. Pacer
David E. Neumeister	Gregory W. Beihl
Mark D. Brent	Douglas W. Lohmar, Jr.

For Complete List of Firm Personnel, See General Section

For full biographical listings, see the Martindale-Hubbell Law Directory

WILSON & MCILVAINE (AV)

500 West Madison, Suite 3700, 60661-2511
Telephone: 312-715-5000
Telecopier: 312-715-5155

PARTNERS

Thomas G. Draths	Kendall R. Meyer
Robert F. Forrer	Dennis J. O'Hara
Timothy S. Harris	Dwight B. Palmer, Jr.
Richard L. Horn	Quinton F. Seamons
Joseph M. Kehoe	Leonard S. Shifflett
Thomas J. Magill	Alexander Terras
	Brian J. Wanca

ASSOCIATES

David B. Altman	Kathleen M. Myalls
Sara E. Elder	Todd A. Rowden
Heather A. Libbey	Kurt T. Temple

For Complete List of Firm Personnel, See General Section

For full biographical listings, see the Martindale-Hubbell Law Directory

COLLINSVILLE, Madison Co.

DUNHAM, BOMAN & LESKERA (AV)

300 West Clay Street, 62234
Telephone: 618-344-7734
Telecopier: 618-344-3853
East St. Louis, Illinois Office: 520 First Illinois Bank Building.
Telephone: 618-271-0535.
Telecopier: 618-271-2800.
Belleville, Illinois Office: 208 North High Street.
Telephone: 618-397-2151.
Telecopier: 618-397-2285.

(See Next Column)

DUNHAM, BOMAN & LESKERA, *Collinsville—Continued*

John W. Leskera   William L. Berry

For full biographical listings, see the Martindale-Hubbell Law Directory

DANVILLE,* Vermilion Co.

GUNN & HICKMAN, P.C. (AV)

220 North Vermilion Street, P.O. Box 706, 61832
Telephone: 217-446-0880
Fax: 217-442-3901

John B. Jenkins   James L. Brougher
                    Fred L. Hubbard

Representative Clients: Insurance Company of North America (INA); Ranger Insurance Co.; ESIS Risk Management; Carolina Casualty Co.; Providence Washington Insurance Group; CNA Insurance Co.; First Midwest Bank/-Danville and Foremost Insurance Group; CIGNA Insurance Cos.; The Prudential Insurance Co.

For Complete List of Firm Personnel, See General Section

For full biographical listings, see the Martindale-Hubbell Law Directory

HUTTON, LAURY, HESSER, LIETZ & WILCOX (AV)

16 West Madison Street, P.O. Box 1128, 61832
Telephone: 217-446-9436
FAX: 217-446-9462

MEMBERS OF FIRM

Everett L. Laury   Gregory G. Lietz
Gary D. Hesser   Roy G. Wilcox

Representative Clients: Pekin Insurance; Prudential Insurance Company; Metropolitan Life Insurance Company; Illinois State Medical Insurance Services, Inc.; Associated Physicians Insurance Company; Employers Reinsurance Corp.; Northwestern National Insurance Company; St. Paul Insurance Companies; Clarendon National Insurance Company; General Motors Corporation.

For Complete List of Firm Personnel, See General Section

For full biographical listings, see the Martindale-Hubbell Law Directory

EAST ST. LOUIS, St. Clair Co.

DUNHAM, BOMAN & LESKERA (AV)

520 First Illinois Bank Building, 327 Missouri Avenue, 62201
Telephone: 618-271-0535
Telecopier: 618-271-2800
Belleville, Illinois Office: 208 North High Street.
Telephone: 618-235-7222.
Telecopier: 618-397-2285.
Collinsville, Illinois Office: 300 West Clay Street.
Telephone: 618-344-7734.
Telecopier: 618-344-3853.

M.F. Oehmke (1887-1963)   Wm. C. Dunham (1893-1975)
            Howard Boman (1917-1985)

MEMBERS OF FIRM

John W. Leskera   Russell K. Scott
William L. Berry   Robert D. Francis
Eric C. Young   John L. Bitzer

Attorneys For: Collinsville School District #10; Hanover Insurance Co.;; Hartford Insurance Group; Home Indemnity Co.; State Farm Insurance Cos.; Transamerica Insurance Group; The Travelers Indemnity Co.; Wausau Insurance Cos.; Nationwide Insurance Co.; Atlantic Mutual Insurance Co..

For full biographical listings, see the Martindale-Hubbell Law Directory

EDWARDSVILLE,* Madison Co.

BURROUGHS, HEPLER, BROOM, MACDONALD & HEBRANK (AV)

Two Mark Twain Plaza, Suite 300, 103 West Vandalia Street, P.O. Box 510, 62025-0510
Telephone: 618-656-0184
Telecopier: 618-656-1364
Email: firm@ilmolaw.com

MEMBERS OF FIRM

George D. Burroughs   G. Gordon Burroughs
  (1873-1977)   (Of Counsel)
William G. Burroughs   Larry E. Hepler
  (1872-1952)   Gordon R. Broom
Mallory L. Burroughs   Theodore J. MacDonald, Jr.
  (1884-1965)   Jeffrey S. Hebrank
Jesse L. Simpson (1884-1973) Gary E. True
David L. Simpson (Retired)   Paul W. Johnson
            William J. Knapp

(See Next Column)

ASSOCIATES

Lisa K. Franke   Daniel W. Farroll
Jack H. Humes, Jr.   David J. Gerber
Melissa Griggs   Donald J. Ohl
L. David Green   D. Scott Rendleman
J. Todd Hayes   Gary A. Meadows
J. Robert Edmonds   T. Scott Stewart

Representative Clients: Ameritech; Travelers Insurance Co.; Fireman's Fund-American Insurance Group; CILCO; Employers Union Insurance Co.; The Hartford; Illinois Power Co.; W.R. Grace; Mark Twain Bank; Prairie Farms.

For full biographical listings, see the Martindale-Hubbell Law Directory

LUCCO BROWN & MUDGE (AV)

224 St. Louis Street, P.O. Box 539, 62025
Telephone: 618-656-2321
Fax: 618-656-2363

Dick H. Mudge, Jr. (1919-1978)   Joseph R. Brown, Jr.
J. William Lucco   William A. Mudge
                    ASSOCIATES
Erin E. Reilly   Michael Shaheen

Reference: Bank of Edwardsville, Edwardsville, Illinois.

For full biographical listings, see the Martindale-Hubbell Law Directory

PEEL, BEATTY & WALTERS (AV)

6100 Center Grove Road, 62025
Telephone: 618-692-0500
Fax: 618-656-4472

MEMBERS OF FIRM

Gary E. Peel   William S. Beatty
                    Gerald R. Walters

Representative Clients: Village of Glen Carbon; Madison County Housing Authority; Madison County Transit District; Alton Police Benevolent and Protective Unit 14; Madison County Sanitary Sewers District; International Laborers Local 397, Granite City.

For full biographical listings, see the Martindale-Hubbell Law Directory

THOMSON & BEHR (AV)

22 B Glen - Ed Professional Park, P.O. Box 538, 62025
Telephone: 618-692-0028
Telecopier: 618-692-0269

MEMBERS OF FIRM

Stephen W. Thomson   Richard J. Behr

Danya L. Johnson

For full biographical listings, see the Martindale-Hubbell Law Directory

FAIRVIEW HEIGHTS, St. Clair Co.

KEEFE & DEPAULI, P.C. (AV)

2 Executive Drive, P.O. Box 3190, 62208
Telephone: 618-624-2444
Fax: 618-624-6031

William L. Rogers   Thomas H. Kuergeleis
                    James K. Keefe

William L. Hanks   Patrick M. Keefe
William Lemp   Richard H. Risse
Andrew T. Nalefski   Dennis O. Douglas
Kevin M. Hazlett   Scott A. White
                    Darren K. Short
                    OF COUNSEL
Thomas Q. Keefe   Frank E. DePauli

Reference: Magna Bank.

For full biographical listings, see the Martindale-Hubbell Law Directory

HARRISBURG,* Saline Co.

JELLIFFE, FERRELL & MORRIS (AV)

108 East Walnut Street, 62946
Telephone: 618-253-7153; 253-7647
Telecopier: 618-252-1843

OF COUNSEL
Charles R. Jelliffe
MEMBERS OF FIRM
DeWitt Twente (1904-1976)   Donald V. Ferrell
                    Walden E. Morris

(See Next Column)

JELLIFFE, FERRELL & MORRIS—*Continued*

ASSOCIATES

Michal Doerge   Thomas J. Foster

Representative Clients: Auto-Owners Insurance; Country Cos; Metropolitan Life Insurance; Ohio Casualty Group; Standard Mutual Insurance Co.; State Farm Cos.; Redland Insurance Co.; Aetna Casualty & Surety Co.; Kerr-McGee Coal Corp.; Sahara Coal Co.

For full biographical listings, see the Martindale-Hubbell Law Directory

JOLIET,* Will Co.

McKEOWN, FITZGERALD, ZOLLNER, BUCK, HUTCHISON & RUTTLE (AV)

2455 Glenwood Avenue, 60435
Telephone: 815-729-4800
Fax: 815-729-4711
Frankfort, Illinois Office: 28 Kansas Street.
Telephone: 815-469-2176.
FAX: 815-469-0295.

MEMBERS OF FIRM

Charles J. McKeown (1908-1985)	Theodore J. Jarz
Paul O. McKeown (1913-1982)	Douglas J. McKeown
Richard T. Buck (1936-1992)	Timothy J. Rathbun
Joseph C. Fitzgerald	James B. Harvey
Max E. Zollner	Kenneth A. Grey
Douglas P. Hutchison	Michael R. Lucas
David L. Ruttle	Christopher N. Wise
	Gary S. Mueller

ASSOCIATES

Frank S. Cservenyak, Jr.	Kurt J. Keller
Arthur J. Wilhelmi	Kelly Kathleen James

OF COUNSEL

George E. Sangmeister   Stewart C. Hutchison

Representative Clients: Caterpillar Tractor Co.; First National Bank of Lockport; Homart Development Co.; First Midwest Bank, N.A.; Silver Cross Hospital; Joliet Township High School District; Villages of: Plainfield and Mokena; Southwest Agency for Risk Management; Joliet Junior College Foundation; Health Service Systems, Inc.

For full biographical listings, see the Martindale-Hubbell Law Directory

KANKAKEE,* Kankakee Co.

ACKMAN, MAREK, BOYD AND WOODRUFF, LTD. (AV)

Suite 400, One Dearborn Square, 60901
Telephone: 815-933-6681
Fax: 815-933-9985
Watseka, Illinois Office: 200 East Walnut Street.
Telephone: 815-432-5215.
Fax: 815-432-3186.
Manteno, Illinois Office: 10 North Locust Street.
Telephone: 815-468-7751.

Richard L. Ackman	Robert W. Boyd
J. Dennis Marek	Deborah A. Woodruff

James A. Devine	John J. Boyd (Also at Manteno Office)

Representative Clients: American States Insurance Co.; Auto Owners Insurance Co.; Consumers Illinois Water Co.; Country Mutual Insurance Co.; Farmers Insurance Group; Martin Boyer Co. Inc.; Medical Protective Co.; Economy Fire & Casualty Co.; Union Ins. Co.

For full biographical listings, see the Martindale-Hubbell Law Directory

MATTOON, Coles Co.

CRAIG & CRAIG (AV)

1807 Broadway, P.O. Box 689, 61938-0689
Telephone: 217-234-6481
Telecopier: 217-234-6486
Mount Vernon, Illinois Office: 227 1/2 South 9th Street.
Telephone: 618-244-7511.

MEMBERS OF FIRM

John H. Armstrong	Gregory C. Ray
John P. Ewart	Paul R. Lynch (Resident, Mount Vernon Office)
Richard F. Record, Jr.	
Stephen L. Corn	Kenneth F. Werts (Resident, Mount Vernon Office)
Richard Charles Hayden	
Robert G. Grierson	John L. Barger

ASSOCIATES

Joshua N. Rosen (Resident, Mount Vernon Office)	Kathleen M. Stockwell

OF COUNSEL

Jack E. Horsley

Representative Clients: Zeigler Coal Co.; Marathon Oil Co.; Illinois Central Railroad Co.; Okaw Building & Loan Association; Travelers Insurance Co.; The Medical Protective Co.; Lloyds Underwriters at London; Aetna Life &

(See Next Column)

Casualty Insurance Co.; Scattering Fork Drainage District of Douglas, Illinois; Mattoon Township Park District of Coles County, Illinois.

For Complete List of Firm Personnel, See General Section

For full biographical listings, see the Martindale-Hubbell Law Directory

HELLER, HOLMES & ASSOCIATES, P.C. (AV)

1101 Broadway, P.O. Box 889, 61938-0889
Telephone: 217-235-2700
FAX: 217-235-0743
Email: Kent@Advant.com

Harlan Heller	Brent D. Holmes
	H. Kent Heller

Teresa K. Righter	David Stevens
	Fred Johnson

Representative Clients: Quantum Chemical Co.; First National Bank of Effingham.
References: First National Bank, Mattoon, Ill.; Central National Bank of Mattoon.

For full biographical listings, see the Martindale-Hubbell Law Directory

MOUNT VERNON,* Jefferson Co.

CAMPBELL, BLACK, CARNINE & HEDIN, P.C. (AV)

P.O. Drawer C, 62864
Telephone: 618-242-3310
Fax: 618-242-3735
Email: cbch@midwest.net *URL:* http://www.cbch.com

David A. Campbell	Carl L. Favreau
Terry R. Black	Howard W. Campbell (1911-1980)
Roy L. Carnine	
Craig R. Hedin	John E. Jacobsen (1922-1985)
Mark J. Ballard	Glenn E. Moore (1911-1991)
Jerome E. McDonald	David E. Furnall (1905-1993)

Fred R. Mann	Brian E. Leach

Representative Clients: Kerr-McGee Coal Corp.; Good Samaritan Hospital; Country Mutual Insurance Co.; Southern Illinois Stone Co; Rend Lake Conservancy District; Consolidation Coal Co.; Illinois State Medical Insurance Services; State Farm Automobile Insurance Co.; John Hancock Mutual Life Insurance Co.

For full biographical listings, see the Martindale-Hubbell Law Directory

NAPERVILLE, Du Page Co.

STEVEN B. LEVY, LTD. (AV)

40 Shuman Boulevard Suite 151, 60563
Telephone: 630-416-6300
Telefax: 630-416-6564
URL: http://www.sblevyltdlaw.com

Steven B. Levy

For full biographical listings, see the Martindale-Hubbell Law Directory

OAK BROOK, Du Page Co.

BOTTI, MARINACCIO & DeLONGIS, LTD. (AV)

720 Enterprise Drive, 60521
Telephone: 708-573-8585
Fax: 708-573-8586
Wheaton, Illinois Office: Suite 401 The Ticor Title Building, 330 Naperville Road.
Telephone: 708-653-2100.

Aldo E. Botti	Mark W. Salkeld
Stephen R. Botti	Peter M. Tumminaro
Andrew Y. Acker	David C. Bruss
Peter M. DeLongis	Jean M. Lasics
Lee A. Marinaccio	Nanette C. Augustin

For full biographical listings, see the Martindale-Hubbell Law Directory

OAKBROOK TERRACE, Du Page Co.

GALLAGHER & JOSLYN (AV)

One Lincoln Centre, Suite 300, 60181
Telephone: 630-916-2600
FAX: 630-916-2606

MEMBERS OF FIRM

Gerard B. Gallagher	Barry E. Garley
David L. Joslyn	Susan B. Shelton
L. Judson Todhunter	Ira E. Sussman

(See Next Column)

GALLAGHER & JOSLYN, *Oakbrook Terrace—Continued*

OF COUNSEL

Peter A. Bauer	Laurie A. Silvestri
Leonard S. DeFranco	Daniel G. McNamara

For full biographical listings, see the Martindale-Hubbell Law Directory

OREGON,* Ogle Co.

WILLIAMS & McCARTHY, A PROFESSIONAL CORPORATION (AV)

607 Washington Street, P.O. Box 339, 61061
Telephone: 815-732-2101
Fax: 815-732-2289
Rockford, Illinois Office: 321 West State Street, P.O. Box 219.
Telephone: 815-987-8900.
Fax: 815-968-0019. ABANET: ABA 5519.

Kari A. Vanderzyl

Representative Clients: Anderson Industries, Inc.; Liberty Mutual Insurance Co.; Atwood Industries, Inc.; The Travelers; American Mutual Insurance Co.; Rockford Memorial Hospital; Chrysler Corp.

For Complete List of Firm Personnel, See General Section

For full biographical listings, see the Martindale-Hubbell Law Directory

PEORIA,* Peoria Co.

CASSIDY & MUELLER (AV)

1510 First Financial Plaza, 61602
Telephone: 309-676-0591
FAX: 309-676-8036

MEMBERS OF FIRM

John E. Cassidy (1896-1984)	John E. Cassidy, III
John E. Cassidy, Jr.	Timothy J. Cassidy
David B. Mueller	Timothy J. Newlin

ASSOCIATES

Andrew D. Cassidy	Christopher F. Cassidy

Representative Clients: Aetna Casualty & Surety Co.; Dow Corning, Inc.; E.I. DuPont-DeNemours & Company; Economy Fire & Casualty Co.; Hartford Insurance Group; Liberty Mutual Insurance Co.; St. Paul Fire and Casualty; Warner-Lambert Company; Squibb & Sons, Inc.; Parke Davis Company.

For full biographical listings, see the Martindale-Hubbell Law Directory

KAVANAGH, SCULLY, SUDOW, WHITE & FREDERICK, P.C. (AV)

301 S.W. Adams Street, Suite 700, 61602
Telephone: 309-676-1381
FAX: 309-676-0324.
East Peoria, Illinois Office: 111 West Washington Street, Suite 206B.
Telephone: 309-694-3707.
Fax: 309-676-0324.

Julian E. Cannell	Douglas S. Slayton
Charles G. Roth	James W. Springer
David J. Dubicki	Mark W. Marlott
Phillip B. Lenzini	David A. Koperski

Counsel for: First of America Bank - Illinois, N.A.; AgriBank, FCB; Construction Equipment Federal Credit Union; Travelers Insurance Co.; Phoenix Mutual Life Insurance Co.; United States Fidelity & Guaranty Co.; Equitable Life Assurance Society of the U.S.; Board of Education of the City of Peoria School District, 150; Anderson State Bank.

For Complete List of Firm Personnel, See General Section

For full biographical listings, see the Martindale-Hubbell Law Directory

KINGERY, DURREE, WAKEMAN & RYAN, ASSOC. (AV)

915 Commerce Bank Building, 61602
Telephone: 309-676-3612
FAX: 309-676-1329

Arthur R. Kingery	Christopher P. Ryan
Edward R. Durree	Craig J. Reiser
Steven A. Wakeman	Philip M. O'Donnell
	James P. Lawson

Reference: Commerce Bank of Peoria.

For full biographical listings, see the Martindale-Hubbell Law Directory

QUINN, JOHNSTON, HENDERSON & PRETORIUS, CHARTERED (AV)

(Formerly McConnell, Kennedy, Quinn & Johnston)
227 N. E. Jefferson Street, 61602
Telephone: 309-674-1133
Telecopier: 309-674-6503
Springfield, Illinois Office: Three North, Old State Capitol Plaza, 62701.
Telephone: 217-753-1133.

(See Next Column)

W. Thomas Johnston	Stephen P. Kelly
R. Michael Henderson	(Resident, Springfield Office)
Murvel Pretorius, Jr.	Stanley L. Morris
Bradley W. Dunham	(Resident, Springfield Office)
Robert H. Jennetten	Julie A. Ward
Charles D. Knell	David Blair Collins
Gregory A. Cerulo	John F. Kamin
Paul P. Gilfillan	Jeanne Wysocki Ballor
John P. Fleming	Scott R. Paulsen
Mary W. McDade	Michael J. Holt
	Laura M. Donahue

Representative Clients: Allstate Insurance Co.; American International Group; Bituminous Insurance Co.; General Motors; Illinois State Medical Insurance Services, Inc.; Pekin Insurance; Peoria Journal Star, Inc.; St. Paul Insurance Co.

For Complete List of Firm Personnel, See General Section

For full biographical listings, see the Martindale-Hubbell Law Directory

ROBERT C. STRODEL, LTD. (AV)

927 Commerce Bank Building, 61602
Telephone: 309-676-4500
Fax: 309-676-4566

Robert C. Strodel

For full biographical listings, see the Martindale-Hubbell Law Directory

SWAIN, HARTSHORN & SCOTT (AV)

411 Hamilton Boulevard, Suite 1806, 61602-1104
Telephone: 309-637-1700; Toll Free (USA): 800-728-1806
Fax: 309-637-1708
URL: http://www.peorialaw.com

MEMBERS OF FIRM

Tim Swain	Donald M. Hartshorn
	Robert W. Scott, Jr.

OF COUNSEL

Timothy W. Swain

For full biographical listings, see the Martindale-Hubbell Law Directory

WINGET & KANE (AV)

807 Commerce Bank Building, 61602
Telephone: 309-674-2310
Fax: 309-674-9722

Walter W. Winget	James F. Kane

Representative Client: Davison-Fulton Ltd.
References: Commerce Bank; Bank One - Peoria.

For full biographical listings, see the Martindale-Hubbell Law Directory

PERU, La Salle Co.

ANTHONY C. RACCUGLIA & ASSOCIATES (AV)

1200 Maple Drive, 61354
Telephone: 815-223-0230
Ottawa, Illinois Office: 633 La Salle Street.
Telephone: 815-434-2003.

ASSOCIATES

James A. McPhedran	Louis L. Bertrand

References: La Salle National Bank; Citizens First National Bank of Peru, Illinois.

For full biographical listings, see the Martindale-Hubbell Law Directory

QUINCY,* Adams Co.

SCHMIEDESKAMP, ROBERTSON, NEU & MITCHELL (AV)

525 Jersey, P.O. Box 1069, 62306
Telephone: 217-223-3030
Telecopier: 217-223-1005

MEMBERS OF FIRM

Delmer R. Mitchell, Jr.	Gena J. Awerkamp

Representative Clients: Mercantile Trust & Savings Bank; Moorman Manufacturing Co.; Travelers Insurance Co.; Hartford Accident & Indemnity Co.; Aetna Casualty & Surety Co.; Knapheide Mfg. Co.; Harris Corp.; Bituminous Casualty Corp.; Quincy Compressor Division of Colt Industries, Inc.

For Complete List of Firm Personnel, See General Section

For full biographical listings, see the Martindale-Hubbell Law Directory

ROCKFORD,* Winnebago Co.

HALDEMAN & ASSOCIATES (AV)

200 Pioneer Centre, 303 North Main Street, 61101
Telephone: 815-965-8840
Fax: 815-965-8355

(See Next Column)

HALDEMAN & ASSOCIATES—*Continued*

Richard R. Haldeman
ASSOCIATE
Michael J. Hedeen

Representative Clients: Pioneer Life Insurance Company of Illinois, Rockford, Ill.; E.D. Etnyre & Co., Rockford, ILL.; Sundstrand Corporation.

For full biographical listings, see the Martindale-Hubbell Law Directory

WILLIAMS & McCARTHY, A PROFESSIONAL CORPORATION (AV)

321 West State Street, P.O. Box 219, 61105-0219
Telephone: 815-987-8900
Fax: 815-968-0019
URL: http://www.wilmac.com
Oregon, Illinois Office: 607 Washington Street. P.O. Box 339.
Telephone: 815-732-2101.
Fax: 815-732-2289.

John R. Kinley	Scott C. Sullivan
Elmer C. Rudy	Carol N. Bailey
Thomas S. Johnson (President, Williams & McCarthy)	Jane E. Durgom-Powers
	James P. Devine
Edward R. Telling, III	J. Mark Doherty
Russell D. Anderson	John J. Holevas
John E. Pfau	Timothy J. Rollins
Richard A. Berman	Clayton L. Lindsey (Resident
John W. Rosenbloom	Partner, Oregon, Illinois
John L. Shepherd	Office)
Terry D. Anderson	Stephen E. Balogh
Kim D. Krahenbuhl (Resident Partner, Oregon, Illinois Office)	Robert E. Luedke
	Marc C. Gravino
	Thomas P. Sandquist

Carl A. Ecklund	Ronald A. Barch
Wendy S. Howarter (Resident, Oregon, Illinois Office)	Troy E. Haggestad
	Kari A. Vanderzyl (Resident, Oregon, Illinois Office)

OF COUNSEL
John C. McCarthy

Representative Clients: Aircraft Gear Corp.; Anderson Industries, Inc.; Gallagher Bassett Insurance Co.; Liberty Mutual Insurance Co.; Atwood Industries, Inc.; The Travelers; American Mutual Insurance Co.; Rockford Health Systems; Chrysler Corp.; USF&G, West Bend.

For full biographical listings, see the Martindale-Hubbell Law Directory

ROCK ISLAND,* Rock Island Co.

KATZ, McHARD, BALCH, LEFSTEIN & FIEWEGER, P.C. (AV)

200 Plaza Office Building, 1705 Second Avenue, P.O. Box 3250, 61204-3250
Telephone: 309-788-5661
Facsimile: 309-788-5688

Stuart R. Lefstein	Samuel S. McHard
Martin H. Katz	Dale G. Haake
Peter C. Fieweger	Linda E. Frischmeyer
Robert T. Park	Brian S. Nelson
	Stephen T. Fieweger

Jonathan J. Heiple

Attorneys for: Augustana College; O'Rourke Bros., Inc.; International Limousines, Ltd.; Reynolds State Bank.
Local Attorneys for: Aetna Casualty & Surety Co.; Maryland Casualty Co.; Liberty Mutual Insurance Co.; CIGNA Cos.; Country Mutual Insurance Co.; Cincinnati Insurance Co.

For Complete List of Firm Personnel, See General Section

For full biographical listings, see the Martindale-Hubbell Law Directory

WINSTEIN, KAVENSKY & WALLACE (AV)

4th Floor, Rock Island Bank Building, 224 18th Street, P.O. Box 4298, 61201
Telephone: 309-794-1515; 800-747-1527
FAX: 309-794-9929

MEMBERS OF FIRM

Stewart R. Winstein	Franklin S. Wallace
Harrison H. Kavensky	Craig L. Kavensky
	Arthur R. Winstein

John Allan Hartsock	David L. Cunningham
James H. Schultz	Brett Andrew Nelson
(Not admitted in IL)	H. J. Pries

Local Regional Counsel for: United Auto Workers.
Reference: First National Bank of Quad Cities.

For full biographical listings, see the Martindale-Hubbell Law Directory

SPRINGFIELD,* Sangamon Co.

GIFFIN, WINNING, COHEN & BODEWES, P.C. (AV)

1 West Old State Capitol Plaza, Suite 600 Myers Building, P.O. Box 2117, 62705
Telephone: 217-525-1571
Facsimile: 217-525-1710
Email: jswartzn@counsel.com

Carol Hansen Posegate	Thomas P. Schanzle-Haskins, III
R. Mark Mifflin	Gregory K. Harris

Representative Clients: Illinois State University Board of Trustees; Allstate Insurance Co.; Grinnell Mutual Reinsurance Company; Horace Mann Insurance Company; Great Central Insurance Cos.; Transamerica Insurance Company; Associated Beer Distributors of Illinois Risk Management Association.

For Complete List of Firm Personnel, See General Section

For full biographical listings, see the Martindale-Hubbell Law Directory

METNICK, WISE, CHERRY & FRAZIER (AV)

Second Floor, Myers Building, 1 West Old State Capitol Plaza, P.O. Box 12140, 62791
Telephone: 217-753-4242
Telefax: 217-753-4642

MEMBERS OF FIRM

Michael B. Metnick	Diana N. Cherry
D. Peter Wise	Richard D. Frazier

ASSOCIATES

Frederick J. Schlosser	Kathryn Saltmarsh
	Thomas W. Patton

For full biographical listings, see the Martindale-Hubbell Law Directory

VANDALIA,* Fayette Co.

BURNSIDE DEES JOHNSTON & CHOISSER (AV)

First National Bank Building, 62471
Telephone: 618-283-3260
Fax: 618-283-2851

MEMBERS OF FIRM

J. G. Burnside (1873-1969)	Joe Dees
Robert G. Burnside	Jack B. Johnston
	Dale F. Choisser

General Counsel for: First National Bank; The First State Bank of St. Peter; State Bank of Farina; South-Central Regional Planning And Development Commission; S&S Urethane, Inc.
Local Counsel for: Pekin Insurance Co.

For full biographical listings, see the Martindale-Hubbell Law Directory

WAUKEGAN,* Lake Co.

DIVER, GRACH, QUADE & MASINI (AV)

First Federal Savings and Loan Building, 111 North County Street, 60085
Telephone: 847-662-8611
FAX: 847-662-2960

MEMBERS OF FIRM

Clarence W. Diver (1883-1962)	David R. Quade
Thomas W. Diver	Robert J. Masini
Brian S. Grach	Sarah P. Lessman

Heidi J. Aavang	Donna-Jo Rodden Vorderstrasse
	Paula Vincich Randall

OF COUNSEL
David L. Hazan

A list of Representative Clients will be furnished upon request.
Reference: First Midwest Bank of Waukegan.

For full biographical listings, see the Martindale-Hubbell Law Directory

WHEATON,* Du Page Co.

DONOVAN & ROBERTS, P.C. (AV)

104 East Roosevelt Road, Suite 202, P.O. Box 417, 60189-0417
Telephone: 630-668-4211
Fax: 630-668-2076

Keith E. Roberts, Sr.	Keith E. (Chuck) Roberts, Jr.
	James J. Konetski

Marie F. Leach	Robert M. Skutt
Mark J. Lyons	Robert J. Lentz
Andrew L. Dryjanski	Rosemarie Calandra

For full biographical listings, see the Martindale-Hubbell Law Directory

Wheaton—Continued

STEVEN B. LEVY, LTD.

(See Naperville)

NORTON AND MANCINI (AV)

109 North Hale Street, P.O. Box 846, 60189-0846
Telephone: 630-668-9440
FAX: 630-668-9489
Chicago, Illinois Office: 111 West Washington Street, Suite 835.
Telephone: 312-807-4999.
FAX: 312-807-4998.

John E. Norton	Thomas R. Weiler
Lorenzo A. Mancini	James L. DeAno
Patricia L. Argentati	Thomas J. Long

Denis K. Sheehan	Joseph M. Polick
Craig D. Queen	Harry E. Bartosiak
Douglas S. Strohm	Jennifer H. Lee
W. Mark Sickles	Dawn C. Didier

OF COUNSEL
Adrianna K. Liber

Representative Clients: Aetna Life & Casualty; Allstate Insurance Company; Chicago Motor Club Insurance Company; County of DuPage; CNA Insurance Company; Hartford Insurance Company; Illinois State Medical Insurance Services, Inc.; St. Paul Insurance Company; Wausau Insurance Companies.

For full biographical listings, see the Martindale-Hubbell Law Directory

SWANSON, MARTIN & BELL (AV)

2100 Manchester Road C-1420, 60187
Telephone: 708-653-2266
Fax: 708-653-2292
Chicago, Illinois Office: Suite 2900, One IBM Plaza.
Telephone: 312-321-9100.
Fax: 312-321-0990.

MEMBERS OF FIRM

Lenard C. Swanson	David J. Cahill (Resident)
	Bruce S. Terlep

ASSOCIATE
Matthew D. Jacobson

For full biographical listings, see the Martindale-Hubbell Law Directory

WOODSTOCK,* McHenry Co.

THEODORE A. E. POEHLMANN (AV)

205 East South Street, P.O. Box 271, 60098-0271
Telephone: 815-337-3337
Fax: 815-337-3340

For full biographical listings, see the Martindale-Hubbell Law Directory

INDIANA

AUBURN,* De Kalb Co.

MEFFORD AND CARPENTER, A PROFESSIONAL CORPORATION (AV)

130 East Seventh Street, P.O. Box 667, 46706-0667
Telephone: 219-925-2300
Facsimile: 219-925-2610
URL: http://www.lawmc.com

Donald T. Mefford	Kirk D. Carpenter
	J. Bryan Nugen

For full biographical listings, see the Martindale-Hubbell Law Directory

BEDFORD,* Lawrence Co.

STEELE, STEELE, McSOLEY & McSOLEY (AV)

Bank One Building, Suite One, 1602 I Street, 47421
Telephone: 812-279-3513
Fax: 812-275-3504

MEMBERS OF FIRM

Ruel W. Steele (1908-1992)	Brent E. Steele
Byron W. Steele	Patrick S. McSoley
	Darlene Steele McSoley

Representative Clients: Bank One, Bloomington, N.A. Bedford Branch; The First National Bank of Mitchell; Bedford Independent Federal Credit Union; The Times Mail (newspaper); Indiana Bell Telephone Co.; Texas Gas Transmission Corporation; U.S. Gypsum Company.

For full biographical listings, see the Martindale-Hubbell Law Directory

BLOOMINGTON,* Monroe Co.

THOMAS A. BERRY & ASSOCIATES (AV)

701 North Walnut Street, 47404
Telephone: 812-336-8300
Fax: 812-336-2343

ASSOCIATE
Michelle Berry Domer

For full biographical listings, see the Martindale-Hubbell Law Directory

BUNGER & ROBERTSON (AV)

226 South College Square, P.O. Box 910, 47402-0910
Telephone: 812-332-9295
Fax: 812-331-8808

MEMBERS OF FIRM

Don M. Robertson	James L. Whitlatch
Joseph D. O'Connor III	Samuel R. Ardery

ASSOCIATES

William J. Beggs	John W. Richards

Representative Clients: Aetna Insurance Companies; Bloomington Hospital; Commercial Union Group; Indiana Insurance Co.; Liberty Mutual Insurance; Medical Protective Co.; Monroe County Community School Corp.; Professional Golf Car, Inc.; Prudential Insurance Company of America; State Farm Automobile Insurance Co.

For Complete List of Firm Personnel, See General Section

For full biographical listings, see the Martindale-Hubbell Law Directory

KELLEY, BELCHER & BROWN, A PROFESSIONAL CORPORATION (AV)

301 West Seventh Street, P.O. Box 3250, 47402-3250
Telephone: 812-336-9963
Telecopier: 812-336-4588

William H. Kelley	Thomas J. Belcher

Shannon L. Robinson	Darla Sue Brown
	Jennifer A. Bauer

For full biographical listings, see the Martindale-Hubbell Law Directory

CARMEL, Hamilton Co.

KNOWLES & ASSOCIATES (AV)

811 South Range Line Road, 46032
Telephone: 317-848-4360
Telecopier: 317-848-4363
URL: http://www.courts9@1x.netcom.com

William W. Knowles

D. Brandon Johnston	Tracy J. Follstad

For full biographical listings, see the Martindale-Hubbell Law Directory

CLARKSVILLE, Clark Co.

MAYER, VOGT, SMITH & PALMQUIST (AV)

501 Eastern Boulevard, 47129
Telephone: 812-288-1235
Louisville, Kentucky: 502-584-5800
Fax: 812-288-1240

MEMBERS OF FIRM

John M. Mayer, Jr.	William E. Smith, III
Samuel H. Vogt, Jr.	Cara Wells Stigger

ASSOCIATES

Susan Wagner Hynes	Kerstin Ann Schuhmann

Representative Clients: First Savings Bank, FSB; PNC Bank Indiana, Inc.
Approved Attorneys for: Commonwealth Land Title Insurance Co.; Ticor Title Insurance Company; Old Republic National Title Insurance Company.
References: First Savings Bank, FSB; PNC Bank Indiana, Inc.

For Complete List of Firm Personnel, See General Section

For full biographical listings, see the Martindale-Hubbell Law Directory

COLUMBUS,* Bartholomew Co.

SHARPNACK, BIGLEY, DAVID & RUMPLE (AV)

321 Washington Street, P.O. Box 310, 47202-0310
Telephone: 812-372-1553
Fax: 812-372-1567

(See Next Column)

SHARPNACK, BIGLEY, DAVID & RUMPLE—*Continued*

MEMBERS OF FIRM

Thomas C. Bigley, Jr.   John A. Stroh
Timothy J. Vrana   Joan Tupin Crites

Representative Clients: Irwin Union Bank and Trust Co.; PSI Energy, Inc.; State Farm Mutual Insurance Cos.; American States Insurance Co.; Home News Enterprises; Centra Federal Credit Union.

For Complete List of Firm Personnel, See General Section

For full biographical listings, see the Martindale-Hubbell Law Directory

---

CROWN POINT,* Lake Co.

EDWARD P. GRIMMER (AV)

603 N. Main Street, 46307-3233
Telephone: 219-662-1661

Representative Clients: Furnished Upon Request.

For full biographical listings, see the Martindale-Hubbell Law Directory

---

ELKHART, Elkhart Co.

COSENTINO, SHEWMAKER & CHRISTOFENO (AV)

115 West Lexington Avenue, P.O. Box 1866, 46515-1866
Telephone: 219-295-6210
Fax: 219-522-5598

MEMBERS OF FIRM

Michael A. Cosentino   Terry C. Shewmaker
Michael A. Christofeno

Reference: KeyBank.

For full biographical listings, see the Martindale-Hubbell Law Directory

---

DANIELS, SANDERS, PIANOWSKI, HAMILTON & TODD (AV)

401 West High Street, 46516
Telephone: 219-294-1499
FAX: 219-294-7277

MEMBERS OF FIRM

Philip E. Byron, Jr. (1911-1977)   Michael A. Pianowski
Robert C. Daniels (1928-1995)   Thomas R. Hamilton
Robert T. Sanders, III   James L. Todd
David G. Thomas

ASSOCIATES

Matthew A. Yeakey   P. Shawn Lewis

Representative Clients: KeyBank Corp.; Commercial Union Insurance Cos.; Aetna Casualty and Surety Co.; Ohio Casualty Insurance Co.; Yoder Oil Co., Inc.; Double Eagle Industries, Inc.; WKJG-TV; Tri-State Coach Lines, Inc.; Tom Naquin Chevrolet, Inc.

For full biographical listings, see the Martindale-Hubbell Law Directory

---

EVANSVILLE,* Vanderburgh Co.

BAMBERGER, FOREMAN, OSWALD AND HAHN (AV)

7th Floor Hulman Building, P.O. Box 657, 47704-0657
Telephone: 812-425-1591
Fax: 812-421-4936

OF COUNSEL

William P. Foreman   Charles E. Oswald, Jr.
Jeffrey R. Kinney

MEMBERS OF FIRM

Frederick P. Bamberger   Fred S. White
  (1903-1983)   R. Thomas Bodkin
Robert H. Hahn   Terry G. Farmer
George A. Porch   Roderick W. Clutter, Jr.
Robert M. Becker   Michele S. Bryant
David D. Bell

ASSOCIATES

J. Herbert Davis   Christopher Lee
Marjorie A. Meeks   Laura A. Scott
Sean M. Georges

General Counsel for: North Park Shopping Center; Southern Indiana Gas and Electric Co.; The Citizens National Bank of Evansville; Welborn Clinic; Welborn HMO.
Representative Clients: Aetna Life and Casualty Group; Medical Protective Insurance Co.; State Farm Mutual Automobile Insurance Co.; The Travelers Insurance Co.; Transamerica Insurance Co.

For Complete List of Firm Personnel, See General Section

For full biographical listings, see the Martindale-Hubbell Law Directory

---

BERGER AND BERGER (AV)

313 Main Street, 47708-1485
Telephone: 812-425-8101;
Indiana Only: 800-622-3604;
Outside Indiana: 800-327-0182
Fax: 812-421-5909

(See Next Column)

MEMBERS OF FIRM

Sydney L. Berger (1917-1988)   Sheila M. Corcoran
Charles L. Berger   Mark W. Rietman
Robert J. Pigman

References: Citizens National Bank of Evansville; Old National Bank in Evansville.

For full biographical listings, see the Martindale-Hubbell Law Directory

---

BOWERS, HARRISON, KENT & MILLER, LLP (AV)

25 N.W. Riverside Drive, P.O. Box 1287, 47706-1287
Telephone: 812-426-1231
Fax: 812-464-3676

MEMBERS OF FIRM

F. Wesley Bowers   Terry Noffsinger
David V. Miller   James P. Casey
Paul E. Black   Thomas A. Massey
Arthur D. Rutkowski   Greg A. Granger
George C. Barnett, Jr.   Joseph H. Harrison, Jr.
Lawrence L. Grimes

Representative Clients: Ameritech Publishing, Inc.; Southern Railway Company; Bootz Manufacturing Company; Indiana Bell Telephone: Company; Black Beauty Resources, Inc.

For Complete List of Firm Personnel, See General Section

For full biographical listings, see the Martindale-Hubbell Law Directory

---

KAHN, DEES, DONOVAN & KAHN (AV)

P.O. Box 3646, 47735-3646
Telephone: 812-423-3183
Fax: 812-423-3841
Email: evvlaw@k2d2.com

MEMBERS OF FIRM

Alan N. Shovers   Jon D. Goldman
Thomas O. Magan   Brian P. Williams
Robert H. Brown   David L. Clark
Jeffrey W. Ahlers

ASSOCIATES

Richard O. Hawley, Jr.   Martha J. Posey
Mark W. Clark

Representative Clients: Atlas Van Lines, Inc.; Sterling Boiler & Mechanical, Inc.; WATS/800, Inc.; University of Southern Indiana; Cresline Plastic Pipe Co., Inc.; Perdue Farms Incorporated; Deaconess Hospital, Inc.

For Complete List of Firm Personnel, See General Section

For full biographical listings, see the Martindale-Hubbell Law Directory

---

WRIGHT, EVANS AND DALY (AV)

425 Main Street, 47708
Telephone: 812-424-3300
Fax: 812-421-5588

MEMBERS OF FIRM

Donald R. Wright   R. Lawrence Daly

Representative Clients: Allstate Insurance Company; Browning-Ferris Industries of Indiana, Inc.; Castle Contracting Co., Inc.; Chrysler Corporation; Home Insurance Companies; Liberty Mutual Insurance Company; Manpower Incorporated of Evansville; The Mortgage Connection of Evansville, Inc.; Orkin Exterminating Company; United Farm Bureau Mutual Insurance Company.

For Complete List of Firm Personnel, See General Section

For full biographical listings, see the Martindale-Hubbell Law Directory

---

FORT WAYNE,* Allen Co.

BARRETT & MCNAGNY (AV)

215 East Berry Street, P.O. Box 2263, 46801-2263
Telephone: 219-423-9551
Telecopier: 219-423-8924

MEMBERS OF FIRM

Ted S. Miller   John D. Walda
J. Michael O'Hara   James P. Fenton
John M. Clifton, Jr.   Alan VerPlanck
Robert S. Walters   Thomas M. Kimbrough
John F. Lyons   Stephen L. Chapman
Gary J. Rickner   Thomas A. Herr
Anthony M. Stites

ASSOCIATES

Kevin K. Fitzharris   Cathleen M. Shrader

Counsel for: Aetna Group; Allen County Motors, Inc.; Fort Wayne National Bank; Northern Indiana Public Service Co.; Omni-Source Corp.; Phelps Dodge Magnet; The Journal-Gazette.
Representative Clients: General Electric; Kemper Insurance Co.; State Farm Mutual Automobile Co.

(See Next Column)

BARRETT & McNAGNY, *Fort Wayne—Continued*

For Complete List of Firm Personnel, See General Section

For full biographical listings, see the Martindale-Hubbell Law Directory

HUNT, SUEDHOFF, BORROR & EILBACHER (AV)

900 Courtside, 803 South Calhoun Street, P.O. Box 11489, 46858-1489
Telephone: 219-423-1311
Telecopier: 219-424-5396

RETIRED
Carl J. Suedhoff, Jr.

MEMBERS OF FIRM

Leigh L. Hunt (1899-1975)	Thomas W. Belleperche
William E. Borror (1932-1989)	Mark W. Baeverstad
Leonard E. Eilbacher	Michael D. Mustard
Robert E. Kabisch	Branch R. Lew
Arthur G. Surguine, Jr.	Carla J. Baird
Thomas C. Ewing	James J. Shea
Carolyn White Spengler	Scott L. Bunnell
Dane L. Tubergen	

ASSOCIATES

Charles H. Bassford, IV	Daniel J. Palmer
Carolyn M. Trier	Brian L. England
Kathleen A. Kilar	Craig J. Bobay
W. Douglas Lemon	

For full biographical listings, see the Martindale-Hubbell Law Directory

ROBY & HOOD (AV)

Standard Federal Plaza, Suite 520, 200 East Main, 46802
Telephone: 219-423-3366
Fax: 219-423-3367
Anderson, Indiana Office: One Citizens Plaza, Suite 305.
Telephone: 317-642-2402.

MEMBERS OF FIRM

Daniel A. Roby	Kathryn J. Roudebush
G. Stanley Hood	Thomas A. Manges
David Joseph Stach	

References: Norwest Bank; NBD Bank.

For full biographical listings, see the Martindale-Hubbell Law Directory

SHAMBAUGH, KAST, BECK & WILLIAMS (AV)

600 Standard Federal Plaza, 46802-2405
Telephone: 219-423-1430
Fax: 219-422-9038

MEMBERS OF FIRM

Michael H. Kast	Daniel E. Serban
Stephen J. Williams	John B. Powell
Edward E. Beck	Timothy L. Claxton
James D. Streit	

Counsel for: Hagerman Construction Corp.; Rogers Markets, Inc.; K & H Realty Corp.; Olive B. Cole Foundation; M. E. Raker Foundation, Inc.; Associates Financial Services Co., of Indiana, Inc.; Professional Federal Credit Union; Fort Wayne Education Association; American Ambassador Casualty Company; CBT Credit Services, Inc.

For Complete List of Firm Personnel, See General Section

For full biographical listings, see the Martindale-Hubbell Law Directory

---

FOWLER,* Benton Co.

BARCE & RYAN (AV)

103 North Jackson Avenue, P.O. Box 252, 47944-0252
Telephone: 317-884-0383
Fax: 317-884-0445
Kentland, Indiana Office: 301 East Graham Street, P.O. Box 338, 47951-0338.
Telephone: 219-474-5158.
Fax: 219-474-6610.

MEMBER OF FIRM
John W. Barce

For Complete List of Firm Personnel, See General Section

For full biographical listings, see the Martindale-Hubbell Law Directory

---

GARY, Lake Co.

STULTS, STULTS, FORSZT & PAWLOWSKI, A PROFESSIONAL ASSOCIATION (AV)

3637 Grant Street, P.O. Box 15050, 46409-5050
Telephone: 219-887-7000
Fax: 219-884-1179

Fred M. Stults, Jr.	Robert P. Forszt
Frederick M. Stults, III	David R. Pawlowski

Representative Clients: American Road Insurance Co.; Employers Casualty Co.; Indiana Insurance Co.; SAFECO Insurance Co.

(See Next Column)

For full biographical listings, see the Martindale-Hubbell Law Directory

---

HAMMOND, Lake Co.

ABRAHAMSON, REED & ADLEY (AV)

200 Russell Street, 46320
Telephone: 219-937-1500
Fax: 219-937-3174

MEMBERS OF FIRM

Harold Abrahamson	Kenneth D. Reed
Michael C. Adley	

ASSOCIATES

Scott R. Bilse	Christopher R. Karsten

References: Calumet National Bank, Hammond; Mercantile National Bank, Hammond.

For full biographical listings, see the Martindale-Hubbell Law Directory

BECKMAN, KELLY & SMITH (AV)

5920 Hohman Avenue, 46320
Telephone: 219-933-6200
Telecopier: 219-933-6201
South Bend, Indiana Office: 300 North Michigan Street, Suite 215.
Telephone: 219-288-2373.
Telecopier: 219-933-6201.

MEMBERS OF FIRM

Richard P. Tinkham (1902-1973)	Andrew J. Fetsch
Daniel F. Kelly (1914-1978)	Randall J. Nye
John F. Beckman, Jr. (1916-1996)	Robert F. Parker
	Daniel W. Glavin
J. B. Smith	Eric L. Kirschner

ASSOCIATES

Melanie Morgan Dunajeski	Christine Hajduch Curosh
Scott A. Bearby	Douglas A. Welp

Representative Clients: Waste Management of North America, Inc.; The Travelers Companies; Bethlehem Steel Corp.; ITT Finance; Northwest Indiana Public Broadcasting, Inc.; Signal Capital Corporation; CIGNA Companies; Sears Roebuck and Co.

For full biographical listings, see the Martindale-Hubbell Law Directory

GALVIN, GALVIN & LEENEY (AV)

5231 Hohman Avenue, 46320
Telephone: 219-933-0380
Fax: 219-933-0471

MEMBERS OF FIRM

Edmond J. Leeney (1897-1978)	Carl N. Carpenter
Timothy P. Galvin, Sr. (1894-1993)	John E. Chevigny
	Timothy P. Galvin, Jr.
Francis J. Galvin, Sr. (1902-1995)	Patrick J. Galvin
	W. Patrick Downes

William G. Crabtree II	Julie A. Rosenwinkel
John H. Lloyd, IV	Amy Galvin Grogan

Attorneys for: Mercantile National Bank of Indiana; Citizens Financial Services, FSB; Auto Owners Insurance Co.; CIGNA; Pepsi-Cola General Bottlers, Inc.; St. Margaret Mercy Healthcare Centers, Inc.; St. Anthony Hospital and Health Centers (Michigan City); Calumet Construction Corp.; Chicago Title Insurance Company; State Farm Insurance Cos.

For full biographical listings, see the Martindale-Hubbell Law Directory

McHIE, MYERS, McHIE & ENSLEN (AV)

53 Muenich Court, 46320
Telephone: 219-931-1707
Telecopier: 219-932-2417

MEMBERS OF FIRM

G. Edward McHie	James E. McHie
Charles A. Myers	Charles Endicott Enslen
Carol M. Green	

Representative Clients: USX Corporation; Ronwal Transportation, Inc.; Hammond Redevelopment Commission; Hammond Economic Development Commission; Raytrans, Inc.; La Salle Steel Co.; Emro Marketing Co., A Division of Marathon Oil; Combined Transport Systems, Inc.

For full biographical listings, see the Martindale-Hubbell Law Directory

---

HIGHLAND, Lake Co.

SMITH & DeBONIS (AV)

Professional Office Building, 9696 Gordon Drive, 46322
Telephone: 219-922-1000
Fax: 219-922-1600
La Porte, Indiana Office: First of America Bank Building, Suite 302, 800 Lincolnway.
Telephone: 219-326-7527.
Wanatah, Indiana office: 105 North Main Street.
Telephone: 219-733-2184.

(See Next Column)

SMITH & DeBONIS—*Continued*

MEMBERS OF FIRM

Terrance L. Smith   Anthony DeBonis, Jr.

Dennis F. Smith

ASSOCIATES

David Stephen Gladish   Krista Smith Mac Lennan

LEGAL SUPPORT PERSONNEL

PARALEGAL ASSISTANTS

Linda A Phillips   Judith S. Evans

For full biographical listings, see the Martindale-Hubbell Law Directory

INDIANAPOLIS,* Marion Co.

BAKER & DANIELS (AV)

300 North Meridian Street, 46204
Telephone: 317-237-0300
FAX: 317-237-1000
Fort Wayne, Indiana Office: 111 East Wayne Street, Suite 800.
Telephone: 219-424-8000.
South Bend, Indiana Office: First Bank Building, 205 West Jefferson Boulevard.
Telephone: 219-234-4149.
Elkhart, Indiana Office: 301 B South Main Street, Suite 307,
Telephone: 219-296-6000.
Washington, D.C. Office: 1701 K Street, N.W., Suite 400.
Telephone: 202-785-1565.

MEMBERS OF FIRM

Norman P. Rowe	Robert Kirk Stanley
Terrill D. Albright	Alan L. McLaughlin
Wendell R. Tucker	Brent D. Taylor
Thomas G. Stayton	Joseph H. Yeager, Jr.
James H. Ham, III	Byron K. Mason
Brian K. Burke	James W. Clark
David K. Herzog	Kevin M. Toner
Christopher G. Scanlon	David A. Given
John R. Schaibley, III	John Joseph Tanner

COUNSEL

Virgil L. Beeler

ASSOCIATES

Scott D. Himsel	Carl R. Pebworth
Andrew Z. Soshnick	Thomas D. Bunton
Nancy G. Tinsley	Patrick S. Cross
Ellen E. Boshkoff	Charles A. Grandy
Mark A. Voigtmann	David P. Scharf

Joseph E. Miller, Jr.

Representative Clients: Anthem Insurance Companies, Inc.; AT&T Corp.; Bank One, Indianapolis, N.A.; Borg-Warner Corp.; City of Indianapolis; Cummins Engine Co.; Eli Lilly and Co.; General Motors Corp.; Indianapolis Public Schools; United Airlines.

For Complete List of Firm Personnel, See General Section

For full biographical listings, see the Martindale-Hubbell Law Directory

BOBERSCHMIDT, MILLER, O'BRYAN & TURNER, A PROFESSIONAL ASSOCIATION (AV)

Bank One Center/Circle, 111 Monument Circle, Suite 302, 46204-5169
Telephone: 317-632-5892
Telecopier: 317-686-3423

Berton W. O'Bryan   L. Craig Turner

A List of Representative Clients will be furnished upon request.

For full biographical listings, see the Martindale-Hubbell Law Directory

BOSE McKINNEY & EVANS (AV)

2700 First Indiana Plaza, 135 North Pennsylvania Street, 46204
Telephone: 317-684-5000
Facsimile: 317-684-5173
Indianapolis North Office: Suite 1201, 8888 Keystone Crossing, 46240.
Telephone: 317-574-3700.
Facsimile: 317-574-3716.

MEMBERS OF FIRM

Wayne C. Ponader	Keith E. White
James P. Seidensticker, Jr.	C. Joseph Russell
Theodore J. Nowacki	Michael A. Trentadue
Ronald E. Elberger	Roderick H. Morgan
Daniel C. Emerson	V. Samuel Laurin III
Stephen E. Arthur	George Thomas Patton, Jr.
George E. Purdy	Debra Linn Burns

ASSOCIATE

William C. Ahrbecker

Representative Clients: Chicago Title Insurance Co.; Duke Construction and Development Cos.; Emmis Broadcasting Corp.; First Indiana Bank; Metropolitan Life Insurance Co.; The Prudential Insurance Company of America; The Travelers Insurance Co.; Indianapolis Colts, Inc.; United Parcel Service, Inc.

(See Next Column)

For Complete List of Firm Personnel, See General Section

For full biographical listings, see the Martindale-Hubbell Law Directory

BRATTAIN & MINNIX (AV)

151 North Delaware Street Suite 760, 46204
Telephone: 317-231-1750
Facsimile: 317-231-1760

Bruce D. Brattain   Larry A. Minnix

Linda Klain

For full biographical listings, see the Martindale-Hubbell Law Directory

BUSCHMANN, CARR & SHANKS, PROFESSIONAL CORPORATION (AV)

1020 Market Tower, 10 West Market Street, 46204-2963
Telephone: 317-636-5511
Fax: 317-636-3661
Email: bcs@indy.net *URL:* http://www.buschmann.com/bcs/

John R. Carr, III   Stephen R. Buschmann

Representative Clients: Archer-Daniels Midland Co.; Ball Corp.; Industrial Valley Title Insurance; Creative Risk Management, Inc.; Deflecto Corporation; Glenfed Mortgage Corp.; Gates McDonald; Merchants National Bank & Trust Company of Muncie; Monumental Life Insurance Co.; National Council on Compensation Insurance.

For full biographical listings, see the Martindale-Hubbell Law Directory

CHRISTOPHER & TAYLOR (AV)

1219 North Delaware Street, P.O. Box 2850, 46206-2850
Telephone: 317-635-9000
Telecopier: 317-686-2200
Fowler, Indiana Office: 306 East Fifth Street, P.O. Box 72.
Telephone: 317-884-0810.

OF COUNSEL

Richard L. Christopher   (Resident at Fowler, Indiana)

MEMBERS OF FIRM

Rodney V. Taylor	David J. Theising
Michael C. Peek	Joseph F. Pieters

John D. Connor

For full biographical listings, see the Martindale-Hubbell Law Directory

CONOUR • DOEHRMAN (AV)

Suite 1725, One Indiana Square, 46204
Telephone: 317-269-3550
Fax: 317-269-3564
Toll Free: 800-269-3443

MEMBERS OF FIRM

William F. Conour   Thomas C. Doehrman

ASSOCIATES

Rex E. Baker   Daniel S. Chamberlain

For full biographical listings, see the Martindale-Hubbell Law Directory

DALE & EKE, PROFESSIONAL CORPORATION (AV)

Suite 400, 9100 Keystone Crossing, 46240
Telephone: 317-844-7400
Fax: 317-574-9426

Joseph W. Eke	Catherine Chambers Kennedy
Deborah J. Caruso	A. Robert Lasich, Jr.

Dawn Michelle Snow

For full biographical listings, see the Martindale-Hubbell Law Directory

DANN PECAR NEWMAN & KLEIMAN, PROFESSIONAL CORPORATION (AV)

Suite 2300, One American Square Box 82008, 46282
Telephone: 317-632-3232; Indiana: 800-622-4799
Telecopy: 317-632-2962

Theodore R. Dann (1907-1993)	Walter E. Wolf, Jr.
Joel Yonover (1932-1995)	Barry E. Beldin
Philip D. Pecar	Robert D. Swhier, Jr.
Norman R. Newman	James P. Moloy
David H. Kleiman	Robert J. Schuckit
Jon B. Abels	Andrew A. Kleiman
Melvin R. Daniel	Michael J. Gabovitch
Lawrence F. Dorocke	Steven M. Pecar
Jeffrey A. Abrams	Benjamin A. Pecar
James H. Schwarz	Richard O. Kissel, II
Robert A. Rose	Joseph D. Calderon

OF COUNSEL

Linda E. Cantor   Anthony J. Rose

(See Next Column)

DANN PECAR NEWMAN & KLEIMAN PROFESSIONAL CORPORATION,
Indianapolis—Continued

Ellen C. Siakotos	Angela L. Mansfield
Stacy L. Hill	Martha M. K. Baird

Karin L. Veatch

Attorneys for: Indianapolis Machinery Co., Inc.; Melvin Simon & Associates, Inc.; Pacers Basketball Corp.; Universal Fire & Casualty Co., Inc.; Bank One, Indianapolis, NA; INB National Bank; Nachi Technology, Inc.; Pharmaceutical Corporation of America; Logo 7, Inc.

For full biographical listings, see the Martindale-Hubbell Law Directory

---

HOLLAND & HOLLAND (AV)

Two Market Square Center, Suite 1011, 251 East Ohio Street, 46204
Telephone: 317-637-4400
Fax: 317-262-9309

C. Warren Holland	Michael W. Holland

ASSOCIATE
Gretchen Holland Etling
OF COUNSEL
Charles G. Reeder

For full biographical listings, see the Martindale-Hubbell Law Directory

---

HUGHES AND SALLEE (AV)

(Not a Partnership)
Two Meridian Plaza, Suite 202, 10401 North Meridian Street, 46290
Telephone: 317-573-2255
Telecopier: 317-573-2266

David B. Hughes	Gary D. Sallee

For full biographical listings, see the Martindale-Hubbell Law Directory

---

ICE MILLER DONADIO & RYAN (AV)

One American Square Box 82001, 46282-0002
Telephone: 317-236-2100
Fax: 317-236-2219
Email: leel@imdr.com *URL:* http://www.imdr.com
South Bend, Indiana Office: 211 West Washington Street, Suite 2420.
Telephone: 219-234-7933.
Fax: 219-234-7965. Internet E-mail: leel@imdr.com. Web Site Address: http://www.imdr.com.

MEMBERS OF FIRM

James V. Donadio	John F. Prescott, Jr.
Alan H. Lobley	Fred R. Biesecker
Jim A. O'Neal	Mary Nold Larimore
Evan E. Steger	Richard A. Smikle
Ralph A. Cohen	L. Alan Whaley
Arthur P. Kalleres	Bonnie L. Gallivan
G. Daniel Kelley, Jr.	John T. Murphy
David M. Mattingly	Debra Hanley Miller
James R. Fisher	Michael A. Wukmer
Cory Brundage	Michael J. Lewinski
David J. Mallon, Jr.	Michael D. Marine
Phillip R. Scaletta, III	Terri Ann Czajka
James L. Petersen	Donald M. Snemis
Gary J. Dankert	Michael A. Wilkins
Philip A. Whistler	Sherry A. Fabina-Abney

OF COUNSEL

Bradley L. Williams	Kathleen K. Shortridge
Nancy Menard Riddle	Diana L. Wann

Kelly Bauman Pitcher
STAFF ATTORNEYS

Suzanne S. Crouch	Edward P. Steegmann

ASSOCIATES

Kristin L. Altice	Jodie L. Miner
Robert A. Anderson	Thomas E. Mixdorf
James Scott Fanzini	Adam Arceneaux
Laure V. Flaniken	Tara L. Schulstad
John J. Morse	Rebecca J. Seamands
Judy Starobin Okenfuss	Christopher S. Sears
Stephanie Alden Smithey	Tracy J. (Vacek) Galbraith
Curtis W. McCauley	Paul N. Alp
Laura B. Daghe	Cindy M. Lott

Melissa S. York

Counsel for: Amax, Inc.; American Cyanamid Co.; Chrysler Corp.; Community Hospitals of Indiana, Inc.; Ford Motor Company; Howard Needles, Tammen & Bergendoff; Indiana Department of Insurance; Parke-Davis; Proctor & Gamble Co.; Liberty Mutual Ins. Co.

For Complete List of Firm Personnel, See General Section

For full biographical listings, see the Martindale-Hubbell Law Directory

---

JOHNSON, SMITH, PENCE, DENSBORN, WRIGHT & HEATH (AV)

One Indiana Square Suite 1800, 46204
Telephone: 317-634-9777
Telecopier: 317-636-9061

MEMBERS OF FIRM

Wayne O Adams, III	G. Ronald Heath
Thomas A. Barnard	Robert B. Hebert
David G. Blachly	David J. Hensel
David J. Carr	John David Hoover
Sean Michael Clapp	Andrew W. Hull
David R. Day	Linda L. Pence
Thomas N. Eckerle	David E. Wright
Mark W. Ford	Sally Franklin Zweig

ASSOCIATES

Thomas G. Burroughs	Bradley C. Morris
Jane Ann Himsel	Michael D. Ramsey
Patricia L. Marshall	David D. Robinson
Alice McKenzie Morical	Ronald G. Sentman

OF COUNSEL
William T. Lawrence

For Complete List of Firm Personnel, See General Section

For full biographical listings, see the Martindale-Hubbell Law Directory

---

KIGHTLINGER & GRAY (AV)

Market Square Center, Suite 660, 151 North Delaware Street, 46204
Telephone: 317-638-4521
Telecopier: 317-636-5917
Evansville, Indiana Office: One Riverfront Place, Suite 210, 20 N.W. First Street, 47708.
Telephone: 812-464-9508.
Telecopier: 812-464-9511.
New Albany, Indiana Office: Pinnacle Centre, Suite 200, 3317 Grant Line Road, P.O. Box 6727, 46151.
Telephone: 812-949-2300.
Telecopier: 812-949-8556.

MEMBERS OF FIRM

Robert J. Wampler	John B. Drummy
Donald L. Dawson	James W. Roehrdanz
Peter G. Tamulonis	Thomas B. Blackwell
Richard A. Young	Peter A. Velde
J. Randall Aikman	Thomas J. Jarzyniecki, Jr.
Michael E. Brown	Jeffrey A. Doty
Mark D. Gerth	Thomas E. Wheeler II
Steven E. Springer	Rodney L. Scott
Joan Fullam Irick	(Resident, New Albany Office)
Richard T. Mullineaux	S. Michael Woodard
(Resident, New Albany Office)	David R. Sauvey
Robert M. Kelso	(Resident, Evansville Office)
Brent R. Weil	Jill Reifinger Marcrum
(Resident, Evansville Office)	(Resident, Evansville Office)
Philip Linnemeier	Van T. Willis
	(Resident, New Albany Office)

OF COUNSEL

Mark William Gray	Roger H. Schmelzer

ASSOCIATES

Mary M. Nord	Diane E. Bluhm
(Resident, New Albany Office)	(Resident, New Albany Office)
William L. O'Connor	David R. Schanker
Scott L. Tyler	Candace L. Sage
(Resident, New Albany Office)	Robert J. Smith
Laura E. Moenning	Marti E. Thurman
Paul F. Lottes	(Resident, New Albany Office)
Christopher C. Hagenow	Jeffrey R. Walker
Eric D. Johnson	(Resident, Evansville Office)
Timothy A. Klingler	Daniel A. Barfield
(Resident, Evansville Office)	(Resident, Evansville Office)
Dirck H. Stahl	Pfenne P. Cantrell
(Resident, Evansville Office)	Marcia A. Mahony
Lowell T. Woods, Jr.	James B. Doyle
Gregory M. Reger	
(Resident, New Albany Office)	

Representative Clients: American Family Mutual Insurance Co.; American International Group; American States; Associated Aviation Underwriters; Black & Decker (U.S., Inc.); Government Employees Insurance Co.; Mack Trucks, Inc.; Reliance Insurance Group.
Reference: INB National Bank.

For Complete List of Firm Personnel, See General Section

For full biographical listings, see the Martindale-Hubbell Law Directory

---

LOCKE REYNOLDS BOYD & WEISELL (AV)

1000 Capital Center South, 201 North Illinois Street, 46204
Telephone: 317-237-3800
Telecopier: 317-237-3900

(See Next Column)

LOCKE REYNOLDS BOYD & WEISELL—*Continued*

Hugh E. Reynolds, Jr.	Terrence L. Brookie
Lloyd H. Milliken, Jr.	Richard A. Huser
William V. Hutchens	Thomas J. Campbell
David S. Allen	Diane Parsons Emswiller
David M. Haskett	Burton M. Harris
Michael A. Bergin	Charles B. Baldwin
David T. Kasper	Thomas W. Farlow
Steven J. Strawbridge	Karl M. Koons, III
Thomas L. Davis	Julia F. Crowe
Robert A. Fanning	James Dimos
Randall R. Riggs	Kristen K. Rollison
Alan S. Brown	Thomas R. Schultz
Mark J. Roberts	Todd J. Kaiser
Kevin Charles Murray	Eric A. Riegner
Julia Blackwell Gelinas	Kevin C. Schiferl
Kim F. Ebert	Ariane Schallwig Johnson

Stephen L. Vaughan	Jerrilyn Powers Ramsey
Peter H. Pogue	Katherine Coble Dassow
John H. Daerr	Mary Margaret Ruth Feldhake
John K. McDavid	Donald B. Kite, Sr.
Robert W. Wright	Thomas F. Bedsole
Jeffrey J. Mortier	Stephanie L. Valadez
Nicholas C. Pappas	David Alexander Sorensen
Mary A. Schopper	Derek S. Burrell
Susan E. Cline	Dean R. Brackenridge

OF COUNSEL

William H. Vobach   Robert C. Riddell

Representative Clients: American Honda Motor Co., Inc; Center for Claims Resolution; Citizens Insurance Company of America; CNA Insurance Cos.; General Motors Corp.; PEPSICO, Inc.; PSI Energy, Inc.; St. Francis Hospital; U.S. Aircraft Insurance Group; Wal-Mart Stores, Inc.

For Complete List of Firm Personnel, See General Section

For full biographical listings, see the Martindale-Hubbell Law Directory

McTURNAN & TURNER (AV)

2400 Market Tower, 10 West Market Street, 46204
Telephone: 317-464-8181
Telecopier: 317-464-8131

Lee B. McTurnan	Jacqueline Bowman Ponder
Wayne C. Turner	Steven M. Badger
Judy L. Woods	Matthew W. Foster
Matthew J. Salzman	

Representative Clients: Ameritech Indiana; Ameritech Services, Inc.; The Dow Chemical Company; Coopers & Lybrand; IPALCO Enterprises Inc.; Prudential Securities Incorporated; National City Bank, Indiana; Western Newspaper Publishing Company; McGraw-Hill Broadcasting Co., Inc., (WRTV-6).

For full biographical listings, see the Martindale-Hubbell Law Directory

MEILS, THOMPSON, DIETZ & CONGLETON (AV)

Suite 830, Two Market Square Center, 251 East Ohio Street, 46204
Telephone: 317-637-1383
Fax: 317-264-2573

MEMBERS OF FIRM

Rick D. Meils	R. Michael Congleton
Scott A. Harkness	

Representative Clients: Indiana Insurance Co.; Consolidated Insurance Cos.; Amerisure Insurance Company; Michigan Mutual Insurance Co.; American Family Insurance Co.; Northwestern Insurance Co.; Northland Insurance Co.; Capitol Indemnity; Acceptance Insurance Co.

For full biographical listings, see the Martindale-Hubbell Law Directory

MILLER MULLER MENDELSON & KENNEDY (AV)

8900 Keystone Crossing Suite 1250, 46240
Telephone: 317-574-4500
1-800-394-3094
Fax: 317-574-4501

MEMBERS OF FIRM

Michael S. Miller	Tilden Mendelson
John Muller	Timothy J. Kennedy

ASSOCIATE

Catherine A. Kling

For full biographical listings, see the Martindale-Hubbell Law Directory

MITCHELL HURST JACOBS & DICK (AV)

152 East Washington Street, 46204
Telephone: 317-636-0808
1-800-636-0808
Fax: 317-633-7680

(See Next Column)

MEMBERS OF FIRM

Marvin H. Mitchell	Richard J. Dick
William W. Hurst	Marshall S. Hanley
Samuel L. Jacobs	Steven K. Huffer
Robert W. Strohmeyer, Jr.	

ASSOCIATES

Danielle A. Takla	Michael T. McNelis
John M. Reames	Jennifer Levin Sinder

General Counsel For: Dr. Tavel's Vision Center; Calderon Bros. Vending Machines, Inc.; Grocers Supply Co., Inc.; Power Train Services, Inc.; Frank E. Irish, Inc.; Bedding Liquidators; Galyan's Trading Co.; Harcourt Management Co., Inc.; Kosene & Kosene Mgt. & Dev. Co., Inc.; Hasten Bancorp.

For full biographical listings, see the Martindale-Hubbell Law Directory

OSBORN HINER LISHER & ORZESKE, P.C. (AV)

Suite 380, One Woodfield, 8330 Woodfield Crossing Boulevard, 46240
Telephone: 317-469-2100
Fax: 317-469-9011

John L. Lisher   Donald G. Orzeske

Donald K. Broad   Christopher Hamilton

OF COUNSEL

William M. Osborn   Edward A. Straith-Miller

For full biographical listings, see the Martindale-Hubbell Law Directory

PRICE & BARKER (AV)

The Hammond Block Building, 301 Massachusetts Avenue, 46204
Telephone: 317-633-8787
Telecopier: 317-633-8797
New Albany, Indiana Office: 409 Bank Street, P.O. Box 785.
Telephone: 812-945-9151.
Fax: 812-945-6131.

PARTNERS

Henry J. Price	Jerry A. Garau
Robert G. Barker	Barbara J. Germano
Mary Arlien Findling	Larry R. Jackson
Deborah K. Pennington	

For full biographical listings, see the Martindale-Hubbell Law Directory

SOMMER & BARNARD, ATTORNEYS AT LAW, PC (AV)

4000 Bank One Tower, 111 Monument Circle, 46204-5140
Telephone: 317-630-4000
FAX: 317-236-9802
North Office: 8900 Keystone Crossing, Suite 1046, Indianapolis, Indiana, 46240-2134.
Telephone: 317-630-4000.
FAX: 317-844-4780.

William C. Barnard	Michael C. Terrell
James E. Hughes	Richard C. Richmond, III
Edward W. Harris, III	Steven C. Shockley
Gordon L. Pittenger	Debra McVicker Lynch
Gayle A. Reindl	

Representative Clients: Comerica Bank; Federal Express; Renault Automation; Kimball International; TRW, Inc.

For Complete List of Firm Personnel, See General Section

For full biographical listings, see the Martindale-Hubbell Law Directory

TABBERT HAHN EARNEST & STARKEY, P.C. (AV)

Suite 2100, One Indiana Square, 46204
Telephone: 317-639-5444
Fax: 317-639-5232

Don A. Tabbert	Lorie A. Brown
Gregory F. Hahn	Mark K. Sullivan
Lante K. Earnest	Judy M. Tyrrell
Martha T. Starkey	Susan L. Abel

OF COUNSEL

James J. Nocon	William D. Lalley
Douglas E. Cregor	

Representative Clients: Indiana National Bank; Coca-Cola Bottling Co.; Atrium Structures, Inc.; Butler Fairman & Suefert, Inc.; G.W. Pierce Auto Parts, Inc.; American Pleasure, Inc.; Daymac Construction; Country Place Apartments; Midland House, Inc.; Filmcraft Color Lab.

For full biographical listings, see the Martindale-Hubbell Law Directory

WARD & WARD (AV)

1014 Circle Tower Building, 55 Monument Circle, 46204
Telephone: 317-639-9501
Fax: 317-637-1919

(See Next Column)

WARD & WARD, *Indianapolis—Continued*

MEMBERS OF FIRM

Donald W. Ward
Charles P. Ward

For full biographical listings, see the Martindale-Hubbell Law Directory

YARLING, ROBINSON, HAMMEL & LAMB (AV)

151 North Delaware, Suite 1535, P.O. Box 44128, 46204
Telephone: 317-262-8800
Fax: 317-262-3046

MEMBERS OF FIRM

Richard W. Yarling
Charles F. Robinson, Jr.
John W. Hammel
Linda Y. Hammel
Edgar H. Lamb
Douglas E. Rogers
Mark S. Gray
Matthew C. Robinson

Representative Clients: Allstate Insurance Co.; American Family Mutual Insurance Company; Chrysler Credit Corporation; Fleet Financenter; General Motors Acceptance Corporation; Household Finance Corporation; Monroe Guaranty Insurance Company; Northbrook Property & Casualty Company; Pafco General Insurance Company; Security Pacific Finance Corporation.

For full biographical listings, see the Martindale-Hubbell Law Directory

YOSHA LADENDORF KRAHULIK & WEDDLE (AV)

Pyramid II, First Floor, 3500 West DePauw Boulevard, Suite 2015, P.O. Box 68979, 46268
Telephone: 317-334-9200
FAX: 317-228-3355

MEMBERS OF FIRM

Louis Buddy Yosha
William Levy
Mark C. Ladendorf
Jon D. Krahulik
Robert G. Weddle

ASSOCIATES

David C. Krahulik
Timothy C. Caress
Angela M. Smith
Jeff D. Oliphant

SENIOR COUNSEL

Jeffrey A. Modisett

OF COUNSEL

Irwin J. Prince
Irving L. Fink

Reference: National Bank of Indianapolis.

For full biographical listings, see the Martindale-Hubbell Law Directory

KENTLAND,* Newton Co.

BARCE & RYAN (AV)

301 East Graham Street, P.O. Box 338, 47951-0338
Telephone: 219-474-5158
Fax: 219-474-6610
Fowler, Indiana Office: 103 North Jackson Avenue, P.O. Box 252, 47944-0252.
Telephone: 317-884-0383.
Fax: 317-884-0445.

MEMBERS OF FIRM

John W. Barce
R. Steven Ryan
J. Edward Barce
(Resident at Fowler Office)

Representative Clients: USX Corporation; Metropolitan Life Insurance Company; Goodland State Bank; State Bank of Oxford; DeMotte State Bank; Newton County Stone; Northern Indiana Public Service Company; DeMeter, Inc; Town of Boswell; Town of Brook.

For Complete List of Firm Personnel, See General Section

For full biographical listings, see the Martindale-Hubbell Law Directory

LAFAYETTE,* Tippecanoe Co.

BALL, EGGLESTON, BUMBLEBURG & McBRIDE (AV)

810 Bank One Building, P.O. Box 1535, 47902
Telephone: 317-742-9046
Fax: 317-742-1966

Cable G. Ball (1904-1981)
Owen Crook (1908-1977)
Warren N. Eggleston
(1923-1991)

MEMBERS OF FIRM

Joseph T. Bumbleburg
John K. McBride
Jack L. Walkey
Michael J. Stapleton
Jeffrey J. Newell
James T. Hodson
Brian Wade Walker
Cheryl M. Knodle
Randy J. Williams

General Counsel for: The Lafayette Union Railway Co.; Bank One, Lafayette, N.A.
Representative Clients: Farmers Insurance Group; General Accident Fire & Life Assurance Corp.; City of Lafayette Board of Parks and Recreation; West Lafayette Community School Corp.; Travelers Insurance Co.; Trustees, West Lafayette Public Library.

For full biographical listings, see the Martindale-Hubbell Law Directory

HANNA & GERDE (AV)

Fifth Floor Bank & Trust Building, P.O. Box 1098, 47902
Telephone: 317-742-5005
Fax: 317-742-6490

Charles H. Robertson (1902-1982)

MEMBERS OF FIRM

George L. Hanna
Cy Gerde

OF COUNSEL

Eric H. Burns

ASSOCIATE

Mary A. Russell

Representative Client: City of Lafayette.
Reference: Lafayette Bank & Trust Co.; Salin Bank & Trust Co.

For full biographical listings, see the Martindale-Hubbell Law Directory

LAYDEN & LAYDEN (AV)

Suite 712, Bank One Building, 201 Main Street, P.O. Box 909, 47902-0909
Telephone: 317-742-7646
Email: cmlayden@holli.com

MEMBERS OF FIRM

Charles Max Layden
Lynn M. Layden

For full biographical listings, see the Martindale-Hubbell Law Directory

STUART & BRANIGIN (AV)

The Life Building, 300 Main Street, Suite 800, 47902
Telephone: 317-423-1561
Telecopier: 317-742-8175

MEMBERS OF FIRM

Allison Ellsworth Stuart
(1886-1950)
Roger D. Branigin (1902-1975)
Russell H. Hart
James V. McGlone
Larry R. Fisher
Stephen R. Pennell
Anthony S. Benton
William E. Emerick
John C. Duffey
Thomas B. Parent
Laura L. Bowker
Kevin D. Nicoson
Susan K. Roberts
John M. Stuckey
Deborah B. Trice

ASSOCIATE

Brent W. Huber

General Counsel for: The Lafayette Life Insurance Co.; INB National Bank, N.W.; Lafayette Home Hospital, Inc.
State Counsel for: Norfolk & Western Railway Co.
Mr. Ryan is Counsel to: The Trustees of Purdue University.
Representative Clients: Aluminum Company of America; Liberty Mutual Insurance Group.

For Complete List of Firm Personnel, See General Section

For full biographical listings, see the Martindale-Hubbell Law Directory

LA PORTE,* La Porte Co.

NEWBY, LEWIS, KAMINSKI & JONES (AV)

916 Lincoln Way, 46350
Telephone: 219-362-1577
Direct Line Michigan City: 219-879-6300
Fax: 219-362-2106
Mailing Address: P.O. Box 1816, La Porte, Indiana, 46352-1816

MEMBERS OF FIRM

John E. Newby (1916-1990)
Daniel E. Lewis, Jr.
Gene M. Jones
John W. Newby
Perry F. Stump, Jr.
Edward L. Volk
Mark L. Phillips
Martin W. Kus
Marsha Schatz Volk
Mark A. Lienhoop
James W. Kaminski

ASSOCIATES

William S. Kaminski
Christine A. Sulewski
David P. Jones

SENIOR COUNSEL

Leon R. Kaminski

OF COUNSEL

Daniel E. Lewis

Counsel for: U. S. F. & G. Co.; State Farm Mutual Insurance Co.; Auto Owners Insurance Co.; Liberty Mutual Insurance Co.; Sullair Corp.; La Porte Community School Corp.; United Farm Bureau Mutual Insurance Co.; Physicians Insurance of Indiana; La Porte Hospital, Inc.; Norwest Bank.

For full biographical listings, see the Martindale-Hubbell Law Directory

MARION,* Grant Co.

KILEY, KILEY, HARKER, MICHAEL & CERTAIN (AV)

300 West Third Street, P.O. Box 899, 46952-0899
Telephone: 317-664-9041
Fax: 317-664-8119

(See Next Column)

KILEY, KILEY, HARKER, MICHAEL & CERTAIN—*Continued*

MEMBERS OF FIRM

Robert Ralph Batton (1890-1963)	David L. Kiley, Sr.
Albert L. Harker (1904-1965)	Michael J. Kiley
Albert Bonner Brown (1911-1981)	Albert C. Harker
	Thomas W. Michael
	Harry J. Certain

ASSOCIATE
Therese McCullough Pryor

Counsel for: Bank One, Marion, N.A.; Liniger Co., Inc.; Atlas Foundry Co. *Local Counsel for:* GenCorp.; CPC Group; General Motors; Indiana Michigan Power Co./AEP; Indiana Bell Telephone Co.; Foster-Forbes, Division of American National Can Corp.

For full biographical listings, see the Martindale-Hubbell Law Directory

---

MERRILLVILLE, Lake Co.

BURKE, MURPHY, COSTANZA & CUPPY (AV)

Suite 600 8585 Broadway, 46410-7064
Telephone: 219-769-1313
Telecopier: 219-769-6806
East Chicago, Indiana Office: First National Bank Building. 720 West Chicago Avenue.
Telephone: 219-397-2401.
Telecopier: 219-397-0508.
Valparaiso, Indiana Office: 15 North Franklin Street, Suite 200.
Telephone: 219-531-0134.
Telecopier: 219-531-0507.
Palm Harbor, Florida Office: Suite 280, 33920 U.S. Highway 19 North.
Telephone: 813-787-7799.
Telecopier: 813-787-7237.

MEMBERS OF FIRM

Lester F. Murphy (Resident, East Chicago, Indiana and Palm Harbor, Florida Offices)	Frederick M. Cuppy
	David K. Ranich
	Kathryn D. Schmidt
David Cerven	

ASSOCIATES

Stacia L. Yoon	Kevin E. Steele

OF COUNSEL
Gregory R. Lyman

Representative Clients: NBD Bank, N.A.; Centier Bank; Whiteco Industries; Lehigh Portland Cement Company; Continental Machine & Engineering Co., Inc.; Gary Steel Products Corp.; Superior Construction Co., Inc.; Federal National Mortgage Association; Morrison Construction Co.; St. Catherine Hospital of East Chicago, Indiana; Travelers/Aetna Casualty Corporation.

For Complete List of Firm Personnel, See General Section

For full biographical listings, see the Martindale-Hubbell Law Directory

---

HODGES & DAVIS, P.C. (AV)

8700 Broadway, 46410
Telephone: 219-641-8700
Fax: 219-641-8710
Portage, Indiana Office: 6082 Lute Road. P.O. Box 1037.
Telephone: 219-762-9129.
Fax: 219-762-2826.

Clyde D. Compton	Bonnie C. Coleman
William B. Davis	Jill M. Madajczyk
Earle F. Hites	Laura B. Frost
R. Lawrence Steele	David H. Kreider
Gregory A. Sobkowski	Robert G. Vann

OF COUNSEL
Edward J. Hussey

Representative Clients: The Associated Group; Metropolitan Life Insurance Co.

For Complete List of Firm Personnel, See General Section

For full biographical listings, see the Martindale-Hubbell Law Directory

---

SPANGLER, JENNINGS & DOUGHERTY, P.C. (AV)

8396 Mississippi Street, 46410-6398
Telephone: 219-769-2323
Facsimile: 219-769-5007
Valparaiso, Indiana Office: 150 Lincolnway, Suite 3001.
Telephone: 219-462-6151.
FAX: 219-477-4935.

Ronald T. Spangler	John P. McQuillan
Harry J. Jennings	Samuel J. Bernardi, Jr. (Valparaiso Office)
Patrick J. Dougherty (Valparaiso Office)	Jon F. Schmoll
Samuel J. Furlin	Robert D. Hawk
Richard A. Mayer	Joseph E. McDonald
Jay A. Charon	Peter G. Koransky

(See Next Column)

David J. Hanson	Harold G. Hagberg
Robert P. Kennedy	Lawrence A. Kalina
Allen B. Zaremba	Robert P. Stoner
James T. McNiece	(Valparaiso Office)
Daniel A. Gioia	Gregory J. Tonner
James D. McQuillan	Kathleen M. Maicher
David L. Abel, II	Paul B. Poracky
	Robert D. Brown

Robert J. Dignam	Anthony F. Tavitas
David R. Phillips	Lloyd P. Mullen
Kristin A. Mulholland	Kisti Good Risse

Representative Clients: Allstate Insurance Cos.; Bank One, Merriville, N.A.; First National Bank of Valparaiso; Ford Motor Credit Co.; Inland Steel Co.; Munster Calumet Shopping Center; School Town of Munster; St. Paul Insurance Cos.; State Farm Cos.; Volkswagen of America.

For Complete List of Firm Personnel, See General Section

For full biographical listings, see the Martindale-Hubbell Law Directory

---

MUNSTER, Lake Co.

LAW OFFICES OF EUGENE M. FEINGOLD (AV)

625 Ridge Road, Suite A, 46321
Telephone: 219-836-8800
Fax: 219-836-8944

ASSOCIATE
Steven P. Kennedy

For full biographical listings, see the Martindale-Hubbell Law Directory

---

LAW OFFICES OF TIMOTHY F. KELLY (AV)

Suite 2A, 9250 Columbia Avenue, 46321
Telephone: 219-836-4062
Telecopier: 219-836-0167
Email: 76325.1505@Compuserve.Com

MEMBERS OF FIRM

Timothy F. Kelly	Karl K. Vanzo

ASSOCIATES

Harvey Karlovac	Steven J. Sersic

For Complete List of Firm Personnel, See General Section

For full biographical listings, see the Martindale-Hubbell Law Directory

---

PORTAGE, Porter Co.

HODGES & DAVIS, P.C. (AV)

6082 Lute Road, P.O. Box 1037, 46368
Telephone: 219-762-9129
Fax: 219-762-2826
Merrillville, Indiana Office: 8700 Broadway.
Telephone: 219-641-8700.
Fax: 219-641-8710.

Clyde D. Compton	R. Lawrence Steele
Earle F. Hites	Gregory A. Sobkowski
	Bonnie C. Coleman

Representative Clients: The Associated Group; Metropolitan Life Insurance Co.

For full biographical listings, see the Martindale-Hubbell Law Directory

---

RUSHVILLE,* Rush Co.

EARNEST, FOSTER, EDER, LEVI & NORTHAM (AV)

114 West Third Street, P.O. Box 430, 46173
Telephone: 317-932-4118
Fax: 317-932-4486

Kenneth L. Earnest (1916-1995)

OF COUNSEL
James S. Foster

MEMBERS OF FIRM

Robert J. Eder	Richard K. Levi
	David E. Northam

Representative Clients: Rush County REMC; First Federal Savings and Loan Association of Rushville; Rush Memorial Hospital; Farm Bureau Insurance Co.; Farmers State Bank; The Sampler, Inc.; Ticor Title Insurance Co.

For full biographical listings, see the Martindale-Hubbell Law Directory

---

SOUTH BEND,* St. Joseph Co.

DORAN BLACKMOND READY HAMILTON & WILLIAMS (AV)

1700 Valley American Bank Building, 211 W. Washington Street, 46601
Telephone: 219-288-1800
Fax: 219-236-4265

(See Next Column)

DORAN BLACKMOND READY HAMILTON & WILLIAMS, *South Bend—Continued*

MEMBERS OF FIRM

M. Edward Doran (1895-1982)	David T. Ready
John E. Doran	John C. Hamilton
Don G. Blackmond	A. Howard Williams

ASSOCIATE
Don Gregory Blackmond

For full biographical listings, see the Martindale-Hubbell Law Directory

JONES, OBENCHAIN, FORD, PANKOW, LEWIS & WOODS (AV)

1800 Valley American Bank Building, P.O. Box 4577, 46634
Telephone: 219-233-1194
Fax: 233-8957; 233-9675

Vitus G. Jones (1879-1951)	Roland Obenchain (Retired)
Roland Obenchain (1890-1961)	Milton A. Johnson (Retired)
Francis Jones (1907-1988)	James H. Pankow (Retired)

MEMBERS OF FIRM

Thomas F. Lewis, Jr.	Robert M. Edwards, Jr.
Timothy W. Woods	John B. Ford
John R. Obenchain	Mark J. Phillipoff
Robert W. Mysliwiec	John W. Van Laere

ASSOCIATES

Edward P. Benchik	Robert S. Sanderson
Thomas F. Lewis, III	

OF COUNSEL
G. Burt Ford

Attorneys for: American Family Insurance; The Equitable Life Assurance Society of the United States; Ohio Casualty Co.; Holy Cross Health Systems; Saint Joseph's Care Group; Koontz-Wagner Electric Co.; Old Kent Bank-Southwest; The Travelers Insurance Co.; H.G. Christman Construction Co., Inc.; Automatic Technologies.

For full biographical listings, see the Martindale-Hubbell Law Directory

EDWARD N. KALAMAROS & ASSOCIATES PROFESSIONAL CORPORATION (AV)

129 North Michigan Avenue, P.O. Box 4156, 46634
Telephone: 219-232-4801
Telecopier: 219-232-9736

Edward N. Kalamaros	Philip E. Kalamaros
Timothy J. Walsh	Sally P. Norton
Thomas F. Cohen	Kevin W. Kearney
Joseph M. Forte	Peter J. Bagiackas
Robert Deane Woods	David A. Wemhoff
Patrick J. Hinkle	Eric G. Ciesielski

Representative Clients: Liberty Mutual Insurance Co.; Employers Mutual of Wausau; Fireman's Fund American Insurance Group; U.S.F. & G.; Cincinnati Insurance Co.; Kemper Group; St. Paul Insurance Companies; Continental Loss Adjusting Services, Inc.; Orion Group.

For full biographical listings, see the Martindale-Hubbell Law Directory

ROWE, ROWE & MAHER (AV)

Suite 900 Keybank Building, 46601
Telephone: 219-233-8200
Fax: 219-234-5987

R. Kent Rowe	R. Kent Rowe, III
Timothy J. Maher	

ASSOCIATES

Gregory J. Haines	Steven D. Groth
Lee Korzan	Marie Anne Hendrie

For full biographical listings, see the Martindale-Hubbell Law Directory

TERRE HAUTE,* Vigo Co.

COX, ZWERNER, GAMBILL & SULLIVAN (AV)

511 Wabash Avenue, P.O. Box 1625, 47808-1625
Telephone: 812-232-6003
Fax: 812-232-6567

MEMBERS OF FIRM

Ernest J. Zwerner (1918-1980)	David W. Sullivan
Benjamin G. Cox (1915-1988)	Robert L. Gowdy
Gilbert W. Gambill, Jr.	Louis F. Britton
James E. Sullivan	Carroll D. Smeltzer
Benjamin G. Cox, Jr.	Jeffry A. Lind

ASSOCIATE
Ronald E. Jumps

OF COUNSEL
Robert D. Hepburn

Counsel for: Terre Haute First National Bank; Farmers Insurance Group; Indiana-American Water Co.; Indiana State University; Merchants National Bank of Terre Haute; Rose-Hulman Institute of Technology; Tribune-Star

(See Next Column)

Publishing Co., Inc.; Weston Paper & Manufacturing Co.; Equitable Life Assurance Society of U.S.; Federated Mutual Insurance Co.; Fireman's Fund; General Accident Group; Guaranty National Insurance; Milwaukee Mutual Insurance Co.; Ohio Casualty Insurance Co.; Hartford Insurance; The Travelers Co.; United Services Auto Assn.; Vernon Insurance Co.

For full biographical listings, see the Martindale-Hubbell Law Directory

WILKINSON, GOELLER, MODESITT, WILKINSON & DRUMMY (AV)

333 Ohio Street, P.O. Box 800, 47808-0800
Telephone: 812-232-4311
Fax: 812-235-5107

MEMBERS OF FIRM

Myrl O. Wilkinson	John C. Wall
Raymond H. Modesitt	Craig M. McKee
B. Curtis Wilkinson	Scott M. Kyrouac
William W. Drummy	Jeffrey A. Boyll
David P. Friedrich	

ASSOCIATE
Anthony R. Jost

Representative Clients: State Farm Mutual Automobile Insurance Company; State Farm Fire & Casualty Co.; Nationwide Insurance Company; The Country Companies; The Medical Protective Company; Physician's Insurance Company of Indiana; Indiana Insurance Companies; United Farm Bureau Mutual Insurance Company; St. Paul Insurance Companies; Prudential Insurance.

For Complete List of Firm Personnel, See General Section

For full biographical listings, see the Martindale-Hubbell Law Directory

VALPARAISO,* Porter Co.

BLACHLY, TABOR, BOZIK & HARTMAN (AV)

Suite 401 Indiana Federal Building, 46383
Telephone: 219-464-1041
Fax: 219-464-0927

MEMBERS OF FIRM

Quentin A. Blachly	David L. Hollenbeck
Glenn J. Tabor	David L. DeBoer
James S. Bozik	Thomas F. Macke
Duane W. Hartman	Randall J. Zromkoski
Richard J. Rupcich	

ASSOCIATES

Roger A. Weitgenant	Craig R. Van Schouwen

Reference: First National Bank.

For Complete List of Firm Personnel, See General Section

For full biographical listings, see the Martindale-Hubbell Law Directory

VERSAILLES,* Ripley Co.

EATON & ROMWEBER (AV)

123 South Main Street, P.O. Box 275, 47042
Telephone: 812-689-5111
Fax: 812-689-5165
Batesville, Indiana Office: 13 East George Street. Telephone 812-934-5735.
Fax: 812-934-6041.

MEMBERS OF FIRM

Larry L. Eaton	Anthony A. Romweber

ASSOCIATES

W. Gregory Coy	Eric E. Wright
	(Not admitted in IN)

For full biographical listings, see the Martindale-Hubbell Law Directory

WARSAW,* Kosciusko Co.

LEMON, ARMEY, HEARN & LEININGER (AV)

210 North Buffalo Street, P.O. Box 770, 46581-0770
Telephone: 219-268-9111
Telecopier: 219-267-8647

MEMBERS OF FIRM

Thomas R. Lemon	Daniel K. Leininger
Michael E. Armey	Jane L. Kauffman
R. Steven Hearn	Ronald B. Cassidente

ASSOCIATE
Andrea E. Halpin

OF COUNSEL
Robert L. Rasor

Representative Clients: Lake City Bank; Zimmer Inc.; The Dalton Foundries, Inc.; Grace Schools, Inc.; Kosciusko Community Hospital, Inc.; Othy, Inc.

For full biographical listings, see the Martindale-Hubbell Law Directory

Warsaw—Continued

ROCKHILL, PINNICK, PEQUIGNOT, HELM, LANDIS & RIGDON (AV)

105 East Main Street, 46580-2742
Telephone: 219-267-6116
Telecopier: 219-269-9264

MEMBERS OF FIRM

Brooks C. Pinnick	Vern K. Landis
Stanley E. Pequignot	Jay A. Rigdon
Richard K. Helm	Jamelyn E. Freeman

OF COUNSEL

Alvin T. Rockhill

Representative Clients: First National Bank of Warsaw, Warsaw, Indiana; Warsaw Times-Union Newspaper and WRSW Radio and Broadcast Station; State Farm Insurance Cos.; Warsaw Chemical Co., Inc.; Little Crow Milling Co., Inc.; Farmers State Bank; C & D Foods, Inc.; Maple Leaf Farms, Inc.; United Farm Bureau Mutual Insurance Co.

For full biographical listings, see the Martindale-Hubbell Law Directory

IOWA

CEDAR RAPIDS,* Linn Co.

LYNCH, DALLAS, SMITH & HARMAN, P.C. (AV)

526 Second Avenue SE, P.O. Box 2457, 52406-2457
Telephone: 319-365-9101
Facsimile: 319-365-9512

Donald G. Ribble	Wilford H. Stone
Scott E. McLeod	Sean W. McPartland
Robert R. Rush	Matthew J. Nagle

Representative Clients: American States Insurance Co.; Blue Cross and Blue Shield of Iowa; Connecticut General Life Insurance Company; Deere & Co.; Rockwell International Corp.; State Farm Insurance Cos.; The Travelers Insurance Cos.

For Complete List of Firm Personnel, See General Section

For full biographical listings, see the Martindale-Hubbell Law Directory

PICKENS, BARNES & ABERNATHY (AV)

Tenth Floor American Building, P.O. Box 74170, 52407-4170
Telephone: 319-366-7621
Fax: 319-366-3158

RETIRED

James F. Pickens

OF COUNSEL

Minor Barnes

MEMBERS OF FIRM

Terry J. Abernathy	Matthew G. Novak

ASSOCIATES

JoAnne M. Lilledahl	Cheryl M. Rosenberg

A list of Representative Clients furnished upon request.

For full biographical listings, see the Martindale-Hubbell Law Directory

SHUTTLEWORTH & INGERSOLL, P.C. (AV)

500 Firstar Bank Building, P.O. Box 2107, 52406-2107
Telephone: 319-365-9461
Fax: 319-365-8443
Email: si-law@inav.net

John M. Bickel	Thomas P. Peffer
Robert D. Houghton	Kevin H. Collins
Richard S. Fry	Diane Kutzko
Richard C. Garberson	Mark L. Zaiger
Steven J. Pace	Douglas R. Oelschlaeger
Glenn L. Johnson	Constance M. Alt
Kurt L. Kratovil	

Christine L. McLaughlin	William H. Courter
Nancy J. Penner	

Representative Clients: Archer-Daniels-Midland Co.; Cargill, Inc.; CIGNA Companies; CNA Insurance Companies; Fireman's Fund Insurance Companies; Firstar Bank Cedar Rapids, N.A.; General Casualty Company of Wisconsin; General Motors Corp.; Grinnell Mutual Insurance Company; IMT Insurance Company.

For Complete List of Firm Personnel, See General Section

For full biographical listings, see the Martindale-Hubbell Law Directory

COUNCIL BLUFFS,* Pottawattamie Co.

PETERS LAW FIRM, P.C. (AV)

233 Pearl Street, P.O. Box 1078, 51502-1078
Telephone: 712-328-3157
FAX: 712-328-9092

Dennis Leu	John M. McHale
Dennis M. Gray	Jacob J. Peters
Lyle W. Ditmars	Scott J. Rogers
Scott H. Peters	Jon E. Heisterkamp

Matthew G. Woods

Representative Clients: Bluffs Run Casino; Mercantile Bank, Council Bluffs, IA; Grinnell Mutual Reinsurance Co.; Iowa West Racing Association; Rockwell International; Shelter Insurance; State Farm Insurance; Kemper Group; The Pillsbury Co.; The Cities of Crescent, Glenwood, Treynor, McClelland, Underwood.

For Complete List of Firm Personnel, See General Section

For full biographical listings, see the Martindale-Hubbell Law Directory

DES MOINES,* Polk Co.

BELIN LAMSON McCORMICK ZUMBACH FLYNN, A PROFESSIONAL CORPORATION (AV)

2000 Financial Center, 50309
Telephone: 515-243-7100
Telecopier: 515-282-7615

Mark McCormick	Dennis P. Ogden
Roger T. Stetson	Edward M. Mansfield
David L. Charles	Margaret C. Callahan
Quentin R. Boyken	Robert D. Sharp
Charles F. Becker	Michael R. Reck
Mark E. Weinhardt	David K. Basler
Danielle Marie Shelton	

For Complete List of Firm Personnel, See General Section

For full biographical listings, see the Martindale-Hubbell Law Directory

FINLEY, ALT, SMITH, SCHARNBERG, MAY & CRAIG, P.C. (AV)

604 Locust Street, Fourth Floor Equitable Building, 50309
Telephone: 515-288-0145
Telecopier: 515-288-2724

Thomas A. Finley	R. Todd Gaffney
Steven K. Scharnberg	V. Glenn Goodwin, Jr.
John D. (Jack) Hilmes	Dawn R. Siebert

Pamela J. Prager	Kerry A. Finley

Representative Clients: Aetna Casualty & Surety Co.; Aetna Life Insurance Co.; ALAS; American Society of Composers, Authors and Publishers; Equitable Life Assurance Society of the U.S.; Federated Insurance Co.; Meredith Corp.
Iowa Attorneys for: Midwest Medical Insurance Co.
District Attorneys for: Norfolk & Southern Railroad; Soo Line Railroad Company.

For Complete List of Firm Personnel, See General Section

For full biographical listings, see the Martindale-Hubbell Law Directory

GREFE & SIDNEY, P.L.C. (AV)

2222 Grand Avenue, P.O. Box 10434, 50306
Telephone: 515-245-4300
Fax: 515-245-4452
Email: GRANDFIRM@AOL.COM

Ross H. Sidney	John Werner
Henry A. Harmon	Patrick J. McNulty
Claude H. Freeman	Mark W. Thomas
Stephen D. Hardy	Guy R. Cook

Andrew D. Hall	Debra L. Scorpiniti
Stephanie L. Glenn	Marcy A. O'Brien
Mark A. Schultheis	Kristin L. Bohlken

Representative Clients: Capitol Communications; Easter Enterprises, Inc.; Freeman Decorating Co.; Koehring Co.; Liberty Mutual Insurance Co.; Otis Elevator Company; Pella Corp.; State Farm Mutual Insurance Companies; United States Fidelity and Guaranty Co.

For Complete List of Firm Personnel, See General Section

For full biographical listings, see the Martindale-Hubbell Law Directory

HANSEN, McCLINTOCK & RILEY (AV)

Eighth Floor - Fleming Building, 218 Sixth Avenue, 50309
Telephone: 515-244-2141
Fax: 515-244-2931

(See Next Column)

HANSEN, McCLINTOCK & RILEY, *Des Moines—Continued*

MEMBERS OF FIRM

Haemer Wheatcraft (1904-1983)	Chester C. Woodburn, III
J. Rudolph Hansen (1904-1995)	William D. Scherle
John A. McClintock	David L. Brown
Ronald A. Riley	John E. Swanson

ASSOCIATE
James M. Ballard

Representative Clients: The St. Paul Companies; Bituminous Insurance Companies; Northwestern National Insurance Co.; The Travelers Insurance Companies; United States Aviation Insurance Group; American International Companies; Iowa Credit Union League; The McAninch Corp.; R. J. Reynolds Tobacco Co.; Brown Bros., Inc. Electrical Contractors.

For full biographical listings, see the Martindale-Hubbell Law Directory

---

HERRICK, LANGDON & LANGDON (AV)

1800 Financial Center, Seventh and Walnut, 50309
Telephone: 515-282-8150
Telecopier: 515-282-8226

MEMBERS OF FIRM

Allan A. Herrick (1896-1989)	William R. Clark, Jr.
Herschel G. Langdon	Richard N. Winders
Richard G. Langdon	Richard A. Steffen

Kermit B. Anderson

ASSOCIATE
Michael B. O'Meara

Representative Clients: Norwest Bank Iowa N.A.; The Principal Financial Group; Hy-Vee Food Stores, Inc.; Farmers Mutual Hail Insurance Co. of Iowa; CNA Health-Pro; Coregis; West Bank; Mercedes Benz; MAPCO, Inc.;

For full biographical listings, see the Martindale-Hubbell Law Directory

---

PATTERSON, LORENTZEN, DUFFIELD, TIMMONS, IRISH, BECKER & ORDWAY, L.L.P. (AV)

729 Insurance Exchange Building, 50309
Telephone: 515-283-2147
Fax: 515-283-1002

MEMBERS OF FIRM

G. O. Patterson (1914-1982)	Gregory J. Wilson
James A. Lorentzen	Jeffrey A. Boehlert
Theodore T. Duffield	Douglas A. Haag
William E. Timmons (Retired)	Charles E. Cutler
Roy M. Irish	Michael D. Huppert
F. H. Becker (Retired)	Martin C. Sprock
Gary D. Ordway	William A. Wickett
Robin L. Hermann	Frederick M. Haskins
Harry Perkins, III	Jeffrey A. Baker
Michael F. Lacey, Jr.	Janice M. Herfkens

ASSOCIATES

Coreen K. Bezdicek	Patrick V. Waldron
Michael S Jones	

Representative Clients: Allied Mutual Insurance Company; CNA Insurance Company; Chubb Insurance Group; Continental Western Insurance Co.; Farmers Insurance Group; Farmland Insurance Company; Grinnell Mutual Reinsurance Company; Hawkeye Security Insurance Company; Iowa Insurance Institute, St. Paul Fire & Marine Insurance Company.

For full biographical listings, see the Martindale-Hubbell Law Directory

---

WASKER, DORR, WIMMER & MARCOUILLER, P.C. (AV)

801 Grand Avenue, Suite 3100, 50309-8036
Telephone: 515-283-1801
Facsimile: 515-283-1802

Fred L. Dorr

Matthew D. Kern

For Complete List of Firm Personnel, See General Section

For full biographical listings, see the Martindale-Hubbell Law Directory

---

WHITFIELD & EDDY, P.L.C. (AV)

317 6th Avenue, Suite 1200 Locust at 6th, 50309-4110
Telephone: 515-288-6041
Fax: 515-246-1474

A. Roger Witke	Robert G. Bridges
Timothy J. Walker	Jaki K. Samuelson
David L. Phipps	Kevin M. Reynolds
Benjamin B. Ullem	Thomas H. Burke
Robert L. Fanter	Thomas Henderson
Bernard L. Spaeth, Jr.	George H. Frampton
Rod Kubat	Megan Manning Antenucci
William L. Fairbank	Wendy L. Carlson

(See Next Column)

Gary A. Norton	Maureen Roach Tobin
Mark V. Hanson	Jeffrey William Courter
August B. Landis	

Richard J. Kirschman	Jason M. Casini

OF COUNSEL
Dean Dutton

General Counsel for: American Life and Casualty Co.; The Statesman Group, Inc.; United Security Insurance Co.; Crum & Forster; General Motors Corp.; Old Republic Surety; Royal Insurance Co.; Tudor Insurance Co.; Western World Insurance Co.

For Complete List of Firm Personnel, See General Section

For full biographical listings, see the Martindale-Hubbell Law Directory

---

HAMPTON,* Franklin Co.

HOBSON, CADY & CADY (AV)

9 First Street S.W., 50441
Telephone: 515-456-2555
Fax: 515-456-3315

MEMBERS OF FIRM

A. J. Hobson (1903-1972)	G. Arthur Cady
	G. A. Cady, III

General Counsel for: Ag Services of America, Inc.
A list of Representative Clients will be furnished upon request.
References: First National Bank of Hampton; Liberty Bank & Trust.

For full biographical listings, see the Martindale-Hubbell Law Directory

---

IOWA CITY,* Johnson Co.

MEARDON, SUEPPEL, DOWNER & HAYES P.L.C. (AV)

122 South Linn Street, 52240
Telephone: 319-338-9222
Fax: 319-338-7250

William L. Meardon	James D. McCarragher
James P. Hayes	Thomas D. Hobart
Paul J. McAndrew, Jr.	

Charles A. Meardon	Steven A. Michalek

Representative Clients: United Technologies-Automotive; Perpetual Savings Bank; Economy Advertising Company; Metro Pavers, Inc.; League of Iowa Municipalities; Hills Bank and Trust Co.; J.M. Swank Co.; City of Muscatine; McComas-Lacina Construction Co., Inc.; Diamond Dave's Taco Company, Inc.

For Complete List of Firm Personnel, See General Section

For full biographical listings, see the Martindale-Hubbell Law Directory

---

MASON CITY,* Cerro Gordo Co.

WINSTON & BYRNE, LAWYERS, A PROFESSIONAL CORPORATION (AV)

119 Second Street, N.W., 50401
Telephone: 515-423-1913
Fax: 515-423-8998

Harold R. Winston	Michael G. Byrne

Representative Clients: Woodharbor Molding & Millworks, Inc.; Winkleman Farms, Inc.; Sparboe Iowa Corporation; Schmidt Family Farms, Inc.; First Citizen's National Bank of Mason City; Norwest Bank Iowa, N.A.

For full biographical listings, see the Martindale-Hubbell Law Directory

---

OSKALOOSA,* Mahaska Co.

POTHOVEN, BLOMGREN & STRAVERS (AV)

1201 High Avenue West, P.O. Box 1066, 52577
Telephone: 515-673-4438
Fax: 515-673-5177
Email: PBSLAW@KDSI.NET

MEMBERS OF FIRM

Marion H. Pothoven	James Q. Blomgren
Randall C. Stravers	

ASSOCIATE
Julie Bond Fisher

For full biographical listings, see the Martindale-Hubbell Law Directory

SIOUX CITY,* Woodbury Co.

HEIDMAN, REDMOND, FREDREGILL, PATTERSON, SCHATZ & PLAZA, L.L.P. (AV)

A Registered Limited Liability Partnership including Professional Corporations
701 Pierce Street, Suite 200, P.O. Box 3086, 51102
Telephone: 712-255-8838
Fax: 712-258-6714

MEMBERS OF FIRM

Marvin F. Heidman	Lance D. Ehmcke
James W. Redmond	Margaret M. Prahl
Alan E. Fredregill (P.C.)	John D. Ackerman
Charles T. Patterson	Gregg E. Williams
Kenneth C. Schatz (P.C.)	Judith A. Higgs
Thomas M. Plaza	John C. Gray
Daniel D. Dykstra	Daniel B. Shuck

Rita C. Grimm

ASSOCIATES

Ryan K. Crayne	Patrick L. Sealey
Charles E. Trullinger	John W. Gleysteen (Retired)
Edward C. Poulsen	Robert R. Eidsmoe (Retired)
Sabra K Craig	Jacob C. Gleysteen (1883-1943)

H. Clifford Harper (1891-1959)

Representative Clients: Aetna Casualty & Surety Co.; Irving F. Jensen Co., Inc.; Marian Health Center; Medical Protective Co.; John Morrell & Co.; Pig Improvement Co.; State Farm Mutual Insurance Co.; Terra International, Inc.; The Security National Bank of Sioux City; Wal-Mart Stores, Inc.

For full biographical listings, see the Martindale-Hubbell Law Directory

MAYNE & MAYNE (AV)

400 Pioneer Bank Building, 701 Pierce Street, P.O. Box 5049, 51102-5049
Telephone: 712-252-3220
Fax: 712-252-1535

MEMBERS OF FIRM

Wiley Mayne	John D. Mayne

Robert J. Pierson

Representative Clients: American Telephone & Telegraph Co.; Amoco Oil Company; Central United Life Insurance Company of America; Credit Bureau of Sioux City; Design Professionals Financial Corp.; Ford Motor Credit Company; Metz Baking Company; Podiatry Insurance Company of America; Shell Chemical Company; U.S. West Communications Company.

For Complete List of Firm Personnel, See General Section

For full biographical listings, see the Martindale-Hubbell Law Directory

WATERLOO,* Black Hawk Co.

SWISHER & COHRT, P.L.C. (AV)

528 West Fourth Street, P.O. Box 1200, 50704
Telephone: 319-232-6555
FAX: 319-232-4835

Benjamin F. Swisher (1878-1959)	J. Douglas Oberman
L. J. Cohrt (1898-1974)	Stephen J. Powell
Charles F. Swisher (1919-1986)	Jim D. DeKoster
Jeffrey J. Greenwood	Samuel C. Anderson
(1953-1995)	Robert C. Griffin
Eldon R. McCann	Kevin R. Rogers
Steven A. Weidner	Beth E. Hansen
Larry J. Cohrt	Mark F. Conway

Natalie Williams Burris

Firm is Counsel for: Koehring Corp.; Clay Equipment; Chamberlain Manufacturing Co.; Waterloo Courier.
Local Counsel for: Allied Group; John Deere Insurance; Liberty Mutual Insurance Co.

For full biographical listings, see the Martindale-Hubbell Law Directory

WEST DES MOINES, Polk Co.

LaMARCA & LANDRY, P.C. (AV)

1300 50th Street, 50266
Telephone: 515-225-2600
Fax: 515-225-8581

George A. LaMarca	Gregory W. Landry

Robert K. DuPuy

Gary G. Mattson

OF COUNSEL

Martin R. Anderson	Samuel S. Duffey

For full biographical listings, see the Martindale-Hubbell Law Directory

KANSAS

DODGE CITY,* Ford Co.

FOULSTON & SIEFKIN L.L.P. (AV)

810 Frontview, P.O. Box 1147, 67801
Telephone: 316-227-8126
Fax: 316-227-8451
Wichita, Kansas Office: 100 North Broadway, 700 Fourth Financial Center, 67202.
Telephone: 316-267-6371.
FAX: 316-267-6345.
Topeka, Kansas Office: 1515 Bank IV Tower, 534 Kansas Avenue, 66603.
Telephone: 913-233-3600.
FAX: 913-233-1610.
Member: Lex Mundi, A Global Association of 126 Independent Firms.

MEMBER OF FIRM

David J. Rebein

For Complete List of Firm Personnel, See General Section

For full biographical listings, see the Martindale-Hubbell Law Directory

KANSAS CITY,* Wyandotte Co.

HOLBROOK, HEAVEN & FAY, P.A. (AV)

757 Armstrong, P.O. Box 171927, 66117
Telephone: 913-342-2500
Fax: 913-342-0603
Merriam, Kansas Office: 6700 Antioch Street.
Telephone: 913-677-1717.
Fax: 913-677-0403.

Reid F. Holbrook	Thomas M. Sutherland
Lewis A. Heaven, Jr.	Thomas S. Busch
(Resident, Merriam Office)	(Resident, Merriam Office)
Ted F. Fay, Jr.	Kurt S. Brack
(Resident, Merriam Office)	(Resident Merriam Office)
Thomas E. Osborn	Sally A. Howard
Robert L. Kennedy	Brent G. Wright
Janet M. Simpson	Douglas G. Peterson
John D. Tongier	Daniel W. Peters
(Resident, Merriam Office)	

For Complete List of Firm Personnel, See General Section

For full biographical listings, see the Martindale-Hubbell Law Directory

McANANY, VAN CLEAVE & PHILLIPS, P.A. (AV)

Fourth Floor, 707 Minnesota Avenue, P.O. Box 171300, 66117
Telephone: 913-371-3838
Facsimile: 913-371-4722
Lenexa, Kansas Office: Suite 200, 11900 West 87th Street Parkway.
Telephone: 913-888-9000.
Facsimile: 913-888-7049.
Kansas City, Missouri Office: Suite 304, 819 Walnut Street.
Telephone: 816-556-9417.

John J. Jurcyk, Jr.	Jeanne Gorman Rau
Robert D. Benham	Robert F. Rowe, Jr.
Clifford T. Mueller	(Resident, Lenexa Office)
(Resident, Lenexa Office)	Lawrence D. Greenbaum
Daniel B. Denk	Douglas M. Greenwald
Charles A. Getto	Daniel F. Church
William P. Coates, Jr.	
(Resident, Lenexa Office)	

OF COUNSEL

Frank D. Menghini

Reference: Guaranty Bank and Trust Co.

For Complete List of Firm Personnel, See General Section

For full biographical listings, see the Martindale-Hubbell Law Directory

LENEXA, Johnson Co.

EVANS & MULLINIX, P.A. (AV)

15301 W. 87th Street, Suite 220, 66219
Telephone: 913-541-1200
Facsimile: 913-541-1010
Kansas City, Kansas Office: 1314 North 38th Street, 66102.
Telephone: 913-621-1200.
Telecopier: 913-621-1263.

Timothy J. Evans	Jo Ann Butaud
Richard C. Wallace	Luis Mata

Kristen F. Heidenreich

OF COUNSEL

Vito C. Barbieri

For full biographical listings, see the Martindale-Hubbell Law Directory

OVERLAND PARK, Johnson Co.

FISHER, PATTERSON, SAYLER & SMITH, L.L.P. (AV)

11050 Roe Avenue, Suite 210, 66211
Telephone: 913-339-6757
FAX: 913-339-6187
Topeka, Kansas Office: 534 South Kansas Avenue, Suite 400, P.O. Box 949, 66601.
Telephone: 913-232-7761.
Fax: 913-232-6604.

MEMBERS OF FIRM

Edwin Dudley Smith (Resident)   Michael K. Seck (Resident)
David P. Madden (Resident)

ASSOCIATE

Patrick G. Reavey (Resident)

For full biographical listings, see the Martindale-Hubbell Law Directory

RISJORD & JAMES, P.C. (AV)

Suite 100, 10680 Barkley, 66212
Telephone: 913-381-5151
Fax: 913-381-2569

Randy W. James   Aaron N. Woods

RETIRED

John C. Risjord

For full biographical listings, see the Martindale-Hubbell Law Directory

SHAMBERG, JOHNSON & BERGMAN, CHARTERED (AV)

Suite 355, 4551 West 107th Street, 66207
Telephone: 913-642-0600
Fax: 913-642-9629
Kansas City, Kansas Office: Suite 860, New Brotherhood Building, 8th and State Streets.
Telephone: 913-281-1900.
Kansas City, Missouri Office: Suite 205, Scarritt Arcade Building, 819 Walnut.
Telephone: 816-556-9431.

Lynn R. Johnson   Victor A. Bergman
John M. Parisi

Steven G. Brown   Anthony L. DeWitt
Steve N. Six   (Not admitted in KS)
Patrick A. Hamilton

OF COUNSEL

John E. Shamberg

For full biographical listings, see the Martindale-Hubbell Law Directory

*TOPEKA,** Shawnee Co.

BENNETT & DILLON, L.L.P. (AV)

1605 Southwest 37th Street, 66611
Telephone: 913-267-5063
Fax: 913-267-2652

MEMBERS OF FIRM

Mark L. Bennett, Jr.   Wilburn Dillon, Jr.
Ann L. Hoover

Representative Clients: St. Louis Southwestern Railway Co.; Denver and Rio Grande Western Railroad Co.; Sears Roebuck and Company; Zenith Electronics, Inc.; St. Paul Insurance Co.; Kansas Medical Mutual Insurance Co.; Kansas Bankers Surety Co.; Burlington Northern Santa Fe Railway Co.; Kyle Railroad Co.
Reference: Silver Lake State Bank.

For Complete List of Firm Personnel, See General Section

For full biographical listings, see the Martindale-Hubbell Law Directory

DAVIS, UNREIN, HUMMER & BUCK, L.L.P. (AV)

100 East Ninth Street, Third Floor, P.O. Box 3575, 66601-3575
Telephone: 913-354-1100
Fax: 913-354-1113

MEMBERS OF FIRM

Byron M. Gray (1901-1986)   J. Franklin Hummer
Maurice D. Freidberg   Mark A. Buck
  (1902-1965)   James B. Biggs
Charles L. Davis, Jr.   Christopher M. Rohrer
  (1921-1992)   Brenda L. Head
Michael J. Unrein   Eric I. Unrein

OF COUNSEL

Gary D. McCallister

Representative Clients: Adams Business Forms; Bettis Asphalt Co., Inc.; Blue Cross & Blue Shield of Kansas; Famous Brands; Jostens, Inc.; Kansas Association of Realtors; McElroys, Inc.; McPherson Contractors; J.R. Nulty Construction.

(See Next Column)

For full biographical listings, see the Martindale-Hubbell Law Directory

FISHER, PATTERSON, SAYLER & SMITH, L.L.P. (AV)

534 South Kansas Avenue, Suite 400, P.O. Box 949, 66601
Telephone: 913-232-7761
Fax: 913-232-6604
Overland Park, Kansas Office: 11050 Roe Avenue, Suite 210, 66211.
Telephone: 913-339-6757.
Fax: 913-339-6187.

MEMBERS OF FIRM

Donald Patterson   Steve R. Fabert
Edwin Dudley Smith (Resident,   Ronald J. Laskowski
  Overland Park Office)   Michael K. Seck (Resident,
Larry G. Pepperdine   Overland Park Office)
James P. Nordstrom   David P. Madden (Resident,
Justice B. King   Overland Park Office)
J. Steven Pigg   Steven K. Johnson

ASSOCIATES

Kristine A. Larscheid   Billy E. Newman
Patrick G. Reavey (Resident,   David R. Cooper
  Overland Park Office)

OF COUNSEL

David H. Fisher

RETIRED

Charles Keith Sayler (Retired)

Representative Clients: Gage Shopping Center, Inc.; Fireman's Fund-American Insurance Cos.; United States Fidelity and Guaranty Co.; The Procter & Gamble Company; American Cyanamid Company; Commercial Union Insurance Companies; National Casualty/Scottsdale Insurance Co.; The Hartford; Berkshire Hathaway Companies.

For full biographical listings, see the Martindale-Hubbell Law Directory

GOODELL, STRATTON, EDMONDS & PALMER, L.L.P. (AV)

515 South Kansas Avenue, 66603-3999
Telephone: 913-233-0593
Telecopier: 913-233-8870
Email: GSEP@CJNETWORKS.COM

MEMBERS OF FIRM

Gerald L. Goodell   Patrick M. Salsbury
Wayne T. Stratton   Les E. Diehl
Arthur E. Palmer   David E. Bruns
Harold S. Youngentob   N. Larry Bork
Charles R. Hay   John D. Ensley
                Catherine M. Walberg

ASSOCIATES

Steve A Schwarm   Anne M. Kindling

SPECIAL COUNSEL

Marta Fisher Linenberger   Curtis J. Waugh

Counsel for: Farm Bureau Mutual Insurance Co.; Metropolitan Life Insurance Co.; St. Paul Fire & Marine Insurance Co.; American Home Life Insurance Co.; Columbian National Title Insurance Co.; The Menninger Foundation; Ford Motor Credit Co.; Kansas Medical Mutual Insurance Co.; National Farmers Union Property and Casualty Co.

For Complete List of Firm Personnel, See General Section

For full biographical listings, see the Martindale-Hubbell Law Directory

EUGENE B. RALSTON & ASSOCIATES, P.A. (AV)

2913 Southwest Maupin Lane, 66614-4139
Telephone: 913-273-8002
FAX: 913-273-0744
Email: ERalston@AOL.Com

Eugene B. Ralston

Kevin L. Diehl   Ronald P. Pope

LEGAL SUPPORT PERSONNEL

PARALEGALS

Barbara Cobuluis   Katrina Windholz
Teresa McLinn   Corri Wecker
                Bonnie Price

PRIVATE INVESTIGATOR

Jack L. Grant

For full biographical listings, see the Martindale-Hubbell Law Directory

WRIGHT, HENSON, SOMERS, SEBELIUS, CLARK & BAKER, LLP (AV)

Commerce Bank Building, 100 Southeast Ninth Street, 2nd Floor, P.O. Box 3555, 66601-3555
Telephone: 913-232-2200
FAX: 913-232-3344

(See Next Column)

WRIGHT, HENSON, SOMERS, SEBELIUS, CLARK & BAKER LLP—*Continued*

MEMBERS OF FIRM

Thomas E. Wright   Bruce J. Clark
K. Gary Sebelius   Anne Lamborn Baker
Evelyn Zabel Wilson

ASSOCIATES

Michael M. Walker   Donald Sutsu Lee

Representative Clients: Continental Insurance Companies; American Family Insurance Companies; Shelter Insurance Companies; Newtek, Inc.; Phico Group; Insurance Co.; Kansas Bankers Association; Western Resources, Inc.; KPL/Gas Service Co.; Payless ShoeSource, Inc.

For Complete List of Firm Personnel, See General Section

For full biographical listings, see the Martindale-Hubbell Law Directory

---

WICHITA,* Sedgwick Co.

ADAMS, JONES, ROBINSON AND MALONE, CHARTERED (AV)

600 Market Centre, 155 North Market, P.O. Box 1034, 67201-1034
Telephone: 316-265-8591
Telecopier: 316-265-9719
Email: ajrm@southwind.net *URL:* http://www2.southwind.net/~ajrm

Clifford L. Malone   Mert F. Buckley
Philip L. Bowman   Monte Vines
Donald W. Bostwick   Teresa J. James
                Larry D. Spurgeon

OF COUNSEL

John S. Seeber

SPECIAL COUNSEL

John T. Conlee   William F. Kluge, III

Representative Clients: Mid Continent Federal Savings Bank; INTRUST Bank, NA; Bank IV, Kansas, NA; First Bank, fsb; Travelers Insurance Co.; Williams Natural Gas Co.; City of Wichita; Ameri-Kart Corp.; A.O. Smith Corp.; Reliance National Insurance Co.

For full biographical listings, see the Martindale-Hubbell Law Directory

---

DEPEW AND GILLEN, L.L.C. (AV)

151 North Main, Suite 700, 67202-1408
Telephone: 316-265-9621
Facsimile: 316-265-3819
Email: d-g@southwind.net

Spencer L. Depew   David W. Nickel
Dennis L. Gillen   Nicholas S. Daily
Randall K. Rathbun   David E. Rogers
Jack Scott McInteer   Charles C. Steincamp

For full biographical listings, see the Martindale-Hubbell Law Directory

---

FOULSTON & SIEFKIN L.L.P. (AV)

700 Fourth Financial Center, 67202
Telephone: 316-267-6371
Facsimile: 316-267-6345
Topeka, Kansas Office: 1515 Bank IV Tower, 534 Kansas Avenue, 66603.
Telephone: 913-233-3600.
Fax: 913-233-1610.
Dodge City, Kansas Office: 810 Frontview, P.O. Box 1147, 67801.
Telephone: 316-227-8126.
Fax: 316-227-8451.
Member: Lex Mundi, A Global Association of 126 Independent Firms.

MEMBERS OF FIRM

Robert L. Howard   Gary L. Ayers
Mikel L. Stout   Wyatt M. Wright
Richard D. Ewy   J. Steven Massoni
Darrell L. Warta   Jeffery A. Jordan
James M. Armstrong   Trisha A. Thelen
Mary Kathleen Babcock   Craig W. West
                Carol A. Beier

For Complete List of Firm Personnel, See General Section

For full biographical listings, see the Martindale-Hubbell Law Directory

---

HERSHBERGER, PATTERSON, JONES & ROTH, L.C. (AV)

600 Hardage Center, 100 South Main, 67202-3779
Telephone: 316-263-7583
Fax: 316-263-7595

Jerome E. Jones   John A. Vetter
Robert J. Roth   David J. Morgan
William R. Smith   Ken W. Dannenberg
J. Michael Kennalley   Tracy A. Applegate

(See Next Column)

OF COUNSEL

H. E. Jones   John L. Kratzer, Jr.

Counsel for: First National Bank in Wichita; Anadarko Petroleum Corporation; Chinese Industries; Mobil Oil Corp.; CNA Insurance; Royal Exchange Group; Central National Insurance Group; Transamerica Insurance Group; Northwestern National Insurance Group.

For Complete List of Firm Personnel, See General Section

For full biographical listings, see the Martindale-Hubbell Law Directory

---

KAHRS, NELSON, FANNING, HITE & KELLOGG, L.L.P. (AV)

Suite 630, 200 West Douglas Street, 67202-3089
Telephone: 316-265-7761
Telecopier: 316-267-7803

MEMBERS OF FIRM

Richard C. Hite   Scott J. Gunderson
Richard L. Honeyman   Randy Troutt
Larry A. Withers   Arthur S. Chalmers
Steven D. Gough   Marc A. Powell
                Forrest James Robinson, Jr.

ASSOCIATES

J. Scott Pohl   Jeffrey R. Emerson
                Lisa Adrian McPherson

OF COUNSEL

H. W. Fanning

Representative Clients: ABF Freight System, Inc.; American Telephone & Telegraph Co.; Amoco Production Co.; General Motors Corp.; Michelin Tire Corp.; St. Paul Insurance Co.; United States Fidelity and Guaranty Co.; Wal-mart Stores, Inc.

For Complete List of Firm Personnel, See General Section

For full biographical listings, see the Martindale-Hubbell Law Directory

---

MORRIS, LAING, EVANS, BROCK & KENNEDY, CHARTERED (AV)

Fourth Floor, 200 West Douglas, 67202-3084
Telephone: 316-262-2671
Fax: 316-262-6226; 262-5991
Topeka, Kansas Office: 800 S.W. Jackson, Suite 914, 66612-2214.
Telephone: 913-232-2662.
Fax: 913-232-9983.

Joseph W. Kennedy   Michael Lennen
Ken M. Peterson   Jana Deines Abbott
Richard D. Greene   Richard F. Hayse
Dennis M. Feeney   (Resident, Topeka Office)
Jeffery L. Carmichael   Thomas R. Docking
Robert W. Coykendall   Diane S. Worth
Susan R. Schrag   Tim J. Moore
Robert E. Nugent   Bruce A. Ney

References: The Emprise Banks of Kansas; Mercantile Bank of Topeka; Southwest National Bank; Twin Lakes National Bank.

For Complete List of Firm Personnel, See General Section

For full biographical listings, see the Martindale-Hubbell Law Directory

---

YOUNG, BOGLE, McCAUSLAND, WELLS & CLARK, P.A. (AV)

106 West Douglas, Suite 923, 67202
Telephone: 316-265-7841
Facsimile: 316-265-3956

Glenn D. Young, Jr.   William A. Wells
Jerry D. Bogle   Kenneth M. Clark
Paul S. McCausland   Patrick C. Blanchard
                Mark R. Maloney

OF COUNSEL

Orlin L. Wagner

Representative Clients: Bridgestone/Firestone, Inc.; Deere & Co.; GAF Corp.; Sears Roebuck & Co.; Deere Credit Services, Inc.; Horace Mann Insurance, Co.; Straightline Manufacturing, Inc.; Lida Advertising.

For full biographical listings, see the Martindale-Hubbell Law Directory

---

KENTUCKY

ASHLAND, Boyd Co.

MARTIN, PICKLESIMER, JUSTICE & VINCENT (AV)

431 Sixteenth Street, P.O. Box 2528, 41105-2528
Telephone: 606-329-8338
Fax: 606-325-8199

Richard W. Martin   David Justice
Max D. Picklesimer   John F. Vincent

(See Next Column)

MARTIN, PICKLESIMER, JUSTICE & VINCENT, *Ashland—Continued*

ASSOCIATES

Thomas Wade Lavender, II   Brian Leslie Hewlett

Representative Clients: City of Ashland; FIVCO Area Development District; Boyd County Sanitation District No. 2; Mid-America Distributors, Inc. *Insurance Counsel for:* State Farm Mutual Automobile Insurance Co.; State Farm Fire and Casualty Co.; Aetna Casualty Insurance Co.; Grange Mutual Insurance Co.; Great American Insurance Co.

For full biographical listings, see the Martindale-Hubbell Law Directory

---

BOWLING GREEN,* Warren Co.

BELL, ORR, AYERS & MOORE, P.S.C. (AV)

1010 College Street, P.O. Box 738, 42102-0738
Telephone: 502-781-8111
Telecopier: 502-781-9027

Chas. R. Bell (1891-1976)	Kevin C. Brooks
Joe B. Orr (1914-1987)	Timothy L. Mauldin
Reginald L. Ayers	Barton D. Darrell
Ray B. Buckberry, Jr.	Timothy L. Edelen
Quinten B. Marquette	Douglas W. Gott
George E. Strickler, Jr.	David T. Sparks

Stacey Johnson Hughes

General Counsel for: First American National Bank of Kentucky; Farm Credit Services of Mid-America, ACA.; Houchens Industries, Inc. (Food Markets and Shopping Centers); Warren County Board of Education; Bowling Green Municipal Utilities.
Representative Clients: Chicago Title Insurance Co.; Commonwealth Land Title Insurance Co.; Kentucky Farm Bureau Mutual Insurance Co.; Martin Automotive Group; Home Insurance Group.

For full biographical listings, see the Martindale-Hubbell Law Directory

---

COLE, MOORE & BAKER (AV)

921 College Street-Phoenix Place, P.O. Box 10240, 42102-7240
Telephone: 502-782-6666
FAX: 502-782-8666

MEMBERS OF FIRM

John David Cole	Frank Hampton Moore, Jr.
	Matthew J. Baker

ASSOCIATES

Dov Moore	John David Cole, Jr.
C. Terrell Miller	Stefan R. Hughes

OF COUNSEL

Frank R. Goad

Counsel for: Western Kentucky Cola-Cola Bottling Co.; Clark Distributing Co., Inc.; Scotty's Contracting & Stone Co.
Local Counsel for: General Electric Co.; Bucyrus-Erie Company; Wal-Mart Stores, Inc.; Kroger/Country Oven.
Representative Insurance Clients: Liberty Mutual Insurance Co.; Travelers Insurance Co.; Wausau Insurance Co.

For full biographical listings, see the Martindale-Hubbell Law Directory

---

ENGLISH, LUCAS, PRIEST & OWSLEY (AV)

1101 College Street, P.O. Box 770, 42102-0770
Telephone: 502-781-6500
Telecopier: 502-782-7782
Email: inquiry@elpo.com

MEMBERS OF FIRM

Charles E. English	Murry A. Raines
James H. Lucas	Kurt W. Maier
Whayne C. Priest, Jr.	Charles E. English, Jr.
Michael A. Owsley	D. Gaines Penn

ASSOCIATES

Robert A. Young	Marc Allen Lovell
W. Cravens Priest, III	Regina Abrams

Jason P. Wright

General Counsel for: Medical Center at Bowling Green; Bowling Green Independent School District; Warren Rural Electric Cooperative Corporation; Trans Financial Bank, N.A.
Representative Clients: Commercial Union Insurance Cos.; Kemper Insurance Group; St. Paul Insurance Co.; Eaton Corp.; Desa International; Sumitomo Electric Wiring Systems, Inc.

For Complete List of Firm Personnel, See General Section

For full biographical listings, see the Martindale-Hubbell Law Directory

---

HARLIN & PARKER, P.S.C. (AV)

519 East Tenth Street, P.O. Box 390, 42102-0390
Telephone: 502-842-5611
Telefax: 502-842-2607

(See Next Column)

William Jerry Parker	Jerry A. Burns
James David Bryant	Scott Charles Marks
Michael Kirby Smith	

OF COUNSEL

Maxey B. Harlin   Jo T. Orendorf

Representative Clients: General Motors Corp.; Ford Motor Co.; Chrysler Corp.; The Goodyear Tire and Rubber Co.; CSX Transportation, Inc.; Bell-South Communications, Inc.; CNA Insurance Companies; Maryland Casualty Company; American International Group; Sears Roebuck & Company.

For Complete List of Firm Personnel, See General Section

For full biographical listings, see the Martindale-Hubbell Law Directory

---

HUDDLESTON & REED (AV)

1032 College Street, P.O. Box 2130, 42102-2130
Telephone: 502-781-9870
Fax: 502-842-1659
Cave City, Kentucky: 210 Broadway, P.O. 810, 42127.
Telephone: 502-773-5511.
Fax: 502-773-5510.

MEMBERS OF FIRM

Philip I. Huddleston	Lee Huddleston
	Jeffrey A. Reed

Representative Clients: Dow Corning Corp.; Borg Warner Corp.; HFC Commercial Realty, Inc.; South Central Banks; Autotruck Federal Credit Union; Acceptance Insurance Company.

For full biographical listings, see the Martindale-Hubbell Law Directory

---

KERRICK, GRISE & STIVERS (AV)

1025 State Street, P.O. Box 9547, 42102-9547
Telephone: 502-782-8160
Fax: 502-782-5856
Elizabethtown, Kentucky Office: 2935 Dolphin Drive, Suite 102.
Telephone: 502-769-5788.
Fax: 502-737-9285.

MEMBERS OF FIRM

Thomas N. Kerrick	Gregory N. Stivers
John R. Grise	H. Brent Brennenstuhl

ASSOCIATES

Lanna Martin Kilgore	Shawn Rosso Alcott
Laura M. Hagan (Resident, Elizabethtown Office)	Jason B. Bell

Representative Clients: Dollar General Corp.; Columbia Greenview Regional Hospital; Hospital Corporation of America; Monarch Environmental, Inc.; Western Kentucky University; Cincinnati Insurance Co.; Kentucky Hospital Association Trust; Kentucky Medical Insurance Co.; Nationwide Insurance Co.; Anthem Casualty Insurance Group.

For full biographical listings, see the Martindale-Hubbell Law Directory

---

COVINGTON, Kenton Co.

ADAMS, BROOKING, STEPNER, WOLTERMANN & DUSING (AV)

421 Garrard Street, P.O. Box 861, 41012
Telephone: 606-291-7270
Fax: 606-291-7902
Florence, Kentucky Office: 8100 Burlington Pike, Suite 400, 41042.
Telephone: 606-371-6220.
Fax: 606-371-8341.

Donald L. Stepner	Dennis R. Williams
James G. Woltermann (Resident at Florence Office)	(Resident at Florence Office)
Gerald F. Dusing (Resident at Florence Office)	James R. Kruer
	Jeffrey C. Mando

ASSOCIATES

Marc D. Dietz (Resident at Florence Office)	John S. "Brook" Brooking (Resident at Florence Office)
Gregory S. Shumate	Stacey L. Graus

Representative Clients: Balluff, Inc., Wampler, Inc., Kisters, Inc., Krauss-Maffei, Inc., A group of German companies; State Automobile Mutual Insurance Co.; Chevron of California; Great American Insurance Co.; Grange Mutual Insurance Co.; Meridian Mutual Insurance Co.; Fifth-Third Bank of Northern Ky.; Northern Kentucky University; ITT Hartford.

For Complete List of Firm Personnel, See General Section

For full biographical listings, see the Martindale-Hubbell Law Directory

---

ROBERT C. CETRULO, P.S.C. (AV)

The Cetrulo Building, 620 Washington Street, 41011
Telephone: 606-491-6200
FAX: 606-491-6201

Robert C. Cetrulo

Representative Clients: Atlanta Casualty Insurance Co.; Celina Insurance Group; Commercial Union Assurance Cos.; Fireman's Fund; Dairyland Insurance Co.; Gates Rubber Co.; Greyhound Lines, Inc.; Kentucky Insurance

(See Next Column)

ROBERT C. CETRULO, P.S.C.—*Continued*

Guaranty Assn.; Universal Underwriters Insurance Co.; Zurich-American Insurance Cos.

For full biographical listings, see the Martindale-Hubbell Law Directory

O'HARA, RUBERG, TAYLOR, SLOAN AND SERGENT (AV)

Suite 209 C, Thomas More Park, P.O. Box 17411, 41017-0411
Telephone: 606-331-2000
Fax: 606-578-3365

MEMBERS OF FIRM

John J. O'Hara	David B. Sloan
Robert E. Ruberg	Gary J. Sergent
Arnold S. Taylor	Michael K. Ruberg
Donald J. Ruberg	Michael O'Hara

ASSOCIATE

Suzanne Cassidy

Representative Clients: Union Light, Heat & Power Co., Legal Dept.; American States Insurance Co.; American Hardware Mutual Indemnity Co.; Hartford Insurance Co.; Ohio Casualty Co.; Kenton County Board of Education; Zurich-American Insurance Co.; Celina Insurance Co.; The Huntington National Bank of Covington, Ky.; Jefferson Insurance Co.

For full biographical listings, see the Martindale-Hubbell Law Directory

ROBERT E. SANDERS AND ASSOCIATES, P.S.C. (AV)

The Charles H. Fisk House, 1017 Russell Street, 41011
Telephone: 606-491-3000
Fax: 606-655-4642
Email: 74762.3055@compuserve.com

Robert E. Sanders

Julie Lippert Duncan	Peggy A. Murphy
Lisa Pruitt Thorner	

LEGAL SUPPORT PERSONNEL

Shirley L. Sanders	Sandra A. Head
Sheila D. Rachal	

For full biographical listings, see the Martindale-Hubbell Law Directory

TALIAFERRO AND MEHLING (AV)

1005 Madison Avenue, P.O. Box 468, 41012-0468
Telephone: 606-291-9900
Fax: 606-291-3014

MEMBERS OF FIRM

Philip Taliaferro, III	Christopher J. Mehling
Lucinda C. Shirooni	

ASSOCIATES

C. Houston Ebert	Howard L. Tankersley
Alice G. Keys	

OF COUNSEL

Robert W. Carran	Norbert J. Bischoff
F. Edward Worland, Jr.	

For full biographical listings, see the Martindale-Hubbell Law Directory

WARE, BRYSON, WEST & KUMMER (AV)

157 Barnwood Drive, 41017
Telephone: 606-341-0255
FAX: 606-341-1876

MEMBERS OF FIRM

Rodney S. Bryson	Greg D. Voss
Larry C. West	Robert B. Cetrulo
John R. Kummer	Susanne M. Cetrulo
Mark W. Howard	David W. Martin

ASSOCIATES

W. L. (Skip) Hammons, Jr.	Orie S. Ware (1882-1974)
James M. West	William O. Ware (1908-1961)
James C. Ware (1913-1991)	

Attorneys for: First National Bank of Northern Ky.; State Farm Insurance Co.; Reliance Insurance Group; Maryland Casualty Insurance Co.; Kemper Insurance Co.; Prudential Insurance Co.; State Farm Fire & Casualty Insurance Co.; Shelby Mutual Insurance Co.; Cincinnati Insurance Co.

For full biographical listings, see the Martindale-Hubbell Law Directory

DANVILLE,* Boyle Co.

LAW OFFICES OF KENT MASTERSON BROWN (AV)

304 West Main Street, Suite 201, 40422
Telephone: 606-238-7383
Fax: 606-238-7442

ASSOCIATE

Christopher J. Shaughnessy

For full biographical listings, see the Martindale-Hubbell Law Directory

FLORENCE, Boone Co.

ADAMS, BROOKING, STEPNER, WOLTERMANN & DUSING (AV)

8100 Burlington Pike, Suite 400, 41042-0576
Telephone: 606-371-6220
Fax: 606-371-8341
Covington, Kentucky Office: 421 Garrard Street.
Telephone: 606-291-7270.
Fax: 606-291-7902.

Donald L. Stepner	Gerald F. Dusing (Resident)
James G. Woltermann	Michael M. Sketch (Resident)
(Resident)	Dennis R. Williams (Resident)

ASSOCIATE

Stacey L. Graus

Representative Clients: State Automobile Mutual Insurance Co.; Standard Oil Co. (Ky.); Great American Insurance Co.; Grange Mutual Insurance Co.; Meridian Mutual Insurance Co.; Fifth-Third Bank of Boone County; Northern Kentucky University.

For Complete List of Firm Personnel, See General Section

For full biographical listings, see the Martindale-Hubbell Law Directory

FRANKLIN,* Simpson Co.

STEERS & STEERS, P.S.C. (AV)

211 South College Street, P.O. Box 447, 42135-0447
Telephone: 502-586-4466
Telecopier: 502-586-4467

Roy L. Steers (1917-1980)	R. Lee Steers, Jr.
Kimberly J. Burns	

For full biographical listings, see the Martindale-Hubbell Law Directory

GLASGOW,* Barren Co.

HERBERT & HERBERT (AV)

135 North Public Square, P.O. Box 1000, 42141
Telephone: 502-651-9000
Fax: 502-651-3317
Email: h&hlaw@glasgow-ky.com

MEMBERS OF FIRM

H. Jefferson Herbert, Jr.	Betty Reece Herbert

Representative Clients: Eaton Corp.; Fireman's Fund Insurance Companies; Glasgow Foods, Inc.; Alliance Corp. (Construction); Indiana Insurance Co.; Kentucky Hospital Association Trust; Wininger Oil Co.; Supreme Mills, Inc.; T.J. Samson Community Hospital, Inc.; Travelers Insurance Co.

For full biographical listings, see the Martindale-Hubbell Law Directory

HENDERSON,* Henderson Co.

DEEP & WOMACK (AV)

790 Bob Posey Street, P.O. Box 50, 42420
Telephone: 502-827-2522
Fax: 502-826-2870
Louisville, Kentucky Office: 1228 Starks Building, 455 South Fourth Avenue. P.O. Box 70033, 40270-0033.
Telephone: 502-589-2530.
Fax: 502-589-9297.

MEMBERS OF FIRM

Charles David Deep	James G. Womack
Zack N. Womack	Toni Cline Renfro
	(Resident, Louisville Office)

For full biographical listings, see the Martindale-Hubbell Law Directory

KING, DEEP AND BRANAMAN (AV)

127 North Main Street, P.O. Box 43, 42420
Telephone: 502-827-1852
FAX: 502-826-7729

MEMBERS OF FIRM

Leo King (1893-1982)	Harry L. Mathison, Jr.
William M. Deep (1920-1990)	W. Mitchell Deep, Jr.
William Branaman	H. Randall Redding
Dorin E. Luck	

ASSOCIATES

Leslie M. Newman	Greg L. Gager

Counsel for: Allstate Insurance; MMI; Community United Methodist Hospital; Thompson International; Reynolds Metals Co.; Scott Lumber Co., Inc.; Westerfield Insurance Cos.; Grange Mutual Insurance Co.; Indiana Lumbermen.

For full biographical listings, see the Martindale-Hubbell Law Directory

LEXINGTON, Fayette Co.

BOEHL STOPHER & GRAVES (AV)

444 West Second Street, 40508
Telephone: 606-252-6721
FAX: 606-253-1445
Louisville, Kentucky Office: Suite 2300, Providian Center, 400 West Market Street.
Telephone: 502-589-5980.
Fax: 502-561-9400.
Paducah, Kentucky Office: Suite 340 Executive Inn Riverfront, One Executive Boulevard.
Telephone: 502-442-4369.
Fax: 502-442-4689.
Prestonsburg, Kentucky Office: 105 West Court Street.
Telephone: 606-886-8004.
Fax: 606-886-9579.
New Albany, Indiana Office: Elsby East, Suite 204, 400 Pearl Street.
Telephone: 812-948-5053.
Fax: 812-948-9233.

RESIDENT PARTNERS

W. T. Adkins	Steven G. Kinkel
Nolan Carter, Jr.	Kim Martin Wilkie
Gregory K. Jenkins	Guillermo A. Carlos
Ronald L. Green	James B. Cooper

RESIDENT ASSOCIATES

Steven R. Armstrong	Patrick J. Murphy, II
Michael J. Cox	Brennen C. Ragone
Fredrick A. Bailey, Jr.	

Counsel for: Ford Motor Co.; Texas Eastern Transmission Corp.; Coca-Cola Bottling Co.; National Collegiate Athletic Assn.; Hartford Accident and Indemnity Co.; Continental Insurance Group; St. Paul Fire & Marine Insurance Co.; Lloyds of London; Old Republic Insurance Co.

For full biographical listings, see the Martindale-Hubbell Law Directory

BROCK, BROCK & BAGBY (AV)

190 Market Street, P.O. Box 1630, 40592-1630
Telephone: 606-255-7000
Fax: 606-255-6198

MEMBERS OF FIRM

Walter L. Brock, Jr. (1918-1995)	Glen S. Bagby
Daniel N. Brock	J. Robert Lyons, Jr.

ASSOCIATES

Bruce A. Rector	Jane Hampton Herrick

LEGAL SUPPORT PERSONNEL
PARALEGALS

Pamela H. Brown	Freda Greer Grubbs

For full biographical listings, see the Martindale-Hubbell Law Directory

KINKEAD & COLLIER (AV)

201 West Vine Street, 40507
Telephone: 606-233-3550
Facsimile: 606-255-1965

MEMBERS OF THE FIRM

Shelby C. Kinkead, Jr.	Wayne F. Collier

Representative Clients: Aetna Life Insurance Co.; CNA Insurance Co.; 3 M Companies; LTD; Florida Power; Bank One Lexington NA; First National Bank and Trust; R.J. Corman Railroad Companies; Maxus Energy Corporation; Kentucky Central Insurance; Shoney's Inc.

For full biographical listings, see the Martindale-Hubbell Law Directory

LANDRUM & SHOUSE (AV)

106 West Vine Street, P.O. Box 951, 40588-0951
Telephone: 606-255-2424
Facsimile: 606-233-0308
Louisville, Kentucky Office: 400 West Market Street, Suite 1550, 40202.
Telephone: 502-589-7616.
Facsimile: 502-589-2119.

MEMBERS OF FIRM

John H. Burrus	Mark J. Hinkel
Thomas M. Cooper	Delores Hill Pregliasco
William C. Shouse	(Resident, Louisville Office)
Pierce W. Hamblin	John Garry McNeill
Mark L. Moseley	Jack E. Toliver
Leslie Patterson Vose	R. Kent Westberry
John R. Martin, Jr.	(Resident, Louisville Office)
(Resident, Louisville Office)	J. Denis Ogburn
Larry C. Deener	(Resident, Louisville Office)
Sandra Mendez Dawahare	Jane Durkin Samuel
Douglas L. Hoots	

(See Next Column)

ASSOCIATES

Stephen D. Milner	Daniel E. Murner
Stephen R. Chappell	Courtney T. Baxter
Dave Whalin	(Resident, Louisville Office)
(Resident, Louisville Office)	Frank M. Jenkins, III

OF COUNSEL

Weldon Shouse

District Attorneys: CSX Transportation, Inc.
Special Trial Counsel: Ford Motor Co. and Affiliates (Eastern Kentucky); Clark Equipment Co.
Representative Clients: The Continental Insurance Cos.; U.S. Insurance Group; U.S. Fidelity & Guaranty Co.; Ohio Casualty Insurance Co.; CIGNA; Royal Insurance Cos.

For Complete List of Firm Personnel, See General Section

For full biographical listings, see the Martindale-Hubbell Law Directory

McCOY, BAKER & WEST (AV)

309 North Broadway, 40507
Telephone: 606-254-6363
FAX: 606-233-4234

MEMBERS OF FIRM

R. Burl McCoy, Jr.	Michael D. Baker
John Kevin West	

Charles E. Beal, II

For full biographical listings, see the Martindale-Hubbell Law Directory

MILLER, GRIFFIN & MARKS, P.S.C. (AV)

Suite 700 Security Trust Building, 271 West Short Street, 40507-1292
Telephone: 606-255-6676
Telecopier: 606-259-1562
URL: http://www.mis.net/mgm/

Harry B. Miller, Jr.	Michael D. Meuser
James M. Marks (1928-1963)	Thomas C. Marks
Robert S. Miller	Theodore E. Cowen
Thomas W. Miller	Judith K. Jones
Catesby Woodford	Stephen G. Amato
Donald R. Rose	Carroll M. Redford, III
Frank T. Becker	Helen M. Marks

Representative Clients: Fifth Third Bank; Lexington Herald-Leader Co.; Kentucky National Insurance Company; Lexington Trots Breeders Association, Inc. d/b/a The Red Mile; Castleton Farm, Inc.; G.F. Vaughan Tobacco Co.; C.V. Whitney Farm; Three Chimneys Farm; Equine Capital Corp.; Belle Reve Farm.
Reference: Bank One Lexington, N.A.

For full biographical listings, see the Martindale-Hubbell Law Directory

PETER PERLMAN LAW OFFICES, P.S.C. (AV)

388 South Broadway, 40508
Telephone: 606-253-3919
FAX: 606-259-0493

Peter Perlman

Bryce D. Franklin, Jr.	Pamela D. Perlman

For full biographical listings, see the Martindale-Hubbell Law Directory

PIPER, WELLMAN & BOWERS (AV)

200 North Upper Street, 40507
Telephone: 606-231-1012
Fax: 606-231-7367
Email: pwb200@uky.campus.mci.net

MEMBERS OF FIRM

George C. Piper	Dean T. Wellman
Barbara J. Bowers	

ASSOCIATE

Johann F. Herklotz

Representative Clients: Kentucky Hospital Association Trust; Woodford Hospital; Garrard Memorial Hospital; Century American Insurance Co.; Guaranty National Insurance Co.; Hillhaven Corp.; Sisters of Charity of Nazareth Health System, Inc. d/b/a/ St. Josephs Hospital; Kentucky River Medical Center; The Reciprocal Alliance.

For full biographical listings, see the Martindale-Hubbell Law Directory

GEORGE F. RABE (AV)

Suite 1004 First National Building, 167 West Main Street, 40507-1708
Telephone: 606-255-2313
Reference: Bank One Lexington, N.A.

For full biographical listings, see the Martindale-Hubbell Law Directory

Lexington—Continued

SAVAGE, GARMER & ELLIOTT, P.S.C. (AV)

Opera House Office Building, 141 North Broadway, 40507
Telephone: 606-254-9351
Fax: 606-233-9769

Joe C. Savage   William R. Garmer
                  Robert L. Elliott

For full biographical listings, see the Martindale-Hubbell Law Directory

STOLL, KEENON & PARK, LLP (AV)

201 E. Main Street, Suite 1000, 40507-1380
Telephone: 606-231-3000
Telecopier: 606-253-1093; 606-253-1027
Frankfort, Kentucky Office: 307 Washington Street, 40601.
Telephone: 502-875-6220.
Telecopier: 502-875-6235.
Louisville, Kentucky Office: 400 West Market Street, Suite 2650, 40202-3377.
Telephone: 502-568-9100.
Telecopier: 502-568-5700.

MEMBERS OF FIRM

Leslie W. Morris II	Lizbeth Ann Tully
Lindsey W. Ingram, Jr.	Eileen M. O'Brien
Bennett Clark	David C. Schwetschenau
Spencer D. Noe	Anita M. Britton
Joseph M. Scott, Jr.	Denise Kirk Ash
Charles E. Shivel, Jr.	Bonnie Hoskins
Robert M. Watt, III	Diane M. Carlton
J. Peter Cassidy, Jr.	Larry A. Sykes
Samuel D. Hinkle IV	P. Douglas Barr
Robert F. Houlihan, Jr.	Perry M. Bentley
William M. Lear, Jr.	Dan M. Rose
Donald P. Wagner	Gregory D. Pavey
Robert W. Kellerman	J. Mel Camenisch, Jr.
	David E. Fleenor

ASSOCIATES

Laura Day DelCotto	Susan Beverly Jones
James L. Thomerson	Todd S. Page
R. Douglas Martin	Palmer G. Vance, II
	William L. Montague, Jr.

Representative Clients: Ashland Oil, Inc.; Bank One, Lexington, NA; International Business Machines Corp.; Keeneland Assn.; Kentucky-American Water Co.; Kentucky Utilities Co.; Lexington Herald-Leader Inc.; Lexmark International, Inc.; MAPCO Coal Inc.; Sisters of Charity of Nazareth Health Corp.

For Complete List of Firm Personnel, See General Section

For full biographical listings, see the Martindale-Hubbell Law Directory

LONDON,* Laurel Co.

FARMER, FARMER, KELLEY AND BROWN (AV)

502 West Fifth Street, Drawer 490, 40743
Telephone: 606-878-7640
Fax: 606-878-2364
Lexington, Kentucky Office: 121 Prosperous Place, Suite 13 B, 40509-1834.
Telephone: 606: 263-2567.
Facsimile: 606: 263-2567.

MEMBERS OF FIRM

F. Preston Farmer	Michael P. Farmer
John F. Kelley, Jr.	Martha L. Brown

ASSOCIATES

Suzanne S. Farmer	Bradford L. Breeding
Jason E. Williams	Estill D. Banks, II

Representative Clients: Bituminous Insurance Co.; State Farm Mutual Automobile Insurance Co.; State Farm Fire & Casualty Insurance; Walmart Stores; Geico; Kentucky National Insurance Co.; Century Claims; National Insurance Association; Shelter Insurance Co.; Crumb & Forester Underwriters Group.

For full biographical listings, see the Martindale-Hubbell Law Directory

TAYLOR, KELLER & DUNAWAY (AV)

802 North Main Street, P.O. Box 905, 40743-0905
Telephone: 606-878-8844
Facsimile: 606-878-5547

Boyd F. Taylor   J. Warren Keller
                  Bridget L. Dunaway

ASSOCIATE

Jason Richardson

OF COUNSEL

Pamela Adams Chesnut

(See Next Column)

LEGAL SUPPORT PERSONNEL

Berneda Baker (Paralegal)   Cynthia K. Taylor (Paralegal)

Representative Clients: Chubb Group; Coronet Insurance Group; ITT Hartford; Mutual of Omaha; American General Property Insurance Co.; State Farm Fire & Casualty; State Farm Mutual Automobile Insurance Co.
Local Counsel for: Multi Line Claims Mgmt.
References: The First National Bank; Cumberland Valley National Bank & Trust Company of London, Kentucky.

For full biographical listings, see the Martindale-Hubbell Law Directory

TOOMS & HOUSE (AV)

310 West Fifth Street, P.O. Box 520, 40743-0520
Telephone: 606-864-4145
FAX: 606-864-4279

MEMBERS OF FIRM

Murray L. Brown (1894-1980)	R. William Tooms
Roy E. Tooms (1917-1986)	Brian C. House

Representative Clients: State Auto Mutual Insurance Co.; Grange Mutual Casualty Co.; Kentucky Farm Bureau Mutual Insurance Co.

For full biographical listings, see the Martindale-Hubbell Law Directory

LOUISVILLE,* Jefferson Co.

BOEHL STOPHER & GRAVES (AV)

Suite 2300 Providian Center, 400 West Market Street, 40202-3354
Telephone: 502-589-5980
FAX: 502-561-9400
Lexington, Kentucky Office: 444 West Second Street.
Telephone: 606-252-6721.
Fax: 606-253-1445.
Paducah, Kentucky Office: Suite 340 Executive Inn Riverfront, One Executive Boulevard.
Telephone: 502-442-4369.
Fax: 502-442-4689.
Prestonsburg, Kentucky Office: 105 West Court Street.
Telephone: 606-886-8004.
Fax: 606-886-9579.
New Albany, Indiana Office: Elsby East, Suite 204, 400 Pearl Street.
Telephone: 812-948-5053.
Fax: 812-948-9233.

OF COUNSEL

Joseph E. Stopher   George R. Effinger
                                       (Resident at Paducah)

MEMBERS OF FIRM

Herbert F. Boehl (1894-1986)	Richard L. Walter
Arthur J. Deindoerfer (1907-1990)	(Resident at Paducah)
	Douglas A. U'Sellis
Raymond O. Harmon (1918-1990)	Steven G. Kinkel
	(Resident at Lexington)
James M. Graves (1912-1994)	John P. Rall
William M. Newman, Jr. (1949-1995)	(Resident at Paducah)
	Kim Martin Wilkie
William O. Guethlein	(Resident at Lexington)
Galen J. White, Jr.	John Harlan Callis, III
William P. Swain	(Resident at Prestonsburg)
Larry L. Johnson	Charles D. Walter
W. T. Adkins	(Resident at Paducah)
(Resident at Lexington)	Janie C. McKenzie
Edward H. Stopher	(Resident at Prestonsburg)
Nolan Carter, Jr.	Guillermo A. Carlos
(Resident at Lexington)	(Resident at Lexington)
Jefferson K. Streepey	William B. Orberson
Wesley G. Gatlin	John F. Parker Jr.
George R. Carter	Jeffrey L. Hansford (Resident at
Robert E. Stopher	New Albany, Indiana)
Philip J. Reverman, Jr.	Matthew Hunter Jones (Resident
Jonathan Freed	at New Albany, Indiana)
(Resident at Paducah)	James B. Cooper
Peter J. Glauber	(Resident at Lexington)
Gregory K. Jenkins	Martin H. Kinney, Jr.
(Resident at Lexington)	Bayard V. Collier
Raymond G. Smith	(Resident at Prestonsburg)
Walter E. Harding	Teresa M. Groves
Robert M. Brooks	(Resident at Paducah)
John W. Phillips	J. Bradley Sanders (Resident at
Susan D. Phillips	New Albany, Indiana)
Ronald L. Green	
(Resident at Lexington)	

ASSOCIATES

Mary Ann Kiwala	David Sean Ragland
Bradley R. Hume	Jenifer A. Tarter
Richard W. Edwards	Daniel S. Stratemeyer
John B. Moore	(Resident at Paducah)
David T. Klapheke	Michael S. Maloney
Robert D. McClure	E. Michael Ooley (Resident at
Michael J. Cox	New Albany, Indiana)
(Resident at Lexington)	John C. Talbott
William J. Crowe	Deron L. Johnson
Denise Basford Askin	(Resident at Prestonburg)

(See Next Column)

BOEHL STOPHER & GRAVES, *Louisville—Continued*

ASSOCIATES (Continued)

Steven R. Armstrong (Resident at Lexington)	Fredrick A. Bailey, Jr. (Resident at Lexington)
Melissa Moore Lewis (Resident at Prestonsburg)	David P. Haick
	Garrett M. Estep
Patrick J. Murphy, II (Resident at Lexington)	Terri E. Kirkpatrick
	Thomas M. Edelen
Brennen C. Ragone (Resident at Lexington)	Tammy C. Snyder
	C. Tom Anderson
Gretchen R. Nunn (Resident at Prestonsburg)	(Resident at Prestonburg)
	Donna Jo Jenkins (Resident at New Albany, Indiana)

Counsel for: Ford Motor Co.; Texas Eastern Transmission Corp.; Coca-Cola Bottling Co.; Hartford Accident and Indemnity Co.; Continental Insurance Group; St. Paul Fire & Marine Insurance Co.; Lloyds of London; Old Republic Insurance Co.

For full biographical listings, see the Martindale-Hubbell Law Directory

EWEN, HILLIARD & BUSH (AV)

The Starks Building Suite 1090, 455 S. 4th Street, 40202
Telephone: 502-584-1090
Fax: 502-584-4707

MEMBERS OF FIRM

Victor W. Ewen (1924-1989)	Frank P. Hilliard
A. Campbell Ewen	John M. Bush

ASSOCIATES

Kevin P. Kinney	Mark McClure Sandmann
Robert J. Rosing	Robin Lynn Burnham

For full biographical listings, see the Martindale-Hubbell Law Directory

FRANKLIN AND HANCE, P.S.C. (AV)

The Speed House, 505 West Ormsby Avenue, 40203
Telephone: 502-637-6000
Fax: 502-637-1413

Larry B. Franklin	Michael R. Hance

David B. Gray	Hope Kathleen Fitzpatrick

Reference: First National Bank.

For full biographical listings, see the Martindale-Hubbell Law Directory

GOLDBERG & SIMPSON, P.S.C. (AV)

3000 National City Tower, 40202
Telephone: 502-589-4440
Telefax: 502-581-1344
Washington, D.C. Office: 1200 G Street, N.W. - Suite 800, 20005.
Telephone: 202-434-8968.
Telefax: 202-737-5822.

Fred M. Goldberg	William J. Hust, III (Not admitted in KY)
David B. Ratterman	
Jonathan D. Goldberg	Mary Alice Maple
James S. Goldberg	Emily L. Lawrence
Mitchell A. Charney	Douglas S. Haynes
Steven A. Goodman	Jan M. West
Edward L. Schoenbaechler	Charles H. Cassis
Cathy S. Pike	Robin Sylvester Craddock
Stephen E. Smith	John Joseph McLaughlin
Cynthia Buss Maddox	Leslie E. Huber
Anthony J Elpers	

OF COUNSEL

Ronald V. Simpson	Kenneth G. Lee (Not admitted in KY; Resident, Washington, D.C. Office)
David A. Brill	

Representative Clients: National City Bank; Liberty Mutual Insurance Co.; Jewish Hospital Healthcare Services, Inc.; Louisville & Jefferson County Board of Health; Providian Corp.

For full biographical listings, see the Martindale-Hubbell Law Directory

HIRN DOHENY & HARPER (AV)

A Partnership including a Professional Service Corporation
2000 Meidinger Tower, 40202
Telephone: 502-585-2450
Telecopiers: 502-585-2207; 585-2529

MEMBERS OF FIRM

Marvin J. Hirn	John E. Selent
Frank P. Doheny, Jr.	B. Todd Thompson
Michael A. Valenti	

ASSOCIATES

Steven A. Edwards	Millicent A. Tanner
Mary R. Harville	Trevor L. Earl
Beverly J. Glascock	(Not admitted in KY)
Michael Marvin Hirn	Audra J. Eckerle

(See Next Column)

Representative Clients: Humana, Inc.; Louisville Gas and Electric Co.; Presbyterian Church (U.S.A.); Mid-America Bank of Louisville; Indiana United Bancorp; National City Bank Kentucky; PNC Bank; Vencor, Inc.; J.J.B. Hilliard, W.L. Lyons, Inc.

For Complete List of Firm Personnel, See General Section

For full biographical listings, see the Martindale-Hubbell Law Directory

MIDDLETON & REUTLINGER, P.S.C. (AV)

2500 Brown and Williamson Tower, 40202-3410
Telephone: 502-584-1135
Fax: 502-561-0442
New Albany, Indiana Office: 2623 Charlestown Road, 47150.
Telephone: 812-944-7215.

O. Grant Bruton	D. Randall Gibson
Kenneth S. Handmaker	G. Kennedy Hall, Jr.
James N. Williams, Jr.	Mark S. Fenzel
Charles G. Middleton, III	Kathiejane Oehler
Charles D. Greenwell	William Jay Hunter, Jr.
John W. Bilby	James E. Milliman
Stewart L. Prather	David J. Kellerman
Edward L. Galloway	

Amy B. Berge	Dennis D. Murrell
Augustus S. Herbert	

For Complete List of Firm Personnel, See General Section

For full biographical listings, see the Martindale-Hubbell Law Directory

J. BRUCE MILLER LAW GROUP (AV)

621 West Main Street, Third Floor, 40202
Telephone: 502-587-0900
Telecopier: 502-587-9008

J. Bruce Miller	Michael J. Kitchen
Norma C. Miller	Jeffrey A. Haeberlin
Anthony L. Schnell	Katherine K. Kitchen
Denis B. Fleming, Jr.	J. Daniel Farrell (Not admitted in KY)

Representative Clients: Advance Machinery Co., Inc.; Anson Machine Mfg. Co.; Biddinger Investment Capital Corp. (Indiana); Carneal Enterprises, Inc. (Kentucky/Florida); MPD Inc. (Owensboro, Kentucky); Motion Picture Association of America; Packaging Unlimited Group (Kentucky/North Carolina); Paducah Medical Supply, Inc. (Kentucky/Tennessee/Florida); Sun Group Broadcasting, Inc. (Indiana/Tennessee); Louisville Gas & Electric Co.

For full biographical listings, see the Martindale-Hubbell Law Directory

MOSLEY, CLARE & TOWNES (AV)

Fifth Floor, Hart Block Building, 730 West Main Street, 40202
Telephone: 502-583-7400
Telecopier: 502-589-4997

MEMBERS OF FIRM

Eugene L. Mosley	Larry C. Ethridge
Dennis M. Clare	Victor L. Baltzell, Jr.
W. Waverley Townes	William J. Nold
Judith E. McDonald-Burkman	

ASSOCIATES

E. Jeffrey Mosley	Eileen L. Minto

For full biographical listings, see the Martindale-Hubbell Law Directory

OLDFATHER & MORRIS (AV)

1330 South Third Street, 40208
Telephone: 502-637-7200
Fax: 502-637-3999
Email: om@ntr.net

Ann B. Oldfather	James Barrett
Douglas H. Morris, II	Jennifer Jordan Hall

For full biographical listings, see the Martindale-Hubbell Law Directory

PEDLEY, ZIELKE & GORDINIER (AV)

1150 Starks Building, 455 South Fourth Avenue, 40202
Telephone: 502-589-4600
Fax: 502-584-0422

MEMBERS OF FIRM

Lawrence L. Pedley	William W. Stodghill
Laurence J. Zielke	P. Stephen Gordinier
John K. Gordinier	Schuyler J. Olt
Frank G. Simpson, III	

OF COUNSEL

Caroline George Meena

(See Next Column)

PEDLEY, ZIELKE & GORDINIER—*Continued*

ASSOCIATE

John H. Dwyer, Jr.

Representative Clients: Kentucky Independent Community Bankers Assoc.; Louisville and Jefferson County Metropolitan Sewer District; Storer Communications of Jefferson County; Gannet Co.; Hitachi Consumer Products of America; Service Painting Co.; Irwin H. Whitehouse & Sons, Inc.; American Marine Service Barge Lines; Aetna Life & Casualty Co.

For full biographical listings, see the Martindale-Hubbell Law Directory

RUBIN HAYS & FOLEY (AV)

First Trust Centre 200 South Fifth Street, 40202
Telephone: 502-569-7550
Telecopier: 502-569-7555

MEMBERS OF FIRM

Wm. Carl Fust	Lisa Koch Bryant
Harry Lee Meyer	Sharon C. Hardy
David W. Gray	Charles S. Musson
Irvin D. Foley	W. Randall Jones
Joseph R. Gathright, Jr.	K. Gail Russell

ASSOCIATES

Christian L. Juckett	Courtney Lynn McCall

OF COUNSEL

James E. Fahey	Newman T. Guthrie

Representative Clients: J.C. Bradford & Co., Inc.; J.J.B. Hilliard, W.L. Lyons, Inc.; Huntington National Bank; Liberty National Bank and Trust Company; National City Bank; PNC Bank; Prudential Bache & Co., Inc.; Prudential Securities, Inc.; Society Bank; Stock Yards Bank and Trust Co.

For full biographical listings, see the Martindale-Hubbell Law Directory

SEILLER & HANDMAKER, LLP (AV)

2200 Meidinger Tower, 40202
Telephone: 502-584-7400
Telecopier: 502-583-2100
Paris, Kentucky Office: Seiller, Handmaker & Blevins, P.S.C., 1431 South Main Street.
Telephone: 606-987-3980.
Telecopier: 606-987-3982.
Cynthiana, Kentucky Office: Seiller, Handmaker & Blevins, P.S.C., 9 South Walnut.
Telephone: 606-234-2880.
New Albany, Indiana Office: 202 Pearl Street.
Telephone: 812-948-8307.
Telecopier: 812-948-8383.

Edward F. Seiller (1897-1990)

MEMBERS OF FIRM

Stuart Allen Handmaker	Maury D. Kommor
Bill V. Seiller	Cynthia Compton Stone
David M. Cantor	Glenn A. Cohen
Neil C. Bordy	Tomi Anne Blevins Pulliam
Kyle Anne Citrynell	(Paris and Cynthiana Offices)

ASSOCIATES

Pamela M. Greenwell	Donna F. Townsend
Michael C. Bratcher	Gregory A. Lindsey
John E. Brengle	Vicki L. Buba
Patrick R. Holland, II	Allen C. Platt III (Resident,
Edwin Jon Wolfe	New Albany, Indiana Office)

OF COUNSEL

Robert S. Frey

For full biographical listings, see the Martindale-Hubbell Law Directory

WOODWARD, HOBSON & FULTON (AV)

2500 National City Tower, 101 South Fifth Street, 40202
Telephone: 502-581-8000
Fax: 502-581-8111
Lexington, Kentucky Office: PNC Bank Plaza, 200 West Vine Street, Suite 500.
Telephone: 606-244-7100.
Telecopier: 606-244-7111.
New Albany, Indiana Office: 611 East Spring Street, P.O. Box 288.
Telephone: 812-941-1800.
Telecopier: 812-941-1855.

MEMBERS OF FIRM

Kenneth L. Anderson	Gregory L. Smith
William D. Grubbs	Gregory A. Bölzle
Harry K. Herren	Elizabeth Ullmer Mendel
David R. Monohan	Jann B. Logsdon
Will H. Fulton	Linsey W. West (Resident,
Richard H. C. Clay	Lexington, Kentucky Office)
Mary Jo Wetzel (Resident, New Albany, Indiana Office)	

(See Next Column)

Representative Clients: CSX Transportation; Fischer Packing Company; Ford Motor Co.; General Motors Corp.; Ralston Purina Co.; Ashland Oil, Inc.; Brown-Forman Corp.; Stock Yards Bank & Trust Co.; Trammell Crow Co.; Ursuline Campus Schools.

For Complete List of Firm Personnel, See General Section

For full biographical listings, see the Martindale-Hubbell Law Directory

WYATT, TARRANT & COMBS (AV)

Citizens Plaza, 40202
Telephone: 502-589-5235
Telecopier: 502-589-0309
URL: http://www.wyattfirm.com
Lexington, Kentucky Office: 1700 Lexington Financial Center.
Telephone: 606-233-2012.
Telecopier: 606-259-0649.
Frankfort, Kentucky Office: The Taylor-Scott Building, 311 West Main Street.
Telephone: 502-223-2104.
Telecopier: 502-227-7681.
New Albany, Indiana Office: The Elsby Building, 117 East Spring Street,
Telephone: 812-945-3561.
Telecopier: 812-949-2524.
Memphis, Tennessee Office: Crescent Center, Suite 650, 6075 Poplar Avenue.
Telephone: 901-537-1000.
Telecopier: 901-537-1010.
Nashville, Tennessee Office: 1500 Nashville City Center, 511 Union Street.
Telephone: 615-244-0020.
Telecopier: 615-256-1726.
Music Row, Nashville Office: 29 Music Square East.
Telephone: 615-255-6161.
Telecopier: 615-254-4490.
Hendersonville, Tennessee Office: 313 E. Main Street, Suite 1.
Telephone: 615-822-8822.
Telecopier: 615-824-4684.

MEMBERS OF FIRM

Edgar A. Zingman	M. Stephen Pitt
Richard W. Iler	Walter M. Jones
Robert C. Ewald	Frank F. Chuppe, Jr.
Samuel G. Bridge, Jr.	Merrill S. Schell
Robert I. Cusick	Virginia Hamilton Snell
John P. Reisz	Byron E. Leet
Jon L. Fleischaker	Mary Ann Main
K. Gregory Haynes	Holliday Hopkins Thacker

Representative Clients: Ashland Oil, Inc.; Churchill Downs, Inc.; E.I. du Pont de Nemours and Company; Ford Motor Co.; Gannett Co., Inc./The Courier-Journal/Louisville Times; General Electric Co.; Kentucky Hospital Assn.; Metropolitan Life Insurance Co.; PNC Bank, Kentucky, Inc. and its affiliates.

For Complete List of Firm Personnel, See General Section

For full biographical listings, see the Martindale-Hubbell Law Directory

OWENSBORO,* Daviess Co.

KAMUF, YEWELL, PACE & CONDON (AV)

Great Financial Federal Building, 322 Frederica Street, 42301
Telephone: 502-685-3901
Fax: 502-926-2005

MEMBERS OF FIRM

Charles J. Kamuf	Patrick D. Pace
David L. Yewell	David C. Condon

ASSOCIATE

John M. Mischel

Representative Clients: Owensboro Municipal Utilities Commission; Lincoln Service Corp.; Hancock County Planning Commission; Daviess County Board of Education; Barmet Aluminum Corp.; Owensboro Sewer Commission; TICOR Title Insurance Co.; Chicago Title Insurance Co.; Owensboro Riverport Authority; Housing Authority of Owensboro.

For full biographical listings, see the Martindale-Hubbell Law Directory

OWINGSVILLE,* Bath Co.

BYRON & ROBERTS (AV)

25 S. Court Street, 40360
Telephone: 606-674-2911

MEMBERS OF FIRM

Roger A. Byron	Winifred Byron Roberts

General Counsel for: Farmers Bank, Owingsville, Kentucky.
Local Counsel for: Delta Natural Gas Co.
Approved Attorneys for: Lawyers Title Insurance Corp.

For full biographical listings, see the Martindale-Hubbell Law Directory

PADUCAH, McCracken Co.

BOEHL STOPHER & GRAVES (AV)

Suite 340 Executive Inn Riverfront, One Executive Boulevard, 42001
Telephone: 502-442-4369
FAX: 502-442-4689
Louisville, Kentucky Office: Providian Center, Suite 2300, 400 West Market Street.
Telephone: 502-589-5980.
Fax: 502-561-9400.
Lexington, Kentucky Office: 444 West Second Street.
Telephone: 606-252-6721.
Fax: 606-253-1445.
Prestonsburg, Kentucky Office: 105 West Court Street.
Telephone: 606-886-8004.
Fax: 606-886-9579.
New Albany, Indiana Office: Elsby East, Suite 204, 400 Pearl Street.
Telephone: 812-948-5053.
Fax: 812-948-9233.

RESIDENT PARTNERS

Jonathan Freed	John P. Rall
Richard L. Walter	Charles D. Walter
	Teresa M. Groves

RESIDENT ASSOCIATE

Daniel S. Stratemeyer

Counsel for: Ford Motor Co.; Texas Eastern Transmission Corp.; Coca-Cola Bottling Co.; National Collegiate Athletic Assn.; Hartford Accident and Indemnity Co.; Continental Insurance Group; St. Paul Fire & Marine Insurance Co.; Lloyds of London; Old Republic Insurance Co.

For Complete List of Firm Personnel, See General Section

For full biographical listings, see the Martindale-Hubbell Law Directory

---

PIKEVILLE, Pike Co.

PRUITT AND DE BOURBON LAW FIRM (AV)

The Call Building, Second Street, P.O. Box 339, 41502
Telephone: 606-437-7366; 437-7367; 237-1280
Fax: 606-432-2367

MEMBERS OF FIRM

James P. Pruitt, Jr.   P. Michael de Bourbon

Reference: The Citizen's Bank of Pikeville.

For full biographical listings, see the Martindale-Hubbell Law Directory

---

SHELBYVILLE, Shelby Co.

NEAL & DAVIS (AV)

931 Main Street, P.O. Box 40, 40066-0040
Telephone: 502-633-6002;
Louisville: 502-589-9888

Gregg Y. Neal   Thomas Todd Davis

Reference: Republic Bank and Trust Co.

For full biographical listings, see the Martindale-Hubbell Law Directory

---

LOUISIANA

ALEXANDRIA, Rapides Parish

NEBLETT, BEARD & ARSENAULT (AV)

A Registered Limited Liability Partnership including Law Corporations
2220 Bonaventure Court, P.O. Box 1190, 71301
Telephone: 318-487-9874; 1-800-256-1050
Fax: 318-443-7887

Robert B. Neblett (1927-1991)	David O. Walker (Law Corporation)
Richard W. Beard (1955-1988)	
Richard J. Arsenault (Law Corporation)	Paul J. Tellarico
	William S. Neblett
C. Michael Bollinger	Michael S. Koch

ASSOCIATES

Galen (Allen) W. McBride	Wesley J. Gralapp
	Gary J. Arsenault

Reference: Guaranty Bank & Trust Co.

For full biographical listings, see the Martindale-Hubbell Law Directory

---

CHRIS J. ROY, SR. (AV)

1100 Tenth Street, 71301
Telephone: 318-487-9537
Fax: 381-482-1353

For full biographical listings, see the Martindale-Hubbell Law Directory

---

BATON ROUGE, East Baton Rouge Parish

BREAZEALE, SACHSE & WILSON, L.L.P. (AV)

Twenty-Third Floor, One American Place, P.O. Box 3197, 70821-3197
Telephone: 504-387-4000
Fax: 504-387-5397
New Orleans, Louisiana Office: LL&E Tower, Suite 2400, 909 Poydras Street.
Telephone: 504-582-1170.
Fax: 504-584-5452.

MEMBERS OF FIRM

Victor A. Sachse, III	Douglas K. Williams
Gordon A. Pugh	John F. Whitney (Resident, New Orleans Office)
Paul M. Hebert, Jr.	
Claude F. Reynaud, Jr.	John E. Heinrich
Christine Lipsey	Michael R. Hubbell
David R. Kelly	John W. Barton, Jr.
Robert L. Atkinson	Jude C. Bursavich
James R. Chastain, Jr.	

ASSOCIATES

Linda Perez Clark	Gwen Petit Harmon
	Jeanne C. Comeaux

Counsel for: Hibernia National Bank; South Central Bell Telephone Co.; Allied-Signal Corp.; Reynolds Metal Co.; Illinois Central Railroad Co.; The Continental Insurance Cos.; Fireman's Fund American Group; Chicago Bridge & Iron Co.; Montgomery Ward & Co.

For Complete List of Firm Personnel, See General Section

For full biographical listings, see the Martindale-Hubbell Law Directory

---

FUNDERBURK & ANDREWS (AV)

329 St. Ferdinand Street, 70802
Telephone: 504-387-2200
Fax: 504-383-0142

MEMBERS OF FIRM

Robert C. Funderburk, Jr.	David T. Butler, Jr.
Arthur H. Andrews	Scott H. Frugé

For full biographical listings, see the Martindale-Hubbell Law Directory

---

KANTROW, SPAHT, WEAVER & BLITZER, A PROFESSIONAL LAW CORPORATION (AV)

Suite 300, City Plaza, 445 North Boulevard, P.O. Box 2997, 70821-2997
Telephone: 504-383-4703
Fax: 504-343-0630; 343-0637

Byron R. Kantrow	Vincent P. Fornias
Carlos G. Spaht	David S. Rubin
Geraldine B. Weaver	Diane L. Crochet
Sidney M. Blitzer, Jr.	Richard F. Zimmerman, Jr.
Paul H. Spaht	Bob D. Tucker
Lee C. Kantrow	Martin E. Golden
John C. Miller	Joseph A. Schittone, Jr.

S. Layne Lee	Connell L. Archey
J. Michael Robinson, Jr.	Randal J. Robert

Representative Clients: CNA Insurance Cos.; Federal Deposit Insurance Corp.; Hartford Insurance Group; Air Products and Chemicals, Inc.; CF Industries, Inc.; AT&T; United Companies Financial Corp.

For full biographical listings, see the Martindale-Hubbell Law Directory

---

KEAN, MILLER, HAWTHORNE, D'ARMOND, McCOWAN & JARMAN, L.L.P. (AV)

22nd Floor, One American Place, P.O. Box 3513, 70821
Telephone: 504-387-0999
Fax: 504-388-9133
New Orleans, Louisiana Office: Energy Centre, Suite 1470, 1100 Poydras Street.
Telephone: 504-585-3050.
Fax: 504-585-3051.
Plaquemine, Louisiana Office: Suite 10, 23425 Railroad Avenue.
Telephone: 504-687-9845.
Fax: 504-382-3445.

MEMBERS OF FIRM

William R. D'Armond	Bradley C. Myers
Charles S. McCowan, Jr.	Melanie M. Hartmann
G. William Jarman	Linda Sarradet Akchin
Leonard L. Kilgore III	James P. Doré
Gary A. Bezet	Erich P. Rapp
Michael C. Garrard	Charles L. Patin, Jr.
Vance A. Gibbs	Mathile W. Abramson
James R. Lackie	Cynthia M. Chemay
David K. Nelson	Gregg R. Kronenberger
J. Carter Wilkinson	Charles S. McCowan III
Sandra L. Edwards	Jay M. Jalenak, Jr.

(See Next Column)

KEAN, MILLER, HAWTHORNE, D'ARMOND, McCOWAN & JARMAN L.L.P.—
Continued

Kelly Wilkinson	Barrye Panepinto Miyagi
Linda G. Rodrigue	Gary P. Graphia
Theresa R. Hagen	Jean Ann Tolleson
Glenn M. Farnet	Gordon D. Polozola
Esteban Herrera, Jr.	Lana D. Davis
Susan Knight Carter (Resident,	Gregory M. Anding
New Orleans Office)	Troy J. Charpentier

Representative Clients: BASF Corporation, Parsippany, NJ; Exxon Company, U.S.A., Baton Rouge, LA; Georgia Gulf Corporation, Atlanta, GA.; Hancock Bank of Louisiana, Baton Rouge, LA; Georgia-Pacific Corporation, Atlanta, GA; Insurance Corporation of America, Houston, TX; Louisiana Medical Mutual Insurance Company, Metairie, LA; Metropolitan Life Insurance Company, New York, NY.

For Complete List of Firm Personnel, See General Section

For full biographical listings, see the Martindale-Hubbell Law Directory

KLEINPETER & KLEINPETER (AV)

1680 South Lobdell Avenue, Suite E, P.O. Box 66443, 70896
Telephone: 504-926-5093
Telecopier: 5048-926-5318

MEMBERS OF FIRM

Robert L. Kleinpeter	R. Loren Kleinpeter

Representative Clients: Argonaut Insurance Co.; American Indemnity Co.; Allstate Insurance Co.; Consolidated American Inc. Co.; South Carolina Insurance Co.; TransAmerica Insurance Group; St. Paul Fire & Marine Insurance Co.; Scottsdale Insurance Co.; Fireman's Fund Insurance Co.; Western Heritage Insurance Co.

For full biographical listings, see the Martindale-Hubbell Law Directory

PHELPS DUNBAR, L.L.P. (AV)

Suite 701, City National Bank Building, P.O. Box 4412, 70821-4412
Telephone: 504-346-0285
Telecopier: 504-381-9197
Email: info@phelps.com
New Orleans, Louisiana Office: Texaco Center, 400 Poydras Street.
Telephone 504-566-1311.
Telecopier: 504-568-9130; 504-568-9007.
Cable Address: "Howspencer."
Telex: 584125 WU.
Telex: 6821155 WUI.
Jackson, Mississippi Office: Suite 500, Mtel Centré, 200 South Lamar Street, P.O. Box 23066.
Telephone: 601-352-2300.
Telecopier: 601-360-9777.
Tupelo, Mississippi Office: Seventh Floor, One Mississippi Plaza, P.O. Box 1220.
Telephone: 601-842-7907.
Telecopier: 601-842-3873.
Houston, Texas Office: Suite 900, 3040 Post Oak Boulevard.
Telephone: 713-626-1386.
Telecopier: 713-626-1388.
London, England Office: Suite 731, Level 7, Lloyd's, 1 Lime Street, London EC3M 7DQ England.
Telephone: 011-44-171-929-4765.
Telecopier: 011-44-171-929-0046.
Telex: 987321.

RESIDENT PARTNERS

H. Alston Johnson, III	Richard E. Matheny
Michael D. Hunt	Steven J. Levine
Jennifer Bowers Zimmerman	Allen D. Darden
F. Scott Kaiser	Thomas H. Kiggans
Marshall M. Redmon	

COUNSEL

E. Jane Sherman	Jane A. Robert

RESIDENT ASSOCIATES

Jane H. Barney	Darrell J. Loup
Rebecca Bellows Crawford	Tricia A. Martinez
Susan W. Furr	Patrick Ragan Richard
Diane Fagan Robinson	

Representative Clients: Blue Cross & Blue Shield of Mississippi; City National Bank of Baton Rouge; Hibernia National Bank; Louisiana Companies; Louisiana Lottery Corporation; Louisiana Workers' Compensation Corporation; Missouri Pacific Railroad Co.; OHM Corporation; The Travelers Insurance Company; Uniroyal Chemical Company.

For Complete List of Firm Personnel, See General Section

For full biographical listings, see the Martindale-Hubbell Law Directory

POWERS, CLEGG & WILLARD (AV)

7967 Office Park Boulevard, P.O. Box 15948, 70895
Telephone: 504-928-1951
Telecopier: 504-929-9834

(See Next Column)

MEMBERS OF FIRM

John Dale Powers	Michael V. Clegg
William E. Willard	

ASSOCIATES

Neil H. Mixon	Robert J. Daigre
Mary A. Cazes	Nicholas Soileau

General Counsel for: Audubon Insurance Co.
Louisiana Counsel for: Hancock Bank & Trust Co.; Hertz Corp.; Ciba-Geigy Corp.; Utica Mutual Insurance Co.

For full biographical listings, see the Martindale-Hubbell Law Directory

SEALE, SMITH, ZUBER & BARNETTE (AV)

Two United Plaza, Suite 200, 8550 United Plaza Boulevard, 70809
Telephone: 504-924-1600
Telecopier: 504-924-6100

Armbrust Gordon Seale (1913-1989)	Ronald A. Seale
Robert W. Smith (1922-1989)	Brent E. Kinchen
Donald S. Zuber	Charles K. Watts
Kenneth E. Barnette	Myron A. Walker, Jr.
William C. Kaufman III	Daniel A. Reed
John W. L. Swanner	William C. Rowe, Jr.
James H. Morgan III	Lawrence R. Anderson, Jr.
	Catherine S. Nobile

ASSOCIATES

Richard T. Reed	Anthony J. Russo, Jr.
Barbara G. Chatelain	Gregory D. Polozola

Representative Clients: Farmers Insurance Group; St. Paul Fire and Marine Insurance Company; United Services Automobile Association; General Motors Acceptance Corporation.
Reference: City National Bank, Baton Rouge, Louisiana.

For full biographical listings, see the Martindale-Hubbell Law Directory

SHOCKEY & ZIOBER, A PROFESSIONAL LAW CORPORATION (AV)

Suite 3-A, 5551 Corporate Boulevard, P.O. Box 80286, 70898-0286
Telephone: 504-929-8929
Telecopier: 504-928-7694

John David Ziober	William C. Shockey

Emily Phillips Ziober	Jennifer R. Treadway Morris
Douglas J. Cochran	James E. Moore, Jr.

For full biographical listings, see the Martindale-Hubbell Law Directory

CROWLEY,* Acadia Parish

BAROUSSE & CRATON (AV)

211 North Parkerson Avenue, P.O. Drawer 1305, 70527-1305
Telephone: 318-785-1000
Facsimile: 318-788-3219

MEMBERS OF FIRM

Homer Ed Barousse, Jr.	John F. Craton

Representative Clients: First Bank, N.A. of Crowley and Lake Charles; Francis Drilling Fluids, Ltd.; Farm Credit Bank of Texas; First South Production Credit Association; J.I. Case Credit Corporation; Louisiana Sheriffs' Association; Broussard Rice Mill, Inc.; Mermentau River Harbor and Terminal District; Farm Service Agency.

For full biographical listings, see the Martindale-Hubbell Law Directory

HOMER,* Claiborne Parish

SHAW, WEAVER, COLVIN & HENRY, L.L.C. (AV)

522 East Main Street, P.O. Box 239, 71040
Telephone: 318-927-6149
Fax: 318-927-2102

William M. Shaw, Sr.	James H. Colvin, Jr.
Charles E. Weaver	Patrick E. Henry

Representative Clients: Bank One; Homer Memorial Hospital; Claiborne Electric Cooperative; Industrial Packaging, Inc.; Gulfco Finance Inc.; The Money Store, Inc.; Louisiana Association of Business and Industry; Dixie Mart, Inc.; Foster Wheeler Corp.

For full biographical listings, see the Martindale-Hubbell Law Directory

LAFAYETTE,* Lafayette Parish

DAVIDSON, MEAUX, SONNIER, McELLIGOTT & SWIFT (AV)

810 South Buchanan Street, P.O. Drawer 2908, 70502
Telephone: 318-237-1660
Fax: 318-237-3676

(See Next Column)

DAVIDSON, MEAUX, SONNIER, McELLIGOTT & SWIFT, *Lafayette—Continued*

MEMBERS OF FIRM

James J. Davidson, Jr.
(1904-1990)
V. Farley Sonnier (1942-1988)
Richard C. Meaux, Sr.
James J. Davidson, III

John E. McElligott, Jr.
John G. Swift
Jeffrey A. Rhoades
Philip A. Fontenot
Kyle L. Gideon

Theodore G. Edwards, IV

ASSOCIATES

Jhan C. Boudreaux Beaullieu

Mark C. Andrus

Representative Clients: Southern Pacific Transportation Co., Wal-Mart Stores, Inc.; Power Rig Drilling Co., Inc.; Southwest Louisiana Electric Membership Corp.; Macro Oil Company; Highlands Insurance Company; United Services Automobile Association; Sears, Roebuck & Company; Lawyers Title Insurance Corporation; Wal-Mart Stores, Inc.; USAA.

For Complete List of Firm Personnel, See General Section

For full biographical listings, see the Martindale-Hubbell Law Directory

---

DOMENGEAUX WRIGHT MOROUX & ROY A PROFESSIONAL LAW CORPORATION (AV)

556 Jefferson Street, Suite 500, P.O. Box 3668, 70502-3668
Telephone: 318-233-3033; 1-800-375-3106
Fax: 318-232-8213

James Domengeaux (1907-1988)
Anthony D. Moroux
(1948-1993)
Bob F. Wright (A Professional
Law Corporation)
James Parkerson Roy (A
Professional Law Corporation)
Thomas R. Edwards (A
Professional Law Corporation)

Frank Edwards
James H. Domengeaux
Gilbert Hennigan Dozier (A
Professional Law Corporation)
Carla Marie Perron
Vivian Veron Neumann
Michael D. Goss

OF COUNSEL

Jerome E. Domengeaux

Reference: Mid-South National Bank; Advocate Financial, L.L.C.

For full biographical listings, see the Martindale-Hubbell Law Directory

---

HILL & BEYER, A PROFESSIONAL LAW CORPORATION (AV)

101 LaRue France, Suite 502, P.O. Box 53006, 70505-3006
Telephone: 318-232-9733
Fax: 1-318-237-2566

John K. Hill, Jr.
Bret C. Beyer
David R. Rabalais

Eugene P. Matherne (1962-1996)
Robert B. Purser
Erin J. Sherburne

Marianna Broussard

For full biographical listings, see the Martindale-Hubbell Law Directory

---

RICHARD R. KENNEDY A PROFESSIONAL LAW CORPORATION (AV)

309 Polk Street, P.O. Box 3243, 70502-3243
Telephone: 318-232-1934
Fax: 318-232-9720
Email: kennedy@net-connect.net

Richard R. Kennedy

For full biographical listings, see the Martindale-Hubbell Law Directory

---

LISKOW & LEWIS, A PROFESSIONAL LAW CORPORATION (AV)

822 Harding Street, P.O. Box 52008, 70505
Telephone: 318-232-7424
Telecopier: 318-267-2399
New Orleans, Louisiana Office: 50th Floor, One Shell Square.
Telephone: 504-581-7979.
Telecopier: 504-592-5108; 504-592-5109.

RESIDENT PERSONNEL

Lawrence P. Simon, Jr.
George H. Robinson, Jr.
Joseph C. Giglio, Jr.
Patrick W. Gray

Thomas M. McNamara
Charles B. Griffis, III
Mark A. Lowe
George Arceneaux III

Matt Jones

Representative Clients: Amerada Hess Corp.; Amoco Corporation; Bank One; BP America Inc.; Hibernia National Bank; Hunt Oil Company; Louisiana Public Service Commission; Mobil Oil Corp.; OXY U.S.A. Inc.; Union Oil Company of California; Union Pacific Resources Company.

For Complete List of Firm Personnel, See General Section

For full biographical listings, see the Martindale-Hubbell Law Directory

---

MANGHAM AND DAVIS (AV)

Suite 1400, First National Bank Towers, 600 Jefferson Street, P.O. Box 93110, 70509-3110
Telephone: 318-233-6200
Fax: 318-233-6521

Michael R. Mangham

Louis R. Davis

ASSOCIATES

Dawn Mayeux Fuqua

Claire A. Fisher

SPECIAL COUNSEL

Michael J. O'Shee

Reference: Hibernia National Bank, Lafayette, Louisiana.

For full biographical listings, see the Martindale-Hubbell Law Directory

---

ONEBANE, BERNARD, TORIAN, DIAZ, McNAMARA & ABELL (AV)

Suite 600, Versailles Centre, 102 Versailles Boulevard, P.O. Box 3507, 70502
Telephone: 318-237-2660
Telecopier: 318-266-1232
Cable Address: "Ondob"
Telex: 311283
Email: info@onebane.com

Joseph Onebane (1917-1987)
John G. Torian, II (1936-1991)
James E. Diaz
Timothy J. McNamara
Edward C. Abell, Jr.
Lawrence L. Lewis, III
Robert M. Mahony
Daniel G. Fournerat
Douglas W. Truxillo
Randall C. Songy
Michael G. Durand
Greg Guidry

Joseph L. Lemoine, Jr.
Mark L. Riley
Graham N. Smith
Gordon T. Whitman
Gary P. Kraus
Richard J. Petre, Jr.
Thomas G. Smart
Roger E. Ishee
John W. Penny, Jr.
John A. Keller
Jennifer McDaniel Kleinpeter
Steven C. Lanza

Joel P. Babineaux
Ted M. Anthony
Carolyn Trahan Bertrand
Alison M. Brumley
Craig A. Davis
Jesse D. Lambert

Charles M. Gordon, Jr.
Brent G. Sonnier
John D. Brouillette
Cristie L. Gautreaux
Elise Mayers Bouchner
(Not admitted in LA)

Cary B. Bryson

Representative Clients: Commercial Union Insurance Co.; Enron Corp.; First National Bank of Lafayette; Flores & Rucks, Inc.; Highlands Insurance Co.; Marathon Oil Co.; Pizza Hut, Inc.; Schering-Plough Corp.; Tenneco, Inc.; Whitney National Bank.

For full biographical listings, see the Martindale-Hubbell Law Directory

---

LAKE CHARLES,* Calcasieu Parish

BERGSTEDT & MOUNT (AV)

Second Floor, Magnolia Life Building, P.O. Drawer 3004, 70602-3004
Telephone: 318-433-3004
Facsimile: 318-433-8080

MEMBERS OF FIRM

Thomas M. Bergstedt

Benjamin W. Mount

ASSOCIATES

Van C. Seneca

Gregory P. Marceaux

Billy E. Loftin, Jr.

OF COUNSEL

Charles S. Ware

Representative Clients: Armstrong World Industries; Ashland Oil Co.; CIGNA Property & Casualty Companies; Homequity; Lake Area Medical Center; Leach Company; Olin Corporation; Terra Corporation; Town of Iowa; R. D. Werner Company.

For full biographical listings, see the Martindale-Hubbell Law Directory

---

JONES, TÊTE, NOLEN, HANCHEY, SWIFT, SPEARS & FONTI, L.L.P. (AV)

First Federal Building, P.O. Box 910, 70602
Telephone: 318-439-8315
Telefax: 436-5606; 433-5536

MEMBERS OF FIRM

Sam H. Jones (1897-1978)
William R. Tête
William M. Nolen
James C. Hanchey
Carl H. Hanchey
William B. Swift

Kenneth R. Spears
Edward J. Fonti
Charles N. Harper
Gregory W. Belfour
Robert J. Tête
Yul D. Lorio

OF COUNSEL

John A. Patin

Edward D. Myrick

(See Next Column)

JONES, TÊTE, NOLEN, HANCHEY, SWIFT, SPEARS & FONTI L.L.P.—*Continued*

ASSOCIATE
Lilynn A. Cutrer

General Counsel for: First Federal Savings & Loan Association of Lake Charles; Beauregard Electric Cooperative, Inc.
Representative Clients: Atlantic Richfield Company; CITGO Petroleum Corp.; Conoco Inc.; MONTELL U.S.A., Inc.; ITT Hartford; Olin Corporation; OXY USA Inc.; Premier Bank, National Association; W.R. Grace & Co.

For full biographical listings, see the Martindale-Hubbell Law Directory

---

PLAUCHÉ SMITH & NIESET, A PROFESSIONAL LAW CORPORATION (AV)

1123 Pithon Street, P.O. Drawer 1705, 70602
Telephone: 318-436-0522
Facsimile: 318-436-9637

S. W. Plauché (1889-1952)	Jeffrey M. Cole
S. W. Plauché, Jr. (1915-1966)	Andrew R. Johnson, IV
A. Lane Plauché	Charles V. Musso, Jr.
Allen L. Smith, Jr.	Christopher P. Ieyoub
James R. Nieset	H. David Vaughan, II
Frank M. Walker, Jr.	Joseph R. Pousson, Jr.
Michael J. McNulty, III	Rebecca S. Young

Representative Clients: CIGNA; CNA Insurance Cos.; Commercial Union Insurance Cos.; Crum & Forster; General Motors Corp.; Reliance Insurance Cos.; Royal Insurance Group; State Farm; U.S. Insurance Group.

For full biographical listings, see the Martindale-Hubbell Law Directory

---

RAGGIO, CAPPEL, CHOZEN & BERNIARD (AV)

500 Magnolia Life Building, P.O. Box 820, 70601
Telephone: 318-436-9481
Fax: 318-436-9499

MEMBERS OF FIRM

Thomas L. Raggio (Retired)	Stephen A. Berniard, Jr.
Richard B. Cappel	Christopher M. Trahan
Frederick L. Cappel	L. Paul Foreman
Richard A. Chozen	Kevin J. Koenig

Counsel for: Aetna Casualty & Surety Co.; Allstate Insurance Co.; Hercules Incorporated; Liberty Mutual Insurance Co.; Southern Pacific Co.; United States Fidelity and Guaranty Co.; Crowley Maritime Corp.; General Motors Corp.; Sabine Towing & Transportation Co.; E. I. duPont de Nemours & Co., Inc.

For Complete List of Firm Personnel, See General Section

For full biographical listings, see the Martindale-Hubbell Law Directory

---

SCOFIELD, GERARD, VERON, SINGLETARY & POHORELSKY, A PROFESSIONAL LAW CORPORATION (AV)

1114 Ryan Street, P.O. Drawer 3028, 70601
Telephone: 318-433-9436
Telefax: 318-436-0306

John B. Scofield	John R. Pohorelsky
Richard E. Gerard, Jr.	Scott J. Scofield
J. Michael Veron	Patrick D. Gallaugher, Jr.
C. Eston Singletary	Robert E. Landry
Russell J. Stutes, Jr.	

Representative Clients: Admiral Insurance Co.; Amoco Production Co.; Banc One; Browning-Ferris Industries, Inc.; Brown & Root Construction Co.; Cosmos Broadcasting Corp.; Dresser Industries, Inc.; Kansas City Southern Railway Co.; Mobil Oil Corp.; Phillips Petroleum Co.

For full biographical listings, see the Martindale-Hubbell Law Directory

---

METAIRIE, Jefferson Parish

CAMPBELL, MCCRANIE, SISTRUNK, ANZELMO & HARDY, P.C. (AV)

3445 North Causeway Boulevard, Suite 802, P.O. Box 7310, 70010-7310
Telephone: 504-831-0946
Fax: 504-831-2492

Frederick R. Campbell	Sidney J. Hardy
Burgess E. McCranie, Jr.	Lisa Miley Geary
Michael R. Sistrunk	Lance S. Ostendorf
Thomas P. Anzelmo	Roy C. Beard

Henry G. Sullivan, Jr.	Charles E. Sutton, Jr.
Adrian F. LaPeyronnie, III	Geoffrey J. Orr
Isidro René DeRojas	Shannon Kenney Lowry
Mark Emerson Hanna	Keith M. Matulich

For full biographical listings, see the Martindale-Hubbell Law Directory

---

*MONROE,** Ouachita Parish

HAYES, HARKEY, SMITH & CASCIO, L.L.P. (AV)

2811 Kilpatrick Boulevard, P.O. Box 8032, 71211-8032
Telephone: 318-387-2422
FAX: 318-388-5809

Thomas M. Hayes, Jr.	Charles S. Smith
(1915-1994)	Thomas M. Hayes, III
Louis D. Smith	Bruce McKamy Mintz
Joseph D. Cascio, Jr.	C. Joseph Roberts, III
John B. Saye	

OF COUNSEL
Haynes L. Harkey, Jr.

Karen L. Hayes	Elizabeth D. Bogan
Harry McClellan Moffett, IV	

Representative Clients: Cigna-Ina; CNA Insurance Group; St. Francis Medical Center, Inc.; St. Paul Insurance Group; Cooper Industries, Inc.; Dresser Industries, Inc.; State Farm Insurance Cos.; Travelers Insurance Cos.; Riverwood International Corp.; Scott Truck and Tractor Co.

For full biographical listings, see the Martindale-Hubbell Law Directory

---

MCLEOD VERLANDER (AV)

A Partnership including Professional Law Corporations
1900 North 18th Street, Suite 610, P.O. Box 2270, 71207-2270
Telephone: 318-325-7000
Telecopier: 318-324-0580
Email: mvlaw@iamerica.net

MEMBERS OF FIRM

Robert P. McLeod (P.L.C.)	Rick W. Duplissey
David E. Verlander, III (P.L.C.)	Pamela G. Nathan
Laurie J. Burkett	

For full biographical listings, see the Martindale-Hubbell Law Directory

---

SNELLINGS, BREARD, SARTOR, INABNETT & TRASCHER (AV)

1503 North 19th Street, P.O. Box 2055, 71207-2055
Telephone: 318-387-8000
Fax: 318-387-8200
Email: sbsit@bayou.com *URL:* http://www.bayou.com/sbsit

MEMBERS OF FIRM

George M. Snellings, Jr.	L. Kent Breard, Jr.
(1910-1984)	Clara Moss Sartor
Daniel Ryan Sartor, Jr.	William Brooks Watson
Carrick R. Inabnett	David C. McMillin
Charles C. Trascher, III	Jon Keith Guice

Representative Clients: Central Bank; Delta Air Lines, Inc.; Federal Deposit Insurance Co.; Glenwood Regional Medical Center; John Hancock Mutual Life Insurance Company; Kemper Insurance Group; Horace Mann Insurance Cos.

For Complete List of Firm Personnel, See General Section

For full biographical listings, see the Martindale-Hubbell Law Directory

---

*NEW ORLEANS,** Orleans Parish

BARHAM & ARCENEAUX, A PROFESSIONAL LAW CORPORATION (AV)

Suite 2700, Poydras Center, 650 Poydras Street, 70130-6101
Telephone: 504-525-4400
Fax: 504-525-6378

Mack E. Barham	Julia C. Symon
Robert E. Arceneaux	Travis Louis Bourgeois
Gail N. Wise	Hansel A. Harlen
Jerry Barfield Jordan	Robert Markle

OF COUNSEL
James A. Comiskey

For full biographical listings, see the Martindale-Hubbell Law Directory

---

BARRIOS, KINGSDORF & CASTEIX, L.L.P. (AV)

36th Floor, One Shell Square, 701 Poydras Street, 70139
Telephone: 504-524-3300
Fax: 504-524-3313

Dawn M. Barrios	Bruce S. Kingsdorf
Barbara Treuting Casteix	

For full biographical listings, see the Martindale-Hubbell Law Directory

---

CAPITELLI & WICKER (AV)

2950 Energy Centre, 1100 Poydras Street, 70163-2950
Telephone: 504-582-2425
FAX: 504-582-2422

(See Next Column)

CAPITELLI & WICKER, New Orleans—Continued

Ralph Capitelli   T. Carey Wicker, III
Paul Michael Elvir, Jr.

OF COUNSEL

Terry Q. Alarcon

For full biographical listings, see the Martindale-Hubbell Law Directory

CARL W. CLEVELAND & ASSOCIATES LLP (AV)

607 St. Charles Avenue, 70130-3411
Telephone: 504-522-7100

Carl W. Cleveland   George P. Vedros

ASSOCIATES

Timothy D. Scandurro   Jean-Paul Layrisson
Stephen O. Scandurro

For full biographical listings, see the Martindale-Hubbell Law Directory

THE GODFREY FIRM A PROFESSIONAL LAW CORPORATION (AV)

2500 Energy Centre, 1100 Poydras Street, 70163-2500
Telephone: 504-585-7538
Fax: 504-585-7535

Jarrell E. Godfrey, Jr.   Cloyd F. Van Hook
Patrick M. Files

For full biographical listings, see the Martindale-Hubbell Law Directory

WARREN A. GOLDSTEIN A PROFESSIONAL LAW CORPORATION (AV)

1515 Poydras Street, Suite 2350, 70112
Telephone: 504-581-7933
FAX: 504-595-3355

Warren A. Goldstein

For full biographical listings, see the Martindale-Hubbell Law Directory

HOUSE, KINGSMILL, RIESS & SEABOLT, L.L.C. (AV)

Place St. Charles, Suite 3300, 201 St. Charles Avenue, 70170
Telephone: 504-581-3300
Houston, Texas Office: Texas Commerce Tower, Suite 6950, 600 Travis Street, 77002.
Telephone: 713-222-6950.
Telecopier: 713-222-6955.

MEMBERS OF FIRM

W. Richard House, Jr.   Michael R.C. Riess
Marguerite K. Kingsmill   Charles F. Seabolt
Michael S. Haddad

OF COUNSEL

Seth J. Riklin (Resident, Houston, Texas Office)

ASSOCIATES

John S. Lawrence, Jr.   Thomas H. Huval
Jeffrey E. Combes   Randal R. Cangelosi
Robert B. Evans, III

For full biographical listings, see the Martindale-Hubbell Law Directory

KOPS, LEE, FUTRELL & PERLES, L.L.P. (AV)

Suite 2409 Place St. Charles 201 St. Charles Avenue, 70170
Telephone: 504-569-1725
Fax: 504-569-1726
Email: 103622.1066@compuserve.com

John Michael Kops   John Maurice Futrell
Gary A. Lee   Richard M. Perles

Representative Clients: Certain Underwriters at Lloyd's, London; Institute of London Underwriters Companies.

For full biographical listings, see the Martindale-Hubbell Law Directory

LADSON, ODOM & DES ROCHES, L.L.P. (AV)

A Partnership including Professional Corporations
35th Floor, Place Saint Charles, 201 Saint Charles Avenue, 70170
Telephone: 504-522-0077
Fax: 504-522-0078
Savannah, Georgia Office: Suite 401, The Realty Building, 24 Drayton Street, 31401.
Telephone: 912-234-1188.
Fax: 912-234-2377.
Hahira, Georgia Office: 217 West Main Street, P.O. Box 523, 31632.
Telephone: 912-794-3412.
Fax: 912-794-3544.

(See Next Column)

John Gregory Odom, PLC   Cary A. Des Roches
M. Brice Ladson, PC (Not   Stuart E. Des Roches
   admitted in LA; Resident,   Christopher J. Thompson (Not
   Savannah, Georgia Office)   admitted in LA; Resident,
                                   Savannah, Georgia Office)

OF COUNSEL

Linda V. Farrer (Not admitted in LA; Resident Of Counsel, Savannah, Georgia Office)

For full biographical listings, see the Martindale-Hubbell Law Directory

LAMOTHE & HAMILTON, A PROFESSIONAL LAW CORPORATION (AV)

Pan American Life Center, 601 Poydras Street, Suite 2750, 70130
Telephone: 504-566-1805
Telecopier: 504-566-1569
MCI Mail: 382-4472
Email: lhplc@neosoft.com

Frank E. Lamothe, III   Galen S. Brown
Charles E. Hamilton, III   M. Lizabeth Talbott
Karen Edginton Milner   Thomas J. Cortazzo

Reference: Jefferson Guaranty Bank, New Orleans, Louisiana.

For full biographical listings, see the Martindale-Hubbell Law Directory

LEA, TYNAN & McGEHEE, P.L.C. (AV)

Southern Marine and Aviation Building, 610 Poydras Street Suite 500, 70130
Telephone: 504-523-4500
Fax: 504-525-7208

Arden J. Lea   Joseph P. Tynan
         W. Clay McGehee

MEXICAN LEGAL ADVISOR

Ricardo Lan (Not admitted in the United States)

For full biographical listings, see the Martindale-Hubbell Law Directory

LEAKE & ANDERSSON, L.L.P. (AV)

1700 Energy Centre, 1100 Poydras Street, 70163-1701
Telephone: 504-585-7500
Telecopier: 504-585-7775
Email: LA1700@aol.com

MEMBERS OF FIRM

Robert E. Leake, Jr.   Kevin O'Bryon
W. Paul Andersson   George D. Fagan
Lawrence A. Mann   Donald E. McKay, Jr.
Marta-Ann Schnabel O'Bryon   Stanton E. Shuler, Jr.

ASSOCIATE

Guy D. Perrier

Representative Clients: Commercial Credit Services Corp.; First Financial Insurance Co.; Government Employees Insurance Co.; National Food Processors, Inc.; National Union Fire Insurance Co.; Nationwide Insurance Co.; Professional Construction Services, Inc.

For Complete List of Firm Personnel, See General Section

For full biographical listings, see the Martindale-Hubbell Law Directory

LISKOW & LEWIS, A PROFESSIONAL LAW CORPORATION (AV)

50th Floor, One Shell Square, 70139
Telephone: 504-581-7979
Telecopier: 504-556-4108; 504-556-4109
Lafayette, Louisiana Office: 822 Harding Street, P.O. Box 52008.
Telephone: 318-232-7424.
Telecopier: 318-267-2399.

Gene W. Lafitte   R. Keith Jarrett
J. Berry St. John, Jr.   Cheryl V. Cunningham
Donald R. Abaunza   Stevia M. Walther
John M. Wilson   Robert L. Theriot
Frederick W. Bradley   Dena L. Olivier
S. Gene Fendler   Marie Breaux
George J. Domas   Jonathan A. Hunter
Robert E. Holden   Thomas P. Diaz
Joe B. Norman   Mary S. Johnson
Philip K. Jones, Jr.   Kathleen Friel Hobson
William W. Pugh   Shaun G. Clarke
David W. Leefe   Scott C. Seiler
George Denegre, Jr.   Cheryl Mollere Kornick
Don K. Haycraft   Mark D. Latham
Wm. Craig Wyman   John C. Anjier
James A. Brown   Guenton C. Slawson, Jr.

(See Next Column)

LISKOW & LEWIS A PROFESSIONAL LAW CORPORATION—Continued

Shannon Skelton Holtzman	Michael D. Rubenstein
Carol Welborn Reisman	Peter C. Muller
Jill Thompson Losch	Susan Tart
David L. Reisman	Kevin P. Horne
Patricia Campbell Smith	Steven P. Crowther
Karen Daniel Ancelet	Harold J. Flanagan

Representative Clients: Atlantic Richfield Co.; Attorneys' Liability Assurance Society, Inc.; BP America, Inc.; Chevron U.S.A.; Federal Deposit Insurance Corporation; Mobil Oil Corp.; Prudential Securities Inc.; Shell Offshore Inc.; Texaco Inc.; Texas Commerce Bank, N.A.

For Complete List of Firm Personnel, See General Section

For full biographical listings, see the Martindale-Hubbell Law Directory

PHELPS DUNBAR, L.L.P. (AV)

Texaco Center, 400 Poydras Street, 70130-3245
Telephone: 504-566-1311
Telecopier: 504-568-9130, 504-568-9007
Cable Address: "Howspencer"
Telex: 584125 WU
Telex: 6821155 WUI
Email: info@phelps.com
Baton Rouge, Louisiana Office: Suite 701, City National Bank Building, P.O. Box 4412.
Telephone: 504-346-0285.
Telecopier: 504-381-9197.
Jackson, Mississippi Office: Suite 500, Mtel Centré, 200 South Lamar Street, P.O. Box 23066.
Telephone: 601-352-2300.
Telecopier: 601-360-9777.
Tupelo, Mississippi Office: Seventh Floor, One Mississippi Plaza, P.O. Box 1220.
Telephone: 601-842-7907.
Telecopier: 601-842-3873.
Houston, Texas Office: Suite 900, 3040 Post Oak Boulevard.
Telephone: 713-626-1386.
Telecopier: 713-626-1388.
London, England Office: Suite 731, Level 7, Lloyd's, 1 Lime Street, London EC3M 7DQ England.
Telephone: 011-44-171-929-4765.
Telecopier: 011-44-171-929-0046.
Telex: 987321.

MEMBERS OF FIRM

Harry Rosenberg	Nancy Scott Degan
Roy C. Cheatwood	M. Nan Alessandra
Danny G. Shaw	Mary Ellen Roy
Brent B. Barriere	Sessions Ault Hootsell III
Bruce V. Schewe	Paul L. Peyronnin
William D. Aaron, Jr.	Gerardo R. Barrios

ASSOCIATES

Thomas M. Beh	Kent A. Lambert
Diane Hollenshead Copes	Skye Henry O'Donnell
Robert S. Eitel	Vanessa A. Richelle
N. Eleanor Graham	Jennifer Burrows Solis
David M. Korn	Tania Tetlow
M. David Kurtz	Michael F. Weiner

Ronald J. White

Representative Clients: Fidelity Investments; First National Bank of Commerce; Hibernia National Bank; Hilton Hotels Corp.; Lawyers Title Insurance Company; Louisiana Gas Service Co., Inc.; Pulitzer Broadcasting Corp.; Texas Gas Transmission Corp.; The Travelers Insurance Company; Witco Corp.

For Complete List of Firm Personnel, See General Section

For full biographical listings, see the Martindale-Hubbell Law Directory

SMITH, JONES & FAWER, L.L.P. (AV)

201 St. Charles Avenue, Suite 3702, 70170
Telephone: 504-525-2200
Telecopier: 504-525-2205

MEMBERS OF FIRM

Randall A. Smith (P.C.)	Gladstone N. Jones, III

Michael S. Fawer

ASSOCIATES

Andrew L. Kramer	L. Tiffany Hawkins

For full biographical listings, see the Martindale-Hubbell Law Directory

ROBERT E. TARCZA (AV)

Thirteen Ten Whitney Building, Two Twenty Eight St. Charles Avenue, 70130
Telephone: 504-525-6696
Fax: 504-525-6701

(See Next Column)

ASSOCIATE

Juliet Puissegur Bland

OF COUNSEL

G. Anthony Gelderman, III

For full biographical listings, see the Martindale-Hubbell Law Directory

WILSON & BOWLING (AV)

A Partnership including Professional Law Corporations
Suite 2411, Place St. Charles, 201 St. Charles Avenue, 70170
Telephone: 504-586-5200
Facsimile: 504-586-5201

Gordon F. Wilson, Jr., (P.L.C.)	Steven F. Grover
David A. Bowling (P.L.C.)	Jeanne B. Roques

LEGAL SUPPORT PERSONNEL

LITIGATION PARALEGALS

Susan Lenfant	Kerry Whiteside

For full biographical listings, see the Martindale-Hubbell Law Directory

---

SHREVEPORT,* Caddo Parish

TROY E. BAIN (AV)

1540 Irving Place, 71101
Telephone: 318-221-0076
Fax: 318-227-8290

Reference: Commercial National Bank of Shreveport.

For full biographical listings, see the Martindale-Hubbell Law Directory

BARLOW AND HARDTNER L.C. (AV)

Tenth Floor, Louisiana Tower, 401 Edwards Street, 71101-3289
Telephone: 318-227-1131
Telecopier: 318-227-1141
Mailing Address: P.O. Box 8, Shreveport, Louisiana, 71161-0008

Malcolm S. Murchison	Clair F. White
Kay Cowden Medlin	Philip E. Downer, III
Joseph L. Shea, Jr.	Michael B. Donald
David R. Taggart	Jay A. Greenleaf

Representative Clients: Anderson Oil & Gas, Inc.; Beaird Industries, Inc.; Kelley Oil Corporation; NorAm Energy Corp. (formerly Arkla, Inc.); Panhandle Eastern Corp.; Southwestern Electric Power Company; Central and South West Corporation; Pennzoil Producing Co.; Johnson Controls, Inc.; First Family Financial Services, Inc.

For Complete List of Firm Personnel, See General Section

For full biographical listings, see the Martindale-Hubbell Law Directory

ROBERT U. GOODMAN, P.L.C. (AV)

Mid South Towers, 416 Travis Street, Suite 1105, 71101-5514
Telephone: 318-221-1601
Fax: 318-221-1749

Robert U. Goodman

OF COUNSEL

Nancy Kay Fox-Reiter

Representative Clients: Trans-World Life Insurance Co.; Aeropres Corp.; Dealers Truck & Equipment Co.; Pioneer Bank & Trust Co.; Steel Erectors, Inc.; Powell Buick, Inc.; Housing Authority of the City of Shreveport; Specht Newspapers, Inc.; Graham Brothers Entertainment, Inc.; Integrated Exploration, Inc.

For full biographical listings, see the Martindale-Hubbell Law Directory

HARGROVE, PESNELL & WYATT, A P.L.C. (AV)

400 Texas Street Suite 1102, 71101
Telephone: 318-429-7200
Fax: 318-429-7201
Mailing Address: P.O. Box 59, Shreveport, Louisiana, 71161-0059

Billy R. Pesnell	David L. Smelley
Thomas James Wyatt	A. L. Wedgeworth, III
Joseph L. Hargrove, Jr.	Paul A. Strickland

Scott C. Sinclair

For full biographical listings, see the Martindale-Hubbell Law Directory

MAYER, SMITH & ROBERTS, L.L.P. (AV)

1550 Creswell, 71101
Telephone: 318-222-2135, 222-2268
Fax: 318-222-6420
Email: (Attorney's First Name)@MSRLAW.COM

(See Next Column)

MAYER, SMITH & ROBERTS L.L.P., *Shreveport—Continued*

MEMBERS OF FIRM

Caldwell Roberts	David Butterfield
Walter O. Hunter, Jr.	Henry N. Bellamy
Mark A. Goodwin	John C. Turnage
Ben Marshall, Jr.	Paul R. Mayer, Jr.
Alexander S. Lyons	Steven E. Soileau
Kim Purdy Thomas	Deborah Shea Baukman

Caldwell Roberts, Jr.

ASSOCIATES

Frank K. Carroll	Dalton Roberts Ross

OF COUNSEL

Charles L. Mayer	Paul R. Mayer

Representative Clients: CNA Insurance Companies; Liberty Mutual Insurance Company; The St. Paul Companies; United States Fidelity and Guaranty Company; Schumpert Medical Center; Travelers Insurance Company; Great American Insurance Company; Insurance Corporation of America; Highlands Insurance Company.

For full biographical listings, see the Martindale-Hubbell Law Directory

MILLS, TIMMONS & FLOWERS, A PROFESSIONAL LAW CORPORATION (AV)

300 Law Center, 331 Milam Street, P.O. Box 1784, 71166-1784
Telephone: 318-222-0337
Fax: 318-222-5400

George H. Mills, Jr.	David C. Turansky
Wayne Timmons	J. Broocks Greer III
Peter R. Flowers	Sandra Lynn Walker

OF COUNSEL

William T. Allison

Reference: Hibernia National Bank.

For full biographical listings, see the Martindale-Hubbell Law Directory

SOCKRIDER, BOLIN & ANGLIN, A PROFESSIONAL LAW CORPORATION (AV)

327 Crockett Street, 71101
Telephone: 318-221-5503
Fax: 318-221-3849

John R. Pleasant (1905-1983)	James E. Bolin, Jr.
H. F. Sockrider, Jr.	D. Rex Anglin

Gregory H. Batte

For full biographical listings, see the Martindale-Hubbell Law Directory

WEEMS, WRIGHT, SCHIMPF, HAYTER & CARMOUCHE, A PROFESSIONAL LAW CORPORATION (AV)

912 Kings Highway, 71104
Telephone: 318-222-2100
Fax: 318-226-5100

Carey T. Schimpf	Paul J. Carmouche
John O. Hayter, III	Mark A. Perkins

Brian D. Landry

Representative Clients: Royal Insurance Co.; Lutheran Benevolent Ins. Co.; Patterson Ins. Co.; Louisiana Indemnity; Louisiana Insurance Guaranty Association; State of Louisiana; Louisiana State University Medical Center; Hibernia National Bank; St. Paul Fire & Marine Insurance Company; Clarendon National Insurance; Commercial Union Insurance Co.; Penn-/American Insurance; Davison Insurance Co.; Davison Transport, Inc.; Stephenson Trucking; Harvest Foods Inc.

For full biographical listings, see the Martindale-Hubbell Law Directory

WILKINSON, CARMODY & GILLIAM (AV)

1700 Beck Building, 400 Travis Street, P.O. Box 1707, 71166
Telephone: 318-221-4196
Telecopier: 318-221-3705

MEMBERS OF FIRM

John D. Wilkinson (1867-1929)	Bobby S. Gilliam
William Scott Wilkinson	Mark E. Gilliam
(1895-1985)	Penny D. Sellers
Arthur R. Carmody, Jr.	Patrick F. Robinson

Michael J. Ryan

Representative Clients: Farmers Insurance Group; Home Federal Savings & Loan Association of Shreveport; The Kansas City Southern Railway Co.; KTAL-TV; Lincoln National Life Insurance Co.; Mobil Oil Co.; Schumpert Medical Center; Sears, Roebuck & Co.; Southern Pacific Transportation Co.; Southwestern Electric Power Co.

For full biographical listings, see the Martindale-Hubbell Law Directory

---

*WINNFIELD,** Winn Parish

SIMMONS AND DERR (AV)

Simmons Building, Church Street, P.O. Box 525, 71483
Telephone: 318-628-3951

MEMBERS OF FIRM

Kermit M. Simmons	Jacque D. Derr

Reference: Bank of Winnfield & Trust Co.

For full biographical listings, see the Martindale-Hubbell Law Directory

MAINE

---

*AUGUSTA,** Kennebec Co.

* indicates certain Bar Register subscribers whose principal office is located elsewhere in the state and who have arranged for representation as a part of the state capital listings that follow

JOHNSON, WEBBERT & LAUBENSTEIN (AV)

160 Capitol Street, P.O. Box 29, 04332-0029
Telephone: 207-623-5110
Fax: 207-622-4160

Phillip E. Johnson	David G. Webbert

William H. Laubenstein, III

Representative Clients: Agway, Inc.; AVEMCO; Central Maine Power Co.; The Doctors Company; ITT/Hartford; Loss Management Services, Inc.; Shand, Morahan & Co.; Union Water Power Company; USAIG.

For full biographical listings, see the Martindale-Hubbell Law Directory

LIPMAN & KATZ, P.A. (AV)

227 Water Street, 04330
Telephone: 207-622-3711
Telecopier: 207-622-7415

Sumner H. Lipman	Robert J. Stolt
David M. Lipman	Keith R. Varner
Roger J. Katz	Ronald E. Colby, III

Laura J.R. Garcia	Walter F. McKee

OF COUNSEL

Joseph B. Campbell

For full biographical listings, see the Martindale-Hubbell Law Directory

* PIERCE ATWOOD (AV)

77 Winthrop Street, 04330
Telephone: 207-622-6311
Fax: 207-623-9367
Email: info@PierceAtwood.com
Portland, Maine Office: One Monument Square.
Telephone: 207-791-1100.
Fax: 207-791-1350.
Newburyport, Massachusetts Office: 6 Harris Street.
Telephone: 508-465-9599.
Fax: 508-465-9945.

MEMBERS OF FIRM

Malcolm L. Lyons	Michael D. Seitzinger

John C. Nivison

ASSOCIATE

Daniel J. Stevens

For Complete List of Firm Personnel, See General Section

For full biographical listings, see the Martindale-Hubbell Law Directory

---

*BANGOR,** Penobscot Co.

EATON, PEABODY, BRADFORD & VEAGUE, P.A. (AV)

Fleet Center-Exchange Street, P.O. Box 1210, 04402-1210
Telephone: 207-947-0111
Telecopier: 207-942-3040
Email: epbv@aol.com
Augusta, Maine Office: 2 Central Plaza.
Telephone: 207-622-3747.
Telecopier: 207-622-9732.
Blue Hill, Maine Office: One East Blue Hill Road.
Telephone: 207-374-2812.
Telecopier: 207-374-2548.
Brunswick, Maine Office: 167 Park Row.
Telephone: 207-729-1144.
Telecopier: 207-729-1140.
Camden, Maine Office: 7-9 Washington Street.
Telephone: 207-236-3325.
Telecopier: 207-236-8611.

(See Next Column)

EATON, PEABODY, BRADFORD & VEAGUE P.A.—*Continued*

Dover-Foxcroft, Maine Office: 30 East Main Street.
Telephone: 207-564-8378.
Telecopier: 207-564-7059.

Thomas M. Brown	Paul L. Gibbons
Bernard J. Kubetz	(Resident, Camden Office)
Stephen G. Morrell	Laurie A. Dart
(Resident, Brunswick Office)	Judy A.S. Metcalf
Glen L. Porter	(Resident, Brunswick Office)
Gordon H. S. Scott	Jonathan B. Huntington
(Resident, Augusta Office)	(Resident, Dover-Foxcroft
William B. Devoe	Office)
Terry W. Calderwood	Thad B. Zmistowski
(Resident, Camden Office)	

OF COUNSEL

Martin L. Wilk (Resident, Brunswick Office)

Dorisann B. W. Wagner (Resident, Augusta Office)

A List of Representative Clients available upon request.

For Complete List of Firm Personnel, See General Section

For full biographical listings, see the Martindale-Hubbell Law Directory

GROSS, MINSKY, MOGUL & SINGAL, P.A. (AV)

Key Plaza, 23 Water Street, P.O. Box 917, 04402-0917
Telephone: 207-942-4644
Telecopier: 207-942-3699
Email: gmm&s-law@atlsysnet.com *URL:*
http://www.atlsysnet.com/gmms

Edward I. Gross (Retired)	George C. Schelling
Jules L. Mogul (1930-1994)	Edward W. Gould
Norman Minsky	Steven J. Mogul
George Z. Singal	James R. Wholly
Louis H. Kornreich	Daniel A. Pileggi
	Philip K. Clarke

Wayne P. Libhart (Retired)	James S. Nixon
Sandra L. Rothera	F. Todd Lowell

Representative Client: Dahl Chase Pathology Associates.
Local Counsel for: The St. Paul Insurance Cos.; Aetna Life & Casualty Co.; Imperial Casualty & Indemnity Co.

For full biographical listings, see the Martindale-Hubbell Law Directory

VAFIADES, BROUNTAS & KOMINSKY (AV)

Key Plaza, 23 Water Street, P.O. Box 919, 04402-0919
Telephone: 207-947-6915
Telecopier: 207-941-0863

MEMBERS OF FIRM

Susan R. Kominsky	Marvin H. Glazier
	Eugene C. Coughlin, III

OF COUNSEL

Lewis V. Vafiades

For Complete List of Firm Personnel, See General Section

For full biographical listings, see the Martindale-Hubbell Law Directory

BAR HARBOR, Hancock Co.

FENTON, CHAPMAN, FENTON, SMITH & KANE, P.A. (AV)

109 Main Street, P.O. Box B, 04609
Telephone: 207-288-3331
FAX: 207-288-9326

Douglas B. Chapman	Nathaniel R. Fenton
	Chadbourn H. Smith

Margaret A. Timothy

Reference: Bar Harbor Banking and Trust Co.

For Complete List of Firm Personnel, See General Section

For full biographical listings, see the Martindale-Hubbell Law Directory

BATH,* Sagadahoc Co.

CONLEY & HALEY (AV)

Thirty Front Street, 04530
Telephone: 207-443-5576
Telefax: 207-443-6665

J. Michael Conley	Laura M. O'Hanlon
Mark L. Haley	Tracey G. Burton
Brian L. Champion	Julie G. Martin

Representative Clients: Bath Iron Works Corporation; Central Maine Power Company; Saco Defense, Inc.; Sugarloaf Mountain Corporation; Maine Public Service Company.

(See Next Column)

References: Key Bank of Maine; First Federal Savings & Loan Association of Bath; Brunswick Federal Savings.

For full biographical listings, see the Martindale-Hubbell Law Directory

ELLSWORTH,* Hancock Co.

HALE & HAMLIN (AV)

10 State Street, P.O. Box 729, 04605
Telephone: 207-667-2561
Telefax: 207-667-8790
Email: http://www.halehaml.com

MEMBER OF FIRM

Barry K. Mills

ASSOCIATE

Laura Yustak Smith

Approved Attorneys for: Lawyers Title Insurance Corp.

For full biographical listings, see the Martindale-Hubbell Law Directory

PORTLAND,* Cumberland Co.

AMERLING & BURNS, A PROFESSIONAL ASSOCIATION (AV)

193 Middle Street, 04101
Telephone: 207-775-3581
Facsimile: 207-775-3814
Affiliated St. Croix Office: Coon & Sanford, P.O. Box 25918, Six Chandlers's Wharf, Suite 202, 00824-0918.

W. John Amerling	Arnold C. Macdonald
George F. Burns	Mary DeLano
David P. Ray	Joanne F. Cole
	A. Robert Ruesch

OF COUNSEL

Bruce M. Jervis

Representative Clients: H.E. Sargent, Inc. (construction); Merrill Trust; J.M. Huber, Inc.; Jackson Laboratories; Hague International (engineering); Aetna Life & Casualty Co.; The Hartford; Great American Insurance Co.; Wausau Insurance Co.

For full biographical listings, see the Martindale-Hubbell Law Directory

BENNETT AND ASSOCIATES, P.A. (AV)

Suite 300, 121 Middle Street, P.O. Box 7799, 04112-7799
Telephone: 207-773-4775
Telecopier: 207-774-2366
Email: 104142.2363@compuserve.com

Herbert H. Bennett (1928-1992)	Frederick B. Finberg
Peter Bennett	Melinda J. Caterine
Jeffrey Bennett	Clare S. Benedict

Counsel for: Associated Grocers of New England; Coca Cola Bottling Company of Northern New England, Inc.; General Star Indemnity Company; Northern Utilities/Bay State Gas; Pratt & Whitney (Division of United Technologies); Primerica Financial Services (The Travelers); Sprague Energy (C.H. Sprague & Son); Perrier Group of America, Inc.; Lepage Bakeries, Inc. (Country Kitchen); Texaco, Inc.

For full biographical listings, see the Martindale-Hubbell Law Directory

FRIEDMAN & BABCOCK (AV)

Suite 400, Six City Center, P.O. Box 4726, 04112-4726
Telephone: 207-761-0900
Telecopier: 207-761-0186

MEMBERS OF FIRM

Harold J. Friedman	Thomas A. Cox
Ernest J. Babcock	Karen Frink Wolf
Martha C. Gaythwaite	Jennifer S. Begel
	Laurence H. Leavitt

ASSOCIATES

Theodore H. Irwin, Jr.	Elizabeth A. Germani
Lee H. Bals	Jonathan Marc Dunitz
Michelle Allott	Darren Blaine Riggle
Arthur J. Lamothe	Tracy D. Hill
	Bruce W. Hepler

For full biographical listings, see the Martindale-Hubbell Law Directory

JENSEN BAIRD GARDNER & HENRY (AV)

Ten Free Street, P.O. Box 4510, 04112
Telephone: 207-775-7271
Telecopier: 207-775-7935
York County Office: 419 Alfred Street, Biddeford, Maine.
Telephone: 207-282-5107.
Telecopier: 207-282-6301.

MEMBERS OF FIRM

James E. Kaplan	Deborah M. Mann
Michael A. Nelson	Keith R. Jacques (Resident,
Joseph H. Groff III	York County Office)

(See Next Column)

JENSEN BAIRD GARDNER & HENRY, Portland—Continued
ASSOCIATES

Julianne Cloutier
Emily A. Bloch

Anne H. Jordan (Resident, York County Office)

Representative Clients: IBM; General Motors Acceptance Corp.; Aetna Life & Casualty; GEICO; Owens Corning Fiberglass; Sedgwick James; Bristol-Myers Squibb Co.; Shaw's Supermarkets.

For Complete List of Firm Personnel, See General Section

For full biographical listings, see the Martindale-Hubbell Law Directory

PERKINS, THOMPSON, HINCKLEY & KEDDY, P.A. (AV)

One Canal Plaza, P.O. Box 426, 04112-0426
Telephone: 207-774-2635

Thomas Schulten
Bruce E. Leddy
Owen W. Wells
Douglas S. Carr
Andrew A. Cadot
John R. Opperman
Philip C. Hunt
John S. Upton

Peggy L. McGehee
Melissa Hanley Murphy
John H. Rich III
John A. Ciraldo
John A. Hobson
Helen I. Muther
Timothy P. Benoit
Fred W. Bopp III

Craig N. Denekas

Mark P. Snow

For Complete List of Firm Personnel, See General Section

For full biographical listings, see the Martindale-Hubbell Law Directory

PETRUCCELLI & MARTIN (AV)

50 Monument Square, P.O. Box 9733, 04104-5033
Telephone: 207-775-0200
Telecopier: 207-775-2360

MEMBERS OF FIRM

Gerald F. Petruccelli
Joel C. Martin

Daniel W. Bates
Michael K. Martin

James B. Haddow

ASSOCIATES

Linda C. Russell

Thomas C. Bradley

John Anderson

Representative Clients: Associated Aviation Underwriters; Bombardier, Inc.; Chicago Title Insurance Co.; Chubb Insurance Co.; Coopers & Lybrand; Cumberland Farms; Granger Northern Construction Co.; Maine Medical Center; Union Mutual Fire Insurance Co.; Vermont Mutual Insurance Co.

For full biographical listings, see the Martindale-Hubbell Law Directory

PIERCE ATWOOD (AV)

One Monument Square, 04101
Telephone: 207-791-1100
Fax: 207-791-1350
Email: info@PierceAtwood.com
Augusta, Maine Office: 77 Winthrop Street.
Telephone: 207-622-6311.
Fax: 207-623-9367.
Newburyport, Massachusetts Office: 6 Harris Street.
Telephone: 508-465-9599.
Fax: 508-465-9945.

MEMBERS OF FIRM

Ralph I. Lancaster, Jr.
Jotham D. Pierce, Jr.
Malcolm L. Lyons
  (Resident, Augusta Office)
John O'Leary
Peter W. Culley
Jeffrey M. White
Louise K. Thomas
Michael D. Seitzinger
  (Resident, Augusta Office)

Daniel M. Snow
William J. Kayatta, Jr.
James R. Erwin, II
John C. Nivison
  (Resident, Augusta Office)
John J. Aromando
Catherine R. Connors
David E. Barry

ASSOCIATES

Daniel J. Stevens
  (Resident, Augusta Office)

Michael N. Ambler, Jr.
Jared S. des Rosiers

Debra L. Brown

COUNSEL

Michael S. Wilson

For Complete List of Firm Personnel, See General Section

For full biographical listings, see the Martindale-Hubbell Law Directory

PRETI, FLAHERTY, BELIVEAU & PACHIOS (AV)

A Limited Liability Company
443 Congress Street, P.O. Box 11410, 04104-7410
Telephone: 207-791-3000
Telecopier: 207-791-3111
Email: admin@pfbpnet.com
Augusta, Maine Office: 45 Memorial Circle, P.O. Box 1058, 04332-1058.
Telephone: 207-623-5300.
Telecopier: 207-623-2914.

MEMBERS OF FIRM

Severin M. Beliveau
  (Augusta Office)
Keith A. Powers
Christopher D. Nyhan
Jonathan S. Piper
Daniel Rapaport
Bruce C. Gerrity
  (Augusta Office)
Jeffrey T. Edwards

Michael G. Messerschmidt
Randall B. Weill
Evan M. Hansen
Edward R. Benjamin, Jr.
Geoffrey K. Cummings
Michael Kaplan
Stephen E. F. Langsdorf
  (Augusta Office)
John P. McVeigh

Elizabeth A. Olivier

OF COUNSEL

Albert J. Beliveau, Jr.

ASSOCIATES

Nelson J. Larkins

Kevin J. Beal

Representative Clients: Crum & Forster; United States Fidelity Guaranty Co.; St. Paul Fire & Marine Insurance Co.; American International Group; PHICO Insurance Company; Dunlap Corp.; Maine Municipal Association; Liberty Group; Key Bank of Maine.

For Complete List of Firm Personnel, See General Section

For full biographical listings, see the Martindale-Hubbell Law Directory

THOMPSON & BOWIE (AV)

Three Canal Plaza, P.O. Box 4630, 04112
Telephone: 207-774-2500
Telecopier: 207-774-3591

MEMBERS OF FIRM

Roy E. Thompson, Jr.
James M. Bowie
Daniel R. Mawhinney
Rebecca H. Farnum
Glenn H. Robinson

Frank W. DeLong, III
Michael E. Saucier
Mark V. Franco
Elizabeth Knox Peck
Cathy S. Roberts

ASSOCIATE

Paul C. Catsos

Representative Clients: Aetna Life & Casualty; Chrysler Corp.; W.R. Grace & Co.; Hertz; Chubb Group; Abbott Laboratories.

For full biographical listings, see the Martindale-Hubbell Law Directory

TROUBH, HEISLER & PIAMPIANO, P.C. (AV)

511 Congress Street, P.O. Box 9711, 04104-5011
Telephone: 207-780-6789
Fax: 207-774-2339

William B. Troubh
Edwin A. Heisler
Robert J. Piampiano
Kevin M. Gillis
Michael P. Boyd

Thomas E. Getchell
Michael Richards
William K. McKinley
Daniel F. Gilligan
Paul S. Bulger

John G. Richardson

Linda L. Sears

Daniel R. Felkel

For full biographical listings, see the Martindale-Hubbell Law Directory

SACO, York Co.

SMITH ELLIOTT SMITH & GARMEY, P.A. (AV)

199 Main Street, P.O. Box 1179, 04072
Telephone: 207-282-1527
Telefax: 207-283-4412
Sanford Telephone: 207-324-1560
Portland Telephone: 207-774-3199
Wells Telephone: 207-646-0970
Kennebunk, Maine Office: Route One South, 9 York Street.
Telephone: 207-985-4464.
Telefax: 207-985-3946.
Portland, Maine Office: 100 Commercial Street, Suite 304.
Telephone: 207-774-3199.
Telefax: 207-774-2235.

Randall E. Smith
Charles W. Smith, Jr.
Terrence D. Garmey
Peter W. Schroeter

Richard P. Romeo
Robert H. Furbish
John H. O'Neil, Jr.
Harry B. Center, II

David S. Abramson

Representative Clients: Town of Waterboro, Maine; City of Biddeford; Saco and Biddeford Savings Institution; Ocean Communities Federal Credit Union.

(See Next Column)

SMITH ELLIOTT SMITH & GARMEY P.A.—*Continued*

Local Counsel for: East Guard Insurance Co.
References: Saco & Biddeford Savings Institution.

For Complete List of Firm Personnel, See General Section

For full biographical listings, see the Martindale-Hubbell Law Directory

---

SKOWHEGAN, * Somerset Co.

WRIGHT & MILLS, P.A. (AV)

218 Water Street, P.O. Box 9, 04976
Telephone: 207-474-3324
Telefax: 207-474-3609

Carl R. Wright   Paul P. Sumberg
S. Peter Mills   Janet T. Mills
Kenneth A. Lexier

Representative Clients: Design Professionals Insurance Co., New Jersey; Solon Manufacturing Co., Solon, Maine; Kleinschmidt Associates-Engineers, Pittsfield, Maine; Acheron Engineering, Newport, Maine; E.W. Littlefield-Contractors, Hartland, Maine; WBRC-Architects, Bangor, Maine; Town of Skowhegan; Town of Norridgewock.

For full biographical listings, see the Martindale-Hubbell Law Directory

---

YORK, York Co.

ERWIN, OTT, CLARK & CAMPBELL (AV)

16A Woodbridge Road, P.O. Box 545, 03909
Telephone: 207-363-5208
Facsimile: 207-363-5322

MEMBERS OF FIRM
Frank E. Hancock (1923-1988)   John P. Campbell
James S. Erwin   David N. Ott
Jeffery J. Clark

For full biographical listings, see the Martindale-Hubbell Law Directory

---

MARYLAND

ANNAPOLIS, * Anne Arundel Co.

BRASSEL & BALDWIN, P.A. (AV)

Suite 501, 116 Defense Highway, 21401
Telephone: 410-224-6600
DC Metro: 301-261-2102
Fax: 410-974-6019
Email: BBLAWYERS@AOL.COM
Baltimore, Maryland Office: The B & O Building, Suite 920. 2 North Charles Street, 21201-3754.
Telephone: 410-974-6000.
Fax: 410-385-2939.

Rignal W. Baldwin, Jr.   Jon W. Brassel

Jonathan P. Kagan   Mary Coale Baldwin
Alexander John May
OF COUNSEL
Richard T. Stansbury (Resident, Baltimore, Maryland Office)

For full biographical listings, see the Martindale-Hubbell Law Directory

---

DALNEKOFF & MASON, P.A. (AV)

Suite 301 West Court Building, 2448 Holly Avenue, 21401-3177
Telephone: 410-841-6500; 266-0544
D.C.: 301-261-8671
Fax: 410-224-4135
Email: 74671.471@compuserve.com
Affiliated with: Morgan and Hendrick, 317 Whitehead Street, Key West, Florida.
Telephone: 305-296-5676.

Carol S. Craig   Leonard E. Moodispaw
Barry J. Dalnekoff   Royal G. Shannonhouse, III
Mark E. Mason   Nelson R. Stewart
Thomas J. Voigt
OF COUNSEL
Matthew S. Evans, Jr.

Reference: NationsBank, Annapolis, Maryland.

For full biographical listings, see the Martindale-Hubbell Law Directory

---

L. VERNON MILLER, JR. (AV)

123 Cathedral Street, 21401
Telephone: 410-268-5570

For full biographical listings, see the Martindale-Hubbell Law Directory

---

WHARTON LEVIN EHRMANTRAUT KLEIN & NASH, A PROFESSIONAL ASSOCIATION (AV)

104 West Street, P.O. Box 551, 21404-0551
Telephone: 800-322-1984; 410-263-5900
Facsimile: 410-280-2230; 410-263-1562
Baltimore, Maryland Office: 400 East Pratt Street.
Telephone: 410-269-7529.
Bethesda, Maryland Office: 7200 Wisconsin Avenue, Suite 308.
Telephone: 301-656-1001.
Facsimile: 301-656-0808.

James T. Wharton   Michael T. Wharton
David A. Levin   Andrew E. Vernick
Robert Dale Klein   D. Lee Rutland
Brian J. Nash   David A. Roling
A. Gwynn Bowie, Jr.   Brian F. Holeman
Jack L. Harvey   (Not admitted in MD)
OF COUNSEL
William A. Ehrmantraut

Debra S. Block   Marian L. Hogan
Daniel C. Costello   Leonard William Dooren, III
Christian A. Lodowski   Mary C. Rice
Douglas K. Schrader   Justine D. Smith
Linda G. Wales   Michael Kevin Wiggins
Stuart N. Herschfeld   Kimberly C. Dumpson
Denise Atkinson Clark   Victoria H. Wink

For full biographical listings, see the Martindale-Hubbell Law Directory

---

BALTIMORE, * (Independent City)

ALBRIGHT BROWN & CAUDILL, LLC (AV)

120 East Baltimore Street Suite 2150, 21202
Telephone: 410-244-0350
Facsimile: 410-244-0356
Elkton, Maryland Office: 151 East Main Street. 21921.
Telephone: 410-398-3850.
Fax: 410-392-5633.

David F. Albright   Karolyn N. Bowe (Resident,
C. Thomas Brown   Elkton, Maryland Office)
Franklin T. Caudill   Cynthia E. Rodgers-Waire

For full biographical listings, see the Martindale-Hubbell Law Directory

---

ALLEN, JOHNSON, ALEXANDER & KARP, P.A. (AV)

Suite 1540, 100 East Pratt Street, 21202
Telephone: 410-727-5000
Fax: 410-727-0861
Washington, D.C. Office: 1707 L Street, N.W., Suite 1050.
Telephone: 202-828-4141.

John D. Alexander, Jr.   D'Ana E. Johnson (Resident,
Daniel Karp   Washington, D.C. Office)
Yvette M. Bryant
OF COUNSEL
Donald C. Allen

Denise Ramsburg Stanley   James X. Crogan, Jr.
George B. Breen (Not admitted   Kevin Bock Karpinski
in MD; Resident, Washington,   Gregory James Dumark
D.C. Office)

Representative Clients: Scottsdale Insurance Co.; Nautilus Insurance Co.; Jefferson Insurance Co.; Liberty Mutual Insurance Co.; Avis Rent-A-Car; Otis Elevator Co.; Montgomery Elevator Co.; Admiral Insurance Co.; Local Government Insurance Trust; Lancer Insurance Co.

For full biographical listings, see the Martindale-Hubbell Law Directory

---

ANDERSON, COE & KING, L.L.P. (AV)

201 North Charles Street, Suite 2000, 21201
Telephone: 410-752-1630
Cable Address: ABKO
Fax: 410-752 0085
Ocean City, Maryland Office: 7904 Coastal Highway, Suite 5, P.O. Box 535.
Telephone: 301-524-6411.
Fax: 301-524-9479.

COUNSEL
G. C. A. Anderson (1898-1985)   Frank J. Vecella
Ward B. Coe, Jr.   John F. King
MEMBERS OF FIRM
Robert H. Bouse, Jr.   G. Macy Nelson
E. Dale Adkins, III   E. Philip Franke, III
James A. Rothschild   Philip C. Jacobson
M. Bradley Hallwig   Lynn B. Malone
J. Michael Sloneker   Gregory L. Van Geison
Barbara McC. Stanley

(See Next Column)

ANDERSON, COE & KING L.L.P., Baltimore—Continued

ASSOCIATES

Matthew T. Angotti	James S. Aist
Hugh Cropper, IV	Russell Sherlock Woodward
(Resident, Ocean City Office)	E. Scott Conover

H. Joy Sharp

Representative Clients: Hartford Accident & Indemnity Co.; The St. Paul Insurance Cos.; Medical Mutual Liability Society of Maryland; Chrysler Corp.; Provident Life and Accident Insurance Co.; Emerson Electric Co.; Pennsylvania Hospital Ins. Co.; Maryland Association of Boards of Education Group Insurance Pool; Pittsburgh Corning Corp.; Sierra Club.

For full biographical listings, see the Martindale-Hubbell Law Directory

---

BALLARD SPAHR ANDREWS & INGERSOLL (AV)

300 East Lombard Street, 19th Floor, 21202-3268
Telephone: 410-528-5600
Fax: 410-528-5650
Philadelphia, Pennsylvania Office: 1735 Market Street, 51st Floor.
Telephone: 215-665-8500.
Fax: 215-864-8999.
Harrisburg, Pennsylvania Office: 105 North Front Street.
Telephone: 717-236-3333.
Fax: 717-236-3884.
Denver, Colorado Office: Seventeenth Street Plaza Building, Suite 2300, 1225 17th Street.
Telephone: 303-292-2400.
Fax: 303-296-3956.
Salt Lake City, Utah Office: One Utah Center, 201 South Main Street, Suite 1200.
Telephone: 801-531-3000.
Fax: 801-531-3001.
Washington, D.C. Office: Suite 900 East, 555 13th Street, N.W.
Telephone: 202-383-8800.
Fax: 202-383-8877; 383-8893.
Camden, New Jersey Office: 800 Hudson Square, 5th Floor.
Telephone: 609-541-5577.
Fax: 609-541-8272.

Susan Souder

For full biographical listings, see the Martindale-Hubbell Law Directory

---

ELLIN AND BAKER (AV)

Second Floor, 1101 St. Paul Street, 21202
Telephone: 410-727-1787
FAX: 410-547-1787
1-800-237-1787

MEMBER OF FIRM

Marvin Ellin	LaVonna Lee Vice

Michael P. Smith

For full biographical listings, see the Martindale-Hubbell Law Directory

---

FREISHTAT & SANDLER (AV)

Suite 1500, One Calvert Plaza, 201 E. Baltimore Street, 21202
Telephone: 410-727-7740
FAX: 410-727-7356

MEMBERS OF FIRM

David Freishtat	Raymond F. Altman
Paul Mark Sandler	Raymond Daniel Burke
William M. Mullen	

Lloyd J. Snow	T. Allen Mott
Lynn Weinberg	Joseph John Coppola
Stacie F. Dubnow	Jeffrey Rosenfeld
Brian A. Zemil	

For full biographical listings, see the Martindale-Hubbell Law Directory

---

GISRIEL & BRUSH, P.A. (AV)

Suite 400 210 East Lexington Street, 21202-3514
Telephone: 410-539-0513
Washington D.C. Area: 301-585-1249
Fax: 410-625-3859

Edward J. Brush	Catherine Chen Hester
Michael U. Gisriel	Paul D. Raschke
H. Dean Bouland, Jr.	Richard K. Abraham

For full biographical listings, see the Martindale-Hubbell Law Directory

---

GLASER & DEROS (AV)

Suite 1717, 201 North Charles Street, 21201
Telephone: 410-244-8822
Toll Free: 1-800-244-8015
Fax: 410-625-1028

(See Next Column)

Harold I. Glaser	John S. Deros

For full biographical listings, see the Martindale-Hubbell Law Directory

---

GORDON & HENESON, P.A. (AV)

Suite 1900, Blaustein Building, One North Charles Street, 21201
Telephone: 410-539-0666
Fax: 410-547-8453
Email: GORHEN@AOL.COM

Michael I. Gordon	Allan Heneson

Stephen R. Robinson
LEGAL SUPPORT PERSONNEL
Shelly Abrams (Administrator)

For full biographical listings, see the Martindale-Hubbell Law Directory

---

ISRAELSON, SALSBURY, CLEMENTS & BEKMAN (AV)

300 West Pratt Street Suite 450, 21201
Telephone: 410-539-6633
FAX: 410-625-9554

MEMBERS OF FIRM

Stuart Marshall Salsbury	Daniel M. Clements
Paul D. Bekman	Matthew Zimmerman
Laurence A. Marder	

Scott R. Scherr	Lauren R. Calia
Carol J. Glover	Andrew David Alpert

COUNSEL TO THE FIRM
Max R. Israelson
OF COUNSEL
Samuel Omar Jackson, Jr. (Semi-Retired)

For full biographical listings, see the Martindale-Hubbell Law Directory

---

KENNY, VETTORI & ROBINSON, P.A. (AV)

Redwood Tower Suite 1500, 217 East Redwood Street, 21202
Telephone: 410-625-0000
Fax: 410-625-0201
Christiansted, St. Croix, Virgin Islands Office: 5025 Anchor Way, Gallows Bay, 00820.
Telephone: 809-773-6955.
Fax: 809-773-3092.

John J. Kenny	Paul M. Vettori
Deborah L. Robinson	

Stacie E. Tobin	Karen J. Detling

OF COUNSEL

Donovan M. Hamm, Jr.	Peter A. Woolson
(Resident, Christiansted, St. Croix, Virgin Islands Office)	

For full biographical listings, see the Martindale-Hubbell Law Directory

---

McDANIEL & MARSH (AV)

118 West Mulberry Street, 21201-3600
Telephone: 410-685-3810
Telecopier: 410-685-0203

William Alden McDaniel, Jr.	Jo Bennett Marsh

ASSOCIATE
Laura M. L. Maroldy

For full biographical listings, see the Martindale-Hubbell Law Directory

---

MEHLMAN & GREENBLATT, LLC (AV)

4 Reservoir Circle, Suite 100, 21208
Telephone: 410-486-4790
Fax: 410-486-4360

Gerson B. Mehlman	Frank W. Spector
Gary R. Greenblatt	Francis X. Leary
Wendy Lozinsky Shiff	Constance M. Hare

LEGAL SUPPORT PERSONNEL

Stephanie A. Ristvey (Paralegal)	Ruth P. Stein

For full biographical listings, see the Martindale-Hubbell Law Directory

---

NEAD, HOFFMAN & KAREY (AV)

Suite 800 W.R. Grace Building, 10 East Baltimore Street, 21202
Telephone: 410-837-1828
FAX: 410-783-5078

MEMBERS OF FIRM

Robert K. Nead	Gilbert A. Hoffman
Joseph N. Karey	

(See Next Column)

NEAD, HOFFMAN & KAREY—*Continued*

Sandra B. Minton   Mark R. Brown

Representative Clients: State Farm Insurance; Horace Mann Insurance Cos.; Consolidated Freightways; Penn Mutual Insurance Co.; Lancer Insurance Co.; Carborundum Co.; Kennecott Industries.
Reference: NationsBank.

For full biographical listings, see the Martindale-Hubbell Law Directory

NILES, BARTON & WILMER (AV)

1400 Legg Mason Tower, 111 South Calvert Street, 21202-6185
Telephone: 410-783-6300
Cable Address: "Nilwo"
Telecopier: 410-783-6363

MEMBERS OF FIRM

Paul B. Lang	John L. Wood
Larry J. Albert	Paul W. Grimm
V. Timothy Bambrick	Steven E. Leder
Robert P. O'Brien	R. Wayne Pierce
	David D. Gilliss

ASSOCIATES

Paul McDermott Finamore	Jeffrey A. Wothers
Tracy A. Mays	Craig D. Roswell
George E. Reede, Jr	Gina M. Harasti
Mary Alice McNamara	Howard A. Wolf-Rodda
	Kevin J. Willging

For Complete List of Firm Personnel, See General Section

For full biographical listings, see the Martindale-Hubbell Law Directory

PHILLIPS P. O'SHAUGHNESSY, P.A. (AV)

1102 Terrace Glen, 21210
Telephone: 410-532-0300
FAX: 410-532-2220

Phillips P. O'Shaughnessy

For Complete List of Firm Personnel, See General Section

For full biographical listings, see the Martindale-Hubbell Law Directory

PIERSON, PIERSON & NOLAN (AV)

Suite 1600 Redwood Tower, 217 East Redwood Street, 21202
Telephone: 410-727-7733
FAX: 410-625-0253

MEMBERS OF FIRM

W. Michel Pierson   James J. Nolan, Jr.
Robert L. Pierson

OF COUNSEL

David S. Sykes

For Complete List of Firm Personnel, See General Section

For full biographical listings, see the Martindale-Hubbell Law Directory

REDMOND, BURGIN & CRUZ, A PROFESSIONAL ASSOCIATION (AV)

Suite 1301 Fidelity Building, 210 North Charles Street, 21202
Telephone: 410-752-1555
Fax: 410-752-1064
Upper Marlboro, Maryland Office: 14746 Main Street.
Telephone: 301-952-1555.

Leonard C. Redmond, III   Harold L. Burgin
Debra B. Cruz

Louise McB. Simpson   Kimberly Brown

OF COUNSEL

Maria Cristina Gutierrez

For full biographical listings, see the Martindale-Hubbell Law Directory

ROLLINS, SMALKIN, RICHARDS & MACKIE (AV)

401 North Charles Street, 21201
Telephone: 410-727-2443
Fax: 410-727-8390

MEMBERS OF FIRM

H. Beale Rollins (1898-1985)	John F. Linsenmeyer
Samuel S. Smalkin (1906-1982)	Thomas C. Gentner
T. Benjamin Weston (1913-1980)	Glenn W. Trimmer
Thomas G. Andrew (1910-1973)	Patrick G. Cullen
Edward C. Mackie	James P. O'Meara
	Dennis J. Sullivan

(See Next Column)

ASSOCIATES

Paul G. Donoghue	Donna Lynn Kolakowski-Hollen
Ralph E. Wilson III	Meg Bantley Whiteford
Kenneth G. Macleay	Anthony G. Lardieri

OF COUNSEL

Raymond A. Richards (Retired)   Hartman J. Miller

For full biographical listings, see the Martindale-Hubbell Law Directory

SCHOCHOR, FEDERICO AND STATON, P.A. (AV)

The Paulton, 1211 St. Paul Street, 21202
Telephone: 410-234-1000
Toll Free: 888-234-0001
Facsimile: 410-234-1010
URL: http://www.sfspa.com
Washington D.C. Office: 750 First Street, N.E., Suite 905.
Telephone: 202-408-3300.

Jonathan Schochor   Philip C. Federico
Kerry D. Staton

Louis G. Close, III   Christopher P. Kennedy

For full biographical listings, see the Martindale-Hubbell Law Directory

BARRY L. STEELMAN, P.A. (AV)

Suite 720, 2 Hopkins Plaza, 21201
Telephone: 410-539-8603
Fax: 410-539-1060

Barry L. Steelman

Nicholas D. Cowie   Stanley Turk

For full biographical listings, see the Martindale-Hubbell Law Directory

THIEBLOT, RYAN, MARTIN & MILLER, P.A. (AV)

4th Floor, The World Trade Center, 21202-3091
Telephone: 410-837-1140
Washington, D.C. Line: 202-628-8223
Fax: 410-837-3282
Towson, Maryland Office: Atlantic Federal Building. Suite 400. 100 West Road. 21204.
Telephone: 410-828-5900.

Robert J. Thieblot	Robert D. Harwick, Jr.
Anthony W. Ryan	Anne M. Hrehorovich
J. Edward Martin, Jr.	Donna Marie Raffaele
Bruce R. Miller	Hamilton Fisk Tyler
	Samuel S. Field III

Representative Clients: American Association of Creditor Attorneys; Allianz Underwriters Insurance Co.; Ford Motor Credit Co.; General Accident Insurance Co.; Nautilus Insurance Co.; Nissan Motor Acceptance Corp.; Scottsdale Insurance Co.; Toyota Motor Credit Co.; Travelers Insurance Co.; USF&G Company.

For full biographical listings, see the Martindale-Hubbell Law Directory

VENABLE ATTORNEYS AT LAW VENABLE, BAETJER AND HOWARD, LLP (AV)

A Partnership including Professional Corporations
1800 Mercantile Bank & Trust Building, 2 Hopkins Plaza, 21201
Telephone: 410-244-7400
Email: INFO@Venable.win.net
Washington, D.C. Office: Venable, Baetjer, Howard & Civiletti LLP. Suite 1000, 1201 New York Avenue, N.W.
Telephone: 202-962-4800.
McLean, Virginia Office: Suite 400, 2010 Corporate Ridge.
Telephone: 703-760-1600.
Rockville, Maryland Office: Suite 500, One Church Street, P. O. Box 1906.
Telephone: 301-217-5600.
Towson, Maryland Office: 210 Allegheny Avenue, P. O. Box 5517.
Telephone: 410-494-6200.

MEMBERS OF FIRM

Benjamin R. Civiletti (P.C.) (Also at Washington, D.C. and Towson, Maryland Offices)	David J. Levenson (Not admitted in MD; Resident, Washington, D.C. Office)
George Cochran Doub (P.C.)	Douglas D. Connah, Jr. (P.C.) (Also at Washington, D.C. Office)
John Henry Lewin, Jr. (P.C.)	
Stanley Mazaroff (P.C.)	Kenneth C. Bass, III (Not admitted in MD; Washington, D.C. and McLean, Virginia Offices)
Roger W. Titus (Resident, Rockville, Maryland Office)	
Thomas J. Madden (Not admitted in MD; Resident, Washington, D.C. Office)	John H. Zink, III (Resident, Towson, Maryland Office)
Ronald R. Glancz (Not admitted in MD; Resident, Washington, D.C. Office)	Bruce E. Titus (Resident, McLean, Virginia Office)
	Paul F. Strain (P.C.)

(See Next Column)

VENABLE ATTORNEYS AT LAW VENABLE, BAETJER AND HOWARD, LLP, *Baltimore—Continued*

MEMBERS OF FIRM (Continued)

William D. Dolan, III (P.C.) (Not admitted in MD; Resident, McLean, Virginia Office)

Paul T. Glasgow (Resident, Rockville, Maryland Office)

Joseph C. Wich, Jr. (Resident, Towson, Maryland Office)

Sondra Harans Block (Resident, Rockville, Maryland Office)

Edward F. Glynn, Jr. (Resident, Washington, D.C. Office)

Craig E. Smith

Robert G. Ames (Also at Washington, D.C. Office)

Michael Schatzow (Also at Washington, D.C. Office)

Nell B. Strachan

David G. Lane (Resident, McLean, Virginia Office)

L. Paige Marvel

N. Frank Wiggins (Not admitted in MD; Resident, Washington, D.C. Office)

G. Stewart Webb, Jr.

James K. Archibald (Also at Washington, D.C. Office)

George W. Johnston (P.C.)

Judson W. Starr (Not admitted in MD; Also at Washington, D.C. and Towson, Maryland Offices)

James R. Myers (Not admitted in MD; Resident, Washington, D.C. Office)

Jana Howard Carey (P.C.)

Jeffrey A. Dunn (also at Washington, D.C. Office)

George F. Pappas (Also at Washington, D.C. Office)

William D. Coston (Not admitted in MD; Resident, Washington, D.C. Office)

James L. Shea (Also at Washington, D.C. Office)

Jeffrey P. Ayres (P.C.)

Elizabeth C. Honeywell

Maurice Baskin (Resident, Washington, D.C. Office)

Amy Berman Jackson (Not admitted in MD; Resident, Washington, D.C. Office)

William D. Quarles (Also at Washington, D.C. and Towson, Maryland Offices)

C. Carey Deeley, Jr. (Also at Towson, Maryland Office)

Kathleen Gallogly Cox (Resident, Towson, Maryland Office)

Christopher R. Mellott

Cynthia M. Hahn (Resident, Towson, Maryland Office)

M. King Hill, III (Resident, Towson, Maryland Office)

James A. Dunbar (Also at Washington, D.C. Office)

Ronald W. Taylor

Thomas J. Kelly, Jr. (Not admitted in MD; Resident, Washington, D. C. Office)

David J. Heubeck

Herbert G. Smith, II (Not admitted in MD; Resident, Washington, D.C. Office)

Patrick J. Stewart (Also at Washington, D.C. Office)

Gary M. Hnath (Resident, Washington, D.C. Office)

Mitchell Y. Mirviss

Geoffrey R. Garinther (Also at Washington, D.C. Office)

Terri L. Turner

Michael W. Robinson (Resident, McLean, Virginia Office)

Elizabeth Marzo Borinsky

OF COUNSEL

A. Samuel Cook (P.C.) (Resident, Towson, Maryland Office)

Todd K. Snyder

Mary T. Flynn (Not admitted in MD; Resident, McLean, Virginia Office)

ASSOCIATES

Paul D. Barker, Jr.

Eric L. Bryant

Daniel William China

Patricia Gillis Cousins (Resident, Rockville, Maryland Office)

Carla Draluck Craft (Resident, Washington, D.C. Office)

Gregory A. Cross

Marina Lolley Dame (Resident, Towson, Maryland Office)

David W. Goewey (Not admitted in MD; Resident, Washington, D.C. Office)

E. Anne Hamel

David R. Hodnett (Not admitted in MD; Resident, McLean, Virginia Office)

J. Scott Hommer, III (Not admitted in MD; Resident, McLean, Virginia Office)

Todd J. Horn

Maria F. Howell

Mary-Dulany James (Resident, Towson, Maryland Office)

Gregory L. Laubach (Resident, Rockville, Maryland Office)

Edward Brendan Magrab (Resident, Washington, D.C. Office)

Patricia A. Malone (Resident, Towson, Maryland Office)

Vicki Margolis (Also at Washington, D.C. Office)

Christine M. McAnney (Not admitted in MD; Resident, McLean, Virginia Office)

John A. McCauley

Traci H. Mundy (Not admitted in MD; Resident, McLean, Virginia Office)

John T. Prisbe

Lawrence C. Renbaum (Resident, Washington, D.C. Office)

John Peter Sarbanes

Melissa Landau Steinman (Resident, Washington, D.C. Office)

Paul N. Wengert (Not admitted in MD; Resident, McLean, Virginia Office)

For Complete List of Firm Personnel, See General Section

For full biographical listings, see the Martindale-Hubbell Law Directory

---

WARD, KERSHAW & MINTON, A PROFESSIONAL ASSOCIATION (AV)

113 West Monument Street, 21201
Telephone: 410-685-6700
Fax: 410-685-6704
Email: wkmfirm@aol.com

(See Next Column)

John T. Ward　　　Robert B. Kershaw
Thomas J. Minton

OF COUNSEL

Richard V. Falcon

For full biographical listings, see the Martindale-Hubbell Law Directory

---

WEINER, ASTRACHAN, GUNST, HILLMAN AND ALLEN, A PROFESSIONAL CORPORATION (AV)

120 East Baltimore Street Suite 2100, 21202
Telephone: 410-783-3500
FAX: 410-783-3510

Arnold M. Weiner　　　Allan P. Hillman
James B. Astrachan　　Steven A. Allen
Peter H. Gunst　　　　Thomas J. Zagami

Bruce L. Mann　　　Donna M.D. Thomas
Heather H. Polzin-Vovakes

For full biographical listings, see the Martindale-Hubbell Law Directory

---

ROBIN PAGE WEST (AV)

110 St. Paul Street, Suite 301, 21202
Telephone: 410-244-0400
Fax: 410-244-0402
Email: robin.west.esq@counsel.com

For full biographical listings, see the Martindale-Hubbell Law Directory

---

WHARTON LEVIN EHRMANTRAUT KLEIN & NASH, A PROFESSIONAL ASSOCIATION (AV)

400 East Pratt Street, 21202
Telephone: 800-322-1984; 410-269-7529
Annapolis, Maryland Office: 104 West Street, P.O. Box 551, Annapolis.
Telephone: 800-322-1984; 410-263-5900.
Facsimile: 410-280-2230; 410-263-1562.
Bethesda, Maryland Office: 7200 Wisconsin Avenue, Suite 308.
Telephone: 301-656-1001.
Facsimile: 301-656-0808.

James T. Wharton　　　Michael T. Wharton
David A. Levin　　　　Andrew E. Vernick
Robert Dale Klein　　　D. Lee Rutland
Brian J. Nash　　　　　David A. Roling
A. Gwynn Bowie, Jr.　　Brian F. Holeman
Jack L. Harvey　　　　　(Not admitted in MD)

OF COUNSEL

William A. Ehrmantraut

Debra S. Block　　　　Marian L. Hogan
Daniel C. Costello　　　Leonard William Dooren, III
Christian A. Lodowski　Mary C. Rice
Douglas K. Schrader　　Justine D. Smith
Linda G. Wales　　　　Michael Kevin Wiggins
Stuart N. Herschfeld　　Kimberly C. Dumpson
Denise Atkinson Clark　Victoria H. Wink

For full biographical listings, see the Martindale-Hubbell Law Directory

---

BEL AIR, * Harford Co.

BROWN, BROWN & BROWN, A PROFESSIONAL ASSOCIATION (AV)

200 South Main Street, 21014
Telephone: 410-838-5500
Baltimore: 410-879-2220
Fax: 410-893-0402

A. Freeborn Brown　　Augustus F. Brown
T. Carroll Brown　　　Albert J. A. Young

A. Frank Carven, III　　Christopher R. vanRoden
Harold Douglas Norton　David E. Carey
Ankur P. Dalal

Attorneys for: Baltimore Gas & Electric Co.; Chesapeake & Potomac Telephone Co.; Aberdeen Proving Ground Federal Credit Union; First Virginia Bank-Central Maryland; First National Bank of Maryland; Bell Atlantic Mobile Systems; First Harbor Securities; Maryland Portable Concrete, Inc.
Approved Counsel for: The Chicago Title Insurance Co. of Maryland, Inc.

For full biographical listings, see the Martindale-Hubbell Law Directory

---

STARK & KEENAN, A PROFESSIONAL ASSOCIATION (AV)

30 Office Street, 21014
Telephone: 410-838-5522
Baltimore: 410-879-2222
Fax: 410-879-0688

(See Next Column)

STARK & KEENAN A PROFESSIONAL ASSOCIATION—*Continued*

Elwood V. Stark, Jr.	Judith Cline-Silverstein
Charles B. Keenan, Jr.	Gregory A. Szoka
Edwin G. Carson	Robert S. Lynch

Claire Prin Blomquist	Paul W. Ishak
Kimberly Kahoe Muenter	Lawrence F. Kreis, Jr.

For full biographical listings, see the Martindale-Hubbell Law Directory

BETHESDA, Montgomery Co.

DECKELBAUM OGENS & FISCHER, CHARTERED (AV)

6701 Democracy Boulevard, 20817
Telephone: 301-564-5100
Washington D.C. Office: 1140 Connecticut Avenue, N.W.
Telephone: 202-223-1474.

Nelson Deckelbaum	Lawrence H. Fischer
Ronald L. Ogens	Deborah E. Reiser

Ronald G. Scheraga	Bryn Hope Sherman
	Darryl Alan Feldman

LEGAL SUPPORT PERSONNEL
Shirley Mostow

Representative Clients: The Charles E. Smith Companies; The Trammell Crow Company.
References: Franklin National Bank; Century National Bank.

For full biographical listings, see the Martindale-Hubbell Law Directory

NELSON & NELSON (AV)

3 Bethesda Metro Center Suite 750, 20814
Telephone: 301-961-1958

MEMBERS OF FIRM

William E. Nelson	Sherlee Stanford Nelson
	(Not admitted in MD)

For full biographical listings, see the Martindale-Hubbell Law Directory

WHARTON LEVIN EHRMANTRAUT KLEIN & NASH, A PROFESSIONAL ASSOCIATION (AV)

7200 Wisconsin Avenue, Suite 308, 20814
Telephone: 301-656-1001
Facsimile: 301-656-0808
Baltimore, Maryland Office: 400 East Pratt Street.
Telephone: 410-269-7529.
Annapolis, Maryland Office: 104 West Street, P.O. Box 551, Annapolis.
Telephone: 800-322-1984; 410-263-5900.
Facsimile: 410-280-2230; 410-263-1562.

James T. Wharton	Michael T. Wharton
David A. Levin	Andrew E. Vernick
Robert Dale Klein	D. Lee Rutland
Brian J. Nash	David A. Roling
A. Gwynn Bowie, Jr.	Brian F. Holeman
Jack L. Harvey	(Not admitted in MD)

OF COUNSEL
William A. Ehrmantraut

Debra S. Block	Marian L. Hogan
Daniel C. Costello	Leonard William Dooren, III
Christian A. Lodowski	Mary C. Rice
Douglas K. Schrader	Justine D. Smith
Linda G. Wales	Michael Kevin Wiggins
Stuart N. Herschfeld	Kimberly C. Dumpson
Denise Atkinson Clark	Victoria H. Wink

For full biographical listings, see the Martindale-Hubbell Law Directory

EDGEWATER, Anne Arundel Co.

JAMES A. McGUIRE (AV)

140 Mayo Road, P.O. Box 57, 21037
Telephone: 410-956-2602
Baltimore Line: 410-269-0825
Washington, D.C. Line: 301-261-4063
FAX: 410-956-3753

OF COUNSEL
Karen R. Carolan
ASSOCIATES

James J. McGuire	Page McGuire Linden

For full biographical listings, see the Martindale-Hubbell Law Directory

ELLICOTT CITY,* Howard Co.

LEWIS STRAUGHN NIPPARD, P.A. (AV)

3701 Court House Drive, 21043-4409
Telephone: 410-465-4700
Fax: 410-461-1329

Lewis Straughn Nippard	E. Josephine Nippard

Reference: Commercial and Farmers Bank.

For full biographical listings, see the Martindale-Hubbell Law Directory

GLEN BURNIE, Anne Arundel Co.

T. JOSEPH TOUHEY, P.A. (AV)

791 Aquahart Road, 21061
Telephone: 410-768-1880
Facsimile: 410-760-1081

T. Joseph Touhey

Thomas C. French

For full biographical listings, see the Martindale-Hubbell Law Directory

GREENBELT, Prince Georges Co.

STANLEY S. PICKETT (AV)

Suite 414 Capital Office Park, 6411 Ivy Lane, 20770
Telephone: 301-513-0613
Fax: 301-513-0618

Stanley Sinclair Pickett
ASSOCIATE
Gordon J. Brumback
LEGAL SUPPORT PERSONNEL

Stacy S. Pickett (Law Clerk)	Vivian W. Wolfe (Paralegal)

Representative Clients: B.F. Saul Co.; McDonald and Eudy Printers, Inc.; Condominium Management, Inc.; Long & Foster Realtors; Mitron Systems Corp.; Coldwell Banker; Glenanden Housing Authority; Koones & Montgomery, Inc.; Community Associations, Inc.

For full biographical listings, see the Martindale-Hubbell Law Directory

REICHELT, NUSSBAUM, LaPLACA & MILLER (AV)

The Maryland Trade Center, Suite 1000, 7500 Greenway Center Drive,
P.O. Box 627, 20768-0627
Telephone: 301-474-9000
Fax: 301-345-0565

MEMBERS OF FIRM

Herbert W. Reichelt (1908-1993)	Sheldon L. Gnatt
Ronald M. Miller	Raymond G. LaPlaca
T. Summers Gwynn, III	Daniel A. LaPlaca
Gary Greenwald	Gail Borjeson Viens
Andrew W. Nussbaum	Roger C. Thomas

ASSOCIATE
Wanda G. Caporaletti
OF COUNSEL

Paul M. Nussbaum	Toni Evon Clarke

Representative Clients: Tower Federal Credit Union; Suburban Bank of Maryland.
Reference: NationsBank of Maryland, N.A.

For full biographical listings, see the Martindale-Hubbell Law Directory

LARGO, Prince Georges Co.

GREENAN, WALKER, TRAINOR & BILLMAN (AV)

Inglewood Business Community, 9200 Basil Court Suite 209, 20774
Telephone: 301-322-7700
Fax: 301-772-0152
Annapolis, Maryland Office: 33 West Street, Suite 200.
Telephone: 410-280-1700. D.C. Line: 301-261-1200.
Fax: 410-268-0031.
Greenbelt, Maryland Office: Capital Office Park, 6411 Ivy Lane, Suite 706.
Telephone: 301-982-1003.
Fax: 301-982-4009.

Thomas E. Walker	Harry J. Trainor, Jr.

For full biographical listings, see the Martindale-Hubbell Law Directory

SHIPLEY & HORNE, P.A. (AV)

1101 Mercantile Lane, Suite 240, 20774
Telephone: 301-925-1800
Fax: 301-925-1803

(See Next Column)

SHIPLEY & HORNE P.A., *Largo—Continued*

Russell W. Shipley   Arthur J. Horne, Jr.

For full biographical listings, see the Martindale-Hubbell Law Directory

OCEAN CITY, Worcester Co.

AYRES, JENKINS, GORDY & ALMAND, P.A. (AV)

5200-B Coastal Highway, 21842
Telephone: 410-723-1400
Fax: 410-723-1861
Berlin, Maryland Office: 11047 Race Track Road (Ocean Pines).
Telephone: 410-641-5033.
FAX: 410-641-6926.

Guy R. Ayres, III   Harold B. Gordy, Jr.
M. Dean Jenkins   (Resident, Berlin Office)
                James W. Almand

Jerome James LaCorte   William E. Esham, III
                Mark S. Cropper

References: Calvin B. Taylor Banking Co.; Peninsula Bank.

For full biographical listings, see the Martindale-Hubbell Law Directory

COURTLAND K. TOWNSEND, JR. CHARTERED (AV)

The Executive Building, Suite 101, 7200 Coastal Highway, 21842
Telephone: 410-524-4300
FAX: 410-524-4953

Courtland K. Townsend, Jr.

For full biographical listings, see the Martindale-Hubbell Law Directory

WILLIAMS, HAMMOND, MOORE, SHOCKLEY & HARRISON, P.A. (AV)

3509 Coastal Highway, P.O. Box 739, 21842
Telephone: 410-289-3553
Fax: 410-289-4157
Email: whmsh@shore.intercom.net
Berlin, Maryland Office: 11070 Cathell Road, Suite 19.
Telephone: 410-641-8080.
Fax: 410-641-8282.

Marcus J. Williams (1923-1995)   Joseph E. Moore
Edward H. Hammond, Jr.   Raymond C. Shockley
            Joseph G. Harrison, Jr.

J. Richard Collins   Jeffrey A. Pilchard
Regan James Reno Smith   Brian D. Shockley

For full biographical listings, see the Martindale-Hubbell Law Directory

ROCKVILLE,* Montgomery Co.

ANDERSON & QUINN (AV)

The Adams Law Center, 25 Wood Lane, 20850
Telephone: 301-762-3303
FAX: 301-762-3776
Other Rockville Maryland Office: 110 North West St., Suite 501, 20850.
Telephone: 301-340-0800.

MEMBERS OF FIRM

Charles C. Collins (1900-1973)   Donald P. Maiberger
Robert E. Anderson (Not   Robert P. Scanlon
  admitted in MD; Retired)   James G. Healy
Francis X. Quinn   John A. Rego

ASSOCIATES

Alice Kelley Scanlon   Mary L. Fellin
Marnie E. Simon   Kelly Ann McInerney
Kerry Patricia Shanahan   Timothy J. Mulreany

Representative Clients: C & P Telephone; Commercial Union Insurance Cos.; Allstate Insurance Co.; State Farm Mutual Automobile Insurance Co.; Liberty Mutual Insurance Co.; Northbrook Insurance Cos.; Travelers Insurance Co.; National General Insurance Co.; American International Adjustment Co.; Marriott Corp.

For full biographical listings, see the Martindale-Hubbell Law Directory

ARMSTRONG, DONOHUE & CEPPOS, CHARTERED (AV)

Suite 101, 204 Monroe Street, 20850
Telephone: 301-251-0440
Telecopier: 301-279-5929

Larry A. Ceppos   H. Kenneth Armstrong
H. Patrick Donohue   Benjamin S. Vaughan
            John C. Monahan

(See Next Column)

Oya S. Oner   Sharon A. Marcial
Pamela Barrow Kincheloe   J. Eric Rhoades
Richard S. Schrager   Garrett V. Williams
            Andrew J. Marter

For full biographical listings, see the Martindale-Hubbell Law Directory

BRAULT, GRAHAM, SCOTT & BRAULT (AV)

101 South Washington Street, 20850
Telephone: 301-424-1060
Fax: 301-424-7991
Washington, D.C. Office: 1906 Sunderland Place, N.W.
Telephone: 202-785-1200.
FAX: 202-785-4301.
Arlington, Virginia Office: Suite 1201, 2300 North Clarendon Boulevard, Courthouse Plaza.
Telephone: 703-358-9200.

OF COUNSEL

Laurence T. Scott   Janet S. Zigler (Resident)

MEMBERS OF FIRM

Denver H. Graham (1922-1987)   Daniel L. Shea (Resident)
Albert E. Brault (Retired)   M. Kathleen Parker (Resident)
Albert D. Brault (Resident)   David G. Mulquin (Resident)
Leo A. Roth, Jr.   James M. Brault (Resident)
James S. Wilson (Resident)   Regina Ann Casey (Resident)
Ronald G. Guziak   Sanford A. Friedman

ASSOCIATES

Holly D. Shupert (Resident)   Joan F. Brault (Resident)
Rhonda Ann Hurwitz (Resident)   Joseph P. Morra (Resident)
            Michael A. Carlo

Representative Clients: American Oil Co.; Crum & Forster Group; Fireman's Fund American Insurance Cos.; Kemper Group; Reliance Insurance Cos.; Safeco Group; Government Employees Insurance Co.; Medical Mutual Insurance Society of Maryland; Legal Mutual Liability Insurance Society of Maryland.

For full biographical listings, see the Martindale-Hubbell Law Directory

ROWAN & QUIRK (AV)

The Adams Law Center, 27 Wood Lane, 20850
Telephone: 301-762-4050
FAX: 301-762-9189

MEMBERS OF FIRM

William J. Rowan, III   Joseph M. Quirk

ASSOCIATE

John G. Nalls

For full biographical listings, see the Martindale-Hubbell Law Directory

SHULMAN, ROGERS, GANDAL, PORDY & ECKER, P.A. (AV)

Third Floor, 11921 Rockville Pike, 20852-2743
Telephone: 301-230-5200
Telecopier: 301-230-2891
Email: litigate@srgpe.com; realprop@srgpe.com
Email: business@srgpe.com
Washington, D.C. Office: 1100 New York Avenue, N.W. West Tower, Suite 500.
Telephone: 202-872-0400.

Lawrence A. Shulman   Lawrence L. Bell
Donald R. Rogers   James M. Kefauver
Larry N. Gandal   Rebecca Oshoway
Karl L. Ecker   Robert B. Canter
David A. Pordy   Edward F. Schiff
David D. Freishtat   Daniel S. Krakower
Martin P. Schaffer   Kevin P. Kennedy
Christopher C. Roberts   Alan B. Sternstein
Edward M. Hanson, Jr.   Nancy P. Regelin
David M. Kochanski   Ashley Joel Gardner
Walter A. Oleniewski   James M. Hoffman

Michael J. Froehlich   Michael V. Nakamura
William C. Davis, III   Paul A. Bellegarde
Elizabeth N. Shomaker   Gregory J. Rupert
            Douglas K. Hirsch

Reference: Maryland National Bank, Montgomery County Regional Office.

For Complete List of Firm Personnel, See General Section

For full biographical listings, see the Martindale-Hubbell Law Directory

STEIN, SPERLING, BENNETT, DE JONG, DRISCOLL, GREENFEIG & METRO, P.A. (AV)

25 West Middle Lane, 20850
Telephone: 301-340-2020; 800-435-5230
Telecopier: 301-340-8217

(See Next Column)

STEIN, SPERLING, BENNETT, DE JONG, DRISCOLL, GREENFEIG & METRO P.A.—*Continued*

David C. Driscoll, Jr.	Jeffrey M. Schwaber
Stuart S. Greenfeig	Paul T. Stein

James D. Dalrymple	Darcy A. Shoop
Jeffrey D. Goldstein	Holly R. Eaton

For Complete List of Firm Personnel, See General Section

For full biographical listings, see the Martindale-Hubbell Law Directory

VENABLE ATTORNEYS AT LAW VENABLE, BAETJER AND HOWARD, LLP (AV)

A Partnership including Professional Corporations
Suite 500, One Church Street, P.O. Box 1906, 20850-4129
Telephone: 301-217-5600
FAX: 301-217-5617
Baltimore, Maryland Office: 1800 Mercantile Bank & Trust Building, 2 Hopkins Plaza.
Telephone: 410-244-7400.
Washington, D.C. Office: Venable, Baetjer, Howard & Civiletti LLP, Suite 1000, 1201 New York Avenue, N.W.
Telephone: 202-962-4800.
McLean, Virginia Office: Suite 400, 2010 Corporate Ridge.
Telephone: 703-760-1600.
Towson, Maryland, Office: 210 Allegheny Avenue, P. O. Box 5517.
Telephone: 410-494-6200.

MEMBERS OF FIRM

Roger W. Titus	Sondra Harans Block

ASSOCIATES

Patricia Gillis Cousins	Gregory L. Laubach

For Complete List of Firm Personnel, See General Section

For full biographical listings, see the Martindale-Hubbell Law Directory

SALISBURY,* Wicomico Co.

ADKINS, POTTS & SMETHURST, L.L.P. (AV)

Suite 600, One Plaza East, P.O. Box 4247, 21803-4247
Telephone: 410-749-0161
Fax: 410-749-5021

MEMBER OF FIRM
Raymond Stevens Smethurst, Jr.

Representative Clients: Atlantic Wood Industries, Inc.; Campbell Soup Company; Delmarva Power & Light Co.; G. E. Capital Mortgage Services, Inc.; Lawyers' Title Insurance Corp.; Mellon Bank (DE); PNC Bank; Proko Industries, Inc.; Shopco Group; WBOC-TV.

For full biographical listings, see the Martindale-Hubbell Law Directory

DUVALL & DUVALL, L.L.P. (AV)

108 East Market Street, P.O. Box 4077, 21803-4077
Telephone: 410-548-1010
Fax: 410-548-1045

MEMBERS OF FIRM

William G. Duvall	Richard M. Duvall

Reference: Nations Bank.

For full biographical listings, see the Martindale-Hubbell Law Directory

WEBB, BURNETT, JACKSON, CORNBROOKS, WILBER, VORHIS & DOUSE, LLP (AV)

115 Broad Street, P.O. Box 910, 21801
Telephone: 410-742-3176
Fax: 410-742-0438
Email: webnett@shore.intercom.net

MEMBERS OF FIRM

Frederick W. C. Webb	W. Newton Jackson, 3rd
(1889-1956)	Ernest I. Cornbrooks, III
John W. T. Webb (1918-1990)	Paul D. Wilber
K. King Burnett	David A. Vorhis
David B. Douse	

ASSOCIATE
Chris Schiller Mason

Counsel for: First National Bank of Maryland (Salisbury branch); K & L Microwave, Inc.; Peninsula General Hospital Medical Center.
Local Attorneys for: State Farm Insurance Cos.; Nationwide Insurance Cos.; Travelers Insurance Co.; United States Fidelity & Guaranty Co.; Aetna Casualty & Surety Co.; Insurance Company of North America.

For full biographical listings, see the Martindale-Hubbell Law Directory

SEABROOK, Prince Georges Co.

FOSSETT & BRUGGER, CHARTERED (AV)

The Aerospace Building, 10210 Greenbelt Road, 20706
Telephone: 301-794-6900
Telecopy: 301-794-7638
La Plata, Maryland Office: 105 LaGrange Avenue, P.O. Box F.
Telephone: 301-934-4200. Washington Line: 301-753-9600.
Fax: 301-870-2884.

George A. Brugger	William M. Shipp
Clarence L. Fossett	John C. Fredrickson
Nancy L. Slepicka	Garland H. Stillwell
Midgett S. Parker, Jr.	Mary A. Liano

LEGAL SUPPORT PERSONNEL
Dean Armstrong (Consulting Land Planner)

Representative Clients: Coscan Washington, Inc.; Citizens Bank & Trust Company of Maryland; The Edward J. DeBartolo Corp.; Ebenezer African Methodist Episcopal Church, Inc.; Greenhorne & O'Mara, Inc.; Kettler Brothers; Michael T. Rose Cos.; The Mutual Life Insurance Company of New York; RE/MAX International, Inc.; Richmond-American Homes; Winchester Homes, Inc.

For full biographical listings, see the Martindale-Hubbell Law Directory

SILVER SPRING, Montgomery Co.

ALEXANDER, BEARDEN, HAIRSTON & MARKS, LLP (AV)

(Formerly, Alexander, Aponte & Marks, LLP)
Lee Plaza-Suite 805, 8601 Georgia Avenue, 20910
Telephone: 301-589-2222
Facsimile: 301-589-2523
Washington, D.C. Office: 2021 L Street, N.W., Suite 300, 20036.
Telephone: 202-293-3700.
Fax: 202-293-7359.
New York, New York Office: 330 Madison Avenue, 36th Floor.
Telephone: 212-808-0008.
Fax: 212-599-1028.

Abbey G. Hairston

Bridnetta D. Edwards	Nihar R. Mohanty
Adrian Van Nelson II	Darius B. Withers

Reference: Riggs National Bank of Washington, D.C.

For full biographical listings, see the Martindale-Hubbell Law Directory

TOWSON,* Baltimore Co.

HOWELL, GATELY, WHITNEY & CARTER, LLP (AV)

401 Washington Avenue, Twelfth Floor, 21204
Telephone: 410-583-8000
Fax: 410-583-8031

MEMBERS OF FIRM

H. Thomas Howell	Daniel W. Whitney
William F. Gately	David A. Carter
Benjamin R. Goertemiller	William R. Levasseur

ASSOCIATES

Una M. Perez	Kathleen D. Leslie
George D. Bogris	Gerard Wm. Wittstadt, Jr.
Laura A. Gregory	

For full biographical listings, see the Martindale-Hubbell Law Directory

NOLAN, PLUMHOFF & WILLIAMS, CHARTERED (AV)

Suite 700 Court Towers, 210 West Pennsylvania Avenue, 21204
Telephone: 410-823-7800
Fax: 410-296-2765

William P. Englehart, Jr.	Stephen M. Schenning
Stephen J. Nolan	Robert E. Cahill, Jr.
Robert L. Hanley, Jr.	C. William Clark
Stuart Alan Schadt	

Representative Clients: Anne Arundel County, Maryland; Baltimore County, Maryland; Board of Education of Anne Arundel County; Board of Education of Baltimore County (Special Counsel in Environmental Cost Recovery Litigation); Bituminous Insurance Companies; Carolina Freight Carriers Corporation; First Fidelity Bank; Humane Society of Baltimore County, Inc.; Keystone Insurance Company; Maryland Automobile Insurance Fund.

For Complete List of Firm Personnel, See General Section

For full biographical listings, see the Martindale-Hubbell Law Directory

Towson—Continued

VENABLE ATTORNEYS AT LAW VENABLE, BAETJER AND HOWARD, LLP (AV)

A Partnership including Professional Corporations
210 Allegheny Avenue, P.O. Box 5517, 21204
Telephone: 410-494-6200
FAX: 410-821-0147
Baltimore, Maryland Office: 1800 Mercantile Bank & Trust Building, 2 Hopkins Plaza.
Telephone: 410-244-7400.
Washington, D.C. Office: Venable, Baetjer, Howard & Civiletti LLP, Suite 1000, 1201 New York Avenue, N.W.
Telephone: 202-962-4800.
McLean, Virginia Office: Suite 400, 2010 Corporate Ridge.
Telephone: 703-760-1600.
Rockville, Maryland Office: Suite 500, One Church Street, P. O. Box 1906.
Telephone: 301-217-5600.

PARTNERS

Benjamin R. Civiletti (P.C.)
(Also at Washington, D.C.
and Baltimore, Maryland
Offices)
John H. Zink, III
Joseph C. Wich, Jr.

William D. Quarles (Also at Washington, D.C. Office)
C. Carey Deeley, Jr. (Also at Baltimore, Maryland Office)
Kathleen Gallogly Cox
Cynthia M. Hahn
M. King Hill, III

ASSOCIATES

Marina Lolley Dame

Mary-Dulany James
Patricia A. Malone

For Complete List of Firm Personnel, See General Section

For full biographical listings, see the Martindale-Hubbell Law Directory

---

UPPER MARLBORO, Prince Georges Co.

KNIGHT, MANZI, BRENNAN, SHAY AND HAM, A PROFESSIONAL ASSOCIATION (AV)

14440 Old Mill Road, 20772
Telephone: 301-952-0100
Annapolis/Baltimore: 410-792-3786
Fax: 301-952-0221
Crofton, Maryland Office: 2411 Crofton Lane, # 26.
Telephone: 301-261-0808.
Fax: 301-261-6945.
Mitchellville, Maryland Office: 12164 Central Avenue, Suite 228.
Telephone: 301-390-0577.
Fax: 301-390-8464.

William E. Knight
Robert A. Manzi
William C. Brennan, Jr.

John F. Shay, Jr.
Richard J. Ham
Martin J. Shuham

Monica M. Haley-Pierson
Daniel F. Lynch III

Norman D. Rivera
Robert L. Lombardo

OF COUNSEL

Stuart R. Hammett

For full biographical listings, see the Martindale-Hubbell Law Directory

MASSACHUSETTS

BOSTON, Suffolk Co.

ATWOOD & CHERNY (AV)

Mason House 211 Commonwealth Avenue, 02116
Telephone: 617-262-6400
Telecopier: 617-421-9482

Jacob M. Atwood

David E. Cherny
Pasquale DeSantis

OF COUNSEL

Margaret F. McGovern

For full biographical listings, see the Martindale-Hubbell Law Directory

BARRON & STADFELD, P.C. (AV)

Two Center Plaza, 02108
Telephone: 617-723-9800
Telecopier: 617-523-8359
Email: PUBLIC@BARRONSTAD.COM *URL:* HTTP://WWW.BARRONSTAD.COM
Hyannis, Massachusetts Office: 258 Winter Street.
Telephone: 617-778-6622.

(See Next Column)

Bernard A. Dwork
Enid M. Starr
Thomas V. Bennett
Edward E. Kelly
Kevin F. Moloney
David P. Dwork

Julie Taylor Moran
Mitchell J. Notis
Robert J. Hoffer
Joseph G. Butler
Denise L. Page
Rosemary Purtell

Dorothy M. Bickford

Alison L. Berman
Roger T. Manwaring
Shawn P. O'Rourke

Kevin P. Scanlon
Kathleen M. Morrissey
Edward J. Fallman

OF COUNSEL

Hertz N. Henkoff

For Complete List of Firm Personnel, See General Section

For full biographical listings, see the Martindale-Hubbell Law Directory

---

BLOOM & BUELL (AV)

1340 Soldiers Field Road, 02135-1020
Telephone: 617-254-4400
Telecopier: 617-254-7610
Email: bloombue@ix.netcom.com

MEMBERS OF FIRM

Laurence J. Bloom

Barbara Hayes Buell
William J. Davenport

ASSOCIATES

Marc J. Gervais

Richard M. Haley
Barry T. Putterman

OF COUNSEL

Victoria L. Polito

LEGAL SUPPORT PERSONNEL

Lisa F. Tuccinardi

For full biographical listings, see the Martindale-Hubbell Law Directory

BROMBERG & SUNSTEIN (AV)

125 Summer Street, 11th Floor, 02110
Telephone: 617-443-9292
Fax: 617-443-0004
Email: IPLAW@BROMSUN.COM

MEMBERS OF FIRM

Bruce D. Sunstein
Lee Carl Bromberg

Robert L. Kann
Timothy M. Murphy
Kerry L. Timbers

ASSOCIATES

Joel R. Leeman
Judith R. S. Stern
Julia Huston
Chinh H. Pham
Samuel J. Petuchowski
(Not admitted in MA)

Steven D. Yates
Erik P. Belt
Seth Z. Kalson
Lisa M. Tittemore

OF COUNSEL

Robert M. Asher

Thomas C. Carey
Edward J. Dailey

LEGAL SUPPORT PERSONNEL

Harriet Strimpel, Ph.D. (Patent Agent)

For full biographical listings, see the Martindale-Hubbell Law Directory

BURNS & LEVINSON LLP (AV)

125 Summer Street, 02110-1624
Telephone: 617-345-3000
Telecopier: 617-345-3299
Email: firm@B-L.com
Rockland, Massachusetts Office: 1001 Hingham Street.
Telephone: 617-982-4100.
Telecopier: 617-982-4141.

MEMBERS OF FIRM

Thomas D. Burns
William H. Clancy
John A. Donovan, Jr.
Charles Mark Furcolo
Traver Clinton Smith, Jr.
Paul E. Stanzler
Michael Weinberg
David P. Rosenblatt
Barbara S. Hamelburg

Michael Ross Gottfried
Dennis J. Kelly
Michael G. Tracy
Darrell Mook
Gary W. Smith
Richard L. Wulsin
Kevin J. Kenneally
Mark Ventola
Maria-Eugenia Recalde

ASSOCIATES

Mark C. DiVincenzo

Ann M. Donovan
Frank C. Muggia

For Complete List of Firm Personnel, See General Section

For full biographical listings, see the Martindale-Hubbell Law Directory

Boston—Continued

CASNER & EDWARDS, LLP (AV)

1 Federal Street, 27th Floor, 02110-2003
Telephone: 617-426-5900
Telecopier: 617-426-8810

MEMBERS OF FIRM

Thomas D. Edwards (1931-1987)	Terrance J. Hamilton
Andrew J. Casner, Jr.	Robert S. Kutner
Walter H. Mayo, III	David J. Chavolla
Martin E. Greenblatt	Robert L. Ciociola
Charles M. Hamann	Stephen M. Perry
Robert A. Murphy	Gary L. Hoff
Robert E. Cowden, III	Anita W. Robboy
John H. Ashby	Robert M. Mendillo
Douglas K. Mansfield	Peter A. Caro
Andrew M. Higgins	Joan M. Griffin

ASSOCIATES

Gaynor D. Casner	Matthew T. Murphy
Donna Brewer MacKenna	Thomas J. Walsh
Gary L. Kemp	Cristina V. Coletta

For full biographical listings, see the Martindale-Hubbell Law Directory

CITY, HAYES, MEAGHER & DISSETTE, P.C. (AV)

50 Congress Street, 02109
Telephone: 617-523-3050
Telecopier: 617-523-5612

Robert D. City	Kieran B. Meagher
James P. Hayes	Michael J. Dissette

Martin R. Fisch	Lewis R. Lear
Philip B. Evans	Philip Di Domenico
Michael N. O'Connell, Jr.	

For full biographical listings, see the Martindale-Hubbell Law Directory

COGAVIN AND WAYSTACK (AV)

2 Center Plaza, 02108
Telephone: 617-742-3340
Telecopier: 617-723-7563

MEMBERS OF FIRM

John J. Cogavin	John P. Fitzgerald
Edward W. Waystack	Gerard A. Butler
Kevin J. McGinty	

ASSOCIATES

David T. Donnelly	Audrey Lewchik Bradley
John J. Jarosak	Daniel S. McInnis
Thomas M. Franco	William P. Hurley
Mark A. Darling	Laura E. Iannetta
Owen Roe O'Neill	Thomas G. Leonard, Jr.
John A. Dolan	

For full biographical listings, see the Martindale-Hubbell Law Directory

CORNELL AND GOLLUB (AV)

75 Federal Street, 02110
Telephone: 617-482-8100
Telecopier: 617-482-3917

MEMBERS OF FIRM

Robert W. Cornell (1910-1988)	Peter M. Durney
Karl L. Gollub (1934-1985)	Paul F. Lynch
David H. Sempert	Jane Treen Brand
Philip J. Foley	Janet J. Bobit

ASSOCIATES

Hugh M. Coxe	Thomas H. Dolan
Thomas A. Pursley	Eric B. Goldberg
David W. McGough	Kelly L. Wilkins
Susan Donaldson Novins	James P. Kerr
Marie Chadeayne Chafe	Patricia A. Hartnett

For full biographical listings, see the Martindale-Hubbell Law Directory

CURLEY & CURLEY, P.C. (AV)

27 School Street, 02108
Telephone: 617-523-2990
Fax: 617-523-7602

Robert A. Curley	Martin J. Rooney
Robert A. Curley, Jr.	Lisabeth A. Ryan-Kundert
Eugene F. Nowell	Stephen J. Gill
David D. Dowd	Marjory D. Robertson

For full biographical listings, see the Martindale-Hubbell Law Directory

DENNIS J. CURRAN (AV)

One State Street, Suite 410, 02109
Telephone: 617-742-3010
Fax: 617-742-1799

For full biographical listings, see the Martindale-Hubbell Law Directory

DEUTSCH WILLIAMS BROOKS DeRENSIS HOLLAND & DRACHMAN, P.C. (AV)

99 Summer Street, 02110-1235
Telephone: 617-951-2300
Fax: 617-951-2323
Email: dwbdhd@ix.netcom.com
Nantucket, Massachusetts Office: 5 Gladlands Avenue.
Telephone: 508-228-8725.
Fax: 508-325-5860.

Burton L. Williams	John Foskett
Steven J. Brooks	Barry L. Mintzer
Paul R. DeRensis	Roger K. Soderberg
Robert E. Holland	Neil R. Schauer
Allan W. Drachman	Michael P. Ridulfo
Roland Gray, III	Daniel R. Deutsch
Richard D. Bickelman	Janet L. Maloof
Valerie Swett	Elliot M. Sherman
Randy J. Kaplan	

Rodney G. Hoffman	Susan A. Moniz
Richard S. Blank	Tristin L. Beard
Marnie Wortzman	Catherine Skahan Reidy
Lawrence R. Holland	Robert D. Hillman
Frank J. Weiner	Andrea Tsacoyeanes
Peter J. Berry	Karen J. Folb
Elizabeth B. Valerio	

OF COUNSEL

Jack Green (P.C.)	Kenneth B. Gould

For full biographical listings, see the Martindale-Hubbell Law Directory

ESDAILE, BARRETT & ESDAILE (AV)

75 Federal Street, 02110
Telephone: 617-482-0333
Fax: 617-426-2978
Email: Esdaile@AOL.COM

MEMBERS OF FIRM

J. Newton Esdaile	Norman I. Jacobs
Charles W. Barrett, Jr.	Michael E. Mone
James N. Esdaile, Jr.	Patricia L. Kelly
Robert J. Rutecki	

ASSOCIATES

Shaun Spencer Forsyth	C. William Barrett
Rhonda Traver Maloney	Mary Moynihan Conneely
Steven J. Ryan	Jon M. Jacobs
Kathryn E. Hand	

OF COUNSEL

Charles J. Murray

For full biographical listings, see the Martindale-Hubbell Law Directory

FINNEGAN, UNDERWOOD, RYAN & TIERNEY (AV)

20 Custom House Street Suite 550, 02110
Telephone: 617-345-0020
Fax: 617-345-0150

MEMBERS OF FIRM

David I. Finnegan	John G. Ryan
Richard J. Underwood	Philip T. Tierney

ASSOCIATES

Peter J. McCue	Kim Beringhause Peacock
Susan E. Ireland	Susan Underwood
Stimpson B. Hubbard	Susan Schramm

For full biographical listings, see the Martindale-Hubbell Law Directory

FRIEDMAN & ATHERTON (AV)

(Formerly Friedman, Atherton, King & Turner)
(Formerly Friedman, Atherton, Sisson & Kozol)
Exchange Place, 53 State Street, 02109-2803
Telephone: 617-227-5540
Telecopier: 617-523-1559

Lee M. Friedman (1895-1957)	Percy A. Atherton (1903-1940)
Frank L. Kozol (1927-1993)	

OF COUNSEL

Frank H. Shapiro

(See Next Column)

FRIEDMAN & ATHERTON, *Boston—Continued*

MEMBERS OF FIRM

Joel A. Kozol	Matthew S. Kozol
Lee H. Kozol	Alan M. Spiro
William I. Cowin	David L. Kelston
Robert D. Kozol	Victor Bass
Richard M. Zinner	David M. Kozol

ASSOCIATES

Andrew D. Cummings	Penny Kozol
Christine P. Deshler	Olive E. Larson
Paula F. Donahue	David A. Rich
Eric J. Kozol	Marie C. Vaccarelli

Herbert Weinberg

COUNSEL

Paul S. Alpert	Debra Dyleski-Najjar
Thomas C. Bailey	Michael P. Morizio

For full biographical listings, see the Martindale-Hubbell Law Directory

GADSBY & HANNAH LLP (AV)

225 Franklin Street, 02110
Telephone: 617-345-7000
Telex: 6817512 GADHAN BSN
Telefax: 617-345-7050
Email: gadsby@ghlaw.com *URL:* http://www.ghlaw.com
Washington, D.C. Office: 1747 Pennsylvania Avenue, N.W.
Telephone: 202-429-9600.

PARTNERS

Richard K. Allen	Stanley A. Martin
Ronald G. Busconi	John M. McKelway, Jr.
Allan R. Curhan	James J. Myers
Robert J. Kaler	Mark E. Schreiber
Daniel J. Kelly	Michael N. Sheetz

William A. Zucker

ASSOCIATES

Joseph A. Barra	John R. Hallal
(Not admitted in MA)	Rosa C. Hallowell
Marjorie E. Boone	Susan J Matthew
Peter M. Coppinger	Risa G. Sorkin
Leigh A. Gilligan	Peter F. Trotter

WASHINGTON, D.C. OFFICE
RESIDENT PARTNERS

Michael A. Hordell	Carol L. B. Matthews
Paul F. Kilmer	(Not admitted in MA)
(Not admitted in MA)	

RESIDENT ASSOCIATES

Thomas W. Brooke	Laura L. Hoffman
(Not admitted in MA)	(Not admitted in MA)

For Complete List of Firm Personnel, See General Section

For full biographical listings, see the Martindale-Hubbell Law Directory

GELB & GELB (AV)

20 Custom House Street, 02110
Telephone: 617-345-0010
Facsimile: 617-345-0009

MEMBERS OF FIRM

Richard M. Gelb	Gail Kleven Gelb

Vanda Marie Khadem	Kathryn A. Thomas

For full biographical listings, see the Martindale-Hubbell Law Directory

GLOVSKY, TARLOW & MILBERG (AV)

Suite 810, 31 Milk Street, 02109-5104
Telephone: 617-423-7100
Telecopier: 617-482-8034
Washington, D.C. Office: 1090 Vermont Avenue, N.W.
Telephone: 202-659-1971.

Richard D. Glovsky	Melinda Milberg

Daniel S. Tarlow

ASSOCIATES

Peter M. Kelley	John F. Tocci

Debra L. Feldstein

OF COUNSEL

Harry M. Carey, Jr.	Lynne K. Zusman (Not
Paul S. Davis	admitted in MA; Resident,
Barry H. Field	Washington, D.C. Office)

For full biographical listings, see the Martindale-Hubbell Law Directory

THE LAW OFFICE OF EDWIN C. HAMADA, P.C. (AV)

88 Broad Street, 02110
Telephone: 617-542-5200
Telecopier: 617-542-5303

(See Next Column)

Edwin C. Hamada

Kevin M. Corr	Pamela B. Lyons

LEGAL SUPPORT PERSONNEL
Reneé M. MacDonald (Office Administrator)

For full biographical listings, see the Martindale-Hubbell Law Directory

HANIFY & KING, PROFESSIONAL CORPORATION (AV)

One Federal Street, 02110-2007
Telephone: 617-423-0400
Telefax: 617-423-0498

James Coyne King	Daniel J. Lyne
John D. Hanify	Donald F. Farrell, Jr.
Harold B. Murphy	Barbara Wegener Pfirrman
David Lee Evans	Gerard P. Richer

Timothy P. O'Neill

Jean A. Musiker	Joseph F. Cortellini
Ann M. Chiacchieri	Eddirland Duncan
Melissa J. Cassedy	Andrew G. Lizotte
Jeffrey J. Upton	Karen A. Whitley
Michael R. Perry	Christopher K. Barry-Smith
Charles A. Dale, III	William T. Harrington
Kathleen E. Cross	Matthew McCue
David M. Wright	Robyn J. Bartlett

Owen P. Kane

For full biographical listings, see the Martindale-Hubbell Law Directory

KERN, ROACH & CARPENTER, P.C. (AV)

24 School Street, 02108
Telephone: 617-720-1800
Telefax: 617-720-0720

Leila R. Kern	Christine M. Roach

M. Ellen Carpenter

Maryaustin Dowd

For full biographical listings, see the Martindale-Hubbell Law Directory

KOPELMAN AND PAIGE, P.C. (AV)

Park Square Building, 31 St. James Avenue, 7th Floor, 02116
Telephone: 617-556-0007
Fax: 617-654-1735

Leonard Kopelman	John W. Giorgio
Donald G. Paige	Barbara J. Saint Andre
Elizabeth A. Lane	Joel B. Bard
Joyce F. Frank	Everett Joseph Marder

Patrick J. Costello

William Hewig, III	Richard Bowen
Judith Chanoux Cutler	Cheryl Ann Banks
Anne-Marie M. Hyland	Brian W. Riley

For Complete List of Firm Personnel, See General Section

For full biographical listings, see the Martindale-Hubbell Law Directory

LANGAN, DEMPSEY AND BRODIGAN (AV)

40 Broad Street Suite 220, 02109
Telephone: 617-542-1871
Telecopier: 617-482-1871

Daniel J. Dempsey (1945-1970)	Joseph J. Brodigan

James M. Langan, Jr.

William D. Gardiner	Joseph J. Brodigan, Jr.

Michael Brodigan

OF COUNSEL
James M. Langan

For full biographical listings, see the Martindale-Hubbell Law Directory

LOONEY & GROSSMAN (AV)

A Partnership including Professional Corporations
101 Arch Street, 02110-1112
Telephone: 617-951-2800
Fax: 617-951-2819

Stewart F. Grossman (P.C.)	Bradley W. Snyder
Richard J. Grahn	Wesley S. Chused
Bertram E. Snyder	Melvin S. Hoffman (P.C.)
Robert Cushman Barber	Joseph H. Matzkin

SENIOR COUNSEL
William F. Looney, Jr.

(See Next Column)

LOONEY & GROSSMAN—*Continued*

OF COUNSEL

Paul D. McCarthy   Sherman H. Starr, Jr.

ASSOCIATES

Seth H. Salinger   Lisa Sternschuss
Erin M. Gilligan   Keir J. Beadling
Maria Galvagna   Lauren K. Heggestad Dillon
                  Adam J. Ruttenberg

For full biographical listings, see the Martindale-Hubbell Law Directory

---

McCormack & Epstein (AV)

One International Place, 02110
Telephone: 617-951-2929
Telecopier: 617-951-2672
New York, N.Y. Office: 330 Madison Avenue, Twenty Seventh Floor.
Telephone: 212-935-0881.

MEMBERS OF FIRM

Robert D. Epstein   Mark E. Cohen
Michael J. McCormack   Joseph H. Aronson

Brian C. Duffey   Amy M. Soisson
George X. Pucci   Stephen D. Rosenberg
Marc L. LaCasse   Mary-Elise Connolly
                  Kjersten Johnsen

Representative Clients: First State Insurance Co.; Crum & Forster Commercial Insurance; Liberty Mutual Insurance Co.; United States Fidelity & Guaranty Co.; Massachusetts Bay Transportation Authority; Technical Aid Corporation.

For full biographical listings, see the Martindale-Hubbell Law Directory

---

Mintz, Levin, Cohn, Ferris, Glovsky and Popeo, P.C. (AV)

One Financial Center, 02111
Telephone: 617-542-6000
FAX: 617-542-2241
Internet: Each Attorney's Internet Address takes the following form: first initial last name @mintz.com (e.g., rmintz@mintz.com)
Washington, D.C. Office: 701 Pennsylvania Avenue, N.W. Suite 900.
Telephone: 202-434-7300.
Fax: 202-434-7400.

R. Robert Popeo   Paul D. Wilson
Peter M. Saparoff   Joseph G. Blute
Thomas R. Murtagh   Jeffrey S. Robbins
Stephen M. Leonard   Samuel M. Starr
Robert M. Gault   Lee H. Glickenhaus
Martha J. Koster   Timothy J. Langella
John K. Markey   David E. Lurie
Michael S. Gardener   Henry A. Sullivan
Cameron F. Kerry   Kim V. Marrkand
Patrick J. Sharkey   William M. Hill
Elizabeth B. Burnett   Tracy A. Miner
Kenneth M. Bello   Rosemary M. Allen
Peter A. Biagetti   Michael F. Connolly
H. Joseph Hameline   Beth I. Z. Boland
Bruce F. Metge   Carleasa A. Coates

OF COUNSEL

Francis X. Bellotti

SPECIAL COUNSEL

John C. Plotkin

For Complete List of Firm Personnel, See General Section

For full biographical listings, see the Martindale-Hubbell Law Directory

---

Nathanson & Goldberg, A Professional Corporation (AV)

10 Union Wharf, 02109
Telephone: 617-742-9350
Fax: 617-742-3559

Alvin S. Nathanson   Valerie S. Carter
Arthur Goldberg   Shannon M. Fitzpatrick

Stuart J. Frank

For full biographical listings, see the Martindale-Hubbell Law Directory

---

Palmer & Dodge LLP (AV)

One Beacon Street, 02108
Telephone: 617-573-0100
Facsimile: 617-227-4420

(See Next Column)

MEMBERS OF FIRM

Acheson H. Callaghan, Jr.   Scott P. Lewis
Ralph D. Gants   Francis C. Lynch
Michael T. Gass   Steven L. Schreckinger
Laurie S. Gill   Thane D. Scott
Jeffrey F. Jones   Craig E. Stewart
Michael J. Lacek   Jeffrey Swope
William L. Lahey   Peter S. Terris
                  Tamara S. Wolfson

COUNSEL

Stephen J. Abarbanel   Jay E. Gruber
                  Cassandra Warshowsky

For Complete List of Firm Personnel, See General Section

For full biographical listings, see the Martindale-Hubbell Law Directory

---

Peabody & Arnold (AV)

A Partnership including Professional Corporations
50 Rowes Wharf, 02110-3342
Telephone: 617-951-2100
Telecopier: 617-951-2125
Providence, Rhode Island Office: One Citizens Plaza, Suite 840.
Telephone: 401-831-8330.
Fax: 401-831-8359.

MEMBERS OF FIRM

Vincent M. Amoroso   Susan Fay Kendall
Kevin C. Cain   Maynard M. Kirpalani
Frederick E. Connelly, Jr.   Robert A. McCall
John P. Connelly   Robert W. Monaghan
William A. Cotter, Jr., (P.C.)   Alexander H. Pratt, Jr.
Philip M. Cronin   George C. Rockas
Allen N. David   E. Macey Russell
Paul R. Devin   Molly Haynes Sherden
Michael P. Duffy   Joseph M. Smick
Thomas Frisardi   Randolph L. Smith
R. Alan Fryer   Vincent M. Tentindo
Robert T. Gill (P.C.)   Harvey Weiner
Deborah S. Griffin   Rebecca J. Wilson
Elizabeth Z. Holmes   Mark E. Young

OF COUNSEL

Dale A. Coggins
Kent A. Willever (Resident,
   Providence, Rhode Island
   Office)

ASSOCIATES

Barry D. Ramsdell   Leonard Louis Spada
Jennifer L. Lauro   Elsie Bennett Kappler
Adam Simms   Kathleen M. Colbert
Christine Hasiotis   Kristin Garner
John J. Canniff   Matthew H. Herndon
Chantal M. Healey   Robin E. Folsom
John J. O'Connor   Rita D. Lu
Sandra P. Criss   William Vance Hoch
Joanne T. Marchi   William M. ("Mo") Cowan
Thomas C. Farrell   Martin S. Ebel
                  Moujan M. Walkow

For Complete List of Firm Personnel, See General Section

For full biographical listings, see the Martindale-Hubbell Law Directory

---

Rackemann, Sawyer & Brewster, Professional Corporation (AV)

One Financial Center, 02111
Telephone: 617-542-2300
Telecopier: 617-542-7437

William B. Tyler   Janet M. Smith
Henry H. Thayer   Peter Friedenberg
Stephen Carr Anderson   Richard S. Novak
Albert M. Fortier, Jr.   J. David Leslie
Michael F. O'Connell   Sanford M. Matathia
Stuart T. Freeland   Richard J. Gallogly
Alan B. Rubenstein   James A. Wachta
James R. Shea, Jr.   Hanson S. Reynolds
Brian M. Hurley   Donald R. Pinto, Jr.

COUNSEL

Ronald S. Duby   Gordon M. Orloff
Lucy West Behymer   Eric A. Smith

OF COUNSEL

Albert B. Wolfe   George V. Anastas
August R. Meyer   Edward M. Condit
Richard H. Lovell   Alexander H. Spaulding

(See Next Column)

RACKEMANN, SAWYER & BREWSTER PROFESSIONAL CORPORATION, *Boston—Continued*

Margaret L. Hayes	Peter A. Alpert
Daniel J. Ossoff	Ellen M. Harrington
Melissa Langer Ellis	Lauren D. Armstrong
Daniel J. Bailey, III	Robert B. Foster
Michael S. Giaimo	Andrew H. Butler
Maura E. Murphy	Gayle E. Parlee
Mary L. Gallant	Elizabeth A. Gibbons
	Melissa Fang

For full biographical listings, see the Martindale-Hubbell Law Directory

REARDON & REARDON (AV)

69 Beacon Street, 02108
Telephone: 617-248-6998
Fax: 617-248-0837
Worcester, Massachusetts Office: One Exchange Place.
Telephone: 508-754-1111.
Fax: 508-797-6176.

MEMBERS OF FIRM

James G. Reardon   Frank S. Puccio, Jr.

References: Mechanics National Bank; Worcester County National Bank; Bank of New England, Worcester.

For full biographical listings, see the Martindale-Hubbell Law Directory

ROPES & GRAY (AV)

One International Place, 02110
Telephone: 617-951-7000
Fax: 617-951-7050
Email: postmaster @ ropesgray.com
Washington, D.C. Office: One Franklin Square, 1301 K Street, NW, Suite 800 East.
Telephone: 202-626-3900.
Telecopy: 202-626-3961.
Providence, Rhode Island Office: 30 Kennedy Plaza.
Telephone: 401-455-4400.
Telecopy: 401-455-4401.

MEMBERS OF FIRM

George C. Caner, Jr.	James L. Sigel
Jerome M. Leonard	Thomas H. Hannigan, Jr.
Thomas G. Dignan, Jr.	John C. Bartenstein
Paul B. Galvani	Douglas H. Meal
William G. Meserve	Steven A. Kaufman
G. Marshall Moriarty	John D. Donovan, Jr.
William L. Patton	John T. Montgomery
John C. Kane, Jr.	Martin J. Newhouse
Robert K. Gad, III	Mark P. Szpak
Kenneth W. Erickson	Michael K. Fee
Harvey J. Wolkoff	Lee Rubin-Collins
Jeffrey B. Storer	Randall W. Bodner

COUNSEL

Clayton S. Marsh (Not admitted in MA)

ASSOCIATES

Laurie R. Wallach	Richard D. Batchelder, Jr.
John R. Baraniak, Jr.	Theodore M. Hess-Mahan
David A. Brown	James W. Matthews
Lisa M. Ropple	Colleen M. Granahan
Kevin J. O'Connor	Michael S. Sher
Thomas P. Smith	Michael P. Allen
Matthew M. Burke	Darlene C. Lynch
	David R. Baron

OF COUNSEL

George H. Lewald   George T. Finnegan
          A. Lane McGovern

For Complete List of Firm Personnel, See General Section

For full biographical listings, see the Martindale-Hubbell Law Directory

SALLY & FITCH (AV)

225 Franklin Street, 02110-2804
Telephone: 617-542-5542
Telecopy: 617-542-1542
Providence, Rhode Island Office: 56 Pine Street, 02903.
Telephone: 401-521-6500.
Fax: 401-274-2780.

MEMBERS OF FIRM

Francis J. Sally	Thomas P. Billings
Jonathan W. Fitch	Andrea Peraner-Sweet
James B. Re	Paul M. McDermott
	Donn A. Randall

(See Next Column)

ASSOCIATES

Samuel J. Gesten	Rory A. Valas
Stephen C. Reilly	Karen S. White

For full biographical listings, see the Martindale-Hubbell Law Directory

SARROUF, TARRICONE & FLEMMING (AV)

95 Commercial Wharf, 02110
Telephone: 617-227-5800
Fax: 617-227-5470

Camille Francis Sarrouf	Daniel J. Gibson
Anthony Tarricone	Sheryl M. Bourbeau
John B. Flemming	Camille F. Sarrouf, Jr.
George J. Leary, Jr.	Donald J. Savery

For full biographical listings, see the Martindale-Hubbell Law Directory

SCHNEIDER, REILLY, ZABIN & COSTELLO, P.C. (AV)

Three Center Plaza, Suite 430, 02108
Telephone: 617-227-7500
Facsimile: 617-722-0286

Joseph Schneider (1924-1985)	Jeffrey D. Woolf
Joseph E. Reilly (1930-1951)	Joanne D'Alcomo
Albert P. Zabin	Marcia J. Allar
Robert V. Costello	Donald L. Liskov
E. L. Schneider (1931-1973)	David A. Goldman

For full biographical listings, see the Martindale-Hubbell Law Directory

SHERIN AND LODGEN LLP (AV)

100 Summer Street, 02110
Telephone: 617-426-5720
Fax: 617-542-5186
Email: lawyers @ sherin.com
Los Angeles, California Office: 11300 W. Olympic Boulevard, Suite 700.
Telephone: 310-914-7891.
Fax: 310-552-5327.

MEMBERS OF FIRM

Arthur L. Sherin (1946-1964)	Mark A. Nowak
George E. Lodgen (1946-1971)	Ronald W. Ruth
Morton B. Brown	Steven D. Eimert
George Waldstein	Barbara A. O'Donnell
John M. Reed	A. Neil Hartzell
Robert J. Muldoon, Jr.	Kenneth J. Mickiewicz
Alette E. Reed	Craig M. Brown
Edward M. Bloom	Andrew Royce
Thomas J. Raftery	Daniel O. Gaquin
Joshua M. Alper	Thomas A. Hippler
Gary M. Markoff	Rhonda B. Parker
Bryan G. Killian	John J. Slater III
David A. Guberman	Philip G. Boyle
Kenneth R. Berman	Nereyda Garcia
Frank J. Bailey	John C. La Liberte
Thomas P. Gorman	Christopher A. Kenney
Dorothy Nelson Stookey	C. Forbes Sargent III

ASSOCIATES

Karen Elise Berman	Michael S. Bloom
Margaret H. Leeson	Carolyn M. Barker
Robert M. Carney	Karen O'Malley
Mary Ellen McDonough	Susanne M. Walsh
Caroline Woodward	Susan S. Sampson
	Anne Marie Dowd

OF COUNSEL

Michael S. Strauss   David M. Franek

LEGAL SUPPORT PERSONNEL

Marilyn J. Stewart (Executive Director)

For full biographical listings, see the Martindale-Hubbell Law Directory

MARK D. SHUMAN (AV)

One Beacon Street 24th Floor, 02108
Telephone: 617-227-6300
Facsimile: 617-723-7236
Concord, Massachusetts Office (Law Office of Henry J. Dane): 37 Main Street, P.O. Box 540.
Telephone: 617-227-6300.

For full biographical listings, see the Martindale-Hubbell Law Directory

SWARTZ & SWARTZ (AV)

10 Marshall Street, 02108
Telephone: 617-742-1900
Fax: 617-367-7193

Edward M. Swartz	Joan E. Swartz
Alan L. Cantor	James A. Swartz
Joseph A. Swartz	Harold David Levine
Victor A. Denaro	David P. Angueira

(See Next Column)

SWARTZ & SWARTZ—*Continued*

OF COUNSEL

Fredric A. Swartz

For full biographical listings, see the Martindale-Hubbell Law Directory

TAYLOR, DUANE, BARTON & GILMAN (AV)

75 Federal Street, 02110
Telephone: 617-654-8208
Fax: 617-482-5350
Providence, Rhode Island Office: The Wilcox Building, 42 Weybosset Street.
Telephone: 401-273-7171.
Fax: 401-273-2904.

MEMBERS OF FIRM

Allan E. Taylor	John J. Barton
James J. Duane, III	Pamela Slater Gilman

ASSOCIATES

Edward D. Shoulkin	Gina Witalec Verdi
Jennifer Ellis Burke	Robert C. Shindell
Francis A. Connor, III	Craig R. Waksler
David G. Bowman	

For full biographical listings, see the Martindale-Hubbell Law Directory

WARNER & STACKPOLE LLP (AV)

75 State Street, 02109
Telephone: 617-951-9000
Telecopier: 617-951-9151
Email: w&s@warstack.com

MEMBERS OF FIRM

Samuel Adams	Joseph J. Leghorn
Deborah E. Barnard	Ralph T. Lepore, III
Judith G. Dein	Keith C. Long
Michael DeMarco	Christopher E. Nolin
Antoinette D. Hubbard	Janice Kelley Rowan
Ronald F. Kehoe	Peter T. Wechsler
Robert A. Whitney	

ASSOCIATES

Christa A. Arcos	Nancy J. Kriegel
James J. Arguin	Christopher G. Lang
Ellen Donahue	Jessica Ferrell Parker
Kristine E. George	Daniel E. Rosenfeld
Alexis Smith Hamdan	Karen R. Sweeney

OF COUNSEL

Norman A. Hubley

For Complete List of Firm Personnel, See General Section

For full biographical listings, see the Martindale-Hubbell Law Directory

WILLCOX, PIROZZOLO AND McCARTHY, PROFESSIONAL CORPORATION (AV)

50 Federal Street, 02110
Telephone: 617-482-5470
Telecopier: 617-423-1572

Harold M. Willcox (1925-1975)	Jack R. Pirozzolo
	Richard F. McCarthy

Richard L. Binder	Richard E. Bennett
	Judith Seplowitz Ziss

OF COUNSEL

Richard P. Crowley

For full biographical listings, see the Martindale-Hubbell Law Directory

WITMER, KARP, WARNER & THUOTTE (AV)

One Joy Street, 02108
Telephone: 617-248-0550
Telefax: 617-248-0607
Email: wkwt@aol.com

Ronald A. Witmer	Mark J. Warner
Eric H. Karp	Robert W. Thuotte

ASSOCIATES

Elisabeth A. Pelletier	Jill E. Zimmerman

For full biographical listings, see the Martindale-Hubbell Law Directory

---

BROCKTON, Plymouth Co.

VINCENT P. CAHALANE, P.C. (AV)

478 Torrey Street, 02401
Telephone: 508-588-1222
Fax: 508-584-4748

(See Next Column)

Vincent P. Cahalane	Julie A. Cahalane Cahill
Robert J. Zullas	John E. Cahill

Representative Clients: General Motors Co.; Quincy Mutual Fire Insurance Co.; American States Insurance Co.; Admiral Insurance Co.; United States Fidelity & Guaranty; Reliance Insurance Co.

For full biographical listings, see the Martindale-Hubbell Law Directory

---

FITCHBURG, Worcester Co.

O'CONNOR AND RYAN, P.C. (AV)

61 Academy Street, 01420
Telephone: 508-345-4166
Fax: 508-343-8416

John M. O'Connor	Edward P. Ryan, Jr.

For full biographical listings, see the Martindale-Hubbell Law Directory

---

FRAMINGHAM, Middlesex Co.

DOMESTICO & BARRY (AV)

The Meadows, 161 Worcester Road, 01701
Telephone: 508-626-9000
Fax: 508-626-9001

MEMBERS OF FIRM

Charles J. Domestico	Susan Moran-Barry
	Timothy E. Maguire

For full biographical listings, see the Martindale-Hubbell Law Directory

STEWART T. HERRICK & ASSOCIATES (AV)

Suite 303, 1661 Worcester Road, 01701
Telephone: 508-875-0021
FAX: 508-875-0029

ASSOCIATE

Lauren P. Smith

For full biographical listings, see the Martindale-Hubbell Law Directory

---

FRANKLIN, Norfolk Co.

ROCHE AND MURPHY (AV)

Franklin Office Park West, 38 Pond Street, Suite 308, P.O. Box 267, 02038
Telephone: 508-528-8300
FAX: 508-528-8889

MEMBERS OF FIRM

Neil J. Roche	Paul G. Murphy

ASSOCIATE

John J. Roche

For full biographical listings, see the Martindale-Hubbell Law Directory

---

LEXINGTON, Middlesex Co.

SALVATORE F. STRAMONDO (AV)

3 Ballard Terrace, 02173
Telephone: 617-862-6422

For full biographical listings, see the Martindale-Hubbell Law Directory

---

MEDFORD, Middlesex Co.

DAVID BERMAN (AV)

100 George P. Hassett Drive, 02155
Telephone: 617-395-7520

Reference: Bay Bank

For full biographical listings, see the Martindale-Hubbell Law Directory

---

MILFORD, Worcester Co.

GREENWALD, GREENWALD & POWERS (AV)

409 Fortune Boulevard Granite Park, 01757-1746
Telephone: 508-478-8611
Fax: 508-634-3959; 478-5937

Alan Greenwald	Anne M. Givens
Steven A. Greenwald	Colleen B. Walker
John D. Powers	Kathleen R. Winsor

OF COUNSEL

Merek S. Rubin

For full biographical listings, see the Martindale-Hubbell Law Directory

NANTUCKET,* Nantucket Co.

DEUTSCH WILLIAMS BROOKS DeRENSIS HOLLAND & DRACHMAN, P.C. (AV)

5 Gladlands Avenue, 02554
Telephone: 508-228-8725
Fax: 508-325-5860
Boston, Massachusetts Office: 99 Summer Street.
Telephone: 617-951-2300.
Fax: 617-951-2323.

Paul R. DeRensis

For full biographical listings, see the Martindale-Hubbell Law Directory

NEW BEDFORD, Bristol Co.

BEAUREGARD & BURKE (AV)

13 Hamilton Street, P.O. Box B-952, 02741
Telephone: 508-993-0333
Fax: 508-990-2045

MEMBERS OF FIRM

Philip N. Beauregard   Richard E. Burke, Jr.

Michael Franco

OF COUNSEL

William H. Carey

For full biographical listings, see the Martindale-Hubbell Law Directory

McLAUGHLIN & FOLAN, P.C. (AV)

401 County Street, P.O. Box 2095, 02741-2095
Telephone: 508-992-9800
Fax: 508-992-9730

David A. McLaughlin   John F. Folan
Mary Alice S. McLaughlin   Michael J. McGlone

John H. Solomito   John A. Leone

OF COUNSEL

Chris Byron

For full biographical listings, see the Martindale-Hubbell Law Directory

NORTHAMPTON,* Hampshire Co.

GROWHOSKI, CALLAHAN & KUZMESKI (AV)

60 State Street, 01060-3099
Telephone: 413-584-1500
Fax: 413-584-1670

MEMBERS OF FIRM

John M. Callahan   Thomas M. Growhoski
            David C. Kuzmeski

ASSOCIATE

Elizabeth C. Mulcahy

For full biographical listings, see the Martindale-Hubbell Law Directory

SPRINGFIELD,* Hampden Co.

PELLEGRINI & SEELEY, P.C. (AV)

1145 Main Street, 01103
Telephone: 413-785-5300
Fax: 413-731-0626

Gilbert W. Baron (1911-1987)   Donald W. Blakesley
Gerard L. Pellegrini   Phyllis P. Ryan
Earlon L. Seeley, Jr.   Paul F. Schneider

Steven D. Rose   Thomas Casartello
Michael J. Chieco   Patrick C. Gable
Charles R. Casartello, Jr.   John J. Dumphy

For full biographical listings, see the Martindale-Hubbell Law Directory

ROBINSON DONOVAN MADDEN & BARRY, P.C. (AV)

Suite 1600, BayBank Tower, 1500 Main Street, 01115
Telephone: 413-732-2301
Fax: 413-785-4658

Homans Robinson (1894-1973)   Milton J. Donovan (1906-1995)
Lawrence M. Sinclair
  (1942-1986)

OF COUNSEL

John H. Madden, Jr.   Victor Rosenberg
Edward J. Barry   Richard S. Milstein

(See Next Column)

Gordon H. Wentworth   John C. Sikorski
James H. Tourtelotte   Nancy Frankel Pelletier
Charles K. Bergin, Jr.   Paul S. Weinberg
Ronald C. Kidd   Frederica H. McCarthy
Jeffrey W. Roberts   Matthew J. King
Jeffrey L. McCormick   Neva Kaufman Rohan
James F. Martin   Douglas F. Boyd
Robert P. Cunningham   James K. Bodurtha
            Keith A. Minoff

E. Paul Amata   Kimberly Davis Crear
  (Not admitted in MA)   John W. Davis
James D. Chadwell   Edmund J. Gorman
Susan L. Cooper   Patricia M. Rapinchuk
            Jonathan P. Rice

Representative Clients: The First National Bank of Boston; United Cooperative Bank; Fleet Bank, N.A.; American Policyholders Insurance Co.; CNA; Commercial Union Insurance Co.; Hanover Insurance Group.

For full biographical listings, see the Martindale-Hubbell Law Directory

RYAN, MARTIN, COSTELLO, LEITER, STEIGER & CASS, P.C. (AV)

Suite 2500, BayBank Tower, 1500 Main Street, P.O. Box 15629, 01115-5629
Telephone: 413-739-6971
Fax: 413-739-1441

Charles V. Ryan   Henry M. Downey
Philip J. Ryan   Joan C. Steiger
Bradford R. Martin, Jr.   Timothy J. Ryan
Mary K. Downey Costello   William J. Cass
Bruce L. Leiter   Michael P. Ryan

For full biographical listings, see the Martindale-Hubbell Law Directory

WORCESTER,* Worcester Co.

CHRISTOPHER, HAYS, WOJCIK & MAVRICOS (AV)

370 Main Street, 01608
Telephone: 508-792-2800
FAX: 508-792-6224

MEMBERS OF FIRM

William W. Hays   David A. Wojcik
            John A. Mavricos

OF COUNSEL

Christopher Christopher   William C. Perrin, Jr.

Reference: Flagship Bank & Trust Co.

For full biographical listings, see the Martindale-Hubbell Law Directory

FULLER, ROSENBERG, PALMER & BELIVEAU (AV)

14 Harvard Street, P.O. Box 764, 01613
Telephone: 508-755-5225
Telecopier: 508-757-1039

MEMBERS OF FIRM

Albert E. Fuller   Peter A. Palmer
Kenneth F. Rosenberg   Thomas W. Beliveau

ASSOCIATES

Robert W. Towle   Michael I. Mutter
Julie Bednarz Russell   Brian F. Welsh
Timothy O. Ribley   John J. Finn
Mark W. Murphy   James C. Crowley, Jr.
Lisa R. Bertonazzi   John P. Donohue
Mark C. Darling   James F. Gettens
William J. Mason   John Arthur Johnson
Antoinette J. Yitchinsky Ann F. Scannell

For full biographical listings, see the Martindale-Hubbell Law Directory

GLICKMAN, SUGARMAN & KNEELAND (AV)

11 Harvard Street, P.O. Box 2917, 01613
Telephone: 508-756-6206
Fax: 508-831-0443

MEMBERS OF FIRM

Melvyn Glickman   David W. Sugarman
            David J. Kneeland, Jr.

ASSOCIATES

Joe Boynton   Wayne M. LeBlanc

Representative Clients: Country Bank for Savings; Clinton Savings Bank.
References: Country Bank for Savings; Shawmut Worcester County Bank N.A.

For full biographical listings, see the Martindale-Hubbell Law Directory

Worcester—Continued

MacCarthy, Pojani & Hurley (AV)

Worcester Plaza, 446 Main Street, 01608
Telephone: 508-798-2480
Fax: 508-797-9561

Philip J. MacCarthy	John F. Hurley, Jr.
Dennis Pojani	Howard E. Stempler

William J. Ritter

Representative Clients: Fleet Bank of Massachusetts, N.A.; Melville Corp.; Travelers Insurance Co.; Liberty Mutual Co.; Commerce Insurance Co.; Worcester Mutual Insurance Co.; Health Plans, Inc.; Marane Oil Corp.

For Complete List of Firm Personnel, See General Section

For full biographical listings, see the Martindale-Hubbell Law Directory

McGuire & McGuire, P.C. (AV)

340 Main Street, Suite 910, 01608
Telephone: 508-754-3291
Fax: 508-752-0553

John K. McGuire (1952-1985)	Joseph E. McGuire

John K. McGuire, Jr.

Penelope A. Kathiwala	Paul Durkee
Christine Griggs Narcisse	Teresa Brooks

John Pedone

For full biographical listings, see the Martindale-Hubbell Law Directory

Reardon & Reardon (AV)

One Exchange Place, 01608
Telephone: 508-754-1111
Fax: 508-797-6176
Boston, Massachusetts Office: 69 Beacon Street.
Telephone: 617-248-6998.
Fax: 617-248-0837.

MEMBERS OF FIRM

James G. Reardon	Margaret Reardon Suuberg
Edward P. Reardon	James G. Reardon, Jr.
Frank S. Puccio, Jr.	Julie E. Reardon
Austin M. Joyce	Michael J. Akerson
James G. Haddad	Francis J. Duggan

References: Mechanics National Bank; Shawmut Worcester County Bank N.A.; Bank of New England, Worcester.

For full biographical listings, see the Martindale-Hubbell Law Directory

Seder & Chandler (AV)

A Partnership including a Professional Corporation
Established 1918
Burnside Building, 339 Main Street, 01608
Telephone: 508-757-7721
Telecopiers: 508-798-1863; 508-831-0955

MEMBERS OF FIRM

Samuel Seder (1918-1964)	Marvin S. Silver, P.C.
Harold Seder (1934-1988)	John L. Pfeffer, Jr.
Burton Chandler	Robert S. Adler
J. Robert Seder	Dawn E. Caccavaro
Darragh K. Kasakoff	Kevin C. McGee

Kurt L. Binder

ASSOCIATES

Paul J. O'Riordan	Jeffrey P. Greenberg

Denise M. Tremblay

OF COUNSEL

Saul A. Seder	Gerald E. Norman

Philip C. Lombardo, Jr.

Reference: First National Bank of Boston; Safety Fund National Bank; Fleet National Bank.

For full biographical listings, see the Martindale-Hubbell Law Directory

MICHIGAN

ANN ARBOR,* Washtenaw Co.

Boothman, Hebert & Eller, P.C. (AV)

300 N. Fifth Avenue, Suite 140, 48108
Telephone: 313-995-9050
Fax: 313-995-8966
Detroit, Michigan Office: Marquette Building, 243 West Congress, Suite 950.
Telephone: 313-964-0150.
Fax: 313-964-2226.

(See Next Column)

Richard C. Boothman (Resident)

For full biographical listings, see the Martindale-Hubbell Law Directory

Davis and Fajen, P.C. (AV)

Suite 400, 320 North Main Street, 48104
Telephone: 313-995-0066
Facsimile: 313-995-0184
West Michigan Office: Davis, Fajen & Miller. Harbourfront Place, 41 Washington Street, Suite 260, Grand Haven, MI, 49417.
Telephone: 616-846-9875.
Facsimile: 616-846-4920.

Peter A. Davis	James A. Fajen

Nelson P. Miller

Richard B. Bailey	Matthew J. Jurson

Reference: First of America Bank-Ann Arbor.

For full biographical listings, see the Martindale-Hubbell Law Directory

Hooper, Hathaway, Price, Beuche & Wallace (AV)

126 South Main Street, 48104
Telephone: 313-662-4426
Fax: 313-662-9559

Joseph C. Hooper (1899-1980)	Gregory A. Spaly
Alan E. Price	Robert W. Southard
James R. Beuche	William J. Stapleton
Bruce T. Wallace	Bruce C. Conybeare, Jr.
Charles W. Borgsdorf	Anthony P. Patti
Mark R. Daane	Marcia J. Major

OF COUNSEL

James A. Evashevski	Roderick K. Daane

Representative Clients: Chem-Trend, Inc.; Dundee Cement Co.; Ervin Industries, Inc.; First Martin Corp.; Group 243 Design, Inc.; Honeywell; Microwave Sensors, Inc.; Shearson Lehman Hutton; O'Neal Construction Co.; Pittsfield Products, Inc.

For Complete List of Firm Personnel, See General Section

For full biographical listings, see the Martindale-Hubbell Law Directory

Hurbis & Clinton (AV)

Fifth Floor, City Center Building, 48104
Telephone: 313-761-8358
Fax: 313-761-3134

Charles J. Hurbis	Mary F. Clinton

Robert Lipnik	Georgette E. David

Representative Clients: General Motors Corp.; ITT Hartford; Insurance Company of North America; The University of Michigan; North Oakland Medical Center; City of Pontiac; Sears Roebuck and Co.; Montgomery Ward and Co., Inc.; Sedjwick-James, Inc.

For full biographical listings, see the Martindale-Hubbell Law Directory

Miller, Canfield, Paddock and Stone, P.L.C. (AV)

A Professional Limited Liability Company
Founded in 1852 by Sidney Davy Miller
101 North Main Street, Seventh Floor, 48104-1400
Telephone: 313-663-2445
Fax: 313-747-7147
Detroit, Michigan Office: 150 West Jefferson, Suite 2500, 48226-4415.
Telephone: 313-963-6420.
Fax: 313-496-7500.
Cable Address: "Stem Detroit."
Bloomfield Hills, Michigan Office: Suite 100, Pinehurst Office Center, 1400 North Woodward, 48303-2014.
Telephone: 313-645-5000.
Fax: 313-645-1917.
Grand Rapids, Michigan Office: 1200 Campau Square Plaza, 99 Monroe, N.W., 49503-2639.
Telephone: 616-454-8656.
Fax: 616-776-6322.
Howell, Michigan Office: 121 South Barnard Street, Suite 4, 48843-2305.
Telephone: 517-546-7600.
Telecopier: 517-546-6974.
Kalamazoo, Michigan Office: 444 West Michigan Avenue, 49007-3752.
Telephone: 616-381-7030.
Fax: 616-382-0244.
Lansing, Michigan Office: One Michigan Avenue, Suite 900, 48933-1609.
Telephone: 517-487-2070.
Fax: 517-374-6304.
Monroe, Michigan Office: The Executive Centre, 214 East Elm Avenue, 48161-2682.
Telephone: 313-243-2000.
Fax: 313-243-0901.

(See Next Column)

MILLER, CANFIELD, PADDOCK AND STONE P.L.C., *Ann Arbor—Continued*

Washington, D.C. Office: 1225 Nineteenth Street, N.W., Suite 400. 20036.
Telephone: 202-429-5575; 785-0600.
Fax: 202-331-1118; 785-1234.
Pensacola, Florida Office: 25 West Cedar, 32501.
Telephone: 904-469-1088.
Fax: 904-432-0677.
St. Petersburg, Florida Office: 100 Second Avenue S., Suite 7045, 33701.
Telephone: 813-982-6000.
Fax: 813-892-6002.
New York, New York Office: Eleventh Floor, 135 East 57th Street, 10022-2087.
Telephone: 212-754-5400.
Fax: 212-754-5401.
Gdansk, Poland Office: Suite 322, Dom Technika Building, UI. Rajska 6, 80-850.
Telephone: 011-485-831-2808.
Fax: 011-485-831-4719.
Warsaw, Poland Office: UI. Marszalkowska 82, Suite 561, 00-517.
Telephone: 011-482-623-6457 and 6458.
Fax: 011-482-623-6459.

RESIDENT PRINCIPALS

Robert E. Gilbert	David A. French
Allyn D. Kantor	Marta A. Manildi

Representative Firm Clients: Chrysler Corporation; Comerica, Incorporated; City of Detroit, Michigan; Detroit Tigers, Inc.; First of Michigan; Ford Motor Company; Ford Motor Credit Company; Great Lakes Bancorp; Henry Ford Hospital; INVETECH Company.

For Complete List of Firm Personnel, See General Section

For full biographical listings, see the Martindale-Hubbell Law Directory

---

PEAR SPERLING EGGAN & MUSKOVITZ, P.C. (AV)

Domino's Farms, 24 Frank Lloyd Wright Drive, 48105
Telephone: 313-665-4441
Fax: 313-665-8788
Ypsilanti, Michigan Offices: 5 South Washington Street.
Telephone: 313-483-3626 and 2164 Bellevue at Washtenaw.
Telephone: 313-483-7177.

Edwin L. Pear	Joel F. Graziani
Lawrence W. Sperling	Paul R. Fransway
Andrew M. Eggan	Francyne Stacey
Melvin J. Muskovitz	Helen Conklin Vick
Thomas E. Daniels	Scott H. Mandel
David E. Kempner	

Counsel for: Domino's Pizza, Inc.; Technical Engineering Consultants, Inc.; Victory Lane Quick Oil Change, Inc.; Citizens Banking Corporation; The Credit Bureau of Ypsilanti; Meadowbrook Insurance Group; Michigan Municipal Liability & Property Pool.

For full biographical listings, see the Martindale-Hubbell Law Directory

---

BATTLE CREEK, Calhoun Co.

SULLIVAN, HAMILTON, SCHULZ, LETZRING, SIMONS, KRETER, TOTH & LEBEUF, P.C. (AV)

One West Michigan Avenue, 49017
Telephone: 616-965-3216
Fax: 616-965-2919

Maxwell B. Allen (1884-1942)	Bert W. Schulz
John M. Allen (1914-1985)	Kurt F. Letzring
Ronald H. Ryan (1901-1988)	Stephen L. Simons
Raymond R. Allen (1919-1996)	Mark E. Kreter
James M. Sullivan	Michael J. Toth
Ronald A. Lebeuf	

OF COUNSEL

Robert P. Hamilton

General Counsel for: Michigan Woodwork and Specialties.
Local Counsel for: The Medical Protective Co.; Gannett, Inc.; Automobile Club of Michigan Insurance Group and Insurance Assn. (AAA); Michigan Physicians Mutual Liability Co.; State Farm Mutual Insurance Co.; Auto Owners Insurance Co.; Cincinnati Insurance Co.; Nationwide Insurance Co.

For full biographical listings, see the Martindale-Hubbell Law Directory

---

BERRIEN SPRINGS, Berrien Co.

BOOTHBY & YINGST (AV)

9047-4 US 31 North, P.O. Box 268, 49103
Telephone: 616-471-7787
Fax: 616-471-7400
Washington, D.C. Office: 4545 42nd Street, N.W.
Telephone: 202-363-1773.
Fax: 202-363-0304.

MEMBERS OF FIRM

Lee Boothby	Robert A. Yingst

For full biographical listings, see the Martindale-Hubbell Law Directory

---

BINGHAM FARMS, Oakland Co.

MEISNER & ASSOCIATES, P.C. (AV)

Suite 467, 30200 Telegraph Road, 48025-4506
Telephone: 810-644-4433

Robert M. Meisner

Robert R. Maxwell

For full biographical listings, see the Martindale-Hubbell Law Directory

---

SMALL, TOTH, BALDRIDGE & VAN BELKUM, P.C. (AV)

30100 Telegraph Road Suite 250, 48025-4516
Telephone: 810-647-9595
Facsimile: 810-647-9599

Richard L. Small	David M. Baldridge
John M. Toth	Thomas G. Van Belkum
Keith P. Felty	

Representative Clients: The Medical Protective Co.; Michigan Physicians Mutual Liability Insurance Co.; Physicians Insurance Company of Michigan; Kemper Insurance Group; AAMOS National; CNA Insurance Group; Anthem Insurance Co.; Oakwood United Hospitals; The Detroit Medical Center Affiliated Hospital; Hastings Mutual Insurance Co.

For full biographical listings, see the Martindale-Hubbell Law Directory

---

SOTIROFF ABRAMCZYK & RAUSS, P.C. (AV)

30400 Telegraph Road, Suite 444, 48025-4541
Telephone: 810-642-6000
Facsimile: 810-642-9001

Philip Sotiroff	Lawrence A. Tower
Lawrence R. Abramczyk	Robert B. Goldi
Dennis M. Rauss	Keith A. Sotiroff

For full biographical listings, see the Martindale-Hubbell Law Directory

---

BIRMINGHAM, Oakland Co.

CARSON FISCHER, P.L.C. (AV)

Third Floor, 300 East Maple Road, 48009-6317
Telephone: 810-644-4840
Facsimile: 810-644-1832

Joseph M. Fischer	Kathleen A. Stibich
James E. Owings	

For full biographical listings, see the Martindale-Hubbell Law Directory

---

HYMAN AND LIPPITT, P.C. (AV)

185 Oakland Avenue, Suite 300, P.O. Box 1750, 48009
Telephone: 810-646-8292
Facsimile: 810-646-8375

J. Leonard Hyman	Kenneth F. Neuman
Norman L. Lippitt	Terry S. Givens
Douglas A. Hyman	Paul J. Fischer
Brian D. O'Keefe	John A. Sellers
H. Joel Newman	Robert H. Lippitt
Nazli G. Sater	Roger L. Myers
David N. Morrell, Jr.	

For full biographical listings, see the Martindale-Hubbell Law Directory

---

KELL & LYNCH, P.C. (AV)

300 East Maple Road, Suite 200, 48009
Telephone: 810-647-2333
Telefax: 810-647-2781

Michael V. Kell	Margaret A. Lynch

Jennifer T. Gilhool	Steven M. Ribiat
(Not admitted in MI)	

OF COUNSEL

M. Andrea Vaughn

Representative Clients: AlliedSignal, Inc.; AMP Inc.; Dow Corning Corp.; Hatteras Yachts; Lectron Products, Inc.; Metromedia Steakhouses, Inc.; Sybron Corp.; Michigan Consolidated Gas Co.; American Natural Resources.

For full biographical listings, see the Martindale-Hubbell Law Directory

---

LACEY & JONES (AV)

600 South Adams Road, Suite 300, 48009-6827
Telephone: 810-433-1414
Fax: 810-433-1241
Grand Rapids, Michigan Office: Suite 430, Ledyard Building, 125 Ottawa Avenue, N.W.
Telephone: 616-776-3641.
Fax: 616-776-3516.

(See Next Column)

LACEY & JONES—*Continued*

Ralph B. Lacey (1885-1966)	Francis L. Sylvester (Retired)
William J. Jones (1908-1991)	Paul Van Hartesveldt (Retired)
Robert B. Lacey (1912-1976)	John A. Hilgendorf (Retired)

MEMBERS OF FIRM

Theodore A. Lughezzani	Dennis E. Zacharski
Steve N. Yardley	T. F. Felker, Jr.
John Hayes	Gerald M. Marcinkoski
Charles E. Mann	William A. Day
Larry P. Beidelman	Kathleen McNichol Behn
Bruce C. Roberts	Richard N. Lovernick
Lawrence G. Kozaruk	Peter M. Roggenbaum
David J. Duthie	
(Resident, Grand Rapids)	

ASSOCIATES

Michael T. Reinholm	Timothy D. Finegan
Johnnie B. Rambus	Robert H. Orlowski, Jr.
Sean J. Powers	J. Patrick O'Neill
Timothy M. McAree	Dawn M. Sutkiewicz
(Resident, Grand Rapids)	D. Michael McCann

OF COUNSEL

Thomas J. Sullivan	Robert L. Beardslee
	William G. Sinn

Representative Clients: Alexsis, Inc.; Ameritech; Chrysler Corporation; CIGNA; Liberty Mutual Insurance Company; Meijer, Inc.; Metropolitan Prop. & Casualty; Michigan Hospital Association; Travelers Insurance Company.

For full biographical listings, see the Martindale-Hubbell Law Directory

MacDonald and Goren, P.C. (AV)

Suite 200, 260 East Brown Street, 48009
Telephone: 810-645-5940
Fax: 810-645-2490

Harold C. MacDonald	Kalman G. Goren
	Cindy Rhodes Victor

Amy L. Glenn	Lawrence C. Atorthy
David D. Marsh	Miriam Blanks-Smart
Glenn G. Ross	John T. Klees
	Rose Marie Karadsheh

OF COUNSEL

Robert L. Biederman

Representative Clients: Beaudin, Gallanis; Beaudin, Incorporated; Orlandi Gear Co., Inc.; Bing Steel, Inc.; Superb Manufacturing, Inc.; Spring Engineering, Inc.; Adrian Steel Co.; Southfield Radiology Associates, P.C.; HDS Services, Inc.; TGI Friday's Inc.; Quality Gold of Cincinnati, Inc.

For full biographical listings, see the Martindale-Hubbell Law Directory

BLOOMFIELD HILLS, Oakland Co.

Dawda, Mann, Mulcahy & Sadler, P.L.C. (AV)

1533 North Woodward Avenue Suite 200, 48304
Telephone: 810-642-3700
Fax: 810-642-7791
Email: EMail@DMMS.Com

Michael D. Mulcahy	Sherwin E. Zamler
Suanne Tiberio Trimmer	John Mucha, III
Susan J. Sadler	Amy Bateson
Tyler D. Tennent	Keith James

Joseph K. Hart, Jr.

Representative Clients: Bally's Total Fitness Corp.; BASF Corporation; Cargill, Inc.; City Management; Home Depot U.S.A., Inc.; Ladbroke Racing Corporation; The Sherwin-Williams Company; Trammell Crow Company; Walker Wire & Steel Corp.; Wal-Mart Stores, Inc.

For full biographical listings, see the Martindale-Hubbell Law Directory

Feeney Kellett Wienner & Bush, Professional Corporation (AV)

950 North Hunter Boulevard, Second Floor, 48304-3927
Telephone: 810-258-1580
Fax: 810-258-0421

James P. Feeney	Cheryl A. Bush
S. Thomas Wienner	Deborah F. Collins
Peter M. Kellett	David N. Goltz

OF COUNSEL

Thomas J. Manganello

(See Next Column)

James J. Majernik	Seth D. Gould
G. Gregory Schuetz	Patrick G. Seyferth
Jeffrey A. Gallant	Mark A. Fisher
	Bryan D. Cross

For full biographical listings, see the Martindale-Hubbell Law Directory

Hardig Parsons & Pedersen (AV)

74 West Long Lake Road, Suite 203, 48304
Telephone: 810-642-3500
Facsimile: 810-645-1128
Charlevoix, Michigan Office: 212 Bridge Street.
Telephone: 616-547-1200.
Facsimile: 616-547-1026.
Pawley's Island, South Carolina Office: 216 Highway 17, P.O. Box 1607, 29585.
Telephone: 803-237-9219.
Facsimile: 803-237-9530.
West Palm Beach, Florida Office: Suite 1450, 515 North Flagler.
Telephone: 407-833-1622.
Facsimile: 407-833-6933.

MEMBERS OF FIRM

Joseph L. Hardig, Jr.	Joseph L. Hardig, III
Donald H. Parsons	Edward C. Pedersen
	Bradley S. Stout

ASSOCIATE

Capri L. Pelshaw

OF COUNSEL

Edward K. Pedersen, Jr.

MEMBER IN SOUTH CAROLINA

John C. Benso

For full biographical listings, see the Martindale-Hubbell Law Directory

Robert Harrison & Associates (AV)

Bloomfield Office Pavilion, 2550 Telegraph Road, Suite 275, 48302
Telephone: 810-253-1800
Fax: 810-253-9446

Robert S. Harrison

ASSOCIATES

Michael J. Rex	Paul M. Newcomer
	Michael James Harrison

References: Comerica Bank, Southfield; Huntington Banks of Michigan, W. Bloomfield.

For full biographical listings, see the Martindale-Hubbell Law Directory

Liss and Associates, P.C. (AV)

The Pinehurst Building, 1400 North Woodward Avenue, Suite 200, 48304
Telephone: 810-647-9700
Facsimile: 810-647-5477; 810-647-0638

Arthur Y. Liss	Christine S. Reiner

Ronald S. Smith	Andrew M. Zack
	Karen E. Seder

For full biographical listings, see the Martindale-Hubbell Law Directory

Meyer, Kirk, Snyder & Safford, PLLC (AV)

Suite 100, 100 West Long Lake Road, 48304
Telephone: 810-647-5111
Telecopier: 810-647-6079
Detroit, Michigan Office: 2500 Penobscot Building.
Telephone: 313-961-1261.

George E. Snyder	Ralph R. Safford
	Patrick K. Rode

Christopher F. Clark	Boyd C. Farnam
	Debra S. Meier

Representative Clients: Available Upon Request.

For Complete List of Firm Personnel, See General Section

For full biographical listings, see the Martindale-Hubbell Law Directory

David D. Patton & Associates, P.C. (AV)

100 Bloomfield Hills Parkway, Suite 110, 48304
Telephone: 810-258-6020
Fax: 810-258-6052
Email: Litigation@Aol.Com

David D. Patton

(See Next Column)

DAVID D. PATTON & ASSOCIATES, P.C., *Bloomfield Hills—Continued*

Ellen Bartman Jannette   Patricia C. White
David H. Patton (1912-1993)

For full biographical listings, see the Martindale-Hubbell Law Directory

PORTNOY, PIDGEON & ROTH, P.C. (AV)

3883 Telegraph, Suite 103, 48302
Telephone: 810-647-4242
Fax: 810-647-8251
Email: DWINNIE103@AOL.COM

Bernard N. Portnoy	Marc S. Berlin
James M. Pidgeon	Berton K. May
Robert P. Roth	Sheila Connor-Heath

Charles A. Harrison III

Representative Clients: North Oakland Medical Center, Pontiac General Hospital Division; Hurley Medical Center, Flint, Michigan; McLaren Regional Medical Center, Flint, Michigan; William Beaumont Hospital, Royal Oak, Michigan; Detroit Osteopathic Hospital, Detroit, Michigan; Bi-County Community Hospital; Riverside Osteopathic Hospital; Lapeer Regional Hospital.

For full biographical listings, see the Martindale-Hubbell Law Directory

ZAMPLAS, JOHNSON, SOPT & CAVANAGH, P.C. (AV)

2550 Telegraph Road, Suite 250, 48302
Telephone: 810-333-2400
Fax: 810-333-7355

Dennis Zamplas	John F. Sopt
Dale E. Johnson	Michael D. Cavanagh

Jeffrey A. McKeever	Ellen Watts Throop

Julie Ann Lyons

For full biographical listings, see the Martindale-Hubbell Law Directory

BRIGHTON, Livingston Co.

BURCHFIELD, PARK & HEDDON, P.C. (AV)

225 East Grand River, Suite 203, 48116
Telephone: 810-227-3100
Facsimile: 810-227-2996

Kenneth E. Burchfield	David L. Park

Shari L. Heddon

Mack T. Spickard
LEGAL SUPPORT PERSONNEL
Janet M. Schillinger

For full biographical listings, see the Martindale-Hubbell Law Directory

DEARBORN, Wayne Co.

ROBERT F. RILEY, P.C. (AV)

Garrison Place East 19855 W. Outer Drive, Suite E-109, 48124
Telephone: 313-565-1330
Facsimile: 313-565-1318

Robert F. Riley

Laura L. Nordberg	Michael D. Dolenga

For full biographical listings, see the Martindale-Hubbell Law Directory

DETROIT,* Wayne Co.

ABBOTT, NICHOLSON, QUILTER, ESSHAKI & YOUNGBLOOD, P.C. (AV)

19th Floor, One Woodward Avenue, 48226
Telephone: 313-963-2500
Telecopier: 313-963-7882

C. Richard Abbott	Carl F. Jarboe
John R. Nicholson	Jay A. Kennedy
Thomas R. Quilter III	Timothy A. Stoepker
Gene J. Esshaki	Timothy J. Kramer
John F. Youngblood	Norbert T. Madison, Jr.
James B. Perry	William D. Gilbride, Jr.

Mary P. Nelson	Kathryn L. Ritchie
Michael R. Blum	Jill A. Bankey
Thomas F. Hatch	Dawn M. Macaddino
Anne Warren Bagno	Casimir J. Swastek
Eric J. Girdler	Daniel G. Kielczewski

George M. Mesrey

(See Next Column)

OF COUNSEL

Thomas C. Shumaker   Karen Smith Kienbaum

For full biographical listings, see the Martindale-Hubbell Law Directory

BARRIS, SOTT, DENN & DRIKER, P.L.L.C. (AV)

211 West Fort Street, Fifteenth Floor, 48226-3281
Telephone: 313-965-9725
Telecopier: 313-965-2493
313-965-5398

Donald E. Barris	Robert E. Kass
Herbert Sott	Daniel M. Share
David L. Denn	Elaine Fieldman
Eugene Driker	Morley Witus
William G. Barris	John A. Libby
Sharon M. Woods	James S. Fontichiaro
Stephen E. Glazek	Daniel J. LaCombe

Robert E. Epstein
COUNSEL
Leon S. Cohan
OF COUNSEL
Stanley M. Weingarden

Dennis M. Barnes	Monique K. Cirelli
Matthew J. Boettcher	Laura Suzanne Laurence
Thomas F. Cavalier	Molly Giles
C. David Bargamian	Eric S. Rosenthal
Michael J. Reynolds	Claudia D. Orr
Elizabeth A. Carrie	Alicia Monique Nails

Representative Clients: Avis Rent A Car System, Inc.; Borman's, Inc.; Consumers Power Co.; County of Wayne, Michigan; Ford Motor Co.; The Great Atlantic & Pacific Tea Company, Inc.; Henry Ford Health System; Michigan Consolidated Gas Co.; NBD Bank, N.A.; Textron, Inc.

For full biographical listings, see the Martindale-Hubbell Law Directory

BENDURE & THOMAS (AV)

577 East Larned, Suite 210, 48226-4392
Telephone: 313-961-1525
Fax: 313-961-1553

MEMBERS OF FIRM

Mark R. Bendure	Marc E. Thomas

ASSOCIATES

J. Christopher Caldwell	Victor S. Valenti

Kevin P. Kavanagh
OF COUNSEL

John A. Lydick	Thomas R. Present

For full biographical listings, see the Martindale-Hubbell Law Directory

BODMAN, LONGLEY & DAHLING LLP (AV)

34th Floor 100 Renaissance Center, 48243
Telephone: 313-259-7777
Fax: 313-393-7579
Email: 2080194@mcimail.com
Troy, Michigan Office: Suite 2020, 755 West Big Beaver Road.
Telephone: 810-362-2110.
Fax: 810-244-0780.
Ann Arbor, Michigan Office: 110 Miller, Suite 300.
Telephone: 313-761-3780.
Fax: 313-930-2494.
Northern Michigan Office: 229 Court Street, P.O. Box 405, Cheboygan.
Telephone: 616-627-4351.
Fax: 616-627-2802.

MEMBERS OF FIRM

Theodore Souris	Lloyd C. Fell
Joseph A. Sullivan	(Northern Michigan Office)
Carson C. Grunewald	Martha Bedsole Goodloe
James A. Smith	(Troy Office)
George G. Kemsley	Harvey W. Berman
James J. Walsh	(Ann Arbor Office)
David G. Chardavoyne	Lawrence P. Hanson
Robert G. Brower	(Northern Michigan Office)
Charles N. Raimi	Diane L. Akers
Thomas Van Dusen	Dennis J. Levasseur
(Troy Office)	Stephen K. Postema
John C. Cashen (Troy Office)	(Ann Arbor Office)

For Representative Client List, See General Section

For Complete List of Firm Personnel, See General Section

For full biographical listings, see the Martindale-Hubbell Law Directory

Detroit—Continued

BOOTHMAN, HEBERT & ELLER, P.C. (AV)

Marquette Building, 243 West Congress, Suite 950, 48226
Telephone: 313-964-0150
Fax: 313-964-2226
Ann Arbor, Michigan Office: 300 N. Fifth Avenue, Suite 140.
Telephone: 313-995-9050.
Fax: 313-995-8966.

Dale L. Hebert	Gary S. Eller
Richard C. Boothman	
(Resident, Ann Arbor Office)	

George D. Moustakas	Marta J. Hoffman
Roy A. Luttmann	Sharon E. Hollins

Joyce E. Taylor
OF COUNSEL

L. Stewart Hastings, Jr.	Kathryn A. Kerka

Representative Clients: University of Michigan; Michigan Physicians Mutual Liability Co.; Emergency Physicians Medical Group; Kaiser Permanente; Physicians Insurance Co. of Michigan.
Reference: Comerica Bank-Detroit.

For full biographical listings, see the Martindale-Hubbell Law Directory

BRADY HATHAWAY, PROFESSIONAL CORPORATION (AV)

1330 Buhl Building, 48226-3602
Telephone: 313-965-3700
Telecopier: 313-965-2830

John F. Brady	Daniel J. Bretz
Thomas M. J. Hathaway	Liliana A. Ciccodicola
Thomas P. Brady	Connie M. Cessante

Representative Clients: Beam Stream, Inc.; Bundy Tubing Company; Energy Conversion Devices, Inc.; Schering Corporation; Warner-Lambert; Wolverine Technologies; ABB Environmental Services; GMIS, Inc.; Marriott Corp.

For Complete List of Firm Personnel, See General Section

For full biographical listings, see the Martindale-Hubbell Law Directory

BUTZEL LONG, A PROFESSIONAL CORPORATION (AV)

Suite 900, 150 West Jefferson, 48226
Telephone: 313-225-7000
Telecopier: 313-225-7080
Email: melnick@butzel.com *URL:* http://www.butzel.com
Birmingham, Michigan Office: Suite 200, 32270 Telegraph Road.
Telephone: 810-258-1616.
Telecopier: 810-258-1439.
Lansing, Michigan Office: 118 West Ottawa Street.
Telephone: 517-372-6622.
Telecopier: 517-372-6672.
Ann Arbor, Michigan Office: Suite 300, 350 South Main Street.
Telephone: 313-995-3110.
Telecopier: 313-995-1777.
Grosse Pointe Farms, Michigan Office: Suite 260, 21 Kercheval.
Telephone: 313-886-5446.
Telecopier: 313-886-2114.

William M. Saxton	Michael J. Lavoie
William R. Ralls (Lansing)	Gordon J. Walker (Birmingham)
Xhafer Orhan	E. William S. Shipman
John H. Dudley, Jr.	Richard P. Saslow
Richard E. Rassel	Gordon W. Didier (Birmingham)
Abba I. Friedman (Birmingham)	Dennis K. Egan
Edward D. Gold (Birmingham)	Bruce L. Sendek
Jack D. Shumate (Birmingham)	Lynne E. Deitch
Edward M. Kronk	Daniel B. Tukel
Philip J. Kessler	Alan S. Levine (Birmingham)
Donald B. Miller	Leonard M. Niehoff
John P. Hancock, Jr.	(Ann Arbor)
Frederick G. Buesser, III	Carey A. DeWitt
(Birmingham)	David H. Oermann
Leonard F. Charla	(Birmingham)
T. Gordon Scupholm II	James Y. Stewart (Birmingham)
(Birmingham)	Eric J. Flessland (Birmingham)
David W. Sommerfeld	Lynn Abraham Sheehy
(Birmingham and Grosse	Robert A. Boonin
Pointe Farms)	Sheldon H. Klein
Thomas B. Radom	Andrea Roumell Dickson
(Birmingham)	J. Michael Huget (Ann Arbor)
David W. Berry (Birmingham)	Anthony J. Saulino, Jr.
Carl Rashid, Jr.	(Birmingham)
D. Stewart Green (Birmingham)	James S. Rosenfeld
Dennis B. Schultz	Clara DeMatteis Mager
Mark T. Nelson	Ronald E. Reynolds
Daniel P. Malone	(Birmingham)
Keefe A. Brooks	Kenneth H. Adamczyk
James E. Wynne	Jordan S. Schreier (Ann Arbor)

(See Next Column)

Representative Clients: Bridgestone/Firestone, Inc.; The Detroit News, Inc.; Kelly Services; Kelsey Hayes Co.; Merrill Lynch Pierce Fenner & Smith, Inc.; Stroh Brewery Co.; Takata Corp.; United Parcel Services of America, Inc.; The University of Michigan.

For Complete List of Firm Personnel, See General Section

For full biographical listings, see the Martindale-Hubbell Law Directory

CLARK HILL P.L.C. (AV)

500 Woodward Avenue, Suite 3500, 48226
Telephone: 313-965-8300
Facsimile: 313-962-4348
Oakland County, Michigan Office: Third Floor, 255 South Woodward Avenue, Birmingham.
Telephone: 810-642-9692.
Facsimile: 810-642-2174.
Lansing, Michigan Office: Suite 600, 200 North Capitol Avenue.
Telephone: 517-484-4481.
Facsimile: 517-484-1246.
Minneapolis, Minnesota Office: Suite 1000, One Financial Plaza, 120 South Sixth Street.
Telephone: 612-332-0102.
Facsimile: 612-332-3225.
Kansas City, Missouri Office: Suite 1400, Bryant Building, 1102 Grand Avenue.
Telephone: 816-221-5578.
Facsimile: 816-221-0303.

Robert B. Webster (Resident, Oakland County Office)	Daniel J. Scully, Jr.
George N. Bashara, Jr.	Michael S. Khoury
Laurence M. Scoville, Jr.	Michael J. Sullivan
J. Walker Henry	Rachelle G. Silberberg
Timothy D. Wittlinger	Cynthia L.M. Johnson
(Resident, Oakland County Office)	LaVern A. Pritchard (Resident, Minneapolis Office)
David M. Hayes	David M. Lawson (Resident, Oakland County Office)
J. Thomas Lenga	Charles G. Goedert (Resident, Oakland County Office)
Richard C. Marsh	
P. Robert Brown, Jr.	Paul E. Scheidemantel
Richard C. Sanders	John E. Berg
Dennis G. Bonucchi	Thomas M. Dixon
James E. Baiers	Judith Greenstone Miller
Kevin S. Hendrick	Edward J. Hood
Charles H. Polzin (Resident, Oakland County Office)	Elizabeth Jolliffe Basten

SENIOR ATTORNEYS

David A. Vorbeck (Resident, Kansas City Office)	Mark W. McInerney

John M. Ketcham	Teresa J. Kimker
Michael I. Conlon	(Resident, Minneapolis Office)
Kevin H. Breck (Resident, Oakland County Office)	M. Maureen McHugh
Patricia Bordman	Jeffrey A. Schultz
Marsha Kay Nettles	Gerald E. Szpotek, Jr.
Katrina I. Crawley	Donald F. Berschback, II
David A. Breuch	Louise B. Sable
Mary Ray Brophy (Resident, Oakland County Office)	Kathleen M. Deegan
Mary C. Dirkes	David Scott Mendelson (Resident, Oakland County Office)

Representative Clients: American Red Cross; Bechtel Corporation; Booth Communications, Inc.; The Budd Co.; Coopers & Lybrand; First Federal of Michigan; R.E. Dailey & Co.; Rouge Steel Company; Scot Ladd Foods.

For Complete List of Firm Personnel, See General Section

For full biographical listings, see the Martindale-Hubbell Law Directory

DICKINSON, WRIGHT, MOON, VAN DUSEN & FREEMAN (AV)

500 Woodward Avenue, Suite 4000, 48226-3425
Telephone: 313-223-3500
Facsimile: 313-223-3598
Bloomfield Hills, Michigan Office: 525 North Woodward Avenue, Suite 2000.
Telephone: 810-433-7200.
Facsimile: 810-433-7274.
Grand Rapids, Michigan Office: 200 Ottawa Avenue, N.W., Suite 900.
Telephone: 616-458-1300.
Facsimile: 616-458-6753.
Lansing, Michigan Office: Suite 200, 215 South Washington Square.
Telephone: 517-371-1730.
Facsimile: 517-487-4700.
Washington, D.C. Office: Suite 800, 1901 L Street, N.W.
Telephone: 202-457-0160.
Facsimile: 202-659-1559.
Chicago, Illinois Office: 225 West Washington, Suite 400.
Telephone: 312-220-0300.
Facsimile: 312-220-0021.

(See Next Column)

DICKINSON, WRIGHT, MOON, VAN DUSEN & FREEMAN, *Detroit—Continued*

MEMBERS OF FIRM

Johanna H. Armstrong
  (Bloomfield Hills Office)
George R. Ashford
William C. Bertrand, Jr.
  (Lansing Office)
James W. Bliss (Lansing Office)
Richard M. Bolton
Andrew S. Boyce
Richard L. Braun, II
David R. Bruegel
  (Bloomfield Hills Office)
William T. Burgess
Maureen H. Burke
  (Bloomfield Hills Office)
Lawrence G. Campbell
James N. Candler, Jr.
Robert E. Carr
  (Bloomfield Hills Office)
Stuart F. Cheney
  (Grand Rapids Office)
Conrad J. Clark
  (Washington, D.C. Office)
Charles F. Clippert
  (Bloomfield Hills Office)
Margaret A. Coughlin
  (Bloomfield Hills Office)
Roger H. Cummings
  (Bloomfield Hills Office)
Michael S. Daar
Julia Donovan Darlow
Stephen E. Dawson
  (Bloomfield Hills Office)
Joseph W. DeLave
  (Bloomfield Hills Office)
David R. Deromedi
Selden S. Dickinson (1892-1964)
Terence M. Donnelly
Dwight D. Ebaugh
  (Lansing Office)
Peter H. Ellsworth
  (Lansing Office)
William E. Elwood
  (Washington, D.C. Office)
Barbara Hughes Erard
John A. Everhardus
Joseph A. Fink (Lansing Office)
Sherisse Eddy Fiorvento
  (Bloomfield Hills Office)
William J. Fisher, III
  (Grand Rapids Office)
Richard A. Glaser
  (Grand Rapids Office)
Daniel F. Gosch
  (Chicago, Illinois Office)
Judith E. Gowing
  (Bloomfield Hills Office)
Kirk E. Grable (Lansing Office)
Deborah L. Grace
  (Bloomfield Hills Office)
Ronald B. Grais
  (Chicago, Illinois Office)
Martin L. Greenberg
  (Chicago, Illinois Office)
Henry M. Grix
  (Bloomfield Hills Office)
K. Scott Hamilton
Michael C. Hammer
Thomas D. Hammerschmidt, Jr.
Craig W. Hammond
Verne C. Hampton, II
Elizabeth Phelps Hardy
  (Bloomfield Hills Office)
Charles T. Harris
  (Bloomfield Hills Office)
Stephen S. Herseth
  (Chicago, Illinois Office)
Mark R. High
Steven H. Hilfinger
Edgar C. Howbert (Detroit,
  Michigan and Chicago, Illinois
  Offices)
Timothy H. Howlett
Robert P. Hurlbert
  (Chicago, Illinois Office)
Maurice G. Jenkins
W. Anthony Jenkins
Jerry L. Johnson
Mary Elizabeth Kelly

Mary Anne Kickham
  (Bloomfield Hills Office)
Thomas G. Kienbaum
Robert S. Krause
John A. Krsul, Jr.
Robert A. LaBelle
  (Bloomfield Hills Office)
Kathleen A. Lang
John K. Lawrence
Patrick J. Ledwidge
Keith J. Lerminiaux
Carl D. Liggio, Sr.
  (Chicago, Illinois Office)
Samuel D. Littlepage
  (Washington, D.C. Office)
Joseph C. Marshall, III
Noel D. Massie
Linda S. McAlpine
  (Bloomfield Hills Office)
Kenneth J. McIntyre
Russell A. McNair, Jr.
Thomas G. McNeill
Richard D McNulty
  (Lansing Office)
Creighton R. Meland, Jr.
  (Chicago, Illinois Office)
Richard J. Meyers
Cynthia A. Moore
  (Bloomfield Hills Office)
Steven C. Nadeau
Sharon R. Newlon
Zan M. Nicolli
  (Bloomfield Hills Office)
John H. Norris
  (Bloomfield Hills Office)
James Gavan O'Connor
  (Grand Rapids Office)
Theodore R. Opperwall
Dustin P. Ordway
  (Grand Rapids Office)
Francis R. Ortiz
Edward H. Pappas
  (Bloomfield Hills Office)
Richard W. Paul
  (Bloomfield Hills Office)
Eric J. Pelton
  (Bloomfield Hills Office)
Robert V. Peterson
  (Bloomfield Hills Office)
Jeffrey M. Petrash
  (Washington, D.C. Office)
Elizabeth M. Pezzetti
  (Bloomfield Hills Office)
David E. Pierson
  (Lansing Office)
Michael T. Platt
  (Washington, D.C. Office)
James A. Plemmons
Michael S. Poulos
  (Chicago, Illinois Office)
Robert W. Powell
Ward Randol, Jr.
  (Bloomfield Hills Office)
Claudia Rast
Mark K. Riashi
Christopher L. Rizik
  (Bloomfield Hills Office)
Douglas D. Roche
  (Bloomfield Hills Office)
James A. Samborn
Jerome M. Schwartz
Susan J. Schwartz
  (Chicago, Illinois Office)
John E. S. Scott
Peter S. Sheldon
  (Lansing Office)
Daniel James Sheridan
  (Chicago, Illinois Office)
Colleen M. Shevnock
William P. Shield, Jr.
Kester K. So (Lansing Office)
Herbert G. Sparrow, III
Jon Robert Steiger
  (Chicago, Illinois Office)
Larry J. Stringer
  (Bloomfield Hills Office)
Jeffery V. Stuckey
  (Lansing Office)

(See Next Column)

MEMBERS OF FIRM (Continued)

John L. Teeples
  (Grand Rapids Office)
Bruce C. Thelen
Richard C. Van Dusen
  (1925-1991)
Margaret Van Meter
  (Bloomfield Hills Office)
Michael Gary Vartanian
Richard A. Wendt
Richard A. Wilhelm

J. Bryan Williams
Rock A. Wood
  (Grand Rapids Office)
Edward P. Wright (1894-1962)
Paul M. Wyzgoski
Thomas V. Yates
Cynthia M. York
Jennifer A. Zinn

CONSULTING PARTNERS

Fred W. Freeman
Ernest Getz
Charles R. Kinnaird

Charles R. Moon
W. Gerald Warren
Judson Werbelow
  (Lansing Office)

OF COUNSEL

Marc A. Bergsman
  (Washington, D.C. Office)
Geoffrey A. Fields
  (Grand Rapids Office)
Paul T. Fitzpatrick
  (Bloomfield Hills Office)
Michael F. Gadola
  (Lansing Office)
David R. Haarz
  (Washington, D.C. Office)
Bethany E. Hawkins
  (Bloomfield Hills Office)
Douglas L. Mann
  (Bloomfield Hills Office)

Thomas D. McLennan
  (Bloomfield Hills Office)
Lucien N. Nedzi
  (Washington, D.C. Office)
Allan G. Sweig
  (Chicago, Illinois Office)
Douglas J. Van Der Aa
  (Grand Rapids Office)
Stephanie Karen Wade
  (Washington, D.C. Office)
Philip F. Wood
  (Grand Rapids Office)
John A. Ziegler, Jr.

ASSOCIATES

Terrence A. Barr
  (Bloomfield Hills Office)
Julia Turner Baumhart
  (Bloomfield Hills Office)
Edward R. Becker
  (Lansing Office)
Harolyn D. Beverly
Rindala Beydoun
Robert F. Boesiger
Shari M. Borsini
Jeffrey J. Brown
  (Bloomfield Hills Office)
Robert B. Brown
Bruce R. Byrd
Stephanie Dawkins Davis
Cynthia L. Della Torre
  (Bloomfield Hills Office)
Mark Alan Densmore
Julie T. Emerick
  (Bloomfield Hills Office)
Sara Anne Engle
  (Bloomfield Hills Office)
Julia L. Ernst
Peter G. Golden
  (Bloomfield Hills Office)
Nanci J. Grant
  (Bloomfield Hills Office)
Erin E. Gravelyn
  (Grand Rapids Office)
Jana L. Henkel-Benjamin
Robert B. Hotchkiss
  (Bloomfield Hills Office)
Kyle M. H. Jones
Kelli L. Kerbawy
  (Bloomfield Hills Office)
Thomas H. Kosik
  (Bloomfield Hills Office)
Monica J. Labe
Judith Fertel Layne
  (Bloomfield Hills Office)

Mi Young Lee
Barbara R. Lentz
Leslee M. Lewis
  (Grand Rapids Office)
Lynne Olman Lourim
Edwin J. Lukas
Elizabeth Virginia Main
Sean D. Major
  (Chicago, Illinois Office)
Amy E. Martin (Lansing Office)
Sarah A. McLaren
Gloria Kay Miller
Ola B. Najar
  (Bloomfield Hills Office)
Kathryn Kraus Nunzio
  (Grand Rapids Office)
Richard W. Paige
John T. Panourgias
  (Bloomfield Hills Office)
Gregory J. Parry
  (Bloomfield Hills Office)
Jeffery M. Peterson
Daniel D. Quick
Jeffrey S. Ruprich
Marian Keidan Seltzer
  (Bloomfield Hills Office)
Kent L. Sevener
Paul L. Sharer
  (Washington, D.C. Office)
Louis Theros
  (Chicago, Illinois Office)
Michelle V. Thurber
Joseph P. Tocco
James M. Toner
Wendy Lee Toolin
  (Chicago, Illinois Office)
Linda J. Truitt
  (Bloomfield Hills Office)
Rhonda D. Welburn
Kathryn S. Wood

LEGAL SUPPORT PERSONNEL

CHIEF INFORMATION OFFICER

Michael W. Harnish

JAPANESE CLIENT SUPPORT

Yukiko Sato (Bloomfield Hills Office)

For Representative Client list, see General Section.

For full biographical listings, see the Martindale-Hubbell Law Directory

Detrot—Continued

DYKEMA GOSSETT PLLC (AV)

400 Renaissance Center, 48243-1668
Telephone: 313-568-6800
Cable Address: "Dyke-Detroit"
Telex: 23-0121
Fax: 313-568-6594
Email: 2084153@mcimail.com
Ann Arbor, Michigan Office: 315 East Eisenhower Parkway, Suite 100, 48108-3306.
Telephone: 313-747-7660.
Fax: 313-747-7696.
Bloomfield Hills, Michigan Office: 1577 North Woodward Avenue, Suite 300, 48304-2820.
Telephone: 810-540-0700.
Fax: 810-540-0763.
Chicago, Illinois Office: 55 East Monroe Street, Suite 3250, 60603-5709.
Telephone: 312-551-4900.
Fax: 312-551-4919.
Grand Rapids, Michigan Office: 200 Oldtown Riverfront Building, 248 Louis Campau Promenade, N.W., 49503-2668.
Telephone: 616-776-7500.
Fax: 616-776-7573.
Lansing, Michigan Office: 800 Michigan National Tower, 48933-1707.
Telephone: 517-374-9100.
Fax: 517-374-9191.
Washington, D.C. Office: Franklin Square, Suite 300 West, 1300 I Street, N.W., 20005-3306.
Telephone: 202-522-8600.
Fax: 202-522-8669.

MEMBERS OF FIRM

Ted T. Amsden	Richard J. Landau (Resident at Ann Arbor Office)
Susan Artinian	
Richard B. Baxter (Resident at Grand Rapids Office)	Kathleen McCree Lewis
	Bonnie L. Mayfield
William J. Brennan (Resident at Grand Rapids Office)	Richard J. McClear
	Derek I. Meier
James M. Cameron, Jr. (Resident at Ann Arbor Office)	Stephen S. Muhich (Resident at Grand Rapids Office)
	Howard E. O'Leary, Jr. (Resident at Washington, D.C. Office)
Laurence D. Connor	
Michael P. Cooney	
J. Terrance Dillon (Resident at Grand Rapids Office)	Marilyn A. Peters (Resident at Bloomfield Hills Office)
	Thomas W. B. Porter
John A. Ferroli (Resident at Grand Rapids Office)	Jack C. Radcliffe, Jr. (Resident at Ann Arbor Office)
Robert J. Franzinger	
Barbara L. Goldman (Resident at Bloomfield Hills Office)	Jonathan D. Rowe (Resident at Ann Arbor Office)
	Mary Elizabeth Royce (Resident at Bloomfield Hills Office)
Dennis M. Haffey (Member in Charge of Bloomfield Hills Office)	
	Suzanne Sahakian
Mark E. Hauck	Lori M. Silsbury (Resident at Lansing Office)
E. Edward Hood (Member in Charge of Ann Arbor Office)	
	Daniel J. Stephenson (Resident at Ann Arbor Office)
Kathryn J. Humphrey	
Craig L. John (Resident at Bloomfield Hills Office)	Mark H. Sutton (Resident at Bloomfield Hills Office)
	Roger K. Timm
Sharon M. Kelly (Resident at Ann Arbor Office)	Stephen D. Winter
	Daniel G. Wyllie
Gregory M. Kopacz (Resident at Bloomfield Hills Office)	Donald S. Young

ASSOCIATES

Laura M. Benitez (Resident at Ann Arbor Office)	Zora E. Johnson
	Steven Marchese (Resident at Ann Arbor Office)
Thomas S. Bishoff	
Kevin J. Bonner	Bryan D. Marcus
Michael J. Brown (Resident at Lansing Office)	Andrew W. Mayoras (Resident at Bloomfield Hills Office)
James R. Bruinsma (Resident at Grand Rapids Office)	Andrew J. McGuinness (Resident at Ann Arbor Office)
Margaret A. Costello	
Joseph K. Erhardt	Ava K. Ortner
Aren L. Fairchild	James C. Partridge
Cheryl Anne Fletcher	Ann Marie Ronchetto
Douglas J. Fryer (Resident at Bloomfield Hills Office)	William R. Schikora
	Bradley L. Smith (Resident at Ann Arbor Office)
Kevin P. Fularczyk	
Kimberly A. Gough (Resident at Bloomfield Hills Office)	Ronald J. Torbert
	Michael Tucker (Resident at Bloomfield Hills Office)
David G. Hagens (Resident at Grand Rapids Office)	
	Jill M. Wheaton
Joseph H. Hickey (Resident at Bloomfield Hills Office)	Marvin Douglas Wilder
	James Zavell
Robert M. Horwitz	Kevin M. Zielke

For Complete List of Firm Personnel, See General Section

For full biographical listings, see the Martindale-Hubbell Law Directory

EAMES WILCOX (AV)

1400 Buhl Building, 48226-3602
Telephone: 313-963-3750
Facsimile: 313-963-8485

MEMBERS OF FIRM

Leonard A. Wilcox, Jr.	Jerry R. Swift
Ronald J. Mastej	Neill T. Riddell
John W. Bryant	Kevin N. Summers
Robert E. Gesell	Keith M. Aretha

OF COUNSEL

Rex Eames	William B. McIntyre, Jr.
	David R. Ritter

Representative Clients: ABF Freight System, Inc.; Chrysler Credit Corp.; City Transfer Co.; Engineered Heat Treat, Inc.; Fetz Engineering Co.; I E & E Industries, Inc.; Schneider Transport; Tank Carrier Employers Association of Michigan; TNT Transport Group, Inc.; Waste Management of Michigan.

For full biographical listings, see the Martindale-Hubbell Law Directory

EGGENBERGER, EGGENBERGER, McKINNEY, WEBER & HOFMEISTER, P.C. (AV)

42nd Floor Penobscot Building, 48226
Telephone: 313-961-9722

William J. Eggenberger (1900-1984)	John P. McKinney
	Stephen L. Weber
William D. Eggenberger	Paul D. Hofmeister
Robert E. Eggenberger	Thomas R. Paxton

Mary T. Humbert	James B. Eggenberger

Representative Clients: Amoco Oil Co.; Central National Insurance Group of Omaha; City of Wayne, Michigan; Clark Oil & Refining Corp.; Country Mutual Casualty Co.; Auto Club Insurance Assn.; General Accident Assurance Co., Ltd.; Great Central Insurance Co.; Inland Mutual Insurance Co.; Midwest Mutual Insurance Co.

For full biographical listings, see the Martindale-Hubbell Law Directory

FEIKENS, VANDER MALE, STEVENS, BELLAMY & GILCHRIST, P.C. (AV)

One Detroit Center Suite 3400, 500 Woodward Avenue, 48226-3406
Telephone: 313-962-5909
Fax: 313-962-3125
Email: FEIKENS@COUNSEL.COM

Jack E. Vander Male	L. Neal Kennedy
	Roger L. Wolcott

Richard G. Koefod	Jeffrey Feikens
Joseph E. Kozely, Jr.	Michael B. Barey

For Complete List of Firm Personnel, See General Section

For full biographical listings, see the Martindale-Hubbell Law Directory

FILDEW HINKS, P.L.L.C. (AV)

3600 Penobscot Building, 645 Griswold Street, 48226-4291
Telephone: 313-961-9700
Telecopier: 313-961-0754

MEMBERS OF FIRM

Stanley L. Fildew (1896-1978)	Randall S. Wangen
Frank T. Hinks (1887-1974)	Mary Jane Ruffley
Richard E. Hinks (1916-1990)	Robert D. Welchli
John H. Fildew	William P. Thorpe
Alan C. Miller	Colleen A. Kramer
Charles D. Todd III	Stephen J. Pokoj

ASSOCIATES

Charles S. Kennedy, III	Walter B. Fisher, Jr.

References: First of America Bank-Detroit, N.A.; Comerica Bank-Detroit; National Bank of Detroit.

For full biographical listings, see the Martindale-Hubbell Law Directory

GARAN, LUCOW, MILLER, SEWARD & BECKER, P.C. (AV)

1000 Woodbridge Place, 48207-3192
Telephone: 313-446-1530
Fax: 313-259-0450
Email: glm@gnn.com
Grand Blanc, Michigan Office: 8332 Office Park Drive.
Telephone: 810-695-3700.
Fax: 810-695-6488.
Port Huron, Michigan Office: Port Huron Office Center, 511 Fort Street, Suite 505.
Telephone: 810-985-4400.
Fax: 810-985-4107.
Ann Arbor, Michigan Office: 101 North Main Street, Suite 801.
Telephone: 313-930-5600.
Fax: 313-930-0043.

(See Next Column)

GARAN, LUCOW, MILLER, SEWARD & BECKER P.C., Detroit—Continued

Troy, Michigan Office: 1111 West Long Lake Road, Suite 300.
Telephone: 810-641-7600.
Fax: 810-641-0222.
Mount Clemens, Michigan Office: Towne Square Development, 10 S. Main Street, Suite 307.
Telephone: 810-954-3800.
Fax: 810-954-3803.
Grand Rapids, Michigan Office: Campau Square Plaza Building, 99 Monroe Avenue N.W., Suite 102.
Telephone: 616-732-5330.
Fax: 616-732-5333.

Matthew A. Seward	James J. Hayes, Jr.
Thomas F. Myers	Thomas W. Emery
Dennis P. Partridge	Joseph Crystal
John E. McSorley	Boyd E. Chapin, Jr.
Lamont E. Buffington	Frederick B. Plumb
Thomas L. Misuraca	Mark C. Smiley
Rosalind Rochkind	James S. Goulding

John J. Gillooly

Daniel S. Saylor	Michael J. DePolo
Peter B. Worden, Jr.	C. David Miller, II
Charlotte H. Johnson	Anne K. Newcomer
David M. Shafer	Eun (Ellen) G. Ha
Lloyd G. Johnson	Timothy J. Jordan
Robert D. Goldstein	Lynn E. Geist
Michael J. Paolucci	Mark T. Rajt

OF COUNSEL

Daniel L. Garan	Beth A. Andrews
Milton Lucow	Nancy J. Bourget
Albert A. Miller	David L. Lattie
Roy E. Castetter	Meri Craver Borin

Counsel for: Allstate Insurance Co.; Sears, Roebuck & Co.; Liberty Mutual Insurance Co.; Continental Insurance Companies.

For Complete List of Firm Personnel, See General Section

For full biographical listings, see the Martindale-Hubbell Law Directory

DAVID GRIEM (AV)

One Woodward Avenue, Suite 2400, 48226
Telephone: 313-961-8380
Mount Clemens, Michigan Office: 14 First Street, 48043.
Telephone: 313-465-4900.

For full biographical listings, see the Martindale-Hubbell Law Directory

HAYDUK, ANDREWS & HYPNAR, P.C. (AV)

1700 Buhl Building, 535 Griswold, 48226
Telephone: 313-962-4500
Fax: 313-964-6577

Mark S. Hayduk	Robin K. Andrews

Mark A. Hypnar

Sean Angus McPhillips	Lynn E. Radke

Representative Clients: Farmers Insurance Group; GameTime, Inc.; Admiral Insurance Co.; Heritage Insurance; Meijer, Inc.; Alexis Condon & Forsyth; Pinkerton's Inc.; Vik Brothers Ins.; American Modern Home Ins.; Scibal Ins. Co.

For full biographical listings, see the Martindale-Hubbell Law Directory

HONIGMAN MILLER SCHWARTZ AND COHN (AV)

A Partnership including Professional Corporations
2290 First National Building, 48226
Telephone: 313-256-7800
Telecopier: 313-962-0176
Telex: 235705
URL: http://law.honigman.com
Lansing, Michigan Office: Phoenix Building, 222 North Washington Square, Suite 400, 48933-1800.
Telephone: 517-484-8282.
West Palm Beach, Florida Office: Suite 800 Esperante Building, 222 Lakeview Avenue, 33401-6112.
Telephone: 561-838-4500.
Tampa, Florida Office: 2700 SunTrust Financial Centre, 401 E. Jackson Street, 33602-5226.
Telephone: 813-221-6600.

MEMBERS OF FIRM

Peter M. Alter	Mark A. Goldsmith
Norman C. Ankers	Daniel G. Helton
Frederick M. Baker, Jr.	Raymond W. Henney
(Lansing, Michigan Office)	Norman Hyman
Richard Bisio	Robert M. Jackson
Jay E. Brant	Sandra L. Jasinski
Robert A. Fineman	(Lansing, Michigan Office)
Herschel P. Fink	John S. Kane
William F. Frey	(Lansing, Michigan Office)

(See Next Column)

MEMBERS OF FIRM (Continued)

Timothy Sawyer Knowlton	Mark A. Stern
(Lansing, Michigan Office)	Stuart H. Teger
Ronald S. Longhofer	Gary A. Trepod
Mark Morton	(Lansing, Michigan Office)
(Lansing, Michigan Office)	Stephen Wasinger
John D. Pirich	Mark R. Werder
(Lansing, Michigan Office)	I. W. Winsten
William D. Sargent	Ruth E. Zimmerman
John Sklar	(Lansing, Michigan Office)

Richard E. Zuckerman

ASSOCIATES

Ann L. Andrews	Gregory D. Hanley
(Lansing, Michigan Office)	Andrea Hansen
David E. Barnes	(Lansing, Michigan Office)
Michael J. Byrnes	Steven E. Mellen
Cameron J. Evans	Lawrence J. Murphy
Amy B. Folbe	Cynthia G. Thomas

Jennifer S. Zbytowski

OF COUNSEL

Milton J. Miller

RESIDENT IN WEST PALM BEACH, FLORIDA OFFICE

MEMBERS

Carla L. Brown (P.A.)	Steven L. Schwarzberg (P.A.)

ASSOCIATE

Jose O. Diaz

RESIDENT IN TAMPA, FLORIDA OFFICE

MEMBERS

Robert W. Boos (P.A.)	Gregory G. Jones (P.A.)
Harry Christopher Goplerud (P.A.)	

ASSOCIATES

Kevin M. Gilhool	Donald A. Mihokovich

Susan M. Salvatore

Representative Clients: Ameritech Michigan; Consumers Power Co.; The Detroit Edison Co.; The Detroit Free Press; Ford Motor Co.; General Motors Corporation, Legal Staff (General Motors Corporation and General Motors Acceptance Corporation); Michigan Hospital Association; The Taubman Company, Inc.; ThornApple Valley, Inc.; Walbridge Aldinger Co.

For Complete List of Firm Personnel, See General Section

For full biographical listings, see the Martindale-Hubbell Law Directory

JAFFE, RAITT, HEUER & WEISS, PROFESSIONAL CORPORATION (AV)

One Woodward Avenue, Suite 2400, 48226
Telephone: 313-961-8380
Telecopier: 313-961-8358
Cable Address: "Jafsni"
Southfield, Michigan Office: Travelers Tower, Suite 1520.
Telephone: 313-961-8380.
Monroe, Michigan Office: 214 East Elm Avenue, Suite 208,
Telephone: 313-241-6470.
Telefacsimile: 313-241-3849.

Christopher A. Andreoff	Steven C. Powell
Julia Blakeslee	Michael A. Rajt
R. Christopher Cataldo	Brian G. Shannon
Wallace H. Glendening	Joseph J. Shannon
Jeffrey G. Heuer	Lawrence R. Shoffner
Sharon J. LaDuke	George A. Sumnik
Melanie LaFave	Nancy L. Waldmann
Susan S. Lichterman	Jeffrey D. Weisserman
Eric A. Linden	Thomas H. Williams

David P. Armstrong	Susan Michelle Bakst

Thomas L. Shaevsky

Representative Clients: Genova Products, Inc.; Honey Baked Ham Co.; Masco Tech, Inc.; McClain Industries, Inc.

For Complete List of Firm Personnel, See General Section

For full biographical listings, see the Martindale-Hubbell Law Directory

JOHNSON & VALENTINE (AV)

4372 Penobscot Building, 48226
Telephone: 313-961-4700

MEMBERS OF FIRM

Edward C. Johnson	Glenn L. Valentine

ASSOCIATE

Dale T. McPherson

OF COUNSEL

Jarvis J. Schmidt

Representative Clients: Huntington Banks of Michigan; The Huntington Mortgage Co.; First of America Bank, Michigan; Sun Bank-Miami, N.A., Coral Gables, Tr. Dpt.; Fifth Third Bank of Toledo, N.A.; Cozadd Rotary

(See Next Column)

JOHNSON & VALENTINE—*Continued*

Foundation Trust; Colonial Hockey League; National Transportation Counsellors.
References: First of America Bank; Southeast Michigan, N.A.

For full biographical listings, see the Martindale-Hubbell Law Directory

KELLER, THOMA, SCHWARZE, SCHWARZE, DUBAY & KATZ, P.C. (AV)

440 East Congress, 5th Floor, 48226
Telephone: 313-965-7610
Bloomfield Hills, Michigan Office: Suite 122, 100 West Long Lake Road.
Telephone: 810-642-5218.

Thomas H. Schwarze	Linda M. Foster
Thomas L. Fleury	Carl F. Schwarze
Terrence J. Miglio	George P. Butler, III
Robert A. Lusk	Brian A. Kreucher

Counsel For: H & H Tube & Manufacturing; Howard Plating Industries, Inc.; Livonia Public Schools; Ludington News Company, Inc.; Northville Public Schools; Ryco Engineering, Inc.; Sign of the Beefcarver, Inc.
Representative Clients: General: Baxter Healthcare Corp.; Borg-Warner Corp.; Detrex Industries, Inc.

For Complete List of Firm Personnel, See General Section

For full biographical listings, see the Martindale-Hubbell Law Directory

LEWIS, CLAY & MUNDAY, A PROFESSIONAL CORPORATION (AV)

(Formerly Lewis, White & Clay, P.C.)
1300 First National Building, 660 Woodward Avenue, 48226-3531
Telephone: 313-961-2550
Troy, Michigan Office: Liberty Center, Suite 200. 100 West Big Beaver Road. 48084.
Telephone: 810-680-6702.
Fax: 810-680-6703.
Washington, D.C. Office: 1000 16th Street, N.W., Suite 401. 20036.
Telephone: 202-835-0616.
Fax: 202-833-3316.
Boston, Massachusetts Office: 10 Post Office Square.
Telephone: 617-422-8646.
Fax: 617-338-5693.

David Baker Lewis	Frank E. Barbee
Eric Lee Clay	Camille Stearns Miller
Reuben A. Munday	Michael T. Raymond
Ulysses Whittaker Boykin	Jacqueline H. Sellers
Carl F. Stafford	David N. Zacks
Helen Francine Strong	Thomas J. Guyer
	Blair A. Person

Karen Kendrick Brown	Hans J. Massaquoi, Jr.
(Resident, Washington, D.C. Office)	Nancy C. Borland
	Tammy L. Terry
J. Taylor Teasdale	Lynn Westfall Gross
Wade Harper McCree	Suzanne P. Pope
Tyrone A. Powell	Matthew R. Halpin
Susan D. Hoffman	Donica Thomas Varner
John J. Walsh	Damon L. White
Andrea L. Powell	(Not admitted in MI)
Althea Lynn Foster	Kathleen L. Royal

COUNSEL

Otis M. Smith (1922-1994)	G. Allen Bass (Resident, Boston,
Herbert O. Reid, Sr. (1915-1991)	Massachusetts Office)

Representative Clients: Omnicare Health Plan; Aetna Life & Casualty Co.; Chrysler Motors Corp.; Chrysler Financial Corp.; MCI Communications Corp.; City of Detroit; City of Detroit Building Authority; City of Detroit Downtown Development Authority; Consolidated Rail Corp. (Conrail); Equitable Life Assurance Society of the United States.

For full biographical listings, see the Martindale-Hubbell Law Directory

MAGER, MERCER, SCOTT & ALBER, P.C. (AV)

500 Woodward Avenue Suite 3400, 48226
Telephone: 313-962-8212
Facsimile: 313-962-5413
Oakland County Office: Top of Troy Building, 755 West Big Beaver, Suite 1700, Troy, Michigan.
Telephone: 810-362-8212.
Facsimile: 810-362-6944.
Macomb County Office: 18285 Ten Mile Road, Suite 100, Roseville, Michigan.
Telephone: 810-771-1100.
Facsimile: 810-775-5170.

George J. Mager, Jr.

Representative Clients: ABB Flakt, Inc.; American States Insurance Co.; CEI Industries; Central Venture Corp.; CIGNA; Construction Management, Inc.

For full biographical listings, see the Martindale-Hubbell Law Directory

MILLER, CANFIELD, PADDOCK AND STONE, P.L.C. (AV)

A Professional Limited Liability Company
Founded in 1852 by Sidney Davy Miller
150 West Jefferson, Suite 2500, 48226-4415
Telephone: 313-963-6420
Fax: 313-496-7500
Cable Address: "Stem Detroit"
Detroit, Michigan Office: 150 West Jefferson, Suite 2500, 48226-4415.
Telephone: 313-963-6420.
Fax: 313-496-7500.
Cable Address: "Stem Detroit."
Ann Arbor, Michigan Office: 101 North Main Street, 7th Floor, 48104-1400.
Telephone: 313-663-2445.
Fax: 313-747-7147.
Bloomfield Hills, Michigan Office: Suite 100, Pinehurst Office Center, 1400 North Woodward, 48303-2014.
Telephone: 313-645-5000.
Fax: 313-645-1917.
Grand Rapids, Michigan Office: 1200 Campau Square Plaza, 99 Monroe, N.W., 49503-2639.
Telephone: 616-454-8656.
Fax: 616-776-6322.
Howell, Michigan Office: 121 South Barnard Street, Suite 4, 48843-2305.
Telephone: 517-546-7600.
Telecopier: 517-546-6974.
Kalamazoo, Michigan Office: 444 West Michigan Avenue, 49007-3752.
Telephone: 616-381-7030.
Fax: 616-382-0244.
Lansing, Michigan Office: One Michigan Avenue, Suite 900, 48933-1609.
Telephone: 517-487-2070.
Fax: 517-374-6304.
Monroe, Michigan Office: The Executive Centre, 214 East Elm Avenue, 48161-2682.
Telephone: 313-243-2000.
Fax: 313-243-0901.
Washington, D.C. Office: 1225 Nineteenth Street, N.W., Suite 400. 20036.
Telephone: 202-429-5575; 785-0600.
Fax: 202-331-1118; 785-1234.
Pensacola, Florida Office: 25 West Cedar, 32501.
Telephone: 904-469-1088.
Fax: 904-432-0677.
St. Petersburg, Florida Office: 100 Second Avenue S., Suite 7045, 33701.
Telephone: 813-982-6000.
Fax: 813-892-6002.
New York, New York Office: Eleventh Floor, 135 East 57th Street, 10022-2087.
Telephone: 212-754-5400.
Fax: 212-754-5401.
Gdansk, Poland Office: Suite 322, Dom Technika Building, UI. Rajska 6, 80-850.
Telephone: 011-485-831-2808.
Fax: 011-485-831-4719.
Warsaw, Poland Office: UI. Marszalkowska 82, Suite 561, 00-517.
Telephone: 011-482-623-6457 and 6458.
Fax: 011-482-623-6459.

PRINCIPALS OF FIRM

Gilbert E. Gove	Marjory G. Basile
Carl H. von Ende	Michael P. Coakley
Allyn D. Kantor	James E. Spurr
(Ann Arbor Office)	(Kalamazoo Office)
Charles E. Ritter	Mark T. Boonstra
(Kalamazoo Office)	David A. French
Gregory L. Curtner	(Ann Arbor Office)
(New York, N.Y. Office)	Le Roy L. Asher, Jr.
Joseph F. Galvin	Richard T. Urbis
Clarence L. Pozza, Jr.	Steven A. Roach
Michael W. Hartmann	Lawrence M. Dudek
Larry J. Saylor	Marta A. Manildi
James G. Vantine, Jr.	(Ann Arbor Office)
(Kalamazoo Office)	

OF COUNSEL

George E. Bushnell, Jr.

ASSOCIATES

Ballard Jay Yelton III	A. Michael Palizzi
(Kalamazoo Office)	Kurt P. McCamman
Thomas R. Cox	(Kalamazoo Office)
Frederick A. Acomb	Scott R. Sikkenga
	(Kalamazoo Office)

Representative Firm Clients: Chrysler Corporation; Comerica, Incorporated; City of Detroit, Michigan; Detroit Tigers, Inc.; First of Michigan; Ford Motor Company; Ford Motor Credit Company; Great Lakes Bancorp; Henry Ford Hospital; INVETECH Company.

For Complete List of Firm Personnel, See General Section

For full biographical listings, see the Martindale-Hubbell Law Directory

Detroit—Continued

PATTERSON, PHIFER & PHILLIPS, P.C. (AV)

L. B. King Building, 1274 Library Street, Suite 500, 48226
Telephone: 313-964-2360

Michael D. Patterson	Randolph D. Phifer
Dwight W. Phillips	

Joseph M. White	Eugene M. Holmes
Lisa A. Cylar	

Representative Clients: Detroit Board of Education; Fireman's Fund Insurance Co.; General Motors Corp.; Home Federal Savings Bank; Liberty Mutual Insurance Co.; Metropolitan Life Insurance Co.; Michigan Basic Property Insurance Assn.; New York Life Insurance Co.; Wayne State University. *Reference:* First of American Bank-Detroit, N.A.

For full biographical listings, see the Martindale-Hubbell Law Directory

SCHUREMAN, FRAKES, GLASS & WULFMEIER (AV)

440 East Congress, Fourth Floor, 48226
Telephone: 313-961-1500
Telecopier: 313-961-1087
Harbor Springs, Michigan Office: One Spring Street Sq., 49740.
Telephone: 616-526-1145.
Telecopier: 616-526-9343.

MEMBERS OF FIRM

Jeptha W. Schureman	LeRoy H. Wulfmeier, III
John C. Frakes, Jr.	Cheryl L. Chandler
Charles F. Glass	David M. Ottenwess

ASSOCIATES

Daniel J. Dulworth	John J. Moran
Paul A. Salyers	

Representative Clients: Michigan Physicians' Mutual Liability Co.; The Medical Protective Co.; Physicians' Insurance Company of Michigan; Michigan Health Care Corp.; Pontiac Osteopathic Hospital; JP Bender & Associates; Insurance Equities Corporation.

For full biographical listings, see the Martindale-Hubbell Law Directory

STRINGARI, FRITZ, KREGER, AHEARN & CRANDALL, P.C. (AV)

510 First National Building, 48226-3538
Telephone: 313-961-6474
Fax: 313-961-5688

Richard J. Fritz	Martin E. Crandall
Conrad W. Kreger	Kenneth S. Wilson
Brian S. Ahearn	Dallas G. Moon

John C. Dickinson
OF COUNSEL

Karl R. Bennett, Jr.	Matt W. Zeigler

For full biographical listings, see the Martindale-Hubbell Law Directory

TIMMIS & INMAN, L.L.P. (AV)

300 Talon Centre, 48207
Telephone: 313-396-4200
Telecopier: 313-396-4228

Robert E. Graziani	Mark W. Peyser
George A. Peck	Bradley J. Knickerbocker
George M. Malis	

Michael F. Wais

Representative Clients: Wash/Blount; Talon, Inc.; Certain Underwriters at Lloyds of London; Gay & Taylor.

For Complete List of Firm Personnel, See General Section

For full biographical listings, see the Martindale-Hubbell Law Directory

VANDEVEER GARZIA, PROFESSIONAL CORPORATION (AV)

Suite 1600, 333 West Fort Street, 48226
Telephone: 313-961-4880
Fax: 313-961-3822
Oakland County Office: 220 Park Street, Suite 300, Birmingham, Michigan.
Telephone: 810-645-0100.
Fax: 810-645-2430.
Macomb County Office: 50 Crocker Boulevard, Mount Clemens, Michigan.
Telephone: 810-468-4880.
Fax: 810-465-7159.
West Michigan Office: 1121 Ottawa Beach Road, Suite 140, Holland Michigan.
Telephone: 616-399-8600.
Fax: 616-786-9095.

(See Next Column)

Thomas P. Rockwell	Gary Alan Miller
James A. Sullivan	William L. Kiriazis
Michael M. Hathaway	Cynthia E. Merry
John J. Lynch, III (Resident, Oakland County Office)	Daniel P. Steele
Thomas M. Peters	Shelley K. Miller (Resident, Oakland County Office)
James K. Thome	Terrance P. Lynch
Ronald L. Cornell (Resident, Macomb County Office)	Dennis B. Cotter

Representative Clients: Aetna Casualty and Surety Co.; Bic Corp.; CNA Insurance Group; Travelers Insurance Co.; United States Aviation Underwriters; Goodyear Tire & Rubber Co.

For Complete List of Firm Personnel, See General Section

For full biographical listings, see the Martindale-Hubbell Law Directory

ZEFF AND ZEFF, P.C. (AV)

The Zeff Building, 607 Shelby, 48226
Telephone: 313-962-3825
Fax: 313-962-6007

Louis Zeff (1896-1966)	A. Robert Zeff

Sheryl L. Berenbaum	Paul W. Broschay
Steven L. Berenbaum	

For full biographical listings, see the Martindale-Hubbell Law Directory

EAST LANSING, Ingham Co.

FARHAT, STORY & KRAUS, P.C. (AV)

Beacon Place, 4572 South Hagadorn Road, Suite 3, 48823
Telephone: 517-351-3700
Fax: 517-332-4122
Email: rkraus@sojourn.com

Leo A. Farhat	Chris A. Bergstrom
James E. Burns (1925-1979)	Kitty L. Groh
Monte R. Story	Charles R. Toy
Richard C. Kraus	David M. Platt
Max R. Hoffman Jr.	Thomas L. Sparks

Lawrence P. Schweitzer	Daniel B. Morgan
Debra A. Geroux	Mary K. Robbins-Kralapp

Representative Clients: Big L. Corp.; Michigan Automotive Wholesalers Association; Hartman-Fabco, Inc.; Lansing Electric Motors, Inc.; Mike Miller Lincoln Mercury; Edward Rose Realty, Inc.; Squires School and Commercial Sales; CBI Copy Products; Lansing School District. *Reference:* City Bank, St. Johns.

For full biographical listings, see the Martindale-Hubbell Law Directory

SMITH HAUGHEY RICE & ROEGGE, P.C. (AV)

1301 North Hagadorn Road, 48823-2320
Telephone: 517-332-3030
Facsimile: 517-332-3468
Grand Rapids, Michigan Office: 200 Calder Plaza Building, 250 Monroe Avenue, N.W., 49503-2251.
Telephone: 616-774-8000.
Facsimile: 616-774-2461.
Traverse City, Michigan Office: 241 East State Street, P.O. Box 848, 49685-0848.
Telephone: 616-929-4878.
Facsimile: 616-929-4182.

Douglas G. Powe

Daniel N. Stephens	James R. Duby, Jr.
Veronica A. Marsich	

Representative Clients: Chevron; Cincinnati Insurance Co.; General Motors Corp.; Kemper Insurance Group; Michigan Hospital Assn.; Navistar International; St. Paul Insurance Cos.; Steelcase, Inc.; Sears Roebuck & Co.; Dow Elanco.

For full biographical listings, see the Martindale-Hubbell Law Directory

FARMINGTON HILLS, Oakland Co.

COUZENS, LANSKY, FEALK, ELLIS, ROEDER & LAZAR, P.C. (AV)

33533 West Twelve Mile Road, Suite 150, P.O. Box 9057, 48333-9057
Telephone: 810-489-8600
Telecopier: 810-489-4156

Sheldon A. Fealk	Renard J. Kolasa
Jack S. Couzens, II	Kathryn Gilson Sussman
Jerry M. Ellis	Jeffrey A. Levine
Donald M. Lansky	Phillip L. Sternberg
Bruce J. Lazar	Marc L. Prey
Alan C. Roeder	Lisa J. Walters

(See Next Column)

COUZENS, LANSKY, FEALK, ELLIS, ROEDER & LAZAR P.C.—*Continued*

Stephen Scapelliti	Mark S. Frankel
Donald A. Wagner	Lynette M. Sheldon
Michael P. Witzke	Roger E. Winkelman
Cyrus Raamin Kashef	David B. Deutsch
Gregg A. Nathanson	Monica Demko Moons

Representative Clients: Provided upon request.
Reference: Comerica Bank-Southfield.

For full biographical listings, see the Martindale-Hubbell Law Directory

MICHAEL H. GOLOB (AV)

30300 Northwestern Highway, Suite 300, 48334
Telephone: 810-855-2626
Fax: 810-932-4009

For full biographical listings, see the Martindale-Hubbell Law Directory

---

FLINT,* Genesee Co.

GAULT DAVISON A PROFESSIONAL SERVICE CORPORATION (AV)

Tenth Floor, Northbank Center, 432 North Saginaw Street, 48502-2032
Telephone: 810-234-3633
Fax: 810-233-3387
Email: GLTDAV@tir.com

F. Robert Schmelzer	Edward B. Davison
Frederick L. Schmoll, III	Richard C. Hohenstein

John R. Moynihan	Timothy D. Batdorf
Michael J. Gildner	Christopher A. Hajek

Representative Clients: Automobile Club Insurance Assn.; State Farm Automobile Mutual Insurance Cos.; State Farm Insurance Companies; Farm Bureau Insurance Group; Al Serra Automobile Cos.; K-Mart Corp.; Harley-Davidson Inc.; Shoney's, Inc.; City of Flint.

For full biographical listings, see the Martindale-Hubbell Law Directory

LAW OFFICES OF PATRICK M. KIRBY A PROFESSIONAL CORPORATION (AV)

G1335 South Linden Road, Suite G, 48532
Telephone: 810-230-0833
Fax: 810-230-8222

Patrick M. Kirby

Todd O. Pope

Representative Clients: Brotherhood Mutual Insurance Co.; City of Flint; K&K Insurance Group; Merchants and Medical Credit Corp.; Nero Plastics; Rent-A-Center.

For full biographical listings, see the Martindale-Hubbell Law Directory

---

GAYLORD,* Otsego Co.

BENSINGER, COTANT, MENKES & AARDEMA, P.C. (AV)

308 West Main Street, P.O. Box 1000, 49735
Telephone: 517-732-7536
Fax: 517-732-4922
Grand Rapids, Michigan Office: 983 Spaulding Avenue, S.E.
Telephone: 616-949-7963.
Fax: 616-949-5264.
Marquette, Michigan Office: 122 West Bluff.
Telephone: 906-225-1000.
Fax: 906-225-0818.

Richard G. Bensinger	James F. Pagels
James C. Cotant	Steven C. Byram
Michael E. Menkes	Michael J. Harrelson
Patrick J. Michaels	William M. Fury
Daniel Joseph Bebble	

Representative Clients: Accident Fund of Michigan; Auto-Owner Insurance Co.; Citizens/Hanover Insurance Co.; Farm Bureau Mutual Insurance Co.; Employers Reinsurance Co,; Lake State Mutual Insurance Co.; Michigan Hospital Association; Michigan Licensed Beverage Association; Physicians Insurance Co. of Michigan; State Farm Mutual Insurance Co.

For full biographical listings, see the Martindale-Hubbell Law Directory

---

GRAND RAPIDS,* Kent Co.

ALLABEN, MASSIE, VANDER WEYDEN & TIMMER (AV)

Suite 850, Commerce Building, 5 Lyon Street, N.W., 49503
Telephone: 616-774-2182
Fax: 616-774-0602

MEMBERS OF FIRM

Fred Roland Allaben	Keith A. Vander Weyden
(1901-1985)	John J. Timmer
Sam F. Massie, Jr.	Robert W. Bandeen

(See Next Column)

John R. Allaben

Representative Clients: Auto Club Insurance Association; American States Insurance Co.; Michigan Mutual Liability Co.; Fidelity & Casualty Company of New York; U.S. Aircraft Insurance Group; Security Mutual Casualty Co.; Nationwide Mutual Insurance Co.; Security Mutual Casualty Co.; Nationwide Mutual Insurance Co.; Union Insurance Co.

For full biographical listings, see the Martindale-Hubbell Law Directory

BORRE, PETERSON, FOWLER & REENS, P.C. (AV)

The Philo C. Fuller House, 44 Lafayette, N.E., P.O. Box 1767, 49501-1767
Telephone: 616-459-1971
Fax: 616-459-2393

James B. Peterson	Frank H. Johnson
William C. Reens	William R. Vander Sluis

References: Old Kent Bank; NBD Bank.

For Complete List of Firm Personnel, See General Section

For full biographical listings, see the Martindale-Hubbell Law Directory

BOS & GLAZIER, P.L.C. (AV)

300 Ottawa N.W., Suite 800, 49503
Telephone: 616-458-6814
Fax: 616-458-0608
Email: BGLAZIOO@counsel.com

Carole D. Bos	Susan Wilson Keener
Bradley K. Glazier	Gwen E. Buday
Anne M. Frye	

For full biographical listings, see the Martindale-Hubbell Law Directory

BREMER, WADE, NELSON, LOHR & COREY, LLP (AV)

600 3 Mile Road, N.W., 49544-1601
Telephone: 616-784-4434
Fax: 616-784-7322

MEMBERS OF FIRM

William M. Bremer	Phillip J. Nelson
Michael D. Wade	James H. Lohr
Michael J. Corey	

ASSOCIATES

Barbara L. Olafsson	Olafur A. Olafsson

LEGAL SUPPORT PERSONNEL

Kathleen A. Fitzpatrick

For full biographical listings, see the Martindale-Hubbell Law Directory

BUCHANAN, SILVER & BECKERING, P.L.C. (AV)

300 Ottawa N.W., Suite 800, 49503
Telephone: 616-458-2464
Fax: 616-458-0608

MEMBERS OF FIRM

John C. Buchanan	Robert J. Buchanan
Lee T. Silver	Jane M. Beckering

Representative Clients: Chrysler Corp.; Clark Equipment Co.; Colt's Manufacturing Company, Inc. (National Defense Counsel); Corning Glass; Excam, Inc.

For full biographical listings, see the Martindale-Hubbell Law Directory

JAMES M. CATCHICK (AV)

200 North Division Avenue, 49503
Telephone: 616-459-3839
Fax: 616-459-4909

References: Union Bank and Trust Co.; Old Kent Bank & Trust Co.; First of Michigan Bank.

For full biographical listings, see the Martindale-Hubbell Law Directory

CHOLETTE, PERKINS & BUCHANAN (AV)

900 Campau Square Plaza Building, 99 Monroe Avenue, N.W., 49503
Telephone: 616-774-2131
Fax: 616-774-7016

MEMBERS OF FIRM

Calvin R. Danhof	Charles H. Worsfold
Frederick W. Bleakley	Michael P. McCasey
Reynolds A. Brander, Jr.	Marc A. Kidder
Edward Malinzak	Michael C. Mysliwiec
Bruce M. Bieneman	Evan L. MacFarlane
William J. Warren	John A. Quinn
Donald C. Exelby	Albert J. Engel, III
Thomas H. Cypher	Stephen C. Oldstrom
William A. Brengle	William E. McDonald, Jr.
Alfred J. Parent	Mark E. Fatum

(See Next Column)

CHOLETTE, PERKINS & BUCHANAN, *Grand Rapids—Continued*

MEMBERS OF FIRM (Continued)

Richard K. Grover, Jr.	Martin W. Buschle
David J. DeGraw	Miles J. Murphy, III

ASSOCIATES

Kenneth L. Block	Martha P. Forman
William J. Yob	Kathrine M. West
Robert E. Attmore	Ilse K. Masselink

John P. Lewis

Counsel for: Aetna Casualty & Surety Co.; Argonaut Insurance Co.; Auto-Owners Insurance Co.; Employers Mutual; Liberty Mutual Insurance Co.; Sentry Group; State Farm Insurance; Eastern Aviation and Marine Underwriters; Home Insurance Co.; Nationwide Insurance.

For Complete List of Firm Personnel, See General Section

For full biographical listings, see the Martindale-Hubbell Law Directory

---

DAY & SAWDEY, A PROFESSIONAL CORPORATION (AV)

200 Monroe Avenue, Suite 500, 49503-2217
Telephone: 616-774-8121
Telefax: 616-774-0168

George B. Kingston (1889-1965)	James B. Frakie
John R. Porter (1915-1975)	Larry A. Ver Merris
Charles E. Day, Jr.	John Boyko, Jr.
Robert W. Sawdey	Jonathan F. Thoits
C. Mark Stoppels	John T. Piggins

Thomas A. DeMeester

Representative Clients: Blodgett Construction and Home Improvement Co.; C.M.S.-North America, Inc.; Heath Mfg. Co.; Heller Financial, Inc.; Michigan National Bank; National Westminster Bank, U.S.A.; Old Kent Bank and Trust Co.; Zurn Industries.

For full biographical listings, see the Martindale-Hubbell Law Directory

---

DE GROOT, KELLER & VINCENT (AV)

300 Michigan Trust Building, 49503
Telephone: 616-459-6251
Fax: 616-459-6352

MEMBERS OF FIRM

Murray B. De Groot	Brian D. Vincent

For full biographical listings, see the Martindale-Hubbell Law Directory

---

GRUEL, MILLS, NIMS AND PYLMAN (AV)

50 Monroe Place, Suite 700 West, 49503
Telephone: 616-235-5500
Fax: 616-235-5550

MEMBERS OF FIRM

Grant J. Gruel	Scott R. Melton
William F. Mills	Brion J. Brooks
J. Clarke Nims	Thomas R. Behm
Norman H. Pylman, II	J. Paul Janes

Representative Clients: Aquinas College; Bell Helmet Co.; Blodgett Memorial Medical Center; Butterworth Hospital; Chem Central, Inc.; Cook Pump Co.; Grove, Inc.; NBDC; Heim Corp.

For full biographical listings, see the Martindale-Hubbell Law Directory

---

GARY J. MCINERNEY, P.C. (AV)

330 East Fulton, 49503
Telephone: 616-458-6111; 800-819-2332
Telecopier: 616-458-6446

Gary J. McInerney

Michael A. McInerney	Adna H. Underhill

For full biographical listings, see the Martindale-Hubbell Law Directory

---

RHOADES, MCKEE, BOER, GOODRICH & TITTA (AV)

161 Ottawa N.W., Suite 600, 49503-2793
Telephone: 616-235-3500
Fax: 616-459-5102
Email: grlaw@grlaw.com *URL:* http://www.grlaw.com

Roger W. Boer	Daniel L. Elve
Peter A. Titta	Thomas L. Saxe
Richard G. Leonard	James L. Schipper
Arthur C. Spalding	Laurie M. Strong
Bruce W. Neckers	Gregory G. Timmer
Robert J. Dugan	Mary Lynette Williams
Terrence L. Groesser	Scott J. Steiner
Mary Ann Cartwright	Douglas P. Vanden Berge

Paul A. McCarthy	Kenneth M. Horjus

Reference: First Michigan Bank.

For full biographical listings, see the Martindale-Hubbell Law Directory

---

ROBERTS, BETZ & BLOSS, P.C. (AV)

555 Riverfront Plaza Building, 55 Campau, 49503
Telephone: 616-235-9955
Telecopier: 616-235-0404

Michael J. Roberts	Ralph M. Reisinger
Michael W. Betz	Henry S. Emrich
David J. Bloss	Allan C. Vander Laan
Gregory A. Block	George J. Quist
Michael T. Small	Marshall W. Grate

For full biographical listings, see the Martindale-Hubbell Law Directory

---

SMITH HAUGHEY RICE & ROEGGE, P.C. (AV)

200 Calder Plaza Building, 250 Monroe Avenue, N.W., 49503-2251
Telephone: 616-774-8000
Facsimile: 616-774-2461
East Lansing, Michigan Office: 1301 North Hagadorn Road, 48823-2320.
Telephone: 517-332-3030.
Facsimile: 517-332-3468.
Traverse City, Michigan Office: 241 East State Street, P.O. Box 848, 49685-0848.
Telephone: 616-929-4878.
Facsimile: 616-929-4182.

Clifford A. Mitts (1902-1962)	Thomas R. Wurst
Laurence D. Smith (1913-1980)	Craig R. Noland
Robert V.V. Rice (1899-1982)	Paul M. Oleniczak
Michael S. Barnes (1944-1989)	Craig S. Neckers
L. Roland Roegge	Thomas E. Kent
Thomas F. Blackwell	Leonard M. Hickey
P. Laurence Mulvihill	John C. O'Loughlin
Lawrence P. Mulligan	Anthony J. Quarto
Thomas R. Tasker	Bruce P. Rissi
Paul H. Reinhardt	John M. Kruis
Lance R. Mather	Paul Van Oostenburg
Charles F. Behler	Dale Ann Iverson
John R. Sparks	William R. Jewell
Gary A. Rowe	Jon D. Vander Ploeg
William W. Jack, Jr.	Patrick F. Geary
William J. Hondorp	Terence J. Ackert
Thomas M. Weibel	Brian J. Kilbane
James G. Black	Dan C. Porter
E. Thomas Mc Carthy, Jr.	Phillip K. Mowers
Glenn W. House, Jr.	Carol D. Carlson

Christopher R. Genther

Kay L. Griffith Hammond	Elizabeth Roberts VerHey
Marilyn S. Nickell	Jennifer Jane Nasser
Beth Suzanne Kromer	Ginny Kaye Mikita
Robert M. Kruse	Karl Werner Butterer, Jr.
John B. Combs	Susan Soon Im
Aileen M. Simet	J. Joseph Rossi
Matthew L. Meyer	Stacie R. Seitz

Dwight K. Hamilton

OF COUNSEL

A. B. Smith, Jr.	Susan Bradley Jakubowski
David O. Haughey	Thomas P. Scholler

Representative Clients: Chevron; Cincinnati Insurance Co.; General Motors Corp.; Kemper Insurance Group; Michigan Hospital Assn.; Navistar International; St. Paul Insurance Cos.; Steelcase, Inc.; Sears Roebuck & Co.; Dow Elanco.

For full biographical listings, see the Martindale-Hubbell Law Directory

---

PETER W. STEKETEE (AV)

660 Cascade West Parkway, S.E., Suite 65, 49546
Telephone: 616-949-6551
Fax: 616-949-8817

For full biographical listings, see the Martindale-Hubbell Law Directory

---

TOLLEY, VANDENBOSCH & WALTON, P.C. (AV)

5650 Foremost Drive, S.E., 49546
Telephone: 616-942-8090
Facsimile: 616-942-4677

Peter R. Tolley	David L. Harrison
Lynwood P. VandenBosch	Richard J. Durden
Michael C. Walton	Robert C. Greene
Lawrence Korolewicz	Miles J. Postema
Todd R. Dickinson	James K. Schepers
Paul L. Nelson	Susan Jasper Stein
James B. Doezema	Mark J. Colon

Scott H. Hogan

Representative Clients: Brunswick Corp.; Citadel Corp.; Erb Lumber Company; Gordon Food Service; First Michigan Bank; Society Bank; State Farm Insurance Co.; Sentry Insurance Co.; Fremont Mutual Insurance Co.

For full biographical listings, see the Martindale-Hubbell Law Directory

Grand Rapids—Continued

VARNUM, RIDDERING, SCHMIDT & HOWLETT LLP (AV)

A Limited Liability Partnership including Professional Corporations
Bridgewater Place, P.O. Box 352, 49501-0352
Telephone: 616-336-6000
800-262-0011
Facsimile: 616-336-7000
Telex: 1561593 VARN
Email: varnum@vrsh.com
Lansing, Michigan Office: The Victor Center, Suite 810, 210 North
Washington Square, 48933.
Telephone: 517-482-6237.
Facsimile: 517-482-6937.
Kalamazoo, Michigan Office: 350 East Michigan Avenue, 49007.
Telephone: 616-382-2300.
Facsimile: 616-382-2382.
Grand Haven, Michigan Office: 321 Washington Street, P.O. Box 288,
49417.
Telephone: 616-846-7100.
Facsimile: 616-846-7101.
Battle Creek, Michigan Office: 4950 West Dickman Road, Suite B-1,
49015.
Telephone: 616-962-7144.
Bingham Farms, Michigan Office: 31600 Telegraph Road, Suite 230,
48025.
Telephone: 810-594-7330.
Facsimile: 810-594- 7331.

MEMBERS OF FIRM

Peter Armstrong	Stephen P. Afendoulis
Robert J. Eleveld	Perrin Rynders
Thomas J. Mulder	Mark S. Allard
Richard A. Kay	Timothy E. Eagle
Bruce A. Barnhart	Michael S. McElwee (Resident
Peter A. Smit	at Kalamazoo Office)
Bruce G. Hudson	Jacqueline D. Scott
(Resident at Lansing Office)	N. Stevenson Jennette III
Teresa S. Decker	Elizabeth Joy Fossel
William E. Rohn	Jeffery S. Crampton
Jeffrey D. Smith (Resident at	
Kalamazoo Office)	

COUNSEL
Terrance R. Bacon

ASSOCIATES

Eric J. Guerin (Resident at	Beverly Holaday
Kalamazoo Office)	(Resident at Lansing Office)
Kevin Abraham Rynbrandt	Eric C. Fleetham
Jon M. Bylsma	Richard B. Evans

STAFF ATTORNEY
Randall J. Groendyk

Representative Clients: Celotex Corporation; Foremost Insurance Co.; Alvey
Corporation; Progressive Engineering.

For Complete List of Firm Personnel, See General Section

For full biographical listings, see the Martindale-Hubbell Law Directory

---

WARNER NORCROSS & JUDD LLP (AV)

900 Old Kent Building, 111 Lyon Street, N.W., 49503-2489
Telephone: 616-752-2000
Fax: 616-752-2500
Muskegon, Michigan Office: 400 Terrace Plaza, P.O. Box 900.
Telephone: 616-727-2600.
Fax: 616-727-2699.
Holland, Michigan Office: Curtis Center, Suite 300, 170 College Avenue.
Telephone: 616-396-9800.
Fax: 616-396-3656.

MEMBERS OF FIRM

Charles E. McCallum	Paul T. Sorensen
John D. Tully	Rodney D. Martin
William K. Holmes	F. William McKee
Roger M. Clark	Louis C. Rabaut
John H. Logie	Douglas A. Dozeman
Jack B. Combs	Stephen B. Grow
Peter L. Gustafson	Daniel R. Gravelyn
J. A. Cragwall, Jr.	Robert J. Jonker
Eugene E. Smary	Devin S. Schindler
Douglas E. Wagner	Valerie Pierre Simmons
Jeffrey O. Birkhold	James Moskal

ASSOCIATES

Kenneth W. Vermeulen	Jeffrey A. Ott

General Counsel for: Bissell Inc.; Blodgett Memorial Medical Center;
Guardsman Products, Inc.; Haworth, Inc.; Kysor Industrial Corp.; Michigan
Bankers Assn.; Old Kent Financial Corp.; Steelcase Inc.; Wolverine World
Wide, Inc.

For Complete List of Firm Personnel, See General Section

For full biographical listings, see the Martindale-Hubbell Law Directory

---

WHEELER UPHAM, A PROFESSIONAL CORPORATION (AV)

Second Floor, Trust Building, 40 Pearl Street, N.W., 49503-3001
Telephone: 616-459-7100
Fax: 616-459-6366

Gordon B. Wheeler (1904-1986)	William H. Heritage, Jr.
Buford A. Upham (Retired)	Kenneth E. Tiews
Robert H. Gillette	Jack L. Hoffman
Geoffrey L. Gillis	Janet C. Baxter
John M. Roels	Peter Kladder, III
Gary A. Maximiuk	James M. Shade
Timothy J. Orlebeke	Thomas A. Kuiper

Counsel For: Prudential Ins. Co.; Metropolitan Life Ins. Co.; Travelers Ins.
Co.; Farmers Ins. Group; Auto-Owners Ins. Co.; Independent Cooperative
Milk Producers Assn.; Medtronic, Inc.; Navistar; Westdale Better Homes
and Gardens; Gospel Films, Inc.

For full biographical listings, see the Martindale-Hubbell Law Directory

---

GROSSE POINTE FARMS, Wayne Co.

JAMES W. GOSS PROFESSIONAL CORPORATION (AV)

230 Punch & Judy Building, 21 Kercheval Avenue, 48236
Telephone: 313-885-7500
Fax: 313-885-2474

James W. Goss

For full biographical listings, see the Martindale-Hubbell Law Directory

---

HANCOCK, Houghton Co.

WISTI & WISTI, P.C. (AV)

101 Quincy Street, 49930
Telephone: 906-482-5220
Fax: 906-482-8800
Iron Mountain, Michigan Office: 623 Stephenson Avenue.
Telephone: 906-779-1280.
Marquette, Michigan Office: 117 South Front Street.
Telephone: 906-228-8204.

Andrew H. Wisti	Mark Wisti
	Daniel J. Wisti

Patricia A. Gotschalk

References: Superior National Bank & Trust Company of Hancock, Michigan; Houghton National Bank, Houghton, Michigan.

For full biographical listings, see the Martindale-Hubbell Law Directory

---

HOLLAND, Ottawa Co.

CUNNINGHAM DALMAN, P.C. (AV)

321 Settlers Road, P.O. Box 1767, 49422-1767
Telephone: 616-392-1821
Fax: 616-392-4769

Gordon H. Cunningham	Kenneth B. Breese
Ronald L. Dalman	Jeffrey K. Helder
Max R. Murphy	Ronald J. Vander Veen
James A. Bidol	David M. Zessin
Andrew J. Mulder	Mark H. Zietlow
Joel G. Bouwens	James W. Bouwens
	Randall S. Schipper

Susan E. Vroegop	Melinda M. Abney

OF COUNSEL

Vernon D. Ten Cate	Kenneth B. Peirce, Jr.

Representative Clients: FMB-First Michigan Bank; Auto Club Insurance
Assn. (AAA); American States Insurance Co.; Board of County Road Com-
missioners; Hope College; Western Theological Seminary; Elzinga & Volkers,
Inc.; TNT Holland Motor Express, Inc.; Gra-Bell Truck Lines.

For full biographical listings, see the Martindale-Hubbell Law Directory

---

KALAMAZOO,* Kalamazoo Co.

DIETRICH, ZODY, HOWARD & VANDERROEST, P.C. (AV)

834 King Highway, Suite 110, 49001
Telephone: 616-344-9236
Fax: 616-344-0412

G. Philip Dietrich	James W. Smith
Richard J. Howard	James E. VanderRoest
	Philip W. Dietrich

OF COUNSEL

Brenda Wheeler Zody

Representative Clients: Amplimedical S.P.A.; Arvco Container Corp; Consolidated Rail Corporation; Day's Molding & Machinery, Inc.; Do-It Corp.;
Langeland Memorial Chapel, Inc.; Jonan, Ltd.; Partnership; Trinity Development Corp.; Rollins, Inc.; Orkin Extermination Co.

For full biographical listings, see the Martindale-Hubbell Law Directory

Kalamazoo—Continued

KREIS, ENDERLE, CALLANDER & HUDGINS, A PROFESSIONAL CORPORATION (AV)

One Moorsbridge, P.O. Box 4010, 49003-4010
Telephone: 616-324-3000
Telecopier: 616-324-3010
Email: kech@sapien.net *URL:* http://www.kech.com

Douglas L. Callander	Thomas G. King
Jeffrey C. O'Brien	Raymond C. Schultz
Stephen J. Hessen	James C. Boerigter

For Complete List of Firm Personnel, See General Section

For full biographical listings, see the Martindale-Hubbell Law Directory

LILLY & LILLY, P.C. (AV)

505 South Park Street, 49007
Telephone: 616-381-7763
Fax: 616-344-6880

Charles M. Lilly (1903-1990)   Terrence J. Lilly

For full biographical listings, see the Martindale-Hubbell Law Directory

MILLER, CANFIELD, PADDOCK AND STONE, P.L.C. (AV)

A Professional Limited Liability Company
Founded in 1852 by Sidney Davy Miller
444 West Michigan Avenue, 49007-3752
Telephone: 616-381-7030
Fax: 616-382-0244
Detroit, Michigan Office: 150 West Jefferson, Suite 2500, 48226-4415.
Telephone: 313-963-6420.
Fax: 313-496-7500.
Cable Address: "Stem Detroit."
Ann Arbor, Michigan Office: 101 North Main Street, 7th Floor, 48104-1400.
Telephone: 313-663-2445.
Fax: 313-747-7147.
Bloomfield Hills, Michigan Office: Suite 100, Pinehurst Office Center, 1400 North Woodward, 48303-2014.
Telephone: 313-645-5000.
Fax: 313-645-1917.
Grand Rapids, Michigan Office: 1200 Campau Square Plaza, 99 Monroe, N.W., 49503-2639.
Telephone: 616-454-8656.
Fax: 616-776-6322.
Howell, Michigan Office: 121 South Barnard Street, Suite 4, 48843-2305.
Telephone: 517-546-7600.
Telecopier: 517-546-6974.
Lansing, Michigan Office: One Michigan Avenue, Suite 900, 48933-1609.
Telephone: 517-487-2070.
Fax: 517-374-6304.
Monroe, Michigan Office: The Executive Centre, 214 East Elm Avenue, 48161-2682.
Telephone: 313-243-2000.
Fax: 313-243-0901.
Washington, D.C. Office: 1225 Nineteenth Street, N.W., Suite 400. 20036.
Telephone: 202-429-5575; 785-0600.
Fax: 202-331-1118; 785-1234.
Pensacola, Florida Office: 25 West Cedar, 32501.
Telephone: 904-469-1088.
Fax: 904-432-0677.
St. Petersburg, Florida Office: 100 Second Avenue S., Suite 7045, 33701.
Telephone: 813-982-6000.
Fax: 813-892-6002.
New York, New York Office: Eleventh Floor, 135 East 57th Street, 10022-2087.
Telephone: 212-754-5400.
Fax: 212-754-5401.
Gdansk, Poland Office: Suite 322, Dom Technika Building, UI. Rajska 6, 80-850.
Telephone: 011-485-831-2808.
Fax: 011-485-831-4719.
Warsaw, Poland Office: UI. Marszalkowska 82, Suite 561, 00-517.
Telephone: 011-482-623-6457 and 6458.
Fax: 011-482-623-6459.

PRINCIPALS OF FIRM

Charles E. Ritter	Ronald E. Baylor
James G. Vantine, Jr.	James E. Spurr

ASSOCIATES

Ballard Jay Yelton, III	Kurt P. McCamman
Scott R. Sikkenga	

Representative Firm Clients: Chrysler Corporation; Comerica, Incorporated; City of Detroit, Michigan; Detroit Tigers, Inc.; First of Michigan; Ford Motor Company; Ford Motor Credit Company; Great Lakes Bancorp; Henry Ford Hospital; INVETECH Company.

For Complete List of Firm Personnel, See General Section

For full biographical listings, see the Martindale-Hubbell Law Directory

LANSING, Ingham Co.

* indicates certain Bar Register subscribers whose principal office is located elsewhere in the state and who have arranged for representation as a part of the state capital listings that follow

DUNNINGS & FRAWLEY, P.C. (AV)

Duncan Building, 530 South Pine Street, 48933-2299
Telephone: 517-487-8222
Fax: 517-487-2026
Email: conrights@voyager.net

Stuart J. Dunnings, Jr.   John J. Frawley

Stuart J. Dunnings, III   Steven D. Dunnings
          Shauna L. Dunnings

Representative Clients: Lansing Board of Education; Lansing Housing Commission; Ford Motor Co.
References: First of America; Michigan National Bank.

For full biographical listings, see the Martindale-Hubbell Law Directory

FOSTER, SWIFT, COLLINS & SMITH, P.C. (AV)

313 South Washington Square, 48933-2193
Telephone: 517-371-8100
Telecopier: 517-371-8200
URL: http://www.fosterswift.com
Farmington Hills, Michigan Office: 32300 Northwestern Highway, Suite 230.
Telephone: 810-539-9900.
Fax: 810-851-7504.

Theodore W. Swift	James B. Jensen, Jr.
John L. Collins	Scott L. Mandel
William K. Fahey	James B. Croom
Stephen O. Schultz	Michael D. Sanders
William R. Schulz	David J. Houston
David H. Aldrich	Kevin T. McGraw
Scott A. Storey	Michael J. Bommarito
Charles E. Barbieri	Brian G. Goodenough

LEGAL SUPPORT PERSONNEL
LEGAL ASSISTANTS

Laurie A. Awad   Theresa G. Solberg

General Counsel: First of America Bank - Central; Michigan Milk Producers Assn.; Story, Inc.; Edward W. Sparrow Hospital; St. Lawrence Hospital; Michigan Financial Corp.; The State Journal; Peninsular Products; Demmer Corp.; Spartan Motors; North Community Health Care.

For Complete List of Firm Personnel, See General Section

For full biographical listings, see the Martindale-Hubbell Law Directory

FRASER TREBILCOCK DAVIS & FOSTER, P.C. (AV)

1000 Michigan National Tower, 48933
Telephone: 517-482-5800
Fax: 517-482-0887

Ronald R. Pentecost	Brett Jon Bean
Peter L. Dunlap	Gary C. Rogers
Michael E. Cavanaugh	Mark A. Bush
C. Mark Hoover	Michael H. Perry
Ronald R. Sutton	Mark R. Fox

Michael S. Ashton	Patrick K. Thornton
Michael James Reilly	Charyn K. Hain

Counsel for: Amtrak; Auto Club Insurance Assn. (A.A.A.); Auto Owners Insurance Co.; Farm Bureau, Inc.; Federated Insurance Co.; State Farm Insurance Companies.

For Complete List of Firm Personnel, See General Section

For full biographical listings, see the Martindale-Hubbell Law Directory

* HONIGMAN MILLER SCHWARTZ AND COHN (AV)

A Partnership including Professional Corporations
222 North Washington Square, Suite 400, 48933-1800
Telephone: 517-484-8282
Telecopier: 517-484-8286
URL: http://law.honigman.com
Detroit, Michigan Office: 2290 First National Building, 48226.
Telephone: 313-256-7800.
West Palm Beach, Florida Office: Suite 800 Esperante Building, 222 Lakeview Avenue, 33401-6112.
Telephone: 561-838-4500.
Tampa, Florida Office: 2700 SunTrust Financial Centre, 401 E. Jackson Street, 33602-5226.
Telephone: 813-221-6600.

(See Next Column)

Honigman Miller Schwartz and Cohn—*Continued*

MEMBERS

Richard J. Aaron	Mark Morton
Frederick M. Baker, Jr.	John D. Pirich
Sandra L. Jasinski	Gary A. Trepod
Timothy Sawyer Knowlton	William C. Whitbeck
	Ruth E. Zimmerman

ASSOCIATES

Ann L. Andrews	Andrew J. Gerdes
	Andrea Hansen

Representative Clients: Ameritech Michigan; American Society of Composers, Authors and Publishers (ASCAP); Garb-Ko, Inc. (7-Eleven Stores); Granger Land Development Co.; Greater Detroit Resource Recovery Authority; Lawyers Title Insurance Company; Michigan Gas Utilities, a division of UtiliCorp United, Inc.; Michigan Health and Hospital Association; ThornApple Valley, Inc.

For Complete List of Firm Personnel, See General Section

For full biographical listings, see the Martindale-Hubbell Law Directory

---

Raymond Joseph (AV)

1602 Michigan National Tower, 48933
Telephone: 517-372-4410
Fax: 517-372-2137

OF COUNSEL

George R. Sidwell (1899-1983)	Michael Bowman
	Bruce C. Blanton

Representative Clients: Ashland Oil, Inc.; Complete Auto Transit, Inc.; Employers Insurance of Wausau; Evans Products Co.; Grain Dealers Mutl.; Harbor Insurance Co.; Interstate Motor Freight System; Lansing Symphony Assn., Inc.; Prudential LMI Insurance Co.

For full biographical listings, see the Martindale-Hubbell Law Directory

---

Smith Haughey Rice & Roegge, P.C.

(See East Lansing)

Timmer, Jamo & O'Leary (AV)

521 Seymour Avenue, 48933
Telephone: 517-371-3500
Fax: 517-371-4514

MEMBERS OF FIRM

James A. Timmer	James S. O'Leary
James S. Jamo	Kathleen A. Lopilato

Representative Clients: Auto-Owners Insurance Co.; National Indemnity Insurance Co.; Pennsylvania Insurance Co.; Travelers Insurance Co.; Ohio Farmers Insurance Co.; Bankers Life & Casualty Co.; Western Casualty & Surety Co.; Indiana Insurance Group; Western Surety Co.; United States Aviation Underwriters, Inc.

For full biographical listings, see the Martindale-Hubbell Law Directory

---

MARQUETTE,* Marquette Co.

Swanson & Dettmann (AV)

Marquette Professional Building, 148 West Washington Street, 49855
Telephone: 906-228-7355
Fax: 906-228-7357

MEMBERS OF FIRM

Keith E. Swanson	Darrell R. Dettmann

Representative Clients: Kemper Insurance Cos.; USF&G Insurance Co.; SETSEG, Inc.; Gallagher Bassett Insurance Service; North Pointe Insurance Co.; Auto Owners Insurance Co.; CoreSource, Inc.; USAA; Upper Peninsula Health Education Corp.; Travelers Insurance Co.
Reference: First of America Bank-Marquette, N.A.

For full biographical listings, see the Martindale-Hubbell Law Directory

---

MOUNT CLEMENS,* Macomb Co.

David Griem (AV)

14 First Street, 48043
Telephone: 810-465-4900
Detroit, Michigan Office: One Woodward Avenue, Suite 2400, 48226.
Telephone: 313-961-8380.

For full biographical listings, see the Martindale-Hubbell Law Directory

---

Martin, Bacon & Martin, P.C. (AV)

44 First Street, 48043
Telephone: 810-979-6500
Fax: 810-468-7016

(See Next Column)

James N. Martin	Michael R. Janes
Jonathan E. Martin	Kevin L. Moffatt
Paul R. VanTol	John W. Crimando
	Victor T. Van Camp

Patrick D. Ball	Amy M. Chauvin

Reference: Old Kent Bank - Mt. Clemens.

For full biographical listings, see the Martindale-Hubbell Law Directory

---

PLYMOUTH, Wayne Co.

Draugelis & Ashton, L.L.P. (AV)

843 Penniman Avenue, 48170-1690
Telephone: 313-453-4044
Clawson, Michigan Office: 380 North Main Street.
Telephone: 810-588-7704.

MEMBERS OF FIRM

Edward F. Draugelis	Lamberto DiStefano
John A. Ashton	David T. Rogers
Donald S. Scully	Joseph R. Conte
Richard T. Haynes	Steven O. Ashton

ASSOCIATES

Dawn E. Clancy	Anne K. Mayer
Timothy M. O'Connor	Sally S. Stauffer
Floyd C. Virant	Darlene M. Germaine
Taras P. Jarema	Joel B. Ashton
Deborah A. Tonelli	Donald E. Walker
Timothy M. McKercher	Kathryn R. Mccool

Representative Clients: State Farm Mutual Automobile Insurance Co.; State Farm Fire and Casualty Co.; Secura Insurance Co.; Westfield Insurance Co.; United States Fidelity and Guaranty Co.; RLI Insurance Co.; United States Automobile Association; Michigan Automobile Insurance Placement Facility; Northville Downs.

For full biographical listings, see the Martindale-Hubbell Law Directory

---

Sempliner, Thomas and Boak (AV)

711 West Ann Arbor Trail, 48170
Telephone: 313-453-6220, 455-4560

MEMBERS OF FIRM

William Sempliner (1908-1985)	John E. Thomas
	Stephen H. Boak

ASSOCIATES

Mark D. Lang	Tracy S. Thomas

OF COUNSEL

Robert P. Tiplady

For full biographical listings, see the Martindale-Hubbell Law Directory

---

PONTIAC,* Oakland Co.

Booth Patterson, P.C. (AV)

1090 West Huron Street, 48328
Telephone: 810-681-1200
Fax: 810-681-1754

Douglas W. Booth (1918-1992)	David J. Lee
Calvin E. Patterson (1913-1987)	Allan T. Motzny
Parvin C. Lee, Jr.	Michael J. Hughes
J. Timothy Patterson	Michael D. Bishop
	Eric S. Meier

For full biographical listings, see the Martindale-Hubbell Law Directory

---

PORT HURON,* St. Clair Co.

Fletcher DeGrow (AV)

522 Michigan Street, 48060-3893
Telephone: 810-987-8444
Facsimile: 810-987-8149

MEMBERS OF FIRM

Gary A. Fletcher	Mark G. Clark

ASSOCIATES

John D. Tomlinson	William L. Fealko, III

Representative Clients: Fremont Mutual Insurance Co.; Westfield Insurance Co.; Michigan Municipal Risk Management Authority; City of Port Huron; City of Marysville; Port Huron Area School District; Marysville Public Schools; Wirtz Manufacturing Co.; Raymond Excavating; Relleum Real Estate Development Co.

For Complete List of Firm Personnel, See General Section

For full biographical listings, see the Martindale-Hubbell Law Directory

ROYAL OAK, Oakland Co.

CARDELLI, SCHAEFER & MASON, P.C. (AV)

322 West Lincoln, 48067
Telephone: 810-544-1100
Toll Free 1-800-411-7774
Telecopier: 810-544-1191

Thomas G. Cardelli
William C. Schaefer
Laura D. Mason

Deborah A. Hebert
Tara Hanley Bratton
Mary Ann J. O'Neil
Diane T. Gorczyca
Lillian C. Pierce
Ronald E. Beier, II
John L. Weston

Representative Clients: Allianz Insurance Company; Coltec Industries (Garlock Inc & Anchor Packing Company); Dana Corporation; Duchossois Industries, Inc.; Fruehauf Trailer Corporation; General Motors Corporation; NBD Bancorp, Inc; Otis Elevator Company; Raymond Corporation; Robert Bosch Power Tool Corporation; Ryobi Power Tool Corporation.

For full biographical listings, see the Martindale-Hubbell Law Directory

SAGINAW,* Saginaw Co.

SMITH & BROOKER, P.C. (AV)

The Gold Building, 4855 State Street, Suite 4, 48603
Telephone: 517-799-1891
Fax: 517-799-1145
Bay City, Michigan Office: 703 Washington Avenue.
Telephone: 517-892-2595.
Flint, Michigan Office: 1309 South Linden Road, Suite C, P.O. Box 315000.
Telephone: 810-733-0140.

RESIDENT ATTORNEYS
Francis B. Drinan
Michael J. Huffman
OF COUNSEL
Carl H. Smith, Jr.
Albert C. Hicks

Representative Clients: CIGNA; Citizens Insurance Co.; City of Saginaw; General Motors Corp.; Saginaw Township Community Schools; Saginaw Intermediate School District; State Farm Mutual Automobile Insurance Co.; Tri-City Airport Commission; CSX Transportation; Tittabawasee Township.

For full biographical listings, see the Martindale-Hubbell Law Directory

ST. JOSEPH,* Berrien Co.

GLOBENSKY, GLEISS, BITTNER & HYRNS, P.C. (AV)

610 Ship Street, P.O. Box 290, 49085
Telephone: 616-983-0551
Fax: 616-983-5858

H. S. Gray (1867-1961)
Rodger V. Bittner
Luman H. Gray (1902-1952)
Randy S. Hyrns
John L. Globensky
J. Joseph Daly
Henry W. Gleiss
Charles T. LaSata
James J. Riemland

General Counsel for: Shoreline Bank; Hanson Cold Storage Co.; Pearson Construction Co., Inc.
Approved Attorneys for: Lawyers Title Insurance Corp.
Reference: Shoreline Bank of Benton Harbor.

For full biographical listings, see the Martindale-Hubbell Law Directory

SAULT STE. MARIE,* Chippewa Co.

MOHER & CANNELLO, P.C. (AV)

150 Water Street, P.O. Box 538, 49783
Telephone: 906-632-3397
Fax: 906-632-0479
Newberry, Michigan Office: 200 East John.
Telephone: 906-293-3600.

Thomas G. Moher
Steven J. Cannello
Timothy S. Moher
LEGAL SUPPORT PERSONNEL
Bridgette A. Moher

Representative Clients: City of Sault Ste. Marie, Michigan; FMB Sault Bank; Sault Ste. Marie Economic Development Corp.; State of Michigan; Michigan Department of Transportation; Tendercare Nursing Homes of Michigan; Chippewa County, Village of De Tour; Pickford Township.

For full biographical listings, see the Martindale-Hubbell Law Directory

SOUTHFIELD, Oakland Co.

COLLINS, EINHORN, FARRELL & ULANOFF, A PROFESSIONAL CORPORATION (AV)

4000 Town Center, Suite 909, 48075-1473
Telephone: 810-355-4141
Facsimile: 810-355-2277

(See Next Column)

Morton H. Collins
Dale J. McLellan
Brian D. Einhorn
Kenneth C. Merritt
Clayton F. Farrell
Noreen L. Slank
Stuart A. Ulanoff
Michael J. Sullivan
Janice G. Hildenbrand

Gerald A. Pawlak
Deborah A. Lujan
Neil W. MacCallum
Barbara H. Goldman
Timothy Orlando
Shannon M. Kos
Theresa M. Asoklis
Kevin P. Moloughney
Karen C. Liddle
Susan P. Saltzman
Lisa L. Fadler
Laura A. Ruckle

For full biographical listings, see the Martindale-Hubbell Law Directory

FIEGER, FIEGER & SCHWARTZ, A PROFESSIONAL CORPORATION (AV)

19390 West Ten Mile Road, 48075-2463
Telephone: 810-355-5555
Fax: 810-355-5148

Bernard J. Fieger (1922-1988)
Todd J. Weglarz
Geoffrey N. Fieger
Rebecca S. Eaton
Michael Alan Schwartz
Ven R. Johnson
William J. McHenry
OF COUNSEL
Barry Fayne
Beverly Hires Brode
Keitha Kay Cowen

For full biographical listings, see the Martindale-Hubbell Law Directory

O'LEARY, O'LEARY, JACOBS, MATTSON, PERRY & MASON, P.C. (AV)

26777 Central Park Boulevard, Suite 275, 48076
Telephone: 810-948-1000
Fax: 810-799-8265
Email: olearyjacobs@michbar.org

John Patrick O'Leary
C. Kenneth Perry, Jr.
Thomas M. O'Leary
Larry G. Mason
John P. Jacobs
D. Jennifer Andreou
Kenneth M. Mattson
Kevin P. Hanbury
Alice A. Zetusky

For full biographical listings, see the Martindale-Hubbell Law Directory

PROVIZER, LICHTENSTEIN & PHILLIPS, P.C. (AV)

4000 Town Center, Suite 1800, 48075
Telephone: 810-352-9080
Facsimile: 810-352-1491

Harold M. Provizer
Deborah Molitz
David S. Lichtenstein
Noel F. Beck
Randall E. Phillips
William J. Selinsky
Marilyn A. Madorsky
Robert I. Brown
Jason Milstone

Representative Clients: Reliance National Ins. Co.; Jefferson Ins. Co.; Jefferson Ins. Group; Blackmoor Group.

For full biographical listings, see the Martindale-Hubbell Law Directory

SCHWARTZ & JALKANEN, P.C. (AV)

Suite 200, 24400 Northwestern Highway, 48075
Telephone: 810-352-2555
Facsimile: 810-352-5963

Melvin R. Schwartz
Arthur W. Jalkanen
Karl Eric Hannum

Deborah L. Laura
Lori A. Barker

For full biographical listings, see the Martindale-Hubbell Law Directory

SOMMERS, SCHWARTZ, SILVER & SCHWARTZ, P.C. (AV)

2000 Town Center, Suite 900, 48075
Telephone: 810-355-0300
Telecopier: 810-746-4001
Plymouth, Michigan Office: 747 South Main Street.
Telephone: 313-455-4250.

Stanley S. Schwartz
Justin C. Ravitz
Leonard B. Schwartz
David L. Nelson
Lawrence Warren
Joseph A. Golden
Jeffrey N. Shillman
Richard D. Fox
Jeremy L. Winer
Frank Mafrice
David R. Getto
James J. Vlasic
Robert H. Darling
Richard L. Groffsky
Paul W. Hines
David J. Winter
Donald J. Gasiorek
David M. Black
Patrick B. McCauley
Daniel D. Swanson

(See Next Column)

SOMMERS, SCHWARTZ, SILVER & SCHWARTZ P.C.—Continued

David A. Kotzian   Andrew Kochanowski
Patricia A. Stamler   David J. Shea

General Counsel for: City of Taylor; Foodland Distributors; C.A. Muer Corporation; Vlasic & Company; Nederlander Corporation; Midwest Health Centers, P.C.
Representative Clients: Crum & Forster Insurance Company; City of Pontiac; Michigan National Bank.

For Complete List of Firm Personnel, See General Section

For full biographical listings, see the Martindale-Hubbell Law Directory

---

YOUNG & ASSOCIATES, P.C. (AV)

Suite 305 Westview Office Center, 26200 American Drive, 48034
Telephone: 810-353-8620
Telecopier: 810-353-6559
Email: youngp@aol.com

Rodger D. Young

Anthony Cho   Steven Susser
Michael J. Fergestrom   Thomas A. Pinch

For full biographical listings, see the Martindale-Hubbell Law Directory

---

TRAVERSE CITY,* Grand Traverse Co.

MURCHIE, CALCUTT & BOYNTON (AV)

109 East Front Street, Suite 300, 49684
Telephone: 616-947-7190
Fax: 616-947-4341

Robert B. Murchie (1894-1975)   William B. Calcutt
Harry Calcutt   Mark A. Burnheimer
Jack E. Boynton   Dawn M. Rogers
ASSOCIATE
Ralph J. Dilley (Not admitted in MI)

General Counsel for: Old Kent Bank-Grand Traverse; Northwestern Savings Bank & Trust; Central-State Bancorp; Traverse City Record Eagle; WPNB-7 & WTOM-4; Emergency Consultants, Inc.; National Guardian Risk Retention Group, Inc.; Farmers Mutual Insurance Co.; Environmental Solutions, Inc.
Local Counsel for: Consumers Power Co.

For full biographical listings, see the Martindale-Hubbell Law Directory

---

ROBB, MESSING, PALMER & DIGNAN, P.C. (AV)

420 East Front Street, P.O. Box 1132, 49684
Telephone: 616-929-1130
Fax: 616-929-7925
Wayne County, Michigan Office: The Annex, 20500 Eureka, Suite 313, Taylor, Michigan 48180.
Telephone: 313-284-5550.

Dean A. Robb   Charles W. Palmer (Resident,
Mark M. Messing   Taylor, Michigan Office)
Thomas J. Dignan

Merritt W. Green, II   Maura N. Brennan
Lucinda Keils   Kirk C. Waibel
(Resident, Taylor, Michigan)
LEGAL SUPPORT PERSONNEL
Blair M. Robb

For full biographical listings, see the Martindale-Hubbell Law Directory

---

RUNNING, WISE, WILSON, FORD AND PHILLIPS, P.L.C. (AV)

326 State Street, P.O. Box 686, 49684
Telephone: 616-946-2700
Tele-Fax: 616-946-0857

Harry T. Running (Deceased)   William L. Wise (Retired)
MEMBERS OF FIRM
Patrick J. Wilson   James C. Adams
Richard W. Ford   Sandra P. Howard
Thomas J. Phillips   Kent E. Gerberding
ASSOCIATES
Shelley A. Kester   Bradley L. Putney
OF COUNSEL
J. Bruce Donaldson   Douglas J. Donaldson

Representative Clients: Peninsula Fruit Exchange; Oleson Food Stores; Munson Healthcare; Munson Medical Center; Grand Traverse County Road Commission; Townships of Peninsula, East Bay, Garfield, Almira, Homestead.

For full biographical listings, see the Martindale-Hubbell Law Directory

---

SMITH HAUGHEY RICE & ROEGGE, P.C. (AV)

241 East State Street, P.O. Box 848, 49685-0848
Telephone: 616-929-4878
Facsimile: 616-929-4182
Grand Rapids, Michigan Office: 200 Calder Plaza Building, 250 Monroe Avenue, N.W., 49503-2251.
Telephone: 616-774-8000.
Facsimile: 616-774-2461.
East Lansing, Michigan Office: 1301 North Hagadorn Road, 48823-2320.
Telephone: 517-332-3030.
Facsimile: 517-332-3468.

George Frederick Bearup   Charles B. Judson
Mark P. Bickel   Robert W. Tubbs
P. David Vinocur   Robert M. Faulkner
R. Jay Hardin   Thomas C. Kates

John R. Vander Veen   Jeffrey R. Wonacott
Mark D. Williams   Todd W. Millar
Erin Eileen Gerrity

Representative Clients: Chevron; Cincinnati Insurance Co.; General Motors Corp.; Kemper Insurance Group; Michigan Hospital Assn.; Navistar International; St. Paul Insurance Cos.; Steelcase, Inc.; Sears Roebuck & Co.; Dow Elanco.

For full biographical listings, see the Martindale-Hubbell Law Directory

---

THOMPSON & O'NEIL, P.C. (AV)

309 East Front Street, P.O. Box 429, 49685
Telephone: 616-929-9700; 1-800-678-1307
Fax: 616-929-7262

George R. Thompson   Daniel P. O'Neil

William J. Brooks

For full biographical listings, see the Martindale-Hubbell Law Directory

---

WALTON, SMITH, PHILLIPS & DIXON, P.C. (AV)

216 Cass Street, P.O. Box 549, 49685
Telephone: 616-947-7410
Fax: 616-947-5112

Geoff G. Smith   L. Kent Walton
Thomas L. Phillips
OF COUNSEL
David S. Dixon

Representative Clients: The Travelers Insurance Cos.; Farm Bureau Insurance Group; First of America-Northern Michigan; State Farm Insurance.
Reference: First of America-Northern Michigan.

For full biographical listings, see the Martindale-Hubbell Law Directory

---

TROY, Oakland Co.

BARLOW & LANGE, P.C. (AV)

3290 West Big Beaver Road Suite 310, 48084
Telephone: 810-649-3150
Facsimile: 810-649-3175

Thomas W. H. Barlow   Craig S. Schwartz
Craig W. Lange   Matthew S. Derby
Paul W. Coughenour   Gary S. Fealk
LEGAL SUPPORT PERSONNEL
Laura L. Russell

For full biographical listings, see the Martindale-Hubbell Law Directory

---

GRASSI & TOERING, P.L.C. (AV)

888 West Big Beaver, Suite 750, 48084
Telephone: 810-269-2020
Fax: 810-269-2025

Sebastian V. Grassi, Jr.   Douglas L. Toering

For full biographical listings, see the Martindale-Hubbell Law Directory

---

HACKETT, MAXWELL & PHILLIPS, P.L.L.C. (AV)

City Center Building, Suite 1470, 888 West Big Beaver Road, 48084
Telephone: 810-362-2600
Fax: 810-362-3610
Email: hackmax@michbar.org

Patrick E. Hackett   Phillip B. Maxwell
Dawn L. Phillips

Mark T. Butler   Lisa Rycus Mikalonis
Jill Tilton Silverman   Jason W. Johnson

For full biographical listings, see the Martindale-Hubbell Law Directory

Troy—Continued

HAINER, DEMOREST & BERMAN, P.C. (AV)

888 West Big Beaver, Suite 1400, 48084
Telephone: 810-244-8424
Fax: 810-244-8455

Michael J. Hainer   Mark S. Demorest
                Leonard K. Berman

James D. Zazakis   Paul S. Miller
                Rae Ann LaFrance
                OF COUNSEL
John P. Charters   Michael A. Kus
Michael A. Heck   Douglas W. Mires

Representative Clients: American Empire Surplus Lines Insurance Co.; Central Distributors of Beer, Inc.; City Management Corp.; Clarklift of Detroit, Inc.; Federal Reserve Bank of Chicago; Hotel Investment Services, Inc.; Michigan Pumping Service; Mid-West Instrument, Inc.; Rockwell International Corp.; Zurich Insurance Co.

For full biographical listings, see the Martindale-Hubbell Law Directory

AUSTIN HIRSCHHORN, P.C. (AV)

Suite 710 Columbia Center, 201 West Big Beaver Road, 48084-4152
Telephone: 810-680-1660
Fax: 810-680-1671

Austin Hirschhorn

For full biographical listings, see the Martindale-Hubbell Law Directory

HOLAHAN, MALLOY, MAYBAUGH & MONNICH (AV)

Suite 100, 2690 Crooks Road, 48084-4700
Telephone: 810-362-4747
Fax: 810-362-4779
East Tawas, Michigan Office: 910 East Bay Street.
Telephone: 517-362-4747.
Fax: 517-362-7331.

MEMBERS OF FIRM
J. Michael Malloy, III   David L. Delie, Jr.
James D. Maybaugh   William J. Kliffel
John R. Monnich   Ingrid Rosvold Kliffel
                OF COUNSEL
Thomas H. O'Connor   Maureen Holahan (Retired;
                Resident, East Tawas Office)

Representative Clients: Johnson & Higgens; Employers Reinsurance; Chubb Companies; American States Insurance Co.; Travelers Insurance; Pontiac Osteopathic Hospital; Michigan Health Care Corporation.

For full biographical listings, see the Martindale-Hubbell Law Directory

KEYWELL AND ROSENFELD (AV)

Suite 600, 2301 West Big Beaver Road, 48084
Telephone: 810-649-3200
Fax: 810-649-0454

MEMBERS OF FIRM
Jimm F. White   Leonard B. Shulman
                ASSOCIATES
Marjorie L. Kolin   Julie D. Abear
Reference: National Bank of Detroit.

For full biographical listings, see the Martindale-Hubbell Law Directory

POLING, McGAW & POLING, P.C. (AV)

Suite 275, 5435 Corporate Drive, 48098
Telephone: 810-641-0500
Telecopier: 810-641-0506

Benson T. Buck (1926-1989)   Richard B. Poling, Jr.
Richard B. Poling   Gregory C. Hamilton
D. Douglas McGaw   Veronica B. O'Haro
                James R. Parker
                OF COUNSEL
                Ralph S. Moore

Representative Clients: County of Oakland; City of Troy; United States Fidelity & Guaranty Co.; Sentry Insurance Co.; Admiral Insurance; DeMaria Construction Co.; Leo Corporation; Aetna Casualty and Surety Co.; Concord Design; Pneumo-Abex.

For full biographical listings, see the Martindale-Hubbell Law Directory

REYNOLDS, BEEBY & MAGNUSON, P.C. (AV)

50 West Big Beaver Road Suite 400, 48084
Telephone: 810-740-9860
Fax: 810-740-9870
Detroit, Michigan Office: Ford Building, Suite 531.
Telephone: 313-961-2720.
Fax: 313-961-5930.

Gregory A. Reynolds   Kenneth M. Zorn
Arnold N. Magnuson, Jr.   Thomas G. Grubba
                Frank K. Mandlebaum

Elizabeth A. Fellows   Joseph J. Wright
Representative Clients: General Motors Corp.; Michelin Tire Co.; Federation Internationale Automotive; Goody; Nissan Automotive; City of Detroit; Wayne County; Uniroyal Goodrich Tire Co.

For full biographical listings, see the Martindale-Hubbell Law Directory

VALENTINE & ASSOCIATES, P.C.

(See West Bloomfield)

WEST BLOOMFIELD, Oakland Co.

CHEATHAM & ACKER, P.C. (AV)

5777 West Maple Road, Suite 130, P.O. Box 255002, 48325-5002
Telephone: 810-932-2000
Fax: 810-932-2008

Charles C. Cheatham   Lawrence J. Acker

Tracy A. Leahy   Mary E. Hollman
                Christopher P. Jelinek
                COUNSEL
                Lynn L. Lower

For full biographical listings, see the Martindale-Hubbell Law Directory

LAW OFFICES OF LEE ESTES (AV)

5777 West Maple Road, Suite 130, P.O. Box 255002, 48325-5002
Telephone: 810-855-0770
Facsimile: 810-932-2008
Email: LESTES@gnn.com

For full biographical listings, see the Martindale-Hubbell Law Directory

VALENTINE & ASSOCIATES, P.C. (AV)

5767 West Maple Road, Suite 400, 48322
Telephone: 810-851-3010

Stephen K. Valentine, Jr.
                OF COUNSEL
                Philip G. Meyer

For full biographical listings, see the Martindale-Hubbell Law Directory

---

YPSILANTI, Washtenaw Co.

PEAR SPERLING EGGAN & MUSKOVITZ, P.C. (AV)

5 South Washington Street, 48197
Telephone: 313-483-3626
Fax: 313-483-1107
Ann Arbor, Michigan Office: Domino's Farms, 24 Frank Lloyd Wright Drive.
Telephone: 313-665-4441
Other Ypsilanti, Michigan Office: 2164 Bellevue at Washtenaw.
Telephone: 313-483-7177.

Lawrence W. Sperling   Thomas E. Daniels
Andrew M. Eggan   Helen Conklin Vick

Counsel for: Domino's Pizza, Inc.; Citizens Banking Corp.; Townsend and Bottum, Inc.; The Credit Bureau of Ypsilanti; City of Ypsilanti (Labor Counsel); Michigan Municipal Worker's Compensation; Self-Insurance Fund.
Approved Attorneys for: Lawyers Title Insurance Corp.

For full biographical listings, see the Martindale-Hubbell Law Directory

COMMERCIAL LAW

ALABAMA

BIRMINGHAM,* Jefferson Co.

BRADLEY, ARANT, ROSE & WHITE (AV)

2001 Park Place, Suite 1400, P.O. Box 830709, 35283-0709
Telephone: 205-521-8000
Facsimile: 205-252-0264
Facsimile (SouthTrust Tower Office): 205-251-9915
URL: http://www.BARW.COM
Huntsville, Alabama Office: 200 Clinton Avenue West, Suite 900, 35801.
Telephone: 205-517-5100.
Facsimile: 205-533-5069.

MEMBERS OF FIRM

Patrick H. Graves, Jr.	Paul S. Ware
(Resident, Huntsville Office)	Sid J. Trant
Laurence Duncan Vinson, Jr.	Stewart M. Cox
Carleta Roberts Hawley	Kenneth T. Wyatt
Bobby C. Underwood	T. Michael Brown
John D. Watson, III	George Bryan Harris
Michael R. Pennington	Susan Donovan Josey

ASSOCIATES

J. Patrick Darby	Helena F. Tozzi
James Tassin	Abdul K. Kallon
(Resident, Huntsville Office)	

For Complete List of Firm Personnel, See General Section

For full biographical listings, see the Martindale-Hubbell Law Directory

GORDON, SILBERMAN, WIGGINS & CHILDS, A PROFESSIONAL CORPORATION (AV)

1400 SouthTrust Tower, 420 North 20th Street, 35203
Telephone: 205-328-0640
Telecopier: 205-254-1500

Wilbur G. Silberman	Augustus J. Beck, Jr.
Bruce L. Gordon	Ray D. Gibbons
Ann C. Robertson	

Paul H. Webb	Timothy D. Davis
Timothy C. Gann	Jon E. Lewis
Brian M. Clark	

For Complete List of Firm Personnel, See General Section

For full biographical listings, see the Martindale-Hubbell Law Directory

HASKELL SLAUGHTER & YOUNG, L.L.C. (AV)

1200 AmSouth/Harbert Plaza, 1901 Sixth Avenue North, 35203
Telephone: 205-251-1000
Facsimile: 205-324-1133
Montgomery, Alabama Office: 305 South Lawrence Street, P.O. Box 4660. 36103-4660.
Telephone: 334-265-8573.
Facsimile: 334-264-7945.

E. Alston Ray	Thomas E. Reynolds
Gwen L. Windle	

Representative Clients: The Equitable Life Assurance Society of the United States; Farm Credit Leasing Services Corporation; Federal Deposit Insurance Corporation; First National Bank of Chicago; NationsCredit Financial Services Corporation; NationsBank Corporation.

For Complete List of Firm Personnel, See General Section

For full biographical listings, see the Martindale-Hubbell Law Directory

SPAIN & GILLON, L.L.C. (AV)

The Zinszer Building, 2117 2nd Avenue North, 35203
Telephone: 205-328-4100
Telecopier: 205-324-8866

MEMBERS OF FIRM

Samuel H. Frazier	Alton B. Parker, Jr.
J. Birch Bowdre	

General Counsel for: Liberty National Life Insurance Co.; Piggly Wiggly Alabama Distributing Co.; Alabama Life and Disability Insurance Guaranty Association; Alabama Insurance Underwriters Association.
Counsel for: America's First Federal Credit Union; Compass Bank; AmSouth Bank; South Trust Bank; The City of Birmingham.

For Complete List of Firm Personnel, See General Section

For full biographical listings, see the Martindale-Hubbell Law Directory

FLORENCE,* Lauderdale Co.

SELF & SELF (AV)

408 West Dr. Hicks Boulevard, P.O. Box 1062, 35631
Telephone: 205-767-2570; 1-800-336-2574
Fax: 205 767-2632

MEMBERS OF FIRM

Henry (Hank) H. Self, Jr.	Gilbert P. Self

Reference: Bank Independent; AmSouth Bank; Compass Bank.

For full biographical listings, see the Martindale-Hubbell Law Directory

GADSDEN,* Etowah Co.

FORD AND ASSOCIATES, P.C. (AV)

The Lancaster Building, 645 Walnut Street, Suite 5, P.O. Box 388, 35902
Telephone: 205-546-5432
Fax: 205-546-5435

George P. Ford

Richard M. Blythe

Reference: AmSouth Bank, N.A.

For Complete List of Firm Personnel, See General Section

For full biographical listings, see the Martindale-Hubbell Law Directory

HUNTSVILLE,* Madison Co.

BERRY, ABLES, TATUM, BAXTER, PARKER & HALL, P.C. (AV)

Legal Building, 315 Franklin Street, S.E., P.O. Box 165, 35804-0165
Telephone: 205-533-3740
Facsimile: 205-533-3751
Email: BAXTERJ@ATTMAIL.COM

William H. Blanton (1889-1973)	James T. Tatum, Jr.
Joe M. Berry	James T. Baxter, III
L. Bruce Ables	Thomas E. Parker, Jr.
Bill G. Hall	

James K. Brabston	Mark Rogers Hunter

Representative Clients: AmSouth Bank; First Alabama Bank; General Shale Products Co.; The Hertz Corp.; Litton Industries, Inc.; Farmers Tractor Co.; Colonial Bank; Farm Credit Bank of Texas; SouthBank; Regions Mortgage.
Reference: First Alabama Bank.

For full biographical listings, see the Martindale-Hubbell Law Directory

MOBILE,* Mobile Co.

FINKBOHNER AND LAWLER, L.L.C. (AV)

169 Dauphin Street Suite 300, P.O. Box 3085, 36652
Telephone: 334-438-5871
Fax: 334-432-8052

MEMBERS OF FIRM

George W. Finkbohner, Jr.	George W. Finkbohner, III
John L. Lawler	Royce A. Ray, III

For full biographical listings, see the Martindale-Hubbell Law Directory

LYONS, PIPES & COOK, P.C. (AV)

2 North Royal Street, P.O. Box 2727, 36652-2727
Telephone: 334-432-4481
Cable Address: "Lysea"
Telecopier: 334-433-1820

Marion A. Quina, Jr.	W. David Johnson, Jr.
Thomas F. Garth	Allen E. Graham
John Patrick Courtney, III	Michael C. Niemeyer
John C. Bell	

Representative Clients: Aetna Life & Casualty Company; Alabama Insurance Guaranty Association; American Family Life Insurance Company; Carrier's Container Council, Inc.; Champion Incorporation; Chubb; Crawford & Company; Crum & Forster Commercial Insurance; Maryland Casualty Company; Massachusetts Mutual Life Insurance Co.

For Complete List of Firm Personnel, See General Section

For full biographical listings, see the Martindale-Hubbell Law Directory

MONTGOMERY,* Montgomery Co.

VOLZ, PRESTWOOD & HANAN, P.C. (AV)

350 Adams Avenue, P.O. Box 1910, 36102-1910
Telephone: 334-264-6401
Fax: 334-834-4954

Charles H. Volz, Jr.	Charles H. Volz, III
Alvin T. Prestwood	Clinton Chadwell Carter
Ellis D. Hanan	Daniel Lewis Feinstein

(See Next Column)

VOLZ, PRESTWOOD & HANAN P.C., *Montgomery—Continued*

LEGAL SUPPORT PERSONNEL

Mark A.W. Turpen

For full biographical listings, see the Martindale-Hubbell Law Directory

TUSCUMBIA,* Colbert Co.

SELF & SELF

(See Florence)

ALASKA

ANCHORAGE,* Third Judicial District

OWENS & TURNER, A PROFESSIONAL CORPORATION (AV)

1500 West 33rd Avenue, Suite 200, 99503-3502
Telephone: 907-276-3963
Facsimile: 907-277-3695

Thomas P. Owens, Jr.	William F. Mede
Terrance A. Turner	Scott J. Nordstrand

Erin R. Brewer	Gregory S. Fisher
Patrick J McCabe	Kimberly K. Geariety

LEGAL SUPPORT PERSONNEL

Susan M. Lamb

Representative Clients: Alaska Finance & Insurance Co., Inc.; Anchorage Sand & Gravel Co., Inc.; BP Exploration (Alaska) Inc.; Baugh Construction & Engineering Company; Cook Inlet Region, Inc.; First National Bank of Anchorage; Merrill Lynch Pierce Fenner & Smith, Inc.; Ounalashka Corporation; Tanadgusix Corporation; Watterson Construction Company.

For full biographical listings, see the Martindale-Hubbell Law Directory

ARIZONA

FLAGSTAFF,* Coconino Co.

ASPEY, WATKINS & DIESEL, P.L.L.C. (AV)

123 North San Francisco, 3rd Floor, 86001
Telephone: 520-774-1478
Facsimile: 520-774-8404
Sedona, Arizona Office: 120 Soldier Pass Road.
Telephone: 520-282-5955.
Facsimile: 520-282-5962.
Page, Arizona Office: 904 North Navajo.
Telephone: 520-645-9694.
Cottonwood, Arizona Office: 2400 E. Highway 89A, Suite C.
Telephone: 520-639-1881.
Facsimile: 520-639-0272.

MEMBERS OF FIRM

Frederick M. Fritz Aspey	Donald H. Bayles, Jr.
Harold L. Watkins	Kaign N. Christy
Louis M. Diesel	John J. Dempsey
Bruce S. Griffen	Zachary J. Markham

James E. Ledbetter	Roger M. Baeurle
Whitney Cunningham	Amy E. Mabius
Pernell Whynn McGuire	Stephen A. Thompson
Joel E. Sannes	

LEGAL SUPPORT PERSONNEL

Karla H. Falls, CLAS (Legal Assistant)	Dominic M. Marino, Jr, (Paralegal Assistant)
Rocky C. Nissen (Paralegal Assistant, Sedona, Arizona Office)	Carrie R. Flynn (Litigation Paralegal, Cottonwood, Arizona Office)
Deborah D. Roberts, CLA (Legal Assistant)	

Representative Clients: Farmer's Insurance Company of Arizona; Pepsi-Cola Bottling Company of Northern Arizona; Bill Luke's Chrysler-Plymouth, Inc.; First American Title Insurance Company; Transnation Title Insurance Co.; Page Electric Utility; Comprehensive Access Health Plan, Inc.; Northern Arizona Healthcare Corporation.
Reference: First Interstate Bank-Arizona, N.A., Flagstaff, Arizona.

For full biographical listings, see the Martindale-Hubbell Law Directory

NOGALES,* Santa Cruz Co.

O'CONNOR, CAVANAGH, ANDERSON, KILLINGSWORTH & BESHEARS, A PROFESSIONAL ASSOCIATION (AV)

1891 North Mastick Way, 85621
Telephone: 520-761-4215
FAX: 520-761-3505
Email: firminfo@arizlaw.com
Phoenix, Arizona Office: One East Camelback Road, Suite 1100, 85012.
Telephone: 602-263-2400.
FAX: 602-263-2900.
Tucson, Arizona Office: O'Connor Cavanagh Molloy Jones, 33 N. Stone, Suite 2100, 85701, P.O. Box 2268, 85702.
Telephone: 520-622-3531.
FAX: 520-624-2816.
Sun City, Arizona Office: 13250 North Del Webb Boulevard, Suite B, 85351.
Telephone: 602-263-2808.
FAX: 602-933-3100.

Hector G. Arana	Kimberly A. Howard Arana

Representative Clients: Omega Produce Co.; Frank's Distributing, Inc.; City of Nogales; Collectron of Ariz., Inc.; James K. Wilson Produce Co.; Agricola Bon, S. de R.L. de C.V.; Angel Demerutis E.; Rene Carrillo C.; Arturo Lomeli; Theojary Crisantes E.

For Complete List of Firm Personnel, See General Section

For full biographical listings, see the Martindale-Hubbell Law Directory

PHOENIX,* Maricopa Co.

APKER, APKER, HAGGARD & KURTZ, P.C. (AV)

2111 East Highland Avenue, Suite 230, 85016
Telephone: 602-381-0085
Telecopier: 602-956-3457

Burton M. Apker	David B. Apker
Jerry L. Haggard	Gerrie Apker Kurtz

Kevin M. Moran

Representative Clients: Ancala Global Company; ASARCO Incorporated; Douglas Land Corp.; Frito-Lay, Inc.; Nevada Power Company; The North West Life Assurance Co.; Phelps Dodge Corporation; Santa Fe Pacific Gold Corporation; Western Federal Savings & Loan Assn.

For full biographical listings, see the Martindale-Hubbell Law Directory

BROWN & BAIN, A PROFESSIONAL ASSOCIATION (AV)

2901 North Central Avenue, P.O. Box 400, 85001-0400
Telephone: 602-351-8000
Telecopier: 602-351-8516
Palo Alto, California Affiliated Office: Brown & Bain, 1755 Embarcadero Road, Suite 200.
Telephone: 415-856-9411.
Telecopier: 415-856-6061.
Tucson, Arizona Affiliated Office: Brown & Bain, A Professional Association. One South Church Avenue, Nineteenth Floor, P.O. Box 2265.
Telephone: 602-798-7900.
Telecopier: 602-798-7945.

Eddward P. Ballinger, Jr.	Brent M. Gunderson
John A. Buttrick	Kyle B. Hettinger
Richard Calvin Cooledge	Philip R. Higdon
Jodi Knobel Feuerhelm	(Resident at Tucson Office)
Douglas Gerlach	Jeanean Kirk
Joseph E. Mais	

COUNSEL

Michael C. Jones	James F. McNulty, Jr.
	(Resident at Tucson Office)

For Complete List of Firm Personnel, See General Section

For full biographical listings, see the Martindale-Hubbell Law Directory

BURCH & CRACCHIOLO, P.A. (AV)

702 East Osborn Road, Suite 200, 85014
Telephone: 602-274-7611
Fax: 602-234-0341
Mailing Address: P.O. Box 16882, Phoenix, AZ, 85011

Stephen E. Silver	Donald W. Lindholm
Jack D. Klausner	F. Michael Carroll
Daryl Manhart	Daniel R. Malinski
David G. Derickson	Edwin D. Fleming
Edwin C. Bull	Ralph D. Harris
Bryan F. Murphy	Stephen M. Hart
David M. Villadolid	

(See Next Column)

BURCH & CRACCHIOLO P.A.—*Continued*

Paul F. Dowdell   Steven M. Serrano
Thomas A. Longfellow   J. Brent Welker

Representative Clients: Bashas' Inc.; Farmers Insurance Group; U-Haul International, Inc.

For Complete List of Firm Personnel, See General Section

For full biographical listings, see the Martindale-Hubbell Law Directory

CRUSE, FIRETAG & BOCK, P.C. (AV)

5611 North 16th Street, 85016
Telephone: 602-279-9411
Facsimile: 602-241-1260

Robert J. Cruse   Jules I. Firetag
Daniel A. Bock

John L. Stoss
OF COUNSEL
Stephen T. Meadow (P.C.)

Reference: Bank One (Sun City/Lakeview Office).

For full biographical listings, see the Martindale-Hubbell Law Directory

FENNEMORE CRAIG, A PROFESSIONAL CORPORATION (AV)

Two North Central, Suite 2200, 85004
Telephone: 602-257-8700
Fax: 602-257-8527
Scottsdale, Arizona Office: 6263 North Scottsdale Road, Suite 290, 85250.
Telephone: 602-257-5400.
Fax: 602-257-5409.
Tucson, Arizona Office: One South Church Avenue, Suite 1030, 85701.
Telephone: 520-791-6800.
Fax: 520-791-6820.

Robert P. Robinson   Mark A. Nesvig
Robert J. Hackett   James R. Huntwork
Ronald L. Ballard   Michael V. Mulchay
Stephen M. Savage   William T. Burghart
Roger T. Hargrove   Jay S. Kramer

W. T. Eggleston, Jr.   Laurel J. Davis
William P. Wichterman

For Complete List of Firm Personnel, See General Section

For full biographical listings, see the Martindale-Hubbell Law Directory

JEROLD KAPLAN (AV)

330 South 1st Avenue, 85003
Telephone: 602-258-8433
FAX: 602-258-4302

Representative Clients: Dillard, Inc.; Citibank, So. Dakota, N.A.; General Electric Credit Corp.; ITT Educational Services; National Bank of Arizona; Monogram Bank; Montgomery Ward.
References: Norwest Bank (Paradise Valley Branch); 1st Interstate Bank.

For full biographical listings, see the Martindale-Hubbell Law Directory

LEWIS AND ROCA, LLP (AV)

A Limited Liability Partnership including a Professional Corporation
40 North Central Avenue, 85004-4429
Telephone: 602-262-5311
Fax: 602-262-5747
Email: mlp@lrlaw.com
Tucson, Arizona Office: One South Church Avenue, Suite 700, 86701-1620.
Telephone: 520-622-2090.
Fax: 520-622-3088. *E-Mail:* mlp@lrlaw.com.

MEMBERS OF FIRM

John P. Frank   Gerald K. Smith
Peter D. Baird   Douglas L. Irish
Tom Galbraith   Marty Harper
Richard N. Goldsmith   Jordan Green
Susan M. Freeman   Randolph J. Haines
Patricia K. Norris   José A. Cárdenas
Dale A. Danneman   Edward F. Novak
Foster Robberson   Thomas H. Campbell
Newman R. Porter   George L. Paul
Thomas G. Ryan   Karen Carter Owens
Jesse B. Simpson   Brent C. Gardner
Mary Ellen Simonson   Cathy M. Holt
James T. Acuff, Jr.   Christopher J. Brelje
Robert H. McKirgan   Pamela B. Petersen
L. Keith Beauchamp   Richard A. Halloran
Deanna Salazar

(See Next Column)

ASSOCIATES
Stephen R. Winkelman   R. Neil Taylor, III
Dawn M. Bergin   Jeff A. Shumway
Randy Papetti
OF COUNSEL
Jeremy E. Butler

Representative Clients: Associates Financial Services; Citibank; The Dial Corp; Digital Equipment Corp.; MCI Communications Corp.; Prudential Securities.

For Complete List of Firm Personnel, See General Section

For full biographical listings, see the Martindale-Hubbell Law Directory

MacLEAN & JACQUES, LTD. (AV)

Suite 202, 40 East Virginia, 85004
Telephone: 602-263-5771
FAX: 602-279-5569

John H. MacLean (1932-1992)   Raoul T. Jacques

Cary T. Inabinet   Macre S. Inabinet
LEGAL SUPPORT PERSONNEL
Sharon Petterson

For full biographical listings, see the Martindale-Hubbell Law Directory

O'CONNOR, CAVANAGH, ANDERSON, KILLINGSWORTH & BESHEARS, A PROFESSIONAL ASSOCIATION (AV)

One East Camelback Road, Suite 1100, 85012-1656
Telephone: 602-263-2400
FAX: 602-263-2900
Email: firminfo@arizlaw.com
Sun City, Arizona Office: 13250 North Del Webb Boulevard, Suite B, 85351.
Telephone: 602-263-2808.
FAX: 602-933-3100.
Tucson, Arizona Office: O'Connor Cavanagh Molloy Jones, 33 N. Stone, Suite 2100, 85701, P.O. Box 2268, 85702.
Telephone: 520-622-3531.
FAX: 520-624-2816.
Nogales, Arizona Office: 1891 North Mastick Way, 85621.
Telephone: 520-761-4215.
FAX: 520-761-3505.

Robert S. Kant   Jean E. Harris
Jeffrey H. Verbin   Michelle S. Monserez
John B. Furman   Frank M. Fox
Richard B. Stagg   Karen L. Liepmann

D. Scott Fehrman   Karl A. Freeburg

Darren L. Brooks   Lisa R. Tsiolis
Jere M. Friedman   Monica D. T. Nguyenduc
OF COUNSEL
Shoshana B. Tancer   Sara R. Ziskin

Representative Clients: Waste Management, Inc.; Rural/Metro Corporation; Three-Five Systems, Inc.; CerProbe Corporation; Main Street & Main Incorporated; American Wireless Systems, Inc.; Maricopa County Sports Authority; Vodavi Communications.

For Complete List of Firm Personnel, See General Section

For full biographical listings, see the Martindale-Hubbell Law Directory

QUARLES & BRADY (AV)

One Camelback Building, One East Camelback Road, Suite 400, 85012-1649
Telephone: 602-230-5500
Fax: 602-230-5598
Milwaukee, Wisconsin Office: 411 East Wisconsin Avenue.
Telephone: 414-277-5000.
Fax: 414-271-3552.
Madison, Wisconsin Office: First Wisconsin Plaza, One South Pinckney Street, P.O. Box 2113.
Telephone: 608-251-5000.
Fax: 608-251-9166.
West Palm Beach, Florida Office: 222 Lakeview Ave., 4th Floor.
Telephone: 407-653-5000.
Fax: 407-653-5333.
Naples, Florida Office: Barnett Center, 4501 Tamiami Trail North, Suite 300.
Telephone: 813-262-5959.
Fax: 813-434-4999.

MEMBERS OF THE FIRM

Robert T. Bailes   Roger K. Spencer
Judith M. Bailey   Peter A. Terry
David G. Beauchamp

(See Next Column)

QUARLES & BRADY, *Phoenix—Continued*

ASSOCIATES

Robert S. Bornhoft   Mark K. Briggs

For Complete List of Firm Personnel, See General Section

For full biographical listings, see the Martindale-Hubbell Law Directory

RENAUD, COOK & DRURY, P.A. (AV)

617 North 2nd Avenue, 85003
Telephone: 602-253-5101
Fax: 602-254-1448
Email: rcdlaw@rcdlaw.com
Scottsdale, Arizona Office: 6991 East Camelback Road, #D-103, 85251.
Telephone: 602-874-9000.
Fax: 602-874-9866.

William W. Drury, Jr.	Cathey L. Joseph
James L. Blair	Mark W. Roth

Diana L. Clarke	Cynthia L. Fulton

For full biographical listings, see the Martindale-Hubbell Law Directory

RIDENOUR, SWENSON, CLEERE & EVANS, P.C. (AV)

40 North Central Avenue, Suite 1400, 85004
Telephone: 602-254-2143
Fax: 602-254-8670

William G. Ridenour	Natalie P. Garth
Gerard R. Cleere	Peter S. Spaw
William D. Fearnow	Alan R. Costello
Tamalyn E. Lewis	Timothy H. Barnes
Joseph A. Kendhammer	Kurt A. Peterson

James R. Hienton

OF COUNSEL

Thomas V. Rawles

David M. Reaves	Scott A. Holden
Jeffrey A. Bernick	Gregory P. Gillis

Representative Clients: American Arbitration Assn.; Biltmore Investors Bank; Citibank (Arizona); Federal Home Life Insurance Co.; Mellon Bank; Guarantee Mutual Life Co.; Indianapolis Life Insurance Co.; Kahler Corp.; Marriott Corp.; Farm Credit Services Southwest.

For full biographical listings, see the Martindale-Hubbell Law Directory

ROBBINS & GREEN, A PROFESSIONAL ASSOCIATION (AV)

1800 Norwest Tower, 3300 North Central Avenue, 85012-9826
Telephone: 602-248-7600
Fax: 602-266-5369

Philip A. Robbins	Janet B. Hutchison
William H. Sandweg III	Alfred W. Ricciardi
Jeffrey P. Boshes	Sarah McGiffert
Brian Imbornoni	Daniel L. Brown

Robert D. Peak

For Complete List of Firm Personnel, See General Section

For full biographical listings, see the Martindale-Hubbell Law Directory

SNELL & WILMER, L.L.P. (AV)

One Arizona Center, 85004-0001
Telephone: 602-382-6000
Fax: 602-382-6070
Tucson, Arizona Office: 1500 Norwest Tower, One South Church Avenue 85701-1612.
Telephone: 520-882-1200.
Fax: 520-884-1294.
Orange County Office: 1920 Main Street, Suite 1200, P.O. Box 57062, Irvine, California, 92619-7062.
Telephone: 714-253-2700.
Fax: 714-955-2507.
Salt Lake City, Utah Office: Broadway Centre, 111 East Broadway, Suite 900, 84111-1004.
Telephone: 801-237-1900.
Fax: 801-237-1950.

MEMBERS OF FIRM

Jon S. Cohen	David A. Sprentall
Terry Morris Roman	Timothy W. Moser

Robert R. Kinas

Representative Clients: Arizona Public Service Co.; Bank One, Arizona, NA.; First Security Bank of Utah, N.A.; Ford Motor Co.; Chrysler Motors Corp.; Toyota Motor Sales U.S.A.; BHP Copper, Inc.; U.S. Home Corp.; Pinnacle West Capital Corp.; Safeway, Inc.

For Complete List of Firm Personnel, See General Section

For full biographical listings, see the Martindale-Hubbell Law Directory

---

PRESCOTT,* Yavapai Co.

FAVOUR, MOORE & WILHELMSEN, A PROFESSIONAL ASSOCIATION (AV)

1580 Plaza West Drive, P.O. Box 1391, 86302
Telephone: 520-445-2444
Fax: 520-771-0450

John M. Favour	Mark M. Moore

David K. Wilhelmsen

Representative Client: Yavapai Title Co.
Reference: Bank of America.

For full biographical listings, see the Martindale-Hubbell Law Directory

---

SCOTTSDALE, Maricopa Co.

PESKIND HYMSON & GOLDSTEIN, P.C. (AV)

14595 North Scottsdale Road, Suite 14, 85254
Telephone: 602-991-9077
Fax: 602-443-8854

E. J. Peskind	David B. Goldstein
Irving Hymson	Marilee Miller Clarke

Eddie A. Pantiliat

For full biographical listings, see the Martindale-Hubbell Law Directory

---

TUCSON,* Pima Co.

CHANDLER, TULLAR, UDALL & REDHAIR (AV)

1700 Bank of America Plaza, 33 North Stone Avenue, 85701
Telephone: 520-623-4353
Telefax: 520-792-3426

MEMBERS OF FIRM

Joe F. Tarver, Jr.	John J. Brady

Representative Clients: Arizona Electric Power Cooperative, Inc.; Atlantic Richfield Co.; CNA Insurance; Farmers Insurance Exchange; MICA; Chubb Insurance Group; Aetna Casualty; State Farm Mutual Insurance Companies; Santa Cruz Valley Water Authority.
Reference: Arizona Bank.

For Complete List of Firm Personnel, See General Section

For full biographical listings, see the Martindale-Hubbell Law Directory

DUFFIELD, MILLER, YOUNG, ADAMSON & ALFRED, P.C. (AV)

Suite 711, Transamerica Building, 177 North Church Avenue, 85701
Telephone: 520-792-1181
FAX: 520-792-2859
Green Valley, Arizona Office: 101-65 South La Canada, Green Valley Mall.
Telephone: 520-625-4404.
Fax: 520-625-4453.
La Paloma Office: La Paloma Corporate Center, 3573 East Sunrise Drive, Suite 115, Tucson, Arizona.
Telephone: 520-577-1135.
Fax: 520-577-1079.

Philip Hawley Smith	Thomas R. Althaus
Arthur H. Miller (1935-1995)	Richard Duffield
Larry R. Adamson	Eugene C. Gieseler
Samuel D. Alfred	K. Alexander Hobson

Michael C. Young

LEGAL SUPPORT PERSONNEL

Cynthia Sargent Althaus	Joan Shelton, CLA
Mary Jane Arnesen	Christine M. Smith
Katrina Hillman	Barbara L. Steimle
Elizabeth Kohl-Sturgeon	Elaine Webb

Representative Clients: San Xavier Rock & Materials; Community Water Company of Green Valley.
Insurance Company Clientele: State Farm Mutual Insurance Cos.; Automobile Club Insurance Co.; Colonial Penn Insurance Co.; Metropolitan Property & Liability Insurance Co.; National Indemnity Ins. Co.

For full biographical listings, see the Martindale-Hubbell Law Directory

MUNGER AND MUNGER, P.L.C. (AV)

333 North Wilmot, Suite 300, 85711
Telephone: 520-721-1900
Fax: 520-747-1550
Northwest Tucson Office: 6700 N. Oracle Road, Suite 411, Tucson 85704.
Telephone: 520-797-7173.
Fax: 520-797-7178.

John F. Munger	Clark W. Munger (Resident, Northwest Tucson Office)

(See Next Column)

MUNGER AND MUNGER P.L.C.—*Continued*

Philip Kimble	Joy Athena
Karen S. Haller	Robert K. Lewis
Susan Gaylord Willis	Craig Wisnom (Resident,
Mark Edward Chadwick	Northwest Tucson Office)

Thomas A. Denker
OF COUNSEL
Doris Bates (Resident, Northwest Tucson Office)

Representative Clients: Jones Intercable; The Nature Conservancy; Tucson Greyhound Park; Tucson Realty and Trust; Associated Dermatologists; Red Rock Cattle Co.; U.S Rentals, Inc.; Nor-Tec Inc.; Grapevine Canyon Ranch; The Winters Co.

For full biographical listings, see the Martindale-Hubbell Law Directory

O'CONNOR CAVANAGH MOLLOY JONES, A PROFESSIONAL ASSOCIATION (AV)

Suite 2100 33 N. Stone, P.O. Box 2268, 85702
Telephone: 520-622-3531
FAX: 520-624-2816
Email: firminfo@arizlaw.com
Phoenix, Arizona Office: O'Connor, Cavanagh, Anderson, Killingsworth & Beshears, One East Camelback Road, Suite 1100, 85012.
Telephone: 602-263-2400.
FAX: 602-263-2900.
Sun City, Arizona Office: O'Connor, Cavanagh, Anderson, Killingsworth & Beshears, 13250 North Del Webb Boulevard, Suite B, 85351.
Telephone: 602-263-2808.
FAX: 602-933-3100.
Nogales, Arizona Office: O'Connor, Cavanagh, Anderson, Killingsworth & Beshears, 1891 North Mastick Way, 85621.
Telephone: 520-761-4215.
FAX: 520-761-3505.

Scott D. Gibson

Chris B. Nakamura

Representative Clients: Three-Five Systems; Main Street & Main; ITT Cannon; Bank of America; The Dial Corp; The Hartford; Dow Corning Corp.; Charles Schwab & Co., Inc.

For Complete List of Firm Personnel, See General Section

For full biographical listings, see the Martindale-Hubbell Law Directory

*YUMA,** Yuma Co.

ROBERT M. COOK (AV)

201 West Second Street, 85364
Telephone: 520-539-0959
Fax: 520-539-0960
1-800 ROBERT M

For full biographical listings, see the Martindale-Hubbell Law Directory

ARKANSAS

*FAYETTEVILLE,** Washington Co.

DAVIS, COX & WRIGHT, PLC (AV)

19 East Mountain Street, P.O. Drawer 1688, 72702-1688
Telephone: 501-521-7600
Fax: 501-521-7661

Sidney P. Davis, Jr.	William Jackson Butt, II
Walter B. Cox	Kelly P. Carithers
Tilden P. Wright, III	Tim E. Howell
Constance G. Clark	Don A. Taylor

Paul H. Taylor

John G. Trice	Mark W. Dossett
Laura J. Andress	David L. McCune

For full biographical listings, see the Martindale-Hubbell Law Directory

*LITTLE ROCK,** Pulaski Co.

ARNOLD, GROBMYER & HALEY, A PROFESSIONAL ASSOCIATION (AV)

875 Union National Plaza, 124 West Capitol Avenue, P.O. Box 70, 72203
Telephone: 501-376-1171
Fax: 501-375-3548

(See Next Column)

Benjamin F. Arnold	Joe A. Polk
James F. Dowden	Richard L. Ramsay
Mark W. Grobmyer	Robert R. Ross
Charles D. McDaniel	Lee S. Thalheimer

Beth Ann Long
OF COUNSEL
John H. Haley

For Complete List of Firm Personnel, See General Section

For full biographical listings, see the Martindale-Hubbell Law Directory

BARBER, McCASKILL, AMSLER, JONES & HALE, P.A. (AV)

2700 First Commercial Building, 400 West Capitol Avenue, 72201-3414
Telephone: 501-372-6175
Telecopier: 501-375-2802

Azro L. Barber (1885-1979)	Richard C. Kalkbrenner
Elbert A. Henry (1889-1966)	G. Spence Fricke
John B. Thurman (1912-1971)	Gail Ponder Gaines
Austin McCaskill, Sr.	Michael J. Emerson
Guy Amsler, Jr.	R. Kenny McCulloch
Glenn W. Jones	Tim A. Cheatham
Michael E. Hale	Joseph F. Kolb
John S. Cherry, Jr.	Scott Michael Strauss
Robert L. Henry, III	Derek J. Edwards
Micheal L. Alexander	Thomas E. Osment, Jr.
William H. Edwards, Jr.	Christopher Gomlicker

Attorneys for: Associated Aviation Underwriters; Canal Insurance Co.; Fireman's Fund Insurance Co.; General Motors Corp.; General Motors Acceptance Corp.; Hanover Insurance Co.; Home Insurance Co.; Royal Insurance; United States Fidelity & Guaranty Co.; Universal Underwriters Insurance Co.

For full biographical listings, see the Martindale-Hubbell Law Directory

HOOVER & KOOISTRA (AV)

111 Center Street, 11th Floor, 72201-4445
Telephone: 501-376-8500
Facsimile: 501-372-3255

MEMBERS OF FIRM

Paul W. Hoover, Jr.	John Kooistra, III
Max C. Mehlburger	

For full biographical listings, see the Martindale-Hubbell Law Directory

HOPKINS LAW FIRM, A PROFESSIONAL ASSOCIATION (AV)

1000 West Second Street, 72201
Telephone: 501-375-1517
Facsimile: 501-375-0231

Gregory M. Hopkins

William P. Allison

Representative Client: PPG Industries, Inc.

For full biographical listings, see the Martindale-Hubbell Law Directory

IVESTER, SKINNER & CAMP, P.A. (AV)

Suite 1200, 111 Center Street, 72201
Telephone: 501-376-7788
FAX: 501-376-8536

Hermann Ivester	Randal B. Frazier
H. Edward Skinner	Laura G. Wiltshire
Charles R. Camp	Todd A. Lewellen

Stan D. Smith

For Complete List of Firm Personnel, See General Section

For full biographical listings, see the Martindale-Hubbell Law Directory

LASER, WILSON, BUFFORD & WATTS, P.A. (AV)

101 S. Spring Street, Suite 300, 72201-2488
Telephone: 501-376-2981
Telecopier: 501-376-2417

Richard N. Watts	Alfred F. Angulo, Jr.
J. Kendal "Ken" Cook	David M. Donovan

Representative Clients: Allstate Insurance Co.; American International Insurance Group; Continental Insurance Cos.; Farm Bureau Insurance Cos. (Casualty & Fire); Farmers Insurance Group; GAB Business Services, Inc.; St. Paul Insurance Cos.; Scottsdale Insurance Co.; State Farm Auto (Fire) Insurance Cos.

For Complete List of Firm Personnel, See General Section

For full biographical listings, see the Martindale-Hubbell Law Directory

Little Rock—Continued

ROSE LAW FIRM, A PROFESSIONAL ASSOCIATION (AV)

120 East Fourth Street, 72201
Telephone: 501-375-9131
Telecopy: 501-375-1309

Herbert C. Rule, III	Thomas P. Thrash
Allen W. Bird, II	John T. Hardin
Garland J. Garrett	Stephen N. Joiner
Brian Rosenthal	

Representative Clients: Arkansas Capital Corp.; The Equitable Life Assurance Society of America; John Hancock Mutual Life Insurance Co.; Harvest Foods, Inc.; International Paper Co.; Mercantile Bank of Central Arkansas; The Prudential Insurance Company of America; Stephens Group Inc.; Trammell Crow Cos.

For Complete List of Firm Personnel, See General Section

For full biographical listings, see the Martindale-Hubbell Law Directory

WALKER & BLACK (AV)

1000 West Third Street, P.O. Box 3780, 72203-3780
Telephone: 501-376-2382
Fax: 501-376-3352

MEMBERS OF FIRM

W. J. Walker	Kendell R. Black

Reference: First Commercial Bank.

For full biographical listings, see the Martindale-Hubbell Law Directory

WILLIAMS & ANDERSON (AV)

Twenty-Second Floor, 111 Center Street, 72201
Telephone: 501-372-0800
FAX: 501-372-6453

MEMBERS OF FIRM

Philip S. Anderson	John E. Tull, III
Peter G. Kumpe	Timothy W. Grooms
Steven W. Quattlebaum	G. Alan Perkins
Thomas G. Williams	

Jeanne L. Seewald	Edie R. Ervin
Katharine R. Cloud	Stephen B. Niswanger

Representative Clients: Arkansas Development Finance Authority; Coca-Cola Enterprises, Inc.; Dean Witter Reynolds Inc.; Entergy Power, Inc.; Little Rock Newspapers, Inc. d/b/a Arkansas Democrat-Gazette; Potlatch Corporation; Texaco Inc.; Roman Catholic Diocese of Little Rock; Wal-Mart Stores, Inc.

For Complete List of Firm Personnel, See General Section

For full biographical listings, see the Martindale-Hubbell Law Directory

SPRINGDALE, Washington Co.

LISLE LAW FIRM, P.C. (AV)

P.O. Box 6877, 72766-6877
Telephone: 501-750-4444
Fax: 501-751-6792

John Lisle

Joe B. Reed	Donnie W. Rutledge, II
Christopher James Lisle	Stephen A. Lisle

For full biographical listings, see the Martindale-Hubbell Law Directory

CALIFORNIA

BAKERSFIELD,* Kern Co.

KLEIN, WEGIS, DENATALE, GOLDNER & MUIR, LLP (AV)

A Partnership including Professional Corporations
(Formerly Di Giorgio, Davis, Klein, Wegis, Duggan & Friedman)
ARCO Tower, 4550 California Avenue, Second Floor, P.O. Box 11172, 93389-1172
Telephone: 805-395-1000
Telecopier: 805-326-0418
Email: kwdgm@kwdgm.com

MEMBERS OF FIRM

Anthony J. Klein (Inc.)	Barry L. Goldner
Thomas V. DeNatale, Jr.	Jay L. Rosenlieb
David J. Cooper	

Representative Clients: Bank of America; California Republic Bank; San Joaquin Bank.

(See Next Column)

For Complete List of Firm Personnel, See General Section

For full biographical listings, see the Martindale-Hubbell Law Directory

BEVERLY HILLS, Los Angeles Co.

DAPEER, ROSENBLIT & LITVAK, LLP (AV)

9460 Wilshire Boulevard, Fifth Floor, 90212
Telephone: 310-203-8200; 310-777-6676
Fax: 310-203-8213; 310-777-6675
Metropolitan Cities Office: 2770 East Slauson Avenue, P.O. Box 2067, Huntington Park, 90255.
Telephone: 213-587-5221.
Fax: 213-587-4190.

William Litvak	Steven H. Rosenblit
Kenneth B. Dapeer	

For full biographical listings, see the Martindale-Hubbell Law Directory

CARLSBAD, San Diego Co.

WEIL & WRIGHT (AV)

1921 Palomar Oaks Way, Suite 301, 92008
Telephone: 619-438-1214
Telefax: 619-438-2666

Paul M. Weil	David A. Ebersole
Archie T. Wright III	John F. Hilbert

For full biographical listings, see the Martindale-Hubbell Law Directory

COSTA MESA, Orange Co.

COULOMBE & KOTTKE, A PROFESSIONAL CORPORATION (AV)

Comerica Bank Tower, 611 Anton Boulevard, Suite 1260, 92626
Telephone: 714-540-1234
Fax: 714-754-0808; 714-754-0707
Email: c-k@coulombe.com

Ronald B. Coulombe	Jon S. Kottke

COUNSEL

Roy B. Woolsey

LEGAL SUPPORT PERSONNEL

PARALEGALS

Vicky M. Pearson	Abeer F. Rider

LEGAL ADMINISTRATOR

Yvonne Mendoza

For full biographical listings, see the Martindale-Hubbell Law Directory

RUTAN & TUCKER, LLP (AV)

A Partnership including Professional Corporations
611 Anton Boulevard, Suite 1400, P.O. Box 1950, 92626
Telephone: 714-641-5100; 213-625-7586
Telecopier: 714-546-9035
Email: rutan&tucker@mcimail.com *URL:* http://www.rutan.com

MEMBERS OF FIRM

William R. Biel	Ira G. Rivin (P.C.)
Clifford E. Frieden	Marcia A. Forsyth
Thomas J. Crane	

ASSOCIATES

Michael K. Slattery	Paul J. Sievers

For Complete List of Firm Personnel, See General Section

For full biographical listings, see the Martindale-Hubbell Law Directory

FRESNO,* Fresno Co.

DOWLING, AARON & KEELER, INCORPORATED (AV)

Suite 200, 6051 North Fresno Street, 93710
Telephone: 209-432-4500
Fax: 209-432-4590
Email: dowling-law.com

Michael D. Dowling	Adolfo M. Corona
Richard M. Aaron	Philip David Kopp
Bruce S. Fraser	Rene Lastreto, II
William J. Keeler, Jr.	Francine Marie Kanne
John C. Ganahl	Christopher A. Brown

Richard E. Heatter	Michael P. Dowling
James C. Sherwood	Daniel T. Fitzpatrick
Mark D. Kruthers	

OF COUNSEL

Daniel K. Whitehurst	Morris M. Sherr
Blaine Pettitt	

Reference: Wells Fargo Bank (Main).

For full biographical listings, see the Martindale-Hubbell Law Directory

Fresno—Continued

JORY, PETERSON, WATKINS & SMITH (AV)

555 West Shaw, Suite C-1, P.O. Box 5394, 93755
Telephone: 209-225-6700
Telecopier: 209-225-3416

MEMBERS OF FIRM

Jay V. Jory	Michael Jens F. Smith
John E. Peterson	Marcia A. Ross
Cal B. Watkins, Jr.	William M. Woolman

ASSOCIATES

John J. Stander	Carla M. McCormack
Jeff W. Reisig	Matthew D. Ruyak

Reference: Valliwide Bank.

For full biographical listings, see the Martindale-Hubbell Law Directory

---

GLENDALE, Los Angeles Co.

LASKIN & GRAHAM (AV)

Suite 840, 800 North Brand Boulevard, 91203
Telephone: 213-665-6955; 818-547-4800; 714-957-3031
Telecopier: 818-547-3100

OF COUNSEL
Richard Laskin

MEMBERS OF FIRM

Arnold K. Graham	Michael Anthony Cisneros
Susan L. Vaage	Gregson M. Perry
John S. Peterson	Lynn I. Ibara

For full biographical listings, see the Martindale-Hubbell Law Directory

---

IRVINE, Orange Co.

HANLEY & PATCH (AV)

A Partnership including Professional Corporations
19900 MacArthur Boulevard, Suite 650, 92715-2445
Telephone: 714-253-0800
Fax: 714-253-0870

William B. Hanley (P.C.)	Ryan Mark Patch (P.C.)
	Joshua M. Wolff

Paul Kim	Johanna Y. Hsu
	Dimitri P. Gross

For full biographical listings, see the Martindale-Hubbell Law Directory

LOBEL & OPERA, PROFESSIONAL CORPORATION (AV)

Suite 1100, 19800 MacArthur Boulevard, P.O. Box 19588, 92713
Telephone: 714-476-7400
Fax: 714-476-7444

William N. Lobel	Tavi Claire Stanley
Robert E. Opera	Metiner G. Kimel
Alan J. Friedman	Edward P. Christian
Pamela Z. Karger	Robert J. Mrofka
Cheryl A. Skigin	Hamid R. Rafatjoo

For full biographical listings, see the Martindale-Hubbell Law Directory

WATT, TIEDER & HOFFAR, L.L.P. (AV⊤)

3 Park Plaza, Suite 1530, 92714
Telephone: 714-852-6700
Telecopier: 714-261-0771
McLean Virginia Office: 7929 Westpark Drive, Suite 400,
Telephone: 703-749-1000.
Telecopier: 703-893-8029.
Washington, D.C. Office: 601 Pennsylvania Avenue, N.W. Suite 900,
Telephone: 202-462-4697.

MEMBERS OF FIRM

John B. Tieder, Jr.	Michael G. Long
(Not admitted in CA)	Christopher P. Pappas
Robert M. Fitzgerald	
(Not admitted in CA)	

ASSOCIATE
Gregory John Dukellis

For full biographical listings, see the Martindale-Hubbell Law Directory

---

LONG BEACH, Los Angeles Co.

RUSSELL & MIRKOVICH (AV)

One World Trade Center, Suite 1450, 90831-1450
Telephone: 310-436-9911
FAX: 310-436-1897

Carlton E. Russell	Joseph N. Mirkovich

For full biographical listings, see the Martindale-Hubbell Law Directory

---

WILLIAMS WOOLLEY COGSWELL NAKAZAWA & RUSSELL (AV)

111 West Ocean Boulevard, Suite 2000, 90802-4614
Telephone: 310-495-6000
Telecopier: 310-435-1359; 310-435-6812
Telex: ITT: 4933872; WU: 984929
Email: wwlaw@msn.com
Rancho Santa Fe, California Office: P.O. Box 9120, 16236 San Dieguito
Road, Building 3, Suite 3-15, 92067.
Telephone: 619-497-0284.
Fax: 619-759-9938.
Port Hueneme, California Office: 237 E. Hueneme Road, Suite A, 93041.
Telephone: 805-488-8560.
Fax: 805-488-7896.

MEMBERS OF FIRM

Reed M. Williams	Alan Nakazawa
David E. R. Woolley	Blake W. Larkin
Forrest R. Cogswell	Thomas A. Russell

ASSOCIATES

Todd A. Valdes	Thomas G. Walsh
	Richard J. Nikas

For full biographical listings, see the Martindale-Hubbell Law Directory

---

LOS ANGELES, * Los Angeles Co.

LAW OFFICES OF DAVID B. BLOOM A PROFESSIONAL CORPORATION (AV)

3325 Wilshire Boulevard, Ninth Floor, 90010
Telephone: 213-938-5248; 384-4088
Telecopier: 213-385-2009

David B. Bloom

Stephen S. Monroe (A	Susan Carole Jay
Professional Corporation)	Edward Idell
Raphael A. Rosemblat	Sandra Kamenir
James E. Adler	Steven Wayne Lazarus
Bonni S. Mantovani	Andrew Edward Briseno
Roy A. Levun	Harold C. Klaskin
Cherie S. Raidy	Shelley M. Gould
Jonathan Udell	Peter O. Israel

For full biographical listings, see the Martindale-Hubbell Law Directory

SANDOR T. BOXER (AV)

Suite 900 2049 Century Park East, 90067-3111
Telephone: 310-282-8118
Fax: 310-282-8077
Email: tedb@themall.net

For full biographical listings, see the Martindale-Hubbell Law Directory

BUCHALTER, NEMER, FIELDS & YOUNGER, A PROFESSIONAL CORPORATION (AV)

24th Floor, 601 South Figueroa Street, 90017
Telephone: 213-891-0700
Fax: 213-896-0400
Email: buchalter@earthlink.net *URL:* http://www.buchalter.com
New York, New York Office: 15th Floor, 605 Third Avenue.
Telephone: 212-490-8600.
Fax: 212-490-6022.
San Francisco, California Office: 29th Floor, 333 Market Street.
Telephone: 415-227-0900.
Fax: 415-227-0770.
Newport Beach, California Office: Suite 1450, 620 Newport Center Drive.
Telephone: 714-760-1121.
Fax: 714-720-0182.

Murray M. Fields	Keith B. Bardellini
Richard Jay Goldstein	Mark A. Bonenfant
Michael L. Wachtell	David S. Kyman
Robert C. Colton	James H. Turken
Gary A. York	Kevin M. Brandt
Arthur Chinski	Jeffrey S. Wruble
Jay R. Ziegler	Randye B. Soref
Michael J. Cereseto	Pamela Kohlman Webster
Bernard E. Le Sage	Matthew W. Kavanaugh
Gregory Keever	Richard S. Angel
Roger D. Loomis, Jr.	Bryan Mashian
Philip J. Wolman	Robert J. Davidson
	Bernard D. Bollinger, Jr.

OF COUNSEL

Ronald E. Gordon	Holly J. Fujie
Stuart D. Buchalter	Elizabeth S. Trussell
Barry A. Smith	Harriet M. Welch
Geoffrey Forsythe Bogeaus	William Mark Levinson
Scott O. Smith	Harriet B. Alexson
	Barry F. Soosman

(See Next Column)

BUCHALTER, NEMER, FIELDS & YOUNGER A PROFESSIONAL CORPORATION, *Los Angeles—Continued*

Janis S. Penton	Kim Allman
Jerry A. Hager	William P. Fong
Jonathan D. Fink	Helen Goldberger Palmer
Julie A. Goren	Brett Michael Broderick
Glenn L. Savard	Robert Alexander Pilmer
Paul S. Arrow	Kirk H. Sharpe
William S. Brody	Nicolas M. Kublicki
Amy L. Rubinfeld	Vincent I.S. Hsieh
Dean Stackel	(Not admitted in CA)
Abraham J. Colman	Simone Margaret Bennett
Monika L. McCarthy	Christina M. Carlson
Mary LePique Dickson	Rachael H. Berman
Shirley Sheau-Lih Lu	Daniel Joseph Kolodziej
Robert A. Willner	Elizabeth H. Murphy
Adam Joel Bass	Lance R. Dixon
David L. Aronoff	Allan R. Mouw

Daniel C. Wong

References: City National Bank; Wells Fargo Bank; Metrobank.

For full biographical listings, see the Martindale-Hubbell Law Directory

CLARK & TREVITHICK, A PROFESSIONAL CORPORATION (AV)

800 Wilshire Boulevard, 12th Floor, 90017
Telephone: 213-629-5700
Telecopier: 213-624-9441
San Francisco, California Office: 456 Montgomery Street, 20th Floor.
Telephone: 415-288-6520.
Fax: 415-398-2820.

Philip W. Bartenetti	Leonard Brazil
Dolores Cordell	Leslie R. Horowitz
Vincent Tricarico	Arturo Santana Jr.

Kerry T. Ryan

OF COUNSEL

Judith Ilene Bloom

References: Wells Fargo Bank (Los Angeles Main Office); National Bank of California.

For Complete List of Firm Personnel, See General Section

For full biographical listings, see the Martindale-Hubbell Law Directory

DEMETRIOU, DEL GUERCIO, SPRINGER & MOYER, LLP (AV)

801 South Grand Avenue, 10th Floor, 90017
Telephone: 213-624-8407
Telecopy: 213-624-0174
Email: ddsm@juno.com *URL:* http://www.ddsm.com

MEMBERS OF FIRM

Chris G. Demetriou (1915-1989)	Laurie E. Davis
Jeffrey Z. B. Springer	Gregory D. Trimarche
Craig A. Moyer	Karen McLaurin Chang
Angela Shanahan	Leslie M. Smario
Stephen A. Del Guercio	Andrew J. Bracker
Michael A. Francis	Kimberly E. Lewand
Regina Liudzius Cobb	Jennifer T. Taggart

Robert P. Silverstein

OF COUNSEL

Ronald J. Del Guercio	Richard A. Del Guercio

James P. Del Guercio

Reference: Bank of America, L.A. Main Office, Los Angeles, Calif.

For full biographical listings, see the Martindale-Hubbell Law Directory

GOLDMAN & GORDON, L.L.P. (AV)

Suite 1920, 1801 Century Park East, 90067
Telephone: 310-277-7171
FAX: 310-277-1547

MEMBERS OF FIRM

A. S. Goldman (1895-1966)	Leonard A. Goldman

Robert P. Gordon

ASSOCIATE

Melody G. Anderson

References: Bank of America, Fourth and Spring Branch, Los Angeles; Bank of America, Wilshire-San Vincente Branch, Beverly Hills.

For full biographical listings, see the Martindale-Hubbell Law Directory

IVANJACK & LAMBIRTH (AV)

A Partnership including Professional Corporations
12301 Wilshire Boulevard, Suite 600, 90025-1000
Telephone: 310-820-7211
Telecopier: 310-820-0687
Email: ivanjack@AOL.com
Irvine, California Office: 5 Park Plaza, Suite 800. 92614.
Telephone: 714-475-4477.
Telecopier: 714-475-4475.

Larry G. Ivanjack (P.C.)	Thomas E. Shuck (P.C.)
Timothy A. Lambirth (P.C.)	Kathryn B. Milstead

Joseph H. Lowther	Gary Tokumori
Elise A. Ross	Mary G. Lee

OF COUNSEL

Robert F. Nichols, Jr.	Camilla N. Andrews

Representative Clients: Bank of America; Citibank N.A.; Union Bank of California, N.A.; Sanwa Bank California; Great Western Bank; Imperial Bank; First Republic Thrift and Loan; General Electric Capital Corp.; Fleet Credit Corp.; Western Bank.

For full biographical listings, see the Martindale-Hubbell Law Directory

KATZ, HOYT, SEIGEL & KAPOR LLP (AV)

A Partnership including a Professional Corporation
Suite 820, 11111 Santa Monica Boulevard, 90025-3342
Telephone: 310-473-1300
Telecopier: 310-473-7138

MEMBERS OF FIRM

Charles J. Katz (1905-1983)	William Schoenholz
Louis C. Hoyt (1905-1994)	Jack R. Lenack
Benjamin S. Seigel (P.C.)	Russell L. Allyn
Jeffrey H. Kapor	Douglas M. Lipstone
Scott H. Jacobs	Moira Doherty
Alan Jay Cohen	Marla Milner

For full biographical listings, see the Martindale-Hubbell Law Directory

MITCHELL, SILBERBERG & KNUPP LLP (AV)

A Partnership including Professional Corporations
11377 West Olympic Boulevard, 90064
Telephone: 310-312-2000
Fax: 310-312-3100

MEMBERS OF FIRM

Chester I. Lappen (A Professional Corporation)	John E. Hatherley (A Professional Corporation)
Marvin Leon (A Professional Corporation)	Anthony A. Adler (A Professional Corporation)
John M. Kuechle (A Professional Corporation)	Laura A. Loftin (A Professional Corporation)
Joseph Ciasulli (A Professional Corporation)	Andrew E. Katz (A Professional Corporation)
Alan L. Pepper (A Professional Corporation)	

OF COUNSEL

Lessing E. Gold (A Professional Corporation)	H. Wayne Taylor
	Richard E. Ackerknecht

ASSOCIATES

David J. Katz	Michael J. Zerman
Harry H.W. Kim	Jeremy A. Lappen

References: Wells Fargo Bank, N.A.; Merrill, Lynch.

For Complete List of Firm Personnel, See General Section

For full biographical listings, see the Martindale-Hubbell Law Directory

O'MELVENY & MYERS LLP (AV)

400 South Hope Street, 90071-2899
Telephone: 213-669-6000
Cable Address: "Moms"
Facsimile: 213-669-6407
Email: omminfo@omm.com
Century City, California Office: 1999 Avenue of the Stars, 90067-6035.
Telephone: 310-553-6700.
Facsimile: 310-246-6779.
Newport Beach, California Office: 610 Newport Center Drive, 92660-6429.
Telephone: 714-760-9600.
Cable Address: "Moms".
Facsimile: 714-669-6994.
San Francisco, California Office: Embarcadero Center West Tower, 275 Battery Street, 94111-3305.
Telephone: 415-984-8700.
Facsimile: 415-984-8701.
New York, New York Office: Citicorp Center, 153 East 53rd Street, 10022-4611.
Telephone: 212-326-2000.
Facsimile: 212-326-2061.

(See Next Column)

O'MELVENY & MYERS LLP—*Continued*

Washington, D.C. Office: 555 13th Street, N.W., 20004-1109.
Telephone: 202-383-5300.
Cable Address: "Moms".
Facsimile: 202-383-5414.
London, England Office: 10 Finsbury Square, London, EC2A 1LA.
Telephone: 0171-256-8451.
Facsimile: 0171-638-8205.
Tokyo, Japan Office: Sanbancho KB-6 Building, 6 Sanbancho, Chiyoda-ku, Tokyo 102, Japan.
Telephone: 03-3239-2900.
Facsimile: 03-3239-2432.
Hong Kong Office: Suite 1905, Peregrine Tower, Lippo Centre, 89 Queensway, Central, Hong Kong.
Telephone: 852-2523-8266.
Facsimile: 852-2522-1760.
Shanghai, Peoples Republic of China Office: Shanghai International Trade Centre, Suite 2011, 2200 Yan An Road West, Shanghai, 200335, PRC.
Telephone: 86-21-6219-5363.
Facsimile: 86-21-6275-4949.

PARTNER
Frederick B. McLane

For Complete List of Firm Personnel, See General Section

For full biographical listings, see the Martindale-Hubbell Law Directory

---

OSTROVE, KRANTZ & OSTROVE, A PROFESSIONAL CORPORATION (AV)

(Successor To: Ostrove and Lancer, A Professional Corporation; David Ostrove, A Professional Corporation)
5757 Wilshire Boulevard, Suite 535, 90036-3600
Telephone: 213-939-3400
Fax: 213-939-3500
Email: OSTROVE@AOL.COM

David Ostrove　　　　　　　David S. Krantz
Kenneth E. Ostrove

Reference: First Business Bank.

For full biographical listings, see the Martindale-Hubbell Law Directory

---

PIZER & MICHAELSON INC. (AV)

2029 Century Park East, Suite 600, 90067
Telephone: 310-843-9729
Fax: 310-843-9619
Santa Ana, California Office: 2122 North Broadway, Suite 100, 92706.
Telephone: 714-558-0535.
Telecopier: 714-550-0841.

Bradley J. Pizer

For full biographical listings, see the Martindale-Hubbell Law Directory

---

RONALD P. SLATES A PROFESSIONAL CORPORATION (AV)

548 South Spring Street, Suite 1012, 90013-2309
Telephone: 213-624-1515; 213-654-1461
Fax: 213-624-7536; 213-654-1463

Ronald P. Slates

G. Michael Jackson

For full biographical listings, see the Martindale-Hubbell Law Directory

---

STUTMAN, TREISTER & GLATT, PROFESSIONAL CORPORATION (AV)

3699 Wilshire Boulevard, Suite 900, 90010
Telephone: 213-251-5100
FAX: 213-251-5288

Jack Stutman (Retired Founder)	Michael H. Goldstein
George M. Treister	Lee R. Bogdanoff
Herman L. Glatt	Frank A. Merola
Richard M. Neiter	K. John Shaffer
Robert A. Greenfield	Mareta C. Hamre
Charles D. Axelrod	Michael L. Tuchin
Theodore B. Stolman	Jeffrey H. Davidson
Isaac M. Pachulski	Ronald L. Fein
Kenneth N. Klee	Mark S. Wallace
Alan Pedlar	Eric D. Goldberg
George C. Webster, II	Eve H. Karasik
Stephan M. Ray	Thomas R. Kreller
Michael A. Morris	Martin R. Barash
Jeffrey C. Krause	James O. Johnston Jr.

Michael C. Standlee

For full biographical listings, see the Martindale-Hubbell Law Directory

---

SULMEYER, KUPETZ, BAUMANN & ROTHMAN, A PROFESSIONAL CORPORATION (AV)

300 South Grand Avenue, 14th Floor, 90071
Telephone: 213-626-2311
Fax: 213-629-4520

Irving Sulmeyer	Israel Saperstein
Arnold L. Kupetz	Victor A. Sahn
Richard G. Baumann	Steven R. Wainess
Don Rothman	David S. Kupetz
Alan G. Tippie	Howard M. Ehrenberg

Kathryn Kerfes

Nathan H. Harris	Mark S. Horoupian
Susan Frances Moley	Stephen C. Seto
Matthew Rothman	Howard N. Madris
Wesley Avery	Tanya M. Vince

OF COUNSEL

Marilyn S. Scheer	Suzanne L. Weakley
Frank Vram Zerunyan	Elissa D. Miller

Representative Clients: General Electric Capital Corp.; Continental Insurance Co.; Litton Industries; North American Phillips Corp.; Ventura Port District; Northwest Financial; Heller Financial Inc.; Transamerica Occidental Life Insurance Co.; Transamerica Realty Services, Inc.; Body Glove International.

For full biographical listings, see the Martindale-Hubbell Law Directory

---

ZIDE & O'BIECUNAS (AV)

Suite 403, 1300 West Olympic Boulevard, 90015
Telephone: 213-487-7550
Fax: 213-382-6095
Mailing Address: P.O. Box 15363, Del Valle Station,
Email: leoatzano@aol.com
Ventura, California Office: 101 South Victoria Avenue.
Telephone: 805-642-2426.
Fax: 805-642-8881.

Thomas Zide　　　　　　　Leo G. O'Biecunas, Jr.

ASSOCIATES
Douglas M. Kaye　　　　　　　Nathan Swedlow

For full biographical listings, see the Martindale-Hubbell Law Directory

---

NEWPORT BEACH, Orange Co.

CAPRETZ & RADCLIFFE (AV)

5000 Birch Street, West Tower Suite 2500, 92660-2139
Telephone: 714-724-3000
Fax: 714-757-2635
Email: CRLAWYERS@AOL.CON *URL:* http://www.CAPRETZ.com

James T. Capretz　　　　　　　Richard J. Radcliffe

ASSOCIATE
Peter A. Martin

OF COUNSEL
William B. Lawless　(Not admitted in CA)

LEGAL SUPPORT PERSONNEL
Rosanna S. Bertheola

For full biographical listings, see the Martindale-Hubbell Law Directory

---

OAKLAND, * Alameda Co.

EDWARD L. BLUM (AV)

1999 Harrison Street, Suite 1333, 94612
Telephone: 510-452-4400
Fax: 510-452-4406

ASSOCIATE
Anne Tremaine

For full biographical listings, see the Martindale-Hubbell Law Directory

---

KORNFIELD, PAUL & BUPP, A PROFESSIONAL CORPORATION (AV)

Suite 800, Lake Merritt Plaza, 1999 Harrison Street, 94612
Telephone: 510-763-1000
Fax: 510-273-8669

Irving J. Kornfield	C. Randall Bupp
Aaron Paul	Merridith A. Schneider

Eric A. Nyberg

Charles D. Novack	Chris D. Kuhner

Gareth M. Chow

For full biographical listings, see the Martindale-Hubbell Law Directory

ORANGE, Orange Co.

FABOZZI, THIERBACH & CALEY (AV)

3111 North Tustin Avenue, Suite 200, 92665
Telephone: 714-637-3385
FAX: 714-637-3489

Dennis F. Fabozzi   Marlene L. Thierbach
          Rebecca A. Caley
ASSOCIATES
Jima Ikegawa   Bruce T. Bauer

For full biographical listings, see the Martindale-Hubbell Law Directory

*SACRAMENTO,** Sacramento Co.

THE BLEIER LAW FIRM (AV)

2100 21st Street, 95818-1708
Telephone: 916-454-2100
Fax: 916-454-2121
Email: tblf@bleier.com *URL:* http://www.bleier.com

Brenton A. Bleier
ASSOCIATES
Alan C. Campbell   Robert W. Hunt
Peter H. Mixon   Bradford A. Bleier

For full biographical listings, see the Martindale-Hubbell Law Directory

*SAN DIEGO,** San Diego Co.

BARNHORST, SCHREINER & GOONAN, A PROFESSIONAL CORPORATION (AV)

550 West C Street, Suite 1350, 92101-3532
Telephone: 619-544-0900
Fax: 619-544-0703
Email: BSG@CTS.COM

Howard J. Barnhorst, II   Gregory P. Goonan
Stephen L. Schreiner   Niles Rice Sharif
          Brian W. DeWitt
OF COUNSEL
          David L. Dick

Representative Clients: Century 21 All Service Realtors; Continental Lawyers Title Co.; Guthy-Renker, Corp.; Heritage Surgical Corp.; Inacom Corp.; James Hardle Industries (USA), Inc.; OASE Pumps, Inc.; Pioneer Liquidating Corp.; Premier Food Services, Inc.; Seaquest, Inc.; USLIFE Corp.

For full biographical listings, see the Martindale-Hubbell Law Directory

CHAPIN, FLEMING & WINET, A PROFESSIONAL CORPORATION (AV)

Library, 501 West Broadway, 15th Floor, 92101
Telephone: 619-232-4261
Telefax: 619-232-4840
Email: cfwlaw@adnc.com *URL:* http://www.sandiego-online.com/cfwlaw
Vista, California Office: 410 South Melrose Drive, Suite 101.
Telephone: 619-758-4261.
Telefax: 619-758-6420.
Los Angeles, California Office: 12121 Wilshire Boulevard, Suite 401.
Telephone: 310-826-0133.
Telefax: 310-207-4236.
Palm Springs, California Office: 225 North El Cielo Road, Suite 470.
Telephone: 619-416-1400.
Telefax: 619-416-1405.

Victor M. Barr, Jr.   Terence L. Greene
Craig H. Bell   Gregory Kevin Hansen
  (Resident, Los Angeles Office) Howard L. Hoffenberg
Darryn L. Berner   (Resident, Los Angeles Office)
Kelli Jean Brooks   Patrick M. Howe
Michael S. Burke   Aaron H. Katz
David H. Bushnell   Elizabeth J. Koumas
  (Resident, Los Angeles Office) Traci Lynn Kuchta
Richard D. Carter   Dana Marie Lawson
  (Resident, Los Angeles Office)   (Resident, Los Angeles Office)
Dean G. Chandler   Jeffrey J. Leist
  (Resident, Vista Office)   (Resident, Los Angeles Office)
Edward D. Chapin   Tonya L. Morgan
Victoria Chen   (Resident, Los Angeles Office)
George Chuang   David A. Myers
  (Resident, Los Angeles Office)   (Resident, Los Angeles Office)
Amber L. Eck   Brenda J. Pannell
Robert Ehrenreich   (Resident, Los Angeles Office)
  (Resident, Los Angeles Office) Kennett L. Patrick
Scott K. Endsley   (Resident, Vista Office)
George E. Fleming   Thomas V. Perea
Antonio Gastelum (Not   (Resident, Los Angeles Office)
  admitted in United States) Roger L. Popeney
Shirley A. Gauvin   Maria C. Roberts
Katherine M. Green   Lawrence W. Shea, II

(See Next Column)

Douglas J. Simpson   Frank L. Tobin
Spencer C. Skeen   Grace I. Wang
  (Resident, Los Angeles Office)   (Resident, Los Angeles Office)
Howard Smith   Peter C. Ward
  (Resident, Los Angeles Office) Jeffrey A. Weaver (Resident,
Patricia L. Sullivan   Palm Springs Office)
Gregory S. Tavill   Randall L. Winet
                             (Resident, Vista Office)
OF COUNSEL
George F. Braun   Irwin Waldman (A P.C.)
Arthur D. Rutledge   (Resident, Los Angeles Office)
  (Resident, Los Angeles Office) James Michael Zimmerman
Jeffrey C. Stodel
  (Resident, Los Angeles Office)

For full biographical listings, see the Martindale-Hubbell Law Directory

DUCKOR SPRADLING & METZGER, A LAW CORPORATION (AV)

401 West A Street, Suite 2400, 92101-7909
Telephone: 619-231-3666
Telecopier: 619-231-6629
Email: dsm@dsmlaw.wanet.com

Michael J. Duckor   K. Michael Garrett
Gary J. Spradling   Patrick L. Prindle
Scott L. Metzger   Li-An C. Leonard
John C. Wynne   Stephen A. Bond
John W. Cutchin   R. Anthony Mahavier
Robert D. Rochelle   Robin Assaf Wofford
Robert L. Kenny   Leslie S. Akins
Laurie J. Orange   Jill Osmars Wolcott
          Thomas R. Darton

Brian A. Barnhorst   Jamie M. Ryan
Catriona M. Cahill   Douglas A. Dube
Robert J. Solis   Gregory P. Olson
John J. Freni   Susan B. Hansen
Jessica M. Amgwerd   Julie D. Wiley
          Laura B. Riesenberg

Representative Clients: Computer Sciences Corp.; E & J Gallo Wineries; General Electric Capital Corp.; Great Western Bank; Pathology Medical Laboratories; Princess Resorts; San Diego Chargers Football; Sedgwick James International; Siemens Credit Corp.; Transamerica Financial Services; Van Camp Seafood Co.; Zevo Golf, Inc.

For full biographical listings, see the Martindale-Hubbell Law Directory

FERRIS & BRITTON, A PROFESSIONAL CORPORATION (AV)

1600 First National Bank Center, 401 West A Street, 92101
Telephone: 619-233-3131
Fax: 619-232-9316

Alfred G. Ferris   Tamara K. Fogg
          Gary T. Moyer
OF COUNSEL
          William M. Winter

Representative Clients: Agouron Pharmaceuticals, Inc.; Cox Communications, Inc.; Enterprise Rent-a-Car; Exxon; Immuno Pharmaceuticals, Inc.; Invitrogen Corporation; Peninsula Bank; Teleport Communications Group; Southwest Airlines.

For Complete List of Firm Personnel, See General Section

For full biographical listings, see the Martindale-Hubbell Law Directory

HOVEY, KIRBY, THORNTON & HAHN, A PROFESSIONAL CORPORATION (AV)

101 West Broadway, Suite 1100, 92101-8297
Telephone: 619-685-4000
Fax: 619-685-4004
Email: 74754.3143@compuserve.com

Dean T. Kirby, Jr.   M. Leslie Hovey
          Geraldine A. Valdez

For full biographical listings, see the Martindale-Hubbell Law Directory

LINDLEY, LAZAR & SCALES, A PROFESSIONAL CORPORATION (AV)

One America Plaza, 600 West Broadway, Suite 1400, 92101-3302
Telephone: 619-234-9181
Fax: 619-234-8475
Email: 104413.1175@compuserve.com

Luke R. Corbett   George C. Lazar
John M. Seitman   James Henry Fox
Michael H. Wexler   R. Gordon Huckins
Richard J. Pekin, Jr.   Kenneth C. Jones

Representative Clients: Bank of Commerce; Resolution Trust Corp.; FDIC; City Chevrolet; Metro Imports; Palomar Savings & Loan Assn.; Northern Trust Bank of California, N.A.

(See Next Column)

LINDLEY, LAZAR & SCALES A PROFESSIONAL CORPORATION—*Continued*

For Complete List of Firm Personnel, See General Section

For full biographical listings, see the Martindale-Hubbell Law Directory

THORSNES, BARTOLOTTA, McGUIRE & PADILLA (AV)

A Partnership including Professional Corporations
Fifth Avenue Financial Center, 11th Floor, 2550 Fifth Avenue, 92103
Telephone: 619-236-9363
Fax: 619-236-9653
Email: TBMP@lawinfo.com *URL:* http://www.tbmp.com

Michael T. Thorsnes (P.C.)	Mitchell S. Golub (P.C.)
Vincent J. Bartolotta, Jr., (P.C.)	Frederic L. Gordon (P.C.)
John F. McGuire (P.C.)	Palma Cesar Hooper (P.C.)
Michael D. Padilla (P.C.)	Neal H. Rockwood (P.C.)
Kevin F. Quinn (P.C.)	Daral B. Mazzarella (P.C.)
C. Brant Noziska (P.C.)	R. Christian Hulburt (P.C.)

ASSOCIATES

Jeffrey F. LaFave	John J. Rice
Stephen D. Lipkin	Robert E. Bright
Rhonda J. Thompson	Douglas J. Billings
Scott A. Kennedy	James T. Atkins

Charles L. Stott

OF COUNSEL

Robert S. Kennedy

For full biographical listings, see the Martindale-Hubbell Law Directory

SAN FRANCISCO,* San Francisco Co.

LAW OFFICES OF KEVIN W. FINCK (AV)

Two Embarcadero Center, Suite 1670, 94111
Telephone: 415-296-9100
Facsimile: 415-394-6446

Michael L. Dobrov

OF COUNSEL

Marla Raucher Osborn

For full biographical listings, see the Martindale-Hubbell Law Directory

LAFAYETTE, KUMAGAI & CLARKE (AV)

100 Spear Street, Suite 400, 94105
Telephone: 415-357-4600
Facsimile: 415-357-4605

MEMBERS OF FIRM

Gary T. Lafayette	Kevin M. Clarke

Susan T. Kumagai

ASSOCIATE

Valerie A. Andersen

For full biographical listings, see the Martindale-Hubbell Law Directory

ROSEN, BIEN & ASARO (AV)

Eighth Floor, 155 Montgomery Street, 94104
Telephone: 415-433-6830
Fax: 415-433-7104
Email: rba@rbalaw.com

Sanford Jay Rosen	Michael W. Bien

Andrea G. Asaro

Thomas Nolan	William H.D. Fernholz
Donna Petrine	Doris Y. Ng
M.J. Tony Paikeday	A. Marie Villafaña

For full biographical listings, see the Martindale-Hubbell Law Directory

SAN JOSE,* Santa Clara Co.

CAMPEAU & THOMAS, A LAW CORPORATION (AV)

Market Post Tower, 55 South Market Street, Suite 1660, 95113
Telephone: 408-295-9555
Fax: 408-295-6606

Kenneth J. Campeau	Wayne H. Thomas

Scott L. Goodsell

Marcie E. Schaap	Kathryn J. Diemer

For full biographical listings, see the Martindale-Hubbell Law Directory

HOPKINS & CARLEY, A LAW CORPORATION (AV)

Fifteenth Floor, 150 Almaden Boulevard, 95113-2089
Telephone: 408-286-9800
Facsimile: 408-998-4790

(See Next Column)

Leon A. Carley (1908-1984)	Ross G. Adler
Garth E. Pickett	Jeffrey E. Essner
Arthur V. Plank	William S. Klein
Stephen J. Kottmeier	Timothy H. Hopkins
Jon Michaelson	Robert O. Whyte

Brenda N. Buonaiuto	Robert W. Ricketson
Kimberly S. Pellissier	Jay M. Ross
Sally A. Reed	Denise Y. Yamamoto

For Complete List of Firm Personnel, See General Section

For full biographical listings, see the Martindale-Hubbell Law Directory

SANTA ANA,* Orange Co.

PIZER & MICHAELSON INC. (AV)

2122 North Broadway, Suite 100, 92706
Telephone: 714-558-0535
Telecopier: 714-550-0841
Los Angeles, California Office: 2029 Century Park East, Suite 600, 90067.
Telephone: 310-843-9729.
Fax: 310-843-9619.

Seymour S. Pizer (1930-1992)	Hugh R. Coffin
Barry S. Michaelson	Bradley J. Pizer
	(Resident, Los Angeles Office)

For full biographical listings, see the Martindale-Hubbell Law Directory

PRENOVOST, NORMANDIN, BERGH & DAWE, A PROFESSIONAL CORPORATION (AV)

2020 East First Street, Suite 500, 92705
Telephone: 714-547-2444
Fax: 714-835-2889
Email: PNBD@worldnet.att.net

Thomas J. Prenovost, Jr.	Steven L. Bergh
Tom Roddy Normandin	Michael G. Dawe

Doris Andree Faust	Paula M. Harrelson
Eric P. Francisconi	Daniel H. McLinden
James Andrew Fraser	Nancy R. Tragarz

Reference: Marine National Bank.

For full biographical listings, see the Martindale-Hubbell Law Directory

SPERLING & PERGANDE (AV)

3 Hutton Centre, Suite 670, 92707
Telephone: 714-540-8500
Facsimile: 714-540-2599

MEMBERS OF FIRM

Dean P. Sperling	K. William Pergande

For full biographical listings, see the Martindale-Hubbell Law Directory

SANTA MONICA, Los Angeles Co.

HAIGHT, BROWN & BONESTEEL (AV)

A Partnership including Professional Corporations
1620 26th Street, Suite 4000 North, P.O. Box 680, 90404
Telephone: 310-449-6000
Telecopier: 310-829-5117
Telex: 705837
Santa Ana, California Office: Suite 900, 5 Hutton Centre Drive.
Telephone: 714-754-1100.
Telecopier: 714-754-0826.
Riverside, California Office: 3750 University Avenue, Suite 650.
Telephone: 909-341-8300.
Fax: 909-341-8309.
San Francisco, California Office: 201 Sansome Street, Suite 300.
Telephone: 415-986-7700.
Fax: 415-986-6954.

MEMBERS OF FIRM

Fulton Haight (A Professional Corporation) (Retired)	Morton Rosen
	Theresa M. Marchlewski
Bruce A. Armstrong (A Professional Corporation)	William E. Ireland
	Tamara Equals Holmes

ASSOCIATE

Jon M. Kasimov

For Complete List of Firm Personnel, See General Section

For full biographical listings, see the Martindale-Hubbell Law Directory

O'NEILL, LYSAGHT & SUN (AV)

100 Wilshire Boulevard, Suite 700, 90401
Telephone: 310-451-5700
Telecopier: 310-399-7201

(See Next Column)

O'NEILL, LYSAGHT & SUN, *Santa Monica—Continued*

Brian O'Neill
Brian C. Lysaght
Frederick D. Friedman
Brian A. Sun

Yolanda Orozco
John M. Moscarino
Harriet Beegun Leva
Edward A. Klein

Robert L. Meylan

David E. Rosen
Ellyn S. Garofalo

Paul D. Murphy
Brian D. Hershman

OF COUNSEL

J. Joseph Connolly

Reference: Wells Fargo Bank, Santa Monica.

For full biographical listings, see the Martindale-Hubbell Law Directory

---

SANTA ROSA,* Sonoma Co.

BELDEN, ABBEY, WEITZENBERG & KELLY, A PROFESSIONAL CORPORATION (AV)

1105 North Dutton Avenue, P.O. Box 1566, 95402
Telephone: 707-542-5050
Telecopier: 707-542-2589

Richard W. Abbey

Timothy W. Hoffman

Peter J. Walls

Representative Clients: Exchange Bank of Santa Rosa; Westamerica Bank; North Bay Title Co.; Northwestern Title Security Co.; Geyser Peak Winery; Santa Rosa City School District; Sonoma National Bank; Arrowood Vineyards & Winery; Arthur & DeVincenzi Concrete; Friedman Bros. Hardware, Inc.

For Complete List of Firm Personnel, See General Section

For full biographical listings, see the Martindale-Hubbell Law Directory

---

TORRANCE, Los Angeles Co.

RONALD D. ELLIS (AV)

4302 Mesa Street, 90012
Telephone: 310-375-9978
Fax: 310-375-5997

For full biographical listings, see the Martindale-Hubbell Law Directory

---

COLORADO

BOULDER,* Boulder Co.

FRENCH & STONE, P.C. (AV)

720 Pearl Street, 80302
Telephone: 303-449-3891
Fax: 303-449-3992

Joseph C. French
Robert W. Stone

Gary S. Mallo
David M. Haynes

Mark M. Haynes

References: Bank One of Boulder; Boulder; Bank of Boulder.

For full biographical listings, see the Martindale-Hubbell Law Directory

---

COLORADO SPRINGS,* El Paso Co.

FLYNN MCKENNA WRIGHT & KARSH (AV)

limited liability company
Plaza of the Rockies 111 South Tejon, Suite 202, 80903
Telephone: 719-578-8444
Fax: 719-578-8836

James T. Flynn
R. Tim McKenna
Bruce M. Wright

Randolph M. Karsh
Brian T. Murphy
Michael C. Potarf

Representative Clients: Western National Bank of Colorado; Tour Ice National, Inc.; Colorado Springs Savings and Loan Association; Chase Manhattan Mortgage Corp.; Colorado Bank and Trust Company of La Junta; Merrill Lynch Credit Corporation.

For full biographical listings, see the Martindale-Hubbell Law Directory

---

DENVER,* Denver Co.

ALEXANDER & CRABTREE, P.C. (AV)

216 16th Street, Suite 1300, 80202-5127
Telephone: 303-825-7307
Fax: 303-825-3202
Email: halexand@alexcrab.com *URL:* http://www.alexcrab.com

(See Next Column)

Hugh Alexander

C. Scott Crabtree

Stephen Fitzsimmons

For full biographical listings, see the Martindale-Hubbell Law Directory

BALLARD SPAHR ANDREWS & INGERSOLL (AV)

Seventeenth Street Plaza Building, Suite 2300, 1225 17th Street, 80202-5596
Telephone: 303-292-2400
Fax: 303-296-3956
Philadelphia, Pennsylvania Office: 1735 Market Street, 51st Floor.
Telephone: 215-665-8500.
Fax: 215-864-8999.
Harrisburg, Pennsylvania Office: 105 North Front Street.
Telephone: 717-236-3333.
Fax: 717-236-3884.
Salt Lake City, Utah Office: One Utah Center, 201 South Main Street, Suite 1200.
Telephone: 801-531-3000.
Fax: 801-531-3001.
Washington, D.C. Office: Suite 900 East, 555 13th Street, N.W.
Telephone: 202-383-8800.
Fax: 202-383-8877; 383-8893.
Baltimore, Maryland Office: 300 East Lombard Street, 19th Floor.
Telephone: 410-528-5600.
Fax: 410-528-5650.
Camden, New Jersey Office: 800 Hudson Square, 5th Floor.
Telephone: 609-541-5577.
Fax: 609-541-8272.

Lyle B. Stewart

Scott W. Hardt
John E. Hayes, III

Darren R. Hensley
Alice Lim Rydberg

For Complete List of Firm Personnel, See General Section

For full biographical listings, see the Martindale-Hubbell Law Directory

---

BENNINGTON JOHNSON & REEVE, A PROFESSIONAL CORPORATION (AV)

2480 Republic Plaza, 370 17th Street, 80202
Telephone: 303-629-5200
Fax: 303-629-5718
Email: krbennington@bjrr.com

Kenneth R. Bennington

Philip E. Johnson

Thomas C. Reeve

SPECIAL COUNSEL

H. Robert Walsh, Jr.

Linda J. Swanson

Kathleen E. Craigmile

For full biographical listings, see the Martindale-Hubbell Law Directory

---

BIRGE & MAYERS, P.C. (AV)

1700 Broadway, Suite 1501, 80290
Telephone: 303-860-7100
Facsimile: 303-860-7338

Thomas D. Birge

Cathryn B. Mayers

Representative Clients: Dean Witter Reynolds, Inc.; Walnut Street Securities.

For full biographical listings, see the Martindale-Hubbell Law Directory

---

BURG & ELDREDGE, P.C. (AV)

P.O. Box 370385, 80237
Telephone: 303-779-5595
Fax: 303-779-0527
Albuquerque, New Mexico Office: 201 Third Street N.W., Suite 1500.
Telephone: 505-242-7020.
Fax: 505-242-7247.

Michael S. Burg
Peter W. Burg
Scott J. Eldredge
David P. Hersh
David M. Houliston

R. Hunter Ellington
Thomas W. Henderson
Janet R. Spies
Tom Van Buskirk
Matthew R. Giacomini

Kerry N. Jardine

Kieth Van Doren
Brendan O'Rourke Powers
Jack D. Robinson
Kirstin G. Lindberg
Bradley W. Howard (Resident, Albuquerque, New Mexico Office)
Matthew S. McElhiney

Christian C. Doherty (Resident, Albuquerque, New Mexico Office)
Rosemary Orsini
Robb A. Nelson
Matthew David Bailis
Christina C. Vigil (Resident, Albuquerque, New Mexico)

(See Next Column)

BURG & ELDREDGE P.C.—*Continued*

Holly S. Baer
James R. Brewster (Resident, Albuquerque, New Mexico Office)

Jonathon P. Brody
Brett Myer Perry

OF COUNSEL
Dale J. Coplan

Representative Clients: AT&T; Budget Rent-A-Car; Communications World International, Inc.; Coors Brewing Co.; CWE, Inc.; Del Webb Commercial Properties Corp.; Douglas Toyota; First Interstate Bank of Denver, N.A.; Independence Funding Company, LLC.; Safeway, Inc.

For full biographical listings, see the Martindale-Hubbell Law Directory

CARPENTER & KLATSKIN, P.C. (AV)

1500 Denver Club Building, 518 Seventeenth Street, 80202
Telephone: 303-534-6315
Telecopier: 303-534-0514

Willis V. Carpenter

Andrew S. Klatskin

Judith C. McNerny

Max A. Minnig, Jr.

LEGAL SUPPORT PERSONNEL
PARALEGAL
Holly S. Hoxeng

Reference: Colorado State Bank.

For full biographical listings, see the Martindale-Hubbell Law Directory

DUFFORD & BROWN, P.C. (AV)

1700 Broadway, Suite 1700, 80290-1701
Telephone: 303-861-8013
Facsimile: 303-832-3804
Affiliated Office: Solomon, Pearl, Blum & Quinn, L.L.P., New York, NY and Denver, Colorado.

Thomas G. Brown
Richard L. Fanyo

Randall J. Feuerstein
S. Kirk Ingebretsen
Edward D. White

OF COUNSEL
Morris B. Hecox, Jr.

Representative Clients: CF&I Steel, L.P.; The Colorado and Wyoming Railway Co.; GT Land Colorado Inc.; Hall and Hall Mortgage Corporation; Hewlett Packard Co.; Reorganized CF&I Steel Corp.

For Complete List of Firm Personnel, See General Section

For full biographical listings, see the Martindale-Hubbell Law Directory

GRUND & BRESLAU, P.C. (AV)

303 East Seventeenth Avenue, Suite 1030, 80203-1260
Telephone: 303-830-7770
Facsimile: 303-830-2313

John W. Grund
Brad W. Breslau

Della S. Nelson
Phillip Jeffrey Frazee

Representative Clients: Amoco Production Co.; Basic Capital Management, Inc.; Chevron U.S.A. Production Co.; Colorado Farm Bureau Mutual Insurance Co.; Figgie International, Inc.; Gallagher, Bassett Services, Inc.; McKesson Corp.

For full biographical listings, see the Martindale-Hubbell Law Directory

KARSH AND FULTON, PROFESSIONAL CORPORATION (AV)

Suite 710, 950 South Cherry Street, 80222
Telephone: 303-759-9669
Fax: 303-782-0902

Alan E. Karsh
Larry C. Fulton

Fred Gabler
J. Terry Wiggins
Seymour Joseph

Antonio T. Ciccarelli

Representative Clients: Commonwealth Land Title Insurance Co.; Lawyers Title Insurance Co.; TransNation Title Insurance Co.; Fidelity National Title Insurance Co.; Karsh and Hagan Advertising; Zeff Properties (Real Estate); CTL/Thompson, Inc. (Engineering); Sport-Haley, Inc. (sport clothing design and distribution); Old Republic National Title Insurance Company; Telecommunications, Inc.

For full biographical listings, see the Martindale-Hubbell Law Directory

MONTGOMERY LITTLE & McGREW, P.C. (AV)

The Quadrant, 5445 DTC Parkway, Suite 800 (Englewood), 80111
Telephone: 303-773-8100
Telecopier: 303-220-0412

(See Next Column)

James J. Soran, III
Michael H. Smith
Debra Piazza

Thomas C. Deline
Rebecca B. Givens
Joel A. Mayo

Representative Clients: Amoco Oil Co.; Bristol-Myers Squibb; Colorado Medical Society; Chrysler Corp.; Cyprus Minerals; Dillon Cos., Inc., d/b/a King Soopers; The St. Paul Insurance Cos.; University of Colorado Health Sciences Center.

For Complete List of Firm Personnel, See General Section

For full biographical listings, see the Martindale-Hubbell Law Directory

MYER, SWANSON, ADAMS & WOLF, P.C. (AV)

The Colorado State Bank Building, 1600 Broadway, Suite 1480, 80202-4915
Telephone: 303-866-9800
Facsimile: 303-866-9818

Rendle Myer
Allan B. Adams

Robert K. Swanson
Thomas J. Wolf

Philip T. Masterson
OF COUNSEL

Robert Swanson

Fred E. Neef (1910-1986)

Representative Clients: The Oppenheimer Funds; Daily Cash Accumulation Fund; The Centennial Trusts; Mile High Chapter of American Red Cross; Master Lease; Heartland Management Co.; Kan-Build of Colorado, Inc.
Reference: The Colorado State Bank of Denver.

For full biographical listings, see the Martindale-Hubbell Law Directory

NETZORG & McKEEVER, PROFESSIONAL CORPORATION (AV)

Republic Plaza, 370 Seventeenth Street, Suite 3590, 80202
Telephone: 303-892-7100
Fax: 303-446-0506

Gordon W. Netzorg
Cecil E. Morris, Jr.

Peter G. Koclanes
Joan M. Collopy

OF COUNSEL
J. Nicholas McKeever, Jr.

For full biographical listings, see the Martindale-Hubbell Law Directory

SENN LEWIS VISCIANO & STRAHLE, PROFESSIONAL CORPORATION (AV)

Suite 4300, 1801 California Street, 80202
Telephone: 303-298-1122
Telecopier: 303-296-9101

Mark A. Senn
Fredric J. Lewis

Wynn E. Strahle
Stephen W. Arent

David C. Camp

Margie J. Titus
Laura B. Redstone

OF COUNSEL
Lawrence A. Atler (P.C.)

SPECIAL COUNSEL
Ellen Kirschenbaum

For Complete List of Firm Personnel, See General Section

For full biographical listings, see the Martindale-Hubbell Law Directory

DURANGO,* La Plata Co.

FRANK J. ANESI (AV)

Suite 220, 835 East Second Avenue, P.O. Box 2185, 81302
Telephone: 970-247-9246
Fax: 970-259-2793

References: First National Bank of Durango; Burns Bank, Durango.

For full biographical listings, see the Martindale-Hubbell Law Directory

FORT COLLINS,* Larimer Co.

FISCHER, HOWARD & FRANCIS, LLP (AV)

125 South Howes, Suite 900, P.O. Box 506, 80522
Telephone: 970-482-4710
Fax: 970-482-4729

MEMBERS OF FIRM
Gene E. Fischer

Stephen E. Howard
Steven G. Francis

Approved Attorneys for: Attorney's Title Guaranty Fund, Inc.
Reference: First National Bank of Fort Collins, N.A.

For full biographical listings, see the Martindale-Hubbell Law Directory

CONNECTICUT

CHESHIRE, New Haven Co.

WINTERS & FORTE (AV)

Waverly Professional Park, 315 Highland Avenue, Suite 102, P.O. Box 844, 06410
Telephone: 203-272-2927
Fax: 203-271-1222

MEMBERS OF FIRM

David Wayne Winters   Michael C. Forte

A List of Representative Clients will be furnished upon request.
References: Bank of Boston, Connecticut; Centerbank; LaFayette American Bank & Trust Co.

For full biographical listings, see the Martindale-Hubbell Law Directory

GREENWICH, Fairfield Co.

IVEY, BARNUM & O'MARA, LLC (AV)

Meridian Building, 170 Mason Street, P.O. Box 1689, 06830
Telephone: 203-661-6000
Telecopier: 203-661-9462

MEMBERS OF FIRM

Michael J. Allen	Donat C. Marchand
Robert C. Barnum, Jr.	Miles F. McDonald, Jr.
Edward D. Cosden, Jr.	Edwin J. O'Mara, Jr.
Wilmot L. Harris, Jr.	Remy A. Rodas
William I. Haslun II	Gregory A. Saum
Michael J. Jones	Lorraine Slavin
Edward T. Krumeich, Jr.	Steven B. Steinmetz

ASSOCIATES

Paul G. Amicucci	Melissa Townsend Klauberg
Stephan B. Grozinger	Cristin L. Rothfuss
Juerg A. Heim	Alan S. Rubenstein
Jennifer B. Kallenbach	Sheryl L. Sensale
	(Not admitted in CT)

OF COUNSEL

James W. Cuminale	Jennifer D. Port
Philip R. McKnight	(Not admitted in CT)

For full biographical listings, see the Martindale-Hubbell Law Directory

HARTFORD,* Hartford Co.

GORDON, MUIR AND FOLEY (AV)

Hartford Square North, Ten Columbus Boulevard, 06106-5123
Telephone: 860-525-5361
Telecopier: 860-525-4849

MEMBERS OF FIRM

William S. Gordon, Jr.	William J. Gallitto
(1946-1956)	Gerald R. Swirsky
George Muir (1939-1976)	Robert J. O'Brien
Edward J. Foley (1955-1983)	Philip J. O'Connor
Peter C. Schwartz	Kenneth G. Williams
John J. Reid	Chester J. Bukowski
John H. Goodrich, Jr.	Mary Ann Santacroce
R. Bradley Wolfe	J. Lawrence Price
Jon Stephen Berk	Mary Anne Alicia Charron
James G. Kelly	

ASSOCIATES

Kevin F. Morin	Andrew J. Hern
Claudia A. Baio	Eileen McCarthy Geel
Patrick T. Treacy	Christopher L. Slack
Renee W. Dwyer	

OF COUNSEL

Stephen M. Riley

Reference: Fleet Bank.

For full biographical listings, see the Martindale-Hubbell Law Directory

SOROKIN SOROKIN GROSS HYDE & WILLIAMS P.C. (AV)

One Corporate Center, 06103
Telephone: 860-525-6645
Fax: 860-522-1781
Simsbury, Connecticut Office: 730 Hopmeadow Street.
Telephone: 860-651-9348.
Rocky Hill, Connecticut Office: 2360 Main Street.
Telephone: 860-563-9305.
Fax: 860-529-6931.

Andrew C. Glassman	Barry D. Greene
Clifford J. Grandjean	Paula G. Pressman
Amelia M. Rugland	

Jeffery P. Apuzzo

(See Next Column)

OF COUNSEL
Joseph D. Hurwitz

For Complete List of Firm Personnel, See General Section

For full biographical listings, see the Martindale-Hubbell Law Directory

NEW HAVEN,* New Haven Co.

BERGMAN, HOROWITZ & REYNOLDS, P.C. (AV)

157 Church Street, 19th Floor, P.O. Box 426, 06502
Telephone: 203-789-1320
Fax: 203-785-8127
Email: mailbox@taxlawyers.com *URL:* http://www.taxlawyers.com
New York, N.Y. Office: 499 Park Avenue, 26th Floor.
Telephone: 212-688-4150.

Melvin Ditman	Jeremy A. Mellitz
Richard M. Porter	Paul J. Stankewich

For full biographical listings, see the Martindale-Hubbell Law Directory

GORMAN & ENRIGHT P.C. (AV)

59 Elm Street, P.O. Box 1961, 06509
Telephone: 203-865-1382
Telecopier: 203-776-7250

John R. Gorman	Brian G. Enright

OF COUNSEL

Patricia King	Earle Giovanniello

References: Bank of New Haven; AT&T Capital Corp.; McGladrey & Pullen.

For full biographical listings, see the Martindale-Hubbell Law Directory

NEW LONDON, New London Co.

WALLER, SMITH & PALMER, P.C. (AV)

52 Eugene O'Neill Drive, P.O. Box 88, 06320
Telephone: 860-442-0367
Telecopier: 860-447-9915
Old Lyme, Connecticut Office: 103-A Halls Road.
Telephone: 860-434-8063.
Telecopier: 860-434-9452.

Birdsey G. Palmer (Retired)	Hughes Griffis
William W. Miner	Edward B. O'Connell
Robert P. Anderson, Jr.	Frederick B. Gahagan
Robert W. Marrion	Mary E. Driscoll
Tracy M. Collins	Valerie Ann Votto
David P. Condon	Charles C. Anderson

General Counsel For: Town of East Lyme; Town of Lebanon.
Counsel For: Citizens Savings Bank; Sonoco/Northeastern, Inc.; The Nature Conservancy; Fleet Bank.
Local Counsel For: McCue Mortgage Co.; Citicorp Mortgage; U.S. Department of Housing and Urban Development.

For Complete List of Firm Personnel, See General Section

For full biographical listings, see the Martindale-Hubbell Law Directory

STAMFORD, Fairfield Co.

WOFSEY, ROSEN, KWESKIN & KURIANSKY (AV)

600 Summer Street, 06901
Telephone: 203-327-2300
Fax: 203-967-9273

MEMBERS OF FIRM

Abraham Wofsey (1915-1944)	Edward M. Kweskin
Michael Wofsey (1927-1951)	David M. Cohen
David M. Rosen (1926-1967)	Marshall Goldberg
Julius B. Kuriansky (1910-1992)	Stephen A. Finn
Monroe Silverman	Judith Rosenberg
Emanuel Margolis	Mark H. Henderson
Howard C. Kaplan	Steven D. Grushkin
Anthony R. Lorenzo	Matthew J. Forstadt

OF COUNSEL

Saul Kwartin	Sydney C. Kweskin (Retired)

ASSOCIATES

Joseph Brachfeld	Eric M. Higgins
John J.L. Chobor	Valerie E. Maze
Steven M. Frederick	Randall M. Skigen
Joy A. Katz	Peter J. Schaffer
Galit Kierkut	Robert W. Finke

Representative Clients: Banque Paribas; Benenson Realty; Cellular Information Systems, Inc.; The Chase Manhattan Bank; First County Bank; Hartford Provision Co.; Louis Dreyfus Corp.; Norwalk Federation of Teachers; People's Bank; Ridgeway Shopping Center.

For full biographical listings, see the Martindale-Hubbell Law Directory

DELAWARE

WILMINGTON,* New Castle Co.

CONNOLLY, BOVE, LODGE & HUTZ (AV)

1220 Market Street, P.O. Box 2207, 19899-2207
Telephone: 302-658-9141
Telecopier: 302-658-5614
URL: http://WWW.CBLHLAW.COM

James M. Mulligan, Jr.	Charles J. Durante
Arthur G. Connolly, Jr.	F. L. Peter Stone
Henry E. Gallagher, Jr.	John C. Kairis
Richard David Levin	Arthur G. Connolly, III
Jeffrey B. Bove	James D. Heisman
Collins J. Seitz, Jr.	Anne Love Barnett

For Complete List of Firm Personnel, See General Section

For full biographical listings, see the Martindale-Hubbell Law Directory

SMITH, KATZENSTEIN & FURLOW (AV)

The Corporate Plaza, 800 Delaware Avenue, P.O. Box 410, 19899
Telephone: 302-652-8400
Fax: 302-652-8405

MEMBERS OF FIRM

Craig B. Smith	Anne E. Bookout
Stephen M. Miller	

Joanne M. Shalk

For Complete List of Firm Personnel, See General Section

For full biographical listings, see the Martindale-Hubbell Law Directory

DISTRICT OF COLUMBIA

WASHINGTON, D.C. Co.

* indicates certain Bar Register subscribers, in cities of comparable size and importance, who maintain an additional office in Washington, D.C. and who have arranged for representation as a part of the Washington, D.C. listings that follow

* BAKER & BOTTS, L.L.P. (AV)

A Registered Limited Liability Partnership
The Warner, 1299 Pennsylvania Avenue, N.W., 20004-2400
Telephone: 202-639-7700
Fax: 202-639-7832
Email: postmaster@bakerbotts.com
Houston, Texas Office: One Shell Plaza, 910 Louisiana.
Telephone: 713-229-1234.
Austin, Texas Office: 1600 San Jacinto Center, 98 San Jacinto Boulevard.
Telephone: 512-322-2500.
Dallas, Texas Office: 2001 Ross Avenue.
Telephone: 214-953-6500.
New York, New York Office: 599 Lexington Avenue.
Telephone: 212-705-5000.
Moscow, Russian Federation Office: 10 ul. Bolshaya Dmitrovka (formerly Pushkinskaya), 103031.
Telephone: 7095/921-5300 (Local); 7501/929-7070 (International).

MEMBERS OF FIRM

James R. Doty	David N. Powers
	Hugh Tucker

ASSOCIATES

Kevin B. Dent	Michael A. Gold

For Complete List of Firm Personnel, See General Section

For full biographical listings, see the Martindale-Hubbell Law Directory

DECKELBAUM OGENS & FISCHER, CHARTERED (AV)

1140 Connecticut Avenue, N.W., 20036
Telephone: 202-223-1474
Fax: 202-293-1471
Bethesda, Maryland Office: 6701 Democracy Boulevard.
Telephone: 301-564-5100.

Nelson Deckelbaum	Deborah E. Reiser
Ronald L. Ogens	Charles A. Moster
Lawrence H. Fischer	Andrew J. Shedlock, III

(See Next Column)

Ronald G. Scheraga	Phyllis Lea Bean
Bryn Hope Sherman	Darryl Alan Feldman
Thomas Peter Mann	(Not admitted in DC)
(Not admitted in DC)	

Representative Clients: The Charles E. Smith Companies; The Trammell Crow Co.
References: Franklin National Bank; Century National Bank.

For full biographical listings, see the Martindale-Hubbell Law Directory

KENNETH R. FEINBERG & ASSOCIATES (AV)

1120 20th Street, N.W. Suite 740 South, 20036
Telephone: 202-371-1110
Fax: 202-962-9290
New York, N.Y. Office: 780 3rd Avenue, Suite 2202.
Telephone: 212-527-9600.
Fax: 212-527-9611.

ASSOCIATES

Deborah E. Greenspan	Peter H. Woodin
Michael K. Rozen	(Not admitted in DC)
(Not admitted in DC)	M. Catherine Faint

OF COUNSEL

Jacqueline E. Zins

For full biographical listings, see the Martindale-Hubbell Law Directory

KROOTH & ALTMAN (AV)

Suite 400, 1850 M Street, N.W., 20036-5803
Telephone: 202-293-8200
Telecopier: 202-872-0145, 202-775-5872
Columbia, Maryland Office: 5401 Twin Knolls Road, Suite 7, 21045.
Telephone: 301-596-1140.
Sterling, Virginia Office: 45591 Shepard Drive, Suite 101J, 20164.
Telephone: 703-450-2755.

MEMBERS OF FIRM

David L. Krooth (1907-1978)	Daniel Randolph Cole, Jr.
Norman S. Altman (Retired)	Patrick J. Clancy
William S. Tennant	James F. Perna
William J. Delany	Harrison C. Smith
Donald F. Libretta	Mario Greszes
E. Joseph Knoll	David A. Barsky
Michael E. Mazer	John E. Vihstadt
Bonnie Hochman Rothell	

OF COUNSEL

Victor A. Altman	Michael J. Milton
J. Stephen Britt	Robert J. Siciliano

ASSOCIATES

Jon I. Opert	Stephen J. Krooth
Felicia M. Groner	(Not admitted in DC)

For full biographical listings, see the Martindale-Hubbell Law Directory

MARY A. MCREYNOLDS, P.C. (AV)

Suite 400, 888 Sixteenth Street, N.W., 20006
Telephone: 202-835-7455
Telecopier: 202-296-8791

Mary A. McReynolds

For full biographical listings, see the Martindale-Hubbell Law Directory

SHAWN, MANN & NIEDERMAYER, L.L.P. (AV)

1850 M Street, N.W., Suite 280, 20036-5803
Telephone: 202-331-7900
Fax: 202-331-0726
Washington, D.C., Government Affairs Office: 499 S. Capitol Street, S.W., Suite 420.
Telephone: 202-842-3000.
Fax: 202-547-7161.
Los Angeles, California Office: 2029 Century Park East, Suite 1690.
Telephone: 310-553-8065.
Fax: 310-557-0729.
San Diego, California Office: 401 West "A" Street, Suite 1850.
Telephone: 619-236-0303.
Fax: 619-238-8181.
San Francisco, California Office: The Fox Plaza, 1390 Market Street, Suite 1204.
Telephone: 415-982-0150.
Fax: 415-522-0513.
Bloomington, Minnesota Office: 2090 West 98th Street.
Telephone: 612-881-6577.
Fax: 612-881-6894.

MEMBERS OF FIRM

William H. Shawn	Roy I. Niedermayer
Kim D. Mann	Joseph L. Steinfeld, Jr.

For full biographical listings, see the Martindale-Hubbell Law Directory

Washington—Continued

STEPTOE & JOHNSON LLP (AV)

1330 Connecticut Avenue, N.W., 20036
Telephone: 202-429-3000
Cable Address: "Stepjohn"
Telex: 89-2503
Telecopier: 202-429-3902
Email: wbatterton@steptoe.com *URL:* http://www.steptoe.com
Phoenix, Arizona Office: Two Renaissance Square, 40 N. Central Avenue, Suite 2400, 85004.
Telephone: 602-257-5200.
Moscow, Russia Office: Steptoe & Johnson International AOZT. 25 Tsvetnoy Boulevard, Building 3 Moscow, Russia 103051.
Telephone: 011-7-501-258-5250.
Fax: 011-7-501-258-5251.
Almaty, Kazakhstan Office: Steptoe & Johnson Company Almaty. 84 Gogol Street, Suite 213, 480083.
Telephones: (3272) 50-11-25, (3272) 32-25-39.

MEMBERS

Calvin H. Cobb, Jr.	Olin L. Wethington
Robert E. McLaughlin	Maureen O'Keefe Ward
Sarah C. Carey	Walter H. White, Jr.
Terence P. Quinn	(Moscow, Russia Office)
John T. Collins	Erik L. Kitchen
Ellen d'Alelio	Scott H. Katzman
Filiberto Agusti	Arthur Randolph Bregman

For Complete List of Firm Personnel, See General Section

For full biographical listings, see the Martindale-Hubbell Law Directory

* VENABLE ATTORNEYS AT LAW VENABLE, BAETJER, HOWARD & CIVILETTI, LLP (AV)

A Partnership including Professional Corporations
Suite 1000, 1201 New York Avenue, N.W., 20005
Telephone: 202-962-4800
Fax: 202-962-8300
Baltimore, Maryland Office: Venable, Baetjer and Howard LLP, 1800 Mercantile Bank & Trust Building, 2 Hopkins Plaza.
Telephone: 410-244-7400.
McLean, Virginia Office: Venable, Baetjer and Howard LLP, Suite 400, 2010 Corporate Ridge.
Telephone: 703-760-1600.
Rockville, Maryland Office: Venable, Baetjer and Howard LLP, Suite 500, One Church Street, P. O. Box 1906.
Telephone: 301-217-5600.
Towson, Maryland Office: Venable, Baetjer and Howard LLP, 210 Allegheny Avenue, P. O. Box 5517.
Telephone: 410-494-6200.

MEMBERS OF FIRM

Benjamin R. Civiletti (P.C.) (Also at Baltimore and Towson, Maryland Offices)	James R. Myers
	Jeffrey A. Dunn (Also at Baltimore, Maryland Office)
Neal D. Borden (Not admitted in DC; Also at Baltimore, Maryland Office)	George F. Pappas (Also at Baltimore, Maryland Office)
	William D. Coston
Douglas D. Connah, Jr. (P.C.) (Also at Baltimore, Maryland Office)	Kenneth S. Slaughter
	James L. Shea (Not admitted in DC; also at Baltimore, Maryland Office)
Joe A. Shull	
Kenneth C. Bass, III (Also at McLean, Virginia Office)	Amy Berman Jackson
	William D. Quarles (Also at Towson, Maryland Office)
Edward F. Glynn, Jr.	
Michael Schatzow (Also at Baltimore, Maryland Office)	James A. Dunbar (Also at Baltimore, Maryland Office)
Bryson L. Cook (P.C.) (Not admitted in DC; Also at Baltimore, Maryland Office)	Robert J. Bolger, Jr. (Not admitted in DC; Also at Baltimore, Maryland Office)
James K. Archibald (Also at Baltimore, Maryland Office)	Bruce H. Jurist (Also at Baltimore, Maryland Office)

Gary M. Hnath

OF COUNSEL

Charles R. Marvin, Jr.

ASSOCIATES

David W. Goewey	Vicki Margolis (Also at Baltimore, Maryland Office)
Fernand A. Lavallee	

For Complete List of Firm Personnel, See General Section

For full biographical listings, see the Martindale-Hubbell Law Directory

VERNER, LIIPFERT, BERNHARD, MCPHERSON AND HAND, CHARTERED (AV)

901 15th Street, N.W., 20005-2301
Telephone: 202-371-6000
Cable Address: "Verlip"
Telex: 1561792 VERLIP UT
Fax: 202-371-6279
Email: verner.com
McLean, Virginia Office: Sixth Floor, 8280 Greensboro Drive, 22102.
Telephone: 703-749-6000.
Fax: 703-749-6027.
Houston, Texas Office: 2600 Texas Commerce Tower, 600 Travis, 77002.
Telephone: 713-237-9034.
Fax: 713-237-1216.
Honolulu, Hawaii Office: Hawaii Times Building, 928 Nuuanu Avenue, Suite 400, 96817.
Telephone: 808-566-0999.
Fax: 808-566-0995.
Austin, Texas Office: Suite 1440 San Jacinto Center, 98 San Jacinto Boulevard, 78701.
Telephone: 512-703-6000.
Fax: 512-703-6003.

Douglas Ochs Adler	Martin Mendelsohn
Berl Bernhard	Lenard M. Parkins (Resident, Houston, Texas Office)
Roy G. Bowman	
Steven A. Buxbaum (Resident, Houston, Texas Office)	William F. Roeder, Jr.
	Frederick J. Tansill
Lawrence N. Cooper	Susan O'Hearn Temkin
Hopewell H. Darneille, III	John D. Waihee, III (Resident, Honolulu, Hawaii Office)
Harold I. Freilich	
Lloyd N. Hand	Buel White
Lawrence E. Levinson (Not admitted in DC)	

SPECIAL COUNSEL

George J. Mitchell

SENIOR COUNSEL

Alvaro Cifuentes de Castro (Not admitted in DC)

OF COUNSEL

Howell E. Begle, Jr.	Frederick J. McConville
David M. Davenport	Francis X. Mellon
Philip R. Hochberg	Mikol S. B. Neilson
James K. Jackson	Renton L. K. Nip (Resident, Honolulu, Hawaii Office)

For Complete List of Firm Personnel, See General Section

For full biographical listings, see the Martindale-Hubbell Law Directory

WATT, TIEDER & HOFFAR, L.L.P. (AV)

601 Pennsylvania Avenue, N.W., Suite 900, 20004
Telephone: 202-462-4697
Telecopier: 703-893-8029
McLean Virginia Office: 7929 Westpark Drive, Suite 400,
Telephone: 703-749-1000.
Telecopier: 703-893-8029.
Irvine California Office: 3 Park Plaza, Suite 1530.
Telephone: 714-852-6700.

MEMBERS OF FIRM

John B. Tieder, Jr.	Robert K. Cox
David C. Romm	

For full biographical listings, see the Martindale-Hubbell Law Directory

FLORIDA

AVENTURA, Dade Co.

BUCHANAN INGERSOLL, PROFESSIONAL CORPORATION (AV©)

One Turnberry Place, 19495 Biscayne Boulevard, Suite 606, 33180
Telephone: 305-933-5600
Telecopier: 305-933-2350
URL: http://www.bipc.com
Pittsburgh, Pennsylvania Office: One Oxford Centre, 301 Grant Street, 20th Floor.
Telephone: 412-562-8800.
Philadelphia, Pennsylvania Office: Two Logan Square, Twelfth Floor, 18th & Arch Streets.
Telephone: 215-665-8700.
Harrisburg, Pennsylvania Office: 30 North Third Street.
Telephone: 717-237-4800.
Miami, Florida Office: NationsBank Tower, 100 S.E. Second Street.
Telephone: 305-347-4080.
Tampa, Florida Office: Suite 2500, 401 East Jackson Street.
Telephone: 813-222-8180.
Princeton, New Jersey Office: Buchanan Ingersoll, A Partnership, College Centre, 500 College Road East.
Telephone: 609-987-6800.
Lexington, Kentucky Office: Suite 600, PNC Bank Plaza, 200 West Vine Street.
Telephone: 606-225-5333.

(See Next Column)

BUCHANAN INGERSOLL PROFESSIONAL CORPORATION—*Continued*

Buffalo, New York Office: 1100 Main Place Tower, 350 Main Street.
Telephone: 716-854-4100.
Fax: 816-854-4227.

Joshua L. Dubin   Mark J. Neuberger
SENIOR ATTORNEY
Ralph B. Bekkevold

Todd A. Bancroft   Randi S. Rothfield
Kevin Carmichael   Richard N. Schermer
Jeffrey M. Goodz   Rebecca S. Trinkler

For full biographical listings, see the Martindale-Hubbell Law Directory

---

BOCA RATON, Palm Beach Co.

WEISS & HANDLER, P.A. (AV)

Suite 218A, One Boca Place, 2255 Glades Road, 33431-7313
Telephone: 407-997-9995
Broward: 954-421-5101
Palm Beach: 407-734-8008
Telecopier: 407-997-5280

Howard I. Weiss   Henry B. Handler

Donald Feldman   Marissa I. Laakso
David K. Friedman   Mark R. Osherow
Carol A. Kartagener   Howard M. Rudolph (Resident,
                             West Palm Beach Office)
OF COUNSEL
Malcolm L. Stein   Stanley E. Preiser
  (Not admitted in FL)   (Not admitted in FL)
Raoul Lionel Felder
  (Not admitted in FL)

For full biographical listings, see the Martindale-Hubbell Law Directory

---

BRADENTON,* Manatee Co.

HARLLEE, PORGES, HAMLIN, KNOWLES, BALD & PROUTY, P.A. (AV)

1205 Manatee Avenue, West, 34205
Telephone: 941-748-3770
Telecopier: 941-748-4160
Email: Law@HarlleePorges.com

John P. Harllee, III   Kimberly Alario Bald
Gregory J. Porges   Steven W. Prouty
Curtis D. Hamlin   Mark A. Nelson
Timothy A. Knowles   Stephen W. Thompson

Joseph L. Najmy   Barrett S. Bell
            Shelly A. Gallagher

For full biographical listings, see the Martindale-Hubbell Law Directory

MCGUIRE, PRATT, MASIO & FARRANCE, P.A. (AV)

Suite 600, 1001 3rd Avenue West, P.O. Box 1866, 34206
Telephone: 941-748-7076
Fax: 941-747-9774

Hugh E. McGuire, Jr.   Carol A. Masio
Charles J. Pratt, Jr.   Robert A. Farrance
            John W. Kaklis
OF COUNSEL
            Carter H. Parry

Reference: Barnett Bank of Manatee County.

For full biographical listings, see the Martindale-Hubbell Law Directory

---

FORT LAUDERDALE,* Broward Co.

DEUSCHLE AND ASSOCIATES, P.A. (AV)

800 Southeast Third Avenue, Suite 500, 33316
Telephone: 954-763-7200
Facsimile: 954-522-7728

            Brian C. Deuschle

            Christopher D. Hale

Representative Clients: Drexel Investments, Inc.; Seabulk Tankers, Ltd.; Seabulk Chemical Carriers, Inc.; Hvide Shipping, Inc.; Eller & Company; American National Bank.
Approved Attorneys for: Attorneys' Title Insurance Fund; American National Bank; Norwest Mortgage, Inc.

For full biographical listings, see the Martindale-Hubbell Law Directory

DOUMAR, CURTIS, CROSS, LAYSTROM & PERLOFF (AV)

A Partnership of Professional Corporations
1177 Southeast Third Avenue, 33316
Telephone: 954-525-3441
Fax: 954-525-3423
Direct Miami Line: 305-945-3172

MEMBERS OF FIRM
Raymond A. Doumar (P.C.)   John W. Perloff (P.C.)
Charles L. Curtis (P.C.)   E. Scott Allsworth (P.C.)
William S. Cross (P.C.)   John D. Voigt (P.C.)
C. William Laystrom, Jr. (P.C.) Jeffrey S. Wachs (P.C.)
            Mark E. Allsworth

Representative Clients: Albertson's, Inc.; Robinson-Humphrey/American Express; Deutsch-Ireland Properties; Massey-Yardley Chrysler Plymouth, Inc.; Waste Management, Inc.; Planned Development Corp.; Toys-R-Us Inc.; Lumbermans Mutual Casualty Co.; Melvin Simon and Associates.

For Complete List of Firm Personnel, See General Section

For full biographical listings, see the Martindale-Hubbell Law Directory

LAW PRACTICE OF J.B. GROSSMAN, P.A. (AV)

2300 East Las Olas Boulevard Fourth Floor, 33301
Telephone: 954-767-3345
Fax: 954-767-3347

J.B. Grossman   Kenneth J. Dunn
Gary Arnold Feder   Blaine H. Hibberd
LEGAL SUPPORT PERSONNEL
            Scott L. Lampert

For full biographical listings, see the Martindale-Hubbell Law Directory

MCGEE, GAINEY & HUSKEY, P.A. (AV)

2455 East Sunrise Boulevard, Penthouse West, 33304
Telephone: 954-563-8200
Fax: 954-566-7754

C. Edward McGee, Jr.   J. David Huskey, Jr.
James P. Gainey   Patricia J. Small

For full biographical listings, see the Martindale-Hubbell Law Directory

MOMBACH, BOYLE & HARDIN, P.A. (AV)

Suite 1950 Broward Financial Centre, 500 East Broward
  Boulevard, 33394-3079
Telephone: 954-467-2200
Telecopier: 954-467-2210

Geoffrey S. Mombach   David C. Hardin
Conrad J. Boyle   Gary S. Singer
            Mitchell D. Adler

Dean A. Brooks   Mark R. Wysocki

Representative Clients: BankAtlantic; Citibank, F.S.B.; Shenandoah Life; National Bank of Canada; NationsBank N.A., (South); SunTrust Bank, South Florida, N.A.; Keenan Development Group; Net Realty Holding Trust; Original Pancake House Restaurants; Cat Cay Yacht Club.

For full biographical listings, see the Martindale-Hubbell Law Directory

MOSKOWITZ, MANDELL & SALIM, P.A. (AV)

Suite 510, 800 Corporate Drive, 33334
Telephone: 954-491-2000; Boca Raton Line: 407-750-7700
FAX: 954-491-2051

Michael W. Moskowitz   Craig J. Mandell
            William G. Salim, Jr.

Greg H. Rosenthal   Scott M. Zaslav
OF COUNSEL
Shirley D. Weisman (P.A.) Monica I. Salis (P.A.)

            Deborah Ann Byles

Representative Clients: Arby's Inc.; BP Oil Co.; Broward Marine, Inc.; Cardinal Atlantic Corp.; Cheney Brothers, Inc.; The Hertz Corp.; Holland Builders, Inc.; Humana, Inc.; Integrated Health Services, Inc.; UDC Homes.

For full biographical listings, see the Martindale-Hubbell Law Directory

OPPENHEIM & PILELSKY, P.A. (AV)

1290 Weston Road, Suite 300, 33326
Telephone: 954-384-6114
Toll Free: 888-384-6114
Fax: 954-384-6115
Email: O&P@oppenheim.com *URL:* http://www.oppenheim.com

Roy D. Oppenheim   Ellen B. Pilelsky

            Monica B. Cunill

Representative Clients: Circle Laboratories, Inc.; Bodwin Ltd.; Intelihomes Development, Inc.; Landmark Building & Design, Inc.; Danro Homes, Inc.; Weston Title & Escrow, Inc.; London & Leeds; Danal Homes Development, Inc.; Seapower Consortium.

For full biographical listings, see the Martindale-Hubbell Law Directory

FORT MYERS, * Lee Co.

PATRICK E. GERAGHTY A PROFESSIONAL ASSOCIATION (AV)

The Courtney Building, Suite 100, 2069 First Street, P.O. Box 1605, 33902-1605
Telephone: 941-334-9500
Fax: 941-334-8930

Patrick E. Geraghty   Thomas M. Dougherty

For full biographical listings, see the Martindale-Hubbell Law Directory

GOLDBERG, GOLDSTEIN & BUCKLEY, P.A. (AV)

1515 Broadway, P.O. Box 2366, 33901-2366
Telephone: 941-334-1146
Fax: 941-334-3039
Naples, Florida Office: 2150 Goodlette Road, Suite 105, Parkway Financial Center, 34102.
Telephone: 941-262-4888.
Fax: 941-262-8716.
Port Charlotte, Florida Office: Emerald Square, Suite 1, 2852 Tamiami Trail, 33952.
Telephone: 941-624-2393.
Fax: 941-624-2155.
Cape Coral, Florida Office: 1603 Hancock Bridge Parkway, 33990.
Telephone: 941-574-5575.
Fax: 941-574-9213.
Lehigh Acres, Florida Office: 1458 Lee Boulevard, Lee Boulevard Shopping Center, 33936.
Telephone: 941-368-6101.
Fax: 941-368-2461.
South Fort Myers, Florida Office: Horizon Plaza, 16050 South Tamiami Trail, Suite 101, 33908.
Telephone: 941-433-6777.
Fax: 941-433-0578.
Bonita Springs, Florida Office: 3431 Bonita Beach Road, Suite 208, 34134.
Telephone: 941-495-0003.
Fax: 941-495-0564.

Ray Goldstein	George J. Mitar
Stephen W. Buckley	Michael J. Ciccarone
Harvey B. Goldberg	Jay Cooper
John B. Cechman	Jonathan D. Conant
J. Jeffrey Rice	Raymond L. Racila
Richard Lee Purtz	Luis E. Insignares
Martin G. Arnowitz	Scot D. Goldberg

Approved Attorneys for: Attorneys' Title Insurance Fund.

For full biographical listings, see the Martindale-Hubbell Law Directory

SMOOT ADAMS EDWARDS & GREEN, P.A. (AV)

One University Park Suite 600, 12800 University Drive, P.O. Box 60259, 33906-6259
Telephone: 941-489-1776
(800) 226-1777 (in Florida)
Fax: 941-489-2444
Email: 71600.2745@compuserve.com

J. Tom Smoot, Jr.	Bruce D. Green
Hal Adams	Steven I. Winer
Franklyn A. (Chip) Johnson (1947-1991)	Mark R. Komray
	Clayton W. Crevasse
Charles B. Edwards	M. Brian Cheffer

Robert S. Forman	C. Berk Edwards, Jr.
Kathleen W. McBride	Melville G. Brinson, III
Lowell Schoenfeld	Samuel J. Hagan, IV.

For full biographical listings, see the Martindale-Hubbell Law Directory

JACKSONVILLE, * Duval Co.

KIRSCHNER, MAIN, GRAHAM, TANNER & DEMONT, PROFESSIONAL ASSOCIATION (AV)

One Independent Drive, Suite 2000, P.O. Box 1559, 32201-1559
Telephone: 904-354-4141
Telecopier: 904-358-2199

Barry C. Averitt	Kenneth M. Kirschner
Babette L. Fletcher	James L. Main
T. Malcolm Graham	John T. Rogerson, III
Lee Stathis Haramis	Michael G. Tanner

Howard L. Alford	Judy Ossi Marko
Robin C. Barco	Charles S. McCall
John F. Germany, Jr.	Beth E. Weitzman
Eric S. Kolar	(Not admitted in FL)

OF COUNSEL

Michael E. Demont	Wyman R. Duggan
G. Stephen Manning	Reese J. Henderson, Jr.

Representative Clients: The Maryland Insurance Group; NationsBank; The Suddath Cos.; Wickes Lumber Co.; BFI, Inc.

For full biographical listings, see the Martindale-Hubbell Law Directory

KISSIMMEE, * Osceola Co.

POHL & SHORT, P.A.

(See Winter Park)

MIAMI, * Dade Co.

CARLSON & BALES, A PROFESSIONAL ASSOCIATION (AV)

First Union Financial Center, 200 South Biscayne Boulevard, Suite 2770, 33131
Telephone: 305-372-9700
Fax: 305-372-8265

Curtis Carlson	Julie Anne Moxley
Richard M. Bales, Jr.	Ronald J. Lewittes

OF COUNSEL

Mara Beth Sommers

For full biographical listings, see the Martindale-Hubbell Law Directory

CLARKE SILVERGLATE WILLIAMS & MONTGOMERY (AV)

A Partnership of Professional Corporations
100 North Biscayne Boulevard Suite 2401, 33132
Telephone: 305-377-0700
Facsimile: 305-377-3001
Chicago, Illinois Office: Williams & Montgomery, Ltd., 20 North Wacker Drive, Suite 2100.
Telephone: 312-443-3200.
Telex: 206598.
Facsimile: 312-443-1323.
Waukegan, Illinois Office: Williams & Montgomery, Ltd., 33 North County Street.
Telephone: 847-360-1220.
Wheaton, Illinois Office: Williams & Montgomery, Ltd., 310 S. County Farm Road.
Telephone: 708-690-3200.
Joliet, Illinois Office: Williams & Montgomery, Ltd., 81 North Chicago Avenue.
Telephone: 815-727-2653.

Mercer K. Clarke   Spencer H. Silverglate

OF COUNSEL

Henry H. Bolz, III

ASSOCIATES

Kelly Anne Luther	Eric L. Lundt
William C. Abruzzo	Carol A. Grant

For full biographical listings, see the Martindale-Hubbell Law Directory

COLSON, HICKS, EIDSON, COLSON & MATTHEWS (AV)

Floor 47 First Union Financial Center, 200 South Biscayne Boulevard, 33131-2351
Telephone: 305-373-5400

MEMBERS OF FIRM

Bill Colson	Tony Korvick
William M. Hicks	Enid Duany Mendoza
Mike Eidson	Newton P. Porter
Dean C. Colson	Julie Braman Kane
Joseph M. Matthews	Robb D. Steinberg
	Brian Scott Yablonski

Reference: Northern Trust Bank of Florida.

For full biographical listings, see the Martindale-Hubbell Law Directory

ANDREW HALL AND ASSOCIATES, P.A. (AV)

Penthouse, 1428 Brickell Avenue, 33131
Telephone: 305-374-5030
Fax: 305-374-5033

Andrew C. Hall

Christopher M. David	William H. Strop
Christopher J. Dawes	Allan A. Joseph
	Douglas M. Horn

For full biographical listings, see the Martindale-Hubbell Law Directory

SIEGFRIED, RIVERA, LERNER DE LA TORRE & SOBEL, P.A. (AV)

Suite 1102, 201 Alhambra Circle (Coral Gables), 33134
Telephone: 305-442-3334
Fax: 305-443-3292

Steven M. Siegfried	Helio De La Torre
Oscar R. Rivera	Peter H. Edwards
Lisa A. Lerner	Stuart H. Sobel

(See Next Column)

SIEGFRIED, RIVERA, LERNER DE LA TORRE & SOBEL P.A.—*Continued*

Maria Victoria Arias	Elisabeth D. Kozlow
Gracian Celaya	Paul J. Layne
James F. Harrington	Samuel A. Persaud

Adrienne F. Promoff
OF COUNSEL
H. Hugh Mc Connell

For full biographical listings, see the Martindale-Hubbell Law Directory

VALLE & CRAIG, P.A. (AV)

Suite 2520 World Trade Center, 80 Southwest Eighth Street, P.O. Box 113009, 33111-3009
Telephone: 305-373-2888; 1800-609-6151
Facsimile: 305-373-2889

Laurence F. Valle	Lawrance B. Craig, III

Timothy Maze Hartley

Frank J. Sioli, Jr.	Nicole F. Ehart

Michael J. Lynott

For full biographical listings, see the Martindale-Hubbell Law Directory

JEFFREY S. WEINER, ATTORNEYS AT LAW, P.A. (AV)

Two Datran Center, Suite 1910, 9130 South Dadeland Boulevard, 33156-7858
Telephone: 305-670-9919
Fax: 305-670-9299
Email: JSWeiner@aol.com
Email: 76440.644@compuserve.com
Boca Raton, Florida Office: Mizner Park. 327 Plaza Real, Suite 215, 33432.

Jeffrey S. Weiner

Mycki L. Ratzan

For full biographical listings, see the Martindale-Hubbell Law Directory

ZACK, SPARBER, KOSNITZKY, SPRATT & BROOKS, P.A. (AV)

International Place, 100 Southeast Second Street, Suite 2800, 33131-2144
Telephone: 305-539-8400
Facsimile: 305-539-1307

Byron L. Sparber	Deborah R. Mayo
Michael Kosnitzky	Nancy E. McCarthy
Marc H. Auerbach	Roland Sanchez-Medina, Jr.
Jorge A. Gonzalez	Heileen Sosa
Debra Weiss Goodstone	Jay A. Steinman

Thomas O. Wells

For Complete List of Firm Personnel, See General Section

For full biographical listings, see the Martindale-Hubbell Law Directory

NAPLES,* Collier Co.

EMERSON & EMERSON, P.A. (AV)

The Aragon Building, 385 Thirteenth Avenue South, 34201
Telephone: 941-261-5200
Telecopier: 941-261-5201

John W. Emerson	Ralph W. Emerson (1932-1989)

Representative Clients: Krehling Industries, Inc.; E-Squared; Chemical Technologys International, Inc.

For full biographical listings, see the Martindale-Hubbell Law Directory

ORLANDO,* Orange Co.

MORAN & SHAMS, P.A. (AV)

111 North Orange Avenue, Suite 1200, P.O. Box 472, 32802-0472
Telephone: 407-841-4141
Fax: 407-841-4148
Email: moran-shams@moran-shams.com

Thomas P. Moran	Robert S. MacDonald
Maurice Shams	Christopher C. Skambis

Representative Clients: Adventist Health System Sunbelt Healthcare Corporation; China Group, Inc.; Florida Hospital; Gencor Industries Inc.; Kvaerner Trafalgar House Construction Co.; Manpower of Cedar Rapids and Central Florida; Medical Artificial Intelligence Inc.; Presbyterian Retirement Communities, Inc.; U.S. Foodservice, Inc.; Vermont American Corporation.

For full biographical listings, see the Martindale-Hubbell Law Directory

O'NEILL, CHAPIN, MARKS, LIEBMAN, COOPER & CARR (AV)

A Partnership including Professional Associations
865 Eola Park Center, 200 East Robinson Street, 32801
Telephone: 407-425-2751
Telex: 407-423-1192

Bernard C. O'Neill, Jr. (P.A.)	John B. Liebman (P.A.)
Bruce E. Chapin (P.A.)	Mark O. Cooper (P.A.)
Robert O. Marks (P.A.)	George E. Carr (P.A.)

ASSOCIATE
Rod C. Lundy

Reference: First Union National Bank.

For full biographical listings, see the Martindale-Hubbell Law Directory

POHL & SHORT, P.A.

(See Winter Park)

SHEPARD, FILBURN & GOODBLATT, P.A. (AV)

First Union Tower, Suite 1107, 20 North Orange Avenue, 32801
Telephone: 407-481-2020
Fax: 407-481-0208
Email: sf2law@aol.com

Clifford B. Shepard, III	Jenna R. Rinehart
Mark C. Filburn	Michael J. Kirwin
Amy E. Goodblatt	(Not admitted in FL)

Representative Clients: Chernoff Silver & Associates; Sovereign Bank; Cintas Corporation; Intercargo Insurance Company; Trade Insurance Services, Inc.; Danella Construction Company; Adventist Health Systems, Inc.; Hersh National Painting & Roofing Company; Team America, Inc.; Sysco Food Services, Inc.

For full biographical listings, see the Martindale-Hubbell Law Directory

ST. PETERSBURG, Pinellas Co.

SKIPPER & DAY (AV)

2600 Ninth Street North Suite 500, 33704
Telephone: 813-821-2889
Fax: 813-823-7478

Chester L. Skipper	John W. Day

Jesse L. Skipper
LEGAL SUPPORT PERSONNEL
Myrna A. Ballard (Legal Assistant)

Representative Clients: N.C.A. Systems, Inc.; Ryder Truck Lines, Inc.; City of Tampa.
Insurance Clients: American Indemnity Co.; Commercial Union Insurance Group; Fireman's Fund American Insurance Co.; Gulf Insurance Co.; Prudential Insurance Co.; Colonial Penn Insurance Co.

For full biographical listings, see the Martindale-Hubbell Law Directory

SARASOTA,* Sarasota Co.

MATTHEWS, HUTTON & EASTMOORE (AV)

Suite 500, 1777 Main Street, P.O. Box 49377, 34230-6377
Telephone: 941-366-8888
Fax: 941-954-7777

MEMBERS OF FIRM
A. Lamar Matthews, Jr.	Jeanne S. Medawar
Steven D. Hutton	Arthur S. Hardy
Theodore C. Eastmoore	Martin Garcia

ASSOCIATE
Edward K. DuBose

For full biographical listings, see the Martindale-Hubbell Law Directory

NELSON ● HESSE (AV)

2070 Ringling Boulevard, P.O. Box 2524, 34230
Telephone: 941-366-7550
Fax: 941-955-3708

MEMBERS OF FIRM
Richard E. Nelson	Omer S. Causey
Ronald Alexander Cyril	William A. Dooley
(1938-1988)	Michael S. Drews
Richard L. Smith	Frederick J. Elbrecht
F. Steven Herb	Gary W. Peal

ASSOCIATES
Philip Sypula	J. Neal Mobley

Stephen M. Walker

General Counsel for: Enterprise National Bank; Dooley Mack Construction Co.
Representative Clients: Wellcraft Marine; Attorneys Title Insurance Fund; Travelers Insurance; SMH Radiology, Inc.; The Carlton Ranch, Inc.
References: Southtrust Bank; Enterprise National Bank.

For full biographical listings, see the Martindale-Hubbell Law Directory

*STUART,** Martin Co.

McCARTHY, SUMMERS, BOBKO, McKEY, WOOD & SAWYER, P.A. (AV)

2081 East Ocean Boulevard, Suite 2-A, 34996
Telephone: 561-286-1700
Fax: 561-283-1803
Email: mcsumm@gate.net *URL:* http://www.gate.net/~mcsumm/

Terence P. McCarthy	John D. McKey, Jr.
Robert P. Summers	Steven J. Wood
Noel A. Bobko	Thomas R. Sawyer

Representative Clients: American Bank of Martin County; First National Bank and Trust Company of the Treasure Coast; Great Western Bank; Hydratech Utilities; Lost Lake at Hobe Sound; Taylor Creek Marina, Inc.; GBS Excavating, Inc.; Seaboard Savings Bank; Gary Player Design Group.

For full biographical listings, see the Martindale-Hubbell Law Directory

---

*TAMPA,** Hillsborough Co.

MORRISON, MORRISON & MILLS, P.A. (AV)

1200 West Platt Street Suite 100, 33606
Telephone: 813-258-3311
Telecopier: 813-258-3209

Thomas K. Morrison	Frederick J. Mills
Susan B. Morrison	James E. Holmes, Jr.

Representative Clients: SouthTrust Bank of West Florida; SouthTrust Bank of Alabama, National Association; NationsBank of Florida, N.A.; Mercantile Bank; Barnett Banks, Inc.; Southern Commerce Bank; Sun Bank of Pasco County; Hillsborough County Industrial Development Authority; Automation Packaging, Inc.; Medical Data Management, Inc.

For full biographical listings, see the Martindale-Hubbell Law Directory

---

RYDBERG & GOLDSTEIN, P.A. (AV)

Suite 200, 500 East Kennedy Boulevard, 33602
Telephone: 813-229-3900
Telecopier: 813-229-6101

Marsha Griffin Rydberg	Bruce S. Goldstein

Peter Baker	Tammy N. Giroux
Brian T. FitzGerald	Cynthia L. Bulan
Susan Greco Tuttle	

For full biographical listings, see the Martindale-Hubbell Law Directory

---

SMITH, WILLIAMS & HUMPHRIES, P.A. (AV)

Old Hyde Park, 712 South Oregon Avenue, 33606
Telephone: 813-253-5400
Fax: 813-254-3459
Orlando, Florida Office: Southeast Bank Building, Suite 701, 201 East Pine Street.
Telephone: 407-849-5151.
Fax: 407-843-4076.

David Lisle Smith	Robert L. Harding
Gregory L. Williams	(Resident, Orlando Office)
J. Gregory Humphries	Gregory E. Mierzwinski
(Resident, Orlando Office)	Carole Taylor Kirkwood
Daniel William King	

For full biographical listings, see the Martindale-Hubbell Law Directory

---

*WEST PALM BEACH,** Palm Beach Co.

BURT & PUCILLO (AV)

Esperanté, Suite 300 East, 222 Lakeview Avenue, 33401
Telephone: 407-835-9400
Telecopier: 407-835-0322

MEMBERS OF FIRM

C. Oliver Burt, III	Michael J. Pucillo
Wendy Hope Zoberman	

ASSOCIATE

Leo W. Desmond

OF COUNSEL

Carol McLean Brewer	Lauren S. Dadario

For full biographical listings, see the Martindale-Hubbell Law Directory

---

QUARLES & BRADY (AV)

222 Lakeview Avenue, 4th Floor, 33401
Telephone: 561-653-5000
Fax: 561-653-5333
Milwaukee, Wisconsin Office: 411 East Wisconsin Avenue, 53202-4497.
Telephone: 414-277-5000.
Fax: 414-271-3552.

(See Next Column)

Madison, Wisconsin Office: Firstar Plaza, One South Pinckney Street, P.O. Box 2113, 53701-2113.
Telephone: 608-251-5000.
Fax: 608-251-9166.
Naples, Florida Office: Barnett Center, 4501 Tamiami Trail North, Suite 300, 33940-3060.
Telephone: 941-262-5959.
Fax: 941-434-4999.
Phoenix, Arizona Office: One Camelback Building, One East Camelback Road, Suite 400, 85012-1649.
Telephone: 602-230-5500.
Fax: 602-230-5598.

PARTNERS

David L. Petersen	Ned R. Nashban

ASSOCIATE

Nancy Berz Colman

For Complete List of Firm Personnel, See General Section

For full biographical listings, see the Martindale-Hubbell Law Directory

---

SEARCY DENNEY SCAROLA BARNHART & SHIPLEY, PROFESSIONAL ASSOCIATION (AV)

2139 Palm Beach Lakes Boulevard, P.O. Drawer 3626, 33402-3626
Telephone: 407-686-6300
800-780-8607
800-220-7006 (Spanish)
Fax: 407-478-0754

John Scarola	William A. Norton
F. Gregory Barnhart	David J. Sales
C. Calvin Warriner, III	William B. King

LEGAL SUPPORT PERSONNEL

Emilio Diamantis	J. Peter Love
(Paralegal/Investigator)	(Paralegal/Investigator)
Marjorie A. Morgan (Paralegal)	

For Complete List of Firm Personnel, See General Section

For full biographical listings, see the Martindale-Hubbell Law Directory

---

WINTER PARK, Orange Co.

POHL & SHORT, P.A. (AV)

280 West Canton Avenue, Suite 410, P.O. Box 3208, 32790
Telephone: 407-647-7645; 407-647-POHL
Telefax: 407-647-2314

Frank L. Pohl	C. Teresa de Arrigoitia
Houston E. Short	George A. Golder
Dwight I. Cool	Norma Stanley
James Everett Shepherd V	Mark W. Garrett
John R. Simpson, Jr.	

Representative Clients: American Pioneer Title Insurance Company; Institute of Internal Auditors, Inc.; Thompson Steel, Inc.; SunTrust, N.A.; The Bank of Winter Park; Bekins Moving and Storage Co., Inc.; Champion Boats, Inc.; KeyCom Telephone Systems, Inc.

For full biographical listings, see the Martindale-Hubbell Law Directory

---

GEORGIA

---

*ATLANTA,** Fulton Co.

BAUER & DEITCH, P.C. (AV)

Building D, 6111 Peachtree-Dunwoody Road, N.E., 30328
Telephone: 770-394-9004
Telecopier: 770-394-8840

Henry R. Bauer, Jr.	Gilbert H. Deitch

For full biographical listings, see the Martindale-Hubbell Law Directory

---

BODKER, RAMSEY & ANDREWS, A PROFESSIONAL CORPORATION (AV)

Suite 615 1800 Peachtree Street, N.W., 30309-2507
Telephone: 404-351-1615
Telecopier: 404-352-1285

Stephen C. Andrews

Thomas Rosseland

For full biographical listings, see the Martindale-Hubbell Law Directory

---

DAVID G. CROCKETT, P.C. (AV)

1950 Equitable Building, 100 Peachtree Street, N.W., 30303
Telephone: 404-522-4280
Telecopier: 404-589-9891

(See Next Column)

DAVID G. CROCKETT, P.C.—*Continued*

David G. Crockett

Tait O. Norton

Approved Attorney for: Chicago Title Insurance Co.
Reference: NationsBank, N.A.

For full biographical listings, see the Martindale-Hubbell Law Directory

---

DREW ECKL & FARNHAM (AV)

880 West Peachtree Street, P.O. Box 7600, 30357
Telephone: 404-885-1400
Facsimile: 404-876-0992
Email: drew@igc.apc.org

MEMBERS OF FIRM

James M. Poe	Benton J. Mathis, Jr.
T. Bart Gary	Dennis M. Hall
Paul W. Burke	J. William Haley

Stephen W. Mooney

ASSOCIATES

Nancy F. Rigby	Peter B. Barlow

OF COUNSEL

Christopher E. Parker

Representative Clients: Chicago Title Insurance Co.; CNA Insurance Companies; Frito-Lay, Inc.; Georgia Pacific Corp.; Southern Water Technologies, Inc.; Advanced Hunting Equipment, Inc.; AGCO Corporation; National Service Industries; Abrams Industries, Inc.; Wachovia Bank of Georgia.

For Complete List of Firm Personnel, See General Section

For full biographical listings, see the Martindale-Hubbell Law Directory

---

GOLDNER, SOMMERS, SCRUDDER & BASS (AV)

900 Circle 75 Parkway Suite 850, 30339
Telephone: 770-612-9200
Facsimile: 770-612-9201

Henry E. Scrudder, Jr.	Glenn S. Bass
	C. G. Jester, Jr.

For Complete List of Firm Personnel, See General Section

For full biographical listings, see the Martindale-Hubbell Law Directory

---

HARMON, SMITH, BRIDGES & WILBANKS (AV)

1795 Peachtree Street, N.E., 30309
Telephone: 404-881-1200
Fax: 404-881-8523

MEMBERS OF FIRM

Archer D. Smith, III	Tyrone M. Bridges
	Marlan B. Wilbanks

ASSOCIATE

Fred Paul Anthony, Jr.

OF COUNSEL

Nolan B. (Joe) Harmon

For full biographical listings, see the Martindale-Hubbell Law Directory

---

HAWKINS & PARNELL (AV)

4000 SunTrust Plaza, 303 Peachtree Street, N.E., 30308-3243
Telephone: 404-614-7400
Fax: 404-614-7500
Email: 73541.1626@compuserve.com

MEMBERS OF FIRM

Howell Hollis, III	Jack N. Sibley
	Kenan G. Loomis

ASSOCIATES

Edwin L. Hall, Jr.	Christine Lupo Mast
Cullen Christie Wilkerson, Jr.	Thomas G. Tidwell
Allen W. Nelson	Jennifer A. Grandoff

Representative Clients: Figgie Acceptance Corp.; Figgie Leasing Corp.; Motel 6; Johnson & Higgins; The Breckenridge Group, Inc.; Warren Sewell Clothing Company; Bremen Bowden Investment Company; Sequa Corporation; Trust Company Bank.

For Complete List of Firm Personnel, See General Section

For full biographical listings, see the Martindale-Hubbell Law Directory

---

HOLT, NEY, ZATCOFF & WASSERMAN (AV)

A Partnership including Professional Corporations
100 Galleria Parkway, Suite 600, 30339
Telephone: 770-956-9600
Facsimile Number: 770-956-1490

(See Next Column)

MEMBERS OF FIRM

Charles D. Vaughn	Richard P. Vornholt
	Brian P. Cain

ASSOCIATE

Thomas K. Anderson

Representative Clients: First Union National Bank of Georgia; NationsBank, N.A. (South); Citibank, N.A.; First National Bank of Chicago.

For Complete List of Firm Personnel, See General Section

For full biographical listings, see the Martindale-Hubbell Law Directory

---

PARKER, HUDSON, RAINER & DOBBS (AV)

1500 Marquis Two Tower, 285 Peachtree Center Avenue, N.E., 30303
Telephone: 404-523-5300
FAX: 404-522-8409
Tallahassee, Florida Office: The Perkins House, 118 North Gadsden Street, 32301.
Telephone: 904-681-0191.
FAX: 904-681-9493.

MEMBERS OF FIRM

C. Edward Dobbs	Robert A. Crosby
Mitchell M. Purvis	Leigh P. Vancil
	Douglas A. Nail

For full biographical listings, see the Martindale-Hubbell Law Directory

---

PETERSON DILLARD YOUNG ASSELIN & POWELL LLP (AV)

Suite 1100, 230 Peachtree Street, N.W., 30303
Telephone: 404-523-3300
Telecopier: 404-522-6000

MEMBERS OF FIRM

Malcolm D. Young, Jr.	David J. Larson
	Susan W. Housen

For full biographical listings, see the Martindale-Hubbell Law Directory

---

PIERCE & YOUNG (AV)

Building 1700, 2255 Cumberland Parkway Northwest, 30339-4575
Telephone: 770-435-0500
Telecopier: 770-435-0362

MEMBERS OF FIRM

J. Wayne Pierce	Richard M. Young

ASSOCIATE

Christy A. Dunkelberger

For full biographical listings, see the Martindale-Hubbell Law Directory

---

STOKES LAZARUS & CARMICHAEL (AV)

80 Peachtree Park Drive, N.E., 30309-1320
Telephone: 404-352-1465
Fax: 404-352-8463

MEMBERS OF FIRM

Marion B. Stokes	William K. Carmichael
Wayne H. Lazarus	Michael J. Ernst

ASSOCIATES

Richard J. Joseph	Gregory Mark Simpson
Douglas L. Brooks	Kevin R. Wolff

For full biographical listings, see the Martindale-Hubbell Law Directory

---

THOMAS, KENNEDY, SAMPSON & PATTERSON (AV)

55 Marietta Street, N.W., Suite 1600, 30303
Telephone: 404-688-4503
Telecopier: 404-681-2950

MEMBERS OF FIRM

John Loren Kennedy (1942-1994)	P. Andrew Patterson
Thomas G. Sampson	Myra H. Dixon
	Jeffrey E. Tompkins

ASSOCIATES

Rosalind T. Drakeford	Adam L. Smith
Melynee C. Leftridge	Thomas G. Sampson, II
La'Sean M. Zilton	Ceasar C. Mitchell, II.

R. E. Thomas, Jr. (1911-1996)

LEGAL SUPPORT PERSONNEL

Gwendolyn C.H. Dixon	Yvonne Torrence
Elbetha (Beth) Martin	Priscilla Yolanda Kelly
Nancy Allen-Haskell	Lureece D. Lewis (Paralegal)

For full biographical listings, see the Martindale-Hubbell Law Directory

---

WEISZ & ASSOCIATES (AV)

Suite 900 Live Oak Center, 3475 Lenox Road, N.E., 30326-1232
Telephone: 404-233-7888
Facsimile: 404-261-1925

Peter R. Weisz

(See Next Column)

WEISZ & ASSOCIATES, *Atlanta—Continued*

ASSOCIATE

Cathy Rae Nash

LEGAL SUPPORT PERSONNEL

PARALEGALS

Jo Anne Gunn

Representative Clients: Marion & Cass Street Corp.; H.K. Brewing Co.; Deerfield Construction Co.; Cee Klein Accessories, LTD; Atlanta Valet, Inc.; Central Bank of Tampa; Aloha Leasing div. of Bennett Funding Group, Inc. *Reference:* First Union National Bank.

For full biographical listings, see the Martindale-Hubbell Law Directory

---

WILSON, BROCK & IRBY, L.L.C. (AV)

999 Peachtree Street, N.E., Suite 2000, 30309
Telephone: 404-853-5050
Fax: 404-853-1812

MEMBERS OF FIRM

Richard W. Wilson, Jr.	Lethco H. Brock, Jr.
Frank L. Wilson, III	John H. Irby

ASSOCIATES

Jerry D. Gerald	James Stuart Teague, Jr.
	Paul Schillawski

OF COUNSEL

L. Robert Lovett

For full biographical listings, see the Martindale-Hubbell Law Directory

---

AUGUSTA,* Richmond Co.

J. BENJAMIN KAY, III (AV)

808 First Union Bank Building, 30901
Telephone: 706-722-2008

Approved Attorney for: Lawyers Title Insurance Corp.
Reference: First Union National Bank of Georgia.
Representative Clients: American National Bank & Trust Company; Biotech Park, Inc.; Caterpillar Financial Services, Inc.; Davis-McGraw, Inc.; Ford Leasing Development Company; Ford Motor Credit Company; Gary Concrete Products, Inc.; Globe Life Insurance Company.

For full biographical listings, see the Martindale-Hubbell Law Directory

---

PAINE, McELREATH & HYDER, P.C. (AV)

301 Wheeler Executive Center, 3540 Wheeler Road, 30909
Telephone: 706-738-9710
Telecopier: 706-738-9761

Travers W. Paine, III	Benjamin F. McElreath
	James D. Hyder, Jr.

For full biographical listings, see the Martindale-Hubbell Law Directory

---

CARROLLTON,* Carroll Co.

TISINGER, TISINGER, VANCE & GREER, A PROFESSIONAL CORPORATION (AV)

100 Wagon Yard Plaza, P.O. Box 2069, 30117
Telephone: 770-834-4467
Fax: 770-834-5426

Richard G. Tisinger, Sr.	G. Gregory Shadrix
J. Thomas Vance	Stacey L. Blackmon
C. David Mecklin, Jr.	Steven T. Minor
	Edith Freeman Rooks

Representative Clients: Carrollton Federal Bank-FSB; Greenway Corporation; Richards Homes, Inc.; Southwire Company; Tanner Medical Center, Inc.

For Complete List of Firm Personnel, See General Section

For full biographical listings, see the Martindale-Hubbell Law Directory

---

COLUMBUS,* Muscogee Co.

JACOB BEIL (AV)

Heritage Tower, Suite 301, 18 - 9th Street, P.O. Box 1126, 31902
Telephone: 706-596-9912
Fax: 706-576-5583

Reference: First Union National Bank of Georgia.

For full biographical listings, see the Martindale-Hubbell Law Directory

---

HATCHER, STUBBS, LAND, HOLLIS & ROTHSCHILD (AV)

A Limited Liability Partnership
Suite 500 The Corporate Center, 233 12th Street, P.O. Box 2707, 31902-2707
Telephone: 706-324-0201
Telecopier: 706-322-7747

(See Next Column)

MEMBERS OF FIRM

Alan F. Rothschild	George W. Mize, Jr.
Morton A. Harris	John M. Tanzine, III
J. Barrington Vaught	Alan F. Rothschild, Jr.
Charles T. Staples	William C. Pound
Joseph L. Waldrep	Mote W. Andrews III

General Counsel for: SunTrust Bank, West Georgia, N.A.; TOM'S Foods Inc.; Kinnett Dairies, Inc.; Georgia Crown Distributing Co.; Bill Heard Enterprises, Inc.
Assistant Division Counsel for: Norfolk Southern Corp.
Local Counsel for: First Union National Bank of Georgia; Ford Motor Credit Corp.; Chrysler Credit Corp.

For Complete List of Firm Personnel, See General Section

For full biographical listings, see the Martindale-Hubbell Law Directory

---

MARIETTA,* Cobb Co.

DUARD R. McDONALD (AV)

214 Roswell Street, Suite 100, 30060-2000
Telephone: 770-424-8414
Fax: 770-590-1231

For full biographical listings, see the Martindale-Hubbell Law Directory

---

NORCROSS, Gwinnett Co.

WALLACE & DE MAYO, P.C. (AV)

6356 Corley Road, 30071-1704
Telephone: 707-446-9996
Fax: 707-368-8331

Richard T. De Mayo

For Complete List of Firm Personnel, See General Section

For full biographical listings, see the Martindale-Hubbell Law Directory

---

SAVANNAH,* Chatham Co.

KARSMAN, BROOKS & CALLAWAY, P.C. (AV)

301 West Congress Street, P.O. Box 9149, 31412
Telephone: 912-238-2750
Cable Address: "Karbro"
Telecopier: 912-238-2767

Stanley M. Karsman	R. Krannert Riddle
Charles C. Brooks	Edward M. Hughes
Timothy F. Callaway, III	Shari Sigman Miltiades
Stanley E. Harris, Jr.	D. Campbell Bowman, Jr.
James L. Drake, Jr.	Timothy J. Haeussler
Dana F. Braun	Tracie Grove Smith

For full biographical listings, see the Martindale-Hubbell Law Directory

---

HAWAII

HONOLULU,* Honolulu Co.

ALSTON, HUNT, FLOYD & ING ATTORNEYS AT LAW, A LAW CORPORATION (AV)

18th Floor Pacific Tower, 1001 Bishop Street, P.O. Box 2281, 96804
Telephone: 808-524-1800
Telecopier: 808-524-4591

Paul D. Alston	Bruce S. Noborikawa
William S. Hunt	Sharon A. Merkle
Shelby Anne Floyd	Everett S. Kaneshige
Louise K. Y. Ing	David A. Nakashima
Ellen Godbey Carson	Neil F. Hulbert

Mei Nakamoto	Marilyn Chung Ushijima
Peter C. Hsieh	Susan Jameson
Mary Martin	Joseph P. Viola
Jade Lynne Holck	Richard A. Yanagi
	Bradford L. Tannen

OF COUNSEL

Bruce H. Wakuzawa	Robert A. Marks

Representative Clients: Kaiser Aluminum and Chemical Co.; Federal Deposit Insurance Corp.; Kaiser Foundation Health Plan, Inc.; Chicago Title Insurance Co.; Amfac, Inc.

For full biographical listings, see the Martindale-Hubbell Law Directory

Honolulu—Continued

GEORGE W. ASHFORD, JR. (AV)

2910 Pacific Tower, 1001 Bishop Street, 96813
Telephone: 808-528-0444
Telecopier: (808) 533-0761
Cable Address: Justlaw

Representative Clients: Lloyds of London; Baker Industries, Inc.; Burns International Security Services; Clark Equipment Co.; Great Lakes Chemical Corporation; California Union Insurance Co.; Great American Insurance Companies; Guaranty National Companies; Horace Mann Insurance Company; Marine Office of America Corp.

For full biographical listings, see the Martindale-Hubbell Law Directory

BAYS, DEAVER, HIATT, LUNG & ROSE (AV)

A Partnership including Professional Corporations
16th Floor, Alii Place, 1099 Alakea Street, P.O. Box 1760, 96806
Telephone: 808-523-9000
Telecopier: 808-533-4184
Telex: RCA 7238976
Kamuela, Hawaii Office: Suite 204 Parker Square, 65-1280 Kawaihae Road.
Telephone: 808-885-3400.
Telecopier: 808-885-6765.

MEMBERS OF FIRM

A. Bernard Bays (A Law Corporation)
Phillip L. Deaver (A Law Corporation)
Jerry Michael Hiatt (A Law Corporation)
Harvey J. Lung (A Law Corporation)
Crystal K. Rose (A Law Corporation)
Jason N. Baba (A Law Corporation)
Carl H. Osaki (A Law Corporation)

ASSOCIATES

Michael W. Thomas
Karin L. Holma
Paul M. Saito
Mahilani Elizabeth Kellett
Donald E. Fisher
Wendy J. Utsumi
Bruce Voss
Robert E. Badger, Jr.
Edward J. Corwin
Ross N. Gushi

For full biographical listings, see the Martindale-Hubbell Law Directory

LAW OFFICES OF DAVID F. DAY (AV)

Grosvenor Center Mauka Tower Suite 1788, 737 Bishop Street, 96813
Telephone: 808-531-8020
Fax: 808-521-0962
Email: ddayofc@lava.net

For full biographical listings, see the Martindale-Hubbell Law Directory

DWYER IMANAKA SCHRAFF KUDO MEYER & FUJIMOTO ATTORNEYS AT LAW, A LAW CORPORATION (AV)

1800 Pioneer Plaza, 900 Fort Street Mall, 96813
Telephone: 808-524-8000
Telecopier: 808-526-1419
Mailing Address: P.O. Box 2727, 96803
Email: hawaiilaw@dwyer-imanaka.com *URL:*
http://www.dwyer-imanaka.com

John R. Dwyer, Jr.
Mitchell A. Imanaka
Paul A. Schraff
Benjamin A. Kudo (Atty. at Law, A Law Corp.)
William G. Meyer, III
Wesley M. Fujimoto
Ronald Van Grant
Jon M. H. Pang
Blake W. Bushnell

Adelbert Green

Richard T. Asato, Jr.
Scott W. Settle
Darcie S. Yoshinaga
Lawrence I. Kawasaki
Stacy E. Uehara
Kris N. Nakagawa
Jeffery S. Werbelow
Lori Ann K. Koseki
Troy T. Fukuhara
Katy Y. Chen
Naomi S. Uyeno
Roger B. McKeague

OF COUNSEL

Randall Y. Iwase
R. Brian Tsujimura

For full biographical listings, see the Martindale-Hubbell Law Directory

KOBAYASHI, SUGITA & GODA (AV)

A Partnership including Professional Corporations
8th Floor, Hawaii Tower, 745 Fort Street, 96813
Telephone: 808-539-8700
Telecopier: 808-539-8799
Telex: 6502396585 MCI
MCI Mail: 23 96585
ABA/Net: ABA2281

(See Next Column)

MEMBERS OF FIRM

Bert T. Kobayashi, Jr., (Atty. at Law, A Law Corp.)
Kenneth Y. Sugita (Atty. at Law, A Law Corp.)
Alan M. Goda (Atty. at Law, A Law Corp.)
Dale W. Lee (Atty. at Law, A Law Corp.)
Lex R. Smith (Atty. at Law, A Law Corp.)
Byron C. Feldman, II (Atty. at Law, A Law Corp.)
David L. Monroy (Atty. at Law, A Law Corp.)
Wendell H. Fuji (Atty. at Law, A Law Corp.)
Robert K. Ichikawa (Atty. at Law, A Law Corp.)
Janeen-Ann A. Olds (Atty. At Law, A Law Corp.)
Clifford K. Higa (Atty. At Law, A Law Corp.)
Charles W. Gall (Atty. At Law, A Law Corp.)
John F. Lezak (Atty. at Law, A Law Corp.)
Larry L. Myers (Atty. at Law, A Law Corp.)

ASSOCIATES

Alan K. Maeda
Wintehn K. T. Park
Burt T. Lau
Rod S. Aoki
Ernest H. Nomura
Joseph N. Kiyose
John A. Kodachi
Christopher T. Kobayashi
Lisa W. Cataldo
Nathan H. Yoshimoto
Jennifer M.L. Chock
Brian T. Nakanishi
Jonathan A. Kobayashi
Bruce A. Nakamura
Gary K. Nakata
Ruth K. Oh

OF COUNSEL

Bert T. Kobayashi, Sr.

Reference: First Hawaiian Bank.

For full biographical listings, see the Martindale-Hubbell Law Directory

LYNCH & FARMER (AV)

Suite 2500, Mauka Tower Grosvenor Center, 737 Bishop Street, 96813
Telephone: 808-528-0100
Facsimile: 808-528-4997

LEGAL SUPPORT PERSONNEL

Doreen C. Watanabe

For full biographical listings, see the Martindale-Hubbell Law Directory

LAW OFFICES OF PETER STARN A LAW CORPORATION (AV)

Suite 1740 Grosvenor Center Mauka Tower, 737 Bishop Street, 96813
Telephone: 808-537-6100
Fax: 808-537-5434

Peter Starn
Duane R. Fisher

Sharon Valentine Lovejoy

For full biographical listings, see the Martindale-Hubbell Law Directory

WATANABE, ING & KAWASHIMA (AV)

A Partnership including Professional Corporations
Hawaii Tower, 5th & 6th Floors, 745 Fort Street, 96813
Telephone: 808-544-8300
Facsimile: 808-544-8399

MEMBERS OF FIRM

Jeffrey N. Watanabe (Atty. at Law, A Law Corp.)
James Kawashima (Atty. at Law, A Law Corp.)
J. Douglas Ing (Atty. at Law, A Law Corp.)
Wray H. Kondo (Atty. at Law, A Law Corp.)
John T. Komeiji (Atty. at Law, A Law Corp.)
Ronald Y. K. Leong (Atty. at Law, A Law Corp.)
Robert T. Takamatsu (Atty. at Law, A Law Corp.)
Cynthia Winegar (Atty. at Law, A Law Corp.)
Randall Y. Yamamoto (Atty. at Law, A Law Corp.)
Lyle Y. Harada (Atty. at Law, A Law Corp.)
Michael A. Lorusso (Atty. at Law, A Law Corp.)
Pamela J. Larson (Atty. At Law, A Law Corp.)
William H. Gilardy, Jr. (Atty. At Law, A Law Corp.)
John R. Aube (Atty. at Law, A Law Corp.)
Jan M.L.Y. Amii (Atty. at Law, A Law Corp.)
Edward B. Rogin (Atty. at Law, A Law Corp.)
Seth M. Reiss
Curtis C. Kim

ASSOCIATES

Donna Y. Kanemaru
George B. Apter
Marcus B. Sierra
Lani Narikiyo
Peter L. Fritz
LLoyd S. Yoshioka
Beth K. Fujimoto
Patsy H. Kirio
Kevin H. Oda
Michael C. Bird
Brian Y. Hiyane
Dennis J. Hwang
Teri Y. Kondo
Jeff N. Miyashiro
John Seiichi Sasaki
Gregory Y.P. Tom

OF COUNSEL

George R. Ariyoshi

ASIA PACIFIC CONSULTANT

Victor Hao Li (Not admitted in HI)

(See Next Column)

WATANABE, ING & KAWASHIMA, *Honolulu—Continued*

LEGAL SUPPORT PERSONNEL
GOVERNMENT AFFAIRS ADVISOR
Millicent M. Y. H. Kim

References: First Hawaiian Bank; American Savings Bank.

For Complete List of Firm Personnel, See General Section

For full biographical listings, see the Martindale-Hubbell Law Directory

---

IDAHO

BOISE,* Ada Co.

ELAM & BURKE, A PROFESSIONAL ASSOCIATION (AV)

Key Financial Center, 702 West Idaho Street, P.O. Box 1539, 83701
Telephone: 208-343-5454
Telecopier: 208-384-5844
Email: eblaw@elamburke.com

M. Allyn Dingel, Jr.	Peter C. K. Marshall
David B. Lincoln	William J. Batt
Randall A. Peterman	Jeffery J. Ventrella
William G. Dryden	Jeffrey A. Thomson

J. Ray Durtschi	Bradlee R. Frazer

Representative Clients: Morrison-Knudsen, Inc.; Texas Instruments, Inc.; Prudential Securities, Inc.; Pechiney Corp.; U.S. West Communications; United Heritage & Mutual Life Insurance Co.; Sinclair Oil Co. d/b/a Sun Valley Co.; Idaho Life & Health Insurance Guaranty Assn.; Boise WestCoast Hotel and Bank of America Centre; Micron Construction.

For Complete List of Firm Personnel, See General Section

For full biographical listings, see the Martindale-Hubbell Law Directory

---

ILLINOIS

BELLEVILLE,* St. Clair Co.

BROWN & GAVIN (AV)

23 Public Square, Suite 410, 62220
Telephone: 618-236-2886
Missouri: 314-231-0953

MEMBERS OF FIRM

Terry N. Brown	William P. Gavin

ASSOCIATES

Gregg N. Johnson	P.K. Johnson, V

For full biographical listings, see the Martindale-Hubbell Law Directory

BLOOMINGTON,* McLean Co.

HARTWEG, MUELLER, TURNER, DRAZEWSKI & WOOD, P.C. (AV)

207 West Jefferson Street, Suite 400, P.O. Box 397, 61701-0397
Telephone: 309-827-0044
Telecopier: 309-829-0328

Darrell L. Hartweg	Ralph T. Turner
William A. Mueller, Jr.	Scott D. Drazewski
	George C Wood

Michael J. Robak
OF COUNSEL
John R. Luedtke

Reference: Magna Bank of McLean County.

For full biographical listings, see the Martindale-Hubbell Law Directory

CHICAGO,* Cook Co.

BATES MECKLER BULGER & TILSON (AV)

8200 Sears Tower, 233 South Wacker, 60606
Telephone: 312-474-7900
Facsimile: 312-474-7898
URL: http://www.bmbt.com

MEMBERS OF FIRM

Robert J. Bates, Jr.	J. Stuart Garbutt
Brian W. Bulger	Paul R. Garry
Janet R. Davis	Francis X. Grossi, Jr.
Maria G. Enriquez	Maryann C. Hayes
Patrick J. Foley	Kathleen H. Jensen

(See Next Column)

MEMBERS OF FIRM (Continued)

Mari Henry Leigh	Bruce R. Meckler
Mary F. Licari	Steven D. Pearson
Michael M. Marick	Scott M. Seaman
	Joseph E. Tilson

ASSOCIATES

Anne L. Blume	Christopher E. Kentra
Dina L. Brantman	Charlene Kittredge
Catherine M. Crisham	Michael I. Leonard
Joseph E. Cwik	Lisa A. Miller
John K. Daly	Felicia Lynn Gerber Perlman
(Not admitted in IL)	John R. Rapasky
Robin Edelstein	Brett G. Rawitz
Mary E. Gootjes	John E. Rodewald
Robert C. Heist	Mark G. Sheridan
Darlene M. Jarzyna-Price	Frederick W. Stein
James H. Kallianis, Jr.	Monica T. Sullivan
	Timothy A. Wolfe

OF COUNSEL

Stanley V. Figura	Matthew M. Murphy
Joseph Frontino	Thomas J. O'Brien
Philip R. King	Brian J. Williams

For full biographical listings, see the Martindale-Hubbell Law Directory

BOEHM, PEARLSTEIN & BRIGHT, LTD. (AV)

33 North La Salle Street Suite 3500, 60602
Telephone: 312-782-7474
Fax: 312-782-0380

Robert I. Boehm	Gary I. Blackman
Mark D. Pearlstein	Roy D. Kessel
Steven Bright	Donna Richman
Konstantinos Armiros	Bryan I. Schwartz
	William Scott Schwartz

Representative Clients: First Bank; Cole Taylor Bank; LaSalle National Bank; LaSalle Bank N.I.; The Northern Trust Company; Firstar Bank of Illinois; First Union National Bank of North Carolina; CB Commerical; Merrill Lynch Business Financial Services, Inc.

For full biographical listings, see the Martindale-Hubbell Law Directory

FOX & GROVE, CHARTERED (AV)

311 South Wacker Drive Suite 6200, 60606
Telephone: 312-876-0500
Telecopier: 312-362-0700
St. Petersburg, Florida Office: Fox, Grove, Abbey, Adams, Byelick & Kiernan, Eleventh Floor, 360 Central Avenue.
Telephone: 813-821-2080.
Tampa, Florida Office: Fox, Grove, Abbey, Adams, Byelick & Kiernan, 500 East Kennedy Boulevard, Suite 200.
Telephone: 813-223-7800.
San Francisco, California Office: 240 Stockton Street, Suite 900.
Telephone: 415-956-1360.

Shayle P. Fox	Marty Denis
Kalvin M. Grove	Steven L. Gillman
Lawrence M. Cohen	William Henry Barrett
S. Richard Pincus	Allison C. Blakley
Russell M. Kofoed	Jeffrey E. Beeson
Jeffrey S. Goldman	Robert M. Mintz
	Joel W. Rice

Mark T. Dabertin	Elisabeth E. Snyder
Tamra S. Domeyer	(Not admitted in IL)
Davi L. Hirsch	Todd D. Steenson
Joshua D. Holleb	Michael L. Sullivan
Daniel A. Kazlauski	Lynn Urkov Thorpe
Daniel R. Madock	Douglas M. Werman
Michael Paull	David Zatuchni

Labor Counsel for: National Association of Independent Insurers; Alliance of American Insurers; Great American Insurance Co.; CNA Financial Corp.; California Casualty Management.
Representative Labor Clients: Liberty Mutual Insurance Co.; Certified Grocers Midwest; Sears Logistics Services; National Wrecking Co.; GAB Business Services, Inc.

For full biographical listings, see the Martindale-Hubbell Law Directory

WILLIAM J. HARTE, LTD. (AV)

Suite 1100, 111 West Washington Street, 60602
Telephone: 312-726-5015
Fax: 312-641-1288

William J. Harte

Sylvia A. Sotiras	Stephen L. Garcia
Erik D. Gruber	Joan M. Mannix
	Cynthia E. Cervini

(See Next Column)

WILLIAM J. HARTE, LTD.—*Continued*

OF COUNSEL

Daniel K. Schlorf	P. A. Sorrentino
David J. Walker	Irving R. Norman
	Robert L. Tucker

For full biographical listings, see the Martindale-Hubbell Law Directory

SCHWARTZBERG, BARNETT & COHEN (AV)

55 West Monroe Street, 2400 Xerox Centre, 60603-5040
Telephone: 312-726-3555
Fax: 312-726-6299
Cable Address: "Justice"
Email: sb&c@twty.chi.il.us

MEMBERS OF FIRM

Ralph M. Schwartzberg	Mark T. Barnett (1939-1970)
(1939-1975)	Hugh J. Schwartzberg
Benjamin H. Cohen	

OF COUNSEL

Eugene P. Thomas Jr.

For full biographical listings, see the Martindale-Hubbell Law Directory

TRIBLER ORPETT PALMER & CRONE, A PROFESSIONAL CORPORATION (AV)

30 North La Salle Street, Suite 2200, 60602
Telephone: 312-201-6400
Fax: 312-201-6401
Schaumburg, Illinois Office: Suite 1260, 1450 East American Lane.
Telephone: 847-517-8400.
Fax: 847-517-8401.

Douglas C. Crone	H. Wesley Sunu
Steven R. McMannon	Willis R. Tribler
Michael J. Meyer	William J. Wall
Mitchell A. Orpett	(Not admitted in IL)
Thomas R. Palmer	
(Resident, Schaumburg Office)	

John W. Carver	Lisa O'Malley
Molly A. Griffin	Christopher J. Ondrula
David P. Hahn	Matthew B. Parker
Kyle J. Kirkham	Stanley D. Sterna
(Resident, Schaumburg Office)	Panos T. Topalis

OF COUNSEL

Daniel D. Drew	John W. Wardell
	(Resident, Schaumburg Office)

For full biographical listings, see the Martindale-Hubbell Law Directory

DANVILLE, * Vermilion Co.

SAIKLEY, GARRISON & COLOMBO, LTD. (AV)

208 West North Street, P.O. Box 6, 61834-0006
Telephone: 217-442-0244
FAX: 217-442-0582

Albert Saikley (1912-1987)	Gilbert H. Saikley
William L. Garrison	Kevin M. Colombo

Jeanette E. Bahnke

References: First Midwest Bank; City National Bank.

For full biographical listings, see the Martindale-Hubbell Law Directory

JOLIET, * Will Co.

HERSCHBACH, TRACY, JOHNSON, BERTANI & WILSON (AV)

Two Rialto Square, 116 North Chicago Street, Sixth Floor, 60432
Telephone: 815-723-8500
Fax: 815-727-4846

Wayne R. Johnson	Kenneth A. Carlson
Thomas R. Wilson	John S. Gallo
A. Michael Wojtak	Richard E. Vogel

OF COUNSEL

Donald J. Tracy

General Counsel for: First National Bank of Joliet; First National Bancorp. *Representative Clients:* Chicago Title Insurance Co.; Vulcan Materials Company; Dow Chemical, U.S.A.; Marathon Oil Co.; Waste Management, Inc.; The Copley Press, Inc.; Citizens Utilities Co.; Empress River Casino Corporation.

For Complete List of Firm Personnel, See General Section

For full biographical listings, see the Martindale-Hubbell Law Directory

KANKAKEE, * Kankakee Co.

BLANKE, NORDEN, BARMANN, KRAMER & BOHLEN, P.C. (AV)

Suite 502, 200 East Court Street, P.O. Box 1787, 60901
Telephone: 815-939-1133
Fax: 815-939-0994

Armen R. Blanke (Deceased)	Glen R. Barmann
Paul F. Blanke (Retired)	Christopher W. Bohlen
Dennis A. Norden	Michael D. Kramer

For full biographical listings, see the Martindale-Hubbell Law Directory

MATTOON, Coles Co.

CRAIG & CRAIG (AV)

1807 Broadway, P.O. Box 689, 61938-0689
Telephone: 217-234-6481
Telecopier: 217-234-6486
Mount Vernon, Illinois Office: 227 1/2 South 9th Street.
Telephone: 618-244-7511.

MEMBERS OF FIRM

Craig Van Meter (1895-1981)	Stephen L. Corn
Fred H. Kelly (1894-1971)	Richard Charles Hayden
Robert M. Werden (1908-1969)	Robert G. Grierson
George N. Gilkerson	Gregory C. Ray
(1911-1985)	Paul R. Lynch (Resident, Mount
John H. Armstrong	Vernon Office)
John P. Ewart	Kenneth F. Werts (Resident,
Richard F. Record, Jr.	Mount Vernon Office)
	John L. Barger

ASSOCIATES

Joshua N. Rosen (Resident,	Theresa M. Thomson
Mount Vernon Office)	Kristine M. Tuttle
Kathleen M. Stockwell	Henry P. Villani (Resident,
	Mount Vernon Office)

OF COUNSEL

Jack E. Horsley

Counsel for: Monterey Coal Co., a Division of Exxon Coal USA, Inc.; Marathon Oil Co.; Illinois Central R.R. Co.; Okaw Building & Loan Assn., Mattoon, Illinois; The Medical Protective Insurance Co.; Consolidated Communications, Inc.; Lloyds Underwriters at London; Hartford Insurance Co.; Coles Together, a Not-For-Profit Corp.; Coles Building Corporation.

For full biographical listings, see the Martindale-Hubbell Law Directory

MOUNT VERNON, * Jefferson Co.

LAW OFFICE OF TERRY SHARP, P.C. (AV)

1115 Harrison Street, P.O. Box 906, 62864
Telephone: 618-242-0246
Fax: 618-242-1170
Benton, Illinois Office: 105 North Main Street.
Telephone: 618-435-5109.
FAX: 618-242-1170.

Terrell Lee Sharp

Brian Thomas McGovern

For full biographical listings, see the Martindale-Hubbell Law Directory

SCHAUMBURG, Cook & Du Page Cos.

TRIBLER ORPETT PALMER & CRONE, A PROFESSIONAL CORPORATION (AV)

Suite 1260 1450 East American Lane, 60173
Telephone: 847-517-8400
Fax: 847-517-8401
Chicago Office: Suite 2200, 30 North LaSalle Street.
Telephone: 312-201-6400.
Fax: 312-201-6401.

Thomas R. Palmer (Resident)	Kyle J. Kirkham (Resident)

OF COUNSEL

John W. Wardell (Resident)

For full biographical listings, see the Martindale-Hubbell Law Directory

INDIANA

ELKHART, Elkhart Co.

CHESTER, PFAFF & BROTHERSON (AV)

317 West Franklin Street, P.O. Box 507, 46515-0507
Telephone: 219-294-5421
Fax: 219-522-1476

(See Next Column)

CHESTER, PFAFF & BROTHERSON, *Elkhart—Continued*

MEMBERS OF FIRM

Robert A. Pfaff   Glenn E. Killoren

OF COUNSEL

James R. Brotherson

ASSOCIATES

Robert C. Whippo   Craig A. Carpenter

For Complete List of Firm Personnel, See General Section

For full biographical listings, see the Martindale-Hubbell Law Directory

---

EVANSVILLE,* Vanderburgh Co.

BOWERS, HARRISON, KENT & MILLER, LLP (AV)

25 N.W. Riverside Drive, P.O. Box 1287, 47706-1287
Telephone: 812-426-1231
Fax: 812-464-3676

MEMBERS OF FIRM

David V. Miller   Timothy J. Hubert
Paul E. Black   Thomas A. Massey
Gary R. Case   Greg A. Granger
Joseph H. Harrison, Jr.

Division Counsel in Indiana for: Southern Railway Co.
Representative Clients: Permanent Federal Savings Bank; Citizens Realty & Insurance, Inc.

For Complete List of Firm Personnel, See General Section

For full biographical listings, see the Martindale-Hubbell Law Directory

---

MATTINGLY, RUDOLPH, FINE & PORTER (AV)

221 N.W. Fifth Street, Second Floor, P.O. Box 1507, 47706
Telephone: 812-422-9444
Fax: 812-421-7459
Email: mrfp@evansville.net

MEMBERS OF FIRM

Ross E. Rudolph   James D. Johnson

ASSOCIATES

Scott S. Stone   Jeffrey W. Henning

Reference: National City Bank of Evansville.

For full biographical listings, see the Martindale-Hubbell Law Directory

---

WRIGHT, EVANS AND DALY (AV)

425 Main Street, 47708
Telephone: 812-424-3300
Fax: 812-421-5588

MEMBERS OF FIRM

Donald R. Wright   R. Lawrence Daly

Representative Clients: Browning-Ferris Industries of Indiana, Inc.; Castle Contracting Co., Inc.; Computing Solutions, Inc.; Happy China Trading Corporation; Manpower Incorporated of Evansville; Need-A-Nurse, Inc.; Mills-Wallace and Associates, Inc. Design Professionals; Servicemaster of Evansville, Inc.; Siemers Glass Company, Inc.; Southwestern Indiana Mental Health Center, Inc.

For Complete List of Firm Personnel, See General Section

For full biographical listings, see the Martindale-Hubbell Law Directory

---

ZIEMER, STAYMAN, WEITZEL & SHOULDERS (AV)

(Formerly Early, Arnold & Ziemer)
One Riverfront Place, 20 N.W. First Street 9th Floor, P.O. Box 916, 47706-0916
Telephone: 812-424-7575
Telecopier: 812-421-5089

MEMBERS OF FIRM

Robert F. Stayman   Marco L. DeLucio
Stephan E. Weitzel   Gregory G. Meyer

Reference: Old National Bank in Evansville.

For full biographical listings, see the Martindale-Hubbell Law Directory

---

FORT WAYNE,* Allen Co.

HUNT, SUEDHOFF, BORROR & EILBACHER (AV)

900 Courtside, 803 South Calhoun Street, P.O. Box 11489, 46858-1489
Telephone: 219-423-1311
Telecopier: 219-424-5396

RETIRED

Carl J. Suedhoff, Jr.

(See Next Column)

MEMBERS OF FIRM

Leigh L. Hunt (1899-1975)   Thomas W. Belleperche
William E. Borror (1932-1989)   Mark W. Baeverstad
Leonard E. Eilbacher   Michael D. Mustard
Robert E. Kabisch   Branch R. Lew
Arthur G. Surguine, Jr.   Carla J. Baird
Thomas C. Ewing   James J. Shea
Carolyn White Spengler   Scott L. Bunnell
Dane L. Tubergen

ASSOCIATES

Charles H. Bassford, IV   Daniel J. Palmer
Carolyn M. Trier   Brian L. England
Kathleen A. Kilar   Craig J. Bobay
W. Douglas Lemon

For full biographical listings, see the Martindale-Hubbell Law Directory

---

SHIPLEY & ASSOCIATES (AV)

130 West Main Street, Suite 25, 46802
Telephone: 219-424-2505
Fax: 219-424-2960

Grant F. Shipley

For full biographical listings, see the Martindale-Hubbell Law Directory

---

SWIFT & FINLAYSON (AV)

803 South Calhoun Street Suite 500, 46802-2480
Telephone: 219-423-4422
Fax: 219-423-4427
Affiliated Law Firm: Leeuw, Plopper & Beeman-Poland, First Indiana Plaza, Suite 2000, 135 North Pennsylvania Street, Indianapolis, Indiana, 46204-2456.

MEMBERS OF FIRM

Frank A. Higgins (1925-1976)   William D. Swift
Craig R. Finlayson

ASSOCIATE

Charles D. Bash

OF COUNSEL

Gene R. Leeuw   Craig D. Doyle
Joseph W. Murphy   Charleyne L. Gabriel
John Michael Mead

For full biographical listings, see the Martindale-Hubbell Law Directory

---

HAMMOND, Lake Co.

BECKMAN, KELLY & SMITH (AV)

5920 Hohman Avenue, 46320
Telephone: 219-933-6200
Telecopier: 219-933-6201
South Bend, Indiana Office: 300 North Michigan Street, Suite 215.
Telephone: 219-288-2373.
Telecopier: 219-933-6201.

MEMBERS OF FIRM

Richard P. Tinkham (1902-1973)   Andrew J. Fetsch
Daniel F. Kelly (1914-1978)   Randall J. Nye
John F. Beckman, Jr.   Robert F. Parker
  (1916-1996)   Daniel W. Glavin
J. B. Smith   Eric L. Kirschner

ASSOCIATES

Melanie Morgan Dunajeski   Christine Hajduch Curosh
Scott A. Bearby   Douglas A. Welp

Representative Clients: Waste Management of North America, Inc.; The Travelers Companies; Bethlehem Steel Corp.; ITT Finance; Northwest Indiana Public Broadcasting, Inc.; Signal Capital Corporation; CIGNA Companies; Sears Roebuck and Co.

For full biographical listings, see the Martindale-Hubbell Law Directory

---

INDIANAPOLIS,* Marion Co.

BACKER & BACKER, A PROFESSIONAL CORPORATION (AV)

101 West Ohio Street, Suite 1500, 46204
Telephone: 317-684-3000
Telecopier: 317-684-3004

Herbert J. Backer (1914-1995)   Stephen A. Backer
David J. Backer

Reference: Bank One, Indianapolis.

For full biographical listings, see the Martindale-Hubbell Law Directory

---

BAMBERGER & FEIBLEMAN (AV)

54 Monument Circle Suite 600, 46204-2947
Telephone: 317-639-5151
FAX: 317-269-2030

(See Next Column)

BAMBERGER & FEIBLEMAN—*Continued*
MEMBERS OF FIRM
A. Thomas Cobb   Edward B. Hopper, II

Representative Clients: C.I.T. Corp.; FFI Corporation; Kipp Brothers, Inc.; BancPlus Mortgage Corp.; Hiway Parts, Inc.; NBD, Indiana; Tube Processing Corp.; Indiana Mortgage Corp.

For full biographical listings, see the Martindale-Hubbell Law Directory

---

BOBERSCHMIDT, MILLER, O'BRYAN & TURNER, A PROFESSIONAL ASSOCIATION (AV)

Bank One Center/Circle, 111 Monument Circle, Suite 302, 46204-5169
Telephone: 317-632-5892
Telecopier: 317-686-3423

Philip F. Boberschmidt   L. Craig Turner

A List of Representative Clients will be furnished upon request.

For full biographical listings, see the Martindale-Hubbell Law Directory

---

BUSCHMANN, CARR & SHANKS, PROFESSIONAL CORPORATION (AV)

1020 Market Tower, 10 West Market Street, 46204-2963
Telephone: 317-636-5511
Fax: 317-636-3661
Email: bcs@indy.net *URL:* http://www.buschmann.com/bcs/

John R. Carr, III   Gary L. Dilk
Stephen R. Buschmann   Lisa T. Hamilton

Representative Clients: Archer-Daniels Midland Co.; Ball Corp.; Industrial Valley Title Insurance; Creative Risk Management, Inc.; Deflecto Corporation; Glenfed Mortgage Corp.; Gates McDonald; Merchants National Bank & Trust Company of Muncie; Monumental Life Insurance Co.; National Council on Compensation Insurance.

For full biographical listings, see the Martindale-Hubbell Law Directory

---

DANN PECAR NEWMAN & KLEIMAN, PROFESSIONAL CORPORATION (AV)

Suite 2300, One American Square Box 82008, 46282
Telephone: 317-632-3232; Indiana: 800-622-4799
Telecopy: 317-632-2962

Theodore R. Dann (1907-1993)   Walter E. Wolf, Jr.
Joel Yonover (1932-1995)   Barry E. Beldin
Philip D. Pecar   Robert D. Swhier, Jr.
Norman R. Newman   James P. Moloy
David H. Kleiman   Robert J. Schuckit
Jon B. Abels   Andrew A. Kleiman
Melvin R. Daniel   Michael J. Gabovitch
Lawrence F. Dorocke   Steven M. Pecar
Jeffrey A. Abrams   Benjamin A. Pecar
James H. Schwarz   Richard O. Kissel, II
Robert A. Rose   Joseph D. Calderon

OF COUNSEL
Linda E. Cantor   Anthony J. Rose

Ellen C. Siakotos   Angela L. Mansfield
Stacy L. Hill   Martha M. K. Baird
            Karin L. Veatch

Attorneys for: Indianapolis Machinery Co., Inc.; Melvin Simon & Associates, Inc.; Pacers Basketball Corp.; Universal Fire & Casualty Co., Inc.; Bank One, Indianapolis, NA; INB National Bank; Nachi Technology, Inc.; Pharmaceutical Corporation of America; Logo 7, Inc.

For full biographical listings, see the Martindale-Hubbell Law Directory

---

FEIWELL & HANNOY, PROFESSIONAL CORPORATION (AV)

251 North Illinois Street, Suite 1700, P.O. Box 44141, 46244-0141
Telephone: 317-237-2727
Facsimile: 317-237-2722

Murray J. Feiwell   Douglas J. Hannoy

John P. Sieger   Michael J. Feiwell
            Laura S. Carafiol

Representative Clients: Fifth Third Bank; Mathews, Click; Revel, Inc.; American Credit Indemnity; Browning Investments, Inc.; Queens Group; Oliver Trucking; Jewelers Board of Trade; A.G. Adjustments, Ltd.; Stanley Tulchin Associates; REI Investments, Inc.

For full biographical listings, see the Martindale-Hubbell Law Directory

---

HOPPER & GALLIHER, P.C. (AV)

Bank One Center/Circle, 111 Monument Circle, Suite 452, 46204-5170
Telephone: 317-635-5005
Facsimile: 317-634-2501

(See Next Column)

George W. Hopper   Jeffrey E. Ramsey
Mark R. Galliher   David G. Pardo

Representative Clients: Bank One, Indianapolis, N.A.; National City Bank, Indiana; Mutual Guaranty Corporation; I.T.T. Financial Services, Commercial Division; ABC Supply Co., Inc.; Sholodge, Inc.

For full biographical listings, see the Martindale-Hubbell Law Directory

---

HOSTETLER & KOWALIK, P.C. (AV)

101 West Ohio Street Suite 2100, 46204
Telephone: 317-262-1001
Fax: 317-262-1010

Gary Lynn Hostetler   David R. Krebs
James S. Kowalik   J. Bradley Schooley

For full biographical listings, see the Martindale-Hubbell Law Directory

---

ICE MILLER DONADIO & RYAN (AV)

One American Square Box 82001, 46282-0002
Telephone: 317-236-2100
Fax: 317-236-2219
Email: leel@imdr.com *URL:* http://www.imdr.com
South Bend, Indiana Office: 211 West Washington Street, Suite 2420.
Telephone: 219-234-7933.
Fax: 219-234-7965. Internet E-mail: leel@imdr.com. Web Site Address: http://www.imdr.com.

MEMBERS OF FIRM
Donald G. Sutherland   Thomas H. Ristine
Berkley W. Duck   John R. Thornburgh
Jack R. Snyder   Richard J. Thrapp
Harry L. Gonso   Henry A. Efroymson

OF COUNSEL
Peggy J. Naile

ASSOCIATES
Dominic F. Polizzotto   Michael E. Schrader

Representative Clients: Amax Coal, Inc.; Bank One, Indianapolis, N.A.; Clark Equipment Co.; Federal Home Loan Bank of Indianapolis; Ford Motor Credit Co.; General Electric Supply Co.; NBD Bank (Trust); National City Bank (Trust); Navistar Financial Corp.; Westinghouse Credit Corp.

For Complete List of Firm Personnel, See General Section

For full biographical listings, see the Martindale-Hubbell Law Directory

---

JOHNSON, SMITH, PENCE, DENSBORN, WRIGHT & HEATH (AV)

One Indiana Square Suite 1800, 46204
Telephone: 317-634-9777
Telecopier: 317-636-9061

MEMBERS OF FIRM
David G. Blachly   Dennis A. Johnson
Peter D. Cleveland   Richard L. Johnson
Jeffrey S. Cohen   Michael J. Kaye
David R. Day   John R. Kirkwood
Donald K. Densborn   David Williams Russell
Thomas N. Eckerle   David E. Wright

ASSOCIATES
Carolyn H. Andretti   Robert T. Buday
            Patricia L. Marshall

OF COUNSEL
William T. Lawrence

For Complete List of Firm Personnel, See General Section

For full biographical listings, see the Martindale-Hubbell Law Directory

---

PRICE & BARKER (AV)

The Hammond Block Building, 301 Massachusetts Avenue, 46204
Telephone: 317-633-8787
Telecopier: 317-633-8797
New Albany, Indiana Office: 409 Bank Street, P.O. Box 785.
Telephone: 812-945-9151.
Fax: 812-945-6131.

PARTNERS
Henry J. Price   Robert G. Barker
            Jerry A. Garau

For full biographical listings, see the Martindale-Hubbell Law Directory

---

ROCAP, WITCHGER & THRELKELD (AV)

One Indiana Square, Suite 2300, 46204
Telephone: 317-639-6281
FAX: 317-637-9056

James E. Rocap, Sr. (1881-1969)   John T. Rocap (1909-1980)
            Keith C. Reese (1920-1993)

(See Next Column)

ROCAP, WITCHGER & THRELKELD, *Indianapolis—Continued*

MEMBERS OF FIRM

James E. Rocap, Jr.	Richard A. Rocap
James D. Witchger	Thomas Todd Reynolds
W. Brent Threlkeld	Robert S. O'Dell

ASSOCIATES

Nancy G. Curless	Mark A. Payne
Robert A. Durham	Kandice L. Kilkelly
Jeffrey V. Crabill	Dionne M. Carroll

OF COUNSEL

Joseph F. Quill

Counsel For: Union Federal Savings Bank; Union Acceptance Corp.; Methodist Hospital FCU; Wolf and Swickard Machine Co., Inc.; Cessna Finance Corp.; Ryland Group; Indiana Materials and Manufacturing, Inc.; Carrier Corp.

For full biographical listings, see the Martindale-Hubbell Law Directory

SOMMER & BARNARD, ATTORNEYS AT LAW, PC (AV)

4000 Bank One Tower, 111 Monument Circle, 46204-5140
Telephone: 317-630-4000
FAX: 317-236-9802
North Office: 8900 Keystone Crossing, Suite 1046, Indianapolis, Indiana, 46240-2134.
Telephone: 317-630-4000.
FAX: 317-844-4780.

James K. Sommer	Eric R. Johnson
William C. Barnard	Gordon L. Pittenger
James E. Hughes	Marlene Reich
Edward W. Harris, III	Richard C. Richmond, III
Jerald I. Ancel	Julianne S. Lis-Milam

Representative Clients: Comerica Bank; Excel Industries; Federal Express; Kimball International; Monsanto; Renault Automation; TRW, Inc.

For Complete List of Firm Personnel, See General Section

For full biographical listings, see the Martindale-Hubbell Law Directory

YARLING, ROBINSON, HAMMEL & LAMB (AV)

151 North Delaware, Suite 1535, P.O. Box 44128, 46204
Telephone: 317-262-8800
Fax: 317-262-3046

MEMBERS OF FIRM

Richard W. Yarling	Edgar H. Lamb
Charles F. Robinson, Jr.	Douglas E. Rogers
John W. Hammel	Mark S. Gray
Linda Y. Hammel	Matthew C. Robinson

Representative Clients: Allstate Insurance Co.; American Family Mutual Insurance Company; Chrysler Credit Corporation; Fleet Financenter; General Motors Acceptance Corporation; Household Finance Corporation; Monroe Guaranty Insurance Company; Northbrook Property & Casualty Company; Pafco General Insurance Company; Security Pacific Finance Corporation.

For full biographical listings, see the Martindale-Hubbell Law Directory

---

LAFAYETTE,* Tippecanoe Co.

STUART & BRANIGIN (AV)

The Life Building, 300 Main Street, Suite 800, 47902
Telephone: 317-423-1561
Telecopier: 317-742-8175

MEMBERS OF FIRM

Allison Ellsworth Stuart (1886-1950)	Stephen R. Pennell
Roger D. Branigin (1902-1975)	Anthony S. Benton
Russell H. Hart	Erik D. Spykman
Roger D. Branigin, Jr.	William E. Emerick
Thomas L. Ryan	John C. Duffey
James V. McGlone	Mark E. DeYoung
Carl W. Kloepfer	Thomas B. Parent
Thomas R. McCully	Laura L. Bowker
Larry R. Fisher	Kevin D. Nicoson
Nina B. Kirkpatrick	Susan K. Roberts
Mark Lillianfeld	John M. Stuckey
	Deborah B. Trice

COUNSEL

John F. Bodle

ASSOCIATES

Brent W. Huber	David A. Starkweather
William P. Kealey	Geoffrey Blazi
A. James Chareq	

General Counsel for: The Lafayette Life Insurance Co.; INB National Bank, N.W.; Lafayette Home Hospital, Inc.
State Counsel for: Norfolk & Western Railway Co.
Mr. Ryan is Counsel to: The Trustees of Purdue University.
Representative Clients: Aluminum Company of America; Liberty Mutual Insurance Group.

For full biographical listings, see the Martindale-Hubbell Law Directory

---

MERRILLVILLE, Lake Co.

BURKE, MURPHY, COSTANZA & CUPPY (AV)

Suite 600 8585 Broadway, 46410-7064
Telephone: 219-769-1313
Telecopier: 219-769-6806
East Chicago, Indiana Office: First National Bank Building. 720 West Chicago Avenue.
Telephone: 219-397-2401.
Telecopier: 219-397-0508.
Valparaiso, Indiana Office: 15 North Franklin Street, Suite 200.
Telephone: 219-531-0134.
Telecopier: 219-531-0507.
Palm Harbor, Florida Office: Suite 280, 33920 U.S. Highway 19 North.
Telephone: 813-787-7799.
Telecopier: 813-787-7237.

MEMBERS OF FIRM

Lester F. Murphy (Resident, East Chicago, Indiana and Palm Harbor, Florida Offices)	Lambert C. Genetos
	David K. Ranich
	Kathryn D. Schmidt
Frederick M. Cuppy	David Cerven
Andrew J. Kopko	Lily M. Schaefer

ASSOCIATES

Stacia L. Yoon	Kevin E. Steele

Representative Clients: Federal National Mortgage Association; Waterfield Mortage Co.; ITT Commercial Financial Corp.; NBD Bank, N.A.; National City Bank/Indiana N.A.; American Trust & Savings Bank of Whiting; Bank One, N.A.; Centier Bank; Transamerica Financial Services; Tech Federal Credit Union.

For Complete List of Firm Personnel, See General Section

For full biographical listings, see the Martindale-Hubbell Law Directory

HODGES & DAVIS, P.C. (AV)

8700 Broadway, 46410
Telephone: 219-641-8700
Fax: 219-641-8710
Portage, Indiana Office: 6082 Lute Road. P.O. Box 1037.
Telephone: 219-762-9129.
Fax: 219-762-2826.

Clyde D. Compton	Bonnie C. Coleman
William B. Davis	Jill M. Madajczyk
Earle F. Hites	Laura B. Frost
R. Lawrence Steele	David H. Kreider
Gregory A. Sobkowski	Robert G. Vann

OF COUNSEL

Edward J. Hussey

Representative Clients: Lake Mortgage Co., Inc.; Nielsen Buick Jeep Eagle; Pine Chevrolet, Inc.; McDonald's Corporation.

For Complete List of Firm Personnel, See General Section

For full biographical listings, see the Martindale-Hubbell Law Directory

---

PORTAGE, Porter Co.

HODGES & DAVIS, P.C. (AV)

6082 Lute Road, P.O. Box 1037, 46368
Telephone: 219-762-9129
Fax: 219-762-2826
Merrillville, Indiana Office: 8700 Broadway.
Telephone: 219-641-8700.
Fax: 219-641-8710.

Clyde D. Compton	R. Lawrence Steele
Earle F. Hites	Gregory A. Sobkowski
	Bonnie C. Coleman

Representative Clients: Lake Mortgage Co., Inc.; Nielson Buick Jeep Eagle; Pine Chevrolet, Inc.; McDonald's Corporation.

For full biographical listings, see the Martindale-Hubbell Law Directory

---

SOUTH BEND,* St. Joseph Co.

DORAN BLACKMOND READY HAMILTON & WILLIAMS (AV)

1700 Valley American Bank Building, 211 W. Washington Street, 46601
Telephone: 219-288-1800
Fax: 219-236-4265

MEMBERS OF FIRM

M. Edward Doran (1895-1982)	David T. Ready
John E. Doran	John C. Hamilton
Don G. Blackmond	A. Howard Williams

ASSOCIATE

Don Gregory Blackmond

For full biographical listings, see the Martindale-Hubbell Law Directory

South Bend—Continued

JONES, OBENCHAIN, FORD, PANKOW, LEWIS & WOODS (AV)

1800 Valley American Bank Building, P.O. Box 4577, 46634
Telephone: 219-233-1194
Fax: 233-8957; 233-9675

Vitus G. Jones (1879-1951)	Roland Obenchain (Retired)
Roland Obenchain (1890-1961)	Milton A. Johnson (Retired)
Francis Jones (1907-1988)	James H. Pankow (Retired)

MEMBERS OF FIRM

Thomas F. Lewis, Jr.	Robert M. Edwards, Jr.
Timothy W. Woods	John B. Ford
John R. Obenchain	Mark J. Phillipoff
Robert W. Mysliwiec	John W. Van Laere

ASSOCIATES

Edward P. Benchik	Robert S. Sanderson

Thomas F. Lewis, III

OF COUNSEL

G. Burt Ford

Attorneys for: American Family Insurance; The Equitable Life Assurance Society of the United States; Ohio Casualty Co.; Holy Cross Health Systems; Saint Joseph's Care Group; Koontz-Wagner Electric Co.; Old Kent Bank-Southwest; The Travelers Insurance Co.; H.G. Christman Construction Co., Inc.; Automatic Technologies.

For full biographical listings, see the Martindale-Hubbell Law Directory

---

IOWA

COUNCIL BLUFFS,* Pottawattamie Co.

SMITH PETERSON LAW FIRM (AV)

35 Main Place, Suite 300, P.O. Box 249, 51502
Telephone: 712-328-1833
Fax: 712-328-8320
Omaha, Nebraska Office: 9290 West Dodge Road, Suite 205.
Telephone: 402-397-8500.
Fax: 402-397-5519.

MEMBERS OF FIRM

Raymond A. Smith (1892-1977)	Lawrence J. Beckman
John LeRoy Peterson	Gregory G. Barntsen
(1895-1969)	W. Curtis Hewett
Harold T. Beckman	Steven H. Krohn
Robert J. Laubenthal	Randy R. Ewing
Richard A. Heininger	Joseph D. Thornton

ASSOCIATES

T. J. Pattermann	Paul M. Shotkoski
Daniel Fretheim	(Not admitted in IA)

Representative Clients: Redland Insurance Group; Iowa Western Community College; Farm Credit Bank of Omaha; Demma Fruit Co.; Peoples National Bank; Council Bluffs Board of Water Works Trustee.

For full biographical listings, see the Martindale-Hubbell Law Directory

DES MOINES,* Polk Co.

SHEARER, TEMPLER & PINGEL, A PROFESSIONAL CORPORATION (AV)

Suite 437 3737 Woodland Avenue (West Des Moines), P.O. Box 1991, 50309
Telephone: 515-225-3737
Fax: 515-225-9510

Ronni F. Begleiter	Leon R. Shearer
Thomas M. Cunningham	Brenton D. Soderstrum
Jeffrey L. Goodman	Jeffrey D. Stone
John R. Perkins	David G. Stork
G. Brian Pingel	John A. Templer, Jr.

For Complete List of Firm Personnel, See General Section

For full biographical listings, see the Martindale-Hubbell Law Directory

WATERLOO,* Black Hawk Co.

SWISHER & COHRT, P.L.C. (AV)

528 West Fourth Street, P.O. Box 1200, 50704
Telephone: 319-232-6555
FAX: 319-232-4835

Benjamin F. Swisher (1878-1959)	Steven A. Weidner
L. J. Cohrt (1898-1974)	Larry J. Cohrt
Charles F. Swisher (1919-1986)	J. Douglas Oberman
Jeffrey J. Greenwood	Stephen J. Powell
(1953-1995)	Jim D. DeKoster
Eldon R. McCann	Samuel C. Anderson

(See Next Column)

Robert C. Griffin	Beth E. Hansen
Kevin R. Rogers	Mark F. Conway

Natalie Williams Burris

Firm is Counsel for: Koehring Corp.; Clay Equipment; Chamberlain Manufacturing Co.; Waterloo Courier.
Local Counsel for: Allied Group; John Deere Insurance; Liberty Mutual Insurance Co.

For full biographical listings, see the Martindale-Hubbell Law Directory

WEST DES MOINES, Polk Co.

LaMARCA & LANDRY, P.C. (AV)

1300 50th Street, 50266
Telephone: 515-225-2600
Fax: 515-225-8581

George A. LaMarca	Gregory W. Landry
	Robert K. DuPuy

Gary G. Mattson

OF COUNSEL

Martin R. Anderson	Samuel S. Duffey

For full biographical listings, see the Martindale-Hubbell Law Directory

---

KANSAS

LENEXA, Johnson Co.

EVANS & MULLINIX, P.A. (AV)

15301 W. 87th Street, Suite 220, 66219
Telephone: 913-541-1200
Facsimile: 913-541-1010
Kansas City, Kansas Office: 1314 North 38th Street, 66102.
Telephone: 913-621-1200.
Telecopier: 913-621-1263.

Timothy J. Evans	John E. Larson
Jo Ann Butaud	Merle E. Parks
	Kristen F. Heidenreich

OF COUNSEL

Vito C. Barbieri

For full biographical listings, see the Martindale-Hubbell Law Directory

OVERLAND PARK, Johnson Co.

FISHER, PATTERSON, SAYLER & SMITH, L.L.P. (AV)

11050 Roe Avenue, Suite 210, 66211
Telephone: 913-339-6757
FAX: 913-339-6187
Topeka, Kansas Office: 534 South Kansas Avenue, Suite 400, P.O. Box 949, 66601.
Telephone: 913-232-7761.
Fax: 913-232-6604.

MEMBERS OF FIRM

Edwin Dudley Smith (Resident)	Michael K. Seck (Resident)
	David P. Madden (Resident)

ASSOCIATE

Patrick G. Reavey (Resident)

For full biographical listings, see the Martindale-Hubbell Law Directory

TOPEKA,* Shawnee Co.

FISHER, PATTERSON, SAYLER & SMITH, L.L.P. (AV)

534 South Kansas Avenue, Suite 400, P.O. Box 949, 66601
Telephone: 913-232-7761
Fax: 913-232-6604
Overland Park, Kansas Office: 11050 Roe Avenue, Suite 210, 66211.
Telephone: 913-339-6757.
Fax: 913-339-6187.

MEMBERS OF FIRM

Donald Patterson	Steve R. Fabert
Edwin Dudley Smith (Resident,	Ronald J. Laskowski
Overland Park Office)	Michael K. Seck (Resident,
Larry G. Pepperdine	Overland Park Office)
James P. Nordstrom	David P. Madden (Resident,
Justice B. King	Overland Park Office)
J. Steven Pigg	Steven K. Johnson

ASSOCIATES

Kristine A. Larscheid	Billy E. Newman
Patrick G. Reavey (Resident,	David R. Cooper
Overland Park Office)	

(See Next Column)

FISHER, PATTERSON, SAYLER & SMITH L.L.P., *Topeka—Continued*

OF COUNSEL
David H. Fisher

RETIRED
Charles Keith Sayler (Retired)

Representative Clients: Gage Shopping Center, Inc.; Fireman's Fund-American Insurance Cos.; United States Fidelity and Guaranty Co.; The Procter & Gamble Company; American Cyanamid Company; Commercial Union Insurance Companies; National Casualty/Scottsdale Insurance Co.; The Hartford; Berkshire Hathaway Companies.

For full biographical listings, see the Martindale-Hubbell Law Directory

---

WRIGHT, HENSON, SOMERS, SEBELIUS, CLARK & BAKER, LLP (AV)

Commerce Bank Building, 100 Southeast Ninth Street, 2nd Floor, P.O. Box 3555, 66601-3555
Telephone: 913-232-2200
FAX: 913-232-3344

MEMBERS OF FIRM
Thomas E. Wright	K. Gary Sebelius
Charles N. Henson	Bruce J. Clark
Dale L. Somers	Anne Lamborn Baker

ASSOCIATE
Theron L. Sims

For Complete List of Firm Personnel, See General Section

For full biographical listings, see the Martindale-Hubbell Law Directory

---

WICHITA,* Sedgwick Co.

ADAMS, JONES, ROBINSON AND MALONE, CHARTERED (AV)

600 Market Centre, 155 North Market, P.O. Box 1034, 67201-1034
Telephone: 316-265-8591
Telecopier: 316-265-9719
Email: ajrm@southwind.net *URL:* http://www.southwind.net,~ajrm

Philip L. Bowman	Monte Vines
Donald W. Bostwick	Teresa J. James
Mert F. Buckley	Laura L. Ice
Larry D. Spurgeon	

SPECIAL COUNSEL
John T. Conlee	William F. Kluge, III

Representative Clients: Mid Continent Federal Saving Bank; INTRUST Bank, NA; Bank IV Kansas, NA; First Bank, fsb; Travelers Insurance Co.; Williams Natural Gas Co.; City of Wichita; Ameri-Kart Corp.; A.O. Smith Corp.; Lease America Corp.

For full biographical listings, see the Martindale-Hubbell Law Directory

---

FOULSTON & SIEFKIN L.L.P. (AV)

700 Fourth Financial Center, 67202
Telephone: 316-267-6371
Facsimile: 316-267-6345
Topeka, Kansas Office: 1515 Bank IV Tower, 534 Kansas Avenue, 66603.
Telephone: 913-233-3600.
Fax: 913-233-1610.
Dodge City, Kansas Office: 810 Frontview, P.O. Box 1147, 67801.
Telephone: 316-227-8126.
Fax: 316-227-8451.
Member: Lex Mundi, A Global Association of 126 Independent Firms.

MEMBERS OF FIRM
Benjamin C. Langel	James D. Oliver
William R. Wood, II	

For Complete List of Firm Personnel, See General Section

For full biographical listings, see the Martindale-Hubbell Law Directory

---

HERSHBERGER, PATTERSON, JONES & ROTH, L.C. (AV)

600 Hardage Center, 100 South Main, 67202-3779
Telephone: 316-263-7583
Fax: 316-263-7595

Jerome E. Jones	J. Michael Kennalley
Robert J. Roth	John A. Vetter
Ken W. Dannenberg	

Counsel for: First National Bank in Wichita; Anadarko Petroleum Corporation; Chinese Industries; Mobil Oil Corp.; CNA Insurance; Royal Exchange Group; Central National Insurance Group; Transamerica Insurance Group; Northwestern National Insurance Group.

For Complete List of Firm Personnel, See General Section

For full biographical listings, see the Martindale-Hubbell Law Directory

---

YOUNG, BOGLE, McCAUSLAND, WELLS & CLARK, P.A. (AV)

106 West Douglas, Suite 923, 67202
Telephone: 316-265-7841
Facsimile: 316-265-3956

Jerry D. Bogle	Kenneth M. Clark
Paul S. McCausland	Patrick C. Blanchard
William A. Wells	Mark R. Maloney

OF COUNSEL
Orlin L. Wagner

Representative Clients: Deere Credit Services, Inc.; Agricredit Acceptance Corp.; Equitable Agri-Business, Inc.; General Mills, Inc.; Straightline Mfg., Inc.

For Complete List of Firm Personnel, See General Section

For full biographical listings, see the Martindale-Hubbell Law Directory

---

KENTUCKY

BOWLING GREEN,* Warren Co.

ENGLISH, LUCAS, PRIEST & OWSLEY (AV)

1101 College Street, P.O. Box 770, 42102-0770
Telephone: 502-781-6500
Telecopier: 502-782-7782
Email: inquiry@elpo.com

MEMBERS OF FIRM
Charles E. English	Whayne C. Priest, Jr.
	Keith M. Carwell

ASSOCIATES
Marc Allen Lovell	Jason P. Wright

For Complete List of Firm Personnel, See General Section

For full biographical listings, see the Martindale-Hubbell Law Directory

---

KERRICK, GRISE & STIVERS (AV)

1025 State Street, P.O. Box 9547, 42102-9547
Telephone: 502-782-8160
Fax: 502-782-5856
Elizabethtown, Kentucky Office: 2935 Dolphin Drive, Suite 102.
Telephone: 502-769-5788.
Fax: 502-737-9285.

MEMBERS OF FIRM
Thomas N. Kerrick	Gregory N. Stivers
John R. Grise	H. Brent Brennenstuhl

ASSOCIATES
Lanna Martin Kilgore	Shawn Rosso Alcott
Laura M. Hagan (Resident, Elizabethtown Office)	Jason B. Bell

Representative Clients: Dollar General Corp.; Columbia Greenview Regional Hospital; Hospital Corporation of America; Hardin Memorial Hospital; Monarch Environmental, Inc.; Mid-South Management Group, Inc.; Trans Financial Bank; TKR Cable.

For full biographical listings, see the Martindale-Hubbell Law Directory

---

LEXINGTON,* Fayette Co.

LANDRUM & SHOUSE (AV)

106 West Vine Street, P.O. Box 951, 40588-0951
Telephone: 606-255-2424
Facsimile: 606-233-0308
Louisville, Kentucky Office: 400 West Market Street, Suite 1550, 40202.
Telephone: 502-589-7616.
Facsimile: 502-589-2119.

MEMBERS OF FIRM
John H. Burrus	Mark L. Moseley
William C. Shouse	Jack E. Toliver

ASSOCIATE
Charles E. Christian

District Attorneys: CSX Transportation, Inc.
Special Trial Counsel: Ford Motor Co. and Affiliates (Eastern Kentucky); Clark Equipment Co.
Representative Clients: The Continental Insurance Cos.; U.S. Insurance Group; U.S. Fidelity & Guaranty Co.; Ohio Casualty Insurance Co.; CIGNA; Royal Insurance Cos.

For Complete List of Firm Personnel, See General Section

For full biographical listings, see the Martindale-Hubbell Law Directory

Lexington—Continued

STOLL, KEENON & PARK, LLP (AV)

201 E. Main Street, Suite 1000, 40507-1380
Telephone: 606-231-3000
Telecopier: 606-253-1093; 606-253-1027
Frankfort, Kentucky Office: 307 Washington Street, 40601.
Telephone: 502-875-6220.
Telecopier: 502-875-6235.
Louisville, Kentucky Office: 400 West Market Street, Suite 2650, 40202-3377.
Telephone: 502-568-9100.
Telecopier: 502-568-5700.

MEMBERS OF FIRM

Samuel D. Hinkle IV	Robert W. Kellerman
R. David Lester	Dan M. Rose
Herbert A. Miller, Jr.	Gregory D. Pavey
Harvie B. Wilkinson	Lea Pauley Goff

ASSOCIATES

Laura Day DelCotto	Culver V. Halliday
R. Douglas Martin	

Representative Clients: Bank One, Lexington, NA; Bank One, Kentucky, NA; Fifth Third Bank; Whitaker Bank Corporation of Kentucky.

For Complete List of Firm Personnel, See General Section

For full biographical listings, see the Martindale-Hubbell Law Directory

---

LOUISVILLE,* Jefferson Co.

STOLL, KEENON & PARK, LLP (AV)

400 West Market Street Suite 2650, 40202-3377
Telephone: 502-568-9100
Telecopier: 502-568-5700
Frankfort, Kentucky Office: 307 Washington Street.
Telephone: 502-875-6220.
Telecopier: 502-875-6235.
Lexington, Kentucky Office: 210 E. Main Street, Suite 1000, 40507-1380.
Telephone: 606-231-3000.
Telecopier: 606-253-1093; 606-253-1380.

MEMBER OF FIRM
Samuel D. Hinkle, IV

For Complete List of Firm Personnel, See General Section

For full biographical listings, see the Martindale-Hubbell Law Directory

---

PIKEVILLE,* Pike Co.

GARY C. JOHNSON, P.S.C. (AV)

104 Caroline Avenue, P.O. Box 231, 41502
Telephone: 606-437-4002
Telecopier: 606-437-0021
Hazard, Kentucky Office: 941 Memorial Drive, P.O. Box 509.
Telephone: 606-436-6059.
Fax: 606-436-4599.
Lexington, Kentucky Office: 101 Prosperous Place, Suite 100.
Telephone: 606-263-4002.

Gary C. Johnson

Anita Johnson	Jeffrey R. Morgan
Roy J. Downey	Jeremy R. Morgan
Timothy D. Belcher	Jimmie G. Orr, Jr.
Julie A. Butcher	Ray Stanley Jones, II
William Hickman, III	Masten Childers, II

For full biographical listings, see the Martindale-Hubbell Law Directory

STRATTON, MAY, HAYS & HOGG, PSC (AV)

232 Second Street Ward Building, P.O. Box 851, 41502
Telephone: 606-437-7300
Fax: 606-437-7569
Whitesburg, Kentucky Office: By-Pass Highway 15. 41858.
Telephone: 606-633-9922.

Henry D. Stratton (1925-1989)	Stephen L. Hogg
Marrs Allen May	H. Edward Maddox
John D. Hays	F. Byrd Hogg (Resident,
David C. Stratton	Whitesburg, Kentucky Office)

LEGAL SUPPORT PERSONNEL
PARALEGALS

Carol Rowe Potter	Rebecca Branham
(Real Estate Paralegal)	(Litigation Paralegal)

General Counsel for: Trans Financial Bank of Pikeville.
Representative Clients: Virginia Iron Coal & Coke Co.; Commercial Union Insurance Co.; The Travelers Insurance Co.; Universal Underwriters Insurance Co.; Bituminous Casualty Co.; Enterprise Coal Company; South Central Bell; Scottsdale Insurance Co.
Reference: Transfinancial Bank, Pikeville.

For full biographical listings, see the Martindale-Hubbell Law Directory

LOUISIANA

BATON ROUGE,* East Baton Rouge Parish

GUGLIELMO, MARKS, SCHUTTE, TERHOEVE & LOVE (AV)

(A Registered Limited Liability Partnership)
320 Somerulos Street, P.O. Box 3177, 70821-3177
Telephone: 504-387-6966
Fax: 504-387-8338

Carey J. Guglielmo	Glen Scott Love
Paul Marks, Jr.	Dawn T. Trabeau-Mire
Charles A. Schutte, Jr.	Joseph W. Mengis
Henry G. Terhoeve	Kevin P. Landreneau

Representative Clients: City National Bank; Greyhound Corp.; The Travelers Insurance Co.; Chrysler Corp.; State Farm Insurance Co's.; Travelers/Aetna Insurance Group; Aetna Life & Casualty Co.

For full biographical listings, see the Martindale-Hubbell Law Directory

---

KANTROW, SPAHT, WEAVER & BLITZER, A PROFESSIONAL LAW CORPORATION (AV)

Suite 300, City Plaza, 445 North Boulevard, P.O. Box 2997, 70821-2997
Telephone: 504-383-4703
Fax: 504-343-0630; 343-0637

Byron R. Kantrow	Vincent P. Fornias
Carlos G. Spaht	David S. Rubin
Geraldine B. Weaver	Diane L. Crochet
Sidney M. Blitzer, Jr.	Richard F. Zimmerman, Jr.
Paul H. Spaht	Bob D. Tucker
Lee C. Kantrow	Martin E. Golden
John C. Miller	Joseph A. Schittone, Jr.

S. Layne Lee	Connell L. Archey
J. Michael Robinson, Jr.	Randal J. Robert

Representative Clients: CNA Insurance Cos.; Federal Deposit Insurance Corp.; Hartford Insurance Group; Air Products and Chemicals, Inc.; CF Industries, Inc.; AT&T; United Companies Financial Corp.

For full biographical listings, see the Martindale-Hubbell Law Directory

---

KEAN, MILLER, HAWTHORNE, D'ARMOND, McCOWAN & JARMAN, L.L.P. (AV)

22nd Floor, One American Place, P.O. Box 3513, 70821
Telephone: 504-387-0999
Fax: 504-388-9133
New Orleans, Louisiana Office: Energy Centre, Suite 1470, 1100 Poydras Street.
Telephone: 504-585-3050.
Fax: 504-585-3051.
Plaquemine, Louisiana Office: Suite 10, 23425 Railroad Avenue.
Telephone: 504-687-9845.
Fax: 504-382-3445.

MEMBERS OF FIRM

Ben R. Miller, Jr.	Isaac M. Gregorie, Jr.
Robert A. Hawthorne, Jr.	G. Blane Clark, Jr.
Carey J. Messina	James R. Lackie
Todd A. Rossi	

Kelly Wilkinson	Stephen M. Robinson
Dean Paul Cazenave	

OF COUNSEL
Reilly L. Stonecipher

Representative Clients: The Lamar Advertising Co., Baton Rouge, LA; Anco Industries, Inc., Baton Rouge, LA; Piccadilly Cafeterias, Inc./Ralph & Kacoo's, Baton Rouge, LA; Amec Engineering, Inc., Houston, TX; Stauffer Chemical, Co., Shelton, CT; Exxon Chemical Americas and Exxon Corporation, Baton Rouge, LA; Mobil Oil Corporation, Fairfax, VA; Hancock Bank of Louisiana, Baton Rouge, LA.

For Complete List of Firm Personnel, See General Section

For full biographical listings, see the Martindale-Hubbell Law Directory

---

SEALE, SMITH, ZUBER & BARNETTE (AV)

Two United Plaza, Suite 200, 8550 United Plaza Boulevard, 70809
Telephone: 504-924-1600
Telecopier: 504-924-6100

Armbrust Gordon Seale (1913-1989)	William C. Kaufman III
	John W. L. Swanner
Robert W. Smith (1922-1989)	James H. Morgan III
Donald S. Zuber	Ronald A. Seale
Kenneth E. Barnette	Brent E. Kinchen

(See Next Column)

SEALE, SMITH, ZUBER & BARNETTE, *Baton Rouge—Continued*

Charles K. Watts	William C. Rowe, Jr.
Myron A. Walker, Jr.	Lawrence R. Anderson, Jr.
Daniel A. Reed	Catherine S. Nobile

ASSOCIATES

Richard T. Reed	Anthony J. Russo, Jr.
Barbara G. Chatelain	Gregory D. Polozola

Representative Clients: Farmers Insurance Group; St. Paul Fire and Marine Insurance Company; United Services Automobile Association; General Motors Acceptance Corporation.
Reference: City National Bank, Baton Rouge, Louisiana.

For full biographical listings, see the Martindale-Hubbell Law Directory

LAFAYETTE, Lafayette Parish

WAYNE A. SHULLAW (AV)

600 Jefferson Street, Fifth Floor, Suite 502, P.O. Box 4815, 70502
Telephone: 318-266-2310
Fax: 318-266-2311

For full biographical listings, see the Martindale-Hubbell Law Directory

METAIRIE, Jefferson Parish

CAMPBELL, McCRANIE, SISTRUNK, ANZELMO & HARDY, P.C. (AV)

3445 North Causeway Boulevard, Suite 802, P.O. Box 7310, 70010-7310
Telephone: 504-831-0946
Fax: 504-831-2492

Frederick R. Campbell	Sidney J. Hardy
Burgess E. McCranie, Jr.	Lisa Miley Geary
Michael R. Sistrunk	Lance S. Ostendorf
Thomas P. Anzelmo	Roy C. Beard

Henry G. Sullivan, Jr.	Charles E. Sutton, Jr.
Adrian F. LaPeyronnie, III	Geoffrey J. Orr
Isidro René DeRojas	Shannon Kenney Lowry
Mark Emerson Hanna	Keith M. Matulich

For full biographical listings, see the Martindale-Hubbell Law Directory

WEIR AND WALLEY (AV)

2721 Division Street, 70002-7084
Telephone: 504-455-7264
Fax: 504-455-7266

Andrew M. Weir	James M. Walley

ASSOCIATE
Mark Needham

References: The Whitney National Bank; First National Bank of Commerce.

For full biographical listings, see the Martindale-Hubbell Law Directory

MONROE, Ouachita Parish

THOMPSON, SPARKS, DEAN & MORRIS (AV)

A Partnership including a Professional Corporation
1401 Royal Street, P.O. Box 2867, 71207
Telephone: 318-388-1440
Fax: 318-322-0887

MEMBERS OF FIRM

M. C. Thompson (1885-1970)	George B. Dean, Jr., (P.C.)
James D. Sparks (1910-1987)	Wood T. Sparks
John C. Morris, III	

Representative Clients: South Central Bell Telephone Co.; Greater Ouachita Water Company; PHH Homequity Corp.; Commonwealth Relocation Services, Inc.; Remax, Monroe; Bell South Advertising & Publishing Corp.; Premier Mortgage Corp.; Countrywide Funding Corp.
Approved Attorneys for: Central Bank; Federal Land Bank.

For full biographical listings, see the Martindale-Hubbell Law Directory

NEW ORLEANS, Orleans Parish

DEUTSCH, KERRIGAN & STILES, L.L.P. (AV)

A Partnership including Professional Law Corporations
755 Magazine Street, 70130-3672
Telephone: 504-581-5141
Cable Address: "Dekest"
Telex: 584358
Telecopier: 504-566-1201
Email: dks@dksno.com *URL:* http://www.dksno.com
St. Tammany Parish Office: 550 Pontchartrain Drive, Suite 200, Slidell, LA. 70458.
Telephone: 504-639-0555.
Fax: 504-639-0550

(See Next Column)

MEMBERS OF FIRM

Frederick R. Bott (P.L.C.)	Darrell K. Cherry (P.L.C.)
William W. Messersmith, III, (P.L.C.)	Richard B. Montgomery III
Peter J. Butler	William E. Wright, Jr.
Charles F. Seemann, Jr., (P.L.C.)	Nancy J. Marshall
Robert E. Kerrigan, Jr., (P.L.C.)	Ellis B. Murov (P.L.C.)
Raymon G. Jones (P.L.C.)	Duris L. Holmes
Victor E. Stilwell, Jr., (P.L.C.)	Joseph L. McReynolds
Matt J. Farley (P.L.C.)	Theodore L. White
Daniel A. Smith	Judy L. Burnthorn
Terrence L. Brennan	Carl A. Butler
Marc J. Yellin (P.L.C.)	Peter J. Butler, Jr.
	Barbara Malik Weller
Karyn J. Vigh	

OF COUNSEL

Marian Mayer Berkett	Malcolm W. Monroe
Ralph L. Kaskell, Jr.	Charles K. Reasonover (P.L.C.)

ASSOCIATES

Herman J. Gesser, III	W. Christopher Beary
Richard G. Passler	Charles F. Seemann III

For Complete List of Firm Personnel, See General Section

For full biographical listings, see the Martindale-Hubbell Law Directory

HEBERT, MOULEDOUX & BLAND, A PROFESSIONAL LAW CORPORATION (AV)

Pan-American Life Center, Suite 1650, 601 Poydras Street, 70130
Telephone: 504-525-3333
Cable Address: "HMBL"
Telex: 588-092;
Fax: 504-523-4224

Maurice C. Hebert, Jr.	André J. Mouledoux
Alan Guy Brackett	

Representative Clients: Archer-Daniels Midland Company; Bisso Marine Company, Inc.; Carline Geismar Fleet, Inc.; Cooper/T. Smith Stevedoring Company, Inc.; Delta Queen Steamboat Co.; Diamond Offshore Drilling, Inc.; LOOP INC.; Marine Equipment Management Corporation; McDermott Incorporated; Olympic Marine Company.

For Complete List of Firm Personnel, See General Section

For full biographical listings, see the Martindale-Hubbell Law Directory

LEAKE & ANDERSSON, L.L.P. (AV)

1700 Energy Centre, 1100 Poydras Street, 70163-1701
Telephone: 504-585-7500
Telecopier: 504-585-7775
Email: LA1700@aol.com

MEMBERS OF FIRM

Robert E. Leake, Jr.	Lawrence A. Mann
W. Paul Andersson	Kevin O'Bryon
George D. Fagan	

ASSOCIATE
Guy D. Perrier

Representative Clients: Trailer Train; KFC; Heller Financial, Inc.; The Kroger Co.; Amway Corporation; Safelite Glass Co.; Secor Bank; F.S.B.; Gerrard Chevrolet.

For Complete List of Firm Personnel, See General Section

For full biographical listings, see the Martindale-Hubbell Law Directory

MIDDLEBERG, RIDDLE & GIANNA (AV)

31st Floor, Place St. Charles, 201 St. Charles Avenue, 70170-3100
Telephone: 504-525-7200
Telecopier: 504-581-5983
Dallas, Texas Office: 2323 Bryan Street, Suite 1600.
Telephone: 214-220-6300;
Telecopier: 214-220-2785.
Austin, Texas Office: 1300 South Mopac Expressway, First Floor.
Telephone: 512-434-8334.

MEMBERS OF FIRM

Ira Joel Middleberg	Dominic J. Gianna
Michael Lee Riddle (Austin and Dallas, Texas)	

Paul J. Mirabile	Tina S. Clark
John D. Person	E. Ralph Lupin
Alan Dean Weinberger	A.J. Herbert, III
L. Marlene Quarles	Marshall J. Simien, Jr.
Ronald J. Vega	Wade P. Webster
Edward T. Suffern, Jr.	Brian G. Meissner
Rebecca J. King	

For full biographical listings, see the Martindale-Hubbell Law Directory

New Orleans—Continued

WAGNER, BAGOT & GLEASON (AV)

Suite 2660, Poydras Center, 650 Poydras Street, 70130-6105
Telephone: 504-525-2141
Telecopier: 504-523-1587
TWX: 5106017673
ELN: 62928850
"INCISIVE"

Thomas J. Wagner	Harvey G. Gleason
Michael H. Bagot, Jr.	Whitney L. Cole
	Eric D. Suben

For full biographical listings, see the Martindale-Hubbell Law Directory

---

SHREVEPORT, * Caddo Parish

BARLOW AND HARDTNER L.C. (AV)

Tenth Floor, Louisiana Tower, 401 Edwards Street, 71101-3289
Telephone: 318-227-1131
Telecopier: 318-227-1141
Mailing Address: P.O. Box 8, Shreveport, Louisiana, 71161-0008

Quintin T. Hardtner, III　　　　　David R. Taggart

Representative Clients: Kelley Oil Corporation; NorAm Energy Corp. (formerly Arkla, Inc.); Central and South West Corporation; Central Louisiana Electric Company; Panhandle Eastern Corp.; Pennzoil Producing Co.; Johnson Controls, Inc.; Ashland Oil, Inc.; Southwestern Electric Power Company; General Electric Co.

For Complete List of Firm Personnel, See General Section

For full biographical listings, see the Martindale-Hubbell Law Directory

---

ROBERT U. GOODMAN, P.L.C. (AV)

Mid South Towers, 416 Travis Street, Suite 1105, 71101-5514
Telephone: 318-221-1601
Fax: 318-221-1749

Robert U. Goodman
OF COUNSEL

James E. Clark　　　　　　　　Nancy Kay Fox-Reiter

Representative Clients: Trans-World Life Insurance Co.; Aeropres Corp.; Dealers Truck & Equipment Co.; Pioneer Bank & Trust Co.; Steel Erectors, Inc.; Powell Buick, Inc.; Housing Authority of the City of Shreveport; Specht Newspapers, Inc.; Graham Brothers Entertainment, Inc.; Integrated Exploration, Inc.

For full biographical listings, see the Martindale-Hubbell Law Directory

---

MAINE

LEWISTON, Androscoggin Co.

PLATZ & THOMPSON, P.A. (AV)

95 Park Street, P.O. Box 960, 04243
Telephone: 207-783-8558
Telecopier: 207-783-9487

John A. Platz (1913-1980)	Roger J. O'Donnell, III
J. Peter Thompson	Robert V. Hoy
Philip K. Hargesheimer	Michael J. LaTorre
Paul S. Douglass	James B. Main

Representative Clients: Key Bank of Maine; Fleet Bank; Androscoggin Savings Bank; Maine Education Assoc.; Pioneer Plastics, Inc.; Getty Oil Co.; Munson Transportation; Livermore Falls Trust; H.P. Cummings Const. Co.

For full biographical listings, see the Martindale-Hubbell Law Directory

---

PORTLAND, * Cumberland Co.

AMERLING & BURNS, A PROFESSIONAL ASSOCIATION (AV)

193 Middle Street, 04101
Telephone: 207-775-3581
Facsimile: 207-775-3814
Affiliated St. Croix Office: Coon & Sanford, P.O. Box 25918, Six Chandlers's Wharf, Suite 202, 00824-0918.

W. John Amerling	Arnold C. Macdonald
George F. Burns	Mary DeLano
David P. Ray	Joanne F. Cole
	A. Robert Ruesch

OF COUNSEL
Bruce M. Jervis

Representative Clients: H.E. Sargent, Inc. (construction); Merrill Trust; J.M. Huber, Inc.; Jackson Laboratories; Hague International (engineering); Aetna Life & Casualty Co.; The Hartford; Great American Insurance Co.; Wausau Insurance Co.

For full biographical listings, see the Martindale-Hubbell Law Directory

---

PIERCE ATWOOD (AV)

One Monument Square, 04101
Telephone: 207-791-1100
Fax: 207-791-1350
Email: info@PierceAtwood.com
Augusta, Maine Office: 77 Winthrop Street.
Telephone: 207-622-6311.
Fax: 207-623-9367.
Newburyport, Massachusetts Office: 6 Harris Street.
Telephone: 508-465-9599.
Fax: 508-465-9945.

MEMBERS OF FIRM

Bruce A. Coggeshall	Christopher E. Howard
James B. Zimpritch	Jacob A. Manheimer
Richard P. Hackett	David J. Champoux
	Gloria A. Pinza

OF COUNSEL
Jeremiah D. Newbury

ASSOCIATES

James M. Saffian	William L. Worden
Foster A. Stewart, Jr	Marcia A. Metcalf

For Complete List of Firm Personnel, See General Section

For full biographical listings, see the Martindale-Hubbell Law Directory

---

PRETI, FLAHERTY, BELIVEAU & PACHIOS (AV)

A Limited Liability Company
443 Congress Street, P.O. Box 11410, 04104-7410
Telephone: 207-791-3000
Telecopier: 207-791-3111
Email: admin@pfbpnet.com
Augusta, Maine Office: 45 Memorial Circle, P.O. Box 1058, 04332-1058.
Telephone: 207-623-5300.
Telecopier: 207-623-2914.

MEMBERS OF FIRM

Harold C. Pachios	Leonard M. Gulino
Michael J. Gentile	Dennis C. Sbrega
(Augusta Office)	Estelle A. Lavoie
Eric P. Stauffer	Susan E. LoGiudice
Jonathan S. Piper	Michael Kaplan
Randall B. Weill	Michael L. Sheehan
James C. Pitney, Jr.	John P. McVeigh
(Augusta Office)	

OF COUNSEL
Jeanne T. Cohn-Connor

ASSOCIATES

James E. Phipps	Scott T. Rodgers

Representative Clients: Key Bank of Maine; Guy Gannett Publishing Co.; Peoples Heritage Savings Bank; Liberty Group Inc.; RECOLL Management Corp.; NRG Barriers, Inc.; Hussey Corp.; Northeast Air Group; The Woodlands Club; P.H. Chadbourne and Co.

For Complete List of Firm Personnel, See General Section

For full biographical listings, see the Martindale-Hubbell Law Directory

---

TROUBH, HEISLER & PIAMPIANO, P.C. (AV)

511 Congress Street, P.O. Box 9711, 04104-5011
Telephone: 207-780-6789
Fax: 207-774-2339

William B. Troubh	Thomas E. Getchell
Edwin A. Heisler	Michael Richards
Robert J. Piampiano	William K. McKinley
Kevin M. Gillis	Daniel F. Gilligan
Michael P. Boyd	Paul S. Bulger

John G. Richardson	Linda L. Sears
	Daniel R. Felkel

For full biographical listings, see the Martindale-Hubbell Law Directory

---

MARYLAND

ANNAPOLIS, * Anne Arundel Co.

STEVEN P. RESNICK (AV)

116-D Cathedral Street, 21401
Telephone: 410-267-8400; Baltimore: 269-8900
Fax: 410-626-6188

(See Next Column)

STEVEN P. RESNICK, *Annapolis—Continued*

ASSOCIATE

W. Kevin Reynolds

Representative Clients: Medlantic Management (d.b.a. Washington Hospital Center); Bell Atlantic Mobile Systems, Inc.; Radar Association Defending Airwave Rights, Inc. (RADAR); Annapolis Housing Authority; Maryland Pest Control Association.

For full biographical listings, see the Martindale-Hubbell Law Directory

BALTIMORE,* (Independent City)

BALLARD SPAHR ANDREWS & INGERSOLL (AV)

300 East Lombard Street, 19th Floor, 21202-3268
Telephone: 410-528-5600
Fax: 410-528-5650
Philadelphia, Pennsylvania Office: 1735 Market Street, 51st Floor.
Telephone: 215-665-8500.
Fax: 215-864-8999.
Harrisburg, Pennsylvania Office: 105 North Front Street.
Telephone: 717-236-3333.
Fax: 717-236-3884.
Denver, Colorado Office: Seventeenth Street Plaza Building, Suite 2300, 1225 17th Street.
Telephone: 303-292-2400.
Fax: 303-296-3956.
Salt Lake City, Utah Office: One Utah Center, 201 South Main Street, Suite 1200.
Telephone: 801-531-3000.
Fax: 801-531-3001.
Washington, D.C. Office: Suite 900 East, 555 13th Street, N.W.
Telephone: 202-383-8800.
Fax: 202-383-8877; 383-8893.
Camden, New Jersey Office: 800 Hudson Square, 5th Floor.
Telephone: 609-541-5577.
Fax: 609-541-8272.

Tracy A. Bacigalupo	James J. Hanks, Jr.
Sophie D. Goetz	Charles R. Moran

S. Nelson Weeks

OF COUNSEL

Douglas M. Fox

For full biographical listings, see the Martindale-Hubbell Law Directory

THIEBLOT, RYAN, MARTIN & MILLER, P.A. (AV)

4th Floor, The World Trade Center, 21202-3091
Telephone: 410-837-1140
Washington, D.C. Line: 202-628-8223
Fax: 410-837-3282
Towson, Maryland Office: Atlantic Federal Building. Suite 400. 100 West Road. 21204.
Telephone: 410-828-5900.

Robert J. Thieblot	Robert D. Harwick, Jr.
Anthony W. Ryan	Anne M. Hrehorovich
J. Edward Martin, Jr.	Donna Marie Raffaele
Bruce R. Miller	Hamilton Fisk Tyler

Samuel S. Field III

Representative Clients: American Association of Creditor Attorneys; Baltimore County Savings Bank, FSB; Bank One National Bank; Carroll County Bank & Trust Co.; Delaware Trust Co.; Ford Motor Credit Company; MBNA America Bank, N.A.; Nissan Motor Acceptance Corp.; Provident Bank of Maryland; Toyota Motor Credit Co.

For full biographical listings, see the Martindale-Hubbell Law Directory

VENABLE ATTORNEYS AT LAW VENABLE, BAETJER AND HOWARD, LLP (AV)

A Partnership including Professional Corporations
1800 Mercantile Bank & Trust Building, 2 Hopkins Plaza, 21201
Telephone: 410-244-7400
Email: INFO@Venable.win.net
Washington, D.C. Office: Venable, Baetjer, Howard & Civiletti LLP. Suite 1000, 1201 New York Avenue, N.W.
Telephone: 202-962-4800.
McLean, Virginia Office: Suite 400, 2010 Corporate Ridge.
Telephone: 703-760-1600.
Rockville, Maryland Office: Suite 500, One Church Street, P. O. Box 1906.
Telephone: 301-217-5600.
Towson, Maryland Office: 210 Allegheny Avenue, P. O. Box 5517.
Telephone: 410-494-6200.

MEMBERS OF FIRM

Thomas P. Perkins, III (P.C.)	Robert A. Shelton
Benjamin R. Civiletti (P.C.) (Also at Washington, D.C. and Towson, Maryland Offices)	Roger W. Titus (Resident, Rockville, Maryland Office)
John Henry Lewin, Jr. (P.C.)	Douglas D. Connah, Jr. (P.C.) (Also at Washington, D.C. Office)
Neal D. Borden (Also at Washington, D.C. Office)	James D. Wright (P.C.)

(See Next Column)

MEMBERS OF FIRM (Continued)

Joe A. Shull (Resident, Washington, D.C. Office)	James L. Shea (Also at Washington, D.C. Office)
Kenneth C. Bass, III (Not admitted in MD; Washington, D.C. and McLean, Virginia Offices)	Jeffrey P. Ayres (P.C.)
	Amy Berman Jackson (Not admitted in MD; Resident, Washington, D.C. Office)
John H. Zink, III (Resident, Towson, Maryland Office)	William D. Quarles (Also at Washington, D.C. and Towson, Maryland Offices)
Bruce E. Titus (Resident, McLean, Virginia Office)	C. Carey Deeley, Jr. (Also at Towson, Maryland Office)
Paul F. Strain (P.C.)	Kathleen Gallogly Cox (Resident, Towson, Maryland Office)
William D. Dolan, III (P.C.) (Not admitted in MD; Resident, McLean, Virginia Office)	Christopher R. Mellott
Paul T. Glasgow (Resident, Rockville, Maryland Office)	M. King Hill, III (Resident, Towson, Maryland Office)
Joseph C. Wich, Jr. (Resident, Towson, Maryland Office)	James A. Dunbar (Also at Washington, D.C. Office)
Edward F. Glynn, Jr. (Resident, Washington, D.C. Office)	John A. Roberts (Also at Rockville, Maryland Office)
Michael Schatzow (Also at Washington, D.C. Office)	Robert J. Bolger, Jr. (Also at Washington, D.C. Office)
Bryson L. Cook (P.C.) (Also at Washington, D.C. Office)	David J. Heubeck
Nell B. Strachan	J. Michael Brennan (Resident, Towson, Maryland Office)
David G. Lane (Resident, McLean, Virginia Office)	Bruce H. Jurist (Also at Washington, D.C. Office)
L. Paige Marvel	Herbert G. Smith, II (Not admitted in MD; Resident, Washington, D.C. Office)
G. Stewart Webb, Jr.	
James K. Archibald (Also at Washington, D.C. Office)	David C. Mancini (Not admitted in MD; Resident, McLean, Virginia Office)
James R. Myers (Not admitted in MD; Resident, Washington, D.C. Office)	Gary M. Hnath (Resident, Washington, D.C. Office)
Edward L. Wender (P.C.)	Kevin L. Shepherd
David M. Fleishman	Newton B. Fowler, III
Jeffrey A. Dunn (also at Washington, D.C. Office)	Michael J. Baader
Mitchell Kolkin	Mitchell Y. Mirviss
George F. Pappas (Also at Washington, D.C. Office)	Michael W. Robinson (Resident, McLean, Virginia Office)
William D. Coston (Not admitted in MD; Resident, Washington, D.C. Office)	Elizabeth Marzo Borinsky
	Robert H. Geis, Jr.
Kenneth S. Slaughter (Not admitted in MD; Resident, Washington, D.C. Office)	

OF COUNSEL

Emried D. Cole, Jr.	Todd K. Snyder
Charles R. Marvin, Jr. (Not admitted in MD; Resident, Washington, D.C. Office)	Mary T. Flynn (Not admitted in MD; Resident, McLean, Virginia Office)

ASSOCIATES

Paul D. Barker, Jr.	Fernand A. Lavallee (Not admitted in MD; Resident, Washington, D. C. Office)
Eric L. Bryant	
Daniel William China	
Wallace E. Christner (Also at Washington, D.C. Office)	Vicki Margolis (Also at Washington, D.C. Office)
David W. Goewey (Not admitted in MD; Resident, Washington, D.C. Office)	John A. McCauley
	Traci H. Mundy (Not admitted in MD; Resident, McLean, Virginia Office)
Maria F. Howell	John T. Prisbe
Mary-Dulany James (Resident, Towson, Maryland Office)	Neal H. Strum
Gregory L. Laubach (Resident, Rockville, Maryland Office)	Brian R. Trumbauer
	Christine J. Warren

Robin L. Zimelman

For Complete List of Firm Personnel, See General Section

For full biographical listings, see the Martindale-Hubbell Law Directory

BETHESDA, Montgomery Co.

DECKELBAUM OGENS & FISCHER, CHARTERED (AV)

6701 Democracy Boulevard, 20817
Telephone: 301-564-5100
Washington D.C. Office: 1140 Connecticut Avenue, N.W.
Telephone: 202-223-1474.

Nelson Deckelbaum	Lawrence H. Fischer
Ronald L. Ogens	Deborah E. Reiser

Ronald G. Scheraga	Bryn Hope Sherman

Darryl Alan Feldman

LEGAL SUPPORT PERSONNEL

Shirley Mostow

Representative Clients: The Charles E. Smith Companies; The Trammell Crow Company.

(See Next Column)

DECKELBAUM OGENS & FISCHER CHARTERED—*Continued*

References: Franklin National Bank; Century National Bank.

For full biographical listings, see the Martindale-Hubbell Law Directory

---

ROCKVILLE,* Montgomery Co.

BRAULT, GRAHAM, SCOTT & BRAULT (AV)

101 South Washington Street, 20850
Telephone: 301-424-1060
Fax: 301-424-7991
Washington, D.C. Office: 1906 Sunderland Place, N.W.
Telephone: 202-785-1200.
FAX: 202-785-4301.
Arlington, Virginia Office: Suite 1201, 2300 North Clarendon Boulevard, Courthouse Plaza.
Telephone: 703-358-9200.

OF COUNSEL

| Laurence T. Scott | Janet S. Zigler (Resident) |

MEMBERS OF FIRM

Denver H. Graham (1922-1987)	Daniel L. Shea (Resident)
Albert E. Brault (Retired)	M. Kathleen Parker (Resident)
Albert D. Brault (Resident)	David G. Mulquin (Resident)
Leo A. Roth, Jr.	James M. Brault (Resident)
James S. Wilson (Resident)	Regina Ann Casey (Resident)
Ronald G. Guziak	Sanford A. Friedman

ASSOCIATES

Holly D. Shupert (Resident)	Joan F. Brault (Resident)
Rhonda Ann Hurwitz (Resident)	Joseph P. Morra (Resident)
Michael A. Carlo	

Representative Clients: American Oil Co.; Crum & Forster Group; Fireman's Fund American Insurance Cos.; Kemper Group; Reliance Insurance Cos.; Safeco Group; Government Employees Insurance Co.; Medical Mutual Insurance Society of Maryland; Legal Mutual Liability Insurance Society of Maryland.

For full biographical listings, see the Martindale-Hubbell Law Directory

SHULMAN, ROGERS, GANDAL, PORDY & ECKER, P.A. (AV)

Third Floor, 11921 Rockville Pike, 20852-2743
Telephone: 301-230-5200
Telecopier: 301-230-2891
Email: litigate@srgpe.com; realprop@srgpe.com
Email: business@srgpe.com
Washington, D.C. Office: 1100 New York Avenue, N.W. West Tower, Suite 500.
Telephone: 202-872-0400.

Lawrence A. Shulman	Lawrence L. Bell
Donald R. Rogers	James M. Kefauver
Larry N. Gandal	Rebecca Oshoway
Karl L. Ecker	Robert B. Canter
David A. Pordy	Edward F. Schiff
David D. Freishtat	Daniel S. Krakower
Martin P. Schaffer	Kevin P. Kennedy
Christopher C. Roberts	Alan B. Sternstein
Edward M. Hanson, Jr.	Nancy P. Regelin
David M. Kochanski	Ashley Joel Gardner
Walter A. Oleniewski	James M. Hoffman

Michael J. Froehlich	Michael V. Nakamura
William C. Davis, III	Paul A. Bellegarde
James A. Powers	Gregory J. Rupert
Elizabeth N. Shomaker	Douglas K. Hirsch

Reference: Maryland National Bank, Montgomery County Regional Office.

For Complete List of Firm Personnel, See General Section
For full biographical listings, see the Martindale-Hubbell Law Directory

STEIN, SPERLING, BENNETT, DE JONG, DRISCOLL, GREENFEIG & METRO, P.A. (AV)

25 West Middle Lane, 20850
Telephone: 301-340-2020; 800-435-5230
Telecopier: 301-340-8217

| Millard S. Bennett | A. Howard Metro |
| Jack A. Garson | Donald N. Sperling |

| Jeffrey D. Goldstein |

For Complete List of Firm Personnel, See General Section
For full biographical listings, see the Martindale-Hubbell Law Directory

---

TOWSON,* Baltimore Co.

VENABLE ATTORNEYS AT LAW VENABLE, BAETJER AND HOWARD, LLP (AV)

A Partnership including Professional Corporations
210 Allegheny Avenue, P.O. Box 5517, 21204
Telephone: 410-494-6200
FAX: 410-821-0147
Baltimore, Maryland Office: 1800 Mercantile Bank & Trust Building, 2 Hopkins Plaza.
Telephone: 410-244-7400.

(See Next Column)

Washington, D.C. Office: Venable, Baetjer, Howard & Civiletti LLP, Suite 1000, 1201 New York Avenue, N.W.
Telephone: 202-962-4800.
McLean, Virginia Office: Suite 400, 2010 Corporate Ridge.
Telephone: 703-760-1600.
Rockville, Maryland Office: Suite 500, One Church Street, P. O. Box 1906.
Telephone: 301-217-5600.

PARTNERS

Benjamin R. Civiletti (P.C.) (Also at Washington, D.C. and Baltimore, Maryland Offices)	William D. Quarles (Also at Washington, D.C. Office)
	C. Carey Deeley, Jr. (Also at Baltimore, Maryland Office)
John H. Zink, III	Kathleen Gallogly Cox
Joseph C. Wich, Jr.	M. King Hill, III
J. Michael Brennan	

ASSOCIATE

Mary-Dulany James

For Complete List of Firm Personnel, See General Section
For full biographical listings, see the Martindale-Hubbell Law Directory

---

UPPER MARLBORO,* Prince Georges Co.

KNIGHT, MANZI, BRENNAN, SHAY AND HAM, A PROFESSIONAL ASSOCIATION (AV)

14440 Old Mill Road, 20772
Telephone: 301-952-0100
Annapolis/Baltimore: 410-792-3786
Fax: 301-952-0221
Crofton, Maryland Office: 2411 Crofton Lane, # 26.
Telephone: 301-261-0808.
Fax: 301-261-6945.
Mitchellville, Maryland Office: 12164 Central Avenue, Suite 228.
Telephone: 301-390-0577.
Fax: 301-390-8464.

William E. Knight	John F. Shay, Jr.
Robert A. Manzi	Richard J. Ham
William C. Brennan, Jr.	Martin J. Shuham

| Monica M. Haley-Pierson | Norman D. Rivera |
| Daniel F. Lynch III | Robert L. Lombardo |

OF COUNSEL

Stuart R. Hammett

For full biographical listings, see the Martindale-Hubbell Law Directory

---

MASSACHUSETTS

AMESBURY, Essex Co.

HAMEL, DESHAIES & GAGLIARDI (AV)

Five Market Square, P.O. Box 198, 01913-0398
Telephone: 508-388-3558
Telecopier: 508-388-0441

MEMBERS OF FIRM

| Richard P. Hamel | Robert J. Deshaies |
| | Paul J. Gagliardi |

ASSOCIATES

| H. Scott Haskell | Roger D. Turgeon |
| Peter R. Ayer, Jr. | John R. Woelfel |

Representative Clients: Essex County Gas Co., Amesbury, MA; First and Ocean National Bank, Newburyport, MA.
Approved Attorneys for: Chicago Title Insurance; Old Republic Title Insurance Co.

For full biographical listings, see the Martindale-Hubbell Law Directory

---

BOSTON,* Suffolk Co.

BADGER, DOLAN, PARKER & COHEN (AV)

Formerly Badger, Sullivan, Kelley & Cole
2 Oliver Street, 02109
Telephone: 617-482-3030
Fax: 617-482-6919
Email: Badger@ma.ultranet.com

MEMBERS OF FIRM

Walter I. Badger (1885-1926)	George F. Parker, III
John J. Sullivan (1926-1979)	James B. Dolan, Jr.
David W. Kelley (1935-1986)	Lawrence J. Cohen

ASSOCIATES

| Audrey LaRowe Nee | Paul J. Barresi |
| John J. Pentz | |

OF COUNSEL

| Joseph E. Rendini | G. Mitchell Eckel, III |

For full biographical listings, see the Martindale-Hubbell Law Directory

Boston—Continued

CHERWIN, GLICKMAN & THEISE, LLP (AV)

A Limited Liability Partnership including Professional Corporations
One International Place, 02110-2622
Telephone: 617-330-1625
Fax: 617-330-1642

Stanley A. Glickman (1937-1994)	Douglas L. Jones (P.C.)
Joel I. Cherwin (P.C.)	David K. Wanger
Jay F. Theise	William O. Rizzo
Marshall D. Stein	Stanley B. Kay
	Lisa Lee Foster

For full biographical listings, see the Martindale-Hubbell Law Directory

HANIFY & KING, PROFESSIONAL CORPORATION (AV)

One Federal Street, 02110-2007
Telephone: 617-423-0400
Telefax: 617-423-0498

James Coyne King	Daniel J. Lyne
John D. Hanify	Donald F. Farrell, Jr.
Harold B. Murphy	Barbara Wegener Pfirrman
David Lee Evans	Gerard P. Richer
	Timothy P. O'Neill

Jean A. Musiker	Joseph F. Cortellini
Ann M. Chiacchieri	Eddirland Duncan
Melissa J. Cassedy	Andrew G. Lizotte
Jeffrey J. Upton	Karen A. Whitley
Michael R. Perry	Christopher K. Barry-Smith
Charles A. Dale, III	William T. Harrington
Kathleen E. Cross	Matthew McCue
David M. Wright	Robyn J. Bartlett
	Owen P. Kane

For full biographical listings, see the Martindale-Hubbell Law Directory

HASSENFELD & LEDERMAN (AV)

An Association including a Professional Corporation
62 Commercial Wharf, 02110
Telephone: 617-367-6400
Fax: 617-367-0280

Merrill I. Hassenfeld, P.C.	Maury E. Lederman

For full biographical listings, see the Martindale-Hubbell Law Directory

PEABODY & ARNOLD (AV)

A Partnership including Professional Corporations
50 Rowes Wharf, 02110-3342
Telephone: 617-951-2100
Telecopier: 617-951-2125
Providence, Rhode Island Office: One Citizens Plaza, Suite 840.
Telephone: 401-831-8330.
Fax: 401-831-8359.

MEMBERS OF FIRM

Paul J. Ayoub	David F. Hendren
Jonathan Bangs	James A. P. Homans
Michael F. Burke	John A. Kessler, Jr.
Philip H. Cahalin	Anil Khosla
Robert J. Coughlin	Andrew R. Menard
Amanda D. Darwin	Frank N. Ray (Resident, Providence, Rhode Island Office)
John K. Dineen	
John R. Gowell, Jr. (Resident, Providence, Rhode Island Office)	Douglas C. Reynolds
Ripley E. Hastings	Suanne C. St. Charles
	Donald E. Vaughan

ASSOCIATES

Frank S. Hamblett	Robert Payne Fox, Jr.
Amelia M. Charamba	John P. Dougherty
	Jane E. Kirk

For Complete List of Firm Personnel, See General Section

For full biographical listings, see the Martindale-Hubbell Law Directory

SHERBURNE, POWERS & NEEDHAM, P.C. (AV)

One Beacon Street, 02108
Telephone: 617-523-2700
Fax: 617-523-6850
Email: @SHERBURNE.COM

William D. Weeks	William V. Tripp III
John T. Collins	Stephen S. Young
Allan J. Landau	William F. Machen
Stephen A. Hopkins	W. Robert Allison
Alan I. Falk	Philip J. Notopoulos
C. Thomas Swaim	Richard J. Hindlian
James Pollock	Paul E. Troy

(See Next Column)

Harold W. Potter, Jr.	James E. McDermott
Philip S. Lapatin	Kenneth P. Brier
Pamela A. Duckworth	Robert V. Lizza
Benjamin Volinski	Miriam Goldstein Altman
Mark Schonfeld	John J. Monaghan
James D. Smeallie	Margaret J. Palladino
Paul Killeen	Mark C. Michalowski
Gordon P. Katz	David Scott Sloan
Joseph B. Darby, III	M. Chrysa Long
Richard M Yanofsky	Lawrence D. Bradley
	Miriam J. McKendall

Cynthia A. Brown	Amy J. Mastrobattista
Cynthia M. Hern	Leslie A. Sprinkle
Meredeth A. Beers	Douglas W. Clapp
Dianne R. Phillips	Jeffrey A. Huebschmann
Paul M. James	Tamara E. Goulston
Theodore F. Hanselman	Paul G. Lannon, Jr.
Joshua C. Krumholz	Nicholas J. Psyhogeos
Ieuan G. Mahony	Edward J. Naughton
Jeffrey J. Nix (Not admitted in MA)	Kathaleen Kelly Cutone
Kenneth L. Harvey	Laurie A. Tribble
Christopher J. Trombetta	Neil C. Higgins
Elise N. Zoli	Deborah Paige Stone
	Brian R. Popiel

COUNSEL

Haig Der Manuelian	Karl J. Hirshman
Mason M. Taber, Jr.	Dale R. Johnson

For full biographical listings, see the Martindale-Hubbell Law Directory

CAMBRIDGE,* Middlesex Co.

WILLIAM M. O'BRIEN (AV)

Suite 216, 186 Alewife Brook Parkway, 02138
Telephone: 617-661-2600
Fax: 617-864-0654

For full biographical listings, see the Martindale-Hubbell Law Directory

PITTSFIELD,* Berkshire Co.

CAIN, HIBBARD, MYERS & COOK, A PROFESSIONAL CORPORATION (AV)

66 West Street, 01201
Telephone: 413-443-4771
Telecopier: 413-443-7694
Great Barrington, Massachusetts Office: 309 Main Street, 01230.
Telephone: 413-528-4771.
Fax: 413-528-5553.

C. Jeffrey Cook	John F. Rogers
Brian J. Quinn (Resident, Great Barrington Office)	Michael E. MacDonald
	William B. Roberts
F. Sydney Smithers, IV	Steven Taylor Smith

Nancy A. Lyon	Bhamati Viswanathan (Not admitted in MA)
Jennifer L. Gerrard	

Representative Clients: Bank of Boston/First Agricultural Bank; Great Barrington Savings Bank; Greylock Credit Union; The Berkshire Gas Company; Berkshire Health Systems, Inc.; Berkshire Physicians & Surgeons, P.C. *Local Counsel for:* General Electric Co.; Boston Symphony Orchestra; Statewide Funding Corporation.

For full biographical listings, see the Martindale-Hubbell Law Directory

SPRINGFIELD,* Hampden Co.

HENDEL, COLLINS & NEWTON, P.C. (AV)

101 State Street, 01103
Telephone: 413-734-6411
Fax: 413-734-8069

Philip J. Hendel	Joseph H. Reinhardt
Joseph B. Collins	Jonathan R. Goldsmith
Carla W. Newton	Henry E. Geberth, Jr.
	George I. Roumeliotis

Representative Clients: Springfield Institution for Savings; United Cooperative Bank.
Reference: Shawmut Bank, N.A.

For full biographical listings, see the Martindale-Hubbell Law Directory

KAMBERG, BERMAN, P.C. (AV)

One Financial Plaza, 1350 Main Street, 01103-1628
Telephone: 413-781-1300
Facsimile: 413-732-0860
ABA/net: KAMBERGB

(See Next Column)

KAMBERG, BERMAN P.C.—*Continued*

    Abraham Kamberg (1895-1981)   Eugene B. Berman
             Kerry David Strayer

References: Fleet Bank of Massachusetts, N.A.; Baybank; Shawmut Bank, N.A.

For full biographical listings, see the Martindale-Hubbell Law Directory

WORCESTER,* Worcester Co.

CHRISTOPHER, HAYS, WOJCIK & MAVRICOS (AV)

370 Main Street, 01608
Telephone: 508-792-2800
FAX: 508-792-6224

MEMBERS OF FIRM

  William W. Hays   David A. Wojcik
        John A. Mavricos

OF COUNSEL

  Christopher Christopher   William C. Perrin, Jr.

Reference: Flagship Bank & Trust Co.

For full biographical listings, see the Martindale-Hubbell Law Directory

MICHIGAN

ANN ARBOR,* Washtenaw Co.

BRAUN KENDRICK FINKBEINER PLC (AV)

700 First National Building, 48104
Telephone: 313-995-4100
Telecopier: 313-995-4798
URL: http://www.bkf-law.com
Bay City, Michigan Office: 201 Phoenix Building, P.O. Box 2039.
Telephone: 517-895-8505.
Telecopier: 517-895-8437.
Saginaw, Michigan Office: 101 N. Washington, Suite 812.
Telephone: 517-753-3461.
Telecopier: 517-753-3951.

Barry M. Levine

Representative Clients: APV Chemical Machinery, Inc.; Bay Health Systems; Berger & Co.; Catholic Federal Credit Union; City of Saginaw; City of Vassar; City of Zilwaukee; Corporate Service; Cox Cable.

For full biographical listings, see the Martindale-Hubbell Law Directory

BIRMINGHAM, Oakland Co.

LOUIS J. BURNETT, P.C. (AV)

255 East Brown, Suite 210, 48009-6782
Telephone: 810-642-4345
Fax: 810-642-2005

Louis J. Burnett

Reference: Comerica, Detroit, Michigan.

For full biographical listings, see the Martindale-Hubbell Law Directory

CARSON FISCHER, P.L.C. (AV)

Third Floor, 300 East Maple Road, 48009-6317
Telephone: 810-644-4840
Facsimile: 810-644-1832

  Joseph M. Fischer   Lawrence A. Lichtman
  Robert A. Weisberg   James E. Owings

For full biographical listings, see the Martindale-Hubbell Law Directory

KELL & LYNCH, P.C. (AV)

300 East Maple Road, Suite 200, 48009
Telephone: 810-647-2333
Telefax: 810-647-2781

  Michael V. Kell   Margaret A. Lynch

  Jennifer T. Gilhool   Steven M. Ribiat
  (Not admitted in MI)

OF COUNSEL

M. Andrea Vaughn

Representative Clients: AlliedSignal, Inc.; AMP Inc.; Dow Corning Corp.; Hatteras Yachts; Lectron Products, Inc.; Metromedia Steakhouses, Inc.; Sybron Corp.; Michigan Consolidated Gas Co.; American Natural Resources.

For full biographical listings, see the Martindale-Hubbell Law Directory

BLOOMFIELD HILLS, Oakland Co.

JON H. BERKEY, P.C. (AV)

1750 South Telegraph Road, Suite 107, 48302-0183
Telephone: 810-332-2100
Fax: 810-332-2190

Jon H. Berkey

Anthony A. Yezbick

For full biographical listings, see the Martindale-Hubbell Law Directory

FEENEY KELLETT WIENNER & BUSH, PROFESSIONAL CORPORATION (AV)

950 North Hunter Boulevard, Second Floor, 48304-3927
Telephone: 810-258-1580
Fax: 810-258-0421

  James P. Feeney   Cheryl A. Bush
  S. Thomas Wienner   Deborah F. Collins
  Peter M. Kellett   David N. Goltz

OF COUNSEL

Thomas J. Manganello

  James J. Majernik   Seth D. Gould
  G. Gregory Schuetz   Patrick G. Seyferth
  Jeffrey A. Gallant   Mark A. Fisher
           Bryan D. Cross

For full biographical listings, see the Martindale-Hubbell Law Directory

HARDIG PARSONS & PEDERSEN (AV)

74 West Long Lake Road, Suite 203, 48304
Telephone: 810-642-3500
Facsimile: 810-645-1128
Charlevoix, Michigan Office: 212 Bridge Street.
Telephone: 616-547-1200.
Facsimile: 616-547-1026.
Pawley's Island, South Carolina Office: 216 Highway 17, P.O. Box 1607, 29585.
Telephone: 803-237-9219.
Facsimile: 803-237-9530.
West Palm Beach, Florida Office: Suite 1450, 515 North Flagler.
Telephone: 407-833-1622.
Facsimile: 407-833-6933.

MEMBERS OF FIRM

  Joseph L. Hardig, Jr.   Joseph L. Hardig, III
  Donald H. Parsons   Edward C. Pedersen
         Bradley S. Stout

ASSOCIATE

Capri L. Pelshaw

OF COUNSEL

Edward K. Pedersen, Jr.

MEMBER IN SOUTH CAROLINA

John C. Benso

For full biographical listings, see the Martindale-Hubbell Law Directory

LEHMAN & VALENTINO, P.C. (AV)

1411 South Woodward Avenue, Suite 200, 48302
Telephone: 810-334-7787
Fax: 810-334-7202

  Richard L. Lehman   Paul G. Valentino
      Victor P. Valentino

OF COUNSEL

Patrick M. Cleary

Reference: NBD.

For full biographical listings, see the Martindale-Hubbell Law Directory

LISS AND ASSOCIATES, P.C. (AV)

The Pinehurst Building, 1400 North Woodward Avenue, Suite 200, 48304
Telephone: 810-647-9700
Facsimile: 810-647-5477; 810-647-0638

  Arthur Y. Liss   Christine S. Reiner

  Ronald S. Smith   Andrew M. Zack
         Karen E. Seder

For full biographical listings, see the Martindale-Hubbell Law Directory

DETROIT, * Wayne Co.

ALLARD & FISH, A PROFESSIONAL CORPORATION (AV)

2600 Buhl Building, 535 Griswold Avenue, 48226
Telephone: 313-961-6141
Facsimile: 313-961-6142
Email: afish@michbar.org

David W. Allard   Ralph R. McKee
Deborah L. Fish   Elias Themistocles Majoros

Rodney M. Glusac

For full biographical listings, see the Martindale-Hubbell Law Directory

BODMAN, LONGLEY & DAHLING LLP (AV)

34th Floor 100 Renaissance Center, 48243
Telephone: 313-259-7777
Fax: 313-393-7579
Email: 2080194@mcimail.com
Troy, Michigan Office: Suite 2020, 755 West Big Beaver Road.
Telephone: 810-362-2110.
Fax: 810-244-0780.
Ann Arbor, Michigan Office: 110 Miller, Suite 300.
Telephone: 313-761-3780.
Fax: 313-930-2494.
Northern Michigan Office: 229 Court Street, P.O. Box 405, Cheboygan.
Telephone: 616-627-4351.
Fax: 616-627-2802.

MEMBERS OF FIRM

Richard D. Rohr   Larry R. Shulman
Theodore Souris   Terrence B. Larkin (Troy Office)
Walter O. Koch (Troy Office)   Thomas Van Dusen
Alfred C. Wortley, Jr.   (Troy Office)
Thomas A. Roach   Robert J. Diehl, Jr.
   (Ann Arbor Office)   James C. Conboy, Jr.
Kenneth R. Lango (Troy Office)   (Northern Michigan Office)
Herold McC. Deason   Martha Bedsole Goodloe
James R. Buschmann   (Troy Office)
George G. Kemsley   Barbara Bowman Bluford
Joseph J. Kochanek   Lawrence P. Hanson
David G. Chardavoyne   (Northern Michigan Office)

COUNSEL
Lewis A. Rockwell

For Representative Client List, See General Section

For Complete List of Firm Personnel, See General Section

For full biographical listings, see the Martindale-Hubbell Law Directory

BUTZEL LONG, A PROFESSIONAL CORPORATION (AV)

Suite 900, 150 West Jefferson, 48226
Telephone: 313-225-7000
Telecopier: 313-225-7080
Email: melnick@butzel.com *URL:* http://www.butzel.com
Birmingham, Michigan Office: Suite 200, 32270 Telegraph Road.
Telephone: 810-258-1616.
Telecopier: 810-258-1439.
Lansing, Michigan Office: 118 West Ottawa Street.
Telephone: 517-372-6622.
Telecopier: 517-372-6672.
Ann Arbor, Michigan Office: Suite 300, 350 South Main Street.
Telephone: 313-995-3110.
Telecopier: 313-995-1777.
Grosse Pointe Farms, Michigan Office: Suite 260, 21 Kercheval.
Telephone: 313-886-5446.
Telecopier: 313-886-2114.

William M. Saxton   Carl Rashid, Jr.
Stephen A. Bromberg   Daniel P. Malone
   (Birmingham)   Keefe A. Brooks
Frank B. Vecchio (Birmingham)   Gordon W. Didier (Birmingham)
Allan Nachman (Birmingham)   Leonard M. Niehoff
William R. Ralls (Lansing)   (Ann Arbor)
C. Peter Theut   David H. Oermann
Richard E. Rassel   (Birmingham)
Abba I. Friedman (Birmingham)   Melvin J. Hollowell, Jr.
Philip J. Kessler   Anthony J. Saulino, Jr.
James C. Bruno   (Birmingham)
Thomas B. Radom   Patrick A. Karbowski
   (Birmingham)   (Birmingham)
                   Kenneth H. Adamczyk

Representative Clients: Bridgestone/Firestone, Inc.; The Detroit News, Inc.;
Kelly Services; Kelsey Hayes Co.; McKechnie PLC; New Venture Gear;
Stroh Brewery Co.; Takata Corp.; United Parcel Services of America, Inc.

For Complete List of Firm Personnel, See General Section

For full biographical listings, see the Martindale-Hubbell Law Directory

CLARK HILL P.L.C. (AV)

500 Woodward Avenue, Suite 3500, 48226
Telephone: 313-965-8300
Facsimile: 313-962-4348
Oakland County, Michigan Office: Third Floor, 255 South Woodward
Avenue, Birmingham.
Telephone: 810-642-9692.
Facsimile: 810-642-2174.
Lansing, Michigan Office: Suite 600, 200 North Capitol Avenue.
Telephone: 517-484-4481.
Facsimile: 517-484-1246.
Minneapolis, Minnesota Office: Suite 1000, One Financial Plaza, 120 South
Sixth Street.
Telephone: 612-332-0102.
Facsimile: 612-332-3225.
Kansas City, Missouri Office: Suite 1400, Bryant Building, 1102 Grand
Avenue.
Telephone: 816-221-5578.
Facsimile: 816-221-0303.

William B. Dunn   Michael S. Khoury
D. Kerry Crenshaw   Peter A. Jackson
John F. Burns   Timothy M. Koltun
Robert L. Weyhing, III   Daniel H. Minkus (Resident,
David E. Nims, III   Oakland County Office)
Thomas S. Nowinski   John J. Hern, Jr.
Duane L. Tarnacki   Andrea M. Kanski
                 Judith Greenstone Miller

Michael I. Conlon   Georgette Borrego Dulworth
Patrice Asimakis   John P. Hensien
                 Margery Siegel Klausner

For Complete List of Firm Personnel, See General Section

For full biographical listings, see the Martindale-Hubbell Law Directory

EAMES WILCOX (AV)

1400 Buhl Building, 48226-3602
Telephone: 313-963-3750
Facsimile: 313-963-8485

MEMBERS OF FIRM

Leonard A. Wilcox, Jr.   Jerry R. Swift
Ronald J. Mastej   Neill T. Riddell
John W. Bryant   Kevin N. Summers
Robert E. Gesell   Keith M. Aretha

OF COUNSEL

Rex Eames   William B. McIntyre, Jr.
                    David R. Ritter

Representative Clients: NationsCredit Commercial Corporation; Chrysler
Credit Corp.; D&B Engineering, Inc.; Engineering Heat Treat, Inc.; Fetz
Engineering Co.; I E & E Industries, Inc.; Macoit Warehouse Co.

For full biographical listings, see the Martindale-Hubbell Law Directory

FEIKENS, VANDER MALE, STEVENS, BELLAMY & GILCHRIST, P.C. (AV)

One Detroit Center Suite 3400, 500 Woodward Avenue, 48226-3406
Telephone: 313-962-5909
Fax: 313-962-3125
Email: FEIKENS@COUNSEL.COM

Robert E. Dice (1922-1983)   Lee A. Stevens
Jon Feikens   William C. Hurley
Jack E. Vander Male   Linda M. Galbraith
Frederick B. Bellamy   Michael S. Cafferty
Alan Gordon Gilchrist   Robert H. Feikens
L. Neal Kennedy   Gerald W. Van Wyke
Bruce A. VandeVusse   Roger L. Wolcott
                 Sharon McPhail

Richard G. Koefod   Keith J. Soltis
Joseph E. Kozely, Jr.   Michael B. Barey
Jeffrey Feikens   Renee T. VanderHagen
                 Michael P. Citrin

OF COUNSEL

Sam W. Thomas (P.C.)   Walter Vincent Bernard III

LEGAL SUPPORT PERSONNEL

PARALEGALS

Robert Westveer   Linda Barthlow

For full biographical listings, see the Martindale-Hubbell Law Directory

Detroit—Continued

MAGER, MERCER, SCOTT & ALBER, P.C. (AV)

500 Woodward Avenue Suite 3400, 48226
Telephone: 313-962-8212
Facsimile: 313-962-5413
Oakland County Office: Top of Troy Building, 755 West Big Beaver, Suite 1700, Troy, Michigan.
Telephone: 810-362-8212.
Facsimile: 810-362-6944.
Macomb County Office: 18285 Ten Mile Road, Suite 100, Roseville, Michigan.
Telephone: 810-771-1100.
Facsimile: 810-775-5170.

George J. Mager, Jr.

Representative Clients: ABB Flakt, Inc.; American States Insurance Co.; CEI Industries; Central Venture Corp.; CIGNA; Construction Management, Inc.

For full biographical listings, see the Martindale-Hubbell Law Directory

PATTERSON, PHIFER & PHILLIPS, P.C. (AV)

L. B. King Building, 1274 Library Street, Suite 500, 48226
Telephone: 313-964-2360

Michael D. Patterson	Randolph D. Phifer
Dwight W. Phillips	

Joseph M. White	Eugene M. Holmes
Lisa A. Cylar	

Representative Clients: Certainteed Corp.; Children's Aid Society of Detroit; Chrysler Corp.; Citizens Insurance Cos.; City of Detroit; County of Wayne; Detroit Board of Education; Detroit Neighborhood Housing Services; General Mills Restaurant, Inc.; General Motors Corp.

For full biographical listings, see the Martindale-Hubbell Law Directory

SHAHEEN, JACOBS & ROSS, P.C. (AV)

585 East Larned, Suite 200, 48226-4316
Telephone: 313-963-1301
Telecopier: 313-963-7123
Email: LAWSJR@AOL.COM

Joseph Shaheen (1920-1984)	Steven P. Ross
Michael A. Jacobs (1949-1992)	Michael J. Thomas
Thomas J. Wall, Jr.	

For full biographical listings, see the Martindale-Hubbell Law Directory

TIMMIS & INMAN, L.L.P. (AV)

300 Talon Centre, 48207
Telephone: 313-396-4200
Telecopier: 313-396-4228

Michael T. Timmis	Henry J. Brennan, III
Robert E. Graziani	Mark W. Peyser
George A. Peck	Richard M. Miettinen
Charles W. Royer	Lisa R. Gorman
Richard L. Levin	Bradley J. Knickerbocker
George M. Malis	

Michael F. Wais	Patrick B. Carey
John P. Kanan	Erich J. D'Andrea
Shannon M. Nichols	

OF COUNSEL

Wayne C. Inman	William B. Fitzgerald
W. Clark Durant, III	

Representative Clients: Stylecraft Printing Co.; Stylerite Label Corp.; Retail Resources, Inc.; Deneb Robotics, Inc.; Applied Process, Inc.; Insilco Corp.; Variety Foods, Inc.; Certain Underwriters at Lloyds of London; Eastpointe Radiologists, P.C.; Talon Automotive Group L.L.C.

For full biographical listings, see the Martindale-Hubbell Law Directory

EAST LANSING, Ingham Co.

FARHAT, STORY & KRAUS, P.C. (AV)

Beacon Place, 4572 South Hagadorn Road, Suite 3, 48823
Telephone: 517-351-3700
Fax: 517-332-4122
Email: rkraus@sojourn.com

Leo A. Farhat	Chris A. Bergstrom
James E. Burns (1925-1979)	Kitty L. Groh
Monte R. Story	Charles R. Toy
Richard C. Kraus	David M. Platt
Max R. Hoffman Jr.	Thomas L. Sparks

(See Next Column)

Lawrence P. Schweitzer	Daniel B. Morgan
Debra A. Geroux	Mary K. Robbins-Kralapp

Representative Clients: Big L. Corp.; Michigan Automotive Wholesalers Association; Hartman-Fabco Inc.; Lansing Electric Motors, Inc.; Mike Miller Lincoln Mercury; Edward Rose Realty, Inc.; GTE Directories Service Corp.; Squires School & Commercial Sales; Commercial Blueprint; Lansing School District.

For full biographical listings, see the Martindale-Hubbell Law Directory

FARMINGTON HILLS, Oakland Co.

COUZENS, LANSKY, FEALK, ELLIS, ROEDER & LAZAR, P.C. (AV)

33533 West Twelve Mile Road, Suite 150, P.O. Box 9057, 48333-9057
Telephone: 810-489-8600
Telecopier: 810-489-4156

Sheldon A. Fealk	Lisa J. Walters
Jack S. Couzens, II	Stephen Scapelliti
Jerry M. Ellis	Donald A. Wagner
Donald M. Lansky	Michael P. Witzke
Bruce J. Lazar	Cyrus Raamin Kashef
Alan C. Roeder	Gregg A. Nathanson
Renard J. Kolasa	Mark S. Frankel
Kathryn Gilson Sussman	Lynette M. Sheldon
Jeffrey A. Levine	Roger E. Winkelman
Phillip L. Sternberg	David B. Deutsch
Marc L. Prey	Monica Demko Moons

Representative Clients: Provided upon request.
Reference: Comerica Bank-Southfield.

For full biographical listings, see the Martindale-Hubbell Law Directory

MICHAEL H. GOLOB (AV)

30300 Northwestern Highway, Suite 300, 48334
Telephone: 810-855-2626
Fax: 810-932-4009

For full biographical listings, see the Martindale-Hubbell Law Directory

HALIW, SICILIANO AND MYCHALOWYCH (AV)

37000 Grand River, Suite 350, 48335
Telephone: 810-442-0510
Fax: 810-442-0518

MEMBERS OF FIRM

Andrew J. Haliw III	Nanette Lynn Korpi
Joseph A. Siciliano	Raymond L. Feul
Andrew W. Mychalowych	Frank E. Henke

For full biographical listings, see the Martindale-Hubbell Law Directory

WRIGHT PENNING (AV)

27655 Middlebelt Road, Suite 170, 48334
Telephone: 810-477-6300
Fax: 810-477-7749

William M. Wright	LeClair L. Flaherty
Dan A. Penning	Dirk A. Beamer
Dale A. Anderson	

For full biographical listings, see the Martindale-Hubbell Law Directory

FLINT,* Genesee Co.

GAULT DAVISON A PROFESSIONAL SERVICE CORPORATION (AV)

Tenth Floor, Northbank Center, 432 North Saginaw Street, 48502-2032
Telephone: 810-234-3633
Fax: 810-233-3387
Email: GLTDAV@tir.com

F. Robert Schmelzer

John R. Moynihan	Christopher A. Hajek

Representative Clients: Al Serra Automobile Co.; Harley-Davidson, Inc.; Harley Owners Group; Shoney's, Inc.; City of Flint; Vic Canever Chevrolet Co.; Genesee Packaging Co.

For full biographical listings, see the Martindale-Hubbell Law Directory

GRAND RAPIDS,* Kent Co.

BORRE, PETERSON, FOWLER & REENS, P.C. (AV)

The Philo C. Fuller House, 44 Lafayette, N.E., P.O. Box 1767, 49501-1767
Telephone: 616-459-1971
Fax: 616-459-2393

(See Next Column)

BORRE, PETERSON, FOWLER & REENS P.C., *Grand Rapids—Continued*

Glen V. Borre	Frank H. Johnson
James B. Peterson	Mark D. Sevald
Ben A. Fowler	Harold E. Nelson
William C. Reens	William R. Vander Sluis

References: Old Kent Bank; NBD Bank; FMB-First Michigan Bank - Grand Rapids.

For Complete List of Firm Personnel, See General Section

For full biographical listings, see the Martindale-Hubbell Law Directory

---

DAY & SAWDEY, A PROFESSIONAL CORPORATION (AV)

200 Monroe Avenue, Suite 500, 49503-2217
Telephone: 616-774-8121
Telefax: 616-774-0168

George B. Kingston (1889-1965)	James B. Frakie
John R. Porter (1915-1975)	Larry A. Ver Merris
Charles E. Day, Jr.	John Boyko, Jr.
Robert W. Sawdey	Jonathan F. Thoits
C. Mark Stoppels	John T. Piggins

Thomas A. DeMeester

For full biographical listings, see the Martindale-Hubbell Law Directory

---

DE GROOT, KELLER & VINCENT (AV)

300 Michigan Trust Building, 49503
Telephone: 616-459-6251
Fax: 616-459-6352

MEMBERS OF FIRM

Murray B. De Groot	Brian D. Vincent

For full biographical listings, see the Martindale-Hubbell Law Directory

---

GRUEL, MILLS, NIMS AND PYLMAN (AV)

50 Monroe Place, Suite 700 West, 49503
Telephone: 616-235-5500
Fax: 616-235-5550

MEMBERS OF FIRM

Grant J. Gruel	Scott R. Melton
William F. Mills	Brion J. Brooks
J. Clarke Nims	Thomas R. Behm
Norman H. Pylman, II	J. Paul Janes

Representative Clients: Aquinas College; Bell Helmet Co.; Blodgett Memorial Medical Center; Butterworth Hospital; Chem Central, Inc.; Cook Pump Co.; Grove, Inc.; NBDC; Heim Corp.

For full biographical listings, see the Martindale-Hubbell Law Directory

---

LAW, WEATHERS & RICHARDSON, P.C. (AV)

Bridgewater Place, Suite 800, 333 Bridge Street, N.W., 49504
Telephone: 616-459-1171
Facsimile: 616-732-1740

OF COUNSEL
W. Fred Hunting, Jr.

Alan C. Bennett	Henry G. Swain
James L. Wernstrom	Anthony P. Gauthier
Stephen D. Turner	Ingrid A. Jensen
Robert A. Buchanan	Ellen S. Carmody

Bruce A. Courtade

David W. Centner

Representative Clients: F.D.I.C.; Ford Motor Credit Co.; Herman Miller, Inc.; Kent County Aeronautics Board; Marriott Corp.; The Procter & Gamble Co.; Peerless Insurance Co.; Ryder Systems, Inc.

For Complete List of Firm Personnel, See General Section

For full biographical listings, see the Martindale-Hubbell Law Directory

---

ROBERTS, BETZ & BLOSS, P.C. (AV)

555 Riverfront Plaza Building, 55 Campau, 49503
Telephone: 616-235-9955
Telecopier: 616-235-0404

Michael J. Roberts	Gregory A. Block
Michael W. Betz	Michael T. Small
David J. Bloss	Ralph M. Reisinger

Henry S. Emrich

For full biographical listings, see the Martindale-Hubbell Law Directory

---

WHEELER UPHAM, A PROFESSIONAL CORPORATION (AV)

Second Floor, Trust Building, 40 Pearl Street, N.W., 49503-3001
Telephone: 616-459-7100
Fax: 616-459-6366

(See Next Column)

Gordon B. Wheeler (1904-1986)	William H. Heritage, Jr.
Buford A. Upham (Retired)	Kenneth E. Tiews
Robert H. Gillette	Jack L. Hoffman
Geoffrey L. Gillis	Janet C. Baxter
John M. Roels	Peter Kladder, III
Gary A. Maximiuk	James M. Shade
Timothy J. Orlebeke	Thomas A. Kuiper

Counsel For: Independent Cooperative Milk Producers Assn.; National Food Processors Assn.; Monsanto Co.; Medtronic, Inc.; Navistar; Westdale Better Homes and Gardens; Gospel Films, Inc.; Michigan Credit Union League.

For full biographical listings, see the Martindale-Hubbell Law Directory

---

KALAMAZOO,* Kalamazoo Co.

DIETRICH, ZODY, HOWARD & VANDERROEST, P.C. (AV)

834 King Highway, Suite 110, 49001
Telephone: 616-344-9236
Fax: 616-344-0412

G. Philip Dietrich	James W. Smith
Richard J. Howard	James E. VanderRoest

Philip W. Dietrich
OF COUNSEL
Brenda Wheeler Zody

Representative Clients: Amplimedical S.P.A.; Arvco Container Corp.; Day's Molding & Machinery, Inc.; The Deaccelerator Corp.; DeLano Foundation; Tremble Foundation; Monroe Foundation; Do-It Corp.; Engineered Stadium Systems, Inc.

For full biographical listings, see the Martindale-Hubbell Law Directory

---

KREIS, ENDERLE, CALLANDER & HUDGINS, A PROFESSIONAL CORPORATION (AV)

One Moorsbridge, P.O. Box 4010, 49003-4010
Telephone: 616-324-3000
Telecopier: 616-324-3010
Email: kech@sapien.net *URL:* http://www.kech.com

Russell A. Kreis	Jeffrey C. O'Brien
Alan G. Enderle	Stephen J. Hessen
C. Reid Hudgins III	Daniel P. McGlinn

For Complete List of Firm Personnel, See General Section

For full biographical listings, see the Martindale-Hubbell Law Directory

---

LEWIS & ALLEN, P.C. (AV)

Old Kent Bank Building, Suite 800, 136 East Michigan Avenue, 49007-3946
Telephone: 616-388-7600
Fax: 616-349-3831

Dean S. Lewis	William A. Redmond
W. Fred Allen, Jr.	Stephen M. Denenfeld
Winfield J. Hollander	Gregory G. St. Arnauld
Bruce W. Martin	Anne McGregor Fries
Daniel L. Conklin	Thomas P. Lewis

Christopher T. Haenicke
LEGAL SUPPORT PERSONNEL
Dorothy B. Kelly

For full biographical listings, see the Martindale-Hubbell Law Directory

---

MILLER, CANFIELD, PADDOCK AND STONE, P.L.C. (AV)

A Professional Limited Liability Company
Founded in 1852 by Sidney Davy Miller
444 West Michigan Avenue, 49007-3752
Telephone: 616-381-7030
Fax: 616-382-0244
Detroit, Michigan Office: 150 West Jefferson, Suite 2500, 48226-4415.
Telephone: 313-963-6420.
Fax: 313-496-7500.
Cable Address: "Stem Detroit."
Ann Arbor, Michigan Office: 101 North Main Street, 7th Floor, 48104-1400.
Telephone: 313-663-2445.
Fax: 313-747-7147.
Bloomfield Hills, Michigan Office: Suite 100, Pinehurst Office Center, 1400 North Woodward, 48303-2014.
Telephone: 313-645-5000.
Fax: 313-645-1917.
Grand Rapids, Michigan Office: 1200 Campau Square Plaza, 99 Monroe, N.W., 49503-2639.
Telephone: 616-454-8656.
Fax: 616-776-6322.
Howell, Michigan Office: 121 South Barnard Street, Suite 4, 48843-2305.
Telephone: 517-546-7600.
Telecopier: 517-546-6974.
Lansing, Michigan Office: One Michigan Avenue, Suite 900, 48933-1609.
Telephone: 517-487-2070.
Fax: 517-374-6304.

(See Next Column)

MILLER, CANFIELD, PADDOCK AND STONE P.L.C.—*Continued*

Monroe, Michigan Office: The Executive Centre, 214 East Elm Avenue, 48161-2682.
Telephone: 313-243-2000.
Fax: 313-243-0901.
Washington, D.C. Office: 1225 Nineteenth Street, N.W., Suite 400. 20036.
Telephone: 202-429-5575; 785-0600.
Fax: 202-331-1118; 785-1234.
Pensacola, Florida Office: 25 West Cedar, 32501.
Telephone: 904-469-1088.
Fax: 904-432-0677.
St. Petersburg, Florida Office: 100 Second Avenue S., Suite 7045, 33701.
Telephone: 813-982-6000.
Fax: 813-892-6002.
New York, New York Office: Eleventh Floor, 135 East 57th Street, 10022-2087.
Telephone: 212-754-5400.
Fax: 212-754-5401.
Gdansk, Poland Office: Suite 322, Dom Technika Building, UI. Rajska 6, 80-850.
Telephone: 011-485-831-2808.
Fax: 011-485-831-4719.
Warsaw, Poland Office: UI. Marszalkowska 82, Suite 561, 00-517.
Telephone: 011-482-623-6457 and 6458.
Fax: 011-482-623-6459.

PRINCIPALS OF FIRM

Eric V. Brown, Jr.	Thomas H. Van Dis
John R. Cook	James E. Spurr
Steven M. Stankewicz	

ASSOCIATES

Ballard Jay Yelton, III	Lori L. Purkey

Representative Firm Clients: Chrysler Corporation; Comerica, Incorporated; City of Detroit, Michigan; Detroit Tigers, Inc.; First of Michigan; Ford Motor Company; Ford Motor Credit Company; Great Lakes Bancorp; Henry Ford Hospital; INVETECH Company.

For Complete List of Firm Personnel, See General Section

For full biographical listings, see the Martindale-Hubbell Law Directory

---

ROCHESTER, Oakland Co.

SHERMETA, CHIMKO AND KILPATRICK, P.C. (AV)

445 South Livernois, Suite 221, P.O. Box 5016, 48308
Telephone: 810-652-8200
Fax: 810-652-1292
Detroit, Michigan Office: Ford Building, 48226.
Telephone: 313-961-4848.
Fax: 313-961-4365.
Grand Rapids, Michigan Office: 169 Louis Campau Prom., Suite 2B.
Telephone: 616-531-6980.
Fax: 616-531-7475.
Sacramento, California Office: 555 Capital Mall, Suite 530.
Telephone: 916-448-5039.
Facsimile: 916-448-7461.
San Leandro, California Office: 777 Davis Street, Suite 100.
Telephone: 510-614-0800.
Facsimile: 510-614-0670.

Douglass H. Shermeta	Barbara L. Adams
Darryl J. Chimko	Karen E. Evangelista
Richardo I. Kilpatrick	Henry J. Mittelstaedt III

Mariana J. Richmond	Julie M. Carroll
Robert D. Dzialo	Mark A. Wolff (Resident, Sacramento, California Office)
Kelly L. Scola	
Karen Lamoreaux Rice	Richard A. Morton (Resident, San Leandro, California Office)
Christopher E. Mcneely	
David R. Shook	
Patrick (Casey) Coston	Mitchell L. Wong (Resident, San Leandro, California Office)
Krispen S. Carroll	
Sheryl S. Zamplas	Kathryn E. Walters (Resident, San Leandro, California Office)
Lisa E. Gocha	

For full biographical listings, see the Martindale-Hubbell Law Directory

---

ROYAL OAK, Oakland Co.

CARDELLI, SCHAEFER & MASON, P.C. (AV)

322 West Lincoln, 48067
Telephone: 810-544-1100
Toll Free 1-800-411-7774
Telecopier: 810-544-1191

Thomas G. Cardelli	William C. Schaefer
Laura D. Mason	

Deborah A. Hebert	Tara Hanley Bratton
Mary Ann J. O'Neil	Diane T. Gorczyca
Lillian C. Pierce	Ronald E. Beier, II
John L. Weston	

(See Next Column)

Representative Clients: Cigarette Service Company; Coltec Industries (Garlock Inc & Anchor Packing Company); Dana Corporation; Duchossois Industries, Inc.; Fruehauf Trailer Corporation; General Motors Corporation; Morton International, Inc.; Otis Elevator Company; Raymond Corporation; T.D. Rowe.

For full biographical listings, see the Martindale-Hubbell Law Directory

---

SAGINAW,* Saginaw Co.

BRAUN KENDRICK FINKBEINER PLC (AV)

101 N. Washington Suite 812, 48607-1297
Telephone: 517-753-3461
Telecopier: 517-753-3951
URL: http://www.bkf-law.com
Bay City, Michigan Office: 201 Phoenix Building, P.O. Box 2039.
Telephone: 517-895-8505.
Telecopier: 517-895-8437.
Ann Arbor, Michigan Office: 700 First National Building.
Telephone: 313-995-4100.
Telecopier: 313-995-4798.

C. Patrick Kaltenbach	Timothy L Curtiss
Michael J. Sauer	Francis J. Keating

OF COUNSEL

Morton E. Weldy

Representative Clients: APV Chemical Machinery, Inc.; Bay Health Systems; Berger & Co.; Catholic Federal Credit Union; City of Saginaw; City of Vassar; City of Zilwaukee; Corporate Service; Cox Cable.

For Complete List of Firm Personnel, See General Section

For full biographical listings, see the Martindale-Hubbell Law Directory

---

SOUTHFIELD, Oakland Co.

COLLINS, EINHORN, FARRELL & ULANOFF, A PROFESSIONAL CORPORATION (AV)

4000 Town Center, Suite 909, 48075-1473
Telephone: 810-355-4141
Facsimile: 810-355-2277

Morton H. Collins	Dale J. McLellan
Brian D. Einhorn	Kenneth C. Merritt
Clayton F. Farrell	Noreen L. Slank
Stuart A. Ulanoff	Michael J. Sullivan
Janice G. Hildenbrand	

Gerald A. Pawlak	Deborah A. Lujan
Neil W. MacCallum	Barbara H. Goldman
Timothy Orlando	Shannon M. Kos
Theresa M. Asoklis	Kevin P. Moloughney
Karen C. Liddle	Susan P. Saltzman
Lisa L. Fadler	Laura A. Ruckle

For full biographical listings, see the Martindale-Hubbell Law Directory

---

MASON, STEINHARDT, JACOBS & PERLMAN, PROFESSIONAL CORPORATION (AV)

Suite 1500, 4000 Town Center, 48075-1415
Telephone: 810-358-2090
Fax: 810-358-3599

John E. Jacobs	Jerome P. Pesick
Michael B. Perlman	Neil S. Silver
L. Jeffrey Zauberman	

Diane Flagg Goldstein	H. Adam Cohen

Representative Clients: Citibank, N.A.; City of Dearborn; DeMattia Development Co.; Forest City Enterprises; Michigan Wholesale Drug Assn.; Mortgage Bankers Association of Michigan; Nationwide Insurance Co.; City of Taylor; Union Labor Life Insurance Co.; Yellow Freight Systems, Inc.

For Complete List of Firm Personnel, See General Section

For full biographical listings, see the Martindale-Hubbell Law Directory

---

PROVIZER, LICHTENSTEIN & PHILLIPS, P.C. (AV)

4000 Town Center, Suite 1800, 48075
Telephone: 810-352-9080
Facsimile: 810-352-1491

Harold M. Provizer	Constance S. Hall
David S. Lichtenstein	Noel F. Beck
Randall E. Phillips	William J. Selinsky
Marilyn A. Madorsky	Robert I. Brown
Deborah Molitz	Todd B. Denenberg
Jason Milstone	

Representative Clients: Investuid Corporation; Mortgage Institute of Michigan.

For full biographical listings, see the Martindale-Hubbell Law Directory

Southfield—Continued

SOMMERS, SCHWARTZ, SILVER & SCHWARTZ, P.C. (AV)

2000 Town Center, Suite 900, 48075
Telephone: 810-355-0300
Telecopier: 810-746-4001
Plymouth, Michigan Office: 747 South Main Street.
Telephone: 313-455-4250.

Steven J. Schwartz	David M. Black
Gary A. Taback	Joseph H. Bourgon
James J. Vlasic	David J Szymanski

Scott C. Hess
OF COUNSEL
Charles S. Farmer

Representative Clients: Foodland Distributors; C.A. Muer Corporation; Vlasic & Company; Nederlander Corporation; Midwest Health Centers, P.C.; Vesco Oil Corporation.
Representative Clients: Michigan National Bank; Bank Hapoalim, B.M.; Bealbank S.A.

For Complete List of Firm Personnel, See General Section

For full biographical listings, see the Martindale-Hubbell Law Directory

---

TRAVERSE CITY,* Grand Traverse Co.

MURCHIE, CALCUTT & BOYNTON (AV)

109 East Front Street, Suite 300, 49684
Telephone: 616-947-7190
Fax: 616-947-4341

Robert B. Murchie (1894-1975)	William B. Calcutt
Harry Calcutt	Mark A. Burnheimer
Jack E. Boynton	Dawn M. Rogers

ASSOCIATE
Ralph J. Dilley (Not admitted in MI)

General Counsel for: Old Kent Bank-Grand Traverse; Northwestern Savings Bank & Trust; Central-State Bancorp; Traverse City Record Eagle; WPNB-7 & WTOM-4; Emergency Consultants, Inc.; National Guardian Risk Retention Group, Inc.; Farmers Mutual Insurance Co.; Environmental Solutions, Inc.
Local Counsel for: Consumers Power Co.

For full biographical listings, see the Martindale-Hubbell Law Directory

---

SMITH, JOHNSON & BRANDT, ATTORNEYS, P.C. (AV)

603 Bay Street, P.O. Box 705, 49685
Telephone: 616-946-0700
Fax: 616-946-1735
Lansing, Michigan Office: Suite 402, 116 West Ottawa Street.
Telephone: 517-482-5142.

Louis A. Smith	Donald A. Brandt
H. Wendell Johnson	Allen G. Anderson

Edgar Roy III

Paul T. Jarboe	Joseph E. Quandt
Thomas A. Pezzetti	Timothy Paul Smith

OF COUNSEL
Barbara Ann Assendelft

Representative Clients: Alden State Bank; Empire National Bank of Traverse City; First of America Bank Michigan, N.A.; Garland; Grand Traverse Mall Limited Partnership; Green Tree Acceptance, Inc.; Lansing Automakers' Federal Credit Union; Michigan Automobile Dealers Association; Cherry Capital Oldsmobile Cadillac L.L.C.; Elmer's Crane and Dozer, Inc.

For full biographical listings, see the Martindale-Hubbell Law Directory

---

TROY, Oakland Co.

AUSTIN HIRSCHHORN, P.C. (AV)

Suite 710 Columbia Center, 201 West Big Beaver Road, 48084-4152
Telephone: 810-680-1660
Fax: 810-680-1671

Austin Hirschhorn

For full biographical listings, see the Martindale-Hubbell Law Directory

---

MORRIS, ROWLAND, PREKEL, FREDERICK, LEWIS & LEWINSKI, P.L.C. (AV)

Suite 921, 2301 West Big Beaver Road, 48084
Telephone: 810-649-2910
Fax: 810-649-4679

MEMBERS OF FIRM

Donald E. Paquette (1932-1983)	Robert B. Frederick
George L. Morris, Jr.	Eugene W. Lewis, III
James W. Rowland	Richard R. Lewinski
Leonard J. Prekel	Gregory M. Frassrand

For full biographical listings, see the Martindale-Hubbell Law Directory

---

POLING, McGAW & POLING, P.C. (AV)

Suite 275, 5435 Corporate Drive, 48098
Telephone: 810-641-0500
Telecopier: 810-641-0506

Benson T. Buck (1926-1989)	Richard B. Poling, Jr.
Richard B. Poling	Gregory C. Hamilton
D. Douglas McGaw	Veronica B. O'Haro

James R. Parker
OF COUNSEL
Ralph S. Moore

Representative Clients: County of Oakland; City of Troy; United States Fidelity & Guaranty Co.; Sentry Insurance Co.; Admiral Insurance; DeMaria Construction Co.; Leo Corporation; Aetna Casualty and Surety Co.; Concord Design; Pneumo-Abex.

For full biographical listings, see the Martindale-Hubbell Law Directory

---

WEST BLOOMFIELD, Oakland Co.

SHEFFERLY & SILVERMAN (AV)

7115 Orchard Lake Road, Suite 500, 48322
Telephone: 810-539-1330
Fax: 810-539-1355

MEMBERS OF FIRM

Phillip J. Shefferly	Geoffrey L. Silverman
Thomas R. Morris	

ASSOCIATES

Karin F. Barto	Kathryn R.S. Spray

Representative Clients: Textron Financial Corp.; Townsend Hotel Corp.; Continental Ins. Co.; Country Home Bakers; D.N.T.; Mr. Bulky Treats & Gifts; Medsker Electric, Inc.; Spartan Finance Company; Neal R. Sutherland, trustee.

For full biographical listings, see the Martindale-Hubbell Law Directory

COMMERCIAL LITIGATION

ALABAMA

GADSDEN, * Etowah Co.

SIMMONS, BRUNSON AND SASSER, ATTORNEYS, P.A. (AV)

1411 Rainbow Drive, P.O. Box 1189, 35902
Telephone: 205-546-9206
Telecopier: 205-546-8091

Clarence Simmons, Jr.	Steve P. Brunson
James T. Sasser	

Rebecca A. Walker	Jeff George Underwood
Jeffrey A. Brown	Scott C. Lloyd
	(Not admitted in AL)

Attorneys for: Preferred Risk Mutual Insurance Co.; ALFA Mutual Insurance Co.; Royal Insurance Cos.
Approved Attorneys for: Lawyers Title Insurance Corp.; Mississippi Valley Title Insurance Co.

For full biographical listings, see the Martindale-Hubbell Law Directory

MOBILE, * Mobile Co.

LOVELESS & LYONS (AV)

28 North Florida Street, 36607
Telephone: 334-476-7857
Fax: 334-476-8510

MEMBERS OF FIRM

Ralph P. Loveless	Beth Marietta Lyons

LEGAL SUPPORT PERSONNEL

Deborah Geiger

For full biographical listings, see the Martindale-Hubbell Law Directory

MONTGOMERY, * Montgomery Co.

GIDIERE & HINTON (AV)

904 Union Bank Building, 60 Commerce Street, 36104
Telephone: 334-834-9950

MEMBERS OF FIRM

Philip S. Gidiere, Jr.	Jack B. Hinton, Jr.
Steven K. Herndon	

Representative Client: The St. Paul Cos.

For full biographical listings, see the Martindale-Hubbell Law Directory

PARNELL, CRUM & ANDERSON, P.A. (AV)

641 South Lawrence Street, P.O. Box 2189, 36102
Telephone: 334-832-4202
Telecopier: 334-832-4703

Charles N. Parnell, III	Charles L. Anderson
G. Barton Crum	Bernard B. Carr

Robert J. Russell, Jr.	Rita L. Hullett
Jennifer M. Chambliss	Kyle Dennis Massingale
Betty B. Byrne	James McCauley Smith

Reference: Colonial Bank of Montgomery.

For full biographical listings, see the Martindale-Hubbell Law Directory

ARIZONA

MESA, Maricopa Co.

JACKSON, WHITE, GARDNER & DECKER, P.C. (AV)

Suite 12000, 1201 S. Alma School Road, 85210
Telephone: 602-464-1111
Fax: 602-464-5692
Statewide: 800-243-1160
Email: JWGD@INDIRECT.COM
Payson, Arizona Office: 260 Building C. Suite E, 108 E. Highway.
Telephone: 520-472-8878.

Roger C. Decker	Michael R. Pruitt
Wayne L. Gardner	Bradley D. Weech
Eric M. Jackson	David L. Weed
J. Grant Walker	Richard A. White
Roger R. Foote	

(See Next Column)

William G. Rood	Hank E. Pearson
Eric K. MacDonald	Christine A. Wigton
Kelly G. Black	

For full biographical listings, see the Martindale-Hubbell Law Directory

PHOENIX, * Maricopa Co.

BEUS, GILBERT & MORRILL, P.L.L.C. (AV)

Suite 1000, Great American Tower 3200 North Central Avenue, 85012-2417
Telephone: 602-274-8229
Fax: 602-234-5893

Leo R. Beus	John V. Berry
Paul E. Gilbert	Michael R. Devitt
K. Layne Morrill	Laurie B. Craig
J. Tyrrell Taber	Anthony H. Misseldine
Martin A. Aronson	Scott D. Larmore
Jeffrey D. Gross	

Joseph M. Leal, III	Quinn C. Wheeler
Christine R. Taradash	Robert A. Miller
Maria Crimi Speth	William D. Cleaveland
Dalon J. Morgan	H. Paul Honsinger
Tony J. Rudman	Richard R. Thomas
Keith A. Call	Michael E. Gottfried
Kelly W. Lewis	Nicholas J. DiCarlo
Brian K. Moll	Michelle C. Lombino
Carol Woods Frazier	Jason Barclay Morris

Representative Clients: Albertsons; Arizona Public Service Co.; Bank of America-Arizona; Bell Atlantic Mobile; Cardon; Carioca Oil Co.; Dillards Department Stores; Estes Homes; First Interstate Bank of Arizona-Trust Department; John C. Lincoln Hospital Foundation.

For full biographical listings, see the Martindale-Hubbell Law Directory

BONN, LUSCHER, PADDEN & WILKINS, CHARTERED (AV)

805 North Second Street, 85004
Telephone: 602-254-5557
Fax: 602-254-0656

Paul V. Bonn	John H. Cassidy
Brian A. Luscher	D. Michael Hall
Jeff C. Padden	Samuel C. Wisotzkey
Randall D. Wilkins	Ronald A. Rice

OF COUNSEL

Marvin Kantor	Ruth Sproull

For full biographical listings, see the Martindale-Hubbell Law Directory

COPPERSMITH & GORDON P.L.C. (AV)

2633 East Indian School Road, Suite 300, 85016-6759
Telephone: 602-224-0999
Fax: 602-224-6020
Email: SAMnANDY@aol.com

Andrew S. Gordon

OF COUNSEL

James J. Belanger

Reference: Norwest Bank Arizona, N.A.

For full biographical listings, see the Martindale-Hubbell Law Directory

GALBUT & CONANT, A PROFESSIONAL CORPORATION (AV)

Camelback Esplanade, Suite 1020, 2425 East Camelback Road, 85016
Telephone: 602-955-1455
Fax: 602-955-1585

Martin R. Galbut	Paul A. Conant

John R. Augustine, Jr.

For full biographical listings, see the Martindale-Hubbell Law Directory

GLOVER & VAN COTT, A PROFESSIONAL ASSOCIATION (AV)

Suite 260, The Brookstone, 2025 North Third Street, 85004
Telephone: 602-257-9160
Telecopier: 602-257-9180

Michael R. Glover	Dari S. Hing
Joyce N. Van Cott	Ryan J. Talamante
Martin A. Tetreault	

Representative Clients: American Bonding Company; Arizona Department of Insurance; Balcor/American Express; United Banks of Colorado; Nu-West, Inc.; FitzGibbons, Tharp and Associates, Inc.; Farm and Home Life Insurance Company; Legacy Life Insurance Company; Underwriters National Assurance Corporation; ISI National Life Insurance Company.

For full biographical listings, see the Martindale-Hubbell Law Directory

Phoenix—Continued

HORNE, KAPLAN AND BISTROW, P.C. (AV)

Renaissance Two, 40 North Central, Suite 2800, 85004
Telephone: 602-253-9700
Fax: 602-258-4805

Thomas C. Horne	Eric J. Bistrow
Martha Bachner Kaplan	Michael S. Dulberg
	Kimball J. Corson

For full biographical listings, see the Martindale-Hubbell Law Directory

KIMERER & LaVELLE, P.L.C. (AV)

100 W. Clarendon Suite 2100, 85013
Telephone: 602-279-5900; 800-220-6817
FAX: 602-264-5566
Email: kimlav@msn.com

Michael D. Kimerer	Clark L. Derrick
Michael J. LaVelle	Merrick B. Firestone

Representative Clients: The National Basketball Association; Aetna Insurance Co.; Kaibab Industries; Centric Jones Constructors; B & B Masonry; Western Block.

For full biographical listings, see the Martindale-Hubbell Law Directory

GUY DAVID KNOLLER, P.C. (AV)

1401 First Interstate Bank Tower, 3550 North Central Avenue, 85012
Telephone: 602-230-1099
Fax: 602-274-0103

Guy David Knoller

LIEBERMAN, DODGE, SENDROW & GERDING, LTD. (AV)

Valley Bank Tower, Suite 1801 3550 North Central Avenue, 85012-2114
Telephone: 602-277-3000
Fax: 602-277-7478
Chicago, Illinois Office: LaSalle Bank Building, Suite 1946, 135 South La Salle Street, 60603.
Telephone: 312-541-8510.
Fax: 312-541-2624.

David D. Dodge	Marc R. Lieberman
Paul S. Gerding	Susan G. Sendrow

Mary K. Farrington-Lorch
Paul S. Gerding, Jr. (Not admitted in AZ; Resident, Chicago, Illinois Office)

OF COUNSEL

Karen L. Kothe	Michael J. Fuller
Robert G. Anderson (P.C.)	Lawrence J. Buckley
	John T. Callan

Representative Clients: John Gardiner's Tennis Ranch; Arizona Education Association; Public Safety Personnel Retirement System; Wells Fargo Bank and Credit Corp.; Regency Savings Bank; Sears, Roebuck and Co.; Baxter Healthcare Corporation; Aetna Life Insurance Company; General Board of Pension and Health Benefits of the United Methodist Church; Anti-Defamation League of B'Nai B'Rith.

For full biographical listings, see the Martindale-Hubbell Law Directory

MARISCAL, WEEKS, McINTYRE & FRIEDLANDER, P.A. (AV)

2901 North Central Avenue Suite 200, 85012-2705
Telephone: 602-285-5000
Fax: 602-285-5100

Richard A. Friedlander	Brian M. Mueller
Michael S. Rubin	P. Bruce Converse
Gary L. Birnbaum	Leonce A. Richard
Robert A. Shull	Scott A. Holcomb
Michael R. Scheurich	David J. Ouimette
Andrew L. Pringle	D. Samuel Coffman
	Scot L. Claus

References: Northern Trust Bank of Arizona; National Bank of Arizona.

For Complete List of Firm Personnel, See General Section

For full biographical listings, see the Martindale-Hubbell Law Directory

MUCHMORE & WALLWORK, A PROFESSIONAL CORPORATION (AV)

2700 North Central Avenue, Suite 1225, 85004-1165
Telephone: 602-240-6699
Data: 602-240-6698
Facsimile: 602-240-6697
Email: muchwork@mmww.com *URL:* http://www.mmww.com

Charles J. Muchmore	Nicholas J. Wallwork

(See Next Column)

COUNSEL

Margaret M. Dean	Fredric D. Bellamy
	Kathy E. Shimpock

Bridget S. Bade	Carolina L. Carver
(Senior Associate)	Margaret Benny Hurst

LEGAL SUPPORT PERSONNEL

Gloria A. Torres (Administrator and Senior Paralegal)	Gale James (Finance Manager and Paralegal)
John A. Bennett (Litigation Support Manager)	

Representative Clients: AgrEvo USA Company; BHP Copper Inc.; City of Scottsdale; Cyprus Amax Minerals Company; General Electric Co.; Homes by Dave Brown, Inc.; National Indemnity Insurance Company; Standard Insurance Company; Washington Mills Electro Minerals Company. *Reference:* M & I Thunderbird Bank.

For full biographical listings, see the Martindale-Hubbell Law Directory

PERRY, PIERSON & SILVER, P.L.C. (AV)

2901 North Central Avenue Suite 300, 85012
Telephone: 602-285-5165
Facsimile: 602-285-5100

Allan R. Perry	Timothy L. Pierson
	Leon B. Silver

For full biographical listings, see the Martindale-Hubbell Law Directory

QUARLES & BRADY (AV)

One Camelback Building, One East Camelback Road, Suite 400, 85012-1649
Telephone: 602-230-5500
Fax: 602-230-5598
Milwaukee, Wisconsin Office: 411 East Wisconsin Avenue.
Telephone: 414-277-5000.
Fax: 414-271-3552.
Madison, Wisconsin Office: First Wisconsin Plaza, One South Pinckney Street, P.O. Box 2113.
Telephone: 608-251-5000.
Fax: 608-251-9166.
West Palm Beach, Florida Office: 222 Lakeview Ave., 4th Floor.
Telephone: 407-653-5000.
Fax: 407-653-5333.
Naples, Florida Office: Barnett Center, 4501 Tamiami Trail North, Suite 300.
Telephone: 813-262-5959.
Fax: 813-434-4999.

MEMBERS OF THE FIRM

William M. Shattuck	Robert C. Houser, Jr.

ASSOCIATE

Colleen A. Scherkenbach

For Complete List of Firm Personnel, See General Section

For full biographical listings, see the Martindale-Hubbell Law Directory

SHERWOOD, KLEIN, DUDLEY & ABRAM, P.A. (AV)

2400 Bank One Center, 201 North Central Avenue, 85073
Telephone: 602-254-7041
Fax: 602-254-7540

Andrew R. Sherwood	Thomas L. Abram
Andrew G. Klein	Hal W. Mack
Gordon E. Dudley	Gregory J. Meell

For full biographical listings, see the Martindale-Hubbell Law Directory

SHIMMEL, HILL, BISHOP & GRUENDER, P.C. (AV)

3700 North 24th Street, 85016
Telephone: 602-224-9500
Telecopier: 602-955-6176

Daniel F. Gruender	Susan M. Swick
Keith F. Overholt	Michael V. Perry
Scott J. Richardson	S. Gregory Jones
Joseph Wm. Kruchek	James H. Hazlewood
	Glenn B. Hotchkiss

OF COUNSEL

Charles A. Finch

Representative Clients: Harkins Amusement Enterprises, Inc.; State of Arizona Property and Casualty Guarantee Fund; Talley Industries; Delta Airlines; Associated General Contractors of America, Inc., Arizona Chapter; Norwest Equipment Finance, Inc.; Rasta Technologies, Inc.; Farmers Insurance Group; Original Apt. Movers; Keystone Graphics, Inc.

For full biographical listings, see the Martindale-Hubbell Law Directory

Phoenix—Continued

SNELL & WILMER, L.L.P. (AV)

One Arizona Center, 85004-0001
Telephone: 602-382-6000
Fax: 602-382-6070
Tucson, Arizona Office: 1500 Norwest Tower, One South Church Avenue 85701-1612.
Telephone: 520-882-1200.
Fax: 520-884-1294.
Orange County Office: 1920 Main Street, Suite 1200, P.O. Box 57062, Irvine, California, 92619-7062.
Telephone: 714-253-2700.
Fax: 714-955-2507.
Salt Lake City, Utah Office: Broadway Centre, 111 East Broadway, Suite 900, 84111-1004.
Telephone: 801-237-1900.
Fax: 801-237-1950.

MEMBERS OF FIRM

John J. Bouma	Warren E. Platt
George H. Lyons	Peter J. Rathwell
Daniel J. McAuliffe	Joel P. Hoxie
James R. Condo	Lonnie J. Williams, Jr.
Vaughn A. Crawford	Heidi L. McNeil
Katherine M. Harmeyer	James J. Sienicki
E. Jeffrey Walsh	George J. Coleman, III
Kevin J. Parker	Steven S. Guy
Barbara J. Dawson	Brian J. Foster
Bob J. McCullough	Patrick G. Byrne
Patricia Lee Refo	

ASSOCIATES

Jennifer Bell Anderson	Andrew S. Ashworth
Jeffery L. Brown	Terri N.A. Buccino
Brian J. Campbell	Nancy J. Caplette
Sarah Chilton	Stephanie R. Derby
Robert M. Kort	Craig Marquiz
David E. Rauch	Heidi J. Richter
Scott D. Sherman	Donald Zavala

Representative Clients: Arizona Public Service Co.; Bank One, Arizona, NA.; First Security Bank of Utah, N.A.; Ford Motor Co.; Chrysler Motors Corp.; Toyota Motor Sales U.S.A.; BHP Copper, Inc.; U.S. Home Corp.; Pinnacle West Capital Corp.; Safeway, Inc.

For Complete List of Firm Personnel, See General Section

For full biographical listings, see the Martindale-Hubbell Law Directory

WARNICKE & LITTLER, P.L.C. (AV)

2020 North Central Avenue, Fifth Floor, 85004-4506
Telephone: 602-256-0400
FAX: 602-256-0345

Ronald E. Warnicke	Ellen B. Davis
Thomas E. Littler	Mark J. Giunta

LEGAL SUPPORT PERSONNEL

Cheryl A. Menefee (Certified Paralegal)

For full biographical listings, see the Martindale-Hubbell Law Directory

PRESCOTT,* Yavapai Co.

MURPHY, LUTEY, SCHMITT & BECK (AV)

Elks Building, 117 East Gurley Street, 86301
Telephone: 520-445-6860
Fax: 520-445-6488
Yuma, Arizona Office: Valley Professional Plaza, 1763 West Twenty-Fourth Street, Suite 200.
Telephone: 520-726-0314.
Fax: 520-341-1079.
Kingman, Arizona Office: 2601 Stockton Hill Road, Suite H8.
Telephone: 520-718-0888; 1-800-281-0822.

MEMBERS OF FIRM

Thelton D. Beck	Selmer D. Lutey
Michael R. Murphy	Robert E. Schmitt

ASSOCIATES

Dan A. Wilson	Bruce E. Rosenberg

OF COUNSEL

Keith F. Quail

Counsel for: State Farm Mutual Automobile Insurance Co.; Allstate Insurance Co.; Farmers Insurance; Western Agricultural Insurance Co.
Local Counsel for: Bank One Arizona, NA; The Stockmen's Bank.
Representative Clients: Prescott College; Galpin Ford, Inc.; Sedona-Oak Creek Airport Authority; Yavapai County Fair Association (Prescott Downs).

For full biographical listings, see the Martindale-Hubbell Law Directory

SCOTTSDALE, Maricopa Co.

SPARKS, TEHAN & RYLEY, P.C. (AV)

7503 First Street, 85251-4573
Telephone: 602-949-1339
Fax: 602-949-7587

Joe P. Sparks	Kevin T. Tehan
	John H. Ryley

References: Bank One, Arizona, Trust Department; Northern Trust Bank of Arizona, N.A.; First Interstate Bank of Arizona.

For full biographical listings, see the Martindale-Hubbell Law Directory

TITUS, BRUECKNER & BERRY, P.C. (AV)

Scottsdale Centre Suite B-252, 7373 North Scottsdale Road, 85253-3527
Telephone: 602-483-9600
Fax: 602-483-3215
Email: TBandB@aol.com

Jon A. Titus	Charles R. Berry
Kurt M. Brueckner	Alex B. Vakula
	Garry S. O'Rafferty
David R. Jordan	K. Scott Reynolds
Scott K. Risley	Michael F. Patterson

LEGAL SUPPORT PERSONNEL

Janice L. Innocenzi	Belle Taylor

Representative Clients: Arizona Department of Insurance; Dickinson & Co. Hancock Homes; McCallum Hill; Heritage Mint, Ltd.; Baukol Construction, Inc.; Office of Special Deputy Receiver, Illinois Department of Insurance; Peacock, Hislop, Staley & Given, Inc.; H.E.R.C. Products., Incorporated; Stewart Title and Trust of Phoenix, Inc.; Beazer Homes.

For full biographical listings, see the Martindale-Hubbell Law Directory

TUCSON,* Pima Co.

DUFFIELD, MILLER, YOUNG, ADAMSON & ALFRED, P.C. (AV)

Suite 711, Transamerica Building, 177 North Church Avenue, 85701
Telephone: 520-792-1181
FAX: 520-792-2859
Green Valley, Arizona Office: 101-65 South La Canada, Green Valley Mall.
Telephone: 520-625-4404.
Fax: 520-625-4453.
La Paloma Office: La Paloma Corporate Center, 3573 East Sunrise Drive, Suite 115, Tucson, Arizona.
Telephone: 520-577-1135.
Fax: 520-577-1079.

Philip Hawley Smith	Thomas R. Althaus
Arthur H. Miller (1935-1995)	Richard Duffield
Larry R. Adamson	Eugene C. Gieseler
Samuel D. Alfred	K. Alexander Hobson
	Michael C. Young

LEGAL SUPPORT PERSONNEL

Cynthia Sargent Althaus	Joan Shelton, CLA
Mary Jane Arnesen	Christine M. Smith
Katrina Hillman	Barbara L. Steimle
Elizabeth Kohl-Sturgeon	Elaine Webb

Representative Clients: San Xavier Rock & Materials; Community Water Company of Green Valley.
Insurance Company Clientele: State Farm Mutual Insurance Cos.; Automobile Club Insurance Co.; Colonial Penn Insurance Co.; Metropolitan Property & Liability Insurance Co.; National Indemnity Ins. Co.

For full biographical listings, see the Martindale-Hubbell Law Directory

WILLIAM G. WALKER, P.C. (AV)

145 South Sixth Avenue, 85701
Telephone: 520-622-3330
Fax: 520-622-0521

William G. Walker

For full biographical listings, see the Martindale-Hubbell Law Directory

YUMA,* Yuma Co.

CLARK & CARTER (AV)

256 South Second Avenue, 85364
Telephone: 520-783-6233
Fax: 520-783-0533

MEMBERS OF FIRM

A. James Clark	Rick K. Carter

ASSOCIATE

Heather D. Burgess

For full biographical listings, see the Martindale-Hubbell Law Directory

ARKANSAS

BATESVILLE, * Independence Co.

GREGG, HART & FARRIS (AV)

262 Boswell Street, P.O. Box 2496, 72501
Telephone: 501-793-7556
Fax: 501-793-6921

MEMBERS OF FIRM

John C. Gregg   Josephine Linker Hart
Phillip B. Farris

For full biographical listings, see the Martindale-Hubbell Law Directory

FAYETTEVILLE, * Washington Co.

DAVIS, COX & WRIGHT, PLC (AV)

19 East Mountain Street, P.O. Drawer 1688, 72702-1688
Telephone: 501-521-7600
Fax: 501-521-7661

Sidney P. Davis, Jr.	William Jackson Butt, II
Walter B. Cox	Kelly P. Carithers
Tilden P. Wright, III	Tim E. Howell
Constance G. Clark	Don A. Taylor
Paul H. Taylor	

John G. Trice	Mark W. Dossett
Laura J. Andress	David L. McCune

Representative Clients: Arkansas Farm Bureau Insurance Cos.; Fireman's Fund Insurance Group; United States Fidelity and Guaranty Co.; St. Paul Insurance Cos; Chrysler Motors Corp.; Kemper Insurance Group; Kawasaki Motors Corp.; CIGNA.

For full biographical listings, see the Martindale-Hubbell Law Directory

FORT SMITH, * Sebastian Co.

HARPER, YOUNG, SMITH & MAURRAS, PLC (AV)

510 North Greenwood Avenue, P.O. Box 10205, 72917
Telephone: 501-782-1001
Telefax: 501-782-1279

Thomas Harper (1908-1989)	Tom Harper, Jr.
R. A. Young, Jr. (1908-1973)	S. Walton Maurras
Don A. Smith	Robert Y. Cohen, II
Michael K. Redd	

Counsel for: Arkansas Best Corp.; ABF Freight System, Inc.; Riverside Furniture Corp.; The City National Bank of Fort Smith; O.K. Industries, Inc.
Insurance Clients: Zurich Insurance Co.; Wausau Insurance Companies.

For full biographical listings, see the Martindale-Hubbell Law Directory

LITTLE ROCK, * Pulaski Co.

RICHARD C. DOWNING, P.A. (AV)

Lafayette Building, Suite 750, 523 South Louisiana, 72201
Telephone: 501-372-2066
FAX: 501-376-6420
Email: RCDown@aol.com

Richard C. Downing

For full biographical listings, see the Martindale-Hubbell Law Directory

WRIGHT, LINDSEY & JENNINGS (AV)

200 West Capitol Avenue, Suite 2200, 72201
Telephone: 501-371-0808
Fax: 501-376-9442
Email: tgraves@wlj.com *URL:* http://www.wlj.com/
Fayetteville, Arkansas Office: 101 West Mountain Street, Suite 206, 72701.
Telephone: 501-575-0808.
Fax: 501-575-0999.
Russellville, Arkansas Office: Suite E, 1110 West B Street.
Telephone: 501-968-7995.

John G. Lile	Roger D. Rowe
David M. Powell	Harry S. Hurst, Jr.
M. Samuel Jones, III	Claire Shows Hancock
H. Keith Morrison	
(Resident, Fayetteville Office)	

Representative Clients: Arkansas Electric Cooperative; General Electric Capital Corp.; Helena Chemical Co.; Murphy Oil U.S.A., Inc.

For full biographical listings, see the Martindale-Hubbell Law Directory

SPRINGDALE, Washington Co.

CYPERT, CROUCH, CLARK & HARWELL (AV)

111 Holcomb Street, P.O. Box 869, 72764-1400
Telephone: 501-751-5222
Fax: 501-751-5777

Courtney C. Crouch (1912-1975)	William M. Clark, Jr.
James E. Crouch	Charles L. Harwell

ASSOCIATES

R. Jeffrey Reynerson   Marcus W. Van Pelt

OF COUNSEL

James D. Cypert	Leslie L. Reid
	Stanley W. Ludwig

General Counsel for: First National Bank of Springdale; Northwest Medical Center; Springdale School District.
Representative Clients: Purina Mills, Inc.; Swift-Eckrich, Inc.
Insurance Clients: Western Casualty & Surety Co.; The John Hancock Cos.; Home Ins. Co.; Liberty Mutual; Fireman's Fund.

For full biographical listings, see the Martindale-Hubbell Law Directory

TEXARKANA, * Miller Co.

DUNN, NUTTER, MORGAN & SHAW (AV)

State Line Plaza, Box 8030, 71854-5945
Telephone: 501-773-5651
Telecopier: 501-772-2037
Email: law@clover.cleaf.com

MEMBERS OF FIRM

R. Gary Nutter	R. David Freeze
	W. David Carter

LEGAL SUPPORT PERSONNEL
LEGAL ASSISTANTS

Myra Conaway Wells   Sonja L. Oliver

Representative Clients: Georgia-Pacific Corp.; FNB Lewisville; S.W. Arkansas Electric Corp.; Southern Greyhound Lines; North American Energy Corp.; Tyson Foods, Inc.; Milway Federal Credit Union.

For Complete List of Firm Personnel, See General Section

For full biographical listings, see the Martindale-Hubbell Law Directory

CALIFORNIA

BEVERLY HILLS, Los Angeles Co.

HERZOG, FISHER & GRAYSON, A LAW CORPORATION (AV)

9460 Wilshire Boulevard Fifth Floor, 90212
Telephone: 310-278-4300
Fax: 310-278-5430

James P. Herzog	David R. Fisher
	Michael A. Grayson

Pamela M. Rosenthal	Eric M. Rosin

OF COUNSEL

Todd I. Grayson

For full biographical listings, see the Martindale-Hubbell Law Directory

CAMARILLO, Ventura Co.

H. ROY JEPPSON A PROFESSIONAL CORPORATION (AV)

1100 Paseo Camarillo, 93010
Telephone: 805-482-3322
FAX: 805-482-6672
Email: roy@vcol.net

H. Roy Jeppson

Robyn F. Stalk

For full biographical listings, see the Martindale-Hubbell Law Directory

COSTA MESA, Orange Co.

LAW OFFICES OF ROBERT J. FELDHAKE (AV)

Plaza Tower, Suite 1730, 600 Anton Boulevard, 92626-7124
Telephone: 714-438-3885
Fax: 714-438-3888
San Diego, California Office: 501 West Broadway, Suite 1600, Koll Center, 92101.
Telephone: 619-235-9443.
Facsimile: 619-235-9449.

(See Next Column)

LAW OFFICES OF ROBERT J. FELDHAKE—*Continued*
ASSOCIATES
Gary W. Dolinski   Lorinda B. Harris
(Resident, San Diego Office)

For full biographical listings, see the Martindale-Hubbell Law Directory

---

EL SEGUNDO, Los Angeles Co.

HOWARD B. MILLER (AV)

2101 Rosecrans Avenue, Suite 5252, 90245
Telephone: 310-607-0003
Fax: 310-607-0005
Email: hbm@netcom.com

Reference: Wells Fargo Bank (Beverly Hills).

For full biographical listings, see the Martindale-Hubbell Law Directory

---

ENCINO, Los Angeles Co.

ALPERT, BARR AND GROSS, A PROFESSIONAL LAW CORPORATION (AV)

Encino Office Park I, Suite 300, 6345 Balboa Boulevard, 91316-1523
Telephone: 818-881-5000
Fax: 818-881-1150

Lee Kanon Alpert   Mark S. Blackman
Gary L. Barr   Michael N. Balikian
Lisa W. Glazener   Judith R. Simon
Mark P. Gross   Jack S. Mack
OF COUNSEL
Charles M. Hughes   Leonard S. Levy (A Professional
                                     Corporation)

For full biographical listings, see the Martindale-Hubbell Law Directory

---

FRESNO,* Fresno Co.

SAGASER, HANSEN, FRANSON & JAMISON, A PROFESSIONAL CORPORATION (AV)

2445 Capitol Street, Second Floor, P.O. Box 1632, 93717-1632
Telephone: 209-233-4800
Fax: 209-233-9330

Eric K. Hansen (1952-1996)   Kimberly A. Gaab
Howard A. Sagaser   Patti L. Williams
Donald R. Franson, Jr.   K. Poncho Baker
Daniel O. Jamison   Kristi R. Culver
Nancy A. Maler   Catherine J. Cerna

For full biographical listings, see the Martindale-Hubbell Law Directory

---

GLENDALE, Los Angeles Co.

IRSFELD, IRSFELD & YOUNGER LLP (AV)

A Partnership including Professional Corporations
Suite 900, 100 West Broadway, 91210-1296
Telephone: 818-242-6859
Fax: 818-240-7728
Email: 104736.1745@compuserver.com
MEMBERS OF FIRM
James B. Irsfeld (1880-1966)   Peter J. Irsfeld (P.C.)
Kenneth C. Younger   James J. Waldorf (P.C.)
(1922-1996)   C. Phillip Jackson (P.C.)
John H. Brink (P.C.)   Norman H. Green (P.C.)
              Kathryn E. Van Houten
ASSOCIATES
Peter C. Wright   Diane L. Walker
RETIRED
              James B. Irsfeld, Jr.

Representative Clients: Lear Sieglar, Inc.; Chrysler Credit Corp.
References: First Interstate Bank (Glendale Main Office); Bank of Hollywood.

For full biographical listings, see the Martindale-Hubbell Law Directory

---

HERMOSA BEACH, Los Angeles Co.

NASH & EDGERTON (AV)

A Limited Liability Partnership
2615 Pacific Coast Highway, Suite 322, 90254
Telephone: 310-937-2066
Fax: 310-937-2063
Torrance, California Office: 3625 Del Amo Boulevard, suite 360.
Telephone: 310-370-8272.
Fax: 310-214-9677.

(See Next Column)

Savery L. Nash   Shelley Nash
Samuel Y. Edgerton, III   David Maurer
              Damon Rubin

For full biographical listings, see the Martindale-Hubbell Law Directory

---

IRVINE, Orange Co.

BARNETT & RUBIN, A PROFESSIONAL CORPORATION (AV)

2 Park Plaza, Suite 980, 92614
Telephone: 714-261-9700
Facsimile: 714-261-9799
Email: Lawyers@Pacbell.net

Richard L. Barnett   Jeffrey D. Rubin

              Kathryn B. Salmond

For full biographical listings, see the Martindale-Hubbell Law Directory

CALLAHAN & BLAINE, A PROFESSIONAL LAW CORPORATION (AV)

Suite 800, 18500 Von Karman, 92612
Telephone: 714-553-1155
Fax: 714-553-0784
Email: info@callahan-law.com

Daniel J. Callahan (A   Stephen E. Blaine
Professional Corporation)

Kathleen L. Dunham   Andrew A. Smits
Jim P. Mahacek   Gary S. Spitzer
Michael J. Sachs   Edward Susolik
              Graig R. Woodburn
OF COUNSEL
Shelley M. Liberto   Walt D. Mahaffa

For full biographical listings, see the Martindale-Hubbell Law Directory

RUS, MILIBAND, WILLIAMS & SMITH (AV)

Suite 700, 2600 Michelson Drive, 92612
Telephone: 714-752-7100
Fax: 714-252-1514

Ronald Rus   J. Scott Williams
Joel S. Miliband   Randall A. Smith
              Laurel Zaeske

M. Peter Crinella   David Edward Hays
Jeffrey H. Sussman   Steven Joseph Kraemer
Cathrine M. Castaldi   Leo J. Presiado

For full biographical listings, see the Martindale-Hubbell Law Directory

SUCHMAN, GALFIN & PASSON, LLP (AV)

18101 Von Karman Avenue, Suite 1400, 92612-1043
Telephone: 714-752-2444
Facsimile: 714-833-8256
Email: sgplaw1@aol.com
Santa Ana, California Office: 2122 North Broadway, Suite 100.
Telephone: 714-752-2444.
MEMBERS OF FIRM
Stewart R. Suchman   Michael R. Adams
Ted A. Galfin   William E. Alsnauer, Jr.
Kenneth D. Passon   Marcelle Suzanne Strauss
Lorraine Kay Smyth   Adam M. Greely

For full biographical listings, see the Martindale-Hubbell Law Directory

---

LAGUNA HILLS, Orange Co.

STETINA BRUNDA & BUYAN, A PROFESSIONAL CORPORATION (AV)

Suite 401, 24221 Calle De La Louisa, 92653
Telephone: 714-855-1246
Telex: 704355
Facsimile: 714-855-6371
Email: 104052.1330@compuserve.com

Kit M. Stetina (Mr.)   Bruce B. Brunda
              Robert Dean Buyan

Mark B. Garred   Thomas C. Naber
William J. Brucker   (Not admitted in CA)
Matthew A. Newboles   Darren S. Rimer
LEGAL SUPPORT PERSONNEL
Norman E. Carte   Kristy Kay Moore

For full biographical listings, see the Martindale-Hubbell Law Directory

LONG BEACH, Los Angeles Co.

FORD, WALKER, HAGGERTY & BEHAR, PROFESSIONAL LAW CORPORATION (AV)

One World Trade Center, Twenty Seventh Floor, 90831
Telephone: 310-983-2500
Telecopier: 310-983-2555

G. Richard Ford	Donna Rogers Kirby
Timothy L. Walker	Tina Ivankovic Mangarpan
William C. Haggerty	Susan D. Berger
Jeffrey S. Behar	Joseph A. Heath
Mark Steven Hennings	Robert J. Chavez

J. Michael McClure

Arthur W. Schultz	Theodore A. Clapp
Jon T. Moseley	Stanley L. Scarlett
Maxine J. Lebowitz	Scott A. Ritsema
Timothy P. McDonald	Michael Guy Martin
K. Michele Williams	Colleen A. Strong
Stephen Ward Moore	Thomas L. Gourde
James D. Savage	Patrick J. Stark
Todd D. Pearl	Shayne L. Wulterin
Patrick J. Gibbs	Charles D. Jarrell
James O. Miller	Charles J. Schmitt
David Huchel	Kyle A. Ostergrad
Robert Reisinger	Todd L. Kessler

OF COUNSEL
Theodore P. Shield, P.L.C.

For full biographical listings, see the Martindale-Hubbell Law Directory

*LOS ANGELES,** Los Angeles Co.

ANDERSON, ABLON, LEWIS & GALE, LLP (AV)

Suite 2000 Equitable Plaza Building, 3435 Wilshire Boulevard, 90010
Telephone: 213-388-3385
Telecopier: 213-388-8432
Thousand Oaks, California Office: 220-H Briarwood Building, 299 West Hillcrest Drive, 91360.
Telephone: 805-373-5273.
Fax: 805-495-1456.

MEMBERS OF FIRM

Robert E. Lewis	Jerald E. Gale

Harris D. Bass

ASSOCIATES

Farhad Kazemzadeh	Candace Connart Bleifer

Robert David Schwartz

OF COUNSEL

Charles R. Anderson (Retired)	Herman Ablon (Retired)

Representative Clients: Maremont Corp.; Chansler & Lyon Co., Inc.
Reference: Bank of America (Wilshire Center Branch).

For full biographical listings, see the Martindale-Hubbell Law Directory

BARBOSA GARCIA & BARNES (AV)

A Partnership including a Professional Corporation
Suite 390, 500 Citadel Drive, 90040
Telephone: 213-889-6600
FAX: 213-889-6605

Henry S. Barbosa (P.C.)	Peter E. Langsfeld
Bonifacio Bonny Garcia	Kenneth T. Fong
Douglas D. Barnes	Jonathan B. Stone

Augustin R. Jimenez	Lorie A. Campos
Rajeev M. Talwani	Charisma T. Tan-Sanchez
Erick L. Solares	Diana M. Carbajal

Sylvia J. Trujillo

OF COUNSEL

Norman Lieberman	John F. Lagle

For full biographical listings, see the Martindale-Hubbell Law Directory

BERMAN, BLANCHARD, MAUSNER & RESSER, A LAW CORPORATION (AV)

4727 Wilshire Boulevard, Suite 500, 90010
Telephone: 213-965-1200
Telecopier: 213-965-1919
Email: BBMR@ix.netcom.com

Laurence M. Berman	Jeffrey N. Mausner
Lonnie C. Blanchard, III	Bernard M. Resser

Paul A. Hoffman	Cary P. Ocon
Eric Levinrad	Lisé Hamilton

For full biographical listings, see the Martindale-Hubbell Law Directory

J. T. CAIRNS & ASSOCIATES (AV)

200 North Larchmont Boulevard, 90004
Telephone: 213-962-5588
Telecopier: 213-463-4412

ASSOCIATE
Deann Hampton

For full biographical listings, see the Martindale-Hubbell Law Directory

CLARK & TREVITHICK, A PROFESSIONAL CORPORATION (AV)

800 Wilshire Boulevard, 12th Floor, 90017
Telephone: 213-629-5700
Telecopier: 213-624-9441
San Francisco, California Office: 456 Montgomery Street, 20th Floor.
Telephone: 415-288-6520.
Fax: 415-398-2820.

Philip W. Bartenetti	Leonard Brazil
Dolores Cordell	Arturo Santana Jr.
Vincent Tricarico	Kerry T. Ryan

References: Wells Fargo Bank (Los Angeles Main Office); National Bank of California.

For Complete List of Firm Personnel, See General Section

For full biographical listings, see the Martindale-Hubbell Law Directory

ENGSTROM, LIPSCOMB & LACK, A PROFESSIONAL CORPORATION (AV)

16th Floor, 10100 Santa Monica Boulevard, 90067
Telephone: 310-552-3800
Telecopier: 310-552-9434
URL: http://www.elllaw.com

Paul W. Engstrom	Brian D. Depew
Lee G. Lipscomb	Jeffrey T. Bolson
Walter J. Lack	Alan B. Nishimura
Jerry A. Ramsey	Gary A. Praglin
Steven C. Shuman	William T. Clemons III
Elizabeth Lane Crooke	Matthew J. Saunders

Robert J. Wolfe

Daniel G. Whalen	Joy L. Robertson
Brian J. Heffernan	Jill P. McDonell
Eric Berg	Laura M. Watkins
Karen-Denise Lee	Mark Evans Millard
Adam D. Miller	Stuart R. Fraenkel
Jill L. Feinberg	Tracy Michelle Tuso
Dawn M. Flores-Oster	David M. Robinson
Paul A. Traina	Karen L. Hindin
Cynthia Jane Emry	Troy H. Slome
Brian J. Leinbach	Daniel J. Padova

Reference: Comerica Bank.

For full biographical listings, see the Martindale-Hubbell Law Directory

GIRARDI AND KEESE (AV)

1126 Wilshire Boulevard, 90017-1904
Telephone: 213-977-0211
FAX: 213-481-1554
San Bernardino, California Office: 596 North Arrowhead.
Telephone: 714-381-1551.
FAX: 714-381-2566.

MEMBERS OF FIRM

Thomas V. Girardi	V. Andre Rekte (Resident, San Bernardino Office)
Robert M. Keese	
John A. Girardi	John K. Courtney
James B. Kropff	Amy Fisch Solomon
Robert W. Finnerty	Thomas C. Morgan
James G. O'Callahan	David N. Bigelow

Carrie J. Rognlien

References: Wells Fargo Bank (Los Angeles Head Office); Bank of Industry.

For full biographical listings, see the Martindale-Hubbell Law Directory

HEDGES & CALDWELL, A PROFESSIONAL CORPORATION (AV)

606 South Olive Street, Suite 500, 90014
Telephone: 213-629-9040
Telecopier: 213-629-9022

Christopher G. Caldwell	Joan Mack
George R. Hedges	Sherryl Elise Michaelson
H. Jay Kallman	Mary Newcombe
Michael R. Leslie	David Pettit

OF COUNSEL

Ralph H. Nutter	Jan B. Norman

For full biographical listings, see the Martindale-Hubbell Law Directory

Los Angeles—Continued

HENNIGAN, MERCER & BENNETT (AV)

601 South Figueroa Street, Suite 3300, 90017
Telephone: 213-694-1200
Fax: 213-694-1234
Email: Silverm@hmb.com

J. Michael Hennigan	Laura Lindgren
James W. Mercer	Bruce R. MacLeod
Bruce Bennett	Elizabeth D. Mann
John L. Amsden	Robert L. Palmer
C. Dana Hobart	Lauren A. Smith
Jeanne E. Irving	Peter J. Most
Pamala J. King	Lee W. Potts

ASSOCIATES

Nichole M. Auden	Linda A. Kontos
Jacqueline Bendy	Jennifer Sulla
Mary H. Chu	Michael Swartz
A. Ann Hered	Shawna L. Ballard
Gregory K. Jones	Claudia Schweikert
Ellen M. Keane	David H. Martin

OF COUNSEL
Anthony Castanares

For full biographical listings, see the Martindale-Hubbell Law Directory

HUANG & MITCHELL, A PROFESSIONAL LAW CORPORATION (AV)

3250 Wilshire Boulevard Suite 1600, 90010
Telephone: 213-251-8199
Fax: 213-251-8188

Patrick K. Huang	Judith M. Mitchell

OF COUNSEL
Stephen S. Duplantis

References: Union Bank, Beverly Hills; First Interstate Bank, Catalina Branch.

For full biographical listings, see the Martindale-Hubbell Law Directory

MAHONEY, COPPENRATH, JAFFE & PEARSON LLP (AV)

A Partnership including Professional Corporations
2049 Century Park East, Suite 2480, 90067-3283
Telephone: 310-557-1919
Telecopier: 310-277-6536

MEMBERS OF FIRM

James E. Mahoney (P.C.)	Ronald C. Pearson
Walter G. Coppenrath, Jr., (P.C.)	Daryl G. Parker
Howard M. Jaffe (P.C.)	Charles L. Grotts
	Arthur L. Martin

OF COUNSEL
Gerald Lee Tahajian

Reference: First Professional Bank, Santa Monica, California.

For full biographical listings, see the Martindale-Hubbell Law Directory

MATTHIAS & BERG LLP (AV)

Seventh Floor, 515 South Flower Street, 90071
Telephone: 213-895-4200
Telecopier: 213-895-4058

Michael R. Matthias	Stuart R. Singer
Jeffrey P. Berg	Kenneth M. H. Hoff
Michael D. Berger	

Representative Clients: Synagro Technologies, Inc.; Mexalit, S.A.; Maxitile, Inc.; Allstar Inns; Chatsworth Products, Inc.; International Meta Systems, Inc.; Residential Resources, Inc.; AVIC Group International, Inc.; AutoBitter Group, Inc. National Quality Care, Inc.; Greater China Corp.; HBO Ole.
Reference: First Professional Bank.

For full biographical listings, see the Martindale-Hubbell Law Directory

PETER J. MCNULTY (AV)

827 Moraga Drive (Bel Air), 90049
Telephone: 310-471-2707
Fax: 310-472-7014
Gilroy, California Office: Suite F-2, 8352 Church Street.
Telephone: 408-848-5900.
Fax: 408-848-1391.
Aurora, Illinois Office: 8 East Galena Street.

ASSOCIATE
Michael L. Oran (A Professional Corporation)
OF COUNSEL

John A. Alvarez (Resident, Gilroy Office)	Robert P. Friedman
Robert M. Foote (Not admitted in CA)	Carl A. McMahan

(See Next Column)

Reference: City National Bank (Beverly Hills, California).

For full biographical listings, see the Martindale-Hubbell Law Directory

HOWARD B. MILLER

(See El Segundo)

THE LAW FIRM OF RICHARD M. MONEYMAKER (AV)

Suite 2102 Broadway Plaza, 700 Flower Street, 90017
Telephone: 213-622-1088
Telecopier: 213-622-7002

Richard M. Moneymaker
ASSOCIATES

Vincent B. Moneymaker	Sheri R. Handel

OF COUNSEL
Frank W. Molloy

Reference: Bank of America (Los Angeles Main Office).

For full biographical listings, see the Martindale-Hubbell Law Directory

MONTELEONE & MCCRORY (AV)

A Partnership including Professional Corporations
725 South Figueroa Street Suite 3750, 90017-5402
Telephone: 213-612-9900
FAX: 213-612-9930
Santa Ana, California Office: Suite 750, 1551 North Tustin Avenue, 92705.
Telephone: 714-565-3170.
Fax: 714-565-3184.

MEMBERS OF FIRM

Stephen Monteleone (1886-1962)	Philip C. Putnam (P.C.)
G. Robert Hale (P.C.)	Joseph A. Miller (P.C.)
Patrick J. Duffy, III (P.C.)	Diana M. Dron
Michael F. Minchella (P.C.)	(Resident, Santa Ana Office)
Thomas P. McGuire (P.C.)	Donald J. Shields
William J. Ingalsbe (P.C.) (Resident, Santa Ana Office)	

ASSOCIATES

David C. Romyn	W. Jeffrey Burch
Barry J. Jensen (Resident, Santa Ana Office)	Andrew W. Hawthorne
	Stephen L. Dubin
Erica S. Behrens	

OF COUNSEL
Darrell P. McCrory

For full biographical listings, see the Martindale-Hubbell Law Directory

THOMAS J. READY (AV)

333 South Grand Avenue, 33rd Floor, 90071-1504
Telephone: 213-229-9009
Facsimile: 213-229-9010
Email: TJRLA@AOL.com

For full biographical listings, see the Martindale-Hubbell Law Directory

ROSSBACHER & ASSOCIATES (AV)

Union Bank Plaza, Twenty-Fourth Floor, 445 South Figueroa Street, 90071
Telephone: 213-895-6500
Fax: 213-895-6161

MEMBER OF FIRM
Henry H. Rossbacher
OF COUNSEL
George M. Snyder
ASSOCIATES

James S. Cahill	Nanci E. Nishimura
Linda L. Griffis	Tracy W. Young
Karen D. Kerner	Julie A. Langslet
David F. Desmond	

LEGAL SUPPORT PERSONNEL

Linda Connell (Legal Administrator)	Joan A. Degenkolb (Paralegal)
	Martha E. Guilmette (Paralegal)

For full biographical listings, see the Martindale-Hubbell Law Directory

SIMKE CHODOS (AV)

A Partnership of Professional Corporation
Suite 1511, 1880 Century Park East, 90067
Telephone: 310-203-3888
Fax: 310-203-3866

Stuart A. Simke	David M. Chodos
Richard A. Fond	Ellen Resinski Rosen
James Robertson Martin	

(See Next Column)

SIMKE CHODOS, *Los Angeles—Continued*

OF COUNSEL
James L. Keane

Reference: City National Bank (Wilshire-La Cienega Branch).

For full biographical listings, see the Martindale-Hubbell Law Directory

STEPHENS, BERG & LASATER, A PROFESSIONAL CORPORATION (AV)

1055 West Seventh Street, Twenty-Ninth Floor, 90017
Telephone: 213-629-3111
Telecopy: 213-629-2302; 213-624-4734

Lawrence M. Berg (1947-1995)	Frederick A. Clark
R. Wicks Stephens II	Joel A. Goldman
Richard W. Lasater II	C. Stephen Davis
Mark G. Ancel	Kenneth A. Feinfield
Dudley M. Lang	Jean-Paul Menard
Joseph F. Butler	Michael J. Kaminsky

John A. Dragonette

OF COUNSEL
Louis R. Baker   J. Lane Tilson

For full biographical listings, see the Martindale-Hubbell Law Directory

LAWRENCE C. TISTAERT (AV)

11766 Wilshire Boulevard, Suite 1580, 90025-6537
Telephone: 310-312-0874
Fax: 310-312-1034
Email: lctist@ix.netcom.com

Representative Clients: Bell Foundry Co.; Brendan Tours; Franklin Telecommunications Corp.; Munro Properties; United States Tour Operators Association.
Reference: Bank of America.

For full biographical listings, see the Martindale-Hubbell Law Directory

MENLO PARK, San Mateo Co.

ENTERPRISE LAW GROUP, INC. (AV)

Menlo Oaks Corporate Center, 4400 Bohannon Drive, Suite 280, 94025-1041
Telephone: 415-462-4700
Facsimile: 415-462-4747
Email: info@enterpriselaw.com

Sherwood M. Sullivan

For full biographical listings, see the Martindale-Hubbell Law Directory

NEWPORT BEACH, Orange Co.

BROKER & O'KEEFE, PROFESSIONAL CORPORATION (AV)

4695 MacArthur Court Suite 1200, 92660
Telephone: 714-222-2000
Fax: 714-222-2022
Email: chpter11@aol.com *URL:* http://wwwbroker-okeefe.com

Jeffrey W. Broker   Sean A. O'Keefe

Lauren B. Lessler   David D. Piper

For full biographical listings, see the Martindale-Hubbell Law Directory

CALLAHAN & ASSOCIATES (AV)

5120 Campus Drive, 92660
Telephone: 714-476-2898
Facsimile: 714-752-8770

Rebecca Callahan
ASSOCIATE
Katherine T. Corrigan
LEGAL SUPPORT PERSONNEL
Sandra A. Thompson (Paralegal)

For full biographical listings, see the Martindale-Hubbell Law Directory

YOUNG & AMUNDSEN (AV)

620 Newport Center Drive, Suite 420, 92660
Telephone: 714-640-4400
Fax: 714-717-4862

MEMBERS OF FIRM
Steven R. Young   Roland J. Amundsen

For full biographical listings, see the Martindale-Hubbell Law Directory

OAKLAND,* Alameda Co.

JOHN O. STANSBURY (AV)

5th Floor, 2030 Franklin Street, 94612
Telephone: 510-444-4022
Fax: 510-444-3667

For full biographical listings, see the Martindale-Hubbell Law Directory

ORINDA, Contra Costa Co.

GILLIN, JACOBSON, ELLIS, LARSEN & DOYLE (AV)

2 Theatre Square Suite 230, 94563
Telephone: 510-258-0800
Fax: 510-848-0266
Email: lawfirm@gjeld.com
San Francisco Office: One Sutter Street, 10th Floor.
Telephone: 415-986-4777.

Andrew R. Gillin	Richard P. Doyle, Jr.
Ralph L. Jacobson	Susan Hunt
Luke Ellis	Mitchell S. Rosenfeld
James Paul Larsen	Catherine T. Doyle

For full biographical listings, see the Martindale-Hubbell Law Directory

OXNARD, Ventura Co.

LAWLER, BONHAM & WALSH (AV)

300 Esplanade Drive, Suite, 1900, P.O. Box 5527, 93031
Telephone: 805-485-8921
MCI Fax: 805-485-3766
Email: LBW@INTERNETMCI.COM

MEMBERS OF FIRM
Byron J. Lawler	Henry J. Walsh
Terrence J. Bonham	Carol A. Woo

Korman Dorsey Ellis
ASSOCIATES
Richard A Shimmel   Maureen M. Houska

For full biographical listings, see the Martindale-Hubbell Law Directory

PASADENA, Los Angeles Co.

OVERLANDER, LEWIS & RUSSELL (AV)

65 North Raymond Avenue, Suite 210, 91103
Telephone: 818-304-0500
Fax: 818-304-9750

Thomas F. Overlander   Edwin A. Lewis
Richard L. Russell, Jr.

Craig J. Miller   Sherri Lynette Woods

For full biographical listings, see the Martindale-Hubbell Law Directory

SAN DIEGO,* San Diego Co.

BARKER, THOMAS, McCOLLOCH & WALTERS, A PROFESSIONAL LAW CORPORATION (AV)

1455 Frazee Road, Suite 800, 92108
Telephone: 619-682-4040
Facsimile: 619-220-7056

Douglas H. Barker	Michael D. Liuzzi
Anastasia E. Thomas	Jeffrey L. Mason
Michael T. McColloch	Jean Detmann Fisher
Elizabeth A. Walters	Joyce R. Dondanville

Douglas V. Fettel

For full biographical listings, see the Martindale-Hubbell Law Directory

BROWN, McDONNELL & ROMAKER, A PROFESSIONAL LAW CORPORATION (AV)

2390 Shelter Island Drive, Suite 210, 92106
Telephone: 619-221-9181
Fax: 619-221-9181

Sampson A. Brown   Michael B. McDonnell
John L. Romaker

Representative Clients: A to Z Marine Service; Knight & Carver Custom Yachts, Inc.; Lester & Lester Marine Survey, Inc.

For full biographical listings, see the Martindale-Hubbell Law Directory

COUGHLAN, SEMMER & LIPMAN (AV)

501 West Broadway, Suite 400, 92101
Telephone: 619-232-0800
Fax: 619-232-0107

MEMBERS OF FIRM
R. J. (Jerry) Coughlan, Jr.   Robert F. Semmer
Michael L. Lipman

(See Next Column)

COUGHLAN, SEMMER & LIPMAN—*Continued*

ASSOCIATES

Cathleen Gilliland Fitch	Barbara Howe Murray
Duane Tyler	Katherine Koransky Pothier
Angela L. Baxter	Daniel A. Kaplan

OF COUNSEL

Alexandra M. Kwoka

Representative Clients: Ernst & Young; U.S. Air; Wells Fargo Bank; Lawyers Mutual Insurance Co.; Prudential-Bache Securities, Inc.; CAMICO; Shell Oil; IBP, Inc.; UST Inc.; San Diego National Bank.

For full biographical listings, see the Martindale-Hubbell Law Directory

HUGHES & NUNN (AV)

A Partnership including a Professional Corporation
450 "B" Street, Suite 2000, 92101
Telephone: 619-231-1661
Telecopier: 619-236-9271

MEMBERS OF FIRM

William D. Hughes (A Professional Corporation)	Randall M. Nunn

ASSOCIATES

E. Kenneth Purviance	Regan Furcolo
Melissa K. Johnson	

For full biographical listings, see the Martindale-Hubbell Law Directory

LINDLEY, LAZAR & SCALES, A PROFESSIONAL CORPORATION (AV)

One America Plaza, 600 West Broadway, Suite 1400, 92101-3302
Telephone: 619-234-9181
Fax: 619-234-8475
Email: 104413.1175@compuserve.com

Luke R. Corbett	Richard J. Pekin, Jr.
John M. Seitman	George C. Lazar
Robert M. McLeod	Raymond L. Heidemann
William E. Johns	James Henry Fox
Stephen F. Treadgold	Elise Streicher Rogerson
Michael H. Wexler	R. Gordon Huckins
Kenneth C. Jones	

Marc A. Geffen

Representative Clients: Palomar Savings & Loan Assn.; McGraw-Hill Broadcasting Co.; Chicago Title Insurance Co.; San Diego Hospital Assn.; Bank of Commerce; City Chevrolet; Ham Bros. Construction Co.; Commonwealth Land Title Insurance Co.; Ponte Builders; Morrison Homes, Inc.

For Complete List of Firm Personnel, See General Section

For full biographical listings, see the Martindale-Hubbell Law Directory

SAN FRANCISCO,* San Francisco Co.

BARTKO, ZANKEL, TARRANT & MILLER, PROFESSIONAL CORPORATION (AV)

900 Front Street, Suite 300, 94111
Telephone: 415-956-1900
Fax: 415-956-1152

John J. Bartko	Randall M. Faccinto
Martin I. Zankel	M. Manuel Fishman
Richard T. Tarrant	Christopher J. Hunt
Charles G. Miller	Theani Christine Louskos
Robert H. Bunzel	Brian McLaughlin
Kim A. Lambert	Howard L Pearlman
Michael D. Welch	C. Griffith Towle
Michael D. Abraham	Mary Elizabeth Trice
Glenn P. Zwang	

P. Craig Cardon	Carissa Shubb
Rita Maria Castro	Christopher D. Sullivan
Cynthia E. King	Ralph J. Sutton
Hussein M. Saffouri	Constance J. Yu

COUNSEL

Thomas A. Lee, Jr.

For full biographical listings, see the Martindale-Hubbell Law Directory

LAW OFFICES OF JOSEPH C. BARTON (AV)

465 California Street, Suite 200, 94104
Telephone: 415-956-3385
Telefax: 415-989-8947
Email: jbartlaw@aol.com

LEGAL SUPPORT PERSONNEL

Nienke A. Lels-Hohmann

Representative Clients: Vinyl Products Manuf., Inc.; Endress & Hauser, Inc.; ONDYNE, Inc.; Transamerica Financial Services, Inc.

(See Next Column)

Reference: Union Bank, San Francisco.

For full biographical listings, see the Martindale-Hubbell Law Directory

BERG, ZIEGLER, ANDERSON & PARKER, LLP (AV)

4 Embarcadero Center, Suite 1400, 94111
Telephone: 415-397-6000
Telecopier: 415-397-9449

MEMBERS OF FIRM

James M. Berg	Robert Ted Parker
William J. Ziegler	David B. Franklin
Robert L. Anderson	David L. Monetta
F. Gale Connor	

Douglas A. Applegate	Jennifer M. Malloy
Jeffrey B. Kirschenbaum	Patrick J. O'Brien

PARALEGALS

David A. Dunbar	Diane E. Gresham
Sharon L. Gostlin	

For full biographical listings, see the Martindale-Hubbell Law Directory

ANTHONY P. DAVID A PROFESSIONAL CORPORATION (AV)

One Montgomery Street, 15th Floor, 94104
Telephone: 415-981-0166
Fax: 415-433-3883

Anthony P. David

For full biographical listings, see the Martindale-Hubbell Law Directory

HOLMAN & O'GRADY (AV)

345 California Street, Suite 1770, 94104-2622
Telephone: 415-352-0500
Facsimile: 415-352-0505
Email: HandOSF@aol.com

Thomas C. Holman	Sharon L. O'Grady

JUNIOR SHAREHOLDER

Kathryn E. McQueen

For full biographical listings, see the Martindale-Hubbell Law Directory

KINDER, WUERFEL & CHOLAKIAN, A PROFESSIONAL CORPORATION (AV)

555 Montgomery Street, Ninth Floor, 94111
Telephone: 415-398-1551; 800-992-5990
FAX: 415-398-3301
URL: http://www.kwcapc.com
Santa Rosa, California Office: 2300 Northpoint Parkway.
Telephones: 707-522-8020; 800-992-5990.
FAX: 707-522-8022.
Costa Mesa, California Office: Avenue of the Arts.
Telephone: 714-825-3590; 800-992-5990.

H. Stuart Kinder	Kevin K. Cholakian
Mark D. Wuerfel	Julian J. Pardini (Resident, Santa Rosa Office)

SPECIAL COUNSEL

Mark A. Koop	Nan R. Hooven
Paul B. Justi	

Robert E. Belshaw	Peter R. Harris
David H. Bennett	(Resident, Santa Rosa Office)
Dean C. Burnick	Kathleen M. Hurly
Cheryl Castrogiovanni	Timothy S. Kirk
Douglas M. Chapman	Bryan A. McBurney
Christopher J. Connell (Resident, Santa Rosa Office)	Steven J. Plas
	Anthony O. Ricucci
Michael J. Estep	Charlene P. Rosack
James M. Gentile	Scott A. Slomiak
Garth A. Gersten	Michael A. Topp
Victor G. Greene	Harold A. Weston

LEGAL SUPPORT PERSONNEL

Gary T. Hall, Legal Administrator

For full biographical listings, see the Martindale-Hubbell Law Directory

LINK & WARHURST (AV)

The Shell Building, 100 Bush Street, Suite 820, 94104
Telephone: 415-788-3600
Facsimile: 415-788-7073

William R. Warhurst

For full biographical listings, see the Martindale-Hubbell Law Directory

San Francisco—Continued

MORGENSTEIN & JUBELIRER, LLP (AV)

A Partnership including a Professional Corporation
One Market Plaza, Spear Street Tower, 32nd Floor, 94105
Telephone: 415-896-0666
Fax: 415-896-5592
Email: jubelirer@aol.com

MEMBERS OF FIRM

Marvin D. Morgenstein (P.C.)	Rocky N. Unruh
Eliot S. Jubelirer	James L. McGinnis
Lee Ann Huntington	Charles W. LaGrave
Jean L. Bertrand	Wendi J. Berkowitz
Jeffrey R. Williams	John S. Worden
James R. Balich	Robert B. Mullen

OF COUNSEL

Laurie K. Anger

Lewis D. Barr	Natasha L. Golding
David H. Bromfield	Stephen M. Hankins
Michael "Cael" S. Davis	Simon E. Kisch
Roberta Nicol Dempster	John J. Petry
Bruce A. Wagman	

For full biographical listings, see the Martindale-Hubbell Law Directory

PREUSS WALKER & SHANAGHER LLP (AV)

595 Market Street, 16th Floor, 94105
Telephone: 415-978-2600
Facsimile: 415-978-2613
Email: pws@pwsllp.com

MEMBERS OF FIRM

Charles F. Preuss	Donald F. Zimmer, Jr.
Gary T. Walker	Sheila Doyle Kelley
Denis F. Shanagher	Thomas W. Pulliam, Jr.
Vernon I. Zvoleff	Alan J. Lazarus
Michael J. Stortz	

John J. Powers	Constance D. Burton
Cynthia C. Roenisch	Paul S. Lecky
Kenneth P. Conour	Catherine M. Leon
Paula R. Lee	Elizabeth L. W. Ewert
Mel M. Negussie	

Representative Clients: Alexander & Alexander; Envision Claims Management Corp.; Federal Deposit Insurance Corp. (FDIC); Grubb & Ellis; Marsh & McLennan; Resolution Trust Corporation (RTC); Westchester Speciality Group; First Colonial Insurance Co.; Franklin Resources.

For full biographical listings, see the Martindale-Hubbell Law Directory

WARTNICK, CHABER, HAROWITZ, SMITH & TIGERMAN, A PROFESSIONAL CORPORATION (AV)

101 California Street, Suite 2200, 94111-5802
Telephone: 415-986-5566
Fax: 415-986-5896

Harry F. Wartnick	Steven M. Harowitz
Madelyn J. Chaber	Audrey A. Smith
Stephen M. Tigerman	

Niromi L. Wijewantha	Christopher C. Lamerdin
Phillip Scott Chan	Garry Cohen
Brenda D. Posada	Cheryl L. White
Gregory M. Sheffer	

For full biographical listings, see the Martindale-Hubbell Law Directory

SAN JOSE,* Santa Clara Co.

BERGESON, ELIOPOULOS, GRADY & GRAY (AV)

Ten Almaden Boulevard, Suite 200, 95113
Telephone: 408-291-6200
Fax: 408-297-6000
Email: BEGG215958@AOL.Com

Daniel J. Bergeson	Richard J. Gray
William T. Eliopoulos	Mary Anne Rodgers
Michael F. Grady	John L. Antracoli

ASSOCIATES

Donald P. Gagliardi	Siobhán Lawlor
Mark E. Waite	John P. Shinn

For full biographical listings, see the Martindale-Hubbell Law Directory

MAHL REHON WALWORTH & ROBERTS, A PROFESSIONAL CORPORATION (AV)

Ten Almaden Boulevard, Suite 1440, 95113
Telephone: 408-494-0900
Fax: 408-494-0909

(See Next Column)

Susan J. Mahl	Janet R. Walworth
Peter M. Rehon	Lisa C. Roberts
Michael T. Parsons	

For full biographical listings, see the Martindale-Hubbell Law Directory

McMANIS, FAULKNER & MORGAN (AV)

160 West Santa Clara Street, 10th Floor, 95113
Telephone: 408-279-8700
Fax: 408-279-3244; 408-279-0494
Email: mfm@mfmlaw.com

MEMBERS OF FIRM

James McManis	William Faulkner
Donelle Morgan	

ASSOCIATES

Nora Rousso	Michael Reedy
Lisa Herrick	Douglas Watanabe
Kelly McHaffie	

For full biographical listings, see the Martindale-Hubbell Law Directory

McPHARLIN, SPRINKLES & THOMAS, LLP (AV)

Ten Almaden Boulevard, Suite 1460, 95113
Telephone: 408-293-1900
Fax: 408-293-1999

MEMBERS OF FIRM

Linda Hendrix McPharlin	Mary Lee Malysz
Catherine C. Sprinkles	Paul M. Hogan
N. David Thomas	Paul S. Avilla

For full biographical listings, see the Martindale-Hubbell Law Directory

ROBINSON & WOOD, INC. (AV)

227 North First Street, 95113
Telephone: 408-298-7120
Fax: 408-298-0477
Email: rw@r-winc.com

Archie S. Robinson	Jonathan L. Lee
Weldon S. Wood	Jon B. Zimmerman
Thomas R. Fellows	Mark B. Schellerup
David S. Henningsen	Andrew W. Olsson
Hugh F. Lennon	Erica R. Yew
Jesse F. Ruiz	Arthur J. Casey
Christian B. Nielsen	Joseph C. Balestrieri

John L. Winchester, III	Wendy Woolpert
Chadney C. Ankele	Ann A. Nguyen
Robert A. Nakamae	Kenneth I. Schumaker
Rebecca L. Moon	Anne C. Bailey
Wendy E. Flockhart	Stephen D. Bays

For full biographical listings, see the Martindale-Hubbell Law Directory

VAN LOUCKS & HANLEY (AV)

160 West Santa Clara Street, Suite 1050, 95113
Telephone: 408-494-0400
Fax: 408-494-0404

Geoffrey Van Loucks	Anthony L. Hanley
Michael K. Budra	

Reference: San Jose National Bank.

For full biographical listings, see the Martindale-Hubbell Law Directory

SAN RAFAEL,* Marin Co.

RAGGHIANTI • FREITAS • MONTOBBIO • WALLACE LLP (AV)

874 Fourth Street, Suite D, 94901
Telephone: 415-453-9433
Fax: 415-453-8269

Gary T. Ragghianti	J. Randolph Wallace
David P. Freitas	Patrick M. Macias
J. Mark Montobbio	Robert F. Epstein
John Ralph Thomas	

For full biographical listings, see the Martindale-Hubbell Law Directory

SANTA ANA,* Orange Co.

MARSHACK & GOE (AV)

Six Hutton Centre Drive, Suite 900, 92707
Telephone: 714-540-5400
Facsimile: 714-540-4330
Email: marshack@mglaw.com *URL:* http://www.mglaw.com

PARTNERS

Richard A. Marshack	Robert P. Goe
Leonard M. Shulman	

(See Next Column)

MARSHACK & GOE—*Continued*

PRINCIPALS

Thomas H. Casey　　　　　　　　Thomas J. Polis

Ronald S. Hodges

ASSOCIATES

Vicki L. Schennum　　　　　　　Judith E. Marshack

Leslie Anne Hawes　　　　　　　James Charles Bastian, Jr.

Stacey D. Sarowatz

TAX COUNSEL

A. Lavar Taylor

LITIGATION COUNSEL

Robert M. Ruben

For full biographical listings, see the Martindale-Hubbell Law Directory

---

SANTA BARBARA,* Santa Barbara Co.

ANGLE, CARLSON, GOLDRICK & ROBERTS (AV)

A Partnership including a Professional Corporation
200 East Carrillo Street, Suite 310, 93101
Telephone: 805-963-7400
Fax: 805-963-7610

Robert O. Angle　　　　　　　　Miles T. Goldrick

Arthur W. Carlson (A P.C.)　　　Paul A. Roberts

OF COUNSEL

Georgia C. McDermott

For full biographical listings, see the Martindale-Hubbell Law Directory

SEED, MACKALL & COLE LLP (AV)

1332 Anacapa Street, Suite 200, 93101
Telephone: 805-963-0669
Fax: 805-962-1404

MEMBERS OF FIRM

John R. Mackall　　　　　　　　Christopher E. Hahn

Joseph L. Cole　　　　　　　　　Sandra Hitchens Thoits

Gregory Canova-Parker　　　　　David E. Reese

Thomas N. Harding　　　　　　　K. Andrew Kent

Peter A. Umoff　　　　　　　　　Alan D. Condren

Barton E. Clemens, Jr.　　　　　Nicholas J. Schneider

Representative Clients: City Commerce Bank; Montecito Bank & Trust; Santa Barbara Bank & Trust; Digital Instruments, Inc.; G & H Technology Inc.; Mission Research Corporation; Bermant Development Company; The Investec Real Estate Companies; STAR Telecommunications, Inc.; TELNET Communications Group.

For full biographical listings, see the Martindale-Hubbell Law Directory

---

SANTA MONICA, Los Angeles Co.

PARIS AND PARIS (AV)

Paris Law Building, 424 Pico Boulevard, 90405-1197
Telephone: 310-392-8722
Telecopier: 310-392-1768
Email: PandP424@aol.com
San Rafael, California Office: 4286 Redwood Highway, Suite, 391. 94903.

Reynold F. Paris　　　　　　　　Jeffrey A. Paris

Bette S. Paris　　　　　　　　　Karen M. Paris

Murray A. Zeffren　　　　　　　Richard E. Paris

J. Robert Force

For full biographical listings, see the Martindale-Hubbell Law Directory

STERN, NEUBAUER, GREENWALD & PAULY, A PROFESSIONAL CORPORATION (AV)

1299 Ocean Avenue, Tenth Floor, 90401-1007
Telephone: 310-451-8001
Telecopier: 310-395-5961

David M. Stern　　　　　　　　　Joshua D. Wayser

Mark A. Neubauer　　　　　　　Richard L. Miller

Dennis L. Greenwald　　　　　　M. Tracy McGeagh

Andrew S. Pauly　　　　　　　　Kirsten Shirley Ellis

Russell F. Wolpert　　　　　　　Owen Scott Solomon

Randall S. Rothschild　　　　　Wendy Angela Loo

Richard M. Foster　　　　　　　Nena W. Wong

David C. Smith　　　　　　　　　Michael F. Donner

Christine Millee Henricks

LEGAL SUPPORT PERSONNEL

Carol Leemom

For full biographical listings, see the Martindale-Hubbell Law Directory

---

WALNUT CREEK, Contra Costa Co.

HINTON & ALFERT, A PROFESSIONAL CORPORATION (AV)

Suite 600, 1646 North California Boulevard, 94596-4113
Telephone: 510-932-6006
Fax: 510-932-3412

Peter J. Hinton　　　　　　　　Peter W. Alfert

Michael P. Clark

Scott H. Z. Sumner　　　　　　　Nancy A. Beninati

For full biographical listings, see the Martindale-Hubbell Law Directory

---

COLORADO

DENVER, Denver Co.

BRENMAN KEY & BROMBERG, P.C. (AV)

Mellon Financial Center Suite 1001, 1775 Sherman Street, 80203
Telephone: 303-894-0234
Fax: 303-839-1633

Albert Brenman　　　　　　　　Donna A. Key

Thomas R. Bromberg　　　　　　Steven W. McDonald

Theresa M. Mehringer　　　　　George D. Kreye

OF COUNSEL

Heather H. S. Sander　　　　　A. Thomas Tenenbaum

D. Elizabeth Wills　　　　　　　Edmund L. Epstein (Inactive)

For full biographical listings, see the Martindale-Hubbell Law Directory

DIXON AND SNOW, P.C. (AV)

425 South Cherry Street, Suite 1000, 80222
Telephone: 303-394-2200
FAX: 303-394-2340

Jerre W. Dixon　　　　　　　　　Rod W. Snow

Steven Janiszewski

For full biographical listings, see the Martindale-Hubbell Law Directory

ELROD, KATZ, PREEO, LOOK, MOISON & SILVERMAN, PROFESSIONAL CORPORATION (AV)

Suite 1100, 1120 Lincoln Street, 80203
Telephone: 303-832-1900
Fax: 303-863-0412

Richard B. Elrod　　　　　　　　Harley K. Look, Jr.

Michael M. Katz　　　　　　　　Peter R. Moison

Robert L. Preeo　　　　　　　　Eldon E. Silverman

Jersey M. Green　　　　　　　　Kathryn A. Reeves

Richard M. Hess, Jr.　　　　　　Gilbert R. Egle

Martin J. Green　　　　　　　　Timothy Kyle Jordan

Marilyn McWilliams　　　　　　Brian E. Onorato

OF COUNSEL

Richard P. Rosen

For full biographical listings, see the Martindale-Hubbell Law Directory

EWING & EWING, P.C. (AV)

8400 East Prentice Avenue, Suite 1115 (Englewood), 80111
Telephone: 303-771-3300
Fax: 303-793-3321

Robert Craig Ewing　　　　　　Mary Ewing

Julie A. Trent

For full biographical listings, see the Martindale-Hubbell Law Directory

KONCILJA & ASSOCIATES, P.C. (AV)

Suite 2050, 1700 Broadway, 80290
Telephone: 303-832-2110
Facsimile: 303-832-2623
Email: koncilja@ix.netcom.com

Frances A. Koncilja

Peter C. Forbes　　　　　　　　Elizabeth A. Woodcock

Dorothy Huysman Dean　　　　　Michael A. Vellone

Julie Leamon Rosen

For full biographical listings, see the Martindale-Hubbell Law Directory

Denver—Continued

MESSNER PAVEK & REEVES, LLC (AV)

600 Seventeenth Street, Suite 2800-South, 80202
Telephone: 303-623-1800
Facsimile: 303-623-0552
Evergreen, Colorado Office: 1202 Bergen Parkway, Suite 300.
Telephone: 303-670-1800.
Facsimile: 303-670-2606.

Bryant S. Messner	Ronald K. Reeves
David D. Pavek	(Resident, Evergreen Office)

SPECIAL COUNSEL
Robert W. Berry (Not admitted in CO)
OF COUNSEL
James R. Everson

John K. Shunk	Mary Jo Dougherty
David A. Reeves	Julia Griffith McVey
Heather Anne Hawker	Montgomery F. Moran

For full biographical listings, see the Martindale-Hubbell Law Directory

MILLER, McCARREN & HELMS, P.C. (AV)

410 Seventeenth Street, Suite 1200, 80202
Telephone: 303-436-1163
Telecopier: 303-436-1143

William J. McCarren	J. Kent Miller
	Thomas J. Helms

For full biographical listings, see the Martindale-Hubbell Law Directory

MYER, SWANSON, ADAMS & WOLF, P.C. (AV)

The Colorado State Bank Building, 1600 Broadway, Suite 1480, 80202-4915
Telephone: 303-866-9800
Facsimile: 303-866-9818

Rendle Myer	Robert K. Swanson
Allan B. Adams	Thomas J. Wolf

Philip T. Masterson
OF COUNSEL
Robert Swanson   Fred E. Neef (1910-1986)

Representative Clients: The Oppenheimer Funds; Daily Cash Accumulation Fund; The Centennial Trusts; Mile High Chapter of American Red Cross; Master Lease; Heartland Management Co.; Kan-Build of Colorado, Inc. *Reference:* The Colorado State Bank of Denver.

For full biographical listings, see the Martindale-Hubbell Law Directory

OTTEN, JOHNSON, ROBINSON, NEFF & RAGONETTI, P.C. (AV)

950 Seventeenth Street, 16th Floor, 80202
Telephone: 303-825-8400
Telecopier: 303-825-6525

William F. Schoeberlein	Kenneth K. Skogg
David W. Stark	Brad W. Schacht
Lawrence W. Marquess	David P. Hutchinson
Darrell G. Waas	Todd A. Fredrickson
Hugh Q. Gottschalk	Darin Mackender
J. Thomas Macdonald	Amy J. Griffin
Edward P. Timmins	Daniel E. Evans
P. Kathleen Lower	Kathryn A. Plonsky
David T. Brennan	Patricia C. Campbell
Terence M. Ridley	Karen L. Brody
Patricia A. Thatcher	

Representative Clients: Aetna Life Insurance Co.; The Broe Companies; Inc.; Colorado National Bank; Connecticut General Life Insurance Co.; First Nationwide Bank; Homart Development Co.; Land Title Guarantee Co.; Trizec Corporation Ltd.; U.S. West Communications, Inc.; The Western Sugar Co.

For Complete List of Firm Personnel, See General Section

For full biographical listings, see the Martindale-Hubbell Law Directory

REIMAN & BAYAZ, P.C. (AV)

1600 Broadway, Suite 1640, 80202
Telephone: 303-860-1500
Fax: 303-839-4380

Jeff Reiman	Marcie K. Bayaz
Darren E. Temkin-Nadel	Eric B. Liebman

For full biographical listings, see the Martindale-Hubbell Law Directory

SENN LEWIS VISCIANO & STRAHLE, PROFESSIONAL CORPORATION (AV)

Suite 4300, 1801 California Street, 80202
Telephone: 303-298-1122
Telecopier: 303-296-9101

Frank W. Visciano

Brian J. Reichel	Margie J. Titus
Christopher R. Alger	Laura B. Redstone
Luis A. Toro	Tad Stephen Rogers

For Complete List of Firm Personnel, See General Section

For full biographical listings, see the Martindale-Hubbell Law Directory

SOLOMON PEARL BLUM & QUINN LLP (AV)

1700 Broadway, Suite 1820, 80290
Telephone: 303-832-6686
Fax: 303-832-6653
Email: SolPearl@aol.com
New York, New York Office: Woolworth Building, 37th Floor, 233 Broadway, 10007.
Charlotte Amalie, St. Thomas, Virgin Islands Affiliated Office: Grunet Stout & Bruch, 24-25 Kongens Gade, P.O. Box 1030, 00804.
Telephone: 809-774-1320.
Fax: 809-774-7839.
Denver, Colorado Affiliated Office: Dufford & Brown, P.C., 1700 Broadway, Suite 1700, 80290.
Telephone: 303-861-8013.
Facsimile: 303-832-3804.

Robert A. Solomon	William L. Blum
Clifford R. Pearl	(Not admitted in CO)
	Thomas F. Quinn

For full biographical listings, see the Martindale-Hubbell Law Directory

TREECE, ALFREY, MUSAT & BOSWORTH, P.C. (AV)

Denver Place, 999 18th Street, Suite 1600, 80202
Telephone: 303-292-2700
Facsimile: 303-295-0414
Email: 73507.2446@compuserve.com

Robert S. Treece	L. Richard Musat
Thomas N. Alfrey	Arthur H. Bosworth, II
	Timothy J. Judson

For full biographical listings, see the Martindale-Hubbell Law Directory

DURANGO, La Plata Co.

McLACHLAN & GOLDMAN, LLC (AV)

850 1/2 Main Avenue, P.O. Box 2270, 81302-2270
Telephone: 970-259-8747
Facsimile: 970-259-8790
Email: LAWMCGLD@FRONTIER.NET

Michael E. McLachlan	Michael A. Goldman
	Jeffery P. Robbins

For full biographical listings, see the Martindale-Hubbell Law Directory

CONNECTICUT

BRIDGEPORT, Fairfield Co.

WEINSTEIN, WEINER, IGNAL, NAPOLITANO & SHAPIRO, P.C. (AV)

350 Fairfield Avenue, P.O. Box 9177, 06601
Telephone: 203-333-1177
Cable Address: "Moot"
Fax: 203-384-9832

Howard Evan Ignal	Roberta Napolitano
Gerald T. Weiner	Richard J. Shapiro
Burton M. Weinstein	Judith A. Mauzaka
	John I. Bolton

For full biographical listings, see the Martindale-Hubbell Law Directory

MILFORD, New Haven Co.

HURWITZ & SAGARIN, P.C. (AV)

147 North Broad Street, P.O. Box 112, 06460
Telephone: 203-877-8000
Fax: 203-878-9800

(See Next Column)

HURWITZ & SAGARIN P.C.—*Continued*

Lewis A. Hurwitz   J. Daniel Sagarin
Christine M. Gonillo

For full biographical listings, see the Martindale-Hubbell Law Directory

DISTRICT OF COLUMBIA

WASHINGTON, D.C. Co.

COHEN, MILSTEIN, HAUSFELD & TOLL, P.L.L.C. (AV)

West Tower, Suite 500, 1100 New York Avenue, N.W., 20005-3964
Telephone: 202-408-4600
Facsimile: 202-408-4699

MEMBERS OF FIRM

Jerry S. Cohen (1925-1995)	Lisa M. Mezzetti
Herbert E. Milstein	Andrew N. Friedman
Michael D. Hausfeld	Richard S. Lewis
Steven J. Toll	Daniel S. Sommers
Ann C. Yahner	Daniel A. Small
	(Not admitted in DC)

ASSOCIATES

Gary E. Mason	Michael J. Flannery
Cyrus Mehri	Paul T. Gallagher
Sharon A. Snyder	Alexander E. Barnett
Mark S. Willis	Angeline G. Chen
(Not admitted in DC)	Victoria C. Arthaud
Lillian S. Hagen	(Not admitted in DC)

OF COUNSEL

Anthony Z. Roisman

For full biographical listings, see the Martindale-Hubbell Law Directory

TROUT & RICHARDS, P.L.L.C. (AV)

1742 N Street, N.W., 4th Floor, 20036
Telephone: 202-463-1920
Fax: 202-463-1925
Alexandria, Virginia Office: 921 King Street, 22314.
Telephone: 703-519-8840.

Robert P. Trout   John Thorpe Richards, Jr.

For full biographical listings, see the Martindale-Hubbell Law Directory

FLORIDA

BARTOW, * Polk Co.

FROST, O'TOOLE & SAUNDERS, P.A. (AV)

395 South Central Avenue, P.O. Box 2188, 33830
Telephone: 941-533-0314; 800-533-0967
Telecopier: 941-533-8985

John W. Frost, II	Robert A. Carr
Neal L. O'Toole	Robert H. Van Hart
Thomas C. Saunders	John Marc Tamayo
Richard E. "Rick" Dantzler	Mark A. Sessums
Robert J. Aranda	

Reference: Community National Bank, Bartow.

For full biographical listings, see the Martindale-Hubbell Law Directory

BOCA RATON, Palm Beach Co.

JOEL H. FELDMAN, P.A. (AV)

Suite 207, Tower D, Sanctuary Centre, 4800 North Federal
Highway, 33431
Telephone: 561-392-4400
Fax: 561-392-1521

Joel H. Feldman

Andrew Merlo

For full biographical listings, see the Martindale-Hubbell Law Directory

WEISS & HANDLER, P.A. (AV)

Suite 218A, One Boca Place, 2255 Glades Road, 33431-7313
Telephone: 407-997-9995
Broward: 954-421-5101
Palm Beach: 407-734-8008
Telecopier: 407-997-5280

(See Next Column)

Howard I. Weiss	Henry B. Handler
Donald Feldman	Marissa I. Laakso
David K. Friedman	Mark R. Osherow
Carol A. Kartagener	Howard M. Rudolph (Resident,
	West Palm Beach Office)

OF COUNSEL

Malcolm L. Stein	Stanley E. Preiser
(Not admitted in FL)	(Not admitted in FL)
Raoul Lionel Felder	
(Not admitted in FL)	

For full biographical listings, see the Martindale-Hubbell Law Directory

BRADENTON, * Manatee Co.

BLALOCK, LANDERS, WALTERS AND VOGLER, P.A. (AV)

802 11th Street West, P.O. Box 469, 34205
Telephone: 941-748-0100
Fax: 941-745-2093

Robert G. Blalock	Edward Vogler, II
Clifford L. Walters, III	Barbara Ann Held
Dana C. Gentry	Michael D. Wyckoff
Charles F. Johnson, III	John E. Wickman
Lisbeth P. Bruce	Lisa E. Bagwell
James R. White	

Representative Client: The Bradenton Herald, Inc.

For full biographical listings, see the Martindale-Hubbell Law Directory

HARLLEE, PORGES, HAMLIN, KNOWLES, BALD & PROUTY, P.A. (AV)

1205 Manatee Avenue, West, 34205
Telephone: 941-748-3770
Telecopier: 941-748-4160
Email: Law@HarlleePorges.com

John P. Harllee, III	Kimberly Alario Bald
Gregory J. Porges	Steven W. Prouty
Curtis D. Hamlin	Mark A. Nelson
Timothy A. Knowles	Stephen W. Thompson
Joseph L. Najmy	Barrett S. Bell
Shelly A. Gallagher	

For full biographical listings, see the Martindale-Hubbell Law Directory

FORT LAUDERDALE, * Broward Co.

ENTIN & MARGULES, P.A. (AV)

200 East Broward Boulevard Suite 1210, 33301
Telephone: 954-761-7201
Dade: 305-935-0242
Fax: 954-767-8343

Alvin E. Entin	Richard F. Della Fera
Leon R. Margules	Jacqueline Perczek
Mario Permuth (Not Admitted	Richard Perlini
in United States)	

OF COUNSEL

Steven E. Goldman

For full biographical listings, see the Martindale-Hubbell Law Directory

OPPENHEIM & PILELSKY, P.A. (AV)

1290 Weston Road, Suite 300, 33326
Telephone: 954-384-6114
Toll Free: 888-384-6114
Fax: 954-384-6115
Email: O&P@oppenheim.com *URL:* http://www.oppenheim.com

Roy D. Oppenheim	Ellen B. Pilelsky
Monica B. Cunill	

Representative Clients: Takara Enterprises, Ltd.; Brody Embroidery, Inc.; Danro Homes, Inc.; Intelihomes Development, Inc.; Ace Schiffli; Danal Homes Development, Inc.; Landmark Building & Design, Inc.

For full biographical listings, see the Martindale-Hubbell Law Directory

FORT MYERS,* Lee Co.

SMOOT ADAMS EDWARDS & GREEN, P.A. (AV)

One University Park Suite 600, 12800 University Drive, P.O. Box 60259, 33906-6259
Telephone: 941-489-1776
(800) 226-1777 (in Florida)
Fax: 941-489-2444
Email: 71600.2745@compuserve.com

J. Tom Smoot, Jr.	Bruce D. Green
Hal Adams	Steven I. Winer
Franklyn A. (Chip) Johnson	Mark R. Komray
(1947-1991)	Clayton W. Crevasse
Charles B. Edwards	M. Brian Cheffer

Robert S. Forman	C. Berk Edwards, Jr.
Kathleen W. McBride	Melville G. Brinson, III
Lowell Schoenfeld	Samuel J. Hagan, IV.

For full biographical listings, see the Martindale-Hubbell Law Directory

JACKSONVILLE,* Duval Co.

FISCHETTE, OWEN & HELD (AV)

1301 Riverplace Boulevard Suite 1916, 32207
Telephone: 904-398-7036
Fax: 904-398-4283

MEMBERS OF FIRM

James A. Fischette	Edwin W. Held, Jr.
Philip C. Owen	Charles W. McBurney, Jr.

ASSOCIATES

Dale R. Campion	R. Joseph Dill
Robert J. Perry, Jr.	

References: First Union National Bank of Florida; Enterprise National Bank of Jacksonville.

For full biographical listings, see the Martindale-Hubbell Law Directory

KIRSCHNER, MAIN, GRAHAM, TANNER & DEMONT, PROFESSIONAL ASSOCIATION (AV)

One Independent Drive, Suite 2000, P.O. Box 1559, 32201-1559
Telephone: 904-354-4141
Telecopier: 904-358-2199

Barry C. Averitt	Kenneth M. Kirschner
Babette L. Fletcher	James L. Main
T. Malcolm Graham	John T. Rogerson, III
Lee Stathis Haramis	Michael G. Tanner

Howard L. Alford	Judy Ossi Marko
Robin C. Barco	Charles S. McCall
John F. Germany, Jr.	Beth E. Weitzman
Eric S. Kolar	(Not admitted in FL)

OF COUNSEL

Michael E. Demont	Wyman R. Duggan
G. Stephen Manning	Reese J. Henderson, Jr.

Representative Clients: The Maryland Insurance Group; NationsBank; The Suddath Cos.; Wickes Lumber Co.; BFI, Inc.

For full biographical listings, see the Martindale-Hubbell Law Directory

LILES, GAVIN & COSTANTINO (AV)

One Enterprise Center, Suite 1500, 225 Water Street, 32202
Telephone: 904-634-1100
Fax: 904-634-1234

Rutledge R. Liles	R. Kyle Gavin
R. Scott Costantino	

ASSOCIATE

Niels P. Murphy

For full biographical listings, see the Martindale-Hubbell Law Directory

LOBRANO & KINCAID (AV)

Suite 1950 Independent Life Building, 1 Independent Drive, 32202
Telephone: 904-359-2100
Facsimile: 904-353-1332

Stephen D. Lobrano	Hope Adams Iseley
Wade McK. Hampton	

OF COUNSEL

Harry G. Kincaid

Representative Clients: New York Life Insurance Co. (Real Estate and Claims Counsel); Fortis Benefits, Inc.; South Pine Associates, Inc.; Duplex Products, Inc.; The Washington Post Co.; Post-Newsweek Stations; Florida, Inc. (WJXT Television); International Effecten En Creditbank, N.V.; Hardage and Sons Estes-Krauss, Inc.; Watson Realty Corp.

(See Next Column)

For full biographical listings, see the Martindale-Hubbell Law Directory

SMITH HULSEY & BUSEY (AV)

1800 First Union National Bank Tower, 225 Water Street, P.O. Box 53315, 32201-3315
Telephone: 904-359-7700
Facsimile: 904-359-7708; 353-9908

Lloyd Smith (1915-1987)

MEMBERS OF FIRM

Dennis L. Blackburn	E. Owen McCuller, Jr.
Stephen D. Busey	James H. Post
Douglas D. Chunn	Bryan L. Putnal
Earl E. Googe, Jr.	E. Lanny Russell
Jeanne E. Helton	Joel Settembrini, Jr.
Cynthia C. Jackson	Tim E. Sleeth
G. Preston Keyes	John R. Smith, Jr.
William E. Kuntz	James J. Taylor, Jr.
M. Richard Lewis, Jr.	Timothy W. Volpe
John F. MacLennan	Waddell A. Wallace, III
Raymond R. Magley	Harry M. Wilson, III

Michael M. Bajalia	R. Leanne McKnight
James A. Bolling, Jr.	Mary E. McManus
E. Lanier Drew	Jeanne M. Miller
Diana Salama Farhat	Stephen D. Moore, Jr.
Martin A. Fitzpatrick	Howard J. Smith
Michael R. Freed	Steven G. Spears
Lee G. Kellison	Melissa Smith Turra
Lauren P. Langham	Herschel T. Vinyard, Jr
Marjorie Conner Makar	Leslie A. Wickes
Bradley R. Markey	Karl A. Zillgitt

OF COUNSEL

Mark Hulsey	John E. Thrasher

Representative Clients: Baptist/St. Vincent's Health System, Inc.; Browning-Ferris Industries, Inc.; Champion Realty Corp. (Florida); First Union National Bank of Florida; Florida Rock Industries, Inc.; PGA Tour, Inc.; KPMG Peat Marwick; The Regency Group, Inc.; The Ritz-Carlton Hotel Co.; University of Florida.

For full biographical listings, see the Martindale-Hubbell Law Directory

LAKELAND, Polk Co.

HAHN, McCLURG, WATSON, GRIFFITH & BUSH, P.A. (AV)

101 South Florida Avenue, P.O. Box 38, 33802
Telephone: 941-688-7747
Telecopier: 941-683-4582

James P. Hahn	Stephen C. Watson
E.V. McClurg	John R. Griffith
Philip H. Bush	

General Counsel: Peoples Bank of Lakeland; First Federal of Florida; Publix Super Markets, Inc.
Approved Attorneys For: Attorneys' Title Insurance Fund; American Title Insurance Co.; Title & Trust Company of Florida; Federal Land Bank of Columbia, Columbia, S.C.
Reference: Peoples Bank of Lakeland.

For full biographical listings, see the Martindale-Hubbell Law Directory

MELBOURNE, Brevard Co.

FRESE, NASH & TORPY, P.A. (AV)

Suite 505, 930 South Harbor City Boulevard, 32901
Telephone: 407-984-3300
FAX: 407-951-3741

Gary B. Frese	Vincent G. Torpy, Jr.
Charles Ian Nash	Gregory S. Hansen
James Patrick Anderson	

Laura L. Anderson	Stephen P. Heuston
Patrick F. Roche	

Reference: First Union National Bank of Florida.

For full biographical listings, see the Martindale-Hubbell Law Directory

GLEASON, BARLOW & BOHNE, P.A. (AV)

121-123 Fifth Avenue (Indialantic), P.O. Box 3648, 32903
Telephone: 407-723-5121
Fax: 407-984-5426

William H. Gleason	Karl W. Bohne, Jr.
T. Mitchell Barlow, Jr.	
(Resident)	

Reference: First Union National Bank of Florida, Melbourne, Florida.

For full biographical listings, see the Martindale-Hubbell Law Directory

MIAMI, Dade Co.

BERMAN WOLFE & RENNERT, P.A. (AV)

35th Floor, International Place, 100 Southeast Second Street, 33131-2130
Telephone: 305-577-4177
Fax: 305-373-6036
Email: 76206.1400@compuserve.com.

Neil J. Berman	Howard J. Vogel
Leon J. Wolfe	Karen J. Orlin
Charles J. Rennert	Jill Nexon Berman

Sheila T. Lynch

For full biographical listings, see the Martindale-Hubbell Law Directory

CARUANA, LANGAN, LORENZEN AND MENDELSOHN, P.A. (AV)

1000 Courthouse Tower, 44 West Flagler Street, 33130
Telephone: 305-371-7972
Fax: 305-358-6907

Albert G. Caruana	Dirk Lorenzen
Elena B. Langan	Stephen A. Mendelsohn

Susan E. Greenberg	Hadas Kohn

LEGAL SUPPORT PERSONNEL
Sheryl Caruana

For full biographical listings, see the Martindale-Hubbell Law Directory

PETER A. COHEN, P.A. (AV)

Penthouse One, 155 South Miami Avenue, 33130
Telephone: 305-358-9251
Fax: 305-358-3412

Peter A. Cohen

For full biographical listings, see the Martindale-Hubbell Law Directory

THE LAW OFFICES OF RONALD S. LOWY (AV)

420 Lincoln Road Penthouse, 7th Floor
Telephone: 305-673-5699
Telecopier: 305-673-9235

ASSOCIATE

Donna J. Riven	Sandra A. Piligian

Representative Clients: Capital Bank; Tate Enterprises; British Airways, PLC; Alleghany Mutual Co.; SunTrust of Miami; Crescent Heights Companies.

For full biographical listings, see the Martindale-Hubbell Law Directory

PODHURST, ORSECK, JOSEFSBERG, EATON, MEADOW, OLIN & PERWIN, P.A. (AV)

Suite 800 City National Bank Building, 25 West Flagler Street, 33130-1780
Telephone: 305-358-2800; Fort Lauderdale: 954-463-4346
Fax: 305-358-2382
Email: 76666.2340@COMPUSERVE.COM *URL:* http://www.turbosales.com/"sfbj/podhurst.html

Aaron Podhurst	Michael S. Olin
Robert Orseck (1934-1978)	Joel S. Perwin
Robert C. Josefsberg	Steven C. Marks
Joel D. Eaton	Victor M. Diaz, Jr.
Barry L. Meadow	Katherine W. Ezell

Karen Podhurst Dern	Xavier Martínez

OF COUNSEL
Walter H. Beckham, Jr.

References: City National Bank of Miami; United National Bank of Miami.

For full biographical listings, see the Martindale-Hubbell Law Directory

RUBINSTEIN, KORNIK, BLOOM & MINSKER, A PROFESSIONAL ASSOCIATION (AV)

800 Brickell Avenue, Suite 1100, 33131
Telephone: 305-371-6800
Telecopier: 305-371-5760

Jeffrey D. Rubinstein	Kenneth M. Bloom
Gary H. Kornik	Joel N. Minsker (P.A.)

Nina Zuckerman Chepp	Stacey Schrage Goldstein
Rowena D. Reich	

Reference: Sun Bank of Miami, N.A.

For full biographical listings, see the Martindale-Hubbell Law Directory

SIMMONS, HART & SHEEHE (AV)

A Partnership of Professional Associations
One Biscayne Tower, 2 South Biscayne Boulevard, Suite 1684, 33131
Telephone: 305-379-3515
Fax: 305-379-5404
Ocala, Florida Office: 125 Northeast First Avenue, Suite 1.
Telephone: 904-732-8121.
Fax: 904-368-2183.

Bryce W. Ackerman	Karl V. Hart
Daniel A. Amat	Phillip J. Sheehe
John B. Fuller	Young J. Simmons
Steven H. Gray	Jeffrey Skates
Timothy D. Haines	Marty Smith
Louis V. Vendittelli	

For full biographical listings, see the Martindale-Hubbell Law Directory

THOMSON MURARO RAZOOK & HART, P.A. (AV)

17th Floor, One Southeast Third Avenue, 33131
Telephone: 305-350-7200
Telecopier: 305-374-1005

Parker Davidson Thomson	Steven W. Davis
Carol A. Licko	Dennis M. Campbell

Gregg H. Metzger

Representative Clients: The Chase Manhattan Bank; Mercedes Benz Credit Corp.; Transamerica Commercial; Stewart Title Guaranty Co.; Wells Fargo Bank, N.A.; TCF Bankruptcy & Savings; Citibank, F.S.B.; First Union National Bank; Lennar Corp.

For Complete List of Firm Personnel, See General Section

For full biographical listings, see the Martindale-Hubbell Law Directory

NAPLES, Collier Co.

EMERSON & EMERSON, P.A. (AV)

The Aragon Building, 385 Thirteenth Avenue South, 34201
Telephone: 941-261-5200
Telecopier: 941-261-5201

John W. Emerson	Ralph W. Emerson (1932-1989)

Representative Clients: Krehling Industries, Inc.; E-Squared; Chemical Technologys International, Inc.

For full biographical listings, see the Martindale-Hubbell Law Directory

GRANT, FRIDKIN & PEARSON, P.A. (AV)

Pelican Bay Corporate Centre, 5551 Ridgewood Drive, Suite 501, 34108
Telephone: 941-514-1000
Fax: 941-514-0377
Email: 76402.3516@compuserve.com
Key West, Florida Office: 422 Fleming Street, 33040.
Telephone: 305-296-4553.
Fax: 305-296-7049.

SHAREHOLDERS

G. Helen Athan	Jeffrey D. Fridkin
Michael A. Feldman	Richard C. Grant
William M. Pearson	

Thomas G. Norsworthy

For full biographical listings, see the Martindale-Hubbell Law Directory

HARDT LAW OFFICES, P.A. (AV)

Suite 705 SunTrust Building, 801 Laurel Oak Drive, 34108
Telephone: 941-598-2900
Fax: 941-598-3785

Frederick R. Hardt

References: Northern Trust Bank of Florida/Naples, N.A.; U.S. Trust Company of Florida; Sun Bank/Naples, N.A.

For full biographical listings, see the Martindale-Hubbell Law Directory

NICEVILLE, Okaloosa Co.

STANLEY BRUCE POWELL, P.A. (AV)

107 North Partin Drive, P.O. Box 400, 32588-0400
Telephone: 904-678-2118
Fax: 904-678-8336
Destin, Florida Office: Suite 21 Commerce Row, 225 Main Street.
Telephone: 904-837-9099.

Stanley Bruce Powell	David R. Swanick III

Representative Clients: Peoples National Bank of Niceville; Destin Bank; D&H Oil Co.
References: Peoples National Bank of Niceville; Destin Bank; Barnett Bank of Northwest Florida; Vanguard Bank and Trust Co.

(See Next Column)

STANLEY BRUCE POWELL, P.A., *Niceville—Continued*

For full biographical listings, see the Martindale-Hubbell Law Directory

NORTH PALM BEACH, Palm Beach Co.

AVIS & AVIS, P.A. (AV)

1201 U.S. Highway One, Suite 435, 33408
Telephone: 407-622-3400
Fax: 407-622-0565
Email: avislaw@gnn.com
Palm Beach, Florida Office: The Island National Bank Building. 180
Royal Palm Way, Suite 203, 33480.
Telephone: 407-659-0200.

Warren E. Avis, Jr.	Deborah K. Avis
Marina D. Petillo	Theodore T. Tarone

For full biographical listings, see the Martindale-Hubbell Law Directory

OCALA,* Marion Co.

SIMMONS, HART & SHEEHE (AV)

A Partnership of Professional Associations
125 Northeast First Avenue, Suite 1, P.O. Box 3310, 34478-3310
Telephone: 352-732-8121
Fax: 352-368-2183
Miami, Florida Office: One Biscayne Tower, Suite 1684, 2 South Biscayne
Boulevard, 33131.
Telephone: 305-379-3515.
Fax: 305-379-5404.

Bryce W. Ackerman	Karl V. Hart
Daniel A. Amat	Young J. Simmons
John B. Fuller	Phillip J. Sheehe
Steven H. Gray	Jeffrey Skates
Timothy D. Haines	Marty Smith
Louis V. Vendittelli	

Representative Clients: Keeneland Association, Inc.; CSX Railroad; Double
Diamond Farm; California Federal Bank.

For full biographical listings, see the Martindale-Hubbell Law Directory

ORLANDO,* Orange Co.

ADAMS & SPEARS, P.A. (AV)

940 Highland Avenue, P.O. Box 3627, 32802
Telephone: 407-422-8116
Fax: 407-648-1044
Email: 74767.2745@compuserve.com

Richard H. Adams, Jr.	Richard D. Connor, Jr.
Douglas C. Spears	Deborah B. Ansbro
Peter C. Vilmos	Elizabeth A. Baker

Joyce R. Adams
OF COUNSEL
Ley H. Smith

General Counsel for: Lochaven Federal Savings & Loan; Independence Mortgage Corporation of America.
Representative Clients: Ensign Property Group, Inc.; Deere Credit Services.

For full biographical listings, see the Martindale-Hubbell Law Directory

ARNOLD, MATHENY & EAGAN, P.A. (AV)

801 North Magnolia Avenue, Suite 201, P.O. Box 2967, 32802
Telephone: 407-841-1550
Facsimile: 407-841-8746

William W. Arnold	Alexander J. Ombres
William L. Eagan	Arthur R. Louv
Lehn E. Abrams	R. Craig Cooley
Barbara Anne Eagan	

Representative Clients: Center Lake Properties, Ltd.; Chase Manhattan of
Florida; Combustion Tec. Inc.; Commonwealth Land Title Insurance Com.;
Contemporary Services; Dillard's Inc. of Florida; Doctor's Home Health
Agency, Inc.; Electro-Science Invest Group, Ltd.; First Union National
Bank; Forbes-Hamilton Management Co.

For full biographical listings, see the Martindale-Hubbell Law Directory

A. CLIFTON BLACK (AV)

126 East Jefferson Street, 32801
Telephone: 407-843-4310
800-433-8149 (Florida Only)
Fax: 407-649-3038

Representative Clients: American Polymers, Inc.; Banc One Leasing Corp.;
Maury L. Carter & Associates, Inc.; Douglass Fertilizer & Chemical, Inc.

For full biographical listings, see the Martindale-Hubbell Law Directory

DeWolf, WARD, O'DONNELL & GLATT, P.A. (AV)

Suite 1750, 111 North Orange Avenue, 32801-2399
Telephone: 407-841-7000
Telecopy: 407-843-6035

Thomas B. DeWolf	John H. Ward
James E. Glatt, Jr.	

Representative Clients: Andover Companies; Deutsche Credit Corp.; Employers Insurance of Wausau; Walt Disney World Co.

For full biographical listings, see the Martindale-Hubbell Law Directory

HARTLEY & WALL (AV)

200 South Orange Avenue, Suite 2810, P.O. Box 2168, 32802
Telephone: 407-422-7992
Fax: 407-425-2182

MEMBERS OF FIRM

Carl W. Hartley, Jr.	Richard F. Wall

ASSOCIATE
Todd K. Norman

Reference: Sun Bank, N.A.

For full biographical listings, see the Martindale-Hubbell Law Directory

KING & BLACKWELL, P.A. (AV)

25 East Pine Street, P.O. Box 1631, 32802-1631
Telephone: 407-422-2472
Fax: 407-648-0161
Email: kbfirm@aol.com

David B. King	Bruce B. Blackwell
	Mayanne Downs
John F. Tannian	Thomas A. Zehnder

For full biographical listings, see the Martindale-Hubbell Law Directory

McGEE & POWERS, P.A. (AV)

201 East Pine Street, Suite 700, P.O. Box 3589, 32801
Telephone: 407-422-5742
Telecopy: 407-423-1377

Patrick A. McGee	Deborah S. Hernandez
James K. Powers	Brenda J. Newman
Melissa Arnold McGee	

For full biographical listings, see the Martindale-Hubbell Law Directory

MORAN & SHAMS, P.A. (AV)

111 North Orange Avenue, Suite 1200, P.O. Box 472, 32802-0472
Telephone: 407-841-4141
Fax: 407-841-4148
Email: moran-shams@moran-shams.com

Kelly T. Blystone	Robert W. Rasch
Brian J. Moran	Christopher C. Skambis
Sidney H. Shams	

Representative Clients: Adventist Health System Sunbelt Healthcare Corporation; All Florida Resorts Management; Dayron, Inc.; Gencor Industries
Inc.; H.J. Heinz Co.; Insurance Office of Florida, Inc.; Kvaerner Trafalgar
House Construction Co.; Photo Chemical Systems of Florida, Inc.; U.S.
Foodservice, Inc.; Vermont American Corporation.

For full biographical listings, see the Martindale-Hubbell Law Directory

O'NEILL, CHAPIN, MARKS, LIEBMAN, COOPER & CARR (AV)

A Partnership including Professional Associations
865 Eola Park Center, 200 East Robinson Street, 32801
Telephone: 407-425-2751
Telex: 407-423-1192

Bernard C. O'Neill, Jr. (P.A.)	John B. Liebman (P.A.)
Bruce E. Chapin (P.A.)	Mark O. Cooper (P.A.)
Robert O. Marks (P.A.)	George E. Carr (P.A.)

ASSOCIATE
Rod C. Lundy

Reference: First Union National Bank.

For full biographical listings, see the Martindale-Hubbell Law Directory

RUSSELL & HULL, P.A. (AV)

537 North Magnolia Avenue, P.O. Box 2751, 32802
Telephone: 407-422-1234
Telecopier: 407-423-2842

Rodney Laird Russell	Norman L. Hull

Representative Clients: BMW Financial Services, N.A., Inc.; BelSouth
Communications Systems, Inc.; Cocoa Inc.; Cross/Tessitore & Associates;
Exeletech, Inc.; Graybar Electric Co., Inc.; Grunau Company; Haley
Construction, Inc.

(See Next Column)

RUSSELL & HULL P.A.—*Continued*

For full biographical listings, see the Martindale-Hubbell Law Directory

SHEPARD, FILBURN & GOODBLATT, P.A. (AV)

First Union Tower, Suite 1107, 20 North Orange Avenue, 32801
Telephone: 407-481-2020
Fax: 407-481-0208
Email: sf2law@aol.com

Clifford B. Shepard, III	Jenna R. Rinehart
Mark C. Filburn	Michael J. Kirwin
Amy E. Goodblatt	(Not admitted in FL)

Representative Clients: Chernoff Silver & Associates; Sovereign Bank; Cintas Corporation; Intercargo Insurance Company; Trade Insurance Services, Inc.; Integon General Insurance Company; Danella Construction Company; Adventist Health Systems, Inc.; Titan Indemnity Company; Hersh National Painting & Roofing Company.

For full biographical listings, see the Martindale-Hubbell Law Directory

STUMP, STOREY & CALLAHAN, P.A. (AV)

28 East Washington Street, P.O. Box 3388, 32802-3388
Telephone: 407-425-2571
Telecopier: 407-425-0827

John R. Stump	Philip D. Storey
W. Scott Callahan	

Donald Paul Dietrich II	Robin L. Hoyle

Representative Clients: Amresco Management, Inc.; Chase Manhattan Service Corp.; Federal Deposit Insurance Corp.; The Huntington National Bank; Jackson Management Group, Inc.; Mobile Home Park Associates, L.P.; NationsBank, N.A.; Orange County, Florida; Seminole Finance Corp.

For full biographical listings, see the Martindale-Hubbell Law Directory

SUBIN, ROSENBLUTH, LOSEY, BRENNAN, BITTMAN & MORSE, PROFESSIONAL ASSOCIATION (AV)

Suite 900, 111 North Orange Avenue, P.O. Box 4950, 32802-4950
Telephone: 407-841-7100
Facsimile: 407-648-0660
Email: lawyer@orlando.com

Eli H. Subin	John M. Brennan
Emery H. Rosenbluth, Jr.	Michael J. Bittman
Ralph C. Losey	Kenneth D. Morse

Stacey R. Littler	Sandra A. Kenny

OF COUNSEL
Philip Frederic Keidaish, Jr.

Representative Clients: Connecticut General Life Insurance Co.; Gilbane Building Company; Subaru of America; Dania JuiAla (Division of the Aragon Group, Inc.); Brice Building Company, Inc.; Trammel Crow Company; Principal Mutual Life Insurance Company; Reynolds Metals Company; SouthTrust Bank of Florida, N.A.; U.S. Foodservice, Inc.

For full biographical listings, see the Martindale-Hubbell Law Directory

PORT CHARLOTTE, Charlotte Co.

SCHWARZ & KAHLE, P.A. (AV)

21229 Olean Boulevard Suite B, 33952
Telephone: 941-625-4158
Facsimile: 941-625-5460

Gary A. Kahle	Stephen deH. Schwarz

Reference: SunTrust Bank/Gulf Coast.

For full biographical listings, see the Martindale-Hubbell Law Directory

ST. AUGUSTINE,* St. Johns Co.

DOBSON & BROWN, P.A. (AV)

66 Cuna Street, Suite B, 32084
Telephone: 904-824-9032
Fax: 904-824-9236

Geoffrey B. Dobson	Ronald W Brown

David C. Reeves

For full biographical listings, see the Martindale-Hubbell Law Directory

ST. PETERSBURG, Pinellas Co.

STEIN, FORD, SCHAAF & TOWZEY, L.L.P. (AV)

501 First Avenue North, Suite 1000, 33701
Telephone: 813-894-4333
Fax: 813-894-0175; 813-822-7222

(See Next Column)

Henry A. Stein	Gary M. Schaaf
Harvey A. Ford	Phyllis J. Towzey
Paul A. Nelson	Sarah E. Williams

For full biographical listings, see the Martindale-Hubbell Law Directory

SARASOTA,* Sarasota Co.

BROWN CLARK & WALTERS, P.A. (AV)

Suite 1100, Sarasota City Center, 1819 Main Street, 34236
Telephone: 941-957-3800
Telefax: 941-957-3888
Email: brownclarkwalters@internetmci.com *URL:*
http://www.prosrv.com/~bcwlaw
Port Charlotte, Florida Office: Murdock Professional Center, Suite 500, 1777 Tamiami Trail.
Telephone: 941-624-2929.
Telecopier: 941-624-4941.

Daryl J. Brown	Stuart Jay Levine
John E. Brown	Carolyn F. McDevitt
Donald D. Clark	Taso Michael Milonas
William G. Christopher	Shane T. Munoz
George J. Dramis, III	(Not admitted in FL)
Elinor E. Erben	Douglas E. Polk, Jr.
Lynn H. Groseclose	Geoffrey F. Rice
Donna L. Kerfoot	Peter Z. Skokos
H. Jack Klingensmith (P.A.)	James Edward Thomison
Conrad J. Lazo	Joel W. Walters

OF COUNSEL
James R. Tario

For full biographical listings, see the Martindale-Hubbell Law Directory

WILLIAMS, PARKER, HARRISON, DIETZ & GETZEN, PROFESSIONAL ASSOCIATION (AV)

200 South Orange Avenue, 34236-6749
Telephone: 941-366-4800
Telecopier: 941-366-5109
Mailing Address: P.O. Box 3258, Sarasota, Florida, 34230-3258
Email: wphdg.law@netsrg.com *URL:*
http://www.sarasota-online.com/williamspa-w

J.J. Williams, Jr. (1886-1968)	Frank Strelec
W. Davis Parker (1920-1982)	Terri Salt Costa
William T. Harrison, Jr.	David A. Wallace
George A. Dietz	Mark A. Schwartz
Monte K. Marshall	Ric Gregoria
James L. Ritchey	Elvin W. Phillips
William G. Lambrecht	Jeffrey A. Grebe
John T. Berteau	John L. Moore
John V. Cannon, III	Morgan R. Bentley
Charles D. Bailey, Jr.	Susan A. Barrett
J. Michael Hartenstine	Carol Ann Kalish
Michele Boardman Grimes	Linda R. Getzen
James L. Turner	Kimberly J. Page
William M. Seider	Phillip D. Eck
Elizabeth C. Marshall	J. Hugh Middlebrooks
Robert W. Benjamin	Robert A. Warram

OF COUNSEL

William E. Getzen	Frazer F. Hilder
Hugh McPheeters, Jr.	

LEGAL SUPPORT PERSONNEL
Mark Loveridge (Land Planner)

General Counsel for: Sarasota County Public Hospital Board; Sarasota-Manatee Airport Authority; Taylor Woodrow Homes Ltd.; FCCI Mutual Insurance Co.
Local Counsel for: NationsBank of Florida; Barnett Bank of Southwest Florida; Northern Trust Bank of Florida; SunTrust Bank, Gulfcoast.

For full biographical listings, see the Martindale-Hubbell Law Directory

STUART,* Martin Co.

McCARTHY, SUMMERS, BOBKO, McKEY, WOOD & SAWYER, P.A. (AV)

2081 East Ocean Boulevard, Suite 2-A, 34996
Telephone: 561-286-1700
Fax: 561-283-1803
Email: mcsumm@gate.net *URL:* http://www.gate.net/~mcsumm/

Terence P. McCarthy	John D. McKey, Jr.
Robert P. Summers	Steven J. Wood
Noel A. Bobko	Thomas R. Sawyer

Representative Clients: American Bank of Martin County; First National Bank and Trust Company of the Treasure Coast; Great Western Bank; Hydratech Utilities; Lost Lake at Hobe Sound; Taylor Creek Marina, Inc.; GBS Excavating, Inc.; Seaboard Savings Bank; Gary Player Design Group.

For full biographical listings, see the Martindale-Hubbell Law Directory

TALLAHASSEE, Leon Co.

RADEY McARTHUR & FREHN (AV)

101 South Monroe Street, 32301
Telephone: 904-681-7766
Fax: 904-681-0160
Email: Radeylaw@aol.com

John Radey Elizabeth Waas McArthur
Jeffrey L. Frehn

Representative Clients: Ringling Bros. Barnum-Bailey Combined Shows; Johnson & Johnson; Electronic Data Systems Corp.; Cubic Automatic Revenue Collection Group, Inc.; Commonwealth Land Title Insurance Co.; First Allmerica Financial Life Insurance Co.; Columbia/HCA Healthcare Corp.

For full biographical listings, see the Martindale-Hubbell Law Directory

TAMPA, Hillsborough Co.

ADKINS, KISE & DIACO, P.A. (AV)

2175 Barnett Plaza, 101 East Kennedy Boulevard, 33602
Telephone: 813-221-2200
Fax: 813-221-8850

Edward C. Adkins Christopher M. Kise
Stephen C. Diaco

For full biographical listings, see the Martindale-Hubbell Law Directory

AMAN & LINS, P.A. (AV)

Paramount Plaza, 14502 North Dale Mabry Highway, Suite 314, P.O. Box 271370, 33688-1370
Telephone: 813-265-0004
Fax: 813-265-9644
Email: amanlaw@aol.com
URL: http://www.members.aol.com/AmanLinsPA

Jeffrey A. Aman D. Michael Lins

For full biographical listings, see the Martindale-Hubbell Law Directory

ANDERSON & ORCUTT, P.A. (AV)

401 East Jackson Street Suite 2400, 33602
Telephone: 813-222-7500
FAX: 813-222-7519
New Port Richey, Florida Office: Hobby, Anderson & Grey, 5709 Tidalwave Drive.
Telephone: 813-847-5854.
Fax: 813-841-8685.

Steven A. Anderson	Robin S. Trupp
Gregory J. Orcutt	B. Herbert Boatner, Jr.
William Kent Ihrig	Beth Anne Cronin
Thomas W. Danaher	Clarke Goode Hobby
Fernando Perez III	Charles E. Klug, Jr.
Samuel R. Mandelbaum	Frederick T. Reeves
Charleen C. Ramus	Mark G. Rodriguez

Kevin J. Fitzsimmons
OF COUNSEL
D. Frank Winkles

For full biographical listings, see the Martindale-Hubbell Law Directory

BARR, MURMAN, TONELLI, HERZFELD & RUBIN (AV)

Enterprise Plaza, Suite 901, 201 East Kennedy Boulevard, P.O. Box 172669, 33672-0669
Telephone: 813-223-3951
Fax: 813-229-2254

James A. Murman	Ellen H. Lorenzen
Michael A. Tonelli	John R. Dixon
Daniel H. Sleet	Michael A. Connolly

Ashley J. McCorvey
OF COUNSEL
Billy R. Barr

Representative Client: CIGNA Insurance Co.
For full biographical listings, see the Martindale-Hubbell Law Directory

BAVOL, BUSH & SISCO, P.A. (AV)

100 South Ashley, Suite 2100, P.O. Box 3423, 33601-3423
Telephone: 813-228-7000
Telefax: 813-273-0091

Charles D. Bavol	Dale R. Sisco
Ronald E. Bush	Ricardo A. Fernandez

Audrey B. Rauchway	Edward M. Rooks
Andrew L. Rosenkranz	Harold L. Sebring, III

For full biographical listings, see the Martindale-Hubbell Law Directory

CAREY, O'MALLEY, WHITAKER & MANSON, P.A. (AV)

Suite 1190, 100 South Ashley Drive, P.O. Box 499, 33601-0499
Telephone: 813-221-8210
Telecopier: 813-221-1430
Email: cowmpa@aol.com

Michael R. Carey	Douglas P. Manson
Andrew M. O'Malley	Randall P. Mueller
Daniel D. Whitaker	Jack R. Pepper, Jr.

Kevin P. O'Brien

For full biographical listings, see the Martindale-Hubbell Law Directory

DE LA PARTE, GILBERT & BALES, PROFESSIONAL ASSOCIATION (AV)

One Tampa City Center, Suite 2300, P.O. Box 2350, 33601-2350
Telephone: 813-229-2775
FAX: 813-229-2712

Louis A. de la Parte	John Calhoun Bales
Richard A. Gilbert	L. David de la Parte
Edward P. de la Parte, Jr.	Patrick J. McNamara

Michael A. Skelton

David M. Caldevilla	David Dallas Dickey
John R. Thomas	Kelli Salem Gustafson

Andrew Klymenko

For full biographical listings, see the Martindale-Hubbell Law Directory

FULLER, SWINDLE & HOLSONBACK, P.A. (AV)

100 North Tampa Street, Suite 2650, 33602
Telephone: 813-229-9119
Fax: Available Upon Request

Jeffery M. Fuller	John P. Holsonback
William R. Swindle	Christina C. Young

For full biographical listings, see the Martindale-Hubbell Law Directory

HOYT, COLGAN & ANDREU, P.A. (AV)

3000 Barnett Plaza, 101 East Kennedy Boulevard, 33602
Telephone: 813-229-6688
Facsimile: 813-229-3331

Brooks P. Hoyt Michael B. Colgan
Timothy A. Andreu

Brian K. French
OF COUNSEL
Louis J. Beltrami

For full biographical listings, see the Martindale-Hubbell Law Directory

KETCHEY HORAN, P.A. (AV)

100 North Tampa Street, Suite 1900, P.O. Box 500, 33601-0500
Telephone: 813-223-9395
Fax: 813-221-1348
Sun City Center, Florida Office: 1647 Sun City Center Plaza, Suite 200.
Telephone: 813-633-1200.

Judith A. English	Alfred A. Colby
Charles F. Ketchey, Jr.	Sarah H. Dennis

John A. Greco

For full biographical listings, see the Martindale-Hubbell Law Directory

JONATHAN C. KOCH, P.A. (AV)

Suite 1290, 100 South Ashley Drive, P.O. Box 2311, 33601-2311
Telephone: 813-273-9311
Fax: 813-273-9611

Jonathan C. Koch

For full biographical listings, see the Martindale-Hubbell Law Directory

MANEY, DAMSKER, HARRIS & JONES, P.A. (AV)

606 Madison Street, P.O. Box 172009, 33672-0009
Telephone: 813-228-7371
Fax: 813-223-4846

Lee S. Damsker	David A. Maney
Nancy Hutcheson Harris	Karen Lynn Jones

Lorena L. Kiely	Patricia F. Kuhlman

Stacey L. Turmel

For full biographical listings, see the Martindale-Hubbell Law Directory

Tampa—Continued

MORRIS LAW FIRM (AV)

4016 Henderson Boulevard, 33629
Telephone: 813-289-4009
Fax: 813-289-7652

MEMBER OF FIRM
Robert E. Morris
ASSOCIATES

Robert A. Bauman   John T. Golding

For full biographical listings, see the Martindale-Hubbell Law Directory

MURNAGHAN, FERGUSON & MAGUIRE, P.A. (AV)

Suite 2600, 100 North Tampa Street, P.O. Box 2937, 33601-2937
Telephone: 813-222-0123
Fax: 813-222-0124

Dennis R. Ferguson   E. Jeanne Maguire
Peter P. Murnaghan

For full biographical listings, see the Martindale-Hubbell Law Directory

SALEM, SAXON & NIELSEN, PROFESSIONAL ASSOCIATION (AV)

Suite 3200, One Barnett Plaza, 101 East Kennedy Boulevard, P.O. Box
3399, 33601
Telephone: 813-224-9000
Telecopier: 813-221-8811

Richard J. Salem	Lisa M. Castellano
Bernice S. Saxon	Beth M. Coleman
Richard A. Nielsen	Roy J. Ford, Jr.
David J. Tong	Marilyn Mullen Healy
Marian B. Rush	Troy M. Lovell
Ricardo L. Gilmore	Evin L. Netzer
Steven M. Berman	Lynn Van Hyning Ramey
C. Graham Carothers, Jr.	Susan K. S. Scarcelli
J. Frazier Carraway	Jacqueline M. Spoto

OF COUNSEL
John Crider

Reference: The Bank of Tampa.

For full biographical listings, see the Martindale-Hubbell Law Directory

SHEAR, NEWMAN, HAHN AND ROSENKRANZ, P.A. (AV)

Suite 1000, 201 East Kennedy Boulevard, 33602
Telephone: 813-228-8530
FAX: 813-221-9122

L. David Shear	Glenn M. Burton
Jerry L. Newman	Roland J. Lamb
William E. Hahn	Bruce Douglas Lamb
Stanley W. Rosenkranz	Jeffrey Drew Butt
James R. Freeman	Mark J. Ragusa
Rodney W. Morgan	Kelly Jo Schmedt

Marilyn Drivas Sandborn	Mildred D. Beam-Rucker
Scott P. Distasio	Joseph F. Diaco, Jr.
Thomas M. Hoeler	Elizabeth (Betsey) Taylor Herd
Christopher J. Schulte	Timothy M. Cerio
Kimberly D. Holladay	Mindy Paige Brostoff
Debra L. Boje	Carl A. Goldman

OF COUNSEL
Daniel J. Gibby   Leonard L. Kleinman

References: NationsBank; First National Bank.

For full biographical listings, see the Martindale-Hubbell Law Directory

SOLOMON & BENEDICT, P.A. (AV)

3000 NationsBank Plaza, 400 North Ashley Drive, 33602
Telephone: 813-225-1818
Telecopier: 813-225-1050

Stanford R. Solomon   Betsy L. McCoy Benedict

Melody E. Altman	John Edgar Booth
Tara Goewert Armstrong	David C. Lanigan
Jennifer M. Tobin	

For full biographical listings, see the Martindale-Hubbell Law Directory

TOWNSEND & BRANNON (AV)

608 West Horatio Street, 33606-2228
Telephone: 813-254-0088
Telecopier: 813-254-0093

MEMBERS OF FIRM
David A. Townsend   Anita C. Brannon

For full biographical listings, see the Martindale-Hubbell Law Directory

YERRID, KNOPIK & MUDANO, P.A. (AV)

Barnett Plaza, Suite 2160, 101 East Kennedy Boulevard, 33602
Telephone: 813-222-8222
Fax: 813-222-8224

C. Steven Yerrid   Christopher S. Knopik
Matthew S. Mudano

Ralph L. Gonzalez   Adam M. Wolfe

For full biographical listings, see the Martindale-Hubbell Law Directory

TAVARES,* Lake Co.

CAUTHEN, OLDHAM & KEOUGH, P.A. (AV)

131 West Main Street, 32778
Telephone: 352-343-3455
Fax: 352-343-8801

Gordon G. Oldham, Jr.   David E. Cauthen
Timothy S. Keough

References: First Union National Bank; First Federal Savings & Loan Association of Lake County.

For full biographical listings, see the Martindale-Hubbell Law Directory

WEST PALM BEACH,* Palm Beach Co.

JONAS & LASORTE (AV)

Suite 1000, United National Bank Tower, 1645 Palm Beach Lakes
Boulevard, 33401
Telephone: 407-684-3000
FAX: 407-684-3004
Email: 75040.1275@compuserve.com

Michael N. Jonas   Alfred A. LaSorte, Jr.

For full biographical listings, see the Martindale-Hubbell Law Directory

THOMAS E. KINGCADE PROFESSIONAL ASSOCIATION (AV)

209 South Olive Avenue, 33401
Telephone: 407-659-7300
FAX: 407-655-1593

Thomas E. Kingcade

William W. Booth

For full biographical listings, see the Martindale-Hubbell Law Directory

LEWIS, VEGOSEN, ROSENBACH & SILBER, P.A. (AV)

500 South Australian Avenue, P.O. Box 4388, 33402-4388
Telephone: 561-659-3300
Fax: 561-832-1991

Robert M. Lewis (1932-1982)	Cynthia J. Jackson
Dean Vegosen	Gary Walk
Dean J. Rosenbach	John B. Levitt
Louis M. Silber	Samuel A. Thomas
Gary M. Dunkel	Marshall J. Osofsky
Kenneth A. Treadwell	John R. Sheppard, Jr.
Cass Walker Christenson	

For full biographical listings, see the Martindale-Hubbell Law Directory

NEWBURGH, BALDWIN & GERSHMAN (AV)

1675 Palm Beach Lakes Boulevard, Suite 700, 33401
Telephone: 561-684-8898; 561-471-0470
Fax: 561-684-8820; 561-471-4222

MEMBERS OF FIRM
Steven S. Newburgh   Fletcher N. Baldwin, III
Robert Scott Gershman
OF COUNSEL
Barry L. Clayton

For full biographical listings, see the Martindale-Hubbell Law Directory

PATRICK M. O'HARA, P.A. (AV)

Commerce Center, Suite 100, 324 Datura Street, 33401
Telephone: 561-659-3771
Fax: 561-659-4224

Patrick M. O'Hara

For full biographical listings, see the Martindale-Hubbell Law Directory

WINTER HAVEN, Polk Co.

CURTIS ALEXANDER & VARNER (AV)

101 6th Street, N.W., P.O. Box 189, 33882-0189
Telephone: 941-297-5111
Telecopier: 941-293-4104

(See Next Column)

CURTIS ALEXANDER & VARNER, *Winter Haven—Continued*

MEMBERS OF FIRM

Clinton A. Curtis   M. David Alexander, III
Joseph H. Varner, III

ASSOCIATE

Angela S. Klug

For full biographical listings, see the Martindale-Hubbell Law Directory

GEORGIA

ATLANTA,* Fulton Co.

SHAPIRO, FUSSELL, WEDGE, SMOTHERMAN & MARTIN (AV)

One Midtown Plaza, Suite 1200, 1360 Peachtree Street, 30309-3214
Telephone: 404-870-2200
Facsimile: 404-870-2222

MEMBERS OF FIRM

J. Ben Shapiro, Jr.	Nicholas S. Papleacos
Ira J. Smotherman, Jr.	Seth Price
Herman L. Fussell	Michael P. Davis
Robert B. Wedge	David L. Tank
H. Fielder Martin	Cyrell E. Lynch
Ronald J. Garber	Scott I. Zucker

Daniel M. Jennings

ASSOCIATES

Connie H. Buffington	Katherine Lynn Freeman
Jason Allen Cooper	Mary L. Hahn

Wade H. Purcell

For full biographical listings, see the Martindale-Hubbell Law Directory

WADE & CAMPBELL, LLP (AV)

Cumberland Center II, 3100 Cumberland Circle, Suite 1500, 30339
Telephone: 770-850-5000
FAX: 770-850-5075
Email: wadecamp@mindspring.com

MEMBERS OF FIRM

Allison Wade   Douglas N. Campbell
Michael S. Thwaites

ASSOCIATES

Nancy P. Parson	Steven W. Hardy
Edward H. Nicholson, Jr.	Steven H. Jackman

Walter Hamberg, III

Representative Clients: American Airlines, Inc.; Apple South, Inc.; British Airports; Columbia/HCA Healthcare Corporation; Delta Air Lines, Inc.; Life Insurance Company of Georgia; Merrill Lynch & Co.; Prudential Securities Incorporated; Southwire Company.

For full biographical listings, see the Martindale-Hubbell Law Directory

AUGUSTA,* Richmond Co.

STANLEY C. HOUSE (AV)

Suite 506 The Lamar Building, 753 Broad Street, P.O. Box 915, 30903-0915
Telephone: 706-722-3341
Fax: 706-722-0471
Email: schouse@counsel.com

Approved Attorney for: Lawyers Title Insurance Corp.
References: First Union Bank & Trust (Augusta); NationsBank (Augusta).

For full biographical listings, see the Martindale-Hubbell Law Directory

SAVANNAH,* Chatham Co.

WOODALL AND MACKENZIE, P.C. (AV)

327 Tattnall Street, P.O. Box 10166, 31412
Telephone: 912-238-9999

John T. Woodall   Malcolm Mackenzie, III

Peter A. Giusti

Representative Clients: Aetna Casualty & Surety Co.; United States Fidelity and Guaranty Co.; The Travelers.

For full biographical listings, see the Martindale-Hubbell Law Directory

IDAHO

BOISE,* Ada Co.

ELLIS, BROWN & SHEILS, CHARTERED (AV)

707 North 8th, P.O. Box 388, 83701
Telephone: 208-345-7832
Fax: 208-345-9564

Allen B. Ellis   Stephen C. Brown
Max M. Sheils, Jr.

Representative Clients: Farm Credit Services Northwest, A.C.A.; Wausau Insurance Cos.; State Insurance Fund; Crawford & Company; Idaho Power Co.; Ada Planning Assn.; Consolidated Supply Co.; Finch-Brown Co.
References: West One Bank; First Interstate Bank.

For full biographical listings, see the Martindale-Hubbell Law Directory

ILLINOIS

BELLEVILLE,* St. Clair Co.

BROWN & GAVIN (AV)

23 Public Square, Suite 410, 62220
Telephone: 618-236-2886
Missouri: 314-231-0953

MEMBERS OF FIRM

Terry N. Brown   William P. Gavin

ASSOCIATES

Gregg N. Johnson   P.K. Johnson, V

For full biographical listings, see the Martindale-Hubbell Law Directory

FREEARK, HARVEY, MENDILLO, DENNIS & WULLER, PROFESSIONAL CORPORATION (AV)

115 West Washington Street, P.O. Box 546, 62222
Telephone: 618-233-2686
Telecopier: 618-233-5677

Ray H. Freeark, Jr.	James R. Mendillo
Ted R. Harvey, Jr.	Ted W. Dennis

Ransom P. Wuller

Jeffery A. Cain	Denise Rusnack
Michael P. Murphy	Anneliesa B. Fierstos

Representative Clients: American Federation of Teachers, Local 434, Belleville, Illinois and 743, Granite City, Illinois.
Local Counsel for: Illinois State Medical Inter-Insurance Exchange, Chicago, Illinois; Sentry Insurance Co., Stevens Point, Wisconsin; General Casualty Cos., Springfield, Illinois and Sun Prairie, Wisconsin; Allstate Insurance Co., St. Louis, Missouri and Arlington Heights, Illinois; St. Paul Fire & Marine Insurance Co.; Safeco Insurance Co., St. Louis, Missouri; Travelers Insurance Co.; Northbrook Insurance Co., Arlington Heights, Illinois; Employers Insurance of Wausau, River Forest, Illinois and St. Louis, Missouri.

For full biographical listings, see the Martindale-Hubbell Law Directory

NEVILLE, RICHARDS, DEFRANCO & WULLER (AV)

5 Park Place, 62221
Telephone: 618-277-0900
Facsimile: 618-277-0970

MEMBERS OF FIRM

James E. Neville	James E. DeFranco
Timothy S. Richards	Robert G. Wuller, Jr.

ASSOCIATES

Shari M. Brunton   Ellen M. Edmonds
Richard Thomas Roustio

For full biographical listings, see the Martindale-Hubbell Law Directory

CHAMPAIGN, Champaign Co.

MEYER, CAPEL, HIRSCHFELD, MUNCY, JAHN & ALDEEN, P.C. (AV)

306 West Church Street, P.O. Box 6750, 61826-6750
Telephone: 217-352-1800
Telecopier: 217-352-1083
Email: attorneys@meyercapel.com *URL:* http://www.meyercapel.com
Urbana, Illinois Office: 300 West Main Street.
Telephone: 217-328-5520.

(See Next Column)

MEYER, CAPEL, HIRSCHFELD, MUNCY, JAHN & ALDEEN P.C.—*Continued*

James L. Capel, Jr. (1933-1991)	Tracy J. Nugent
John C. Hirschfeld	Richard T. West
Dennis K. Muncy	Rusty W. Freeland
Francis J. Jahn	Lorna K. Geiler
Donald R. Aldeen	Patrick T. Fitzgerald
John H. Elder	Todd J. Black
David B. Sholem	Mark P. Miller
Mark D. Lipton	Joseph Dwyer Murphy

Neil R. Rafferty	Patricia L. Gruber
James M. Mullady	William B. Moore
Adam B. Hirschfeld	Rochelle A. Funderburg
	Evan D. Coobs

OF COUNSEL

August C. Meyer, Jr.	Richard J. Winkel, Jr.

Representative Clients: Bank of Illinois in Champaign; Bell Foods, Inc.; Champaign News-Gazette; Christie Clinic; Federal Deposit Insurance Corp.; Illini Cablevision, Inc.; Kuck & Associates, Inc.; Midwest Television, Inc.; Parkland College.

For full biographical listings, see the Martindale-Hubbell Law Directory

---

CHICAGO,* Cook Co.

BECKER ASSOCIATES (AV)

19 South La Salle Street Suite 1500, 60603
Telephone: 312-621-9500
Fax: 312-621-9011
Email: Firm@becker-law.com *URL:* http://www.becker-law.com

Theodore M. Becker	Daniel Steven Kaplan
	Michael Jeffrey Boxerman

OF COUNSEL

Ira J. Marcus	Anthony C. Campanale
Lee Scott Perres	Steven J. Gross
	John P. Connell

For full biographical listings, see the Martindale-Hubbell Law Directory

---

BERMAN & YOTIS, A PROFESSIONAL ASSOCIATION (AV)

(A Professional Association comprised of Professional Corporations)
Suite 2215, 100 North La Salle Street, 60602
Telephone: 312-726-0531
Fax: 312-726-4928

Michael H. Berman (P.C.)	William W. Yotis, III, (P.C.)

Joy C. Airaudi	Dean J. Papadakis
Eric D. Kaplan	Dean Gournis

OF COUNSEL
Karen C. Yotis

For full biographical listings, see the Martindale-Hubbell Law Directory

---

BLATT, HAMMESFAHR & EATON (AV)

333 W. Wacker Drive, Suite 1900, 60606
Telephone: 312-357-1277
FAX: 312-357-0198
Email: BHE@BHELAW.COM *URL:* HTTP://WWW.BHELAW.COM

MEMBERS OF FIRM

Richard Lee Blatt	Lori S. Nugent
Larry R. Eaton	Peter M. Page
Bruce M. Engel	William F. Richardson
Brent J. Graber	Gregory G. Smith
Robert W. Hammesfahr	Leonard S. Surdyk
Gregory D. Hopp	Patrick T. Walsh
Joanne J. Matousek	Judith M. Wexler
	Scott W. Wright

ASSOCIATES

David W. Alberts	Kathleen A. McQueeny
David Hollingshead Anderson	Stephen R. Meinertzhagen
Christopher R. Barth	Hallie J. Miller
Julie S. Bender	Ziyad I. Naccasha
Kristin M. Buchholz	Kevin J. Rielley
Andrea L. Caplan	Stephen J. Rosenfeld
Susan J. Cheney	Scott V. Scarpelli
Lisa A. Dunsky	Dana L. Schmitt
Mary E. Fechtig	Susan B. Shulman
S. William Grimes	George Matthew Silvers
Josh M. Kantrow	Janet B. Stern
Jill Ann Kaplan	Timothy L. Swabb
Andrea C. Kenealey	Matthew T. Walsh
Elizabeth E. Kim	Laura R. Zaroski

OF COUNSEL
Shane V. Nugent

For full biographical listings, see the Martindale-Hubbell Law Directory

---

CARNEY & BROTHERS, LTD. (AV)

30 North La Salle Street, Suite 3100, 60602
Telephone: 312-372-2909
Fax: 312-704-6693

Demetrius E. Carney	Ellen E. Douglass
Alan W. Brothers	Lori A. Owens
Hubert O. Thompson	James L. Bebley

Cheryl J Colston	Andre Gamble
Trasha A. Embry	Angela M. Williams
	Oswald G. Lewis

OF COUNSEL

Joyce A. Hughes	Henry I. Thomas

Representative Clients: Allstate Life Insurance Co.; Amoco Oil Co.; Commonwealth Edison Co.; First National Bank of Chicago; General Motors Corp.; McDonald's Corp.; New York Life Insurance Co.; Pathway Financial; Seaway National Bank.

For full biographical listings, see the Martindale-Hubbell Law Directory

---

CLIFFORD LAW OFFICES, P.C. (AV)

120 North La Salle Street, 31st Floor, 60602
Telephone: 312-899-9090
1-800-899-0410
Fax: 312-251-1160
Email: 102554.2453@compuserve.com

Robert A. Clifford	Keith A. Hebeisen
	Kevin P. Durkin

Robert P. Walsh, Jr.	Richard L. Pullano
Susan A. Capra	Patricia C. Durkin
Jeffrey J. Kroll	Matthew I. Baker
Thomas K. Prindable	Timothy P. Rhatigan
Richard F. Burke, Jr.	Isobel S. Thomas

OF COUNSEL
Robert P. Sheridan

For full biographical listings, see the Martindale-Hubbell Law Directory

---

CONNELLY & SCHROEDER (AV)

One North Franklin Street, Suite 1200, 60606
Telephone: 312-251-9600
FAX: 312-251-9601
Geneva, Illinois Office: 1250 Executive Place, Suite 201.
Telephone: 708-232-6440.
FAX: 708-232-6450

MEMBERS OF FIRM

Michael P. Connelly	Charles H. Cole
John L. Schroeder	Daniel F. Konicek
(Resident, Geneva Office)	(Resident, Geneva Office)
Thomas F. Tobin	Eugene S. Kraus
Raymond E. Stachnik	Patrick G. Donnelly

OF COUNSEL
John W. Hough

ASSOCIATES

Michelle L. Adams	Colleen Konicek
(Resident, Geneva Office)	Charina de los Reyes
Matthew Patrick Connelly	Abbey Fishman Romanek
Thomas W. Dillon	Martha Swatek
(Resident, Geneva Office)	(Resident, Geneva Office)
Mary Lisa Kamins	Carla A. Summers
John Michael Kelly	(Resident, Geneva Office)

For full biographical listings, see the Martindale-Hubbell Law Directory

---

FIELD GOLAN & SWIGER (AV)

Three First National Plaza Twenty-First Floor, 60602-4206
Telephone: 312-263-2300
Fax: 312-263-0939

MEMBERS OF FIRM

Robert E. Field	Cynthia G. Swiger
Stephen L. Golan	Margaret A. Christie

ASSOCIATES

William J. Arendt	Margaret A. Gisch
Peter C. Quigley	Matthew J. Cozzi

OF COUNSEL

Leonard W. Golan	Stephen Edward Smith
Donna F. Hartl	Frank J. Dolan

For full biographical listings, see the Martindale-Hubbell Law Directory

---

FREEMAN, FREEMAN & SALZMAN, P.C. (AV)

401 North Michigan Avenue, Suite 3200, 60611-4207
Telephone: 312-222-5100
Facsimile: 312-822-0870
Email: freeman@wwa.com

(See Next Column)

FREEMAN, FREEMAN & SALZMAN P.C., *Chicago—Continued*

Lee A. Freeman (1909-1995)	James T. Malysiak
Lee A. Freeman, Jr.	Glynna W. Freeman
Jerrold E. Salzman	Phillip L. Stern
John F. Kinney	Albert F. Ettinger
	Chris C. Gair

Christopher M. Kelly	Michelle Reese Andrew
Derek J. Meyer	Kevin P. Kappock

For full biographical listings, see the Martindale-Hubbell Law Directory

GESSLER, HUGHES & SOCOL, LTD. (AV)

Three First National Plaza, Suite 2200, 60602
Telephone: 312-580-0100
Telecopy: 312-580-1994

Mark S. Dym	Terence J. Moran
George W. Gessler	Mark D. Olson
John K. Hughes	Matthew J. Piers
William P. Jones	David J. Pritchard
Peter M. Katsaros	Kalman D. Resnick
Mark A. LaRose	Frederick S. Rhine
Kimberley Marsh	Jonathan A. Rothstein
	Donna Kaner Socol

Benjamin P. Beringer	Alex W. Miller
Darilyn W. Bock	Belkis Cervantes Muldoon
Gary Chodorow	Jonathan D. Rosenblum
Anjali Dayal	Marci S. Sperling
Ruth M. Dunning	Dana H. Sukenik
Adam D. Ingber	J. Eric Vander Arend
Michael J. Klein	Maria L. Vertuno
Laura C. Liu	Mark B. Weiner
	Charles H. Wintersteen

OF COUNSEL

James T. Derico, Jr.	Darius S. Francescatti, M.D.
	Susan R. Gzesh

For full biographical listings, see the Martindale-Hubbell Law Directory

MICHAEL T. HANNAFAN & ASSOCIATES, LTD. (AV)

Three First National Plaza, Suite 4040, 60602
Telephone: 312-782-7490
FAX: 312-782-9440

Michael T. Hannafan

Cory A. Johnson	Gregory M. Jordan

LEGAL SUPPORT PERSONNEL

Tracy D. Hannafan

Reference: The Northern Trust Co.

For full biographical listings, see the Martindale-Hubbell Law Directory

HELLER, SHAPIRO, FRISONE & FERLEGER, LTD. (AV)

111 West Washington Street, Suite 1650, 60602-2779
Telephone: 312-236-3644
FAX: 312-236-3595

Paul M. Heller	Nicholas J. Frisone
Bruce K. Shapiro	Eric P. Ferleger

David S. Ruskin	Michelle Gold Seifman

Representative Clients: The Peoples Gas Light & Coke Co.; North Shore Gas Co.; Jewel Food Stores, Inc.; City of Chicago; Great American Finance Co.; The Community Bank of Lawndale; State Farm Insurance Co.; Eagle Finance Co.; Price Waterhouse; N I C E Federal Credit Union.

For full biographical listings, see the Martindale-Hubbell Law Directory

NORMAN J. LERUM (AV)

Suite 2100, 100 West Monroe Street, 60603
Telephone: 312-782-1087
Facsimile: 312-332-6020

For full biographical listings, see the Martindale-Hubbell Law Directory

McCONNELL & MENDELSON (AV)

140 South Dearborn Street, 9th Floor, 60603
Telephone: 312-263-1212
Telecopier: 312-263-0402

Thomas C. McConnell	Francis J. McConnell
(1943-1972)	Michael Sweig Mendelson
	Peter S. Lubin

(See Next Column)

OF COUNSEL

Diane Hudson Andersen	John K. Chatz
Dennis A. Bell	Anne C. Keays
Elizabeth J. Caprini	Synde B. Keywell

ASSOCIATE

Sheryl Jafee Halpern

Reference: The Northern Trust Co., Chicago, Illinois.

For full biographical listings, see the Martindale-Hubbell Law Directory

McFADDEN & DILLON, A PROFESSIONAL CORPORATION (AV)

135 South La Salle Street, Suite 2110, 60603
Telephone: 312-201-8300
Facsimile: 312-201-0535

Roger J. McFadden	Thomas J. Dillon

Tyrrel J. Penn

For full biographical listings, see the Martindale-Hubbell Law Directory

MORA & BAUGH, LTD. (AV)

55 West Monroe Street, Suite 600, 60603
Telephone: 312-759-1400
Facsimile: 312-759-0402
West Palm Beach, Florida Office: Mora, Baugh & Derrevere, 224 Datura Street, Suite 1102.
Telephone: 407-835-3753.
Facsimile: 407-835-9831.

Steven H. Mora	David A. Baugh
	David R. Carlson

Ellen L. Flannigan

OF COUNSEL

Robert M. Greco	Frank W. Nagorka

For full biographical listings, see the Martindale-Hubbell Law Directory

NISEN & ELLIOTT (AV)

200 West Adams Street, Suite 2500, 60606
Telephone: 312-346-7800
Telecopier: 312-346-9316

MEMBERS OF FIRM

Paul F. Gerbosi	John Foster Lesch
Edward B. Mueller	John K. Kneafsey
Anthony Packard	Michael H. Moirano
Donald C. Shine	Robert O. Middleton
Mark F. Zaenger	William G. Daluga, Jr.
Michael J. Daley	Kenneth J. Rojc
	Thomas V. McCauley

Robert Christie	Michael J. Pavlicek
Daniel P. Dawson	Brian D. Proctor
Donald F. Froehlke	Jeffrey S. Torosian
Helen M. Jensen	William A. Walker
Thomas K. Juffernbruch	Gregory C. Ward
Adam O. Kirwan	Eric R. Wilen
(Not admitted in IL)	

OF COUNSEL

Charles M. Nisen

For full biographical listings, see the Martindale-Hubbell Law Directory

RICHARD J. PRENDERGAST, LTD. (AV)

111 West Washington-Suite 1100, 60602-2768
Telephone: 312-641-0881

Richard J. Prendergast	James Prendergast

Ellen M. Murphy	Michael T. Layden
	Deirdre Ann Close

For full biographical listings, see the Martindale-Hubbell Law Directory

MERLE L. ROYCE, II (AV)

111 West Washington Street Suite 1710, 60606
Telephone: 312-553-1233
Fax: 312-372-4700

ASSOCIATE

Marshall J. Burt

OF COUNSEL

James J. Macchitelli	Khurram Hussain

For full biographical listings, see the Martindale-Hubbell Law Directory

Chicago—Continued

SIEGEL, MOSES, SCHOENSTADT & WEBSTER, P.C. (AV)

111 East Wacker Drive Suite 2800, 60601-4801
Telephone: 312-658-2000
Fax: 312-658-2022

Morton Siegel	Richard G. Schoenstadt
Michael A. Moses	James L. Webster
	Jennifer G. Hoff

For full biographical listings, see the Martindale-Hubbell Law Directory

PETER R. SONDERBY, P.C. (AV)

135 South La Salle Street Suite 1424, 60603
Telephone: 312-201-0999
Fax: 312-201-0749; 641-1930

Peter R. Sonderby

For full biographical listings, see the Martindale-Hubbell Law Directory

STACK & FILPI, CHARTERED (AV)

Suite 411, 140 South Dearborn Street, 60603-5298
Telephone: 312-782-0690; 236-5032
Telecopier: 312-782-0936

Paul F. Stack	Robert A. Filpi

Christine R. Norgle-Loewer
OF COUNSEL

John H. Shurtleff	James A. McGurk

For full biographical listings, see the Martindale-Hubbell Law Directory

SUGAR, FRIEDBERG & FELSENTHAL (AV)

30 North La Salle Street, Suite 2600, 60602
Telephone: 312-704-9400
Telecopier: 312-372-7951
Cable: "SUGARFREE"

MEMBERS OF FIRM

Richard A. Sugar	Ira S. Neiman
Michael R. Friedberg	Jonathan L. Mills
Steven A. Felsenthal	Etahn M. Cohen
Andrew B. David	Howard M. Helsinger
Leslie J. Weiss	Robert F. Simon
	Martin M. Weinstein

ASSOCIATES

Kathryn A. Erickson	Jay R. Hoffman
Norman J. Ginsparg	Sophia Stergianis
	Jonathan W. Michael

For full biographical listings, see the Martindale-Hubbell Law Directory

TORSHEN, SPREYER & GARMISA, LTD. (AV)

105 West Adams Street, Suite 3200, 60603
Telephone: 312-372-9282
Fax: 312-372-7914

Jerome H. Torshen	Steven P. Garmisa
Abigail Kay Spreyer	Robert J. Slobig
James K. Genden	Eric James Rietz
Zoran Dragutinovich	Thomas J. Ramsdell

For full biographical listings, see the Martindale-Hubbell Law Directory

WILDMAN, HARROLD, ALLEN & DIXON (AV)

225 West Wacker Drive, 30th Floor, 60606-1229
Telephone: 312-201-2000
Cable Address: "Whad"
Fax: 312-201-2555
URL: http://www.whad.com
Aurora, Illinois Office: 1851 W. Galena Boulevard, Suite 210.
Telephone: 630-892-7021.
Fax: 630-892-7158.
Waukegan, Illinois Office: 404 West Water, P. O. Box 890.
Telephone: 847-623-0700.
Fax: 847-244-5273.
Lisle, Illinois Office: 4300 Commerce Court.
Telephone: 630-955-0555.
New York, New York Office: Wildman, Harrold, Allen, Dixon & Smith. The International Building, 45 Rockefeller Plaza, Suite 353.
Telephone: 212-632-5500.
Fax: 212-632-3858.
Toronto, Ontario affiliated Office: Keel Cottrelle. 36 Toronto Street, Ninth Floor, Suite 920.
Telephone: 416-367-2900.
Telefax: 416-367-2791.
Telex: 062-18660.

(See Next Column)

Mississauga, Ontario affiliated Office: Keel Cottrelle. 100 Matatson Avenue East, Suite 104.
Telephone: 416-890-7700.
Fax: 416-890-8006.

MEMBERS OF FIRM

Thomas D. Allen	Anne Giddings Kimball
John J. Arado	Brian W. Lewis
Richard C. Bartelt	Thomas M. Lynch
Michael R. Blankshain	Michael L. McCluggage
Cal R. Burnton	Mark J. McCombs
Douglas R. Carlson	Donald R. McGarrah
Paul S. Chervin	Mark P. Miller
(Waukegan Office)	James R. Morrin
Michael Dockterman	Richard D. Murphy Jr.
Jerald P. Esrick	Timothy G. Nickels
Ira C. Feldman	James T. Nyeste
James D. Fiffer	David J. Parsons
Donald Flayton	Douglas L. Prochnow
Kathy Pinkstaff Fox	Fred E. Schulz
Peter H. Fritts	Robert L. Shuftan
Richard P. Glovka	Lisa S. Simmons
Robert E. Haley	R. John Street
Bernard Harrold	Peter A. Tomaras
H. Roderic Heard	Thomas J. Verticchio
Anthony G. Hopp	Louis P. Vitullo
Robert E. Kehoe, Jr.	Craig M. White

John T. Benz	Stephanie B. Miller
Eric P. Berlin	W. Scott Nehs
Stacey V. Bowers	Martha D. Owens
Leland H. Chait	Kevin B. Reid
David J. Chroust (Lisle Office)	John A. Roberts
Jeffrey W. Eich	Elizabeth A. Sanders
Lawrence W. Falbe	Jeannine Y. Sano
Michael A. Glackin	David M. Simon
Adam J. Glazer	Andrew E. Skopp
Kenneth M. Gorenberg	Ada Skyles
Scott Z. Hochfelder	Paul A. Slager
James C. James, III	Lauren S. Tashma
(Aurora Office)	John A. Terselic
Elizabeth Keiley	(Waukegan Office)
Michael J. Lotus	Jennifer K. Walter
Jeffrey A. McIntyre	Joleen S. Willis
Jeffrey E. Michel	Robin L. Wolkoff
	Jonathan W. Young

For Complete List of Firm Personnel, See General Section

For full biographical listings, see the Martindale-Hubbell Law Directory

DECATUR,* Macon Co.

TIETZ & RICHARDSON (AV)

444 Millikin Court Building, P.O. Box 1664, 62525
Telephone: 217-425-1515
Telecopier: 217-425-4077

Christopher M. Tietz	Jeffrey D. Richardson

Representative Clients: Industrial Process Control Engineering Company; Dectra, Ltd.; Custom Computer Services, Inc.; Dover Elevator Co.; Craftmasters, Inc.; ICAL, Inc.; Farmers Insurance Group, Standard Mutual Insurance Co.; American Investment Bank; AgriBank, FCB.

For full biographical listings, see the Martindale-Hubbell Law Directory

GALESBURG,* Knox Co.

MUSTAIN LINDSTROM & HENSON (AV)

1865 North Henderson Street, Suite 11B, 61401
Telephone: 309-344-5252
Telecopier: 309-344-3939

MEMBERS OF FIRM

Douglas D. Mustain	Ronald Henson
Robert Lindstrom	Christopher Henson
	Carl E. Hawkinson

References: The Farmers and Mechanics Bank; Norwest Bank Illinois, N.A.; First Bank; First Financial Bank; Farmers State Bank of Western Illinois; McGladrey and Pullen.

For full biographical listings, see the Martindale-Hubbell Law Directory

OAK BROOK, Du Page Co.

BOTTI, MARINACCIO & DeLONGIS, LTD. (AV)

720 Enterprise Drive, 60521
Telephone: 708-573-8585
Fax: 708-573-8586
Wheaton, Illinois Office: Suite 401 The Ticor Title Building, 330 Naperville Road.
Telephone: 708-653-2100.

(See Next Column)

BOTTI, MARINACCIO & DELONGIS LTD., *Oak Brook—Continued*

Aldo E. Botti	Mark W. Salkeld
Stephen R. Botti	Peter M. Tumminaro
Andrew Y. Acker	David C. Bruss
Peter M. DeLongis	Jean M. Lasics
Lee A. Marinaccio	Nanette C. Augustin

For full biographical listings, see the Martindale-Hubbell Law Directory

---

*PEORIA,** Peoria Co.

HOWARD & HOWARD ATTORNEYS, P.C. (AV)

The Creve Coeur Building, Suite 200, 321 Liberty Street, 61602-1403
Telephone: 309-672-1483
Telecopier: 309-672-1568
Kalamazoo, Michigan Office: The Kalamazoo Building, Suite 400, 107
West Michigan Avenue.
Telephone: 616-382-1483.
Telecopier: 616-382-1568.
Bloomfield Hills, Michigan Office: The Pinehurst Office Center, Suite 101,
1400 North Woodward Avenue.
Telephone: 810-645-1483.
Telecopier: 810-645-1568.
Lansing, Michigan Office: Suite 500, The Phoenix Building, 222
Washington Square, North.
Telephone: 517-485-1483.
Telecopier: 517-485-1568.
Tampa, Florida Office: First of America Plaza, Suite 2000, 201 East
Kennedy Boulevard.
Telephone: 813-229-1483.
Telecopier: 813-229-1568.

Stephen C. Ferlmann	Timothy J. Howard
Frederick G. Hoffman	Leonard W. Sachs
	Jeffrey G. Sorenson

Representative Clients: For Representative Client list, see General Practice,
Peoria, IL.

For Complete List of Firm Personnel, See General Section

For full biographical listings, see the Martindale-Hubbell Law Directory

---

*URBANA,** Champaign Co.

WEBBER & THIES, P.C. (AV)

202 Lincoln Square, P.O. Box 189, 61803-0189
Telephone: 217-367-1126
FAX: 217-367-3752

Richard L. Thies	David C. Thies
Craig R. Webber	Holten D. Summers
Carl M. Webber	Daniel P. Wurl
	John E. Thies

Alan R. Singleton	Phillip R. Van Ness
	Tammy Koester Parks

For Complete List of Firm Personnel, See General Section

For full biographical listings, see the Martindale-Hubbell Law Directory

---

VERNON HILLS, Lake Co.

RICHARDS, RALPH & SCHWAB, CHTD. (AV)

Suite 345, One Hawthorn Place, 175 East Hawthorn Parkway, 60061
Telephone: 708-367-9699
FAX: 708-367-9621

Michael L. Ralph	Alan E. Richards
	David J. Schwab

For full biographical listings, see the Martindale-Hubbell Law Directory

---

*WHEATON,** Du Page Co.

DONOVAN & ROBERTS, P.C. (AV)

104 East Roosevelt Road, Suite 202, P.O. Box 417, 60189-0417
Telephone: 630-668-4211
Fax: 630-668-2076

Keith E. Roberts, Sr.	Keith E. (Chuck) Roberts, Jr.
	James J. Konetski

Marie F. Leach	Robert M. Skutt
Mark J. Lyons	Robert J. Lentz
Andrew L. Dryjanski	Rosemarie Calandra

For full biographical listings, see the Martindale-Hubbell Law Directory

---

LAW OFFICES OF ROGER KEVIN O'REILLY (AV)

1776 South Naperville Road, Suite 206-A, 60189-5039
Telephone: 708-665-4444
Telecopier: 708-665-4442

(See Next Column)

Molly M. O'Reilly

For full biographical listings, see the Martindale-Hubbell Law Directory

---

INDIANA

---

*CROWN POINT,** Lake Co.

EDWARD P. GRIMMER (AV)

603 N. Main Street, 46307-3233
Telephone: 219-662-1661

Representative Clients: Furnished Upon Request.

For full biographical listings, see the Martindale-Hubbell Law Directory

---

ELKHART, Elkhart Co.

CHESTER, PFAFF & BROTHERSON (AV)

317 West Franklin Street, P.O. Box 507, 46515-0507
Telephone: 219-294-5421
Fax: 219-522-1476

MEMBERS OF FIRM

Robert A. Pfaff	Edward J. Chester

ASSOCIATES

Robert C. Whippo	Craig A. Carpenter

LEGAL SUPPORT PERSONNEL

Laura L. Ezzell (Paralegal)

For Complete List of Firm Personnel, See General Section

For full biographical listings, see the Martindale-Hubbell Law Directory

---

*FORT WAYNE,** Allen Co.

ROTHBERG & LOGAN (AV)

(Formerly, Rothberg, Gallmeyer, Fruechtenicht & Logan)
2100 Fort Wayne National Bank Building, 110 West Berry Street, P.O.
Box 11647, 46859-1647
Telephone: 219-422-9454
Telefax: 219-422-1622

MEMBERS OF FIRM

Martin T. Fletcher, Sr.	Catherine C. Ediger
Scott T. Niemann	Gregory Martin Cole

ASSOCIATES

James A. Butz	Brian L. Nehrig

Counsel for: Parkview Memorial Hospital; Cameron Memorial Community
Hospital; Norwest Bank Indiana, N.A.; NBD Bank, N.A.; Parkview Health
System; Azar's, Incorporated; Fort Wayne-Allen County Airport Authority;
Fort Wayne Public Transportation Corporation; Avis Industrial Corp.; Farm
Credit Services of Mid-America, ASA; Slater Fort Wayne Federal Credit
Union.

For Complete List of Firm Personnel, See General Section

For full biographical listings, see the Martindale-Hubbell Law Directory

---

HAMMOND, Lake Co.

ABRAHAMSON, REED & ADLEY (AV)

200 Russell Street, 46320
Telephone: 219-937-1500
Fax: 219-937-3174

MEMBERS OF FIRM

Harold Abrahamson	Kenneth D. Reed
	Michael C. Adley

ASSOCIATES

Scott R. Bilse	Christopher R. Karsten

References: Calumet National Bank, Hammond; Mercantile National Bank,
Hammond.

For full biographical listings, see the Martindale-Hubbell Law Directory

---

*INDIANAPOLIS,** Marion Co.

CLARK, QUINN, MOSES & CLARK (AV)

One Indiana Square, Suite 2200, 46204-2011
Telephone: 317-637-1321
Fax: 317-687-2344

MEMBERS OF FIRM

Alex M. Clark (1916-1991)	John M. Moses
James C. Clark	J. Murray Clark
Thomas Michael Quinn	Matthew R. Clark

(See Next Column)

CLARK, QUINN, MOSES & CLARK—*Continued*

ASSOCIATES

Michael D. Keele   Cameron F. Clark

L. Michael Koch

OF COUNSEL

David M. Brooks   Robert C. Bruner

Representative Clients: Justus; The Shorewood Corporation; Marina Limited Partnership; Lafarge Corporation; Meijer Realty, Inc.; Lowe's; Kite Development; U-Stor Self Storage Warehouses; Mechanic's Laundry; Davis Homes.

For full biographical listings, see the Martindale-Hubbell Law Directory

---

COLLIER-MAGAR & KIRAGES, P.C. (AV)

Market Square Center, Suite 1460 151 North Delaware Street, 46204-2957
Telephone: 317-261-1885
Facsimile: 317-261-1887

Kenneth Collier-Magar   Christopher Kirages

For full biographical listings, see the Martindale-Hubbell Law Directory

---

DANN PECAR NEWMAN & KLEIMAN, PROFESSIONAL CORPORATION (AV)

Suite 2300, One American Square Box 82008, 46282
Telephone: 317-632-3232; Indiana: 800-622-4799
Telecopy: 317-632-2962

Theodore R. Dann (1907-1993)	Walter E. Wolf, Jr.
Joel Yonover (1932-1995)	Barry E. Beldin
Philip D. Pecar	Robert D. Swhier, Jr.
Norman R. Newman	James P. Moloy
David H. Kleiman	Robert J. Schuckit
Jon B. Abels	Andrew A. Kleiman
Melvin R. Daniel	Michael J. Gabovitch
Lawrence F. Dorocke	Steven M. Pecar
Jeffrey A. Abrams	Benjamin A. Pecar
James H. Schwarz	Richard O. Kissel, II
Robert A. Rose	Joseph D. Calderon

OF COUNSEL

Linda E. Cantor   Anthony J. Rose

Ellen C. Siakotos	Angela L. Mansfield
Stacy L. Hill	Martha M. K. Baird
	Karin L. Veatch

Attorneys for: Indianapolis Machinery Co., Inc.; Melvin Simon & Associates, Inc.; Pacers Basketball Corp.; Universal Fire & Casualty Co., Inc.; Bank One, Indianapolis, NA; INB National Bank; Nachi Technology, Inc.; Pharmaceutical Corporation of America; Logo 7, Inc.

For full biographical listings, see the Martindale-Hubbell Law Directory

---

LAFAYETTE, * Tippecanoe Co.

PEARLMAN AND CHOSNEK, P.C. (AV)

316 Ferry Street, P.O. Box 708, 47902-0708
Telephone: 317-742-9081
Fax: 317-742-4379

Louis Pearlman, Jr. (1930-1992)   Edward Chosnek

David W. Haniford   Christopher Paul Hopson

Michael A. Morrissey

Representative Clients: Tippecanoe Memory Gardens, Inc.; Industrial Federal Credit Union; Farmers and Merchants Bank, Boswell, Indiana; Biggs Pump & Supply, Inc; Brummett Elec. Co. Inc.; Klooz Plumbing, Inc.; Gene B. Glick Mgmt. Co; Chauncey Hill Mall; Von Tobel Lumber & Hardware; Purdue Employees Federal Credit Union.
Reference: NBD Bank, N.W.

For full biographical listings, see the Martindale-Hubbell Law Directory

---

MARION, * Grant Co.

KILEY, KILEY, HARKER, MICHAEL & CERTAIN (AV)

300 West Third Street, P.O. Box 899, 46952-0899
Telephone: 317-664-9041
Fax: 317-664-8119

MEMBERS OF FIRM

Robert Ralph Batton (1890-1963)	David L. Kiley, Sr.
Albert L. Harker (1904-1965)	Michael J. Kiley
Albert Bonner Brown (1911-1981)	Albert C. Harker
	Thomas W. Michael
	Harry J. Certain

(See Next Column)

ASSOCIATE

Therese McCullough Pryor

Counsel for: Bank One, Marion, N.A.; Liniger Co., Inc.; Atlas Foundry Co. *Local Counsel for:* GenCorp.; CPC Group; General Motors; Indiana Michigan Power Co./AEP; Indiana Bell Telephone Co.; Foster-Forbes, Division of American National Can Corp.

For full biographical listings, see the Martindale-Hubbell Law Directory

---

SOUTH BEND, * St. Joseph Co.

SOPKO & FIRTH (AV)

Plaza Building, 5th Floor, 210 South Michigan Street, P.O. Box 300, 46624
Telephone: 219-234-3000
Telecopier: 219-234-4220

MEMBERS OF FIRM

Thomas C. Sopko   John C. Firth

ASSOCIATE

Brent E. Inabnit

OF COUNSEL

Ronald J. Jaicomo

References: 1st Source Bank; 1st Interstate Bank; Notre Dame Federal Credit Union.

For full biographical listings, see the Martindale-Hubbell Law Directory

---

IOWA

DAVENPORT, * Scott Co.

NOYES & GOSMA, L.L.P. (AV)

400 North Main Street, Suite 106, 52801
Telephone: 319-322-8223
Fax: 319-322-8234

MEMBERS OF FIRM

Michael L. Noyes   John S. Gosma

ASSOCIATE

Marie R. Rolling-Tarbox

OF COUNSEL

Clay LeGrand   Charles G. Rehling

Reference: Quad City Bank and Trust Company.

For full biographical listings, see the Martindale-Hubbell Law Directory

---

KENTUCKY

LOUISVILLE, * Jefferson Co.

MORGAN & POTTINGER, P.S.C. (AV)

601 West Main Street, 40202
Telephone: 502-589-2780
Telecopier: 502-585-3498
Lexington, Kentucky Office: 133 West Short Street.
Telephone: 606-253-1900.
Telecopier: 606-255-2038.
New Albany, Indiana Office: 400 Pearl Street, Suite 100.
Telephone: 812-948-0008.
Telecopier: 812-944-6215.

John T. McGarvey	Douglas Gene Sharp
James I. Murray	John A. Majors
(Resident, Lexington Office)	J. Jeffrey Cooke
	Hal D. Friedman

For Complete List of Firm Personnel, See General Section

For full biographical listings, see the Martindale-Hubbell Law Directory

---

SOMERSET, * Pulaski Co.

ADAMS & ADAMS (AV)

35 Public Square, P.O. Box 35, 42502-0035
Telephone: 606-679-6741; 678-4916
Fax: 606-679-3691

MEMBERS OF FIRM

Charles C. Adams   Norma B. Adams

ASSOCIATE

Jane Adams Venters

Counsel for: First and Farmers Bank of Somerset, Inc.; Aluminum Wheel Technology, Inc.

(See Next Column)

ADAMS & ADAMS, *Somerset—Continued*

Representative Clients: Community Trust Bank, FSB; Aluminum Wheel Technology, Inc.; Food Fair Cos.; Kentucky Farm Bureau Mutual Insurance Cos.; Cumberland Valley Communications; Shamrock Coal Co.; Railum, Inc.; Hartco Flooring Co.

For full biographical listings, see the Martindale-Hubbell Law Directory

LOUISIANA

BATON ROUGE,* East Baton Rouge Parish

GUGLIELMO, MARKS, SCHUTTE, TERHOEVE & LOVE (AV)

(A Registered Limited Liability Partnership)
320 Somerulos Street, P.O. Box 3177, 70821-3177
Telephone: 504-387-6966
Fax: 504-387-8338

Carey J. Guglielmo	Glen Scott Love
Paul Marks, Jr.	Dawn T. Trabeau-Mire
Charles A. Schutte, Jr.	Joseph W. Mengis
Henry G. Terhoeve	Kevin P. Landreneau

Representative Clients: City National Bank; Greyhound Corp.; The Travelers Insurance Co.; Chrysler Corp.; State Farm Insurance Co's.; Travelers/Aetna Insurance Group; Aetna Life & Casualty Co.

For full biographical listings, see the Martindale-Hubbell Law Directory

POWERS, CLEGG & WILLARD (AV)

7967 Office Park Boulevard, P.O. Box 15948, 70895
Telephone: 504-928-1951
Telecopier: 504-929-9834

MEMBERS OF FIRM

John Dale Powers	Michael V. Clegg
	William E. Willard

ASSOCIATES

Neil H. Mixon	Robert J. Daigre
Mary A. Cazes	Nicholas Soileau

General Counsel for: Audubon Insurance Co.
Louisiana Counsel for: Hancock Bank & Trust Co.; Hertz Corp.; Ciba-Geigy Corp.; Utica Mutual Insurance Co.

For full biographical listings, see the Martindale-Hubbell Law Directory

WATSON, BLANCHE, WILSON & POSNER (AV)

505 North Boulevard, P.O. Drawer 2995, 70821-2995
Telephone: 504-387-5511
Fax: 504-387-5972

Warren O. Watson (1893-1973)	Felix R. Weill
Fred A. Blanche (1898-1977)	Richard S. Dunn
Charles W. Wilson (1910-1981)	William E. Scott, III
Harvey H. Posner	Michael M. Remson
Robert L. Roland	P. Chauvin Wilkinson, Jr.
Alton J. Reine, Jr.	Randall L. Champagne
Peter T. Dazzio	René J. Pfefferle

ASSOCIATES

P. Scott Jolly	David G. Koch
Linda Orlansky Posner	Chris J. LeBlanc

Representative Clients: Citizens Savings and Loan Association; Community Coffee Company, Inc.; Louisiana Hospital Association; Prudential Insurance Company of America (The).

For full biographical listings, see the Martindale-Hubbell Law Directory

LAFAYETTE,* Lafayette Parish

DAVIDSON, MEAUX, SONNIER, MCELLIGOTT & SWIFT (AV)

810 South Buchanan Street, P.O. Drawer 2908, 70502
Telephone: 318-237-1660
Fax: 318-237-3676

MEMBERS OF FIRM

James J. Davidson, Jr. (1904-1990)	John E. McElligott, Jr.
	John G. Swift
V. Farley Sonnier (1942-1988)	Jeffrey A. Rhoades
Richard C. Meaux, Sr.	Philip A. Fontenot
James J. Davidson, III	Kyle L. Gideon
Theodore G. Edwards, IV	

ASSOCIATES

Jhan C. Boudreaux Beaullieu	Mark C. Andrus

(See Next Column)

OF COUNSEL

Jan Whitehead Swift

General Counsel: Southwest Louisiana Electric Membership Corp., Inc.; Macro Oil Co., Inc.; Dwight W. Andrus Insurance Agency; Lafayette Airport Commission.
Local Counsel: Southern Pacific Transportation Co.
Representative Clients: Highlands Insurance Co.; Wal-Mart Stores, Inc.; USAA.

For full biographical listings, see the Martindale-Hubbell Law Directory

LAKE CHARLES,* Calcasieu Parish

LORENZI, SANCHEZ & ROSTEET, L.L.P. (AV)

518 Pujo Street, P.O. Drawer 3305, 70602-3305
Telephone: 318-436-8401
Facsimile: 318-439-3216
Email: lorsanrost@linknet.net

MEMBERS OF FIRM

Thomas L. Lorenzi	Walter M. Sanchez
	Sidney J. Rosteet

For full biographical listings, see the Martindale-Hubbell Law Directory

MONROE,* Ouachita Parish

DOLLAR, LAIRD & SCOTT, L.L.P. (AV)

A Partnership including a Professional Law Corporation
700 Premier Plaza, 1900 North 18th Street, P.O. Box 14310, 71207-4310
Telephone: 318-387-9000
Telecopier: 318-387-9494

PARTNERS

Johnny E. Dollar (P.L.C.)	John C. Laird
	John T. Scott

R. Nicolas Anderson

For full biographical listings, see the Martindale-Hubbell Law Directory

NEW ORLEANS,* Orleans Parish

THE BAGERT LAW FIRM (AV)

Suite 2055 Pan-American Life Center, 601 Poydras Street, 70130
Telephone: 504-523-1117
Facsimile: 504-522-5406
Email: bagertlf@ix.netcom.com

Bernard J. Bagert, Jr., (A P.L.C.)

For full biographical listings, see the Martindale-Hubbell Law Directory

LEA, TYNAN & MCGEHEE, P.L.C. (AV)

Southern Marine and Aviation Building, 610 Poydras Street Suite 500, 70130
Telephone: 504-523-4500
Fax: 504-525-7208

Arden J. Lea	Joseph P. Tynan
	W. Clay McGehee

MEXICAN LEGAL ADVISOR

Ricardo Lan (Not admitted in the United States)

For full biographical listings, see the Martindale-Hubbell Law Directory

SLIDELL, St. Tammany Parish

PATRICK J. BERRIGAN (P.L.C.) (AV)

770 Gause Boulevard, Suite B, P.O. Box 220, 70459
Telephone: 504-641-1070
Fax: 504-641-1073
Email: pjbplc@comm.net

Patrick J. Berrigan

Jenifer B. Besh	Judith Otero
	Rodney J. Lacoste, Jr.

For full biographical listings, see the Martindale-Hubbell Law Directory

MAINE

AUGUSTA,* Kennebec Co.

LIPMAN & KATZ, P.A. (AV)

227 Water Street, 04330
Telephone: 207-622-3711
Telecopier: 207-622-7415

(See Next Column)

LIPMAN & KATZ P.A.—*Continued*

Sumner H. Lipman	Robert J. Stolt
David M. Lipman	Keith R. Varner
Roger J. Katz	Ronald E. Colby, III

Laura J.R. Garcia	Walter F. McKee

OF COUNSEL

Joseph B. Campbell

For full biographical listings, see the Martindale-Hubbell Law Directory

PORTLAND,* Cumberland Co.

PETRUCCELLI & MARTIN (AV)

50 Monument Square, P.O. Box 9733, 04104-5033
Telephone: 207-775-0200
Telecopier: 207-775-2360

MEMBERS OF FIRM

Gerald F. Petruccelli	Daniel W. Bates
Joel C. Martin	Michael K. Martin
James B. Haddow	

ASSOCIATES

Linda C. Russell	Thomas C. Bradley
John Anderson	

Representative Clients: Bangor Hydro-Electric Co.; Chubb Insurance Co.; Coopers & Lybrand; Cumberland Farms; General Electric Capital Corp.; Maine Medical Center; Pine Tree Telephone & Telegraph Co.; KPMG Peat Marwick; Union Mutual Fire Insurance Co.; Vermont Mutual Insurance Co.

For full biographical listings, see the Martindale-Hubbell Law Directory

MARYLAND

BALTIMORE,* (Independent City)

McDANIEL & MARSH (AV)

118 West Mulberry Street, 21201-3600
Telephone: 410-685-3810
Telecopier: 410-685-0203

William Alden McDaniel, Jr.	Jo Bennett Marsh

ASSOCIATE

Laura M. L. Maroldy

For full biographical listings, see the Martindale-Hubbell Law Directory

EASTON,* Talbot Co.

THOMAS T. ALSPACH (AV)

295 Bay Street, Suite One, P.O. Box 1358, 21601
Telephone: 410-822-9100
Fax: 410-822-2550

For full biographical listings, see the Martindale-Hubbell Law Directory

MASSACHUSETTS

BOSTON,* Suffolk Co.

KERN, ROACH & CARPENTER, P.C. (AV)

24 School Street, 02108
Telephone: 617-720-1800
Telefax: 617-720-0720

Leila R. Kern	Christine M. Roach
M. Ellen Carpenter	

Maryaustin Dowd

For full biographical listings, see the Martindale-Hubbell Law Directory

FRAMINGHAM, Middlesex Co.

DOMESTICO & BARRY (AV)

The Meadows, 161 Worcester Road, 01701
Telephone: 508-626-9000
Fax: 508-626-9001

MEMBERS OF FIRM

Charles J. Domestico	Susan Moran-Barry
Timothy E. Maguire	

For full biographical listings, see the Martindale-Hubbell Law Directory

DAVID I. SHORR (AV)

24 Union Avenue, 01701
Telephone: 508-879-4412
Fax: 508-872-2888

Marlene Kerble

References: Shawmut Bank; Framingham Savings Bank.

For full biographical listings, see the Martindale-Hubbell Law Directory

WORCESTER,* Worcester Co.

BOURGEOIS, DRESSER & WHITE (AV)

Worcester Plaza, 20th Floor, 446 Main Street, 01608
Telephone: 508-798-8801
Telecopier: 508-754-1943

MEMBERS OF FIRM

Bennett C. Wilson (1928-1988)	George L. Dresser
Roy A. Bourgeois	Robert Scott White

ASSOCIATES

Amato J. Bocchino, Jr.	Nadia R. Totino Beard

For full biographical listings, see the Martindale-Hubbell Law Directory

CHRISTOPHER, HAYS, WOJCIK & MAVRICOS (AV)

370 Main Street, 01608
Telephone: 508-792-2800
FAX: 508-792-6224

MEMBERS OF FIRM

William W. Hays	David A. Wojcik
John A. Mavricos	

OF COUNSEL

Christopher Christopher	William C. Perrin, Jr.

Reference: Flagship Bank & Trust Co.

For full biographical listings, see the Martindale-Hubbell Law Directory

WILLIAM J. LeDOUX (AV)

446 Main Street, 01608
Telephone: 508-792-5448
Fax: 508-792-5449
Email: WILEDOUX@BILLYLEDOUX.COM

For full biographical listings, see the Martindale-Hubbell Law Directory

MOUNTAIN, DEARBORN & WHITING (AV)

370 Main Street, 01608
Telephone: 508-756-2423
Fax: 508-755-6640

MEMBERS OF FIRM

Alfred N. Whiting (1920-1989)	Francis J. Russell
Thomas R. Mountain	Dale R. Harger
Richard W. Dearborn	Mark W. Bloom
Samuel R. DeSimone	Donald J. O'Neil
Henry W. Beth	Lawrence S. Delaney
Ann K. Molloy	

ASSOCIATE

Richard M. Freije

For full biographical listings, see the Martindale-Hubbell Law Directory

MICHIGAN

ANN ARBOR,* Washtenaw Co.

HOOPER, HATHAWAY, PRICE, BEUCHE & WALLACE (AV)

126 South Main Street, 48104
Telephone: 313-662-4426
Fax: 313-662-9559

Joseph C. Hooper (1899-1980)	Gregory A. Spaly
John R. Hathaway (Retired)	Robert W. Southard
Alan E. Price	William J. Stapleton
James R. Beuche	Bruce C. Conybeare, Jr.
Bruce T. Wallace	Anthony P. Patti
Charles W. Borgsdorf	Marcia J. Major
Mark R. Daane	Angela L. Jackson

OF COUNSEL

James A. Evashevski	Roderick K. Daane

Representative Clients: Chem-Trend, Inc.; Dundee Cement Co.; Ervin Industries, Inc.; First Martin Corp.; Group 243 Design, Inc.; Honeywell; Microwave Sensors, Inc.; Shearson Lehman Hutton; O'Neal Construction Co.; Pittsfield Products, Inc.

For full biographical listings, see the Martindale-Hubbell Law Directory

Ann Arbor—Continued

MAGILL AND RUMSEY, P.C. (AV)

Seventh Floor, First National Building, 201 South Main Street, 48104
Telephone: 313-995-2500
Fax: 313-995-4798

Robert F. Magill, Jr.　　　　　　　　　Ralph S. Rumsey

For full biographical listings, see the Martindale-Hubbell Law Directory

BINGHAM FARMS, Oakland Co.

HARNISCH & HOHAUSER, P.C. (AV)

30700 Telegraph Road, Suite 3475, 48025-4527
Telephone: 810-644-8600
Fax: 810-644-8344

Alan C. Harnisch　　　　　　　　　　Michael S. Hohauser

Lawrence S. Gadd　　　　　　　　　William J. Yochim, Jr.
OF COUNSEL
Debra C. Holt

Representative Clients: Dealers Financial Service, Inc.; Eaton Corporation; Edgewood Electric, Inc.; ITT Commercial Finance; Jeffrey C. Harrell, Builder, Inc.; Johnson Controls, Inc.

For full biographical listings, see the Martindale-Hubbell Law Directory

BIRMINGHAM, Oakland Co.

HYMAN AND LIPPITT, P.C. (AV)

185 Oakland Avenue, Suite 300, P.O. Box 1750, 48009
Telephone: 810-646-8292
Facsimile: 810-646-8375

J. Leonard Hyman	Kenneth F. Neuman
Norman L. Lippitt	Terry S. Givens
Douglas A. Hyman	Paul J. Fischer
Brian D. O'Keefe	John A. Sellers
H. Joel Newman	Robert H. Lippitt
Nazli G. Sater	Roger L. Myers

David N. Morrell, Jr.

For full biographical listings, see the Martindale-Hubbell Law Directory

KELL & LYNCH, P.C. (AV)

300 East Maple Road, Suite 200, 48009
Telephone: 810-647-2333
Telefax: 810-647-2781

Michael V. Kell　　　　　　　　　Margaret A. Lynch

Jennifer T. Gilhool　　　　　　　Steven M. Ribiat
(Not admitted in MI)
OF COUNSEL
M. Andrea Vaughn

Representative Clients: AlliedSignal, Inc.; AMP Inc.; Dow Corning Corp.; Hatteras Yachts; Lectron Products, Inc.; Metromedia Steakhouses, Inc.; Sybron Corp.; Michigan Consolidated Gas Co.; American Natural Resources.

For full biographical listings, see the Martindale-Hubbell Law Directory

BLOOMFIELD HILLS, Oakland Co.

ADKISON NEED (AV)

1533 North Woodward Avenue, Suite 210, 48304
Telephone: 810-540-7400
Fax: 810-540-7401
Email: AdkisNeed@aol.com

MEMBERS OF FIRM
Phillip G. Adkison	Paul Green
Gregory K. Need	Kelly A. Allen

Deborah M. Schneider
ASSOCIATES
Richard D. Kuhn, Jr.	Ann D. Christ
Kathryn N. Nichols	Laura B. Andoni

For full biographical listings, see the Martindale-Hubbell Law Directory

BEIER HOWLETT, PROFESSIONAL CORPORATION (AV)

200 East Long Lake Road, Suite 110, 48304-2361
Telephone: 810-645-9400
Fax: 810-645-9344

Dean G. Beier	Lawrence R. Ternan
James L. Howlett	Stephen W. Jones
Daniel C. Devine	Frank S. Galgan
Gerald G. White	Kenneth J. Sorensen

(See Next Column)

Thomas J. Trenta	Robert R. Shuman
Mark W. Hafeli	John D. Staran
Timothy J. Currier	Joseph F. Yamin
Mary T. Schmitt Smith	Phyllis Aiuto Zimmerman

P. Daniel Christ	Amy D. Comito
Richard A. Joslin, Jr.	Michael C. Gibbons
Lauren M. Underwood	George S. Fish

Nicole D. Bogard
OF COUNSEL
Robert G. Waddell

Representative Clients: Automobile Club Insurance Association (AAA); City of Birmingham; City of Lake Angelus; City of Rochester Hills; C.J. Edwards, Inc.; Dundee Community Schools; First of America Bank; Lake States Insurance Company; MAC Values; Troy School District.

For full biographical listings, see the Martindale-Hubbell Law Directory

DAWDA, MANN, MULCAHY & SADLER, P.L.C. (AV)

1533 North Woodward Avenue Suite 200, 48304
Telephone: 810-642-3700
Fax: 810-642-7791
Email: EMail@DMMS.Com

Michael D. Mulcahy	Sherwin E. Zamler
Suanne Tiberio Trimmer	John Mucha, III
Susan J. Sadler	Amy Bateson
Tyler D. Tennent	Keith James

Joseph K. Hart, Jr.

Representative Clients: AEGON USA Realty Advisors, Inc.; AMB Institutional Realty Advisors, Inc.; Bally's Total Fitness Corp.; BASF Corporation; Cardell Corporation; Cargill, Inc.; CB Commercial Real Estate; City Management; Ford Motor Company; G.E. Capital Realty Group.

For full biographical listings, see the Martindale-Hubbell Law Directory

FEDERLEIN & KERANEN, P.C. (AV)

6895 Telegraph Road, 48301
Telephone: 810-647-9653
Fax: 810-647-9683
Email: 102416.1133@COMPUSERVE.COM
Detroit, Michigan Office: 407 East Fort, Suite 350.
Telephone: 313-965-6090.

Walter J. Federlein　　　　　　Thomas M. Keranen

Frederick F. Butters　　　　　　Maria J. Bernard
Peter J. Cavanaugh

For full biographical listings, see the Martindale-Hubbell Law Directory

THE GOOGASIAN FIRM, P.C. (AV)

6895 Telegraph Road, 48301-3138
Telephone: 810-540-3333
Fax: 810-540-7213

George A. Googasian　　　　　　Craig Weber
Steven G. Googasian

For full biographical listings, see the Martindale-Hubbell Law Directory

HOWARD & HOWARD ATTORNEYS, P.C. (AV)

The Pinehurst Office Center, Suite 101, 1400 North Woodward Avenue, 48304-2856
Telephone: 810-645-1483
Telecopier: 810-645-1568
Kalamazoo, Michigan Office: The Kalamazoo Building, Suite 400, 107 West Michigan Avenue.
Telephone: 616-382-1483.
Telecopier: 616-382-1568.
Lansing, Michigan Office: The Phoenix Building, Suite 500, 222 Washington Square, North.
Telephone: 517-485-1483.
Telecopier: 517-485-1568.
Peoria, Illinois Office: The Creve Coeur Building, Suite 200, 321 Liberty Street.
Telephone: 309-672-1483.
Telecopier: 309-672-1568.
Tampa, Florida Office: First of America Plaza, Suite 2000, 201 East Kennedy Boulevard.
Telephone: 813-229-1483.
Telecopier: 813-229-1568.

(See Next Column)

HOWARD & HOWARD ATTORNEYS P.C.—*Continued*

William G. Asimakis, Jr.	Steven C. Kohl
Daniel L. Baker	Patrick M. McCarthy
Philip T. Carter	Jeffrey G. Raphelson
Christopher A. Chekan	Todd M. Stenerson
Kevin M. Chudler	Thomas J. Tallerico
Roger M. Groves	Donald F. Tucker
Jon H. Kingsepp	Marla Gottlieb Zwas

Representative Clients: For Representative Client list, see General Practice, Bloomfield Hills, MI.

For Complete List of Firm Personnel, See General Section

For full biographical listings, see the Martindale-Hubbell Law Directory

---

SCHAFER AND WEINER, P.C. (AV)

2050 North Woodward Avenue Suite 100, 48304
Telephone: 810-540-3340
Facsimile: 810-642-2127

Arnold Schafer	Daniel J. Weiner
	Michael E. Baum

Elaine Temesan	Max J. Newman
Robert S. McWhorter	James C. Lamb

For full biographical listings, see the Martindale-Hubbell Law Directory

---

*DETROIT,** Wayne Co.

FEIKENS, VANDER MALE, STEVENS, BELLAMY & GILCHRIST, P.C. (AV)

One Detroit Center Suite 3400, 500 Woodward Avenue, 48226-3406
Telephone: 313-962-5909
Fax: 313-962-3125
Email: FEIKENS@COUNSEL.COM

Robert E. Dice (1922-1983)	Lee A. Stevens
Jon Feikens	William C. Hurley
Jack E. Vander Male	Linda M. Galbraith
Frederick B. Bellamy	Michael S. Cafferty
Alan Gordon Gilchrist	Robert H. Feikens
L. Neal Kennedy	Gerald W. Van Wyke
Bruce A. VandeVusse	Roger L. Wolcott
	Sharon McPhail

Richard G. Koefod	Keith J. Soltis
Joseph E. Kozely, Jr.	Michael B. Barey
Jeffrey Feikens	Renee T. VanderHagen
	Michael P. Citrin

OF COUNSEL

Sam W. Thomas (P.C.)	Walter Vincent Bernard III

LEGAL SUPPORT PERSONNEL
PARALEGALS

Robert Westveer	Linda Barthlow

For full biographical listings, see the Martindale-Hubbell Law Directory

---

MAGER, MERCER, SCOTT & ALBER, P.C. (AV)

500 Woodward Avenue Suite 3400, 48226
Telephone: 313-962-8212
Facsimile: 313-962-5413
Oakland County Office: Top of Troy Building, 755 West Big Beaver, Suite 1700, Troy, Michigan.
Telephone: 810-362-8212.
Facsimile: 810-362-6944.
Macomb County Office: 18285 Ten Mile Road, Suite 100, Roseville, Michigan.
Telephone: 810-771-1100.
Facsimile: 810-775-5170.

George J. Mager, Jr.

Representative Clients: ABB Flakt, Inc.; American States Insurance Co.; CEI Industries; Central Venture Corp.; CIGNA; Construction Management, Inc.

For full biographical listings, see the Martindale-Hubbell Law Directory

---

R.H. PYTELL & ASSOCIATES, P.C. (AV)

18580 Mack Avenue, 48236
Telephone: 313-343-9200
Fax: 313-343-0207
Email: 103161.221@compuserve.com
URL: http://www.lawinfo.com/law/mi/pytell.html

Robert H. Pytell	Henry C. Pytell (1903-1988)
	Paul E. Varchetti

Representative Clients: J & N Fabrications, Inc.; Walton-Pierce, Inc.; Yorkshire Market; U.S. Amada Ltd.; Hickeys Inc.; Midwest Underwriters Insurance Agency, Inc.; Cassens Transport Co.; Mr. B's Tire; Mr. B's Car Wash; New Roots Landscape, Inc.

(See Next Column)

For full biographical listings, see the Martindale-Hubbell Law Directory

FARMINGTON HILLS, Oakland Co.

WRIGHT PENNING (AV)

27655 Middlebelt Road, Suite 170, 48334
Telephone: 810-477-6300
Fax: 810-477-7749

William M. Wright	LeClair L. Flaherty
Dan A. Penning	Dirk A. Beamer
	Dale A. Anderson

For full biographical listings, see the Martindale-Hubbell Law Directory

---

*GRAND RAPIDS,** Kent Co.

BORRE, PETERSON, FOWLER & REENS, P.C. (AV)

The Philo C. Fuller House, 44 Lafayette, N.E., P.O. Box 1767, 49501-1767
Telephone: 616-459-1971
Fax: 616-459-2393

Glen V. Borre	William C. Reens
James B. Peterson	Frank H. Johnson
Ben A. Fowler	Harold E. Nelson
	William R. Vander Sluis

References: Old Kent Bank; NBD Bank; FMB-First Michigan Bank - Grand Rapids.

For Complete List of Firm Personnel, See General Section

For full biographical listings, see the Martindale-Hubbell Law Directory

---

BUCHANAN, SILVER & BECKERING, P.L.C. (AV)

300 Ottawa N.W., Suite 800, 49503
Telephone: 616-458-2464
Fax: 616-458-0608

MEMBERS OF FIRM

John C. Buchanan	Robert J. Buchanan
Lee T. Silver	Jane M. Beckering

For full biographical listings, see the Martindale-Hubbell Law Directory

---

DE GROOT, KELLER & VINCENT (AV)

300 Michigan Trust Building, 49503
Telephone: 616-459-6251
Fax: 616-459-6352

MEMBERS OF FIRM

Murray B. De Groot	Brian D. Vincent

ASSOCIATE
Ingrid W. Erickson

For full biographical listings, see the Martindale-Hubbell Law Directory

---

GRUEL, MILLS, NIMS AND PYLMAN (AV)

50 Monroe Place, Suite 700 West, 49503
Telephone: 616-235-5500
Fax: 616-235-5550

MEMBERS OF FIRM

Grant J. Gruel	Scott R. Melton
William F. Mills	Brion J. Brooks
J. Clarke Nims	Thomas R. Behm
Norman H. Pylman, II	J. Paul Janes

Representative Clients: Aquinas College; Bell Helmet Co.; Blodgett Memorial Medical Center; Butterworth Hospital; Chem Central, Inc.; Cook Pump Co.; Grove, Inc.; NBDC; Heim Corp.

For full biographical listings, see the Martindale-Hubbell Law Directory

---

GUIKEMA & HULBERT, P.C. (AV)

Suite 410, Ledyard Building, 125 Ottawa, N.W., 49503
Telephone: 616-235-2601
Fax: 616-458-7548

Henry L. Guikema	James R. Hulbert

For full biographical listings, see the Martindale-Hubbell Law Directory

---

*KALAMAZOO,** Kalamazoo Co.

HOWARD & HOWARD ATTORNEYS, P.C. (AV)

The Kalamazoo Building, Suite 400, 107 West Michigan Avenue, 49007-3956
Telephone: 616-382-1483
Telecopier: 616-382-1568
Bloomfield Hills, Michigan Office: The Pinehurst Office Center, Suite 101, 1400 North Woodward Avenue.
Telephone: 810-645-1483.
Telecopier: 810-645-1568.

(See Next Column)

HOWARD & HOWARD ATTORNEYS P.C., *Kalamazoo—Continued*

Lansing, Michigan Office: The Phoenix Building, Suite 500, 222 Washington Square North.
Telephone: 517-485-1483.
Telecopier: 517-485-1568.
Peoria, Illinois Office: The Creve Coeur Building, Suite 200, 321 Liberty Street.
Telephone: 309-672-1483.
Telecopier: 309-672-1568.
Tampa, Florida Office: First of America Plaza, Suite 2000, 201 East Kennedy Boulevard.
Telephone: 813-229-1483.
Telecopier: 813-229-1568.

John W. Allen	James H. Geary
Robert C. Beck	Myra L. Willis

Representative Clients: For Representative Client list, see General Practice, Kalamazoo, MI.

For Complete List of Firm Personnel, See General Section

For full biographical listings, see the Martindale-Hubbell Law Directory

---

LANSING, Ingham Co.

HOWARD & HOWARD ATTORNEYS, P.C. (AV)

The Phoenix Building, Suite 500, 222 Washington Square, North, 48933-1817
Telephone: 517-485-1483
Telecopier: 517-485-1568
Kalamazoo, Michigan Office: The Kalamazoo Building, Suite 400, 107 West Michigan Avenue.
Telephone: 616-382-1483.
Telecopier: 616-382-1568.
Bloomfield Hills, Michigan Office: The Pinehurst Office Center, Suite 101, 1400 North Woodward Avenue.
Telephone: 810-645-1483.
Telecopier: 810-645-1568.
Peoria, Illinois Office: The Creve Coeur Building, Suite 200, 321 Liberty Street.
Telephone: 309-672-1483.
Telecopier: 309-672-1568.
Tampa, Florida Office: First of America Plaza, Suite 2000, 201 East Kennedy Boulevard.
Telephone: 813-229-1483.
Telecopier: 813-229-1568.

David C. Coey	Ellen M. Harvath
Patrick D. Hanes	James E. Lozier
C. Douglas Moran	

Representative Clients: For Representative Client list, see General Practice, Lansing, MI.

For Complete List of Firm Personnel, See General Section

For full biographical listings, see the Martindale-Hubbell Law Directory

---

SOUTHFIELD, Oakland Co.

PROVIZER, LICHTENSTEIN & PHILLIPS, P.C. (AV)

4000 Town Center, Suite 1800, 48075
Telephone: 810-352-9080
Facsimile: 810-352-1491

Harold M. Provizer	Constance S. Hall
David S. Lichtenstein	Noel F. Beck
Randall E. Phillips	William J. Selinsky
Marilyn A. Madorsky	Robert I. Brown
Deborah Molitz	Todd B. Denenberg
Jason Milstone	

For full biographical listings, see the Martindale-Hubbell Law Directory

YOUNG & ASSOCIATES, P.C. (AV)

Suite 305 Westview Office Center, 26200 American Drive, 48034
Telephone: 810-353-8620
Telecopier: 810-353-6559
Email: youngp@aol.com

Rodger D. Young

Anthony Cho	Steven Susser
Michael J. Fergestrom	Thomas A. Pinch

For full biographical listings, see the Martindale-Hubbell Law Directory

HARVEY J. ZAMECK (AV)

3000 Town Center, Suite 2990, 48075
Telephone: 810-355-4130

For full biographical listings, see the Martindale-Hubbell Law Directory

---

TROY, Oakland Co.

RANDALL J. GILLARY, P.C. (AV)

Suite 1020 Columbia Center, 201 W. Big Beaver, 48084
Telephone: 810-528-0440
Fax: 810-528-3412

Randall J. Gillary

Kevin P. Albus

For full biographical listings, see the Martindale-Hubbell Law Directory

HACKETT, MAXWELL & PHILLIPS, P.L.L.C. (AV)

City Center Building, Suite 1470, 888 West Big Beaver Road, 48084
Telephone: 810-362-2600
Fax: 810-362-3610
Email: hackmax@michbar.org

Patrick E. Hackett	Phillip B. Maxwell
	Dawn L. Phillips

Mark T. Butler	Lisa Rycus Mikalonis
Jill Tilton Silverman	Jason W. Johnson

For full biographical listings, see the Martindale-Hubbell Law Directory

COMMUNICATIONS LAW

ALABAMA

BIRMINGHAM, * Jefferson Co.

BRADLEY, ARANT, ROSE & WHITE (AV)

2001 Park Place, Suite 1400, P.O. Box 830709, 35283-0709
Telephone: 205-521-8000
Facsimile: 205-252-0264
Facsimile (SouthTrust Tower Office): 205-251-9915
URL: http://www.BARW.COM
Huntsville, Alabama Office: 200 Clinton Avenue West, Suite 900, 35801.
Telephone: 205-517-5100.
Facsimile: 205-533-5069.

MEMBERS OF FIRM

Gary C. Huckaby
　(Resident, Huntsville Office)
E. Cutter Hughes, Jr.
　(Resident, Huntsville Office)
G. Rick Hall
　(Resident, Huntsville Office)

Counsel for: SouthTrust Bank of Alabama, National Association; Energen, Corporation (formerly Alagasco, Inc.); Blount, Inc.; Torchmark Corp.; Russell Corp.; Coca-Cola Bottling Company United, Inc.; Ford Motor Co.; Walter Industries, Inc.; The Birmingham Post Co. (Post-Herald); The New York Times Co.

For Complete List of Firm Personnel, See General Section

For full biographical listings, see the Martindale-Hubbell Law Directory

BURR & FORMAN (AV)

3100 SouthTrust Tower, 420 North 20th Street, 35203
Telephone: 205-251-3000
Telecopier: 205-458-5100
Huntsville, Alabama Office: Suite 204, Regency Center, 400 Meridian Street.
Telephone: 205-551-0010.
Atlanta, Georgia Office: Suite 1800, One Georgia Center, 600 West Peachtree Street, 30308.
Telephone: 404-817-3536.
Facsimile: 404-817-3244.

MEMBERS OF FIRM

John D. Clements

John F. DeBuys, Jr.

For Complete List of Firm Personnel, See General Section

For full biographical listings, see the Martindale-Hubbell Law Directory

JOHNSTON, BARTON, PROCTOR & POWELL (AV)

2900 AmSouth/Harbert Plaza, 1901 Sixth Avenue North, 35203-2618
Telephone: 205-458-9400
Telecopier: 205-458-9500

MEMBERS OF FIRM

Harvey Deramus (1904-1970)	James C. Barton, Jr.
Alfred M. Naff (1923-1993)	Thomas E. Walker
Gilbert E. Johnston (1916-1994)	Anne P. Wheeler
G. Burns Proctor, Jr.	Barry V. Frederick
Sydney L. Lavender	Hollinger F. Barnard
Charles A. Powell, III	William D. Jones III
Jerome K. Lanning	David W. Proctor
Don B. Long, Jr.	Oscar M. Price III
Charles L. Robinson	W. Hill Sewell
J. William Rose, Jr.	Robert S. Vance, Jr.
Gilbert E. Johnston, Jr.	Richard J. Brockman
Ralph H. Smith II	Anthony A. Joseph

William G. Somerville, III

COUNSEL

Josh Mullins, Jr.

Paul E. Toppins

R. Marcus Givhan

OF COUNSEL

James C. Barton

Alfred Swedlaw

Alan W. Heldman

ASSOCIATES

William K. Hancock	Helen Kathryn Downs
James P. Pewitt	Jennifer Fox Swain
Scott Wells Ford	Spencer A. Kinderman
David M. Hunt	Scott R. McLaughlin
Lee M. Pope	Bradley C. Mayhew
John W. Sheffield	W. Jonathan Daniel
Haskins W. Jones	J. Vincent Edge
Russell L. Irby, III	Allison Powell

General Counsel for: Anderson News Co.; The Birmingham News Co. (Publishers of The Birmingham News and owner of the Huntsville Times Co.); Bookland Stores, Inc.

(See Next Column)

Counsel for: BellSouth Services, Inc.; Broadcast Music, Inc.; Times-Mirror Broadcasting (WVTM-TV, Channel 13); WAPI, Inc.; Tucker Wayne/Luckie & Co.

For full biographical listings, see the Martindale-Hubbell Law Directory

HUNTSVILLE, * Madison Co.

BRADLEY, ARANT, ROSE & WHITE (AV)

200 Clinton Avenue West, Suite 900, 35801
Telephone: 205-517-5100
Facsimile: 205-533-5069
URL: http://www.BARW.COM
Birmingham, Alabama Office: 2001 Park Place, Suite 1400, P.O. Box 830709.
Telephone: 205-521-8000.
Facsimile: 205-251-8611, 251-8665, 252-0264. Facsimile (SouthTrust Tower Office): 205-251-9915.

RESIDENT PARTNERS

Gary C. Huckaby

E. Cutter Hughes, Jr.

G. Rick Hall

For Complete List of Firm Personnel, See General Section

For full biographical listings, see the Martindale-Hubbell Law Directory

MONTGOMERY, * Montgomery Co.

BRANTLEY & WILKERSON, P.C. (AV)

405 South Hull Street, P.O. Box 830, 36101-0830
Telephone: 334-265-1500
Fax: 334-265-0319

Paul A. Brantley

Mark D. Wilkerson

Leah Snell Stephens

Representative Clients: ALLTEL; The Birmingham News; TDS; Southeastern Cellular; USA Mobile Communications, Inc.; U.S. Long Distance, Inc.; Technologies Management, Inc.

For full biographical listings, see the Martindale-Hubbell Law Directory

ARIZONA

PHOENIX, * Maricopa Co.

BROWN & BAIN, A PROFESSIONAL ASSOCIATION (AV)

2901 North Central Avenue, P.O. Box 400, 85001-0400
Telephone: 602-351-8000
Telecopier: 602-351-8516
Palo Alto, California Affiliated Office: Brown & Bain, 1755 Embarcadero Road, Suite 200.
Telephone: 415-856-9411.
Telecopier: 415-856-6061.
Tucson, Arizona Affiliated Office: Brown & Bain, A Professional Association. One South Church Avenue, Nineteenth Floor, P.O. Box 2265.
Telephone: 602-798-7900
Telecopier: 602-798-7945.

Daniel C. Barr	Paul F. Eckstein
Charles A. Blanchard	Douglas Gerlach
Alan H. Blankenheimer	Philip R. Higdon
Jack E. Brown	(Resident at Tucson Office)
H. Michael Clyde	Kelly A. O'Connor

Michael W. Patten

COUNSEL

Bernard Petrie (Resident at Palo Alto Office)

For Complete List of Firm Personnel, See General Section

For full biographical listings, see the Martindale-Hubbell Law Directory

ARKANSAS

LITTLE ROCK, * Pulaski Co.

IVESTER, SKINNER & CAMP, P.A. (AV)

Suite 1200, 111 Center Street, 72201
Telephone: 501-376-7788
FAX: 501-376-8536

Hermann Ivester	Charles R. Camp
H. Edward Skinner	Stan D. Smith

For Complete List of Firm Personnel, See General Section

For full biographical listings, see the Martindale-Hubbell Law Directory

Little Rock—*Continued*

ROSE LAW FIRM, A PROFESSIONAL ASSOCIATION (AV)

120 East Fourth Street, 72201
Telephone: 501-375-9131
Telecopy: 501-375-1309

| W. Wilson Jones | David L. Williams |
| Jerry C. Jones | Jackson Farrow Jr. |

COUNSEL
Phillip Carroll

———————————

| John P. Fletcher | Michael N. Shannon |

Counsel for: ALLTEL Corporation; Aluminum Company of America; Donrey Media Group Inc.; The Equitable Life Assurance Society of The United States; Bridgestone/Firestone Inc.; General Motors Corp.; The Prudential Insurance Company of America; Stephens Group, Inc.; Tyson Foods, Inc.; WEHCO Media Inc.

For Complete List of Firm Personnel, See General Section

For full biographical listings, see the Martindale-Hubbell Law Directory

———————————

CALIFORNIA

COSTA MESA, Orange Co.

RUTAN & TUCKER, LLP (AV)

A Partnership including Professional Corporations
611 Anton Boulevard, Suite 1400, P.O. Box 1950, 92626
Telephone: 714-641-5100; 213-625-7586
Telecopier: 714-546-9035
Email: rutan&tucker@mcimail.com *URL:* http://www.rutan.com
MEMBER OF FIRM
William M. Marticorena

For Complete List of Firm Personnel, See General Section

For full biographical listings, see the Martindale-Hubbell Law Directory

———————————

LOS ANGELES,* Los Angeles Co.

O'MELVENY & MYERS LLP (AV)

400 South Hope Street, 90071-2899
Telephone: 213-669-6000
Cable Address: "Moms"
Facsimile: 213-669-6407
Email: omminfo@omm.com
Century City, California Office: 1999 Avenue of the Stars, 90067-6035.
Telephone: 310-553-6700.
Facsimile: 310-246-6779.
Newport Beach, California Office: 610 Newport Center Drive, 92660-6429.
Telephone: 714-760-9600.
Cable Address: "Moms".
Facsimile: 714-669-6994.
San Francisco, California Office: Embarcadero Center West Tower, 275 Battery Street, 94111-3305.
Telephone: 415-984-8700.
Facsimile: 415-984-8701.
New York, New York Office: Citicorp Center, 153 East 53rd Street, 10022-4611.
Telephone: 212-326-2000.
Facsimile: 212-326-2061.
Washington, D.C. Office: 555 13th Street, N.W., 20004-1109.
Telephone: 202-383-5300.
Cable Address: "Moms".
Facsimile: 202-383-5414.
London, England Office: 10 Finsbury Square, London, EC2A 1LA.
Telephone: 0171-256-8451.
Facsimile: 0171-638-8205.
Tokyo, Japan Office: Sanbancho KB-6 Building, 6 Sanbancho, Chiyoda-ku, Tokyo 102, Japan.
Telephone: 03-3239-2900.
Facsimile: 03-3239-2432.
Hong Kong Office: Suite 1905, Peregrine Tower, Lippo Centre, 89 Queensway, Central, Hong Kong.
Telephone: 852-2523-8266.
Facsimile: 852-2522-1760.
Shanghai, Peoples Republic of China Office: Shanghai International Trade Centre, Suite 2011, 2200 Yan An Road West, Shanghai, 200335, PRC.
Telephone: 86-21-6219-5363.
Facsimile: 86-21-6275-4949.

PARTNER
John H. Beisner (Washington, D.C. Office)

For Complete List of Firm Personnel, See General Section

For full biographical listings, see the Martindale-Hubbell Law Directory

SAN DIEGO,* San Diego Co.

FERRIS & BRITTON, A PROFESSIONAL CORPORATION (AV)

1600 First National Bank Center, 401 West A Street, 92101
Telephone: 619-233-3131
Fax: 619-232-9316

| Alfred G. Ferris | Christopher Q. Britton |
| | Michael R. Weinstein |

OF COUNSEL
William M. Winter

Representative Clients: California Cable Television Assoc.; Cox Communications, Inc.; Immuno Pharmaceutics, Inc.; Invitrogen Corporation; Par Broadcasting; Peninsula Bank; Teleport Communications Group; Southwest Airlines.

For Complete List of Firm Personnel, See General Section

For full biographical listings, see the Martindale-Hubbell Law Directory

———————————

DISTRICT OF COLUMBIA

WASHINGTON, D.C. Co.

* indicates certain Bar Register subscribers, in cities of comparable size and importance, who maintain an additional office in Washington, D.C. and who have arranged for representation as a part of the Washington, D.C. listings that follow

ALEXANDER, BEARDEN, HAIRSTON & MARKS, LLP (AV)

Limited Liability Partnership
2021 L Street, N.W., Suite 300, 20036
Telephone: 202-293-3700
Fax: 202-293-7359
Silver Spring, Maryland Office: Lee Plaza, Suite 805, 8601 Georgia Avenue, 20910.
Telephone: 301-589-2222.
Facsimile: 301-539-2523.
New York, New York Office: 330 Madison Avenue, 36th Floor.
Telephone: 212-808-0008.
Fax: 212-599-1028.

| Koteles Alexander | James L. Bearden |

———————————

Darius B. Withers (Not admitted in DC)
Reference: Riggs National Bank of Washington, D.C.

For full biographical listings, see the Martindale-Hubbell Law Directory

———————————

BAKER & HOSTETLER (AV)

Washington Square, Suite 1100, 1050 Connecticut Avenue, N.W., 20036-5304
Telephone: 202-861-1500
In Cleveland, Ohio: 3200 National City Center, 1900 East Ninth Street.
Telephone: 216-621-0200.
In Columbus, Ohio: Capitol Square, Suite 2100, 65 East State Street.
Telephone: 614-228-1541.
In Denver, Colorado: 303 East 17th Avenue, Suite 1100.
Telephone: 303-861-0600.
In Houston, Texas: 1000 Louisiana, Suite 2000.
Telephone: 713-751-1600.
In Long Beach, California: 300 Oceangate, Suite 620.
Telephone: 310-432-2827.
In Los Angeles, California: 600 Wilshire Boulevard.
Telephone: 213-624-2400.
In Orlando, Florida: SunBank Center, Suite 2300, 200 South Orange Avenue.
Telephone: 305-841-1111.
In College Park, Maryland: 9658 Baltimore Boulevard, Suite 206.
Telephone: 301-441-2781.
In Alexandria, Virginia: 437 North Lee Street.
Telephone: 703-549-1294.
In San Francisco, California: One Sansome Street, Suite 2000.
Telephone: 415-951-4705.

PARTNERS
| Kenneth C. Howard, Jr. | Donald P. Zeifang |

ASSOCIATE
Michael C. Ruger

For Complete List of Firm Personnel, See General Section

For full biographical listings, see the Martindale-Hubbell Law Directory

Washington—Continued

* BELL, BOYD & LLOYD (AV)

1615 L Street, N.W., 20036
Telephone: 202-466-6300
FAX: 202-463-0678
Chicago, Illinois Office: Three First National Plaza, Suite 3300, 70 West Madison Street.
Telephone: 312-372-1121.
FAX: 312-372-2098.

RESIDENT PARTNERS

A. Thomas Carroccio   Charles A. Zielinski
Thomas R. Gibbon   (Not admitted in DC)

For Complete List of Firm Personnel, See General Section

For full biographical listings, see the Martindale-Hubbell Law Directory

BLOOSTON, MORDKOFSKY, JACKSON & DICKENS (AV)

2120 L Street, N.W., Suite 300, 20037
Telephone: 202-659-0830
Fax: 202-828-5568

MEMBERS OF FIRM

Arthur Blooston (Retired)   Benjamin H. Dickens, Jr.
Harold Mordkofsky   John A. Prendergast
Robert M. Jackson   Gerard J. Duffy

OF COUNSEL

Jeremiah Courtney (1910-1994)   Perry W. Woofter
     (Not admitted in DC)

ASSOCIATES

Richard D. Rubino   Susan J. Bahr
  (Not admitted in DC)   David Cary Mitchell

For full biographical listings, see the Martindale-Hubbell Law Directory

COHN AND MARKS (AV)

Suite 600, 1333 New Hampshire Avenue, N.W., 20036
Telephone: 202-293-3860
Fax: 202-293-4827
URL: http://www.cohnmarks.com

MEMBERS OF FIRM

Joel H. Levy   Richard A. Helmick
Robert B. Jacobi   Wayne Coy, Jr.
Roy R. Russo   Mark L. Pelesh
Ronald A. Siegel   J. Brian De Boice
Lawrence N. Cohn   Edward N. Leavy

ASSOCIATES

Susan Valerie Sachs   Kevin M. Goldberg
John R. Przypszny   Michael A. McVicker
A. Sheba Chacko   (Not admitted in DC)

OF COUNSEL

Marcus Cohn   Stanley S. Neustadt
Leonard H. Marks   Stanley B. Cohen
     Richard M. Schmidt, Jr.

LEGAL SUPPORT PERSONNEL
SPECIALIST (NON-LAWYER)

Sharon H. Bob (Higher Education Specialist on Policy and Regulation)

For full biographical listings, see the Martindale-Hubbell Law Directory

COLE, RAYWID & BRAVERMAN, L.L.P. (AV)

1919 Pennsylvania Avenue, N.W., 20006
Telephone: 202-659-9750
Cable Address: "Crab"
Telecopier: 202-452-0067
URL: http://www.crblaw.com

John P. Cole, Jr.   Paul Glist
Alan Raywid (1930-1991)   David M. Silverman
Burt A. Braverman   James F. Ireland, III
Robert L. James   Steven Jay Horvitz
Joseph R. Reifer   Christopher W. Savage
Frances J. Chetwynd   Ann E. Flowers
John D. Seiver   Robert G. Scott, Jr.
Wesley R. Heppler   Susan Whelan Westfall

Theresa A. Zeterberg   Robert N. Walton
John Dodge   T. Scott Thompson
Frederick W. Giroux   Sandra Greiner
John Davidson Thomas   Navid C. Haghighi
Maria T. Browne   (Not admitted in DC)
Donna Carrie Rattley   Lisa A. Leventhal
     (Not admitted in DC)

For full biographical listings, see the Martindale-Hubbell Law Directory

DOW, LOHNES & ALBERTSON, PLLC (AV)

1200 New Hampshire Avenue, N.W. Suite 800, 20036-6802
Telephone: 202-776-2000
Facsimile: 202-776-2222
Email: postmaster@dla.com *URL:* http://www.dlalaw.com
Atlanta, Georgia Office: One Ravinia Drive, Suite 1600.
Telephone: 770-901-8800.
Telecopier: 770-901-8874.

MEMBERS OF THE FIRM

Michael D. Basile   Leonard Jervey Kennedy
Leonard J. Baxt   (Not admitted in DC)
Raymond G. Bender, Jr.   John S. Logan
Peter H. Feinberg   B. Dwight Perry
John R. Feore, Jr.   (Managing Director)
Ralph W. Hardy, Jr.   Laura Hathaway Phillips
J.G. Harrington   J. Christopher Redding
Werner K. Hartenberger   Kevin F. Reed
Thomas J. Hutton   Michael S. Schooler

Christina Hosp Burrow   H. Anthony Lehv
Richard S. Denning   Christopher D. Libertelli
Andrew C. Fish   Elizabeth Anne McGeary
  (Not admitted in DC)   Frank S. Murray
Jennifer L. Keefe   (Not admitted in DC)
     Suzanne M. Perry

For Complete List of Firm Personnel, See General Section

For full biographical listings, see the Martindale-Hubbell Law Directory

FISHER WAYLAND COOPER LEADER & ZARAGOZA L.L.P (AV)

A Registered Limited Liability Partnership
Suite 400, 2001 Pennsylvania Avenue, N.W., 20006-1851
Telephone: 202-659-3494
Facsimile: 202-296-6518
Email: fwclz@fwclz.com *URL:* http://www.fwclz.com

Ben S. Fisher (1890-1954)   David D. Oxenford
Charles V. Wayland (1910-1980)   Barry H. Gottfried
Ben C. Fisher   Bruce D. Jacobs
Martin R. Leader   Eliot J. Greenwald
Richard R. Zaragoza   Carroll John Yung
Clifford M. Harrington   Glenn S. Richards
Joel R. Kaswell   Barrie Debra Berman
Kathryn R. Schmeltzer   Francisco R. Montero
Douglas Woloshin   Robert C. Fisher
     Scott R. Flick

OF COUNSEL

Grover C. Cooper   John Q. Hearne

ASSOCIATES

Gregory L. Masters   Brooks B. Gracie III
  (Not admitted in DC)   (Not admitted in DC)
Lauren Lynch Flick   Colette M. Capretz
Kevin M. Walsh   Jason S. Roberts
  (Not admitted in DC)   (Not admitted in DC)
Miles S. Mason   Heidi Atassi Gaffney
Robert L. Galbreath   (Not admitted in DC)
  (Not admitted in DC)   Stephen J. Berman
Dawn M. Sciarrino   (Not admitted in DC)
  (Not admitted in DC)   Veronica D. McLaughlin
Karen C. Rindner   Stephanie Blessey Lilley
     Jaqualin Friend Peterson

For full biographical listings, see the Martindale-Hubbell Law Directory

FLETCHER, HEALD & HILDRETH, P.L.C. (AV)

2000 L Street, NW, Suite 200, 20036
Telephone: 202-828-5700
Email: office@fhh-telcomlaw.com
Arlington, Virginia Office: 1300 North 17th Street, 11th Floor.
Telephone: 703-812-0400.
Fax: 703-812-0486.

Paul D. P. Spearman   Russell Rowell (1910-1994)
  (1898-1962)   Robert L. Heald (1917-1994)
Frank Roberson (1882-1961)   Frank U. Fletcher (1912-1995)
     Edward F. Kenehan (Retired)

MEMBERS OF FIRM

Richard Hildreth   Frank R. Jazzo
James P. Riley   Howard M. Weiss
Leonard R. Raish   Harry C. Martin
Vincent J. Curtis, Jr.   Eric Fishman
George Petrutsas   Paul J. Feldman
     Kathleen Victory

SENIOR ASSOCIATES

Ann Bavender   Anne Goodwin Crump
     Andrew S. Kersting

ASSOCIATES

Kathryn A. Kleiman   Richard J. Estevez
  (Not admitted in DC)   (Not admitted in DC)

(See Next Column)

FLETCHER, HEALD & HILDRETH P.L.C., *Washington—Continued*

OF COUNSEL

Edward A. Caine   Eugene M. Lawson, Jr.
          (Not admitted in DC)

For full biographical listings, see the Martindale-Hubbell Law Directory

GURMAN, BLASK & FREEDMAN, CHARTERED (AV)

Suite 500, 1400 16th Street, N.W., 20036
Telephone: 202-328-8200
Fax: 202-462-1784; 462-1786

Louis Gurman   William D. Freedman
Jerome K. Blask   Doane F. Kiechel, III

Andrea S. Miano   Daniel E. Smith
Nadja S. Sodos   Stephen E. Holsten

For full biographical listings, see the Martindale-Hubbell Law Directory

HOGAN & HARTSON L.L.P. (AV)

Columbia Square, 555 13th Street, N.W., 20004-1109
Telephone: 202-637-5600
Telex: 89-2757
Cable Address: "Hogander Washington"
Fax: 202-637-5910
Email: HHINFO@DC4.HHLAW.COM
Brussels, Belgium Office: Avenue des Arts 41, 1040.
Telephone: (32.2) 505.09.11.
Fax: (32.2) 505.09.96.
Budapest, Hungary Office: Bank Center, Granite Tower, 9th Floor, 1944
Budapest, Hungary.
Telephone: (36-1) 302-9050.
Fax: (36-1) 302-9060.
London, England Office: 21 Garlick Hill, EC4V 2AU.
Telephone: (44 171) 815 1200.
Fax: (44 171) 329 0299.
Moscow, Russia Office: 33/2 Usacheva Street, Building 3, 119048.
Telephone: (7095) 245-5190. Int'l
Telephone: (7501-907-0451).
Fax: (7095) 245-5192.
Fax: (7501) 907-0462 (International).
Paris, France (Affiliated Office): Cariddi, Mee, Rué, Avocats Associés à la
Cour de Paris, 12, rue de la Paix, 75002.
Telephone: (33-1) 42.61.57.71.
Fax: (33-1) 42.61.79.21.
Prague, Czech Republic Office: Opletalova 37, 110 00.
Telephone: (42-2) 2422-9009.
Fax: (42-2) 2421-5105.
Warsaw, Poland Office: Marszalkowska 6/6, 00-590.
Telephone: (48 22) 628 0201; Int'l (48) 3912 1413.
Fax: (48 22) 628 7787; Int'l (48) 3912 1511.
Baltimore, Maryland Office: 111 South Calvert Street, 16th Floor.
Telephone: 410-659-2700.
Fax: 410-539-6981.
Bethesda, Maryland Office: Two Democracy Center, Suite 720, 6903
Rockledge Drive.
Telephone: 301-564-5000.
Fax: 301-493-5169.
Colorado Springs, Colorado Office: Two North Cascade Avenue, Suite
1300.
Telephone: 719-448-5900.
Fax: 719-448-5922.
Denver, Colorado Office: One Tabor Center, Suite 1500, 1200 Seventeenth
Street.
Telephone: 303-899-7300.
Fax: 303-899-7333.
McLean, Virginia Office: 8300 Greensboro Drive.
Telephone: 703-848-2600.
Fax: 703-448-7650.

MEMBERS OF FIRM

Robert L. Corn-Revere   William S. Reyner, Jr.
Gardner F. Gillespie   Richard S. Rodin
Gerald E. Oberst, Jr. (Resident, Peter A. Rohrbach
 Brussels, Belgium Office) Mace J. Rosenstein
Linda L. Oliver   David J. Saylor
    Joel S. Winnik

COUNSEL

Jacquelyn E. Grillon   Marissa G. Repp

OF COUNSEL

Marvin J. Diamond

ASSOCIATES

Jacqueline P. Cleary   Karis A. Hastings
Tia Cudahy   Michelle M. Shanahan
Kyle D. Dixon
 (Not admitted in DC)

For Complete List of Firm Personnel, See General Section

For full biographical listings, see the Martindale-Hubbell Law Directory

JOHN H. MIDLEN, JR. CHARTERED (AV)

3238 Prospect Street, N.W., 20007-3214
Telephone: 202-333-1500
Facsimile: 202-333-6852
Email: john@midlen.com *URL:* http://www.midlen.com

John H. Midlen, Jr.

For full biographical listings, see the Martindale-Hubbell Law Directory

MOIR & HARDMAN (AV)

2000 L Street, N.W., Suite 512, 20036-4907
Telephone: 202-331-9852
Fax: 202-331-9854

Brian R. Moir   Kenneth E. Hardman

For full biographical listings, see the Martindale-Hubbell Law Directory

O'MELVENY & MYERS LLP (AV)

555 13th Street, N.W. Suite 500 West, 20004-1109
Telephone: 202-383-5300
Cable Address: "Moms"
Facsimile: 202-383-5414
Email: ommifo@omm.com
Los Angeles, California Office: 400 South Hope Street.
Telephone: 213-669-6000.
Cable Address: "Moms."
Facsimile: 213-669-6407.
Century City Office: 1999 Avenue of the Stars, 7th Floor.
Telephone: 310-553-6700.
Facsimile: 310-246-6779.
Newport Beach, California Office: 610 Newport Center Drive, Suite 1700.
Telephone: 714-760-9600.
Cable Address: "Moms."
Facsimile: 714-669-6994.
San Francisco, California Office: Embarcadero Center West Tower, 275
Battery Street, Suite 2600.
Telephone: 415-984-8700.
Facsimile: 415-984-8701.
New York, N.Y. Office: Citicorp Center, 153 East 53rd Street, 54th Floor.
Telephone: 212-326-2000.
Facsimile: 212-326-2061.
London, England Office: 10 Finsbury Square, London, EC2A 1LA.
Telephone: 44-171-256-8451
Facsimile: 44-171-638-8205.
Tokyo, Japan Office: Sanbancho KB-6 Building, 6 Sanbancho, Chiyoda-ku,
Tokyo 102, Japan.
Telephone: 81-3-3239-2800.
Facsimile: 81-3-3239-2432.
Hong Kong Office: Suite 1905, Peregrine Tower, Lippo Centre, 89
Queensway, Central, Hong, Kong.
Telephone: 852-2523-8266.
Facsimile: 852-2522-1760.
Shanghai, People's Republic of China Office: Shanghai International Trade
Centre, Suite 2011, 2200 Yan An Road West.
Telephone: 86-21-6219-5363.
Facsimile: 86-21-6275-4949.

WASHINGTON, D.C.
MEMBERS OF FIRM

Brian C. Anderson   Donald T. Bliss, Jr.
John H. Beisner   F. Amanda DeBusk
Ben E. Benjamin   John E. Welch

RESIDENT ASSOCIATES

Jeffrey J. Carlisle   Nina Shafran
 (Not admitted in DC)

For full biographical listings, see the Martindale-Hubbell Law Directory

PEPPER & CORAZZINI (AV)

1776 K Street, N.W., 20006
Telephone: 202-296-0600
Telecopier: 202-296-5572
Email: pepcor@commlaw.com *URL:* http://www.commlaw.com/pepper

MEMBERS OF FIRM

Vincent A Pepper   Frederick W. Ford (1909-1986)
Robert D. L'Heureux   Peter Gutmann
 (1912-1969)   John F. Garziglia
Robert F. Corazzini   Howard J. Barr

ASSOCIATES

Neal J. Friedman   Suzanne Catherine Spink
Ellen S. Mandell   (Not admitted in DC)
Michael J. Lehmkuhl   Michael H. Shacter
 (Not admitted in DC)

OF COUNSEL

Gregg P. Skall   E. Theodore Mallyck

For full biographical listings, see the Martindale-Hubbell Law Directory

Washington—Continued

TIERNEY & SWIFT (AV)

Suite 350, 1001 22nd Street, N.W., 20037
Telephone: 202-293-7979
Telecopier: 202-659-5711

John L. Tierney   Richard F. Swift

* VENABLE ATTORNEYS AT LAW VENABLE, BAETJER, HOWARD & CIVILETTI, LLP (AV)

A Partnership including Professional Corporations
Suite 1000, 1201 New York Avenue, N.W., 20005
Telephone: 202-962-4800
Fax: 202-962-8300
Baltimore, Maryland Office: Venable, Baetjer and Howard LLP, 1800
Mercantile Bank & Trust Building, 2 Hopkins Plaza.
Telephone: 410-244-7400.
McLean, Virginia Office: Venable, Baetjer and Howard LLP, Suite 400,
2010 Corporate Ridge.
Telephone: 703-760-1600.
Rockville, Maryland Office: Venable, Baetjer and Howard LLP, Suite 500,
One Church Street, P. O. Box 1906.
Telephone: 301-217-5600.
Towson, Maryland Office: Venable, Baetjer and Howard LLP, 210
Allegheny Avenue, P. O. Box 5517.
Telephone: 410-494-6200.

MEMBERS OF FIRM

Ian D. Volner   James R. Myers
Edward F. Glynn, Jr.   Jeffrey D. Knowles

OF COUNSEL

Frank Horton   Barbara L. Waite

For Complete List of Firm Personnel, See General Section

For full biographical listings, see the Martindale-Hubbell Law Directory

VERNER, LIIPFERT, BERNHARD, MCPHERSON AND HAND, CHARTERED (AV)

901 15th Street, N.W., 20005-2301
Telephone: 202-371-6000
Cable Address: "Verlip"
Telex: 1561792 VERLIP UT
Fax: 202-371-6279
Email: verner.com
McLean, Virginia Office: Sixth Floor, 8280 Greensboro Drive, 22102.
Telephone: 703-749-6000.
Fax: 703-749-6027.
Houston, Texas Office: 2600 Texas Commerce Tower, 600 Travis, 77002.
Telephone: 713-237-9034.
Fax: 713-237-1216.
Honolulu, Hawaii Office: Hawaii Times Building, 928 Nuuanu Avenue,
Suite 400, 96817.
Telephone: 808-566-0999.
Fax: 808-566-0995.
Austin, Texas Office: Suite 1440 San Jacinto Center, 98 San Jacinto
Boulevard, 78701.
Telephone: 512-703-6000.
Fax: 512-703-6003.

Thomas J. Keller   Lawrence E. Levinson
Erwin G. Krasnow   (Not admitted in DC)
                      Lawrence R. Sidman
OF COUNSEL
Michael D. Berg   Julian L. Shepard

For Complete List of Firm Personnel, See General Section

For full biographical listings, see the Martindale-Hubbell Law Directory

WILMER, CUTLER & PICKERING (AV)

2445 M Street, N.W., 20037-1420
Telephone: 202-663-6000
Fax: 202-663-6363
Email: Law@Wilmer.Com
Baltimore, Maryland Office: 100 Light Street, 21202.
Telephone: 410-986-2800.
Fax: 410-986-2828.
European Offices:
4 Carlton Gardens, London, SW1Y 5AA, England. Telephone: +44 (171)
872-1000.
Fax: +44 (171) 839-3537.
Rue de la Loi 15Wetstraat, B-1040 Brussels, Belgium. Telephone: +32 (2)
285-4900.
Fax: +32 (2) 285-4949.
Friedrichstrasse 95, D-10117 Berlin, Germany. Telephone: +49 (30)
2022-6400.
Fax: +49 (30)2022-6500.

(See Next Column)

MEMBERS OF FIRM

Joel Rosenbloom   William R. Richardson, Jr.
Daniel Marcus   W. Scott Blackmer
William T. Lake   Thomas P. Olson
John H. Harwood II   Patrick J. Carome

SENIOR COUNSEL
J. Roger Wollenberg
OF COUNSEL
Robert A. Hammond, III   Timothy N. Black

For Complete List of Firm Personnel, See General Section

For full biographical listings, see the Martindale-Hubbell Law Directory

FLORIDA

JACKSONVILLE, * Duval Co.

GABEL & HAIR (AV)

76 South Laura Street, Suite 1600, 32202-3421
Telephone: 904-353-7329
Fax: 904-358-1637
Email: lawoffcs@gabelhair.com

MEMBERS OF FIRM

George D. Gabel, Jr.   Sheldon Boney Forte
Mattox S. Hair   Timothy J. Conner
Joel B. Toomey   Suzanne Meyer Judas
Robert M. Dees   Karen Harris Williams

ASSOCIATES

Michael L. Berry, Jr.   Karl B. Hanson, III
Robert Blaine Birthisel   Brooks Charles Rathet

Scott M. Loftin (1878-1953)   Harold B. Wahl (1907-1993)

Representative Clients: Florida Publishing Co. (Florida Times-Union); Southern Bell Telephone & Telegraph Co.; American District Telegraph Co.; Employers Reinsurance Co.; WTLV Channel 12 TV; Gannett, Inc.; Capital Cities/ABC, Inc.; The New York Times Company; Jacksonville Business Journal; Media/Professional Insurance, Inc.

For full biographical listings, see the Martindale-Hubbell Law Directory

MIAMI, * Dade Co.

MILLEDGE IDEN & HELD (AV)

Suite 600, 2100 Ponce de Leon Boulevard (Coral Gables), 33134
Telephone: 305-445-1500
Facsimile: 305-446-9972

MEMBERS OF FIRM

Allan Milledge   Bruce F. Iden
                      Gary M. Held
ASSOCIATE
Dana J. McElroy
OF COUNSEL
John M. Milledge   Patricia Fields Anderson

Reference: Northern Trust Bank.

For full biographical listings, see the Martindale-Hubbell Law Directory

THOMSON MURARO RAZOOK & HART, P.A. (AV)

17th Floor, One Southeast Third Avenue, 33131
Telephone: 305-350-7200
Telecopier: 305-374-1005

Parker Davidson Thomson   Carol A. Licko

Representative Clients: Community Television Foundation of South Florida; Florida Society of Newspaper Editors; First Amendment Foundation.

For Complete List of Firm Personnel, See General Section

For full biographical listings, see the Martindale-Hubbell Law Directory

TALLAHASSEE, * Leon Co.

HOPPING GREEN SAMS & SMITH, PROFESSIONAL ASSOCIATION (AV)

123 South Calhoun Street, P.O. Box 6526, 32314
Telephone: 904-222-7500
Fax: 904-224-8551

James S. Alves   Ralph A. DeMeo
Brian H. Bibeau   Thomas M. DeRose
Kathleen L. Blizzard   William H. Green
Elizabeth C. Bowman   Wade L. Hopping
Richard S. Brightman   Frank E. Matthews
Peter C. Cunningham   Richard D. Melson

(See Next Column)

HOPPING GREEN SAMS & SMITH PROFESSIONAL ASSOCIATION, *Tallahassee—Continued*

David L. Powell	Douglas S. Roberts
William D. Preston	Gary P. Sams
Carolyn S. Raepple	Robert P. Smith
	Cheryl G. Stuart

Gary K. Hunter, Jr.	Karen Peterson
Jonathan T. Johnson	Michael P. Petrovich
Robert A. Manning	R. Scott Ruth
Angela R. Morrison	W. Steve Sykes
Gary V. Perko	T. Kent Wetherell, II

OF COUNSEL

W. Robert Fokes

Representative Clients: Atlantic Gulf Communities; Dunes and Viera East Community Development Districts; Florida Electric Power Coordinating Group; Florida Power & Light Co.; MCI Telecommunications; Seminole Electric Co.; Sugar Cane Growers Cooperative of Florida; UPS; Waste Management, Inc.; Wheelabrator.

For full biographical listings, see the Martindale-Hubbell Law Directory

GEORGIA

ATLANTA,* Fulton Co.

ALSTON & BIRD (AV)

A Partnership including Professional Corporations
One Atlantic Center, 1201 West Peachtree Street, 30309-3424
Telephone: 404-881-7000
Telecopier: 404-881-7777
Cable Address: AMGRAM GA
Telex: 54-2996
Easylink: 62985848
Washington, D.C. Office: 601 Pennsylvania Ave., N.W., North Building, Suite 250 20004.
Telephone: 202-508-3300.
Telecopier: 202-508-3333.

MEMBERS OF FIRM

L. Clifford Adams, Jr.	Martin J. Elgison
Oscar N. Persons	Patrick J. Flinn
Timothy S. Perry	H. Stephen Harris, Jr.
Peter Kontio	George M. Maxwell, Jr.
William H. Avery	Robert J. Middleton, Jr.
Judson Graves	Michael P. Kenny

ASSOCIATES

Stephen P. Berke	Elise Kirban
(Not admitted in GA)	(Not admitted in GA)
Cynthia L. Counts	Kristen P. Mersereau
Robert B. Cunningham	Lori L. Pruitt Rowland
Kristen K. Darnell	David J. Stewart
Christopher D. Ford	M. Russell Wofford, Jr.
John P. Fry	(Not admitted in GA)
James M. Jordan III	Robert Y. Wood III
James M. Kapenstein	Susan L. Wright
(Not admitted in GA)	

COUNSEL

Janet E. Witt

Representative Clients: Codecomm (Inc.); GTE Mobilnet Incorporated; GTE Personal Communications Services; National Data Corporation.

For Complete List of Firm Personnel, See General Section

For full biographical listings, see the Martindale-Hubbell Law Directory

---

BODKER, RAMSEY & ANDREWS, A PROFESSIONAL CORPORATION (AV)

Suite 615 1800 Peachtree Street, N.W., 30309-2507
Telephone: 404-351-1615
Telecopier: 404-352-1285

Stephen C. Andrews	Harry J. Winograd

For full biographical listings, see the Martindale-Hubbell Law Directory

---

CHOREY, TAYLOR & FEIL, A PROFESSIONAL CORPORATION (AV)

Suite 1700, The Lenox Building, 3399 Peachtree Road, N.E., 30326
Telephone: 404-841-3200
Facsimile: 404-841-3221

Thomas V. Chorey, Jr.	John L. Taylor, Jr.

(See Next Column)

OF COUNSEL

Charles V. Gerkin, Jr.

For Complete List of Firm Personnel, See General Section

For full biographical listings, see the Martindale-Hubbell Law Directory

KILPATRICK & CODY LLP (AV)

Suite 2800, 1100 Peachtree Street, 30309-4530
Telephone: 404-815-6500
Telephone Copier: 404-815-6555
Telex: 54-2307
Washington, D.C. Office: Suite 800, 700 13th Street, N.W., 20005.
Telephone: 202-508-5800. Telephone Copier: 202-508-5858.
Brussels, Belgium Office: Avenue Louise 65, BTE 3, 1050 Brussels.
Telephone: (32) (2) 533-03-00.
Telecopier: (32) (2) 534-86-38.
London, England Office: 68 Pall Mall, London, SW1Y 5ES, England.
Telephone: (44) (71) 321 0477.
Telecopier: (44) (71) 930 9733.
Augusta, Georgia Office: Suite 1400 First Union Bank Building, P.O. Box 2043, 30903. Telephone (706) 724-2622. Telecopier (706) 722-0219.

OF COUNSEL

George B. Haley

MEMBERS OF FIRM

Harold E. Abrams	R. Alexander Bransford, Jr.
W. Stanley Blackburn	Jerre B. Swann
	Frederick H. von Unwerth

For Complete List of Firm Personnel, See General Section

For full biographical listings, see the Martindale-Hubbell Law Directory

LONG ALDRIDGE & NORMAN, LLP (AV)

A Limited Liability Partnership including Professional Corporations
One Peachtree Center, Suite 5300, 303 Peachtree Street, 30308
Telephone: 404-527-4000
Telecopier: 404-527-4198
Washington, D.C. Office: Suite 600, 701 Pennsylvania Avenue, N.W., 20004.
Telephone: 202-624-1200.
FAX: 202-624-1298.

MEMBERS OF FIRM

Stephen L. Camp	Clay C. Long
Jeffrey K. Haidet	Albert G. Norman, Jr.

SENIOR COUNSEL

F. T. Davis, Jr., (P.C.)

ASSOCIATES

Wayne N. Bradley	H. Franklin Layson
	Briggs L. Tobin

For Complete List of Firm Personnel, See General Section

For full biographical listings, see the Martindale-Hubbell Law Directory

---

ILLINOIS

CHICAGO,* Cook Co.

SAUNDERS & MONROE (AV)

Suite 4201, 205 North Michigan Avenue, 60601
Telephone: 312-946-9000
Facsimile: 312-946-0528

MEMBERS OF FIRM

George L. Saunders, Jr.	Thomas F. Bush, Jr.
Lee A. Monroe	Matthew E. Van Tine
	Thomas A. Doyle

Gwen A. Niedbalski

OF COUNSEL

Kenneth K. Howell	Victoria S. Kaplan

For full biographical listings, see the Martindale-Hubbell Law Directory

---

PEORIA,* Peoria Co.

HOWARD & HOWARD ATTORNEYS, P.C. (AV)

The Creve Coeur Building, Suite 200, 321 Liberty Street, 61602-1403
Telephone: 309-672-1483
Telecopier: 309-672-1568
Kalamazoo, Michigan Office: The Kalamazoo Building, Suite 400, 107 West Michigan Avenue.
Telephone: 616-382-1483.
Telecopier: 616-382-1568.

(See Next Column)

HOWARD & HOWARD ATTORNEYS, P.C.—*Continued*

Bloomfield Hills, Michigan Office: The Pinehurst Office Center, Suite 101, 1400 North Woodward Avenue.
Telephone: 810-645-1483.
Telecopier: 810-645-1568.
Lansing, Michigan Office: Suite 500, The Phoenix Building, 222 Washington Square, North.
Telephone: 517-485-1483.
Telecopier: 517-485-1568.
Tampa, Florida Office: First of America Plaza, Suite 2000, 201 East Kennedy Boulevard.
Telephone: 813-229-1483.
Telecopier: 813-229-1568.

Frederick G. Hoffman

Representative Clients: For Representative Client list, see General Practice, Peoria, IL.

For Complete List of Firm Personnel, See General Section

For full biographical listings, see the Martindale-Hubbell Law Directory

INDIANA

*INDIANAPOLIS,** Marion Co.

BOSE MCKINNEY & EVANS (AV)

2700 First Indiana Plaza, 135 North Pennsylvania Street, 46204
Telephone: 317-684-5000
Facsimile: 317-684-5173
Indianapolis North Office: Suite 1201, 8888 Keystone Crossing, 46240.
Telephone: 317-574-3700.
Facsimile: 317-574-3716.

MEMBERS OF FIRM

Kendall C. Crook	David L. Wills
Ronald E. Elberger	Alan W. Becker
Dwight L. Miller	

Representative Clients: David Letterman Companies; Columbia Management, Inc.; Emmis Broadcasting Corp.; Apollo Communications Corporation; Hebdo Mag International; LeSea Broadcasting Corp.; Atlanta Magazine; Nuvo News-Weekly; Indianapolis Monthly.

For Complete List of Firm Personnel, See General Section

For full biographical listings, see the Martindale-Hubbell Law Directory

ICE MILLER DONADIO & RYAN (AV)

One American Square Box 82001, 46282-0002
Telephone: 317-236-2100
Fax: 317-236-2219
Email: leel@imdr.com *URL:* http://www.imdr.com
South Bend, Indiana Office: 211 West Washington Street, Suite 2420.
Telephone: 219-234-7933.
Fax: 219-234-7965. Internet E-mail: leel@imdr.com. Web Site Address: http://www.imdr.com.

MEMBERS OF FIRM

Donald G. Sutherland	Thomas H. Ristine
Jack R. Snyder	Marcus B. Chandler
Michael A. Wilkins	

OF COUNSEL

James B. Burroughs

ASSOCIATE

Paul H. Sinclair

Representative Clients: Indiana Broadcasters Assn.; Fairbanks Communications, Inc.; VideoIndiana, Inc.; Michiana Telecasting Corp.; National Broadcasting Co.; Wabash Valley Broadcasting Corp.; IMS Broadcasting; Butler University; Taylor University; Great American Television & Radio Co.

For Complete List of Firm Personnel, See General Section

For full biographical listings, see the Martindale-Hubbell Law Directory

KANSAS

*TOPEKA,** Shawnee Co.

GOODELL, STRATTON, EDMONDS & PALMER, L.L.P. (AV)

515 South Kansas Avenue, 66603-3999
Telephone: 913-233-0593
Telecopier: 913-233-8870
Email: GSEP@CJNETWORKS.COM

(See Next Column)

MEMBERS OF FIRM

Gerald L. Goodell	Michael W. Merriam
Arthur E. Palmer	John H. Stauffer, Jr.
Charles R. Hay	John D. Ensley

SPECIAL COUNSEL

Curtis J. Waugh

Counsel for: Morris Communications; Media Professional Insurance; Topeka Capital Journal; WIBW-AM, FM, TV; Associated Press; Libel Defense Resource Center; Kansas Association of Broadcasters; Kansas Press Association; Reporters Committee for Freedom of the Press.

For Complete List of Firm Personnel, See General Section

For full biographical listings, see the Martindale-Hubbell Law Directory

KENTUCKY

*LEXINGTON,** Fayette Co.

STOLL, KEENON & PARK, LLP (AV)

201 E. Main Street, Suite 1000, 40507-1380
Telephone: 606-231-3000
Telecopier: 606-253-1093; 606-253-1027
Frankfort, Kentucky Office: 307 Washington Street, 40601.
Telephone: 502-875-6220.
Telecopier: 502-875-6235.
Louisville, Kentucky Office: 400 West Market Street, Suite 2650, 40202-3377.
Telephone: 502-568-9100.
Telecopier: 502-568-5700.

MEMBERS OF FIRM

Robert F. Houlihan, Jr.	Dan M. Rose

ASSOCIATE

James L. Thomerson

Representative Clients: Lexington Herald Leader Co.; Knight-Ridder; GTE Of The South, GTE Products Corp.; BellSouth Mobility; Kentucky Press Assn.; Thompson Newspapers Inc.; Thoroughbred Racing Communications, Inc.; The Jockey Club.

For Complete List of Firm Personnel, See General Section

For full biographical listings, see the Martindale-Hubbell Law Directory

*LOUISVILLE,** Jefferson Co.

WYATT, TARRANT & COMBS (AV)

Citizens Plaza, 40202
Telephone: 502-589-5235
Telecopier: 502-589-0309
URL: http://www.wyattfirm.com
Lexington, Kentucky Office: 1700 Lexington Financial Center.
Telephone: 606-233-2012.
Telecopier: 606-259-0649.
Frankfort, Kentucky Office: The Taylor-Scott Building, 311 West Main Street.
Telephone: 502-223-2104.
Telecopier: 502-227-7681.
New Albany, Indiana Office: The Elsby Building, 117 East Spring Street,
Telephone: 812-945-3561.
Telecopier: 812-949-2524.
Memphis, Tennessee Office: Crescent Center, Suite 650, 6075 Poplar Avenue.
Telephone: 901-537-1000.
Telecopier: 901-537-1010.
Nashville, Tennessee Office: 1500 Nashville City Center, 511 Union Street.
Telephone: 615-244-0020.
Telecopier: 615-256-1726.
Music Row, Nashville Office: 29 Music Square East.
Telephone: 615-255-6161.
Telecopier: 615-254-4490.
Hendersonville, Tennessee Office: 313 E. Main Street, Suite 1.
Telephone: 615-822-8822.
Telecopier: 615-824-4684.

MEMBERS OF FIRM

Edgar A. Zingman	Kimberly K. Greene
Jon L. Fleischaker	William H. Hollander

Representative Clients: Alpha Cellular Telephone Co.; BellSouth Telecommunications, Inc./South Central Bell; Data Courier, Inc.; Gannett Co., Inc./The Courier-Journal/Louisville Times; Kentucky Press Assn.; Kentucky Cable Television Assn.; McCann-Erickson of Louisville, Inc.; Telecable of Lexington; Thomas Nelson Publishers, Inc.; WHAS and WHAS T.V.

For Complete List of Firm Personnel, See General Section

For full biographical listings, see the Martindale-Hubbell Law Directory

LOUISIANA

SHREVEPORT,* Caddo Parish

BARLOW AND HARDTNER L.C. (AV)

Tenth Floor, Louisiana Tower, 401 Edwards Street, 71101-3289
Telephone: 318-227-1131
Telecopier: 318-227-1141
Mailing Address: P.O. Box 8, Shreveport, Louisiana, 71161-0008

Joseph L. Shea, Jr.   Jay A. Greenleaf
OF COUNSEL
Paula Hazelrig Hickman

Representative Clients: AmCom General Corporation; NorAm Energy Corp. (formerly Arkla, Inc.); Panhandle Eastern Corp.; Pennzoil Producing Co.; Johnson Controls, Inc.; Ashland Oil, Inc.

For Complete List of Firm Personnel, See General Section

For full biographical listings, see the Martindale-Hubbell Law Directory

MAINE

PORTLAND,* Cumberland Co.

PETRUCCELLI & MARTIN (AV)

50 Monument Square, P.O. Box 9733, 04104-5033
Telephone: 207-775-0200
Telecopier: 207-775-2360

MEMBER OF FIRM
Joel C. Martin
ASSOCIATE
John Anderson

Representatives Clients: The Camden Herald; Journal Transcript Newspapers, Inc.; Northeast Cellular Telephone Co., L.P.; Pine Tree Tel & Tel Co.

For full biographical listings, see the Martindale-Hubbell Law Directory

PRETI, FLAHERTY, BELIVEAU & PACHIOS (AV)

A Limited Liability Company
443 Congress Street, P.O. Box 11410, 04104-7410
Telephone: 207-791-3000
Telecopier: 207-791-3111
Email: admin@pfbpnet.com
Augusta, Maine Office: 45 Memorial Circle, P.O. Box 1058, 04332-1058.
Telephone: 207-623-5300.
Telecopier: 207-623-2914.

MEMBERS OF FIRM
Severin M. Beliveau   Edward R. Benjamin, Jr.
(Augusta Office)   Ann R. Robinson
Jonathan S. Piper   (Augusta Office)
OF COUNSEL
Mark B. LeDuc (Augusta Office)

Representative Clients: Guy Gannett Publishing Company; Maine Association of Broadcasters; Brunswick Publishing Co.; The Maine Times; State Cable T.V. Corporation; Bee Line Cable, Inc.; Better Cable Television; Public Cable Co.; New England Cable Television Association.

For Complete List of Firm Personnel, See General Section

For full biographical listings, see the Martindale-Hubbell Law Directory

MARYLAND

BALTIMORE,* (Independent City)

VENABLE ATTORNEYS AT LAW VENABLE, BAETJER AND HOWARD, LLP (AV)

A Partnership including Professional Corporations
1800 Mercantile Bank & Trust Building, 2 Hopkins Plaza, 21201
Telephone: 410-244-7400
Email: INFO@Venable.win.net
Washington, D.C. Office: Venable, Baetjer, Howard & Civiletti LLP. Suite 1000, 1201 New York Avenue, N.W.
Telephone: 202-962-4800.
McLean, Virginia Office: Suite 400, 2010 Corporate Ridge.
Telephone: 703-760-1600.
Rockville, Maryland Office: Suite 500, One Church Street, P. O. Box 1906.
Telephone: 301-217-5600.
Towson, Maryland Office: 210 Allegheny Avenue, P. O. Box 5517.
Telephone: 410-494-6200.

(See Next Column)

MEMBERS OF FIRM
Thomas P. Perkins, III (P.C.)   James R. Myers (Not admitted
James A. Cole   in MD; Resident, Washington,
Ian D. Volner (Not admitted in   D.C. Office)
MD; Resident, Washington,   Jeffrey D. Knowles (Not
D.C. Office)   admitted in MD; Resident,
Edward F. Glynn, Jr. (Resident,   Washington, D.C. Office)
Washington, D.C. Office)
OF COUNSEL
Frank Horton (Not admitted in MD; Resident, Washington, D.C. Office)

For Complete List of Firm Personnel, See General Section

For full biographical listings, see the Martindale-Hubbell Law Directory

MASSACHUSETTS

BOSTON,* Suffolk Co.

MINTZ, LEVIN, COHN, FERRIS, GLOVSKY AND POPEO, P.C. (AV)

One Financial Center, 02111
Telephone: 617-542-6000
FAX: 617-542-2241
Internet: Each Attorney's Internet Address takes the following form: first initial last name @mintz.com (e.g., rmintz@mintz.com)
Washington, D.C. Office: 701 Pennsylvania Avenue, N.W. Suite 900.
Telephone: 202-434-7300.
Fax: 202-434-7400.

Charles D. Ferris (Resident,   Bruce D. Sokler (Resident,
Washington, D.C. Office)   Washington, D.C. Office)
Frank W. Lloyd (Resident,   Howard J. Symons (Resident,
Washington, D.C. Office)   Washington, D.C. Office)

For Complete List of Firm Personnel, See General Section

For full biographical listings, see the Martindale-Hubbell Law Directory

PALMER & DODGE LLP (AV)

One Beacon Street, 02108
Telephone: 617-573-0100
Facsimile: 617-227-4420

MEMBERS OF FIRM
F. Andrew Anderson   Jeffrey F. Jones
F. Kingston Berlew   Stanley Keller
Robert Duggan   David R. Pokross, Jr.
Lynnette C. Fallon   George Ticknor
Mark A. Fischer   William T. Whelan
Nathaniel S. Gardiner   John Taylor Williams
Laurie S. Gill   William Williams II
Peter Wirth
COUNSEL
Jay E. Gruber

For Complete List of Firm Personnel, See General Section

For full biographical listings, see the Martindale-Hubbell Law Directory

MICHIGAN

BLOOMFIELD HILLS, Oakland Co.

ADKISON NEED (AV)

1533 North Woodward Avenue, Suite 210, 48304
Telephone: 810-540-7400
Fax: 810-540-7401
Email: AdkisNeed@aol.com

MEMBERS OF FIRM
Phillip G. Adkison   Paul Green
Gregory K. Need   Kelly A. Allen
Deborah M. Schneider
ASSOCIATES
Kathryn N. Nichols   Laura B. Andoni

For Complete List of Firm Personnel, See General Section

For full biographical listings, see the Martindale-Hubbell Law Directory

DETROIT, * Wayne Co.

BODMAN, LONGLEY & DAHLING LLP (AV)

34th Floor 100 Renaissance Center, 48243
Telephone: 313-259-7777
Fax: 313-393-7579
Email: 2080194@mcimail.com
Troy, Michigan Office: Suite 2020, 755 West Big Beaver Road.
Telephone: 810-362-2110.
Fax: 810-244-0780.
Ann Arbor, Michigan Office: 110 Miller, Suite 300.
Telephone: 313-761-3780.
Fax: 313-930-2494.
Northern Michigan Office: 229 Court Street, P.O. Box 405, Cheboygan.
Telephone: 616-627-4351.
Fax: 616-627-2802.

MEMBERS OF FIRM

Theodore Souris	Kenneth R. Lango (Troy Office)
Carson C. Grunewald	James A. Smith
	James J. Walsh

For Representative Client List, See General Section

For Complete List of Firm Personnel, See General Section

For full biographical listings, see the Martindale-Hubbell Law Directory

BUTZEL LONG, A PROFESSIONAL CORPORATION (AV)

Suite 900, 150 West Jefferson, 48226
Telephone: 313-225-7000
Telecopier: 313-225-7080
Email: melnick@butzel.com *URL:* http://www.butzel.com
Birmingham, Michigan Office: Suite 200, 32270 Telegraph Road.
Telephone: 810-258-1616.
Telecopier: 810-258-1439.
Lansing, Michigan Office: 118 West Ottawa Street.
Telephone: 517-372-6622.
Telecopier: 517-372-6672.
Ann Arbor, Michigan Office: Suite 300, 350 South Main Street.
Telephone: 313-995-3110.
Telecopier: 313-995-1777.
Grosse Pointe Farms, Michigan Office: Suite 260, 21 Kercheval.
Telephone: 313-886-5446.
Telecopier: 313-886-2114.

William R. Ralls (Lansing)	Leonard M. Niehoff
Richard E. Rassel	(Ann Arbor)
	J. Michael Huget (Ann Arbor)

Eugene H. Boyle, Jr.	Barbara L. McQuade
Robin K. Luce	Laurie J. Michelson

Representative Clients: Booth Newspapers, Inc.; CBS, Inc.; Crain Communications, Inc.; The Detroit News, Inc.; Gannett Co., Inc.; Infinity Broadcasting; Paramount Pictures; Stroh Brewery Co.; United Parcel Services of America, Inc.; The University of Michigan.

For Complete List of Firm Personnel, See General Section

For full biographical listings, see the Martindale-Hubbell Law Directory

CLARK HILL P.L.C. (AV)

500 Woodward Avenue, Suite 3500, 48226
Telephone: 313-965-8300
Facsimile: 313-962-4348
Oakland County, Michigan Office: Third Floor, 255 South Woodward Avenue, Birmingham.
Telephone: 810-642-9692.
Facsimile: 810-642-2174.
Lansing, Michigan Office: Suite 600, 200 North Capitol Avenue.
Telephone: 517-484-4481.
Facsimile: 517-484-1246.
Minneapolis, Minnesota Office: Suite 1000, One Financial Plaza, 120 South Sixth Street.
Telephone: 612-332-0102.
Facsimile: 612-332-3225.
Kansas City, Missouri Office: Suite 1400, Bryant Building, 1102 Grand Avenue.
Telephone: 816-221-5578.
Facsimile: 816-221-0303.

David E. Nims, III

Representative Clients: Booth American Company.

For Complete List of Firm Personnel, See General Section

For full biographical listings, see the Martindale-Hubbell Law Directory

HONIGMAN MILLER SCHWARTZ AND COHN (AV)

A Partnership including Professional Corporations
2290 First National Building, 48226
Telephone: 313-256-7800
Telecopier: 313-962-0176
Telex: 235705
URL: http://law.honigman.com
Lansing, Michigan Office: Phoenix Building, 222 North Washington Square, Suite 400, 48933-1800.
Telephone: 517-484-8282.
West Palm Beach, Florida Office: Suite 800 Esperante Building, 222 Lakeview Avenue, 33401-6112.
Telephone: 561-838-4500.
Tampa, Florida Office: 2700 SunTrust Financial Centre, 401 E. Jackson Street, 33602-5226.
Telephone: 813-221-6600.

MEMBER OF FIRM
Herschel P. Fink
RESIDENT IN WEST PALM BEACH, FLORIDA OFFICE
MEMBER
Steven L. Schwarzberg (P.A.)
RESIDENT IN TAMPA, FLORIDA OFFICE
MEMBER
Gregory G. Jones (P.A.)

Representative Clients: The Detroit Free Press; Knight-Ridder Inc.; Capital Cities/ABC, Inc.; Crain Communications; Heritage Media Corp. (Mellus Newspapers, Dearborn Press and Guide, and News Herald Newspapers); National Broadcasting Co.; Fox, Inc.; New World Television, Paramount Group Stations; American Society of Composers, Authors and Publishers (ASCAP).

For Complete List of Firm Personnel, See General Section

For full biographical listings, see the Martindale-Hubbell Law Directory

MILLER, CANFIELD, PADDOCK AND STONE, P.L.C. (AV)

A Professional Limited Liability Company
Founded in 1852 by Sidney Davy Miller
150 West Jefferson, Suite 2500, 48226-4415
Telephone: 313-963-6420
Fax: 313-496-7500
Cable Address: "Stem Detroit"
Detroit, Michigan Office: 150 West Jefferson, Suite 2500, 48226-4415.
Telephone: 313-963-6420.
Fax: 313-496-7500.
Cable Address: "Stem Detroit."
Ann Arbor, Michigan Office: 101 North Main Street, 7th Floor, 48104-1400.
Telephone: 313-663-2445.
Fax: 313-747-7147.
Bloomfield Hills, Michigan Office: Suite 100, Pinehurst Office Center, 1400 North Woodward, 48303-2014.
Telephone: 313-645-5000.
Fax: 313-645-1917.
Grand Rapids, Michigan Office: 1200 Campau Square Plaza, 99 Monroe, N.W., 49503-2639.
Telephone: 616-454-8656.
Fax: 616-776-6322.
Howell, Michigan Office: 121 South Barnard Street, Suite 4, 48843-2305.
Telephone: 517-546-7600.
Telecopier: 517-546-6974.
Kalamazoo, Michigan Office: 444 West Michigan Avenue, 49007-3752.
Telephone: 616-381-7030.
Fax: 616-382-0244.
Lansing, Michigan Office: One Michigan Avenue, Suite 900, 48933-1609.
Telephone: 517-487-2070.
Fax: 517-374-6304.
Monroe, Michigan Office: The Executive Centre, 214 East Elm Avenue, 48161-2682.
Telephone: 313-243-2000.
Fax: 313-243-0901.
Washington, D.C. Office: 1225 Nineteenth Street, N.W., Suite 400. 20036.
Telephone: 202-429-5575; 785-0600.
Fax: 202-331-1118; 785-1234.
Pensacola, Florida Office: 25 West Cedar, 32501.
Telephone: 904-469-1088.
Fax: 904-432-0677.
St. Petersburg, Florida Office: 100 Second Avenue S., Suite 7045, 33701.
Telephone: 813-982-6000.
Fax: 813-892-6002.
New York, New York Office: Eleventh Floor, 135 East 57th Street, 10022-2087.
Telephone: 212-754-5400.
Fax: 212-754-5401.
Gdansk, Poland Office: Suite 322, Dom Technika Building, UI. Rajska 6, 80-850.
Telephone: 011-485-831-2808.
Fax: 011-485-831-4719.

(See Next Column)

MILLER, CANFIELD, PADDOCK AND STONE P.L.C., *Detroit—Continued*

Warsaw, Poland Office: UI. Marszalkowska 82, Suite 561, 00-517.
Telephone: 011-482-623-6457 and 6458.
Fax: 011-482-623-6459.

PRINCIPALS OF FIRM

John J. Collins, Jr.   (Bloomfield Hills Office)

OF COUNSEL

Nicholas P. Miller   (Washington, D.C. Office)

Representative Firm Clients: Chrysler Corporation; Comerica, Incorporated; City of Detroit, Michigan; Detroit Tigers, Inc.; First of Michigan; Ford Motor Company; Ford Motor Credit Company; Great Lakes Bancorp; Henry Ford Hospital; INVETECH Company.

For Complete List of Firm Personnel, See General Section

For full biographical listings, see the Martindale-Hubbell Law Directory

---

KALAMAZOO,* Kalamazoo Co.

HOWARD & HOWARD ATTORNEYS, P.C. (AV)

The Kalamazoo Building, Suite 400, 107 West Michigan
   Avenue, 49007-3956
Telephone: 616-382-1483
Telecopier: 616-382-1568
Bloomfield Hills, Michigan Office: The Pinehurst Office Center, Suite 101, 1400 North Woodward Avenue.
Telephone: 810-645-1483.
Telecopier: 810-645-1568.
Lansing, Michigan Office: The Phoenix Building, Suite 500, 222 Washington Square North.
Telephone: 517-485-1483.
Telecopier: 517-485-1568.
Peoria, Illinois Office: The Creve Coeur Building, Suite 200, 321 Liberty Street.
Telephone: 309-672-1483.
Telecopier: 309-672-1568.
Tampa, Florida Office: First of America Plaza, Suite 2000, 201 East Kennedy Boulevard.
Telephone: 813-229-1483.
Telecopier: 813-229-1568.

Eric E. Breisach   D. Craig Martin

Representative Clients: For Representative Client list, see General Practice, Kalamazoo, MI.

For Complete List of Firm Personnel, See General Section

For full biographical listings, see the Martindale-Hubbell Law Directory

---

LANSING, Ingham Co.

HOWARD & HOWARD ATTORNEYS, P.C. (AV)

The Phoenix Building, Suite 500, 222 Washington Square,
   North, 48933-1817
Telephone: 517-485-1483
Telecopier: 517-485-1568
Kalamazoo, Michigan Office: The Kalamazoo Building, Suite 400, 107 West Michigan Avenue.
Telephone: 616-382-1483.
Telecopier: 616-382-1568.
Bloomfield Hills, Michigan Office: The Pinehurst Office Center, Suite 101, 1400 North Woodward Avenue.
Telephone: 810-645-1483.
Telecopier: 810-645-1568.
Peoria, Illinois Office: The Creve Coeur Building, Suite 200, 321 Liberty Street.
Telephone: 309-672-1483.
Telecopier: 309-672-1568.
Tampa, Florida Office: First of America Plaza, Suite 2000, 201 East Kennedy Boulevard.
Telephone: 813-229-1483.
Telecopier: 813-229-1568.

Christopher C. Cinnamon   Kim D. Crooks

Representative Clients: For Representative Client list, see General Practice, Lansing, MI.

For Complete List of Firm Personnel, See General Section

For full biographical listings, see the Martindale-Hubbell Law Directory

---

TROY, Oakland Co.

HACKETT, MAXWELL & PHILLIPS, P.L.L.C. (AV)

City Center Building, Suite 1470, 888 West Big Beaver Road, 48084
Telephone: 810-362-2600
Fax: 810-362-3610
Email: hackmax@michbar.org

Patrick E. Hackett   Phillip B. Maxwell
                    Dawn L. Phillips

Mark T. Butler   Lisa Rycus Mikalonis
Jill Tilton Silverman   Jason W. Johnson

For full biographical listings, see the Martindale-Hubbell Law Directory

COMPUTER LAW

ALABAMA

*BIRMINGHAM,** Jefferson Co.

BRADLEY, ARANT, ROSE & WHITE (AV)

2001 Park Place, Suite 1400, P.O. Box 830709, 35283-0709
Telephone: 205-521-8000
Facsimile: 205-252-0264
Facsimile (SouthTrust Tower Office): 205-251-9915
URL: http://www.BARW.COM
Huntsville, Alabama Office: 200 Clinton Avenue West, Suite 900, 35801.
Telephone: 205-517-5100.
Facsimile: 205-533-5069.

MEMBER OF FIRM
David Glenn Hymer

For Complete List of Firm Personnel, See General Section

For full biographical listings, see the Martindale-Hubbell Law Directory

CALIFORNIA

COSTA MESA, Orange Co.

RUTAN & TUCKER, LLP (AV)

A Partnership including Professional Corporations
611 Anton Boulevard, Suite 1400, P.O. Box 1950, 92626
Telephone: 714-641-5100; 213-625-7586
Telecopier: 714-546-9035
Email: rutan&tucker@mcimail.com *URL:* http://www.rutan.com
MEMBERS OF FIRM
Edward D. Sybesma, Jr., (P.C.)   Michael T. Hornak
Thomas J. Crane

For Complete List of Firm Personnel, See General Section

For full biographical listings, see the Martindale-Hubbell Law Directory

GLENDALE, Los Angeles Co.

HAGENBAUGH & MURPHY (AV)

A Partnership including Professional Corporations
700 North Central Avenue, Suite 500, 91203
Telephone: 818-240-2600
Fax: 818-240-1253
Email: hmurphy@interserv.com *URL:* http://www.seamless.com/hm/
Orange County, California Office: 701 South Parker Street, Suite 8200, Orange.
Telephone: 714-835-5406.
Fax: 714-835-5949.
San Bernardino, California Office: 301 Vanderbilt Way, Suite 220.
Telephone: 909-884-5331.
FAX: 909-889-1250.

Van A. Hagenbaugh (1914-1980)	Daniel A. Leipold (Resident,
Sigurd E. Murphy (1903-1976)	Orange County Office)
William D. Stewart (A P.C.)	Craig D. Aronson
John J. Tary (A P.C.)	Paul G. Szumiak
Raymond R. Moore (A P.C.)	Robert F. Donohue (Resident,
Neil R. Gunny (Resident,	Orange County Office)
Orange County Office)	Katharine L. Spaniac (Resident,
Alan R. Zuckerman	San Bernardino Office)
David L. Winter	Alan H. Boon (Resident, Orange
Mary E. Porter	County Office)
	Jamie B. Skebba

Raymond T. Gail (Resident, San	Cathy L. Shipe (Resident,
Bernardino Office)	Orange County Office)
Kirk G. Neiberger	Keri Lynn Bush
Meredith A. Musicant	Michael A. Tonya
David M. Chute (Resident,	Laura C. McLennan
Orange County Office)	Graciela L. Freixes
Luanne Walsh	Melinda W. Ebelhar
Rhonda L. Etzwiler	Kirk N. Sullivan
Steven M. Schuetze	Gary P. Simonian
Thomas J. Heatly	Mark Habeeb
Matthew R. Rungaitis	Howard J. Hirsch (Resident,
Stephen Barry	Orange County Office)
Julie M. DeRose	Michelle Mann
Randal A. Whitecotton	
(Resident, San Bernardino	
Office)	

(See Next Column)

Representative Clients: Farmers Insurance Group; Truck Insurance Exchange; Fire Insurance Exchange.

For full biographical listings, see the Martindale-Hubbell Law Directory

LAGUNA HILLS, Orange Co.

STETINA BRUNDA & BUYAN, A PROFESSIONAL CORPORATION (AV)

Suite 401, 24221 Calle De La Louisa, 92653
Telephone: 714-855-1246
Telex: 704355
Facsimile: 714-855-6371
Email: 104052.1330@compuserve.com

Kit M. Stetina (Mr.)	Bruce B. Brunda
	Robert Dean Buyan

Mark B. Garred	Thomas C. Naber
William J. Brucker	(Not admitted in CA)
Matthew A. Newboles	Darren S. Rimer

LEGAL SUPPORT PERSONNEL

Norman E. Carte	Kristy Kay Moore

For full biographical listings, see the Martindale-Hubbell Law Directory

*LOS ANGELES,** Los Angeles Co.

BERMAN, BLANCHARD, MAUSNER & RESSER, A LAW CORPORATION (AV)

4727 Wilshire Boulevard, Suite 500, 90010
Telephone: 213-965-1200
Telecopier: 213-965-1919
Email: BBMR@ix.netcom.com

Laurence M. Berman	Jeffrey N. Mausner
Lonnie C. Blanchard, III	Bernard M. Resser

Paul A. Hoffman	Cary P. Ocon
Eric Levinrad	Lisé Hamilton

For full biographical listings, see the Martindale-Hubbell Law Directory

STEVEN J. STANWYCK (AV)

1900 Avenue of the Stars, Suite 1700, 90067-4403
Telephone: 310-557-8390
Telecopier: 310-557-8391

For full biographical listings, see the Martindale-Hubbell Law Directory

*OAKLAND,** Alameda Co.

PEZZOLA & REINKE, A PROFESSIONAL CORPORATION (AV)

Suite 1300, Lake Merritt Plaza, 1999 Harrison Street, 94612
Telephone: 510-273-8750
Telecopier: 510-834-7440
San Francisco, California Office: 650 California Street, 32nd Floor, 94111.
Telephone: 415-989-9710.
Menlo Park, California Office: 3000 Sand Hill Road, Building 4, Suite 160, 94025.
Telephone: 415-854-8797.

Stephen P. Pezzola	Donald C. Reinke
	Bruce D. Whitley

OF COUNSEL
Robert E. Krebs

Representative Clients: Vertisoft Systems, Inc.; Ultimate Media Enterprises; Tom Sawyer Software, Inc.; TA Engineering, Inc.; Vision Software, Inc.; Ubique, Ltd.; Midwest Microelectronics, Inc.

For full biographical listings, see the Martindale-Hubbell Law Directory

*SAN DIEGO,** San Diego Co.

LINDLEY, LAZAR & SCALES, A PROFESSIONAL CORPORATION (AV)

One America Plaza, 600 West Broadway, Suite 1400, 92101-3302
Telephone: 619-234-9181
Fax: 619-234-8475
Email: 104413.1175@compuserve.com

Luke R. Corbett	Richard J. Pekin, Jr.
John M. Seitman	George C. Lazar
Robert M. McLeod	Raymond L. Heidemann
William E. Johns	James Henry Fox
Stephen F. Treadgold	Elise Streicher Rogerson
Michael H. Wexler	R. Gordon Huckins
	Kenneth C. Jones

(See Next Column)

LINDLEY, LAZAR & SCALES A PROFESSIONAL CORPORATION, *San Diego—Continued*

Marc A. Geffen

Representative Clients: Palomar Savings & Loan Assn.; McGraw-Hill Broadcasting Co.; Chicago Title Insurance Co.; San Diego Hospital Assn.; Bank of Commerce; City Chevrolet; Ham Bros. Construction Co.; Commonwealth Land Title Insurance Co.; Ponte Builders; Morrison Homes, Inc.

For Complete List of Firm Personnel, See General Section

For full biographical listings, see the Martindale-Hubbell Law Directory

DISTRICT OF COLUMBIA

WASHINGTON, D.C. Co.

DOW, LOHNES & ALBERTSON, PLLC (AV)

1200 New Hampshire Avenue, N.W. Suite 800, 20036-6802
Telephone: 202-776-2000
Facsimile: 202-776-2222
Email: postmaster@dla.com *URL:* http://www.dlalaw.com
Atlanta, Georgia Office: One Ravinia Drive, Suite 1600.
Telephone: 770-901-8800.
Telecopier: 770-901-8874.

MEMBER OF THE FIRM
Richard D. Marks

For Complete List of Firm Personnel, See General Section

For full biographical listings, see the Martindale-Hubbell Law Directory

MILLER, CANFIELD, PADDOCK AND STONE, P.L.C. (AV)

A Professional Limited Liability Company
Founded in 1852 by Sidney Davy Miller
1225 Nineteenth Street, N.W., Suite 400, 20036
Telephone: 202-429-5575; 785-0600
Fax: 202-331-1118; 785-1234
URL: http://www.millercanfield.com
Detroit, Michigan Office: 150 West Jefferson, Suite 2500, 48226-4415.
Telephone: 313-963-6420.
Fax: 313-496-7500.
Cable Address: "Stem Detroit."
Ann Arbor, Michigan Office: 101 North Main Street, 7th Floor, 48104-1400.
Telephone: 313-663-2445.
Fax: 313-747-7147.
Bloomfield Hills, Michigan Office: Suite 100, Pinehurst Office Center, 1400 North Woodward, 48303-2014.
Telephone: 313-645-5000.
Fax: 313-645-1917.
Grand Rapids, Michigan Office: 1200 Campau Square Plaza, 99 Monroe, N.W., 49503-2639.
Telephone: 616-454-8656.
Fax: 616-776-6322.
Howell, Michigan Office: 121 South Barnard Street, Suite 4, 48843-2305.
Telephone: 517-546-7600.
Telecopier: 517-546-6974.
Kalamazoo, Michigan Office: 444 West Michigan Avenue, 49007-3752.
Telephone: 616-381-7030.
Fax: 616-382-0244.
Lansing, Michigan Office: One Michigan Avenue, Suite 900, 48933-1609.
Telephone: 517-487-2070.
Fax: 517-374-6304.
Monroe, Michigan Office: The Executive Centre, 214 East Elm Avenue, 48161-2682.
Telephone: 313-243-2000.
Fax: 313-243-0901.
Pensacola, Florida Office: 25 West Cedar 32501.
Telephone: 904-469-1088.
Fax: 904-432-0677.
St. Petersburg, Florida Office: 100 Second Avenue S., Suite 7045, 33701.
Telephone: 813-982-6000.
Fax: 813-892-6002.
New York, New York Office: Eleventh Floor, 135 East 57th Street, 10022-2087.
Telephone: 212-754-5400.
Fax: 212-754-5401.
Gdansk, Poland Office: Suite 322, Dom Technika Building, UI. Rajska 6, 80-850.
Telephone: 011-485-831-2808.
Fax: 011-485-831-4719.
Warsaw, Poland Office: UI. Marszalkowska 82, Suite 561, 00-517.
Telephone: 011-482-623-6457 and 6458.
Fax: 011-482-623-6459.

(See Next Column)

OF COUNSEL

Nicholas P. Miller   Tillman L. Lay
Joseph Van Eaton   William R. Malone

For full biographical listings, see the Martindale-Hubbell Law Directory

GEORGIA

*ATLANTA,** Fulton Co.

HICKS, MALOOF & CAMPBELL, A PROFESSIONAL CORPORATION (AV)

Suite 2200 Marquis Two Tower, 285 Peachtree Center Avenue, 30303-1234
Telephone: 404-588-1100
Telecopy: 404-420-7474

Robert E. Hicks   Steven K. Bender
Maurice Ted Maloof   Lisa W. Wannamaker
James E. Meadows

For full biographical listings, see the Martindale-Hubbell Law Directory

LOUIS T. ISAF, P.C. (AV)

6445 Powers Ferry Road, Suite 230, 30339-2909
Telephone: 770-951-2623
Fax: 770-612-9713

Louis T. Isaf

For full biographical listings, see the Martindale-Hubbell Law Directory

ROSWELL, Fulton Co.

FREDERICK L. COOPER, III A PROFESSIONAL CORPORATION (AV)

2370 Roxburgh Drive, Suite 100, 30076
Telephone: 770-664-8555
Facsimile: 770-667-9203

Frederick L. Cooper, III

Reference: Bank Atlanta.

For full biographical listings, see the Martindale-Hubbell Law Directory

ILLINOIS

*CHICAGO,** Cook Co.

DAVIS, MANNIX & McGRATH (AV)

125 South Wacker Drive, Suite 1700, 60606
Telephone: 312-332-3033
Fax: 312-332-6376

David C. Bogan (1946-1995)   Julia D. Mannix
Champ W. Davis, Jr.   Gini S. Marziani
Marsha K. Hoover   William T. McGrath

John B. Alsterda   J. Thomas Warlick, IV
Richard R. Danis, Jr.   (Not admitted in IL)
OF COUNSEL
Celeste Ebers Kralovec   Margaret F. Woulfe

For full biographical listings, see the Martindale-Hubbell Law Directory

KEGAN & KEGAN, LTD. (AV)

79 West Monroe Street, Suite 1320, 60603-4969
Telephone: 312-782-6495
Telecopier: (fax) 312-782-6494
Email: ElanKegan@aol.com

Albert I. Kegan (1908-1963)   Esther O. Kegan
Daniel L. Kegan

Cynthia L. Scott   Diane Lidman Prendiville
OF COUNSEL
Marvin N. Benn

For full biographical listings, see the Martindale-Hubbell Law Directory

McCONNELL & MENDELSON (AV)

140 South Dearborn Street, 9th Floor, 60603
Telephone: 312-263-1212
Telecopier: 312-263-0402

(See Next Column)

McCONNELL & MENDELSON—*Continued*

Francis J. McConnell   Michael Sweig Mendelson
OF COUNSEL
Elizabeth J. Caprini   Anne C. Keays

Reference: The Northern Trust Co., Chicago, Illinois.

For full biographical listings, see the Martindale-Hubbell Law Directory

---

LOMBARD, Du Page Co.

ARTHUR FAKES, P.C. (AV)

929 South Main Street, Suite 109, 60148
Telephone: 630-268-0600
Telecopier: 630-268-0642
Email: ARTFAKES@AOL.COM

Arthur Fakes

For full biographical listings, see the Martindale-Hubbell Law Directory

---

INDIANA

INDIANAPOLIS, * Marion Co.

BAKER & DANIELS (AV)

300 North Meridian Street, 46204
Telephone: 317-237-0300
FAX: 317-237-1000
Fort Wayne, Indiana Office: 111 East Wayne Street, Suite 800.
Telephone: 219-424-8000.
South Bend, Indiana Office: First Bank Building, 205 West Jefferson Boulevard.
Telephone: 219-234-4149.
Elkhart, Indiana Office: 301 B South Main Street, Suite 307,
Telephone: 219-296-6000.
Washington, D.C. Office: 1701 K Street, N.W., Suite 400.
Telephone: 202-785-1565.

FORT WAYNE OFFICE
MEMBERS OF FIRM
John F. Hoffman   Anthony Niewyk
Kevin R. Erdman

ASSOCIATES
Jeffrey O. Davidson   Brian C. Pauls
(Not admitted in IN)

Representative Clients: Anthem Insurance Companies, Inc.; AT&T Corp.; Bank One, Indianapolis, N.A.; Borg-Warner Corp.; City of Indianapolis; Cummins Engine Co.; Eli Lilly and Co.; General Motors Corp.; Indianapolis Public Schools; United Airlines.

For Complete List of Firm Personnel, See General Section

For full biographical listings, see the Martindale-Hubbell Law Directory

---

SOMMER & BARNARD, ATTORNEYS AT LAW, PC (AV)

4000 Bank One Tower, 111 Monument Circle, 46204-5140
Telephone: 317-630-4000
FAX: 317-236-9802
North Office: 8900 Keystone Crossing, Suite 1046, Indianapolis, Indiana, 46240-2134.
Telephone: 317-630-4000.
FAX: 317-844-4780.

William C. Barnard   Edward W. Harris, III
Gordon L. Pittenger

Representative Clients: Comerica Bank; Excel Industries; Federal Express; Kimball International; Monsanto; Renault Automation; TRW, Inc.

For Complete List of Firm Personnel, See General Section

For full biographical listings, see the Martindale-Hubbell Law Directory

---

LOUISIANA

NEW ORLEANS, * Orleans Parish

NATIONAL LAW OFFICES OF PUGH/ASSOCIATES PATENT & TRADEMARK ATTORNEYS (AV)

4917 St. Charles Avenue, 70115-4927
Telephone: 504-587-0000
Telecopier: 504-899-5360;
Cable Address: Pat. Pend. New Orleans
Email: epugh@patentlaw.com

(See Next Column)

C. Emmett Pugh

For full biographical listings, see the Martindale-Hubbell Law Directory

---

MASSACHUSETTS

BOSTON, * Suffolk Co.

PALMER & DODGE LLP (AV)

One Beacon Street, 02108
Telephone: 617-573-0100
Facsimile: 617-227-4420

MEMBER OF FIRM
Peter Wirth

For Complete List of Firm Personnel, See General Section

For full biographical listings, see the Martindale-Hubbell Law Directory

---

MICHIGAN

BLOOMFIELD HILLS, Oakland Co.

ADKISON NEED (AV)

1533 North Woodward Avenue, Suite 210, 48304
Telephone: 810-540-7400
Fax: 810-540-7401
Email: AdkisNeed@aol.com

MEMBERS OF FIRM
Phillip G. Adkison   Paul Green
Gregory K. Need   Kelly A. Allen
Deborah M. Schneider
ASSOCIATES
Richard D. Kuhn, Jr.   Ann D. Christ
Kathryn N. Nichols   Laura B. Andoni

For full biographical listings, see the Martindale-Hubbell Law Directory

---

DETROIT, * Wayne Co.

MILLER, CANFIELD, PADDOCK AND STONE, P.L.C. (AV)

A Professional Limited Liability Company
Founded in 1852 by Sidney Davy Miller
150 West Jefferson, Suite 2500, 48226-4415
Telephone: 313-963-6420
Fax: 313-496-7500
Cable Address: "Stem Detroit"
Detroit, Michigan Office: 150 West Jefferson, Suite 2500, 48226-4415.
Telephone: 313-963-6420.
Fax: 313-496-7500.
Cable Address: "Stem Detroit."
Ann Arbor, Michigan Office: 101 North Main Street, 7th Floor, 48104-1400.
Telephone: 313-663-2445.
Fax: 313-747-7147.
Bloomfield Hills, Michigan Office: Suite 100, Pinehurst Office Center, 1400 North Woodward, 48303-2014.
Telephone: 313-645-5000.
Fax: 313-645-1917.
Grand Rapids, Michigan Office: 1200 Campau Square Plaza, 99 Monroe, N.W., 49503-2639.
Telephone: 616-454-8656.
Fax: 616-776-6322.
Howell, Michigan Office: 121 South Barnard Street, Suite 4, 48843-2305.
Telephone: 517-546-7600.
Telecopier: 517-546-6974.
Kalamazoo, Michigan Office: 444 West Michigan Avenue, 49007-3752.
Telephone: 616-381-7030.
Fax: 616-382-0244.
Lansing, Michigan Office: One Michigan Avenue, Suite 900, 48933-1609.
Telephone: 517-487-2070.
Fax: 517-374-6304.
Monroe, Michigan Office: The Executive Centre, 214 East Elm Avenue, 48161-2682.
Telephone: 313-243-2000.
Fax: 313-243-0901.
Washington, D.C. Office: 1225 Nineteenth Street, N.W., Suite 400. 20036.
Telephone: 202-429-5575; 785-0600.
Fax: 202-331-1118; 785-1234.
Pensacola, Florida Office: 25 West Cedar, 32501.
Telephone: 904-469-1088.
Fax: 904-432-0677.
St. Petersburg, Florida Office: 100 Second Avenue S., Suite 7045, 33701.
Telephone: 813-982-6000.
Fax: 813-892-6002.

(See Next Column)

MILLER, CANFIELD, PADDOCK AND STONE P.L.C., *Detroit—Continued*

New York, New York Office: Eleventh Floor, 135 East 57th Street, 10022-2087.
Telephone: 212-754-5400.
Fax: 212-754-5401.
Gdansk, Poland Office: Suite 322, Dom Technika Building, Ul. Rajska 6, 80-850.
Telephone: 011-485-831-2808.
Fax: 011-485-831-4719.
Warsaw, Poland Office: Ul. Marszalkowska 82, Suite 561, 00-517.
Telephone: 011-482-623-6457 and 6458.
Fax: 011-482-623-6459.

PRINCIPALS OF FIRM
Marjory G. Basile
OF COUNSEL

Edward F. Langs   Raphael A. Monsanto
                                   (Not admitted in MI)
ASSOCIATE
Robert R. Lech

Representative Firm Clients: Chrysler Corporation; Comerica, Incorporated; City of Detroit, Michigan; Detroit Tigers, Inc.; First of Michigan; Ford Motor Company; Ford Motor Credit Company; Great Lakes Bancorp; Henry Ford Hospital; INVETECH Company.

For Complete List of Firm Personnel, See General Section

For full biographical listings, see the Martindale-Hubbell Law Directory

---

GRAND RAPIDS, Kent Co.

MILLER, CANFIELD, PADDOCK AND STONE, P.L.C. (AV)

A Professional Limited Liability Company
Founded in 1852 by Sidney Davy Miller
1200 Campau Square Plaza, 99 Monroe, N.W., P.O. Box 329, 49503-2639
Telephone: 616-454-8656
Fax: 616-776-6322
Detroit, Michigan Office: 150 West Jefferson, Suite 2500, 48226-4415.
Telephone: 313-963-6420.
Fax: 313-496-7500.
Cable Address: "Stem Detroit."
Ann Arbor, Michigan Office: 101 North Main Street, 7th Floor, 48104-1400.
Telephone: 313-663-2445.
Fax: 313-747-7147.
Bloomfield Hills, Michigan Office: Suite 100, Pinehurst Office Center, 1400 North Woodward, 48303-2014.
Telephone: 313-645-5000.
Fax: 313-645-1917.
Howell, Michigan Office: 121 South Barnard Street, Suite 4, 48843-2305.
Telephone: 517-546-7600.
Telecopier: 517-546-6974.
Kalamazoo, Michigan Office: 444 West Michigan Avenue, 49007-3752.
Telephone: 616-381-7030.
Fax: 616-382-0244.
Lansing, Michigan Office: One Michigan Avenue, Suite 900, 48933-1609.
Telephone: 517-487-2070.
Fax: 517-374-6304.
Monroe, Michigan Office: The Executive Centre, 214 East Elm Avenue, 48161-2682.
Telephone: 313-243-2000.
Fax: 313-243-0901.
Washington, D.C. Office: 1225 Nineteenth Street, N.W., Suite 400. 20036.
Telephone: 202-429-5575; 785-0600.
Fax: 202-331-1118; 785-1234.
Pensacola, Florida Office: 25 West Cedar 32501.
Telephone: 904-469-1088.
Fax: 904-432-0677.
St. Petersburg Florida Office: 100 Second Avenue S., Suite 7045, 33701.
Telephone: 813-982-6000.
Fax: 813-892-6002.
New York, New York Office: Eleventh Floor, 135 East 57th Street, 10022-2087.
Telephone: 212-754-5400.
Fax: 212-754-5401.
Gdansk, Poland Office: Suite 322, Dom Technika Building, Ul. Rajska 6, 80-850.
Telephone: 011-485-831-2808.
Fax: 011-485-831-4719.
Warsaw, Poland Office: Ul. Marszalkowska 82, Suite 561, 00-517.
Telephone: 011-482-623-6457 and 6458.
Fax: 011-482-623-6459.

PRINCIPALS OF FIRM
Mark E. Putney (Resident Director, Grand Rapids Office)

Representative Firm Clients: Chrysler Corporation; Comerica, Incorporated; City of Detroit, Michigan; Detroit Tigers, Inc.; First of Michigan; Ford Motor Company; Ford Motor Credit Company; Great Lakes Bancorp; Henry Ford Hospital; INVETECH Company.

For Complete List of Firm Personnel, See General Section

For full biographical listings, see the Martindale-Hubbell Law Directory

CONSTITUTIONAL LAW

CALIFORNIA

*LOS ANGELES,** Los Angeles Co.

ROSSBACHER & ASSOCIATES (AV)

Union Bank Plaza, Twenty-Fourth Floor, 445 South Figueroa
  Street, 90071
Telephone: 213-895-6500
Fax: 213-895-6161

MEMBER OF FIRM
Henry H. Rossbacher
OF COUNSEL
George M. Snyder
ASSOCIATES

James S. Cahill	Nanci E. Nishimura
Linda L. Griffis	Tracy W. Young
Karen D. Kerner	Julie A. Langslet
David F. Desmond	

LEGAL SUPPORT PERSONNEL

Linda Connell	Joan A. Degenkolb (Paralegal)
(Legal Administrator)	Martha E. Guilmette (Paralegal)

For full biographical listings, see the Martindale-Hubbell Law Directory

*SAN FRANCISCO,** San Francisco Co.

REMCHO, JOHANSEN AND PURCELL (AV)

Suite 800, 220 Montgomery Street, 94104
Telephone: 415-398-6230
Fax: 415-398-7256
Email: Info@RJP.com
Sacramento, California Office: Suite 625, 555 Capitol Mall.
Telephone: 916-264-1818.
Fax: 916-264-1824.

MEMBERS OF FIRM

Joseph Remcho	Robin B. Johansen
Kathleen J. Purcell	

Janet Sommer	Deborah L. Breiner

LEGAL SUPPORT PERSONNEL

Douglas Denton (Paralegal)	Ruth Fridhandler
	(Legal Administrator)

For full biographical listings, see the Martindale-Hubbell Law Directory

CONNECTICUT

WESTPORT, Fairfield Co.

ANDREW B. BOWMAN (AV)

1804 Post Road East, 06880
Telephone: 203-259-0599
Fax: 203-255-2570

Reference: Peoples Bank.

For full biographical listings, see the Martindale-Hubbell Law Directory

ILLINOIS

*CHICAGO,** Cook Co.

SIEGEL, MOSES, SCHOENSTADT & WEBSTER, P.C. (AV)

111 East Wacker Drive Suite 2800, 60601-4801
Telephone: 312-658-2000
Fax: 312-658-2022

Morton Siegel	Richard G. Schoenstadt
Michael A. Moses	James L. Webster
Jennifer G. Hoff	

For full biographical listings, see the Martindale-Hubbell Law Directory

*EDWARDSVILLE,** Madison Co.

REED, ARMSTRONG, GORMAN, COFFEY, GILBERT & MUDGE, PROFESSIONAL CORPORATION (AV)

One Mark Twain Plaza, Suite 300, P.O. Box 368, 62025
Telephone: 618-656-0257
Facsimile: 618-692-4416
Other Edwardsville Office: 125 North Buchanan, P.O. Box 247.
Telephone: 618-656-2244.
Fax: 618-658-1307.
Springfield, Illinois Office: One West Old State Capital Plaza, Suite 400,
Myers Building.
Telephone: 217-525-1366.
Fax: 217-525-0986.

Harry C. Armstrong	Martin K. Morrissey
James E. Gorman	Charles C. Compton
Stephen C. Mudge	Kevin J. Babb

Michael J. Bedesky	Bryan L. Skelton
David Laurent	Michelle A. Kunin
Ronald D. Robinson	

Representative Clients: State Farm Insurance Cos; Country Companies; Standard Mutual Casualty Co.; General Casualty Co. Of Wisconsin; Lloyds of London; Hawkeye Security Insurance Co.; Shelter Insurance Companies; Pekin Insurance Cos.; American International Adjusting Co.; Employers Reinsurance Corp.

For full biographical listings, see the Martindale-Hubbell Law Directory

MICHIGAN

*DETROIT,** Wayne Co.

BUTZEL LONG, A PROFESSIONAL CORPORATION (AV)

Suite 900, 150 West Jefferson, 48226
Telephone: 313-225-7000
Telecopier: 313-225-7080
Email: melnick@butzel.com *URL:* http://www.butzel.com
Birmingham, Michigan Office: Suite 200, 32270 Telegraph Road.
Telephone: 810-258-1616.
Telecopier: 810-258-1439.
Lansing, Michigan Office: 118 West Ottawa Street.
Telephone: 517-372-6622.
Telecopier: 517-372-6672.
Ann Arbor, Michigan Office: Suite 300, 350 South Main Street.
Telephone: 313-995-3110.
Telecopier: 313-995-1777.
Grosse Pointe Farms, Michigan Office: Suite 260, 21 Kercheval.
Telephone: 313-886-5446.
Telecopier: 313-886-2114.

William M. Saxton	Mark T. Nelson
John H. Dudley, Jr.	Keefe A. Brooks
Richard E. Rassel	Leonard M. Niehoff
Philip J. Kessler	(Ann Arbor)
Donald B. Miller	Robert A. Boonin

Representative Clients: Detroit Newspapers; Bridgestone/Firestone; Dayton Walther Corp.; General Dynamics; General Electric; Kelsey Hayes Co.; Mobil Oil; Stroh Brewery Co.; United Parcel Service.

For Complete List of Firm Personnel, See General Section

For full biographical listings, see the Martindale-Hubbell Law Directory

CONSTRUCTION LAW

ALABAMA

BIRMINGHAM,* Jefferson Co.

BRADLEY, ARANT, ROSE & WHITE (AV)

2001 Park Place, Suite 1400, P.O. Box 830709, 35283-0709
Telephone: 205-521-8000
Facsimile: 205-252-0264
Facsimile (SouthTrust Tower Office): 205-251-9915
URL: http://www.BARW.COM
Huntsville, Alabama Office: 200 Clinton Avenue West, Suite 900, 35801.
Telephone: 205-517-5100.
Facsimile: 205-533-5069.

MEMBERS OF FIRM

A. H. Gaede, Jr.	David Glenn Hymer
E. Mabry Rogers	G. Rick Hall
Andrew J. Noble, III	(Resident, Huntsville Office)
Walter J. Sears, III	Axel Bolvig III
Michael D. McKibben	J. David Pugh

Susan Donovan Josey

COUNSEL

Stanley D. Bynum	Walter H. Monroe, III

ASSOCIATES

Matthew H. Lembke	Douglas E. Eckert
James F. Archibald, III	Rodney L. Moss

For Complete List of Firm Personnel, See General Section

For full biographical listings, see the Martindale-Hubbell Law Directory

LONDON & YANCEY (AV)

1000 Park Place Tower, 2001 Park Place, 35203
Telephone: 205-251-2531
FAX: 205-251-8929

MEMBERS OF FIRM

Alex T. London (1847-1908)	Thomas R. Elliott, Jr.
John London (1848-1935)	Bert S. Nettles
George W. Yancey (1883-1962)	Richard W. Lewis

ASSOCIATES

Allen R. Trippeer, Jr.	Laura Ellison Proctor
Mark David Hess	Paige Elliott-Pinson
Lisa Wright Borden	F. Daniel Wood, Jr.
A. David Fawal	C. Dennis Hughes

Michael J. Velezis

OF COUNSEL

Robert W. Norris

Representative Clients: State of Alabama; Cincinnati Ins. Co.; Lloyd's of London; Blue Cross/Blue Shield; Attorney's Mutual of Alabama; State Farm; CIGNA; Royal Ins. Co. of America; Paul Revere Ins. Co.; Chubb Group.

For full biographical listings, see the Martindale-Hubbell Law Directory

SCHOEL, OGLE, BENTON AND CENTENO (AV)

600 Financial Center, 505 North 20th Street, P.O. Box 1865, 35201-1865
Telephone: 205-521-7000
Telecopier: 205-521-7007

MEMBERS OF FIRM

Jerry W. Schoel	Douglas J. Centeno
Richard F. Ogle	Melinda Murphy Dionne
Lee R. Benton	Gilbert M. Sullivan, Jr.
Paul A. Liles	David O. Upshaw

Reference: National Bank of Commerce; First Alabama Bank.

For full biographical listings, see the Martindale-Hubbell Law Directory

STARNES & ATCHISON (AV)

100 Brookwood Place, P.O. Box 598512, 35259-8512
Telephone: 205-868-6000
Telecopier: 205-868-6099

MEMBERS OF FIRM

W. Stancil Starnes	William Anthony Davis, III
W. Michael Atchison	L. Graves Stiff, III

Thomas Lawson Selden

ASSOCIATES

Steven T. McMeekin	Joe L. Leak

Representative Clients: Harbert International; Brice Building Co., Inc.; Ellard Cont. Co., Inc.; Hallmark Builders, Inc.; Brasfield & Gorrie General Contractor, Inc.; Rives Construction Co.; Morris Shea Bridge Co.; Cowin & Company, Inc.; Daniel International.

For full biographical listings, see the Martindale-Hubbell Law Directory

HUNTSVILLE,* Madison Co.

BERRY, ABLES, TATUM, BAXTER, PARKER & HALL, P.C. (AV)

Legal Building, 315 Franklin Street, S.E., P.O. Box 165, 35804-0165
Telephone: 205-533-3740
Facsimile: 205-533-3751
Email: BAXTERJ@ATTMAIL.COM

William H. Blanton (1889-1973)	James T. Tatum, Jr.
Joe M. Berry	James T. Baxter, III
L. Bruce Ables	Thomas E. Parker, Jr.

Bill G. Hall

James K. Brabston	Mark Rogers Hunter

Representative Clients: AmSouth Bank; First Alabama Bank; General Shale Products Co.; The Hertz Corp.; Litton Industries, Inc.; Farmers Tractor Co.; Colonial Bank; Farm Credit Bank of Texas; SouthBank; Regions Mortgage.
Reference: First Alabama Bank.

For full biographical listings, see the Martindale-Hubbell Law Directory

MOBILE,* Mobile Co.

JOHNSTONE, ADAMS, BAILEY, GORDON AND HARRIS, L.L.C. (AV)

Royal St. Francis Building, 104 St. Francis Street, P.O. Box 1988, 36633
Telephone: 334-432-7682
Facsimile: 334-432-2800
Telex: 782040

MEMBERS OF FIRM

I. David Cherniak	William Alexander Gray, Jr.

ASSOCIATE

Lawrence J. Seiter

General Counsel for: First Alabama Bank, Mobile; Infirmary Health System/Mobile Infirmary Medical Center/Rotary Rehabilitation Hospital (Multi-Hospital System).
Counsel for: Oil and Gas: Exxon Corp. Business and Corporate: Bell South Telecommunications, Inc.; Aluminum Co. of America; Michelin North America, Inc.; Metropolitan Life Insurance Co.; The Travelers Insurance Cos. Marine: The West of England Ship Owners Mutual Protection and Indemnity Association (Luxembourg); The Standard Steamship Owners' Protection and Indemnity Association (Bermuda) Ltd.

For Complete List of Firm Personnel, See General Section

For full biographical listings, see the Martindale-Hubbell Law Directory

ARIZONA

FLAGSTAFF,* Coconino Co.

ASPEY, WATKINS & DIESEL, P.L.L.C. (AV)

123 North San Francisco, 3rd Floor, 86001
Telephone: 520-774-1478
Facsimile: 520-774-8404
Sedona, Arizona Office: 120 Soldier Pass Road.
Telephone: 520-282-5955.
Facsimile: 520-282-5962.
Page, Arizona Office: 904 North Navajo.
Telephone: 520-645-9694.
Cottonwood, Arizona Office: 2400 E. Highway 89A, Suite C.
Telephone: 520-639-1881.
Facsimile: 520-639-0272.

MEMBERS OF FIRM

Frederick M. Fritz Aspey	Donald H. Bayles, Jr.
Harold L. Watkins	Kaign N. Christy
Louis M. Diesel	John J. Dempsey
Bruce S. Griffen	Zachary J. Markham

James E. Ledbetter	Roger M. Baeurle
Whitney Cunningham	Amy E. Mabius
Pernell Whynn McGuire	Stephen A. Thompson

Joel E. Sannes

LEGAL SUPPORT PERSONNEL

Karla H. Falls, CLAS (Legal Assistant)	Dominic M. Marino, Jr. (Paralegal Assistant)
Rocky C. Nissen (Paralegal Assistant, Sedona, Arizona Office)	Carrie R. Flynn (Litigation Paralegal, Cottonwood, Arizona Office)
Deborah D. Roberts, CLA (Legal Assistant)	

Representative Clients: Farmer's Insurance Company of Arizona; Pepsi-Cola Bottling Company of Northern Arizona; Bill Luke's Chrysler-Plymouth, Inc.; First American Title Insurance Company; Transnation Title Insurance Co.; Page Electric Utility; Comprehensive Access Health Plan, Inc.; Northern Arizona Healthcare Corporation.

(See Next Column)

ASPEY, WATKINS & DIESEL P.L.L.C., *Flagstaff—Continued*

Reference: First Interstate Bank-Arizona, N.A., Flagstaff, Arizona.

For full biographical listings, see the Martindale-Hubbell Law Directory

---

PHOENIX,* Maricopa Co.

CARMICHAEL & POWELL, PROFESSIONAL CORPORATION (AV)

7301 North 16th Street, 85020-5224
Telephone: 602-861-0777
Facsimile: 602-870-0296

Ronald W. Carmichael	Donald W. Powell
Sid A. Horwitz	

Stephen Manes	Brian A. Hatch
Richard C. Gramlich	

Representative Clients: Kawasaki Motors Corp., U.S.A.; Home Builders Association of Central Arizona; Firstar Metropolitan Bank & Trust; Wendy's International, Inc.; Associates National Bank; The Ryland Group, Inc.; Innsuites International; Bank of America Nevada; JWJ Contracting Company; Gold Key Homes.

For full biographical listings, see the Martindale-Hubbell Law Directory

FENNEMORE CRAIG, A PROFESSIONAL CORPORATION (AV)

Two North Central, Suite 2200, 85004
Telephone: 602-257-8700
Fax: 602-257-8527
Scottsdale, Arizona Office: 6263 North Scottsdale Road, Suite 290, 85250.
Telephone: 602-257-5400.
Fax: 602-257-5409.
Tucson, Arizona Office: One South Church Avenue, Suite 1030, 85701.
Telephone: 520-791-6800.
Fax: 520-791-6820.

Calvin H. Udall	Andrew M. Federhar
John G. Ryan	John Randall Jefferies

Keith L. Hendricks

For Complete List of Firm Personnel, See General Section

For full biographical listings, see the Martindale-Hubbell Law Directory

HORNE, KAPLAN AND BISTROW, P.C. (AV)

Renaissance Two, 40 North Central, Suite 2800, 85004
Telephone: 602-253-9700
Fax: 602-258-4805

Thomas C. Horne	Eric J. Bistrow
Martha Bachner Kaplan	Michael S. Dulberg
Kimball J. Corson	

For full biographical listings, see the Martindale-Hubbell Law Directory

JENNINGS & HAUG (AV)

2800 North Central Avenue Suite Eighteen Hundred, 85004-1019
Telephone: 602-234-7800
Fax: 602-277-5595
Email: jhlaw@syspac.com
Irvine, California Office: 1920 Main Street, Suite Eight-Thirty, 92714.
Telephone: 714-250-7800.
Fax: 714-250-4913.

MEMBERS OF FIRM

Curtis A. Jennings	Chad L. Schexnayder
William F. Haug	Mark E. Barker
Robert A. Scheffing	John G. Sinodis
Robert O. Dyer	James L. Csontos
Jack R. Cunningham	Robert J. Berens
Jay M. Mann	Jeff R. Wilhelm
Carolyn M. Kaluzniacki	Edward Rubacha
Dean Kim Lough	Larry J. Crown
Christopher C. Wooten	

ASSOCIATES

Paul D. Kramer (Resident, Irvine, California Office)	Laurence R. Sharlot
	Lori A. Metcalf
Paul S. Ruderman	Stacey A. Dowdell
Neal H. Bookspan	

OF COUNSEL

James W. Washington (Not admitted in AZ)

For full biographical listings, see the Martindale-Hubbell Law Directory

ROBERT J. NOVAK & ASSOCIATES (AV)

1440 E. Washington Street Suite 100, 85034
Telephone: 602-253-8000
Fax: 602-271-4733

(See Next Column)

ASSOCIATE

Herbert T. Swafford

Representative Clients: SouthTrust Mortgage, BancBoston; L.V. Associates, Ltd.; AEI Real Estate Fund Limited Partnership; Heron North American Property Trust; Tippmann Construction, Inc.; Sun World Corporation; G.B. Mannisto, Inc.; Phoenix Computer Systems, Inc.; Pasternack Architect, Inc.; Phoenix Plastics, Inc.

For full biographical listings, see the Martindale-Hubbell Law Directory

O'CONNOR, CAVANAGH, ANDERSON, KILLINGSWORTH & BESHEARS, A PROFESSIONAL ASSOCIATION (AV)

One East Camelback Road, Suite 1100, 85012-1656
Telephone: 602-263-2400
FAX: 602-263-2900
Email: firminfo@arizlaw.com
Sun City, Arizona Office: 13250 North Del Webb Boulevard, Suite B, 85351.
Telephone: 602-263-2808.
FAX: 602-933-3100.
Tucson, Arizona Office: O'Connor Cavanagh Molloy Jones, 33 N. Stone, Suite 2100, 85701, P.O. Box 2268, 85702.
Telephone: 520-622-3531.
FAX: 520-624-2816.
Nogales, Arizona Office: 1891 North Mastick Way, 85621.
Telephone: 520-761-4215.
FAX: 520-761-3505.

Stephen E. Richman

Representative Clients: McCarthy; Pulte Home Corporation; L.M.B. Construction; Glendale Union High School District; Gilpin's Construction; Mike Greenberg Construction; The Fishel Company; Kleven Construction, Inc.

For Complete List of Firm Personnel, See General Section

For full biographical listings, see the Martindale-Hubbell Law Directory

RENAUD, COOK & DRURY, P.A. (AV)

617 North 2nd Avenue, 85003
Telephone: 602-253-5101
Fax: 602-254-1448
Email: rcdlaw@rcdlaw.com
Scottsdale, Arizona Office: 6991 East Camelback Road, #D-103, 85251.
Telephone: 602-874-9000.
Fax: 602-874-9866.

J. Gordon Cook	Steven G. Mesaros
William W. Drury, Jr.	Mark W. Roth

Diane Mihalsky

For full biographical listings, see the Martindale-Hubbell Law Directory

RHEES & HOPKINS (AV)

100 West Clarendon Suite 710, 85013
Telephone: 602-263-6010
Fax: 602-263-6016

Michael L. Rhees	Stephen M. Hopkins
Richard B. Murphy	

For full biographical listings, see the Martindale-Hubbell Law Directory

SNELL & WILMER, L.L.P. (AV)

One Arizona Center, 85004-0001
Telephone: 602-382-6000
Fax: 602-382-6070
Tucson, Arizona Office: 1500 Norwest Tower, One South Church Avenue 85701-1612.
Telephone: 520-882-1200.
Fax: 520-884-1294.
Orange County Office: 1920 Main Street, Suite 1200, P.O. Box 57062, Irvine, California, 92619-7062.
Telephone: 714-253-2700.
Fax: 714-955-2507.
Salt Lake City, Utah Office: Broadway Centre, 111 East Broadway, Suite 900, 84111-1004.
Telephone: 801-237-1900.
Fax: 801-237-1950.

MEMBERS OF FIRM

Richard K. Mallery	Jay D. Wiley
Robert J. Deeny	Gerard Morales
James R. Condo	James J. Sienicki
E. Jeffrey Walsh	Bob J. McCullough

OF COUNSEL

Jarril F. Kaplan

ASSOCIATE

Scott D. Sherman

Representative Clients: Pinnacle West Capital Corp.; Richmond American Homes; U.S. Home Corp.; Del Webb Corp.; McCarthy West; W.E. O'Neil Construction Co.; Central Arizona Water Conservative District.

(See Next Column)

SNELL & WILMER L.L.P.—*Continued*

For Complete List of Firm Personnel, See General Section

For full biographical listings, see the Martindale-Hubbell Law Directory

---

WARNICKE & LITTLER, P.L.C. (AV)

2020 North Central Avenue, Fifth Floor, 85004-4506
Telephone: 602-256-0400
FAX: 602-256-0345

Ronald E. Warnicke
Thomas E. Littler

Ellen B. Davis
Mark J. Giunta

LEGAL SUPPORT PERSONNEL
Cheryl A. Menefee (Certified Paralegal)

For full biographical listings, see the Martindale-Hubbell Law Directory

---

SCOTTSDALE, Maricopa Co.

PESKIND HYMSON & GOLDSTEIN, P.C. (AV)

14595 North Scottsdale Road, Suite 14, 85254
Telephone: 602-991-9077
Fax: 602-443-8854

E. J. Peskind

For full biographical listings, see the Martindale-Hubbell Law Directory

---

TUCSON, * Pima Co.

O'CONNOR CAVANAGH MOLLOY JONES, A PROFESSIONAL ASSOCIATION (AV)

Suite 2100 33 N. Stone, P.O. Box 2268, 85702
Telephone: 520-622-3531
FAX: 520-624-2816
Email: firminfo@arizlaw.com
Phoenix, Arizona Office: O'Connor, Cavanagh, Anderson, Killingsworth & Beshears, One East Camelback Road, Suite 1100, 85012.
Telephone: 602-263-2400.
FAX: 602-263-2900.
Sun City, Arizona Office: O'Connor, Cavanagh, Anderson, Killingsworth & Beshears, 13250 North Del Webb Boulevard, Suite B, 85351.
Telephone: 602-263-2808.
FAX: 602-933-3100.
Nogales, Arizona Office: O'Connor, Cavanagh, Anderson, Killingsworth & Beshears, 1891 North Mastick Way, 85621.
Telephone: 520-761-4215.
FAX: 520-761-3505.

Scott D. Gibson
Peter Akmajian
Drue A. Morgan-Birch
Russell E. Jones

Richard T. Coolidge
David K. Gray
George O. Krauja
William W. Pearson

Benjamin W. Bauer

Chris B. Nakamura

Thomas E. Laursen
Paul A. Relich
Nathan B. Hannah
Michael W. Baldwin

Jennifer M. Dubay
Amy M. Samberg
Dale F. Regelman
James D. Campbell

OF COUNSEL
John F. Molloy (Retired)
John L. Donahue Jr.

Representative Clients: Three-Five Systems; Main Street & Main; ITT Cannon; Bank of America; The Dial Corp; The Hartford; Dow Corning Corp.; Charles Schwab & Co., Inc.

For full biographical listings, see the Martindale-Hubbell Law Directory

---

ARKANSAS

LITTLE ROCK, * Pulaski Co.

HOOVER & KOOISTRA (AV)

111 Center Street, 11th Floor, 72201-4445
Telephone: 501-376-8500
Facsimile: 501-372-3255

MEMBERS OF FIRM
Paul W. Hoover, Jr.
John Kooistra, III
Max C. Mehlburger

For full biographical listings, see the Martindale-Hubbell Law Directory

---

CALIFORNIA

ALAMO, Contra Costa Co.

LAW OFFICES OF DAVID M. BIRKA-WHITE (AV)

3240 Stone Valley Road West, Suite 102, 94507
Telephone: 510-838-2090
Facsimile: 510-820-5592

For full biographical listings, see the Martindale-Hubbell Law Directory

---

BAKERSFIELD, * Kern Co.

KLEIN, WEGIS, DeNATALE, GOLDNER & MUIR, LLP (AV)

A Partnership including Professional Corporations
(Formerly Di Giorgio, Davis, Klein, Wegis, Duggan & Friedman)
ARCO Tower, 4550 California Avenue, Second Floor, P.O. Box 11172, 93389-1172
Telephone: 805-395-1000
Telecopier: 805-326-0418
Email: kwdgm@kwdgm.com

MEMBERS OF FIRM
Anthony J. Klein (Inc.)
Barry L. Goldner

Representative Clients: Findley Construction; Kern High School District; Renfro-Russell & Associates, Inc.

For Complete List of Firm Personnel, See General Section

For full biographical listings, see the Martindale-Hubbell Law Directory

---

COSTA MESA, Orange Co.

COULOMBE & KOTTKE, A PROFESSIONAL CORPORATION (AV)

Comerica Bank Tower, 611 Anton Boulevard, Suite 1260, 92626
Telephone: 714-540-1234
Fax: 714-754-0808; 714-754-0707
Email: c-k@coulombe.com

Ronald B. Coulombe
Jon S. Kottke
COUNSEL
Roy B. Woolsey
LEGAL SUPPORT PERSONNEL
PARALEGALS
Vicky M. Pearson
Abeer F. Rider
LEGAL ADMINISTRATOR
Yvonne Mendoza

For full biographical listings, see the Martindale-Hubbell Law Directory

---

DUKE, GERSTEL, SHEARER & BREGANTE, LLP (AV)

3200 Park Center Drive, Suite 1000, 92626
Telephone: 714-551-8664
800-405-0816
Email: dgsb@lawinfo.com *URL:* url:http://www.dgsb.com
San Diego, California Office: 101 West Broadway, Suite 600, Sixth Floor, 92186-5470.
Telephone: 619-232-0816.
San Jose, California Office: 1740 Technology Drive, Suite 250, 95110.
Telephone: 408-441-7800, 800-405-0816.
Fax: 408-441-7302.

MEMBERS OF FIRM
Stephen V. Rupp (A Professional Corporation)
Robert K. Goff (A Professional Corporation)

Bryan R. Snyder (A Professional Corporation)

ASSOCIATE
Eric W. Sachrison

Reference: Bank of Commerce.

RUTAN & TUCKER, LLP (AV)

A Partnership including Professional Corporations
611 Anton Boulevard, Suite 1400, P.O. Box 1950, 92626
Telephone: 714-641-5100; 213-625-7586
Telecopier: 714-546-9035
Email: rutan&tucker@mcimail.com *URL:* http://www.rutan.com

MEMBERS OF FIRM
Thomas S. Salinger (P.C.)
David C. Larsen (P.C.)
Michael D. Rubin
David J. Aleshire
Marcia A. Forsyth

Philip D. Kohn
Stephen A. Ellis
Robert Owen
Adam N. Volkert
F. Kevin Brazil

ASSOCIATES
David H. Hochner
Patrick D. McCalla

Robert Elliot Adel II
Steven John Goon

(See Next Column)

RUTAN & TUCKER LLP, *Costa Mesa—Continued*

For Complete List of Firm Personnel, See General Section

For full biographical listings, see the Martindale-Hubbell Law Directory

---

FRESNO,* Fresno Co.

KIMBLE, MACMICHAEL & UPTON, A PROFESSIONAL CORPORATION (AV)

Fig Garden Financial Center, 5260 North Palm Avenue, Suite 221, P.O. Box 9489, 93792-9489
Telephone: 209-435-5500
Telecopier: 209-435-1500
Email: kmu@primenet.com

Joseph C. Kimble (1910-1972)	Robert H. Scribner
Thomas A. MacMichael (1920-1990)	Michael E. Moss
	Mark D. Miller
Jon Wallace Upton	Michael F. Tatham
Robert E. Bergin	W. Richard Lee
Jeffrey G. Boswell	D. Tyler Tharpe
Steven D. McGee	Sylvia Halkousis Coyle
Robert E. Ward	S. Brett Sutton
John P. Eleazarian	Michael J. Jurkovich

Douglas V. Thornton	Susan King Hatmaker
Robert William Branch	Lawrence J. Salisbury
Donald J. Pool	Daniel R. Foster

Meredith E. Allen

OF COUNSEL
Mary Ann Bluhm

For full biographical listings, see the Martindale-Hubbell Law Directory

---

LANG, RICHERT & PATCH, A PROFESSIONAL CORPORATION (AV)

Fig Garden Financial Center, 5200 North Palm Avenue, 4th Floor, P.O. Box 40012, 93755
Telephone: 209-228-6700
Fax: 209-228-6727

Frank H. Lang	Victoria J. Salisch
William T. Richert (1937-1993)	Bradley A. Silva
Robert L. Patch, II	Charles Trudrung Taylor
Val W. Saldaña	Mark L. Creede
Douglas E. Noll	Peter N. Zeitler
Michael T. Hertz	Charles L. Doerksen

Laurie L. Quigley	Nabil E. Zumout
Douglas E. Griffin	Shawn H. Alikian

Thomas E. Gauthier

References: Wells Fargo Bank (Fresno Main Office).

For full biographical listings, see the Martindale-Hubbell Law Directory

---

GLENDALE, Los Angeles Co.

GILL AND BALDWIN (AV)

130 North Brand Boulevard Fourth Floor, 91203
Telephone: 818-500-7755; 213-245-3131
Fax: 818-242-4305

MEMBERS OF FIRM

Samuel S. Gill (1912-1965)	Joseph C. Malpasuto
John M. Carmack	Kirk S. MacDonald

OF COUNSEL
Ernest R. Baldwin

Representative Clients: Kasler Corp.; Bireley Foundation.
Reference: American West Bank.

For full biographical listings, see the Martindale-Hubbell Law Directory

---

IRSFELD, IRSFELD & YOUNGER LLP (AV)

A Partnership including Professional Corporations
Suite 900, 100 West Broadway, 91210-1296
Telephone: 818-242-6859
Fax: 818-240-7728
Email: 104736.1745@compuserver.com

MEMBERS OF FIRM

James B. Irsfeld (1880-1966)	Peter J. Irsfeld (P.C.)
Kenneth C. Younger (1922-1996)	James J. Waldorf (P.C.)
	C. Phillip Jackson (P.C.)
John H. Brink (P.C.)	Norman H. Green (P.C.)

Kathryn E. Van Houten

ASSOCIATES

Peter C. Wright	Diane L. Walker

(See Next Column)

RETIRED
James B. Irsfeld, Jr.

Representative Clients: Lear Sieglar, Inc.; Chrysler Credit Corp.
References: First Interstate Bank (Glendale Main Office); Bank of Hollywood.

For full biographical listings, see the Martindale-Hubbell Law Directory

---

O'ROURKE, ALLAN & FONG (AV)

3rd Floor, 104 North Belmont, P.O. Box 10220, 91209-3220
Telephone: 818-247-4303
Fax: 818-247-1451

MEMBERS OF FIRM

Denis M. O'Rourke	Joan H. Allan
	Roderick D. Fong

ASSOCIATE
Denise Michelle O'Rourke

References: Verdugo Banking Co. (Glendale, California); Community Bank (Glendale, California).

For full biographical listings, see the Martindale-Hubbell Law Directory

---

THOMAS & PRICE (AV)

535 North Brand Boulevard, 7th Floor, 91203
Telephone: 213-387-4800; 818-500-4800
FAX: 818-500-4822
Ventura, California Office: 1655 Mesa Verde Avenue, Suite 230.
Telephone: 805-642-6255.
Fax: 805-642-4580.

MEMBERS OF FIRM

Michael Thomas	Craig R. Donahue
Bonnie R. Louis	Maureen F. Thomas

ASSOCIATES

John P. DeGomez	Christian E. Sanne
Timothy A. Hodge	Benjimin M. Brees
Linda B. Hurevitz	Janet L. Keuper

Kevin M. McCormick

OF COUNSEL
Lawrence E. Price

For full biographical listings, see the Martindale-Hubbell Law Directory

---

IRVINE, Orange Co.

ANDRADE & MUZI (AV)

Marine National Bank Building, 18401 Von Karman, Suite 350, 92715
Telephone: 714-553-1951
Telecopier: 714-553-0655
San Diego, California Office: Tokia Bank Building, 3111 Camino Del Rio North, Suite 1100.
Telephone: 619-291-2481.

MEMBERS OF FIRM

Richard B. Andrade	Abilio Tavares, Jr.
Andrew C. Muzi	Samuel G. Broyles, Jr.
Ronald G. Holbert	Frank A. Satalino

OF COUNSEL
Kurt Kupferman

Representative Clients: Advanco Constructor's, Inc.; American Insurance Company of North America; Fireman's Fund Insurance Co.; CIGNA Insurance Co.; Gentosi Bros., Inc.; Griffith Co.; Steve Bubalo Construction Co.; Sukut Construction, Inc.; U.S. Rentals, Inc.; Veco International, Inc.

For full biographical listings, see the Martindale-Hubbell Law Directory

---

BARNES, CROSBY, FITZGERALD & ZEMAN (AV)

2030 Main Street, Suite 1050, 92614
Telephone: 714-852-1100
Fax: 714-852-1501

MEMBERS OF FIRM

Robert Samuel Barnes	Larry S. Zeman
William M. Crosby	Mark H. Cheung
Michael J. FitzGerald	Alka N. Patel

OF COUNSEL
Frederick J. Stemmler

For full biographical listings, see the Martindale-Hubbell Law Directory

---

BROWN, PISTONE, HURLEY & VAN VLEAR, A PROFESSIONAL CORPORATION (AV)

Suite 900 AT&T Building, 8001 Irvine Center Drive, 92618-2921
Telephone: 714-727-0559
Fax: 714-727-0656
Email: BPHVLAW@AOL.COM
Phoenix, Arizona Office: 2999 North 44th Street, Suite 300.
Telephone: 602-968-2427.
Fax: 602-840-0794.

(See Next Column)

BROWN, PISTONE, HURLEY & VAN VLEAR A PROFESSIONAL CORPORATION—
Continued

San Diego, California Office: 4350 La Jolla Village Drive, Suite 300.
Telephone: 619-546-4368.
Fax: 619-453-2839.
Sacramento, California Office: 980 Ninth Street, 16th Floor.
Telephone: 916-449-9541.
Fax: 916-446-7104.

Ernest C. Brown	Gregory F. Hurley
Thomas A. Pistone	John E. Van Vlear
	Michael K. Wolder

Francis T. Donohue, III	Sheila I. Patterson
Robert C. Schneider (Resident,	Michael R. Gandee
Phoenix, Arizona Office)	Julia E. Kress

OF COUNSEL

Robert G. Mahan	Brian A. Runkel
Stephen M. Wontrobski	(Not admitted in CA)

For full biographical listings, see the Martindale-Hubbell Law Directory

CALLAHAN & BLAINE, A PROFESSIONAL LAW CORPORATION (AV)

Suite 800, 18500 Von Karman, 92612
Telephone: 714-553-1155
Fax: 714-553-0784
Email: info@callahan-law.com

Daniel J. Callahan (A	Stephen E. Blaine
Professional Corporation)	

Kathleen L. Dunham	Andrew A. Smits
Jim P. Mahacek	Gary S. Spitzer
Michael J. Sachs	Edward Susolik
	Graig R. Woodburn

OF COUNSEL

Shelley M. Liberto	Walt D. Mahaffa

For full biographical listings, see the Martindale-Hubbell Law Directory

CONNOR, CULVER, BLAKE & GRIFFIN LLP (AV)

2600 Michelson Drive, Suite 1450, 92612
Telephone: 714-622-2600
Fax: 714-622-2626

Edmond M. Connor	Laura Lee Blake
Marilyn Martin Culver	Craig L. Griffin

Roma R. Hanlon	David J. Hasseltime

For full biographical listings, see the Martindale-Hubbell Law Directory

LAWRENCE J. GALARDI (AV)

Wells Fargo Tower, 2030 Main Street Suite 1050, 92714
Telephone: 714-852-1100
Telecopier: 714-252-7780

For full biographical listings, see the Martindale-Hubbell Law Directory

KASDAN, SIMONDS, McINTYRE, EPSTEIN & MARTIN (AV)

2600 Michelson Drive, Tenth Floor, 92715
Telephone: 714-851-9000
Fax: 714-833-9455

MEMBERS OF FIRM

Kenneth S. Kasdan	David G. Epstein
Vance C. Simonds, Jr.	Ronald B. Martin
R. Donald McIntyre	Andrew D. Weiss

ASSOCIATE

Henry P. Schrenker	Steven S. Hanagami

Reference: Commerce Bank.

For full biographical listings, see the Martindale-Hubbell Law Directory

WATT, TIEDER & HOFFAR, L.L.P. (AV①)

3 Park Plaza, Suite 1530, 92714
Telephone: 714-852-6700
Telecopier: 714-261-0771
McLean Virginia Office: 7929 Westpark Drive, Suite 400,
Telephone: 703-749-1000.
Telecopier: 703-893-8029.
Washington, D.C. Office: 601 Pennsylvania Avenue, N.W. Suite 900,
Telephone: 202-462-4697.

MEMBERS OF FIRM

John B. Tieder, Jr.	Michael G. Long
(Not admitted in CA)	Christopher P. Pappas
Robert M. Fitzgerald	
(Not admitted in CA)	

(See Next Column)

ASSOCIATE
Gregory John Dukellis

For full biographical listings, see the Martindale-Hubbell Law Directory

---

LONG BEACH, Los Angeles Co.

FORD, WALKER, HAGGERTY & BEHAR, PROFESSIONAL LAW CORPORATION (AV)

One World Trade Center, Twenty Seventh Floor, 90831
Telephone: 310-983-2500
Telecopier: 310-983-2555

G. Richard Ford	Donna Rogers Kirby
Timothy L. Walker	Tina Ivankovic Mangarpan
William C. Haggerty	Susan D. Berger
Jeffrey S. Behar	Joseph A. Heath
Mark Steven Hennings	Robert J. Chavez
	J. Michael McClure

Arthur W. Schultz	Theodore A. Clapp
Jon T. Moseley	Stanley L. Scarlett
Maxine J. Lebowitz	Scott A. Ritsema
Timothy P. McDonald	Michael Guy Martin
K. Michele Williams	Colleen A. Strong
Stephen Ward Moore	Thomas L. Gourde
James D. Savage	Patrick J. Stark
Todd D. Pearl	Shayne L. Wulterin
Patrick J. Gibbs	Charles D. Jarrell
James O. Miller	Charles J. Schmitt
David Huchel	Kyle A. Ostergrad
Robert Reisinger	Todd L. Kessler

OF COUNSEL
Theodore P. Shield, P.L.C.

For full biographical listings, see the Martindale-Hubbell Law Directory

---

LOS ANGELES,* Los Angeles Co.

BERGMAN & WEDNER, INC. (AV)

Suite 900, 10880 Wilshire Boulevard, 90024
Telephone: 310-470-6110
Fax: Available on Request

Gregory M. Bergman	Robert M. Mason III
Gregory A. Wedner	Kristi Anne Sjoholm-Sierchio
Mark E. Fingerman	Keith A. Robinson
Alan Harvey Mittelman	John P. Dacey

John V. Tamborelli	Lisa S. Shukiar
Blithe Ann Smith	Daphne M. Humphreys
	Suzanne Z. Shbaro

OF COUNSEL

Lloyd A. Bergman (1923-1994)	Jacob A. Wedner

SPECIAL COUNSEL
Richard V. Godino

For full biographical listings, see the Martindale-Hubbell Law Directory

LAW OFFICES OF DAVID B. BLOOM A PROFESSIONAL CORPORATION (AV)

3325 Wilshire Boulevard, Ninth Floor, 90010
Telephone: 213-938-5248; 384-4088
Telecopier: 213-385-2009

David B. Bloom

Stephen S. Monroe (A	Susan Carole Jay
Professional Corporation)	Edward Idell
Raphael A. Rosemblat	Sandra Kamenir
James E. Adler	Steven Wayne Lazarus
Bonni S. Mantovani	Andrew Edward Briseno
Roy A. Levun	Harold C. Klaskin
Cherie S. Raidy	Shelley M. Gould
Jonathan Udell	Peter O. Israel

For full biographical listings, see the Martindale-Hubbell Law Directory

BOTTUM & FELITON, A PROFESSIONAL CORPORATION (AV)

Suite 1500, South Tower, 3200 Wilshire Boulevard, 90010
Telephone: 213-487-0402
Fax: 213-386-9803
San Diego, California Office: Suite 400 Emerald Plaza, 402 West Broadway.
Telephone: 619-595-4857.
Fax: 619-595-4863.

John R. Feliton, Jr.	Steve Johnson
Robert A. Wooten, Jr.	Mark A. Oertel
	Alexander F. Giovanniello

(See Next Column)

BOTTUM & FELITON A PROFESSIONAL CORPORATION, *Los Angeles—Continued*

Kenneth C. Feldman
Jerry Garcia
Paul K. Schrieffer
Scott A. Hampton
Gregg S. Garfinkel
Brian E. Cooper

Julie A. Covell
Karl R. Loureiro
Sean T. Hamada
Gary F. Werner
Victor I. King
Andrea J. Lang

Linwood Warren, Jr.

For full biographical listings, see the Martindale-Hubbell Law Directory

CHAPMAN & GLUCKSMAN, A PROFESSIONAL CORPORATION (AV)

11900 West Olympic Boulevard, Suite 800, 90064-0704
Telephone: 310-207-7722
Facsimile: 310-207-6550

Richard H. Glucksman
Arthur J. Chapman
Randall J. Dean

Wendy M. Housman
James C. Earle
Craig A. Roeb

Thomas L. Halliwell
Dominic J. Fote
Christopher R. Kent
Andrew B. Cohn
Jeffrey A. Cohen
Glenn T. Barger

Christine L. Vanderbilt
Gregory Sabo
Rita Mongoven Miller
Todd M. Mobley
D. Scott Dodd
Jon A. Turigliatto

Karen S. Danto

OF COUNSEL

Thomas J. Pabst

Reference: First Professional Bank, Santa Monica.

For full biographical listings, see the Martindale-Hubbell Law Directory

CRAWFORD & REIMANN LLP (AV)

15th Floor, 11755 Wilshire Boulevard, 90025
Telephone: 310-478-7442
Fax: 310-575-4575

MEMBERS OF FIRM

Thomas W. Crawford

David W. Reimann

ASSOCIATES

Robert C. Cartwright

Glenn D. Hamovitz

Reference: Santa Monica Bank, Brentwood Office.

For full biographical listings, see the Martindale-Hubbell Law Directory

DANIELS, BARATTA & FINE (AV)

A Partnership including a Professional Corporation
1801 Century Park East, 9th Floor, 90067
Telephone: 310-556-7900
Telecopier: 310-556-2807
Bakersfield, California Office: 5201 California Avenue, Suite 400.
Telephone: 805-335-7788.
Telecopier: 805-324-3660.

MEMBERS OF FIRM

John P. Daniels (Inc.)
James M. Baratta
Paul R. Fine
Nathan B. Hoffman

Mary Hulett
Michael B. Geibel
James I. Montgomery, Jr.
Lance D. Orloff

Mark R. Israel

ASSOCIATES

Ilene Wendy Kurtzman
Janet Sacks
Michael N. Schonbuch
Scott M. Leavitt
Michelle R. Press
Scott Ashford Brooks
Craig A. Laidig
Robin A. Webb
Craig S. Momita

Spencer A. Schneider
Angelo A. Du Plantier, III
Leslie E. Wright, III.
Erin B. Hallissy
Kena B. Chin
Dean Bengston
Peter Anders Nyquist
Jeannie Masse
Lori Chotiner

Maureen M. Michail

OF COUNSEL

Timothy J. Hughes

Drew T. Hanker

Mark A. Vega

For full biographical listings, see the Martindale-Hubbell Law Directory

GORDON, EDELSTEIN, KREPACK, GRANT, FELTON & GOLDSTEIN (AV)

A Partnership including a Professional Corporation
Suite 1800, 3580 Wilshire Boulevard, 90010
Telephone: 213-739-7000
Fax: 213-386-1671

(See Next Column)

Roger L. Gordon
Mark Edelstein
Howard D. Krepack
Sherry E. Grant

Richard I. Felton
Irwin L. Goldstein (A Professional Corporation)
Steven J. Kleifield

ASSOCIATES

Joshua M. Merliss

David A. Goldstein

Eugenia L. Steele

For full biographical listings, see the Martindale-Hubbell Law Directory

GRAY, YORK, DUFFY & RATTET (AV)

15760 Ventura Boulevard, 16th Floor (Encino), 91436
Telephone: 818-907-4000; 310-553-0445
FAX: 818-783-4551

MEMBERS OF FIRM

Gary S. Gray
James R. York

John J. Duffy
Arlene A. Colman

ASSOCIATES

Amalia L. Taylor
Kenneth A. Hearn
Gabriel H. Wainfeld

Michael S. Eisenbaum
Eric J. Erickson
Carol G. Arnold

Reference: Marathon National Bank, Los Angeles, California.

For full biographical listings, see the Martindale-Hubbell Law Directory

HORNBERGER & CRISWELL (AV)

444 South Flower, 31st Floor, 90071
Telephone: 213-488-1655
Facsimile: 213-488-1255
Email: kbranch0@counsel.com

MEMBERS OF FIRM

Nicholas W. Hornberger
Leslie E. Criswell

Ann M. Ghazarians
Michael A. Brewer

Scott Alan Freedman

ASSOCIATES

Marlin E. Howes
Christopher T. Olsen
Scott B. Cloud

James M. Slominski
Michael C. Denlinger
Gayle L. Eskridge

OF COUNSEL

David E. Bower

William P. Driscoll

For full biographical listings, see the Martindale-Hubbell Law Directory

KERN, STREETER & GONZALEZ (AV)

601 West 5th Street, Suite 1100, 90071
Telephone: 213-629-8100
Facsimile: 213-627-8765

MEMBERS OF FIRM

René J. Kern, Jr.

John W. Streeter

Michael D. Gonzalez

ASSOCIATES

Tina L. Gentile
Claudia T. Beightol

Angela J. Armitage
Christina L. Young

Representative Clients: Farmers Insurance Group; The Hahn Co.; The Home Insurance Co.; Scottsdale Insurance Co.; TM Claims Service, Inc.; United States Fidelity and Guaranty Co.

For full biographical listings, see the Martindale-Hubbell Law Directory

KNOPFLER & ROBERTSON, A PROFESSIONAL LAW CORPORATION (AV)

Suite 500, 21650 Oxnard Street (Woodland Hills), 91367
Telephone: 818-227-0770; 213-624-1111
Telefax: 818-227-0777

George Knopfler
Alexander Robertson, IV
Deborah Broom

Richard A. Capella
Edward D. Vaisbort
Jonathan S. Vick

OF COUNSEL

James H. Patton, Jr.

Arlen Ross Gunner

Scott C. Haith

Kevin Matthew Davis
Richard P. Riley
Christina S. Robertson
Janice M. Michaels
William G. Kelsberg
Ernesto F. Aldover
Jeanine M. St. Pierre-Kumar
Terri Eileen Hilliard

James M. Pazos
Lisa Bondy Dunn
Brian I. Glicker
Colin E. Barr
Cynthia Coulter Mulvihill
Christopher J. Bagnaschi
Cheryl A. Kirkpatrick
Peter C. Brown

For full biographical listings, see the Martindale-Hubbell Law Directory

KOSLOV & MEDLEN (AV)

30141 Agoura Road, Suite 200, 91301-4334
Telephone: 818-597-9996
FAX: 818-597-8848

(See Next Column)

KOSLOV & MEDLEN—*Continued*

MEMBERS OF FIRM

John Koslov   William P. Medlen

ASSOCIATE

Sabrina Simmons-Brill

For full biographical listings, see the Martindale-Hubbell Law Directory

MAGUIRE & ORBACH, LAW CORPORATION (AV)

Suite 300, 10866 Wilshire Boulevard, 90024-4311
Telephone: 310-470-2929
Fax: 310-474-4710

Everett W. Maguire   Jeffrey D. Pearlman
David M. Orbach   David M. Huff
           Michael D. Germain

For full biographical listings, see the Martindale-Hubbell Law Directory

MONTELEONE & McCRORY (AV)

A Partnership including Professional Corporations
725 South Figueroa Street Suite 3750, 90017-5402
Telephone: 213-612-9900
FAX: 213-612-9930
Santa Ana, California Office: Suite 750, 1551 North Tustin Avenue, 92705.
Telephone: 714-565-3170.
Fax: 714-565-3184.

MEMBERS OF FIRM

Stephen Monteleone (1886-1962)   Philip C. Putnam (P.C.)
G. Robert Hale (P.C.)   Joseph A. Miller (P.C.)
Patrick J. Duffy, III (P.C.)   Diana M. Dron
Michael F. Minchella (P.C.)   (Resident, Santa Ana Office)
Thomas P. McGuire (P.C.)   Donald J. Shields
William J. Ingalsbe (P.C.)
   (Resident, Santa Ana Office)

ASSOCIATES

David C. Romyn   W. Jeffrey Burch
Barry J. Jensen   Andrew W. Hawthorne
   (Resident, Santa Ana Office)   Stephen L. Dubin
         Erica S. Behrens

OF COUNSEL

Darrell P. McCrory

For full biographical listings, see the Martindale-Hubbell Law Directory

OCHOA & SILLAS (AV)

444 South, Flower Street, 18th Floor, 90071
Telephone: 213-362-1400
Fax: 213-622-0162
Sacramento, California Office: Wells Fargo Center, 400 Capitol Mall, Suite 1850.
Telephone: 916-447-3383.
FAX: 916-447-3495.
Mexico City, Mexico Office: Bosques de Duraznos, No. 65-507-B, Bosques de Las Lomas, 11700 Mexico, D.F.
Telephone: 905-596-68-48.

MEMBERS OF FIRM

Ralph M. Ochoa   Jesse M. Jauregui
Herman Sillas   Jacqueline Rich Moore

ASSOCIATES

Jack T. Molodanof   Evan F. Hadnot
Joyce E. Earl   Thomas J. Joy
Christopher Gonzalez   Mario Cordero

OF COUNSEL

Cochran & Lotkin, , Washington, D.C.

LEGAL SUPPORT PERSONNEL

Manuel Tejeda (Paralegal)   Jeanette M. Palma (Paralegal)
        Lori Lee Marino (Paralegal)

For full biographical listings, see the Martindale-Hubbell Law Directory

O'MELVENY & MYERS LLP (AV)

400 South Hope Street, 90071-2899
Telephone: 213-669-6000
Cable Address: "Moms"
Facsimile: 213-669-6407
Email: omminfo@omm.com
Century City, California Office: 1999 Avenue of the Stars, 90067-6035.
Telephone: 310-553-6700.
Facsimile: 310-246-6779.
Newport Beach, California Office: 610 Newport Center Drive, 92660-6429.
Telephone: 714-760-9600.
Cable Address: "Moms".
Facsimile: 714-669-6994.

(See Next Column)

San Francisco, California Office: Embarcadero Center West Tower, 275 Battery Street, 94111-3305.
Telephone: 415-984-8700.
Facsimile: 415-984-8701.
New York, New York Office: Citicorp Center, 153 East 53rd Street, 10022-4611.
Telephone: 212-326-2000.
Facsimile: 212-326-2061.
Washington, D.C. Office: 555 13th Street, N.W., 20004-1109.
Telephone: 202-383-5300.
Cable Address: "Moms".
Facsimile: 202-383-5414.
London, England Office: 10 Finsbury Square, London, EC2A 1LA.
Telephone: 0171-256-8451.
Facsimile: 0171-638-8205.
Tokyo, Japan Office: Sanbancho KB-6 Building, 6 Sanbancho, Chiyoda-ku, Tokyo 102, Japan.
Telephone: 03-3239-2900.
Facsimile: 03-3239-2432.
Hong Kong Office: Suite 1905, Peregrine Tower, Lippo Centre, 89 Queensway, Central, Hong Kong.
Telephone: 852-2523-8266.
Facsimile: 852-2522-1760.
Shanghai, Peoples Republic of China Office: Shanghai International Trade Centre, Suite 2011, 2200 Yan An Road West, Shanghai, 200335, PRC.
Telephone: 86-21-6219-5363.
Facsimile: 86-21-6275-4949.

PARTNER

Ralph J. Shapira

For Complete List of Firm Personnel, See General Section

For full biographical listings, see the Martindale-Hubbell Law Directory

JACK PAUL (AV)

1801 Avenue of the Stars Suite 932, 90067
Telephone: 310-277-1322
Facsimile: 310-277-1333

For full biographical listings, see the Martindale-Hubbell Law Directory

RADCLIFF, FRANDSEN & DONGELL (AV)

40th Floor, 777 South Figueroa Street, 90017
Telephone: 213-614-1990
Facsimile: 213-489-9263
San Francisco, California Office: 88 Kearny Street, Suite 1475.
Telephone: 415-399-8393.
Facsimile: 415-989-5465.
Rome, Italy Office: Via Tacito, 7.
Telephone: (39) 06-323-5588.
Facsimile: (39) 06-324-3392.

MEMBERS OF FIRM

Jules G. Radcliff, Jr.   Russell Mackay Frandsen
         Richard A. Dongell

OF COUNSEL

Tal Clifton Finney

ASSOCIATES

Francis P. Aspessi   Jeffrey C. Mayes
Ruben A. Castellon   Marisa A. Moret
William W. Funderburk, Jr.   Daniel E. Park
Jeffrey A. Gagliardi   Scott D. Pinsky
David K. Lee   Eric H. Saiki
Maria Anna Mancini   Steve R. Segura
        Glenn M. White

For full biographical listings, see the Martindale-Hubbell Law Directory

SCHELL & DELAMER, LLP (AV)

A Partnership including Professional Corporations
865 South Figueroa Street Suite 2750, 90017
Telephone: 213-622-8181
Fax: 213-627-5252
Thousand Oaks, California Office: 100 East Thousand Oaks Boulevard, Suite 142.
Telephone: 805-496-9533.
Fax: 805-496-3424.

Gerald F. H. Delamer   Garrin James Shaw (Professional
   (1892-1955)   Corporation)
Walter O. Schell (1895-1981)   Robert S. Hamrick (Professional
Roland R. Kaspar (Professional   Corporation)
   Corporation)   Jeffrey F. Briskin
        Katherine B. Pene

ASSOCIATES

Candace E. Ahrens Kallberg   John J. Latzanich, II. (Resident
Denise A. Nardi   at Thousand Oaks Office)
Randy A. Berg   Lori M. Levine
Kenneth S. Markson   Sylvia Havens
Joseph P. Sepikas   Roman Y. Nykolyshyn
Gregory J. Amantia (Resident at
   Thousand Oaks Office)

(See Next Column)

SCHELL & DELAMER LLP, *Los Angeles—Continued*

Representative Clients: Hartford Insurance Group; Liberty Mutual Group; Travelers Insurance Co.
References: Los Angeles: First Interstate Bank; Merrill-Lynch.

For full biographical listings, see the Martindale-Hubbell Law Directory

SELMAN ● BREITMAN (AV)

11766 Wilshire Boulevard, Sixth Floor, 90025-6538
Telephone: 310-445-0800
Fax: 310-473-2525
San Diego, California Office: Emerald Plaza, 402 W. Broadway, Suite 400.
Telephone: 619-595-4880.
Facsimile: 619-595-4890.
San Francisco, California Office: Citicorp Center, One Sansome Street, Suite 1900.
Telephone: 415-951-4646.
Fax: 415-951-4676.

MEMBERS OF FIRM

Neil H. Selman	Elaine K. Fresch
Craig R. Breitman	Nicholas Banko
Robert A. Steller	Brad D. Bleichner
(Partner, San Diego Office)	David L. Jones
Alan B. Yuter	Mark L. Jubelt
Nancy W. Shokohi	Monica Cruz Thornton
Jeffrey C. Segal	David T. Bamberger
A. Scott Goldberg	Sterling Tao
	(Partner, San Francisco Office)

Lynette Klawon	James B. Kamanski
Ramon Z. Bacerdo (Resident, San Francisco Office)	Michael L. Mengoli
	Rita H. Issagholian
John S. Knowlton	Sarah F. Burke
Murray M. Sinclair	(Resident, San Diego Office)
Jeffrey A. Simmons	Darcy D. Jorgensen
Mark S. Gruskin	Linda S. Wendell (Resident, San Francisco Office)
Anthony L. Cione	
Christopher J. Harrington	Jeffrey S. Bolender
Sheryl W. Leichenger	Jeffrey T. Briggs
Theresa Ann Loss	Marcie A. Keenan
Jerry C. Popovich	Lisa M. Dyson (Resident, San Francisco Office)
Lisa Hannah Kahn	
David H. Oken	Aimee Y. Wong
Katy A. Nelson	Grace Horoupian
Jan Long Pocaterra	Kathleen T. Deeley
Kim Karelis	Christopher A. Petrovic
Asim K. Desai	Kimberly D. Allario
Pauline A. New	(Resident, San Diego Office)
Dianne M. Costales	Wendy Wen Yun Chang
Eldon S. Edson	Jack M. Zakariaie

OF COUNSEL

Thomas A. Leary (Of Counsel, San Diego Office)

Reference: City National Bank (Beverly Hills Branch).

For full biographical listings, see the Martindale-Hubbell Law Directory

NEWPORT BEACH, Orange Co.

KELEGIAN & THOMAS (AV)

4685 MacArthur Court, Suite 400, 92660
Telephone: 714-553-1200
Fax: 714-553-1013
Email: KelThomLaw@aol.com

Mark A. Kelegian	James P. Habel
Michael Paul Thomas	Jeri E. Tabback
Joseph P. Gallo	Dean H. McVay
Bruce A. Thomason	Erik R. Musurlian
Steven M. Hepps	William N. Villard

For full biographical listings, see the Martindale-Hubbell Law Directory

FRANK B. MYERS (AV)

Suite 720, 4400 MacArthur Boulevard, 92660
Telephone: 714-752-2001
Facsimile: 714-955-3670

For full biographical listings, see the Martindale-Hubbell Law Directory

YOUNG & AMUNDSEN (AV)

620 Newport Center Drive, Suite 420, 92660
Telephone: 714-640-4400
Fax: 714-717-4862

MEMBERS OF FIRM

Steven R. Young	Roland J. Amundsen

For full biographical listings, see the Martindale-Hubbell Law Directory

---

*OAKLAND,** Alameda Co.

AIKEN, KRAMER & CUMMINGS, INCORPORATED (AV)

Suite 550 Ordway Building, One Kaiser Plaza, 94612
Telephone: 510-834-6800
Fax: 510-834-9017
Email: aikenkrame@aol.com

Benj. R. Aiken (1879-1955)	John A. Harkavy
Bauer E. Kramer (Retired)	Elizabeth M. Engh
Benj. R. Aiken, Jr. (Retired)	Matthew F. Graham
Fred V. Cummings (Retired)	Steven J. Cramer
Richard A. Sipos	

OF COUNSEL

Russell L. Barlow	Bruce G. Herold
Michael A. Coan	

Ellen Suzanne Wyatt	Michael S. Treppa

Reference: Union Bank of California, Oakland, California.

For full biographical listings, see the Martindale-Hubbell Law Directory

HAIMS, JOHNSON, MACGOWAN & McINERNEY (AV)

490 Grand Avenue, 94610
Telephone: 510-835-0500
Facsimile: 510-835-2833

MEMBERS OF FIRM

Arnold B. Haims	Randy M. Marmor
Gary R. Johnson	John K. Kirby
Clyde L. MacGowan	Robert J. Frassetto
Thomas McInerney	Caroline N. Valentino
Lawrence A. Baker	Dianne D. Peebles

ASSOCIATES

Joseph Y. Ahn	Anne M. Michaels
Edward D. Baldwin	Michelle Diane Perry
Marc P. Bouret	Edward C. Schroeder, Jr.

For full biographical listings, see the Martindale-Hubbell Law Directory

RYAN, ANDRADA & LIFTER, A PROFESSIONAL CORPORATION (AV)

Tenth Floor, Kaiser Center Building, 300 Lakeside Drive, Suite 1045, 94612-3536
Telephone: 510-763-6510
Fax: 510-763-3921

Joseph D. Ryan, Jr.	Charles E. Kallgren
J. Randall Andrada	Rhonda D. Shelton
Jill J. Lifter	Lora Vail French
Jolie Krakauer	Vikki L. Barron
Glenn Gould	Bruce A. McIntosh
Michael J. Daley	Michael J. Thomas
Laura E. Ozak	

Representative Clients: Alameda Contra Costa County Transit District; CNA Insurance Companies; Truck Insurance Exchange; Liberty Mutual Insurance Group; Safeway Stores, Inc.

For full biographical listings, see the Martindale-Hubbell Law Directory

PALO ALTO, Santa Clara Co.

HANNA & VAN ATTA (AV)

A Partnership of Professional Corporations
525 University Avenue, Suite 705, 94301
Telephone: 415-321-5700
Fax: 415-321-5639

John Paul Hanna	David M. Van Atta

For full biographical listings, see the Martindale-Hubbell Law Directory

PASADENA, Los Angeles Co.

BURNS, AMMIRATO, PALUMBO, MILAM & BARONIAN, A PROFESSIONAL LAW CORPORATION (AV)

65 North Raymond Avenue, 2nd Floor, 91103-3919
Telephone: 818-796-5053; 213-258-8282
Fax: 818-792-3078
Long Beach, California Office: One World Trade Center, Suite 1200.
Telephone: 310-436-8338; 714-952-1047.
Fax: 310-432-6049.

Michael A. Burns	Bruce Palumbo
Vincent A. Ammirato, Resident, Long Bch	Jeffrey L. Milam
	Robert H. Baronian

(See Next Column)

BURNS, AMMIRATO, PALUMBO, MILAM & BARONIAN A PROFESSIONAL LAW CORPORATION—*Continued*

Normand A. Ayotte
Colleen Clark
Valerie Julien-Peto
Susan E. Luhring
Grace C. Mori,
    Resident, Long Bch

Michael P. Vicencia,
    Resident, LOng Bch
Michael E. Wenzel,
    Resident, Long Bch

Reference: First Los Angeles Bank.

For full biographical listings, see the Martindale-Hubbell Law Directory

COLLINS, COLLINS, MUIR & TRAVER (AV)

Successor to Collins & Collins
Suite 300, 265 North Euclid, 91101
Telephone: 818-793-1163
FAX: 818-793-5982
Newport Beach, California Office: 333 Bayside Drive, 92660.
Telephone: 714-723-6284.
Fax: 714-723-7701.

MEMBERS OF FIRM

James E. Collins (1910-1987)
John J. Collins
Samuel J. Muir

Robert J. Traver
Frank J. D'Oro
Brian K. Stewart

ASSOCIATES

Paul L. Rupard
Robert H. Stellwagen, Jr.
Tomas A. Guterres

Christine E. Drage
Peter L. Stacy
Stephen W. Olson

For full biographical listings, see the Martindale-Hubbell Law Directory

SCOTT C. TURNER (AV)

301 North Lake Avenue Suite 700, 91101
Telephone: 818-440-1822
FAX: 818-440-9409
Carmel, California Office: P.O. Box 1671, 93921.
Telephone: 408-626-5626.
FAX: 408-626-5634.

For full biographical listings, see the Martindale-Hubbell Law Directory

RANCHO CORDOVA, Sacramento Co.

HERRIG & VOGT (AV(T))

2724 Kilgore Road, 95670
Telephone: 916-631-7000
Telecopier: 916-631-7717
Kennewick, Washington Office: 3104 West Kennewick Avenue, Suite D.
Telephone: 509-943-6691.
Fax: 509-783-8808.
Redmond, Washington Office: 7981 168th Avenue, N.E.
Telephone: 206-3129.
Fax: 206-556-0595.
Los Angeles, California Office: 100 Wilshire Boulevard, #950, Santa Monica.
Telephone: 310-260-5088.
Fax: 310-260-5089.

MEMBERS OF FIRM

John R. Herrig

George F. Vogt, Jr. (Resident)

ASSOCIATES

C. Patrick Stoll
Hazel Bergtholdt (Resident)
Heidi Susan Hart (Resident, Los
    Angeles, California Office)

David D. Hilton (Resident,
    Kennewick, Washington
    Office)

LEGAL SUPPORT PERSONNEL

CONSTRUCTION ANALYST

Gregg T. Gottgetreu

For full biographical listings, see the Martindale-Hubbell Law Directory

REDWOOD CITY,* San Mateo Co.

LOW, BALL & LYNCH, A PROFESSIONAL CORPORATION (AV)

10 Twin Dolphin, Suite B-500, 94065
Telephone: 415-591-8822
Fax: 415-591-8884
San Francisco, California Office: 601 California Street, Suite 2100, 94108.
Telephone: 415-981-6630.
Monterey, California Office: 10 Ragsdale Drive, Suite 175, 93940.
Telephone: 408-655-8822.

Raymond Coates
Chester G. Moore, III
James D. Miller
William H. Holsinger

David L. Blinn
Janet Kulig
Thomas E. Mulvihill
Jennifer Elizabeth Acheson

(See Next Column)

John R. Baumann

Joseph M. Fenech

Michael E. Sandgren

For full biographical listings, see the Martindale-Hubbell Law Directory

SACRAMENTO,* Sacramento Co.

CAULFIELD, DAVIES & DONAHUE (AV)

3500 American River Drive, Suite 100, 95864
Telephone: 916-487-7700
Fairfield, California Office: Fairfield West Plaza, 1455 Oliver Road, Suite 130.
Telephone: 707-426-0223.

MEMBERS OF FIRM

Richard Hyland Caulfield
Robert E. Davies

James R. Donahue
Bruce E. Leonard

ASSOCIATES

David N. Tedesco
Matthew Paul Donahue
Brian C. Haydon

Jennifer Gittisriboongul
John T. Stralen
David D. Poland

Shannon Spellacy

For full biographical listings, see the Martindale-Hubbell Law Directory

HARDY ERICH BROWN & WILSON, A PROFESSIONAL CORPORATION (AV)

1000 G Street, 95814
Telephone: 916-449-3800
Fax: 916-449-3888
Mailing Address: P.O. Box 13530, Sacramento, California, 95853-4530

Anthony D. Osmundson
Thomas C. Richards
David S. Worthington
L. Kent Wyatt

Bruce E. Salenko
Brian H. Charter
Whitney A. Davis
John C. Miller, Jr.

Kristine E. Balough

Representative Clients: The Chubb Insurance Company; Risk Administration & Management Company; Royal Insurance Company.

For full biographical listings, see the Martindale-Hubbell Law Directory

HARMATA LAW OFFICES (AV)

2201 Q Street, 95816
Telephone: 916-442-2842
Fax: 916-442-2015

Donald D. Harmata

LEGAL SUPPORT PERSONNEL
PARALEGAL

Debra D. Morrow

Representative Clients: Control Data Corp.; Deloitte & Touche; General Electric Co.; Myers Electric, Inc.; Syblon-Reid Co.; Systemhouse Inc.; TRW, Inc.

For full biographical listings, see the Martindale-Hubbell Law Directory

NAGELEY, MEREDITH & RAMSEY, INC. (AV)

8001 Folsom Boulevard, Suite 200, P.O. Box 276270, 95827-6270
Telephone: 916-386-8282
Fax: 916-386-8952

Sam R. Nageley

Gregory A. Meredith

Joe Ramsey

Drew M. Johnson
Craig S. MacGlashan
Michael B. O'Harra
Lawrence N. Hensley

Carole Sharples
L. Alan Warwick
Janet M. Meredith
Debbie J. Vorous

James C. Keowen

OF COUNSEL

Andrea M. Miller

For full biographical listings, see the Martindale-Hubbell Law Directory

SAN DIEGO,* San Diego Co.

DUKE, GERSTEL, SHEARER & BREGANTE, LLP (AV)

A Registered Limited Liability Partnership
Sixth Floor, 101 West Broadway, P.O. Box 85470, 92186-5470
Telephone: 619-232-0816
800-405-0816
Fax: 619-232-4661
Email: dgsb@lawinfo.com *URL:* http://www.dgsb.com
Costa Mesa, California Office: 3200 Park Center Drive, Suite 1000, 92626.
Telephone: 714-551-8664, 800-405-0816.
San Jose, California Office: 1740 Technology Drive, Suite 250, 95110.
Telephone: 408-441-7800, 800-405-0816.
Fax: 408-441-7302.

(See Next Column)

DUKE, GERSTEL, SHEARER & BREGANTE LLP, San Diego—Continued

MEMBERS OF FIRM

Clifford L. Duke, Jr.
(1921-1989)
Bryan R. Gerstel (A Professional
Corporation)
William K. Shearer (A
Professional Corporation)
Richard D. Bregante (A
Professional Corporation)
Stephen V. Rupp (A
Professional Corporation)
Andrew F. Lloyd (A
Professional Corporation)
David T. Pursiano (A
Professional Corporation)

Daniel J. Perwich (A
Professional Corporation)
Alan R. Johnston (A
Professional Corporation)
Robert K. Goff (A Professional
Corporation)
Bryan R. Snyder (A Professional
Corporation)
Robert D. Shoecraft
Michael S. Woodlock
Dawn R. Brennan
Carolyn J. Kaye

ASSOCIATES

Ronald M. Green
Eric W. Sachrison

Steven L. Weisenberg
Jeffrey A. French

Trinette S. Kosmas

OF COUNSEL

Jeffrey A. Barnett

Reference: Bank of Commerce.

For full biographical listings, see the Martindale-Hubbell Law Directory

HOVEY, KIRBY, THORNTON & HAHN, A PROFESSIONAL CORPORATION (AV)

101 West Broadway, Suite 1100, 92101-8297
Telephone: 619-685-4000
Fax: 619-685-4004
Email: 74754.3143@compuserve.com

Gregg B. Hovey
Cynthia K. Thornton

M. Leslie Hovey
Jane Hahn

Patrick R. Kitchin

For full biographical listings, see the Martindale-Hubbell Law Directory

LINDLEY, LAZAR & SCALES, A PROFESSIONAL CORPORATION (AV)

One America Plaza, 600 West Broadway, Suite 1400, 92101-3302
Telephone: 619-234-9181
Fax: 619-234-8475
Email: 104413.1175@compuserve.com

Luke R. Corbett
Robert M. McLeod
Richard J. Pekin, Jr.

Representative Clients: Southern California Soil & Testing, Inc.; Westana Builders-Developers; Ham Bros. Construction; Shapell Industries, Inc.; Pointe Builders; Morrison Homes, Inc.

For Complete List of Firm Personnel, See General Section

For full biographical listings, see the Martindale-Hubbell Law Directory

SPARBER, FERGUSON, PONDER & RYAN, A PROFESSIONAL LAW CORPORATION (AV)

Imperial Bank Building, 701 "B" Street, Tenth Floor, 92101-8103
Telephone: 619-239-3600
Facsimile: 619-239-5601

Richard E. Sparber
James P. Ferguson
John E. Ponder

Greg J. Ryan
Richard J. Annen
Daniel F. Morrin

Gary B. Rudolph

Todd R. Gabriel
Carol R. McGinnis

William P. Fennell
James E. Highsmith

OF COUNSEL

Mark P. Mandell

LEGAL SUPPORT PERSONNEL

LEGAL ADMINISTRATOR

Beverly K. Driscoll

For full biographical listings, see the Martindale-Hubbell Law Directory

SAN FRANCISCO,* San Francisco Co.

BREON, O'DONNELL, MILLER, BROWN & DANNIS (AV)

19th Floor, Stevenson Place, 71 Stevenson Street, 94105
Telephone: 415-543-4111
Fax: 415-543-4384
Palos Verdes Estates, California Office: Suite 3A, 2550 Via Tejon, 90274.
Telephone: 310-373-6857.
FAX: 310-373-6808.
Salinas, California Office: Suite H120, 17842 Moro Road, Suite F120, 93907.
Telephone: 408-663-0470.

(See Next Column)

MEMBERS OF FIRM

Keith V. Breon
Margaret E. O'Donnell
David G. Miller (Resident, Palos
Verdes Estates Office)
Priscilla Brown
Gregory J. Dannis

Emi R. Uyehara
Bridget A. Flanagan
Nancy B. Bourne
Kathryn Luhe
Marilyn J. Cleveland
Laurie S. Juengert

Joan Birdt (Resident, Palos
Verdes Estates Office)
David A. Wolf
Claudia L. Madrigal
Peter W. Sturges
Laurie E. Reynolds
Guy A. Bryant
Jane Mitchell Weston

Aaron Kaufmann
SueAnn Salmon Evans
(Resident, Palos Verdes
Estates Office)
Janet L. Mueller (Resident,
Palos Verdes Estates Office)
Ivette Peña (Resident, Palos
Verdes Estates Office)

SPECIAL COUNSEL

Martha Buell Scott

Marilyn Kaplan

Representative Clients: Monterey Peninsula Unified School Dist.; Mt. Diablo Unified School Dist.; Palo Alto Unified School Dist.; Santa Cruz City Schools.

For full biographical listings, see the Martindale-Hubbell Law Directory

FELDMAN, WALDMAN & KLINE, A PROFESSIONAL CORPORATION (AV)

3 Embarcadero Center, Suite 2800, 94111
Telephone: 415-981-1300
Fax: 415-981-1350
Email: info@fwk.com
Stockton, California Office: Sperry Building, 146-148 West Weber Avenue.
Telephone: 209-943-2004.
Fax: 209-943-0905.

Murry J. Waldman
Leland R. Selna, Jr.
Michael L. Korbholz
Howard M. Wexler
Patricia S. Mar
Kenneth W. Jones
Paul J. Dion
Vern S. Bothwell
L.J. Chris Martiniak

Martha Jeanne Shaver
(Resident, Stockton Office)
Robert Cedric Goodman
Laura Grad
William F. Adams
Elizabeth A. Thompson
Julie A. Jones
David L. Kanel
Abram S. Feuerstein

Linda Sorensen

Laura J. Dawson
Joanne M. Lafreniere
Paul A. Weiss

Dana A. Suntag
(Resident, Stockton Office)
Danielle Ochs-Tillotson

OF COUNSEL

Richard L. Jaeger

Gerald A. Sherwin
(Resident, Stockton Office)

For full biographical listings, see the Martindale-Hubbell Law Directory

THE LAW OFFICE OF RONALD H. KAHN (AV)

353 Sacramento Street, Suite 460, 94111
Telephone: 415-274-0880
FAX: 415-274-0889

ASSOCIATE

Christopher Dyas

OF COUNSEL

Kelly S. Hise

For full biographical listings, see the Martindale-Hubbell Law Directory

KINDER, WUERFEL & CHOLAKIAN, A PROFESSIONAL CORPORATION (AV)

555 Montgomery Street, Ninth Floor, 94111
Telephone: 415-398-1551; 800-992-5990
FAX: 415-398-3301
URL: http://www.kwcapc.com
Santa Rosa, California Office: 2300 Northpoint Parkway.
Telephones: 707-522-8020; 800-992-5990.
FAX: 707-522-8022.
Costa Mesa, California Office: Avenue of the Arts.
Telephone: 714-825-3590; 800-992-5990.

H. Stuart Kinder
Mark D. Wuerfel

Kevin K. Cholakian
Julian J. Pardini
(Resident, Santa Rosa Office)

SPECIAL COUNSEL

Mark A. Koop

Nan R. Hooven
Paul B. Justi

Robert E. Belshaw
David H. Bennett
Dean C. Burnick
Cheryl Castrogiovanni
Douglas M. Chapman

Christopher J. Connell
(Resident, Santa Rosa Office)
Michael J. Estep
James M. Gentile
Garth A. Gersten

(See Next Column)

KINDER, WUERFEL & CHOLAKIAN A PROFESSIONAL CORPORATION—
Continued

Victor G. Greene	Steven J. Plas
Peter R. Harris	Anthony O. Ricucci
(Resident, Santa Rosa Office)	Charlene P. Rosack
Kathleen M. Hurly	Scott A. Slomiak
Timothy S. Kirk	Michael A. Topp
Bryan A. McBurney	Harold A. Weston

LEGAL SUPPORT PERSONNEL
Gary T. Hall, Legal Administrator

For full biographical listings, see the Martindale-Hubbell Law Directory

LEACH, McGREEVY & BAUTISTA (AV)

1735 Pacific Avenue, 94109
Telephone: 415-775-4455
Telefax: 415-775-7435
Southern California Office: 13643 Fifth Street, Chino, CA. 91710.
Telephone: 909-590-2224.

Theodore Tamba (1900-1973)	Teresa A. Cunningham
John T. Harmon (1928-1993)	J. Curtis Cox
David G. Leach	Robert W. Shinnick
Richard E. McGreevy	Philip T. Kilduff
A. Marquez Bautista	Paul David Katerndahl

ASSOCIATE
John C. Connolly
OF COUNSEL

Roger G. Eliassen	Lloyd F. Postel

For full biographical listings, see the Martindale-Hubbell Law Directory

MURPHY, PEARSON, BRADLEY & FEENEY, A PROFESSIONAL CORPORATION (AV)

88 Kearny Street, 11th Floor, 94108
Telephone: 415-788-1900
Telecopier: 415-393-8087
Sacramento, California Office: Suite 200, 3600 American River Drive, 95864.
Telephone: 916-483-6074.
Telecopier: 916-483-6088.

Karen M. Goodman	Mark S. Perelman
(Resident, Sacramento Office)	

For Complete List of Firm Personnel, See General Section

For full biographical listings, see the Martindale-Hubbell Law Directory

ROGERS, JOSEPH, O'DONNELL & QUINN, A PROFESSIONAL CORPORATION (AV)

311 California Street, 94104
Telephone: 415-956-2828
Fax: 415-956-6457

Allan J. Joseph	Anna M. Rossi
Martin Quinn	Connie M. Teevan
Neil H. O'Donnell	Allen Samelson
Margot Wenger	Suzanne M. Mellard
Pamela Phillips	Neil H. Weinstein
Renée D. Wasserman	Patricia A. Meagher
Merri A. Baldwin	

OF COUNSEL

Joseph W. Rogers	William Bennett Turner
Kyra A. Subbotin	

David F. Innis	Ian K. Sweedler
Jennifer M. Kawamura	Matthew D. Levett
Sean M. SeLegue	E. Sean McLoughlin
Aaron P. Silberman	

SPECIAL COUNSEL
Valerie Ackerman

For full biographical listings, see the Martindale-Hubbell Law Directory

SELTZER LAW GROUP (AV)

Suite 1300, Steuart Street Tower, One Market Plaza, 94105-1402
Telephone: 415-281-2154
Fax: 415-281-2194
Email: mseltzoo@counsel.com

Margaret A. Seltzer

For full biographical listings, see the Martindale-Hubbell Law Directory

STUBBS, HITTIG & LEONE, A PROFESSIONAL CORPORATION (AV)

Fox Plaza, Suite 818, 1390 Market Street, 94102-5399
Telephone: 415-861-8200
Telecopier: 415-861-6700
Email: SHLSF@aol.com

Gregory E. Stubbs	Louis A. Leone
H. Christopher Hittig	Marina B. Pitts

For full biographical listings, see the Martindale-Hubbell Law Directory

WELCH, OLRICH & MORI, A PROFESSIONAL CORPORATION (AV)

Four Embarcadero Center, 37th Floor, 94111
Telephone: 415-397-4100
Telecopier: 415-986-0245
Santa Rosa, California Office: 50 Courthouse Square, Suite 602.
Telephone: 707-577-0220.

Vernon D. Stokes (Retired)	Denise L. Olrich
Craig K. Welch	James S. Mori

Jan C. Nielsen

For full biographical listings, see the Martindale-Hubbell Law Directory

SAN JOSE, * Santa Clara Co.

DUKE, GERSTEL, SHEARER & BREGANTE, LLP (AV)

1740 Technology Drive, Suite 250, 95110
Telephone: 408-441-7800
800-405-0816
Fax: 408-441-7302
Email: dgsb@lawinfo.com *URL:* http://www.dgsb.com
San Diego, California Office: 101 West Broadway, P.O. Box 85470, 92186-5470.
Telephone: 619-232-0816; 800-405-0816.
Fax: 619-232-4661. Costa Mesa, California Office: 3200 Park Center Drive, Suite 1000, 92626.
Telephone: 714-551-8664, 800-405-0816.

MEMBER OF FIRM
Robert K. Goff (A Professional Corporation)
ASSOCIATES

Ronald M. Green	Jeffrey A. French

OF COUNSEL
Jeffrey A. Barnett

Reference: Bank of Commerce.

LAW OFFICES OF THOMAS R. HOGAN (AV)

60 South Market Street, Suite 1125, 95113-2332
Telephone: 408-292-7600
Facsimile: 408-292-7611

ASSOCIATE
Kelly W. Bhirdo
PARALEGAL
Leslie Holmes

For full biographical listings, see the Martindale-Hubbell Law Directory

MAHL REHON WALWORTH & ROBERTS, A PROFESSIONAL CORPORATION (AV)

Ten Almaden Boulevard, Suite 1440, 95113
Telephone: 408-494-0900
Fax: 408-494-0909

Susan J. Mahl	Janet R. Walworth
Peter M. Rehon	Lisa C. Roberts
Michael T. Parsons	

For full biographical listings, see the Martindale-Hubbell Law Directory

McMANIS, FAULKNER & MORGAN (AV)

160 West Santa Clara Street, 10th Floor, 95113
Telephone: 408-279-8700
Fax: 408-279-3244; 408-279-0494
Email: mfm@mfmlaw.com

MEMBERS OF FIRM

James McManis	William Faulkner
Donelle Morgan	

ASSOCIATES

Nora Rousso	Michael Reedy
Lisa Herrick	Douglas Watanabe
Kelly McHaffie	

For full biographical listings, see the Martindale-Hubbell Law Directory

San Jose—Continued

MILLER, MORTON, CAILLAT & NEVIS (AV)

50 West San Fernando Street, Suite 1300, 95113-2413
Telephone: 408-292-1765
Telecopier: 408-292-4484

Richard W. Morton (1916-1975)   Charles V. Caillat (1920-1990)
Harvey C. Miller (1906-1993)

MEMBERS OF FIRM

David L. Nevis	Joseph A. Scanlan, Jr.
Francis J. Hughes	Carolyn Tobiason Stuart
Peter A. Kline	William K. Hurley
Stevan C. Adelman	Peter V. Dessau
	Eric Mogensen

OF COUNSEL

Nancy F. Symons   Susan L. Sutton
Pamela J. Silberstein

ASSOCIATES

Kathryn E. Barrett	David I. Kornbluh
Katherine S. Pak	Kimberly Holtz MacMillan

Representative Clients: Trammell Crow Residential Services; Yamaoka Builders, Inc.; B. T. Mancini Co., Inc.; Lennox International, Inc.; Greenbriar Homes Company; Webcor Builders, Inc.; Hensel Phelps Construction Co.; Ray Helwig Plumbing & Heating Co.; Builders Exchange.

For full biographical listings, see the Martindale-Hubbell Law Directory

SAN RAFAEL,* Marin Co.

RAGGHIANTI • FREITAS • MONTOBBIO • WALLACE LLP (AV)

874 Fourth Street, Suite D, 94901
Telephone: 415-453-9433
Fax: 415-453-8269

Gary T. Ragghianti	J. Randolph Wallace
David P. Freitas	Patrick M. Macias
J. Mark Montobbio	Robert F. Epstein
	John Ralph Thomas

For full biographical listings, see the Martindale-Hubbell Law Directory

SANTA ANA,* Orange Co.

HORTON BARBARO & REILLY (AV)

A Partnership including Professional Corporations
Second Floor, 200 North Main Street, 92701
Telephone: 714-835-2122
Fax: 714-973-4892
Email: HBR@Hortonetal.com *URL:* http://www.Hortonetal.com

MEMBERS OF FIRM

Jay Cordell Horton (A Professional Corporation)	Geoffrey S. Gray
	John R. Hanna
Frank P. Barbaro (A Professional Corporation)	William O. Humphreys
	Karen L. Karavatos
Ned P. Reilly (A Professional Corporation)	John E. O'Brien, Jr.

ASSOCIATES

Malena R. LeClair	Timothy V. Kassouni
Robert J. Younger	Richard E. Donahoo

For full biographical listings, see the Martindale-Hubbell Law Directory

SANTA MONICA, Los Angeles Co.

GERALD T. YOSHIDA (AV)

100 Wilshire Boulevard, Suite 1000, 90401
Telephone: 310-393-9212
Telecopier: 310-395-2132

Representative Clients: Vido Artukovich & Sons Construction; McKean Construction; Spiess Construction; Gierlich-Mitchell, Inc.; Ullibarri Construction; Hill Crane Service, Inc.; ACI General Engineering Contractors; A.A. Portanova & Sons, Inc.; Rough Terraih, Inc.; Altfillisch Construction.

For full biographical listings, see the Martindale-Hubbell Law Directory

SANTA ROSA,* Sonoma Co.

BELDEN, ABBEY, WEITZENBERG & KELLY, A PROFESSIONAL CORPORATION (AV)

1105 North Dutton Avenue, P.O. Box 1566, 95402
Telephone: 707-542-5050
Telecopier: 707-542-2589

Thomas P. Kelly, Jr.   W. Barton Weitzenberg
Wayne R. Wolski

Representative Clients: Exchange Bank of Santa Rosa; Westamerica Bank; North Bay Title Co.; Northwestern Title Security Co.; Geyser Peak Winery; Santa Rosa City School District; Sonoma National Bank; Arrowood Vineyards & Winery; Arthur & DeVincenzi Concrete; Friedman Bros. Hardware, Inc.

(See Next Column)

For Complete List of Firm Personnel, See General Section

For full biographical listings, see the Martindale-Hubbell Law Directory

SHERMAN OAKS, Los Angeles Co.

SCHIMMEL, HILLSHAFER & LOEWENTHAL (AV)

15250 Ventura Boulevard Penthouse, Suite 1210, 91403-3110
Telephone: 818-905-6283
Fax: 818-905-6372
URL: http://www.shllaw.com
Ventura, California Office: 290 Maple Court, Suite 200. Telephone 805-289-1430.

MEMBERS OF FIRM

Alan I. Schimmel	David A. Loewenthal
Robert D. Hillshafer	Glenn T. Rosenblatt
	Jeff B. Domine

LEGAL SUPPORT PERSONNEL

Blanca L. Saltos (Paralegal)	Claudia A. Galati
Cynthia G. Carter (Paralegal)	(Office Administrator)

For full biographical listings, see the Martindale-Hubbell Law Directory

STOCKTON,* San Joaquin Co.

MAYALL, HURLEY, KNUTSEN, SMITH & GREEN, A PROFESSIONAL CORPORATION (AV)

2453 Grand Canal Boulevard, Second Floor, 95207-8253
Telephone: 209-477-3833
Fax: 209-473-4818

Edwin Mayall (1907-1980)	William W. Hale
John J. Hurley (Retired)	Mark Stephen Adams
Clarence D. Knutsen	J. Anthony Abbott
Alan E. Smith	Peter J. Whipple
Dennis J. Green	Kristen M. Hegge
	Vladimir F. Kozina

William L. Anderson	William J. Gorham, III
Donald W. West	Matthew Christopher Felix
Robert E. Laubengayer	Joseph A. Salazar, Jr.
Mark E. Berry	Steven A. Malcoun
	Lesley Solomon

Representative Clients: Allstate Insurance Co.; California State Automobile Assn.; Fireman's Fund Insurance Co.; General Motors Corp.; Texaco, Inc; State Farm Mutual Insurance Cos.; Beck Development, Inc; HD Arnaiz, Ltd; Vito Transporation; The Alpine Group.

For full biographical listings, see the Martindale-Hubbell Law Directory

WALNUT CREEK, Contra Costa Co.

FIELD, RICHARDSON & WILHELMY (AV)

Peri Executive Centre, 2033 North Main Street, Suite 900, 94596-3729
Telephone: 510-934-7700
Telecopier: 510-934-6090

MEMBERS

Robert C. Field   Robert W. Richardson
Alan J. Wilhelmy

ASSOCIATE

Emelyn Jewett Carothers

OF COUNSEL

Donald L. Edgar

Reference: Civic Bank of Commerce (Walnut Creek Regional Office).

For full biographical listings, see the Martindale-Hubbell Law Directory

JACKL & KATZEN (AV)

2033 North Main Street, Suite 700, 94596
Telephone: 510-932-8500
Fax: 510-932-1961
Email: jklawfirm@aol.com

MEMBERS OF FIRM

V. James Jackl   Linda R. Katzen

Andrew N. Contopoulos

For full biographical listings, see the Martindale-Hubbell Law Directory

COLORADO

COLORADO SPRINGS,* El Paso Co.

BELTZ, EDWARDS & SABO, L.L.P. (AV)

729 South Cascade, 80903
Telephone: 719-473-4444; 719-634-6620
Fax: 719-444-0186

W. Thomas Beltz	Daniel P. Edwards
John W. Sabo, III	

Daniel A. West

Representative Clients: Dows Investments, Inc.; Douglas Veltri Contracting; HBS, Inc.; Holmes Plumbing & Heating, Inc.; Jones Plumbing & Heating, LLC; Midway Development Company; Moldrite Products, Inc.; Newport Company; Nighthawk Industries, Inc.; RMG Engineers.

For full biographical listings, see the Martindale-Hubbell Law Directory

DENVER,* Denver Co.

DAVIS & WEINSTEIN (AV)

Suite 2600, 1600 Broadway, 80202
Telephone: 303-861-4166

Jo Ann Weinstein

For full biographical listings, see the Martindale-Hubbell Law Directory

OTTEN, JOHNSON, ROBINSON, NEFF & RAGONETTI, P.C. (AV)

950 Seventeenth Street, 16th Floor, 80202
Telephone: 303-825-8400
Telecopier: 303-825-6525

Thomas J. Ragonetti	Darrell G. Waas

Representative Clients: Aetna Life Insurance Co.; The Broe Companies; Inc.; Colorado National Bank; Connecticut General Life Insurance Co.; First Nationwide Bank; Homart Development Co.; Land Title Guarantee Co.; Trizec Corporation Ltd.; U.S. West Communications, Inc.; The Western Sugar Co.

For Complete List of Firm Personnel, See General Section

For full biographical listings, see the Martindale-Hubbell Law Directory

REIMAN & BAYAZ, P.C. (AV)

1600 Broadway, Suite 1640, 80202
Telephone: 303-860-1500
Fax: 303-839-4380

Jeff Reiman	Marcie K. Bayaz
Darren E. Temkin-Nadel	Eric B. Liebman

For full biographical listings, see the Martindale-Hubbell Law Directory

GOLDEN,* Jefferson Co.

HOLLEY, ALBERTSON & POLK, P.C. (AV)

Suite 100, 1667 Cole Boulevard, 80401
Telephone: 303-233-7838
Fax: 303-233-2860

George Alan Holley	Scott D. Albertson
Dennis B. Polk	
Eric E. Torgersen	Thomas A. Walsh
Howard R. Stone	

Reference: First Bank of Wheat Ridge.

For full biographical listings, see the Martindale-Hubbell Law Directory

CONNECTICUT

GREENWICH, Fairfield Co.

ALBERT, WARD & JOHNSON, P.C. (AV)

125 Mason Street, P.O. Box 1668, 06836
Telephone: 203-661-8600
Telecopier: 203-661-8051

OF COUNSEL

David Albert	C. Robton Perelli-Minetti

(See Next Column)

Tom S. Ward, Jr.	Howard R. Wolfe
Scott R. Johnson	Christopher A. Kristoff
Jane D. Hogeman	Vicki K. Comberiati

For full biographical listings, see the Martindale-Hubbell Law Directory

HARTFORD,* Hartford Co.

GORDON, MUIR AND FOLEY (AV)

Hartford Square North, Ten Columbus Boulevard, 06106-5123
Telephone: 860-525-5361
Telecopier: 860-525-4849

MEMBERS OF FIRM

William S. Gordon, Jr.	William J. Gallitto
(1946-1956)	Gerald R. Swirsky
George Muir (1939-1976)	Robert J. O'Brien
Edward J. Foley (1955-1983)	Philip J. O'Connor
Peter C. Schwartz	Kenneth G. Williams
John J. Reid	Chester J. Bukowski
John H. Goodrich, Jr.	Mary Ann Santacroce
R. Bradley Wolfe	J. Lawrence Price
Jon Stephen Berk	Mary Anne Alicia Charron
	James G. Kelly

ASSOCIATES

Kevin F. Morin	Andrew J. Hern
Claudia A. Baio	Eileen McCarthy Geel
Patrick T. Treacy	Christopher L. Slack
	Renee W. Dwyer

OF COUNSEL

Stephen M. Riley

Reference: Fleet Bank.

For full biographical listings, see the Martindale-Hubbell Law Directory

SOROKIN SOROKIN GROSS HYDE & WILLIAMS P.C. (AV)

One Corporate Center, 06103
Telephone: 860-525-6645
Fax: 860-522-1781
Simsbury, Connecticut Office: 730 Hopmeadow Street.
Telephone: 860-651-9348.
Rocky Hill, Connecticut Office: 2360 Main Street.
Telephone: 860-563-9305.
Fax: 860-529-6931.

Clifford J. Grandjean	Richard C. Robinson

For Complete List of Firm Personnel, See General Section

For full biographical listings, see the Martindale-Hubbell Law Directory

WALLINGFORD, New Haven Co.

DELANEY, ZEMETIS, DONAHUE, DURHAM & NOONAN, P.C. (AV)

111 South Main Street, P.O. Box 747, 06492
Telephone: 203-269-1441
Fax: 203-284-9428

Joseph M. Delaney	Timothy W. Donahue
Terence A. Zemetis	Michael G. Durham
Patrick M. Noonan	
Edward W. Mayer, Jr.	Edward T. Falsey, III
Thomas J. Flanagan	Mark Popolizio

For full biographical listings, see the Martindale-Hubbell Law Directory

DELAWARE

WILMINGTON,* New Castle Co.

WARREN B. BURT & ASSOCIATES (AV)

1700 Mellon Bank Center, 919 Market Street, 19801-3023
Telephone: 302-429-9430
Fax: 302-429-9427

ASSOCIATES

Richard D. Abrams	Michael F. Duggan

For full biographical listings, see the Martindale-Hubbell Law Directory

DISTRICT OF COLUMBIA

WASHINGTON, D.C. Co.

* indicates certain Bar Register subscribers, in cities of comparable size and importance, who maintain an additional office in Washington, D.C. and who have arranged for representation as a part of the Washington, D.C. listings that follow

* BELL, BOYD & LLOYD (AV)

1615 L Street, N.W., 20036
Telephone: 202-466-6300
FAX: 202-463-0678
Chicago, Illinois Office: Three First National Plaza, Suite 3300, 70 West Madison Street.
Telephone: 312-372-1121.
FAX: 312-372-2098.

RESIDENT PARTNERS

Francis J. Pelland	Joel S. Rubinstein
	Robert J. Sciaroni

OF COUNSEL
Marvin P. Sadur

RESIDENT ASSOCIATES

Brian Cohen	Andrew N. Cook
(Not admitted in DC)	

For Complete List of Firm Personnel, See General Section

For full biographical listings, see the Martindale-Hubbell Law Directory

BRAUDE & MARGULIES, P.C. (AV)

The Brawner Building, 888 Seventeenth Street, N.W., Suite 500, 20006
Telephone: 202-293-2993
Fax: 202-331-7916
Email: Braudemarg@aol.com
Riyadh, Saudi Arabia Office: Mohammed A. Al-Abdullah, P.O. Box 59446, Nuzha Building, Sixth Floor, 11525.
Telephone: 966-1-405-1291.
Fax: 966-1-405-1291.
Abu Dhabi, United Arab Emirates Office: P.O. Box 43908.
Telephone: (971-2) 787222.
Fax: (971-2) 784001.

Herman M. Braude

Samuel M. Morrison, Jr.	Conrad Christopher Ledoux
Robert D. Windus	Stuart H. Sakwa
John P. McGowan, Jr. (Not	(Not admitted in DC)
admitted in DC; Resident,	James D. Finn, Jr.
Abu Dhabi, U.A.E. Office)	

OF COUNSEL
J. Richard Margulies

For full biographical listings, see the Martindale-Hubbell Law Directory

KENNETH R. FEINBERG & ASSOCIATES (AV)

1120 20th Street, N.W. Suite 740 South, 20036
Telephone: 202-371-1110
Fax: 202-962-9290
New York, N.Y. Office: 780 3rd Avenue, Suite 2202.
Telephone: 212-527-9600.
Fax: 212-527-9611.

ASSOCIATES

Deborah E. Greenspan	Peter H. Woodin
Michael K. Rozen	(Not admitted in DC)
(Not admitted in DC)	M. Catherine Faint

OF COUNSEL
Jacqueline E. Zins

For full biographical listings, see the Martindale-Hubbell Law Directory

ROBERT E. LOSCH, P.C. (AV)

1716 New Hampshire Avenue, N.W., 20009
Telephone: 202-296-4222

Robert E. Losch

SELTZER AND ROSEN, P.C. (AV)

One Franklin Square, Suite 310 East 1301 K Street, N.W., 20005-3307
Telephone: 202-682-4585
Telecopier: 202-682-4599

E. Manning Seltzer	Harold I. Rosen
	Mark E. Davis

ENGINEER ADVISOR
John W. Morris

For full biographical listings, see the Martindale-Hubbell Law Directory

* VENABLE ATTORNEYS AT LAW VENABLE, BAETJER, HOWARD & CIVILETTI, LLP (AV)

A Partnership including Professional Corporations
Suite 1000, 1201 New York Avenue, N.W., 20005
Telephone: 202-962-4800
Fax: 202-962-8300
Baltimore, Maryland Office: Venable, Baetjer and Howard LLP, 1800 Mercantile Bank & Trust Building, 2 Hopkins Plaza.
Telephone: 410-244-7400.
McLean, Virginia Office: Venable, Baetjer and Howard LLP, Suite 400, 2010 Corporate Ridge.
Telephone: 703-760-1600.
Rockville, Maryland Office: Venable, Baetjer and Howard LLP, Suite 500, One Church Street, P. O. Box 1906.
Telephone: 301-217-5600.
Towson, Maryland Office: Venable, Baetjer and Howard LLP, 210 Allegheny Avenue, P. O. Box 5517.
Telephone: 410-494-6200.

MEMBERS OF FIRM

Benjamin R. Civiletti (P.C.)	Jeffrey A. Dunn (Also at
(Also at Baltimore and	Baltimore, Maryland Office)
Towson, Maryland Offices)	George F. Pappas (Also at
Thomas J. Kenney, Jr. (P.C.)	Baltimore, Maryland Office)
(Not admitted in DC; Also at	James L. Shea (Not admitted in
Baltimore, Maryland Office)	DC; also at Baltimore,
James K. Archibald (Also at	Maryland Office)
Baltimore, Maryland Office)	Maurice Baskin

For Complete List of Firm Personnel, See General Section

For full biographical listings, see the Martindale-Hubbell Law Directory

WATT, TIEDER & HOFFAR, L.L.P. (AV)

601 Pennsylvania Avenue, N.W., Suite 900, 20004
Telephone: 202-462-4697
Telecopier: 703-893-8029
McLean Virginia Office: 7929 Westpark Drive, Suite 400,
Telephone: 703-749-1000.
Telecopier: 703-893-8029.
Irvine California Office: 3 Park Plaza, Suite 1530.
Telephone: 714-852-6700.

MEMBERS OF FIRM

John B. Tieder, Jr.	Robert K. Cox
	David C. Romm

For full biographical listings, see the Martindale-Hubbell Law Directory

FLORIDA

AVENTURA, Dade Co.

BUCHANAN INGERSOLL, PROFESSIONAL CORPORATION (AV(T))

One Turnberry Place, 19495 Biscayne Boulevard, Suite 606, 33180
Telephone: 305-933-5600
Telecopier: 305-933-2350
URL: http://www.bipc.com
Pittsburgh, Pennsylvania Office: One Oxford Centre, 301 Grant Street, 20th Floor.
Telephone: 412-562-8800.
Philadelphia, Pennsylvania Office: Two Logan Square, Twelfth Floor, 18th & Arch Streets.
Telephone: 215-665-8700.
Harrisburg, Pennsylvania Office: 30 North Third Street.
Telephone: 717-237-4800.
Miami, Florida Office: NationsBank Tower, 100 S.E. Second Street.
Telephone: 305-347-4080.
Tampa, Florida Office: Suite 2500, 401 East Jackson Street.
Telephone: 813-222-8180.
Princeton, New Jersey Office: Buchanan Ingersoll, A Partnership, College Centre, 500 College Road East.
Telephone: 609-987-6800.
Lexington, Kentucky Office: Suite 600, PNC Bank Plaza, 200 West Vine Street.
Telephone: 606-225-5333.
Buffalo, New York Office: 1100 Main Place Tower, 350 Main Street.
Telephone: 716-854-4100.
Fax: 816-854-4227.

Joshua L. Dubin	Mark J. Neuberger

SENIOR ATTORNEY
Ralph B. Bekkevold

Todd A. Bancroft	Randi S. Rothfield
Kevin Carmichael	Richard N. Schermer
Jeffrey M. Goodz	Rebecca S. Trinkler

For full biographical listings, see the Martindale-Hubbell Law Directory

BOCA RATON, Palm Beach Co.

MICHAUD, BUSCHMANN, FOX, FERRARA & MITTELMARK, P.A. (AV)

33 Southeast 8th Street, 33432
Telephone: 561-392-0540
Fax: 561-392-0582
Email: Bocalaw@MBFFM.com

Scott H. Michaud	Brian S. Fox
Paul Buschmann	James T. Ferrara
Michael K. Mittelmark	

Marc T. Millian

For full biographical listings, see the Martindale-Hubbell Law Directory

---

FORT MYERS, * Lee Co.

GOLDBERG, GOLDSTEIN & BUCKLEY, P.A. (AV)

1515 Broadway, P.O. Box 2366, 33901-2366
Telephone: 941-334-1146
Fax: 941-334-3039
Naples, Florida Office: 2150 Goodlette Road, Suite 105, Parkway Financial Center, 34102.
Telephone: 941-262-4888.
Fax: 941-262-8716.
Port Charlotte, Florida Office: Emerald Square, Suite 1, 2852 Tamiami Trail, 33952.
Telephone: 941-624-2393.
Fax: 941-624-2155.
Cape Coral, Florida Office: 1603 Hancock Bridge Parkway, 33990.
Telephone: 941-574-5575.
Fax: 941-574-9213.
Lehigh Acres, Florida Office: 1458 Lee Boulevard, Lee Boulevard Shopping Center, 33936.
Telephone: 941-368-6101.
Fax: 941-368-2461.
South Fort Myers, Florida Office: Horizon Plaza, 16050 South Tamiami Trail, Suite 101, 33908.
Telephone: 941-433-6777.
Fax: 941-433-0578.
Bonita Springs, Florida Office: 3431 Bonita Beach Road, Suite 208, 34134.
Telephone: 941-495-0003.
Fax: 941-495-0564.

Ray Goldstein	George J. Mitar
Stephen W. Buckley	Michael J. Ciccarone
Harvey B. Goldberg	Jay Cooper
John B. Cechman	Jonathan D. Conant
J. Jeffrey Rice	Raymond L. Racila
Richard Lee Purtz	Luis E. Insignares
Martin G. Arnowitz	Scot D. Goldberg

Approved Attorneys for: Attorneys' Title Insurance Fund.

For full biographical listings, see the Martindale-Hubbell Law Directory

---

SMOOT ADAMS EDWARDS & GREEN, P.A. (AV)

One University Park Suite 600, 12800 University Drive, P.O. Box 60259, 33906-6259
Telephone: 941-489-1776
(800) 226-1777 (in Florida)
Fax: 941-489-2444
Email: 71600.2745@compuserve.com

J. Tom Smoot, Jr.	Bruce D. Green
Hal Adams	Steven I. Winer
Franklyn A. (Chip) Johnson (1947-1991)	Mark R. Komray
	Clayton W. Crevasse
Charles B. Edwards	M. Brian Cheffer

Robert S. Forman	C. Berk Edwards, Jr.
Kathleen W. McBride	Melville G. Brinson, III
Lowell Schoenfeld	Samuel J. Hagan, IV.

For full biographical listings, see the Martindale-Hubbell Law Directory

---

JACKSONVILLE, * Duval Co.

HEDRICK, DEWBERRY & REGAN, P.A. (AV)

50 North Laura Street, Suite 2225, 32202
Telephone: 904-356-1300
Fax: 904-356-8050

Michael J. Dewberry	Alexandra Krueger Hedrick
Jeffrey C. Regan	

Clinton Allen Wright, III	Evan G. Frayman

For full biographical listings, see the Martindale-Hubbell Law Directory

---

KISSIMMEE, * Osceola Co.

POHL & SHORT, P.A.

(See Winter Park)

MIAMI, * Dade Co.

DANIELS, KASHTAN & FORNARIS, P.A. (AV)

241 Sevilla Avenue, Penthouse 2, 33134
Telephone: 305-448-7988
Telecopier: 305-448-7978

Richard G. Daniels	Martha D. Fornaris
Michael F. Kashtan	Angel Garcia
	John E. Oramas

Albert Blair	David N. Gambach
Elizabeth M. Touma	Camille D. Riviere
Ana M. Latour	Katherine Lamas
	Tracey A. Wright

Reference: Barnett Bank.

For full biographical listings, see the Martindale-Hubbell Law Directory

---

ELDER & KURZMAN, P.A. (AV)

Courvoisier Centre II, Suite 401 601 Brickell Key Drive, 33131
Telephone: 305-373-6065
Broward: 954-763-5304
Fax: 305-373-6066

David R. Elder	Vincent F. Vaccarella
Michael J. Kurzman	Sharon A. Hornett

OF COUNSEL
Fredrica B. Elder

For full biographical listings, see the Martindale-Hubbell Law Directory

---

KEITH, MACK, LEWIS, COHEN & LUMPKIN (AV)

First Union Financial Center, Twentieth Floor, 200 South Biscayne Boulevard, 33131-2310
Telephone: 305-358-7605
Fax: 305-358-4755
Email: PREVAIL@KEITHMACK.COM

MEMBERS OF FIRM

Edgar Lewis	Jan Carson Cheezem
Robert A. Cohen	Loren S. Granoff
R. Hugh Lumpkin	Jack S. Lewis
Gregg S. Ahrens	Alan Rosenthal
	Norman S. Segall

ASSOCIATES

Michael J. Hogsten	Michele S. Primeau
Felix M. Lasarte	Cynthia Ramos
Dawn Marshall	Jack R. Reiter
Mercedes Padin	Karl J. Schumer
	Jeffrey P. Shapiro

OF COUNSEL

Seymour D. Keith	James L. Mack

Representative Clients: CitiBank, F.S.B.; Attorneys Title Insurance Fund, Inc.; Barnett Bank, N.A.
Approved Counsel: First American Title Insurance Co.; Attorneys Title Insurance Fund, Inc.; Commonwealth Title Insurance Co.
Reference: CitiBank, F.S.B.

For full biographical listings, see the Martindale-Hubbell Law Directory

---

SIEGFRIED, RIVERA, LERNER DE LA TORRE & SOBEL, P.A. (AV)

Suite 1102, 201 Alhambra Circle (Coral Gables), 33134
Telephone: 305-442-3334
Fax: 305-443-3292

Steven M. Siegfried	Helio De La Torre
Oscar R. Rivera	Peter H. Edwards
Lisa A. Lerner	Stuart H. Sobel

Maria Victoria Arias	Elisabeth D. Kozlow
Gracian Celaya	Paul J. Layne
James F. Harrington	Samuel A. Persaud
	Adrienne F. Promoff

OF COUNSEL
H. Hugh Mc Connell

For full biographical listings, see the Martindale-Hubbell Law Directory

Miami—Continued

Welbaum, Guernsey, Hingston, Greenleaf & Gregory, L.L.P. (AV)

Penthouse Suite, 901 Ponce de Leon Boulevard (Coral Gables), 33134-3009
Telephone: 305-441-8900
Fax: 305-441-2255

MEMBERS OF FIRM

R. Earl Welbaum	Robert A. Hingston
Dan B. Guernsey	W. Frank Greenleaf
	John H. Gregory

ASSOCIATES

Michael Yates	Mark D. Greenwell

OF COUNSEL

Alice E. Warwick	René Sacasas

For full biographical listings, see the Martindale-Hubbell Law Directory

NAPLES,* Collier Co.

Quarles & Brady (AV)

Barnett Center, 4501 Tamiami Trail North Suite 300, 33940-3060
Telephone: 941-262-5959
Fax: 941-434-4999
Milwaukee, Wisconsin Office: 411 East Wisconsin Avenue, 53202-4497.
Telephone: 414-277-5000.
Fax: 414-271-3552.
Madison, Wisconsin Office: Firstar Plaza, One South Pinckney Street, P.O. Box 2113, 53701-2113.
Telephone: 608-251-5000.
Fax: 608-251-9166.
West Palm Beach, Florida Office: 222 Lakeview Avenue, 4th Floor, 33401.
Telephone: 561-653-5000.
Fax: 561-653-5333.
Phoenix, Arizona Office: One Camelback Building, One East Camelback Road, Suite 400, 85012-1649.
Telephone: 602-230-5500.
Fax: 602-230-5598.

PARTNER
Robert E. Doyle, Jr.

ASSOCIATES

Mark Hubert Muller	James T. Demarest

For Complete List of Firm Personnel, See General Section

For full biographical listings, see the Martindale-Hubbell Law Directory

ORLANDO,* Orange Co.

Baker & Hostetler (AV)

SunBank Center, Suite 2300, 200 South Orange Avenue, 32802-3432
Telephone: 407-649-4000
In Cleveland, Ohio: 3200 National City Center, 1900 East Ninth Street.
Telephone: 216-621-0200.
In Columbus, Ohio: Capitol Square, Suite 2100, 65 East State Street.
Telephone: 614-228-1541.
In Denver, Colorado: 303 East 17th Avenue, Suite 1100.
Telephone: 303-861-0600.
In Houston, Texas: 1000 Louisiana, Suite 2000.
Telephone: 713-751-1600.
In Long Beach, California: 300 Oceangate, Suite 620.
Telephone: 310-432-2827.
In Los Angeles, California: 600 Wilshire Boulevard.
Telephone: 213-624-2400.
In Washington, D.C.: Washington Square, Suite 1100, 1050 Connecticut Avenue, N.W., Suite 1100.
Telephone: 202-861-1500.
In College Park, Maryland: 9658 Baltimore Boulevard, Suite 206.
Telephone: 301-441-2781.
In Alexandria, Virginia: 437 North Lee Street.
Telephone: 703-549-1294.
In San Francisco, California: One Sansome Street, Suite 2000.
Telephone: 415-951-4705.

PARTNER
John W. Foster, Sr.

For Complete List of Firm Personnel, See General Section

For full biographical listings, see the Martindale-Hubbell Law Directory

Brown & Van Leuven, P.A. (AV)

111 North Orange Avenue, Suite 875, P.O. Box 2873, 32802-2873
Telephone: 407-425-9566
Fax: 407-425-9596
Kissimmee, Florida Office: 201 East Ruby Avenue, Suite A, 34741.
Telephone: 407-870-9998.
Fax: 407-870-5510.

Usher L. Brown	Mary B. Van Leuven

(See Next Column)

Suzanne D'Agresta	Sandra J. Pomerantz
	Mark A. Tittle

For full biographical listings, see the Martindale-Hubbell Law Directory

Moye, O'Brien, O'Rourke, Hogan & Pickert (AV)

Suite 710, 201 East Pine Street, 32801
Telephone: 407-843-3341
Fax: 407-843-3048
Chicago, Illinois Office: O'Brien, O'Rourke, & Hogan, Suite 830, 135 South La Salle Street.
Telephone: 312-372-1462.
Fax: 312-372-8029.
Atlanta, Georgia Office: 999 Peachtree Street, Northeast, Suite 2020.
Telephone: 404-875-6300.

James Elton Moye (Resident)	Stephen W. Pickert (Resident)

ASSOCIATES

Bryan L. Capps (Resident)	Gregory S. Martin (Resident)
Patrick J. Kennedy (Resident)	Nathan E. Minear (Resident, Atlanta, Georgia Office)

Representative Clients: Allied Data Communications, Inc.; Applied Concepts; Archer-Western Contractors, Ltd.; Atlanta Testing & Engineering, Inc.; Belfour Beatty, Inc.; Balfour Beatty Construction, Inc.; Barnett Banks, Inc.; Bell-Mann, Inc.; Cannon Sline; Clinton Technical Institute.

For full biographical listings, see the Martindale-Hubbell Law Directory

Pohl & Short, P.A.

(See Winter Park)

Russell & Hull, P.A. (AV)

537 North Magnolia Avenue, P.O. Box 2751, 32802
Telephone: 407-422-1234
Telecopier: 407-423-2842

Rodney Laird Russell	Norman L. Hull

Reference: First Union National Bank, N.A.

For full biographical listings, see the Martindale-Hubbell Law Directory

Shepard, Filburn & Goodblatt, P.A. (AV)

First Union Tower, Suite 1107, 20 North Orange Avenue, 32801
Telephone: 407-481-2020
Fax: 407-481-0208
Email: sf2law@aol.com

Clifford B. Shepard, III	Jenna R. Rinehart
Mark C. Filburn	Michael J. Kirwin
Amy E. Goodblatt	(Not admitted in FL)

Representative Clients: Danella Construction Company; Titan Indemnity Company; Hersh National Painting & Roofing Company; ABC Supply Company; Seminole Walls & Ceilings Corporation; Unique Scaffolding, Inc.; American Contractors Indemnity Company; Quinn Contractors, Inc.

For full biographical listings, see the Martindale-Hubbell Law Directory

Subin, Rosenbluth, Losey, Brennan, Bittman & Morse, Professional Association (AV)

Suite 900, 111 North Orange Avenue, P.O. Box 4950, 32802-4950
Telephone: 407-841-7100
Facsimile: 407-648-0660
Email: lawyer@orlando.com

Eli H. Subin	Emery H. Rosenbluth, Jr.
	Kenneth D. Morse

Sandra A. Kenny

Representative Clients: Connecticut General Life Insurance Co.; Gilbane Building Company; Subaru of America; Dania JuiAla (Division of the Aragon Group, Inc.); Brice Building Company, Inc.; Trammel Crow Company; Principal Mutual Life Insurance Company; Reynolds Metals Company; SouthTrust Bank of Florida, N.A.; U.S. Foodservice, Inc.

For full biographical listings, see the Martindale-Hubbell Law Directory

PENSACOLA,* Escambia Co.

B. Richard Young, P.A. (AV)

309B South Palafox Place, 32501
Telephone: 904-432-2222
Fax: 904-432-1444

B. Richard Young

Penny L. Hendrix	Michael T. Bill

For full biographical listings, see the Martindale-Hubbell Law Directory

SARASOTA,* Sarasota Co.

BROWN CLARK & WALTERS, P.A. (AV)

Suite 1100, Sarasota City Center, 1819 Main Street, 34236
Telephone: 941-957-3800
Telefax: 941-957-3888
Email: brownclarkwalters@internetmci.com *URL:*
http://www.prosrv.com/~bcwlaw
Port Charlotte, Florida Office: Murdock Professional Center, Suite 500, 1777 Tamiami Trail.
Telephone: 941-624-2929.
Telecopier: 941-624-4941.

Daryl J. Brown	Stuart Jay Levine
John E. Brown	Carolyn F. McDevitt
Donald D. Clark	Taso Michael Milonas
William G. Christopher	Shane T. Munoz
George J. Dramis, III	(Not admitted in FL)
Elinor E. Erben	Douglas E. Polk, Jr.
Lynn H. Groseclose	Geoffrey F. Rice
Donna L. Kerfoot	Peter Z. Skokos
H. Jack Klingensmith (P.A.)	James Edward Thomison
Conrad J. Lazo	Joel W. Walters

OF COUNSEL
James R. Tario

For full biographical listings, see the Martindale-Hubbell Law Directory

TAMPA,* Hillsborough Co.

MICHAEL C. ADDISON (AV)

Suite 2175, 100 North Tampa Street, 33602-5145
Telephone: 813-223-2000
Facsimile: 813-228-6000
Mailing Address: P.O. Box 2175, Tampa, Florida, 33601-2175
Email: 72100.337@compuserve.com

For full biographical listings, see the Martindale-Hubbell Law Directory

ADKINS, KISE & DIACO, P.A. (AV)

2175 Barnett Plaza, 101 East Kennedy Boulevard, 33602
Telephone: 813-221-2200
Fax: 813-221-8850

Edward C. Adkins	Christopher M. Kise
Stephen C. Diaco	

For full biographical listings, see the Martindale-Hubbell Law Directory

CAREY, O'MALLEY, WHITAKER & MANSON, P.A. (AV)

Suite 1190, 100 South Ashley Drive, P.O. Box 499, 33601-0499
Telephone: 813-221-8210
Telecopier: 813-221-1430
Email: cowmpa@aol.com

Michael R. Carey	Douglas P. Manson
Andrew M. O'Malley	Randall P. Mueller
Daniel D. Whitaker	Jack R. Pepper, Jr.
Kevin P. O'Brien	

For full biographical listings, see the Martindale-Hubbell Law Directory

HOYT, COLGAN & ANDREU, P.A. (AV)

3000 Barnett Plaza, 101 East Kennedy Boulevard, 33602
Telephone: 813-229-6688
Facsimile: 813-229-3331

Brooks P. Hoyt	Michael B. Colgan
Timothy A. Andreu	

Brian K. French
OF COUNSEL
Louis J. Beltrami

For full biographical listings, see the Martindale-Hubbell Law Directory

MORRIS LAW FIRM (AV)

4016 Henderson Boulevard, 33629
Telephone: 813-289-4009
Fax: 813-289-7652

MEMBER OF FIRM
Robert E. Morris
ASSOCIATES

Robert A. Bauman	John T. Golding

For full biographical listings, see the Martindale-Hubbell Law Directory

WEST PALM BEACH,* Palm Beach Co.

QUARLES & BRADY (AV)

222 Lakeview Avenue, 4th Floor, 33401
Telephone: 561-653-5000
Fax: 561-653-5333
Milwaukee, Wisconsin Office: 411 East Wisconsin Avenue, 53202-4497.
Telephone: 414-277-5000.
Fax: 414-271-3552.
Madison, Wisconsin Office: Firstar Plaza, One South Pinckney Street, P.O. Box 2113, 53701-2113.
Telephone: 608-251-5000.
Fax: 608-251-9166.
Naples, Florida Office: Barnett Center, 4501 Tamiami Trail North, Suite 300, 33940-3060.
Telephone: 941-262-5959.
Fax: 941-434-4999.
Phoenix, Arizona Office: One Camelback Building, One East Camelback Road, Suite 400, 85012-1649.
Telephone: 602-230-5500.
Fax: 602-230-5598.

PARTNERS

David L. Petersen	Paul M. Platte

For Complete List of Firm Personnel, See General Section

For full biographical listings, see the Martindale-Hubbell Law Directory

WINTER PARK, Orange Co.

DEMPSEY & ASSOCIATES, P.A. (AV)

Suite 200, 1031 West Morse Boulevard, 32789
Telephone: 407-740-7778
Telecopier: 407-740-0911

Bernard H. Dempsey, Jr.	Michael C. Sasso

Frederick C. Barnes	Daniel N. Brodersen
Peter Francis Carr, Jr.	

For full biographical listings, see the Martindale-Hubbell Law Directory

POHL & SHORT, P.A. (AV)

280 West Canton Avenue, Suite 410, P.O. Box 3208, 32790
Telephone: 407-647-7645; 407-647-POHL
Telefax: 407-647-2314

Frank L. Pohl	C. Teresa de Arrigoitia
Houston E. Short	George A. Golder
Dwight I. Cool	Norma Stanley
James Everett Shepherd V	Mark W. Garrett
John R. Simpson, Jr.	

Representative Clients: American Pioneer Title Insurance Company; Institute of Internal Auditors, Inc.; Thompson Steel, Inc.; SunTrust, N.A.; The Bank of Winter Park; Bekins Moving and Storage Co., Inc.; Champion Boats, Inc.; KeyCom Telephone Systems, Inc.

For full biographical listings, see the Martindale-Hubbell Law Directory

GEORGIA

ATLANTA,* Fulton Co.

BOVIS, KYLE & BURCH (AV)

A Partnership including Professional Corporations
Third Floor, 53 Perimeter Center East, 30346
Telephone: 770-391-9100
Telecopier: 770-668-0878

MEMBERS OF FIRM

John V. Burch (P.C.)	Gregory R. Veal
Timothy J. Burson	

ASSOCIATES

Christina A. Craddock	Kenneth W. Sheppard

For full biographical listings, see the Martindale-Hubbell Law Directory

DREW ECKL & FARNHAM (AV)

880 West Peachtree Street, P.O. Box 7600, 30357
Telephone: 404-885-1400
Facsimile: 404-876-0992
Email: drew@igc.apc.org

MEMBERS OF FIRM

Arthur H. Glaser	T. Bart Gary

(See Next Column)

DREW ECKL & FARNHAM, *Atlanta—Continued*

ASSOCIATES

April Rich   Robert J. Moye III

Representative Clients: Southern Water Technologies, Inc.; CNA Insurance Co.; Abrams Industries; C.W. Matthews Contracting Co., Inc.; National Services Industries, Inc.; AGCO Corporation; Hanover Insurance Company; DPIC Insurance Companies; United Forming, Inc.

For Complete List of Firm Personnel, See General Section

For full biographical listings, see the Martindale-Hubbell Law Directory

---

GOLDNER, SOMMERS, SCRUDDER & BASS (AV)

900 Circle 75 Parkway Suite 850, 30339
Telephone: 770-612-9200
Facsimile: 770-612-9201

C. G. Jester, Jr.

For Complete List of Firm Personnel, See General Section

For full biographical listings, see the Martindale-Hubbell Law Directory

---

GRIFFIN COCHRANE & MARSHALL, A PROFESSIONAL CORPORATION (AV)

191 Peachtree Street, N.E. Suite 2000, 30303
Telephone: 404-523-2000
Fax: 404-523-9655

Harry L. Griffin, Jr.   John Dean Marshall, Jr.
Robert D. Marshall   Michael C. Castellon
Curtis W. Martin   Robert Thomas Tifverman
Lee C. Davis   Craig Alan Courville
Jennifer Wheatley Fletcher   Melissa S. Harben
W. Henry Parkman   Todd S. Barton
            Christine S. Mayo

OF COUNSEL

John F. Elger

For full biographical listings, see the Martindale-Hubbell Law Directory

---

PETERSON DILLARD YOUNG ASSELIN & POWELL LLP (AV)

Suite 1100, 230 Peachtree Street, N.W., 30303
Telephone: 404-523-3300
Telecopier: 404-522-6000

MEMBERS OF FIRM

Malcolm D. Young, Jr.   Thomas H. Asselin
            David J. Larson

For full biographical listings, see the Martindale-Hubbell Law Directory

---

JAMES B. RITCHIE A PROFESSIONAL CORPORATION (AV)

Suite 201, West Wieuca Square, 90 West Wieuca Road, N.E., 30342-3200
Telephone: 404-255-8900
Fax: 404-255-9267

James B. Ritchie

LEGAL SUPPORT PERSONNEL

Deborah M. Clague

Representative Clients: Britton and Associates, Inc.; Douglas & Associates, Architects, Inc.; Henry Electric Co., Inc.; J & A Pipeline Co., Inc.; Kennedy Electrical, Inc.; Lewis Construction & Consulting, Inc.; McClure Electrical Constructors, Inc.; Sunbelt Structures, Inc.; Willow Construction, Inc.; W. L. Carey, General Contractor, Inc.

For full biographical listings, see the Martindale-Hubbell Law Directory

---

SHAPIRO, FUSSELL, WEDGE, SMOTHERMAN & MARTIN (AV)

One Midtown Plaza, Suite 1200, 1360 Peachtree Street, 30309-3214
Telephone: 404-870-2200
Facsimile: 404-870-2222

MEMBERS OF FIRM

J. Ben Shapiro, Jr.   Nicholas S. Papleacos
Ira J. Smotherman, Jr.   Seth Price
Herman L. Fussell   Michael P. Davis
Robert B. Wedge   David L. Tank
H. Fielder Martin   Cyrell E. Lynch
Ronald J. Garber   Scott I. Zucker
            Daniel M. Jennings

ASSOCIATES

Connie H. Buffington   Katherine Lynn Freeman
Jason Allen Cooper   Mary L. Hahn
            Wade H. Purcell

For full biographical listings, see the Martindale-Hubbell Law Directory

---

SMITH, CURRIE & HANCOCK (AV)

2600 Harris Tower-Peachtree Center, 233 Peachtree Street, N.E., 30303-1530
Telephone: 404-521-3800
Telecopier: 404-688-0671

MEMBERS OF FIRM

G. Maynard Smith (1907-1992).   Ronald G. Robey
Overton A. Currie   William E. Dorris
E. Reginald Hancock (Retired)   Brian G. Corgan
Luther P. House, Jr.   Charles W. Surasky
Glower W. Jones   Robert N. Godfrey
Robert B. Ansley, Jr.   John T. Flynn
George K. McPherson, Jr.   James F. Butler, III
Bert R. Oastler   Joseph C. Staak
James Allan Smith   Hubert J. Bell, Jr.
John G. Skinner   Philip E. Beck
J. Thomas Kilpatrick   Neal J. Sweeney
Aubrey L. Coleman, Jr.   Frederick L. Wright
Larry E. Forrester   James K. Bidgood, Jr.
Thomas E. Abernathy, IV   Randall F. Hafer
Philip L. Fortune   S. Gregory Joy
John C. Stout, Jr.   Fredric W. Stearns
Daniel M. Shea   Robert C. Chambers
Thomas J. Kelleher, Jr.   Karl Dix, Jr.
Frank E. Riggs, Jr.   William R. Poplin, Jr.

OF COUNSEL

James E. Stephenson   John E. Menechino, Jr.
Joseph Paul Henner   Marty N. Martenson

ASSOCIATES

Daniel F. DuPré   Ronald G. Polly, Jr.
Catherine M. Hobart   William L. Baggett, Jr.
George Papaioanou   R. Lee Mann, III
Christine M. MacIver   J. Cletus McGinty
Craig P. Siegenthaler   Steven C. Ellingson
Suzanne J. Mulliken   Veronica J. Cherniak
R. Randy Edwards   Kimmberly M. Bulkley
J. Chadwick Hatmaker   Scott C. Casey
Jennifer R. Williams   Kathryn B. Vargo

Labor Relations Clients: Echlin, Inc.; Genuine Parts Co. (NAPA); Proctor & Gamble Co.; First Union Corp.
Construction Clients: P.J. Dick, Inc.; Jacobs Engineering; Kitchell Contractors; Robertson-Ceco Corp.

For full biographical listings, see the Martindale-Hubbell Law Directory

---

SUMNER & ANDERSON (AV)

A Limited Liability Company
Suite 700, The Hurt Building, 50 Hurt Plaza, 30303
Telephone: 404-588-9000
Fax: 404-525-1116
Orlando, Florida Office: 940 Highland Avenue, 32802.
Telephone: 407-841-3000.
Fax: 407-841-0022.
Beaufort, South Carolina Office: 1001 Bay Street, Suite 102, 29902.
Telephone: 803-986-1000.
Fax: 803-986-1002.

MEMBERS OF FIRM

William E. Sumner   Steven E. Harbour
Stephen J. Anderson   David A. Webster

ASSOCIATES

Gerald Kirk Domescik   Anne S. Douds (Resident,
Kathleen M. Fischer   Beaufort, South Carolina)
Everrette V. Snotherly, III   Elizabeth A. Green (Resident,
Jerry P. Doyle   Orlando, Florida Office)

For full biographical listings, see the Martindale-Hubbell Law Directory

---

SUTHERLAND, ASBILL & BRENNAN, L.L.P. (AV)

999 Peachtree Street, N.E., 30309-3996
Telephone: 404-853-8000
Facsimile: 404-853-8806
Email: postmaster@sablaw.com
Washington, D.C. Office: 1275 Pennsylvania Avenue, N.W., 20004-2404.
Telephone: 202-383-0100.
New York, N.Y. Office: 600 Madison Avenue, 11th Floor, 10022-1615.
Telephone: 212-605-6400.
Austin, Texas Office: 111 Congress Avenue, 23rd Floor, 78701-4079.
Telephone: 512-469-3350.

James P. Groton   Alfred A. Lindseth
Charles T. Lester, Jr.   George Anthony Smith

COUNSEL OF THE FIRM IN ATLANTA, GEORGIA

William R. Wildman

For Complete List of Firm Personnel, See General Section

For full biographical listings, see the Martindale-Hubbell Law Directory

Atlanta—Continued

WEISZ & ASSOCIATES (AV)

Suite 900 Live Oak Center, 3475 Lenox Road, N.E., 30326-1232
Telephone: 404-233-7888
Facsimile: 404-261-1925

Peter R. Weisz
ASSOCIATE
Cathy Rae Nash
LEGAL SUPPORT PERSONNEL
PARALEGALS
Jo Anne Gunn

Representative Clients: Marion & Cass Street Corp.; H.K. Brewing Co.; Deerfield Construction Co.; Cee Klein Accessories, LTD; Atlanta Valet, Inc.; Central Bank of Tampa; Aloha Leasing div. of Bennett Funding Group, Inc. *Reference:* First Union National Bank.

For full biographical listings, see the Martindale-Hubbell Law Directory

---

MICHAEL WELCH (AV)

The Lenox Building, Suite 910, 3399 Peachtree Road N.E., 30326
Telephone: 404-239-9100
Fax: 404-364-6294

For full biographical listings, see the Martindale-Hubbell Law Directory

---

*AUGUSTA,** Richmond Co.

CAPERS, DUNBAR, SANDERS & BRUCKNER (AV)

Fifteenth Floor, First Union Bank Building, 30901-1454
Telephone: 706-722-7542
Telecopier: 706-724-7776

MEMBERS OF FIRM

John D. Capers	E. Frederick Sanders
Paul H. Dunbar, III	Ziva P. Bruckner

ASSOCIATE
Carl P. Dowling

For full biographical listings, see the Martindale-Hubbell Law Directory

---

*NEWNAN,** Coweta Co.

GLOVER & DAVIS, P.A. (AV)

10 Brown Street, P.O. Box 1038, 30264
Telephone: 770-253-4330
Fax: 770-251-7152
Peachtree City, Georgia Office: Suite 130, 200 Westpark Drive.
Telephone: 770-487-5834.
Fax: 770-487-3492.

J. Littleton Glover, Jr.

Representative Clients: Newnan Savings Bank; Batson-Cook Company, General Corporate and Construction Divisions; Coweta County, Georgia. *Local Counsel for:* International Latex Corp.; First Union National Bank of Georgia; West Georgia Farm Credit, ACA.

For Complete List of Firm Personnel, See General Section

For full biographical listings, see the Martindale-Hubbell Law Directory

---

HAWAII

---

*HONOLULU,** Honolulu Co.

AYABE, CHONG, NISHIMOTO, SIA & NAKAMURA (AV)

A Partnership including a Professional Corporation
Pauahi Tower, Suite 2500, 1001 Bishop Street, 96813
Telephone: 808-537-6119
Telecopier: 808-526-3491

MEMBERS OF FIRM

Sidney K. Ayabe (P.C.)	Richard F. Nakamura
Ann H. Aratani	

Representative Clients: Travelers Insurance Co.; St. Paul Fire and Marine Insurance Co.; The Employers Group of Insurance Companies; TIG Insurance Co.; Pacific Insurance Co.; Hartford Accident and Indemnity Co.; Continental Casualty Co.; CNA Insurance Co.

For Complete List of Firm Personnel, See General Section

For full biographical listings, see the Martindale-Hubbell Law Directory

---

BAYS, DEAVER, HIATT, LUNG & ROSE (AV)

A Partnership including Professional Corporations
16th Floor, Alii Place, 1099 Alakea Street, P.O. Box 1760, 96806
Telephone: 808-523-9000
Telecopier: 808-533-4184
Telex: RCA 7238976
Kamuela, Hawaii Office: Suite 204 Parker Square, 65-1280 Kawaihae Road.
Telephone: 808-885-3400.
Telecopier: 808-885-6765.

MEMBERS OF FIRM

A. Bernard Bays (A Law Corporation)	Crystal K. Rose (A Law Corporation)
Phillip L. Deaver (A Law Corporation)	Jason N. Baba (A Law Corporation)
Jerry Michael Hiatt (A Law Corporation)	Carl H. Osaki (A Law Corporation)
Harvey J. Lung (A Law Corporation)	

ASSOCIATES

Michael W. Thomas	Wendy J. Utsumi
Karin L. Holma	Bruce Voss
Paul M. Saito	Robert E. Badger, Jr.
Mahilani Elizabeth Kellett	Edward J. Corwin
Donald E. Fisher	Ross N. Gushi

For full biographical listings, see the Martindale-Hubbell Law Directory

---

LAW OFFICES OF DAVID F. DAY (AV)

Grosvenor Center Mauka Tower Suite 1788, 737 Bishop Street, 96813
Telephone: 808-531-8020
Fax: 808-521-0962
Email: ddayofc@lava.net

For full biographical listings, see the Martindale-Hubbell Law Directory

---

DWYER IMANAKA SCHRAFF KUDO MEYER & FUJIMOTO ATTORNEYS AT LAW, A LAW CORPORATION (AV)

1800 Pioneer Plaza, 900 Fort Street Mall, 96813
Telephone: 808-524-8000
Telecopier: 808-526-1419
Mailing Address: P.O. Box 2727, 96803
Email: hawaiilaw@dwyer-imanaka.com *URL:* http://www.dwyer-imanaka.com

John R. Dwyer, Jr.	William G. Meyer, III
Mitchell A. Imanaka	Wesley M. Fujimoto
Paul A. Schraff	Ronald Van Grant
Benjamin A. Kudo (Atty. at Law, A Law Corp.)	Jon M. H. Pang
	Blake W. Bushnell

Adelbert Green

Richard T. Asato, Jr.	Jeffery S. Werbelow
Scott W. Settle	Lori Ann K. Koseki
Darcie S. Yoshinaga	Troy T. Fukuhara
Lawrence I. Kawasaki	Katy Y. Chen
Stacy E. Uehara	Naomi S. Uyeno
Kris N. Nakagawa	Roger B. McKeague

OF COUNSEL

Randall Y. Iwase	R. Brian Tsujimura

For full biographical listings, see the Martindale-Hubbell Law Directory

---

ROBBINS & RHODES ATTORNEYS AT LAW, A LAW CORPORATION (AV)

Suite 2200 Davies Pacific Center, 841 Bishop Street, 96813
Telephone: 808-524-2355
Fax: 808-526-0290

Kenneth S. Robbins	Shinken Naitoh

Representative Clients: Aetna Casualty & Surety, Inc.; Argonaut Insurance Co.; American Reinsurance Co.; Crum & Forster Insurance; Farmers Insurance Group; Industrial Underwriters Insurance Co.; North Hawaii Community Hospital; State of Hawaii; Western Indemnity Insurance Co.; Westin Hotel Company.

For full biographical listings, see the Martindale-Hubbell Law Directory

ILLINOIS

CHICAGO,* Cook Co.

BELL, BOYD & LLOYD (AV)

Three First National Plaza Suite 3300, 70 West Madison Street, 60602
Telephone: 312-372-1121
FAX: 312-372-2098
Email: bbl@bbl.com
Washington, D.C. Office: 1615 L Street, N.W.
Telephone: 202-466-6300.
FAX: 202-463-0678.

MEMBERS OF FIRM

Gregory R. Andre   Margery Newman
Stanley P. Sklar

ASSOCIATE

Josh M. Leavitt

For Complete List of Firm Personnel, See General Section

For full biographical listings, see the Martindale-Hubbell Law Directory

FORAN & SCHULTZ (AV)

Suite 3000, 30 North La Salle Street, 60602
Telephone: 312-368-8330
Fax: 312-580-2600

MEMBERS OF FIRM

Thomas A. Foran	Jack J. Carriglio
Richard G. Schultz	Steven H. Gistenson
James R. Figliulo	Brooke R. Whitted
Stephen A. Gorman	Jeffrey C. Blumenthal
Jeff D. Harris	Carl A. Gigante
Carmen D. Caruso	

ASSOCIATES

Teresa F. Frisbie	Brian P. Liston
Peter A. Silverman	Paul A. Henmueller
Marla B. Wilneff	James J. Sipchen, Jr.
Daniel D. Kasten	Mitchell S. Chaban
Patrick R. Gabrione	Dana L. Romaniuk
Jessica Dickstein	

OF COUNSEL

Harry G. Comerford

For full biographical listings, see the Martindale-Hubbell Law Directory

KAPLAN & BEGY (AV)

One First National Plaza 51st Floor, 60603
Telephone: 312-345-3000
Fax: 312-345-3119

MEMBERS OF FIRM

Fred C. Begy, III	Joseph A. Bosco
Larry S. Kaplan	Martin K. LaPointe
James D. Solon	Richard A. Walker
Robert C. von Ohlen, Jr.	Mitchell J. Kanaan

ASSOCIATES

John B. Austin	Michael J. Vint
Donald F. Brosnan	Maritoni Derecho Kane
(Not admitted in IL)	Adriana Gardella
J. Peter Martin	Michael J. Frazier
Neal J. Moglin	John T. Midgett
Jeffrey E. Margulis	Keith S. Yamaguchi
Kevin R. Davis	Rose Jagust
Patrick J. Keating	Thomas C. Sokol
Terrill Elise Pierce	

For full biographical listings, see the Martindale-Hubbell Law Directory

LAWRENCE, KAMIN, SAUNDERS & UHLENHOP (AV)

208 South La Salle Street, Suite 1750, 60604
Telephone: 312-372-1947
Telecopier: 312-372-2389

MEMBERS OF FIRM

Howard P. Kamin	David E. Muschler
Kent Lawrence	Lawrence A. Rosen
Randall B. Gold	

ASSOCIATE

David L. Reich

Representative Clients: Blount, Inc.; Pepper Construction Co.; Corrigan Construction Co.; O'Neil Construction Co.; United States Fidelity and Guaranty; Lyons Electric Co.; St. Paul Financial Marine Insurance Co.; Seaboard Surety Co; Mellon Stuart Co.

For full biographical listings, see the Martindale-Hubbell Law Directory

MURPHY, SMITH & POLK, A PROFESSIONAL CORPORATION (AV)

Twenty-Fifth Floor, Two First National Plaza 20 South Clark Street, 60603-1891
Telephone: 312-558-1220
Telecopier: 807-3619
Email: msp@pg.net

Charles E. Murphy

For full biographical listings, see the Martindale-Hubbell Law Directory

O'BRIEN, O'ROURKE & HOGAN (AV)

135 South La Salle Street Suite 830, 60603
Telephone: 312-372-1462
Fax: 312-372-8029
Orlando, Florida Office: Moye, O'Brien, O'Rourke, Hogan & Pickert, 201 East Pine Street, Suite 710.
Telephone: 407-843-3341.
Fax: 407-843-3048.
Atlanta, Georgia Office: Moye, O'Brien, O'Rourke, Hogan & Pickert, 999 Peachtree Street, Northeast, Suite 2020.
Telephone: 404-875-6300.

MEMBERS OF FIRM

James Elton Moye (Resident at Orlando, Florida Office)	John C. O'Rourke, Jr.
Donald V. O'Brien	Stephen W. Pickert (Resident at Orlando, Florida Office)

For full biographical listings, see the Martindale-Hubbell Law Directory

SCHWARTZBERG, BARNETT & COHEN (AV)

55 West Monroe Street, 2400 Xerox Centre, 60603-5040
Telephone: 312-726-3555
Fax: 312-726-6299
Cable Address: "Justice"
Email: sb&c@twty.chi.il.us

MEMBERS OF FIRM

Ralph M. Schwartzberg (1939-1975)	Mark T. Barnett (1939-1970)
	Hugh J. Schwartzberg
Benjamin H. Cohen	

OF COUNSEL

Eugene P. Thomas Jr.

For full biographical listings, see the Martindale-Hubbell Law Directory

PEORIA,* Peoria Co.

HOWARD & HOWARD ATTORNEYS, P.C. (AV)

The Creve Coeur Building, Suite 200, 321 Liberty Street, 61602-1403
Telephone: 309-672-1483
Telecopier: 309-672-1568
Kalamazoo, Michigan Office: The Kalamazoo Building, Suite 400, 107 West Michigan Avenue.
Telephone: 616-382-1483.
Telecopier: 616-382-1568.
Bloomfield Hills, Michigan Office: The Pinehurst Office Center, Suite 101, 1400 North Woodward Avenue.
Telephone: 810-645-1483.
Telecopier: 810-645-1568.
Lansing, Michigan Office: Suite 500, The Phoenix Building, 222 Washington Square, North.
Telephone: 517-485-1483.
Telecopier: 517-485-1568.
Tampa, Florida Office: First of America Plaza, Suite 2000, 201 East Kennedy Boulevard.
Telephone: 813-229-1483.
Telecopier: 813-229-1568.

Frederick G. Hoffman   Jeffrey G. Sorenson

Representative Clients: For Representative Client list, see General Practice, Peoria, IL.

For Complete List of Firm Personnel, See General Section

For full biographical listings, see the Martindale-Hubbell Law Directory

INDIANA

EVANSVILLE,* Vanderburgh Co.

ZIEMER, STAYMAN, WEITZEL & SHOULDERS (AV)

(Formerly Early, Arnold & Ziemer)
One Riverfront Place, 20 N.W. First Street 9th Floor, P.O. Box 916, 47706-0916
Telephone: 812-424-7575
Telecopier: 812-421-5089

MEMBER OF FIRM

Robert F. Stayman

(See Next Column)

ZIEMER, STAYMAN, WEITZEL & SHOULDERS—*Continued*

ASSOCIATE

Mary Lee Franke

Reference: Old National Bank in Evansville.

For full biographical listings, see the Martindale-Hubbell Law Directory

---

INDIANAPOLIS,* Marion Co.

BACKER & BACKER, A PROFESSIONAL CORPORATION (AV)

101 West Ohio Street, Suite 1500, 46204
Telephone: 317-684-3000
Telecopier: 317-684-3004

Herbert J. Backer (1914-1995)   Stephen A. Backer
David J. Backer

Reference: Bank One, Indianapolis.

For full biographical listings, see the Martindale-Hubbell Law Directory

---

HOFFMAN DREWRY HANCOCK & SIMMONS (AV)

9100 Keystone Crossing, Suite 350, 46240
Telephone: 317-580-4848
Telecopier: 317-580-4855

Robert J. Hoffman	Richard S. Pitts
Michael F. Drewry	Joseph R. Pitcher
William J. Hancock	Thomas A. Pastore
David L. Simmons	David B. Vornehm

For full biographical listings, see the Martindale-Hubbell Law Directory

---

ICE MILLER DONADIO & RYAN (AV)

One American Square Box 82001, 46282-0002
Telephone: 317-236-2100
Fax: 317-236-2219
Email: leel@imdr.com *URL:* http://www.imdr.com
South Bend, Indiana Office: 211 West Washington Street, Suite 2420.
Telephone: 219-234-7933.
Fax: 219-234-7965. Internet E-mail: leel@imdr.com. Web Site Address: http://www.imdr.com.

MEMBERS OF FIRM

Alan H. Lobley	Gary J. Dankert
Arthur P. Kalleres	Phillip L. Bayt
Michael H. Boldt	Fred R. Biesecker
	Zeff A. Weiss

ASSOCIATES

Kristin L. Altice	Stephanie Alden Smithey
	Curtis W. McCauley

Representative Clients: Howard Needles Tammen & Bergendoff; Geupel De-Mars, Inc.; Browning Day Mullins Dierdorf, Inc.; F.A. Wilhelm Construction Company, Inc.; CSO Architects, Inc.; Ratio Architects, Inc.; Shiel-Sexton Co., Inc.

For Complete List of Firm Personnel, See General Section

For full biographical listings, see the Martindale-Hubbell Law Directory

---

LOCKE REYNOLDS BOYD & WEISELL (AV)

1000 Capital Center South, 201 North Illinois Street, 46204
Telephone: 317-237-3800
Telecopier: 317-237-3900

Hugh E. Reynolds, Jr.	Julia Blackwell Gelinas
Steven J. Strawbridge	Terrence L. Brookie
	James Dimos

John K. McDavid	Nelson D. Alexander

Representative Clients: American States Insurance Co.; Badger Engineers; CNA Insurance; Fidelity & Deposit Co. of Maryland; Hagerman Construction; MSE Corp.; Miller Pipeline Corporation; PSI Energy; United States Fidelity & Guaranty Co.

For Complete List of Firm Personnel, See General Section

For full biographical listings, see the Martindale-Hubbell Law Directory

---

RICHMOND,* Wayne Co.

HARRINGTON, MALEY, GARDNER & SAYRE (AV)

Third Floor, Harrington Bank Building, Two North Eighth, 47374-3090
Telephone: 317-966-6643
FAX: 317-966-6799

MEMBERS OF FIRM

Alonzo M. Gardner (1886-1941)	Robert J. Maley
Wilfred Jessup (1900-1944)	Gayle W. Gardner
Frank K. Chambers (1938-1955)	John M. Sayre, III
Floyd W. Gardner (1933-1965)	Kirk A. Weikart
Clifford M. Haworth (1923-1967)	

(See Next Column)

OF COUNSEL

John R. Harrington

General Counsel for: Harrington Bank, FSB.
Local Counsel for: Belden Manufacturing Co.; CIGNA.

For full biographical listings, see the Martindale-Hubbell Law Directory

---

IOWA

DES MOINES,* Polk Co.

FINLEY, ALT, SMITH, SCHARNBERG, MAY & CRAIG, P.C. (AV)

604 Locust Street, Fourth Floor Equitable Building, 50309
Telephone: 515-288-0145
Telecopier: 515-288-2724

Jerry P. Alt

Representative Clients: Aetna Casualty & Surety Co.; Aetna Life Insurance Co.; ALAS; American Society of Composers, Authors and Publishers; Equitable Life Assurance Society of the U.S.; Federated Insurance Co.; Meredith Corp.
Iowa Attorneys for: Midwest Medical Insurance Co.
District Attorneys for: Norfolk & Southern Railroad; Soo Line Railroad Company.

For Complete List of Firm Personnel, See General Section

For full biographical listings, see the Martindale-Hubbell Law Directory

---

SHEARER, TEMPLER & PINGEL, A PROFESSIONAL CORPORATION (AV)

Suite 437 3737 Woodland Avenue (West Des Moines), P.O. Box 1991, 50309
Telephone: 515-225-3737
Fax: 515-225-9510

Jeffrey L. Goodman	Brenton D. Soderstrum
John R. Perkins	Jeffrey D. Stone
Leon R. Shearer	John A. Templer, Jr.

For Complete List of Firm Personnel, See General Section

For full biographical listings, see the Martindale-Hubbell Law Directory

---

KANSAS

WICHITA,* Sedgwick Co.

FOULSTON & SIEFKIN L.L.P. (AV)

700 Fourth Financial Center, 67202
Telephone: 316-267-6371
Facsimile: 316-267-6345
Topeka, Kansas Office: 1515 Bank IV Tower, 534 Kansas Avenue, 66603.
Telephone: 913-233-3600.
Fax: 913-233-1610.
Dodge City, Kansas Office: 810 Frontview, P.O. Box 1147, 67801.
Telephone: 316-227-8126.
Fax: 316-227-8451.
Member: Lex Mundi, A Global Association of 126 Independent Firms.

MEMBERS OF FIRM

Robert L. Howard	Charles P. Efflandt
Mikel L. Stout	Wyatt A. Hoch

For Complete List of Firm Personnel, See General Section

For full biographical listings, see the Martindale-Hubbell Law Directory

---

KENTUCKY

BOWLING GREEN,* Warren Co.

HARLIN & PARKER, P.S.C. (AV)

519 East Tenth Street, P.O. Box 390, 42102-0390
Telephone: 502-842-5611
Telefax: 502-842-2607

William Jerry Parker   Jerry A. Burns
Scott Charles Marks

Insurance Clients: CNA Insurance Companies.
Railroad and Utilities Clients: District Attorneys for BellSouth Telecommunications, Inc.; CSX Transportation, Inc.

(See Next Column)

HARLIN & PARKER P.S.C., *Bowling Green—Continued*

Representative Clients: Jim Walter Homes, Inc.; Morrison & Knuteson.
Local Counsel for: General Motors Corp.; News Publishing Co.

For Complete List of Firm Personnel, See General Section

For full biographical listings, see the Martindale-Hubbell Law Directory

---

LEXINGTON, * Fayette Co.

VIMONT & WILLS (AV)

Suite 300, 155 East Main Street, 40507-1317
Telephone: 606-252-2202
Telecopier: 606-259-2927

MEMBERS OF FIRM

Richard E. Vimont   Bernard F. Lovely, Jr.

ASSOCIATES

Barbara Booker Wills   J. Thomas Rawlings

For full biographical listings, see the Martindale-Hubbell Law Directory

---

LOUISIANA

BATON ROUGE, * East Baton Rouge Parish

JAMES S. HOLLIDAY, JR. A PROFESSIONAL CORPORATION (AV)

3538 Cole Drive, P.O. Box 65203, 70896
Telephone: 504-344-2100
Fax: 504-344-4005
Email: shobli03@counsel.com *URL:* http.//www.hollidaylaw.com

James S. Holliday, Jr.

Susan Wall Griffin   Stephen J. Holliday

For full biographical listings, see the Martindale-Hubbell Law Directory

---

WRAY & KRACHT, L.L.P. (AV)

5643 Corporate Boulevard, P.O. Box 80239, 70898-0239
Telephone: 504-928-3200
Telecopier: 504-928-3266

MEMBERS OF FIRM

W. P. Wray, Jr.   Russel W. Wray
Eric A. Kracht   Christopher P. Pierce

ASSOCIATES

E. Allen Graves, Jr.   Randall C. Gregory

OF COUNSEL

Charles Wm. Roberts   M. J. Bodenhamer

LEGAL SUPPORT PERSONNEL

James W. Cox (Construction   Kim Bergeron Perkins
  Claims Consultant)   (Paralegal)

Representative Clients: The Louisiana Associated General Contractors, Inc.; Coastal Contractors, Inc.; T. L. James & Company, Inc.; Clearly Canadian Beverage Corporation (Canada).
Reference: City National Bank.

For full biographical listings, see the Martindale-Hubbell Law Directory

---

NEW ORLEANS, * Orleans Parish

DEUTSCH, KERRIGAN & STILES, L.L.P. (AV)

A Partnership including Professional Law Corporations
755 Magazine Street, 70130-3672
Telephone: 504-581-5141
Cable Address: "Dekest"
Telex: 584358
Telecopier: 504-566-1201
Email: dks@dksno.com *URL:* http://www.dksno.com
St. Tammany Parish Office: 550 Pontchartrain Drive, Suite 200, Slidell, LA. 70458.
Telephone: 504-639-0555.
Fax: 504-639-0550

MEMBERS OF FIRM

Frederick R. Bott (P.L.C.)   Terrence L. Brennan
Charles F. Seemann, Jr., (P.L.C.)   Howard L. Murphy
Raymon G. Jones (P.L.C.)   William E. Wright, Jr.
Victor E. Stilwell, Jr., (P.L.C.)   Joseph L. McReynolds
Matt J. Farley (P.L.C.)   W. Lee Kohler
               Theodore L. White

OF COUNSEL

Ralph L. Kaskell, Jr.

(See Next Column)

ASSOCIATE

Herman J. Gesser, III

For Complete List of Firm Personnel, See General Section

For full biographical listings, see the Martindale-Hubbell Law Directory

LEAKE & ANDERSSON, L.L.P. (AV)

1700 Energy Centre, 1100 Poydras Street, 70163-1701
Telephone: 504-585-7500
Telecopier: 504-585-7775
Email: LA1700@aol.com

MEMBERS OF FIRM

Robert E. Leake, Jr.   Marta-Ann Schnabel O'Bryon
W. Paul Andersson   Donald E. McKay, Jr.
               Stanton E. Shuler, Jr.

Representative Clients: L.B. Hebert & Co.; Montgomery Elevator Co.; Solvation Services, Inc.; Professional Construction Services, Inc.; R.F. Varley Co., Inc.

For Complete List of Firm Personnel, See General Section

For full biographical listings, see the Martindale-Hubbell Law Directory

---

SHREVEPORT, * Caddo Parish

BARLOW AND HARDTNER L.C. (AV)

Tenth Floor, Louisiana Tower, 401 Edwards Street, 71101-3289
Telephone: 318-227-1131
Telecopier: 318-227-1141
Mailing Address: P.O. Box 8, Shreveport, Louisiana, 71161-0008

Malcolm S. Murchison   Clair F. White
Joseph L. Shea, Jr.   Philip E. Downer, III
David R. Taggart   Michael B. Donald
               Jay A. Greenleaf

Representative Clients: The Brinkman Corporation; T.L. James & Company, Inc.; NorAm Energy Corp. (formerly Arkla, Inc.); Central and South West Corporation; Panhandle Eastern Corp.; Pennzoil Producing Co.; Johnson Controls, Inc.; Ashland Oil, Inc.; The Centex Construction Group; Southwestern Electric Power Company.

For Complete List of Firm Personnel, See General Section

For full biographical listings, see the Martindale-Hubbell Law Directory

WEEMS, WRIGHT, SCHIMPF, HAYTER & CARMOUCHE, A PROFESSIONAL LAW CORPORATION (AV)

912 Kings Highway, 71104
Telephone: 318-222-2100
Fax: 318-226-5100

John O. Hayter, III

Brian D. Landry

Representative Clients: Hand Construction Co., Inc.; Max Foote Construction Co., Inc.; La Quinta Inns, Inc.; Don M. Barron Contractor, Inc.; Northwest Louisiana Construction, Inc.; Jabar, Inc.; Con-Fab Welding, Inc.; Air-Ref, Inc.; Melvin Butler, Inc.; MONCLA Construction Co., Inc.; Reynolds Industrial Coatings, Inc.

For full biographical listings, see the Martindale-Hubbell Law Directory

---

MAINE

PORTLAND, * Cumberland Co.

AMERLING & BURNS, A PROFESSIONAL ASSOCIATION (AV)

193 Middle Street, 04101
Telephone: 207-775-3581
Facsimile: 207-775-3814
Affiliated St. Croix Office: Coon & Sanford, P.O. Box 25918, Six Chandlers's Wharf, Suite 202, 00824-0918.

W. John Amerling   Arnold C. Macdonald
George F. Burns   Mary DeLano
David P. Ray   Joanne F. Cole
               A. Robert Ruesch

OF COUNSEL

Bruce M. Jervis

Representative Clients: H.E. Sargent, Inc. (construction); Merrill Trust; J.M. Huber, Inc.; Jackson Laboratories; Hague International (engineering); Aetna Life & Casualty Co.; The Hartford; Great American Insurance Co.; Wausau Insurance Co.

For full biographical listings, see the Martindale-Hubbell Law Directory

Portland—Continued

PETRUCCELLI & MARTIN (AV)

50 Monument Square, P.O. Box 9733, 04104-5033
Telephone: 207-775-0200
Telecopier: 207-775-2360

MEMBERS OF FIRM

Gerald F. Petruccelli   Michael K. Martin

Representative Clients: Granger Northern Construction Co.; Seppala & Aho Construction Co.

For full biographical listings, see the Martindale-Hubbell Law Directory

---

THOMPSON & BOWIE (AV)

Three Canal Plaza, P.O. Box 4630, 04112
Telephone: 207-774-2500
Telecopier: 207-774-3591

MEMBERS OF FIRM

Roy E. Thompson, Jr.	Frank W. DeLong, III
James M. Bowie	Michael E. Saucier
Daniel R. Mawhinney	Mark V. Franco
Rebecca H. Farnum	Elizabeth Knox Peck
Glenn H. Robinson	Cathy S. Roberts

ASSOCIATE
Paul C. Catsos

For full biographical listings, see the Martindale-Hubbell Law Directory

MARYLAND

BALTIMORE,* (Independent City)

FERGUSON, SCHETELICH, HEFFERNAN & MURDOCK, P.A. (AV)

1300 NationsBank Center 1, 100 South Charles Street, 21201
Telephone: 410-837-2200
Fax: 410-837-1188
Email: fshm@ix.netcom

Robert L. Ferguson, Jr.	Christopher J. Heffernan
Thomas J. Schetelich	M. Brooke Murdock

Michael N. Russo, Jr.	Peter Joseph Basile
Jodi K. Ebersole	Ann D. Ware

For full biographical listings, see the Martindale-Hubbell Law Directory

---

FREISHTAT & SANDLER (AV)

Suite 1500, One Calvert Plaza, 201 E. Baltimore Street, 21202
Telephone: 410-727-7740
FAX: 410-727-7356

MEMBERS OF FIRM

David Freishtat	Raymond F. Altman
Paul Mark Sandler	Raymond Daniel Burke
William M. Mullen	

Lloyd J. Snow	T. Allen Mott
Lynn Weinberg	Joseph John Coppola
Stacie F. Dubnow	Jeffrey Rosenfeld
Brian A. Zemil	

For full biographical listings, see the Martindale-Hubbell Law Directory

---

KOLLMAN & SHEEHAN, P.A. (AV)

Sun Life Building, 20 South Charles Street, 21201
Telephone: 410-727-4300
Telecopier: 410-727-4391

Frank L. Kollman	Peter S. Saucier
David M. Sheehan	Francis R. Laws
Darrell R. VanDeusen	

Bruce M. Luchansky	Jonathan J. Biedron
Clifford B. Geiger	Randi A. Klein
Charles J. Kresslein	

For full biographical listings, see the Martindale-Hubbell Law Directory

---

SOMMER & STEELE, L.L.C. (AV)

The B & O Building, Suite 930, Two North Charles Street, 21201
Telephone: 410-783-2790
Fax: 410-783-2797

Peter J. Sommer   Deborah Williams Steele

(See Next Column)

ASSOCIATE
Samuel Joseph Mangione

For Complete List of Firm Personnel, See General Section

For full biographical listings, see the Martindale-Hubbell Law Directory

---

THIEBLOT, RYAN, MARTIN & MILLER, P.A. (AV)

4th Floor, The World Trade Center, 21202-3091
Telephone: 410-837-1140
Washington, D.C. Line: 202-628-8223
Fax: 410-837-3282
Towson, Maryland Office: Atlantic Federal Building. Suite 400. 100 West Road. 21204.
Telephone: 410-828-5900.

Robert J. Thieblot	Robert D. Harwick, Jr.
Anthony W. Ryan	Anne M. Hrehorovich
J. Edward Martin, Jr.	Donna Marie Raffaele
Bruce R. Miller	Hamilton Fisk Tyler
Samuel S. Field III	

Representative Clients: City of Frederick; Board of Education for Frederick County; Brundage Bone Concrete Pumping, Inc.; Fidelity Engineering Co.; Hardin-Huber, Inc.; Castle & Cooke Properties, Inc.; USF&G Company; Constitution State Insurance Co.; The Travelers Companies; General Accident Insurance Co.

For full biographical listings, see the Martindale-Hubbell Law Directory

---

VENABLE ATTORNEYS AT LAW VENABLE, BAETJER AND HOWARD, LLP (AV)

A Partnership including Professional Corporations
1800 Mercantile Bank & Trust Building, 2 Hopkins Plaza, 21201
Telephone: 410-244-7400
Email: INFO@Venable.win.net
Washington, D.C. Office: Venable, Baetjer, Howard & Civiletti LLP. Suite 1000, 1201 New York Avenue, N.W.
Telephone: 202-962-4800.
McLean, Virginia Office: Suite 400, 2010 Corporate Ridge.
Telephone: 703-760-1600.
Rockville, Maryland Office: Suite 500, One Church Street, P. O. Box 1906.
Telephone: 301-217-5600.
Towson, Maryland Office: 210 Allegheny Avenue, P. O. Box 5517.
Telephone: 410-494-6200.

MEMBERS OF FIRM

James A. Cole	Jeffrey A. Dunn (also at Washington, D.C. Office)
Benjamin R. Civiletti (P.C.) (Also at Washington, D.C. and Towson, Maryland Offices)	George F. Pappas (Also at Washington, D.C. Office)
John Henry Lewin, Jr. (P.C.)	Peter P. Parvis
Thomas J. Kenney, Jr. (P.C.) (Also at Washington, D.C. Office)	James L. Shea (Also at Washington, D.C. Office)
Roger W. Titus (Resident, Rockville, Maryland Office)	Maurice Baskin (Resident, Washington, D.C. Office)
Daniel O'C. Tracy, Jr. (Also at Rockville, Maryland Office)	C. Carey Deeley, Jr. (Also at Towson, Maryland Office)
John H. Zink, III (Resident, Towson, Maryland Office)	Christopher R. Mellott
Bruce E. Titus (Resident, McLean, Virginia Office)	Cynthia M. Hahn (Resident, Towson, Maryland Office)
Paul T. Glasgow (Resident, Rockville, Maryland Office)	M. King Hill, III (Resident, Towson, Maryland Office)
Joseph C. Wich, Jr. (Resident, Towson, Maryland Office)	J. Michael Brennan (Resident, Towson, Maryland Office)
Craig E. Smith	Herbert G. Smith, II (Not admitted in MD; Resident, Washington, D.C. Office)
David G. Lane (Resident, McLean, Virginia Office)	David C. Mancini (Not admitted in MD; Resident, McLean, Virginia Office)
G. Stewart Webb, Jr.	
James K. Archibald (Also at Washington, D.C. Office)	Michael W. Robinson (Resident, McLean, Virginia Office)

OF COUNSEL

Mary T. Flynn (Not admitted in MD; Resident, McLean, Virginia Office)

ASSOCIATES

Paul D. Barker, Jr.	Mary-Dulany James (Resident, Towson, Maryland Office)
Daniel William China	
David R. Hodnett (Not admitted in MD; Resident, McLean, Virginia Office)	Patricia A. Malone (Resident, Towson, Maryland Office)
Todd J. Horn	Christine L. M. McAnney (Not admitted in MD; Resident, McLean, Virginia Office)

For Complete List of Firm Personnel, See General Section

For full biographical listings, see the Martindale-Hubbell Law Directory

ROCKVILLE,* Montgomery Co.

STEIN, SPERLING, BENNETT, DE JONG, DRISCOLL, GREENFEIG & METRO, P.A. (AV)

25 West Middle Lane, 20850
Telephone: 301-340-2020; 800-435-5230
Telecopier: 301-340-8217

Millard S. Bennett   David C. Driscoll, Jr.

For Complete List of Firm Personnel, See General Section

For full biographical listings, see the Martindale-Hubbell Law Directory

TOWSON,* Baltimore Co.

VENABLE ATTORNEYS AT LAW VENABLE, BAETJER AND HOWARD, LLP (AV)

A Partnership including Professional Corporations
210 Allegheny Avenue, P.O. Box 5517, 21204
Telephone: 410-494-6200
FAX: 410-821-0147
Baltimore, Maryland Office: 1800 Mercantile Bank & Trust Building, 2 Hopkins Plaza.
Telephone: 410-244-7400.
Washington, D.C. Office: Venable, Baetjer, Howard & Civiletti LLP, Suite 1000, 1201 New York Avenue, N.W.
Telephone: 202-962-4800.
McLean, Virginia Office: Suite 400, 2010 Corporate Ridge.
Telephone: 703-760-1600.
Rockville, Maryland Office: Suite 500, One Church Street, P. O. Box 1906.
Telephone: 301-217-5600.

PARTNERS

Benjamin R. Civiletti (P.C.) Joseph C. Wich, Jr.
 (Also at Washington, D.C. C. Carey Deeley, Jr. (Also at
 and Baltimore, Maryland   Baltimore, Maryland Office)
 Offices)   Cynthia M. Hahn
John H. Zink, III   M. King Hill, III
    J. Michael Brennan

ASSOCIATES

Mary-Dulany James   Corie L. Williams

For Complete List of Firm Personnel, See General Section

For full biographical listings, see the Martindale-Hubbell Law Directory

MASSACHUSETTS

BOSTON,* Suffolk Co.

CITY, HAYES, MEAGHER & DISSETTE, P.C. (AV)

50 Congress Street, 02109
Telephone: 617-523-3050
Telecopier: 617-523-5612

Robert D. City   Kieran B. Meagher
James P. Hayes   Michael J. Dissette

Martin R. Fisch   Lewis R. Lear
Philip B. Evans   Philip Di Domenico
   Michael N. O'Connell, Jr.

For full biographical listings, see the Martindale-Hubbell Law Directory

NATHANSON & GOLDBERG, A PROFESSIONAL CORPORATION (AV)

10 Union Wharf, 02109
Telephone: 617-742-9350
Fax: 617-742-3559

Alvin S. Nathanson   Valerie S. Carter
Arthur Goldberg   Shannon M. Fitzpatrick

Stuart J. Frank

For full biographical listings, see the Martindale-Hubbell Law Directory

PALMER & DODGE LLP (AV)

One Beacon Street, 02108
Telephone: 617-573-0100
Facsimile: 617-227-4420

MEMBERS OF FIRM

Michael J. Lacek   Craig E. Stewart
David R. Rodgers   Peter S. Terris

For Complete List of Firm Personnel, See General Section

For full biographical listings, see the Martindale-Hubbell Law Directory

SHERBURNE, POWERS & NEEDHAM, P.C. (AV)

One Beacon Street, 02108
Telephone: 617-523-2700
Fax: 617-523-6850
Email: @SHERBURNE.COM

William D. Weeks   Benjamin Volinski
John T. Collins   Mark Schonfeld
Allan J. Landau   James D. Smeallie
Stephen A. Hopkins   Paul Killeen
Alan I. Falk   Gordon P. Katz
C. Thomas Swaim   Joseph B. Darby, III
James Pollock   Richard M Yanofsky
William V. Tripp III   James E. McDermott
Stephen S. Young   Kenneth P. Brier
William F. Machen   Robert V. Lizza
W. Robert Allison   Miriam Goldstein Altman
Philip J. Notopoulos   John J. Monaghan
Richard J. Hindlian   Margaret J. Palladino
Paul E. Troy   Mark C. Michalowski
Harold W. Potter, Jr.   David Scott Sloan
Philip S. Lapatin   M. Chrysa Long
Pamela A. Duckworth   Lawrence D. Bradley
   Miriam J. McKendall

Cynthia A. Brown   Amy J. Mastrobattista
Cynthia M. Hern   Leslie A. Sprinkle
Meredeth A. Beers   Douglas W. Clapp
Dianne R. Phillips   Jeffrey A. Huebschmann
Paul M. James   Tamara E. Goulston
Theodore F. Hanselman Paul G. Lannon, Jr.
Joshua C. Krumholz   Nicholas J. Psyhogeos
Ieuan G. Mahony   Edward J. Naughton
Jeffrey J. Nix   Kathaleen Kelly Cutone
 (Not admitted in MA) Laurie A. Tribble
Kenneth L. Harvey   Neil C. Higgins
Christopher J. Trombetta Deborah Paige Stone
Elise N. Zoli   Brian R. Popiel

COUNSEL

Haig Der Manuelian   Karl J. Hirshman
Mason M. Taber, Jr.   Dale R. Johnson

For full biographical listings, see the Martindale-Hubbell Law Directory

VENA, TRUELOVE & RILEY (AV)

253 Summer Street, 02210
Telephone: 617-737-8700
Fax: 617 737-0440

MEMBERS OF FIRM

Edward F. Vena   Paul Lane
Robert E. Riley   Joseph F. Leighton, Jr.

John J. McNamara

For full biographical listings, see the Martindale-Hubbell Law Directory

BROCKTON, Plymouth Co.

VINCENT P. CAHALANE, P.C. (AV)

478 Torrey Street, 02401
Telephone: 508-588-1222
Fax: 508-584-4748

Vincent P. Cahalane

For full biographical listings, see the Martindale-Hubbell Law Directory

PITTSFIELD,* Berkshire Co.

CAIN, HIBBARD, MYERS & COOK, A PROFESSIONAL CORPORATION (AV)

66 West Street, 01201
Telephone: 413-443-4771
Telecopier: 413-443-7694
Great Barrington, Massachusetts Office: 309 Main Street, 01230.
Telephone: 413-528-4771.
Fax: 413-528-5553.

C. Jeffrey Cook   Michael E. MacDonald

Jennifer L. Gerrard   Benjamin Smith

Representative Clients: Bank of Boston/First Agricultural Bank; Great Barrington Savings Bank; Greylock Credit Union; The Berkshire Gas Company; Berkshire Health Systems, Inc.; Berkshire Physicians & Surgeons, P.C.
Local Counsel for: General Electric Co.; Boston Symphony Orchestra; Statewide Funding Corporation.

For full biographical listings, see the Martindale-Hubbell Law Directory

SPRINGFIELD,* Hampden Co.

ANNINO, DRAPER & MOORE, P.C. (AV)

Suite 1818 BayBank Tower, 1500 Main Street, P.O. Box 15428, 01115
Telephone: 413-732-6400
Fax: 413-732-3339
Westfield, Massachusetts Office: 52 Court Street.
Telephone: 413-562-9829.

Calvin W. Annino, Jr.	Louis S. Moore
Mark E. Draper	Michael R. Siddall

For full biographical listings, see the Martindale-Hubbell Law Directory

---

MICHIGAN

ANN ARBOR,* Washtenaw Co.

HURBIS & CLINTON (AV)

Fifth Floor, City Center Building, 48104
Telephone: 313-761-8358
Fax: 313-761-3134

Charles J. Hurbis	Mary F. Clinton

Robert Lipnik	Georgette E. David

Representative Clients: General Motors Corp.; ITT Hartford; Insurance Company of North America; The University of Michigan; North Oakland Medical Center; City of Pontiac; Sears Roebuck and Co.; Montgomery Ward and Co., Inc.; Sedjwick-James, Inc.

For full biographical listings, see the Martindale-Hubbell Law Directory

---

BIRMINGHAM, Oakland Co.

CARSON FISCHER, P.L.C. (AV)

Third Floor, 300 East Maple Road, 48009-6317
Telephone: 810-644-4840
Facsimile: 810-644-1832

Peter L. Wanger

For full biographical listings, see the Martindale-Hubbell Law Directory

---

BLOOMFIELD HILLS, Oakland Co.

FEDERLEIN & KERANEN, P.C. (AV)

6895 Telegraph Road, 48301
Telephone: 810-647-9653
Fax: 810-647-9683
Email: 102416.1133@COMPUSERVE.COM
Detroit, Michigan Office: 407 East Fort, Suite 350.
Telephone: 313-965-6090.

Walter J. Federlein	Thomas M. Keranen

Frederick F. Butters	Maria J. Bernard
Peter J. Cavanaugh	

For full biographical listings, see the Martindale-Hubbell Law Directory

---

DETROIT,* Wayne Co.

BODMAN, LONGLEY & DAHLING LLP (AV)

34th Floor 100 Renaissance Center, 48243
Telephone: 313-259-7777
Fax: 313-393-7579
Email: 2080194@mcimail.com
Troy, Michigan Office: Suite 2020, 755 West Big Beaver Road.
Telephone: 810-362-2110.
Fax: 810-244-0780.
Ann Arbor, Michigan Office: 110 Miller, Suite 300.
Telephone: 313-761-3780.
Fax: 313-930-2494.
Northern Michigan Office: 229 Court Street, P.O. Box 405, Cheboygan.
Telephone: 616-627-4351.
Fax: 616-627-2802.

MEMBERS OF FIRM

Walter O. Koch (Troy Office)	James R. Buschmann
Thomas A. Roach	Robert J. Diehl, Jr.
(Ann Arbor Office)	John C. Cashen (Troy Office)
Gary D. Reeves (Troy Office)	

For Representative Client List, See General Section

For Complete List of Firm Personnel, See General Section

For full biographical listings, see the Martindale-Hubbell Law Directory

---

BUTZEL LONG, A PROFESSIONAL CORPORATION (AV)

Suite 900, 150 West Jefferson, 48226
Telephone: 313-225-7000
Telecopier: 313-225-7080
Email: melnick@butzel.com *URL:* http://www.butzel.com
Birmingham, Michigan Office: Suite 200, 32270 Telegraph Road.
Telephone: 810-258-1616.
Telecopier: 810-258-1439.
Lansing, Michigan Office: 118 West Ottawa Street.
Telephone: 517-372-6622.
Telecopier: 517-372-6672.
Ann Arbor, Michigan Office: Suite 300, 350 South Main Street.
Telephone: 313-995-3110.
Telecopier: 313-995-1777.
Grosse Pointe Farms, Michigan Office: Suite 260, 21 Kercheval.
Telephone: 313-886-5446.
Telecopier: 313-886-2114.

Robert J. Battista	Michael J. Lavoie
William R. Ralls (Lansing)	Gordon W. Didier (Birmingham)
Abba I. Friedman (Birmingham)	Marissa W. Pollick (Ann Arbor)
Dennis B. Schultz	Eric J. Flessland (Birmingham)
	Kenneth H. Adamczyk

David K. Tillman	James J. Urban (Lansing)
Richard T. Hewlett	Daniel R. W. Rustmann
	Robert E. Norton II

Representative Clients: Albert Kahn Associates, Inc.; Associated General Contractors; Associated Underground Contractors; Barton Malow Co.; Kajima International, Inc.; Michigan Road Builders Assn.; Perini Building Co.; Stroh Brewery Co.; The University of Michigan; William Beaumont Hospital.

For Complete List of Firm Personnel, See General Section

For full biographical listings, see the Martindale-Hubbell Law Directory

---

CLARK HILL P.L.C. (AV)

500 Woodward Avenue, Suite 3500, 48226
Telephone: 313-965-8300
Facsimile: 313-962-4348
Oakland County, Michigan Office: Third Floor, 255 South Woodward Avenue, Birmingham.
Telephone: 810-642-9692.
Facsimile: 810-642-2174.
Lansing, Michigan Office: Suite 600, 200 North Capitol Avenue.
Telephone: 517-484-4481.
Facsimile: 517-484-1246.
Minneapolis, Minnesota Office: Suite 1000, One Financial Plaza, 120 South Sixth Street.
Telephone: 612-332-0102.
Facsimile: 612-332-3225.
Kansas City, Missouri Office: Suite 1400, Bryant Building, 1102 Grand Avenue.
Telephone: 816-221-5578.
Facsimile: 816-221-0303.

Laurence M. Scoville, Jr.	Kevin S. Hendrick
J. Walker Henry	Timothy M. Koltun
David M. Hayes	John E. Berg
Frank T. Mamat	Thomas M. Dixon
James E. Baiers	Edward J. Hood

SENIOR ATTORNEY
Mark W. McInerney

David A. Breuch	Mary C. Dirkes
	Kathleen M. Deegan

Representative Clients: The Robert Carter Corporation; The Christman Co.; Bechtel Group, Inc.; Centex Bateson Construction Co. Inc.; Centel Corporation; Blount, Inc.; Smith, Hinchman & Grylls; Commercial Contracting Corp.; Fidelity & Deposit Co. Maryland.

For Complete List of Firm Personnel, See General Section

For full biographical listings, see the Martindale-Hubbell Law Directory

---

MAGER, MERCER, SCOTT & ALBER, P.C. (AV)

500 Woodward Avenue Suite 3400, 48226
Telephone: 313-962-8212
Facsimile: 313-962-5413
Oakland County Office: Top of Troy Building, 755 West Big Beaver, Suite 1700, Troy, Michigan.
Telephone: 810-362-8212.
Facsimile: 810-362-6944.
Macomb County Office: 18285 Ten Mile Road, Suite 100, Roseville, Michigan.
Telephone: 810-771-1100.
Facsimile: 810-775-5170.

George J. Mager, Jr.

Representative Clients: ABB Flakt, Inc.; American States Insurance Co.; CEI Industries; Central Venture Corp.; CIGNA; Construction Management, Inc.

(See Next Column)

MAGER, MERCER, SCOTT & ALBER P.C., *Detroit—Continued*

For full biographical listings, see the Martindale-Hubbell Law Directory

MILLER, CANFIELD, PADDOCK AND STONE, P.L.C. (AV)

A Professional Limited Liability Company
Founded in 1852 by Sidney Davy Miller
150 West Jefferson, Suite 2500, 48226-4415
Telephone: 313-963-6420
Fax: 313-496-7500
Cable Address: "Stem Detroit"
Detroit, Michigan Office: 150 West Jefferson, Suite 2500, 48226-4415.
Telephone: 313-963-6420.
Fax: 313-496-7500.
Cable Address: "Stem Detroit."
Ann Arbor, Michigan Office: 101 North Main Street, 7th Floor, 48104-1400.
Telephone: 313-663-2445.
Fax: 313-747-7147.
Bloomfield Hills, Michigan Office: Suite 100, Pinehurst Office Center, 1400 North Woodward, 48303-2014.
Telephone: 313-645-5000.
Fax: 313-645-1917.
Grand Rapids, Michigan Office: 1200 Campau Square Plaza, 99 Monroe, N.W., 49503-2639.
Telephone: 616-454-8656.
Fax: 616-776-6322.
Howell, Michigan Office: 121 South Barnard Street, Suite 4, 48843-2305.
Telephone: 517-546-7600.
Telecopier: 517-546-6974.
Kalamazoo, Michigan Office: 444 West Michigan Avenue, 49007-3752.
Telephone: 616-381-7030.
Fax: 616-382-0244.
Lansing, Michigan Office: One Michigan Avenue, Suite 900, 48933-1609.
Telephone: 517-487-2070.
Fax: 517-374-6304.
Monroe, Michigan Office: The Executive Centre, 214 East Elm Avenue, 48161-2682.
Telephone: 313-243-2000.
Fax: 313-243-0901.
Washington, D.C. Office: 1225 Nineteenth Street, N.W., Suite 400. 20036.
Telephone: 202-429-5575; 785-0600.
Fax: 202-331-1118; 785-1234.
Pensacola, Florida Office: 25 West Cedar, 32501.
Telephone: 904-469-1088.
Fax: 904-432-0677.
St. Petersburg, Florida Office: 100 Second Avenue S., Suite 7045, 33701.
Telephone: 813-982-6000.
Fax: 813-892-6002.
New York, New York Office: Eleventh Floor, 135 East 57th Street, 10022-2087.
Telephone: 212-754-5400.
Fax: 212-754-5401.
Gdansk, Poland Office: Suite 322, Dom Technika Building, Ul. Rajska 6, 80-850.
Telephone: 011-485-831-2808.
Fax: 011-485-831-4719.
Warsaw, Poland Office: Ul. Marszalkowska 82, Suite 561, 00-517.
Telephone: 011-482-623-6457 and 6458.
Fax: 011-482-623-6459.

PRINCIPALS OF FIRM

Michael W. Hartmann	Lawrence M. Dudek
Richard A. Gaffin	Ronald E. Hodess
(Grand Rapids Office)	(Bloomfield Hills Office)
James E. Spurr	Don M. Schmidt
(Kalamazoo Office)	(Kalamazoo Office)

ASSOCIATES

James R. Lancaster, Jr.	Scott R. Sikkenga
(Lansing Office)	(Kalamazoo Office)
Kurt P. McCamman	
(Kalamazoo Office)	

Representative Firm Clients: Chrysler Corporation; Comerica, Incorporated; City of Detroit, Michigan; Detroit Tigers, Inc.; First of Michigan; Ford Motor Company; Ford Motor Credit Company; Great Lakes Bancorp; Henry Ford Hospital; INVETECH Company.

For Complete List of Firm Personnel, See General Section

For full biographical listings, see the Martindale-Hubbell Law Directory

ROSEN & LOVELL, P.C. (AV)

Penobscot Building, 645 Griswold Street, Suite 3080, 48226-4224
Telephone: 313-961-7510
Fax: 313-961-2905

Paul A. Rosen	Joan Lovell

For full biographical listings, see the Martindale-Hubbell Law Directory

STEINBERG, O'CONNOR, PATON & BURNS, P.L.L.C. (AV)

1724 Ford Building, 615 Griswold Street, 48226-3901
Telephone: 313-962-3738
Telefax: 313-962-3779

Richard L. Steinberg	Alison L. Paton
Doyle O'Connor	Janice L. Burns

For full biographical listings, see the Martindale-Hubbell Law Directory

---

GRAND RAPIDS, * Kent Co.

DAY & SAWDEY, A PROFESSIONAL CORPORATION (AV)

200 Monroe Avenue, Suite 500, 49503-2217
Telephone: 616-774-8121
Telefax: 616-774-0168

George B. Kingston (1889-1965)	James B. Frakie
John R. Porter (1915-1975)	Larry A. Ver Merris
Charles E. Day, Jr.	John Boyko, Jr.
Robert W. Sawdey	Jonathan F. Thoits
C. Mark Stoppels	John T. Piggins
Thomas A. DeMeester	

For full biographical listings, see the Martindale-Hubbell Law Directory

ROBERTS, BETZ & BLOSS, P.C. (AV)

555 Riverfront Plaza Building, 55 Campau, 49503
Telephone: 616-235-9955
Telecopier: 616-235-0404

Michael J. Roberts	Gregory A. Block
Michael W. Betz	Michael T. Small
David J. Bloss	Ralph M. Reisinger
Henry S. Emrich	

For full biographical listings, see the Martindale-Hubbell Law Directory

TOLLEY, VANDENBOSCH & WALTON, P.C. (AV)

5650 Foremost Drive, S.E., 49546
Telephone: 616-942-8090
Facsimile: 616-942-4677

Peter R. Tolley	Michael C. Walton
Paul L. Nelson	

For full biographical listings, see the Martindale-Hubbell Law Directory

---

HANCOCK, Houghton Co.

WISTI & WISTI, P.C. (AV)

101 Quincy Street, 49930
Telephone: 906-482-5220
Fax: 906-482-8800
Iron Mountain, Michigan Office: 623 Stephenson Avenue.
Telephone: 906-779-1280.
Marquette, Michigan Office: 117 South Front Street.
Telephone: 906-228-8204.

Andrew H. Wisti	Mark Wisti
Daniel J. Wisti	

Patricia A. Gotschalk

References: Superior National Bank & Trust Company of Hancock, Michigan; Houghton National Bank, Houghton, Michigan.

For full biographical listings, see the Martindale-Hubbell Law Directory

---

KALAMAZOO, * Kalamazoo Co.

KREIS, ENDERLE, CALLANDER & HUDGINS, A PROFESSIONAL CORPORATION (AV)

One Moorsbridge, P.O. Box 4010, 49003-4010
Telephone: 616-324-3000
Telecopier: 616-324-3010
Email: kech@sapien.net *URL:* http://www.kech.com

Alan G. Enderle	Stephen J. Hessen
Jeffrey D. Swenarton	

For Complete List of Firm Personnel, See General Section

For full biographical listings, see the Martindale-Hubbell Law Directory

MILLER, CANFIELD, PADDOCK AND STONE, P.L.C. (AV)

A Professional Limited Liability Company
Founded in 1852 by Sidney Davy Miller
444 West Michigan Avenue, 49007-3752
Telephone: 616-381-7030
Fax: 616-382-0244
Detroit, Michigan Office: 150 West Jefferson, Suite 2500, 48226-4415.
Telephone: 313-963-6420.
Fax: 313-496-7500.
Cable Address: "Stem Detroit."

(See Next Column)

MILLER, CANFIELD, PADDOCK AND STONE P.L.C.—*Continued*

Ann Arbor, Michigan Office: 101 North Main Street, 7th Floor, 48104-1400.
Telephone: 313-663-2445.
Fax: 313-747-7147.
Bloomfield Hills, Michigan Office: Suite 100, Pinehurst Office Center, 1400 North Woodward, 48303-2014.
Telephone: 313-645-5000.
Fax: 313-645-1917.
Grand Rapids, Michigan Office: 1200 Campau Square Plaza, 99 Monroe, N.W., 49503-2639.
Telephone: 616-454-8656.
Fax: 616-776-6322.
Howell, Michigan Office: 121 South Barnard Street, Suite 4, 48843-2305.
Telephone: 517-546-7600.
Telecopier: 517-546-6974.
Lansing, Michigan Office: One Michigan Avenue, Suite 900, 48933-1609.
Telephone: 517-487-2070.
Fax: 517-374-6304.
Monroe, Michigan Office: The Executive Centre, 214 East Elm Avenue, 48161-2682.
Telephone: 313-243-2000.
Fax: 313-243-0901.
Washington, D.C. Office: 1225 Nineteenth Street, N.W., Suite 400. 20036.
Telephone: 202-429-5575; 785-0600.
Fax: 202-331-1118; 785-1234.
Pensacola, Florida Office: 25 West Cedar, 32501.
Telephone: 904-469-1088.
Fax: 904-432-0677.
St. Petersburg, Florida Office: 100 Second Avenue S., Suite 7045, 33701.
Telephone: 813-982-6000.
Fax: 813-892-6002.
New York, New York Office: Eleventh Floor, 135 East 57th Street, 10022-2087.
Telephone: 212-754-5400.
Fax: 212-754-5401.
Gdansk, Poland Office: Suite 322, Dom Technika Building, UI. Rajska 6, 80-850.
Telephone: 011-485-831-2808.
Fax: 011-485-831-4719.
Warsaw, Poland Office: UI. Marszalkowska 82, Suite 561, 00-517.
Telephone: 011-482-623-6457 and 6458.
Fax: 011-482-623-6459.

PRINCIPALS OF FIRM

James E. Spurr   Don M. Schmidt

ASSOCIATES

Kurt P. McCamman   Scott R. Sikkenga

Representative Firm Clients: Chrysler Corporation; Comerica, Incorporated; City of Detroit, Michigan; Detroit Tigers, Inc.; First of Michigan; Ford Motor Company; Ford Motor Credit Company; Great Lakes Bancorp; Henry Ford Hospital; INVETECH Company.

For Complete List of Firm Personnel, See General Section

For full biographical listings, see the Martindale-Hubbell Law Directory

---

SOUTHFIELD, Oakland Co.

DE VINE & KOHN (AV)

29800 Telegraph Road, 48034
Telephone: 810-353-6500
Fax: 810-353-2514

Clifford J. De Vine   Sheldon B. Kohn

For full biographical listings, see the Martindale-Hubbell Law Directory

---

PROVIZER, LICHTENSTEIN & PHILLIPS, P.C. (AV)

4000 Town Center, Suite 1800, 48075
Telephone: 810-352-9080
Facsimile: 810-352-1491

Harold M. Provizer   Constance S. Hall
David S. Lichtenstein   Noel F. Beck
Randall E. Phillips   William J. Selinsky
Marilyn A. Madorsky   Robert I. Brown
Deborah Molitz   Todd B. Denenberg
Jason Milstone

Representative Clients: Royal Ins. Group; Thomas Howell Group; Jefferson Ins. Co.

For full biographical listings, see the Martindale-Hubbell Law Directory

---

TROY, Oakland Co.

POLING, McGAW & POLING, P.C. (AV)

Suite 275, 5435 Corporate Drive, 48098
Telephone: 810-641-0500
Telecopier: 810-641-0506

Benson T. Buck (1926-1989)   Richard B. Poling, Jr.
Richard B. Poling   Gregory C. Hamilton
D. Douglas McGaw   Veronica B. O'Haro
James R. Parker

OF COUNSEL

Ralph S. Moore

Representative Clients: County of Oakland; City of Troy; United States Fidelity & Guaranty Co.; Sentry Insurance Co.; Admiral Insurance; DeMaria Construction Co.; Leo Corporation; Aetna Casualty and Surety Co.; Concord Design; Pneumo-Abex.

For full biographical listings, see the Martindale-Hubbell Law Directory

---

SCHIER, DENEWETH & PARFITT, P.C. (AV)

888 West Big Beaver Road, Suite 610, 48084-4737
Telephone: 810-362-5600
Telecopier: 810-362-0073

Carl F. Schier   Timothy P. Dugan
Ronald A. Deneweth   Janette E. Frank
Chris Parfitt   Mark D. Sassak

OF COUNSEL

Edward A. Ryder

References: Armond Cassil Company; Best Wrecking Company; Capital Contracting Co.; John Carlo, Inc.; Long Mechanical; Nagle Paving Company; P.K. Contracting, Inc.; R.W. Mead Company; Rainbow Construction Co. Inc.; Sunset Excavating.

For full biographical listings, see the Martindale-Hubbell Law Directory

CRIMINAL TRIAL PRACTICE

ALABAMA

BIRMINGHAM, * Jefferson Co.

BAXLEY, DILLARD, DAUPHIN & McKNIGHT (AV)

2000 Sixteenth Avenue South, 35205
Telephone: 205-939-0995
Telecopier: 205-939-5025

MEMBERS OF FIRM

William J. Baxley
Joel E. Dillard

Charles A. Dauphin
Stewart D. McKnight, III

ASSOCIATES

Donald R. James, Jr
Mary Margaret Bailey

Paul R. Ellis

For full biographical listings, see the Martindale-Hubbell Law Directory

GORHAM & WALDREP, P.C. (AV)

2101 6th Avenue North, Suite 700, 35203
Telephone: 205-254-3216; 251-9166
Telecopier: 205-324-3802
Email: info@gorham-waldrep.com
Montgomery, Alabama Office: 250 Commerce Street, P.O. Box 4837,
36103-4837.
Telephone: 334-262-0777.
Telecopier: 334-262-0742.

Charles W. Gorham
Charlie D. Waldrep
Thomas L. Stewart
Michael G. Kendrick
William J. Bryant

LaVeeda Morgan Battle
John T. Natter
Frank G. Alfano
Kay L. McNabb Cason
Victor Kelley

K. Mark Parnell

Victoria Franklin-Sisson
Karen Brown Evans
Mary H. Thompson

Leslie Miller Klasing
Brian Dennis Turner, Jr.
Anne D. Lamkin

Representative Clients: Jefferson County Personnel Board; Birmingham-Jefferson Civic Center Authority; The Water Works and Sewer Board of the City of Birmingham; City of Homewood; American Federation of Government Employees Local #1945; City of Pelham; Town of Kimberly; Alabama Tire Dealers Assn.; Southern States Body Shop Assn.

For full biographical listings, see the Martindale-Hubbell Law Directory

RICHARD S. JAFFE, P.C. (AV)

1905 Fourteenth Avenue South, 35205
Telephone: 205-930-9800
Telecopier: 205-930-9809

Richard S. Jaffe

Stephen A. Strickland

Cecilie Russell Beasley

For full biographical listings, see the Martindale-Hubbell Law Directory

DAVID CROMWELL JOHNSON (AV)

The Land Title Building, Suite 200, 600 20th Street, North, 35203
Telephone: 205-327-5223

ASSOCIATES

J. Flint Liddon

Barry R. Tuggle

For full biographical listings, see the Martindale-Hubbell Law Directory

REDDEN, MILLS & CLARK (AV)

940 First Alabama Bank Building, 417 North 20th Street, 35203
Telephone: 205-322-0457
Fax: 205-322-8481

MEMBERS OF FIRM

L. Drew Redden
William H. Mills

William N. Clark
Gerald L. Miller

Stephen W. Shaw

ASSOCIATE

Maxwell H. Pulliam, Jr.

References: SouthTrust Bank; First Alabama Bank.

For full biographical listings, see the Martindale-Hubbell Law Directory

CHATOM, * Washington Co.

TURNER, ONDERDONK, KIMBROUGH & HOWELL, P.A. (AV)

100 Central Avenue, P.O. Drawer 1389, 36518
Telephone: 334-847-2237
Fax: 334-847-3115
Mobile, Alabama Office: 1359 Dauphin Street.
Telephone: 334-432-2855.
Fax: 334-432-2863.

Edward P. Turner, Jr.
A. Michael Onderdonk
William A. Kimbrough, Jr.
(Resident, Mobile Office)

Gordon K. Howell
Marc E. Bradley
(Resident, Mobile Office)

Halron W. Turner
Frank Woodson
(Resident, Mobile Office)

David M. Huggins
(Resident, Mobile Office)
E. Tatum Turner

For full biographical listings, see the Martindale-Hubbell Law Directory

GADSDEN, * Etowah Co.

FLOYD, KEENER, CUSIMANO & ROBERTS, P.C. (AV)

816 Chestnut Street, P.O. Box 49, 35902
Telephone: 205-547-6328
Fax: 205-546-8173

Jack Floyd

Larry H. Keener

John D. Floyd

For Complete List of Firm Personnel, See General Section

For full biographical listings, see the Martindale-Hubbell Law Directory

HUNTSVILLE, * Madison Co.

MORRIS, CLOUD AND CONCHIN, P.C. (AV)

521 Madison Street, P.O. Box 248, 35804
Telephone: 205-534-0065
Fax: 205-539-0741

Harvey B. Morris (P.C.)

Joseph M. Cloud

Gary V. Conchin

Maureen "Mike" K. Cooper

Daniel B. Banks, Jr.

For full biographical listings, see the Martindale-Hubbell Law Directory

MOBILE, * Mobile Co.

BRISKMAN & BINION, P.C. (AV)

205 Church Street, P.O. Box 43, 36601
Telephone: 334-433-7600
Fax: 334-433-4485

Donald M. Briskman

Christ N. Coumanis

Walter G. (Stoney) Chavers

A List of Representative Clients will be furnished upon request.
References: First Alabama Bank; AmSouth Bank, N.A.; Southtrust Bank of Mobile.

For full biographical listings, see the Martindale-Hubbell Law Directory

THOMAS M. HAAS (AV)

258 State Street, 36603
Telephone: 334-432-0457

ASSOCIATE

N. Ruth Haas

HESS & ATCHISON (AV)

301 St. Joseph Street, P.O. Box 1706, 36633
Telephone: 334-432-4546
Fax: 334-433-6635

Barry Hess
James E. Atchison

Mona Ann Vivar
Donald C. Partridge

Lori Brown Meadows

Reference: Bank of Mobile.

For full biographical listings, see the Martindale-Hubbell Law Directory

MONTGOMERY, * Montgomery Co.

BECK & TRAVIS, P.C. (AV)

22 Scott Street, P.O. Box 5019, 36103-5019
Telephone: 334-832-4878
Fax: 334-832-4704

George L. Beck, Jr.

(See Next Column)

BECK & TRAVIS P.C., Montgomery—Continued

OF COUNSEL
W. Terry Travis

David Bryson Byrne, III

For full biographical listings, see the Martindale-Hubbell Law Directory

WETUMPKA,* Elmore Co.

ENSLEN, JOHNSTON & PINKSTON, L.L.C. (AV)

499 South Main Street, 36092
Telephone: 334-567-2545
Fax: 334-567-2547

John E. Enslen   Parker C. Johnston
Patrick D. Pinkston

References: Elmore County National Bank; First National Bank of Wetumpka.

For full biographical listings, see the Martindale-Hubbell Law Directory

ARIZONA

CASA GRANDE, Pinal Co.

FITZGIBBONS LAW OFFICES, P.L.C. (AV)

Suite E, 711 East Cottonwood Lane, P.O. Box 11208, 85230-1208
Telephone: 520-426-3824
Fax: 520-426-9355

David A. Fitzgibbons   Denis M. Fitzgibbons
David A. Fitzgibbons, III   Robert M. Yates
Kevin D. White
OF COUNSEL
E.D. "Bud" McBryde

Representative Clients: Bank of Casa Grande Valley; Charlie Case Tire Co., Inc.; Fletcher's Cobre Tire; M&O Agencies; Maricopa Turf, Inc. a/b/a Western Sod; Vaquero Foundation; Sun Life Family Health Center, Inc.; Casa Grande Regional Medical Center; Verde Grande Vineyards.

For full biographical listings, see the Martindale-Hubbell Law Directory

FLAGSTAFF,* Coconino Co.

ASPEY, WATKINS & DIESEL, P.L.L.C. (AV)

123 North San Francisco, 3rd Floor, 86001
Telephone: 520-774-1478
Facsimile: 520-774-8404
Sedona, Arizona Office: 120 Soldier Pass Road.
Telephone: 520-282-5955.
Facsimile: 520-282-5962.
Page, Arizona Office: 904 North Navajo.
Telephone: 520-645-9694.
Cottonwood, Arizona Office: 2400 E. Highway 89A, Suite C.
Telephone: 520-639-1881.
Facsimile: 520-639-0272.

MEMBERS OF FIRM
Frederick M. Fritz Aspey   Donald H. Bayles, Jr.
Harold L. Watkins   Kaign N. Christy
Louis M. Diesel   John J. Dempsey
Bruce S. Griffen   Zachary J. Markham

James E. Ledbetter   Roger M. Baeurle
Whitney Cunningham   Amy E. Mabius
Pernell Whynn McGuire   Stephen A. Thompson
Joel E. Sannes

LEGAL SUPPORT PERSONNEL
Karla H. Falls, CLAS   Dominic M. Marino, Jr,
  (Legal Assistant)   (Paralegal Assistant)
Rocky C. Nissen (Paralegal   Carrie R. Flynn (Litigation
  Assistant, Sedona, Arizona   Paralegal, Cottonwood,
  Office)   Arizona Office)
Deborah D. Roberts, CLA
  (Legal Assistant)

Representative Clients: Farmer's Insurance Company of Arizona; Pepsi-Cola Bottling Company of Northern Arizona; Bill Luke's Chrysler-Plymouth, Inc.; First American Title Insurance Company; Transnation Title Insurance Co.; Page Electric Utility; Comprehensive Access Health Plan, Inc.; Northern Arizona Healthcare Corporation.
Reference: First Interstate Bank-Arizona, N.A., Flagstaff, Arizona.

For full biographical listings, see the Martindale-Hubbell Law Directory

PHOENIX,* Maricopa Co.

BLACK & GOTTLIEB (AV)

3101 North Central Avenue, Suite 530, 85012
Telephone: 602-265-7200
Fax: 602-265-2431

Michael V. Black   Stacey F. Gottlieb

For full biographical listings, see the Martindale-Hubbell Law Directory

BURCH & CRACCHIOLO, P.A. (AV)

702 East Osborn Road, Suite 200, 85014
Telephone: 602-274-7611
Fax: 602-234-0341
Mailing Address: P.O. Box 16882, Phoenix, AZ, 85011

Stephen E. Silver   Jess A. Lorona
David G. Derickson   Stephen M. Hart

Representative Clients: Bashas' Inc.; Farmers Insurance Group; U-Haul International, Inc.

For Complete List of Firm Personnel, See General Section

For full biographical listings, see the Martindale-Hubbell Law Directory

O. JOSEPH CHORNENKY, P.C. (AV)

Suite A209, 301 East Bethany Home Road, 85012
Telephone: 602-264-3289
Fax: 602-264-3779

O. Joseph Chornenky

Christopher D. Lonn   Elliot H. Wernick

For full biographical listings, see the Martindale-Hubbell Law Directory

CROWE & SCOTT, A PROFESSIONAL ASSOCIATION (AV)

1100 East Washington Suite 200, 85034
Telephone: 602-252-2570
Fax: 602-252-1939

Tom Crowe   Michael B. Scott

For full biographical listings, see the Martindale-Hubbell Law Directory

DEBUS & KAZAN, LTD. (AV)

335 East Palm Lane, 85004
Telephone: 602-257-8900
Fax: 602-257-0723

Larry L. Debus   Lawrence Ian Kazan

Tracey Westerhausen

References: Firstar Metropolitan Bank; Citibank, Arizona.

For full biographical listings, see the Martindale-Hubbell Law Directory

RICHARD J. HERTZBERG (AV)

16 Luhrs Arcade 11 West Jefferson, 85003
Telephone: 602-253-1781
Fax: 602-253-0928

For full biographical listings, see the Martindale-Hubbell Law Directory

JOE KEILP, P.C. (AV)

1440 East Washington, Suite 100, 85034
Telephone: 602-252-0100
Fax: 602-271-4733

Joe Keilp

For full biographical listings, see the Martindale-Hubbell Law Directory

KIMERER & LAVELLE, P.L.C. (AV)

100 W. Clarendon Suite 2100, 85013
Telephone: 602-279-5900; 800-220-6817
FAX: 602-264-5566
Email: kimlav@msn.com

Michael D. Kimerer   Clark L. Derrick

For full biographical listings, see the Martindale-Hubbell Law Directory

Phoenix—Continued

LEWIS AND ROCA, LLP (AV)

A Limited Liability Partnership including a Professional Corporation
40 North Central Avenue, 85004-4429
Telephone: 602-262-5311
Fax: 602-262-5747
Email: mlp@lrlaw.com
Tucson, Arizona Office: One South Church Avenue, Suite 700, 86701-1620.
Telephone: 520-622-2090.
Fax: 520-622-3088. E-Mail: mlp@lrlaw.com.

MEMBERS OF FIRM

Jordan Green   Dale A. Danneman
                Edward F. Novak

For Complete List of Firm Personnel, See General Section

For full biographical listings, see the Martindale-Hubbell Law Directory

MATHEW & MATHEW (AV)

2425 East Camelback Road, Suite 880, 85016
Telephone: 602-381-8556
Fax: 602-957-2137
Email: SATMATHEW@aol.com; IVANM5A@ad.com
(IVANM5A@aol.com)

Ivan K. Mathew   Susan Turner Mathew

Reference: Biltmore Investors Bank.

For full biographical listings, see the Martindale-Hubbell Law Directory

MEHRENS AND WILEMON, P.A. (AV)

1005 North Second Street, 85004
Telephone: 602-258-5151
FAX: 602-257-8316

Craig Mehrens   Amy Wilemon

Reference: Firstar Metropolitan Bank & Trust.

For full biographical listings, see the Martindale-Hubbell Law Directory

ELEANOR L. MILLER (AV)

1010 East Jefferson Street, 85034
Telephone: 602-253-1010
Fax: 602-253-1048

For full biographical listings, see the Martindale-Hubbell Law Directory

MILLER & MILLER, LTD. (AV)

Suite 2250, 3200 North Central Avenue, 85012
Telephone: 602-266-8440
Fax: 602-266-8453

Murray Miller   Robert M. Miller
                Marcus Westervelt

For full biographical listings, see the Martindale-Hubbell Law Directory

LAW OFFICES OF RICHARD L. STROHM, P.C. (AV)

1136 East Campbell, 85014
Telephone: 602-279-6316
Mobile: 602-616-7094
Facsimile: 602-279-7102
Email: 102442.1444@compuserve.com

Richard L. Strohm
OF COUNSEL

Brad K. Keogh   Nedra J. Bates
LEGAL SUPPORT PERSONNEL

Mindy L. Raymond   Barbara A. Shore
(Legal Assistant)   (Nurse Paralegal)
Richard M. Knaeble
(Licensed Private Investigator)

For full biographical listings, see the Martindale-Hubbell Law Directory

THOMAS A. THINNES, P.A. (AV)

1005 North Second Street, 85004
Telephone: 602-257-8408
Fax: 602-257-8316

Thomas A. Thinnes

Gregory L. Harding
Reference: Firstar Metropolitan Bank & Trust.

For full biographical listings, see the Martindale-Hubbell Law Directory

TOLES & ASSOCIATES, P.C. (AV)

1010 East Jefferson Street, 85034
Telephone: 602-253-1010
Fax: 602-253-1048

M. Jeremy Toles

Richard M. Gerry   Craig C. Gillespie
Rosann K. Johnson   M. L. (Les) Weatherly, Jr.
OF COUNSEL
Barbara A. Jarvis

For full biographical listings, see the Martindale-Hubbell Law Directory

TUCSON,* Pima Co.

DONAU & BOLT (AV)

Suite 501, 3505 North Campbell Avenue, 85719-2033
Telephone: 520-795-8710
Fax: 520-795-0308

MEMBER OF FIRM
Alfred S. Donau III
ASSOCIATE
Sharon M. Wolfkiel

For full biographical listings, see the Martindale-Hubbell Law Directory

HIRSH, DAVIS & PICCARRETA, P.C. (AV)

145 South Sixth Avenue, 85701-2007
Telephone: 520-622-6900
Fax: 520-622-0521

Robert J. Hirsh   JoJene E. Mills
Barry M. Davis   David L. Bjorgaard
Michael L. Piccarreta   Jefferson Keenan
Carl A. Piccarreta   Jeffrey J. Rogers

For full biographical listings, see the Martindale-Hubbell Law Directory

THE LAW OFFICE OF ROBERT HOOKER (AV)

2525 East Broadway Boulevard, Suite 102, 85716-5303
Telephone: 520-881-2333
800-280-2333
Telecopier: 520-325-0150

For full biographical listings, see the Martindale-Hubbell Law Directory

LAW OFFICES OF WALTER B. NASH III, P.C. (AV)

Suite 4297, Guadalajara Building, La Placita, P.O. Box 2310, 85702-2310
Telephone: 520-792-1613
Fax: 520-628-1079

Walter B. Nash III   Cari M. Dangerfield
LEGAL SUPPORT PERSONNEL
Vicki L. Covey (Legal Assistant)

Reference: Bank One.

For full biographical listings, see the Martindale-Hubbell Law Directory

WILLIAM G. WALKER, P.C. (AV)

145 South Sixth Avenue, 85701
Telephone: 520-622-3330
Fax: 520-622-0521

William G. Walker

For full biographical listings, see the Martindale-Hubbell Law Directory

ARKANSAS

LITTLE ROCK,* Pulaski Co.

HATFIELD & LASSITER (AV)

401 West Capitol, Suite 502, 72201
Telephone: 501-374-9010
FAX: 501-374-8510

MEMBERS OF FIRM
Richard F. Hatfield   Jack T. Lassiter

Karen DeLayne Miller

For full biographical listings, see the Martindale-Hubbell Law Directory

WILSON, ENGSTROM, CORUM & COULTER (AV)

809 West Third Street, P.O. Box 71, 72203
Telephone: 501-375-6453
FAX: 501-375-5914

(See Next Column)

WILSON, ENGSTROM, CORUM & COULTER, *Little Rock—Continued*

MEMBERS OF FIRM

Roxanne Wilson (1947-1992) Gary D. Corum
Stephen Engstrom Nate Coulter

For full biographical listings, see the Martindale-Hubbell Law Directory

CALIFORNIA

BEVERLY HILLS, Los Angeles Co.

HOCHMAN, SALKIN AND DEROY, A PROFESSIONAL CORPORATION (AV)

9150 Wilshire Boulevard Suite 300, 90212-3414
Telephone: 310-281-3200; 273-1181
Fax: 310-859-1430

Bruce I. Hochman Charles P. Rettig
Avram Salkin Dennis Perez
Steven R. Toscher

OF COUNSEL
George DeRoy

Stuart A. Simon Michael W. Popoff
Frederic J. Adam

Reference: Union Bank of California.

For full biographical listings, see the Martindale-Hubbell Law Directory

COSTA MESA, Orange Co.

SCHULMAN & McMILLAN, INCORPORATED (AV)

3200 Park Center Drive, Suite 600, 92626-7148
Telephone: 714-434-9596
Telecopier: 714-434-1823

Marshall M. Schulman

For full biographical listings, see the Martindale-Hubbell Law Directory

FRESNO, * Fresno Co.

NUTTALL BERMAN ATTORNEYS (AV)

A Partnership including a Professional Corporation
2333 Merced Street, 93721
Telephone: 209-233-2333
Fax: 209-233-6947
Email: dfndr@cybergate.com

MEMBERS OF FIRM
Roger T. Nuttall (Inc.) Richard P. Berman

ASSOCIATE
Mark W. Coleman

For full biographical listings, see the Martindale-Hubbell Law Directory

FULLERTON, Orange Co.

CURRAN AND WATSON (AV)

Suite 290, 1235 North Harbor Boulevard, 92632
Telephone: 714-871-1138
Facsimile: 714-871-5620

MEMBERS OF FIRM
Richard J. Curran William G. Watson

For full biographical listings, see the Martindale-Hubbell Law Directory

GLENDALE, Los Angeles Co.

FLANAGAN, BOOTH, UNGER & MOSES (AV)

1156 North Brand Boulevard, 91202-2582
Telephone: 818-244-8694
Fax: 818-244-1852
Santa Ana, California Office: 1851 East First Street, Suite 805. 92705.
Telephone: 714-835-2607.
Fax: 714-835-4825.

MEMBERS OF FIRM
J. Michael Flanagan Charles J. Unger
Douglas M. Booth J. Barry Moses

ASSOCIATES
Michael T. Danis James A. Grover

For full biographical listings, see the Martindale-Hubbell Law Directory

IRVINE, Orange Co.

JACK M. EARLEY (AV)

19100 Von Karman Avenue, Suite 950, 92715
Telephone: 714-476-8900
Fax: 714-476-0900

For full biographical listings, see the Martindale-Hubbell Law Directory

LAW OFFICES OF JENNIFER L. KELLER (AV)

19100 Von Karman Avenue, Suite 950, 92612
Telephone: 714-476-8700
Fax: 714-476-0900
Email: HVDE71A@PRODIGY.COM

For full biographical listings, see the Martindale-Hubbell Law Directory

LONG BEACH, Los Angeles Co.

EDWARD P. GEORGE, JR., INC. A PROFESSIONAL CORPORATION (AV)

Suite 430, 5000 East Spring Street, 90815
Telephone: 310-497-2900
Facsimile: 310-497-2904

Edward P. George, Jr. Timothy L. O'Reilly
OF COUNSEL
Albert C. S. Ramsey

Reference: Harbor Bank, Long Beach.

For full biographical listings, see the Martindale-Hubbell Law Directory

MOORE, RUTTER & EVANS (AV)

A Partnership including a Professional Corporation
555 East Ocean Boulevard, Suite 500, 90802-5090
Telephone: 310-494-6667; 435-4499
Facsimile: 310-495-4229
Huntington Beach, California Office: 2100 Main Street, Suite 280, 92648.
Telephone: 714-374-3333.

RESIDENT PARTNERS
Neal Moore Mark D. Rutter
William D. Evans (P.C.)
OF COUNSEL
Michael J. Emling

For full biographical listings, see the Martindale-Hubbell Law Directory

LOS ANGELES, * Los Angeles Co.

BECK, DE CORSO, DALY, BARRERA & OH, A PROFESSIONAL LAW CORPORATION (AV)

601 West Fifth Street, 12th Floor, 90071-2025
Telephone: 213-688-1198
Fax: 213-489-7532
Email: beckdecorso@earthlink.net *URL:*
http://www.earthlink.net/~beckdecorso

Mark E. Beck Bryan D. Daly
Anthony A. De Corso Teresa R. Barrera
Angela E. Oh

Peter J. Diedrich Joan M. Steinmann
Evan Scheffel
OF COUNSEL
Godfrey Isaac

For full biographical listings, see the Martindale-Hubbell Law Directory

COLEMAN & RICHARDS, A PROFESSIONAL CORPORATION (AV)

Suite 810, 1801 Avenue of the Stars (Century City), 90067
Telephone: 310-277-2700

Richard M. Coleman Laurie J. Richards

For full biographical listings, see the Martindale-Hubbell Law Directory

GERAGOS & GERAGOS (AV)

201 N. Figueroa Street 5th Floor, 90012-2628
Telephone: 213-250-5055
Fax: 213-250-2828

Paul J. Geragos Mark J. Geragos
Matthew J. Geragos
OF COUNSEL
Susan P. Strick

For full biographical listings, see the Martindale-Hubbell Law Directory

Los Angeles—Continued

KIRKLAND & ELLIS (AV)

A Partnership including Professional Corporations
300 South Grand Avenue, Suite 3000, 90071
Telephone: 213-680-8400
Facsimile: 213-626-0010
URL: http://www.kirkland.com
Washington, D.C. Office: 655 Fifteenth Street, N.W.
Telephone: 202-879-5000.
Facsimile: (202)-879-5200.
Chicago, Illinois Office: 200 East Randolph Drive.
Telephone: 312-861-2000.
Telex: 25-4361.
New York, New York Office: Citicorp Center, 153 East 53rd Street.
Telephone: 212-446-4800.
Facsimile: (212)-446-4900.
London England Office: 199 Bishopsgate, London EC2M 3TY England.
Telephone: 171 814 6682.
Facsimile: 171 814 6622.

MEMBER OF FIRM
Jan Lawrence Handzlik

For full biographical listings, see the Martindale-Hubbell Law Directory

JOSÉ Y. LAUCHENGCO, JR. (AV)

3545 Wilshire Boulevard, Suite 247, 90010
Telephone: 213-380-9897

OF COUNSEL
Paul J. Estuar

For full biographical listings, see the Martindale-Hubbell Law Directory

MICHAELSON & LEVINE (AV)

1901 Avenue of the Stars, Suite 1708, 90067
Telephone: 310-278-4984
Fax: 310-286-9969

MEMBERS OF FIRM
Alvin S. Michaelson   Janet I. Levine
ASSOCIATE
Brenda Ligorsky
OF COUNSEL
Roger L. Cossack

Reference: City National Bank (Century City Branch).

For full biographical listings, see the Martindale-Hubbell Law Directory

O'MELVENY & MYERS LLP (AV)

400 South Hope Street, 90071-2899
Telephone: 213-669-6000
Cable Address: "Moms"
Facsimile: 213-669-6407
Email: omminfo@omm.com
Century City, California Office: 1999 Avenue of the Stars, 90067-6035.
Telephone: 310-553-6700.
Facsimile: 310-246-6779.
Newport Beach, California Office: 610 Newport Center Drive, 92660-6429.
Telephone: 714-760-9600.
Cable Address: "Moms".
Facsimile: 714-669-6994.
San Francisco, California Office: Embarcadero Center West Tower, 275 Battery Street, 94111-3305.
Telephone: 415-984-8700.
Facsimile: 415-984-8701.
New York, New York Office: Citicorp Center, 153 East 53rd Street, 10022-4611.
Telephone: 212-326-2000.
Facsimile: 212-326-2061.
Washington, D.C. Office: 555 13th Street, N.W., 20004-1109.
Telephone: 202-383-5300.
Cable Address: "Moms".
Facsimile: 202-383-5414.
London, England Office: 10 Finsbury Square, London, EC2A 1LA.
Telephone: 0171-256-8451.
Facsimile: 0171-638-8205.
Tokyo, Japan Office: Sanbancho KB-6 Building, 6 Sanbancho, Chiyoda-ku, Tokyo 102, Japan.
Telephone: 03-3239-2900.
Facsimile: 03-3239-2432.
Hong Kong Office: Suite 1905, Peregrine Tower, Lippo Centre, 89 Queensway, Central, Hong Kong.
Telephone: 852-2523-8266.
Facsimile: 852-2522-1760.
Shanghai, Peoples Republic of China Office: Shanghai International Trade Centre, Suite 2011, 2200 Yan An Road West, Shanghai, 200335, PRC.
Telephone: 86-21-6219-5363.
Facsimile: 86-21-6275-4949.

(See Next Column)

PARTNER
James R. Asperger

For Complete List of Firm Personnel, See General Section

For full biographical listings, see the Martindale-Hubbell Law Directory

MICHAEL I. SIDLEY (AV)

1900 Avenue of the Stars, Suite 1450, 90067
Telephone: 310-551-1295
Fax: 310- 277-5953

TALCOTT, LIGHTFOOT, VANDEVELDE & SADOWSKY (AV)

Thirteenth Floor 655 South Hope Street, 90017
Telephone: 213-622-4750
Fax: 213-622-2690

MEMBERS OF FIRM
Robert M. Talcott   Stephen B. Sadowsky
Michael J. Lightfoot   John S. Crouchley
John D. Vandevelde   John P. Martin
          Melissa N. Widdifield
ASSOCIATE
James H. Locklin

Reference: Sterling Bank, Los Angeles, California.

For full biographical listings, see the Martindale-Hubbell Law Directory

LAW OFFICES OF BARRY TARLOW A PROFESSIONAL CORPORATION (AV)

9119 Sunset Boulevard, 90069
Telephone: 310-278-2111
Cable Address: "Habeas"
Fax: 310-550-7055
Email: lobt@earthlink.net

Barry Tarlow

Mark O. Heaney   Evan A. Jenness
A. Blair Bernholz   Paul J. Loh

For full biographical listings, see the Martindale-Hubbell Law Directory

DONALD R. WAGER (AV)

10960 Wilshire Boulevard, Suite 1000, 90024
Telephone: 310-235-3939
Fax: 310-325-3949

Reference: Bank of America, Santa Monica, California.

For full biographical listings, see the Martindale-Hubbell Law Directory

LAW OFFICES OF MARK J. WERKSMAN (AV)

601 West Fifth Street, Twelfth Floor, 90071
Telephone: 213-688-0460
Fax: 213-624-1942

ASSOCIATE
Donna Tryfman

For full biographical listings, see the Martindale-Hubbell Law Directory

ANDREW RUSSELL WILLING (AV)

Promenade West, 880 West First Street Suite 302, 90012
Telephone: 213-626-6600
Facsimile: 213-626-0488

Reference: Wells Fargo Bank (Pasadena Main Office).

For full biographical listings, see the Martindale-Hubbell Law Directory

OAKLAND,* Alameda Co.

ROBERT J. BELES (AV)

#1 Kaiser Plaza, Suite 1750, 94612
Telephone: 510-836-0100
FAX: 510-832-3690

For full biographical listings, see the Martindale-Hubbell Law Directory

PALO ALTO, Santa Clara Co.

NOLAN & ARMSTRONG (AV)

600 University Avenue, 94301
Telephone: 415-326-2980
Fax: 415-326-9704

MEMBERS OF FIRM
Thomas J. Nolan   Michael W. Armstrong
          Daniel L. Barton
ASSOCIATE
Rebecca Laibson

(See Next Column)

NOLAN & ARMSTRONG, *Palo Alto—Continued*
LEGAL SUPPORT PERSONNEL
LEGAL ASSISTANTS

Lynn M. Memolo   Marguerite Giuliano

For full biographical listings, see the Martindale-Hubbell Law Directory

---

PASADENA, Los Angeles Co.

W. MICHAEL MAYOCK (AV)

The Braley Building, Fourth Floor, 35 South Raymond Avenue, 91105
Telephone: 818-405-1465; 310-552-1465
FAX: 818-578-0768

Reference: Union Bank.

For full biographical listings, see the Martindale-Hubbell Law Directory

---

REDWOOD CITY,* San Mateo Co.

M. GERALD SCHWARTZBACH (AV)

601 Brewster Avenue, P.O. Box 3389, 94103
Telephone: 415-367-6811
Fax: 415-368-0367

For full biographical listings, see the Martindale-Hubbell Law Directory

SMITH & BENTLEY (AV)

777 Marshall Street, 94063
Telephone: 415-568-2820
Fax: 415-568-2823

MEMBERS OF FIRM

Charles J. Smith   Joshua M. Bentley
Jim Hartnett

OF COUNSEL
Lee W. Clark

For full biographical listings, see the Martindale-Hubbell Law Directory

---

RIVERSIDE,* Riverside Co.

STEVEN L. HARMON (AV)

The Loring Building, 3685 Main Street, Suite 250, 92501
Telephone: 909-787-6800
Fax: 909-787-6700

For full biographical listings, see the Martindale-Hubbell Law Directory

---

SACRAMENTO,* Sacramento Co.

BLACKMON, DROZD & SNELLINGS (AV)

U.S. Bank Plaza, 980 9th Street, Suite 2080, 95814
Telephone: 916-441-0824
Fax: 916-441-0970

MEMBERS OF FIRM

Clyde M. Blackmon   Dale A. Drozd
Hill C. Snellings

For full biographical listings, see the Martindale-Hubbell Law Directory

ROTHSCHILD, WISHEK & SANDS (AV)

901 "F" Street, Suite 200, 95814
Telephone: 916-444-9845

MEMBERS OF FIRM

Michael Rothschild   M. Bradley Wishek
Stacy Elaine Boulware

OF COUNSEL
Michael S. Sands

For full biographical listings, see the Martindale-Hubbell Law Directory

---

SAN BERNARDINO,* San Bernardino Co.

KASSEL & KASSEL (AV)

A Group of Independent Law Offices
Suite 207, Wells Fargo Bank Building, 334 West Third Street, 92401
Telephone: 909-884-6455
Fax: 909-884-8032

Philip Kassel   Gregory H. Kassel

References: Wells Fargo Bank; Bank of America; Bank of San Bernardino.

For full biographical listings, see the Martindale-Hubbell Law Directory

---

SAN DIEGO,* San Diego Co.

DOUGLAS C. BROWN (AV)

501 West Broadway, Suite 800, 92101-3547
Telephone: 619-230-7254
Fax: 619-231-9754

For full biographical listings, see the Martindale-Hubbell Law Directory

JOHN G. COTSIRILOS (AV)

2442 Fourth Avenue, 92101
Telephone: 619-232-6022
Fax: 619-232-6052

For full biographical listings, see the Martindale-Hubbell Law Directory

COUGHLAN, SEMMER & LIPMAN (AV)

501 West Broadway, Suite 400, 92101
Telephone: 619-232-0800
Fax: 619-232-0107

MEMBERS OF FIRM

R. J. (Jerry) Coughlan, Jr.   Robert F. Semmer
Michael L. Lipman

ASSOCIATES

Cathleen Gilliland Fitch   Barbara Howe Murray
Duane Tyler   Katherine Koransky Pothier
Angela L. Baxter   Daniel A. Kaplan

OF COUNSEL
Alexandra M. Kwoka

Representative Clients: Ernst & Young; U.S. Air; Wells Fargo Bank; Lawyers Mutual Insurance Co.; Prudential-Bache Securities, Inc.; CAMICO; Shell Oil; IBP, Inc.; UST Inc.; San Diego National Bank.

For full biographical listings, see the Martindale-Hubbell Law Directory

JOHN A. CRAWFORD, JR. (AV)

1010 Second Avenue, Suite 2000, 92101
Telephone: 619-233-7012
Fax: 619-233-3172

For full biographical listings, see the Martindale-Hubbell Law Directory

GOLDBERG & HALL (AV)

2100 Symphony Towers, 750 B Street, 92101
Telephone: 619-297-1111
Fax: 619-297-1150

MEMBERS OF FIRM

Charles L. Goldberg   Patrick Q. Hall

For full biographical listings, see the Martindale-Hubbell Law Directory

GRIMES & WARWICK (AV)

2664 Fourth Avenue, 92103
Telephone: 619-232-2014
Fax: 619-232-8857

MEMBERS OF FIRM

Robert L. Grimes   Thomas J. Warwick, Jr.

ASSOCIATES

Linda K. Grimes   Jennifer J. Sinex
Antonio F. Yoon

For full biographical listings, see the Martindale-Hubbell Law Directory

PETER J. HUGHES A PROFESSIONAL CORPORATION (AV)

1010 Second Avenue, Suite 1917, 92101
Telephone: 619-234-6695
Fax: 619-696-0155

Peter J. Hughes

For full biographical listings, see the Martindale-Hubbell Law Directory

SELTZER CAPLAN WILKINS & McMAHON, A PROFESSIONAL CORPORATION (AV)

2100 Symphony Towers, 750 B Street, 92101
Telephone: 619-685-3003
Fax: 619-685-3100

OF COUNSEL

Charles L. Goldberg   Patrick Q. Hall

Representative Clients: Chicago Title; Girard Savings Bank; Goodyear Tire & Rubber Co.; W.R. Grace & Co--Conn.; McDonnell-Douglas Corp.; McMillin Communities; Philip Morris Incorporated; Western Financial Savings Bank.

For Complete List of Firm Personnel, See General Section

For full biographical listings, see the Martindale-Hubbell Law Directory

SAN FRANCISCO, San Francisco Co.

LADAR & KNAPP (AV)

Suite 310, 507 Polk Street, 94102
Telephone: 415-928-2333
Fax: 415-928-4499

Jerrold M. Ladar   Joyce B. Ladar
Bernard L. Knapp
ASSOCIATE
Gregory T. Powell

For full biographical listings, see the Martindale-Hubbell Law Directory

HARRIET ROSS (AV)

One Sansome Street, Suite 2000, 94104
Telephone: 415-956-7655
Fax: 415-673-8172

For full biographical listings, see the Martindale-Hubbell Law Directory

JOHN M. RUNFOLA (AV)

One Maritime Plaza, Suite 1040, 94111
Telephone: 415-391-4243
Fax: 415-394-0222

Reference: First Interstate Bank.

For full biographical listings, see the Martindale-Hubbell Law Directory

GEORGE G. WALKER, INC. (AV)

Suite 635, 633 Battery Street, 94111
Telephone: 415-421-6911
Fax: 415-788-6787

George G. Walker

For full biographical listings, see the Martindale-Hubbell Law Directory

SAN JOSE, Santa Clara Co.

CRAIG M. BROWN, INC. (AV)

333 West Santa Clara Street, Suite 618, 95113
Telephone: 408-286-8844
Fax: 408-286-6699
Email: cmbtrialaw@aol.com

Craig M. Brown

For full biographical listings, see the Martindale-Hubbell Law Directory

GUYTON N. JINKERSON (AV)

50 West San Fernando Street Suite 400, 95113
Telephone: 408-297-8555
Fax: 408-295-6375
Email: gnj__law@compuserve.com

For full biographical listings, see the Martindale-Hubbell Law Directory

MANCHESTER & WILLIAMS (AV)

An Association of Attorneys including Professional Corporations
100 Park Center Plaza, Suite 525, 95113
Telephone: 408-287-6193
Fax: 408-287-1554
Email: mwslaw@ix.netcom.com

Steven R. Manchester (Inc.)   John L. Williams (Inc.)
Kurt J. Seibert
LEGAL SUPPORT PERSONNEL
Sylvia M. Cole (Administrative Assistant)

For full biographical listings, see the Martindale-Hubbell Law Directory

McMANIS, FAULKNER & MORGAN (AV)

160 West Santa Clara Street, 10th Floor, 95113
Telephone: 408-279-8700
Fax: 408-279-3244; 408-279-0494
Email: mfm@mfmlaw.com
MEMBERS OF FIRM
James McManis   William Faulkner
Donelle Morgan
ASSOCIATES
Nora Rousso   Michael Reedy
Lisa Herrick   Douglas Watanabe
Kelly McHaffie

For full biographical listings, see the Martindale-Hubbell Law Directory

THOMAS F. MUELLER A PROFESSIONAL CORPORATION (AV)

255 North Market Street, Suite 190, 95110
Telephone: 408-292-2434
Fax: 408-292-1264

Thomas F. Mueller

For full biographical listings, see the Martindale-Hubbell Law Directory

TYNDALL & CAHNERS (AV)

An Association of Attorneys including a Professional Corporation
96 North Third Street, Suite 580, 95112
Telephone: 408-297-3700
Fax: 408-297-3721

John G. Tyndall III (P.C.)   John D. Cahners

Michael Francis Brown

For full biographical listings, see the Martindale-Hubbell Law Directory

SAN RAFAEL, Marin Co.

RAGGHIANTI • FREITAS • MONTOBBIO • WALLACE LLP (AV)

874 Fourth Street, Suite D, 94901
Telephone: 415-453-9433
Fax: 415-453-8269

Gary T. Ragghianti   J. Randolph Wallace
David P. Freitas   Patrick M. Macias
J. Mark Montobbio   Robert F. Epstein
John Ralph Thomas

For full biographical listings, see the Martindale-Hubbell Law Directory

SANTA BARBARA, Santa Barbara Co.

ESKIN & JACKSON (AV)

1111 Chapala Street, Suite 310, 93101
Telephone: 805-965-8550
Fax: 805-564-2170
Ventura, California Office: 830 East Santa Clara Street.
Telephone: 805-641-5888.
Fax: 805-641-5877.

MEMBERS OF FIRM
George C. Eskin   Hannah-Beth Jackson
ASSOCIATE
Joanne S. Sumalpong

For full biographical listings, see the Martindale-Hubbell Law Directory

SANTA MONICA, Los Angeles Co.

LAW OFFICES OF ROBERT BERKE (AV)

1717 Fourth Street, Third Floor, 90401
Telephone: 310-917-5599
Fax: 310-395-3884; 310-393-0405
Email: lawservices@earthlink.net

Jeanne J. Kim   Deborah A. Nolan
LEGAL SUPPORT PERSONNEL
Sonja K. Renz

Representative Clients: L.A. County Bar Association Lawyer Referral Service; Santa Monica Bar Association Lawyer Referral Service.

For full biographical listings, see the Martindale-Hubbell Law Directory

CHALEFF & ENGLISH (AV)

Garden Suite, 1337 Ocean Avenue, 90401
Telephone: 310-458-1691
Fax: 310-393-6937

MEMBERS OF FIRM
Gerald L. Chaleff   Audrey Winograde
Charles R. English   Gigi Gordon

For full biographical listings, see the Martindale-Hubbell Law Directory

NASATIR, HIRSCH & PODBERESKY (AV)

2115 Main Street, 90405
Telephone: 310-399-3259
Fax: 310-392-9029

Michael D. Nasatir   Richard G. Hirsch
Vicki I. Podberesky

For full biographical listings, see the Martindale-Hubbell Law Directory

O'NEILL, LYSAGHT & SUN (AV)

100 Wilshire Boulevard, Suite 700, 90401
Telephone: 310-451-5700
Telecopier: 310-399-7201

(See Next Column)

O'NEILL, LYSAGHT & SUN, *Santa Monica—Continued*

Brian O'Neill	Yolanda Orozco
Brian C. Lysaght	John M. Moscarino
Frederick D. Friedman	Harriet Beegun Leva
Brian A. Sun	Edward A. Klein

Robert L. Meylan

David E. Rosen	Paul D. Murphy
Ellyn S. Garofalo	Brian D. Hershman

OF COUNSEL

J. Joseph Connolly

Reference: Wells Fargo Bank, Santa Monica.

For full biographical listings, see the Martindale-Hubbell Law Directory

---

TORRANCE, Los Angeles Co.

BIRD & BIRD, A LAW CORPORATION (AV)

3555 Torrance Boulevard, Suite 200, 90503-4816
Telephone: 310-316-2285
Fax: 310-316-7930

George Francis Bird, Jr.   Karen Hunter Bird

Kimberly Gay Anderson

For full biographical listings, see the Martindale-Hubbell Law Directory

---

VENTURA,* Ventura Co.

ESKIN & JACKSON (AV)

830 East Santa Clara Street, 93001
Telephone: 805-641-5888
Fax: 805-641-5877
Santa Barbara, California Office: 1111 Chapala Street, Suite 310.
Telephone: 805-965-8550.
Fax: 805-564-2170.

MEMBERS OF FIRM

George C. Eskin   Hannah-Beth Jackson

ASSOCIATE

Joanne S. Sumalpong

For full biographical listings, see the Martindale-Hubbell Law Directory

WHIPPLE AND VIELE, A PROFESSIONAL LAW CORPORATION (AV)

60 South California Street, 93001
Telephone: 805-643-8658; 643-8422
Fax: 805-653-6079

Edward A. Whipple

References: Wells Fargo Bank; American Commercial Bank.

For full biographical listings, see the Martindale-Hubbell Law Directory

---

COLORADO

BOULDER,* Boulder Co.

HOWARD BITTMAN (AV)

1406 Pearl Street, Suite 200, 80302
Telephone: 303-443-2281
Fax: 303-443-2862

For full biographical listings, see the Martindale-Hubbell Law Directory

LAW OFFICES OF MICHAEL R. ENWALL (AV)

720 Pearl Street, 80302
Telephone: 303-449-3891
FAX: 303-449-3992
Email: Enwall@nilenet.com

ASSOCIATE

Barbara K. Grant

For full biographical listings, see the Martindale-Hubbell Law Directory

McCORMICK AND CHRISTOPH, P.C. (AV)

1406 Pearl Street, Suite 200, 80302-5307
Telephone: 303-443-2281
Fax: 303-443-2862

G. Paul McCormick   James R. Christoph

For full biographical listings, see the Martindale-Hubbell Law Directory

---

MILLER AND HARRISON, LLC (AV)

2305 Broadway, 80304-4106
Telephone: 303-449-2830
Fax: 303-449-2198

MEMBERS OF FIRM

Robert Bruce Miller   David B. Harrison

ASSOCIATE

Joan Clifford

OF COUNSEL

Steven Taffet

Reference: Norwest Bank.

For full biographical listings, see the Martindale-Hubbell Law Directory

PETER SCHILD (AV)

1720 14th Street, #100, 80302
Telephone: 303-444-8720
Fax: 303-444-8720
Mailing Address: 259 E. Kelly Road, Boulder, CO, 80302

For full biographical listings, see the Martindale-Hubbell Law Directory

---

COLORADO SPRINGS,* El Paso Co.

ELVIN L. GENTRY, P.C. (AV)

Suite 201, 405 South Cascade, 80903
Telephone: 719-632-4647
Fax: 719-578-9311

Elvin L. Gentry

For full biographical listings, see the Martindale-Hubbell Law Directory

DENNIS W. HARTLEY, P.C. PROFESSIONAL CORPORATION (AV)

1749 S. 8th Street, Suite 5, 80906-1968
Telephone: 719-635-5521
FAX: 719-635-5760

Dennis W. Hartley

Reference: First American Bank.

For full biographical listings, see the Martindale-Hubbell Law Directory

THE TEGTMEIER LAW FIRM, P.C. (AV)

518 North Nevada, 80903
Telephone: 719-473-5757
Telefax: 719-473-6767

Richard L. Tegtmeier

Bradley S. Taylor

For full biographical listings, see the Martindale-Hubbell Law Directory

---

DENVER,* Denver Co.

MICHAEL L. BENDER, P.C. (AV)

Suite 1160, 1660 Wynkoop Street, 80202-1146
Telephone: 303-893-8000
Fax: 303-893-8055
Email: MLBends@AOL.COM

Michael L. Bender

For full biographical listings, see the Martindale-Hubbell Law Directory

BIRGE & MAYERS, P.C. (AV)

1700 Broadway, Suite 1501, 80290
Telephone: 303-860-7100
Facsimile: 303-860-7338

Thomas D. Birge   Cathryn B. Mayers

For full biographical listings, see the Martindale-Hubbell Law Directory

BREGA & WINTERS, P.C. (AV)

One Norwest Center, 1700 Lincoln Street, Suite 2222, 80203
Telephone: 303-866-9400
Fax: 303-861-9109
Email: bwpc@indra.com
Greeley, Colorado Office: 1100 Tenth Street, Suite 402, 80631.
Telephone: 303-352-4805.
Fax: 303-352-6547.

James W. Bain	Brian A. Magoon
Stuart N. Bennett	Loren L. Mall
Charles F. Brega	Pamela A. Shaddock
Robert R. Dormer	(Resident, Greeley Office)
Robert C. Kaufman	Jay John Schnell
Ronald S. Loser	Jerry D. Winters
	(Resident, Greeley Office)

(See Next Column)

BREGA & WINTERS P.C.—*Continued*

Peter A. Gergely
Wesley B. Howard, Jr.
Yvonne Marie Kreye
S. Scott Lasher

Bradley D. Laue
  (Resident, Greeley Office)
Jack R. Luellen
  (Not admitted in CO)

OF COUNSEL

Carolyn Jane Hariton   Mark Spitalnik

COUNSEL

Jay W. Enyart

For full biographical listings, see the Martindale-Hubbell Law Directory

CANGES, IWASHKO & BETHKE, A PROFESSIONAL CORPORATION (AV)

303 East 17th Avenue Suite 400, 80203-1261
Telephone: 303-860-1900
Fax: 303-860-1665

E. Michael Canges   Nina A. Iwashko
Erich L. Bethke

Stephen R. Fatzinger   James S. Bailey

Reference: Norwest Bank Denver.

For full biographical listings, see the Martindale-Hubbell Law Directory

DIXON AND SNOW, P.C. (AV)

425 South Cherry Street, Suite 1000, 80222
Telephone: 303-394-2200
FAX: 303-394-2340

Jerre W. Dixon   Rod W. Snow
Steven Janiszewski

For full biographical listings, see the Martindale-Hubbell Law Directory

JERALYN E. MERRITT (AV)

303 East Seventeenth Avenue, Suite 400, 80203
Telephone: 303-837-1837
Fax: 303-860-1665
Email: jem96@aol.com

For full biographical listings, see the Martindale-Hubbell Law Directory

NEWELL & MARTENS (AV)

A Partnership including a Professional Corporation
226 West Twelfth Avenue, 80204
Telephone: 303-573-5253
FAX: 303-573-5257

Steven R. Newell (P.C.)   Steven P. Martens
Kevin C. Massaro

Reference: Vectra Bank.

For full biographical listings, see the Martindale-Hubbell Law Directory

DAVID A. OGILVIE, P.C. (AV)

Suite 3901, One Norwest Center, 1700 Lincoln Street, 80203
Telephone: 303-837-9991
Fax: 303-832-5010
Email: DAO9991@aol.com

David A. Ogilvie

LEGAL SUPPORT PERSONNEL

Sherry R. Shults

Representative Clients: Dwight Deere Carter Trust; Sean Deere Carter Trust; Charles W. Swanson Trust.
Reference: Norwest Bank Denver, N.A.

For full biographical listings, see the Martindale-Hubbell Law Directory

POZNER & KAPLAN, P.C. (AV)

1890 Gaylord Street, 80206-1211
Telephone: 303-333-1890
Fax: 303-333-1041

Larry S. Pozner   David S. Kaplan

Reference: Guaranty Bank.

For full biographical listings, see the Martindale-Hubbell Law Directory

JOHN M. RICHILANO P.C. (AV)

1660 Wynkoop Suite 1160, 80202
Telephone: 303-893-8000
Telecopier: 303-893-8055

John M. Richilano

For full biographical listings, see the Martindale-Hubbell Law Directory

ARTHUR M. SCHWARTZ, P.C. (AV)

Dominion Plaza, Suite 2250 South Tower 600 Seventeenth Street, 80202
Telephone: 303-893-2500
Fax: 303-893-3349

Arthur M. Schwartz

Michael W. Gross   Cindy D. Schwartz
Gary M. Kramer

Reference: First Interstate Bank of Denver.

For full biographical listings, see the Martindale-Hubbell Law Directory

DANIEL T. SMITH (AV)

Suite 200, 430 East 7th Avenue, 80203
Telephone: 303-860-8100
Fax: 303-860-8018

For full biographical listings, see the Martindale-Hubbell Law Directory

SPRINGER & STEINBERG, A PROFESSIONAL CORPORATION (AV)

Suite 1500, 1600 Broadway, 80202
Telephone: 303-861-2800
Fax: 303-832-7116

Jeffrey A. Springer   Susan Fuller
Harvey A. Steinberg   Amy Mandel Springer

Reference: Norwest Bank of Denver.

For full biographical listings, see the Martindale-Hubbell Law Directory

CRAIG L. TRUMAN, P.C. (AV)

Suite 205, 1444 Wazee Street, 80202
Telephone: 303-595-8008
Fax: 303-595-9505

Craig L. Truman

For full biographical listings, see the Martindale-Hubbell Law Directory

LAKEWOOD, Jefferson Co.

POLIDORI, GEROME, FRANKLIN AND JACOBSON, L.L.C. (AV)

Suite 300, 550 South Wadsworth Boulevard, 80226
Telephone: 303-936-3300
Fax: 303-936-0125

Dennis J. Jacobson

Barry J. Seidenfeld

Representative Clients: Lakewood City Center; Treeforms, Inc.; Lakewood Chrysler-Plymouth, Inc.; Western Fasteners U.S.A., Inc.; Horizon Glass and Glazing Co., Inc.; Grif-Fab Corp.; Commercial Architectural Products, Inc.; Voyaguers International, Inc.; 1st Bank, Villa Italia.

For full biographical listings, see the Martindale-Hubbell Law Directory

CONNECTICUT

*BRIDGEPORT,** Fairfield Co.

GASTON & RUANE (AV)

Suite 403 350 Fairfield Avenue, 06604
Telephone: 203-334-1656
Fax: 203-333-4532

James J. Ruane

JohnPatrick C. O'Brien

For full biographical listings, see the Martindale-Hubbell Law Directory

MEEHAN & MEEHAN (AV)

76 Lyon Terrace, 06604
Telephone: 203-333-1888
Fax: 203-331-0107

Richard T. Meehan, Sr.   Richard T. Meehan, Jr.
Edward J. Gavin

For full biographical listings, see the Martindale-Hubbell Law Directory

Bridgeport—Continued

WEINSTEIN, WEINER, IGNAL, NAPOLITANO & SHAPIRO, P.C. (AV)

350 Fairfield Avenue, P.O. Box 9177, 06601
Telephone: 203-333-1177
Cable Address: "Moot"
Fax: 203-384-9832

Howard Evan Ignal	Roberta Napolitano
Gerald T. Weiner	Richard J. Shapiro
Burton M. Weinstein	Judith A. Mauzaka
John I. Bolton	

For full biographical listings, see the Martindale-Hubbell Law Directory

---

HARTFORD,* Hartford Co.

BROWN, PAINDIRIS & ZARELLA, LLP (AV)

100 Pearl Street, 06103
Telephone: 860-522-3343
Telecopier: 860-522-2490
Glastonbury, Connecticut Office: 7 Sycamore Street.
Telephone: 860-659-6668.
Fax: 860-658-6671.
East Hampton, Connecticut Office: 42 East High Street.
Telephone: 860-267-2044.

MEMBERS OF FIRM

Richard R. Brown	Ronald T. Scott
Nicholas Paindiris	John D. Maxwell
Peter T. Zarella	Kate W. Haakonsen
Steven W. Varney	

ASSOCIATES

Christopher J. McCarthy	Sean M. Peoples
Robert T. Rimmer	

For full biographical listings, see the Martindale-Hubbell Law Directory

---

NEW HAVEN,* New Haven Co.

LAW OFFICES OF JOHN R. WILLIAMS (AV)

51 Elm Street, 06510
Telephone: 203-562-9931
Fax: 203-776-9494

ASSOCIATES

Diane Polan	Norman A. Pattis
Katrena Engstrom	William S. Palmieri

References: Webster Bank; Bank of New Haven.

For full biographical listings, see the Martindale-Hubbell Law Directory

---

STAMFORD, Fairfield Co.

SILVER, GOLUB & TEITELL (AV)

184 Atlantic Street, P.O. Box 389, 06904
Telephone: 203-325-4491
Fax: 203-325-3769

MEMBERS OF FIRM

David S. Golub	Ernest F. Teitell

For full biographical listings, see the Martindale-Hubbell Law Directory

---

VERNON,* Tolland Co.

FLAHERTY, MEISLER & COURTNEY (AV)

30 Lafayette Square, P.O. Box 508, 06066
Telephone: 860-872-7200
Fax: 860-875-6594
Email: FMACATTY@aol.com

MEMBERS OF FIRM

Leo B. Flaherty Jr.	Arthur P. Meisler
Joseph D. Courtney	

ASSOCIATE

Elizabeth C. Foran

Reference: Savings Bank of Rockville.

For full biographical listings, see the Martindale-Hubbell Law Directory

---

WESTPORT, Fairfield Co.

ANDREW B. BOWMAN (AV)

1804 Post Road East, 06880
Telephone: 203-259-0599
Fax: 203-255-2570

Reference: Peoples Bank.

For full biographical listings, see the Martindale-Hubbell Law Directory

---

STUART A. McKEEVER (AV)

155 Post Road, East, 06880
Telephone: 203-227-4756
Fax: 203-454-2031

Reference: Fleet Bank.

For full biographical listings, see the Martindale-Hubbell Law Directory

---

DELAWARE

WILMINGTON,* New Castle Co.

BIGGS AND BATTAGLIA (AV)

1800 Mellon Bank Center, P.O. Box 1489, 19899-1489
Telephone: 302-655-9677

MEMBERS OF FIRM

Victor F. Battaglia	Philip B. Bartoshesky
Robert D. Goldberg	Victor F. Battaglia, Jr.
Charles Slanina	Christopher J. Battaglia

For Complete List of Firm Personnel, See General Section

For full biographical listings, see the Martindale-Hubbell Law Directory

---

JOSEPH A. HURLEY, P.A. (AV)

1215 King Street, 19801
Telephone: 302-658-8980

Joseph A. Hurley

For full biographical listings, see the Martindale-Hubbell Law Directory

---

EUGENE J. MAURER, JR., P.A. (AV)

1201-A King Street, 19801
Telephone: 302-652-7900
Fax: 302-652-2173

Eugene J. Maurer, Jr.

LEGAL SUPPORT PERSONNEL

Carol Rende (Paralegal)

For full biographical listings, see the Martindale-Hubbell Law Directory

---

DISTRICT OF COLUMBIA

WASHINGTON, D.C. Co.

* indicates certain Bar Register subscribers, in cities of comparable size and importance, who maintain an additional office in Washington, D.C. and who have arranged for representation as a part of the Washington, D.C. listings that follow

---

ASBILL, JUNKIN & MOFFITT, CHTD. (AV)

1615 New Hampshire Avenue, N.W., 20009
Telephone: 202-234-9000
Facsimile: 202-332-6480

Henry W. Asbill	William B. Moffitt
Timothy deForest Junkin	(Not admitted in DC)

OF COUNSEL

Oscar I. Dodek, Jr.	Matthew L. Myers

For full biographical listings, see the Martindale-Hubbell Law Directory

---

CACHERIS & TREANOR (AV)

Suite 730, 1100 Connecticut Avenue, North West, 20036
Telephone: 202-775-8700
Fax: 202-775-8702; 202-775-8722
Alexandria, Virginia Office: 705 Prince Street.
Telephone: 703-549-8181.

Plato Cacheris	Gerard Treanor
	Philip T. Inglima

ASSOCIATES

Judith L. Wheat	Karl A. Racine
	John F. Hundley

OF COUNSEL

Philip T. White

For full biographical listings, see the Martindale-Hubbell Law Directory

Washington—Continued

CAPLIN & DRYSDALE, CHARTERED (AV)

One Thomas Circle, N.W., 20005
Telephone: 202-862-5000
Cable Address: "Capdale"
Telex: 904001 CAPL UR WSH
Fax: 202-429-3301
New York, N.Y. Office: 399 Park Avenue.
Telephone: 212-319-7125.
Fax: 212-644-6755.

Mortimer M. Caplin	Douglas D. Drysdale
Robert A. Klayman	Thomas A. Troyer
Ralph A. Muoio	David N. Webster
Elihu Inselbuch	H. David Rosenbloom
(Resident, New York Office)	Peter Van N. Lockwood
Ronald B. Lewis	Cono R. Namorato
Richard W. Skillman	Daniel B. Rosenbaum
Patricia G. Lewis	Richard E. Timbie
Bernard S. Bailor	Graeme W. Bush
Stafford Smiley	Albert G. Lauber, Jr.
Sally A. Regal	Scott D. Michel
Julie W. Davis	Kent A. Mason
Carl S. Kravitz	Trevor W. Swett III
Robert A. Boisture	Robert E. Culbertson
James Sottile, IV	Charles T. Plambeck
Harry J. Hicks, III	James E. Salles
Milton Cerny	Craig A. Sharon
Paul G. Cellupica	Matthew W. Frank
Michael T. Doran	Christian R. Pastore
Nathan D. Finch	(Not admitted in DC)
Jessica L. Goldstein	Elizabeth M. Sellers
Laura J. Kerrigan	Douglas N. Varley
	(Not admitted in DC)

OF COUNSEL

Robert H. Elliott, Jr.	Myron C. Baum
Vivian L. Cavalieri	C. Sanders McNew
Ann C. McMillan	(Resident, New York Office)

Janne G. Gallagher

For full biographical listings, see the Martindale-Hubbell Law Directory

---

JANIS, SCHUELKE & WECHSLER (AV)

1728 Massachusetts Avenue, N.W., 20036
Telephone: 202-861-0600
Telecopier: 202-223-7230

N. Richard Janis	Lawrence H. Wechsler
Henry F. Schuelke, III	S. Robert Sutton

John W. Kern

For full biographical listings, see the Martindale-Hubbell Law Directory

---

* JONES, DAY, REAVIS & POGUE (AV)

Metropolitan Square, 1450 G Street, N.W., 20005-2088
Telephone: 202-879-3939
Cable Address: "Attorneys Washington"
Telex: W.U. (Domestic) 89-2410 ATTORNEYS WASH (International)
64363 ATTORNEYS WASH
Telecopier: 202-737-2832
In Atlanta, Georgia: 3500 One Peachtree Center, 303 Peachtree Street, N.E
.
Telephone: 404-521-3939.
Cable Address: "Attorneys Atlanta".
Telex: 54-2711.
Telecopier: 404-581-8330.
In Brussels, Belgium: Avenue Louise 480, 7th Floor, B-1050 Brussels.
Telephone: 32-2-645-14-11.
Telecopier: 32-2-645-14-45.
In Chicago, Illinois: 77 West Wacker.
Telephone: 312-782-3939.
Telecopier: 312-782-8585.
In Cleveland, Ohio: North Point, 901 Lakeside Avenue.
Telephone: 216-586-3939.
Cable Address: "Attorneys Cleveland."
Telex: 980389.
Telecopier: 216-579-0212.
In Columbus, Ohio: 1900 Huntington Center.
Telephone: 614-469-3939.
Cable Address: "Attorneys Columbus."
Telecopier: 614-461-4198.
In Dallas, Texas: 2300 Trammell Crow Center, 2001 Ross Avenue.
Telephone: 214-220-3939.
Cable Address: "Attorneys Dallas."
Telex: 730852.
Telecopier: 214-969-5100.
In Frankfurt, Germany: Triton Haus, Bockenheimer Landstrasse 42, 60323 Frankfurt am Main.
Telephone: 49-69-9726-3939.
Telecopier: 49-69-9726-3993.
In Geneva, Switzerland: 20, rue de Candolle.
Telephone: 41-22-320-2339.
Telecopier: 41-22-320-1232.

(See Next Column)

In Hong Kong: 29th Floor, Entertainment Building, 30 Queen's Road Central.
Telephone: 852-2526-6895.
Telecopier: 852-2868-5871.
In Irvine, California: 2603 Main Street, Suite 900 .
Telephone: 714-851-3939.
Telex: 194911 Lawyers LSA.
Telecopier: 714-553-7539.
In London, England: One Mount Street.
Telephone: 44-71-493-9361.
Cable Address: "Surgoe London WI."
Telecopier: 44-71-493-9666.
In Los Angeles, California: 555 West Fifth Street, Suite 4600.
Telephone: 213-489-3939.
Telex: 181439 UD.
Telecopier: 213-243-2539.
In New Delhi, India: Pathak & Associates, 13th Floor, Dr. Gopal Das Bhaven, 28 Barakhamba Road.
Telephone: 91-11-373-8793.
Telecopier: 91-11-335-3761.
In New York, New York: 599 Lexington Avenue.
Telephone: 212-326-3939.
Cable Address: "JONESDAY NEWYORK."
Telex: 237013 JDRP UR.
Telecopier: 212-755-7306.
In Paris, France: 62, rue du Faubourg Saint-Honore.
Telephone: 33-1-44-71-3939.
Cable Address: "Surgoe Paris."
Telex: 290156 Surgoe.
Telecopier: 33-1-49-24-0471.
In Pittsburgh, Pennsylvania: 500 Grant Street, 31st Floor.
Telephone: 412-391-3939.
Cable Address: "Attorneys Pittsburgh".
Telecopier: 412-394-7959.
In Riyadh, Saudi Arabia: Law Offices of Saud M.A. Shawwaf, P.O. Box 22166.
Telephone: (966-1) 462-8866.
Telex: 401831 SAUCON SJ.
Telecopier: (966-1) 462-9001.
In Taipai, Taiwan: 8th Floor, 2 Tun Hwa South Road, Section 2.
Telephone: (886-2) 704-6808.
Telecopier: (886-2) 704-6791.
In Tokyo, Japan: Toranomon MT Building, 4th Floor, 10-3, Toranomon 3-Chome, Minato-Ku, Tokyo 105, Japan.
Telephone: 81-3-3433-3939.
Telecopier: 81-3-5401-2725.

MEMBER OF FIRM IN WASHINGTON, D.C.

George T. Manning

For Complete List of Firm Personnel, See General Section

For full biographical listings, see the Martindale-Hubbell Law Directory

---

JOHN A. McCAHILL

(See Alexandria, Virginia)

MILLER, CASSIDY, LARROCA & LEWIN, L.L.P. (AV)

2555 M Street, N.W., 20037
Telephone: 202-293-6400
Telecopier: 202-293-1827

MEMBERS OF FIRM

Herbert J. Miller, Jr.	Scott L. Nelson
John Joseph Cassidy	Julia E. Guttman
Raymond G. Larroca	Niki Kuckes
Nathan Lewin	Jay L. Alexander
Martin D. Minsker	Cynthia Thomas Calvert
William H. Jeffress, Jr.	Paul F. Enzinna
R. Stan Mortenson	Douglas F. Curtis
Thomas B. Carr	Michael J. Barta
James E. Rocap, III	Bradford M. Berry
Randall J. Turk	Stuart A. Levey
Stephen L. Braga	David S. Cohen
Joe R. Caldwell, Jr.	David R. Fontaine

J. Bradley Bennett

ASSOCIATES

Ellen Fels Berkman	Katherine L. Pringle
Hugh P. Quinn	Robert J. McGahan
Barry J. Pollack	Daniel J. Cloherty
James R. Heavner, Jr.	Jody A. Manier
Mathew S. Nosanchuk	(Not admitted in DC)
Alison E. Grossman	Timothy J. Preso
Kirsten D. Levingston	(Not admitted in DC)

OF COUNSEL

Courtney A. Evans

For full biographical listings, see the Martindale-Hubbell Law Directory

Washington—Continued

THE ROBINSON LAW FIRM (AV)

Market Square, 717 D Street, N.W., 4th Floor, 20004
Telephone: 202-347-6100
Fax: 202-347-0081
Email: RLAW@aol.com

MEMBERS OF FIRM

Kenneth Michael Robinson　　　　Nicholas H. Hantzes

ASSOCIATES

Randall W. Roy　　　　　　Stacey Papa
　　　　　　　　　　　　　(Not admitted in DC)

OF COUNSEL

Daniel E. Ellenbogen　　　　Dennis M. Hart

For full biographical listings, see the Martindale-Hubbell Law Directory

---

SCHWALB, DONNENFELD, BRAY & SILBERT, A PROFESSIONAL CORPORATION (AV)

1025 Thomas Jefferson Street, N.W. Suite 300 East, 20007
Telephone: 202-965-7910
Telecopier: 202-337-0676

Burton A. Schwalb	Lucinda J. Bach
John M. Bray	Cary M. Feldman
Earl J. Silbert	Joseph M. Jones
David J. Curtin	Adam S. Hoffinger
Charles B. Wayne	Kevin M. Dinan
Steven Sarfatti	Patricia L. Maher

SENIOR COUNSEL

Charles R. Donnenfeld

OF COUNSEL

Debra Ornstein

Robert A. Salerno	James T. Phalen
Carmen R. Kelley	Robert J. McAuliffe
Richard J. Oparil	Jeffrey D. Clark

For full biographical listings, see the Martindale-Hubbell Law Directory

---

TROUT & RICHARDS, P.L.L.C. (AV)

1742 N Street, N.W., 4th Floor, 20036
Telephone: 202-463-1920
Fax: 202-463-1925
Alexandria, Virginia Office: 921 King Street, 22314.
Telephone: 703-519-8840.

Robert P. Trout　　　　　John Thorpe Richards, Jr.

For full biographical listings, see the Martindale-Hubbell Law Directory

---

* VENABLE ATTORNEYS AT LAW VENABLE, BAETJER, HOWARD & CIVILETTI, LLP (AV)

A Partnership including Professional Corporations
Suite 1000, 1201 New York Avenue, N.W., 20005
Telephone: 202-962-4800
Fax: 202-962-8300
Baltimore, Maryland Office: Venable, Baetjer and Howard LLP, 1800 Mercantile Bank & Trust Building, 2 Hopkins Plaza.
Telephone: 410-244-7400.
McLean, Virginia Office: Venable, Baetjer and Howard LLP, Suite 400, 2010 Corporate Ridge.
Telephone: 703-760-1600.
Rockville, Maryland Office: Venable, Baetjer and Howard LLP, Suite 500, One Church Street, P. O. Box 1906.
Telephone: 301-217-5600.
Towson, Maryland Office: Venable, Baetjer and Howard LLP, 210 Allegheny Avenue, P. O. Box 5517.
Telephone: 410-494-6200.

MEMBERS OF FIRM

Benjamin R. Civiletti (P.C.) (Also at Baltimore and Towson, Maryland Offices)	William D. Coston
	Amy Berman Jackson
Joseph G. Block	William D. Quarles (Also at Towson, Maryland Office)
Michael Schatzow (Also at Baltimore, Maryland Office)	Thomas J. Kelly, Jr.
	Gary M. Hnath
Judson W. Starr (Also at Baltimore and Towson, Maryland Offices)	Geoffrey R. Garinther (Not admitted in DC; Also at Baltimore, Maryland Office)

ASSOCIATE

David W. Goewey

For Complete List of Firm Personnel, See General Section

For full biographical listings, see the Martindale-Hubbell Law Directory

---

WEHNER & YORK (AV)

513 Capitol Court, N.E. Suite 200, 20002
Telephone: 202-543-2700
Facsimile: 202-543-2023
Email: litigation@wehner-york-law.com
Philadelphia, Pennsylvania Office: 2650 Provident Mutual, 1600 Market Street.
Telephone: 215-569-8777.
Facsimile: 215-569-8884. *E-Mail:* litigation@wehner-york-law.com.
Bridgeport, West Virginia Office: Grande Meadows, Saltwell Road and Route 73, Suite 230.
Telephone: 304-592-3400. *E-Mail:* litigation@wehner-york-law.com.

MEMBERS OF FIRM

Stephen V. Wehner　　　　　Michael M. York
　　　　　　Kay Millicent Brown

LEGAL SUPPORT PERSONNEL

Lela Rao (Paralegal)

For full biographical listings, see the Martindale-Hubbell Law Directory

---

WILLIAMS & CONNOLLY (AV)

725 Twelfth Street, N.W., 20005
Telephone: 202-434-5000

MEMBERS OF FIRM

Vincent J. Fuller	Michael S. Sundermeyer
Raymond W. Bergan	James T. Fuller, III
Jeremiah C. Collins	David D. Aufhauser
David Povich	Bruce R. Genderson
Steven M. Umin	Carolyn H. Williams
John W. Vardaman	Frank Lane Heard III
Paul Martin Wolff	Steven R. Kuney
J. Alan Galbraith	Gerson A. Zweifach
John G. Kester	Paul Mogin
William E. McDaniels	Howard W. Gutman
Brendan V. Sullivan, Jr.	Nancy F. Lesser
Aubrey M. Daniel, III	Richard S. Hoffman
Richard M. Cooper	Steven A. Steinbach
Gerald A. Feffer	Mark S. Levinstein
Robert P. Watkins	Mary Greer Clark
Jerry L. Shulman	Daniel F. Katz
Lawrence Lucchino	Nicole K. Seligman
Lewis H. Ferguson, III	Robert M. Krasne
Robert B. Barnett	Kathleen L. Beggs
David E. Kendall	William R. Murray, Jr.
Gregory B. Craig	Eva Petko Esber
John J. Buckley, Jr.	Stephen D. Raber
Douglas R. Marvin	David C. Kiernan
John K. Villa	Lon E. Musslewhite
Barry S. Simon	Robin E. Jacobsohn
Kevin T. Baine	Charles A. Sweet
Stephen L. Urbanczyk	Glenn J. Pfadenhauer
Philip J. Ward	George A. Borden
Peter J. Kahn	Robert J. Shaughnessy
Lon S. Babby	Jonathan P. Graham
	Allen P. Waxman

Eric M. Braun	Joseph D. Piorkowski, Jr.
David S. Blatt	Dane H. Butswinkas
Ari S. Zymelman	Laurie S. Fulton

OF COUNSEL

Lyman G. Friedman

For Complete List of Firm Personnel, See General Section

For full biographical listings, see the Martindale-Hubbell Law Directory

---

WILMER, CUTLER & PICKERING (AV)

2445 M Street, N.W., 20037-1420
Telephone: 202-663-6000
Fax: 202-663-6363
Email: Law@Wilmer.Com
Baltimore, Maryland Office: 100 Light Street, 21202.
Telephone: 410-986-2800.
Fax: 410-986-2828.
European Offices:
4 Carlton Gardens, London, SW1Y 5AA, England. Telephone: +44 (171) 872-1000.
Fax: +44 (171) 839-3537.
Rue de la Loi 15Wetstraat, B-1040 Brussels, Belgium. Telephone: +32 (2) 285-4900.
Fax: +32 (2) 285-4949.
Friedrichstrasse 95, D-10117 Berlin, Germany. Telephone: +49 (30) 2022-6400.
Fax: +49 (30)2022-6500.

MEMBERS OF FIRM

Daniel K. Mayers	Paul J. Mode, Jr.
Stephen H. Sachs	Stephen F. Black
Arthur F. Mathews	Gary D. Wilson
Louis R. Cohen	James A. Rogers
Michael R. Klein	Michael L. Burack

(See Next Column)

WILMER, CUTLER & PICKERING—*Continued*

MEMBERS OF FIRM (Continued)

Robert B. McCaw	Bruce M. Berman
William J. Kolasky, Jr.	Thomas F. Connell
A. Stephen Hut, Jr.	Charles E. Davidow
John Rounsaville, Jr.	Philip D. Anker
Roger M. Witten	Joseph K. Brenner
David M. Becker	Carol Clayton
Andrew B. Weissman	Thomas P. Olson
Lynn Bregman	Patrick J. Carome
Bruce E. Coolidge	David P. Donovan
Juanita A. Crowley	Stephen M. Cutler
John Payton	Roger W. Yoerges

OF COUNSEL

Howard P. Willens   Max O. Truitt, Jr.

For Complete List of Firm Personnel, See General Section

For full biographical listings, see the Martindale-Hubbell Law Directory

FLORIDA

*BARTOW,** Polk Co.

RICHARD D. MARS, P.A. (AV)

343 West Davidson Street, Suite 103, P.O. Box 1276, 33830
Telephone: 941-533-0855
Telecopier: 941-534-3500

Richard D. Mars

For full biographical listings, see the Martindale-Hubbell Law Directory

*BRADENTON,** Manatee Co.

MULOCK, THOMPSON & LITTLE (AV)

A Partnership of Professional Associations
519 13th Street West, 34205
Telephone: 941-748-2104
Fax: 941-748-6588

Edwin T. Mulock (P.A.)   W. Wade Thompson (P.A.)
Melton H. Little (P.A.)

Donald E. Grieco

Representative Client: Clerk of Circuit Court of Manatee County.
Approved Attorneys for: Attorneys' Title Insurance Fund.

For full biographical listings, see the Martindale-Hubbell Law Directory

*CLEARWATER,** Pinellas Co.

BAUER, CRIDER & PELLEGRINO (AV)

1550 South Highland Avenue, Suite C, 34616-2353
Telephone: 813-446-4800
Email: RonnieC291@aol.com
Email: RBauer5012@aol.com
Tampa, Florida Office: One Urban Centre. Suite 750. 4830 West Kennedy Boulevard. 33609.
Telephone: 813-286-4300. E-Mail: RonnieC291@aol.com.

MEMBERS OF FIRM

Robert O. Bauer, Jr.   Victor J. Pellegrino
Ronnie G. Crider   (Resident, Tampa Office)

For full biographical listings, see the Martindale-Hubbell Law Directory

MICHAEL C. CHEEK (AV)

814 Chestnut Street, 34616
Telephone: 813-443-7659

For full biographical listings, see the Martindale-Hubbell Law Directory

JOHN D. FERNANDEZ, P.A. (AV)

918 Drew Street, 34615
Telephone: 813-461-4441
Email: fernand@gate.net

John D. Fernandez

Connie R. Stephens

For full biographical listings, see the Martindale-Hubbell Law Directory

LEE FUGATE (AV)

Suite 108 Icot Center, 13630 58th Street North, 34620
Telephone: 813-539-6536
Tampa: 813-855-9115

For full biographical listings, see the Martindale-Hubbell Law Directory

KWALL & SHOWERS, P.A. (AV)

133 North Fort Harrison Avenue, 34615
Telephone: 813-441-4947
Telecopier: 813-447-3158
Email: Kwall133@MSN.com

Louis Kwall   Gregory K. Showers

For full biographical listings, see the Martindale-Hubbell Law Directory

GEORGE E. TRAGOS (AV)

600 Cleveland Street Suite 700, 34615
Telephone: 813-441-9030; Tampa: 813-223-6405
Fax: 813-441-9254

For full biographical listings, see the Martindale-Hubbell Law Directory

*DADE CITY,** Pasco Co.

GREENFELDER, MANDER, HANSON, MURPHY & DWYER (AV)

14217 Third Street, 33523
Telephone: 352-567-0411
Fax: 352-567-7758

MEMBERS OF FIRM

Albert R. Mander, III   T. Philip Hanson, Jr.

For full biographical listings, see the Martindale-Hubbell Law Directory

DAYTONA BEACH, Volusia Co.

LANDIS, GRAHAM, FRENCH, HUSFELD, SHERMAN & FORD, P.A. (AV)

Formerly Hull, Landis, Graham & French
543 South Ridgewood Avenue, 32114
Telephone: 904-252-4717
Fax: 904-253-7352
De Land, Florida Office: 145 East Rich Avenue, P.O. Box 48.
Telephone: 904-734-3451.
Deltona, Florida Office: 204 Medical Arts Center, 1555 Saxon Boulevard.
Telephone: 407-574-1461.
Fax: 407-574-0242.

Erskine W. Landis (1900-1967)	Richard S. Graham
John L. Graham (1905-1978)	William E. Sherman
Thorwald J. Husfeld (1926-1995)	Sam N. Masters

OF COUNSEL

J. Compton French

Counsel for: Barnett Bank of Volusia County; State Farm Mutual Automobile Insurance Co.; West Volusia Hospital Authority; Central Florida Fern Cooperative, Inc.; General Motors Corp.; South Florida Natural Gas Co.; Florida Public Utilities Co.; Volusia County Industrial Development Authority; Florida United Methodist Children's Home: Volusia County Educational Facilities Authority.

For full biographical listings, see the Martindale-Hubbell Law Directory

*FORT LAUDERDALE,** Broward Co.

BOGENSCHUTZ & DUTKO, P.A. (AV)

600 South Andrews Avenue, Suite 500, 33301
Telephone: 954-764-2500
Fax: 954-764-5040

J. David Bogenschutz   Michael E. Dutko
Mary H. McCleary

For full biographical listings, see the Martindale-Hubbell Law Directory

ENTIN & MARGULES, P.A. (AV)

200 East Broward Boulevard Suite 1210, 33301
Telephone: 954-761-7201
Dade: 305-935-0242
Fax: 954-767-8343

Alvin E. Entin	Richard F. Della Fera
Leon R. Margules	Jacqueline Perczek

Mario Permuth (Not Admitted   Richard Perlini
in United States)

OF COUNSEL

Steven E. Goldman

For full biographical listings, see the Martindale-Hubbell Law Directory

Fort Lauderdale—Continued

RICHARD L. ROSENBAUM (AV)

Suite 1500 - Barnett Bank Plaza, One East Broward Boulevard, 33301
Telephone: 954-522-7000
Facsimile: 954-522-7003
Email: rlrappeal@aol.com

For full biographical listings, see the Martindale-Hubbell Law Directory

FORT MYERS,* Lee Co.

PETER D. RINGSMUTH (AV)

2215 First Street, 33901
Telephone: 941-332-2500
FAX: 941-332-2795

Larry D. Justham

For full biographical listings, see the Martindale-Hubbell Law Directory

WILBUR C. SMITH, III (AV)

The Courtney Building, Suite 100, 2069 First Street, 33902
Telephone: 941-334-7696
FAX: 941-334-3669

For full biographical listings, see the Martindale-Hubbell Law Directory

GAINESVILLE,* Alachua Co.

THOMAS W. KURRUS (AV)

Suite 11, 204 West University Avenue, P.O. Box 508, 32602
Telephone: 352-377-2332 or 1-800-781-2332
Fax: 352-375-6249

For full biographical listings, see the Martindale-Hubbell Law Directory

TURNER & GRISCTI, PROFESSIONAL ASSOCIATION (AV)

Suite 6, 204 West University Avenue, P.O. Box 508, 32602
Telephone: 352-375-4460
Fax: 352-375-6249

Larry G. Turner   Robert S. Griscti

Reference: Barnett Bank.

For full biographical listings, see the Martindale-Hubbell Law Directory

JACKSONVILLE,* Duval Co.

SUZANNE BASS (AV)

3974 Woodcock Drive, Suite 100, 32207
Telephone: 904-396-2277
Fax: 904-396-5730
Email: bass@southeast.net

For full biographical listings, see the Martindale-Hubbell Law Directory

HUGH COTNEY, P.A. (AV)

905 Blackstone Building, 233 East Bay Street, 32202
Telephone: 904-356-0162
FAX: 904-355-5170

Hugh Cotney

Representative Clients: First Insuramerica of Florida, Inc.; Deaf Services Center, Inc.

For full biographical listings, see the Martindale-Hubbell Law Directory

SHEPPARD & WHITE, P.A. (AV)

215 Washington Street, 32202
Telephone: 904-356-9661
Facsimile: 904-356-9667

Wm. J. Sheppard   Elizabeth L. White

D. Gray Thomas   Richard W. Smith
Adam Benjamin Allen

For full biographical listings, see the Martindale-Hubbell Law Directory

MIAMI,* Dade Co.

WILLIAM AARON (AV)

Suite 202, Grove Forest Plaza, 2937 Southwest 27th Avenue, 33133
Telephone: 305-443-1600
Cable Address: "Worldlaw"
Fax: 305-445-9666

For full biographical listings, see the Martindale-Hubbell Law Directory

JOSEPH BEELER, P.A. (AV)

Suite 300, 3050 Biscayne Boulevard, 33137
Telephone: 305-576-3050
Facsimile: 305-576-8080
Email: jbeeler@counsel.com

Joseph Beeler

H. Eugene Lindsey (Not admitted in FL)

For full biographical listings, see the Martindale-Hubbell Law Directory

BIERMAN, SHOHAT, LOEWY, PERRY & KLEIN, PROFESSIONAL ASSOCIATION (AV)

Penthouse Two, 800 Brickell Avenue, 33131-2944
Telephone: 305-358-7000
Facsimile: 305-358-4010
Email: BSLPK@AOL.COM

Donald I. Bierman   Pamela I. Perry
Edward R. Shohat   Theodore Klein
Ira N. Loewy   Maria Beguiristain Shohat

Reference: United National Bank of Miami.

For full biographical listings, see the Martindale-Hubbell Law Directory

BLACK, SREBNICK & KORNSPAN, P.A. (AV)

201 South Biscayne Boulevard Suite 1300, 33131
Telephone: 305-371-6421
Email: blacklaw@black-law.com

Roy Black   Christine Metcalf Ng
Scott A. Kornspan   Paul D. Petruzzi
Maria Neyra   Timothy W. Schulz
          Howard M. Srebnick

For full biographical listings, see the Martindale-Hubbell Law Directory

WILLIAM P. CAGNEY, III, P.A. (AV)

Suite 3400 First Union Financial Center, 200 South Biscayne Boulevard, 33131-2393
Telephone: 305-371-1411
Fax: 305-371-3810
Chicago, Illinois Office: Suite 1800, 100 West Monroe Street.

William P. Cagney, III

For full biographical listings, see the Martindale-Hubbell Law Directory

ESSEN, ESSEN, SUSANECK, CANET & LIPSON, P.A. (AV)

18305 Biscayne Boulevard, Suite 400 (North Miami Beach), 33160
Telephone: 305-935-6680
Fax: 305-935-2314
Email: RESSEN@AOL.COM
West Palm Beach, Florida Office: Commerce Centre, 324 Datura Street, Suite 145.
Telephone: 407-833-0626.

Ben Essen (Retired)   Carlos A. Canet
Richard Essen   Alan T. Lipson
Fredrick R. Susaneck (Resident,
  West Palm Beach Office)

Jose L. Fernandez   Lloyd H. Goldburg
          L. Edwin Saar

For full biographical listings, see the Martindale-Hubbell Law Directory

FERRELL & FERTEL, P.A. (AV)

Suite 1920 Miami Center, 201 South Biscayne Boulevard, 33131-2305
Telephone: 305-371-8585
Telecopier: 305-371-5732

Milton M. Ferrell, Jr.   Alan K. Fertel

Reference: City National Bank of Florida.

For full biographical listings, see the Martindale-Hubbell Law Directory

FERRO & LEHR, P.A. (AV)

1401 Brickell, Suite 1040, 33131
Telephone: 305-377-1777
Fax: 305-377-0087

Henry G. Ferro   Bruce H. Lehr

For full biographical listings, see the Martindale-Hubbell Law Directory

DAVID M. GARVIN, P.A. (AV)

1401 Brickell Avenue, 33131
Telephone: 305-371-8101
Fax: 305-371-8848

(See Next Column)

DAVID M. GARVIN, P.A.—*Continued*

David M. Garvin

For full biographical listings, see the Martindale-Hubbell Law Directory

---

ALBERT J. KRIEGER, P.A. (AV)

1899 South Bayshore Drive, 33133
Telephone: 305-854-0050
Fax: 305-285-1761
Email: AJKRIEGERLAW@WORLDNET.ATT.NET

Albert J. Krieger

OF COUNSEL

Susan W. Van Dusen   Scott A. Srebnick

For full biographical listings, see the Martindale-Hubbell Law Directory

---

CLARK D. MERVIS (AV)

Grove Forest Plaza, Suite 202, 2937 Southwest 27th Avenue (Coconut Grove), 33133-3703
Telephone: 305-443-1600

For full biographical listings, see the Martindale-Hubbell Law Directory

---

NEIL M. NAMEROFF PROFESSIONAL ASSOCIATION (AV)

1221 Brickell Avenue Suite 1020, 33131
Telephone: 305-536-8700
Fax: 305-536-8304

Neil M. Nameroff

For full biographical listings, see the Martindale-Hubbell Law Directory

---

PODHURST, ORSECK, JOSEFSBERG, EATON, MEADOW, OLIN & PERWIN, P.A. (AV)

Suite 800 City National Bank Building, 25 West Flagler Street, 33130-1780
Telephone: 305-358-2800; Fort Lauderdale: 954-463-4346
Fax: 305-358-2382
Email: 76666.2340@COMPUSERVE.COM *URL:*
http://www.turbosales.com/"sfbj/podhurst.html

Robert C. Josefsberg

References: City National Bank of Miami; United National Bank of Miami.

For Complete List of Firm Personnel, See General Section

For full biographical listings, see the Martindale-Hubbell Law Directory

---

RASKIN & RASKIN, P.A. (AV)

Grove Forest Plaza, Suite 206, 2937 Southwest 27th Avenue, 33133-3703
Telephone: 305-444-3400
Telefax: 305-445-0266

Martin R. Raskin   Jane Serene Raskin

Robert John Becerra   Elissa D. Grodd

For full biographical listings, see the Martindale-Hubbell Law Directory

---

RICHEY & DIAZ, P.A. (AV)

3100 First Union Financial Center, 200 South Biscayne Boulevard, 33131-2327
Telephone: 305-372-8808
Telefax: 305-372-3669; 374-4652
Email: richdiaz@netrunner.net

William L. Richey   Michael Diaz, Jr.
OF COUNSEL
Kirk W. Munroe

For full biographical listings, see the Martindale-Hubbell Law Directory

---

ROBBINS, TUNKEY, ROSS, AMSEL, RABEN & WAXMAN, P.A. (AV)

2250 Southwest Third Avenue, Fourth Floor, 33129
Telephone: Dade County 305-858-9550; Broward County 954-522-6244 (All Telephones Open 24 Hours); 1-800-226-9550
Fax: 305-858-7491

Frederick S. Robbins   Robert G. Amsel
William R. Tunkey   David Raben
Alan S. Ross   Benjamin S. Waxman

Alan L. Quiles   Mark R. Eiglarsh
Marco A. Vazquez (1968-1995)

Reference: United National Bank, Miami, Florida.

For full biographical listings, see the Martindale-Hubbell Law Directory

---

MARK SEIDEN, P.A. (AV)

Suite 100, SunTrust Building, 777 Brickell Avenue, 33131
Telephone: 305-577-4981
Fax: 305-577-8376

Mark Seiden

Representative Clients: Florida Association of State Troopers; Hispanic Police Officers Association; Hispanic Public Safety Coalition.

For full biographical listings, see the Martindale-Hubbell Law Directory

---

NEAL R. SONNETT, P.A. (AV)

Twenty Sixth Floor, One Biscayne Tower, Two South Biscayne Boulevard, 33131-1802
Telephone: 305-358-2000
Fax: 305-358-1233

Neal R. Sonnett
OF COUNSEL

David K. Tucker   David Everett Marko
Miguel M. de la O   Kenneth J. Kukec

For full biographical listings, see the Martindale-Hubbell Law Directory

---

THORNTON & ROTHMAN, P.A. (AV)

200 South Biscayne Boulevard, Suite 3420 First Union Financial Center, 33131
Telephone: 305-358-9000
Fax: 305-374-5747

John W. Thornton, Jr.   David B. Rothman

For full biographical listings, see the Martindale-Hubbell Law Directory

---

JEFFREY S. WEINER, ATTORNEYS AT LAW, P.A. (AV)

Two Datran Center, Suite 1910, 9130 South Dadeland Boulevard, 33156-7858
Telephone: 305-670-9919
Fax: 305-670-9299
Email: JSWeiner@aol.com
Email: 76440.644@compuserve.com
Boca Raton, Florida Office: Mizner Park. 327 Plaza Real, Suite 215, 33432.

Jeffrey S. Weiner

Mycki L. Ratzan
LEGAL SUPPORT PERSONNEL

Duchess Weiner   Bernice Lopez (Legal
(Law Office Administrator)   Translator/Interpreter: Spanish)

For full biographical listings, see the Martindale-Hubbell Law Directory

---

NAPLES, * Collier Co.

FAERBER, HISSAM, CLIFF & PEREZ-BENITOA (AV)

Suite 505 Moorings Professional Building, 2335 Tamiami Trail North, 33940-4482
Telephone: 941-262-6161
Telecopier: 941-262-2627

MEMBERS OF FIRM

Nelson A. Faerber, Jr.   Cary Alan Cliff
Christine P. Hissam Greider   Antonio J. Perez-Benitoa
Aimee Melton Peeples

References: Barnett Bank of Naples; First National Bank of Naples.

For full biographical listings, see the Martindale-Hubbell Law Directory

---

VEGA, STANLEY, ZELMAN & HANLON, P.A. (AV)

2660 Airport Road South, 34112
Telephone: 941-774-3333
Fax: 941-776-6420

George Vega, Jr.

Paula J. Rhoads

General Counsel for: Lely Estates; Naples Community Hospital.
Local Counsel: Quail Creek Developments.

For full biographical listings, see the Martindale-Hubbell Law Directory

---

NORTH PALM BEACH, Palm Beach Co.

CRAIG R. WILSON (AV)

Crystal Tree Office Centre, Suite 415, 1201 U.S. Highway 1, 33408-3581
Telephone: 407-626-6300
FAX: 407-627-2288

Reference: First Union Bank of Palm Beach County.

For full biographical listings, see the Martindale-Hubbell Law Directory

OCALA, * Marion Co.

CHARLES R. HOLLOMAN, P.A. (AV)

1515 East Silver Springs Boulevard, Suite 120 East, 34470
Telephone: 904-867-0766
Fax: 352-351-9217
Email: rguh56a@prodigy.com

Charles R. Holloman, Jr.

For full biographical listings, see the Martindale-Hubbell Law Directory

ORLANDO, * Orange Co.

BARNETT, BARCLAY & SPRINGMANN, P.A. (AV)

501 Mariposa Street, P.O. Box 1667, 32802
Telephone: 407-425-4245
Telecopier: 407-423-4332

William B. Barnett	Bert W. Barclay
Henry B. Rothblatt (1916-1985)	Franz F. Springmann

For full biographical listings, see the Martindale-Hubbell Law Directory

ROBERT J. BUONAURO, P.A. (AV)

390 North Orange Avenue, Suite 1630, 32801
Telephone: 407-841-1940
Fax: 407-649-1936

Robert J. Buonauro

For full biographical listings, see the Martindale-Hubbell Law Directory

W. FORD DUANE (AV)

Suite 505 Landmark Center II, 225 East Robinson Street, 32801-4303
Telephone: 407-849-1122
Fax: 407-422-5310
(Also Of Counsel to Hannah, Marsee & Voght, P.A.)

For full biographical listings, see the Martindale-Hubbell Law Directory

THOMAS F. EGAN, P.A. (AV)

56 East Pine, Suite 300, P.O. Box 204, 32802-0204
Telephone: 407-246-1055

Thomas F. Egan

For full biographical listings, see the Martindale-Hubbell Law Directory

LAW OFFICES OF HORWITZ & FUSSELL A PROFESSIONAL ASSOCIATION (AV)

17 East Pine Street, 32801
Telephone: 407-843-7733
Fax: 407-849-1321

Mark L. Horwitz	David Dean Fussell

For full biographical listings, see the Martindale-Hubbell Law Directory

LEVENTHAL & SLAUGHTER, P.A. (AV)

Suite 700, 111 North Orange Avenue, 32801
Telephone: 407-849-6161
Telecopier: 407-843-3738

Robert A. Leventhal	Harrison T. Slaughter, Jr.

For full biographical listings, see the Martindale-Hubbell Law Directory

J. CHENEY MASON, P.A. (AV)

Barnett Bank Center, 390 North Orange Avenue, Suite 2100, 32801
Telephone: 407-843-5785
Fax: 407-422-6858

J. Cheney Mason

For full biographical listings, see the Martindale-Hubbell Law Directory

NEJAME & HYMAN, P.A. (AV)

1520 East Amelia Street, 32803-5490
Telephone: 407-896-0536
Fax: 407-896-0540

Mark Elias NeJame	Stuart I. Hyman

For full biographical listings, see the Martindale-Hubbell Law Directory

LAW OFFICES OF JAMES M. RUSS, P.A. (AV)

Tinker Building, 18 West Pine Street, 32801
Telephone: 407-849-6050
Fax: 407-849-6059

James M. Russ

Tad A. Yates

(See Next Column)

LEGAL SUPPORT PERSONNEL
M.Cherie Heckford
Reference: First Union National Bank of Orlando.

For full biographical listings, see the Martindale-Hubbell Law Directory

SARASOTA, * Sarasota Co.

JAMES R. DIRMANN, P.A. (AV)

2180 Main Street, Suite A, 34237
Telephone: 941-366-7997
FAX: 941-955-7797

James R. Dirmann

Reference: First Union National Bank.

For full biographical listings, see the Martindale-Hubbell Law Directory

JOHN M. FITZGIBBONS (AV)

SouthTrust Bank Plaza, Suite 880, 1800 Second Street, 34236
Telephone: 941-953-5697
Tampa, Florida Office: 707 North Franklin Street, Suite 700.
Telephone: 813-221-8800.
Fax: Available upon request.

OF COUNSEL
B. Kay Neiss

STUART, * Martin Co.

FRIERSON & WATSON (AV)

A Partnership of Professional Associations
3601 S.E. Ocean Boulevard, Suite 4, 34996
Telephone: 561-288-1880
Fax: 561-288-1887
Port St. Lucie, Florida Office: 1920 S.E. Port St. Lucie Boulevard.
Telephone: 561-337-1203.
Fax: 561-337-1206.

Robert J. Watson (P.A.)
Robin Wesley Frierson (P.A.)
(Resident, Port St. Lucie
Office)

Reference: Sun Bank of Martin County.

For full biographical listings, see the Martindale-Hubbell Law Directory

TAMPA, * Hillsborough Co.

ADKINS, KISE & DIACO, P.A. (AV)

2175 Barnett Plaza, 101 East Kennedy Boulevard, 33602
Telephone: 813-221-2200
Fax: 813-221-8850

Edward C. Adkins	Christopher M. Kise
	Stephen C. Diaco

For full biographical listings, see the Martindale-Hubbell Law Directory

BAUER, CRIDER & PELLEGRINO (AV)

One Urban Centre, Suite 750, 4830 West Kennedy Boulevard, 33609
Telephone: 813-286-4300
Email: RonnieC291@aol.com
Email: RBauer5012@aol.com
Clearwater, Florida Office: 1550 South Highland Avenue, Suite C. 34616-2353.
Telephone: 813-446-4800.

Victor J. Pellegrino

For full biographical listings, see the Martindale-Hubbell Law Directory

RONALD K. CACCIATORE, P.A. (AV)

100 North Tampa Street, Suite 2835, 33602
Telephone: 813-223-4831
Facsimile: 813-223-2737

Ronald K. Cacciatore

Reference: The Bank of Tampa.

For full biographical listings, see the Martindale-Hubbell Law Directory

THE LAW FIRM OF COHEN, JAYSON & FOSTER, P.A. (AV)

First of America Plaza, Suite 1700, 201 East Kennedy Boulevard, P.O. Box 172538, 33672
Telephone: 813-225-1655
Fax: 813-225-1921

Barry A. Cohen	Christopher P. Jayson
Todd Foster	Mark H. Wright
	Michelle Lee Pickett

(See Next Column)

THE LAW FIRM OF COHEN, JAYSON & FOSTER, P.A.—*Continued*

E. Patrick Buntz

For full biographical listings, see the Martindale-Hubbell Law Directory

JOHN M. FITZGIBBONS (AV)

707 North Franklin Street, Suite 700, 33602-4441
Telephone: 813-221-8800
Fax: Available upon request
Sarasota, Florida Office: SouthTrust Bank Plaza, Suite 880, 1800 Second Street.
Telephone: 941-953-5697.

OF COUNSEL
B. Kay Neiss

For full biographical listings, see the Martindale-Hubbell Law Directory

MARCELINO J. HUERTA, III, P.A. (AV)

201 East Kennedy Boulevard Suite 1108, 33602
Telephone: 813-229-7623
Telefax: 813-228-0903

Marcelino J. Huerta, III

For full biographical listings, see the Martindale-Hubbell Law Directory

KYNES, MARKMAN & FELMAN, P.A. (AV)

P.O. Box 3396, 33601
Telephone: 813-229-1118
Facsimile: 813-221-6750

James H. Kynes (1953-1993)   James E. Felman
Stuart C. Markman   Susan H. Freemon

For full biographical listings, see the Martindale-Hubbell Law Directory

ANTHONY J. LaSPADA, P.A. (AV)

1802 North Morgan Street, 33602
Telephone: 813-223-6048
Pinellas Line: 813-894-1788
Fax: 813-228-9471

Anthony J. LaSpada

Joseph A. Eustace, Jr.

For full biographical listings, see the Martindale-Hubbell Law Directory

LEVINE, HIRSCH & SEGALL, P.A. (AV)

First Union Center, 100 South Ashley Drive, Suite 1600, P.O. Box 3429, 33601-3429
Telephone: 813-229-6585
Telecopier: 813-229-7210

Arnold D. Levine   Richard A. Hirsch
Stephen L. Segall

Edward M. Brennan

For full biographical listings, see the Martindale-Hubbell Law Directory

MANEY, DAMSKER, HARRIS & JONES, P.A. (AV)

606 Madison Street, P.O. Box 172009, 33672-0009
Telephone: 813-228-7371
Fax: 813-223-4846

David A. Maney

For full biographical listings, see the Martindale-Hubbell Law Directory

ROBERT P. POLLI, P.A. (AV)

Barnett Bank Plaza, 101 East Kennedy Boulevard, Suite 3130, 33602
Telephone: 813-222-8350
Fax: Available Upon Request

Robert P. Polli

For full biographical listings, see the Martindale-Hubbell Law Directory

ROCHELLE A. REBACK (AV)

405 West Azeele Street, 33606
Telephone: 813-251-9660
Fax: 813-251-9662

For full biographical listings, see the Martindale-Hubbell Law Directory

WEST PALM BEACH,* Palm Beach Co.

LUBIN AND GANO, P.A. (AV)

Second Floor, Flagler Plaza, 1217 South Flagler Drive, 33401
Telephone: 407-655-2040
Fax: 407-655-2182

Richard G. Lubin   Nancy H. Hamill (1938-1980)
Thomas C. Gano

John Olea

For full biographical listings, see the Martindale-Hubbell Law Directory

NEWBURGH, BALDWIN & GERSHMAN (AV)

1675 Palm Beach Lakes Boulevard, Suite 700, 33401
Telephone: 561-684-8898; 561-471-0470
Fax: 561-684-8820; 561-471-4222

MEMBERS OF FIRM
Steven S. Newburgh   Fletcher N. Baldwin, III
Robert Scott Gershman
OF COUNSEL
Barry L. Clayton

For full biographical listings, see the Martindale-Hubbell Law Directory

ROTH AND DUNCAN, P.A. (AV)

Northbridge Centre, Suite 325, 515 North Flagler Drive, 33401
Telephone: 407-655-5529
Telecopier: 407-655-7818
Mailing Address: P.O. Box 770, 33402

David Roth   Douglas Duncan

For full biographical listings, see the Martindale-Hubbell Law Directory

WINTER PARK, Orange Co.

DEMPSEY & ASSOCIATES, P.A. (AV)

Suite 200, 1031 West Morse Boulevard, 32789
Telephone: 407-740-7778
Telecopier: 407-740-0911

Bernard H. Dempsey, Jr.   Michael C. Sasso

Frederick C. Barnes   Daniel N. Brodersen
Peter Francis Carr, Jr.

For full biographical listings, see the Martindale-Hubbell Law Directory

GEORGIA

ATHENS,* Clarke Co.

COOK, NOELL, TOLLEY & WIGGINS (AV)

304 East Washington Street, P.O. Box 1927, 30603
Telephone: 706-549-6111
Fax: 706-548-0956

MEMBERS OF FIRM
J. Vincent Cook   Morton M. Wiggins, III
John S. Noell, Jr.   Robert B. Bates
Edward D. Tolley   M. Kim Michael

For full biographical listings, see the Martindale-Hubbell Law Directory

ATLANTA,* Fulton Co.

C. MICHAEL ABBOTT, P.C. (AV)

One Atlantic Center, Suite 3410, 1201 West Peachtree Street, 30309-3400
Telephone: 404-885-1994
Fax: 404-885-1677

Michael Abbott

For full biographical listings, see the Martindale-Hubbell Law Directory

JAKE ARBES (AV)

2300 Harris Tower, 233 Peachtree Street, N.E., 30303
Telephone: 404-522-1980
FAX: 404-588-0648

For full biographical listings, see the Martindale-Hubbell Law Directory

BEDFORD, KIRSCHNER AND VENKER, P.C. (AV)

Suite 450, 600 West Peachtree Street, N.W., 30308
Telephone: 404-872-6646

(See Next Column)

BEDFORD, KIRSCHNER AND VENKER P.C., *Atlanta—Continued*

T. Jackson Bedford, Jr.

For full biographical listings, see the Martindale-Hubbell Law Directory

BONDURANT, MIXSON & ELMORE, LLP (AV)

1201 W. Peachtree Street Suite 3900, 30309
Telephone: 404-881-4100
FAX: 404-881-4111

MEMBERS OF FIRM

Emmet J. Bondurant II	Dirk G. Christensen
H. Lamar Mixson	Jane E. Fahey
M. Jerome Elmore	John E. Floyd
Edward B. Krugman	Michael A. Sullivan
Jeffrey O. Bramlett	Michael B. Terry

Representative Clients: The Aetna Casualty and Surety Company; Blue Circle of America; Circle K; Conoco, Inc.; Delta Air Lines, Inc.; Queen Carpets, Inc.; Sanifill, Inc.; Ticketmaster; Trammell Crow Co.; Wyle Laboratories.

For full biographical listings, see the Martindale-Hubbell Law Directory

R. DAVID BOTTS (AV)

152 Nassau Street, N.W., 30303
Telephone: 404-524-0606
FAX: 404-524-0607

For full biographical listings, see the Martindale-Hubbell Law Directory

CHILIVIS, COCHRAN, LARKINS & BEVER (AV)

3127 Maple Drive, N.E., 30305
Telephone: 404-233-4171
Facsimile: 404-261-2842

Nickolas P. Chilivis	Daniel P. Griffin
Anthony L. Cochran	John D. Dalbey
John K. Larkins, Jr.	Merrilee Aynes Gober
Thomas D. Bever	James D. Durham

For full biographical listings, see the Martindale-Hubbell Law Directory

ENGLAND & McKNIGHT (AV)

Suite 410 River Ridge, 9040 Roswell Road, 30350
Telephone: 770-641-6010
FAX: 770-641-6003

MEMBERS OF FIRM

J. Melvin England	Robert H. McKnight, Jr.

Reference: Nations Bank N.A.

For full biographical listings, see the Martindale-Hubbell Law Directory

GARLAND, SAMUEL & LOEB, P.C. (AV)

3151 Maple Drive, N.E., 30305
Telephone: 404-262-2225
Fax: 404-365-5041
Email: TrialLaw@aol.com

Edward T. M. Garland	Donald F. Samuel

For full biographical listings, see the Martindale-Hubbell Law Directory

THOMAS E. MADDOX, JR., P.C. (AV)

3521 Habersham at Northlake (Tucker), 30084-4001
Telephone: 770-414-8055
Telecopier: 770-414-8755

Thomas E. Maddox, Jr.

LEGAL SUPPORT PERSONNEL

Matthew K. Johnson, Jr.

For full biographical listings, see the Martindale-Hubbell Law Directory

STEVEN H. SADOW, P.C. (AV)

800 Grant Building, 44 Broad Street, N.W., 30303
Telephone: 404-577-1400
Fax: 404-577-3600
Email: steve8300@aol.com *URL:* http://www.steve8300@msn.com

Steven H. Sadow

For full biographical listings, see the Martindale-Hubbell Law Directory

AUGUSTA,* Richmond Co.

RICHARD E. ALLEN (AV)

440 Greene Street, 30901
Telephone: 706-724-4466

For full biographical listings, see the Martindale-Hubbell Law Directory

GARRETT & GILLIARD (AV)

SunTrust Bank Building, 801 Broad Street, Suite 1001, 30901
Telephone: 706-724-1896
Fax: 706-724-0047

MEMBERS OF FIRM

Michael C. Garrett	Kirk Emerson Gilliard

ASSOCIATE

Melissa S. Padgett

For full biographical listings, see the Martindale-Hubbell Law Directory

DECATUR,* De Kalb Co.

JOHN W. STOKES, JR. (AV)

125 Trinity Place, Suite 214, 30030
Telephone: 404-377-9358
Fax: 404-377-7713

OCILLA,* Irwin Co.

WALTERS, DAVIS & PUJADAS, P.C. (AV)

South Cherry Street, P.O. Box 247, 31774
Telephone: 912-468-7472; 468-9433
Fax: 912-468-9022

W. Emory Walters	Thomas E. Pujadas
J. Harvey Davis	C. Vinson Walters, II

Attorneys for: Irwin County Board of Education; First State Bank of Ocilla; Irwin County; Wilcox County.
Local Counsel for: Georgia Farm Bureau Mutual Insurance Co.
Approved Attorneys for: Kaiser Aluminum & Chemical Sales, Inc.; Lawyers Title Insurance Corp.; Ticor Title Insurance Co.; Farmers Home Administration; Federal Land Bank of Columbia.

For Complete List of Firm Personnel, See General Section

For full biographical listings, see the Martindale-Hubbell Law Directory

SUMMERVILLE,* Chattooga Co.

COOK & CONNELLY (AV)

128 South Commerce Street, P.O. Box 370, 30747
Telephone: 706-857-3421
Fax: 706-857-1520

MEMBERS OF FIRM

Bobby Lee Cook	L. Branch S. Connelly
A. Cecil Palmour (1913-1980)	Todd Johnson
Bobby Lee Cook, Jr. (1950-1995)	

For full biographical listings, see the Martindale-Hubbell Law Directory

VALDOSTA,* Lowndes Co.

J. CONVERSE BRIGHT (AV)

The McKey Building, 101 E. Central Avenue, P.O. Box 5889, 31603
Telephone: 912-247-7846
Telecopier: 912-245-0693

For full biographical listings, see the Martindale-Hubbell Law Directory

DODD AND DENNIS, P.C. (AV)

613 N. Patterson Street, P.O. Box 1066, 31603-1066
Telephone: 912-242-4470
Telefax: 912-245-7731
Email: doddlaw@mail.datasys.net *URL:* http://www.doddlaw.com

Roger J. Dodd	Sam D. Dennis

References: First Union Bank; First State Bank and Trust Co.; Park Avenue Bank.

For full biographical listings, see the Martindale-Hubbell Law Directory

HAWAII

HONOLULU,* Honolulu Co.

BENJAMIN B. CASSIDAY, III (AV)

2440 Mauka Tower, Grosvenor Center, 737 Bishop Street, 96813-3215
Telephone: 808-523-9007
Fax: 808-531-8898

For full biographical listings, see the Martindale-Hubbell Law Directory

Honolulu—Continued

DAVID W. HALL ATTORNEY AT LAW, A LAW CORPORATION (AV)

Dillingham Transportation Building, Suite 237, 735 Bishop Street, 96813
Telephone: 808-526-0402
Fax: 808-526-0404

David W. Hall

For full biographical listings, see the Martindale-Hubbell Law Directory

MICHAEL A. WEIGHT ATTORNEY AT LAW, A LAW CORPORATION (AV)

Suite 430 Dillingham Transportation Building, 735 Bishop Street, 96813
Telephone: 808-528-3255
Fax: 800-521-5346

Michael A. Weight

Reference: City Bank.

For full biographical listings, see the Martindale-Hubbell Law Directory

RENEE M. L. YUEN ATTORNEY AT LAW, A LAW CORPORATION (AV)

Haseko Center, 820 Mililani Street, Suite 702A, 96813-2937
Telephone: 808-523-0125
Facsimile: 808-523-0127

Renee M. L. Yuen

For full biographical listings, see the Martindale-Hubbell Law Directory

ILLINOIS

BELLEVILLE,* St. Clair Co.

DUNHAM, BOMAN & LESKERA (AV)

208 North High Street, 62220
Telephone: 618-235-7222
Telecopier: 618-397-2285
East St. Louis, Illinois Office: 520 First Illinois Bank Building.
Telephone: 618-271-0535.
Telecopier: 618-271-2800.
Collinsville, Illinois Office: 300 West Clay Street.
Telephone: 618-344-7734.
Telecopier: 618-344-3853.

John W. Leskera	Russell K. Scott
William L. Berry	Robert D. Francis
Eric C. Young	John L. Bitzer

Attorneys For: Collinsville School District #10; Hanover Insurance Co.; Hartford Insurance Group; Home Indemnity Co.; State Farm Insurance Cos.; Transamerica Insurance Group; The Travelers Indemnity Co.; Wausau Insurance Cos.; Nationwide Insurance Co.; Atlantic Mutual Insurance Co..

For full biographical listings, see the Martindale-Hubbell Law Directory

CHICAGO,* Cook Co.

ALLAN A. ACKERMAN, P.C. (AV)

2000 North Clifton Avenue, 60614
Telephone: 312-332-2891; 332-2863
Fax: 312-871-3304

Allan A. Ackerman

For full biographical listings, see the Martindale-Hubbell Law Directory

ROBERT H. ARONSON (AV)

Suite 714, 100 West Monroe Street, 60603
Telephone: 312-372-7123
FAX: 312-372-7125

For full biographical listings, see the Martindale-Hubbell Law Directory

SUSAN BOGART (AV)

10 South La Salle Street, Suite 3505, 60603
Telephone: 312-726-9060
Fax: 312-726-9248
(Also Of Counsel to Sulzer & Shopiro)

For full biographical listings, see the Martindale-Hubbell Law Directory

FORAN & SCHULTZ (AV)

Suite 3000, 30 North La Salle Street, 60602
Telephone: 312-368-8330
Fax: 312-580-2600

(See Next Column)

MEMBERS OF FIRM

Thomas A. Foran	Jack J. Carriglio
Richard G. Schultz	Steven H. Gistenson
James R. Figliulo	Brooke R. Whitted
Stephen A. Gorman	Jeffrey C. Blumenthal
Jeff D. Harris	Carl A. Gigante

Carmen D. Caruso

ASSOCIATES

Teresa F. Frisbie	Brian P. Liston
Peter A. Silverman	Paul A. Henmueller
Marla B. Wilneff	James J. Sipchen, Jr.
Daniel D. Kasten	Mitchell S. Chaban
Patrick R. Gabrione	Dana L. Romaniuk

Jessica Dickstein

OF COUNSEL

Harry G. Comerford

For full biographical listings, see the Martindale-Hubbell Law Directory

JONES, DAY, REAVIS & POGUE (AV)

77 West Wacker, 60601-1692
Telephone: 312-782-3939
Telecopier: 312-782-8585
In Atlanta, Georgia: 3500 One Peachtree Center, 303 Peachtree Street, N.E.
Telephone: 404-521-3939.
Cable Address: "Attorneys Atlanta".
Telex: 54-2711.
Telecopier: 404-581-8330.
In Brussels, Belgium: Avenue Louise 480, 7th Floor, B-1050 Brussels.
Telephone: 32-2-645-14-11.
Telecopier: 32-2-645-14-45.
In Cleveland, Ohio: North Point, 901 Lakeside Avenue.
Telephone: 216-586-3939.
Cable Address: "Attorneys Cleveland."
Telex: 980389.
Telecopier: 216-579-0212.
In Columbus, Ohio: 1900 Huntington Center.
Telephone: 614-469-3939.
Cable Address: "Attorneys Columbus."
Telecopier: 614-461-4198.
In Dallas, Texas: 2300 Trammell Crow Center, 2001 Ross Avenue.
Telephone: 214-220-3939.
Cable Address: "Attorneys Dallas."
Telex: 730852.
Telecopier: 214-969-5100.
In Frankfurt, Germany: Triton Haus, Bockenheimer Landstrasse 42, 60323 Frankfurt am Main.
Telephone: 49-69-9726-3939.
Telecopier: 49-69-9726-3993.
In Geneva, Switzerland: 20, rue de Candolle.
Telephone: 41-22-320-2339.
Telecopier: 41-22-320-1232.
In Hong Kong: 29th Floor, Entertainment Building, 30 Queen's Road Central.
Telephone: 852-2526-6895.
Telecopier: 852-2868-5871 or 852-2868-5699.
In Irvine, California: 2603 Main Street, Suite 900.
Telephone: 714-851-3939.
Telex: 194911 Lawyers LSA.
Telecopier: 714-553-7539.
In London, England: One Mount Street.
Telephone: 44-71-493-9361.
Cable Address: "Surgoe London WI."
Telecopier: 44-71-493-9666.
In Los Angeles, California: 555 West Fifth Street, Suite 4600.
Telephone: 213-489-3939.
Telex: 181439 UD.
Telecopier: 213-243-2539.
In New Delhi, India: Pathak & Associates, 9th Floor, Dr. Gopal Das Bhaven, 28 Barakhamba Road.
Telephone: 91-11-331-9719.
Telecopier: 91-11-331-7802.
In New York, New York: 599 Lexington Avenue.
Telephone: 212-326-3939.
Cable Address: "JONESDAY NEWYORK."
Telex: 237013 JDRP UR.
Telecopier: 212-755-7306.
In Paris, France: 62, rue du Faubourg Saint-Honore.
Telephone: 33-1-44-71-3939.
Cable Address: "Surgoe Paris."
Telex: 290156 Surgoe.
Telecopier: 33-1-49-24-0471.
In Pittsburgh, Pennsylvania: 500 Grant Street, 31st Floor.
Telephone: 412-391-3939.
Cable Address: "Attorneys Pittsburgh."
Telecopier: 412-394-7959.
In Riyadh, Saudi Arabia: Law Offices of Saud M.A. Shawwaf, P.O. Box 22166.
Telephone: (966-1) 462-8866.
Telex: 401831 SAUCON SJ.
Telecopier: (966-1) 462-9001.

(See Next Column)

JONES, DAY, REAVIS & POGUE, *Chicago—Continued*

In Taipei, Taiwan: 8th Floor, 2 Tun Hwa South Road, Section 2.
Telephone: (886-2) 704-6808.
Telecopier: (886-2) 704-6791.
In Tokyo, Japan: Toranomon MT Building, 4th Floor, 10-3, Toranomon 3-Chome, Minato-ku, Tokyo 105, Japan.
Telephone: 81-3-3433-3939.
Telecopier: 81-3-5401-2725.
In Washington, D.C.: Metropolitan Square, 1450 G Street, N.W.
Telephone: 202-879-3939.
Cable Address: "Attorneys Washington."
Telex: 89-2410 ATTORNEYS WASH.
Telecopier: 202-737-2832.

MEMBER OF FIRM IN CHICAGO
Daniel E. Reidy

For Complete List of Firm Personnel, See General Section

For full biographical listings, see the Martindale-Hubbell Law Directory

---

KANE OBBISH PROPES & GARIPPO (AV)

19th Floor, 100 West Monroe Street, 60603
Telephone: 312-346-8355
Fax: 312-346-6549

MEMBERS OF FIRM

Michael J. Kane	Lorna E. Propes
James M. Obbish	Louis B. Garippo
Susan G. Feibus	

For full biographical listings, see the Martindale-Hubbell Law Directory

---

LAW OFFICES OF KOMIE AND ASSOCIATES (AV)

Suite 3500 Avondale Centre, 20 North Clark Street, 60602-5002
Telephone: 312-263-4383
Fax: 312-263-2803

Stephen M. Komie

ASSOCIATES

Julia A. McConnahy	Terrance McWhorter
Mark A. Walwyn	

OF COUNSEL

Douglas W. Godfrey	Marc D. Wolfe

LEGAL SUPPORT PERSONNEL
Paul J. Ciolino

For full biographical listings, see the Martindale-Hubbell Law Directory

---

STONE, McGUIRE & BENJAMIN (AV)

Suite 3230, 55 East Monroe Street, 60603
Telephone: 312-372-4100
Fax: 312-372-9461
Northbrook, Illinois Office: 801 Skokie Boulevard.
Telephone: 847-205-9700.
FAX: 847-205-9492.

MEMBERS OF FIRM

Howard L. Stone	Lee E. Gussin
David A. McGuire	(Resident, Northbrook Office)
Marc A. Benjamin	Michael L. Siegel
(Resident, Northbrook Office)	Edward C. Richard

ASSOCIATES

Carl E. Poli	Michael A. Harsch
	(Resident, Northbrook Office)

For full biographical listings, see the Martindale-Hubbell Law Directory

---

CRAIG D. TOBIN & ASSOCIATES (AV)

Three First National Plaza, Suite 535, 60602
Telephone: 312-641-1321
FAX: 312-641-5220

OF COUNSEL
Robert J. Collins

Tomas Petkus	Thomas C. Crooks

For full biographical listings, see the Martindale-Hubbell Law Directory

---

COLLINSVILLE, Madison Co.

DUNHAM, BOMAN & LESKERA (AV)

300 West Clay Street, 62234
Telephone: 618-344-7734
Telecopier: 618-344-3853
East St. Louis, Illinois Office: 520 First Illinois Bank Building.
Telephone: 618-271-0535.
Telecopier: 618-271-2800.
Belleville, Illinois Office: 208 North High Street.
Telephone: 618-397-2151.
Telecopier: 618-397-2285.

(See Next Column)

John W. Leskera	William L. Berry

For full biographical listings, see the Martindale-Hubbell Law Directory

---

EAST ST. LOUIS, St. Clair Co.

DUNHAM, BOMAN & LESKERA (AV)

520 First Illinois Bank Building, 327 Missouri Avenue, 62201
Telephone: 618-271-0535
Telecopier: 618-271-2800
Belleville, Illinois Office: 208 North High Street.
Telephone: 618-235-7222.
Telecopier: 618-397-2285.
Collinsville, Illinois Office: 300 West Clay Street.
Telephone: 618-344-7734.
Telecopier: 618-344-3853.

M.F. Oehmke (1887-1963)	Wm. C. Dunham (1893-1975)
	Howard Boman (1917-1985)

MEMBERS OF FIRM

John W. Leskera	Russell K. Scott
William L. Berry	Robert D. Francis
Eric C. Young	John L. Bitzer

Attorneys For: Collinsville School District #10; Hanover Insurance Co.;; Hartford Insurance Group; Home Indemnity Co.; State Farm Insurance Cos.; Transamerica Insurance Group; The Travelers Indemnity Co.; Wausau Insurance Cos.; Nationwide Insurance Co.; Atlantic Mutual Insurance Co..

For full biographical listings, see the Martindale-Hubbell Law Directory

---

MARION,* Williamson Co.

HARRIS, LAMBERT, HOWERTON & DORRIS (AV)

300 West Main Street, 62959
Telephone: 618-993-2616
Fax: 618-997-1845

MEMBERS OF FIRM

Ralph W. Harris (1904-1982)	Robert H. Howerton
Richard Gordon Lambert	Douglas N. Dorris

ASSOCIATE
Kelley Ray Phelps

For full biographical listings, see the Martindale-Hubbell Law Directory

---

OAK BROOK, Du Page Co.

BOTTI, MARINACCIO & DeLONGIS, LTD. (AV)

720 Enterprise Drive, 60521
Telephone: 708-573-8585
Fax: 708-573-8586
Wheaton, Illinois Office: Suite 401 The Ticor Title Building, 330 Naperville Road.
Telephone: 708-653-2100.

Aldo E. Botti	Mark W. Salkeld
Stephen R. Botti	Peter M. Tumminaro
Andrew Y. Acker	David C. Bruss
Peter M. DeLongis	Jean M. Lasics
Lee A. Marinaccio	Nanette C. Augustin

For full biographical listings, see the Martindale-Hubbell Law Directory

---

SPRINGFIELD,* Sangamon Co.

METNICK, WISE, CHERRY & FRAZIER (AV)

Second Floor, Myers Building, 1 West Old State Capitol Plaza, P.O. Box 12140, 62791
Telephone: 217-753-4242
Telefax: 217-753-4642

MEMBERS OF FIRM

Michael B. Metnick	D. Peter Wise
Richard D. Frazier	

ASSOCIATE
Frederick J. Schlosser

For full biographical listings, see the Martindale-Hubbell Law Directory

---

INDIANA

CARMEL, Hamilton Co.

KNOWLES & ASSOCIATES (AV)

811 South Range Line Road, 46032
Telephone: 317-848-4360
Telecopier: 317-848-4363
URL: http://www.courts9@1x.netcom.com

William W. Knowles

(See Next Column)

KNOWLES & ASSOCIATES—*Continued*

D. Brandon Johnston   Tracy J. Follstad

For full biographical listings, see the Martindale-Hubbell Law Directory

ELKHART, Elkhart Co.

CHESTER, PFAFF & BROTHERSON (AV)

317 West Franklin Street, P.O. Box 507, 46515-0507
Telephone: 219-294-5421
Fax: 219-522-1476

MEMBERS OF FIRM

Robert A. Pfaff   Edward J. Chester

For Complete List of Firm Personnel, See General Section

For full biographical listings, see the Martindale-Hubbell Law Directory

EVANSVILLE,* Vanderburgh Co.

JEFFERY L. LANTZ (AV)

525 Sycamore Street, P.O. Box 1087, 47706-1087
Telephone: 812-464-0044
Fax: 812-426-0779

References: Citizens National Bank of Evansville; Old National Bank of Evansville.

For full biographical listings, see the Martindale-Hubbell Law Directory

GREENFIELD,* Hancock Co.

BRAND & ALLEN (AV)

Five Courthouse Plaza, P.O. Box 455, 46140
Telephone: 317-462-3455
Fax: 317-467-6109

Waldo C. Ging (1892-1971)   James L. Brand (1938-1996)

MEMBERS OF FIRM

Eric N. Allen   Dawn E. Wellman
James W. McNew

ASSOCIATES

Gregory A. Brand   Nicole A. Zelin
Mary G. Willis   Jeffrey W. Eakins

For full biographical listings, see the Martindale-Hubbell Law Directory

INDIANAPOLIS,* Marion Co.

TABBERT HAHN EARNEST & STARKEY, P.C. (AV)

Suite 2100, One Indiana Square, 46204
Telephone: 317-639-5444
Fax: 317-639-5232

Don A. Tabbert   Lorie A. Brown
Gregory F. Hahn   Mark K. Sullivan
Lante K. Earnest   Judy M. Tyrrell
Martha T. Starkey   Susan L. Abel

OF COUNSEL

James J. Nocon   William D. Lalley
Douglas E. Cregor

For full biographical listings, see the Martindale-Hubbell Law Directory

IOWA

DES MOINES,* Polk Co.

THE ROSENBERG LAW FIRM (AV)

1010 Insurance Exchange Building, 505 Fifth Avenue, 50309
Telephone: 515-243-7600

MEMBERS OF FIRM

Raymond Rosenberg   Brent D. Rosenberg
Dean A. Stowers   Carole L. Hunt

Reference: Firstar Bank, Des Moines, Iowa.

For full biographical listings, see the Martindale-Hubbell Law Directory

KANSAS

TOPEKA,* Shawnee Co.

BENNETT & DILLON, L.L.P. (AV)

1605 Southwest 37th Street, 66611
Telephone: 913-267-5063
Fax: 913-267-2652

MEMBERS OF FIRM

Mark L. Bennett, Jr.   Wilburn Dillon, Jr.

References: Silver Lake State Bank; Columbian National Bank and Trust.

For Complete List of Firm Personnel, See General Section

For full biographical listings, see the Martindale-Hubbell Law Directory

WICHITA,* Sedgwick Co.

YOUNG, BOGLE, MCCAUSLAND, WELLS & CLARK, P.A. (AV)

106 West Douglas, Suite 923, 67202
Telephone: 316-265-7841
Facsimile: 316-265-3956

Paul S. McCausland   Patrick C. Blanchard
Kenneth M. Clark   Mark R. Maloney

Representative Client: CJA Panel, D.Kan.

For Complete List of Firm Personnel, See General Section

For full biographical listings, see the Martindale-Hubbell Law Directory

KENTUCKY

BOWLING GREEN,* Warren Co.

ENGLISH, LUCAS, PRIEST & OWSLEY (AV)

1101 College Street, P.O. Box 770, 42102-0770
Telephone: 502-781-6500
Telecopier: 502-782-7782
Email: inquiry@elpo.com

MEMBERS OF FIRM

Charles E. English   Charles E. English, Jr.

ASSOCIATE

Robert A. Young

For Complete List of Firm Personnel, See General Section

For full biographical listings, see the Martindale-Hubbell Law Directory

MILLIKEN LAW FIRM (AV)

426 East Main Street, P.O. Box 1640, 42102-1640
Telephone: 502-843-0800
Fax: 502-842-1237

W. Currie Milliken   Wesley V. Milliken

Reference: Trans Financial Bank, Bowling Green, Kentucky.

For full biographical listings, see the Martindale-Hubbell Law Directory

COVINGTON, Kenton Co.

ROBERT E. SANDERS AND ASSOCIATES, P.S.C. (AV)

The Charles H. Fisk House, 1017 Russell Street, 41011
Telephone: 606-491-3000
Fax: 606-655-4642
Email: 74762.3055@compuserve.com

Robert E. Sanders

Julie Lippert Duncan   Peggy A. Murphy
Lisa Pruitt Thorner

LEGAL SUPPORT PERSONNEL

Shirley L. Sanders   Sandra A. Head
Sheila D. Rachal

For full biographical listings, see the Martindale-Hubbell Law Directory

TALIAFERRO AND MEHLING (AV)

1005 Madison Avenue, P.O. Box 468, 41012-0468
Telephone: 606-291-9900
Fax: 606-291-3014

MEMBERS OF FIRM

Philip Taliaferro, III   Christopher J. Mehling
Lucinda C. Shirooni

(See Next Column)

TALIAFERRO AND MEHLING, *Covington—Continued*

ASSOCIATES

C. Houston Ebert   Howard L. Tankersley
                Alice G. Keys

OF COUNSEL

Robert W. Carran   Norbert J. Bischoff
                F. Edward Worland, Jr.

For full biographical listings, see the Martindale-Hubbell Law Directory

---

LEXINGTON,* Fayette Co.

KINKEAD & COLLIER (AV)

201 West Vine Street, 40507
Telephone: 606-233-3550
Facsimile: 606-255-1965

MEMBERS OF THE FIRM

Shelby C. Kinkead, Jr.   Wayne F. Collier

For full biographical listings, see the Martindale-Hubbell Law Directory

McCoy, BAKER & WEST (AV)

309 North Broadway, 40507
Telephone: 606-254-6363
FAX: 606-233-4234

MEMBERS OF FIRM

R. Burl McCoy, Jr.   Michael D. Baker
                John Kevin West

Charles E. Beal, II

For full biographical listings, see the Martindale-Hubbell Law Directory

ROBERTS & SMITH (AV)

167 West Main Street Suite 200, 40507
Telephone: 606-233-1104

MEMBERS OF FIRM

Larry S. Roberts   Kenneth W. Smith

For full biographical listings, see the Martindale-Hubbell Law Directory

---

LONDON,* Laurel Co.

TOOMS & HOUSE (AV)

310 West Fifth Street, P.O. Box 520, 40743-0520
Telephone: 606-864-4145
FAX: 606-864-4279

MEMBERS OF FIRM

Murray L. Brown (1894-1980)   R. William Tooms
Roy E. Tooms (1917-1986)   Brian C. House

Representative Clients: State Auto Mutual Insurance Co.; Grange Mutual Casualty Co.; Kentucky Farm Bureau Mutual Insurance Co.

For full biographical listings, see the Martindale-Hubbell Law Directory

---

LOUISVILLE,* Jefferson Co.

JAY LAMBERT (AV)

Suite 200, Second Floor, Morrissey Building, 304 West Liberty
  Street, 40202
Telephone: 502-583-2831
FAX: 502-583-3701

For full biographical listings, see the Martindale-Hubbell Law Directory

FRANK MASCAGNI, III (AV)

Suite 200, Second Floor, Morrissey Building, 304 West Liberty
  Street, 40202-3012
Telephone: 502-583-2831
Fax: 502-583-3701

Reference: PNC Bank, Ky.

For full biographical listings, see the Martindale-Hubbell Law Directory

SEILLER & HANDMAKER, LLP (AV)

2200 Meidinger Tower, 40202
Telephone: 502-584-7400
Telecopier: 502-583-2100
Paris, Kentucky Office: Seiller, Handmaker & Blevins, P.S.C., 1431 South
Main Street.
Telephone: 606-987-3980.
Telecopier: 606-987-3982.
Cynthiana, Kentucky Office: Seiller, Handmaker & Blevins, P.S.C., 9 South
Walnut.
Telephone: 606-234-2880.
New Albany, Indiana Office: 202 Pearl Street.
Telephone: 812-948-8307.
Telecopier: 812-948-8383.

(See Next Column)

Edward F. Seiller (1897-1990)

MEMBERS OF FIRM

Stuart Allen Handmaker   Maury D. Kommor
Bill V. Seiller   Cynthia Compton Stone
David M. Cantor   Glenn A. Cohen
Neil C. Bordy   Tomi Anne Blevins Pulliam
Kyle Anne Citrynell   (Paris and Cynthiana Offices)

ASSOCIATES

Pamela M. Greenwell   Donna F. Townsend
Michael C. Bratcher   Gregory A. Lindsey
John E. Brengle   Vicki L. Buba
Patrick R. Holland, II   Allen C. Platt III (Resident,
Edwin Jon Wolfe   New Albany, Indiana Office)

OF COUNSEL

Robert S. Frey

For full biographical listings, see the Martindale-Hubbell Law Directory

---

MOUNT VERNON,* Rockcastle Co.

CLONTZ & COX (AV)

Courthouse, 205 Main Street, P.O. Box 1350, 40456
Telephone: 606-256-5111
Fax: 606-256-2036

MEMBERS OF FIRM

Carl R. Clontz   Jerry J. Cox
                John E. Clontz

Representative Clients: The Bank of Mt. Vernon; Citizens Bank, Brodhead, Kentucky; Kentucky Farm Bureau Mutual Insurance Co.; Louisville Title Division of Commonwealth Land Title Insurance Co.
Reference: The Bank of Mt. Vernon, Mt. Vernon, Kentucky.

For full biographical listings, see the Martindale-Hubbell Law Directory

---

OWENSBORO,* Daviess Co.

KAMUF, YEWELL, PACE & CONDON (AV)

Great Financial Federal Building, 322 Frederica Street, 42301
Telephone: 502-685-3901
Fax: 502-926-2005

MEMBERS OF FIRM

Charles J. Kamuf   David L. Yewell

Representative Clients: Owensboro Municipal Utilities Commission; Lincoln Service Corp.; Hancock County Planning Commission; Daviess County Board of Education; Barmet Aluminum Corp.; Owensboro Sewer Commission; TICOR Title Insurance Co.; Chicago Title Insurance Co.; Owensboro Riverport Authority; Housing Authority of Owensboro.

For Complete List of Firm Personnel, See General Section

For full biographical listings, see the Martindale-Hubbell Law Directory

---

PADUCAH,* McCracken Co.

LEN W. OGDEN, JR. (AV)

The Sinnott House, 228 North 9th Street, 42001-1850
Telephone: 502-444-0232
Fax: 502-444-0239

For full biographical listings, see the Martindale-Hubbell Law Directory

---

RICHMOND,* Madison Co.

SHUMATE, FLAHERTY & EUBANKS (AV)

Formerly Shumate, Shumate & Flaherty
225 West Irvine Street, P.O. Box 157, 40476-0157
Telephone: 606-623-3049
Fax: 606-623-6406

MEMBERS OF FIRM

Hunter M. Shumate (1893-1971)   Peter J. Flaherty (1920-1978)
Thomas D. Shumate (1906-1978)   Peter J. Flaherty III
                Michael F. Eubanks

General Counsel for: Peoples Rural Telephone Cooperative Corp., McKee, Ky.

For full biographical listings, see the Martindale-Hubbell Law Directory

---

LOUISIANA

ALEXANDRIA,* Rapides Parish

LAW OFFICE OF J. MICHAEL SMALL (AV)

1412 Centre Court Drive, Suite 201, P.O. Box 1470, 71309
Telephone: 318-487-8963
Fax: 318-442-3062

For full biographical listings, see the Martindale-Hubbell Law Directory

BATON ROUGE, East Baton Rouge Parish

UNGLESBY & KOCH (AV)

246 Napoleon Street, 70802
Telephone: 504-387-0120
Fax: 504-336-4355
Email: unglkoch@premier.net

Lewis O. Unglesby	Deborah H. Baer
Karl J. Koch	Aidan C. Reynolds

For full biographical listings, see the Martindale-Hubbell Law Directory

LAKE CHARLES, Calcasieu Parish

LORENZI, SANCHEZ & ROSTEET, L.L.P. (AV)

518 Pujo Street, P.O. Drawer 3305, 70602-3305
Telephone: 318-436-8401
Facsimile: 318-439-3216
Email: lorsanrost@linknet.net

MEMBERS OF FIRM

Thomas L. Lorenzi	Walter M. Sanchez
Sidney J. Rosteet	

For full biographical listings, see the Martindale-Hubbell Law Directory

MONROE, Ouachita Parish

DAVENPORT, FILES & KELLY, L.L.P. (AV)

1509 Lamy Lane, P.O. Box 4787, 71211-4787
Telephone: 318-387-6453
FAX: 318-323-6533

Thos. W. Davenport (1909-1962)	Jack B. Files
Wm. G. Kelly, Jr.	Mike C. Sanders
Thomas W. Davenport, Jr.	Ramsey L. Ogg
Michael J. Fontenot	

M. Shane Craighead	W. David Hammett
Carey B. Underwood	

STAFF ATTORNEY
Stacy L. Guice

Representative Clients: American International Group (AIG); Burlington Motor Carriers; Chubb Group; Crum & Forster Group; Delta Airlines, Inc.; GAINSCO; GEICO; Highlands Ins. Co.; Trinity Universal Ins. Co.; Zurich-American Insurance Companies.

For full biographical listings, see the Martindale-Hubbell Law Directory

NEW ORLEANS, Orleans Parish

THE BAGERT LAW FIRM (AV)

Suite 2055 Pan-American Life Center, 601 Poydras Street, 70130
Telephone: 504-523-1117
Facsimile: 504-522-5406
Email: bagertlf@ix.netcom.com

Bernard J. Bagert, Jr., (A P.L.C.)

For full biographical listings, see the Martindale-Hubbell Law Directory

CAPITELLI & WICKER (AV)

2950 Energy Centre, 1100 Poydras Street, 70163-2950
Telephone: 504-582-2425
FAX: 504-582-2422

Ralph Capitelli	T. Carey Wicker, III
Paul Michael Elvir, Jr.	

OF COUNSEL
Terry Q. Alarcon

For full biographical listings, see the Martindale-Hubbell Law Directory

GAINSBURGH, BENJAMIN, DAVID, MEUNIER, NORIEA & WARSHAUER (AV)

2800 Energy Centre, 1100 Poydras, 70163-2800
Telephone: 504-522-2304
Telecopier: 504-528-9973
Email: GAINSBEN@IAMERICA.NET

MEMBERS OF FIRM

Nick F. Noriea, Jr.	Irving J. Warshauer
Madeleine M. Landrieu	

For full biographical listings, see the Martindale-Hubbell Law Directory

HABANS, BOLOGNA & CARRIERE, A PROFESSIONAL LAW CORPORATION (AV)

Suite 2323, 1515 Poydras Street, 70112
Telephone: 504-524-2323
Telex: 151514 HABA M UT
Telecopier: 504-522-7224
Cable Address: HABOL

Robert N. Habans, Jr.	John C. McNeese
William F. Bologna	Aimée Carriere
James D. Carriere	Dwight L. Acomb
Julien F. Jurgens	

For full biographical listings, see the Martindale-Hubbell Law Directory

SMITH, JONES & FAWER, L.L.P. (AV)

201 St. Charles Avenue, Sute 3702, 70170
Telephone: 504-525-2200
Telecopier: 504-525-2205

MEMBERS OF FIRM

Randall A. Smith (P.C.)	Gladstone N. Jones, III
Michael S. Fawer	

ASSOCIATES

Andrew L. Kramer	L. Tiffany Hawkins

For full biographical listings, see the Martindale-Hubbell Law Directory

SHREVEPORT, Caddo Parish

WELLBORN JACK, JR. (AV)

101 Milam Street, 71101
Telephone: 318-227-9637
Fax: 318-221-6076

For full biographical listings, see the Martindale-Hubbell Law Directory

MILLS, TIMMONS & FLOWERS, A PROFESSIONAL LAW CORPORATION (AV)

300 Law Center, 331 Milam Street, P.O. Box 1784, 71166-1784
Telephone: 318-222-0337
Fax: 318-222-5400

George H. Mills, Jr.	David C. Turansky
Wayne Timmons	J. Broocks Greer III
Peter R. Flowers	Sandra Lynn Walker

OF COUNSEL
William T. Allison

Reference: Hibernia National Bank.

For full biographical listings, see the Martindale-Hubbell Law Directory

MAINE

AUGUSTA, Kennebec Co.

* indicates certain Bar Register subscribers whose principal office is located elsewhere in the state and who have arranged for representation as a part of the state capital listings that follow

* PIERCE ATWOOD (AV)

77 Winthrop Street, 04330
Telephone: 207-622-6311
Fax: 207-623-9367
Email: info@PierceAtwood.com
Portland, Maine Office: One Monument Square.
Telephone: 207-791-1100.
Fax: 207-791-1350.
Newburyport, Massachusetts Office: 6 Harris Street.
Telephone: 508-465-9599.
Fax: 508-465-9945.

MEMBER OF FIRM
Malcolm L. Lyons

For Complete List of Firm Personnel, See General Section

For full biographical listings, see the Martindale-Hubbell Law Directory

BANGOR, Penobscot Co.

GROSS, MINSKY, MOGUL & SINGAL, P.A. (AV)

Key Plaza, 23 Water Street, P.O. Box 917, 04402-0917
Telephone: 207-942-4644
Telecopier: 207-942-3699
Email: gmm&s-law@atlsysnet.com *URL:*
http://www.atlsysnet.com/gmms

(See Next Column)

GROSS, MINSKY, MOGUL & SINGAL P.A., Bangor—Continued

Edward I. Gross (Retired)	George C. Schelling
Jules L. Mogul (1930-1994)	Edward W. Gould
Norman Minsky	Steven J. Mogul
George Z. Singal	James R. Wholly
Louis H. Kornreich	Daniel A. Pileggi
	Philip K. Clarke

Wayne P. Libhart (Retired)	James S. Nixon
Sandra L. Rothera	F. Todd Lowell

Representative Client: Dahl Chase Pathology Associates.
Local Counsel for: The St. Paul Insurance Cos.; Aetna Life & Casualty Co.; Imperial Casualty & Indemnity Co.

For full biographical listings, see the Martindale-Hubbell Law Directory

VAFIADES, BROUNTAS & KOMINSKY (AV)

Key Plaza, 23 Water Street, P.O. Box 919, 04402-0919
Telephone: 207-947-6915
Telecopier: 207-941-0863

MEMBERS OF FIRM

Marvin H. Glazier	Eugene C. Coughlin, III

ASSOCIATES

Terence M. Harrigan	James C. Munch, III

OF COUNSEL
Lewis V. Vafiades

For Complete List of Firm Personnel, See General Section

For full biographical listings, see the Martindale-Hubbell Law Directory

---

PORTLAND, * Cumberland Co.

DANIEL G. LILLEY, P.A. (AV)

39 Portland Pier, P.O. Box 4803, 04112
Telephone: 207-774-6206
Telecopier: 207-774-2257
Email: DGLilley@ AOL.com

Daniel G. Lilley

Mark L. Randall	Karen L. Morgan
Mary Davis	(Not admitted in ME)

OF COUNSEL
William A. Fogel

For full biographical listings, see the Martindale-Hubbell Law Directory

PIERCE ATWOOD (AV)

One Monument Square, 04101
Telephone: 207-791-1100
Fax: 207-791-1350
Email: info@PierceAtwood.com
Augusta, Maine Office: 77 Winthrop Street.
Telephone: 207-622-6311.
Fax: 207-623-9367.
Newburyport, Massachusetts Office: 6 Harris Street.
Telephone: 508-465-9599.
Fax: 508-465-9945.

MEMBERS OF FIRM

Ralph I. Lancaster, Jr.	Peter W. Culley
Malcolm L. Lyons	James R. Erwin, II
(Resident, Augusta Office)	Kevin F. Gordon

For Complete List of Firm Personnel, See General Section

For full biographical listings, see the Martindale-Hubbell Law Directory

---

SACO, York Co.

SMITH ELLIOTT SMITH & GARMEY, P.A. (AV)

199 Main Street, P.O. Box 1179, 04072
Telephone: 207-282-1527
Telefax: 207-283-4412
Sanford Telephone: 207-324-1560
Portland Telephone: 207-774-3199
Wells Telephone: 207-646-0970
Kennebunk, Maine Office: Route One South, 9 York Street.
Telephone: 207-985-4464.
Telefax: 207-985-3946.
Portland, Maine Office: 100 Commercial Street, Suite 304.
Telephone: 207-774-3199.
Telefax: 207-774-2235.

Charles W. Smith, Jr.	John H. O'Neil, Jr.
	Harry B. Center, II

References: Saco & Biddeford Savings Institution.

(See Next Column)

For Complete List of Firm Personnel, See General Section

For full biographical listings, see the Martindale-Hubbell Law Directory

---

SKOWHEGAN, * Somerset Co.

WRIGHT & MILLS, P.A. (AV)

218 Water Street, P.O. Box 9, 04976
Telephone: 207-474-3324
Telefax: 207-474-3609

S. Peter Mills	Janet T. Mills
Paul P. Sumberg	Kenneth A. Lexier

Representative Clients: Design Professionals Insurance Co., New Jersey; Solon Manufacturing Co., Solon, Maine; Kleinschmidt Associates-Engineers, Pittsfield, Maine; Acheron Engineering, Newport, Maine; E.W. Littlefield-Contractors, Hartland, Maine; WBRC-Architects, Bangor, Maine; Town of Skowhegan; Town of Norridgewock.

For Complete List of Firm Personnel, See General Section

For full biographical listings, see the Martindale-Hubbell Law Directory

---

MARYLAND

BALTIMORE, * (Independent City)

ALBRIGHT BROWN & CAUDILL, LLC (AV)

120 East Baltimore Street Suite 2150, 21202
Telephone: 410-244-0350
Facsimile: 410-244-0356
Elkton, Maryland Office: 151 East Main Street. 21921.
Telephone: 410-398-3850.
Fax: 410-392-5633.

David F. Albright	Karolyn N. Bowe (Resident,
C. Thomas Brown	Elkton, Maryland Office)
Franklin T. Caudill	Cynthia E. Rodgers-Waire

For full biographical listings, see the Martindale-Hubbell Law Directory

FERGUSON, SCHETELICH, HEFFERNAN & MURDOCK, P.A. (AV)

1300 NationsBank Center 1, 100 South Charles Street, 21201
Telephone: 410-837-2200
Fax: 410-837-1188
Email: fshm@ix.netcom

Robert L. Ferguson, Jr.	Christopher J. Heffernan
Thomas J. Schetelich	M. Brooke Murdock

Michael N. Russo, Jr.	Peter Joseph Basile
Jodi K. Ebersole	Ann D. Ware

For full biographical listings, see the Martindale-Hubbell Law Directory

FREISHTAT & SANDLER (AV)

Suite 1500, One Calvert Plaza, 201 E. Baltimore Street, 21202
Telephone: 410-727-7740
FAX: 410-727-7356

MEMBERS OF FIRM

David Freishtat	Raymond Daniel Burke
Paul Mark Sandler	William M. Mullen

Lloyd J. Snow	Stacie F. Dubnow
Lynn Weinberg	T. Allen Mott

For full biographical listings, see the Martindale-Hubbell Law Directory

GLASER & DEROS (AV)

Suite 1717, 201 North Charles Street, 21201
Telephone: 410-244-8822
Toll Free: 1-800-244-8015
Fax: 410-625-1028

Harold I. Glaser	John S. Deros

For full biographical listings, see the Martindale-Hubbell Law Directory

PAUL R. KRAMER, P.A. (AV)

231 St. Paul Place, 21202-2003
Telephone: 410-727-5531
FAX: 410-727-2186

Paul R. Kramer

For full biographical listings, see the Martindale-Hubbell Law Directory

Baltimore—Continued

MARTIN, JUNGHANS, SNYDER & BERNSTEIN, P.A. (AV)

Redwood Tower, Suite 2000, 217 East Redwood Street, 21202
Telephone: 410-547-7163
Facsimile: 410-547-1605

Gerard P. Martin
Paula M. Junghans

David L. Snyder
Gregg L. Bernstein

Kimberly Dunn Spelman   William S. Heyman
OF COUNSEL
Steven J. Sibel
LEGAL SUPPORT PERSONNEL
Linda S. Baker (Administrator)   Meg L. Zimmerman (Paralegal)

For full biographical listings, see the Martindale-Hubbell Law Directory

McDANIEL & MARSH (AV)

118 West Mulberry Street, 21201-3600
Telephone: 410-685-3810
Telecopier: 410-685-0203

William Alden McDaniel, Jr.   Jo Bennett Marsh
ASSOCIATE
Laura M. L. Maroldy

For full biographical listings, see the Martindale-Hubbell Law Directory

PHILLIP M. SUTLEY (AV)

116 West Mulberry Street, 21201-3687
Telephone: 410-727-2040
Fax: 410-727-0343

For full biographical listings, see the Martindale-Hubbell Law Directory

VENABLE ATTORNEYS AT LAW VENABLE, BAETJER AND HOWARD, LLP (AV)

A Partnership including Professional Corporations
1800 Mercantile Bank & Trust Building, 2 Hopkins Plaza, 21201
Telephone: 410-244-7400
Email: INFO@Venable.win.net
Washington, D.C. Office: Venable, Baetjer, Howard & Civiletti LLP. Suite 1000, 1201 New York Avenue, N.W.
Telephone: 202-962-4800.
McLean, Virginia Office: Suite 400, 2010 Corporate Ridge.
Telephone: 703-760-1600.
Rockville, Maryland Office: Suite 500, One Church Street, P. O. Box 1906.
Telephone: 301-217-5600.
Towson, Maryland Office: 210 Allegheny Avenue, P. O. Box 5517.
Telephone: 410-494-6200.

MEMBERS OF FIRM

Benjamin R. Civiletti (P.C.) (Also at Washington, D.C. and Towson, Maryland Offices)
John Henry Lewin, Jr. (P.C.)
Bruce E. Titus (Resident, McLean, Virginia Office)
Joseph G. Block (Not admitted in MD; Resident, Washington, D.C. Office)
Michael Schatzow (Also at Washington, D.C. Office)
L. Paige Marvel
Judson W. Starr (Not admitted in MD; Also at Washington, D.C. and Towson, Maryland Offices)
William D. Coston (Not admitted in MD; Resident, Washington, D.C. Office)

Amy Berman Jackson (Not admitted in MD; Resident, Washington, D.C. Office)
William D. Quarles (Also at Washington, D.C. and Towson, Maryland Offices)
Kathleen Gallogly Cox (Resident, Towson, Maryland Office)
Thomas J. Kelly, Jr. (Not admitted in MD; Resident, Washington, D. C. Office)
Gary M. Hnath (Resident, Washington, D.C. Office)
Mitchell Y. Mirviss
Geoffrey R. Garinther (Also at Washington, D.C. Office)
Terri L. Turner

ASSOCIATES

Paul D. Barker, Jr.
David W. Goewey (Not admitted in MD; Resident, Washington, D.C. Office)

David R. Hodnett (Not admitted in MD; Resident, McLean, Virginia Office)

For Complete List of Firm Personnel, See General Section

For full biographical listings, see the Martindale-Hubbell Law Directory

WEINER, ASTRACHAN, GUNST, HILLMAN AND ALLEN, A PROFESSIONAL CORPORATION (AV)

120 East Baltimore Street Suite 2100, 21202
Telephone: 410-783-3500
FAX: 410-783-3510

(See Next Column)

Arnold M. Weiner
James B. Astrachan
Peter H. Gunst

Allan P. Hillman
Steven A. Allen
Thomas J. Zagami

Bruce L. Mann   Donna M.D. Thomas
Heather H. Polzin-Vovakes

For full biographical listings, see the Martindale-Hubbell Law Directory

BEL AIR,* Harford Co.

BROWN, BROWN & BROWN, A PROFESSIONAL ASSOCIATION (AV)

200 South Main Street, 21014
Telephone: 410-838-5500
Baltimore: 410-879-2220
Fax: 410-893-0402

A. Freeborn Brown
T. Carroll Brown

Augustus F. Brown
Albert J. A. Young

A. Frank Carven, III
Harold Douglas Norton

Christopher R. vanRoden
David E. Carey

Ankur P. Dalal

Attorneys for: Baltimore Gas & Electric Co.; Chesapeake & Potomac Telephone Co.; Aberdeen Proving Ground Federal Credit Union; First Virginia Bank-Central Maryland; First National Bank of Maryland; Bell Atlantic Mobile Systems; First Harbor Securities; Maryland Portable Concrete, Inc. *Approved Counsel for:* The Chicago Title Insurance Co. of Maryland, Inc.

For full biographical listings, see the Martindale-Hubbell Law Directory

GREENBELT, Prince Georges Co.

STANLEY S. PICKETT (AV)

Suite 414 Capital Office Park, 6411 Ivy Lane, 20770
Telephone: 301-513-0613
Fax: 301-513-0618

Stanley Sinclair Pickett
ASSOCIATE
Gordon J. Brumback
LEGAL SUPPORT PERSONNEL
Stacy S. Pickett (Law Clerk)   Vivian W. Wolfe (Paralegal)

Representative Clients: B.F. Saul Co.; McDonald and Eudy Printers, Inc.; Condominium Management, Inc.; Long & Foster Realtors; Mitron Systems Corp.; Coldwell Banker; Glenanden Housing Authority; Koones & Montgomery, Inc.; Community Associations, Inc.

For full biographical listings, see the Martindale-Hubbell Law Directory

OCEAN CITY, Worcester Co.

AYRES, JENKINS, GORDY & ALMAND, P.A. (AV)

5200-B Coastal Highway, 21842
Telephone: 410-723-1400
Fax: 410-723-1861
Berlin, Maryland Office: 11047 Race Track Road (Ocean Pines).
Telephone: 410-641-5033.
FAX: 410-641-6926.

Guy R. Ayres, III
M. Dean Jenkins

Harold B. Gordy, Jr. (Resident, Berlin Office)

James W. Almand

Jerome James LaCorte   William E. Esham, III
Mark S. Cropper

References: Calvin B. Taylor Banking Co.; Peninsula Bank.

For full biographical listings, see the Martindale-Hubbell Law Directory

COURTLAND K. TOWNSEND, JR. CHARTERED (AV)

The Executive Building, Suite 101, 7200 Coastal Highway, 21842
Telephone: 410-524-4300
FAX: 410-524-4953

Courtland K. Townsend, Jr.

For full biographical listings, see the Martindale-Hubbell Law Directory

ROCKVILLE,* Montgomery Co.

ARMSTRONG, DONOHUE & CEPPOS, CHARTERED (AV)

Suite 101, 204 Monroe Street, 20850
Telephone: 301-251-0440
Telecopier: 301-279-5929

Larry A. Ceppos   Benjamin S. Vaughan
John C. Monahan

For full biographical listings, see the Martindale-Hubbell Law Directory

MASSACHUSETTS

Rockville—Continued

CATTERTON, KEMP & DONOHUE (AV)

Suite 215, 200 A Monroe Street, 20850
Telephone: 301-294-0460
FAX: 301-294-6406

MEMBERS OF FIRM

Judith R. Catterton
Paul F. Kemp
Sara M. Donohue

ASSOCIATE

Anne Marie Jackson

OF COUNSEL

Jane Macht

For full biographical listings, see the Martindale-Hubbell Law Directory

HEENEY, ARMSTRONG & HEENEY (AV)

Adams Law Center, 29 Wood Lane, 20850
Telephone: 301-762-8585
Fax: 301-309-1461

MEMBERS OF FIRM

Robert C. Heeney (1922-1981)
Thomas L. Heeney
Philip H. Armstrong

ASSOCIATES

Matthew W. Black Jr.
Ronald A. Rubloff

Reference: Citizen Bank of Maryland, Rockville, Maryland.

For full biographical listings, see the Martindale-Hubbell Law Directory

STEIN, SPERLING, BENNETT, DE JONG, DRISCOLL, GREENFEIG & METRO, P.A. (AV)

25 West Middle Lane, 20850
Telephone: 301-340-2020; 800-435-5230
Telecopier: 301-340-8217

David C. Driscoll, Jr.
Paul T. Stein

For Complete List of Firm Personnel, See General Section

For full biographical listings, see the Martindale-Hubbell Law Directory

SALISBURY,* Wicomico Co.

DUVALL & DUVALL, L.L.P. (AV)

108 East Market Street, P.O. Box 4077, 21803-4077
Telephone: 410-548-1010
Fax: 410-548-1045

MEMBERS OF FIRM

William G. Duvall
Richard M. Duvall

Reference: Nations Bank.

For full biographical listings, see the Martindale-Hubbell Law Directory

TOWSON,* Baltimore Co.

NOLAN, PLUMHOFF & WILLIAMS, CHARTERED (AV)

Suite 700 Court Towers, 210 West Pennsylvania Avenue, 21204
Telephone: 410-823-7800
Fax: 410-296-2765

Stephen M. Schenning
Stuart Alan Schadt

For Complete List of Firm Personnel, See General Section

For full biographical listings, see the Martindale-Hubbell Law Directory

UPPER MARLBORO,* Prince Georges Co.

KNIGHT, MANZI, BRENNAN, SHAY AND HAM, A PROFESSIONAL ASSOCIATION (AV)

14440 Old Mill Road, 20772
Telephone: 301-952-0100
Annapolis/Baltimore: 410-792-3786
Fax: 301-952-0221
Crofton, Maryland Office: 2411 Crofton Lane, # 26.
Telephone: 301-261-0808.
Fax: 301-261-6945.
Mitchellville, Maryland Office: 12164 Central Avenue, Suite 228.
Telephone: 301-390-0577.
Fax: 301-390-8464.

William E. Knight
John F. Shay, Jr.
Robert A. Manzi
Richard J. Ham
William C. Brennan, Jr.
Martin J. Shuham

Monica M. Haley-Pierson
Norman D. Rivera
Daniel F. Lynch III
Robert L. Lombardo

OF COUNSEL

Stuart R. Hammett

For full biographical listings, see the Martindale-Hubbell Law Directory

---

BOSTON,* Suffolk Co.

MINTZ, LEVIN, COHN, FERRIS, GLOVSKY AND POPEO, P.C. (AV)

One Financial Center, 02111
Telephone: 617-542-6000
FAX: 617-542-2241
Internet: Each Attorney's Internet Address takes the following form: first initial last name @mintz.com (e.g., rmintz@mintz.com)
Washington, D.C. Office: 701 Pennsylvania Avenue, N.W. Suite 900.
Telephone: 202-434-7300.
Fax: 202-434-7400.

R. Robert Popeo
John K. Markey
Thomas R. Murtagh
Michael S. Gardener
Tracy A. Miner

For Complete List of Firm Personnel, See General Section

For full biographical listings, see the Martindale-Hubbell Law Directory

OTERI, WEINBERG & LAWSON (AV)

The Statler Building, 20 Park Plaza, Suite 905, 02116
Telephone: 617-227-3700
Fax: 617-338-9538

Joseph S. Oteri
Martin G. Weinberg
James W. Lawson

REARDON & REARDON (AV)

69 Beacon Street, 02108
Telephone: 617-248-6998
Fax: 617-248-0837
Worcester, Massachusetts Office: One Exchange Place.
Telephone: 508-754-1111.
Fax: 508-797-6176.

MEMBERS OF FIRM

James G. Reardon
Frank S. Puccio, Jr.

References: Mechanics National Bank; Worcester County National Bank; Bank of New England, Worcester.

For full biographical listings, see the Martindale-Hubbell Law Directory

SHEKETOFF & HOMAN (AV)

84 State Street, 02109
Telephone: 617-367-3449
Fax: 617-723-1710

MEMBERS OF FIRM

Robert L. Sheketoff
Kimberly Homan

For full biographical listings, see the Martindale-Hubbell Law Directory

SHERBURNE, POWERS & NEEDHAM, P.C. (AV)

One Beacon Street, 02108
Telephone: 617-523-2700
Fax: 617-523-6850
Email: @SHERBURNE.COM

William D. Weeks
Benjamin Volinski
John T. Collins
Mark Schonfeld
Allan J. Landau
James D. Smeallie
Stephen A. Hopkins
Paul Killeen
Alan I. Falk
Gordon P. Katz
C. Thomas Swaim
Joseph B. Darby, III
James Pollock
Richard M Yanofsky
William V. Tripp III
James E. McDermott
Stephen S. Young
Kenneth P. Brier
William F. Machen
Robert V. Lizza
W. Robert Allison
Miriam Goldstein Altman
Philip J. Notopoulos
John J. Monaghan
Richard J. Hindlian
Margaret J. Palladino
Paul E. Troy
Mark C. Michalowski
Harold W. Potter, Jr.
David Scott Sloan
Philip S. Lapatin
M. Chrysa Long
Pamela A. Duckworth
Lawrence D. Bradley
Miriam J. McKendall

Cynthia A. Brown
Jeffrey J. Nix
Cynthia M. Hern
(Not admitted in MA)
Meredeth A. Beers
Kenneth L. Harvey
Dianne R. Phillips
Christopher J. Trombetta
Paul M. James
Elise N. Zoli
Theodore F. Hanselman
Amy J. Mastrobattista
Joshua C. Krumholz
Leslie A. Sprinkle
Ieuan G. Mahony
Douglas W. Clapp

(See Next Column)

SHERBURNE, POWERS & NEEDHAM P.C.—*Continued*

Jeffrey A. Huebschmann	Kathaleen Kelly Cutone
Tamara E. Goulston	Laurie A. Tribble
Paul G. Lannon, Jr.	Neil C. Higgins
Nicholas J. Psyhogeos	Deborah Paige Stone
Edward J. Naughton	Brian R. Popiel

COUNSEL

Haig Der Manuelian	Karl J. Hirshman
Mason M. Taber, Jr.	Dale R. Johnson

For full biographical listings, see the Martindale-Hubbell Law Directory

ZALKIND, RODRIGUEZ, LUNT & DUNCAN (AV)

65A Atlantic Avenue, 02110
Telephone: 617-742-6020

MEMBERS OF FIRM

Norman S. Zalkind	Elizabeth A. Lunt
	David Duncan

ASSOCIATES

Inga S. Bernstein	William B. Van lonkhuyzen

OF COUNSEL

Barbara Equen Rodriguez	John Ward

For full biographical listings, see the Martindale-Hubbell Law Directory

CAMBRIDGE,* Middlesex Co.

GORMLEY & COLUCCI, P.C. (AV)

One Main Street, P.O. Box 965, 02142-0900
Telephone: 617-349-3750
Fax: 617-661-2576

George F. Gormley	John D. Colucci

For full biographical listings, see the Martindale-Hubbell Law Directory

FRAMINGHAM, Middlesex Co.

STEWART T. HERRICK & ASSOCIATES (AV)

Suite 303, 1661 Worcester Road, 01701
Telephone: 508-875-0021
FAX: 508-875-0029

ASSOCIATE
Lauren P. Smith

For full biographical listings, see the Martindale-Hubbell Law Directory

FRANKLIN, Norfolk Co.

PAUL A. CATALDO & ASSOCIATES (AV)

55 West Central Street, P.O. Box 435, 02038
Telephone: 508-528-2400
Fax: 508-520-0699

Paul A. Cataldo
ASSOCIATES

Cheryl A. Tracy	Joseph P. Cataldo

References: The Benjamin Franklin Savings Bank; Bank of Boston.

For full biographical listings, see the Martindale-Hubbell Law Directory

WORCESTER,* Worcester Co.

McGUIRE & McGUIRE, P.C. (AV)

340 Main Street, Suite 910, 01608
Telephone: 508-754-3291
Fax: 508-752-0553

John K. McGuire (1952-1985)	Joseph E. McGuire
	John K. McGuire, Jr.

Penelope A. Kathiwala	Paul Durkee
Christine Griggs Narcisse	Teresa Brooks
	John Pedone

For full biographical listings, see the Martindale-Hubbell Law Directory

REARDON & REARDON (AV)

One Exchange Place, 01608
Telephone: 508-754-1111
Fax: 508-797-6176
Boston, Massachusetts Office: 69 Beacon Street.
Telephone: 617-248-6998.
Fax: 617-248-0837.

MEMBERS OF FIRM

James G. Reardon	Margaret Reardon Suuberg
Edward P. Reardon	James G. Reardon, Jr.
Frank S. Puccio, Jr.	Julie E. Reardon
Austin M. Joyce	Michael J. Akerson
James G. Haddad	Francis J. Duggan

(See Next Column)

References: Mechanics National Bank; Shawmut Worcester County Bank N.A.; Bank of New England, Worcester.

For full biographical listings, see the Martindale-Hubbell Law Directory

MICHIGAN

ANN ARBOR,* Washtenaw Co.

HOOPER, HATHAWAY, PRICE, BEUCHE & WALLACE (AV)

126 South Main Street, 48104
Telephone: 313-662-4426
Fax: 313-662-9559

Joseph C. Hooper (1899-1980)	Gregory A. Spaly
Alan E. Price	Robert W. Southard
James R. Beuche	William J. Stapleton
Bruce T. Wallace	Bruce C. Conybeare, Jr.
Charles W. Borgsdorf	Anthony P. Patti
Mark R. Daane	Marcia J. Major

OF COUNSEL

James A. Evashevski	Roderick K. Daane

Representative Clients: Chem-Trend, Inc.; Dundee Cement Co.; Ervin Industries, Inc.; First Martin Corp.; Group 243 Design, Inc.; Honeywell; Microwave Sensors, Inc.; Shearson Lehman Hutton; O'Neal Construction Co.; Pittsfield Products, Inc.

For Complete List of Firm Personnel, See General Section

For full biographical listings, see the Martindale-Hubbell Law Directory

BINGHAM FARMS, Oakland Co.

HARNISCH & HOHAUSER, P.C. (AV)

30700 Telegraph Road, Suite 3475, 48025-4527
Telephone: 810-644-8600
Fax: 810-644-8344

Alan C. Harnisch	Michael S. Hohauser

Lawrence S. Gadd	William J. Yochim, Jr.

OF COUNSEL
Debra C. Holt

Representative Clients: Dealers Financial Service, Inc.; Eaton Corporation; Edgewood Electric, Inc.; ITT Commercial Finance; Jeffrey C. Harrell, Builder, Inc.; Johnson Controls, Inc.

For full biographical listings, see the Martindale-Hubbell Law Directory

BLOOMFIELD HILLS, Oakland Co.

BAUM & ASSOCIATES (AV)

200 East Long Lake Road Suite 180, 48304
Telephone: 810-647-6890

MEMBER OF FIRM
Martin S. Baum
ASSOCIATE
Margo S. Apple

For full biographical listings, see the Martindale-Hubbell Law Directory

ROBERT HARRISON & ASSOCIATES (AV)

Bloomfield Office Pavilion, 2550 Telegraph Road, Suite 275, 48302
Telephone: 810-253-1800
Fax: 810-253-9446

Robert S. Harrison
ASSOCIATES

Michael J. Rex	Paul M. Newcomer
	Michael James Harrison

References: Comerica Bank, Southfield; Huntington Banks of Michigan, W. Bloomfield.

For full biographical listings, see the Martindale-Hubbell Law Directory

DETROIT,* Wayne Co.

DAVID F. DuMOUCHEL, P.C. (AV)

150 West Jefferson, Suite 900, 48226-4430
Telephone: 313-225-7004

David F. DuMouchel

For full biographical listings, see the Martindale-Hubbell Law Directory

Detroit—Continued

DAVID GRIEM (AV)

One Woodward Avenue, Suite 2400, 48226
Telephone: 313-961-8380
Mount Clemens, Michigan Office: 14 First Street, 48043.
Telephone: 313-465-4900.

For full biographical listings, see the Martindale-Hubbell Law Directory

HONIGMAN MILLER SCHWARTZ AND COHN (AV)

A Partnership including Professional Corporations
2290 First National Building, 48226
Telephone: 313-256-7800
Telecopier: 313-962-0176
Telex: 235705
URL: http://law.honigman.com
Lansing, Michigan Office: Phoenix Building, 222 North Washington
Square, Suite 400, 48933-1800.
Telephone: 517-484-8282.
West Palm Beach, Florida Office: Suite 800 Esperante Building, 222
Lakeview Avenue, 33401-6112.
Telephone: 561-838-4500.
Tampa, Florida Office: 2700 SunTrust Financial Centre, 401 E. Jackson
Street, 33602-5226.
Telephone: 813-221-6600.

MEMBERS OF FIRM

Jay E. Brant	Mark R. Werder

Richard E. Zuckerman

For Complete List of Firm Personnel, See General Section

For full biographical listings, see the Martindale-Hubbell Law Directory

MARK J. KRIGER (AV)

One Kennedy Square, Suite 1938, 48226
Telephone: 313-963-7222
Southfield, Michigan Office: 29800 Telegraph Road.
Telephone: 810-353-6500.

For full biographical listings, see the Martindale-Hubbell Law Directory

KENNETH M. MOGILL (AV)

One Kennedy Square Building, Suite 1930, 719 Griswold, 48226
Telephone: 313-962-7210
Fax: 313-961-7799

For full biographical listings, see the Martindale-Hubbell Law Directory

STRINGARI, FRITZ, KREGER, AHEARN & CRANDALL, P.C. (AV)

510 First National Building, 48226-3538
Telephone: 313-961-6474
Fax: 313-961-5688

Martin E. Crandall	Kenneth S. Wilson

John C. Dickinson

For full biographical listings, see the Martindale-Hubbell Law Directory

---

EAST LANSING, Ingham Co.

FARHAT, STORY & KRAUS, P.C. (AV)

Beacon Place, 4572 South Hagadorn Road, Suite 3, 48823
Telephone: 517-351-3700
Fax: 517-332-4122
Email: rkraus@sojourn.com

Leo A. Farhat	Chris A. Bergstrom
James E. Burns (1925-1979)	Kitty L. Groh
Monte R. Story	Charles R. Toy
Richard C. Kraus	David M. Platt
Max R. Hoffman Jr.	Thomas L. Sparks
Lawrence P. Schweitzer	Daniel B. Morgan
Debra A. Geroux	Mary K. Robbins-Kralapp

Reference: City Bank, St. Johns.

For full biographical listings, see the Martindale-Hubbell Law Directory

---

FARMINGTON HILLS, Oakland Co.

CLYDE B. PRITCHARD (AV)

31420 Northwestern Highway, Suite 110, 48334
Telephone: 810-737-7003
Fax: 810-737-8205

GRAND RAPIDS, * Kent Co.

DAVID A. DODGE, P.C. (AV)

200 North Division Avenue, 49503
Telephone: 616-459-3850
Fax: 616-459-4909

David A. Dodge

For full biographical listings, see the Martindale-Hubbell Law Directory

---

WILLEY & CHAMBERLAIN, L.L.P. (AV)

940 Trust Building, 40 Pearl Street, N.W., 49503
Telephone: 616-458-2212
Fax: 616-458-1158

Larry C. Willey	Charles E. Chamberlain, Jr.

ASSOCIATE
Raymond E. Beckering, III

For full biographical listings, see the Martindale-Hubbell Law Directory

---

HANCOCK, Houghton Co.

WISTI & WISTI, P.C. (AV)

101 Quincy Street, 49930
Telephone: 906-482-5220
Fax: 906-482-8800
Iron Mountain, Michigan Office: 623 Stephenson Avenue.
Telephone: 906-779-1280.
Marquette, Michigan Office: 117 South Front Street.
Telephone: 906-228-8204.

Andrew H. Wisti	Mark Wisti

Daniel J. Wisti

Patricia A. Gotschalk

References: Superior National Bank & Trust Company of Hancock, Michigan; Houghton National Bank, Houghton, Michigan.

For full biographical listings, see the Martindale-Hubbell Law Directory

---

LANSING, Ingham Co.

DUNNINGS & FRAWLEY, P.C. (AV)

Duncan Building, 530 South Pine Street, 48933-2299
Telephone: 517-487-8222
Fax: 517-487-2026
Email: conrights@voyager.net

Stuart J. Dunnings, Jr.	John J. Frawley
Stuart J. Dunnings, III	Steven D. Dunnings

Shauna L. Dunnings

For full biographical listings, see the Martindale-Hubbell Law Directory

---

MOUNT CLEMENS, * Macomb Co.

DAVID GRIEM (AV)

14 First Street, 48043
Telephone: 810-465-4900
Detroit, Michigan Office: One Woodward Avenue, Suite 2400, 48226.
Telephone: 313-961-8380.

For full biographical listings, see the Martindale-Hubbell Law Directory

---

SOUTHFIELD, Oakland Co.

FIEGER, FIEGER & SCHWARTZ, A PROFESSIONAL CORPORATION (AV)

19390 West Ten Mile Road, 48075-2463
Telephone: 810-355-5555
Fax: 810-355-5148

Bernard J. Fieger (1922-1988)	Todd J. Weglarz
Geoffrey N. Fieger	Rebecca S. Eaton
Michael Alan Schwartz	Ven R. Johnson

William J. McHenry
OF COUNSEL

Barry Fayne	Beverly Hires Brode

Keitha Kay Cowen

For full biographical listings, see the Martindale-Hubbell Law Directory

SOMMERS, SCHWARTZ, SILVER & SCHWARTZ, P.C. (AV)

2000 Town Center, Suite 900, 48075
Telephone: 810-355-0300
Telecopier: 810-746-4001
Plymouth, Michigan Office: 747 South Main Street.
Telephone: 313-455-4250.

Lawrence Warren	David M. Black
Justin C. Ravitz	Matthew G. Curtis

General Counsel for: City of Taylor; Township of Van Buren.
Representative Clients: City of Pontiac.

For Complete List of Firm Personnel, See General Section

For full biographical listings, see the Martindale-Hubbell Law Directory

EMPLOYMENT BENEFITS LAW

ALABAMA

*BIRMINGHAM,** Jefferson Co.

BRADLEY, ARANT, ROSE & WHITE (AV)

2001 Park Place, Suite 1400, P.O. Box 830709, 35283-0709
Telephone: 205-521-8000
Facsimile: 205-252-0264
Facsimile (SouthTrust Tower Office): 205-251-9915
URL: http://www.BARW.COM
Huntsville, Alabama Office: 200 Clinton Avenue West, Suite 900, 35801.
Telephone: 205-517-5100.
Facsimile: 205-533-5069.

MEMBERS OF FIRM

John James Coleman, Jr.	James Walker May
Robert G. Johnson	James S. Christie, Jr.

ASSOCIATES

Kevin J. Henderson	Abdul K. Kallon
T. Matthew Miller	Kelly Hubbard Estes

For Complete List of Firm Personnel, See General Section

For full biographical listings, see the Martindale-Hubbell Law Directory

GORDON, SILBERMAN, WIGGINS & CHILDS, A PROFESSIONAL CORPORATION (AV)

1400 SouthTrust Tower, 420 North 20th Street, 35203
Telephone: 205-328-0640
Telecopier: 205-254-1500

Wilbur G. Silberman	C. Michael Quinn
Bruce L. Gordon	Dennis George Pantazis
Robert L. Wiggins, Jr.	Terrill W. Sanders
Robert F. Childs, Jr.	James Mendelsohn
Augustus J. Beck, Jr.	Richard J. Ebbinghouse
Harvey L. Wachsman	Ann K. Wiggins
Ray D. Gibbons	Samuel Fisher
	Ann C. Robertson

Paul H. Webb	Byron R. Perkins
Mark P. Williams	Jon C. Goldfarb
Timothy C. Gann	Gregory O. Wiggins
Timothy D. Davis	Lee Winston
Joseph H. Calvin, III	Jon E. Lewis
Linda J. Peacock	Deborah A. Mattison
Elizabeth Evans Courtney	Rocco Calamusa, Jr.

OF COUNSEL
Robert H. Loeb

For Complete List of Firm Personnel, See General Section

For full biographical listings, see the Martindale-Hubbell Law Directory

LONDON & YANCEY (AV)

1000 Park Place Tower, 2001 Park Place, 35203
Telephone: 205-251-2531
FAX: 205-251-8929

MEMBERS OF FIRM

Alex T. London (1847-1908)	Thomas R. Elliott, Jr.
John London (1848-1935)	Bert S. Nettles
George W. Yancey (1883-1962)	Richard W. Lewis

ASSOCIATES

Allen R. Trippeer, Jr.	Laura Ellison Proctor
Mark David Hess	Paige Elliott-Pinson
Lisa Wright Borden	F. Daniel Wood, Jr.
A. David Fawal	C. Dennis Hughes
	Michael J. Velezis

OF COUNSEL
Robert W. Norris

Representative Clients: State of Alabama; Cincinnati Ins. Co.; Lloyd's of London; Blue Cross/Blue Shield; Attorney's Mutual of Alabama; State Farm; CIGNA; Royal Ins. Co. of America; Paul Revere Ins. Co.; Chubb Group.

For full biographical listings, see the Martindale-Hubbell Law Directory

*MOBILE,** Mobile Co.

ARMBRECHT, JACKSON, DeMOUY, CROWE, HOLMES & REEVES, L.L.C. (AV)

1300 AmSouth Center, P.O. Box 290, 36601
Telephone: 334-405-1300
Facsimile: 334-432-6843; 433-3821

(See Next Column)

MEMBERS OF FIRM

Broox G. Holmes, Jr.	William B. Harvey
	James Donald Hughes

Representative Clients: Cooper/T. Smith Stevedoring Co., Inc.; Loyal American Life Insurance Co.; Mobile Gas Service Corp.; Mobile Steamship Ass'n -- International Longshoremen's Pension, Welfare & Vacation Plans; Southern Pine Inspection Bureau; United Bank; WKRG-TV, Inc.

For Complete List of Firm Personnel, See General Section

For full biographical listings, see the Martindale-Hubbell Law Directory

JOHNSTONE, ADAMS, BAILEY, GORDON AND HARRIS, L.L.C. (AV)

Royal St. Francis Building, 104 St. Francis Street, P.O. Box 1988, 36633
Telephone: 334-432-7682
Facsimile: 334-432-2800
Telex: 782040

MEMBERS OF FIRM

Brock B. Gordon	Wade B. Perry, Jr.
Ben H. Harris, Jr.	Gregory C. Buffalow
E. Watson Smith	Celia J. Collins
Joseph M. Allen, Jr.	R. Gregory Watts

ASSOCIATE
Tracy P. Turner

General Counsel for: First Alabama Bank, Mobile; Infirmary Health System/Mobile Infirmary Medical Center/Rotary Rehabilitation Hospital (Multi-Hospital System).
Counsel for: Oil and Gas: Exxon Corp. Business and Corporate: Bell South Telecommunications, Inc.; Aluminum Co. of America; Michelin North America, Inc.; Metropolitan Life Insurance Co.; The Travelers Insurance Cos. Marine: The West of England Ship Owners Mutual Protection and Indemnity Association (Luxembourg); The Standard Steamship Owners' Protection and Indemnity Association (Bermuda) Ltd.

For Complete List of Firm Personnel, See General Section

For full biographical listings, see the Martindale-Hubbell Law Directory

ARIZONA

*PHOENIX,** Maricopa Co.

FENNEMORE CRAIG, A PROFESSIONAL CORPORATION (AV)

Two North Central, Suite 2200, 85004
Telephone: 602-257-8700
Fax: 602-257-8527
Scottsdale, Arizona Office: 6263 North Scottsdale Road, Suite 290, 85250.
Telephone: 602-257-5400.
Fax: 602-257-5409.
Tucson, Arizona Office: One South Church Avenue, Suite 1030, 85701.
Telephone: 520-791-6800.
Fax: 520-791-6820.

Cynthia L. Shupe	David N. Heap

For Complete List of Firm Personnel, See General Section

For full biographical listings, see the Martindale-Hubbell Law Directory

SHIMMEL, HILL, BISHOP & GRUENDER, P.C. (AV)

3700 North 24th Street, 85016
Telephone: 602-224-9500
Telecopier: 602-955-6176

Daniel F. Gruender	Keith F. Overholt
	James L. Person

Representative Clients: Harkins Amusement Enterprises, Inc.; Citizen Auto Stage Line; Delta Airlines; Grayline Sightseeing Association.

For full biographical listings, see the Martindale-Hubbell Law Directory

SNELL & WILMER, L.L.P. (AV)

One Arizona Center, 85004-0001
Telephone: 602-382-6000
Fax: 602-382-6070
Tucson, Arizona Office: 1500 Norwest Tower, One South Church Avenue 85701-1612.
Telephone: 520-882-1200.
Fax: 520-884-1294.
Orange County Office: 1920 Main Street, Suite 1200, P.O. Box 57062, Irvine, California, 92619-7062.
Telephone: 714-253-2700.
Fax: 714-955-2507.

(See Next Column)

SNELL & WILMER L.L.P., Phoenix—Continued

Salt Lake City, Utah Office: Broadway Centre, 111 East Broadway, Suite 900, 84111-1004.
Telephone: 801-237-1900.
Fax: 801-237-1950.

MEMBERS OF FIRM

Robert J. Deeny
Gerard Morales

William R. Hayden
Rebecca A. Winterscheidt

Charles P. Keller

SENIOR ATTORNEY

William P. Allen

ASSOCIATE

Joseph E. Lambert

Representative Clients: ABF Freight System, Inc.; Apollo Group, Inc.; Banc One Corp.; Brown & Root; Centex Corp.; Del Webb; Intel Corp.; Mayo Clinic; Remington Arms Company, Inc.; Service Corporation International.

For Complete List of Firm Personnel, See General Section

For full biographical listings, see the Martindale-Hubbell Law Directory

---

TUCSON,* Pima Co.

DANIEL H. O'CONNELL, P.C. (AV)

Suite 510, 6245 East Broadway, 85711
Telephone: 520-790-2535
Telefax: 520-571-8148

Daniel H. O'Connell

Benjamin J. Burnside

OF COUNSEL

Rosanne F. Lapan

Representative Clients: Empire West Cos.; Southwest Energy, Inc.; Alban Medical Associates; Industrial Motor & Control, Inc.; Allergy Asthma Associates, P.C.
Reference: Bank of America.

For full biographical listings, see the Martindale-Hubbell Law Directory

---

SNELL & WILMER, L.L.P. (AV)

1500 Norwest Tower, One South Church Avenue, 85701-1612
Telephone: 520-882-1200
Fax: 520-884-1294
Phoenix, Arizona Office: One Arizona Center, 85004-0001.
Telephone: 602-382-6000.
Fax: 602-382-6070.
Orange County Office: 1920 Main Street, Suite 1200, P.O. Box 57062, Irvine, California, 92619-7062.
Telephone: 714-253-2700
Fax: 714-955-2507.
Salt Lake City, Utah Office: Broadway Centre, 111 East Broadway, Suite 900, 84111- 1004.
Telephone: 801-237-1900.
Fax: 801-237-1950.

MEMBERS OF FIRM

John A. Robertson

Sandra S. Froman

Representative Clients: Apache Nitrogen Products, Inc.; Arizona Electric Power Cooperative, Inc.; ASARCO; Association of Universities for Research in Astronomy, Inc.; BHP Copper, Inc. (formerly Magna Copper Company); Insight Distribution Network, Inc.; Lockheed-Martin Corp.; McDonnell Douglas Helicopter Systems; State of Arizona; Transit Management of Tucson, Inc.

For full biographical listings, see the Martindale-Hubbell Law Directory

---

ARKANSAS

LITTLE ROCK,* Pulaski Co.

PLASTIRAS, HYDEN & MIRON (AV)

A Partnership of Professional Associations
200 Louisiana, 72201
Telephone: 501-376-8222
Fax: 501-376-7047
1-800-467-8297
Hot Springs Village, Arkansas Office: Village Square, Suite "G", 4501 North Highway 7.
Telephone: 501-984-6366.
Fax: 501-984-6366. 1-800-467-8297.
Pine Bluff, Arkansas Office: 620 South Laurel.
Telephone: 501-536-8222. 1-800-467-8297.

MEMBERS OF FIRM

George N. Plastiras (P.A.)

James W. Hyden (P.A.)

Philip Miron (P.A.)

(See Next Column)

OF COUNSEL

James F. Goodhart

ASSOCIATES

Lyle D. Foster

Anthony A. Hilliard

For full biographical listings, see the Martindale-Hubbell Law Directory

ROSE LAW FIRM, A PROFESSIONAL ASSOCIATION (AV)

120 East Fourth Street, 72201
Telephone: 501-375-9131
Telecopy: 501-375-1309

Tim Boe

James Hunter Birch

James M. Gary

Mark Alan Peoples

David P. Martin

Kathryn Bennett Perkins

Counsel for: Aluminum Company of America; Bridgestone/Firestone, Inc.; The Equitable Life Assurance Society of The United States; General Motors Corp.; The Prudential Insurance Company of America; Stephens Group Inc.; TCBY Enterprises, Inc.; Tyson Foods, Inc.

For Complete List of Firm Personnel, See General Section

For full biographical listings, see the Martindale-Hubbell Law Directory

---

CALIFORNIA

COSTA MESA, Orange Co.

RUTAN & TUCKER, LLP (AV)

A Partnership including Professional Corporations
611 Anton Boulevard, Suite 1400, P.O. Box 1950, 92626
Telephone: 714-641-5100; 213-625-7586
Telecopier: 714-546-9035
Email: rutan&tucker@mcimail.com *URL:* http://www.rutan.com

MEMBER OF FIRM

David C. Larsen (P.C.)

For Complete List of Firm Personnel, See General Section

For full biographical listings, see the Martindale-Hubbell Law Directory

---

FRESNO,* Fresno Co.

KIMBLE, MACMICHAEL & UPTON, A PROFESSIONAL CORPORATION (AV)

Fig Garden Financial Center, 5260 North Palm Avenue, Suite 221, P.O. Box 9489, 93792-9489
Telephone: 209-435-5500
Telecopier: 209-435-1500
Email: kmu@primenet.com

Joseph C. Kimble (1910-1972)
Thomas A. MacMichael (1920-1990)
Jon Wallace Upton
Robert E. Bergin
Jeffrey G. Boswell
Steven D. McGee
Robert E. Ward
John P. Eleazarian

Robert H. Scribner
Michael E. Moss
Mark D. Miller
Michael F. Tatham
W. Richard Lee
D. Tyler Tharpe
Sylvia Halkousis Coyle
S. Brett Sutton
Michael J. Jurkovich

Douglas V. Thornton
Robert William Branch
Donald J. Pool

Susan King Hatmaker
Lawrence J. Salisbury
Daniel R. Foster

Meredith E. Allen

OF COUNSEL

Mary Ann Bluhm

For full biographical listings, see the Martindale-Hubbell Law Directory

---

GLENDALE, Los Angeles Co.

HAGENBAUGH & MURPHY (AV)

A Partnership including Professional Corporations
700 North Central Avenue, Suite 500, 91203
Telephone: 818-240-2600
Fax: 818-240-1253
Email: hmurphy@interserv.com *URL:* http://www.seamless.com/hm/
Orange County, California Office: 701 South Parker Street, Suite 8200, Orange.
Telephone: 714-835-5406.
Fax: 714-835-5949.
San Bernardino, California Office: 301 Vanderbilt Way, Suite 220.
Telephone: 909-884-5331.
FAX: 909-889-1250.

(See Next Column)

HAGENBAUGH & MURPHY—*Continued*

Van A. Hagenbaugh (1914-1980)
Sigurd E. Murphy (1903-1976)
William D. Stewart (A P.C.)
John J. Tary (A P.C.)
Raymond R. Moore (A P.C.)
Neil R. Gunny (Resident,
  Orange County Office)
Alan R. Zuckerman
David L. Winter
Mary E. Porter

Daniel A. Leipold (Resident,
  Orange County Office)
Craig D. Aronson
Paul G. Szumiak
Robert F. Donohue (Resident,
  Orange County Office)
Katharine L. Spaniac (Resident,
  San Bernardino Office)
Alan H. Boon (Resident, Orange
  County Office)

Jamie B. Skebba

Raymond T. Gail (Resident, San
  Bernardino Office)
Kirk G. Neiberger
Meredith A. Musicant
David M. Chute (Resident,
  Orange County Office)
Luanne Walsh
Rhonda L. Etzwiler
Steven M. Schuetze
Thomas J. Heatly
Matthew R. Rungaitis
Stephen Barry
Julie M. DeRose
Randal A. Whitecotton
  (Resident, San Bernardino
  Office)

Cathy L. Shipe (Resident,
  Orange County Office)
Keri Lynn Bush
Michael A. Tonya
Laura C. McLennan
Graciela L. Freixes
Melinda W. Ebelhar
Kirk N. Sullivan
Gary P. Simonian
Mark Habeeb
Howard J. Hirsch (Resident,
  Orange County Office)
Michelle Mann

Representative Clients: Farmers Insurance Group; Truck Insurance Exchange; Fire Insurance Exchange.

For full biographical listings, see the Martindale-Hubbell Law Directory

---

IRVINE, Orange Co.

BARNES, CROSBY, FITZGERALD & ZEMAN (AV)

2030 Main Street, Suite 1050, 92614
Telephone: 714-852-1100
Fax: 714-852-1501

MEMBERS OF FIRM

Robert Samuel Barnes
William M. Crosby
Michael J. FitzGerald

Larry S. Zeman
Mark H. Cheung
Alka N. Patel

OF COUNSEL
Frederick J. Stemmler

For full biographical listings, see the Martindale-Hubbell Law Directory

GAUNTLETT & ASSOCIATES (AV)

18400 Von Karman, Suite 300, 92612
Telephone: 714-553-1010
Fax: 714-553-2050
Email: ugauntlett@aol.com

David A. Gauntlett

David A. Stall
Leo E. Lundberg, Jr.
Michael Danton Richardson
William P. Warden
Stanley H. Shure

Elizabeth A. Gillis
  (Not admitted in CA)
Mark H. Plager
  (Not admitted in CA)
Jeffrey S. Allison

OF COUNSEL

Gary L. Hinman

Jose Zorrilla, Jr.

For full biographical listings, see the Martindale-Hubbell Law Directory

---

LOS ANGELES, * Los Angeles Co.

ANTIN & TAYLOR (AV)

1875 Century Park East, Suite 700, 90067
Telephone: 310-788-2733
Fax: 310-788-0754
Email: mantin@ix.netcom.com

MEMBERS OF FIRM

Michael Antin

Michael L. Taylor

For full biographical listings, see the Martindale-Hubbell Law Directory

ALEX M. BRUCKER A LAW CORPORATION (AV)

10880 Wilshire Boulevard, Suite 2210, 90024
Telephone: 310-475-7540
Fax: 310-470-4806
URL: http://www.pensionlawyers.com

Alex M. Brucker

(See Next Column)

Linda Russano Morra

Michael L. Cotter

Scott E. Hiltunen

For full biographical listings, see the Martindale-Hubbell Law Directory

O'MELVENY & MYERS LLP (AV)

400 South Hope Street, 90071-2899
Telephone: 213-669-6000
Cable Address: "Moms"
Facsimile: 213-669-6407
Email: omminfo@omm.com
Century City, California Office: 1999 Avenue of the Stars, 90067-6035.
Telephone: 310-553-6700.
Facsimile: 310-246-6779.
Newport Beach, California Office: 610 Newport Center Drive, 92660-6429.
Telephone: 714-760-9600.
Cable Address: "Moms".
Facsimile: 714-669-6994.
San Francisco, California Office: Embarcadero Center West Tower, 275 Battery Street, 94111-3305.
Telephone: 415-984-8700.
Facsimile: 415-984-8701.
New York, New York Office: Citicorp Center, 153 East 53rd Street, 10022-4611.
Telephone: 212-326-2000.
Facsimile: 212-326-2061.
Washington, D.C. Office: 555 13th Street, N.W., 20004-1109.
Telephone: 202-383-5300.
Cable Address: "Moms".
Facsimile: 202-383-5414.
London, England Office: 10 Finsbury Square, London, EC2A 1LA.
Telephone: 0171-256-8451.
Facsimile: 0171-638-8205.
Tokyo, Japan Office: Sanbancho KB-6 Building, 6 Sanbancho, Chiyoda-ku, Tokyo 102, Japan.
Telephone: 03-3239-2900.
Facsimile: 03-3239-2432.
Hong Kong Office: Suite 1905, Peregrine Tower, Lippo Centre, 89 Queensway, Central, Hong Kong.
Telephone: 852-2523-8266.
Facsimile: 852-2522-1760.
Shanghai, Peoples Republic of China Office: Shanghai International Trade Centre, Suite 2011, 2200 Yan An Road West, Shanghai, 200335, PRC.
Telephone: 86-21-6219-5363.
Facsimile: 86-21-6275-4949.

PARTNER
David E. Gordon

For Complete List of Firm Personnel, See General Section

For full biographical listings, see the Martindale-Hubbell Law Directory

REISH & LUFTMAN, A PROFESSIONAL CORPORATION (AV)

11755 Wilshire Boulevard 10th Floor, 90025
Telephone: 310-478-5656
Facsimile: 310-478-5831
URL: http://www.benefitslink.com/reish/
Washington, D.C. Office: One Massachusetts Avenue, N.W., Suite 800, 20001.
Telephone: 202-745-0024.
Facsimile: 202-745-0005.

Bruce L. Ashton
Roland M. Attenborough
Joseph C. Faucher
Martin M. Heming

James R. McDaniel
C. Frederick Reish
Mark E. Terman
Michael A. Vanic

Lynn B. Witte

Fernando L. Delmendo

Ilene Hirsch Ferenczy

For full biographical listings, see the Martindale-Hubbell Law Directory

SCHWARTZ, STEINSAPIR, DOHRMANN & SOMMERS (AV)

6300 Wilshire Boulevard, Suite 2000, 90048
Telephone: 213-655-4700
Fax: 213-655-4488
Pittsburgh, Pennsylvania Office: 3600 One Oxford Centre.
Telephone: 412-456-2008.
Fax: 412-456-2020.

MEMBERS OF FIRM

Laurence D. Steinsapir
Robert M. Dohrmann
Richard D. Sommers
Stuart Libicki
Michael R. Feinberg
Michael D. Four

Margo A. Feinberg
Henry M. Willis
Dennis J. Murphy
D. William Heine, Jr.
Claude Cazzulino
Dolly M. Gee

ASSOCIATE
Erika A. Zucker

For full biographical listings, see the Martindale-Hubbell Law Directory

MONTEREY, Monterey Co.

HARRAY, MASUDA & LINKER (AV)

80 Garden Court, Suite 260, 93940
Telephone: 408-373-3101
Fax: 408-373-6712

Richard K. Harray   Michael P. Masuda
Stan L. Linker

For full biographical listings, see the Martindale-Hubbell Law Directory

NEWPORT BEACH, Orange Co.

YOUNG & AMUNDSEN (AV)

620 Newport Center Drive, Suite 420, 92660
Telephone: 714-640-4400
Fax: 714-717-4862

MEMBERS OF FIRM

Steven R. Young   Roland J. Amundsen

For full biographical listings, see the Martindale-Hubbell Law Directory

ONTARIO, San Bernardino Co.

COVINGTON & CROWE (AV)

1131 West Sixth Street, P.O. Box 1515, 91762
Telephone: 909-983-9393
Fax: 909-391-6762
Email: covcrowe@ix.netcom.com

MEMBERS OF FIRM

Harold A. Bailin (1930-1988)	Stephen R. Wade
Samuel P. Crowe	Jette R. Anderson
George W. Porter	Audrey A. Perri
Robert E. Dougherty	Tracy L. Tibbals
Donald G. Haslam	Melanie Fisch
Robert F. Schauer	Robert H. Reeder
Edward A. Hopson	R. Doug Donesky

Tammy S. Jager

ASSOCIATES

Howard S. Borenstein	Richard R. Muir
Denise Matthey	Kimberly A. Rohn
Katrina West	J. Michael Kaler

Eric S. Vail

For full biographical listings, see the Martindale-Hubbell Law Directory

SACRAMENTO,* Sacramento Co.

MATHENY POIDMORE LINKERT & SEARS (AV)

3638 American River Drive, P.O. Box 13711, 95853-4711
Telephone: 916-978-3434
Fax: 916-978-3430
Email: mpls1@netcom.com

MEMBERS OF FIRM

Henry G. Matheny (1933-1984)	James C. Damir
Anthony J. Poidmore	Michael A. Bishop
Douglas A. Sears	Ernest A. Long
Richard S. Linkert	Joann Georgallis

Kent M. Luckey

ASSOCIATES

Matthew C. Jaime	Cathy A. Reynolds
Robert B. Berrigan	Eric R. Wiesel
Stephen J. Nardine	Reed R. Johnson
Ronald E. Enabnit	Danielle M. Guard

Andrea M. Croak

LEGAL SUPPORT PERSONNEL

PARALEGALS

Karen D. Fisher	Lynell Rae Steed
Fran Studer	Jennifer Bachman

Debbie Sue Miller

For full biographical listings, see the Martindale-Hubbell Law Directory

SAN DIEGO,* San Diego Co.

STEPHENSON WORLEY GARRATT SCHWARTZ HEIDEL & PRAIRIE (AV)

A Limited Liability Partnership
101 West Broadway, Suite 1300, 92101-8214
Telephone: 619-696-3500
Fax: 619-696-3555
Email: SDLAW@swgshp.com

MEMBERS OF FIRM

Gary J. Stephenson	Michael W. Prairie
Donald R. Worley	Timothy K. Garfield
Gregory C. M. Garratt	Lori A. Chamberlain
William J. Schwartz, Jr.	Jennifer Treese Wilson
Lynne L. Heidel	Amy Rosen

James B. MacRobbie

(See Next Column)

OF COUNSEL

Kent H. Foster   Elaine L. Chan
Reference: Bank of Commerce.

For full biographical listings, see the Martindale-Hubbell Law Directory

SAN FRANCISCO,* San Francisco Co.

LUDWIG GOLDBERG & KRENZEL, A PROFESSIONAL CORPORATION (AV)

36th Floor, 50 California Street, 94111
Telephone: 415-788-7200
Fax: 415-433-6496

Ronald L. Ludwig	Jeffrey F. Krenzel
Laurence A. Goldberg	Karen D. Ng

For full biographical listings, see the Martindale-Hubbell Law Directory

SUSAN RUBENSTEIN (AV)

351 California Street, Suite 700, 94104
Telephone: 415-434-9800
Fax: 415-434-0513

For full biographical listings, see the Martindale-Hubbell Law Directory

SAN MATEO, San Mateo Co.

QUADROS & JOHNSON (AV)

1400 Fashion Island Boulevard, Suite 800, 94404
Telephone: 415-377-4300
Telecopier: 415-573-1387

Katherine M. Quadros   Benjamin A. Johnson

SENIOR ASSOCIATE

Kenyon Mark Lee

ASSOCIATES

Leslie A. Eberhardt   Michael D. Wood

OF COUNSEL

Arthur L. Hillman, Jr.

Representative Clients: Anning Johnson Co. (national gypsum board and asbestos abatement contractor); Bechtel Corporation; Blue Cross of California (major health benefits insurer); Browning-Ferris Industries, Inc. (national waste management company); Los Angeles County Metropolitan Transportation Authority; Mutual Savings & Loan; Pacific Gas and Electric Co.; Safeway, Inc.; Santa Clara County Transit District; Sasco Electric.

For full biographical listings, see the Martindale-Hubbell Law Directory

---

COLORADO

DENVER,* Denver Co.

ALEXANDER & CRABTREE, P.C. (AV)

216 16th Street, Suite 1300, 80202-5127
Telephone: 303-825-7307
Fax: 303-825-3202
Email: halexand@alexcrab.com *URL:* http://www.alexcrab.com

Hugh Alexander   C. Scott Crabtree

Stephen Fitzsimmons

For full biographical listings, see the Martindale-Hubbell Law Directory

WHITE AND STEELE, PROFESSIONAL CORPORATION (AV)

1225 17th Street, Suite 2800, 80202
Telephone: 303-296-2828
Telecopier: 303-296-3131
Email: law@wsteele.com
Cheyenne, Wyoming Office: 1912 Capital Avenue, Suite 416, 82003.
Telephone: 307-778-4160.
Telecopier: 307-778-7041.

James M. Dieterich   Sandra L. Spencer

Michelle R. Magruder   Frank D. Sledge

OF COUNSEL

Kevin W. Hecht

Colorado Tort Counsel for: Goodyear Tire and Rubber Co.; The Dow Chemical Co.; Firestone Tire and Rubber Co.
Insurance Clients: Allied Insurance Co.; CNA; Kemper Insurance Group; Massachusetts Mutual Life Insurance Co.; Underwriters at Lloyds; U.S.A.A.

For Complete List of Firm Personnel, See General Section

For full biographical listings, see the Martindale-Hubbell Law Directory

CONNECTICUT

GROTON, New London Co.

MOUKAWSHER & WALSH LLC (AV)

328 Mitchell Street, P.O. Box 966, 06340
Telephone: 860-445-1809
Fax: 860-446-8161
Email: moukwals@mail.snet.net
Hartford, Connecticut Office: 21 Oak Street.
Telephone: 860-549-8440.
Fax: 860-549-8443.

Joseph E. Moukawsher	Thomas G. Moukawsher
Michael J. Walsh	Ann W. Henderson

Reference: Fleet Bank.

For full biographical listings, see the Martindale-Hubbell Law Directory

*HARTFORD,** Hartford Co.

SOROKIN SOROKIN GROSS HYDE & WILLIAMS P.C. (AV)

One Corporate Center, 06103
Telephone: 860-525-6645
Fax: 860-522-1781
Simsbury, Connecticut Office: 730 Hopmeadow Street.
Telephone: 860-651-9348.
Rocky Hill, Connecticut Office: 2360 Main Street.
Telephone: 860-563-9305.
Fax: 860-529-6931.

Barrie K. Wetstone

Sharon Kowal Freilich

For Complete List of Firm Personnel, See General Section

For full biographical listings, see the Martindale-Hubbell Law Directory

SOUTHPORT, Fairfield Co.

BRODY AND OBER, P.C. (AV)

135 Rennell Drive, P.O. Box 572, 06490-0572
Telephone: 203-259-7405
Fax: 203-255-8572

Charles S. Brody (1894-1976)	S. Giles Payne
Seth O. L. Brody	William J. Britt
Stanley B. Garrell	Barbara S. Miller
Frank F. Ober	Ronald B. Noren

Diane F. Martucci	Seth L. Cooper
Douglas R. Brown	

OF COUNSEL

James M. Thorburn	John F. Merchant

For full biographical listings, see the Martindale-Hubbell Law Directory

DELAWARE

*WILMINGTON,** New Castle Co.

POTTER ANDERSON & CORROON (AV)

350 Delaware Trust Building, P.O. Box 951, 19899-0951
Telephone: 302-984-6000
FAX: 302-658-1192
URL: HTTP://ATTYS.PACDELAWARE.COM

MEMBER OF FIRM
Mary E. Copper

Representative Clients: KOA Corporation of America; The Andrew Jergens Company; Delaware Trust Capital Management, Inc.; Delmarva Power & Light Company; E.I. du Pont de Nemours & Co.; The Equitable Life Assurance Society of the United States; Winterthur Museum.

For Complete List of Firm Personnel, See General Section

For full biographical listings, see the Martindale-Hubbell Law Directory

DISTRICT OF COLUMBIA

WASHINGTON, D.C. Co.

* indicates certain Bar Register subscribers, in cities of comparable size and importance, who maintain an additional office in Washington, D.C. and who have arranged for representation as a part of the Washington, D.C. listings that follow

ALEXANDER, BEARDEN, HAIRSTON & MARKS, LLP (AV)

Limited Liability Partnership
2021 L Street, N.W., Suite 300, 20036
Telephone: 202-293-3700
Fax: 202-293-7359
Silver Spring, Maryland Office: Lee Plaza, Suite 805, 8601 Georgia Avenue, 20910.
Telephone: 301-589-2222.
Facsimile: 301-539-2523.
New York, New York Office: 330 Madison Avenue, 36th Floor.
Telephone: 212-808-0008.
Fax: 212-599-1028.

Koteles Alexander

Reference: Riggs National Bank of Washington, D.C.

For full biographical listings, see the Martindale-Hubbell Law Directory

KENNETH R. FEINBERG & ASSOCIATES (AV)

1120 20th Street, N.W. Suite 740 South, 20036
Telephone: 202-371-1110
Fax: 202-962-9290
New York, N.Y. Office: 780 3rd Avenue, Suite 2202.
Telephone: 212-527-9600.
Fax: 212-527-9611.

ASSOCIATES

Deborah E. Greenspan	Peter H. Woodin
Michael K. Rozen	(Not admitted in DC)
(Not admitted in DC)	M. Catherine Faint

OF COUNSEL
Jacqueline E. Zins

For full biographical listings, see the Martindale-Hubbell Law Directory

GROOM AND NORDBERG, CHARTERED (AV)

1701 Pennsylvania Avenue, N.W., Suite 1200, 20006
Telephone: 202-857-0620
Telecopier: 202-659-4503

Theodore R. Groom	William G. Schiffbauer
Carl A. Nordberg, Jr.	Charles W. Sherman, Jr.
Robert B. Harding	Thomas F. Fitzgerald
Louis T. Mazawey	William J. Flanagan
Michael F. Kelleher	Lonie Hassel
Irene Price	Linda K. Shore
Gary M. Ford	Thomas S. Gigot
Daniel Horowitz	Holly K. Hemphill
Robert P. Gallagher	Robin L. Greenhouse
Stephen M. Saxon	Ian D. Lanoff
Douglas W. Ell	Lynda Joy Striegel
William F. Hanrahan	Brenda R. Viehe-Naess
John P. McAllister	William M. Evans
Alan L. Fischl	Andrée M. St. Martin
(Not admitted in DC)	Jon W. Breyfogle
	(Not admitted in DC)

NON-ATTORNEY MEMBER
Peter E. Holmes
COUNSEL

John F. Murray	David W. Powell
Lincoln D. Weed	Edward B. Horahan III
Michael A. Thrasher	
(Not admitted in DC)	

Steven D. Jensen	J. René Toadvine
(Not admitted in DC)	Angela C. Montez
Regina M. Pizzonia	(Not admitted in DC)
(Not admitted in DC)	Brigen Lee Winters
Roberta J. Ufford	Mary Ann Dominy Edgar
Kevin M. O'Toole	Carl R. Erdmann
L. Richard Winchester	(Not admitted in DC)
(Not admitted in DC)	Kathryn A. English
Mark L. Lofgren	Patrick J. Morgan
(Not admitted in DC)	(Not admitted in DC)
Maria O'Toole Jones	Elizabeth Thomas Dold
Edward R. Horkan	(Not admitted in DC)

LEGAL SUPPORT PERSONNEL
CONSULTANTS
Jill Leonhardt

(See Next Column)

GROOM AND NORDBERG CHARTERED, *Washington—Continued*
FINANCIAL ECONOMIST
Stephen C. Oakley

For full biographical listings, see the Martindale-Hubbell Law Directory

SCHMELTZER, APTAKER & SHEPARD, P.C. (AV)

The Watergate, Suite 1000, 2600 Virginia Avenue, N.W., 20037-1905
Telephone: 202-333-8800
Cable Address: "Ship"
Telex: 440517
Facsimile: 202-342-3434
Email: sas@saslaw.com *URL:* http://www.saspc.com
Los Angeles, California Office: 1999 Avenue of the Stars, Twenty-Seventh Floor, 90067-4095.
Telephone: 310-557-2966.
FAX: 310-286-6610.

Ira M. Shepard　　　　　　Paul M. Heylman
Scott Robins

For full biographical listings, see the Martindale-Hubbell Law Directory

* VENABLE ATTORNEYS AT LAW VENABLE, BAETJER, HOWARD & CIVILETTI, LLP (AV)

A Partnership including Professional Corporations
Suite 1000, 1201 New York Avenue, N.W., 20005
Telephone: 202-962-4800
Fax: 202-962-8300
Baltimore, Maryland Office: Venable, Baetjer and Howard LLP, 1800 Mercantile Bank & Trust Building, 2 Hopkins Plaza.
Telephone: 410-244-7400.
McLean, Virginia Office: Venable, Baetjer and Howard LLP, Suite 400, 2010 Corporate Ridge.
Telephone: 703-760-1600.
Rockville, Maryland Office: Venable, Baetjer and Howard LLP, Suite 500, One Church Street, P. O. Box 1906.
Telephone: 301-217-5600.
Towson, Maryland Office: Venable, Baetjer and Howard LLP, 210 Allegheny Avenue, P. O. Box 5517.
Telephone: 410-494-6200.

MEMBERS OF FIRM
Douglas D. Connah, Jr. (P.C.)　　Maurice Baskin
(Also at Baltimore, Maryland　　James A. Dunbar (Also at
Office)　　　　　　　　　　Baltimore, Maryland Office)
George F. Pappas (Also at
Baltimore, Maryland Office)

For Complete List of Firm Personnel, See General Section

For full biographical listings, see the Martindale-Hubbell Law Directory

FLORIDA

FORT MYERS,* Lee Co.

SMOOT ADAMS EDWARDS & GREEN, P.A. (AV)

One University Park Suite 600, 12800 University Drive, P.O. Box 60259, 33906-6259
Telephone: 941-489-1776
(800) 226-1777 (in Florida)
Fax: 941-489-2444
Email: 71600.2745@compuserve.com

J. Tom Smoot, Jr.　　　　　Bruce D. Green
Hal Adams　　　　　　　　Steven I. Winer
Franklyn A. (Chip) Johnson　　Mark R. Komray
(1947-1991)　　　　　　　Clayton W. Crevasse
Charles B. Edwards　　　　　M. Brian Cheffer

Robert S. Forman　　　　　C. Berk Edwards, Jr.
Kathleen W. McBride　　　　Melville G. Brinson, III
Lowell Schoenfeld　　　　　Samuel J. Hagan, IV.

For full biographical listings, see the Martindale-Hubbell Law Directory

MIAMI,* Dade Co.

CLARKE SILVERGLATE WILLIAMS & MONTGOMERY (AV)

A Partnership of Professional Corporations
100 North Biscayne Boulevard Suite 2401, 33132
Telephone: 305-377-0700
Facsimile: 305-377-3001
Chicago, Illinois Office: Williams & Montgomery, Ltd., 20 North Wacker Drive, Suite 2100.
Telephone: 312-443-3200.
Telex: 206598.
Facsimile: 312-443-1323.

(See Next Column)

Waukegan, Illinois Office: Williams & Montgomery, Ltd., 33 North County Street.
Telephone: 847-360-1220.
Wheaton, Illinois Office: Williams & Montgomery, Ltd., 310 S. County Farm Road.
Telephone: 708-690-3200.
Joliet, Illinois Office: Williams & Montgomery, Ltd., 81 North Chicago Avenue.
Telephone: 815-727-2653.

Mercer K. Clarke　　　　　Spencer H. Silverglate
OF COUNSEL
Henry H. Bolz, III
ASSOCIATES
Kelly Anne Luther　　　　　Eric L. Lundt
William C. Abruzzo　　　　　Carol A. Grant

For full biographical listings, see the Martindale-Hubbell Law Directory

TAMPA,* Hillsborough Co.

ANTHONY F. GONZALEZ (AV)

701 North Franklin Street Mall, Franklin and Zack Streets, 33602
Telephone: 813-224-0431

For full biographical listings, see the Martindale-Hubbell Law Directory

GEORGIA

ATLANTA,* Fulton Co.

ELARBEE, THOMPSON & TRAPNELL (AV)

800 Peachtree-Cain Tower, 229 Peachtree Street, N.E., 30303
Telephone: 404-659-6700
Fax: 404-222-9718

MEMBERS OF FIRM
Fred W. Elarbee, Jr. (1925-1986)　Robert J. Martin, Jr.
Robert L. Thompson　　　　　Joseph M. Freeman
John R. Trapnell　　　　　　Stanford G. Wilson
David M. Vaughan　　　　　Brent L. Wilson
John Lewis Sapp　　　　　　Victor A. Cavanaugh
William M. Earnest　　　　　Nancy F. Reynolds
Charles K. Howard, Jr.　　　　Sharon Parker Morgan
Walter O. Lambeth, Jr.　　　　Mark D. Halverson
R. Read Gignilliat
ASSOCIATES
Douglas H. Duerr　　　　　Kenneth N. Winkler
Victor J. Maya　　　　　　Frederick L. Douglas
Jan M. Jacobson　　　　　Catherine M. Norman
William Drummond Deveney　　Laura K. Johnson
Patrick L. Lail　　　　　　Scott E. Atwood
Kelly Michael Hundley　　　　(Not admitted in GA)
Stephanie E. Meyerson

Representative Clients: Cox Communications, Inc.; Dunlop Tire Corp.; National Service Industries; Atlanta Gas Light Co.; Brown & Williamson Tobacco Corp.; Engelhard Corp.; Louisiana-Pacific Corp.; MCI Communications Corp.; Florida Power and Light Co.; Southwire Co.

For full biographical listings, see the Martindale-Hubbell Law Directory

FISHER & PHILLIPS (AV)

A Partnership including Professional Corporations and Associations
1500 Resurgens Plaza, 945 East Paces Ferry Road, N.E., 30326
Telephone: 404-231-1400
Telecopier: 404-240-4249;
Telex: 54-2331
Fort Lauderdale, Florida Office: Suite 2300 NationsBank Tower, One Financial Plaza, 33394.
Telephone: 954-525-4800.
Telecopier: 954-525-8739.
Redwood City, California Office: Suite 345, Three Lagoon Drive, 94065.
Telephone: 415-592-6160.
Telecopier: 415-592-6385.
Newport Beach, California Office: 4675 MacArthur Court, Suite 550, 92660.
Telephone: 714-851-2424.
Telecopier: 714-851-0152.
New Orleans, Louisiana Office: 3710 Place St. Charles, 201 St. Charles Avenue, 70170.
Telephone: 504-522-3303.
Telecopier: 504-529-3850.

(See Next Column)

FISHER & PHILLIPS—*Continued*

MEMBERS OF FIRM

Robert C. Christenson
Sandra Mills Feingerts (Resident
Partner, New Orleans,
Louisiana Office)

Representative Clients: Arvida/JMB Partners; Atlantic Gulf Communities Corp.; Eastern Asiatic Corp.; The Flagler System, Inc.; Hyatt Corp.; Johnstown America Corp.; Pneumo Abex Corp.

For full biographical listings, see the Martindale-Hubbell Law Directory

KILPATRICK & CODY LLP (AV)

Suite 2800, 1100 Peachtree Street, 30309-4530
Telephone: 404-815-6500
Telephone Copier: 404-815-6555
Telex: 54-2307
Washington, D.C. Office: Suite 800, 700 13th Street, N.W., 20005.
Telephone: 202-508-5800. Telephone Copier: 202-508-5858.
Brussels, Belgium Office: Avenue Louise 65, BTE 3, 1050 Brussels.
Telephone: (32) (2) 533-03-00.
Telecopier: (32) (2) 534-86-38.
London, England Office: 68 Pall Mall, London, SW1Y 5ES, England.
Telephone: (44) (71) 321 0477.
Telecopier: (44) (71) 930 9733.
Augusta, Georgia Office: Suite 1400 First Union Bank Building, P.O. Box 2043, 30903. Telephone (706) 724-2622. Telecopier (706) 722-0219.

MEMBERS OF FIRM

Sally Cotter Baxter
A. Kimbrough Davis
Mark P. Kelly
Steven J. Sacher
  (Washington, D.C. Office)

William J. Vesely, Jr.
Martha Jo Wagner
  (Washington, D.C. Office)
Mark D. Wincek
  (Washington, D.C. Office)

COUNSEL

William L. Sollee, Jr.
  (Washington, D.C. Office)

Kathryn B. Solley

ASSOCIATES

Josephine M. Hammack
  (Washington, D.C. Office)
Devon Lee Miller
  (Washington, D.C. Office)

David Pickle
  (Washington, D.C. Office)
Jennifer S. Schumacher

For Complete List of Firm Personnel, See General Section

For full biographical listings, see the Martindale-Hubbell Law Directory

LONG ALDRIDGE & NORMAN, LLP (AV)

A Limited Liability Partnership including Professional Corporations
One Peachtree Center, Suite 5300, 303 Peachtree Street, 30308
Telephone: 404-527-4000
Telecopier: 404-527-4198
Washington, D.C. Office: Suite 600, 701 Pennsylvania Avenue, N.W., 20004.
Telephone: 202-624-1200.
FAX: 202-624-1298.

MEMBERS OF FIRM

Phillip A. Bradley
Bruce H. Wynn

Patricia E. Tate

For Complete List of Firm Personnel, See General Section

For full biographical listings, see the Martindale-Hubbell Law Directory

SUTHERLAND, ASBILL & BRENNAN, L.L.P. (AV)

999 Peachtree Street, N.E., 30309-3996
Telephone: 404-853-8000
Facsimile: 404-853-8806
Email: postmaster@sablaw.com
Washington, D.C. Office: 1275 Pennsylvania Avenue, N.W., 20004-2404.
Telephone: 202-383-0100.
New York, N.Y. Office: 600 Madison Avenue, 11th Floor, 10022-1615.
Telephone: 212-605-6400.
Austin, Texas Office: 111 Congress Avenue, 23rd Floor, 78701-4079.
Telephone: 512-469-3350.

William M. Hames   Walter H. Wingfield

For Complete List of Firm Personnel, See General Section

For full biographical listings, see the Martindale-Hubbell Law Directory

COLUMBUS,* Muscogee Co.

HATCHER, STUBBS, LAND, HOLLIS & ROTHSCHILD (AV)

A Limited Liability Partnership
Suite 500 The Corporate Center, 233 12th Street, P.O. Box 2707, 31902-2707
Telephone: 706-324-0201
Telecopier: 706-322-7747

(See Next Column)

MEMBERS OF FIRM

Morton A. Harris
Charles T. Staples

James E. Humes, II
Alan F. Rothschild, Jr.

General Counsel for: SunTrust Bank, West Georgia, N.A.; TOM'S Foods Inc.; Muscogee County Board of Education; Kinnett Dairies, Inc.; St. Francis Hospital, Inc.; Georgia Crown Distributing Co.
Local Counsel for: First Union National Bank of Georgia.

For Complete List of Firm Personnel, See General Section

For full biographical listings, see the Martindale-Hubbell Law Directory

ILLINOIS

CHICAGO,* Cook Co.

BRITTAIN SLEDZ MORRIS & SLOVAK, A PROFESSIONAL CORPORATION (AV)

500 Marquette Building, 140 South Dearborn, 60603
Telephone: 312-346-4515
Fax: 312-346-4523

E. Allan Kovar (1927-1987)
Max G. Brittain, Jr.
James F. Hendricks, Jr.
Gabriel J. Minc

Ralph A. Morris
John J. Murphy, Jr.
Mary Aileen O'Callaghan
Henry W. Sledz, Jr.

Patricia Costello Slovak

Christine Greener
John Joseph Lynch

Jane M. McFetridge
Wendy L. Nutt

OF COUNSEL

Kearney W. Kilens
Mary J. McNichols

John B. Murnighan
P. Neill Petronella

For full biographical listings, see the Martindale-Hubbell Law Directory

HOWARD GORDON KAPLAN, LTD. (AV)

180 North La Salle Street, 28th Floor, 60601
Telephone: 312-641-2555
Facsimile No.: 312-641-6265
Email: howie641@aol.com

Howard Gordon Kaplan

Leonard J. Brenner   Rhonda D. Kaplan-Katz

For full biographical listings, see the Martindale-Hubbell Law Directory

LANER, MUCHIN, DOMBROW, BECKER, LEVIN AND TOMINBERG, LTD. (AV)

515 North State Street, Suite 2800, 60610
Telephone: 312-467-9800
Fax: 312-467-9479

Richard W. Laner
Lawrence F. Doppelt
  (1935-1979)
Arthur B. Muchin
Anthony E. Dombrow
William L. Becker
Alan M. Levin
Carl S. Tominberg
Mark L. Juster
Gary Alan Wincek
Michael Klupchak

Joseph H. Yastrow
Joseph M. Gagliardo
Robert H. Brown
James J. Convery
Robert S. Letchinger
Violet M. Clark
James F. Vanek
Jeffrey P. Carren
Jane E. Shaffer
Jill P. O'Brien
Neil P. Stern

Thomas Vasiljevich

Robert T. Bernstein
Thomas Bradley
Beth A. Clukey
Jeffrey S. Fowler
Scott A. Gore

Maureen A. Gorman
Stefanie W. Kohen
Linda J. Lemel
Clifford R. Perry, III
Shavaun Adams-Taylor

OF COUNSEL

Isaiah S. Dorfman

Herman J. De Koven
Seymour Cohen

References: NBD Bank Chicago; Illinois; La Salle National Bank & Trust Co.

For full biographical listings, see the Martindale-Hubbell Law Directory

MATKOV, SALZMAN, MADOFF & GUNN (AV)

Suite 2900, 55 East Monroe Street, 60603-5709
Telephone: 312-332-0777
Telecopier: 312-332-6130

(See Next Column)

MATKOV, SALZMAN, MADOFF & GUNN, *Chicago—Continued*

MEMBERS OF FIRM

George J. Matkov, Jr.	Jay G. Swardenski
James John Salzman	John N. Raudabaugh
Jeffrey L. Madoff	(Not admitted in IL)
Allan Gunn	Julia A. Martin
Larry G. Hall	Frank J. Saibert
Kenneth T. Lopatka	Steven L. Brenneman
Michael W. Duffee	Elliot H. Goldman

Deborah Lee Smith

ASSOCIATES

Mark J. Mahoney	Tammy D. McCutchen
Beth Elaine Koch	Karen J. Fellows
Christopher A. Johlie	Thomas M. Dugard
John D. Nelson	Jacqueline M. Damm
Lisa A. Wetzel	Jennifer L. Levi
Craig R. Thorstenson	Rachel B. Cowen
Kenneth F. Sparks	Susan A. Pipal
(Not admitted in IL)	Daniel B. Pasternak

For full biographical listings, see the Martindale-Hubbell Law Directory

McBRIDE BAKER & COLES (AV)

500 West Madison Street 40th Floor, 60661
Telephone: 312-715-5700
Cable Address: "Chilaw"
Telex: 270258
Telecopier: 312-993-9350
Email: lastname@mbc.com *URL:* http://www.mbc.com
Oakbrook Terrace, Illinois Office: Suite 1000, One Mid America Plaza, 60181-4710.
Telephone: 630-954-2100.
Telecopier: 630-954-2112.

MEMBERS OF FIRM

David Ackerman	Thomas J. Kinasz
Martin J. Campanella	Patrick W. Kocian
William J. Cooney	Steven R. Lifson
Kenneth A. Jenero	Anne Hamblin Schiave

Larry M. Zanger

ASSOCIATES

Eric E. Mennel	Jonathan E. Strouse

For Complete List of Firm Personnel, See General Section

For full biographical listings, see the Martindale-Hubbell Law Directory

TIMOTHY M. MLSNA & ASSOCIATES, LTD. (AV)

360 N. Michigan Avenue, Suite 906, 60601
Telephone: 312-845-3540
Fax: 312-845-1010
Oak Brook, Illinois Office: 2100 Clearwater Drive, Suite 107.
Telephone: 630-954-0041.
Fax: 630-954-3801.

Timothy M. Mlsna

For full biographical listings, see the Martindale-Hubbell Law Directory

MURPHY, SMITH & POLK, A PROFESSIONAL CORPORATION (AV)

Twenty-Fifth Floor, Two First National Plaza 20 South Clark Street, 60603-1891
Telephone: 312-558-1220
Telecopier: 807-3619
Email: msp@pg.net

Charles E. Murphy	Peter M. Kelly, II
Arthur B. Smith, Jr.	Richard L. Samson
Lee T. Polk	Carol A. Poplawski
Robert P. Casey	Dwight D. Pancottine
Michael T. Roumell	Daniel J. Ashley

Tracey L. Truesdale	Joseph E. Burke
Julia A. Donnelly	Charles R. Marcordes
Peter A. Steinmeyer	Sandra K. Carolina

OF COUNSEL

Karl W. Grabemann

For full biographical listings, see the Martindale-Hubbell Law Directory

SCARIANO, KULA, ELLCH AND HIMES, CHARTERED (AV)

Two Prudential Plaza 180 North Stetson Suite 3100, 60601-6224
Telephone: 312-565-3100
Facsimile: 312-565-0000
Chicago Heights, Illinois Office: 1450 Aberdeen.
Telephone: 708-755-1900.
Facsimile: 708-755-0000.

(See Next Column)

Anthony G. Scariano	Kathleen Field Orr
David P. Kula	John M. Izzo
Robert H. Ellch	Raymond A. Hauser
Alan T. Sraga	Kathleen Roche Hirsman
A. Lynn Himes	Joanne W. Schochat
Justino D. Petrarca	Anthony Ficarelli
Lawrence Jay Weiner	G. Robb Cooper

Daniel M. Boyle

OF COUNSEL

Max A. Bailey	John B. Kralovec

Patrick J. Broncato	Kelly A. Hayden
Rosanne Ciambrone	Todd K. Hayden
Jon G. Crawford	David A. Hemenway
Joel R. DeTella	Sarah E. Joyce
Teri E. Engler	Christopher L. Petrarca
Andrew C. Eulass	Shelia C. Riley

Janet L. Schwieters

For full biographical listings, see the Martindale-Hubbell Law Directory

INDIANA

INDIANAPOLIS, * Marion Co.

ICE MILLER DONADIO & RYAN (AV)

One American Square Box 82001, 46282-0002
Telephone: 317-236-2100
Fax: 317-236-2219
Email: leel@imdr.com *URL:* http://www.imdr.com
South Bend, Indiana Office: 211 West Washington Street, Suite 2420.
Telephone: 219-234-7933.
Fax: 219-234-7965. Internet E-mail: leel@imdr.com. Web Site Address: http://www.imdr.com.

MEMBERS OF FIRM

James D. Kemper	E. Van Olson
Terry A. M. Mumford	Marc W. Sciscoe
Michael H. Boldt	Mary Beth Braitman
Gary J. Dankert	Melissa Proffitt Reese

OF COUNSEL

Catherine R. Reese

ASSOCIATES

Brian G. Steinkamp	George A. Norwood
Stephanie Alden Smithey	Tara L. Schulstad
Craig C. Burke	Margaret R. Bernardin

For Complete List of Firm Personnel, See General Section

For full biographical listings, see the Martindale-Hubbell Law Directory

LAFAYETTE, * Tippecanoe Co.

STUART & BRANIGIN (AV)

The Life Building, 300 Main Street, Suite 800, 47902
Telephone: 317-423-1561
Telecopier: 317-742-8175

MEMBERS OF FIRM

Allison Ellsworth Stuart	Stephen R. Pennell
(1886-1950)	Anthony S. Benton
Roger D. Branigin (1902-1975)	Erik D. Spykman
Russell H. Hart	William E. Emerick
Roger D. Branigin, Jr.	John C. Duffey
Thomas L. Ryan	Mark E. DeYoung
James V. McGlone	Thomas B. Parent
Carl W. Kloepfer	Laura L. Bowker
Thomas R. McCully	Kevin D. Nicoson
Larry R. Fisher	Susan K. Roberts
Nina B. Kirkpatrick	John M. Stuckey
Mark Lillianfeld	Deborah B. Trice

COUNSEL

John F. Bodle

ASSOCIATES

Brent W. Huber	David A. Starkweather
William P. Kealey	Geoffrey Blazi

A. James Chareq

General Counsel for: The Lafayette Life Insurance Co.; INB National Bank, N.W.; Lafayette Home Hospital, Inc.
State Counsel for: Norfolk & Western Railway Co.
Mr. Ryan is Counsel to: The Trustees of Purdue University.
Representative Clients: Aluminum Company of America; Liberty Mutual Insurance Group.

For full biographical listings, see the Martindale-Hubbell Law Directory

MUNSTER, Lake Co.

PINKERTON AND FRIEDMAN, PROFESSIONAL CORPORATION (AV)

The Fairmont, 9245 Calumet Avenue Suite 201, 46321
Telephone: 219-836-3050
Fax: 219-836-2955

Milton Roth (1925-1996)	Jeffrey F. Gunning
Kirk A. Pinkerton	Gail Oosterhof
Stuart J. Friedman	Richard N. Shapiro

Reference: Calumet National Bank of Hammond.

For full biographical listings, see the Martindale-Hubbell Law Directory

*VALPARAISO,** Porter Co.

HOEPPNER WAGNER AND EVANS (AV)

103 East Lincolnway, P.O. Box 2357, 46384-2357
Telephone: 219-464-4961; 800-879-2246 (IN,IL)
Fax: 219-465-0603
Merrillville, Indiana Office: Twin Towers, Suite 606 South, 1000 East 80th Place, 46410.
Telephone: 219-769-6552; 800-263-1466. (IN,IL,).
Fax: 219-738-2349.

MEMBERS OF FIRM

Larry G. Evans   Mark E. Schmidtke

Attorneys for: Bethlehem Steel Corp.; Chester, Inc.; Hunt-Wesson Foods, Inc.; NBD Bank, N.A.; Owens-Corning Fiberglas Corp.; Valparaiso University; State Farm Insurance; Allstate Insurance Co.; Indiana Federal Bank for Savings.

For Complete List of Firm Personnel, See General Section

For full biographical listings, see the Martindale-Hubbell Law Directory

IOWA

*DES MOINES,** Polk Co.

ROXANNE B. CONLIN AND ASSOCIATES, P.C. (AV)

The Plaza, 300 Walnut Street - Suite 5, 50309-2239
Telephone: 515-282-3333
Fax: 515-282-0318

Roxanne B. Conlin

Melinda Kaye Ellwanger   Thomas J. Duff

For full biographical listings, see the Martindale-Hubbell Law Directory

FINLEY, ALT, SMITH, SCHARNBERG, MAY & CRAIG, P.C. (AV)

604 Locust Street, Fourth Floor Equitable Building, 50309
Telephone: 515-288-0145
Telecopier: 515-288-2724

Lorraine J. May   David C. Craig

Representative Clients: Aetna Casualty & Surety Co.; Aetna Life Insurance Co.; ALAS; American Society of Composers, Authors and Publishers; Equitable Life Assurance Society of the U.S.; Federated Insurance Co.; Meredith Corp.
Iowa Attorneys for: Midwest Medical Insurance Co.
District Attorneys for: Norfolk & Southern Railroad; Soo Line Railroad Company.

For Complete List of Firm Personnel, See General Section

For full biographical listings, see the Martindale-Hubbell Law Directory

KANSAS

*TOPEKA,** Shawnee Co.

FOULSTON & SIEFKIN L.L.P. (AV)

1515 Bank IV Tower, 534 Kansas Avenue, 66603
Telephone: 913-233-3600
Fax: 913-233-1610
Wichita, Kansas Office: 100 North Broadway, 700 Fourth Financial Center, 67202.
Telephone: 316-267-6371.
Fax: 316-267-6345.
Dodge City, Kansas Office: 810 Frontview, P.O. Box 1147, 67801.
Telephone: 316-227-8126.
Fax: 316-227-8451.
Member: Lex Mundi, A Global Association of 126 Independent Firms.

(See Next Column)

MEMBER OF FIRM
James P. Rankin

For full biographical listings, see the Martindale-Hubbell Law Directory

*WICHITA,** Sedgwick Co.

FOULSTON & SIEFKIN L.L.P. (AV)

700 Fourth Financial Center, 67202
Telephone: 316-267-6371
Facsimile: 316-267-6345
Topeka, Kansas Office: 1515 Bank IV Tower, 534 Kansas Avenue, 66603.
Telephone: 913-233-3600.
Fax: 913-233-1610.
Dodge City, Kansas Office: 810 Frontview, P.O. Box 1147, 67801.
Telephone: 316-227-8126.
Fax: 316-227-8451.
Member: Lex Mundi, A Global Association of 126 Independent Firms.

MEMBERS OF FIRM

James P. Rankin (Resident, Topeka Office)	Douglas L. Hanisch
	Kevin J. Arnel

For Complete List of Firm Personnel, See General Section

For full biographical listings, see the Martindale-Hubbell Law Directory

HERSHBERGER, PATTERSON, JONES & ROTH, L.C. (AV)

600 Hardage Center, 100 South Main, 67202-3779
Telephone: 316-263-7583
Fax: 316-263-7595

A. W. Hershberger (1897-1976)	J. Michael Kennalley
J. B. Patterson (1895-1957)	John A. Vetter
Richard Jones (1914-1988)	Edward L. Keeley
Jerome E. Jones	Bryce A. Abbott
Robert J. Roth	David J. Morgan
William R. Smith	Ken W. Dannenberg
	Tracy A. Applegate

T. Lynn Ward	Gary K. Albin

OF COUNSEL

H. E. Jones	John L. Kratzer, Jr.

Counsel for: First National Bank in Wichita; Anadarko Petroleum Corporation; Chinese Industries; Mobil Oil Corp.; CNA Insurance; Royal Exchange Group; Central National Insurance Group; Transamerica Insurance Group; Northwestern National Insurance Group.

For full biographical listings, see the Martindale-Hubbell Law Directory

KENTUCKY

*LEXINGTON,** Fayette Co.

STOLL, KEENON & PARK, LLP (AV)

201 E. Main Street, Suite 1000, 40507-1380
Telephone: 606-231-3000
Telecopier: 606-253-1093; 606-253-1027
Frankfort, Kentucky Office: 307 Washington Street, 40601.
Telephone: 502-875-6220.
Telecopier: 502-875-6235.
Louisville, Kentucky Office: 400 West Market Street, Suite 2650, 40202-3377.
Telephone: 502-568-9100.
Telecopier: 502-568-5700.

MEMBERS OF FIRM

Richard C. Stephenson   C. Joseph Beavin

Representative Clients: Lexmark International, Inc.; Bank One, Lexington, NA; Farmers Capital Bank Corp.; International Business Machines Corp.; Keeneland Association; ATR Wire & Cable; Christian Appalachian Project; Link-Belt Construction Equipment Co.; Whitaker Bank Corporation of Kentucky; VicWest Steel.

For Complete List of Firm Personnel, See General Section

For full biographical listings, see the Martindale-Hubbell Law Directory

*LOUISVILLE,** Jefferson Co.

MACKENZIE & PEDEN, P.S.C. (AV)

650 Starks Building, 455 South Fourth Avenue, 40202-2509
Telephone: 502-589-1110
Fax: 502-589-1117
Other Louisville, Kentucky Office: 8311 Shelbyville Road.
Telephone: 502-426-6688.
Fax: 502-425-0561.

(See Next Column)

MacKENZIE & PEDEN P.S.C., Louisville—Continued

William B. Peden (Retired)
Thomas G. Mooney (1939-1991)
Wm. A. MacKenzie (Resident)
John G. Crutchfield
Wayne J. Carroll
James C. Hickey
B. Carlton Neat, III
Robert W. Dickey
William B. Bardenwerper
(Resident)

James T. Lobb
Valerie T. Mayer (Resident)
Edward H. Bartenstein
Judith B. Hoge
Sidney L. Hymson
Lee Ann Risner
Charles T. Baxter
John Patrick Hamm

OF COUNSEL

Walker C. Cunningham, Jr.
Lawrence J. Phillips

Robert W. Riley (Resident)
Stephen A. Schwager

Representative Clients: Allstate Insurance Co.; American States Insurance Co.; The Fund Insurance Companies; State Automobile Mutual Insurance Co..

For full biographical listings, see the Martindale-Hubbell Law Directory

LOUISIANA

BATON ROUGE,* East Baton Rouge Parish

SCHMIDT & KUEHNE, A PROFESSIONAL LAW CORPORATION (AV)

10935 Perkins Road, P.O. Box 80317, 70898
Telephone: 504-767-7093
Telecopier: 504-767-7096

Robert C. Schmidt

G. Bruce Kuehne

For full biographical listings, see the Martindale-Hubbell Law Directory

MAINE

PORTLAND,* Cumberland Co.

PIERCE ATWOOD (AV)

One Monument Square, 04101
Telephone: 207-791-1100
Fax: 207-791-1350
Email: info@PierceAtwood.com
Augusta, Maine Office: 77 Winthrop Street.
Telephone: 207-622-6311.
Fax: 207-623-9367.
Newburyport, Massachusetts Office: 6 Harris Street.
Telephone: 508-465-9599.
Fax: 508-465-9945.

MEMBER OF FIRM
William H. Nichols
ASSOCIATE
Eric D. Altholz

For Complete List of Firm Personnel, See General Section

For full biographical listings, see the Martindale-Hubbell Law Directory

MARYLAND

BALTIMORE,* (Independent City)

VENABLE ATTORNEYS AT LAW VENABLE, BAETJER AND HOWARD, LLP (AV)

A Partnership including Professional Corporations
1800 Mercantile Bank & Trust Building, 2 Hopkins Plaza, 21201
Telephone: 410-244-7400
Email: INFO@Venable.win.net
Washington, D.C. Office: Venable, Baetjer, Howard & Civiletti LLP. Suite 1000, 1201 New York Avenue, N.W.
Telephone: 202-962-4800.
McLean, Virginia Office: Suite 400, 2010 Corporate Ridge.
Telephone: 703-760-1600.
Rockville, Maryland Office: Suite 500, One Church Street, P. O. Box 1906.
Telephone: 301-217-5600.
Towson, Maryland Office: 210 Allegheny Avenue, P. O. Box 5517.
Telephone: 410-494-6200.

(See Next Column)

MEMBERS OF FIRM

Douglas D. Connah, Jr. (P.C.)
(Also at Washington, D.C. Office)
Barbara E. Schlaff
G. Stewart Webb, Jr.
Jana Howard Carey (P.C.)
George F. Pappas (Also at Washington, D.C. Office)

Jeffrey P. Ayres (P.C.)
Maurice Baskin (Resident, Washington, D.C. Office)
James A. Dunbar (Also at Washington, D.C. Office)
Robert L. Waldman
Michael W. Robinson (Resident, McLean, Virginia Office)

OF COUNSEL

A. Samuel Cook (P.C.)
(Resident, Towson, Maryland Office)

John A. Wilhelm (Not admitted in MD; Resident, McLean, Virginia Office)

ASSOCIATES

Louis B. Barr
Todd J. Horn

John A. McCauley
Linda Marotta Thomas

For Complete List of Firm Personnel, See General Section

For full biographical listings, see the Martindale-Hubbell Law Directory

MASSACHUSETTS

BOSTON,* Suffolk Co.

PALMER & DODGE LLP (AV)

One Beacon Street, 02108
Telephone: 617-573-0100
Facsimile: 617-227-4420

MEMBERS OF FIRM
Ralph C. Derbyshire

Malcolm E. Hindin

For Complete List of Firm Personnel, See General Section

For full biographical listings, see the Martindale-Hubbell Law Directory

SIMONDS, WINSLOW, WILLIS & ABBOTT, A PROFESSIONAL ASSOCIATION (AV)

50 Congress Street, 02109
Telephone: 617-367-4747
Fax: 617-227-1961

William S. Abbott
Marc A. Elfman
Robert S. Gulick
Brenda G. Levy

Robert Torrence Morrison
Hugh V. A. Starkey
Dudley H. Willis
John L. Worden III

Edward J. Wynne III

For full biographical listings, see the Martindale-Hubbell Law Directory

CAMBRIDGE,* Middlesex Co.

MERVIN M. WILF, LTD. (AV)

2 Berkeley Place, 02138
Telephone: 617-876-5200
Philadelphia, Pennsylvania Office: 3901 Mellon Bank Center. 1735 Market Street.
Telephone: 215-994-1430. 215- 568-4842.
Facsimile: 215-994-1432.

Mervin M. Wilf

A list of Representative Clients and References will be furnished upon request.

For full biographical listings, see the Martindale-Hubbell Law Directory

SPRINGFIELD,* Hampden Co.

RYAN, MARTIN, COSTELLO, LEITER, STEIGER & CASS, P.C. (AV)

Suite 2500, BayBank Tower, 1500 Main Street, P.O. Box 15629, 01115-5629
Telephone: 413-739-6971
Fax: 413-739-1441

Charles V. Ryan
Philip J. Ryan
Bradford R. Martin, Jr.
Mary K. Downey Costello
Bruce L. Leiter

Henry M. Downey
Joan C. Steiger
Timothy J. Ryan
William J. Cass
Michael P. Ryan

For full biographical listings, see the Martindale-Hubbell Law Directory

MICHIGAN

ANN ARBOR,* Washtenaw Co.

FERGUSON & WIDMAYER, P.C. (AV)

505 East Huron Street, Suite 202, 48104
Telephone: 313-662-0222
Fax: 313-662-8884

Larry J. Ferguson   Warren J. Widmayer

Marlo A. Bakris

For full biographical listings, see the Martindale-Hubbell Law Directory

BINGHAM FARMS, Oakland Co.

KORNEY & HELDT (AV)

30700 Telegraph Road, Suite 1551, 48025
Telephone: 810-646-1050
Fax: 810-646-1054

J. Douglas Korney   Jeffrey A. Heldt

For full biographical listings, see the Martindale-Hubbell Law Directory

BIRMINGHAM, Oakland Co.

MacDONALD AND GOREN, P.C. (AV)

Suite 200, 260 East Brown Street, 48009
Telephone: 810-645-5940
Fax: 810-645-2490

Harold C. MacDonald   Kalman G. Goren
                Cindy Rhodes Victor

Amy L. Glenn   Lawrence C. Atorthy
David D. Marsh   Miriam Blanks-Smart
Glenn G. Ross   John T. Klees
                Rose Marie Karadsheh
                OF COUNSEL
                Robert L. Biederman

Representative Clients: Beaudin, Gallanis; Beaudin, Incorporated; Orlandi Gear Co., Inc.; Bing Steel, Inc.; Superb Manufacturing, Inc.; Spring Engineering, Inc.; Adrian Steel Co.; Southfield Radiology Associates, P.C.; HDS Services, Inc.; TGI Friday's Inc.; Quality Gold of Cincinnati, Inc.

For full biographical listings, see the Martindale-Hubbell Law Directory

DETROIT,* Wayne Co.

ABBOTT, NICHOLSON, QUILTER, ESSHAKI & YOUNGBLOOD, P.C. (AV)

19th Floor, One Woodward Avenue, 48226
Telephone: 313-963-2500
Telecopier: 313-963-7882

C. Richard Abbott   Carl F. Jarboe
John R. Nicholson   Jay A. Kennedy
Thomas R. Quilter III   Timothy A. Stoepker
Gene J. Esshaki   Timothy J. Kramer
John F. Youngblood   Norbert T. Madison, Jr.
James B. Perry   William D. Gilbride, Jr.

Mary P. Nelson   Kathryn L. Ritchie
Michael R. Blum   Jill A. Bankey
Thomas F. Hatch   Dawn M. Macaddino
Anne Warren Bagno   Casimir J. Swastek
Eric J. Girdler   Daniel G. Kielczewski
                George M. Mesrey
                OF COUNSEL
Thomas C. Shumaker   Karen Smith Kienbaum

For full biographical listings, see the Martindale-Hubbell Law Directory

BUTZEL LONG, A PROFESSIONAL CORPORATION (AV)

Suite 900, 150 West Jefferson, 48226
Telephone: 313-225-7000
Telecopier: 313-225-7080
Email: melnick@butzel.com *URL:* http://www.butzel.com
Birmingham, Michigan Office: Suite 200, 32270 Telegraph Road.
Telephone: 810-258-1616.
Telecopier: 810-258-1439.
Lansing, Michigan Office: 118 West Ottawa Street.
Telephone: 517-372-6622.
Telecopier: 517-372-6672.
Ann Arbor, Michigan Office: Suite 300, 350 South Main Street.
Telephone: 313-995-3110.
Telecopier: 313-995-1777.

(See Next Column)

Grosse Pointe Farms, Michigan Office: Suite 260, 21 Kercheval.
Telephone: 313-886-5446.
Telecopier: 313-886-2114.

Paul L. Triemstra (Birmingham)   Mark T. Nelson
        Jordan S. Schreier (Ann Arbor)

Nicholas J. Stasevich

Representative Clients: Central Michigan University; Detroit Diesel Corp.; The Detroit News, Inc.; Kelly Services; Kelsey Hayes Co.; Merrill Lynch Pierce Fenner & Smith, Inc.; Stroh Brewery Co.; Takata Corp.; United Parcel Services of America, Inc.; The University of Michigan.

For Complete List of Firm Personnel, See General Section

For full biographical listings, see the Martindale-Hubbell Law Directory

CLARK HILL P.L.C. (AV)

500 Woodward Avenue, Suite 3500, 48226
Telephone: 313-965-8300
Facsimile: 313-962-4348
Oakland County, Michigan Office: Third Floor, 255 South Woodward Avenue, Birmingham.
Telephone: 810-642-9692.
Facsimile: 810-642-2174.
Lansing, Michigan Office: Suite 600, 200 North Capitol Avenue.
Telephone: 517-484-4481.
Facsimile: 517-484-1246.
Minneapolis, Minnesota Office: Suite 1000, One Financial Plaza, 120 South Sixth Street.
Telephone: 612-332-0102.
Facsimile: 612-332-3225.
Kansas City, Missouri Office: Suite 1400, Bryant Building, 1102 Grand Avenue.
Telephone: 816-221-5578.
Facsimile: 816-221-0303.

Robert G. Buydens   Edward C. Hammond
Kevin M. Bernys (Resident,
    Oakland County Office)

Kerry A. Anderson   Amy Malone

Representative Clients: American Automobile Manufacturers Association; Booth American Company; Compass Group USA, Inc.; Detroit-Macomb Hospital Corporation; Detroit Symphony Orchestra Hall, Inc.; First Federal of Michigan; Fletcher Paper Corporation; La-Z-Boy Chair Company; Peoples State Bank; United Way Community Services of Metropolitan Detroit.

For Complete List of Firm Personnel, See General Section

For full biographical listings, see the Martindale-Hubbell Law Directory

JAFFE, RAITT, HEUER & WEISS, PROFESSIONAL CORPORATION (AV)

One Woodward Avenue, Suite 2400, 48226
Telephone: 313-961-8380
Telecopier: 313-961-8358
Cable Address: "Jafsni"
Southfield, Michigan Office: Travelers Tower, Suite 1520.
Telephone: 313-961-8380.
Monroe, Michigan Office: 214 East Elm Avenue, Suite 208,
Telephone: 313-241-6470.
Telefacsimile: 313-241-3849.

Alexander B. Bragdon   Arthur A. Weiss
Michael A. Rajt   Thomas H. Williams
Joseph J. Shannon   Janet G. Witkowski

Representative Clients: Masco Tech, Inc.; Sisters of Mercy - Province of Detroit; The Stroh Brewery Company; Unisys Corporation.

For Complete List of Firm Personnel, See General Section

For full biographical listings, see the Martindale-Hubbell Law Directory

KELLER, THOMA, SCHWARZE, SCHWARZE, DuBAY & KATZ, P.C. (AV)

440 East Congress, 5th Floor, 48226
Telephone: 313-965-7610
Bloomfield Hills, Michigan Office: Suite 122, 100 West Long Lake Road.
Telephone: 810-642-5218.

Anthony J. Heckemeyer

Counsel for: Livonia Public Schools; Ludington News Co., Inc.
Representative Clients: Borg-Warner Corp.; E & L Transport Co.; The Kroger Co.; Holnam, Inc.
Public Employer Clients: City of Farmington Hills; City of Flint; City of Grosse Pointe Woods; Saginaw Public Schools.

For Complete List of Firm Personnel, See General Section

For full biographical listings, see the Martindale-Hubbell Law Directory

Detroit—Continued

STRINGARI, FRITZ, KREGER, AHEARN & CRANDALL, P.C. (AV)

510 First National Building, 48226-3538
Telephone: 313-961-6474
Fax: 313-961-5688

Richard J. Fritz	Martin E. Crandall
Conrad W. Kreger	Kenneth S. Wilson
Brian S. Ahearn	Dallas G. Moon

John C. Dickinson
OF COUNSEL
Karl R. Bennett, Jr.　　　　　　　Matt W. Zeigler

For full biographical listings, see the Martindale-Hubbell Law Directory

GRAND RAPIDS,* Kent Co.

WARNER NORCROSS & JUDD LLP (AV)

900 Old Kent Building, 111 Lyon Street, N.W., 49503-2489
Telephone: 616-752-2000
Fax: 616-752-2500
Muskegon, Michigan Office: 400 Terrace Plaza, P.O. Box 900.
Telephone: 616-727-2600.
Fax: 616-727-2699.
Holland, Michigan Office: Curtis Center, Suite 300, 170 College Avenue.
Telephone: 616-396-9800.
Fax: 616-396-3656.

MEMBERS OF FIRM

Jack B. Combs　　　　　　　　Sue O. Conway
John H. McKendry, Jr.
　(Resident at Muskegon Office)

For Complete List of Firm Personnel, See General Section

For full biographical listings, see the Martindale-Hubbell Law Directory

WHEELER UPHAM, A PROFESSIONAL CORPORATION (AV)

Second Floor, Trust Building, 40 Pearl Street, N.W., 49503-3001
Telephone: 616-459-7100
Fax: 616-459-6366

Gordon B. Wheeler (1904-1986)	William H. Heritage, Jr.
Buford A. Upham (Retired)	Kenneth E. Tiews
Robert H. Gillette	Jack L. Hoffman
Geoffrey L. Gillis	Janet C. Baxter
John M. Roels	Peter Kladder, III
Gary A. Maximiuk	James M. Shade
Timothy J. Orlebeke	Thomas A. Kuiper

Counsel For: Prudential Ins. Co.; Metropolitan Life Ins. Co.; Travelers Ins. Co.; Auto-Owners Ins. Co.; Independent Cooperative Milk Producers Assn.; American Premier Underwriters, Inc.; Navistar; Westdale Better Homes and Gardens; Gospel Films, Inc.; Michigan Credit Union League.

For full biographical listings, see the Martindale-Hubbell Law Directory

KALAMAZOO,* Kalamazoo Co.

KREIS, ENDERLE, CALLANDER & HUDGINS, A PROFESSIONAL CORPORATION (AV)

One Moorsbridge, P.O. Box 4010, 49003-4010
Telephone: 616-324-3000
Telecopier: 616-324-3010
Email: kech@sapien.net *URL:* http://www.kech.com

Douglas L. Callander	John F. Koryto
C. Reid Hudgins III	Janice Roark Peters

For Complete List of Firm Personnel, See General Section

For full biographical listings, see the Martindale-Hubbell Law Directory

LILLY & LILLY, P.C. (AV)

505 South Park Street, 49007
Telephone: 616-381-7763
Fax: 616-344-6880

Charles M. Lilly (1903-1990)　　　Terrence J. Lilly

For full biographical listings, see the Martindale-Hubbell Law Directory

LANSING, Ingham Co.

FOSTER, SWIFT, COLLINS & SMITH, P.C. (AV)

313 South Washington Square, 48933-2193
Telephone: 517-371-8100
Telecopier: 517-371-8200
URL: http://www.fosterswift.com
Farmington Hills, Michigan Office: 32300 Northwestern Highway, Suite 230.
Telephone: 810-539-9900.
Fax: 810-851-7504.

(See Next Column)

Stephen I. Jurmu	Patricia A. Calore
Sherry A. Stein	Eric E. Doster
Stephen J. Lowney	Matt G. Hrebec

LEGAL SUPPORT PERSONNEL
LEGAL ASSISTANTS
Jaxine L. Wintjen, CLA

Representative Clients: Edward W. Sparrow Hospital; Michigan Milk Producers Assn.; Industrial Metal Products Co. (IMPCO); Spartan Motors; Community First Bank; Physicians Insurance Company of Michigan.

For Complete List of Firm Personnel, See General Section

For full biographical listings, see the Martindale-Hubbell Law Directory

FRASER TREBILCOCK DAVIS & FOSTER, P.C. (AV)

1000 Michigan National Tower, 48933
Telephone: 517-482-5800
Fax: 517-482-0887

Darrell A. Lindman　　　　　　David D. Waddell

Counsel for: Michigan Capital Medical Center; Michigan Catholic Conference; Michigan Farm Bureau; Weyco, Inc.; Michigan State University; Physicians Health Plan of Mid-Michigan, Inc.

For Complete List of Firm Personnel, See General Section

For full biographical listings, see the Martindale-Hubbell Law Directory

SOUTHFIELD, Oakland Co.

MADDIN, HAUSER, WARTELL, ROTH, HELLER & PESSES, P.C. (AV)

Third Floor Essex Center, 28400 Northwestern Highway, P.O. Box 215, 48037
Telephone: 810-354-4030, 355-5200
Telefax: 810-354-1422

Milton M. Maddin (1902-1984)	Robert D. Kaplow
Michael W. Maddin	William E. Sigler
Mark R. Hauser	Stewart C. W. Weiner
C. Robert Wartell	Charles M. Lax
Richard J. Maddin	Stuart M. Bordman
Richard F. Roth	Steven D. Sallen
Harvey R. Heller	Joseph M. Fazio
Ian D. Pesses	Gregory J. Gamalski
Michael S. Leib	Julie Chenot Mayer

Nathaniel H. Simpson	Lowell D. Salesin
Ronald A. Sollish	Marc J. Mendelson
Mark H. Fink	Joseph W. Girardot
Steven M. Wolock	Lori E. Talsky

OF COUNSEL
Joel D. Kellman

Reference: Comerica Bank.

For full biographical listings, see the Martindale-Hubbell Law Directory

PROVIZER, LICHTENSTEIN & PHILLIPS, P.C. (AV)

4000 Town Center, Suite 1800, 48075
Telephone: 810-352-9080
Facsimile: 810-352-1491

Harold M. Provizer	Marilyn A. Madorsky
David S. Lichtenstein	Robert I. Brown

For full biographical listings, see the Martindale-Hubbell Law Directory

JACK M. SCHULTZ, P.C. (AV)

3000 Town Center, Suite 2990, 48075-1365
Telephone: 810-354-3440
Facsimile: 810-355-5608

Jack M. Schultz

For full biographical listings, see the Martindale-Hubbell Law Directory

TROY, Oakland Co.

POLING, McGAW & POLING, P.C. (AV)

Suite 275, 5435 Corporate Drive, 48098
Telephone: 810-641-0500
Telecopier: 810-641-0506

Benson T. Buck (1926-1989)	Richard B. Poling, Jr.
Richard B. Poling	Gregory C. Hamilton
D. Douglas McGaw	Veronica B. O'Haro

James R. Parker

(See Next Column)

POLING, McGAW & POLING P.C.—*Continued*

OF COUNSEL
Ralph S. Moore

Representative Clients: County of Oakland; City of Troy; United States Fidelity & Guaranty Co.; Sentry Insurance Co.; Admiral Insurance; DeMaria Construction Co.; Leo Corporation; Aetna Casualty and Surety Co.; Concord Design; Pneumo-Abex.

For full biographical listings, see the Martindale-Hubbell Law Directory

ENERGY LAW

COLORADO

DENVER, * Denver Co.

JONES & KELLER, A PROFESSIONAL CORPORATION (AV)

Suite 1600, 1625 Broadway, 80202
Telephone: 303-573-1600
Fax: 303-893-6506

Marion F. Jones (1898-1978)	Thomas J. Burke, Jr.
Alec J. Keller (1913-1995)	Samuel E. Wing
Alvin J. Meiklejohn, Jr.	Reid A. Godbolt
Leslie R. Kehl	Rodney D. Knutson
Edward T. Lyons, Jr.	Kevin L. Brown
David E. Driggers	Barry L. Wilkie

Howard R. Hertzberg	Brent Nicholls
David A. Thayer	Michael Brian Cavanaugh
	Nathan D. Simmons

Reference: Colorado State Bank; Union Bank & Trust.

For full biographical listings, see the Martindale-Hubbell Law Directory

DISTRICT OF COLUMBIA

WASHINGTON, D.C. Co.

BRICKFIELD, BURCHETTE & RITTS, P.C. (AV)

8th Floor, West Tower, 1025 Thomas Jefferson Street, N.W., 20007-0805
Telephone: 202-342-0800
Fax: 202-342-0807
Austin, Texas Office: Suite 1050, 1005 Congress Avenue.
Telephone: 512-472-1081.

Peter J. P. Brickfield	Michael N. McCarty
William H. Burchette	Frederick H. Ritts
Mark C. Davis (Not admitted in DC; Resident, Austin, Texas Office)	Fernando Rodriguez (Not admitted in DC; Resident, Austin, Texas Office)
Michael E. Kaufmann	Christine C. Ryan
Peter J. Mattheis	Garrett A. Stone

COUNSEL

James W. Brew (Not admitted in DC)	Robert L. McCarty A. Hewitt Rose

Dean S. Brockbank (Not admitted in DC)	Julie B. Greenisen
Elizabeth Grieco Cunningham (Resident, Austin, Texas Office)	Stephen J. Karina (Not admitted in DC) Christopher C. O'Hara
Vincent P. Duane	Sonnet C. Schmidt Damon E. Xenopoulos

For full biographical listings, see the Martindale-Hubbell Law Directory

BRUDER, GENTILE & MARCOUX, L.L.P. (AV)

1100 New York Avenue, N.W., Suite 510 East, 20005-3934
Telephone: 202-783-1350
Telecopiers: 202-737-9117; 347-2644
Email: brugen@ix.netcom.com

MEMBERS OF FIRM

George F. Bruder	David E. Goroff
Carmen L. Gentile	Gary E. Guy
Albert R. Simonds, Jr.	James H. McGrew
J. Michel Marcoux	Thomas L. Blackburn
	Arlene Pianko Groner

ASSOCIATE

Cheryl Lynn Belkowitz

For full biographical listings, see the Martindale-Hubbell Law Directory

CUTLER & STANFIELD, L.L.P. (AV)

700 Fourteenth Street, N.W., 20005-2010
Telephone: 202-624-8400
Fax: 202-624-8410
Denver, Colorado Office: 1675 Broadway, 80202.
Telephone: 303-825-7000.
FAX: 303-825-7005.

(See Next Column)

MEMBERS OF FIRM

Eliot R. Cutler	Peter J. Kirsch
Jeffrey L. Stanfield	Barry Conaty
Sheila D. Jones	Stephen H. Kaplan
Perry M. Rosen	(Not admitted in DC)

OF COUNSEL

Byron Keith Huffman, Jr.	Sarah M. Rockwell (Not admitted in DC)

ASSOCIATES

Katherine Boonin Andrus	Dana C. Nifosi
Françoise M. Carrier	Barbara Paley
Christopher M. Kamper (Not admitted in DC)	W. Eric Pilsk
	Timothy A. Pohle
William G. Malley	Thomas D. Roth

For full biographical listings, see the Martindale-Hubbell Law Directory

DUNCAN & ALLEN (AV)

1575 Eye Street, N.W., 20005-1105
Telephone: 202-289-8400
Facsimile: 202-289-8450
Email: ENERGY@DUNCAN.ALLEN.COM

MEMBERS OF FIRM

C. Emerson Duncan, II	Gregg D. Ottinger
Donald R. Allen	John P. Williams
	John P. Coyle

For full biographical listings, see the Martindale-Hubbell Law Directory

GOLDBERG, FIELDMAN & LETHAM, P.C. (AV)

Suite 200, 1100 15th Street, N.W., 20005
Telephone: 202-463-8300
Telecopier: 202-463-8309
Email: 72727.1161@compuserve.com

Arnold Fieldman	Channing D. Strother, Jr.
Glenn W. Letham	Joshua L. Menter

OF COUNSEL

Reuben Goldberg	David C. Hjelmfelt

For full biographical listings, see the Martindale-Hubbell Law Directory

KENTUCKY

LEXINGTON, * Fayette Co.

KINKEAD & COLLIER (AV)

201 West Vine Street, 40507
Telephone: 606-233-3550
Facsimile: 606-255-1965

MEMBERS OF THE FIRM

Shelby C. Kinkead, Jr.	Wayne F. Collier

For full biographical listings, see the Martindale-Hubbell Law Directory

LOUISIANA

LAKE CHARLES, * Calcasieu Parish

THE CARMOUCHE LAW FIRM A PROFESSIONAL CORPORATION (AV)

Bank One Tower, 901 Lakeshore Drive, Suite 900, P.O. Drawer 2001, 70601-5270
Telephone: 318-433-0355
Telecopier: 318-433-1274
Email: clf@carmouche.com

John F. Robichaux	W. Joseph Mize

For full biographical listings, see the Martindale-Hubbell Law Directory

NEW IBERIA, * Iberia Parish

CAFFERY, OUBRE, DUGAS & CAMPBELL, L.L.P. (AV)

420 Iberia Street, P.O. Drawer 12410, 70562-2410
Telephone: 318-364-1816
Fax: 318-364-9822

MEMBERS OF FIRM

Patrick T. Caffery	Michael W. Campbell
Jerry A. Oubre	Charles C. Garrison
David R. Dugas	Michael M. Caffery
	Michelle E. Oubre

For full biographical listings, see the Martindale-Hubbell Law Directory

NEW ORLEANS, * Orleans Parish

KOPS, LEE, FUTRELL & PERLES, L.L.P. (AV)

Suite 2409 Place St. Charles 201 St. Charles Avenue, 70170
Telephone: 504-569-1725
Fax: 504-569-1726
Email: 103622.1066@compuserve.com

John Michael Kops	John Maurice Futrell
Gary A. Lee	Richard M. Perles

Representative Clients: Certain Underwriters at Lloyd's, London; Institute of
London Underwriters Companies.

For full biographical listings, see the Martindale-Hubbell Law Directory

MICHIGAN

DETROIT, * Wayne Co.

CLARK HILL P.L.C. (AV)

500 Woodward Avenue, Suite 3500, 48226
Telephone: 313-965-8300
Facsimile: 313-962-4348
Oakland County, Michigan Office: Third Floor, 255 South Woodward
Avenue, Birmingham.
Telephone: 810-642-9692.
Facsimile: 810-642-2174.
Lansing, Michigan Office: Suite 600, 200 North Capitol Avenue.
Telephone: 517-484-4481.
Facsimile: 517-484-1246.
Minneapolis, Minnesota Office: Suite 1000, One Financial Plaza, 120 South
Sixth Street.
Telephone: 612-332-0102.
Facsimile: 612-332-3225.
Kansas City, Missouri Office: Suite 1400, Bryant Building, 1102 Grand
Avenue.
Telephone: 816-221-5578.
Facsimile: 816-221-0303.

Douglas H. West	Robert A. W. Strong
Richard C. Marsh	Louis J. Porter
Roderick S. Coy	(Resident, Lansing Office)
(Resident, Lansing Office)	

Stewart A. Binke	Stephen J. Videto
(Resident, Lansing Office)	(Resident, Lansing Office)

Representative Clients: Booth Communications, Inc.; LCI International Telecom Corp.; Chrysler Corp.; Ford Motor Co.; General Motors Corp.; National Steel Corp.

For Complete List of Firm Personnel, See General Section

For full biographical listings, see the Martindale-Hubbell Law Directory

ENVIRONMENTAL LAW

ALABAMA

BIRMINGHAM,* Jefferson Co.

BRADLEY, ARANT, ROSE & WHITE (AV)

2001 Park Place, Suite 1400, P.O. Box 830709, 35283-0709
Telephone: 205-521-8000
Facsimile: 205-252-0264
Facsimile (SouthTrust Tower Office): 205-251-9915
URL: http://www.BARW.COM
Huntsville, Alabama Office: 200 Clinton Avenue West, Suite 900, 35801.
Telephone: 205-517-5100.
Facsimile: 205-533-5069.

MEMBERS OF FIRM

Macbeth Wagnon, Jr.	Andrew Robert Greene
Gary C. Huckaby	Bobby C. Underwood
(Resident, Huntsville Office)	Joseph S. Bird, III
John E. Hagefstration, Jr.	

COUNSEL

Robert R. Reid, Jr.	Walter H. Monroe, III

ASSOCIATES

Michael S. Denniston	James Tassin
John W. Smith T	(Resident, Huntsville Office)

For Complete List of Firm Personnel, See General Section

For full biographical listings, see the Martindale-Hubbell Law Directory

BURR & FORMAN (AV)

3100 SouthTrust Tower, 420 North 20th Street, 35203
Telephone: 205-251-3000
Telecopier: 205-458-5100
Huntsville, Alabama Office: Suite 204, Regency Center, 400 Meridian Street.
Telephone: 205-551-0010.
Atlanta, Georgia Office: Suite 1800, One Georgia Center, 600 West Peachtree Street, 30308.
Telephone: 404-817-3536.
Facsimile: 404-817-3244.

MEMBERS OF FIRM

John F. DeBuys, Jr.	D. Frank Davis
James Ross Forman, III	Mark McCarroll Lawson
Harri J. Haikala	

For Complete List of Firm Personnel, See General Section

For full biographical listings, see the Martindale-Hubbell Law Directory

COOPER, MITCH, CRAWFORD, KUYKENDALL & WHATLEY, L.L.C. (AV)

1100 Financial Center, 505 20th Street North, 35203-2605
Telephone: 205-328-9576
Telecopier: 205-328-9669

MEMBERS OF FIRM

Jerome A. Cooper	Frederick T. Kuykendall, III
William E. Mitch	Joe R. Whatley, Jr.
Thomas N. Crawford, Jr.	Glen M. Connor
Patricia Guthrie Fraley	

ASSOCIATES

Candis A. McGowan	Maureen Kane Berg
Andrew C. Allen	Gerald B. Taylor, Jr.
William Z. Cullen	Peter H. Burke
Samuel H. Heldman	Charlene Cullen
Hilary E. Ball-Walker	William Todd Harvey
Richard Paul Rouco	

OF COUNSEL

W. Braxton Schell, Jr.	Russell Jackson Drake

Counsel for: United Steelworkers of America, AFL-CIO; Birmingham Plumbers & Steamfitters Local Union No. 91 Pension Fund.
Reference: AMSouth Bank of Birmingham.

For full biographical listings, see the Martindale-Hubbell Law Directory

HOGAN, SMITH & ALSPAUGH, P.C. (AV)

2323 Second Avenue, North, 35203
Telephone: 205-324-5635
Telecopier: 205-324-5637

William W. Smith	David J. Guin
M. Clay Alspaugh	Ronald R. Crook
R. Benjamin Hogan, III	Richard D. Stratton
David R. Donaldson	Pamela D. Beard

(See Next Column)

Reference: First Alabama Bank.

For full biographical listings, see the Martindale-Hubbell Law Directory

DAVID CROMWELL JOHNSON (AV)

The Land Title Building, Suite 200, 600 20th Street, North, 35203
Telephone: 205-327-5223

ASSOCIATES

J. Flint Liddon	Barry R. Tuggle

For full biographical listings, see the Martindale-Hubbell Law Directory

LIGHTFOOT, FRANKLIN & WHITE, L.L.C. (AV)

300 Financial Center, 505 20th Street North, 35203-2706
Telephone: 205-581-0700
Facsimile: 205-581-0799

John M. Johnson	Adam K. Peck
William S. Cox, III	

Sarah Bruce Jackson	Sabrina A. Simon
Jackson R. Sharman, III	
(Not admitted in AL)	

Counsel for: AT&T; Ford Motor Co.; Emerson Electric Co.; Monsanto Co.; Chrysler Corp.; Unocal Corp.; The Upjohn Co.; Bristol-Myers Squibb Co.; Kimberly-Clark Corp.; Chevron Chemical Co.

For full biographical listings, see the Martindale-Hubbell Law Directory

SPAIN & GILLON, L.L.C. (AV)

The Zinszer Building, 2117 2nd Avenue North, 35203
Telephone: 205-328-4100
Telecopier: 205-324-8866

MEMBERS OF FIRM

Samuel H. Frazier	Alton B. Parker, Jr.

General Counsel for: Liberty National Life Insurance Co.; Piggly Wiggly Alabama Distributing Co.; Alabama Insurance Guaranty Association; Alabama Life and Disability Insurance Guaranty Association; Alabama Insurance Underwriters Association.
Counsel for: Alabama Department of Environmental Management, Inc.; City of Birmingham; Jefferson County Health Department.

For Complete List of Firm Personnel, See General Section

For full biographical listings, see the Martindale-Hubbell Law Directory

STARNES & ATCHISON (AV)

100 Brookwood Place, P.O. Box 598512, 35259-8512
Telephone: 205-868-6000
Telecopier: 205-868-6099

MEMBERS OF FIRM

W. Stancil Starnes	L. Graves Stiff, III
W. Michael Atchison	Robert P. Mackenzie, III
William Anthony Davis, III	Jeffrey E. Friedman
Thomas Lawson Selden	

ASSOCIATES

Steven T. McMeekin	P. Thomas Dazzio, Jr.
Joe L. Leak	Rik S. Tozzi

Representative Clients: Ciba-Geigy Corp.; Wyerhaeuser, Inc.; Browning-Ferris Industries, Inc.; Nobel Insurance Co.; Drummond Co., Inc.; Mobile Infirmary Medical Center; Hoffman-La Roche, Inc.

For full biographical listings, see the Martindale-Hubbell Law Directory

HUNTSVILLE,* Madison Co.

BRADLEY, ARANT, ROSE & WHITE (AV)

200 Clinton Avenue West, Suite 900, 35801
Telephone: 205-517-5100
Facsimile: 205-533-5069
URL: http://www.BARW.COM
Birmingham, Alabama Office: 2001 Park Place, Suite 1400, P.O. Box 830709.
Telephone: 205-521-8000.
Facsimile: 205-251-8611, 251-8665, 252-0264. Facsimile (SouthTrust Tower Office): 205-251-9915.

RESIDENT PARTNERS

Gary C. Huckaby	Patrick H. Graves, Jr.
G. Rick Hall	

RESIDENT ASSOCIATE

James Tassin

For Complete List of Firm Personnel, See General Section

For full biographical listings, see the Martindale-Hubbell Law Directory

LIVINGSTON, * Sumter Co.

PRUITT, PRUITT AND WATKINS, P.A. (AV)

105 Washington Street, P.O. Box 1037, 35470
Telephone: 205-652-9627
Fax: 205-652-9620

Ira D. Pruitt (1904-1984)   Ira D. Pruitt, Jr.
Nathan G. Watkins, Jr.

OF COUNSEL

Nathan G. Watkins

Representative Clients Banks: First Alabama Bank; Alabama Power Co. Corporations: Waste Management, Inc.; McGregor Printing Corp.; Liv Lite Corp., A division of Big River Industries. Insurance: Hartford Insurance Co.; St. Paul Insurance Co.; Standard Guaranty Insurance Co.

For full biographical listings, see the Martindale-Hubbell Law Directory

MOBILE, * Mobile Co.

JOHNSTONE, ADAMS, BAILEY, GORDON AND HARRIS, L.L.C. (AV)

Royal St. Francis Building, 104 St. Francis Street, P.O. Box 1988, 36633
Telephone: 334-432-7682
Facsimile: 334-432-2800
Telex: 782040

MEMBERS OF FIRM

Brock B. Gordon   Ben H. Harris, Jr.
Alan C. Christian

ASSOCIATE

Tracy P. Turner

General Counsel for: First Alabama Bank, Mobile; Infirmary Health System/Mobile Infirmary Medical Center/Rotary Rehabilitation Hospital (Multi-Hospital System).
Counsel for: Oil and Gas: Exxon Corp. Business and Corporate: Bell South Telecommunications, Inc.; Aluminum Co. of America; Michelin North America, Inc.; Metropolitan Life Insurance Co.; The Travelers Insurance Cos. Marine: The West of England Ship Owners Mutual Protection and Indemnity Association (Luxembourg); The Standard Steamship Owners' Protection and Indemnity Association (Bermuda) Ltd.

For Complete List of Firm Personnel, See General Section

For full biographical listings, see the Martindale-Hubbell Law Directory

LYONS, PIPES & COOK, P.C. (AV)

2 North Royal Street, P.O. Box 2727, 36652-2727
Telephone: 334-432-4481
Cable Address: "Lysea"
Telecopier: 334-433-1820

Wesley Pipes   Walter M. Cook, Jr.
Norton W. Brooker, Jr.   John Patrick Courtney, III
W. David Johnson, Jr.

Representative Clients: Esenjay Petroleum Corporation; Shell Oil Company; Spectacor Management Group.

For Complete List of Firm Personnel, See General Section

For full biographical listings, see the Martindale-Hubbell Law Directory

VICKERS, RIIS, MURRAY AND CURRAN, L.L.C. (AV)

8th Floor, First Alabama Bank Building, 106 Saint Francis Street, P.O. Box 2568, 36652
Telephone: 334-432-9772
Fax: 334-432-9781

MEMBERS OF FIRM

Edwin J. Curran, Jr.   Thomas E. Sharp, III
J. Marshall Gardner

For Complete List of Firm Personnel, See General Section

For full biographical listings, see the Martindale-Hubbell Law Directory

MONTGOMERY, * Montgomery Co.

NIX, HOLTSFORD & VERCELLI, P.C. (AV)

300 A Water Street, Suite 300, P.O. Box 4128, 36103
Telephone: 334-262-2006
Fax: 334-834-3616

H. E. Nix, Jr.   Floyd R. Gilliland

Representative Clients: Alabama Chemical Association; Alabama League of Municipalities; Coastal Chemical Co.; Dupont Chemical Co.; Gay & Taylor; Tennessee Farmers Cooperative; Terra International; Ranger Insurance Co.; United States Fidelity & Guaranty Co.

For full biographical listings, see the Martindale-Hubbell Law Directory

ALASKA

ANCHORAGE, * Third Judicial District

DELANEY, WILES, HAYES, GERETY & ELLIS, INC. (AV)

1007 West Third Avenue, Suite 400, 99501
Telephone: 907-279-3581
Fax: 907-277-1331

Stephen M. Ellis   Marc D. Bond
Clyde E. Sniffen, Jr.

Representative Clients: Carr-Gottstein Foods Co.; Chevron Corporation; Arco Alaska Inc.; Alyeska Pipeline Service Co.; Phillips Petroleum Company; Matanuska Electric Association; Nana Regional Corporation; Bering Straits Native Corporation; Mobil Oil Company; Seibu, Inc.

For Complete List of Firm Personnel, See General Section

For full biographical listings, see the Martindale-Hubbell Law Directory

ARIZONA

PHOENIX, * Maricopa Co.

BESS & DYSART, P.C. (AV)

7210 North 16th Street, 82020-5201
Telephone: 602-331-4600
Telecopier: 602-331-8600

Robert L. Dysart   William M. Demlong

For full biographical listings, see the Martindale-Hubbell Law Directory

BROWN & BAIN, A PROFESSIONAL ASSOCIATION (AV)

2901 North Central Avenue, P.O. Box 400, 85001-0400
Telephone: 602-351-8000
Telecopier: 602-351-8516
Palo Alto, California Affiliated Office: Brown & Bain, 1755 Embarcadero Road, Suite 200.
Telephone: 415-856-9411.
Telecopier: 415-856-6061.
Tucson, Arizona Affiliated Office: Brown & Bain, A Professional Association. One South Church Avenue, Nineteenth Floor, P.O. Box 2265.
Telephone: 602-798-7900
Telecopier: 602-798-7945.

Michael P. Berman   Michael W. Patten
Paul F. Eckstein   Lawrence G. D. Scarborough
Kim E. Williamson

For Complete List of Firm Personnel, See General Section

For full biographical listings, see the Martindale-Hubbell Law Directory

BURCH & CRACCHIOLO, P.A. (AV)

702 East Osborn Road, Suite 200, 85014
Telephone: 602-274-7611
Fax: 602-234-0341
Mailing Address: P.O. Box 16882, Phoenix, AZ, 85011

Daniel Cracchiolo   Edwin D. Fleming
Ralph D. Harris

Representative Clients: Bashas' Inc.; Farmers Insurance Group; U-Haul International, Inc.

For Complete List of Firm Personnel, See General Section

For full biographical listings, see the Martindale-Hubbell Law Directory

FENNEMORE CRAIG, A PROFESSIONAL CORPORATION (AV)

Two North Central, Suite 2200, 85004
Telephone: 602-257-8700
Fax: 602-257-8527
Scottsdale, Arizona Office: 6263 North Scottsdale Road, Suite 290, 85250.
Telephone: 602-257-5400.
Fax: 602-257-5409.
Tucson, Arizona Office: One South Church Avenue, Suite 1030, 85701.
Telephone: 520-791-6800.
Fax: 520-791-6820.

John D. Everroad   Douglas E. McAllister
James W. Johnson   Christopher L. Callahan
Phillip F. Fargotstein   Robert D. Anderson
Robert J. Kramer

(See Next Column)

FENNEMORE CRAIG A PROFESSIONAL CORPORATION—*Continued*

Scott H. Thomas   Douglas C. Northup

Marc H. Lamber

For Complete List of Firm Personnel, See General Section

For full biographical listings, see the Martindale-Hubbell Law Directory

JENNINGS, STROUSS AND SALMON, P.L.C. (AV)

A Professional Limited Liability Company
One Renaissance Square, Two North Central, 85004-2393
Telephone: 602-262-5911
Fax: 602-253-3255

Richard N. Morrison   George Esahak-Gage

For Complete List of Firm Personnel, See General Section

For full biographical listings, see the Martindale-Hubbell Law Directory

LEWIS AND ROCA, LLP (AV)

A Limited Liability Partnership including a Professional Corporation
40 North Central Avenue, 85004-4429
Telephone: 602-262-5311
Fax: 602-262-5747
Email: mlp@lrlaw.com
Tucson, Arizona Office: One South Church Avenue, Suite 700, 86701-1620.
Telephone: 520-622-2090.
Fax: 520-622-3088. E-Mail: mlp@lrlaw.com.

MEMBERS OF FIRM

Edward F. Novak	Newman R. Porter
Amy R. Porter	James K. Kloss
Robert F. Roos	Steven J. Burr
Deanna Salazar	

Representative Clients: Arizona Hospital Assn.; ASARCO Inc.; Digital Equipment Corp.; Intel Corp.; Lockheed Aeromod Center, Inc.; Woodstuff Manufacturing.

For Complete List of Firm Personnel, See General Section

For full biographical listings, see the Martindale-Hubbell Law Directory

MITTEN, GOODWIN & RAUP, A PROFESSIONAL CORPORATION (AV)

One Columbus Plaza, 3636 North Central, Suite 1200, 85012
Telephone: 602-650-2000
Fax: 602-264-7033
Email: mgr@starlink.com

Roger C. Mitten   Edward R. Glady, Jr.

OF COUNSEL

Richard M. Davis

For full biographical listings, see the Martindale-Hubbell Law Directory

MUCHMORE & WALLWORK, A PROFESSIONAL CORPORATION (AV)

2700 North Central Avenue, Suite 1225, 85004-1165
Telephone: 602-240-6699
Data: 602-240-6698
Facsimile: 602-240-6697
Email: muchwork@mmww.com *URL:* http://www.mmww.com

Charles J. Muchmore   Nicholas J. Wallwork

COUNSEL

Margaret M. Dean   Fredric D. Bellamy

Kathy E. Shimpock

Bridget S. Bade   Carolina L. Carver
(Senior Associate)   Margaret Benny Hurst

LEGAL SUPPORT PERSONNEL

Gloria A. Torres (Administrator   Gale James (Finance Manager
and Senior Paralegal)   and Paralegal)
John A. Bennett
(Litigation Support Manager)

Representative Clients: AgrEvo USA Company; BHP Copper Inc.; City of Scottsdale; Cyprus Amax Minerals Company; General Electric Co.; Homes by Dave Brown, Inc.; National Indemnity Insurance Company; Standard Insurance Company; Washington Mills Electro Minerals Company.
Reference: M & I Thunderbird Bank.

For full biographical listings, see the Martindale-Hubbell Law Directory

O'CONNOR, CAVANAGH, ANDERSON, KILLINGSWORTH & BESHEARS, A PROFESSIONAL ASSOCIATION (AV)

One East Camelback Road, Suite 1100, 85012-1656
Telephone: 602-263-2400
FAX: 602-263-2900
Email: firminfo@arizlaw.com
Sun City, Arizona Office: 13250 North Del Webb Boulevard, Suite B, 85351.
Telephone: 602-263-2808.
FAX: 602-933-3100.
Tucson, Arizona Office: O'Connor Cavanagh Molloy Jones, 33 N. Stone, Suite 2100, 85701, P.O. Box 2268, 85702.
Telephone: 520-622-3531.
FAX: 520-624-2816.
Nogales, Arizona Office: 1891 North Mastick Way, 85621.
Telephone: 520-761-4215.
FAX: 520-761-3505.

Richard J. Woods   Scott A. Salmon
       Lucas J. Narducci

Troy B. Froderman

Carla A. Wortley   Eric A. Mark

Representative Clients: ITT Cannon; W.P.P., Inc.; Chemical Waste Management, Inc.; Granite Construction Company; City of Nogales; Continental Waste; Sentry Insurance and Great American Insurance Co.; Home Insurance Co.; Citation Insurance Co.

For Complete List of Firm Personnel, See General Section

For full biographical listings, see the Martindale-Hubbell Law Directory

QUARLES & BRADY (AV)

One Camelback Building, One East Camelback Road, Suite 400, 85012-1649
Telephone: 602-230-5500
Fax: 602-230-5598
Milwaukee, Wisconsin Office: 411 East Wisconsin Avenue.
Telephone: 414-277-5000.
Fax: 414-271-3552.
Madison, Wisconsin Office: First Wisconsin Plaza, One South Pinckney Street, P.O. Box 2113.
Telephone: 608-251-5000.
Fax: 608-251-9166.
West Palm Beach, Florida Office: 222 Lakeview Ave., 4th Floor.
Telephone: 407-653-5000.
Fax: 407-653-5333.
Naples, Florida Office: Barnett Center, 4501 Tamiami Trail North, Suite 300.
Telephone: 813-262-5959.
Fax: 813-434-4999.

MEMBERS OF THE FIRM

James D. Vieregg   David G. Beauchamp
       Daniel L. Muchow

ASSOCIATE

Jennifer B. Wuamett

For Complete List of Firm Personnel, See General Section

For full biographical listings, see the Martindale-Hubbell Law Directory

SNELL & WILMER, L.L.P. (AV)

One Arizona Center, 85004-0001
Telephone: 602-382-6000
Fax: 602-382-6070
Tucson, Arizona Office: 1500 Norwest Tower, One South Church Avenue 85701-1612.
Telephone: 520-882-1200.
Fax: 520-884-1294.
Orange County Office: 1920 Main Street, Suite 1200, P.O. Box 57062, Irvine, California, 92619-7062.
Telephone: 714-253-2700.
Fax: 714-955-2507.
Salt Lake City, Utah Office: Broadway Centre, 111 East Broadway, Suite 900, 84111-1004.
Telephone: 801-237-1900.
Fax: 801-237-1950.

MEMBERS OF FIRM

Steven M. Wheeler	Robert B. Hoffman
Richard W. Shapiro	G. Van Velsor Wolf, Jr.
Martha E. Gibbs	E. Jeffrey Walsh

SENIOR ATTORNEY

Thomas L. Mumaw

(See Next Column)

SNELL & WILMER L.L.P., Phoenix—Continued

ASSOCIATES

Jeffrey Webb Crockett	Robert Henry
Carlos D. Ronstadt	Lisa A. Schuh

Representative Clients: Arizona Public Service Co.; Bank One, Arizona, NA.; First Security Bank of Utah, N.A.; Ford Motor Co.; Chrysler Motors Corp.; Toyota Motor Sales U.S.A.; BHP Copper, Inc.; U.S. Home Corp.; Pinnacle West Capital Corp.; Safeway, Inc.

For Complete List of Firm Personnel, See General Section

For full biographical listings, see the Martindale-Hubbell Law Directory

---

SCOTTSDALE, Maricopa Co.

SPARKS, TEHAN & RYLEY, P.C. (AV)

7503 First Street, 85251-4573
Telephone: 602-949-1339
Fax: 602-949-7587

Joe P. Sparks	Kevin T. Tehan
	John H. Ryley

References: Bank One, Arizona, Trust Department; Northern Trust Bank of Arizona, N.A.; First Interstate Bank of Arizona.

For full biographical listings, see the Martindale-Hubbell Law Directory

---

*TUCSON,** Pima Co.

O'CONNOR CAVANAGH MOLLOY JONES, A PROFESSIONAL ASSOCIATION (AV)

Suite 2100 33 N. Stone, P.O. Box 2268, 85702
Telephone: 520-622-3531
FAX: 520-624-2816
Email: firminfo@arizlaw.com
Phoenix, Arizona Office: O'Connor, Cavanagh, Anderson, Killingsworth & Beshears, One East Camelback Road, Suite 1100, 85012.
Telephone: 602-263-2400.
FAX: 602-263-2900.
Sun City, Arizona Office: O'Connor, Cavanagh, Anderson, Killingsworth & Beshears, 13250 North Del Webb Boulevard, Suite B, 85351.
Telephone: 602-263-2808.
FAX: 602-933-3100.
Nogales, Arizona Office: O'Connor, Cavanagh, Anderson, Killingsworth & Beshears, 1891 North Mastick Way, 85621.
Telephone: 520-761-4215.
FAX: 520-761-3505.

Scott D. Gibson	Richard T. Coolidge
Peter Akmajian	David K. Gray
Drue A. Morgan-Birch	George O. Krauja
Russell E. Jones	William W. Pearson
	Benjamin W. Bauer

Chris B. Nakamura

Thomas E. Laursen	Jennifer M. Dubay
Paul A. Relich	Amy M. Samberg
Nathan B. Hannah	Dale F. Regelman
Michael W. Baldwin	James D. Campbell

OF COUNSEL

John F. Molloy (Retired)	John L. Donahue Jr.

Representative Clients: Three-Five Systems; Main Street & Main; ITT Cannon; Bank of America; The Dial Corp; The Hartford; Dow Corning Corp.; Charles Schwab & Co., Inc.

For full biographical listings, see the Martindale-Hubbell Law Directory

---

SNELL & WILMER, L.L.P. (AV)

1500 Norwest Tower, One South Church Avenue, 85701-1612
Telephone: 520-882-1200
Fax: 520-884-1294
Phoenix, Arizona Office: One Arizona Center, 85004-0001.
Telephone: 602-382-6000.
Fax: 602-382-6070.
Orange County Office: 1920 Main Street, Suite 1200, P.O. Box 57062, Irvine, California, 92619-7062.
Telephone: 714-253-2700
Fax: 714-955-2507.
Salt Lake City, Utah Office: Broadway Centre, 111 East Broadway, Suite 900, 84111- 1004.
Telephone: 801-237-1900.
Fax: 801-237-1950.

MEMBERS OF FIRM

Michael S. Milroy	Marjorie R. Perry
Marc G. Simon	Tibor Nagy, Jr.
Curt D. Reimann	William N. Poorten, III
John A. Robertson	Timothy E. Pickrell
Sandra S. Froman	Kathleen Brown Corey
	Patrick E. Broom

(See Next Column)

OF COUNSEL

Clague A. Van Slyke

ASSOCIATES

Steven Adamczyk	Annemarie Hennelly
Eric S. Baker	Todd V. Jones
Rolando Ballesteros	Mark E. Konrad
Dawn Brewer	James K. (Jim) Mackie
Joan S. Caplan	Regina L. Nassen
David R. Cohen	Kathryn B. Nelson
J. Matthew Derstine	Russell B. Stowers
Rosalind R. Greene	M. Roxanne Veliz

Representative Clients: Transit Management, Inc.; Tucson Airport Authority; Allstate Insurance Co.; Bank One, Arizona, NA; Southern Pacific Railroad Co.; Ford Motor Co.; Chrysler Motors Corp.; Toyota Motor Sales, U.S.A., Inc.; BHP Copper, Inc.; Pinnacle West Capital Corp.; Safeway Inc.; Honeywell, Inc.; Wells Fargo Bank, N.A.

For full biographical listings, see the Martindale-Hubbell Law Directory

STRICKLAND & STRICKLAND, P.C. (AV)

4400 E. Broadway, Suite 700, 85711-3517
Telephone: 520-795-8727
Fax: 520-795-5649

William E. Strickland	William E. Strickland, Jr.
	Robert F. Palmquist

Representative Client: AkChin Indian Community.
Reference: Bank One (formerly Valley National Bank).

ARKANSAS

---

*LITTLE ROCK,** Pulaski Co.

ROSE LAW FIRM, A PROFESSIONAL ASSOCIATION (AV)

120 East Fourth Street, 72201
Telephone: 501-375-9131
Telecopy: 501-375-1309

Herbert C. Rule, III	Thomas P. Thrash
Allen W. Bird, II	Stephen N. Joiner
Garland J. Garrett	Amy Lee Stewart
Jerry C. Jones	Brian Rosenthal

COUNSEL

John A. Davis, III

Grant E. Fortson	Kathryn Bennett Perkins
David P. Martin	Michael N. Shannon

Counsel for: ALLTEL Corporation; Aluminum Company of America; Bridgestone/Firestone, Inc.; The Equitable Life Assurance Society of The United States; General Motors Corp.; The Prudential Insurance Company of America; Stephens Group Inc.; Tyson Foods, Inc.

For Complete List of Firm Personnel, See General Section

For full biographical listings, see the Martindale-Hubbell Law Directory

---

CALIFORNIA

APTOS, Santa Cruz Co.

DENNIS J. KEHOE A LAW CORPORATION (AV)

311 Bonita Drive, 95003
Telephone: 408-662-8444
Fax: 408-662-0227

Dennis J. Kehoe

For full biographical listings, see the Martindale-Hubbell Law Directory

---

*BAKERSFIELD,** Kern Co.

KLEIN, WEGIS, DeNATALE, GOLDNER & MUIR, LLP (AV)

A Partnership including Professional Corporations
(Formerly Di Giorgio, Davis, Klein, Wegis, Duggan & Friedman)
ARCO Tower, 4550 California Avenue, Second Floor, P.O. Box 11172, 93389-1172
Telephone: 805-395-1000
Telecopier: 805-326-0418
Email: kwdgm@kwdgm.com

MEMBERS OF FIRM

Anthony J. Klein (Inc.)	David J. Cooper

(See Next Column)

KLEIN, WEGIS, DENATALE, GOLDNER & MUIR LLP—*Continued*

ASSOCIATES

Christopher P. Burger   Melvin L. Ehrlich

Representative Clients: JACO Oil Company; City of Visalia; City of Farmersville; Destec, Inc.; Sandyland Nursery; Boggiato Produce, Inc.

For Complete List of Firm Personnel, See General Section

For full biographical listings, see the Martindale-Hubbell Law Directory

CARLSBAD, San Diego Co.

GATZKE, MISPAGEL & DILLON (AV)

A Partnership including a Professional Law Corporation
Suite 200, 1921 Palomar Oaks Way, P.O. Box 1636, 92009
Telephone: 619-431-9501
Fax: 619-431-9512

MEMBERS OF FIRM

Michael Scott Gatzke   Mark J. Dillon
Mark F. Mispagel   Lori D. Ballance

ASSOCIATES

David P. Hubbard   Kristin Beth White

For full biographical listings, see the Martindale-Hubbell Law Directory

COSTA MESA, Orange Co.

McCORMICK, KIDMAN & BEHRENS, LLP (AV)

A Partnership of Professional Corporations
Imperial Bank Building, 695 Town Center Drive Suite 1400, 92626-1924
Telephone: 714-755-3100
Fax: 714-755-3110; 1-800-755-3125
Email: mkb1@ix.netcom.com

MEMBERS OF FIRM

Homer L. (Mike) McCormick,   Russell G. Behrens (P.C.)
  Jr., (P.C.)   Suzanne M. Tague (P.C.)
Arthur G. Kidman (P.C.)   Janet R. Morningstar (P.C.)
          Keith E. McCullough (P.C.)

ASSOCIATES

David D. Boyer   John O. Clune
Robert A. Johnson   Bradley D. Pierce

For full biographical listings, see the Martindale-Hubbell Law Directory

RUTAN & TUCKER, LLP (AV)

A Partnership including Professional Corporations
611 Anton Boulevard, Suite 1400, P.O. Box 1950, 92626
Telephone: 714-641-5100; 213-625-7586
Telecopier: 714-546-9035
Email: rutan&tucker@mcimail.com *URL:* http://www.rutan.com

MEMBERS OF FIRM

Leonard A. Hampel, Jr.   Richard Montevideo
Michael D. Rubin   Elizabeth L. Martyn
Robert S. Bower   Kim D. Thompson
David J. Aleshire   Hans Van Ligten
Philip D. Kohn   Adam N. Volkert
Joel D. Kuperberg   F. Kevin Brazil
Mary M. Green   Layne H. Melzer
Mark B. Frazier   Lien Ski Harrison

ASSOCIATES

Patrick D. McCalla   S. Daniel Harbottle

For Complete List of Firm Personnel, See General Section

For full biographical listings, see the Martindale-Hubbell Law Directory

FRESNO,* Fresno Co.

DOWLING, AARON & KEELER, INCORPORATED (AV)

Suite 200, 6051 North Fresno Street, 93710
Telephone: 209-432-4500
Fax: 209-432-4590
Email: dowling-law.com

Philip David Kopp   Francine Marie Kanne
          Christopher A. Brown

Reference: Wells Fargo Bank (Main).

For Complete List of Firm Personnel, See General Section

For full biographical listings, see the Martindale-Hubbell Law Directory

LANG, RICHERT & PATCH, A PROFESSIONAL CORPORATION (AV)

Fig Garden Financial Center, 5200 North Palm Avenue, 4th Floor, P.O. Box 40012, 93755
Telephone: 209-228-6700
Fax: 209-228-6727

(See Next Column)

Frank H. Lang   Victoria J. Salisch
William T. Richert (1937-1993) Bradley A. Silva
Robert L. Patch, II   Charles Trudrung Taylor
Val W. Saldaña   Mark L. Creede
Douglas E. Noll   Peter N. Zeitler
Michael T. Hertz   Charles L. Doerksen

Laurie L. Quigley   Nabil E. Zumout
Douglas E. Griffin   Shawn H. Alikian
          Thomas E. Gauthier

References: Wells Fargo Bank (Fresno Main Office).

For full biographical listings, see the Martindale-Hubbell Law Directory

GLENDALE, Los Angeles Co.

BRIGHT AND BROWN (AV)

550 North Brand Boulevard, Suite 2100, 91203
Telephone: 818-243-2121; 213-489-1414
Facsimile: 818-243-3225

James S. Bright   Maureen J. Bright
Gregory C. Brown   John Quirk
          Brian L. Becker

ASSOCIATES

Anthony S. Brill   Doris A. Mendenhall

For full biographical listings, see the Martindale-Hubbell Law Directory

IRVINE, Orange Co.

BROWN, PISTONE, HURLEY & VAN VLEAR, A PROFESSIONAL CORPORATION (AV)

Suite 900 AT&T Building, 8001 Irvine Center Drive, 92618-2921
Telephone: 714-727-0559
Fax: 714-727-0656
Email: BPHVLAW@AOL.COM
Phoenix, Arizona Office: 2999 North 44th Street, Suite 300.
Telephone: 602-968-2427.
Fax: 602-840-0794.
San Diego, California Office: 4350 La Jolla Village Drive, Suite 300.
Telephone: 619-546-4368.
Fax: 619-453-2839.
Sacramento, California Office: 980 Ninth Street, 16th Floor.
Telephone: 916-449-9541.
Fax: 916-446-7104.

Ernest C. Brown   Gregory F. Hurley
Thomas A. Pistone   John E. Van Vlear
          Michael K. Wolder

Francis T. Donohue, III   Sheila I. Patterson
Robert C. Schneider (Resident, Michael R. Gandee
  Phoenix, Arizona Office)   Julia E. Kress

OF COUNSEL

Robert G. Mahan   Brian A. Runkel
Stephen M. Wontrobski   (Not admitted in CA)

For full biographical listings, see the Martindale-Hubbell Law Directory

CALLAHAN & BLAINE, A PROFESSIONAL LAW CORPORATION (AV)

Suite 800, 18500 Von Karman, 92612
Telephone: 714-553-1155
Fax: 714-553-0784
Email: info@callahan-law.com

Daniel J. Callahan (A   Stephen E. Blaine
  Professional Corporation)

Kathleen L. Dunham   Andrew A. Smits
Jim P. Mahacek   Gary S. Spitzer
Michael J. Sachs   Edward Susolik
          Graig R. Woodburn

OF COUNSEL

Shelley M. Liberto   Walt D. Mahaffa

For full biographical listings, see the Martindale-Hubbell Law Directory

JACK M. EARLEY (AV)

19100 Von Karman Avenue, Suite 950, 92715
Telephone: 714-476-8900
Fax: 714-476-0900

For full biographical listings, see the Martindale-Hubbell Law Directory

Irvine—Continued

GAUNTLETT & ASSOCIATES (AV)

18400 Von Karman, Suite 300, 92612
Telephone: 714-553-1010
Fax: 714-553-2050
Email: ugauntlett@aol.com

David A. Gauntlett

David A. Stall	Elizabeth A. Gillis
Leo E. Lundberg, Jr.	(Not admitted in CA)
Michael Danton Richardson	Mark H. Plager
William P. Warden	(Not admitted in CA)
Stanley H. Shure	Jeffrey S. Allison

OF COUNSEL

Gary L. Hinman   Jose Zorrilla, Jr.

For full biographical listings, see the Martindale-Hubbell Law Directory

MAHER, LEE & GODDARD, LLP (AV)

18500 Von Karman Avenue, Suite 700, 92715
Telephone: 714-721-7555
Facsimile: 714-721-7444

Michael K. Maher	Cynthia R. Maher
Raymond A. Lee	Sherman O. Halstead, Jr.
William A. Goddard, IV	Maureen M. Alpin

For full biographical listings, see the Martindale-Hubbell Law Directory

SNELL & WILMER, L.L.P. (AV)

1920 Main Street, Suite 1200, 92614
Telephone: 714-253-2700
FAX: 714-955-2507
URL: http://www.swlaw.com
Phoenix, Arizona Office: One Arizona Center, 85004-0001.
Telephone: 602-382-6000.
Fax: 602-382-6070.
Tucson, Arizona Office: Norwest Tower, Suite 1500, One South Church Avenue, 85701-1612.
Telephone: 520-882-1200.
Fax: 520-884-1294.
Salt Lake City, Utah Office: Broadway Centre, 111 East Broadway, Suite 900, 84111-1004.
Telephone: 801-237-1900.
Fax: 801-237-1950.

MEMBER OF FIRM
Diane R. Smith (Resident)
ASSOCIATE
Sean Michael Sherlock

For Complete List of Firm Personnel, See General Section

For full biographical listings, see the Martindale-Hubbell Law Directory

LAW OFFICES OF SUSAN M. TRAGER A PROFESSIONAL CORPORATION (AV)

The Landmark Building, Suite 104, 2100 S. E. Main Street, 92614
Telephone: 714-752-8971
Telefax: 714-863-9804

Susan M. Trager

Michele A. Staples   Laura Pavloff Couch

Representative Client: San Luis Rey Municipal Water District.
Reference: Sanwa Bank California.

For full biographical listings, see the Martindale-Hubbell Law Directory

WATT, TIEDER & HOFFAR, L.L.P. (AV⊤)

3 Park Plaza, Suite 1530, 92714
Telephone: 714-852-6700
Telecopier: 714-261-0771
McLean Virginia Office: 7929 Westpark Drive, Suite 400,
Telephone: 703-749-1000.
Telecopier: 703-893-8029.
Washington, D.C. Office: 601 Pennsylvania Avenue, N.W. Suite 900,
Telephone: 202-462-4697.

MEMBERS OF FIRM

John B. Tieder, Jr.	Michael G. Long
(Not admitted in CA)	Christopher P. Pappas
Robert M. Fitzgerald	
(Not admitted in CA)	

ASSOCIATE
Gregory John Dukellis

For full biographical listings, see the Martindale-Hubbell Law Directory

---

LONG BEACH, Los Angeles Co.

CAMERON, MADDEN, PEARLSON, GALE & SELLARS (AV)

One World Trade Center Suite 1600, 90831-1600
Telephone: 310-436-3888
Telecopier: 310-437-1967

MEMBERS OF THE FIRM

Timothy C. Cameron	Patrick T. Madden
Charles M. Gale	Paul R. Pearlson
James D. Sellars	

ASSOCIATE
Lillian D. Salinger

For full biographical listings, see the Martindale-Hubbell Law Directory

FISHER & PORTER, A LAW CORPORATION (AV)

110 Pine Avenue, 11th Floor, P.O. Box 22686, 90801-5686
Telephone: 310-435-5626
Telex: 284549 FPKLAW UR
Fax: 310-432-5399

Gerald M. Fisher	Therese G. Groff
David S. Porter	Michael W. Lodwick
George P. Hassapis	

OF COUNSEL

Stephen C. Klausen	Stephen Chace Bass
Anthony P. Lombardo	

Vicki L. Hassman	Michael J. McLaughlin
Linda A. Mancini	Sandra L. Gryder
Kenneth F. Mattfeld	

For full biographical listings, see the Martindale-Hubbell Law Directory

RUSSELL & MIRKOVICH (AV)

One World Trade Center, Suite 1450, 90831-1450
Telephone: 310-436-9911
FAX: 310-436-1897

Carlton E. Russell   Joseph N. Mirkovich

For full biographical listings, see the Martindale-Hubbell Law Directory

TAUBMAN, SIMPSON, YOUNG & SULENTOR (AV)

249 East Ocean Boulevard, Suite 700, P.O. Box 22670, 90801-5670
Telephone: 310-436-9201
FAX: 310-590-9695

E. C. Denio (1864-1952)	Richard G. Wilson (1928-1993)
Geo. A. Hart (1881-1967)	Roger W. Young
Geo. P. Taubman, Jr.	William J. Sulentor
(1897-1970)	Peter M. Williams
Matthew C. Simpson	Scott R. Magee
(1900-1988)	Maria M. Rohaidy
Stuart C. Talley	

Attorneys for: Bixby Land Co.; Renick Cadillac, Inc.; Oil Operators Inc.
Local Counsel: Crown Cork & Seal Co., Inc.

For full biographical listings, see the Martindale-Hubbell Law Directory

WILLIAMS WOOLLEY COGSWELL NAKAZAWA & RUSSELL (AV)

111 West Ocean Boulevard, Suite 2000, 90802-4614
Telephone: 310-495-6000
Telecopier: 310-435-1359; 310-435-6812
Telex: ITT: 4933872; WU: 984929
Email: wwlaw@msn.com
Rancho Santa Fe, California Office: P.O. Box 9120, 16236 San Dieguito Road, Building 3, Suite 3-15, 92067.
Telephone: 619-497-0284.
Fax: 619-759-9938.
Port Hueneme, California Office: 237 E. Hueneme Road, Suite A, 93041.
Telephone: 805-488-8560.
Fax: 805-488-7896.

MEMBERS OF FIRM

Reed M. Williams	Alan Nakazawa
David E. R. Woolley	Blake W. Larkin
Forrest R. Cogswell	Thomas A. Russell

ASSOCIATES

Todd A. Valdes	Thomas G. Walsh
Richard J. Nikas	

For full biographical listings, see the Martindale-Hubbell Law Directory

LOS ANGELES, * Los Angeles Co.

BAKER & HOSTETLER (AV)

600 Wilshire Boulevard, 90017-3212
Telephone: 213-624-2400
FAX: 213-975-1740
In Cleveland, Ohio: 3200 National City Center, 1900 East Ninth Street.
Telephone: 216-621-0200.
In Columbus, Ohio: Capitol Square, Suite 2100, 65 East State Street.
Telephone: 614-228-1541.
In Denver, Colorado: 303 East 17th Avenue, Suite 1100.
Telephone: 303-861-0600.
In Houston, Texas: 1000 Louisiana, Suite 2000.
Telephone: 713-236-0020.
In Long Beach, California: 300 Oceangate, Suite 620.
Telephone: 310-432-2827.
In Orlando, Florida: SunBank Center, Suite 2300, 200 South Orange Avenue.
Telephone: 407-649-4000.
In Washington, D. C.: Washington Square, Suite 1100, 1050 Connecticut Avenue, N. W.
Telephone: 202-861-1500.
In College Park, Maryland: 9658 Baltimore Boulevard, Suite 206.
Telephone: 301-441-2781.
In Alexandria, Virginia: 437 North Lee Street.
Telephone: 703-549-1294.
In San Francisco, California: One Sansome Street, Suite 2000.
Telephone: 415-951-4705.

PARTNERS

Bradley R. Hogin   John C. Mueller

ASSOCIATE

Marc I. Seltzer

For Complete List of Firm Personnel, See General Section

For full biographical listings, see the Martindale-Hubbell Law Directory

BOTTUM & FELITON, A PROFESSIONAL CORPORATION (AV)

Suite 1500, South Tower, 3200 Wilshire Boulevard, 90010
Telephone: 213-487-0402
Fax: 213-386-9803
San Diego, California Office: Suite 400 Emerald Plaza, 402 West Broadway.
Telephone: 619-595-4857.
Fax: 619-595-4863.

Robert A. Wooten, Jr.   Steve Johnson

Scott A. Hampton

For full biographical listings, see the Martindale-Hubbell Law Directory

CLARK & TREVITHICK, A PROFESSIONAL CORPORATION (AV)

800 Wilshire Boulevard, 12th Floor, 90017
Telephone: 213-629-5700
Telecopier: 213-624-9441
San Francisco, California Office: 456 Montgomery Street, 20th Floor.
Telephone: 415-288-6520.
Fax: 415-398-2820.

Philip W. Bartenetti   Leonard Brazil
Dolores Cordell   Arturo Santana Jr.
Vincent Tricarico   Kerry T. Ryan

References: Wells Fargo Bank (Los Angeles Main Office); National Bank of California.

For Complete List of Firm Personnel, See General Section

For full biographical listings, see the Martindale-Hubbell Law Directory

DAVIS & FOX (AV)

1901 Avenue of the Stars, Suite 400, 90067
Telephone: 310-286-2915
Fax: 310-286-2916

MEMBERS OF FIRM

Calvin E. Davis   Steven A. Fox

ASSOCIATES

Brian Aronson   Amy L. Freisleben
Susan R. Peck

OF COUNSEL

Herbert D. Meyers

For full biographical listings, see the Martindale-Hubbell Law Directory

DEMETRIOU, DEL GUERCIO, SPRINGER & MOYER, LLP (AV)

801 South Grand Avenue, 10th Floor, 90017
Telephone: 213-624-8407
Telecopy: 213-624-0174
Email: ddsm@juno.com *URL:* http://www.ddsm.com

(See Next Column)

MEMBERS OF FIRM

Craig A. Moyer   Leslie M. Smario
Stephen A. Del Guercio   Andrew J. Bracker
Michael A. Francis   Kimberly E. Lewand
Regina Liudzius Cobb   Jennifer T. Taggart

OF COUNSEL

Ronald J. Del Guercio

Reference: Bank of America, L.A. Main Office, Los Angeles, Calif.

For full biographical listings, see the Martindale-Hubbell Law Directory

HANNA AND MORTON (AV)

A Partnership including Professional Corporations
Seventeenth Floor, Wilshire-Grand Building, 600 Wilshire Boulevard, 90017
Telephone: 213-628-7131
Facsimile: 213-623-3379

MEMBERS OF FIRM

Edward S. Renwick (A   James P. Lower
   Professional Corporation)   David A. Ossentjuk

ASSOCIATE

Robert J. Roche

Representative Clients: AlliedSignal, Inc.; Atlantic Richfield Co.; Air Liquide America Corp.; Carrier Corp.; Mobil Oil Corp.; Shell Oil Corp.; Texaco, Inc.; Unocal; Witco Corp.

For Complete List of Firm Personnel, See General Section

For full biographical listings, see the Martindale-Hubbell Law Directory

HORNBERGER & CRISWELL (AV)

444 South Flower, 31st Floor, 90071
Telephone: 213-488-1655
Facsimile: 213-488-1255
Email: kbranch0@counsel.com

MEMBERS OF FIRM

Nicholas W. Hornberger   Ann M. Ghazarians
Leslie E. Criswell   Michael A. Brewer
Scott Alan Freedman

ASSOCIATES

Marlin E. Howes   James M. Slominski
Christopher T. Olsen   Michael C. Denlinger
Scott B. Cloud   Gayle L. Eskridge

OF COUNSEL

David E. Bower   William P. Driscoll

For full biographical listings, see the Martindale-Hubbell Law Directory

LOEB & LOEB LLP (AV)

A Limited Liability Partnership including Professional Corporations
Suite 1800, 1000 Wilshire Boulevard, 90017-2475
Telephone: 213-688-3400
Facsimile: 213-688-3460; 688-3461; 688-3462
Century City, California Office: Suite 2200, 10100 Santa Monica Boulevard, Los Angeles, 90067-4164.
Telephone: 310-282-2000.
Facsimile: 310-282-2191; 282-2192.
New York, N.Y. Office: 345 Park Avenue, 10154-0037.
Telephone: 212-407-4000.
Facsimile: 212-407-4990.
Washington, D.C. Office: Suite 601, 2100 M Street N.W., 20037-1207.
Telephone: 202-223-5700.
Facsimile: 202-223-5704.
Nashville, Tennessee Office: 45 Music Square West, 37203-3205.
Telephone: 615-749-8300;
Facsimile: 615-749-8308.
Rome, Italy Office: Piazza Digione 1, 00197.
Telephone: 011-396-808-8456.
Facsimile: 011-396-808-8288.

MEMBERS OF FIRM

Malissa Hathaway McKeith   Raymond W. Thomas
                             (Century City Office)

ASSOCIATES

Nina B. Luban   Michelle Oyler Saifer
                            (New York City Office)

For Complete List of Firm Personnel, See General Section

For full biographical listings, see the Martindale-Hubbell Law Directory

MITCHELL, SILBERBERG & KNUPP LLP (AV)

A Partnership including Professional Corporations
11377 West Olympic Boulevard, 90064
Telephone: 310-312-2000
Fax: 310-312-3100

(See Next Column)

MITCHELL, SILBERBERG & KNUPP LLP, *Los Angeles—Continued*

MEMBERS OF FIRM

Marvin Leon (A Professional
    Corporation)
Arthur Fine (A Professional
    Corporation)

Jean Pierre Nogues (A
    Professional Corporation)
John E. Hatherley (A
    Professional Corporation)

OF COUNSEL
Douglas W. Bordewieck

References: Wells Fargo Bank, N.A.; Merrill, Lynch.

For Complete List of Firm Personnel, See General Section

For full biographical listings, see the Martindale-Hubbell Law Directory

OLIVER, VOSE, SANDIFER, MURPHY & LEE, A PROFESSIONAL CORPORATION (AV)

The Park, Second Floor, 281 South Figueroa Street, 90012
Telephone: 213-621-2000
Telecopier: 213-621-2211

Charles S. Vose
Connie Cooke Sandifer

James Duff Murphy
Edward W. Lee

Roger W. Springer

Mary L. McMaster
Arthur J. Hazarabedian

Bradley E. Wohlenberg
Timothy J. Chung

Kristin B. Mendenhall

OF COUNSEL
William B. Barr

Representative Clients: Cities of Covina, Hermosa Beach, South Pasadena and Calabasas; Los Angeles County North Valley Building Corp.; Los Angeles County Coroner's Building Corp.; Los Angeles County Montrose Sheriff's Station Corp.
Special Counsel: Anaheim Redevelopment Agency; Arcadia Redevelopment Agency; City of Brea; Brea Redevelopment Agency; Calleguas Municipal Water District; City of Anaheim.

For full biographical listings, see the Martindale-Hubbell Law Directory

O'MELVENY & MYERS LLP (AV)

400 South Hope Street, 90071-2899
Telephone: 213-669-6000
Cable Address: "Moms"
Facsimile: 213-669-6407
Email: omminfo@omm.com
Century City, California Office: 1999 Avenue of the Stars, 90067-6035.
Telephone: 310-553-6700.
Facsimile: 310-246-6779.
Newport Beach, California Office: 610 Newport Center Drive, 92660-6429.
Telephone: 714-760-9600.
Cable Address: "Moms".
Facsimile: 714-669-6994.
San Francisco, California Office: Embarcadero Center West Tower, 275 Battery Street, 94111-3305.
Telephone: 415-984-8700.
Facsimile: 415-984-8701.
New York, New York Office: Citicorp Center, 153 East 53rd Street, 10022-4611.
Telephone: 212-326-2000.
Facsimile: 212-326-2061.
Washington, D.C. Office: 555 13th Street, N.W., 20004-1109.
Telephone: 202-383-5300.
Cable Address: "Moms".
Facsimile: 202-383-5414.
London, England Office: 10 Finsbury Square, London, EC2A 1LA.
Telephone: 0171-256-8451.
Facsimile: 0171-638-8205.
Tokyo, Japan Office: Sanbancho KB-6 Building, 6 Sanbancho, Chiyoda-ku, Tokyo 102, Japan.
Telephone: 03-3239-2900.
Facsimile: 03-3239-2432.
Hong Kong Office: Suite 1905, Peregrine Tower, Lippo Centre, 89 Queensway, Central, Hong Kong.
Telephone: 852-2523-8266.
Facsimile: 852-2522-1760.
Shanghai, Peoples Republic of China Office: Shanghai International Trade Centre, Suite 2011, 2200 Yan An Road West, Shanghai, 200335, PRC.
Telephone: 86-21-6219-5363.
Facsimile: 86-21-6275-4949.

PARTNER
Mitchell B. Menzer

For Complete List of Firm Personnel, See General Section

For full biographical listings, see the Martindale-Hubbell Law Directory

RADCLIFF, FRANDSEN & DONGELL (AV)

40th Floor, 777 South Figueroa Street, 90017
Telephone: 213-614-1990
Facsimile: 213-489-9263
San Francisco, California Office: 88 Kearny Street, Suite 1475.
Telephone: 415-399-8393.
Facsimile: 415-989-5465.
Rome, Italy Office: Via Tacito, 7.
Telephone: (39) 06-323-5588.
Facsimile: (39) 06-324-3392.

MEMBERS OF FIRM

Jules G. Radcliff, Jr.

Russell Mackay Frandsen

Richard A. Dongell

OF COUNSEL
Tal Clifton Finney

ASSOCIATES

Francis P. Aspessi
Ruben A. Castellon
William W. Funderburk, Jr.
Jeffrey A. Gagliardi
David K. Lee
Maria Anna Mancini

Jeffrey C. Mayes
Marisa A. Moret
Daniel E. Park
Scott D. Pinsky
Eric H. Saiki
Steve R. Segura

Glenn M. White

For full biographical listings, see the Martindale-Hubbell Law Directory

RODI, POLLOCK, PETTKER, GALBRAITH & CAHILL, A LAW CORPORATION (AV)

Suite 400 801 South Grand Avenue, 90017
Telephone: 213-895-4900; 680-0823
Telecopiers: 213-895-4921; 895-4922; 895-4750

Karl B. Rodi (1908-1982)
John D. Cahill
John D. Pettker
Daniel C. Bond (1942-1977)
William R. Christian
Henry P. Pramov, Jr.
Robert A. Yahiro

Elizabeth B. Blakely
Robert C. Norton
John F. Cermak, Jr.
Tim G. Ceperley
Coralie Kupfer
Cris K. O'Neall
John S. Cha

Scott E. Adamson

Sonja A. Inglin
Thomas J. Yoo

Richard Nessary
Mark McCleary

OF COUNSEL
John P. Pollock

Margaret Rosenthal

For full biographical listings, see the Martindale-Hubbell Law Directory

SCHELL & DELAMER, LLP (AV)

A Partnership including Professional Corporations
865 South Figueroa Street Suite 2750, 90017
Telephone: 213-622-8181
Fax: 213-627-5252
Thousand Oaks, California Office: 100 East Thousand Oaks Boulevard, Suite 142.
Telephone: 805-496-9533.
Fax: 805-496-3424.

Gerald F. H. Delamer
    (1892-1955)
Walter O. Schell (1895-1981)
Roland R. Kaspar (Professional
    Corporation)

Garrin James Shaw (Professional
    Corporation)
Robert S. Hamrick (Professional
    Corporation)
Jeffrey F. Briskin

Katherine B. Pene

ASSOCIATES

Candace E. Ahrens Kallberg
Denise A. Nardi
Randy A. Berg
Kenneth S. Markson
Joseph P. Sepikas
Gregory J. Amantia (Resident at
    Thousand Oaks Office)

John J. Latzanich, II. (Resident
    at Thousand Oaks Office)
Lori M. Levine
Sylvia Havens
Roman Y. Nykolyshyn

Representative Clients: Hartford Insurance Group; Liberty Mutual Group; Travelers Insurance Co.
References: Los Angeles: First Interstate Bank; Merrill-Lynch.

For full biographical listings, see the Martindale-Hubbell Law Directory

SHEPPARD, MULLIN, RICHTER & HAMPTON LLP (AV)

A Limited Liability Partnership including Professional Corporations
Forty-Eighth Floor, 333 South Hope Street, 90071-1448
Telephone: 213-620-1780
Telecopier: 213-620-1398
Cable Address: "Sheplaw"
Email: info@smrh.com *URL:* http://www.smrh.com
Orange County, California Office: 650 Town Center Drive, 4th Floor, Costa Mesa.
Telephone: 714-513-5100.
Telecopier: 714-513-5130. Home Page Address: http://www.smrh.com.

(See Next Column)

SHEPPARD, MULLIN, RICHTER & HAMPTON LLP—*Continued*

San Francisco, California Office: Seventeenth Floor, Four Embarcadero Center.
Telephone: 415-434-9100.
Telecopier: 415-434-3947. Home Page Address: http://www.smrh.com.
San Diego, California Office: Nineteenth Floor, 501 West Broadway.
Telephone: 619-338-6500.
Telecopier: 619-234-3815. Home Page Address: http://www.smrh.com.

MEMBERS OF FIRM

Joseph A. Darrell	Stephen C. Taylor *
(San Francisco Office)	Timothy B. Taylor
M. Elizabeth McDaniel	(San Diego Office)
Stephen J. O'Neil	Roy G. Wuchitech

*Professional Corporation

For full biographical listings, see the Martindale-Hubbell Law Directory

---

NEWPORT BEACH, Orange Co.

DAVIS, PUNELLI, KEATHLEY & WILLARD (AV)

610 Newport Center Drive, Suite 1000, P.O. Box 7920, 92658-7920
Telephone: 714-640-0700
Telecopier: 714-640-0714
San Diego, California Office: 501 West Broadway, Suite 900, 92101.
Telephone: 619-558-2581.

MEMBERS OF FIRM

Robert E. Willard	H. James Keathley
S. Eric Davis	Eric G. Anderson
Frank Punelli, Jr.	Katherine D. Keathley

OF COUNSEL
Lewis K. Uhler

For full biographical listings, see the Martindale-Hubbell Law Directory

---

OAKLAND,* Alameda Co.

AIKEN, KRAMER & CUMMINGS, INCORPORATED (AV)

Suite 550 Ordway Building, One Kaiser Plaza, 94612
Telephone: 510-834-6800
Fax: 510-834-9017
Email: aikenkrame@aol.com

Benj. R. Aiken (1879-1955)	John A. Harkavy
Bauer E. Kramer (Retired)	Elizabeth M. Engh
Benj. R. Aiken, Jr. (Retired)	Matthew F. Graham
Fred V. Cummings (Retired)	Steven J. Cramer
Richard A. Sipos	

OF COUNSEL

Russell L. Barlow	Bruce G. Herold
Michael A. Coan	

Ellen Suzanne Wyatt	Michael S. Treppa

Reference: Union Bank of California, Oakland, California.

For full biographical listings, see the Martindale-Hubbell Law Directory

---

HAIMS, JOHNSON, MACGOWAN & MCINERNEY (AV)

490 Grand Avenue, 94610
Telephone: 510-835-0500
Facsimile: 510-835-2833

MEMBERS OF FIRM

Arnold B. Haims	Randy M. Marmor
Gary R. Johnson	John K. Kirby
Clyde L. MacGowan	Robert J. Frassetto
Thomas McInerney	Caroline N. Valentino
Lawrence A. Baker	Dianne D. Peebles

ASSOCIATES

Joseph Y. Ahn	Anne M. Michaels
Edward D. Baldwin	Michelle Diane Perry
Marc P. Bouret	Edward C. Schroeder, Jr.

For full biographical listings, see the Martindale-Hubbell Law Directory

---

HARDIN, COOK, LOPER, ENGEL & BERGEZ (AV)

1999 Harrison Street, 18th Floor, 94612-3541
Telephone: 510-444-3131
Telecopier: 510-839-7940

MEMBERS OF FIRM

Raymond J. Bergez	Matthew S. Conant
Willard L. Alloway	Chris P. Lavdiotis
Gennaro A. Filice, III	Robert D. Eassa
Stephen McKae	Nicholas D. Kayhan
Bruce E. McLeod	John A. De Pasquale
Eugene Brown, Jr.	Peter A. Strotz

(See Next Column)

Amber L. Kelly	Margaret L. Kotzebue
Elsa M. Baldwin	Amee A. Mikacich
Marshall A. Johnson	Timothy J. McCaffery
Diane R. Stanton	Stephen J. Valen
Jennifer M. Walker	Troy D. McMahan
Richard V. Normington III	

Representative Clients: Firemans Fund Insurance Cos.; City of Piedmont; The Dow Chemical Co.; Nissan Motor Corp.; Subaru of America; Weyerhauser Co.; Bay Area Rapid Transit District; Diamond Shamrock; Home Indemnity Co.; Rhone-Poulenc.

For Complete List of Firm Personnel, See General Section

For full biographical listings, see the Martindale-Hubbell Law Directory

---

ORANGE, Orange Co.

WALSWORTH, FRANKLIN, BEVINS & MCCALL (AV)

1 City Boulevard West, Suite 308, 92668
Telephone: 714-634-2522
LAW-FAX: 714-634-0686
San Francisco, California Office: 580 California Street, Suite 1335.
Telephone: 415-781-7072.
Fax: 415-391-6258.
Santa Barbara, California Office: 4520 Via Esperanza.
Telephone: 805-569-3100
Fax: 805-569-1906.
Houston, Texas Office: 2425 West Loop South, Suite 200.
Telephone: 713-787-9009.
Fax: 713-787-9010.

Jeffrey P. Walsworth	Randall J. Lee (Resident, San
Ferdie F. Franklin	Francisco Office)
Ronald H. Bevins, Jr.	Kevin Pegan
Michael T. McCall	Allan W. Ruggles
Noel Edlin (Resident, San	Laurie E. Sherwood
Francisco Office)	Cindy R. Hughes
Lawrence E. Duffy, Jr.	Stephen M. Nichols
James A. Anton	Cyrian B. Tabuena (Resident,
Ingrid K. Campagne (Resident,	San Francisco Office)
San Francisco Office)	Mary A. Watson
Robert M. Channel (Resident,	Alisa A. Shorago
San Francisco Office)	Deidre F. Cohen
Nicholas A. Cipiti	Demetrius D. Shelton
Sharon L. Clisham (Resident,	Jennifer A. Johnson
San Francisco Office)	Mark J. Mulkerin
Richard M. Hills (Resident, San	John S. Murray
Francisco Office)	Allyson B. Fox
Sandra G. Kennedy	(Resident, Houston Office)

For full biographical listings, see the Martindale-Hubbell Law Directory

---

PASADENA, Los Angeles Co.

CAIRNS, DOYLE, LANS, NICHOLAS & SONI, A LAW CORPORATION (AV)

Ninth Floor, 225 South Lake Avenue, 91101
Telephone: 818-683-3111
Telecopier: 818-683-4999

John D. Cairns	Stephen M. Lans
John C. Doyle	Francisco J. Nicholas
Rohini Soni (1956-1994)	

Representative Clients: Allstate Insurance Companies; Burger King Corp.; California Insurance Guarantee Assn.; California United Bank; CIGNA Insurance Companies; City of Pasadena; Cumis Insurance Society, Inc.; Employer's Mutual Insurance Companies; State Farm Insurance Companies; Tokio Marine Insurance.

For full biographical listings, see the Martindale-Hubbell Law Directory

---

FREEBURG, JUDY & NETTELS (AV)

600 South Lake Avenue, 91106
Telephone: 818-585-4150
FAX: 818-585-0718
Santa Ana, California Office: Xerox Centre. 1851 East First Street, Suite 120. 92705-4017.
Telephone: 714-569-0950.
Facsimile: 714-569-0955.

Steven J. Freeburg	J. Lawrence Judy
Charles F. Nettels	

ASSOCIATES

Ingall W. Bull, Jr.	Holly A. McNulty
Richard B. Castle	Karen S. Freeburg
Cynthia B. Schaldenbrand	Jennifer D. Helsel
(Resident, Santa Ana Office)	William R. Francis
Robert S. Brody	Fred W. Brandt
Carla Crochet	

For full biographical listings, see the Martindale-Hubbell Law Directory

Pasadena—Continued

LAGERLOF, SENECAL, BRADLEY & SWIFT, LLP (AV)

301 North Lake Avenue, 10th Floor, 91101-4108
Telephone: 818-793-9400
FAX: 818-793-5900

MEMBERS OF FIRM

Joseph J. Burris (1913-1980)	John F. Bradley
Stanley C. Lagerlof (Retired)	Timothy J. Gosney
H. Melvin Swift, Jr.	William F. Kruse
H. Jess Senecal	Thomas S. Bunn, III
Jack T. Swafford	Andrew D. Turner

Rebecca J. Thyne

ASSOCIATES

James D. Ciampa	Robert W. Renken

Representative Clients: Anchor Glass Container Corp.; Bethlehem Steel Corp.; Orthopaedic Hospital; Palmdale Water District; Public Water Agencies Group; Ventura Port District; Walnut Valley Water District; Metric Construction Co., Inc.

For full biographical listings, see the Martindale-Hubbell Law Directory

---

REDWOOD CITY,* San Mateo Co.

LOW, BALL & LYNCH, A PROFESSIONAL CORPORATION (AV)

10 Twin Dolphin, Suite B-500, 94065
Telephone: 415-591-8822
Fax: 415-591-8884
San Francisco, California Office: 601 California Street, Suite 2100, 94108.
Telephone: 415-981-6630.
Monterey, California Office: 10 Ragsdale Drive, Suite 175, 93940.
Telephone: 408-655-8822.

Raymond Coates	David L. Blinn
Chester G. Moore, III	Janet Kulig
James D. Miller	Thomas E. Mulvihill
William H. Holsinger	Jennifer Elizabeth Acheson

John R. Baumann	Joseph M. Fenech

Michael E. Sandgren

For full biographical listings, see the Martindale-Hubbell Law Directory

---

SACRAMENTO,* Sacramento Co.

THE BLEIER LAW FIRM (AV)

2100 21st Street, 95818-1708
Telephone: 916-454-2100
Fax: 916-454-2121
Email: tblf@bleier.com *URL:* http://www.bleier.com

Brenton A. Bleier

ASSOCIATES

Alan C. Campbell	Robert W. Hunt
Peter H. Mixon	Bradford A. Bleier

For full biographical listings, see the Martindale-Hubbell Law Directory

---

DIEPENBROCK & COSTA (AV)

455 University Avenue, Suite 300, 95825
Telephone: 916-565-6222
Fax: 916-565-6220

MEMBERS OF FIRM

Anthony C. Diepenbrock	Daniel P. Costa

ASSOCIATES

John P. Cotter	Nora E. Dwyer
Steven H. Schultz	Jeanne M. Carroll

Representative Clients: American Nuclear Insurer; Caldwell International; Central States of Omaha; Century Surety Co.; CIGNA; Citation; Colonial Penn; Connecticut Speciality Insurance Co.; Federated Mutual; Fleming & Hall.

For full biographical listings, see the Martindale-Hubbell Law Directory

---

DOWNEY, BRAND, SEYMOUR & ROHWER (AV)

Suite 1050, 555 Capitol Mall, 95814
Telephone: 916-441-0131
FAX: 916-441-4021
Email: downey@dbsr.com *URL:* http://www.dbsr.com

MEMBERS OF FIRM

Stephen J. Meyer	Steven H. Goldberg
George L. O'Connell	Katharine E. Wagner
Judy Holzer Hersher	Patrick G. Mitchell

ASSOCIATES

Adisa M. Abudu-Davis	Craig C. Allison
David R.E. Aladjem	Gordon B. Burns

Robert C. Bylsma

Counsel for: Roseburg Forest Products Co.; California Department of Conservation; Sunsweet Growers, Inc.; Cargill, Inc.; Diamond Lands; Procter & Gamble Co.; Raley's; Sacramento-Yolo Port District; The Hertz Corp.

(See Next Column)

For Complete List of Firm Personnel, See General Section

For full biographical listings, see the Martindale-Hubbell Law Directory

---

HARDY ERICH BROWN & WILSON, A PROFESSIONAL CORPORATION (AV)

1000 G Street, 95814
Telephone: 916-449-3800
Fax: 916-449-3888
Mailing Address: P.O. Box 13530, Sacramento, California, 95853-4530

Anthony D. Osmundson	Brian H. Charter
Thomas C. Richards	Larry Caldwell
John Quincy Brown, III	Richard L. Alley
David S. Worthington	Whitney A. Davis
L. Kent Wyatt	John C. Miller, Jr.
Bruce E. Salenko	Michael J. Nelson

Kristine E. Balough

Representative Clients: The Dexter Corporation; Fireman's Fund Insurance Company; Liberty Mutual Insurance Company; Goodyear Tire & Rubber Company; Royal Insurance Company; Travelers Insurance Company; Wausau Insurance Company.

For full biographical listings, see the Martindale-Hubbell Law Directory

---

HUNTER RICHEY DI BENEDETTO & BREWER, LLP (AV)

A Limited Liability Partnership
Renaissance Tower, 801 K Street, 23rd Floor, 95814-3525
Telephone: 916-491-3000
Facsimile: 916-491-3080
Email: hrdb@hrdb.com *URL:* http://www.hrdb.com

MEMBERS OF FIRM

William S. Hunter	James F. Geary
Win R. Richey	Janet C. Eisenbeis
Florence L. Di Benedetto	Jeffery D. Harris
Roy E. Brewer	Stephen C. Ruehmann
Anne E. Ferguson	Ralph T. Ferguson
Judith J. Citko	Sharon K. Sandeen

Kathryn T. Papalia

LEGAL SUPPORT PERSONNEL

Lori J. Kelly (Paralegal)	Michele L. Nickell
Deborah M. Romero (Paralegal)	(Legal Assistant)
Linda Jane Hall	Dawn Krein (Legal Assistant)
(Legal Assistant)	Stephanie L. Neumann
Jennifer E. Mueller	(Legal Assistant)
(Legal Assistant)	

For full biographical listings, see the Martindale-Hubbell Law Directory

---

LIVINGSTON & MATTESICH, LAW CORPORATION (AV)

1201 K Street, Suite 1100, 95814
Telephone: 916-442-1111
Fax: 916-448-1709
Email: liv-matt@gvn.net

Gene Livingston	Carol Livingston
James M. Mattesich	Rebecca M. Ceniceros

Steven P. Belzer	Trisha M. McAlmond

Reference: Bank of California.

For full biographical listings, see the Martindale-Hubbell Law Directory

---

SAN DIEGO,* San Diego Co.

HOVEY, KIRBY, THORNTON & HAHN, A PROFESSIONAL CORPORATION (AV)

101 West Broadway, Suite 1100, 92101-8297
Telephone: 619-685-4000
Fax: 619-685-4004
Email: 74754.3143@compuserve.com

Gregg B. Hovey	Jane Hahn
Cynthia K. Thornton	Geraldine A. Valdez

For full biographical listings, see the Martindale-Hubbell Law Directory

---

LUCE, FORWARD, HAMILTON & SCRIPPS LLP (AV)

A Partnership including Professional Corporations
600 West Broadway, Suite 2600, 92101
Telephone: 619-236-1414
Fax: 619-232-8311
URL: http://www.luce.com
La Jolla, California Office: 4275 Executive Square, Suite 800, 92037.
Telephone: 619-535-2639.
Fax: 619-453-2812.
Los Angeles, California Office: 777 South Figueroa, Suite 3600, 90017.
Telephone: 213-892-4992.
Fax: 213-892-7731.

(See Next Column)

LUCE, FORWARD, HAMILTON & SCRIPPS LLP—*Continued*

San Francisco, California Office: 100 Bush Street, 20th Floor, 94104.
Telephone: 415-395-7900.
Fax: 415-395-7949.
New York, N.Y. Office: Citicorp Center, 153 East 53rd Street, 26th Floor, 10022.
Telephone: 212-754-1414.
Fax: 212-644-9727.
Chicago, Illinois Office: 180 North La Salle Street, Suite 1125, 60601.
Telephone: 312-641-0580.
Fax: 312-641-0380.

MEMBERS OF FIRM

Steven P. McDonald	Stephen L. Marsh
John W. Leslie	Jon K. Wactor (Resident, San
Christopher J. Healey	Francisco Office)

ASSOCIATES

James G. Waian	Michael A. M. Lauffer

For Complete List of Firm Personnel, See General Section

For full biographical listings, see the Martindale-Hubbell Law Directory

---

SAN FRANCISCO,* San Francisco Co.

ALDEN ARONOVSKY & SAX (AV)

235 Montgomery Street, 28th Floor, 94104-2902
Telephone: 415-732-5820
Facsimile: 415-732-5840
Email: law@aaslaw.com

MEMBERS OF FIRM

David W. Alden	Ronald G. Aronovsky
	Brian M. Sax

ASSOCIATES

Jeffrey S. Koppelmaa	Sherry A. Glassman

For full biographical listings, see the Martindale-Hubbell Law Directory

---

BISHOP, BARRY, HOWE, HANEY & RYDER, A PROFESSIONAL CORPORATION (AV)

Embarcadero Center West, 12th Floor, 275 Battery Street, 94111-3333
Telephone: 415-421-8550
FAX: 415-362-4730

Ross R. Ryder (1940-1989)	Thomas O. Haran
Nelson C. Barry	Rebecca B. Aherne
Drayton F. Howe, Jr.	Michael W. Bolechowski
Jeffrey N. Haney	Mark C. Raskoff
Patricia S. Lakner	

William R. Brown	Stacey A. Kuch
J. Scott Wood	Marco R. Sumarriva
Mitchell J. Alward	Curtis A. Canfield
Lawrence S. Molton	Gregory R. de la Peña
Susan Knell Bumbalo	Paul Andrew Herp
Brook Bernard Bond	Rebecca E. Thomson
Marisa D'Amico	Jane E. Carey

OF COUNSEL

Woodrow W. Denney

Reference: The Redwood Bank.

For full biographical listings, see the Martindale-Hubbell Law Directory

---

LEACH, McGREEVY & BAUTISTA (AV)

1735 Pacific Avenue, 94109
Telephone: 415-775-4455
Telefax: 415-775-7435
Southern California Office: 13643 Fifth Street, Chino, CA. 91710.
Telephone: 909-590-2224.

Theodore Tamba (1900-1973)	Teresa A. Cunningham
John T. Harmon (1928-1993)	J. Curtis Cox
David G. Leach	Robert W. Shinnick
Richard E. McGreevy	Philip T. Kilduff
A. Marquez Bautista	Paul David Katerndahl

ASSOCIATE

John C. Connolly

OF COUNSEL

Roger G. Eliassen	Lloyd F. Postel

For full biographical listings, see the Martindale-Hubbell Law Directory

---

LIEFF, CABRASER, HEIMANN & BERNSTEIN, LLP (AV)

Embarcadero Center West, 30th Floor, 275 Battery Street, 94111
Telephone: 415-956-1000
Telecopier: 415-956-1008
Email: mail@lchb.com

(See Next Column)

Robert L. Lieff	Michael F. Ram
Elizabeth J. Cabraser	Joseph R. Saveri
Richard M. Heimann	Donald C. Arbitblit
William Bernstein	Robert J. Nelson
William B. Hirsch	Jacqueline E. Mottek
James M. Finberg	Morris A. Ratner
Karen E. Karpen	Melanie M. Piech

Richard L. Akel	Anthony K. Lee
Christine J. Anderson	Fabrice V. Nijhof
Kelly M. Dermody	Trina N. Parker
Eric B. Fastiff	Jonathan D. Selbin
Richard M. Franco	Mark N. Todzo
Heather A. Woodard	

For full biographical listings, see the Martindale-Hubbell Law Directory

---

VOGL & MEREDITH (AV)

456 Montgomery Street, 20th Floor, 94104
Telephone: 415-398-0200
Facsimile: 415-398-2820

Samuel E. Meredith	Jean N. Yeh
David R. Vogl	Janet Brayer
John P. Walovich	Thomas S. Clifton

Jill M. Thayer	Mark Ginalski
	Nicole L. Meredith

For full biographical listings, see the Martindale-Hubbell Law Directory

---

SAN JOSE,* Santa Clara Co.

THE ALEXANDER LAW FIRM (AV)

55 South Market Street, Suite 1080, 95113
Telephone: 408-289-1776
Fax: 408-287-1776
Email: access@alexanderlaw.com *URL:* http://www.alexanderlaw.com/
Cincinnati, Ohio Office: The Alexander Law Firm, 1300 Mercantile Library Building, 414 Walnut Street.
Telephone: 513-723-1776.
Fax: 513-421-1776.

Richard Alexander

ASSOCIATES

Michael T. Alexander (Resident,	Michael McShane
Cincinnati, Ohio Office)	Amanda Hawes
Jonathan D. Pendleton	Ann Saponara
Tyler A. Shaw	

OF COUNSEL

William M. Audet

For full biographical listings, see the Martindale-Hubbell Law Directory

---

HOPKINS & CARLEY, A LAW CORPORATION (AV)

Fifteenth Floor, 150 Almaden Boulevard, 95113-2089
Telephone: 408-286-9800
Facsimile: 408-998-4790

Leon A. Carley (1908-1984)	William S. Klein

For Complete List of Firm Personnel, See General Section

For full biographical listings, see the Martindale-Hubbell Law Directory

---

McMANIS, FAULKNER & MORGAN (AV)

160 West Santa Clara Street, 10th Floor, 95113
Telephone: 408-279-8700
Fax: 408-279-3244; 408-279-0494
Email: mfm@mfmlaw.com

MEMBERS OF FIRM

James McManis	William Faulkner
	Donelle Morgan

ASSOCIATES

Nora Rousso	Michael Reedy
Lisa Herrick	Douglas Watanabe
Kelly McHaffie	

For full biographical listings, see the Martindale-Hubbell Law Directory

---

TYNDALL & CAHNERS (AV)

An Association of Attorneys including a Professional Corporation
96 North Third Street, Suite 580, 95112
Telephone: 408-297-3700
Fax: 408-297-3721

John G. Tyndall III (P.C.)	John D. Cahners
	Michael Francis Brown

For full biographical listings, see the Martindale-Hubbell Law Directory

SAN RAFAEL, Marin Co.

RAGGHIANTI • FREITAS • MONTOBBIO • WALLACE LLP (AV)

874 Fourth Street, Suite D, 94901
Telephone: 415-453-9433
Fax: 415-453-8269

Gary T. Ragghianti	J. Randolph Wallace
David P. Freitas	Patrick M. Macias
J. Mark Montobbio	Robert F. Epstein

John Ralph Thomas

For full biographical listings, see the Martindale-Hubbell Law Directory

SANTA ANA, Orange Co.

CASSIDY, WARNER, THURBER & LANE, A PROFESSIONAL CORPORATION (AV)

600 West Santa Ana Boulevard, Suite 700, 92701
Telephone: 714-835-9431
Fax: 714-835-5264

Alvin M. Cassidy	David K. Thurber
B. Kent Warner	Timothy X. Lane

Bruce A. Winstead

Lloyd W. Felver	David C. Olson

Glen A. Stebens

For full biographical listings, see the Martindale-Hubbell Law Directory

FERRUZZO & FERRUZZO (AV)

A Partnership of Professional Corporations
2114 North Broadway, 92706
Telephone: 714-834-9322
Telecopier: 714-834-9358

MEMBERS OF FIRM

Thomas G. Ferruzzo (A Professional Corporation)	James K. Leese (A Professional Corporation)
James J. Ferruzzo (A Professional Corporation)	

ASSOCIATES

John R. Pelle	Maria Ann Newkirk
Dirk E. Petchul	Paul A. Madruga
Gregory J. Ferruzzo	Lisa L. Schultz

OF COUNSEL
M. Susan Watson

For full biographical listings, see the Martindale-Hubbell Law Directory

SANTA MONICA, Los Angeles Co.

HAIGHT, BROWN & BONESTEEL (AV)

A Partnership including Professional Corporations
1620 26th Street, Suite 4000 North, P.O. Box 680, 90404
Telephone: 310-449-6000
Telecopier: 310-829-5117
Telex: 705837
Santa Ana, California Office: Suite 900, 5 Hutton Centre Drive.
Telephone: 714-754-1100.
Telecopier: 714-754-0826.
Riverside, California Office: 3750 University Avenue, Suite 650.
Telephone: 909-341-8300.
Fax: 909-341-8309.
San Francisco, California Office: 201 Sansome Street, Suite 300.
Telephone: 415-986-7700.
Fax: 415-986-6954.

MEMBERS OF FIRM

Steven L. Hoch (A Professional Corporation)	William J. Sayers

ASSOCIATE
Farah Sohaili Nicol

For Complete List of Firm Personnel, See General Section

For full biographical listings, see the Martindale-Hubbell Law Directory

STOCKTON, San Joaquin Co.

MAYALL, HURLEY, KNUTSEN, SMITH & GREEN, A PROFESSIONAL CORPORATION (AV)

2453 Grand Canal Boulevard, Second Floor, 95207-8253
Telephone: 209-477-3833
Fax: 209-473-4818

(See Next Column)

Edwin Mayall (1907-1980)	William W. Hale
John J. Hurley (Retired)	Mark Stephen Adams
Clarence D. Knutsen	J. Anthony Abbott
Alan E. Smith	Peter J. Whipple
Dennis J. Green	Kristen M. Hegge

Vladimir F. Kozina

William L. Anderson	William J. Gorham, III
Donald W. West	Matthew Christopher Felix
Robert E. Laubengayer	Joseph A. Salazar, Jr.
Mark E. Berry	Steven A. Malcoun

Lesley Solomon

Representative Clients: Allstate Insurance Co.; California State Automobile Assn.; Fireman's Fund Insurance Co.; General Motors Corp.; Texaco, Inc; State Farm Mutual Insurance Cos.; Beck Development, Inc; HD Arnaiz, Ltd; Vito Transporation; The Alpine Group.

For full biographical listings, see the Martindale-Hubbell Law Directory

TORRANCE, Los Angeles Co.

FINER, KIM & STEARNS (AV)

An Association of Professional Corporations
City National Bank Building, 3424 Carson Street, Suite 500, 90503
Telephone: 310-214-1477
Telecopier: 310-214-0764

W. A. Finer (A Professional Corporation)	Robert David Ciaccio
	Robert B. Parsons

OF COUNSEL
Bennett A. Rheingold	Ryan E. Stearns

For Complete List of Firm Personnel, See General Section

For full biographical listings, see the Martindale-Hubbell Law Directory

VENTURA, Ventura Co.

FAIRFIELD, STRAUSS, URITZ & KINIGSTEIN, A PROFESSIONAL CORPORATION (AV)

290 Maple Court, Suite 200, 93003
Telephone: 805-644-7458
Fax: 805-644-4325
Email: mail@venturalaw.com *URL:* http://www.venturalaw.com

William D. Fairfield	Curt W. Uritz
Anthony R. Strauss	Terry Kinigstein

Wilfred J. Freeman	Bruce P. Crary

For full biographical listings, see the Martindale-Hubbell Law Directory

TAYLOR McCORD, A LAW CORPORATION (AV)

721 East Main Street, P.O. Box 1477, 93002
Telephone: 805-648-4700
Fax: 805-653-6124

Richard L. Taylor	Robert L. McCord, Jr.

David L. Praver

Patrick Cherry	Susan D. Siple

Rebbecca F. Calderwood

LEGAL SUPPORT PERSONNEL
PARALEGALS
Stephanie Gibson	Adele Rubino

Diane Lovato

For full biographical listings, see the Martindale-Hubbell Law Directory

COLORADO

ASPEN, Pitkin Co.

PATRICK & STOWELL, P.C. (AV)

Suite 300, 205 South Mill Street, 81611
Telephone: 970-920-1028
Fax: 970-925-6847
URL: http://www.waterlaw.com

Kevin L. Patrick	Brian L. Stowell

Scott Carpenter Miller	Thomas Edward Kinney

LEGAL SUPPORT PERSONNEL
Jennifer R. Santa Barbara (Paralegal)

For full biographical listings, see the Martindale-Hubbell Law Directory

BOULDER, * Boulder Co.

VRANESH AND RAISCH, L.L.C. (AV)

1720 14th Street, P.O. Box 871, 80306
Telephone: 303-443-6151
Telecopier: 303-443-9586

MEMBERS OF FIRM

Jerry W. Raisch	Eugene J. Riordan
John R. Henderson	Paul J. Zilis
Michael D. Shimmin	George Vranesh (Retired)

Thomas Morris	Margaret J. Woods

Representative Clients: Cyprus Climax Metals Co.; City of Fort Collins; Colorado Association of Commerce and Industry; County of Arapahoe; Eastman Kodak Company; Hendricks Mining Company; Horizon Gold Corporation, Inc.; Metro Wastewater Reclamation District; Phillips Petroleum Company; Waste Management of North America.

For full biographical listings, see the Martindale-Hubbell Law Directory

WILLIAMS & TRINE, P.C. (AV)

1435 Arapahoe Avenue, 80302-6390
Telephone: 303-442-0173
Fax: 303-443-7677

William A. Trine	J. Conard Metcalf
Joel H. Greenstein (1933-1984)	Mari C. Bush

Michael A. Patrick
OF COUNSEL
Charles E. Williams

Reference: Norwest Bank of Boulder.

For full biographical listings, see the Martindale-Hubbell Law Directory

DENVER, * Denver Co.

BAKER & HOSTETLER (AV)

303 East 17th Avenue, Suite 1100, 80203-1264
Telephone: 303-861-0600
FAX: 303-861-7805
In Cleveland, Ohio: 3200 National City Center, 1900 East Ninth Street.
Telephone: 216-621-0200.
In Columbus, Ohio: Capitol Square, Suite 2100, 65 East State Street.
Telephone: 614-228-1541.
In Houston, Texas: 1000 Louisiana, Suite 2000.
Telephone: 713-751-1600.
In Long Beach, California: 300 Oceangate, Suite 620.
Telephone: 310-432-2827.
In Los Angeles, California: 600 Wilshire Boulevard. Telephone 213-624-2400.
In Orlando, Florida: SunBank Center, Suite 2300, 200 South Orange Avenue.
Telephone: 305-841-1111.
In Washington, D. C.: Washington Square, Suite 1100, 1050 Connecticut Avenue, N.W.
Telephone: 202-861-1500.
In College Park, Maryland: 9658 Baltimore Boulevard, Suite 206.
Telephone: 301-441-2781.
In Alexandria, Virginia: 437 North Lee Street.
Telephone: 703-549-1294.
In San Francisco, California: One Sansome Street, Suite 2000.
Telephone: 415-951-4705.

PARTNER
Kenneth J. Burke

For Complete List of Firm Personnel, See General Section

For full biographical listings, see the Martindale-Hubbell Law Directory

BALLARD SPAHR ANDREWS & INGERSOLL (AV)

Seventeenth Street Plaza Building, Suite 2300, 1225 17th Street, 80202-5596
Telephone: 303-292-2400
Fax: 303-296-3956
Philadelphia, Pennsylvania Office: 1735 Market Street, 51st Floor.
Telephone: 215-665-8500.
Fax: 215-864-8999.
Harrisburg, Pennsylvania Office: 105 North Front Street.
Telephone: 717-236-3333.
Fax: 717-236-3884.
Salt Lake City, Utah Office: One Utah Center, 201 South Main Street, Suite 1200.
Telephone: 801-531-3000.
Fax: 801-531-3001.
Washington, D.C. Office: Suite 900 East, 555 13th Street, N.W.
Telephone: 202-383-8800.
Fax: 202-383-8877; 383-8893.
Baltimore, Maryland Office: 300 East Lombard Street, 19th Floor.
Telephone: 410-528-5600.
Fax: 410-528-5650.

(See Next Column)

Camden, New Jersey Office: 800 Hudson Square, 5th Floor.
Telephone: 609-541-5577.
Fax: 609-541-8272.

Elizabeth H. Temkin

Scott W. Hardt	Denise S. Maes

For Complete List of Firm Personnel, See General Section

For full biographical listings, see the Martindale-Hubbell Law Directory

BROWNSTEIN HYATT FARBER & STRICKLAND, P.C. (AV)

Twenty-Second Floor, 410 Seventeenth Street, 80202-4437
Telephone: 303-534-6335
Telecopier: 303-623-1956
Washington, D.C. Office: 601 Pennsylvania Avenue, N.W., Suite 900.
Telephone: 202-434-8377.
Telecopier: 202-393-7864.

Thomas L. Strickland	Stanley L. Garnett
Andrew W. Loewi	Wayne F. Forman

Hubert A. Farbes, Jr.

Mark J. Mathews	Beth Doherty Quinn

David S. Chipman

Representative Clients: Boston Chicken, Inc.; FCR, Inc.; Great American Insurance Co.; The Hertz Corporation; Kohlberg & Co.; Mid-American Waste Systems, Inc.; The Prudential Insurance Company of America; Trammell Crow Company.

For Complete List of Firm Personnel, See General Section

For full biographical listings, see the Martindale-Hubbell Law Directory

CARLSON, HAMMOND & PADDOCK, L.L.C. (AV)

1700 Lincoln Street, Suite 3900, 80203
Telephone: 303-861-9000
Telefax: 303-861-9026

MEMBERS OF FIRM

John Undem Carlson	Mary Mead Hammond
(1940-1992)	William A. Paddock

Lee Heinrick Johnson

Melanie Kopperud Backes	Peter C. Fleming

K. Gwen Beacham

Representative Clients: Atlantic Richfield Co.; Board of Water Works of Pueblo Colorado; D.C. Burns Realty & Trust Company; City of Colorado Springs; Colorado Water Resources & Power Development Authority; Forbes Inc.; OXY USA, Inc.; Rio Grande Water Users Assn.; San Luis Valley Water Conservancy District; City of Westminster.

For full biographical listings, see the Martindale-Hubbell Law Directory

DUFFORD & BROWN, P.C. (AV)

1700 Broadway, Suite 1700, 80290-1701
Telephone: 303-861-8013
Facsimile: 303-832-3804
Affiliated Office: Solomon, Pearl, Blum & Quinn, L.L.P., New York, NY and Denver, Colorado.

William C. Robb	Eugene F. Megyesy, Jr.
Richard L. Fanyo	Craig B. Shaffer

Joanne Herlihy

Representative Clients: A. O. Smith Corp.; CF&I Steel, L.P.; Chemical Waste Management, Inc.; Chevron Shale Oil Company; Coors Brewing Company; Echo Bay-Sunnyside Gold; Homestake Mining Company; Kerr Coal Company; Trapper Mining Inc.; WMX Technologies, Inc.

For Complete List of Firm Personnel, See General Section

For full biographical listings, see the Martindale-Hubbell Law Directory

FRIEDLOB SANDERSON RASKIN PAULSON & TOURTILLOTT, LLC (AV)

1400 Glenarm Place, 80202-5099
Telephone: 303-571-1400
Fax: 303-595-3159; 303-595-3970; 303-615-5472
Email: 72731.505@Compuserve.Com
Englewood, Colorado Office: 8400 East Prentice Avenue, 80111-2918.
Telephone: 303-571-1400.

James W. Sanderson	Christopher R. Paulson

W. B. Tourtillott

For full biographical listings, see the Martindale-Hubbell Law Directory

Denver—Continued

HOLME ROBERTS & OWEN LLP (AV)

Suite 4100, 1700 Lincoln, 80203
Telephone: 303-861-7000
Telecopier: 303-866-0200
Email: hro@hro.com *URL:* http://www.hro.com
Boulder, Colorado Office: Suite 400, 1401 Pearl Street.
Telephone: 303-444-5955.
Telecopier: 303-444-1063.
Colorado Springs, Colorado Office: Suite 1300, 90 South Cascade Avenue.
Telephone: 719-473-3800.
Telecopier: 719-633-1518.
Salt Lake City, Utah Office: Suite 1100, 111 East Broadway.
Telephone: 801-521-5800.
Telecopier: 801-521-9639.
London, England Office: Mellier House, 26a Albemarle Street.
Telephone: 44-171-499-8776.
Telecopier: 44-171-499-7769.
Moscow, Russia Office: Kosmodamianskaya Nab. #52/1, Suite 9100, 113054.
Telephone: 7095-961-3000.
Telecopier: 7095-961-3001.
Kiev, Ukraine Office: Terestchenkovskaya #19, Suite 2, 252004.
Telephone: 380-44-224-1348.
Telecopier: 380-44-224-4986.

PARTNERS OF FIRM

Edward J. McGrath	Nick Nimmo
Henry W. Ipsen	Charlotte Louise Neitzel
Brent V. Manning	Daniel J. Dunn
(Salt Lake City Office)	Linnea Brown
Phillip R. Clark	Robert Tuchman
Thomas F. Cope	John D. McCarthy
John Leonard Watson	Colin G. Harris

Kenneth W. Lund

OF COUNSEL

A. Edgar Benton

SPECIAL COUNSEL

Richard A. Oertli

ASSOCIATES

Loretta (Laurie) A. Cahill	Matthew J. Lepore
Katheryn Jarvis Coggon	Edward E. Stevenson

For Complete List of Firm Personnel, See General Section

For full biographical listings, see the Martindale-Hubbell Law Directory

MYERS, BRADLEY AND DEVITT, P.C. (AV)

Suite 420, 4704 Harlan Street, 80212
Telephone: 303-433-8527
Fax: 303-433-8219

Frederick J. Myers	Jerald J. Devitt
Jon T. Bradley	Randall C. Arp

OF COUNSEL

Kent E. Hanson

Reference: Bank One Lakeside Banking Center.

For full biographical listings, see the Martindale-Hubbell Law Directory

PARCEL, MAURO, HULTIN & SPAANSTRA, P.C. (AV)

Suite 3600, 1801 California Street, 80202
Telephone: 303-292-6400
Telecopier: 303-295-3040

David A. Bailey	Dean R. Massey
Jeffrey H. Desautels	Linda L. Rockwood
William J. Duffy	Kenneth L. Salazar
William A. Hillhouse II	James R. Spaanstra
Robert W. Lawrence	Christopher J. Sutton

OF COUNSEL

Mark N. Semenoff

Jodi S. Coviello	Laurie L. Korneffel
Michelle J. Hirth	Jeffrey K. Reeser
Susan J. Keller	Jeffrey W. Schwarz

Kimberly Ann Tempel

Reference: 1st Interstate, Denver, Colorado.

For Complete List of Firm Personnel, See General Section

For full biographical listings, see the Martindale-Hubbell Law Directory

REES & ASSOCIATES, P.C. (AV)

1675 Broadway, Suite 1400, 80202
Telephone: 303-592-5392
Fax: 303-892-3882

David K. Rees

For full biographical listings, see the Martindale-Hubbell Law Directory

ROOT & SCHINDLER, P.C. (AV)

410 17th Street, Suite 840, 80202
Telephone: 303-572-1235
Fax: 303-572-1256
Email: rootschi@ix.netcom.com

Thomas E. Root	Ronald I. Schindler

OF COUNSEL

F. Alan Fletcher

For full biographical listings, see the Martindale-Hubbell Law Directory

TREECE, ALFREY, MUSAT & BOSWORTH, P.C. (AV)

Denver Place, 999 18th Street, Suite 1600, 80202
Telephone: 303-292-2700
Facsimile: 303-295-0414
Email: 73507.2446@compuserve.com

Robert S. Treece	Thomas N. Alfrey

Arthur H. Bosworth, II

For full biographical listings, see the Martindale-Hubbell Law Directory

WELBORN SULLIVAN MECK & TOOLEY, P.C. (AV)

1775 Sherman Street, Suite 1800, 80203-4318
Telephone: 303-830-2500
Facsimile: 303-832-2366
Email: wsmt.denver@mep-1.sprint.com
Republic of Kazakstan Branch Office: 480100 Almaty 38 Dostyk Prospect, Suite 703.
Telephone: +7-3272 617-422; 616-509; 616-642.
Fax: +7-3272 615-840. *Email:* wsmt.welborn@mep-1.sprint.com.

John F. Welborn

Scott L. Sells

For Complete List of Firm Personnel, See General Section

For full biographical listings, see the Martindale-Hubbell Law Directory

CONNECTICUT

GREENWICH, Fairfield Co.

IVEY, BARNUM & O'MARA, LLC (AV)

Meridian Building, 170 Mason Street, P.O. Box 1689, 06830
Telephone: 203-661-6000
Telecopier: 203-661-9462

MEMBERS OF FIRM

Michael J. Allen	Donat C. Marchand
Robert C. Barnum, Jr.	Miles F. McDonald, Jr.
Edward D. Cosden, Jr.	Edwin J. O'Mara, Jr.
Wilmot L. Harris, Jr.	Remy A. Rodas
William I. Haslun II	Gregory A. Saum
Michael J. Jones	Lorraine Slavin
Edward T. Krumeich, Jr.	Steven B. Steinmetz

ASSOCIATES

Paul G. Amicucci	Melissa Townsend Klauberg
Stephan B. Grozinger	Cristin L. Rothfuss
Juerg A. Heim	Alan S. Rubenstein
Jennifer B. Kallenbach	Sheryl L. Sensale
	(Not admitted in CT)

OF COUNSEL

James W. Cuminale	Jennifer D. Port
Philip R. McKnight	(Not admitted in CT)

For full biographical listings, see the Martindale-Hubbell Law Directory

HARTFORD, * Hartford Co.

AUSTIN CAREY, JR., P.C. (AV)

Gothic Park, Suite 200, 43 Woodland Street, 06105-2340
Telephone: 860-724-0012
Fax: 860-724-1211
Email: acarey@counsel.com

Austin Carey, Jr.	Margaret Rausch Appicelli

For full biographical listings, see the Martindale-Hubbell Law Directory

KENNY, BRIMMER, MELLEY & MAHONEY (AV)

5 Grand Street, 06106
Telephone: 860-527-4226
FAX: 860-527-0214

(See Next Column)

KENNY, BRIMMER, MELLEY & MAHONEY—*Continued*

Joseph P. Kenny (1920-1993)

MEMBERS OF FIRM

Leslie R. Brimmer	William J. Melley, III

Richard C. Mahoney

ASSOCIATES

Anita M. Varunes	Beverly Johns
Dennis F. McCarthy	Edward J. Fitzgerald

For full biographical listings, see the Martindale-Hubbell Law Directory

SHIPMAN & GOODWIN LLP (AV)

One American Row, 06103-2819
Telephone: 860-251-5000
Telecopier: 860-251-5099
Email: first initial last name @goodwin.com
Email: www@goodwin.com *URL:* http://shipman-goodwin.com
Lakeville, Connecticut Office: Porter Street.
Telephone: 203-435-2539.
Stamford, Connecticut Office: One Landmark Square.
Telephone: 203-324-8100.

MEMBERS OF FIRM

Coleman H. Casey	John E. Wertam
Charles L. Howard	Timothy S. Hollister

ASSOCIATE

Timothy Patrick Brady

Representative Clients: Hartford Hospital; Lego Systems; Shawmut Bank, Connecticut, N.A.; The Napier Co.

For Complete List of Firm Personnel, See General Section

For full biographical listings, see the Martindale-Hubbell Law Directory

DELAWARE

DOVER, * Kent Co.

PARKOWSKI, NOBLE & GUERKE, PROFESSIONAL ASSOCIATION (AV)

116 West Water Street, P.O. Box 598, 19903
Telephone: 302-678-3262
Telecopier: 302-678-9415

F. Michael Parkowski	Jeremy W. Homer
John W. Noble	John C. Andrade
I. Barry Guerke	Jonathan Eisenberg
Clay T. Jester	Dana J. Schaefer

Mark F. Dunkle

OF COUNSEL

George F. Gardner, III

Representative Clients: Delaware Solid Waste Authority; Cabe Associates (Consulting Engineers).
Approved Attorneys for: Ticor Title Insurance Co.
Reference: First National Bank of Wyoming.

For full biographical listings, see the Martindale-Hubbell Law Directory

WILMINGTON, * New Castle Co.

WARREN B. BURT & ASSOCIATES (AV)

1700 Mellon Bank Center, 919 Market Street, 19801-3023
Telephone: 302-429-9430
Fax: 302-429-9427

ASSOCIATES

Richard D. Abrams	Michael F. Duggan

For full biographical listings, see the Martindale-Hubbell Law Directory

POTTER ANDERSON & CORROON (AV)

350 Delaware Trust Building, P.O. Box 951, 19899-0951
Telephone: 302-984-6000
FAX: 302-658-1192
URL: HTTP://ATTYS.PACDELAWARE.COM

MEMBERS OF FIRM

W. Harding Drane, Jr.	Harold I. Salmons, III

COUNSEL

David L. Baumberger

Representative Clients: Delmarva Power & Light Co.; U.S. Generating Co.; International Petroleum Corporation; KAO Infosystems Company; The Andrew Jergens Company; High Point Chemical Corporation; Rodel, Inc.; Hercules, Incorporated; Conrail; Amtrak.

For Complete List of Firm Personnel, See General Section

For full biographical listings, see the Martindale-Hubbell Law Directory

DISTRICT OF COLUMBIA

WASHINGTON, D.C. Co.

* indicates certain Bar Register subscribers, in cities of comparable size and importance, who maintain an additional office in Washington, D.C. and who have arranged for representation as a part of the Washington, D.C. listings that follow

ALEXANDER, BEARDEN, HAIRSTON & MARKS, LLP (AV)

Limited Liability Partnership
2021 L Street, N.W., Suite 300, 20036
Telephone: 202-293-3700
Fax: 202-293-7359
Silver Spring, Maryland Office: Lee Plaza, Suite 805, 8601 Georgia Avenue, 20910.
Telephone: 301-589-2222.
Facsimile: 301-539-2523.
New York, New York Office: 330 Madison Avenue, 36th Floor.
Telephone: 212-808-0008.
Fax: 212-599-1028.

Koteles Alexander

Reference: Riggs National Bank of Washington, D.C.

For full biographical listings, see the Martindale-Hubbell Law Directory

* BAKER & BOTTS, L.L.P. (AV)

A Registered Limited Liability Partnership
The Warner, 1299 Pennsylvania Avenue, N.W., 20004-2400
Telephone: 202-639-7700
Fax: 202-639-7832
Email: postmaster @bakerbotts.com
Houston, Texas Office: One Shell Plaza, 910 Louisiana.
Telephone: 713-229-1234.
Austin, Texas Office: 1600 San Jacinto Center, 98 San Jacinto Boulevard.
Telephone: 512-322-2500.
Dallas, Texas Office: 2001 Ross Avenue.
Telephone: 214-953-6500.
New York, New York Office: 599 Lexington Avenue.
Telephone: 212-705-5000.
Moscow, Russian Federation Office: 10 ul. Bolshaya Dmitrovka (formerly Pushkinskaya), 103031.
Telephone: 7095/921-5300 (Local); 7501/929-7070 (International).

MEMBERS OF FIRM

J. Patrick Berry	Steven R. Hunsicker
William M. Bumpers	Bruce F. Kiely
Charles M. Darling, IV	Steven L. Leifer
Thomas J. Eastment	Randolph Quaile McManus

ASSOCIATES

Debra Raggio Bolton	Jennifer S. Leete
Debra J. Jezouit	Mark K. Lewis

For Complete List of Firm Personnel, See General Section

For full biographical listings, see the Martindale-Hubbell Law Directory

BAKER & HOSTETLER (AV)

Washington Square, Suite 1100, 1050 Connecticut Avenue, N.W., 20036-5304
Telephone: 202-861-1500
In Cleveland, Ohio: 3200 National City Center, 1900 East Ninth Street.
Telephone: 216-621-0200.
In Columbus, Ohio: Capitol Square, Suite 2100, 65 East State Street.
Telephone: 614-228-1541.
In Denver, Colorado: 303 East 17th Avenue, Suite 1100.
Telephone: 303-861-0600.
In Houston, Texas: 1000 Louisiana, Suite 2000.
Telephone: 713-751-1600.
In Long Beach, California: 300 Oceangate, Suite 620.
Telephone: 310-432-2827.
In Los Angeles, California: 600 Wilshire Boulevard.
Telephone: 213-624-2400.
In Orlando, Florida: SunBank Center, Suite 2300, 200 South Orange Avenue.
Telephone: 305-841-1111.
In College Park, Maryland: 9658 Baltimore Boulevard, Suite 206.
Telephone: 301-441-2781.
In Alexandria, Virginia: 437 North Lee Street.
Telephone: 703-549-1294.
In San Francisco, California: One Sansome Street, Suite 2000.
Telephone: 415-951-4705.

PARTNER

Richard J. Leon

(See Next Column)

BAKER & HOSTETLER, *Washington—Continued*
ASSOCIATE
Kenneth D. Woodrow (Not admitted in DC)

For Complete List of Firm Personnel, See General Section

For full biographical listings, see the Martindale-Hubbell Law Directory

---

CARR GOODSON LEE & WARNER, A PROFESSIONAL CORPORATION (AV)

1301 K Street, N.W., Suite 400, East Tower, 20005-3300
Telephone: 202-310-5500
Telecopier: 202-310-5555
Email: info@cglw.com *URL:* http://www.cglw.com
Fairfax, Virginia Office: Tycon Towers, 8000 Towers Crescent Drive, Suite 1350, Vienna, Virginia, 22182.
Telephone: 703-691-8818.
Baltimore, Maryland Office: 201 North Charles St., 21201.
Telephone: 410-752-1570.
Rockville, Maryland Office: 31 Wood Lane, 20850.
Telephone: 301-424-7024.

Lawrence E. Carr, Jr.	William J. Carter
Margaret H. Warner	Kyle A. Kane
M. Miller Baker	Gregory A. Krauss
Charles E. Leasure, III	

SENIOR COUNSEL
Peter K. Tompa

Mark A. Collins	Patricia Ann Smith
Kent G. Huntington	Brian M. Tauscher
Michelle L. Melin	Karen E. Torrent
Karen A. Rosenthal	Bruce K. Trauben

For Complete List of Firm Personnel, See General Section

For full biographical listings, see the Martindale-Hubbell Law Directory

---

COHEN, MILSTEIN, HAUSFELD & TOLL, P.L.L.C. (AV)

West Tower, Suite 500, 1100 New York Avenue, N.W., 20005-3964
Telephone: 202-408-4600
Facsimile: 202-408-4699

MEMBERS OF FIRM

Jerry S. Cohen (1925-1995)	Lisa M. Mezzetti
Herbert E. Milstein	Andrew N. Friedman
Michael D. Hausfeld	Richard S. Lewis
Steven J. Toll	Daniel S. Sommers
Ann C. Yahner	Daniel A. Small
	(Not admitted in DC)

ASSOCIATES

Gary E. Mason	Michael J. Flannery
Cyrus Mehri	Paul T. Gallagher
Sharon A. Snyder	Alexander E. Barnett
Mark S. Willis	Angeline G. Chen
(Not admitted in DC)	Victoria C. Arthaud
Lillian S. Hagen	(Not admitted in DC)

OF COUNSEL
Anthony Z. Roisman

For full biographical listings, see the Martindale-Hubbell Law Directory

---

CUTLER & STANFIELD, L.L.P. (AV)

700 Fourteenth Street, N.W., 20005-2010
Telephone: 202-624-8400
Fax: 202-624-8410
Denver, Colorado Office: 1675 Broadway, 80202.
Telephone: 303-825-7000.
FAX: 303-825-7005.

MEMBERS OF FIRM

Eliot R. Cutler	Peter J. Kirsch
Jeffrey L. Stanfield	Barry Conaty
Sheila D. Jones	Stephen H. Kaplan
Perry M. Rosen	(Not admitted in DC)

OF COUNSEL

Byron Keith Huffman, Jr.	Sarah M. Rockwell
	(Not admitted in DC)

ASSOCIATES

Katherine Boonin Andrus	Dana C. Nifosi
Françoise M. Carrier	Barbara Paley
Christopher M. Kamper	W. Eric Pilsk
(Not admitted in DC)	Timothy A. Pohle
William G. Malley	Thomas D. Roth

For full biographical listings, see the Martindale-Hubbell Law Directory

---

FREEDMAN, LEVY, KROLL & SIMONDS (AV)

Suite 825, 1050 Connecticut Avenue, N.W., 20036-5366
Telephone: 202-457-5100
Cable Address: "Attorneys"
Telecopier: 202-457-5151
Email: flks@flks.com *URL:* http://www.flks.com/home/flks

MEMBERS OF FIRM

Richard G. Stoll	Karen M. Wardzinski
David P. Novello	

ASSOCIATE
Serena P. Wiltshire

For Complete List of Firm Personnel, See General Section

For full biographical listings, see the Martindale-Hubbell Law Directory

---

FRANK W. FRISK, JR., P.C. (AV)

Suite 125, Canal Square, 1054 Thirty-First Street, N.W., 20007
Telephone: 202-333-8433
Fax: 202-333-8431

Frank W. Frisk, Jr.

For full biographical listings, see the Martindale-Hubbell Law Directory

---

KELLY & WEAVER, A PROFESSIONAL CORPORATION (AV)

Suite 700, 11 Dupont Circle, 20036
Telephone: 202-797-7100
Fax: 202-939-6969

William G. Kelly, Jr.	Robert C. Weaver

NON-ATTORNEY MEMBER AND REGULATORY ADVISOR
Jim J. Tozzi

For full biographical listings, see the Martindale-Hubbell Law Directory

---

* LEWIS, CLAY & MUNDAY, A PROFESSIONAL CORPORATION (AV)

(Formerly Lewis, White & Clay, P.C.)
1000 16th Street, N.W., Suite 401, 20036
Telephone: 202-835-0616
Fax: 202-833-3316
Detroit, Michigan Office: 1300 First National Building, 660 Woodward Avenue. 48226-3531.
Telephone: 313-961-2550.
Troy, Michigan Office: Liberty Center, Suite 200. 100 West Big Beaver Road, 48084.
Telephone: 810-680-6702.
Fax: 810-680-6703.
Boston, Massachusetts Office: 10 Post Office Square. 02109.
Telephone: 617-422-8646.
Fax: 617-338-5693.

Karen Kendrick Brown (Resident)

For full biographical listings, see the Martindale-Hubbell Law Directory

---

STEPTOE & JOHNSON LLP (AV)

1330 Connecticut Avenue, N.W., 20036
Telephone: 202-429-3000
Cable Address: "Stepjohn"
Telex: 89-2503
Telecopier: 202-429-3902
Email: wbatterton@steptoe.com *URL:* http://www.steptoe.com
Phoenix, Arizona Office: Two Renaissance Square, 40 N. Central Avenue, Suite 2400, 85004.
Telephone: 602-257-5200.
Moscow, Russia Office: Steptoe & Johnson International AOZT. 25 Tsvetnoy Boulevard, Building 3 Moscow, Russia 103051.
Telephone: 011-7-501-258-5250.
Fax: 011-7-501-258-5251.
Almaty, Kazakhstan Office: Steptoe & Johnson Company Almaty. 84 Gogol Street, Suite 213, 480083.
Telephones: (3272) 50-11-25, (3272) 32-25-39.

MEMBERS

Robert E. Jordan III	Seth Goldberg
J. A. Bouknight, Jr.	Gary A. Morgans
F. Michael Kail	Steven Reed
Steven H. Brose	John D. Graubert
Douglas G. Green	Steven J. Ross
Samuel T. Perkins	Jane I. Ryan
James B. Vasile	David H. Coburn

OF COUNSEL

Sara Beth Watson	Joseph E. Stubbs
Scott A. Harman	Edward J. Twomey

For Complete List of Firm Personnel, See General Section

For full biographical listings, see the Martindale-Hubbell Law Directory

Washington—Continued

DANIEL R. THOMPSON, P.C. (AV)

Suite 925, 1620 I Street, N.W., 20006
Telephone: 202-293-5800
Facsimile: 202-463-8998

Daniel R. Thompson	Gregory E. Thompson
	John B. Hallagan

Reference: NationsBank, Washington, D.C.

For full biographical listings, see the Martindale-Hubbell Law Directory

* VENABLE ATTORNEYS AT LAW VENABLE, BAETJER, HOWARD & CIVILETTI, LLP (AV)

A Partnership including Professional Corporations
Suite 1000, 1201 New York Avenue, N.W., 20005
Telephone: 202-962-4800
Fax: 202-962-8300
Baltimore, Maryland Office: Venable, Baetjer and Howard LLP, 1800
Mercantile Bank & Trust Building, 2 Hopkins Plaza.
Telephone: 410-244-7400.
McLean, Virginia Office: Venable, Baetjer and Howard LLP, Suite 400,
2010 Corporate Ridge.
Telephone: 703-760-1600.
Rockville, Maryland Office: Venable, Baetjer and Howard LLP, Suite 500,
One Church Street, P. O. Box 1906.
Telephone: 301-217-5600.
Towson, Maryland Office: Venable, Baetjer and Howard LLP, 210
Allegheny Avenue, P. O. Box 5517.
Telephone: 410-494-6200.

MEMBERS OF FIRM

Benjamin R. Civiletti (P.C.) (Also at Baltimore and Towson, Maryland Offices)	James K. Archibald (Also at Baltimore, Maryland Office)
Anthony M. Carey (Not admitted in DC; Also at Baltimore, Maryland Office)	Judson W. Starr (Also at Baltimore and Towson, Maryland Offices)
Dennis J. Whittlesey	Jeffrey A. Dunn (Also at Baltimore, Maryland Office)
John G. Milliken (Also at McLean, Virginia Office)	James L. Shea (Not admitted in DC; also at Baltimore, Maryland Office)
Joseph G. Block	
Michael Schatzow (Also at Baltimore, Maryland Office)	John J. Pavlick, Jr.
John F. Cooney	James A. Dunbar (Also at Baltimore, Maryland Office)
	Thomas J. Kelly, Jr.

OF COUNSEL

Richard H. Mays (Not admitted in DC; Also at McLean, Virginia Office)

ASSOCIATES

Gregory S. Braker	Andrew R. Herrup
	Valerie K. Mann

For Complete List of Firm Personnel, See General Section

For full biographical listings, see the Martindale-Hubbell Law Directory

VERNER, LIIPFERT, BERNHARD, McPHERSON AND HAND, CHARTERED (AV)

901 15th Street, N.W., 20005-2301
Telephone: 202-371-6000
Cable Address: "Verlip"
Telex: 1561792 VERLIP UT
Fax: 202-371-6279
Email: verner.com
McLean, Virginia Office: Sixth Floor, 8280 Greensboro Drive, 22102.
Telephone: 703-749-6000.
Fax: 703-749-6027.
Houston, Texas Office: 2600 Texas Commerce Tower, 600 Travis, 77002.
Telephone: 713-237-9034.
Fax: 713-237-1216.
Honolulu, Hawaii Office: Hawaii Times Building, 928 Nuuanu Avenue,
Suite 400, 96817.
Telephone: 808-566-0999.
Fax: 808-566-0995.
Austin, Texas Office: Suite 1440 San Jacinto Center, 98 San Jacinto
Boulevard, 78701.
Telephone: 512-703-6000.
Fax: 512-703-6003.

Roy G. Bowman	Paul E. Nordstrom
R. Stuart Broom	Neil T. Proto
Gary J. Klein	Sherry A. Quirk
	Clinton A. Vince

OF COUNSEL

James K. Jackson	Stanley W. Legro

For Complete List of Firm Personnel, See General Section

For full biographical listings, see the Martindale-Hubbell Law Directory

WATT, TIEDER & HOFFAR, L.L.P. (AV)

601 Pennsylvania Avenue, N.W., Suite 900, 20004
Telephone: 202-462-4697
Telecopier: 703-893-8029
McLean Virginia Office: 7929 Westpark Drive, Suite 400,
Telephone: 703-749-1000.
Telecopier: 703-893-8029.
Irvine California Office: 3 Park Plaza, Suite 1530.
Telephone: 714-852-6700.

MEMBERS OF FIRM

John B. Tieder, Jr.	Robert K. Cox
	David C. Romm

For full biographical listings, see the Martindale-Hubbell Law Directory

WILMER, CUTLER & PICKERING (AV)

2445 M Street, N.W., 20037-1420
Telephone: 202-663-6000
Fax: 202-663-6363
Email: Law@Wilmer.Com
Baltimore, Maryland Office: 100 Light Street, 21202.
Telephone: 410-986-2800.
Fax: 410-986-2828.
European Offices:
4 Carlton Gardens, London, SW1Y 5AA, England. *Telephone:* +44 (171)
872-1000.
Fax: +44 (171) 839-3537.
Rue de la Loi 15Wetstraat, B-1040 Brussels, Belgium. *Telephone:* +32 (2)
285-4900.
Fax: +32 (2) 285-4949.
Friedrichstrasse 95, D-10117 Berlin, Germany. *Telephone:* +49 (30)
2022-6400.
Fax: +49 (30)2022-6500.

MEMBERS OF FIRM

C. Boyden Gray	Daniel H. Squire
James A. Rogers	Carol Clayton
Neil J. King	Laura B. Ahearn
	James R. Wrathall

For Complete List of Firm Personnel, See General Section

For full biographical listings, see the Martindale-Hubbell Law Directory

ZEVNIK HORTON GUIBORD & McGOVERN, P.C. (AV)

Ninth Floor, 1299 Pennsylvania Avenue, N.W., 20004
Telephone: 202-824-0950
FAX: 202-824-0955
Chicago, Illinois Office: Suite 3300, 77 West Wacker Drive.
Telephone: 312-977-2500.
Telefax: 312-977-2560.
Los Angeles, California Office: 333 South Grand Avenue, Twenty First
Floor.
Telephone: 213-437-5200.
Telefax: 213-437-5222.
New York, N.Y. Office: 745 Fifth Avenue, Twenty-Fifth Floor.
Telephone: 212-935-2735.
Telefax: 212-935-0614.
Palo Alto, California Office: 5 Palo Alto Square, 3000 El Camino Real.
Telephone: 415-842-5900.
Facsimile: 415-855-9226.
London, England Office: 4 Kings Bench Walk, Temple, London EC4Y
7DL.
Telephone: 071-353-0478.
Facsimile: 071-583-3549.
Norfolk, Virginia Office: Main Street Tower, 300 East Main Street, 13th
Floor.
Telephone: 757-624-3480.
Fax: 757-624-3479.

Paul Anton Zevnik	Joseph G. Homsy
Michel Yves Horton	(Not admitted in DC)
Barbara B. Guibord	John W. Roberts
(Not admitted in DC)	(Not admitted in DC)
Patrick Michael McGovern	John K. Crossman
(Not admitted in DC)	(Not admitted in DC)
	Jonathan L. Osborne

Yolanda C. Griffin	Michael J. Wilson
(Not admitted in DC)	

For full biographical listings, see the Martindale-Hubbell Law Directory

FLORIDA

BRADENTON,* Manatee Co.

GRIMES GOEBEL GRIMES HAWKINS & GLADFELTER, P.A. (AV)

The Professional Building, 1023 Manatee Avenue West, P.O. Box
1550, 34206
Telephone: 941-748-0151
Fax: 941-748-0158

Caleb J. Grimes   Leslie Horton Gladfelter
William S. Galvano

Counsel for: Schroeder Manatee Inc. (Agriculture and Land Development);
Pursley, Inc., (Horticulture, Retail and Land Development); Lombardo &
Skipper, Inc. (Civil Engineers); CCI Environmental Services, Inc. (Environmental Consultants); Creekwood Investors, Ltd.; Old Hyde Park Village
Center, Ltd.; First Federal Savings & Loan Association of Florida.
Approved Attorneys for: Lawyers Title Insurance Corp.; Chicago Title Insurance Co.; Attorneys Title Insurance Fund.

For Complete List of Firm Personnel, See General Section

For full biographical listings, see the Martindale-Hubbell Law Directory

McGUIRE, PRATT, MASIO & FARRANCE, P.A. (AV)

Suite 600, 1001 3rd Avenue West, P.O. Box 1866, 34206
Telephone: 941-748-7076
Fax: 941-747-9774

Hugh E. McGuire, Jr.   Carol A. Masio
Charles J. Pratt, Jr.   Robert A. Farrance
           John W. Kaklis
           OF COUNSEL
           Carter H. Parry

Reference: Barnett Bank of Manatee County.

For full biographical listings, see the Martindale-Hubbell Law Directory

FORT LAUDERDALE,* Broward Co.

TRIPP, SCOTT, CONKLIN & SMITH (AV)

28th Floor, 110 Tower, 110 S.E. 6th Street, P.O. Box 14245, 33301
Telephone: 954-525-7500
Telecopier: 954-761-8475

Norman D. Tripp   Timothy J. McDermott
James A. Scott   Kimberly A. Gilmour
Howard L. Conklin   Richard D. Heller
Dennis Dustin Smith   Gregory A. McLaughlin
Peter G. Herman   Steven C. Elkin
Garry W. Johnson   Drake M. Batchelder
           OF COUNSEL
Robert E. Huebner   Welcom H. Watson, Jr.
           ASSOCIATES
O. Mason Hurst, II   Heidi E. Davis
Matthew Zifrony   Jeffrey S. Wood
Grant J. Smith   Scott J. Jordan
William J. Gross   Jason A. Diamond
Paul Octavio Lopez   Christopher L. Smith
Daniel E. Taylor   Angelia Maria Baldwin

Representative Clients: Alamo Rent A Car, Inc.; The Sports Authority, Inc.;
Atlas Waste Magic Recyclers, Inc.; Broward County.

For full biographical listings, see the Martindale-Hubbell Law Directory

JACKSONVILLE,* Duval Co.

SMITH HULSEY & BUSEY (AV)

1800 First Union National Bank Tower, 225 Water Street, P.O. Box
53315, 32201-3315
Telephone: 904-359-7700
Facsimile: 904-359-7708; 353-9908

Lloyd Smith (1915-1987)
MEMBERS OF FIRM

Dennis L. Blackburn   E. Owen McCuller, Jr.
Stephen D. Busey   James H. Post
Douglas D. Chunn   Bryan L. Putnal
Earl E. Googe, Jr.   E. Lanny Russell
Jeanne E. Helton   Joel Settembrini, Jr.
Cynthia C. Jackson   Tim E. Sleeth
G. Preston Keyes   John R. Smith, Jr.
William E. Kuntz   James J. Taylor, Jr.
M. Richard Lewis, Jr.   Timothy W. Volpe
John F. MacLennan   Waddell A. Wallace, III
Raymond R. Magley   Harry M. Wilson, III

(See Next Column)

Michael M. Bajalia   R. Leanne McKnight
James A. Bolling, Jr.   Mary E. McManus
E. Lanier Drew   Jeanne M. Miller
Diana Salama Farhat   Stephen D. Moore, Jr.
Martin A. Fitzpatrick   Howard J. Smith
Michael R. Freed   Steven G. Spears
Lee G. Kellison   Melissa Smith Turra
Lauren P. Langham   Herschel T. Vinyard, Jr
Marjorie Conner Makar Leslie A. Wickes
Bradley R. Markey   Karl A. Zillgitt
           OF COUNSEL
Mark Hulsey   John E. Thrasher

Representative Clients: Baptist/St. Vincent's Health System, Inc.; Browning-Ferris Industries, Inc.; Champion Realty Corp. (Florida); First Union National Bank of Florida; Florida Rock Industries, Inc.; PGA Tour, Inc.;
KPMG Peat Marwick; The Regency Group, Inc.; The Ritz-Carlton Hotel
Co.; University of Florida.

For full biographical listings, see the Martindale-Hubbell Law Directory

KISSIMMEE,* Osceola Co.

POHL & SHORT, P.A.

(See Winter Park)

LAKELAND, Polk Co.

PETERSON & MYERS, P.A. (AV)

100 East Main Street, P.O. Box 24628, 33802-4628
Telephone: 941-683-6511; 676-6934
Telecopier: 941-682-8031
Lake Wales, Florida Office: 130 East Central Avenue, P.O. Box 1079.
Telephones: 941-676-7611; 683-8942.
Winter Haven, Florida Office: Suite 300, 141 5th Street, N.W., P.O.
Drawer 7608.
Telephone: 941-294-3360.

Philip O. Allen   Peter J. Munson
Jack P. Brandon   Corneal B. Myers
Beach A Brooks, Jr.   Cornelius B. Myers, III
Kristen Marie Buzzanca E. Blake Paul
J. Davis Connor   Robert E. Puterbaugh
Michael S. Craig   Abel A. Putnam
Roy A. Craig, Jr.   Thomas B. Putnam, Jr.
Jacob C. Dykxhoorn   Deborah A. Ruster
Dennis P. Johnson   Stephen R. Senn
Kevin C. Knowlton   Andrea Teves Smith
Douglas A. Lockwood, III Keith H. Wadsworth
M. Craig Massey   Kerry M. Wilson

General Counsel for: Barnett Bank of Polk County.
Representative Clients: Mutual Wholesale Co.; Barnett Banks, Inc.; Ben Hill
Griffin, Inc.; Alcoma Association, Inc.
Approved Attorneys for: Equitable Life Assurance Society of the United
States; Federal Land Bank, Columbia, South Carolina; Attorneys' Title Insurance Fund.

For full biographical listings, see the Martindale-Hubbell Law Directory

LAKE WALES, Polk Co.

PETERSON & MYERS, P.A. (AV)

130 East Central Avenue, P.O. Box 1079, 33853
Telephone: 941-676-7611; 683-8942
Telecopier: 941-676-0643
Lakeland, Florida Office: 100 East Main Street, P.O. Box 24628.
Telephones: 941-683-6511; 676-6934.
Winter Haven, Florida Office: Suite 300, 141 5th Street, N.W., P.O.
Drawer 7608.
Telephone: 941-294-3360.

Philip O. Allen   Peter J. Munson
Jack P. Brandon   Corneal B. Myers
Beach A Brooks, Jr.   Cornelius B. Myers, III
Kristen Marie Buzzanca E. Blake Paul
J. Davis Connor   Robert E. Puterbaugh
Michael S. Craig   Abel A. Putnam
Roy A. Craig, Jr.   Thomas B. Putnam, Jr.
Jacob C. Dykxhoorn   Deborah A. Ruster
Dennis P. Johnson   Stephen R. Senn
Kevin C. Knowlton   Andrea Teves Smith
Douglas A. Lockwood, III Keith H. Wadsworth
M. Craig Massey   Kerry M. Wilson

General Counsel for: Barnett Bank of Polk County.
Representative Clients: Mutual Wholesale Co.; Sun Bank/Mid-Florida, N.A.;
Chase Commercial Corp.; Barnett Banks, Inc.; Ben Hill Griffin, Inc.; Alcoma
Association, Inc.
Approved Attorneys for: Equitable Life Assurance Society of the United
States; Federal Land Bank, Columbia, South Carolina; Attorneys' Title Insurance Fund.

For full biographical listings, see the Martindale-Hubbell Law Directory

*MIAMI,** Dade Co.

EARL, BLANK, KAVANAUGH & STOTTS, PROFESSIONAL ASSOCIATION (AV)

Suite 3636, One Biscayne Tower, Two South Biscayne Boulevard, 33131
Telephone: 305-358-3000
FAX: 305-358-5079
Email: ebks@aol.com
Sarasota, Florida Office: 1800 Second Street.
Telephone: 941-366-1180.
Fax: 941-366-1183. E-Mail: ebkssrq@aol.com.

William L. Earl	Dennis M. Stotts
Robert H. Blank	Mark T. Kobelinski
Judith Smith Kavanaugh	Stephen R. Verbit

Reference: NationsBank, N.A.

For full biographical listings, see the Martindale-Hubbell Law Directory

DOUGLAS M. HALSEY, P.A. (AV)

First Union Financial Center, Suite 4980, 200 South Biscayne
  Boulevard, 33131-5309
Telephone: 305-375-0077
Telecopier: 305-375-0020
Email: DMHPA@aol.com

Douglas M. Halsey	Kirk Lee Burns
Judith J. Chorlog	Evan M. Goldenberg

Reference: United National Bank.

For full biographical listings, see the Martindale-Hubbell Law Directory

KEITH, MACK, LEWIS, COHEN & LUMPKIN (AV)

First Union Financial Center, Twentieth Floor, 200 South Biscayne
  Boulevard, 33131-2310
Telephone: 305-358-7605
Fax: 305-358-4755
Email: PREVAIL@KEITHMACK.COM

MEMBERS OF FIRM

Edgar Lewis	Jan Carson Cheezem
Robert A. Cohen	Loren S. Granoff
R. Hugh Lumpkin	Jack S. Lewis
Gregg S. Ahrens	Alan Rosenthal
Norman S. Segall	

ASSOCIATES

Michael J. Hogsten	Michele S. Primeau
Felix M. Lasarte	Cynthia Ramos
Dawn Marshall	Jack R. Reiter
Mercedes Padin	Karl J. Schumer
Jeffrey P. Shapiro	

OF COUNSEL

Seymour D. Keith	James L. Mack

Representative Clients: CitiBank, F.S.B.; Attorneys Title Insurance Fund, Inc.; Barnett Bank, N.A.
Approved Counsel: First American Title Insurance Co.; Attorneys Title Insurance Fund, Inc.; Commonwealth Title Insurance Co.
Reference: CitiBank, F.S.B.

For full biographical listings, see the Martindale-Hubbell Law Directory

*ORLANDO,** Orange Co.

BEST & ANDERSON, P.A. (AV)

20 North Orange Avenue, Suite 505, 32801
Telephone: 407-425-2985
Crystal River, Florida Office: 7655 West Gulf to Lake Highway, Suite 6.
Telephone: 352-795-1107.
Melbourne, Florida Office: Marina Towers, 709 South Harbor City
Boulevard, Suite 220, 32901.
Telephone: 407-727-9923.

David R. Best	Lawrence I. Hauser
George H. "Dutch" Anderson, III	
G. Clay Morris	Angela O'Neil
Natt O. Reifler	

For full biographical listings, see the Martindale-Hubbell Law Directory

POHL & SHORT, P.A.

(See Winter Park)

LAW OFFICE OF IRBY G. PUGH (AV)

218 Annie Street, 32806
Telephone: 407-843-5840
Reference: Upon Request.

For full biographical listings, see the Martindale-Hubbell Law Directory

WILSON, LEAVITT & SMALL, P.A. (AV)

Nations Bank Tower, 111 North Orange Avenue, Suite 1575, 32801
Telephone: 407-843-4321
Fax: 407-423-1505

J. Christy Wilson, III	Jay W. Small
Mark R. Leavitt	Lauren B. Shapiro

Representative Clients: Circle K; Cumberland Farms; Hardee's Food Systems; Mobil Oil; Public Storage; Southland Corp.; NationsBank, N.A.; U.S.F.& G.; Oerther Foods; Seventh Day Adventists.

For full biographical listings, see the Martindale-Hubbell Law Directory

PALM BEACH GARDENS, Palm Beach Co.

SCOTT, ROYCE, HARRIS, BRYAN, BARRA & JORGENSEN, PROFESSIONAL ASSOCIATION (AV)

4400 PGA Boulevard, Suite 800, 33410
Telephone: 561-624-3900
Fax: 561-624-3533

Raymond W. Royce

Representative Clients: John D. & Catherine T. MacArthur Foundation; First Union National Bank of Florida, N.A.; The Realtors Association of the Palm Beaches, Inc.; Lost Tree Village; Jupiter Hills, Pappalardo Contractors, Inc.; Art Moran Pontiac, Inc.; John D. and Catherine T. MacArthur Foundation; Wal-Mart Stores, Inc.; Whitworth Farms.

For Complete List of Firm Personnel, See General Section

For full biographical listings, see the Martindale-Hubbell Law Directory

*ST. AUGUSTINE,** St. Johns Co.

DOBSON & BROWN, P.A. (AV)

66 Cuna Street, Suite B, 32084
Telephone: 904-824-9032
Fax: 904-824-9236

Geoffrey B. Dobson	Ronald W Brown
David C. Reeves	

For full biographical listings, see the Martindale-Hubbell Law Directory

*SARASOTA,** Sarasota Co.

EARL, BLANK, KAVANAUGH & STOTTS, PROFESSIONAL ASSOCIATION (AV)

1800 Second Street, Suite 888, 34236
Telephone: 941-366-1180
FAX: 941-366-1183
Email: ebkssrq@aol.com
Miami, Florida Office: Suite 3636, One Biscayne Tower, Two South
Biscayne Boulevard.
Telephone: 305-358-3000.
Fax: 305-358-5079. E-Mail: ebks@aol.com.

William L. Earl	Dennis M. Stotts
Robert H. Blank	Mark T. Kobelinski
Judith Smith Kavanaugh	Stephen R. Verbit

Reference: NationsBank, N.A.

For full biographical listings, see the Martindale-Hubbell Law Directory

*TALLAHASSEE,** Leon Co.

HOPPING GREEN SAMS & SMITH, PROFESSIONAL ASSOCIATION (AV)

123 South Calhoun Street, P.O. Box 6526, 32314
Telephone: 904-222-7500
Fax: 904-224-8551

James S. Alves	Wade L. Hopping
Brian H. Bibeau	Frank E. Matthews
Kathleen L. Blizzard	Richard D. Melson
Elizabeth C. Bowman	David L. Powell
Richard S. Brightman	William D. Preston
Peter C. Cunningham	Carolyn S. Raepple
Ralph A. DeMeo	Douglas S. Roberts
Thomas M. DeRose	Gary P. Sams
William H. Green	Robert P. Smith
Cheryl G. Stuart	

(See Next Column)

HOPPING GREEN SAMS & SMITH PROFESSIONAL ASSOCIATION, *Tallahassee—Continued*

Gary K. Hunter, Jr.	Karen Peterson
Jonathan T. Johnson	Michael P. Petrovich
Robert A. Manning	R. Scott Ruth
Angela R. Morrison	W. Steve Sykes
Gary V. Perko	T. Kent Wetherell, II

OF COUNSEL
W. Robert Fokes

Representative Clients: Atlantic Gulf Communities; Dunes and Viera East Community Development Districts; Florida Electric Power Coordinating Group; Florida Power & Light Co.; MCI Telecommunications; Seminole Electric Co.; Sugar Cane Growers Cooperative of Florida; UPS; Waste Management, Inc.; Wheelabrator.

For full biographical listings, see the Martindale-Hubbell Law Directory

RADEY MCARTHUR & FREHN (AV)

101 South Monroe Street, 32301
Telephone: 904-681-7766
Fax: 904-681-0160
Email: Radeylaw@aol.com

John Radey	Elizabeth Waas McArthur
	Jeffrey L. Frehn

Representative Clients: Lee County Mosquito Control District; Agrifos.

For full biographical listings, see the Martindale-Hubbell Law Directory

ROSE, SUNDSTROM & BENTLEY (AV)

A Partnership including Professional Associations
2548 Blairstone Pines Drive, P.O. Box 1567, 32302-1567
Telephone: 904-877-6555
Telecopier: 904-656-4029

MEMBERS OF FIRM

Chris H. Bentley (P.A.)	John R. Jenkins (P.A.)
Martin S. Friedman (P.A.)	William E. Sundstrom (P.A.)
	Diane D. Tremor (P.A.)

Representative Clients: Aloha Utilities, Inc.; Autry Petroleum Company; Bonita Springs Utility, Inc; Destec Energy; East Central Florida Services, Inc.; Hydratech Utilities, Inc.; Utility Board of Key West; Clay County Water and Sewer Authority.
Reference: Barnett Bank, Tallahassee.

For full biographical listings, see the Martindale-Hubbell Law Directory

TAMPA, * Hillsborough Co.

DE LA PARTE, GILBERT & BALES, PROFESSIONAL ASSOCIATION (AV)

One Tampa City Center, Suite 2300, P.O. Box 2350, 33601-2350
Telephone: 813-229-2775
FAX: 813-229-2712

Louis A. de la Parte	John Calhoun Bales
Richard A. Gilbert	L. David de la Parte
Edward P. de la Parte, Jr.	Patrick J. McNamara
	Michael A. Skelton

David M. Caldevilla	David Dallas Dickey
John R. Thomas	Kelli Salem Gustafson
	Andrew Klymenko

For full biographical listings, see the Martindale-Hubbell Law Directory

HONIGMAN MILLER SCHWARTZ AND COHN (AV)

A Partnership including Professional Associations
2700 SunTrust Financial Centre, 401 E. Jackson Street, 33602-5226
Telephone: 813-221-6600
Telecopier: 813-223-4410
URL: http://law.honigman.com
West Palm Beach, Florida Office: Suite 800 Esperante Building, 222 Lakeview Avenue, 33401-6112.
Telephone: 561-838-4500.
Detroit, Michigan Office: 2290 First National Building, 48226.
Telephone: 313-256-7800.
Lansing, Michigan Office: 222 North Washington Square, Suite 400, 48933-1800.
Telephone: 517-484-8282.

MEMBERS

Michael G. Cooke (P.A.)	John W. Voelpel

For Complete List of Firm Personnel, See General Section

For full biographical listings, see the Martindale-Hubbell Law Directory

RYDBERG & GOLDSTEIN, P.A. (AV)

Suite 200, 500 East Kennedy Boulevard, 33602
Telephone: 813-229-3900
Telecopier: 813-229-6101

Marsha Griffin Rydberg	Bruce S. Goldstein

Peter Baker	Tammy N. Giroux
Brian T. FitzGerald	Cynthia L. Bulan
	Susan Greco Tuttle

For full biographical listings, see the Martindale-Hubbell Law Directory

WILLIAMS, REED, WEINSTEIN, SCHIFINO & MANGIONE, P.A. (AV)

One Tampa City Center, 201 North Franklin Street, Suite 2600, P.O. Box 380, 33601
Telephone: 813-221-2626
Telefax: 813-221-7335

Robert V. Williams	Ralph P. Mangione
James M. Reed	Scott I. Steady
David B. Weinstein	R. Marshall Rainey
William J. Schifino, Jr.	David S. Jennis
	Russell S. Thomas

Kenneth G. Turkel	Robert R. Hearn
Aminie Mohip	John A. Schifino
Ricardo A. Roig	Jennifer A. Powers
V. Stephen Cohen	Elizabeth S. Hoskins

FIRM ADMINISTRATOR
Joseph C. Simmons

For full biographical listings, see the Martindale-Hubbell Law Directory

VERO BEACH, * Indian River Co.

COLLINS, BROWN, CALDWELL, BARKETT, ROSSWAY, GARAVAGLIA & MOORE, CHARTERED (AV)

756 Beachland Boulevard, P.O. Box 3686, 32964
Telephone: 561-231-4343
FAX: 561-234-5213

George G. Collins, Jr.	Bradley W. Rossway
Calvin B. Brown	Michael J. Garavaglia
William W. Caldwell	John E. Moore, III
Bruce D. Barkett	Lisa N. Thompson

Reference: First Union Bank of Indian River County, Vero Beach, Florida.

For full biographical listings, see the Martindale-Hubbell Law Directory

WEST PALM BEACH, * Palm Beach Co.

BURT & PUCILLO (AV)

Esperanté, Suite 300 East, 222 Lakeview Avenue, 33401
Telephone: 407-835-9400
Telecopier: 407-835-0322

MEMBERS OF FIRM

C. Oliver Burt, III	Michael J. Pucillo
	Wendy Hope Zoberman

ASSOCIATE
Leo W. Desmond

OF COUNSEL

Carol McLean Brewer	Lauren S. Dadario

For full biographical listings, see the Martindale-Hubbell Law Directory

HONIGMAN MILLER SCHWARTZ AND COHN (AV)

A Partnership including Professional Associations
Suite 800 Esperante Building, 222 Lakeview Avenue, 33401-6112
Telephone: 561-838-4500
Telecopier: 561-832-3036; 832-2645
URL: http://law.honigman.com
Tampa, Florida Office: 2700 SunTrust Financial Centre, 401 E. Jackson Street, 33602-5226.
Telephone: 813-221-6600.
Detroit, Michigan Office: 2290 First National Building, 48226.
Telephone: 313-256-7800.
Lansing, Michigan Office: 222 North Washington Square, Suite 400, 48933-1800.
Telephone: 517-484-8282.

MEMBERS

Carla L. Brown (P.A.)	E. Lee Worsham (P.A.)

Representative Clients: Adler Group, Inc.; Chiquita Brands, Inc.; E. Llwyd Ecclestone, Jr.; Forbes/Cohen Properties; ITT-Rayonier, Inc.; National Advertising Company; Pulte Corporation (Pulte Home Corp.); Thos. J. White Development Corp.; Linpro, Inc.; Rubin Periodical Group-FEC News.

(See Next Column)

HONIGMAN MILLER SCHWARTZ AND COHN—*Continued*

For Complete List of Firm Personnel, See General Section

For full biographical listings, see the Martindale-Hubbell Law Directory

WINTER HAVEN, Polk Co.

PETERSON & MYERS, P.A. (AV)

Suite 300, 141 5th Street N.W., P.O. Drawer 7608, 33883-7608
Telephone: 941-294-3360
Lake Wales, Florida Office: 130 East Central Avenue, P.O. Box 1079.
Telephones: 941-676-7611; 683-8942.
Lakeland, Florida Office: 100 East Main Street, P.O. Box 24628.
Telephones: 941-683-6511; 676-6934.

Philip O. Allen	Peter J. Munson
Jack P. Brandon	Corneal B. Myers
Beach A Brooks, Jr.	Cornelius B. Myers, III
Kristen Marie Buzzanca	E. Blake Paul
J. Davis Connor	Robert E. Puterbaugh
Michael S. Craig	Abel A. Putnam
Roy A. Craig, Jr.	Thomas B. Putnam, Jr.
Jacob C. Dykxhoorn	Deborah A. Ruster
Dennis P. Johnson	Stephen R. Senn
Kevin C. Knowlton	Andrea Teves Smith
Douglas A. Lockwood, III	Keith H. Wadsworth
M. Craig Massey	Kerry M. Wilson

General Counsel for: Barnett Bank of Polk County.
Representative Clients: Mutual Wholesale Co.; Barnett Banks, Inc.; Ben Hill Griffin, Inc.; Alcoma Association, Inc.
Approved Attorneys for: Attorneys' Title Insurance Fund; Federal Land Bank, Columbia, South Carolina; Equitable Life Assurance Society of the United States.

For full biographical listings, see the Martindale-Hubbell Law Directory

WINTER PARK, Orange Co.

POHL & SHORT, P.A. (AV)

280 West Canton Avenue, Suite 410, P.O. Box 3208, 32790
Telephone: 407-647-7645; 407-647-POHL
Telefax: 407-647-2314

Frank L. Pohl	C. Teresa de Arrigoitia
Houston E. Short	George A. Golder
Dwight I. Cool	Norma Stanley
James Everett Shepherd V	Mark W. Garrett
John R. Simpson, Jr.	

Representative Clients: American Pioneer Title Insurance Company; Institute of Internal Auditors, Inc.; Thompson Steel, Inc.; SunTrust, N.A.; The Bank of Winter Park; Bekins Moving and Storage Co., Inc.; Champion Boats, Inc.; KeyCom Telephone Systems, Inc.

For full biographical listings, see the Martindale-Hubbell Law Directory

GEORGIA

*ATLANTA,** Fulton Co.

ALSTON & BIRD (AV)

A Partnership including Professional Corporations
One Atlantic Center, 1201 West Peachtree Street, 30309-3424
Telephone: 404-881-7000
Telecopier: 404-881-7777
Cable Address: AMGRAM GA
Telex: 54-2996
Easylink: 62985848
Washington, D.C. Office: 601 Pennsylvania Ave., N.W., North Building, Suite 250 20004.
Telephone: 202-508-3300.
Telecopier: 202-508-3333.

MEMBERS OF FIRM

William C. Humphreys, Jr.	R. Wayne Thorpe
James S. Stokes	Richard T. Fulton
Lee A. DeHihns III	Elizabeth A. Gilley
Nill V. Toulme	Douglas E. Cloud
Robert D. Mowrey	

ASSOCIATES

Douglas S. Arnold	William W. Sapp
Nicole Fletcher O'Connor	Robyn Ice Sosebee
Amy R. Wolverton	

Representative Clients: Anheuser-Busch Companies; Atlantic Steel Industries, Inc.; E.I. DuPont de Nemours; Georgia-Pacific Corporation; Philips Electronics North America Corp.; Prudential Insurance Co. of America; The Goodyear Tire & Rubber Co.; Vulcan Materials Co.; Wachovia Corporation; Weyerhauser Company.

(See Next Column)

For Complete List of Firm Personnel, See General Section

For full biographical listings, see the Martindale-Hubbell Law Directory

BONDURANT, MIXSON & ELMORE, LLP (AV)

1201 W. Peachtree Street Suite 3900, 30309
Telephone: 404-881-4100
FAX: 404-881-4111

MEMBERS OF FIRM

Emmet J. Bondurant II	Dirk G. Christensen
H. Lamar Mixson	Jane E. Fahey
M. Jerome Elmore	John E. Floyd
Edward B. Krugman	Michael A. Sullivan
Jeffrey O. Bramlett	Michael B. Terry

Representative Clients: The Aetna Casualty and Surety Company; Blue Circle of America; Circle K; Conoco, Inc.; Delta Air Lines, Inc.; Queen Carpets, Inc.; Sanifill, Inc.; Ticketmaster; Trammell Crow Co.; Wyle Laboratories.

For full biographical listings, see the Martindale-Hubbell Law Directory

BOVIS, KYLE & BURCH (AV)

A Partnership including Professional Corporations
Third Floor, 53 Perimeter Center East, 30346
Telephone: 770-391-9100
Telecopier: 770-668-0878

MEMBERS OF FIRM

John M. Bovis (P.C.)	James E. Singer
William S. Allred	

ASSOCIATES

Charles M. Medlin	John H. Peavy Jr.
Nicholas P. Garcia	

For full biographical listings, see the Martindale-Hubbell Law Directory

HAWKINS & PARNELL (AV)

4000 SunTrust Plaza, 303 Peachtree Street, N.E., 30308-3243
Telephone: 404-614-7400
Fax: 404-614-7500
Email: 73541.1626@compuserve.com

MEMBERS OF FIRM

J. Bruce Welch	Stephen M. Lore
Albert H. Parnell	William H. Major, III
A. Timothy Jones	Edward M. Newsom
Alan F. Herman	Jack N. Sibley
H. Lane Young, II	Warner S. Fox
Joseph R. Cullens	Robert U. Wright
Frank C. Bedinger, III	Michael E. Hutchins
Julia Bennett Jagger	Ollie M. Harton

ASSOCIATES

Kevin J. Bahr	Allen L. Broughton
Edwin L. Hall, Jr.	Kristen K. Duggan
Robert Rache Elarbee	Jennifer A. Grandoff
Dennis J. Manganiello	Debra L. Dewar

Representative Clients: Ashland Oil, Inc.; Georgia-Pacific Corp.; Ericsson, Inc.; Monsanto Corporation; Commercial Union Insurance Co.; Terminix; Mobay Corp.; Apollo Industries.

For Complete List of Firm Personnel, See General Section

For full biographical listings, see the Martindale-Hubbell Law Directory

HOLT, NEY, ZATCOFF & WASSERMAN (AV)

A Partnership including Professional Corporations
100 Galleria Parkway, Suite 600, 30339
Telephone: 770-956-9600
Facsimile Number: 770-956-1490

MEMBERS OF FIRM

J. Scott Jacobson	Richard P. Vornholt

ASSOCIATE

Jay Frank Castle

Representative Clients: Safety-Kleen Corp.; Cummins South, Inc.; Gables Residential Trust; The University Financing Foundation, Inc.; Trammell Crow Residential; NationsBank N.A. (South).

For Complete List of Firm Personnel, See General Section

For full biographical listings, see the Martindale-Hubbell Law Directory

KILPATRICK & CODY LLP (AV)

Suite 2800, 1100 Peachtree Street, 30309-4530
Telephone: 404-815-6500
Telephone Copier: 404-815-6555
Telex: 54-2307
Washington, D.C. Office: Suite 800, 700 13th Street, N.W., 20005.
Telephone: 202-508-5800. *Telephone Copier:* 202-508-5858.
Brussels, Belgium Office: Avenue Louise 65, BTE 3, 1050 Brussels.
Telephone: (32) (2) 533-03-00.
Telecopier: (32) (2) 534-86-38.

(See Next Column)

KILPATRICK & CODY, *Atlanta—Continued*

London, England Office: 68 Pall Mall, London, SW1Y 5ES, England.
Telephone: (44) (71) 321 0477.
Telecopier: (44) (71) 930 9733.
Augusta, Georgia Office: Suite 1400 First Union Bank Building, P.O. Box 2043, 30903. Telephone (706) 724-2622. Telecopier (706) 722-0219.

MEMBERS OF FIRM

Thomas K. Bick	J. Vance Hughes
(Washington, D.C. Office)	Edward A. Kazmarek
Kurt E. Blase	Elliott H. Levitas
(Washington, D.C. Office)	Ronald L. Raider
Richard A. Horder	(Washington, D.C. Office)

Ann Marie Stack

ASSOCIATES

Steven I. Addlestone	W. Scott Laseter
Wilburn L. Chesser	Kenneth J. Markowitz
(Washington, D.C. Office)	(Washington, D.C. Office)
Vicki Arroyo Cochran	Newton G. Quantz, III
(Washington, D.C. Office)	Edwin S. Schwartz
Elizabeth P. Cowie	Charles T. Simmons
Matt Dillard	(Washington, D.C. Office)
Ciannat M. Howett	Lisa G. Youngblood

For Complete List of Firm Personnel, See General Section

For full biographical listings, see the Martindale-Hubbell Law Directory

---

LONG ALDRIDGE & NORMAN, LLP (AV)

A Limited Liability Partnership including Professional Corporations
One Peachtree Center, Suite 5300, 303 Peachtree Street, 30308
Telephone: 404-527-4000
Telecopier: 404-527-4198
Washington, D.C. Office: Suite 600, 701 Pennsylvania Avenue, N.W., 20004.
Telephone: 202-624-1200.
FAX: 202-624-1298.

MEMBERS OF FIRM

Phillip A. Bradley	Gordon D. Giffin

ASSOCIATE

William E. Rice

For Complete List of Firm Personnel, See General Section

For full biographical listings, see the Martindale-Hubbell Law Directory

---

SUTHERLAND, ASBILL & BRENNAN, L.L.P. (AV)

999 Peachtree Street, N.E., 30309-3996
Telephone: 404-853-8000
Facsimile: 404-853-8806
Email: postmaster@sablaw.com
Washington, D.C. Office: 1275 Pennsylvania Avenue, N.W., 20004-2404.
Telephone: 202-383-0100.
New York, N.Y. Office: 600 Madison Avenue, 11th Floor, 10022-1615.
Telephone: 212-605-6400.
Austin, Texas Office: 111 Congress Avenue, 23rd Floor, 78701-4079.
Telephone: 512-469-3350.

C. Christopher Hagy	Randall D. Quintrell

Teresa Wynn Roseborough

COUNSEL OF THE FIRM
IN ATLANTA, GEORGIA
Elizabeth W. Boswell

Representative Clients: Blue Circle, Inc.; Chemical Products Corp.; China Clay Producers Association, Inc.; Ellis & Everard (J.S.) Holdings, Inc.; General Motors Corporation; LWD Inc.; Martin Marietta Corporation; Mobil Land Development Corporation; Southern Mills, Inc.; ECC International, Inc.

For Complete List of Firm Personnel, See General Section
For full biographical listings, see the Martindale-Hubbell Law Directory

---

SAVANNAH,* Chatham Co.

HUNTER, MACLEAN, EXLEY & DUNN, P.C. (AV)

200 East St. Julian Street, P.O. Box 9848, 31412
Telephone: 912-236-0261
Cable Address: "Ancan"
Telecopier: 912-236-4936
Telex: 54-6483
Atlanta, Georgia Office: The Peachtree, 1355 Peachtree Street, N.E., Suite 1050.
Telephone: 404-876-3611.
Fax: 404-870-2025.

John M. Hewson, III	Andrew H. Ernst

Ronnie D. Talley

Representative Clients: Great Dane Trailers, Inc.; Atlantic Wood Industries, Inc.; CSX, Inc.; Savannah Economic Developments Authority; TIC Southeast.

(See Next Column)

For Complete List of Firm Personnel, See General Section

For full biographical listings, see the Martindale-Hubbell Law Directory

---

HAWAII

HONOLULU,* Honolulu Co.

DWYER IMANAKA SCHRAFF KUDO MEYER & FUJIMOTO ATTORNEYS AT LAW, A LAW CORPORATION (AV)

1800 Pioneer Plaza, 900 Fort Street Mall, 96813
Telephone: 808-524-8000
Telecopier: 808-526-1419
Mailing Address: P.O. Box 2727, 96803
Email: hawaiilaw@dwyer-imanaka.com *URL:*
http://www.dwyer-imanaka.com

John R. Dwyer, Jr.	William G. Meyer, III
Mitchell A. Imanaka	Wesley M. Fujimoto
Paul A. Schraff	Ronald Van Grant
Benjamin A. Kudo (Atty. at	Jon M. H. Pang
Law, A Law Corp.)	Blake W. Bushnell

Adelbert Green

Richard T. Asato, Jr.	Jeffery S. Werbelow
Scott W. Settle	Lori Ann K. Koseki
Darcie S. Yoshinaga	Troy T. Fukuhara
Lawrence I. Kawasaki	Katy Y. Chen
Stacy E. Uehara	Naomi S. Uyeno
Kris N. Nakagawa	Roger B. McKeague

OF COUNSEL

Randall Y. Iwase	R. Brian Tsujimura

For full biographical listings, see the Martindale-Hubbell Law Directory

---

IDAHO

BOISE,* Ada Co.

ELAM & BURKE, A PROFESSIONAL ASSOCIATION (AV)

Key Financial Center, 702 West Idaho Street, P.O. Box 1539, 83701
Telephone: 208-343-5454
Telecopier: 208-384-5844
Email: eblaw@elamburke.com

Carl P. Burke	William G. Dryden
John Magel	Scott L. Campbell

Harry M. Lane, Jr.

Representative Clients: Morrison-Knudsen, Inc.; Texas Instruments, Inc.; Pechiney Corp.; Dow Corning Corporation; State Farm Insurance Cos.; Sinclair Oil Co. d/b/a/ Sun Valley Co.; Farmers Insurance Group; Thompson Creek Mining Co.

For Complete List of Firm Personnel, See General Section

For full biographical listings, see the Martindale-Hubbell Law Directory

---

MOFFATT, THOMAS, BARRETT, ROCK & FIELDS, CHARTERED (AV)

101 South Capitol Boulevard, P.O. Box 829, 83702
Telephone: 208-345-2000
FAX: 208-385-5384
Email: info@moffatt.com
Idaho Falls Office: 525 Park Avenue, Suite 2D, P.O. Box 1367, 83403.
Telephone: 208-522-6700.
FAX: 208-522-5111.
Pocatello, Idaho Office: 845 West Center, Suite C, P.O. Box 4941, 83201.
Telephone: 208-233-2001.

Jon S. Gorski	James C. deGlee
Gary T. Dance (Resident, Idaho	
Falls and Pocatello Offices)	

Representative Clients: BMC West Corporation; Chevron, U.S.A.; First Security Bank of Idaho, N.A.; General Motors Corp.; Idaho Potato Commission; Intermountain Gas Co.; John Alden Life Insurance Co.; Micron Technology, Inc.; Royal Insurance Cos.; St. Luke's Regional Medical Center & Mountain States Tumor Institute.

For Complete List of Firm Personnel, See General Section

For full biographical listings, see the Martindale-Hubbell Law Directory

KETCHUM, Blaine Co.

JAMES L. KENNEDY, JR. (AV)

340 Second Street East, P.O. Box 2165, 83340
Telephone: 208-726-8255

Reference: First Interstate Bank of Idaho, N.A. (Ketchum-Sun Valley Branch); First Security Bank of Idaho, N.A. (Ketchum Branch)

For full biographical listings, see the Martindale-Hubbell Law Directory

---

ILLINOIS

AURORA, Kane Co.

MURPHY, HUPP, FOOTE, MIELKE AND KINNALLY (AV)

North Island Center, P.O. Box 5030, 60507
Telephone: 708-844-0056
FAX: 708-844-1905

MEMBERS OF FIRM

William C. Murphy	Patrick M. Kinnally
Robert B. Hupp	Paul G. Krentz
Robert M. Foote	Joseph C. Loran
Craig S. Mielke	Gerald K. Hodge

Timothy D. O'Neil
OF COUNSEL
Robert T. Olson

Representative Clients: American Telephone & Telegraph Co.; Fox Valley Park District; Lyon Metal Products; Kane County Forest Preserve District; Hollywood Casino; Employers Mutual Insurance Co.; Forty-Eight Insulations, Inc.; UNR Asbestos Disease Trust; Richards-Wilcox Co.; National Bank & Trust Company of Syracuse.

For full biographical listings, see the Martindale-Hubbell Law Directory

---

BELLEVILLE,* St. Clair Co.

BROWN & GAVIN (AV)

23 Public Square, Suite 410, 62220
Telephone: 618-236-2886
Missouri: 314-231-0953

MEMBERS OF FIRM

Terry N. Brown	William P. Gavin

ASSOCIATES

Gregg N. Johnson	P.K. Johnson, V

For full biographical listings, see the Martindale-Hubbell Law Directory

---

CHICAGO,* Cook Co.

ANSPACH & DALTON (AV)

111 West Washington Street, Suite 1435, 60602
Telephone: 312-407-7888
Facsimile: 312-407-7889
Email: KANSPACH@counsel.com

Kenneth G. Anspach	John D. Dalton

Representative Clients: A. H. Harris & Sons, Inc.; Caprel Consulting; Cooper Tire & Rubber Company; Chase Products Co.; Deerfield Federal Savings; Graham Paint & Varnish Co., Inc.; James Cape & Sons Co.; Mid-City National Bank of Chicago; Monarch Tile, Inc.; W. R. Meadows, Inc.

For full biographical listings, see the Martindale-Hubbell Law Directory

BELL, BOYD & LLOYD (AV)

Three First National Plaza Suite 3300, 70 West Madison Street, 60602
Telephone: 312-372-1121
FAX: 312-372-2098
Email: bbl@bbl.com
Washington, D.C. Office: 1615 L Street, N.W.
Telephone: 202-466-6300.
FAX: 202-463-0678.

MEMBERS OF FIRM

Michael K. Ohm	Neal H. Weinfield

ASSOCIATES

Thomas R. Carey	Bryan E. Keyt

For Complete List of Firm Personnel, See General Section

For full biographical listings, see the Martindale-Hubbell Law Directory

BLATT, HAMMESFAHR & EATON (AV)

333 W. Wacker Drive, Suite 1900, 60606
Telephone: 312-357-1277
FAX: 312-357-0198
Email: BHE@BHELAW.COM *URL:* HTTP://WWW.BHELAW.COM

MEMBERS OF FIRM

Richard Lee Blatt	Lori S. Nugent
Larry R. Eaton	Peter M. Page
Bruce M. Engel	William F. Richardson
Brent J. Graber	Gregory G. Smith
Robert W. Hammesfahr	Leonard S. Surdyk
Gregory D. Hopp	Patrick T. Walsh
Joanne J. Matousek	Judith M. Wexler

Scott W. Wright

ASSOCIATES

David W. Alberts	Kathleen A. McQueeny
David Hollingshead Anderson	Stephen R. Meinertzhagen
Christopher R. Barth	Hallie J. Miller
Julie S. Bender	Ziyad I. Naccasha
Kristin M. Buchholz	Kevin J. Rielley
Andrea L. Caplan	Stephen J. Rosenfeld
Susan J. Cheney	Scott V. Scarpelli
Lisa A. Dunsky	Dana L. Schmitt
Mary E. Fechtig	Susan B. Shulman
S. William Grimes	George Matthew Silvers
Josh M. Kantrow	Janet B. Stern
Jill Ann Kaplan	Timothy L. Swabb
Andrea C. Kenealey	Matthew T. Walsh
Elizabeth E. Kim	Laura R. Zaroski

OF COUNSEL
Shane V. Nugent

For full biographical listings, see the Martindale-Hubbell Law Directory

BROWNMARTIN, P.C. (AV)

35 East Wacker Drive Suite 1356, 60601
Telephone: 312-236-1450
Fax: 312-236-1451

Johnine J. Brown	Maureen Martin
Ann Parisi Messer	Stacey Rubin Silver

Representative Clients: Acme Refining Scrap Iron & Metal Co.; Benjamin Moore & Co.; Chicago Trust Co.; Deere & Co.; Gallagher & Henry; Hartz Construction Co.; Heidelberg Harris, Inc.; Metropolitan Water Reclamation District of Greater Chicago; Midas Realty Corp.; United Companies Lending Corporation.

For full biographical listings, see the Martindale-Hubbell Law Directory

CHERRY & FLYNN (AV)

30 North La Salle Street, Suite 2300, 60602
Telephone: 312-372-2100
Telecopier: 312-853-0279

Myron M. Cherry	William R. Coulson
Peter Flynn	David D. Merritt

Adam J. Levitt

For full biographical listings, see the Martindale-Hubbell Law Directory

GUNTY & McCARTHY (AV)

150 South Wacker Drive, Suite 1025, 60606
Telephone: 312-541-0022
Facsimile: 312-541-0033
St. Louis, Missouri Office: 1515 North Warson Road, Suite 137.
Telephone: 314-427-7262.
Facsimile: 314-427-7268.

Susan Gunty	James P. McCarthy
Stephen K. Milott	Kirk Austin
Paul D. Van Lysebettens	Karyn S. Glennon

For full biographical listings, see the Martindale-Hubbell Law Directory

JOHNSON & BELL, LTD. (AV)

Suite 2200, 222 North La Salle Street, 60601
Telephone: 312-372-0770
Facsimile: 312-372-9818
Wheaton, Illinois Office: Suite 1640, 2100 Manchester Road.
Telephone: 630-510-0880.
Facsimile: 630-510-0939.

John W. Bell	Frederick S. Mueller

Daniel C. Murray

William J. Anaya

References available upon request.

For full biographical listings, see the Martindale-Hubbell Law Directory

Chicago—Continued

WILDMAN, HARROLD, ALLEN & DIXON (AV)

225 West Wacker Drive, 30th Floor, 60606-1229
Telephone: 312-201-2000
Cable Address: "Whad"
Fax: 312-201-2555
URL: http://www.whad.com
Aurora, Illinois Office: 1851 W. Galena Boulevard, Suite 210.
Telephone: 630-892-7021.
Fax: 630-892-7158.
Waukegan, Illinois Office: 404 West Water, P. O. Box 890.
Telephone: 847-623-0700.
Fax: 847-244-5273.
Lisle, Illinois Office: 4300 Commerce Court.
Telephone: 630-955-0555.
New York, New York Office: Wildman, Harrold, Allen, Dixon & Smith. The International Building, 45 Rockefeller Plaza, Suite 353.
Telephone: 212-632-3850.
Fax: 212-632-3858.
Toronto, Ontario affiliated Office: Keel Cottrelle. 36 Toronto Street, Ninth Floor, Suite 920.
Telephone: 416-367-2900.
Telefax: 416-367-2791.
Telex: 062-18660.
Mississauga, Ontario affiliated Office: Keel Cottrelle. 100 Matatson Avenue East, Suite 104.
Telephone: 416-890-7700.
Fax: 416-890-8006.

MEMBERS OF FIRM

Michael R. Blankshain	Joseph F. Madonia
Thomas W. Daggett	Michael L. McCluggage
Steven E. Danekas	Donald R. McGarrah
Michael Dockterman	James R. Morrin
James P. Dorr	Sarah L. Olson
John E. Frey	Richard C. Palmer
Bernard Harrold	Robert L. Shuftan
H. Roderic Heard	Linda E. Spring
Anthony G. Hopp	(Waukegan Office)
David A. Kanter	Sanford M. Stein
Brian W. Lewis	Peter A. Tomaras
	James B. Vogts

Leo P. Dombrowski	Scott Z. Hochfelder
Lawrence W. Falbe	Padmavati G. Klejwa
Louise M. Goodwin	Patricia Lynn McCarthy
	David M. Simon

For Complete List of Firm Personnel, See General Section

For full biographical listings, see the Martindale-Hubbell Law Directory

MATTOON, Coles Co.

CRAIG & CRAIG (AV)

1807 Broadway, P.O. Box 689, 61938-0689
Telephone: 217-234-6481
Telecopier: 217-234-6486
Mount Vernon, Illinois Office: 227 1/2 South 9th Street.
Telephone: 618-244-7511.

MEMBERS OF FIRM

Craig Van Meter (1895-1981)	Stephen L. Corn
Fred H. Kelly (1894-1971)	Richard Charles Hayden
Robert M. Werden (1908-1969)	Robert G. Grierson
George N. Gilkerson	Gregory C. Ray
(1911-1985)	Paul R. Lynch (Resident, Mount
John H. Armstrong	Vernon Office)
John P. Ewart	Kenneth F. Werts (Resident,
Richard F. Record, Jr.	Mount Vernon Office)
	John L. Barger

ASSOCIATES

Joshua N. Rosen (Resident,	Theresa M. Thomson
Mount Vernon Office)	Kristine M. Tuttle
Kathleen M. Stockwell	Henry P. Villani (Resident,
	Mount Vernon Office)

OF COUNSEL

Jack E. Horsley

Counsel for: Monterey Coal Co., a Division of Exxon Coal USA, Inc.; Marathon Oil Co.; Illinois Central R.R. Co.; Okaw Building & Loan Assn., Mattoon, Illinois; The Medical Protective Insurance Co.; Consolidated Communications, Inc.; Lloyds Underwriters at London; Hartford Insurance Co.; Coles Together, a Not-For-Profit Corp.; Coles Building Corporation.

For full biographical listings, see the Martindale-Hubbell Law Directory

PEORIA,* Peoria Co.

HOWARD & HOWARD ATTORNEYS, P.C. (AV)

The Creve Coeur Building, Suite 200, 321 Liberty Street, 61602-1403
Telephone: 309-672-1483
Telecopier: 309-672-1568
Kalamazoo, Michigan Office: The Kalamazoo Building, Suite 400, 107 West Michigan Avenue.
Telephone: 616-382-1483.
Telecopier: 616-382-1568.
Bloomfield Hills, Michigan Office: The Pinehurst Office Center, Suite 101, 1400 North Woodward Avenue.
Telephone: 810-645-1483.
Telecopier: 810-645-1568.
Lansing, Michigan Office: Suite 500, The Phoenix Building, 222 Washington Square, North.
Telephone: 517-485-1483.
Telecopier: 517-485-1568.
Tampa, Florida Office: First of America Plaza, Suite 2000, 201 East Kennedy Boulevard.
Telephone: 813-229-1483.
Telecopier: 813-229-1568.

Jon S. Faletto	Frederick G. Hoffman
	Diana M. Jagiella

Representative Clients: For Representative Client list, see General Practice, Peoria, IL.

For Complete List of Firm Personnel, See General Section

For full biographical listings, see the Martindale-Hubbell Law Directory

SPRINGFIELD,* Sangamon Co.

MOHAN, ALEWELT, PRILLAMAN & ADAMI (AV)

First of America Center, Suite 325, 1 North Old Capitol Plaza, 62701-1323
Telephone: 217-528-2517
Telecopier: 217-528-2553
Email: fprillam@counsel.com.

MEMBERS

Fred C. Prillaman	Stephen F. Hedinger

ASSOCIATES

Becky S. McCray	Patrick D. Shaw
	Joel A. Benoit

Representative Clients: Amoco Oil Company; Andrews Environmental Engineering, Inc.; Federal Deposit Insurance Corp.; PCS Phosphate Company, Inc.; Viacom, Inc.

For Complete List of Firm Personnel, See General Section

For full biographical listings, see the Martindale-Hubbell Law Directory

URBANA,* Champaign Co.

WEBBER & THIES, P.C. (AV)

202 Lincoln Square, P.O. Box 189, 61803-0189
Telephone: 217-367-1126
FAX: 217-367-3752

David C. Thies

Phillip R. Van Ness

For Complete List of Firm Personnel, See General Section

For full biographical listings, see the Martindale-Hubbell Law Directory

INDIANA

ELKHART, Elkhart Co.

CHESTER, PFAFF & BROTHERSON (AV)

317 West Franklin Street, P.O. Box 507, 46515-0507
Telephone: 219-294-5421
Fax: 219-522-1476

MEMBER OF FIRM

Robert A. Pfaff

ASSOCIATE

Craig A. Carpenter

For Complete List of Firm Personnel, See General Section

For full biographical listings, see the Martindale-Hubbell Law Directory

EVANSVILLE,* Vanderburgh Co.

FINE & HATFIELD (AV)

520 N.W. Second Street, P.O. Box 779, 47705-0779
Telephone: 812-425-3592
Telecopier: 812-421-4269
Email: Fine@Fine-Hatfield.com *URL:* http://www.Fine-Hatfield.com

MEMBER OF FIRM
Thomas H. Bryan

A List of Representative Clients Furnished Upon Request.

For full biographical listings, see the Martindale-Hubbell Law Directory

KAHN, DEES, DONOVAN & KAHN (AV)

P.O. Box 3646, 47735-3646
Telephone: 812-423-3183
Fax: 812-423-3841
Email: evvlaw@k2d2.com

MEMBERS OF FIRM

Alan N. Shovers	G. Michael Schopmeyer
Brian P. Williams	Jeffrey K. Helfrich

ASSOCIATES

Kent A. Brasseale, II	Martha J. Posey
	Mark L. Boos

Representative Clients: Enviro Group, Inc.; D. Patrick, Inc.; Deaconess Hospital, Inc.; Geo. Koch Sons, Inc.; Red Spot Paint & Varnish Co., Inc.; Sterling Boiler & Mechanical, Inc.; Windsor Plastics, Inc.; CSX Transporation, Inc.

For Complete List of Firm Personnel, See General Section

For full biographical listings, see the Martindale-Hubbell Law Directory

FORT WAYNE,* Allen Co.

BARRETT & McNAGNY (AV)

215 East Berry Street, P.O. Box 2263, 46801-2263
Telephone: 219-423-9551
Telecopier: 219-423-8924

MEMBERS OF FIRM

Richard E. Fox	James P. Fenton
John D. Walda	Alan VerPlanck
	Thomas A. Herr

ASSOCIATE
David R. Steiner

Representative Clients: City of New Haven; Fort Wayne National Bank; Franklin Electric Co.; Lake George Regional Sewer District; Lincoln Food Service Products, Inc.; OmniSource Corp.

For Complete List of Firm Personnel, See General Section

For full biographical listings, see the Martindale-Hubbell Law Directory

HAMMOND, Lake Co.

BECKMAN, KELLY & SMITH (AV)

5920 Hohman Avenue, 46320
Telephone: 219-933-6200
Telecopier: 219-933-6201
South Bend, Indiana Office: 300 North Michigan Street, Suite 215.
Telephone: 219-288-2373.
Telecopier: 219-933-6201.

MEMBERS OF FIRM

Richard P. Tinkham (1902-1973)	Andrew J. Fetsch
Daniel F. Kelly (1914-1978)	Randall J. Nye
John F. Beckman, Jr.	Robert F. Parker
(1916-1996)	Daniel W. Glavin
J. B. Smith	Eric L. Kirschner

ASSOCIATES

Melanie Morgan Dunajeski	Christine Hajduch Curosh
Scott A. Bearby	Douglas A. Welp

Representative Clients: Waste Management of North America, Inc.; The Travelers Companies; Bethlehem Steel Corp.; ITT Finance; Northwest Indiana Public Broadcasting, Inc.; Signal Capital Corporation; CIGNA Companies; Sears Roebuck and Co.

For full biographical listings, see the Martindale-Hubbell Law Directory

INDIANAPOLIS,* Marion Co.

BAKER & DANIELS (AV)

300 North Meridian Street, 46204
Telephone: 317-237-0300
FAX: 317-237-1000
Fort Wayne, Indiana Office: 111 East Wayne Street, Suite 800.
Telephone: 219-424-8000.
South Bend, Indiana Office: First Bank Building, 205 West Jefferson Boulevard.
Telephone: 219-234-4149.

(See Next Column)

Elkhart, Indiana Office: 301 B South Main Street, Suite 307,
Telephone: 219-296-6000.
Washington, D.C. Office: 1701 K Street, N.W., Suite 400.
Telephone: 202-785-1565.

MEMBERS OF FIRM

Michael J. Huston	Christopher G. Scanlon
Lewis D. Beckwith	Anne Slaughter Andrew
	James W. Clark

COUNSEL
Joseph B. Carney

ASSOCIATES

Sharon A. Hilmes	Charles A. Grandy

Representative Clients: Anthem Insurance Companies, Inc.; AT&T Corp.; Bank One, Indianapolis, N.A.; Borg-Warner Corp.; City of Indianapolis; Cummins Engine Co.; Eli Lilly and Co.; General Motors Corp.; Indianapolis Public Schools; United Airlines.

For Complete List of Firm Personnel, See General Section

For full biographical listings, see the Martindale-Hubbell Law Directory

BOSE MCKINNEY & EVANS (AV)

2700 First Indiana Plaza, 135 North Pennsylvania Street, 46204
Telephone: 317-684-5000
Facsimile: 317-684-5173
Indianapolis North Office: Suite 1201, 8888 Keystone Crossing, 46240.
Telephone: 317-574-3700.
Facsimile: 317-574-3716.

MEMBERS OF FIRM

Theodore J. Nowacki	C. Joseph Russell
James C. Carlino	Kathleen G. Lucas

ASSOCIATES

Lisa C. McKinney	Daniel P. McInerny

Representative Clients: Amoco Corp.; Duke Realty Investments Inc.; First Indiana Bank; Prudential Life Insurance Co.; USX Corp.; Indiana Pork Producers Association; Valeo Engine Cooling, Inc.; White River Environmental Partnership; Carolina Freight Carriers Corp.; United Parcel Service, Inc.

For Complete List of Firm Personnel, See General Section

For full biographical listings, see the Martindale-Hubbell Law Directory

CLARK, QUINN, MOSES & CLARK (AV)

One Indiana Square, Suite 2200, 46204-2011
Telephone: 317-637-1321
Fax: 317-687-2344

MEMBERS OF FIRM

Alex M. Clark (1916-1991)	John M. Moses
James C. Clark	J. Murray Clark
Thomas Michael Quinn	Matthew R. Clark

ASSOCIATES

Michael D. Keele	Cameron F. Clark
	L. Michael Koch

OF COUNSEL

David M. Brooks	Robert C. Bruner

Representative Clients: Justus; The Shorewood Corporation; Marina Limited Partnership; Lafarge Corporation; Meijer Realty, Inc.; Lowe's; Kite Development; U-Stor Self Storage Warehouses; Mechanic's Laundry; Davis Homes.

For full biographical listings, see the Martindale-Hubbell Law Directory

DANN PECAR NEWMAN & KLEIMAN, PROFESSIONAL CORPORATION (AV)

Suite 2300, One American Square Box 82008, 46282
Telephone: 317-632-3232; Indiana: 800-622-4799
Telecopy: 317-632-2962

Theodore R. Dann (1907-1993)	Walter E. Wolf, Jr.
Joel Yonover (1932-1995)	Barry E. Beldin
Philip D. Pecar	Robert D. Swhier, Jr.
Norman R. Newman	James P. Moloy
David H. Kleiman	Robert J. Schuckit
Jon B. Abels	Andrew A. Kleiman
Melvin R. Daniel	Michael J. Gabovitch
Lawrence F. Dorocke	Steven M. Pecar
Jeffrey A. Abrams	Benjamin A. Pecar
James H. Schwarz	Richard O. Kissel, II
Robert A. Rose	Joseph D. Calderon

OF COUNSEL

Linda E. Cantor	Anthony J. Rose

Ellen C. Siakotos	Angela L. Mansfield
Stacy L. Hill	Martha M. K. Baird
	Karin L. Veatch

(See Next Column)

Dann Pecar Newman & Kleiman Professional Corporation,
Indianapolis—Continued

Attorneys for: Indianapolis Machinery Co., Inc.; Melvin Simon & Associates, Inc.; Pacers Basketball Corp.; Universal Fire & Casualty Co., Inc.; Bank One, Indianapolis, NA; INB National Bank; Nachi Technology, Inc.; Pharmaceutical Corporation of America; Logo 7, Inc.

For full biographical listings, see the Martindale-Hubbell Law Directory

Ice Miller Donadio & Ryan (AV)

One American Square Box 82001, 46282-0002
Telephone: 317-236-2100
Fax: 317-236-2219
Email: leel@imdr.com *URL:* http://www.imdr.com
South Bend, Indiana Office: 211 West Washington Street, Suite 2420.
Telephone: 219-234-7933.
Fax: 219-234-7965. Internet E-mail: leel@imdr.com. Web Site Address: http://www.imdr.com.

MEMBERS OF FIRM

Phillip R. Scaletta, III	Terri Ann Czajka

ASSOCIATES

Jodie L. Miner	James V. Hetzel
Jared L. Burden	(Not admitted in IN)

Representative Clients: Amax Coal Co.; Amoco Oil Corp.; Avesta-Sheffield, Inc.; Citizens Gas and Coke Utility; Chrysler Corp.; Dana Corp.; Lehigh Portland Cement Co.; Phelps Dodge Corp.; Reilly Industries, Inc.; United Dominion Industries, Inc.

For Complete List of Firm Personnel, See General Section

For full biographical listings, see the Martindale-Hubbell Law Directory

Johnson, Smith, Pence, Densborn, Wright & Heath (AV)

One Indiana Square Suite 1800, 46204
Telephone: 317-634-9777
Telecopier: 317-636-9061

MEMBERS OF FIRM

Robert M. Baker, III	David R. Day
Thomas A. Barnard	G. Ronald Heath
Peter D. Cleveland	Linda L. Pence

ASSOCIATE

David A. Tucker

OF COUNSEL

John K. Smeltzer

For Complete List of Firm Personnel, See General Section

For full biographical listings, see the Martindale-Hubbell Law Directory

Plews Shadley Racher & Braun (AV)

1346 North Delaware Street, 46202-2415
Telephone: 317-637-0700
Telecopier: 317-637-0710

MEMBERS OF FIRM

George M. Plews	Peter M. Racher
Sue A. Shadley	Christopher J. Braun
Jeffrey D. Claflin	

ASSOCIATES

Harinder Kaur	Jeffrey D. Featherstun
Leonardo D. Robinson	Donna C. Marron
Frederick D. Emhardt	Michael A. Myers
S. Curtis DeVoe	Julie E. Polizzotto

OF COUNSEL

Christine C. H. Plews	Timothy J. Paris

For full biographical listings, see the Martindale-Hubbell Law Directory

Sommer & Barnard, Attorneys at Law, PC (AV)

4000 Bank One Tower, 111 Monument Circle, 46204-5140
Telephone: 317-630-4000
FAX: 317-236-9802
North Office: 8900 Keystone Crossing, Suite 1046, Indianapolis, Indiana, 46240-2134.
Telephone: 317-630-4000.
FAX: 317-844-4780.

Frank J. Deveau	Lawrence A. Vanore
	Donald C. Biggs

OF COUNSEL

Robert R. Clark	Verl L. Myers

Representative Clients: Comerica Bank; Excel Industries; Federal Express; Kimball International; Monsanto; Renault Automation; TRW, Inc.

For Complete List of Firm Personnel, See General Section

For full biographical listings, see the Martindale-Hubbell Law Directory

Stark Doninger & Smith (AV)

Suite 700, 50 South Meridian Street, 46204
Telephone: 317-638-2400
Fax: 317-633-6618; 633-6619

MEMBERS OF FIRM

John C. Stark	Patricia Seasor Bailey
Bruce E. Smith	Brian J. Tuohy
John W. Van Buskirk	Mark A. Bailey
Richard W. Dyar	Lewis E. Willis, Jr.

ASSOCIATES

Thomas A. Brodnik	Richard B. Kaufman
Neil E. Lucas	Patrick J. Dietrick

COUNSEL

Clarence H. Doninger	Robert D. Maas
Gregory S. Fehribach	William K. Byrum

Representative Clients: ATEC Environmental Consultants; ATEC Associates, Inc.; American Environmental Corp.; Douglass Environmental Services, Inc.

For full biographical listings, see the Martindale-Hubbell Law Directory

Tabbert Hahn Earnest & Starkey, P.C. (AV)

Suite 2100, One Indiana Square, 46204
Telephone: 317-639-5444
Fax: 317-639-5232

Mark K. Sullivan

OF COUNSEL

Douglas E. Cregor

For full biographical listings, see the Martindale-Hubbell Law Directory

LAFAYETTE,* Tippecanoe Co.

Stuart & Branigin (AV)

The Life Building, 300 Main Street, Suite 800, 47902
Telephone: 317-423-1561
Telecopier: 317-742-8175

MEMBERS OF FIRM

Allison Ellsworth Stuart (1886-1950)	Stephen R. Pennell
Roger D. Branigin (1902-1975)	Anthony S. Benton
Russell H. Hart	Erik D. Spykman
Roger D. Branigin, Jr.	William E. Emerick
Thomas L. Ryan	John C. Duffey
James V. McGlone	Mark E. DeYoung
Carl W. Kloepfer	Thomas B. Parent
Thomas R. McCully	Laura L. Bowker
Larry R. Fisher	Kevin D. Nicoson
Nina B. Kirkpatrick	Susan K. Roberts
Mark Lillianfeld	John M. Stuckey
	Deborah B. Trice

COUNSEL

John F. Bodle

ASSOCIATES

Brent W. Huber	David A. Starkweather
William P. Kealey	Geoffrey Blazi
A. James Chareq	

General Counsel for: The Lafayette Life Insurance Co.; INB National Bank, N.W.; Lafayette Home Hospital, Inc.
State Counsel for: Norfolk & Western Railway Co.
Mr. Ryan is Counsel to: The Trustees of Purdue University.
Representative Clients: Aluminum Company of America; Liberty Mutual Insurance Group.

For full biographical listings, see the Martindale-Hubbell Law Directory

MERRILLVILLE, Lake Co.

Burke, Murphy, Costanza & Cuppy (AV)

Suite 600 8585 Broadway, 46410-7064
Telephone: 219-769-1313
Telecopier: 219-769-6806
East Chicago, Indiana Office: First National Bank Building. 720 West Chicago Avenue.
Telephone: 219-397-2401.
Telecopier: 219-397-0508.
Valparaiso, Indiana Office: 15 North Franklin Street, Suite 200.
Telephone: 219-531-0134.
Telecopier: 219-531-0507.
Palm Harbor, Florida Office: Suite 280, 33920 U.S. Highway 19 North.
Telephone: 813-787-7799.
Telecopier: 813-787-7237.

MEMBERS OF FIRM

Joseph E. Costanza	Frederick M. Cuppy
	Gerald K. Hrebec

(See Next Column)

BURKE, MURPHY, COSTANZA & CUPPY—*Continued*

ASSOCIATE

Paula E. Neff

Representative Clients: Whiteco Industries; Continental Machine & Engineering Co., Inc.; Gary Steel Products Corp.; Superior Construction Co., Inc.; Federal National Mortgage Association; Morrison Construction Co.; Welsh Oil, Inc.

For Complete List of Firm Personnel, See General Section

For full biographical listings, see the Martindale-Hubbell Law Directory

---

*SOUTH BEND,** St. Joseph Co.

DORAN BLACKMOND READY HAMILTON & WILLIAMS (AV)

1700 Valley American Bank Building, 211 W. Washington Street, 46601
Telephone: 219-288-1800
Fax: 219-236-4265

MEMBERS OF FIRM

M. Edward Doran (1895-1982)	David T. Ready
John E. Doran	John C. Hamilton
Don G. Blackmond	A. Howard Williams

ASSOCIATE

Don Gregory Blackmond

For full biographical listings, see the Martindale-Hubbell Law Directory

---

KANSAS

OVERLAND PARK, Johnson Co.

SHAMBERG, JOHNSON & BERGMAN, CHARTERED (AV)

Suite 355, 4551 West 107th Street, 66207
Telephone: 913-642-0600
Fax: 913-642-9629
Kansas City, Kansas Office: Suite 860, New Brotherhood Building, 8th and State Streets.
Telephone: 913-281-1900.
Kansas City, Missouri Office: Suite 205, Scarritt Arcade Building, 819 Walnut.
Telephone: 816-556-9431.

Lynn R. Johnson	Victor A. Bergman
	John M. Parisi

Steven G. Brown	Anthony L. DeWitt
Steve N. Six	(Not admitted in KS)
	Patrick A. Hamilton

OF COUNSEL

John E. Shamberg

For full biographical listings, see the Martindale-Hubbell Law Directory

---

*TOPEKA,** Shawnee Co.

GOODELL, STRATTON, EDMONDS & PALMER, L.L.P. (AV)

515 South Kansas Avenue, 66603-3999
Telephone: 913-233-0593
Telecopier: 913-233-8870
Email: GSEP@CJNETWORKS.COM

MEMBERS OF FIRM

Gerald L. Goodell	David E. Bruns
Wayne T. Stratton	N. Larry Bork

SPECIAL COUNSEL

Curtis J. Waugh

Local Counsel for: Farm Bureau Mutual Insurance Co.; St. Paul Fire & Marine Insurance Co.; Washburn University of Topeka; HydroFlex, Inc.; Bartlett & West Engineers.
General Counsel for: American Home Life Insurance Co.; Columbian National Title Insurance Co.; The Menninger Foundation; Kansas Medical Society; Kansas Hospital Association.

For Complete List of Firm Personnel, See General Section

For full biographical listings, see the Martindale-Hubbell Law Directory

---

*WICHITA,** Sedgwick Co.

DEPEW AND GILLEN, L.L.C. (AV)

151 North Main, Suite 700, 67202-1408
Telephone: 316-265-9621
Facsimile: 316-265-3819
Email: d-g@southwind.net

(See Next Column)

Spencer L. Depew	David W. Nickel
Dennis L. Gillen	Nicholas S. Daily
Randall K. Rathbun	David E. Rogers
Jack Scott McInteer	Charles C. Steincamp

For full biographical listings, see the Martindale-Hubbell Law Directory

---

FOULSTON & SIEFKIN L.L.P. (AV)

700 Fourth Financial Center, 67202
Telephone: 316-267-6371
Facsimile: 316-267-6345
Topeka, Kansas Office: 1515 Bank IV Tower, 534 Kansas Avenue, 66603.
Telephone: 913-233-3600.
Fax: 913-233-1610.
Dodge City, Kansas Office: 810 Frontview, P.O. Box 1147, 67801.
Telephone: 316-227-8126.
Fax: 316-227-8451.
Member: Lex Mundi, A Global Association of 126 Independent Firms.

MEMBERS OF FIRM

Charles P. Efflandt	Wyatt A. Hoch

SPECIAL COUNSEL

Nancy M. Clifton	David M. Traster

For Complete List of Firm Personnel, See General Section

For full biographical listings, see the Martindale-Hubbell Law Directory

---

YOUNG, BOGLE, MCCAUSLAND, WELLS & CLARK, P.A. (AV)

106 West Douglas, Suite 923, 67202
Telephone: 316-265-7841
Facsimile: 316-265-3956

Glenn D. Young, Jr.	Paul S. McCausland
	Mark R. Maloney

Representative Clients: Bridgestone/Firestone Inc.; Deere & Co.; Citibank; Metropolitan Life Insurance Co.; Equitable Assurance Society of the United States; Geotechnical Services, Inc.; Greif Bros. Corp.; Geotechnical Services, Inc.

For Complete List of Firm Personnel, See General Section

For full biographical listings, see the Martindale-Hubbell Law Directory

---

KENTUCKY

---

*BOWLING GREEN,** Warren Co.

ENGLISH, LUCAS, PRIEST & OWSLEY (AV)

1101 College Street, P.O. Box 770, 42102-0770
Telephone: 502-781-6500
Telecopier: 502-782-7782
Email: inquiry@elpo.com

MEMBER OF FIRM

Charles E. English

ASSOCIATE

Jason P. Wright

For Complete List of Firm Personnel, See General Section

For full biographical listings, see the Martindale-Hubbell Law Directory

---

COVINGTON, Kenton Co.

ROBERT E. SANDERS AND ASSOCIATES, P.S.C. (AV)

The Charles H. Fisk House, 1017 Russell Street, 41011
Telephone: 606-491-3000
Fax: 606-655-4642
Email: 74762.3055@compuserve.com

Robert E. Sanders

Julie Lippert Duncan	Peggy A. Murphy
	Lisa Pruitt Thorner

LEGAL SUPPORT PERSONNEL

Shirley L. Sanders	Sandra A. Head
	Sheila D. Rachal

For full biographical listings, see the Martindale-Hubbell Law Directory

---

*LEXINGTON,** Fayette Co.

BUCHANAN INGERSOLL, PROFESSIONAL CORPORATION (AV)

Suite 600, PNC Bank Plaza, 200 West Vine Street, 40507
Telephone: 606-225-5333
Telecopier: 606-225-5334
Pittsburgh, Pennsylvania Office: One Oxford Centre, 301 Grant Street, 20th Floor.
Telephone: 412-562-8800.

(See Next Column)

BUCHANAN INGERSOLL PROFESSIONAL CORPORATION, *Lexington—Continued*

Philadelphia, Pennsylvania Office: Two Logan Square, Twelfth Floor, 18th & Arch Streets.
Telephone: 215-665-8700.
Harrisburg, Pennsylvania Office: 30 North Third Street.
Telephone: 717-237-4800.
Tampa, Florida Office: 101 East Kennedy Boulevard, Suite 1030.
Telephone: 813-222-8180.
North Miami Beach, Florida Office: 19495 Biscayne Boulevard, Suite 606.
Telephone: 305-933-5600.
Miami, Florida Office: Nationsbank Tower, 100 S.E. Second Street.
Telephone: 305-347-4080.
Princeton, New Jersey Office: Buchanan Ingersoll, A Partnership, College Centre, 500 College Road East.
Telephone: 609-987-6800.
Buffalo, New York Office: 1100 Main Place Tower, 350 Main Street.
Telephone: 716-854-4100.
Fax: 716-854-4227.

John R. Leathers

Stephen G. Allen

For full biographical listings, see the Martindale-Hubbell Law Directory

LANDRUM & SHOUSE (AV)

106 West Vine Street, P.O. Box 951, 40588-0951
Telephone: 606-255-2424
Facsimile: 606-233-0308
Louisville, Kentucky Office: 400 West Market Street, Suite 1550, 40202.
Telephone: 502-589-7616.
Facsimile: 502-589-2119.

MEMBER OF FIRM
John H. Burrus

District Attorneys: CSX Transportation, Inc.
Special Trial Counsel: Ford Motor Co. and Affiliates (Eastern Kentucky); Clark Equipment Co.
Representative Clients: The Continental Insurance Cos.; U.S. Insurance Group; U.S. Fidelity & Guaranty Co.; Ohio Casualty Insurance Co.; CIGNA; Royal Insurance Cos.

For Complete List of Firm Personnel, See General Section

For full biographical listings, see the Martindale-Hubbell Law Directory

STOLL, KEENON & PARK, LLP (AV)

201 E. Main Street, Suite 1000, 40507-1380
Telephone: 606-231-3000
Telecopier: 606-253-1093; 606-253-1027
Frankfort, Kentucky Office: 307 Washington Street, 40601.
Telephone: 502-875-6220.
Telecopier: 502-875-6235.
Louisville, Kentucky Office: 400 West Market Street, Suite 2650, 40202-3377.
Telephone: 502-568-9100.
Telecopier: 502-568-5700.

MEMBERS OF FIRM
Charles E. Shivel, Jr.	Diane M. Carlton
Samuel D. Hinkle IV	David E. Fleenor
Lea Pauley Goff	

ASSOCIATES
Culver V. Halliday	John Browning Park

Representative Clients: Bank One, Lexington, NA; C. Lee Cook; Cintech Industrial Coatings; Farmers Capital Bank Corp.; FOSROC; Link Belt Construction Equipment Co.; General Motors Corp.; International Business Machines Corp.; Rockwell International Corp.; Swifty Oil Co.

For Complete List of Firm Personnel, See General Section

For full biographical listings, see the Martindale-Hubbell Law Directory

LOUISVILLE,* Jefferson Co.

MIDDLETON & REUTLINGER, P.S.C. (AV)

2500 Brown and Williamson Tower, 40202-3410
Telephone: 502-584-1135
Fax: 502-561-0442
New Albany, Indiana Office: 2623 Charlestown Road, 47150.
Telephone: 812-944-7215.

Charles G. Middleton, III	Stewart L. Prather
John W. Bilby	Kathiejane Oehler
James E. Milliman	

For Complete List of Firm Personnel, See General Section

For full biographical listings, see the Martindale-Hubbell Law Directory

WOODWARD, HOBSON & FULTON (AV)

2500 National City Tower, 101 South Fifth Street, 40202
Telephone: 502-581-8000
Fax: 502-581-8111
Lexington, Kentucky Office: PNC Bank Plaza, 200 West Vine Street, Suite 500.
Telephone: 606-244-7100.
Telecopier: 606-244-7111.
New Albany, Indiana Office: 611 East Spring Street, P.O. Box 288.
Telephone: 812-941-1800.
Telecopier: 812-941-1855.

MEMBERS OF FIRM
Harry K. Herren	Gregory L. Smith
Thomas A. Hoy	Arthur L. Williams

ASSOCIATE
Christopher R. Fitzpatrick

Representative Clients: Custom Resins; Sun Refining and Marketing; Koppers Industries, Inc.; Concord Custom Cleaners; Hechingers; OPTA Food Ingredients; Owensboro Grain; Rumpke Waste Systems; United Waste.

For Complete List of Firm Personnel, See General Section

For full biographical listings, see the Martindale-Hubbell Law Directory

LOUISIANA

*BATON ROUGE,*** East Baton Rouge Parish

KEAN, MILLER, HAWTHORNE, D'ARMOND, McCOWAN & JARMAN, L.L.P. (AV)

22nd Floor, One American Place, P.O. Box 3513, 70821
Telephone: 504-387-0999
Fax: 504-388-9133
New Orleans, Louisiana Office: Energy Centre, Suite 1470, 1100 Poydras Street.
Telephone: 504-585-3050.
Fax: 504-585-3051.
Plaquemine, Louisiana Office: Suite 10, 23425 Railroad Avenue.
Telephone: 504-687-9845.
Fax: 504-382-3445.

MEMBERS OF FIRM
Charles S. McCowan, Jr.	J. Carter Wilkinson
G. William Jarman	Sandra L. Edwards
Leonard L. Kilgore III	James P. Doré
Maureen N. Harbourt	Katherine W. King
M. Dwayne Johnson	Charles S. McCowan III

Esteban Herrera, Jr.	J. Randy Young
Susan Knight Carter (Resident, New Orleans Office)	Robert M. Hoyland
	Murray A. Greene

Representative Clients: Amoco Production Company, Houston, TX; BASF Corporation, Parsippany, NJ; Exxon Company, U.S.A., Baton Rouge, LA; Georgia-Pacific Corporation, Atlanta, GA; Louisiana Chemical Association, Baton Rouge, LA; PPG Industries, Inc., Pittsburgh, PA; Tenneco, Inc., Houston, TX; Transcontinental Gas Pipe Line Company, Houston, TX; Willamette Industries, Inc., Portland, OR.

For Complete List of Firm Personnel, See General Section

For full biographical listings, see the Martindale-Hubbell Law Directory

SHOCKEY & ZIOBER, A PROFESSIONAL LAW CORPORATION (AV)

Suite 3-A, 5551 Corporate Boulevard, P.O. Box 80286, 70898-0286
Telephone: 504-929-8929
Telecopier: 504-928-7694

John David Ziober	William C. Shockey

Emily Phillips Ziober	Jennifer R. Treadway Morris
Douglas J. Cochran	James E. Moore, Jr.

For full biographical listings, see the Martindale-Hubbell Law Directory

SIMONEAUX & CARLETON (AV)

8555 United Plaza Boulevard Suite 402, 70809
Telephone: 504-928-6880
Fax: 504-928-6881

MEMBERS OF FIRM
Frank P. Simoneaux	Stephen C. Carleton

ASSOCIATE
Timothy J. Poche

Representative Clients: ARKLA, Inc.; Borden Chemicals & Plastics Operating Limited Partnership; Cabot Corp.; Mazda Motor of America, Inc.; Mobil Oil Corp; Murphy Oil USA Inc.; Penzoil Exploration & Production Co.;

(See Next Column)

SIMONEAUX & CARLETON—*Continued*

Schuylkill Metals Corp.; CITGO Petroleum Corp.; Kaiser Aluminum and Chemical Corp.

For full biographical listings, see the Martindale-Hubbell Law Directory

LAFAYETTE,* Lafayette Parish

HILL & BEYER, A PROFESSIONAL LAW CORPORATION (AV)

101 LaRue France, Suite 502, P.O. Box 53006, 70505-3006
Telephone: 318-232-9733
Fax: 1-318-237-2566

John K. Hill, Jr.	Eugene P. Matherne (1962-1996)
Bret C. Beyer	Robert B. Purser
David R. Rabalais	Erin J. Sherburne
Marianna Broussard	

For full biographical listings, see the Martindale-Hubbell Law Directory

MANGHAM AND DAVIS (AV)

Suite 1400 First National Bank Towers, 600 Jefferson Street, P.O. Box 93110, 70509-3110
Telephone: 318-233-6200
Fax: 318-233-6521

Michael R. Mangham	Louis R. Davis

ASSOCIATES

Dawn Mayeux Fuqua	Claire A. Fisher

SPECIAL COUNSEL

Michael J. O'Shee

Reference: Hibernia National Bank, Lafayette, Louisiana.

For full biographical listings, see the Martindale-Hubbell Law Directory

NEW ORLEANS,* Orleans Parish

BOGGS, LOEHN & RODRIGUE (AV)

A Partnership including Law Corporations
Suite 1800 Lykes Center, 300 Poydras Street, 70130-3597
Telephone: 504-523-7090
Fax: 504-581-6822

Charles A. Boggs (A Law Corporation)	Edward A. Rodrigue, Jr., (A Law Corporation)
Thomas E. Loehn (A Law Corporation)	Robert I. Baudouin
	Jedd S. Malish

Reference: First National Bank of Commerce, New Orleans, La.

For full biographical listings, see the Martindale-Hubbell Law Directory

DEUTSCH, KERRIGAN & STILES, L.L.P. (AV)

A Partnership including Professional Law Corporations
755 Magazine Street, 70130-3672
Telephone: 504-581-5141
Cable Address: "Dekest"
Telex: 584358
Telecopier: 504-566-1201
Email: dks@dksno.com *URL:* http://www.dksno.com
St. Tammany Parish Office: 550 Pontchartrain Drive, Suite 200, Slidell, LA. 70458.
Telephone: 504-639-0555.
Fax: 504-639-0550

MEMBERS OF FIRM

Charles F. Seemann, Jr., (P.L.C.)	Janet L. MacDonell
Robert E. Kerrigan, Jr., (P.L.C.)	Theodore L. White
A. Wendel Stout, III	William C. Harrison, Jr.
Marc J. Yellin (P.L.C.)	Gary B. Roth
Nancy J. Marshall	Lisa C. Winter

OF COUNSEL

David C. Treen	Charles K. Reasonover (P.L.C.)

ASSOCIATE

Victor J. Franckiewicz, Jr.

For Complete List of Firm Personnel, See General Section

For full biographical listings, see the Martindale-Hubbell Law Directory

GAINSBURGH, BENJAMIN, DAVID, MEUNIER, NORIEA & WARSHAUER (AV)

2800 Energy Centre, 1100 Poydras, 70163-2800
Telephone: 504-522-2304
Telecopier: 504-528-9973
Email: GAINSBEN@IAMERICA.NET

MEMBERS OF FIRM

Gerald E. Meunier	Stevan C. Dittman
Nick F. Noriea, Jr.	Madeleine M. Landrieu
Darryl M. Phillips	

For full biographical listings, see the Martindale-Hubbell Law Directory

GORDON, ARATA, McCOLLAM & DUPLANTIS, L.L.P. (AV)

A Partnership including Professional Law Corporations
Place St. Charles, Suite 4000, 201 St. Charles Avenue, 70170-4000
Telephone: 504-582-1111
Fax: 504-582-1121
Lafayette, Louisiana Office: 625 East Kaliste Saloom Road.
Telephone: 318-237-0132.
Fax: 318-237-3451.
Baton Rouge, Louisiana Office: 1420 One American Place.
Telephone: 504-381-9643.
Fax: 504-336-9763.

MEMBERS OF FIRM

John A. Gordon (A P.L.C.)	Guy E. Wall
John M. McCollam (A P.L.C.)	James L. Weiss

ASSOCIATE

Elizabeth L. Gordon

LAFAYETTE OFFICE

RESIDENT MEMBER OF FIRM

William F. Bailey

RESIDENT ASSOCIATE

Denis C. Swords

Representative Clients: Amoco Production Co.; McMoran Oil & Gas Co., Inc.; First National Bank of Commerce of New Orleans; Universal Health Services, Inc.; Cox Cable Communications, Inc.; W.R. Grace & Co.; Lorillard, Inc.; First City Bancorporation; Enron Oil and Gas Co.

For Complete List of Firm Personnel, See General Section

For full biographical listings, see the Martindale-Hubbell Law Directory

HABANS, BOLOGNA & CARRIERE, A PROFESSIONAL LAW CORPORATION (AV)

Suite 2323, 1515 Poydras Street, 70112
Telephone: 504-524-2323
Telex: 151514 HABA M UT
Telecopier: 504-522-7224
Cable Address: HABOL

Robert N. Habans, Jr.	John C. McNeese
William F. Bologna	Aimée Carriere
James D. Carriere	Dwight L. Acomb
Julien F. Jurgens	

For full biographical listings, see the Martindale-Hubbell Law Directory

HEBERT, MOULEDOUX & BLAND, A PROFESSIONAL LAW CORPORATION (AV)

Pan-American Life Center, Suite 1650, 601 Poydras Street, 70130
Telephone: 504-525-3333
Cable Address: "HMBL"
Telex: 588-092;
Fax: 504-523-4224

Maurice C. Hebert, Jr.	Alan Guy Brackett
André J. Mouledoux	John H. Musser, V

Representative Clients: Archer-Daniels Midland Company; Bisso Marine Company, Inc.; Carline Geismar Fleet, Inc.; Cooper/T. Smith Stevedoring Company, Inc.; Delta Queen Steamboat Co.; Diamond Offshore Drilling, Inc.; LOOP INC.; Marine Equipment Management Corporation; McDermott Incorporated; Olympic Marine Company.

For Complete List of Firm Personnel, See General Section

For full biographical listings, see the Martindale-Hubbell Law Directory

LISKOW & LEWIS, A PROFESSIONAL LAW CORPORATION (AV)

50th Floor, One Shell Square, 70139
Telephone: 504-581-7979
Telecopier: 504-556-4108; 504-556-4109
Lafayette, Louisiana Office: 822 Harding Street, P.O. Box 52008.
Telephone: 318-232-7424.
Telecopier: 318-267-2399.

J. Berry St. John, Jr.	Mary S. Johnson
Robert E. Holden	Scott C. Seiler
Wm. Craig Wyman	Guenton C. Slawson, Jr.

Patricia Campbell Smith

Representative Clients: American Petroleum Institute; Cabot Corporation; City of New Orleans; Columbian Chemicals Company; Exxon Company; Mobil Oil Corporation; Olin Corporation; Pennzoil Company; Star Enterprise.

For Complete List of Firm Personnel, See General Section

For full biographical listings, see the Martindale-Hubbell Law Directory

New Orleans—Continued

PHELPS DUNBAR, L.L.P. (AV)

Texaco Center, 400 Poydras Street, 70130-3245
Telephone: 504-566-1311
Telecopier: 504-568-9130, 504-568-9007
Cable Address: "Howspencer"
Telex: 584125 WU
Telex: 6821155 WUI
Email: info@phelps.com
Baton Rouge, Louisiana Office: Suite 701, City National Bank Building,
P.O. Box 4412.
Telephone: 504-346-0285.
Telecopier: 504-381-9197.
Jackson, Mississippi Office: Suite 500, Mtel Centré, 200 South Lamar
Street, P.O. Box 23066.
Telephone: 601-352-2300.
Telecopier: 601-360-9777.
Tupelo, Mississippi Office: Seventh Floor, One Mississippi Plaza, P.O. Box
1220.
Telephone: 601-842-7907.
Telecopier: 601-842-3873.
Houston, Texas Office: Suite 900, 3040 Post Oak Boulevard.
Telephone: 713-626-1386.
Telecopier: 713-626-1388.
London, England Office: Suite 731, Level 7, Lloyd's, 1 Lime Street,
London EC3M 7DQ England.
Telephone: 011-44-171-929-4765.
Telecopier: 011-44-171-929-0046.
Telex: 987321.

MEMBER OF FIRM
Steven J. Levine (Resident, Baton Rouge, Louisiana Office)
ASSOCIATES

Patrick O'Hara (Resident, Baton Rouge, Louisiana Office)
Sheila T. Walet

John Whitney Pesnell (Resident, Baton Rouge, Louisiana Office)

Representative Clients: Energy Development Corp.; GATX Terminals Corp.; Liquid Carbonics; Missouri Pacific Railroad Co.; Rubicon Inc.; Underwriters at Lloyd's, London; Union Tank Car Company, Inc.; Western Waste Industries, Inc.

For Complete List of Firm Personnel, See General Section

For full biographical listings, see the Martindale-Hubbell Law Directory

PULASKI, GIEGER & LABORDE, L.L.C. (AV)

Suite 4800, One Shell Square, 701 Poydras Street, 70139
Telephone: 504-561-0400
Telecopier: 504-561-1011

Michael T. Pulaski (P.C.)	Leo R. McAloon, III
Ernest P. Gieger, Jr., (P.C.)	John P. Gonzalez
Kenneth H. Laborde (P.C.)	J. Jeffery Raborn
Robert W. Maxwell (P.C.)	Lance Blake Williams
Keith W. McDaniel (P.C.)	James E. Swinnen
Sharon D. Smith (P.C.)	Gina S. Montgomery
Gary G. Hebert	Mary Beth Meyer
	Julianne T. Echols

For full biographical listings, see the Martindale-Hubbell Law Directory

SMITH, JONES & FAWER, L.L.P. (AV)

201 St. Charles Avenue, Sute 3702, 70170
Telephone: 504-525-2200
Telecopier: 504-525-2205

MEMBERS OF FIRM
Randall A. Smith (P.C.)
Gladstone N. Jones, III
Michael S. Fawer
ASSOCIATES
Andrew L. Kramer
L. Tiffany Hawkins

For full biographical listings, see the Martindale-Hubbell Law Directory

WAGNER, BAGOT & GLEASON (AV)

Suite 2660, Poydras Center, 650 Poydras Street, 70130-6105
Telephone: 504-525-2141
Telecopier: 504-523-1587
TWX: 5106017673
ELN: 62928850
"INCISIVE"

Thomas J. Wagner	Harvey G. Gleason
Michael H. Bagot, Jr.	Whitney L. Cole
	Eric D. Suben

For full biographical listings, see the Martindale-Hubbell Law Directory

SHREVEPORT, Caddo Parish

BARLOW AND HARDTNER L.C. (AV)

Tenth Floor, Louisiana Tower, 401 Edwards Street, 71101-3289
Telephone: 318-227-1131
Telecopier: 318-227-1141
Mailing Address: P.O. Box 8, Shreveport, Louisiana, 71161-0008

Malcolm S. Murchison	Clair F. White
Joseph L. Shea, Jr.	Philip E. Downer, III
	Michael B. Donald

Representative Clients: Ashland Oil, Inc.; The Brinkmann Corporation; Central Louisiana Electric Co., Inc.; NorAm Energy Corp. (formerly Arkla, Inc.); Central and South West Corporation; Panhandle Eastern Corp.; Texas Eastern Corp.; Pennzoil Producing Co.; Ashland Oil, Inc.; TE Products Pipeline Company.

For Complete List of Firm Personnel, See General Section

For full biographical listings, see the Martindale-Hubbell Law Directory

MILLS, TIMMONS & FLOWERS, A PROFESSIONAL LAW CORPORATION (AV)

300 Law Center, 331 Milam Street, P.O. Box 1784, 71166-1784
Telephone: 318-222-0337
Fax: 318-222-5400

George H. Mills, Jr.	David C. Turansky
Wayne Timmons	J. Broocks Greer III
Peter R. Flowers	Sandra Lynn Walker

OF COUNSEL
William T. Allison

Reference: Hibernia National Bank.

For full biographical listings, see the Martindale-Hubbell Law Directory

WILKINSON, CARMODY & GILLIAM (AV)

1700 Beck Building, 400 Travis Street, P.O. Box 1707, 71166
Telephone: 318-221-4196
Telecopier: 318-221-3705

MEMBERS OF FIRM

John D. Wilkinson (1867-1929)	Bobby S. Gilliam
William Scott Wilkinson (1895-1985)	Mark E. Gilliam
	Penny D. Sellers
Arthur R. Carmody, Jr.	Patrick F. Robinson
	Michael J. Ryan

Representative Clients: Farmers Insurance Group; Home Federal Savings & Loan Association of Shreveport; The Kansas City Southern Railway Co.; KTAL-TV; Lincoln National Life Insurance Co.; Mobil Oil Co.; Schumpert Medical Center; Sears, Roebuck & Co.; Southern Pacific Transportation Co.; Southwestern Electric Power Co.

For full biographical listings, see the Martindale-Hubbell Law Directory

MAINE

BANGOR, Penobscot Co.

EATON, PEABODY, BRADFORD & VEAGUE, P.A. (AV)

Fleet Center-Exchange Street, P.O. Box 1210, 04402-1210
Telephone: 207-947-0111
Telecopier: 207-942-3040
Email: epbv@aol.com
Augusta, Maine Office: 2 Central Plaza.
Telephone: 207-622-3747.
Telecopier: 207-622-9732.
Blue Hill, Maine Office: One East Blue Hill Road.
Telephone: 207-374-2812.
Telecopier: 207-374-2548.
Brunswick, Maine Office: 167 Park Row.
Telephone: 207-729-1144.
Telecopier: 207-729-1140.
Camden, Maine Office: 7-9 Washington Street.
Telephone: 207-236-3325.
Telecopier: 207-236-8611.
Dover-Foxcroft, Maine Office: 30 East Main Street.
Telephone: 207-564-8378.
Telecopier: 207-564-7059.

Edward D. Leonard, III
P. Andrew Hamilton
OF COUNSEL
Martin L. Wilk (Resident, Brunswick Office)

Dorisann B. W. Wagner (Resident, Augusta Office)
Roger Lang Huber

A List of Representative Clients available upon request.

(See Next Column)

EATON, PEABODY, BRADFORD & VEAGUE P.A.—*Continued*

For Complete List of Firm Personnel, See General Section

For full biographical listings, see the Martindale-Hubbell Law Directory

---

BAR HARBOR, Hancock Co.

FENTON, CHAPMAN, FENTON, SMITH & KANE, P.A. (AV)

109 Main Street, P.O. Box B, 04609
Telephone: 207-288-3331
FAX: 207-288-9326

William Fenton	Chadbourn H. Smith
Douglas B. Chapman	Daniel H. Kane (1940-1995)
Nathaniel R. Fenton	Hancock Griffin, Jr. (1912-1980)

Margaret A. Timothy	Eric Lindquist

OF COUNSEL
Edwin R. Smith

Reference: Bar Harbor Banking and Trust Co.

For full biographical listings, see the Martindale-Hubbell Law Directory

---

BATH, * Sagadahoc Co.

CONLEY & HALEY (AV)

Thirty Front Street, 04530
Telephone: 207-443-5576
Telefax: 207-443-6665

Mark L. Haley	Tracey G. Burton

Representative Clients: Bath Iron Works Corporation; Central Maine Power Company; Saco Defense, Inc.; Sugarloaf Mountain Corporation.
References: Key Bank of Maine; First Federal Savings & Loan Association of Bath; Brunswick Federal Savings.

For Complete List of Firm Personnel, See General Section

For full biographical listings, see the Martindale-Hubbell Law Directory

---

PORTLAND, * Cumberland Co.

AMERLING & BURNS, A PROFESSIONAL ASSOCIATION (AV)

193 Middle Street, 04101
Telephone: 207-775-3581
Facsimile: 207-775-3814
Affiliated St. Croix Office: Coon & Sanford, P.O. Box 25918, Six Chandlers's Wharf, Suite 202, 00824-0918.

W. John Amerling	Arnold C. Macdonald
George F. Burns	Mary DeLano
David P. Ray	Joanne F. Cole
	A. Robert Ruesch

OF COUNSEL
Bruce M. Jervis

Representative Clients: H.E. Sargent, Inc. (construction); Merrill Trust; J.M. Huber, Inc.; Jackson Laboratories; Hague International (engineering); Aetna Life & Casualty Co.; The Hartford; Great American Insurance Co.; Wausau Insurance Co.

For full biographical listings, see the Martindale-Hubbell Law Directory

FRIEDMAN & BABCOCK (AV)

Suite 400, Six City Center, P.O. Box 4726, 04112-4726
Telephone: 207-761-0900
Telecopier: 207-761-0186

MEMBERS OF FIRM

Harold J. Friedman	Thomas A. Cox
Ernest J. Babcock	Karen Frink Wolf
Martha C. Gaythwaite	Jennifer S. Begel
	Laurence H. Leavitt

ASSOCIATES

Theodore H. Irwin, Jr.	Elizabeth A. Germani
Lee H. Bals	Jonathan Marc Dunitz
Michelle Allott	Darren Blaine Riggle
Arthur J. Lamothe	Tracy D. Hill
	Bruce W. Hepler

For full biographical listings, see the Martindale-Hubbell Law Directory

JENSEN BAIRD GARDNER & HENRY (AV)

Ten Free Street, P.O. Box 4510, 04112
Telephone: 207-775-7271
Telecopier: 207-775-7935
York County Office: 419 Alfred Street, Biddeford, Maine.
Telephone: 207-282-5107.
Telecopier: 207-282-6301.

MEMBERS OF FIRM

Walter E. Webber	Leslie E. Lowry, III
Nicholas S. Nadzo	James N. Katsiaficas

(See Next Column)

ASSOCIATE
Emily A. Bloch

Representative Clients: Steego Auto Parts Co.; St. Lawrence & Atlantic Railroad; Regional Waste Systems; Mid-Maine Waste Action Corp.; Pratt & Whitney; Shaw's Supermarkets.

For Complete List of Firm Personnel, See General Section

For full biographical listings, see the Martindale-Hubbell Law Directory

PETRUCCELLI & MARTIN (AV)

50 Monument Square, P.O. Box 9733, 04104-5033
Telephone: 207-775-0200
Telecopier: 207-775-2360

MEMBERS OF FIRM

Gerald F. Petruccelli	Joel C. Martin

ASSOCIATES

Linda C. Russell	Thomas C. Bradley

Representative Clients: Brunswick Associates Trust; Cumberland Farms; Town of Jay, Maine.

For full biographical listings, see the Martindale-Hubbell Law Directory

PIERCE ATWOOD (AV)

One Monument Square, 04101
Telephone: 207-791-1100
Fax: 207-791-1350
Email: info@PierceAtwood.com
Augusta, Maine Office: 77 Winthrop Street.
Telephone: 207-622-6311.
Fax: 207-623-9367.
Newburyport, Massachusetts Office: 6 Harris Street.
Telephone: 508-465-9599.
Fax: 508-465-9945.

MEMBERS OF FIRM

Daniel E. Boxer	Philip F. W. Ahrens, III
John O'Leary	Kenneth Fairbanks Gray
John D. Delahanty	William E. Taylor
Thomas R. Doyle	Dixon P. Pike

ASSOCIATES

Kate L. Geoffroy	David P. Littell
Matthew D. Manahan	Abigail M. Holman
Adam H. Steinman	Helen L. Edmonds
	(Not admitted in ME)

For Complete List of Firm Personnel, See General Section

For full biographical listings, see the Martindale-Hubbell Law Directory

PRETI, FLAHERTY, BELIVEAU & PACHIOS (AV)

A Limited Liability Company
443 Congress Street, P.O. Box 11410, 04104-7410
Telephone: 207-791-3000
Telecopier: 207-791-3111
Email: admin@pfbpnet.com
Augusta, Maine Office: 45 Memorial Circle, P.O. Box 1058, 04332-1058.
Telephone: 207-623-5300.
Telecopier: 207-623-2914.

MEMBERS OF FIRM

Severin M. Beliveau (Augusta Office)	Michael Kaplan
Harold C. Pachios	Joseph G. Donahue (Augusta Office)
Michael J. Gentile (Augusta Office)	David B. Van Slyke
Anthony W. Buxton (Augusta Office)	Ann R. Robinson (Augusta Office)
Virginia E. Davis (Augusta Office)	John P. McVeigh

OF COUNSEL

Mark B. LeDuc (Augusta Office)	Jeanne T. Cohn-Connor

ASSOCIATE
Deirdre M. O'Callaghan (Augusta Office)

Representative Clients: Bangor Hydroelectric Co.; Maine Turnpike Authority; Guy Gannett Publishing Co.; Maine Low-Level Waste Authority; Industrial Energy Consumer Group; James River Corp.; Maine Oil Dealers Assn.; LCP Chemicals; Wheelabrator Environmental Systems; The Maine Alliance.

For Complete List of Firm Personnel, See General Section

For full biographical listings, see the Martindale-Hubbell Law Directory

TROUBH, HEISLER & PIAMPIANO, P.C. (AV)

511 Congress Street, P.O. Box 9711, 04104-5011
Telephone: 207-780-6789
Fax: 207-774-2339

(See Next Column)

TROUBH, HEISLER & PIAMPIANO P.C., *Portland—Continued*

William B. Troubh	Thomas E. Getchell
Edwin A. Heisler	Michael Richards
Robert J. Piampiano	William K. McKinley
Kevin M. Gillis	Daniel F. Gilligan
Michael P. Boyd	Paul S. Bulger

John G. Richardson	Linda L. Sears

Daniel R. Felkel

For full biographical listings, see the Martindale-Hubbell Law Directory

WRIGHT, COON & CUNNINGHAM, P.A. (AV)

377 Fore Street, P.O. Box 7526, 04112
Telephone: 207-775-7722
Fax: 207-772-7045
Email: lexfori@lexfori.com

Steven F. Wright	John R. Coon

Gregory M. Cunningham

For full biographical listings, see the Martindale-Hubbell Law Directory

MARYLAND

BALTIMORE, * (Independent City)

FERGUSON, SCHETELICH, HEFFERNAN & MURDOCK, P.A. (AV)

1300 NationsBank Center 1, 100 South Charles Street, 21201
Telephone: 410-837-2200
Fax: 410-837-1188
Email: fshm@ix.netcom

Robert L. Ferguson, Jr.	Christopher J. Heffernan
Thomas J. Schetelich	M. Brooke Murdock

Michael N. Russo, Jr.	Peter Joseph Basile
Jodi K. Ebersole	Ann D. Ware

For full biographical listings, see the Martindale-Hubbell Law Directory

VENABLE ATTORNEYS AT LAW VENABLE, BAETJER AND HOWARD, LLP (AV)

A Partnership including Professional Corporations
1800 Mercantile Bank & Trust Building, 2 Hopkins Plaza, 21201
Telephone: 410-244-7400
Email: INFO@Venable.win.net
Washington, D.C. Office: Venable, Baetjer, Howard & Civiletti LLP. Suite 1000, 1201 New York Avenue, N.W.
Telephone: 202-962-4800.
McLean, Virginia Office: Suite 400, 2010 Corporate Ridge.
Telephone: 703-760-1600.
Rockville, Maryland Office: Suite 500, One Church Street, P. O. Box 1906.
Telephone: 301-217-5600.
Towson, Maryland Office: 210 Allegheny Avenue, P. O. Box 5517.
Telephone: 410-494-6200.

MEMBERS OF FIRM

Benjamin R. Civiletti (P.C.) (Also at Washington, D.C. and Towson, Maryland Offices)	Jeffrey A. Dunn (also at Washington, D.C. Office)
Anthony M. Carey (Also at Washington, D.C. Office)	James L. Shea (Also at Washington, D.C. Office)
John Henry Lewin, Jr. (P.C.)	Brigid E. Kenney
Dennis J. Whittlesey (Not admitted in MD; Resident, Washington, D.C. Office)	John J. Pavlick, Jr. (Not admitted in MD; Resident, Washington, D. C. Office)
Robert G. Smith (P.C.)	Kathleen Gallogly Cox (Resident, Towson, Maryland Office)
John G. Milliken (Not admitted in MD; Washington, D.C. and McLean, Virginia Offices)	Christopher R. Mellott
Joseph C. Wich, Jr. (Resident, Towson, Maryland Office)	M. King Hill, III (Resident, Towson, Maryland Office)
Joseph G. Block (Not admitted in MD; Resident, Washington, D.C. Office)	James A. Dunbar (Also at Washington, D.C. Office)
Michael Schatzow (Also at Washington, D.C. Office)	Ronald W. Taylor
John F. Cooney (Not admitted in MD; Resident, Washington, D.C. Office)	Thomas J. Kelly, Jr. (Not admitted in MD; Resident, Washington, D. C. Office)
James K. Archibald (Also at Washington, D.C. Office)	David C. Mancini (Not admitted in MD; Resident, McLean, Virginia Office)
Judson W. Starr (Not admitted in MD; Also at Washington, D.C. and Towson, Maryland Offices)	Kevin L. Shepherd
	Mitchell Y. Mirviss
	Thomas M. Lingan

(See Next Column)

OF COUNSEL

Richard H. Mays (Not admitted in MD; Washington, D.C. and McLean, Virginia Offices)	Judith A. Armold

ASSOCIATES

Gregory S. Braker (Resident, Washington, D.C. Office)	Valerie K. Mann (Not admitted in MD; Resident, Washington, D.C. Office)
Andrew R. Herrup (Resident, Washington, D.C. Office)	Christine M. McAnney (Not admitted in MD; Resident, McLean, Virginia Office)
Mary-Dulany James (Resident, Towson, Maryland Office)	
Thomas H. Strong	

For Complete List of Firm Personnel, See General Section

For full biographical listings, see the Martindale-Hubbell Law Directory

SALISBURY, * Wicomico Co.

ADKINS, POTTS & SMETHURST, L.L.P. (AV)

Suite 600, One Plaza East, P.O. Box 4247, 21803-4247
Telephone: 410-749-0161
Fax: 410-749-5021

MEMBER OF FIRM

Raymond Stevens Smethurst, Jr.

Representative Clients: Atlantic Wood Industries, Inc.; Campbell Soup Company; Delmarva Power & Light Co.; G. E. Capital Mortgage Services, Inc.; Lawyers' Title Insurance Corp.; Mellon Bank (DE); PNC Bank; Proko Industries, Inc.; Shopco Group; WBOC-TV.

For full biographical listings, see the Martindale-Hubbell Law Directory

SILVER SPRING, Montgomery Co.

LIPSHULTZ AND HONE, CHARTERED (AV)

Suite 108 Montgomery Center, 8630 Fenton Street, 20910
Telephone: 301-587-8500
Fax: 301-495-9759
Washington, D.C. Office: Suite 200, 2000 L Street, N.W.
Telephone: 202-872-0909.

John Llewellyn Hone

For Complete List of Firm Personnel, See General Section

For full biographical listings, see the Martindale-Hubbell Law Directory

MASSACHUSETTS

BOSTON, * Suffolk Co.

BARRON & STADFELD, P.C. (AV)

Two Center Plaza, 02108
Telephone: 617-723-9800
Telecopier: 617-523-8359
Email: PUBLIC@BARRONSTAD.COM *URL:* HTTP://WWW.BARRONSTAD.COM
Hyannis, Massachusetts Office: 258 Winter Street.
Telephone: 617-778-6622.

Bernard A. Dwork	David P. Dwork

Julie Taylor Moran

Judith C. Knight

For Complete List of Firm Personnel, See General Section

For full biographical listings, see the Martindale-Hubbell Law Directory

KOPELMAN AND PAIGE, P.C. (AV)

Park Square Building, 31 St. James Avenue, 7th Floor, 02116
Telephone: 617-556-0007
Fax: 617-654-1735

Leonard Kopelman	John W. Giorgio
Donald G. Paige	Barbara J. Saint Andre
Elizabeth A. Lane	Joel B. Bard
Joyce F. Frank	Everett Joseph Marder

Patrick J. Costello

William Hewig, III	Anne-Marie M. Hyland
Deborah Eliason	Richard Bowen
Judith Chanoux Cutler	Cheryl Ann Banks

Brian W. Riley

For Complete List of Firm Personnel, See General Section

For full biographical listings, see the Martindale-Hubbell Law Directory

Boston—Continued

McGregor & Shea, P.C. (AV)

80 Temple Place, 02111
Telephone: 617-237-1961
URL: http://www.thespotlight.com/bostonlaw/mcgregorshea/

Gregor I. McGregor   John F. Shea

Cheryl Blaine   David S. Blackmar

OF COUNSEL

H. Theodore Cohen   Carolyn W. Baldwin
           (Not admitted in MA)

LEGAL SUPPORT PERSONNEL

Ralph R. Willmer, A.I.C.P. Heidi M. Zisch
 (Environmental Planner)

For full biographical listings, see the Martindale-Hubbell Law Directory

Palmer & Dodge LLP (AV)

One Beacon Street, 02108
Telephone: 617-573-0100
Facsimile: 617-227-4420

MEMBERS OF FIRM

Charles E. DeWitt, Jr.   Scott P. Lewis
William L. Lahey   Raymond M. Murphy

COUNSEL

Stephen J. Abarbanel

For Complete List of Firm Personnel, See General Section

For full biographical listings, see the Martindale-Hubbell Law Directory

Rackemann, Sawyer & Brewster, Professional Corporation (AV)

One Financial Center, 02111
Telephone: 617-542-2300
Telecopier: 617-542-7437

William B. Tyler   Janet M. Smith
Henry H. Thayer   Peter Friedenberg
Stephen Carr Anderson   Richard S. Novak
Albert M. Fortier, Jr.   J. David Leslie
Michael F. O'Connell   Sanford M. Matathia
Stuart T. Freeland   Richard J. Gallogly
Alan B. Rubenstein   James A. Wachta
James R. Shea, Jr.   Hanson S. Reynolds
Brian M. Hurley   Donald R. Pinto, Jr.

COUNSEL

Ronald S. Duby   Gordon M. Orloff
Lucy West Behymer   Eric A. Smith

OF COUNSEL

Albert B. Wolfe   George V. Anastas
August R. Meyer   Edward M. Condit
Richard H. Lovell   Alexander H. Spaulding

Margaret L. Hayes   Peter A. Alpert
Daniel J. Ossoff   Ellen M. Harrington
Melissa Langer Ellis   Lauren D. Armstrong
Daniel J. Bailey, III   Robert B. Foster
Michael S. Giaimo   Andrew H. Butler
Maura E. Murphy   Gayle E. Parlee
Mary L. Gallant   Elizabeth A. Gibbons
    Melissa Fang

For full biographical listings, see the Martindale-Hubbell Law Directory

Swartz & Swartz (AV)

10 Marshall Street, 02108
Telephone: 617-742-1900
Fax: 617-367-7193

Edward M. Swartz   Joan E. Swartz
Alan L. Cantor   James A. Swartz
Joseph A. Swartz   Harold David Levine
Victor A. Denaro   David P. Angueira

OF COUNSEL

Fredric A. Swartz

For full biographical listings, see the Martindale-Hubbell Law Directory

Warner & Stackpole LLP (AV)

75 State Street, 02109
Telephone: 617-951-9000
Telecopier: 617-951-9151
Email: w&s@warstack.com

(See Next Column)

MEMBERS OF FIRM

Deborah E. Barnard   Ralph T. Lepore, III
Paul C. Bauer   Janice Kelley Rowan
Judith G. Dein   James G. Ward
Joseph J. Leghorn   Peter T. Wechsler
Michael A. Leon   Robert A. Whitney

ASSOCIATES

James J. Arguin   Michael E. Scott
Fannie Iselin Minot   Karen R. Sweeney

For Complete List of Firm Personnel, See General Section

For full biographical listings, see the Martindale-Hubbell Law Directory

---

PITTSFIELD,* Berkshire Co.

Cain, Hibbard, Myers & Cook, A Professional Corporation (AV)

66 West Street, 01201
Telephone: 413-443-4771
Telecopier: 413-443-7694
Great Barrington, Massachusetts Office: 309 Main Street, 01230.
Telephone: 413-528-4771.
Fax: 413-528-5553.

F. Sydney Smithers, IV   Michael E. MacDonald
   Steven Taylor Smith

Representative Clients: Bank of Boston/First Agricultural Bank; Great Barrington Savings Bank; Greylock Credit Union; The Berkshire Gas Company; Berkshire Health Systems, Inc.; Berkshire Physicians & Surgeons, P.C.
Local Counsel for: General Electric Co.; Boston Symphony Orchestra; Statewide Funding Corporation.

For full biographical listings, see the Martindale-Hubbell Law Directory

---

SPRINGFIELD,* Hampden Co.

Annino, Draper & Moore, P.C. (AV)

Suite 1818 BayBank Tower, 1500 Main Street, P.O. Box 15428, 01115
Telephone: 413-732-6400
Fax: 413-732-3339
Westfield, Massachusetts Office: 52 Court Street.
Telephone: 413-562-9829.

Calvin W. Annino, Jr.   Louis S. Moore
Mark E. Draper   Michael R. Siddall

For full biographical listings, see the Martindale-Hubbell Law Directory

Robinson Donovan Madden & Barry, P.C. (AV)

Suite 1600, BayBank Tower, 1500 Main Street, 01115
Telephone: 413-732-2301
Fax: 413-785-4658

Homans Robinson (1894-1973) Milton J. Donovan (1906-1995)
Lawrence M. Sinclair
 (1942-1986)

OF COUNSEL

John H. Madden, Jr.   Victor Rosenberg
Edward J. Barry   Richard S. Milstein

Gordon H. Wentworth   John C. Sikorski
James H. Tourtelotte   Nancy Frankel Pelletier
Charles K. Bergin, Jr.   Paul S. Weinberg
Ronald C. Kidd   Frederica H. McCarthy
Jeffrey W. Roberts   Matthew J. King
Jeffrey L. McCormick   Neva Kaufman Rohan
James F. Martin   Douglas F. Boyd
Robert P. Cunningham   James K. Bodurtha
   Keith A. Minoff

E. Paul Amata   Kimberly Davis Crear
 (Not admitted in MA)   John W. Davis
James D. Chadwell   Edmund J. Gorman
Susan L. Cooper   Patricia M. Rapinchuk
   Jonathan P. Rice

Representative Clients: The First National Bank of Boston; United Cooperative Bank; Fleet Bank, N.A.; American Policyholders Insurance Co.; CNA; Commercial Union Insurance Co.; Hanover Insurance Group.

For full biographical listings, see the Martindale-Hubbell Law Directory

MICHIGAN

ANN ARBOR, Washtenaw Co.

BRAUN KENDRICK FINKBEINER PLC (AV)

700 First National Building, 48104
Telephone: 313-995-4100
Telecopier: 313-995-4798
URL: http://www.bkf-law.com
Bay City, Michigan Office: 201 Phoenix Building, P.O. Box 2039.
Telephone: 517-895-8505.
Telecopier: 517-895-8437.
Saginaw, Michigan Office: 101 N. Washington, Suite 812.
Telephone: 517-753-3461.
Telecopier: 517-753-3951.

Barry M. Levine

Representative Clients: The Dow Chemical Co.; General Motors Corp.; Lobdell Emery Manufacturing Co.; Merrill, Lynch, Inc.; Saginaw General Hospital; Saginaw News; The Wickes Foundation.

For full biographical listings, see the Martindale-Hubbell Law Directory

HOOPER, HATHAWAY, PRICE, BEUCHE & WALLACE (AV)

126 South Main Street, 48104
Telephone: 313-662-4426
Fax: 313-662-9559

Bruce T. Wallace   William J. Stapleton

Representative Clients: Chem-Trend, Inc.; Dundee Cement Co.; Ervin Industries, Inc.; First Martin Corp.; Group 243 Design, Inc.; Honeywell; Microwave Sensors, Inc.; Shearson Lehman Hutton; O'Neal Construction Co.; Pittsfield Products, Inc.

For Complete List of Firm Personnel, See General Section

For full biographical listings, see the Martindale-Hubbell Law Directory

MILLER, CANFIELD, PADDOCK AND STONE, P.L.C. (AV)

A Professional Limited Liability Company
Founded in 1852 by Sidney Davy Miller
101 North Main Street, Seventh Floor, 48104-1400
Telephone: 313-663-2445
Fax: 313-747-7147
Detroit, Michigan Office: 150 West Jefferson, Suite 2500, 48226-4415.
Telephone: 313-963-6420.
Fax: 313-496-7500.
Cable Address: "Stem Detroit."
Bloomfield Hills, Michigan Office: Suite 100, Pinehurst Office Center, 1400 North Woodward, 48303-2014.
Telephone: 313-645-5000.
Fax: 313-645-1917.
Grand Rapids, Michigan Office: 1200 Campau Square Plaza, 99 Monroe, N.W., 49503-2639.
Telephone: 616-454-8656.
Fax: 616-776-6322.
Howell, Michigan Office: 121 South Barnard Street, Suite 4, 48843-2305.
Telephone: 517-546-7600.
Telecopier: 517-546-6974.
Kalamazoo, Michigan Office: 444 West Michigan Avenue, 49007-3752.
Telephone: 616-381-7030.
Fax: 616-382-0244.
Lansing, Michigan Office: One Michigan Avenue, Suite 900, 48933-1609.
Telephone: 517-487-2070.
Fax: 517-374-6304.
Monroe, Michigan Office: The Executive Centre, 214 East Elm Avenue, 48161-2682.
Telephone: 313-243-2000.
Fax: 313-243-0901.
Washington, D.C. Office: 1225 Nineteenth Street, N.W., Suite 400. 20036.
Telephone: 202-429-5575; 785-0600.
Fax: 202-331-1118; 785-1234.
Pensacola, Florida Office: 25 West Cedar, 32501.
Telephone: 904-469-1088.
Fax: 904-432-0677.
St. Petersburg, Florida Office: 100 Second Avenue S., Suite 7045, 33701.
Telephone: 813-982-6000.
Fax: 813-892-6002.
New York, New York Office: Eleventh Floor, 135 East 57th Street, 10022-2087.
Telephone: 212-754-5400.
Fax: 212-754-5401.
Gdansk, Poland Office: Suite 322, Dom Technika Building, UI. Rajska 6, 80-850.
Telephone: 011-485-831-2808.
Fax: 011-485-831-4719.
Warsaw, Poland Office: UI. Marszalkowska 82, Suite 561, 00-517.
Telephone: 011-482-623-6457 and 6458.
Fax: 011-482-623-6459.

(See Next Column)

RESIDENT PRINCIPALS
Robert E. Gilbert

Representative Firm Clients: Chrysler Corporation; Comerica, Incorporated; City of Detroit, Michigan; Detroit Tigers, Inc.; First of Michigan; Ford Motor Company; Ford Motor Credit Company; Great Lakes Bancorp; Henry Ford Hospital; INVETECH Company.

For Complete List of Firm Personnel, See General Section

For full biographical listings, see the Martindale-Hubbell Law Directory

BAY CITY, Bay Co.

BRAUN KENDRICK FINKBEINER PLC (AV)

201 Phoenix Building, P.O. Box 2039, 48708
Telephone: 517-895-8505
Telecopier: 517-895-8437
URL: http://www.bkf-law.com
Saginaw, Michigan Office: 101 N. Washington, Suite 812. 8th Floor Second National Bank Building.
Telephone: 517-753-3461.
Telecopier: 517-753-3951.
Ann Arbor, Michigan Office: 700 First National Building.
Telephone: 313-995-4100.
Telecopier: 313-995-4798.

Ralph J. Isackson   Gregory E. Meter
George F. Gronewold, Jr.   Daniel S. Opperman
Frank M. Quinn   Gregory T. Demers

OF COUNSEL
Patrick D. Neering

Representative Clients: APV Chemical Machinery, Inc.; Bay Health Systems; Catholic Federal Credit Union; City of Saginaw; City of Vassar; City of Milwaukee; Corporate Service; Cox Cable.

For Complete List of Firm Personnel, See General Section

For full biographical listings, see the Martindale-Hubbell Law Directory

BIRMINGHAM, Oakland Co.

CARSON FISCHER, P.L.C. (AV)

Third Floor, 300 East Maple Road, 48009-6317
Telephone: 810-644-4840
Facsimile: 810-644-1832

Peter L. Wanger   Todd M. Fink

For full biographical listings, see the Martindale-Hubbell Law Directory

MACDONALD AND GOREN, P.C. (AV)

Suite 200, 260 East Brown Street, 48009
Telephone: 810-645-5940
Fax: 810-645-2490

Harold C. MacDonald   Kalman G. Goren
                Cindy Rhodes Victor

Amy L. Glenn   Lawrence C. Atorthy
David D. Marsh   Miriam Blanks-Smart
Glenn G. Ross   John T. Klees
                Rose Marie Karadsheh
OF COUNSEL
Robert L. Biederman

Representative Clients: Beaudin, Gallanis; Beaudin, Incorporated; Orlandi Gear Co., Inc.; Bing Steel, Inc.; Superb Manufacturing, Inc.; Spring Engineering, Inc.; Adrian Steel Co.; Southfield Radiology Associates, P.C.; HDS Services, Inc.; TGI Friday's Inc.; Quality Gold of Cincinnati, Inc.

For full biographical listings, see the Martindale-Hubbell Law Directory

WILLIAMS, SCHAEFER, RUBY & WILLIAMS, PROFESSIONAL CORPORATION (AV)

Suite 300, 380 North Woodward Avenue, 48009
Telephone: 810-642-0333
Telecopy: 810-642-0856

James A. Williams   Thomas G. Plunkett
                Richard D. Rattner
OF COUNSEL
Robert A. Jacobs

Representative Clients: Beachum & Roeser Development Corporation; Clare County; Deerfield Township; Groveland Township; Huron Township; KinderCare Learning Centers; Lapeer County; Mundy Township; Sanilac County; Western Development Company.

For full biographical listings, see the Martindale-Hubbell Law Directory

BLOOMFIELD HILLS, Oakland Co.

DAWDA, MANN, MULCAHY & SADLER, P.L.C. (AV)

1533 North Woodward Avenue Suite 200, 48304
Telephone: 810-642-3700
Fax: 810-642-7791
Email: EMail@DMMS.Com

Susan J. Sadler	John Mucha, III
Tyler D. Tennent	William L. Rosin
Sherwin E. Zamler	Amy Bateson

Joseph K. Hart, Jr.

Representative Clients: BASF Corporation; Cardell Corporation; Cargill, Inc.; City Management; Home Depot U.S.A., Inc.; Ladbroke Racing Corporation; Lockheed Martin, Corp.; The Sherwin-Williams Company; Trammell Crow Company; Wal-Mart Stores, Inc.

For full biographical listings, see the Martindale-Hubbell Law Directory

HOWARD & HOWARD ATTORNEYS, P.C. (AV)

The Pinehurst Office Center, Suite 101, 1400 North Woodward
Avenue, 48304-2856
Telephone: 810-645-1483
Telecopier: 810-645-1568
Kalamazoo, Michigan Office: The Kalamazoo Building, Suite 400, 107
West Michigan Avenue.
Telephone: 616-382-1483.
Telecopier: 616-382-1568.
Lansing, Michigan Office: The Phoenix Building, Suite 500, 222
Washington Square, North.
Telephone: 517-485-1483.
Telecopier: 517-485-1568.
Peoria, Illinois Office: The Creve Coeur Building, Suite 200, 321 Liberty
Street.
Telephone: 309-672-1483.
Telecopier: 309-672-1568.
Tampa, Florida Office: First of America Plaza, Suite 2000, 201 East
Kennedy Boulevard.
Telephone: 813-229-1483.
Telecopier: 813-229-1568.

Antoinette Beuche	Susan E. Padley
Tammy L. Brown	Gary A. Peters
Chris T. Danikolas	Dorene M. Price
Charles E. Dunn	Brian J. Renaud
Steven C. Kohl	Laura A. Talt

Representative Clients: For Representative Client list, see General Practice, Bloomfield Hills, MI.

For Complete List of Firm Personnel, See General Section

For full biographical listings, see the Martindale-Hubbell Law Directory

DETROIT, * Wayne Co.

BODMAN, LONGLEY & DAHLING LLP (AV)

34th Floor 100 Renaissance Center, 48243
Telephone: 313-259-7777
Fax: 313-393-7579
Email: 2080194@mcimail.com
Troy, Michigan Office: Suite 2020, 755 West Big Beaver Road.
Telephone: 810-362-2110.
Fax: 810-244-0780.
Ann Arbor, Michigan Office: 110 Miller, Suite 300.
Telephone: 313-761-3780.
Fax: 313-930-2494.
Northern Michigan Office: 229 Court Street, P.O. Box 405, Cheboygan.
Telephone: 616-627-4351.
Fax: 616-627-2802.

MEMBERS OF FIRM

James A. Smith	R. Craig Hupp
Fredrick J. Dindoffer	Henry N. Carnaby (Troy Office)
Michael A. Stack	
(Northern Michigan Office)	

For Representative Client List, See General Section

For Complete List of Firm Personnel, See General Section

For full biographical listings, see the Martindale-Hubbell Law Directory

BUTZEL LONG, A PROFESSIONAL CORPORATION (AV)

Suite 900, 150 West Jefferson, 48226
Telephone: 313-225-7000
Telecopier: 313-225-7080
Email: melnick@butzel.com *URL:* http://www.butzel.com
Birmingham, Michigan Office: Suite 200, 32270 Telegraph Road.
Telephone: 810-258-1616.
Telecopier: 810-258-1439.
Lansing, Michigan Office: 118 West Ottawa Street.
Telephone: 517-372-6622.
Telecopier: 517-372-6672.

(See Next Column)

Ann Arbor, Michigan Office: Suite 300, 350 South Main Street.
Telephone: 313-995-3110.
Telecopier: 313-995-1777.
Grosse Pointe Farms, Michigan Office: Suite 260, 21 Kercheval.
Telephone: 313-886-5446.
Telecopier: 313-886-2114.

John H. Dudley, Jr.	Leonard F. Charla
Jack D. Shumate (Birmingham)	James E. Wynne
Donald B. Miller	Michael J. Lavoie
Steven D. Weyhing (Lansing)	

Paul S. Lewandowski	Elizabeth A. DuMouchelle
James A. Gray, III	

Representative Clients: Associated General Contractors; The Dow Chemical Co.; General Dynamics Corp.; General Electric Co.; Indian Head Industries, Inc.; Kelsey Hayes Co.; McKesson Corp.; McLouth Steel.

For Complete List of Firm Personnel, See General Section

For full biographical listings, see the Martindale-Hubbell Law Directory

CLARK HILL P.L.C. (AV)

500 Woodward Avenue, Suite 3500, 48226
Telephone: 313-965-8300
Facsimile: 313-962-4348
Oakland County, Michigan Office: Third Floor, 255 South Woodward
Avenue, Birmingham.
Telephone: 810-642-9692.
Facsimile: 810-642-2174.
Lansing, Michigan Office: Suite 600, 200 North Capitol Avenue.
Telephone: 517-484-4481.
Facsimile: 517-484-1246.
Minneapolis, Minnesota Office: Suite 1000, One Financial Plaza, 120 South
Sixth Street.
Telephone: 612-332-0102.
Facsimile: 612-332-3225.
Kansas City, Missouri Office: Suite 1400, Bryant Building, 1102 Grand
Avenue.
Telephone: 816-221-5578.
Facsimile: 816-221-0303.

Richard C. Marsh	Thomas M. Dixon

Donald F. Berschback, II

Representative Clients: The Budd Company.

For Complete List of Firm Personnel, See General Section

For full biographical listings, see the Martindale-Hubbell Law Directory

DICKINSON, WRIGHT, MOON, VAN DUSEN & FREEMAN (AV)

500 Woodward Avenue, Suite 4000, 48226-3425
Telephone: 313-223-3500
Facsimile: 313-223-3598
Bloomfield Hills, Michigan Office: 525 North Woodward Avenue, Suite
2000.
Telephone: 810-433-7200.
Facsimile: 810-433-7274.
Grand Rapids, Michigan Office: 200 Ottawa Avenue, N.W., Suite 900.
Telephone: 616-458-1300.
Facsimile: 616-458-6753.
Lansing, Michigan Office: Suite 200, 215 South Washington Square.
Telephone: 517-371-1730.
Facsimile: 517-487-4700.
Washington, D.C. Office: Suite 800, 1901 L Street, N.W.
Telephone: 202-457-0160.
Facsimile: 202-659-1559.
Chicago, Illinois Office: 225 West Washington, Suite 400.
Telephone: 312-220-0300.
Facsimile: 312-220-0021.

MEMBERS OF FIRM

David R. Bruegel	Sharon R. Newlon
(Bloomfield Hills Office)	James Gavan O'Connor
Margaret A. Coughlin	(Grand Rapids Office)
(Bloomfield Hills Office)	Dustin P. Ordway
Keith J. Lerminiaux	(Grand Rapids Office)
Linda S. McAlpine	Claudia Rast
(Bloomfield Hills Office)	Herbert G. Sparrow, III
Steven C. Nadeau	John L. Teeples
	(Grand Rapids Office)

ASSOCIATES

Julia L. Ernst	Elizabeth Virginia Main
Jana L. Henkel-Benjamin	John T. Panourgias
Kyle M. H. Jones	(Bloomfield Hills Office)
Barbara R. Lentz	Gregory J. Parry
	(Bloomfield Hills Office)

For Representative Client list, see General Section.

For Complete List of Firm Personnel, See General Section

For full biographical listings, see the Martindale-Hubbell Law Directory

Detroit—Continued

DYKEMA GOSSETT PLLC (AV)

400 Renaissance Center, 48243-1668
Telephone: 313-568-6800
Cable Address: "Dyke-Detroit"
Telex: 23-0121
Fax: 313-568-6594
Email: 2084153@mcimail.com
Ann Arbor, Michigan Office: 315 East Eisenhower Parkway, Suite 100, 48108-3306.
Telephone: 313-747-7660.
Fax: 313-747-7696.
Bloomfield Hills, Michigan Office: 1577 North Woodward Avenue, Suite 300, 48304-2820.
Telephone: 810-540-0700.
Fax: 810-540-0763.
Chicago, Illinois Office: 55 East Monroe Street, Suite 3250, 60603-5709.
Telephone: 312-551-4900.
Fax: 312-551-4919.
Grand Rapids, Michigan Office: 200 Oldtown Riverfront Building, 248 Louis Campau Promenade, N.W., 49503-2668.
Telephone: 616-776-7500.
Fax: 616-776-7573.
Lansing, Michigan Office: 800 Michigan National Tower, 48933-1707.
Telephone: 517-374-9100.
Fax: 517-374-9191.
Washington, D.C. Office: Franklin Square, Suite 300 West, 1300 I Street, N.W., 20005-3306.
Telephone: 202-522-8600.
Fax: 202-522-8669.

MEMBERS OF FIRM

Joseph C. Basta
James W. Collier
John A. Ferroli (Resident at Grand Rapids Office)

Mark D. Jacobs
Jerome I. Maynard (Member in Charge of Chicago, Illinois Office)

David L. Tripp

ASSOCIATES

Scott D. Broekstra (Resident at Grand Rapids Office)
Grant P. Gilezan
Steven J. Rollins (Not admitted in MI; Resident at Chicago, Illinois Office)

William R. Schikora
Nicholas G. Zotos

For Complete List of Firm Personnel, See General Section

For full biographical listings, see the Martindale-Hubbell Law Directory

HONIGMAN MILLER SCHWARTZ AND COHN (AV)

A Partnership including Professional Corporations
2290 First National Building, 48226
Telephone: 313-256-7800
Telecopier: 313-962-0176
Telex: 235705
URL: http://law.honigman.com
Lansing, Michigan Office: Phoenix Building, 222 North Washington Square, Suite 400, 48933-1800.
Telephone: 517-484-8282.
West Palm Beach, Florida Office: Suite 800 Esperante Building, 222 Lakeview Avenue, 33401-6112.
Telephone: 561-838-4500.
Tampa, Florida Office: 2700 SunTrust Financial Centre, 401 E. Jackson Street, 33602-5226.
Telephone: 813-221-6600.

MEMBERS OF FIRM

Christopher J. Dunsky
Kenneth C. Gold
Philip A. Grashoff, Jr.
Robert A. Hykan
Norman Hyman
Brian J. Negele
John D. Pirich
(Lansing, Michigan Office)

Joseph M. Polito
Paul Revere, III
Gary A. Trepod
(Lansing, Michigan Office)
Grant R. Trigger
William A. Wichers II
Jeffrey L. Woolstrum
Ruth E. Zimmerman
(Lansing, Michigan Office)

ASSOCIATES

S. Lee Johnson

Walter J. Kramarz

RESIDENT IN WEST PALM BEACH, FLORIDA OFFICE

MEMBER

E. Lee Worsham (P.A.)

RESIDENT IN TAMPA, FLORIDA OFFICE

MEMBERS

Michael G. Cooke (P.A.)

John W. Voelpel

Representative Clients: Auto Alliance International Inc. (formerly Mazda Motor Manufacturing (USA) Corporation); Consumers Power Company; The Detroit Edison Company; Ford Motor Company; General Motors Corporation; Edw. C. Levy Co.; Masco Corporation and its affiliates; McLouth Steel Products Corporation; Morton International, Inc.

(See Next Column)

For Complete List of Firm Personnel, See General Section

For full biographical listings, see the Martindale-Hubbell Law Directory

JAFFE, RAITT, HEUER & WEISS, PROFESSIONAL CORPORATION (AV)

One Woodward Avenue, Suite 2400, 48226
Telephone: 313-961-8380
Telecopier: 313-961-8358
Cable Address: "Jafsni"
Southfield, Michigan Office: Travelers Tower, Suite 1520.
Telephone: 313-961-8380.
Monroe, Michigan Office: 214 East Elm Avenue, Suite 208,
Telephone: 313-241-6470.
Telefacsimile: 313-241-3849.

Jeffrey G. Heuer
Arthur H. Siegal

Eric A. Linden

For Complete List of Firm Personnel, See General Section

For full biographical listings, see the Martindale-Hubbell Law Directory

LEWIS, CLAY & MUNDAY, A PROFESSIONAL CORPORATION (AV)

(Formerly Lewis, White & Clay, P.C.)
1300 First National Building, 660 Woodward Avenue, 48226-3531
Telephone: 313-961-2550
Troy, Michigan Office: Liberty Center, Suite 200. 100 West Big Beaver Road. 48084.
Telephone: 810-680-6702.
Fax: 810-680-6703.
Washington, D.C. Office: 1000 16th Street, N.W., Suite 401. 20036.
Telephone: 202-835-0616.
Fax: 202-833-3316.
Boston, Massachusetts Office: 10 Post Office Square.
Telephone: 617-422-8646.
Fax: 617-338-5693.

David Baker Lewis
Eric Lee Clay
Reuben A. Munday
Ulysses Whittaker Boykin
Carl F. Stafford
Helen Francine Strong

Frank E. Barbee
Camille Stearns Miller
Michael T. Raymond
Jacqueline H. Sellers
David N. Zacks
Thomas J. Guyer

Blair A. Person

Karen Kendrick Brown
(Resident, Washington, D.C. Office)
J. Taylor Teasdale
Wade Harper McCree
Tyrone A. Powell
Susan D. Hoffman
John J. Walsh
Andrea L. Powell
Althea Lynn Foster

Hans J. Massaquoi, Jr.
Nancy C. Borland
Tammy L. Terry
Lynn Westfall Gross
Suzanne P. Pope
Matthew R. Halpin
Donica Thomas Varner
Damon L. White
(Not admitted in MI)
Kathleen L. Royal

COUNSEL

Otis M. Smith (1922-1994)
Herbert O. Reid, Sr. (1915-1991)

G. Allen Bass (Resident, Boston, Massachusetts Office)

Representative Clients: Omnicare Health Plan; Aetna Life & Casualty Co.; Chrysler Motors Corp.; Chrysler Financial Corp.; MCI Communications Corp.; City of Detroit; City of Detroit Building Authority; City of Detroit Downtown Development Authority; Consolidated Rail Corp. (Conrail); Equitable Life Assurance Society of the United States.

For full biographical listings, see the Martindale-Hubbell Law Directory

MILLER, CANFIELD, PADDOCK AND STONE, P.L.C. (AV)

A Professional Limited Liability Company
Founded in 1852 by Sidney Davy Miller
150 West Jefferson, Suite 2500, 48226-4415
Telephone: 313-963-6420
Fax: 313-496-7500
Cable Address: "Stem Detroit"
Detroit, Michigan Office: 150 West Jefferson, Suite 2500, 48226-4415.
Telephone: 313-963-6420.
Fax: 313-496-7500.
Cable Address: "Stem Detroit."
Ann Arbor, Michigan Office: 101 North Main Street, 7th Floor, 48104-1400.
Telephone: 313-663-2445.
Fax: 313-747-7147.
Bloomfield Hills, Michigan Office: Suite 100, Pinehurst Office Center, 1400 North Woodward, 48303-2014.
Telephone: 313-645-5000.
Fax: 313-645-1917.
Grand Rapids, Michigan Office: 1200 Campau Square Plaza, 99 Monroe, N.W., 49503-2639.
Telephone: 616-454-8656.
Fax: 616-776-6322.

(See Next Column)

MILLER, CANFIELD, PADDOCK AND STONE P.L.C.—*Continued*

Howell, Michigan Office: 121 South Barnard Street, Suite 4, 48843-2305.
Telephone: 517-546-7600.
Telecopier: 517-546-6974.
Kalamazoo, Michigan Office: 444 West Michigan Avenue, 49007-3752.
Telephone: 616-381-7030.
Fax: 616-382-0244.
Lansing, Michigan Office: One Michigan Avenue, Suite 900, 48933-1609.
Telephone: 517-487-2070.
Fax: 517-374-6304.
Monroe, Michigan Office: The Executive Centre, 214 East Elm Avenue, 48161-2682.
Telephone: 313-243-2000.
Fax: 313-243-0901.
Washington, D.C. Office: 1225 Nineteenth Street, N.W., Suite 400. 20036.
Telephone: 202-429-5575; 785-0600.
Fax: 202-331-1118; 785-1234.
Pensacola, Florida Office: 25 West Cedar, 32501.
Telephone: 904-469-1088.
Fax: 904-432-0677.
St. Petersburg, Florida Office: 100 Second Avenue S., Suite 7045, 33701.
Telephone: 813-982-6000.
Fax: 813-892-6002.
New York, New York Office: Eleventh Floor, 135 East 57th Street, 10022-2087.
Telephone: 212-754-5400.
Fax: 212-754-5401.
Gdansk, Poland Office: Suite 322, Dom Technika Building, UI. Rajska 6, 80-850.
Telephone: 011-485-831-2808.
Fax: 011-485-831-4719.
Warsaw, Poland Office: UI. Marszalkowska 82, Suite 561, 00-517.
Telephone: 011-482-623-6457 and 6458.
Fax: 011-482-623-6459.

PRINCIPALS OF FIRM

Allyn D. Kantor
(Ann Arbor Office)
Frank L. Andrews (Detroit and
Bloomfield Hills Offices)
Thomas C. Phillips
(Lansing Office)

Ronald E. Baylor
(Kalamazoo Office)
Douglas W. Crim
(Grand Rapids Office)
Ronald E. Hodess
(Bloomfield Hills Office)

OF COUNSEL

Steven E. Chester (Resident, Lansing Office)

ASSOCIATES

James R. Lancaster, Jr.
(Lansing Office)

Anna M. Maiuri
(Bloomfield Hills Office)

Representative Firm Clients: Chrysler Corporation; Comerica, Incorporated; City of Detroit, Michigan; Detroit Tigers, Inc.; First of Michigan; Ford Motor Company; Ford Motor Credit Company; Great Lakes Bancorp; Henry Ford Hospital; INVETECH Company.

For Complete List of Firm Personnel, See General Section

For full biographical listings, see the Martindale-Hubbell Law Directory

---

TIMMIS & INMAN, L.L.P. (AV)

300 Talon Centre, 48207
Telephone: 313-396-4200
Telecopier: 313-396-4228

Robert E. Graziani
Mark W. Peyser

Richard M. Miettinen
Bradley J. Knickerbocker

OF COUNSEL

Wayne C. Inman

Representative Clients: CNA Insurance Companies; Continental Insurance; Transamerica Insurance.

For Complete List of Firm Personnel, See General Section

For full biographical listings, see the Martindale-Hubbell Law Directory

---

VANDEVEER GARZIA, PROFESSIONAL CORPORATION (AV)

Suite 1600, 333 West Fort Street, 48226
Telephone: 313-961-4880
Fax: 313-961-3822
Oakland County Office: 220 Park Street, Suite 300, Birmingham, Michigan.
Telephone: 810-645-0100.
Fax: 810-645-2430.
Macomb County Office: 50 Crocker Boulevard, Mount Clemens, Michigan.
Telephone: 810-468-4880.
Fax: 810-465-7159.
West Michigan Office: 1121 Ottawa Beach Road, Suite 140, Holland Michigan.
Telephone: 616-399-8600.
Fax: 616-786-9095.

(See Next Column)

James A. Sullivan
John J. Lynch, III (Resident,
Oakland County Office)

James K. Thorne

Representative Clients: Aetna Casualty and Surety Co.; Bic Corp.; CNA Insurance Group; Travelers Insurance Co.; United States Aviation Underwriters; Goodyear Tire & Rubber Co.

For Complete List of Firm Personnel, See General Section

For full biographical listings, see the Martindale-Hubbell Law Directory

---

EAST LANSING, Ingham Co.

FARHAT, STORY & KRAUS, P.C. (AV)

Beacon Place, 4572 South Hagadorn Road, Suite 3, 48823
Telephone: 517-351-3700
Fax: 517-332-4122
Email: rkraus@sojourn.com

Leo A. Farhat
James E. Burns (1925-1979)
Monte R. Story
Richard C. Kraus
Max R. Hoffman Jr.

Chris A. Bergstrom
Kitty L. Groh
Charles R. Toy
David M. Platt
Thomas L. Sparks

Lawrence P. Schweitzer
Debra A. Geroux

Daniel B. Morgan
Mary K. Robbins-Kralapp

Representative Clients: Big L. Corp.; Michigan Automotive Wholesalers Association; Hartman-Fabco, Inc.; Lansing Electric Motors, Inc.; Mike Miller Lincoln Mercury; Michigan Coalition of Radioactive Material Users, Inc.; Environmental Quality Co.; Michigan Aquatic Managers Association.
Reference: City Bank, St. Johns.

For full biographical listings, see the Martindale-Hubbell Law Directory

---

FARMINGTON HILLS, Oakland Co.

FINK ZAUSMER, P.C. (AV)

31700 Middlebelt Road, Suite 150, 48334
Telephone: 810-851-4111
Telefax: 810-851-0100
Detroit, Michigan Office: 1917 Penobscot Building.
Telephone: 313-963-3873.
Telefax: 313-961-6879.
Lansing, Michigan Office: One Michigan Avenue, Suite 1050.
Telephone: 517-372-2020.
Telefax: 517-371-3207.

David H. Fink

Avery K. Williams

Michael L. Caldwell

OF COUNSEL

Alan D. Wasserman

For full biographical listings, see the Martindale-Hubbell Law Directory

---

*FLINT,** Genesee Co.

GAULT DAVISON A PROFESSIONAL SERVICE CORPORATION (AV)

Tenth Floor, Northbank Center, 432 North Saginaw Street, 48502-2032
Telephone: 810-234-3633
Fax: 810-233-3387
Email: GLTDAV@tir.com

Frederick L. Schmoll, III

Kevin A. Lavalle

Representative Clients: Al Serra Automobile Cos.; Shoney's, Inc.; City of Flint; Vic Canever Chevrolet Co.; Oil Chem, Inc.; Richfield Iron Works, Inc.; Wakeland Oil Co.

For full biographical listings, see the Martindale-Hubbell Law Directory

---

*GRAND RAPIDS,** Kent Co.

BORRE, PETERSON, FOWLER & REENS, P.C. (AV)

The Philo C. Fuller House, 44 Lafayette, N.E., P.O. Box 1767, 49501-1767
Telephone: 616-459-1971
Fax: 616-459-2393

Mark D. Sevald

References: NBD Bank; FMB-First Michigan Bank - Grand Rapids.

For Complete List of Firm Personnel, See General Section

For full biographical listings, see the Martindale-Hubbell Law Directory

Grand Rapids—Continued

Bos & Glazier, P.L.C. (AV)

300 Ottawa N.W., Suite 800, 49503
Telephone: 616-458-6814
Fax: 616-458-0608
Email: BGLAZIOO@counsel.com

Carole D. Bos	Susan Wilson Keener
Bradley K. Glazier	Gwen E. Buday
	Anne M. Frye

For full biographical listings, see the Martindale-Hubbell Law Directory

Day & Sawdey, A Professional Corporation (AV)

200 Monroe Avenue, Suite 500, 49503-2217
Telephone: 616-774-8121
Telefax: 616-774-0168

George B. Kingston (1889-1965)	James B. Frakie
John R. Porter (1915-1975)	Larry A. Ver Merris
Charles E. Day, Jr.	John Boyko, Jr.
Robert W. Sawdey	Jonathan F. Thoits
C. Mark Stoppels	John T. Piggins
	Thomas A. DeMeester

For full biographical listings, see the Martindale-Hubbell Law Directory

Gruel, Mills, Nims and Pylman (AV)

50 Monroe Place, Suite 700 West, 49503
Telephone: 616-235-5500
Fax: 616-235-5550

MEMBERS OF FIRM

Grant J. Gruel	Scott R. Melton
William F. Mills	Brion J. Brooks
J. Clarke Nims	Thomas R. Behm
Norman H. Pylman, II	J. Paul Janes

Representative Clients: Aquinas College; Bell Helmet Co.; Blodgett Memorial Medical Center; Butterworth Hospital; Chem Central, Inc.; Cook Pump Co.; Grove, Inc.; NBDC; Heim Corp.

For full biographical listings, see the Martindale-Hubbell Law Directory

Roberts, Betz & Bloss, P.C. (AV)

555 Riverfront Plaza Building, 55 Campau, 49503
Telephone: 616-235-9955
Telecopier: 616-235-0404

Michael W. Betz	Michael T. Small
David J. Bloss	Ralph M. Reisinger

For full biographical listings, see the Martindale-Hubbell Law Directory

Peter W. Steketee (AV)

660 Cascade West Parkway, S.E., Suite 65, 49546
Telephone: 616-949-6551
Fax: 616-949-8817

For full biographical listings, see the Martindale-Hubbell Law Directory

Varnum, Riddering, Schmidt & Howlett LLP (AV)

A Limited Liability Partnership including Professional Corporations
Bridgewater Place, P.O. Box 352, 49501-0352
Telephone: 616-336-6000
800-262-0011
Facsimile: 616-336-7000
Telex: 1561593 VARN
Email: varnum@vrsh.com
Lansing, Michigan Office: The Victor Center, Suite 810, 210 North Washington Square, 48933.
Telephone: 517-482-6237.
Facsimile: 517-482-6937.
Kalamazoo, Michigan Office: 350 East Michigan Avenue, 49007.
Telephone: 616-382-2300.
Facsimile: 616-382-2382.
Grand Haven, Michigan Office: 321 Washington Street, P.O. Box 288, 49417.
Telephone: 616-846-7100.
Facsimile: 616-846-7101.
Battle Creek, Michigan Office: 4950 West Dickman Road, Suite B-1, 49015.
Telephone: 616-962-7144.
Bingham Farms, Michigan Office: 31600 Telegraph Road, Suite 230, 48025.
Telephone: 810-594-7330.
Facsimile: 810-594-7331.

(See Next Column)

MEMBERS OF FIRM

Jon F. DeWitt	Matthew D. Zimmerman
Peter A. Smit	Charles M. Denton II
Mark C. Hanisch	Mark S. Allard
Bruce Goodman	George B. Davis
Teresa S. Decker	David E. Preston
Richard W. Butler, Jr.	Michael F. Kelly

ASSOCIATES

Andrew J. Kok	Mark M. Davis
Michael X. Hidalgo	Linda L. Bunge
Alfred L. Schubkegel, Jr.	
(Resident at Kalamazoo Office)	

Counsel for: CMI International; Donnelly Corporation; FKI Industries; Great Lakes Casting Corporation; HM Holdings, Inc.; Harrow Industries; Kent County; Outboard Marine Corporation; Safety-Kleen; Sparton Corporation.

For Complete List of Firm Personnel, See General Section

For full biographical listings, see the Martindale-Hubbell Law Directory

Warner Norcross & Judd LLP (AV)

900 Old Kent Building, 111 Lyon Street, N.W., 49503-2489
Telephone: 616-752-2000
Fax: 616-752-2500
Muskegon, Michigan Office: 400 Terrace Plaza, P.O. Box 900.
Telephone: 616-727-2600.
Fax: 616-727-2699.
Holland, Michigan Office: Curtis Center, Suite 300, 170 College Avenue.
Telephone: 616-396-9800.
Fax: 616-396-3656.

MEMBERS OF FIRM

John D. Tully	Paul T. Sorensen
Peter L. Gustafson	John D. Dunn
Michael L. Robinson	John V. Byl
Eugene E. Smary	Tracy T. Larsen

For Complete List of Firm Personnel, See General Section

For full biographical listings, see the Martindale-Hubbell Law Directory

Wheeler Upham, A Professional Corporation (AV)

Second Floor, Trust Building, 40 Pearl Street, N.W., 49503-3001
Telephone: 616-459-7100
Fax: 616-459-6366

Gordon B. Wheeler (1904-1986)	William H. Heritage, Jr.
Buford A. Upham (Retired)	Kenneth E. Tiews
Robert H. Gillette	Jack L. Hoffman
Geoffrey L. Gillis	Janet C. Baxter
John M. Roels	Peter Kladder, III
Gary A. Maximiuk	James M. Shade
Timothy J. Orlebeke	Thomas A. Kuiper

Counsel For: Prudential Ins. Co.; Metropolitan Life Ins. Co.; Travelers Ins. Co.; John Hancock Mutual Life Insurance Co.; Farmers Ins. Group; Auto-Owners Ins. Co.; Farm Bureau Ins. Co.; Countrywide Services; Global Claims Services; American Premier Underwriters, Inc.

For full biographical listings, see the Martindale-Hubbell Law Directory

HOLLAND, Ottawa Co.

Cunningham Dalman, P.C. (AV)

321 Settlers Road, P.O. Box 1767, 49422-1767
Telephone: 616-392-1821
Fax: 616-392-4769

Gordon H. Cunningham	Kenneth B. Breese
Ronald L. Dalman	Jeffrey K. Helder
Max R. Murphy	Ronald J. Vander Veen
James A. Bidol	David M. Zessin
Andrew J. Mulder	Mark H. Zietlow
Joel G. Bouwens	James W. Bouwens
	Randall S. Schipper

Susan E. Vroegop	Melinda M. Abney

OF COUNSEL

Vernon D. Ten Cate	Kenneth B. Peirce, Jr.

Representative Clients: Waste Management of Michigan; FMB-First Michigan Bank; First of America Bank-Holland, N.A.; Ottawa Savings Bank; City of Holland; The Title Office; Donnelly Corp.

For full biographical listings, see the Martindale-Hubbell Law Directory

KALAMAZOO, Kalamazoo Co.

HOWARD & HOWARD ATTORNEYS, P.C. (AV)

The Kalamazoo Building, Suite 400, 107 West Michigan
  Avenue, 49007-3956
Telephone: 616-382-1483
Telecopier: 616-382-1568
Bloomfield Hills, Michigan Office: The Pinehurst Office Center, Suite 101,
1400 North Woodward Avenue.
Telephone: 810-645-1483
Telecopier: 810-645-1568.
Lansing, Michigan Office: The Phoenix Building, Suite 500, 222
Washington Square North.
Telephone: 517-485-1483
Telecopier: 517-485-1568.
Peoria, Illinois Office: The Creve Coeur Building, Suite 200, 321 Liberty
Street.
Telephone: 309-672-1483.
Telecopier: 309-672-1568.
Tampa, Florida Office: First of America Plaza, Suite 2000, 201 East
Kennedy Boulevard.
Telephone: 813-229-1483.
Telecopier: 813-229-1568.

John W. Allen	Michael L. Chojnowski
Robert C. Beck	James H. Geary
	Myra L. Willis

Representative Clients: For Representative Client list, see General Practice,
Kalamazoo, MI.

For Complete List of Firm Personnel, See General Section

For full biographical listings, see the Martindale-Hubbell Law Directory

KREIS, ENDERLE, CALLANDER & HUDGINS, A PROFESSIONAL CORPORATION (AV)

One Moorsbridge, P.O. Box 4010, 49003-4010
Telephone: 616-324-3000
Telecopier: 616-324-3010
Email: kech@sapien.net *URL:* http://www.kech.com

Alan G. Enderle	Jeffrey D. Swenarton

For Complete List of Firm Personnel, See General Section

For full biographical listings, see the Martindale-Hubbell Law Directory

MILLER, CANFIELD, PADDOCK AND STONE, P.L.C. (AV)

A Professional Limited Liability Company
Founded in 1852 by Sidney Davy Miller
444 West Michigan Avenue, 49007-3752
Telephone: 616-381-7030
Fax: 616-382-0244
Detroit, Michigan Office: 150 West Jefferson, Suite 2500, 48226-4415.
Telephone: 313-963-6420.
Fax: 313-496-7500.
Cable Address: "Stem Detroit."
Ann Arbor, Michigan Office: 101 North Main Street, 7th Floor,
48104-1400.
Telephone: 313-663-2445.
Fax: 313-747-7147.
Bloomfield Hills, Michigan Office: Suite 100, Pinehurst Office Center, 1400
North Woodward, 48303-2014.
Telephone: 313-645-5000.
Fax: 313-645-1917.
Grand Rapids, Michigan Office: 1200 Campau Square Plaza, 99 Monroe,
N.W., 49503-2639.
Telephone: 616-454-8656.
Fax: 616-776-6322.
Howell, Michigan Office: 121 South Barnard Street, Suite 4, 48843-2305.
Telephone: 517-546-7600.
Telecopier: 517-546-6974.
Lansing, Michigan Office: One Michigan Avenue, Suite 900, 48933-1609.
Telephone: 517-487-2070.
Fax: 517-374-6304.
Monroe, Michigan Office: The Executive Centre, 214 East Elm Avenue,
48161-2682.
Telephone: 313-243-2000.
Fax: 313-243-0901.
Washington, D.C. Office: 1225 Nineteenth Street, N.W., Suite 400. 20036.
Telephone: 202-429-5575; 785-0600.
Fax: 202-331-1118; 785-1234.
Pensacola, Florida Office: 25 West Cedar, 32501.
Telephone: 904-469-1088.
Fax: 904-432-0677.
St. Petersburg, Florida Office: 100 Second Avenue S., Suite 7045, 33701.
Telephone: 813-982-6000.
Fax: 813-892-6002.
New York, New York Office: Eleventh Floor, 135 East 57th Street,
10022-2087.
Telephone: 212-754-5400.
Fax: 212-754-5401.

(See Next Column)

Gdansk, Poland Office: Suite 322, Dom Technika Building, UI. Rajska 6,
80-850.
Telephone: 011-485-831-2808.
Fax: 011-485-831-4719.
Warsaw, Poland Office: UI. Marszalkowska 82, Suite 561, 00-517.
Telephone: 011-482-623-6457 and 6458.
Fax: 011-482-623-6459.

PRINCIPALS OF FIRM

Eric V. Brown, Jr.	John R. Cook
	Ronald E. Baylor

Representative Firm Clients: Chrysler Corporation; Comerica, Incorporated;
City of Detroit, Michigan; Detroit Tigers, Inc.; First of Michigan; Ford Mo-
tor Company; Ford Motor Credit Company; Great Lakes Bancorp; Henry
Ford Hospital; INVETECH Company.

For Complete List of Firm Personnel, See General Section

For full biographical listings, see the Martindale-Hubbell Law Directory

LANSING, Ingham Co.

✱ indicates certain Bar Register subscribers whose principal office is
located elsewhere in the state and who have arranged for representation
as a part of the state capital listings that follow

FOSTER, SWIFT, COLLINS & SMITH, P.C. (AV)

313 South Washington Square, 48933-2193
Telephone: 517-371-8100
Telecopier: 517-371-8200
URL: http://www.fosterswift.com
Farmington Hills, Michigan Office: 32300 Northwestern Highway, Suite
230.
Telephone: 810-539-9900.
Fax: 810-851-7504.

Webb A. Smith	James B. Jensen, Jr.
Stephen O. Schultz	James B. Croom
Charles E. Barbieri	Brent A. Titus
	Nancy L. Kahn

OF COUNSEL
Kenneth T. Brooks

General Counsel for: First American Bank-Central; Story, Inc.; Michigan
Milk Producers Assn.; Edward W. Sparrow Hospital; St. Lawrence Hospital;
Demmer Corp.; Michigan Financial Corp.
Local Counsel for: Shell Oil Co.; Michigan-Mutual Insurance Co.; Century
Telephone.

For Complete List of Firm Personnel, See General Section

For full biographical listings, see the Martindale-Hubbell Law Directory

FRASER TREBILCOCK DAVIS & FOSTER, P.C. (AV)

1000 Michigan National Tower, 48933
Telephone: 517-482-5800
Fax: 517-482-0887

Douglas J. Austin	Michael H. Perry
Stephen L. Burlingame	Thomas J. Waters

Charyn K. Hain
OF COUNSEL
Donald A. Hines

Counsel for: Texaco, Federated Insurance Co.; Snell Environmental Group;
Mason Family Enterprises; STRATA Environmental Services; RCO Engineering, Inc.; Livingston County.

For Complete List of Firm Personnel, See General Section

For full biographical listings, see the Martindale-Hubbell Law Directory

✱ HONIGMAN MILLER SCHWARTZ AND COHN (AV)

A Partnership including Professional Corporations
222 North Washington Square, Suite 400, 48933-1800
Telephone: 517-484-8282
Telecopier: 517-484-8286
URL: http://law.honigman.com
Detroit, Michigan Office: 2290 First National Building, 48226.
Telephone: 313-256-7800.
West Palm Beach, Florida Office: Suite 800 Esperante Building, 222
Lakeview Avenue, 33401-6112.
Telephone: 561-838-4500.
Tampa, Florida Office: 2700 SunTrust Financial Centre, 401 E. Jackson
Street, 33602-5226.
Telephone: 813-221-6600.

MEMBERS

Frederick M. Baker, Jr.	John D. Pirich
Mark Morton	Gary A. Trepod

General Counsel for: Dart Container Corp; Forbes-Cohen Properties (The
Lansing Mall); Granger Land Development Co.; Michigan Hospital Association.

(See Next Column)

HONIGMAN MILLER SCHWARTZ AND COHN, *Lansing—Continued*

Legal or Special Counsel for: Champion International; Greater Detroit Resource Recovery Authority; First American Title Insurance Company of the Midwest.

For Complete List of Firm Personnel, See General Section

For full biographical listings, see the Martindale-Hubbell Law Directory

MONROE,* Monroe Co.

BRAUNLICH, RUSSOW & BRAUNLICH, A PROFESSIONAL CORPORATION (AV)

111 South Macomb Street, 48161
Telephone: 313-241-8300
Fax: 313-241-7715

William J. Braunlich, Jr. (1924-1992)	Thomas P. Russow
	William H. Braunlich

Philip A. Costello	Marie C. Kennedy
Patricia M. Poupard	Susan J. Mehregan
Ann L. Nickel	Robert Wetzel
Michael G. Roehrig	

LEGAL SUPPORT PERSONNEL
Ruth G. Flint

Representative Clients: State Farm Mutual Insurance Co.; Auto Club Insurance Assn.; Farm Bureau Insurance Co.; Home Mutual Insurance Co.; Cincinnati Insurance Co.; Board of Road Commissioners, Monroe County; Port of Monroe; Monroe County Community College; City of Luna Pier; City of Petersburg.

For full biographical listings, see the Martindale-Hubbell Law Directory

MOUNT PLEASANT,* Isabella Co.

LYNCH, GALLAGHER, LYNCH & MARTINEAU, P.L.L.C. (AV)

555 North Main Street, P.O. Box 446, 48858
Telephone: 517-773-9961
Fax: 517-773-2107
Lansing, Michigan Office: 2400 Lake Lansing Road, Suite B.
Telephone: 517-485-0400.
Fax: 517-485-0402.

MEMBERS OF FIRM

Edward N. Lynch (1908-1984)	Paula K. Manis
Byron P. Gallagher	(Resident at Lansing Office)
John J. Lynch	Michael J. Hackett
Steven W. Martineau	Byron P. Gallagher, Jr.
Sue A. Jeffers	Nancy E. Gallagher
Jennifer M. Galloway	

OF COUNSEL
Richard J. Garcia

Representative Clients: Amoco Production, Co.; Liquid Transport, Inc.; Central Concrete Products; Central Michigan University; Northern Michigan Oil and Gas Corp.

For full biographical listings, see the Martindale-Hubbell Law Directory

PONTIAC,* Oakland Co.

BOOTH PATTERSON, P.C. (AV)

1090 West Huron Street, 48328
Telephone: 810-681-1200
Fax: 810-681-1754

Douglas W. Booth (1918-1992)	David J. Lee
Calvin E. Patterson (1913-1987)	Allan T. Motzny
Parvin C. Lee, Jr.	Michael J. Hughes
J. Timothy Patterson	Michael D. Bishop
Eric S. Meier	

For full biographical listings, see the Martindale-Hubbell Law Directory

PORT HURON,* St. Clair Co.

FLETCHER DeGROW (AV)

522 Michigan Street, 48060-3893
Telephone: 810-987-8444
Facsimile: 810-987-8149

MEMBERS OF FIRM

Gary A. Fletcher	Dan L. DeGrow

ASSOCIATES

John D. Tomlinson	William L. Fealko, III

Representative Clients: Fremont Mutual Insurance Co.; Westfield Insurance Co.; Michigan Municipal Risk Management Authority; City of Port Huron; City of Marysville; Port Huron Area School District; Marysville Public Schools; Wirtz Manufacturing Co.; Raymond Excavating; Relleum Real Estate Development Co.

(See Next Column)

For Complete List of Firm Personnel, See General Section

For full biographical listings, see the Martindale-Hubbell Law Directory

SAGINAW,* Saginaw Co.

BRAUN KENDRICK FINKBEINER PLC (AV)

101 N. Washington Suite 812, 48607-1297
Telephone: 517-753-3461
Telecopier: 517-753-3951
URL: http://www.bkf-law.com
Bay City, Michigan Office: 201 Phoenix Building, P.O. Box 2039.
Telephone: 517-895-8505.
Telecopier: 517-895-8437.
Ann Arbor, Michigan Office: 700 First National Building.
Telephone: 313-995-4100.
Telecopier: 313-995-4798.

James V. Finkbeiner	John A. Decker
Thomas R. Luplow	Barry M. Levine

Brian S. Makaric	Glenn L. Fitkin

OF COUNSEL
J. Richard Kendrick

Representative Clients: The Dow Chemical Co.; General Motors Corp.; Lobdell Emery Manufacturing Co.; Merrill, Lynch, Inc.; Saginaw General Hospital; Saginaw News; The Wickes Foundation.

For Complete List of Firm Personnel, See General Section

For full biographical listings, see the Martindale-Hubbell Law Directory

SOUTHFIELD, Oakland Co.

COLLINS, EINHORN, FARRELL & ULANOFF, A PROFESSIONAL CORPORATION (AV)

4000 Town Center, Suite 909, 48075-1473
Telephone: 810-355-4141
Facsimile: 810-355-2277

Morton H. Collins	Dale J. McLellan
Brian D. Einhorn	Kenneth C. Merritt
Clayton F. Farrell	Noreen L. Slank
Stuart A. Ulanoff	Michael J. Sullivan
Janice G. Hildenbrand	

Gerald A. Pawlak	Deborah A. Lujan
Neil W. MacCallum	Barbara H. Goldman
Timothy Orlando	Shannon M. Kos
Theresa M. Asoklis	Kevin P. Moloughney
Karen C. Liddle	Susan P. Saltzman
Lisa L. Fadler	Laura A. Ruckle

For full biographical listings, see the Martindale-Hubbell Law Directory

MASON, STEINHARDT, JACOBS & PERLMAN, PROFESSIONAL CORPORATION (AV)

Suite 1500, 4000 Town Center, 48075-1415
Telephone: 810-358-2090
Fax: 810-358-3599

John E. Jacobs	Michael B. Perlman
Neil S. Silver	

Representative Clients: Citibank, N.A.; City of Dearborn; DeMattia Development Co.; Forest City Enterprises; Michigan Wholesale Drug Assn.; Mortgage Bankers Association of Michigan; Nationwide Insurance Co.; City of Taylor; Union Labor Life Insurance Co.; Yellow Freight Systems, Inc.

For Complete List of Firm Personnel, See General Section

For full biographical listings, see the Martindale-Hubbell Law Directory

PROVIZER, LICHTENSTEIN & PHILLIPS, P.C. (AV)

4000 Town Center, Suite 1800, 48075
Telephone: 810-352-9080
Facsimile: 810-352-1491

Harold M. Provizer	Constance S. Hall
Randall E. Phillips	Noel F. Beck
Marilyn A. Madorsky	William J. Selinsky
Deborah Molitz	Jason Milstone

Representative Clients: Jefferson Ins. Co.; Reliance National Ins. Group; Ken Modell (Personal Representative); Mort Novak (Personal Representative of the Estate of Garavaglia).

For full biographical listings, see the Martindale-Hubbell Law Directory

SOMMERS, SCHWARTZ, SILVER & SCHWARTZ, P.C. (AV)

2000 Town Center, Suite 900, 48075
Telephone: 810-355-0300
Telecopier: 810-746-4001
Plymouth, Michigan Office: 747 South Main Street.
Telephone: 313-455-4250.

(See Next Column)

SOMMERS, SCHWARTZ, SILVER & SCHWARTZ P.C.—*Continued*

James J. Vlasic	David M. Black

Saulius K. Mikalonis

General Counsel for: City of Taylor; Foodland Distributors; C.A. Muer Corporation; Vlasic & Company; Nederlander Corporation; Midwest Health Centers, P.C.
Representative Clients: Crum & Forster Insurance Company; City of Pontiac; Michigan National Bank.

For Complete List of Firm Personnel, See General Section

For full biographical listings, see the Martindale-Hubbell Law Directory

TRAVERSE CITY,* Grand Traverse Co.

OLSON, NOONAN, URSU & RINGSMUTH, P.C. (AV)

Suite 200, 161 East Front Street, P.O. Box 2358, 49685-2358
Telephone: 616-946-0044
Fax: 616-946-4807
Email: jnoonan@igc.apc.org

James M. Olson	Joan Cowley Ursu
John D. Noonan	Blake K. Ringsmuth

OF COUNSEL
Barry L. Levine

For full biographical listings, see the Martindale-Hubbell Law Directory

SMITH, JOHNSON & BRANDT, ATTORNEYS, P.C. (AV)

603 Bay Street, P.O. Box 705, 49685
Telephone: 616-946-0700
Fax: 616-946-1735
Lansing, Michigan Office: Suite 402, 116 West Ottawa Street.
Telephone: 517-482-5142.

Louis A. Smith

Joseph E. Quandt

Representative Clients: Alden State Bank; Empire National Bank of Traverse City; First of America Bank Michigan, N.A.; Garland; Grand Traverse Mall Limited Partnership; Green Tree Acceptance, Inc.; Lansing Automakers' Federal Credit Union; Michigan Automobile Dealers Association; Cherry Capital Oldsmobile Cadillac L.L.C.; Elmer's Crane and Dozer, Inc.

For Complete List of Firm Personnel, See General Section

For full biographical listings, see the Martindale-Hubbell Law Directory

TROY, Oakland Co.

HAINER, DEMOREST & BERMAN, P.C. (AV)

888 West Big Beaver, Suite 1400, 48084
Telephone: 810-244-8424
Fax: 810-244-8455

Michael J. Hainer	Mark S. Demorest

Leonard K. Berman

James D. Zazakis	Paul S. Miller

Rae Ann LaFrance
OF COUNSEL
John P. Charters	Michael A. Kus
Michael A. Heck	Douglas W. Mires

Representative Clients: American Empire Surplus Lines Insurance Co.; Central Distributors of Beer, Inc.; City Management Corp.; Clarklift of Detroit, Inc.; Federal Reserve Bank of Chicago; Hotel Investment Services, Inc.; Michigan Pumping Service; Mid-West Instrument, Inc.; Rockwell International Corp.; Zurich Insurance Co.

For full biographical listings, see the Martindale-Hubbell Law Directory

POLING, McGAW & POLING, P.C. (AV)

Suite 275, 5435 Corporate Drive, 48098
Telephone: 810-641-0500
Telecopier: 810-641-0506

Benson T. Buck (1926-1989)	Richard B. Poling, Jr.
Richard B. Poling	Gregory C. Hamilton
D. Douglas McGaw	Veronica B. O'Haro

James R. Parker
OF COUNSEL
Ralph S. Moore

Representative Clients: County of Oakland; City of Troy; United States Fidelity & Guaranty Co.; Sentry Insurance Co.; Admiral Insurance; DeMaria Construction Co.; Leo Corporation; Aetna Casualty and Surety Co.; Concord Design; Pneumo-Abex.

For full biographical listings, see the Martindale-Hubbell Law Directory

WEST BLOOMFIELD, Oakland Co.

CHEATHAM & ACKER, P.C. (AV)

5777 West Maple Road, Suite 130, P.O. Box 255002, 48325-5002
Telephone: 810-932-2000
Fax: 810-932-2008

Charles C. Cheatham	Lawrence J. Acker

Tracy A. Leahy	Mary E. Hollman

Christopher P. Jelinek
COUNSEL
Lynn L. Lower

For full biographical listings, see the Martindale-Hubbell Law Directory

FAMILY LAW

ALABAMA

BIRMINGHAM,* Jefferson Co.

BARNETT, HANES, O'NEAL, DUFFEE & GARFIELD, LLC (AV)

850 Park Place Tower, 2001 Park Place North, 35203
Telephone: 205-322-0471; 205-322-0484

MEMBERS OF FIRM

Robert C. Barnett	Cecil G. Duffee
Thomas B. Hanes	Frederick Mott Garfield, Jr.
James P. O'Neal	Janice G. Formato

OF COUNSEL

Arthur J. Hanes

Counsel for: City of Gardendale; State of Alabama Highway Department.
Approved Attorneys for: Alabama Title Co., Inc.

For full biographical listings, see the Martindale-Hubbell Law Directory

BRADLEY, ARANT, ROSE & WHITE (AV)

2001 Park Place, Suite 1400, P.O. Box 830709, 35283-0709
Telephone: 205-521-8000
Facsimile: 205-252-0264
Facsimile (SouthTrust Tower Office): 205-251-9915
URL: http://www.BARW.COM
Huntsville, Alabama Office: 200 Clinton Avenue West, Suite 900, 35801.
Telephone: 205-517-5100.
Facsimile: 205-533-5069.

MEMBER OF FIRM

Patrick H. Graves, Jr. (Resident, Huntsville Office)

For Complete List of Firm Personnel, See General Section

For full biographical listings, see the Martindale-Hubbell Law Directory

DAVID CROMWELL JOHNSON (AV)

The Land Title Building, Suite 200, 600 20th Street, North, 35203
Telephone: 205-327-5223

ASSOCIATES

J. Flint Liddon	Barry R. Tuggle

For full biographical listings, see the Martindale-Hubbell Law Directory

NAJJAR DENABURG, P.C. (AV)

2125 Morris Avenue, 35203
Telephone: 205-250-8400
Telecopier: 205-326-3837

Charles L. Denaburg	L. Stephen Wright, Jr.
Thomas C. Najjar, Jr. (1931-1995)	

Denise J. Pomeroy

General Counsel: Acousti Engineering of Alabama, Inc.
Representative Client: Compass Bank.
Approved Attorneys for: Mississippi Valley Title Insurance Co.
Reference: Compass Bank.

For Complete List of Firm Personnel, See General Section

For full biographical listings, see the Martindale-Hubbell Law Directory

REDDEN, MILLS & CLARK (AV)

940 First Alabama Bank Building, 417 North 20th Street, 35203
Telephone: 205-322-0457
Fax: 205-322-8481

MEMBERS OF FIRM

L. Drew Redden	William N. Clark
William H. Mills	Gerald L. Miller
Stephen W. Shaw	

ASSOCIATE

Maxwell H. Pulliam, Jr.

References: SouthTrust Bank; First Alabama Bank.

For full biographical listings, see the Martindale-Hubbell Law Directory

HUNTSVILLE,* Madison Co.

BERRY, ABLES, TATUM, BAXTER, PARKER & HALL, P.C. (AV)

Legal Building, 315 Franklin Street, S.E., P.O. Box 165, 35804-0165
Telephone: 205-533-3740
Facsimile: 205-533-3751
Email: BAXTERJ@ATTMAIL.COM

(See Next Column)

William H. Blanton (1889-1973)	James T. Tatum, Jr.
Joe M. Berry	James T. Baxter, III
L. Bruce Ables	Thomas E. Parker, Jr.
Bill G. Hall	

James K. Brabston	Mark Rogers Hunter

Representative Clients: AmSouth Bank; First Alabama Bank; General Shale Products Co.; The Hertz Corp.; Litton Industries, Inc.; Farmers Tractor Co.; Colonial Bank; Farm Credit Bank of Texas; SouthBank; Regions Mortgage.
Reference: First Alabama Bank.

For full biographical listings, see the Martindale-Hubbell Law Directory

DAVID B. BLANKENSHIP ATTORNEY-AT-LAW, P.C. (AV)

229 East Side Square, 35801
Telephone: 205-517-1550
Telecopier: 205-517-1559

David B. Blankenship

For full biographical listings, see the Martindale-Hubbell Law Directory

STEPHENS, MILLIRONS, HARRISON & GAMMONS, P.C. (AV)

333 Franklin Street, P.O. Box 307, 35801
Telephone: 205-533-7711
Telecopier: 205-536-9388

Arthur M. Stephens	James G. Harrison
Paul L. Millirons	Robert C. Gammons

Attorneys for: Lomas Mortgage USA, Inc.; AmSouth Mortgage Co., Inc.

For full biographical listings, see the Martindale-Hubbell Law Directory

MOBILE,* Mobile Co.

BRISKMAN & BINION, P.C. (AV)

205 Church Street, P.O. Box 43, 36601
Telephone: 334-433-7600
Fax: 334-433-4485

Donald M. Briskman	Christ N. Coumanis
Walter G. (Stoney) Chavers	

A List of Representative Clients will be furnished upon request.
References: First Alabama Bank; AmSouth Bank, N.A.; Southtrust Bank of Mobile.

For full biographical listings, see the Martindale-Hubbell Law Directory

MONTGOMERY,* Montgomery Co.

J. FLOYD MINOR (AV)

458 South Lawrence Street, P.O. Box 164, 36101-0164
Telephone: 334-265-6200
Fax: 334-265-6270

ASSOCIATE

John L. Olszewski

For full biographical listings, see the Martindale-Hubbell Law Directory

TURNER, WILSON & SAWYER (AV)

428 South Lawrence Street, P.O. Box 98, 36104
Telephone: 334-262-2756
Fax: 334-262-2759

MEMBERS OF FIRM

Wayne P. Turner	Terry P. Wilson
William P. Sawyer	

For full biographical listings, see the Martindale-Hubbell Law Directory

ARIZONA

FLAGSTAFF,* Coconino Co.

ASPEY, WATKINS & DIESEL, P.L.L.C. (AV)

123 North San Francisco, 3rd Floor, 86001
Telephone: 520-774-1478
Facsimile: 520-774-8404
Sedona, Arizona Office: 120 Soldier Pass Road.
Telephone: 520-282-5955.
Facsimile: 520-282-5962.
Page, Arizona Office: 904 North Navajo.
Telephone: 520-645-9694.
Cottonwood, Arizona Office: 2400 E. Highway 89A, Suite C.
Telephone: 520-639-1881.
Facsimile: 520-639-0272.

(See Next Column)

ASPEY, WATKINS & DIESEL P.L.L.C., *Flagstaff—Continued*

MEMBERS OF FIRM

Frederick M. Fritz Aspey	Donald H. Bayles, Jr.
Harold L. Watkins	Kaign N. Christy
Louis M. Diesel	John J. Dempsey
Bruce S. Griffen	Zachary J. Markham

James E. Ledbetter	Roger M. Baeurle
Whitney Cunningham	Amy E. Mabius
Pernell Whynn McGuire	Stephen A. Thompson

Joel E. Sannes

LEGAL SUPPORT PERSONNEL

Karla H. Falls, CLAS (Legal Assistant)	Dominic M. Marino, Jr. (Paralegal Assistant)
Rocky C. Nissen (Paralegal Assistant, Sedona, Arizona Office)	Carrie R. Flynn (Litigation Paralegal, Cottonwood, Arizona Office)
Deborah D. Roberts, CLA (Legal Assistant)	

Representative Clients: Farmer's Insurance Company of Arizona; Pepsi-Cola Bottling Company of Northern Arizona; Bill Luke's Chrysler-Plymouth, Inc.; First American Title Insurance Company; Transnation Title Insurance Co.; Page Electric Utility; Comprehensive Access Health Plan, Inc.; Northern Arizona Healthcare Corporation.
Reference: First Interstate Bank-Arizona, N.A., Flagstaff, Arizona.

For full biographical listings, see the Martindale-Hubbell Law Directory

---

PHOENIX,* Maricopa Co.

DAVID W. ADLER (AV)

4141 West Bethany Home Road, 85019
Telephone: 602-266-6010
Fax: 602-841-7684

For full biographical listings, see the Martindale-Hubbell Law Directory

---

BURCH & CRACCHIOLO, P.A. (AV)

702 East Osborn Road, Suite 200, 85014
Telephone: 602-274-7611
Fax: 602-234-0341
Mailing Address: P.O. Box 16882, Phoenix, AZ, 85011

Donald W. Lindholm	Jess A. Lorona

Representative Clients: Bashas' Inc.; Farmers Insurance Group; U-Haul International, Inc.

For Complete List of Firm Personnel, See General Section

For full biographical listings, see the Martindale-Hubbell Law Directory

---

COHEN AND FROMM, P.C. (AV)

2198 East Camelback Road, Suite 365, 85016-4742
Telephone: 602-955-1515
Facsimile: 602-955-0509

Bruce R. Cohen	Sandra J. Fromm

Stephen R. Smith	Lesley C. Abelsohn

LEGAL SUPPORT PERSONNEL
PARALEGALS

Karen L. Wilhelm	Kelly S. Gilliland

For full biographical listings, see the Martindale-Hubbell Law Directory

---

HIRSCH LAW OFFICE, P.C. (AV)

4614 E. Shea Boulevard Suite D250, 85028
Telephone: 602-996-9544
Fax: 602-494-0815

Lawrence D. Hirsch	Iva S. Hirsch

For full biographical listings, see the Martindale-Hubbell Law Directory

---

MacLEAN & JACQUES, LTD. (AV)

Suite 202, 40 East Virginia, 85004
Telephone: 602-263-5771
FAX: 602-279-5569

John H. MacLean (1932-1992)	Raoul T. Jacques

Cary T. Inabinet	Macre S. Inabinet

LEGAL SUPPORT PERSONNEL

Sharon Petterson

For full biographical listings, see the Martindale-Hubbell Law Directory

---

MARISCAL, WEEKS, McINTYRE & FRIEDLANDER, P.A. (AV)

2901 North Central Avenue Suite 200, 85012-2705
Telephone: 602-285-5000
Fax: 602-285-5100

Mark J. Robens	Robert L. Schwartz

Cindra L. White

OF COUNSEL

Phillip Weeks

References: Northern Trust Bank of Arizona; National Bank of Arizona.

For Complete List of Firm Personnel, See General Section

For full biographical listings, see the Martindale-Hubbell Law Directory

---

MARK & PEARLSTEIN, P.A. (AV)

Suite 150 The Brookstone, 2025 North Third Street, 85004
Telephone: 602-257-0200
Fax: 602-271-4711

Leonard J. Mark	Mr. Lynn M. Pearlstein

OF COUNSEL

Stephen G. Campbell

For full biographical listings, see the Martindale-Hubbell Law Directory

---

MUELLER & GALLIOS, P.C. (AV)

Country Club Manor, 1221 East Osborn Road, Suite 200, 85014
Telephone: 602-274-7272
Telecopier: 602-279-0863

James W. Mueller	Aris J. Gallios

Jodi Lynd Lawrence

Reference: Bank of America, Arizona.

For full biographical listings, see the Martindale-Hubbell Law Directory

---

SHIMMEL, HILL, BISHOP & GRUENDER, P.C. (AV)

3700 North 24th Street, 85016
Telephone: 602-224-9500
Telecopier: 602-955-6176

Daniel F. Gruender	Susan M. Swick

Representative Clients: Harkins Amusement Enterprises, Inc.; Citizen Auto Stage Line; Delta Airlines; Grayline Sightseeing Association.

For full biographical listings, see the Martindale-Hubbell Law Directory

---

SKARECKY, CALES & HOLDER, A PROFESSIONAL ASSOCIATION (AV)

Suite 300, 3130 North Third Avenue, 85013
Telephone: 602-248-0393
Fax: 602-266-4991

Gloria L. Cales

Reference: First National Bank of Arizona.

For full biographical listings, see the Martindale-Hubbell Law Directory

---

TOLES & ASSOCIATES, P.C. (AV)

1010 East Jefferson Street, 85034
Telephone: 602-253-1010
Fax: 602-253-1048

M. Jeremy Toles

Richard M. Gerry	Craig C. Gillespie
Rosann K. Johnson	M. L. (Les) Weatherly, Jr.

OF COUNSEL

Barbara A. Jarvis

For full biographical listings, see the Martindale-Hubbell Law Directory

---

TUCSON,* Pima Co.

DONAU & BOLT (AV)

Suite 501, 3505 North Campbell Avenue, 85719-2033
Telephone: 520-795-8710
Fax: 520-795-0308

MEMBER OF FIRM

John R. Bolt

ASSOCIATE

Sharon M. Wolfkiel

For full biographical listings, see the Martindale-Hubbell Law Directory

Tucson—Continued

KARP, HEURLIN & WEISS, P.L.C. (AV)

Suite 2120 33 North Stone Avenue, 85701-1415
Telephone: 520-882-9705
Fax: 520-798-3339
Email: khaw@azstarnet.com

Leonard Karp

Reference: National Bank of Arizona.

For full biographical listings, see the Martindale-Hubbell Law Directory

DAVID H. LIEBERTHAL (AV)

Bank of America Building, 33 North Stone Avenue, Suite 2100, 85701
Telephone: 520-622-6793
Fax: 520-624-2816

For full biographical listings, see the Martindale-Hubbell Law Directory

STOMPOLY, STROUD, GIDDINGS & GLICKSMAN, P.C. (AV)

1820 Citibank Tower, One South Church Avenue, 85702
Telephone: 520-628-8300
Telefax: 520-628-9948
Mailing Address: P.O. Box 190, Tucson, AZ, 85702-0190

James L. Stroud

For Complete List of Firm Personnel, See General Section

For full biographical listings, see the Martindale-Hubbell Law Directory

CALIFORNIA

ARCADIA, Los Angeles Co.

HELMS, HANRAHAN & MYERS (AV)

Suite 685 Towne Centre Building, 150 North Santa Anita Avenue, 91006
Telephone: 818-445-1177
Email: helmsj@aol.com

Sterling E. Myers

Reference: Bank of America National Trust & Savings Assn. (Arcadia Branch).

For Complete List of Firm Personnel, See General Section

For full biographical listings, see the Martindale-Hubbell Law Directory

BEVERLY HILLS, Los Angeles Co.

ROBERT A. ADELMAN, A LAW CORPORATION (AV)

9454 Wilshire Boulevard Suite PH-29, 90212-2937
Telephone: 310-858-1201
Fax: 310-858-6558

Robert A. Adelman

Reference: City National Bank.

For full biographical listings, see the Martindale-Hubbell Law Directory

HARRY M. FAIN (AV)

121 South Beverly Drive, 90212
Telephone: 310-275-5132; 213-272-7807
Fax: 310-271-5269

Reference: City National Bank (Beverly Hills Main Office).

For full biographical listings, see the Martindale-Hubbell Law Directory

JAFFE & CLEMENS (AV)

A Partnership including Professional Corporations
Suite 1000, 433 North Camden Drive, 90210
Telephone: 310-550-7477
Telecopier: 310-271-8313

Daniel J. Jaffe (A Professional Corporation)	Bruce A. Clemens (A Professional Corporation)
William S. Ryden	

ASSOCIATES

Judy Bogen	Gretchen Wellman Taylor
David M. Luboff	Richard Mackay
Mark L. Levinson	(Not admitted in CA)
Cynthia S. Monaco (On Leave)	

For full biographical listings, see the Martindale-Hubbell Law Directory

KAUFMAN & YOUNG, A PROFESSIONAL CORPORATION (AV)

121 South Beverly Drive, 90212-3002
Telephone: 310-275-5132
Los Angeles: 213-272-7807
Fax: 310-275-2919

Robert S. Kaufman	Marcy L. Kenerson
Kenneth M. Young	Scott K. Robinson

OF COUNSEL

Lance S. Spiegel

Reference: City National Bank (Beverly Hills Main Office Branch).

For full biographical listings, see the Martindale-Hubbell Law Directory

KOLODNY & ANTEAU (AV)

9100 Wilshire Boulevard Suite 900, 90212
Telephone: 310-271-5533
FAX: 310-271-3918

MEMBERS OF FIRM

Stephen A. Kolodny	Ronald W. Anteau
Harlee M. Gasmer	

William P. Glavin IV	Peter T. Hermes
William J. Glucksman	Terry Levich Ross
Lauren S. Petkin	Erin L. Grey

Reference: Wells Fargo Bank, Los Angeles, CA.

For full biographical listings, see the Martindale-Hubbell Law Directory

ENCINO, Los Angeles Co.

ALPERT, BARR AND GROSS, A PROFESSIONAL LAW CORPORATION (AV)

Encino Office Park I, Suite 300, 6345 Balboa Boulevard, 91316-1523
Telephone: 818-881-5000
Fax: 818-881-1150

Lee Kanon Alpert	Mark S. Blackman
Gary L. Barr	Michael N. Balikian
Lisa W. Glazener	Judith R. Simon
Mark P. Gross	Jack S. Mack

OF COUNSEL

Charles M. Hughes	Leonard S. Levy (A Professional Corporation)

For full biographical listings, see the Martindale-Hubbell Law Directory

*FAIRFIELD,** Solano Co.

WILLIAM H. McPHERSON (AV)

825 Webster Street, 94533
Telephone: 707-422-7706
Fax: 707-425-9331

For full biographical listings, see the Martindale-Hubbell Law Directory

GLENDALE, Los Angeles Co.

O'ROURKE, ALLAN & FONG (AV)

3rd Floor, 104 North Belmont, P.O. Box 10220, 91209-3220
Telephone: 818-247-4303
Fax: 818-247-1451

MEMBERS OF FIRM

Denis M. O'Rourke	Joan H. Allan
Roderick D. Fong	

ASSOCIATE

Denise Michelle O'Rourke

References: Verdugo Banking Co. (Glendale, California); Community Bank (Glendale, California).

For full biographical listings, see the Martindale-Hubbell Law Directory

IRVINE, Orange Co.

RAY HENDRICKSON (AV)

University Tower, Suite 700, 4199 Campus Drive, 92612
Telephone: 714-833-0101; 854-8800
Fax: 714-854-4897

References: Mitsui Manufacturers Bank, Newport Beach, California; Bank of California, Newport Beach, California; Home Fed, Irvine, California.

For full biographical listings, see the Martindale-Hubbell Law Directory

GEORGE M. KORNIEVSKY A PROFESSIONAL CORPORATION (AV)

18881 Von Karman Avenue, Suite 1260, 92612-1578
Telephone: 714-724-0888
Fax: 714-752-7035
Email: gmkapc@quick.com

(See Next Column)

GEORGE M. KORNIEVSKY A PROFESSIONAL CORPORATION, *Irvine—Continued*

George M. Kornievsky

For full biographical listings, see the Martindale-Hubbell Law Directory

LA HABRA, Orange Co.

C. LARRY FANCHER (AV)

440 East La Habra Boulevard, 90631
Telephone: 714-870-9972; 310-691-1300

For full biographical listings, see the Martindale-Hubbell Law Directory

LONG BEACH, Los Angeles Co.

CAMERON, MADDEN, PEARLSON, GALE & SELLARS (AV)

One World Trade Center Suite 1600, 90831-1600
Telephone: 310-436-3888
Telecopier: 310-437-1967

MEMBERS OF THE FIRM
Timothy C. Cameron   Patrick T. Madden
Charles M. Gale   Paul R. Pearlson
James D. Sellars
ASSOCIATE
Lillian D. Salinger

For full biographical listings, see the Martindale-Hubbell Law Directory

LOS ALTOS, Santa Clara Co.

MALOVOS & KONEVICH (AV)

Los Altos Plaza, 5150 El Camino Real, Suite A-22, 94022
Telephone: 415-988-9700
Facsimile: 415-988-9639

Marian Malovos Konevich   Robert W. Konevich
RETIRED FOUNDING PARTNER
Kenneth R. Malovos

For full biographical listings, see the Martindale-Hubbell Law Directory

LOS ANGELES,* Los Angeles Co.

PATRICK DeCAROLIS, JR. A PROFESSIONAL LAW CORPORATION (AV)

2029 Century Park East, Suite 2860, 90067
Telephone: 310-552-3312
Telecopier: 310-552-0441

Patrick DeCarolis, Jr.

For full biographical listings, see the Martindale-Hubbell Law Directory

DEUTSCH & RUBIN (AV)

Second Floor, West Tower, 11377 West Olympic Boulevard, 90064-1683
Telephone: 310-312-3222
FAX: 310-312-3205

MEMBERS OF FIRM
Miles J. Rubin (A Professional   Wendy A. Herzog
Corporation)   Lauri A. Kritt
OF COUNSEL
Linda Cukier

For full biographical listings, see the Martindale-Hubbell Law Directory

NORMAN M. DOLIN (AV)

Suite 2200, 1925 Century Park East (Century City), 90067-2723
Telephone: 310-552-9338
Fax: 310-552-1922

ASSOCIATES
Lynn Langley   Ani M. Garikian

For full biographical listings, see the Martindale-Hubbell Law Directory

LAW OFFICES OF ROBERT W. EISFELDER, P.C. (AV)

Suite 400, 11726 San Vicente Boulevard, 90049-5047
Telephone: 310-820-4500

Robert W. Eisfelder

For full biographical listings, see the Martindale-Hubbell Law Directory

FREID AND GOLDSMAN, A PROFESSIONAL LAW CORPORATION (AV)

2029 Century Park East, Suite 860, 90067
Telephone: 310-552-2700
Telecopier: 310-552-2770

(See Next Column)

Manley Freid   Marci R. Levine
Melvin S. Goldsman   Joanne D. Ratinoff
Gary J. Cohen   Heather Rickett Graham
          Lori A. Loo

Janet Kaplan   Reuel M. Baluyot

For full biographical listings, see the Martindale-Hubbell Law Directory

GOLDMAN & KAGON, LAW CORPORATION (AV)

1801 Century Park East, Suite 2222, 90067
Telephone: 310-552-1707
Telecopier: 310-552-7938

Terry Mc Niff   Jared Laskin
COUNSEL
A. David Kagon

For Complete List of Firm Personnel, See General Section

For full biographical listings, see the Martindale-Hubbell Law Directory

JOHNSON, POULSON, COONS & SLATER (AV)

10880 Wilshire Boulevard, Suite 1800, 90024
Telephone: 310-475-0611
Telecopier: 310-475-0143

MEMBERS OF FIRM
Jonathan E. Johnson   Lynn O. Poulson (Mr.)
Michael H. Coons
OF COUNSEL
Martin R. Slater

For full biographical listings, see the Martindale-Hubbell Law Directory

LEVINSON, MILLER, JACOBS & PHILLIPS, A PROFESSIONAL CORPORATION (AV)

Suite 2000, 1875 Century Park East, 90067-2534
Telephone: 310-557-2455
Cable Address: "Levrom"
Facsimile: 310-282-0472

Paul Levinson   Stanton Lee Phillips
Gary S. Jacobs   Samuel M. Robin

Sharon Jill Sandler   Fern S. Nisen
J. Bennett Friedman   Erin L. Prouty
OF COUNSEL
Milton Louis Miller   Stephen I. Halper
References: First Charter Bank; Wells Fargo Trust (Trust Dept., Southern California Headquarters).

For full biographical listings, see the Martindale-Hubbell Law Directory

MOSTEN & TUFFIAS (AV)

10990 Wilshire Boulevard, Suite 940, 90024
Telephone: 310-473-7611
Facsimile: 310-473-7422
Email: FMosten@counsel.com

MEMBERS OF FIRM
Forrest S. Mosten   Heidi S. Tuffias

For full biographical listings, see the Martindale-Hubbell Law Directory

F. PATRICIA MUDIE A PROFESSIONAL CORPORATION (AV)

12100 Wilshire Boulevard, Suite 1900, 90025-1506
Telephone: 310-820-5505
Fax: 310-207-1030

F. Patricia Mudie

For full biographical listings, see the Martindale-Hubbell Law Directory

NACHSHIN & WESTON (AV)

A Partnership including Professional Corporations
Suite 2240, 11755 Wilshire Boulevard, 90025
Telephone: 310-478-6868
Telefax: 310-473-8112

Robert J. Nachshin (A   Scott N. Weston (A Professional
Professional Corporation)   Corporation)
ASSOCIATE
Joseph A. Langlois

For full biographical listings, see the Martindale-Hubbell Law Directory

Los Angeles—Continued

BEATRICE H. NEMLAHA, P.C. (AV)

11377 West Olympic Boulevard, 90064-1683
Telephone: 310-914-7911
Fax: 310-312-3787

Beatrice H. Nemlaha

For full biographical listings, see the Martindale-Hubbell Law Directory

HARVEY STRASSMAN (AV)

1875 Century Park East, 15th Floor, 90067
Telephone: 310-277-6775
Fax: 310-552-3228

For full biographical listings, see the Martindale-Hubbell Law Directory

JOSEPH TABACK, P.C. (AV)

Suite 2860, 2029 Century Park East (Century City), 90067-3014
Telephone: 310-557-1200
Fax: 310-286-3147

Joseph Taback

Marci A. Taback

Reference: Union Bank (Century City Branch).

For full biographical listings, see the Martindale-Hubbell Law Directory

TROPE AND TROPE (AV)

12121 Wilshire Boulevard, Suite 801, 90025
Telephone: 310-207-8228
Fax: 310-826-1122

MEMBERS OF FIRM

Sorrell Trope	Steven Knowles
Eugene L. Trope	Mark S. Patt
Maryanne La Guardia	Bruce E. Cooperman
Mark Vincent Kaplan	

ASSOCIATES

Thomas Paine Dunlap	Leslie M. Jordon
Donna Beck Weaver	Nancy Cronenwalt
Carolyn J. Kozuch	Andrea A. Fugate
Anne Campbell Kiley	Jeff M. Sturman
Roger B. Peikin	Susan E. Wiesner
Salvador P. Laviña	Fahi Takesh
Lori A. Howe	Derek Jon Reeve
Warren D. Camp	Geniveve Joan Ruskus
Robert B. Clayton	Daniel B. Rubanowitz

OF COUNSEL
Roland L. Trope (Not admitted in CA)

For full biographical listings, see the Martindale-Hubbell Law Directory

LAW OFFICES OF PETER M. WALZER (AV)

Suite 2610, 2029 Century Park East, 90067
Telephone: 310-557-0915
Email: peterlaw@aol.com

For full biographical listings, see the Martindale-Hubbell Law Directory

WASSER, ROSENSON & CARTER (AV)

Suite 1200, One Century Plaza, 2029 Century Park East (Century City), 90067
Telephone: 310-277-7117
Fax: 310-553-1793

MEMBERS OF FIRM

Dennis M. Wasser	S. David Rosenson
Susan K. Carter	

ASSOCIATES

John A. Foley	Laura Landesman
Laura Allison Wasser	

For full biographical listings, see the Martindale-Hubbell Law Directory

ZOLLA AND MEYER (AV)

A Partnership including a Professional Corporation
Suite 1020, 2029 Century Park East, 90067
Telephone: 310-277-0725
Facsimile: 310-277-3784
Email: familylaw@zmlalaw.com *URL:*
http://www.zmlalaw.com/familylaw

MEMBERS OF FIRM

Marshall S. Zolla (A P.C.)	Lisa Helfend Meyer

(See Next Column)

ASSOCIATES

Doreen Marie Olson	Dana Lowy
Gregory M. Marsh	

Reference: Bank of California, Beverly Hills.

For full biographical listings, see the Martindale-Hubbell Law Directory

---

MOUNTAIN VIEW, Santa Clara Co.

J. NORMAN BAKER (AV)

San Antonio Center, 2570 El Camino Real West, Suite 504, 94040
Telephone: 415-941-0604
Fax: 415-941-4697

Reference: Bank of the West (Los Altos Branch).

For full biographical listings, see the Martindale-Hubbell Law Directory

---

NEWPORT BEACH, Orange Co.

THOMAS A. BERNAUER A PROFESSIONAL CORPORATION (AV)

500 Newport Center Drive, Suite 950, 92660
Telephone: 714-720-1313
Fax: 714-720-7457

Thomas A. Bernauer
LEGAL SUPPORT PERSONNEL
Michael Minick

For full biographical listings, see the Martindale-Hubbell Law Directory

DOUGLAS C. LIECHTY (AV)

Suite 520 Newport Financial Plaza, 500 Newport Center Drive, 92660-7005
Telephone: 714-644-8600
Fax: 714-759-6832

LEGAL SUPPORT PERSONNEL
Rosemary K. Buchan (Legal Assistant)

For full biographical listings, see the Martindale-Hubbell Law Directory

JOHN R. SCHILLING A PROFESSIONAL CORPORATION (AV)

4675 MacArthur Court Suite 590, Tower One, 92660-1839
Telephone: 714-833-8833
Fax: 714-833-3883

John R. Schilling

References: Union Bank (Airport Branch); City National Bank (Newport Beach); Bank of America (Newport Beach).

For full biographical listings, see the Martindale-Hubbell Law Directory

---

OAKLAND,* Alameda Co.

LAW OFFICES OF LORIN B. BLUM (AV)

1939 Harrison Street, Suite 618, 94612-3533
Telephone: 510-465-3927
Fax: 510-465-4222
Email: lbblum@ix.netcom.com
Walnut Creek, California Office: 1850 Mt. Diablo Boulevard, Suite 605, 94596.
Telephone: 510-933-6125.

ASSOCIATE
Sharon M. Braz
LEGAL SUPPORT PERSONNEL

Sandra L. Kellum	Stephanie Snyder

For full biographical listings, see the Martindale-Hubbell Law Directory

GARRETT C. DAILEY (AV)

519 - 17th Street, 7th Floor, 94612
Telephone: 510-465-3920
Fax: 510-465-7348
Email: BriefCase@aol.com

Reference: Wells Fargo Bank (Oakland City Center Office).

For full biographical listings, see the Martindale-Hubbell Law Directory

---

ONTARIO, San Bernardino Co.

COVINGTON & CROWE (AV)

1131 West Sixth Street, P.O. Box 1515, 91762
Telephone: 909-983-9393
Fax: 909-391-6762
Email: covcrowe@ix.netcom.com

(See Next Column)

COVINGTON & CROWE, *Ontario—Continued*

MEMBERS OF FIRM

Harold A. Bailin (1930-1988)	Stephen R. Wade
Samuel P. Crowe	Jette R. Anderson
George W. Porter	Audrey A. Perri
Robert E. Dougherty	Tracy L. Tibbals
Donald G. Haslam	Melanie Fisch
Robert F. Schauer	Robert H. Reeder
Edward A. Hopson	R. Doug Donesky

Tammy S. Jager

ASSOCIATES

Howard S. Borenstein	Richard R. Muir
Denise Matthey	Kimberly A. Rohn
Katrina West	J. Michael Kaler

Eric S. Vail

For full biographical listings, see the Martindale-Hubbell Law Directory

---

ORANGE, Orange Co.

JAMES K. BATCHELOR A PROFESSIONAL CORPORATION (AV)

765 South The City Drive Suite 270, 92668
Telephone: 714-750-8388; 714-542-2333
Fax: 714-750-8002

James K. Batchelor

Reference: Wells Fargo Bank

For full biographical listings, see the Martindale-Hubbell Law Directory

WILLIAM P. BENNETT, A P.L.C. (AV)

333 City Boulevard West, Suite 1810, 92668
Telephone: 714-978-3293
FAX: 714-634-3688

William P. Bennett

OF COUNSEL

Kelly A. Bennett

LEGAL SUPPORT PERSONNEL

Andrea D. Everage (Paralegal)

For full biographical listings, see the Martindale-Hubbell Law Directory

---

PALM DESERT, Riverside Co.

LAW OFFICES OF VIRGINIA S. CRISTE (AV)

74-075 El Paseo, Suite A-14, 92260
Telephone: 619-776-1770
Fax: 619-776-1775

For full biographical listings, see the Martindale-Hubbell Law Directory

---

PALM SPRINGS, Riverside Co.

SCHLECHT, SHEVLIN & SHOENBERGER, A LAW CORPORATION (AV)

Suite 100, 801 East Tahquitz Canyon Way, P.O. Box 2744, 92263-2744
Telephone: 619-320-7161
Facsimile: 619-323-1758; 619-325-4623

James M. Schlecht	Jon A. Shoenberger
John C. Shevlin	Daniel T. Johnson

David Darrin	Elizabeth A. Dreier

OF COUNSEL

Donald B. McNelley	Allen O. Perrier (Retired)

Representative Clients: Outdoor Resorts of America; The Escrow Connection; Wells Fargo Bank; Canyon Country Club; Waste Management Co.

For full biographical listings, see the Martindale-Hubbell Law Directory

---

PALO ALTO, Santa Clara Co.

FLICKER & KERIN (AV)

Suite 460, 285 Hamilton, P.O. Box 840, 94302
Telephone: 415-321-0947
Fax: 415-326-9722

MEMBERS OF FIRM

Michael R. Flicker	Anthony J. Kerin, III

ASSOCIATES

Rhesa C. Rubin	Cheri A. Bell

For full biographical listings, see the Martindale-Hubbell Law Directory

JOHN E. MILLER (AV)

250 Cambridge Avenue, Suite 102, 94306-1504
Telephone: 415-321-8886
Fax: 415-321-8998

(See Next Column)

ASSOCIATES

Annalisa C Wood	Kerre R. Dubinsky

Reference: Bank of the West.

For full biographical listings, see the Martindale-Hubbell Law Directory

LINCOLN A. MITCHELL (AV)

Suite 300, 550 Hamilton Avenue, 94301
Telephone: 415-321-5003
Fax: 415-326-2404

For full biographical listings, see the Martindale-Hubbell Law Directory

NANETTE SCHULZE STRINGER (AV)

430 Cowper Street, 94301
Telephone: 415-617-4540
Fax: 415-617-4541

For full biographical listings, see the Martindale-Hubbell Law Directory

---

PASADENA, Los Angeles Co.

GARY W. KEARNEY (AV)

Suite 410, 225 South Lake Avenue, 91101-3005
Telephone: 818-796-9621
Telecopier: 818-796-6839

ASSOCIATE

Ronald K. Ziff

For full biographical listings, see the Martindale-Hubbell Law Directory

WILLSEY LAW OFFICES OWNED BY A PROFESSIONAL CORPORATION (AV)

553 S. Marengo Avenue, 91101
Telephone: 818-577-1086
Fax: 818-304-2959

Burke W. Willsey	Daniel P. Willsey (A Professional Corporation)

Reference: Sanwa Bank.

For full biographical listings, see the Martindale-Hubbell Law Directory

---

PLEASANTON, Alameda Co.

STALEY, JOBSON & WETHERELL, A PROFESSIONAL CORPORATION (AV)

5776 Stoneridge Mall Road, Suite 310, 94588
Telephone: 510-463-0750
Fax: 510-463-0407

John F. Staley	Bruce Jobson
	Joan M. Wetherell

For full biographical listings, see the Martindale-Hubbell Law Directory

---

SACRAMENTO,* Sacramento Co.

BARTHOLOMEW, WASZNICKY & MOLINARO, LLP (AV)

1006 Fourth Street, 8th Floor, 95814
Telephone: 916-443-2055
Fax: 916-443-8287
Email: SACFAMLAW@AOL.COM

MEMBERS OF FIRM

Hal D. Bartholomew	Diane Wasznicky
	Mary C. Molinaro

ASSOCIATE

Patricia Huberty

For full biographical listings, see the Martindale-Hubbell Law Directory

JAMES M. MIZE (AV)

3620 American River Drive, Suite 250, 95864
Telephone: 916-485-2211
FAX: 916-485-1934

For full biographical listings, see the Martindale-Hubbell Law Directory

WOODRUFF, O'HAIR & POSNER, INC. A LAW CORPORATION (AV)

2251 Fair Oaks Boulevard, Suite 100, 95825
Telephone: 916-920-0211
Telecopier: 916-920-0241

(See Next Column)

WOODRUFF, O'HAIR & POSNER INC. A LAW CORPORATION—*Continued*

D. Thomas Woodruff   Robert J. O'Hair
Jeffrey J. Posner

For full biographical listings, see the Martindale-Hubbell Law Directory

---

SAN BERNARDINO,* San Bernardino Co.

STEVEN A. BECKER A PROFESSIONAL LAW CORPORATION (AV)

315 West Sixth Street, 92401
Telephone: 909-888-2211
Fax: 909-381-0586

Steven A. Becker

For full biographical listings, see the Martindale-Hubbell Law Directory

---

SAN DIEGO,* San Diego Co.

E. GREGORY ALFORD (AV)

1551 Fourth Avenue, Suite 301, 92101
Telephone: 619-232-4734
FAX: 619-239-3345

Charles Wesley Kim, Jr.

For full biographical listings, see the Martindale-Hubbell Law Directory

LUCE, FORWARD, HAMILTON & SCRIPPS LLP (AV)

A Partnership including Professional Corporations
600 West Broadway, Suite 2600, 92101
Telephone: 619-236-1414
Fax: 619-232-8311
URL: http://www.luce.com
La Jolla, California Office: 4275 Executive Square, Suite 800, 92037.
Telephone: 619-535-2639.
Fax: 619-453-2812.
Los Angeles, California Office: 777 South Figueroa, Suite 3600, 90017.
Telephone: 213-892-4992.
Fax: 213-892-7731.
San Francisco, California Office: 100 Bush Street, 20th Floor, 94104.
Telephone: 415-395-7900.
Fax: 415-395-7949.
New York, N.Y. Office: Citicorp Center, 153 East 53rd Street, 26th Floor, 10022.
Telephone: 212-754-1414.
Fax: 212-644-9727.
Chicago, Illinois Office: 180 North La Salle Street, Suite 1125, 60601.
Telephone: 312-641-0580.
Fax: 312-641-0380.

MEMBER OF FIRM
Susanne J. Stanford
ASSOCIATE
Frank J. Kros

For Complete List of Firm Personnel, See General Section

For full biographical listings, see the Martindale-Hubbell Law Directory

OLINS, FOERSTER & HAYES (AV)

A Legal Liability Partnership including Professional Corporation
2214 Second Avenue, 92101
Telephone: 619-238-1601
Fax: 619-238-1613
Email: ofh@cts.com
Santa Ana, California Office: 1314 West Fifth Street, Suite C, 92703.
Telephone: 714-836-9777.
Fax: 714-954-1156.
Riverside, California Office: 4361 Latham Street, Suite 240, 92501.
Telephone: 909-683-2485.
Fax: 909-683-1064.

MEMBERS OF FIRM
Douglas F. Olins   Barrett J. Foerster (A P.C.)
Dennis J. Hayes
ASSOCIATES
Laura H. Miller   Karen L. Cote
John C. Zucconi   (Resident, Riverside Office)
Barbara J. Ginsberg
  (Resident, Santa Ana Office)

For full biographical listings, see the Martindale-Hubbell Law Directory

PIKE & SUMNER, A PROFESSIONAL CORPORATION (AV)

520 West Ash Street, Suite 200, 92101
Telephone: 619-238-1234
Telecopier: 619-238-0127
Email: info@pslaw.com *URL:* http://www.pslaw.com

(See Next Column)

Gary E. Pike   Leann A. Sumner

For full biographical listings, see the Martindale-Hubbell Law Directory

VELTMANN & LETO (AV)

1620 Fifth Avenue, Suite 700, 92101-2743
Telephone: 619-232-7384
FAX: 619-232-2236

MEMBERS OF FIRM
James S. Veltmann   Nicholas A. Leto, Jr.
ASSOCIATES
Stephen R. Murphy   Neill M. Marangi
Reference: Bank of Southern California.

For full biographical listings, see the Martindale-Hubbell Law Directory

---

SAN FRANCISCO,* San Francisco Co.

G. WILLIAM FILLEY (AV)

115 Sansome Street, Suite 1100, 94104
Telephone: 415-956-5912
Fax: 415-982-3181
Email: scottorino@aol.com

For full biographical listings, see the Martindale-Hubbell Law Directory

MACINNIS, DONNER & KOPLOWITZ (AV)

Suite 222, 465 California Street, 94104
Telephone: 415-434-2400
FAX: 415-433-1917

MEMBERS OF FIRM
James Martin MacInnis   Conrad Donner
(1914-1979)   Edward A. Koplowitz

For full biographical listings, see the Martindale-Hubbell Law Directory

LAW OFFICES OF LAWRENCE W. THORPE (AV)

115 Sansome, Suite 1100, 94104
Telephone: 415-981-3111
Telecopier: 415-982-3181
Email: LWTHORPE@AOL.COM

Julia M. Tracy
LEGAL SUPPORT PERSONNEL
PARALEGAL/CONSULTANT
Jan Caldwell Thorpe, M.F.C.C.

For full biographical listings, see the Martindale-Hubbell Law Directory

---

SAN JOSE,* Santa Clara Co.

DOK, LEVY & PERRIN (AV)

An Association of Attorneys including a Professional Corporation
1550 The Alameda, Suite 300, 95126
Telephone: 408-287-7790
Fax: 408-280-5748

William L. Dok (Inc.)   Michael R. Levy
Lawrence J. Perrin

For full biographical listings, see the Martindale-Hubbell Law Directory

HAMMER JACOBS & THROGMORTON (AV)

10 Almaden Boulevard, 10th Floor, 95113-2237
Telephone: 408-297-8400
Fax: 408-297-8488

Philip L. Hammer   Jamie J. Throgmorton
Paul E. Jacobs   Natalie T. Daprile
Jane Meredith Ohringer

For full biographical listings, see the Martindale-Hubbell Law Directory

McMANIS, FAULKNER & MORGAN (AV)

160 West Santa Clara Street, 10th Floor, 95113
Telephone: 408-279-8700
Fax: 408-279-3244; 408-279-0494
Email: mfm@mfmlaw.com

MEMBERS OF FIRM
James McManis   William Faulkner
Donelle Morgan
ASSOCIATES
Nora Rousso   Michael Reedy
Lisa Herrick   Douglas Watanabe
Kelly McHaffie

For full biographical listings, see the Martindale-Hubbell Law Directory

SAN MATEO, San Mateo Co.

NORRIS & ROSSI (AV)

777 Mariners Island Boulevard, Suite 575, P.O. Box 5446, 94404-1588
Telephone: 415-571-0600
Fax: 415-571-0835

MEMBERS OF FIRM
Lana L. Norris   Anne Marie Rossi
ASSOCIATES
Audrey Braker Fox   Julie A. Flynn
Kerry L. Moorhead

For full biographical listings, see the Martindale-Hubbell Law Directory

*SAN RAFAEL,** Marin Co.

RICHARD BARRY AND SHARON MAH (AV)

An Association - Not a Partnership
Courthouse Square, 1000 Fourth Street, Suite 350, P.O. Box 151257, 94915-1257
Telephone: 415-453-0360
Fax: 415-453-9193

Richard F. Barry   Sharon F. Mah

For full biographical listings, see the Martindale-Hubbell Law Directory

RAGGHIANTI • FREITAS • MONTOBBIO • WALLACE LLP (AV)

874 Fourth Street, Suite D, 94901
Telephone: 415-453-9433
Fax: 415-453-8269

Gary T. Ragghianti   J. Randolph Wallace
David P. Freitas   Patrick M. Macias
J. Mark Montobbio   Robert F. Epstein
John Ralph Thomas

For full biographical listings, see the Martindale-Hubbell Law Directory

SAN RAMON, Contra Costa Co.

LEONARD D. WEILER A PROFESSIONAL CORPORATION (AV)

Suite 200, Two Annabel Lane, 94583
Telephone: 510-275-0855
Telecopier: 510-830-8787

Leonard D. Weiler

Thomas G. Borst

For full biographical listings, see the Martindale-Hubbell Law Directory

*SANTA ANA,** Orange Co.

FERRUZZO & FERRUZZO (AV)

A Partnership of Professional Corporations
2114 North Broadway, 92706
Telephone: 714-834-9322
Telecopier: 714-834-9358

MEMBERS OF FIRM
Thomas G. Ferruzzo (A Professional Corporation)   James K. Leese (A Professional Corporation)
James J. Ferruzzo (A Professional Corporation)
ASSOCIATES
John R. Pelle   Maria Ann Newkirk
Dirk E. Petchul   Paul A. Madruga
Gregory J. Ferruzzo   Lisa L. Schultz
OF COUNSEL
M. Susan Watson

For full biographical listings, see the Martindale-Hubbell Law Directory

*SANTA BARBARA,** Santa Barbara Co.

ANGLE, CARLSON, GOLDRICK & ROBERTS (AV)

A Partnership including a Professional Corporation
200 East Carrillo Street, Suite 310, 93101
Telephone: 805-963-7400
Fax: 805-963-7610

Robert O. Angle   Miles T. Goldrick
Arthur W. Carlson (A P.C.)   Paul A. Roberts
OF COUNSEL
Georgia C. McDermott

For full biographical listings, see the Martindale-Hubbell Law Directory

ESKIN & JACKSON (AV)

1111 Chapala Street, Suite 310, 93101
Telephone: 805-965-8550
Fax: 805-564-2170
Ventura, California Office: 830 East Santa Clara Street.
Telephone: 805-641-5888.
Fax: 805-641-5877.

MEMBERS OF FIRM
George C. Eskin   Hannah-Beth Jackson
ASSOCIATE
Joanne S. Sumalpong

For full biographical listings, see the Martindale-Hubbell Law Directory

SANTA MONICA, Los Angeles Co.

J. MICHAEL KELLY & ASSOCIATES A PROFESSIONAL CORPORATION (AV)

233 Wilshire Boulevard, Suite 400, P.O. Box 1490, 90406-1490
Telephone: 310-393-0236
Email: JMK@clfi.com *URL:* http://www.cfli.com

J. Michael Kelly

For full biographical listings, see the Martindale-Hubbell Law Directory

TORRANCE, Los Angeles Co.

McGAUGHEY & SPIRITO (AV)

2377 Crenshaw Boulevard, Suite 310, 90501
Telephone: 310-787-8783
Fax: 310-787-9937

MEMBERS OF FIRM
Terence C. McGaughey   Joseph P. Spirito Jr.
ASSOCIATE
Steven Spitzer

Reference: Bay Cities National Bank.

For full biographical listings, see the Martindale-Hubbell Law Directory

CHRISTOPHER M. MOORE & ASSOCIATES A LAW CORPORATION (AV)

Suite 490 Union Bank Tower, 21515 Hawthorne Boulevard, 90503
Telephone: 310-540-8855
Fax: 310-316-1307
Email: chrismesq@aol.com

Christopher M. Moore

Sharon A. Bryan   Rebecca Lee Tomlinson Schroff
Julia A. Stanton

For full biographical listings, see the Martindale-Hubbell Law Directory

TUSTIN, Orange Co.

STAPLETON & STAPLETON, A PROFESSIONAL ASSOCIATION (AV)

Irvine Plaza Building, Suite 114, 17621 Irvine Boulevard, 92680-3130
Telephone: 714-832-8003
Fax: 714-832-2007

Marlin G. Stapleton   Marlin G. Stapleton, Jr.

For full biographical listings, see the Martindale-Hubbell Law Directory

*VENTURA,** Ventura Co.

ESKIN & JACKSON (AV)

830 East Santa Clara Street, 93001
Telephone: 805-641-5888
Fax: 805-641-5877
Santa Barbara, California Office: 1111 Chapala Street, Suite 310.
Telephone: 805-965-8550.
Fax: 805-564-2170.

MEMBERS OF FIRM
George C. Eskin   Hannah-Beth Jackson
ASSOCIATE
Joanne S. Sumalpong

For full biographical listings, see the Martindale-Hubbell Law Directory

SMITH AND NOWLIN (AV)

950 County Square Drive, Suite 108, 93003
Telephone: 805-650-8188
FAX: 805-650-0741

Leonard H. Smith   Herbert D. Nowlin

For full biographical listings, see the Martindale-Hubbell Law Directory

Ventura—Continued

TAYLOR MCCORD, A LAW CORPORATION (AV)

721 East Main Street, P.O. Box 1477, 93002
Telephone: 805-648-4700
Fax: 805-653-6124

Richard L. Taylor   Robert L. McCord, Jr.
                    David L. Praver

Patrick Cherry   Susan D. Siple
                    Rebbecca F. Calderwood
LEGAL SUPPORT PERSONNEL
PARALEGALS
Stephanie Gibson   Adele Rubino
                    Diane Lovato

For full biographical listings, see the Martindale-Hubbell Law Directory

WHIPPLE AND VIELE, A PROFESSIONAL LAW CORPORATION (AV)

60 South California Street, 93001
Telephone: 805-643-8658; 643-8422
Fax: 805-653-6079

Terry James Viele

References: Wells Fargo Bank; American Commercial Bank.

For full biographical listings, see the Martindale-Hubbell Law Directory

VICTORVILLE, San Bernardino Co.

LYNN E. ZUMBRUNN A LAW CORPORATION (AV)

14335 Park Avenue, Suite A, 92392-2365
Telephone: 619-245-5333
Fax: 619-245-2000

Lynn Edward Zumbrunn

James Bruce Minton   Gregory L. Zumbrunn
References: Wells Fargo Bank; Desert Community Bank.

For full biographical listings, see the Martindale-Hubbell Law Directory

VISTA, San Diego Co.

JAMES A. HENNENHOEFER A PROFESSIONAL CORPORATION (AV)

316 South Melrose Drive, Suite 200, 92083-6618
Telephone: 619-941-2260
Facsimile: 619-945-1805
Email: jahesq@aol.com

James A. Hennenhoefer   Rolf G. Steeve, Jr.
LEGAL SUPPORT PERSONNEL
Claudia Vess   Hanne Mallard

For full biographical listings, see the Martindale-Hubbell Law Directory

WALNUT CREEK, Contra Costa Co.

R. KENT BREWER (AV)

1981 North Broadway, Suite 405, 94596
Telephone: 510-934-8988
Fax: 510-943-6894

For full biographical listings, see the Martindale-Hubbell Law Directory

WOODLAND HILLS, Los Angeles Co.

LAURENCE R. GOLDMAN (AV)

21700 Oxnard Street, Suite 1750, 91367
Telephone: 818-888-0299
Facsimile: 818-888-5602

For full biographical listings, see the Martindale-Hubbell Law Directory

COLORADO

*BOULDER,** Boulder Co.

HOWARD BITTMAN (AV)

1406 Pearl Street, Suite 200, 80302
Telephone: 303-443-2281
Fax: 303-443-2862

For full biographical listings, see the Martindale-Hubbell Law Directory

THORBURN, SAKOL & THRONE (AV)

A Partnership of Professional Corporations
255 Canyon Boulevard at Cloud Creek, Suite 100, 80302-4920
Telephone: 303-449-1873
Fax: 303-447-9840

MEMBER OF FIRM
Barre M. Sakol (P.C.)

Reference: Bank One of Boulder.

For full biographical listings, see the Martindale-Hubbell Law Directory

*DELTA,** Delta Co.

THE WENDT LAW OFFICE, P.C. (AV)

540 Main Street, Suite 101, P.O. Box 94, 81416
Telephone: 970-874-8744
Fax: 970-874-3470

John A. F. Wendt, Jr.

Representative Clients: Western Community Bank; Century 21-Paradise Valley Realty; DuFon Land & Cattle Co.; Hellman Motor Co.; Uncompahgre Development Corp.; Colorado West Orthopaedics and Sports Medicine.

*DENVER,** Denver Co.

CANGES, IWASHKO & BETHKE, A PROFESSIONAL CORPORATION (AV)

303 East 17th Avenue Suite 400, 80203-1261
Telephone: 303-860-1900
Fax: 303-860-1665

E. Michael Canges   Nina A. Iwashko
                    Erich L. Bethke

Stephen R. Fatzinger   James S. Bailey
Reference: Norwest Bank Denver.

For full biographical listings, see the Martindale-Hubbell Law Directory

DAVIS & WEINSTEIN (AV)

Suite 2600, 1600 Broadway, 80202
Telephone: 303-861-4166

Wendy W. Davis   Erica Richardson Kemmerley

For full biographical listings, see the Martindale-Hubbell Law Directory

DIXON AND SNOW, P.C. (AV)

425 South Cherry Street, Suite 1000, 80222
Telephone: 303-394-2200
FAX: 303-394-2340

Jerre W. Dixon   Rod W. Snow
                    Steven Janiszewski

For full biographical listings, see the Martindale-Hubbell Law Directory

STEPHEN J. HARHAI (AV)

1928 East Eighteenth Avenue, 80206
Telephone: 303-329-8300
Fax: 303-329-8119
Email: harhai@msn.com

ASSOCIATE
Suzzanne Griffiths

For full biographical listings, see the Martindale-Hubbell Law Directory

ROBERT T. HINDS, JR. AND ASSOCIATES, P.C. (AV)

600 South Cherry Street Penthouse Suite 1400, 80222-1714
Telephone: 303-320-0300
Fax: 303-321-1121

Robert T. Hinds, Jr.

Ray L. Weaver   Lucy Hojo Denson
                    Robert T. Hinds, III
OF COUNSEL
Dr. Howard I. Rosenberg

For full biographical listings, see the Martindale-Hubbell Law Directory

STANLEY G. LIPKIN (AV)

1380 Lawrence Street, Suite 300, 80204
Telephone: 303-446-8300
FAX: 303-572-7804

ASSOCIATE
Kerry D. Mason

For full biographical listings, see the Martindale-Hubbell Law Directory

Denver—Continued

THOMAS P. MALONE & ASSOCIATES, P.C. (AV)

Suite 1502, 950 South Cherry Street, 80222
Telephone: 303-757-8300
Fax: 303-757-8001

Thomas P. Malone

Judith C. Bregman

For full biographical listings, see the Martindale-Hubbell Law Directory

FRANK McGUANE & ASSOCIATES, P.C. (AV)

Suite 910-N, The Galleria, 720 South Colorado Boulevard, 80222
Telephone: 303-691-9600
Fax: 303-691-9900
Email: McGuaneAsc@AOL.com

Frank L. McGuane, Jr.

Kathleen A. Hogan

For full biographical listings, see the Martindale-Hubbell Law Directory

MYERS, BRADLEY AND DEVITT, P.C. (AV)

Suite 420, 4704 Harlan Street, 80212
Telephone: 303-433-8527
Fax: 303-433-8219

| Frederick J. Myers | Jerald J. Devitt |
| Jon T. Bradley | Randall C. Arp |

OF COUNSEL
Kent E. Hanson

Reference: Bank One Lakeside Banking Center.

For full biographical listings, see the Martindale-Hubbell Law Directory

---

LAKEWOOD, Jefferson Co.

POLIDORI, GEROME, FRANKLIN AND JACOBSON, L.L.C. (AV)

Suite 300, 550 South Wadsworth Boulevard, 80226
Telephone: 303-936-3300
Fax: 303-936-0125

| Gary L. Polidori | Dennis J. Jacobson |
| Peter L. Franklin | |

| Lesleigh W. Monahan | Barry J. Seidenfeld |

For full biographical listings, see the Martindale-Hubbell Law Directory

---

LITTLETON, * Arapahoe Co.

COX, MUSTAIN-WOOD, WALKER & SCHUMACHER, LLC (AV)

6601 South University Boulevard, 80121
Telephone: 303-730-0067
Fax: 303-730-0344

MEMBERS OF FIRM
| Mary Jane Truesdell Cox | Randall C. Mustain-Wood |
| James C. Schumacher | |

J. Brita Darling
OF COUNSEL
Timothy B. Walker (P.C.)

For full biographical listings, see the Martindale-Hubbell Law Directory

---

MONTROSE, * Montrose Co.

EDWARD D. DURHAM (AV)

524 South First Street, P.O. Box 1721, 81402
Telephone: 970-249-2274
Fax: 970-249-6482

Reference: Norwest Bank of Montrose.

For full biographical listings, see the Martindale-Hubbell Law Directory

---

CONNECTICUT

GREENWICH, Fairfield Co.

COHEN & MARLOW (AV)

779 North Street, 06831
Telephone: 203-622-8787
Fax: 203-622-8798
New Haven, Connecticut Office: 157 Church Street, P.O. Box 1800.
Telephone: 203-782-9440.

(See Next Column)

| Gary I. Cohen | Lee Marlow |

For full biographical listings, see the Martindale-Hubbell Law Directory

HOLLAND KAUFMANN & BARTELS, LLC (AV)

289 Greenwich Avenue, 06830-6595
Telephone: 203-869-5600
Fax: 203-869-4648

Alexander J. Holland	Amy K. Wilfert
Charles B. Kaufmann, III	Harold R. Burke
Philip H. Bartels	Jean Mills Aranha
Beth K. Hansson	Lori E. Romano
	John C. Fusco

For full biographical listings, see the Martindale-Hubbell Law Directory

IVEY, BARNUM & O'MARA, LLC (AV)

Meridian Building, 170 Mason Street, P.O. Box 1689, 06830
Telephone: 203-661-6000
Telecopier: 203-661-9462

MEMBERS OF FIRM
Michael J. Allen	Donat C. Marchand
Robert C. Barnum, Jr.	Miles F. McDonald, Jr.
Edward D. Cosden, Jr.	Edwin J. O'Mara, Jr.
Wilmot L. Harris, Jr.	Remy A. Rodas
William I. Haslun II	Gregory A. Saum
Michael J. Jones	Lorraine Slavin
Edward T. Krumeich, Jr.	Steven B. Steinmetz

ASSOCIATES
Paul G. Amicucci	Melissa Townsend Klauberg
Stephan B. Grozinger	Cristin L. Rothfuss
Juerg A. Heim	Alan S. Rubenstein
Jennifer B. Kallenbach	Sheryl L. Sensale
	(Not admitted in CT)

OF COUNSEL
| James W. Cuminale | Jennifer D. Port |
| Philip R. McKnight | (Not admitted in CT) |

For full biographical listings, see the Martindale-Hubbell Law Directory

---

HARTFORD, * Hartford Co.

JACKSON, O'KEEFE AND PHELAN (AV)

36 Russ Street, 06106-1571
Telephone: 860-278-4040
Fax: 860-527-2500
West Hartford, Connecticut Office: 62 LaSalle Road.
Telephone: 860-521-7500.
Fax: 860-561-5399.
Bethlehem, Connecticut Office: 423 Munger Lane. Telephone/ *Fax:* 203-266-5255.

MEMBERS OF FIRM
Jay W. Jackson	Michael E. Riley
Andrew J. O'Keefe	Peter K. O'Keefe
Denise Martino Phelan	Philip R. Dunn, Jr.
Matthew J. O'Keefe	Kathryn M. Cunningham
	Joseph M. Busher, Jr.

Representative Clients: Travelers Aetna Property Casualty Co.; ITT Hartford; Liberty Mutual Insurance Co.; Connecticut Medical Insurance Co.

For full biographical listings, see the Martindale-Hubbell Law Directory

SOROKIN SOROKIN GROSS HYDE & WILLIAMS P.C. (AV)

One Corporate Center, 06103
Telephone: 860-525-6645
Fax: 860-522-1781
Simsbury, Connecticut Office: 730 Hopmeadow Street.
Telephone: 860-651-9348.
Rocky Hill, Connecticut Office: 2360 Main Street.
Telephone: 860-563-9305.
Fax: 860-529-6931.

John J. Bracken III	Lewis Rabinovitz
Lisa A. Magliochetti	Richard D. Tulisano
	(Resident, Rocky Hill Office)

OF COUNSEL
Ethel Silver Sorokin

For Complete List of Firm Personnel, See General Section

For full biographical listings, see the Martindale-Hubbell Law Directory

---

NEW HAVEN, * New Haven Co.

COHEN & MARLOW (AV)

157 Church Street, P.O. Box 1800, 06507-1800
Telephone: 203-782-9440
Facsimile: 203-772-0583
Greenwich, Connecticut Office: 779 North Street.
Telephone: 203-622-8787.

(See Next Column)

COHEN & MARLOW—*Continued*

MEMBERS OF FIRM

Gary I. Cohen   Lee Marlow

For full biographical listings, see the Martindale-Hubbell Law Directory

GREENFIELD AND MURPHY (AV)

234 Church Street, P.O. Box 1103, 06504-1103
Telephone: 203-787-6711
Telecopier: 203-777-6442

MEMBERS OF FIRM

James R. Greenfield   Helen D. Murphy
Maureen M. Murphy

Reference: First Fidelity Bank.

For full biographical listings, see the Martindale-Hubbell Law Directory

GERALD H. KAHN, P.C. (AV)

261 Bradley Street, 06511
Telephone: 203-777-0506
Facsimile: 203-776-1107

Gerald H. Kahn

For full biographical listings, see the Martindale-Hubbell Law Directory

ROSEN & DOLAN, P.C. (AV)

400 Orange Street, 06511
Telephone: 203-787-3513
Fax: 203-789-1605
Email: davidrosen@counsel.com
Email: spincus@counsel.com

Edward J. Dolan

Reference: Peoples Bank.

For Complete List of Firm Personnel, See General Section

For full biographical listings, see the Martindale-Hubbell Law Directory

JEAN L. WELTY (AV)

385 Orange Street, P.O. Box 1662, 06507
Telephone: 203-781-0877
Fax: 203-781-0899

Reference: Peoples Bank.

For full biographical listings, see the Martindale-Hubbell Law Directory

STAMFORD, Fairfield Co.

COHEN & MARLOW

(See New Haven)

PIAZZA & MELMED (AV)

112 Prospect Street, P.O. Box 15390, 06901
Telephone: 203-348-2465
Fax: 203-964-9509

MEMBERS OF FIRM

Anthony A. Piazza   Julian K. Melmed

Alan Scott Pickel   Angela M. Trombly
Tara C. F. Ryan

For full biographical listings, see the Martindale-Hubbell Law Directory

SILVER, GOLUB & TEITELL (AV)

184 Atlantic Street, P.O. Box 389, 06904
Telephone: 203-325-4491
Fax: 203-325-3769

MEMBERS OF FIRM

Richard A. Silver   Elaine T. Silver

For full biographical listings, see the Martindale-Hubbell Law Directory

WOFSEY, ROSEN, KWESKIN & KURIANSKY (AV)

600 Summer Street, 06901
Telephone: 203-327-2300
Fax: 203-967-9273

MEMBERS OF FIRM

Abraham Wofsey (1915-1944)   Edward M. Kweskin
Michael Wofsey (1927-1951)   David M. Cohen
David M. Rosen (1926-1967)   Marshall Goldberg
Julius B. Kuriansky (1910-1992)   Stephen A. Finn
Monroe Silverman   Judith Rosenberg
Emanuel Margolis   Mark H. Henderson
Howard C. Kaplan   Steven D. Grushkin
Anthony R. Lorenzo   Matthew J. Forstadt

(See Next Column)

OF COUNSEL

Saul Kwartin   Sydney C. Kweskin (Retired)

ASSOCIATES

Joseph Brachfeld   Eric M. Higgins
John J.L. Chobor   Valerie E. Maze
Steven M. Frederick   Randall M. Skigen
Joy A. Katz   Peter J. Schaffer
Galit Kierkut   Robert W. Finke

Representative Clients: Banque Paribas; Benenson Realty; Cellular Information Systems, Inc.; The Chase Manhattan Bank; First County Bank; Hartford Provision Co.; Louis Dreyfus Corp.; Norwalk Federation of Teachers; People's Bank; Ridgeway Shopping Center.

For full biographical listings, see the Martindale-Hubbell Law Directory

WEST HARTFORD, Hartford Co.

BERMAN, BOURNS & CURRIE, LLC (AV)

970 Farmington Avenue, P.O. Box 271837, 06127-1837
Telephone: 860-232-4471
Fax: 860-523-4605

John A. Berman   Courtney B. Bourns
John K. Currie

Mary Beth Anderson   Robert W. Storm, Jr.

For full biographical listings, see the Martindale-Hubbell Law Directory

WESTPORT, Fairfield Co.

LESLIE BYELAS (AV)

1804 Post Road East, 06880
Telephone: 203-259-0599
Fax: 203-255-2570

For full biographical listings, see the Martindale-Hubbell Law Directory

NUSBAUM & PARRINO, P.C. (AV)

212 Post Road West, 06880
Telephone: 203-226-8181
Fax: 203-454-9937

Edward Nusbaum   Thomas P. Parrino

Laura J. Lewis

OF COUNSEL

Susan A. Moch

For full biographical listings, see the Martindale-Hubbell Law Directory

RUTKIN AND OLDHAM, L.L.C (AV)

323 Riverside Avenue, P.O. Box 295, 06881
Telephone: 203-227-7301
Fax: 203-222-9295

Arnold H. Rutkin   Sarah S. Oldham

OF COUNSEL

Kathleen A. Hogan

For full biographical listings, see the Martindale-Hubbell Law Directory

WEISMAN & LUBELL (AV)

5 Sylvan Road South, P.O. Box 3184, 06880
Telephone: 203-226-8307
Telecopier: 203-221-7279

MEMBERS OF FIRM

Lawrence P. Weisman   Ellen B. Lubell

Debra B. Wolfert-Marino

For full biographical listings, see the Martindale-Hubbell Law Directory

DELAWARE

WILMINGTON,* New Castle Co.

TRZUSKOWSKI, KIPP, KELLEHER & PEARCE, P.A. (AV)

1020 North Bancroft Parkway, P.O. Box 429, 19899-0429
Telephone: 302-571-1782
Fax: 302-571-1638

Daniel F. Kelleher

For full biographical listings, see the Martindale-Hubbell Law Directory

DISTRICT OF COLUMBIA

WASHINGTON, D.C. Co.

DECKELBAUM OGENS & FISCHER, CHARTERED (AV)

1140 Connecticut Avenue, N.W., 20036
Telephone: 202-223-1474
Fax: 202-293-1471
Bethesda, Maryland Office: 6701 Democracy Boulevard.
Telephone: 301-564-5100.

Nelson Deckelbaum	Deborah E. Reiser
Ronald L. Ogens	Charles A. Moster
Lawrence H. Fischer	Andrew J. Shedlock, III

Ronald G. Scheraga	Phyllis Lea Bean
Bryn Hope Sherman	Darryl Alan Feldman
Thomas Peter Mann	(Not admitted in DC)
(Not admitted in DC)	

Representative Clients: The Charles E. Smith Companies; The Trammell Crow Co.
References: Franklin National Bank; Century National Bank.

For full biographical listings, see the Martindale-Hubbell Law Directory

---

FELDESMAN, TUCKER, LEIFER, FIDELL & BANK (AV)

2001 L Street, N.W., Suite 300, 20036
Telephone: 202-466-8960
Telefax: 202-293-8103
Rockville, Maryland Office: One Church Street, Suite 800.
Telephone: 301-279-6770.
Arlington, Virginia Office: 2009 North 14th Street, Suite 610.
Telephone: 703-841-4245.

Margaret H. Long (1940-1990)
MEMBERS OF FIRM

James L. Feldesman	Pamela Borland Forbes
Marna Susan Tucker	Mary S. Pence
Jacqueline C. Leifer	Jonathan M. Dana
Eugene R. Fidell	Martha JP McQuade
Rita M. Bank	Roger A. Schwartz

Beth Goodman
ASSOCIATES

Tanya Ann Harvey	Bruce F. Hoffmeister
Michael B. Glomb	David P. Sheldon
Edward T. Waters	(Not admitted in DC)
Margaret J. McKinney	Robin Ann Clark
Lisa V. Terry	(Not admitted in DC)
(Not admitted in DC)	Nancy Joan Sardeson
Deborah Lynn Pollock	(Not admitted in DC)
Karen Burke	Garrett Lamont Lee
Kelly A. Sweeney	(Not admitted in DC)
(Not admitted in DC)	Nancy Evert

Maria-Cristina Fernandez

For full biographical listings, see the Martindale-Hubbell Law Directory

---

KUDER, SMOLLAR & FRIEDMAN, P.C. (AV)

Suite 200, 1925 K Street, N.W., 20006
Telephone: 202-331-7522
Fax: 202-331-0388
Email: ksflaw@lchange.com
Rockville, Maryland Office: 414 Hungerford Drive, Suite 456.
Telephone: 301-340-9090.

Armin U. Kuder	Susan Meyers Friedman
Paul R. Smollar	Theresa M. Mihalik

Jeffrey L. Poersch
OF COUNSEL
John V. Long

For full biographical listings, see the Martindale-Hubbell Law Directory

---

THE LEWIS LAW FIRM A PROFESSIONAL CORPORATION (AV)

Suite 900 One Thousand Connecticut Avenue, N.W., 20036
Telephone: 202-429-9400
Fax: 202-775-0836
Fairfax, Virginia Office: Suite 500, 10306 Eaton Place.
Telephone: 703-691-8686.
Rockville, Maryland Office: Suite 1700, 51 Monroe Street.

Glenn C. Lewis	Leslie Weber Hoffman

Edouard Jean-Pierre Bouquet	Keira Lynne Schwartz
Wendy Helene Schwartz	Kristen E. Timpf
Daniel G. Dannenbaum	John A. Wasowicz (Resident,
Hadrian N. Hatfield	Fairfax, Virginia Office)
Linda D. Regenhardt	Robin L. Robb

(See Next Column)

LEGAL SUPPORT PERSONNEL

Carol L. Andrews (Paralegal)	Dion Elizabeth Lapham
	(Paralegal)

OF COUNSEL
David L. Good

For full biographical listings, see the Martindale-Hubbell Law Directory

---

LIOTTA, DRANITZKE & ENGEL (AV)

Suite 250, 1666 Connecticut Avenue, N.W., 20009
Telephone: 202-797-7700
Facsimile: 202-797-2354

MEMBERS OF FIRM

Alan Dranitzke	Robert Case Liotta

Diana R. Engel
ASSOCIATE
Alisa A. Wilkins

For full biographical listings, see the Martindale-Hubbell Law Directory

---

WITT, NOLAN & BINDEMAN (AV)

Suite 600, 1140 Connecticut Avenue, N.W., 20036
Telephone: 202-296-3333
Telecopier: 202-296-0416
Chevy Chase, Maryland Office: Suite 801, 5530 Wisconsin Avenue.
Telephone: 202-296-3333.

MEMBERS OF FIRM

Hal Witt	James G. Nolan

Sherry A. Bindeman
ASSOCIATE
Marjorie Just

For full biographical listings, see the Martindale-Hubbell Law Directory

---

FLORIDA

BOCA RATON, Palm Beach Co.

JOEL H. FELDMAN, P.A. (AV)

Suite 207, Tower D, Sanctuary Centre, 4800 North Federal Highway, 33431
Telephone: 561-392-4400
Fax: 561-392-1521

Joel H. Feldman

Andrew Merlo

For full biographical listings, see the Martindale-Hubbell Law Directory

---

FURR AND COHEN, P.A. (AV)

Suite 412, 1499 W. Palmetto Park Road, 33486
Telephone: 407-395-0500
Broward: 954-421-0300 0
Fax: 407-338-7532

Robert C. Furr	Charles I. Cohen

Leslie Scott Osborne	Jordi Guso
Lisa Judith Chaiklin	Brendan A. Barry

OF COUNSEL
C. William Berger

For full biographical listings, see the Martindale-Hubbell Law Directory

---

WEISS & HANDLER, P.A. (AV)

Suite 218A, One Boca Place, 2255 Glades Road, 33431-7313
Telephone: 407-997-9995
Broward: 954-421-5101
Palm Beach: 407-734-8008
Telecopier: 407-997-5280

Howard I. Weiss	Henry B. Handler

Donald Feldman	Marissa I. Laakso
David K. Friedman	Mark R. Osherow
Carol A. Kartagener	Howard M. Rudolph (Resident,
	West Palm Beach Office)

OF COUNSEL

Malcolm L. Stein	Stanley E. Preiser
(Not admitted in FL)	(Not admitted in FL)
Raoul Lionel Felder	
(Not admitted in FL)	

For full biographical listings, see the Martindale-Hubbell Law Directory

BRADENTON,* Manatee Co.

LARRY K. COLEMAN (AV)

The Riverview Center, Suite 100, 1111 Third Avenue West, 34205
Telephone: 941-747-1234
Fax: 941-747-1236

LEGAL SUPPORT PERSONNEL
Nancy A. Martin (Certified Legal Assistant)

For full biographical listings, see the Martindale-Hubbell Law Directory

GRIMES GOEBEL GRIMES HAWKINS & GLADFELTER, P.A. (AV)

The Professional Building, 1023 Manatee Avenue West, P.O. Box 1550, 34206
Telephone: 941-748-0151
Fax: 941-748-0158

John D. Hawkins   William S. Galvano
            Douglas A. Peebles

Counsel for: Schroeder Manatee Inc. (Agriculture and Land Development); Pursley, Inc., (Horticulture, Retail and Land Development); Lombardo & Skipper, Inc. (Civil Engineers); CCI Environmental Services, Inc. (Environmental Consultants); Creekwood Investors, Ltd.; Old Hyde Park Village Center, Ltd.; First Federal Savings & Loan Association of Florida.
Approved Attorneys for: Lawyers Title Insurance Corp.; Chicago Title Insurance Co.; Attorneys Title Insurance Fund.

For Complete List of Firm Personnel, See General Section

For full biographical listings, see the Martindale-Hubbell Law Directory

McGUIRE, PRATT, MASIO & FARRANCE, P.A. (AV)

Suite 600, 1001 3rd Avenue West, P.O. Box 1866, 34206
Telephone: 941-748-7076
Fax: 941-747-9774

Hugh E. McGuire, Jr.   Carol A. Masio
Charles J. Pratt, Jr.   Robert A. Farrance
            John W. Kaklis
            OF COUNSEL
            Carter H. Parry

Reference: Barnett Bank of Manatee County.

For full biographical listings, see the Martindale-Hubbell Law Directory

BROOKSVILLE,* Hernando Co.

MERRITT & MASON, P.A. (AV)

101 South Main Street, P.O. Box 1900, 34605-1900
Telephone: 352-796-0795
Telecopier: 352-796-0235
Spring Hill, Florida Office: 4074 Commercial Way (U.S. 19).
Telephone: 352-686-1028.

Daniel B. Merritt, Sr.   Joseph M. Mason, Jr.

John M. Keller   Daniel B. Merritt, Jr.

For full biographical listings, see the Martindale-Hubbell Law Directory

CLEARWATER,* Pinellas Co.

WAYNE J. BOYER, P.A. (AV)

P.O. Box 10655, 34617-8655
Telephone: 813-733-2154
Fax: 813-734-0333

            Wayne J. Boyer

            Joann Rowe Divito
            LEGAL SUPPORT PERSONNEL
Linda D. Abbott   Patricia A. Miller
(Certified Legal Assistant)   (Certified Legal Assistant)

For full biographical listings, see the Martindale-Hubbell Law Directory

ANN LOUGHRIDGE KERR (AV)

425 South Garden Avenue, 34616
Telephone: 813-443-6787
Fax: 813-442-1251
Tampa, Florida Office: 601 East Twiggs Street, Suite 200.
Telephone: 813-229-7251.
Fax: 813-442-1251.

For full biographical listings, see the Martindale-Hubbell Law Directory

N. DAVID KORONES ATTORNEY AT LAW, P.A. (AV)

Plymouth Plaza, Suite 104, 26750 U.S. 19 North, 34623
Telephone: 813-724-1011
Fax: 813-724-3708

(See Next Column)

N. David Korones
LEGAL SUPPORT PERSONNEL
Jacqueline Hardy (Legal Assistant)
Reference: Citizens Bank.

For full biographical listings, see the Martindale-Hubbell Law Directory

FORT LAUDERDALE,* Broward Co.

AMLONG & AMLONG, P.A. (AV)

Second Floor, 500 Northeast Fourth Street, 33301
Telephone: 954-462-1983
FAX: 954-523-3192

Karen Coolman Amlong   William R. Amlong

Robyn S. Hankins   Sheryl T. Simon
Walter W. Palmer   Lisa Beth Stern

For full biographical listings, see the Martindale-Hubbell Law Directory

SHELLEY M. MITCHELL (AV)

Suite 103, 212 S.E. 8th Street, 33316
Telephone: 954-523-8311
Fax: 954-523-4707

For full biographical listings, see the Martindale-Hubbell Law Directory

OPPENHEIM & PILELSKY, P.A. (AV)

1290 Weston Road, Suite 300, 33326
Telephone: 954-384-6114
Toll Free: 888-384-6114
Fax: 954-384-6115
Email: O&P@oppenheim.com *URL:* http://www.oppenheim.com

Roy D. Oppenheim   Ellen B. Pilelsky

            Monica B. Cunill

For full biographical listings, see the Martindale-Hubbell Law Directory

FORT MYERS,* Lee Co.

SHELDON E. FINMAN, P.A. (AV)

2215 First Street, P.O. Drawer 1380, 33902-1380
Telephone: 941-332-4543

            Sheldon E. Finman

For full biographical listings, see the Martindale-Hubbell Law Directory

JACKSONVILLE,* Duval Co.

MAHON & FARLEY, P.A. (AV)

350 East Adams Street, 32202
Telephone: 904-354-4300
Fax: 904-354-4658

Lacy Mahon (1891-1968)   Harry B. Mahon
            Joseph S. Farley, Jr.

References: First Union National Bank; First Guaranty Bank & Trust Co.

For full biographical listings, see the Martindale-Hubbell Law Directory

WILLIAM C. A. MOULDER, P.A. (AV)

One San Jose Place, Suite 20, 32257
Telephone: 904-262-7600
Fax: 904-262-7608

            William C. A. Moulder

References: First Guaranty Bank & Trust Company of Jacksonville; First Union Bank of Jacksonville.

For full biographical listings, see the Martindale-Hubbell Law Directory

LAW OFFICE OF BARRY S. SINOFF, P.A. (AV)

6960 Bonneval Road, Suite 202, 32216-6076
Telephone: 904-296-2299
Telecopier: 904-296-8900

            Barry S. Sinoff
            LEGAL SUPPORT PERSONNEL
            Patricia J. Abraham (Paralegal)

For full biographical listings, see the Martindale-Hubbell Law Directory

LAKE WORTH, Palm Beach Co.

RENICK, SINGER AND KAMBER (AV)

1530 North Federal Highway, 33460
Telephone: 561-582-6644
Fax: 561-533-7975

(See Next Column)

RENICK, SINGER AND KAMBER, *Lake Worth—Continued*

    Kenneth H. Renick   Cathy L. Kamber

LARGO, Pinellas Co.

LAW OFFICE MARGOT PEQUIGNOT, P.A. (AV)

1501A Belcher Road South, 34641
Telephone: 813-531-3400
Fax: 813-535-2765

        Margot Pequignot

        Rebecca A. Graham

For full biographical listings, see the Martindale-Hubbell Law Directory

---

*MIAMI,** Dade Co.

MARILYN J. W. CESARANO, P.A. (AV)

Suite 550, 999 Ponce de Leon Boulevard (Coral Gables), 33134
Telephone: 305-446-2020
Facsimile: 305-442-4371

        Marilyn J. W. Cesarano

For full biographical listings, see the Martindale-Hubbell Law Directory

IRA L. DUBITSKY, P.A. (AV)

Courthouse Tower, Suite 300, 44 West Flagler Street, 33130
Telephone: 305-374-8919
Telecopier: 305-375-0097

        Ira L. Dubitsky, Esq.

For full biographical listings, see the Martindale-Hubbell Law Directory

ANDREW HALL AND ASSOCIATES, P.A. (AV)

Penthouse, 1428 Brickell Avenue, 33131
Telephone: 305-374-5030
Fax: 305-374-5033

        Andrew C. Hall

Christopher M. David   William H. Strop
Christopher J. Dawes   Allan A. Joseph
      Douglas M. Horn

For full biographical listings, see the Martindale-Hubbell Law Directory

RUBINSTEIN, KORNIK, BLOOM & MINSKER, A PROFESSIONAL ASSOCIATION (AV)

800 Brickell Avenue, Suite 1100, 33131
Telephone: 305-371-6800
Telecopier: 305-371-5760

Jeffrey D. Rubinstein   Kenneth M. Bloom
Gary H. Kornik   Joel N. Minsker (P.A.)

Nina Zuckerman Chepp   Stacey Schrage Goldstein
      Rowena D. Reich
Reference: Sun Bank of Miami, N.A.

For full biographical listings, see the Martindale-Hubbell Law Directory

---

*NAPLES,** Collier Co.

ASBELL, COLEMAN & HO, P.A. (AV)

365 5th Avenue South, Suite 202, 34102
Telephone: 941-775-2888
Telefax: 941-775-2821

John R. Asbell   J. Michael Coleman
      Victoria M. Ho

Kristine Kennedy-Rieger   Edmond E. Koester

For full biographical listings, see the Martindale-Hubbell Law Directory

VEGA, STANLEY, ZELMAN & HANLON, P.A. (AV)

2660 Airport Road South, 34112
Telephone: 941-774-3333
Fax: 941-776-6420

        George Vega, Jr.

        Paula J. Rhoads
General Counsel for: Lely Estates; Naples Community Hospital.
Local Counsel: Quail Creek Developments.

For full biographical listings, see the Martindale-Hubbell Law Directory

---

NORTH MIAMI BEACH, Dade Co.

YOUNG, BERMAN & KARPF, PROFESSIONAL ASSOCIATION (AV)

17071 West Dixie Highway, 33160
Telephone: 305-945-1851
Fax: 305-940-4616

Burton Young   Andrew S. Berman
      Mitchell K. Karpf

Maria C. Mitropoulos-Gonzalez   Douglas P. Fremont
      OF COUNSEL
      Pedro V. Roig

For full biographical listings, see the Martindale-Hubbell Law Directory

---

NORTH PALM BEACH, Palm Beach Co.

AVIS & AVIS, P.A. (AV)

1201 U.S. Highway One, Suite 435, 33408
Telephone: 407-622-3400
Fax: 407-622-0565
Email: avislaw@gnn.com
Palm Beach, Florida Office: The Island National Bank Building. 180 Royal Palm Way, Suite 203, 33480.
Telephone: 407-659-0200.

Warren E. Avis, Jr.   Deborah K. Avis

Marina D. Petillo   Theodore T. Tarone

For full biographical listings, see the Martindale-Hubbell Law Directory

MARTIN L. HAINES, III CHARTERED (AV)

501 North Federal Highway, P.O. Box 14790, 33408
Telephone: 561-863-5400
Fax: 561-863-3420

        Martin L. Haines, III

Jon D. Newman   John F. Schutz
Approved Attorney for: Lawyers Title Guaranty Fund.

For full biographical listings, see the Martindale-Hubbell Law Directory

---

*ORLANDO,** Orange Co.

BARNETT, BARCLAY & SPRINGMANN, P.A. (AV)

501 Mariposa Street, P.O. Box 1667, 32802
Telephone: 407-425-4245
Telecopier: 407-423-4332

William B. Barnett   Bert W. Barclay
Henry B. Rothblatt (1916-1985) Franz F. Springmann

For full biographical listings, see the Martindale-Hubbell Law Directory

LAW FIRM OF STANTON L. COBB, P.A. (AV)

1617 Woodward Street, 32803
Telephone: 407-895-6966
Fax: 407-895-6955

        Stanton L. Cobb

For full biographical listings, see the Martindale-Hubbell Law Directory

J. CHENEY MASON, P.A. (AV)

Barnett Bank Center, 390 North Orange Avenue, Suite 2100, 32801
Telephone: 407-843-5785
Fax: 407-422-6858

        J. Cheney Mason

For full biographical listings, see the Martindale-Hubbell Law Directory

MICHAEL R. WALSH (AV)

326 North Fern Creek Avenue, 32803
Telephone: 407-896-9431
Fax: 407-898-2724

Reference: The First Union National Bank of Orlando, Florida.

For full biographical listings, see the Martindale-Hubbell Law Directory

---

*PENSACOLA,** Escambia Co.

JAMES D. SWEARINGEN (AV)

201 East Government Street, 32501
Telephone: 904-432-7723

For full biographical listings, see the Martindale-Hubbell Law Directory

ST. PETERSBURG, Pinellas Co.

STEIN, FORD, SCHAAF & TOWZEY, L.L.P. (AV)

501 First Avenue North, Suite 1000, 33701
Telephone: 813-894-4333
Fax: 813-894-0175; 813-822-7222

Henry A. Stein	Gary M. Schaaf
Harvey A. Ford	Phyllis J. Towzey
Paul A. Nelson	Sarah E. Williams

For full biographical listings, see the Martindale-Hubbell Law Directory

SHALIMAR, Okaloosa Co.

STEPHEN S. POCHÉ, P.A. (AV)

1270 North Eglin Parkway, Suite C-11, P.O. Box 130, 32579
Telephone: 904-651-4466
Fax: 904-651-3499

Stephen S. Poché

Tonya C. Wells

For full biographical listings, see the Martindale-Hubbell Law Directory

MICHAEL T. WEBSTER, P.A. (AV)

12 Old Ferry Road, P.O. Box 876, 32579
Telephone: 904-651-0354
Fax: 904-651-5958

Michael T. Webster

Curtis W. Brannon
LEGAL SUPPORT PERSONNEL

Hunter Webster	Rochelle Mathews
(Litigation Support)	(Legal Assistant)

For full biographical listings, see the Martindale-Hubbell Law Directory

STUART,* Martin Co.

RUSSELL J. FERRARO, JR. AND ASSOCIATES, P.A. (AV)

3601 East Ocean Boulevard, Suite 201 (Sewall's Point), 34996-6737
Telephone: 561-221-0600
FAX: 561-220-0640

Russell J. Ferraro, Jr.

Mary T. Laasanen
LEGAL SUPPORT PERSONNEL

Dorthea M. Duncan	Barbara A. Hopkins
(Certified Legal Assistant)	(Certified Legal Assistant)

For full biographical listings, see the Martindale-Hubbell Law Directory

McCARTHY, SUMMERS, BOBKO, McKEY, WOOD & SAWYER, P.A. (AV)

2081 East Ocean Boulevard, Suite 2-A, 34996
Telephone: 561-286-1700
Fax: 561-283-1803
Email: mcsumm@gate.net *URL:* http://www.gate.net/~mcsumm/

Terence P. McCarthy	John D. McKey, Jr.
Robert P. Summers	Steven J. Wood
Noel A. Bobko	Thomas R. Sawyer

Representative Clients: American Bank of Martin County; First National Bank and Trust Company of the Treasure Coast; Great Western Bank; Hydratech Utilities; Lost Lake at Hobe Sound; Taylor Creek Marina, Inc.; GBS Excavating, Inc.; Seaboard Savings Bank; Gary Player Design Group.

For full biographical listings, see the Martindale-Hubbell Law Directory

TALLAHASSEE,* Leon Co.

McFARLAIN, WILEY, CASSEDY & JONES, PROFESSIONAL ASSOCIATION (AV)

215 South Monroe Street, Suite 600, P.O. Box 2174, 32316-2174
Telephone: 904-222-2107
Telecopier: 904-222-8475

Richard C. McFarlain	Charles A. Stampelos
William B. Wiley	Linda McMullen
Marshall R. Cassedy	H. Darrell White, Jr.
Douglas P. Jones	Christopher Barkas

Harold R. Mardenborough, Jr.	Rogelio J. Fontela
Robert A. McNeely	Patrick John McGinley

For full biographical listings, see the Martindale-Hubbell Law Directory

NOVEY, MENDELSON & ADAMSON (AV)

851 East Park Avenue, 32301
Telephone: 904-224-2000
FAX: 904-222-4951
Email: jmnovey@polaris.net

Jerome M. Novey	Robert D. Mendelson
	Kristin Adamson

For full biographical listings, see the Martindale-Hubbell Law Directory

TAMPA,* Hillsborough Co.

RAYMOND A. ALLEY, JR., P.A. (AV)

805 West Azeele, 33606
Telephone: 813-251-8778
Fax: 813-254-3892

Raymond A. Alley, Jr.

Regina L. Milam
LEGAL SUPPORT PERSONNEL
Linda R. Albrecht

For full biographical listings, see the Martindale-Hubbell Law Directory

GARCIA & FIELDS, P.A. (AV)

Suite 2560 Barnett Plaza, 101 East Kennedy Boulevard, 33602
Telephone: 813-222-8500
FAX: 813-222-8520

Joseph Garcia	Lesley J. Friedsam
Robert W. Fields	Victor D. Ines
	Kristina J. Jones

Reference: Barnett Bank of Tampa.

For full biographical listings, see the Martindale-Hubbell Law Directory

MANEY, DAMSKER, HARRIS & JONES, P.A. (AV)

606 Madison Street, P.O. Box 172009, 33672-0009
Telephone: 813-228-7371
Fax: 813-223-4846

Nancy Hutcheson Harris	David A. Maney

Lorena L. Kiely	Patricia F. Kuhlman
	Stacey L. Turmel

For full biographical listings, see the Martindale-Hubbell Law Directory

SESSUMS & MASON, P.A. (AV)

307 South Magnolia Avenue, 33606
Telephone: 813-251-9200
FAX: 813-254-6841

Stephen W. Sessums	Miriam E. Mason
	Caroline Kapusta Black

LEGAL SUPPORT PERSONNEL

Mary L. McGinnis, CLA	Linda M. Kaufmann, CLA

For full biographical listings, see the Martindale-Hubbell Law Directory

TAVARES,* Lake Co.

WILLIAMS, SMITH & SUMMERS, P.A. (AV)

380 West Alfred Street, 32778
Telephone: 352-343-6655
Fax: 352-343-4267

Robert Q. Williams	Christopher J. Smith
	Gary L. Summers

Approved Attorneys for: Attorneys' Title Insurance Fund.
Reference: Sun Bank, N.A.

For full biographical listings, see the Martindale-Hubbell Law Directory

VERO BEACH,* Indian River Co.

G. RUSSELL PETERSEN, P.A. (AV)

3426 Ocean Drive, 32963
Telephone: 561-234-1501
Fax: 561-231-3923
Email: 76635.2572@compuserve.com

G. Russell Petersen

Representative Clients: General Motors Corp.; General Motors Acceptance Corp.
Reference: Sun Bank of Indian River County.

For full biographical listings, see the Martindale-Hubbell Law Directory

WEST PALM BEACH,* Palm Beach Co.

CHRISTIANSEN & JACKNIN (AV)

Suite 1010, NationsBank Tower, 1555 Palm Beach Lakes Boulevard, P.O. Box 3346, 33402
Telephone: 561-689-1888
Fax: 561-689-0586

MEMBERS OF FIRM

| John T. Christiansen | Neil B. Jagolinzer |
| Jay R. Jacknin | Eric Ash |

Clients and References Furnished by Request.

For full biographical listings, see the Martindale-Hubbell Law Directory

FARISH, FARISH & ROMANI (AV)

316 Banyan Boulevard, P.O. Box 4118, 33402
Telephone: 561-659-3500
1-800-401-4LAW
Fax: 561-655-3158

MEMBERS OF FIRM

| Joseph D. Farish (1892-1977) | Joseph D. Farish, Jr. |
| Robert V. Romani | |

ASSOCIATES

| S. Emory Rogers | Peter M. Bassaline |
| Keith R. Taylor | |

LEGAL SUPPORT PERSONNEL

Ken P. Beelner

References: 1st Union Bank; Clewiston National Bank; Barnett Bank of Palm Beach County.

For full biographical listings, see the Martindale-Hubbell Law Directory

FISHER & BENDECK, P.A. (AV)

222 Lakeview Avenue, Suite 960, 33401
Telephone: 561-832-1005
Telefax: 561-820-9375

| Jeffrey D. Fisher | Odette Marie Bendeck |

OF COUNSEL

James P. O'Flarity

For full biographical listings, see the Martindale-Hubbell Law Directory

GAMOT & FREEMAN (AV)

315 Fifth Street, 33401-3709
Telephone: 561-655-6025
Fax: 561-655-5759
Palatka, Florida Office: 415 St. Johns Avenue.
Telephone: 904-325-6239.
Fax: 904-329-9626.

| Melinda Penney Gamot | Terry N. Freeman |
| Albert J. Gamot, Jr. | |

For full biographical listings, see the Martindale-Hubbell Law Directory

LEWIS KAPNER, P.A. (AV)

Suite 1402, One Clearlake Centre, 250 Australian Avenue South, P.O. Box 1428, 33402
Telephone: 561-655-3000
Delray/Ft. Lauderdale: 305-930-9191
Fax: 561-655-8899
Email: KAPNER1@AOL.COM
Boca Raton, Florida Office: 621 Northwest 53rd Street.
Telephone: 305-930-9191.

| Lewis Kapner | Victoria A. Calebrese |
| Michael C. Spain | |

For full biographical listings, see the Martindale-Hubbell Law Directory

PRUITT & PRUITT, P.A. (AV)

Suite 400 Flagler Tower, 505 South Flagler Drive, 33401
Telephone: 407-655-8080
Fax: 407-655-4134

| William H. Pruitt | William E. Pruitt |

Reference: Flagler National Bank.

For full biographical listings, see the Martindale-Hubbell Law Directory

DONALD J. SASSER, P.A. (AV)

1800 Australian Avenue, South, Suite 203, P.O. Box 2907, 33402
Telephone: 561-689-4378
Fax: 561-689-4652

Donald J. Sasser

(See Next Column)

| Jorge M. Cestero | Thomas J. Sasser |

Reference: First Union National Bank of Florida.

For full biographical listings, see the Martindale-Hubbell Law Directory

LAW OFFICES OF ROBERT M.W. SHALHOUB, P.A. (AV)

Suite 1107, One Clearlake Center, 250 Australian Avenue South, 33401
Telephone: 561-835-1102
FAX: 561-835-1777

| Robert M. W. Shalhoub | C. Debra Welch |

For full biographical listings, see the Martindale-Hubbell Law Directory

MICHAEL P. WALSH, P.A. (AV)

501 South Flagler Drive, Suite 504, 33401
Telephone: 407-659-3989
Fax: 407-659-3822

Michael P. Walsh

For full biographical listings, see the Martindale-Hubbell Law Directory

WINTER HAVEN, Polk Co.

PETERSON & MYERS, P.A. (AV)

Suite 300, 141 5th Street N.W., P.O. Drawer 7608, 33883-7608
Telephone: 941-294-3360
Lake Wales, Florida Office: 130 East Central Avenue, P.O. Box 1079.
Telephones: 941-676-7611; 683-8942.
Lakeland, Florida Office: 100 East Main Street, P.O. Box 24628.
Telephones: 941-683-6511; 676-6934.

Philip O. Allen	Peter J. Munson
Jack P. Brandon	Corneal B. Myers
Beach A Brooks, Jr.	Cornelius B. Myers, III
Kristen Marie Buzzanca	E. Blake Paul
J. Davis Connor	Robert E. Puterbaugh
Michael S. Craig	Abel A. Putnam
Roy A. Craig, Jr.	Thomas B. Putnam, Jr.
Jacob C. Dykxhoorn	Deborah A. Ruster
Dennis P. Johnson	Stephen R. Senn
Kevin C. Knowlton	Andrea Teves Smith
Douglas A. Lockwood, III	Keith H. Wadsworth
M. Craig Massey	Kerry M. Wilson

General Counsel for: Barnett Bank of Polk County.
Representative Clients: Mutual Wholesale Co.; Barnett Banks, Inc.; Ben Hill Griffin, Inc.; Alcoma Association, Inc.
Approved Attorneys for: Attorneys' Title Insurance Fund; Federal Land Bank, Columbia, South Carolina; Equitable Life Assurance Society of the United States.

For full biographical listings, see the Martindale-Hubbell Law Directory

GEORGIA

ATLANTA,* Fulton Co.

ALEMBIK & ALEMBIK (AV)

3033 Maple Drive, N.E., 30305
Telephone: 404-261-7565
Fax: 404-264-0639

MEMBERS OF FIRM

| Judith M. Alembik | Gary M. Alembik |

References: Trust Company of Georgia; Wachovia Bank, Bank South.

For full biographical listings, see the Martindale-Hubbell Law Directory

ALEMBIK, FINE & CALLNER, P.A. (AV)

Marquis One Tower, Fourth Floor, 245 Peachtree Center Avenue, N.E., 30303
Telephone: 404-688-8800
Telecopier: 404-420-7191

Michael D. Alembik (1936-1993)	Ronald T. Gold
Lowell S. Fine	G. Michael Banick
Bruce W. Callner	Mark E. Bergeson
Kathy L. Portnoy	Russell P. Love

Z. Ileana Martinez	Janet Lichiello Franchi
Susan M. Lieppe	Heidi Koch Martin
Bruce R. Steinfeld	Janet Caroline Moja
John H. Zwald	

For full biographical listings, see the Martindale-Hubbell Law Directory

Atlanta—Continued

BAUER & DEITCH, P.C. (AV)

Building D, 6111 Peachtree-Dunwoody Road, N.E., 30328
Telephone: 770-394-9004
Telecopier: 770-394-8840

Henry R. Bauer, Jr.　　　　　Gilbert H. Deitch

For full biographical listings, see the Martindale-Hubbell Law Directory

BIVENS, HOFFMAN & FOWLER (AV)

A Partnership of Professional Corporations
5040 Roswell Road, N.E., 30342
Telephone: 404-256-6464
FAX: 404-256-1422

MEMBER OF FIRM
L. Brown Bivens (P.C.)

For full biographical listings, see the Martindale-Hubbell Law Directory

DAVIS, MATTHEWS & QUIGLEY, P.C. (AV)

Fourteenth Floor, Lenox Towers II, 3400 Peachtree Road, 30326
Telephone: 404-261-3900
Telecopier: 404-261-0159
Email: dmq@interserv.com

Baxter L. Davis　　　　　Frank A. DeVincent
Richard W. Schiffman, Jr.　　　Elizabeth Green Lindsey

Sylvia A. Martin

Approved Attorneys for: Lawyers Title Insurance Corp.

For Complete List of Firm Personnel, See General Section

For full biographical listings, see the Martindale-Hubbell Law Directory

HARRY P. HALL (AV)

Ten Piedmont Center, Suite 500, 3495 Piedmont Road, N.E., 30305
Telephone: 404-231-0060
Fax: 404-231-3731

For full biographical listings, see the Martindale-Hubbell Law Directory

HARMON, SMITH, BRIDGES & WILBANKS (AV)

1795 Peachtree Street, N.E., 30309
Telephone: 404-881-1200
Fax: 404-881-8523

MEMBER OF FIRM
Archer D. Smith, III

For full biographical listings, see the Martindale-Hubbell Law Directory

KAUFMAN, CHAIKEN, RICKERTSEN, KREVOLIN, MILLER & HORST, A PROFESSIONAL CORPORATION (AV)

400 Perimeter Center Terrace, N.E., Suite 720, 30346-1234
Telephone: 770-390-9200
Facsimile: 770-395-6720
Email: rkaufm03@counsel.com

Robert J. Kaufman

References: Gulf States Mortgage Co., Inc.; Dyer & Dyer Volvo, Inc.; Trust Company Bank; Wachovia Bank of Georgia.

For Complete List of Firm Personnel, See General Section

For full biographical listings, see the Martindale-Hubbell Law Directory

JAMES J. MACIE (AV)

400 Colony Square, Suite 1940, 1201 Peachtree Street, 30361
Telephone: 770-478-4155
Fax: 770-471-2053
Jonesboro, Georgia Office: 2212 Emerald Drive.
Telephone: 770-478-4155.
Fax: 770-471-2053.

For full biographical listings, see the Martindale-Hubbell Law Directory

STERN & EDLIN, P.C. (AV)

225 West Wieuca Road, N.E., 30342
Telephone: 404-256-0010
FAX: 404-851-9081

George S. Stern　　　　　Shiel G. Edlin

Janis Y. Dickman　　　　　Jeri L. Kagel
Carla F. Stern　　　　　Heidi Geiger

Reference: NationsBank.

For full biographical listings, see the Martindale-Hubbell Law Directory

TURNAGE & CHAMBERS (AV)

999 Peachtree Street, N.E., Suite 1750, 30309
Telephone: 404-872-0000
Fax: 404-873-2748

Kirby L. Turnage　　　　　Eugene P. Chambers, III

OF COUNSEL
Carol A. Paulk

For full biographical listings, see the Martindale-Hubbell Law Directory

TURNER, TURNER & TURNER, P.C. (AV)

1445 Resurgens Plaza, 945 East Paces Ferry Road, N.E., 30326
Telephone: 404-237-0045
Fax: 404-237-4989

Russell G. Turner, Sr.　　　　Nelson Goss Turner
(1896-1981)　　　　　　Anne H. Jarrett
Jack P. Turner　　　　　Gregory R. Miller

For full biographical listings, see the Martindale-Hubbell Law Directory

WARNER, MAYOUE & BATES, P.C. (AV)

100 Galleria Parkway, Suite 1300, 30339
Telephone: 770-951-2700
Telecopier: 770-951-2200

C. Wilbur Warner, Jr.　　　J. Matthew Anthony
John C. Mayoue　　　　　John Lind Collar, Jr.
Edward E. Bates, Jr.　　　Richard M. Nolen
Alvah O. Smith　　　　　Teresa R. Wenke
Robert D. Boyd　　　　　Catherine Knight Quackenboss
　　　　Margaret R. Martin

For full biographical listings, see the Martindale-Hubbell Law Directory

WILSON, STRICKLAND & BENSON, P.C. (AV)

1100 One Midtown Plaza, 1360 Peachtree Street, N.E., 30309
Telephone: 404-870-1800
Telecopier: 404-870-1808

OF COUNSEL
Robert G. Wellon

For Complete List of Firm Personnel, See General Section

For full biographical listings, see the Martindale-Hubbell Law Directory

AUGUSTA,* Richmond Co.

SURRETT & COLEMAN, P.A. (AV)

901 Suntrust Bank Building, P.O. Box 1497, 30903
Telephone: 706-722-3301
Telecopier: 706-722-3318

Carl J. Surrett　　　　　Edward J. Coleman, III

Representative Clients: Sears, Roebuck & Co.; American Home Assurance Co.; Great Southwest Fire Insurance Co.; Duke Buick, Inc.; American Southern Insurance Co.; Scottsdale Insurance Co.; Providence Washington Insurance Co.; Nautilus Insurance Co.

For full biographical listings, see the Martindale-Hubbell Law Directory

BUFORD, Gwinnett Co.

JOSEPH E. CHEELEY, JR., P.C. (AV)

345 East Main Street, 30518-5718
Telephone: 770-945-1442
Fax: 770-945-1444

Joseph E. Cheeley, Jr.

For full biographical listings, see the Martindale-Hubbell Law Directory

COLUMBUS,* Muscogee Co.

HARP & JOHNSON, P.C. (AV)

936 Second Avenue, P.O. Box 1172, 31902
Telephone: 706-323-2761
Fax: 706-323-0182

Beverly R. Keil (1924-1983)　　　B. Seth Harp, Jr.
　　　　Gary L. Johnson

Reference: Trust Company Bank of Columbus.

For full biographical listings, see the Martindale-Hubbell Law Directory

HIRSCH, PARTIN, GROGAN & GROGAN, P.C. (AV)

1021 Third Avenue, P.O. Box 469, 31993
Telephone: 706-323-6581
Fax: 706-323-6585

(See Next Column)

HIRSCH, PARTIN, GROGAN & GROGAN P.C., *Columbus—Continued*

Milton Hirsch
John P. Partin

Lynn L. Grogan
Lee R. Grogan, Jr.

Approved Attorneys: Lawyers Title Insurance Corp.
Reference: Columbus Bank & Trust Co.

For full biographical listings, see the Martindale-Hubbell Law Directory

DECATUR,* De Kalb Co.

SIMMONS, WARREN, SZCZECKO & McFEE, PROFESSIONAL ASSOCIATION (AV)

315 West Ponce de Leon Avenue, Suite 850, 30030
Telephone: 404-378-1711
Fax: 404-377-6101

M. T. Simmons, Jr.

Joseph Szczecko

Representative Clients: David Hocker & Associates (Shopping Center Development); Julian LeCraw & Company (Real Estate); Intown Suites, Inc.; Preferred Lodging Systems, Inc.; Royal Oldsmobile,; Cotter & Co.; Atlanta Neurosurgical Associates, P.A.; Troncalli Motors, Inc.

For Complete List of Firm Personnel, See General Section

For full biographical listings, see the Martindale-Hubbell Law Directory

JONESBORO,* Clayton Co.

JAMES J. MACIE (AV)

2212 Emerald Drive, 30236
Telephone: 770-478-4155
Fax: 770-471-2053
Atlanta, Georgia Office: 400 Colony Square, Suite 1940, 1201 Peachtree Street.
Telephone: 770-478-4155.
Fax: 770-471-2053.

For full biographical listings, see the Martindale-Hubbell Law Directory

MACON,* Bibb Co.

THE STONE LAW FIRM, P.C. (AV)

720 North Avenue, P.O. Box 56701, 31208
Telephone: 912-741-0060
FAX: 912-741-7971

Kice H. Stone, Jr.

Lise Kaplan

Claire C. Chapman

Reference: Wachovia.

For full biographical listings, see the Martindale-Hubbell Law Directory

MARIETTA,* Cobb Co.

BARNES, BROWNING, TANKSLEY & CASURELLA (AV)

Suite 225, 166 Anderson Street, 30060
Telephone: 770-424-1500
Fax: 770-424-1740

MEMBERS OF FIRM

Roy E. Barnes

Thomas J. Browning

OF COUNSEL

George T. Smith

For full biographical listings, see the Martindale-Hubbell Law Directory

CUSTER & HILL, P.C. (AV)

241 Washington Avenue, P.O. Box 1224, 30061
Telephone: 770-429-8300
Fax: 770-429-8338

Lawrence B. Custer

Douglas A. Hill

Reference: First Union National Bank.

For Complete List of Firm Personnel, See General Section

For full biographical listings, see the Martindale-Hubbell Law Directory

ROBERT E. FLOURNOY, III (AV)

236 Washington Avenue, P.O. Box 1183, 30060-1959
Telephone: 770-422-4115
Computer Fax: 770-426-9594

For full biographical listings, see the Martindale-Hubbell Law Directory

DUARD R. McDONALD (AV)

214 Roswell Street, Suite 100, 30060-2000
Telephone: 770-424-8414
Fax: 770-590-1231

For full biographical listings, see the Martindale-Hubbell Law Directory

W. R. ROBERTSON, III (AV)

244 Roswell Street, Suite 600, 30060-2000
Telephone: 770-422-0200
Fax: 770-424-1322
Email: wrobert244@aol.com

For full biographical listings, see the Martindale-Hubbell Law Directory

MCDONOUGH,* Henry Co.

SMITH, WELCH, STUDDARD & BRITTAIN (AV)

200 The Commerce Building, 235 Keys Ferry Street, P.O. Box 31, 30253
Telephone: 770-957-3937
Fax: 770-957-9165
Stockbridge, Georgia Office: 1231-A Eagle's Landing Parkway.
Telephone: 770-389-4864.
Fax: 770-389-5157.

MEMBERS OF FIRM

Ernest M. Smith (1911-1992)
A. J. Welch, Jr.

Ben W. Studdard, III
J. Mark Brittain
(Resident, Stockbridge Office)

ASSOCIATES

Patrick D. Jaugstetter
E. Gilmore Maxwell

Shawn Marie Story
Arthur Scully Barbee

Representative Clients: Alliance Corp.; Atlanta Motor Speedway, Inc.; Bellamy-Strickland Chevrolet, Inc.; Ceramic and Metal Coatings Corp.; City of Hampton; City of Locust Grove; City of Stockbridge.

For full biographical listings, see the Martindale-Hubbell Law Directory

VALDOSTA,* Lowndes Co.

DODD AND DENNIS, P.C. (AV)

613 N. Patterson Street, P.O. Box 1066, 31603-1066
Telephone: 912-242-4470
Telefax: 912-245-7731
Email: doddlaw@mail.datasys.net *URL:* http://www.doddlaw.com

Roger J. Dodd

Sam D. Dennis

References: First Union Bank; First State Bank and Trust Co.; Park Avenue Bank.

For full biographical listings, see the Martindale-Hubbell Law Directory

HAWAII

HONOLULU,* Honolulu Co.

LYNCH & FARMER (AV)

Suite 2500, Mauka Tower Grosvenor Center, 737 Bishop Street, 96813
Telephone: 808-528-0100
Facsimile: 808-528-4997

David C. Farmer

Paul A. Lynch

LEGAL SUPPORT PERSONNEL

Linda L. Tauotaba

For full biographical listings, see the Martindale-Hubbell Law Directory

STIRLING & KLEINTOP (AV)

20th Floor, 1100 Alakea Street, 96813
Telephone: 808-524-5183
FAX: 808-528-0261

MEMBERS OF FIRM

Thomas L. Stirling, Jr.
Charles T. Kleintop
(Managing Partner)

Sara Robbins Harvey

Carolyn E. Ogami

Ellen T. Nomura

For full biographical listings, see the Martindale-Hubbell Law Directory

MICHAEL J. Y. WONG (AV)

2222 Central Pacific Plaza, 220 South King Street, 96813
Telephone: 808-536-1855
Fax: 808-536-1857

ASSOCIATE

R. Malia Taum

For full biographical listings, see the Martindale-Hubbell Law Directory

ILLINOIS

CHICAGO,* Cook Co.

MARSHALL J. AUERBACH & ASSOCIATES, LTD. (AV)

180 North La Salle Street, Suite 2307, 60601
Telephone: 312-853-3300
Fax: 312-853-1043

Marshall J. Auerbach

For full biographical listings, see the Martindale-Hubbell Law Directory

THEODORE BIRNDORF (AV)

33 North La Salle Street, Suite 2500, 60602-2604
Telephone: 312-726-7331
Fax: 312-641-3031

For full biographical listings, see the Martindale-Hubbell Law Directory

OWEN L. DOSS, P.C. (AV)

Suite 3800, Three First National Plaza, 70 West Madison Street, 60602
Telephone: 312-726-3060

Owen L. Doss

FEINBERG & BARRY, P.C. (AV)

Three First National Plaza, Suite 1250, 60602
Telephone: 312-444-1050

Joy M. Feinberg   Carroll A. Barry

For full biographical listings, see the Martindale-Hubbell Law Directory

GRUND & STARKOPF, A PROFESSIONAL CORPORATION (AV)

28th Floor One Illinois Center, 111 East Wacker Drive, 60601-4801
Telephone: 312-616-6600
FAX: 312-616-6606

David I. Grund   Lawrence S. Starkopf

Robert S. Kipnis   Richard S. Zachary

For full biographical listings, see the Martindale-Hubbell Law Directory

SUSAN CHRISTINE HADDAD (AV)

Suite 3600, Three First National Plaza, 60602
Telephone: 312-236-2298
FAX: 312-236-0089

For full biographical listings, see the Martindale-Hubbell Law Directory

KALCHEIM, SCHATZ & BERGER (AV)

A Partnership including Professional Corporations
161 North Clark Street, 28th Floor, 60601
Telephone: 312-782-3456
FAX: 312-782-8463
Lake Forest, Illinois Office: 920 South Waukegan Road.
Telephone: 847-295-0550.
Fax: 847-295-0560.

MEMBERS OF FIRM

Michael W. Kalcheim (P.C.)   David H. Levy (P.C.)
Barry A. Schatz (P.C.)   Michael S. Cohen
Michael J. Berger (P.C.)   Leon I. Finkel
          Andrew D. Eichner

Jennifer Cantrell   Tara Gordon Kochman
David M. Goldman   Robert D. Segal
Cecilia A. Hynes   Zisl Taub Loventhal

For full biographical listings, see the Martindale-Hubbell Law Directory

LAW OFFICES OF KOMIE AND ASSOCIATES (AV)

Suite 3500 Avondale Centre, 20 North Clark Street, 60602-5002
Telephone: 312-263-4383
Fax: 312-263-2803

Stephen M. Komie
ASSOCIATES
Julia A. McConnahy   Terrance McWhorter
        Mark A. Walwyn
OF COUNSEL
Douglas W. Godfrey   Marc D. Wolfe
LEGAL SUPPORT PERSONNEL
Paul J. Ciolino

For full biographical listings, see the Martindale-Hubbell Law Directory

LAKE, TOBACK & YAVITZ (AV)

A Partnership including a Professional Corporation
Chicago Title Tower, Suite 2200, 161 North Clark Street, 60601
Telephone: 312-726-7111
Fax: 312-726-2385

MEMBERS OF FIRM

Steven R. Lake   Theresa J. Meyers
Alan Jay Toback   Ross S. Levey
David B. Yavitz, Ltd.   Debra J. Reinstein

For full biographical listings, see the Martindale-Hubbell Law Directory

MANDEL, LIPTON AND STEVENSON LIMITED (AV)

Suite 2900, 120 North La Salle Street, 60602
Telephone: 312-236-7080
Facsimile: 312-236-0781

Richard L. Mandel   Richard A. Lifshitz
Alfred R. Lipton   Terry Yale Feiertag
Leonard M. Malkin   Kathleen Hogan Morrison
R. Peter Carey   Uve R. Jerzy
Henry A. Waller   Carolyn E. Winter
Kathleen Roseborough   Audrey L. Gaynor

Andrés J. Gallegos   Megan Kennedy Riordan
                       (Not admitted in IL)
OF COUNSEL
Nicholas Stevenson   Mark R. Ordower
LEGAL SUPPORT PERSONNEL
Jacqueline Steffens (Paralegal)

References: Northern Trust Co.; American National Bank of Chicago.

For full biographical listings, see the Martindale-Hubbell Law Directory

THE MINTON FIRM (AV)

Suite 1950, 222 North La Salle Street, 60601
Telephone: 312-641-2500
Fax: 312-641-6688
Inverness, Illinois Office: 1600 Colonial Parkway, 60067.
Telephone: 847-358-7767.
Fax: 847-991-0219.

Michael Harry Minton   James P. Powers

Anthony D'Agostino

For full biographical listings, see the Martindale-Hubbell Law Directory

NOTTAGE AND WARD (AV)

Ten North Dearborn Street, Penthouse, 60602
Telephone: 312-332-2915
Fax: 312-332-3075

MEMBERS OF FIRM
Rosaire M. Nottage   Eunice Ward
ASSOCIATES
Doris Schumacher McMorrow   Richard Allen Wilson
       Anne Margaret Coladarci

For full biographical listings, see the Martindale-Hubbell Law Directory

JAMES ANTHONY PALMISANO, LTD. (AV)

180 North La Salle Street, Suite 2400, 60601
Telephone: 312-332-7247
FAX: 312-332-7247

James A. Palmisano

For full biographical listings, see the Martindale-Hubbell Law Directory

RINELLA AND RINELLA, LTD. (AV)

Suite 3400, One North La Salle Street, 60602
Telephone: 312-236-5454
Fax: 312-236-6975
Lake Forest, Illinois Office: 207 East Westminster Avenue - 200.
Telephone: 847-234-5486.
Fax: 847-234-6978.

Samuel A. Rinella (1906-1982)   Walter J. Monco
Kathryn B. Rinella (1906-1991)   Steven S. Russo
Bernard B. Rinella   Leslie L. Veon
Richard A. Rinella   Steven D. Gerage
Joseph G. Phelps   Brian M. Livermore

For full biographical listings, see the Martindale-Hubbell Law Directory

Chicago—Continued

SCHILLER, DU CANTO AND FLECK (AV)

200 North La Salle Street, Suite 2700, 60601
Telephone: 312-641-5560
Fax: 312-641-6361
Lake Forest, Illinois Office: Suite 201, 207 East Westminster Avenue.
Telephone: 708-615-8300.
Fax: 708-615-8284.
Wheaton, Illinois Office: 300 South County Farm Road, Suite A.
Telephone: 630-665-5800.
Fax: 630-665-6082.

MEMBERS OF FIRM

Joseph N. Du Canto	Carlton R. Marcyan
Donald C. Schiller	Sarane Crowther Siewerth
Charles J. Fleck	Timothy M. Daw
David H. Hopkins	(Resident, Wheaton Office)
Arnold B. Stein	Ilene Beth Goldstein
James B. O'Brien	Harold G. Field
Burton S. Hochberg	(Resident, Wheaton Office)
Stephen H. Katz	
(Resident, Lake Forest Office)	

ASSOCIATES

Todd R. Warren	Karen Pinkert-Lieb
(Resident, Lake Forest Office)	Daniel R. Stefani
Anita Bolaños	Sharon M. Warning
Andrea K. Muchin	Melinda C. Rogers
David A. King	(Resident, Lake Forest Office)
(Resident, Wheaton Office)	

OF COUNSEL

Sidney S. Schiller   David Linn

For full biographical listings, see the Martindale-Hubbell Law Directory

SCHWARTZBERG, BARNETT & COHEN (AV)

55 West Monroe Street, 2400 Xerox Centre, 60603-5040
Telephone: 312-726-3555
Fax: 312-726-6299
Cable Address: "Justice"
Email: sb&c@twty.chi.il.us

MEMBERS OF FIRM

Ralph M. Schwartzberg	Mark T. Barnett (1939-1970)
(1939-1975)	Hugh J. Schwartzberg
Benjamin H. Cohen	

OF COUNSEL

Eugene P. Thomas Jr.

For full biographical listings, see the Martindale-Hubbell Law Directory

---

CRYSTAL LAKE, McHenry Co.

ZUKOWSKI, ROGERS, FLOOD & McARDLE (AV)

50 Virginia Street, 60014
Telephone: 815-459-2050
Facsimile: 815-459-9057
Chicago, Illinois Office: 100 South Wacker Drive, Suite 1502.
Telephone: 312-407-7700.
Facsimile: 312-332-1901.

PARTNERS

H. David Rogers	David W. McArdle
Richard G. Flood	Jeannine A. Thoms
Stuart D. Gordon	

ASSOCIATES

William P. Stanton	Michael J. Chmiel
Melissa J. Cooney	Maureen T. Murphy
Kelly A. Cahill	E. Regan Shepley
Michael J. Smoron	Stuart M. Nagel
Kevin J. O'Brien	

OF COUNSEL

Timothy J. Curran   Francis S. Lorenz

For full biographical listings, see the Martindale-Hubbell Law Directory

---

EDWARDSVILLE,* Madison Co.

PEEL, BEATTY & WALTERS (AV)

6100 Center Grove Road, 62025
Telephone: 618-692-0500
Fax: 618-656-4472

MEMBERS OF FIRM

Gary E. Peel	William S. Beatty
Gerald R. Walters	

Representative Clients: Village of Glen Carbon; Madison County Housing Authority; Madison County Transit District; Alton Police Benevolent and Protective Unit 14; Madison County Sanitary Sewers District; International Laborers Local 397, Granite City.

For full biographical listings, see the Martindale-Hubbell Law Directory

---

LAKE FOREST, Lake Co.

SCHILLER, DU CANTO AND FLECK (AV)

Suite 201, 207 East Westminster Avenue, 60045-1857
Telephone: 708-615-8300
Fax: 708-615-8284
Chicago, Illinois Office: 200 North La Salle Street, Suite 2700.
Telephone: 312-641-5560.
Fax: 312-641-6361.
Wheaton, Illinois Office: 300 South County Farm Road, Suite A.
Telephone: 630-665-5800.
Fax: 630-665-6082.

RESIDENT PARTNER

Stephen H. Katz

RESIDENT ASSOCIATES

Todd R. Warren   Melinda C. Rogers

For full biographical listings, see the Martindale-Hubbell Law Directory

---

OAK BROOK, Du Page Co.

BOTTI, MARINACCIO & DeLONGIS, LTD. (AV)

720 Enterprise Drive, 60521
Telephone: 708-573-8585
Fax: 708-573-8586
Wheaton, Illinois Office: Suite 401 The Ticor Title Building, 330 Naperville Road.
Telephone: 708-653-2100.

Aldo E. Botti	Mark W. Salkeld
Stephen R. Botti	Peter M. Tumminaro
Andrew Y. Acker	David C. Bruss
Peter M. DeLongis	Jean M. Lasics
Lee A. Marinaccio	Nanette C. Augustin

For full biographical listings, see the Martindale-Hubbell Law Directory

---

PEORIA,* Peoria Co.

WINGET & KANE (AV)

807 Commerce Bank Building, 61602
Telephone: 309-674-2310
Fax: 309-674-9722

Walter W. Winget   James F. Kane

Representative Client: Davison-Fulton Ltd.
References: Commerce Bank; Bank One - Peoria.

For full biographical listings, see the Martindale-Hubbell Law Directory

---

SPRINGFIELD,* Sangamon Co.

METNICK, WISE, CHERRY & FRAZIER (AV)

Second Floor, Myers Building, 1 West Old State Capitol Plaza, P.O. Box 12140, 62791
Telephone: 217-753-4242
Telefax: 217-753-4642

MEMBERS OF FIRM

Michael B. Metnick   Diana N. Cherry

ASSOCIATE

Kathryn Saltmarsh

For full biographical listings, see the Martindale-Hubbell Law Directory

---

INDIANA

COLUMBUS,* Bartholomew Co.

SHARPNACK, BIGLEY, DAVID & RUMPLE (AV)

321 Washington Street, P.O. Box 310, 47202-0310
Telephone: 812-372-1553
Fax: 812-372-1567

MEMBERS OF FIRM

John A. Stroh   Joan Tupin Crites

For Complete List of Firm Personnel, See General Section

For full biographical listings, see the Martindale-Hubbell Law Directory

---

CRAWFORDSVILLE,* Montgomery Co.

BERRY, CAPPER, DONALDSON & TULLEY (AV)

131 North Green Street, P.O. Box 429, 47933
Telephone: 317-362-7340
Fax: 317-362-5023

(See Next Column)

BERRY, CAPPER, DONALDSON & TULLEY—*Continued*

Andrew N. Foley (1909-1963)
John R. Berry (1907-1986)
Richard G. Tulley
John S. Capper, IV
S. Bryan Donaldson

Representative Clients: Elston Bank & Trust Co.; R. R. Donnelley & Sons Co. (Crawfordsville Division); Linden State Bank; City of Crawfordsville, Ind.

For full biographical listings, see the Martindale-Hubbell Law Directory

ELKHART, Elkhart Co.

CHESTER, PFAFF & BROTHERSON (AV)

317 West Franklin Street, P.O. Box 507, 46515-0507
Telephone: 219-294-5421
Fax: 219-522-1476

MEMBERS OF FIRM

Robert A. Pfaff   Glenn E. Killoren

ASSOCIATE

Craig A. Carpenter

For Complete List of Firm Personnel, See General Section

For full biographical listings, see the Martindale-Hubbell Law Directory

FORT WAYNE,* Allen Co.

HAYES & HAYES (AV)

Second Floor, Courtside Building, 803 South Calhoun Street, 46802
Telephone: 219-420-1800
Facsimile: 219-420-1809

C. Byron Hayes (1891-1975)   J. Byron Hayes (1920-1986)
Cornelius B. (Neil) Hayes

For full biographical listings, see the Martindale-Hubbell Law Directory

STANLEY A. LEVINE (AV)

Fort Wayne National Bank Building, Suite 2008, 110 West Berry Street, 46802
Telephone: 219-422-7431
Facsimile: 219-422-7433

For full biographical listings, see the Martindale-Hubbell Law Directory

ROTHBERG & LOGAN (AV)

(Formerly, Rothberg, Gallmeyer, Fruechtenicht & Logan)
2100 Fort Wayne National Bank Building, 110 West Berry Street, P.O. Box 11647, 46859-1647
Telephone: 219-422-9454
Telefax: 219-422-1622

MEMBERS OF FIRM

Sol Rothberg (1910-1993)
Thomas A. Gallmeyer
(1922-1981)
George E. Fruechtenicht
(1925-1996)
Thomas D. Logan
Martin T. Fletcher, Sr.
F. L. Dennis Logan
Scott T. Niemann
David R. Smelko
Dennis F. Dykhuizen
Catherine C. Ediger
Anne Carney
Gregory Martin Cole
Michael T. Deam

ASSOCIATES

James A. Butz
Brian L. Nehrig
Daniel G. McNamara
J. Rickard Donovan
N. Jean Schendel
Samuel J. Talarico, Jr.

OF COUNSEL

John H. Heiney   Loren K. Allison

Counsel for: Parkview Memorial Hospital; Cameron Memorial Community Hospital; Norwest Bank Indiana, N.A.; NBD Bank, N.A.; Parkview Health System; Azar's, Incorporated; Fort Wayne-Allen County Airport Authority; Fort Wayne Public Transportation Corporation; Avis Industrial Corp.; Farm Credit Services of Mid-America, ASA; Slater Fort Wayne Federal Credit Union.

For full biographical listings, see the Martindale-Hubbell Law Directory

INDIANAPOLIS,* Marion Co.

BOBERSCHMIDT, MILLER, O'BRYAN & TURNER, A PROFESSIONAL ASSOCIATION (AV)

Bank One Center/Circle, 111 Monument Circle, Suite 302, 46204-5169
Telephone: 317-632-5892
Telecopier: 317-686-3423

Philip F. Boberschmidt
Jerald L. Miller
Berton W. O'Bryan
L. Craig Turner
William B. Powers

(See Next Column)

OF COUNSEL

John Thomas Drics

A List of Representative Clients will be furnished upon request.

For full biographical listings, see the Martindale-Hubbell Law Directory

DANN PECAR NEWMAN & KLEIMAN, PROFESSIONAL CORPORATION (AV)

Suite 2300, One American Square Box 82008, 46282
Telephone: 317-632-3232; Indiana: 800-622-4799
Telecopy: 317-632-2962

Theodore R. Dann (1907-1993)
Joel Yonover (1932-1995)
Philip D. Pecar
Norman R. Newman
David H. Kleiman
Jon B. Abels
Melvin R. Daniel
Lawrence F. Dorocke
Jeffrey A. Abrams
James H. Schwarz
Robert A. Rose
Walter E. Wolf, Jr.
Barry E. Beldin
Robert D. Swhier, Jr.
James P. Moloy
Robert J. Schuckit
Andrew A. Kleiman
Michael J. Gabovitch
Steven M. Pecar
Benjamin A. Pecar
Richard O. Kissel, II
Joseph D. Calderon

OF COUNSEL

Linda E. Cantor   Anthony J. Rose

Ellen C. Siakotos
Stacy L. Hill
Angela L. Mansfield
Martha M. K. Baird
Karin L. Veatch

Attorneys for: Indianapolis Machinery Co., Inc.; Melvin Simon & Associates, Inc.; Pacers Basketball Corp.; Universal Fire & Casualty Co., Inc.; Bank One, Indianapolis, NA; INB National Bank; Nachi Technology, Inc.; Pharmaceutical Corporation of America; Logo 7, Inc.

For full biographical listings, see the Martindale-Hubbell Law Directory

MIROFF, CROSS & KLINEMAN (AV)

An Association, Not a Partnership
Suite 1000, Two Market Square Center, 251 East Ohio Street, 46204-2133
Telephone: 317-264-1040
Telecopier: 317-264-1039

Franklin I. Miroff
Nancy L. Cross
Monty K. Woolsey
Penny R. Ritenour

OF COUNSEL

James M. Klineman   Stephen J. Klineman

For full biographical listings, see the Martindale-Hubbell Law Directory

PHELPS & FARA (AV)

Indiana Bar Center, 230 East Ohio, Sixth Floor, 46204-2149
Telephone: 317-637-7575
Facsimile: 317-685-1106
Email: pandf@iquest.net

MEMBERS OF FIRM

Gale M. Phelps   Thomas A. Fara
Michael Cheerva

For full biographical listings, see the Martindale-Hubbell Law Directory

LAFAYETTE,* Tippecanoe Co.

PEARLMAN AND CHOSNEK, P.C. (AV)

316 Ferry Street, P.O. Box 708, 47902-0708
Telephone: 317-742-9081
Fax: 317-742-4379

Louis Pearlman, Jr. (1930-1992)   Edward Chosnek

David W. Haniford   Christopher Paul Hopson
Michael A. Morrissey

Representative Clients: Tippecanoe Memory Gardens, Inc.; Industrial Federal Credit Union; Farmers and Merchants Bank, Boswell, Indiana; Biggs Pump & Supply, Inc; Brummett Elec. Co. Inc.; Klooz Plumbing, Inc.; Gene B. Glick Mgmt. Co; Chauncey Hill Mall; Von Tobel Lumber & Hardware; Purdue Employees Federal Credit Union.
Reference: NBD Bank, N.W.

For full biographical listings, see the Martindale-Hubbell Law Directory

MARION,* Grant Co.

KILEY, KILEY, HARKER, MICHAEL & CERTAIN (AV)

300 West Third Street, P.O. Box 899, 46952-0899
Telephone: 317-664-9041
Fax: 317-664-8119

(See Next Column)

KILEY, KILEY, HARKER, MICHAEL & CERTAIN, *Marion—Continued*

MEMBERS OF FIRM

Robert Ralph Batton	David L. Kiley, Sr.
(1890-1963)	Michael J. Kiley
Albert L. Harker (1904-1965)	Albert C. Harker
Albert Bonner Brown	Thomas W. Michael
(1911-1981)	Harry J. Certain

ASSOCIATE

Therese McCullough Pryor

Counsel for: Bank One, Marion, N.A.; Liniger Co., Inc.; Atlas Foundry Co.
Local Counsel for: GenCorp.; CPC Group; General Motors; Indiana Michigan Power Co./AEP; Indiana Bell Telephone Co.; Foster-Forbes, Division of American National Can Corp.

For full biographical listings, see the Martindale-Hubbell Law Directory

---

SOUTH BEND, St. Joseph Co.

SOPKO & FIRTH (AV)

Plaza Building, 5th Floor, 210 South Michigan Street, P.O. Box 300, 46624
Telephone: 219-234-3000
Telecopier: 219-234-4220

MEMBERS OF FIRM

Thomas C. Sopko	John C. Firth

ASSOCIATE

Brent E. Inabnit

OF COUNSEL

Ronald J. Jaicomo

References: 1st Source Bank; 1st Interstate Bank; Notre Dame Federal Credit Union.

For full biographical listings, see the Martindale-Hubbell Law Directory

---

IOWA

SIOUX CITY, Woodbury Co.

GILES AND GILES (AV)

322 Frances Building, 505 Fifth Street, 51101
Telephone: 712-252-4458
FAX: 712-252-3400
Crofton, Nebraska Office: P. O. Box 88.
Telephone: 402-388-4215.

MEMBERS OF FIRM

W. Jefferson Giles, III	William J. Giles, IV

Representative Clients: Security National Bank, Firstar Bank, Boatmen's Bank, all in Sioux City, Iowa; Live Stock State Bank, Yankton, SD.

For Complete List of Firm Personnel, See General Section

For full biographical listings, see the Martindale-Hubbell Law Directory

---

KANSAS

OVERLAND PARK, Johnson Co.

SHORT & BORTH (AV)

32 Corporate Woods, Suite 1111, 9225 Indian Creek Parkway, 66210
Telephone: 913-491-4400
Facsimile: 913-491-6550

MEMBERS OF FIRM

J. Bradley Short	Ray L. Borth

Reference: Boatmen's Bank of Kansas, Overland Park, Kansas.

For full biographical listings, see the Martindale-Hubbell Law Directory

---

TOPEKA, Shawnee Co.

WRIGHT, HENSON, SOMERS, SEBELIUS, CLARK & BAKER, LLP (AV)

Commerce Bank Building, 100 Southeast Ninth Street, 2nd Floor, P.O. Box 3555, 66601-3555
Telephone: 913-232-2200
FAX: 913-232-3344

MEMBERS OF FIRM

Dale L. Somers	Evelyn Zabel Wilson

For Complete List of Firm Personnel, See General Section

For full biographical listings, see the Martindale-Hubbell Law Directory

---

WICHITA, Sedgwick Co.

LAMBDIN HERLOCKER & SODERBERG, CHARTERED (AV)

830 North Main, P.O. Box 797, 67201-0797
Telephone: 316-265-3285
Fax: 316-265-1303

Donald E. Lambdin	Lucy L. Herlocker
Ann Gottberg Soderberg	Lisa L. Lamdin

Reference: INTRUST Bank, NA.

For full biographical listings, see the Martindale-Hubbell Law Directory

---

KENTUCKY

COVINGTON, Kenton Co.

O'HARA, RUBERG, TAYLOR, SLOAN AND SERGENT (AV)

Suite 209 C, Thomas More Park, P.O. Box 17411, 41017-0411
Telephone: 606-331-2000
Fax: 606-578-3365

MEMBERS OF FIRM

John J. O'Hara	David B. Sloan
Robert E. Ruberg	Gary J. Sergent
Arnold S. Taylor	Michael K. Ruberg
Donald J. Ruberg	Michael O'Hara

ASSOCIATE

Suzanne Cassidy

Representative Clients: Cincinnati Bell; American Transportation Enterprises; Union Light, Heat & Power Co.; Crum & Forster; American States Insurance Co.; Ohio Casualty Co.; Monticello Insurance Co.; United States Aviation Underwriters, Inc.
Local Counsel for: Lloyds of London.

For full biographical listings, see the Martindale-Hubbell Law Directory

---

TALIAFERRO AND MEHLING (AV)

1005 Madison Avenue, P.O. Box 468, 41012-0468
Telephone: 606-291-9900
Fax: 606-291-3014

MEMBERS OF FIRM

Philip Taliaferro, III	Christopher J. Mehling
Lucinda C. Shirooni	

ASSOCIATES

C. Houston Ebert	Howard L. Tankersley
Alice G. Keys	

OF COUNSEL

Robert W. Carran	Norbert J. Bischoff
F. Edward Worland, Jr.	

For full biographical listings, see the Martindale-Hubbell Law Directory

---

GLASGOW, Barren Co.

HERBERT & HERBERT (AV)

135 North Public Square, P.O. Box 1000, 42141
Telephone: 502-651-9000
Fax: 502-651-3317
Email: h&hlaw@glasgow-ky.com

MEMBERS OF FIRM

H. Jefferson Herbert, Jr.	Betty Reece Herbert

For full biographical listings, see the Martindale-Hubbell Law Directory

---

LEXINGTON, Fayette Co.

BROCK, BROCK & BAGBY (AV)

190 Market Street, P.O. Box 1630, 40592-1630
Telephone: 606-255-7000
Fax: 606-255-6198

MEMBERS OF FIRM

Walter L. Brock, Jr. (1918-1995)	Glen S. Bagby
Daniel N. Brock	J. Robert Lyons, Jr.

ASSOCIATES

Bruce A. Rector	Jane Hampton Herrick

LEGAL SUPPORT PERSONNEL

PARALEGALS

Pamela H. Brown	Freda Greer Grubbs

For full biographical listings, see the Martindale-Hubbell Law Directory

Lexington—Continued

LANDRUM & SHOUSE (AV)

106 West Vine Street, P.O. Box 951, 40588-0951
Telephone: 606-255-2424
Facsimile: 606-233-0308
Louisville, Kentucky Office: 400 West Market Street, Suite 1550, 40202.
Telephone: 502-589-7616
Facsimile: 502-589-2119.

MEMBERS OF FIRM

John H. Burrus	Sandra Mendez Dawahare
William C. Shouse	Delores Hill Pregliasco
Mark L. Moseley	(Resident, Louisville Office)

ASSOCIATES

Stephen D. Milner	Charles E. Christian

OF COUNSEL

Weldon Shouse

District Attorneys: CSX Transportation, Inc.
Special Trial Counsel: Ford Motor Co. and Affiliates (Eastern Kentucky); Clark Equipment Co.
Representative Clients: The Continental Insurance Cos.; U.S. Insurance Group; U.S. Fidelity & Guaranty Co.; Ohio Casualty Insurance Co.; CIGNA; Royal Insurance Cos.

For Complete List of Firm Personnel, See General Section

For full biographical listings, see the Martindale-Hubbell Law Directory

MILLER, GRIFFIN & MARKS, P.S.C. (AV)

Suite 700 Security Trust Building, 271 West Short Street, 40507-1292
Telephone: 606-255-6676
Telecopier: 606-259-1562
URL: http://www.mis.net/mgm/

Harry B. Miller, Jr.	Michael D. Meuser
James M. Marks (1928-1963)	Thomas C. Marks
Robert S. Miller	Theodore E. Cowen
Thomas W. Miller	Judith K. Jones
Catesby Woodford	Stephen G. Amato
Donald R. Rose	Carroll M. Redford, III
Frank T. Becker	Helen M. Marks

Representative Clients: Central Kentucky Anesthesia, PSC.; Central Radiology Associates; Lexington Herald-Leader Co.; Paul Miller Ford, Inc.; WDKY-TV; WKYT-TV.
Reference: Bank One Lexington, N.A.

For full biographical listings, see the Martindale-Hubbell Law Directory

STOLL, KEENON & PARK, LLP (AV)

201 E. Main Street, Suite 1000, 40507-1380
Telephone: 606-231-3000
Telecopier: 606-253-1093; 606-253-1027
Frankfort, Kentucky Office: 307 Washington Street, 40601.
Telephone: 502-875-6220.
Telecopier: 502-875-6235.
Louisville, Kentucky Office: 400 West Market Street, Suite 2650, 40202-3377.
Telephone: 502-568-9100.
Telecopier: 502-568-5700.

MEMBER OF FIRM

Anita M. Britton

ASSOCIATE

Susan Beverly Jones

For Complete List of Firm Personnel, See General Section

For full biographical listings, see the Martindale-Hubbell Law Directory

LOUISVILLE,* Jefferson Co.

LANDRUM & SHOUSE (AV)

400 West Market Street Suite 1550, 40202
Telephone: 502-589-7616
Facsimile: 502-589-2119
Lexington, Kentucky Office: 106 West Vine Street, P.O. Box 951.
Telephone: 606-255-2424.
Facsimile: 606-233-0308.

RESIDENT MEMBERS OF THE FIRM

John R. Martin, Jr.	Delores Hill Pregliasco

RESIDENT ASSOCIATE

Melanie Lee Straw-Boone

For Complete List of Firm Personnel, See General Section

For full biographical listings, see the Martindale-Hubbell Law Directory

MOSLEY, CLARE & TOWNES (AV)

Fifth Floor, Hart Block Building, 730 West Main Street, 40202
Telephone: 502-583-7400
Telecopier: 502-589-4997

(See Next Column)

MEMBERS OF FIRM

Eugene L. Mosley	Larry C. Ethridge
Dennis M. Clare	Victor L. Baltzell, Jr.
W. Waverley Townes	William J. Nold
Judith E. McDonald-Burkman	

ASSOCIATES

E. Jeffrey Mosley	Eileen L. Minto

For full biographical listings, see the Martindale-Hubbell Law Directory

OLDFATHER & MORRIS (AV)

1330 South Third Street, 40208
Telephone: 502-637-7200
Fax: 502-637-3999
Email: om@ntr.net

Ann B. Oldfather

For Complete List of Firm Personnel, See General Section

For full biographical listings, see the Martindale-Hubbell Law Directory

RUBIN HAYS & FOLEY (AV)

First Trust Centre 200 South Fifth Street, 40202
Telephone: 502-569-7550
Telecopier: 502-569-7555

MEMBERS OF FIRM

Wm. Carl Fust	Lisa Koch Bryant
Harry Lee Meyer	Sharon C. Hardy
David W. Gray	Charles S. Musson
Irvin D. Foley	W. Randall Jones
Joseph R. Gathright, Jr.	K. Gail Russell

ASSOCIATES

Christian L. Juckett	Courtney Lynn McCall

OF COUNSEL

James E. Fahey	Newman T. Guthrie

Representative Clients: J.C. Bradford & Co., Inc.; J.J.B. Hilliard, W.L. Lyons, Inc.; Huntington National Bank; Liberty National Bank and Trust Company; National City Bank; PNC Bank; Prudential Bache & Co., Inc.; Prudential Securities, Inc.; Society Bank; Stock Yards Bank and Trust Co.

For full biographical listings, see the Martindale-Hubbell Law Directory

SEILLER & HANDMAKER, LLP (AV)

2200 Meidinger Tower, 40202
Telephone: 502-584-7400
Telecopier: 502-583-2100
Paris, Kentucky Office: Seiller, Handmaker & Blevins, P.S.C., 1431 South Main Street.
Telephone: 606-987-3980.
Telecopier: 606-987-3982.
Cynthiana, Kentucky Office: Seiller, Handmaker & Blevins, P.S.C., 9 South Walnut.
Telephone: 606-234-2880.
New Albany, Indiana Office: 202 Pearl Street.
Telephone: 812-948-8307.
Telecopier: 812-948-8383.

Edward F. Seiller (1897-1990)

MEMBERS OF FIRM

Stuart Allen Handmaker	Maury D. Kommor
Bill V. Seiller	Cynthia Compton Stone
David M. Cantor	Glenn A. Cohen
Neil C. Bordy	Tomi Anne Blevins Pulliam
Kyle Anne Citrynell	(Paris and Cynthiana Offices)

ASSOCIATES

Pamela M. Greenwell	Donna F. Townsend
Michael C. Bratcher	Gregory A. Lindsey
John E. Brengle	Vicki L. Buba
Patrick R. Holland, II	Allen C. Platt III (Resident,
Edwin Jon Wolfe	New Albany, Indiana Office)

OF COUNSEL

Robert S. Frey

For full biographical listings, see the Martindale-Hubbell Law Directory

OWENSBORO,* Daviess Co.

KAMUF, YEWELL, PACE & CONDON (AV)

Great Financial Federal Building, 322 Frederica Street, 42301
Telephone: 502-685-3901
Fax: 502-926-2005

MEMBERS OF FIRM

Charles J. Kamuf	Patrick D. Pace
David L. Yewell	David C. Condon

(See Next Column)

KAMUF, YEWELL, PACE & CONDON, *Owensboro—Continued*

ASSOCIATE

John M. Mischel

Representative Clients: Owensboro Municipal Utilities Commission; Lincoln Service Corp.; Hancock County Planning Commission; Daviess County Board of Education; Barmet Aluminum Corp.; Owensboro Sewer Commission; TICOR Title Insurance Co.; Chicago Title Insurance Co.; Owensboro Riverport Authority; Housing Authority of Owensboro.

For full biographical listings, see the Martindale-Hubbell Law Directory

LOUISIANA

*MONROE,** Ouachita Parish

McLEOD VERLANDER (AV)

A Partnership including Professional Law Corporations
1900 North 18th Street, Suite 610, P.O. Box 2270, 71207-2270
Telephone: 318-325-7000
Telecopier: 318-324-0580
Email: mvlaw@iamerica.net

MEMBERS OF FIRM

Robert P. McLeod (P.L.C.)	Rick W. Duplissey
David E. Verlander, III (P.L.C.)	Pamela G. Nathan
Laurie J. Burkett	

For full biographical listings, see the Martindale-Hubbell Law Directory

*SHREVEPORT,** Caddo Parish

MILLS, TIMMONS & FLOWERS, A PROFESSIONAL LAW CORPORATION (AV)

300 Law Center, 331 Milam Street, P.O. Box 1784, 71166-1784
Telephone: 318-222-0337
Fax: 318-222-5400

George H. Mills, Jr.	David C. Turansky
Wayne Timmons	J. Broocks Greer III
Peter R. Flowers	Sandra Lynn Walker

OF COUNSEL

William T. Allison

Reference: Hibernia National Bank.

For full biographical listings, see the Martindale-Hubbell Law Directory

SOCKRIDER, BOLIN & ANGLIN, A PROFESSIONAL LAW CORPORATION (AV)

327 Crockett Street, 71101
Telephone: 318-221-5503
Fax: 318-221-3849

John R. Pleasant (1905-1983)	James E. Bolin, Jr.
H. F. Sockrider, Jr.	D. Rex Anglin
Gregory H. Batte	

For full biographical listings, see the Martindale-Hubbell Law Directory

MARYLAND

*ANNAPOLIS,** Anne Arundel Co.

ROGER A. PERKINS (AV)

Suite 202, The Courtyards, 133 Defense Highway, 21401
Telephone: 410-266-3558
Baltimore: 410-841-6368
FAX: 410-841-6466

For full biographical listings, see the Martindale-Hubbell Law Directory

*BALTIMORE,** (Independent City)

LAW OFFICE OF JULIE ELLEN LANDAU (AV)

201 North Charles Street, Suite 1330, 21201
Telephone: 410-625-1100
Fax: 410-576-0140

ASSOCIATE

Julie Klein Cutler

For full biographical listings, see the Martindale-Hubbell Law Directory

THOMAS & LIBOWITZ, A PROFESSIONAL ASSOCIATION (AV)

USF&G Tower, Suite 1100, 100 Light Street, 21202-1053
Telephone: 410-752-2468
Telecopier: 410-752-2046

Michael S. Libowitz

For full biographical listings, see the Martindale-Hubbell Law Directory

VENABLE ATTORNEYS AT LAW VENABLE, BAETJER AND HOWARD, LLP (AV)

A Partnership including Professional Corporations
1800 Mercantile Bank & Trust Building, 2 Hopkins Plaza, 21201
Telephone: 410-244-7400
Email: INFO@Venable.win.net
Washington, D.C. Office: Venable, Baetjer, Howard & Civiletti LLP. Suite 1000, 1201 New York Avenue, N.W.
Telephone: 202-962-4800.
McLean, Virginia Office: Suite 400, 2010 Corporate Ridge.
Telephone: 703-760-1600.
Rockville, Maryland Office: Suite 500, One Church Street, P. O. Box 1906.
Telephone: 301-217-5600.
Towson, Maryland Office: 210 Allegheny Avenue, P. O. Box 5517.
Telephone: 410-494-6200.

MEMBERS OF FIRM

John H. Zink, III (Resident, Towson, Maryland Office)	L. Paige Marvel
Paul T. Glasgow (Resident, Rockville, Maryland Office)	Christopher R. Mellott
Craig E. Smith	Mitchell Y. Mirviss
Michael Schatzow (Also at Washington, D.C. Office)	Michael W. Robinson (Resident, McLean, Virginia Office)

ASSOCIATES

Carla Draluck Craft (Resident, Washington, D.C. Office)	Patricia A. Malone (Resident, Towson, Maryland Office)
Mary-Dulany James (Resident, Towson, Maryland Office)	Vicki Margolis (Also at Washington, D.C. Office)
Gregory L. Laubach (Resident, Rockville, Maryland Office)	John A. McCauley

For Complete List of Firm Personnel, See General Section

For full biographical listings, see the Martindale-Hubbell Law Directory

*BEL AIR,** Harford Co.

BROWN, BROWN & BROWN, A PROFESSIONAL ASSOCIATION (AV)

200 South Main Street, 21014
Telephone: 410-838-5500
Baltimore: 410-879-2220
Fax: 410-893-0402

A. Freeborn Brown	Augustus F. Brown
T. Carroll Brown	Albert J. A. Young

A. Frank Carven, III	Christopher R. vanRoden
Harold Douglas Norton	David E. Carey
Ankur P. Dalal	

Attorneys for: Baltimore Gas & Electric Co.; Chesapeake & Potomac Telephone Co.; Aberdeen Proving Ground Federal Credit Union; First Virginia Bank-Central Maryland; First National Bank of Maryland; Bell Atlantic Mobile Systems; First Harbor Securities; Maryland Portable Concrete, Inc. *Approved Counsel for:* The Chicago Title Insurance Co. of Maryland, Inc.

For full biographical listings, see the Martindale-Hubbell Law Directory

BETHESDA, Montgomery Co.

DECKELBAUM OGENS & FISCHER, CHARTERED (AV)

6701 Democracy Boulevard, 20817
Telephone: 301-564-5100
Washington D.C. Office: 1140 Connecticut Avenue, N.W.
Telephone: 202-223-1474.

Nelson Deckelbaum	Lawrence H. Fischer
Ronald L. Ogens	Deborah E. Reiser

Ronald G. Scheraga	Bryn Hope Sherman
Darryl Alan Feldman	

LEGAL SUPPORT PERSONNEL

Shirley Mostow

Representative Clients: The Charles E. Smith Companies; The Trammell Crow Company.
References: Franklin National Bank; Century National Bank.

For full biographical listings, see the Martindale-Hubbell Law Directory

Bethesda—Continued

MOSS, STRICKLER & SACHITANO, P.A. (AV)

Suite 700 N, 4550 Montgomery Avenue, 20814
Telephone: 301-657-8805
Facsimile: 301-657-8815

| Stephen E. Moss | Scott Michael Strickler |
| | Nancy A. Sachitano |

| Joel Weinshank | Penelope A. Lantz |

For full biographical listings, see the Martindale-Hubbell Law Directory

---

CHEVY CHASE, Montgomery Co.

GRONER AND GRONER, CHARTERED (AV)

The Chevy Chase Building, 5530 Wisconsin Avenue, Suite 1208, 20815-4301
Telephone: 301-657-2828
Fax: 301-657-2450

| Beverly Anne Groner | Samuel B. Groner |
| | (On Leave of Absence) |

Reference: Nation's Bank, Bethesda, Maryland Branch.

For full biographical listings, see the Martindale-Hubbell Law Directory

---

GREENBELT, Prince Georges Co.

STANLEY S. PICKETT (AV)

Suite 414 Capital Office Park, 6411 Ivy Lane, 20770
Telephone: 301-513-0613
Fax: 301-513-0618

Stanley Sinclair Pickett
ASSOCIATE
Gordon J. Brumback
LEGAL SUPPORT PERSONNEL
Stacy S. Pickett (Law Clerk)   Vivian W. Wolfe (Paralegal)

Representative Clients: B.F. Saul Co.; McDonald and Eudy Printers, Inc.; Condominium Management, Inc.; Long & Foster Realtors; Mitron Systems Corp.; Coldwell Banker; Glenanden Housing Authority; Koones & Montgomery, Inc.; Community Associations, Inc.

For full biographical listings, see the Martindale-Hubbell Law Directory

---

ROCKVILLE,* Montgomery Co.

JO BENSON FOGEL, P.A. (AV)

Georgetowne Park, 5900 Hubbard Drive, 20852
Telephone: 301-468-2288
FAX: 301-881-9074

Jo Benson Fogel

Farida Moreau Robinson

For full biographical listings, see the Martindale-Hubbell Law Directory

---

MILLER, STEINBERG & HESSLER (AV)

Suite 414, 414 Hungerford Drive, 20850
Telephone: 301-424-1180
Fax: 301-424-8459

MEMBERS OF FIRM
| James Robert Miller | Harvey B. Steinberg |
| | Kevin G. Hessler |

Reference: NationsBank, Rockville Branch.

For full biographical listings, see the Martindale-Hubbell Law Directory

---

STEIN, SPERLING, BENNETT, DE JONG, DRISCOLL, GREENFEIG & METRO, P.A. (AV)

25 West Middle Lane, 20850
Telephone: 301-340-2020; 800-435-5230
Telecopier: 301-340-8217

| David C. Driscoll, Jr. | Stuart S. Greenfeig |
| | Paul T. Stein |

Darcy A. Shoop

For Complete List of Firm Personnel, See General Section

For full biographical listings, see the Martindale-Hubbell Law Directory

---

TOWSON,* Baltimore Co.

BREGEL, KERR, DAVIS & DANTES (AV)

101 East Chesapeake Avenue, Suite 200A, 21204
Telephone: 410-828-6818
FAX: 410-494-1035

(See Next Column)

Howard C. Bregel (1903-1976)
OF COUNSEL
Calvert Ross Bregel
MEMBERS OF FIRM
| William T. Kerr | Phillip G. Dantes |
| | Michael Hart Davis |
ASSOCIATES
| Shirley A. Lindsey | Beverly A. Wallace |

For full biographical listings, see the Martindale-Hubbell Law Directory

---

UPPER MARLBORO,* Prince Georges Co.

KNIGHT, MANZI, BRENNAN, SHAY AND HAM, A PROFESSIONAL ASSOCIATION (AV)

14440 Old Mill Road, 20772
Telephone: 301-952-0100
Annapolis/Baltimore: 410-792-3786
Fax: 301-952-0221
Crofton, Maryland Office: 2411 Crofton Lane, # 26.
Telephone: 301-261-0808.
Fax: 301-261-6945.
Mitchellville, Maryland Office: 12164 Central Avenue, Suite 228.
Telephone: 301-390-0577.
Fax: 301-390-8464.

William E. Knight	John F. Shay, Jr.
Robert A. Manzi	Richard J. Ham
William C. Brennan, Jr.	Martin J. Shuham

| Monica M. Haley-Pierson | Norman D. Rivera |
| Daniel F. Lynch III | Robert L. Lombardo |
OF COUNSEL
Stuart R. Hammett

For full biographical listings, see the Martindale-Hubbell Law Directory

---

MASSACHUSETTS

BOSTON, Suffolk Co.

ATWOOD & CHERNY (AV)

Mason House 211 Commonwealth Avenue, 02116
Telephone: 617-262-6400
Telecopier: 617-421-9482

| Jacob M. Atwood | David E. Cherny |
| | Pasquale DeSantis |
OF COUNSEL
Margaret F. McGovern

For full biographical listings, see the Martindale-Hubbell Law Directory

---

CUDDY BIXBY (AV)

One Financial Center, 02111
Telephone: 617-348-3600
Telecopier: 617-348-3643
Wellesley, Massachusetts Office: 60 Walnut Street.
Telephone: 617-235-1034.

| Brian D. Bixby | Robert J. O'Regan |

For Complete List of Firm Personnel, See General Section

For full biographical listings, see the Martindale-Hubbell Law Directory

---

FRIEDMAN & ATHERTON (AV)

(Formerly Friedman, Atherton, King & Turner)
(Formerly Friedman, Atherton, Sisson & Kozol)
Exchange Place, 53 State Street, 02109-2803
Telephone: 617-227-5540
Telecopier: 617-523-1559

| Lee M. Friedman (1895-1957) | Percy A. Atherton (1903-1940) |
| | Frank L. Kozol (1927-1993) |
OF COUNSEL
Frank H. Shapiro
MEMBERS OF FIRM
Joel A. Kozol	Matthew S. Kozol
Lee H. Kozol	Alan M. Spiro
William I. Cowin	David L. Kelston
Robert D. Kozol	Victor Bass
Richard M. Zinner	David M. Kozol

(See Next Column)

FRIEDMAN & ATHERTON, *Boston—Continued*

ASSOCIATES

Andrew D. Cummings	Penny Kozol
Christine P. Deshler	Olive E. Larson
Paula F. Donahue	David A. Rich
Eric J. Kozol	Marie C. Vaccarelli
Herbert Weinberg	

COUNSEL

Paul S. Alpert	Debra Dyleski-Najjar
Thomas C. Bailey	Michael P. Morizio

For full biographical listings, see the Martindale-Hubbell Law Directory

GELB & GELB (AV)

20 Custom House Street, 02110
Telephone: 617-345-0010
Facsimile: 617-345-0009

MEMBER OF FIRM
Gail Kleven Gelb

For full biographical listings, see the Martindale-Hubbell Law Directory

PACKENHAM, SCHMIDT & FEDERICO, P.C. (AV)

Four Longfellow Place, 35th Floor, 02114-2832
Telephone: 617-742-6565
Fax: 617-742-0292

Richard D. Packenham	Mary H. Schmidt
Phyllis E. Federico	

David A. Schwartz

For full biographical listings, see the Martindale-Hubbell Law Directory

PEABODY & ARNOLD (AV)

A Partnership including Professional Corporations
50 Rowes Wharf, 02110-3342
Telephone: 617-951-2100
Telecopier: 617-951-2125
Providence, Rhode Island Office: One Citizens Plaza, Suite 840.
Telephone: 401-831-8330.
Fax: 401-831-8359.

MEMBER OF FIRM
Samuel S. Robinson

For Complete List of Firm Personnel, See General Section

For full biographical listings, see the Martindale-Hubbell Law Directory

SHERBURNE, POWERS & NEEDHAM, P.C. (AV)

One Beacon Street, 02108
Telephone: 617-523-2700
Fax: 617-523-6850
Email: @SHERBURNE.COM

William D. Weeks	Benjamin Volinski
John T. Collins	Mark Schonfeld
Allan J. Landau	James D. Smeallie
Stephen A. Hopkins	Paul Killeen
Alan I. Falk	Gordon P. Katz
C. Thomas Swaim	Joseph B. Darby, III
James Pollock	Richard M Yanofsky
William V. Tripp III	James E. McDermott
Stephen S. Young	Kenneth P. Brier
William F. Machen	Robert V. Lizza
W. Robert Allison	Miriam Goldstein Altman
Philip J. Notopoulos	John J. Monaghan
Richard J. Hindlian	Margaret J. Palladino
Paul E. Troy	Mark C. Michalowski
Harold W. Potter, Jr.	David Scott Sloan
Philip S. Lapatin	M. Chrysa Long
Pamela A. Duckworth	Lawrence D. Bradley
Miriam J. McKendall	

Cynthia A. Brown	Amy J. Mastrobattista
Cynthia M. Hern	Leslie A. Sprinkle
Meredeth A. Beers	Douglas W. Clapp
Dianne R. Phillips	Jeffrey A. Huebschmann
Paul M. James	Tamara E. Goulston
Theodore F. Hanselman	Paul G. Lannon, Jr.
Joshua C. Krumholz	Nicholas J. Psyhogeos
Ieuan G. Mahony	Edward J. Naughton
Jeffrey J. Nix	Kathaleen Kelly Cutone
(Not admitted in MA)	Laurie A. Tribble
Kenneth L. Harvey	Neil C. Higgins
Christopher J. Trombetta	Deborah Paige Stone
Elise N. Zoli	Brian R. Popiel

(See Next Column)

COUNSEL

Haig Der Manuelian	Karl J. Hirshman
Mason M. Taber, Jr.	Dale R. Johnson

For full biographical listings, see the Martindale-Hubbell Law Directory

WHITE, INKER, ARONSON, P.C. (AV)

One Washington Mall, 02108
Telephone: 617-367-7700
Telecopier: 617-523-5085

Monroe L. Inker	Laura J. Cervizzi
Martin L. Aronson	Kevin R. Connelly
John P. White, Jr.	Libby G. Fulgione, II
Leilah Anne Keamy	James D. Takacs
Ann E. Wagner	Patricia A. Kindregan
Frances M. Giordano	Martha W. Carroll
Laura Davis Smith	

For full biographical listings, see the Martindale-Hubbell Law Directory

WITMER, KARP, WARNER & THUOTTE (AV)

One Joy Street, 02108
Telephone: 617-248-0550
Telefax: 617-248-0607
Email: wkwt@aol.com

Ronald A. Witmer	Mark J. Warner
Eric H. Karp	Robert W. Thuotte

ASSOCIATES

Elisabeth A. Pelletier	Jill E. Zimmerman

For full biographical listings, see the Martindale-Hubbell Law Directory

*CAMBRIDGE,** Middlesex Co.

BENJAMIN & BENSON (AV)

Bulfinch Square, 43 Thorndike Street, 02141
Telephone: 617-577-1515
Fax: 617-577-0595

Roberta F. Benjamin	Jon Benson

ASSOCIATE
Phyllis K. Kolman

For full biographical listings, see the Martindale-Hubbell Law Directory

FITCHBURG, Worcester Co.

O'CONNOR AND RYAN, P.C. (AV)

61 Academy Street, 01420
Telephone: 508-345-4166
Fax: 508-343-8416

John M. O'Connor	Edward P. Ryan, Jr.

For full biographical listings, see the Martindale-Hubbell Law Directory

FRANKLIN, Norfolk Co.

PAUL A. CATALDO & ASSOCIATES (AV)

55 West Central Street, P.O. Box 435, 02038
Telephone: 508-528-2400
Fax: 508-520-0699

Paul A. Cataldo

ASSOCIATES

Cheryl A. Tracy	Joseph P. Cataldo

References: The Benjamin Franklin Savings Bank; Bank of Boston.

For full biographical listings, see the Martindale-Hubbell Law Directory

NEWTON, Middlesex Co.

SHARYN T. SOOHO (AV)

Two Newton Place, Suite 200, 02158-1634
Telephone: 617-969-1400
Telecopier: 617-964-1694
URL: http://www.DivorceNet.com

Steven L. Fuchs

LEGAL SUPPORT PERSONNEL
Steven J. Steinmetz

For full biographical listings, see the Martindale-Hubbell Law Directory

PLYMOUTH,* Plymouth Co.

MILES AND MILES, A PROFESSIONAL ASSOCIATION (AV)

7 South Park Avenue, 02360
Telephone: 508-746-2660
Fax: 508-830-0395
Duxbury, Massachusetts Office: 907 Tremont Street, P.O. Box 1686, 02331
-1686.
Telephone: 617-934-5474

Frankland W. L. Miles	Frankland W. L. Miles, Jr.
(1897-1974)	John Grother Miles

For full biographical listings, see the Martindale-Hubbell Law Directory

MICHIGAN

ANN ARBOR,* Washtenaw Co.

HOOPER, HATHAWAY, PRICE, BEUCHE & WALLACE (AV)

126 South Main Street, 48104
Telephone: 313-662-4426
Fax: 313-662-9559

Joseph C. Hooper (1899-1980)	Gregory A. Spaly
John R. Hathaway (Retired)	Robert W. Southard
Alan E. Price	William J. Stapleton
James R. Beuche	Bruce C. Conybeare, Jr.
Bruce T. Wallace	Anthony P. Patti
Charles W. Borgsdorf	Marcia J. Major
Mark R. Daane	Angela L. Jackson

OF COUNSEL

James A. Evashevski	Roderick K. Daane

Representative Clients: Chem-Trend, Inc.; Dundee Cement Co.; Ervin Industries, Inc.; First Martin Corp.; Group 243 Design, Inc.; Honeywell; Microwave Sensors, Inc.; Shearson Lehman Hutton; O'Neal Construction Co.; Pittsfield Products, Inc.

For full biographical listings, see the Martindale-Hubbell Law Directory

MILLER, CANFIELD, PADDOCK AND STONE, P.L.C. (AV)

A Professional Limited Liability Company
Founded in 1852 by Sidney Davy Miller
101 North Main Street, Seventh Floor, 48104-1400
Telephone: 313-663-2445
Fax: 313-747-7147
Detroit, Michigan Office: 150 West Jefferson, Suite 2500, 48226-4415.
Telephone: 313-963-6420.
Fax: 313-496-7500.
Cable Address: "Stem Detroit."
Bloomfield Hills, Michigan Office: Suite 100, Pinehurst Office Center, 1400 North Woodward, 48303-2014.
Telephone: 313-645-5000.
Fax: 313-645-1917.
Grand Rapids, Michigan Office: 1200 Campau Square Plaza, 99 Monroe, N.W., 49503-2639.
Telephone: 616-454-8656.
Fax: 616-776-6322.
Howell, Michigan Office: 121 South Barnard Street, Suite 4, 48843-2305.
Telephone: 517-546-7600.
Telecopier: 517-546-6974.
Kalamazoo, Michigan Office: 444 West Michigan Avenue, 49007-3752.
Telephone: 616-381-7030.
Fax: 616-382-0244.
Lansing, Michigan Office: One Michigan Avenue, Suite 900, 48933-1609.
Telephone: 517-487-2070.
Fax: 517-374-6304.
Monroe, Michigan Office: The Executive Centre, 214 East Elm Avenue, 48161-2682.
Telephone: 313-243-2000.
Fax: 313-243-0901.
Washington, D.C. Office: 1225 Nineteenth Street, N.W., Suite 400. 20036.
Telephone: 202-429-5575; 785-0600.
Fax: 202-331-1118; 785-1234.
Pensacola, Florida Office: 25 West Cedar, 32501.
Telephone: 904-469-1088.
Fax: 904-432-0677.
St. Petersburg, Florida Office: 100 Second Avenue S., Suite 7045, 33701.
Telephone: 813-982-6000.
Fax: 813-892-6002.
New York, New York Office: Eleventh Floor, 135 East 57th Street, 10022-2087.
Telephone: 212-754-5400.
Fax: 212-754-5401.
Gdansk, Poland Office: Suite 322, Dom Technika Building, UI. Rajska 6, 80-850.
Telephone: 011-485-831-2808.
Fax: 011-485-831-4719.

(See Next Column)

Warsaw, Poland Office: UI. Marszalkowska 82, Suite 561, 00-517.
Telephone: 011-482-623-6457 and 6458.
Fax: 011-482-623-6459.

RESIDENT PRINCIPALS
Robert E. Gilbert

Representative Firm Clients: Chrysler Corporation; Comerica, Incorporated; City of Detroit, Michigan; Detroit Tigers, Inc.; First of Michigan; Ford Motor Company; Ford Motor Credit Company; Great Lakes Bancorp; Henry Ford Hospital; INVETECH Company.

For Complete List of Firm Personnel, See General Section

For full biographical listings, see the Martindale-Hubbell Law Directory

PEAR SPERLING EGGAN & MUSKOVITZ, P.C. (AV)

Domino's Farms, 24 Frank Lloyd Wright Drive, 48105
Telephone: 313-665-4441
Fax: 313-665-8788
Ypsilanti, Michigan Offices: 5 South Washington Street.
Telephone: 313-483-3626 and 2164 Bellevue at Washtenaw.
Telephone: 313-483-7177.

Edwin L. Pear	Paul R. Fransway
Andrew M. Eggan	Francyne Stacey
Thomas E. Daniels	Helen Conklin Vick

Counsel For: Domino's Pizza, Inc.; Townsend and Bottum, Inc.; The Credit Bureau of Ypsilanti; Margolis Nursery, Inc.; Wiards Orchards.

For Complete List of Firm Personnel, See General Section

For full biographical listings, see the Martindale-Hubbell Law Directory

BINGHAM FARMS, Oakland Co.

SHELDON G. LARKY (AV)

Suite 3350, 30600 Telegraph Road, 48025-4533
Telephone: 810-642-4660

For full biographical listings, see the Martindale-Hubbell Law Directory

BIRMINGHAM, Oakland Co.

BUTZEL LONG, A PROFESSIONAL CORPORATION (AV)

Suite 200, 32270 Telegraph Road, 48025
Telephone: 810-258-1616
Telecopier: 810-258-1439
Email: melnick@butzel.com *URL:* http://www.butzel.com
Detroit, Michigan Office: Suite 900, 150 West Jefferson.
Telephone: 313-225-7000.
Telecopier: 313-225-7080.
Lansing, Michigan Office: 118 West Ottawa Street.
Telephone: 517-372-6622.
Telecopier: 517-372-6672.
Ann Arbor, Michigan Office: Suite 300, 350 South Main Street.
Telephone: 313-995-3110.
Telecopier: 313-995-1777.
Grosse Pointe Farms, Michigan Office: Suite 260, 21 Kercheval.
Telephone: 313-886-5446.
Telecopier: 313-886-2114.

Edward D. Gold (Resident)	T. Gordon Scupholm II
Frederick G. Buesser, III	(Resident)
(Resident)	

Patricia E. Nessel (Resident)

For full biographical listings, see the Martindale-Hubbell Law Directory

CARSON FISCHER, P.L.C. (AV)

Third Floor, 300 East Maple Road, 48009-6317
Telephone: 810-644-4840
Facsimile: 810-644-1832

Robert M. Carson

For full biographical listings, see the Martindale-Hubbell Law Directory

HYMAN AND LIPPITT, P.C. (AV)

185 Oakland Avenue, Suite 300, P.O. Box 1750, 48009
Telephone: 810-646-8292
Facsimile: 810-646-8375

J. Leonard Hyman	Kenneth F. Neuman
Norman L. Lippitt	Terry S. Givens
Douglas A. Hyman	Paul J. Fischer
Brian D. O'Keefe	John A. Sellers
H. Joel Newman	Robert H. Lippitt
Nazli G. Sater	Roger L. Myers
David N. Morrell, Jr.	

For full biographical listings, see the Martindale-Hubbell Law Directory

Birmingham—Continued

WEINGARDEN & HAUER, P.C. (AV)

30100 Telegraph Road, Suite 221, 48025
Telephone: 810-258-0800
Telecopier: 810-258-2750

Harvey I. Hauer

Reference: Security Bank & Trust.

For full biographical listings, see the Martindale-Hubbell Law Directory

WILLIAMS, SCHAEFER, RUBY & WILLIAMS, PROFESSIONAL CORPORATION (AV)

Suite 300, 380 North Woodward Avenue, 48009
Telephone: 810-642-0333
Telecopy: 810-642-0856

Thomas G. Plunkett	Richard D. Rattner
James P. Cunningham	

OF COUNSEL

John F. Schaefer	Mark A. Bank

For full biographical listings, see the Martindale-Hubbell Law Directory

BLOOMFIELD HILLS, Oakland Co.

BEIER HOWLETT, PROFESSIONAL CORPORATION (AV)

200 East Long Lake Road, Suite 110, 48304-2361
Telephone: 810-645-9400
Fax: 810-645-9344

Dean G. Beier	Thomas J. Trenta
James L. Howlett	Mark W. Hafeli
Daniel C. Devine	Timothy J. Currier
Gerald G. White	Mary T. Schmitt Smith
Lawrence R. Ternan	Robert R. Shuman
Stephen W. Jones	John D. Staran
Frank S. Galgan	Joseph F. Yamin
Kenneth J. Sorensen	Phyllis Aiuto Zimmerman

P. Daniel Christ	Amy D. Comito
Richard A. Joslin, Jr.	Michael C. Gibbons
Lauren M. Underwood	George S. Fish
Nicole D. Bogard	

OF COUNSEL

Robert G. Waddell

Representative Clients: Automobile Club Insurance Association (AAA); City of Birmingham; City of Lake Angelus; City of Rochester Hills; C.J. Edwards, Inc.; Dundee Community Schools; First of America Bank; Lake States Insurance Company; MAC Values; Troy School District.

For full biographical listings, see the Martindale-Hubbell Law Directory

HARDIG PARSONS & PEDERSEN (AV)

74 West Long Lake Road, Suite 203, 48304
Telephone: 810-642-3500
Facsimile: 810-645-1128
Charlevoix, Michigan Office: 212 Bridge Street.
Telephone: 616-547-1200.
Facsimile: 616-547-1026.
Pawley's Island, South Carolina Office: 216 Highway 17, P.O. Box 1607, 29585.
Telephone: 803-237-9219.
Facsimile: 803-237-9530.
West Palm Beach, Florida Office: Suite 1450, 515 North Flagler.
Telephone: 407-833-1622.
Facsimile: 407-833-6933.

MEMBERS OF FIRM

Joseph L. Hardig, Jr.	Joseph L. Hardig, III
Donald H. Parsons	Edward C. Pedersen
Bradley S. Stout	

ASSOCIATE

Capri L. Pelshaw

OF COUNSEL

Edward K. Pedersen, Jr.

MEMBER IN SOUTH CAROLINA

John C. Benso

For full biographical listings, see the Martindale-Hubbell Law Directory

MEYER, KIRK, SNYDER & SAFFORD, PLLC (AV)

Suite 100, 100 West Long Lake Road, 48304
Telephone: 810-647-5111
Telecopier: 810-647-6079
Detroit, Michigan Office: 2500 Penobscot Building.
Telephone: 313-961-1261.

George E. Snyder

(See Next Column)

Boyd C. Farnam

Representative Clients: Available Upon Request.

For Complete List of Firm Personnel, See General Section

For full biographical listings, see the Martindale-Hubbell Law Directory

DETROIT,* Wayne Co.

BEVERLY CLARK, P.C. (AV)

440 East Congress, Suite 4R, 48226-2917
Telephone: 313-961-4440

Beverly Clark

For full biographical listings, see the Martindale-Hubbell Law Directory

JAFFE, RAITT, HEUER & WEISS, PROFESSIONAL CORPORATION (AV)

One Woodward Avenue, Suite 2400, 48226
Telephone: 313-961-8380
Telecopier: 313-961-8358
Cable Address: "Jafsni"
Southfield, Michigan Office: Travelers Tower, Suite 1520.
Telephone: 313-961-8380.
Monroe, Michigan Office: 214 East Elm Avenue, Suite 208,
Telephone: 313-241-6470.
Telefacsimile: 313-241-3849.

Joel S. Golden	Sharon J. LaDuke
	Susan S. Lichterman

For Complete List of Firm Personnel, See General Section

For full biographical listings, see the Martindale-Hubbell Law Directory

MEYER, KIRK, SNYDER & SAFFORD, PLLC (AV)

2500 Penobscot Building, 48226
Telephone: 313-961-1261
Fax: 810-647-6079
Bloomfield Hills, Michigan Office: Suite 100, 100 West Long Lake Road.
Telephone: 313-647-5111.
Telecopier: 313-647-6079.

George E. Snyder

Representative Clients: Available Upon Request.

For Complete List of Firm Personnel, See General Section

For full biographical listings, see the Martindale-Hubbell Law Directory

MILLER, CANFIELD, PADDOCK AND STONE, P.L.C. (AV)

A Professional Limited Liability Company
Founded in 1852 by Sidney Davy Miller
150 West Jefferson, Suite 2500, 48226-4415
Telephone: 313-963-6420
Fax: 313-496-7500
Cable Address: "Stem Detroit"
Detroit, Michigan Office: 150 West Jefferson, Suite 2500, 48226-4415.
Telephone: 313-963-6420.
Fax: 313-496-7500.
Cable Address: "Stem Detroit."
Ann Arbor, Michigan Office: 101 North Main Street, 7th Floor, 48104-1400.
Telephone: 313-663-2445.
Fax: 313-747-7147.
Bloomfield Hills, Michigan Office: Suite 100, Pinehurst Office Center, 1400 North Woodward, 48303-2014.
Telephone: 313-645-5000.
Fax: 313-645-1917.
Grand Rapids, Michigan Office: 1200 Campau Square Plaza, 99 Monroe, N.W., 49503-2639.
Telephone: 616-454-8656.
Fax: 616-776-6322.
Howell, Michigan Office: 121 South Barnard Street, Suite 4, 48843-2305.
Telephone: 517-546-7600.
Telecopier: 517-546-6974.
Kalamazoo, Michigan Office: 444 West Michigan Avenue, 49007-3752.
Telephone: 616-381-7030.
Fax: 616-382-0244.
Lansing, Michigan Office: One Michigan Avenue, Suite 900, 48933-1609.
Telephone: 517-487-2070.
Fax: 517-374-6304.
Monroe, Michigan Office: The Executive Centre, 214 East Elm Avenue, 48161-2682.
Telephone: 313-243-2000.
Fax: 313-243-0901.
Washington, D.C. Office: 1225 Nineteenth Street, N.W., Suite 400. 20036.
Telephone: 202-429-5575; 785-0600.
Fax: 202-331-1118; 785-1234.

(See Next Column)

MILLER, CANFIELD, PADDOCK AND STONE P.L.C.—*Continued*

Pensacola, Florida Office: 25 West Cedar, 32501.
Telephone: 904-469-1088.
Fax: 904-432-0677.
St. Petersburg, Florida Office: 100 Second Avenue S., Suite 7045, 33701.
Telephone: 813-982-6000.
Fax: 813-892-6002.
New York, New York Office: Eleventh Floor, 135 East 57th Street, 10022-2087.
Telephone: 212-754-5400.
Fax: 212-754-5401.
Gdansk, Poland Office: Suite 322, Dom Technika Building, UI. Rajska 6, 80-850.
Telephone: 011-485-831-2808.
Fax: 011-485-831-4719.
Warsaw, Poland Office: UI. Marszalkowska 82, Suite 561, 00-517.
Telephone: 011-482-623-6457 and 6458.
Fax: 011-482-623-6459.

PRINCIPALS OF FIRM

James W. Williams (Bloomfield Hills Office)

ASSOCIATE

Dawn M. Schluter (Bloomfield Hills Office)

Representative Firm Clients: Chrysler Corporation; Comerica, Incorporated; City of Detroit, Michigan; Detroit Tigers, Inc.; First of Michigan; Ford Motor Company; Ford Motor Credit Company; Great Lakes Bancorp; Henry Ford Hospital; INVETECH Company.

For Complete List of Firm Personnel, See General Section

For full biographical listings, see the Martindale-Hubbell Law Directory

---

SCHUREMAN, FRAKES, GLASS & WULFMEIER (AV)

440 East Congress, Fourth Floor, 48226
Telephone: 313-961-1500
Telecopier: 313-961-1087
Harbor Springs, Michigan Office: One Spring Street Sq., 49740.
Telephone: 616-526-1145.
Telecopier: 616-526-9343.

MEMBERS OF FIRM

Jeptha W. Schureman   LeRoy H. Wulfmeier, III
John C. Frakes, Jr.   Cheryl L. Chandler
Charles F. Glass   David M. Ottenwess

ASSOCIATES

Daniel J. Dulworth   John J. Moran
Paul A. Salyers

Reference: Comerica.

For full biographical listings, see the Martindale-Hubbell Law Directory

---

EAST LANSING, Ingham Co.

FARHAT, STORY & KRAUS, P.C. (AV)

Beacon Place, 4572 South Hagadorn Road, Suite 3, 48823
Telephone: 517-351-3700
Fax: 517-332-4122
Email: rkraus@sojourn.com

Leo A. Farhat   Chris A. Bergstrom
James E. Burns (1925-1979) Kitty L. Groh
Monte R. Story   Charles R. Toy
Richard C. Kraus   David M. Platt
Max R. Hoffman Jr.   Thomas L. Sparks

Lawrence P. Schweitzer   Daniel B. Morgan
Debra A. Geroux   Mary K. Robbins-Kralapp

Reference: City Bank, St. Johns.

For full biographical listings, see the Martindale-Hubbell Law Directory

---

FARMINGTON HILLS, Oakland Co.

MICHAEL H. GOLOB (AV)

30300 Northwestern Highway, Suite 300, 48334
Telephone: 810-855-2626
Fax: 810-932-4009

For full biographical listings, see the Martindale-Hubbell Law Directory

---

GRAND RAPIDS,* Kent Co.

VARNUM, RIDDERING, SCHMIDT & HOWLETT LLP (AV)

A Limited Liability Partnership including Professional Corporations
Bridgewater Place, P.O. Box 352, 49501-0352
Telephone: 616-336-6000
800-262-0011
Facsimile: 616-336-7000
Telex: 1561593 VARN
Email: varnum@vrsh.com
Lansing, Michigan Office: The Victor Center, Suite 810, 210 North Washington Square, 48933.
Telephone: 517-482-6237.
Facsimile: 517-482-6937.
Kalamazoo, Michigan Office: 350 East Michigan Avenue, 49007.
Telephone: 616-382-2300.
Facsimile: 616-382-2382.
Grand Haven, Michigan Office: 321 Washington Street, P.O. Box 288, 49417.
Telephone: 616-846-7100.
Facsimile: 616-846-7101.
Battle Creek, Michigan Office: 4950 West Dickman Road, Suite B-1, 49015.
Telephone: 616-962-7144.
Bingham Farms, Michigan Office: 31600 Telegraph Road, Suite 230, 48025.
Telephone: 810-594-7330.
Facsimile: 810-594- 7331.

MEMBERS OF FIRM

Bruce A. Barnhart   N. Stevenson Jennette III

For Complete List of Firm Personnel, See General Section

For full biographical listings, see the Martindale-Hubbell Law Directory

---

ZERRENNER & ROANE (AV)

Grand Plaza Place, Suite 450, 220 Lyon Square, N.W., 49503
Telephone: 616-774-4414
Fax: 616-774-8203

James W. Zerrenner   Richard A. Roane

For full biographical listings, see the Martindale-Hubbell Law Directory

---

HOLLAND, Ottawa Co.

CUNNINGHAM DALMAN, P.C. (AV)

321 Settlers Road, P.O. Box 1767, 49422-1767
Telephone: 616-392-1821
Fax: 616-392-4769

Gordon H. Cunningham   Kenneth B. Breese
Ronald L. Dalman   Jeffrey K. Helder
Max R. Murphy   Ronald J. Vander Veen
James A. Bidol   David M. Zessin
Andrew J. Mulder   Mark H. Zietlow
Joel G. Bouwens   James W. Bouwens
              Randall S. Schipper

Susan E. Vroegop   Melinda M. Abney

OF COUNSEL

Vernon D. Ten Cate   Kenneth B. Peirce, Jr.

Representative Clients: FMB-First Michigan Bank; First of America Bank-Holland, N.A.; Ottawa Savings Bank; City of Holland; Auto Club Insurance Assn. (AAA); American States Insurance Co.; Holland Economic Development Corp.; Hope College; Western Theological Seminary.
Reference: FMB-First Michigan Bank.

For full biographical listings, see the Martindale-Hubbell Law Directory

---

KALAMAZOO,* Kalamazoo Co.

KREIS, ENDERLE, CALLANDER & HUDGINS, A PROFESSIONAL CORPORATION (AV)

One Moorsbridge, P.O. Box 4010, 49003-4010
Telephone: 616-324-3000
Telecopier: 616-324-3010
Email: kech@sapien.net *URL:* http://www.kech.com

Russell A. Kreis   Jeffery S. Rubel
         James C. Boerigter

For Complete List of Firm Personnel, See General Section

For full biographical listings, see the Martindale-Hubbell Law Directory

Kalamazoo—Continued

MILLER, CANFIELD, PADDOCK AND STONE, P.L.C. (AV)

A Professional Limited Liability Company
Founded in 1852 by Sidney Davy Miller
444 West Michigan Avenue, 49007-3752
Telephone: 616-381-7030
Fax: 616-382-0244
Detroit, Michigan Office: 150 West Jefferson, Suite 2500, 48226-4415.
Telephone: 313-963-6420.
Fax: 313-496-7500.
Cable Address: "Stem Detroit."
Ann Arbor, Michigan Office: 101 North Main Street, 7th Floor, 48104-1400.
Telephone: 313-663-2445.
Fax: 313-747-7147.
Bloomfield Hills, Michigan Office: Suite 100, Pinehurst Office Center, 1400 North Woodward, 48303-2014.
Telephone: 313-645-5000.
Fax: 313-645-1917.
Grand Rapids, Michigan Office: 1200 Campau Square Plaza, 99 Monroe, N.W., 49503-2639.
Telephone: 616-454-8656.
Fax: 616-776-6322.
Howell, Michigan Office: 121 South Barnard Street, Suite 4, 48843-2305.
Telephone: 517-546-7600.
Telecopier: 517-546-6974.
Lansing, Michigan Office: One Michigan Avenue, Suite 900, 48933-1609.
Telephone: 517-487-2070.
Fax: 517-374-6304.
Monroe, Michigan Office: The Executive Centre, 214 East Elm Avenue, 48161-2682.
Telephone: 313-243-2000.
Fax: 313-243-0901.
Washington, D.C. Office: 1225 Nineteenth Street, N.W., Suite 400. 20036.
Telephone: 202-429-5575; 785-0600.
Fax: 202-331-1118; 785-1234.
Pensacola, Florida Office: 25 West Cedar, 32501.
Telephone: 904-469-1088.
Fax: 904-432-0677.
St. Petersburg, Florida Office: 100 Second Avenue S., Suite 7045, 33701.
Telephone: 813-982-6000.
Fax: 813-892-6002.
New York, New York Office: Eleventh Floor, 135 East 57th Street, 10022-2087.
Telephone: 212-754-5400.
Fax: 212-754-5401.
Gdansk, Poland Office: Suite 322, Dom Technika Building, UI. Rajska 6, 80-850.
Telephone: 011-485-831-2808.
Fax: 011-485-831-4719.
Warsaw, Poland Office: UI. Marszalkowska 82, Suite 561, 00-517.
Telephone: 011-482-623-6457 and 6458.
Fax: 011-482-623-6459.

PRINCIPALS OF FIRM
Eric V. Brown, Jr.
SENIOR ATTORNEY
John G. VanSlambrouck

Representative Firm Clients: Chrysler Corporation; Comerica, Incorporated; City of Detroit, Michigan; Detroit Tigers, Inc.; First of Michigan; Ford Motor Company; Ford Motor Credit Company; Great Lakes Bancorp; Henry Ford Hospital; INVETECH Company.

For Complete List of Firm Personnel, See General Section

For full biographical listings, see the Martindale-Hubbell Law Directory

---

LANSING, Ingham Co.

DUNNINGS & FRAWLEY, P.C. (AV)

Duncan Building, 530 South Pine Street, 48933-2299
Telephone: 517-487-8222
Fax: 517-487-2026
Email: conrights@voyager.net

Stuart J. Dunnings, Jr.	John J. Frawley

Stuart J. Dunnings, III	Steven D. Dunnings
Shauna L. Dunnings	

For full biographical listings, see the Martindale-Hubbell Law Directory

---

MOUNT CLEMENS,* Macomb Co.

DANIEL T. STEPEK (AV)

76 South Main Street, Suite 100, 48043
Telephone: 810-463-3800
Fax: 810-463-7428

For full biographical listings, see the Martindale-Hubbell Law Directory

---

PONTIAC,* Oakland Co.

BOOTH PATTERSON, P.C. (AV)

1090 West Huron Street, 48328
Telephone: 810-681-1200
Fax: 810-681-1754

Douglas W. Booth (1918-1992)	David J. Lee
Calvin E. Patterson (1913-1987)	Allan T. Motzny
Parvin C. Lee, Jr.	Michael J. Hughes
J. Timothy Patterson	Michael D. Bishop
	Eric S. Meier

For full biographical listings, see the Martindale-Hubbell Law Directory

---

ROYAL OAK, Oakland Co.

KATHERINE L. BARNHART, P.C. (AV)

Sixth Floor Washington Square Plaza, 48067
Telephone: 810-543-2400
Fax: 810-543-2403
Email: KLBarnhart@aol.com

Katherine L. Barnhart	Karen S. Sendelbach

For full biographical listings, see the Martindale-Hubbell Law Directory

---

ST. JOSEPH,* Berrien Co.

TROFF, PETZKE & AMMESON (AV)

Law and Title Building, 811 Ship Street, P.O. Box 67, 49085
Telephone: 616-983-0161
Facsimile: 616-983-0166

MEMBERS OF FIRM

Theodore E. Troff	Roger A. Petzke
	Charles F. Ammeson

ASSOCIATES

Bennett S. Schwartz	Daniel G. Lambrecht
	Deborah L. Berecz

For full biographical listings, see the Martindale-Hubbell Law Directory

---

SOUTHFIELD, Oakland Co.

SOMMERS, SCHWARTZ, SILVER & SCHWARTZ, P.C. (AV)

2000 Town Center, Suite 900, 48075
Telephone: 810-355-0300
Telecopier: 810-746-4001
Plymouth, Michigan Office: 747 South Main Street.
Telephone: 313-455-4250.

Lawrence Warren	William M. Brukoff

General Counsel for: City of Taylor; Foodland Distributors; C.A. Muer Corporation; Vlasic & Company; Nederlander Corporation; Midwest Health Centers, P.C.
Representative Clients: Crum & Forster Insurance Company; City of Pontiac; Michigan National Bank.

For Complete List of Firm Personnel, See General Section

For full biographical listings, see the Martindale-Hubbell Law Directory

---

TROY, Oakland Co.

BOOKHOLDER, BASSETT, GORNBEIN & COHEN, P.L.L.C. (AV)

Long Lake Crossings, 1301 West Long Lake Road, Suite 355, 48098
Telephone: 810-641-0100
Fax: 810-641-0109

Ronald M. Bookholder	Henry S. Gornbein
Scott Bassett	Susan E. Cohen

For full biographical listings, see the Martindale-Hubbell Law Directory

POLING, McGAW & POLING, P.C. (AV)

Suite 275, 5435 Corporate Drive, 48098
Telephone: 810-641-0500
Telecopier: 810-641-0506

Benson T. Buck (1926-1989)	Richard B. Poling, Jr.
Richard B. Poling	Gregory C. Hamilton
D. Douglas McGaw	Veronica B. O'Haro
	James R. Parker

OF COUNSEL
Ralph S. Moore

Representative Clients: County of Oakland; City of Troy; United States Fidelity & Guaranty Co.; Sentry Insurance Co.; Admiral Insurance; DeMaria Construction Co.; Leo Corporation; Aetna Casualty and Surety Co.; Concord Design; Pneumo-Abex.

For full biographical listings, see the Martindale-Hubbell Law Directory

GENERAL PRACTICE

ALABAMA

ALBERTVILLE, Marshall Co.

GULLAHORN & HARE, P.C. (AV)

310 West Main Street, P.O. Box 1669, 35950
Telephone: 205-878-1891
Fax: 205-878-1965

Charles R. Hare, Jr.   John C. Gullahorn

Jeffrey B. Carr

Representative Clients: First Bank of Boaz; The Home Bank; Peoples Independent Bank of Boaz; AmSouth Bank; Compass Bank; Albertville Industrial Development Board; Boaz Industrial Development Board; Marshall-Dekalb Electric Cooperative; Olympia Construction, Inc.

For full biographical listings, see the Martindale-Hubbell Law Directory

ANDALUSIA,* Covington Co.

W. SIDNEY FULLER (AV)

28 South Court Square, P.O. Drawer 1637, 36420
Telephone: 334-222-4196
Fax: 334-222-4197

LEGAL SUPPORT PERSONNEL
Lenora O'Neal (Legal Assistant)

Representative Client: Covington County Bank.

For full biographical listings, see the Martindale-Hubbell Law Directory

ANNISTON,* Calhoun Co.

BURNHAM & KLINEFELTER, P.C. (AV)

South Trust Bank Building, Suite 401, P.O. Box 1618, 36202
Telephone: 205-237-8515
Fax: 205-236-5150

Herbert D. Jones, Jr. (1945-1988)	J. L. Klinefelter
William S. Halsey (Retired)	Patrick S. Burnham
H. R. Burnham	Thomas M. Sowa
	Polly D. Enger

Representative Clients: Alfa Insurance Cos.; United Services Auto Assn.; Motors Insurance Corp.; Fireman's Fund; SouthTrust Bank of Calhoun County, N.A.; America's First Credit Union; First South Production Credit; Calhoun County Board of Education; Calhoun County Commission; Coca-Cola Enterprises, Inc.

For full biographical listings, see the Martindale-Hubbell Law Directory

MERRILL, PORCH, DILLON & FITE, P.A. (AV)

Formerly Knox, Jones, Woolf & Merrill
5th Floor SouthTrust Bank, P.O. Box 580, 36202
Telephone: 205-237-2871
Fax: 205-237-3022

Robert C. Dillon	George A. Monk
Robert M. Field	Brenda S. Stedham
Arthur F. Fite, III	William J. Miller

OF COUNSEL

Walter J. Merrill   Ralph D. Porch

General Counsel for: Farmers & Merchants Bank; Northeast Alabama Regional Medical Center; City of Anniston.
Assistant Division Counsel: Norfolk Southern Corp.
Attorneys for: Alabama Power Co.; Browning Ferris Industries of Alabama, Inc.; Nationwide Mutual Insurance Co.; Maryland Casualty Co.; Lawyers Title Insurance Corp.; Monsanto Co.

For full biographical listings, see the Martindale-Hubbell Law Directory

ASHLAND,* Clay Co. — (Refer to Talladega)

ATHENS,* Limestone Co.

PATTON, LATHAM, LEGGE & COLE (AV)

Professional Building, 315 West Market Street, P.O. Box 470, 35611
Telephone: 205-232-2010
Fax: 205-230-0610

MEMBERS OF FIRM

Roy B. Patton (1885-1954)	Byrd R. Latham
David U. Patton (Retired)	Winston V. Legge, Jr.
P. Michael Cole	

(See Next Column)

Local Counsel for: Auto-Owners Insurance Co.; Avis; Blue Cross and Blue Shield of Alabama; CIGNA Insurance Cos.; Gold Kist, Inc.; State Farm Life Insurance Co.; State Farm Mutual Automobile Insurance Co.; Travelers Insurance Co.; United States Fidelity and Guaranty Co.; Wausau Insurance Company.

For full biographical listings, see the Martindale-Hubbell Law Directory

BESSEMER, Jefferson Co. — (Refer to Birmingham)

BIRMINGHAM,* Jefferson Co.

BAINBRIDGE, MIMS, ROGERS & SMITH (AV)

The Luckie Building, Suite 415, 600 Luckie Drive, P.O. Box 530886, 35253
Telephone: 205-879-1100
Fax: 205-879-4300

MEMBERS OF FIRM

Frank Bainbridge (1895-1980)	Frank M. Bainbridge
Walter L. Mims (1910-1993)	Bruce F. Rogers
Alfred F. Smith, Jr.	

For full biographical listings, see the Martindale-Hubbell Law Directory

BALCH & BINGHAM (AV)

1710 Sixth Avenue North, P.O. Box 306, 35201
Telephone: 205-251-8100
Facsimile: 205-226-8798
URL: http://www.balch.com
Other Birmingham, Alabama Office: 1901 Sixth Avenue North, 35203.
Telephone: 205-251-8100.
Facsimile: 205-226-8799.
Montgomery, Alabama Office: The Winter Building, 2 Dexter Avenue, 36101.
Telephone: 334-834-6500.
Facsimile: 334-269-3115.
Huntsville, Alabama Office: 204 Gates Avenue, 35801.
Telephone: 205-551-0171.
Facsimile: 205-551-0174.
Washington, D.C. Office: Suite 800, 1101 Connecticut Avenue, N.W., 20036.
Telephone: 202-296-0387.
Facsimile: 202-452-8180.

William Logan Martin (1883-1959)	Schuyler A. Baker (1915-1990)

COUNSEL

S. Eason Balch	Edward M. Rogers, Jr.
John Bingham	(Resident, Washington, D.C.
Joseph M. Farley	Office)
M. Roland Nachman, Jr. (Resident, Montgomery Office)	

MEMBERS OF FIRM

Maury D. Smith (Resident, Montgomery Office)	Richard L. Pearson
Harold A. Bowron, Jr.	James A. Bradford
A. Key Foster, Jr.	Dan H. McCrary
John S. Bowman (Resident, Montgomery Office)	William P. Cobb, II (Resident, Montgomery Office)
Charles M. Crook (Resident, Montgomery Office)	Alan T. Rogers
Sterling G. Culpepper, Jr. (Resident, Montgomery Office)	James A. Byram, Jr. (Resident, Montgomery Office)
Edward S. Allen	William S. Wright
Warren H. Goodwyn (Resident, Montgomery Office)	Susan B. Bevill
H. Hampton Boles	John J. Coleman, III
Michael L. Edwards	John F. Mandt
Marshall Timberlake	M. Stanford Blanton
Walter M. Beale, Jr.	T. Kurt Miller
Rodney O. Mundy	J. Thomas Francis, Jr.
James F. Hughey, Jr.	Timothy J. Tracy
S. Eason Balch, Jr.	Clark R. Hammond
John P. Scott, Jr.	W. Joseph McCorkle, Jr. (Resident, Montgomery Office)
S. Allen Baker, Jr.	
J. Foster Clark	Karl R. Moor (Resident, Washington, D.C. Office)
Randolph H. Lanier	
David R. Boyd (Resident, Montgomery Office)	Patrick J. McCormick, III (Resident, Washington, D.C. Office)
John Richard Carrigan	
Lee H. Zell	Will Hill Tankersley, Jr.
William E. Shanks, Jr.	Suzanne Ashe
T. Dwight Sloan	Mark A. Crosswhite
S. Revelle Gwyn (Resident, Huntsville Office)	Leonard Charles Tillman
	Dorman Walker (Resident, Montgomery Office)
William H. Satterfield	Alex B. Leath, III
Steven G. McKinney	Cavender Crosby Kimble
Steven F. Casey	Daniel M. Wilson (Resident, Huntsville Office)
Malcolm N. Carmichael (Resident, Montgomery Office)	Michael D. Freeman
	James H. Hancock, Jr.
	Robin G. Laurie (Resident, Montgomery Office)

(See Next Column)

BALCH & BINGHAM, *Birmingham—Continued*
MEMBERS OF FIRM (Continued)

Jesse Stringer Vogtle, Jr.	John S. Bowman, Jr. (Resident,
David B. Champlin	Montgomery Office)
Donald R. Jones, Jr. (Resident,	Gregory S. Curran
Montgomery Office)	

ASSOCIATES

Lois Smith Woodward	Randall D. McClanahan
John D. Buchanan	C. Grady Moore, III
Felton W. Smith	Lisa Johnson Sharp
Glenn G. Waddell	Rebecca J. Michael (Resident,
Suzanne Alldredge	Washington, D.C. Office)
Leslie M. Allen (Resident,	Teresa G. Minor
Montgomery Office)	G. Scott Morris
James Ernest Bridges, III	Ed R. Haden
(Resident, Montgomery	N. DeWayne Pope
Office)	Joseph B. Cartee
Gregory Carl Cook	John W. McCullough
Lyle David Larson	(Not admitted in AL)
Phillip Anthony Nichols	Andrew W. Tunnell
John Russell Campbell	Timothy John Segers
Paul B. Seeley	Anna C. Northington (Resident,
(Resident, Huntsville Office)	Montgomery Office)
Marcel L. Debruge	Cynthia G. Burnside
R. Bruce Barze, Jr.	Tom S. Roper
David B. Block	Katherine E. Griffith (Resident,
(Resident, Huntsville Office)	Washington, D.C. Office)
Matthew W. Bowden	John D Pickering
Leigh Anne Hodge	Martin E. Burke (Resident,
Cynthia H. Torbert (Resident,	Montgomery Office)
Montgomery Office)	William W. Stewart (Resident,
	Montgomery Office)

OF COUNSEL
Harold Williams

Counsel for: Alabama Power Co.; Blue Cross and Blue Shield of Alabama; The Boeing Company; Brasfield & Gorrie, Inc.; Compass Bancshares, Inc.; Harbert Corp.; Kimberly-Clark Corp.; Southern Company Services, Inc.; Southern Research Institute; Vesta Insurance Group, Inc.

For full biographical listings, see the Martindale-Hubbell Law Directory

---

BERKOWITZ, LEFKOVITS, ISOM & KUSHNER, A PROFESSIONAL CORPORATION (AV)

1600 SouthTrust Tower, 420 North Twentieth Street, 35203
Telephone: 205-328-0480
Telecopier: 205-322-8007

A. Berkowitz (1907-1985)	Frank S. James III
Arnold K. Lefkovits	D. J. Simonetti
Chervis Isom	W. Clark Goodwin
Harold B. Kushner	Patricia Clotfelter
B. G. Minisman, Jr.	Wesley C. Redmond
Henry I. Frohsin	Denise W. Killebrew
David A. Larsen	Thomas O. Kolb
A. Lee Martin, Jr.	Thomas J. Mahoney, Jr.
Barry S. Marks	Richard A. Pizitz, Jr.
Anne W. Mitchell	Andrew J. Potts
Susan S. Wagner	Walton E. Williams III

Nancy C. Hughes

Michael R. Silberman	Ellen Elizabeth Henderson
Judy P. Hamer	Hewes T. Hull
Robin L. Tucker	Lori L. Duwve
N. Andrew Rotenstreich	Elise Beth May

Frederick M. Thurman

Representative Clients: AlaTenn Resources, Inc.; AlaTenn Natural Gas Co.; B.A.S.S., Inc.; Hanna Steel Co., Inc.; Liberty Trouser Co., Inc.; McDonald's Corp.; Parisian, Inc.; Southern Pipe & Supply Co., Inc.

For full biographical listings, see the Martindale-Hubbell Law Directory

---

BISHOP, COLVIN, JOHNSON & KENT (AV)

317-20th Street, North, P.O. Box 370404, 35237
Telephone: 205-251-2881
Fax: 205-254-3987

MEMBERS OF FIRM

Maurice F. Bishop (1913-1982)	Burgin H. Kent
Gerald D. Colvin, Jr.	Gerald DeWitt (Whit) Colvin,
Carl E. Johnson, Jr.	III

Representative Clients: Miller Transporters, Inc.; United Van Lines, Inc.; Western Steel, Inc.; Alabama Building Products, Inc.; The City of Trussville, Alabama; Utilities Board of the City of Trussville, Alabama; Jefferson County Board of Education; University of Montevallo; Milan Express, Inc.
Reference: AmSouth Bank, N.A.

For full biographical listings, see the Martindale-Hubbell Law Directory

---

BRADLEY, ARANT, ROSE & WHITE (AV)

2001 Park Place, Suite 1400, P.O. Box 830709, 35283-0709
Telephone: 205-521-8000
Facsimile: 205-252-0264
Facsimile (SouthTrust Tower Office): 205-251-9915
URL: http://www.BARW.COM
Huntsville, Alabama Office: 200 Clinton Avenue West, Suite 900, 35801.
Telephone: 205-517-5100.
Facsimile: 205-533-5069.

MEMBERS OF FIRM

Douglas Arant (1897-1987)	John K. Molen
Wm. Alfred Rose (1900-1981)	Charles A. J. Beavers, Jr.
Ellene Winn (1911-1986)	Lant B. Davis
William W. Johnson, Jr.	Kenneth O. Simon
(1943-1984)	Carleta Roberts Hawley
Mary Louise Ahearn	James Walker May
(1934-1985)	M. Williams Goodwyn, Jr.
Bernard A. Monaghan	Bobby C. Underwood
(1916-1987)	Norman Jetmundsen, Jr.
Wm. Allen Smyly (1954-1993)	Joseph S. Bird, III
Lee C. Bradley, Jr. (Retired)	John B. Grenier
John James Coleman, Jr.	J. David Dresher
Edward M. Selfe	John D. Watson, III
Thomas Neely Carruthers, Jr.	Jay D. St. Clair
John H. Morrow	Ralph Howard Yeilding
Hobart A. McWhorter, Jr.	Scott E. Ludwig
Macbeth Wagnon, Jr.	(Resident, Huntsville Office)
Thad Gladden Long	G. Edward Cassady, III
John P. Adams	Michael R. Pennington
A. H. Gaede, Jr.	Michael D. McKibben
William L. Hinds, Jr.	David Glenn Hymer
Gary C. Huckaby	John William Hargrove
(Resident, Huntsville Office)	G. Rick Hall
James W. Gewin	(Resident, Huntsville Office)
Charles Larimore Whitaker	John E. Hagefstration, Jr.
John G. Harrell	Stuart Joseph Frentz
James Patrick Alexander	Paul S. Ware
Robert G. Johnson	Virginia Calvert Patterson
Robert C. Walthall	Sid J. Trant
Brittin Turner Coleman	Stewart M. Cox
Charles R. Smith, Jr.	Axel Bolvig III
(Resident, Huntsville Office)	Forrest K. Covington
E. Cutter Hughes, Jr.	Philip J. Carroll III
(Resident, Huntsville Office)	James S. Christie, Jr.
Andrew Robert Greene	Sherri Tucker Freeman
P. Nicholas Greenwood	Stephen K. Greene
James E. Rotch	J. David Pugh
Patrick H. Graves, Jr.	Kenneth T. Wyatt
(Resident, Huntsville Office)	Denson Nauls Franklin III
Laurence Duncan Vinson, Jr.	John E. Goodman
E. Mabry Rogers	T. Michael Brown
John P. Whittington	J. Paul Compton, Jr.
Alan K. Zeigler	Deane K. Corliss
Andrew J. Noble, III	L. Susan Doss
Walter J. Sears, III	George Bryan Harris
Linda A. Friedman	Warne S. Heath
Robert K. Spotswood	(Resident, Huntsville Office)
Joseph B. Mays, Jr.	Anne R. Yuengert

Susan Donovan Josey

COUNSEL

Wm. Bew White, Jr. (Retired)	John N. Wrinkle
J. Reese Murray	Stanley D. Bynum
Romaine S. Scott, Jr.	Walter H. Monroe, III
Robert R. Reid, Jr.	Scott M. Phelps
J. Robert Fleenor	Joan Crowder Ragsdale

K. Wood Herren

ASSOCIATES

Frank C. Galloway, III	Carolyn Reed Douglas
Michael S. Denniston	(Resident, Huntsville Office)
J. Patrick Darby	Douglas E. Eckert
Kevin J. Henderson	Kenneth M. Perry
Denise Avery Dodson	Fred M. Haston, III
Matthew H. Lembke	Richard L. Sharff, Jr.
Paige Maddox Davis	T. Matthew Miller
Richard H. Monk III	Charles K. Hamilton
Hall B, Bryant III	Rodney L. Moss
(Resident, Huntsville Office)	Kimberly A. Bessiere
Amy K. Myers	(Resident, Huntsville Office)
Paul D. Gilbert	Dorothy C. Daigle
Arnold W. Umbach, III	Helena F. Tozzi
John W. Smith T	Abdul K. Kallon
Jennifer Byers McLeod	Lauren E. Wagner
James W. Davis	David E. Roth
James Tassin	Kelly Hubbard Estes
(Resident, Huntsville Office)	Joseph E. Smith
James F. Archibald, III	Hugh Chester Boston, III
Jay R. Bender	Steven Austin King
Justin T. McDonald	Julie Scharfenberg Elmer

David M. Lawson

(See Next Column)

BRADLEY, ARANT, ROSE & WHITE—*Continued*

Counsel for: SouthTrust Bank of Alabama, National Association; Energen, Corporation; Blount, Inc.; Torchmark Corp.; Russell Corp.; Coca-Cola Bottling Company United, Inc.; Ford Motor Co.; Walter Industries, Inc.; The Birmingham Post Co. (Post-Herald); The New York Times Co.

For full biographical listings, see the Martindale-Hubbell Law Directory

BURR & FORMAN (AV)

3100 SouthTrust Tower, 420 North 20th Street, 35203
Telephone: 205-251-3000
Telecopier: 205-458-5100
Huntsville, Alabama Office: Suite 204, Regency Center, 400 Meridian Street.
Telephone: 205-551-0010.
Atlanta, Georgia Office: Suite 1800, One Georgia Center, 600 West Peachtree Street, 30308.
Telephone: 404-817-3536.
Facsimile: 404-817-3244.

Borden H. Burr (1876-1952)	Andrew J. Thomas (1897-1984)
James R. Forman (1880-1942)	Mark L. Taliaferro (1906-1981)

MEMBERS OF FIRM

C. V. Stelzenmuller	Bruce A. Rawls
Robert G. Tate	F. A. Flowers, III
J. Fred Powell	Michael L. Hall
L. Tennent Lee, III (Resident, Huntsville, Alabama Office)	Michael L. Lucas
	Dwight L. Mixson, Jr.
Samuel W. Oliver, Jr.	J. Hunter Phillips, III
Paul O. Woodall	David D. Dowd, III
J. Fredric Ingram	Carol H. Stewart
Louis H. Anders, Jr.	Robert H. Rutherford, Jr.
Robert B. Rubin	Gene T. Price
William C. Knight, Jr.	Henry Graham Beene
Joseph G. Stewart	Deborah P. Fisher
John D. Clements	Gail Livingston Mills
John F. DeBuys, Jr.	John C. Morrow
Mark Taliaferro, Jr.	Victor L. Hayslip
John W. Evans (Resident, Huntsville, Alabama Office)	W. Benjamin Johnson
	E. Clayton Lowe, Jr.
James Ross Forman, III	George F. Maynard (Resident, Atlanta, Georgia Office)
D. Frank Davis	
A. Brand Walton	Robert S. W. Given
John T. Mooresmith	Marvin Glenn Perry, Jr.
William F. Murray, Jr.	Mark McCarroll Lawson
Jack P. Stephenson, Jr.	Dent M. Morton
Eric L. Carlton	Jeffrey T. Baker
S. Dagnal Rowe (Resident, Huntsville, Alabama Office)	Paul P. Bolus
	David A. Elliott
W. Lee Thuston	Gary W. Farris (Resident, Atlanta, Georgia Office)
James J. Robinson	
Joseph W. Letzer	William S. Hereford
T. Thomas Cottingham, III	Jill Verdeyen Deer
J. Patrick Logan	Nancy L. Carter (Resident, Huntsville, Alabama Office)
George M. Taylor, III	
Gary M. London	Harri J. Haikala

OF COUNSEL

James R. Forman, Jr.	Samuel H. Burr
William K. Murray	A. Jackson Noble, Jr.

ASSOCIATES

Jennifer M. Busby	Howard E. Bogard
Allan G. Overton (Resident, Atlanta, Georgia Office)	William K. Holbrook
	John E. Norris
Warren C. Matthews	Cary Tynes Wahlheim
Gerald P. Gillespy	Clark A. Cooper
Timothy M. Lupinacci	Pamela Morse Arenberg
Alan P. Judge	D. Christopher Carson
S. Mark Burr (Resident, Atlanta, Georgia Office)	Gary Lane Howard
	Richard C. Keller
R. Michael Yarbro	James Earnest Fleenor, Jr.
Peter A. Grammas	Charles A. Hardin
Patricia Powell Burke	Reid Stephens Manley
William C. Byrd, II	Patrick G. Nelson (Resident, Huntsville, Alabama Office)
Darin W. Collier	
Allyson L. Edwards	Edward R. Christian
Eric Franz	Harlan F. Winn, III
Gregory F. Harley (Resident, Atlanta, Georgia Office)	Wendy Cornett
	Catherine A. Loveless
Jeffrey S. Miller	Shannon G. Marty
C. Gregory Burgess	

LEGAL SUPPORT PERSONNEL

J. Michael Tarpley (Director of Administration)

For full biographical listings, see the Martindale-Hubbell Law Directory

CABANISS, JOHNSTON, GARDNER, DUMAS & O'NEAL (AV)

Park Place Tower, 2001 Park Place North, Suite 700, P.O. Box 830612, 35283-0612
Telephone: 205-716-5200
Telecopier: 205-716-5200
Email: CabJohnston@aol.com
Mobile, Alabama Office: 700 AmSouth Center, P.O. Box 2906.
Telephone: 334-433-6961.
Telecopier: 334-433-1060.

Edward H. Cabaniss (1857-1936)	Lucien D. Gardner, Jr.
Forney Johnston (1879-1965)	(1903-1988)
M. Camper O'Neal (1907-1989)	

MEMBERS OF FIRM

William F. Gardner	F. Gerald Burnett
Crawford S. McGivaren, Jr.	David S. Dunkle
Sydney F. Frazier, Jr.	David L. Kane
Benjamen T. Rowe (Resident, Mobile Office)	(Resident, Mobile Office)
	R. Boyd Miller
William A. Robinson (Resident, Mobile Office)	(Resident, Mobile Office)
	R. Carlton Smyly
Patrick H. Sims (Resident, Mobile Office)	Steve A. Tucker
	Sandy G. Robinson
Donald J. Stewart (Resident at Mobile Office)	(Resident, Mobile Office)
	R. Taylor Abbot, Jr.
Roy J. Crawford	Herbert H. West, Jr.
William K. Thomas	Richard Eldon Davis

COUNSEL

L. Murray Alley

OF COUNSEL

Joseph F. Johnston	E. T. Brown, Jr.

ASSOCIATES

Melanie Merkle Bass	Douglas B. Kauffman
Cathryn Anne Berryman	Lisa J. Wathey
John M. Graham	David C. Skinner
Samuel D. Payne	James T. Pugh
Diane H. Crawley	

Counsel for: Alabaster Industries, Inc.; Schuler Industries, Inc.; Carraway Methodist Hospitals of Alabama; Doster Construction Co., Inc.; Liberty Mutual Insurance Co.; John Alden Life Insurance Co.; MacMillan Bloedel Packaging, Inc.; Norfolk Southern Corp.; O'Neal Steel, Inc.

For full biographical listings, see the Martindale-Hubbell Law Directory

COOPER, MITCH, CRAWFORD, KUYKENDALL & WHATLEY, L.L.C. (AV)

1100 Financial Center, 505 20th Street North, 35203-2605
Telephone: 205-328-9576
Telecopier: 205-328-9669

MEMBERS OF FIRM

Jerome A. Cooper	Frederick T. Kuykendall, III
William E. Mitch	Joe R. Whatley, Jr.
Thomas N. Crawford, Jr.	Glen M. Connor
Patricia Guthrie Fraley	

ASSOCIATES

Candis A. McGowan	Maureen Kane Berg
Andrew C. Allen	Gerald B. Taylor, Jr.
William Z. Cullen	Peter H. Burke
Samuel H. Heldman	Charlene Cullen
Hilary E. Ball-Walker	William Todd Harvey
Richard Paul Rouco	

OF COUNSEL

W. Braxton Schell, Jr.	Russell Jackson Drake

Counsel for: United Steelworkers of America, AFL-CIO; Birmingham Plumbers & Steamfitters Local Union No. 91 Pension Fund.
Reference: AMSouth Bank of Birmingham.

For full biographical listings, see the Martindale-Hubbell Law Directory

CORLEY, MONCUS & WARD, P.C. (AV)

400 Shades Creek Parkway, Suite 100, P.O. Box 59807, 35259
Telephone: 205-879-5959
Telecopier: 205-871-4411

Dale Corley (1942-1989)	James S. Ward
Claude McCain Moncus	Ezra B. Perry, Jr.

Christopher P. Moseley

For full biographical listings, see the Martindale-Hubbell Law Directory

DOMINICK, FLETCHER, YEILDING, WOOD & LLOYD, P.A. (AV)

2121 Highland Avenue, 35205
Telephone: 205-939-0033

(See Next Column)

DOMINICK, FLETCHER, YEILDING, WOOD & LLOYD P.A., *Birmingham—Continued*

Frank Dominick	J. Terrell McElheny
Walter Fletcher	Sammye Oden Kok
Manly Yeilding	Brian T. Williams
J. Fred Wood, Jr.	C. Clark Collier
Harold L. Ferguson, Jr.	B. Boozer Downs, Jr.
C. Fred Daniels	Mary P. Thornton
Susan Dominick Doughton	J. Mitchell Frost, Jr.

Judy Bateman Shepura

John W. Dodson	L. Hunter Compton, Jr.
Jim G. McLaughlin	Peter McKeever Wright

OF COUNSEL

Lee B. Lloyd

Counsel for: Citizens Federal Savings Bank; St. Vincent's Hospital; Birmingham-Southern College; Castle Mortgage Corporation; Methodist Homes for the Aging; Integrated Health Services, Inc.; American Home Assurance Co.; New Hampshire Insurance Group; The Cigna Cos.; Amerisure Companies.

For full biographical listings, see the Martindale-Hubbell Law Directory

---

GORDON, SILBERMAN, WIGGINS & CHILDS, A PROFESSIONAL CORPORATION (AV)

1400 SouthTrust Tower, 420 North 20th Street, 35203
Telephone: 205-328-0640
Telecopier: 205-254-1500

Louis Silberman (1889-1976)	Ray D. Gibbons
Robert S. Gordon (1914-1983)	C. Michael Quinn
Wilbur G. Silberman	Dennis George Pantazis
Bruce L. Gordon	Terrill W. Sanders
Robert L. Wiggins, Jr.	James Mendelsohn
Robert F. Childs, Jr.	Richard J. Ebbinghouse
Augustus J. Beck, Jr.	Ann K. Wiggins
Harvey L. Wachsman	Samuel Fisher

Ann C. Robertson

Paul H. Webb	Brian M. Clark
Mark P. Williams	Joel S. Isenberg
Timothy C. Gann	Rebecca J. Anthony
Timothy D. Davis	Craig L. Lowell
Joseph H. Calvin, III	Sandra B. Reiss
Linda J. Peacock	C. Paige Williams
Elizabeth Evans Courtney	N. Ronald Downey, III
Byron R. Perkins	Laura M. Hitt
Jon C. Goldfarb	Kyle T. Smith
Gregory O. Wiggins	Alan Garber
Lee Winston	(Not admitted in AL)
Jon E. Lewis	Amy W. Sinnott
Deborah A. Mattison	Paul O. Woodall, Jr.
Rocco Calamusa, Jr.	Christian E. Roberson

OF COUNSEL

Robert H. Loeb

For full biographical listings, see the Martindale-Hubbell Law Directory

---

GORHAM & WALDREP, P.C. (AV)

2101 6th Avenue North, Suite 700, 35203
Telephone: 205-254-3216; 251-9166
Telecopier: 205-324-3802
Email: info@gorham-waldrep.com
Montgomery, Alabama Office: 250 Commerce Street, P.O. Box 4837, 36104-4837.
Telephone: 334-262-0777.
Telecopier: 334-262-0742.

Charles W. Gorham	LaVeeda Morgan Battle
Charlie D. Waldrep	John T. Natter
Thomas L. Stewart	Frank G. Alfano
Michael G. Kendrick	Kay L. McNabb Cason
William J. Bryant	Victor Kelley

K. Mark Parnell

Victoria Franklin-Sisson	Leslie Miller Klasing
Karen Brown Evans	Brian Dennis Turner, Jr.
Mary H. Thompson	Anne D. Lamkin

Representative Clients: Jefferson County Personnel Board; Birmingham-Jefferson Civic Center Authority; The Water Works and Sewer Board of the City of Birmingham; City of Homewood; American Federation of Government Employees Local #1945; City of Pelham; Town of Kimberly; Alabama Tire Dealers Assn.; Southern States Body Shop Assn.

For full biographical listings, see the Martindale-Hubbell Law Directory

---

HASKELL SLAUGHTER & YOUNG, L.L.C. (AV)

1200 AmSouth/Harbert Plaza, 1901 Sixth Avenue North, 35203
Telephone: 205-251-1000
Facsimile: 205-324-1133
Montgomery, Alabama Office: 305 South Lawrence Street, P.O. Box 4660. 36103-4660.
Telephone: 334-265-8573.
Facsimile: 334-264-7945.

Wyatt Rushton Haskell	Mark Edward Ezell
William M. Slaughter	Stephen L. Poer
Frank M. Young, III	Thomas E. Reynolds
Benjamin B. Spratling III	Beverly P. Baker
Thomas T. Gallion, III	Ross N. Cohen
(Resident, Montgomery Office)	Richard H. Walston
Robert D. Shattuck, Jr.	Constance A. Caldwell
E. Alston Ray	(Resident, Montgomery Office)
James C. Huckaby, Jr.	Gwen L. Windle

Michael K. K. Choy

Carter H. Dukes	Barry D. Woodham
Paula B. Carroll	Georgia S. Roberson
Frank Hampton McFadden, Jr.	Susan E. Kennedy
John W. Scott	Rebecca Higgins Hunt

Representative Clients: The Bradford Group, Inc.; City of Birmingham; The Equitable Life Assurance Society of the United States; Exxon Corporation; Federal Deposit Insurance Corporation/Resolution Trust Corporation; HEALTHSOUTH Corporation/HEALTHSOUTH Medical Centers; Hughes Missile Systems; Montgomery County, Alabama; NationsBank Corporation; USX Corporation.

For full biographical listings, see the Martindale-Hubbell Law Directory

---

JOHNSTON, BARTON, PROCTOR & POWELL (AV)

2900 AmSouth/Harbert Plaza, 1901 Sixth Avenue North, 35203-2618
Telephone: 205-458-9400
Telecopier: 205-458-9500

MEMBERS OF FIRM

Harvey Deramus (1904-1970)	James C. Barton, Jr.
Alfred M. Naff (1923-1993)	Thomas E. Walker
Gilbert E. Johnston (1916-1994)	Anne P. Wheeler
G. Burns Proctor, Jr.	Barry V. Frederick
Sydney L. Lavender	Hollinger F. Barnard
Charles A. Powell, III	William D. Jones III
Jerome K. Lanning	David W. Proctor
Don B. Long, Jr.	Oscar M. Price III
Charles L. Robinson	W. Hill Sewell
J. William Rose, Jr.	Robert S. Vance, Jr.
Gilbert E. Johnston, Jr.	Richard J. Brockman
Ralph H. Smith II	Anthony A. Joseph

William G. Somerville, III

COUNSEL

Josh Mullins, Jr.	Paul E. Toppins

R. Marcus Givhan

OF COUNSEL

James C. Barton	Alfred Swedlaw

Alan W. Heldman

ASSOCIATES

William K. Hancock	Helen Kathryn Downs
James P. Pewitt	Jennifer Fox Swain
Scott Wells Ford	Spencer A. Kinderman
David M. Hunt	Scott R. McLaughlin
Lee M. Pope	Bradley C. Mayhew
John W. Sheffield	W. Jonathan Daniel
Haskins W. Jones	J. Vincent Edge
Russell L. Irby, III	Allison Powell

General Counsel for: The Birmingham News Co.
Counsel for: General Motors Corp.; General Electric Capital Corp.; Goldome Credit Corp.

For full biographical listings, see the Martindale-Hubbell Law Directory

---

LEITMAN, SIEGAL & PAYNE, P.C. (AV)

Suite 400 The Land Title Building, 600 North 20th Street, 35203
Telephone: 205-251-5900
Telecopier: 205-323-2098

F. Don Siegal	Phillip G. Stutts
Eddie Leitman	Bradley G. Siegal
Jackson M. Payne	Virginia K. Hopper
Lynne Stephens O'Neal	John J. Kubiszyn

Thomas A. Edenbaum

For full biographical listings, see the Martindale-Hubbell Law Directory

---

McDANIEL, HALL & CONERLY, P.C. (AV)

1400 Financial Center, 505 North 20th Street, 35203-2626
Telephone: 205-251-8143

(See Next Column)

McDANIEL, HALL & CONERLY P.C.—*Continued*

William J. McDaniel	William A. Mudd
Jack J. Hall	C. Peter Bolvig
Edward O. Conerly	Jack J. Hall, Jr.

Jack Martin Bains, Jr.	Patrick R. Norris
Matthew W. Veal	Christy Lynn Campbell Osborne
Paul C Garrison	

Counsel for: Alabama Farm Bureau Insurance Cos.; Allstate Insurance Co.; Insurance Company of North America; Crum & Forster Insurance Co.; Canal Insurance Co.; Argonaut Insurance Co.; Chubb Pacific Indemnity Group; Commercial Union Cos.; General Accident Group.

For full biographical listings, see the Martindale-Hubbell Law Directory

NAJJAR DENABURG, P.C. (AV)

2125 Morris Avenue, 35203
Telephone: 205-250-8400
Telecopier: 205-326-3837

Charles L. Denaburg	Douglas L. McWhorter
Thomas C. Najjar, Jr.	Gary S. Schiff
(1931-1995)	Robert H. Adams
Edward P. Meyerson	Marvin E. Franklin
Ben L. Zarzaur	Marvin L. Stewart, Jr.
L. Stephen Wright, Jr.	Jesse P. Evans III
David A. (Chip) Schwartz	Hub Harrington
Richard W. Theibert	

Keith J. Nadler	Denise J. Pomeroy
Walter F. McArdle	Rachel Jackson Moore
Laurie B. Sharp	

General Counsel: Acousti Engineering of Alabama, Inc.
Representative Client: Compass Bank.
Approved Attorneys for: Mississippi Valley Title Insurance Co.
Reference: Compass Bank.

For full biographical listings, see the Martindale-Hubbell Law Directory

PARSONS, LEE & JULIANO, P.C. (AV)

2200 AmSouth/Harbert Plaza, 1901 Sixth Avenue, North, P.O. Box 371088, 35237-1088
Telephone: 205-326-6600
Fax: 205-324-7097

Robert E. Parsons	David A. Lee
Jasper P. Juliano	John M. Bergquist
Marcus W. Lee	Paul J. DeMarco
Marda W. Sydnor	Deborah Ann Payne
Tracy Toussaint	

OF COUNSEL
Dorothy A. Powell

For full biographical listings, see the Martindale-Hubbell Law Directory

REDDEN, MILLS & CLARK (AV)

940 First Alabama Bank Building, 417 North 20th Street, 35203
Telephone: 205-322-0457
Fax: 205-322-8481

MEMBERS OF FIRM

L. Drew Redden	William N. Clark
William H. Mills	Gerald L. Miller
Stephen W. Shaw	

ASSOCIATES
Maxwell H. Pulliam, Jr.

References: SouthTrust Bank; First Alabama Bank.

For full biographical listings, see the Martindale-Hubbell Law Directory

SCHOEL, OGLE, BENTON AND CENTENO (AV)

600 Financial Center, 505 North 20th Street, P.O. Box 1865, 35201-1865
Telephone: 205-521-7000
Telecopier: 205-521-7007

MEMBERS OF FIRM

Jerry W. Schoel	Douglas J. Centeno
Richard F. Ogle	Melinda Murphy Dionne
Lee R. Benton	Gilbert M. Sullivan, Jr.
Paul A. Liles	David O. Upshaw

Reference: National Bank of Commerce; First Alabama Bank.

For full biographical listings, see the Martindale-Hubbell Law Directory

SPAIN & GILLON, L.L.C. (AV)

The Zinszer Building, 2117 2nd Avenue North, 35203
Telephone: 205-328-4100
Telecopier: 205-324-8866

(See Next Column)

MEMBERS OF FIRM

H. Hobart Grooms, Jr.	Elizabeth Ann McMahan
Ollie L. Blan, Jr.	Glenn E. Estess, Jr.
John P. McKleroy, Jr.	J. Sanford Mullins, III
Eugene P. Stutts	Harold H. Goings
Samuel H. Frazier	Thomas M. Eden, III
Alton B. Parker, Jr.	Paul S. Leonard
Charles D. Stewart	Paul L. Sotherland
J. Birch Bowdre	Robert L. Williams
W. Gregory Smith	

OF COUNSEL

Richard S. Riley	John P. Ansley
Ralph B. Tate	Ira L. Burleson
J. W. Gillon (1900-1992)	

ASSOCIATES

Gary A. Parker	Howard K. Glick
Steve R. Burford	Damon P. Denney
Earl H. Lawson, Jr.	Sally A. Broatch
Joey D. Duke	Karen Joy Pugh
Anthony C. Harlow	David Lawrence Faulkner, Jr.
Philip G. Piggott	Kimberly Keefer Boone

LEGAL SUPPORT PERSONNEL
Landis H. Munkus

General Counsel for: Liberty National Life Insurance Co.; Piggly Wiggly Alabama Distributing Co.; Alabama Insurance Guaranty Association; Alabama Life and Disability Insurance Guaranty Association; Alabama Insurance Underwriters Association.
Counsel for: The Minnesota Mutual Insurance Company of America; Government Employees Insurance Co.; Massachusetts Mutual Life Insurance Co.

For full biographical listings, see the Martindale-Hubbell Law Directory

WALSTON, STABLER, WELLS, ANDERSON & BAINS (AV)

Suite 500 Financial Center, 505 20th Street North, 35203
Telephone: 205-251-9600
Telecopier: 205-251-0700
Mailing Address: P.O. Box 830642, Birmingham, AL, 35283-0642

Robert H. Walston	David B. Anderson
Frank C. Galloway, Jr.	Larry B. Childs
L. Vastine Stabler, Jr.	Kay K. Bains
Charles L. Hayes	Heyward C. Hosch III
Lawrence Dumas, III	Helen Currie Foster
C. Henry Marston	Elizabeth Champlin Bishop
Vernon L. Wells, II	C. Ellis Brazeal, III
James L. Birchall	David B. Walston
Michael C. Quillen	Anne Byrne Stone

OF COUNSEL
Edward J. Ashton

ASSOCIATES

Emily Sides Bonds	Randall D. Quarles
Julia Boaz Cooper	N. Christian Glenos
Jerry Dean Hillman	Dawn Helms Sharff

For full biographical listings, see the Martindale-Hubbell Law Directory

---

BREWTON,* Escambia Co.

THOMPSON, GARRETT & HINES (AV)

218 Belleville Avenue, P.O. Box 387, 36427-0387
Telephone: 334-867-6063
Fax: 334-867-6067
Atmore, Alabama Office: 101 3rd Avenue, P.O. Box 737.
Telephone: 205-368-4999.

MEMBERS OF FIRM

Joe B. Thompson, Jr.	Broox G. Garrett, Jr.
Edward T. Hines	

Counsel for: First National Bank, Brewton, Alabama; Alabama Power Co.; St. Louis-San Francisco Railway; State Farm Insurance Co.; Royal-Liverpool Insurance Group; Southern Guaranty Insurance Cos.; Home Insurance Co.; Federated Insurance Co.; Hartford Accident & Indemnity Co.; First National Bank of Atmore.

For full biographical listings, see the Martindale-Hubbell Law Directory

---

CAMDEN,* Wilcox Co. — (Refer to Selma)

CARROLLTON,* Pickens Co. — (Refer to Tuscaloosa)

CENTRE,* Cherokee Co.

KEENER & KEENER (AV)

150 East Main Street, P.O. Box 604, 35960
Telephone: 205-927-5518

Irby A. Keener (1900-1965)	Irby A. Keener, Jr.

CENTREVILLE,* Bibb Co. — (Refer to Tuscaloosa)

CLANTON,* Chilton Co. — (Refer to Montgomery)

CLAYTON,* Barbour Co. — (Refer to Troy)

COLUMBIANA,* Shelby Co. — (Refer to Birmingham)

DADEVILLE,* Tallapoosa Co. — (Refer to Opelika)

DECATUR,* Morgan Co.

EYSTER, KEY, TUBB, WEAVER & ROTH (AV)

Eyster Building, 402 East Moulton Street, S.E., P.O. Box 1607, 35602
Telephone: 205-353-6761
Fax: 205-353-6767

John C. Eyster (1863-1926)   Wm. B. Eyster (1921-1995)
Charles H. Eyster, Sr.
  (1888-1964)

MEMBERS OF FIRM

John S. Key   Nicholas B. Roth
J. Glynn Tubb   J. Witty Allen
Laurence C. Weaver   William L. Middleton, III
James G. Adams, Jr.

ASSOCIATES

Jenny L. Mcleroy   John R. Baggette, Jr.

General Counsel for: Alabama Farmers Cooperative.
Regional Counsel for: AmSouth Bank.
Local Counsel for: Allstate Insurance Co.; Liberty Mutual Insurance Co.; Maryland Casualty Co.; Saginaw Steering Gear Division, General Motors Corp.; State Farm Mutual Automobile Insurance Co.; The Travelers.

For full biographical listings, see the Martindale-Hubbell Law Directory

HARRIS, CADDELL & SHANKS, P.C. (AV)

214 Johnston Street, S.E., P.O. Box 2688, 35602-2688
Telephone: 205-340-8000
Telecopier: 205-340-8040

Julian Harris (1904-1994)   Thomas A. Caddell
Norman W. Harris (P.C.)   William E. Shinn, Jr.
  (Retired)   Gary A. Phillips
Philip T. Shanks (Retired)   Dow M. Perry, Jr.
Charles L. Murphree (Retired)   Barnes F. Lovelace, Jr.
John A. Caddell (P.A.)   Arthur W. Orr
Robert H. Harris   J. Noel King
Jon H. Moores   Jeffrey S. Brown

Attorneys for: First American Bank, Decatur, Alabama; SouthTrust Bank of Morgan County; Morgan County Commission; The Industrial Development Board of the City of Decatur, Alabama; Amoco Chemical Co.; South Central Bell Telephone Co.; Auto-Owners Insurance Co.; ALFA Insurance Cos.; American General Life & Accident Insurance Co.; U.S.F. & G. Co.

For full biographical listings, see the Martindale-Hubbell Law Directory

DEMOPOLIS, Marengo Co. — (Refer to Selma)

DOTHAN,* Houston Co.

COBB & SHEALY, P.A. (AV)

206 North Lena Street, P.O. Box 6346, 36302
Telephone: 334-794-8526
Fax: 334-677-0030

Herman W. Cobb   Richard Elder Crum
Steadman S. Shealy, Jr.   James H. Pike
Raymond Todd Derrick   Joseph A. Morris
A. Gary Jones

OF COUNSEL

Joey Hornsby

Representative Clients: Travelers Insurance; Nationwide Insurance; Auto-Owners Insurance; Employers Casualty of Texas; Safeco Insurance; Federated Insurance; Universal Underwriters; National Security Insurance; Great Central Insurance.
Approved Title Attorneys for: Lawyers Title Insurance Corp.

For full biographical listings, see the Martindale-Hubbell Law Directory

HARDWICK, HAUSE & SEGREST (AV)

212 North Lena Street, P.O. Box 1469, 36302
Telephone: 334-794-4144
Fax: 334-671-9330

W. G. Hardwick (1910-1993)   William G. Hause (Retired)

MEMBERS OF FIRM

Jere C. Segrest   Kevin Walding
Tina Whitehead Stamps

ASSOCIATE

G. Ward Beeson, III

Counsel for: Dothan City Board of Education; American General Life & Accident Ins. Co.; General Motors Acceptance Corp.; Alabama Power Co.; Liberty NAtional Life Ins. Co.; CBI-Equifax, Inc.

For full biographical listings, see the Martindale-Hubbell Law Directory

LEE & McINISH (AV)

238 West Main Street, P.O. Box 1665, 36302
Telephone: 334-792-4156
Facsimile: 334-794-8342

MEMBERS OF FIRM

W. L. Lee (1873-1944)   William C. Carn, III
Alto V. Lee, III (1915-1987)   Peter A. McInish
William L. Lee, III   Jerry M. White
Alan C. Livingston   William L. Lee, IV

OF COUNSEL

H. Dwight McInish

Counsel for: Seaboard Coast Line Railroad Co.; Atlanta & St. Andrews Bay Railroad Co.; ALFA; U. S. F. & G. Co.; Maryland Casualty Co.; Continental Insurance Cos.; Royal-Globe Group; Slocomb National Bank; The Federal Land Bank of Jackson; GTE South.

For full biographical listings, see the Martindale-Hubbell Law Directory

DOUBLE SPRINGS,* Winston Co. — (Refer to Decatur)

ELBA,* Coffee Co. — (Refer to Enterprise)

ENTERPRISE, Coffee Co.

CASSADY, FULLER & MARSH (AV)

203 East Lee Avenue, P.O. Box 780, 36331
Telephone: 334-347-2626
Telecopier: 334-393-1396

MEMBERS OF FIRM

Joe C. Cassady   M. Dale Marsh
Kenneth T. Fuller   Joe C. Cassady, Jr.
Mark E. Fuller

ASSOCIATES

R. Rainer Cotter, III   J.P. Sawyer

Representative Clients: First Alabama Bank; Enterprise Hospital Board; Sessions Co., Inc.; Allstate; State Farm Mutual Insurance Co.; Community Bank & Trust Co.; Conagra, Inc.
Approved Attorneys for: First American Title Insurance Co.

For full biographical listings, see the Martindale-Hubbell Law Directory

J. E. SAWYER, JR. (AV)

203 South Edwards Street, P.O. Box 720, 36331-0720
Telephone: 334-347-6447
Fax: 334-347-8217

For full biographical listings, see the Martindale-Hubbell Law Directory

EUFAULA, Barbour Co.

WILLIAM V. NEVILLE, JR. (AV)

302 East Broad Street, P.O. Box 337, 36072-0337
Telephone: 334-687-5183
Fax: 334-687-6602

For full biographical listings, see the Martindale-Hubbell Law Directory

EUTAW,* Greene Co. — (Refer to Tuscaloosa)

EVERGREEN,* Conecuh Co.

WILLIAM D. MELTON (AV)

Melton Building, 100 Liberty Hill, P.O. Drawer 800, 36401-0800
Telephone: 334-578-2423

Reference: Bank of Evergreen, Evergreen, Alabama.

For full biographical listings, see the Martindale-Hubbell Law Directory

FAYETTE,* Fayette Co. — (Refer to Tuscaloosa)

FLORENCE,* Lauderdale Co.

POTTS & YOUNG (AV)

107 East College Street, 35630
Telephone: 205-764-7142
Fax: 205-764-7717

OF COUNSEL

Doyle R. Young (Retired)   Robert L. Potts

MEMBERS OF FIRM

Frank V. Potts   Frank B. Potts

ASSOCIATES

Robert W. Beasley   Debra H. Coble

Representative Clients: E. A. Nelson Co., Inc.; Nelco, Inc.; American Abrasive Air & Service Co., Inc.; Diversified Products, Inc.; Big Deli Stores, Inc.; Spry Funeral Homes of Russellville, Sheffield & Florence; Americans United for the Separation of Church & State; Colbert County Community Economic Development Corp.

(See Next Column)

POTTS & YOUNG—*Continued*

Reference: Bank Independent.

For full biographical listings, see the Martindale-Hubbell Law Directory

FORT PAYNE,* De Kalb Co.

KELLETT & KELLETT, P.A. (AV)

106 Alabama Avenue, S.W., P.O. Box 715, 35967
Telephone: 205-845-4541

Joseph C. Kellett   Patricia C. Kellett

Attorneys for: V.I. Prewett & Son, Inc.; AmSouth Bank, N.A.; St. Paul Insurance Cos.; DeKalb-Cherokee Counties Gas District; Home Insurance Co.; Johnson Hosiery Mills, Inc.; Cherokee Hosiery Mills, Inc.; Alfa Mutual Insurance Co.

For full biographical listings, see the Martindale-Hubbell Law Directory

SCRUGGS, JORDAN, DODD & DODD, P.A. (AV)

207 Alabama Avenue, South, P.O. Box 1109, 35967
Telephone: 205-845-5932
Fax: 205-845-4325

William D. Scruggs, Jr.   David Dodd
Robert K. Jordan   E. Allen Dodd, Jr.

Representative Clients: State Farm Insurance Company; Allstate Insurance Co., Inc.; USF&G Insurance Co.; Nucor, Inc.; Ladd Engineering, Inc.; ALABAMA Band; First Federal Savings & Loan Association of Dekalb County; Fritz Structural Steel, Inc.; Williamson Oil Co., Inc.

For full biographical listings, see the Martindale-Hubbell Law Directory

GADSDEN,* Etowah Co.

DORTCH, WRIGHT & WRIGHT (AV)

239 College Street, P.O. Box 405, 35902
Telephone: 205-546-4616

MEMBERS OF FIRM

Walter R. Dortch (1847-1926)   William B. Dortch (1892-1983)
G. C. Allen (1872-1935)   Curtis Wright
     Curtis Wright, II

Attorneys for: St. Paul Insurance Cos.; Employers Insurance of Wausau; Mutual Assurance Society of Alabama; State Farm Insurance Cos.; Alabama Hospital Association Trust; Mutual Savings Life Insurance Co.; Lawyers Title Insurance Corp.; Nationwide Mutual Insurance Co.; Government Employees Insurance Co.; CSX Transportation Systems.

For full biographical listings, see the Martindale-Hubbell Law Directory

FLOYD, KEENER, CUSIMANO & ROBERTS, P.C. (AV)

816 Chestnut Street, P.O. Box 49, 35902
Telephone: 205-547-6328
Fax: 205-546-8173

Jack Floyd   Gregory S. Cusimano
Larry H. Keener   Michael L. Roberts
    David A. Kimberley

John D. Floyd   Elizabeth Ragsdole Howard
Philip E. Miles   Jane V. Floyd

For full biographical listings, see the Martindale-Hubbell Law Directory

FORD AND ASSOCIATES, P.C. (AV)

The Lancaster Building, 645 Walnut Street, Suite 5, P.O. Box 388, 35902
Telephone: 205-546-5432
Fax: 205-546-5435

George P. Ford

Richard M. Blythe   H. Edgar Howard
   Bradley Williams Cornett

Reference: AmSouth Bank, N.A.

For full biographical listings, see the Martindale-Hubbell Law Directory

INZER, STIVENDER, HANEY & JOHNSON, P.A. (AV)

(Inzer, Suttle, Swann & Stivender)
Second Floor, Compass Bank Building, 601 Broad Street, P.O. Drawer 287, 35999-0287
Telephone: 205-546-1656
Telecopier: 205-546-1093

(See Next Column)

James C. Inzer (1887-1967)   James C. Inzer, Jr. (Of Counsel)
John A. Lusk, Jr. (1891-1970)   James C. Stivender (Of Counsel)
Hubert Burns (1915-1975)   W. Roscoe Johnson, III
Julius S. Swann, Sr. (1907-1989)   James C. Inzer, III
Frank J. Martin (1905-1992)   F. Michael Haney
Roger C. Suttle (Of Counsel)   Robert D. McWhorter, Jr.

James W. McGlaughn   Elizabeth Golson McGlaughn

Assistant Division Counsel for: Southern Railway System.
Attorneys for: General Motors Corp.; Goodyear Tire and Rubber Co.; Alabama Power Co.; Southern Natural Gas Co.; Allstate Insurance Co.; Travelers Insurance Co.; Central Bank of the South.

For full biographical listings, see the Martindale-Hubbell Law Directory

GREENSBORO,* Hale Co. — (Refer to Selma)

GUNTERSVILLE,* Marshall Co.

LUSK & LUSK (AV)

452 Gunter Avenue, P.O. Box 609, 35976
Telephone: 205-582-3248
Fax: 205-582-3215

MEMBERS OF FIRM

Marion F. Lusk (1896-1986)   Louis B. Lusk

Representative Clients: AmSouth Bank of Alabama, Guntersville; United States Fidelity & Guaranty Co.; The Travelers Insurance Co.; St. Paul Cos.; ALFA Mutual Insurance Cos.; Hartford Group; Liberty Mutual Insurance Co.; Allstate Insurance Co.; Home of New York Group.

For full biographical listings, see the Martindale-Hubbell Law Directory

WRIGHT AND WRIGHT, A PROFESSIONAL CORPORATION (AV)

Worth Street, P.O. Box 70, 35976-0070
Telephone: 205-582-3721; 582-8590; 582-8411
Fax: 205-582-3733

T. Harvey Wright (1890-1972)   Harvey J. Wright
     Wade K. Wright

Approved Attorneys for: Commonwealth Land Title Insurance Co.; Lawyers Title Insurance Corp.

HEADLAND, Henry Co. — (Refer to Abbeville)

HEFLIN,* Cleburne Co. — (Refer to Anniston)

HUNTSVILLE,* Madison Co.

BERRY, ABLES, TATUM, BAXTER, PARKER & HALL, P.C. (AV)

Legal Building, 315 Franklin Street, S.E., P.O. Box 165, 35804-0165
Telephone: 205-533-3740
Facsimile: 205-533-3751
Email: BAXTERJ@ATTMAIL.COM

William H. Blanton (1889-1973)   James T. Tatum, Jr.
Joe M. Berry   James T. Baxter, III
L. Bruce Ables   Thomas E. Parker, Jr.
     Bill G. Hall

James K. Brabston   Mark Rogers Hunter

Representative Clients: AmSouth Bank; First Alabama Bank; General Shale Products Co.; The Hertz Corp.; Litton Industries, Inc.; Farmers Tractor Co.; Colonial Bank; Farm Credit Bank of Texas; SouthBank; Regions Mortgage.
Reference: First Alabama Bank.

For full biographical listings, see the Martindale-Hubbell Law Directory

BRADLEY, ARANT, ROSE & WHITE (AV)

200 Clinton Avenue West, Suite 900, 35801
Telephone: 205-517-5100
Facsimile: 205-533-5069
URL: http://www.BARW.COM
Birmingham, Alabama Office: 2001 Park Place, Suite 1400, P.O. Box 830709.
Telephone: 205-521-8000.
Facsimile: 205-251-8611, 251-8665, 252-0264. Facsimile (SouthTrust Tower Office): 205-251-9915.

RESIDENT PARTNERS

Gary C. Huckaby   Patrick H. Graves, Jr.
Charles R. Smith, Jr.   Scott E. Ludwig
E. Cutter Hughes, Jr.   G. Rick Hall
    Warne S. Heath

RESIDENT ASSOCIATES

James Tassin   Carolyn Reed Douglas
Hall B, Bryant III   Kimberly A. Bessiere

Counsel for: SouthTrust Bank of Alabama, National Association; Energen, Corporation; Blount, Inc.; Torchmark Corp.; Russell Corp.; Coca-Cola Bottling Company United, Inc.; Ford Motor Co.; Walter Industries, Inc.; The Birmingham Post Co. (Post-Herald); The New York Times Co.

(See Next Column)

BRADLEY, ARANT, ROSE & WHITE, *Huntsville—Continued*

For full biographical listings, see the Martindale-Hubbell Law Directory

LANIER FORD SHAVER & PAYNE, P.C. (AV)

200 West Court Square, Suite 5000, P.O. Box 2087, 35804
Telephone: 205-535-1100
FAX: 205-533-9322

M. H. Lanier (1878-1946)	J. R. Brooks
Earle Raymond Ford	William Blanton Tatum
(1890-1973)	William W. Sanderson, Jr.
Ralph H. Ford (1916-1986)	H. Harold Stephens
James L. Caldwell (1914-1991)	Joe W. Campbell
Charles E. Shaver (1907-1993)	D. Edward Starnes, III
M. H. Lanier	Donna S. Pate
Joe L. Payne	Robert E. Ledyard, III
William T. Galloway, Jr.	Ronald F. Suber
Jerry B. Ange	Elizabeth W. Abel
W. Stanley Rodgers	Y. Albert Moore, III
James E. Davis, Jr.	Claude E. Hundley, III
John M. Heacock, Jr.	George E. Knox, Jr.
Charles E. Shaver, Jr.	Frank M. Caprio
John R. Wynn	Jeffrey T. Kelly
Thomas R. Robinson	Paul A. Pate

Edward E. Wilson, Jr.	P. Scott Arnston
Rodney C. Lewis	Greg Taube
Jamie Manasco Brabston	Phillip Gibson
Melissa J. Long	

OF COUNSEL
Frank McRight

Representative Clients: Aetna Life & Casualty Company; General Motors Corp.; Huntsville Coca-Cola Bottling Co.; Huntsville Hospital; Royal Insurance; St. Paul Insurance Co.; The Travelers Insurance Co.; United States Fidelity & Guaranty.

For full biographical listings, see the Martindale-Hubbell Law Directory

---

LANETT, Chambers Co. — (Refer to Lafayette)

---

*LINDEN,** Marengo Co. — (Refer to Selma)

---

*MARION,** Perry Co. — (Refer to Selma)

---

*MOBILE,** Mobile Co.

ARMBRECHT, JACKSON, DeMOUY, CROWE, HOLMES & REEVES, L.L.C. (AV)

1300 AmSouth Center, P.O. Box 290, 36601
Telephone: 334-405-1300
Facsimile: 334-432-6843; 433-3821

MEMBERS OF FIRM

Wm. H. Armbrecht (1908-1991)	Donald C. Radcliff
Theodore K. Jackson	Christopher I. Gruenewald
(1910-1981)	James Donald Hughes
F.M. Keeling (1943-1993)	M. Kathleen Miller
Marshall J. DeMouy	Dabney Bragg Foshee
Wm. H. Armbrecht, III	Edward A. Dean
Rae M. Crowe	Reggie Copeland, Jr.
Broox G. Holmes, Jr.	David E. Hudgens
W. Boyd Reeves	Ray Morgan Thompson
E. B. Peebles III	James Dale Smith
William B. Harvey	Duane A. Graham
Kirk C. Shaw	Robert J. Mullican
Norman E. Waldrop, Jr.	Wm. Steele Holman II
Conrad P. Armbrecht	Coleman F. Meador
Edward G. Hawkins	Broox G. Holmes
Grover E. Asmus II	James E. Robertson, Jr.
David A. Bagwell	Scott G. Brown
Douglas L. Brown	Clifford C. Brady
Richard W. Franklin	

ASSOCIATES

Stephen Russell Copeland	P. Vincent Gaddy
Rodney R. Cate	Richard G. Brock
James F. Watkins	Timothy D. Ryan

Representative Clients: American Surety Group (Regional Counsel); AmSouth Bank of Alabama (Regional Counsel); Burlington Northern Railroad Co. (District Counsel); Loyal American Life Insurance Co.; Kimberly Clark Corporation; Travelers Insurance Co.

For full biographical listings, see the Martindale-Hubbell Law Directory

---

CABANISS, JOHNSTON, GARDNER, DUMAS & O'NEAL (AV)

700 AmSouth Center, P.O. Box 2906, 36652
Telephone: 334-433-6961
Telecopier: 334-433-1060
Birmingham, Alabama Office: Park Place Tower. 2001 Park Place North, Suite 700. P.O. Box 830612.
Telephone: 205-716-5200.
Telecopier: 205-716-5389.

(See Next Column)

MEMBERS OF FIRM

Benjamen T. Rowe (Resident)	William K. Thomas
William A. Robinson (Resident)	David L. Kane (Resident)
Patrick H. Sims (Resident)	R. Boyd Miller (Resident)
Donald J. Stewart (Resident)	Sandy G. Robinson (Resident)

Representative Clients: American Marine Underwriters, Inc.; Liberty Mutual Insurance Co.; Union Carbide Corp.; Rohr, Inc.

For full biographical listings, see the Martindale-Hubbell Law Directory

CUNNINGHAM, BOUNDS, YANCE, CROWDER & BROWN (AV)

1601 Dauphin Street, P.O. Box 66705, 36660
Telephone: 334-471-6191
Fax: 334-479-1031

Richard Bounds	Joseph M. Brown, Jr.
James A. Yance	Gregory B. Breedlove
John T. Crowder, Jr.	Andrew T. Citrin
Robert T. Cunningham, Jr.	Michael A. Worel

David G. Wirtes, Jr.	Mitchell K. Shelly
Toby D. Brown	Kelli Denise Taylor

OF COUNSEL

Robert T. Cunningham	Valentino D. B. Mazzia

References: First Alabama Bank; AmSouth Bank, N.A.

For full biographical listings, see the Martindale-Hubbell Law Directory

---

FINKBOHNER AND LAWLER, L.L.C. (AV)

169 Dauphin Street Suite 300, P.O. Box 3085, 36652
Telephone: 334-438-5871
Fax: 334-432-8052

MEMBERS OF FIRM

George W. Finkbohner, Jr.	George W. Finkbohner, III
John L. Lawler	Royce A. Ray, III

For full biographical listings, see the Martindale-Hubbell Law Directory

---

HELMSING, LYONS, SIMS & LEACH, P.C. (AV)

The Laclede Building, 150 Government Street, P.O. Box 2767, 36652
Telephone: 334-432-5521
Telecopy: 334-432-0633

Larry U. Sims	Robert H. Rouse
Champ Lyons, Jr.	Charles H. Dodson, Jr.
Frederick G. Helmsing	Richard E. Davis
John N. Leach, Jr.	Joseph P. H. Babington
Warren C. Herlong, Jr.	John J. Crowley, Jr.
James B. Newman	Joseph D. Steadman

Todd S. Strohmeyer	John Townsend Dukes
William R. Lancaster	P. Bradley Murray
Robin Kilpatrick Fincher	Leslie T. Fields

For full biographical listings, see the Martindale-Hubbell Law Directory

JOHNSTONE, ADAMS, BAILEY, GORDON AND HARRIS, L.L.C. (AV)

Royal St. Francis Building, 104 St. Francis Street, P.O. Box 1988, 36633
Telephone: 334-432-7682
Facsimile: 334-432-2800
Telex: 782040

MEMBERS OF FIRM

Charles B. Bailey, Jr.	Wade B. Perry, Jr.
Brock B. Gordon	Thomas S. Rue
Ben H. Harris, Jr.	Alan C. Christian
William H. Hardie, Jr.	Gregory C. Buffalow
E. Watson Smith	Celia J. Collins
Joseph M. Allen, Jr.	R. Gregory Watts
I. David Cherniak	William Alexander Gray, Jr.
David C. Hannan	Robert S. Frost

ASSOCIATES

Tracy P. Turner	E. Erich Bergdolt
Lawrence J. Seiter	E. Russell March, III
Benjamin H. Harris, III	Scott Alton Browning
W. Andrew Wing, II	Craig Bryant Morris
John Robert Parker	

OF COUNSEL

C. A. L. Johnstone, Jr.	Robert F. Adams

General Counsel for: First Alabama Bank, Mobile; Infirmary Health System/Mobile Infirmary Medical Center/Rotary Rehabilitation Hospital (Multi-Hospital System).
Counsel for: Oil and Gas: Exxon Corp. Business and Corporate: Bell South Telecommunications, Inc.; Aluminum Co. of America; Michelin North America, Inc.; Metropolitan Life Insurance Co.; The Travelers Insurance Cos. Marine: The West of England Ship Owners Mutual Protection and Indemnity Association (Luxembourg); The Standard Steamship Owners' Protection and Indemnity Association (Bermuda) Ltd.

(See Next Column)

JOHNSTONE, ADAMS, BAILEY, GORDON AND HARRIS L.L.C.—*Continued*

For full biographical listings, see the Martindale-Hubbell Law Directory

LOVELESS & LYONS (AV)

28 North Florida Street, 36607
Telephone: 334-476-7857
Fax: 334-476-8510

MEMBERS OF FIRM

Ralph P. Loveless   Beth Marietta Lyons

LEGAL SUPPORT PERSONNEL

Deborah Geiger

For full biographical listings, see the Martindale-Hubbell Law Directory

LYONS, PIPES & COOK, P.C. (AV)

2 North Royal Street, P.O. Box 2727, 36652-2727
Telephone: 334-432-4481
Cable Address: "Lysea"
Telecopier: 334-433-1820

Joseph H. Lyons (1874-1957)	Caroline C. McCarthy
Sam W. Pipes, III (1916-1982)	William E. Shreve, Jr.
Walter M. Cook (1915-1988)	R. Mark Kirkpatrick
Wesley Pipes	Kenneth A. Nixon
Norton W. Brooker, Jr.	Daniel S. Cushing
Cooper C. Thurber	Allen E. Graham
Marion A. Quina, Jr.	Michael C. Niemeyer
Thomas F. Garth	John C. Bell
Claude D. Boone	M. Warren Butler
Walter M. Cook, Jr.	Christopher Lee George
John Patrick Courtney, III	M. Lauren Lemmon
W. David Johnson, Jr.	J. Murphy McMillan, III
Joseph J. Minus, Jr.	S. Wesley Pipes, V

General Counsel: Inchcape Shipping Services.
Counsel: The Hertz Corp.; McKenzie Tank Lines, Inc.; SCNO Barge Lines, Inc.; Scott Paper Co.; Shell Oil Corp.
Trial Counsel: Aetna Life & Casualty Co.; Chubb Group of Insurance Companies.

For full biographical listings, see the Martindale-Hubbell Law Directory

AUGUSTINE MEAHER, III, P.C. (AV)

Suite 2118, First National Bank Building, 36602
Telephone: 334-432-9971
FAX: 334-432-9978

Augustine Meaher, III

References: Bank of Mobile, Mobile, Alabama; AmSouth Bank, Mobile, Alabama.

For full biographical listings, see the Martindale-Hubbell Law Directory

REAMS, PHILIPS, BROOKS, SCHELL, GASTON & HUDSON, P.C. (AV)

The Pillans Building, 3662 Dauphin Street, P.O. Box 8158, 36608
Telephone: 334-344-4721
Telex: 78-2025
Telecopier: 334-343-9760

Harry Pillans (1847-1940)	Sidney H. Schell
William Cowley (1880-1948)	Geary A. Gaston
Palmer Pillans (1876-1976)	Victor T. Hudson
John H. Tappan (1916-1995)	C. Robert Gottlieb, Jr.
W. Dewitt Reams (Retired)	John R. Nix
George F. Wood (Retired)	Richard L. Reed
Bonnerrae H. Roberts (Retired)	William W. Watts, III
Abe L. Philips, Jr.	David M. O'Brien
James D. Brooks	A. Lewis Philips, III
	Kenneth A. Watson

Attorneys for: Assuranceforeningen Gard; Assuranceforeningen Skuld; The Brittania Steamship Insurance Association, Ltd.; Ciba Corp.; Degussa Corp., Inc.; Hartford Insurance Co.; Japan Ship Owners' Mutual Protection and Insurance Association; Olin Corp.; Springhill Memorial Hospital; State Farm Insurance Cos.; The Swedish P. & I. Club; The United Kingdom Mutual Steam Ship Assurance Assn. (Bermuda) Ltd.

For full biographical listings, see the Martindale-Hubbell Law Directory

VICKERS, RIIS, MURRAY AND CURRAN, L.L.C. (AV)

8th Floor, First Alabama Bank Building, 106 Saint Francis Street, P.O. Box 2568, 36652
Telephone: 334-432-9772
Fax: 334-432-9781

(See Next Column)

MEMBERS OF FIRM

Marion R. Vickers (1901-1995)	J. W. Goodloe, Jr.
Marion R. Vickers, Jr. (1935-1989)	Zebulon M. P. Inge, Jr.
	Thomas E. Sharp, III
Erling Riis, Jr.	Ronald P. Davis
J. Manson Murray	J. Marshall Gardner
Edwin J. Curran, Jr.	C. Richard Wilkins

Representative Clients: Mobile Forest Products, Inc.; Azalea Aviation, Inc.; Midstream Fuel Services; McPhillips Manufacturing Co.; Spring Hill College; Steiner Shipyard, Inc.; Homeowners Marketing Services, Inc.; Marine Office of America Corp.; Cummins Alabama, Inc.; Ben M. Radcliff Contractor, Inc.

For full biographical listings, see the Martindale-Hubbell Law Directory

---

MONROEVILLE, * Monroe Co. — (Refer to Evergreen)

MONTGOMERY, * Montgomery Co.

BALL, BALL, MATTHEWS & NOVAK, P.A. (AV)

Suite 1100, 60 Commerce Street, P.O. Box 2148, 36102-2148
Telephone: 334-834-7680
Fax: 334-265-3222

Fred S. Ball (1866-1942)	C. Winston Sheehan, Jr.
Charles A. Ball (1904-1969)	William H. Brittain II
Fred S. Ball, Jr. (1896-1974)	Joana S. Ellis
Richard A. Ball (1906-1983)	E. Hamilton Wilson, Jr.
John R. Matthews, Jr.	Richard E. Broughton
Richard A. Ball, Jr.	T. Cowin Knowles
Tabor R. Novak, Jr.	Gerald C. Swann, Jr.
Clyde C. Owen, Jr.	Mark T. Davis
	James A. Rives

Fred B. Matthews   Allison L. Alford

Counsel for: Beech Aircraft Corporation; Bell Helicopter Co.; John Deere Co.; Government Employees Insurance Co.; Chubb & Son; Cigna Co.; Chrysler Corp.; Associated Aviation Underwriters.

For full biographical listings, see the Martindale-Hubbell Law Directory

BECK & TRAVIS, P.C. (AV)

22 Scott Street, P.O. Box 5019, 36103-5019
Telephone: 334-832-4878
Fax: 334-832-4704

George L. Beck, Jr.

OF COUNSEL

W. Terry Travis

David Bryson Byrne, III

For full biographical listings, see the Martindale-Hubbell Law Directory

HASKELL SLAUGHTER & YOUNG, L.L.C. (AV)

305 South Lawrence Street, P.O. Box 4660, 36103-4660
Telephone: 334-265-8573
Facsimile: 334-264-7945
Birmingham, Alabama Office: 1200 AmSouth/Harbert Plaza, 1901 Sixth Avenue North. 35203
Telephone: 205-251-1000.
Facsimile: 205-324-1133.

Thomas T. Gallion, III   Constance A. Caldwell

Barry D. Woodham   Susan E. Kennedy

Representative Clients: The Bradford Group, Inc.; City of Birmingham; The Equitable Life Assurance Society of the United States; Exxon Corporation; Federal Deposit Insurance Corporation; HEALTHSOUTH Corporation/-HEALTHSOUTH Medical Centers; Hughes Missile Systems; Montgomery County, Alabama; USX Corporation.

For full biographical listings, see the Martindale-Hubbell Law Directory

HILL, HILL, CARTER, FRANCO, COLE & BLACK, P.C. (AV)

425 South Perry Street, P.O. Box 116, 36101-0116
Telephone: 334-834-7600
Fax: 334-263-5969

Thomas B. Hill, Jr. (1903-1984)	John M. Milling, Jr.
Wm. Inge Hill (1911-1995)	William Inge Hill, Jr.
James T. Stovall (1905-1972)	Gerald W. Hartley
James J. Carter (1913-1985)	Randall Morgan
William A. Oldacre (1932-1973)	Robert W. Bradford, Jr.
Ralph A. Franco	David E. Allred
T. Bowen Hill, III	Laura L. Crum
Harry Cole	Mark A. Franco
Robert C. Black, Sr.	Terry A. Sides
William I. Hill, II	John R. Bradwell
	William C. McGowin

(See Next Column)

HILL, HILL, CARTER, FRANCO, COLE & BLACK P.C., *Montgomery—Continued*

Robert C. Black, Jr.
Pamela Pelekis Swan
Elizabeth K. Brannen

Jeffrey Joseph Bradwell
Thomas C. Tankersley
Doy Leale McCall, III

Representative Clients: The Aetna Group; The State Farm Group; ALFA; General Electric Co.; General Motors Corp; Blue Cross and Blue Shield of Alabama; Allstate Insurance Co.; Winn-Dixie Stores, Inc.; Scottsdale Insurance Co.; National Casualty Co.

For full biographical listings, see the Martindale-Hubbell Law Directory

VOLZ, PRESTWOOD & HANAN, P.C. (AV)

350 Adams Avenue, P.O. Box 1910, 36102-1910
Telephone: 334-264-6401
Fax: 334-834-4954

Charles H. Volz, Jr.
Alvin T. Prestwood
Ellis D. Hanan

Charles H. Volz, III
Clinton Chadwell Carter
Daniel Lewis Feinstein

LEGAL SUPPORT PERSONNEL
Mark A.W. Turpen

For full biographical listings, see the Martindale-Hubbell Law Directory

---

MOULTON,* Lawrence Co. — (Refer to Decatur)

OPELIKA,* Lee Co.

SAMFORD, DENSON, HORSLEY, PETTEY & MARTIN (AV)

709 Avenue A, P.O. Box 2345, 36803-2345
Telephone: 334-745-3504
Fax: 334-745-3506

MEMBERS OF FIRM
N. D. Denson (1856-1927)
John V. Denson (1885-1940)
N. D. Denson, Jr. (1887-1958)
Yetta G. Samford, Jr.

John V. Denson
William F. Horsley
Robert H. Pettey, Jr.
Stanley A. Martin

ASSOCIATE
Amy J. Himmelwright

Attorneys for: The Farmers National Bank; BellSouth Communications, Inc.; International Paper Co.; Liberty National Life Insurance Co.; The First National Bank.

For full biographical listings, see the Martindale-Hubbell Law Directory

WALKER, HILL, ADAMS, UMBACH, MEADOWS & WALTON (AV)

Walker Building, 205 South 9th Street, P.O. Box 2069, 36803
Telephone: 334-745-6466
Fax: 334-749-2800

MEMBERS OF FIRM
Jacob A. Walker (1889-1973)
Phillip E. Adams, Jr.
Arnold W. Umbach, Jr.

Robert T. Meadows, III
Will O. (Trip) Walton, III
Jacob A. Walker, III

ASSOCIATES
Russell K. Bush

Robbie A. Hyde

OF COUNSEL
Jacob Walker

Hoyt W. Hill

Local Counsel for: Liberty Mutual Insurance Co.; Aetna Casualty & Surety Co.; Fireman's Fund Insurance Group; U.S.F. & G. Co.; Bituminous Insurance Group; American Interstate Insurance Company of Georgia; Carolina Casualty Insurance Co.; Cotton States Insurance Co.; Kemper Insurance Group; The Hartford Insurance Co.

For full biographical listings, see the Martindale-Hubbell Law Directory

---

PELL CITY, St. Clair Co.

BLAIR, HOLLADAY AND PARSONS (AV)

St. Clair Land Title Building, 1711 Cogswell Avenue, 35125
Telephone: 205-884-3440
Fax: 205-884-3442

MEMBERS OF FIRM
A. Dwight Blair

Hugh E. Holladay
Elizabeth S. Parsons

Representative Clients: Colonial Bank; Metro Bank; Am South Bank; St. Clair Federal Savings Bank; State Farm Mutual Insurance Cos; ALFA Mutual Insurance Co.; Allstate Insurance Co.; St. Paul Insurance Cos.; Auto Owners Insurance Co.; Reliance Insurance Cos.

For full biographical listings, see the Martindale-Hubbell Law Directory

---

ROCKFORD,* Coosa Co. — (Refer to Opelika)

RUSSELLVILLE,* Franklin Co.

FINE & MCDOWELL (AV)

507 North Jackson, P.O. Box 818, 35653
Telephone: 205-332-1660
Fax: 205-332-0318

Joe Fine

Daniel G. McDowell

ASSOCIATES
Eddie Beason

John F. Pilati

Representative Clients: Citizens Bank & Savings Co. of Russellville; Citigroup; City of Phil Campbell; Russellville City Board of Education; Franklin County Board of Education; Mutual Savings Life Insurance Co.; State Farm Fire & Casualty Co.; State Farm Mutual Automobile Ins. Co.; Franklin County Board of Commissioners; Marshall Durbin Co.

For full biographical listings, see the Martindale-Hubbell Law Directory

---

SELMA,* Dallas Co.

HOBBS & HAIN, P.C. (AV)

707 Selma Avenue, P.O. Box 1190, 36701
Telephone: 334-874-6683
Facsimile: 334-872-8435

Samuel Earle Hobbs (1917-1994)
Bruce V. Hain (1915-1995)

Ralph N. Hobbs
Barry R. Bennett
James B. McNeill, Jr.

Counsel for: Industrial Development Board of the City of Selma; Roy S. Jones Realty Co., Inc.; Jones Oil Co., Inc.

For full biographical listings, see the Martindale-Hubbell Law Directory

REEVES & STEWART, P.C. (AV)

First Alabama Bank Building, 101 Church Street, P.O. Box 457, 36702-0457
Telephone: 334-875-7236
Fax: 205-875-7625

Edgar A. Stewart (Retired)
Archie T. Reeves, Jr.

B. Kincey Green, Jr.
Robert E. Armstrong, III

Local Attorneys for: State Farm Mutual Insurance Cos.; St. Paul Insurance Cos.; International Paper Co.; First Alabama Bank; Alabama Power Co.; South Central Bell Telephone; Alabama Gas Corp.; HealthTrust, Inc.

Assistant Division Counsel for: Norfolk Southern Corp.

For full biographical listings, see the Martindale-Hubbell Law Directory

---

TROY,* Pike Co.

CALHOUN, FAULK, WATKINS & CLOWER, L.L.C. (AV)

78 South Court Square, P.O. Box 489, 36081
Telephone: 334-566-7200
Fax: 334-566-7584

Richard F. Calhoun
Joseph E. Faulk

William Keith Watkins
James G. Clower (Retired)

Robert Curry Faircloth

General Counsel for: City of Troy; City of Brundidge; First Alabama Bank, Troy; First National Bank of Brundidge; Troy City Board of Education; Pike County Board of Education; South Alabama Electric Cooperative, Inc.; B & D Plastics, Inc.; Battery Marketing Corporation.

For full biographical listings, see the Martindale-Hubbell Law Directory

---

TUSCALOOSA,* Tuscaloosa Co.

DAVIDSON, WIGGINS & CROWDER, P.C. (AV)

2625 Eighth Street, P.O. Box 1939, 35403
Telephone: 205-759-5771
Fax: 205-752-8259

M. McCoy Davidson
G. Stephen Wiggins

A. Courtney Crowder
David Ryan

OF COUNSEL
Hugh W. Roberts, Jr.

Brett Ross

Attorneys for: Canal Insurance Co.; Government Employees Insurance Co.; The Travelers Group; Auto-Owners Insurance Co.; Continental National American Group; Federated Insurance; Lynn Insurance Group; The Trinity Cos.; The PMA Group; Nationwide Ins. Co.; Colonial Ins. Co. of California.

For full biographical listings, see the Martindale-Hubbell Law Directory

Tuscaloosa—Continued

PHELPS, JENKINS, GIBSON & FOWLER (AV)

1201 Greensboro Avenue, P.O. Box 020848, 35402-0848
Telephone: 205-345-5100
Fax: 205-758-4394
Fax: 205-391-6658

MEMBERS OF FIRM

Sam M. Phelps	Randolph M. Fowler
James J. Jenkins	Michael S. Burroughs
Johnson Russell Gibson, III	C. Barton Adcox
Farley A. Poellnitz	

ASSOCIATES

Karen C. Welborn	Stephen E. Snow
Sandra C. Guin	Thomas W. Davis
Lisa Paul Hodges	M. Kristi Wallace

LEGAL SUPPORT PERSONNEL

Alicia Suzanne Wilson	Ashley D. Sparks
Cathey Raye Hartline	Kimberly Susan Wright

Attorneys for: Aetna Insurance Co.; Allstate Insurance Co.; Carolina Casualty Insurance Co.; Continental Insurance Cos.; Fireman's Fund-American Insurance Cos.; Great American Insurance Co.; Hanover Insurance Co.

For full biographical listings, see the Martindale-Hubbell Law Directory

ZEANAH, HUST, SUMMERFORD, DAVIS & JONES, L.L.C. (AV)

Seventh Floor, AmSouth Bank Building, P.O. Box 1310, 35403
Telephone: 205-349-1383
Fax: 205-391-1319

MEMBERS OF FIRM

Olin W. Zeanah (1922-1987)	Kenneth D. Davis
Wilbor J. Hust, Jr.	Christopher H. Jones
E. Clark Summerford	Beverly A. Smith

OF COUNSEL

Marvin T. Ormond

Representative Clients: Alfa Insurance Cos.; Hartford Insurance Group; Home Insurance Co.; Nationwide Insurance Co.; Alabama Power Co.; Liberty Mutual Insurance Co.; The Uniroyal Goodrich Tire Co.

For full biographical listings, see the Martindale-Hubbell Law Directory

---

UNION SPRINGS, * Bullock Co. — (Refer to Tuskegee)

VERNON, * Lamar Co. — (Refer to Tuscaloosa)

WETUMPKA, * Elmore Co.

ENSLEN, JOHNSTON & PINKSTON, L.L.C. (AV)

499 South Main Street, 36092
Telephone: 334-567-2545
Fax: 334-567-2547

John E. Enslen	Parker C. Johnston
Patrick D. Pinkston	

References: Elmore County National Bank; First National Bank of Wetumpka.

For full biographical listings, see the Martindale-Hubbell Law Directory

ALASKA

ANCHORAGE, * Third Judicial District

DELANEY, WILES, HAYES, GERETY & ELLIS, INC. (AV)

1007 West Third Avenue, Suite 400, 99501
Telephone: 907-279-3581
Fax: 907-277-1331

Daniel A. Gerety	Donald C. Thomas
Stephen M. Ellis	Timothy J. Lamb
Clay A. Young	Cynthia L. Ducey
William E. Moseley	Donna M. Meyers
Marc D. Bond	Jeffrey P. Stark
J. D. Cellars	Eugene F. Wiles (1922-1990)
James B. Friderici	John K. Brubaker (1937-1992)
Andrew Guidi	Clyde E. Sniffen, Jr.
Howard A. Lazar	Elise M. Hsieh

OF COUNSEL

James J. Delaney	George N. Hayes
Stanley H. Reitman	

Representative Clients: Carr-Gottstein Foods Co.; Chevron Corporation; Arco Alaska Inc.; Alyeska Pipeline Service Co.; Phillips Petroleum Company; Matanuska Electric Association; Nana Regional Corporation; Bering Straits Native Corporation; Mobil Oil Company; Seibu, Inc.

For full biographical listings, see the Martindale-Hubbell Law Directory

FAULKNER, BANFIELD, DOOGAN & HOLMES, A PROFESSIONAL CORPORATION (AV)

550 West Seventh Avenue, Suite 1000, 99501
Telephone: 907-274-0666
Telecopier: 907-277-4657
Email: fbdhjno@ptialaska.net
Juneau, Alaska Office: 302 Gold Street, 99801.
Telephone: 907-586-2210.
Telecopier: 907-586-8090.
Seattle, Washington Office: 999 Third Avenue, Suite 2600, 98104.
Telephone: 206-292-8008.
Telecopier: 206-340-0289.

Herbert L. Faulkner (1882-1972)	Richard B. Brown (Resident)
Frank M. Doogan (1923-1977)	Timothy A. McKeever
Michael M. Holmes (Resident at the Seattle, Washington Office)	(Resident)
	James E. Hutchins (Resident)
	Constance E. Livsey (Resident)
Randall J. Weddle (Resident)	Theresa M. Hennemann
William B. Rozell (Resident at the Juneau Office)	(Resident)
	Norman C. Banfield (Retired)
Michael A. Barcott (Resident at the Seattle, Washington Office)	Lawrence T. Feeney (Retired)

Elizabeth D. Goudreau (Resident)	Suzanne H. Lombardi (Resident)
Matthew D. Regan (Resident)	Suzanne K. Ishii-Regan (Resident)
Michael A. Barnhill (Resident)	Paul J. Niewiadomski (Resident)

For full biographical listings, see the Martindale-Hubbell Law Directory

ROBERTSON, MONAGLE & EASTAUGH, A PROFESSIONAL CORPORATION (AV)

Suite 1200 The Bank of America Building, 550 West Seventh Avenue, 99501
Telephone: 907-277-6693
Telecopy: 907-279-1959
Juneau, Alaska Office: Goldbelt Place Office Building, 801 West 10th Street, Suite 300.
Telephone: 907-586-3340.
Telecopy: 907-586-6818.
Arlington, Virginia Office: Arlington Courthouse Plaza II, 2300 Clarendon Boulevard, Suite 1010.
Telephone: 703-527-4414.
Telecopy: 703-527-0421.

Royal Arch Gunnison (1873-1918)	Bradley D. Gilman (Resident at Arlington, Virginia Office)
R. E. Robertson (1885-1961)	Robert Blasco
M. E. Monagle (1902-1985)	(Resident at Juneau Office)
Frederick O. Eastaugh (1913-1992)	Julia Barrows Bockmon
Leroy J. Barker	Terry L. Thurbon
James F. Clark (Resident at Juneau Office)	(Resident at Juneau Office)
	Margaret Ogden Dullanty
Paul M. Hoffman (Resident at Juneau Office)	Daniel J. Boone (Resident at Juneau Office)
L. G. Berry	Ruth R. Hamilton
Harold E. Snow, Jr.	(Resident at Juneau Office)
Steven W. Silver (Resident at Arlington, Virginia Office)	Stacie L. Kraly (Resident at Juneau Office)
Carl Winner (Resident at Arlington, Virginia Office)	Nelson E. Hubbell

LEGAL SUPPORT PERSONNEL
LEGAL ASSISTANTS

Chloe Clark-Berry	Deborah Sims

Representative Clients: Alaska Pulp Corp.; Associated Aviation Underwriters; Brunswick Corp.; Fireman's Fund Insurance Group; U.S. Aviation Insurance Group; U.S. Borax Chemical Corp.

For full biographical listings, see the Martindale-Hubbell Law Directory

---

FAIRBANKS, * Fourth Judicial District

CALL, BARRETT & BURBANK, A PROFESSIONAL CORPORATION (AV)

711 Gaffney Road, 99701
Telephone: 907-452-2211
Fax: 907-456-1137

David H. Call	Michael P. McConahy
Winston S. Burbank	Christopher E. Zimmerman
John Foster Wallace	

OF COUNSEL

Paul A. Barrett

Reference: Denali State Bank.

For full biographical listings, see the Martindale-Hubbell Law Directory

JUNEAU,* First Judicial District

FAULKNER, BANFIELD, DOOGAN & HOLMES, A PROFESSIONAL CORPORATION (AV)

302 Gold Street, 99801
Telephone: 907-586-2210
Telecopier: 907-586-8090
Email: fbdhjno@ptialaska.net
Anchorage, Alaska Office: 550 West Seventh Avenue, Suite 1000, 99501.
Telephone: 907-274-0666.
Telecopier: 907-277-4657.
Seattle, Washington Office: 999 Third Avenue, Suite 2600, 98104.
Telephone: 206-292-8008.
Telecopier: 206-340-0289.

Herbert L. Faulkner (1882-1972)	Eric A. Kueffner (Resident)
Frank M. Doogan (1923-1977)	Bethann Boudah Chapman
William B. Rozell (Resident)	(Resident)
Anthony M. Sholty (Resident)	Bruce B. Weyhrauch (Resident)
Leon T. Vance (Resident)	Norman C. Banfield (Retired)
Elizabeth Ann Gifford	Lawrence T. Feeney (Retired)
(Resident)	James R. Webb (Retired)

Mala J. Reges (Resident)	Mary H. Zemp (Resident)
F. Lachicotte Zemp, Jr	
(Resident)	

For full biographical listings, see the Martindale-Hubbell Law Directory

KODIAK, Third Judicial District

JAMIN, EBELL, BOLGER & GENTRY, A PROFESSIONAL CORPORATION (AV)

323 Carolyn Street, 99615
Telephone: 907-486-6024
Telecopier: 907-486-6112
Seattle, Washington Office: 300 Mutual Life Building, 605 First Avenue.
Telephone: 206-622-7634.
Telecopier: 206-623-7521.

Matthew D. Jamin	Joel H. Bolger
C. Walter Ebell	Dianna R. Gentry
(Resident, Seattle, Office)	Alan L. Schmitt

Walter W. Mason	Duncan S. Fields
(Resident, Seattle Office)	Karen E. Bendler

For full biographical listings, see the Martindale-Hubbell Law Directory

ARIZONA

BISBEE,* Cochise Co. — (Refer to Nogales)

CASA GRANDE, Pinal Co.

FITZGIBBONS LAW OFFICES, P.L.C. (AV)

Suite E, 711 East Cottonwood Lane, P.O. Box 11208, 85230-1208
Telephone: 520-426-3824
Fax: 520-426-9355

David A. Fitzgibbons	Denis M. Fitzgibbons
David A. Fitzgibbons, III	Robert M. Yates
	Kevin D. White

OF COUNSEL
E.D. "Bud" McBryde

Representative Clients: Bank of Casa Grande Valley; Charlie Case Tire Co., Inc.; Fletcher's Cobre Tire; M&O Agencies; Maricopa Turf, Inc. a/b/a Western Sod; Vaquero Foundation; Sun Life Family Health Center, Inc.; Casa Grande Regional Medical Center; Verde Grande Vineyards.

For full biographical listings, see the Martindale-Hubbell Law Directory

CHANDLER, Maricopa Co. — (Refer to Mesa)

COOLIDGE, Pinal Co. — (Refer to Casa Grande)

COTTONWOOD, Yavapai Co.

ASPEY, WATKINS & DIESEL, P.L.L.C. (AV)

2400 East Highway 89A, Suite C, 86326
Telephone: 520-639-1881
Facsimile: 520-639-0272
Flagstaff, Arizona Office: 123 North San Francisco, 3rd Floor.
Telephone: 520-774-1478.
Facsimile: 520-774-8404.
Sedona, Arizona Office: 120 Soldier Pass Road.
Telephone: 520-282-5955.
Facsimile: 520-282-5962.

(See Next Column)

Page, Arizona Office: 904 North Navajo.
Telephone: 520-645-9694.

MEMBERS OF FIRM

Harold L. Watkins	Kaign N. Christy

ASSOCIATES

James E. Ledbetter	Stephen A. Thompson

LEGAL SUPPORT PERSONNEL
Carrie R. Flynn (Litigation Paralegal)

For full biographical listings, see the Martindale-Hubbell Law Directory

DOUGLAS, Cochise Co. — (Refer to Tucson)

FLAGSTAFF,* Coconino Co.

ASPEY, WATKINS & DIESEL, P.L.L.C. (AV)

123 North San Francisco, 3rd Floor, 86001
Telephone: 520-774-1478
Facsimile: 520-774-8404
Sedona, Arizona Office: 120 Soldier Pass Road.
Telephone: 520-282-5955.
Facsimile: 520-282-5962.
Page, Arizona Office: 904 North Navajo.
Telephone: 520-645-9694.
Cottonwood, Arizona Office: 2400 E. Highway 89A, Suite C.
Telephone: 520-639-1881.
Facsimile: 520-639-0272.

MEMBERS OF FIRM

Frederick M. Fritz Aspey	Donald H. Bayles, Jr.
Harold L. Watkins	Kaign N. Christy
Louis M. Diesel	John J. Dempsey
Bruce S. Griffen	Zachary J. Markham

James E. Ledbetter	Roger M. Baeurle
Whitney Cunningham	Amy E. Mabius
Pernell Whynn McGuire	Stephen A. Thompson
	Joel E. Sannes

LEGAL SUPPORT PERSONNEL

Karla H. Falls, CLAS	Dominic M. Marino, Jr,
(Legal Assistant)	(Paralegal Assistant)
Rocky C. Nissen (Paralegal	Carrie R. Flynn (Litigation
Assistant, Sedona, Arizona	Paralegal, Cottonwood,
Office)	Arizona Office)
Deborah D. Roberts, CLA	
(Legal Assistant)	

Representative Clients: Farmer's Insurance Company of Arizona; Pepsi-Cola Bottling Company of Northern Arizona; Bill Luke's Chrysler-Plymouth, Inc.; First American Title Insurance Company; Transnation Title Insurance Co.; Page Electric Utility; Comprehensive Access Health Plan, Inc.; Northern Arizona Healthcare Corporation.
Reference: First Interstate Bank-Arizona, N.A., Flagstaff, Arizona.

For full biographical listings, see the Martindale-Hubbell Law Directory

MANGUM, WALL, STOOPS & WARDEN, P.L.L.C. (AV)

222 East Birch Avenue, P.O. Box 10, 86002
Telephone: 520-779-6951
Fax: 520-773-1312

H. Karl Mangum (1908-1993)

OF COUNSEL

Douglas J. Wall	Robert W. Warden

MEMBERS OF FIRM

Daniel J. Stoops	Stephen K. Smith
A. Dean Pickett	Melinda L. Garrahan

ASSOCIATES

Deborah M. Fine	Annette Star Lustgarten
Michael L. Transier	David L. Anderson
	Michael H. Hinson

Representative Clients: Northern Arizona University; Flagstaff Unified School District; Museum of Northern Arizona; City of Sedona; Arizona School Board Association.
Local Counsel for: Bank of America-Arizona; Arizona Public Service; U.S.-A.A.; State Farm Fire & Casualty Ins. Co.; Property Development Co.

For full biographical listings, see the Martindale-Hubbell Law Directory

GLOBE,* Gila Co. — (Refer to Coolidge)

GREEN VALLEY, Pima Co.

DUFFIELD, MILLER, YOUNG, ADAMSON & ALFRED, P.C. (AV)

101-65 South La Canada, Green Valley Mall, 85614
Telephone: 520-625-4404
FAX: 520-625-4453
Tucson, Arizona Office: Suite 711, Transamerica Building, 177 North Church Avenue.
Telephone: 520-792-1181.
Fax: 520-792-2859.

(See Next Column)

DUFFIELD, MILLER, YOUNG, ADAMSON & ALFRED P.C.—*Continued*

La Paloma Office: La Paloma Corporate Center, 3573 East Sunrise Drive, Suite 115, Tucson, Arizona.
Telephone: 520-577-1135.
Fax: 520-577-1079.

Richard Duffield	Larry R. Adamson
Michael C. Young	K. Alexander Hobson
	Eugene C. Gieseler

Representative Clients: San Xavier Rock & Materials, Inc.; Mobat-Adamson Tire Co.; Community Water Company of Green Valley.
Insurance Company Clientele: State Farm Mutual Insurance Cos.; Automobile Club Insurance Co.; Colonial Penn Insurance Co.; Crum & Forster Group; National Indemnity Insurance Co.

For full biographical listings, see the Martindale-Hubbell Law Directory

---

HOLBROOK,* Navajo Co. — (Refer to Flagstaff)

LAKE HAVASU CITY, Mohave Co.

WACHTEL, BIEHN & MALM (AV)

Suite A, 2240 McCulloch Boulevard, 86403
Telephone: 520-855-5115
Fax: 520-855-5211

OF COUNSEL
Wing Wachtel

MEMBERS OF FIRM

Don Biehn	James B. Wyss
Denis R. Malm	Steven A. Biehn
	Rex L. Martin

For full biographical listings, see the Martindale-Hubbell Law Directory

---

MESA, Maricopa Co.

KILLIAN, NICHOLAS, FISCHER, WIRKEN, COOK & PEW, P.L.C. (AV)

40 North Center Street, Suite 200, 85201
Telephone: 602-461-4600
Facsimile: 602-461-4763
Mailing Address: P.O. Box 1467, Mesa, Arizona, 85211-1467

Vernon L. Nicholas	Douglas K. Cook
M. Paul Fischer	W. Ralph Pew
Charles W. Wirken	Gail M. Ledward

OF COUNSEL
C. Max Killian

Thomas J. Griggs	Michael G. Delgado
Wilford L. Taylor	John E. Rooney, IV
David R. Baker	(Not admitted in AZ)
Ezra T. Clark, III	Kent M. Nicholas

Representative Clients: Dunkin' Donuts Incorporated; Pulte Home Corp.; Tempe Life Care Village, Inc.; Voit Development Co.; Bingham Equipment Company; Queen Creek Irrigation District; Mesa United Way; Del Webb Corporation; Heraeus Incorporated; A.G. Spanos Construction, Inc.

For full biographical listings, see the Martindale-Hubbell Law Directory

---

NOGALES,* Santa Cruz Co.

O'CONNOR, CAVANAGH, ANDERSON, KILLINGSWORTH & BESHEARS, A PROFESSIONAL ASSOCIATION (AV)

1891 North Mastick Way, 85621
Telephone: 520-761-4215
FAX: 520-761-3505
Email: firminfo@arizlaw.com
Phoenix, Arizona Office: One East Camelback Road, Suite 1100, 85012.
Telephone: 602-263-2400.
FAX: 602-263-2900.
Tucson, Arizona Office: O'Connor Cavanagh Molloy Jones, 33 N. Stone, Suite 2100, 85701, P.O. Box 2268, 85702.
Telephone: 520-622-3531.
FAX: 520-624-2816.
Sun City, Arizona Office: 13250 North Del Webb Boulevard, Suite B, 85351.
Telephone: 602-263-2808.
FAX: 602-933-3100.

Hector G. Arana	Kimberly A. Howard Arana
Brian G. Larson	Ann Katherine Shell

Representative Clients: Omega Produce Co.; Frank's Distributing, Inc.; City of Nogales; Collectron of Ariz., Inc.; James K. Wilson Produce Co.; Agricola Bon, S. de R.L. de C.V.; Angel Demerutis E.; Rene Carrillo C.; Arturo Lomeli; Theojary Crisantes E.

For full biographical listings, see the Martindale-Hubbell Law Directory

---

PAGE, Coconino Co.

ASPEY, WATKINS & DIESEL, P.L.L.C. (AV)

904 North Navajo, 86040
Telephone: 520-645-9694
Flagstaff, Arizona Office: 123 North San Francisco, 3rd Floor.
Telephone: 520-774-1478.
Facsimile: 520-774-8404.
Sedona, Arizona Office: 120 Soldier Pass Road.
Telephone: 520-282-5955.
Facsimile: 520-282-5962.
Cottonwood, Arizona Office: 2400 E. Highway 89A Suite C.
Telephone: 520-639-1881.
Facsimile: 520-639-0272.

MEMBERS OF FIRM

Bruce S. Griffen	Zachary J. Markham

ASSOCIATES

Roger M. Baeurle	Amy E. Mabius

Representative Clients: Page Electric Utility.
Reference: First Interstate Bank.

For full biographical listings, see the Martindale-Hubbell Law Directory

---

PHOENIX,* Maricopa Co.

ANDERSON, BRODY, LEVINSON, WEISER & HORWITZ, P.A. (AV)

1112 West Camelback Road, 85013
Telephone: 602-234-0563
Fax: 602-234-2952

Donald E. Anderson	Ronald M. Horwitz
Jeffrey H. Levinson	Bradley D. Gardner
Paul M. Weiser	Alan M. Levinsky
Jamie A. Brody	Mark Bohn
	Carrie M. Beasley

OF COUNSEL
Stephen A. Myers

For full biographical listings, see the Martindale-Hubbell Law Directory

---

BEER & TOONE, P.C. (AV)

76 East Mitchell, 85012
Telephone: 602-263-0900
Fax: 602-263-0917

Paul Beer	Michael C. Sheedy
Thomas L. Toone	Matthew F. Winter

LEGAL SUPPORT PERSONNEL

Ruth M. Murphy	Sandra Alcumbrac
(Legal Assistant)	(Legal Assistant)

Attorneys for: AIG Aviation, Inc.; AVEMCO Insurance Company; Beech Aircraft Corporation; Cessna Aircraft Company; Loss Management Services, Inc.; Mercury Insurance Group; The Southland Corporation dba 7-Eleven Food Stores; State of Arizona; Underwriters at Lloyds, London; Thrifty Car Rental.

For full biographical listings, see the Martindale-Hubbell Law Directory

---

JAMES T. BIALAC (AV)

Suite 8 Luhrs Arcade, 11 West Jefferson Street, 85003
Telephone: 602-258-8441
Fax: 602-258-8443
Mailing Address: P.O. Box 4095, 85030

BROWN & BAIN, A PROFESSIONAL ASSOCIATION (AV)

2901 North Central Avenue, P.O. Box 400, 85001-0400
Telephone: 602-351-8000
Telecopier: 602-351-8516
Palo Alto, California Affiliated Office: Brown & Bain, 1755 Embarcadero Road, Suite 200.
Telephone: 415-856-9411.
Telecopier: 415-856-6061.
Tucson, Arizona Affiliated Office: Brown & Bain, A Professional Association. One South Church Avenue, Nineteenth Floor, P.O. Box 2265.
Telephone: 602-798-7900
Telecopier: 602-798-7945.

Lois W. Abraham	David P. Brooks
(Resident at Palo Alto Office)	Jack E. Brown
Lynne Christensen Adams	John A. Buttrick
C. Randall Bain	Howard Ross Cabot
Eddward P. Ballinger, Jr.	H. Michael Clyde
Daniel C. Barr	William S. Coats
Michael P. Berman	(Resident at Palo Alto Office)
Charles A. Blanchard	Richard Calvin Cooledge
Alan H. Blankenheimer	Stephen W. Craig

(See Next Column)

BROWN & BAIN A PROFESSIONAL ASSOCIATION, *Phoenix—Continued*

Paul F. Eckstein	Joseph E. Mais
Terry E. Fenzl	Anthony L. Marks
Jodi Knobel Feuerhelm	Michael F. McNulty
Douglas Gerlach	(Resident at Tucson Office)
Amy J. Gittler	Joel W. Nomkin
Brent M. Gunderson	Kelly A. O'Connor
Richard H. Harvey	Michael W. Patten
(Resident at Palo Alto Office)	Frank M. Placenti
Kyle B. Hettinger	Joseph P. Richardson
Philip R. Higdon	John W. Rogers
(Resident at Tucson Office)	Lawrence G. D. Scarborough
Patricia A. Hubbard	Sarah R. Simmons
Jonathan M. James	(Resident at Tucson Office)
Jeanean Kirk	Lex J. Smith
Roy W. Kyle	Craig W. Soland
(Resident at Tucson Office)	Samuel A. Thumma
Stephen E. Lee	Antonio T. Viera
Ronald E. Lowe	Judith K. Weiss
Diane L. Madenci	Kim E. Williamson
(Resident at Tucson Office)	

Dan L. Bagatell	Todd R. Kerr
Daniel D. Barnowski	Dennis R. Kiker
Eric S. Beane	Jin Sun Kim
(Resident at Palo Alto Office)	C. Mark Kittredge
Michael K. Ben-Horin	Chad H. Kolodisner
Susan D. Berney-Key	Deborah Henscheid Lyon
(Resident at Palo Alto Office)	Jolene L. McCaleb
Timothy P. Boudreau	Rebecca B. Merritt
Elizabeth P. Chase	Douglas D. Metcalf
(Resident at Tucson Office)	(Resident at Tucson Office)
Mala D. Clancey	Cheryl L. Nackino
Benjamin G. Clark	Timothy A. Nelson
Alan R. Davis	Sarah Ellison Porter
Christopher J. Day	Steven R. Rodgers
James A. Fassold	Kristen B. Rosati
Timothy J. Franks	Phaedra Tanner
Michael R. Johnson	John J. Tuchi
Lisa M. Kaplan	Rachel R. Weiss
Shirley Ann Kaufman	Karen M. Wilkinson

COUNSEL

Ian C. Ballon	Douglas Clark Neilsson
(Resident at Palo Alto Office)	(Resident at Palo Alto Office)
Michael C. Jones	Bernard Petrie
Victoria S. Lewis	(Resident at Palo Alto Office)
James F. McNulty, Jr.	
(Resident at Tucson Office)	

For full biographical listings, see the Martindale-Hubbell Law Directory

BURCH & CRACCHIOLO, P.A. (AV)

702 East Osborn Road, Suite 200, 85014
Telephone: 602-274-7611
Fax: 602-234-0341
Mailing Address: P.O. Box 16882, Phoenix, AZ, 85011

Daniel Cracchiolo	Linda A. Finnegan
Stephen E. Silver	Andrew Abraham
Brian Kaven	Clare H. Abel
Jack D. Klausner	Donald W. Lindholm
Guadalupe Iniguez	F. Michael Carroll
Brad S. Ostroff	Daniel R. Malinski
Daryl Manhart	Edwin D. Fleming
Ian Neale	Ralph D. Harris
David G. Derickson	Jess A. Lorona
Edwin C. Bull	Stephen M. Hart
Bryan F. Murphy	David M. Villadolid

Marvin Davis	Judy M. Miller
Paul F. Dowdell	Martha C. Patrick
Theodore (Todd) Julian	Steven M. Serrano
Steven J. Lippman	James M. Stipe
Thomas A. Longfellow	J. Brent Welker

OF COUNSEL

Frank Haze Burch	Donna Platt
Howard C. Meyers	

Representative Clients: Bashas' Inc.; Farmers Insurance Group; U-Haul International, Inc.

For full biographical listings, see the Martindale-Hubbell Law Directory

RONALD G. COOLEY (AV)

322 West Roosevelt Street, 85003
Telephone: 602-258-1684
Fax: 602-252-2864

Representative Clients: Arizona Estate Administration, Inc. (A Private Fiduciary); Process Equipment Co., Inc.; Eastlake Mortuary.
Reference: Bank of America.

For full biographical listings, see the Martindale-Hubbell Law Directory

FENNEMORE CRAIG, A PROFESSIONAL CORPORATION (AV)

Two North Central, Suite 2200, 85004
Telephone: 602-257-8700
Fax: 602-257-8527
Scottsdale, Arizona Office: 6263 North Scottsdale Road, Suite 290, 85250.
Telephone: 602-257-5400.
Fax: 602-257-5409.
Tucson, Arizona Office: One South Church Avenue, Suite 1030, 85701.
Telephone: 520-791-6800.
Fax: 520-791-6820.

Calvin H. Udall	Cynthia L. Shupe
James Powers	Michael V. Mulchay
James M. Bush	Phillip F. Fargotstein
Arthur D. Ehrenreich	Paul J. Mooney
C. Webb Crockett	David A. Weatherwax
Kenneth J. Sherk	Graeme E. M. Hancock
Neal Kurn	Rita A. Eisenfeld
Robert P. Robinson	David N. Heap
Michael Preston Green	Ray K. Harris
Philip A. Edlund	Margaret R. Gallogly
John D. Everroad	Kaye L. McCarthy
James W. Johnson	Scott M. Finical
F. Pendleton Gaines, III	William T. Burghart
Robert J. Hackett	Andrew M. Federhar
Jay S. Ruffner	Douglas E. McAllister
Louis F. Comus, Jr.	Cathy L. Reece
Donald R. Gilbert	Gregg Hanks
Ronald L. Ballard	Karen Ciupak McConnell
Timothy J. Burke	Jay S. Kramer
Ronald J. Stolkin	Christopher L. Callahan
Stephen M. Savage	Rebecca L. Burnham
Roger T. Hargrove	Loral Deatherage
Mark A. Nesvig	Jim L. Wright
James R. Huntwork	Bryan A. Albue
David T. Maddox	David E. Vieweg
George T. Cole	J. Barry Shelley
John G. Ryan	Lesa J. Storey
Lauren J. Caster	Christopher P. Staring
Leland M. Jones	Janet W. Lord
Timothy Berg	John Randall Jefferies
C. Owen Paepke	Robert D. Anderson
William L. Thorpe	John J. Balitis, Jr.
Charles M. King	James J. Trimble
David T. Cox	Janice Procter-Murphy
	Robert J. Kramer

Marc L. Spitzer	Dewain D. Fox
Karen A. Curosh	Jeffrey S. Silvyn
Theresa Dwyer	Brett L Hopper
Mark H. Brain	Alan S. Hall
Scott H. Thomas	Scott T. Ashby
Jean Marie Sullivan	Laurel J. Davis
Keith L. Hendricks	James D. Burgess
Selma F. Baharoglu	Jeffrey C. Thacker
Elizabeth M. Behnke	Scott L. Altes
W. T. Eggleston, Jr.	Sandra L. Bierman
M. Virginia Perry	Erin E. Flaharty
Anna Pawlik Winsett	William P. Wichterman
(Not admitted in AZ)	Jane E. Birge
Douglas C. Northup	Susan L. Bostock
Marc H. Lamber	Janna B. Day
Richard A. Kasper	Susan M. Hassig
Kendis K. Muscheid	David M. Call
Stephen A. Good	Vera E. Muñoz
Susan Marie Ciupak	Sal J. Rivera
Christopher W. Zaharis	Carey J. Fox
Stacie K. Smith	Joel B. Shapiro
	Pamela J. Crane

For full biographical listings, see the Martindale-Hubbell Law Directory

GAMMAGE & BURNHAM, P.L.C. (AV)

One Renaissance Square, Two North Central Avenue, Suite 1800, 85004
Telephone: 602-256-0566
Fax: 602-256-4475

MEMBERS OF FIRM

Richard B. Burnham	James A. Craft
Grady Gammage, Jr.	Ellen Harris Hoff
F. William Sheppard	Kevin R. Merritt
Michael R. King	Randall S. Dalton
Richard K. Mahrle	Kevin J. Blakley
Shawn E. Tobin	John R. Dacey
Curtis A. Ullman	Jeffrey J. Miller
Mary B. Artigue	Cameron C. Artigue
Michael B. Withey	Susan L. Watchman
Thomas J. McDonald	Stephen W. Anderson

(See Next Column)

GAMMAGE & BURNHAM P.L.C.—*Continued*
MEMBERS OF FIRM (Continued)

Mark J.A. Hughes	Margo S. Kirchner
Colleen E. Grant	Christopher A. Womack
	David J. Kolbe

For full biographical listings, see the Martindale-Hubbell Law Directory

GOODSON, MANLEY & DURFEE, P.L.C. (AV)

The Brookstone Building, 2025 North 3rd Street, Suite 200, 85004-1471
Telephone: 602-252-5110
Fax: 602-257-1883

John F. Goodson	Colleen C. Manley
	Richard E. Durfee, Jr.

Lawrence F. Scaringelli	Bryan C. Moody

A list of Representative Clients will be furnished upon request.
Reference: First National Bank of Arizona.

For full biographical listings, see the Martindale-Hubbell Law Directory

HOFMANN, SALCITO & STEVENS (AV)

302 East Coronado Road, 85004
Telephone: 602-254-5341
Fax: 602-258-6192

Leroy W. Hofmann	Daniel R. Salcito
	Gene C. Stevens

For full biographical listings, see the Martindale-Hubbell Law Directory

JENNINGS, STROUSS AND SALMON, P.L.C. (AV)

A Professional Limited Liability Company
One Renaissance Square, Two North Central, 85004-2393
Telephone: 602-262-5911
Fax: 602-253-3255

Irving A. Jennings (1896-1972)	Gary L. Lassen
Charles L. Strouss (1891-1958)	Richard N. Morrison
Riney B. Salmon (1902-1970)	Barry E. Lewin
J. A. Riggins, Jr. (1912-1986)	Anne L. Kleindienst
Rex H. Moore (1906-1971)	Joen M. Schaefer
Charles R. Esser (1929-1972)	Jay A. Fradkin
John R. Christian	Michael R. Palumbo
Gary G. Keltner	David W. Kash
Lee E. Esch	Glenn J. Carter
Richard L. Lassen	H. Christian Bode
T. Patrick Flood	James M. Ackerman
W. Michael Flood	George Esahak-Gage
I. Douglas Dunipace	Robert J. Werner
Gary L. Stuart	Ernest Calderon
Douglas G. Zimmerman	Jon D. Schneider
Gerald W. Alston	Wendy D. Woodrow
George C. Spilsbury	Robert P. Solliday
John G. Sestak, Jr.	Brian N. Spector
Philip J. MacDonnell	Michael J. O'Connor
David J. Calverley	Katherine M. Cooper
Kenneth C. Sundlof, Jr.	John J. Egbert
Rita A. Meiser	Charles D. Onofry
Gerrit M. Steenblik	Robert D. Haws
	Shiela B. Schmidt

OF COUNSEL

Douglas F. Behm	James O. Ehinger

Michael J. Farrell	Gordon Lewis
Jennifer M. Bligh	Stephanie McRae
Margaret A. Gillespie	Tracye R. Grinnage
Kim D. Steinmetz	Brian A. Cabianca
Cody M. Hall	Brad Denton
David B. Earl	Gregory J. Stanton
Lisa A. Frey	Andrew Borders Turk

Representative Clients: Best Western International, Inc.; Chemical Waste Management, Inc.; CNA Insurance; Salt River Project; Southwest Gas Corp.; St. Joseph's Hospital and Medical Center; Karsten Manufacturing; Mutual Insurance of Arizona; Shamrick Foods Co.; Smitty's Super Valu, Inc.

For full biographical listings, see the Martindale-Hubbell Law Directory

LEWIS AND ROCA, LLP (AV)

A Limited Liability Partnership including a Professional Corporation
40 North Central Avenue, 85004-4429
Telephone: 602-262-5311
Fax: 602-262-5747
Email: mlp@lrlaw.com
Tucson, Arizona Office: One South Church Avenue, Suite 700, 86701-1620.
Telephone: 520-622-2090.
Fax: 520-622-3088. E-Mail: mlp@lrlaw.com.

(See Next Column)

MEMBERS OF FIRM

Orme Lewis (1903-1990)	Paul M. Roca (1911-1979)
Edwin Beauchamp (1916-1964)	John P. Frank
Joseph E. McGarry	Gerald K. Smith
Peter D. Baird	Douglas L. Irish
Merton E. Marks (P.C.)	Douglas R. Chandler
Tom Galbraith	Marty Harper
Richard N. Goldsmith	R. Kent Klein
Richard S. Cohen	Jordan Green
Susan M. Freeman	Barry Fish
David E. Manch	Randolph J. Haines
Judith E. Sirkis	Patricia K. Norris
José A. Cárdenas	Patrick Derdenger
Dale A. Danneman	Edward F. Novak
Foster Robberson	Thomas H. Campbell
Michael J. Holden	Beth J. Schermer
Kevin L. Olson	David J. Cantelme
David M. Bixby	Newman R. Porter
Amy R. Porter	Sheila Carmody
George L. Paul	D. Randall Stokes
Thomas G. Ryan	Betty L. Hum
Steven J. Labensky	Stephen M. Bressler
Thomas Klinkel	Barbara J. Muller
Allen R. Clarke	Karen Carter Owens
Jesse B. Simpson	Scott DeWald
James K. Kloss	Robert F. Roos
Brent C. Gardner	Mary Ellen Simonson
Cathy M. Holt	James T. Acuff, Jr.
Steven J. Hulsman	Rosemarie Christofolo
Carl F. Mariano	Bryant D. Barber
Christopher J. Brelje	Bret A. Maidman
Kenneth Van Winkle, Jr.	Robert H. McKirgan
Steven J. Burr	Pamela B. Petersen
L. Keith Beauchamp	Jane E. Reddin
Thomas J. Kennedy	Hope Leibsohn
J. Tyler Haahr	Craig W. Phillips
Douglas L. Christian	Kim C. Stanger
Greg S. Como	Richard A. Halloran
	Deanna Salazar

ASSOCIATES

Barbara Anstey Hoerner	Stephen R. Winkelman
R. Neil Taylor, III	Kevin G. Hunter
Margaret R. Russell	Thel W. Casper
Dawn M. Bergin	Anthony J. Blackwell
Jeff A. Shumway	Julie M. Arvo MacKenzie
Janell M. Adams-Vogl	Todd A. Rigby
Jeffrey T. Bergin	Cynthia A. Coates
Julie Mathis Nelson	Randy Papetti
David B. Gass	Marc D. McCain
Ann-Martha Andrews	Todd E. Hale
Bruce E. Samuels	Robert A. Strent
Glenn D. Forcucci	Rebecca L. Story

OF COUNSEL

Lyman A. Manser	Jeremy E. Butler
James L. Hohnbaum	Deborah A. Nye
Lance J. Rose	Hui Tian
	James F. Mahoney

Representative Clients: Arizona Public Service; Blood Systems, Inc.; CIT Corp.; City of Phoenix; The Dial Corp.; E.I. du Pont de Nemours and Co.; MCI Communications, Corp.; The Prudential Insurance Company of America; Samaritan Health System; Smith Barney Shearson, Inc.

For full biographical listings, see the Martindale-Hubbell Law Directory

MARISCAL, WEEKS, McINTYRE & FRIEDLANDER, P.A. (AV)

2901 North Central Avenue Suite 200, 85012-2705
Telephone: 602-285-5000
Fax: 602-285-5100

Rudolph Mariscal	James T. Braselton
Richard A. Friedlander	Leslie A. Kresin
Gerald Gaffaney	Leonce A. Richard
William L. Novotny	Scott A. Holcomb
Michael S. Rubin	David J. Ouimette
Gary L. Birnbaum	D. Samuel Coffman
Robert A. Shull	Mark J. Robens
Peter A. Winkler	Kenneth A. Hodson
Robert V. Kerrick	Franklin D. Dodge
Michael R. Scheurich	Michael D. Hool
Fred C. Fathe	Robert L. Schwartz
Les S. Raatz	Cindra L. White
Andrew L. Pringle	Steven D. Wolfson
Brian M. Mueller	John B. Even
Anne L. Tiffen	Scot L. Claus
P. Bruce Converse	Mary Grace Blasko
Terry L. Tedesco	David D. Rodgers

OF COUNSEL

Phillip Weeks

References: Northern Trust Bank of Arizona; National Bank of Arizona.

For full biographical listings, see the Martindale-Hubbell Law Directory

Phoenix—Continued

MOHR, HACKETT, PEDERSON, BLAKLEY, RANDOLPH & HAGA, P.C. (AV)

2800 North Central Avenue, Suite 1100, 85004-1043
Telephone: 602-240-3000
Fax: 602-240-6600

William C. Blakley (1946-1987)	M. Maureen Anders
Robert C. Hackett	Gregory W. Falls
Gordon A. Mohr	Azim Q. Hameed
Arthur W. Pederson	Thomas C. Axelsen
John M. Randolph	John J. Nicgorski
David L. Haga, Jr.	Cathy L. Knapp
Thomas K. Chenal	Thomas M. Quigley
Charles I. Kelhoffer	Daniel P. Beeks
John R. Hoopes	Ronald P. Adams
Peter N. Spiller	Carolyn Ratti Matthews
David W. Dow	Nathaniel B. Rose
Michele M. Feeney	Karen L. Karr

For full biographical listings, see the Martindale-Hubbell Law Directory

O'CONNOR, CAVANAGH, ANDERSON, KILLINGSWORTH & BESHEARS, A PROFESSIONAL ASSOCIATION (AV)

One East Camelback Road, Suite 1100, 85012-1656
Telephone: 602-263-2400
FAX: 602-263-2900
Email: firminfo@arizlaw.com
Sun City, Arizona Office: 13250 North Del Webb Boulevard, Suite B, 85351.
Telephone: 602-263-2808.
FAX: 602-933-3100.
Tucson, Arizona Office: O'Connor Cavanagh Molloy Jones, 33 N. Stone, Suite 2100, 85701, P.O. Box 2268, 85702.
Telephone: 520-622-3531.
FAX: 520-624-2816.
Nogales, Arizona Office: 1891 North Mastick Way, 85621.
Telephone: 520-761-4215.
FAX: 520-761-3505.

James H. O'Connor (1922-1978)	Scott A. Salmon
Harry J. Cavanagh	Richard B. Stagg
Wilbert G. Anderson (Retired)	Steven L. Lisker
John H. Killingsworth (1922-1993)	Peter C. Guild
	Glenn M. Feldman
Robert G. Beshears	Richard M. Lorenzen
Ralph E. Hunsaker	Gilbert L. Rudolph
Gerald L. Jacobs	Jean E. Harris
George H. Mitchell	Max K. Boyer
Richard J. Woods	Daniel W. Peters
Richard E. Mitchell	David L. Kurtz
Mayor Shanken	Stephen E. Richman
Jeffrey B. Smith	David A. Van Engelhoven
Jolyon Grant	Paul J. Giancola
Harding B. Cure	Pamela M. Overton
Richard C. Smith	Michelle S. Monserez
Steven D. Smith	Frank M. Fox
Robert S. Kant	David L. Lansky
Henry L. Timmerman	Michael Cafiso
Michael E. Woolf	Christina S. Hamilton
Philip C. Gerard	Lisa M. Sommer
Jeffrey H. Verbin	Lucas J. Narducci
John B. Furman	Philip G. Mitchell
Charles F. Myers	Christopher Robbins
Carol N. Cure	Karen L. Liepmann
Scott A. Rose	Donald J. Lenkszus
	Lawrence J. Rosenfeld

Leigh A. Kaylor	Timothy F. Bolden
Robert J. Itri	Mark J. DePasquale
Craig J. Bolton	Troy B. Froderman
D. Scott Fehrman	Karl A. Freeburg
Robert L. Ehmann	Mark W. Daliere
R. Corey Hill	Robert H. Nagle
	Jonathan R. Feldman

Barbara L. Bolin	Eric A. Mark
John D. Titus	Jeffrey G. Pollitt
David A. Kelly	Jere M. Friedman
Helen Rubenstein Holden	Lisa R. Tsiolis
Thomas W. Bade	Michael L. Kaplan
Ashley D. Adams	Bradley J. Johnston
Carla A. Wortley	Lisa M. Ashbrook
Carl O. Wortley, III	Becky L. Brooks
Dawn Grove	David J. Wood
Timothy P. Stallcup	Brian P. Dolasinski
Mark D. Dillon	Christopher A. Coury
Frank W. Moskowitz	Kerry M. Griggs
Steven J. German	Jill E.C. Freret
Darren L. Brooks	David M. Klein

(See Next Column)

Robert S. Miller	Mary G. Pryor
Monica D. T. Nguyenduc	James Nelson Smith, Jr.

OF COUNSEL

Shoshana B. Tancer	Sara R. Ziskin

Representative Clients: Three-Five Systems; Main Street and Main Incorporated; ITT Cannon; Bank of America; The Dial Corp.; The Hartford; Dow Corning Corp.; Charles Schwab & Co., Inc.

For full biographical listings, see the Martindale-Hubbell Law Directory

QUARLES & BRADY (AV)

One Camelback Building, One East Camelback Road, Suite 400, 85012-1649
Telephone: 602-230-5500
Fax: 602-230-5598
Milwaukee, Wisconsin Office: 411 East Wisconsin Avenue.
Telephone: 414-277-5000.
Fax: 414-271-3552.
Madison, Wisconsin Office: First Wisconsin Plaza, One South Pinckney Street, P.O. Box 2113.
Telephone: 608-251-5000.
Fax: 608-251-9166.
West Palm Beach, Florida Office: 222 Lakeview Ave., 4th Floor.
Telephone: 407-653-5000.
Fax: 407-653-5333.
Naples, Florida Office: Barnett Center, 4501 Tamiami Trail North, Suite 300.
Telephone: 813-262-5959.
Fax: 813-434-4999.

MEMBERS OF THE FIRM

P. Robert Fannin	Jon E. Pettibone
Charles W. Herf	Roger K. Spencer
P. Robert Moya	Peter A. Terry
William M. Shattuck	Glenn Spencer Bacal
James D. Vieregg	David G. Beauchamp
Robert C. Houser, Jr.	Daniel L. Muchow
Robert T. Bailes	Paul M. Gales
Judith M. Bailey	Steven P. Emerick
	Gerald L. Shelley

ASSOCIATES

Michael G. Galloway	Jennifer N. MacLennan
Robert S. Bornhoft	Sean D. Garrison
Benjamin R. Norris	David T. Barton
Colleen A. Scherkenbach	Mark N. Rogers
Jose L. Martinez	Amy O'Melia-Endres
Tracy D. Taylor	Russell Mancuso
Wendy L. Gerlach	Mark K. Briggs
William D. O'Neal	Jeffrey A. Sandquist
Mary Beth Miller	Ronald M. Goldberg
	Jennifer B. Wuamett

GOVERNMENT RELATIONS ADVISOR

G. Michael Williams

BUSINESS MANAGEMENT SUPPORT PERSONNEL

Linda J. Hornbeck

LEGAL ASSISTANTS

Lydia G.K. Butler	Elizabeth Hibbs
Patricia M. Fairfield	Teri L. Glaser
Linda A. McDermott	Jamie Tuccio
Dianne L. Lash	Kristi A. Lyons

For full biographical listings, see the Martindale-Hubbell Law Directory

ROBBINS & GREEN, A PROFESSIONAL ASSOCIATION (AV)

1800 Norwest Tower, 3300 North Central Avenue, 85012-9826
Telephone: 602-248-7600
Fax: 602-266-5369

Philip A. Robbins	Janet B. Hutchison
Richard W. Abbuhl	Ronald G. Wilson
Wayne A. Smith	Bradley J. Stevens
Edmund F. Richardson	Dwayne Ross
William H. Sandweg III	Alfred W. Ricciardi
Jack N. Rudel	Sarah McGiffert
Jeffrey P. Boshes	Peter W. Sorensen
Brian Imbornoni	Daniel L. Brown
	Robert D. Peak

For full biographical listings, see the Martindale-Hubbell Law Directory

SACKS TIERNEY P.A. (AV)

2929 North Central Avenue, Fourteenth Floor, 85012-2742
Telephone: 602-279-4900
Fax: 602-279-2027

(See Next Column)

SACKS TIERNEY P.A.—*Continued*

Seymour Sacks	Marcia J. Busching
Marvin S. Cohen	Scot C. Stirling
David C. Tierney	Randall S. Yavitz
Stephen Aron Benson	Sharon Brook Shively
Michael R. Rooney	James W. Armstrong
Robert G. Kimball	Steven M. Goldstein

Judith M. Dworkin

Sharon S. Moyer	Candess J. Hunter
Samuel J. Cohen	Brian de Vallance
Sandra E. Price	Margaret E. Koppen

Reference: M&I Thunderbird Bank.

For full biographical listings, see the Martindale-Hubbell Law Directory

SNELL & WILMER, L.L.P. (AV)

One Arizona Center, 85004-0001
Telephone: 602-382-6000
Fax: 602-382-6070
Tucson, Arizona Office: 1500 Norwest Tower, One South Church Avenue 85701-1612.
Telephone: 520-882-1200.
Fax: 520-884-1294.
Orange County Office: 1920 Main Street, Suite 1200, P.O. Box 57062, Irvine, California, 92619-7062.
Telephone: 714-253-2700.
Fax: 714-955-2507.
Salt Lake City, Utah Office: Broadway Centre, 111 East Broadway, Suite 900, 84111-1004.
Telephone: 801-237-1900.
Fax: 801-237-1950.

MEMBERS OF FIRM

John J. Bouma	Richard K. Mallery
Robert C. Bates	Jon S. Cohen
Warren E. Platt	Jay D. Wiley
William A. Hicks, III	George H. Lyons
Peter J. Rathwell	Daniel J. McAuliffe
Steven M. Wheeler	Donald D. Colburn
Douglas W. Seitz	Robert J. Deeny
Joseph T. Melczer, III	William R. Hayden
Gerard Morales	Robert B. Hoffman
Barry D. Halpern	Joel P. Hoxie
James R. Condo	Lonnie J. Williams, Jr.
Richard W. Sheffield	Vaughn A. Crawford
Arthur P. Greenfield	David A. Sprentall
Thomas R. Hoecker	Suzanne McCann
Charles A. Pulaski, Jr.	Terry Morris Roman
Matthew P. Feeney	Donald L. Gaffney
Arthur T. Anderson	Patrick E. Hoog
Joyce Kline Wright	Quinn Williams
Rebecca A. Winterscheidt	Richard W. Shapiro
Craig K. Williams	Jody Kathleen Pokorski
Timothy G. O'Neill	Heidi L. McNeil
G. Van Velsor Wolf, Jr.	Alex B. Marconi
Martha E. Gibbs	Katherine M. Harmeyer
James J. Sienicki	E. Jeffrey Walsh
George J. Coleman, III	Janet E. Barton
Kevin J. Parker	Donald H. Smith
Peter M. Wittekind	Timothy W. Moser
Charles E. James, Jr.	Steven S. Guy
Christopher H. Bayley	David E. Weiss, Jr.
Nicholas J. Wood	Robert R. Kinas
Samuel C. Cowley	Richard D. Blau
Sherman O. Parrett	Steven D. Pidgeon
Michael K. Kelly	Charles P. Keller
Thea Foglietta Silverstein	Patrick X. Fowler
Barbara J. Dawson	Brian J. Foster
Bob J. McCullough	Patrick G. Byrne
Prithviraj S. Sivananthan	Marvin S. Swift, Jr.
Charles F. Hauff, Jr.	Patricia Lee Refo

OF COUNSEL

Edward Jacobson	Jarril F. Kaplan
John A. Greene	Jose P. Ceppi

SENIOR ATTORNEYS

Bruce P. White	Lisa M. Coulter
Cheryl A. Ikegami	William P. Allen

Thomas L. Mumaw

ASSOCIATES

Benjamin D. Aguilera	Sondri Allison
Jennifer Bell Anderson	Andrew S. Ashworth
John K. Ausdemore	Mark D. Becker
Jeffery L. Brown	Terri N.A. Buccino
Lon A. Burke	Brian J. Campbell
Nancy Kay Campbell	Nancy J. Caplette
Timothy J. Casey	Sarah Chilton
J. Michael Christopher	Sharon K. Coleman
Jeffrey Webb Crockett	Roger D. Curley
Stephanie R. Derby	Michael M. Donahey
Elisabeth B. Donnovin	Stacy Gabriel

(See Next Column)

ASSOCIATES (Continued)

Greg R. Hall	Brian Hegardt
Robert Henry	Chad W. Hilyard
Moon Yung Kim	Robert M. Kort
Joseph C. Kreamer	Paul A. Krulisky
Joseph E. Lambert	Kevin T. LeMond
David Lewis	Christopher J. Littlefield
Christine Broghammer Long	Deborah Jill Lotstein
Craig Marquiz	Mishka L. Marshall
Andrew G. Miller	Kevin T. Miller
Daniel J. Noblitt	Maria Nutile
Eugene F. O'Connor II	Patrick J. Paul
Daren W. Perkins	Stephanie Quincy
David E. Rauch	David S. Reid
Heidi J. Richter	Carlos D. Ronstadt
GinaMarie Rossano	Philip Randolph Rudd
Lisa A. Schuh	Darrell C. Sherman
Scott D. Sherman	Howard Sobelman
Barrie E. Stachel	Victoria M. Stevens
Mark M. Takahashi	Gregg J. Tucek
Catherine Wehling	(Not admitted in AZ)

Donald Zavala

Representative Clients: Arizona Public Service Co.; Bank One, Arizona, NA.; First Security Bank of Utah, N.A.; Ford Motor Co.; Chrysler Motors Corp.; Toyota Motor Sales U.S.A.; BHP Copper, Inc.; U.S. Home Corp.; Pinnacle West Capital Corp.; Safeway, Inc.

For full biographical listings, see the Martindale-Hubbell Law Directory

SQUIRE, SANDERS & DEMPSEY (AV)

Two Renaissance Square, 40 North Central Avenue, Suite 2700, 85004-4441
Telephone: 602-528-4000
Fax: 602-253-8129
Cleveland, Ohio Office: 4900 Key Tower, 127 Public Square, Cleveland, Ohio 44114-1304.
Telephone: 216-479-8500. *Fax's:* 216-479-8780, 216-479-8781, 216-479-8787, 216-479-8795, 216-479-8793, 216-479-8776, 216-479-8788.
Columbus, Ohio Offices: 1300 Huntington Center, 41 South High Street, Columbus, Ohio 43215.
Telephone: 614-365-2700.
Fax: 614-365-2499.
Jacksonville, Florida Office: One Enterprise Center, Suite 2100, 225 Water Street, Jacksonville, Florida 32202.
Telephone: 904-353-1264.
Fax: 904-356-2986.
Miami, Florida Office: 201 South Biscayne Boulevard, Suite 2900 Miami Center, Miami, Florida 33131.
Telephone: 305-577-8700.
Fax: 305-358-1425.
New York, New York Office: 520 Madison Avenue, 32nd Floor, New York, New York 10022.
Telephone: 212-872-9800.
Fax: 212-872-9815.
Washington, D.C. Office: 1201 Pennsylvania Avenue, N.W., P.O. Box 407, Washington, D.C. 20044.
Telephone: 202-626-6600.
Fax: 202-626-6780.
London, England Office: 4th Floor, Royex House, Aldermanbury Square, London EC2V 7HR.
Telephone: 011-44-171-830-0055.
Fax: 011-44-171-830-0056.
Brussels, Belgium Office: Avenue Louise, 165-Box 15, 1050 Brussels, Belgium.
Telephone: 011-32-2-648-1717.
Fax: 011-32-2-648-1064.
Prague Czech Republic Office: Vaclavska Namesti 57, 11000 PRAHA 1, Czech Republic.
Telephone: 011-42-2-216-62111.
Fax: 011-42-2-216-62222.
Bratislava Slovakia Office: Mudronova 37, 811 01 Bratislava, Slovak Republic.
Telephone: 011-42-7-580-2210.
Fax: 011-42-7-580-2212.
Budapest, Hungary Office: Deak Ferenc Ut. 10, Office 304, H-1052 Budapest V., Hungary.
Telephone: 011-36-1-226-2024.
Fax: 011-361-226-2025.
Kiev, Ukraine Office: vul. Prorizna 9, KV 20, Kiev 252030, Ukraine.
Telephone: 011-380-44-244-3452.
Fax: 011-380-44-228-4938.
Moscow, Russian Federation Office: 28 Pokrovka Street, No. 4-4A, Moscow 103062, Russian Federation.
Telephone: 7-503-956-3750.
Fax: 7-503-956-3635.

(See Next Column)

SQUIRE, SANDERS & DEMPSEY, *Phoenix—Continued*

RESIDENT MEMBERS

James L. Adler, Jr.	Mark A. Nadeau
Craig D. Hansen	William L. Nelson
Christopher D. Johnson	Robert H. Olson, Jr.
Karen T. Kahler	Richard F. Ross
David W. Kreutzberg	Thomas J. Salerno
Michael A. Lechter	Norman C. Storey
Robert L. Matia	Christopher D. Thomas
	Donald A. Wall

RESIDENT ASSOCIATES

Rawle Andrews, Jr.	John G. Loughrey
(Not admitted in AZ)	Hugh H. Marthinsen
Christine A. Aguilera	Timothy C. Nash
Carl M. Bennett	(Not admitted in AZ)
Curtis L. Bowe, III	Steven D. Nemecek
(Not admitted in AZ)	Bradley S. Paulson
Steven J. Brown	Karen L. Peters
Sheila M. Castilla	Cynthia A. Ricketts
Joseph M. Crabb	Renée E. Tetreault
Timothy B. Evans	Kathleen T. Tobin
John J. Fetters	Ann Thompson Uglietta
Julie A. Inderlied	Stephen B. White

OF COUNSEL

Liana C. Cocanower	Hugh A. Madden
	James H. Phillips

For full biographical listings, see the Martindale-Hubbell Law Directory

STEPTOE & JOHNSON LLP (AV)

Two Renaissance Square, 40 N. Central, Suite 2400, 85004
Telephone: 602-257-5200
Telecopier: 602-257-5299
Washington, D.C. Office: 1330 Connecticut Avenue, N.W.
Telephone: 202-429-3000.
Cable Address: "Stepjohn".
Telex: 89-2503.
Telecopier: 202-429-9204.
Moscow, Russia Office: Steptoe & Johnson International Affiliate in Moscow. 25 Tsvetnoy Boulevard, Building 3 Moscow Russia.
Telephone: 011-7-501-258-5250.
Fax: 011-7-501-258-5251.
Almaty, Kazakhstan Office: Steptoe & Johnson Company Almaty, 84 Gogol Street, Suite 213, 480083.
Telephones: (3272) 50-11-25, (3272) 32-25-39.

PARTNERS

Lawrence A. Katz	Barry J. Dale
James G. Derouin	David J. Bodney
Bruce E. Meyerson	Floyd P. Bienstock
Francis J. Burke, Jr.	David A. Selden

ASSOCIATES

Bennett Evan Cooper	R. Michael Dunnigan
Monica L. Goebel	Mark G. Kisicki
Kevin M. Judiscak	Julie A. Pace
Kimberly A. Fatica	Emily R. Froimson
Lisa L. Glow	Andrew J. Sweet
Peter B. Swann	Tracy Lorenz Wareing
Lisa Morganstern Bickel	Michael B. Gerdes
Kathryn E. Underwood	Steven D. Wheeless
	Elizabeth A. Schallop Call

For full biographical listings, see the Martindale-Hubbell Law Directory

LAW OFFICES OF DAVID WM. WEST, P.C. (AV)

1300 E. Missouri Avenue, Suite B-200, 85014
Telephone: 602-263-7891
Fax: 602-263-5031

David Wm. West

For full biographical listings, see the Martindale-Hubbell Law Directory

---

PRESCOTT, * Yavapai Co.

FAVOUR, MOORE & WILHELMSEN, A PROFESSIONAL ASSOCIATION (AV)

1580 Plaza West Drive, P.O. Box 1391, 86302
Telephone: 520-445-2444
Fax: 520-771-0450

John M. Favour	Mark M. Moore
	David K. Wilhelmsen

Representative Client: Yavapai Title Co.
Reference: Bank of America.

For full biographical listings, see the Martindale-Hubbell Law Directory

MURPHY, LUTEY, SCHMITT & BECK (AV)

Elks Building, 117 East Gurley Street, 86301
Telephone: 520-445-6860
Fax: 520-445-6488
Yuma, Arizona Office: Valley Professional Plaza, 1763 West Twenty-Fourth Street, Suite 200.
Telephone: 520-726-0314.
Fax: 520-341-1079.
Kingman, Arizona Office: 2601 Stockton Hill Road, Suite H8.
Telephone: 520-718-0888; 1-800-281-0822.

MEMBERS OF FIRM

Thelton D. Beck	Selmer D. Lutey
Michael R. Murphy	Robert E. Schmitt

ASSOCIATES

Dan A. Wilson	Bruce E. Rosenberg

OF COUNSEL

Keith F. Quail

Counsel for: State Farm Mutual Automobile Insurance Co.; Allstate Insurance Co.; Farmers Insurance; Western Agricultural Insurance Co.
Local Counsel for: Bank One Arizona, NA; The Stockmen's Bank.
Representative Clients: Prescott College; Galpin Ford, Inc.; Sedona-Oak Creek Airport Authority; Yavapai County Fair Association (Prescott Downs).

For full biographical listings, see the Martindale-Hubbell Law Directory

---

ST. JOHNS, * Apache Co. — (Refer to Flagstaff)

SCOTTSDALE, Maricopa Co.

FENNEMORE CRAIG, A PROFESSIONAL CORPORATION (AV)

6263 North Scottsdale Road, Suite 290, 85250
Telephone: 602-257-5400
Fax: 602-945-4932
TWX: 910-950-4608
Phoenix, Arizona Office: Two North Central Avenue, Suite 2200, 85004.
Telephone: 602-257-8700.
Fax: 602-257-8527.
Tucson, Arizona Office: One South Church Avenue, Suite 1030, 85701.
Telephone: 520-791-6800.
Fax: 520-791-6820.

Philip A. Edlund	George T. Cole
Alan S. Hall	Susan Marie Ciupak

For full biographical listings, see the Martindale-Hubbell Law Directory

---

SEDONA, Coconino & Yavapai Cos.

ASPEY, WATKINS & DIESEL, P.L.L.C. (AV)

120 Soldier Pass Road, 86336
Telephone: 520-282-5955
Facsimile: 520-282-5962
Flagstaff, Arizona Office: 123 North San Francisco, 3rd Floor.
Telephone: 520-774-1478.
Facsimile: 520-774-8404.
Page, Arizona Office: 904 North Navajo.
Telephone: 520-645-9694.
Cottonwood, Arizona Office: 2400 E. Highway 89A, Suite C.
Telephone: 520-639-1881.
Facsimile: 520-639-0272.

MEMBERS OF FIRM

Harold L. Watkins	Kaign N. Christy
James E. Ledbetter	Stephen A. Thompson

LEGAL SUPPORT PERSONNEL

Rocky C. Nissen (Paralegal Assistant)

Representative Clients: Sedona-Verde Valley Board of Realtors, Inc.; Sedona Physician Center; Sedona Center Development Group; Foothills North Homeowners Association; Shadows Estates Homeowners Assn., Inc.
References: Security Pacific Bank- Arizona; First Interstate Bank.

For full biographical listings, see the Martindale-Hubbell Law Directory

---

SIERRA VISTA, Cochise Co.

RILEY, CARDINAL & FLORES, P.C. (AV)

Suite M-12 Haymore Plaza, 500 E. Fry Boulevard, 85635
Telephone: 520-458-0130
FAX: 520-459-5181

Richard J. Riley	Laura A. Cardinal
	Adela Maria Flores

Deron B. Knoner

LEGAL SUPPORT PERSONNEL

Yvonne Morris (Senior Paralegal)

For full biographical listings, see the Martindale-Hubbell Law Directory

TUCSON, * Pima Co.

BROWN & BAIN, A PROFESSIONAL ASSOCIATION (AV)

One South Church Avenue, Nineteenth Floor, P.O. Box 2265, 85702-2265
Telephone: 520-798-7900
Telecopier: 520-798-7945
Phoenix, Arizona Affiliated Office: Brown & Bain, A Professional
Association, 2901 North Central Avenue, P.O. Box 400.
Telephone: 602-351-8000.
Telecopier: 602-351-8516.
Palo Alto, California Affiliated Office: Brown & Bain, 1755 Embarcadero
Road, Suite 200.
Telephone: 415-856-9411.
Telecopier: 415-856-6061.

RESIDENT PERSONNEL

Philip R. Higdon	Diane L. Madenci
Roy W. Kyle	Michael F. McNulty
Sarah R. Simmons	

Elizabeth P. Chase	Douglas D. Metcalf
	(Not admitted in AZ)

COUNSEL
James F. McNulty, Jr.

For full biographical listings, see the Martindale-Hubbell Law Directory

CHANDLER, TULLAR, UDALL & REDHAIR (AV)

1700 Bank of America Plaza, 33 North Stone Avenue, 85701
Telephone: 520-623-4353
Telefax: 520-792-3426

MEMBERS OF FIRM

Thomas Chandler	Dwight M. Whitley, Jr.
D. B. Udall	E. Hardy Smith
Jack Redhair	John J. Brady
Joe F. Tarver, Jr.	Christopher J. Smith
Steven Weatherspoon	Charles V. Harrington
Edwin M. Gaines, Jr.	Bruce G. MacDonald
Christopher C. Browning	

ASSOCIATES

Joel T. Ireland	Kurt Kroese
Mark Fredenberg	Sean C. Chapman
Mariann T. Shinoskie	Anne M. Fulton

Representative Clients: Arizona Electric Power Cooperative, Inc.; Atlantic
Richfield Co.; CNA Insurance; Farmers Insurance Exchange; MICA; Chubb
Insurance Group; Aetna Casualty; State Farm Mutual Insurance Companies;
Santa Cruz Valley Water Authority.
Reference: Arizona Bank.

For full biographical listings, see the Martindale-Hubbell Law Directory

DUFFIELD, MILLER, YOUNG, ADAMSON & ALFRED, P.C. (AV)

Suite 711, Transamerica Building, 177 North Church Avenue, 85701
Telephone: 520-792-1181
FAX: 520-792-2859
Green Valley, Arizona Office: 101-65 South La Canada, Green Valley
Mall.
Telephone: 520-625-4404.
Fax: 520-625-4453.
La Paloma Office: La Paloma Corporate Center, 3573 East Sunrise Drive,
Suite 115, Tucson, Arizona.
Telephone: 520-577-1135.
Fax: 520-577-1079.

Philip Hawley Smith	Thomas R. Althaus
Arthur H. Miller (1935-1995)	Richard Duffield
Larry R. Adamson	Eugene C. Gieseler
Samuel D. Alfred	K. Alexander Hobson
Michael C. Young	

LEGAL SUPPORT PERSONNEL

Cynthia Sargent Althaus	Joan Shelton, CLA
Mary Jane Arnesen	Christine M. Smith
Katrina Hillman	Barbara L. Steimle
Elizabeth Kohl-Sturgeon	Elaine Webb

Representative Clients: San Xavier Rock & Materials; Community Water
Company of Green Valley.
Insurance Company Clientele: State Farm Mutual Insurance Cos.; Automobile Club Insurance Co.; Colonial Penn Insurance Co.; Metropolitan Property & Liability Insurance Co.; National Indemnity Ins. Co.

For full biographical listings, see the Martindale-Hubbell Law Directory

FENNEMORE CRAIG, A PROFESSIONAL CORPORATION (AV)

Suite 1030, One South Church Avenue, 85701-1620
Telephone: 520-791-6800
Fax: 520-791-6820
Phoenix, Arizona Office: Two North Central Avenue, Suite 2200, 85004.
Telephone: 602-257-8700.
Fax: 602-257-8527.

(See Next Column)

Scottsdale, Arizona Office: 6263 North Scottsdale Road, Suite 290, 85250.
Telephone: 602-257-5400.
Fax: 602-257-5409.

Ronald J. Stolkin	Andrew M. Federhar
Christopher P. Staring	

Jeffrey S. Silvyn

For full biographical listings, see the Martindale-Hubbell Law Directory

GABROY, ROLLMAN & BOSSÉ, P.C. (AV)

Suite 201, 2195 East River Road, 85718
Telephone: 520-577-1300
Telefax: 520-577-0717

Steven L. Bossé	Ronald M. Lehman
Richard M. Rollman	Fred A. Farsjo
John Gabroy	Lyle D. Aldridge
Ronna L. Fickbohm	

Richard A. Brown

For full biographical listings, see the Martindale-Hubbell Law Directory

PETER T. GIANAS, P.C. (AV)

4400 East Broadway, Suite 800, 85711
Telephone: 520-795-6630
Fax: 520-327-1922

Peter T. Gianas

For full biographical listings, see the Martindale-Hubbell Law Directory

GOERING, ROBERTS, BERKMAN, RUBIN & BROGNA, P.C. (AV)

Suite 302, 1840 East River Road, 85718
Telephone: 520-577-9300
Fax: 520-577-0848

Scott Goering	David L. Berkman
Howard T. Roberts, Jr.	William L. Rubin
Carmine A. Brogna	

Christopher L. Enos

Representative Clients: Fireman's Fund Insurance; Safeco Insurance; Royal
Insurance; Sentry Insurance; American International Group; Farmers Insur-
ance; USAA; Country Companies; Cigna.
Reference: Bank One.

For full biographical listings, see the Martindale-Hubbell Law Directory

HAZLETT & WILKES (AV)

310 South Williams Boulevard, Suite 305, 85711
Telephone: 520-790-9663
Fax: 520-790-9616

MEMBERS OF FIRM

Carl E. Hazlett	James M. Wilkes

ASSOCIATES
Thomas M. Bayham

For full biographical listings, see the Martindale-Hubbell Law Directory

KIMBLE, GOTHREAU & NELSON, P.C. (AV)

5285 East Williams Circle, Suite 3500, 85711-7411
Telephone: 520-748-2440
Fax: 520-748-2469

Michael J. Gothreau (1943-1990)	David F. Toone
Darwin J. Nelson	Michelle T. Lopez
Daryl A. Audilett	Negatu Molla
Lawrence McDonough	Michael E. Medina
Andrew J. Petersen	

OF COUNSEL
William Kimble

Representative Clients: State of Arizona; General Motors Corp.; Procter &
Gamble Co.; St. Paul Fire and Marine Insurance Co.; City of Tucson; Tucson
Electric Power Co.; United States Fidelity & Guaranty Co.; Coriegis Co.;
Allstate Insurance Co.

For full biographical listings, see the Martindale-Hubbell Law Directory

LESHER & LESHER, A PROFESSIONAL CORPORATION (AV)

3773 East Broadway, 85716
Telephone: 520-795-4800
Telefax: 520-325-7609

Stephen H. Lesher	Robert O. Lesher

Representative Clients: Associated Aviation Underwriters; Empire Fire and
Marine Insurance Co.; Merck and Co., Inc.; Underwriters at Lloyd's, London.

(See Next Column)

LESHER & LESHER A PROFESSIONAL CORPORATION, *Tucson—Continued*

For full biographical listings, see the Martindale-Hubbell Law Directory

MILLER, PITT & MCANALLY, P.C. (AV)

111 South Church Avenue, 85701-1680
Telephone: 520-792-3836
Telecopier: 520-624-5080
Nogales, Arizona Office: 272 West View Point, 85621.
Telephone: 520-281-1361.
Correspondent Office: Lizarraga, Robles, Savinon & Tapia, S.C. Boulevard Hidalgo 64, Colonia Centenario. CP 83000 Hermosillo, Sonora, Mexico.
Telephone: (62) 17-27-28, 12-79-89, 13-47-10, 12-79-18, 13-33-25, 12-77-70.

Barry N. Akin (1939-1988)	Philip J. Hall
G. Eugene Isaak	Grace McIlvain
Gerald Maltz	Thomas G. Cotter
Janice A. Wezelman	Lindsay E. Brew
T. Patrick Griffin	Armando Rivera
Gus Aragón, Jr.	

Carole A. Summers	Bradley P. Miller

OF COUNSEL
Richard L. McAnally
RETIRED

Robert F. Miller	Donald Pitt

Representative Clients: Bell Atlantic Metro Mobile; Evergreen International Aviation; Farmers Investment Co.; Forest City Enterprises; Vince Granatelli Racing; KVOA Channel 4 TV; Newmont Mining Corp.; S.L. Industries, Inc.; Tucson Unified School District; University of Arizona Foundation.

For full biographical listings, see the Martindale-Hubbell Law Directory

O'CONNOR CAVANAGH MOLLOY JONES, A PROFESSIONAL ASSOCIATION (AV)

Suite 2100 33 N. Stone, P.O. Box 2268, 85702
Telephone: 520-622-3531
FAX: 520-624-2816
Email: firminfo@arizlaw.com
Phoenix, Arizona Office: O'Connor, Cavanagh, Anderson, Killingsworth & Beshears, One East Camelback Road, Suite 1100, 85012.
Telephone: 602-263-2400.
FAX: 602-263-2900.
Sun City, Arizona Office: O'Connor, Cavanagh, Anderson, Killingsworth & Beshears, 13250 North Del Webb Boulevard, Suite B, 85351.
Telephone: 602-263-2808.
FAX: 602-933-3100.
Nogales, Arizona Office: O'Connor, Cavanagh, Anderson, Killingsworth & Beshears, 1891 North Mastick Way, 85621.
Telephone: 520-761-4215.
FAX: 520-761-3505.

Scott D. Gibson	Richard T. Coolidge
Peter Akmajian	David K. Gray
Drue A. Morgan-Birch	George O. Krauja
Russell E. Jones	William W. Pearson
Benjamin W. Bauer	

Chris B. Nakamura

Thomas E. Laursen	Jennifer M. Dubay
Paul A. Relich	Amy M. Samberg
Nathan B. Hannah	Dale F. Regelman
Michael W. Baldwin	James D. Campbell

OF COUNSEL

John F. Molloy (Retired)	John L. Donahue Jr.

Representative Clients: Three-Five Systems; Main Street & Main; ITT Cannon; Bank of America; The Dial Corp; The Hartford; Dow Corning Corp.; Charles Schwab & Co., Inc.

For full biographical listings, see the Martindale-Hubbell Law Directory

RAVEN, KIRSCHNER & NORELL, P.C. (AV)

Suite 1600, One South Church Avenue, 85701-1612
Telephone: 520-628-8700
Telefax: 520-798-5200

Donald T. Awerkamp	Andrew Oldland Norell
Dennis J. Clancy	Lane D. Oden
L. Anthony Fines	Mark B. Raven
Susan M. Freund	S. Leonard Scheff
Ronald N. Hatcher, Jr.	Theodore Harper Sinclair
Barry Kirschner	Stephen A. Thomas

LEGAL SUPPORT PERSONNEL
Elizabeth G. O'Hara (Administrator)

Representative Clients: Continental Medical Systems, Inc.; El Paso Natural Gas Co.; Norwest Bank Arizona; El Rio-Santa Cruz Neighborhood Health Center, Inc.; Resolution Trust Corp.; Sierra Vista Community Hospital;

(See Next Column)

Southern Arizona Rehabilitation Hospital; Northern Cochise Community Hospital.

For full biographical listings, see the Martindale-Hubbell Law Directory

STOMPOLY, STROUD, GIDDINGS & GLICKSMAN, P.C. (AV)

1820 Citibank Tower, One South Church Avenue, 85702
Telephone: 520-628-8300
Telefax: 520-628-9948
Mailing Address: P.O. Box 190, Tucson, AZ, 85702-0190

John G. Stompoly	Charles E. Giddings
James L. Stroud	Elliot A. Glicksman
George Erickson	

For full biographical listings, see the Martindale-Hubbell Law Directory

TAYLOR & CAWTHORNE, LTD. (AV)

7400 North Oracle Road Suite 243, 85704
Telephone: 520-742-2500
Fax: 520-742-6953
Other Tucson Office: Mountain View Plaza, 1171 Rancho Vistoso Boulevard, Suite 117, 85737.
Telephone: 520-825-0981.

Roger W. Taylor	Hugh Cawthorne
	Jackson G. Gallup

Donald A. Doran	D. Stephen Wallin
Peter A. Nielsen	Jixiang (Jennifer) Huang
Helena R. Bish	

For full biographical listings, see the Martindale-Hubbell Law Directory

ARKANSAS

*ARKADELPHIA,** Clark Co.

WRIGHT, CHANEY, BERRY & DANIEL, P.A. (AV)

303 Professional Park Drive, P.O. Drawer 947, 71923
Telephone: 501-246-6796
Telefax: 501-246-2178
Email: chaneyd@iocc.com

William G. Wright	LeAnne Daniel
Donald P. Chaney, Jr.	Eric G. Hughes
Travis R. Berry	Edward M. Slaughter
Rodney Moore	

Counsel for: Elk Horn Bank and Trust Co.; Farm Bureau Mutual Insurance Company of Arkansas, Inc.; Southern Farm Bureau Casualty Insurance Co.; Underwriters Adjustment Co.; Nationwide Insurance Co.; Central Production Credit Assn.; Shelter Insurance Co.; Colonial Insurance Co.
Approved Attorneys for: Farmers Home Administration; American Title Insurance Co.

For full biographical listings, see the Martindale-Hubbell Law Directory

*ASHDOWN,** Little River Co.

BISHOP & BISHOP (AV)

171 West Main Street, P.O. Box 609, 71822
Telephone: 501-898-5058
Fax: 501-898-8110

MEMBERS OF FIRM

Eric W. Bishop	Eric T. Bishop

Representative Clients: Bank of Ashdown; First National Bank of De Queen; Citizens National Bank of Nashville; Little River County Rural Development Authority; Ashdown Clinic, Ltd.; E-Z Mart Stores, Inc.; Little River Memorial Hospital.
Approved Agents for: Lawyers Title Insurance Corp.

For full biographical listings, see the Martindale-Hubbell Law Directory

*ASH FLAT,** Sharp Co. — (Refer to Batesville)

*AUGUSTA,** Woodruff Co. — (Refer to Newport)

*BATESVILLE,** Independence Co.

BLAIR & STROUD (AV)

Suite 201, 500 East Main, P.O. Box 2135, 72501
Telephone: 501-793-8350
FAX: 501-793-3989

MEMBERS OF FIRM

H. David Blair	Robert D. Stroud
J. Scott Davidson	

Counsel for: Boatmen's National Bank, Batesville, Ark.; Boatmen's National Bank, Newark, Arkansas; First National Bank of Izard County, Arkansas.

(See Next Column)

BLAIR & STROUD—*Continued*

For full biographical listings, see the Martindale-Hubbell Law Directory

---

GREGG, HART & FARRIS (AV)

262 Boswell Street, P.O. Box 2496, 72501
Telephone: 501-793-7556
Fax: 501-793-6921

MEMBERS OF FIRM

John C. Gregg   Josephine Linker Hart
Phillip B. Farris

For full biographical listings, see the Martindale-Hubbell Law Directory

---

WALMSLEY LAW FIRM (AV)

398 Barnett, P.O. Box 2535, 72503
Telephone: 501-793-6818
Fax: 501-793-6977

Bill H. Walmsley
ASSOCIATES
Timothy M. Weaver

For full biographical listings, see the Martindale-Hubbell Law Directory

---

BENTON, Saline Co.

ELLIS LAW FIRM (AV)

126 North Main Street, P.O. Box 1259, 72015
Telephone: 501-776-3916; Little Rock: 375-5210
Fax: 501-776-2278
Email: ellislaw@aol.com
Email: 76403.507@compuserve.com

MEMBER OF FIRM
George D. Ellis
LEGAL SUPPORT PERSONNEL
Rhonda Beck Malone (Paralegal)

References: The Union Bank of Benton; Benton State Bank.

For full biographical listings, see the Martindale-Hubbell Law Directory

---

BERRYVILLE, Carroll Co. — (Refer to Springdale)

BLYTHEVILLE, Mississippi Co.

OSCAR FENDLER (AV)

104 North Sixth Street, P.O. Box 548, 72316-0548
Telephone: 501-763-6891
Facsimile: 501-763-6892

Representative Clients: Farmers Bank & Trust Co., Blytheville; Drainage District No. 16, Miss. Co., Ark.; Lee Wilson & Co.; S.J. Cohen Co.; Ashmore Bros. & Brown, Inc.; Skyline Steel Corp.; Arkansas Steel Processing, Inc.; Merchants & Planters Bank, Manila; Manila Depot, Inc.

BOONEVILLE, Logan Co. — (Refer to Fort Smith)

BRINKLEY, Monroe Co. — (Refer to Clarendon)

CAMDEN, Ouachita Co.

BRAMBLETT & PRATT (AV)

146 Washington Street., N.W., P.O. Box 938, 71701
Telephone: 501-836-7328
Fax: 501-836-4442

MEMBERS OF FIRM
Eugene D. Bramblett   James M. Pratt, Jr.

Representative Clients: Hartford Accident and Indemnity Co.; Liberty Mutual Insurance Co.; International Paper Co.; Stephens Security Bank.

For full biographical listings, see the Martindale-Hubbell Law Directory

---

ALLEN P. ROBERTS, P.A. (AV)

119 Van Buren Street, NW, P.O. Box 280, 71701
Telephone: 501-836-5310
FAX: 501-836-9662

Allen P. Roberts

Representative Clients: International Paper Co.; Camden Fairview School District; The City of Camden; Byars Oil Co.; American Fuel Cell & Coated Fabrics Co.; Star City School District; Highland Resources, Inc.; Circle B Logging Co.; First National Bank, Magnolia, Arkansas.

For full biographical listings, see the Martindale-Hubbell Law Directory

---

CHARLESTON, Franklin Co. — (Refer to Fort Smith)

CLARKSVILLE, Johnson Co. — (Refer to Fort Smith)

CLINTON, Van Buren Co. — (Refer to Conway)

CORNING, Clay Co. — (Refer to Pocahontas)

DANVILLE, Yell Co. — (Refer to Russellville)

DE QUEEN, Sevier Co. — (Refer to Ashdown)

DE WITT, Arkansas Co. — (Refer to Pine Bluff)

EL DORADO, Union Co.

COMPTON, PREWETT, THOMAS & HICKEY, P.A. (AV)

423 North Washington Avenue, P.O. Box 1917, 71731-1917
Telephone: 501-862-3478
Fax: 501-862-7228

Walter L. Brown (1893-1972)   Floyd M. Thomas, Jr.
Robert C. Compton   Joseph Hickey
William I. Prewett   Cathleen V. Compton
Roger W. Landes

LEGAL SUPPORT PERSONNEL
Jerri L. Agerton (Paralegal)

General Counsel for: National Bank of Commerce of El Dorado.
Local Counsel for: Shelter Insurance Co.; Farmers Insurance Group; Employers Mutual Companies; Murphy Oil Corp.; Figgie International, Inc.; Waite-Hill Services, Inc.
Representative Clients: Medical Center of South Arkansas; South Arkansas Oil Co.; El Dorado Industrial Development Corp.

For full biographical listings, see the Martindale-Hubbell Law Directory

---

CRUMPLER O'CONNOR & WYNNE (AV)

308 National Bank of Commerce Building, 71730
Telephone: 501-863-8118
FAX: 501-863-8110
Email: WJWGSW@aol.com

Claude B. Crumpler (1890-1978)   William J. Wynne
John A. O'Connor, Jr.
(1913-1988)

A list of Representative Clients will be furnished upon request.

For full biographical listings, see the Martindale-Hubbell Law Directory

---

SHACKLEFORD, PHILLIPS, WINELAND & RATCLIFF, P.A. (AV)

100 East Church Street, P.O. Box 1718, 71731-1718
Telephone: 501-862-5523
FAX: 501-862-9443

John M. Shackleford   Dennis L. Shackleford
(1896-1968)   Norwood Phillips
John M. Shackleford, Jr.   Teresa Wineland
Brian H. Ratcliff

Representative Insurance Clients: CIGNA Cos.; Commercial Union Insurance Co.; Fireman's Fund Insurance Co.; ITT Hartford Insurance Co.; Kemper Insurance Co.; Liberty Mutual Insurance Co.; Maryland-American General Insurance Co.; The St. Paul Cos.; Wausau Insurance Co.

For full biographical listings, see the Martindale-Hubbell Law Directory

---

EUREKA SPRINGS, Carroll Co. — (Refer to Springdale)

FAYETTEVILLE, Washington Co.

BALL & MOURTON, LTD., PLLC (AV)

A Professional Limited Liability Company
Suite 700, E.J. Ball Plaza, P.O. Box 1948, 72702
Telephone: 501-442-6213
Fax: 501-442-6233
Siloam Springs, Arkansas Office: 106 South Broadway. P.O. Box 1348, 72761.
Telephone: 501-524-2337.
Fax: 501-524-3693.

E. J. Ball   Neal R. Pendergraft
Kenneth R. Mourton   John T. Lee

Rayburn W. Green   Dee A. Bailey

Representative Clients: Arkansas Western Gas Co.; Coors of Western Arkansas, Inc.; Rebel Enterprises, Inc.; Southwestern Energy Co.; Stephens Production Co.; Ohlendorf Investment Co.; Norman Lures; Central Health Corporation; McIlroy Bank & Trust.

For full biographical listings, see the Martindale-Hubbell Law Directory

---

BASSETT LAW FIRM (AV)

221 North College Avenue, P.O. Box 3618, 72702-3618
Telephone: 501-521-9996
Fax: 501-521-9600

(See Next Column)

Bassett Law Firm, *Fayetteville—Continued*
MEMBERS OF FIRM

Woodson W. Bassett, Jr.	Angela M. Doss
Woodson W. Bassett, III	Gary V. Weeks
Tod C. Bassett	J. David Wall
Wm. Robert Still, Jr.	Shawn David Twing
Walker Dale Garrett	Vincent O. Chadick
Curtis L. Nebben	Michael W. Langley
Earl Buddy Chadick, Jr.	James M. Graves

Patricia A. Hines

Representative Clients: The Home Insurance Co.; Hartford Insurance Group; Tyson Foods, Inc.; CIGNA; Scottsdale Insurance Co.; St. Paul Fire and Marine Insurance Co.; AIG Aviation Ins. Co.; WAUSAU; USAA.

For full biographical listings, see the Martindale-Hubbell Law Directory

CONNER & WINTERS, P.L.L.C. (AV)

100 West Center Street, Suite 200, 72701-6081
Telephone: 501-582-5711
Facsimile: 501-587-7426
Tulsa, Oklahoma Office: Conner & Winters, A Professional Corporation, 15 East 5th Street, Suite 2400, 74103.
Telephone: 918-586-5711.
Facsimile: 918-586-8982.
Oklahoma City, Oklahoma Office: Conner & Winters, A Professional Corporation, One Leadership Square, 211 North Robinson, Suite 1700, 73102-7101.
Telephone: 405-272-5711.
Facsimile: 405-232-2695.
Washington, D.C. Office: Conner & Winters, A Professional Corporation, Suite 450 North, The Homer Building, 601 Thirteenth Street, N.W., 20005-3807.
Telephone: 202-783-3880.
Facsimile: 202-783-3899.

John R. Elrod	D. Westbrook Doss, Jr.
Greg S. Scharlau	
(Not admitted in AR)	

ASSOCIATE
Ruth Ann Wisener
OF COUNSEL
D. Randy Laney
OFFICE PERSONNEL
TULSA, OKLAHOMA

John E. Barry	Judith A. McCoy
John S. Athens	Douglas M. Rather
Henry G. Will	Gentra Abbey Sorem
Joseph J. McCain, Jr.	R. Kevin Redwine
Russell H. Harbaugh, Jr.	Deirdre O'Neil E. Dexter
Lynnwood R. Moore, Jr.	Tony W. Haynie
Robert A. Curry	Bruce W. Freeman
Steven W. McGrath	David R. Cordell
John T. Schmidt	G. W. Turner, III
D. Richard Funk	Paul E. Braden
Randolph L. Jones, Jr.	Robert J. Melgaard
P. David Newsome, Jr.	R. Mark Solano
Martin R. Wing	C. Kevin Morrison
John W. Ingraham	P. Scott Hathaway
Andrew R. Turner	John A. Bugg

Katherine Gallagher Coyle	Lawrence A. Hall
Anne B. Sublett	R. Richard Love, III
Rebecca Sellers Woodward	Steven G. Heinen
Beverly K. Smith	John M. Matheson

Christopher S. Thrutchley
OF COUNSEL

Robert L. McGowen	James R. Ryan
Charles C. Killin	David J. Hyman

Debbie L. Blackwell
OFFICE PERSONNEL
OKLAHOMA CITY, OKLAHOMA

Peter B. Bradford	John W. Funk
Raymond E. Tompkins	Kiran A. Phansalkar
Irwin H. Steinhorn	Timothy J. Bomhoff

Mitchell D. Blackburn	Patrick F. Summers

OF COUNSEL
David O. Cordell
OFFICE PERSONNEL
WASHINGTON, D.C.
G. Daniel Miller

Erica L. Summers

For full biographical listings, see the Martindale-Hubbell Law Directory

DAVIS, COX & WRIGHT, PLC (AV)

19 East Mountain Street, P.O. Drawer 1688, 72702-1688
Telephone: 501-521-7600
Fax: 501-521-7661

Sidney P. Davis, Jr.	William Jackson Butt, II
Walter B. Cox	Kelly P. Carithers
Tilden P. Wright, III	Tim E. Howell
Constance G. Clark	Don A. Taylor

Paul H. Taylor

John G. Trice	Mark W. Dossett
Laura J. Andress	David L. McCune

Representative Clients: Arkansas Farm Bureau Insurance Cos.; Fireman's Fund Insurance Group; United States Fidelity and Guaranty Co.; St. Paul Insurance Cos; Chrysler Motors Corp.; Kemper Insurance Group; Kawasaki Motors Corp.; CIGNA.

For full biographical listings, see the Martindale-Hubbell Law Directory

GREENHAW & GREENHAW (AV)

P.O. Box 4276, 72702
Telephone: 501-442-2562
Fax: 501-442-8479

Karl Greenhaw (1892-1967)	William K. Greenhaw
Leonard F. Greenhaw	John F. Greenhaw

Representative Clients: Southwestern Electric Power Co.; Commonwealth Theatres, Inc.; Federal Deposit Insurance Corp.; Foremost Dairies, Inc.; Pillsbury Mills, Inc.; Burlington Northern Railroad; Royal-Globe Insurance Group; St. Paul-Mercury Indemnity Co.; Government Employees Insurance Co.; General Electric Co.

For full biographical listings, see the Martindale-Hubbell Law Directory

FORREST CITY,* St. Francis Co.

BUTLER, HICKY & LONG (AV)

2216 North Washington Street, P.O. Box 989, 72335
Telephone: 501-633-4611
FAX: 501-633-6848

MEMBERS OF FIRM
Philip Hicky	Fletcher Long, Jr.

ASSOCIATES
Gary J. Mitchusson	Rita Reed Harris

Representative Clients: First National Bank of Eastern Arkansas; Southern Farm Bureau Insurance Cos.; United States Aviation Underwriters Group; National Aviation Underwriters; Hartford Accident and Indemnity Co.; Peoples Implement Co.

For full biographical listings, see the Martindale-Hubbell Law Directory

FORT SMITH,* Sebastian Co.

BETHELL, CALLAWAY, ROBERTSON, BEASLEY & COWAN (AV)

615 North "B" Street, P.O. Box 23, 72902
Telephone: 501-782-7911
Fax: 501-782-7964
Waldron, Arkansas Office: 80 West Second Street, 72958.
Telephone: 501-637-1197.
Fax: 501-782-7964.

MEMBERS OF FIRM
Donald P. Callaway (1935-1984)	John R. Beasley
Thomas E. Robertson, Jr.	Kenneth W. Cowan

J. Michael Fitzhugh
ASSOCIATE
Matthew J. Ketcham
OF COUNSEL
Edgar E. Bethell

Representative Clients: The Aetna Casualty & Surety Co.; James River - Dixie Cup; Arkansas-Oklahoma Gas Corp.; Beverage Products Corp. (Pepsi-Cola); The Prudential Insurance Company of America; Sentry - Dairyland Insurance Co; General Tire and Rubber; Quanex Corp.; The Fort Smith Municipal Airport Commission; Southern Steel & Wire Co.

For full biographical listings, see the Martindale-Hubbell Law Directory

DAILY, WEST, CORE, COFFMAN & CANFIELD (AV)

Stephens Office Building, 623 Garrison Avenue, P.O. Box 1446, 72902
Telephone: 501-782-0361
Fax: 501-782-6160

MEMBERS OF FIRM
Ben Core	Wyman R. Wade, Jr.
Eldon F. Coffman	Stanley A. Leasure
Jerry L. Canfield	Douglas M. Carson
Thomas A. Daily	Robert W. Bishop

(See Next Column)

DAILY, WEST, CORE, COFFMAN & CANFIELD—*Continued*

OF COUNSEL

James E. West

Counsel for: Claims Management, Inc. (Wal-Mart); Arkla, Inc.; City of Fort Smith; Commercial Union Insurance Cos.; Pennzoil Exploration and Production Co.; Silvey Cos., Inc.; Metropolitan Life Insurance Co.; Chevron U.S.A., Inc.

For full biographical listings, see the Martindale-Hubbell Law Directory

HARDIN, DAWSON & TERRY (AV)

Suite 500, Superior Federal Tower, 5000 Rogers Avenue, P.O. Box 10127, 72917-0127
Telephone: 501-452-2200
FAX: 501-452-9097

MEMBERS OF FIRM

G. C. Hardin (1884-1964)	Robert M. Honea
P. H. Hardin	J. Leslie Evitts III
Robert T. Dawson	J. Rodney Mills
Rex M. Terry	Kirkman T. Dougherty
	J. Gregory Magness

Counsel for: Superior Federal Bank, FSB; The Kansas City Southern Railway Co.; KFSM-TV; Johnson & Johnson; Ortho Pharmaceutical Corp; ASARCO Inc.; Allstate Insurance Co.; Southern Farm Bureau Insurance Co.; Dodson Insurance Group.

For full biographical listings, see the Martindale-Hubbell Law Directory

SHAW, LEDBETTER, HORNBERGER, COGBILL & ARNOLD (AV)

South Seventh and Parker, P.O. Box 185, 72902-0185
Telephone: 501-782-7294
FAX: 501-782-1493

Bruce H. Shaw (1904-1990)   Richard B. Shaw (1927-1988)

MEMBERS OF FIRM

Charles R. Ledbetter	James A. Arnold, II
Robert E. Hornberger	Ronald D. Harrison
J. Michael Cogbill	E. Diane Graham
	R. Ray Fulmer, II

ASSOCIATE

Rebecca D. Hattabaugh

OF COUNSEL

J. Michael Shaw

Representative Clients: General: First National Bank of Fort Smith; Bank of Mansfield; Commercial Bank at Alma; Mid-South Dredging Co.
Local Attorneys for: Liberty Mutual Insurance Co.; St Paul Insurance Cos.

For full biographical listings, see the Martindale-Hubbell Law Directory

WARNER, SMITH & HARRIS, PLC (AV)

214 North Sixth Street, P.O. Box 1626, 72901
Telephone: 501-782-6041
Fax: 501-782-0841

Harry Preston Warner (1885-1969)	Lillard Cody Hayes
Cecil Randolph Warner (1890-1955)	G. Alan Wooten
	James Melvin Dunn
Thomas G. Graves (1939-1971)	John Alan Lewis
Douglas O. Smith, Jr.	Joel D. Johnson
C. Wayne Harris	Gary W. Udouj
Gerald L. DeLung	J. Randall McGinnis
Patrick Neill Moore	Kathryn Stocks Campbell
	R. Gregory Aclin

OF COUNSEL

C. R. Warner, Jr.

District Attorneys for: Burlington Northern Railroad Co.
Counsel for: Fairfield Communities, Inc.; Sparks Regional Medical Center.
Local Counsel for: Planters Division, Nabisco Brands, Inc.; Gerber Products Co.; United States Fidelity & Guaranty Co.; Aetna Group; Fireman's Fund-American Insurance Cos.; Hiram Walker & Sons, Inc.; Continental National American Group.

For full biographical listings, see the Martindale-Hubbell Law Directory

HARRISBURG,* Poinsett Co. — (Refer to Jonesboro)

HOPE,* Hempstead Co.

McKENZIE, GRAVES, McRAE & VASSER (AV)

201 South Elm, P.O. Box 458, 71801
Telephone: 501-777-2391
Fax: 501-777-8699
Prescott, Arkansas Office: 122 East Second South, 71857.
Telephone: 501-887-2601.
Fax: 501-887-5504.

(See Next Column)

MEMBERS OF FIRM

William V. Tompkins (1861-1953)	Duncan L. McRae
O. A. Graves (1876-1968)	Albert Graves, Jr.
Charles H. Tompkins (1889-1975)	James H. McKenzie
	Albert Glenn Vasser
Horace H. McKenzie	Barry D. Barber
Albert Graves	Duncan McRae Culpepper
	M. Chad Trammell

Attorneys for: The Citizens National Bank, Hope; Bank of Prescott; Bank of Delight; Farm Credit Services of Southwest, Arkansas; Arkla, Inc.; McLarty Cos.; United States Fidelity & Guaranty Co.; The Travelers; Fireman's Fund American Insurance Cos.; Hudson Foods, Inc.

For full biographical listings, see the Martindale-Hubbell Law Directory

PILKINTON, PILKINTON & YOCOM (AV)

116-118 East Second Street, P.O. Box 583, 71801
Telephone: 501-777-8871
Fax: 501-777-2781

MEMBERS OF FIRM

James H. Pilkinton (1914-1994)   James H. Pilkinton, Jr.
Tony Lynn Yocom

Representative Clients: First National Bank of Hope; Pioneer Washington Restoration Foundation; Pyramid Plastics, Inc.; John Hays Chevrolet Co.; Michigan Chrome & Chemical; Bank of Blevins, Ark.
Approved Attorneys for: Commonwealth Land Title Insurance Co.; Lawyers Title Insurance Corp.

For full biographical listings, see the Martindale-Hubbell Law Directory

HOT SPRINGS NATIONAL PARK,* Garland Co.

RICHARD H. WOOTTON, P.A. (AV)

Rix Professional Center, 1401 Malvern, Suite 180, 71901
Telephone: 501-623-2593
Fax: 501-623-1485

Richard H. Wootton

Attorney for: American Surety Co.; Jefferson Standard Life Insurance Co.; Zurich American Insurance Co.; Western Surety Co; National Life & Accident Co.
Approved Attorneys for: Lawyers Title Insurance Corp.; Chicago Title Insurance Co.; Chubb Insurance Co.

For full biographical listings, see the Martindale-Hubbell Law Directory

HUNTSVILLE,* Madison Co. — (Refer to Fayetteville)

JASPER,* Newton Co. — (Refer to Fayetteville)

JONESBORO,* Craighead Co.

BARRETT & DEACON (AV)

Union Planters Bank Building, 300 South Church Street, P.O. Box 1700, 72403
Telephone: 501-931-1700
FAX: 501-931-1800

MEMBERS OF FIRM

Joe C. Barrett (1897-1980)	David W. Cahoon
John C. Deacon	Ralph W. Waddell
J. Barry Deacon	Paul D. Waddell
	D. Price Marshall, Jr.

ASSOCIATES

James D. Bradbury	Kevin W. Cole
	Anita S. Perkins

For full biographical listings, see the Martindale-Hubbell Law Directory

MOONEY LAW FIRM (AV)

214 East Washington, P.O. Box 1423, 72403-1423
Telephone: 501-935-5847
Fax: 501-935-4438

MEMBERS OF FIRM

Charles M. Mooney   Charles M (Skip) Mooney, Jr.
Mary Lile Broadaway

Representative Clients: Simmons First Bank of Jonesboro; The Bert Cruse Agency, Inc.; Prudential Insurance Company of America.
Approved Attorneys for: Chicago Title Co.; Chelsea Title & Guaranty Co.; Commerce Title Guaranty Co.; Lawyers Title Insurance Corp.
References: Citizens Bank of Jonesboro; The Mercantile Bank of Jonesboro.

For full biographical listings, see the Martindale-Hubbell Law Directory

PENIX, PENIX, LUSBY AND NIX (AV)

401 South Main Street, P.O. Box 1306, 72403-1306
Telephone: 501-932-7449
Fax: 501-933-7281

(See Next Column)

PENIX, PENIX, LUSBY AND NIX, *Jonesboro—Continued*

MEMBERS OF FIRM

Roy Penix (1891-1978)　　　　　　Bill Penix
Marian F. Penix (1924-1991)　　　Richard A. Lusby
J. Robin Nix, II

Representative Clients: American Policyholders Ins. Co.; CIGNA Cos.; K-Mart Corp.; Liberty Mutual Insurance Co.; Sentry and Dairyland Insurance; Southwestern Bell Telephone Co.; The Jonesboro Sun.

For full biographical listings, see the Martindale-Hubbell Law Directory

SNELLGROVE, LASER, LANGLEY, LOVETT & CULPEPPER (AV)

Second Floor, 111 East Huntington, P.O. Box 1346, 72403-1346
Telephone: 501-932-8357
Fax: 501-932-5488

MEMBERS OF FIRM

G. D. Walker (1910-1989)　　　Glenn Lovett, Jr.
Frank Snellgrove, Jr.　　　　　Malcolm Culpepper
David N. Laser　　　　　　　　D. Todd Williams
Stanley R. Langley　　　　　　Michael E. Mullally
P. Sanders Huckabee

Representative Clients: Union Planters Bank of Northeast Arkansas (formerly Mercantile Bank); First Bank of Arkansas; Travelers Insurance Co.; Aetna Insurance Co.; ITT Hartford Insurance Co.; Commercial Union Insurance Co.; CNA Insurance Group; State Farm Insurance Cos.; Columbia Mutual Insurance Co.; Bituminous Insurance Co.

For full biographical listings, see the Martindale-Hubbell Law Directory

WOMACK, LANDIS, PHELPS, McNEILL & McDANIEL, A PROFESSIONAL ASSOCIATION (AV)

Century Center, Washington at Madison, P.O. Box 3077, 72403
Telephone: 501-932-0900
Fax: 501-932-2553

Tom D. Womack　　　　　　John V. Phelps
Carl David Landis　　　　　Paul D. McNeill
Lucinda McDaniel

Brant Perkins　　　　　　　Jeffrey W. Puryear
Donald L. Parker II　　　　Mark Alan Mayfield
David Christopher Gardner

Representative Clients: Arkansas State University; Bank of Trumann; E.C. Barton & Co.; Kraft General Foods Corp.; Home Indemnity Company of N.Y.; St. Paul Insurance Cos.; Shelter Insurance Co.; United States Fidelity & Guaranty Co.

For full biographical listings, see the Martindale-Hubbell Law Directory

LAKE VILLAGE, * Chicot Co. — (Refer to Hamburg)

LEWISVILLE, * Lafayette Co. — (Refer to Magnolia)

LITTLE ROCK, * Pulaski Co.

ARNOLD, GROBMYER & HALEY, A PROFESSIONAL ASSOCIATION (AV)

875 Union National Plaza, 124 West Capitol Avenue, P.O. Box 70, 72203
Telephone: 501-376-1171
Fax: 501-375-3548

Erwin M. Arnold (1906-1985)　　Joe A. Polk
Benjamin F. Arnold　　　　　　Richard L. Ramsay
James F. Dowden　　　　　　　Robert R. Ross
Mark W. Grobmyer　　　　　　Lee S. Thalheimer
Charles D. McDaniel　　　　　Beth Ann Long

OF COUNSEL

Robert A. Blair (P.C.)　　　　Scott E. Slaughter
　(Not admitted in AR)　　　　　(Not admitted in AR)
John H. Haley　　　　　　　　Lloyd S. Wolf
G. Hite McLean, Jr.　　　　　　(Not admitted in AR)
　(Not admitted in AR)

For full biographical listings, see the Martindale-Hubbell Law Directory

BARBER, McCASKILL, AMSLER, JONES & HALE, P.A. (AV)

2700 First Commercial Building, 400 West Capitol Avenue, 72201-3414
Telephone: 501-372-6175
Telecopier: 501-375-2802

Azro L. Barber (1885-1979)　　Micheal L. Alexander
Elbert A. Henry (1889-1966)　　William H. Edwards, Jr.
John B. Thurman (1912-1971)　　Richard C. Kalkbrenner
Austin McCaskill, Sr.　　　　　G. Spence Fricke
Guy Amsler, Jr.　　　　　　　Gail Ponder Gaines
Glenn W. Jones　　　　　　　Michael J. Emerson
Michael E. Hale　　　　　　　R. Kenny McCulloch
John S. Cherry, Jr.　　　　　Tim A. Cheatham
Robert L. Henry, III　　　　　Joseph F. Kolb

(See Next Column)

Scott Michael Strauss　　　　Thomas E. Osment, Jr.
Derek J. Edwards　　　　　　Christopher Gomlicker

Attorneys for: Associated Aviation Underwriters; Canal Insurance Co.; Fireman's Fund Insurance Co.; General Motors Corp.; General Motors Acceptance Corp.; Hanover Insurance Co.; Home Insurance Co.; Royal Insurance; United States Fidelity & Guaranty Co.; Universal Underwriters Insurance Co.

For full biographical listings, see the Martindale-Hubbell Law Directory

CEARLEY LAW FIRM (AV)

Centre Place, Second Floor, 212 Center Street, 72201
Telephone: 501-375-9451
Fax: 501-374-3463
Email: 102574.227@compuserve.com

Robert M. Cearley, Jr.

Counsel for: Arkansas Bankers Association; Greyhound Lines, Inc.

For full biographical listings, see the Martindale-Hubbell Law Directory

DOVER & DIXON, P.A. (AV)

425 West Capitol, Suite 3700, 72201
Telephone: 501-375-9151
Telecopier: 501-375-6484

Darrell D. Dover　　　　　　Gary B. Rogers
Philip E. Dixon　　　　　　　Michael R. Johns
Thomas S. Stone　　　　　　W. Michael Reif
Steve L. Riggs　　　　　　　David A. Couch
Joseph H. Purvis　　　　　　M. Darren O'Quinn
Charles W. Reynolds　　　　Monte D. Estes
John B. Peace　　　　　　　Patrick E. Hollingsworth
Wm. Dean Overstreet　　　　Derrick Davidson
Jennifer M. Browne

Representative Clients: Wood Manufacturing Company, Inc. (Ranger Boats); J.B. Hunt; Affiliated Foods; St. Vincent Infirmary; First Commercial Bank; Arkansas Teacher Retirement System; Assurance Alliance, Inc.; City of Little Rock; Connecticut Mutual Life Insurance; Old Republic National Title Insurance Company.

For full biographical listings, see the Martindale-Hubbell Law Directory

FRIDAY, ELDREDGE & CLARK (AV)

A Partnership including Professional Associations
Formerly, Smith, Williams, Friday, Eldredge & Clark
2000 First Commercial Building, 400 West Capitol Avenue, 72201-3493
Telephone: 501-376-2011
Telecopier: 501-376-2147; 376-6369
Email: fecmh@fec.sprint.com

MEMBERS OF FIRM

William H. Sutton (P.A.)　　　　Joseph B. Hurst, Jr., (P.A.)
James W. Moore　　　　　　　Elizabeth Robben Murray (P.A.)
Byron M. Eiseman, Jr., (P.A.)　Christopher J. Heller (P.A.)
Joe D. Bell (P.A.)　　　　　　Laura Hensley Smith (P.A.)
John C. Echols (P.A.)　　　　Robert S. Shafer (P.A.)
James A. Buttry (P.A.)　　　　William Mell Griffin III, (P.A.)
Frederick S. Ursery (P.A.)　　Thomas N. Rose (P.A.)
H. T. Larzelere, Jr., (P.A.)　　Michael Scott Moore (P.A.)
Oscar E. Davis, Jr., (P.A.)　　Diane S. Mackey (P.A.)
James C. Clark, Jr., (P.A.)　　Walter M. Ebel, III, (P.A.)
Thomas P. Leggett, (P.A.)　　Kevin A. Crass (P.A.)
John Dewey Watson (P.A.)　　William A. Waddell, Jr., (P.A.)
Paul B. Benham, III, (P.A.)　　M. Gayle Corley (P.A.)
Larry W. Burks (P.A.)　　　　Robert B. Beach, Jr., (P.A.)
A. Wyckliff Nisbet, Jr., (P.A.)　Scott J. Lancaster (P.A.)
James E. Harris (P.A.)　　　　J. Lee Brown (P.A.)
J. Phillip Malcom (P.A.)　　　James C. Baker (P.A.)
James M. Simpson, Jr., (P.A.)　Harry A. Light (P.A.)
Meredith P. Catlett (P.A.)　　Scott H. Tucker (P.A.)
James M. Saxton (P.A.)　　　John Clayton Randolph (P.A.)
J. Shepherd Russell, III, (P.A.)　Guy Alton Wade (P.A.)
Donald H. Bacon (P.A.)　　　Price C. Gardner (P.A.)
W. Thomas Baxter (P.A.)　　J. Michael Pickens (P.A.)
Walter A. Paulson, II, (P.A.)　Tonia P. Jones (P.A.)
Barry E. Coplin (P.A.)　　　　David D. Wilson (P.A.)
Richard D. Taylor (P.A.)　　　Jeffrey H. Moore (P.A.)

ASSOCIATES

Andrew T. Turner　　　　　　Fran C. Hickman
David M. Graf　　　　　　　Betty J. Demory
Carla G. Spainhour　　　　　Barbara J. Rand
John C. Fendley, Jr　　　　　　(Not admitted in AR)
Allison Graves　　　　　　　James W. Smith
Jonann C. Roosevelt　　　　Will Bond
R. Christopher Lawson　　　Daniel Lee Herrington
Gregory D. Taylor　　　　　Clifford W. Plunkett
Tony L. Wilcox　　　　　　　Allison Cornwell

(See Next Column)

FRIDAY, ELDREDGE & CLARK—*Continued*

COUNSEL

William J. Smith	B. S. Clark
John T. Williams (1909-1988)	William L. Terry
Herschel H. Friday (1922-1994)	William L. Patton, Jr.
William A. Eldredge, Jr., (P.A.)	Robert V. Light (1930-1996)

Counsel for: Union Pacific System; St. Paul Insurance Co.; Liberty Mutual Insurance Co.; Cigna Property & Casualty Co.; Arkansas Power & Light Co.; Dillard Department Stores, Inc.; First Commercial Corp.; Browning Arms Co.; Phillips Petroleum Co.; Aetna Casualty & Surety Co.

For full biographical listings, see the Martindale-Hubbell Law Directory

---

GILL LAW FIRM, A PROFESSIONAL ASSOCIATION (AV)

3801 TCBY Tower, Capitol and Broadway, 72201
Telephone: 501-376-3800
Fax: 501-372-3359

John P. Gill	Heartsill Ragon III, (P.A.)
Charles C. Owen (P.A.)	Joseph D. Calhoun III
W. W. Elrod, II	W. Bradford Sherman
Victor A. Fleming	Glenn E. Kelley

Judy P. McNeil	C. Tad Bohannon

Robert B. Holitik

OF COUNSEL

John A. Fogleman

For full biographical listings, see the Martindale-Hubbell Law Directory

---

HILBURN, CALHOON, HARPER, PRUNISKI & CALHOUN, LTD. (AV)

P.O. Box 1256, 72203-1256
Telephone: 501-372-0110
Fax: 501-372-2029
North Little Rock, Arkansas Office: Eighth Floor, Mercantile Bank Building, One Riverfront Place, P.O. Box 5551, 72119.
Telephone: 501-372-0110.
Fax: 501-372-2029.

Sam Hilburn	Phil Campbell
Ken F. Calhoon	J. Maurice Rogers
Ernest H. Harper, Jr.	Paula Jamell Storeygard
John E. Pruniski, III	Scott E. Daniel
John C. Calhoun, Jr.	Carrold E. Ray
David M. Fuqua	Scott Thomas Vaughn
James H. McHaney, Jr.	Susan Gordon Gunter

James D. Lawson

Dorcy Kyle Corbin	Bruce D. Eddy
Graham F. Sloan	Pamela A. Moseley
Mark K. Halter	Randy L. Grice
Michael E. Hartje, Jr.	Harry John Chakales (Resident, North Little Rock Office)

Representative Clients: Mercantile Bank of Central Arkansas; Merrill Lynch Pierce Fenner & Smith, Inc.; Allstate Insurance Company.

For full biographical listings, see the Martindale-Hubbell Law Directory

---

HOOVER & KOOISTRA (AV)

111 Center Street, 11th Floor, 72201-4445
Telephone: 501-376-8500
Facsimile: 501-372-3255

MEMBERS OF FIRM

Paul W. Hoover, Jr.	John Kooistra, III

Max C. Mehlburger

For full biographical listings, see the Martindale-Hubbell Law Directory

---

HORNE, HOLLINGSWORTH & PARKER, A PROFESSIONAL ASSOCIATION (AV)

401 West Capitol, Suite 501, P.O. Box 3363, 72203
Telephone: 501-376-4731
FAX: 501-372-7142

Walter W. Davidson (Retired)	Mark H. Allison
Allan W. Horne	Frank J. Wills, III
Cyril Hollingsworth	Joyce Bradley Babin
Michael O. Parker	Bradley Sean Chafin
James P. Beachboard	Ed M. Koon

OF COUNSEL

Garland W. Binns, Jr.

Representative Clients: Associated Industries of Arkansas, Inc.; Arkansas Blue Cross and Blue Shield; Boatmen's National Bank of Arkansas; J.B. Hunt Transport, Inc.; American Insurance Association; Arkansas Kraft Corp.; Gaylord Container Corp.; Southern Pioneer Life Insurance Co.; Robinette-Burnett Construction Co.

For full biographical listings, see the Martindale-Hubbell Law Directory

---

IVESTER, SKINNER & CAMP, P.A. (AV)

Suite 1200, 111 Center Street, 72201
Telephone: 501-376-7788
FAX: 501-376-8536

Hermann Ivester	Laura G. Wiltshire
H. Edward Skinner	Todd A. Lewellen
Charles R. Camp	Stan D. Smith
Randal B. Frazier	Michael H. Massey

For full biographical listings, see the Martindale-Hubbell Law Directory

---

KEMP, DUCKETT, HOPKINS & SPRADLEY (AV)

A Partnership including Professional Associations
Suite 1300, 111 Center Street, 72201
Telephone: 501-372-7243
Fax: 501-372-5553

Hal Joseph Kemp (P.A.)	J. Mark Spradley
James M. Duckett	Stephen L. Curry
Randolph B. Hopkins (P.A.)	Rhonda K. Slayden

Representative Clients: Ticor Title Insurance Co.; Chicago Title Insurance Co.; Beach Enterprises, Inc.

For full biographical listings, see the Martindale-Hubbell Law Directory

---

LASER, WILSON, BUFFORD & WATTS, P.A. (AV)

101 S. Spring Street, Suite 300, 72201-2488
Telephone: 501-376-2981
Telecopier: 501-376-2417

Sam Laser	Walter A. Kendel, Jr.
Dan F. Bufford	Brian A. Brown
Richard N. Watts	Karen J. Hughes
J. Kendal "Ken" Cook	Gena Gregory
Kevin J. Staten	Keith Martin McPherson
Alfred F. Angulo, Jr.	Thomas J. Diaz
David M. Donovan	Frank B. Newell

OF COUNSEL

Ralph R. Wilson

Representative Clients: Allstate Insurance Co.; American International Insurance Group; Continental Insurance Cos.; Farm Bureau Insurance Cos. (Casualty & Fire); Farmers Insurance Group; GAB Business Services, Inc.; St. Paul Insurance Cos.; Scottsdale Insurance Co.; State Farm Auto (Fire) Insurance Cos.

For full biographical listings, see the Martindale-Hubbell Law Directory

---

ROSE LAW FIRM, A PROFESSIONAL ASSOCIATION (AV)

120 East Fourth Street, 72201
Telephone: 501-375-9131
Telecopy: 501-375-1309

George E. Campbell	Les R. Baledge
Herbert C. Rule, III	James Hunter Birch
W. Wilson Jones	Kevin R. Burns
Allen W. Bird, II	Richard T. Donovan
William E. Bishop	Richard N. Massey
C. Brantly Buck	John T. Hardin
Tim Boe	Stephen N. Joiner
M. Jane Dickey	James M. Gary
William H. Kennedy, III	James H. Druff
Ronald M. Clark	Gordon M. Wilbourn
Garland J. Garrett	Amy Lee Stewart
Jerry C. Jones	David A. Smith
Thomas P. Thrash	Brian Rosenthal
Charles W. Baker	J. Scott Schallhorn
David L. Williams	Jeffrey J. Gearhart
Jackson Farrow Jr.	James L. Harris

Clay H. Davis

COUNSEL

J. Gaston Williamson	W. Dane Clay
Phillip Carroll	John A. Davis, III

Mark Alan Peoples	Kathryn Bennett Perkins
Franklin M. Faust	John P. Fletcher
Bryant K. Cranford	Goodloe M. Partee
Grant E. Fortson	Michael N. Shannon
David P. Martin	Craig S. Lair

Deanna J. Weisse

Counsel for: ALLTEL Corporation; Aluminum Company of America; Bridgestone/Firestone, Inc.; The Equitable Life Assurance Society of The United States; General Motors Corp.; The Prudential Insurance Company of America; Stephens Group Inc.; Tyson Foods, Inc.

For full biographical listings, see the Martindale-Hubbell Law Directory

Little Rock—*Continued*

WILLIAM F. SHERMAN (AV)

Suite 504, Pyramid Place, 221 West Second Street, 72201
Telephone: 501-372-3148
FAX: 501-372-2630

For full biographical listings, see the Martindale-Hubbell Law Directory

WILLIAMS & ANDERSON (AV)

Twenty-Second Floor, 111 Center Street, 72201
Telephone: 501-372-0800
FAX: 501-372-6453

MEMBERS OF FIRM

W. Jackson Williams	John E. Tull, III
Philip S. Anderson	Rush B. Deacon
Peter G. Kumpe	J. Leon Holmes
David F. Menz	Timothy W. Grooms
Steven W. Quattlebaum	G. Alan Perkins
James E. Hathaway III	Thomas G. Williams

J. Cal McCastlain	Katharine R. Cloud
Jeanne L. Seewald	Edie R. Ervin
Stephen B. Niswanger	

Representative Clients: Arkansas Development Finance Authority; Coca-Cola Enterprises, Inc.; Dean Witter Reynolds Inc.; Entergy Power, Inc.; Little Rock Newspapers, Inc. d/b/a Arkansas Democrat-Gazette; Metrocentre Improvement District No. 1 of the City of Little Rock; Potlatch Corporation; Texaco Inc.; Roman Catholic Diocese of Little Rock; Wal-Mart Stores, Inc.

For full biographical listings, see the Martindale-Hubbell Law Directory

WOOD & LOCKHART, A PROFESSIONAL ASSOCIATION (AV)

809 West Second Street, 72201
Telephone: 501-375-0200
FAX: 501-375-0218
Email: woodlaw@cei.net

David J. Wood   W. Kirby Lockhart

Counsel for: Arkansas Motor Carriers Assn.

For full biographical listings, see the Martindale-Hubbell Law Directory

---

MAGNOLIA,* Columbia Co.

WOODWARD & EPLEY (AV)

105 West Calhoun Street, P.O. Box 765, 71753
Telephone: 501-234-4781
FAX: 501-234-7751

Joe D. Woodward   Michael G. Epley

David P. Price

Representative Clients: American Fuel Cell and Coated Fabrics Co.; The Banner News Publishing Co.; First National Bank of Lewisville; Peoples Bank, Waldo, Arkansas; Boatmen's National Bank; Unit Structures Systems, Inc.; Prescott Land & Timber Company, Inc.; Harold Rogers Logging, Inc.; J. W. Miller Timber Co., Inc.; Miller Hardwood, Inc.

For full biographical listings, see the Martindale-Hubbell Law Directory

---

MALVERN,* Hot Spring Co. — (Refer to Hot Springs National Park)

MARIANNA,* Lee Co. — (Refer to Helena)

MARSHALL,* Searcy Co. — (Refer to Mountain Home)

MELBOURNE,* Izard Co. — (Refer to Batesville)

MENA,* Polk Co. — (Refer to Ashdown)

MONTICELLO,* Drew Co.

BALL, BARTON & HOFFMAN (AV)

North Main at Oakland, P.O. Box 507, 71655
Telephone: 501-367-6288
Fax: 501-367-7851

MEMBERS OF FIRM

Lamar Williamson (1887-1974)	William K. Ball
Adrian Williamson (1892-1982)	Walter W. Barton
David D. Hoffman	

Representative Clients: Crossett Division of Georgia-Pacific Corp.; Union Bank & Trust Co.; Sea Ark Marine, Inc.; Monticello School District; Southern Farm Bureau Casualty Insurance Co.; R. A. Pickens & Son; Arkansas Land & Cattle Co.; State Auto Insurance; U.S.A.A.

ROSS & ROSS (AV)

115 East Shelton Avenue, P.O. Box 209, 71655
Telephone: 501-367-5351
FAX: 501-367-2221

(See Next Column)

James A. Ross (1911-1983)   James A. Ross, Jr.
Reference: Heritage Bank, A Federal Savings Bank, Monticello, Ark.

For full biographical listings, see the Martindale-Hubbell Law Directory

---

MORRILTON,* Conway Co. — (Refer to Russellville)

MOUNTAINBURG, Crawford Co. — (Refer to Fort Smith)

MOUNTAIN HOME,* Baxter Co.

POYNTER & GEARHART, P.A. (AV)

123 East Seventh Street, P.O. Box 370, 72653
Telephone: 501-425-2196
FAX: 501-425-2198

Terry M. Poynter   Van A. Gearhart

Representative Clients: First National Bank & Trust Co.; Mercantile Bank; United States Fidelity & Guaranty Co.
Approved Attorneys for: Farmers Home Administration; Chicago Title Insurance Co.; Mid-South Title Insurance Co.
References: First National Bank and Trust Co.; The Peoples Bank & Trust Co.; Farmers Home Administration; Mercantile Bank.

For full biographical listings, see the Martindale-Hubbell Law Directory

---

MOUNTAIN VIEW,* Stone Co. — (Refer to Batesville)

MURFREESBORO,* Pike Co. — (Refer to Nashville)

NASHVILLE,* Howard Co.

STEEL & STEEL (AV)

102 North Main Street, 71852
Telephone: 501-845-1870
Fax: 501-845-3355

MEMBERS OF FIRM

George E. Steel   George E. Steel, Jr.

Attorneys for: First National Bank, Nashville; Pike County Bank, Murfreesboro and Mineral Springs, Nashville; Weyerhaeuser Co.; Nashville Trucking ; R.D. Plant Contracting Co.; Bank of Amity, Amity; Southwestern Electric Power Co.; M & P Paving Company; Walmart Stores, Inc.

NEWPORT,* Jackson Co.

BOYCE & BOYCE, A PROFESSIONAL ASSOCIATION (AV)

515 Second Street, P.O. Box 948, 72112
Telephone: 501-523-5242
FAX: 501-523-5196

Wayne Boyce   Edward W. Boyce, III

For full biographical listings, see the Martindale-Hubbell Law Directory

BOYCE LAW FIRM (AV)

307 Main, P.O. Box 38, 72112
Telephone: 501-523-3626; Jonesboro: 501-932-7189
Fax: 501-523-4839

Sam H. Boyce   Henry H. Boyce

LEGAL SUPPORT PERSONNEL
Betty Butler (Paralegal)

Reference: Merchants & Planters Bank, Newport, Arkansas.

For full biographical listings, see the Martindale-Hubbell Law Directory

---

OZARK,* Franklin Co. — (Refer to Fort Smith)

PARAGOULD,* Greene Co. — (Refer to Jonesboro)

PARIS,* Logan Co. — (Refer to Fort Smith)

PIGGOTT,* Clay Co. — (Refer to Jonesboro)

PINE BLUFF,* Jefferson Co.

BRIDGES, YOUNG, MATTHEWS & DRAKE PLC (AV)

315 East Eighth Avenue, P.O. Box 7808, 71611
Telephone: 501-534-5532
Fax: 501-534-5582

F. G. Bridges (1866-1959)	Terry F. Wynne
Frank G. Bridges, Jr.	James L. (Lee) Moore, III
(1906-1973)	Michael J. Dennis
Stephen A. Matthews	David L. Sims
Ted N. Drake	R. Scott Morgan
Joseph A. Strode	Jeffrey H. Dixon
Jack A. McNulty	Carrington E. (Cary) Young

James C. Moser, Jr.

(See Next Column)

BRIDGES, YOUNG, MATTHEWS & DRAKE PLC—*Continued*
OF COUNSEL
Paul B. Young

Representative Clients: Corporate: Central Moloney, Inc.; International Paper Co.; Boatmen's National Bank of Pine Bluff, Arkansas. Insurance: Hartford Insurance Group; The Travelers; United States Fidelity & Guaranty Co. Other: Jefferson Regional Medical Center.

For full biographical listings, see the Martindale-Hubbell Law Directory

RAMSAY, BRIDGFORTH, HARRELSON & STARLING (AV)

11th Floor, Simmons First National Building, P.O. Drawer 8509, 71611
Telephone: 501-535-9000
FAX: 501-535-8544

MEMBERS OF FIRM

William Franklin Coleman (1870-1956)	F. Daniel Harrelson
Nicholas J. Gantt, Jr. (1879-1975)	Spencer F. Robinson
	Phillip A. Raley
Marion J. Starling, Jr. (1941-1990)	Patrick A. Burrow
	Rosalind M. Mouser
William C. Bridgforth	William M. Bridgforth
	David R. Bridgforth

ASSOCIATES

William Jay Harrelson   John Thomas Starling

OF COUNSEL
Louis L. Ramsay, Jr.

Representative Clients: Simmons First National Bank; Pine Bluff Sand & Gravel Co.; Stant, Inc.; McGeorge Contracting Co., Inc.; Television Station KATV.

For full biographical listings, see the Martindale-Hubbell Law Directory

*RISON,** Cleveland Co. — (Refer to Pine Bluff)

*RUSSELLVILLE,** Pope Co.

LAWS & MURDOCH, P.A. (AV)

2nd & South Arkansas, 72801
Telephone: 501-968-1168
Fax: 501-968-5590

Ike Allen Laws, Jr.	Ike Allen Laws, III
Timothy W. Murdoch	Hugh R. Laws

Representative Clients: Delhi Gas Pipeline Corp.; Boatmen's National Bank; Bibler Bros., Inc.; Pope County Levee District; Dixon Poultry, Inc.; Sonat Exploration Company.
Approved Attorneys for: Old Republic Title Co.

For full biographical listings, see the Martindale-Hubbell Law Directory

*SALEM,** Fulton Co. — (Refer to Batesville)

*SHERIDAN,** Grant Co. — (Refer to Little Rock)

SPRINGDALE, Washington Co.

CYPERT, CROUCH, CLARK & HARWELL (AV)

111 Holcomb Street, P.O. Box 869, 72764-1400
Telephone: 501-751-5222
Fax: 501-751-5777

Courtney C. Crouch (1912-1975)	William M. Clark, Jr.
James E. Crouch	Charles L. Harwell

ASSOCIATES

R. Jeffrey Reynerson	Marcus W. Van Pelt

OF COUNSEL

James D. Cypert	Leslie L. Reid
Stanley W. Ludwig	

General Counsel for: First National Bank of Springdale; Northwest Medical Center; Springdale School District.
Representative Clients: Purina Mills, Inc.; Swift-Eckrich, Inc.
Insurance Clients: Western Casualty & Surety Co.; The John Hancock Cos.; Home Ins. Co.; Liberty Mutual; Fireman's Fund.

For full biographical listings, see the Martindale-Hubbell Law Directory

ROY & LAMBERT (AV)

2706 South Dividend Drive, P.O. Drawer 7030, 72766-7030
Telephone: 501-756-8510
Fax: 501-756-8562

MEMBERS OF FIRM

James M. Roy, Jr.	Robert J. Lambert, Jr.

ASSOCIATES

Jerry L. Lovelace	Jon P. Robinson
Brian D. Wood	James H. Bingaman

(See Next Column)

OF COUNSEL
John D. Copeland

Representative Clients: State Farm Mutual Automobile Insurance Co.; State Farm Fire and Casualty Co.; Shelter Mutual Insurance Co.; Silvey Insurance Companies; Columbia Mutual Insurance Co.; State Volunteer Mutual Insurance Co.; Farmers Insurance Group; Springdale Bank & Trust; 4-State Poultry Supply, Inc.; Commerce Construction Co.

For full biographical listings, see the Martindale-Hubbell Law Directory

*STAR CITY,** Lincoln Co. — (Refer to Pine Bluff)

*STUTTGART,** Arkansas Co. — (Refer to Pine Bluff)

*TEXARKANA,** Miller Co.

DUNN, NUTTER, MORGAN & SHAW (AV)

State Line Plaza, Box 8030, 71854-5945
Telephone: 501-773-5651
Telecopier: 501-772-2037
Email: law@clover.cleaf.com

MEMBERS OF FIRM

Willis B. Smith (1926-1980)	Charles A. Morgan
Charles M. Conway (1925-1976)	James N. Nutt (1949-1983)
Winford L. Dunn, Jr.	Nelson V. Shaw
R. Gary Nutter	R. David Freeze
W. David Carter	

ASSOCIATES

Mark A. Daniels	Tina R. Green
Jeff M. Addison	Christie G. Adams (Not admitted in AR)

OF COUNSEL

Alex G. Sanderson	Hayes C. McClerkin

LEGAL SUPPORT PERSONNEL
LEGAL ASSISTANTS

Myra Conaway Wells	Sonja L. Oliver

Representative Clients: North American Energy Corporation (NorAm); The State First National Bank of Texarkana; Prudential Insurance Company of America; CNA Insurance Cos.; Cigna Insurance Cos.; First Federal Savings & Loan Assn.; St. Michael Hospital; Southwest Arkansas Water District; Mobil Oil Co.; Southwest Arkansas Electric Cooperative Corp.

For full biographical listings, see the Martindale-Hubbell Law Directory

*VAN BUREN,** Crawford Co. — (Refer to Fort Smith)

*WALDRON,** Scott Co. — (Refer to Fort Smith)

*WALNUT RIDGE,** Lawrence Co. — (Refer to Jonesboro)

*WARREN,** Bradley Co. — (Refer to Monticello)

WEST MEMPHIS, Crittenden Co.

HALE, FOGLEMAN & ROGERS (AV)

108 Dover Road, P.O. Box 1666, 72301
Telephone: 501-735-1900
FAX: 501-735-1662

MEMBERS OF FIRM

Julian B. Fogleman	Joe M. Rogers
Thomas F. Donaldson, Jr.	

General Counsel for: Drainage Districts # 2, 3 and 8 of Crittenden County; Edmondson Hotel Service, Inc.; Heath & House Construction Co.
Local Counsel for: Southern Farm Bureau Casualty Insurance Co.; Shelby Mutual Insurance Co.; Greyhound Lines, Inc.; American Justice Insurance Reciprocal.

For full biographical listings, see the Martindale-Hubbell Law Directory

RIEVES & MAYTON (AV)

304 East Broadway, P.O. Box 1359, 72303
Telephone: 501-735-3420
Telecopier: 501-735-4678

MEMBERS OF FIRM

Elton A. Rieves, Jr. (1909-1984)	Michael R. Mayton
Elton A. Rieves, III	Elton A. Rieves, IV
Martin W. Bowen	

ASSOCIATES

William Terrell Smith, Jr.	David S. Wilson, III

For full biographical listings, see the Martindale-Hubbell Law Directory

SLOAN, RUBENS & PEEPLES (AV)

600 North Missouri Street, P.O. Box 768, 72303
Telephone: 501-735-5500
Telecopy: 501-735-2624

MEMBERS OF FIRM

Edward J. Rubens (1913-1977)	Kent J. Rubens
David C. Peeples	

(See Next Column)

SLOAN, RUBENS & PEEPLES, *West Memphis—Continued*

ASSOCIATES

J. Michael Stephenson   James A. Davis

OF COUNSEL

Ralph W. Sloan   Edward B. Johnson
(Not admitted in AR)

General Counsel for: Bank of West Memphis; Crittenden Publishing Co., Inc.; West Memphis School District; Razorback Concrete; Flash Markets, Inc.

Representative Clients: Earle School District; Crawfordsville School District; Citizens Bank Marion; Marion School District; AgriBank, FCB.

For full biographical listings, see the Martindale-Hubbell Law Directory

---

WYNNE,* Cross Co. — (Refer to Forrest City)

YELLVILLE,* Marion Co. — (Refer to Harrison)

CALIFORNIA

ALAMEDA, Alameda Co. — (Refer to Oakland)

ALHAMBRA, Los Angeles Co. — (Refer to Pasadena)

ALTURAS,* Modoc Co. — (Refer to Redding)

ARCADIA, Los Angeles Co.

HELMS, HANRAHAN & MYERS (AV)

Suite 685 Towne Centre Building, 150 North Santa Anita Avenue, 91006
Telephone: 818-445-1177
Email: helmsj@aol.com

James R. Helms, Jr.   James J. Hanrahan
Sterling E. Myers

LEGAL SUPPORT PERSONNEL

PARALEGALS

Michelle L. Upp   Josephine Phillips

Reference: Bank of America National Trust & Savings Assn. (Arcadia Branch).

For full biographical listings, see the Martindale-Hubbell Law Directory

---

AUBURN,* Placer Co. — (Refer to Sacramento)

BAKERSFIELD,* Kern Co.

BORTON, PETRINI & CONRON (AV)

The Borton, Petrini & Conron Building, 1600 Truxtun Avenue, P.O. Box 2026, 93303
Telephone: 805-322-3051
Voice Mail: 805-395-6700
Fax: 805-322-4628
Email: bpcbak@bpclaw.com
San Luis Obispo, California Office: 1114 Marsh Street.
Telephone: 805-541-4340.
Fax: 805-541-4558. Email: bpcslo@bpclaw.com.
Visalia, California Office: 206 South Mooney Boulevard, P.O. Box 1028.
Telephone: 209-627-5600.
Fax: 209-627-4309. Email: bpcvis@bpclaw.com.
Fresno, California Office: T. W. Patterson Building, 2014 Tulare Street, Suite 830.
Telephone: 209-268-0117.
Fax: 209-237-7995. Email: bpcfrs@bpclaw.com.
Sacramento, California Office: 2233 Watt Avenue, Suite 290.
Telephone: 916-484-3555.
Fax: 916-484-3550. Email: bpcsac@bpclaw.com.
Santa Barbara, California Office: 211 East Victoria Street, Suite D.
Telephone: 805-564-2404.
Fax: 805-564-2176. Email: bpcsb@bpclaw.com.
Los Angeles, California Office: 707 Wilshire Boulevard, Suite 5100.
Telephone: 213-624-2869.
Fax: 213-489-3930. Email: bpcla@bpclaw.com.
San Diego, California Office: John Burnham Building, 610 West Ash Street, 9th Floor.
Telephone: 619-232-2424.
Fax: 619-531-0794. Email: bpcsd@bpclaw.com.
Newport Beach, California Office: 4675 MacArthur Court, Suite 1150.
Telephone: 714-752-2333.
Fax: 714-752-2854. Email: bpcnb@bpclaw.com.
Modesto, California Office: The Turner Building, 900 "H" Street, Suite D.
Telephone: 209-576-1701.
Fax: 209-527-9753. Email: bpcmod@bpclaw.com.
San Francisco, California Office: 111 Pine Street, Suite 730.
Telephone: 415-981-4415.
Fax: 415-391-5538. Email: bpcsf@bpclaw.com.
Redding, California Office: 280 Hemsted Drive, Suite 100.
Telephone: 916-222-1530.
Fax: 916-222-4498. Email: bpcred@bpclaw.com.

(See Next Column)

San Bernardino, California Office: 290 North "D" Street, Suite 500.
Telephone: 909-381-0527.
Fax: 909-381-0658. Email: bpcsbdo@bpclaw.com.
San Jose, California Office: 2 North Second Street.
Telephone: 408-298-3997.
Fax: 408-298-3365. Email: bpcsj@bpclaw.com.
Ventura, California Office: 1000 Hill Road, Suite 310.
Telephone: 805-650-9994.
Fax: 805-650-7125. Email: bpcvta@bpclaw.com.
Santa Rosa, California Office: 50 Santa Rosa Avenue, Suite 300.
Telephone: 707-527-9477.
Fax: 707-527-9488. Email: bpcsr@bpclaw.com.

MEMBERS OF FIRM

Fred E. Borton (1877-1948)
James Petrini (1897-1978)
Harry M. Conron (1907-1971)
Kenneth D. Pinsent (1953-1984)
Richard E. Hitchcock
John F. Petrini

George F. Martin
Stephen M. Dake
Paul Lafranchise
Steven M. Karcher
Mark Alan Jones
Victoria R. Allard

ASSOCIATES

Craig N. Beardsley
Randall Steven Joyce
Wendy E. Coulston
Greg L. Ferrari
Brian E. Bisol
Tobias A. Dorsey
Richard E. Morton
Andrew C. Thomson
Joe W. Whittington
Elizabeth M. Giesick
Timothy C. Hale
J. David Bournazian
Linda M. Marschang
William H. Cantrell (Resident Member, Newport Beach Office)
J. David Petrie (Resident Member, Fresno Office)
Daniel L. Ferguson (Resident Member, San Bernardino Office)
Rocky K. Copley (Resident Member, San Diego Office)
Craig R. McCollum (Resident Member, San Luis Obispo Office)
Mark S. Newman (Resident Member, Sacramento Office)
James M. McKanna (Resident Member, San Luis Obispo, Office)
Richard M. Macias (Resident Member, Los Angeles Office)
Dale M. Dorfmeier (Resident Member, Fresno Office)
Phillip B. Greer (Resident Member, Newport Beach Office)
Robert H. Grove (Resident Member, Ventura Office)
Steven M. Shewry (Resident Member, San Diego Office)
Robert J. Gundert (Resident Member, San Luis Obispo Office)
Randall L. Harr (Resident Member, Redding Office)
George J. Hernandez, Jr. (Resident Member, Los Angeles Office)
Robert N. Ridenour (Resident Member, Los Angeles Office)
Rick D. Hardin (Resident Member, Santa Barbara Office)
Paul Kissel (Resident Member, San Diego Office)
Carla J. Hartley (Resident Member, San Francisco Office)
Sharon G. Pratt (Resident Member, San Jose Office)
Bradley A. Post (Resident Member, Modesto Office)
Michael J. Macko (Resident Member, Modesto Office)
Tracy W. Goldberg (Resident Member, San Bernardino Office)
Samuel L. Phillips (Resident Member, Modesto Office)
Calvin R. Stead (Resident Member, Santa Rosa Office)

Gary C. Harvey (Resident Member, Fresno Office)
Michael F. Long (Resident Member, Newport Beach Office)
Thomas A. Gifford (Resident Member, Sacramento Office)
Thomas J. Stoddard (Resident Member, San Diego Office)
Kenneth B. Arthofer (Resident Member, Redding Office)
Darlene M. Ball (Resident Member, Visalia Office)
Steven G. Gatley (Resident Member, Los Angeles Office)
Rosemarie Suazo Lewis (Resident Member, Los Angeles Office)
Dennis D. Resh (Resident Associate, Los Angeles Office)
R. Stephen Kinnaird (Resident Associate, Santa Barbara Office)
Thomas F. Brooks (Resident Member, Ventura Office)
Richard E. Korb (Resident Associate, San Francisco Office)
Nelson H. Chan (Resident Associate, Sacramento Office)
J. Albert Boada (Resident Associate, San Luis Obispo Office)
Tuvana B. Jeffrey (Resident Associate, San Francisco Office)
Gary A. Bixler (Resident Associate, San Luis Obispo Office)
Michael V. Peros (Resident Associate, San Bernardino Office)
Christopher Der Manuelian, Jr. (Resident Associate, San Jose Office)
Lynne L. Bentley (Resident Member, San Jose Office)
Barton C. Merrill (Resident Member, Santa Barbara Office)
Marc C. Gessford (Resident Associate, Sacramento Office)
Paige M. Hibbert (Resident Member, Sacramento Office)
Donald A. Diebold (Resident Associate, Newport Beach Office)
William F. Klausner (Resident Member, San Bernardino Office)
Arcangelo Clarizio (Resident Associate, Ventura Office)
Paul T. McBride (Resident Associate, Newport Beach Office)
Mark T. Coffin (Resident Associate, Santa Barbara Office)
Michelle L. Van Dyke (Resident Associate, San Diego Office)
Steven P. Owen (Resident Associate, Los Angeles Office)

(See Next Column)

BORTON, PETRINI & CONRON—Continued

ASSOCIATES (Continued)

Paul C. Clauss (Resident Associate, Santa Rosa Office)
Michael J. Boyajian (Resident Associate, Fresno Office)
Daniel J. Tekunoff (Resident Associate, Fresno Office)
Guy Chirinian (Resident Associate, Los Angeles Office)
Sharon P. McAleenan (Resident Associate, Los Angeles Office)
Alfred W. Mondorf (Resident Associate, Redding Office)
Robert D. Reed (Resident Associate, San Luis Obispo Office)
Carol D. Janssen (Resident Associate, San Luis Obispo Office)
Eric J. Larson (Resident Associate, San Diego Office)

Cari S. Baum (Resident Associate, Newport Beach Office)
Carolyn M. Kern (Resident Associate, Newport Beach Office)
Joyce M. Stovall (Resident Associate, San Bernardino Office)
Kari L. Rutherford (Resident Associate, San Bernardino Office)
Barton F. Hoey (Resident Associate, San Luis Obispo Office)
Janice K. Lachman (Resident Associate, Sacramento Office)
Greg Rubinoff (Resident Associate, Sacramento Office)

OF COUNSEL

Roy J. Gargano   Jere N. Sullivan, Sr.

Representative Clients: Castle and Cooke; Wells Fargo Bank; Pacific Gas & Electric.

For full biographical listings, see the Martindale-Hubbell Law Directory

KLEIN, WEGIS, DENATALE, GOLDNER & MUIR, LLP (AV)

A Partnership including Professional Corporations
(Formerly Di Giorgio, Davis, Klein, Wegis, Duggan & Friedman)
ARCO Tower, 4550 California Avenue, Second Floor, P.O. Box 11172, 93389-1172
Telephone: 805-395-1000
Telecopier: 805-326-0418
Email: kwdgm@kwdgm.com

Thomas R. Davis (1920-1990)

MEMBERS OF FIRM

Anthony J. Klein (Inc.)
Ralph B. Wegis (Inc.)
Thomas V. DeNatale, Jr.
Gregory A. Muir

Barry L. Goldner
Jay L. Rosenlieb
David J. Cooper
Claude P. Kimball

William A. Bruce

ASSOCIATES

Denise Martin
David L. Saine
Laurence C. Hall
William H. Slocumb
Ned E. Dunphy
Barry E. Rosenberg
Kirk S. Tracey
Christopher P. Burger

Kevin C. Findley
Carol J. Grogan
Jose Benavides
Michael S. Abril
Melvin L. Ehrlich
Krystyna L. Jamieson
Stacy Henry Bowman
Thomas J. Jamieson, Jr.

Jeffrey W. Noe

OF COUNSEL

Bruce F. Bunker

Representative Clients: Bank of America; Great Western Bank; Mojave Pipeline Co.; Transamerican Title Insurance Co.; Dean Whittier Reynolds, Inc.; California Republic Bank; San Joaquin Bank; Nahama & Weagant Energy Co.; Freymiller Trucking, Inc.; Westinghouse Electric Co.

For full biographical listings, see the Martindale-Hubbell Law Directory

ROBINSON, PALMER & LOGAN (AV)

Suite 150, 3434 Truxtun Avenue, 93301
Telephone: 805-323-8277
Fax: 805-323-4205

MEMBERS OF FIRM

Oliver U. Robinson   William D. Palmer

Gary L. Logan

ASSOCIATES

Luke A. Foster   Marshall S. Fontes

For full biographical listings, see the Martindale-Hubbell Law Directory

LAW OFFICES OF YOUNG WOOLDRIDGE (AV)

1800 30th Street, Fourth Floor, 93301
Telephone: 805-327-9661
Facsimile: 805-327-1087

MEMBERS OF FIRM

Joseph Wooldridge
A. Cameron Paulden (1927-1984)
Robert J. Self
G. Neil Farr

Michael R. Young
Ernest A. Conant
Steve W. Nichols
Larry R. Cox
Scott K. Kuney

Michael A. Kaia

(See Next Column)

ASSOCIATES

Russell B. Hicks
Vickie Y. Songer
Steven M. Torigiani

Scott D. Howry
David F. Leon
Todd A. Gall

OF COUNSEL

John B. Young   Edward M. Carpenter

James E. Millar

Representative Clients: Arvin-Edison Water Storage District; Motor City Truck Sales and Service.
References: Wells Fargo Bank; First Interstate Bank; California Republic Bank.

For full biographical listings, see the Martindale-Hubbell Law Directory

---

BEVERLY HILLS, Los Angeles Co.

NORMINTON & WIITA (AV)

A Partnership of Professional Corporations
433 North Camden Drive Twelfth Floor, 90210
Telephone: 310-288-5900
Facsimile: 310-288-5901
Email: norminton@aol.com

Thomas M. Norminton (P.C.)
Douglas P. Wiita (P.C.)

Kathleen Dority Fuster (P.C.).
A. Rick Atwood, Jr.

For full biographical listings, see the Martindale-Hubbell Law Directory

TURNER, GERSTENFELD, WILK, AUBERT & YOUNG, LLP (AV)

Formerly Turner, Gerstenfeld, Wilk & Tigerman
Suite 510, 8383 Wilshire Boulevard, 90211
Telephone: 213-653-3900
Facsimile: 213-653-3021

MEMBERS OF FIRM

Rubin M. Turner
Gerald F. Gerstenfeld
Barry R. Wilk
Ronald D. Aubert

Steven E. Young
Edward Friedman
Michael J. Hanna
Linda Wight Mazur

ASSOCIATES

Dortha Larene Pyles
Steven A. Morris

Diane H. Pappas
Vicki L. Cresap

OF COUNSEL

Bert Z. Tigerman

For full biographical listings, see the Martindale-Hubbell Law Directory

---

BURLINGAME, San Mateo Co.

CARR, MCCLELLAN, INGERSOLL, THOMPSON & HORN, PROFESSIONAL CORPORATION (AV)

216 Park Road, P.O. Box 513, 94011-0513
Telephone: 415-342-9600
Telecopier: 415-342-7685
Email: cmith@cmithlaw.com
San Francisco, California Office: Suite 1120, Four Embarcadero Center.
Telephone: 415-362-1400.
Telecopier: 415-362-5149.

E. H. Cosgriff (1880-1947)
J. Ed McClellan (1895-1985)
Robert R. Thompson (1921-1995)
Norman I. Book, Jr.
Robert A. Nebrig
Marion L. Brown
L. Michael Telleen
Lage E. Andersen
Keith P. Bartel
Mark A. Cassanego
Laurence M. May
Michael J. McQuaid

Penelope Creasey Greenberg
James R. Cody
Edward J. Willig, III
Sarah J. DiBoise
W. George Wailes
Carol B. Schwartz
Lori A. Lutzker
Moira C. Walsh
Jeremy W. Katz
Lisa Hayhurst Stalteri
Elizabeth A. Franklin
Steven D. Anderson
James F. Blood

SENIOR COUNSEL

Denny S. Roja

Todd L. Burlingame
Michele G. Dulsky

Michael D. Liberty
Wendy L. MacIlwaine

Terese M. Raddie

CHAIRMAN EMERITUS

Albert J. Horn

OF COUNSEL

Luther M. Carr (Retired)
Frank B. Ingersoll, Jr. (Retired)

Cyrus J. McMillan (Retired)
David C. Carr (Retired)

For full biographical listings, see the Martindale-Hubbell Law Directory

CHICO, Butte Co.

LEONARD & LYDE (AV)

A Partnership including Professional Corporations
1600 Humboldt Road, Suite 1, 95927
Telephone: 916-345-3494
Fax: 916-345-0460
Oroville, California Office: 1453 Huntoon Street.
Telephone: 916-533-2662.
Fax: 916-533-3843.

Raymond A. Leonard	C. Keith Lyde (Inc.)
(1961-1981)	Dorsett Marc Lyde

ASSOCIATES

Sharon A. Stone	Maria Lathrop Winter
	Larry S. Buckley

LEGAL SUPPORT PERSONNEL
Diana C. Berexa

For full biographical listings, see the Martindale-Hubbell Law Directory

PETERS, FULLER, RUSH, FARNSWORTH & HABIB (AV)

414 Salem Street, P.O. Box 3509, 95928
Telephone: 916-342-3593
FAX: 916-342-4272

MEMBERS OF FIRM

Jerome D. Peters, Jr.	James C. Farnsworth
David H. Rush	Mark A. Habib

ASSOCIATES

James P. McKenna	Harley A. Merritt

Local Counsel: Pacific Gas & Electric Co.; Southern Pacific Co.; Helena Chemical Co.; California Water Service Co. Insurance Companies: Great American Insurance Co.; Industrial Indemnity; Lloyds of London; Zurich Insurance Co.; U.S.F. & G.; Progressive Insurance Co.

For full biographical listings, see the Martindale-Hubbell Law Directory

CHULA VISTA, San Diego Co.

ATHERTON & ALLEN (AV)

210 Towne Centre Professional Building, 345 "F" Street, 91910
Telephone: 619-420-6869

MEMBERS OF FIRM

Harvey H. Atherton (1881-1972)	Keith Atherton (Retired)
	David R. Allen

For full biographical listings, see the Martindale-Hubbell Law Directory

*COLUSA,** Colusa Co. — (Refer to Marysville)

CORONA, Riverside Co.

CLAYSON, MANN & YAEGER, A PROFESSIONAL LAW CORPORATION (AV)

Clayson Law Building, 601 South Main Street, P.O. Box 1447, 91718-1447
Telephone: 909-737-1910
Riverside: 909-689-7241
Fax: 909-737-4384

Walter S. Clayson (1887-1972)	Gary K. Rosenzweig
E. Spurgeon Rothrock	Elisabeth Sichel
(1918-1979)	Kent A. Hansen
Roy H. Mann	Roland C. Bainer
Derrill E. Yaeger	David R. Saunders
	Sallie Barnett

Scott Carleton Brenner

Counsel for: Citizens Business Bank; Lee Lake Municipal Water District; Palo Verde Irrigation District; Loma Linda University.
Local Counsel: Minnesota Mining & Manufacturing Co.; Western Waste Industries.

For full biographical listings, see the Martindale-Hubbell Law Directory

COSTA MESA, Orange Co.

ELY, FRITZ & HOGAN (AV)

3100 Bristol Street #200, 92626
Telephone: 714-556-1480
Telecopier: 714-556-2863

MEMBERS OF FIRM

Thomas W. Ely	Michael G. Hogan
James H. Fritz	Jerome D. Rybarczyk

Charles A. Correia	Ronald F. Templer
	Allen D. MacNeil

(See Next Column)

OF COUNSEL
Gerald W. Mouzis

For full biographical listings, see the Martindale-Hubbell Law Directory

LAW OFFICES OF ROBERT J. FELDHAKE (AV)

Plaza Tower, Suite 1730, 600 Anton Boulevard, 92626-7124
Telephone: 714-438-3885
Fax: 714-438-3888
San Diego, California Office: 501 West Broadway, Suite 1600, Koll Center, 92101.
Telephone: 619-235-9443.
Facsimile: 619-235-9449.

ASSOCIATES

Gary W. Dolinski	Lorinda B. Harris
(Resident, San Diego Office)	

For full biographical listings, see the Martindale-Hubbell Law Directory

McCORMICK, KIDMAN & BEHRENS, LLP (AV)

A Partnership of Professional Corporations
Imperial Bank Building, 695 Town Center Drive Suite 1400, 92626-1924
Telephone: 714-755-3100
Fax: 714-755-3110; 1-800-755-3125
Email: mkb1@ix.netcom.com

MEMBERS OF FIRM

Homer L. (Mike) McCormick,	Russell G. Behrens (P.C.)
Jr., (P.C.)	Suzanne M. Tague (P.C.)
Arthur G. Kidman (P.C.)	Janet R. Morningstar (P.C.)
	Keith E. McCullough (P.C.)

ASSOCIATES

David D. Boyer	John O. Clune
Robert A. Johnson	Bradley D. Pierce

For full biographical listings, see the Martindale-Hubbell Law Directory

PAUL, HASTINGS, JANOFSKY & WALKER LLP (AV)

A Limited Liability Partnership including Professional Corporations
Firm Established in 1951; Office in 1974
Seventeenth Floor, 695 Town Center Drive, 92626-1924
Telephone: 714-668-6200
Fax: 714-979-1921
Email: info@PHJW.com *URL:* http://www.phjw.com
Los Angeles, California Office: Twenty-Third Floor, 555 South Flower Street.
Telephone: 213-683-6000.
Washington, D.C. Office: Tenth Floor, 1299 Pennsylvania Avenue, N.W.
Telephone: 202-508-9500.
Atlanta, Georgia Office: 24th Floor, 600 Peachtree Street, N.E.
Telephone: 404-815-2400.
Santa Monica, California Office: Fifth Floor, 1299 Ocean Avenue.
Telephone: 310-319-3300.
Stamford, Connecticut Office: Ninth Floor, 1055 Washington Boulevard.
Telephone: 203-961-7400.
New York, New York Office: 31st Floor, 399 Park Avenue.
Telephone: 212-318-6000.
Tokyo, Japan Office: Ark Mori Building, 30th Floor, 12-32 Akasaka, P.O. Box 577, 1-Chome, Minato-Ku.
Telephone: (03) 3586-4711.

COUNSEL

Oliver F. Green	Lee G. Paul

MEMBERS OF FIRM

Stephen D. Cooke	Michael A. Hood
Glenn D. Dassoff	Donald L. Morrow
Janet Toll Davidson	Douglas A. Schaaf
John F. Della Grotta	William J. Simpson
Howard C. Hay	Peter J. Tennyson
Matthew A. Hodel	John E. Trinnaman

SENIOR COUNSEL

Robert R. Burge	James W. Hamilton

OF COUNSEL

Mary L. Cornwell	Scott N. Leslie
Jason O. Engel	Sean A. O'Brien
	Darla L. Yancey

ASSOCIATES

Terry Jon Allen	Violet F. Fiacco
Steven D. Allison	Laura A. Forbes
Brent R. Bohn	Andrew P. Hanson
Glenn L. Briggs	Jarret L. Johnson
Robert P. Bryant	Lisa M. LaFourcade
Barbara R. Danz	Vincent D. Lowder
Jessica S. Dorman-Davis	Scott R. Miller
Malinda A. Faber	John B. Stephens

For full biographical listings, see the Martindale-Hubbell Law Directory

Costa Mesa—Continued

THE RUDOLPH LAW GROUP A PROFESSIONAL CORPORATION (AV)

3200 Park Center Drive, Suite 1370, 92626
Telephone: 714-545-7272; 714-757-7272
Fax: 714-545-7273

George C. Rudolph

For full biographical listings, see the Martindale-Hubbell Law Directory

RUTAN & TUCKER, LLP (AV)

A Partnership including Professional Corporations
611 Anton Boulevard, Suite 1400, P.O. Box 1950, 92626
Telephone: 714-641-5100; 213-625-7586
Telecopier: 714-546-9035
Email: rutan&tucker@mcimail.com *URL:* http://www.rutan.com

MEMBERS OF FIRM

James R. Moore (P.C.)	Philip D. Kohn
Paul Frederic Marx	Joel D. Kuperberg
William R. Biel	Steven A. Nichols
Richard A. Curnutt	Thomas G. Brockington
Leonard A. Hampel, Jr.	William W. Wynder
John B. Hurlbut, Jr.	Evridiki (Vicki) Dallas
Michael W. Immell	Randall M. Babbush
Milford W. Dahl, Jr.	Mary M. Green
Theodore I. Wallace, Jr., (P.C.)	Thomas J. Crane
Richard P. Sims	Mark B. Frazier
Robert C. Braun	M. Katherine Jenson
Edward D. Sybesma, Jr., (P.C.)	Duke Wahlquist
Thomas S. Salinger (P.C.)	Richard Montevideo
David C. Larsen (P.C.)	Lori Sarner Smith
Clifford E. Frieden	Ernest W. Klatte III
Michael D. Rubin	Elizabeth L. Martyn
Ira G. Rivin (P.C.)	Kim D. Thompson
Jeffrey M. Oderman (P.C.)	Jayne Taylor Kacer
Joseph D. Carruth	David B. Cosgrove
Stan Wolcott (P.C.)	Hans Van Ligten
Robert S. Bower	Stephen A. Ellis
David J. Aleshire	Matthew K. Ross
Marcia A. Forsyth	Jeffrey Wertheimer
William M. Marticorena	Robert Owen
James L. Morris	Adam N. Volkert
Anne Nelson Lanphar	Jeffrey A. Goldfarb
William J. Caplan	F. Kevin Brazil
Michael T. Hornak	Layne H. Melzer

Lien Ski Harrison

ASSOCIATES

Michael K. Slattery	Jennifer White-Sperling
Debra Dunn Steel	Robert Elliot Adel II
David H. Hochner	Anward Li
Elise K. Traynum	Steven M. Coleman
Dan Slater	Steven John Goon
James S. Weisz	Douglas J. Dennington
Carol Landis Demmler	Kara S. Carlson
Patrick D. McCalla	Sue Lee Collins
Richard K. Howell	Eric L. Dunn
A. Patrick Muñoz	Todd Owen Litfin
Paul J. Sievers	Steven M. Muldowney
S. Daniel Harbottle	Deborah J. Chuang
Joseph Louis Maga III	Natalie Sibbald Dundas
Kraig C. Kilger	Sean P. Farrell
Scott R. Santagata	Fred A. Jenkins
Sandra J. Young	Marlene Pose
Allen C. Ostergar III	April Lee Walter
Julia L. Bond	Karen E. Walter

OF COUNSEL

Garvin F. Shallenberger	David J. Garibaldi III

For full biographical listings, see the Martindale-Hubbell Law Directory

---

DOWNEY, Los Angeles Co.

TREDWAY, LUMSDAINE & DOYLE, LLP (AV)

10841 Paramount Boulevard, 90241-3397
Telephone: 310-923-0971; 714-750-0141
Telecopier: 310-869-4607
Irvine, California Office: Suite 1000, 1920 Main Street.
Telephone: 714-756-0684.
Telecopier: 714-756-0596.

MEMBERS OF FIRM

Joseph A. Lumsdaine	Michael A. Lanphere
Mark C. Doyle	(Resident, Irvine Office)
(Resident, Irvine Office)	Harold T. Tredway (Retired)
Jeffrey B. Singer	Matthew L. Kinley
(Resident, Irvine Office)	Lynn L. Walker (1951-1994)
Michele S. Ahrens	Gary Lieberman
Cheri A. Kadotani	Daniel R. Gold
(Resident, Irvine Office)	

(See Next Column)

Sharisse E. Molyneux	Joseph A. Maleki
	(Resident, Irvine Office)

OF COUNSEL

David A. Pasqualini (Resident, Irvine Office)
Reference: Southern California Bank.

For full biographical listings, see the Martindale-Hubbell Law Directory

---

EL CAJON, San Diego Co. — (Refer to San Diego)

EL CENTRO, Imperial Co.

EWING & JOHNSON, A PROFESSIONAL LAW CORPORATION (AV)

636 State Street, P.O. Box 2568, 92244
Telephone: 619-352-6371
Telecopier: 619-353-5355

William J. Ewing	Charles G. Johnson
	James K. Graves

Michael C. Cotugno

Representative Clients: Bonanza Farms, Inc.; Kandal Insurance Agency; Imperial Printers; Robert Hawk Farming; Foss Accountancy Corp.; T. C. Worthy Cash & Carry, Inc.; Val Rock, Inc.; Southland Geotechnical; I.V. Radiology Group; Phillips Cattle Co.

For full biographical listings, see the Martindale-Hubbell Law Directory

GRAY CARY WARE & FREIDENRICH, A PROFESSIONAL CORPORATION (AV)

Gray Cary Established in 1927
Ware & Freidenrich Established in 1969
1224 State Street, P.O. Box 2890, 92244
Telephone: 619-353-6140
Telecopier: 619-353-6228
Email: info@gcwf.com *URL:* http://www.gcwf.com
San Diego, California Office: 401 "B" Street, Suite 1700.
Telephone: 619-699-2700.
San Diego/Golden Triangle, California Office: 4365 Executive Drive, Suite 1600, 92121.
Telephone: 619-677-1400.
Fax: 619-677-1477.
Palo Alto, California Office: 400 Hamilton Avenue.
Telephone: 415-328-6561.
La Jolla, California Office: Suite 575, 1200 Prospect Street.
Telephone: 619-454-9101.

Jay W. Jeffcoat	Merrill F. Storms, Jr.

Representative Clients: American Bankers Life; Asgrow Seed; Boise Cascade; California State Automobile Assn.; Helena Chemical Co.; Hospital Council of San Diego and Imperial Counties; Imperial Valley Press/Brawley News; Unocal; Valley Independent Bank.

For full biographical listings, see the Martindale-Hubbell Law Directory

HORTON, KNOX, CARTER & FOOTE (AV)

Suite 101 Law Building, 895 Broadway, 92243
Telephone: 619-352-2821
Telefax: 619-352-8540
Email: hkcf@QUIX.net
Brawley, California Office: 195 South Second Street.
Telephone: 619-344-2360.
Fax: 619-344-9778.

MEMBERS OF FIRM

Harry W. Horton (1892-1966)	Frank A. Oswalt, III
James H. Carter (1918-1978)	Dennis H. Morita
Orlando B. Foote, III	Philip J. Krum, Jr.
John Penn Carter, III	Mercedes Z. Wheeler
	(Resident, Brawley Office)

ASSOCIATES

Thomas V. Barrington	Ruth Bermudez Montenegro
Bradley S. Ellis	Jeffrey M. Garber
Patrick M. Pace	Mathew M. McCormick

OF COUNSEL

Paul D. Engstrand

Representative Clients: Automobile Club of Southern Calif.; Imperial Irrigation District; Southern Pacific Co.; Reliance Insurance Cos.; Surplus Lines Adjusting Co.; Pioneer Memorial Hospital District; City of Imperial; San Diego Gas & Electric Co.; Chevron U.S.A.; Bixby Land Co.

For full biographical listings, see the Martindale-Hubbell Law Directory

---

EL TORO, Orange Co. — (Refer to Santa Ana)

EMERYVILLE, Alameda Co.

LEGAL STRATEGIES GROUP (AV)

5905 Christie Avenue, 94608
Telephone: 510-450-9600
Fax: 510-450-9601
URL: http://www.legalstrategies.com/lsgdemoindex3.html

Timothy R. Cahn	Peter H. Goldsmith
Joshua R. Floum	Vincent L. Johnson
Karen S. Frank	Leigh A. Kirmssé
Gregory S. Gilchrist	Louise E. Ma

Heather A. Young
OF COUNSEL
Robert J. Vizas

For full biographical listings, see the Martindale-Hubbell Law Directory

ESCONDIDO, San Diego Co.

LOUNSBERY, FERGUSON, ALTONA & PEAK, LLP (AV)

613 West Valley Parkway, Suite 345, 92025-2552
Telephone: 619-743-1201
Facsimile: 619-743-9926
Email: LFAPllp@aol.com

Kenneth H. Lounsbery	Erick R. Altona
David W. Ferguson	Helen Holmes Peak

Michelle J. Brown	Charles A. LePla
Kevin P. Sullivan	Daniel Lounsbery

OF COUNSEL

Garth O. Reid, Jr.	Curtis M. Fitzpatrick

For full biographical listings, see the Martindale-Hubbell Law Directory

EUREKA,* Humboldt Co.

HUBER & GOODWIN (AV)

Huber-Goodwin Building, 550 "I" Street, P.O. Box 23, 95502-0023
Telephone: 707-443-4573
Fax: 707-443-7182
Email: prior@humboldt1.com
Email: carson@humboldt1.com

MEMBERS OF FIRM

Milton L. Huber (1914-1994)	Norman C. Cissna (1923-1989)
G. Edward Goodwin (Retired)	Robert D. Prior
Dayton D. Murray, Jr.	William H. Carson, Jr.
(1923-1981)	

Representative Clients: D & B Cattle Co. (livestock); Simpson Timber Co.; Miller & Rellim Redwood Cos.; The Pacific Lumber Co.; Western Self Insurance Service (Workers Compensation); Hilfiker Pipe Co.

For full biographical listings, see the Martindale-Hubbell Law Directory

MITCHELL, BRISSO, DELANEY & VRIEZE (AV)

814 Seventh Street, P.O. Drawer 1008, 95502
Telephone: 707-443-5643
Fax: 707-444-9586

MEMBERS OF FIRM

Clifford B. Mitchell	Paul A. Brisso
Nancy K. Delaney	John M. Vrieze

C. Todd Endres
ASSOCIATES

William F. Mitchell	Cherie L. Evans

Russell Scott Gans
RETIRED PARTNER
Robert C. Dedekam

Representative Clients: Louisiana-Pacific Corp.; City of Eureka; Housing Authority; St. Joseph Health Systems; California Automobile Assn.; K Mart; Hertz Corp.; Walmart; StairMaster Sports/Medical Products, Inc.; Montgomery Ward.

For full biographical listings, see the Martindale-Hubbell Law Directory

FREMONT, Alameda Co. — (Refer to Hayward)

FRESNO,* Fresno Co.

BAKER, MANOCK & JENSEN, A PROFESSIONAL CORPORATION (AV)

5260 North Palm, Suite 421, 93704
Telephone: 209-432-5400
Fax: 209-432-5620

John H. Baker	Robert G. Fishman
Kendall L. Manock	Howard M. Zidenberg
Douglas B. Jensen	John L. B. Smith
Donald R. Fischbach	George L. Strasser

(See Next Column)

Joseph M. Marchini	Jeffrey A. Jaech
Craig A. Houghton	David M. Camenson
Andrew R. Weiss	Lisa M. Martin
Mark W. Snauffer	Gayle D. Hearst
James E. Shekoyan	Glenn J. Holder
Carl R. Refuerzo	Mark B. Canepa
John G. Michael	William S. Barcus
Christopher L. Campbell	Douglas M. Larsen
Robert D. Wilkinson	Michael W. Goldring

Randall J. Krause

Michele A. Engnath	Glenn A. Rowley
William M. White	Matthew Earl Hoffman
Kathleen A. Meehan	Colleen Schulthies
Gary B. Wells	James M. Cipolla
Richard S. Salinas	Mark E. Crone
Richard A. Ryan	Paul B. Mello
David E. Holland	Kristine R. Cerro
Glen F. Dorgan	Lisa A. Travis
Charles K. Manock	Jeffrey R. Ahronian

OF COUNSEL

Michelle T. Tutelian	Leonard I. Meyers

James E. Ganulin

Representative Clients: Bank of America NT&SA; Challenge Dairy Products, Inc.; Fresno Metropolitan Flood Control District; Metropolitan Life Insurance Co.; Norcal Mutual Insurance Co.; Wells Fargo Bank, N.A.; Sun-Maid Growers of California.

For full biographical listings, see the Martindale-Hubbell Law Directory

DOWLING, AARON & KEELER, INCORPORATED (AV)

Suite 200, 6051 North Fresno Street, 93710
Telephone: 209-432-4500
Fax: 209-432-4590
Email: dowling-law.com

Michael D. Dowling	Adolfo M. Corona
Richard M. Aaron	Philip David Kopp
Bruce S. Fraser	Rene Lastreto, II
William J. Keeler, Jr.	Francine Marie Kanne
John C. Ganahl	Christopher A. Brown

Richard E. Heatter	Michael P. Dowling
James C. Sherwood	Daniel T. Fitzpatrick

Mark D. Kruthers
OF COUNSEL

Daniel K. Whitehurst	Morris M. Sherr

Blaine Pettitt

Reference: Wells Fargo Bank (Main).

For full biographical listings, see the Martindale-Hubbell Law Directory

LANG, RICHERT & PATCH, A PROFESSIONAL CORPORATION (AV)

Fig Garden Financial Center, 5200 North Palm Avenue, 4th Floor, P.O. Box 40012, 93755
Telephone: 209-228-6700
Fax: 209-228-6727

Frank H. Lang	Victoria J. Salisch
William T. Richert (1937-1993)	Bradley A. Silva
Robert L. Patch, II	Charles Trudrung Taylor
Val W. Saldaña	Mark L. Creede
Douglas E. Noll	Peter N. Zeitler
Michael T. Hertz	Charles L. Doerksen

Laurie L. Quigley	Nabil E. Zumout
Douglas E. Griffin	Shawn H. Alikian

Thomas E. Gauthier

References: Wells Fargo Bank (Fresno Main Office).

For full biographical listings, see the Martindale-Hubbell Law Directory

THOMAS, SNELL, JAMISON, RUSSELL AND ASPERGER, A PROFESSIONAL CORPORATION (AV)

2445 Capitol Street, P.O. Box 1461, 93716
Telephone: 209-442-0600; 800-559-9009
Telecopier: 209-442-5078
Email: tsnell@cybergate.com

Howard B. Thomas (1912-1993)	Robert J. Tyler
Fenton Williamson, Jr.	Gerald D. Vinnard
(1926-1993)	E. Robert Wright
Roger E. Fipps	David M. Gilmore
Samuel C. Palmer, III	Russell O. Wood
James O. Demsey	Scott R. Shewan

Hilary A. Chittick

(See Next Column)

THOMAS, SNELL, JAMISON, RUSSELL AND ASPERGER A PROFESSIONAL CORPORATION—*Continued*

OF COUNSEL

William N. Snell
T. Newton Russell

Charles E. Small
James E. LaFollette

RETIRED

Paul Asperger (Retired)

Oliver M. Jamison (Retired)

Marcus Don Magness

Angela E. Taylor

Representative Clients: California Table Grape Commission; Gottschalk's, Inc.
Local Counsel for: Metropolitan Life Insurance Co.; PPG Industries; The Vendo Co.

For full biographical listings, see the Martindale-Hubbell Law Directory

---

GLENDALE, Los Angeles Co.

THOMAS & PRICE (AV)

535 North Brand Boulevard, 7th Floor, 91203
Telephone: 213-387-4800; 818-500-4800
FAX: 818-500-4822
Ventura, California Office: 1655 Mesa Verde Avenue, Suite 230.
Telephone: 805-642-6255.
Fax: 805-642-4580.

MEMBERS OF FIRM

Michael Thomas
Bonnie R. Louis

Craig R. Donahue
Maureen F. Thomas

ASSOCIATES

John P. DeGomez
Timothy A. Hodge
Linda B. Hurevitz

Christian E. Sanne
Benjimin M. Brees
Janet L. Keuper

Kevin M. McCormick

OF COUNSEL

Lawrence E. Price

For full biographical listings, see the Martindale-Hubbell Law Directory

---

HANFORD,* Kings Co.

GRISWOLD, LASALLE, COBB, DOWD & GIN, L.L.P. (AV)

311 North Douty Street, 93230
Telephone: 209-584-6656
Facsimile: 209-582-3106

Lyman D. Griswold (Retired)

Steven W. Cobb (1947-1993)

MEMBERS OF FIRM

Michael E. LaSalle
Robert M. Dowd

Robert W. Gin
Randy L. Edwards

Craig Griswold

ASSOCIATES

Jack G. Willis
Jim D. Lee

Jeffrey L. Levinson
A. David Medeiros

OF COUNSEL

Julienne L. Rynda

Representative Clients: Badasci Land Leveling, Inc.; David A. Bush, Inc.; Calcot, Ltd.; Kings County Housing Authority; Kings County Water District; Silvas Oil Co.; Stone Land Co.; Western Waste Industries; World Wide Sires, Inc.

For full biographical listings, see the Martindale-Hubbell Law Directory

---

HAYWARD, Alameda Co.

HALEY, PURCHIO, SAKAI & SMITH (AV)

P.O. Box 450, 22320 Foothill Boulevard, Suite 620, 94543
Telephone: 510-538-6400
Oakland: 510-351-1932

MEMBERS OF FIRM

J. Kenneth Birchfield
(1920-1978)

John K. Smith
Robert Sakai

Cynthia K. Smith

OF COUNSEL

John J. Purchio

Donald A. Pearce (1898-1982)

Marlin W. Haley (1910-1993)

Representative Clients: City Center Commercial (Shopping Center); Oak Hills, Walnut Hills, Creekwood (Apartment Complexes); R. Zaballos & Sons (General Contractors); Hospital Associates; Wolf Investment Co.; Chicago Title Company of Alameda County; Sunnyside Nurseries, Inc.; Mission Valley Rock Co. (quarry); LaVista Quarry.

For full biographical listings, see the Martindale-Hubbell Law Directory

---

HOLLISTER,* San Benito Co. — (Refer to Salinas)

INDIO, Riverside Co.

THOMAS T. ANDERSON, P.C. (AV)

45-926 Oasis Street, 92201
Telephone: 619-347-3364
Fax: 619-347-5572

Thomas T. Anderson

David M. Chapman

Samuel F. Trussell

Gregory T. Anderson

Reference: City National Bank.

For full biographical listings, see the Martindale-Hubbell Law Directory

---

IRVINE, Orange Co.

ALLEN, MATKINS, LECK, GAMBLE & MALLORY LLP (AV)

A Limited Liability Partnership including Professional Corporations
Fourth Floor, 18400 Von Karman, 92715
Telephone: 714-553-1313
Telecopier: 714-553-8354
Los Angeles, California Office: Seventh Floor, 515 South Figueroa Street, 90071.
Telephone: 213-622-5555.
Telecopier: 213-620-8816.
San Diego, California Office: 501 West Broadway, Suite 900, 92101.
Telephone: 619-233-1155.
Facsimile: 619-233-1158.
West Los Angeles, California Office: 1999 Avenue of the Stars, 90067.
Telephone: 310-788-2400.
Fax: 310-788-2410.

PARTNERS

John C. Gamble (Resident)
Thomas C. Foster (Resident)
R. Michael Joyce (Resident)
Lawrence D. Lewis (P.C.)
   (Resident)
Monica E. Olson (Resident)
Thomas E. Gibbs (Resident)
Dwight L. Armstrong (Resident)
Paul D. O'Connor (Resident)

S. Lee Hancock (Resident)
Richard E. Stinehart (Resident)
Stephen R. Thames (Resident)
Anne E. Klokow (Resident)
David W. Wensley (Resident)
Gary S. McKitterick (Resident)
Patrick J. Grady (Resident)
Robert M. Hamilton (Resident)
Vincent M. Coscino

RESIDENT ASSOCIATES

Bradley N. Schweitzer
Alan J. Gordee
Pamela L. Andes
Catherine M. Page
Leslie Tucker Fischer
Ralph H. Winter
Michael S. Greger
A. Kristine Floyd

Stephen J. Kepler
Michael A. Alvarado
Mary Kay Ruck
Susan E. Graham
Christopher G. Lund
Sally S. Costanzo
Allison Fong Greenberg
Jeffrey Mannisto

Tracy L Silva

For full biographical listings, see the Martindale-Hubbell Law Directory

---

BORCHARD & WILLOUGHBY, A PROFESSIONAL CORPORATION (AV)

18881 Von Karman Avenue, Suite 1400, 92612
Telephone: 714-644-6161
Fax: 714-263-1913

Michael D. Borchard

Michael L. Willoughby

Mark A. Rodriguez

Stephanie A. Pittaluga

For full biographical listings, see the Martindale-Hubbell Law Directory

---

CALLAHAN & BLAINE, A PROFESSIONAL LAW CORPORATION (AV)

Suite 800, 18500 Von Karman, 92612
Telephone: 714-553-1155
Fax: 714-553-0784
Email: info@callahan-law.com

Daniel J. Callahan (A
   Professional Corporation)

Stephen E. Blaine

Kathleen L. Dunham
Jim P. Mahacek
Michael J. Sachs

Andrew A. Smits
Gary S. Spitzer
Edward Susolik

Graig R. Woodburn

OF COUNSEL

Shelley M. Liberto

Walt D. Mahaffa

For full biographical listings, see the Martindale-Hubbell Law Directory

Irvine—Continued

CROWELL & MORING LLP (AV)

2010 Main Street, Suite 1200, 92714-7217
Telephone: 714-263-8400
Fax: 714-263-8414
Washington, D.C. Office: 1001 Pennsylvania Avenue, N.W.
Telephone: 202-624-2500.
Fax: 202-628-5116.
London, England Office: 180 Fleet Street, EC4A 2HD.
Telephone: 011-44-171-413-0011.
Fax: 011-44-171-413-0333.

MEMBERS OF FIRM

Donald E. Sovie   Randall L. Erickson
Michael D. Newman

OF COUNSEL

Linda M. Cipriani   Steven A. Fink
Steven P. Rice

ASSOCIATES

Cecelia A. Tripi   Diane Smith Daruty
Donald E. Bradley   Deborah E. Colaner
Stuart Einbinder   John F. Walsh

For full biographical listings, see the Martindale-Hubbell Law Directory

JONES, DAY, REAVIS & POGUE (AV)

2603 Main Street, Suite 900, 92714-6232
Telephone: 714-851-3939
Telex: 194911 Lawyers LSA
Telecopier: 714-553-7539
In Los Angeles, California: 555 West Fifth Street, Suite 4600.
Telephone: 213-489-3939.
Telex: 181439 UD.
Telecopier: 213-243-2539.
In Atlanta, Georgia: 3500 One Peachtree Center, 303 Peachtree Street, N.E.
Telephone: 404-521-3939.
Cable Address: "Attorneys Atlanta".
Telex: 54-2711.
Telecopier: 404-581-8330.
In Brussels, Belgium: Avenue Louise 480, 7th Floor, B-1050 Brussels.
Telephone: 32-2-645-14-11.
Telecopier: 32-2-645-14-45.
In Chicago, Illinois: 77 West Wacker.
Telephone: 312-782-3939.
Telecopier: 312-782-8585.
In Cleveland, Ohio: North Point, 901 Lakeside Avenue.
Telephone: 216-586-3939.
Cable Address: "Attorneys Cleveland."
Telex: 980389.
Telecopier: 216-579-0212.
In Columbus, Ohio: 1900 Huntington Center.
Telephone: 614-469-3939.
Cable Address: "Attorneys Columbus."
Telecopier: 614-461-4198.
In Dallas, Texas: 2300 Trammell Crow Center, 2001 Ross Avenue.
Telephone: 214-220-3939.
Cable Address: "Attorneys Dallas."
Telex: 730852.
Telecopier: 214-969-5100.
In Frankfurt, Germany: Triton Haus, Bockenheimer Landstrasse 42, 60323 Frankfurt am Main.
Telephone: 49-69-9726-3939.
Telecopier: 49-69-9726-3993.
In Geneva, Switzerland: 20, rue de Candolle.
Telephone: 41-22-320-2339.
Telecopier: 41-22-320-1232.
In Hong Kong: 29th Floor, Entertainment Building, 30 Queen's Road Central.
Telephone: 852-2526-6895.
Telecopier: 852-2868-5871.
In London, England: Bucklersbury House, 3 Queen Victoria Street.
Telephone: 44-171-236-3939.
Telecopier: 44-171-236-1113.
In New Delhi, India: Pathak & Associates, 13th Floor, Dr. Gopal Das Bhavan, 28 Barakhamba Road.
Telephone: 91-11-373-8793.
Telecopy: 91-11-335-3761.
In New York, New York: 599 Lexington Avenue.
Telephone: 212-326-3939.
Cable Address: "JONESDAY NEWYORK."
Telex: 237013 JDRP UR.
Telecopier: 212-755-7306.
In Paris, France: 62, rue du Faubourg Saint-Honore.
Telephone: 33-1-44-71-3939.
Telex: 290156 Surgoe.
Telecopier: 33-1-49-24-0471.
In Pittsburgh, Pennsylvania: 500 Grant Street, 31st Floor.
Telephone: 412-391-3939.
Cable Address: "Attorneys Pittsburgh."
Telecopier: 412-394-7959.

(See Next Column)

In Riyadh, Saudi Arabia: The International Law Firm, Sulaymaniyah Center, Tahlia Street, P.O. Box 22166.
Telephone: (966-1) 462-8866.
Telecopier: (966-1) 462-9001.
In Taipei, Taiwan: 8th Floor, 2 Tun Hwa South Road, Section 2.
Telephone: (886-2) 704-6808.
Telecopier: (886-2) 704-6791.
In Tokyo, Japan: Toranomon MT Building, 4th Floor, 10-3, Toranomon 3-Chome, Minato-ku, Tokyo 105, Japan.
Telephone: 81-3-3433-3939.
Telecopier: 81-3-5401-2725.
In Washington, D.C.: Metropolitan Square, 1450 G Street, N.W.
Telephone: 202-879-3939.
Cable Address: "Attorneys Washington."
Telex: 89-2410 ATTORNEYS WASH.
Telecopier: 202-737-2832.

MEMBERS OF FIRM IN IRVINE

Thomas R. Malcolm   Dulcie D. Brand
Richard J. Grabowski

ASSOCIATES

J. Scott Schoeffel   Jeffrey B. Kirzner
Mark D. Kemple   Michelle M. Nuszkiewicz
William E. Halle   Michael D. Fabiano
Marc K. Callahan   James L. Poth
Heather A. McConnell

For full biographical listings, see the Martindale-Hubbell Law Directory

LOBEL & OPERA, PROFESSIONAL CORPORATION (AV)

Suite 1100, 19800 MacArthur Boulevard, P.O. Box 19588, 92713
Telephone: 714-476-7400
Fax: 714-476-7444

William N. Lobel   Tavi Claire Stanley
Robert E. Opera   Metiner G. Kimel
Alan J. Friedman   Edward P. Christian
Pamela Z. Karger   Robert J. Mrofka
Cheryl A. Skigin   Hamid R. Rafatjoo

For full biographical listings, see the Martindale-Hubbell Law Directory

MAHER, LEE & GODDARD, LLP (AV)

18500 Von Karman Avenue, Suite 700, 92715
Telephone: 714-721-7555
Facsimile: 714-721-7444

Michael K. Maher   Cynthia R. Maher
Raymond A. Lee   Sherman O. Halstead, Jr.
William A. Goddard, IV   Maureen M. Alpin

For full biographical listings, see the Martindale-Hubbell Law Directory

MESERVE, MUMPER & HUGHES (AV)

A Partnership
2301 Dupont Drive, Suite 410, 92612
Telephone: 714-474-8995
Telecopier: 714-975-1065
Email: mmhir@ix.netcom.com
Los Angeles, California Office: 555 South Flower Street, 18th Floor.
Telephone: 213-620-0300.
Telecopier: 213-625-1930.
San Diego, California Office: 701 "B" Street, Suite 1080.
Telephone: 619-237-0500.
Telecopier: 619-237-0073.

MEMBERS OF FIRM

Edwin A. Meserve (1863-1955)   Bernard A. Leckie
Shirley E. Meserve (1889-1959)   David R. Eichten
Hewlings Mumper (1889-1968)   Timothy A. Gravitt
Clifford E. Hughes (1894-1981)   E. Avery Crary
Lisa A. Roquemore

OF COUNSEL

J. Robert Meserve   Gary V. Spencer

ASSOCIATES

Joseph B. McGinley   Wendy C. Satuloff

For full biographical listings, see the Martindale-Hubbell Law Directory

PALMIERI, TYLER, WIENER, WILHELM & WALDRON, LLP (AV)

A Limited Liability Partnership including Professional Corporations
East Tower - Suite 1300, 2603 Main Street, P.O. Box 19712, 92614-6228
Telephone: 714-851-9400
Telecopier: 714-851-1554; 851-3844; 757-1225
Email: general@ptwww.com

MEMBERS OF FIRM

Angelo J. Palmieri (A Professional Corporation) (1926-1996)   Alan H. Wiener (A Professional Corporation)
Robert F. Waldron (A Professional Corporation)   Robert C. Ihrke (A Professional Corporation)

(See Next Column)

PALMIERI, TYLER, WIENER, WILHELM & WALDRON LLP—*Continued*

MEMBERS OF FIRM (Continued)

James E. Wilhelm (A Professional Corporation)	George J. Wall
Dennis G. Tyler (A Professional Corporation)	L. Richard Rawls
	Patrick A. Hennessey
Michael J. Greene (A Professional Corporation)	Don Fisher
	Gregory N. Weiler
Frank C. Rothrock (A Professional Corporation)	Warren A. Williams
	John R. Lister
Dennis W. Ghan (A Professional Corporation)	Bruce W. Dannemeyer
	Cynthia M. Wolcott
David D. Parr (A Professional Corporation)	Joel P. Kew
	Michelle M. Fujimoto
Charles H. Kanter (A Professional Corporation)	Gary C. Weisberg
	Michael H. Leifer

Norman J. Rodich	Cynthia B. Paulsen
Michele D. Murphy	Sean P. O'Connor
Scott R. Carpenter	Susan T. Sakura
Richard A. Salus	Jennifer Anne Kim
D. Susan Wiens	Matthew W. Paskerian
Ronald M. Cole	Paul B. La Scalla

For full biographical listings, see the Martindale-Hubbell Law Directory

SIKORA AND PRICE, INCORPORATED (AV)

10 Corporate Park Suite 300, 92606
Telephone: 714-261-2233
Telecopier: 714-261-6935

Warren Sikora	Steven C. Crooke
Donald R. Price	Bruce J. Gary

For full biographical listings, see the Martindale-Hubbell Law Directory

SNELL & WILMER, L.L.P. (AV)

1920 Main Street, Suite 1200, 92614
Telephone: 714-253-2700
FAX: 714-955-2507
URL: http://www.swlaw.com
Phoenix, Arizona Office: One Arizona Center, 85004-0001.
Telephone: 602-382-6000.
Fax: 602-382-6070.
Tucson, Arizona Office: Norwest Tower, Suite 1500, One South Church Avenue, 85701-1612.
Telephone: 520-882-1200.
Fax: 520-884-1294.
Salt Lake City, Utah Office: Broadway Centre, 111 East Broadway, Suite 900, 84111-1004.
Telephone: 801-237-1900.
Fax: 801-237-1950.

MEMBERS OF FIRM

Robert J. Gibson (Resident)	Gilbert N. Kruger (Resident)
Arthur P. Greenfield	Charles W. Hurst (Resident)
Creighton D. Mills (Resident)	David W. Evans (Resident)
Steven T. Graham (Resident)	Richard A. Derevan
Christy D. Joseph	Randolph T. Moore
William S. O'Hare, Jr. (Resident)	Nanette D. Sanders
	Luke A. Torres (Resident)
Diane R. Smith (Resident)	Gregg Amber
Gary A. Wolensky (Resident)	Penelope Parmes
Frank Cronin	

ASSOCIATES

Shara C. Beral	Ronald T. Labriola
Tiffanny Brosnan	Cristy G. Lomenzo
Larry A. Cerutti	Jeffrey Scott Marks
Kent M. Clayton	Michael B. Reynolds
Alexander L. Conti	Daniel S. Rodman
Ellen L. Darling	Gerda M. Roy
Lisa M. Farrington	Julianne Sartain
Jon J. Janecek	Sean Michael Sherlock
Martin W. Taylor	

For full biographical listings, see the Martindale-Hubbell Law Directory

WATT, TIEDER & HOFFAR, L.L.P. (AV①)

3 Park Plaza, Suite 1530, 92714
Telephone: 714-852-6700
Telecopier: 714-261-0771
McLean Virginia Office: 7929 Westpark Drive, Suite 400,
Telephone: 703-749-1000.
Telecopier: 703-893-8029.
Washington, D.C. Office: 601 Pennsylvania Avenue, N.W. Suite 900,
Telephone: 202-462-4697.

MEMBERS OF FIRM

John B. Tieder, Jr. (Not admitted in CA)	Michael G. Long
	Christopher P. Pappas
Robert M. Fitzgerald (Not admitted in CA)	

(See Next Column)

ASSOCIATE
Gregory John Dukellis

For full biographical listings, see the Martindale-Hubbell Law Directory

JACKSON,* Amador Co. — (Refer to Stockton)

LAGUNA BEACH, Orange Co.

WARREN FINLEY (AV)

564 Vista Lane, 92651
Telephone: 714-494-8960
Facsimile: 714-497-8477
Email: WFinley@SurEmail.com *URL:* http://www.SurEmail.com/finley

For full biographical listings, see the Martindale-Hubbell Law Directory

LA JOLLA, San Diego Co.

GRAY CARY WARE & FREIDENRICH, A PROFESSIONAL CORPORATION (AV)

Suite 575, 1200 Prospect Street, 92037
Telephone: 619-454-9101
Telecopier: 619-456-3075
Email: info@gcwf.com *URL:* http://www.gcwf.com
San Diego, California Office: 401 "B" Street, Suite 1700.
Telephone: 619-699-2700.
San Diego/Golden Triangle, California Office: 4365 Executive Drive, Suite 1600, 92121.
Telephone: 619-677-1400.
Fax: 619-677-1477.
Palo Alto, California Office: 400 Hamilton Avenue.
Telephone: 415-328-6561.
El Centro, California Office: 1224 State Street, P.O. Box 2890.
Telephone: 619-353-6140.

Theodore J. Cranston (Resident, San Diego/Golden Triangle Office)	Ellen H. Whelan (Resident, San Diego/Golden Triangle Office)
	Karl Zobell
Melitta Fleck (Resident, San Diego/Golden Triangle Office)	(Resident, La Jolla Office)

Mildred Basden, Resident, San Diego/Golden Triangle Office)

Representative Clients: The Copley Press, Inc.; Home Capital Corp.; Dr. Seuss Foundation; Ernest W. Hahn, Inc.; Imperial Corporation of America; La Jolla Bank & Trust Co.; La Jolla Real Estate Brokers Association; Merrill, Lynch, Pierce, Fenner & Smith; Scripps Clinic and Research Foundation; Timkin-Sturgis Foundation.

For full biographical listings, see the Martindale-Hubbell Law Directory

LUCE, FORWARD, HAMILTON & SCRIPPS LLP (AV)

A Partnership including Professional Corporations
La Jolla Golden Triangle, 4275 Executive Square, Suite 800, 92037
Telephone: 619-535-2639
Fax: 619-453-2812
URL: http://www.luce.com
San Diego, California Office: 600 West Broadway, Suite 2600, 92101.
Telephone: 619-236-1414.
Fax: 619-232-8311.
Los Angeles, California Office: 777 South Figueroa, Suite 3600, 90017.
Telephone: 213-892-4992.
Fax: 213-892-7731.
San Francisco, California Office: 100 Bush Street, 20th Floor, 94104.
Telephone: 415-395-7900.
Fax: 415-395-7949.
New York, N.Y. Office: Citicorp Center, 153 East 53rd Street, 26th Floor, 10022.
Telephone: 212-754-1414.
Fax: 212-644-9727.
Chicago, Illinois Office: 180 North La Salle Street, Suite 1125, 60601.
Telephone: 312-641-0580.
Fax: 312-641-0380.

MEMBERS OF FIRM

Jack G. Charney	Frederick R. Vandeveer
Robert J. Durham, Jr.	Mary F. Gillick
Daniel N. Riesenberg	

ASSOCIATES

Carol K. Kao	Philip J. Sullivan

For full biographical listings, see the Martindale-Hubbell Law Directory

LANCASTER, Los Angeles Co.

COSGROVE, MICHELIZZI, SCHWABACHER, WARD & BIANCHI, A PROFESSIONAL CORPORATION (AV)

767 West Lancaster Boulevard, 93534-3135
Telephone: 805-948-5021
Telecopier: 805-948-5395

(See Next Column)

COSGROVE, MICHELIZZI, SCHWABACHER, WARD & BIANCHI A PROFESSIONAL CORPORATION, *Lancaster—Continued*

Philip M. Schwabacher (1913-1993)	Frank G. Michelizzi
Leonard A. Cosgrove	Thomas J. Ward
	David W. Bianchi
David T. Collins	

James Lillicrap   Kevin L. Von Tungeln

For full biographical listings, see the Martindale-Hubbell Law Directory

---

LODI, San Joaquin Co. — (Refer to Stockton)

LONG BEACH, Los Angeles Co.

LAW OFFICES OF JAMES H. ACKERMAN (AV)

Suite 1440, One World Trade Center, 90831-1440
Telephone: 310-436-9911
Cable Address: "Jimack"
Telecopier: 310-436-1897

References: Farmers and Merchants Bank (Long Beach Main Office); Sumitomo Bank of California (Long Beach Main Office).

For full biographical listings, see the Martindale-Hubbell Law Directory

BAKER & HOSTETLER (AV)

300 Oceangate, Suite 620, 90802-6807
Telephone: 310-432-2827
FAX: 310-432-6698
In Cleveland, Ohio: 3200 National City Center, 1900 East Ninth Street.
Telephone: 216-621-0200.
In Columbus, Ohio: Capitol Square, Suite 2100, 65 East State Street.
Telephone: 614-228-1541.
In Denver, Colorado: 303 East 17th Avenue, Suite 1100.
Telephone: 303-861-0600.
In Houston, Texas: 1000 Louisiana, Suite 2000.
Telephone: 713-236-0020.
In Los Angeles, California: 600 Wilshire Boulevard.
Telephone: 213-624-2400.
In Orlando, Florida: SunBank Center, Suite 2300, 200 South Orange Avenue.
Telephone: 407-649-4000.
In Washington, D. C.: Washington Square, Suite 1100, 1050 Connecticut Avenue, N. W.
Telephone: 202-861-1500.
In College Park, Maryland: 9658 Baltimore Boulevard, Suite 206.
Telephone: 301-441-2781.
In Alexandria, Virginia: 437 North Lee Street.
Telephone: 703-549-1294.
In San Francisco, California: One Sansome Street, Suite 2000.
Telephone: 415-951-4705.

MEMBERS OF FIRM IN LONG BEACH, CALIFORNIA
Sheldon A. Gebb (Managing Partner, Los Angeles and Long Beach, California and Houston, Texas Offices)

PARTNERS
Robert E. Coppola (Partner in Charge)	David A. Kettel
	George T. Mooradian
Christina L. Owen	

ASSOCIATES
Kenneth E. Johnson	Steven Y. Otera
George M. Jones	Robert M. White, Jr.

OF COUNSEL
Herbert W. Kalmbach

For full biographical listings, see the Martindale-Hubbell Law Directory

CAYER, KILSTOFTE & CRATON, A PROFESSIONAL LAW CORPORATION (AV)

Suite 700, 444 West Ocean Boulevard, 90802
Telephone: 310-435-6008
Fax: 310-435-3704
Email: CKCCRC@AOL.COM

John J. Cayer	Stephen R. Kilstofte
	Curt R. Craton

Cortlen R. Hauge

For full biographical listings, see the Martindale-Hubbell Law Directory

FISHER & PORTER, A LAW CORPORATION (AV)

110 Pine Avenue, 11th Floor, P.O. Box 22686, 90801-5686
Telephone: 310-435-5626
Telex: 284549 FPKLAW UR
Fax: 310-432-5399

(See Next Column)

Gerald M. Fisher	Therese G. Groff
David S. Porter	Michael W. Lodwick
	George P. Hassapis

OF COUNSEL
Stephen C. Klausen	Stephen Chace Bass
	Anthony P. Lombardo

Vicki L. Hassman	Michael J. McLaughlin
Linda A. Mancini	Sandra L. Gryder
	Kenneth F. Mattfeld

For full biographical listings, see the Martindale-Hubbell Law Directory

FORD, WALKER, HAGGERTY & BEHAR, PROFESSIONAL LAW CORPORATION (AV)

One World Trade Center, Twenty Seventh Floor, 90831
Telephone: 310-983-2500
Telecopier: 310-983-2555

G. Richard Ford	Donna Rogers Kirby
Timothy L. Walker	Tina Ivankovic Mangarpan
William C. Haggerty	Susan D. Berger
Jeffrey S. Behar	Joseph A. Heath
Mark Steven Hennings	Robert J. Chavez
J. Michael McClure	

Arthur W. Schultz	Theodore A. Clapp
Jon T. Moseley	Stanley L. Scarlett
Maxine J. Lebowitz	Scott A. Ritsema
Timothy P. McDonald	Michael Guy Martin
K. Michele Williams	Colleen A. Strong
Stephen Ward Moore	Thomas L. Gourde
James D. Savage	Patrick J. Stark
Todd D. Pearl	Shayne L. Wulterin
Patrick J. Gibbs	Charles D. Jarrell
James O. Miller	Charles J. Schmitt
David Huchel	Kyle A. Ostergrad
Robert Reisinger	Todd L. Kessler

OF COUNSEL
Theodore P. Shield, P.L.C.

For full biographical listings, see the Martindale-Hubbell Law Directory

RUSSELL & MIRKOVICH (AV)

One World Trade Center, Suite 1450, 90831-1450
Telephone: 310-436-9911
FAX: 310-436-1897

Carlton E. Russell   Joseph N. Mirkovich

For full biographical listings, see the Martindale-Hubbell Law Directory

TAUBMAN, SIMPSON, YOUNG & SULENTOR (AV)

249 East Ocean Boulevard, Suite 700, P.O. Box 22670, 90801-5670
Telephone: 310-436-9201
FAX: 310-590-9695

E. C. Denio (1864-1952)	Richard G. Wilson (1928-1993)
Geo. A. Hart (1881-1967)	Roger W. Young
Geo. P. Taubman, Jr. (1897-1970)	William J. Sulentor
	Peter M. Williams
Matthew C. Simpson (1900-1988)	Scott R. Magee
	Maria M. Rohaidy
Stuart C. Talley	

Attorneys for: Bixby Land Co.; Renick Cadillac, Inc.; Oil Operators Inc.
Local Counsel: Crown Cork & Seal Co., Inc.

For full biographical listings, see the Martindale-Hubbell Law Directory

WILLIAMS WOOLLEY COGSWELL NAKAZAWA & RUSSELL (AV)

111 West Ocean Boulevard, Suite 2000, 90802-4614
Telephone: 310-495-6000
Telecopier: 310-435-1359; 310-435-6812
Telex: ITT: 4933872; WU: 984929
Email: wwlaw@msn.com
Rancho Santa Fe, California Office: P.O. Box 9120, 16236 San Dieguito Road, Building 3, Suite 3-15, 92067.
Telephone: 619-497-0284.
Fax: 619-759-9938.
Port Hueneme, California Office: 237 E. Hueneme Road, Suite A, 93041.
Telephone: 805-488-8560.
Fax: 805-488-7896.

MEMBERS OF FIRM
Reed M. Williams	Alan Nakazawa
David E. R. Woolley	Blake W. Larkin
Forrest R. Cogswell	Thomas A. Russell

(See Next Column)

WILLIAMS WOOLLEY COGSWELL NAKAZAWA & RUSSELL—*Continued*

ASSOCIATES

Todd A. Valdes
Thomas G. Walsh
Richard J. Nikas

For full biographical listings, see the Martindale-Hubbell Law Directory

WISE, WIEZOREK, TIMMONS & WISE, A PROFESSIONAL CORPORATION (AV)

3700 Santa Fe Avenue, Suite 300, P.O. Box 2190, 90810
Telephone: 310-834-5028
Fax: 310-834-8018
Redding, California Office: 443 Redcliff Drive, Suite 230.
Telephone: 916-221-7632.
Fax: 916-221-8832.

George E. Wise
Duane H. Timmons
Anthony F. Wiezorek
Susan E. Anderson Wise
Albert F. Padley, III
Michael J. Pearce
Mark C. Allen, III

Richard P. Dieffenbach
Steven C. Rice
Stephen M. Smith
Thomas J. Yocis
James M. Cox
Mathew J. Vande Wydeven
Tae J. Im

For full biographical listings, see the Martindale-Hubbell Law Directory

---

LOS ALTOS, Santa Clara Co.

MALOVOS & KONEVICH (AV)

Los Altos Plaza, 5150 El Camino Real, Suite A-22, 94022
Telephone: 415-988-9700
Facsimile: 415-988-9639

Marian Malovos Konevich
Robert W. Konevich

RETIRED FOUNDING PARTNER
Kenneth R. Malovos

For full biographical listings, see the Martindale-Hubbell Law Directory

---

LOS ANGELES,* Los Angeles Co.

ALLEN, MATKINS, LECK, GAMBLE & MALLORY LLP (AV)

A Limited Liability Partnership including Professional Corporations
Seventh Floor, 515 South Figueroa Street, 90071
Telephone: 213-622-5555
Telecopier: 213-620-8816
Irvine, California Office: Fourth Floor, 18400 Von Karman, 92715.
Telephone: 714-553-1313.
Telecopier: 714-553-8354.
San Diego, California Office: 501 West Broadway, Suite 900, 92101.
Telephone: 619-233-1155.
Facsimile: 619-233-1158.
West Los Angeles, California Office: 1999 Avenue of the Stars, Suite 1800, 90067.
Telephone: 310-788-2400.
Fax: 310-788-2410.

PARTNERS

Frederick L. Allen
John C. Gamble
  (Resident, Irvine Office)
Brian C. Leck
Richard C. Mallory
Michael L. Matkins
Marvin E. Garrett
Michael E. Gleason (P.C.)
  (Resident, San Diego Office)
Thomas C. Foster
  (Resident, Irvine Office)
Robert J. Cathcart
R. Michael Joyce
  (Resident, Irvine Office)
Gerben Hoeksma
Thomas W. Henning
Patrick E. Breen
Lawrence D. Lewis (P.C.)
  (Resident, Irvine Office)
George T. McDonnell
Michael F. Sfregola
David A. B. Burton (P.C.)
Monica E. Olson
  (Resident, Irvine Office)
Thomas E. Gibbs
  (Resident, Irvine Office)
Vernon C. Gauntt
  (Resident, San Diego Office)
Dwight L. Armstrong
  (Resident, Irvine Office)
Paul D. O'Connor
  (Resident, Irvine Office)
S. Lee Hancock
  (Resident, Irvine Office)
David L. Osias

William R. Harmsen
Debra Dison Hall
Anton N. Natsis
George J. Berger
  (Resident, San Diego Office)
Michael C. Pruter
  (Resident, San Diego Office)
Michael H. Cerrina
Richard E. Stinehart
  (Resident, Irvine Office)
Stephen R. Thames
  (Resident, Irvine Office)
John K. McKay
Dana I. Schiffman
  (Resident, San Diego Office)
Anne E. Klokow
  (Resident, Irvine Office)
Neil N. Gluck
David W. Wensley
  (Resident, Irvine Office)
Gary S. McKitterick
  (Resident, Irvine Office)
Patrick J. Grady
  (Resident, Irvine Office)
Ray B. Gliner
  (Resident, San Diego Office)
Anthony S. Bouza
Charles N. Kenworthy
  (Resident, West Los Angeles Office)
Anthony J. Oliva
Robert M. Hamilton
  (Resident, Irvine Office)
David R. Zaro
Janet A. Winnick

(See Next Column)

PARTNERS (Continued)

Robert R. Barnes
  (Resident, San Diego Office)
Vincent M. Coscino
Jeffrey R. Patterson
  (Resident, San Diego Office)

Mark R. Hartney
John M. Tipton (Resident, West Los Angeles Office)

ASSOCIATES

Cheryl S. Rivers
Craig D. Swanson
  (Resident, San Diego Office)
Bradley N. Schweitzer
  (Resident, Irvine Office)
Gregory G. Gorman
Alan J. Gordee
  (Resident, Irvine Office)
Pamela L. Andes
  (Resident, Irvine Office)
Rebecca L. Gundzik
Adela Carrasco (Resident, West Los Angeles Office)
Martha K. Guy
  (Resident, San Diego Office)
George W. Kuney
  (Resident, San Diego Office)
Daniel L. Goodkin
Catherine M. Page
  (Resident, Irvine Office)
Scott P. Schomer
Kelli L. Fuller
  (Resident, San Diego Office)
Leslie Tucker Fischer
  (Resident, Irvine Office)
Michael J. Kiely
David Adam Swartz (Resident, West Los Angeles Office)
Ralph H. Winter
  (Resident, Irvine Office)
Michael S. Greger
  (Resident, Irvine Office)
A. Kristine Floyd
  (Resident, Irvine Office)
Robert A. Lurie (Resident, West Los Angeles Office)
Susan G. Spira
Cynthia Ann Eder
Michael A. Alvarado
  (Resident, Irvine Office)
Hadar Gonen Goldstein
Mary Kay Ruck
  (Resident, Irvine Office)

Eric J. Shelby (Resident, West Los Angeles Office)
Susan E. Graham
  (Resident, Irvine Office)
Martin L. Togni
  (Resident, San Diego Office)
David T. Hathaway
Christopher G. Lund
  (Resident, Irvine Office)
Loraine L. Pedowitz
  (Resident, San Diego Office)
Randy J. Myricks
John G. Piano
Mark J. Hattam
  (Resident, San Diego Office)
Michael R. Farrell
Stephen J. Kepler
  (Resident, Irvine Office)
Steve Wellington
  (Resident, San Diego Office)
Sally S. Costanzo
  (Resident, Irvine Office)
Ann Marie Maas
  (Resident, San Diego Office)
Todd E. Whitman
Allison L. Malin (Resident, West Los Angeles Office)
Reon Roski-Amendola
  (Resident, West Los Angeles Office)
Allison Fong Greenberg
  (Resident, Irvine Office)
Jeffrey Mannisto
  (Resident, Irvine Office)
Pamela M. Everett
Jeffrey N. Strug
Kathryn D. Horning
Jordan Fishman (Resident, West Los Angeles Office)
Tracy L Silva
  (Resident, Irvine Office)
Francis N. Scollan
Darren A. Manibog

Veena D. Persaud

OF COUNSEL

John G. Davies
  (Resident, San Diego Office)
Joe M. Davidson
  (Resident, San Diego Office)

Michael J. Murphy

Reference: Wells Fargo Bank (Los Angeles Main Office).

For full biographical listings, see the Martindale-Hubbell Law Directory

---

ALSCHULER GROSSMAN & PINES LLP (AV)

2049 Century Park East, Thirty-Ninth Floor, 90067-3213
Telephone: 310-277-1226
Fax: 310-552-6077
Email: info@agplaw.com *URL:* http://www.agplaw.com

MEMBERS OF FIRM

Leon S. Alschuler (1910-1987)
Daniel Alberstone
Bruce D. Andelson
Jeffrey C. Briggs
Michael J. Brill (P.C.)
Michael L. Cypers
Melvyn B. Fliegel (P.C.)
Andrew D. Friedman
Bruce A. Friedman (P.C.)
Dale J. Goldsmith
Marshall B. Grossman (P.C.)
Carole E. Handler
Gerald B. Kagan (P.C.)
Frank Kaplan (P.C.)

Karen Kaplowitz (P.C.)
Dana N. Levitt (P.C.)
Kenneth S. Meyers
Burt Pines (P.C.)
Gwyn Quillen
Paul H. Rochmes
John A. Schwimmer
Michael A. Sherman
Sandra G. Slon
William S. Small (P.C.)
Pierre Vogelenzang (P.C.)
Bruce Warner (P.C.)
Karen Africk Wolfen
Joan A. Wolff

ASSOCIATES

M. Cris Armenta
Betty Bales
Julian Brew
Rebecca Edelson
Yael Feinreich
Grant E. Finkle

Donald P. Harris
Johnnie A. James
Caroline S. Lee
Jonathan A. Loeb
Dana Milmeister
Jeffrey H. Mintz

Michael A. Taitelman

OF COUNSEL

Stanley S. Arkin
Eric van Ginkel

(See Next Column)

ALSCHULER GROSSMAN & PINES LLP, *Los Angeles—Continued*

LEGAL SUPPORT PERSONNEL

Denise J. Grigst (Librarian)   W. Jack Kessler
(Executive Director)

For full biographical listings, see the Martindale-Hubbell Law Directory

ANDREWS & KURTH L.L.P. (AV)

Suite 4200, 601 S. Figueroa Street, 90017
Telephone: 213-896-3100
Telecopier: 213-896-3137
Houston, Texas Office: Suite 4200, 600 Travis, 77002.
Telephone: 713-220-4200.
Telecopier: 713-220-4285. E-Mail: webmaster@andrews-kurth.com.
Washington, D.C. Office: Suite 200, 1701 Pennsylvania Avenue, N.W.
Telephone: 202-662-2700.
Telecopier: 213-896-3137.
Dallas, Texas Office: Suite 4400, 1601 Elm Street.
Telephone: 214-979-4400.
Telecopier: 214-979-4401.
The Woodlands, Texas Office: Suite 150, 2170 Buckthorne Place, 77380.
Telephone: 713-220-4801.
Telecopier: 713-364-9538. E-Mail: hightech@andrews-kurth.com.
New York, N.Y. Office: 425 Lexington Avenue.
Telephone: 212-850-2800.
Telecopier: 212-850-2929.
London, England Office: 2 Creed Court, 5-11 Ludgate Hill, EC4M 7AA.
Telephone: 0171-236-3456.
Telefax: 0171-236-4276.

MEMBERS OF FIRM

Steven H. Haney   Carl B. Phelps
David J. Johnson, Jr.   Shelly Rothschild
William H. Lancaster   Ralph W. Tarr
Michael T. Williams

OF COUNSEL

Marta Thoerner Kurland   Diane C. Weil

ASSOCIATES

Damon C. Anastasia   Gregg J. Loubier
Graeme Lawrence Currie   David W. Meadows
Jon L. R. Dalberg   Gabriela Mejia
John L. House   Audra M. Mori
Diana J. Hunt   Rebecca O'Malley
Charles Gustaf Klink   Daniel F. Passage
(Not admitted in CA)   (Not admitted in CA)
Steven L. Satz

For full biographical listings, see the Martindale-Hubbell Law Directory

ARTER & HADDEN (AV)

700 South Flower Street, 30th Floor, 90017-4101
Telephone: 213-629-9300
Cable Address: "Oslaw"
Facsimile: 213-617-9255
In Cleveland, Ohio: 1100 Huntington Building, 925 Euclid Avenue.
Telephone: 216-696-1100.
Fax: 216-696-2645.
In Columbus, Ohio: 21st Floor, One Columbus, 10 West Broad Street.
Fax: 614-221-0479.
Telephone: 614-221-3155.
In Washington, D.C.: 1801 K Street, N.W., Suite 400K.
Telephone: 202-775-7100.
Fax: 202-857-0172.
In Dallas, Texas: 1717 Main Street, Suite 4100.
Telephone: 214-761-2100.
Fax: 214-741-7139.
In Irvine, California: Five Park Plaza, 10th Floor, Jamboree Center.
Telephone: 714-252-7500.
Fax: 714-833-9604.
In Austin, Texas: 100 Congress Avenue, Suite 1800.
Telephone: 512-479-6403.
Fax: 512-469-5505.
In San Antonio, Texas: 7710 Jones Maltsberger, Harte-Hanks Tower, Suite 540.
Telephone: 210-805-8497.
Fax: 210-805-8519.
In San Francisco, California: 201 California Street, 14th Floor, 94111.
Telephone: 415-912-3600.
Fax: 415-912-3636.
In San Diego, California: 402 West Broadway, Fourth Floor, 92101.
Telephone: 619-238-0001.
Fax: 619-238-8333.
In Woodland Hills, California: 5959 Topanga Canyon Boulevard, Suite 244, 91367.
Telephone: 818-712-0036.
Fax: 818-346-6502.

MEMBERS OF FIRM

Robert P. Andreani   Jay M. Davis
Kathleen M. K. Brahn   William S. Davis
James S. Bryan   Eric D. Dean
Steven J. Coté   David R. Decker

(See Next Column)

Richard D. De Luce   Julie Dean Larsen
Edwin W. Duncan   Kenneth J. Murphy
James E. Durbin   Bruce H. Newman
Richard N. Ellner   Richard R. Pace
Donald C. Erickson   J. Douglas Post
Jack Goldman   Kay Rustand
Wayne S. Grajewski   Andrea Y. Slade
John L. Hosack   Stephen T. Swanson
Curtiss L. Isler   John R. Tate
John E. James   Jacqueline I. Valenzuela
Bart L. Kessel   Ronald Warner
Craig G. Kline   Kim W. West
Michael S. Kogan   Michael C. Zellers

RETIRED PARTNERS

Robert Henigson   Richard F. Outcault, Jr.
Reed A. Stout

OF COUNSEL

Michael L. Coates   Judith A. Gilbert
Barbara R. Diamond   Ronald M. Griffith
Steven T. Gubner

ASSOCIATES

Julian Bach   Mary Devereaux Mackey
Victor M. Bartholetti   Michelle McAloon
Susan C. Bergemann   Maura B. O'Connor
Linley Clare Bizik   John M. Orr
Katessa M. Charles   Jane H. Root
Robert M. Forester   Alexander G. Rufus-Isaacs
Adam Gubner   Helen A. Sabo
Holly A. Hayes   Michael D. Schwarzmann
David M. Hershorin   Robert G. Soper
Tammy L. Kahane   Juliana Stamato
Kathryn L. Kempton   Karen M. Stuckey
Wendy L. Linder   Neil M. Sunkin
Brenda J. Logan   Daniel R. Villegas
David B. Zolkin

Representative Clients: Chevron Corp.; American International Group; ADT, Inc.; PacTel Properties; The Bank of California, N.A.; Brunswick Corp.; Reliance Steel & Aluminum Co.; Scope Industries; National Railroad Passenger Car; Boral Industries, Inc.

For full biographical listings, see the Martindale-Hubbell Law Directory

BAKER & HOSTETLER (AV)

600 Wilshire Boulevard, 90017-3212
Telephone: 213-624-2400
FAX: 213-975-1740
In Cleveland, Ohio: 3200 National City Center, 1900 East Ninth Street.
Telephone: 216-621-0200.
In Columbus, Ohio: Capitol Square, Suite 2100, 65 East State Street.
Telephone: 614-228-1541.
In Denver, Colorado: 303 East 17th Avenue, Suite 1100.
Telephone: 303-861-0600.
In Houston, Texas: 1000 Louisiana, Suite 2000.
Telephone: 713-236-0020.
In Long Beach, California: 300 Oceangate, Suite 620.
Telephone: 310-432-2827.
In Orlando, Florida: SunBank Center, Suite 2300, 200 South Orange Avenue.
Telephone: 407-649-4000.
In Washington, D. C.: Washington Square, Suite 1100, 1050 Connecticut Avenue, N. W.
Telephone: 202-861-1500.
In College Park, Maryland: 9658 Baltimore Boulevard, Suite 206.
Telephone: 301-441-2781.
In Alexandria, Virginia: 437 North Lee Street.
Telephone: 703-549-1294.
In San Francisco, California: One Sansome Street, Suite 2000.
Telephone: 415-951-4705.

MEMBERS OF FIRM IN LOS ANGELES, CALIFORNIA

Edward J. McCutchen   Harold A. Black (1895-1970)
(1857-1933)   George Harnagel (1903-1962)
G. William Shea (1911-1986) Sheldon A. Gebb (Managing
Partner-Los Angeles, Long
Beach, California and
Houston, Texas Offices)

PARTNERS

Angela C. Agrusa   William P. Barry
Patrick J. Cain   Penny M. Costa
Richard A. Deeb   David A. Destino
Jack D. Fudge   Richard A. Goette
Byron Hayes, Jr.   Emil W. Herich
Dennis F. Hernandez   Bradley R. Hogin
Joseph B. Hudson, Jr.   Peter W. James
Michael M. Johnson   Anthony M. Keats
Lynn S. Loeb   Larry W. McFarland
John C. Mueller   Dean G. Rallis Jr.
Jill Sarnoff Riola   Thomas G. Roberts
Jack I. Samet   David C. Sampson
Bill E. Schroeder   Diane C. Stanfield
Teresa R. Tracy   Ralph Zarefsky

(See Next Column)

BAKER & HOSTETLER—*Continued*

ASSOCIATES

Steve W. Ackerman	David W. Ammons
Roger L. Armstrong	(Not admitted in CA)
Kathleen E. Bailey	David Caplan
Maria T. CeloCruz	Norman C. Davis
Andrew J. Durkovic	Keith A. Fink
Megan E. Gray	James E. Houpt
Lisa F. Hinchliffe	(Not admitted in CA)
Susan Horwitz	Thomas Johnson
(Not admitted in CA)	Jeffrey K. Joyner
Kirstin M. Larson	Marcia T. Law
Stephen Nakata	Peggy A. Propper

ASSOCIATES (Continued)

Gregg A. Rapoport	Marc I. Seltzer
Cranston J. Williams	Dennis L. Wilson

OF COUNSEL

Janet S. Hoffman	Glen A. Smith
	John R. Sommer

For full biographical listings, see the Martindale-Hubbell Law Directory

BELCHER, HENZIE & BIEGENZAHN, A PROFESSIONAL CORPORATION (AV)

333 South Hope Street, Suite 3650, 90071-1479
Telephone: 213-624-8293
Telecopier: 213-895-6082

Frank B. Belcher (1891-1979)	E. Lee Horton
David Bernard (1931-1978)	William T. DelHagen
John S. Curtis	Julia Azrael

Jeffrey L. Horwith	James C. Hildebrand
Georgette Renata Herget	Robert S. Cooper
David L. Bonar	Wun-ee Chelsea Chen
Raymond E. Hane, III	John Erin McOsker
	Mary E. Gram

OF COUNSEL

George M. Henzie	Leo J. Biegenzahn
	James M. Derr

Reference: Bank of America (Los Angeles Main Office).

For full biographical listings, see the Martindale-Hubbell Law Directory

MARTIN H. BLANK, JR. (AV)

11755 Wilshire Boulevard, Suite 1400, 90025-1520
Telephone: 310-477-5455
Fax: 310-444-9203
Email: marty@general.net

For full biographical listings, see the Martindale-Hubbell Law Directory

LAW OFFICES OF DAVID B. BLOOM A PROFESSIONAL CORPORATION (AV)

3325 Wilshire Boulevard, Ninth Floor, 90010
Telephone: 213-938-5248; 384-4088
Telecopier: 213-385-2009

David B. Bloom

Stephen S. Monroe (A Professional Corporation)	Susan Carole Jay
	Edward Idell
Raphael A. Rosemblat	Sandra Kamenir
James E. Adler	Steven Wayne Lazarus
Bonni S. Mantovani	Andrew Edward Briseno
Roy A. Levun	Harold C. Klaskin
Cherie S. Raidy	Shelley M. Gould
Jonathan Udell	Peter O. Israel

For full biographical listings, see the Martindale-Hubbell Law Directory

BROBECK, PHLEGER & HARRISON LLP (AV)

A Partnership including a Professional Corporation
550 South Hope Street, 90071-2604
Telephone: 213-489-4060
Facsimile: 213-745-3345
Cable Address: "Brobeck"
Telex: 181164 BPH LSA
San Francisco, California Office: Spear Street Tower, One Market.
Telephone: 415-442-0900.
Facsimile: 415-442-1010.
Palo Alto, California Office: Two Embarcadero Place, 2200 Geng Road.
Telephone: 415-424-0160.
Facsimile: 415-496-2885.
San Diego, California Office: 550 West C Street, Suite 1300.
Telephone: 619-234-1966.
Facsimile: 619-236-1403.

(See Next Column)

Orange County, California Office: 4675 MacArthur Court, Suite 1000, Newport Beach.
Telephone: 714-752-7535.
Facsimile: 714-752-7522.
Austin, Texas Office: Brobeck, Phleger & Harrison LLP, 301 Congress Avenue, Suite 1200.
Telephone: 512-477-5495.
Facsimile: 512-477-5813.
Denver, Colorado Office: Brobeck, Phleger & Harrison LLP, 1125 Seventeenth Street, 25th Floor.
Telephone: 303-293-0760.
Facsimile: 303-299-8819.
New York, N.Y. Office: Brobeck, Phleger & Harrison LLP, 1633 Broadway, 47th Floor.
Telephone: 212-581-1600.
Facsimile: 212-586-7878.
Brobeck Hale and Dorr International Office:
London, England Office: Veritas House, 125 Finsbury Pavement, London EC2A 1NQ.
Telephone: 44 071 638 6688.
Facsimile: 44 071 638 5888.

MANAGING PARTNER

Thomas P. Burke

RESIDENT PARTNERS

Laurie A. Allen	Albert R. Karel
Kenneth R. Bender	George H. Link
Linda J. Bozung	Debra E. Pole
Edmond R. Davis	Todd B. Serota
Gregg A. Farley	V. Joseph Stubbs
William B. Fitzgerald	William K. Swank
David M. Halbreich	Jeffrey S. Turner
Susan B. Hall	Daniel J. Tyukody
Jeffery D. Hermann	Kenneth L. Waggoner
David M. Higgins	Gerard J. Walsh
John Francis Hilson	John J. Wasilczyk
Drew Jones	Michael S. Whalen
	Michael T. Zarro

OF COUNSEL

Tom Bradley	Earle Miller
Chris Steven Jacobsen	John A. Payne, Jr.
	Thomas H. Petrides

RESIDENT ASSOCIATES

Michael L. Armstrong	Braden W. Penhoet
David W. Berry	Howard M. Privette
Kara L. Bue	Douglas C. Rawles
Richard L. Daniels	Steven J. Renshaw
Paul M. Gleason	Eddie Rodriguez
Marcia Z. Gordon	David L. Schrader
John Hameetman	Konrad F. Schreier, III
Bruce W. Hepler	Jody L. Spiegel
(Not admitted in CA)	Raymond T. Sung
Bernard C. Jasper	Edward D. Totino
Jamie L. Johnson	David R. Venderbush
Wayne E. Johnson	Daniel I. Villapando
Brian W. Kasell	Todd W. Walker
Patty H. Le	Perrie M. Weiner
Howard L. Magee	Daniel Weisberg
Christopher J. Menjou	Pamela J. Yates
Cynthia M. Patton	Thomas B. Youth
	Gregg Zucker

CONTRACT ATTORNEY

Gary D. Rothstein

For full biographical listings, see the Martindale-Hubbell Law Directory

BRONSON, BRONSON & McKINNON LLP (AV)

A Partnership including Professional Corporations
444 South Flower Street, 24th Floor, 90071
Telephone: 213-627-2000
Fax: 213-627-2277
San Francisco, California Office: 505 Montgomery Street.
Telephone: 415-986-4200.
San Jose, California Office: 10 Almaden Boulevard, Suite 600.
Telephone: 408-293-0599.

RESIDENT PARTNERS

Eric A. Amador	Elizabeth A. Erskine
Donna P. Arlow	Edwin W. Green
Stephen L. Backus	Claudia L. Greenspoon
Charles N. Bland, Jr.	Stuart I. Koenig
Breton August Bocchieri	Ralph S. LaMontagne, Jr.
John D. Boyle	Richard C. Macias
Thomas T. Carpenter	Dani H. Rogers
William B. Creim	Manuel Saldaña
L. Morris Dennis (A Professional Corporation)	David M. Walsh
	Sheldon J. Warren
Lucinda Dennis (A Professional Corporation)	

OF COUNSEL

David L. Horgan	Robert Weber, Jr.

(See Next Column)

BRONSON, BRONSON & McKINNON LLP, *Los Angeles—Continued*

RESIDENT ASSOCIATES

Janet Andrea	Kathleen R. O'Laughlin
Raymon B. Bilbeaux, III	Hayley L. Sneiderman
Laurie K. Jones	John F. Stephens
Laurie S. Julien	Nancy L. Tetreault
Charles E. Koro	James B. Yobski

REGISTERED PATENT AGENT
David Alexander

For full biographical listings, see the Martindale-Hubbell Law Directory

BROWN, WINFIELD & CANZONERI, INCORPORATED (AV)

Suite 1500 California Plaza, 300 South Grand Avenue, 90071-3125
Telephone: 213-687-2100
Fax: 213-687-2149

J. Kenneth Brown	Christopher Norgaard
Thomas F. Winfield, III	C. Geoffrey Mitchell
Anthony Canzoneri	Scott H. Campbell
Vicki E. Land	Joshua C. Gottheim
James C. Camp	Donald Paul Ries
Steven Abram	Muira K. Sethi
Dennis S. Roy	Seth I. Weissman
Mark Steres	John H. Holloway
Katharine Araujo Miller	Rafael E. Alfonzo
Sonya L. Karpowich	

Reference: Wells Fargo Bank.

For full biographical listings, see the Martindale-Hubbell Law Directory

BUCHALTER, NEMER, FIELDS & YOUNGER, A PROFESSIONAL CORPORATION (AV)

24th Floor, 601 South Figueroa Street, 90017
Telephone: 213-891-0700
Fax: 213-896-0400
Email: buchalter@earthlink.net *URL:* http://www.buchalter.com
New York, New York Office: 15th Floor, 605 Third Avenue.
Telephone: 212-490-8600.
Fax: 212-490-6022.
San Francisco, California Office: 29th Floor, 333 Market Street.
Telephone: 415-227-0900.
Fax: 415-227-0770.
Newport Beach, California Office: Suite 1450, 620 Newport Center Drive.
Telephone: 714-760-1121.
Fax: 714-720-0182.

Murray M. Fields	Keith B. Bardellini
Richard Jay Goldstein	Mark A. Bonenfant
Michael L. Wachtell	David S. Kyman
Robert C. Colton	James H. Turken
Gary A. York	Kevin M. Brandt
Arthur Chinski	Jeffrey S. Wruble
Jay R. Ziegler	Randye B. Soref
Michael J. Cereseto	Pamela Kohlman Webster
Bernard E. Le Sage	Matthew W. Kavanaugh
Gregory Keever	Richard S. Angel
Roger D. Loomis, Jr.	Bryan Mashian
Philip J. Wolman	Robert J. Davidson
Bernard D. Bollinger, Jr.	

OF COUNSEL

Ronald E. Gordon	Holly J. Fujie
Stuart D. Buchalter	Elizabeth S. Trussell
Barry A. Smith	Harriet M. Welch
Geoffrey Forsythe Bogeaus	William Mark Levinson
Scott O. Smith	Harriet B. Alexson
Barry F. Soosman	

Janis S. Penton	Kim Allman
Jerry A. Hager	William P. Fong
Jonathan D. Fink	Helen Goldberger Palmer
Julie A. Goren	Brett Michael Broderick
Glenn L. Savard	Robert Alexander Pilmer
Paul S. Arrow	Kirk H. Sharpe
William S. Brody	Nicolas M. Kublicki
Amy L. Rubinfeld	Vincent I.S. Hsieh
Dean Stackel	(Not admitted in CA)
Abraham J. Colman	Simone Margaret Bennett
Monika L. McCarthy	Christina M. Carlson
Mary LePique Dickson	Rachael H. Berman
Shirley Sheau-Lih Lu	Daniel Joseph Kolodziej
Robert A. Willner	Elizabeth H. Murphy
Adam Joel Bass	Lance R. Dixon
David L. Aronoff	Allan R. Mouw
Daniel C. Wong	

References: City National Bank; Wells Fargo Bank; Metrobank.

For full biographical listings, see the Martindale-Hubbell Law Directory

CARLSMITH BALL WICHMAN CASE & ICHIKI (AV)

A Partnership including Law Corporations
555 South Flower Street, 25th Floor, 90071
Telephone: 213-955-1200
Cable Address: CWCMI LOSANGELESCALIFORNIA
Fax: 213-623-0032; 213-624-7183
Honolulu, Hawaii Office: Suite 2200, Pacific Tower, 1001 Bishop Street. P.O. Box 656.
Telephone: 808-523-2500.
Kapolei, Hawaii Office: Kapolei Building, Suite 318, 1001 Kamokila Boulevard.
Telephone: 808-523-2500.
Wailuku, Maui Hawaii Office: One Main Plaza, Suite 400, 2200 Main Street, P.O. Box 1086.
Telephone: 808-242-4535.
Kailua-Kona, Hawaii Office: Second Floor, Bank of Hawaii Annex Building, P.O. Box 1720.
Telephone: 808-329-6464.
Hilo, Hawaii Office: 121 Waianuenue Avenue, P.O. Box 686.
Telephone: 808-935-6644.
Agana, Guam Office: 4th Floor, Bank of Hawaii Building, P.O. Box BF.
Telephone: 671-472-6813.
Saipan, Commonwealth of the Northern Mariana Islands Office: Carlsmith Building, Capitol Hill, P.O. Box 5241.
Telephone: (011) 670-322-3455.
Washington, D.C. Office: 700 14th Street, N.W., 9th Floor.
Telephone: 202-508-1025.
Mexico City, Mexico Office: Monte Pelvous 111, Piso 1, Col. Lomas de Chapultepec 11000, Mexico, D.F.
Telephone: (011-52-5) 520-8514.
Fax: (011-52-5) 540-1545.
Mexico, D.F. Office of Carlsmith Ball Garcia Cacho y Asociados, S.C. (Authorized to practice Mexican Law): Monte Pelvoux 111, Piso 1, Col. Lomas de Chapultepec, 11000 Mexico, D.F.
Telephone: (011-52-5) 520-8514.
Fax: (011-52-5) 540-1545.

MEMBERS OF FIRM

Annie Kun Baker	John R. McDonough
Joseph A. Ball	Randolph G. Muhlestein
Roger B. Baymiller	Joseph D. Mullender, Jr.
Nancy M. Beckner	David S. Olson
Stephen L. Bradford	James M. Polish
Albert H. Ebright	Jonathan L. Smoller
Terrence A. Everett	Allan Edward Tebbetts
Jonathan R. Hodes	Donald C. Williams
Robert F. Kull	Duane H. Zobrist

RESIDENT ASSOCIATES

Peter N. Greenfeld	Ann Luotto Wolf

RESIDENT OF COUNSEL

Herbert G. Baerwitz	Tom K. Houston
Dagmar V. Halamka	Robert R. Thornton

For full biographical listings, see the Martindale-Hubbell Law Directory

CHADBOURNE & PARKE LLP (AV)

601 South Figueroa Street, 90017
Telephone: 213-892-1000
Facsimile: 213-622-9865
New York, N.Y. Office: 30 Rockefeller Plaza, 10112.
Telephone: 212-408-5100.
Facsimile: 212-541-5369.
Washington, D.C. Office: 1101 Vermont Avenue, N.W., 20005.
Telephone: 202-289-3000.
Facsimile: 202-289-3002.
London, England Office: 86 Jermyn Street, SW1 6JD.
Telephone: 44-171-925-7400.
Facsimile: 44-171-839-3393.
Moscow, Russia Office: 38 Kosmodamianskaya Naberezhnaya, 113035.
Telephone: 7095-974-2424.
Facsimile: 7095-974-2425. International satellite lines via U.S.:
Telephone: 212-408-1190.
Facsimile: 212-408-1199.
Hong Kong Office: Suite 3704, Peregrine Tower, Lippo Centre, 89 Queensway.
Telephone: 852-2842-5400.
Facsimile: 852-2521-7527.

PARTNERS

Richard J. Ney	Peter R. Chaffetz
Jonathan F. Bank	Jay R. Henneberry
Harvey I. Saferstein	Linda Dakin-Grimm
Kenneth J. Langan	

RESIDENT COUNSEL
William J. Kelley, III

(See Next Column)

CHADBOURNE & PARKE LLP—*Continued*

RESIDENT ASSOCIATES

Robin D. Ball
Glenn R. Bronson
Peter M. DelVecchio
 (Not admitted in CA)
Anahid Gharakhanian
Armen K. Hovannisian

Kevin D. Hughes
 (Not admitted in CA)
George Lasko
Marvin D. Mohn
Ann K. Penners
Mary Louise Serafine

For full biographical listings, see the Martindale-Hubbell Law Directory

CLARK & TREVITHICK, A PROFESSIONAL CORPORATION (AV)

800 Wilshire Boulevard, 12th Floor, 90017
Telephone: 213-629-5700
Telecopier: 213-624-9441
San Francisco, California Office: 456 Montgomery Street, 20th Floor.
Telephone: 415-288-6520.
Fax: 415-398-2820.

Donald P. Clark
Alexander C. McGilvray, Jr.
Philip W. Bartenetti
Kevin P. Fiore
Dolores Cordell
Vincent Tricarico
John A. Lapinski
Leonard Brazil

Dean I. Friedman
Robert F. DeMeter
Michael K. Wofford
Leslie R. Horowitz
Brent A. Reinke
Arturo Santana Jr.
Kerry T. Ryan
James S. Arico

OF COUNSEL

John A. Tucker, Jr.

Judith Ilene Bloom

References: Wells Fargo Bank (Los Angeles Main Office); National Bank of California.

For full biographical listings, see the Martindale-Hubbell Law Directory

CORINBLIT & SELTZER, A PROFESSIONAL CORPORATION (AV)

Suite 820 Wilshire Park Place, 3700 Wilshire Boulevard, 90010-3085
Telephone: 213-380-4200
Telecopier: 213-385-7503; 385-4560
Email: mseltzer@AOL.com

Marc M. Seltzer

Christina A. Snyder

OF COUNSEL

Jack Corinblit, A Law
 Corporation

Earl P. Willens

Gretchen M. Nelson

George A. Shohet
Moses Garcia

For full biographical listings, see the Martindale-Hubbell Law Directory

COTKIN & COLLINS, A PROFESSIONAL CORPORATION (AV)

1055 West Seventh Street, Suite 1900, 90017-2503
Telephone: 213-688-9350
FAX: 213-688-9351
Email: cotkinla@sprynet.com
Santa Ana, California Office: 200 West Santa Ana Boulevard, Suite 800.
Telephone: 714-835-2330.
FAX: 714-835-2209.

Raphael Cotkin
James P. Collins, Jr.
 (Resident, Santa Ana Office)
Steven L. Paine
William D. Naeve
 (Resident, Santa Ana Office)
Terry C. Leuin
Roger W. Simpson

Joan M. Dolinsky
Robert G. Wilson
David A. Winkle
 (Resident, Santa Ana Office)
Philip S. Gutierrez
 (Resident, Santa Ana Office)
Karen C. Freitas
Brian R. Hill
 (Resident, Santa Ana Office)

Lori S. Blitstien
Carrie F. Smith
Gregory A. Sargenti
 (Resident, Santa Ana Office)
Terry L. Kesinger
 (Resident, Santa Ana Office)

Bradley W. Jacks
Scott P. Ward
Ellen M. Tipping
 (Resident, Santa Ana Office)

References: American City Bank (Downtown Branch); Security Pacific Bank (7th and Grand Branch); Bank of America.

For full biographical listings, see the Martindale-Hubbell Law Directory

DAAR & NEWMAN, PROFESSIONAL CORPORATION (AV)

Suite 2500, 865 South Figueroa Street, 90017-2567
Telephone: 213-892-0999
FAX: 213-892-1066

David Daar
Michael R. Newman

Jeffery J. Daar
Marsha McLean-Utley
Michael J. White

(See Next Column)

OF COUNSEL

Rodney W. Loeb

William F. White, Jr.
Samuel T. Rees

LEGAL SUPPORT PERSONNEL

Joe A. Morton

Frank E. Raab

Representative Clients: Allianz Insurance Co.; American Income Life Insurance Co.; American Life and Casualty Insurance Co.; Balboa Insurance Co.; California Casualty Insurance Co.; National Benefit Life Insurance Co.; Capital Life Insurance Co.; Charter National Life; Columbian Mutual Life; Connecticut Mutual Life Insurance Co.

For full biographical listings, see the Martindale-Hubbell Law Directory

DAVIS & FOX (AV)

1901 Avenue of the Stars, Suite 400, 90067
Telephone: 310-286-2915
Fax: 310-286-2916

MEMBERS OF FIRM

Calvin E. Davis

Steven A. Fox

ASSOCIATES

Brian Aronson

Amy L. Freisleben
Susan R. Peck

OF COUNSEL

Herbert D. Meyers

For full biographical listings, see the Martindale-Hubbell Law Directory

GIBSON, DUNN & CRUTCHER LLP (AV)

333 South Grand Avenue, 90071-3197
Telephone: 213-229-7000
Telex: 188171 GIBTRASK LSA (TRT), 674930 GIBTRASK LSA (WUT)
Telecopier: 213-229-7520; 213-229-7268
Cable Address: GIBTRASK LOS ANGELES
Century City, Los Angeles, California Office: 2029 Century Park East, Suite 4000.
Telephone: 310-552-8500.
Telecopier: 310-551-8741.
Cable Address: GIBTRASKCC LOS ANGELES.
Irvine, California Office: 4 Park Plaza, Suites 1400, 1500, 1700 and 1800.
Telephone: 714-451-3800.
Telecopier: 714-451-4220.
San Diego, California Office: 750 B Street, Suite 3300.
Telephone: 619-544-8000.
Telecopier: 619-544-8190; 619-544-8191.
San Francisco, California Office: One Montgomery Street, 26th Floor and 31st Floor.
Telephone: 415-393-8200.
Telecopier: 415-986-5309.
Palo Alto, California Office: 525 University Avenue, Suite 220.
Telephone: 415-463-7300.
Telecopier: 415-463-7333.
Denver, Colorado Office: 1801 California Street, Suite 4100.
Telephone: 303-298-5700.
Telecopier: 303-296-5310.
Washington, D.C. Office: 1050 Connecticut Avenue, N.W.
Telephone: 202-955-8500.
Telex: 197659 GIBTRASK WSH (TRT), 892501 GIBTRASK WSH (WUT).
Telecopier: 202-467-0539.
Cable Address: GIBTRASK WASHINGTON DC.
New York, New York Office: 200 Park Avenue.
Telephone: 212-351-4000.
Telecopier: 212-351-4035.
Cable Address: GIBTRASK NEWYORK.
Dallas, Texas Office: 1717 Main Street, Suite 5400.
Telephone: 214-698-3100.
Telecopier: 214-698-3400.
Paris, France Office: 104 Avenue Raymond Poincare, 75116.
Telephone: 011-33-1-45-01-93-83.
Telecopier: 011-33-1-45-00-69-59.
Cable Address: GIBTRAK PARIS.
London, England Office: 30/35 Pall Mall, SW1Y 5LP.
Telephone: 011-44-171-925-0440.
Telex: 27731 GIBTRK G; 916176 GIBTRK G.
Telecopier: 011-44-171-925-2465.
Cable Address: GIBTRASK LONDON W1.
Affiliated Jeddah, Saudi Arabia Office: Law Office of Abdulaziz Fahad, Sixth Floor, Haji Hussein Alireza Building, Bab Makkah, Post Office Box 16206, Jeddah, 21464.
Telephone: 011-966-2-644-2663.
Telecopier: 011-966-2-643-5401.
Affiliated Riyadh, Saudi Arabia Office: Law Office of Abdulaziz Fahad, Jarir Plaza, 4th Floor, Olaya Street, Post Office Box 15870, Riyadh, 11454.
Telephone: 011-966-1-464-8081.
Telex: 406176 LAWS SJ.
Telecopier: 011-966-1-462-4968.

(See Next Column)

GIBSON, DUNN & CRUTCHER LLP, *Los Angeles—Continued*

Hong Kong Office: 10th Floor, Two Pacific Place, 88 Queensway.
Telephone: 011-852-2526-6816.
Telex: 65665 GIBTK HX.
Telecopier: 011-852-2845-9144.

Jas. A. Gibson (1852-1922)　　W. E. Dunn (1861-1925)
Albert Crutcher (1860-1931)

PARTNERS

Norman B. Barker
Robert S. Warren
Ronald E. Gother
Stephen E. Tallent (Los Angeles and Washington, D.C. Offices)
Robert E. Cooper
Ronald S. Beard
John H. Sharer
Wesley G. Howell, Jr. (New York City and Los Angeles, California Offices)
John F. Olson (Washington, D.C. Office)
Andrew E. Bogen
Robert K. Montgomery (Century City and Los Angeles Offices)
Theodore B. Olson (Washington, D.C. Office)
John J. Swenson
John T. Behrendt (Los Angeles and New York City Offices)
Charles K. Marquis (New York City and Los Angeles Offices)
William J. Kilberg (Washington, D.C. Office)
Charles S. Battles, Jr.
Robert T. Gelber
Kenneth E. Ristau, Jr. (Irvine Office)
Bruce L. Gitelson (San Francisco and Palo Alto Offices)
Dean Stern
Jack H. Halgren
Roy J. Schmidt, Jr. (Century City Office)
Richard G. Duncan, Jr. (Irvine Office)
John A. Ruskey
Fred F. Gregory
Kenneth W. Anderson
Stephen M. Blitz (Denver, Colorado Office)
Ralph C. Wintrode (Irvine Office)
Dwight L. Nye (Dallas, Texas Office)
James G. Phillipp
Blake T. Franklin (New York City and Irvine Offices)
David A. Cathcart
Robert C. Bonner (Washington, D.C. and Los Angeles, California Offices)
Steven Alan Meiers
Arthur L. Sherwood
John C. Wells (Irvine Office)
James R. Martin
Richard A. Strong
Richard D. Hall
William Stinehart, Jr. (Century City Office)
R. Randall Huff
Lawrence Calof (San Francisco Office)
John Edd Stepp, Jr.
Robert Forgnone
Charles C. Ivie
Bruce D. Meyer
Meldon E. Levine (Los Angeles and Washington, D.C. Offices)
C. Ransom Samuelson II
J. Anthony Sinclitico, III (San Diego Office)
Peter J. Wallison (Washington, D.C. Office)
J. Michael Brennan (Irvine Office)
Don Parris (Century City Office)
Joseph H. Price (Washington, D.C. Office)
Marc R. Isaacson
Michael D. Ryan

James C. Opel
Martin Carl Washton
Cantwell Faulkner Muckenfuss III (Washington, D.C. Office)
Scott August Kruse
Wayne W. Smith (Los Angeles and Irvine Offices)
Peter L. Baumbusch (Washington, D.C. Office)
Richard Paul Levy
Robert D. Sack (New York City Office)
Dennis A. Gladwell (Irvine Office)
S. David Blinn (Los Angeles and Irvine Offices)
Ronald S. Orr
Jonathan M. Landers (San Francisco Office)
Irwin F. Sentilles, III (Dallas, Texas Office)
Aulana L. Peters (Los Angeles and Washington, D.C. Offices)
Fred Gilbert Bennett
Gerard J. Kenny (Irvine Office)
James P. Clark (Century City Office)
John A. Herfort (New York City Office)
Lawrence J. Hohlt (New York City Office)
Jerry J. Strochlic (New York City Office)
Bennett L. Silverman
Kirk A. Patrick
Thomas E. Holliday
Peter F. Ziegler
Stephen C. Johnson (Dallas, Texas Office)
Christopher H. Buckley, Jr. (Washington, D.C. Office)
Gordon A. Schaller (Irvine Office)
David R. Johnson (Washington, D.C. Office)
Donald Harrison (Washington, D.C. Office)
David G. Palmer (Denver, Colorado Office)
Pamela A. Ray (Denver, Colorado Office)
Gaynell C. Methvin (Dallas, Texas Office)
Richard Michael Russo (Denver, Colorado Office)
Phillip L. Bosl
Wayne A. Schrader (Washington, D.C. Office)
William F. Highberger
Rex S. Heinke
Robert W. Loewen (Irvine Office)
Anthony Bonanno (London, England Office)
Peter H. Turza (Washington, D.C. Office)
Jonathan L. Sulds (New York City Office)
Charles F. Feldman (New York City Office)
Conor D. Reilly (New York City Office)
Dennis B. Arnold
Steven R. Finley (New York City Office)
John J. A. Hossenlopp (New York City Office)
Martin B. McNamara (Dallas, Texas Office)
Michael L. Denger (Washington, D.C. Office)
F. Joseph Warin (Washington, D.C. Office)

(See Next Column)

PARTNERS (Continued)

Charles M. Schwartz (Dallas, Texas Office)
Lawrence J. Ulman
Jane Lindsey Wingfield
Robert Everett Dean (Irvine Office)
Thomas D. Magill (Irvine Office)
George B. Curtis (Denver, Colorado Office)
William D. Claster (Irvine Office)
Joseph P. Busch III (Irvine Office)
Pamela Lynn Hemminger
Donald E. Sloan (San Francisco Office)
Daniel Q. Callister (Washington, D.C. Office)
Fred L. Pillon (San Francisco Office)
Denis R. Salmon (Palo Alto Office)
Scott Blake Harris (Washington, D.C. Office)
Larry C. Boyd (Irvine Office)
E. Michael Greaney (Irvine, California and New York, N.Y. Offices)
Nancy P. McClelland
Mary Laura Davis (Century City Office)
H. Richard Dallas (New York City Office)
John D. Fognani (Denver, Colorado Office)
Howard B. Adler (Washington, D.C. Office)
Karen H. Clark (Irvine Office)
Dhiya El-Saden
Dean J. Kitchens
Jeffrey Reid Hudson
Charles A. Larson (Century City Office)
Mark W. Shurtleff (Irvine Office)
Christopher J. Martin (San Francisco and Palo Alto Offices)
Lesley Sara Wolf
Peter Sullivan
Shari Leinwand (Century City Office)
Gary L. Justice
Jonathan K. Layne
Scott A. Fink (San Francisco Office)
William D. Connell (San Francisco Office)
Gail Ellen Lees
Marjorie Ehrich Lewis
Timothy L. Dickinson (Washington, D.C. Office)
David West
Russell C. Hansen (Century City Office)
Walter L. Schindler (Irvine Office)
William Edward Wegner (Los Angeles and Century City Offices)
Meryl L. Young (San Diego Office)
Larry L. Simms (Washington, D.C. Office)
John H. Sturc (Washington, D.C. Office)
Jonathan C. Dickey (Palo Alto Office)
Scott R. Hoyt (Dallas, Texas Office)
Rhonda S. Wagner (San Diego Office)
Elizabeth A. Grimes
Paul D. Inman (Dallas, Texas Office)
Mitchell A. Karlan (New York City Office)
Thomas C. McGraw (Dallas, Texas Office)
Michael A. Barrett (Washington, D.C. Office)
Hatef Behnia
Joel A. Feuer

Kenneth M. Doran (Los Angeles and Century City Offices)
J. Nicholson Thomas
Michael A. Monahan
Michele C. Coyle (Irvine Office)
Susan Erburu Reardon
Karen E. Bertero
Robert C. Eager (Washington, D.C. Office)
Ray T. Khirallah (Dallas, Texas Office)
Robert L. Weigel (New York City Office)
Mark E. Weber
Todd H. Baker (San Francisco Office)
Stephen L. Tolles
Cheryl D. Justice
Jeffrey T. Thomas (Irvine Office)
Steven Eugene Sletten
Baruch A. Fellner (Washington, D.C. Office)
Patrick W. Dennis
Craig H. Millet (Irvine Office)
Robert Bruce Vernon (New York City Office)
Michael A. Rosenthal (Dallas, Texas Office)
Mitri J. Najjar (London, England Office)
Jennifer Bellah
Joel S. Sanders (San Francisco Office)
Phillip Howard Rudolph (Washington, D.C. Office)
Rory Michael Hernandez
Arthur David Pasternak (Washington, D.C. Office)
Paul R. Harter (London, England Office)
Terence P. Ross (Washington, D.C. Office)
Kathryn Anne Coleman (San Francisco Office)
John C. Millian (Washington, D.C. Office)
Brian D. Kilb
Robert B. Krakow (Dallas, Texas Office)
Thomas Satrom
M. Byron Wilder (Dallas, Texas Office)
Robert E. Palmer (Irvine Office)
Steven P. Buffone (New York City Office)
Mark S. Pécheck
Daniel G. Swanson
Gregory J. Kerwin (Denver, Colorado Office)
Scott A. Edelman (Los Angeles and Century City Offices)
David B. Pendarvis (San Diego Office)
David B. Rosenauer (New York City Office)
Raymond B. Ludwiszewski (Washington, D.C. Office)
Amy R. Forbes
David I. Schiller (Dallas, Texas Office)
John R. Crews (Dallas, Texas Office)
Kenneth R. Lamb (San Francisco Office)
Joerg H. Esdorn (New York City Office)
Daniel S. Floyd
William R. Lindsay
Clay A. Halvorsen (Century City Office)
Robert Francis Serio (New York City Office)
Kimmarie Sinatra (New York City Office)
Steven A. Ruben
Thomas R. Denison (Denver, Colorado Office)
Paul S. Issler
Kay Ellen Kochenderfer
Joseph M. Salamunovich
Richard J. Doren
Jesse Sharf

(See Next Column)

GIBSON, DUNN & CRUTCHER LLP—*Continued*

PARTNERS (Continued)

Sean P. Griffiths
(New York City Office)
Julia A. Dahlberg
(Washington, D.C. Office)
Patricia S. Radez
(San Francisco Office)
Timothy J. Hatch
Bradford P. Weirick
James P. Ricciardi
(New York City Office)
David Alan Battaglia
Theodore J. Boutrous, Jr.
(Washington, D.C. Office)
Brian W. Copple (Irvine Office)
James Edward Bass
(Hong Kong Office)
Kevin S. Rosen
Hsiao-chiung Li
(Hong Kong Office)
Janet Popofsky Vance
(New York City Office)
Steven Mark Schultz
Judith A. Lee
(Washington, D.C. Office)
A. James Isbester
(San Francisco Office)

Bernard Grinspan
(Paris, France Office)
Jeffrey M. Trinklein
(Dallas, Texas Office)
Ronald O. Mueller
(Washington, D.C. Office)
Timothy J. Kay (Irvine Office)
Douglas R. Cox
(Washington, D.C. Office)
Geniene B. Stillwell
(Irvine Office)
Chad S. Hummel
Steven R. Shoemate
(New York City Office)
Gregory Toll Davidson
(San Francisco Office)
John Novak
(New York City Office)
Kimberly S. McGovern
(San Francisco Office)
Susan M. Marcella
Thomas G. Hungar
(Washington, D.C. Office)
Wendy M. Singer (London,
England and Paris, France
Offices) (European Partner)

ADVISORY COUNSELS

Sherman Seymour Welpton, Jr.
Julian O. von Kalinowski
F. Daniel Frost
Sharp Whitmore
(San Diego Office)
Francis M. Wheat
Arthur W. Schmutz
William F. Spalding
James R. Hutter
Robert D. Burch
(Century City Office)
John L. Endicott
John J. Hanson
Jerome C. Byrne
George W. Bermant
(Denver, Colorado Office)
Willard Z. Carr, Jr.
G. Edward Fitzgerald
Russell L. Johnson
Thomas B. Pitcher
(Irvine Office)

George H. Whitney
Frank L. Mallory (Irvine Office)
John T. Pigott
(Century City Office)
Raymond L. Curran
Dean C. Dunlavey
Roy D. Miller
Guy K. Claire (Irvine Office)
Herbert Kraus
Irwin F. Woodland
James M. Murphy
Paul G. Bower
Charles R. Collins
(San Francisco Office)
Leo G. Ziffren
(Century City Office)
Bruce A. Toor
Lester Ziffren
(Century City Office)
Michael E. Alpert
(San Diego Office)

OF COUNSELS

John A. Arguelles (Irvine Office)
Peter J. Arturo
Kevin W. Barrett
(New York City Office)
Paul Blankenstein
(Washington, D.C. Office)
Susan B. Burr (Palo Alto Office)
Sheila R. Caudle
Ellen J. Curnes
(Dallas, Texas Office)
Michael J. Eliasberg
(Century City Office)
Deborah S. Feinerman
(Century City Office)
Cynthia Leap Goldman
(Denver, Colorado Office)
Mark A. Grannis
(Washington, D.C. Office)
Xuhua Huang (New York City
and Hong Kong Offices)
Joanne Franzel
(New York City Office)
David W. Jackson
(Jeddah, Saudi Arabia Office)
Gary M. Joye
Sungyong Kang
David H. Kennedy
(Washington, D.C. Office)
Richard G. Lyon
(Dallas, Texas Office)

Robert A. McConnell
(Washington, D.C. Office)
Robert E. Mellor
(San Francisco Office)
John A. Mintz
(Washington, D.C. Office)
Nathan I. Nahm
(New York City Office)
John O'Halloran
(Century City Office)
Gonzalo Pardo de Zela
(New York City Office)
Malcolm R. Pfunder
(Washington, D.C. Office)
Thomas M. Piccone
(Denver, Colorado Office)
Therese D. Pritchard
(Washington, D.C. Office)
Amy G. Rudnick
(Washington, D.C. Office)
W. Richard Smith, Jr.
(Irvine Office)
Lawrence W. Treece
(Denver, Colorado Office)
Stephanie Tsacoumis
(Washington, D.C. Office)
William M. Wiltshire
(Washington, D.C. Office)

SPECIAL COUNSELS

Deborah E. Miller
(New York City Office)
Josiah O. Hatch III
(Denver, Colorado Office)
David Andrew Cheit
(San Francisco Office)
Derry Dean Sparlin Jr.
(Washington, D.C. Office)
Teresa Joanning Farrell
(Irvine Office)

April McGandy Evans
Marilyn G. McDowell
Brent M. Cohen
(San Francisco Office)
David C. Mahaffey
(Washington, D.C. Office)
I. Richard Levy
(Dallas, Texas Office)
Laura Ben-Porat
(Century City Office)

(See Next Column)

SPECIAL COUNSELS (Continued)

Thomas D. Boyle
(Dallas, Texas Office)
Stephen H. Willard
(Washington, D.C. Office)
Steven James Johnson
(San Francisco Office)

Kevin R. Nowicki
(San Diego Office)
John Masao Iino
Gary M. Roberts

ASSOCIATES

Deborah Ann Aiwasian
Adam S. Bendell
Marianne Shipp (Irvine Office)
Markus U. Diethelm
(New York City Office)
D. Eric Remensperger
Gregory L. Surman
Michael J. Keliher
(Dallas, Texas Office)
Alicia J. Bentley
Lawrence M. Isenberg
Mitchell Steven Cohen
Liisa Anselmi Stith
(Irvine Office)
Riaz A. Karamali
(Palo Alto Office)
Jeffrey David Dintzer
Carl Timothy Crow
Gregory J. Conklin
(San Francisco Office)
Peter C. D'Apice
(Dallas, Texas Office)
Leonard H. Hersh
(New York City Office)
Duncan T. O'Brien
(New York City Office)
Deborah J. Clarke
Vivienne Angela Vella
Margaret B. Graham
(Denver, Colorado Office)
Lawrence S. Achorn
(San Francisco Office)
Gunnar Blaise Gooding
(Irvine Office)
Cynthia L. Salmen
Scott Monro Dreyer
Adam H. Offenhartz
(New York City Office)
Gareth T. Evans
Jeffrey F. Webb
Rodney J. Stone
Desmond Cussen
(San Francisco Office)
Mark Snyderman
(Washington, D.C. Office)
Christopher J. Bellini
(Washington, D.C. Office)
David W. Mayo
(New York City Office)
Lawrence Byrne
(New York City Office)
Janet M. Weiss
(New York City Office)
Walter J. Scott, Jr.
(Dallas, Texas Office)
Margaret C. McCulla
(Washington, D.C. Office)
Diana Gale Richard
(Washington, D.C. Office)
Linda L. Curtis
Seeley Ann Brooks
J. Mark Dunbar
(San Diego Office)
Meredith C. Braxton
(New York City Office)
Stanton P. Eigenbrodt
(Dallas, Texas Office)
Oscar Garza (Irvine Office)
Alan N. Bick (Irvine Office)
John W. Fricks
Jeffrey T. Gilleran
(Washington, D.C. Office)
Kim A. Thompson
(San Francisco Office)
Cheryl Wright Olsen
Michael F. Flanagan
(Washington, D.C. Office)
Andrea E. Neuman
(Irvine Office)
John Andrew Yu-Cheng Chang
Clark D. Stith (Irvine Office)
Eugene Scalia
(Washington, D.C. Office)
Robert E. Malchman
(New York City Office)

Henry A. Thompson (Jeddah,
Riyadh and Washington, D.C.
Offices)
Christopher L. Thorne
(Denver, Colorado Office)
J. Fred Neuman (Irvine Office)
Jerry S. Fowler, Jr.
(Washington, D.C. Office)
M. Sean Royall
(Washington, D.C. Office)
Ralph H. Blakeney
(Dallas, Texas Office)
Eben Paul Perison
(Century City Office)
Peter J. Beshar
(New York City Office)
Richard D. Gluck
(San Diego Office)
Jeffrey B. Conner
(Not admitted in CA)
Noël C. Lohr
Frédérique Sauvage (Not
admitted in CA; Not admitted
in United States)
Scott M. Knutson (Irvine Office)
Karl G. Nelson
(Dallas, Texas Office)
William A. MacArthur
Jeffrey H. Reeves (Irvine Office)
William J. Gallagher
(New York City Office)
Marshall R. King
(New York City Office)
Scott J. Calfas
Jodi M. Newberry
J. Mitchell Dolloff
(New York City Office)
Mark R. Dunn
(Dallas, Texas Office)
Kristine D. Ristaino
Michael S. Udovic
Robert H. Wright
Laura A. Zwicker
John M. Williams, III
(Irvine Office)
Gregg P. Goldman
(Irvine Office)
David A. Levine
(Washington, D.C. Office)
Steven K. Talley
(Denver, Colorado Office)
Holly B. Windham
(Dallas, Texas Office)
Audrey S. Trundle
(New York City Office)
W. James Biederman
(Washington, D.C. Office)
Antoinette D. Paglia
Shahin Rezai
(Washington, D.C. Office)
Peter M. Stone (Irvine Office)
Tracey Nelson Tiedman
(Denver, Colorado Office)
Mark J. Payne (Irvine Office)
Charles F. Kester
Tanya S. McVeigh
Brian L. Duffy
(Denver, Colorado Office)
Rebecca A. Womeldorf
(Washington, D.C. Office)
James C. Dougherty
(Washington, D.C. Office)
Mark A. Perry
(Washington, D.C. Office)
Michele L. Sheldon
(New York City Office)
Leeanna Izuel
Preeta D. Bansal
(New York City Office)
Dara L. Freedman
Alan R. Struble
(Dallas, Texas Office)
James P. Fogelman
Cori L. MacDonneil

(See Next Column)

GIBSON, DUNN & CRUTCHER LLP, *Los Angeles—Continued*

ASSOCIATES (Continued)

Craig V. Richardson
(Denver, Colorado Office)
Timothy L. Alger
Stella S. Leung (Hong Kong and
Dallas, Texas Offices)
Michael P. De Simone
(New York City Office)
Trygve M. Thoresen
(Irvine Office)
Richard B. Levy
Ignacio M. Foncillas
(New York City Office)
Maryn L. Miller (Irvine Office)
Leslie Ellen Moore
(New York City Office)
Patricia E. Foley
(Denver, Colorado Office)
Jody L. Johnson
Michelle D. Lustig
(Irvine Office)
William L. Menard
(Washington, D.C. Office)
Elise D. Charbonnet
(New York City Office)
Maya R. Crone
(Washington, D.C. Office)
Sharyl P. Bilas (Irvine Office)
Michael A. Levy
(San Francisco Office)
Chris D. Biondi
(New York City Office)
Brian E. Casey
(Denver, Colorado Office)
Lawrence J. La Sala
(New York City Office)
Matthew Ben Hinerfeld
(San Francisco Office)
David A. Segal (Irvine Office)
Alan Lawhead
(San Diego Office)
Boyd M. Johnson III
(New York City Office)
Peter P. Murphy
(Washington, D.C. Office)
Steven N. Gofman
H. Mark Lyon
(Palo Alto Office)
Paul J. Collins
(Palo Alto Office)
Linda Greif
(New York City Office)
Timothy D. Blanton
(Palo Alto Office)
Daniel W. Nelson
(Washington, D.C. Office)
Leslie Y. Kim
Debra Alligood White
Jeffrey A. Fiarman
(Washington, D.C. Office)
Monique Michal Drake
(Denver, Colorado Office)
T. Michael Crimmins
(Denver, Colorado Office)
Timothy J. Hart
Leslie R. Olson (Irvine Office)
Peter E. Seley
(Washington, D.C. Office)
Lisa A. Sleboda
(New York City Office)
Lindsey F. Buss
(Washington, D.C. Office)
Lisa M. Landmeier
(Washington, D.C. Office)
D. Jarrett Arp
(Washington, D.C. Office)
Lincoln D. Bandlow
Jeffrey D. Goldstein
Kathleen M. Vanderziel
Jon G. Shepherd
(Dallas, Texas Office)
Jason C. Murray (Los Angeles
and Century City Offices)
Donna M. Bigi (Irvine Office)
Jonathan K. Tycko
(Washington, D.C. Office)
Kimberly Ann Udovic
Thomas S. Jones (Irvine Office)
Stephanie Yost Cameron
Jonathan L. Israel
(New York City Office)

O. Rey Rodriguez
(Dallas, Texas Office)
Jeanette M. Bazis
(Century City Office)
Jessica Bolger Lee
(Denver, Colorado Office)
Deborah A. Hulse
(Washington, D.C. Office)
Torrey A. Olins (Irvine Office)
Georgiana G. Rodiger
Stephen B. Dorrough
Catherine Herrin Gorecki
(Washington, D.C. Office)
Paul B. Lackey
(Dallas, Texas Office)
Charles R. Bogle
(New York City Office)
Stacy V. Brown
(New York City Office)
Corinne A. Franzen
Thomas G. Mackey
Frederick A. Walters
(New York City Office)
Rebecca Sanhueza
(San Francisco Office)
Cosmas N. Lykos (Irvine Office)
Shelley R. Meacham
William M. Rustum
(Century City Office)
Mary Sikra Thomas
Michelle M. Brissette
(Denver, Colorado Office)
Laura C. Roche
(Palo Alto Office)
Mary K. Porter
(Denver, Colorado Office)
Brian Jaywoo Kim
David N. King
Lila E. Rogers
Hilary Joy Hatch
Michael L. Reed
(Century City Office)
Lara M. Krieger
(New York City Office)
Albert R. Morales
(New York City Office)
Theodore A. Russell
Todd M. Noonan
(San Francisco Office)
Tracey M. Whitney
Christopher D. Dusseault
Jeffrey E. Oraker
(Denver, Colorado Office)
Simone Procas
(New York City Office)
Christina L. Rooke
(San Francisco Office)
Alex E. Sadler
(Washington, D.C. Office)
Adam E. Muchnick
(Irvine Office)
Ellen L. Farrell
Sue J. Nam
(New York City Office)
Pauline H. Yoo
(New York City Office)
C. Glen Morris
(Dallas, Texas Office)
Sabrina Y. T. Fang
(Hong Kong Office)
Sean E. Andrussier
(Washington, D.C. Office)
Helgard C. Walker
(Washington, D.C. Office)
Hillary S. Zilz
(New York City Office)
Brette S. Simon
Sahily H. Feliciano
Robert R. Stark, Jr.
(Denver, Colorado Office)
Andrew H. Caudal
(Dallas, Texas Office)
Kelby D. Hagar
(Dallas, Texas Office)
John C. Conway
Arun Jha
Mark N. Mazda (Irvine Office)
Natalie Kay Sidles
(Dallas, Texas Office)

ASSOCIATES (Continued)

(See Next Column)

Paul A. Andronico
(Irvine Office)
James P. Maniscalco
Michael E. Sanders
(Irvine Office)
Todd D. Kantorezyk
(Washington, D.C. Office)
Connie J. Rand
(San Diego Office)
Dylan K. Remley
(New York City Office)
Lisa A. Alfaro
(New York City Office)
Rachael A. Simonoff
Douglas C. Freeman
(New York City Office)
Sean C. Carr
(Washington, D.C. Office)
Jeff Augustini (Irvine Office)
Wendy A. Lutzker
Jennifer R. Poe
(Dallas, Texas Office)
Tiffany Doon Silva
Walker J. Wallace III
(New York City Office)
Daniel H. Baren (Irvine Office)
Todd S. Cohen
(New York City Office)
Michele J. Herschkowitz
(New York City Office)
Laurie McLaughlin
(New York City Office)
Stacy S. Shibao
(Washington, D.C. Office)
Samuel G. Liversidge
Timothy S. Lykowski
Stewart L. McDowell
(New York City Office)
Hassan A. Zavareei
(Washington, D.C. Office)
Julie S. Zebrak
(Washington, D.C. Office)
Richard F. Romero
Joanne S. Field
Michael Pierovich
Kevin F. Mabrey
Holli H. Payne
(San Diego Office)

Sachin D. Adarkar
(San Francisco Office)
Jay P. Srinivasan
Thomas R. Greenberg
Robert H. Pritchard, Jr.
(New York City Office)
Daniel N. Shallman
Karin L. Wolff
(New York City Office)
Gavin A. Beske
(San Francisco Office)
Jeffrey L. Mengoli
(San Diego Office)
S. Elizabeth Foster
(New York City Office)
Michael D. Newton
Phillip F. Smith, Jr.
(Denver, Colorado Office)
Jesse S. Finlayson (Irvine Office)
Allison C. Goodman
(Washington, D.C. Office)
Raymond Ku
(Washington, D.C. Office)
Linda Richichi Stahl
(Dallas, Texas Office)
Michael A. Barmettler
(Irvine Office)
Kate Jeffery Stoia
(San Francisco Office)
Jill M. Dennis
(Washington, D.C. Office)
Colleen R. McMillin
(Dallas, Texas Office)
Seth M. M. Stodder
Inna Idelchik
(New York City Office)
Roger P. Capriotti
Daisy C. Wu
Daniel T. Perini
(Denver, Colorado Office)
Jean De Forest Billyou
(Irvine Office)
Jonathan M. Fingeret
(Denver, Colorado Office)
Abdul Aziz I. Al-Ajlan
(Riyadh, Saudi Arabia Office)
Abdullah A. Al Habardi
(Riyadh, Saudi Arabia Office)

STAFF ATTORNEYS

William H. Boyles
(Dallas, Texas Office)
Margaret Ann Garner
(Washington, D.C. Office)
Sally Novak Janin
(Washington, D.C. Office)
Brian R. Kirchoff (Irvine Office)
Sharon W. Koplan
(Dallas, Texas Office)
Christine Naylor
Linda Noonan
(Washington, D.C. Office)
Irene M. Ramirez
(Dallas, Texas Office)

Roberto Redondo
(New York City Office)
Randy Rhodes
Kenneth A. Schagrin
(Washington, D.C. Office)
Anna C. Silva
(San Francisco Office)
Sydney M. Smith
(Washington, D.C. Office)
Mark Oneal Suttle
Kathleen G. Vagt
(Washington, D.C. Office)
Melinda Dalton Waterman
(Irvine Office)

For full biographical listings, see the Martindale-Hubbell Law Directory

---

GOLDMAN & KAGON, LAW CORPORATION (AV)

1801 Century Park East, Suite 2222, 90067
Telephone: 310-552-1707
Telecopier: 310-552-7938

Mark A. Goldman
Barry Felsen
Richard D. Goldman
Charles D. Meyer

Christopher B. Fagan
Terry Mc Niff
Jared Laskin
Marco F. Weiss

Edmund S. Schaffer

COUNSEL

A. David Kagon

For full biographical listings, see the Martindale-Hubbell Law Directory

---

GRAHAM & JAMES LLP (AV)

14th Floor, 801 South Figueroa Street, 90017
Telephone: 213-624-2500
Telex: 4720414 GRJAUI
Telecopier: 213-623-4581
Email: dmiyamoto@gj.com *URL:* http://www.gj.com
Other offices located in: San Francisco, Orange County, Palo Alto,
Sacramento and Fresno, California; Seattle, Washington; Washington,
D.C.; New York, New York; Milan, Italy; Beijing, China; Tokyo, Japan;
London, England; Dusseldorf, Germany.

(See Next Column)

GRAHAM & JAMES LLP—*Continued*

Associated Offices: Deacons Graham & James, Hong Kong, Sydney, Melbourne, Brisbane, Perth and Canberra, Australia.
Affiliated Offices: Deacons Graham & James, Hanoi and Ho Chi Minh City, Vietnam; Taipei, Taiwan and Bangkok, Thailand; In association with Dewi Soeharto & Rekan, Jakarta, Indonesia; Graham & James in affiliation with Taylor Joynson Garrett, London, England, Bucharest, Romania and Brussels, Belgium; Mishare M. Al-Ghazali & Partners, Safat, Kuwait; Law Firm of Salah Al-Hejailan, Jeddah and Riyadh, Saudi Arabia.

John J. Allen	Michael R. Lindsay
Jorge Arciniega	Thomas T. Liu
Hidetoshi Asakura	David A. Livdahl
Vincent J. Belusko	Joseph T. Lynyak, III
James H. Broderick, Jr.	Thomas J. Masenga
Jeffrey A. Chester	Stuart L. Merkadeau
Hillel T. Cohn	David T. Miyamoto
Henry S. David	John T. Nagai
Craig J. de Recat	Stephen T. Owens
Steven S. Doi	Denis H. Oyakawa
David L. Fehrman	Charles Paturick
Rodney A. Fujii	Steven G. Polard
Benjamin E. Goldman	Pamela K. Prickett
Randolph H. Gustafson	Don A. Proudfoot, Jr.
Yasuhiro Hagihara	Edwin B. Reeser, III
(Not admitted in CA)	James C. Roberts
David L. Henty	William J. Robinson
John C. Holberton	Minda R. Schechter
J. Eric Isken	Brian E. Schield
William J. James	Allan A. Shenoi
Cheryl Lee Johnson	Wayne M. Smith
Wolfgang M. Kau	Brian A. Sullivan
Joon Yong Kim	Derrick K. Takeuchi
Stan H. Koyanagi	Martin J. Trupiano
Ken M. Kurosu	Les J. Weinstein

Barry Leigh Weissman

SPECIAL COUNSEL

William G. Anderson	Everitt G. Beers
Larry W. Mitchell	

SENIOR COUNSEL

Daniel E. Champion	Patrick J. Fields

OF COUNSEL

David A. Hayden	William W. Wells
Richard P. Manson	Eric E. Younger

COUNSEL

Merrill J. Baumann, Jr.

ASSOCIATES

David B. Abel	Jonathan E. Johnson III
Michael B. Annis	Allen Choo Kim
Martha L. Applebaum	Hyunu Lee
Alison M. Barbarosh	Jeanne M. Malitz
Brian M. Berliner	David J. Meyer
Kenneth N. Burraston	Rie Miyake
Lynn D. Cantor	Hisako Muramatsu
(Not admitted in CA)	Martin M. Noonen
Pei-Wen Chang	David K. Ritenour
JoAn H. Cho	Bin Xue Sang
Marcus Delgado	Thomas P. Schmidt
Victor de Gyarfas	Eric Shih
Marjorie Turk Desmond	Nao S. Shimato
Robert Desmond	Kristi Miki Springer
Peter R. Duchesneau	Jennifer M. Tsao
Shivbir S. Grewal	Brian Van Vleck
Jennifer R. Hasbrouck	Kimberly G. Winer
Gerard A. Hekker	Rami S. Yanni

For full biographical listings, see the Martindale-Hubbell Law Directory

GREENBERG GLUSKER FIELDS CLAMAN & MACHTINGER LLP (AV)

21st Floor, 1900 Avenue of the Stars (Century City), 90067
Telephone: 310-553-3610
Fax: 310-553-0687

MEMBERS OF FIRM

Arthur N. Greenberg	Norman H. Levine
Philip Glusker	William A. Halama
Sidney J. Machtinger	James E. Hornstein
Stephen Claman	Robert S. Chapman
Bertram Fields	Robert F. Marshall
Harvey R. Friedman	Robert E. Bennett, Jr.
Bernard Shearer	Marc S. Cohen
Jon J. Gallo	Charles N. Shephard
Paula J. Peters	Dennis B. Ellman
Michael K. Collins	Gary L. Kaplan
John L. Child	Robert W. Barnes
C. Bruce Levine	Lawrence Y. Iser
Michael A. Greene	E. Barry Haldeman
Joseph M. Cahn	Mark Stankevich
Garrett L. Hanken	Martin H. Webster

(See Next Column)

Michael V. Bales	Mark A. Gochman
Henry D. Finkelstein	Eve H. Wagner
Diane J. Crumpacker	Gerald L. Sauer
Jean Morris	Nancy A. Bertrando
Elizabeth Watson	Bonnie E. Eskenazi
Jill A. Cossman	Glenn A. Dryfoos
Peter J. Niemiec	Richard E. Posell
Roger L. Funk	Jeffrey Spitz
Richard A. Kale	Steven J. Lurie
Debby R. Zurzolo	Brian L. Edwards
Arnold D. Kahn	Stanley W. Levy

Michael K. Grace

ASSOCIATES

Lee A. Dresie	Matthew M. Johnson
Nancy C. Hsieh	Wendy M. Mesnick
Nanette Lynn Klein	Stephen S. Smith
David R. Mersten	Marc M. Stern
Patricia A. Millett	Curtis P. Holdsworth
Elisabeth A. Basini	Karen E. Pointer
Jeffrey A. Krieger	Paul A. Blechner
Carla M. Roberts	Stephen P. Clark
Edward N. Sabin	Nathanael M. Cousins
Michael W. Scholtz	Patrick P. de Gravelles
Joan E. Smiles	Kristen L. Jacobsmeyer
Mark S. Weinstock	Barry D. Kellman
Kevin L. James	Kelly L. Sather
Sheri E. Porath	Bradley Small
Stephanie H. Gold	Douglas G. Crowell

Gregory J. Sater

Reference: Wells Fargo Bank, 1801 Century Park East, Los Angeles, CA 90067.

For full biographical listings, see the Martindale-Hubbell Law Directory

HANNA AND MORTON (AV)

A Partnership including Professional Corporations
Seventeenth Floor, Wilshire-Grand Building, 600 Wilshire Boulevard, 90017
Telephone: 213-628-7131
Facsimile: 213-623-3379

MEMBERS OF FIRM

Byron C. Hanna (1887-1951)	Robert M. Newell, Jr.
Harold C. Morton (1895-1978)	James P. Modisette
John H. Blake (1916-1971)	Michael I. Blaylock
Edward S. Renwick (A Professional Corporation)	David A. Ossentjuk
	Judith A. Lower
James P. Lower	John A. Belcher

OF COUNSEL

William N. Greene	Milo V. Olson
David A. Thomas	

ASSOCIATES

Thomas N. Campbell	Michael P. Wippler
Robert J. Roche	Daniel Y. Zohar

For full biographical listings, see the Martindale-Hubbell Law Directory

HILL, FARRER & BURRILL LLP (AV)

A Limited Liability Partnership including Professional Corporations
35th Floor, Union Bank Square, 445 South Figueroa Street, 90071
Telephone: 213-620-0460
Fax: 213-624-4840

William M. Farrer (1894-1971)	Alfred J. Hill (1881-1953)
Stanley S. Burrill (1902-1957)	

MEMBERS OF FIRM

Leon S. Angvire (P.C.)	Alfred M. Clark, III
Stanley E. Tobin (P.C.)	Daniel J. McCarthy
Jack R. White (P.C.)	Ronald W. Novotny (P.C.)
Kyle D. Brown (P.C.)	David E. Parry
William M. Bitting (P.C.)	Benjamin B. Salvaty
Stuart H. Young, Jr., (P.C.)	Dean E. Dennis
Steven W. Bacon (P.C.)	Thomas F. Reed
Wm. Harold Borthwick (P.C.)	Suzanne J. Holland
Arthur B. Cook, II, (P.C.)	William A. White
James G. Johnson (P.C.)	R. Curtis Ballantyne
George Koide (P.C.)	James R. Evans, Jr.
Jonathan M. Brandler (P.C.)	G. Cresswell Templeton III
Scott L. Gilmore	Curtis A. Westfall
Kevin H. Brogan	Jennifer Cook Lewis
James A. Bowles (P.C.)	Michael S. Turner
Neil D. Martin	Michelle A. Meghrouni
Michael J. DiBiase	Jennifer L. Pancake

Barry Van Sickle

OF COUNSEL

Edwin H. Franzen (P.C.)	Darlene Fischer Phillips (P.C.)

RETIRED

Carl M. Gould	Vincent C. Page
William C. Farrer (P.C.)	

(See Next Column)

HILL, FARRER & BURRILL LLP, *Los Angeles—Continued*

ASSOCIATES

Ian M. Green	Leslie G. Van Zyl
Byron T. Ball	Arnold D. Woo
Dean A. Reeves	Karen S. Seigel
Paul M. Porter	Stacey A. Sullivan

For full biographical listings, see the Martindale-Hubbell Law Directory

---

HOLLEY & GALEN (AV)

800 South Figueroa, Suite 1100, 90017
Telephone: 213-629-1880
Fax: 213-895-0363

MEMBERS OF FIRM

Clyde E. Holley (1891-1980)	W. Michael Johnson
Albert J. Galen (Retired)	A. Steven Brown

ASSOCIATES

Debra Burchard Coffeen	Charles A. Jordan

For full biographical listings, see the Martindale-Hubbell Law Directory

---

HOWARTH & SMITH (AV)

Suite 2900, 700 South Flower Street, 90017
Telephone: 213-955-9400
Fax: 213-622-0791

MEMBERS OF FIRM

Don Howarth	David K. Ringwood
Suzelle M. Smith	Kenneth S. Tune

Brian D. Bubb

Marcus J. Berger	Katy Jacobs
Patricia Lee-Gulley	Sheila M. Bradley
Thomas F. Vandenburg	Julia S. Swanson
Gregory S. Tamkin	Kimberly L. Honus

Randall Boese

For full biographical listings, see the Martindale-Hubbell Law Directory

---

HUGHES HUBBARD & REED LLP (AV)

350 South Grand Avenue, Suite 3600, 90071-3442
Telephone: 213-613-2800
Telecopier: 213-613-2950
New York, New York Office: One Battery Park Plaza, 10004.
Telephone: 212-837-6000.
Telex: 427120.
Telecopier: 212-422-4726.
Miami, Florida Office: 201 South Biscayne Boulevard, Suite 2500,
33131-4332.
Telephone: 305-358-1666.
Fax: 305-371-8759.
Telex: 518785.
Paris, France Office: 47, Avenue Georges Mandel, 75116.
Telephone: 33 (0)1 44 05 80 00.
Telecopier: 33 (0)1 45 53 15 04.
Washington, D.C. Office: 1300 I Street, N.W., Suite 900 West, 20005.
Telephone: 202-408-3600.
Telex: 89-2674.
Telecopier: 202-408-3636.

RESIDENT PARTNERS

Charles Avrith	Richard J. Kaplan
William T. Bisset	Peter M. Langenberg
John A. Blue	Theodore H. Latty
Richard S. Friedman	Charles D. Schoor
George A. Furst	Daniel H. Slate
Rita M. Haeusler	Mark R. Moskowitz

John R. Zebrowski

SPECIAL COUNSEL

Andrea H. Bricker	Randy B. Holman

OF COUNSEL

Howard F. Hart

For full biographical listings, see the Martindale-Hubbell Law Directory

---

IRELL & MANELLA LLP (AV)

A Law Partnership including Professional Corporations
Suite 900, 1800 Avenue of the Stars (Century City), 90067-4276
Telephone: 310-277-1010
Cable Address: "Irella LSA"
Telecopier: 310-203-7199
URL: http://www.irell.com
Downtown Los Angeles Office: Suite 3300, 333 South Hope Street,
90071-3042.
Telephone: 213-620-1555.
Telecopier: 213-229-0515.
Newport Beach, California Office: Suite 500, 840 Newport Center Drive,
92660-6324.
Telephone: 714-760-0991.
Telecopier: 714-760-5200.

(See Next Column)

MEMBERS OF FIRM

Eugene M. Berger (1892-1944)	Sandra Gerson Kanengiser
Allan J. Abshez	Edmund M. Kaufman (P.C.)
James N. Adler (P.C.)	(Downtown Los Angeles
Scott D. Baskin (P.C.)	Office)
(Resident at Newport Beach)	Kyle S. Kawakami
Cary J. A. Berger (Downtown	(Resident at Newport Beach)
Los Angeles Office)	J. Christopher Kennedy
Richard L. Bernacchi (P.C.)	(Downtown Los Angeles
Sheri A. Bluebond (Downtown	Office)
Los Angeles Office)	Bruce D. Kuyper
Richard H. Borow (P.C.)	Henry Lesser (Downtown Los
Derrick O. Boston	Angeles Office)
Christine W. S. Byrd	Joan L. Lesser (P.C.)
Frank A. Caput	Ronald M. Loeb (P.C.)
(Resident at Newport Beach)	Steven A. Marenberg
Louis M. Castruccio (P.C.)	C. Kevin McGeehan
Daniel G. Christopher	Richard J. McNeil
Morgan Chu	(Resident at Newport Beach)
Richard de Bodo	Ashok W. Mukhey
David A. Dull	Layn R. Phillips
James F. Elliott	(Resident at Newport Beach)
Michael G. Ermer	Anthony W. Pierotti
(Resident at Newport Beach)	(Resident at Newport Beach)
Dorette S. Feit	S. Thomas Pollack
John C. Fossum (P.C.)	Joel Rabinovitz (P.C.)
(Resident at Newport Beach)	Susan Sakai
Elliot G. Freier	Lois J. Scali
Paul N. Frimmer (P.C.)	Alvin G. Segel
Gary N. Frischling	Marvin S. Shapiro (P.C.)
Roy S. Geiger (Downtown Los	Richard M. Sherman, Jr.,(P.C.)
Angeles Office)	(Resident at Newport Beach)
Martin N. Gelfand	Henry Shields, Jr., (P.C.)
Andra Barmash Greene	David Siegel
(Resident at Newport Beach)	Steven P. Sim
Peter J. Gregora	Steven L. Sloca
Andrew W. Gross	Gregory R. Smith
Theodore E. Guth	Howard J. Steinberg (Downtown
Kenneth R. Heitz	Los Angeles Office)
Catherine H. Helm	Jonathan H. Steinberg
Brian J. Hennigan (Downtown	Robert Steinberg
Los Angeles Office)	Steven E. Thomas
Louis A. Huskins (P.C.)	Ronald B. Tischler (P.C.)
Milton B. Hyman (P.C.)	Bruce A. Wessel
Edebeatu C. Ibekwe (Downtown	Alexander F. Wiles
Los Angeles Office)	Richard C. Wirthlin (Downtown
Anthony T. Iler (Downtown Los	Los Angeles Office)
Angeles Office)	Werner F. Wolfen (P.C.)
Thomas W. Johnson, Jr.	Rob C. Zeitinger
(Resident at Newport Beach)	Edward Zeldow

OF COUNSEL

Charles A. Collier, Jr.	Alvaro Pascotto
John J. Cost (P.C.) (Downtown	Steven H. Shiffrin
Los Angeles Office)	Robert W. Stedman (P.C.)
Lawrence E. Irell	(Resident at Newport Beach)
Thomas A. Kirschbaum	Lawrence M. Stone (P.C.)
Arthur Manella (P.C.)	William D. Warren
David Nimmer	(Not admitted in CA)

ASSOCIATES

Jeffrey L. Arrington	Peter M. Juzwiak (Downtown
Spencer E. Bendell	Los Angeles Office)
Richard M. Birnholz	Jonathan S. Kagan
Elliot N. Brown	Gregory B. Klein
André J. Brunel	Michael Krakovsky
Elizabeth A. Camacho	Brian D. Ledahl
Nancy J. Cohen	Richard Ung-Jin Lee
Leigh Taylor Combs	(Downtown Los Angeles
(Resident at Newport Beach)	Office)
Graham L. W. Day	Daniel P. Lefler
Jerald B. Dotson	Francine J. Lipman
Charles E. Elder	(Resident at Newport Beach)
Scott M. Epstein	Joseph M. Lipner
Marc A. Fenster	Wen Liu
Kevin L. Finch	Michael S. Lowe
Robert J. Flachs	Samuel Kai Lu
Joseph M. Freeman	Marc S. Maister
Melissa R. Gleiberman	(Resident at Newport Beach)
Darren J. Gold	Benjamin R. Martin
Perry M. Goldberg	Jennifer E. Meier
Philip J. Graves	Roman Melnik
Michael Grizzi (Downtown Los	Philip H. Miller
Angeles Office)	Harry A. Mittleman
Craig A. Grossman	Joanna Moore
Benjamin Hattenbach	David Z. Moss
Stephanie Kaufman Hernand	Maurine M. Murtagh
John W. Holcomb (Downtown	John M. Nakashima
Los Angeles Office)	(Resident at Newport Beach)
Steven W. Hopkins	Ben D. Orlanski (Downtown
(Resident at Newport Beach)	Los Angeles Office)
Patrick O. Hunnius	

(See Next Column)

IRELL & MANELLA LLP—Continued

ASSOCIATES (Continued)

Elizabeth K. Penfil (Resident at Newport Beach)	Douglas K. Sugimoto
David J. Richter	Mary-Christine (M.C.) Sungaila (Resident at Newport Beach)
Flavio Rose	Sana Swe
David J. Rosmann	Craig Varnen
Kathryn Schaefer	Eric A. Webber (Downtown Los Angeles Office)
David A. Schwarz	
Alan D. Sege	Toni Weinstein
Laura A. Seigle	Jessica Weisel
Jeffrey N. Shapiro	Ian C. Wiener
Gail J. Standish	Wendy A. Wolf
Ethan G. Stone	Christopher F. Wong

Juliette Youngblood

For full biographical listings, see the Martindale-Hubbell Law Directory

---

IVERSON, YOAKUM, PAPIANO & HATCH (AV)

One Wilshire Building, 27th Floor 624 South Grand Avenue, 90017
Telephone: 213-624-7444
Telecopier: 213 629-4563

Paul E. Iverson (1907-1975)	Frank B. Yoakum, Jr. (1906-1991)

MEMBERS OF FIRM

Neil Papiano	Patrick M. Mc Adam
Dennis A. Page	Arnold D. Larson

John M. Garrick

ASSOCIATES

Douglas C. Pease	Barbara Lee Berkowitz
Andrew K. Doty	Mark Pearson
Melissa A. Immel	Frederick Brevard Hayes
Mary P. Lightfoot	Gioia M. Fasi

Denise Renee Byrnes

OF COUNSEL

R. Noel Hatch

Representative Clients: Lockheed Corp.; International Paper; Bridgestone/-Firestone, Inc.
Reference: Security Pacific National Bank (Los Angeles Head Office).

For full biographical listings, see the Martindale-Hubbell Law Directory

---

JONES, DAY, REAVIS & POGUE (AV)

555 West Fifth Street Suite 4600, 90013-1025
Telephone: 213-489-3939
Telex: 181439 UD
Telecopier: 213-243-2539
In Irvine, California: 2603 Main Street, Suite 900.
Telephone: 714-851-3939.
Telex: 194911 Lawyers LSA.
Telecopier: 714-553-7539.
In Atlanta, Georgia: 3500 One Peachtree Center, 303 Peachtree Street, N.E.
Telephone: 404-521-3939.
Cable Address: "Attorneys Atlanta".
Telex: 54-2711.
Telecopier: 404-581-8330.
In Brussels, Belgium: Avenue Louise 480, 7th Floor, B-1050 Brussels.
Telephone: 32-2-645-14-11.
Telecopier: 32-2-645-14-45.
In Chicago, Illinois: 77 West Wacker.
Telephone: 312-782-3939.
Telecopier: 312-782-8585.
In Cleveland, Ohio: North Point, 901 Lakeside Avenue.
Telephone: 216-586-3939.
Cable Address: "Attorneys Cleveland."
Telex: 980389.
Telecopier: 216-579-0212.
In Columbus, Ohio: 1900 Huntington Center.
Telephone: 614-469-3939.
Cable Address: "Attorneys Columbus."
Telecopier: 614-461-4198.
In Dallas, Texas: 2300 Trammell Crow Center, 2001 Ross Avenue.
Telephone: 214-220-3939.
Cable Address: "Attorneys Dallas."
Telex: 730852.
Telecopier: 214-969-5100.
In Frankfurt, Germany: Triton Haus, Bockenheimer Landstrasse 42, 60323 Frankfurt am Main.
Telephone: 49-69-9726-3939.
Telecopier: 49-69-9726-3993.
In Geneva, Switzerland: 20, rue de Candolle.
Telephone: 41-22-320-2339.
Telecopier: 41-22-320-1232.
In Hong Kong: 29th Floor, Entertainment Building, 30 Queen's Road Central.
Telephone: 852-2526-6895.
Telecopier: 852-2868-5871.

(See Next Column)

In London England: Bucklersbury House, 3 Queen Victoria Street.
Telephone: 44-171-236-3939.
Telecopier: 44-171-236-1113.
In New Delhi, India: Pathak & Associates, 13th Floor, Dr. Gopal Das Bhaven, 28 Barakhamba Road.
Telephone: 91-11-373-8793.
Telecopier: 91-11-335-3761.
In New York, New York: 599 Lexington Avenue.
Telephone: 212-326-3939.
Cable Address: "JONESDAY NEWYORK."
Telex: 237013 JDRP UR.
Telecopier: 212-755-7306.
In Paris, France: 62, rue du Faubourg Saint-Honore.
Telephone: 33-1-44-71-3939.
Telex: 290156 Surgoe.
Telecopier: 33-1-49-24-0471.
In Pittsburgh, Pennsylvania: 500 Grant Street, 31st Floor.
Telephone: 412-391-3939.
Cable Address: "Attorneys Pittsburgh".
Telecopier: 412-394-7959.
In Riyadh, Saudi Arabia: The International Law Firm, Sulaymaniyah Center, Tahlia Street, P.O. Box 22166.
Telephone: (966-1) 462-8866.
Telecopier: (966-1) 462-9001.
In Taipei, Taiwan: 8th Floor, 2 Tun Hwa South Road, Section 2.
Telephone: (886-2) 704-6808.
Telecopier: (886-2) 704-6791.
In Tokyo, Japan: Toranomon MT Building, 4th Floor, 10-3, Toranomon 3-Chome, Minato-ku, Tokyo 105, Japan.
Telephone: 81-3-3433-3939.
Telecopier: 81-3-5401-2725.
In Washington, D.C.: Metropolitan Square, 1450 G Street, N.W.
Telephone: 202-879-3939.
Cable Address: "Attorneys Washington."
Telex: 89-2410 ATTORNEYS WASH.
Telecopier: 202-737-2832.

MEMBERS OF FIRM IN LOS ANGELES

Bertram R. Zweig	Norman A. Pedersen
James F. Childs, Jr.	David S. Boyce
Ronald S. Rizzo	Andrew J. Demetriou
William G. Wilson	Thomas R. Mueller
Ross E. Stromberg	Thomas M. McMahon
Gerald W. Palmer	Eric V. Rowen
Victor G. Savikas	Louis L. Touton
Gerry D. Osterland (Not admitted in CA)	Daniel J. McLoon
Elwood Lui	Scott D. Bertzyk
Robert Dean Avery	Sarah Heck Griffin
Donald D. Gralnek	Jeffrey A. LeVee
James L. Baumoel	Lester O. Brown
Frederick L. McKnight	Kevin G. McBride (Not admitted in CA)
Dean B. Allison	David J. DiMeglio

Daniel D. McMillan

OF COUNSEL

Richard H. Koppes	Richard J. Frick
David C. Zucker	Patricia A. Van Dyke

SENIOR ATTORNEY

Douglas F. Landrum	Lynn Leversen Kambe

ASSOCIATES

Marsha E. Durko	Sharon L. Faris
Peter G. McAllen	Jeffrey S. Koenig
Thomas Botz	Susanne L. Meline
Mary J. Garnett	Elizabeth G. Moreno
Craig S. Gatarz (Not admitted in CA)	Sophia Friedman Roslin
	Alonzo B. Wickers, IV
Robert M. Gilchrest	Jinshu Zhang
Kevin A. Dorse	David B. Fischer
Catherine A. Ehrgott	Erin E. Nolan
Katherine M. Elwood	Kirstin D. Poirier-Whitley
Kevin R. Lussier	Karen R. Thorland
Jeffrey A. Miller	Jacqueline M. Aguilera
Kenneth A. Remson	Kathryn Blagden
Bruce J. Shih	Amy R. Brownstein
Philip E. Cook	Katarzyna A. Buchen (Not admitted in CA)
Jane M. Nowotny	
Ricky L. Shackelford	Marc D. Field
Valerie A. Brown	Jocelyn M. Gutiérrez
Mary K. Hartigan	C. Megan Laurance
Mark M. Kassabian	Vick K. Mansourian
Stanley C. Morris	Ashley S.H. Sim
Maria K. Nelson	Susanne E. Stamey
Gary W. Nugent	Allan Z. Litovsky
Wendy L. Thomas	Eugenia L. Castruccio
Eugene Y. T. Won	Vince L. Farhat
B. Maria Dennis	C. Steve Hagemeister
Miwon Yi	Gregory S.G. Klatt

Tristan B.L. Siegel

For full biographical listings, see the Martindale-Hubbell Law Directory

Los Angeles—Continued

KAYE, SCHOLER, FIERMAN, HAYS & HANDLER, LLP (AV)

A New York Limited Liability Partnership
1999 Avenue of the Stars, Suite 1600, 90067-6048
Telephone: 310-788-1000
Facsimile: 310-788-1200
New York, N.Y.: 425 Park Avenue, 10022-3598.
Telephone: 212-836-8000.
Telex: 234860 KAY UR.
Facsimile: 212-836-8689.
Washington, D.C.: McPherson Building, 901 Fifteenth Street, N.W., Suite 1100, 20005-2327.
Telephone: 202-682-3500.
Facsimile: 202-682-3580.
Hong Kong: 9 Queen Road Centre, 18th Floor.
Telephone: 852-28458989.
Facsimile: 852-28453682; 2389.

MEMBERS OF FIRM

Gary Apfel	Kenneth A. Freeling
Aton Arbisser	Jeffrey S. Gordon
Robert Barnes	Channing D. Johnson
T. Brent Costello	Barry H. Lawrence
(Not admitted in CA)	Ronald L. Leibow
Barry L. Dastin	Hushmand Sohaili
Michael D. Fernhoff	William E. Thomson, Jr.

SPECIAL COUNSEL
Cruz Reynoso

COUNSEL

Susan A. Grode	Sheri Jeffrey
Peter L. Haviland	Anthony R. Salandra
	M. Kenneth Suddleson

ASSOCIATES

Ivy Kagan Bierman	Ronald E. Levinson
Russ Alan Cashdan	Gina LiMandri
Brian T. Corrigan	Mitchell J. Steinberger
Alan L. Friel	Bonnie Stylides
Brian M. Hoye	Rhonda Renee Trotter
Lillie Hsu	Kym R. Wulfe
Liza Ilona Karsai	John A. Zecca

For full biographical listings, see the Martindale-Hubbell Law Directory

KNAPP, MARSH, JONES & DORAN (AV)

Suite 1400, Manulife Plaza, 515 South Figueroa Street, 90071-3329
Telephone: 213-627-8471
Telecopier: 213-627-7897

MEMBERS OF FIRM

B. Richard Marsh	Gary H. Giesler
Thomas A. Doran	Wesley G. Beverlin
James G. Jones	Patricia M. Schnegg
Daniel V. Hyde	Janette Sarmiento Knowlton

ASSOCIATES

Eileen M. Whalen	Scott M. Olken
Paul J. Beck	Mario A. Pichardo
Alexander Shipman	Wendy W. Huang

For full biographical listings, see the Martindale-Hubbell Law Directory

LAGERLOF, SENECAL, BRADLEY & SWIFT, LLP

(See Pasadena)

LATHAM & WATKINS (AV)

633 West Fifth Street, Suite 4000, 90071
Telephone: 213-485-1234
Telecopier: 213-891-8763
TWX: 910-321-3733
Cable Address: "Lathwat"
URL: http://www.lw.com
Costa Mesa, California Office: Suite 2000, 650 Town Center Drive.
Telephone: 714-540-1235.
San Diego, California Office: Suite 2100, 701 B Street.
Telephone: 619-236-1234.
San Francisco, California Office: 505 Montgomery Street, Suite 1990.
Telephone: 415-391-0600.
Washington, D.C. Office: Suite 1300, 1001 Pennsylvania Avenue, N.W.
Telephone: 202-637-2200.
Chicago, Illinois Office: Suite 5800 Sears Tower.
Telephone: 312-876-7700.
Newark, New Jersey Office: One Newark Center.
Telephone: 201-639-1234.
Fax: 201-639-7298.
New York, N.Y. Office: Suite 1000, 885 Third Avenue.
Telephone: 212-906-1200.
London, England Office: One Angel Court, EC2R 7HJ.
Telephone: +-44-171-374 4444.
Telecopier: +-44-171-374 4460.

(See Next Column)

Moscow, Russia Office: Suite C200, 113/1 Leninsky Prospeckt, 117198.
Telephone: +-7 503 956-5555.
Fax: +-7 503 956-5556.
Hong Kong Office: 11th Floor Central Building, Number One Pedder Street, Central Hong Kong.
Telephone: 011-852-2841-7779.
Fax: 011-852-2841-7749.
Tokyo, Japan Office: Infini Akasaka, 8-7-15 Akasaka, Minato-Ku, Tokyo 107, Japan.
Telephone: 011 81 3 3423-3970.
Fax: 011 81 3 3423-3971.

MEMBERS OF FIRM

Paul R. Watkins (1899-1973)	William C. Bottger, Jr.
Dana Latham (1898-1974)	Laurence H. Levine
Ira M. Price, II (1919-1968)	(Chicago, Illinois Office)
Philip F. Belleville	John F. Walker, Jr.
Irving Salem	Robert A. Long
(New York City Office)	William J. Gibbons
William R. Nicholas	(Chicago, Illinois Office)
John P. McLoughlin	Gary M. Epstein
Alan I. Rothenberg	(Washington, D.C. Office)
Francis K. Decker, Jr.	Roger H. Kimmel
(New York City Office)	(New York City Office)
David H. Vena	Job Taylor, III
Donald P. Newell	(New York City Office)
(San Diego Office)	Jeffrey T. Pero
Joseph A. Wheelock Jr.	(Costa Mesa Office)
(Costa Mesa Office)	Betty-Jane Kirwan
Kenneth Conboy	William J. Meeske
(New York City Office)	John J. Clair, Jr.
J. Thomas Rosch	Stephen S. Bowen
(San Francisco Office)	(Chicago, Illinois Office)
Kenneth M. Poovey	Erica H. Steinberger
(San Francisco Office)	(New York City Office)
John J. Kirby, Jr.	Robert A. Greenspon
(New York City Office)	(New York City Office)
Takashi Matsumoto	Gene A. Lucero
(Tokyo, Japan Office)	Richard L. Chadakoff
Robert E. Currie	(New York City Office)
(Costa Mesa Office)	Bruce A. Tester
Michael J. Shockro	(Costa Mesa Office)
John R. Light	Barbara A. Caulfield
James G. Hunter, Jr.	(San Francisco Office)
(Chicago, Illinois Office)	Donald P. Baker
John P. Lynch	James A. Cherney
(Chicago, Illinois Office)	(Chicago, Illinois Office)
Thomas W. Dobson	Paul I. Meyer (San Diego Office)
Bruce R. Lederman	Robert M. Sussman
Thomas G. Bost	(Washington, D.C. Office)
Selvyn Seidel	James V. Kearney
(New York City Office)	(New York City Office)
Alan W. Pettis	Geoffrey K. Hurley
(Costa Mesa Office)	(New York City Office)
George Vradenburg III	Thomas L. Pfister
Joseph I. Bentley	Alan B. Clark
(Costa Mesa Office)	Dale K. Neal
Fredric J. Zepp	Donald L. Schwartz
(San Francisco Office)	(Chicago Office)
Gary Olson	David L. Mulliken
George A. Rice	(San Diego Office)
(Chicago, Illinois Office)	Robert K. Break
Thomas L. Patten	(Costa Mesa Office)
(Washington, D.C. Office)	Joel E. Krischer
Randall C. Bassett	James D. C. Barrall
A. Victor Antola	Ronald W. Hanson
James W. Daniels	(Chicago, Illinois Office)
(Costa Mesa Office)	Leonard A. Zax
Ernest J. Getto	(Washington, D.C. Office)
Philip E. Coviello	John J. Lyons
(New York City Office)	John J. Huber
Hendrik de Jong	(Washington, D.C. Office)
Roger M. Zaitzeff	W. Harrison Wellford
(New York City Office)	(Washington, D.C. Office)
Barry A. Sanders	Walter P. Loughlin
Morris A. Thurston	(New York City Office)
(Costa Mesa Office)	Miles N. Ruthberg
Peter H. Benzian	Jon D. Anderson
(San Diego Office)	(Costa Mesa Office)
David V. Lee	John B. Sherrell
Michael S. Lurey	Carl E. Witschy
McGee Grigsby	(Chicago, Illinois Office)
(Washington, D.C. Office)	Robert M. Dell
Robert J. Rosenberg	(San Francisco Office)
(New York City Office)	Mary B. Ruhl
Paul H. Dawes	Patrick T. Seaver
(San Francisco Office)	(Costa Mesa Office)
Christopher L. Kaufman	Thomas G. Gallatin, Jr.
(San Francisco Office)	(New York City Office)
Hugh Steven Wilson	Victoria E. Marmorstein
(San Diego Office)	Peter A. Wald
Eric L. Bernthal	(San Francisco Office)
(Washington, D.C. Office)	Gary L. Dickson
William C. Kelly, Jr.	Scott N. Wolfe
(Washington, D.C. Office)	(San Diego Office)

(See Next Column)

LATHAM & WATKINS—*Continued*

MEMBERS OF FIRM (Continued)

Gregory P. Lindstrom
(Costa Mesa Office)
Joseph J. Wheeler
(San Diego Office)
Maureen E. Mahoney
(Washington, D.C. Office)
David J. Hayes
(Washington, D.C. Office)
Bruce P. Howard
(Costa Mesa Office)
Michael Chertoff (Newark, New
Jersey, New York City and
Washington, D.C. Offices)
Jon D. Demorest
(San Diego Office)
Virginia Sollenberger Grogan
Kelley Michael Gale
(San Diego Office)
Karen Smith Bryan
Deanne P. George
(San Diego Office)
Edward Sonnenschein, Jr.
Milton A. Miller
Martin N. Flics
(New York City Office)
Paul R. DeMuro
(Also at San Francisco Office)
Robert A. Waterman
(San Francisco Office)
Shelley B. O'Neill
(New York City Office)
Terrence J. Connolly
(New York City Office)
James F. Rogers
(Washington, D.C. Office)
George J. Mihlsten
Peter L. Winik
(Washington, D.C. Office)
Russell F. Sauer, Jr.
Steven Della Rocca
(New York City Office)
Jed W. Brickner
(New York City Office)
Elizabeth A. Blendell
Kevin A. Russell
(Chicago, Illinois Office)
Marc W. Rappel
Mary K. Westbrook
(Costa Mesa Office)
Mark S. Pulliam
(San Diego Office)
Robert A. Wyman, Jr.
Roger S. Goldman
(Washington, D.C. Office)
Bruce E. Rosenblum
(Washington, D.C. Office)
Brian G. Cartwright
Charles Stephen Treat
(San Francisco Office)
Marc D. Bassewitz
(Chicago, Illinois Office)
Kevin M. Murphy
(Chicago, Illinois Office)
Bryant B. Edwards
Christopher W. Garrett
(San Diego Office)
Everett C. Johnson, Jr.
(Washington, D.C. Office)
Paul D. Tosetti
William K. Rawson
(Washington, D.C. Office)
Mark W. Smith
(San Francisco Office)
David R. Hazelton
(Washington, D.C. Office)
G. Andrew Lundberg
Mark E. Newell
(Washington, D.C. Office)
John D. Shyer
(New York City Office)
Joshua Stein
(New York City Office)
John C. Hart
(New York City Office)
Edward J. Shapiro
(Washington, D.C. Office)
Samuel A. Fishman
(New York City Office)
Tomoaki Ikenaga
(New York City Office)

David C. Boatwright
(San Diego Office)
Mark A. Harris
(Chicago, Illinois Office)
Mark A. Stegemoeller
(Chicago, Illinois Office)
Robert P. Dahlquist
(San Diego Office)
Robert D. Crockett
David J. McLean
Thomas C. Sadler
Richard A. Levy
(Chicago, Illinois Office)
James E. Brandt
(New York City Office)
Sharon Y. Bowen
(New York City Office)
John L. Sachs
(Washington, D.C. Office)
Jerry R. Peters
(San Francisco Office)
Kenneth A. Wolfson
(Costa Mesa Office)
Pamela S. Palmer
Karl S. Lytz
(San Francisco Office)
William H. Voge
(New York City Office)
Nancy Scheurwater Hunter
(Chicago, Illinois Office)
Ursula H. Hyman
Martha Barnhart Jordan
Thomas A. Edwards
(San Diego Office)
David Booth Rogers
John D. Watson, Jr.
(Washington, D.C. Office)
Richard A. Conn, Jr.
(Washington, D.C. Office)
David S. Foster
(Chicago, Illinois Office)
Bennett J. Murphy
Eric A. Stern
(Washington, D.C. Office)
Lori E. Simon
(Chicago, Illinois Office)
Nancy L. Schimmel
(Chicago, Illinois Office)
J. Douglas Bacon
(Chicago, Illinois Office)
Cary K. Hyden
(Costa Mesa Office)
Peter W. Devereaux
Mark A. Flagel
Bruce P. Shepherd
(San Diego Office)
Edith R. Perez
David W. Barby
(Costa Mesa Office)
Juli Wilson Marshall
(Chicago, Illinois Office)
Robert G. Goldman
(Chicago, Illinois Office)
Michael J. Brody
Mary Ellen Kanoff
Peter F. Kerman
(San Francisco Office)
Kirk A. Davenport
(New York City Office)
Lucinda Starrett
Scott R. Haber
(San Francisco Office)
Kristine L. Wilkes
(San Diego Office)
Joel H. Mack (San Diego Office)
Raymond Yung Lin
(New York City Office)
Robert J. Gunther, Jr.
(New York City Office)
Geoffrey S. Berman
(New York City Office)
Joseph D. Sullivan
(Washington, D.C. Office)
Richard S. Zbur
Douglas A. Freedman
(Chicago, Illinois Office)
John M. Jameson
John M. Newell
Linda S. Schurman
(Chicago, Illinois Office)

MEMBERS OF FIRM (Continued)

(See Next Column)

Glenda Sanders
(Costa Mesa Office)
Peter J. Wilson
(Costa Mesa Office)
Laurence J. Stein
(Chicago, Illinois Office)
Joseph Blum
(London, England Office)
Patricia Timko Sinclair
Kirk A. Wilkinson
Allen D. Haynie
(San Diego Office)
Reba W. Thomas
Kevin C. Blauch
(New York City Office)
David A. Hahn
(San Diego Office)
Richard L. Wirthlin
(Moscow, Russia Office)
Linda M. Inscoe
(San Francisco Office)
James F. Ritter
(Washington, D.C. Office)
David A. Gordon
(New York City Office)
Robert A. Koenig
Pamela Brown Kelly
Dennis B. Nordstrom
(London, England Office)
Paul A. Galleberg
Kevin Charles Boyle
(Washington, D.C. Office)
Glen B. Collyer
Richard W. Raushenbush
(San Francisco Office)
William J. Cernius
(Costa Mesa Office)
David K. Rathgeber
(Chicago, Illinois Office)
John H. Kenney
(San Francisco Office)
David T. I. Vong
(Hong Kong Office)
Andrew D. Singer
(San Diego Office)
Michael Bruce Abelson
Julia A. Hatcher
(Washington, D.C. Office)
Joseph A. Bevash
(Hong Kong Office)
Samuel R. Weiner
(San Francisco Office)
Dena L. Bloom
Cynthia H. Cwik
(San Diego Office)
Philip J. Perzek
(Chicago, Illinois Office)
Carolyne R. Hathaway
(Washington, D.C. Office)
Cary R. Perlman
(Chicago, Illinois Office)

OF COUNSEL

John S. Welch
Clinton R. Stevenson
H. Randall Stoke
Richard Carver
John R. Stahr
(Costa Mesa Office)
Alan N. Halkett
Robert B. Wessling
Philip L. Reynolds
Warren B. Elterman
(New York City Office)
David A. York
(San Francisco Office)
Frederick M. Danziger
(New York City Office)
Beth R. Neckman
(New York City Office)
Patrick W. Duval
(New York City Office)
Regina M. Schlatter
(Costa Mesa Office)
Jeffrey S. Haber
Michael P. Vandenbergh
(Washington, D.C. Office)
Andrea L. Mersel
(Costa Mesa Office)
John P. Coffey
(New York City Office)
Austin H. Peck, Jr.

Michael Scott Feeley
John P. Janka
(Washington, D.C. Office)
Steven M. Bauer
(San Francisco Office)
Linda Schilling
(Costa Mesa Office)
Brian C. Krisberg
(New York City Office)
Michael K. Hertz
(New York City Office)
Joseph B. Farrell
(Costa Mesa Office)
R. Ronald Hopkinson
(New York City Office)
Scott O. Bowie
David L. Shapiro
(Chicago, Illinois Office)
Tracy K. Edmonson
(San Francisco Office)
David S. Raab
(Washington, D.C. Office)
Anthony J. Richmond
Mark S. Mester
(Chicago, Illinois Office)
Michael G. Romey
Jeffrey R. Holmstead
(Washington, D.C. Office)
Scott P. Klein
Sosi Biricik Klijian
(San Diego Office)
Timothy B. Hardwicke
(Chicago, Illinois Office)
Robert A. Klyman
Ian B. Blumenstein
(New York City Office)
Barry J. Shotts
(San Diego Office)
Susan S. Azad
A. Brent Truitt
(New York City Office)
Timothy P. Crudo
(San Francisco Office)
Gay L. Bronson
(New York City Office)
Michael J. Carroll
Hyun Park (Hong Kong Office)
Mary Rose Alexander
(Chicago, Illinois Office)
J. Drew Page (San Diego Office)
Robert M. Howard
(San Diego Office)
Susan Paulsrud Welch
Nicholas W. Allard
(Washington, D.C. Office)
James I. Hisiger
(New York City Office)
Russell Hayman
David Miles
(London, England Office)
Mark D. Gerstein
(Chicago Office)

Scott R. Smith
(New York City Office)
Gerald J. Lewis
(San Diego Office)
Mark S. Fowler
(Washington, D.C. Office)
Stephen M. Burgin
David E. Novitski
David W. Fleming
Thomas B. Trimble
(Washington, D.C. Office)
Gordon Simonds
(San Francisco Office)
David M. Leive
(Washington, D.C. Office)
Desiree Icaza Kellogg
(San Diego Office)
Jean M. Donnelly
(Costa Mesa Office)
Yanlei Wu
(Washington, D.C. Office)
Hervé Gouraige (Newark, New
Jersey and New York City
Offices)
Richard B. Ulmer Jr.
(San Francisco Office)
Daniel K. Settelmayer
Dean G. Dunlavey
(Costa Mesa Office)

(See Next Column)

LATHAM & WATKINS, *Los Angeles—Continued*

OF COUNSEL (Continued)

James O. Copley
(New York City Office)
Gregory K. Miller
(San Francisco Office)
Jonathan S. Berck
(London Office)
Kenneth R. Whiting, Jr.
(San Francisco Office)
Bruce J. Prager
(New York City Office)

Bernard C. Byrnes
(New York City Office)
Lev S. Simkin
(Moscow, Russia Office)
Louise Zeitzew
(New York City Office)
Christopher R. Plaut
(New York City Office)
Jiyeon Lee Lim
(New York City Office)

ASSOCIATES

Christopher D. Lueking
(Chicago, Illinois Office)
Carlos Alvarez
(New York City Office)
Adele K. Cardoza
(Costa Mesa Office)
Elissa Ganbarg Benudis
(New York City Office)
Gail A. Matthews
(New York City Office)
Jeffrey T. Wald
(New York City Office)
Mark D. Beckett
(New York City Office)
Marc J. Veilleux
(New York City Office)
Katherine A. Lauer
(San Diego Office)
Marla S. Becker
(New York City Office)
J. Wesley Skow
(San Francisco Office)
Gregory A. Ezring
(New York City Office)
Kimberly M. McCormick
(San Diego Office)
Amos M. Levy
(Not admitted in CA)
Jeffrey G. Moran
(Chicago, Illinois Office)
John T. Brennan
(New York City Office)
Patrick J. Carty
(New York City Office)
Jeffrey M. Goodman
(New York City Office)
Elisabeth L. Goot
(New York City Office)
Dean T. Janis (San Diego Office)
David C. Meckler
(Costa Mesa Office)
Jennifer C. Archie
(Washington, D.C. Office)
Mark I. Michigan
(New York City Office)
E. William Cattan, Jr.
(New York City Office)
Kenneth M. Fitzgerald
(San Diego Office)
Dorn G. Bishop
(San Diego Office)
Kim Natalie Alicia Boras
(New York City Office)
L. Susan McGinnis
Marian A. Harvey
Steven Atlee
James L. Arnone
Jeff D. Wesselkamper
(San Francisco Office)
Marcus A. McDaniel
Daniel T. Lennon
(Washington, D.C. Office)
Anya Goldin
(Moscow, Russia Office)
Eva Herbst Davis
David C. Flattum
(Costa Mesa Office)
Gregory N. Pimstone
Steven J. Levine
(San Diego Office)
Wayne S. Flick
Maureen Smith
(New York City Office)
Peter M. Gilhuly
Cynthia A. Rotell
Mark Bruce Abbott
Peter Huston
(San Francisco Office)

Andrew Marc Paley
Gregory M. Pettigrew
Ann K. O'Brien
Donna J. Williams
(San Diego Office)
William J. Caldarelli
(San Diego Office)
Jon L. Praed
(Washington, D.C. Office)
David F. Randell
(Chicago, Illinois Office)
James H. Barker, III
(Washington, D.C. Office)
Curtis P. Lu
(Washington, D.C. Office)
Jennifer Upham Saunders
Teresa D. Baer
(Washington, D.C. Office)
Jeffrey H. Koppele
(New York City Office)
David L. Schwartz
(Washington, D.C. Office)
S. H. Spencer Compton
(New York City Office)
David A. Barrett
(Washington, D.C. Office)
John R. Tinkham
(Chicago, Illinois Office)
Rebecca D. Roberts
(Not admitted in CA)
Scott R. McCaw
(New York City Office)
Regina L. Scinta
(New York City Office)
Andrew D. Richman
(New York City Office)
James S. Blank
(New York City Office)
Corinne M. Plummer
(London, England Office)
Howard A. Matalon
(Newark, New Jersey Office)
Kathryn Shaw Collins
(Chicago, Illinois Office)
Joseph M. Kronsnoble
(Chicago, Illinois Office)
Diana L. Day (San Diego Office)
R. Brian Timmons
(Costa Mesa Office)
Ora T. Fruehauf
(San Francisco Office)
David Judson Barrett
(San Diego Office)
Ellen L. Marks
(Chicago, Illinois Office)
Scott C. Herlihy
(Washington, D.C. Office)
Robin D. Dal Soglio
Scott B. Garner
(Costa Mesa Office)
James P. Beaubien
Philip J. Perry
(Washington, D.C. Office)
Richard M. Trobman
(New York City Office)
Lisa A. Von Eschen
James R. Barrett
(Washington, D.C. Office)
Michael W. Sturrock
Kimberly L. Wilkinson
(San Francisco Office)
Robin M. Hulshizer
(Chicago Office)
Amy G. Nefouse
(San Diego Office)
Deborah A. Bigbee
Bruce D. Gellman
(San Francisco Office)

(See Next Column)

ASSOCIATES (Continued)

Paul J. Hunt
(Washington, D.C. Office)
Anthony I. Fenwick
(San Francisco Office)
Maria P. Hoye
Kathleen M. O'Prey Truman
Vivian Clara Strache
(Washington, D.C. Office)
Christopher J. Peters
(Chicago, Illinois Office)
Melissa A. Roper
(New York City Office)
Gwyn Goodson Timms
(San Diego Office)
Charles W. Cox, II
(Costa Mesa Office)
David T. Kraska
(San Francisco Office)
Marci L. Smith
Annette L. Hayes
(Washington, D.C. Office)
Scott C. Lewis
Whitney E. Peterson
(San Diego Office)
Charles K. Ruck
(Costa Mesa Office)
Julian Y. Kim
(Washington, D.C. Office)
Michael J. Guzman
(Washington, D.C. Office)
Kimberly Arouh
(San Diego Office)
Kenneth A. Schuhmacher
(London, England Office)
Paul N. Singarella
(Costa Mesa Office)
Maureen A. Riley
(New York City Office)
Greg S. Slater
(Washington, D.C. Office)
Maureen C. Shay
(New York City Office)
Peter J. Falconer
(Chicago, Illinois Office)
Dennis M. Walsh
(New York City Office)
Christopher Harrison
(London, England Office)
Tracy M. Preston
(San Francisco Office)
Stephen K. Phillips
(San Francisco Office)
James W. Baker
(San Diego Office)
J. Scott Hodgkins
David A. Nelson
(Chicago, Illinois Office)
Michael S. Wroblewski
(Washington, D.C. Office)
Hugh L. Burns
(New York City Office)
David M. Hernand
Michael A. Bell
(Washington, D.C. Office)
Dean M. Kato
Craig M. Garner
(San Diego Office)
Minh N. Vu
(Washington, D.C. Office)
Eric A. Gaynor
Andrew Han
Amy N. Keroes
Teri L. Witteman
Linda Harrison Edwards
Simon J. Dickens
(Chicago, Illinois Office)
Marc D. Jaffe
(New York City Office)
Daniel J. Ross
(New York City Office)
Peter M. Labonski
(New York City Office)
Michèle O. Penzer
(New York City Office)
Robert F. Kennedy
(New York City Office)
Kenneth D. Crews
(Chicago, Illinois Office)
Gary R. Ignatin
Jeffrey L. Kateman
Joseph A. Sullivan
(Chicago, Illinois Office)

Anat Hakim
(New York City Office)
Michelle M. Carroll
Eric J. Custer
Brian H. Levey
Stuart L. Leviton
Susan M. Marsch
Parris J. Sanz
John B. Duer
(New York City Office)
C. Chad Johnson
(New York City Office)
Lee D. Hwang
Darci A. Lanphere
Andrea S. Matiauda
(Costa Mesa Office)
Daniel A. Thomson
(Costa Mesa Office)
Pilar S. Parducci
Bruce R. Ledesma
(San Francisco Office)
Mary E. Britton
(Washington, D.C. Office)
Steven D. McKenney
David L. Kuiper
(Costa Mesa Office)
Kenneth G. Schuler
(Chicago, Illinois Office)
Daniel Scott Schecter
Susan P. Flattum
Daniel W. Burke
(Costa Mesa Office)
Michael J. Malecek
(San Francisco Office)
William C. Tayler
(San Diego Office)
Laura Gabriel
(San Francisco Office)
Sylvia A. Stein
(Chicago, Illinois Office)
John H. Gomez
William A. Voxman
(Washington, D.C. Office)
Naomi H. Kobayashi
Jerianne E. Mancini
(New York City Office)
Anton Leof
(San Francisco Office)
Randall D. Roth
(New York City Office)
Michael A. Bond
(New York City Office)
David N. Fong
(New York City Office)
Gary A. Kashar
Michael D. Smith
(Chicago, Illinois Office)
Deidre L. Schneider
(San Diego Office)
Jill H. Silfen
Alice S. Fisher
(Washington, D.C. Office)
Neil Cummings
(New York City Office)
Julia E. Parry (San Diego Office)
Dawn D. Schiller
(Chicago, Illinois Office)
Marsha Y. Reeves
(Washington, D.C. Office)
Richard S. Davis
Ted Fikre
Francis Y. Park
Eric A. Richardson
(New York City Office)
Steven H. Schulman
(Washington, D.C. Office)
Claudia M. O'Brien
(Washington, D.C. Office)
Ian H. Fisher
(Chicago, Illinois Office)
Gregory O. Lunt
Daniel L. Martens
Christine LeGrand Lehman
(San Francisco Office)
James R. Dutro
(San Francisco Office)
Carolyn R. Worsley
(New York City Office)
Assaf J. Henig
Robert S. Michitarian
(San Francisco Office)

(See Next Column)

LATHAM & WATKINS—*Continued*

ASSOCIATES (Continued)

Matthew W. Walch
(Chicago, Illinois Office)
Jens H. Hillen
Kathleen Kilourie
Michael G. Mishik
Mary C. Tesh
Dominic K.L. Yoong
Tad J. Freese
(San Francisco Office)
Sony Ben-Moshe
(San Diego Office)
Michelle Duncan Bergman
(New York City Office)
JoAnn Laurentino
(New York City Office)
Denise R. Ben-Attar
(New York City Office)
Carole Ferguson Johnson
(New York City Office)
Rose Greenberg
(New York City Office)
Theodore K. Smith
(Moscow, Russia Office)
Roland S. Young
(New York City Office)
Christian B. McGrath
(Chicago, Illinois Office)
Lynne S. Hoffenberg
(Chicago, Illinois Office)
Andrew B. Munro
Laura I. Bushnell
(Costa Mesa Office)
R. Scott Shean
(Costa Mesa Office)
Malu S. Mercado
(San Francisco Office)
Donald A. Fishman
(Washington, D.C. Office)
Oswald B. Cousins, II
(San Francisco Office)
Hyen-ae Jane Sung
(San Francisco Office)
Lauren E. Passmore
(New York City Office)
Ian A. Gerard
(New York City Office)
Miriam T. Jona
(Chicago, Illinois Office)
Michael R. Etzioni
Vincent H. Herron
Blair G. Connelly
Mark A. Finkelstein
(Costa Mesa Office)
Debra N. Michelson
(New York City Office)
Mary A. Donovan
(Costa Mesa Office)
Lino J. Lauro
(Chicago, Illinois Office)
Wayne G. Nitti
David O. Kahn
Carol M. Mauch
John G. Holland
(Washington, D.C. Office)
Kyle W. Hoffman
(San Diego Office)
David Pitman
(Costa Mesa Office)
Kevin T. Kerns
(Chicago, Illinois Office)
Robert E. Burwell
(San Diego Office)
Sandra A. Muhlenbeck
(Chicago, Illinois Office)
Patrick Gibbs
(Chicago, Illinois Office)
Lane H. Blumenfeld
(Washington, D.C. Office)
Jacklyn Kay Bartlett
(New York City Office)
Scott R. Raber
(New York City Office)
David S. Dantzic
(Washington, D.C. Office)
Will B. Fitton
(San Francisco Office)
Elena C. Norman
(New York City Office)
Matthew D. Moren
(New York City Office)

Katharine M. Albright
Richard D. Strulson
John W. Creighton, III
(Washington, D.C. Office)
Craig D. Solar
(New York City Office)
Joseph M. Yaffe
(Costa Mesa Office)
Jared W. Johnson
(Washington, D.C. Office)
Scott B. Cooper
(Costa Mesa Office)
David L. London
(Washington, D.C. Office)
Eva Izsak-Niimura
(New York City Office)
Don Robert Spellmann
(New York City Office)
Grace Won
Jeffrey A. Brandon
(New York City Office)
Robert Braumuller
(Washington, D.C. Office)
Monica Yung-Min Kim
Leslie A. Pereira
David A. Kass
(Washington, D.C. Office)
Katherine M. Rollins
(Washington, D.C. Office)
Michele T. Blay
(Chicago, Illinois Office)
Sarah M. Ekdahl
(Chicago, Illinois Office)
Audrey Lee
Jacques Youssefmir
Ronit D. Earley
(Costa Mesa Office)
Mark W. Seneca
(Costa Mesa Office)
Bradley E. Kotler
(Chicago, Illinois Office)
Lenora Smith
(Chicago, Illinois Office)
Daniel P. Dillon
(San Diego Office)
Barbara L. Cammarata
(San Diego Office)
John C. Marchese
(Washington, D.C. Office)
Lynley A. Ogilvie
(Washington, D.C. Office)
Thomas R. Pappas
(New York City Office)
J. Erik Sandstedt
(New York City Office)
Shane M. Spradlin
(New York City Office)
Virginia C. Edwards
(San Francisco Office)
Rowland I. Cheng
Michael J. Lawrence
Jacklyn J. Park
Sally Shekou
Stephen F. Case
(San Diego Office)
Diana L. Strauss
(San Diego Office)
Fred B. Jacobsen
(Chicago, Illinois Office)
Clifford Mentrup
(Chicago, Illinois Office)
Peter J. Millones, Jr.
(New York City Office)
Mark D. Spoto
(Washington, D.C. Office)
Susan Finch Moore
(Washington, D.C. Office)
David E. Ross
(Washington, D.C. Office)
Patrick J. Devine
(Washington, D.C. Office)
Daniel S. Duane
(New York City Office)
Daniel McCray
(New York City Office)
Jennifer R. Fonner
(San Francisco Office)
Deborah C. Lambe
Holly M. Holt
(San Diego Office)

ASSOCIATES (Continued)

(See Next Column)

M. Michelle Alvarez
William C. Davisson, III
Robert M. O'Shea
Hoyt Sze
David M. Taub
Vivian W. Yang
Stefanie B. Isser
(New York City Office)
Chris Burt
Jamie L. Wine
(Costa Mesa Office)
Martin A. Sabarsky
Stephen R. Tetro, II
(Chicago, Illinois Office)
John D. Whipple
(San Francisco Office)
Karen E. Humphreys
(San Francisco Office)
Sangyeup Lee
(New York City Office)
Donna Herzing
(New York City Office)
Stephen D. Blevit
Joshua R. Frieman
Michael D. Lewis
Kelly J. Sosnow
Cheryl Miller Coe
(Washington, D.C. Office)
Eric Whitaker
(San Francisco Office)
Catherine S. Bridge
John M. Kuriyama
Ellen C. Waggoner
Sarah K. Freeman
(San Diego Office)
Thomas M. Reiter
(Moscow Office)
David E. Christensen
Stephen J. Newman
Susan E. McNeil
(Washington, D.C. Office)
James R. Hanna
(Washington, D.C. Office)
Martha Ann Mazzone
(Washington, D.C. Office)
Carter H. Strickland, Jr.
(New York City Office)
Maria E. Platsis
(Washington, D.C. Office)
Stephanie Switzer Brule
(San Francisco Office)
Christopher L. Elwell
T. Edward Smith
Steven J. Olson
Lauren G. Krasnow
(New York City Office)
Bradd L. Williamson
(New York City Office)
Marilyn M. Singleton
(San Francisco Office)
Mara I. Kapelovitz
(San Francisco Office)
Sanjay Bhandari
(San Francisco Office)
Maurine J. Neiberg
(Chicago, Illinois Office)
Eric A. Rosand
(Washington, D.C. Office)
Chunlin Leonhard
(Chicago Office)
Alan S. Adler
Randy R. Merritt
Brian E. Cromer
(San Diego Office)
Louis G. Alonso
(San Diego Office)
Meera Joshi Cattafesta
(New York City Office)
Stephanie H. Knutson
(Costa Mesa Office)
Gregory M. Saylin
(Costa Mesa Office)
Heidi E. Klein
(Washington, D.C. Office)
Monique Valbuena Pertchik
(Washington, D.C. Office)
Diana S. Doyle (Chicago Office)
Matthew Fradin
(Chicago Office)
Katharine P. Moir
(Chicago Office)
Guy Giberson
(New York City Office)

Jena Kirsch (San Diego Office)
Jill M. Houlahan
(San Diego Office)
Brett Rosenblatt
(San Diego Office)
David A. Becker
(Washington, D.C. Office)
Chris Carr
(Washington, D.C. Office)
Nandan M. Joshi
(Washington, D.C. Office)
Joseph M. Boyle
(Washington, D.C. Office)
Alyssa R. Harvey
(Washington, D.C. Office)
Paul M. Winters
(Washington, D.C. Office)
Arthur S. Landerholm
(Washington, D.C. Office)
Elizabeth T. Carlson
(Washington, D.C. Office)
Jocelyn M. Seitzman
(Washington, D.C. Office)
Meredith A. Berlin
(Chicago Office)
Katharine A. Wolanyk
(Chicago Office)
Adel F. Bebawy
Connie C. Chen
Scott Gluck
Eric M. Lanyard
Jason T. Miller
Jonn R. Beeson
(Costa Mesa Office)
Julie Vigil King
(Costa Mesa Office)
Stephen J. Venuto
(Costa Mesa Office)
Eric L. Czech
(New York City Office)
M. Christopher Hall
(New York City Office)
Perry J. Hindin
(New York City Office)
Anna C. Lincoln
(New York City Office)
Michael S. Winderman
(New York City Office)
Kevin C. May (Chicago Office)
Steven J. Novatney
(Chicago Office)
Micaela H. Martín
(San Francisco Office)
Karen A. Merkle
(New York City Office)
Judy D. Stratton
(New York City Office)
Derek D. Dundas
Angelee Fox
Jeffrey B. Greenberg
Daniel W. S. Lawrence
Susan E. Leckrone
Deborah T. Lee
Lisa S. Prange
Nadia A. Shabaik
Mary J. Yoo
Jeannette M. Hill-Yonis
Stacey Sternberg
Amos E. Hartston
Loren M. Montgomery
Eyal Gamliel
Julie Vaughan
(London, England Office)
Dru Greenhalgh
(San Diego Office)
Melinda A. Pfeiffer
(San Francisco Office)
Scott K. Milsten
(San Francisco Office)
Dana N. Linker
(San Francisco Office)
Randall K. H. Ching
(San Francisco Office)
Clay Shevlin (Costa Mesa Office)
Catherine Lamb
(San Francisco Office)
David B. Allen
(Costa Mesa Office)
Sharadchandra A. Samy
(New York City Office)
Matthew J. Rossman
(New York City Office)

ASSOCIATES (Continued)

(See Next Column)

LATHAM & WATKINS, *Los Angeles—Continued*

Alexander S. Pesic
(San Francisco Office)
David A. Levitt
(New York City Office)
Lisa K. Eastwood
(New York City Office)
Theresa J. McPherson
(San Francisco Office)

Kenneth R. Morris
(San Francisco Office)
Dmitri A. Kounitsa
(Moscow, Russian Office)
Ivan A. Smolin
(Moscow, Russia Office)
Lisa Binder

For full biographical listings, see the Martindale-Hubbell Law Directory

LEWIS, D'AMATO, BRISBOIS & BISGAARD (AV)

A Partnership including Professional Corporations
Suite 1200, 221 North Figueroa Street, 90012
Telephone: 213-250-1800
Telex: 194508
Facsimile: 213-250-7900
Lewis, D'Amato, Brisbois & Bisgaard California Offices:
Costa Mesa Office: 650 Town Center, Suite 1400, Costa Mesa, California, 92626.
Telephone: 714-545-9200.
Facsimile: 714-850-1030.
Sacramento Office: 2500 Venture Oaks Way, Sacramento, California 95833.
Telephone: 916-564-5400.
Facsimile: 916-564-5444.
San Bernardino Office: 650 East Hospitality Lane, Suite 600, San Bernardino, California 92408.
Telephone: 909-387-1130.
Facsimile: 909-387-1138.
San Diego Office: 550 West C Street, Suite 800, San Diego California 92101.
Telephone: 619-233-1006.
Facsimile: 619-233-8627.
San Francisco Office: 601 California Street, Suite 1900, San Francisco, California 94108.
Telephone: 415-362-2580.
Facsimile: 415-434-0882.
Affiliated Offices:
Jakarta, Indonesia Affiliated Office: Mulya Lubis and Partners, Wisma Bank Dharmala, 16th Floor, Jendral, Sudirman, Kav. 28, Jakarta 12920, Indonesia.
Telephone: (62)(21) 521-1931/521-1932.
Facsimile: (62)(21) 521-1930.
Bangkok, Thailand Affiliated Office: Kanung & Partners Law Offices, Raintree Office Garden, 272 Japanese School Lane, Rama IX Road, Bangkok 10310, Thailand.
Telephone: (662) 319-7571/319-7574.
Facsimile: (662) 319-6372.

MEMBERS OF FIRM

Robert F. Lewis (P.C.)
Christopher P. Bisgaard (P.C.)
Roy M. Brisbois (P.C.)
R. Gaylord Smith
(Resident, San Diego Office)
David E. Reynolds (P.C.)
Duane C. Musfelt (Resident, San Francisco Office)
Barry G. Kaiman (P.C.)
Raul L. Martinez (P.C.)
Steven Mark Levy
B. Casey Yim (P.C.)
Alan E. Greenberg
(Resident, San Diego Office)
Mary G. Whitaker (P.C.)
Scott Lichtig
Donald A. Ruston
(Resident, Costa Mesa Office)
James D. Fraser
David B. Paynter (Resident, San Francisco Office)
Dennis R. Kasper
Ernest Slome
(Resident, San Diego Office)
Keith D. Taylor
(Resident, Costa Mesa Office)
Douglas R. Reynolds
(Resident, San Diego Office)
Marilyn R. Moriarty
(Resident, San Diego Office)
Jeffrey B. Barton
(Resident, San Diego Office)
Robert K. Wrede
Timothy R. Graves
Peter L. Garchie
(Resident, San Diego Office)
Steven R. Lewis
David N. Makous
Randall L. Mason
(Resident, San Diego Office)
Eric C. Castro

Lawrence N. Halperin
Jeffrey R. Kurtock (P.C.)
(Resident, San Francisco Office)
Gary M. Lape
(Resident, Costa Mesa Office)
Shawn K. Deasy
(Resident, San Diego Office)
Thomas Rittenburg
Bartley L. Becker
Lance A. Selfridge
Sharon S. Chandler (Resident, San Francisco Office)
Nancy E. Zeltzer
(Resident, Costa Mesa Office)
John H. Shimada
Gary L. Effron
Kenneth T. Kreeble (Resident, San Bernardino Office)
Joseph K. Hegedus
Judith A. Zipkin
Gordon J. Calhoun
Richard B. Wolf
Paul Y. Lee
David E. Long
Roger S. Raphael (Resident, San Francisco Office)
Cathey A. Stricker
Thomas L. Vazakas
(Resident, San Diego Office)
Elise D. Klein
Joseph C. Owens
William John Rea, Jr.
Lee A. Wood
(Resident, Costa Mesa Office)
Dennis G. Seley
(Resident, Sacramento Office)
Jana I. Lubert
Judith M. Tishkoff
Thomas M. Diachenko
(Resident, San Diego Office)

(See Next Column)

MEMBERS OF FIRM (Continued)

R. Anthony Moya
(Resident, San Diego Office)
Thomas E. Francis
(Resident, Costa Mesa Office)
Susan E. Leonard
(Resident, San Diego Office)
H. Gilbert Jones
(Resident, Costa Mesa Office)
Howard G. Rath, Jr., (P.C.)
Frankie Fook-Lun Leung
Michael W. Connally
(Resident, Costa Mesa Office)
Annie Verdries
(Resident, Costa Mesa Office)
Stephen T. Waimey
Mercedes Cruz
Armen Hairapetian
Claudia J. Robinson
(Resident, Sacramento Office)
Leon M. Cooper
James G. Bohm
(Resident, Costa Mesa Office)
George A. Boland (Resident, San Bernardino Office)
Joan L. Danielsen
(Resident, San Diego Office)
Richard L. Antognini
(Resident, Sacramento Office)
Laura S. Inlow
Douglas R. Irvine
Scott W. Monson
(Resident, Costa Mesa Office)
Michael C. Olson
(Resident, Costa Mesa Office)
James J. Wallace
(Resident, San Diego Office)
Timothy J. Watson
Louis Robert De Stefano
David M. Reeder
Peter F. Harris
John F. Davis
(Resident, Sacramento Office)
David E. Isenberg
(Resident, Costa Mesa Office)

Russell J. Callison
(Resident, Sacramento Office)
Paul N. Phillips
(Resident, Sacramento Office)
Brad D. Krasnoff
(Resident, Costa Mesa Office)
Penny Paxton
Raul B. Garcia
(Resident, Costa Mesa Office)
Michael J. Lancaster
(Resident, Costa Mesa Office)
Bruce Legernes (Resident, San Francisco Office)
Bruce L. Shaffer
(Resident, Sacramento Office)
Gregory P. Matzen
(Resident, Sacramento Office)
Joseph Arias (Resident, San Bernardino Office)
Richard W. Bane (Resident, San Bernardino Office)
Roger L. Bellows (Resident, San Bernardino Office)
Henry W. Crowle
(Resident, Sacramento Office)
Charles S. Haughey, Jr.
(Resident, San Diego Office)
Janelle F. Garchie
(Resident, San Diego Office)
Robert V. Closson
(Resident, San Diego Office)
Thomas M. Correll
(Resident, San Diego Office)
Kenneth E. Goates
(Resident, San Diego Office)
Howard A. Slavin
Edward F. Morrison, Jr.
Jack D. Tomlinson (Resident, San Francisco Office)
Kenneth D. Huston
(Resident, San Diego Office)
Gerald R Judson

ASSOCIATES

Kelly D. Akins
Sarira D. Alexander
Norman E. Allen (Resident, San Francisco Office)
Lee M. Amidon (Resident, San Bernardino Office)
Paul Ellis Baron (Resident, San Francisco Office)
Mark A. Birmingham
(Resident, San Diego Office)
Leslie S. Bowen
(Resident, Costa Mesa Office)
Larry J. Brock
Joseph C. Campo
Cindy Merten Cardullo
(Resident, Sacramento Office)
John S. Christopher
G. Russell Clark,
Resident, San Diego Office)
David S. Cohn (Resident, San Bernardino Office)
Lori Creasey
(Resident, Costa Mesa Office)
Troy A. Edwards
(Resident, Costa Mesa Office)
Lawrence A. Eugenio
Karen A. Feld (Resident, San Bernardino Office)
Tina Fisher
Kelly M. Flanagan
(Resident, Costa Mesa Office)
James E. Friedhofer
(Resident, San Diego Office)
J. Albert Garcia
(Resident, San Diego Office)
Robert H. Garnett
Christopher R. Green
Allison A. Greene
(Resident, Costa Mesa Office)
Christopher J. Greenleaf
Patrick P. Gunn
Jay D. Harker
(Resident, Costa Mesa Office)
Heather Anne Henderson
(Resident, Costa Mesa Office)

Paula F. Henry
(Resident, Costa Mesa Office)
Helen E. Hesse
(Resident, Costa Mesa Office)
Madonna L. Hultman
(Resident, Costa Mesa Office)
Charles J. Hyland
(Resident, Costa Mesa Office)
April M. Johnson
(Resident, San Diego Office)
Raimo H. Kaasik
Laura B. Kaliser
Jonathon Kaplan
Jenifer L. Kienle
(Resident, San Diego Office)
Catherine J. Kim
(Resident, Costa Mesa Office)
Harry T. Kozak
(Resident, Costa Mesa Office)
Jacqueline S. LaScala
(Resident, San Diego Office)
Sharon M. Lawrence
(Resident, San Diego Office)
Valerie L. Leatherwood
Douglas W. Lewis
(Resident, San Diego Office)
Judith A. Lewis
(Resident, San Diego Office)
Joan Creigh. Little
(Resident, San Diego Office)
Michael S. Little
Christopher D. Lockwood
(Resident, San Bernardino Office)
Dennis J. Mahoney (Resident, San Bernardino Office)
Gregory P. Martin
James P. Mayo
(Resident, Sacramento Office)
John H. McCardle
(Resident, Sacramento Office)
Steven E. Meyer
Gail F. Montgomery (Resident, San Bernardino Office)
Raffi A. Nahabedian

(See Next Column)

LEWIS, D'AMATO, BRISBOIS & BISGAARD—*Continued*

ASSOCIATES (Continued)

Paul F. O'Brien
  (Resident, San Diego Office)
Terrell A. Quealy
  (Resident, San Diego Office)
Catherine J. Quinn
Lisa K. Roberts
  (Resident, San Diego Office)
James F. B. Sawyer
Larry R. Schmadeka
Robert M. Shannon
  (Resident, Sacramento Office)

Christina M. Slatton
Christine Graves Thoene
  (Resident, San Diego Office)
Karen E. Vaughey
Julie A. Veltkamp
Jamie E. Walters
Kenneth D. Watnick
Susan West
Cary L. Wood
Beth E. Yoffie
John Yong-Jin Yoon

For full biographical listings, see the Martindale-Hubbell Law Directory

---

LOEB & LOEB LLP (AV)

A Limited Liability Partnership including Professional Corporations
Suite 1800, 1000 Wilshire Boulevard, 90017-2475
Telephone: 213-688-3400
Facsimile: 213-688-3460; 688-3461; 688-3462
Century City, California Office: Suite 2200, 10100 Santa Monica
Boulevard, Los Angeles, 90067-4164.
Telephone: 310-282-2000.
Facsimile: 310-282-2191; 282-2192.
New York, N.Y. Office: 345 Park Avenue, 10154-0037.
Telephone: 212-407-4000.
Facsimile: 212-407-4990.
Washington, D.C. Office: Suite 601, 2100 M Street N.W., 20037-1207.
Telephone: 202-223-5700.
Facsimile: 202-223-5704.
Nashville, Tennessee Office: 45 Music Square West, 37203-3205.
Telephone: 615-749-8300;
Facsimile: 615-749-8308.
Rome, Italy Office: Piazza Digione 1, 00197.
Telephone: 011-396-808-8456.
Facsimile: 011-396-808-8288.

MEMBERS OF FIRM

Joseph P. Loeb (1883-1974)
Edwin J. Loeb (1886-1970)
Mortimer H. Hess (1889-1968)
Phillip E. Adler (A P.C.)
Christopher K. Aidun
  (New York City Office)
Kenneth B. Anderson
  (New York City Office)
John Arao
Roger M. Arar
  (Century City Office)
Donald L. B. Baraf
  (New York City Office)
Robert S. Barry, Jr.
Harold A. Barza
Michael D. Beck
  (New York City Office)
Carol Laurene Belfield
Kenneth R. Benbassat
Maribeth A. Borthwick
  (Century City Office)
David H. Carlin
  (New York City Office)
Marc Chamlin
  (New York City Office)
Alex Chartove
  (Washington, D.C. Office)
Andrew S. Clare (A P.C.)
Richard J. Codding
  (Century City Office)
Kenneth R. Costello
Terence F. Cuff
John J. Dellaverson
  (Century City Office)
Lorenzo De Sanctis
  (Rome, Italy Office)
David B. Eizenman
  (New York City Office)
Frank E. Feder (A P.C.)
  (Century City and New York
  Offices)
Martin D. Fern
David L. Ficksman
Evan Finkel
  (Century City Office)
Jay M. Finkelstein
  (Washington, D.C. Office)
David C. Fischer
  (New York City Office)
John T. Frankenheimer (A P.C.)
  (Century City Office)
Kenneth D. Freeman
  (New York City Office)
James D. Friedman

Andrew S. Garb (A P.C.)
David W. Grace
Fred B. Griffin
Philip J. Grosz
  (Century City Office)
Lawrence B. Gutcho
Joseph P. Heffernan (A P.C.)
Irv Hepner
  (New York City Office)
Joyce S. Jun
  (Century City Office)
Lance N. Jurich
Michael Bryce Kinney
  (New York City Office)
William K. Konrad
  (Century City Office)
Richard W. Kopenhefer
  (Century City Office)
Mary D. Lane
John F. Lang
  (New York City Office)
Michael Langs
Jerome L. Levine
  (New York City Office)
Andrew E. Lippmann
  (New York City Office)
Don F. Livornese
  (Century City Office)
Jeffrey M. Loeb
Stuart Lubitz
  (Century City Office)
Gary D. Mann
  (Century City Office)
William J. Marlow
  (New York City Office)
Michael A. Mayerson
  (Century City Office)
Malissa Hathaway McKeith
Robert A. Meyer
Stephen R. Mick
Charles H. Miller
  (New York City Office)
Malcolm L. Mimms, Jr.
  (Nashville, Tennessee Office)
Douglas E. Mirell
Daniel G. Murphy
Anthony Murray
David C. Nelson
Susan V. Noonoo
Diane B. Paul
Alden G. Pearce (A P.C.)
Robert L. Pelz
  (New York City Office)

(See Next Column)

MEMBERS OF FIRM (Continued)

Martin R. Pollner
  (New York City Office)
Guendalina Ponti
  (Rome, Italy Office)
Shirley M. Price
Robert S. Reich
  (New York City Office)
Victor A. Rodgers
Thomas E. Rohlf (A P.C.)
Andrew M. Ross
  (New York City Office)
Jonathan P. Roth
Stanford K. Rubin (A P.C.)
  (Century City Office)
Stephen L. Saltzman
  (Century City Office)
Fredric M. Sanders
  (New York City Office)
David M. Satnick
  (New York City Office)
David S. Schaefer
  (New York City Office)
P. Gregory Schwed
  (New York City Office)
Paul A. Sczudlo
Peter S. Selvin
David B. Shontz
  (New York City Office)
Clark B. Siegel
  (Century City Office)

David M. Simon
  (Century City Office)
Michael F. Sitzer
Lee N. Steiner
  (New York City Office)
Rebel R. Steiner, Jr.
  (Century City Office)
Bruce M. Stiglitz (A P.C.)
Richard P. Streicher
  (New York City Office)
James D. Taylor
  (New York City Office)
Raymond W. Thomas
  (Century City Office)
Robert N. Treiman
William P. Wasserman (A P.C.)
Ronald Weinstein (A P.C.)
Bruce J. Wexler
  (New York City Office)
Rebecca E. White
  (New York City Office)
Alan W. Wilken
Roger R. Wise
  (Century City Office)
Susan A. Wolf
William S. Woods, II
Richard H. Zaitlen
  (Century City Office)
Michael P. Zweig
  (New York City Office)

OF COUNSEL

Harold D. Berkowitz (A P.C.)
  (Century City Office)
James R. Birnberg
Morton R. Field
Harry First
  (New York City Office)
Howard I. Friedman (A P.C.)
Marvin Greene (A P.C.)
Abraham S. Guterman
  (New York City Office)
Robert A. Holtzman (A P.C.)
Harold I. Kahen
  (New York City Office)
Gerald D. Kleinman (A P.C.)
  (Century City Office)

Jay Adams Knight
Saul N. Rittenberg (A P.C.)
  (Century City Office)
Alfred I. Rothman (A P.C.)
Arthur A. Segall
  (New York City Office)
Alan D. Shulman
  (Century City Office)
Bernard M. Silbert
  (Century City Office)
Harvey L. Silbert
  (Century City Office)
Myron L. Slobodien (A P.C.)
  (Century City Office)
John S. Warren (A P.C.)

SENIOR COUNSEL

Miriam J. Golbert
  (Century City Office)
Adrienne Halpern
  (New York City Office)
Louis A. Mok
  (Century City Office)

Laurie S. Ruckel
  (New York City Office)
John P. Scherlacher
  (Century City Office)

ASSOCIATES

Paula G. Atkinson
Curtis W. Bajak
  (Century City Office)
Jeremy W. Barber
  (Century City Office)
Roberta S. Bell
  (New York City Office)
Michele E. Beuerlein
Elana C. Bloom
  (New York City Office)
Stephen Bongini
  (Century City Office)
Marguerite L. Bui
Matthew Clark Bures
David A. Byrnes
  (Century City Office)
Steve S. Chahine
Ying Chen (Century City Office)
Paula K. Colbath
  (New York City Office)
Marco D. Costales
Marita T. Covarrubias
  (Century City Office)
Anne P. Donovan
  (New York City Office)
Brant H. Dveirin
Linda F. Edell
  (Nashville, Tennessee Office)
Philippe O. Erwin
  (Century City Office)
Jay Fenster
  (New York City Office)
David A. Fleissig
  (New York City Office)

Kenneth R. Florin
  (New York City Office)
Richard J. Frey
  (Century City Office)
Bruce Friedman
Daniel J. Friedman
Randall Collins Furlong
  (Century City Office)
Raul Carl Galaz
  (Century City Office)
Helen Gavaris
  (New York City Office)
James P. Goodkind
  (Century City Office)
Karen A. Greenstein
  (New York City Office)
Kurtiss Lee Grossman
James R. Guerette
  (New York City Office)
Karen Nielsen Higgins
Jonathan Y. Kang
  (Century City Office)
David D. Kim
  (New York City Office)
John W. Kittleson
Amir I. Kornblum
  (New York City Office)
Paul H. Kovelman
  (Century City Office)
Robert B. Lachenauer
  (New York City Office)
Lynda C. Loigman
  (New York Office)
Nina B. Luban

(See Next Column)

LOEB & LOEB LLP, *Los Angeles—Continued.*

ASSOCIATES (Continued)

David L. Lubitz	Scott I. Schneider
Linda McCauley Mack	(New York City Office)
(Century City Office)	Rachel Schwartz
David Alan Makman	(New York City Office)
(Century City Office)	Terri J. Seligman
Sonya Makunga	(New York City Office)
Jonathan S. Marshall	Edward H. Shapiro
(Century City Office)	(Nashville, Tennessee Office)
Denise Marie McIntosh	Riccardo Siciliani
(Century City Office)	(Rome, Italy Office)
Sharon S. Mequet	Brian R. Socolow
Beth R. Meyers	(New York City Office)
(New York City Office)	Adam F. Streisand
Paul G. Nagy	Gerald J. Strenio
(Century City Office)	Claudia M. Taylor
Lloyd Charles Nathan	(New York City Office)
(Century City Office)	Arya Towfighi
Theotis F. Oliphant	(Century City Office)
Giovanni A. Pedde	David W. Victor
(Rome, Italy Office)	(Century City Office)
Chris P. Perque	Joseph F. von Sauers
(Century City Office)	(Century City Office)
Harry S. Prawer	Courtney I. Williams
(New York City Office)	(New York City Office)
Ted Rittmaster	Susan Z. Williams
(Century City Office)	(Century City Office)
Allison Klayman Rosenthal	Weining Yang
(New York City Office)	(Century City Office)
Michael E. Ross	Wendy W. Yang
Glen A. Rothstein	(Century City Office)
Michelle Oyler Saifer	Richard Kon Yoon
(New York City Office)	Maria L. Zanfini
Deborah L. Saltzman	(New York City Office)
(New York City Office)	Andrew D. Zuckerman
Jay D. Sanders	(New York City Office)
Roni Schneider	Richard S. Zuniga
(New York City Office)	(Century City Office)

For full biographical listings, see the Martindale-Hubbell Law Directory

---

LONG & LEVIT LLP (AV)

A Limited Liability Partnership including a Professional Corporation
601 S. Figueroa, 25th Floor, 90071
Telephone: 213-356-5900
Facsimile: 213-613-0664
San Francisco, California Office: 101 California Street, Suite 2300.
Telephone: 415-397-2222.
Telex: 340924 HOME OFC SFO-LONG & LEVIT.
Facsimile: 415-397-6392.

RESIDENT PARTNERS

Randall A. Miller	Gretchen S. Carner

Cyril E. "Ted" Armbrister, Jr.

RESIDENT ASSOCIATES

B. Gerard Cordelli	David M. Morrow
Patricia M. De La Peña	Susan Andrews O'Neal
J. Andrew Douglas	JoLynn M. Pollard
Jeffrey A. Evans	Roni Reed
Douglas H. Galt	Stephen E. Ronk
Christina Katris-Michael	Valerie J. Wiles

For full biographical listings, see the Martindale-Hubbell Law Directory

---

LORD, BISSELL & BROOK (AV)

300 South Grand Avenue, 90071-3200
Telephone: 213-485-1500
Telecopy: 213-485-1200
Telex: 18-1135
Chicago, Illinois Office: Suites 2600-3600 Harris Bank Building, 115 South LaSalle Street, 60603.
Telephone: 312-443-0700.
Telecopy: 312-443-0570.
Cable Address: "Lowirco".
Telex: 25-0336.
Atlanta, Georgia Office: One Atlantic Center, 1201 West Peachtree Street, N.W., Suite 3700, 30309.
Telephone: 404-870-4600.
Telecopy: 404-872-5547.
Rockford, Illinois Office: 120 West State Street, Suite 200, 61101.
Telephone: 815-963-8050.

RESIDENT PARTNERS

Charles A. Adamek	David F. Hauge
Gail M. Baev	Jeffrey S. Kravitz
C. Guerry Collins	Rudolf H. Schroeter
Charles L. Crouch, III	Keith G. Wileman

OF COUNSEL
Marguerite L. Brown

(See Next Column)

RESIDENT ASSOCIATES

Brenda Adams Bissett	John M. Hochhausler
Jacqueline C. Brown	Barbara J. Klass
John D. Buchanan	Jacqueline Redin Klein
Stephen L. Cope	LouCinda Laughlin
Charissa Dorian	Jeri Rouse Looney
Franklin T. Dunn	George D. Lozano
Mark Scott Fall	Mitchell J. Popham
Cynthia M. Frey	Karen A. Soomekh

Anthony F. Witteman

For full biographical listings, see the Martindale-Hubbell Law Directory

---

MANATT, PHELPS & PHILLIPS, LLP (AV)

A Limited Liability Partnership
Trident Center, East Tower, 11355 West Olympic Boulevard, 90064
Telephone: 310-312-4000
Fax: 310-312-4224
Telex: 21-5653
Email: mpp@manatt.com
Washington, D.C. Office: 1500 M Street, N.W., Suite 700.
Telephone: 202-463-4300.
Fax: 202-463-4394.
Nashville, Tennessee Office: 1233 17th Avenue South.
Telephone: 615-327-2600.
Fax: 615-327-2044.

MEMBERS OF FIRM

Charles T. Manatt (P.C.)	L. Lee Phillips (P.C.)
Thomas D. Phelps (P.C.)	Ronald S. Barak

Gordon M. Bava (P.C.)

Irwin P. Altschuler (Resident, Washington, D.C. Office)	George David Kieffer
David R. Amerine (Resident, Washington, D.C. Office)	Sandra R. King
	David M. Klaus (Resident, Washington, D.C. Office)
George M. Belfield	Kenneth L. Kraus (Resident, Nashville, Tennessee Office)
Geoffrey A. Berkin	
Ellen Berkowitz	Barry S. Landsberg
Donna R. Black	David H. Larry (Resident, Washington, D.C. Office)
Robert A. Blair (P.C.) (Resident, Washington, D.C. Office)	John P. LeCrone
Lawrence J. Blake	Mark S. Lee
T. Hale Boggs	Tin Kin Lee
Diana K. Brown	Margaret Levy
Richard A. Brown	John F. Libby
William S. Brunsten (P.C.)	Edward L. Lublin (Resident, Washington, D.C. Office)
Alan M. Brunswick	Eileen Lyon
Jack W. Buechner (Resident, Washington, D.C. Office)	Barry E. Mallen
Cara R. Burns	Laurence M. Marks
Chris A. Carlson	Gerald A. Margolis
Catherine A. Conway	Thomas J. McDermott Jr.
Jay L. Cooper	Thomas R. McMorrow
June Langston (Walton) DeHart (Resident, Washington, D.C. Office)	Sherwin L. Memel (P.C.)
	Peter M. Menard
Neal Dittersdorf (Resident, Washington, D.C. Office)	Alan E. Morelli
	James P. Mulkeen
Gene R. Elerding	Kevin O'Connell
Roger Ellison	Thomas P. Ondeck (Resident, Washington, D.C. Office)
David Elson	
Andrew Erskine	Robert H. Platt
Diane L. Faber	William T. Quicksilver (P.C.)
Paul H. Falon (Resident, Washington, D.C. Office)	B. Michael Rauh (Resident, Washington, D.C. Office)
Donald J. Fitzgerald	John L. Ray (Resident, Washington, D.C. Office)
Judith R. Forman (P.C.)	Harold P. Reichwald
Howard M. Frumes	James H. Roberts III (Resident, Washington, D.C. Office)
Cynthia Futter	
Peter R. Gilbert (Resident, Washington, D.C. Office)	Christopher L. Rudd
	Alan U. Schwartz
Donna Fields Goldstein	Brad William Seiling
Andrea Jane Grefe	Martin Shulman (Resident, Washington, D.C. Office)
Rick L. Grossman	
Carl Grumer	Laurie L. Soriano
Scott D. Harrington	Lisa Specht
Robert E. Hinerfeld	Donald S. Stein (Resident, Washington, D.C. Office)
Paul S. Hoffman	Robert L. Sullivan (Resident, Nashville, Tennessee Office)
Maria D. Hummer (P.C.)	
Phalen G. Hurewitz	Timothy M. Thornton
Linda M. Iannone (Resident, Washington, D.C. Office)	Ronald B. Turovsky
	Leonard D. Venger
Paul H. Irving	Vincent M. Waldman
Clarence L. James (Resident, Washington, D.C. Office)	Charles E. Washburn Jr.
	H. Lee Watson
Rosalyn Evelyn Jones	Nancy H. Wojtas
Robert J. Kabel (Resident, Washington, D.C. Office)	Shari Mulrooney Wollman
	Steven J. Younger
Andrew M. Katzenstein	Steven L. Zelinger (Resident, Washington, D.C. Office)

(See Next Column)

MANATT, PHELPS & PHILLIPS LLP—*Continued*

OF COUNSEL

Dennis B. Franks	Robert A. Pallemon
Joseph Horacek III, (P.C.)	Martin E. Steere
Arnold D. Kassoy	Abby B. Wayne
Kevin Keenan	Gail Anderson Windisch
Spencer L. Kimball	(Firm General Counsel)
(Not admitted in CA)	Angela Wong
Elliot B. Kristal	Thomas A. Zaccaro

ASSOCIATES

Erin K. Atkins	Suzanne K. List
Matthew D. Berger	Lisa Cathleen McArthur
Katrina L. Breuner	Craig D. Miller
Donald Brown	Jay M. Miller
Cynthia F. Catalino	Vibiana Molina
Andrew Cushnir	Eugene E. Mueller
Leah E. Delancey	Brenda B. Nelson
Kathleen D. De Vaney	Seema L. Nene
Katia T. Diehl	John P. Phillips
Dan Forman	Jill M. Pietrini
Seth Gold	Adam Pines
Marc P. Goodman	Steven J. Plinio
Jay R. Grant	Harvey Rochman
Allison B. Gruettner	Ciema Lili Salem
Daniel B. Hayes	Kelley L. Sbarbaro
Terri Donna Keville	Marlene R. Schwartz
Brian S. Keys	Laurie Jill Slosberg
Coby A. King	Allen Z. Sussman
John I. Lazar	Mary E. Wright
Monte M. Lemann II	Candace Anne Younger

For full biographical listings, see the Martindale-Hubbell Law Directory

---

MARKS & MURASE L.L.P. (AV)

The Wells Fargo Center, 333 South Grand Avenue Suite 1570, 90071-1535
Telephone: 213-620-9690
FAX: 213-617-9109
New York, New York Office: 399 Park Avenue.
Telephone: 212-318-7700.
Washington, D.C. Office: Suite 750, 2001 L Street, N.W.
Telephone: 202-955-4900.

PARTNERS IN LOS ANGELES, CALIFORNIA

Shu Tokuyama	Matthew E. Digby

ASSOCIATES IN LOS ANGELES, CALIFORNIA

Tanya K. Danforth	John J. Del Propost
(Not admitted in CA)	Craig L. Sheldon

For full biographical listings, see the Martindale-Hubbell Law Directory

---

MAYER, BROWN & PLATT (AV)

350 South Grand Avenue, 25th Floor, 90071-1503
Telephone: 213-229-9500
Facsimile: 213-625-0248
Telex: 188089
Cable: LEMAYLA
URL: http://www.mayerbrown.com
Chicago, Illinois Office: 190 South La Salle Street, 60603-3441.
Telephone: (312) 782-0600.
Facsimile: (312) 701-7711.
Telex: 190404.
Cable: LEMAY.
Berlin, Germany Office: Spreeufer 5, 10178.
Telephone: 011-49-30-247-3800.
Facsimile: 011-49-30-247-38044.
Brussels, Belgium Office: Square de Meeûs 19/20, Bte. 4, 1050.
Telephone: 011-32-2-512-9878. Facsimile : 011-3 2-2-511-3305.
Houston, Texas Office: 700 Louisiana Street, Suite 3600, 77002-2730.
Telephone: (713) 221-1651.
Facsimile: (723) 224-6410.
Telex: 775809.
Cable: LEMAYHOU.
London, England Office: 162 Queen Victoria Street, EC4V 4DB.
Telephone: 011-44-171-248-1465.
Facsimile: 011-44-171-329-4465.
Telex: 8811095.
Cable: LEMAYLDN.
New York, New York Office: 1675 Broadway, 10019-5820.
Telephone: (212) 506-2500.
Facsimile: (212) 262-1910.
Telex: 701842.
Cable: LEMAYEN.
Washington, D.C. Office: 2000 Pennsylvania Avenue, N.W., 20006-1882.
Telephone: (202) 463-2000.
Facsimile: (202) 861-0473.
Telex: 892603.
Cable: LEMAYDC.
Representative Offices:
Almaty, Republic of Kazakhstan: 162 Tulebaev Street #32.
Telephone: 011-7-3272-636388.
Facsimile: 011-7-3272-507828.

(See Next Column)

Bishkek, Kyrgyz Republic: Suite 405, Prospekt Manasa 55, 720001.
Telephone: 011-7-3312-222970.
Facsimile: 011-7-3312-620980.
Köln, Germany: An Lyskirchen 14, 50676.
Telephone: 011-49-221-921-5210.
Facsimile: 011-49-221-921-5514.
Tashkent, Republic of Uzbekistan: 5th Floor, 1 Turab Tula Street, 700003.
Telephone: 011-7-3712-891179.
Facsimile: 011-7-3712-891178.
Mexico City, Mexico, D.F., Independent Mexico Correspondent: Jáuregui, Navarrete, Nader y Rojas, S.C. Abogados, Paseo de la Reforma 199, Pisos 15, 16 y 17, 06500, Mexico.
Telephone: 011-525-591-16-55.
Facsimile: 011-525-535-80-62, 011-525-703-22-47.
Cable: JANANE.

PARTNERS

Teresa A. Beaudet	M. Ellen Robb
Louis P. Eatman	Kevin L. Shaw
L. Bruce Fischer	Neil M. Soltman
Michael F. Kerr	Robert A. Southern
Kenneth E. Kohler	(Not admitted in CA)
Alec G. Nedelman	James R. Walther
Brian E. Newhouse	Don L. Weaver

SPECIAL COUNSEL

John Shepard Wiley, Jr.

COUNSEL

Christopher P. Murphy

ASSOCIATES

Andrei A. Baev	Jerome M.F.J. Jauffret
David C. Bolstad	Fredrick S. Levin
Jacqueline R. Brady	(Not admitted in CA)
Christopher D. Chen	Bruce H. Levine
Boise A. Ding	John Nadolenco
Henry Einar Fink	A. Ken Okamoto
Douglas B. Frank	Maria M. Rabassa
Anthony G. Graham	Mary Beth Rhoden
Richard Greta	Nina E. Scholtz
Lorie S. Griffen	Carl J. Thomas
	Kimberly S. Winick

For full biographical listings, see the Martindale-Hubbell Law Directory

---

McCUTCHEN, DOYLE, BROWN & ENERSEN (AV)

355 South Grand Avenue Suite 4400, 90071-1560
Telephone: 213-680-6400
Facsimile: 213-680-6499
Email: postmaster@mdbe.com *URL:* http://www.mccutchen.com
San Francisco, California Office: Three Embarcadero Center, 94111-4066.
Telephone: 415-393-2000.
Facsimile: 415-393-2286 (G I, II, III).
Telex: 340817 MACPAG SFO.
San Jose, California Office: Market Post Tower, Suite 1500, 55 South Market Street, 95113-2327.
Telephone: 408-947-8400.
Facsimile: 408-947-4750.
Telex: 910 250 2931 MACPAG SJ.
Walnut Creek, California Office: 1331 North California Boulevard, Post Office Box V, 94596-4502.
Telephone: 510-937-8000.
Facsimile: 510-975-5390.
Palo Alto, California Office: One Embarcadero Place, 2100 Geng Road, 94303-0913.
Telephone: 415-846-4000.
Fax: 415-846-4086.
Washington, D.C. Office: The Evening Star Building, Suite 800, 1101 Pennsylvania Avenue, N.W., 20004-2514.
Telephone: 202-628-4900.
Facsimile: 202-628-4912.
Taipei, Taiwan Republic of China Office: International Trade Building, Tenth Floor, 333 Keelung Road, Section 1, 110.
Telephone: 886-2-723-5000.
Facsimile: 886-2-757-6070.
Affiliated Offices In: Bangkok, Thailand; Beijing, China; Shanghai, China.

MEMBERS OF FIRM

Joseph R. Austin	Melinda L. Hayes
Colleen P. Doyle	Susan L. Hoffman
James J. Dragna	Michael B. Lubic
Debra L. Fischer	John C. Morrissey
Karla A. Francken	James Franklin Owens
William H. Freedman	Rick R. Rothman
	Patricia L. Shanks

COUNSEL

Karen A. Caffee	Douglas R. Painter
Peter Hsiao	Clayton J. Vreeland
Diana Pfeffer Martin	Pamela F. Worth

(See Next Column)

McCutchen, Doyle, Brown & Enersen, *Los Angeles—Continued*

ASSOCIATES

Jeffrey M. Anderson	Micah R. Jacobs
P. Scott Burton	Jerilyn López Mendoza
Greg A. Christianson	Neal A. Rubin
Jill F. Cooper	John D. Schlotterbeck
I-Fan Ching Go	Allyson W. Sonenshine
Tiffany R. Hedgpeth	Charles E. Shelton, II
Heather Hoecherl	Sandra Hughes Waddell
Asher D. Issacs	Cory Wurtzel
Kenneth J. Yood	

For full biographical listings, see the Martindale-Hubbell Law Directory

---

MESERVE, MUMPER & HUGHES (AV)

A Partnership
555 South Flower Street, 18th Floor, 90071-2319
Telephone: 213-620-0300
Telecopier: 213-625-1930
Email: mmhla@ix.netcom.com
Irvine, California Office: 2301 Dupont Drive, Suite 410.
Telephone: 714-474-8995.
Telecopier: 714-975-1065.
San Diego, California Office: 701 "B" Street, Suite 1080.
Telephone: 619-237-0500.
Telecopier: 619-237-0073.

MEMBERS OF FIRM

Edwin A. Meserve (1863-1955)	William E. von Behren
Shirley E. Meserve (1889-1959)	Joan E. Aarestad
Hewlings Mumper (1889-1968)	Timothy A. Gravitt (Los
Clifford E. Hughes (1894-1981)	Angeles, Irvine and San Diego
Dennett F. Kouri	Offices)
Bernard A. Leckie (Irvine Office)	E. Avery Crary (Irvine Office)
Linda M. Lawson	Patricia A. Ellis
David R. Eichten	Lisa A. Roquemore
(San Diego and Irvine Offices)	(Irvine Office)

OF COUNSEL

J. Robert Meserve (Irvine Office)	Julian Scheiner
Thomas E. Kellett	Gary V. Spencer (Irvine Office)

ASSOCIATES

Joseph B. McGinley	Matthew T. Currie
(Irvine Office)	Kendra S. Meinert Hodson
Brian K. Mazen	Andrew L. Satenberg
Carol B. Burney	Wendy C. Satuloff
Geoffrey T. Tong	(Irvine Office)
Christopher M. Stevens	Becky J. Belke
Brian M. Holbrook	Dennett F. Kouri, Jr.

For full biographical listings, see the Martindale-Hubbell Law Directory

---

MILBANK, TWEED, HADLEY & McCLOY (AV)

601 South Figueroa Street, 90017
Telephone: 213-892-4000
Fax: 213-629-5063 ABA/net: MilbankLA
New York, New York Office: 1 Chase Manhattan Plaza, 10005.
Telephone: 212-530-5000.
Fax: 212- 530-5219. ABA/net: MilbankNY; MCI Mail: MilbankTweed.
Midtown Office: 50 Rockefeller Plaza, 10020.
Telephone: 212-530-5800.
Fax: 212-530-0158.
Washington, D.C. Office: International Square Building, Suite 1100, 1825 Eye Street, N.W., 20006.
Telephone: 202-835-7500.
Fax: 202-835-7586. ABA/net: MilbankDC.
Tokyo, Japan Office: Nippon Press Center Building, 2-1, Uchisaiwai-cho 2-chome, Chiyoda-ku, Tokyo 100.
Telephone: 011-81-3-3504-1050.
Fax: 011-81-3-3595-2790, 011-81-3-3502-5192.
London, England Office: Dashwood House, 69 Old Broad Street, London, EC2M 1Q5.
Telephone: 011-44-171-448-3000.
Fax: 011-44-171-448-3029.
Hong Kong Office: 3007 Alexandra House, 16 Charter Road.
Telephone: 011-852-2571-4888.
Fax: 011-852-2840-0792, 011-8522-845-9046. ABA/net: MilbankHK.
Singapore Office: 14-02 Caltex House, 30 Raffles Place, 048622.
Telephone: 011-65-534-1700.
Fax: 011-65-534-2733. ABA/net: EDNANG.
Moscow, Russia Office: 24/27 Sadovaya-Samotyochnya, Moscow, 103051.
Telephone: 011-7-501-258-5015.
Fax: 011-7-501-258-5014.
Jakarta, Indonesia Correspondent Office: Makarim & Taira S., 17th Floor, Summitmas Tower, Jl, Jend. Sudirman 61, Jakarta.
Telephone: 011-62-21-252-1839 or 1272.
Fax: 011-62-21-252-4740 or 2750.

(See Next Column)

RESIDENT PARTNERS

Kenneth J. Baronsky	David A. Lamb
Paul S. Aronzon	Ted Obrzut
Edwin F. Feo	Eric H. Schunk
David C. L. Frauman	Peter P. Wallace
C. Stephen Howard	Karen B. Wong

OF COUNSEL

Alan M. Fenning

SENIOR COUNSEL

Neil J Wertlieb	Harry L. Usher

RESIDENT ASSOCIATES

Taline A. Aharonian	Melainie K. Mansfield
Dino Barajas	Allan T. Marks
Devan D. Beck	Jeffrey D. McFarland
Amy Bersch	Eddy Ching-Liang Meng
Scott M. Brown	John A. Mitchell
Gregory L. Call	Fred Neufeld
Veronica Davies	Gloria M. Noh
Michael Dayen	William J. Peters
Jose M. Deetjan	Eric R. Reimer
Ada E. Ejikeme	Kendrick F. Royer
R. Lee Garner III	Eileen Driscoll Rubens
Lawrence B. Gill	Deborah Ruosch
David J. Impastato	Roger K. Smith
(Not admitted in CA)	Scot Tucker
Patricia K Jones	Scott Vick
Nicholas L. Kondoleon	Paul T. Wrycha
Andrew H.T. Wu	

For full biographical listings, see the Martindale-Hubbell Law Directory

---

MITCHELL, SILBERBERG & KNUPP LLP (AV)

A Partnership including Professional Corporations
11377 West Olympic Boulevard, 90064
Telephone: 310-312-2000
Fax: 310-312-3100

MEMBERS OF FIRM

Shepard Mitchell (1908-1979)	John E. Hatherley (A Professional Corporation)
M. B. Silberberg (1908-1965)	Lawrence A. Ginsberg (A Professional Corporation)
Guy Knupp (1907-1970)	Daniel M. Petrocelli (A Professional Corporation)
Arthur Groman (A Professional Corporation)	Mark A. Wasserman (A Professional Corporation)
Chester I. Lappen (A Professional Corporation)	Allen J. Gross (A Professional Corporation)
Harold Friedman (A Professional Corporation)	Anthony A. Adler (A Professional Corporation)
Allan E. Biblin (A Professional Corporation)	Elia Weinbach (A Professional Corporation)
Edward M. Medvene (A Professional Corporation)	Allan B. Cutrow (A Professional Corporation)
Russell J. Frackman (A Professional Corporation)	Laura A. Loftin (A Professional Corporation)
Thomas P. Lambert (A Professional Corporation)	Peter B. Gelblum (A Professional Corporation)
Eugene H. Veenhuis (A Professional Corporation)	David P. Schack (A Professional Corporation)
Philip Davis (A Professional Corporation)	Lawrence A. Michaels (A Professional Corporation)
Roy L. Shults (A Professional Corporation)	Ronald A. DiNicola (A Professional Corporation)
Steven M. Schneider (A Professional Corporation)	Andrew E. Katz (A Professional Corporation)
Marvin Leon (A Professional Corporation)	James O. Thoma (A Professional Corporation)
Patricia H. Benson (A Professional Corporation)	Kevin Gaut (A Professional Corporation)
Arthur Fine (A Professional Corporation)	Danna L. Cook (A Professional Corporation)
Hayward J. Kaiser (A Professional Corporation)	Larry C. Drapkin (A Professional Corporation)
Deborah P. Koeffler (A Professional Corporation)	Steven E. Shapiro
John M. Kuechle (A Professional Corporation)	Lucia E. Coyoca (A Professional Corporation)
William L. Cole (A Professional Corporation)	Regina T. Shanney-Saborsky (A Professional Corporation)
Richard S. Hessenius (A Professional Corporation)	Robert C. Welsh (A Professional Corporation)
Joseph Ciasulli (A Professional Corporation)	J. Eugene Salomon, Jr. (A Professional Corporation)
Frida Popik Glucoft (A Professional Corporation)	John L. Segal (A Professional Corporation)
Jean Pierre Nogues (A Professional Corporation)	George M. Borkowski (A Professional Corporation)
David Wheeler Newman (A Professional Corporation)	David A. Steinberg (A Professional Corporation)
Roger Sherman (A Professional Corporation)	Christopher B. Leonard (A Professional Corporation)
Alan L. Pepper (A Professional Corporation)	

(See Next Column)

MITCHELL, SILBERBERG & KNUPP LLP—Continued

OF COUNSEL

Edward Rubin (A Professional
Corporation)
William M. Kaplan (A
Professional Corporation)
Lessing E. Gold (A Professional
Corporation)
Douglas R. Ring (A Professional
Corporation)
Stephen D. Marks (A
Professional Corporation)

H. Wayne Taylor
Marvin A. Demoff (A
Professional Corporation)
Jeffrey B. Wheeler
Bernard Donnenfeld (A
Professional Corporation)
Douglas W. Bordewieck
A. Catherine Norian
Kim H. Swartz
Richard E. Ackerknecht

Christian L. Castle

ASSOCIATES

Yvette Molinaro
Richard B. Sheldon, Jr.
Yakub Hazzard
Mary Courtney Burke
Jeffrey D. Goldman
Ann S. Lee
Brenda S. Barton
Brian S. Arbetter
Michelle Abend Bauman
Jeffrey L. Richardson
Matt J. Railo
Adam Levin
Tammy Cain Bloomfield
Michael Tsao
David J. Katz
Jeffrey D. Davine
Jeffrey K. Eisen
Tracy L. Thornburg
Howard D. Shapiro

Jeannette Hahm
Jeffrey M. Lowy
Timothy R. Collins, Jr.
Kim Y. Richardson
Jennifer Lightman Wessels
Wayne Kazan
Habib A. Balian
Harry H.W. Kim
Michael J. Zerman
Carolyn S. Javier
Sheri E. Cohen
Karl J. de Costa
Lee Anne Steinberg
Stefano G. Moscato
Stacie L. Feldman
Jason Krischer
Suzanne M. Steinke
Jeremy A. Lappen
D. James Chung

References: Wells Fargo Bank, N.A.; Merrill, Lynch.

For full biographical listings, see the Martindale-Hubbell Law Directory

---

MONTELEONE & McCRORY (AV)

A Partnership including Professional Corporations
725 South Figueroa Street Suite 3750, 90017-5402
Telephone: 213-612-9900
FAX: 213-612-9930
Santa Ana, California Office: Suite 750, 1551 North Tustin Avenue,
92705.
Telephone: 714-565-3170.
Fax: 714-565-3184.

MEMBERS OF FIRM

Stephen Monteleone (1886-1962)
G. Robert Hale (P.C.)
Patrick J. Duffy, III (P.C.)
Michael F. Minchella (P.C.)
Thomas P. McGuire (P.C.)
William J. Ingalsbe (P.C.)
(Resident, Santa Ana Office)

Philip C. Putnam (P.C.)
Joseph A. Miller (P.C.)
Diana M. Dron
(Resident, Santa Ana Office)
Donald J. Shields

ASSOCIATES

David C. Romyn
Barry J. Jensen
(Resident, Santa Ana Office)

W. Jeffrey Burch
Andrew W. Hawthorne
Stephen L. Dubin

Erica S. Behrens

OF COUNSEL

Darrell P. McCrory

For full biographical listings, see the Martindale-Hubbell Law Directory

---

MORRIS, POLICH & PURDY (AV)

1055 West Seventh Street Suite 2400, 90017
Telephone: 213-891-9100
Facsimile: 213-488-1178
Orange County Office: 500 North State College Boulevard, 11th Floor,
Orange, California.
Telephone: 714-939-1100.
Facsimile: 714-939-9261.
San Diego County Office: 501 W. Broadway, Suite 500, San Diego,
California.
Telephone: 619-557-0404.
Facsimile: 619-557-0460.

MEMBERS OF FIRM

Jeffrey S. Barron
Anthony G. Brazil
James M. Chantland
Michael T. Colliau
Douglas J. Collodel
Steven M. Crane
Carol Ann Humiston
Marc S. Katz

Theodore D. Levin
Walter J. Lipsman
Landon Morris (1904-1991)
Dean A. Olson
Theodore P. Polich, Jr.
Douglas C. Purdy
Donald L. Ridge
Nicholas M. Wieczorek

(See Next Column)

ASSOCIATES

Michael F. Avila
Mark C. Carlson
Penelope D. Doherty
Philip M. Drewry
Michael A. Fox
Hal D. Goldflam
Brian G. Hanneman
Carla M. Hoffman
Christine A. Hull
Beth A. Kahn
Cynthia L. Keener

Katherine E. Klima Liner
Jason Levin
Corrine L. Mix
Marilyn Muir
Richard H. Nakamura Jr.
Derrick H. Nguyen
David B. Olson
Lee I. Petersil
Janet M. Richardson
Jeffrey T. Woodruff
Megan S. Wynne

ORANGE COUNTY OFFICE
MEMBERS OF FIRM

Gary L. Hoffman
Randall F. Koenig

John P. Miller
Steven C. Miller

ORANGE COUNTY OFFICE
ASSOCIATES

William M. Betley
Kay Ann Connelly
Stephen J. McGreevy
Daniel J. McNamee

Thierry R. Montoya
Kristen Kay Nelson
Carlos A. Prietto, III
Paul S. Sienski

SAN DIEGO OFFICE
MEMBERS OF FIRM

Gary L. Jacobsen

Gerald P. Schneeweis

SAN DIEGO OFFICE
ASSOCIATES

Diana L. Cuomo
William C. Getty
Mark Hellenkamp

Joseph C. Lavelle
Matthew J. Liedle
Margot Sanguinetti

William C. Wilson

Reference: Security Pacific National Bank (6th & Flower Branch Office).

For full biographical listings, see the Martindale-Hubbell Law Directory

---

MUNGER, TOLLES & OLSON (AV)

A Law Partnership including Professional Corporations
355 South Grand Avenue 35th Floor, 90071
Telephone: 213-683-9100
Cable Address: "Muntoll"
Telex: 677574
Telecopier: 213-687-3702
San Francisco, California Office: 33 New Montgomery Street, Suite 1900.
Telephone: 415-512-4000.
FAX: 415-512-4077.

MEMBERS OF FIRM

Richard D. Esbenshade (A
Professional Corporation)
Frederick B. Warder, Jr.
(1932-1972)
Peter R. Taft (A Professional
Corporation)
Robert K. Johnson (A
Professional Corporation)
Alan V. Friedman (A
Professional Corporation)
Ronald L. Olson (A Professional
Corporation)
Dennis E. Kinnaird (A
Professional Corporation)
Richard S. Volpert
Dennis C. Brown (A
Professional Corporation)
Jeffrey I. Weinberger
Melvyn H. Wald (1947-1992)
Edwin V. Woodsome, Jr., (A
Professional Corporation)
Robert L. Adler
Cary B. Lerman
William L. Cathey
Charles D. Siegal
Ronald K. Meyer
Gregory P. Stone
Vilma S. Martinez
Lucy T. Eisenberg
Brad D. Brian
Bradley S. Phillips
George M. Garvey
Rita J. Miller
D. Barclay Edmundson
William D. Temko
Steven L. Guise (A Professional
Corporation)
Robert B. Knauss
R. Gregory Morgan

Stephen M. Kristovich
John W. Spiegel
Terry E. Sanchez
Steven M. Perry
Ruth E. Fisher
Mark B. Helm
Joseph D. Lee
Michael R. Doyen
Michael E. Soloff
Gregory D. Phillips
John B. Frank
Lawrence C. Barth
Kathleen M. McDowell
Glenn D. Pomerantz
Thomas B. Walper
Ronald C. Hausmann (Resident,
San Francisco Office)
Patrick J. Cafferty, Jr. (Resident,
San Francisco Office)
Jay Masa Fujitani
O'Malley M. Miller
Sandra A. Seville-Jones
Mark H. Epstein
Henry Weissmann
Kevin S. Allred
Marc A. Becker
Cynthia L. Burch
Bart H. Williams
Jeffrey A. Heintz
Judith T. Kitano
Kristin A. Linsley
Marc T. G. Dworsky
Jerome C. Roth (Resident, San
Francisco Office)
Steven D. Rose
Jeffrey L. Bleich (Resident, San
Francisco Office)
Garth T. Vincent
Ted Dane

ASSOCIATES

Marsha Hymanson
Stuart N. Senator
Eva Orlebeke Caldera
Monica Wahl Shaffer

Leonard P. Leichnitz
Andrew J. Thomas
Robert L. DellAngelo
Bruce A. Abbott

(See Next Column)

MUNGER, TOLLES & OLSON, *Los Angeles—Continued*

ASSOCIATES (Continued)

Martin D. Bern (Resident, San Francisco Office)
Margaret Elizabeth Deane (Resident, San Francisco Office)
Deanne B. Kyle
Susan R. Szabo
Inez D. Hope
Bernardo Silva
Kristin Sherratt Escalante
Manuel A. Abascal
Jonathan E. Altman
Gregg W. Kettles
Steven B. Weisburd
Ilana B. Rubenstein
Mary Ann Lyman
Carla N. Jones
John C. Ulin
James H. Ellis
Burton A. Gross (Resident, San Francisco Office)
Andrea J. Weiss
Steven W. Hawkins
David M. Rosenzweig
David C. Dinielli

Peter A. Detre
Elizabeth Earle Beske (Resident, San Francisco Office)
Edward C. Hagerott, Jr.
Kevin S. Masuda
Daniel P. Collins
Robert E. Holo (Not admitted in CA)
Michael J. O'Sullivan
Steven Usdan
Paul J. Watford
Timothy P. Grieve
Hojoon Hwang (Resident, San Francisco Office)
Jennifer R. Scullion
Devon A. Gold
Jose F. Sanchez
Sean A. Monroe
Jonathan R. Levey (Not admitted in CA)
Kelly M. Klaus (Resident, San Francisco Office)
Dennis M. Woodside
Douglas A. Axel
Rachel M. Capoccia

Bruce Hamilton Searby

Reference: The Bank of California.

For full biographical listings, see the Martindale-Hubbell Law Directory

---

TIMOTHY D. NAEGELE & ASSOCIATES (AVⓉ)

Suite 2430, 1900 Avenue of the Stars, 90067
Telephone: 310-557-2300
Facsimile: 310-457-4014
Email: naegelewdc@aol.com *URL:* http://www.naegele.com
Washington, D.C. Office: Suite 300, 1250 24th Street, N.W., 20037.
Telephone: 202-466-7500.
Facsimile: 202-466-3079 or 466-2888. Internet Web Site:
http://www.naegele.com. Internet E-mail: naegelewdc@aol.com.

For full biographical listings, see the Martindale-Hubbell Law Directory

---

O'MELVENY & MYERS LLP (AV)

400 South Hope Street, 90071-2899
Telephone: 213-669-6000
Cable Address: "Moms"
Facsimile: 213-669-6407
Email: omminfo@omm.com
Century City, California Office: 1999 Avenue of the Stars, 90067-6035.
Telephone: 310-553-6700.
Facsimile: 310-246-6779.
Newport Beach, California Office: 610 Newport Center Drive, 92660-6429.
Telephone: 714-760-9600.
Cable Address: "Moms".
Facsimile: 714-669-6994.
San Francisco, California Office: Embarcadero Center West Tower, 275 Battery Street, 94111-3305.
Telephone: 415-984-8700.
Facsimile: 415-984-8701.
New York, New York Office: Citicorp Center, 153 East 53rd Street, 10022-4611.
Telephone: 212-326-2000.
Facsimile: 212-326-2061.
Washington, D.C. Office: 555 13th Street, N.W., 20004-1109.
Telephone: 202-383-5300.
Cable Address: "Moms".
Facsimile: 202-383-5414.
London, England Office: 10 Finsbury Square, London, EC2A 1LA.
Telephone: 0171-256-8451.
Facsimile: 0171-638-8205.
Tokyo, Japan Office: Sanbancho KB-6 Building, 6 Sanbancho, Chiyoda-ku, Tokyo 102, Japan.
Telephone: 03-3239-2900.
Facsimile: 03-3239-2432.
Hong Kong Office: Suite 1905, Peregrine Tower, Lippo Centre, 89 Queensway, Central, Hong Kong.
Telephone: 852-2523-8266.
Facsimile: 852-2522-1760.
Shanghai, Peoples Republic of China Office: Shanghai International Trade Centre, Suite 2011, 2200 Yan An Road West, Shanghai, 200335, PRC.
Telephone: 86-21-6219-5363.
Facsimile: 86-21-6275-4949.

SENIOR PARTNER

Warren Christopher (Century City Office; also in Los Angeles and Washington, D.C. Offices)

(See Next Column)

PARTNERS

Douglas W. Abendroth (Newport Beach Office)
William G. Adams (Newport Beach Office)
Wallace M. Allan
Russell G. Allen (Newport Beach Office)
Kermit W. Almstedt (Washington, D.C. Office)
John L. Altieri, Jr. (New York, N.Y. Office)
Brian C. Anderson (Washington, D.C. Office)
D. Stephen Antion
Dale M. Araki (Tokyo, Japan Office; may also be contacted at the Los Angeles Office)
Seth Aronson
James R. Asperger
Gary Barnett (New York, N.Y. Office)
George M. Bartlett
Thomas W. Baxter
John H. Beisner (Washington, D.C. Office)
Charles W. Bender
Ben E. Benjamin (Washington, D.C. Office)
Kendall R. Bishop (Century City and Los Angeles Offices)
Leah Margaret Bishop (Century City Office)
Robert D. Blashek, III (Century City Office)
Donald T. Bliss, Jr. (Not admitted in CA; Washington, D.C. Office)
Richard A. Boehmer
Daniel H. Bookin (San Francisco Office)
Brian David Boyle (Washington, D.C. Office)
Greyson Lee Bryan
Francis J. Burgweger, Jr. (New York, N.Y. Office)
Joseph A. Calabrese (Century City Office)
Jerry W. Carlton (Newport Beach Office)
Cormac J. Carney (Newport Beach Office)
David W. Cartwright (Century City Office)
Dale M. Cendali (New York, N.Y. Office)
Theresa A. Cerezola (New York, N.Y. Office)
Howard Chao (Hong Kong and Shanghai Offices; may also be contacted at the Los Angeles Office)
Martin S. Checov (San Francisco Office)
Denise M. Clolery (New York, N.Y. Office and Century City, California Offices)
Alan M. Cohen (New York, N.Y. Office)
James W. Colbert, III
William N. Cooney
Bertrand M. Cooper
Stephen A. Cowan (San Francisco Office)
Arthur B. Culvahouse, Jr. (Washington, D.C. Office)
Michael A. Curley (New York, N.Y. Office)
Brian S. Currey
John F. Daum (Washington, D.C. Office)
F. Amanda DeBusk (Washington, D.C. Office)
James H. De Meules
Daniel A. Deshon, IV (San Francisco Office)
Charles P. Diamond (Century City Office)
Thomas E. Donilon (Washington, D.C. Office)
Robert S. Draper
Karen K. Dreyfus (Newport Beach Office)
Scott H. Dunham

Robert N. Eccles (Washington, D.C. Office)
Steven L. Edwards (Newport Beach Office)
Michael J. Fairclough
Robert E. Ferdon (New York, N.Y. Office)
José W. Fernandez (New York, N.Y. Office)
Richard N. Fisher
Cliff H. Fonstein (New York, N.Y. Office)
Andrew J. Frackman (New York, N.Y. Office)
Patricia Frobes (Newport Beach and Los Angeles Offices)
Travis C. Gibbs
Martin Glenn (New York, N.Y. Office)
Richard B. Goetz
Gregory W. Goff
David E. Gordon
Kent V. Graham (Century City Office)
Pamela C. Gray (Newport Beach and Los Angeles Offices)
Linda Boyd Griffey
Steven L. Grossman (New York, N.Y. Office)
Catherine Burcham Hagen (Newport Beach and Los Angeles Office)
Christopher D. Hall (London, England and New York Offices)
Theodore C. Hamilton (Newport Beach Office)
Marc P. Hanrahan (New York, N.Y. Office)
Stephen J. Harburg (Washington, D.C. Office)
John D. Hardy, Jr. (San Francisco Office and Los Angeles Office)
Adam C. Harris (New York, N. Y. Office)
Robert D. Haymer (Century City Office)
Peter T. Healy (San Francisco Office)
Howard M. Heitner
Joseph J. Herron (Newport Beach Office)
Jack B. Hicks III
B. Boyd Hight
Bruce A. Hiler (Washington, D.C. Office)
Michael S. Hobel (Century City Office)
Gary N. Horlick (Washington, D.C. Office)
Sandra Segal Ikuta
Robert S. Insolia (New York, N.Y. Office)
Philip D. Irwin
Wayne Jacobsen (Newport Beach Office)
Tom A. Jerman (Washington, D.C. Office)
Evan M. Jones
Richard M. Jones
Phillip R. Kaplan (Newport Beach Office)
Peter C. Kelley (Century City Office)
Holly E. Kendig
David E. Killough (San Francisco and Los Angeles Offices)
Joseph K. Kim
Louis B. Kimmelman (New York, N.Y. Office)
James H. Kinney
Matthew T. Kirby (Los Angeles, California and New York, N.Y. Offices)
F. Curt Kirschner, Jr. (San Francisco Office)
Paul R. Koepff (New York, N.Y. Office)
Jeffrey I. Kohn (New York, N.Y. Office)

(See Next Column)

O'MELVENY & MYERS LLP—Continued

PARTNERS (Continued)

C. Douglas Kranwinkle (New York, N.Y. and Los Angeles, California Offices)
David A. Krinsky (Newport Beach Office)
Gordon E. Krischer
Thomas J. Leary
Perry A. Lerner (New York, N.Y. and Century City, California Offices)
C. James Levin
Douglas P. Ley (San Francisco Office)
Charles C. Lifland
Ben H. Logan, III
Warren R. Loui (Century City Office)
Patrick Lynch
Joseph M. Malkin (San Francisco Office)
James P. Marlin (New York, N.Y. Office)
Lowell C. Martindale, Jr. (Newport Beach Office)
Marie L. Martineau (New York, N.Y. and Los Angeles California Offices)
Cheryl White Mason (San Francisco and Los Angeles Offices)
Jill H. Matichak (San Francisco and Los Angeles Offices)
Edward J. McAniff (Los Angeles and San Francisco Offices)
Michael G. McGuinness
Frederick B. McLane
Julie A. McMillan (San Francisco Office)
Paul G. McNamara
Mitchell B. Menzer
Scott A. Meyerhoff (Newport Beach Office)
Paul E. Mosley (Newport Beach Office)
F. Thomas Muller, Jr.
Christopher C. Murray (Century City Office)
Michael Newman
Charles F. Niemeth (New York, N.Y. and Century City, California Offices)
John G. Niles
Jeffery L. Norton (New York, N.Y. Office)
Christine M. Olsen
M. Randall Oppenheimer (Century City Office)
Kenneth R. O'Rourke
Peter V. Pantaleo (New York, N.Y. Office)
Richard G. Parker (Washington, D.C. Office)
Stephen P. Pepe (Newport Beach and Los Angeles Offices)
Donald V. Petroni (Century City Office)
David G. Pommerening (Washington, D. C. Office)
John B. Power
Laurence G. Preble (New York, N.Y. and Los Angeles, California Offices)
Alan Rader (Century City Office)
Ira H. Raphaelson (Washington, D.C. Office)
Gilbert T. Ray
Charles C. Read
Frederick A. Richman (Century City Office)
George A. Riley (San Francisco Office)
Robert A. Rizzi (Washington, D.C. Office)
Jeffrey J. Rosen (Washington, D.C. and New York, N.Y. Offices)
Richard R. Ross (Century City Office)
Frank L. Rugani (Newport Beach Office)
Mark A. Samuels
Kathryn A. Sanders
William H. Satchell (Washington, D.C. and New York, N.Y. Offices)
Stephen Scharf (Century City Office)
Carl R. Schenker, Jr. (Washington, D.C. Office)
Patricia A. Schmiege (San Francisco Office)
Robert M. Schwartz (Century City Office)
James V. Selna (Newport Beach Office)
Ralph J. Shapi
Robert A. Siegel
Gary J. Singer (Newport Beach Office)
Linda Jane Smith (Century City and Los Angeles Offices)
Steven L. Smith (San Francisco Office)
Darin W. Snyder (San Francisco Office)
Masood Sohaili
Stephanie I. Splane (New York, N.Y. and Newport Beach, California Offices)
John W. Stamper
Stephen J. Stern
Drake S. Tempest (New York, N.Y. Office)
Gregory B. Thorpe
Henry C. Thumann
Stuart P. Tobisman (Century City and Los Angeles Offices)
Lawrence P. Tu (Not admitted in CA; Hong Kong Office)
Ko-Yung Tung (New York, N.Y. Office)
Suzzanne Uhland
James R. Ukropina
Robert C. Vanderet
Framroze M. Virjee
Ulrich Wagner (New York, N.Y. Office)
Diana L. Walker
Richard C. Warmer (San Francisco Office)
Stephen H. Warren
David D. Watts
David I. Weil (Century City Office)
Dean M. Weiner
Jacqueline A. Weiss (New York, N.Y. Office)
John E. Welch (Washington, D.C. Office)
Pamela Lynne Westhoff
Robert J. White
Robert E. Willett
Jonathan P. Williams (New York, N.Y. and Los Angeles, California Offices)
Michael A. Wisnev
Charles C. Wolf
Thomas E. Wolfe (Newport Beach Office)
W. Mark Wood
Michael G. Yoder (Newport Beach Office)
Joel B. Zweibel (New York, N. Y. Office)

SENIOR COUNSELLOR
William T. Coleman, Jr. (Washington, D.C. Office)

SENIOR COUNSEL
Edward W. Hieronymus

(See Next Column)

OF COUNSEL

Barton Beek (Newport Beach Office)
R. Bradbury Clark
Owen Olpin
Lawrence J. Sheehan (Century City Office)
Clyde E. Tritt
William W. Vaughn

SPECIAL COUNSEL

Peter B. Ackerman
Susan E. Akens (Century City Office)
Kevin Ray Baker (Newport Beach Office)
David T. Beddow (Washington, D.C. Office)
Stan Blumenfeld
Rosemary B. Boller (New York, N.Y. Office)
Jennifer L. Borow (Century City Office)
Mark L. Bradshaw (San Francisco and Los Angeles Offices)
Avery R. Brown
Deborah J. Brown (Century City Office)
Richard W. Buckner
Donald G. Carden (New York, N.Y. Office)
Thomas G. Carruthers (New York, N.Y. Office)
K. Leigh Chapman
Christine E. Coleman (Century City Office)
Fiona M. Connell (Hong Kong Office)
Steven M. Cooper
Reginam (Ginger) Covitt (Century City Office)
John A. Crose, Jr.
George C. Demos (Newport Beach Office)
Douglas E. Dexter (San Francisco Office)
Marian J. Dillon (New York, N.Y. and Los Angeles, California Offices)
Suzanne F. Duff
David P. Enzminger
David G. Estes (San Francisco Office)
Thomas A. Ferrigno (Washington, D.C. Office)
Charles W. Fournier (New York, N.Y. Office)
Daniel M. Freedman (Not admitted in CA; Century City Office)
David R. Garcia
James H. Gianninoto (New York, N.Y. Office)
Joseph G. Giannola (New York, N.Y. Office)
Robert A. Grauman (New York, N.Y. Office)
Edward G. Gregory
Allan I. Grossman
Karen R. Growdon
Harold Henderson (Washington, D. C. Office)
Margaret C. Henry (New York, N.Y. Office)
David A. Hollander
Chris Hollinger
Mark C. Holscher
David I. Hurwitz (Not admitted in CA)
Kenneth E. Johnson
Carol A. Johnston (Century City Office)
Jeffrey M. Judd (San Francisco Office)
Christopher N. Kandel (London, England Office)
Jeffrey W. Kilduff (Washington, D.C. Office)
Malcolm M. Kratzer (New York, N. Y. Office)
Stanford G. Ladner (New York, N.Y. Office)
Elizabeth A. Leckie (New York, N. Y. Office)
David G. Litt (Washington, D.C. Office)
Frances Elizabeth Lossing
Helen P. Mac Donald (London, England Office; may also be contacted at Los Angeles Office)
Marcy Jo Mandel
Joseph G. McHugh
Gregory R. Oxford
Achilles M. Perry (New York, N.Y. Office)
Diane E. Pritchard
Eric A. S. Richards
John A. Rogovin (Washington, D.C. Office)
Tancred V. Schiavoni, III (New York, N.Y. Office)
Peter O. Shinevar (New York, N.Y. Office)
Edward J. Szczepkowski
Todd R. Triller (New York, N.Y. Office)
Brett J. Williamson (Newport Beach Office)
Alfred M. Wurglitz (Washington, D.C. Office)

ASSOCIATES

Christine M. Adams
Paul M. Alfieri (New York, N.Y. Office)
Hubert L. Allen (San Francisco Office)
Terrence R. Allen
Eric E. Amdursky
Iman Anabtawi (Century City Office)
K. Allen Anderson (Newport Beach Office)
Martine N. Apollon (Washington, D.C. Office)
James D. Arbogast (New York, N.Y. Office)
Barton S. Aronson (Washington, D.C. Office)
Felipe J. Arroyo
Christine L. Bacon (New York, N.Y. Office)
Linda A. Bagley (San Francisco Office)
Patrick J. Bannon (San Francisco Office)
Bernard C. Barmann, Jr.
Alfredo Barrios, Jr.
Steven Basileo
Evelyn Becker (Washington, D.C. Office)
Angela M. Bellanca
Richard D. Beller
Carla J. Bennett
Laura B. Berger (Century City Office)
Jay Blaivas (New York, N.Y. Office)
Corey A. Boock
Michael G. Bosko (Newport Beach and San Francisco Offices)
Lisa M. Bossetti
Debra L. Boyd
Laura C. Bremer (San Francisco and Los Angles Offices)
Brian P. Brooks (Washington, D.C. Office)
George H. Brown
J. Taylor Browning
Sharon Bunzel (San Francisco Office)
Nadia St. George Burgard (New York, N.Y. Office)
Walter R. Burkley, III

(See Next Column)

O'MELVENY & MYERS LLP, *Los Angeles—Continued*

ASSOCIATES (Continued)

Andrea L. Campbell
(New York, N.Y. Office)
Bruce L. Campbell
Cannon Quigley Campbell
William A. Candelaria
Paul P. Canfield
(New York, N.Y. Office)
Jeffrey J. Carlisle
(Washington, D.C. Office)
Sean M. Carney
Christine L. Carr
Kevin B. Carter
Pinaki Chakravorty
John B. Chang
(San Francisco Office)
Gary A. Chodosh
(New York, N.Y. Office)
Apalla U. Chopra
Carla J. Christofferson
(Century City Office)
Peggy Ann Clarke
(Washington, D.C. Office)
Craig J. Coleman
Charles F. Connolly
(Washington, D.C. Office)
Craig A. Corman
(Century City Office)
Colleen Cox
(Newport Beach Office)
Frank M. Crance
(Newport Beach Office)
Andrea L. Crowe
(New York, N.Y. Office)
Brian Daly
(New York, N.Y. Office)
Scott J. Daruty
(Newport Beach Office)
Robert L. Davis
(Newport Beach Office)
Teresa E. Dawson
(Washington, D.C. Office)
Elizabeth A. Delaney
(Washington, D.C. Office)
Antonio A. Del Pino
(New York, N.Y. Office)
Ralph P. DeSanto
(New York, N.Y. Office)
Rafael Diaz-Granados
(New York, N.Y. Office)
Thomas J. Di Resta
(New York, N.Y. Office)
Mary P. Donlevy
(Newport Beach Office)
Erica K. Doran
(New York, N.Y. Office)
Kate W. Duchene
Bradford David Duea
(Century City Office)
Daniel M. Dunn
(New York, N.Y. Office)
Loryn D. Dunn
Martha Dye
(Washington, D.C. Office)
Mark C. Easton
Steven G. Eisner
John M. Farrell
(Century City Office)
Stephen P. Fattman
(Washington, D.C. Office)
Marcia A. Fay
(San Francisco Office)
John M. Fedorko
(New York, N.Y. Office)
Marc F. Feinstein
Aaron F. Fishbein
(New York, N.Y. Office)
Jeanne Morales Flynn
(Century City Office)
Suzanne Rich Folsom
(Washington, D.C. Office)
Michael Friedman
(New York, N.Y. Office)
Jess B. Frost
Lisa E. Funk
(New York, N.Y. Office)
Anne Elizabeth Garrett
Katherine E. Garrett
Neil K. Gilman
(Washington, D.C. Office)

John A. Gliedman
(New York, N.Y. Office)
Robin L. Gohlke
Gary R. Gold
(Washington, D.C. Office)
David B. Goldman
Jason P. Gonzalez
(San Francisco Office)
Victoria A. Graff
Todd A. Green
(Newport Beach Office)
Dionne C. Greene
(New York, N.Y. Office)
Jennifer G. Grenert
(New York, N.Y. Office)
Jonathan L. Griffith
(Washington, D.C. Office)
Alyssa A. Grikscheit
(New York, N.Y. Office)
Lawrence M. Hadley
Afshin Hakim
Andrea Hanneman
(New York, N.Y. Office)
Clint M. Hanni
Maria Snyder Hardy
(Century City Office)
Kevin M. Harr
David L. Hayes
(Newport Beach Office)
Judith A. Heinz
Krista Helfferich
David L. Herron
Lawrence J. Hilton
(Newport Beach Office)
Bruce R. Hirsh
(Washington, D.C. Office)
Mark Ho (Shanghai Office;
China Counsel)
Bonnie L. Hobbs
(Hong Kong Office)
Michael J. Holden
(New York, N.Y. Office)
Richard J. Holmstrom
(New York, N.Y. Office)
Carl D. Howard
(New York, N.Y. Office)
Lane Huang (Shanghai Office;
China Counsel)
Yongjin Im (New York, N.Y.
and Los Angeles, California
Offices)
Mary A. Inman
(San Francisco Office)
Jill Irvin
(New York, N.Y. Office)
Bruce Gen Iwasaki
Neil Scot Jahss
Lynn A. Jansen
James Paul Jenal
Tonya Jenerette
(Washington, D.C. Office)
Nicholas G. Jenkins
Victor Jih (Century City Office)
Teresa L. Johnson
(London, England Office)
Thomas J. Karr
(Washington, D. C. Office)
Allison M. Keller
(Century City Office)
Alice J. Kim (Not admitted in
CA; Century City Office)
Jonathan J. Kim
Patricia H. Kim
(New York, N.Y. Office)
Stuart Y. Kim
Susanna M. Kim
(Newport Beach Office)
Kathleen E. Kinney
(Newport Beach Office)
David S. Kitchen
Sandra R. Klein
Stephanie I. Klein
(New York, N.Y. Office)
Lonnie L. Kocontes
Hayley J. Kondon
Stephen V. Kovarik
(New York, N.Y. Office)
Peter Kozinets
(San Francisco Office)

Lisa E. Krim
Teresa Kwong
(District of Columbia Office)
John A. Laco
John M. Lambros
Jose Lau Dan
(New York, N.Y. Office)
Courtney A. Lederer
(New York, N.Y. Office)
James C. Lee
Mimi Lee
(New York, N.Y. Office)
Michelle M. Leonard
(Century City Office)
Michael Cary Levine
Barry P. Levinson
(New York, N.Y. Office)
Alfred P. Levitt
(New York, N.Y. Office)
Warren H. Lilien
(San Francisco Office)
George C. Lin
Barry Littman
(Century City Office)
Lisa Litwiller
(Newport Beach Office)
Robert G. Loewy
(Newport Beach Office)
Joseph C. Lombard
(Washington, D.C. Office)
Monique Janelle London
(San Francisco Office)
Eva M. Luchini
Michael M. Maddigan
Andrew S. Mansfield
Lisa H. Marino
(Washington, D.C. Office)
Dennis J. Martin
(New York, N.Y. Office)
Carlos M. Matos
(Newport Beach Office)
Greg K. Matson
Lori A. Mazur
(New York, N.Y. Office)
Marion K. McDonald
(Washington, D.C. Office)
Patricia A. McKenna
(New York, N.Y. Office)
Susan M. McNeill
(New York, N.Y. Office)
Ann Catherine Menard
Michael A. Meyer
(Washington, D.C. Office)
John F. Milani
Eric S. Miller
(San Francisco Office)
Jessica Davidson Miller
(Washington, D.C. Office)
Angela C. Mok
(San Francisco Office)
Luc Moritz
Robert C. Murray
Vicki A. Nash
(Newport Beach Office)
David B. Newdorf
(San Francisco Office)
John F. Niblock
Anthony R. G. Nolan
(New York, N.Y. Office)
Brent J. North
(Newport Beach Office)
Peter Obstler
(San Francisco Office)
Arthur J. Ochoa
John C. Oehmke
Geoffrey D. Oliver
(Washington, D.C. Office)
Kevin Oliver
David L. Orlic
Dean Pappas
(Century City Office)
Troy A. Paredes
Jeehye Park
(New York, N.Y. Office)
Kenneth G. Parker
(Newport Beach Office)
Lisa J. Parnell
(Century City Office)
Lynn E. Parseghian
(Washington, D.C. Office)
Gregory P. Patti, Jr.
(New York, N.Y. Office)

Mark D. Peterson
(Newport Beach Office)
George R. Phillips, Jr.
Claire J. Philpott
(San Francisco Office)
Steven Lee Pickering
(San Francisco Office)
Annette L. Poblete
(New York, N.Y. Office)
Stuart S. Poloner
(New York, N.Y. Office)
Karen Craig Poltrock
(Newport Beach Office)
Sean H. Porter
(New York, N.Y. Office)
Henry K. Prempeh
(Washington, D.C. Office)
Mark R. Pronk
(New York, N.Y. Office)
Yash A. Rana
(New York, N.Y. Office)
Anthony D. Ratner
(San Francisco Office)
Claudia E. Ray
(New York, N.Y. Office)
Michael C. Ray
(Newport Beach Office)
David J. Reis
(San Francisco Office)
Jendi B. Reiter
(New York, N.Y. Office)
Donald M. Remy
(Washington, D.C. Office)
Laurel A. Remington
Ramon E. Reyes, Jr.
(New York, N.Y. Office)
Thomas M. Riordan
Patrick R. Rizzi
(Washington, D.C. Office)
James Gerard Rizzo
(New York, N.Y. Office)
Deborah Rogers
(Century City Office)
Lori E. Romley
(San Francisco Office)
Allison M. Rose
Eric N. Roth
(Century City Office)
Valerie Granfield Roush
(Washington, D.C. Office)
Lynda M. Ruiz
(San Francisco Office)
Rogelio M. Ruíz
(San Francisco Office)
Carlos P. Salas
Deborah J. Saltzman
Paul Salvaty
Pamela D. Samuels
Philip C. Scheurer
(Washington, D.C. Office)
Christine A. Schnabel
(Washington, D.C. Office)
Scott Schrader
(New York Office)
Daniel A. Schulze
(New York, N.Y. Office)
Nancy L. Shackleton
(Newport Beach Office)
Nina Shafran
(Washington, D.C. Office)
Sam S. Shaulson
(New York, N.Y. Office)
Gregory B. Shean
Katherine Sieck
(Newport Beach Office)
James P. Sileneck
(New York, N.Y. Office)
Gulwinder S. Singh
(Newport Beach Office)
Thomas Singher
(New York, N.Y. Office)
John F. Slusher
(Century City Office)
Craig W. Smith
Ellen M. Smith
(New York, N.Y. Office)
Gary M. Smith
(New York, N.Y. Office)
Valerie A. Smith
Albert J. Solecki, Jr.
(New York, N.Y. Office)
Steven E. Soule

ASSOCIATES (Continued)

(See Next Column)

ASSOCIATES (Continued)

(See Next Column)

O'MELVENY & MYERS LLP—*Continued*

Geoffrey J. Spolyar
Irene E. Stewart
William J. Stuckwisch
  (Washington, D.C. Office)
Christine H. Suh
Dean Sussman
Nancy E. Sussman
  (Century City Office)
Janet I. Swerdlow
Christine Tam
Jadene M.W. Tamura
  (Newport Beach Office)
Mark Christopher Teuton
  (Newport Beach Office)
Mark E. Thierfelder
  (New York, N.Y. Office)
Diana M. Torres
Glenn A. Trager
Gloria Trattles
  (New York, N.Y. Office)
Dana S. Treister
Kenneth J. Turnbull
  (New York, N.Y. Office)
George A.H. Turner
  (Newport Beach Office)
Harry E. Turner
  (San Francisco Office)
Mark T. Uyeda
Debra J. Vella
Scott M. Voelz
Karen Mary Wahle
  (Washington, D.C. Office)
Kent D. Wakeford
  (Century City Office)

Jeffrey W. Walbridge
  (Newport Beach Office)
Ellen R. Waldorf
  (Washington, D.C. Office)
Larry A. Walraven
  (Newport Beach Office)
Stephanie M. Walter
Todd R. Watkins
Stephen J. Watson
  (New York, N.Y. Office)
Aimee S. Weisner
  (Newport Beach Office)
Kevin M. Wernick
Heather G. White
Molly M. White
Ronan M. Wicks
  (New York, N.Y. Office)
Michael A. Williamson
David A. Wimmer
Robert Winter
  (New York, N.Y. Office)
Jeffrey A. Wortman
Todd R. Wulffson
  (Newport Beach Office)
Richard Xu (Hong Kong Office;
  China Counsel)
Kevin Yamaga-Karns
Masami Yamamoto
Keith K. Yang
  (Century City Office)
Stephanie K. Yonekura
Spencer H.C. Yu

For full biographical listings, see the Martindale-Hubbell Law Directory

---

OSTROVE, KRANTZ & OSTROVE, A PROFESSIONAL CORPORATION (AV)

(Successor To: Ostrove and Lancer, A Professional Corporation; David Ostrove, A Professional Corporation)
5757 Wilshire Boulevard, Suite 535, 90036-3600
Telephone: 213-939-3400
Fax: 213-939-3500
Email: OSTROVE@AOL.COM

David Ostrove   David S. Krantz
Kenneth E. Ostrove

Reference: First Business Bank.

For full biographical listings, see the Martindale-Hubbell Law Directory

---

PAUL, HASTINGS, JANOFSKY & WALKER LLP (AV)

A Limited Liability Partnership including Professional Corporations
Twenty-Third Floor, 555 South Flower Street, 90071-2371
Telephone: 213-683-6000
FAX: 213-627-0705
Email: info@PHJW.com *URL:* http://www.phjw.com
Orange County, California Office: Seventeenth Floor, 695 Town Center Drive, Costa Mesa.
Telephone: 714-668-6200.
Washington, D.C. Office: Tenth Floor, 1299 Pennsylvania Avenue, N.W.
Telephone: 202-508-9500.
Atlanta, Georgia Office: 24th Floor, 600 Peachtree Street, N.E.
Telephone: 404-815-2400.
Santa Monica, California Office: Fifth Floor, 1299 Ocean Avenue.
Telephone: 310-319-3300.
Stamford, Connecticut Office: Ninth Floor, 1055 Washington Boulevard.
Telephone: 203-961-7400.
New York, New York Office: 31st Floor, 399 Park Avenue.
Telephone: 212-318-6000.
Tokyo, Japan Office: Ark Mori Building, 30th Floor, 12-32 Akasaka, P.O. Box 577, 1-Chome, Minato-Ku.
Telephone: (03) 3586-4711.

Robert Pusey Hastings (1910-1996)
COUNSEL

Oliver F. Green
  (Costa Mesa, California)
Leonard S. Janofsky
  (Santa Monica, California)

Lee G. Paul
  (Costa Mesa, California)
Charles M. Walker
  (Santa Monica, California)

MEMBERS OF FIRM

Nancy L. Abell
  (Santa Monica, California)
Carl T. Anderson
  (Stamford, Connecticut)
Toshiyuki Arai
Richard M. Asbill
  (Atlanta, Georgia)

R. Lawrence Ashe, Jr., (P.C.)
  (Atlanta, Georgia)
Mark W. Atkinson
Jesse H. Austin, III
  (Atlanta, Georgia)
E. Lawrence Barcella, Jr.
  (Washington, D.C.)

(See Next Column)

Christopher A. Barreca
  (Stamford, Connecticut)
Alan J. Barton
Keith W. Berglund
  (Atlanta, Georgia)
Daniel G. Bergstein
  (New York, New York)
Stephen L. Berry
Woodson Toliver Besson (P.C.)
  (Santa Monica, California)
Jonathan Birenbaum
  (Stamford, Connecticut)
Thomas P. Brennan (P.C.)
John H. Brinsley
Jamie Broder
Barry A. Brooks
  (New York, New York)
Barbara Berish Brown
  (Washington D.C.)
Daryl R. Buffenstein
  (Atlanta, Georgia)
Thomas G. Burch, Jr.
  (Atlanta, Georgia)
Siobhan McBreen Burke
Paul W. Cane, Jr.
Robert E. Carlson
Grace A. Carter
Eve Mary Coddon
Ronald T. Coleman, Jr.
  (Atlanta, Georgia)
Kevin Conboy
  (Atlanta, Georgia)
Paul J. Connell
  (Atlanta, Georgia)
Douglas C. Conroy
  (Stamford, Connecticut)
Stephen D. Cooke
  (Costa Mesa, California)
James H. Cox
  (Atlanta, Georgia)
Victoria A. Cundiff
  (New York, New York)
Glenn D. Dassoff
  (Costa Mesa, California)
Donald A. Daucher
Janet Toll Davidson
  (Costa Mesa, California)
Barbra L. Davis
John F. Della Grotta
  (Costa Mesa, California)
Nicholas DeWitt
Robert A. DeWitt (P.C.)
R. Bruce Dickson (Washington.
  D.C. and New York, New
  York)
Robert M. Dudnik
  (Santa Monica, California)
William E. Eason, Jr.
  (Atlanta, Georgia)
E. Donald Elliott
  (Washington, D.C.)
Ralph B. Everett
  (Washington, D.C.)
Zachary D. Fasman
  (Washington, D.C.)
Philip N. Feder
Hydee R. Feldstein
Alfred G. Feliu
  (New York, New York)
Esteban A. Ferrer, III
  (Stamford, Connecticut)
Bruce W. Fraser
John C. Funk
Norman A. Futami
John J. Gallagher
  (Washington, D.C.)
Jon A. Geier
  (Washington, D.C.)
David L. Gersh
John S. Gibson
Michael Glazer
George L. Graff
  (New York, New York)
Paul Grossman
William M. Hart
  (New York, New York)
Lawrence J. Hass
  (Washington, D.C.)
John D. Hawkins, Jr.
  (Stamford, Connecticut)
Howard C. Hay
  (Costa Mesa, California)

William B. Hill, Jr.
  (Atlanta, Georgia)
Matthew A. Hodel
  (Costa Mesa, California)
Michael A. Hood
  (Costa Mesa, California)
Judith Richards Hope
  (Washington, D.C.)
John P. Howitt
  (New York, New York)
Mario J. Ippolito
  (Stamford, Connecticut)
Nancy L. Iredale (P.C.)
Euclid A. Irving
  (New York, New York)
John Griffith Johnson, Jr.
  (Washington, D.C.)
Weyman T. Johnson, Jr.
  (Atlanta, Georgia)
Eric H. Joss
  (Santa Monica, California)
Marguerite R. Kahn
  (New York, New York)
James W. Kennedy
  (New York, New York)
Ronald Kreismann
  (New York, New York)
Thomas R. Lamia (New York,
  New York and Washington,
  D.C.)
J. Al Latham, Jr.
Charles T. Lee
  (Stamford, Connecticut)
Michael K. Lindsey
Ethan Lipsig
G. Hamilton Loeb
  (Washington, D.C.)
Kevin C. Logue
  (New York, New York)
M. Guy Maisnik
Philip J. Marzetti
  (Atlanta, Georgia)
John S. McGeeney
  (Stamford, Connecticut)
Roger M. Milgrim
  (New York, New York)
Nancy Kennerly Miller
Robert A. Miller, Jr.
Chris D. Molen
  (Atlanta, Georgia)
Donald L. Morrow
  (Costa Mesa, California)
Julian D. Nealy
  (Atlanta, Georgia)
Greg M. Nitzkowski
Carl W. Northrop
  (Washington, D.C.)
Belinda K. Orem
Brendan J. O'Rourke
  (New York, New York)
Charles B. Ortner
  (New York, New York)
Kevin J. O'Shea
  (New York, New York)
Ronald M. Oster (P.C.)
Michael L. Owen
John G. Parker
  (Atlanta, Georgia)
Charles A. Patrizia
  (Washington, D.C.)
Paul L. Perito
  (Washington, D.C.)
Thomas R. Pollock
  (New York, New York)
John E. Porter
Patrick A. Ramsey
Clayton S. Reynolds
  (Stamford, Connecticut)
David M. Roberts
Samuel D. Rosen
  (New York, New York)
Bruce D. Ryan
  (Washington, D.C.)
Leigh P. Ryan
  (New York, New York)
Cheryl R. Saban
  (New York, New York)
Douglas A. Schaaf
  (Costa Mesa, California)
William A. Schmidt
  (Washington, D.C.)

(See Next Column)

PAUL, HASTINGS, JANOFSKY & WALKER LLP, *Los Angeles—Continued*

MEMBERS OF FIRM (Continued)

William F. Schwitter, Jr.
(New York, New York)
W. Andrew Scott
(Atlanta, Georgia)
Charles T. Sharbaugh
(Atlanta, Georgia)
Patrick W. Shea
(Stamford, Connecticut)
Robert L. Sherman
(New York, New York)
Andrew M. Short
(New York, New York)
Wayne H. Shortridge
(Atlanta, Georgia)
Marc L. Silverman
(New York, New York)
Joel M. Simon
(New York, New York)
William J. Simpson
(Costa Mesa, California)
David E. Snediker
(Stamford, Connecticut)
Robert S. Span
(Santa Monica, California)
John H. Steed (Tokyo, Japan)
Alan K. Steinbrecher
George E. Stephens, Jr., (P.C.)
Harvey A. Strickon
(New York, New York)

Kaoruhiko Suzuki
Peter J. Tennyson
(Costa Mesa, California)
Geoffrey L. Thomas (P.C.)
Charles V. Thornton
Neil A. Torpey
(New York, New York)
Gary F. Torrell
John E. Trinnaman
(Costa Mesa, California)
Dennis H. Vaughn
(Santa Monica, California)
William Stewart Waldo
Elizabeth W. Walker
Paul R. Walker
Robert F. Walker
(Santa Monica, California)
Alan Wade Weakland
Lawrence I. Weinstein
(New York, New York)
C. Geoffrey Weirich
(Atlanta, Georgia)
Michael A. Wiegard
(Washington, D.C.)
Thomas S. Wisialowski
Seth M. Zachary
(New York, New York)
James A. Zapp
Harry A. Zinn
(Santa Monica, California)

SENIOR COUNSEL

Robert R. Burge
(Costa Mesa, California)

James W. Hamilton
(Costa Mesa, California)

OF COUNSEL

John M. Bergin
(New York, New York)
Theodore W. Browne, II
(New York, New York)
Roxanne E. Christ
Edwin I. Colodny
(Washington, D.C.)
Mary L. Cornwell
(Costa Mesa, California)
Jonathan C. Curtis
Julian B. Decyk
William D. DeGrandis
(Washington, D.C.)
Leslie A. Dent
(Atlanta, Georgia)
Brian J. Donnelly
Jane Elizabeth Eakins
(Santa Monica, California)
Jason O. Engel
(Costa Mesa, California)
Elliot K. Gordon
(Santa Monica, California)
Anna M. Graves
Kurt W. Hansson
(Stamford, Connecticut)
Andrew S. Holmes
(Stamford Connecticut)
Gage Randolph Johnson
(Washington, D.C.)
Steven D. Johnson
(New York, New York)
Rick S. Kirkbride
Thomas J. Knapp
(Washington, D.C.)
Peter W. LaVigne
(New York, New York)
Scott N. Leslie
(Costa Mesa, California)
A. Alan Manning
Deborah A. Marlowe
(Atlanta, Georgia)
Neal D. Mollen
(Washington, D.C.)

Robert C. Moot, Jr.
(Atlanta, Georgia)
Sean A. O'Brien
(Costa Mesa, California)
Tetsuya Ogawa (Tokyo, Japan)
Craig K. Pendergrast
(Atlanta, Georgia)
Gloria C. Phares
(New York, New York)
David S. Phelps
Robert S. Plotkin
(Washington, D.C.)
Robert E. Pokusa
(Washington, D.C.)
Lucy Prashker
(New York, New York)
David E. Rabin
(Stamford, Connecticut)
William Thomas Reeder, Jr.
(Washington, D.C.)
Anthony J. Rossi
Christine A. Scheuneman
Charles A. Shanor (Atlanta,
Georgia and Washington,
D.C.)
Margaret H. Spurlin
(Washington, D.C.)
Takashi Suzuki (Tokyo, Japan)
Jeffrey G. Varga
William P. Wade
Philip R. Weingold
(New York, New York)
Patrick J. Whittle
(Washington, D.C.)
Kenneth M. Willner
(Washington, D.C.)
Michael S. Woodward
Gerald H. Yamada
(Washington, D.C.)
Darla L. Yancey
(Costa Mesa, California)
Clarisse W. J. Young

ASSOCIATES

Leslie Abbott
(Santa Monica, California)
George W. Abele
Eliot J. Abt (Atlanta, Georgia)
Elizabeth A. Adolff
(Stamford, Connecticut)
Terry Jon Allen
(Costa Mesa, California)
Steven D. Allison
(Costa Mesa, California)

Kenneth T. Araki
Peter Aronson
Elena R. Baca
Jennifer Stivers Baldocchi
Tracey T. Barbaree
(Atlanta, Georgia)
Michele L. Barber
Kirby D. Behre
(Washington, D.C.)

(See Next Column)

ASSOCIATES (Continued)

Brent J. Belnap
(New York, New York)
David S. Benyacar
(New York, New York)
Patricia M. Berry
James R. Bliss
(Stamford, Connecticut)
Stephanie A. Bohm
(Atlanta, Georgia)
Brent R. Bohn
(Costa Mesa, California)
David B. Booker
(New York, New York)
Robert L. Boyd
(New York, New York)
Deborah M. Bradley
(Atlanta, Georgia)
Marian L. Brancaccio
(New York, New York)
Glenn L. Briggs
(Costa Mesa, California)
Mark Bronson
Sheryl J. Brown
(Washington, D.C.)
Robert P. Bryant
(Costa Mesa, California)
David D. Burns
(Washington, D.C.)
Christine E. Cahill
(Atlanta, Georgia)
Joseph A. Callari
(Stamford, Connecticut)
Gwyneth A. Campbell
Robert R. Carlson
Dianne C. Carraway
(Washington, D.C.)
Patricia M. Carroll
(New York, New York)
Marie Censoplano
(New York, New York)
Sarka Cerna-Fagan
(New York, New York)
Veronica J. Cherniak
(Atlanta, Georgia)
Alpa Patel Chernof
TanYee Cheung
(New York, New York)
Justin C. Choi
(New York, New York)
John H. Clayton
(New York, New York)
A. Craig Cleland
(Atlanta, Georgia)
Michelle Weisberg Cohen
(Washington, D.C.)
Christopher H. Craig
(Stamford, Connecticut)
Sandra A. Crawshaw
(New York, New York)
Christine M. Crowe
(Washington, D.C.)
Kathleen O. Currey
(Atlanta, Georgia)
Marc A. Daniel
(New York, New York)
Barbara R. Danz
(Costa Mesa, California)
Cindy J.K. Davis
(Atlanta, Georgia)
Eric B. Davis
(New York, New York)
Jeanne R. Dawson
Behnam Dayanim
(Washington, D.C.)
Daniel P. Delaney
S. Mark Denham
Alejandro J. Diaz
(Stamford, Connecticut)
Kristina H. Dinerman
Mary C. Dollarhide
(Stamford, Connecticut)
Jessica S. Dorman-Davis
(Costa Mesa, California)
Patricia A. Driscoll
(Stamford, Connecticut)
Michael W. Dubus
(Atlanta, Georgia)
John C. Dworkin
(New York, New York)
Harold N. Eddy, Jr.
(Stamford, Connecticut)
Linda M. Edwards
(Santa Monica, California)

Susan Langley Elliot
(Atlanta, Georgia)
Dennis S. Ellis
Jewell L. Esposito
(Washington, D.C.)
William P. Ewing
(Atlanta, Georgia)
Malinda A. Faber
(Costa Mesa, California)
Wendell M. Faria
(Washington, D.C.)
Elizabeth A. Fealy
(New York, New York)
Alan M. Feld
(New York, New York)
Benjamin J. Ferron
(New York, New York)
Violet F. Fiacco
(Costa Mesa, California)
Regina M. Flaherty
(Stamford, Connecticut)
Scott M. Flicker
(Washington, D.C.)
Laura A. Forbes
(Costa Mesa, California)
Michele Freedenthal
Margo E. Freedman
Philip E. Fried
(New York, New York)
Intra L. Germanis
(Washington, D.C.)
David E. Gevertz
(Atlanta, Georgia)
Lisa M. Gigliotti
(New York, New York)
Ronald K. Giller
Margaret A. Gilleran
(New York, New York)
Mark A. Gloade
(New York, New York)
Karen K. Greenwalt
E. Jeffrey Grube
Delia Guevara
John W. Hamlin
(Stamford, Connecticut)
Andrew P. Hanson
(Costa Mesa, California)
Susan E. Himmer
(Atlanta, Georgia)
Eric J. Hoffman
Stacy M. Hopkins
Alan B. Horowitz
(Washington, D.C.)
James Che-Ming Hsu
(New York, New York)
Scott N. Hudson
(New York, New York)
Lisa G. Huffiness
(New York, New York)
James Judson Jackson
(Stamford, Connecticut)
Marcia N. Jackson
(Santa Monica, California)
Michael B. Jaffe
(Stamford, Connecticut)
Edward S. Johnson, Jr.
(Atlanta, Georgia)
Jarret L. Johnson
(Costa Mesa, California)
E. Ashton Johnston
(Washington, D.C.)
George R.A. Jones
(Washington, D.C.)
Karen E. Jorik
(Atlanta, Georgia)
Michael B. Kaufman
(New York, New York)
Deidre M. Kelly
Tara K. Kelly
Ann T. Kenny
(New York, New York)
Marc E. Kenny
Jong Han Kim
Ken Kimura
(New York, New York)
Eileen M. King
(New York, New York)
Rosemary Mahar Kirbach
Janet L. Kishbaugh
(Atlanta, Georgia)
Karen L. Kleiderman
Judith M. Kline

(See Next Column)

PAUL, HASTINGS, JANOFSKY & WALKER LLP—*Continued*

ASSOCIATES (Continued)

Cheryl L. Kopitzke
(Santa Monica, California)
Lisa M. LaFourcade
(Costa Mesa, California)
Douglas E. Lahammer
Gregory F. Lang
(Stamford, Connecticut)
Lisa J. Laplace
(New York, New York)
Aric H. Lasky
David S. Levin
(New York, New York)
Eric T. Levine
(Stamford, Connecticut)
Brigitte P. Lippmann
(New York, New York)
Katherine B. Lipton
(New York, New York)
Vincent D. Lowder
(Costa Mesa, California)
Robert L. Madok
Jenifer A. Magyar
(Stamford, Connecticut)
Christopher J. Manfredi
Paul C. Marazita
(Stamford, Connecticut)
Michael S. Marx
Andrew M. Mayer
(New York, New York)
Kathleen L. McAchran
P. Casey McGannon
Denise Marie McGorrin
Sarah M. McWilliams
(Washington, D.C.)
Martin C. Mead
Jon Douglas Meer
Michael T. Mervis
(New York, New York)
Ingrid M. Mesa
(New York, New York)
Cara D. Miller
(Santa Monica, California)
J. Clark Miller
Scott R. Miller
(Costa Mesa, California)
Haruki Minaki
Heather Morgan
(Santa Monica, California)
Jay A. Morrison
(Washington, D.C.)
Melinda L. Moseley
(Atlanta, Georgia)
John J. Neely, III
(Atlanta, Georgia)
Elizabeth A. Newell
(New York, New York)
Elizabeth Hardy Noe
(Atlanta, Georgia)
J. Yoheved Novogroder
(New York, New York)
Robert J. Odson
John C. O'Malley
Maureen E. O'Neill
(Atlanta, Georgia)
Joseph P. Opich
(New York, New York)
DeAnne H. Ozaki
Vincent J. Pasquariello
(New York, New York)
Susan M. Pavlin
(Atlanta, Georgia)
Joseph D. Penachio
(New York, New York)
Suzanne Marie Pepe-Robbins
(Stamford, Connecticut)
Bonnie Pierson-Murphy
(Stamford, Connecticut)
Alexis Pinto
(New York, New York)
Sara Rabinowitz Pinto
(New York, New York Office)
Leslie A. Plaskon
(Stamford, Connecticut)
Tracy S. Plott (Atlanta, Georgia)
Lisa A. Popovich
Nancy E. Rafuse
(Atlanta, Georgia)

Philip J. Ragona
(New York, New York)
Lynne H. Rambo
(Atlanta, Georgia)
T. Robert Reid
(Atlanta, Georgia)
Ellen C. Rice
(Washington, D.C.)
Peter J. Roth
Joel H. Rothstein
Dena T. Sacco
(Washington, D.C.)
Alfred Sanchez, Jr.
Allyson G. Saunders
Mathew Anthony Schuh
(Atlanta, Georgia)
Glori J. Schultz
Susan E. Schwartz
Craig S. Seligman
Lee R. Seltman
Nancy E. Shallow
(Washington, D.C.)
Joseph C. Sharp
(Atlanta, Georgia)
Eric M. Sherbet
(New York, New York)
Glenn C. Shrader
Betty M. Shumener
Derek E. Smith
Naomi Weyand Smith
(Atlanta, Georgia)
Nancy L. Sommer
(New York, New York)
Stephen P. Sonnenberg
E. Gary Spitko
(Atlanta, Georgia)
David H. Steinberg
(New York, New York)
John B. Stephens
(Costa Mesa, California)
Joshua H. Sternoff
(Washington, D.C.)
Randall M. Stone
(Washington, D.C.)
Brian D. Sullivan
(Atlanta, Georgia)
Kristen K. Swartz
(Atlanta, Georgia)
Gregory J. Swedelson
Erin M. Sweeney
(Washington, D.C.)
Eric Jon Taylor
(Atlanta, Georgia)
Katherine A. Traxler
Michael W. Traynham
Richard M. Vicenzi
(Stamford, Connecticut)
Michael T. Voytek
(Atlanta, Georgia)
Stanley F. Wasowski
(Atlanta, Georgia)
L. Kent Webb
(Atlanta, Georgia)
Deborah S. Weiser
(Santa Monica, California)
Timothy J. Wellman
(Washington, D.C.)
Elise M. Whitaker
(Atlanta, Georgia)
Crystal L. Williams
(Atlanta, Georgia)
S. Reginald Williams
(New York, New York)
Jonathan B. Wilson
(Atlanta, Georgia)
Ivan J. Wolpert
(New York, New York)
Scott M. Wornow
(New York, New York)
Shannon P. Wright
Joshua G. Wrobel
Jenny C. Wu
(Washington, D.C.)
Stephen A. Yamaguchi
Julie Arias Young
Arthur L. Zwickel

For full biographical listings, see the Martindale-Hubbell Law Directory

PILLSBURY MADISON & SUTRO LLP (AV)

Citicorp Plaza, 725 South Figueroa Street, Suite 1200, 90017-2513
Telephone: 213-488-7100
Fax: 213-629-1033
Costa Mesa, California Office: Plaza Tower, Suite 1100, 600 Anton Boulevard, 92626.
Telephone: 714-436-6800.
Fax: 714-662-6999.
Silicon Valley Office: 2700 San Hill Road, Menlo Park, 94025.
Telephone: 415-233-4500.
Fax: 415-233-4545.
Sacramento, California Office: 400 Capitol Mall, Suite 1700, 95814.
Telephone: 916-329-4700.
Fax: 916-441-3583.
San Diego, California Office: 101 West Broadway, Suite 1800, 92101.
Telephone: 619-234-5000.
Fax: 619-236-1995.
San Francisco, California Office: 235 Montgomery Street, 94104.
Telephone: 415-983-1000.
Fax: 415-983-1200.
Washington, D.C. Office: 1100 New York Avenue, N.W., Ninth Floor, 20005.
Telephone: 202-861-3000.
Fax: 202-822-0944.
New York, New York Office: 520 Madison Avenue, 40th Floor, 10022.
Telephone: 212-328-4810.
Fax: 212-328-4824. One Liberty Plaza, 165 Broadway, 51st Floor.
Telephone: 212-374-1890.
Fax: 212-374-1852.
Hong Kong Office: 6/F Asia Pacific Finance Tower, Citibank Plaza, 3 Garden Road, Central.
Telephone: 011-852-2509-7100.
Fax: 011-852-2509-7188.
Tokyo, Japan Office: Pillsbury Madison & Sutro, Gaikokuho Jimu Bengoshi Jimusho, 5th Floor, Samon Eleven Building, 3-1, Samon-cho, Shinjuku-ku, Tokyo 160 Japan.
Telephone: 800-729-9830; 011-813-3354-3531.
Fax: 011-813-3354-3534.

MEMBERS OF FIRM

Lawrence D. Bradley, Jr.
Anthon S. Cannon, Jr.
Anthony R. Delling
Blase P. Dillingham
Jerone J. English
L. Gail Gordon
T.J. (Mick) Grasmick
Jeffrey W. Hill
Carolyn M. Huestis
Sidney K. Kanazawa
Steven O. Kramer
Thomas R. Larmore
John Y. Liu
Donald W. Meaders
Michael E. Meyer
Nancy G. Morrison
J. Richard Morrissey
F. John Nyhan
Jackie K. Park
Edward A. Perron
James M. Rishwain, Jr.
Matthew R. Rogers
Karl A. Schmidt
Robert V. Slattery Jr.
William E. Stoner
Reed S. Waddell
William S. Waller
John W. Whitaker
Thomas E. Workman, Jr.

John R. Cadarette, Jr.
Kenneth R. Chiate
William K. Dial
John J. Duffy
Michael J. Finnegan
Kent B. Goss
David L. Hayutin
Amy D. Hogue
Yuji Iwanaga
Ralph D. Kirwan
Jennie L. La Prade
Peter V. Leparulo
Christopher J. McNevin
Catherine D. Meyer
Ruth Modisette
Robert L. Morrison
Dana P. Newman
Henry Y. Ota
Charles E. Patterson
Teresa M. Quinn
Patrick G. Rogan
Kenneth N. Russak
Faisal Shah
Sheryl E. Stein
Marshall M. Taylor
Robert L. Wallan
Don R. Weigandt
John G. Wigmore
Gordon K. Wright

OF COUNSEL

Charles E. Anderson
Deborah S. Thoren-Peden

Roland G. Simpson

SENIOR COUNSEL

A. Todd Littleworth

Steven M. Nakasone

ASSOCIATES

Keith A. Allen-Niesen
Brett H. Bailey
J. Keith Biancamano
J. Douglas Bishop
Jan H. Cate
Barbara L. Croutch
Douglas H. Deems
Julie G. Duffy
Douglas C. Emhoff
Michael J. Erlinger
Eric B. Foker
Jeffrey D. Frost
Tracy Birnkrant Gray
L. Keven Hayworth
Karen L. Hermann
Kelly A. Kightlinger
Tohru Masago
Mary T. Michelena-Monroe

Farhad Bahar
Ian R. Barrett
Dimitrios P. Biller
Dawn S. Brookey
J. Mark Childs
Michael J. Crowley
Sybille Dreuth
Sheri F. Eisner
Jason R. Erb
Alyssa First
William B. Freeman
William T. Gillespie
Stewart S. Harrison
Sabina A. Helton
Julia R. Johnson
Lynne E. Mallya
Jennifer E. Mayo
Margaret L. Milam

(See Next Column)

PILLSBURY MADISON & SUTRO LLP, *Los Angeles—Continued*

ASSOCIATES (Continued)

David S. Rauch	Jeffrey A. Rich
Julia Ellen Richards	Lori A. Ridley
Susan M. St. Denis	Kalman Steinberg
John T. Vangel	David J. Westgor
Marcus G. Whittle	Christopher T. Williams
Andrew M. Winograd	

For full biographical listings, see the Martindale-Hubbell Law Directory

PROSKAUER ROSE GOETZ & MENDELSOHN LLP (AV)

2121 Avenue of the Stars, Suite 2700, 90067-3003
Telephone: 310-557-2900
FAX: 310-557-2193
Email: info@proskauer.com *URL:* http://www.proskauer.com
New York, N.Y. Office: 1585 Broadway.
Telephone: 212-969-3000.
Washington, D.C. Office: 1233 Twentieth Street, N.W., Suite 800.
Telephone: 202-416-6800.
Boca Raton, Florida Office: One Boca Place, Suite 340 West, 2255 Glades Road.
Telephone: 407-241-7400.
Clifton, New Jersey Office: 1373 Broad Street, P.O. Box 4444.
Telephone: 201-779-6300.
Paris, France Office: Proskauer Rose Goetz & Mendelsohn, 9 rue Le Tasse.
Telephone: (33-1) 44 30 25 30.

RESIDENT PARTNERS

Howard D. Behar	Mitchell M. Gaswirth
Henry Ben-Zvi	Bernard D. Gold
Jeffrey A. Berman	Barry C. Groveman
Harold M. Brody	Paul D. Rubenstein
Scott P. Cooper	David R. Scheidemantle
Thomas W. Dollinger	Marvin Sears
Howard D. Fabrick	Lois D. Thompson
Martin S. Zohn	

SPECIAL COUNSEL

Walter Cochran-Bond	Kenneth Krug
W. Herbert Young	

RESIDENT ASSOCIATES

Aaron P. Allan	Dana Hirsch Lipman
Christopher M. Brock	David S. Lippman
Yun Y. Choi	Seth A. Miller
Nicholas P. Connon	Gregory J. Patterson
James F. Dunn	Mary H. Rose
Daniel E. Eaton	Jane E. Rudofsky
Steven J. Elkins	Lori E. Sambol
Alan H. Finkel	Christopher J. Tricarico
Maria E. Grecky	Tal O. Vigderson
Gloria Ching-hua Jan	Hao-Nhien Q. Vu
Elizabeth J. Kruger	James M. Wakefield
Carol E. Kurtz	Leslie A. Wederich
Erick Kwak	Scott J. Witlin

For full biographical listings, see the Martindale-Hubbell Law Directory

ROGERS & WELLS (AV)

444 South Flower Street, 90071-2901
Telephone: 213-689-2900
Facsimile: 213-689-2999
New York, N.Y. Office: Two Hundred Park Avenue, New York, N.Y. 10166-0153.
Telephone: 212-878-8000.
Facsimile: 212-878-8375.
Telex: 234493 RKWUR. E-Mail: email@rw.com.
Washington, D.C. Office: 607 Fourteenth Street, N.W., Washington, D.C. 20005-2018.
Telephone: 202-434-0700.
Facsimile: 202-434-0800.
Paris, France Office: 47, Avenue Hoche, 75008-Paris, France.
Telephone: 33-1-44-09-46-00.
Facsimile: 33-1-42-67-50-81.
Telex: 651617 EURLAW.
London, England Office: 40 Basinghall Street, London EC2V 5DE, England.
Telephone: 44-171-628-0101.
Facsimile: 44-171-628-6111.
Frankfurt, Germany Office: Westendstrasse 16-22, 60325 Frankfurt/Main, Federal Republic of Germany.
Telephone: 49-69-97-14-78-0.
Facsimile: 49-69-97-14-78-33.
Hong Kong: One Exchange Square, 8 Connaught Place, Central, Hong Kong.
Telephone: 852-2844-3500.
Facsimile: 852-2844-3555.

(See Next Column)

PARTNERS

Allan E. Ceran	Terry O. Kelly
John I. Forry	Eugene Y. C. Lu
John A. Karaczynski	Richard A. Shortz
John K. Keitt, Jr.	Carl W. Sonne
(Not admitted in CA)	I. Bruce Speiser

ASSOCIATES

Christopher R. Baker	Steven M. Ruskin
David B. Cohen	Julie A. Shepard
Alan H. Fairley	Steven S. Spitz
Richard C. Jun	
(Not admitted in CA)	

For full biographical listings, see the Martindale-Hubbell Law Directory

ROPERS, MAJESKI, KOHN & BENTLEY, A PROFESSIONAL CORPORATION (AV)

550 South Hope Street, Suite 1900, 90071
Telephone: 213-312-2000
Fax: 213-312-2001
Redwood City, California Office: 1001 Marshall Street.
Telephone: 415-364-8200.
Fax: 415-367-0997.
San Jose, California Office: 80 North 1st Street.
Telephone: 408-287-6262.
Fax: 408-297-6819.
San Francisco, California Office: 670 Howard Street.
Telephone: 415-543-4800.
Fax: 415-512-1574.
Santa Rosa, California Office: Fountaingrove Center, Suite 300, 3558 Round Barn Boulevard.
Telephone: 707-524-4200.
Fax: 707-523-4610.
Sacramento, California Office: 1000 G. Street, Suite 400.
Telephone: 916-556-3100.
Fax: 916-442-7121.

Stephen J. Erigero	Sue Carol Rokaw
Frank T. Sabaitis (Resident)	Carol Kurke Lucas
Marta B. Arriandiaga	Allan E. Anderson (Resident)

Michael W. Parks	I. Paul Bae (Resident)
Sean S. Varner	Bradley P. Boyer
Ernest E. Price	Michael T. O'Callaghan
Andrew D. Castricone	Robin L Jacobs
Charlene Rudio Culver	Gerald B. Malanga
Robin J. Devereux	

For full biographical listings, see the Martindale-Hubbell Law Directory

SCHELL & DELAMER, LLP (AV)

A Partnership including Professional Corporations
865 South Figueroa Street Suite 2750, 90017
Telephone: 213-622-8181
Fax: 213-627-5252
Thousand Oaks, California Office: 100 East Thousand Oaks Boulevard, Suite 142.
Telephone: 805-496-9533.
Fax: 805-496-3424.

Gerald F. H. Delamer (1892-1955)	Garrin James Shaw (Professional Corporation)
Walter O. Schell (1895-1981)	Robert S. Hamrick (Professional Corporation)
Roland R. Kaspar (Professional Corporation)	Jeffrey F. Briskin
Katherine B. Pene	

ASSOCIATES

Candace E. Ahrens Kallberg	John J. Latzanich, II. (Resident at Thousand Oaks Office)
Denise A. Nardi	Lori M. Levine
Randy A. Berg	Sylvia Havens
Kenneth S. Markson	Roman Y. Nykolyshyn
Joseph P. Sepikas	
Gregory J. Amantia (Resident at Thousand Oaks Office)	

Representative Clients: Hartford Insurance Group; Liberty Mutual Group; Travelers Insurance Co.
References: Los Angeles: First Interstate Bank; Merrill-Lynch.

For full biographical listings, see the Martindale-Hubbell Law Directory

SHEARMAN & STERLING (AV)

777 South Figueroa Street, 34th Floor, 90017-5418
Telephone: (213) 239-0300
Fax: (213) 239-0381, 614-0936
New York, N.Y. Office: 599 Lexington Avenue, New York, New York 10022-6069 and Citicorp Center, 153 East 53rd Street, New York, New York 10022-4676.
Telephone: (212) 848-4000.
Telex: 667290 Num Lau.
Fax: 599 Lexington Avenue: (212) 848-7179. Citicorp Center: (212) 848-5252.

(See Next Column)

SHEARMAN & STERLING—*Continued*

Abu Dhabi, United Arab Emirates Office: P.O. Box 2948.
Telephone: (971-2) 324477.
Fax: (971-2) 774533.
Beijing, People's Republic of China Office: Suite #2205, Capital Mansion, No. 6, Xin Yuan Nan Lu. Chao Yang District, Beijing, 100004.
Telephone: (86-10)6465-4574.
Fax: (86-10) 6465-4578.
Budapest, Hungary Office: Szerb utca 17-19, 1056 Budapest.
Telephone: (36-1) 266-3522.
Fax: (36-1) 266-3523.
Düsseldorf, Federal Republic of Germany Office: Couvenstrasse 8 40211 Düsseldorf.
Telephone: (49 211) 178 88-0.
Fax: (49 211) 178 88-88.
Telex: 8588294 NYLO.
Frankfurt, Federal Republic of Germany Office: Bockenheimer Landstrasse 55, 60325 Frankfurt am Main.
Telephone: (49-69) 97107-0.
Fax: (49-69) 97107-100.
Hong Kong Office: Standard Chartered Bank Building, 4 Des Voeux Road, Central.
Telephone: (852) 2978-8000.
Fax: (852) 2978-8099.
London, England Office: 199 Bishopsgate, London EC2M 3TY.
Telephone: (44-171) 920-9000.
Fax: (44-171) 920-9020.
Paris, France Office: 114 avenue des Champs-Elysées, 75008.
Telephone: (33-1) 53-89-7000.
Fax: (33-1) 53-89-7070.
Telex: 282964 ROYALE.
San Francisco, California Office: 555 California Street, 94104-1522.
Telephone: (415) 616-1100.
Fax: (415) 616-1199.
Singapore Office: 80 Raffles Place #16-21, UOB Plaza 2. Singapore 048624. Telephone (65) 230-3800.
Fax: (65) 230-3899.
Tokyo, Japan Office: Shearman & Sterling (Grant Finlayson Gaikokuho-Jimu-Bengoshi Jimusho), Fukoku Seimei Building, 5th Fl. 2-2-2, Uchisaiwaicho, Chiyoda-ku, Tokyo 100, Japan.
Telephone: (81 3) 5251-1601.
Fax: (81 3) 5251-1602.
Toronto, Ontario, Canada Office: Commerce Court West, Suite 4405, P.O. Box 247, M5L 1E8.
Telephone: (416) 360-8484.
Fax: (416) 360-2958.
Washington, D.C. Office: 801 Pennsylvania Avenue, N.W., 20004-2604.
Telephone: (202) 508-8000.
Fax: (202) 508-8100.

RESIDENT PARTNERS

Ronald M. Bayer	Jaculin Aaron
(Managing Partner)	Richard B. Kendall
Darryl Snider	

For full biographical listings, see the Martindale-Hubbell Law Directory

SIDLEY & AUSTIN (AV)

A Partnership including Professional Corporations
555 West Fifth Street, 40th Floor, 90013-1010
Telephone: 213-896-6000
Telecopier: 213-896-6600
Chicago, Illinois Office: One First National Plaza 60603.
Telephone: 312-853-7000.
Telecopier: 312-853-7036.
New York, New York Office: 875 Third Avenue 10022.
Telephone: 212-906-2022.
Telecopier: 212-906-2021.
Washington, D.C. Office: 1722 Eye Street, N.W. 20006.
Telephone: 202-736-8000.
Telecopier: 202-736-8711.
Dallas, Texas Office: 4500 Renaissance Tower, 1201 Elm Street 75270.
Telephone: 214-939-4500.
Telecopier: 214-939-4600.
London, England Office: Royal Exchange, EC3V 3LE.
Telephone: 011-44-171-360-3600.
Telecopier: 011-44-171-626-7937.
Tokyo, Japan Office: Taisho Seimei Hibiya Building, 7th Floor, 9-1, Yurakucho, 1 Chome, Chiyoda-ku, 100.
Facsimile: 011-81-3-3218-5900.
Facsimile: 011-81-3-3218-5922.
Singapore Office: 36 Robinson Road, #18-01 City House, Singapore 0106.
Telephone: 011-65-224-5000.
Telecopier: 011-65-224-0530.

RESIDENT PARTNERS

Amy L. Applebaum	Lori Huff Dillman
Philip M. Battaglia	Edward D. Eddy III
David W. Burhenn	Bradley H. Ellis
Gary J. Cohen	Robert Fabrikant
Ronald C. Cohen	Howard D. Gest
Stephen G. Contopulos	Richard J. Grad
M. Scott Cooper	Johnny D. Griggs
George Deukmejian	Larry G. Gutterridge

(See Next Column)

RESIDENT PARTNERS (Continued)

Jennifer C. Hagle	Sally Schultz Neely
Kent A. Halkett	Edwin L. Norris
Adam M. Handler	Peter I. Ostroff
Thomas P. Hanrahan	Thomas E. Patterson
James M. Harris	Richard T. Peters
Richard W. Havel	Linda S. Peterson
Marc I. Hayutin	Judith M. Praitis
Michael C. Kelley	Howard J. Rubinroit
Moshe J. Kupietzky	Joel G. Samuels
Perry L. Landsberg	Sherwin L. Samuels
Kenneth H. Levin	Ronie M. Schmelz
George M. Means	D. William Wagner
Theodore N. Miller	Michael D. Wright

COUNSEL

James F. Donlan	Richard Schauer
Stuart L. Kadison	Yee-Yoong Yong

RESIDENT ASSOCIATES

Mark Anchor Albert	Jefferson K. Logan
Alan Au	Aimee D. Long
Lee L. Auerbach	Susanne M. MacIntosh
Randee J. Barak	Thomas A. McWatters III
Leslie Kent Beckhart	Cathy Ostiller
Ellie Mask Bertwell	Octavio A. Pedroz
Jonathan M. Brenner	John E. Polich
Steven A. Ellis	Scott Preston
Adam G. Engelskirchen	John V. Pridjian
Jeffrey M. Fisher	James Robertson
Lisa A. Fontenot	Jay D. Rockey
John E. Friedrichs	Matthew E. Sloan
Stephen W. Geary	Glenn E. Solomon
Marlo Ann Goldstein	Sarah V. J. Spyksma
Robert A. Holland	Sonya Sud
Robert W. Kadlec	Holly L. Sutton
Jennifer Landau	Laurine E. Tuleja
Kevin T. Lantry	Catherine M. Valerio Barrad
Joel K. Liberson	Stanley J. Wallach
	Daron Watts

For full biographical listings, see the Martindale-Hubbell Law Directory

SONNENSCHEIN NATH & ROSENTHAL (AV)

601 South Figueroa Street, Suite 1500, 90017
Telephone: 213-623-9300
Telecopier: 213-623-9924
Chicago, Illinois Office: Suite 8000 Sears Tower, 233 South Wacker Drive.
Telephone: 312-876-8000.
Cable Address: "Sonberk".
Telex: 25-3526.
Facsimile: 312-876-7934.
New York, N.Y. Office: 1221 Avenue of the Americas, 24th Floor.
Telephone: 212-768-6700.
Facsimile: 212-391-1247.
Washington, D.C. Office: 1301 K Street, N.W., Suite 600 East Tower.
Telephone: 202-408-6400.
Fax: 202-408-6399.
San Francisco, California Office: 685 Market Street, 10th Floor.
Telephone: 415-882-5000.
Facsimile: 415-543-5472.
St. Louis, Missouri Office: One Metropolitan Square, Suite 3000.
Telephone: 314-241-1800.
Facsimile: 314-259-5959.
Kansas City, Missouri Office: Suite 1100, 4520 Main Street, 64111.
Telephone: 816-932-4400.
Facsimile: 816-531-7545.
London, England Office: Sonnenscheins, Royex House, Aldermanbury Square, EC2V 7HR.
Telephone: 0171-600-2222.
Facsimile: 0171-600-2221.

Percy Anderson	Sue L. Himmelrich
Michael J. Bayard	Ronald D. Kent
Ernest P. Burger	Lee T. Paterson
Charles R. Campbell, Jr.	Laura R. Petroff
Martin J. Foley	Andria K. Richey
Matthew C. Fragner	Michael W. Ring
Brent Matthew Giddens	Robert F. Scoular
Peter J. Gurfein	Norbert M. Seifert
Elliott J. Hahn	J. A. Shafran
Mark T. Hansen	Arthur F. Silbergeld
	Susan M. Walker

OF COUNSEL

Neal R. Marder	Grace Ellen Mueller
	Henry S. Zangwill

ASSOCIATES

Jeffry Butler	Jonathan F. Golding
Anthony Capobianco	Charles W. Hokanson
Nargis Choudhry	Bryan C. Jackson
Stephen J. Curran	Scott L. Jones
Weston A. Edwards	Suzanne Cate Jones

(See Next Column)

SONNENSCHEIN NATH & ROSENTHAL, *Los Angeles—Continued*
ASSOCIATES (Continued)

Matthew I. Kaplan	Leonora M. Schloss
Namyon Kim	David Simantob
Jessie A. Kohler	Steven R. Smith
Pauline Ng Lee	T. Mark Smith
John R. Miller	David W. Tufts
Duncan E. Montgomery	John E. Walker
Terrence R. Pace	Vivian L. Williams
Michael E. Pappas	Lauren M. Yu
Stacie S. Polashuk	Consuelo A. Zermeno

For full biographical listings, see the Martindale-Hubbell Law Directory

---

STROOCK & STROOCK & LAVAN LLP (AV)

Suite 1800, 2029 Century Park East, 90067-3086
Telephone: 310-556-5800
Telecopier: (310) 556-5959
Cable Address: "Plastroock, L.A."
Telex: Plastroock LSA 677190 (Domestic and International)
New York, N.Y. Office: 180 Maiden Lane, New York, N.Y., 10038.
Telephone: 212-806-5400.
Telecopiers: (212) 806-5919; (212) 806-6006; (212) 806-6086; (212) 425-9509; (212) 806-6176.
New York Conference Center: 767 Third Avenue, New York, N.Y., 10017-2023.
Telephones: 212-806-5767; 5768; 5769; 5770.
Telecopier: (212) 421-6234.
Boston, Massachusetts Office: 100 Federal Street, 02110.
Telephone: 617-482-6800.
Fax: 617-330-5111.
Budapest, Hungary Office: East-West Business Center, Rákóczi ut 1-3, H-1088.
Telephone: 011-361-266-9520 or 011-361-266-7770.
Telecopier: 011-361-266-9279.
Miami, Florida Office: 200 South Biscayne Boulevard, Suite 3300, First Union Financial Center, 33131-2385.
Telephone: 305-358-9900.
Telecopier: (305) 789-9302.
Washington, D.C. Office: 1150 Seventeenth Street, N.W., Suite 600, 20036-4652.
Telephone: 202-452-9250.
Telecopier: (202) 293-2293.

RESIDENT PARTNERS

Richard S. Forman	Michael F. Perlis
Schuyler M. Moore	Julia B. Strickland
Margaret A. Nagle	Michael M. Umansky

OF COUNSEL
Gerald J. Mehlman

RETIRED PARTNERS

Merrill E. Jenkins	William H. Levit (P.C.)
Robert M. Shafton	

Judith L. Anderson	Mary D. Manesis
Maryanne Carson	Andrew J. Matosich
Wrenn E. Chais	Scott M. Pearson
James W. Denison	Lisa M. Simonetti
Karen R. Dinino	Glenn D. Smith
Joseph W. Dung	Chauncey M. Swalwell
D. Wayne Jeffries	Matthew C. Thompson
Nicholas F. Klein	Karynne G. Weiss
David S. Lippes	
(Not admitted in CA)	

For full biographical listings, see the Martindale-Hubbell Law Directory

---

SULLIVAN & CROMWELL (AV)

444 South Flower Street, 90071-2901
Telephone: 213-955-8000
Telecopier: 213-683-0457
New York City Office: 125 Broad Street, 10004-2498.
Telephone: 212-558-4000.
Telex: 62694.
Telecopier: 212-558-3588.
Washington, D.C. Office: 1701 Pennsylvania Avenue, N.W., 20006-5805.
Telephone: 202-956-7500.
Telecopier: 202-293-6330.
Paris Office: 8, Place Vendôme, Paris 75001, France.
Telephone: (011)(331)4450-6000.
Telex: 240654.
Telecopier: (011)(331)4450-6060.
London Office: St. Olave's House, 9a Ironmonger Lane, London EC2V 8EY, England.
Telephone: (011)(44171)710-6500.
Telecopier: (011)(44171)710-6565.
Melbourne Office: 101 Collins Street, Melbourne, Victoria 3000, Australia.
Telephone: (011)(613)9654-1500.
Telecopier: (011)(613)9654-2422.

(See Next Column)

Tokyo Office: Sullivan & Cromwell, Gaikokuho Jimu Bengoshi Jimusho, Akai Law Offices (Registered Associated Offices), Tokio Kaijo Building Shinkan, 2-1, Marunouchi 1-chome, Chiyoda-ku, Tokyo 100, Japan.
Telephone: (011)(813)3213-6140.
Telecopier: (011)(813)3213-6470.
Hong Kong Office: 28th Floor, Nine Queen's Road, Central, Hong Kong.
Telephone: (011)(852)2826-8688.
Telecopier: (011)(852)2522-2280.
Frankfurt Office: Oberlindau 54-56, 60323 Frankfurt am Main, Germany.
Telephone: (011)(4969)7191-260.
Telecopier: (011)(4969)7191-2610.

PARTNERS IN LOS ANGELES

Stanley F. Farrar	Alison S. Ressler
Frank H. Golay, Jr.	Michael H. Steinberg
Robert A. Sacks	John L. Savva

ASSOCIATES IN LOS ANGELES

Elizabeth S. Bluestein	Michael L. Preston
Patrick S. Brown	Stevie Pyon
Julius G. Christensen	Daniel E. Sobelsohn
Valerie C. Edwards	Thaddeus G. Stephens
Ken Ikari	Steven B. Stokdyk
Brian P.Y. Liu	Steven W. Thomas

For full biographical listings, see the Martindale-Hubbell Law Directory

---

SULLIVAN LAW CORPORATION (AV)

545 South Figueroa Street, Suite 1216, 90071-1599
Telephone: 213-488-9200
Telecopier: 213-488-9664

Michael R. Sullivan

Douglas G. Carroll

For full biographical listings, see the Martindale-Hubbell Law Directory

---

SULLIVAN, WORKMAN & DEE (AV)

A Partnership including a Professional Corporation
Twelfth Floor, 800 Figueroa Street, 90017
Telephone: 213-624-5544
Fax: 213-627-7128

PARTNERS

Roger M. Sullivan (A Professional Corporation)	Charles F. Callanan
	Gary A. Kovacic
Henry K. Workman	Joseph S. Dzida, Jr.
John J. Dee	John E. Mackel, III
Charles D. Cummings	Paul C. Epstein
Christopher K. Cooper	

Susan Mapel Kahn	Emil J. Wohl

OF COUNSEL

Henry G. Bodkin, Jr.	Thomas E. O'Sullivan

Reference: First Business Bank.

For full biographical listings, see the Martindale-Hubbell Law Directory

---

TUTTLE & TAYLOR, A LAW CORPORATION (AV)

355 South Grand Avenue Fortieth Floor, 90071-3102
Telephone: 213-683-0600
Facsimile: 213-683-0225
Washington, D.C. Office: Tuttle, Taylor & Heron, 1025 Thomas Jefferson Street, N.W. 20007-5201.
Telephone: 202-342-1300.
Facsimile: 202-342-5880.
Sacramento, California Office: 1521 I Street, 95814-2016.
Telephone: 916-441-2249.
Facsimile: 916-441-2910.

Edward W. Tuttle (1877-1960)	Mark A. Borenstein
Edward E. Tuttle (1907-1996)	Nancy E. Howard
Robert G. Taylor	Marc L. Brown
Merlin W. Call	Michael H. Bierman
Frank C. Christl	Louis E. Kempinsky
Patrick L. Shreve	Gordon A. Goldsmith
C. David Anderson	Gregory D. Schetina
Richard S. Berger	Diann H. Kim
John R. Liebman	Marla J. Aspinwall
Alan E. Friedman	Robin D. Wiener (Resident, Sacramento, California Office)
Timi Anyon Hallem	
Charles L. Woltmann	Laura J. Carroll
Marjorie S. Steinberg	Edward A. Mendoza
Douglas W. Beck	Jeffrey D. Wexler
John Arthur Moe, II	Julio A. Thompson
Robert L. Shuler (Resident, Sacramento, California Office)	

(See Next Column)

TUTTLE & TAYLOR A LAW CORPORATION—*Continued*

John R. Dent	Sherry L. Appel
Sung H. Shin	Malissia R. Lennox
Marnie S. Carlin	Kathryn E. Olson
Kate Schneider Gold	Thomas I. Dupuis
Dahni K. Tsuboi	Shannon Sullivan Martinez
Andrea V. Ramos	Dean A. Bochner
Sam S. Oh	Steven M. Rogers

Jeffrey S. Karr

OF COUNSEL

Julian B. Heron, Jr. (Resident, Washington, D.C. Office)   Phillip L. Fraas (Resident, Washington, D.C. Office)

Pamela G. Bothwell

Reference: Union Bank, 455 South Figueroa Street, Main Office (Los Angeles, California).

For full biographical listings, see the Martindale-Hubbell Law Directory

MANHATTAN BEACH, Los Angeles Co.

STEINBERG BARNESS GLASGOW & FOSTER LLP (AV)

1334 Park View Avenue, Suite 100, 90266
Telephone: 310-546-5838
Telecopier: 310-546-5630
Email: SGBF@ix.netcom.com

MEMBERS OF FIRM

Alex Steinberg	Jordan G. Barness
Daniel I. Barness	Paul J. Laurin
Donna Glasgow	Shannon M. Foley
(Not admitted in CA)	Richard L. Weiner
Douglas B. Foster	William R. (Randy) Kirkpatrick

Jeffrey Michael Lee

OF COUNSEL

Roanld D. Harari (Not admitted in CA)

References: Home Bank; Imperial Bank; Citizens Commerical Trust & Savings Bank; Bank of America.

For full biographical listings, see the Martindale-Hubbell Law Directory

MARTINEZ,* Contra Costa Co.

BERNARD F. CUMMINS (AV)

917 Las Juntas Street, P.O. Box 351, 94553
Telephone: 510-228-3001
Fax: 510-228-6825

For full biographical listings, see the Martindale-Hubbell Law Directory

MARYSVILLE,* Yuba Co.

RICH, FUIDGE, MORRIS & IVERSON, INC. (AV)

1129 D Street, P.O. Box "A", 95901
Telephone: 916-742-7371
Fax: 916-742-5982

William P. Rich (1880-1965)	David R. Lane
Richard H. Fuidge (1906-1976)	Brant J. Bordsen
Chester Morris	Stephen W. Berrier
Roland K. Iverson, Jr.	Jill Ceruda Hall

General Counsel: Linda Fire Protection District; City of Yuba City; County of Yuba; City of Live Oak.
Local Counsel: California State Automobile Assn.; State Farm Insurance Cos.

For full biographical listings, see the Martindale-Hubbell Law Directory

MENLO PARK, San Mateo Co.

JORGENSON, SIEGEL, McCLURE & FLEGEL (AV)

Suite 210, 1100 Alma Street, 94025-3392
Telephone: 415-324-9300
Fax: 415-324-0227

MEMBERS OF FIRM

John D. Jorgenson	William L. McClure
Marvin S. Siegel	John L. Flegel

Margaret A. Sloan

ASSOCIATES

Dan K. Siegel

Counsel for: City of Menlo Park.
References: Mid-Peninsula Bank (Palo Alto); Bank of America National Trust & Savings Assn.

For full biographical listings, see the Martindale-Hubbell Law Directory

MERCED,* Merced Co.

ALLEN, POLGAR, PROIETTI & FAGALDE (AV)

A Partnership including a Professional Corporation
1640 "N" Street, Suite 200, P.O. Box 2184, 95344
Telephone: 209-723-4372
Fax: 209-723-7397
Mariposa, California Office: 5079 Highway 140. P.O. Box 1907.
Telephone: 209-966-3007.
Fax: 209-742-6353.

MEMBERS OF FIRM

Terry L. Allen (P.C.)	Jeffrey S. Kaufman
Gary B. Polgar	F. Dana Walton
Donald J. Proietti	(Resident, Mariposa Office)
Michael A. Fagalde	Brian L. McCabe

Paul C. Lo

For full biographical listings, see the Martindale-Hubbell Law Directory

MISSION VIEJO, Orange Co.

THE BUCKLEY FIRM, P.C. (AV)

Suite 200, 26522 La Alameda, 92691
Telephone: 714-348-8300
Facsimile: 714-348-8310
Email: TBF__law@ix.netcom.com
Email: 73321.331@compuserve.com

Lawrence J. Buckley	John W. Klein
John Thomas Callan	Paula Scotland
Jeffrey W. Griffith	Edgar C. Smith, III
Stephen J. Kane	Adam H. Springel

OF COUNSEL

Timothy D. Carlyle	Jonathan C. Cavett

Reference: Bank of California.

For full biographical listings, see the Martindale-Hubbell Law Directory

MODESTO,* Stanislaus Co.

CRABTREE, SCHMIDT, ZEFF, JACOBS & FARRAR (AV)

1100 14th Street, Second Floor, P.O. Box 3307, 95353
Telephone: 209-522-5231
Fax: 209-526-0632

MEMBERS OF FIRM

Robert W. Crabtree	Thomas D. Zeff
Walter J. Schmidt	Nan Cohan Jacobs

E. Daniel Farrar

ASSOCIATE

Helen M. Calverley

Counsel for: Great American Insurance Co.; United Pacific/Reliance Insurance Co.; Hahn Property Management Corp.; Kemper Insurance Co.; State Farm Fire & Casualty; National Can Co.; Central Valley Production Credit Assn.; WestAmerica Bank.

For full biographical listings, see the Martindale-Hubbell Law Directory

DAMRELL, NELSON, SCHRIMP, PALLIOS & LADINE, A PROFESSIONAL CORPORATION (AV)

1601 I Street, Fifth Floor, 95354
Telephone: 209-526-3500
Fax: 209-526-3534
Email: dnsp1@ix.netcom.com
Sacramento, California Office: Suite 200, 1100 K Street.
Telephone: 916-447-2909.
Fax: 916-447-0552.
Oakdale, California Office: 703 West "F" Street, P.O. Drawer C.
Telephone: 209-848-3500.
Fax: 209-848-3400.

Frank C. Damrell (1898-1988)	Steven G. Pallios
Frank C. Damrell, Jr.	Wray F. Ladine
Duane L. Nelson	Matthew O. Pacher
Roger M. Schrimp	Fred A. Silva

Craig W. Hunter	Wendelin Z. Warwick
John K. Peltier	Lisa L. Gillispie
Brian J. Bartow	Amy E. Elliott
Jefferey A. Wooten	Kristine L. Burks
C. Kelley Evans	Michelle Luisa Christian

OF COUNSEL

Surendra J. Sood, M.D.	Cressey H. Nakagawa

Representative Clients: American Honda Motor Co., Inc.; Bronco Wine Co.; E. & J. Gallo Winery; Gallo Glass Co.; The Luckey Co.; Norfolk Southern Corp.; Pep Boys of California, Inc.; W. R. Grace & Co.; National Medical Enterprises, Inc.; Ogden Corp.

For full biographical listings, see the Martindale-Hubbell Law Directory

Modesto—Continued

GIANELLI & FORES, A PROFESSIONAL LAW CORPORATION (AV)

1014 16th Street, P.O. Box 3212, 95353
Telephone: 209-521-6260
Telecopier: 209-521-5971

Louis F. Gianelli	Robert P. Fores
Michael L. Gianelli	David L. Gianelli
Lisa B. Williams	

For full biographical listings, see the Martindale-Hubbell Law Directory

NEUMILLER & BEARDSLEE, A PROFESSIONAL CORPORATION (AV)

611 Thirteenth Street, 95354-2435
Telephone: 209-577-8200
Fax: 209-577-4910
Stockton, California Office: 5th Floor, Waterfront Office Towers II, 509 West Weber Avenue, P.O. Box 20, 95201-3020.
Telephone: 209-948-8200.
Fax: 209-948-4910.

Thomas J. Shephard, Sr.	Steven A. Herum
Robert C. Morrison	Michael J. Dyer
James R. Dyke	Jeanne Marie Zolezzi
Thomas H. Terpstra	

| Clifford W. Stevens | Matthew I. Friedrich |
| Karna E. Harrigfeld | Patrick M. McGrath |

Representative Clients: Roman Catholic Bishop of Stockton; Doctors Medical Center of Modesto; Farmland Management Services; J.C. Williams Co.; Kaufman & Broad Central Valley, Inc.; Morrison Homes; Stanislaus Area Association of Governments; Stanislaus Food Products; Teichert Aggregate; The Westside Irrigation District.

For full biographical listings, see the Martindale-Hubbell Law Directory

STOCKTON & SADLER (AV)

1034 Twelfth Street, P.O. Box 3153, 95353
Telephone: 209-523-6416
Fax: 209-523-2315

MEMBERS OF FIRM

| Cleveland J. Stockton | James L. Sadler |

ASSOCIATES

Karen Tall Sadler

Representative Clients: Dan Mellis Liquors; American Lumber Co.; Paul's Rexall Drug Stores; American Distributing Co.; Tro-Pic-Kal Mfg. Co.; Pete Pappas Broadcasting Co.; Pete Pappas Broadcasting, Inc.; Sanders Construction Co.; Goldrush Broadcasting, Inc.; Paul M. Zagaris Realtor, Inc.

For full biographical listings, see the Martindale-Hubbell Law Directory

---

MONROVIA, Los Angeles Co. — (Refer to Arcadia)

MORRO BAY, San Luis Obispo Co.

OGLE & MERZON (AV)

A Partnership including a Professional Corporation
770 Morro Bay Boulevard, P.O. Box 720, 93443-0720
Telephone: 805-772-7353
Fax: 805-772-7713
San Luis Obispo, California Office: P.O. Box 1855, 93406.
Telephone: 805-543-0295.

| Charles E. Ogle (A Professional Corporation) | James B. Merzon |

| Charles G. Kirschner | Charles Patrick Ogle |

For full biographical listings, see the Martindale-Hubbell Law Directory

---

NAPA, * Napa Co.

COOMBS & DUNLAP (AV)

1211 Division Street, 94559
Telephone: 707-252-9100
Fax: 707-252-8516
St. Helena, California Office: 1110 Adams Street.
Telephone: 707-963-5202; 944-8779.

| Frank L. Coombs (1853-1934) | Nathan F. Coombs (1881-1973) |
| Frank L. Dunlap (1913-1984) | |

MEMBERS OF FIRM

Malcolm A. Mackenzie	Diane L. Dillon
C. Preston Shackelford	L. Randolph Skidmore
Diane M. Price	Charles P. Kuntz

| Donald M. Davis | Rafael Rios, III |

(See Next Column)

OF COUNSEL

June E. Moroney

Representative Clients: City of St. Helena; Napa Sanitation District; Saintsbury; Napa Valley Family Medical Group, Inc.; California Council of the Blind; Havens Wine Cellars; Coldwell-Banker, Brokers of the Valley; ZD Winery; Anderson's Conn Valley Vineyards; Corison Wines.

For full biographical listings, see the Martindale-Hubbell Law Directory

DICKENSON, PEATMAN & FOGARTY, A PROFESSIONAL LAW CORPORATION (AV)

809 Coombs Street, 94559-2977
Telephone: 707-252-7122
Telecopier: 707-255-6876

Joseph G. Peatman	Joseph M. Keebler
David W. Meyers	Cathy A. Roche
C. Richard Lemon	Jonathan P. Dyer
Francis J. Collin, Jr.	James W. Terry
David B. Gilbreth	Katherine Ohlandt
Charles H. Dickenson	Stanley D. Blyth
Paul G. Carey	Linda Emerson
Richard P. Mendelson	Thomas F. Carey
Grace Goodman Ross	

OF COUNSEL

| Walter J. Fogarty, Jr. | Howard G. Dickenson (Retired) |

For full biographical listings, see the Martindale-Hubbell Law Directory

---

NEWPORT BEACH, Orange Co.

BROBECK, PHLEGER & HARRISON LLP (AV)

A Partnership including a Professional Corporation
4675 MacArthur Court, Suite 1000, 92660
Telephone: 714-752-7535
Facsimile: 714-752-7522
San Francisco, California Office: Spear Street Tower, One Market.
Telephone: 415-442-0900.
Facsimile: 415-442-1010.
Palo Alto, California Office: Two Embarcadero Place, 2200 Geng Road.
Telephone: 415-424-0160.
Facsimile: 415-496-2885.
Los Angeles, California Office: 550 South Hope Street.
Telephone: 213-489-4060.
Facsimile: 213-745-3345.
San Diego, California Office: 550 West C Street, Suite 1300.
Telephone: 619-234-1966.
Facsimile: 619-236-1403.
Austin, Texas Office: Brobeck, Phleger & Harrison LLP, 301 Congress Avenue, Suite 1200.
Telephone: 512-477-5495.
Facsimile: 512-477-5813.
Denver, Colorado Office: Brobeck, Phleger & Harrison LLP, 1125 Seventeenth Street, 25th Floor.
Telephone: 303-293-0760.
Facsimile: 303-299-8819.
New York, N.Y. Office: Brobeck, Phleger & Harrison LLP, 1633 Broadway, 47th Floor.
Telephone: 212-581-1600.
Facsimile: 212-586-7878.
Brobeck Hale and Dorr International Office:
London, England Office: Veritas House, 125 Finsbury Pavement, London EC2A 1NQ.
Telephone: 44 071 638 6688.
Facsimile: 44 071 638 5888.

MANAGING PARTNER

Bruce R. Hallett

RESIDENT PARTNERS

R. Patrick Arrington	Laura B. Hunter
Roger M. Cohen	Kathlene W. Lowe
Richard A. Fink	Frederic Alport Randall, Jr.
Gabrielle M. Wirth	

OF COUNSEL

Jeffrey S. Rovner

ASSOCIATES

Jonathan F. Atzen	Dana E. Frost
Richard J. Babcock	Lisa Schechter Goon
John S. Baker	Neel Grover
Ellen S. Bancroft	Anita Gruettke
James S. Brennan	Elizabeth T. Hall
Susan N. Cayley	Lee J. Leslie
Kevin D. DeBré	Gregory T. May
Scott S. Draeker	Barbara J. Miller
Ethan D. Feffer	Daniel E. Roston
R. Scott Feldmann	Matthew V. Waterman
Greg T. Williams	

For full biographical listings, see the Martindale-Hubbell Law Directory

Newport Beach—Continued

BUCHALTER, NEMER, FIELDS & YOUNGER, A PROFESSIONAL CORPORATION (AV)

Suite 1450, 620 Newport Center Drive, 92660
Telephone: 714-760-1121
Fax: 714-720-0182
Email: buchalter@earthlink.net *URL:* http://www.buchalter.com
Los Angeles, California Office: 24th Floor, 601 South Figueroa Street.
Telephone: 213-891-0700.
Fax: 213-896-0400.
New York, New York Office: 15th Floor, 605 Third Avenue.
Telephone: 212-490-8600.
Fax: 212-490-6022.
San Francisco, California Office: 29th Floor, 333 Market Street.
Telephone: 415-227-0900.
Fax: 415-227-0770.

Clifford John Meyer   Debra Solle Healy
            Kirk S. Rense

Lori S. Ross   Mark M. Scott

References: City National Bank; Wells Fargo Bank; Metrobank.

For full biographical listings, see the Martindale-Hubbell Law Directory

CAPRETZ & RADCLIFFE (AV)

5000 Birch Street, West Tower Suite 2500, 92660-2139
Telephone: 714-724-3000
Fax: 714-757-2635
Email: CRLAWYERS@AOL.CON *URL:* http://www.CAPRETZ.com

James T. Capretz   Richard J. Radcliffe
            ASSOCIATES
            Peter A. Martin
            OF COUNSEL
William B. Lawless (Not admitted in CA)
            LEGAL SUPPORT PERSONNEL
            Rosanna S. Bertheola

For full biographical listings, see the Martindale-Hubbell Law Directory

DAVIS, PUNELLI, KEATHLEY & WILLARD (AV)

610 Newport Center Drive, Suite 1000, P.O. Box 7920, 92658-7920
Telephone: 714-640-0700
Telecopier: 714-640-0714
San Diego, California Office: 501 West Broadway, Suite 900, 92101.
Telephone: 619-558-2581.

            MEMBERS OF FIRM
Robert E. Willard   H. James Keathley
S. Eric Davis   Eric G. Anderson
Frank Punelli, Jr.   Katherine D. Keathley
            OF COUNSEL
            Lewis K. Uhler

For full biographical listings, see the Martindale-Hubbell Law Directory

EADINGTON, MERHAB & EADINGTON, A PROFESSIONAL CORPORATION (AV)

Suite 600, South Tower, 3501 Jamboree Road, P.O. Box 9408, 92658-9408
Telephone: 714-854-5000
Telecopier: 714-854-5138

George Eadington   Marla Merhab Robinson
            Debra L. Klevatt

References: Orange National Bank.

For full biographical listings, see the Martindale-Hubbell Law Directory

RICHARD J. SCHWARZSTEIN (AV)

Second Floor, Redstone Plaza, 1300 Dove Street, 92660
Telephone: 714-752-9152
Fax: 714-752-0651

For full biographical listings, see the Martindale-Hubbell Law Directory

STRADLING, YOCCA, CARLSON & RAUTH, A PROFESSIONAL CORPORATION (AV)

660 Newport Center Drive, Suite 1600, 92660-6441
Telephone: 714-725-4000
Facsimile: 714-725-4100
Mailing Address: P.O. Box 7680, 92658-7680
San Francisco, California Office: 44 Montgomery Street, Suite 2950, 94104-4803.
Telephone: 415-765-9180.
Facsimile: 415-765-9187.

(See Next Column)

Fritz R. Stradling   David G. Casnocha (Resident,
Nick E. Yocca   San Francisco Office)
C. Craig Carlson   Karen A. Ellis
William R. Rauth III   Bruce D. May
K. C. Schaaf   Andrew F. Puzder
Richard C. Goodman   Donald J. Hamman
John J. Murphy   John J. Swigart, Jr.
Thomas P. Clark, Jr.   Celeste Stahl Brady
Ben A. Frydman   Christopher J. Kilpatrick
David R. McEwen   Douglas S. Brown
Paul L. Gale   Julie McCoy Akins
Rudolph C. Shepard   Lawrence B. Cohn
Robert J. Kane   Stephen T. Freeman
Bruce C. Stuart   Carol L. Lew
E. Kurt Yeager   Michael E. Flynn
Robert J. Whalen   Julie M. Porter
Robert E. Rich   Gary A. Pemberton
Randall J. Sherman   Denise Harbaugh Hering
Bruce Feuchter   Jon E. Goetz
Mark J. Huebsch   Russell A. Miller (Resident, San
                                    Francisco Office)

Michael A. Zablocki   John David Vaughan
Neila R. Bernstein   Steven M. Hanle
Nicholas J. Yocca   Michael Hennessey Mulroy
J. Michael Vaughn   Mary Anne Wagner
John D. Ireland   Matthew McQueen
David H. Mann   Holly A. Ellis
Douglas J. Evertz   William E. Garrett
Sean Tierney (Resident, San   Christopher D. Ivey
    Francisco Office)   H. Lee Kolodny
Darryl S. Gibson   Gerald J. Ramiza
Jee Hi Park   Daniel Glassman
Richard T. Needham   David E. Outwater
Robert Craig Wallace   Joy Heuser Otsuki
John F. Cannon   Numan J. Siddiqi
David A. Hoffer   David E. Lafitte
Douglas P. Feick   Teri N. Hollander
Mark L. Skaist   Marc G. Alcser
Jeffrey B. Coyne   Ryan E. Davis
John E. Woodhead, IV   Brent N. Triff
Matthew P. Thullen   Michele McCormick Troyan
Andrea Levitan Reeves   Gary J. Vyneman
            Thomas M. Williams
            OF COUNSEL
John E. Breckenridge   Douglas J. Rovens
Rena C. Stone   Robert J. Matthews

For full biographical listings, see the Martindale-Hubbell Law Directory

*OAKLAND,** Alameda Co.

BERRY & BERRY, A PROFESSIONAL CORPORATION (AV)

1300 Clay Street, Ninth Floor, P.O. Box 70250, Station D, 94520
Telephone: 510-835-8330
Fax: 510-835-5117

Samuel H. Berry (1904-1990)   Leonardo J. Vacchina
Phillip S. Berry   Peter R. Gilbert
Carolyn Collins   Lynne P. Blair

Evanthia Spanos   Ellen D. Berris
Gregory D. Meronek   Laura Przetak

Representative Clients: Parke-Davis; Warner-Lambert; St. Paul Insurance Co.; Fireman's Fund Insurance Co.; American International Underwriters; Lloyd's of London; Celina Insurance Group; American Optical; Biomet, Inc.

For full biographical listings, see the Martindale-Hubbell Law Directory

FITZGERALD, ABBOTT & BEARDSLEY LLP (AV)

A Partnership including Professional Corporations
1221 Broadway, 21st Floor, P.O. Box 12867, 94602-2867
Telephone: 510-451-3300
Telecopy: 510-451-1527

            MEMBERS OF FIRM
Robert M. Fitzgerald   Michael P. Walsh
    (1858-1934)   J. Brittain Habegger
Carl H. Abbott (1867-1933)   Virginia Palmer
Charles A. Beardsley   Timothy H. Smallsreed
    (1882-1963)   Stephen M. Judson
James C. Soper (Inc.)   Stephen M. Williams
Philip M. Jelley (Inc.)   Jonathan W. Redding
Gerald C. Smith   Beth E. Aspedon
Lawrence R. Shepp   Kristin A. Pace
Richard T. White   Michael M.K. Sebree
            Antonia L. More

(See Next Column)

FITZGERALD, ABBOTT & BEARDSLEY LLP, *Oakland—Continued*

ASSOCIATES

Sarah Robertson McCuaig	Carlo C. Mormorunni
Philip E. Drysdale	Michael S. Ward
Kristen Thall Peters	Jean Buo-lin Chen Fung
Jay M. Goldman	Fatima Michon Brunson

Attorneys for: Peterson Tractor Co.; Sunset View Cemetery Assn.; Bigge Crane & Rigging Corp.; Gillig Corp.
Local Counsel for: Exxon Corp.

For full biographical listings, see the Martindale-Hubbell Law Directory

HAIMS, JOHNSON, MACGOWAN & MCINERNEY (AV)

490 Grand Avenue, 94610
Telephone: 510-835-0500
Facsimile: 510-835-2833

MEMBERS OF FIRM

Arnold B. Haims	Randy M. Marmor
Gary R. Johnson	John K. Kirby
Clyde L. MacGowan	Robert J. Frassetto
Thomas McInerney	Caroline N. Valentino
Lawrence A. Baker	Dianne D. Peebles

ASSOCIATES

Joseph Y. Ahn	Anne M. Michaels
Edward D. Baldwin	Michelle Diane Perry
Marc P. Bouret	Edward C. Schroeder, Jr.

For full biographical listings, see the Martindale-Hubbell Law Directory

HARDIN, COOK, LOPER, ENGEL & BERGEZ (AV)

1999 Harrison Street, 18th Floor, 94612-3541
Telephone: 510-444-3131
Telecopier: 510-839-7940

MEMBERS OF FIRM

J. Marcus Hardin (1905-1993)	Stephen McKae
L. S. Fletcher (1905-1964)	Bruce P. Loper
Herman Cook (1914-1982)	Bruce E. McLeod
John C. Loper	Eugene Brown, Jr.
(Partner Emeritus)	Linda C. Roodhouse
Barrie Engel	Matthew S. Conant
Raymond J. Bergez	Chris P. Lavdiotis
George S. Peyton, Jr.	Robert D. Eassa
Ralph A. Lombardi	Peter O. Glaessner
Sandra F. Wagner	Nicholas D. Kayhan
Willard L. Alloway	John A. De Pasquale
Gennaro A. Filice, III	Peter A. Strotz

Amber L. Kelly	Troy D. McMahan
Elsa M. Baldwin	GayLynn Renee Kirn
Marshall A. Johnson	Richard V. Normington III
Diane R. Stanton	Lisa M. Brown
Jennifer M. Walker	Jason J. Curliano
Margaret L. Kotzebue	Rachel L. Barack
Amee A. Mikacich	Lynn S. Samuels
Timothy J. McCaffery	Gary S. Alexander
Stephen J. Valen	James S. Knopf

Jonathan M. Cohen

OF COUNSEL

Ronald A. Wagner	Rachel K. Angress

Representative Clients: Firemans Fund Insurance Cos.; City of Piedmont; The Dow Chemical Co.; Nissan Motor Corp.; Subaru of America; Weyerhauser Co.; Bay Area Rapid Transit District; Diamond Shamrock; Home Indemnity Co.; Rhone-Poulenc.

For full biographical listings, see the Martindale-Hubbell Law Directory

LARSON & BURNHAM, A PROFESSIONAL CORPORATION (AV)

1901 Harrison Street, 11th Floor, P.O. Box 119, 94604
Telephone: 510-444-6800
Fax: 510-835-6666

A. Hubbard Moffitt, Jr.	Monica Dell'Osso
(1908-1969)	Jeffrey G. Bairey
Howard S. Rode (1907-1973)	Susan Feldsted Halman
Arthur Jay Moore, Jr.	Patrick K. M. McCarthy
(1918-1984)	Gary R. Selvin
David O. Larson	H. Wayne Goodroe
Clark J. Burnham	Robert A. Ford
Gregory D. Brown	David R. Pinelli
George J. Ziser	Michael R. Reynolds
Robert J. Lyman	James L. Wraith
Eric R. Haas	Richard J. Finn
Scott C. Finch	John J. Verber
Steven M. Marden	Cathy L. Arias
Ralph A. Zappala	Thomas M. Downey
Peter Dixon	Michael K. Johnson

(See Next Column)

John P. Bevan	Frank C. Liuzzi
Tara D. Bodden	Pelayo Antonio Llamas, Jr.
Caryn Bortnick	Joanna MacQueen
Paul D. Caleo	Randolph G. McCalla
John D. Colombo	Michael T. McKeeman
Vera C. De Martini	Steven A. Nielsen
Matthew G. Dudley	Gustavo Peña
Pamela Fastiff Ellman	Noreen N. Quan
Susan E. Firtch	James J. Rosati
Douglas S. Free	Stephen Q. Rowell
Beth S. Freedman	Walter C. Rundin, III
Alison F. Greene	Bryan K. Stainfield
Anne Cobbledick Gritzer	Anjali Talwar
Ayesha Z. Hassan	Darrell T. Thompson
James F. Hodgkins	Shawn A. Toliver
Nancy E. Hooten	Jedediah Wakefield
Julie Jardine	David H. Waters
Julie Hwang Kim	David S. Webster
Peter Leo Lagasse	Bradley M. Zamczyk

Barry Zoller

OF COUNSEL

James H. Riggs

Representative Clients: The Travelers Insurance Co.; Wholesale Building Supply Co.; U.S. Fidelity & Guaranty Co.; Home Insurance Co.; County of Alameda; City of Livermore; Shell Oil Co.; Exxon; Allied-Signal Inc.; Rohm and Haas Co.

For full biographical listings, see the Martindale-Hubbell Law Directory

HARVEY W. STEIN A PROFESSIONAL CORPORATION (AV)

Suite 600 Transpacific Centre, 1000 Broadway, 94607
Telephone: 510-763-6233
Fax: 510-832-1717

Harvey W. Stein

For full biographical listings, see the Martindale-Hubbell Law Directory

ONTARIO, San Bernardino Co.

COVINGTON & CROWE (AV)

1131 West Sixth Street, P.O. Box 1515, 91762
Telephone: 909-983-9393
Fax: 909-391-6762
Email: covcrowe@ix.netcom.com

MEMBERS OF FIRM

Harold A. Bailin (1930-1988)	Stephen R. Wade
Samuel P. Crowe	Jette R. Anderson
George W. Porter	Audrey A. Perri
Robert E. Dougherty	Tracy L. Tibbals
Donald G. Haslam	Melanie Fisch
Robert F. Schauer	Robert H. Reeder
Edward A. Hopson	R. Doug Donesky

Tammy S. Jager

ASSOCIATES

Howard S. Borenstein	Richard R. Muir
Denise Matthey	Kimberly A. Rohn
Katrina West	J. Michael Kaler

Eric S. Vail

For full biographical listings, see the Martindale-Hubbell Law Directory

OXNARD, Ventura Co.

ENGLAND & COHEN (AV)

300 Esplanade Drive Financial Plaza Tower, Suite 380, 93030
Telephone: 805-983-8181; California Toll Free: 800-675-6166
FAX: 805-983-8813

MEMBERS OF FIRM

Robert B. England	Randall A. Cohen

OF COUNSEL

Stanley E. Cohen

For full biographical listings, see the Martindale-Hubbell Law Directory

ENGLAND, WHITFIELD, SCHRÖEDER & TREDWAY, L.L.P. (AV)

300 Esplanade Drive, 6th Floor, 93030
Telephone: 805-485-9627
Ventura: 647-8237
Southern California Toll Free: 800-255-3485
Fax: 805-983-0297
URL: http://www.tsurf.com/ewst/
Thousand Oaks, California Office: Rolling Oaks Office Center, 351 Rolling Oaks Drive.
Telephone: Southern California Toll Free: 800-255-3485.

(See Next Column)

ENGLAND, WHITFIELD, SCHRÖEDER & TREDWAY L.L.P.—Continued
MEMBERS OF FIRM

Theodore J. England
Anson M. Whitfield
Robert W. Schröeder
David W. Tredway
Robert A. McSorley
Stuart A. Comis
Mitchel B. Kahn

Mark A. Nelson
Eric J. Kananen
Mary E. Schröeder
Oscar C. Gonzalez
Steven K. Perrin
Andrew S. Hughes
Madison M. Christian

Kurt Edward Kananen

ASSOCIATES

William J. Kesatie
Melissa E. Cohen

Linda Kathryn Ash
Mark T. Barney

Representative Clients: Seneca Resources Corp. (oil & gas); Cal-Sun Produce Co.; Waste Management of California, Inc; Dah Chong Hong (Honda, Toyota, Mazda, Lexus, Acura, Saturn automobile dealerships); Willamette Industries; Oxnard Harbor Association of Realtors; Port of Hueneme; Conejo Valley Association of Realtors; Power-One, Inc.

For full biographical listings, see the Martindale-Hubbell Law Directory

LOWTHORP, RICHARDS, McMILLAN, MILLER, CONWAY & TEMPLEMAN, A PROFESSIONAL CORPORATION (AV)

300 Esplanade Drive, Suite 850, P.O. Box 5167, 93031
Telephone: 805-981-8555
FAX: 805-983-1967

Carl F. Lowthorp, Jr.
(1933-1992)
Richard A. Richards
Robert C. McMillan
Paul A. Miller
Charles J. Conway, Jr.

Alan R. Templeman
Patrick T. Loughman
Glenn J. Campbell
John Q. Masteller
E.P. Michael Karcis
Gregory J. Ramirez

LEGAL SUPPORT PERSONNEL
Elizabeth T. Ladiana, CLA

Reference: Ventura County National Bank.

For full biographical listings, see the Martindale-Hubbell Law Directory

NORDMAN, CORMANY, HAIR & COMPTON (AV)

1000 Town Center Drive, Sixth Floor, P.O. Box 9100, 93031-9100
Telephone: 805-485-1000
Ventura: 805-656-3304
Telecopier: 805-988-8387
805-988-7790
Westlake Village, California Office: 920 Hampshire Road, Suite A-17, 91361.
Telephone: 805-497-2795.

Ben E. Nordman, Founder (1913-1985)
MEMBERS OF FIRM

William H. Hair
Robert L. Compton (Also at Westlake Village Office)
Marc L. Charney
Ronald H. Gill
Larry L. Hines
Kenneth M. High, Jr.
Michael C. O'Brien
Laura K. McAvoy
Randall H. George
Janet Anne Reese (Also at Westlake Village Office)

Paul W. Kurzeka
Anthony H. Trembley
Jonathan Fraser Light
Kent M. Kellegrew (Also at Westlake Village Office)
William E. Winfield
Gerald M. Etchingham
Chris K. Kitasaki
Scott B. Samsky
Guy C. Parvex, Jr.
Robert J. Lent (Also at Westlake Village Office)

Susan Westeen Novatt

OF COUNSEL

Ralph L. Cormany

John A. Slezak

ASSOCIATES

Susan M. Seemiller
John M. Andersen (Also at Westlake Village Office)

Laurel A. McLaughlin
Glenn J. Dickinson
Nancy Miller

Representative Clients: Berry Petroleum Co.; Real Estate Investment Trust of California; Amgen; Kmart Corp.; Saticoy Lemon Assn.; The Procter & Gamble Paper Products Co.; Halliburton Services; Schlumberger; The Prudential Insurance Company of America; Laguna Pacific Development.

For full biographical listings, see the Martindale-Hubbell Law Directory

PALM SPRINGS, Riverside Co.

SCHLECHT, SHEVLIN & SHOENBERGER, A LAW CORPORATION (AV)

Suite 100, 801 East Tahquitz Canyon Way, P.O. Box 2744, 92263-2744
Telephone: 619-320-7161
Facsimile: 619-323-1758; 619-325-4623

James M. Schlecht
John C. Shevlin

Jon A. Shoenberger
Daniel T. Johnson

David Darrin

Elizabeth A. Dreier

(See Next Column)

OF COUNSEL

Donald B. McNelley

Allen O. Perrier (Retired)

Representative Clients: Outdoor Resorts of America; The Escrow Connection; Wells Fargo Bank; Canyon Country Club; Waste Management Co.

For full biographical listings, see the Martindale-Hubbell Law Directory

PALO ALTO, Santa Clara Co.

BAKER & McKENZIE (AV)

660 Hansen Way, P.O. Box 60309, 94304-0309
Telephone: (415) 856-2400
Intn'l. Dialing: (1-415) 856-2400
Facsimile: (1-415) 856-9299
Associated Offices of Baker & McKenzie in: Almaty, Amsterdam, Bangkok, Barcelona, Beijing, Berlin, Bogotá, Brasília, Brussels, Budapest, Buenos Aires, Cairo, Caracas, Chicago, Dallas, Frankfurt, Geneva, Hanoi, Ho Chi Minh City, Hong Kong, Juárez, Kiev, Lausanne, London, Madrid, Manila, Melbourne, México City, Miami, Milan, Monterrey, Moscow, Münich, New York, Paris, Prague, Rio de Janeiro, Riyadh, Rome, St. Petersburg, San Diego, San Francisco, Santiago, São Paulo, Singapore, Stockholm, Sydney, Taipei, Tijuana, Tokyo, Toronto, Valencia, Warsaw, Washington, D.C. and Zürich.
Correspondent Law Firm: Hadiputranto, Hadinoto & Partners, Jakarta.

MEMBERS OF FIRM

Maurice S. Emmer
Tod L. Gamlen
John C. Klotsche
(Not admitted in CA)
Michael J. Madda

Susan H. Nycum
John M. Peterson, Jr.
J. Pat Powers
André M. Saltoun
Gary D. Sprague

LOCAL PARTNER
Robin L. Filion

ASSOCIATES

Jon M. Appleton
Michael Bumbaca
Robin A. Chesler
Brian Geoghegan
Stewart R. Lipeles
(Not admitted in CA)
Owen P. Martikan

Louise C. Ober
Taylor S. Reid
(Not admitted in CA)
James C. Ross
Michelle J. Wachs
Andrew D. Zeif
(Not admitted in CA)

For full biographical listings, see the Martindale-Hubbell Law Directory

BROBECK, PHLEGER & HARRISON LLP (AV)

A Partnership including a Professional Corporation
Two Embarcadero Place, 2200 Geng Road, 94303
Telephone: 415-424-0160
Facsimile: 415-496-2885
San Francisco, California Office: Spear Street Tower, One Market.
Telephone: 415-442-0900.
Facsimile: 415-442-0900.
Los Angeles, California Office: 550 South Hope Street.
Telephone: 213-489-4060.
Facsimile: 213-745-3345.
San Diego, California Office: 550 West C Street, Suite 1300.
Telephone: 619-234-1966.
Facsimile: 619-236-1403.
Orange County, California Office: 4675 MacArthur Court, Suite 1000, Newport Beach.
Telephone: 714-752-7535.
Facsimile: 714-752-7522.
Austin, Texas Office: Brobeck, Phleger & Harrison LLP, 301 Congress Avenue, Suite 1200.
Telephone: 512-477-5495.
Facsimile: 512-477-5813.
Denver, Colorado Office: Brobeck, Phleger & Harrison LLP, 1125 Seventeenth Street, 25th Floor.
Telephone: 303-293-0760.
Facsimile: 303-299-8819.
New York, N.Y. Office: Brobeck, Phleger & Harrison LLP, 1633 Broadway, 47th Floor.
Telephone: 212-581-1600.
Facsimile: 212-586-7878.
Brobeck Hale and Dorr International Office:
London, England Office: Veritas House, 125 Finsbury Pavement, London EC2A 1NQ.
Telephone: 44 071 638 6688.
Facsimile: 44 071 638 5888.

MANAGING PARTNER
Thomas W. Kellerman

PARTNERS

William C. Anderson
William L. Anthony, Jr.
Thomas A. Bevilacqua
Michael J. Casey
Gari L. Cheever
Robert DeBerardine
S. James DiBernardo

J. Stephan Dolezalek
David M. Furbush
Noemi Espinosa Hayes
Karen N. Ikeda
Meredith Nelson Landy
John W. Larson
Warren T. Lazarow

(See Next Column)

BROBECK, PHLEGER & HARRISON LLP, *Palo Alto—Continued*

PARTNERS (Continued)

Gregory S. Lemmer	Therese A. Mrozek
Edward M. Leonard	Luther Kent Orton
	Ronald S. Wynn

OF COUNSEL

Thomas H. Carlson	Zaitun Poonja

RESIDENT ASSOCIATES

Craig Y. Allison	James N. Kramer
Charles K. Ashley II	Peter C. Ku
Andrew Baw	Sara M. Kurlich
Timothy S. Bergreen	Elaine Llewelyn
Robert J. Blanch, Jr.	Taraneh Maghamé
(Not admitted in CA)	Sharon E. Meieran
Patricia G. Copeland	Margaret T. Miles
Jacqueline Cowden	Patricia Montalvo
Timothy R. Curry	Benjamin P. Oelsner
Michael F. Cyran	Michael A. Plumleigh
Thomas P. Dennedy	Magan Ray
Michael C. Doran	Christine L. Richardson
Amr A. El-Bayoumi	Melinda Collins Riechert
Helen G.F. Fields	Christina Baker Robinson
Carol R. Freeman	Maura Roe
Tamar Fruchtman	Anna A. Ruiz
William P. Garvey	Valerie L. Russell
Hanna Casper George	Kevin A. Smith
Nora L. Gibson	Karen Y. Spencer
Susan Giordano	David W. Stevens
Scot A. Griffin	Andrew N. Thomases
Rodrigo M. Guidero	Candace M. Tillman
Ramesh Hamadani	Tomas C. Tovar
Daniel R. Hansen	Peter Vaughan
Kimberley Erin Henningsen	Craig R. Venable
Jeffrey P. Higgins	Roburt J. Waldow
Franklin P. Huang	(Not admitted in CA)
H. Richard Hukari	Craig E. Walker
Gregory C. Jackson	Stephen G. Wanderer
Andrew B. Koslow	Sarah H. Whittle
	Elizabeth A. R. Yee

For full biographical listings, see the Martindale-Hubbell Law Directory

---

BROWN & BAIN (AV)

1755 Embarcadero Road, Suite 200, 94306
Telephone: 415-856-9411
Telecopier: 415-856-6061
Phoenix, Arizona Affiliated Office: Brown & Bain, A Professional
Association, 2901 North Central Avenue, P.O. Box 400.
Telephone: 602-351-8000.
Telecopier: 602-351-8516.
Tucson, Arizona Affiliated Office: Brown & Bain, A Professional
Association. One South Church Avenue, Nineteenth Floor, P.O. Box
2265.
Telephone: 602-798-7900
Telecopier: 602-798-7945.

RESIDENT PERSONNEL

Richard H. Harvey

COUNSEL

Lois W. Abraham	Douglas Clark Neilsson
Ian C. Ballon	Bernard Petrie

For full biographical listings, see the Martindale-Hubbell Law Directory

---

COOLEY GODWARD LLP (AV)

Five Palo Alto Square, 3000 El Camino Real, 94306
Telephone: 415-843-5000
Telex: 380816 COOLEY PA
Fax: 415-857-0663
Email: webmaster@cooley.com *URL:* http://www.cooley.com
San Francisco, California Office: 20th Floor, One Maritime Plaza.
Telephone: 415-693-2000.
Telex: 380815 COOLEY SFO
Fax: 415-951-3698 or 415-951-3699.
Menlo Park, California Office: 3000 Sand Hill Road, Building 3, Suite
230.
Telephone: 415-843-5000.
Telex: 380816 COOLEY PA.
Fax: 415-854-2691.
San Diego, California Office: 4365 Executive Drive, Suite 1100.
Telephone: 619-550-6000.
Fax: 619-453-3555.
Boulder, Colorado Office: 2595 Canyon Boulevard, Suite 250.
Telephone: 303-546-4000.
Fax: 303-546-4099.
Denver, Colorado Office: One Tabor Center, 1200 17th Street, Suite 2100.
Telephone: 303-606-4800.
Fax: 303-606-4899.

(See Next Column)

MEMBERS OF FIRM

James R. Batchelder	Martin L. Lagod
Lois K. Benes	David M. Madrid
Lee F. Benton	Andrei M. Manoliu
Robert J. Brigham	Deborah A. Marshall
Craig Hill Casebeer	Pamela J. Martinson
Paul Churchill	Herbert W. McGuire
Richard E. Climan	Alan C. Mendelson
Janet L. Cullum	Webb B. Morrow, III
Brian C. Cunningham	Stephen C. Neal
Julia Loewy Davidson	Richard L. Neeley
Lloyd R. Day, Jr.	Timothy G. Patterson
Stephen W. Fackler	Anne Harris Peck
William S. Freeman	Mark B. Pitchford
John W. Girvin, Jr.	Patrick A. Pohlen
Willis E. Higgins	(Not admitted in CA)
Michael R. Jacobson	Anna B. Pope
Ronald L. Jacobson	Jeffrey G. Randall
Daniel Johnson, Jr.	Diane Wilkins Savage
Robert L. Jones	Gregory C. Smith
James C. Kitch	Michael Stern
Barbara A. Kosacz	Daniel P. Westman
	John F. Young

SPECIAL COUNSEL

Elisa Clowes	Gary H. Ritchey
Ann Habernigg	Deidre Lynn Sparks
James R. Jones	Gretchen R. Stroud
Tom M. Moran	Andrea H. Vachss
	Christopher O. B. Wright

ASSOCIATES

Gregg H. Alton	Julie C. Lythcott-Haims
Kevin C. Austin	Matthew E. Marquis
Suzanne A. Barr	Barbara J. McGeoch
Alex H. Benn	Gerald T. McLaughlin
Laura A. Berezin	John D. Mendlein
Judith E. Brown	Wm. Bradford Middlekauff
Terrence J. Carroll	Jana R. Miller
Salvador A. Casente Jr.	Darren B. Mitchell
Theodore A. Chen	Shawn N. Molodow
Troy F. Christmas	Donald J. Morrissey, Jr.
Patricia Louise Cox	Tahir J. Naim
Linda DeMelis	Jackie N. Nakamura
Scott D. Devereaux	Glenn Gerard Nash
Tracy Friedman Dobmeier	Keith C. Nashawaty
Chuck Ebertin	Craig P. Opperman
David T. Emerson	Laura M. Owen
David J. Estrada	Stephanie J. Parr
Melissa A. Finocchio	Mehul T. Patel
Jason D. Firth	Mary-Alice Pomputius
(Not admitted in CA)	Kelvin P. Quan
Keith A. Flaum	Ruth Reitman
Molly Brown Forstall	Matthew F. Roberts
Michelle Greer Galloway	Julie M. Robinson
Robert M. Galvin	Ricardo Rodriguez
Karen A. Gibbs	Stephen N. Rosenfield
Michele K. Granaada	Gurjeev K. Sachdeva
Bradley A. Handler	Eric Schlachter
Judith A. Hasko	Joanne Marshall Shea
Lana K. Hawkins	Myles B. Silton
(Not admitted in CA)	(Not admitted in CA)
Matthew B. Hemington	Matthew W. Sonsini
Paula Holm Jensen	Seksom N. Suriyapa
Suzanne Sawochka Hooper	Jonathan H. Takei
Jeffrey N. Hyman	Barbara E. Tanzillo
Viraj D. Jha	Gregory C. Tenhoff
(Not admitted in CA)	Vicki Ting
Dan S. Johnston	William S. Veatch
Barclay J. Kamb	Julie A. Vehrenkamp
Anthony R. Klein	Erin M. Verneris
Judith Landis	Laurie A. Webb
(Not admitted in CA)	Michael L. Weiner
T. Gregory Lanier	Brett D. White
Eleonora Leznik	Lara A. Williams
David M. Lisi	Kevin James Zimmer

PATENT AGENTS

Melya J. Hughes

LEGAL SUPPORT PERSONNEL

ADMINISTRATOR

Susan Y. Chen-Wong

SECURITIES SPECIALIST

Linda M. Rigas

SENIOR LEGAL ASSISTANTS

J. Paul Armstrong	Karon Pasos
Susan P. Bermel	Eric J. Steiner
C. Kim Miller	Gary A. Thunell

For full biographical listings, see the Martindale-Hubbell Law Directory

Palo Alto—Continued

GRAHAM & JAMES LLP (AV)

600 Hansen Way, 94304
Telephone: 415-856-6500
Telecopier: 415-856-3619
Email: dgross@gj.com *URL:* http://www.gj.com
Other offices located in: San Francisco, Los Angeles, Orange County,
Sacramento and Fresno, California; Seattle, Washington; Washington,
D.C.; New York, New York; Milan, Italy; Beijing, China; Tokyo, Japan;
London, England; Dusseldorf, Germany.
Associated Offices: Deacons Graham & James, Hong Kong, Sydney,
Melbourne, Brisbane, Perth and Canberra, Australia.
Affiliated Offices: Deacons Graham & James, Hanoi and Ho Chi Minh
City, Vietnam; Taipei, Taiwan and Bangkok, Thailand; In association with
Dewi Soeharto & Rekan, Jakarta, Indonesia; Graham & James in
affiliation with Taylor Joynson Garrett, London, England, Bucharest,
Romania and Brussels, Belgium; Mishare M. Al-Ghazali & Partners,
Safat, Kuwait; Law Firm of Salah Al-Hejailan, Jeddah and Riyadh, Saudi
Arabia.

MEMBERS OF FIRM

Donald R. Davis	Alan B. Kalin
James E. Eakin	Michael H. Kalkstein
Chris Scott Graham	Ronald S. Lemieux
Lawrence W. Granatelli	Ralph M. Pais
David F. Gross	Robert E. Patterson
Timothy T. Huber	Thomas R. Radcliffe

Joe C. Sorenson

RESIDENT ASSOCIATES

Michele Z. Allen	Brien B. Kirk
Douglas A. Carlen	Jill F. Kopeikin
Deborah M. Chang	Laura A. Majerus
W. Clay Deanhardt	Thomas A. M'Guinness
David S. Elkins	Andrew Y. Piatnicia
U. P. Peter Eng	Perpetua B. Tranlong
Jenny J. Kim	Harold T. Tsiang

Valerie M. Wagner

For full biographical listings, see the Martindale-Hubbell Law Directory

---

GRAY CARY WARE & FREIDENRICH, A PROFESSIONAL CORPORATION (AV)

Gray Cary Established in 1927
Ware & Freidenrich Established in 1969
400 Hamilton Avenue, 94301-1825
Telephone: 415-328-6561
Telex: 348-372
Telecopier: 415-327-3699
Email: info@gcwf.com *URL:* http://www.gcwf.com
San Diego, California Office: 401 B Street, Suite 1700.
Telephone: 619-699-2700.
San Diego/Golden Triangle, California Office: 4365 Executive Drive, Suite
1600, 92121.
Telephone: 619-677-1400.
Fax: 619-677-1477.
La Jolla, California Office: 1200 Prospect Street, Suite 575.
Telephone: 619-454-9101.
El Centro, California Office: 1224 State Street, P.O. Box 2890.
Telephone: 619-353-6140.

Peter M. Astiz	Jeffrey J. Lederman
Cynthia Beth Carlson	Patrick J. McGaraghan
John Howard Clowes	Marvin Meisel
Lawrence A. Cogan	Mark F. Radcliffe
Steven G. Cohen	Jonathan E. Rattner
David Henry Dolkas	Arthur C. Rinsky
Ian N. Feinberg	J. Martin Robertson
Mark Fowler	Bradley J. Rock
Diane Holt Frankle	Robert T. Russell
Thomas M. French	Bruce E. Schaeffer
Thomas W. Furlong	Daniel K. Seubert
Gregory M. Gallo	John R. Shuman, Jr.
Penny Howe Gallo	Stacy Snowman
Hugh Goodwin, Jr.	Jay M. Spitzen
John B. Hale	Lillian G. Stenfeldt
William H. Hoffman	Dennis C. Sullivan
Rodrigo J. Howard	R. Allyn Taylor
Joan S. Kato	Craig M. Tighe
Margaret H. Kavalaris	Jeffrey A. Trant
James M. Koshland	Elizabeth H. Ward
Eric J. Lapp	Richard I. Yankwich
Mary LaVigne-Butler	Barry N. Young
	(Not admitted in CA)

James E. Anderson	Kathleen K. Bryski
Jeffrey D. Ball	Pamela B. Burke
Marilyn M. Bautista	Kelly Lynn Canady
Marcy Berkman	Hope A. Case
Mary Elizabeth Berry	Amanda Castillo
Paul A. Blumenstein	Kathleen Cattani
Larry J. Bradfish	Julia L. Cochrane
Todd Samuel Brecher	Janet M. Craycroft

(See Next Column)

Gary L. Dahlby	Ginger L. Levy
M. Elizabeth Day	(Not admitted in CA)
Eric H. Dorf	Timothy W. Lohse
Maureen S. Dorney	Charles M. Miller
Charles M. Dyke	Martin H. Myers
John W. Easterbrook	Nels Raymond Nelsen
Russell S. Elmer	Denise Woodson Ofria
Melanie E. Erasmus	L. Scott Oliver
John M. Fogg	Frank H. Pao
Barbara Friedrich	Pamela Pasti
Gilbert Gallardo	Jamie C. Pawliczek
Vanessa R Gonzalez	Darren J. Pittenger
David R. Graham	David J. Plewa
Christina Groll	Margaret M. Powers
Wilma (Woody) Growney	Douglas J. Renert
Michelle R. Harbottle	William A. Rodoni
Daniel Ross Harris	Dianne B. Salesin
(Not admitted in CA)	Jason Schaumberg
Sharon W. Hawkins	Eileen Evans Schefsky
Linda M. Hayes	Jim A. Scheinman
Cheryl K. House	William R. Schreiber
David Alan Hubb	Mary E. Shallman
Mark Huppin	M. Andrew Sherman
Christopher J. Hurley	Scott M. Stanton
Jeffrey R. Ii	Marilyn N. Taketa
Andrew M. Jacobson	Don Thornburgh
Paul B. Johnson	Andrew Paul Valentine
Lawrence C. King	Karen K. Williams
Victoria W-Y Lee	Kirk Orlando Williams

OF COUNSEL

Adrian Arima	Albert F. Knorp

Marta L. Morando

RETIRED PARTNERS

John Freidenrich	Leonard Ware

Representative Clients: Automobile Club of South California; Bank of America; Brooktree Corp.; C. A. Parr (Agencies), Ltd.; IMED; Pacific Bell;
McMillin Development Co.; Scripps Clinic and Research Found.; SeaWorld,
Inc.; Underwriters at Lloyds.

For full biographical listings, see the Martindale-Hubbell Law Directory

---

WILSON, SONSINI, GOODRICH & ROSATI, PROFESSIONAL CORPORATION (AV)

650 Page Mill Road, 94304-1050
Telephone: 415-493-9300
Internet: postmaster@wsgr.com
Telex: 345500 wilson pla
Fax: 415-493-6811
Email: wsgr@wsgr.com *URL:* http://www.wsgr.com

Aaron J. Alter	Andrew J. Hirsch
Denise M. Amantea	Ivan H. Humphreys
Aileen L. Arrieta	Gail Clayton Husick
Alan K. Austin	Robert B. Jack
Jonathan Axelrad	Meredith S. Jackson
Michael Barclay	Terry T. Johnson
Henry V. Barry	Thomas Christopher Klein
Suzanne Y. Bell	Jared L. Kopel
David J. Berger	Martin W. Korman
Steven L. Berson	Peter LaBoskey
Mark A. Bertelsen	Michael A. Ladra
Jerome F. Birn, Jr.	David L. Larson
Steven E. Bochner	Robert P. Latta
Mark E. Bonham	Douglas M. Laurice
Donald E. Bradley	Nina Locker
Tor Braham	Page Mailliard
Harry B. Bremond	Henry P. Massey, Jr.
Andrew P. Bridges	J. Casey McGlynn
Robert D. Brownell	Christopher D. Mitchell
Richard J. Char	Allen L. Morgan
Peter P. Chen	Bradford C. O'Brien
Douglas J. Clark	Judith Mayer O'Brien
Kenneth A. Clark	Michael J. O'Donnell
Douglas H. Collom	Mark Parnes
Charles T. C. Compton	Donna M. Petkanics
Susan A. Creighton	Michael S. Rabson
Francis S. Currie	Gary L. Reback
Michael J. Danaher	John V. Roos
Paul Davis	Mario M. Rosati
Thomas C. DeFilipps	Ronald M. Roth
James A. DiBoise	Jeffrey D. Saper
Stephen C. Durant	Elizabeth M. Saunders
Boris Feldman	Steven M. Schatz
Robert P. Feldman	Arthur F. Schneiderman
Chris F. Fennell	Patrick J. Schultheis
Elizabeth R. Flint	Timothy T. Scott
Herbert P. Fockler	David J. Segre
John A. Fore	John T. Sheridan
John B. Goodrich	Ron E. Shulman
Dana Haviland	Kenneth M. Siegel
Mark A. Haynes	Laurie B. Smilan

(See Next Column)

WILSON, SONSINI, GOODRICH & ROSATI PROFESSIONAL CORPORATION, *Palo Alto—Continued*

Larry W. Sonsini
Timothy J. Sparks
Roger D. Stern
David S. Steuer
Blair W. Stewart, Jr.
James Neilson Strawbridge
Debra S. Summers

Barry E. Taylor
Bruce G. Vanyo
Ann Yvonne Walker
Kenneth B. Wilson
Lloyd Winawer
Neil Jay Wolff
Howard S. Zeprun

COUNSEL

Douglas Keith Krohn
Thomas L. Cronan, III
Francis W. Dubreuil
(Not admitted in CA)

Kathleen Borrero Bloch
David M. Hoffmeister
Richard A. Shupack

Paul D. Anawalt
Richard S. Arnold, Jr.
J. Michael Arrington
Ronald A. Baker
Colleen Bal
John P. Bartholomay
(Not admitted in CA)
Mark B. Baudler
Marilyn U. Bauriedel
Julie Ann Bell
Bradley A. Benbrook
Steven J. Benerofe
Peter H. Bergman
(Not admitted in CA)
Steven V. Bernard
Kurt J. Berney
(Not admitted in CA)
Jeffrey M. Bloom
(Not admitted in CA)
Ira J. Blumberg
Lauren I. Boro
Susan Bower
Christopher F. Boyd
Jason M. Brady
Carmine J. Broccole
Ivan J. Brockman
Thomas G. Brown
Michelle Brownlee
Jason P. Bucha
Bradley A. Bugdanowitz
Brett D. Byers
Gidon M. Caine
(Not admitted in CA)
David M. Campbell
Megan J. Carroll
Charles C. Cary
(Not admitted in CA)
Bernard James Cassidy
Armando Castro
Jeff Cattalini
Marta Cervantes
Alex Chachkes
Daniel M. Chambers
H.C. Chan
Carmen I-Hua Chang
Williana Chang
Warren Chao
Trevor J. Chaplick
Theodore C. Chen
(Not admitted in CA)
Hanley Chew
(Not admitted in CA)
Roger J. Chin
Sandra Chutorian
Robert Claassen
(Not admitted in CA)
Todd Cleary
Olabisi L. Clinton
Anton Theodore Commissaris
(Not admitted in the United States)
Gregory T. Cox
Brandyn Criswell
Linda M. Cuny
Brian D. Danella
(Not admitted in CA)
Jill Daniels
Lisa A. Davis
Robert G. Day
Harold R. DeGraff
Cecilia M. de Leon
Laura Miller de Petra
Martha L. Dienes
Bret M. DiMarco
Vivian B. Distler

Adam R. Dolinko
Stephen A. Donovan
Stephen G. Driggers
David C. Drummond
Cynthia A. Dy
Ian B. Edvalson
Keith E. Eggleton
Nevan C. Elam
Vera M. Elson
Rebecca L. Epstein
Brian C. Erb
Craig H. Factor
Janice Leyrer Fall
Dorothy L. Fernandez
Eric J. Finseth
Diane Jean Fong
Deborah S. Fox
Brenda R. Frank
Karen P. Fredericks
(Not admitted in CA)
Adele C. Freedman
Kevin M. Galligan
W. H. Baird Garrett
Roger Edward George
Stephen E. Gillette
Selwyn B. Goldberg
Jon C. Gonzales
(Not admitted in CA)
Sarah Ann Good
Marc E. Gottschalk
Linda S. Grais
Monica L. Greenberg
(Not admitted in CA)
Irwin R. Gross
Geoffrey B. Hale
Ramsey Hanna
Sara Duval Harrington
Richard J. Hart
Susan Heaney
Peter S. Heinecke
Jeffrey A. Herbst
Michael Hetherington
Charles D. Holland
Bruce Robert Hopenfeld
Frank I. Hoppe
John Mathias Horan
Anna Itoi
Barbara A. Izzo
James L. Jacobs
Raju S. Judge
Christine Kendrick
Adit M. Khorana
David A. Killam
Nan H. Kim
(Not admitted in CA)
Stephen E. Kim
(Not admitted in CA)
W. Brian Kinard
David R. King
Catherine S. Kirkman
Christopher M. Koa
Robert F. Kornegay, Jr.
David H. Kramer
Susan P. Krause
Elizabeth M. Kurr
Gilbert M. Labrucherie, Jr.
Joan E. Lambert
Marthe LaRosiliere
Thomas G. LaWer
Andrew Leibnitz
Michael B. Levin
Adam D. Levy
Michael J. Levy
John R. Lewis
Joshua A. Lipp

(See Next Column)

Bridget Logterman
Laurie-Ann Mei Inn Look
Thomas J. Lorr
Tiffany Lyon
Jose F. Macias
Matthew MacKenzie
Thomas J. Martin
Nancy D. Martindale
Tamara Gail Mattison
Thomas E. McKeever
Bruce M. McNamara
Ruth Ann McNees
Lisa G. Meckfessel
Heather Meeker
Millicent S. Meroney
Noah D. Mesel
Harold J. Milstein
Rebecca A. Mitchells
Daniel R. Mitz
Robert Moll
Kelly Ames Morehead
Diana M. Morrow
Caine T. Moss
Monica Mucchetti
Michael J. Murphy
Usha Narayanan
Neil Nathanson
Marnia Nichols
Christopher G. Nicholson
John C. Nishi
Donna Katherine Norman
Craig D. Norris
Burke F. Norton
David P. O'Brien
(Not admitted in CA)
Michael Occhiolini
Robert G. O'Connor
Michael Okada
James C. Otteson
William B. Owens, Jr.
Christopher J. Ozburn
Agnes Pak
(Not admitted in CA)
Michael J. Panepucci
A. Richard Park
John A. Pearce
Sarah Preisler
David Priebe
Stacey G. Prochaska
Soraya N. Rashid
Amy E. Rees
Julia Reigel
Rosemary G. Reilly
(Not admitted in CA)
Mark L. Reinstra
Susan Pasquinelli Reinstra
Gene Rhough
Kent R. Richardson
Erik F. Riegler
Michele E. Rose
Eric Jon Rosenzweig
Debra B. Rosler
Jeremy Rossen
RoseAnn Marie Rotandaro
(Not admitted in CA)
Alisande M. Rozynko
Rachel L. Ruskin
Christopher K. Sadeghian
Ignacio E. Salceda

Robert D. Sanchez
Leslie S. Santos
Vahe H. Sarrafian
David J. Saul
Thomas I. Savage
(Not admitted in CA)
Richard J. Schachtili
Valerie Schulthies
Peter M. Schwab
Joanne Renée Scully
Kaivan M. Shakib
(Not admitted in CA)
Behrooz Shariati
Stephanie Sharron
Craig A. Shelburne
Laura Lewis Shelburne
Sungbo Shim
Victor Sim
S. Dawn Smith
Ellen Solomon-Gonzales
(Not admitted in CA)
Noga Devecseri Spira
Susan L. Stapleton
Richard G. Steele
Vadim D. Stepanchenko
Thomas N. Stephens
Timothy J. Stevens
Rodney G. Strickland, Jr.
Betsey Sue
J. Robert Suffoletta, Jr.
Matthew B. Swartz
Ahmed E. Taha
Yoichiro Taku
Tomer Tal
Robert M. Tarkoff
Romy S. Taubman
Bruce A. Telkamp
Susan Stuermer Thomas
Richard H. Thompson
(Not admitted in CA)
Susan Tien
Paul R. Tobias
(Not admitted in CA)
Tracy L. Tosh
Jennifer Tsay
Daniel W. Turbow
Diane E. Turriff
David M. Urso
Jan-Marc van der Schee
Alicia J. Vasquez
Daniel F. Vaughn
(Not admitted in CA)
Issac J. Vaughn
Jason B. Wacha
Don M. Wade
Victoria M. Walter
(Not admitted in CA)
David C. Wang
David J. Weitz
Martin Wellington
Shannon D. Whisenant
Don S. Williams
George A. Willman
Richard L. Woodworth
Eric W. Wright
James C. Yoon
Christopher J. Younger
Stacey A. Zartler
Lior Zorea
(Not admitted in CA)

For full biographical listings, see the Martindale-Hubbell Law Directory

---

WISE & SHEPARD, LLP (AV)

3030 Hansen Way, Suite 100, 94304
Telephone: 415-856-1200
Telecopier: 415-856-1344

PARTNERS

Lisa B. Armando
Thomas L. Barton
M. Scott Donahey
David R. Foley
Amy L. Gilson

David W. Herbst
Jerrold F. Petruzzelli
Edward L. Quevedo
James M. Smith
Priscilla Wheeler

ASSOCIATES

Sanjiv S. Dhawan
Timothy R. Fulkerson
Joseph D. Hernandez
Michelle E. Lentzner
Daniel H. Kern
Michael G. McClory

Deborah L. Livornese
Tina M. Singh
Alison E. Spong
Joi C. True
Christopher L. Wanger
Susan F. Wegner

(See Next Column)

WISE & SHEPARD LLP—*Continued*

COUNSEL

Neal M. Williams

Representative Clients: City of San Jose; Insight Development Corp.; Pilkington Visioncare, Inc.; Sola Optical U.S.A.; Syntex Corp.; Wells Fargo Bank, N.A.; Varian Associates, Inc.; Videonics, Inc.

For full biographical listings, see the Martindale-Hubbell Law Directory

---

PASADENA, Los Angeles Co.

FRANSCELL, STRICKLAND, ROBERTS & LAWRENCE, A PROFESSIONAL CORPORATION (AV)

Penthouse, 225 South Lake Avenue, 91101-3005
Telephone: 818-304-7830; 213-684-7830
Fax: 818-795-7460
Santa Ana, California Office: Suite 800, 401 Civic Center Drive West.
Telephone: 714-543-6511.
Fax: 714-543-6711.
Riverside, California Office: Suite 670, 3801 University Avenue.
Telephone: 909-686-1000.
Fax: 909-686-2565.

George J. Franscell	Donald C. McFarlane
Tracy Strickland	(Resident, Santa Ana Office)
(Resident, Santa Ana Office)	Libby Wong
Barbara E. Roberts	Cindy S. Lee
(Resident, Riverside Office)	Martin J. De Vries
David D. Lawrence	(Resident, Riverside Office)
Carol Ann Rohr	Ann Marie Sanders
Scott D. MacLatchie	Priscilla F. Slocum
S. Frank Harrell	Garth Matthew Drozin
(Resident, Santa Ana Office)	

For full biographical listings, see the Martindale-Hubbell Law Directory

---

HAHN & HAHN (AV)

A Partnership including Professional Corporations
Ninth Floor, 301 East Colorado Boulevard, 91101
Telephone: 818-796-9123
Los Angeles: 213-681-6948
Orange Co.: 714-971-5590
Cable Address: "Hahnlaw"
Telecopier: 818-449-7357

MEMBERS OF FIRM

David K. Robinson (P.C.)	Susan T. House (P.C.)
Loren H. Russell (P.C.)	Dianne H. Bukata
Leonard M. Marangi (P.C.)	Gene E. Gregg, Jr. (P.C.)
William S. Johnstone, Jr., (P.C.)	R. Scott Jenkins (P.C.)
George R. Baffa (P.C.)	Charles J. Greaves (P.C.)
Don Mike Anthony (P.C.)	Dale R. Pelch
Robert W. Anderson	William S. Garr (P.C.)
William K. Henley (P.C.)	Karl I. Swaidan
Clark R. Byam (P.C.)	Sandra K. Murphy
Richard L. Hall (P.C.)	Laura V. Farber
	Tali Shaddow

OF COUNSEL

Stanley L. Hahn (P.C.)	George E. Zillgitt
	Emrys J. Ross

Representative Clients: Becton Dickinson & Co.; California Institute of Technology; City of Glendale; City of Pasadena, City of Long Beach; Flint Ink Corp.; Pasadena Tournament of Roses Assn.; Symes Cadillac, Inc.

For full biographical listings, see the Martindale-Hubbell Law Directory

---

THROCKMORTON, BECKSTROM, OAKES & TOMASSIAN LLP (AV)

Corporate Center Pasadena, 225 South Lake Avenue, Suite 500, 91101-3005
Telephone: 818-568-2500; 213-681-2321
Fax: 818-405-0786
Irvine, California Office: Suite 350, 19800 MacArthur Boulevard 92715.
Telephone: 714-955-2280.
Fax: 714-467-8081.

MEMBERS OF FIRM

A. Robert Throckmorton	Serge Tomassian
(Resident, Irvine Office)	(Resident, Irvine Office)
Spencer S. Beckstrom	David Alan Huffaker
George A. Oakes	Robert S. Throckmorton

References Available Upon Request.

For full biographical listings, see the Martindale-Hubbell Law Directory

---

WITTER AND HARPOLE (AV)

Wells Fargo Building, 350 W. Colorado Boulevard, Suite 400, 91105
Telephone: 213-624-1311, 818-440-1111
FAX: 213-620-0430
Email: 102444.2117@compuserve.com
Newport Beach, California Office: Suite 1050, 610 Newport Center Drive.
Telephone: 714-644-7600.
Fax: 714-759-1014.

MEMBERS OF FIRM

Myron E. Harpole	Eugene Harpole (1896-1987)
George G. Witter (1895-1978)	Debra M. Olsen (Resident, Newport Beach Office)

OF COUNSEL

James D. Harris (A Professional Corporation)

Reference: Union Bank (Newport Beach, Calif.).

For full biographical listings, see the Martindale-Hubbell Law Directory

---

PETALUMA, Sonoma Co. — (Refer to Santa Rosa)

RED BLUFF,* Tehama Co. — (Refer to Redding)

REDDING,* Shasta Co.

CARR, KENNEDY, PETERSON & FROST, A LAW CORPORATION (AV)

420 Redcliff Drive, P.O. Box 492396, 96049
Telephone: 916-222-2100
Fax: 916-222-0504

Francis Carr (1875-1944)	Daniel S. Frost
Lawrence J. Kennedy, Sr. (1883-1975)	Robert M. Harding
	Evan L. Delgado
Laurence J. Kennedy, Jr. (1918-1986)	Stephen H. Baker
	Michael P. Ashby
Laurence W. Carr (1912-1991)	Randall C. Nelson
R. Russ Peterson	Robert A. West

Representative Clients: Chicago Title Insurance Co.; CH2M Hill California, Inc.; Fruit Growers Supply Co.; ITT Rayonier, Inc.; Louisiana-Pacific Corp.; Minnesota Mining & Manufacturing; Northbrook Insurance Co.; Roseburg Lumber Co.; Security Union Title Insurance Co.; Stewart Title Insurance Co.

For full biographical listings, see the Martindale-Hubbell Law Directory

---

MOSS & ENOCHIAN, A LAW CORPORATION (AV)

2701 Park Marina Drive, P.O. Drawer 994608, 96099-4608
Telephone: 916-225-8990
Fax: 916-241-5734

Steven R. Enochian	Stewart C. Altemus
Larry B. Moss	John S. Kenny
Todd E. Slaughter	Robert A. Spano

Sandra L. Johnson	Monica M. Balavage
Mark D. Norcross	Gustavo L. Martinez
Eric A. Omstead	Gary E. Haslerud
Darryl L. Wagner	Monique Grandaw

Reference: Tri Counties Bank.

For full biographical listings, see the Martindale-Hubbell Law Directory

---

REDWOOD CITY,* San Mateo Co.

LOW, BALL & LYNCH, A PROFESSIONAL CORPORATION (AV)

10 Twin Dolphin, Suite B-500, 94065
Telephone: 415-591-8822
Fax: 415-591-8884
San Francisco, California Office: 601 California Street, Suite 2100, 94108.
Telephone: 415-981-6630.
Monterey, California Office: 10 Ragsdale Drive, Suite 175, 93940.
Telephone: 408-655-8822.

Raymond Coates	David L. Blinn
Chester G. Moore, III	Janet Kulig
James D. Miller	Thomas E. Mulvihill
William H. Holsinger	Jennifer Elizabeth Acheson

John R. Baumann	Joseph M. Fenech
	Michael E. Sandgren

For full biographical listings, see the Martindale-Hubbell Law Directory

---

OWEN & MELBYE, A PROFESSIONAL CORPORATION (AV)

700 Jefferson Street, 94063
Telephone: 415-364-6500
Fax: 415-365-7036
Tahoe City, California Office: P.O. Box 1524.
Telephone: 916-546-2473.

(See Next Column)

OWEN & MELBYE A PROFESSIONAL CORPORATION, *Redwood City—Continued*

William H. Owen	Edmund M. Scott
Richard B. Melbye	Pamela J. Helmer
Norman J. Roger	John S. Posthauer
	Paul R. Mangiantini

Albert P. Blake, Jr.	Conor A. Meyers
Dawn M. Patterson	Mary P. Derner

Representative Clients: Aetna Cravens Dargan Co.; Avco Lycoming; Beech Aircraft Corp.; California Casualty Indemnity Exchange; K & K Claims Service; Kemper Insurance Cos.; Mutual Service Insurance Co.; State Farm Mutual Insurance Cos.; Underwriters at Lloyds; United States Aviation Insurance Group.

For full biographical listings, see the Martindale-Hubbell Law Directory

ROPERS, MAJESKI, KOHN & BENTLEY, A PROFESSIONAL CORPORATION (AV)

1001 Marshall Street, 94063
Telephone: 415-364-8200
Fax: 415-367-0997
San Jose, California Office: 80 North 1st Street.
Telephone: 408-287-6262.
Fax: 408-297-6819.
San Francisco, California Office: 670 Howard Street.
Telephone: 415-543-4800.
Fax: 415-512-1574.
Santa Rosa, California Office: Fountaingrove Center, Suite 300, 3558 Round Barn Boulevard.
Telephone: 707-524-4200.
Fax: 707-523-4610.
Los Angeles, California Office: 550 South Hope Street, Suite 1900.
Telephone: 213-312-2000.
Fax: 213-312-2001.
Sacramento, California Office: 1000 G Street, Suite 400.
Telephone: 916-556-3100.
Fax: 916-442-7121.

Harold Ropers (1905-1966)	David A. Levy
John M. Rubens (1936-1993)	Colin R. Campbell
Eugene J. Majeski	Brad W. Blocker
John M. Bentley	Marc D. Rosati
Michael J. Brady	Thomas H. Clarke, Jr.
Frank J. Pagliaro, Jr.	Robert P. Andris, II
John S. Simonson	Todd A. Roberts
Stephen A. Scott	Michael Ropers (Resident)
Daniel E. Alberti	David M. McLaughlin
Mark G. Bonino	William R. Garrett
Richard K. Wilson	Raymond A. Greene III
Stephen M. Hayes	Robert G. Ittig
Katherine S. Clark	V. Raymond Swope, III
Lawrence M. Guslani	Ralph Tortorella III
Ted J. Hannig	Francois G. Laugier
Theodore C. Zayner	Susan H. Handelman
David J. Miclean	Kevin G. McCurdy
Pamela E. Cogan	Stephen P. Ellingson

OF COUNSEL

Ron W. Fields	Chi-Hung A. Chan
Walter C. Kohn	James H. McKibben

Michael E. Pitts	Ida Samawi Skikos
Linda J. Dvorak	Jennifer C. Coates
Peter C. Suhr	Bruce M. MacKay
Allison Lindley Dobbrow	Stacy Ann Smith (Resident)
Justice C. McPherson	Michael David Morehead
JoAnna R. Reichel	Mark Casper
Kathryn C. Curry	Bridget C. Hopkins Ivanov
Richard Fisher	Roxanne R. Rapson
Laura L. Reidenbach	Robert S. McLay
Brian R. Davis	Terry Anastassiou
Kimberly A. Donovan	Dennis Alan Duchene
Robert P. Soran	Roger B. Frederickson
Kelly Franks	Neda Navabpour
Anthony Joseph Hoglund	H. Ann Liroff
Hans Stephen Steinhoffer	Tara Jane Walsh
Kevin Hunsaker	Denise A. Cole
	Michael R. Solomon

For full biographical listings, see the Martindale-Hubbell Law Directory

RICHMOND, Contra Costa Co. — (Refer to Walnut Creek)

RIVERSIDE,* Riverside Co.

AKLUFI AND WYSOCKI (AV)

3403 Tenth Street, Suite 610, 92501
Telephone: 909-682-5480
Telecopier: 909-682-2619

(See Next Column)

MEMBERS OF FIRM

Joseph S. Aklufi	David L. Wysocki

ASSOCIATE

Daniel R. Aklufi

For full biographical listings, see the Martindale-Hubbell Law Directory

BEST BEST & KRIEGER LLP (AV)

A California Limited Liability Partnership including Professional Corporations
400 Mission Square, 3750 University Avenue, P.O. Box 1028, 92502
Telephone: 909-686-1450
Fax: 909-686-3083; 909-682-4612
Rancho Mirage, California Office: Hope Square Professional Centre, 39700 Bob Hope Drive, Suite 312, P.O. Box 1555.
Telephone: 619-568-2611.
Fax: 619-340-6698; 619-341-7039.
Ontario, California Office: 800 North Haven, Suite 120.
Telephone: 909-989-8584.
Fax: 909-944-1441.
San Diego, California Office: 402 West Broadway, 13th Floor.
Telephone: 619-525-1300.
Fax: 619-233-6118.
Victorville, California Office: High Desert Corporate Pointe Building, 14350 Civic Drive, Suite 270.
Telephone: 619-245-4127.
Fax: 619-245-6437.

MEMBERS OF FIRM

Raymond Best (1868-1957)	Daniel E. Olivier
James H. Krieger (1913-1975)	(Rancho Mirage Office)
Eugene Best (1893-1981)	Howard B. Golds
Arthur L. Littleworth (P.C.)	Stephen P. Deitsch
Glen E. Stephens (P.C.)	(Ontario Office)
William R. DeWolfe (P.C.)	Marc E. Empey
Christopher L. Carpenter (P.C.)	(Rancho Mirage Office)
Richard T. Anderson (P.C.)	John R. Rottschaefer
John D. Wahlin (P.C.)	Martin A. Mueller
Michael D. Harris (P.C.)	(Rancho Mirage Office)
(Rancho Mirage Office)	J. Michael Summerour
John E. Brown (P.C.)	Scott C. Smith
Michael T. Riddell (P.C.)	(San Diego Office)
Meredith A. Jury (P.C.)	Brian M. Lewis
(Ontario Office)	(Rancho Mirage Office)
Michael Grant (P.C.)	Jack B. Clarke, Jr.
Francis J. Baum (P.C.)	Bradley E. Neufeld
Anne T. Thomas (P.C.)	Peter M. Barmack
D. Martin Nethery (P.C.)	(Ontario Office)
(Rancho Mirage Office)	Matt H. Morris
George M. Reyes	(Rancho Mirage Office)
William W. Floyd, Jr.	Jeffrey V. Dunn
Gregory L. Hardke	Steven C. DeBaun
Kendall H. MacVey	Eric L. Garner
Clark H. Alsop	Dennis M. Cota (Ontario Office)
David J. Erwin (P.C.)	Patrick H.W.F. Pearce
(Rancho Mirage Office)	Robert W. Hargreaves
Michael J. Andelson (P.C.)	(Rancho Mirage Office)
(Rancho Mirage Office)	C. Michael Cowett
Douglas S. Phillips (P.C.)	(San Diego Office)
(Rancho Mirage Office)	Bruce W. Beach
Gregory K. Wilkinson	(San Diego Office)
Wynne S. Furth (Ontario Office)	Arlene Prater (San Diego Office)
Gene Tanaka	Jason D. Dabareiner
Basil T. Chapman	(Rancho Mirage Office)
(Rancho Mirage Office)	Mark A. Easter
Victor L. Wolf	Michelle Ouellette

ASSOCIATES

William D. Dahling, Jr.	Juliann Anderson
Kirk W. Smith	Susan Dumouchel Wilson
Kyle A. Snow	Jacqueline E. Bailey
Bernie L. Williamson	(Rancho Mirage Office)
Kevin K. Randolph	David Cabral (San Diego Office)
(Ontario Office)	David J. Hancock
Mary E. Gilstrap	Marc T. Rasich
(Rancho Mirage Office)	Philip M. Savage, IV
Cynthia M. Germano	Ana Maria Z. Fredgren
Kim A. Byrens	(Rancho Mirage Office)
James B. Gilpin	Karen M. Lewis (Ontario Office)
(San Diego Office)	Hayley Elizabeth Peterson
G. Henry Welles	(San Diego Office)
(Rancho Mirage Office)	Michael J. Schaefer
Dina O. Harris	Zachary R. Walton
Barbara R. Baron	Sandy A. Jacobson
(Rancho Mirage Office)	(Rancho Mirage Office)
Richard T. Egger	Jeffrey S. Flashman
(Ontario Office)	(Rancho Mirage Office)
Dean Derleth	Jeffrey T. Melching
Helene P. Dreyer	(Ontario Office)
(Rancho Mirage Office)	Scott D. Howie
Sonia Rubio Carvalho	Marguerite S. Strand
(Ontario Office)	(San Diego Office)
Patricia Byars Cisneros	Roger K. Crawford

(See Next Column)

Best Best & Krieger LLP—*Continued*

ASSOCIATES (Continued)

Keith L. Higgins	Pedro C. Dallarda
(Victorville Office)	Kristi Lynn Gudoski
John R. Perry	Caryn Leigh Craig
Shawn Hagerty	(San Diego Office)
(San Diego Office)	Kevin Collins
Mitchell L. Norton	James P. Morris

Dwight M. Montgomery

OF COUNSEL

John C. Tobin	Henry R. Kraft (P.C.)
Donald F. Zimmer	(Victorville Office)

For full biographical listings, see the Martindale-Hubbell Law Directory

BUTTERWICK, BRIGHT & O'LAUGHLIN, INC., A PROFESSIONAL LAW CORPORATION (AV)

4000 Tenth Street, P.O. Box 1229, 92502
Telephone: 909-686-3092
Telefax: 909-684-5743

J. D. Butterwick	John F. O'Laughlin
Michael T. Bright	Robert J. Mitchell

Reference: Riverside National Bank.

For full biographical listings, see the Martindale-Hubbell Law Directory

---

SACRAMENTO,* Sacramento Co.

DOWNEY, BRAND, SEYMOUR & ROHWER (AV)

Suite 1050, 555 Capitol Mall, 95814
Telephone: 916-441-0131
FAX: 916-441-4021
Email: downey@dbsr.com *URL:* http://www.dbsr.com

MEMBERS OF FIRM

Stephen W. Downey (1926-1959)	Fred A. Dawkins
Clyde H. Brand (1926-1964)	Roberta Lee Franklin
Harry B. Seymour (1926-1977)	James L. Deeringer
John F. Downey (1930-1991)	Kevin M. O'Brien
Otto Rohwer (1931—)	R. Dale Ginter
George Basye	David E. Lindgren
James A. Willett	Dan L. Carroll
John J. Hamlyn, Jr.	Stephen G. Stwora-Hail
Philip A. Stohr	Anthony A. Arostegui
Brian R. Van Camp	Judy Holzer Hersher
Henry E. Rodegerdts	Steven P. Saxton
D. Steven Blake	Julie A. Carter
James M. Day, Jr.	Lisa Lauritzen Ditora
Thomas N. Cooper	Steven H. Goldberg
Stephen J. Meyer	Julia L. Jenness
Daniel James McVeigh	Jeffrey M. Koewler
George L. O'Connell	Katharine E. Wagner
Michael A. Kvarme	William R. Warne

Patrick G. Mitchell

COUNSEL

Barbara L. Berg	Ronald F. Lipp

ASSOCIATES

Adisa M. Abudu-Davis	Stacey H. Leong
David R.E. Aladjem	JudyAnne McGinley
Craig C. Allison	Sean B. Murphy
Steven Benjamin	David H. Read
Gordon B. Burns	Lisa L. Ruth
Robert C. Bylsma	Scott L. Shapiro
Betty Chang	Helen Singmaster-Hernández
Joseph G. De Angelis	Peter Keller Southworth
Janlynn Robinson Fleener	Robert G. Strauch
William L. Keane	Richard K. Sueyoshi
Heather B. Lee	Robin Raff Taylor

Representative Clients: Hertz Corp.; Raley's Supermarkets; Sacramento Municipal Utility District; Steelcase, Inc.

For full biographical listings, see the Martindale-Hubbell Law Directory

---

FRIEDMAN, COLLARD, CUTTER & PANNETON, PROFESSIONAL CORPORATION (AV)

Suite 300, 7750 College Town Drive, 95826
Telephone: 916-381-9011
Telecopier: 916-381-7048

Morton L. Friedman	John Panneton
William H. Collard	Eric J. Ratinoff
C. Brooks Cutter	Ron Winters

For full biographical listings, see the Martindale-Hubbell Law Directory

GREVE, CLIFFORD, WENGEL & PARAS, LLP (AV)

980 Ninth Street, Suite 1900, 95814-2739
Telephone: 916-443-2011
Telecopier: 916-441-7457
Email: GREVEetal@aol.com
San Francisco, California Office: First Market Tower, 525 Market Street, Suite 3680.
Telephone: 415-274-3345.
FAX: 415-392-7349.

MEMBERS OF FIRM

Edward T. Clifford	Maureen A. Lenihan
Lawrence A. Wengel	William L. Baker
Gary L. Vinson	Robert L. Collins
Bradley R. Larson	Scott E. Cofer

William J. Barcellona

ASSOCIATES

Bradley W. Kragel	Amy L. Dobberteen
Craig L. Scott	John D. Broghammer

OF COUNSEL

Claire H. Greve	Irving H. Perluss

RETIRED

George E. Paras

Representative Clients: Allstate Insurance Co.; Atlantic Richfield, Corp.; Commercial Union Insurance Co.; Design Professionals Insurance Co.; E & O Professionals; Great American Insurance Cos.; Perini Corp.; State of California; Union Oil Co.; United Pacific/Reliance Insurance Cos.

For full biographical listings, see the Martindale-Hubbell Law Directory

HARMATA LAW OFFICES (AV)

2201 Q Street, 95816
Telephone: 916-442-2842
Fax: 916-442-2015

Donald D. Harmata

LEGAL SUPPORT PERSONNEL
PARALEGAL

Debra D. Morrow

Representative Clients: Control Data Corp.; Deloitte & Touche; General Electric Co.; Myers Electric, Inc.; Syblon-Reid Co.; Systemhouse Inc.; TRW, Inc.

For full biographical listings, see the Martindale-Hubbell Law Directory

LIVINGSTON & MATTESICH, LAW CORPORATION (AV)

1201 K Street, Suite 1100, 95814
Telephone: 916-442-1111
Fax: 916-448-1709
Email: liv-matt@gvn.net

Gene Livingston	Carol Livingston
James M. Mattesich	Rebecca M. Ceniceros

Steven P. Belzer	Trisha M. McAlmond

Reference: Bank of California.

For full biographical listings, see the Martindale-Hubbell Law Directory

McDONOUGH, HOLLAND & ALLEN, A PROFESSIONAL CORPORATION (AV)

9th Floor, 555 Capitol Mall, 95814
Telephone: 916-444-3900
Fax: 916-444-8334
Yuba City, California Office: 422 Century Park Drive, Suite A, P.O. Box 776.
Telephone: 916-674-9761.
Fax: 916-671-0990.
Oakland, California Office: 1999 Harrison Street, Suite 1300.
Telephone: 510-273-8780.
Fax: 510-839-9104.

Martin McDonough (1915-1987)	Jeffry R. Jones
Alfred E. Holland (Retired)	T. Brent Hawkins
Bruce F. Allen (Retired)	James M. Ruddick
Joseph E. Coomes, Jr.	(Resident, Yuba City Office)
David J. Spottiswood	Dawn H. Cole
Richard W. Nichols	Sharon Day Roseme
Donald C. Poole	Susan L. Schoenig
Richard W. Osen	James L. Leet
Richard E. Brandt	Mark A. Wasser
G. Richard Brown	David S. Salem
David W. Post	Virginia A. Cahill
Susan K. Edling	Harriet A. Steiner
David F. Beatty	William A. Lichtig
Michael T. Fogarty	Edward J. Quinn, Jr.
Natalie E. West	Mark Gorton
(Resident, Oakland Office)	Robert R. Rubin
Ann H. O'Connell	Patricia D. Elliott
Robert W. O'Connor	William C. Hilson, Jr.

(See Next Column)

McDONOUGH, HOLLAND & ALLEN A PROFESSIONAL CORPORATION,
Sacramento—Continued

Iris P. Yang	Stephen L. Goff
Mary Powers Antoine	Michael K. Iwahiro
Cathy Deubel Salenko	Glenn W. Peterson
Craig Labadie	David L. Krotine
(Resident, Oakland Office)	Julie E. Green
Jack D. Brown	Timothy P. Hayes
(Resident, Yuba City Office)	(Resident, Yuba City Office)
Thomas L. Hill	Todd M. Bailey
(Resident, Yuba City Office)	Marcia L. Augsburger
Nancy P. Lee	Nancy T. Templeton
Mary E. Olden	David E. Macchiavelli
Edward J. Wright, Jr.	Kent William Silvester
Michelle Marchetta Kenyon	Daniel V. Martinez
(Resident, Oakland Office)	(Resident, Yuba City Office)
Michele M. Clark	Steven A. Lamon

Michael V. Brady	Paul C. Anderson
L. Stuart List	(Resident, Oakland Office)
Jan Patrick Sherry	Torene L.M. Schwab
Don F. Harris	Wesley C.J. Ehlers
Douglas A. Potts	Terry L. Thomas
Clyde T. Ogata	Julie Raney
C. Nicole Murphy	Michelle Rudd
Madeline K. Davis	(Resident, Oakland Office)
Jeremy S. Millstone	Stacey N. Sheston
Jennifer Smith Davis	Dean J. Sioukas

OF COUNSEL

V. Barlow Goff	Seth P. Brunner
Ann Taylor Schwing	Zachary M. Smith

Clement J. Dougherty, Jr.

Representative Clients: Sutter Health/California Health Systems; California Public Employees Retirement System; Robert C. Powell Properties; Martin Media, L.P.; Las Vegas, Nevada Redevelopment Agency; NEC Electronics; The Money Store;Weyerhaeuser Venture Co.; City of Davis.

For full biographical listings, see the Martindale-Hubbell Law Directory

MOORE, MEEGAN, HANSCHU & KASSENBROCK (AV)

1545 River Park Drive, Suite 550, 95815
Telephone: 916-925-1800

MEMBERS OF FIRM

John M. Moore	James L. Hanschu
David M. Meegan	Mark R. Kassenbrock

Roberta Lindsey-Scott	Peter J. Pullen
Mary Clarke Ver Hoef	Wendy S. Dezzani

For full biographical listings, see the Martindale-Hubbell Law Directory

ROPERS, MAJESKI, KOHN & BENTLEY, A PROFESSIONAL CORPORATION (AV)

1000 G Street, Suite 400, 95814
Telephone: 916-556-3100
Fax: 916-442-7121
Redwood City, California Office: 1001 Marshall Street.
Telephone: 415-364-8200.
Fax: 415-367-0997.
San Jose, California Office: 80 North 1st Street.
Telephone: 408-287-6262.
Fax: 408-297-6819.
San Francisco, California Office: 670 Howard Street.
Telephone: 415-543-4800.
Fax: 415-512-1574.
Santa Rosa, California Office: Fountaingrove Center, Suite 300, 3558 Round Barn Boulevard.
Telephone: 707-524-4200.
Fax: 707-523-4610.
Los Angeles, California Office: 550 South Hope Street, Suite 1900.
Telephone: 213-312-2000.
Fax: 213-312-2001.

Gigi M. Knudtson

Ellen C. Arabian	Scott D. McElhern

Todd J. Rahimi

For full biographical listings, see the Martindale-Hubbell Law Directory

TUTTLE & TAYLOR, A LAW CORPORATION (AV)

1521 I Street, 95814-2016
Telephone: 916-441-2249
Facsimile: 916-441-2910
Los Angeles, California Office: Tuttle & Taylor, A Law Corporation, 355 South Grand Avenue, 40th Floor, 90071-3102.
Telephone: 213-683-0600.
Facsimile: 213-683-0225.

(See Next Column)

Washington, D.C. Office: Tuttle, Taylor & Heron, 1025 Thomas Jefferson Street, N.W., 20007-5201.
Telephone: 202-342-1300.
Facsimile: 202-342-5880.

Robert L. Shuler	Robin D. Wiener

For full biographical listings, see the Martindale-Hubbell Law Directory

---

SALINAS,* Monterey Co.

NOLAND, HAMERLY, ETIENNE & HOSS, A PROFESSIONAL CORPORATION (AV)

333 Salinas Street, P.O. Box 2510, 93902
Telephone: 408-424-1414; 372-7525
Fax: 408-424-1975
Monterey, California Office: Heritage Harbor, 99 Pacific Street, Building 200, Suite C.
Telephone: 408-373-4427.
Fax: 408-373-4797.
King City, California Office: 104 South Vanderhurst, Suite D, 93930.
Telephone: 408-386-1080.
Fax: 408-386-1083.

Harry L. Noland (1904-1991)	Lloyd W. Lowrey, Jr.
Paul M. Hamerly	Anne K. Secker
Myron E. Etienne, Jr.	Paula Robinson
Peter T. Hoss	Jerome F. Politzer, Jr.
James D. Schwefel, Jr.	Werner D. ("Randy") Meyenberg
Martin J. May	Christine P. Gianascol
Stephen W. Pearson	Lisa Nakata

Laura A. Davis

OF COUNSEL

Blanca E. Zarazua

Representative Clients: Quail Lodge, Inc.; J. M. Smucker Company; McCormick & Co.; Tanimura & Antle; Fresh Express; Mann Packing Co.; First National Bank of Central California; Household International; Robert Talbott, Inc.; El Aguila Food Products, Inc.

For full biographical listings, see the Martindale-Hubbell Law Directory

---

SAN BERNARDINO,* San Bernardino Co.

KASSEL & KASSEL (AV)

A Group of Independent Law Offices
Suite 207, Wells Fargo Bank Building, 334 West Third Street, 92401
Telephone: 909-884-6455
Fax: 909-884-8032

Philip Kassel	Gregory H. Kassel

References: Wells Fargo Bank; Bank of America; Bank of San Bernardino.

For full biographical listings, see the Martindale-Hubbell Law Directory

WILSON, BORROR, DUNN & DAVIS (AV)

Suite 307, The Bank of California Building, 255 North D Street, 92401
Telephone: 909-884-8855
Fax: 909-884-5161

MEMBERS OF FIRM

Fred A. Wilson (1886-1973)	James R. Dunn
Wm. H. Wilson (1915-1981)	Thomas M. Davis

Keith D. Davis

ASSOCIATES

Timothy P. Prince	Sarah L. Overton

OF COUNSEL

Caywood J. Borror

Representative Clients: Travelers Insurance Co.; Rockwell International; Westinghouse Air Brake Co.; Goodyear Tire and Rubber Co.; Home Insurance Co.; Cities of: Redlands, Chino, Colton, San Bernardino and Upland; The Canadian Insurance Co.

For full biographical listings, see the Martindale-Hubbell Law Directory

---

SAN BRUNO, San Mateo Co. — (Refer to Burlingame)

SAN DIEGO,* San Diego Co.

ALLEN, MATKINS, LECK, GAMBLE & MALLORY LLP (AV)

A Limited Liability Partnership including Professional Corporations
501 West Broadway, Suite 900, 92101
Telephone: 619-233-1155
Facsimile: 619-233-1158
Los Angeles, California Office: Seventh Floor, 515 South Figueroa Street, 90071.
Telephone: 213-622-5555.
Telecopier: 213-620-8816.
Irvine, California Office: Fourth Floor, 18400 Von Karman, 92715.
Telephone: 714-553-1313.
Telecopier: 714-553-8354.

(See Next Column)

ALLEN, MATKINS, LECK, GAMBLE & MALLORY LLP—*Continued*

West Los Angeles, California Office: 1999 Avenue of the Stars, 90067.
Telephone: 310-788-2400.
Fax: 310-788-2410.

PARTNERS

Michael E. Gleason (P.C.) (Resident)	Dana I. Schiffman (Resident)
Vernon C. Gauntt (Resident)	David L. Osias
George J. Berger (Resident)	Ray B. Gliner (Resident)
Michael C. Pruter (Resident)	Robert R. Barnes (Resident)
	Jeffrey R. Patterson (Resident)

RESIDENT ASSOCIATES

Craig D. Swanson	Loraine L. Pedowitz
Martha K. Guy	Ann Marie Maas
George W. Kuney	Mark J. Hattam
Kelli L. Fuller	Kathryn D. Horning
Steve Wellington	Pamela M. Everett
Martin L. Togni	

OF COUNSEL

John G. Davies	Joe M. Davidson

Reference: Wells Fargo Bank (Los Angeles Main Office).

For full biographical listings, see the Martindale-Hubbell Law Directory

BAKER & McKENZIE (AV)

The Wells Fargo Plaza Twelfth Floor, 101 West Broadway, 92101
Telephone: (619) 236-1441; (800) 786-1022
Intl. Dialing: (1-619) 236-1441
Cable Address: ABOGADO SD
Telex: 9102503468
Answer Back: ABOGADO SD
Facsimile: (1-619) 236-0429
Associated Offices of Baker & McKenzie in: Almaty, Amsterdam, Bangkok, Barcelona, Beijing, Berlin, Bogotá, Brasília, Brussels, Budapest, Buenos Aires, Cairo, Caracas, Chicago, Dallas, Frankfurt, Geneva, Hanoi, Ho Chi Minh City, Hong Kong, Juárez, Kiev, Lausanne, London, Madrid, Manila, Melbourne, México City, Miami, Milan, Monterrey, Moscow, Münich, New York, Palo Alto, Paris, Prague, Rio de Janeiro, Riyadh, Rome, St. Petersburg, San Francisco, Santiago, São Paulo, Singapore, Stockholm, Sydney, Taipei, Tijuana, Tokyo, Toronto, Valencia, Warsaw, Washington, D.C. and Zürich.
Correspondent Law Firm: Hadiputranto, Hadinoto & Partners, Jakarta.

MEMBERS OF FIRM

Charles H. Dick, Jr.	Donald McGrath II
David C. Doyle	Ali M. M. Mojdehi
Thomas W. Ferrell	Pamela J. Naughton
John J. Hentrich	Thomas M. Shoesmith
Clark H. Libenson	Abby B. Silverman

LOCAL PARTNERS

Ernest Cordero, Jr.	Maria E. Nuñez
Ian L. Kessler	Claire Wright

OF COUNSEL

Randall K. Broberg	Edward T. Butler
J. Michael Roake	

ASSOCIATES

Mitchell P. Brook	Robert M. Harkins, Jr.
Lauren S. Cartwright	Carlos D. Heredia
Craig I. Celniker (Not admitted in CA)	Ronald F. Hoffman
	Cynthia G. Iliff
Wanda W. H. Chang	Michael P. McCloskey
Michael S. Christian	Laura L. Peterson
Andrea J. Clapp	Eric M. Robinson
Steven E. Comer	Renee S. Schor
Cynthia A. Freeland	Vincent Li-Cheng Shih (Not admitted in United States)
Rachel A. Gonzalez	

For full biographical listings, see the Martindale-Hubbell Law Directory

BROBECK, PHLEGER & HARRISON LLP (AV)

A Partnership including a Professional Corporation
550 West C Street Suite 1300, 92101
Telephone: 619-234-1966
Facsimile: 619-236-1403 (13th Floor); 619-234-3848 (12th Floor)
San Francisco, California Office: Spear Street Tower, One Market.
Telephone: 415-442-0900.
Facsimile: 415-442-0900.
Palo Alto, California Office: Two Embarcadero Place, 2200 Geng Road.
Telephone: 415-424-0160.
Facsimile: 415-496-2885.
Los Angeles, California Office: 550 South Hope Street.
Telephone: 213-489-4060.
Facsimile: 213-745-3345.
Orange County, California Office: 4675 MacArthur Court, Suite 1000, Newport Beach.
Telephone: 714-752-7535.
Facsimile: 714-752-7522.

(See Next Column)

Austin, Texas Office: Brobeck, Phleger & Harrison LLP, 301 Congress Avenue, Suite 1200.
Telephone: 512-477-5495.
Facsimile: 512-477-5813.
Denver, Colorado Office: Brobeck, Phleger & Harrison LLP, 1125 Seventeenth Street, 25th Floor.
Telephone: 303-293-0760.
Facsimile: 303-299-8819.
New York, N.Y. Office: Brobeck, Phleger & Harrison LLP, 1633 Broadway, 47th Floor.
Telephone: 212-581-1600.
Facsimile: 212-586-7878.
Brobeck Hale and Dorr International Office:
London, England Office: Veritas House, 125 Finsbury Pavement, London EC2A 1NQ.
Telephone: 44 071 638 6688.
Facsimile: 44 071 638 5888.

MANAGING PARTNER

Todd J. Anson

RESIDENT PARTNERS

Craig S. Andrews	Richard L. Parker
John A. de Groot	Maria K. Pum
John A. Denniston	Ellen B. Spellman
Theodore W. Graham	William F. Sullivan
Jennifer A. Kearns	(Firm Managing Partner)
Richard L. Kintz	Hayden J. Trubitt
Daniel G. Lamb, Jr.	Mary L. Walker

ASSOCIATES

Shelley E. Bennett	Mary Kathryn Kelley
William S. Biel	Chris A. Knudsen
Ross L. Burningham	Lance S. Kurata
Kristen E. Caverly	Christopher H. McGrath
John R. Cook	Beth Newman
Wayne Fong	Martin Clark Nichols
Jeffrey Garfinkle	Elizabeth E. Reed
Thomas E. Hornish (Not admitted in CA)	Faye H. Russell
	Jason Schauer
Ellen E. Jamason	Joan B. Stafslien
Michael S. Kagnoff	Kimberly S. Steckling

For full biographical listings, see the Martindale-Hubbell Law Directory

DETISCH & CHRISTENSEN (AV)

444 West C Street, Suite 200, 92101
Telephone: 619-236-9343
Fax: 619-236-8307

MEMBERS OF FIRM

Charles B. Christensen	Donald W. Detisch

ASSOCIATE

Sean D. Schwerdtfeger

For full biographical listings, see the Martindale-Hubbell Law Directory

FERRIS & BRITTON, A PROFESSIONAL CORPORATION (AV)

1600 First National Bank Center, 401 West A Street, 92101
Telephone: 619-233-3131
Fax: 619-232-9316

Alfred G. Ferris	Tamara K. Fogg
Christopher Q. Britton	Michael R. Weinstein
Steven J. Pynes	Gary T. Moyer

OF COUNSEL

James J. Granby	William M. Winter

Representative Clients: Agouron Pharmaceuticals, Inc.; Cox Communications, Inc.; Enterprise Rent-a-Car; Exxon; Invitrogen Corp.; Peninsula Bank; Structural Bioinformatics, Inc.; Teleport Communications Group; Southwest Airlines.

For full biographical listings, see the Martindale-Hubbell Law Directory

LOUIS E. GOEBEL (AV)

The Historic "Britt-Scripps" House, 406 Maple Street, 92103
Telephone: 619-239-2611
Fax: 619-239-4269
Email: goebellaw@aol.com

For full biographical listings, see the Martindale-Hubbell Law Directory

San Diego—Continued

GRAY CARY WARE & FREIDENRICH, A PROFESSIONAL CORPORATION (AV)

Gray Cary Established in 1927
Ware & Freidenrich Established in 1969
401 "B" Street, Suite 1700, 92101
Telephone: 619-699-2700
Telecopier: 619-236-1048
Email: info@gcwf.com *URL:* http://www.gcwf.com
San Diego/Golden Triangle, California Office: 4365 Executive Drive, Suite 1600, 92121.
Telephone: 619-677-1400.
Fax: 619-677-1477.
Palo Alto, California Office: 400 Hamilton Avenue.
Telephone: 415-328-6561.
La Jolla, California Office: Suite 575, 1200 Prospect Street.
Telephone: 619-454-9101.
El Centro, California Office: 1224 State Street, P.O. Box 2890.
Telephone: 619-353-6140.

John Allcock
Louis G. Arnell
Robert W. Ayling
Neil P. Balmert (Resident, San Diego/Golden Triangle Office)
Robert W. Bell, Jr.
T. Knox Bell (Resident, San Diego/Golden Triangle Office)
Cathy A. Bencivengo
J. Rod Betts
Charles E. Black
William S. Boggs
Robert W. Brownlie
Theodore J. Cranston (Resident, San Diego/Golden Triangle and La Jolla Offices)
Guylyn R. Cummins
Jeffry A. Davis
Charles L. Deem
Joseph A. Delaney
Nancy O. Dix
L. B. Chip Edleson
Elisabeth Eisner (Resident, San Diego/Golden Triangle Office)
Melitta Fleck (Resident, San Diego/Golden Triangle and La Jolla Offices)
Brian L. Forbes
Brian A. Foster
David B. Geerdes (Resident, San Diego/Golden Triangle Office)
William E. Grauer (Resident, San Diego/Golden Triangle Office)
James T. Hannink
Jay D. Hanson
Paul E. Hurdlow (Resident, San Diego/Golden Triangle Office)
James W. Huston
Therese H. Hymer
Jay W. Jeffcoat
William N. Kammer
Paul E. Kreutz (Resident, San Diego/Golden Triangle Office)

Robert C. Longstreth
Richard F. Luther
Guillermo Marrero
William McCurine, Jr.
Lisa C. Merrill
Andrea E. Migdal (Resident, San Diego/Golden Triangle Office)
Marcelle E. Mihaila
David E. Monahan
J. Terence O'Malley
Barbara Jean Orr
Richard A. Paul
Fred M. Plevin
Cameron Jay Rains (Resident, San Diego/Golden Triangle Office)
Douglas J. Rein (Resident, San Diego/Golden Triangle Office)
Paul H. Roeder
Alexander H. Rogers
Terry D. Ross
Don G. Rushing
William B. Sailer (Resident, San Diego/Golden Triangle Office)
Rebecca K. Schmitt (Resident, San Diego/Golden Triangle Office)
Dennis A. Schoville
Jeffrey M. Shohet
James K. Smith
Jonathan B. Sokol
Merrill F. Storms, Jr.
Lawrence I. Tannenbaum
Michael S. Tracy
Shirli Fabbri Weiss
Ellen H. Whelan (Resident, San Diego/Golden Triangle and La Jolla Offices)
Mark C. Zebrowski
Karl Zobell (Resident, La Jolla Office)

Maria R. Acker
Marta B. Almli
Jeffrey T. Baglio (Resident, San Diego/Golden Triangle Office)
Marnie Wright Barnhorst
Mildred Basden (Resident, San Diego/Golden Triangle Office)
Charles W. Becker
Brian L. Behmer
Christopher P. Bifone (Resident, San Diego/Golden Triangle Office)
Nader Bitar (Resident, San Diego/Golden Triangle Office)
Ann K. Bradley
Lorna Alksne Brown
Stewart M. Brown
Eric P. Campbell (Resident, San Diego/Golden Triangle Office)
Jackson Chen
Cindy M. Cipriani
Sara L. Cohen
E. Joseph Connaughton
Sean C. Cunningham
Emily Durkee
Rodney S. Edmonds
Janis S. Fagan

John E. Fitzsimmons
Andrew M. Greene
Mark H. Hamer
Duane S. Horning
Noel C. Howe (Resident, San Diego/Golden Triangle Office)
Benjamin P. Jones
Kathryn E. Karcher
Nancy Kawano
Randall Evan Kay
Matt A. Kirmayer (Resident, San Diego/Golden Triangle Office)
David Kleinsmith (Resident, San Diego/Golden Triangle Office)
Cynthia R. Kok
Mary A. Lehman
Diane L. Levitsky
Deborah H. Lyon (Not admitted in CA)
Jonathan D. Mack
Douglas B. Martin
Tracy L. Nation
Sharon D. Newman
Daniel T. Pascucci
Dayna J. Pineda (Resident, San Diego/Golden Triangle Office)

(See Next Column)

Paul A. Reynolds
Ian N. Rose
Leslie T. Rubin
Sharon B. Spivak
Nancy L. Stagg
Heather M. Stearns
Donald J. Sullivan

Helena Wallentin
David E. Watson
Kevin Wechter
Amy T. Wintersheimer
Christopher M. Young
David R. Young (Resident, San Diego/Golden Triangle Office)

Troy Zander

CONSULTING PARTNERS

Robert Ames
Richard Alexander Burt
Frederick P. Crowell (Consulting Partner)

R. Reaves Elledge, Jr.
Sterling Hutcheson
Browning E. Marean, III
Ralph M. Pray, III

OF COUNSEL

H. Cushman Dow

Representative Clients: Automobile Club of South California; Bank of America; Brooktree Corp.; C. A. Parr (Agencies), Ltd.; IMED; Pacific Bell; McMillin Development Co.; Scripps Clinic and Research Found.; SeaWorld, Inc.; Underwriters at Lloyds.

For full biographical listings, see the Martindale-Hubbell Law Directory

HARRIGAN, RUFF, SBARDELLATI & MOORE, A PROFESSIONAL CORPORATION (AV)

101 West Broadway, Suite 1600, 92101
Telephone: 619-233-1511
Fax: 619-233-1537
Email: hrsmsd@aol.com

James G. Harrigan
Joseph W. Ruff (Retired)
Robert G. Sbardellati
Michael R. Moore
F. Gregory Pyke
Susan A. Mercure
Stephen T. Landuyt

Steven K. Ewald
William D. Hoshaw
Michael L. Madgett
Jon R. Pearce
Marco F. Garavaglia
Eleanor L. Blais
Patrick W. Martin

John F. Golembesky

For full biographical listings, see the Martindale-Hubbell Law Directory

HIGGS, FLETCHER & MACK LLP (AV)

2000 First National Bank Building, 401 West "A" Street, 92101
Telephone: 619-236-1551
Telecopier: 619-696-1410
Email: info@higgslaw.com

MEMBERS OF FIRM

Henry Pitts Mack (1909-1974)
DeWitt A. Higgs (1907-1994)
John W. Netterblad
Joe N. Turner
Craig D. Higgs
J. Tim Konold
Harry L. Carter
Ronald E. Null
Franklin T. Lloyd
Michael F. Boyle
Steven B. Davis
John Morris

Kurt L. Kicklighter
John L. Morrell
Steven H. Kruis
David R. Clark
Jeanne S. Gallagher
M. Cory Brown
Patricia P. Hollenbeck
Thomas P. Sayer, Jr.
James M. Peterson
Greg A. McAtee
Charles V. Berwanger
Susan Moriarty Hack

Bernard L. Kleinke

OF COUNSEL

Ferdinand T. Fletcher

Margaret Anne Payne

SPECIAL COUNSEL

Andrew S. Albert (P.C.)

ASSOCIATES

Martin A. Eliopulos
Phillip C. Samouris
Dolores E. Gonzales
Daniel C. Herbert
Liong Lie Gan Penfield
Jeff G. Harmeyer

Debra G. Kaufman
Michael T. Quinn
James E. Fox
Scott D. Kumpf
Lauren F. Weidner
Peter P. Scott

Representative Clients: Frazee Industries; Kawasaki Motors Corp.; Rohr Industries; Allstate Insurance Co.; Associated Aviation Underwriters; Physicians & Surgeons Insurance Exchange.

For full biographical listings, see the Martindale-Hubbell Law Directory

KING & BALLOW (AV)

2700 Symphony Towers, 750 B Street, 92101
Telephone: 619-236-9401
Fax: 619-236-9437
URL: http://www.king-ballow.com
Nashville, Tennessee Office: 1200 Noel Place, 200 Fourth Avenue, North, 37219.
Telephone: 615-259-3456.
Fax: 615-254-7907.

(See Next Column)

King & Ballow—*Continued*

MEMBERS OF FIRM

Frank S. King, Jr. (Not admitted in CA)	R. Eddie Wayland (Not admitted in CA)
Robert L. Ballow (Not admitted in CA)	Paul H. Duvall (Resident)
Richard C. Lowe (Not admitted in CA)	Mark E. Hunt (Not admitted in CA)
	Lynn Siegel

ASSOCIATES

Leslie E. Lewis	Bruce C. Young

Representative Clients: City of Chula Vista, Chula Vista, California; Ingram Micro, Inc., Santa Ana, California; KNSD-TV, San Diego, California; San Diego Daily Transcript, San Diego, California; Sullivan Graphics, Inc., Brentwood, Tennessee; Union-Tribune Publishing Co., San Diego, California.

For full biographical listings, see the Martindale-Hubbell Law Directory

---

LINDLEY, LAZAR & SCALES, A PROFESSIONAL CORPORATION (AV)

One America Plaza, 600 West Broadway, Suite 1400, 92101-3302
Telephone: 619-234-9181
Fax: 619-234-8475
Email: 104413.1175@compuserve.com

Fred E. Lindley (1876-1971)	Michael H. Wexler
George A. Lazar (1909-1992)	Richard J. Pekin, Jr.
Leon W. Scales (1908-1983)	George C. Lazar
Luke R. Corbett	Raymond L. Heidemann
John M. Seitman	James Henry Fox
Robert M. McLeod	Elise Streicher Rogerson
William E. Johns	R. Gordon Huckins
Stephen F. Treadgold	Kenneth C. Jones

Marc A. Geffen

OF COUNSEL

Maurice T. Watson	Philip P. Martin, Jr.

Representative Clients: Palomar Savings & Loan Assn.; McGraw-Hill Broadcasting Co.; Chicago Title Insurance Co.; San Diego Hospital Assn.; Bank of Commerce; City Chevrolet; Ham Bros. Construction Co.; Commonwealth Land Title Insurance Co.; Ponte Builders; Morrison Homes, Inc.

For full biographical listings, see the Martindale-Hubbell Law Directory

---

LUCE, FORWARD, HAMILTON & SCRIPPS LLP (AV)

A Partnership including Professional Corporations
600 West Broadway, Suite 2600, 92101
Telephone: 619-236-1414
Fax: 619-232-8311
URL: http://www.luce.com
La Jolla, California Office: 4275 Executive Square, Suite 800, 92037.
Telephone: 619-535-2639.
Fax: 619-453-2812.
Los Angeles, California Office: 777 South Figueroa, Suite 3600, 90017.
Telephone: 213-892-4992.
Fax: 213-892-7731.
San Francisco, California Office: 100 Bush Street, 20th Floor, 94104.
Telephone: 415-395-7900.
Fax: 415-395-7949.
New York, N.Y. Office: Citicorp Center, 153 East 53rd Street, 26th Floor, 10022.
Telephone: 212-754-1414.
Fax: 212-644-9727.
Chicago, Illinois Office: 180 North La Salle Street, Suite 1125, 60601.
Telephone: 312-641-0580.
Fax: 312-641-0380.

MEMBERS OF FIRM

Edgar A. Luce (1881-1958)	Mark L. Mann
F. Tudor Scripps, Jr. (1908-1963)	John B. McNeece III
Charles H. Forward (1886-1981)	Robert J. Durham, Jr.
Thomas M. Hamilton (Retired)	Mark Hagarty
Robert G. Steiner	Frederick R. Vandeveer
Gerald S. Davee	Lawrence J. Kouns
John W. Brooks	Mikel R. Bistrow
Steven S. Wall	Margaret M. Mann
Thomas M. Murray	Darryl Steinhause
Ronald W. Rouse	Craig A. Schloss
Charles L. Hellerich	Richard R. Spirra
Jack G. Charney	Vickie E. Turner
Charles A. Bird	Nancy T. Scull
Craig K. Beam	R. William Bowen
Susanne J. Stanford	John W. Leslie
Scott W. Sonne (Managing Partner)	Robert A. Levy
	Mark W. Hansen
Robert J. Bell	Peter H. Klee
G. Edward Arledge	Christopher J. Healey
George S. Howard, Jr.	Thomas A. May
Steven P. McDonald	Stephen T. Toohill
	Mary F. Gillick

(See Next Column)

MEMBERS OF FIRM (Continued)

Robert D. Buell	Jeffrey L. Fillerup (Resident, San Francisco Office)
Daniel N. Riesenberg	Kimball Ann Lane (Resident, New York, N.Y. Office)
Stephen L. Marsh	
Marjorie J. Burchett	Craig R. Brown (Resident, New York, N.Y. Office)
Valentine S. Hoy, VIII	
R. Randal Crispen	Daniel I. Simon (Resident, Los Angeles Office)
Edward Patrick "Pat" Swan, Jr.	
Dennis J. Doucette	Christopher Celentino
Kathryn A. Bernert	Phillip L. Jelsma
Mitchell L. Lathrop (Resident, New York, N.Y. Office)	Timothy R. Pestotnik
	Robert G. Copeland
Terrence L. Bingman	Christopher K. Barnette
Otto E. Sorensen	David M. Hymer
Robert H. Roe	Jeffrey A. Chine
Kathy P. Waring	Cary W. Miller
John L. Riedl	Debra A. Chong (Resident, San Francisco Office)
Jon K. Wactor (Resident, San Francisco Office)	
	Nancy J. Gleason (Resident, Chicago, Illinois Office)
Mary L. Russell	
Rex Heeseman (Resident, Los Angeles Office)	Charles A. Danaher
	William T. Earley
James E. Fitzgerald (Resident, Los Angeles Office)	Roger C. Haerr
	Peter K. Hahn
Andrew J. Waxler (Resident, Los Angeles Office)	Robin Craig-Olson (Resident, San Francisco Office)
Cathy L. Croshaw (Resident, San Francisco Office)	

OF COUNSEL

Michael T. Andrew	Robert E. McGinnis
Stephen R. Brown	Gregory D. Roper
	William A. Yale

SPECIAL COUNSEL

Richard T. Forsyth	Philip J. McGuire (Resident, Chicago, Illinois Office)
Harvey T. Elam (Resident, San Francisco Office)	

ASSOCIATES

Callie A. Bjurstrom	Richard C. Turner
Marc J. Feldman	Christopher H. Findley
Pamela Ewers Wagner	Cindy Dobler Davis
Michael L. Branch	Christine M. Megna (Resident, New York, N.Y. Office)
Teryl Murabayashi (Resident, Los Angeles Office)	
	Helen T. Chao
Kathryn M. S. Catherwood	Philip J. Sullivan
Jane P. Bahnson	Sean C. Sheely (Resident, New York, N.Y. Office)
Carol K. Kao	
Maria C. Heredia	Cathie A. Childs
Valerie R. Cardenas	Ronald D. Getchey
John P. Cooley	Julie A. Vogelzang
Michael G. Fraunces	Christina Bull Arndt (Resident, Los Angeles Office)
Nancy Fuller-Jacobs	
Frank J. Kros	Matthew C. Elstein (Resident, Los Angeles Office)
Roger D. Brown	
James G. Waian	Eric Todd Jorgensen (Resident, Los Angeles Office)
Sonia S. Waisman	
Nancy L. Beattie	Greg R Groeneveld (Resident, Los Angeles Office)
Armin R. Callo	
Roger S. Sampson (Resident, San Francisco Office)	Jana Ford-Harder
	Robert L. Young
James A. Goniea (Resident, San Francisco Office)	Leticia Olivarez Cadena
	Russell A. Gold
Patricia Dee-Bilka (Resident, New York, N.Y. Office)	Blaze D. Waleski (Resident, New York, N.Y. Office)
	Michael G. Ramsey
Joseph F. Bermudez (Resident, New York, N.Y. Office)	Michael A. M. Lauffer
	Gregory H. King (Resident, Los Angeles Office)
Huhnsik Chung (Resident, New York, N.Y. Office)	
	Allan R. Gutkin
Frances J. Phillips (Resident, New York, N.Y. Office)	Marjorie A. Waltrip
	William G. Peterson (Not admitted in CA)
Richard J. Fabian (Resident, New York, N.Y. Office)	
	Deborah A. Primps (Resident, New York, N.Y. Office)
Julie B. Pollack (Resident, New York, N.Y. Office)	
	Patrick J. McGuire (Resident, Chicago, Illinois Office)
Lourdes M. Slater (Resident, New York, N.Y. Office)	
	Jessica Hausknecht (Not admitted in CA)
Lisa J. Greene (Resident, New York, N.Y. Office)	
	Robert C. Thurston (Resident, Chicago, Illinois Office)
Richard J. Bergstrom	
James A. Mercer III	Elizabeth R. Potter
Tami Johnson Penner	Stephanie E. Kish
Kelly Capen Douglas	Brian C. Fish
Bridget Klein Moorhead	Kourosh Vossoughi
John T. Brooks	Steven J. Davis
Lynne D. Kaelin	David J. Smith
Laura L. Jackson (Resident, San Francisco Office)	David N. Ruben (Resident, Los Angeles Office)

For full biographical listings, see the Martindale-Hubbell Law Directory

San Diego—Continued

PAGE, POLIN & BUSCH, A PROFESSIONAL CORPORATION (AV)

350 West Ash Street, Suite 900, 92101-3436
Telephone: 619-231-1822
Fax: 619-231-1877
Fax: 619-231-1875
Email: pagepolin@pagepolin.com

Michael E. Busch	Richard W. Page
Kathleen A. Cashman-Kramer	Kenneth D. Polin
Richard L. Moskitis	Steven G. Rowles

Rod S. Fiori	Michael G. Rowles
Dorothy A. Johnson	(Not admitted in CA)
Jolene L. Parker	Barry M. Taira

For full biographical listings, see the Martindale-Hubbell Law Directory

PILLSBURY MADISON & SUTRO LLP (AV)

101 West Broadway, Suite 1800, 92101
Telephone: 619-234-5000
FAX: 619-236-1995
Costa Mesa, California Office: Plaza Tower, 600 Anton Boulevard, Suite 1100, 92626.
Telephone: 714-436-6800.
Fax: 714-662-6999.
Los Angeles, California Office: Citicorp Plaza, 725 South Figueroa, Suite 1200, 90017.
Telephone: 213-488-7100.
Fax: 213-629-1033.
New York, New York Office: 520 Madison Avenue, 40th Floor, 10022.
Telephone: 212-328-4810.
Fax: 212-328-4824.
Silicon Valley Office: 2700 Sand Hill Road, Menlo Park, 94025.
Telephone: 415-233-4500.
Fax: 415-233-4545.
Sacramento, California Office: 400 Capitol Mall, Suite 1700, 95814.
Telephone: 916-329-4700.
Fax: 916-441-3583.
San Francisco, California Office: 235 Montgomery Street, 94104.
Telephone: 415-983-1000.
Fax: 415-983-1200.
Washington, D.C. Office: 1100 New York Avenue, N.W., Ninth Floor, 20005.
Telephone: 202-861-3000.
Fax: 202-822-0944.
Hong Kong Office: 6/F Asia Pacific Finance Tower, Citibank Plaza, 3 Garden Road, Central.
Telephone: 011-852-2509-7100.
Fax: 011-852-2509-7188.
Tokyo, Japan Office: Pillsbury Madison & Sutro, Gaikokuho Jimu Bengoshi Jimusho, 5th Floor, Samon Eleven Building, 3-1, Samon-cho, Shinjuku-ku, Tokyo 160 Japan.
Telephone: 800-729-9830; 011-813-3354-3531.
Fax: 011-813-3354-3534.

MEMBERS OF FIRM

John M. Dunn	Daniel C. Minteer
P. Garth Gartrell	Patrick C. Shea
Sue J. Hodges	David R. Snyder
David E. Kleinfeld	Jo Ann Taormina
Eric A. Kremer	Douglas R. Tribble
James H. Mayer	Mark R. Wicker

Angela M. Yates

OF COUNSEL

Matthew S. Walker

SENIOR COUNSEL

Eric C. Young

ASSOCIATES

Karen M. Buttemer	Cheryl H. Picker
T. Michael Hird	(Not admitted in CA)
Christopher B. Latham	Richard M. Segal
Laura K. Licht	Daniel S. Silverman
David M. Logan	John E. Timmons
Kimberly A. Mc Donnell	Barry J. Tucker
Daniel P. Murphy	Jan H. Webster
Kathryn L. Partrick	Augustine G. Yee

For full biographical listings, see the Martindale-Hubbell Law Directory

SELTZER CAPLAN WILKINS & MCMAHON, A PROFESSIONAL CORPORATION (AV)

2100 Symphony Towers, 750 B Street, 92101
Telephone: 619-685-3003
Fax: 619-685-3100

Floyd Wilkins, Jr. (Retired)	Gerald L. McMahon
James B. Person (1947-1991)	Reginald A. Vitek
Norman T. Seltzer	James B. Franklin
Robert Caplan	Stephen D. Royer

(See Next Column)

David J. Dorne	Adrienne Jeffrey
James R. Dawe	Daniel A. Andrist
Brian T. Seltzer	J. Scott Scheper
Elizabeth A. Smith	David J. Zubkoff
Julie P. Dubick	Andrew M. Kaplan
Joyce A. McCoy	Elisa A. Brandes
Dennis J. Wickham	Virginia C. Pearson
Frederick J. Stocker	Patricia Garcia
John H. Alspaugh	Gregory E. Flynn
Michael H. Riney	Tamara L. Reed
James P. Delphey	Kelly Rae Waggonner
Craig E. Courter	Lee E. Hejmanowski
Karen M. ZoBell	Christine M. Dabrowski
Elinor T. Merideth	David P. Chiappetta
Michael G. Nardi	Daniel W. Negroni
Thomas F. Steinke	Michael A. Leone
Neal P. Panish	Christopher J. Weaver
Janice Patrice Brown	Laura H. Roppe
Sean T. Hargaden	Margaret Evans
Vera P. Pardee	Genevieve Chesnut
Michael J. Snider	Debra D. B. Deck
Michael R. Seyle	Steven M. Weiss
David S. Minton	Scott W. Sigman
Julie Genthner Simon	Jeffrey A. Junge

Jeanie Mae Branham

OF COUNSEL

Elizabeth C. Eldridge	Patrick Q. Hall
Charles L. Goldberg	John D. Hershberger

Representative Clients: Chicago Title; Girard Savings Bank; Goodyear Tire & Rubber Co.; W.R. Grace & Co.-Conn.; McDonnell-Douglas Corp.; McMillin Communities; Philip Morris Incorporated; Western Financial Savings Bank.

For full biographical listings, see the Martindale-Hubbell Law Directory

THORSNES, BARTOLOTTA, MCGUIRE & PADILLA (AV)

A Partnership including Professional Corporations
Fifth Avenue Financial Center, 11th Floor, 2550 Fifth Avenue, 92103
Telephone: 619-236-9363
Fax: 619-236-9653
Email: TBMP@lawinfo.com *URL:* http://www.tbmp.com

Michael T. Thorsnes (P.C.)	Mitchell S. Golub (P.C.)
Vincent J. Bartolotta, Jr., (P.C.)	Frederic L. Gordon (P.C.)
John F. McGuire (P.C.)	Palma Cesar Hooper (P.C.)
Michael D. Padilla (P.C.)	Neal H. Rockwood (P.C.)
Kevin F. Quinn (P.C.)	Daral B. Mazzarella (P.C.)
C. Brant Noziska (P.C.)	R. Christian Hulburt (P.C.)

ASSOCIATES

Jeffrey F. LaFave	John J. Rice
Stephen D. Lipkin	Robert E. Bright
Rhonda J. Thompson	Douglas J. Billings
Scott A. Kennedy	James T. Atkins

Charles L. Stott

OF COUNSEL

Robert S. Kennedy

For full biographical listings, see the Martindale-Hubbell Law Directory

SAN FRANCISCO,* San Francisco Co.

BAKER & MCKENZIE (AV)

Two Embarcadero Center 24th Floor, 94111-3909
Telephone: (415) 576-3000
Intl. Dialing: (1-415) 576-3000
Cable: ABOGADO
Telex: 278588
Answer Back: 278588 ABOG UR
Facsimiles: (1-415) 576-3099; 576-3098
Associated Offices of Baker & McKenzie in: Almaty, Amsterdam, Bangkok, Barcelona, Beijing, Berlin, Bogotá, Brasília, Brussels, Budapest, Buenos Aires, Cairo, Caracas, Chicago, Dallas, Frankfurt, Geneva, Hanoi, Ho Chi Minh City, Hong Kong, Juárez, Kiev, Lausanne, London, Madrid, Manila, Melbourne, México City, Miami, Milan, Monterrey, Moscow, Münich, New York, Palo Alto, Paris, Prague, Rio de Janeiro, Riyadh, Rome, St. Petersburg, San Diego, Santiago, São Paulo, Singapore, Stockholm, Sydney, Taipei, Tijuana, Tokyo, Toronto, Valencia, Warsaw, Washington, D.C. and Zürich.
Correspondent Law Firm: Hadiputranto, Hadinoto & Partners, Jakarta.

MEMBERS OF FIRM

Michael E. Arruda	John L. Fruth
Russell Baker (1901-1979)	Virginia L. Gibson
Frank S. Bayley	Bruce H. Jackson
Edward D. Burmeister	Dennis Keeley
Klaus H. Burmeister	Jonathan S. Kitchen
Judy V. Davidoff	John F. McKenzie
Howard F. Fine	Timothy A. Tosta

Robert T. Yahng

LOCAL PARTNERS

Peter J. Engstrom	Kent F. Wisner

(See Next Column)

BAKER & McKENZIE—*Continued*

OF COUNSEL

Bonnie K. Levitt

ASSOCIATES

Kathleen Stewart Anderson	Mark J. Jarrett
Edward S. Atkinson, Jr.	Chirag Karia
Bartley B. Baer	Charles V. Moseley
Regine W. Corrado	Tyrrell M. Prosser
Timothy D. Cremin	Richard H. Rahm
Thao H. Cung	Raymond J. Ramsey
Peter R. Denwood	Seth B. Rosen
Valerie Diamond	C. Matthew Schulz
William F. Dietrich	Kerry Shapiro
Rebecca Fruchtman	Joyce Y. Smith
Kim Gelman	Elena V. Speed
Bill O. Hing	A. Alyce Werdel
Maurice L. Hoo	Joyce T. Whitaker

Sharon P. Yau

For full biographical listings, see the Martindale-Hubbell Law Directory

---

BEVERIDGE & DIAMOND (AV)

One Sansome Street, Suite 3400, 94104-4438
Telephone: 415-397-0100
Telecopier: 415-397-4238
Washington, D.C. Office: Beveridge & Diamond, P.C. 1350 I Street, N.W.,
Suite 700, 20005-3311.
Telephone: 202-789-6000.
Telecopier: 202-789-6190.
New York, N.Y. Office: Beveridge & Diamond, P.C. 40th Floor, 437
Madison Avenue, 10022-7380.
Telephone: 212-702-5400.
Telecopier: 212-702-5450.
Fort Lee, New Jersey Office: Suite 400, One Bridge Plaza, 07024-7502.
Telephone: 201-585-8162.
Telecopier: 201-592-7720.

Lawrence S. Bazel	James L. Meeder
David D. Cooke	Daniel J. O'Hanlon
Jennifer L. Hernandez	Gary J. Smith

Robert D. Wyatt

SENIOR ATTORNEY

Eileen M. Nottoli

Stuart I. Block	Kimberly Martin McMorrow
Robert P. Doty	Katherine B. Reilly
Janet C. Loduca	Katherine B. Steuer

Julie K. Walters

For full biographical listings, see the Martindale-Hubbell Law Directory

---

BROBECK, PHLEGER & HARRISON LLP (AV)

A Partnership including a Professional Corporation
Spear Street Tower, One Market, 94105
Telephone: 415-442-0900
Cable Address: "Brobeck"
Telex: 34228 BPH SFO
Facsimile: 415-442-1010
Email: info@brobeck.com *URL:* http://www.brobeck.com
Los Angeles, California Office: 550 South Hope Street.
Telephone: 213-489-4060.
Facsimile: 213-745-3345.
Palo Alto, California Office: Two Embarcadero Place, 2200 Geng Road.
Telephone: 415-424-0160.
Facsimile: 415-496-2885.
San Diego, California Office: 550 West C Street, Suite 1300.
Telephone: 619-234-1966.
Facsimile: 619-236-1403 (13th Floor); 619-234-3848 (12th Floor).
Orange County, California Office: 4675 MacArthur Court, Suite 1000,
Newport Beach.
Telephone: 714-752-7535.
Facsimile: 714-752-7522.
Austin, Texas Office: Brobeck, Phleger & Harrison LLP, 301 Congress
Avenue, Suite 1200.
Telephone: 512-477-5495.
Facsimile: 512-477-5813.
Denver, Colorado Office: Brobeck, Phleger & Harrison LLP, 1125
Seventeenth Street, 25th Floor.
Telephone: 303-293-0760.
Facsimile: 303-299-8819.
New York, N.Y. Office: Brobeck, Phleger & Harrison LLP, 1633
Broadway, 47th Floor.
Telephone: 212-581-1600.
Facsimile: 212-586-7878.
Brobeck Hale and Dorr International Office:
London, England Office: Veritas House, 125 Finsbury Pavement, London
EC2A 1NQ.
Telephone: 44 071 638 6688.
Facsimile: 44 071 638 5888.

(See Next Column)

CHAIRMAN

Stephen M. Snyder

MANAGING PARTNER

Cecily A. Waterman

MEMBERS OF FIRM

Grady M. Bolding	Scott D. Lester
Donald J. Bouey	F. Daniel Leventhal
William S. Boyd	William A. Levin
Sara B. Brody	Robert C. Livsey
David J. Brown	Robert N. Lowry
Donald W. Brown	Mark E. McKeen
James E. Burns, Jr.	Roderick A. McLeod
John E. Carlson	Timothy A. Meltzer
Rollin B. Chippey, II	James L. Miller
Roy E. Crawford, III	John B. Missing
Robert S. Daggett	Michael E. Molland
Susan R. Diamond	Ronald B. Moskovitz
Brendan G. Dolan	Kevin P. Muck
Rebecca D. Eisen	James N. Penrod
G. Larry Engel	Thomas M. Peterson
Gary S. Fergus	Barbara Pletcher
Vincent P. Finigan, Jr.	James H. Quirk
Stephen R. Finn	Laura J. Remington
Kevin B. Fisher	Diane S. Rice
Tom M. Freeman	Kent M. Roger
Anthony O. Garvin	J. Michael L. Shepherd
A. Bruce Gilmore	Douglas D. Smith
Lawrence J. Gornick	Tower C. Snow, Jr.
Franklin Brockway Gowdy	John E. Sparks
William B. Griffin	Michael P. Stanley
Max Gutierrez, Jr.	W. Scott Thomas
George A. Hisert	Michael D. Torpey
Frederick D. Holden, Jr.	William E. Trautman
Barry W. Homer	George D. Tuttle
William L. Hudson	Douglas G. Van Gessel
William R. Irwin	Robert P. Varian
Karen Johnson-McKewan	L. Christopher Vejnoska
Eric W. Jorgensen	Nicholas B. Waranoff
Jeffrey S. Kingston	Thomas A. Welch

Kelly C. Wooster

SENIOR COUNSEL

Caleb J. (Jeff) Brinton, IV	Karen H. Peteros
Jayne Loughry	Tracy Thompson

OF COUNSEL

Hamilton W. Budge	Jean C. Gaskill
Wiebke L. Buxbaum	Ivan M. Gold
Peter C. Coleman	J. Stewart Harrison
(Not admitted in CA)	Edward E. Kallgren
John J. Corrigan	David N. Lillevand, Jr.
George T. Cronin	Neil C. Ludman
Gordon E. Davis	Eileen M. Malley
E. Judge Elderkin	John D. Muller
Marilyn Fisher	Alvin J. Rockwell

Hart H. Spiegel

ASSOCIATES

Paul R. Bessette	Kahala J. Lee
V. Elise Bigelow	James A. Lico
Mark H. Boxer	Thomas J. Lima
John A. Burke	Gregory L. Lippetz
Bridget A. Clarke	Renée T. Machi
Delphine S. Damon	Pamela B. Marostica
David Daniels	Richard Marquez
David F. Dedyo	Carrie M. McIntyre
Joshua S. Evett	Nikki S. McKennedy
Lisa Feldman	Leslie McKnew
Samuel J. Fleischmann	Amy M. McNamer
Jeff B. Furchtenicht	Eric Meckley
Barbara Skaggs Gallagher	Andrea Syran Meghrouni-Brown
David R. Gilbert	Amy Anne Meldrum
Theodore Goldin	Rachael E. Meny
Michael A. Graham	Lauren M. Michals
Michael B. Green	Rosalyn P. Mitchell
Christina M. Greenway	Lisa J. Morelli
Mortimer H. Hartwell	Janet J. Mullinax
Renata Bianca Hesse	Patrick T. Murphy
Edith M. Hofmeister	Michael J. Penner
Howard Holderness III	Jon C. Perry
Otto C. Holz	Peter M. Phleger
Valerie J. Horwitz	Michael F. Potter
Elizabeth A. Howard	Margo N. Rabinovitz
Rolf B. Johnson	A. Michelle Ramirez
Jeffrey A. Kaiser	Keith M. Roberts
Roberto J. Kampfner	Robyn Diane Roberts
Scott D. Karchmer	Shari Sacks
(Not admitted in CA)	Véronique Sanchez Scalzo
Elizabeth M. Khachgian	Amy E. Scheffler
Elizabeth M. Khachigian	Robert C. Sepucha Jr.
Stephen M. Knaster	Peter V. Shackter
Randall Lake	Daniel P. Shenkman
Molly Moriarty Lane	Michelle Sicula
Jeanine Marie Larrea	Erika B. Smith

(See Next Column)

BROBECK, PHLEGER & HARRISON LLP, San Francisco—Continued

ASSOCIATES (Continued)

Jennifer E. Smith	Kay Tittle
Craig C. Stevens	Dana P. Veeder
Teresa L. Stricker	Susan P. Vomund
Wendy Theophilos	David E. Weiss
Tamara L. Thompson	Isabella A. Whitaker

Michael A. Zuercher

CONTRACT ATTORNEY

Judy Lynn Paraventi

For full biographical listings, see the Martindale-Hubbell Law Directory

BRONSON, BRONSON & MCKINNON LLP (AV)

A Partnership including Professional Corporations
505 Montgomery Street, 94111-2514
Telephone: 415-986-4200
Fax: 415-982-1394
Telex: 255921 KINBR UR
Email: moreinfo@bronson.com *URL:* http://www.bronson.com
Los Angeles, California Office: 444 South Flower Street, 24th Floor.
Telephone: 213-627-2000.
San Jose, California Office: 10 Almaden Boulevard, Suite 600.
Telephone: 408-293-0599.

MEMBERS OF FIRM

Michael H. Ahrens	Maureen McQuaid
Richard A. Ardoin	Julia A. Molander
Jack Berman (1957-1993)	A. John Murphy, Jr.
Lynn A. Bersch	Leo J. Murphy, Jr.
Alexander L. Brainerd	William H. G. Norman
E. D. Bronson (1893-1976)	William P. O'Connell, Jr.
Roy A. Bronson (1889-1977)	Robert N. Phillips
Lawrence M. Cirelli	Terrence V. Ponsford
Zela G. Claiborne	Mary Eileen Reilley
Carlyn Clause	Stan G. Roman
Ronald K. Clausen	Donald P. Rubenstein
Bonnie R. Cohen	Richard A. Saffir
Robert W. Crockett	Jay P. Sanders
Patricia H. Cullison	Paul J. Sanner
Edwin L. Currey, Jr.	Charles Schug
Gilmore F. Diekmann, Jr.	Janine S. Simerly
Grant P. DuBois (1937-1990)	Thomas H. Sloan, Jr.
Stephen H. Dye	Madeleine E. Sloane
David Eiseman	Kymberly E. Speer
Frederick S. Fields	Richard J. Stratton
Robert C. Gebhardt	Robert J. Stumpf
Heidi Kohn Hugo	Craig Stuppi
Lawrence R. Katzin	Sarah M. Stuppi
Bernard C. Kearns (1930-1987)	T. Scott Tate
Kenneth E. Keller	Stephen C. Tausz (1946-1989)
James C. Krieg	Robert William Tollen
William T. Manierre	Michele K. Trausch
Joseph G. Mason	Richard P. Walker
Harold R. McKinnon	Keith R. Weed
(1894-1977)	

OF COUNSEL

Joan B. Breen	Rongjie Ma
John W. Carr	John H. Sears
Elizabeth A. England	Charles W. Tuckman
Marvin M. Grove	Max Weingarten

RESIDENT ASSOCIATES

Albert P. Bedecarre	Craig A. Livingston
Greg Boller	Ellen F. McDonald
Raymond A. Chenault	Paul R. Mohun
Kristina H. Chung	Debora A. Morrison
Erika C. Collins	Patricia J. Porter
Richard C. Darwin	Nancy N. Potter
Adam M. Dodek	Jeffrey K. Rehfeld
Cheryl M.L. Doo	(Not admitted in CA)
Jason A. Doren	Linda B. Ross
Clifford J. Gleicher	Susan L. Sakmar
Carl R. Goldberg	Abraham A. Simmons
Anne M. Lawlor Goyette	Timothy C. Smith
Julie C. Grollmus Gruber	Ann C. Springgate
Andrea L. Hackett	Christopher J. Sundermeier
Mary Bossart Halfpenny	Steven H. Winick

Jennifer R. Woods

For full biographical listings, see the Martindale-Hubbell Law Directory

BUCHALTER, NEMER, FIELDS & YOUNGER, A PROFESSIONAL CORPORATION (AV)

29th Floor, 333 Market Street, 94105
Telephone: 415-227-0900
Fax: 415-227-0770
Email: buchalter@earthlink.net *URL:* http://www.buchalter.com
Los Angeles, California Office: 24th Floor, 601 South Figueroa Street.
Telephone: 213-891-0700.
Fax: 213-896-0400.

(See Next Column)

New York, New York Office: 15th Floor, 605 Third Avenue.
Telephone: 212-490-8600.
Fax: 212-490-6022.
Newport Beach, California Office: Suite 1450, 620 Newport Center Drive.
Telephone: 714-760-1121.
Fax: 714-720-0182.

Roxani M. Gillespie	Robert E. Izmirian
Richard de Saint Phalle	James B. Wright
William McC. Wright	Peter G. Bertrand
Gary Nemer	Shawn M. Christianson

OF COUNSEL

Jared A. Goldin	Robert A. Zadek

Stephen W. Sommerhalter	Aron Mark Oliner
Denise H. Field	Mark C. Goodman
Mary E. Jameson (Resident)	Marie G. Quashnock
David C. Powell	Ethan Allen Miller
Dennis D. Miller	Marlene I. Camacho
Mark G. Crawford	David M. Serepca
David Sturgeon-Garcia	Elizabeth A. Fox

K. Todd Shollenbarger

References: City National Bank; Wells Fargo Bank; Metrobank.

For full biographical listings, see the Martindale-Hubbell Law Directory

COOLEY GODWARD LLP (AV)

20th Floor, One Maritime Plaza, 94111
Telephone: 415-693-2000
Telex: 380815 COOLEY SFO
Fax: 415-951-3698 or 415-951-3699
Email: webmaster@cooley.com *URL:* http://www.cooley.com
Palo Alto, California Office: Five Palo Alto Square, 3000 El Camino Real.
Telephone: 415-843-5000.
Telex: 380816 COOLEY PA.
Fax: 415-857-0663.
Menlo Park, California Office: 3000 Sand Hill Road, Building 3 Suite 230.
Telephone: 415-843-5000.
Telex: 380816 COOLEY PA.
Fax: 415-854-2691.
Boulder, Colorado Office: 2595 Canyon Boulevard, Suite 250.
Telephone: 303-546-4000.
Fax: 303-546-4099.
San Diego, California Office: 4365 Executive Drive, Suite 1100.
Telephone: 619-550-6000.
Fax: 619-453-3555.
Denver, Colorado Office: One Tabor Center, 1200 17th Street, Suite 2100.
Telephone: 303-606-4800.
Fax: 303-606-4899.

MEMBERS OF FIRM

Augustus Castro (1911-1995)	William G. Gaede, III
Edwin E. Huddleson, Jr.	James C. Gaither
(1914-1995)	Kenneth L. Guernsey
Arthur E. Cooley (1882-1972)	J. Michael Kelly
Louis V. Crowley (1887-1971)	Karen J. Kubin
H. Rowan Gaither, Jr.	Paul J. Laveroni
(1909-1961)	Samuel M. Livermore
Thomas A. H. Hartwell	Lance Director Nagel
(1927-1990)	Susan Cooper Philpot
Andrew Kopperud (1924-1973)	Paul A. Renne
Kenneth J. Adelson	James A. Richman
Gordon C. Atkinson	Benjamin K. Riley
John L. Cardoza	Joseph P. Russoniello
Peter H. Carson	Joseph A. Scherer
Paul Churchill	Myron G. Sugarman
John W. Crittenden	Michael Traynor
Robert L. Eisenbach III	Christopher A. Westover
Howard G. Ervin, III	Vernon M. Winters
Daniel W. Frank	John F. Young
Richard H. Frank	Jeffrey S. Zimman

OF COUNSEL

William W. Godward	Erving Sodos
Paul M. Little	Frank D. Tatum, Jr.

SPECIAL COUNSEL

Cydney S. Posner	Sandra B. Price

Paul Startz

ASSOCIATES

Jodie M. Bourdet	Phillip Kirk Hobbs
Deborah L. Budach	Kathleen A. Howard
Thea M. Chester	Noel C. Johnson
Ann Chiga	Isobel Ann Jones
Jamie E. Chung	Tracy S. Kaplan
Christina G. Cordoza	Marina Landau
Bradley C. Crawford	Felice P. Liang
James Donato	Jeffrey T. Lindgren
Nancy E. Egan	Martin J. Lobdell
Kimberly D. Fanning	Bradley P. MacMillin
Eric R. Fleming	Alice A. McTighe
Steven L. Friedlander	Ann M. Mooney
Yvonne Gonzalez-Rogers	Quang D. Nguyen
Philip M. Guess	Laura M. Randall

(See Next Column)

COOLEY GODWARD LLP—*Continued*

ASSOCIATES (Continued)

Charles M. Schaible	Rita E. Tautkus
Randi Silverman	Mitchell R. Truelock
Karyn R. Smith	John W. Vander Vort
Anita F. Stork	James R. Vidano
Christopher E. Stretch	Patrick Walravens
Alan Tafapolsky	Kathryn M. Wheble
(Not admitted in CA)	(Not admitted in CA)

LEGAL SUPPORT PERSONNEL

ADMINISTRATOR

Susan Y. Chen-Wong

SENIOR PARALEGALS

Tomoko T. Flynn	Laura D. Herrera

For full biographical listings, see the Martindale-Hubbell Law Directory

---

FABRIS, BURGESS & RING, A PROFESSIONAL CORPORATION (AV)

456 Montgomery Street, Suite 1800, 94104
Telephone: 415-982-6393
Fax: 415-982-2429

Alvin J. Fabris (1912-1983)	Barri Kaplan Bonapart
David D. Ring	James H. Duncan, Jr.
Joseph I. Burgess	Deborah Daniloff
Edward F. Mitchell	Karen M. Porter

Kevin A. Mills

LEGAL SUPPORT PERSONNEL

PARALEGALS

Susan E. R. Parker	Katherine A. O'Connell
Noah Hawley	

For full biographical listings, see the Martindale-Hubbell Law Directory

---

FELDMAN, WALDMAN & KLINE, A PROFESSIONAL CORPORATION (AV)

3 Embarcadero Center, Suite 2800, 94111
Telephone: 415-981-1300
Fax: 415-981-1350
Email: info@fwk.com
Stockton, California Office: Sperry Building, 146-148 West Weber Avenue.
Telephone: 209-943-2004.
Fax: 209-943-0905.

Murry J. Waldman	Martha Jeanne Shaver
Leland R. Selna, Jr.	(Resident, Stockton Office)
Michael L. Korbholz	Robert Cedric Goodman
Howard M. Wexler	Laura Grad
Patricia S. Mar	William F. Adams
Kenneth W. Jones	Elizabeth A. Thompson
Paul J. Dion	Julie A. Jones
Vern S. Bothwell	David L. Kanel
L.J. Chris Martiniak	Abram S. Feuerstein
Linda Sorensen	

Laura J. Dawson	Dana A. Suntag
Joanne M. Lafreniere	(Resident, Stockton Office)
Paul A. Weiss	Danielle Ochs-Tillotson

OF COUNSEL

Richard L. Jaeger	Gerald A. Sherwin
	(Resident, Stockton Office)

For full biographical listings, see the Martindale-Hubbell Law Directory

---

FOLGER LEVIN & KAHN LLP (AV)

Embarcadero Center West, 275 Battery Street, 23rd Floor, 94111
Telephone: 415-986-2800
FAX: 415-986-2827
Los Angeles, California Office: 28th Floor, 1900 Avenue of the Stars.
Telephone: 310-556-3700.
FAX: 310-556-3770.

MEMBERS OF FIRM

John P. Levin	Margaret R. Dollbaum
Peter M. Folger	James Goldberg
Michael A. Kahn	Lisa McCabe van Krieken
Donald E. Kelley, Jr.	Gregory D. Call
Thomas P. Laffey	Janice B. Lawrence
Scott W. Bowen	Susan W. Ansberry
Samuel R. Miller	Thomas F. Koegel
Mary C. Castle	Katharine Livingston
Richard Keenan	Adam Sachs
Roger B. Mead	Wesley D. Hurst
Douglas W. Sullivan	J. Daniel Sharp
Teressa K. Lippert	Margaret E. Murray

(See Next Column)

ASSOCIATES

Deborah Harrawood	Theresa A. Nagle
Charles R. Perry	Karen Jensen Petrulakis
Brian C. Bunger	Jennifer L. Wright
Christopher B. Conner	Kelvin T. Wyles
M. Kay Martin	Robert A. McFarlane
Julie M. Kennedy	Beatrice B. Nguyen
Roland Valayre	Ernst A. Halperin
Frieda A. Taylor	Jessica M. Karner
Kenneth R. Hillier	Kimberly A. Simpson
Theresa I. McFarland	Nancy E. Yaffe
Michael F. Kelleher	Lynne S. Bourgault
Raquel L. Wilkening	Stuart J. Mackey
G. Jiyun Lee	Maxwell S. Peltz
Angela C. Miller	

For full biographical listings, see the Martindale-Hubbell Law Directory

---

GRAHAM & JAMES LLP (AV)

One Maritime Plaza, Suite 300, 94111
Telephone: 415-954-0200
Cable Address: "Chalgray"
Telex: WU 340143; WUI 67565
Telecopier: 415-391-2493
Email: mlevin@gj.com *URL:* http://www.gj.com
Other offices located in: Los Angeles, Orange County, Palo Alto, Sacramento and Fresno, California; Seattle, Washington; Washington, D.C.; New York, New York; Milan, Italy; Beijing, China; Tokyo, Japan; London, England; Dusseldorf, Germany.
Associated Offices: Deacons Graham & James, Hong Kong, Sydney, Melbourne, Brisbane, Perth and Canberra, Australia.
Affiliated Offices: Deacons Graham & James, Hanoi and Ho Chi Minh City, Vietnam; Taipei, Taiwan and Bangkok, Thailand; In association with Dewi Soeharto & Rekan, Jakarta, Indonesia; Graham & James in affiliation with Taylor Joynson Garrett, London, England, Bucharest, Romania and Brussels, Belgium; Mishare M. Al-Ghazali & Partners, Safat, Kuwait; Law Firm of Salah Al-Hejailan, Jeddah and Riyadh, Saudi Arabia.

Bruce W. Belding	Michael D. Levin
David V. Biesemeyer	David M. Lofholm
John L. Boos	Lawrence B. Low
David Colker	Nancy Lundeen
Eric M. Danoff	Douglas D. Mancill
Mark C. Dosker	Martin A. Mattes
Jill Feldman	Caroline H. Mead
Diane L. Gibson	Michael R. Moyle
Peter W. Hanschen	Rodney R. Patula
Kevin Hobgood-Brown	Andrew I. Port
Bruce W. Hyman	Susan M. Reid
David R. Johanson	Thomas F. Smegal, Jr.
Kent Jonas	Lisa Petricone Sullivan
David C. Kenny	James E. Topinka
James P. Kleier	Gilda R. Turitz
Michael Kross	Nicholas Unkovic
Nathan Lane III	Thomas H. Woofter
Philip R. Zender	

OF COUNSEL

Alexander D. Calhoun	F. Conger Fawcett
Thomas Y. Yasuda	

ASSOCIATES

Julie A. Aguilar	Ellen A. O'Donnell
Maureen Bennett	Angela Lauer Polk
Janine D. Bloch	Yvonne P. Ranieri
Mark S. Burton	Jennifer J. Sam
Carrie M. Callaway	Serafina Sands
Priscilla J. Cortez	Noriyuki Shimoda
Quoc-Hay D. Do	Michael E. Sobel
Spencer M. Gusick	Kevin E. Solliday
Remsen M. Kinne, IV	Eric Stein
Warren P. Kujawa	Kristen J. Thorsness
Cheree L. McAlpine	Kenneth C. Webster
Robert M. Monti	Elizabeth A. Willes
Victor C. Murphy	Alisa Won

For full biographical listings, see the Martindale-Hubbell Law Directory

---

HANCOCK ROTHERT & BUNSHOFT LLP (AV)

10th Floor, Four Embarcadero Center, 94111-4168
Telephone: 415-981-5550
Telecopy: 415-955-2599
Los Angeles, California Office: 17th Floor, 515 South Figueroa Street, 90071-3334.
Telephone: 213-623-7777.
Telecopy: 213-623-5405.
Tahoe City, California Office: Lighthouse Center, 850 North Lake Boulevard, Suite 15, P.O. Box 7199, 96145-7199.
Telephone: 916-583-7767.
Telecopy: 916-581-3215.

(See Next Column)

HANCOCK ROTHERT & BUNSHOFT LLP, *San Francisco—Continued*

London Office: Forum House, 15/18 Lime Street, Sixth Floor, London EC3M 7AP, England.
Telephone: 071-220-7567.
Telecopy: 071-220-7609.
Associated Office: Staiger, Schwald & Sauter. Genferstrasse 24, 8002 Zurich, Switzerland.
Telephone: 01-282-8686.
Telecopy: 01-283-8787.
Telex: 813-273-GND.

MEMBERS OF FIRM

Barry L. Bunshoft	W. Andrew Miller
George L. Waddell	Michael L. Donovan
James P. Barber	William J. Casey
Paul D. Nelson	Eric J. Sinrod
Aubin K. Barthold	Nancy B. Ranney
Richard L. Seabolt	Brian A. Kelly
Patrick A. Cathcart	Dominica Cortum Anderson
(Resident, Los Angeles Office)	Paul J. Killion
Patricia Shuler Schimbor	Devin F. O'Brien
(Resident, Los Angeles Office)	Michael A. Gevertz
Philip R. Matthews	Lisa J. Evans
Ray L. Wong	Daniel J. Crawford
David L. Suddendorf	Peter J. Koenig
Earl J. Imhoff, Jr.	Peter J. Whalen
(Resident, Los Angeles Office)	Yvette D. Roland
Deborah Pitts	(Resident, Los Angeles Office)
(Resident, Los Angeles Office)	Marc J. Derewetzky
Paul S. Rosenlund	(Resident, Los Angeles Office)
Robert C. Hendrickson	William J. Baron
Ernest J. Beffel, Jr.	Robert V. Richter
Andrew K. Gordon	(Resident, Los Angeles Office)
Ronald E. Ruma	Douglas T. Gneiser
Vito C. Peraino	Mary L. Guilfoyle
(Resident, Los Angeles Office)	William K. Enger
John E. Fagan	(Resident, Los Angeles Office)
(Resident, Tahoe City Office)	David J. Potkul

SENIOR COUNSEL

Albert I. Moon, Jr.	L. Savannah Lichtman
(Resident, Los Angeles Office)	

ASSOCIATES

Stephanie L. Choy	Melissa M. Harnett
Kenneth D. Ayers	(Resident, Los Angeles Office)
Andrea J. Schoeneman	Laura A. Pace
Mark D. Tokunaga	(Resident, Los Angeles Office)
(Resident, Tahoe City Office)	Charles M. Fontana
M. Elisabeth Huettner	Paul F. Donsbach
Linda B. Carr	Beth Pennington
(Resident, Los Angeles Office)	John T. Clappison
Brian Gearinger	Lisa Ann Mango
Mark A. Robbins	Monica M. Slakey
(Resident, Los Angeles Office)	Charles E. Webb
Colleen A. Cassidy	Eve F. Lynch
Eileen M. Hansen	Kelli Andrew Close-Smith
Reginald D. Davis	(Resident, London, England
Heidi Honora Frenzel	Office)
Jonathan U. Lee	Frank A. Yokoyama
Kelly Lynn Quigley	(Resident, Los Angeles Office)
Lorraine P. Ocheltree	Jennifer D. McKee
Jennifer A. Vane	(Resident, Los Angeles Office)
(Resident, Los Angeles Office)	John E. Breen
Patricio T.D. Barrera	(Resident, Los Angeles Office)
(Resident, Los Angeles Office)	Brian T. Hafter
Mary Cavins Anderson	Samantha Mitty
Joan N. D'Ambrosio	Bruce J. Rome
Katherine A. Knopoff	Stephen H. Sutro
Suzanne Ryder Fogarty	Stephen D. Gillespie
Maximilian H. Stern	Daniel W. Nugent
David A. Greene	(Resident, Los Angeles Office)
Vipal J. Patel	B. Otis Felder
(Resident, Los Angeles Office)	(Resident, Los Angeles Office)
Dominique R. Shelton	Peter T. Imhof
(Resident, Los Angeles Office)	(Resident, Los Angeles Office)
John R. Garnett	Julie A. Porte-Vega
John L. Slebir	Steven C. Uribe
David A. Gabianelli	(Resident, Los Angeles Office)
Joseph P. Collins	Louisa G. Weix
(Resident, Tahoe City Office)	Christopher J. Keene
Arthur J. Friedman	(Resident, Los Angeles Office)
Kevin M. Haithcox	Thomas S. Kim
Merton A. Howard	Jennifer L. Pruski
Sarah K. Chang	(Resident, Tahoe City Office)
R. Christopher Rhody	Jennifer Zelikson
(Resident, Los Angeles Office)	

For full biographical listings, see the Martindale-Hubbell Law Directory

HANSON, BRIDGETT, MARCUS, VLAHOS & RUDY, LLP (AV)

23rd Floor, 333 Market Street, 94105
Telephone: 415-777-3200
Facsimile: 415-541-9366
Telex: 6502628734 MCI
Email: hanson@hbmvr.com

MEMBERS OF FIRM

Raymond L. Hanson	Allan D. Jergesen
(1912-1996)	Kim T. Schoknecht
Gerald D. Marcus	Robert L. Rusky
John J. Vlahos	Bonnie Kathleen Gibson
Sidney Rudy	Howard W. Ashcraft, Jr.
William J. Bush	Joel S. Goldman
Ronald C. Peterson	Rory J. Campbell
Richard N. Rapoport	Jacquelyn J. Garman
David J. Miller	David W. Baer
Laurence W. Kessenick	Madeline Chun
Ray E. McDevitt	Lora J. Thielbar
Douglas H. Barton	Linda E. Klamm
Jerrold C. Schaefer	Paul F. Goldsmith
James D. Holden	Peter Dmytryk
Paul A. Gordon	Jane Siegel Woodside
Michael A. Duncheon	Susan G. O'Neill
William D. Taylor	Patrick M. Glenn
Fred B. Weil	W. Daniel Clinton
Craig J. Cannizzo	David C. Longinotti
Steven V. Schnier	Pamela S. Kaufmann
Theodore A. Hellman	Diane Marie O'Malley
Kevin M. O'Donnell	Jeffrey M. Chu
Stephen L. Taber	Michael N. Conneran
Joan L. Cassman	Matthew J. Dulka
Stephen B. Peck	Jonathan S. Storper

Lee Ann M. La France

ASSOCIATES

William A. Hickey	Philip E. Fagone
Steven J. Levine	Sandra L. Rappaport
Lynn Tracy Nerland	Lisa K. Puntillo
Andrew G. Giacomini	Bettina E. Moore
Debra L. Watanuki	Eric V. Tao
James A. Napoli	Allison M. Woodall
Patrick T. Miyaki	Glenda M. Zarbock
Dana B. Wolf	Amy R. Ratner
Charles L. Thompson IV	Rosy H. Cho
Laura L. Hauck	Leah S. Goldberg
Lisa M. Pooley	Walter R. Schneider
Michael B. McNaughton	Carole R. Rossi
Amy L. Brown	Jennifer Bergstrom
Meredith E. Brown	Gilson S. Riecken

Janet Lee

OF COUNSEL

Arthur T. Bridgett (Retired)	John W. Broad
Jack P. Wong	Ted Carleton Krumland
Daniel W. Baker	Sarah D. Mott
Robert E. Simms	Peter Franck

Gary T. Giacomini

Representative Clients: Blue Cross and Blue Shield Assn.; Blue Diamond Growers; California Association of Homes for the Aging; CH2M Hill; Consolidated Freightways; Golden Gate Bridge; Levi Strauss & Co.; Santa Cruz Medical Clinic; University of California; Wells Fargo Bank, N.A.

For full biographical listings, see the Martindale-Hubbell Law Directory

LAW OFFICES OF CHRISTOPHER HAYS (AV)

580 California Street, Suite 1500, 94104
Telephone: 415-398-0848
Facsimile: 415-982-6700

OF COUNSEL

Louise M. Quintard

For full biographical listings, see the Martindale-Hubbell Law Directory

JACKSON TUFTS COLE & BLACK, LLP (AV)

A Registered Limited Liability Partnership
650 California Street Thirty-Second Floor, 94108
Telephone: 415-433-1950
Fax: 415-392-3494
Email: info@jtcb.com
San Jose, California Office: 60 South Market Street, 10th Floor.
Telephone: 408-998-1952.
Fax: 408-998-4889.

MEMBERS OF FIRM

Bartlett A. Jackson (A	Carl J. Stoney, Jr.
Professional Corporation)	Kenneth J. Philpot
Robert R. Tufts	Michael J. Baker
George H. Cole, Jr.	David Ayers Thompson
J. David Black	Ellen McGinty King
Templeton C. Peck	Peter S. Muñoz
Charles G. Stephenson	Dennis V. Swanson
John S. Siamas	Debra S. Belaga
David T. Alexander	Emil G. Pesiri

(See Next Column)

JACKSON TUFTS COLE & BLACK LLP—*Continued*

MEMBERS OF FIRM (Continued)

D. D. Hughmanick	Martin S. Schenker
William H. Booth	Michael F. McCabe
Twila L. Foster	Debra L. Kasper
Nicole A. Dillingham	Paul H. Goldstein
George R. Theofel	Lynn M. McLean
Jeffrey J. Cole	Jane M. Hawkins
Roy M. Bartlett, Jr.	Patrick S. Hallinan
Richard Scudellari	Lynn Acker Starr
Donna M. Mezias	Stephen M. Debenham

Shane M. Byrne

OF COUNSEL

Eric T. Sullivan	Gerald Z. Marer
Wayne W. Lew	Breck E. Milde

Jesse W. Markham, Jr.

ASSOCIATES

Marily Peatman Lerner	Marion C. Ingersoll
Robert G. White	Ki D. Ingersol
Gretchen Dean Hug	Elizabeth A. Barton
Benjamin B. Quinones	Erin L. McPherson
Eric S. Walters	Jason W. Kuhns
Steven N. Sherr	Joseph M. Quinn, III
John J. Sciortino	Jonathan M. Eisenberg
Daniel L. Rabago	Anne Hayes Hartman
Amy E. Margolin	Mark A. Sheft

For full biographical listings, see the Martindale-Hubbell Law Directory

---

LANDELS, RIPLEY & DIAMOND, LLP (AV)

Hills Plaza, 350 The Embarcadero, 94105
Telephone: 415-512-8700
Fax: 415-512-8750

MEMBERS OF FIRM

Edward D. Landels (1899-1991)	Robert J. Breakstone
Earl M. Ripley (Retired)	Michael H. Zischke
Philip E. Diamond (Retired)	Margaret Hart Edwards
John H. Bickel	Howard A. Simon
Yaroslav Sochynsky	Beth Aboulafia
James A. Bruen	Daniel W. McGovern
Jon Enscoe	Neil L. Shapiro
Stephen C. Lewis	Stafford Matthews
Richard C. Coffin	Kathleen M. Meagher
Bruce W. Laidlaw	R. Morgan Gilhuly
Geoffrey M. Dugan	Preston P. DuFauchard, Jr.
Thomas D. Trapp	Paul P. Spaulding, III
Deborah J. Schmall	Peter C. Pang
John F. Barg	Peter S. Modlin
Deborah K. Miller	Jennifer G. Redmond
Paul Zieff	Melinda L. Haag
Scott D. Rogers	Burton F. Boltuch
R. Christopher Locke	Theodore A. Griffinger, Jr.
Matthew J. Geyer	Karen A. Cook
Gregory L. Germain	Stewart H. Foreman
Beth S. Jordan	Jonathan A. Funk
Sanford Svetcov	Peter S. Fishman
Robert L. Hines	Jonathan Polland
Brian S. Haughton	Dinah L. Szander
Raymond F. Lynch	John D. Fiero
Deborah K. Tellier	Mark J. Klaiman

Michele S. Benson	Amy L. Keyser
Ligi Coleen Yee	Davina Pujari
Barbara Cohen Stikker	Steven R. Charno
Deborah C. Brown	Richard S. Winer
Mark D. Johnson	Robert L. Wishner
Ross D. Tillman	Alison J. Morbey
James H. Colopy	M.D. Moye
Chad D. Naylor	Ted Stevens
Ariana N. Sarabia	Matthew Paul

Helen H. Surh

Representative Clients: Bank of America; California Mortgage Bankers Association; Catellus Development Corp.; General Electric Co.; Metropolitan Life Insurance Co.; Occidental Petroleum Corp.; Sega of America; Union Oil Co.; WMX Technologies, Inc.; Weyerhauser Corp.

For full biographical listings, see the Martindale-Hubbell Law Directory

---

LELAND, PARACHINI, STEINBERG, FLINN, MATZGER & MELNICK, L.L.P. (AV)

27th Floor, 333 Market Street, 94105
Telephone: 415-957-1800
FAX: 415-974-1520
Los Angeles, California Office: 500 South Grand Avenue, Suite 1100.
Telephone: 213-623-7505;
Fax: 213-623-7595

Herbert A. Leland (1907-1984)

(See Next Column)

PARTNERS

James M. Allen	Paul J. Matzger
Nick A. Boodrookas	David H. Melnick
David B. Flinn	Teresa Viskovich Pahl
Harvey L. Gould	Donald G. Parachini
Nina P. Kwan	Merrill E. Steinberg
Steven B. Mains	Neil E. Taxy

Kenneth R. Wachtel

ASSOCIATES

N.L. Rafferty Atha	Lissa L. Rapoport
Christopher J. Donnelly	Adam P. Siegman
Christopher J. Hunter	Anna M. Simmons
Craig A. Kepler	Michael L. Violanti

Peter K. Wolff, Jr.

OF COUNSEL

David J. Block	Gayle Nin Rosenkrantz

Stephan R. Silen

For full biographical listings, see the Martindale-Hubbell Law Directory

---

LITTLER, MENDELSON, FASTIFF, TICHY & MATHIASON, A PROFESSIONAL CORPORATION (AV)

650 California Street, 20th Floor, 94108
Telephone: 415-433-1940
Facsimile: 415-399-8490
URL: http://www.littler.com
Offices located in: California -- Bakersfield, Fresno, Long Beach, Los Angeles, Menlo Park, Oakland, Sacramento, San Diego, San Jose, Santa Maria, Santa Rosa and Stockton; Denver, Colorado; Washington, D.C.; Atlanta, Georgia; Baltimore, Maryland; Reno and Las Vegas, Nevada (a partnership with the Law Offices of Hicks & Walt); Morristown, New Jersey; New York, New York; and Dallas and Houston, Texas.

Arthur Mendelson (Retired)	Michele J. Silak
Wesley J. Fastiff	Karen E. Ford
George J. Tichy, II	Judy S. Coffin
J. Richard Thesing	Wendy L. Tice-Wallner
Allen W. Teagle	Joseph A. Schwachter
Robert M. Lieber	Steven B. Berlin
Jordan L. Bloom	Lindbergh Porter, Jr.
Garry G. Mathiason	Patricia A. Shepherd
Alan S. Levins	Jeffrey M. Tanenbaum
Randolph C. Roeder	Jennifer J. Walt
Gary P. Scholick	Scott D. Rechtschaffen
William F. Terheyden	James P. Baker
Nancy L. Ober	Nancy E. Pritikin
John M. Skonberg	Joseph P. Ryan
Robert G. Hulteng	Maria G. Narayan
Robert Kelton Carrol	Eric A. Grover
R. Brian Dixon	Stephen C. Tedesco
David S. Durham	Philip L. Ross
Paula Champagne	Marjorie S. Fochtman
Richard N. Hill	David F. Byrnes

OF COUNSEL

Dennis T. Daniels

G. J. Stillson MacDonnell	Salimé Samii
Ronald J. Holland II	Kenneth B. Stratton
Carolyn Sue Petrouski	Carolyn Colton Frantz
Daniel A. Croley	Michael Hoffman
Robert Leinwand	Joni B. Vogel
Carolann Gee Hinkle	Adam Ratner
John C. Fish, Jr.	Tram-Anh T. Frank
C. Robert Sturm	Chris Baker
Arthur M. Eidelhoch	David S. Warner
Ann M. Wicks	Terry Chapko
Geoffrey J.L. Brown	Jodie Jones
Andrew E. Burrows	John C. Corcoran
Robert T. Landau	Frank F. Martinez
David Y. Otsuka	Lori J. Bien
	(Not admitted in CA)

For full biographical listings, see the Martindale-Hubbell Law Directory

---

LONG & LEVIT LLP (AV)

A Limited Liability Partnership including a Professional Corporation
101 California Street, Suite 2300, 94111
Telephone: 415-397-2222
Telex: 340924 HOME OFC SFO-LONG & LEVIT
Facsimile: 415-397-6392
Los Angeles, California Office: 601 S. Figueroa, 25th Floor.
Telephone: 213-356-5900.
Facsimile: 213-613-0664.

RESIDENT PARTNERS

Percy V. Long (1870-1953)	Joseph P. McMonigle
Bert W. Levit (1903-1980)	Donald W. Carlson
John B. Hook	Marsha Lee Morrow
Ronald E. Mallen (Professional Corporation)	Russell S. Roeca
Howard M. Garfield	Guy D. Calladine
	Robert M. Peterson

(See Next Column)

Long & Levit LLP, *San Francisco—Continued*

RESIDENT PARTNERS (Continued)

Edward F. Donohue, III	Burton C. "Skip" Allyn, IV
Don A. Lesser	Gerald Gamliel Weisbach
Robert C. Chiles	J. Michael Higginbotham
David I. Dalby	Gary A. Hernandez
Joyce C. Wang	Robert J. Romero
Michael A. Vasquez	Steven M. Sharafian
Michael C. Cooper	Jeanette Traverso
	Glenn A. Friedman

RESIDENT ASSOCIATES

Natalie A. Balfour	John H. Quinn
Corey Shapiro Cherkas	Stephen Patrick Randall
Sherri J. Conrad	Eliza M. Rodrigues
Marc A. Eckardt	Ryan T. Russell
Kathleen M. Ewins	Richard J. Sciaroni
John M. Farrell, Jr.	Mark M. Smith
Peter L. Isola	Terry Ann Smith
Amy Tollakson Jeter	Ann L. Strayer
Allison Lane	Jennifer Wong Suzuki
Jeffrey P. Miller	Elizabeth A. Tosaris
Christopher R. Moore	Paul E. Vallone
Kim Morimoto	William E. Waddell
Mark L. Nissenbaum	Thomas Weathers

SENIOR COUNSEL

Jeffrey D. Livingston

OF COUNSEL

Edward D. Haas

SPECIAL COUNSEL

Alan E. Lacy	Karen L. Uno

For full biographical listings, see the Martindale-Hubbell Law Directory

---

LAW OFFICES OF WAYNE LUTTRINGER (AV)

311 California Street, Suite 500, 94104
Telephone: 415-421-2583
Fax: 415-421-2584

ASSOCIATE

James A. Glimme

OF COUNSEL

M. Francis Brass	Patrick M.K. Richardson

For full biographical listings, see the Martindale-Hubbell Law Directory

---

McCUTCHEN, DOYLE, BROWN & ENERSEN (AV)

Three Embarcadero Center, 94111-4066
Telephone: 415-393-2000
Facsimile: 415-393-2286 (G I, II, III)
Telex: 340817 MACPAG SFO
Email: postmaster@mdbe.com *URL:* http://www.mccutchen.com
Los Angeles, California Office: 355 South Grand Avenue, Suite 4400, 90071-1560.
Telephone: 213-680-6400.
Facsimile: 213-680-6499.
San Jose, California Office: Market Post Tower, Suite 1500, 55 South Market Street, 95113-2327.
Telephone: 408-947-8400.
Facsimile: 408-947-4750.
Telex: 9102502931 MACPAG SJ.
Walnut Creek, California Office: 1331 North California Boulevard, Post Office Box V, 94596-4502.
Telephone: 510-937-8000.
Facsimile: 510-975-5390.
Palo Alto, California Office: One Embarcadero Place, 2100 Geng Road, 94303-0913.
Telephone: 415-846-4000.
Fax: 415-846-4086.
Washington, D.C. Office: The Evening Star Building, Suite 800, 1101 Pennsylvania Avenue, N.W., 20004-2514.
Telephone: 202-628-4900.
Facsimile: 202-628-4912.
Taipei, Taiwan Republic of China Office: International Trade Building, Tenth Floor, 333 Keelung Road, Section 1, 110.
Telephone: 886-2-723-5000.
Facsimile: 886-2-757-6070.
Affiliated Offices In: Bangkok, Thailand; Beijing, China; Shanghai, China.

MEMBERS OF FIRM

David R. Andrews	Michael A. Brown (Not admitted in CA; Resident, Washington, D.C. Office)
Joseph R. Austin	
David M. Balabanian	
Dale E. Barnes, Jr.	Robert Minge Brown (1911-1994)
William Bates, III	
Michael I. Begert	Ross E. Campbell
Christopher P. Berka (Resident, San Jose Office)	(Resident, San Jose Office)
	Patrick O. Cavanaugh
Gilbert C. Berkeley (Resident, Walnut Creek Office)	(Not admitted in CA)
	Byde W. Clawson
Susan S. Briggs	(Resident, San Jose Office)

(See Next Column)

MEMBERS OF FIRM (Continued)

Cynthia A. Coe (Resident, Washington, D.C. Office)	James Boyd Lewis
	Robert A. Lewis
Daniel Cooperman	Jane Elizabeth Lovell
Robert E. Cox (San Francisco and San Jose Offices)	John B. Lowry
	Michael B. Lubic (Resident, Los Angeles Office)
Charles William Craycroft (Resident, San Jose Office)	
Charles S. Crompton, III	Palmer Brown Madden (Resident, Walnut Creek Office)
Philip T. Cummings (Not admitted in CA; Resident, Washington, D.C. Office)	
	Raymond Charles Marshall
	Loyd W. McCormick
Daniel J. Curtin, Jr. (Resident, Walnut Creek Office)	Edward J. McCutchen (1857-1933)
Barry J. Cutler (Not admitted in CA; Resident, Washington, D.C. Office)	Edward S. Merrill
	Robert E. Merritt (Resident, Walnut Creek Office)
Bartley C. Deamer	Randy Michelson
Carol K. Dillon (At San Jose and Palo Alto Offices)	Robert A. Mills
	Gary H. Moore (Resident, Palo Alto Office)
Colleen P. Doyle (Resident, Los Angeles Office)	
	John C. Morrissey (Resident, Los Angeles Office)
James J. Dragna (Resident, Los Angeles Office)	
	David E. Moser
Kenta K. Duffey	Karen J. Nardi
Michael P. Durkee	William J. Newell (Resident, Palo Alto Office)
Robert L. Ebe	
Roger D. Ehlers	Lior O. Nuchi
James B. Ellis (Resident, Walnut Creek Office)	James Franklin Owens (Resident, Los Angeles Office)
Henry D. Evans, Jr.	Beth H. Parker (Resident, Taipei Office)
Pecos Bill Field	
Debra L. Fischer (Resident, Los Angeles Office)	Robert P. Parker
	Lynn H. Pasahow
James C. Fowler	Sara Louise Peterson
John W. Fowler (Resident, San Jose Office)	Alfred C. Pfeiffer, Jr.
	Donn P. Pickett
William H. Freedman (Resident, Los Angeles Office)	Michael J. Plishner
	Thomas G. Reddy
Warren E. George	John R. Reese
Sandra A. Golze	Geoffrey L. Robinson (Resident, Walnut Creek Office)
Barry P. Goode	
Michael L. Greene (Resident, Walnut Creek Office)	Ulrico S. Rosales (Resident and Managing Partner, Palo Alto Office)
Melinda L. Hayes (Resident, Los Angeles Office)	
	Rick R. Rothman (Resident, Los Angeles Office)
David M. Heilbron	
Daniel B. Higgins	Jonathan H. Sakol
Christopher B. Hockett	James Severson
Susan L. Hoffman (Resident, Los Angeles Office)	Patricia L. Shanks
	Charlene Sachi Shimada
Terry J. Houlihan	Sanford M. Skaggs (Resident and Managing Partner, Walnut Creek Office)
Holly A. House	
James L. Hunt	
John Edward Hurley, Jr.	Robert H. Solomon
Mary T. Huser	Edward L. Strohbehn, Jr.
Mark O. Kasanin	Cecily T. Talbert
Karen L. Kennard	Daniel M. Wall
William D. Kissinger	George J. Weiner (Resident, Washington, D.C. Office)
James P. Kleinberg	
Stephen L. Kostka (Resident, Walnut Creek Office)	Harlan Wendell
	Gayl A. Westendorf
Leslie G. Landau	Michael C. White (Resident, Washington, D.C. Office)
Ronald S. Laurie	
Rebecca A. Lenaburg	Thomas B. Worth
Donald M. Levy Jr. (Resident, Palo Alto Office)	Gordon T. Yamate (Resident, San Jose Office)
	Stephen A. Zovickian

COUNSEL

Brent M. Abel (Retired Partner)	Susan Herald (Resident, Palo Alto Office)
Marilee J. Allan	
Denise Savoie Blocker	Stephen D. Hibbard (Not admitted in CA)
Neil Boorstyn	
Gregory L. Bowling	Susan K. Hoerger (Resident, Palo Alto Office)
Karen A. Caffee (Resident, Los Angeles Office)	
	Peter Hsiao (Resident, Los Angeles Office)
Joan C. Y. Chen (Resident, Taipei, Taiwan Office)	
	M. Thomas Jacobson (Resident, Walnut Creek Office)
David D. Chow (Resident, Taipei, Taiwan Office)	
	Owen Jameson
Henry A. Cirillo	Jack G. Knebel
Marie A. Cooper (Resident, Walnut Creek Office)	Diana Pfeffer Martin (Resident, Los Angeles Office)
Anne M. Deibert	
Morris M. Doyle	Maria T. Mascaro
Sally A. Drach	Kathleen A. McDonald (Resident, San Jose Office)
Burnham Enersen	
Margaret A. Freeston (Resident, Washington, D.C. Office)	Beth A. McGowen (Resident, San Jose Office)
	Barry R. Ogilby
Jacqueline C. Fu (Resident, Taipei Office)	Douglas R. Painter (Resident, Los Angeles Office)
John N. Hauser	

(See Next Column)

McCUTCHEN, DOYLE, BROWN & ENERSEN—*Continued*

COUNSEL (Continued)

Elizabeth A. Pierce (Resident,
    Washington, D.C. Office)
Marco Quazzo
Norman B. Richards
James M. Rockett
Christine E. Sherry
Joseph K. Siino

Karen E. Silverman-Johnson
Beverly A. Tiffany
Keith D. Ungles
Clayton J. Vreeland
    (Resident, Los Angeles Office)
Pamela F. Worth
    (Resident, Los Angeles Office)

ASSOCIATES

Rajesh A. Aji
    (Resident, Palo Alto Office)
Jeffrey M. Anderson
Brandt Andersson (Resident,
    Walnut Creek Office)
Asha Lata Badrinath
Christine Banks
Page R. Barnes
Eric J. Baysinger
Kristin K. Bear
    (Resident, San Jose Office)
Margaret Bielak
Robert A. Brundage
P. Scott Burton
    (Resident, Los Angeles Office)
William Carpenter
William W. Choe
    (Resident, San Jose Office)
Greg A. Christianson
    (Resident, Los Angeles Office)
William Wei-Li Chuang
Jill F. Cooper
    (Resident, Los Angeles Office)
Claire T. Cormier
    (Resident, San Jose Office)
Nora C. Cregan
Anthony E. Davis
Shashikala Deb
Krystal N. Denley
Mitchell L. DeStigter
    (Not admitted in CA)
Kevin M. Epstein
David Fallek
Elizabeth Meinert Fielder
Karla A. Francken
    (Resident, Los Angeles Office)
Angel A. Garganta
David J. Gershon
David C. Getzinger (Resident,
    Taipei, Taiwan Office)
Haywood S. Gilliam, Jr
I-Fan Ching Go
    (Resident, Los Angeles Office)
Kathleen M. Graber (Resident,
    Washington, D.C. Office)
Grant A. Guerra (Resident,
    Walnut Creek Office)
J. David Hadden
Karen A. Hall
Michael D. Hartogs
    (Resident, Palo Alto Office)
Tiffany R. Hedgpeth
Peter S. Hayes (Resident,
    Walnut Creek Office)
Frank M. Hinman
Heather Hoecherl
Geoffrey M. Howard
Flora M. Hsu (Resident, Taipei,
    Taiwan Office)
Asher D. Issacs
    (Resident, Los Angeles Office)
Micah R. Jacobs
    (Resident, Los Angeles Office)
Paige K. Kaplan
Steven S. Kaufhold
Frank B. Kennamer

Erica L. Kuerbis
Thomas Eilif Kuhnle
    (Resident, San Jose Office)
Andrew Kumamoto
    (Resident, Palo Alto Office)
Elizabeth A. Lake
Adria Y. La Rose
Tienne Elissa Lee
Adam U. Lindgren (Resident,
    Walnut Creek Office)
Matthew A. Lesnick
Laura Mazzerella
Kirstie A. McCornock
Jerilyn López Mendoza
    (Resident, Los Angeles Office)
Daniel D. Meyers
Michael J. Morris
Elan Q.G. Nguyen
    (Palo Alto Office)
Trenton H. Norris
Julia A. Oas (Resident,
    Washington, D.C. Office)
Rajiv Suresh Parikh (Resident,
    Walnut Creek Office)
Michael T. Pyle
Gregory A. Randall (Resident,
    Walnut Creek Office)
Carolyn L. Reid
Steven G. Rosen
Neal A. Rubin
    (Resident, Los Angeles Office)
Jenifer P. Schatten
Jacob J. Schatz
John D. Schlotterbeck
    (Resident, Los Angeles Office)
Hope A. Schmeltzer
Caitlin A. Schneider
Barbara J. Schussman (Resident,
    Walnut Creek Office)
Charles E. Shelton, II
    (Resident, Los Angeles Office)
Sindy Jill Siegel
Carissa M. Smith
    (Resident, Palo Alto Office)
James Grant Snell
    (Resident, San Jose Office)
Allyson W. Sonenshine
Ann D. Springer
Nina K. Srejovic
Duy Thai
Peter Tong
    (Resident, Palo Alto Office)
Han N. Tran
Sandra Hughes Waddell
    (Resident, Los Angeles Office)
John V. Wadsworth
Colin West
Robert J. Wierenga
Julia C. Wo
Cory Wurtzel
Dr. Joseph Yang
    (Resident, Palo Alto Office)
Mallun Yen
Kenneth J. Yood
    (Resident, Los Angeles Office)
Russ K. Yoshinaka

LEGAL SUPPORT PERSONNEL

SCIENTIFIC STAFF

Michael J. Shuster

For full biographical listings, see the Martindale-Hubbell Law Directory

MILLER, MAILLIARD & CULVER, LLP (AV)

A Partnership including Professional Corporations
155 Montgomery Street, Suite 1212, 94104
Telephone: 415-391-4291
Fax: 415-391-4292
Email: mmc@sirius.com
Santa Rosa, California Office: 100 B Street, Suite 200. P.O. Box 5257.
Telephone: 707-571-8112.
Fax: 707-575-9116. Email: milmaicul@aol.com.

(See Next Column)

Christopher R. Miller (P.C.)
William S. Mailliard, Jr.
David C. Culver
R. W. Achor (P.C.) (Retired)
Phyllis E. Andelin

Kevin F. Barrett
William D. Evers
Jay P. Hendrickson
Paul E. Manasian
Philip J. Nicholsen, P.C.

Chigusa Saotome

OF COUNSEL

Stephen T. Kong

Representative Clients: BioZone Laboratories; California Dept. of Insurance;
Dover Elevator Co.; Pacific Coast Apparel; Red Rose Collections; Sanwa
Bank; Schug Carneros Estate Winery; TransMotive Technologies; Veriflo
Corporation; Wyse Technology, Inc.

For full biographical listings, see the Martindale-Hubbell Law Directory

MORGENSTEIN & JUBELIRER, LLP (AV)

A Partnership including a Professional Corporation
One Market Plaza, Spear Street Tower, 32nd Floor, 94105
Telephone: 415-896-0666
Fax: 415-896-5592
Email: jubelirer@aol.com

MEMBERS OF FIRM

Marvin D. Morgenstein (P.C.)
Eliot S. Jubelirer
Lee Ann Huntington
Jean L. Bertrand
Jeffrey R. Williams
James R. Balich

Rocky N. Unruh
James L. McGinnis
Charles W. LaGrave
Wendi J. Berkowitz
John S. Worden
Robert B. Mullen

OF COUNSEL

Laurie K. Anger

Lewis D. Barr
David H. Bromfield
Michael "Cael" S. Davis
Roberta Nicol Dempster

Natasha L. Golding
Stephen M. Hankins
Simon E. Kisch
John J. Petry

Bruce A. Wagman

For full biographical listings, see the Martindale-Hubbell Law Directory

MORRISON & FOERSTER LLP (AV)

425 Market Street, 94105-2482
Telephone: 415-268-7000
Facsimile: 415-268-7522
URL: http://www.mofo.com
Other offices located in: Los Angeles, New York, Washington, D.C.,
London, Brussels, Hong Kong, Tokyo, Sacramento, Palo Alto, Walnut
Creek, Orange County and Denver.

MEMBERS OF FIRM

Peter Aitelli
Rochelle D. Alpert
William Alsup
Carl E. Anduri, Jr.
David E. Baudler
James P. Bennett
Kenneth E. Blohm
Roland E. Brandel
James J. Brosnahan
John W. Campbell, III
Annette P. Carnegie
Cedric C. Chao
Vincent J. Chiarello
Michèle B. Corash (San
    Francisco and Los Angeles
    Offices)
Mark W. Danis
Gregory P. Dresser
Gordon P. Erspamer (San
    Francisco and Walnut Creek
    Offices)
Jordan Eth
Craig B. Etlin
Marc P. Fairman
Robert L. Falk
Kathleen V. Fisher
Paul Flum
Paul T. Friedman
James J. Garrett (San Francisco
    and Walnut Creek Offices)
David A. Gold (San Francisco
    and Walnut Creek Offices)
Melvin R. Goldman
Arturo J. Gonzalez
Zane O. Gresham
Gavin B. Grover
Kevin T. Haroff
Nancy L. Hayes
Douglas L. Hendricks
Michael A. Jacobs

Joseph M. Karp
Raoul D. Kennedy
Grant L. Kim
Richard S. Kinyon
Thomas F. Kostic
Rachel Krevans
Ray Larroca
Adam A. Lewis
Jack W. Londen
Ann T. MacLeod
Bruce Alan Mann
Rachel Markun
Harold J. McElhinny
James E. Merritt
Charles J. Moll III
Andrew E. Monach
Portia R. Moore
Preston Moore
R. Clark Morrison (San
    Francisco and Walnut Creek
    Offices)
Carla B. Oakley
Stuart J. Offer
James C. Paras
Peter J. Pfister
Michael S. Powlen
Penelope Athene Preovolos
Darryl P. Rains
Pamela J. Reed (San Francisco
    and Walnut Creek Offices)
David G. Robertson
Barry S. Sandals
Lori A. Schechter
William I. Schwartz
Carl J. (Kim) Seneker II
Linda E. Shostak
J. Michael Stusiak
Tamu K. Sudduth
James M. Tobin
Robert S. Townsend

(See Next Column)

MORRISON & FOERSTER LLP, San Francisco—Continued

MEMBERS OF FIRM (Continued)

Keith C. Wetmore	Prentiss Willson, Jr.
M. Kirby C. Wilcox	Michael L. Zigler

SENIOR OF COUNSEL

Paul E. Homrighausen	Robert D. Raven
David E. Nelson	Marshall L. Small

OF COUNSEL

Lee S. Adams	Michael R. Goldstein
Elizabeth P. Allor	Paul Goldstein
James E. Boddy, Jr.	Philip J. McConnaughay
Ruth N. Borenstein	Ross D. Meador
Chieko Eda	Michael G. O'Bryan
Robert M. Frieden	C. Jean Ryan
(Not admitted in CA)	Robert A. Saltzberg

ASSOCIATES

Michael J. Agoglia	Matthew I. Kreeger
Joan C. Aguado	William L. Leschensky
Lisa E. Alexander	(Not admitted in CA)
Julia Alloggiamento	Diane Y. Lewis
Edwin P. Antolin	David A. Lorie
Khin Mai Aung	April Madison-Ramsey
D. Cameron Baker	Sean M. Mahoney
Philip T. Besirof	Craig D. Martin
Susan S. Boranian	David J. Martz
James L. S. Bouldin	Patrick R. McCabe
Tracie L. Brown	Constance T. Y. McComb
Tamra D. Browne	Sheryl C. Medeiros
William R. Burford	Elizabeth H. Miller
Scott C. Burrell	Kimberley Milligan
Carolyn Beasley Burton	John M. Moynihan
Raymond E. Cannon	Jill Neiman
Maria Chedid	Annemarie C. O'Shea
(Not admitted in CA)	Wesley E. Overson, Jr.
Connie L. Chen	Angela L. Padilla
Perry S. Chen	Aaron Persky
Christina W. Chi	J. Edgar Pew
Frederick S. Chung	Kathi J. Pugh
Christopher C. Cooke	Clare Rathbone
Michael James Cordero	Julie C. Reagin
Laura M. Craska	D. Anthony Rodriguez
Jill K. DeGraff	James M. Schurz
Eric L. Dupré	Tessa I. Schwartz
Marc J. Fagel	Amy L. Silverstein
Matthew K. Fawcett	Anders E. Stenstedt
Daniel F. Feldman	Malcolm A. H. Stewart
Ronald P. Flynn	Anita Taff-Rice
Terri A. Garland	Eda Su Ling Tan
Lynn M. Garney	Raj Tanden
Sallie P. Gibson	H. Perry Taubman
Sue C. Hansen	Jennifer Lee Taylor
Francine M. Hanson	Jill Teitelbaum
James C. Harrison	Olive L. Thaler
Michelle D. Hilleary	Stephen B. Thau
Elena Kondos Hillman (San	David W. Tollen
Francisco and Sacramento	Elizabeth E. Tweedie
Offices)	A. James Vazquez-Azpiri
Barry R. Himmelstein	James M. Vickery
Katharine A. Hobin	Valerie A. Villanueva
John Hou	Carolyn J. Vondriska
Michelle Howard	Mary E. Wand
Lynn M. Humphreys	Karin H. Wang
David A. Hyman	Kathleen M. Wardlaw
Carolyn A. Johnston	Gail D. Weiswasser
Stuart P. Kaler	Claudia D. Westin
Peter B. Kanter	Kristian E. Wiggert
Robert F. Kramer	Carolyn M. Wiggin

Haidee Kathleen Winter

LEGAL SUPPORT PERSONNEL

ENVIRONMENTAL ANALYSTS

Lynne F. Anderson	Susan Prentice Linder

Robert J. Reinhard

PATENT AGENT

Gary A. Green

For full biographical listings, see the Martindale-Hubbell Law Directory

---

MURPHY, PEARSON, BRADLEY & FEENEY, A PROFESSIONAL CORPORATION (AV)

88 Kearny Street, 11th Floor, 94108
Telephone: 415-788-1900
Telecopier: 415-393-8087
Sacramento, California Office: Suite 200, 3600 American River Drive, 95864.
Telephone: 916-483-6074.
Telecopier: 916-483-6088.

(See Next Column)

James A. Murphy	Timothy J. Halloran
Arthur V. Pearson	Karen M. Goodman
Michael P. Bradley	(Resident, Sacramento Office)
John H. Feeney	Mark S. Perelman
Gregory A. Bastian	Mark Ellis
(Resident, Sacramento Office)	(Resident, Sacramento Office)

William S. Kronenberg

Gregg Anthony Thornton	Veronica E. Rendon
Anne F. Marchant	Mikel C. Deimler
Antoinette Waters Farrell	Erica Brachfeld
Michael K. Pazdernik	(Resident, Sacramento Office)
(Resident, Sacramento Office)	Kristina L. Thornton
Alexander J. Berline	(Resident, Sacramento Office)
Alec Hunter Boyd	Joan E. Low
Jane L. O'Hara Gamp	Dennis J. Priolo
Joseph E. Addiego, III	(Resident, Sacramento Office)
Maretta D. Ward	Anthony O. Ayeni
Brett M. Witter	(Resident, Sacramento Office)
Brad S. Parker	Farzad Tabatabai
Barbara A. Cotter	(Resident, Sacramento Office)
Margaret M. Schneck	Randall L. Thompson
Gregory W. McCracken	Maria S. Magaros
Steven L. Jawgiel	(Resident, Sacramento Office)

For full biographical listings, see the Martindale-Hubbell Law Directory

---

ORRICK, HERRINGTON & SUTCLIFFE LLP (AV)

Old Federal Reserve Bank Building, 400 Sansome Street, 94111
Telephone: 415-392-1122
Telecopier: 415-773-5759
URL: http://www.orrick.com
Los Angeles, California Office: 777 South Figueroa Street.
Telephone: 213-629-2020.
Telecopier: 213-612-2499.
New York, New York Office: 666 Fifth Avenue.
Telephone: 212-505-5000.
Telecopier: 212-506-5151.
Sacramento, California Office: 400 Capitol Mall.
Telephone: 916-447-9200.
Telecopier: 916-329-4900.
Singapore Office: 10 Collyer Quay, #23-08 Ocean Building, Singapore.
Telephone: 011-65-538-6116.
Telecopier: 011-65-538-0606.
Washington, D.C. Office: Washington Harbour, 3050 K Street, N.W.
Telephone: 202-339-8400.
Telecopier: 202-339-8500.
Menlo Park, California Office: 1020 Marsh Road.
Telephone: 415-833-7800.
Telecopier: 415-614-7401.

SAN FRANCISCO, CALIFORNIA
MEMBERS OF FIRM

John E. Aguirre	Dana M. Ketcham
William F. Alderman	John H. Knox
Ralph H. Baxter, Jr.	Geoffrey P. Leonard
Elaine R. Bayus	Mark R. Levie
Daniel R. Bedford	Michael H. Liever
Michael J. Bettinger	Peter Lillevand
Steven A. Brick	Dora Mao
Frederick Brown	John E. McInerney, III
Charles Cardall	Michael R. Meyers
Thomas Y. Coleman	Thomas C. Mitchell
Mary A. Collins	William G. Murray, Jr.
Dean E. Criddle	Noel W. Nellis
Roger L. Davis	M. J. Pritchett
Stanley J. Dirks	Greg R. Riddle
William M. Doyle	Marie B. Riehle
Raymond G. Ellis	William L. Riley
Robert P. Feyer	Paul J. Sax
Carlo S. Fowler	John F. Seegal
David S. Fries	Thomas R. Shearer, Jr.
Richard A. Gilbert	Gary R. Siniscalco
Robert J. Gloistein	Richard V. Smith
Richard E. V. Harris	Stephen A. Spitz
Richard D. Harroch	Alan Talkington
Gary A. Herrmann	Ralph C. Walker
Patricia K. Hershey	Jeffrey S. White
Richard I. Hiscocks	Kenneth G. Whyburn
William L. Hoisington	Jeffrey D. Wohl
Leslie P. Jay	George G. Wolf
John H. Kanberg	Cameron W. Wolfe, Jr.
Lawrence T. Kane	George A. Yuhas

OF COUNSEL

Bruce S. Klafter	Douglas C. Sands
Philip C. Morgan	Samuel A. Sperry
Catherine K. O'Connell	Timothy P. Walker

ASSOCIATES

Melody A. Barker	Paul C. Borden
Pamela H. Bennett	Kerry Anne Bresnahan
Gregory D. Bibbes	Susan J. Briscoe
Scott D. Blickenstaff	Jessica L. Cahen

(See Next Column)

ORRICK, HERRINGTON & SUTCLIFFE LLP—*Continued*

ASSOCIATES (Continued)

David J. Castillo	Thomas P. Klein
Kevin Shih-Chun Chou	William J. Kramer
Brett E. Cooper	Kathleen Hughes Leak
Mark Davis	Nancy M. Lee
Kirsten J. Day	Gary Louie
Ana Marie del Rio	Ashley E. Lowe
Mary Patricia Dooley	Steven C. Malvey
Scott D. Elliott	Douglas D. Mandell
Gabriela Franco	Karen L. Marangi
David K. F. Gillis	George P. Miller
Carlos E. Gonzalez	James W. Miller Jr.
Mary Elizabeth Grant	Genevieve M. Moore
Maria Gray	Lowell D. Ness
Adam J. Gutride	Mark F. Parcella
John M. Hartenstein	Anthony B. Pearsall
Dolph M. Hellman	David C. Ritchey
Mats F. Hellsten	Peter E. Root
Tanya Herrera	Christian J. Rowley
Lynne T. Hirata	Paul I. Rubin
Laura A. Izon	Dave A. Sanchez
Stephen J. Jackson, Jr.	Michelle W. Sexton
Andrew P. Johnson	Usha Rengachary Smerdon
Daniel Judge	David Sobul
Susan R. Kelley	Lawrence N. Tonomura
Hera Lie Kim	Adrienne Diamant Weil

Stephen E. Whittaker

LOS ANGELES, CALIFORNIA
MEMBERS OF FIRM

Alan G. Benjamin	W. Douglas Kari
William W. Bothwell	Michael A. McAndrews
Lori A. Bowman	Richard C. Mendelson
William B. Campbell	Lawrence Peitzman
Eugene J. Carron	Gary D. Samson
Robert E. Freitas	Larry D. Sobel
Earl A. Glick	Payne L. Templeton
Todd E. Gordinier	Paul A. Webber
Greg Harrington	Howard J. Weg

OF COUNSEL

Jeffrey S. Allen	Mary H. Neale
John P. Kreis	Michael E. Silver

ASSOCIATES

Ella L. Brown	Lisa Girand Mann
Diana K. Chuang	Paul T. Martin
Christopher L. Davis	Antonio D. Martini
Andrew D. Garelick	Bradley Scott Miller
Margaret H. Gillespie	Melanie Murakami
Owen P. Gross	William W. Oxley
Brett L. Healy	Luan Phan
Victor Hsu	Georgiana Rosenkranz
Alisa Jardine	Christopher S. Ruhland
Julie E. Knipstein	John P. Sharkey
Linda S. Koffman	David B. Shemano
Scott G. Lawson	Bridgette M. Smith
Victoria A. Levin	Winnie Tsien
Douglas E. Love	Bradley S. White

MENLO PARK, CALIFORNIA
MEMBERS OF FIRM

W. Reece Bader	Terrence P. McMahon
G. Hopkins Guy, III	Christopher R. Ottenweller
Lynne C. Hermle	Jon B. Streeter

Gary E. Weiss

ASSOCIATES

David J. Anderman	Sean A. Lincoln
Carl W. Chamberlin	Alexandra McClure
Erin Farrell	Peter C. McMahon
Kenneth J. Halpern	Matthew H. Poppe
Leslie Y. Kimball	Eve T. Saltman
Wendy Kosanovich	Shelley J. Sandusky
Amy L. Landers	Graeme Ellis Sharpe
Joseph C. Liburt	Eric L. Wesenberg

Thomas H. Zellerbach

NEW YORK, NEW YORK
MEMBERS OF FIRM

Paul B. Abramson	Adam W. Glass
Charles W. Bradley	Lawrence B. Goodwin
Bradford S. Breen	F. Susan Gottlieb
Peter R. Bucci	William A. Gray
Charles N. Burger	Arnold Gulkowitz
Colman J. Burke	Eileen B. Heitzler
Fred C. Byers, Jr.	Robyn A. Huffman
Richard Chirls	Laurence Bryan Isaacson
Katharine I. Crost	Robert M. Isackson
Bruce S. Cybul	John J. Keohane
Duncan N. Darrow	Alan M. Knoll
Michael Delikat	Peter J. Korda
Edward M. De Sear	Jeffrey A. Lenobel
Rubi Finkelstein	Herbert J. Levine
Robert A. Fippinger	Carl F. Lyon, Jr.
Lawrence B. Fisher	Daniel A. Mathews

(See Next Column)

NEW YORK, NEW YORK
MEMBERS OF FIRM (Continued)

Sam Scott Miller	Stephen K. Sawyier
Kathleen H. Moriarty	Albert Simons, III
Barbara Moses	Louis H. Singer
David Z. Nirenberg	Michael Voldstad
Joshua E. Raff	Richard Weidman
Jill L. Rosenberg	Neil T. Wolk

SPECIAL COUNSEL
Donald J. Robinson

OF COUNSEL

Stanley L. Amberg	John A. MacKerron
Thomas Barr, IV	Robert B. Michel
Susan L. Barry	Martin R. Miller
Michael E. Emrich	Amy Moskowitz
William H. Horton, Jr.	Richard H. Nicholls

ASSOCIATES

Craig T. Beazer	David A. Marple
Jonathan K. Bender	Edward Mayfield
Thomas J. Benison	Lisa K. McClelland
Leon J. Bijou	Thomas N. McManus
Colette Bonnard	James H. McQuade
Patti Lynn Boss	Aimee B. Meltzer
Eric R. Bothwell	Ronald Millet
Whitney R. Bradshaw	Bradford E. Monks
Karen M. Braun	Christopher J. Moore
Jarrett D. Bruhn	C. Rochelle Moorehead
Juliet F. Buck	P. Quinn Moss
Benjamin C. Burkhart	Bryan Jay Neilinger
Lawton M. Camp	William O'Brien
Anthony Carabba, Jr.	John F. Olsen
Michael B. Carlinsky	Edwin Gerard Oswald
Jennifer M. Clapp	Scott M. Pasternack
Joseph M. Cohen	Marc J. Pensabene
Caterina A. Conti	Sheryl Lynn Pereira
Robert A. Cote	Gail Pflederer
Kyle W. Drefke	Nanci Prado
Joseph Evall	Ruth D. Raisfeld
Marguerite J. Felsenfeld	Marlene Watts Reed
Jeffrey J. Fessler	Marni J. Roder
John D. Giansello, III	Ira G. Rosenstein
Michael A. Gilbert	Sidney M. Ruthenberg
Howard M. Goldwasser	Hooman Sabeti-Rahmati
Meryl A. Griff	David J. Sack
Tzvi Hirshaut	Al B. Sawyers
Kiran J. Kamboj	Martin L. Schmelkin
René A. Kathawala	Patricia A. Seddon
Joseph T. Kennedy	William C. Seligman
Jaemin Kim	Ronit Setton
Steven L. Kopp	Katherine A. Simmons
Diane Krebs	Corey A. Tessler
Kenneth R. Linsk	David M. Traitel
Christopher Locke	Sandra L. Tsang
Jonathan B. Lurvey	Robert A. Villani
Michael D. Maline	Steven I. Weinberger
Joseph E. Maloney	Bradley E. Wolf

Michael J. Zeidel

SACRAMENTO, CALIFORNIA
MEMBERS OF FIRM

R. Michael Bacon	Marc A. Levinson
Norman C. Hile	Timothy J. Long
Perry E. Israel	John R. Myers
Cynthia J. Larsen	Cynthia L. Remmers

SPECIAL COUNSEL
William E. Donovan

OF COUNSEL
E. Randolph Hooks   Iain Mickle

ASSOCIATES

Jennifer P. Brown	Kelcie M. Gosling
Jordon Lee Burch	Trish Higgins
James T. Cahalan	Christopher E. Krueger
Virginia M. Christianson	Constance L. LeLouis
John P. Cook	Kim Mueller
William T. Darden	Charles W. Nugent
Stephen L. Davis	Andrew W. Stroud
Edward P. Dudensing	Susan R. Thompson
Lynn T. Ernce	Margaret Carew Toledo
Eric J. Glassman	Thomas J. Welsh

SINGAPORE
MEMBER OF FIRM
William R. Campbell

ASSOCIATES

Kenneth S. Aboud	Bruce R. Schulberg
M. Tamara Box	David Z. Vance
Nicholas Chan Kei Cheong	Eleanor Wong

(See Next Column)

ORRICK, HERRINGTON & SUTCLIFFE LLP, *San Francisco—Continued*

WASHINGTON, D.C.
MEMBERS OF FIRM

Cameron L. Cowan	Keith W. Kriebel
Felicia B. Graham	Lorraine S. McGowen
Paul Weiffenbach	

OF COUNSEL

David S. Katz	Dianne Loennig Stoddard

ASSOCIATES

Michele E. Beasley	Rohit H. Kirpalani
Mark S. Dola	Douglas Madsen
Michael H. Freedman	Thomas D. Salus
Adam B. Tankel	

For full biographical listings, see the Martindale-Hubbell Law Directory

---

PILLSBURY MADISON & SUTRO LLP (AV)

235 Montgomery Street, 94104
Telephone: 415-983-1000
FAX: 415-983-1200
Costa Mesa, California Office: Plaza Tower, Suite 1100, 600 Anton Boulevard, Costa Mesa, California, 92626.
Telephone: 714-436-6800.
Fax: 714-662-6999.
Los Angeles, California Office: Citicorp Plaza, 725 South Figueroa Street, Suite 1200, 90017.
Telephone: 213-488-7100.
Fax: 213-629-1033.
Silicon Valley Office: 2700 Sand Hill Road, 94025.
Telephone: 415-233-4500.
Fax: 415-233-4545.
New York, New York Office: 520 Madison Avenue, 40th Floor, 10022.
Telephone: 212-328-4810.
Fax: 212-328-4824.
Sacramento, California Office: 400 Capitol Mall, Suite 1700, 95814.
Telephone: 916-329-4700.
Fax: 916-441-3583.
San Diego, California Office: 101 West Broadway, Suite 1800, 92101.
Telephone: 619-234-5000.
Fax: 619-236-1995.
Washington, D.C. Office: 1100 New York Avenue, N.W., Ninth Floor, 20005.
Telephone: 202-861-3000.
Fax: 202-822-0944.
Hong Kong Office: 6/F Asia Pacific Finance Tower, Citibank Plaza, 3 Garden Road, Central.
Telephone: 011-852-2509-7100.
Fax: 011-852-2509-7188.
Tokyo, Japan Office: Pillsbury Madison & Sutro, Gaikokuho Jimu Bengoshi Jimusho, 5th Floor, Samon Eleven Building, 3-1, Samon-cho, Shinjuku-ku, Tokyo 160 Japan.
Telephone: 800-729-9830; 011-813-3354-3531.
Fax: 011-813-3354-3534.

MEMBERS OF FIRM

William G. Alberti	John M. Grenfell
Walter R. Allan	Richard S. Grey
Fred W. Alvarez	Paul R. Griffin
Gary H. Anderson	George P. Haley
Rebeca P. Anderson	Willis D. Hannawalt
Christopher R. Ball	John T. Hansen
Michael R. Barr	Shawn E. Hanson
John B. Bates	John E. Hartman
William D. Berry	Kirke M. Hasson
Ronald E. Bornstein	Robert L. Heimbichner
Gary E. Botto	Robert C. Herr
James F. Brown	William J. Hoehler
Christopher L. Byers	Lawrence L. Hoenig
Terrence A. Callan	John R. Hofmann, Jr.
James M. Canty	John O'Hara Horsley
Nathaniel M. Cartmell III	Philip Hudner
Mark J. Coleman	Timothy R. Jacobs
Robert W. Cosby	Robert A. James
Mary B. Cranston	Jonathan D. Joseph
Barbara B. Creed	Philip L. Judson
Karen A. Dempsey	Mary Ellen Kazimer
Julie A. Divola	Terry M. Kee
John L. Donahue	Alson R. Kemp, Jr.
Noel J. Dyer	James F. Kirkham
Bartly A. Dzivi	David L. Klott
William I. Edlund	Anne E. Libbin
Richard M. Eigner	Allan N. Littman
Bruce A. Ericson	Thomas V. Loran III
David R. Farabee	Frederick K. Lowell
Patrick L. Finley	Parker A. Maddux
William O. Fisher	Richard Maggio
Sarah G. Flanagan	Patrick C. Marshall
Kevin M. Fong	Stephen J. Martin
Maurice D. L. Fuller	William J. Martin, Jr.
William Gaus	Bruce W. McDiarmid
Robert B. Gex IV	Jason McDonell
Robert A. Gordon, Jr.	John F. McLean

(See Next Column)

MEMBERS OF FIRM (Continued)

T. Neal McNamara	Michael J. Steel
William C. Miller	Reginald D. Steer
Frederick D. Minnes	David T. Steffen
M. David Minnick	Craig E. Stewart
Robert A. Mittelstaedt	Stephen Stublarec
James C. Olson	Robert E. Sullivan
Rodney R. Peck	Chinin Tana
Alfred L. Pepin, Jr.	Graham R. Taylor
Robert C. Phelps	Roderick M. Thompson
Marcia L. Pope	Joseph R. Tiffany II
Jay E. Powell	James O'M. Tingle
Charles R. Ragan	Ronald E. Van Buskirk
Toni Rembe	Jeffrey M. Vesely
Ina J. Risman	Gregg F. Vignos
Frank H. Roberts	C. Brian Wainwright
Walter J. Robinson III	James J. Walsh
Margaret N. Rosegay	Philip S. Warden
Jerry W. Ross	Paula M. Weber
Steven L. Saxe	Robert M. Westberg
Mark Schallert	Blair W. White
James M. Seff	Carole V. White
Elisa W. Smith	Mark N. White
Glenn Q. Snyder	Linda C. Williams
Sharon M. Solomon	Andrea A. Wirum
Thomas E. Sparks, Jr.	Stanton D. Wong
Robert J. Spjut	James B. Young
Emmett C. Stanton	Benjamin C. Zuraw

OF COUNSEL

William E. Bonano	D. Kirk Jamieson
James T. Caleshu	Cameo F. Jones
Maureen E. Corcoran	Teresa C. Lahaderne
C. Douglas Floyd	Richard E. Nielsen

SENIOR COUNSEL

Mark A. Beskind	Victoria R. Nuetzel
Teresa M. Corbin	Robert S. Rosborough
James B. Duncan	David W. Trotter
Gabriella A. Lombardi	Cydney A. Tune
Warren H. Nelson, Jr.	David S. Winton

ASSOCIATES

Stephanie M. Alexander	Barbara M. Lange
Gregor Baer	Lindy M. Lilien
Kristen M. Bamford	Jean I. Liu
Marte J. Bassi	Courtney M. Lynch
Craig A. Becker	James K. Lynch
Marta Y. Beckwith	Dale C. Lysak
Jesse Berg	Melissa M. Manwaring
Thomas G. Blomberg, Jr.	Andrew D. Mastin
Roger E. Booth	Kerne H. Matsubara
Sally A. Brammell	Ann Colter Matthews
Brent W. Brougher	Anita D. Mayo
Timothy P. Burns	Peter D. McCabe
Brian C. Burr	Christina A. McCormick
Paula F. Carney	Caroline N. Mitchell
Lisa F. Cetlin	Theresa G. Moran
Matthew S. Crowley	Andrew T. Mortl
Joanne Crowther	Margaret M. Niver
J. Daniel Davis	Darren L. Nunn
Margaret A. de Lisser	(Not admitted in CA)
David A. DeGroot	Roxane Alicia Polidora
Maureen C. Dellinger	Ann E. Polus
Matthew D. Disco	Adam D. Pressman
David A. Eligator	Richard P. Rados
Steven W. Frank	Jesus G. Roman
Ellyn Freed	Elizabeth K. Roodner
Patricia A. Furlong	Jeffrey S. Ross
Gilbert J. Garcia-Pumento	Katherine M. Salo
Ruth E. Gaube	Jennifer T. Sanders
Christopher S. Gibson	Rona H. Sandler
Emily J. Gould	Margaret S. Schroeder
Andrea L. Gross	Luma C. Serrano
George A. Gucker	Sally K. Smith
Laura E. Hannusch	Morgan R. Smock
Alice K. Hayashi	Scott C. Taylor
Henry A. Hernandez	Patrick S. Thompson
Constance M. Hiatt	Catherine L. Thornberry
Curt Holbreich	Marina C. Tsatalis
Victoria N. Kaempf	Laura E. Watts
Alexa K. King	Joseph A. Whitecavage
Ed Kolto	Laura A. Woodman
Judith B. Kridle	Monique L. Wright
Michael F. LaBianca	Bruce L. Yonehiro
David R. Lamarre	Kim Zeldin

For full biographical listings, see the Martindale-Hubbell Law Directory

---

ROGERS, JOSEPH, O'DONNELL & QUINN, A PROFESSIONAL CORPORATION (AV)

311 California Street, 94104
Telephone: 415-956-2828
Fax: 415-956-6457

(See Next Column)

ROGERS, JOSEPH, O'DONNELL & QUINN A PROFESSIONAL CORPORATION—
Continued

Allan J. Joseph	Anna M. Rossi
Martin Quinn	Connie M. Teevan
Neil H. O'Donnell	Allen Samelson
Margot Wenger	Suzanne M. Mellard
Pamela Phillips	Neil H. Weinstein
Renée D. Wasserman	Patricia A. Meagher

Merri A. Baldwin

OF COUNSEL

Joseph W. Rogers   William Bennett Turner

Kyra A. Subbotin

David F. Innis	Ian K. Sweedler
Jennifer M. Kawamura	Matthew D. Levett
Sean M. SeLegue	E. Sean McLoughlin

Aaron P. Silberman

SPECIAL COUNSEL

Valerie Ackerman

For full biographical listings, see the Martindale-Hubbell Law Directory

---

ROPERS, MAJESKI, KOHN & BENTLEY, A PROFESSIONAL CORPORATION (AV)

670 Howard Street, 94105
Telephone: 415-543-4800
Fax: 415-512-1574
Redwood City, California Office: 1001 Marshall Street.
Telephone: 415-364-8200.
Fax: 415-367-0997.
San Jose, California Office: 80 North 1st Street.
Telephone: 408-287-6262.
Fax: 408-297-6819.
Santa Rosa, California Office: Fountaingrove Center, Suite 300, 3558 Round Barn Boulevard.
Telephone: 707-524-4200.
Fax: 707-523-4610.
Los Angeles, California Office: 550 South Hope Street, Suite 1900.
Telephone: 213-312-2000.
Fax: 213-312-2001.
Sacramento, California Office: 1000 G Street, Suite 400.
Telephone: 916-556-3100.
Fax: 916-442-7121.

John A. Koeppel (Resident)	David C. Anderson (Resident)
John A. Rowland (Resident)	Dennis D. Strazulo (Resident)
Charles M. Louderback (Resident)	John Curran Ladd (Resident)
James A. Lassart (Resident)	Stacey L. Pratt (Resident)
Jeffrey W. Allen (Resident)	Lawrence O. Monin
Gail Y. Norton (Resident)	Adrian G. Driscoll (Resident)
Paul D. Herbert (Resident)	Robert J. Intner
	George G. Weickhardt

Carol P. La Plant (Resident)	Larry A. Reback
Bruce Hunter Hinze (Resident)	Joleen C. Lenihan
Maurice J. Fitzgerald (Resident)	Heidi Quinn
Mary Ellen Gambino	Ilene Hoffman Goldberg
Narendra B. Patel	Kathleen Clark
Timothy Joseph Lucey	Andrew Wanger
Joseph P. Breen	Michelle Elig

OF COUNSEL

Ronald F. Sullivan   Stephen S. Austin

For full biographical listings, see the Martindale-Hubbell Law Directory

---

ROBERT G. SCHUCHARDT (AV)

Four Embarcadero Center, Suite 1700, 94111
Telephone: 415-986-5000
Fax: 415-434-3947

LEGAL SUPPORT PERSONNEL

Susanne Beilicke

Reference: Bank of America (Main Office).

For full biographical listings, see the Martindale-Hubbell Law Directory

---

SEDGWICK, DETERT, MORAN & ARNOLD (AV)

A Partnership including Professional Corporations
16th Floor, One Embarcadero Center, 94111-3765
Telephone: 415-781-7900
Cable Address: "SEDMA"
Fax: 415-781-2635
Email: E-Mail@SDMA.com
Los Angeles, California Office: 801 South Figueroa Street, 18th Floor.
Telephone: 213-426-6900.
Fax: 213-426-6921.

(See Next Column)

New York, New York Office: 41st Floor, 59 Maiden Lane.
Telephone: 212-422-0202.
Fax: 212-422-0925.
Telex: 141027.
Irvine, California Office: 3 Park Plaza, 17th Floor.
Telephone: 714-852-8200.
Fax: 714-852-8282.
Chicago, Illinois Office: The Rookery Building, Seventh Floor, 209 South La Salle Street.
Telephone: 312-641-9050.
Fax: 312-641-9530.
London, England Office: Lloyds Avenue House, 6 Lloyds Avenue, EC3N 3AX.
Telephone: 0171-929-1829.
Fax: 0171-929-1808.
Telex: 927037.
Zurich, Switzerland Office: Spluegenstrasse 3, CH-8002.
Telephone: 011-411-201-1730.
Fax: 011-411-201-4404.

MEMBERS OF FIRM

Andrew J. Collins *	Steven D. Wasserman
P. Beach Kuhl *	Scott D. Mroz
Roger W. Sleight *	David De Busschere
William C. Judge *	Paul J. Riehle
Kevin J. Dunne *	Stuart W. Miller
Stephen W. Jones *	Kathleen D. Patterson
Gregory C. Read *	Frederick D. Baker
David E. Bordon *	Martin J. O'Leary
Mark W. Hudson *	Eugene V. Elsbree III
W. Bruce Wold *	Christopher A. Nedeau
Cynthia H. Plevin *	Alan H. Packer
Warren J. Krauss	Ann L. Wilson
Paul B. Lahaderne	Stephanie A. Sheridan
Berridge R. Marsh	Steven P. Burke
Michael B. McGeehon	James S. Brown
Nicholas W. Heldt	Tod I. Zuckerman
Michael F. Healy	Anthony J. Anscombe
Rebecca A. Hull	Earl L. Hagström
Marilyn Klinger	Annette C. Warfield Hughes
Steven D. Roland	Micki S. Singer

SPECIAL COUNSEL

Daniel T. Bernhard	Kathryn H. Edwards
Randall G. Block	James L. Gault *

Ann J. Reavis

ASSOCIATES

Gary A. Cerio	James V. Weixel, Jr.
Marie J. Giardina	William E. Adams
Judy S. Ireland	Nicola Erbe
Shelley L. Brittman	Sean H. Gallagher
Constance A. Leahy	Gayle L. Gough
Kathleen A. McKinley	Matthew H. Haberkorn
Alicia J. Donahue	R. Peter Rittling
Barbara H. Clement	Charles T. Sheldon
Kirk Christopher Jenkins	Ingrid E. von Kaschnitz
Melinda Knupp Walker	Jeanine M. Donohue
Holly A. Harris	David E. Faliszek
Carol V. Holland	Elizabeth Yelland Lara
Sigrid Owczarek	Eric W. Schnurpfeil
Stephen A. Schram	Wayne A. Wolff
Denise Trani-Morris	B. Scott Douglass
James Yuanxin Li	Matthew S. Collins
Diane D. Papan	Peter J. Messrobian
James P. Diwik	R. Scott Diaz
Janet M. Alexander	Linh N. Ha
Elizabeth A. Collier	Michael McDonnell
Craig S. Jones	Ritu Patel
Shannon Ball Jones	Denis S. Kenny
Sarah E. Lucas	David McClure
Nadine Permutt Lauren	Michael F. Ehrlich
Noreen E. McDermott	Geoffrey M. Ezgar
Maureen Mulligan	Robert E. Tonn

Representative Clients: Aetna Casualty & Surety Co.; Bristol Meyers Squibb; Chrysler Corp.; Lockheed Missiles & Space Co.; Underwriters at Lloyd's.
*A Professional Corporation

For full biographical listings, see the Martindale-Hubbell Law Directory

---

SEVERSON & WERSON, A PROFESSIONAL CORPORATION (AV)

Twenty-Fifth Floor, 1 Embarcadero Center, 94111
Telephone: 415-398-3344
Telecopier: 415-956-0439
Newport Beach, California Office: 4675 MacArthur Court, Suite 370.
Telephone: 714-442-7110.
Facsimile: 714-442-7118.

Nathan R. Berke (1912-1985)	Lawrence A. Callaghan
Walter R. Severson (1903-1986)	Jan T. Chilton
Carole F. Barrett	Ransom S. Cook
John W. Bergholt	Paul N. Dubrasich
Michael J. Bertinetti	Loraine P. Eber
Gerald J. Buchwald	David A. Ericksen

(See Next Column)

SEVERSON & WERSON A PROFESSIONAL CORPORATION, *San Francisco—Continued*

John H. Feldmann, III	Michael B. Murphy
Allan L. Fink	Donald J. Querio
Duane M. Geck	Roberta V. Romberg
Edward A. Giedgowd	Ernest Y. Sevier
Mark Joseph Kenney	Michael J. Steiner
Edmund T. King, II	William L. Stern
Robert L. Lofts	John B. Sullivan
Mark D. Lonergan	Dennis M. Talbott
Patricia L. McClaran	Larry W. Telford
William T. McGivern, Jr.	Steven W. Waldo
Scott H. McNutt	James B. Werson
Roger S. Mertz	Donald J. Yellon

Christopher S. Chen	Gregory C. Nuti
Joel L. Halverson	Jasmin N. Patel
Edward P. Heartney	Carolyn Powell (Resident at Newport Beach Office)
Christina G. Hong	
Karen S. Hull	William C. Ruettinger
Scott J. Hyman	Andrew P. Rush
Kristine H. Kim	Jeffrey C. Selman
Kimberly A. Kralowec	Daniel B. Siegel
Peter C. Lyon	Kimberly D. Taylor (Resident at Newport Beach Office)
Colleen H. McDonald	

SPECIAL COUNSEL

William E. Hannan, III	Joseph Louis Kish
Rebecca U. Litteneker	

For full biographical listings, see the Martindale-Hubbell Law Directory

SHARTSIS, FRIESE & GINSBURG, LLP (AV)

One Maritime Plaza, Eighteenth Floor, 94111
Telephone: 415-421-6500
FAX: 415-421-2922

Robert Charles Friese	Tracy L. Salisbury
Arthur J. Shartsis	Jeffrey A. O'Connell
Mary Jo Shartsis	Susan York Janin
Robert D. Evans	Carolyn R. Klasco
Douglas L. Hammer	Jeffrey J. Goodrich
Ronald Hayes Malone	Eric Sippel
Joel Zeldin	Jonathan M. Kennedy
John P. Broadhurst	Adam K. Elsesser
David H. Kremer	Steven O. Gasser
Charles R. Rice	Barbara W. Staman
Anthony B. Leuin	Zesara C. Chan
Douglas Mo	M. Greg Allio
Robert E. Schaberg	Geoffrey W. Haynes

Christopher J. Rupright	Michael B. Schwarz
Carolyn S. Reiser	James P. Martin
Ellen S. Mouchawar	Frank A. Cialone
Robert Charles Ward	Lara Orsi McCarthy
Carl D. Ciochon	Benjamin L. Douglas
Christina M. O'Brien	

SENIOR COUNSEL

Paul M. Ginsburg

OF COUNSEL

Adam C. Belsky	Mary R. Montella
Monique A. van Yzerlooy	

For full biographical listings, see the Martindale-Hubbell Law Directory

SHEARMAN & STERLING (AV)

555 California Street, 94104-1522
Telephone: (415) 616-1100
Fax: (415) 616-1199
New York, N.Y. Office: 599 Lexington Avenue, New York, New York 10022-6069 and Citicorp Center, 153 East 53rd Street, New York, New York 10022-4676.
Telephone: (212) 848-4000.
Telex: 667290 Num Lau.
Fax: 599 Lexington Avenue: (212) 848-7179. Citicorp Center: (212) 848-5252.
Abu Dhabi, United Arab Emirates Office: P.O. Box 2948.
Telephone: (971-2) 324477.
Fax: (971-2) 774533.
Beijing, People's Republic of China Office: Suite #2205, Capital Mansion, No. 6, Xin Yuan Nan Lu. Chao Yang District, Beijing, 100004.
Telephone: (86-10)6465-4574.
Fax: (86-10) 6465-4578.
Budapest, Hungary Office: Szerb utca 17-19, 1056 Budapest.
Telephone: (36-1) 266-3522.
Fax: (36-1) 266-3523.
Düsseldorf, Federal Republic of Germany Office: Couvenstrasse 8 40211 Düsseldorf.
Telephone: (49 211) 178 88-0.
Fax: (49 211) 178 88-88.
Telex: 8588294 NYLO.

(See Next Column)

Frankfurt, Federal Republic of Germany Office: Bockenheimer Landstrasse 55, 60325 Frankfurt am Main.
Telephone: (49-69) 97107-0.
Fax: (49-69) 97107-100.
Hong Kong Office: Standard Chartered Bank Building, 4 Des Voeux Road, Central.
Telephone: (852) 2978-8000.
Fax: (852) 2978-8099.
London, England Office: 199 Bishopsgate, London EC2M 3TY.
Telephone: (44-171) 920-9000.
Fax: (44-171) 920-9020.
Los Angeles, California Office: 777 South Figueroa Street, 34th Floor, 90017-5418.
Telephone: (213) 239-0300.
Fax: (213) 239-0381, 614-0936.
Paris, France Office: 114 avenue des Champs-Elysées, 75008.
Telephone: (33-1) 53-89-7000.
Fax: (33-1) 53-89-7070.
Telex: 282964 ROYALE.
Singapore Office: 80 Raffles Place #16-21, UOB Plaza 2. Singapore 048624. Telephone (65) 230-3800.
Fax: (65) 230-3899.
Tokyo, Japan Office: Shearman & Sterling (Grant Finlayson Gaikokuho-Jimu-Bengoshi Jimusho), Fukoku Seimei Building, 5th Fl. 2-2-2, Uchisaiwaicho, Chiyoda-ku, Tokyo 100, Japan.
Telephone: (81 3) 5251-1601.
Fax: (81 3) 5251-1602.
Toronto, Ontario, Canada Office: Commerce Court West, Suite 4405, P.O. Box 247, M5L 1E8.
Telephone: (416) 360-8484.
Fax: (416) 360-2958.
Washington, D.C. Office: 801 Pennsylvania Avenue, N.W., 20004-2604.
Telephone: (202) 508-8000.
Fax: (202) 508-8100.

RESIDENT PARTNERS

William H. Hinman (Not admitted in CA; Managing Partner)	Alfred C. Groff
	Michael J. Kennedy
	Dean S. Krystowski
Jeffrey S. Facter	Susan S. Muck
Steven E. Sherman	

OTHER COUNSEL

Robert L. Nelson, Jr.	Douglas M. Young

For full biographical listings, see the Martindale-Hubbell Law Directory

SKJERVEN, MORRILL, MACPHERSON, FRANKLIN & FRIEL LLP (AV)

Suite 800, 601 California Street, 94108
Telephone: 415-986-8383
Telecopier: 415-982-7372
San Jose, California Office: Suite 700, 25 Metro Drive.
Telephone: 408-453-9200.
Telecopier: 408-453-7979.
Austin, Texas Office: Suite 300 West, 9600 Great Hills Trail.
Telephone: 512-794-3600.
Telecopier: 512-794-3601.

MEMBERS OF FIRM

Richard H. Skjerven (At San Jose, California and Austin, Texas Offices)	Charles D. Chalmers (Also at San Jose and Austin, Texas Offices)
Robert B. Morrill (Also at San Jose Office)	Kenneth E. Leeds (Resident, San Jose Office)
Alan H. MacPherson (Resident, San Jose Office)	Brian D. Ogonowsky (Resident, San Jose Office)
Richard K. Franklin (Resident, San Jose Office)	David E. Steuber (Resident, San Jose Office)
Thomas J. Friel, Jr. (Also at San Jose Office)	Laura Terlizzi (Resident, San Jose Office)
Marc David Freed (Also at San Jose Office)	Edward V. Anderson (Resident, San Jose Office)
Anthony de Alcuaz (Resident, San Jose Office)	Edward C. Kwok (Resident, San Jose Office)
Justin T. Beck (Resident, San Jose Office)	Michelle G. Breit (Resident, San Jose Office)
Joseph A. Greco (Resident, San Jose Office)	Stephen A. Terrile (Resident, Austin, Texas Office)
David W. Heid (Resident, San Jose Office)	Russell L. Johnson (Resident, San Jose Office)
Forrest E. Gunnison (Resident, San Jose Office)	Kimberly Paul Zapata (Resident, San Jose Office)
Norman R. Klivans, Jr. (Resident, San Jose Office)	Ken J. Koestner (Resident, Austin, Texas Office)

ASSOCIATES

Michael Shenker (Resident, San Jose Office)	T. Lester Wallace (Resident, San Jose Office)
Scott R. Brown (Resident, San Jose Office)	Peter H. Kang (Resident, San Jose Office)
Patrick T. Bever (Resident, San Jose Office)	Alexandra J. Horne (Resident, San Jose Office)
James E. Parsons (Resident, San Jose Office)	David T. Millers (Resident, San Jose Office)

(See Next Column)

SKJERVEN, MORRILL, MACPHERSON, FRANKLIN & FRIEL LLP—*Continued*

ASSOCIATES (Continued)

E. Eric Hoffman
(Resident, San Jose Office)
Omkarmurthy K. Suryadevara
(Resident, San Jose Office)
Emily M. Haliday
(Resident, San Jose Office)
Elizabeth Ann Hemphill
(Resident, San Jose Office)
William L. Paradice III
(Resident, San Jose Office)
L. Scott Primak
(Resident, San Jose Office)
Thomas E. Rossmeissl
(Resident, San Jose Office)
Steven M. Levitan
(Resident, San Jose Office)
Arthur J. Behiel
(Resident, San Jose Office)
Michael J. Halbert
(Resident, San Jose Office)
Jennifer A. Ochs
(Resident, San Jose Office)

Serge J. Hodgson
(Resident, San Jose Office)
Edward S. Mao
(Resident, San Jose Office)
Scott D. Minden
(Resident, San Jose Office)
Lisa Lee Pate
(Resident, San Jose Office)
Matthew T. Powers
(Resident, San Jose Office)
Leanne Price
(Resident, San Jose Office)
Jeffrey C. Whitley
(Resident, San Jose Office)
Paul Yang
(Resident, San Jose Office)
Juergen Krause-Polstorff
(Resident, San Jose Office)
Bryan K. Anderson
(Resident, San Jose Office)
Kent B. Chambers (Resident,
Austin, Texas Office)

OF COUNSEL

Thomas S. MacDonald
(Resident, San Jose Office)

H. Donald Nelson
(Resident, San Jose Office)

TECHNICAL COUNSEL

Ronald J. Meetin (Resident, San Jose Office)

PATENT AGENT

Anthony G. Dervan (Resident, San Jose Office)

Reference: Bank of America.

For full biographical listings, see the Martindale-Hubbell Law Directory

---

SONNENSCHEIN NATH & ROSENTHAL (AV)

10th Floor, 685 Market Street, 94105
Telephone: 415-882-5000
Telecopier: 415-543-5472
Chicago, Illinois Office: Suite 8000 Sears Tower, 233 South Wacker Drive.
Telephone: 312-876-8000.
Cable Address: "Sonberk".
Telex: 25-3526.
Facsimile: 312-876-7934.
New York, N.Y. Office: 1221 Avenue of the Americas, 24th Floor.
Telephone: 212-768-6700.
Facsimile: 212-391-1247.
Washington, D.C. Office: 1301 K Street, N.W., Suite 600, East Tower.
Telephone: 202-408-6400.
Facsimile: 202-408-6399.
Los Angeles, California Office: Suite 1500, 601 South Figueroa Street.
Telephone: 213-623-9300.
Facsimile: 213-623-9924.
St. Louis, Missouri Office: One Metropolitan Square, Suite 3000.
Telephone: 314-241-1800.
Facsimile: 314-259-5959.
Kansas City, Missouri Office: Suite 1100, 4520 Main Street, 64111.
Telephone: 816-932-4400.
Facsimile: 816-531-7545.
London, England Office: Sonnenscheins, Royex House, Aldermanbury Square, EC2V 7HR.
Telephone: 0171-600-2222.
Facsimile: 0171-600-2221.

RESIDENT PARTNERS

Gayle M. Athanacio
Michael A. Barnes
Robin M. Edwards
Steven H. Frankel
Paul E. B. Glad
Oliver L. Holmes
Curtis E. A. Karnow
H. Sinclair Kerr, Jr.
Mark J. Linderman

Sandra R. McCandless
Cynthia L. Mellema
Philip A. O'Connell, Jr.
Ivor E. Samson
Arnold P. Schuster
Peter A. Smalbach
Charles Spiegel
John Leland Williams
Nicholas C. Yost

OF COUNSEL

Jon K. Adams

RESIDENT ASSOCIATES

Terence M. Abad
Cheryl Dyer Berg
Susan E. Bloch
Kevin M. Christensen
Theodore Correl
Kenneth G. Downs
Deborah F. Dubin
Thomas E. Duley
Terri Marie Esparza
Bryce P. Goeking

James L. Heideman
Mary Kay Lacey
Matthew F. Lintner
Rhonda V. Magee
J. Robert Maxwell
Sean McEneaney
Anuja Guleria Purohit
Gregory L. Smith
Phyllis T. Solomon
Christopher P. Sonderby

(See Next Column)

RESIDENT ASSOCIATES (Continued)

Diane Sovereign
Craig A. Sterling

Kelly B. Valen
Michael J. von Loewenfeldt

Paula M. Yost

For full biographical listings, see the Martindale-Hubbell Law Directory

---

STEEFEL, LEVITT & WEISS, A PROFESSIONAL CORPORATION (AV)

30th Floor, One Embarcadero Center, 94111
Telephone: 415-788-0900
Fax: 415-788-2019
Email: slw@steefel.com

Edward R. Steefel
Alvin T. Levitt
Lenard G. Weiss
Richard A. Kramer
Harvey S. Schochet
Michael J. Lawson
Christine A. Murphy
Janet C. Norris
Marvin B. Pearlstein
Harvey L. Leiderman
Laura R. Craft
Bruce E. Prigoff

Frank T. Pepler
Leonard R. Stein
Michael D. Early
Marc A. Lackner
Clayton B. Gantz
Craig P. Wood
Barry W. Lee
Jordan P. Rose
James F. Eastman
Stephen S. Mayne
Brenda Jansen
Daryl S. Landy

Sheldon H. Wolfe

Richard Aiello
Mario L. Albert
Andrew A. Bassak
Jay H. Bhatt
Kenneth A. Brunetti
Lisa M. Carvalho
Brian J. Danzig
Jill S. Dodd
Adriana Estrada
Joseph E. Floren
Karen Frasier-Kolligs
John P. Halfpenny
E. Venessa Henlon
Anthony J. Justman
Christine Garcia Kolm
(Not admitted in CA)

Ralph T. Kokka
Julie B. Landau
Peter N. Larson
William L. Lowery
Vladislav V. Luskin
Peter A. Mastromonaco
Elaine B. Michetti
Robert B. Mison
Eugene M. Pak
Kevin Reese
Teresa A. Rice
Sarah Richards
Lisa R. Sattler
Michael G. Schinner
Karen F. Smart
Erica J. Teasley

Pamela A. Weeks

OF COUNSEL

Ronald Larson
Gary J. Shapiro

Richard J. Tannenbaum
(Not admitted in CA)

For full biographical listings, see the Martindale-Hubbell Law Directory

---

SAN JOSE, * Santa Clara Co.

CAMPBELL, WARBURTON, FITZSIMMONS, SMITH, MENDELL & PASTORE, A PROFESSIONAL CORPORATION (AV)

111 West St. John Street, Suite 440, P.O. Box 1867, 95113
Telephone: 408-295-7701
Fax: 408-295-1423

Frank Valpey Campbell
(1892-1971)
Frank L. Custer (1902-1962)
Alfred B. Britton, Jr.
(1919-1991)
Austen D. Warburton
(1917-1995)

John R. Fitzsimmons, Jr.
C. Michael Smith
Ralph E. Mendell
Nicholas Pastore
J. Michael Fitzsimmons

William R. Colucci

Carolyn M. Rose

LEGAL SUPPORT PERSONNEL

Susan Frederick

Representative Corporate Clients: Helene Curtis, Inc.; Viking Freight System, Inc.
Representative Insurance Clients: California State Automobile Assn.; Farmers Insurance Group; Travelers Insurance Co.; Westfield Insurance Cos.; Michelin Tire Corp. (Self Insured).

For full biographical listings, see the Martindale-Hubbell Law Directory

---

LAW OFFICES OF THOMAS R. HOGAN (AV)

60 South Market Street, Suite 1125, 95113-2332
Telephone: 408-292-7600
Facsimile: 408-292-7611

ASSOCIATES

Kelly W. Bhirdo

PARALEGAL

Leslie Holmes

For full biographical listings, see the Martindale-Hubbell Law Directory

San Jose—Continued

HOPKINS & CARLEY, A LAW CORPORATION (AV)

Fifteenth Floor, 150 Almaden Boulevard, 95113-2089
Telephone: 408-286-9800
Facsimile: 408-998-4790

Leon A. Carley (1908-1984)	Jon Michaelson
John F. Hopkins	James M. Hager
Robert D. Wenzel	Charles H. Packer
Garth E. Pickett	Ross G. Adler
Dunham B. Sherer	Robert V. Hawn
Arthur V. Plank	Jeffrey E. Essner
Stephen J. Kottmeier	William S. Klein
Anthony J. McCarthy	Timothy H. Hopkins

Robert O. Whyte

OF COUNSEL

Clarence A. Kellogg Jr.	Theodore J. Biagini

Donald J. Pagel

Brenda N. Buonaiuto	Robert W. Ricketson
Jennifer M. Cunneen	Jay M. Ross
Brian C. Finerty	Jessica M. Schwedner
H. Katerina Hertzog	Suzanne F. Seavello
David R. McDonald	Russell K. Smith
Kimberly S. Pellissier	Linda Larson Usoz
Christine Baddell Redfield	Susan L. Walker
Sally A. Reed	Sharon L. Wong

Denise Y. Yamamoto

For full biographical listings, see the Martindale-Hubbell Law Directory

JACKSON TUFTS COLE & BLACK, LLP (AV)

A Registered Limited Liability Partnership
60 South Market Street, 10th Floor, 95113
Telephone: 408-998-1952
Fax: 408-998-4889
Email: info@jtcb.com
San Francisco, California Office: 650 California Street, Thirty-Second Floor.
Telephone: 415-433-1950.
Fax: 415-392-3494.

MEMBERS OF FIRM

Bartlett A. Jackson (A Professional Corporation)	D. D. Hughmanick
	William H. Booth
Robert R. Tufts	Twila L. Foster
George H. Cole, Jr.	Nicole A. Dillingham
J. David Black	George R. Theofel
Templeton C. Peck	Jeffrey J. Cole
Charles G. Stephenson	Roy M. Bartlett, Jr.
John S. Siamas	Richard Scudellari
David T. Alexander	Donna M. Mezias
Carl J. Stoney, Jr.	Martin S. Schenker
Kenneth J. Philpot	Michael F. McCabe
Michael J. Baker	Debra L. Kasper
David Ayers Thompson	Paul H. Goldstein
Ellen McGinty King	Lynn M. McLean
Peter S. Muñoz	Jane M. Hawkins
Dennis V. Swanson	Patrick S. Hallinan
Debra S. Belaga	Lynn Acker Starr
Emil G. Pesiri	Stephen M. Debenham

Shane M. Byrne

OF COUNSEL

Eric T. Sullivan	Gerald Z. Marer
Wayne W. Lew	Breck E. Milde

ASSOCIATES

Marily Peatman Lerner	Marion C. Ingersoll
Robert G. White	Ki D. Ingersol
Gretchen Dean Hug	Elizabeth A. Barton
Benjamin B. Quinones	Erin L. McPherson
Eric S. Walters	Jason W. Kuhns
Steven N. Sherr	Joseph M. Quinn, III
John J. Sciortino	Jonathan M. Eisenberg
Daniel L. Rabago	Anne Hayes Hartman
Amy E. Margolin	Mark A. Sheft

For full biographical listings, see the Martindale-Hubbell Law Directory

McCUTCHEN, DOYLE, BROWN & ENERSEN (AV)

Market Post Tower, Suite 1500, 55 South Market Street, 95113-2327
Telephone: 408-947-8400
Facsimile: 408-947-4750
Telex: 910 250 2931 MACPAG SJ
Email: postmaster@mdbe.com
San Francisco, California Office: Three Embarcadero Center, 94111-4066.
Telephone: 415-393-2000.
Facsimile: 415-393-2286 (G I, II, III).
Telex: 340817 MACPAG SFO.

(See Next Column)

Los Angeles, California Office: 355 South Grand Avenue, Suite 4400, 90071-1560.
Telephone: 213-680-6400.
Facsimile: 213-680-6499.
Walnut Creek, California Office: 1331 North California Boulevard, Post Office Box V, 94596-4502.
Telephone: 510-937-8000.
Facsimile: 510-975-5390.
Palo Alto, California Office: One Embarcadero Place, 2100 Geng Road, 94303-0913.
Telephone: 415-846-4000.
Fax: 415-846-4086.
Washington, D.C. Office: The Evening Star Building, Suite 800, 1101 Pennsylvania Avenue, N.W., 20004-2514.
Telephone: 202-628-4900.
Facsimile: 202-628-4912.
Taipei, Taiwan Republic of China Office: International Trade Building, Tenth Floor, 333 Keelung Road, Section 1, 110.
Telephone: 886-2-723-5000.
Facsimile: 886-2-757-6070.
Affiliated Offices In: Bangkok, Thailand; Beijing, China; Shanghai, China.

MEMBERS OF FIRM

Christopher P. Berka	Charles William Craycroft
Ross E. Campbell	Carol K. Dillon
Byde W. Clawson	John W. Fowler
Daniel Cooperman	James P. Kleinberg
Robert E. Cox	Ronald S. Laurie

Gordon T. Yamate

OF COUNSEL

Kathleen A. McDonald (Resident)	Beth A. McGowen
	Christine E. Sherry

Beverly A. Tiffany

ASSOCIATES

Kristin K. Bear	Claire T. Cormier
William W. Choe	Michael T. Pyle

James Grant Snell

For full biographical listings, see the Martindale-Hubbell Law Directory

MILLER, MORTON, CAILLAT & NEVIS (AV)

50 West San Fernando Street, Suite 1300, 95113-2413
Telephone: 408-292-1765
Telecopier: 408-292-4484

Richard W. Morton (1916-1975)	Charles V. Caillat (1920-1990)

Harvey C. Miller (1906-1993)

MEMBERS OF FIRM

David L. Nevis	Joseph A. Scanlan, Jr.
Francis J. Hughes	Carolyn Tobiason Stuart
Peter A. Kline	William K. Hurley
Stevan C. Adelman	Peter V. Dessau

Eric Mogensen

OF COUNSEL

Nancy F. Symons	Susan L. Sutton

Pamela J. Silberstein

ASSOCIATES

Kathryn E. Barrett	David I. Kornbluh
Katherine S. Pak	Kimberly Holtz MacMillan

Representative Clients: Trammell Crow Residential Services; Joe Kerley Lincoln Mercury Co.; Milligan News Co.; Joseph George Distributors; The Frozen Food Employees Pension Trust; Santa Clara Dental Society; New West Foods; Bay Apartment Communities; Guy F. Atkinson Company; A. Hathaway Co.

For full biographical listings, see the Martindale-Hubbell Law Directory

ROPERS, MAJESKI, KOHN & BENTLEY, A PROFESSIONAL CORPORATION (AV)

80 North 1st Street, 95113
Telephone: 408-287-6262
Fax: 408-297-6819
Redwood City, California Office: 1001 Marshall Street.
Telephone: 415-364-8200.
Fax: 415-367-0997.
San Francisco, California Office: 670 Howard Street.
Telephone: 415-543-4800.
Fax: 415-512-1574.
Santa Rosa, California Office: Fountaingrove Center, Suite 300, 3558 Round Barn Boulevard.
Telephone: 707-524-4200.
Fax: 707-523-4610.
Los Angeles, California Office: 550 South Hope Street, Suite 1900.
Telephone: 213-312-2000.
Fax: 213-312-2001.
Sacramento, California Office: 1000 G Street, Suite 400.
Telephone: 916-556-3100.
Fax: 916-442-7121.

(See Next Column)

ROPERS, MAJESKI, KOHN & BENTLEY A PROFESSIONAL CORPORATION—
Continued

Robert S. Luft (Resident)	George E. Clause (Resident)
Dennis J. Ward (Resident)	Curtis R. Tingley (Resident)
Richard M. Williams (Resident)	Mary L. Scharrenberg (Resident)
Michael J. Ioannou (Resident)	Dean A. Pappas (Resident)
Stephan A. Barber (Resident)	Jo Ann DeRuvo (Resident)
Kevin P. Cody (Resident)	James C. Hyde

David B. Draper

Christopher J. Cox (Resident)	Eva Yablonsky
Daniel R. Kirwan (Resident)	Anne S. Hilleary
J. Mark Thacker (Resident)	Lita Monique Verrier
Carol Seidler Golbranson	Mary H. Atwell (Resident)
(Resident)	Bruce Piontkowski
John Komar	Jonathan M. Schwartz
Douglas W. Dal Cielo	Judy B. Shaw
Martin Dioli	Nicole E. Rossi

For full biographical listings, see the Martindale-Hubbell Law Directory

---

RUBY & SCHOFIELD (AV)

A Partnership of Law Corporations
60 South Market Street, Suite 1500, 95113-2379
Telephone: 408-998-8500
Fax: 408-998-8503

Allen Ruby (L.C.)   Glen W. Schofield (L.C.)

For full biographical listings, see the Martindale-Hubbell Law Directory

---

SKJERVEN, MORRILL, MACPHERSON, FRANKLIN & FRIEL LLP (AV)

Suite 700, 25 Metro Drive, 95110
Telephone: 408-453-9200
Telecopier: 408-453-7979
San Francisco, California Office: Suite 800, 601 California Street.
Telephone: 415-986-8383.
Telecopier: 415-982-7372.
Austin, Texas Office: Suite 300 West, 9600 Great Hills Trail.
Telephone: 512-794-3600.
Telecopier: 512-794-3601.

MEMBERS OF FIRM

Richard H. Skjerven	Kenneth E. Leeds
(Also at Austin, Texas Office)	Brian D. Ogonowsky
Robert B. Morrill	David E. Steuber
Alan H. MacPherson	Laura Terlizzi
Richard K. Franklin	Edward V. Anderson
Thomas J. Friel, Jr.	Edward C. Kwok
Marc David Freed	Michelle G. Breit
Anthony de Alcuaz	Stephen A. Terrile (Resident,
Justin T. Beck	Austin, Texas Office)
Joseph A. Greco	Russell L. Johnson
David W. Heid	Kimberly Paul Zapata
Forrest E. Gunnison	Ken J. Koestner (Resident,
Norman R. Klivans, Jr.	Austin, Texas Office)
Charles D. Chalmers (Also at	
San Francisco and Austin,	
Texas Offices)	

ASSOCIATES

Michael Shenker	Thomas E. Rossmeissl
Scott R. Brown	Steven M. Levitan
Patrick T. Bever	Arthur J. Behiel
James E. Parsons	Michael J. Halbert
T. Lester Wallace	Jennifer A. Ochs
Peter H. Kang	Serge J. Hodgson
Alexandra J. Horne	Edward S. Mao
David T. Millers	Scott D. Minden
E. Eric Hoffman	Lisa Lee Pate
Omkarmurthy K. Suryadevara	Matthew T. Powers
Emily M. Haliday	Leanne Price
Elizabeth Ann Hemphill	Jeffrey C. Whitley
William L. Paradice III	Paul Yang
L. Scott Primak	Juergen Krause-Polstorff

Bryan K. Anderson

OF COUNSEL

Thomas S. MacDonald   H. Donald Nelson

TECHNICAL COUNSEL

Ronald J. Meetin

PATENT AGENT

Anthony G. Dervan

Reference: Bank of America.

For full biographical listings, see the Martindale-Hubbell Law Directory

---

VAN LOUCKS & HANLEY (AV)

160 West Santa Clara Street, Suite 1050, 95113
Telephone: 408-494-0400
Fax: 408-494-0404

Geoffrey Van Loucks   Anthony L. Hanley

Michael K. Budra

Reference: San Jose National Bank.

For full biographical listings, see the Martindale-Hubbell Law Directory

---

SAN LEANDRO, Alameda Co. — (Refer to Hayward)

SAN MATEO, San Mateo Co.

QUADROS & JOHNSON (AV)

1400 Fashion Island Boulevard, Suite 800, 94404
Telephone: 415-377-4300
Telecopier: 415-573-1387

Katherine M. Quadros   Benjamin A. Johnson

SENIOR ASSOCIATE

Kenyon Mark Lee

ASSOCIATES

Leslie A. Eberhardt   Michael D. Wood

OF COUNSEL

Arthur L. Hillman, Jr.

Representative Clients: Anning Johnson Co. (national gypsum board and asbestos abatement contractor); Bechtel Corporation; Blue Cross of California (major health benefits insurer); Browning-Ferris Industries, Inc. (national waste management company); Los Angeles County Metropolitan Transportation Authority; Mutual Savings & Loan; Pacific Gas and Electric Co.; Safeway, Inc.; Santa Clara County Transit District; Sasco Electric.

For full biographical listings, see the Martindale-Hubbell Law Directory

---

SANTA ANA,* Orange Co.

BEAM, BROBECK & WEST (AV)

600 West Santa Ana Boulevard, Suite 1000, 92701
Telephone: 714-558-3944
Fax: 714-568-0129

MEMBERS OF FIRM

Byron J. Beam	Kirk H. Nakamura
David J. Brobeck, Jr.	Robert H. McMillan
John E. West	Daniel R. Sullivan

ASSOCIATES

Betsey J. Jeffery	Donald S. Zalewski
Charles W. Matheis, Jr.	Geralyn L. Skapik
Robert C. Hastie	David R. Rosenberg
Gregory L. Rippetoe	Louise M. Douville
Jennifer J. Miller	Kermit D. Marsh

Representative Clients: Aetna Insurance Co.; American General Life Insurance Co.; American Hospital Supply; Carl Warren & Co.; Casualty Insurance Co.; City of Anaheim; City of Fullerton; City of Newport Beach; Empire Insurance Cos.; Physicians Interindemnity.

For full biographical listings, see the Martindale-Hubbell Law Directory

---

COTKIN & COLLINS, A PROFESSIONAL CORPORATION (AV)

200 West Santa Ana Boulevard, Suite 800, 92701
Telephone: 714-835-2330
FAX: 714-835-2209
Email: cotkinoc@sprynet.com
Los Angeles, California Office: 1055 West Seventh Street, Suite 1900.
Telephone: 213-688-9350.
FAX: 213-688-9351.

Raphael Cotkin	Joan M. Dolinsky
(Resident, Los Angeles Office)	(Resident, Los Angeles Office)
James P. Collins, Jr.	Robert G. Wilson
Steven L. Paine	(Resident, Los Angeles Office)
(Resident, Los Angeles Office)	David A. Winkle
William D. Naeve	Philip S. Gutierrez
Terry C. Leuin	Karen C. Freitas
(Resident, Los Angeles Office)	(Resident, Los Angeles Office)
Roger W. Simpson	Brian R. Hill
(Resident, Los Angeles Office)	

Lori S. Blitstien	Terry L. Kesinger
(Resident, Los Angeles Office)	Bradley W. Jacks
Carrie F. Smith	(Resident, Los Angeles Office)
(Resident, Los Angeles Office)	Scott P. Ward
Gregory A. Sargenti	(Resident, Los Angeles Office)

Ellen M. Tipping

References: American City Bank (Downtown Branch); Security Pacific Bank (7th and Grand Branch); Bank of America.

For full biographical listings, see the Martindale-Hubbell Law Directory

Santa Ana—Continued

HAIGHT, BROWN & BONESTEEL (AV)

A Partnership including Professional Corporations
Suite 900, 5 Hutton Centre Drive, 92707
Telephone: 714-754-1100
Telecopier: 714-754-0826
Santa Monica, California Office: 1620 26th Street, Suite 4000 North, P.O. Box 680.
Telephone: 310-449-6000.
Telecopier: 310-829-5117.
Telex: 705837.
Riverside, California Office: 3750 University Avenue, Suite 650.
Telephone: 909-341-8300.
Fax: 909-341-8309.
San Francisco, California Office: 20 Sansome Street, Suite 300.
Telephone: 415-986-7700.
Fax: 415-986-6954.

RESIDENT MEMBERS

Bruce L. Cleeland — Jay T. Thompson

ASSOCIATES

Laura M. Knox (Resident) — John M. Choi
Jeffrey S. Gerardo (Resident) — Elizabeth A. Livesay Fry
Susan A. Streit — Wendy L.R. Miele

Counsel for: Orange County: Aetna Casualty and Surety Co.; Zurich-American Insurance Cos.; Industrial Indemnity Co.; Professional Liability Claims Managers; Maryland Casualty Insurance Co.; Royal Insurance Company of America.

For full biographical listings, see the Martindale-Hubbell Law Directory

SPERLING & PERGANDE (AV)

3 Hutton Centre, Suite 670, 92707
Telephone: 714-540-8500
Facsimile: 714-540-2599

MEMBERS OF FIRM

Dean P. Sperling — K. William Pergande

For full biographical listings, see the Martindale-Hubbell Law Directory

SANTA ANA HEIGHTS, Orange Co. — (Refer to Santa Ana)

SANTA BARBARA,* Santa Barbara Co.

ALLEN AND KIMBELL (AV)

317 East Carrillo Street, 93101
Telephone: 805-963-8611
Fax: 805-962-1940
Email: ank@worldnet.att.net

MEMBERS OF FIRM

W. Joe Bush — Paul A. Graziano
Charles D. Kimbell — Steven K. McGuire
John H. Parke

ASSOCIATES

Jennifer J. Tice

OF COUNSEL

George H. Allen

Reference: Santa Barbara Bank.

For full biographical listings, see the Martindale-Hubbell Law Directory

ARCHBALD & SPRAY (AV)

505 Bath Street, 93101
Telephone: 805-564-2070
Telecopier: 805-564-2081
Email: arch@silcom.com

MEMBERS OF FIRM

Malcolm Archbald (Retired) — Karen T. Burgett
Joseph L. Spray (1927-1985) — Edwin K. Loskamp
Kenneth L. Moes — Wm. Brennan Lynch
J. William McLafferty — Michael A. Colton
Douglas B. Large — Ann Gormican Anderson

SENIOR ATTORNEYS

Peri Maziarz — Katherine H. Bower

ASSOCIATE

Cheryl A. Shaw

OF COUNSEL

John W. Warnock

Representative Clients: Aetna; Caldwell International, Inc.; Crawford & Company; Hyundai Motors America, Inc.; Jackson National Life Insurance Co.; Chevron, Inc.; Reliance National; Safeco Insurance Companies; City of San Buenaventura.

For full biographical listings, see the Martindale-Hubbell Law Directory

HOLLISTER & BRACE, A PROFESSIONAL CORPORATION (AV)

1126 Santa Barbara Street, P.O. Box 630, 93101
Telephone: 805-963-6711
Fax: 805-965-0329

William A. Brace (Retired) — Bradford F. Ginder
J. James Hollister, III (Retired) — John G. Busby
John S. Poucher — Susan H. McCollum
Richard C. Monk — Richard G. Kravetz
George A. Rempe, III — Robert L. Brace
Steven Evans Kirby — Marcus Scott Bird
David Frank Hubbard

OF COUNSEL

Julie A. Turner

Attorneys for: First American Title Insurance Co.; Celite Corp.; Chevron, U.S.A., Inc.; Mission Industries; Gaviota Marine Terminal Co.; Hyatt Hotels; Occidential Petroleum Corp.; Great Universal Capital Corp; Mobil Oil Corp.; Texaco Inc.

For full biographical listings, see the Martindale-Hubbell Law Directory

MULLEN & HENZELL, L.L.P. (AV)

A California registered limited liability partnership
112 East Victoria Street, Post Office Drawer 789, 93102-0789
Telephone: 805-966-1501
FAX: 805-966-9204

MEMBERS OF FIRM

Thomas M. Mullen (1915-1991) — Robert A. Zeavin
Arthur A. Henzell (Retired) — Joseph F. Green
J. Robert Andrews — Gary W. Robinson
James W. Brown — Lawrence T. Sorensen
Dennis W. Reilly — Gregory F. Faulkner
Jeffrey C. Nelson — Richard G. Battles
Charles S. Bargiel — Edward C. Thoits
Jay L. Beckerman — William E. Degen
Michael E. Cage

OF COUNSEL

Kim A. Harley Seefeld

ASSOCIATES

Andrew M. Polinsky — Paul K. Wilcox
Catherine Perlman — Thomas Y. Chen
Richard E. Fogg

Representative Clients: Goleta Sanitary District; Interinsurance Exchange of the Automobile Club of Southern California; State Farm Fire & Casualty Co.; State Farm Mutual Automobile Insurance Co.

For full biographical listings, see the Martindale-Hubbell Law Directory

SANTA CRUZ,* Santa Cruz Co.

BOSSO, WILLIAMS, LEVIN, SACHS & BOOK, A PROFESSIONAL CORPORATION (AV)

133 Mission Street, Suite 280, P.O. Box 1822, 95061-1822
Telephone: 408-426-8484
Fax: 408-458-9172; 423-2839
Email: admin@sclawfirm.com

Robert E. Bosso — Dennis R. Book
Lloyd R. Williams — Charlene B. Atack
Philip M. Sachs — John M. Gallagher

Catherine A. Rodoni — Jason R. Book

Representative Clients: Santa Cruz Seaside Co.; World Savings & Loan; Coast Dairies & Land Co.; Sunset Farms, Inc.; Valley Packing Service, Inc.; Soquel Creek Water District.
References: Coast Commercial Bank (Santa Cruz); Pacific Western Bank.

For full biographical listings, see the Martindale-Hubbell Law Directory

SANTA MARIA, Santa Barbara Co.

TWITCHELL AND RICE (AV)

215 North Lincoln Street, P.O. Box 520, 93456-0520
Telephone: 805-925-2611
Telecopier: 805-925-1635

MEMBERS OF FIRM

T. A. Twitchell (1902-1955) — Maurice F. Twitchell
William C. Rice (1924-1960) — Burton J. Twitchell
W. Kenneth Rice

A list of Representative Clients and References will be furnished upon request.

For full biographical listings, see the Martindale-Hubbell Law Directory

SANTA MONICA, Los Angeles Co.

GEORGE W. COLLINS, INC. A PROFESSIONAL CORPORATION (AV)

520 Broadway, Suite 300, P.O. Box 2133, 90407-2133
Telephone: 310-451-5584
Fax: 310-458-2907

George W. Collins

Camille J. Everett   Jonathan Eoyang

General Counsel for: Santa Monica Bank, Santa Monica, California; Bowman Merritt Associates.
Reference: Santa Monica Bank, Santa Monica, California.

For full biographical listings, see the Martindale-Hubbell Law Directory

HAIGHT, BROWN & BONESTEEL (AV)

A Partnership including Professional Corporations
1620 26th Street, Suite 4000 North, P.O. Box 680, 90404
Telephone: 310-449-6000
Telecopier: 310-829-5117
Telex: 705837
Santa Ana, California Office: Suite 900, 5 Hutton Centre Drive.
Telephone: 714-754-1100.
Telecopier: 714-754-0826.
Riverside, California Office: 3750 University Avenue, Suite 650.
Telephone: 909-341-8300.
Fax: 909-341-8309.
San Francisco, California Office: 201 Sansome Street, Suite 300.
Telephone: 415-986-7700.
Fax: 415-986-6954.

MEMBERS OF FIRM

Sidney A. Moss (1893-1963)
Gerald C. Dunn (1911-1980)
George C. Lyon (1906-1990)
Charles B. Smith (1908-1990)
Fulton Haight (A Professional Corporation) (Retired)
Harold Hansen Brown (A Professional Corporation)
Michael J. Bonesteel (A Professional Corporation)
Gary C. Ottoson (A Professional Corporation)
Roy G. Weatherup
Peter Q. Ezzell (A Professional Corporation)
Dennis K. Wheeler (A Professional Corporation)
Steven L. Hoch (A Professional Corporation)
John W. Sheller (A Professional Corporation)
William G. Baumgaertner (A Professional Corporation)
Bruce A. Armstrong (A Professional Corporation)
Morton Rosen
Peter A. Dubrawski
Michael J. Leahy
Lori R. Behar
Robert L. Kaufman

William J. Sayers
Michael McCarthy
Barry Z. Brodsky
Gary A. Bague
J. R. Seashore
Kevin R. Crisp
Lee Marshall
George Christensen
Steven E. Moyer
Denis J. Moriarty
Desmond J. Hinds, Jr.
Jules Solomon Zeman
Thomas N. Charchut
Neil G. McNiece
Thomas M. Moore
Rita (Sucharita) Gunasekaran
Kenneth G. Anderson
Victor Anderson III
William O. Martin, Jr.
Theresa M. Marchlewski
Jennifer K. Saunders
Timothy B. Bradford
Amor A. Esteban
William E. Ireland
Jay T. Thompson
Lyn Skinner Foster
Valerie A. Moore
David C. McGovern
Richard E. Wirick
Jeffrey B. Margulies

Tamara Equals Holmes

ASSOCIATES

Susan Lerner
Kelly C. McSpadden
Cynthia A. Robins
Marsha L. Kempson
Birgit Sale
Jon M. Kasimov
Alicia E. Taylor
Dorothy B. Ceccon
Andrew J Marton
Nancy E. Lucas
Cynthia R. Thompson
Robin Zukin
Tamra Lee Bowman
Nancy Doyle
Margaret Johnson Wiley
Jodi L. Girten
Maureen Haight Gee
Robert D. Wilson
Frances Mary O'Meara
Holly M. Teel
Christopher I. Ritter
Sean E. Judge
Lisa J. Golden
Daniel J. Kelly
David E. Stanley

Charles T. Calix
Teresa M. Wainman
S. Christian Stouder
Michael J. Sipos
Cary D. Glassner
Caroline E. Chan
Thomas A. Moore
Charles C. W. Brown
Nancy E. Dunne
Caroline Craddock Raggio
Michael H. Gottschlich
Joanne Lembert Rosen
Kristine J. Westhaver
Michael S. Kelly
Michael Mark McMahon
Susan A. Streit
John T. Burnite, Jr.
Caroline Kelley Hunt
Farah Sohaili Nicol
Christopher Kendrick
Erica Krikorian
Barbara Z. Safechuck
Cynthia Weingart Venuti
Suzanne M. VanDer Meulen
Cynthi F. Hizami

(See Next Column)

ASSOCIATES (Continued)

Yvette Cano
Amy E. Moffett
Caroline M. Dee
Derrick F. Coleman
George Joseph MacKoul
Karen Sinkhorn
  (Resident, Riverside Office)
Damon B. Bonesteel
Shanna R. Davis
Lisa Marie Schinnerer

John C. Rogers
Eric L. Barnum
D. Barry Khan
Jason D. Carter
David I. Reiner
Cynthia M. Holbrook
William C. Saacke
Deborah Yoon
John A. Safyurtlu
Siobhan A. Cullen

OF COUNSEL

William M. Fitzhugh
Ira E. Bilson
Richard F. Runkle
R. Roy Finkle
Mitchell J. Albert

George C. Rudolph
Robert B. Leck III
Robert A. West
Donald S. Ralphs
Edwin J. Richards

Kathryn M. Forgie

For full biographical listings, see the Martindale-Hubbell Law Directory

PAUL, HASTINGS, JANOFSKY & WALKER LLP (AV)

A Limited Liability Partnership including Professional Corporations
Firm Established in 1951; Office in 1981
Fifth Floor, 1299 Ocean Avenue, 90401-1078
Telephone: 310-319-3300
Fax: 310-393-3652
Email: info@PHJW.comm *URL:* http://www.phjw.com
Los Angeles, California Office: Twenty-Third Floor, 555 South Flower Street.
Telephone: 213-683-6000.
Orange County, California Office: Seventeenth Floor, 695 Town Center Drive, Costa Mesa.
Telephone: 714-668-6200.
Washington, D.C. Office: Tenth Floor, 1299 Pennsylvania Avenue, N.W.
Telephone: 202-508-9500.
Atlanta, Georgia Office: 24th Floor, 600 Peachtree Street, N.E.
Telephone: 404-815-2400.
Stamford, Connecticut Office: Ninth Floor, 1055 Washington Boulevard.
Telephone: 203-961-7400.
New York, New York Office: 31st Floor, 399 Park Avenue.
Telephone: 212-318-6000.
Tokyo, Japan Office: Ark Mori Building, 30th Floor, 12-32 Akasaka, P.O. Box 577, 1-Chome, Minato-Ku.
Telephone: (03) 3586-4711.

COUNSEL

Leonard S. Janofsky   Charles M. Walker

MEMBERS OF FIRM

Nancy L. Abell
Woodson Toliver Besson (P.C.)
Robert M. Dudnik
Eric H. Joss

Robert S. Span
Dennis H. Vaughn
Robert F. Walker
Harry A. Zinn

OF COUNSEL

Jan Elizabeth Eakins   Elliot K. Gordon

ASSOCIATES

Leslie Abbott
Linda M. Edwards
Marcia N. Jackson

Cheryl L. Kopitzke
Cara D. Miller
Heather Morgan

Deborah S. Weiser

For full biographical listings, see the Martindale-Hubbell Law Directory

SACKS ZWEIG & BURRIS, LLP (AV)

100 Wilshire Building, Suite 1300, 100 Wilshire Boulevard, 90401
Telephone: 310-451-3113
Facsimile: 310-451-0089
San Francisco, California Office: 100 Pine Street, 21st Floor.
Telephone: 415-788-6794.
Facsimile: 415-788-7009.

MEMBERS

Donald S. Burris   Lee Sacks
            Michael K. Zweig

ASSOCIATES

Les Bradford Hairrell   Filomena E. Meyer

OF COUNSEL

Dennis Holahan   Barton S. Selden

For full biographical listings, see the Martindale-Hubbell Law Directory

SANTA ROSA, * Sonoma Co.

ANDERSON, ZEIGLER, DISHAROON, GALLAGHER & GRAY, PROFESSIONAL CORPORATION (AV)

50 Old Courthouse Square, 5th Floor, P.O. Box 1498, 95404
Telephone: 707-545-4910
Fax: 707-544-0260
Other Santa Rosa, California Office: 6641 Oakmont Drive, 95409.
Telephone: 707-539-3880.

(See Next Column)

ANDERSON, ZEIGLER, DISHAROON, GALLAGHER & GRAY PROFESSIONAL CORPORATION, *Santa Rosa—Continued*

Petaluma, California Office: 715 Southpoint Boulevard, 94952.
Telephone: 707-763-0937.

Edwin C. Anderson, Jr.	Margaret M. Elliott
Kirt F. Zeigler	David G. Bjornstrom
Robert Disharoon	Robert S. Rutherfurd
Barbara Detrich Gallagher	Christopher M. Mazzia
	Tricia A. Shindledecker

Jeremy L. Olsan	Daniel E. Post
Wendy D. Whitson	Mary Catherine Doherty
	Gloria K. Park

OF COUNSEL
John J. King, Jr.
LEGAL SUPPORT PERSONNEL
Daniel B. Flock (Director of Information)

For full biographical listings, see the Martindale-Hubbell Law Directory

BELDEN, ABBEY, WEITZENBERG & KELLY, A PROFESSIONAL CORPORATION (AV)

1105 North Dutton Avenue, P.O. Box 1566, 95402
Telephone: 707-542-5050
Telecopier: 707-542-2589

Clarendon W. Anderson (1895-1987)	W. Barton Weitzenberg
Lester M. Belden (1927-1993)	Candace H. Shirley
Thomas P. Kelly, Jr.	Timothy W. Hoffman
Richard W. Abbey	Wayne R. Wolski
	Lewis R. Warren

Peter J. Walls	Craig M. Stainbrook

OF COUNSEL
Patrick W. Emery

Representative Clients: Exchange Bank of Santa Rosa; Westamerica Bank; North Bay Title Co.; Northwestern Title Security Co.; Geyser Peak Winery; Santa Rosa City School District; Sonoma National Bank; Arrowwood Vineyards & Winery; Arthur & DeVincenzi Concrete; Friedman Bros. Hardware, Inc.

For full biographical listings, see the Martindale-Hubbell Law Directory

MILLER, MAILLIARD & CULVER, LLP (AV)

A Partnership including Professional Corporations
100 B Street, Suite 200, P.O. Box 5257, 95402
Telephone: 707-571-8112
Fax: 707-575-9116
Email: milmaicul@aol.com
San Francisco, California Office: 155 Montgomery Street, Suite 1212.
Telephone: 415-391-4291.
Fax: 415-391-4292. Email: mmc@sirius.com.

Christopher R. Miller (P.C.)	Kevin F. Barrett
William S. Mailliard, Jr.	William D. Evers
David C. Culver	Jay P. Hendrickson
R. W. Achor (P.C.) (Retired)	Paul E. Manasian
Phyllis E. Andelin	Philip J. Nicholsen, P.C.
	Chigusa Saotome

OF COUNSEL
Stephen T. Kong

Representative Clients: BioZone Laboratories; California Dept. of Insurance; Dover Elevator Co.; Pacific Coast Apparel; Red Rose Collections; Sanwa Bank; Schug Carneros Estate Winery; TransMotive Technologies; Veriflo Corporation; Wyse Technology, Inc.

For full biographical listings, see the Martindale-Hubbell Law Directory

ROPERS, MAJESKI, KOHN & BENTLEY, A PROFESSIONAL CORPORATION (AV)

Fountaingrove Center, Suite 300, 3558 Round Barn Boulevard, 95403
Telephone: 707-524-4200
Fax: 707-523-4610
Redwood City, California Office: 1001 Marshall Street.
Telephone: 415-364-8200.
Fax: 415-367-0997.
San Jose, California Office: 80 North 1st Street.
Telephone: 408-287-6262.
Fax: 408-297-6819.
San Francisco, California Office: 670 Howard Street.
Telephone: 415-543-4800.
Fax: 415-512-1574.
Los Angeles, California Office: 550 South Hope Street, Suite 1900.
Telephone: 213-312-2000.
Fax: 213-312-2001.
Sacramento, California Office: 1000 G Street, Suite 400.
Telephone: 916-556-3100.
Fax: 916-442-7121.

(See Next Column)

Robert J. Intner	Cynthia Ribas-Rosen
Deanna J. Shirley	John Charles Willsie

For full biographical listings, see the Martindale-Hubbell Law Directory

SONORA,* Tuolumne Co. — (Refer to Modesto)

STOCKTON,* San Joaquin Co.

BRAY, GEIGER, RUDQUIST & NUSS (AV)

400 Bank of Stockton Building, 311 East Main Street, 95202
Telephone: 209-948-0434
Fax: 209-948-9451

MEMBERS OF FIRM

Dennis D. Geiger	Alan R. Coon
John B. Rudquist	Anthony S. Guerriero
James T. C. Nuss	Steven P. Emrick

ASSOCIATES

Mark S. Bray	Laureen J. Keen
	Peter A. Viri

Representative Clients: Bank of Stockton; Stockton Savings Bank, F.S.B.; Georgia-Pacific Corp.; South San Joaquin Irrigation District; Stockton Newspapers Inc.; University of the Pacific.

For full biographical listings, see the Martindale-Hubbell Law Directory

DIEHL, STEINHEIMER, RIGGIO, HAYDEL & MORDAUNT, A PROFESSIONAL LAW CORPORATION (AV)

400 East Main Street, Suite 600, 95290-0600
Telephone: 209-464-8732
Fax: 209-464-9165
Email: 104714.654@compuserve.com
Sonora, California Office: 38 North Washington Street, Suite A.
Telephone: 209-532-1424.
Fax: 209-532-4233.
Affiliated Office: Law Offices of M. Max Steinheimer and P. Gary Cassel, 301 Flint Street, Reno, Nevada 89505-3295.
Telephone: 702-322-2240.

M. Max Steinheimer	Joseph H. Fagundes
Donald M. Riggio	William D. Johnson
Douglas A. Haydel	Frank J. Enright
Michael R. Mordaunt	Kate Powell Segerstrom
Peter J. Kelly	(Resident, Sonora Office)
P. Gary Cassel	Kevin M. Seibert
Scott Malm	Scott A. Ginns
Mark F. Ornellas	Tamara M. Polley

Elizabeth R. Bogart	Corinne K. Reynolds
Darin T. Judd	Edward P. Murphy
Frank R. Perrott	Bruce J. Boehm
Rachelle C. Sanchez	Maria E. Gutierrez

OF COUNSEL
Joseph W. Diehl

Counsel for: Pacific Gas and Electric Co.; Kleinfelder Inc.; Turlock Irrigation District.
Insurance Clients: Allied Insurance Group; Design Professional Insurance Co.; The Doctors Co.; Kemper Insurance Co.; Norcal Mutual Insurance Co.; The Travelers.

For full biographical listings, see the Martindale-Hubbell Law Directory

KROLOFF, BELCHER, SMART, PERRY & CHRISTOPHERSON (AV)

7540 Shoreline Drive, P.O. Box 692050, 95269-2050
Telephone: 209-478-2000
Fax: 209-478-0354
Email: kroloff@inreach.com

FOUNDING PARTNERS

Yale S. Kroloff (1907-1987)	Richard Belcher (Retired)

MEMBERS OF FIRM

Claude H. Smart, Jr.	Christopher H. Engh
Thomas O. Perry	Elizabeth Humphreys
Gary Christopherson	Velma K. Lim
J. Douglas Van Sant	Robert J. Harrington
John F. Strangman	Kim A. Smith
Orlie L. Curtis	Randy G. Lockwood

ASSOCIATES

Kathleen M. Abdallah	Michael J. Christian
Ron A. Northup	Patricia K. Almon
	Alfred L. Sanderson, Jr.

Counsel for: Bank of America; Equitable Agri-Business, Inc.; Foster Farms; The Grupe Company; Tudor Construction.
Representative Clients: Allstate Insurance Co.; California Casualty Indemnity Exchange; Nationwide Insurance; TIG Insurance Co.; Truck Insurance Exchange.

For full biographical listings, see the Martindale-Hubbell Law Directory

Stockton—Continued

NEUMILLER & BEARDSLEE, A PROFESSIONAL CORPORATION (AV)

5th Floor, Waterfront Office Towers II, 509 West Weber Avenue, P.O. Box 20, 95201-3020
Telephone: 209-948-8200
Fax: 209-948-4910
Modesto, California Office: 611 Thirteenth Street, 95354-2435.
Telephone: 209-577-8200.
Fax: 209-577-4910.

Charles L. Neumiller (1873-1933)	James R. Dyke
George A. Ditz (1889-1971)	John W. Stovall
Irving L. Neumiller (1899-1970)	Steven A. Herum
Thomas J. Shephard, Sr.	Michael J. Dyer
Duncan R. McPherson	Paul N. Balestracci
Rudy V. Bilawski	Steven D. Crabtree
Robert C. Morrison	Jeanne Marie Zolezzi
	Thomas E. Jeffry, Jr.

Thomas H. Terpstra

OF COUNSEL

Robert L. Beardslee | Christopher A. Greene

Daniel J. Schroeder	Desiree A. Brown
Clifford W. Stevens	Patrick M. McGrath
Daniel S. Truax	Darren M. Schreiber
Karna E. Harrigfeld	K. Robert Foster
Matthew I. Friedrich	Scott R. Weaver

Representative Clients: Roman Catholic Bishop of Stockton; Equitable Insurance Co.; The Grupe Cos.; Kaufman & Broad Central Valley, Inc.; St. Joseph's Regional Health System & Medical Center; Solano County Water Agency; Stockton-East Water District; Teichert Aggregate.

For full biographical listings, see the Martindale-Hubbell Law Directory

---

TARZANA, Los Angeles Co.

WASSERMAN, COMDEN & CASSELMAN L.L.P. (AV)

5567 Reseda Boulevard, Suite 330, P.O. Box 7033, 91357-7033
Telephone: 818-705-6800; 213-872-0995
Fax: 818-345-0162; 996-8266

MEMBERS OF FIRM

Steve K. Wasserman	Jay N. Rosenwald
Leonard J. Comden	Daniel E. Lewis
David B. Casselman	Crystal A. Zarpas
Clifford H. Pearson	Gary S. Soter
Rebecca J. Schroer	Catherine Stevenson Garcia

Glenn A. Brown, Jr.

ASSOCIATES

Joel Fischman	Richard A. Brownstein
Jeffrey K. Jayson	Albert G. Turner, Jr.
Lloyd S. Mann	Kenneth M. Jones
J. Christopher Bennington	Sharon Zemel
Norman L. Pearl	L. Stephen Albright
Todd A. Chamberlain	John A. Raymond
Howard S. Blum	Michael E. Garner

Marina N. Vitek

OF COUNSEL

Cecilia S. Wu

Representative Clients: Toplis & Harding; Appalachian Insurance; Lumbermens Mutual Insurance Co.; State Farm Fire and Casualty Co.; Factory Mutual Engineering; Cravens, Dargan & Co.; Lloyd's of London.

For full biographical listings, see the Martindale-Hubbell Law Directory

---

TEMPLE CITY, Los Angeles Co. — (Refer to Arcadia)

THOUSAND OAKS, Ventura Co.

ENGLAND, WHITFIELD, SCHRÖEDER & TREDWAY, L.L.P. (AV)

Rolling Oaks Office Center, 351 Rolling Oaks Drive, 91360
Telephone: 805-485-9627; Southern California Toll Free: 800-255-3485
Oxnard, California Office: 300 Esplanade Drive, 6th Floor.
Telephones: 805-485-9627; Ventura: 647-8237; Southern California Toll Free: 800-255-3485.
Fax: 805-983-0297.

MEMBERS OF FIRM

Robert W. Schröeder	Mitchel B. Kahn
Stuart A. Comis	Eric J. Kananen

For full biographical listings, see the Martindale-Hubbell Law Directory

---

TORRANCE, Los Angeles Co.

FINER, KIM & STEARNS (AV)

An Association of Professional Corporations
City National Bank Building, 3424 Carson Street, Suite 500, 90503
Telephone: 310-214-1477
Telecopier: 310-214-0764

Harry J. Kim (A Professional Corporation)	Robert David Ciaccio
W. A. Finer (A Professional Corporation)	Robert B. Parsons

OF COUNSEL

Bennett A. Rheingold | Ryan E. Stearns

LEGAL SUPPORT PERSONNEL

Marcia E. Talbert | Daphne Fenwick

For full biographical listings, see the Martindale-Hubbell Law Directory

---

UKIAH,* Mendocino Co. — (Refer to Lakeport)

UPLAND, San Bernardino Co.

ALTHOUSE & McDONOUGH (AV)

Second Floor, Metro Commerce Bank Building, 188 North Euclid Avenue, P.O. Box 698, 91785
Telephone: 909-985-9828
Telecopier: 909-985-3282

Charles S. Althouse	James E. Bamber (1947-1989)

Elizabeth A. McDonough

References: Security Pacific National Bank, Upland Branch; First National Bank & Trust Company, Upland Branch.

For full biographical listings, see the Martindale-Hubbell Law Directory

---

VALLEJO, Solano Co.

DUNN, ROGASKI, PREOVOLOS & WEBER (AV)

241 Georgia Street, P.O. Box 1072, 94590
Telephone: 707-553-1555

MEMBERS OF FIRM

Robert C. Dunn	Michael J. Preovolos
Chester A. Rogaski, Jr.	Howard R. Weber

ASSOCIATES

Jill Noonan	Jeffrey S. Olds
Stephen J. Liberatore	Leeanne Y. Patterson

Representative Clients: Norcal Mutual Insurance Co.; Nationwide Insurance Co.; Medical Insurance Exchange of California; California Insurance Guarantee Assn.; Scottsdale Insurance Co.; CAP/MPT; Kaiser Foundation Hospitals.
Reference: Bank of America, NT & SA.

For full biographical listings, see the Martindale-Hubbell Law Directory

---

VENTURA,* Ventura Co.

BENTON, ORR, DUVAL & BUCKINGHAM, A PROFESSIONAL CORPORATION (AV)

39 North California Street, P.O. Box 1178, 93002
Telephone: 805-648-5111; 656-1166
Fax: 805-648-7218
Email: BentonOrr@usa.net

James T. Sherren	Thomas E. Olson
Ronald L. Colton	Dean W. Hazard
Robert A. Davidson	Brenda L. DeHart

Mark S. Borrell

Counsel for: American Commercial Bank; Petoseed Co., Inc.
Trial Counsel for: Southern California Edison Co.; Shell Oil Co.; Automobile Club of Southern California.

For full biographical listings, see the Martindale-Hubbell Law Directory

---

ENGLE & BRIDE (AV)

353 San Jon Road, 93001
Telephone: 805-643-2200
Fax: 805-643-3062

MEMBERS OF FIRM

Benjamin J. Engle | Robert F. Bride

ASSOCIATES

Daniel J. Carobine	Gary M. Schumacher
Matthew P. Guasco	

For full biographical listings, see the Martindale-Hubbell Law Directory

Ventura—Continued

NORMAN, DOWLER, SAWYER, ISRAEL & HANCOCK (AV)

A Limited Liability Partnership
840 County Square Drive, 93003
Telephone: 805-654-0911
Fax: 805-654-1902

Richard M. Norman	Eugenia M. Bernacchi
Peter C. Dowler	William J. Corbett
Robert M. Sawyer	Michael G. Walker
Michael M. Israel	Loye M. Barton
Diana G. Hancock	Jack Beebe

OF COUNSEL
James D. Loebl
RETIRED
Margaret Keller

For full biographical listings, see the Martindale-Hubbell Law Directory

---

VISTA, San Diego Co.

ERNEST L. HUNT, JR. (AV)

630 Alta Vista Drive, Suite 103, P.O. Box 640, 92085-0640
Telephone: 619-726-3839
Fax: 619-726-5491

For full biographical listings, see the Martindale-Hubbell Law Directory

---

WALNUT CREEK, Contra Costa Co.

McCUTCHEN, DOYLE, BROWN & ENERSEN (AV)

1331 North California Boulevard, P.O. Box Post Office Box
V, 94596-4502
Telephone: 510-937-8000
Facsimile: 510-975-5390
Email: postmaster@mdbe.com
San Francisco, California Office: Three Embarcadero Center, 94111-4066.
Telephone: 415-393-2000.
Facsimile: 415-393-2286 (G I, II, III).
Telex: 340817 MACPAG SFO.
Los Angeles, California Office: 355 South Grand Avenue, Suite 4400,
90071-1560.
Telephone: 213-680-6400.
Facsimile: 213-680-6499.
San Jose, California Office: Market Post Tower, Suite 1500, 55 South
Market Street, 95113-2327.
Telephone: 408-947-8400.
Facsimile: 408-947-4750.
Telex: 910 250 2931 MACPAG SJ.
Palo Alto, California Office: One Embarcadero Place, 2100 Geng Road,
94303-0913.
Telephone: 415-846-4000.
Fax: 415-846-4086.
Washington, D.C. Office: The Evening Star Building, Suite 800, 1101
Pennsylvania Avenue, N.W., 20004-2514.
Telephone: 202-628-4900.
Facsimile: 202-628-4912.
Taipei, Taiwan Republic of China Office: International Trade Building,
Tenth Floor, 333 Keelung Road, Section 1, 110.
Telephone: 886-2-723-5000.
Facsimile: 886-2-757-6070.
Affiliated Offices In: Bangkok, Thailand; Beijing, China; Shanghai, China.

MEMBERS OF FIRM

Gilbert C. Berkeley	Palmer Brown Madden
Daniel J. Curtin, Jr.	Robert E. Merritt
James B. Ellis	Geoffrey L. Robinson
Michael L. Greene	Sanford M. Skaggs (Managing
Stephen L. Kostka	Partner, Walnut Creek Office)

COUNSEL

Marie A. Cooper	M. Thomas Jacobson

ASSOCIATES

Brandt Andersson	Adam U. Lindgren
Grant A. Guerra	Rajiv Suresh Parikh
Peter S. Hayes	Gregory A. Randall
Barbara J. Schussman	

For full biographical listings, see the Martindale-Hubbell Law Directory

---

WATSONVILLE, Santa Cruz Co.

GRUNSKY, EBEY, FARRAR & HOWELL, A PROFESSIONAL CORPORATION (AV)

240 Westgate Drive, 95076
Telephone: 408-722-2444
Fax: 408-722-6153
Email: gefh@grunskylaw.com
Salinas, California Office: 238 Capitol Street, P.O. Box 1451.
Telephone: 408-754-0611.
Fax: 408-754-0614.

(See Next Column)

Donald L. Grunsky (Retired)	Thomas N. Griffin
Frederick H. Ebey	Alan J. Smith
James S. Farrar	Robert E. Wall, III
Dennis P. Howell	Mark E. Myers
(Resident, Salinas Office)	

Leslie J. Karst	Kathleen Ann Franke
Patricia McKenzie	Michael Tunink
Elaine Richelieu	Deborah Mall
(Resident, Salinas Office)	William J. Taylor, III
David S. Spini	(Resident, Salinas Office)

OF COUNSEL
Bruce A. Richardson

Local Counsel for: Farmers Insurance Group; California-State Automobile
Assn.; State Farm Insurance Cos.; Granite Construction Co.; Berman Steel
Co.; Watsonville Community Hospital; Bassi Distributing Co.; Great Lakes
Chemical Co., Inc.; First American Title Insurance Co.; California Straw-
berry Advisory Board.

For full biographical listings, see the Martindale-Hubbell Law Directory

---

WHITTIER, Los Angeles Co.

BEWLEY, LASSLEBEN & MILLER (AV)

13215 East Penn Street, Suite 510, 90602-1797
Telephone: 310-698-9771
Fax: 310-696-6357

MEMBERS OF FIRM

Thomas W. Bewley (1903-1986)	Ernie Zachary Park
William M. Lassleben, Jr.	Robert H. Dewberry
(Retired)	Richard L. Dewberry
Edward L. Miller	Jeffrey S. Baird
J. Terrence Mooschekian	Kevin P. Duthoy
Joseph A. Vinatieri	

ASSOCIATES

Jason C. Demille	John P. Godsil
Suzanne R. Kramer	Peter B. Fan

Representative Clients: Quaker City Federal Savings & Loan Assn.; Whittier
College; Presbyterian Intercommunity Hospital; Bank of Whittier; Circuit
Systems, Inc.; Lockhart Industries, Inc.; Subdivided Land, Inc.; United Ad-
Label Co., Inc.
References: Bank of America National Trust & Savings Assn. (Whittier Main
Office); Southern California Bank.

For full biographical listings, see the Martindale-Hubbell Law Directory

---

THOMSON & NELSON, A PROFESSIONAL LAW CORPORATION (AV)

15111 East Whittier Boulevard, Suite 400, 90603-2189
Telephone: 310-945-3536
714-680-0674
Telecopier: 310-693-2866

Alexander D. Thomson	John G. Nelson

Michael A. Rule	Karl V. Matthews

Representative Clients: Blue Hills Nursery; Great Western Hotels Corp.;
ICBO Evaluation Service, Inc.; International Conference of Building Offi-
cials; Shima Pearl, Inc.; Sunset Tropicals, Inc.; Trico Trading Co.

For full biographical listings, see the Martindale-Hubbell Law Directory

---

*WILLOWS,** Glenn Co. — (Refer to Chico)

*YUBA CITY,** Sutter Co. — (Refer to Marysville)

COLORADO

---

*ASPEN,** Pitkin Co.

AUSTIN, PEIRCE & SMITH, P.C. (AV)

Suite 205, 600 East Hopkins Avenue, 81611
Telephone: 970-925-2600
FAX: 970-925-4720
Email: apspc@rof.net

Ronald D. Austin	Frederick F. Peirce
	Thomas Fenton Smith

Michael P. Fossenier	

Counsel for: Chase Manhattan of Colorado, Inc.; Clark's Market; Cootes,
Reid & Waldron Property Management, Inc.; Crystal Palace Corp.; Snow-
mass Shopping Center; Coldwell Banker The Aspen Brokers, Ltd.; William
Poss & Assoc., Architects; Snowmass Resort Association; Aspen/Pitkin
County Housing Authority; Nations Title Insurance, Inc.

(See Next Column)

AUSTIN, PEIRCE & SMITH P.C.—*Continued*

For full biographical listings, see the Martindale-Hubbell Law Directory

J. NICHOLAS McGRATH, P.C. (AV)

Suite 203, 600 East Hopkins Avenue, 81611
Telephone: 970-925-2612
Telecopier: 970-925-4402
Email: nicklaw@csn.net *URL:* http://www.aspenlink.com/nicklaw

J. Nicholas McGrath

Susan W. Laatsch   Diana L. Godwin

Representative Clients: Alpine Surveys, Inc.; Aspen Alps Condominium Assn.; Aspen Center for Physics; Gant Condominium Assn.; Hotel Jerome Associates, Ltd. Partners; Redstone Investments, Inc. (Cleveholm Castle).

For full biographical listings, see the Martindale-Hubbell Law Directory

OATES, HUGHES, KNEZEVICH & GARDENSWARTZ, P.C. (AV)

Aspen Plaza Building, 3rd Floor, 533 East Hopkins Avenue, 81611
Telephone: 970-920-1700
Telecopier: 970-920-1121
Email: ohkg@rof.net

Leonard M. Oates   Richard A. Knezevich
Ted D. Gardenswartz

David B. Kelly   Rich Orman
OF COUNSEL
Robert W. Hughes   John Thomas Kelly

Counsel for: Stapleton Insurance Agency; Pitkin County Title, Inc.

For full biographical listings, see the Martindale-Hubbell Law Directory

BOULDER,* Boulder Co.

HOLME ROBERTS & OWEN LLP (AV)

Suite 400, 1401 Pearl Street, 80302
Telephone: 303-444-5955
Telecopier: 303-444-1063
Email: hro@hro.com *URL:* http://www.hro.com
Denver, Colorado Office: Suite 4100, 1700 Lincoln.
Telephone: 303-861-7000.
Telecopier: 303-866-0200.
Colorado Springs, Colorado Office: Suite 1300, 90 South Cascade Avenue.
Telephone: 719-473-3800.
Telecopier: 719-633-1518.
Salt Lake City, Utah Office: Suite 1100, 111 East Broadway.
Telephone: 801-521-5800.
Telecopier: 801-521-9639.
London, England Office: Mellier House, 26a Albemarle Street.
Telephone: 44-171-499-8776.
Telecopier: 44-171-499-7769.
Moscow, Russia Office: Kosmodamianskaya Nab. #52/1, Suite 9100, 113054.
Telephone: 7095-961-3000.
Telecopier: 7095-961-3001.
Kiev, Ukraine Office: Terestchenkovskaya #19, Suite 2, 252004.
Telephone: 380-44-224-1348.
Telecopier: 380-44-224-4986.

PARTNERS OF FIRM
William R. Roberts   Jill K. Rood
  (Managing Partner)   James R. Ghiselli
Paul E. Smith   Patrick K. Perrin
OF COUNSEL
Kay M. Small (Resident)
SPECIAL COUNSEL
Christopher D. Ozeroff   John B. Wood
RESIDENT ASSOCIATES
Rebecca Hall   Cynthia A. Mitchell
Peter-Christian Olivo

For full biographical listings, see the Martindale-Hubbell Law Directory

HURTH, YEAGER & SISK (AV)

4860 Riverbend Road, P.O. Box 17850, 80308
Telephone: 303-443-7900
Telecopier: 303-443-8733

MEMBERS OF FIRM
John M. Yeager   Christopher W. Blakemore
Charles L. Sisk   Beverly C. Nelson
Erik A. Johnson

(See Next Column)

OF COUNSEL
Charles A. Hurth, Jr.   Edward R. Kellenberger

Representative Clients: Colorado National Bank, Boulder; Boulder Valley Bank and Trust; Bank of Louisville; Commonwealth Land Title Insurance Co.; Data Storage Marketing, Inc.; Ugland USA, Inc.; Dovatron International, Inc.; First Northern Savings Bank.
References: Colorado National Bank, Boulder; Boulder Valley Bank & Trust.

For full biographical listings, see the Martindale-Hubbell Law Directory

BRUSH, Morgan Co. — (Refer to Greeley)

CANON CITY,* Fremont Co.

FREDRICKSON & JOHNSON, P.C. (AV)

3rd Floor, First National Bank Building, Suite 329, 831 Royal Gorge Boulevard, P.O. Box 889, 81215-0889
Telephone: 719-275-4161
Fax: Available upon request

Robert G. Fredrickson   Bruce Johnson
Bryan T. Fredrickson

Attorneys for: I.O.O.F. of Colorado; Fremont County Board of Realtors; Canon City Area Fire Protection District; St. Thomas More Hospital, Canon City; Royal Gorge Company of Colorado.
References: The First National Bank of Canon City; Fremont National Bank.

For full biographical listings, see the Martindale-Hubbell Law Directory

CASTLE ROCK,* Douglas Co.

FOLKESTAD & FAZEKAS, P.C. (AV)

316 Wilcox Street, 80104-2495
Telephone: 303-688-3045
FAX: 303-688-3189

James B. Folkestad   Ernest F. Fazekas, II

Susan B. Shoemaker

Representative Clients: Bank of Douglas County; Johnson & Sons Construction, Inc.; B & W Construction Co.; Proto Construction & Paving, Inc.; Grimm Construction Co.; Ashcroft Homes of Denver LLC.
References: Bank of Douglas County; First National Bank of Castle Rock; First Bank of Castle Rock; Colorado National Bank.

For full biographical listings, see the Martindale-Hubbell Law Directory

COLORADO SPRINGS,* El Paso Co.

BELTZ, EDWARDS & SABO, L.L.P. (AV)

729 South Cascade, 80903
Telephone: 719-473-4444; 719-634-6620
Fax: 719-444-0186

W. Thomas Beltz   Daniel P. Edwards
John W. Sabo, III

Daniel A. West

Representative Clients: A.M.I. Industries, Inc.; Analytical Surveys, Inc.; A.C. Israel Enterprises, Inc.; Boddington Lumber Co., Inc.; Cardiovascular Surgeons of Colorado Springs, P.C.; Colorado Springs Radiologists, P.C.; Digital, Inc.; Music Semi-Conductors, Inc.; Schlage Lock Co.; Texas Instruments.

For full biographical listings, see the Martindale-Hubbell Law Directory

HALL & EVANS, L.L.C. (AV)

Suite 600, 102 South Tejon Street, 80903
Telephone: 719-578-5600; Toll-Free From Denver Telephone: 303-628-3400
Telecopier: 719-635-7458
Denver
Email: hallevans@hallevans.com
Denver, Colorado Office: Suite 1700, 1200 Seventeenth Street, 80202.
Telephone: 303-628-3300.
Telecopier: 303-628-3368.
COLORADO SPRINGS RESIDENT ATTORNEYS
MEMBERS
Miles M. Dewhirst   S. Kent Karber
ASSOCIATES
Jeffrey L. Bodily   Daniel L. Rosenberg
Meredith L. Kendziorski   Cornelia P. Weiss
Consuelo Williams

Representative Clients: American International Group (A.I.G.); American Insurance Association; Chrysler Corporation; Continental Airlines, Inc.; Jacor Broadcasting Corporation of Colorado, Inc.; Monfort, Inc.; National Railroad Passenger Corporation (AMTRAK); Northern Telecom Inc. (NORTEL); Safeco Insurance Company of America; Sandoz Pharmaceuticals Corporation.

For full biographical listings, see the Martindale-Hubbell Law Directory

Colorado Springs—Continued

HOLME ROBERTS & OWEN LLP (AV)

Suite 1300, 90 South Cascade Avenue, 80903
Telephone: 719-473-3800
Telecopier: 719-633-1518
Email: hro@hro.com URL: http://www.hro.com
Denver, Colorado Office: Suite 4100, 1700 Lincoln.
Telephone: 303-861-7000.
Telecopier: 303-866-0200.
Boulder, Colorado Office: Suite 400, 1401 Pearl Street.
Telephone: 303-444-5955.
Telecopier: 303-444-1063.
Salt Lake City, Utah Office: Suite 1100, 111 East Broadway.
Telephone: 801-521-5800.
Telecopier: 801-521-9639.
London, England Office: Mellier House, 26a Albemarle Street.
Telephone: 44-171-499-8776.
Telecopier: 44-171-499-7769.
Moscow, Russia Office: Kosmodamianskaya Nab. #52/1, Suite 9100, 113054.
Telephone: 7095-961-3000.
Telecopier: 7095-961-3001.
Kiev, Ukraine Office: Terestchenkovskaya #19, Suite 2, 252004.
Telephone: 380-44-224-1348.
Telecopier: 380-44-224-4986.

PARTNERS OF FIRM

Richard R. Young (Managing Partner)	Thomas M. James
Richard L. Nagl	Brent E. Rychener
Steve L. Gaines	Susan E. Duffey Campbell
	John R. Wylie

Christopher Cipoletti

SPECIAL COUNSEL

Charles E. Berry	David W. Isbell

ASSOCIATES

G. Leland Dutcher, Jr.	Timothy G. Pfeifer
Brent P. Karasiuk	Dominic Jude Ricotta
Stuart J. Lark	Steven B. Smith
Deborah S. Menkins	Sharon A. Thomas

For full biographical listings, see the Martindale-Hubbell Law Directory

KANE & DONLEY, P.C. (AV)

90 South Cascade Avenue, Suite 830, 80903
Telephone: 719-471-1650
Fax: 719-471-1663
Mailing Address: P.O. Box 1119, Colorado Springs, CO, 80901

Jerry A. Donley	Mark H. Kane
	Jack E. Donley

William A. Palmer	Hayden W. Kane, II

OF COUNSEL

Hayden W. Kane

Representative Clients: American International Companies; Shelter Insurance Co.; Metropolitan Insurance Co.
Reference: Norwest Bank of Colorado Springs.

For full biographical listings, see the Martindale-Hubbell Law Directory

RETHERFORD, MULLEN, JOHNSON & BRUCE, L.L.C. (AV)

415 South Sahwatch, P.O. Box 1580, 80901
Telephone: 719-475-2014
Fax: 719-630-1267

MEMBERS OF FIRM

Jerry A. Retherford	Neil C. Bruce
J. Stephen Mullen	Patrick R. Salt
Anthony A. Johnson	J. Ronald Voss
	Lori M. Moore

ASSOCIATES

Amelia L. Klemme	Debra A. Long
M. James Zendejas	Patricia Richardson

OF COUNSEL

E. William Shaffer, Jr.	Carla M. Albers

Reference: Norwest Banks; Colorado Springs Memorial Hospital.

For full biographical listings, see the Martindale-Hubbell Law Directory

SHERMAN & HOWARD L.L.C. (AV)

Attorneys and Counselors at Law
Suite 1500, 90 South Cascade Avenue, 80903
Telephone: 719-475-2440
Telecopier: 719-635-4576
Denver, Colorado Office: 633 17th Street, Suite 3000, 80202.
Telephone: 303-297-2900.
Las Vegas, Nevada Office: Swendseid & Stern a member in Sherman & Howard L.L.C., 317 Sixth Street, 89101.
Telephone: 702-387-6073

(See Next Column)

Reno, Nevada Office: Swendseid & Stern, a member in Sherman & Howard L.L.C., 50 West Liberty Street, Suite 660, 89501.
Telephone: 702-323-1980.

Ben S. Wendelken (1899-1991)	Durward E. Timmons, Jr.
William A. Baker (1913-1991)	N. Dawn Webber
Raymond M. Deeny	Glenn H. Schlabs
	Bruce A. Kolbezen

Wayne W. Williams	Jennifer R. George
Milton L. "Skip" Smith, III	Brenda K. Buege

Representative Clients: El Pomar Foundation Co.; Ampex, Inc.; Broadmoor Hotel, Inc.; Signal Processing Technologies, Inc.; Colorado Springs Gazette-Telegraph.
References: Colorado National Bank-Exchange; First National Bank, Colorado Springs; United Bank of Colorado Springs.

For full biographical listings, see the Martindale-Hubbell Law Directory

---

CORTEZ,* Montezuma Co. — (Refer to Durango)

DEL NORTE,* Rio Grande Co. — (Refer to Alamosa)

DENVER,* Denver Co.

BAKER & HOSTETLER (AV)

303 East 17th Avenue, Suite 1100, 80203-1264
Telephone: 303-861-0600
FAX: 303-861-7805
In Cleveland, Ohio: 3200 National City Center, 1900 East Ninth Street.
Telephone: 216-621-0200.
In Columbus, Ohio: Capitol Square, Suite 2100, 65 East State Street.
Telephone: 614-228-1541.
In Houston, Texas: 1000 Louisiana, Suite 2000.
Telephone: 713-751-1600.
In Long Beach, California: 300 Oceangate, Suite 620.
Telephone: 310-432-2827.
In Los Angeles, California: 600 Wilshire Boulevard. Telephone 213-624-2400.
In Orlando, Florida: SunBank Center, Suite 2300, 200 South Orange Avenue.
Telephone: 305-841-1111.
In Washington, D. C.: Washington Square, Suite 1100, 1050 Connecticut Avenue, N.W.
Telephone: 202-861-1500.
In College Park, Maryland: 9658 Baltimore Boulevard, Suite 206.
Telephone: 301-441-2781.
In Alexandria, Virginia: 437 North Lee Street.
Telephone: 703-549-1294.
In San Francisco, California: One Sansome Street, Suite 2000.
Telephone: 415-951-4705.

MEMBERS OF FIRM IN DENVER, COLORADO

Raymond L. Sutton, Jr.

PARTNERS

Steven Reed Armstrong (Not admitted in CO)	Phillip S. Lorenzo
Timothy R. Beyer	Todd L. Lundy
Mary Price Birk	Richard S. Mandelson
Gregory S. Brown	James R. Martin
Kenneth J. Burke	Michael G. Martin
Alfred C. Chidester	Thomas H. Maxfield
James A. Clark (Managing Partner-Denver Office)	John B. Moorhead
Kathryn A. Elzi	Stuart G. Rifkin
Marc D. Flink	Cassandra G. Sasso
	Marjorie N. Sloan
	David L. Starbuck
	Victor L. Wallace, II

ASSOCIATES

Fay Chu Fong	Demetrie E. (Rico) Munn
L. Andrew Cooper	David J. Ringelman
Raymond L. Gifford	Michael J. Roche
Gerald H. Hansen	Mary Beth Searles
Peter J. Korneffel, Jr.	Michelle M. St. Pierre
Rebecca C. Lovell	Margaret M. Williams

OF COUNSEL

Winchester Cooley, III (Not admitted in CO)	Roger M. Morris

For full biographical listings, see the Martindale-Hubbell Law Directory

BALLARD SPAHR ANDREWS & INGERSOLL (AV)

Seventeenth Street Plaza Building, Suite 2300, 1225 17th Street, 80202-5596
Telephone: 303-292-2400
Fax: 303-296-3956
Philadelphia, Pennsylvania Office: 1735 Market Street, 51st Floor.
Telephone: 215-665-8500.
Fax: 215-864-8999.
Harrisburg, Pennsylvania Office: 105 North Front Street.
Telephone: 717-236-3333.
Fax: 717-236-3884.

(See Next Column)

BALLARD SPAHR ANDREWS & INGERSOLL—*Continued*

Salt Lake City, Utah Office: One Utah Center, 201 South Main Street, Suite 1200.
Telephone: 801-531-3000.
Fax: 801-531-3001.
Washington, D.C. Office: Suite 900 East, 555 13th Street, N.W.
Telephone: 202-383-8800.
Fax: 202-383-8877; 383-8893.
Baltimore, Maryland Office: 300 East Lombard Street, 19th Floor.
Telephone: 410-528-5600.
Fax: 410-528-5650.
Camden, New Jersey Office: 800 Hudson Square, 5th Floor.
Telephone: 609-541-5577.
Fax: 609-541-8272.

Leslie A. Eaton	Lyle B. Stewart
Loring E. Harkness III	Elizabeth H. Temkin
Beverly J. Quail	Roger P. Thomasch
Kevin Michael Shea	Mark Wielga

OF COUNSEL
Thomas H. Duncan

Anita Shakeh Agajanian	Kaye A. Jacuzzi
Erika Zimmer Enger	Karen Samuels Jones
Barbara A. Grandjean	Nathan M. Longenecker
Scott W. Hardt	Denise S. Maes
John E. Hayes, III	Judith I. Meyka
Darren R. Hensley	Alice Lim Rydberg
Matthew J. Hogan	William T. Slamkowski

Terri S. Winter

For full biographical listings, see the Martindale-Hubbell Law Directory

BERENBAUM, WEINSHIENK & EASON, P.C. (AV)

Suite 2600 Republic Plaza, 370 17th Street, 80202
Telephone: 303-825-0800
Facsimile: 303-629-7610
Durango, Colorado Office: 2815 Main.
Telephone: 303-247-1333.

Mandel Berenbaum (1914-1993)	Kenneth S. Kramer
Hubert T. Weinshienk	James L. Kurtz-Phelan
(1931-1983)	Charles P. Leder
Joseph Berenbaum	A. Elizabeth Meyers
Charles A. Bewley	H. Michael Miller
Joseph S. Borus	Neil B. Oberfeld
Martin D. Buckley	Dean G. Panos
M. Frances Cetrulo	Edwin G. Perlmutter
Daniel S. Duggan	Barry M. Permut
David R. Eason	Keith M. Pockross
Richard L. Eason	Dan A. Sciullo
Steven C. Hoth	Edward L. Sperry
James A. Jacobson	Eugene M. Sprague
I. H. Kaiser	Robert G. Wilson, Jr.

Ronald I. Zall

J. Hunter Banbury	Amy L. Durfee
Patricia Bellac	Heather Scheel Hagemann

Stephen K. Schutte
SPECIAL COUNSEL
John E. Bush

Representative Clients: Stanley Works; Columbine Venture Funds; The Home Depot; Karman, Inc.; Lomas Mortgage; Southwest State Bank; The Bank of Boulder; Teamsters; Trinity Ventures; The David Johnson Group.

For full biographical listings, see the Martindale-Hubbell Law Directory

BREGA & WINTERS, P.C. (AV)

One Norwest Center, 1700 Lincoln Street, Suite 2222, 80203
Telephone: 303-866-9400
Fax: 303-861-9109
Email: bwpc@indra.com
Greeley, Colorado Office: 1100 Tenth Street, Suite 402, 80631.
Telephone: 303-352-4805.
Fax: 303-352-6547.

James W. Bain	Brian A. Magoon
Stuart N. Bennett	Loren L. Mall
Charles F. Brega	Pamela A. Shaddock
Robert R. Dormer	(Resident, Greeley Office)
Robert C. Kaufman	Jay John Schnell
Ronald S. Loser	Jerry D. Winters
	(Resident, Greeley Office)

Peter A. Gergely	Bradley D. Laue
Wesley B. Howard, Jr.	(Resident, Greeley Office)
Yvonne Marie Kreye	Jack R. Luellen
S. Scott Lasher	(Not admitted in CO)

OF COUNSEL

Carolyn Jane Hariton	Mark Spitalnik

(See Next Column)

COUNSEL
Jay W. Enyart

For full biographical listings, see the Martindale-Hubbell Law Directory

BROWNSTEIN HYATT FARBER & STRICKLAND, P.C. (AV)

Twenty-Second Floor, 410 Seventeenth Street, 80202-4437
Telephone: 303-534-6335
Telecopier: 303-623-1956
Washington, D.C. Office: 601 Pennsylvania Avenue, N.W., Suite 900.
Telephone: 202-434-8377.
Telecopier: 202-393-7864.

Norman Brownstein	Michael J. Sternick
Steven W. Farber	Gary M. Reiff
Mark F. Leonard	Michael R. McGinnis
Edward N. Barad	Lisa Hogan
John R. Call	Wayne F. Forman
Steven M. Sommers	Bruce A. James
Thomas L. Strickland	Thomas J. Mancuso
Ronald B. Merrill	Cole Finegan
Lynda A. McNeive	Jeffrey M. Knetsch
Laura Jean Christman	Hubert A. Farbes, Jr.
Andrew W. Loewi	John R. Garrett
Wayne H. Hykan	Terence C. Gill
Stanley L. Garnett	Steven S. Siegel

John L. Ruppert
OF COUNSEL

Jack N. Hyatt	Steven C. Demby
Ann B. Riley	William T. Brack (Resident, Washington, D.C. Office)

Robert Kaufmann	Jill E. Murray
Brent T. Slosky	Gregory W. Berger
Anne M. Murphy	Howard J. Pollack
Jay F. Kamlet	Peter Q. Murphy
Robert C. Troyer	Stephen D. Gurr
Patrick F Carrigan	Ellen O. Kauffmann
Ana Lazo Tenzer	Joshua J. Widoff
Mark J. Mathews	Beth Doherty Quinn
David M. Brown	Lea Ann T. Groesser

David S. Chipman

Representative Clients: Alfalfa's Inc.; Colorado National Bank; Columbia/HCA Healthcare Corp.; The Denver Nuggets; The Hertz Corporation; SunAmerica Inc.; Trammell Crow Company; United Airlines; U.S. Home Corporation; Vail Associates, Inc.

For full biographical listings, see the Martindale-Hubbell Law Directory

BURNS WALL SMITH AND MUELLER, A PROFESSIONAL CORPORATION (AV)

303 East Seventeenth Avenue Suite 800, 80203-1260
Telephone: 303-830-7000
Telecopier: 303-830-6708
Email: BWSM@MCIMAIL.COM

Peter J. Wall	James E. Bosik
Gregory J. Smith	Steven F. Mueller
George W. Mueller	Robert T. Cosgrove

Gretchen L. Aultman	Donald D. Farlow

OF COUNSEL

Thomas M. Burns	Darrell C. Miller
Frank H. Houck	Anthony van Westrum

SPECIAL COUNSEL

John D. Amen	Robert Neece

Jack M. Merritts

Representative Clients: IBM Credit Corp.; Landmark Graphics Corp.; Snyder Oil Corp.; Colorado Chapter of the American Physical Therapy Assn; Ford Motor Co.; QC Data Inc.

For full biographical listings, see the Martindale-Hubbell Law Directory

DAVIS, GRAHAM & STUBBS LLP (AV)

A Limited Liability Partnership
Suite 4700, 370 Seventeenth Street, P.O. Box 185, 80201-0185
Telephone: 303-892-9400
Fax: (303) 893-1379
Cable Address: "Davgram, Denver"
Telex: 413726 DGS DVR UD
Email: dgs@dgslaw.com
Washington, D.C. Office: 1314 19th Street, N.W.
Telephone: 202-822-8660.
Fax: 202-293-4794.
Telex: 248260 DGSW.
Houston, Texas Office: 515 Post Oak Boulevard, Suite 870.
Telephone: 713-850-9400.
Facsimile: 713-850-0807.

(See Next Column)

DAVIS, GRAHAM & STUBBS LLP, *Denver—Continued*

PARTNERS

Wanda J. Abel	Ronald R. Levine, II
Glenn K. Beaton	Alan M. Loeb
Thomas C. Bell	Andrew M. Low
William A. Bianco	Paula J. Martin
Charles L. Casteel	Judith M. Matlock
James E. Culhane	John L. McCabe
Brian T. Dolan	John G. McGrath
Thomas C. Folsom	Thomas B. McNamara
John A. Francis	Joseph P. McMahon, Jr.
Roger L. Freeman	Gale T. Miller
Daniel E. D. Friesen	Zach C. Miller
Michael J. Gallagher	Laura J. Nagle
Christopher J. Hagan (Not	Laurence E. Nemirow
admitted in CO; Resident,	Thomas S. Nichols
Washington, D.C. Office)	Donald J. O'Connor
David R. Hammond	Neil Peck
Felicity Hannay	Kurt M. Petersen
Dale R. Harris	Patricia Peterson
Paul Hilton	Jeffrey R. Pilkington
Richard P. Holme	Robert S. Rich
Marcia Chadwick Holt	Christopher L. Richardson
Randall E. Hubbard	John M. Roche
John R. Jacus	Anthony J. Shaheen
Carole K. Jeffery	Jean Justyn Sirkin
Thomas P. Johnson	Sheldon H. Smith
Lisa S. Kahn	Randall Weeks
Charles L. Kaiser	John R. Wilson
Glen E. Keller, Jr.	Lester R. Woodward
J. Hovey Kemp (Resident,	Gail L. Wurtzler
Washington, D.C. Office)	

OF COUNSEL

Richard Marden Davis	George M. Hopfenbeck, Jr.
(1912-1987)	Alvin J. LaCabe
Donald S. Graham	Clyde O. Martz
Donald S. Stubbs (1908-1996)	Quigg Newton, Jr.
Janet N. Harris	John M. Sayre
Robert H. Harry	Lorna A. Schnase (Resident,
Donald W. Hoagland	Houston, Texas Office)
	James D. Voorhees

ASSOCIATES

Barry C. Bartel	Martin J. Katz
Joel Benson	Horace Anthony Lowe
Jonathan D. Bergman	Laura M. Metcalfe
Mark D. Bingham	Sara A. Moon
Charles A. Breer	Barbara J. Mueller
Karen Renfree Clark (Resident,	Meredith A. Munro
Washington, D.C. Office)	Brett C. Painter
Kristin W. Dale	Peter J. Perla
Ronald K. Edquist	Bruce L. Plotkin
Laura B. Gill	Chris Reiss
Barbara Schuldt Heikoff	Michael Nikolaos Stefanoudakis
Arturo G. Hernandez	Kevin P. Stichter
James A. Hutchinson (Resident,	Mark Taylor
Washington, D.C. Office)	Mark T. Urban
Patrick A. Jackman	Paul Washington
N. Anthony Jeffries	Peter F. Weinberg
	Ezekiel J. Williams

For full biographical listings, see the Martindale-Hubbell Law Directory

DeMuth & DeMuth (AV)

1660 Tower Building Suite 222, 1660 South Albion Street, 80222
Telephone: 303-759-2755
Fax: 303-759-3255

MEMBERS OF FIRM

Lael S. DeMuth	Alan C. DeMuth

Representative Clients: Mount Evans Co.; Jefferson Standard Life Insurance Co.; H.W. Stewart, Inc.; Colorado State Employees Credit Union; Bellco First Federal Credit Union; Fidelity Union Life Insurance Co.; Decals, Inc.; Jefferson Pilot Communications.

For full biographical listings, see the Martindale-Hubbell Law Directory

Dufford & Brown, P.C. (AV)

1700 Broadway, Suite 1700, 80290-1701
Telephone: 303-861-8013
Facsimile: 303-832-3804
Affiliated Office: Solomon, Pearl, Blum & Quinn, L.L.P., New York, NY and Denver, Colorado.

(See Next Column)

Philip G. Dufford	Jack F. Ross
Thomas G. Brown	Eugene F. Megyesy, Jr.
Dale Tooley (1933-1985)	Randall J. Feuerstein
David W. Furgason	S. Kirk Ingebretsen
William C. Robb	Edward D. White
Richard L. Fanyo	Peggy J. Anderson
Phillip D. Barber	Craig B. Shaffer
	Scott J. Mikulecky

Terry Jo Epstein	David L. Smith
Thomas E. J. Hazard	Lisa A. Varriale
Thomas M. Stern	Joanne Herlihy
Michael Goodman	Lisa Ann Lee
Douglas A. Thomas	Michael Roch

SPECIAL COUNSEL

Lawrence D. Stone

OF COUNSEL

Morris B. Hecox, Jr.	Claude M. Maer, Jr.

Representative Clients: CF&I Steel L.P.; The Colorado and Wyoming Railway Co.; Echo Bay-Sunnyside Gold; Hall and Hall Mortgage Corp.; Hewlett-Packard Co.; Coors Brewing Co.; Reorganized CF&I Steel Corp.; Starbucks Coffee Co.; Stewart & Stevenson Services, Inc.

For full biographical listings, see the Martindale-Hubbell Law Directory

Faegre & Benson LLP (AV)

2500 Republic Plaza, 370 Seventeenth Street, 80202-4004
Telephone: 303-592-9000
Facsimile: 303-820-0600
Email: postmaster@faegre.com *URL:* http://www.faegre.com
Minneapolis, Minnesota Office: 2200 Norwest Center, 90 South Seventh Street, 55402-3901.
Telephone: 612-336-3000.
Facsimile: 612-336-3026.
Des Moines, Iowa Office: 400 Capital Square, 400 Locust Street, 50309-2335.
Telephone: 515-248-9000.
Facsimile: 515-248-9010.
London, England Office: 10 EastCheap, EC3M 1ET.
Telephone: 171-623-6163.
Facsimile: 171-623-3227.
Frankfurt, Germany Office: Wiesenau 1, 60323 Frankfurt am Main.
Telephone: 011-49-69-971-227-0.
Facsimile: 011-49-69-971-227-70.
Almaty, Republic of Kazakhstan Office: 597 Seifullin Street, Suite 310, 480072.
Telephone: 7-3272-64-79-79.
Facsimile: 7-3272-64-79-79,

RESIDENT MEMBERS

Joseph M. Montano	Michael J. Cook
Frederic K. Conover, II	Gerald A. Niederman
John D. Shively	Christian Carl Onsager
Bruce W. Sattler	Leslie A. Fields
Dirk W. De Roos	Catherine A. Lemon
William J. Campbell	Elizabeth A. MacDonald
Thomas B. Kelley	Russell O. Stewart
Michael S. McCarthy	Diane B. Davies
	Charlotte Wiessner

SPECIAL COUNSEL

J. David Arkell	Jo Frances Walsh
	Ann C. McCullough

RESIDENT ASSOCIATES

Adrienne O'Connell McNamara	Jack R. Sperber
Natalie Hanlon-Leh	Laury E. Bowman
Michael J. Pankow	Bret R. Gunnell
Michel L. Singer	Steven D. Zansberg
Matthew Nelson	Mark W. Oveson
Jeanne M. Coleman	Christopher G. Penny
(Not admitted in CO)	K. Megan Doberneck
	(Not admitted in CO)

For full biographical listings, see the Martindale-Hubbell Law Directory

Fairfield and Woods, P.C. (AV)

One Norwest Center, Suite 2400, 1700 Lincoln Street, 80203-4524
Telephone: 303-830-2400
Telecopier: 303-830-1033
Email: sseifert@fwlaw.com *URL:* http://www.fwlaw.com/

Peter F. Breitenstein	Mary Jo Gross
Charlton H. Carpenter	Robert A. Holmes
Howard Holme	John J. Silver
Robert S. Slosky	Thomas P. Kearns
James L. Stone	Rocco A. Dodson
Michael M. McKinstry	Mary E. Moser
Robert L. Loeb, Jr.	Brent T. Johnson
Daniel R. Frost	Stephen H. Leonhardt
Stephen W. Seifert	Caroline C. Fuller

(See Next Column)

FAIRFIELD AND WOODS P.C.—*Continued*

Gregory C. Smith	Neil T. Duggan
John M. Tanner	Douglas J. Becker

SPECIAL COUNSEL

John S. Pfeiffer

Thomas M. Pierce	Jacalyn W. Peter
Suzanne R. Kalutkiewicz	David L. Joeris
Philip J. Roselli	Christine E. Payne

Sean D. Baker

Representative Clients: American Web, Inc.; Copper Mountain, Inc.; Denver Metropolitan Major League Baseball Stadium District; Deutsche Financial Services Corp.; Gates Foundation; Security Title Guaranty Co.; Southeastern Colorado Water Conservancy District.

For full biographical listings, see the Martindale-Hubbell Law Directory

GUTHERY & RICKLES, P.C. (AV)

Cherry Creek Plaza II, 650 South Cherry Street Suite 1000, 80222
Telephone: 303-320-5889
Fax: 303-320-5890

Peter C. Guthery	Stephen P. Rickles

A list of Representative Clients that have provided written authorization will be furnished upon request.

For full biographical listings, see the Martindale-Hubbell Law Directory

HALABY CROSS LIECHTY & SCHLUTER (AV)

Suite 1400, 1873 South Bellaire Street, 80222
Telephone: 303-691-5300
Fax: 303-691-5307

Theodore S. Halaby	Robert M. Liechty
Jonathan A. Cross	Leslie L. Schluter

ASSOCIATES

Jon A. Halaby	R. Craig Hess

Heidi A. Harpowiski

For full biographical listings, see the Martindale-Hubbell Law Directory

HALL & EVANS, L.L.C. (AV)

Suite 1700, 1200 Seventeenth Street, 80202
Telephone: 303-628-3300
Telecopier: 303-628-3368
Email: hallevans@hallevans.com
Colorado Springs, Colorado Office: Suite 600, 102 South Tejon Street, 80903.
Telephone: 719-578-5600. Toll-Free From Denver
Telephone: 303-628-3400.
Telecopier: 719-635-7458.

MEMBERS

Ronald V. Yegge (1905-1970)	Alan Epstein
Don R. Evans (1925-1976)	Paul R. Franke, III
John D. Phillips, Jr.	Charles Greenhouse
Eugene O. Daniels	Marilyn Sterrenberg-Rose
Edward H. Widmann	John E. Bolmer, II
Richard A. Hanneman	Barbara A. Duff
David R. Brougham	Linda S. Comer
Samuel David Cheris	Kenneth H. Lyman
Peter F. Jones	Clinton P. Swift
John P. Mitzner	Joyce H. Nakamura
Michael W. Jones	Michael R. McCurdy
Bruce A. Menk	Cathy Havener Greer
Jeffery B. Stalder	Thomas R. Dolven
James W. Britt	Robert J. McCormick
Eugene R. Commander	Alan J. Schmitz
Daniel R. Satriana, Jr.	Dominic A. Lloyd
Kevin E. O'Brien	Matthew Y. Biscan
C. Willing Browne	Thomas J. Lyons
Chris A. Mattison	Anthony L. Joseph
Robert M. Ferm	Sean R. Gallagher

Patricia Jean Clisham

SPECIAL COUNSEL

David N. Schachter	H. F. Riebesell, Jr.
Stephen M. Bailey	Larry R. Martinez
F. Gregory McKenna	Richard F. Busch II

OF COUNSEL

Richard D. Hall	Brooke Wunnicke

ASSOCIATES

Laura B. Alms	Barbara Schuman Heckler
Robert D. Baker	Joyce L. Jenkins
Robin Lee Beattie	Todd K. Lanting
LaDonne Bush	Thomas M. List
Brian A. Carpenter	Michael L. Luchetta
Laura B. Embleton	Josh A. Marks
Scott V. Goettelman	Malcolm S. Mead
Steven M. Gutierrez	S. Jane Mitchell
Laurie M. Hawley	Kevin Derek Pernell

(See Next Column)

ASSOCIATES (Continued)

Marianne E. Pierce	Pamela Skelton
Andrew D. Ringel	Susan J. Trout
Tracey P. Robinson	James R. Waite
Kimberlie K. Ryan	
(Not admitted in CO)	

Representative Clients: American International Group (A.I.G.); American Insurance Association; Chrysler Corporation; Continental Airlines, Inc.; Jacor Braodcasting Corporation of Colorado, Inc.; Monfort, Inc.; National Railroad Passenger Corporation (AMTRAK); Northern Telecom Inc. (NORTEL); Safeco Insurance Company of America; Sandoz Pharmaceuticals Corporation.

For full biographical listings, see the Martindale-Hubbell Law Directory

HAMILTON AND FAATZ, A PROFESSIONAL CORPORATION (AV)

Suite 500 Colorado State Bank Building, 1600 Broadway, 80202-4988
Telephone: 303-830-0500
Facsimile: 303-860-7855

Pierpont Fuller (1906-1983)	John T. Willson
John M. Evans (1911-1984)	Michael E. Gurley
Dwight Alan Hamilton	James H. Marlow
Clyde A. Faatz, Jr.	Jan E. Montgomery

Gregory W. Smith

Robert L. Bartholic	Christopher J.W. Forrest

Meghan Welch Martinez

OF COUNSEL

Kenneth W. Caughey

Representative Clients: PPG Industries, Inc.; Public Employees Retirement Association of Colorado; Masonic Temple Association of Denver; Lockton Silversmith, Inc.; Muller, Sirhall and Associates, Inc.; South Denver Cardiology Associates, P.C.; Landmark Reclamation, Inc.; Stone's Farm Supply, Inc.; Heather Gardens Association; DCX, Inc.

For full biographical listings, see the Martindale-Hubbell Law Directory

HOLLAND & HART LLP (AV)

Suite 3200, 555 Seventeenth Street, P.O. Box 8749, 80201
Telephone: 303-295-8000
Cable Address: "Holhart Denver"
Telecopier: 303-295-8261
TWX: 910-931-0568
Regional Offices:
Denver Tech Center, Colorado
Aspen, Colorado
Boulder, Colorado
Colorado Springs, Colorado
Boise, Idaho
Billings, Montana
Salt Lake City, Utah
Cheyenne, Wyoming, Holland & Hart, A Partnership including Professional Corporations
Jackson, Wyoming, Holland & Hart, A Partnership including Professional Corporations

MEMBERS OF FIRM

Josiah G. Holland (1900-1975)	Joseph W. Halpern
Stephen H. Hart (1908-1993)	John F. Shepherd
William C. McClearn	John M. Vaught
Gordon G. Greiner	Davis O. O'Connor
William E. Murane	Brian Muldoon
H. Gregory Austin	Jeffrey T. Johnson
John S. Castellano	Mark D. Safty
Dennis M. Jackson	Kathleen J. Shima
Robert E. Benson	(Not admitted in CO)
Stephen H. Foster	Kevin S. Crandell
(Not admitted in CO)	Jeanine Feriancek
Richard M. Koon	Elizabeth A. Sharrer
Robert T. Connery	Mary Ellen Scanlan
Michael D. Martin	Scott S. Barker
Haradon Beatty	Anne J. Castle
Jack L. Smith	Timothy M. Rastello
Jesse B. Heath, Jr.	John C. Tredennick, Jr.
Mark R. Levy	Maureen Reidy Witt
R. Brooke Jackson	Elizabeth Ann Phelan
Wiley E. Mayne, Jr.	Jack M. Englert, Jr.
Frederick G. Meyer	A. Bruce Jones
Paul J. Schlauch	John R. Maxfield
Gregory A. Eurich	Holly Stein Sollod
Ronald M. Martin	Geraldine A. Brimmer
Gregory Russell Piché	Sandra R. Goldman
John Arthur Ramsey	Marcy G. Glenn
Jane Michaels	Denise W. Kennedy
James E. Hartley	William J. Kubida
W. Harold Flowers, Jr.	Christopher H. Toll
Peter C. Houtsma	Renée W. O'Rourke
Gregg I. Anderson	Steven C. Choquette
Betty Carter Arkell	David E. Crandall
Paul D. Phillips	Debra S. Fagan
John M. Husband	Karen Sweeney

(See Next Column)

HOLLAND & HART LLP, *Denver—Continued*

MEMBERS OF FIRM (Continued)

Risa L. Wolf-Smith	David D. Powell, Jr.
Michael S. Quinn	Craig E. Stewart
J. Kevin Bridston	Judith A. (Jude) Biggs

OF COUNSEL

John L. J. Hart (1904-1986)	Robert R. Keatinge
David Butler	Homer L. Knearl
Alan W. Cathcart	Lawrence E. Volmert
(Not admitted in CO)	John R. Wahl
William Dean Embree, Jr.	John F. Walsh
Susan N.H. Dixon	William W. Cochran II

SPECIAL COUNSEL

Jane Oglesby Francis	James J. Gonzales
	Brian M. Mumaugh

ASSOCIATES

Douglas L. Abbott	Karol L. Kahalley
Steven W. Black	William L. Lawrence
Virginia L. Briggs	Shari R. Lefkoff
Carol W. Burton	Andrea J. Levitt
Elizabeth Carney	(Not admitted in CO)
Steven E. Christoffersen	Teresa D. Locke
Elizabeth Schuler Cohen	Ginger E. Margolin
Steven M. Cohen	Stephen Masciocchi
Elizabeth Loring Crane	Veronica J. May
Patricia Dean	Billi R. McCullough
Donald A. Degnan	Nicole R. Morbach
Lynn Bolinske Dolven	Michael Noone
Mark D. Ebel	Fiona W. Ong
Stephanie C. Evans	Lee R. Osman
Maria Teresa (Terry) Fox	Lawrence L. Ostema
Timothy P. Getzoff	Stephanie Sue Padilla
Heidi S. Glance	James A. Pinto
Daniel J. Glivar	Andrew D. Sorensen
Jimmy Goh	Alan N. Stern
Stephen P. Gottesfeld	Jacqueline Sandoval Tahsuda
Eric L. Hilty	John Tahsuda
Laura S. Hundley	Monique A. Tuttle
(Not admitted in CO)	Valerie W. Tyler
Elizabeth R. Jones	Stephanie D. Welsh

DENVER TECH CENTER, COLORADO PARTNERS

Paul J. Schlauch	Maureen Reidy Witt
Robert M. Pomeroy, Jr.	Michael S. Beaver
Robert Alan Poe	Perry L. Glantz
William W. Maywhort	Todd W. Miller

DENVER TECH CENTER RESIDENT OF COUNSEL

Mary D. Metzger

DENVER TECH CENTER, COLORADO RESIDENT ASSOCIATES

C. William Groscup	Montez L. Horne
(Not admitted in CO)	Rachel A. Yates

ASPEN, COLORADO RESIDENT PARTNERS

Charles T. Brandt	Arthur B. Ferguson, Jr.
Arthur C. Daily	Harry Shulman
	Thomas J. Todd

ASPEN, COLORADO RESIDENT ASSOCIATE

Michael Feigenbaum

BOULDER, COLORADO PARTNERS

Betty Carter Arkell	Scott Havlick
Camron R. Kuelthau	Judith A. (Jude) Biggs

OF COUNSEL

Earl C. Hancock	Homer L. Knearl
	Francis A. Sirr

BOULDER, COLORADO ASSOCIATES

Rita S. Heimes	Donald A. Degnan
(Not admitted in CO)	Beth N. Nesis

COLORADO SPRINGS, COLORADO PARTNERS

Ronald M. Martin	Edward H. Flitton (Resident)
Ronald A. Lehmann (Resident)	William K. Brown (Resident)
	William J. Kubida

COLORADO SPRINGS, COLORADO RESIDENT SPECIAL COUNSEL

Elaine Holland Turner

COLORADO SPRINGS, COLORADO RESIDENT OF COUNSEL

Richard A. Bachand

RESIDENT ASSOCIATES

Wendy J. Pifher	David Scott Prince

BOISE, IDAHO RESIDENT PARTNERS

Walter H. Bithell	B. Newal Squyres
J. Frederick Mack	Steven B. Andersen
Larry E. Prince	Linda B. Jones

BOISE, IDAHO RESIDENT ASSOCIATES

Steven C. Bowman	Robert A. Faucher
Amanda K. Brailsford	Murray D. Feldman
Kim J. Dockstader	Kurt D. Holzer
Debra K. Ellers	Bradley J. Wiskirchen

(See Next Column)

BILLINGS, MONTANA PARTNERS

Stephen H. Foster	Jeanne Matthews Bender
Paul D. Miller	James M. Ragain
Donald W. Quander	David R. Chisholm

BILLINGS, MONTANA SPECIAL COUNSEL

Kyle A. Gray	Robert A. Lorenz

BILLINGS, MONTANA RESIDENT ASSOCIATES

W. Scott Mitchell	Elizabeth A. Nedrow

SALT LAKE CITY UTAH RESIDENT PARTNERS

Lawrence J. Jensen	David R. Rudd
Bruce N. Lemons	David G. Angerbauer
	Brent E. Johnson

RESIDENT ASSOCIATES

Robert H. Cutler	Yvonne R. Hogle
Brian T. Hansen	H. Matthew Horlacher
	Stan E. Soper

CHEYENNE, WYOMING PARTNERS

Jack D. Palma, II (P.C.)	Lawrence J. Wolfe (P.C.)
Donald I. Schultz (P.C.)	Richard Schneebeck (P.C.)
Patrick R. Day (P.C.)	Thomas L. Sansonetti (P.C.)
Edward W. Harris	Ronald M. Martin
Joe M. Teig (P.C.)	James R. Belcher
	Bradley T. Cave

CHEYENNE, WYOMING OF COUNSEL

Teresa Burkett Buffington

CHEYENNE, WYOMING RESIDENT ASSOCIATES

William R. Dabney	David G. Ditto

JACKSON, WYOMING PARTNERS

John L. Gallinger (P.C.)	Marilyn S. Kite (P.C.)
	Michael J. Brennan

JACKSON RESIDENT OF COUNSEL

Stephen R. Duerr

JACKSON, WYOMING ASSOCIATE

Paula Fleck

LEGAL SUPPORT PERSONNEL

Regis P. Malloy	Shannon S. Davis
(Legal Assistant)	

For full biographical listings, see the Martindale-Hubbell Law Directory

---

HOLME ROBERTS & OWEN LLP (AV)

Suite 4100, 1700 Lincoln, 80203
Telephone: 303-861-7000
Telecopier: 303-866-0200
Email: hro@hro.com *URL:* http://www.hro.com
Boulder, Colorado Office: Suite 400, 1401 Pearl Street.
Telephone: 303-444-5955.
Telecopier: 303-444-1063.
Colorado Springs, Colorado Office: Suite 1300, 90 South Cascade Avenue.
Telephone: 719-473-3800.
Telecopier: 719-633-1518.
Salt Lake City, Utah Office: Suite 1100, 111 East Broadway.
Telephone: 801-521-5800.
Telecopier: 801-521-9639.
London, England Office: Mellier House, 26a Albemarle Street.
Telephone: 44-171-499-8776.
Telecopier: 44-171-499-7769.
Moscow, Russia Office: Kosmodamianskaya Nab. #52/1, Suite 9100, 113054.
Telephone: 7095-961-3000.
Telecopier: 7095-961-3001.
Kiev, Ukraine Office: Terestchenkovskaya #19, Suite 2, 252004.
Telephone: 380-44-224-1348.
Telecopier: 380-44-224-4986.

PARTNERS OF FIRM

James E. Bye	Richard R. Young (Managing
James C. Owen Jr.	Partner, Colorado Springs
Richard G. Wohlgenant	Office)
Joseph W. Morrisey, Jr.	Donald J. Hopkins
Donald K. Bain	John R. Webb
G. Kevin Conwick	Bruce L. Likoff
Paul D. Holleman	Spencer T. Denison
Robert J. Welter	Henry W. Ipsen
Judson W. Detrick	Brent V. Manning
W. Dean Salter	(Salt Lake City Office)
Lawrence L. Levin	Richard L. Nagl
Edward J. McGrath	(Colorado Springs Office)
Frank Erisman	William R. Roberts (Managing
Thomas A. Richardson	Partner, Boulder Office)
William D. Watson	Phillip R. Clark
David T. Mitzner	Carolyn E. Daniels
Charles A. Ramunno	Martha Traudt Collins
William S. Huff	David K. Detton
Bruce R. Kohler (Co-Resident	(Salt Lake City Office)
Managing Partner, London,	Thomas F. Cope
England Office)	John Leonard Watson

(See Next Column)

HOLME ROBERTS & OWEN LLP—*Continued*

PARTNERS OF FIRM (Continued)

Francis R. Wheeler
K. Preston Oade, Jr.
Lynn Parker Hendrix
Nick Nimmo
Charlotte Louise Neitzel
Steve L. Gaines
　(Colorado Springs Office)
David S. Steefel
Judith L. L. Roberts
　(Co-Director, Moscow Office;
　London Office)
Jan N. Steiert
R. Bruce Johnson
　(Salt Lake City Office)
Nancy J. Gegenheimer
Mark K. Buchi
　(Salt Lake City Office)
Bruce F. Black
LeGrand R. Curtis, Jr.
　(Managing Partner, Salt Lake
　City Office)
P. Christian Anderson
　(Salt Lake City Office)
Mary L. Groves
Manuel L. Martinez
Patricia C. Tisdale
Dennis L. Arfmann
Paul E. Smith (Boulder Office)
Marla J. Williams
Daniel J. Dunn
Linnea Brown
Steven B. Richardson
Boyd N. Boland
Thomas M. James
　(Colorado Springs Office)
McKay Marsden
　(Salt Lake City Office)
Martha Dugan Rehm
Robert Tuchman
John F. Knoeckel
Anne Stark Walker
Katherine Jean Peck
Jill K. Rood (Boulder Office)

Brent E. Rychener
　(Colorado Springs Office)
Susan E. Duffey Campbell
　(Colorado Springs Office)
David R. Child
John R. Wylie
　(Colorado Springs Office)
David Harold Little
　(Salt Lake City Office)
Stephanie M. Tuthill
Robert H. Bach
David B. Wilson
James R. Ghiselli
　(Boulder Office)
Alan C. Bradshaw
　(Salt Lake City Office)
Garth B. Jensen
John D. McCarthy
Eric E. Johnson
Duncan E. Barber
Paul V. Timmins
Richard L. Gabriel
Margaret B. McLean (Resident
　Managing Partner, Moscow,
　Russia Office and Co-Resident
　Managing Partner, London,
　England Office)
Mary Hurley Stuart
James F. Cress
Colin G. Harris
Kenneth W. Lund
Paul G. Thompson
Kevin P. Block (Managing
　Partner, Kiev Office)
George G. Matava
Edwin P. Aro
Steven C. Bednar
　(Salt Lake City Office)
Christopher Cipoletti
　(Colorado Springs Office)
Mark M. Hrenya
Patrick K. Perrin
　(Boulder Office)

OF COUNSEL

Ted P. Stockmar
A. Edgar Benton
Harold S. Bloomenthal
Richard L. Schrepferman

Kay M. Small (Boulder Office)
Richard G. Wilkins
　(Salt Lake City Office)
John P. Babb

SPECIAL COUNSEL

Charles E. Berry
　(Colorado Springs Office)
Richard A. Oertli
Frank J Schuchat
　(Not admitted in CO)
David H. Goldberg
Diane S. Barrett

David W. Isbell
　(Colorado Springs Office)
Christopher D. Ozeroff
　(Boulder Office)
Laurence B. James
John B. Wood (Boulder Office)
Gary R. Thorup
　(Salt Lake City Office)

SENIOR COUNSEL

Stephen C. Rench
Kathryn P. Beller
Michael W. Bruzga

Kathryn Stoker Worford
Lawrence M. Zavadil
Erin Marie Smith

ASSOCIATES

Edward E. Abels, Jr.
Marat Ametov (Moscow Office)
Daron J. Arnold
　(Not admitted in CO)
Blaine J. Benard
　(Salt Lake City Office)
Christopher Boffey (Resident,
　Moscow, Russia Office)
Charles B. Bruce, Jr.
Loretta (Laurie) A. Cahill
Katheryn Jarvis Coggon
Kelly M. Condon
Denise M. DeForest
Susan B. Dussault
　(Not admitted in CO)
G. Leland Dutcher, Jr.
　(Colorado Springs Office)
Adam R. Eaton
　(Not admitted in CO)
Denise Pino Erwin
Valery Fedichin (Kiev Office)
Cody Winchester Field
　(Salt Lake City Office)
Elizabeth M. Flores
Sherry A. Gonzales
Mary C. Gordon
　(Salt Lake City Office)

Harriet M. Hageman
Rebecca Hall (Boulder Office)
Peter O. Hansen
Lisa Anne Hawkins
Sherri A. Heckel
Shuang Hu
Brent P. Karasiuk
　(Colorado Springs Office)
Elena Kuryatnikova
　(Moscow, Russia Office)
Stuart J. Lark
　(Colorado Springs Office)
Matthew J. Lepore
William C. Letzsch, III
Martin D. Litt
Maria Mashenka Lundberg
Daniel P. Maguire
Deborah S. Menkins
　(Colorado Springs Office)
Joli A. Messer
Adrian Miller
Cynthia A. Mitchell
　(Boulder Office)
Neil F. O'Donnell
　(Moscow Office)
Felicity A. O'Herron

(See Next Column)

ASSOCIATES (Continued)

Peter-Christian Olivo
　(Boulder Office)
Sandra Orihuela
Timothy G. Pfeifer
　(Colorado Springs Office)
Thad W. Renaud
Dominic Jude Ricotta
　(Colorado Springs Office)
Matthew J. Rita
Alan Romero
　(Salt Lake City Office)
Michelle M. Rose-Hughes
Nikita O. Sergeyev
　(Moscow, Russia Office)
Rashid Sharipov (Resident,
　Moscow, Russia Office)

J. Alison Shelton
Steven B. Smith
　(Colorado Springs Office)
Edward E. Stevenson
Sharon A. Thomas
　(Colorado Springs Office)
Alexander Udovenko
　(Moscow, Russia Office)
Anna B. Veiksha (Kiev Office)
Jeffrey M. Vincent
　(Salt Lake City Office)
Maria V. Woods
Thomas E. Yearout
Masahiro Max Yoshimura
Steven P. Young
　(Salt Lake City Office)

LEGAL SUPPORT PERSONNEL

Mark E. Estes (Librarian)

For full biographical listings, see the Martindale-Hubbell Law Directory

JONES & KELLER, A PROFESSIONAL CORPORATION (AV)

Suite 1600, 1625 Broadway, 80202
Telephone: 303-573-1600
Fax: 303-893-6506

Marion F. Jones (1898-1978)
Alec J. Keller (1913-1995)
Alvin J. Meiklejohn, Jr.
Leslie R. Kehl
Edward T. Lyons, Jr.
David E. Driggers

Thomas J. Burke, Jr.
Samuel E. Wing
Reid A. Godbolt
Rodney D. Knutson
Kevin L. Brown
Barry L. Wilkie

Howard R. Hertzberg
David A. Thayer

Brent Nicholls
Michael Brian Cavanaugh

Nathan D. Simmons

Reference: Colorado State Bank; Union Bank & Trust.

For full biographical listings, see the Martindale-Hubbell Law Directory

---

KUTAK ROCK (AV)

A Partnership including Professional Corporations
Suite 2900, 717 Seventeenth Street, 80202-3329
Telephone: 303-297-2400
Fax: 303-292-7799
URL: http://www.kutakrock.com
Atlanta, Georgia Office: Suite 2100, 225 Peachtree Street, NE, 30303-1731.
Telephone: 404-222-4600.
Facsimile: 404-222-4654.
Little Rock, Arkansas Office: Suite 1770, 124 West Capitol Avenue,
72201-3719.
Telephone: 501-376-9208.
Facsimile: 501-375-3749.
Kansas City, Missouri Office: United Missouri Bank Building, Third Floor,
9201 Ward Parkway.
Telephone: 816-361-3363.
Telecopier: 816-361-8397.
New York, New York Office: 767 Third Avenue.
Telephone: 212-752-0800.
Facsimile: 212-752-2281.
Oklahoma City, Oklahoma Office: Suite 475, 6305 Waterford Boulevard,
73118-1116.
Telephone: 405-848-2475.
Facsimile: 405-842-5748.
Omaha, Nebraska Office: The Omaha Building, 1650 Farnam Street,
68102-2186.
Telephone: 402-346-6000.
Facsimile: 402-346-1148.
Phoenix, Arizona Office: 16th Floor, 3300 North Central Avenue,
85012-2516.
Telephone: 602-285-1700.
Facsimile: 602-285-1868.
Pittsburgh, Pennsylvania Office: 1214 Frick Building, 437 Grant Street,
15219-6002.
Telephone: 412-261-6720.
Facsimile: 412-261-6717.
Washington, D.C. Office: Suite 1000, 1101 Connecticut Avenue, NW,
20036-4374.
Telephone: 202-828-2400.
Facsimile: 202-828-2488.

MEMBERS OF FIRM

James D. Arundel
Paul E. Belitz
Robert D. Irvin
Warren L. Troupe
Michael K. Reppe
John H. Bernstein
James C. Ruh
Larry L. Carlile
Robert J. Ahrenholz

Timothy J. Flanagan, P.C.
Robert C. Roth, Jr.
Thane R. Hodson
Frederic H. Marienthal III
Michael R. Johnson
Peter D. Willis
David A. Caprera
John V. McDermott
M. Lou Raders

(See Next Column)

KUTAK ROCK, *Denver—Continued*

MEMBERS OF FIRM (Continued)

William C. Gorham
Diana C. Fields
Scott H. Beck
Richard L. Buddin

Brian V. Caid
Peggy Ann Richter
Tana K. Simard
William S. Martin

Lydia A. Mangan

SPECIAL COUNSEL

Michael T. Lambert
Thomas M. Peltz

Saranne K Maxwell

ASSOCIATES

Sam S. Balisy
(Not admitted in CO)
Donald R. Stover
John P. Jones
Anne M. Gish
Stephen J. Ismert
Craig N. Johnson
Deborah A. Schultz

Brian D. Lewandowski
Wendy Win Wolfe
Mark A. Adams
Keith L. Henderson
(Not admitted in CO)
Trenton H. Johnson
(Not admitted in CO)
David G. Thatcher

For full biographical listings, see the Martindale-Hubbell Law Directory

---

LONG & JAUDON, P.C. (AV)

The Bailey Mansion, 1600 Ogden Street, 80218-1414
Telephone: 303-832-1122
FAX: 303-832-1348

Lawrence A. Long (1908-1992)
Joseph C. Jaudon, Jr.
David B. Higgins
James A. Dierker
Frederick W. Long
Gary B. Blum
Michael T. McConnell
Stephen P. Hopkins
Michael T. DePinto (1956-1995)
Robert M. Baldwin
Dennis Woodfin Brown
Celine Lillie
Alan D. Avery

Cecelia A. Fleischner
Walter N. Houghtaling
Ellen Rubright Ivy
Christine Anne Craigmile
Carla M. LaRosa
Sheri Lyn Hood
Thomas C. Kearns, Jr.
Margaret J. Walton
David H. Yun
James Michael Miletich
Richard T. D'Ambrosio
Jennifer Joe Miller
Traci L. Van Pelt
(Not admitted in CO)

Representative Clients: Goodman Buick-GMC Trucks, Inc.; Keystone Resorts, Inc.; King Soopers, Inc. (Dillon Companies, Inc.); St. Joseph Hospital; Watersaver; Aetna Life & Casualty Co.; The Doctors Co.; Home Insurance Co.; Baxter Healthcare; CNA.

For full biographical listings, see the Martindale-Hubbell Law Directory

---

MONTGOMERY LITTLE & McGREW, P.C. (AV)

The Quadrant, 5445 DTC Parkway, Suite 800 (Englewood), 80111
Telephone: 303-773-8100
Telecopier: 303-220-0412

Roy E. Montgomery
(1907-1986)
Robert R. Montgomery
David C. Little
Dan McGrew
James J. Soran, III
Richard L. Murray, Jr.
Kevin J. Kuhn
David A. Burlage
Robert J. Beattie
Brian K. Stutheit
Michael H. Smith
William H. ReMine, III

Debra Piazza
William H. Knapp
Daniel P. Murphy
Thomas C. Deline
Karen B. Best
John R. Riley
Rebecca B. Givens
Christopher B. Little
Melinda L. Sanders
Timothy M. Schulte
Carole Salamaha
Patrick T. O'Rourke
Joel A. Mayo

OF COUNSEL

J. Bayard Young

LEGAL SUPPORT PERSONNEL

Rodney R. Germeroth (Director
of Administration and
Finance)
Mary Kay Ackley
(Legal Assistant)
Carmen L. Antonio
(Legal Assistant)
Margaret M. Green
(Legal Assistant)
Debbie L. Kirke
(Legal Assistant)

Lynne M. Thill (Legal Assistant)
Ginny A. Leiker
(Legal Assistant)
Anna M. Krigger
(Legal Assistant)
Allyson K. Snyder-Mueller
(Legal Assistant)
Kelly J. Roberge
(Legal Assistant)
Monica L. Sharp
(Legal Assistant)

Representative Clients: Amoco Oil Co.; Bristol-Myers Squibb; Colorado Medical Society; Chrysler Corp.; Cyprus Minerals; Dillon Cos., Inc., d/b/a King Soopers; The St. Paul Insurance Cos.; University of Colorado Health Sciences Center.

For full biographical listings, see the Martindale-Hubbell Law Directory

---

MOYE, GILES, O'KEEFE, VERMEIRE & GORRELL LLP (AV)

A Limited Liability Partnership of Professional Corporations
29th Floor, 1225 Seventeenth Street, 80202
Telephone: 303-292-2900
Telecopier: 303-292-4510
URL: http://www.mgovg.com

PARTNERS

John E. Moye (P.C.)
Edward M. Giles (P.C.)
Edward F. O'Keefe (P.C.)
Richard S. Vermeire (P.C.)
Teryl R. Gorrell (P.C.)
James T. Burghardt (P.C.)
Edwin A. Naylor (P.C.)
Patricia M. Nagel (P.C.)
Charles F. Luce, Jr., (P.C.)
J. William Callison (P.C.)
John R. Paddock, Jr., (P.C.)

Paul F. Lewis (P.C.)
Susan M. Rogers (P.C.)
Erik K. Foster (P.C.)
Jerry N. Jones (P.C.)
Dwight K. Shellman III (P.C.)
William C. Jensen (P.C.)
Elaine G. Edinburg (P.C.)
Thomas H. Keyse (P.C.)
Jeffrey C. Pond (P.C.)
Chesley "Bud" K. Culp III (P.C.)

ASSOCIATES

Patrick E. Meyers
Laura G. Kastetter
Kevin E. Burr
Vincent G. Toenjes

Sherlyn K. Visani
Cynthia L. McNeill
Sean S. Hogle
Kevin P. Hein

Charles T. Mitchell

For full biographical listings, see the Martindale-Hubbell Law Directory

---

MYER, SWANSON, ADAMS & WOLF, P.C. (AV)

The Colorado State Bank Building, 1600 Broadway, Suite
1480, 80202-4915
Telephone: 303-866-9800
Facsimile: 303-866-9818

Rendle Myer
Allan B. Adams

Robert K. Swanson
Thomas J. Wolf

Philip T. Masterson

OF COUNSEL

Robert Swanson
Fred E. Neef (1910-1986)

Representative Clients: The Oppenheimer Funds; Daily Cash Accumulation Fund; The Centennial Trusts; Mile High Chapter of American Red Cross; Master Lease; Heartland Management Co.; Kan-Build of Colorado, Inc.
Reference: The Colorado State Bank of Denver.

For full biographical listings, see the Martindale-Hubbell Law Directory

---

OTTEN, JOHNSON, ROBINSON, NEFF & RAGONETTI, P.C. (AV)

950 Seventeenth Street, 16th Floor, 80202
Telephone: 303-825-8400
Telecopier: 303-825-6525

Arthur E. Otten, Jr.
William F. Schoeberlein
Frank L. Robinson
Bruce B. Johnson
A. Bruce Campbell
William R. Neff
Thomas J. Ragonetti
David W. Stark
Lawrence W. Marquess
Darrell G. Waas
Robert C. Fisher, Jr.
Neil M. Goff
Blair L. Lockwood
Hugh Q. Gottschalk
J. Thomas Macdonald
John D. Sternberg
Michael Westover
Edward P. Timmins
Daniel M. Minzer
Kevin A. Gliwa
Henry I. Lowe
P. Kathleen Lower
David T. Brennan
Kathleen M. Bottagaro
Terence M. Ridley

Kenneth K. Skogg
David W. Fell
Karen L. Barsch
Brad W. Schacht
R. Michael Shomo
David P. Hutchinson
Michael C. Villano
Alex Iskenderian
James D. Leonard
Todd A. Fredrickson
Darin Mackender
Amy J. Griffin
Mark F. Copertino
William H. Brierly
Victoria L. Hellmer
Lisa A. Osman
Daniel E. Evans
Daniel J. Culhane
Kathryn A. Plonsky
Patricia C. Campbell
Christopher T. Toll
J. Bart Johnson
Richard C. Jennings
Karen L. Brody
James C. Ellenberger

Patricia A. Thatcher

OF COUNSEL

Kenneth M. Robins
William J. Baum, Jr.

Barbara J. Kelley

SPECIAL COUNSEL

Marguerite L. Sadler

Representative Clients: Aetna Life Insurance Co.; The Broe Companies; Inc.; Colorado National Bank; Connecticut General Life Insurance Co.; First Nationwide Bank; Homart Development Co.; Land Title Guarantee Co.; Trizec Corporation Ltd.; U.S. West Communications, Inc.; The Western Sugar Co.

For full biographical listings, see the Martindale-Hubbell Law Directory

Denver—Continued

PARCEL, MAURO, HULTIN & SPAANSTRA, P.C. (AV)

Suite 3600, 1801 California Street, 80202
Telephone: 303-292-6400
Telecopier: 303-295-3040

Randall G. Alt	Randy L. Parcel
James K. Aronstein	Douglas A. Pluss
David A. Bailey	Lori L. Roberts
James D. Butler	Linda L. Rockwood
Steven A. Cohen	Kenneth L. Salazar
Jeffrey H. Desautels	Don H. Sherwood
William J. Duffy	Rodney L. Smith
William A. Hillhouse II	James R. Spaanstra
Paul F. Hultin	Leslie Bokee Speed
Robert B. Hunter	Marcus L. Squarrell
Mark F. Kennedy	David H. Stacy
James M. King	Edward W. Stern
Robert W. Lawrence	Bruce D. Stocks
William R. Marsh	Christopher J. Sutton
Raymond W. Martin	John R. Trigg
Dean R. Massey	Joseph B. Valentine
Brian E. McGee	(Not admitted in CO)
Christopher J. Meyer	Gary Wagner
Habib Nasrullah	Malcolm E. Wheeler
Michael L. O'Donnell	Douglas R. Wright
Michael M. Page	Gwen Jarahian Young

OF COUNSEL

Richard P. Barkley	Peggy E. Montaño
John H. Feiner	Scott M. Reed
Richard F. Mauro	Susan M. Schaecher
Mark N. Semenoff	

Nancy E. Berman	Lee A. Mickus
Angella K. Bond	Andrew J. Mihalick
Susan D. Brienza	(Not admitted in CO)
Cheryl Burnside	Scott D. Peterson
Martha J. Cardi	Jeffrey K. Reeser
Theresa J. Collier	Jeffrey W. Schwarz
Jodi S. Coviello	Geoffrey H. Simon
David A. Greher	Edward C. Stewart
Michelle J. Hirth	Stephanie Stimpson
Paul F. Hodapp	(Not admitted in CO)
James E. Hooper, Jr.	Kimberly Ann Tempel
Polly B. Jessen	Michael C. Thompson
Susan J. Keller	(Not admitted in CO)
Laurie L. Korneffel	David F. White
Jennifer G. Krolik	(Not admitted in CO)
John R. Marcil	
(Not admitted in CO)	

Reference: 1st Interstate, Denver, Colorado.

For full biographical listings, see the Martindale-Hubbell Law Directory

SENN LEWIS VISCIANO & STRAHLE, PROFESSIONAL CORPORATION (AV)

Suite 4300, 1801 California Street, 80202
Telephone: 303-298-1122
Telecopier: 303-296-9101

Mark A. Senn	Frank W. Visciano
Fredric J. Lewis	Wynn E. Strahle
Stephen W. Arent	

Brian J. Reichel	Luis A. Toro
Christopher R. Alger	Margie J. Titus
David C. Camp	Laura B. Redstone
Tad Stephen Rogers	

OF COUNSEL

Lawrence A. Atler (P.C.)

SPECIAL COUNSEL

Ellen Kirschenbaum

For full biographical listings, see the Martindale-Hubbell Law Directory

SHERMAN & HOWARD L.L.C. (AV)

Attorneys and Counselors at Law
633 Seventeenth Street, Suite 3000, 80202
Telephone: 303-297-2900
Telecopier: 303-298-0940
Colorado Springs, Colorado Office: Suite 1500, 90 South Cascade Avenue, 80903.
Telephone: 719-475-2440.
Las Vegas, Nevada Office: Swendseid & Stern a member in Sherman & Howard L.L.C., 317 Sixth Street, 89101.
Telephone: 702-387-6073.
Reno, Nevada Office: Swendseid & Stern, a member in Sherman & Howard L.L.C., 50 West Liberty Street, Suite 660, 89501.
Telephone: 702-323-1980.

(See Next Column)

James H. Pershing (1863-1948)	Theodore A. Olsen
Robert Graham Bosworth	Manuel D. Savage
(1888-1954)	Paul Curtis Daw
Lewis A. Dick (1889-1954)	Ronald M. Eddy
Fritz A. Nagel (1891-1978)	Durward E. Timmons, Jr.
Clyde C. Dawson (1905-1979)	(Colorado Springs Office)
Samuel S. Sherman, Jr.	Rebecca Anderson Fischer
(1909-1988)	Steven D. Miller
Winston S. Howard (Retired)	Peggy Berning Knight
James E. Hautzinger	B. Scott Pullara
James L. Cunningham	Jennifer Stern (Las Vegas and
Douglas M. Cain	Reno, Nevada Offices)
Duane F. Wurzer	Ann Marie (Amy) Kennedy
E. Lee Dale	Richard N. Baer
Christopher Lane	Leanne B. DeVos
Hugh J. McClearn	William T. Diss
R. Michael Sanchez	Edmond F. Noel, Jr.
Andrew L. Blair, Jr.	Richard K. Parks
Howard B. Gelt	Calvin T. Hanson
Charles W. Newcom	N. Dawn Webber
Mark L. Fulford	(Colorado Springs Office)
James F. Wood	Glenn H. Schlabs
Robert P. Mitchell	(Colorado Springs Office)
Kenneth B. Siegel	Cynthia P. Delaney
David Thomas III	Leslie A. Nichols
Cynthia C. Benson	Bruce A. Kolbezen
Joseph J. Bronesky	(Colorado Springs Office)
John O. Swendseid (Las Vegas	Carol V. Berger
and Reno, Nevada Offices)	James P. Lane
Charles Y. Tanabe	Kathleen A. Odle
Robert L. Brown	Joanne F. Norris
Dee P. Wisor	Diana M. Wendel
Arlene S. Bobrow	Doran L. Matzke
Alan J. Gilbert	Maria L. Prevedel
Raymond M. Deeny	Andrew W. Volin
(Colorado Springs Office)	Stephanie J. Griffin
W.V. Bernie Siebert	Stefan D. Stein
Stanley M. Raine	Robert Mintz

COUNSEL

John W. Low	Amy L. Hirter
Raymond J. Turner	Jane R. Levine
Garth C. Grissom	(Not admitted in CO)
Michael D. Groshek	Barbara Weil Gall
Gary L. Greer	Joan Blaik
Paul E. Roberts	James R. McMaster
Stephen S. Halasz	Carolyn Lubchenco

Carol Hildebrand	John J. Cyran
Wayne W. Williams	Clark G. Malak
(Colorado Springs Office)	(Not admitted in CO)
Bridget K. Sullivan	Heather Fox Vickles
Donna K. McNamara	Sheilah M. Rogers
Milton L. "Skip" Smith, III	Devona J. Futch
(Colorado Springs Office)	Michael J. Angus
John W. Mill	Maria L. Sepúlveda
Dominick Sekich	Heather L. Mitchell
Monica T. Langley	Jennifer M. Mardosz
Leslie A. Petri	Cherry J. Hearn
Deborah L. Land Buckley	J. David Varley
Christopher R. Mosley	(Not admitted in CO)
Sarah J. Kilgore	Ronald M. Pierce
Kimberley H. Tyson	Dawn A. Leporati
Jennifer R. George	(Not admitted in CO)
(Colorado Springs Office)	Christopher McCabe
Kendra S. Follett (Las Vegas	Carol Deanne Harper
and Reno, Nevada Offices)	Susan Lee Lipson
Paul J. McCue	Lisa K. McGee
Joseph M. Dencker	William A. Wright
Jeffrey S. Lyons	Brenda K. Buege
(Not admitted in CO)	(Colorado Springs Office)
James T. Giel	
(Not admitted in CO)	

Representative Clients: AT&T Corp.; Hathaway Corp.; Keystone Resort; Newmont Gold Corp.; Public Service Company of Colorado; Public Employees' Retirement Assn.; Tele-Communications, Inc.

For full biographical listings, see the Martindale-Hubbell Law Directory

WALDBAUM, CORN, KOFF, BERGER AND COHEN, P.C. (AV)

303 East Seventeenth Avenue, Suite 940, 80203
Telephone: 303-861-1166
Telecopier: 303-861-0601

Leonard N. Waldbaum	Michael H. Berger
Douglas B. Koff	Nancy L. Cohen
Robert O. Corn	Scot M. Peterson

Representative Clients: Bestop, Inc.; CIMA Energy Corporation; Contact Lens Association of Ophthalmologists, Inc. (CLAO); First Winthrop Properties, Inc.; Hayashida Farms, Inc.; J.A. Balistreri Farms, Inc.; Premier Enterprises, Inc.; Raintree Homes, Inc.; Sevo-Miller, Inc.; Western Optical, Inc.

For full biographical listings, see the Martindale-Hubbell Law Directory

Denver—Continued

WALTERS & JOYCE, P.C. (AV)

2015 York Street, 80205
Telephone: 303-322-1404
FAX: 303-377-5668

William E. Walters, III   Craig D. Joyce

Anne Baudino Holton
OF COUNSEL
Julia T. Waggener

Reference: Norwest Bank of Buckingham Square; Mountain States Bank.

For full biographical listings, see the Martindale-Hubbell Law Directory

WELBORN SULLIVAN MECK & TOOLEY, P.C. (AV)

1775 Sherman Street, Suite 1800, 80203-4318
Telephone: 303-830-2500
Facsimile: 303-832-2366
Email: wsmt.denver@mep-1.sprint.com
Republic of Kazakstan Branch Office: 480100 Almaty 38 Dostyk Prospect, Suite 703.
Telephone: +7-3272 617-422; 616-509; 616-642.
Fax: +7-3272 615-840. Email: wsmt.welborn@mep-1.sprint.com.

John F. Welborn   Kendor P. Jones
Stephen J. Sullivan   Molly Sommerville
John F. Meck   Marla E. Valdez
Keith D. Tooley   Karen Ostrander-Krug
Brian S. Tooley

Scott L. Sells
OF COUNSEL
Robert F. Welborn
SPECIAL COUNSEL
Hugh V. Schaefer   Jan G. Laitos

For full biographical listings, see the Martindale-Hubbell Law Directory

WHITE AND STEELE, PROFESSIONAL CORPORATION (AV)

1225 17th Street, Suite 2800, 80202
Telephone: 303-296-2828
Telecopier: 303-296-3131
Email: law@wsteele.com
Cheyenne, Wyoming Office: 1912 Capital Avenue, Suite 416, 82003.
Telephone: 307-778-4160.
Telecopier: 307-778-7041.

Lowell White (1897-1983)   Sandra L. Spencer
Walter A. Steele   John M. Palmeri
R. Eric Peterson   Frederick W. Klann
Stephen K. Gerdes   Richard M. Kaudy
Michael W. Anderson   Peter W. Rietz
James M. Dieterich   Thomas B. Quinn
Glendon L. Laird   Michael J. Daugherty
John Lebsack   Ted A. Krumreich
Stephen G. Sparr   William F. Campbell, Jr.
John P. Craver   Kurt A. Horton
David J. Nowak   Stewart J. Rourke
Robert R. Carlson

Christopher P. Kenney   Kimberly A. Viergever
Robert H. Coate   J. Barton Maxwell
Michelle R. Magruder   Sherri L. Sweers
Monty L. Barnett   Shanise M. Black
Joseph R. King   Matthew W. Tills
Frank D. Sledge   Claire Diaz
Kristi Blumhardt   Charles W. Yett
Keith R. Olivera   Laura E. David Fuller
A.W. Victoria Poley
OF COUNSEL
Fred L. Witsell   Kevin W. Hecht

Colorado Tort Counsel for: Goodyear Tire and Rubber Co.; The Dow Chemical Co.; Firestone Tire and Rubber Co.
Insurance Clients: Allied Insurance Co.; CNA; Kemper Insurance Group; Massachusetts Mutual Life Insurance Co.; Underwriters at Lloyds; U.S.A.A.

For full biographical listings, see the Martindale-Hubbell Law Directory

DURANGO,* La Plata Co.

FRANK J. ANESI (AV)

Suite 220, 835 East Second Avenue, P.O. Box 2185, 81302
Telephone: 970-247-9246
Fax: 970-259-2793

References: First National Bank of Durango; Burns Bank, Durango.

For full biographical listings, see the Martindale-Hubbell Law Directory

DUTHIE & TATE (AV)

A Partnership of Professional Corporations
835 East Second Avenue, Suite 444, P.O. Box 219, 81302
Telephone: 970-247-4545
Fax: 970-247-2471

Alonzo M. Emigh (1915-1971)   Frederic B. Emigh (1910-1987)
MEMBERS OF FIRM
Harry G. Tate (P.C.)   Robert C. Duthie, III (P.C.)

Counsel for: The First National Bank of Durango; Basin Properties, Inc.; Strater Hotel; Bula.
Local Counsel: State Farm Mutuals; United Fire & Casualty Co.; U.S.A.A. and Commercial Union Insurance Companies.

For full biographical listings, see the Martindale-Hubbell Law Directory

MAYNES, BRADFORD, SHIPPS & SHEFTEL (AV)

West Building, Suite 123, 835 East Second Avenue, P.O. Box 2717, 81302
Telephone: 970-247-1755
Fax: 970-247-8827
Email: mbss@frontier.net

MEMBERS OF FIRM
Frank E. (Sam) Maynes   Sam W. Maynes
Byron V. Bradford (1907-1985) Patricia A. Hall
Thomas H. Shipps   John Barlow Spear
Janice C. Sheftel   Geoffrey M. Craig

Counsel for: Southwestern Water Conservation District; San Miguel and La Plata Water Conservancy Districts; La Plata Electric Association, Inc. (REA); Southern Ute Indian Tribe; South Durango Water District; Dolores Water Conservancy District; Animas-La Plata Water Conservancy District; State Farm Insurance.

For full biographical listings, see the Martindale-Hubbell Law Directory

ENGLEWOOD, Arapahoe Co.

BANTA, HOYT, EVERALL & FARRINGTON, L.L.C. (AV)

Suite 240E, 5690 DTC Boulevard, 80111
Telephone: 303-220-8000
Fax: 303-220-0153

Richard L. Banta, Jr.   Richard J. Banta
  (1912-1993)   Stephen G. Everall
Darryl L. Farrington
OF COUNSEL
R. Val Hoyt   Richard D. Greene
Craig E. Wagner

Representative Clients: American Institute of Timber Construction; Cherry Creek School District No. 5; City of Greenwood Village; Colorado School District Self Insurance Pool; Intermountain Rural Electric Association; Kiewit Western Co.; Littleton Public Schools; National Union Fire Insurance Co. (local); Southgate Sanitation and Water Districts.

For full biographical listings, see the Martindale-Hubbell Law Directory

FORT COLLINS,* Larimer Co.

ALLEN, ROGERS AND VAHRENWALD (AV)

Eleventh Floor, Key Bank Building, 125 South Howes, P.O. Box 608, 80522
Telephone: 970-482-5058
Fax: 970-482-5175

MEMBERS OF FIRM
William H. Allen (1917-1990) Donald E. Johnson, Jr.
Garth W. Rogers   J. Brian McMahill
Jack D. Vahrenwald   Russell B. Sanford
Allan S. Massey
ASSOCIATE
Todd W. Rogers

Representative Clients: Everitt Enterprises, Inc. (Real Estate Development); LaPorte Water and Sanitation District; Foothills Fashion Mall (Shopping Center); Poudre Valley Bank, Fort Collins.
References: First National Bank of Fort Collins, N.A.; Poudre Valley Bank, Fort Collins.

For full biographical listings, see the Martindale-Hubbell Law Directory

DWYER, HUDDLESON & RAY, P.C. (AV)

Tenth Floor, First Tower, 215 West Oak Street Drawer J, 80522
Telephone: 970-482-1056
Facsimile: 970-482-3840
URL: http://www.fornet.ort/~ded/dhr.html

(See Next Column)

DWYER, HUDDLESON & RAY P.C.—*Continued*

David E. Dwyer	T. Thomas Metier
Charles R. Huddleson	Stephen J. Jouard
Steven B. Ray	Clinton L. Hubbard
James E. Ringenberg	Joel M. Funk

Jon-Mark C. Patterson

General Counsel for: First National Bank; Advanced Energy Industries, Co.; Columbine Management Services, Inc.; Steele's Market, Inc.; Orthopaedic Center of the Rockies.
Counsel for: Hewlett-Packard Co.; Leggett & Platt Inc.; Platte River Power Authority; Woodward Governor Co.; Stelbar Oil Corp.

For full biographical listings, see the Martindale-Hubbell Law Directory

FISCHER, BROWN & GUNN, P.C. (AV)

8th Floor, First Tower, 215 West Oak Street, P.O. Box Q, 80521
Telephone: 970-407-9000
Facsimile: 970-407-1055
Email: FBG@FR11.COM

Ward H. Fischer	William C. Gunn
William H. Brown	William R. Fischer

Margaret A. Brown

General Counsel for: First National Bank; The Water Supply and Storage Co.; Cache La Poudre Water Users Assn.
Counsel for: Eastman Kodak Co.; The City of Northglenn; The City of Littleton; The City of Brighton.

For full biographical listings, see the Martindale-Hubbell Law Directory

FISCHER, HOWARD & FRANCIS, LLP (AV)

125 South Howes, Suite 900, P.O. Box 506, 80522
Telephone: 970-482-4710
Fax: 970-482-4729

MEMBERS OF FIRM

Gene E. Fischer	Stephen E. Howard

Steven G. Francis

Approved Attorneys for: Attorney's Title Guaranty Fund, Inc.
Reference: First National Bank of Fort Collins, N.A.

For full biographical listings, see the Martindale-Hubbell Law Directory

MARCH & MYATT, P.C. (AV)

110 East Oak Street, Suite 200, P.O. Box 469, 80522
Telephone: 970-482-4322
Fax: 970-482-3038

Arthur E. March (1909-1981)	Richard Shaeffer Gast
Arthur E. March, Jr.	Lucia A. Liley
Ramsey D. Myatt	J. Brad March
Robert W. Brandes, Jr.	Linda S. Miller

Jeffrey J. Johnson	Matthew J. Douglas

Local Counsel for: Union Colony Bank (Fort Collins); Bank One of Colorado (Fort Collins, Loveland).
General Counsel for: Schrader Oil Co.; First State Bank of Fort Collins; Fort Collins Downtown Development Authority; Factual Data Corp.; Connell Resources, Inc.

For full biographical listings, see the Martindale-Hubbell Law Directory

FORT LUPTON, Weld Co. — (Refer to Brighton)

FORT MORGAN,* Morgan Co. — (Refer to Greeley)

GLENWOOD SPRINGS,* Garfield Co.

DELANEY & BALCOMB, P.C. (AV)

818 Colorado Avenue, P.O. Drawer 790, 81602
Telephone: 970-945-6546, 945-2371
Fax: 970-945-8902

John A. Thulson	Robert M. Noone
Edward Mulhall, Jr.	Timothy A. Thulson
Scott M. Balcomb	Lori J.M. Satterfield
Lawrence R. Green	Edward Bryan Olszewski

Karl J. Hanlon

OF COUNSEL

Robert Delaney	Kenneth Balcomb

General Counsel for: Ski Sunlight, Inc.
Local Counsel for: Farm Credit Services.

For full biographical listings, see the Martindale-Hubbell Law Directory

GOLDEN,* Jefferson Co.

BRADLEY, CAMPBELL, CARNEY & MADSEN, PROFESSIONAL CORPORATION (AV)

1717 Washington Avenue, 80401-1994
Telephone: 303-278-3300
Fax: 303-278-3379
Email: firm@bccm.com

Leo N. Bradley	Russell Carparelli
Tim L. Campbell	T. J. Carney
Earl K. Madsen	Gary W. Truman
Thomas A. Nolan	Kent R. Saraceno

David F. Murray

OF COUNSEL

Laura J. Vogelgesang	Thomas J. Carney

Counsel for: Coors Brewing Co.; Coors Ceramics Co.; Evergreen National Bank, Evergreen, Colorado; Clear Creek National Bank, Georgetown, Colorado; ASARCO, Inc.; Morrison-Knudsen; Westinghouse Electric Corp.
Local Counsel for: Public Service Company of Colorado.
Reference: Colorado National Bank, Denver, Colorado.

For full biographical listings, see the Martindale-Hubbell Law Directory

FLEMING, PATTRIDGE & RUNNERSTROM, P.C. (AV)

1200 Arapahoe Street, 80401-1198
Telephone: 303-279-2563
Fax: 303-279-2677

Robert G. Fleming (Retired)	Frederick J. Pattridge (Retired)

Lars R. Runnerstrom

Michelle A. Dobbins	Marilana S. "Marnie" Walsh

Counsel for: Metrolist, Inc.; Ardourel Construction Co.; The Foss Co.; Meyer Home Center, Inc.; Mesa Meadows Land Co.

For full biographical listings, see the Martindale-Hubbell Law Directory

GRAND JUNCTION,* Mesa Co.

HOSKIN, FARINA, ALDRICH & KAMPF, PROFESSIONAL CORPORATION (AV)

Bank of Colorado Building, 200 Grand Avenue, Suite 400, P.O. Box 40, 81502
Telephone: 970-242-4903
FAX: 970-241-3760

William H. Nelson (1926-1992)	Gregg K. Kampf
Gregory K. Hoskin	Curtis G. Taylor
Terrance L. Farina	David M. Scanga
Frederick G. Aldrich	David A. Younger

Michael J. Russell

John T. Howe	John Siddeek
Matthew G. Weber	Darrel Linn Moss

Attorneys for: Great American First Savings Bank, FSB; Central Bank of Grand Junction; Grand Valley National Bank; City Market, Inc.; Rangely School District RE-4; Rocky Mountain Health Maintenance Organization; Unocal Corp.; Equitable Life Assurance Society; Grand Valley Rural Power Lines, Inc.; Pepsi-Cola Bottling Group.

For full biographical listings, see the Martindale-Hubbell Law Directory

GREELEY,* Weld Co.

HOUTCHENS, DANIEL & GREENFIELD, LLC (AV)

1007 Ninth Avenue, 80631
Telephone: 970-353-9195
Facsimile: 970-353-0151

OF COUNSEL

Barnard Houtchens

MEMBERS OF FIRM

S. Robert Houtchens (1917-1989)	John B. Houtchens
Rodger I. Houtchens (1921-1988)	Jerry C. Daniel
	Kim R. Houtchens
	Thomas A. Houtchens

Dallas D. Greenfield

ASSOCIATES

Julie Christine Hoskins	Mark J. Geil

Counsel for: Norwest Bank Greeley; Miner and Miner, Consulting Engineers; State Farm Insurance Cos.; Home Builders Association of Northern Colorado; Noffsinger Manufacturing Co., Inc.; Cornerstone Builders, Inc.; Farmers Insurance Cos.

For full biographical listings, see the Martindale-Hubbell Law Directory

Greeley—Continued

WITWER, OLDENBURG, BARRY & BEDINGFIELD, LLP (AV)

Suite 760, 822 7th Street, 80631
Telephone: 970-352-3161
Facsimile: 970-352-3165

MEMBERS OF FIRM

Stow L. Witwer, Jr.   John J. Barry
R. Sam Oldenburg   Jeffrey T. Bedingfield

OF COUNSEL

Marilyn J. David

ASSOCIATES

Jacqueline Johnson   Curtis R. Sears
Charles A. Karowsky (Retired)

Representative Clients: Bank One-Greely; Greeley School District; Aims Junior College; John Hancock Mutual Life Insurance Co.; United Power Co.; Phelps-Tointon, Inc.

For full biographical listings, see the Martindale-Hubbell Law Directory

---

JULESBURG, * Sedgwick Co. — (Refer to Greeley)

LA JUNTA, * Otero Co. — (Refer to Lamar)

LAKEWOOD, Jefferson Co.

ROBERT G. BUSCH (AV)

Suite C-400, 12600 West Colfax Avenue, 80215
Telephone: 303-232-0362
Fax: 303-742-2396
Email: rgbuschesq@aol.com

For full biographical listings, see the Martindale-Hubbell Law Directory

---

LAMAR, * Prowers Co.

SHINN LAWYERS (AV)

200 West Elm Street, P.O. Box 390, 81052
Telephone: 719-336-4313
Fax: 719-336-4315

MEMBERS OF FIRM

Carl M. Shinn   Wendy S. Shinn

ASSOCIATES

Donald L. Steerman

Counsel for: Amity Canal; Lamar Canal; District 67 Ditch Assn.; County of Cheyenne, Colorado; County of Kiowa, Colorado; Ragsdale Farms, Inc.; Sherler Farms; Hatcher Farms, Inc.; Young Bros. Equipment Co., Inc.; Buffalo Canal Co.

For full biographical listings, see the Martindale-Hubbell Law Directory

---

LITTLETON, * Arapahoe Co.

JAMES S. KIMMEL (AV)

Suite 207 Norwest Bank Building, 5601 South Broadway, 80121
Telephone: 303-794-2036
Fax: 303-794-2073

Representative Clients: KDL Gaming, Inc.; Sunrise International Trading, Ltd.; Radco Technical Sales; Bicycle Villages of Colorado; Infotel Telecommunications, Inc.; Crestwood Restaurant, Inc.; Land Aide, Inc.; Las Delicias Restaurants; Madison Engineering Co.
Reference: Norwest Bank Littleton, N.A.

For full biographical listings, see the Martindale-Hubbell Law Directory

---

LONGMONT, Boulder Co.

FLANDERS, SONNESYN & STOVER, LLP (AV)

Suite 1 First National Bank Building, 401 Main Street, 80501
Telephone: 303-776-5380
Fax: 303-440-0638

MEMBERS OF FIRM

David N. Sonnesyn   John C. Flanders
Thomas L. Stover

ASSOCIATES

Kathleen A. Ellis   Scott W. Dunn

OF COUNSEL

L. B. Flanders

Representative Clients: The First National Bank of Longmont; The Boulder & White Rock Ditch & Reservoir Co.; The Animal Hospital; The Charles L. Hover Family Foundation; Longmont Realty & Insurance Co.; Longmont United Hospital; Plasco, Inc.; Longmont Toyota, Inc.

For full biographical listings, see the Martindale-Hubbell Law Directory

---

GRANT, BERNARD, LYONS & GADDIS, A PROFESSIONAL CORPORATION (AV)

515 Kimbark Street, P.O. Box 978, 80502-0978
Telephone: 303-776-9900 Denver: 303-571-5506
Telecopier: 303-772-6105
Email: info@gblg.com

Wallace H. Grant   H. William Sims, Jr.
Daniel F. Bernard   John W. Gaddis
Richard N. Lyons, II   Bradley A. Hall
Jeffrey J. Kahn   Steven P. Jeffers

Cameron A. Grant   Wendy S. Rudnik

Representative Clients: Avedon Engineering; Eagle County School District RE-50J (Vail); Economic Development Association of Longmont, Inc.; Golden's Concrete; Longmont Foods; Murphy Cattle Company (Colorado and New Mexico); Scripps Howard Cable Company; St. Vrain & Left Hand Water Conservancy District; West Metro Fire Protection District.

For full biographical listings, see the Martindale-Hubbell Law Directory

---

LOVELAND, Larimer Co.

HAMMOND, CLARK AND WHITE (AV)

Suite 418 Bank One Building, 200 East 7th Street, 80537
Telephone: 970-667-1023
Fax: 970-669-9380

MEMBERS OF FIRM

Lynn A. Hammond   Roger E. Clark
Gregory A. White

Representative Clients: Hewlett-Packard Co.; Hach Co.; Bank One, Colorado, N.A.; Town of Estes Park; Loveland Rural Fire Protection District; Colorado Crystal Corp.; Loveland Economic Development Council, Inc.; City of Loveland (Water Matters).
Reference: Bank One, Colorado, N.A.

For full biographical listings, see the Martindale-Hubbell Law Directory

---

MONTE VISTA, Rio Grande Co.

GORDON H. ROWE, JR. (AV)

40 North Washington Street, P.O. Box 208, 81144
Telephone: 719-852-5162
Fax: 719-852-5163
Albuquerque, New Mexico Office: 1520 Tramway NE, Suite F, 87112.
Telephone: 505-293-7100.
Fax: 505-293-3736.

Representative Clients: Tri-Me Potato Co.; Lariat Irrigation Co.; Rio Grande & San Luis Irrigation Co.; Rio Grande & Piedra Ditch Co.; Emerald Ranch.
Counsel for: Bank of Monte Vista.
Approved Attorney for: Attorneys Title Guaranty Fund, Inc.
Reference: Bank of Monte Vista.

For full biographical listings, see the Martindale-Hubbell Law Directory

---

MONTROSE, * Montrose Co.

EDWARD D. DURHAM (AV)

524 South First Street, P.O. Box 1721, 81402
Telephone: 970-249-2274
Fax: 970-249-6482

Reference: Norwest Bank of Montrose.

For full biographical listings, see the Martindale-Hubbell Law Directory

WOODROW & ROUSHAR (AV)

144 South Uncompahgre Avenue, P.O. Box 327, 81401
Telephone: 970-249-4531
Fax: 970-249-3102

MEMBERS OF FIRM

Frank J. Woodrow   Victor T. Roushar

Representative Clients: Allstate Insurance Co.; Uncompahgre Valley Water Users Association; Farm Credit Services.

For full biographical listings, see the Martindale-Hubbell Law Directory

---

ROCKY FORD, Otero Co. — (Refer to Lamar)

STERLING, * Logan Co. — (Refer to Greeley)

TRINIDAD, * Las Animas Co. — (Refer to Canon City)

VAIL, Eagle Co.

DUNN, ABPLANALP & CHRISTENSEN, P.C. (AV)

Suite 300 Vail Bank Building, 108 South Frontage Road
    West, 81657-5087
Telephone: 970-476-0300
Telecopier: 970-476-4765

(See Next Column)

DUNN, ABPLANALP & CHRISTENSEN P.C.—*Continued*

John W. Dunn   Allen C. Christensen
Arthur A. Abplanalp, Jr.   Diane L. Herman
Randelle C. Stephenson

SPECIAL COUNSEL
Jerry W. Hannah

LEGAL SUPPORT PERSONNEL
Karen M. Dunn (Paralegal)

Representative Clients: Towns of Avon, Minturn and Red Cliff, Colorado.

For full biographical listings, see the Martindale-Hubbell Law Directory

OTTO, PORTERFIELD & POST, LLC (AV)

51 Eagle Road, P.O. Box 3149, 81658-3149
Telephone: 970-949-5380
Fax: 970-845-9135

Frederick S. Otto   Wendell B. Porterfield, Jr.
William J. Post

References: 1st Bank of Vail; WestStar Bank.

For full biographical listings, see the Martindale-Hubbell Law Directory

WALSENBURG,* Huerfano Co. — (Refer to Canon City)

WHEAT RIDGE, Jefferson Co. — (Refer to Golden)

CONNECTICUT

BRIDGEPORT,* Fairfield Co.

COHEN AND WOLF, P.C. (AV)

1115 Broad Street, P.O. Box 1821, 06601
Telephone: 203-368-0211
Facsimile: 203-576-8504
Danbury, Connecticut Office: 158 Deer Hill Avenue.
Telephone: 203-792-2771.
Facsimile: 203-791-8149.
Stamford, Connecticut Office: 112 Prospect Street.
Telephone: 203-964-9907.
Facsimile: 203-576-8504.

Herbert L. Cohen (1905-1983)   Richard L. Newman
Austin K. Wolf   (Resident at Danbury Office)
Martin F. Wolf   Richard Slavin
Richard L. Albrecht   Daniel S. Nagel
Jonathan S. Bowman   Richard J. Di Marco
Irving J. Kern   David B. Zabel
Martin J. Albert   Mark A. Kirsch
Stewart I. Edelstein   Neil W. Sutton
Neil R. Marcus   David M. Levine
   (Resident at Danbury Office)   Joseph G. Walsh
David L. Grogins   (Resident at Danbury Office)
   (Resident at Danbury Office)   Mary Ann Connors
Robert B. Adelman   David A. Ball
Michael S. Rosten   Michael F. Ewing
Greta E. Solomon   Jennifer Landsman Chobor
Joram Hirsch   Jocelyn B. Hurwitz
Robin A. Kahn   Stuart M. Katz
   (Resident at Danbury Office)   Monte Frank
Richard G. Kent   (Resident at Danbury Office)
Ellen A. Jawitz

OF COUNSEL
Robert J. Ashkins   Stuart A. Epstein
Jack E. McGregor

LEGAL SUPPORT PERSONNEL
Sherry E. Sopin

For full biographical listings, see the Martindale-Hubbell Law Directory

GOLDSTEIN AND PECK, P.C. (AV)

955 Main Street, P.O. Box 1538, 06601
Telephone: 203-334-9421
Telecopier: 203-334-6949
Westport, Connecticut Office: 190 Main Street. P.O. Box 5031.
Telephone: 203-226-7488.
Telecopier: 203-226-6403.

David Goldstein (1898-1992)   John G. Dzurik
William J. Kupinse, Jr.   Dennis M. Laccavole
Walter A. Flynn, Jr.   Peter L. Leepson
G. Kenneth Bernhard   Kathleen H. Allsup
Eugene E. Cederbaum   Patricia E. Curtin
Peter B. O'Connell   Lisa Kasden Kent
John H. Kane

(See Next Column)

Representative Clients: Bee Publishing Co., Inc.; The Chase Manhattan Bank, N.A.; Fairfield County Medical Assn.; Great American Insurance Companies; Sequa Corp.; Inco, Ltd.; Physicians Health Services, Inc.; Town of Westport.

For full biographical listings, see the Martindale-Hubbell Law Directory

MARSH, DAY & CALHOUN (AV)

955 Main Street, 06604
Telephone: 203-259-8993
Fax: 203-254-1772
Southport, Connecticut Office: 2507 Post Road.
Telephone: 203-259-8993.
Fax: 203-254-1772.

MEMBER OF FIRM
Thomas F. Maxwell, Jr.

Counsel for: Chase Manhattan Bank, N.A.; Southern Connecticut Gas Co.; Metropolitan Life Insurance Co.; General Electric Co.; Sturm Ruger & Co., Inc.; The Producto Machine Co.

For full biographical listings, see the Martindale-Hubbell Law Directory

WILLIAMS, COONEY & SHEEHY (AV)

One Lafayette Circle, 06604
Telephone: 203-331-0888
Telecopier: 203-331-0896

MEMBERS OF FIRM
Ronald D. Williams   Peter J. Dauk
Robert J. Cooney   Dion W. Moore
Edward Maum Sheehy   Ronald D. Williams, Jr.
Peter D. Clark   Francis A. Smith, Jr.
              (1951-1989)

Michael P. Bowler   Paul Sean Curtin
Michael Cuff Deakin   Suzannah Kim Nigro

Representative Clients: Aetna Life & Casualty Co.; Nationwide Insurance Co.; Connecticut Medical Insurance Co.; Zimmer Manufacturing Co.; Textron-Lycoming; The Stop & Shop Companies, Inc.; Shawmut Bank Connecticut, N.A.; Podiatry Insurance Company of America; Town of Easton, Conn.

For full biographical listings, see the Martindale-Hubbell Law Directory

ZELDES, NEEDLE & COOPER, A PROFESSIONAL CORPORATION (AV)

1000 Lafayette Boulevard, P.O. Box 1740, 06601-1740
Telephone: 203-333-9441
Telecopiers: 203-333-1489; 579-2933

Jacob D. Zeldes   Paul F. Thomas
Elaine S. Amendola   Gregory J. Cava
Charles M. Needle   David P. Atkins
Robert S. Cooper   Maximino Medina, Jr.
Alfred J. Jennings, Jr.   Jonathan B. Orleans
Stuart Bear   Shelley R. Sadin
Frank J. Silvestri, Jr.   Edward R. Scofield
William C. Longa   David P. Friedman
Robert A. Harris   Leslie Paier Aceto

Ann M. VanDeventer   Marcy Tench Stovall
Patrick J. Fitzgerald   Brian E. Spears
Caryn L. Mullin   James K. Filan, Jr.
Martin L. McCann   Thomas M. Nolan
S. Dave Vatti   Diane M. Juffras

Representative Clients: Pace Motor Lines, Inc.; Rudel Machinery Co., Inc.; C.W. Pond Contractors, Inc.; Jeneric/Pentron, Inc.; The H.L. Hayden Co.; U.S. Surgical Corp.

For full biographical listings, see the Martindale-Hubbell Law Directory

DANBURY, Fairfield Co.

WANDERER, HANNA & TALARICO (AV)

142 Deer Hill Avenue, 06810-7727
Telephone: 203-792-8333
Telecopier: 203-778-9570

MEMBERS OF FIRM
Herbert B. Wanderer   Richard W. Hanna
   (1902-1979)   Robert N. Talarico

For full biographical listings, see the Martindale-Hubbell Law Directory

DANIELSON, Windham Co.

JACKSON, HARRIS, BURLINGAME & HUBERT (AV)

245 Main Street, 06239
Telephone: 860-774-9627
Fax: 860-774-5784

(See Next Column)

JACKSON, HARRIS, BURLINGAME & HUBERT, *Danielson—Continued*

MEMBERS OF FIRM

George H. Jackson, III	Stephen J. Burlingame
John K. Harris, Jr.	David M. Hubert

Representative Client: New London Trust, F.S.B.

For full biographical listings, see the Martindale-Hubbell Law Directory

---

DARIEN, Fairfield Co.

MILLAR & AMBRETTE (AV)

23 Old King's Highway South, 06820-1267
Telephone: 203-655-7931
FAX: 203-656-2055

MEMBERS OF FIRM

Samuel D. B. Millar, Jr.	L. Conrad Ambrette

OF COUNSEL

Peter M. Ryan

ASSOCIATES

Patricia Moreland Gross	Carolyn C. Swiggart

For full biographical listings, see the Martindale-Hubbell Law Directory

---

FARMINGTON, Hartford Co. — (Refer to Hartford)

GLASTONBURY, Hartford Co.

POMERANZ, DRAYTON & STABNICK (AV)

95 Glastonbury Boulevard, 06033-4412
Telephone: 860-657-8000; 800-246-5541
Fax: 860-657-9838

Douglas L. Drayton	Jason M. Dodge
James L. Pomeranz	Anne Kelly Zovas
Richard T. Stabnick	Richard L. Aiken, Jr.
Lucas D. Strunk	Margaret E. Corrigan

ASSOCIATES

Michael J. McAuliffe	Stephen G. Ekern

For full biographical listings, see the Martindale-Hubbell Law Directory

---

GREENWICH, Fairfield Co.

ALBERT, WARD & JOHNSON, P.C. (AV)

125 Mason Street, P.O. Box 1668, 06836
Telephone: 203-661-8600
Telecopier: 203-661-8051

OF COUNSEL

David Albert	C. Robton Perelli-Minetti

Tom S. Ward, Jr.	Howard R. Wolfe
Scott R. Johnson	Christopher A. Kristoff
Jane D. Hogeman	Vicki K. Comberiati

For full biographical listings, see the Martindale-Hubbell Law Directory

---

EPSTEIN FOGARTY COHEN & SELBY LLC (AV)

88 Field Point Road, P.O. Box 2508, 06830
Telephone: 203-661-1000
Telefax: 203-629-7300
Stamford, Connecticut Office: 733 Summer Street, 06901.
Telephone: 201-661-1000.
Telefax: 203-629-7300.

PARTNERS

James R. Fogarty	Leland C. Selby
Bruce F. Cohen	Andrew P. Nemiroff

COUNSEL

Robert A. Epstein	Everett Fisher
	Jennifer N. Boyd

ASSOCIATES

William Bradford Smith, Jr.	Jennifer Paul Cohen
Joseph T. O'Connor	Jacqueline J. Coyle
Carolyn Alexander Collins	Stephanie Budlong Paul

For full biographical listings, see the Martindale-Hubbell Law Directory

---

HEAGNEY, LENNON & SLANE (AV)

248 Greenwich Avenue, P.O. Box 7910, 06836
Telephone: 203-661-8400
Fax: 203-661-7496

MEMBERS OF FIRM

John G. Heagney (1925-1982)	John F. Slane, Jr.
Francis X. Lennon, Jr.	Thomas J. Heagney

For full biographical listings, see the Martindale-Hubbell Law Directory

---

HOLLAND KAUFMANN & BARTELS, LLC (AV)

289 Greenwich Avenue, 06830-6595
Telephone: 203-869-5600
Fax: 203-869-4648

Alexander J. Holland	Amy K. Wilfert
Charles B. Kaufmann, III	Harold R. Burke
Philip H. Bartels	Jean Mills Aranha
Beth K. Hansson	Lori E. Romano
	John C. Fusco

For full biographical listings, see the Martindale-Hubbell Law Directory

---

IVEY, BARNUM & O'MARA, LLC (AV)

Meridian Building, 170 Mason Street, P.O. Box 1689, 06830
Telephone: 203-661-6000
Telecopier: 203-661-9462

MEMBERS OF FIRM

Michael J. Allen	Donat C. Marchand
Robert C. Barnum, Jr.	Miles F. McDonald, Jr.
Edward D. Cosden, Jr.	Edwin J. O'Mara, Jr.
Wilmot L. Harris, Jr.	Remy A. Rodas
William I. Haslun II	Gregory A. Saum
Michael J. Jones	Lorraine Slavin
Edward T. Krumeich, Jr.	Steven B. Steinmetz

ASSOCIATES

Paul G. Amicucci	Melissa Townsend Klauberg
Stephan B. Grozinger	Cristin L. Rothfuss
Juerg A. Heim	Alan S. Rubenstein
Jennifer B. Kallenbach	Sheryl L. Sensale
	(Not admitted in CT)

OF COUNSEL

James W. Cuminale	Jennifer D. Port
Philip R. McKnight	(Not admitted in CT)

For full biographical listings, see the Martindale-Hubbell Law Directory

---

WHITMAN BREED ABBOTT & MORGAN (AV)

100 Field Point Road, 06830
Telephone: 203-869-3800
Telecopier: 203-869-1951
New York, N.Y. Office: 200 Park Avenue.
Telephone: 212-351-3000.
Los Angeles, California Office: 633 West Fifth Street.
Telephone: 213-896-2400.
Sacramento, California Office: Senator Hotel Building, 1121 L Street.
Telephone: 916-441-4242.
Newark, New Jersey Office: One Gateway Center.
Telephone: 201-621-2230.
Palm Beach, Florida Office: 220 Sunrise Avenue.
Telephone: 407-832-5458.
London, England Office: 11 Waterloo Place.
Telephone: 71-839-3226.
Telex: 917881.
Tokyo, Japan Office: Suite 450, New Otemachi Building, 2-2-1 Otemachi, Chiyoda-Ku, Tokyo 100.
Telephone: 81-3-3242-1289.
Associated with: Tyan & Associes, 22, La Sagesse Street-Rmeil, Beirut, Lebanon.
Telephone: 337968.
Fax: 200969.
Telex: 43928.

PARTNERS

Charles E. Coates, III	Harry E. Peden, III
James A. Fulton	James C. Riley
Richard F. Lawler	Christopher A. Stack
Anthony M. Macleod	(Not admitted in CT)
Robert C. O'Brien	David P. Tuttle
Harry E. Peden, Jr.	Kevin A. Walsh

RETIRED PARTNER

Jacob R. Lynch

ASSOCIATES

Ann Dudley Belknap	Richard E. Mancuso
Margaret E. Conboy	Teresa V. Triglia
Joseph C. Gasparrini	Margaret Ann Triolo

For full biographical listings, see the Martindale-Hubbell Law Directory

---

GROTON, New London Co.

O'BRIEN, SHAFNER, STUART, KELLY & MORRIS, P.C. (AV)

475 Bridge Street, P.O. Drawer 929, 06340
Telephone: 860-445-2463
Fax: 860-445-4539
Norwich, Connecticut Office: 2 Courthouse Square.
Telephone: 860-889-3855.
Fax: 860-886-6352.

(See Next Column)

O'BRIEN, SHAFNER, STUART, KELLY & MORRIS P.C.—*Continued*

John C. O'Brien	Lloyd L. Langhammer
Matthew Shafner	Mark W. Oberlatz
Peter F. Stuart	Nathan J. Shafner
Carolyn P. Kelly	Richard J. Pascal
Granville R. Morris	Amy M. Stone
Frank N. Eppinger	Eric M. Janney
Mark E. Block	Katherine M. Dempski
(Resident at Norwich Office)	

For full biographical listings, see the Martindale-Hubbell Law Directory

---

HARTFORD, * Hartford Co.

* indicates certain Bar Register subscribers whose principal office is located elsewhere in the state and who have arranged for representation as a part of the state capital listings that follow

---

BINGHAM, DANA & GOULD LLP (AV)

100 Pearl Street, 06103
Telephone: 860-244-3770
Telefax: 860-527-5188
Email: info@bingham.com
Boston, Massachusetts Office: 150 Federal Street.
Telephone: 617-951-8000.
Telecopy: 617-951-8736.
London, England Office: 39 Victoria Street, SWIH 0EE.
Telephone: 011-44-71-799-2646.
Telecopy: 011-44-71-799-2654.
Washington, D.C. Office: 1200 19th Street, N.W., Suite 400.
Telephone: 202-778-6150.
Telecopy: 202-778-6155.

RESIDENT PARTNERS

Robert M. Dombroff	Stuart D. Rosen
F. Mark Fucci	James G. Scantling
Ben M. Krowicki	Scott M. Schooley
Mark Oland	Bruce C. Silvers
Judy K. Weinstein	

RESIDENT OF COUNSEL

Catherine E. LaMarr	Peter H. Levine

RESIDENT ASSOCIATES

Jonathan B. Alter	Daniel I. Papermaster
Frank A. Appicelli	Andrew H. Pinkowski
Robert M. Borden	James Scott Rollins
Marianne M. Downie	James W. Shaughnessy
Gerald B. Goldberg	Ann M. Siczewicz
Jeffrey B. Zeman	

For full biographical listings, see the Martindale-Hubbell Law Directory

---

BROWN, PAINDIRIS & ZARELLA, LLP (AV)

100 Pearl Street, 06103
Telephone: 860-522-3343
Telecopier: 860-522-2490
Glastonbury, Connecticut Office: 7 Sycamore Street.
Telephone: 860-659-6668.
Fax: 860-658-6671.
East Hampton, Connecticut Office: 42 East High Street.
Telephone: 860-267-2044.

MEMBERS OF FIRM

Richard R. Brown	Ronald T. Scott
Nicholas Paindiris	John D. Maxwell
Peter T. Zarella	Kate W. Haakonsen
Steven W. Varney	

ASSOCIATES

Christopher J. McCarthy	Sean M. Peoples
Robert T. Rimmer	

For full biographical listings, see the Martindale-Hubbell Law Directory

---

DAY, BERRY & HOWARD (AV)

CityPlace I, 06103-3499
Telephone: 860-275-0100
Telecopier: 860-275-0343
Email: postmaster@dbh.com
Stamford, Connecticut Office: One Canterbury Green.
Telephone: 203-977-7300.
Telecopier: 203-977-7301.
Boston, Massachusetts Office: 260 Franklin Street.
Telephone: 617-345-4600.
Telecopier: 617-345-4745.

MEMBERS OF FIRM IN HARTFORD

Edward M. Day (1872-1947)	Robert A. Brooks
Joseph Francis Berry	Harold C. Buckingham, Jr.
(1880-1953)	Dean M. Cordiano
Lawrence Augustus Howard	William H. Cuddy
(1881-1960)	Rodney J. Dillman
J. Danford Anthony, Jr.	David T. Doot
C. Duane Blinn	David J. Elliott

(See Next Column)

MEMBERS OF FIRM IN HARTFORD (Continued)

Michael W. Elsass	Joseph A. Moniz
Steven M. Fast	Francis H. Morrison III
Daniel L. FitzMaurice	John B. Nolan
Gerald Garfield	Thomas Z. Reicher
John C. Glezen	Richard M. Reynolds
Raymond B. Green	James H. Rotondo
Steven M. Greenspan	Edmund M. See
Thomas J. Groark, Jr.	James Sicilian
Jeffrey G. Grody	Robert G. Siegel
Michael F. Halloran	Felix J. Springer
J. Roger Hanlon	James J. Tancredi
Thomas F. Harrison	Allan B. Taylor
Paula Lacey Herman	Robert M. Taylor III
Robert P. Knickerbocker, Jr.	M. Louise Turilli
Charles H. Lenore	Lyn Gammill Walker
Timothy R. Lyman	Philip S. Walker
Richard C. MacKenzie	Richard J. Wasserman
Daniel S. Matos	Thomas R. Wildman
Ernest J. Mattei	Paul D. Williams
Paul F. McAlenney	Martin Wolman
James A. McGraw	Albert Zakarian

ASSOCIATES OF FIRM IN HARTFORD

Elizabeth A. Alquist	Richard D. Harris
J. Michael Amrein	Tricia A. Haught
Esther R. Aronson	Peter M. Holland
John B. Ashmeade	C. J. Karbowicz
Rosemary G. Ayers	Joseph Kershenbaum
John G. Balboni	Mark B. Leach
Thomas E. Bartell	Robin S. Linker
Sarah C. Baskin	Judy S. Loitherstein
Gary M. Becker	Regina A. Long
Matthew J. Becker	Leah A. Martin
Diane C. Bellantoni	Carolyn B. Martino
Martha S. Berek	Kathleen M. McFadden
Gail Bonner	Edward F. McHugh
Michael A. Bucci	Laurie K. Molinari
Susan Busby-Mott	Kathleen Dondero Monnes
Mary Beth Cardin	Scott P. Myers
Victoria Woodin Chavey	Robert J. O'Hara
Sara Discepolo	Rebecca Matthews Parent
Glenn W. Dowd	John J. Phillips
Peter J. Duffy	David C. Robinson
Dean A. Dulchinos	Daniel A. Schwartz
Kenneth H. Eagle	Mary Lou Scofield
Charles W. Fortune	Kent I. Scott-Smith
Glenn A. Frankel	Robin L. Smith
Merrily A. Gere	James F. Sullivan
Ronald A. Gonzalez	Athena R. Tsakanikas
Lauren R. Greenspoon	Cristi C. Walker
Laurie A. Hall	Philip S. Wellman
Mitchell R. Harris	Jean E. Winn

OF COUNSEL

George H. Cain	A. Peter Quinn, Jr.
Palmer S. McGee, Jr.	(Not admitted in CT)
James R. McIntosh	Olcott D. Smith

COUNSEL

Douglas W. Gillette	Edward F. Krzanowski
Joseph L. Hammer	Stephen B. Middlebrook

RESIDENT PARTNERS IN BOSTON OFFICE

James L. Ackerman	Lisa J. Damon
Joseph W. Ambash	Charles Donelan
Glenn E. Brace	William A. Hunter
David B. Broughel	J. Charles Mokriski
Lewis A. Burleigh	Ross A. Pascal
Daniel J. Carragher	William Shields
Jeffrey A. Clopeck	H. Lawrence Tafe III
Nancy M. Cullen	Kenneth E. Werner
George L. Cushing	Cynthia J. Williams

RESIDENT PARTNERS IN STAMFORD OFFICE

Jerome Berkman	Robert J. Miller
Martin L. Budd	Kenneth W. Ritt
Michael P. Byrne	Sabino Rodriguez III
Patricia A. Carpenter	James F. Stapleton
Ronald Osburn Dederick	David A. Swerdloff
Thomas D. Goldberg	Stanley A. Twardy, Jr.
F. Lee Griffith III	Stefan R. Underhill
Gregory A. Hayes	Carla R. Walworth
Michael S. Leo	
(Not admitted in CT)	

RESIDENT COUNSEL IN BOSTON OFFICE

Richard C. Csaplar, Jr.	Ellen Jo Levesque
Kenneth A. Reich	

RESIDENT COUNSEL IN STAMFORD OFFICE

Michael G. Considine	Emil H. Frankel
John Crosskey	Andrew P. Gaillard
Ellen B. Wells	

(See Next Column)

DAY, BERRY & HOWARD, *Hartford—Continued*

RESIDENT ASSOCIATES IN BOSTON OFFICE

Laurie C. Buck	David Nersessian
Colin Hugh Buckley	Kenneth B. Newton
Allan C. Cave, Jr.	Faith B. Nirenstein
Sean R. Gatewood	Kenneth C. Pickering
Edward J. Goddard	Nancy M. Reimer
Jonathan I. Handler	Mark C. Rosenthal
Bruce D. Hickey	Jeffrey M. Rosin
Jocelyn Lee	Karen E. Schneck
Rina M. Mayman	Jan M. Siok
Carol M. Merchasin	Gerald M. Slater
Kathleen S. Moore	Maura D. Sullivan
Mary Theresa Moran	Mark C. Wilson
Jason R. Morgan	G. Perry Wu

RESIDENT ASSOCIATES IN STAMFORD OFFICE

Marsha L. Anastasia	Marcia R. Ginsberg
R. Scott Beach	Craig A. Goldberg
Joy Beane	Deborah S. Gordon
Eileen R. Becker	Sarah E. Graves
Paul N. Belval	Lynn A. Kappelman
J. Bradley Britton	Vincent Laurentino
Keith P. Carroll	Catherine Dugan O'Connor
M. Kate Curran	Philip J. Paseltiner
Martha C. Deneen	Daniel L. Schwartz
Wendy D. DiChristina	James A. Shapiro
Brian P. Donovan	Terri L. Stein
Andrea Falcione	Steven M. Torkelsen
Kristina A. Fisher	Jonathan B. Tropp
Kenneth W. Gage	Theodore J. Whitehead

For full biographical listings, see the Martindale-Hubbell Law Directory

---

GORDON, MUIR AND FOLEY (AV)

Hartford Square North, Ten Columbus Boulevard, 06106-5123
Telephone: 860-525-5361
Telecopier: 860-525-4849

MEMBERS OF FIRM

William S. Gordon, Jr.	William J. Gallitto
(1946-1956)	Gerald R. Swirsky
George Muir (1939-1976)	Robert J. O'Brien
Edward J. Foley (1955-1983)	Philip J. O'Connor
Peter C. Schwartz	Kenneth G. Williams
John J. Reid	Chester J. Bukowski
John H. Goodrich, Jr.	Mary Ann Santacroce
R. Bradley Wolfe	J. Lawrence Price
Jon Stephen Berk	Mary Anne Alicia Charron
James G. Kelly	

ASSOCIATES

Kevin F. Morin	Andrew J. Hern
Claudia A. Baio	Eileen McCarthy Geel
Patrick T. Treacy	Christopher L. Slack
Renee W. Dwyer	

OF COUNSEL

Stephen M. Riley

Reference: Fleet Bank.

For full biographical listings, see the Martindale-Hubbell Law Directory

---

GOULD, KILLIAN & WYNNE (AV)

One Commercial Plaza, 25th Floor, 06103-3595
Telephone: 860-278-1270
Telecopier: 860-244-9290

MEMBERS OF FIRM

Samuel Gould (1905-1994)	Mark W. Baronas
Robert K. Killian	William F. Healey
Francis J. Wynne	Nancy E. Gould
Martin A. Gould	Robert O. Wynne

For full biographical listings, see the Martindale-Hubbell Law Directory

---

HALLORAN & SAGE (AV)

One Goodwin Square, 225 Asylum Street, 06103
Telephone: 860-522-6103
Fax: 860-548-0006
URL: http://www.halloran-sage.com
Middletown, Connecticut Office: 300 Plaza Middlesex, 06457.
Telephone: 860-346-8641.
Fax: 860-344-1641.
Westport, Connecticut Office: 315 Post Road West, 06880-4739.
Telephone: 203-227-2855.
Fax: 203-227-6992.

MEMBERS OF FIRM

Joseph G. Lynch	Robert C. Engstrom
Joseph T. Sweeney	Vincent M. Marino
George D. Royster, Jr.	(Middletown Office)
Arthur P. McGowan, Jr.	Richard C. Tynan
John W. Lemega	William P. Borchert

(See Next Column)

MEMBERS OF FIRM (Continued)

Thomas J. Hagarty, Jr.	Peter G. Boucher
Paul V. Knopf	Jean M. D'Aquila
Brian J. Donnell	Steven H. Malitz
James J. Szerejko	Michael J. Gustafson
Mark B. Seiger	Erin M. Kallaugher
William J. McGrath, Jr.	John B. Farley
Dennis C. Cavanaugh	Mark R. Cramer
Christopher J. Lynch	David B. Losee
Paul D. Meade	Michael A. Pease
Joseph G. Fortner, Jr.	Harris B. Appelman
Stephen P. Fogerty	Mark T. Altermatt
(Westport Office)	

COUNSEL

Milford F. Rhines	Henry M. Beck, Jr.
Irwin D. Mittelman	Peter B. Prestey
(Middletown Office)	Robert B. Cox
Janet L. Lawler	

ASSOCIATES

Susan O'Donnell	John W. Dietz
Bruce H. Raymond	Deborah L. Dorio
Kevin M. Roche	Jill Hartley
David G. Hill	Michael J. Whalen
Daniel P. Scapellati	Brian P. Leaming
James M. Sconzo	Paul S. McCarthy
Donna-Maria Lonergan	Amy M. Fauver
Janet M. Helmke	Michael S. Taylor
Thomas P. O'Dea, Jr.	Kelly A. Peters
(Westport Office)	Mark T. Livesay
Robert M. Barrack	Robert A. Rhodes
Richard P. Roberts	(Westport Office)
Steven M. Barry	Heather M. Dubian
Gregory R. Faulkner	James F. Shea
John S. Rosania	James V. Somers
Lynda A. Barry	E. Amanda Sayers
Jennifer A. Butler	

Representative Clients: Beech Aircraft Corp.; Catholic Mutual Relief Society; LWP Claims Services, Inc.; Guardian Life Insurance Co.; Hertz Cos.; State Farm; The Travelers; Western World Insurance Co.

For full biographical listings, see the Martindale-Hubbell Law Directory

---

HEBB & GITLIN, A PROFESSIONAL CORPORATION (AV)

One State Street, 06103-3178
Telephone: 860-240-2700
Telecopier: 860-278-8968
Email: 5111037@MCIMail.com
London, England Office: York House, 199 Westminster Bridge Road, London SE1 7UT, U.K.
Telephone: 011-44-171-395-9400.
Telecopier: 011-44-171-395-9409.

MEMBERS OF FIRM

G. Eric Brunstad, Jr.	William E. Kelly
David M. Cain	Jeffery S. Kuperstock
Richard F. Casher	Thomas J. Love, Jr.
John B. D'Agostino	George A. McKeon
Chester L. Fisher III	(Of Counsel)
Douglas E. Fiske	M. Bree Nesbitt
Evan D. Flaschen	Peter M. Nolin
John J. Gillies, Jr.	Gregory W. Nye
Richard A. Gitlin	Michael J. Reilly
James Greenfield	Barry G. Russell (Resident
Gary S. Hammersmith	Member, London Office)
Edwin Gordon Hebb, Jr.	R. Jeffrey Smith
Harold S. Horwich	Lorraine Murphy Weil
Eric W. Johnson	Jeffrey L. Williams

COUNSEL

Thomas H. Day	Deborah Samuels Freeman
Garrett J. Delehanty, Jr.	John D. Inwood
Timothy B. DeSieno	James P. Maher
Scott A. Falk	Joyce M. Resnick

ASSOCIATES

Claude M. Brouillard	Michael B. Nadolski
Mark E. Chavey	Thomas F. O'Connor
Laura Gonzalez Ciabarra	Thomas J. O'Shea
Jane M. Domboski	Brenda J. Page
William H. Erickson	Peter C.L. Roth
Judith H. Friedman	Joseph L. Scibilia
(Not admitted in CT)	Patricia Ann Shackelford
Brad Christian Gustafson	David Silber
Jonathan A. Harris	Ronald J. Silverman
James P. Juliano	J. Dormer Stephen
Gregory W. Kulak	Oscar Urizar
R. Michael Meo, Jr.	Brian N. Watkins
Theodore C. Morris	William J. Yoo

For full biographical listings, see the Martindale-Hubbell Law Directory

Hartford—Continued

HORTON, SHIELDS & CORMIER, P.C. (AV)

90 Gillett Street, 06105
Telephone: 860-522-8338
Email: kmurdo01@counsel.com

Wesley W. Horton	Susan M. Cormier
Robert M. Shields, Jr.	Kimberly A. Knox
	Karen L. Murdoch

John A. Reed	Kenneth J. Bartschi

For full biographical listings, see the Martindale-Hubbell Law Directory

HOWD & LUDORF (AV)

65 Wethersfield Avenue, 06114
Telephone: 860-249-1361
Telecopier: 860-543-7155
Email: handl@ix.netcom.com

MEMBERS OF FIRM

John R. Lilliendahl, III	Linda Gray MacDonald
John J. Bogdanski	John P. Majewski
Philip T. Newbury, Jr.	Kimberly B. McCarthy
Thomas R. Gerarde	Jane E. Hugo
Mark J. Claflin	Susan D. Giacalone
William F. Corrigan	Michael J. Rose
Christopher M. Vossler	David S. Monastersky
	Mark Sheehan

RETIRED

Edward S. Ludorf

Representative Clients: CIGNA; Reliance; Chrysler; Toyota; Harsco; Ladder Management; Baxter International; Black & Decker; Texaco; Windsor Insurance Co.

For full biographical listings, see the Martindale-Hubbell Law Directory

JACKSON, O'KEEFE AND PHELAN (AV)

36 Russ Street, 06106-1571
Telephone: 860-278-4040
Fax: 860-527-2500
West Hartford, Connecticut Office: 62 LaSalle Road.
Telephone: 860-521-7500.
Fax: 860-561-5399.
Bethlehem, Connecticut Office: 423 Munger Lane. Telephone/ *Fax:* 203-266-5255.

MEMBERS OF FIRM

Jay W. Jackson	Michael E. Riley
Andrew J. O'Keefe	Peter K. O'Keefe
Denise Martino Phelan	Philip R. Dunn, Jr.
Matthew J. O'Keefe	Kathryn M. Cunningham
	Joseph M. Busher, Jr.

Representative Clients: Travelers Aetna Property Casualty Co.; ITT Hartford; Liberty Mutual Insurance Co.; Connecticut Medical Insurance Co.

For full biographical listings, see the Martindale-Hubbell Law Directory

KENNY, BRIMMER, MELLEY & MAHONEY (AV)

5 Grand Street, 06106
Telephone: 860-527-4226
FAX: 860-527-0214

Joseph P. Kenny (1920-1993)

MEMBERS OF FIRM

Leslie R. Brimmer	William J. Melley, III
	Richard C. Mahoney

ASSOCIATES

Anita M. Varunes	Beverly Johns
Dennis F. McCarthy	Edward J. Fitzgerald

Representative Clients: Allstate Insurance Co.; Peerless Insurance Co.; Berkshire Mutual Fire Insurance Co.; Dorchester Mutual Fire Insurance Co.; Abington Mutual Fire Insurance Co.

For full biographical listings, see the Martindale-Hubbell Law Directory

MOLLER, DIPENTIMA, PECK AND O'BRIEN, LLC (AV)

1010 Wethersfield Avenue, 06114
Telephone: 860-296-1010
Fax: 860-947-3236

William R. Moller	Michael Ruben Peck
Anthony F. DiPentima	John J. O'Brien, Jr.

For full biographical listings, see the Martindale-Hubbell Law Directory

O'BRIEN, TANSKI, TANZER & YOUNG (AV)

CityPlace II, 06103
Telephone: 860-525-2700
Telefax: 860-247-7861

(See Next Column)

MEMBERS OF FIRM

Donald W. O'Brien	Roland F. Young, III
James M. Tanski	Robert E. Kiley
Lois B. Tanzer	Thomas O. Anderson
	Nancy Phillips Maxwell

OF COUNSEL

Hilary Fisher Nelson	Donna R. Zito

ASSOCIATES

Caroline Schnog	P. Jo Anne Burgh
Robert D. Silva	Jennifer L. Cox
Albert G. Danker, Jr.	Tanya Feliciano

References: Shawmut National Bank; New England Bank.

For full biographical listings, see the Martindale-Hubbell Law Directory

REID AND RIEGE, P.C. (AV)

One State Street, 06103
Telephone: 860-278-1150
FAX: 860-240-1002
West Hartford, Connecticut Office: 65 LaSalle Road.
Telephone: 203-232-6565.
FAX: 203-232-6066.

Clifford S. Burdge, Jr.	Neil P. Coughlan
William R. Judy	Edmund A. Mikolowsky
Robert C. McNally	Robert U. Sattin
James C. Ervin, Jr.	John M. Horak
Andrew J. Howat	Edward F. Spinella
Travers T. Auburn	Craig L. Sylvester
Maurice T. FitzMaurice	Robert M. Mulé
Bruce M. Lutsk	Paul B. Sonoski, Jr.
Maynard R. Miller, Jr.	Eileen M. Marks
Michael L. Coyle	Earl F. McMahon
Suzanne S. Bocchini	Thomas C. Lee, Jr.
John J. Jacobson	Christopher J. Sowden
John E. D'Amico	Jon P. Newton
Lawrence H. Lissitzyn	Mark X. Ryan
Frederick J. Mullen, Jr.	John D. Newman
	Joseph K. Fortier

Karen L. Brand	Michael T. Wade
Robert C. Reichert	Frank R. Virnelli, Jr.
John R. Ivimey	Sherri McKelvey
Carolyn A. Magnan	Amy C. Matthews
Douglas K. Knight	Erica S. Gregg
Eric A. Henzy	Richard H. Lugli
Theodore A. Donahue, Jr.	Elaine C. Philis
	Jennifer Ventres Filler

OF COUNSEL

John H. Riege	Suzanne M. Batchelor
Raymond J. Payne	Thomas M. Armstrong

For full biographical listings, see the Martindale-Hubbell Law Directory

ROGIN, NASSAU, CAPLAN, LASSMAN & HIRTLE, LLC (AV)

CityPlace I, 22nd Floor, 185 Asylum Street, 06103-3460
Telephone: 860-278-7480
Fax: 860-278-2179

MEMBERS OF FIRM

Jerome E. Caplan	David J. Heinlein
Edwin A. Lassman	Lewis K. Wise
Robert L. Hirtle	Joan G. Engel
William R. Breetz	Mark A. Rosenblum
Steven D. Bartelstone	Barry S. Feigenbaum
David M. Call	Donald G. Gaudreau
Paul B. Zolan	Peter S. Sorokin
	Iris June Brown

ASSOCIATES

Jeffrey W. Stein	Brendan T. Flynn
Mark J. Lassman	Elizabeth R. Houde
Benjamin Engel	Jonathan M. Starble

OF COUNSEL

Arthur M. Nassau

RETIRED

Edward S. Rogin (Retired)	Louis E. Nassau (Retired)

For full biographical listings, see the Martindale-Hubbell Law Directory

SHIPMAN & GOODWIN LLP (AV)

One American Row, 06103-2819
Telephone: 860-251-5000
Telecopier: 860-251-5099
E-Mail: first initial last name @goodwin.com
Email: www@goodwin.com *URL:* http://shipman-goodwin.com
Lakeville, Connecticut Office: Porter Street.
Telephone: 203-435-2539.
Stamford, Connecticut Office: One Landmark Square.
Telephone: 203-324-8100.

(See Next Column)

SHIPMAN & GOODWIN LLP, *Hartford—Continued*

MEMBERS OF FIRM

Paul W. Orth	Charles L. Howard
Robert J. Cathcart	John H. Lawrence, Jr.
Francis M. Dooley	James W. Bergenn
(Lakeville Office)	Paul D. Sanson
Theodore M. Space	Saranne P. Murray
Stuyvesant K. Bearns	Alan E. Lieberman
(Lakeville Office)	William George Rock
Alex Lloyd	Donna L. Brooks
Daniel P. Brown, Jr.	Linda L. Yoder
James T. Betts	John E. Wertam
Brian Clemow	Richard I. Cohen
Ira H. Goldman	Timothy S. Hollister
Scott L. Murphy	Joan W. Feldman
Coleman H. Casey	Richard A. Mills, Jr.
Brenda A. Eckert	Deborah Smith Frisone
John E. Kreitler	Stephen J. Geissler
Peter W. Benner	Mark K. Ostrowski
Thomas B. Mooney	Michael P. Meotti
Thomas F. Tresselt	Paul R. Pescatello
John T. Harris	Stephen K. Gellman
Robert L. Wyld	Thomas P. Flynn
Frank J. Marco (Hartford and	Louis B. Schatz
Stamford Offices)	Charles B. Spadoni

Janet S. Stulting

ASSOCIATES

Leslie L. Davenport	Paul A. Hughes
Timothy Patrick Brady	Deirdre M. Tymann
Mary Jo Blain Andrews	Maria A. Gulluni
John W. Mahoney	Natalie W. Welsh
Clare E. Kindall	Joseph P. Williams
Patrick J. McHale	Stephanie M. Gitlin
Glenn M. Cunningham	Joseph W. McQuade
Michael J. Palmieri	Andrew J. Cohen
Susan C. Freedman	Aline B. Goldbach
Christine S. Horrigan	Jessica G. Elliott
Richard M. Borden	Nancy V. Gifford
Christine L. Chinni	Kevin M. McGlinchey
Donna M. Mattiello	Brian R. Haskell
Kimberly A. Mango	Anne H. Littlefield
Scott D. Macdonald	Nastasha M. Lipcan
Julie A. Manning	Scott H. Rothstein
Sheila A. Huddleston	Joseph T. Olecki
Kay K. Tolbert	(Not admitted in CT)
Maureen J. Anderson	Raymond M. Bernstein
Howard L. Pierce	Henry J. Zaccardi
Gerald P. Stergio	Jennifer Brown Mailly
Karen H. Simmonds	Michael J. Andreana

COUNSEL

Warren S. Randall	Robert L. Rosensweig
Charles B. Milliken	William H. Wood, Jr.

Robert Ewing

Representative Clients: Aetna Casualty & Surety Co.; Agri-Mark, Inc.; Blue Cross & Blue Shield of Connecticut, Inc.; City of Hartford; The Dexter Corp.; The First National Bank of Boston; Hartford Hospital; Shawmut Bank, Connecticut, N.A.; United Technologies Corp.; Yankee Energy System, Inc.

For full biographical listings, see the Martindale-Hubbell Law Directory

SOROKIN SOROKIN GROSS HYDE & WILLIAMS P.C. (AV)

One Corporate Center, 06103
Telephone: 860-525-6645
Fax: 860-522-1781
Simsbury, Connecticut Office: 730 Hopmeadow Street.
Telephone: 860-651-9348.
Rocky Hill, Connecticut Office: 2360 Main Street.
Telephone: 860-563-9305.
Fax: 860-529-6931.

Morris W. Banks	Charles R. Moore, Jr.
John J. Bracken III	Paula G. Pressman
James G. Dowling, Jr.	Lewis Rabinovitz
Andrew C. Glassman	Richard C. Robinson
Clifford J. Grandjean	Amelia M. Rugland
Barry D. Greene	Richard D. Tulisano
Lisa A. Magliochetti	(Resident, Rocky Hill Office)
Jeffrey R. Martin	Barrie K. Wetstone

Jeffery P. Apuzzo	Sharon Kowal Freilich

Joshua A. Hawks-Ladds

OF COUNSEL

Joseph D. Hurwitz	Ethel Silver Sorokin

For full biographical listings, see the Martindale-Hubbell Law Directory

TYLER COOPER & ALCORN (AV)

CityPlace, 06103-3488
Telephone: 860-725-6200
Telecopier: 860-278-3802
New Haven, Connecticut Office: 205 Church Street.
Telephone: 203-784-8200.
Telecopier: 203-789-2133.
Stamford, Connecticut Office: One Landmark Square.
Telephone: 203-348-5555.
Telecopier: 203-348-3875.
Greenwich, Connecticut Office: 675 Steamboat Road.
Telephone: 203-869-2000.
Telecopier: 203-869-2001.
Madison, Connecticut Office: 23 Woodland Road.
Telephone: 203-318-3600.
Telecopier: 203-218-3609.

MEMBERS OF FIRM

William S. Rogers	Mark V. Connolly
Ralph G. Elliot	William S. Fish, Jr.
Lewis Segal	Kevin McCann
William H. Champlin III	David J. Wiese
Robert J. Metzler II	Fillis W. Stober
William W. Bouton III	Thomas S. Marrion

Kevin G. Ferrigno

COUNSEL

Kurt W. Johnson

RESIDENT ASSOCIATES

Barry M. Winnick	Glory Martyn Lena
William F. Cummings	Kevin S. Murphy

Representative Clients: Purolator Courier Corp.; American Society of Composers, Authors and Publishers (ASCAP); The Hartford Courant Co.; Sears, Roebuck & Co.; Shearson Lehman Brothers; Prudential Securities Inc.; Aetna Life and Casualty Co.; The Travelers Companies.

For full biographical listings, see the Martindale-Hubbell Law Directory

* WIGGIN & DANA (AV)

One CityPlace, 06103-3402
Telephone: 860-297-3700
Fax: 860-525-9380
New Haven, Connecticut Office: One Century Tower.
Telephone: 203-498-4400.
Telefax: 203-782-2889.
Stamford, Connecticut Office: Three Stamford Plaza, 301 Tresser Boulevard.
Telephone: 203-363-7600.
Telefax: 203-363-7676.

PARTNERS

Robert F. Cavanagh	Valerie A. Seiling
Peter J. Lefeber	Patrick J. Monahan, II

Robert M. Langer

ASSOCIATES

Lynn F. Guelzow	Marcia Kenny Keegan
Stephen B. Harris	Eric P. Neff
Marcella Ann Hourihane	Karen E. Overchuk
Bernard E. Jacques	Thomas J. Witt

For full biographical listings, see the Martindale-Hubbell Law Directory

LAKEVILLE, Litchfield Co.

SHIPMAN & GOODWIN LLP (AV)

Porter Street, 06039
Telephone: 860-435-2539
Telecopier: 860-435-0011
E.Mail: first initial last name @goodwin.com
Email: www@goodwin.com *URL:* http://shipman-goodwin.com
Hartford, Connecticut Office: One American Row.
Telephone: 203-251-5000.
Stamford, Connecticut Office: One Landmark Square.
Telephone: 203-324-8100.

MEMBERS

Francis M. Dooley	Stuyvesant K. Bearns

Representative Clients: American Title Insurance Co.; Berkshire Construction Co.; Colonial Bank and Trust Co., Sharon; Lakeville Journal, Inc.; Lawyers Title Insurance Co.; Salisbury Bank & Trust Co., Lakeville, Conn.

For full biographical listings, see the Martindale-Hubbell Law Directory

LITCHFIELD,* Litchfield Co.

CRAMER & ANDERSON (AV)

46 West Street, P.O. Box 278, 06759-0278
Telephone: 860-567-8718
Telecopier: 860-567-4531
New Milford, Connecticut Office: 51 Main Street, P.O. Box 330.
Telephone: 860-355-2631.
Kent, Connecticut Office: Kent Green, P.O. Box 333.
Telephone: 860-927-3568.

(See Next Column)

CRAMER & ANDERSON—*Continued*

Washington Depot, Connecticut Office: 2 Green Hill Road, P.O. Box 321.
Telephone: 860-868-0527.

MEMBERS OF FIRM

David Cramer (1928-1981)	Robert L. Fisher, Jr.
Henry B. Anderson (Resident at New Milford Office)	Reginald William H. Fairbairn (Resident at Washington Depot Office)
Clayton L. Blick	
Robert M. FitzGerald	William C. Franklin
Paul B. Altermatt (Resident at New Milford Office)	Arthur C. Weinshank (Resident at New Milford Office)
Maurice A. Goldstein (Resident at New Milford Office)	David P. Burke (Resident at New Milford Office)
Grant J. Nelson (Resident at Kent Office)	Jeffrey W. Reinen (Resident at New Milford Office)
Perley H. Grimes, Jr.	Barry S. Moller

ASSOCIATES

James D. Hirschfield	John D. Tower (Resident at New Milford Office)
Mitchell J. Melnick (Resident at New Milford Office)	

OF COUNSEL
Stephen N. Hume

Counsel for: Town of Cornwall; First National Bank of Litchfield; Lindstedt Oil; Neeltran, Inc.; New Milford Hospital, Inc.; New Milford Bank & Trust; Canterbury School; Cologne Reinsurance Company of America.

For full biographical listings, see the Martindale-Hubbell Law Directory

GUION, STEVENS & RYBAK (AV)

93 West Street, P.O. Box 338, 06759-0338
Telephone: 860-567-0821
Telecopier: 860-567-0825

H. Gibson Guion (1908-1994)

MEMBERS OF FIRM

E. Seward Stevens	Michael D. Rybak

Brian M. Yard

Counsel for: Town of Thomaston; Town of Harwinton.
References: Thomaston Savings Bank; The First National Bank of Litchfield; First Pioneer Farm Credit; ACA, Claverack, NY.

MIDDLETOWN,* Middlesex Co.

HALLORAN & SAGE (AV)

300 Plaza Middlesex, 06457
Telephone: 860-346-8641
Fax: 860-344-1641
Hartford, Connecticut Office: One Goodwin Square, 225 Asylum Street, 06103.
Telephone: 860-522-6103.
Fax: 860-548-0006.
Westport, Connecticut Office: 315 Post Road West, 06880-4739.
Telephone: 203-227-2855.
Fax: 203-227-6992.

RESIDENT PARTNER
Vincent M. Marino
COUNSEL
Irwin D. Mittelman

MILFORD, New Haven Co.

HARLOW, ADAMS & FRIEDMAN, P.C. (AV)

300 Bic Drive, 06460-3508
Telephone: 203-878-0661
Fax: 203-878-9568
Email: attorney@quidproquo.com

William D. Harlow (1921-1988)	Michael P. A. Williams
George W. Adams, III	Eric R. Gaynor
Dana Eric Friedman	Joseph A. Kubic
Theodore H. Shumaker	Elizabeth Stuckal
Stephen P. Wright	James M. Nugent

For full biographical listings, see the Martindale-Hubbell Law Directory

NEW BRITAIN, Hartford Co.

JANUSZEWSKI, MCQUILLAN AND DENIGRIS (AV)

165 West Main Street, P.O. Box 150, 06050-0150
Telephone: 860-225-7667
Fax: 860-826-1814

MEMBERS OF FIRM

Edward Januszewski	John C. Matulis, Jr.
Paul J. McQuillan	Steven D. Anderson
Nicholas E. DeNigris	Martin McQuillan

Representative Clients: The Peoples Savings Bank of New Britain, Inc.; Tilcon, Inc.; Acmat, Inc.

For full biographical listings, see the Martindale-Hubbell Law Directory

NEW CANAAN, Fairfield Co.

HAWTHORNE, ACKERLY & DORRANCE (AV)

25 South Avenue, P.O. Box 937, 06840
Telephone: 203-966-9583
Fax: 203-966-1296

MEMBERS OF FIRM

Dana C. Ackerly	Michelle R. Hubbard
Jeremiah S. Miller	Robert M. Di Scipio

George W. Baker

ASSOCIATES

Timothy H. Throckmorton	Lawrence S. Mannix

OF COUNSEL

Samuel R. Dorrance	Louis S. Pryor

Paul L. Rathblott

References: First Union Bank; Fleet Bank; U.S. Trust Co. of Connecticut.

For full biographical listings, see the Martindale-Hubbell Law Directory

NEW HAVEN,* New Haven Co.

CARMODY & TORRANCE (AV)

195 Church Street, P.O. Box 1950, 06509
Telephone: 203-777-5501
Facsimile: 203-784-3199
Waterbury, Connecticut Office: 50 Leavenworth Street. P.O. Box 1110, 06721.
Telephone: 203-573-1200.
Facsimile: 203-575-2600.

MEMBERS OF FIRM

Anthony M. Fitzgerald	Ann Harris Rubin
Charles F. Corcoran, III	Thomas J. Sansone
Thomas R. Candrick, Jr.	Ann Hedges Zucker
William P. Yelenak	Christopher Rooney
Susan Seidler Chambers	Steven G. Mednick

ASSOCIATES

Joseph J. Packtor	Donna M. Rigg
Kevin C. Doyle	Kevin S. Russo
Heena Kapadia	Suzanne H. Nathanson

Representative Clients: Algonquin Gas Transmission Co.; Bank of Boston Connecticut; Blue Cross & Blue Shield of Connecticut, Inc.; City of Waterbury; Northeast Utilities; T. Sendzimir, Inc.; Timex Corp.; Waterbury Hospital.
Trial Counsel for: Aetna Life and Casualty; Stop & Shop Companies.

For full biographical listings, see the Martindale-Hubbell Law Directory

WILLIAM H. CLENDENEN, JR. A PROFESSIONAL CORPORATION (AV)

400 Orange Street, P.O. Box 301, 06502-0301
Telephone: 203-787-1183
Fax: 203-787-2847

William H. Clendenen, Jr.

James E. Clifford	Nancy L. Walker

Thomas C. Pellegrino

For full biographical listings, see the Martindale-Hubbell Law Directory

GALLAGHER GALLAGHER & CALISTRO (AV)

1377 Boulevard, P.O. Box 1925, 06509
Telephone: 203-624-4165
Fax: 203-865-5598

William F. Gallagher	Cynthia C. Bott
Elizabeth A. Gallagher	Barbara L. Cox
Roger B. Calistro	Kurt D. Koehler

Thomas J. Airone

Approved Attorneys for: Chicago Title Insurance Co.; Centerbank; Dime Savings Bank of Wallingford; New Haven Savings Bank; Bank of Boston Connecticut; Fleet Bank; People's Bank; Bank of New Haven.
References: Bank of New Haven; Prime Bank.

For full biographical listings, see the Martindale-Hubbell Law Directory

GARRISON PHELAN LEVIN-EPSTEIN & PENZEL, P.C. (AV)

405 Orange Street, 06511
Telephone: 203-777-4425
Fax: 203-776-3965

Joseph D. Garrison	Robert A. Richardson
Gary E. Phelan	Lewis H. Chimes
Ethan A. Levin-Epstein	Deborah J. Krauss
Markus L. Penzel	Michele Lang Palter

Monika Lahiri Escoriaza

(See Next Column)

GARRISON PHELAN LEVIN-EPSTEIN & PENZEL P.C., *New Haven—Continued*

Reference: Bank of New Haven.

For full biographical listings, see the Martindale-Hubbell Law Directory

GREENFIELD AND MURPHY (AV)

234 Church Street, P.O. Box 1103, 06504-1103
Telephone: 203-787-6711
Telecopier: 203-777-6442

MEMBERS OF FIRM

James R. Greenfield	Helen D. Murphy
	Maureen M. Murphy

Reference: First Fidelity Bank.

For full biographical listings, see the Martindale-Hubbell Law Directory

JACOBS, GRUDBERG, BELT & DOW, P.C. (AV)

350 Orange Street, P.O. Box 606, 06503
Telephone: 203-772-3100
Fax: 203-772-1691
Email: jacobslaw@jacobslaw.com *URL:* http://www.jacobslaw.com

Israel J. Jacobs (1918-1963)	Alice S. Miskimin
Howard A. Jacobs	Charles B. Price, Jr.
Ira B. Grudberg	F. Herbert Gruendel
David L. Belt	William M. Bloss
William F. Dow, III	Shirley V. Hoogstra
Jonathan Katz	Mark R. Soboslai
Susan H. Bartholomew	David T. Grudberg

Steven J. DeFrank	Alinor C. Sterling
David A. Leff	Phillip A. Escoriaza
	Marybeth C. Gauthier

For full biographical listings, see the Martindale-Hubbell Law Directory

LYNCH, TRAUB, KEEFE AND ERRANTE, A PROFESSIONAL CORPORATION (AV)

52 Trumbull Street, P.O. Box 1612, 06506
Telephone: 203-787-0275
Fax: 203-782-0278
Email: ltke@snet.com *URL:* http://www.ltke.com

Stephen I. Traub	Donn A. Swift
Hugh F. Keefe	Charles E. Tiernan, III
Steven J. Errante	Robert W. Lynch
John J. Keefe, Jr.	Richard W. Lynch
	John M. Walsh, Jr.

Suzanne L. McAlpine	Lee Kennedy Tiernan
Christopher M. Licari	William F. Clark
Eric P. Smith	James A. Mongillo

OF COUNSEL
William C. Lynch

Local Counsel for: Transport Insurance Co., Dallas, Texas; American Trucking Associations; Roadway Express, Inc., Akron, Ohio; A.R.A. Philadelphia, Penn.; Consolidated Freightways, Menlo Park, California; Ogden Corp.
Labor Counsel: Coca-Cola, U.S.A., Atlanta, Georgia (Private Truck Operation); The Dow Chemical Co.; Cincinnati Milacron.

For full biographical listings, see the Martindale-Hubbell Law Directory

ROSEN & DOLAN, P.C. (AV)

400 Orange Street, 06511
Telephone: 203-787-3513
Fax: 203-789-1605
Email: davidrosen@counsel.com
Email: spincus@counsel.com

David N. Rosen	Edward J. Dolan
	Stephen M. Pincus

Reference: Peoples Bank.

For full biographical listings, see the Martindale-Hubbell Law Directory

SUSMAN, DUFFY & SEGALOFF, P.C. (AV)

55 Whitney Avenue, 06510-1300
Telephone: 203-624-9830
Telecopier: 203-562-8430
Mailing Address: P.O. Box 1684, New Haven, Connecticut, 06507-1684

(See Next Column)

Allen H. Duffy (1931-1986)	Susan W. Wolfson
Michael Susman	Laura M. Sklaver
James H. Segaloff	Andrew R. Lubin
David A. Reif	James J. Perito
Joseph E. Faughnan	Matthew C. Susman
	Thomas E. Katon

Jennifer L. Schancupp	Peter G. Kruzynski
Donna Decker Morris	Joshua W. Cohen
	Vincent J. Candelora

OF COUNSEL

Diana C. Ballard	David P. Hambleton

For full biographical listings, see the Martindale-Hubbell Law Directory

TYLER COOPER & ALCORN (AV)

205 Church Street, P.O. Box 1936, 06509-1910
Telephone: 203-784-8200
Telecopier: 203-789-2133
Hartford, Connecticut Office: CityPlace.
Telephone: 860-725-6200.
Telecopier: 860-278-3802.
Stamford, Connecticut Office: One Landmark Square.
Telephone: 203-348-5555.
Telecopier: 203-348-3875.
Greenwich, Connecticut Office: 675 Steamboat Road.
Telephone: 203-869-2000.
Telecopier: 203-869-2001.
Madison, Connecticut Office: 23 Woodland Road.
Telephone: 203-318-3600.
Telecopier: 203-318-3609.

MEMBERS OF FIRM

William R. Murphy	Ronald J. Cohen
Richard G. Bell (Managing Partner of the Firm)	Margaret P. Mason
	William W. Bouton III
William S. Rogers (Resident at Hartford Office)	(Resident at Hartford Office)
	Anthony B. Casareale
Ralph G. Elliot (Resident at Hartford Office)	(Resident at Stamford Office)
	Mark V. Connolly
Michael J. Dorney	(Resident at Hartford Office)
Samuel W. Bowlby	William S. Fish, Jr.
Bruce Lewellyn	(Resident at Hartford Office)
Joseph C. Lee	Kevin McCann
James G. Kenefick, Jr.	(Resident at Hartford Office)
Lewis Segal	David J. Wiese
(Resident at Hartford Office)	(Resident at Hartford Office)
Irving S. Schloss	Emmett E. Brown III
Jon T. Hirschoff	(Resident at Stamford Office)
William H. Champlin III	Margaret A. Little
(Resident at Hartford Office)	Ben A. Solnit
Timothy W. Bingham	Jacqueline DeAndrus Bucar
David W. Schneider	Fillis W. Stober
Robert W. Allen	(Resident at Hartford Office)
Robert L. Teicher	Thomas S. Marrion
Richard W. Bowerman	(Resident at Hartford Office)
George E. O'Brien, Jr.	Christopher P. McCormack
Robert J. Metzler II	Kevin G. Ferrigno
(Resident at Hartford Office)	(Resident at Hartford Office)

OF COUNSEL
Milton P. DeVane

SENIOR COUNSEL
Henry W. Pascarella (Resident at Greenwich Office)

COUNSEL

Nan Budde Chequer (Resident at Stamford Office)	Kurt W. Johnson (Resident at Hartford Office)
	Kathleen A. Maher

ASSOCIATES

Christopher L. Ulrich (Resident at Stamford Office)	Robert B. Flynn
	Ellen M. Fusco
Charles R. Andres	Renee M. Reed
Shawn L. O'Sullivan	Steven L. Elbaum
Lori B. Alexander	(Resident at Stamford Office)
Greg R. Barringer	Niclas A. Ferland
Patricia E. Reilly	Kevin S. Murphy
Barry M. Winnick	(Resident at Hartford Office)
(Resident at Hartford Office)	Timothy P. Pothin
William F. Cummings	Brian O'Donnell
(Resident at Hartford Office)	Joseph R. Tiano, Jr.
Noble F. Allen	Robert C. Hinton
Glory Martyn Lena	
(Resident at Hartford Office)	

Counsel for: Echlin, Inc.; Hospital of St. Raphael; The Stanley Works; The Southern Connecticut Gas Co.; Southern New England Telephone Co.; Science Park Development Corp.; Connecticut American Water Co.; General Electric Co.

For full biographical listings, see the Martindale-Hubbell Law Directory

New Haven—Continued

WIGGIN & DANA (AV)

One Century Tower, 06508-1832
Telephone: 203-498-4400
Telefax: 203-782-2889
Hartford, Connecticut Office: One CityPlace.
Telephone: 203-297-3700.
FAX: 203-525-9380.
Stamford, Connecticut Office: Three Stamford Plaza, 301 Tresser Boulevard.
Telephone: 203-363-7600.
Telefax: 203-363-7676.

MEMBERS OF FIRM

Frederick H. Wiggin (1882-1963)	Peter J. Lefeber
J. Dwight Dana (1889-1951)	John G. Zandy
John Q. Tilson	Sherry L. Dominick
John W. Barnett	Alan G. Schwartz
William C. Baskin, Jr.	Penny Quinn Seaman
Robert F. Cavanagh	Valerie A. Seiling
Charles C. Kingsley	(Resident at Hartford)
William J. Doyle	Bennett J. Bernblum
David P. Faulkner	Susan J. Bryson
William E. Craig	William G. Millman, Jr.
Noel E. Hanf	Jeanette Carpenter Schreiber
Shaun S. Sullivan	Patrick J. Monahan, II
Jeremy G. Zimmermann	(Resident at Hartford)
J. Michael Eisner	Peter H. Gruen
Norman Fineberg	Mary R. Norris
Michael K. Brown	Maureen Weaver
William H. Prout, Jr.	Robert M. Langer
J. Drake Turrentine	(Resident at Hartford)
(Resident at Stamford)	James F. Farrington, Jr.
Linda L. Randell	(Resident at Hartford)
D. Terence Jones	Karen L. Clute
Mark R. Kravitz	John F. Conway
Melinda A. Agsten	Abbie Eremich
Edward Wood Dunham	Leonard Leader
Norman J. Fleming	(Resident at Stamford)

SENIOR COUNSEL

S. Robert Jelley	Charles N. Schenck, III
Robert M. McAnerney	
(Resident at Stamford)	

COUNSEL

Sidney R. Bresnick	Gregory S. Rosenblatt
(Not admitted in CT)	(Not admitted in CT)
Dale L. Carlson	William A. Simons
	(Not admitted in CT)

ASSOCIATES

Joan M. Allen	Nicole M. Hoffmeister
Ann K. Anderson	Marcella Ann Hourihane
Catherine P. Baatz	(Resident at Hartford)
Jeffrey R. Babbin	Bernard E. Jacques
Dean W. Baker	(Resident at Hartford)
Penelope I. Bellamy	Marcia Kenny Keegan
Ian E. Bjorkman	(Resident at Hartford)
Joaquina L. Borges	Lisa Dougherty Kenna
John E. Buerkert, Jr.	Kevin M. Kennedy
Andrew J. Cappel	Daniel J. Klau
Julie Behm Carter	Matthew A. Lieberman
Thomas L. Casagrande	Patricia Kavee Melick
Isabel E. Chenoweth	(Resident at Stamford)
Patrick J. Corcoran	Steven D. Meyers
Michelle Wilcox DeBarge	(Not admitted in CT)
Eleanor Stuart Devane	Christine Owens Morgan
Inez M. Diaz	M. Veronica Mullally
Francis J. Duffin	Richard F. Nace, Jr.
Elise R. Epner	Eric P. Neff
Andrea Frankl	(Resident at Hartford)
Todd E. Garabedian	Susan M. Neilson
(Not admitted in CT)	Karen E. Overchuk
Robert A. Geckle, Jr.	(Resident at Hartford)
Jessie A. Gilbert	Phyllis M. Pari
(Resident at Stamford)	Bonnie Lynne Patten
Merton G. Gollaher	Colleen Beth Pernerewski
David C. Grigsby	Mumtaza Malaika Rahi
Michael Grundei	Charles P. Reed
Lynn F. Guelzow	Meredith Gordon Remigino
(Resident at Hartford)	George H. Richards II
Stephen B. Harris	Eric J. Stockman
(Resident at Hartford)	Peter M. Wendzel
Robert S. Hauser	Thomas J. Witt
Mark W. Heaphy	(Resident at Hartford)
Lisa Page Heslin	Laura Wright Wooton
Claudia Damsky Heyman	(Resident at Stamford)

For full biographical listings, see the Martindale-Hubbell Law Directory

---

NEW LONDON, New London Co.

GREENBERG & PARENTEAU, P.C. (AV)

130 Eugene O'Neill Drive, 06320
Telephone: 860-442-5373
Fax: 860-443-8131

Lawrence J. Greenberg	Philip M. Johnstone
Jacques J. Parenteau	Frank J. Liberty
	Karen Reilly

Representative Clients: Stonington Community Credit Union; Tri County Distributors; United Builders Supply; Waterford Hotel Group, Inc.; General Dynamics Co.; Electric Boat Division.

For full biographical listings, see the Martindale-Hubbell Law Directory

---

WALLER, SMITH & PALMER, P.C. (AV)

52 Eugene O'Neill Drive, P.O. Box 88, 06320
Telephone: 860-442-0367
Telecopier: 860-447-9915
Old Lyme, Connecticut Office: 103-A Halls Road.
Telephone: 860-434-8063.
Telecopier: 860-434-9452.

Tracy Waller (1862-1947)	Robert W. Marrion
J. Rodney Smith (1906-1979)	Hughes Griffis
Birdsey G. Palmer (Retired)	Edward B. O'Connell
William W. Miner	Frederick B. Gahagan
Robert P. Anderson, Jr.	Mary E. Driscoll

Tracy M. Collins	Valerie Ann Votto
Edward B. Potter	Charles C. Anderson
David P. Condon	Ames B. Shea

General Counsel For: Town of East Lyme; Town of Lebanon.
Counsel For: Citizens Savings Bank; Sonoco/Northeastern, Inc.; The Nature Conservancy; Fleet Bank.
Local Counsel For: McCue Mortgage Co.; Citicorp Mortgage; U.S. Department of Housing and Urban Development.

For full biographical listings, see the Martindale-Hubbell Law Directory

---

NORWALK, Fairfield Co.

KEOGH, BURKHART & VETTER (AV)

34 Wall Street, P.O. Box 126, 06852
Telephone: 203-866-2535, 866-2536
Fax: 203-855-9016

MEMBERS OF FIRM

John Keogh (1871-1960)	Alfred W. Burkhart
John Keogh, Jr. (1910-1992)	Thomas J. Vetter
	Stephen B. Keogh

Local Counsel for: Metropolitan Life Insurance Co.

For full biographical listings, see the Martindale-Hubbell Law Directory

---

TIERNEY, ZULLO, FLAHERTY & MURPHY, P.C. (AV)

134 East Avenue, P.O. Box 2028-Belden Station, 06852
Telephone: 203-853-7000
Fax: 203-838-4829
Other Norwalk Office: 401 Merritt 7, First Floor.
Telephone: 203-853-7000.
Fax: 203-849-1452.

Thomas Tierney	Gary Lorusso
Frank N. Zullo	Andrew F. Kordas
Thomas A. Flaherty	Barbara Coughlan
Frank W. Murphy	Elizabeth A.B. Suchy
Reuben S. Midler	Creighton M. English

OF COUNSEL

Thomas A. Keating, Jr.	Vincent Gallogly

References: First Union Bank of Connecticut; Fleet Bank.

For full biographical listings, see the Martindale-Hubbell Law Directory

---

*NORWICH,** New London Co.

BROWN, JACOBSON, TILLINGHAST, LAHAN & KING, P.C. (AV)

Uncas-Merchants National Bank Building, 22 Courthouse Square, 06360
Telephone: 860-889-3321
Fax: 860-886-0673

Milton L. Jacobson	John C. Wirzbicki
Vincent A. Laudone	Michael D. Colonese
Wayne G. Tillinghast	Karl-Erik Sternlof
P. Michael Lahan	Michael P. Carey
Michael E. Driscoll	Jeffrey R. Godley
David S. Williams	Michael E. Kennedy
Michael A. Blanchard	Doreen A. West

(See Next Column)

BROWN, JACOBSON, TILLINGHAST, LAHAN & KING P.C., *Norwich—Continued*

Elizabeth Conway	Gerald M. Smith, Jr.
John F. Duggan	Jeffrey F. Buebendorf

OF COUNSEL

Allyn L. Brown, Jr.	James J. Dutton, Jr.
Charles W. Jewett	Jackson T. King, Jr.

Representative Clients: Nationwide Insurance Co.; Aetna Casualty & Surety Co.; Chelsea-Groton Savings Bank; Norwich Community Development Corp.

For full biographical listings, see the Martindale-Hubbell Law Directory

O'BRIEN, SHAFNER, STUART, KELLY & MORRIS, P.C. (AV)

2 Courthouse Square, P.O. Box 310, 06360
Telephone: 860-889-3855
Fax: 860-886-6352
Groton, Connecticut Office: 475 Bridge Street.
Telephone: 860-445-2463.
Fax: 860-445-4539.

Mark E. Block (Resident)	Lloyd L. Langhammer
Richard J. Pascal	

For full biographical listings, see the Martindale-Hubbell Law Directory

OLD LYME, New London Co.

WALLER, SMITH & PALMER, P.C. (AV)

103-A Halls Road, 06371
Telephone: 860-434-8063
Telecopier: 860-434-9452
New London, Connecticut Office: 52 Eugene O'Neill Drive.
Telephone: 860-442-0367.
Telecopier: 860-447-9915.

Robert W. Marrion	Frederick B. Gahagan

Valerie Ann Votto
OF COUNSEL
Suzanne Donnelly Kitchings

For full biographical listings, see the Martindale-Hubbell Law Directory

PUTNAM,* Windham Co. — (Refer to Willimantic)

SOUTHBURY, New Haven Co.

SECOR, CASSIDY & McPARTLAND, P.C. (AV)

Successors to Bronson, Lewis, Upson & Secor; Lewis, Hart, Upson & Secor; Upson, Secor, Greene & Cassidy and Upson, Secor, Cassidy & McPartland, P.C.
900 Main Street South, 06488
Telephone: 203-264-8223
Fax: 203-264-6730
Waterbury, Connecticut Office: 41 Church Street, P.O. Box 2818.
Telephone: 203-757-9261.
Fax: 203-756-5762.

James R. Healey

Attorneys for: The Mattatuck Museum; American Republican, Inc.; Hubbard-Hall, Inc.; The Siemon Co.; Engineered Sinterings and Plastics, Inc.; Boutin Industries; County Line Buick-Nissan, Inc.

For full biographical listings, see the Martindale-Hubbell Law Directory

SOUTHPORT, Fairfield Co.

MARSH, DAY & CALHOUN (AV)

2507 Post Road, 06490
Telephone: 203-259-8993
Fax: 203-254-1772
Bridgeport, Connecticut Office: 955 Main Street.
Telephone: 203-259-8993.
Fax: 203-254-1772.

MEMBERS OF FIRM

Peter Wilkinson	James E. Rice
Robert J. Berta	Peter T. Mott
Thomas F. Maxwell, Jr.	Roy W. Moore, III
Thomas J. Walsh, Jr.	

ASSOCIATES

Tracey C. Kammerer	Tracy Wheeler Lennon
John R. Mitola	Matthew M. Hausman
Stephen M. Carruthers	

SPECIAL COUNSEL

Bruce E. Dillingham	David S. Maclay
Muriel E. Zacharias	

Counsel for: Chase Manhattan Bank, N.A.; Southern Connecticut Gas Co.; Metropolitan Life Insurance Co.; General Electric Co.; Sturm Ruger & Co., Inc.; The Producto Machine Co.

(See Next Column)

For full biographical listings, see the Martindale-Hubbell Law Directory

STAMFORD, Fairfield Co.

CURTIS, BRINCKERHOFF & BARRETT, P.C. (AV)

666 Summer Street, 06901-1416
Telephone: 203-324-6777
Telecopier: 203-324-9621

T. Ward Cleary (1916-1988)	John Wayne Fox
John D. Hertz	Ward Frank Cleary
Frederick M. Tobin	James D'Alton Murphy
Randolph T. Lovallo	

OF COUNSEL

Richard L. Brinckerhoff	Jane F. Donovan

Susan L. Stratton	Derek Gilman
Michael P. Murray	

Counsel for: The F. A. Bartlett Tree Expert Co.; Town of Darien; Miller Automobile Corp.; Bolliger, Inc.; Titan Sports; People's Bank, Bridgeport; Fleet Bank; Federal Deposit Insurance Co.; William Pitt Foundation; Wood Logan Associates.

For full biographical listings, see the Martindale-Hubbell Law Directory

DAY, BERRY & HOWARD (AV)

One Canterbury Green, 06901
Telephone: 203-977-7300
Telecopier: 203-977-7301
Email: postmaster@dbh.com
Hartford, Connecticut Office: CityPlace I.
Telephone: 860-275-0100.
Telecopier: 860-275-0343.
Boston, Massachusetts Office: 260 Franklin Street.
Telephone: 617-345-4600.
Telecopier: 617-439-4453.

MEMBERS OF FIRM IN STAMFORD

Jerome Berkman	Robert J. Miller
Martin L. Budd	Kenneth W. Ritt
Michael P. Byrne	Sabino Rodriguez III
Patricia A. Carpenter	James F. Stapleton
Ronald Osburn Dederick	David A. Swerdloff
Thomas D. Goldberg	Stanley A. Twardy, Jr.
F. Lee Griffith III	Stefan R. Underhill
Gregory A. Hayes	Carla R. Walworth
Michael S. Leo	
(Not admitted in CT)	

ASSOCIATES OF FIRM IN STAMFORD

Marsha L. Anastasia	Marcia R. Ginsberg
R. Scott Beach	Craig A. Goldberg
Joy Beane	Deborah S. Gordon
Eileen R. Becker	(Not admitted in CT)
Paul N. Belval	Sarah E. Graves
J. Bradley Britton	Lynn A. Kappelman
Keith P. Carroll	Vincent Laurentino
Martha C. Deneen	Philip J. Paseltiner
Wendy D. DiChristina	Daniel L. Schwartz
Brian P. Donovan	James A. Shapiro
(Not admitted in CT)	Terri L. Stein
Andrea Falcione	Steven M. Torkelsen
Kenneth W. Gage	Jonathan B. Tropp
Theodore J. Whitehead	

OF COUNSEL IN STAMFORD

John Crosskey	Emil H. Frankel
Ellen B. Wells	

COUNSEL IN STAMFORD

Michael G. Considine	Andrew P. Gaillard
(Not admitted in CT)	

For full biographical listings, see the Martindale-Hubbell Law Directory

HEALY & BAILLIE, LLP (AV⊤)

Stamford Harbor Park, 333 Ludlow Street, 06902-6987
Telephone: 203-961-7250
Telecopier: 203-357-7909
Email: RECEPTION@HEALY.COM
New York, N.Y. Office: 29 Broadway, 10006-3293.
Telephone: 212-943-3980.
Telecopier: 212-425-0131. INTERNET E-MAIL: RECEPTION@HEALY.COM.
Hong Kong Office: Healy & Baillie, Luk Hoi Tong Building, Suite 1301, 31 Queen's Road Central.
Telephone: 852-2537-8628.
Telecopier: 852-2521-9072. INTERNET E-MAIL: 6412689@MCIMAIL.COM.

RESIDENT PARTNER
John W. Wall

For full biographical listings, see the Martindale-Hubbell Law Directory

Stamford—Continued

PAUL, HASTINGS, JANOFSKY & WALKER LLP (AV)

A Limited Liability Partnership including Professional Corporations
Ninth Floor, 1055 Washington Boulevard, 06901-2217
Telephone: 203-961-7400
Fax: 203-359-3031
Email: info@PHJW.com *URL:* http://www.PHJW.com
Los Angeles, California Office: Twenty-Third Floor, 555 South Flower Street.
Telephone: 213-683-6000.
Orange County, California Office: Seventeenth Floor, 695 Town Center Drive, Costa Mesa.
Telephone: 714-668-6200.
Washington, D.C. Office: Tenth Floor, 1299 Pennsylvania Avenue, N.W.
Telephone: 202-508-9500.
Atlanta, Georgia Office: 24th Floor, 600 Peachtree Street, N.E.
Telephone: 404-815-2400.
Santa Monica, California Office: Fifth Floor, 1299 Ocean Avenue.
Telephone: 310-319-3300.
New York, New York Office: 31st Floor, 399 Park Avenue.
Telephone: 212-318-6000.
Tokyo, Japan Office: Ark Mori Building, 30th Floor, 12-32 Akasaka, P.O. Box 577, 1-Chome, Minato-Ku.
Telephone: (03) 3556-4711.

MEMBERS OF FIRM

Carl T. Anderson	Mario J. Ippolito
Christopher A. Barreca	Charles T. Lee
Jonathan Birenbaum	John S. McGeeney
Douglas C. Conroy	Clayton S. Reynolds
Esteban A. Ferrer, III	(Not admitted in CT)
John D. Hawkins, Jr.	Patrick W. Shea
(Not admitted in CT)	David E. Snediker

OF COUNSEL

Kurt W. Hansson	David E. Rabin
Andrew S. Holmes	(Not admitted in CT)

ASSOCIATES

Elizabeth A. Adolff	John W. Hamlin
James R. Bliss	James Judson Jackson
Joseph A. Callari	Michael B. Jaffe
(Not admitted in CT)	(Not admitted in CT)
Christopher H. Craig	Gregory F. Lang
(Not admitted in CT)	Eric T. Levine
Alejandro J. Diaz	Paul C. Marazita
Mary C. Dollarhide	Suzanne Marie Pepe-Robbins
Patricia A. Driscoll	Bonnie Pierson-Murphy
Harold N. Eddy, Jr.	Leslie A. Plaskon
Regina M. Flaherty	Richard M. Vicenzi
	(Not admitted in CT)

For full biographical listings, see the Martindale-Hubbell Law Directory

RYAN, RYAN, JOHNSON, McCAGHEY & DELUCA, LLP (AV)

80 Fourth Street, P.O. Box 3057, 06905
Telephone: 203-357-9200
FAX: 203-357-7915
Email: cdelucoo@counsel.com
New York, New York Office: Park Avenue Atrium, 237 Park Avenue.
Telephone: 212-949-0722.

MEMBERS OF FIRM

Daniel E. Ryan, Jr.	Michael T. Ryan
W. Patrick Ryan	Charles M. McCaghey
J. Paul Johnson	John W. Mullin
Charles A. Deluca	Elizabeth W. Carter
Daniel E. Ryan, III	Holly K. Dustin

ASSOCIATES

Beverly J. Hunt	Robert C.E. Laney
Richard P. Colbert	Catherine S. Nietzel
John F. Leydon, Jr.	Darren R. Renner
Barbara J. Pulaski	Kieran M. Ryan
Thomas J. O'Neill	Joseph P. Sargent

For full biographical listings, see the Martindale-Hubbell Law Directory

SHIPMAN & GOODWIN LLP (AV)

One Landmark Square, 06901
Telephone: 203-324-8100
Telecopier: 203-324-8199
E.Mail: first initial last name @goodwin.com
Email: www@goodwin.com *URL:* http://shipman-goodwin.com
Hartford, Connecticut Office: One American Row.
Telephone: 203-251-5000.
Lakeville, Connecticut Office: Porter Street.
Telephone: 203-435-2539.

PARTNERS

Michael L. Widland	Lewis G. Schwartz
Frank J. Marco (Stamford and	Frederick S. Gold
Hartford Offices)	Steven M. Gold
Barry C. Hawkins	Donald R. Gustafson

(See Next Column)

ASSOCIATES

Cathy S. Satz	Lisa J. Kerner
Robin G. Frederick	Jennifer A. Hauhuth
Karla P. Ray	Michael Montecalvo

For full biographical listings, see the Martindale-Hubbell Law Directory

TYLER COOPER & ALCORN (AV)

One Landmark Square, 06901-2501
Telephone: 203-348-5555
Telecopier: 203-348-3875
Hartford, Connecticut Office: CityPlace.
Telephone: 860-725-6200.
Telecopier: 860-278-3802.
New Haven, Connecticut Office: 205 Church Street.
Telephone: 203-784-8200.
Telecopier: 203-789-2133.
Greenwich, Connecticut Office: 675 Steamboat Road.
Telephone: 203-869-2000.
Telecopier: 203-869-2001.
Madison, Connecticut Office: 23 Woodland Road.
Telephone: 203-318-3600.
Telecopier: 203-318-3609.

MEMBERS OF FIRM

Anthony B. Casareale (Resident)   Emmett E. Brown III (Resident)
Robert L. Teicher

COUNSEL

Nan Budde Chequer (Resident)

RESIDENT ASSOCIATES

Christopher L. Ulrich	Steven L. Elbaum

For full biographical listings, see the Martindale-Hubbell Law Directory

WINTHROP, STIMSON, PUTNAM & ROBERTS (AV)

Financial Centre, 695 East Main Street, P.O. Box 6760, 06904-6760
Telephone: 203-348-2300
Telefax: 203-965-8226
New York, N.Y. Office: One Battery Park Plaza, 10004.
Telephone: 212-858-1000.
Fax: 212-858-1500.
Washington, D.C. Office: 1133 Connecticut Avenue, N.W., 20036.
Telephone: 202-775-9800.
Fax: 202-833-8491.
Palm Beach, Florida Office: 125 Worth Avenue, 33480.
Telephone: 407-655-7297.
Fax: 407-833-6726.
London, England Office: 2 Throgmorton Avenue, London, EC2N 2DL, England.
Telephone: O11-44171-628-4931.
Fax: 011-44171-638-0443.
Brussels, Belgium Office: Rue Du Taciturne 42, B-1040 Brussels, Belgium.
Telephone: 011-322-230-1392.
Fax: 011-322-230-9288.
Tokyo, Japan Office: 608 Atagoyama Bengoshi Building 6-7, Atago 1-chome, Minato-ku, Tokyo 105 Japan.
Telephone: 011-813-3437-9740.
Fax: 011-813-3437-9261.
Hong Kong Office: 2505 Asia Pacific Finance Tower, Citibank Plaza, 3 Garden Road, Central.
Telephone: 011-852-2530-3400.
Fax: 011-852-2530-3355.

MEMBERS OF FIRM

Thomas F. Clauss, Jr.	Arthur W. Hooper, Jr.
Elizabeth H. W. Fry	Frode Jensen, III
Francis W. Hogan III	G. William Sisley

COUNSEL

Kent S. Nevins	Thomas R. Trowbridge, III

SENIOR COUNSEL

Endicott P. Davison	David M. Payne
Richard B. Tweedy	

ASSOCIATES

Marjorie Hennigan Alutto	Kelly J. McClure
Eric X. Fishman	Sheila A. Ozalis
Steven Kapiloff	Robert J. Rawn
Seth L. Kaplan	Paul A. Sherrington

For full biographical listings, see the Martindale-Hubbell Law Directory

VERNON,* Tolland Co.

FLAHERTY, MEISLER & COURTNEY (AV)

30 Lafayette Square, P.O. Box 508, 06066
Telephone: 860-872-7200
Fax: 860-875-6594
Email: FMACATTY@aol.com

MEMBERS OF FIRM

Leo B. Flaherty Jr.	Arthur P. Meisler
Joseph D. Courtney	

(See Next Column)

FLAHERTY, MEISLER & COURTNEY, *Vernon—Continued*

ASSOCIATES

Elizabeth C. Foran

Reference: Savings Bank of Rockville.

For full biographical listings, see the Martindale-Hubbell Law Directory

WALLINGFORD, New Haven Co.

FARRELL & LESLIE (AV)

375 Center Street, P.O. Box 369, 06492
Telephone: 203-269-7756
Fax: 203-269-1927

MEMBERS OF FIRM

Gerald E. Farrell	Ann Farrell Leslie
Gerald E. Farrell, Jr.	Brian J. Leslie

References: Dime Savings Bank of Wallingford; Shawmut Bank (Wallingford Office).

For full biographical listings, see the Martindale-Hubbell Law Directory

WATERBURY, New Haven Co.

CARMODY & TORRANCE (AV)

50 Leavenworth Street, P.O. Box 1110, 06721
Telephone: 203-573-1200
Facsimile: 203-575-2600
New Haven, Connecticut Office: 195 Church Street, P.O. Box 1950, 06509.
Telephone: 203-777-5501.
Facsimile: 203-784-3199.

MEMBERS OF FIRM

Timothy R. Carmody	Susan Seidler Chambers
Joseph F. Budny	(Resident, New Haven Office)
Anthony M. Fitzgerald	D. Charles Stohler
(Resident, New Haven Office)	Ann Harris Rubin
Norman K. Jellinghaus	(Resident, New Haven Office)
Kenneth J. Pocius	Marianne Barbino Dubuque
Burton Z. Alter	William I. Garfinkel
Charles F. Corcoran, III	Thomas J. Sansone
(Resident, New Haven Office)	(Resident, New Haven Office)
James K. Robertson, Jr.	Joseph A. Wellington
Thomas R. Candrick, Jr.	Joseph L. Kinsella
(Resident, New Haven Office)	Ann Hedges Zucker
Trudie Ross Hamilton	(Resident, New Haven Office)
James Wu	Kathleen Lenehan Nastri
David L. Sfara	Christopher Rooney
William P. Yelenak	(Resident, New Haven Office)
(Resident, New Haven Office)	Joseph E. Dornfried
John D. Yarbrough, Jr.	M. Anne Peters
Maureen Danehy Cox	Michael J. Reardon
Mark J. Malaspina	Steven G. Mednick
	(Resident, New Haven Office)

OF COUNSEL

G. Bradford Palmer	Walter F. Torrance, Jr.

Thomas L. Brayton

ASSOCIATES

Brian T. Henebry	Jennifer E. Sills
Paul S. Tagatac	Richard L. Street
Rona C. Lynch	Viktoria K. Cech
Joseph J. Packtor	George Monteiro Moreira
(Resident, New Haven Office)	Kevin S. Russo
Brian L. Smith	(Resident, New Haven Office)
Kevin C. Doyle	Mariella LaRosa
(Resident, New Haven Office)	Ronald E. Lyles
Giovanna Tiberii Weller	Matthew C. McGrath
Heena Kapadia	William M. O'Donnell, III
(Resident, New Haven Office)	Suzanne H. Nathanson
Nicholas G. Kokis	(Resident, New Haven Office)
Donna M. Rigg	
(Resident, New Haven Office)	

Representative Clients: Algonquin Gas Transmission Co.; Bank of Boston Connecticut; Blue Cross & Blue Shield of Connecticut, Inc.; City of Waterbury; Northeast Utilities; T. Sendzimir, Inc.; Timex Corp.; Waterbury Hospital.
Trial Counsel for: Aetna Life and Casualty; Stop & Shop Companies.

For full biographical listings, see the Martindale-Hubbell Law Directory

GAGER & PETERSON (AV)

(Formerly Gager & Henry)
One Exchange Place, P.O. Box 2480, 06722
Telephone: 203-597-5100
Telecopier: 203-757-7888
Danbury, Connecticut Office: 100 Mill Plain Road.
Telephone: 203-792-7525.
Telecopier: 203-757-7888.
Sharon, Connecticut Office: 25 West Main Street, P.O. Box 158.
Telephone: 860-364-5531.
Telecopier: 860-364-5805.

(See Next Column)

Southbury, Connecticut Office: 325 Main Street South.
Telephone: 203-262-6600.
Telecopier: 203-262-6780.
Litchfield, Connecticut Office: 49 Commons Drive, P.O. Box 1544.
Telephone: 860-567-0828.
Fax: 860-567-5844.

MEMBERS OF FIRM

William W. Gager (1892-1967)	J. Michael Sconyers
Carl A. Peterson	(Sharon & Litchfield Offices)
Curtis V. Titus	John V. Galiette
William C. Crutcher	Thomas M. Rickart
Alan Birmingham	Jo E. Friday
Thomas J. McHale	(Sharon & Litchfield Offices)
Richard A. Hoppe	Edward M. Rosenblatt
Edward S. Hill	C. Robert Zelinger
Richard L. Emerson	Frank J. Scinto
Augustus R. Southworth, III	Edward J. Kelleher
Louise F. Brown (Sharon Office)	Kathy S. Bower
Mary M. Ackerly	
(Litchfield Office)	

ASSOCIATES

Ann Martindale	Kristin C. Cunningham
Thomas A. Kaelin	Robert L. Cavanaugh, Jr.
Regina Duchin Kraus	Alisa N. Fay
John R. Horvack, Jr.	James B. Schomburg

James J. Flaherty, Jr.

Counsel for: Bank of Boston Connecticut; Centerbank; The Eastern Co.; Risdon Corp.; Anamet, Inc.; Timex Corp.; The Platt Brothers & Co.; Caradon, Inc.
Trial Counsel for: Aetna Casualty and Surety Co.; Continental National Assurance Co.

For full biographical listings, see the Martindale-Hubbell Law Directory

SECOR, CASSIDY & McPARTLAND, P.C. (AV)

Successors to Bronson, Lewis, Upson & Secor; Lewis, Hart, Upson & Secor; Upson, Secor, Greene & Cassidy and Upson, Secor, Cassidy & McPartland, P.C.
41 Church Street, P.O. Box 2818, 06723-2818
Telephone: 203-757-9261
Fax: 203-756-5762
Southbury, Connecticut Office: 900 Main Street South.
Telephone: 203-264-8223.
Fax: 203-264-6730.

Nath'l R. Bronson (1860-1949)	Gail E. McTaggart
Lawrence L. Lewis (1881-1965)	Thomas G. Parisot
Charles E. Hart (1884-1972)	Elizabeth A. Bozzuto
J. Warren Upson (1903-1992)	Patrick W. Finn
John H. Cassidy, Jr.	Eric R. Brown
Donald McPartland	David J. Bozzuto
W. Fielding Secor	Victor E. Gatti
James R. Healey	
(Resident, Southbury Office)	

SPECIAL TAX COUNSEL

Bruce C. Johnson

COUNSEL

William J. Secor, Jr.	Milton A. Seymour

Attorneys for: The Mattatuck Museum; American Republican, Inc.; Hubbard-Hall, Inc.; The Siemon Co.; Engineered Sinterings and Plastics, Inc.; Boutin Industries; County Line Buick-Nissan, Inc.

For full biographical listings, see the Martindale-Hubbell Law Directory

TINLEY, NASTRI, RENEHAN & DOST (AV)

161 North Main Street, 06702
Telephone: 203-596-9030
Fax: 203-596-9036

Jeffrey J. Tinley	Richard P. Renehan
Robert Nastri, Jr.	Mark W. Dost

William T. Blake, Jr.

ASSOCIATE

Barbara W. Reynolds

Representative Clients: Center Capital Corp.; Gar-San Corp.; General Electric Capital Commercial Automotive Finance, Inc.; Mobil Oil Corp.; Teikyo Post University; The May Department Stores Company; Watertown Construction Company, Inc.

For full biographical listings, see the Martindale-Hubbell Law Directory

WEST HARTFORD, Hartford Co.

BERMAN, BOURNS & CURRIE, LLC (AV)

970 Farmington Avenue, P.O. Box 271837, 06127-1837
Telephone: 860-232-4471
Fax: 860-523-4605

(See Next Column)

BERMAN, BOURNS & CURRIE LLC—*Continued*

John A. Berman   Courtney B. Bourns
                    John K. Currie

Mary Beth Anderson   Robert W. Storm, Jr.

For full biographical listings, see the Martindale-Hubbell Law Directory

JOHN C. PETERS, P.C. (AV)

61 South Main Street, Suite 204, 06107
Telephone: 860-313-0255
Facsimile: 860-313-0257

John C. Peters

For full biographical listings, see the Martindale-Hubbell Law Directory

WESTPORT, Fairfield Co.

BLAZZARD, GRODD & HASENAUER, P.C. (AV)

943 Post Road East, P.O. Box 5108, 06881
Telephone: 203-226-7866
Telecopier: 203-454-4855
Hollywood, Florida Office: Suite 213, Oceanwalk Mall, 101 North Ocean Drive, 33019.
Telephone: 954-920-4864.
Facsimile: 954-920-6902. E-Mail: BGHFL@AOL.COM

Norse N. Blazzard   William E. Hasenauer
Leslie E. Grodd   Raymond A. O'Hara, III
Judith A. Hasenauer   Lynn Korman Stone
                Maureen M. Murphy

For full biographical listings, see the Martindale-Hubbell Law Directory

GOLDSTEIN AND PECK, P.C. (AV)

190 Main Street, P.O. Box 5031, 06881
Telephone: 203-226-7488
Telecopier: 203-226-6403
Bridgeport, Connecticut Office: 955 Main Street.
Telephone: 203-334-9421.
Telecopier: 203-334-6949.

William J. Kupinse, Jr.   G. Kenneth Bernhard
Walter A. Flynn, Jr.   Eugene E. Cederbaum

Representative Clients: Bee Publishing Co., Inc.; The Chase Manhattan Bank, N.A.; Fairfield County Medical Assn.; Great American Insurance Companies; Sequa Corporation; Inco, Ltd.; Physicians Health Services, Inc.; Town of Westport.

For full biographical listings, see the Martindale-Hubbell Law Directory

LEVETT, ROCKWOOD & SANDERS, PROFESSIONAL CORPORATION (AV)

33 Riverside Avenue, P.O. Box 5116, 06881
Telephone: 203-222-0885
Telecopier: 203-226-8025

David R. Levett   Sharon M. Schweitzer
John Sanders   Barbara A. Young
B. Lance Sauerteig   Steven M. Siegelaub
Madeleine F. Grossman   Marc J. Kurzman
James M. Barton   Suzanne B. Albani
Judy A. Rabkin   Peter H. Struzzi
Dorit Schutzengel Heimer   Edward B. Chansky
                Cheryl L. Johnson
                    OF COUNSEL
                William O. Rockwood, Jr.

Robin K. Higgins   Ernest C. Mysogland
                Patricia D. Weitzman

Representative Clients: Bankers Trust Company; Cannondale Corp.; Caradon, Inc.; Electrolux Corporation; Exxon Chemical Corporation; HealthSouth Corp.; Heyman Properties; Hospital of Saint Raphael; Marketing Corporation of America; St. Vincent's Medical Center.

For full biographical listings, see the Martindale-Hubbell Law Directory

STUART A. MCKEEVER (AV)

155 Post Road, East, 06880
Telephone: 203-227-4756
Fax: 203-454-2031
Reference: Fleet Bank.

For full biographical listings, see the Martindale-Hubbell Law Directory

WEISMAN & LUBELL (AV)

5 Sylvan Road South, P.O. Box 3184, 06880
Telephone: 203-226-8307
Telecopier: 203-221-7279

(See Next Column)

MEMBERS OF FIRM
Lawrence P. Weisman   Ellen B. Lubell

Debra B. Wolfert-Marino

For full biographical listings, see the Martindale-Hubbell Law Directory

WILLIMANTIC, Windham Co.

LANE, ROSEN AND STARKEY, P.C. (AV)

433 Valley Street, 06226
Telephone: 860-423-7761
Fax: 860-423-7764

Herbert A. Lane (1915-1989)   Jerome A. Rosen
                Noah H. Starkey

Reference: Fleet Bank.

For full biographical listings, see the Martindale-Hubbell Law Directory

WINSTED, Litchfield Co.

HOWD, LAVIERI & FINCH (AV)

682 Main Street, P.O. Box 1080, 06098
Telephone: 860-379-2761; 860-496-0889
1-800-556-9998
Fax: 860-379-5187; 860-738-4393
                MEMBERS OF FIRM
Hadleigh H. Howd (1896-1971)   Frank H. Finch, Jr.
Carmine R. Lavieri (1918-1984) Douglas K. O'Connell
David M. Cusick   Patrick E. Power, Jr.
                Bruce C. Schmidt

Representative Clients: Shawmut Bank, Connecticut, N.A.; Squire Hill Condominium Assn.; PTC Aerospace; D&M Construction Corp.; New England Bark Mulch; Winsted Savings Bank; Litchfield Bancorp.; Standard Cycle and Auto Supply Co.; Town of Norfolk Planning & Zoning Commission; Winsted Memorial Hospital.

For full biographical listings, see the Martindale-Hubbell Law Directory

DELAWARE

DOVER,* Kent Co.

* indicates certain Bar Register subscribers whose principal office is located elsewhere in the state and who have arranged for representation as a part of the state capital listings that follow

* MORRIS, JAMES, HITCHENS & WILLIAMS (AV)

Suite 202, 32 West Loockerman Street, 19904
Telephone: 302-678-8815
Telecopier: 302-678-9063
URL: http://www.morrisjames.com
Wilmington, Delaware Office: 222 Delaware Avenue. P.O. Box 2306, 19899-2306.
Telephone: 302-888-6800.
Telecopier: 302-571-1750.

RESIDENT PARTNER
Glenn E. Hitchens
RESIDENT ASSOCIATE
Mary L. Sutherland

For full biographical listings, see the Martindale-Hubbell Law Directory

PARKOWSKI, NOBLE & GUERKE, PROFESSIONAL ASSOCIATION (AV)

116 West Water Street, P.O. Box 598, 19903
Telephone: 302-678-3262
Telecopier: 302-678-9415

F. Michael Parkowski   Jeremy W. Homer
John W. Noble   John C. Andrade
I. Barry Guerke   Jonathan Eisenberg
Clay T. Jester   Dana J. Schaefer
                Mark F. Dunkle
                    OF COUNSEL
                George F. Gardner, III

Representative Clients: Delaware Solid Waste Authority; Cabe Associates (Consulting Engineers).
Approved Attorneys for: Ticor Title Insurance Co.
Reference: First National Bank of Wyoming.

For full biographical listings, see the Martindale-Hubbell Law Directory

Dover—Continued

* PRICKETT, JONES, ELLIOTT, KRISTOL & SCHNEE (AV)

26 The Green, 19901
Telephone: 302-674-3841
Telecopier: 302-674-5864
Email: attorneys@prickett.com *URL:* http://www.prickett.com
Wilmington, Delaware Office: 1310 King Street.
Telephone: 302-888-6500.
Kennett Square, Pennsylvania Office: 217 West State Street.
Telephone: 610-444-1573.

RESIDENT MEMBERS

Gary F. Dalton　　　　　　　　　Kevin M. Howard
William L. Witham, Jr.　　　　　　Gary F. Traynor

RESIDENT ASSOCIATES

John W. Paradee　　　　　　　　Rebecca D. Batson

For full biographical listings, see the Martindale-Hubbell Law Directory

SCHMITTINGER & RODRIGUEZ, PROFESSIONAL ASSOCIATION (AV)

414 South State Street, 19901
Telephone: 302-674-0140
FAX: 302-674-1830
Wilmington, Delaware Office: Suite 205, 1300 North Market Street.
Telephone: 302-652-3676.
Rehoboth Beach, Delaware Office: 4602 Highway One.
Telephone: 302-227-1400.
Odessa, Delaware Office: Odessa Professional Park, P.O. Box 626.
Telephone: 302-378-1697.
Telecopier: 302-378-1659.

Harold Schmittinger　　　　　　William W. Pepper, Sr.
Nicholas H. Rodriguez　　　　　Craig T. Eliassen
Paul H. Boswell　　　　　　　　Crystal L. Carey
John J. Schmittinger　　　　　　Scott E. Chambers
Bruce C. Ennis　　　　　　　　Mardi F. Pyott
Larry W. Fifer (Resident,　　　　John J. Sullivan, Jr. (Resident,
　Rehoboth Beach, Delaware)　　　Wilmington, Delaware)
Douglas B. Catts　　　　　　　Noel E. Primos
William D. Fletcher, Jr.　　　　　David A. Boswell (Resident,
William A. Denman　　　　　　　Wilmington, Delaware Office)
James T. Vaughn, Jr.　　　　　　Michele L. Procino
Catherine T. Hickey　　　　　　Walt F. Schmittinger
　　　　　　　Jeffrey J Clark

Representative Clients: CoreStates; Chesapeake Utilities Corp.; Travelers Insurance Co.; Dover Downs, Inc.; City of Dover.

For full biographical listings, see the Martindale-Hubbell Law Directory

GEORGETOWN,* Sussex Co.

YOUNG, CONAWAY, STARGATT & TAYLOR (AV)

110 West Pine Street, 19947
Telephone: 302-856-3571
Telecopy: 302-856-9338
Wilmington, Delaware Office: 11th Floor, Rodney Square North, P.O. Box 391.
Telephone: 302-571-6600.
Telecopy: 302-571-1253.

MEMBERS OF FIRM

H. James Conaway, Jr.　　　　　Craig A. Karsnitz (Resident)
　(1922-1990)

ASSOCIATES

E. Scott Bradley

For full biographical listings, see the Martindale-Hubbell Law Directory

WILMINGTON,* New Castle Co.

ASHBY & GEDDES (AV)

One Rodney Square, P.O. Box 1150, 19899
Telephone: 302-654-1888
Fax: 302-654-2067

MEMBERS OF FIRM

Lawrence C. Ashby　　　　　　Randall E. Robbins
James McC. Geddes　　　　　　Steven J. Balick
Stephen E. Jenkins　　　　　　Regina A. Iorii
　　　　　William P. Bowden

ASSOCIATES

Richard D. Heins　　　　　　　Steven T. Margolin
Philip Trainer, Jr.　　　　　　　Christopher S. Sontchi
Amy Arnott Quinlan　　　　　　John S. Grimm

For full biographical listings, see the Martindale-Hubbell Law Directory

BIGGS AND BATTAGLIA (AV)

1800 Mellon Bank Center, P.O. Box 1489, 19899-1489
Telephone: 302-655-9677

(See Next Column)

MEMBERS OF FIRM

Victor F. Battaglia　　　　　　Jeffrey S. Marlin
Alan W. Behringer　　　　　　Charles Slanina
Francis S. Babiarz　　　　　　Philip B. Bartoshesky
Robert D. Goldberg　　　　　　Victor F. Battaglia, Jr.
Robert K. Beste, Jr.　　　　　　Christopher J. Battaglia
　　　　　Linda F. Shopland

OF COUNSEL

John Biggs, III　　　　　　　　Gerard P. Kavanaugh, Sr.
　　　　　S. Bernard Ableman

For full biographical listings, see the Martindale-Hubbell Law Directory

CONNOLLY, BOVE, LODGE & HUTZ (AV)

1220 Market Street, P.O. Box 2207, 19899-2207
Telephone: 302-658-9141
Telecopier: 302-658-5614
URL: http://WWW.CBLHLAW.COM

Arthur G. Connolly (Emeritus)　　James J. Woods, Jr.
James M. Mulligan, Jr.　　　　　Collins J. Seitz, Jr.
Arthur G. Connolly, Jr.　　　　　Edward F. Eaton
Rudolf E. Hutz　　　　　　　　Charles J. Durante
Harold Pezzner　　　　　　　　Patricia Smink Rogowski
John D. Fairchild　　　　　　　Mary W. Bourke
　(Not admitted in DE)　　　　　Robert G. McMorrow, Jr.
Richard M. Beck　　　　　　　　(Not admitted in DE)
　(Not admitted in DE)　　　　　F. L. Peter Stone
Paul E. Crawford　　　　　　　R. Eric Hutz
Stanley C. Macel, III　　　　　　John C. Kairis
Thomas M. Meshbesher　　　　　Arthur G. Connolly, III
Henry E. Gallagher, Jr.　　　　　James D. Heisman
George Pazuniak　　　　　　　Ashley I. Pezzner
N. Richard Powers　　　　　　　William E. McShane
Richard David Levin　　　　　　　(Not admitted in DE)
John A. Clark, III　　　　　　　Anne Love Barnett
Jeffrey B. Bove　　　　　　　　Gerard M. O'Rourke

ASSOCIATES

Patricia L. Kelly　　　　　　　Julie S. Dvorak
　(Not admitted in DE)　　　　　Oleh V. Bilynski
　　　　　　　　　　　　　　　(Not admitted in DE)

OF COUNSEL

William E. Lambert　(Not admitted in DE)

For full biographical listings, see the Martindale-Hubbell Law Directory

DUANE, MORRIS & HECKSCHER (AV)

1201 Market Street, 19801
Telephone: 302-571-5550
Fax: 302-571-5560
Philadelphia, Pennsylvania Office: Suite 4200, One Liberty Place.
Telephone: 215-979-1000.
Fax: 215-979-1020.
Harrisburg, Pennsylvania Office: 305 North Front Street, 5th Floor, P.O. Box 1003.
Telephone: 717-237-5500.
Fax: 717-232-4015.
New York, N.Y. Office: Suite 3300, 122 East 42nd Street.
Telephone: 212-692-1000.
Fax: 212-692-1020.
Newark, New Jersey Office: Suite 1210, One Gateway Center.
Telephone: 201-733-9880.
Fax: 201-733-9881.
Wayne, Pennsylvania Office: Suite 300, 735 Chesterbrook Boulevard.
Telephone: 610-647-3555.
Fax: 610-640-2619.
Allentown, Pennsylvania Office: Suite 200, 968 Postal Road.
Telephone: 610-266-3650.
Fax: 610-266-3651.
Cherry Hill, New Jersey Office: Suite 340, 51 Haddonfield Road.
Telephone: 609-488-7300.
Fax: 609-488-7021.
Dover, Delaware Office: 314 South State Street.
Telephone: 302-736-0156.
Fax: 302-736-0336.

RESIDENT PARTNERS

David S. Swayze　　　　　　　James S. Green
Thomas P. Preston　　　　　　Joseph A. Fillip, Jr.
William E. Manning　　　　　　David C. Weiss
Daniel F. Lindley　　　　　　　Teresa K. D. Currier
Judith Nichols Renzulli　　　　　Carl J. Fernandes

RESIDENT ASSOCIATES

Richard A. Forsten　　　　　　Daniel B. Rath
Robert J. Valihura, Jr.　　　　　Adam G. Landis
Mark A. Morton　　　　　　　Mary Catherine Biondi
Bonnie Lynne Wolfgang　　　　Richard S. Cobb
Mary F. Caloway　　　　　　　Linda Joy Jennings
　　　　　Teri L. Thompson

For full biographical listings, see the Martindale-Hubbell Law Directory

Wilmington—Continued

McCARTER & ENGLISH (AV)

Mellon Bank Center, 919 Market Street, 19899
Telephone: 302-654-8010
Telecopier: 302-654-0795
Newark, New Jersey Office: Four Gateway Center, 100 Mulberry Street.
P.O. Box 652.
Telephone: 201-622-4444.
Telecopier: 201-624-7070.
Cable Address: "McCarter" Newark.
Cherry Hill, New Jersey Office: 1820 Chapel Avenue West, Suite 380.
Telephone: 609-662-8444.
Telecopier: 609-662-6203.
New York, New York Office: Suite 2247, One World Trade Center.
Telephone: 212-466-9018.
Telecopier: 212-432-6568.
Boca Raton, Florida Office: 2255 Glades Road, Suite 319-A.
Telephone: 407-994-6262.
Telecopier: 407-241-0798.
Philadelphia, Pennsylvania Office: One Commerce Square, 20005 Market Street, Suite 3250.
Telephone: 215-557-7700.
Telecopier: 215-557-6544.

RESIDENT PARTNERS

Robert B. Anderson   Paul A. Bradley

For full biographical listings, see the Martindale-Hubbell Law Directory

MORRIS, JAMES, HITCHENS & WILLIAMS (AV)

222 Delaware Avenue, P.O. Box 2306, 19899-2306
Telephone: 302-888-6800
Telecopier: 302-571-1750
URL: http://www.morrisjames.com
Dover, Delaware Office: Suite 202, 32 West Loockerman Street, 19904.
Telephone: 302-678-8815.
Telecopier: 302-678-9063.

MEMBERS OF FIRM

Henry N. Herndon, Jr.	Richard Galperin
George C. Hering, III	Steven R. Director
Grover C. Brown	Richard D. Kirk
Arden B. Engebretsen	Lewis H. Lazarus
William R. Hitchens, Jr.	Michael M. Ledyard
Richard P. Beck	Francis J. Jones, Jr.
Glenn E. Hitchens	Daniel P. McCollom
(Resident at Dover)	Barbara MacDonald
Edward M. McNally	Kent A. Jordan
Norris P. Wright	Robert L. Symonds, Jr.
James W. Semple	John D. Demmy
David H. Williams	Mary M. Culley
P. Clarkson Collins, Jr.	Joseph R. Slights, III

ASSOCIATES

Sherry C. McReynolds	Joseph C. Schoell
Michael J. Maimone	Eric D. Schwartz
(Not admitted in DE)	John T. Meli, Jr.
Neal C. Belgam	Matthew J. O'Toole
Norman M. Powell	Paul P. Rooney
Eileen K. Andersen	Michael A. Weidinger
Gretchen S. Knight	Mary L. Sutherland
Peter A. Pietra	(Resident at Dover)
Lewis C. Ledyard, III	Nancy Shane Rappaport

OF COUNSEL

Howard L. Williams   William F. Lynch, II
Alfred M. Isaacs

For full biographical listings, see the Martindale-Hubbell Law Directory

MORRIS, NICHOLS, ARSHT & TUNNELL (AV)

1201 North Market Street, P.O. Box 1347, 19899-1347
Telephone: 302-658-9200
Telecopier: 302-658-3989

MEMBERS OF FIRM

Richard L. Sutton	Donald F. Parsons, Jr.
Johannes R. Krahmer	Jack B. Blumenfeld
O. Francis Biondi	Donald Nelson Isken
Lewis S. Black, Jr.	Donald E. Reid
Paul P. Welsh	Denison H. Hatch, Jr.
William O. LaMotte, III	Thomas C. Grimm
Douglas E. Whitney	Kenneth J. Nachbar
William H. Sudell, Jr.	Andrew M. Johnston
Martin P. Tully	Mary B. Graham
Thomas Reed Hunt, Jr.	Michael Houghton
A. Gilchrist Sparks, III	Matthew B. Lehr
Richard D. Allen	John S. McDaniel
David Ley Hamilton	Thomas R. Pulsifer
John F. Johnston	Jon E. Abramczyk
Walter C. Tuthill	Alan J. Stone
	Louis G. Hering

(See Next Column)

ASSOCIATES

Rachel A. Dwares	Jeffrey R. Wolters
Frederick H. Alexander	Kendra S. Baker
R. Judson Scaggs, Jr.	Maryellen Noreika
William M. Lafferty	David J. Teklits
Andrea L. Rocanelli	S. Mark Hurd
Karen Jacobs Louden	Lucinda Cole Cucuzzella
Karen L. Pascale	(Not admitted in DE)
Elaine C. Reilly	Lisa K. Crossland
Donna L. Culver	(Not admitted in DE)
Julia Heaney	Stanford L. Stevenson, III
Jonathan I. Lessner	Katherine Randolph
Lisa B. Baeurle	Witherspoon
Robert J. Dehney	J. Andrew Huffman
(Not admitted in DE)	(Not admitted in DE)
Derek C. Abbott	

COUNSEL

S. Samuel Arsht	Hugh M. Morris (1878-1966)
Andrew B. Kirkpatrick, Jr.	Alexander L. Nichols
David A. Drexler	(1906-1985)
Walter L. Pepperman, II	James M. Tunnell, Jr.
S. Maynard Turk	(1910-1986)

Representative Clients: The Coca Cola Co.; Delaware River and Bay Authority; Ford Motor Co.; J.P. Morgan Delaware; Longwood Foundation, Inc.; Rollins, Inc.; Texaco Inc.

For full biographical listings, see the Martindale-Hubbell Law Directory

PEPPER, HAMILTON & SCHEETZ (AV)

1201 Market Street, Suite 1600, P.O. Box 1709, 19899-1709
Telephone: 302-777-6500
Telecopy: 302-656-8865
Philadelphia, Pennsylvania Office: 3000 Two Logan Square, Eighteenth and Arch Streets, 19103-2799.
Telephone: 215-981-4000.
Fax: 215-981-4750.
Washington, D.C. Office: 1300 Nineteenth Street, N.W., 20036-1685.
Telephone: 202-828-1200.
Fax: 202-828-1665.
Detroit, Michigan Office: 100 Renaissance Center, 36th Floor, 48243-1157.
Telephone: 313-259-7110.
Fax: 313-259-7926.
New York, New York Office: 450 Lexington Avenue, Suite 1600, 10017-3904.
Telephone: 212-878-3800.
Fax: 212-878-3835.
Pittsburgh, Pennsylvania Office: One Mellon Bank Center, 50th Floor, 500 Grant Street, 15219-2502.
Telephone: 412-454-5000.
Fax: 412-281-0717.
Harrisburg, Pennsylvania Office: 200 One Keystone Plaza, North Front and Market Streets, P.O. Box 1181, 17108-1181.
Telephone: 717-255-1155.
Fax: 717-238-0575.
Berwyn, Pennsylvania Office: 1235 Westlakes Drive, Suite 400, 19312-2401.
Telephone: 610-640-7800.
Fax: 610-640-7835.
Cherry Hill, New Jersey Office: LibertyView Building, Suite 500, 457 Haddonfield Road, 08002-2002.
Telephone: 609-317-9530.
Fax: 609-317-9238.
London, England Office: 9 Haywards Place, EC1R 0EE.
Telephone: 011-44-171-628-1122.
Fax: 011-44-171-628-6010.
Moscow, Russia Office: 19-27 Grokholsky Pereulok, 129010.
Telephone: 011-7-095-280-4493.
Fax: 011-7-095-280-5518.

PARTNERS

Alfred J. D'Angelo, Jr.	Richard P. Eckman
(Managing Partner,	M. Duncan Grant
Wilmington Office)	David B. Stratton
James J. Sullivan, Jr.	

ASSOCIATES

Daniel V. Folt	Christopher J. Lamb
David M. Fournier	Sean P. McDevitt
Lia S. Grassi	Barbara E. McDonald
(Not admitted in DE)	(Not admitted in DE)
Kathryn A. Kelly	Benjamin Strauss

For full biographical listings, see the Martindale-Hubbell Law Directory

POTTER ANDERSON & CORROON (AV)

350 Delaware Trust Building, P.O. Box 951, 19899-0951
Telephone: 302-984-6000
FAX: 302-658-1192
URL: HTTP://ATTYS.PACDELAWARE.COM

(See Next Column)

POTTER ANDERSON & CORROON, *Wilmington—Continued*

MEMBERS OF FIRM

Charles S. Crompton, Jr.	John E. James
Robert K. Payson	W. Harding Drane, Jr.
Leonard S. Togman	Mary E. Copper
Richard E. Poole	W. Laird Stabler, III
Michael D. Goldman	Richard L. Horwitz
James F. Burnett	William J. Marsden, Jr.
Daniel F. Wolcott, Jr.	Michael B. Tumas
David J. Garrett	Kathleen Furey McDonough
Charles S. McDowell	Laurie Selber Silverstein
David B. Brown	Peter J. Walsh, Jr.
Somers S. Price, Jr.	Stephen C. Norman
Donald J. Wolfe, Jr.	Arthur L. Dent
Gregory A. Inskip	Harold I. Salmons, III
David J. Baldwin	William R. Denny

COUNSEL

Robert P. Barnett	W. Laird Stabler, Jr.

David L. Baumberger

OF COUNSEL

William Poole	Hugh Corroon
John P. Sinclair	Joseph H. Geoghegan
Blaine T. Phillips	Richard L. McMahon

SENIOR ATTORNEY

Frederick H. Altergott

ASSOCIATES

Philip A. Rovner	Michael A. Pittenger
Peter L. Tracey	Colleen E. Hicks
Jennifer Gimler Brady	Michael S. McGinniss
Scott E. Waxman	Andrew McK. Jefferson
Joanne Ceballos	William A. Hazeltine
Wendy K. Voss	Eileen M. Filliben
Kevin R. Shannon	(Not admitted in DE)
Linda S. Kranitz	Judy Royer May
Todd L. Goodman	Emilie Rajaratnam

Andrew T. O'Neill

Counsel for: Delaware Trust Capital Management, Inc.; ConRail; Delmarva Power & Light Co.; Diamond State Telephone Co.; Hercules Inc.; Corporation Trust Co.; General Motors Corp.; Chrysler Corp.; Citicorp.

For full biographical listings, see the Martindale-Hubbell Law Directory

---

PRICKETT, JONES, ELLIOTT, KRISTOL & SCHNEE (AV)

1310 King Street, P.O. Box 1328, 19899-1328
Telephone: 302-888-6500
Telecopier: 302-658-8111; 658-7257
Email: attorneys@prickett.com *URL:* http://www.prickett.com
Dover, Delaware Office: 26 The Green.
Telephone: 302-674-3841.
Kennett Square, Pennsylvania Office: 217 West State Street.
Telephone: 610-444-1573.

MEMBERS OF FIRM

William S. Prickett (1862-1926)	David E. Brand
William Prickett (1894-1964)	William L. Witham, Jr.
William Prickett	(Resident at Dover Office)
Richard I. G. Jones	Dennis Spivack
Wayne L. Elliott	Timothy A. Casey
Daniel M. Kristol	Wayne J. Carey
Carl Schnee	Paul M. Lukoff
Walter P. McEvilly, Jr.	Elizabeth M. McGeever
Mason E. Turner, Jr.	Kevin M. Howard
James L. Holzman	(Resident at Dover Office)
John H. Small	William J. Martin, III
Richard P. S. Hannum	Ralph K. ("Dirk") Durstein, III
George H. Seitz, III	W. Wade W. Scott
Gary F. Dalton	Joseph Grey
(Resident at Dover Office)	Ellisa Opstbaum Habbart
Michael Hanrahan	Gary F. Traynor
	(Resident at Dover Office)

COUNSEL

Benjamin J. Berger

ASSOCIATES

Chandlee Johnson Kuhn	Thomas A. Mullen
April Caso Ishak	Patricia Ann Pyles
John W. Paradee	Rebecca D. Batson
(Resident at Dover Office)	(Resident at Dover Office)
J. Kate Stickles	Julie Ann Sandler
Ronald A. Brown, Jr.	F. Peter Conaty, Jr.
Bruce E. Jameson	Daniel P. Conneen
Gretchen Ann Bender	Catherine M. Behl
John E. Tracey	Heather D. Jefferson

Representative Clients: Browning-Ferris Industries; Computer Associates International; Delmarva Power & Light; Nationwide.

For full biographical listings, see the Martindale-Hubbell Law Directory

---

RICHARDS, LAYTON & FINGER, P.A. (AV)

One Rodney Square, P.O. Box 551, 19899
Telephone: 302-658-6541
Telecopier: 302-658-6548

Richard J. Abrams	Samuel A. Nolen
Charles F. Richards, Jr.	Thomas A. Beck
Thomas P. Sweeney	John A. Parkins, Jr.
Pierre S. du Pont	Gregory P. Williams
Robert H. Richards, III	Paul M. Altman
R. Franklin Balotti	Gregory V. Varallo
Martin I. Lubaroff	Mark J. Gentile
Richard G. Elliott, Jr.	Robert J. Krapf
Wendell Fenton	Kevin G. Abrams
Allen M. Terrell, Jr.	Eric A. Mazie
Glenn C. Kenton	Robert W. Whetzel
Richard G. Bacon	W. Donald Sparks, II
Stephen E. Herrmann	C. Stephen Bigler
Julian H. Baumann, Jr.	Charles Malcolm Cochran, IV
Daniel L. Klein	Anne C. Foster
Donald A. Bussard	Cynthia Deans Kaiser
William J. Wade	Daniel A. Dreisbach
Thomas L. Ambro	James Gerard Leyden, Jr.
Jesse A. Finkelstein	Frederick L. Cottrell, III

Bernard J. Kelley

Karen C. Bifferato	Joseph G. Lisicky
Mark D. Collins	Jeffrey L. Moyer
Doneene Keemer Damon	Kimberly Konrad Murphy
Claudia A. DelGross	Jon L. Peterson
Raymond J. DiCamillo	Srinivas M. Raju
Francis DiGiovanni	David L. Renauld
John T. Dorsey	Helen M. Richards
Matthew J. Ferretti	Janine M. Salomone
David A. Firn	Todd Schiltz
Matthew E. Fischer	Lisa A. Schmidt
Brigitte V. Fresco	Russell C. Silberglied
William J. Haubert	Robert J. Stearn, Jr.
Jennifer Lahn Janss	Hillary C. Steinberg
(Not admitted in DE)	Saul D. Treiman
Richard I.G. Jones, Jr.	Catherine G. Wagner
Peter S. Kirsh	Helen L. Winslow
Gregory W. Ladner	William A. Yemc

General Counsel for: Wilmington Trust Co.
Local Counsel for: General Motors Corp.; Shell Oil Co.; Aetna Group; Dean Witter Reynolds, Inc.; Gulf & Western Industries Inc.

For full biographical listings, see the Martindale-Hubbell Law Directory

---

SKADDEN, ARPS, SLATE, MEAGHER & FLOM (AV)

One Rodney Square, P.O. Box 636, 19899
Telephone: 302-651-3000
Fax: 302-651-3001
New York, New York Office: 919 Third Avenue, 10022.
Telephone: 212-735-3000.
Fax: 212-735-2000; 212-735-2001.
Telex: 645899 Skarslaw.
Boston, Massachusetts Office: One Beacon Street, 02108.
Telephone: 617-573-4800.
Fax: 617-573-4822.
Washington, D.C. Office: 1440 New York Avenue, N.W., 20005.
Telephone: 202-371-7000.
Fax: 202-393-5760.
Los Angeles, California Office: 300 South Grand Avenue, 90071.
Telephone: 213-687-5000.
Fax: 213-687-5600.
Chicago, Illinois Office: 333 West Wacker Drive, 60606.
Telephone: 312-407-0700.
Fax: 312-407-0411.
San Francisco, California Office: Four Embarcadero Center, 94111.
Telephone: 415-984-6400.
Fax: 415-984-2698.
Houston, Texas Office: 1600 Smith Street, Suite 4460, 77002.
Telephone: 713-655-5100.
Fax: 713-655-5181.
Newark, New Jersey Office: One Newark Center, 07102.
Telephone: 201-639-6800.
Fax: 201-639-6858.
Tokyo, Japan Office: 403, ABS Building, 2-4-16 Kudan Minami, Chiyoda-ku, Tokyo 102.
Telephone: 81-3-3221-9738.
Fax: 81-3-3221-9753.
London, England Office: 25 Bucklersbury EC4N 8DA.
Telephone: 011-44-171-248-9929.
Fax: 011-44-171-489-8533.
Hong Kong Office: 30/F Peregrine Tower, Lippo Centre, 89 Queensway, Central.
Telephone: 011-852-2820-0700.
Fax: 011-852-2820-0727.
Sydney, New South Wales, 2000, Australia Office: Level 26-State Bank Centre, 52 Martin Place.
Telephone: 011-61-2-9224-6000.
Fax: 011-61-2-9224-6044.

(See Next Column)

SKADDEN, ARPS, SLATE, MEAGHER & FLOM—*Continued*

Toronto, Ontario Office: Suite 1820, North Tower, P.O. Box 189, Royal Bank Plaza, M5J 2J4.
Telephone: 416-777-4700.
Fax: 416-777-4747.
Paris, France Office: 105 rue du Faubourg Saint-Honoré, 75008.
Telephone: 011-33-1-40-75-44-44.
Fax: 011-33-1-49-53-09-99.
Brussels, Belgium Office: 523 avenue Louise, Box 30, 1050.
Telephone: 011-32-2-648-7666.
Fax: 011-32-2-640-3032.
Frankfurt, am Main, Germany Office: MesseTurm, 27th Floor, 60308.
Telephone: 011-49-69-9757-3000.
Fax: 011-49-69-9757-3050.
Beijing, China Office: East Wing Office, Level 4, China World Trade Center, No. 1 Jian Guo Men Wai Avenue, 100004.
Telephone: 011-86-10-6505-5511.
Fax: 011-86-10-6505-5522.
Prague, Czech Republic Office: Husova 5, 110 00, Prague 1.
Telephone: 011-42-2-2424-8526.
Fax: 011-42-2-2424-8566.
Moscow, Russia Office: Pleteshkovsky, Pereulok 3/2, 107005.
Telephone: 011-7-501-940-2304.
Fax: 011-7-501-940-2511.
Singapore, Singapore Office: 9 Temasek Boulevard, Suite 29-01, Suntec City Tower Two, Singapore, 038989.
Telephone: 011-65-434-2900.
Fax: 011-65-434-2988.

PARTNERS

Steven J. Rothschild	Thomas J. Allingham II
Rodman Ward, Jr.	Anthony W. Clark
Richard L. Easton	Robert B. Pincus
Edward P. Welch	Marc B. Tucker

Patricia Moran Chuff

OF COUNSEL

Irving S. Shapiro

SPECIAL COUNSEL

Randolph K. Herndon	Andrew J. Turezyn

ASSOCIATES

Curtis S. Alva	Gregg M. Galardi
Allison L. Amorison	Jaya B. Gokhalé
Joseph M. Asher	R. Michael Lindsey
Karen M. Bab	Thomas G Macauley
Kevin F. Brady	Kevin Michael Maloy
Mark S. Chehi	Kathleen T. Miller
Anne E. Connolly	Herbert W. Mondros
(Not admitted in DE)	Jeanene F. Patterson
Ronald J. Fisher	Cathy L. Reese
(Not admitted in DE)	Robert S. Saunders

For full biographical listings, see the Martindale-Hubbell Law Directory

---

SMITH, KATZENSTEIN & FURLOW (AV)

The Corporate Plaza, 800 Delaware Avenue, P.O. Box 410, 19899
Telephone: 302-652-8400
Fax: 302-652-8405

MEMBERS OF FIRM

Craig B. Smith	Susan L. Parker
Robert J. Katzenstein	Laurence V. Cronin
David A. Jenkins	Brett D. Fallon
Anne E. Bookout	Stephen M. Miller

Joanne M. Shalk	Kathleen M. Miller

COUNSEL

Charles E. Butler

OF COUNSEL

Clark W. Furlow

For full biographical listings, see the Martindale-Hubbell Law Directory

---

THEISEN, LANK, MULFORD & GOLDBERG, P.A. (AV)

Ninth Floor, One Commerce Center, P.O. Box 1470, 19899
Telephone: 302-656-7712
Fax: 302-655-0923
Email: Theisen@delcorp.com *URL:* http://www.delcorp.theisen.com

Aubrey B. Lank	Steven D. Goldberg
John G. Mulford	Michael J. Goodrick

David S. Lank

Richard L. Abbott

OF COUNSEL

Vincent A. Theisen (Retired)

References: Wilmington Trust Co.; PNC Bank.

For full biographical listings, see the Martindale-Hubbell Law Directory

---

WILLIAMS, HERSHMAN & WISLER, P.A. (AV)

Suite 600, One Commerce Center, Twelfth and Orange Streets, P.O. Box 511, 19899-0511
Telephone: 302-575-0873
Telecopier: 302-575-1642

David Nicol Williams	Jeffrey C. Wisler
Douglas M. Hershman	Barbara Snapp Danberg

References: Wilmington Trust Co.; PNC Bank.

For full biographical listings, see the Martindale-Hubbell Law Directory

---

YOUNG, CONAWAY, STARGATT & TAYLOR (AV)

Eleventh Floor, Rodney Square North, P.O. Box 391, 19899-0391
Telephone: 302-571-6600
Telecopy: 302-571-1253
Georgetown, Delaware Office: 110 West Pine Street.
Telephone: 302-856-3571.
Telecopy: 302-856-9338.

MEMBERS OF FIRM

H. Albert Young (1904-1982)	Barry M. Willoughby
H. James Conaway, Jr.	Josy W. Ingersoll
(1922-1990)	Anthony G. Flynn
Bruce M. Stargatt	Jerome K. Grossman
Richard H. May	Eugene A. DiPrinzio
Stuart B. Young	James L. Patton, Jr.
Ben T. Castle	Robert L. Thomas
Edward B. Maxwell, 2nd	William D. Johnston
Sheldon A. Weinstein	Timothy J. Snyder
Arthur Inden	Laura Davis Jones
Sheldon N. Sandler	Bruce L. Silverstein
Richard A. Levine	William W. Bowser
Richard A. Zappa	Larry J. Tarabicos
Frederick William Iobst	Richard A. DiLiberto, Jr.
David C. McBride	Melanie K. Sharp
Richard H. Morse	Cassandra Faline Kaminski
Joseph M. Nicholson	Richard J. A. Popper
John Vincent Alexander	Jan R. Jurden

David W. O'Connor

OF COUNSEL

William F. Taylor

ASSOCIATES

Robert S. Brady	James P. Hughes, Jr.
Janet Z. Charlton	Martin S. Lessner
Scott D. Cousins	Omar Y. McNeill
Matthew P. Denn	Brian R. Murphy
Mark I. Duedall	Sasson David Peress
Teresa C. Fariss	Brent C. Shaffer
Lisa B. Goodman	Brendan Linehan Shannon
Craig D. Grear	John W. Shaw
Edwin J. Harron	Donna L. Smith
Scott A. Holt	Joel A. Waite
Timothy Jay Houseal	Neilli Mullen Walsh

Natalie S. Wolf

GEORGETOWN, DELAWARE OFFICE

RESIDENT PARTNERS

Craig A. Karsnitz

ASSOCIATES

E. Scott Bradley

For full biographical listings, see the Martindale-Hubbell Law Directory

---

DISTRICT OF COLUMBIA

WASHINGTON, D.C. Co.

* indicates certain Bar Register subscribers, in cities of comparable size and importance, who maintain an additional office in Washington, D.C. and who have arranged for representation as a part of the Washington, D.C. listings that follow

---

*** AKIN, GUMP, STRAUSS, HAUER & FELD, L.L.P.** (AV)

A Registered Limited Liability Partnership including Professional Corporations
1333 New Hampshire Avenue, N.W., Suite 400, 20036
Telephone: 202-887-4000
FAX: 202-887-4288
Dallas, Texas Office: 1700 Pacific Avenue, Suite 4100.
Telephone: 214-969-2800.
FAX: 214-969-4343.
Austin, Texas Office: 1900 Frost Bank Plaza, 816 Congress Avenue.
Telephone: 512-499-6200.
Fax: 512-499-6290.
San Antonio, Texas Office: 300 Convent Street, Suite 1500.
Telephone: 210-270-0800.

(See Next Column)

AKIN, GUMP, STRAUSS, HAUER & FELD L.L.P., *Washington—Continued*

Houston, Texas Office: 1900 Pennzoil Place-South Tower, 711 Louisiana Street.
Telephone: 713-220-5800.
New York, New York Office: 399 Park Avenue, 22nd Floor.
Telephone: 212-872-1000.
Fax: 212-872-1002.
Philadelphia, Pennsylvania Office: Suite 3600, One Liberty Place, 1650 Market Street.
Telephone: 215-979-1980.
Fax: 215-979-1981.
Brussels, Belgium Office: Akin, Gump, Strauss, Hauer & Feld, 65 Avenue Louise, P.B. #7, 1050.
Telephone: (+32 2) 535-29-11.
Moscow, Russia Office: Bolshoi Sukharevsky Pereulok 26, Building 1.
Telephone: 011/7-095-974-2411.
Fax: 011/7-095-974-2412.

MEMBERS OF FIRM

Donald C. Alexander	Roy P. Lessy, Jr.
David C. Allen (P.C.)	Lawrence D. Levien (P.C.)
Edward John Allera (P.C.)	Donald R. Livingston
Richard N Appel (P.C.)	Jorge Lopez, Jr. (P.C.)
Clinton R. Batterton	Terence J. Lynam (P.C.)
Andrew G. Berg	Mark J. MacDougall
Janet C. Boyd (P.C.)	Patrick F. J. Macrory (P.C.)
Cheryl C. Burke (P.C.)	Michael J. Madigan (P.C.)
David P. Callet (P.C.)	Michael S. Mandel
Patricia A. Casey (P.C.)	Michael S. Marcus (P.C.)
James W. Cicconi (P.C.)	Roger J. Marzulla (P.C.)
Joel M. Cohn (P.C.)	R. Bruce McLean
Warren E. Connelly (P.C.)	Bruce S. Mendelsohn
Tom W. Davidson (P.C.)	Michael J. Mueller (P.C.)
Smith W. Davis (P.C.)	Daniel L. Nash
Sylvia A. de Leon (P.C.)	L. Kirk O'Donnell
James P. Denvir, III	David B. Palmer (P.C.)
Frank J. Donatelli	Russell W. Parks, Jr., (P.C.)
David A. Donohoe (P.C.)	Duane H. Pellervo
Marilyn L. Doria	Anthony T. Pierce
John M. Dowd (P.C.)	Robert G. Pinco (P.C.)
Jeffry R. Dwyer (P.C.)	Alexander Hartley Platt
David H. Eisenstat	Donald R. Pongrace (P.C.)
Courtenay Ellis	Michael Quigley
Joseph P. Esposito (P.C.)	Dennis M. Race (P.C.)
Cheryl Adams Falvey	Franz R. Rassman (P.C.)
Mark P. Fitzsimmons (P.C.)	Richard R. Rivers (P.C.)
Thomas S. Foley	Steven R. Ross
David Geanacopoulos	Jerry E. Rothrock
Avrum M. Goldberg (P.C.)	Edward L. Rubinoff (P.C.)
Larry S. Gondelman	George R. Salem (P.C.)
Spencer S. Griffith	Stanley J. Samorajczyk (P.C.)
Paul E. Gutermann	Dianne H. Sanford
Scott M. Heimberg (P.C.)	Randall L. Sarosdy
Frank H. Henneburg	Sanford M. Saunders, Jr. (P.C.)
Paul B. Hewitt (P.C.)	Donald E. Segal (P.C.)
Laurence J. Hoffman	Earl L. Segal (P.C.)
Helen M. Hubbard	Jeffrey K. Sherwood (P.C.)
William G. Hundley	Valerie A. Slater
Howard B. Jacobson (P.C.)	Roxane N. Sokolove
Joel Jankowsky (P.C.)	Jonathan S. Spaeth
Owen M. Johnson, Jr., (P.C.)	C. Fairley Spillman (P.C.)
Ronald M. Johnson (P.C.)	Robert S. Strauss (P.C.)
Vernon E. Jordan, Jr.	Larry E. Tanenbaum (P.C.)
Daniel Joseph (P.C.)	L. Kay Tatum
Donald Michael Kaye	Henry A. Terhune
Sukhan Kim	W. Randolph Teslik (P.C.)
Merrill L. Kramer (P.C.)	Margaret L. Tobey (P.C.)
James C. Langdon, Jr., (P.C.)	Charles L. Warren (P.C.)
Malcolm Lassman (P.C.)	Richard L. Wyatt, Jr. (P.C.)
Clifford J. Zatz (P.C.)	

ASSOCIATES

Sam J. Alberts	Michael L. Converse
Paige S. Anderson	Colleen M. Coyle
Todd S. Babbitz	Julie J. Crain
Connie N. Bertram	Anita M. Cream
William A. Bianco	John C. Crespo
William F. Birchfield III	Sean G. D'Arcy
John M. Bradham	Barbara J. Deakin
Cindy M. Bryton	Stacy R. Dees
Kris O. Carter	(Not admitted in DC)
David A. Catania	Jacqueline R. Depew
(Not admitted in DC)	Thomas E. Digan
Kimberly Hincken Chamberlain	Alexander Drew
Margaret D. Chisholm	Dmitri I. Dubograev
Anne Clark Christman	Eugene E. Elder
Patrick J. Christmas, II	William J. Farah
Kerwin Chung	Robin A. Fastenau
Robert J. Cicero	Shari L. Fleishman
(Not admitted in DC)	Vicki Scheer Foster
M. Lisbeth Coen	Edwin P. Geils
Robert S. Collins	Brian S. Gleicher
Marlene M. Colucci	Alison Leigh Gray
Maryellen Connor	Tracy Greer

(See Next Column)

ASSOCIATES (Continued)

Kelly Compton Grems	Tracy B. McKibben
Stefan A. Hagerup	(Not admitted in DC)
Naomi Joy Levan Halpern	Thomas P. McLish
Sarah L. Harpham	Melissa Heitmann McNiven
Michele L. Harrington	Luis R. Mejia
Gary A. Heimberg	James E. Mendenhall
Brian A. Heller	Robert L. Miller
(Not admitted in DC)	Margaret K. Minister
Nick A. Henderson	John N. Moore
Andrew M. Herzig	Jill Morganbesser
(Not admitted in DC)	(Not admitted in DC)
Steven M. Hilton	Alfred E. Mottur
Katherine M. Ho	James J. Murphy
Gary S. Hulsey	Rebecca A. Naser
Cynthia C. Humphries	Robin M. Nuschler
Michael J. Huppe	David J. Ohrenstein
(Not admitted in DC)	James C. Osborne, Jr.
John R. Jacob	Amy E. Overton
Jennifer Jacobsen	Michael P. Panagrossi
(Not admitted in DC)	Evangeline Paschal
Charles W. Johnson, IV	(Not admitted in DC)
James L. Johnson, Jr.	J. Steven Patterson
Craig Naveen Kakarla	(Not admitted in DC)
(Not admitted in DC)	Laurent C. Pavageau
Elizabeth A. Kandravy	Phuong N. Pham
Jonathan E. Kapp	Richard J. Rabin
Kathleen A. Kenealy	Georgia C. Ravitz
C. Michele Kirk	Michael S. Ray
(Not admitted in DC)	Laura M. Reifschneider
Julie A. Klusza	William F. Reynolds, Jr.
(Not admitted in DC)	Lee Harriss Roberts
Alexander Kogan	Edward M. Rogers
Dionne L. Koller	Matthew A. Rossi
David C. Kully	Paul D. Rubin
Rajat Kumar	Robert Salcido
Imtiaz T. Ladak	Richard P. Schlegel
Lisa F. Lazarus	Wynn H. Segall
Michael T. Lempres	Wendy E. Sheldon
Robert G. Lian, Jr.	(Not admitted in DC)
Alan S. Macdonald	Lara K. Shelesky
Kathryn D. MacKinnon	Elizabeth Wells Skaggs
Lori A. Manca	Anthony W. Swisher
Jennifer Abbe Manner	Joseph A. Turzi
Demetrios J. Marantis	T. Cy Walker
Mark D. Marderosian	Mary Somerville Welch
Stephanie J. Markiewicz	Neil J. Welch, Jr.
Daniel F. McInnis	F. Robert Wheeler III

OF COUNSEL

Ronald R. Adee	Stark Ritchie
Micha Barach	Michael Schwarz
Linda S. Broyhill	Barney J. Skladany, Jr.
George H. Lawrence	Dawn E. Starr
(Not admitted in DC)	Rosemary Stewart
Vladimir Lechtman	Steven A. Weiler
William E. Potts, Jr.	Samuel Wolff

Mark M. Yacura

SENIOR COUNSEL

Kenneth D. Alderfer	Richard P. Bonsignore

Mary Beth Rosenthal

SENIOR ADVISOR

Harry H. Schwarz

For full biographical listings, see the Martindale-Hubbell Law Directory

ALLEN, JOHNSON, ALEXANDER & KARP, P.A. (AV)

1707 L Street, N.W., Suite 1050, 20036
Telephone: 202-828-4141
Fax: 202-429-8798
Baltimore, Maryland Office: Suite 1540, 100 East Pratt Street.
Telephone: 410-727-5000.

D'Ana E. Johnson

George B. Breen	Gregory James Dumark

Representative Clients: Scottsdale Insurance Co.; Nautilus Insurance Co.; Jefferson Insurance Co.; Liberty Mutual Insurance Co.; Avis Rent-A-Car; Otis Elevator Co.; Montgomery Elevator Co.; Admiral Insurance Co.; Local Government Insurance Trust; Lancer Insurance Co.

For full biographical listings, see the Martindale-Hubbell Law Directory

＊ ANDERSON KILL & OLICK, L.L.P. (AV)

2000 Pennsylvania Avenue, N.W. Suite 7500, 20006
Telephone: 202-728-3100
Telecopier: 202-728-3199
Email: akodc@andersonkill.com *URL:* http://www.andersonkill.com
New York, N.Y. Office: Anderson Kill & Olick, P.C., 1251 Avenue of the Americas.
Telephone: 212-278-1000.
Fax: 212-278-1733 and 212-953-7249.

(See Next Column)

ANDERSON KILL & OLICK L.L.P.—*Continued*

Philadelphia, Pennsylvania Office: Anderson Kill & Olick, P.C., 1600 Market Street.
Telephone: 215-568-4202.
Fax: 215-568-4573.
Newark, New Jersey Office: Anderson Kill & Olick. One Gateway Center, Suite 901.
Telephone: 201-642-5858.
Fax: 201-621-6361.
San Francisco, California Office: Anderson Kill & Olick. One Sansome Street, Suite 1610.
Telephone: 415-677-1450.
Fax: 415-677-1475.
Phoenix, Arizona Office: Anderson Kill & Olick. One Renaissance Square, Two North Central, Suite 1910.
Telephone: 602-252-0002.
Fax: 602-252-0003.
Tucson, Arizona Office: Anderson Kill & Olick. Bank of America Plaza, 33 North Stone Avenue, Suite 1825.
Telephone: 520-822-8299.
Fax: 520-882-9299.

Michael P. Allen	Rhonda D. Orin
(Not admitted in DC)	Lorelie S. Masters
Koorosh Talieh	

For full biographical listings, see the Martindale-Hubbell Law Directory

* ANDREWS & KURTH L.L.P. (AV)

A Registered Limited Liability Partnership
Suite 200, 1701 Pennsylvania Avenue, N.W., 20006
Telephone: 202-662-2700
Telecopier: 202-662-2739
Houston, Texas Office: Suite 4200, 600 Travis, 77002.
Telephone: 713-220-4200.
Telecopier: 713-220-4285. E-Mail: webmaster@andrews-kurth.com.
Dallas, Texas Office: Suite 4400, 1601 Elm Street.
Telephone: 214-979-4400.
Telecopier: 214-979-4401.
The Woodlands, Texas Office: Suite 150, 2170 Buckthorne Place, 77380.
Telephone: 713-220-4801.
Telecopier: 713-364-9538. E-Mail: hightech@andrews-kurth.com.
Los Angeles, California Office: Suite 4200, 601 South Figueroa Street.
Telephone: 213-896-3100.
Telecopier: 213-896-3137.
New York, N.Y. Office: 425 Lexington Avenue, 10017.
Telephone: 212-850-2800.
Telecopier: 212-850-2929.
London, England Office: 2 Creed Court, 5-11 Ludgate Hill, EC4M 7AA.
Telephone: 0171-236-3456.
Telefax: 0171-236-4276.

MEMBERS OF FIRM

James A. Blalock III	Gregory J. Marich
Constance Collins Davis	Jay G. Martin
Michael J. Fremuth	Mary Anne Mason
Catherine S. Gallagher	T. Rush Moody, Jr.
Richard C. Green	Jennifer M. Porter
Anthony J. Ivancovich	Thomas R. Salley, III
Judy A. Johnson	Gilbert P. Sperling
Michael L. Kessler	Mark F. Sundback
Thomas R. Kline	Bruce A. Templeton
Kenneth L. Wiseman	

SENIOR COUNSEL

C. Howard Hardesty, Jr.

OF COUNSEL

Hu A. Benton	Thomas E. Starnes
Douglas V. Rigler	Craig B. Young
Robert D. Simon	
(Not admitted in DC)	

ASSOCIATES

Dawn M. Becker	Kristina Ann Mack
Christine R. Bianchine	(Not admitted in DC)
A. Lindsey Crawford	Kenneth M. Minesinger
Charles M. Crout	(Not admitted in DC)
(Not admitted in DC)	Julie Nolan Papa
Matthew T. Gould	(Not admitted in DC)
(Not admitted in DC)	Shemin V. Proctor
Maureen Z. Hurley	Scott A. Richie
Amy C. Kwak	Sheila F. Rock
Robert M. Lamkin	(Not admitted in DC)
(Not admitted in DC)	Peter J. Thompson

For full biographical listings, see the Martindale-Hubbell Law Directory

ARENT FOX KINTNER PLOTKIN & KAHN (AV)

1050 Connecticut Avenue, N.W., 20036-5339
Telephone: 202-857-6000
Fax: 202-857-6395
Bethesda, Maryland Office: Suite 700, 7475 Wisconsin Avenue.
Telephone: 301-654-3070.
Fax: 202-857-6395.

(See Next Column)

McLean, Virginia Office: Suite 460, 2010 Corporate Ridge.
Telephone: 703-847-5800.
Fax: 202-857-6395.
New York City Office: 1675 Broadway, 25th Floor.
Telephone: 212-484-3900.
Telecopier: 212-484-3990.
Budapest Representative Office: EMKE Building, Rakoczi utca 42, 1072 Budapest, Hungary.
Telephones: (36-1) 269 0596; 269 0597.
Fax: (36-1) 269 0599.
Kingdom of Saudi Arabia Office: Law Offices of His Royal Highness Prince Saad Al Faisel Bin Abdul Aziz, P.O. Box 15836, Jeddah 21454, Kingdom of Saudi Arabia.
Telephone: (966-2) 651-9373.
Facsimile: (966-2) 651-9465.

MEMBERS OF FIRM

Henry J. Fox (1911-1990)	John B. Madden, Jr. (Resident,
Earl W. Kintner (1912-1992)	New York, N.Y. Office)
Jerome P. Akman	Alan R. Malasky
Jennifer A. Albert	Stewart S. Manela
Mark E. Alberta	Eugene A. Massey
David J. Bardin	Wayne H. Matelski
Donald M. Barnes	Gerald P. McCartin
Evan R. Berlack	John C. McCoy, Jr.
Richard L. Brand	Donald C. McLean
Ronald L. Castle	Eugene J. Meigher
William R. Charyk	James P. Mercurio
Earl M. Colson	Steven R. Miles
John C. Culver	Donald B. Mitchell, Jr.
David T. Dekker	Gerald L. Mitchell
Mary Joanne Dowd	Henry Morris, Jr.
Alan S. Dubin	Jeffrey B. Newman (Resident,
Michael M. Eaton	Budapest, Hungary Office)
Arlene Fine	Richard A. Newman
Marc L. Fleischaker	David M. Osnos
Carol Connor Flowe	Rodney F. Page
Stephen B. Forman	James P. Parker
Jeremy B. Fox	Lynn K. Pearle
Theodore D. Frank	Matthew S. Perlman
Andre H. Friedman (Budapest,	Howard B. Possick
Hungary and New York, N.Y.	Deborah A. Randall
Offices)	Marc Rauch (Resident, New
Joseph M. Fries	York, N.Y. Office)
Richard N. Gale	Peter S. Reichertz
Stephen L. Gibson	Alan E. Reider
Coralyn G. Goode	Paul Jackson Rice
William W. Goodrich, Jr.	John R. Risher, Jr.
Hendrik Gordenker	Salvatore A. Romano
Michael A. Gordon	Lewis Rose
Michael A. Grow	Thomas Schattenfield
David C. Haas	Joanne Schehl
James B. Halpern	George H. Shapiro
Ben I. Haraguchi (Resident,	Allen G. Siegel
New York, N.Y. Office)	Joel N. Simon
C. Stephen Heard, Jr. (Resident,	Howard V. Sinclair
New York, N.Y. Office)	Sheryl L. Sklorman
Lawrence F. Henneberger	Christopher Smith
Robert B. Hirsch	Timothy J. Smith
Peter Hoagland	Marilyn D. Sonn
R. Steven Holt	Michael L. Stevens
James H. Hulme	Carter Strong
Michael Evan Jaffe	Gary C. Tepper
Jeffrey E. Jordan	Carl A. Valenstein
Stephen D. Kahn	Barbara S. Wahl
Mark M. Katz	Robert J. Waters
David L. Kelleher	Richard J. Webber
Craig S. King	Marsha C. Wertzberger
George R. Kucik	Arnold R. Westerman
Michael J. Kurman	Burton V. Wides
Michael H. Leahy	Breckinridge L. Willcox
Bernice K. Leber (Resident,	David N. Wynn (Resident, New
New York, N.Y. Office)	York, N.Y. Office)
Gerard Leval	Harvey A. Yampolsky
Lawrence A. Levit	John J. Yurow
Jerome T. Levy (Resident, New	Lynda S. Zengerle
York, N.Y. Office)	Gerald Zingone

COUNSEL

Albert E. Arent (Retired)	Patrick F. O'Leary
William C. Basil	Harry M. Plotkin (Retired)
Robert A. Bauman	Carson P. Porter
Ronald H. Clark	(Not admitted in DC)
Samuel Efron	Karen Maloy Sprecher
John D. Hushon	Angela E. Vallot (Resident, New
Edwin L. Kahn (Retired)	York, N.Y. Office)
John N. Nassikas III	Kathleen E. Voelker
Jinhee Kim Wilde	

ASSOCIATES

Eduardo Acosta, II	Hallie M. Bastian
Beth-Sherri Akyereko	Attila Beczner (Resident,
(Not admitted in DC)	Budapest, Hungary Office)
Nancy Susan Appel	Laurel A. Bedig

(See Next Column)

ARENT FOX KINTNER PLOTKIN & KAHN, *Washington—Continued*

ASSOCIATES (Continued)

Margo S. Block
Emerson V. Briggs, III
Jonathan T. Brohard
　(Not admitted in DC)
Eric B. Bruce
　(Not admitted in DC)
Douglas R. Bush
Tenley A. Carp
Hunter T. Carter
Samuel K. Charnoff
Todd Chase
　(Not admitted in DC)
Elizabeth H. Cohen
　(Not admitted in DC)
Fabienne M. Clermont
　(Not admitted in DC)
Andrew C. Cooper
Michael S. Cryan (Resident,
　New York, N.Y. Office)
Debra M. Daumit
　(Not admitted in DC)
Idris M. Diaz
　(Not admitted in DC)
Kendra L. Dimond
D. Jeffrey Disbrow
Ákos Erős (Resident, Budapest,
　Hungary Office)
John P. Feldman
John P. Foley
　(Not admitted in DC)
Sean W. Glynn
Deborah B. Goldman
Anne M. Hamilton
Rebecca S. Hartley
　(Not admitted in DC)
Lisa Goekjian Henneberry
George C. Hlavac
Kenneth S. Jacob
Quana C. Jew
Susan V. Kayser (Resident, New
　York, N.Y. Office)
Emese Korányi (Resident,
　Budapest, Hungary Office)
Rachel G. Lattimore
Noreen M. Lavan (Resident,
　New York, N.Y. Office)
Mitchell Lazarus
Melissa Callahan Lesmes
Karen M. Litsinger
Anthony V. Lupo
Susan A. Marshall
Alvaro J. Mestre
　(Not admitted in DC)

John J. Meyer
　(Not admitted in DC)
Alison J. Micheli
John T. Mitchell
Patrick J. Morrisey
　(Not admitted in DC)
Jill R. Newman
José M. Ochoa
Paul A. O'Hop, Jr.
Christopher E. Ondeck
　(Not admitted in DC)
Deanne M. Ottaviano
Jennifer R. Pitarresi
Robert T. Plesnarski
　(Not admitted in DC)
Elliott I. Portnoy
Connie A. Raffa (Resident, New
　York, N.Y. Office)
Deborah M. Rochkind
C. Mario Russell (Resident,
　New York, N.Y. Office)
William A. Sarraille
Sonya Savkar
Steven F. Schroeder
Larri A. Short
Lynn Frendt Shotwell
Bryan J. Sinclair
Christopher J. Smart
D. Jacques Smith
　(Not admitted in DC)
Nada S. Sulaiman
Kerry S. Sullivan (Resident,
　New York, N.Y. Office)
Peter L. Sultan
John E. Thomas
Stephen F. Thurber
Ernest A. Tuckett, III
　(Not admitted in DC)
Christopher Van Hollen, Jr.
Kimberly A. Wachen
Brian P. Waldman
G.T. Franklin Walker
Jeffrey Walker (Resident, New
　York, N.Y. Office)
Molly B.F. Walls
Ivan J. Wasserman
Ronald L. Wisor, Jr.
Jeanine M. Worden
Ellen C. Wright (Resident,
　Budapest, Hungary Office)
Howard J. Young

For full biographical listings, see the Martindale-Hubbell Law Directory

---

ARNOLD & PORTER (AV)

Thurman Arnold Building, 555 Twelfth Street, N.W., 20004-1202
Telephone: 202-942-5000
Cable Address: "Arfopo"
Telecopy: 202-942-5999
Los Angeles, California Office: 44th Floor, 777 Figueroa Street,
90017-2513.
Telephone: 213-243-4000.
Telecopy: 213-243-4199.
Denver, Colorado Office: 1700 Lincoln Street, 80203-4540.
Telephone: 303-863-1000.
Telecopy: 303-832-0428.
New York, New York Office: 399 Park Avenue, 10022-4690.
Telephone: 212-715-1000.
Telecopy: 212-715-1399.
The United Kingdom Office: One, St. Paul's Churchyard, London,
England, EC4M 8SH.
Telephone: 011-44-171-236-3626.
FAX: 011-44-171-236-3610.

WASHINGTON, D.C. OFFICE
MEMBERS OF FIRM

Thurman Arnold (1891-1969)
Paul A. Porter (1904-1975)
William L. McGovern
　(1913-1977)
B. Howell Hill (1922-1977)
James R. McAlee (1931-1985)
David H. Lloyd (1938-1988)
Mason C. Brown (1945-1994)
Thomas J. McGrew (1942-1995)
Nancy K. Mintz (1942-1996)
Bruce A. Adams
Richard M. Alexander
David B. Apatoff

Donald O. Beers
Alexander E. Bennett
Paul S. Berger
Blake A. Biles
Edward E. Bintz
Peter K. Bleakley
Jeffrey S. Bromme
Jeffrey A. Burt
Howard Neil Cayne
Bruce M. Chadwick
Jerome I. Chapman
Lynda M. Clarizio
Charles H. Cochran

(See Next Column)

WASHINGTON, D.C. OFFICE
MEMBERS OF FIRM (Continued)

Martha L. Cochran
William Edro Cook, Jr.
George E. Covucci
Patricia Ann Dean
Eli Whitney Debevoise, II
Paul T. Denis
Jacqueline R. Denning
Norman Diamond
Steven S. Diamond
James A. Dobkin
A. Patrick Doyle
Douglas A. Dworkin
Thomas R. Dwyer
David S. Eggert
Richard S. Ewing
Melanie L. Fein
Deborah L. Feinstein
Roger P. Fendrich
Richard M. Firestone
James F. Fitzpatrick
Samuel A. Flax
Sonia (Turcotte) Fois
David F. Freeman, Jr.
Milton V. Freeman
Melvin C. Garbow
Murray R. Garnick
Robert A. Garrett
David P. Gersch
Neil M. Goodman
Michael D. Goodwin
Richard M. Graf
Patrick J. Grant
Julius M. Greisman
Peter T. Grossi, Jr.
Drew A. Harker
Althea L. Harlin
Vivian Lee Hobbs
Cathy Hoffman
Philip W. Horton
Roberta Lazarus Horton
Richard L. Hubbard
Gary E. Humes
Even Hurwitz
Darryl W. Jackson
Richard A. Johnson
Robert J. Jones
Kenneth I. Juster
Steven Kaplan
Andrew T. Karron
Hadrian R. Katz
David R. Kentoff
Abe Krash
Werner Kronstein
Kenneth J. Krupsky
M. Sean Laane
Stuart J. Land

J. Stephen Lawrence, Jr.
Kenneth A. Letzler
Arthur N. Levine
Daniel Martin Lewis
Jack L. Lipson
Steven P. Lockman
Dennis G. Lyons
Helene B. Madonick
Robert E. Mannion
Catherine Collins McCoy
Mark R. Merley
Michael B. Mierzewski
Thomas H. Milch
Bruce L. Montgomery
Susan T. Morita
S. Lee Narrow
Irvin B. Nathan
Fern Phillips O'Brian
Robert B. Ott
L. Stevenson Parker
Donna E. Patterson
Stephanie M. Phillipps
Stephen W. Porter
Claire E. Reade
Steven G. Reade
Walter J. Rockler
William D. Rogers
Richard L. Rosen
Robert D. Rosenbaum
Stanford G. Ross
Stephen M. Sacks
James J. Sandman
Ronald A. Schechter
K. Peter Schmidt
Lawrence A. Schneider
Scott B. Schreiber
Matthew J. Seiden
Cary Howard Sherman
Michael T. Shor
Thomas E. Silfen
Norman M. Sinel
Jeffrey H. Smith
Michael N. Sohn
Lester Sotsky
Melvin Spaeth
Mary Gabrielle Sprague
Mark H. Stumpf
Bryan J. Tomasek
G. Duane Vieth
William W. Vodra
Douglas L. Wald
Robert N. Weiner
Joseph D. West
Leslie Wharton
Robert H. Winter
Jay Kelly Wright

OF COUNSEL

J. Bradway Butler
Myron P. Curzan
Michael A. Lee
Anne J. O'Brien

Andrew Pace
Jennifer S. Perkins
Richard P. Schifter
James T. Walsh

SPECIAL COUNSEL

Waltraut Susanne Addy
Richard E. Baltz
Mary E. Cassidy
March Coleman
Marcia Ann Cranberg
Lawrence E. Culleen

Beth S. DeSimone
Lisa B. Horowitz
Howard L. Hyde
David E. Korn
Joan G. Ochs
Randal M. Shaheen

ASSOCIATES

David A. Ashmore
Michael C. Augustini
　(Not admitted in DC)
Elizabeth Hecht Baus
Kathleen A. Behan
Deena R. Bernstein
Michael L. Bernstein
Judith Bernstein-Gaeta
Theodore S. Boone
L. Elizabeth Bowles
Katherine M. Breaks
　(Not admitted in DC)
Michael Caglioti
Joseph S. Carlin
William J. Carmody
Susan Booth Cassidy
Linda B. Coe
Robert B. Conley
James L. Cooper
Robert M. Cooper

Katherine Culliton
　(Not admitted in DC)
Michael D. Daneker
Jodi Danis
　(Not admitted in DC)
Jeffrey R. Denman
　(Not admitted in DC)
Kari Mason Desgalier
Ranjit S. Dhindsa
　(Not admitted in DC)
Rajeev P. Duggal
　(Not admitted in DC)
Steven R. Englund
Michael D. Farber
Jill T. Feeney
Paul S. Feira
Samuel Figler
　(Not admitted in DC)
Holly R. Fogler
Johnathan M. Frenkel

(See Next Column)

ARNOLD & PORTER—*Continued*

ASSOCIATES (Continued)

Paul D. Freshour	Anthony J. O'Donnell
Tracey K. Friedlander	Nancy M. Olson
Matthew Frumin	Mary B. Percifull
Michael R. Geske	Nancy L. Perkins
Jonathan Gleklen	Annalisa Pizzarello
Jeffrey L. Handwerker	Erica Frohman Plave
Jason D. Hanson	Laurie A. Plessala
Thomas B. Heinemann	(Not admitted in DC)
(Not admitted in DC)	Kenneth L. Pollack
Scott D. Helsel	(Not admitted in DC)
(Not admitted in DC)	Daniel A. Raskas
Susan E. Hendrickson	Thomas W. Richardson
Steven A. Hetcher	Jeff Richman
Laura Jean Hines	John D. Roesser
Susan E. Huhta	(Not admitted in DC)
(Not admitted in DC)	Julie B. Rottenberg
Aimee L. Imundo	Melissa A. Scanlan
James P. Joseph	Charles Wylie Scarborough
Matthew Harris Joseph	Catherine A. Schmidt
Sarah Elizabeth Kahn	(Not admitted in DC)
Jamieson Lee Kase	Kenneth L. Schwartz
Robert J. Kulperger	Rebecca Testa Simpson
Brian E. J. Lam	(Not admitted in DC)
Charles C. Lemley	Edward H. Sisson
Joel Garner Levi	Darren C. Skinner
Jaimy M. Levine	(Not admitted in DC)
(Not admitted in DC)	Carey W. Smith
Franklin R. Liss	(Not admitted in DC)
Richard M. Lucas	Jennifer C. Smith
Jennifer C. Maloney	Michael S. Solender
Steven M. Marks	Brian Joseph Sonfield
Jonathan S. Martel	Charles E. Spicknall
Robert E. Mascola	Jonathan R. Streeter
John C. Massaro	Thomas D. Sydnor, II
Duane J. Mauney	Sharon L. Taylor
(Not admitted in DC)	Tracy M. Thomas
Rosemary Maxwell	Joseph G. Tirone
Laura K. McNally	Joseph Turitz
(Not admitted in DC)	(Not admitted in DC)
Mark A. Merva	Asim Varma
Leslie A. Nickel	Anne McBride Walker
David F. Noteware	Jonathan B. Werther
Ellen T. Noteware	Kevin A. Zambrowicz
	Walter F. Zenner

For full biographical listings, see the Martindale-Hubbell Law Directory

---

* ARTER & HADDEN (AV)

1801 K Street, N.W., Suite 400K, 20006
Telephone: 202-775-7100
Cable Address: "Stem Washington";
Telex: 6502156242-MCI
In Cleveland, Ohio: 1100 Huntington Building, 925 Euclid Avenue, 44115-1475.
Telephone: 216-696-1100.
Fax: 216-696-2645.
In Columbus, Ohio: One Columbus, 10 West Broad Street, 43215-3422.
Telephone: 614-221-3155.
Fax: 614-221-0479.
In Dallas, Texas: 1717 Main Street, Suite 4100, 75201-4605.
Telephone: 214-761-2100.
Fax: 214-741-7139.
In Los Angeles, California: 700 South Flower Street, 30th Floor, 90017-4101.
Telephone: 213-629-9300.
Fax: 213-617-9255.
In Irvine, California: Five Park Plaza, Jamboree Center, 92714.
Telephone: 714-252-7500.
Fax: 714-833-9604.
In Austin, Texas: 100 Congress Avenue, Suite 1800, 78701.
Telephone: 512-479-6403.
Fax: 512-469-3552.
In San Antonio, Texas: 7710 Jones Maltsberger, Harte-Hanks Tower, Suite 540, 78216.
Telephone: 210-805-8497.
Fax: 210-805-8519.
In San Francisco, California: 201 California Street, 14th Floor, 94111.
Telephone: 415-912-3600.
Fax: 415-912-3636.
In San Diego, California: 401 West "A" Street, Suite 2600, 92101.
Telephone: 619-238-0001.
Fax: 619-238-8333.
In Woodland Hills, California: 5959 Topanga Canyon Boulevard, Suite 244, 91367.
Telephone: 818-712-0036.
Fax: 818-346-6502.

(See Next Column)

MEMBERS OF FIRM

Charles K. Arter (1875-1957)	Paul H. Friedman
John A. Hadden (1886-1979)	Laura Metcoff Klaus
Jerome A. Hochberg	William L. Gehrig
Francis R. Snodgrass	Laurence E. Bensignor
James L. Bikoff	Michael P. Murphy
David I. Wilson	H. John Steele
David L. Miller	Peter L. Canzano
Mark E. Solomons	Mary Jane Saunders
William K. Dabaghi	Roger P. Furey
Richard A. Dean	Lawrence H. Gesner
Philip M. Horowitz	David J. Shaffer
Allan J. Weiner	Douglas M. Mangel
Howard M. Liberman	James U. Troup
John D. Maddox	John C. Hockenbury
Dennis E. Eckart	Thomas G. Loeffler
(Not admitted in DC)	Thomas C. Barbuti
Jerry A. Moore III	(Not admitted in DC)
James Wm. Morrison	Adele Baker
	W. James Jonas, III

OF COUNSEL

N. Barr Miller	Reta J. Lewis
Sol Schildhause	Gerald Stevens-Kittner
	Robert J. Ungar

ASSOCIATES

Jodi Mintzer Krame	Jennifer L. Blum
James Grier Hoyt	(Not admitted in DC)
Joseph V. Gatti	Denise L. Diaz
Dominick M. Valencia, Jr.	(Not admitted in DC)
(Not admitted in DC)	Naomi S. Travers
Karen Rapaport Esser	(Not admitted in DC)
Michael J. Pollack	Joanna Sambrook Kutler
Thomas H. Odom	(Not admitted in DC)
Michael R. Goodstein	Steven J. Hamrick
Patricia Adams McQuillen	(Not admitted in DC)
Thomas K. Slattery	Cynthia J. Larose
Marsha M. Baumgarner	(Not admitted in DC)
(Not admitted in DC)	Terri L. Bowman
Bryan A. Sims	Jeffrey R. Johnson
Courtney H. Bailey	Aimee M. Cook
(Not admitted in DC)	(Not admitted in DC)
Curtis D. McKenzie	
(Not admitted in DC)	

Reference: The Century Bank, Washington, D.C.

For full biographical listings, see the Martindale-Hubbell Law Directory

---

* BAKER & BOTTS, L.L.P. (AV)

A Registered Limited Liability Partnership
The Warner, 1299 Pennsylvania Avenue, N.W., 20004-2400
Telephone: 202-639-7700
Fax: 202-639-7832
Email: postmaster@bakerbotts.com
Houston, Texas Office: One Shell Plaza, 910 Louisiana.
Telephone: 713-229-1234.
Austin, Texas Office: 1600 San Jacinto Center, 98 San Jacinto Boulevard.
Telephone: 512-322-2500.
Dallas, Texas Office: 2001 Ross Avenue.
Telephone: 214-953-6500.
New York, New York Office: 599 Lexington Avenue.
Telephone: 212-705-5000.
Moscow, Russian Federation Office: 10 ul. Bolshaya Dmitrovka (formerly Pushkinskaya), 103031.
Telephone: 7095/921-5300 (Local); 7501/929-7070 (International).

MEMBERS OF FIRM

James A. Baker IV	William D. Kramer
James Addison Baker, III	Steven L. Leifer
(Not admitted in DC)	John B. McDaniel
J. Patrick Berry	Randolph Quaile McManus
William M. Bumpers	Scott F. Partridge
O. Donaldson Chapoton	B. Donovan Picard
(Not admitted in DC)	David N. Powers
Charles M. Darling, IV	Daniel J. Riley
James R. Doty	(Not admitted in DC)
Thomas J. Eastment	Rodger L. Tate
Steven R. Hunsicker	Hugh Tucker
Bruce F. Kiely	Kirk K. Van Tine

ASSOCIATES

Susan E. Aldrich	Jon A. Dyck
James B. Arpin	(Not admitted in DC)
Wendy Barrett	Kristin Gracen Francis
(Not admitted in DC)	(Not admitted in DC)
Debra Raggio Bolton	James G. Gatto
Christopher C. Campbell	Michael A. Gold
Wendy L. Cox	Wendy K.L. Harvel
Kevin B. Dent	(Not admitted in DC)
Kelly Riley Donovan	Debra J. Jezouit

(See Next Column)

BAKER & BOTTS L.L.P., *Washington—Continued*

ASSOCIATES (Continued)

Jane Boland Keough	Laurence H. Posorske
Steven P. Klocinski	James Remenick
(Not admitted in DC)	Edward B. Rowe
Jennifer S. Leete	(Not admitted in DC)
Estee S. Levine	Martin Schaefermeier
Mark K. Lewis	Gregory D. Shorin
Paul T. Luther	Tamar C. Snyder
Martin T. Lutz	Clifford E. Stevens, Jr.
Stacy B. Margolies	(Not admitted in DC)
Michael X. Marinelli	Jeffrey A. Stonerock
Nikesh R. Patel	David A. Super
(Not admitted in DC)	O. Kevin Vincent
Mary Ann Poirier	Jennifer J. Yi
(Not admitted in DC)	(Not admitted in DC)

For full biographical listings, see the Martindale-Hubbell Law Directory

BAKER & HOSTETLER (AV)

Washington Square, Suite 1100, 1050 Connecticut Avenue, N.W., 20036-5304
Telephone: 202-861-1500
In Cleveland, Ohio: 3200 National City Center, 1900 East Ninth Street.
Telephone: 216-621-0200.
In Columbus, Ohio: Capitol Square, Suite 2100, 65 East State Street.
Telephone: 614-228-1541.
In Denver, Colorado: 303 East 17th Avenue, Suite 1100.
Telephone: 303-861-0600.
In Houston, Texas: 1000 Louisiana, Suite 2000.
Telephone: 713-751-1600.
In Long Beach, California: 300 Oceangate, Suite 620.
Telephone: 310-432-2827.
In Los Angeles, California: 600 Wilshire Boulevard.
Telephone: 213-624-2400.
In Orlando, Florida: SunBank Center, Suite 2300, 200 South Orange Avenue.
Telephone: 305-841-1111.
In College Park, Maryland: 9658 Baltimore Boulevard, Suite 206.
Telephone: 301-441-2781.
In Alexandria, Virginia: 437 North Lee Street.
Telephone: 703-549-1294.
In San Francisco, California: One Sansome Street, Suite 2000.
Telephone: 415-951-4705.

MEMBERS OF FIRM IN WASHINGTON, D.C.

William H. Schweitzer (Managing Partner, Washington, D.C. Office)

PARTNERS

Edward Jay Beckwith	Thomas Hylden
Joseph M. Berl	E. Andrew Keeney
Ralph G. Blasey, III	Richard J. Leon
Gaspare J. Bono	David L. Marshall
Frederick W. Chockley, III	Charles B. Mathias
Gerald A. Connell	Mario V. Mirabelli
William F. Conroy	Shelby F. Mitchell
William J. Conti	Thomas R. Mounteer
Mark A. Cymrot	Betty Southard Murphy
Matthew J. Dolan	Robert H. Neuman
Lee T. Ellis, Jr.	Bruce W. Sanford
Ann K. Ford	Belinda Jayne Scrimenti
Frederick H. Graefe	Louis R. Sernoff
David Alistair Grant	Lee H. Simowitz
Leonard C. Greenebaum	John Lewis Smith, III
Brian S. Harvey	Alan S. Ward
Richard A. Hauser	Joanne W. Young (Resident)
Henry S. Hoberman	Donald P. Zeifang
Kenneth C. Howard, Jr.	H. Karl Zeswitz, Jr.

ASSOCIATES

Marc A. Antonetti	Robert D. Lystad
Thomas E. Arend, Jr.	Kent W. McAllister
(Not admitted in DC)	(Not admitted in DC)
Jenifer M. Brown	Michael J. Myers
Mareza I. Estevez	(Not admitted in DC)
John S. Farrington	Wendy Norris
(Not admitted in DC)	(Not admitted in DC)
Paul O. Gagnier, Jr.	Dawn M. Porter
Eric J. Geppert	Michael C. Ruger
Kelly Matthews Gerber	Lisa K. Rushton
David Morgan Giles	(Not admitted in DC)
(Not admitted in DC)	Tara C. Schoff
Margaret E. Goss	(Not admitted in DC)
Julie E. Hawkins	Theodore N. Stern
Rebekah J. Kinnett	Mark H. Tidman
Kevin J. Krist	Ronald F. Wick
Sean H. Lane	Kenneth D. Woodrow
Michael J. Lorenger	(Not admitted in DC)
(Not admitted in DC)	

(See Next Column)

OF COUNSEL

E. Mark Braden	David M. Kirstein
Jack Evans	G. Michael Richwine
Luis A. Galliani (Not admitted in United States)	David E. Short
	Guy Vander Jagt

RETIRED PARTNERS

Samuel K. Abrams	Harlan Pomeroy

For full biographical listings, see the Martindale-Hubbell Law Directory

★ BAKER & McKENZIE (AV)

815 Connecticut Avenue, N.W., 20006-4078
Telephone: (202) 452-7000
Intn'l. Dialing: (1-202) 452-7000
Facsimiles: (1-202) 452-7074, 452-7073, 452-7072
Email: washington.info@bakernet.com
Associated Offices of Baker & McKenzie in: Almaty, Amsterdam, Bangkok, Barcelona, Beijing, Berlin, Bogotá, Brasília, Brussels, Budapest, Buenos Aires, Cairo, Caracas, Chicago, Dallas, Frankfurt, Geneva, Hanoi, Ho Chi Minh City, Hong Kong, Juárez, Kiev, Lausanne, London, Madrid, Manila, Melbourne, México City, Miami, Milan, Monterrey, Moscow, München, New York, Palo Alto, Paris, Prague, Rio de Janeiro, Riyadh, Rome, St. Petersburg, San Diego, San Francisco, Santiago, São Paulo, Singapore, Stockholm, Sydney, Taipei, Tijuana, Tokyo, Toronto, Valencia, Warsaw and Zürich.
Correspondent Law Firm: Hadiputranto, Hadinoto & Partners, Jakarta.

MEMBERS OF FIRM

Joseph L. Andrus	Dennis I. Meyer
Mary C. Bennett	Philip D. Morrison
David A. Clanton	Kevin M. O'Brien
Nicholas F. Coward	Thomas A. O'Donnell
Robert H. Dilworth	William D. Outman, II
Edward E. Dyson	Marc R. Paul
Thomas J. Egan, Jr.	B. Thomas Peele III
Daniel L. Goelzer	C. David Swenson
Lafayette G. Harter, III	Leonard B. Terr
Bradford E. Kile	Eugene Theroux
	A. Duane Webber

LOCAL PARTNERS

W. Warren Crowdus, III	Teresa A. Gleason
(Not admitted in DC)	Jeffrey M. O'Donnell
Steven F. Fabry	(Not admitted in DC)

OF COUNSEL

David N. Bowen	John W. Polk
	John R. Reilly

RESIDENT ASSOCIATES

Jonathan A. Beckham	Francisco C. Martínez
(Not admitted in DC)	(Not admitted in DC)
Daniel S. Berger	Marie C. Milnes-Vasquez
Sandra E. Chavez	Eleanor Pelta
Paul A. DiSangro	Darren G. Pratt
Andrei J. Dorenbaum	(Not admitted in DC)
(Not admitted in DC)	Laura F. Reiff
Sara E. Hagigh	William L. Richter
(Not admitted in DC)	(Not admitted in DC)
Janet K. Kim	Diane U. Mage Roberts
David J. Laing	Richard L. Slowinski
Rachel Laro	Kimberly J. Tan Majure
(Not admitted in DC)	Kirsten B. Wielobob
	Jacob R. Wyatt

For full biographical listings, see the Martindale-Hubbell Law Directory

★ BALLARD SPAHR ANDREWS & INGERSOLL (AV)

Suite 900 East, 555 13th Street, N.W., 20004-1112
Telephone: 202-383-8800
Fax: 202-383-8877
Philadelphia, Pennsylvania Office: 1735 Market Street, 51st Floor.
Telephone: 215-665-8500.
Fax: 215-864-8999.
Harrisburg, Pennsylvania Office: 105 North Front Street.
Telephone: 717-236-3333.
Fax: 717-236-3884.
Denver, Colorado Office: Seventeenth Street Plaza Building, Suite 2300, 1225 17th Street.
Telephone: 303-292-2400.
Fax: 303-296-3956.
Salt Lake City, Utah Office: One Utah Center, 201 South Main Street, Suite 1200.
Telephone: 801-531-3000.
Fax: 801-531-3001.
Baltimore, Maryland Office: 300 East Lombard Street, 19th Floor.
Telephone: 410-528-5600.
Fax: 410-528-5650.
Camden, New Jersey Office: 800 Hudson Square, 5th Floor.
Telephone: 609-541-5577.
Fax: 609-541-8272.

(See Next Column)

BALLARD SPAHR ANDREWS & INGERSOLL—*Continued*

Nancy V. Alquist
  (Not admitted in DC)
Frederic L. Ballard, Jr.
Paul K. Casey
Joseph A. Fanone
Mary Jo George
  (Not admitted in DC)

Charles S. Henck
Justin P. Klein
F. Joseph Nealon
Howard H. Shafferman
Allan R. Winn

COUNSEL
Kelly Mitchell Wrenn

C. Vaughan Gibson
  (Not admitted in DC)
Jeffrey W. Larroca
  (Not admitted in DC)
Eric C. Lund
Bryan Myers
  (Not admitted in DC)

Constantinos G. Panagopoulos
  (Not admitted in DC)
David A. Pesel
  (Not admitted in DC)
John A. Washington, Jr.
  (Not admitted in DC)
S. Elizabeth Weaver

Deborah A. Wisnowski

For full biographical listings, see the Martindale-Hubbell Law Directory

* BELL, BOYD & LLOYD (AV)

1615 L Street, N.W., 20036
Telephone: 202-466-6300
FAX: 202-463-0678
Chicago, Illinois Office: Three First National Plaza, Suite 3300, 70 West Madison Street.
Telephone: 312-372-1121.
FAX: 312-372-2098.

RESIDENT PARTNERS

Edward A. Bloom
A. Thomas Carroccio
Raymond C. Fay
Thomas R. Gibbon
Christopher G. Mackaronis
Francis J. Pelland
Dante J. Picciano

Henry M. Polmer
Phillip L. Robinson
Joel S. Rubinstein
Donald E. Santarelli
Robert S. Sciaroni
Watson T. Scott
Charles A. Zielinski
  (Not admitted in DC)

OF COUNSEL

Andrew I. Gavil
Richard E. Hill

Marvin P. Sadur
Edward J. Smith, Jr.

RESIDENT ASSOCIATES

Anthony M. Black
Ross A. Buntrock
  (Not admitted in DC)
Brian Cohen
  (Not admitted in DC)

Andrew N. Cook
Michael W. Fleming
  (Not admitted in DC)
Timothy W. Seaver
  (Not admitted in DC)

For full biographical listings, see the Martindale-Hubbell Law Directory

BEVERIDGE & DIAMOND, P.C. (AV)

1350 I Street, N.W., Suite 700, 20005-3311
Telephone: 202-789-6000
Telecopier: 202-789-6190
New York, N.Y. Office: 40th Floor, 437 Madison Avenue, 10022-7380.
Telephone: 212-702-5400.
Telecopier: 212-702-5450.
San Francisco, California Office: Beveridge & Diamond, Suite 3400, One Sansome Street, 94104-4438.
Telephone: 415-397-0100.
Telecopier: 415-397-4238.
Fort Lee, New Jersey Office: Beveridge & Diamond, Suite 400, One Bridge Plaza, 07024-7502.
Telephone: 201-585-8162.
Telecopier: 201-592-7720.

Virginia S. Albrecht
Lawrence S. Bazel (Resident, San Francisco, CA Office)
Karl S. Bourdeau
Robert Brager
Dean H. Cannon
David D. Cooke (Resident, San Francisco, CA Office)
Devarieste Curry
Richard S. Davis
Henry L. Diamond
David M. Friedland
Aaron H. Goldberg
Stephen L. Gordon (New York, N.Y. and Fort Lee, N.J. Offices)
John S. Guttmann, Jr.
John N. Hanson
Jennifer L. Hernandez (Resident, San Francisco, CA Office)
Harold Himmelman

Steven M. Jawetz
David S. Krakoff
Cynthia Ann Lewis
Christopher W. Mahoney
Brenda Mallory
James L. Meeder (Resident, San Francisco, CA Office)
Andrew E. Mishkin
Daniel J. O'Hanlon (Resident, San Francisco, CA Office)
Donald J. Patterson, Jr.
Alan Charles Raul
Thomas Richichi
Harold L. Segall
Paul E. Shorb, III
Gary J. Smith
Kathryn E. Szmuszkovicz
Mark A. Turco
Benjamin F. Wilson
Robert D. Wyatt (Resident, San Francisco, CA Office)

(See Next Column)

OF COUNSEL

Gus Bauman
Albert J. Beveridge, III

John French III (Resident, New York, N.Y. Office)

SPECIAL COUNSEL
A. James Barnes

SENIOR ATTORNEYS

Sy Gruza (Resident, New York, N.Y. Office)

Terry F. Quill
Eileen M. Nottoli (Resident, San Francisco, CA Office)

Laurie G. Ballenger
  (Not admitted in DC)
Scott F. Belcher
Stuart I. Block (Resident, San Francisco, CA Office)
Steven N. Brautigam (Resident, New York, N.Y. Office)
Robert W. Chamberlin
  (Not admitted in DC)
Robert P. Doty (Resident, San Francisco, CA Office)
Michael Goldstein (Resident, New York, N.Y. Office)
Paul E. Hagen
Timothy J. Hagerty
David S. Langer (New York, N.Y. and Fort Lee, N.J. Offices)
Janet C. Loduca (Resident, San Francisco, CA Office)
Laura K. McAfee
  (Not admitted in DC)
David A. McKay
Christopher J. McKenzie
  (Resident, New York, N.Y. Office)

Kimberly Martin McMorrow
  (Resident, San Francisco, CA Office)
Christopher F. Regan
James B. Slaughter
Adam D. Snyder
Joseph C. Stanko, Jr.
Katherine B. Steuer (Resident, San Francisco, CA Office)
Caroline Tipton
  (Not admitted in DC)
Alec I. Ugol
  (Not admitted in DC)
Jennifer L. Vogdes
  (Not admitted in DC)
Fred R. Wagner
John D. Walke
Julie K. Walters (Resident, San Francisco, CA Office)
Bernard A. Weintraub (Resident, New York, N.Y. Office)
Michelle A. Wenzel
  (Not admitted in DC)
Sharmian L. White
  (Not admitted in DC)
Nancy N. Young

For full biographical listings, see the Martindale-Hubbell Law Directory

* BINGHAM, DANA & GOULD LLP (AV)

1200 19th Street, N.W. Suite 400, 20005
Telephone: 202-778-6150
Telecopy: 202-778-6155
Email: info@bingham.com
Boston, Massachusetts Office: 150 Federal Street.
Telephone: 617-951-8000.
Telecopy: 617-951-8736.
Hartford, Connecticut Office: 100 Pearl Street.
Telephone: 203-244-3770.
Telefax: 203-527-5188.
London, England Office: 39 Victoria Street, SWIH 0EE.
Telephone: 011-44-71-799-2646.
Telecopy: 011-44-71-799-2654.

RESIDENT PARTNERS

David M. Astrove
Paul J. Lambert

Barry P. Rosenthal
Peter D. Schellie

RESIDENT ASSOCIATES

Teresa Burke
MaryEllen S. Dolan
Gerard P. Finn
Joseph P. Pelican

J. Michael Pickett
Melissa R. Sarke
  (Not admitted in DC)
Deborah G. Segal

Erica H. Weiss

For full biographical listings, see the Martindale-Hubbell Law Directory

* BROWN & WOOD LLP (AV)

815 Connecticut Avenue, N.W., Suite 701, 20006-4004
Telephone: 202-973-0600
Telecopier: 202-223-0495
Los Angeles, California Office: 10900 Wilshire Boulevard, 90024-3959.
Telephone: 310-443-0200.
New York, New York Office: One World Trade Center, 10048-0557.
Telephone: 212-839-5300.
San Francisco, California Office: 555 California Street, 94104-1715.
Telephone: 415-772-1200.
London, England Office: Blackwell House, Guildhall Yard.
Telephone: 011-44-171-778-1800.
Hong Kong Office: 2606 Asia Pacific Finance Tower, Citibank Plaza, 3 Garden Road, Central.
Telephone: 011-852-2509-7888.
Sao Paulo, Brazil Office: Rua da Consolacao, 247 - 5° Andar.
Telephone: 011-55-11-256-9785.
Beijing, China Office: 2315, China World Tower, 1 Jian Guo Men Wai Avenue.
Telephone: 011-8610-6505-5359; 011-8610-6505-1807.

RESIDENT PARTNER
John Arnholz

OF COUNSEL
James E. Murray

(See Next Column)

BROWN & WOOD LLP, *Washington—Continued*

RESIDENT ASSOCIATES

Matthew J. Fitzgerald	Erinn Harley-Lewis
Edward E. Gainor	(Not admitted in DC)
Samir A. Gandhi	Timothy Sadler
	Robert Charles Torch

For full biographical listings, see the Martindale-Hubbell Law Directory

* BUTLER & BINION, L.L.P. (AV)

A Partnership including Professional Corporations
1747 Pennsylvania Avenue, N.W., 20006
Telephone: 202-466-6900
Telecopier: 202-833-1274
Houston, Texas Office: 1000 Louisiana, Suite 1600.
Telephone: 713-237-3111.
Telecopier: 713-237-3202.
Dallas, Texas Office: 750 N. St. Paul, Suite 1800.
Telephone: 214-220-3100.
Telecopiers: 214-969-7013; 214-954-4245.
San Antonio, Texas Office: 112 East Pecan, 27th Floor.
Telephone: 210-227-2200.
Telecopier: 210-223-6730.

RESIDENT MEMBERS
Richard E. Powers, Jr. (P.C.)
ASSOCIATES
Steven A. Adducci

For full biographical listings, see the Martindale-Hubbell Law Directory

* CAHILL GORDON & REINDEL (AV)

A Partnership including a Professional Corporation
1990 K Street, N.W., 20006-1103
Telephone: 202-862-8900
Facsimile: 202-862-8958.
Cable Address: "Cottofrank Washington"
New York, N.Y. Office: 80 Pine Street.
Telephone: 212-701-3000.
European Office: 19 rue François 1er, 75008, Paris, France.
Telephone: 33.1-47.20.10.50.

RESIDENT PARTNERS
Donald J. Mulvihill
COUNSEL
Corydon B. Dunham
RESIDENT ASSOCIATES

Barbara O. Brincefield	Kathy Silberthau Strom
Paul W. Butler	
(Not admitted in DC)	

For full biographical listings, see the Martindale-Hubbell Law Directory

CARLSMITH BALL WICHMAN CASE & ICHIKI (AV)

A Partnership including Law Corporations
700 14th Street, N.W., 9th Floor, 20005
Telephone: 202-508-1025
Telecopier: 202-508-1026
Honolulu, Hawaii Office: Suite 2200, Pacific Tower, 1001 Bishop Street.
P.O. Box 656.
Telephone: 808-523-2500.
Kapolei, Hawaii Office: Kapolei Building, Suite 318, 1001 Kamokila Boulevard.
Telephone: 808-523-2500.
Wailuku, Maui Hawaii Office: One Main Plaza, Suite 400, 2200 Main Street, P.O. Box 1086.
Telephone: 808-242-4535.
Kailua-Kona, Hawaii Office: Second Floor, Bank of Hawaii Annex Building, P.O. Box 1720.
Telephone: 808-329-6464.
Hilo, Hawaii Office: 121 Waianuenue Avenue, P.O. Box 686.
Telephone: 808-935-6644.
Agana, Guam Office: 4th Floor, Bank of Hawaii Building, P.O. Box BF.
Telephone: 671-472-6813.
Saipan, Commonwealth of the Northern Mariana Islands Office: Carlsmith Building, Capitol Hill, P.O. Box 5241.
Telephone: (011) 670-322-3455.
Los Angeles, California Office: 555 South Flower Street, 25th Floor.
Telephone: 213-955-1200.
Mexico City, Mexico Office: Monte Pelvoux 111, Piso 1, Col. Lomas de Chapultepec 11000, Mexico, D.F.
Telephone: (011-52-5) 520-8514.
Fax: (011-52-5) 540-1545.
Mexico, D.F. Office of Carlsmith Ball Garcia Cacho y Asociados, S.C. (Authorized to practice Mexican Law): Monte Pelvoux 111, Piso 1, Col. Lomas de Chapultepec, 11000 Mexico, D.F.
Telephone: (011-52-5) 520-8514.
Fax: (011-52-5) 540-1545.

RESIDENT PARTNERS

Anne Price Fortney	Renee L. Stransky

(See Next Column)

OF COUNSEL
Aaron Schildhaus

For full biographical listings, see the Martindale-Hubbell Law Directory

CARR GOODSON LEE & WARNER, A PROFESSIONAL CORPORATION (AV)

1301 K Street, N.W., Suite 400, East Tower, 20005-3300
Telephone: 202-310-5500
Telecopier: 202-310-5555
Email: info@cglw.com *URL:* http://www.cglw.com
Fairfax, Virginia Office: Tycon Towers, 8000 Towers Crescent Drive, Suite 1350, Vienna, Virginia, 22182.
Telephone: 703-691-8818.
Baltimore, Maryland Office: 201 North Charles St., 21201.
Telephone: 410-752-1570.
Rockville, Maryland Office: 31 Wood Lane, 20850.
Telephone: 301-424-7024.

Lawrence E. Carr, Jr.	Robert E. Madden
Robert W. Goodson	Paul J. Maloney
James F. Lee, Jr.	Thomas L. McCally
Margaret H. Warner	Terrence M. McShane
M. Miller Baker	Kevin M. Murphy
William J. Carter	Walter J. Murphy, Jr.
Catherine A. Hanrahan	Brian H. Rhatigan
Kyle A. Kane	Alexander D. Shoaibi
Gregory A. Krauss	Jan E. Simonsen
Charles E. Leasure, III	James A. Welch

SENIOR COUNSEL
Peter K. Tompa
OF COUNSEL
Edward J. Krill

Tracy J. Allen	Ngoc H. Lam
Janette M. Blee	(Not admitted in DC)
(Not admitted in DC)	Michelle L. Melin
Mark A. Collins	Howard D. Reitz, Jr.
Matthew J. Cuccias	Karen A. Rosenthal
(Not admitted in DC)	Patricia Ann Smith
Teresa Grace Fay	James P. Steele
Pamela Diane Gilman	Spencer K. Stephens
Richard S. Gordon	Ki Jun Sung
(Not admitted in DC)	(Not admitted in DC)
Shadonna E. Hale	Brian M. Tauscher
Mary Margaret Hogans-Ott	Karen E. Torrent
Timothy R. Hughes	Bruce K. Trauben
Kent G. Huntington	Clifton B. Welch
David H. Jacobs	Douglas V. Wolfe
(Not admitted in DC)	

For full biographical listings, see the Martindale-Hubbell Law Directory

* CHADBOURNE & PARKE LLP (AV)

1101 Vermont Avenue, N.W., 20005
Telephone: 202-289-3000
Telex: WU 904256
Facsimile: 202-289-3002
New York, N.Y. Office: 30 Rockefeller Plaza, 10112.
Telephone: 212-408-5100.
Facsimile: 212-541-5369.
Los Angeles, California Office: 601 South Figueroa Street, 90017.
Telephone: 213-892-1000.
Facsimile: 213-622-9865.
London, England Office: 86 Jermyn Street, SW1 6JD.
Telephone: 44-171-925-7400.
Facsimile: 44-171-839-3393.
Moscow, Russia Office: 38 Kosmodamianskaya, 113035.
Telephone: 7095-974-2424.
Facsimile: 7095-974-2425. International satellite via US:
Telephone: 212-408-1190.
Facsimile: 212-408-1199.
Hong Kong Office: Suite 3704, Peregrine Tower, Lippo Centre, 89 Queensway.
Telephone: 852-2842-5400.
Facsimile: 852-2521-7527.
New Delhi, India Office: Chadbourne & Parke Associates, Paharpur Business Center, 21 Nehru Place, 6th Floor.
Telephone: 91-11-644-3709.
Facsimile: 91-11-643-2486.

PARTNERS

William S. D'Amico	Peter F. Fitzgerald
John B. O'Sullivan	(Not admitted in DC)
Keith Martin	William K. Perry
Cornelius J. Golden, Jr.	(Not admitted in DC)
Robert F. Shapiro	Ellen H. Woodbury
Russell S. Frye	(Not admitted in DC)
David M. Raim	Andrew A. Giaccia
Nancy M. Persechino	Kenneth R. Pierce

(See Next Column)

CHADBOURNE & PARKE LLP—*Continued*

RESIDENT COUNSEL

Lynn N. Hargis	Kathy Bailey
Don J. Mros	Thomas P. Hechl
	(Not admitted in DC)

RESIDENT OF COUNSEL

Edmund E. Harvey

RESIDENT ASSOCIATES

Todd E. Alexander	Martin W. Gitlin
(Not admitted in DC)	Philip J. Goodman
Roy S. Belden	Chris Groobey
Steven A. Bennett	Kenneth R. Hayduk
Erin Buckley Bradley	Heléna M. Klumpp
Kerian Bunch	(Not admitted in DC)
Carey G. Child	Joy Langford
Daniel J. Cohen	Tracey W. Laws
(Not admitted in DC)	Ellen M. MacDonald
Kenneth J. Diamond	(Not admitted in DC)
Timothy J. DiCintio	S. Kelly Myers
Lisa C. Dorr	Kristin Oelstrom
Lynne E. Gedanken	Maura B. Perry
Barbara Gibian	David K. Schumacher
	Sheila V. Malkani Walsh

For full biographical listings, see the Martindale-Hubbell Law Directory

---

* CLEARY, GOTTLIEB, STEEN & HAMILTON (AV)

1752 N Street, N.W., 20036-2806
Telephone: 202-728-2700
Facsimile: 202-429-0946
New York, New York Office: One Liberty Plaza, New York, N.Y. 10006.
Telephone: 212-225-2000.
Paris, France Office: 41, Avenue de Friedland, 75008 Paris, France.
Telephone: 33-1-4074-6800.
Brussels, Belgium Office: Rue de la Loi 23, 1040 Brussels, Belgium.
Telephone: 32-2-287-2000.
London, England Office: City Place House, 55 Basinghall Street, London EC2V 5EH England.
Telephone: 44-71-614-2200.
Hong Kong Office: 56th Floor, Bank of China Tower, One Garden Road, Hong Kong.
Telephone: 852-2521-4122.
Tokyo, Japan Office: Cleary, Gottlieb, Steen & Hamilton Gaikokuho Jimu Bengoshi Jimusho, 20th Floor, Shin Kasumigaseki Building, 3-2, Kasumigaseki 3-Chome, Chiyoda-Ku, Tokyo 100, Japan.
Telephone: 81-3-3595-3911.
Frankfurt, Germany Office: Ulmenstrasse 37-39, 60325 Frankfurt am Main, Germany.
Telephone: 49-69-971-03-0.

COUNSEL

Robert C. Barnard	Fred D. Turnage

WASHINGTON, D.C. PARTNERS

J. Eugene Marans	Henry J. Plog, Jr.
Douglas E. Kliever	Dana L. Trier
Daniel B. Silver	Eugene M. Goott
Kenneth L. Bachman, Jr.	Janet L. Weller
Charles F. Lettow	Mitchell S. Dupler
Richard deC. Hinds	Linda J. Soldo
Sara D. Schotland	Giovanni P. Prezioso
Mark Leddy	John T. Byam
John C. Murphy, Jr.	Steven N. Robinson
	Michael R. Lazerwitz

SPECIAL COUNSEL

W. Richard Bidstrup	Linda S. Matlack
Scott N. Benedict	Kevin A. Griffin

ASSOCIATES

Ricardo A. Anzaldúa-Montoya	Jean E. Kalicki
Robin M. Bergen	Elizabeth L. Katkin
Barbara W. Bernstein	Karen A. Kerr
Robert T. Bradford	Daniel C. Kolb
Marcilynn A. Burke	Paul D. Marquardt
(Not admitted in DC)	(Not admitted in DC)
Derek M. Bush	Michael A. Mazzuchi
(Not admitted in DC)	Joyce E. McCarty
Brian Byrne	David H. McClain
Robert W. Cook	Patrick J. McDermott
Jeffrey R. Costello	Michael F. O'Connor
(Not admitted in DC)	Mitchell L. Rabinowitz
Onnig H. Dombalagian	David K. Richardson
Thomas M. Doyle II	(Not admitted in DC)
Michael G. Egge	Scott E. Schang
David I. Gelfand	Mark A. Singley
Brandt J. Goldstein	Michael S. Steele
Debra Gatison Hatter	(Not admitted in DC)
Steven J. Kaiser	Sandra E. Trimble
(Not admitted in DC)	

(See Next Column)

ASSOCIATES (Continued)

Mark E. Van Der Weide	Michael W. Waldron
(Not admitted in DC)	Amy Deen Westbrook
James G. Votaw	Carla L. Wheeler

For full biographical listings, see the Martindale-Hubbell Law Directory

---

CONNERTON & RAY (AV)

Fourth Floor, 1920 L Street, N.W., 20036-5004
Telephone: 202-466-6790
Telecopier: 202-659-3458

MEMBERS OF FIRM

Robert J. Connerton	Tèrese M. Connerton
James S. Ray	John McN. Broaddus
Phillis Payne	Daniel S. Kozma
	Michael Barrett

NON-ATTORNEY MEMBER

David L. Mallino

NON-ATTORNEY LEGISLATIVE DIRECTOR

Jack Curran

ASSOCIATE

Jennifer M. Roof

For full biographical listings, see the Martindale-Hubbell Law Directory

---

H. CLAYTON COOK, JR. (AV)

1133 21st Street, N.W., Suite 500, 20036
Telephone: 202-338-8088
Facsimile: 202-338-1843
McLean, Virginia Office: 1011 Langley Hill Drive. 22101.
Telephone: 703-821-2468.
Facsimile: 703-821-2469.
(Also Of Counsel, Bastianelli, Brown, Touhey & Kelley, Chartered)

For full biographical listings, see the Martindale-Hubbell Law Directory

---

* COUDERT BROTHERS (AV)

1627 I Street, N.W., 20006
Telephone: 202-775-5100
Telecopier: 202-775-1168
Cable Address: "Treduoc"
URL: http://www.coudert.com
New York, New York 10036-7703: 1114 Avenue of the Americas.
San Francisco, California 94111: 4 Embarcadero Center, Suite 3300.
Los Angeles, California 90017: 1055 West Seventh Street, Twentieth Floor.
San Jose, California 95113: Suite 1250, Ten Almaden Boulevard.
Denver, Colorado 80202: 1999 Broadway, Suite 2235.
Paris 75008, France: Coudert Frères, 52, Avenue des Champs-Elysées.
London EC4M 7JP England: 20 Old Bailey.
Brussels B-1050, Belgium: Tour Louise-Box 8, 149 Avenue Louise.
Berlin 10707, Germany: Kurfürstendamm 52.
Beijing, People's Republic of China 100020: Suite 2708-09, Jing Guang Centre, Hu Jia Lou, Chao Yang Qu.
Hong Kong: 25th Floor, Nine Queen's Road Central.
Singapore 049319: Tung Centre, #21-00, 20 Collyer Quay.
Sydney N.S.W. 2000, Australia: Suite 2202, Colonial Centre, 52 Martin Place.
Tokyo 107, Japan: 1355 West Tower, Aoyama Twin Towers, 1-1-1 Minami-Aoyama, Minato-Ku.
Moscow 109004, Russia: Ul. Nikoloyamskaya 54 (formerly Ulyanovskaya).
St. Petersburg 191011, Russia: U1. Italianskaya 5, Office 56/57.
Bangkok 10550, Thailand: Bubhajit Building, 20 North Sathorn Road, 10th Floor.
Ho Chi Minh City, Vietnam: 58 Dong Khoi Street, Suite 3B, District 1.
Hanoi, Vietnam: 38 Bui Thi Xuan Street, Hai Ba Trung District.

MEMBERS OF THE FIRM

Wendy L. Addiss	Tara Kalagher Giunta
(Not admitted in DC)	Tedson J. Meyers
Richard N. Dean	Robert F. Pietrowski, Jr.
(Not admitted in DC)	Arthur F. Sampson, III
	(Resident)

RETIRED PARTNER

Milo G. Coerper (Resident)

RESIDENT ASSOCIATES

Kay Georgi

Gonzalo de Dios	Susan M. Muchmore
Jonathan Hangartner	Nancy J. Rosenfeld
(Not admitted in DC)	Robert J. Thomsen
Mary E. Hartnett	(Not admitted in DC)
	Craig Alan Wilson

For full biographical listings, see the Martindale-Hubbell Law Directory

Washington—Continued

COVINGTON & BURLING (AV)

1201 Pennsylvania Avenue, N.W., P.O. Box 7566, 20044-7566
Telephone: 202-662-6000
Fax: 202-662-6291
Email: postmaster@cov.com
London, England Office: Leconfield House, Curzon Street, W1Y 8A5.
Telephone: 011-44-71-495-5655.
Fax: 011-44-71-495-3101.
Brussels, Belgium Office: 44 Avenue des Arts (Bte. 8), 1040.
Telephone: 011-32-2-549-5230.
Fax: 011-32-2-502-1598.

PARTNERS

Roberts B. Owen	Richard A. Meserve
Henry P. Sailer	Gregg H. Levy
Edgar F. Czarra, Jr.	Robert J. Gage
David B. Isbell	Carolyn F. Corwin
John L. Ellicott	Arvid E. Roach II
David E. McGiffert	Oscar M. Garibaldi
Paul R. Duke	Ellen J. Flannery
H. Edward Dunkelberger, Jr.	John G. Buchanan, III
Philip R. Stansbury	William M. Paul
Brice M. Clagett	Scott D. Gilbert
Charles A. Miller	Bobby R. Burchfield
Richard A. Brady	Andrew H. Friedman
Peter Barton Hutt	Steven J. Rosenbaum
Herbert Dym	Barry E. Kabalkin
Eugene I. Lambert	Saul B. Goodman
John Vanderstar	Charles F. (Rick) Rule
Mark A. Weiss	Keith A. Teel
Newman T. Halvorson, Jr.	Phyllis D. Thompson
Harris Weinstein	Michael E. Cutler
Harvey M. Applebaum	Mitchell F. Dolin
John B. Denniston	William F. Greaney
Michael S. Horne	D. Jean Veta
Peter J. Nickles	James C. Snipes
Jonathan D. Blake	Corinne A. Goldstein
Charles E. Buffon	Bruce N. Kuhlik
Bingham B. Leverich	David L. Harfst (Resident,
Robert N. Sayler	Brussels, Belgium Office)
Allan J. Topol	Michael St. Patrick Baxter
E. Edward Bruce	Sonya D. Winner
David N. Brown	Timothy C. Hester
Richard D. Copaken	Mark H. Lynch
Ronald A. Pearlman	Bruce A. Baird
Charles E. Lister (Resident,	Amy N. Moore
London, England Office)	D. Michael Lefever
Andrew W. Singer	Edward C. Britton
Peter D. Trooboff	Henriette A. Tielemans (Not
David H. Hickman	admitted in United States)
Wesley S. Williams, Jr.	(Resident, Brussels, Belgium
Russell H. Carpenter, Jr.	Office)
Doris Blazek-White	Frances M. Horner
Nicholas W. Fels	Bradford L. Smith (On leave of
William D. Iverson	absence) (Resident, London,
Theodore L. Garrett	England Office)
S. William Livingston, Jr.	Neil K. Roman
Dana T. Ackerly II	Richard C. Shea
James R. Atwood	Rebecca Snow
John M. Vine	Bruce Sandess Wilson
John Thomas Smith, II	Jay T. Smith
Stuart C. Stock	David Lawrence Meyer
Eugene D. Gulland	Anthony Herman
Clausen Ely, Jr.	John C. Dugan
O. Thomas Johnson, Jr.	Deborah A. Garza
Richard F. Kingham (Resident,	Eric C. Bosset
London, England Office)	Lanny A. Breuer
Patricia A. Barald	Evan R. Cox (Resident, London,
Michael R. Levy	England Office)
Roderick Allen DeArment	Ivan K. Fong
Reeves C. Westbrook	Marialuisa S. Gallozzi
Theodore Voorhees, Jr.	Robert A. Long, Jr.
Thomas S. Williamson, Jr.	Richard D. Shore
Jeffrey G. Huvelle	Kurt A. Wimmer
Paul J. Berman	David H. Remes
Joanne B. Grossman	Peter W. L. Bogaert (Resident,
William P. Skinner	Brussels, Belgium Office)
J. Michael Hemmer	Mark E. Plotkin
George M. Chester, Jr.	Seth A. Tucker

SENIOR COUNSEL

Charles A. Horsky	James C. McKay
Daniel M. Gribbon	J. Randolph Wilson
Stanley L. Temko	Edwin M. Zimmerman
Edwin S. Cohen	John H. Schafer

(See Next Column)

OF COUNSEL

Brian E. Lebowitz	Robert B. Stevens (Resident,
Alan A. Pemberton	London, England Office)
Ruth S. Epstein	Rachel S. Kronowitz
R. Laird Hart	Serena Gray Simons (Resident,
Elliott Schulder	London, England Office)
James A. Goold	Herbert Estreicher
David R. Grace	Douglas E. Phillips
	Sarah E. Taylor

SPECIAL COUNSEL

Richard A. Merrill	Gerard J. Waldron
Karen K. Schwartz	(Not admitted in DC)

ASSOCIATE COUNSEL

Joseph K. Doss	Joyce Payne Yette
William H. Fitz	Bette M. Orr
W. Andrew Jack	Patrick S. Davies
Michael Gary Michaelson	Elizabeth Kluger Cooper
Robert Edward Shaw	Scott David Feldstein

ASSOCIATES

Julie Abbate	Olga Hartwell
David W. Addis	Mark R. Hoffenberg
E. Jason Albert	Marta Hoilman
George E. Anhang	Victoria Huber
(Not admitted in DC)	John A. Hurvitz
Dennis B. Auerbach	Michael X. Imbroscio
Rene I. Augustine	H. Stuart Irvin, Jr.
Thomas O. Barnett	Robin Jacobson
Michael D. Bergman	Gail H. Javitt
Michael R. Bergmann	Laura Jehl
Stephanos (Steve) Bibas	Jennifer Anne Johnson
Caroline M. Brown	Michael J. Karlan
Susan L. Burke	Georgia Kazakis
Deron Cornell Burton	Talfourd Kemper
(Not admitted in DC)	Karen Kramer
Camille Caesar	(Not admitted in DC)
Kurt G. Calia	Thomas W. Krause
Rebecca Stack Campbell	Joan L. Kutcher
Michael A. Carrier	Michael Scott Labson
Ellen L. Chubin	Vicki J. Larson
Michael J. Cicero	Eric G. Lasker
Kipp A. Coddington	Kurt L.P. Lawson
Kenneth P. Cohen	Benedict M. Lenhart
Deanna Conn	Emily Leonard
Karen D. Coombs	M. Elizabeth Leverage
(Not admitted in DC)	(Not admitted in DC)
Angela M. Cooper	Jason A. Levine
Daniel P. Cooper	Benjamin Lieber
Jeffrey B. Coopersmith	Michael A. Listgarten
Manal S. Corwin	Michael S. Long
Thomas L. Cubbage III	Johnathan E. Mansfield
Estelina L. Dallett	Susan A. Maxson
Catherine Janine Dargan	Jennifer R. Meron
Michael S. Dawson	Julie Simon Miller
David B. Deitch	Jonathan Benjamin Mirsky
Nancy Dickinson	(Not admitted in DC)
Edward H. Dixon	Maneesha Mithal
Stacey L. Dogan	Allan B. Moore
Ronald G. Dove	David G. Nason
Kenneth J. Drexler	Dawn C. Nunziato
Jonathan C. Drimmer	Frank Partnoy
Richard Dulik	Ethan M. Posner
Thomasenia P. Duncan	Laura Quinter
James Louis Eastman	Neil A. Riemann
(Not admitted in DC)	Edward Holden Rippey
Erin M. Egan	Jennifer Ronnell
Anna Engh	(Not admitted in DC)
Donna Maria Epps	Michael L. Rosenthal
Michael J. Fanelli	Kristina Rosette
(Not admitted in DC)	Lewis Rosman
Wendy L. Feng	Simone Elizabeth Ross
Peter L. Flanagan	Salvatore G. Rotella, Jr.
Sean F. Foley	Anthony Saldana
Samuel M. Forstein	(Not admitted in DC)
James W. Fox, Jr.	A. Christopher Sega
Lawrence Stewart Fox	Laurie C. Self
Michael J. Francese	Andrew J. Shapiro
Andrew C. Friedman	(Not admitted in DC)
Kathleen T. Gallagher-Duff	William J. Shieber
Jonathan Galst	Kevin Shortill
Laura B. Gasho	Noah J. Silverman
Alex Gendzier	Christopher N. Sipes
Marc S. Gerber	Bruce P. Smith
Douglas G. Gibson	Geralyn G. Smitherman
Teresa Gillis	Kit Strauss
Douglas M. Gleason	(Not admitted in DC)
Ellen P. Goodman	Philipp Tamussino
Michael D. Granston	Tracy A. Thomas
Eric D. Greenberg	Lee J. Tiedrich
Lewis Grossman	Kimberly Vasconi
Gideon Y. Grunfeld	Martin Wald

(See Next Column)

COVINGTON & BURLING—*Continued*

ASSOCIATES (Continued)

William C. Waller	Ann-Kelley Yelverton
George L. Washington, Jr.	(Not admitted in DC)
Alane C. Weixel	Matthew Yeo
Robert Wick	(Not admitted in DC)
Jarrett Williams	Ernest A. Young
Michele J. Woods	(Not admitted in DC)

For full biographical listings, see the Martindale-Hubbell Law Directory

CROWELL & MORING LLP (AV)

1001 Pennsylvania Avenue, N.W., 20004-2595
Telephone: 202-624-2500
Fax: 202-628-5116
Email: info%c&m@mcimail.com
Irvine, California Office: 2010 Main Street, Suite 1200.
Telephone: 714-263-8400.
Fax: 714-263-8414.
London, England Office: 180 Fleet Street, EC4A 2HD.
Telephone: 011-44-171-413-0011.
Fax: 011-44-171-413-0333.

MEMBERS OF FIRM

Jerry W. Ryan	Peter J. Romatowski
Philip A. Fleming	Wm. Randolph Smith
Roger N. Boyd	Fred S. Souk
Frederick Moring	John I. Stewart, Jr.
Brian C. Elmer	Frederick W. Claybrook, Jr.
Patrick W. Lee	Robert T. Ebert
W. Stanfield Johnson	Thomas P. Gies
Peter B. Work	Andrew H. Marks
Victor E. Schwartz	William P. O'Neill
Ridgway M. Hall, Jr.	James J. Regan
Harold J. Heltzer	Jennifer N. Waters
Richard L. Beizer	Rosemary M. Collyer
Donald L. Flexner	Kenneth M. Bruntel
R. Bruce Keiner, Jr.	Robert C. Davis, Jr.
Joseph N. Onek	Warren J. DeVecchio
Steven P. Quarles	Clifford B. Hendler
Jeffrey H. Howard	Thomas C. Means
Thomas P. Humphrey	John T. Scott, III
Michael M. Levy	Shauna E. Alonge
John A. Macleod	Clifton S. Elgarten
Kent R. Morrison	Laurel Pyke Malson
Barry E. Cohen	Stuart H. Newberger
Marc F. Efron	David B. Siegel
Joseph M. Oliver, Jr.	Robert M. Halperin
Timothy M. Biddle	Raymond F. Monroe
Herbert J. Martin	Robert L. Willmore
Joseph I. Goldstein	Alan W.H. Gourley
Richard McMillan, Jr.	Mark D. Plevin
Dana C. Contratto	David Z. Bodenheimer
George D. Ruttinger	R. Timothy McCrum
Richard E. Schwartz	M. Lisanne Crowley
Jean-Pierre Swennen	Kent A. Gardiner
Howard M. Weinman	Mark E. Baker
Karen Hastie Williams	Ellen Moran Dwyer
Terry L. Albertson	Lawrence J. Gotts
James J. Maiwurm	Luther Zeigler
Richard J. Morvillo	J. Michael Klise
Nancy S. Bryson	William D. Wallace
JoAnn E. Macbeth	Scott L. Winkelman

Kathryn Dean Kirmayer

OF COUNSEL

Eldon H. Crowell	Anne M. ("Nancy") Wheeler
Richard J. Bednar	Daryl A. Lander
Paul Shnitzer	Jeffrey M. Villet
Edward M. Green	Kathryn A. Underhill
L. Graeme Bell, III	Paul William Kalish
Robert P. Charrow	Edward M. Barberic
Lloyd M. Weinerman	William L. Anderson
Thomas J. Plotz	Edward Jackson
Linda S. Bruggeman	Amy J. Mauser
Lorraine Berman Halloway	Ramona E. Romero
Bonnie A. Sullivan	Steven C. Schnitzer

Thomas R. Lundquist (Special Counsel)

ASSOCIATES

Susan M. Hoffman	Christopher C. Fennell
Jay A. Stephens	John E. McCarthy, Jr.
Richard J. Mannix	Stephanie B. N. Renzi
Joan H. Moosally	David M. Schnorrenberg
Brian E. Sweeney	(Not admitted in DC)
Janine L. Gregory	Jeane A. Thomas
(Not admitted in DC)	Michael J. Zoeller
Elizabeth M. Roesel	Aslan Baghdadi
Steven P. Taub	Mark A. Behrens
Charles C. Hwang	Terence F. Flynn
Cary Hastings Plamondon	Alexandre de Gramont

(See Next Column)

ASSOCIATES (Continued)

Glenn D. Grant	David M. Pfefferkorn
Kathleen E. Karelis	(Not admitted in DC)
Kris David Meade	Jeffrey F. Robertson
Jonathan Hale Pittman	(Not admitted in DC)
Robert D. Rowe	Jeffrey A. Spector
John W. Sither	(Not admitted in DC)
Caryl Lazzaro Flannery	Joseph W. C. Warren
Javier M. Guzman	(Not admitted in DC)
(Not admitted in DC)	Robert D. Wing
Kelly J. Harris	(Not admitted in DC)
Todd Hutchen	Christopher H. Wood
Karen M. Johnston	Lorraine J. Adler
Jamie W. Klein	(Not admitted in DC)
Mark R. Koehn	Tara Weinstock Blanchard
Christopher McGuire	Gina Cattalini
Colleen Rachel Olszowy	(Not admitted in DC)
Sandy L. Roth	Karen A. Deakins
(Not admitted in DC)	(Not admitted in DC)
Ellen B. Steen	C. Carnot Evans III
Mark D. Taylor	(Not admitted in DC)
Matthew S. Bewig	Scott E. Gant
Stephen M. Byers	(Not admitted in DC)
Christopher M. Farris	James Anthony Garcia
Lisa Taeko Greenlees	(Not admitted in DC)
Pamela J. Hicks	Rodrigo "Diego" Garcia, Jr.
Douglas T. Kendall	(Not admitted in DC)
Bonita F. Lewis	Jessica Rae Herrera
David D. McCurdy	Rachel Carlson Lieber
Steven A. Mirmina	(Not admitted in DC)
Patricia M. Connally	Andy Liu (Not admitted in DC)
(Not admitted in DC)	Bennett J. Matelson
Nabil W. Istafanous	(Not admitted in DC)
Ann H. Kim	Dawn Michelle Millman
Kent E. Lewis	(Not admitted in DC)
Monica G. Parham	Barry M. Parsons
Michael A. Valerio	(Not admitted in DC)
Jamie Ann Yavelberg	David A. Sadoff
Bradley S. Albert	(Not admitted in DC)
(Not admitted in DC)	Michele T. St. Mary
Andrew W. Bagley	(Not admitted in DC)
Kerry A. Dolan	Felicia Goldberg Schweitzer
Sarah Buchanan Dorsey	(Not admitted in DC)
Jacqueline E. Hand	Cheryl A. Solomon
Leah Lorber	(Not admitted in DC)
(Not admitted in DC)	Matthew Tuchband
Elizabeth L. Pearl	(Not admitted in DC)
(Not admitted in DC)	

For full biographical listings, see the Martindale-Hubbell Law Directory

* CURTIS, MALLET-PREVOST, COLT & MOSLE (AV)

Suite 1205L, 1801 K Street, N.W., 20006
Telephone: 202-452-7373
Telecopier: 202-452-7333
Cable Address: "Migniard Washington, D.C."
Telex: ITT 440379 CMPUI
New York, N.Y. Office: 101 Park Avenue.
Telephone: 212-696-6000.
Telecopier: 212-697-1559.
Cable Address: "Migniard New York".
Telex: 12-6811 Migniard; ITT 422127 MGND.
Newark, New Jersey Office: One Gateway Center, Suite 403.
Telephone: 201-622-0605.
Telecopier: 201-622-5646.
Houston, Texas Office: 2 Houston, Center, 909 Fannin Street, Suite 3725.
Telephone: 713-759-9555.
Telecopier: 713-759-0712.
Mexico City, D.F., Mexico Office: Torre Chapultepec, Ruben Dario 281, Col. Bosques de Chapultepec, 11530 Mexico, D.F.
Telephone: 525-282-0444.
Telecopier: 525-282-0637.
Paris, France Office: 15 rue d'Astorg, 75008.
Telephone: 42-66-39-10.
Telecopier: 42-66-39-62 .
London, England Office: Two Throgmorton Avenue, EC2N 2DL.
Telephone: 71-638-7957.
Telecopier: 71-638-5512.
Frankfurt am Main 1 Office: Staufenstrasse 42.
Telephone: 069-971-4420.
Telecopier: 69-17 33 99.
Hong Kong Office: 401 St. George's Building, 2 Ice House Street, Central Hong Kong.
Telephone: (852) 2845-0200.
Telecopier: (852) 2868-2801.

RESIDENT PARTNERS

Preston Brown	Samuel Rosenthal
	Jeffrey I. Zuckerman

For full biographical listings, see the Martindale-Hubbell Law Directory

Washington—Continued

DAVID, HAGNER, KUNEY & KRUPIN, P.C. (AV)

1120 Nineteenth Street, N.W., 20036
Telephone: 202-467-6900
Telecopier: 202-467-6910

Richard G. David	Pamela V. Rothenberg
John D. Hagner	Christine M. Carstens
David R. Kuney	Janet M. Meiburger
Dennis A. Davison	Jeffrey L. Tarkenton
Jay P. Krupin	Janis B. Schiff
Stanley J. Wrobel	Cameron Cohick
Paul A. Kaplan	Jonathan W. Greenbaum
Kenneth W. Logwood	Elizabeth C. Lee
Desmond D. Connall, Jr.	Robert P. Goodridge
Stuart A. Kruger	James J. O'Brien
Howard N. Solodky	Erik D. Bolog

Caryn G. Pass	John G. Nahajzer
Timothy R. Epp	Jeffrey A. Liesemer
Tara A. Scanlon	Alison J. Hurewitz
Carolyn D. Chabrow	Jennifer L. Kocher
Jeffrey A. Spector	(Not admitted in DC)

For full biographical listings, see the Martindale-Hubbell Law Directory

* DAVIS, GRAHAM & STUBBS LLP (AV)

A Limited Liability Partnership
1314 19th Street, N.W., 20036
Telephone: 202-822-8660
Fax: 202-293-4794
Telex: 248260 DGSW
Email: dgs@dgslaw.com
Denver, Colorado Office: Suite 4700, 370 Seventeenth Street, P.O. Box 185.
Telephone: 303-892-9400.
Fax: 303-893-1379.
Cable Address: "Davgram, Denver."
Telex: 413726 DGS DVR UD.
Houston, Texas Office: 515 Post Oak Boulevard, Suite 870.
Telephone: 713-850-9400.
Facsimile: 713-850-0807.

RESIDENT PARTNERS

Christopher J. Hagan	J. Hovey Kemp

ASSOCIATE

Karen Renfree Clark	James A. Hutchinson

For full biographical listings, see the Martindale-Hubbell Law Directory

* DAVIS POLK & WARDWELL (AV)

1300 I Street, N.W., 20005
Telephone: 202-962-7000
Fax: 202-962-7111
New York, N.Y. Office: 450 Lexington Avenue, 10017.
Telephone: 212-450-4000.
Fax: 212-450-4800.
Paris, France Office: 4, Place de la Concorde, 75008.
Telephone: 011.33.01.40.17.36.00.
Fax: 011.33.01.42.65.22.34.
London, England Office: 1 Frederick's Place, EC2R 8AB.
Telephone: 011-44-171-418-1300.
Telex: 888238.
Fax: 011-44-171-418-1400.
Tokyo, Japan Office: Akasaka Twin Tower East 13F, 17-22, Akasaka 2-Chome, Minato-ku, Tokyo 107, Japan.
Telephone: 011-81-3-5561-4421. Fax (main): 011-81-3-5561-4425.
Frankfurt, Germany Office: MesseTurm, 60308 Frankfurt am Main, Germany.
Telephone: 011-49-69-97-57-03-0.
Fax: 011-49-69-74-77-44.
Hong Kong Office: The Hong Kong Club Building, 3A Chater Road.
Telephone: 011-852-2533-3300.
Fax: 011-852-2533-3388.

MEMBERS OF FIRM

Stephen H. Case	Scott W. Muller

RESIDENT COUNSEL

Theodore A. Doremus, Jr.	Kathleen L. Ferrell
	Jordan Luke

SENIOR ATTORNEYS

Margaret M. Ayres	Robert W. Weaver

RESIDENT ASSOCIATES

Jeanine P. McGuinness

For full biographical listings, see the Martindale-Hubbell Law Directory

* DEBEVOISE & PLIMPTON (AV)

555 13th Street N.W., 20004
Telephone: 202-383-8000
Telecopier: 202-383-8118
New York, N.Y. Office: 875 Third Avenue, 10022.
Telephone: 212-909-6000.
Telex: (Domestic) 148377 DEBSTEVE NYK.
Telecopier: (212) 909-6836.
Paris, France Office: 21 Avenue George V 75008.
Telephone: (33-1) 40 73 12 12.
Telecopier: (33-1) 47 20 50 82.
Telex: 648141F DPPAR.
London, England Office: 1 Creed Court, 5 Ludgate Hill, EC4M 7AA.
Telephone: (44-71) 329-0779.
Telex: 884569 DPLON G.
Telecopier: (44-71) 329-0860.
Budapest, Hungary Office: 1065 Budapest, Révay Köz 2 III.
Telephone: (36-1) 131-0845.
Telecopier: (36-1) 132-7995.
Hong Kong Office: 13/F Entertainment Building, 30 Queen's Road Central.
Telephone: 852-2810-7918.
Fax: 852-2810-9828.

MEMBERS OF FIRM

Judah Best	Eric D. Roiter
Ralph C. Ferrara	Marcia L. MacHarg
Loren Kieve	Jeffrey P. Cunard

COUNSEL

Ann M. Ashton	Paul C. Palmer
Matthew A. Chambers	Phillip D. Parker

RETIRED PARTNER

Robert J. Geniesse

ASSOCIATES

Kevin T. Abikoff	Ariadne Dawn Makris
Scott N. Auby	Brett I. Miller
Barton B. Clark	(Not admitted in DC)
Roberta R. W. Kameda	Margaret E. Miniter
Elizabeth N. Kaplan	Douglas B. Paul
Philip S. Khinda	Brian A. Stern
Lothar A. Kneifel	Herbert C. Thomas
Jonathan R. Tuttle	

For full biographical listings, see the Martindale-Hubbell Law Directory

* DECHERT PRICE & RHOADS (AV)

1500 K Street, N. W., 20005-1208
Telephone: 202-626-3300
Telefax: 202-626-3334
Philadelphia, Pennsylvania: 4000 Bell Atlantic Tower, 1717 Arch Street, 19103-2793.
Telephone: 215-994-4000.
New York, New York: 30 Rockefeller Plaza, 10112.
Telephone: 212-698-3500.
Harrisburg, Pennsylvania: Thirty North Third Street, 17101-1603.
Telephone: 717-237-2000.
Princeton, New Jersey: Princeton Pike Corporate Center, P.O. Box 5218, 08543-5218.
Telephone: 609-520-3200.
Boston, Massachusetts: Ten Post Office Square South, 12th Floor, 02109-4603.
Telephone: 617-728-7100.
Hartford, Connecticut: 90 State House Square, 06103-3702.
Telephone: 860-524-3999.
London, England: 2 Serjeants' Inn, EC4Y 1LT.
Telephone: (0171) 583-5353. (Also see Titmuss Sainer Dechert).
Brussels, Belgium: 65 Avenue Louise, 1050.
Telephone: (02) 535-5411.
Paris, France: 151, Boulevard Haussmann, 75008.
Telephone: (33-1) 53 83 84 70.

RESIDENT PARTNERS

Sander M. Bieber	I. Lewis Libby
Ronald S. Cohn	Allan S. Mostoff
Frank J. Eisenhart	Jeffrey S. Puretz
Robert W. Helm	Paul F. Roye
Bettina M. Lawton	Theodore Sonde
Arthur W. Leibold Jr.	Jeffrey L. Steele
Donald Zarin	

RESIDENT COUNSEL

Joseph J. Aronica	Leonard Garment
David K. Diebold	Ralph Oman
Alan Rosenblat	

RESIDENT ASSOCIATES

Olivia P. Adler	Brendan C. Fox
Edie R. Albert	Hilary J. Gettman
Karen L. Anderberg	(Not admitted in DC)
Catherine Botticelli	David J. Harris
Douglas P. Dick	Jennifer L. Kim
(Not admitted in DC)	William J. Kotapish

(See Next Column)

DECHERT PRICE & RHOADS—*Continued*

RESIDENT ASSOCIATES (Continued)

Dennis J. Lawson	Sonya M. Tsiros
Jennifer Buehler McHugh	Patrick W.D. Turley
Keith T. Robinson	Jonathan P. Willmott
Meha Shah	(Not admitted in DC)

For full biographical listings, see the Martindale-Hubbell Law Directory

✳ DEWEY BALLANTINE (AV)

1775 Pennsylvania Avenue, N.W., 20006-4605
Telephone: 202-862-1000; *Telecopier:* 202-862-1093
Cable Address: "Dewbalaw"
N.Y., N.Y., L.A., Calif., Budapest, Hungary, Prague, Czech Republic & Warsaw, Poland
Other offices: New York, New York; Los Angeles, California; London, England; Hong Kong; Budapest, Hungary; Prague, Czech Republic; Warsaw and Kraków, Poland.

RESIDENT PARTNERS

James F. Bowe, Jr.	Kevin G. McAnaney
David H. Brockway	W. Clark McFadden II
Joseph K. Dowley	Earle H. O'Donnell
Matt E. Egger	Joseph M. Pari
Zori G. Ferkin	John A. Ragosta
Thomas R. Howell	Howard J. Rosenstock
Gerald A. Kafka	John J. Salmon
Andrew W. Kentz	Michael H. Stein
Felix B. Laughlin	Martha J. Talley
Myles V. Lynk	Alan Wm. Wolff

COUNSEL

Laurel W. Glassman	B. Thomas Mansbach
John K. Hughes	Timothy M. Reif
	O. Julia Weller

OF COUNSEL

Philip W. Buchen

For full biographical listings, see the Martindale-Hubbell Law Directory

✳ DICKINSON, WRIGHT, MOON, VAN DUSEN & FREEMAN (AV)

Suite 800, 1901 L Street, N.W., 20036-3506
Telephone: 202-457-0160
Facsimile: 202-659-1559
Detroit, Michigan Office: 500 Woodward Avenue, Suite 4000.
Telephone: 313-223-3500.
Facsimile: 313-223-3598.
Bloomfield Hills, Michigan Office: 525 North Woodward Avenue, Suite 2000.
Telephone: 810-433-7200.
Facsimile: 810-433-7274.
Grand Rapids, Michigan Office: 200 Ottawa Avenue, N.W., Suite 900.
Telephone: 616-458-1300.
Facsimile: 616-458-6753.
Lansing, Michigan Office: Suite 200, 215 South Washington Square.
Telephone: 517-371-1730.
Facsimile: 517-487-4700.
Chicago, Illinois Office: 225 West Washington, Suite 400.
Telephone: 312-220-0300.
Facsimile: 312-220-0021.

RESIDENT PARTNERS

Conrad J. Clark	Samuel D. Littlepage
William E. Elwood	Jeffrey M. Petrash
	Michael T. Platt

RESIDENT OF COUNSEL

Marc A. Bergsman	Lucien N. Nedzi
David R. Haarz	Stephanie Karen Wade

RESIDENT ASSOCIATE

Paul L. Sharer

For full biographical listings, see the Martindale-Hubbell Law Directory

DICKSTEIN SHAPIRO MORIN & OSHINSKY LLP (AV)

2101 L Street, N.W., 20037-1526
Telephone: 202-785-9700
New York, New York Office: 598 Madison Avenue.
Telephone: 212-832-1900.
Correspondent Office, St. Petersburg, Russia: Russian-American Law Firm, Lermontovsky Prospect 7/12, 190008. Local
Telephone: 114-5660. International
Telephone: 850-1430.

MEMBERS OF FIRM

Kenneth L. Adams	Leslie R. Cohen
John Agar	Robin L. Cohen (Resident, New
Lee A. Alexander	York, N.Y. Office)
Angelo V. Arcadipane	Richard J. Conway
George T. Boggs	Thomas J. D'Amico
James W. Brady, Jr.	Sidney Dickstein
Paul Bennett Bran	Deborah Swindells Donovan
Karen L. Bush	Stephen A. Dvorkin (Resident,
Henry C. Cashen II	New York, N.Y. Office)

(See Next Column)

MEMBERS OF FIRM (Continued)

Larry F. Eisenstat	Kenneth M. Lyons
David L. Elkind	Thomas W. Mack
Emanuel Faust, Jr.	Matthew G. Maloney
Howard N. Feldman	Elaine Metlin
Barry J. Fleishman	Andrew P. Miller
Lawrence D. Garr	G. Joseph Minetti (1907-1993)
Seymour Glanzer	M. J. Mintz
Allan B. Goldstein	Ira R. Mitzner
G. Michael Green	Peter W. Morgan
Donald A. Gregory	David M. Nadler
John W. Griffin	Michael E. Nannes
Jon David Grossman	Bernard Nash
Sallie H. Helm	Jerold Oshinsky
Robert J. Higgins	Mark A. Packman
Gary M. Hoffman	Lewis J. Paper
R. Bruce Holcomb	Woody N. Peterson
Timothy C. Hutchens	George R. Pitts
James Andrew Jackson	Ira H. Polon
Howard S. Jatlow	Frank C. Razzano (Resident)
Jeffrey M. Johnson	William M. Rosen
Peter Hafner Jost	Charles W. Saber
Peter J. Kadzik	Murray D. Sacks
Leslie A. Kaplan	Howard Schiffman
George Kaufmann (1931-1990)	Richard Schramm (1941-1991)
Leon B. Kellner	Elizabeth A. Sherwin (Resident,
William D. Kingery, Jr.	New York, N.Y. Office)
Joel B. Kleinman	Justin D. Simon
Joseph E. Kolick, Jr.	Kenneth M. Simon
Mark H. Kolman	James vanR. Springer
John T. Kotelly	Paul R. Taskier
Albert H. Kramer	Edward Tessler (Resident, New
Arthur J. Lafave III	York, N.Y. Office)
Neil Lefkowitz	Joseph D. Tydings
Richard J. Leveridge	Beth L. Webb
Barry Wm. Levine	Stephan G. Weil
Daniel M. Litt	Andrew D. Weissman
Frederick M. Lowther	Rebecca Wright
Patrick Winston Lynch	L. Andrew Zausner
	Victor J. Zupa

OF COUNSEL

Robert F. Aldrich	Michael A. Nardolilli
Laura Hamilton Calaluca	Amy Marmer Nice
(Not admitted in DC)	David Patton Parker
Linda J. Chase	Stanford E. Parris
Maura J. Condon	Mark L. Perlis
Katherine J. Henry	Janet M. Robins
Kimberly Hill Hoover	Francis J. Sailer
George E. Johnson	David I. Shapiro
Edward G. Modell	Nancie A. Thomas
Charles H. Morin	Walter J. Walvick

SPECIAL COUNSEL

Isaac Lyumkis

PRINCIPALS

Hilary Stephen Cairnie	David B. Killalea
(Not admitted in DC)	Kenneth R. Morrow
Margaret Feinstein	Adam Proujansky
Deborah P. Kelly	Mark J. Thronson
James D. Kelly	Kent T. Withycombe
	(Not admitted in DC)

ASSOCIATES

Therman A. Baker, Jr.	Keisha A. Gary
Ansu Nath Banerjee	(Not admitted in DC)
Lynda A. Bennett (Resident,	Yoav Karel Gery
New York, N.Y. Office)	Michael I. Gilman
Matthew Steven Bergman	Seena D. Gressin
Julia A. Bronson	Robert L. Hails, Jr.
Susan L. Buckingham	Jenifer N. Hartog
Bret A. Campbell	Teresa L. Harvey
Douglas M. Chapin, Jr.	(Not admitted in DC)
(Not admitted in DC)	Maria Colsey Heard
Frank M. Dale, Jr.	Jennifer Tara Geter Holubar
(Not admitted in DC)	(Not admitted in DC)
Joan M. Darby	Douglas N. Jacobson
Lauren A. Degnan	(Not admitted in DC)
(Not admitted in DC)	David M. Janas
Merle Miller DeLancey, Jr.	Samuel L. Jefferson, Jr.
Dana M. Dicarlo	Alan R. Jenkins
Jennifer M. Eck	Joshua S. Kans
Charles Ernest Edgar, IV	Catherine L. Kello
David L. Engelhardt	Michael S. Kimberling
Jacob S. Farber	(Not admitted in DC)
(Not admitted in DC)	Jorge Kotelanski
Laura Beth Feigin	(Not admitted in DC)
Laurence E. Fisher	Mark Kotlarsky
Leticia E. Flores	Stefan M. Krantz
Kendrick C. Fong	Deborah Kravitz (Resident)
Michele A. Gallagher	Karen Lau
(Not admitted in DC)	(Not admitted in DC)

(See Next Column)

DICKSTEIN SHAPIRO MORIN & OSHINSKY LLP, *Washington—Continued*

ASSOCIATES (Continued)

Susan Lee (Not admitted in DC)	Michael J. Rustum
Tricia J. Long	Gretchen Schott
Carla M. Marcolin	Reed P. Sexter
Charles L. Miller, Jr.	Michael T. Sharkey
Robert J. Moss	(Not admitted in DC)
(Not admitted in DC)	Michelle D. Smith
Charles S. Murray, Jr.	Joshua H. Soven
Guy S. Neal	Patricia M. Steele
Bridget O'Connor	Laura J. V. Szabo
Jonathan C. Odell	Edna Vassilovski
Richard P. Perrin	(Not admitted in DC)
Robert W. Pommer, III	Alice Aragonés Vergara
R. Edward Poole	Laura A. Vikander
(Not admitted in DC)	James R. Wagner
William E. Powell III	John A. Wasleff
Jody Meier Reitzes	Steven M. Weinstein
George C. Rogers	Karen E. Weiss
(Not admitted in DC)	(Not admitted in DC)
Gabrielle S. Roth	Christopher A. Wilson

Lois Casaleggi Wolf

For full biographical listings, see the Martindale-Hubbell Law Directory

DOW, LOHNES & ALBERTSON, PLLC (AV)

1200 New Hampshire Avenue, N.W. Suite 800, 20036-6802
Telephone: 202-776-2000
Facsimile: 202-776-2222
Email: postmaster@dla.com *URL:* http://www.dlalaw.com
Atlanta, Georgia Office: One Ravinia Drive, Suite 1600.
Telephone: 770-901-8800.
Telecopier: 770-901-8874.

MEMBERS OF THE FIRM

Marion H. Allen III (Chairman, Board of Partners) (Resident, Atlanta, Georgia Office)	Thomas J. Hutton
	John C. Jost
	Timothy J. Kelley
Corinne M. Antley	Leonard Jervey Kennedy
Michael D. Basile	(Not admitted in DC)
Leonard J. Baxt	Paul R. Lang
Raymond G. Bender, Jr.	John S. Logan
Richard L. Braunstein	Bernard J. Long, Jr.
Lisa C. Bureau	Richard D. Marks
Blain B. Butner	Judith A. Mather
John T. Byrnes, Jr.	Richard P. McHugh
Peter C. Canfield (Resident, Atlanta, Georgia Office)	David E. Mills
	Edward J. O'Connell
J. Eric Dahlgren (Resident, Atlanta, Georgia Office)	Timothy J. O'Rourke
	B. Dwight Perry
James A. Demetry (Resident, Atlanta, Georgia Office)	(Managing Director)
	Thomas J. Peters IV (Resident, Atlanta, Georgia Office)
Peter H. Feinberg	
John R. Feore, Jr.	Laura Hathaway Phillips
Michael P. Fisher (Resident, Atlanta, Georgia Office)	John H. Pomeroy
	Mary K. Qualiana
Linda A. Fritts	J. Christopher Redding
Yolanda R. Gallegos	Kevin F. Reed
Michael B. Goldstein	Curtis A. Ritter
Todd D. Gray	Kenneth D. Salomon
Joyce Trimble Gwadz	Michael S. Schooler
Ralph W. Hardy, Jr.	Stuart A. Sheldon
J.G. Harrington	James A. Treanor, III
Jonathan D. Hart	John D. Ward
Werner K. Hartenberger	Leslie H. Wiesenfelder
Michael D. Hays	David Daniel Wild
David A. Hildebrandt	Richard A. Wilhelm (Resident, Atlanta, Georgia Office)
Jonathan B. Hill	
J. Michael Hines	David J. Wittenstein
R. Dale Hughes (Resident, Atlanta, Georgia Office)	

J. Clark Armitage	Jonathon C. Glass
Kevin P. Brandon	David R. Goldberg
Christina Hosp Burrow	Sadhna Govindarajulu
Thomas M. Clyde (Resident, Atlanta, Georgia Office)	Michael A. Hepburn
	Peter D. Horkitz
Joan M. Corcoran	Sean D. Hughto
(Not admitted in DC)	Karen Hunter
Scott D. Dailard	Kelli J. Jareaux
Richard S. Denning	Jennifer L. Keefe
William S. Dudzinsky, Jr.	James W. Kimmell, Jr.
(Not admitted in DC)	Michael Kovaka
Terri L. Evans	Kevin J. Kuzas
(Not admitted in DC)	H. Anthony Lehv
Andrew C. Fish	Elizabeth J. Levensohn
(Not admitted in DC)	Christopher D. Libertelli
Patricia I. Folan	Ramie C. Little (Resident, Atlanta, Georgia Office)
Craig A. Folds (Resident, Atlanta, Georgia Office)	
	Stephen E. Lopez
Patricia A. Francis	(Not admitted in DC)
Andrew Givens	Stephanie M. Loughlin
(Not admitted in DC)	

(See Next Column)

Courtney G. Lytle (Resident, Atlanta, Georgia Office)	Deborah L. Reichle (Resident, Atlanta, Georgia Office)
Sherry Booth Mastrostefano	Elisa P. Rosen
Elizabeth Anne McGeary	James R. Saxenian
Margaret L. Miller	Randall R. Smith (Resident, Atlanta, Georgia Office)
J. Kevin Mills	
Frank S. Murray	Sean R. Smith (Resident, Atlanta, Georgia Office)
(Not admitted in DC)	
Carlos M. Nalda	Natacha Steimer
Charles M. Oliver	(Not admitted in DC)
Sharon S. Y. Park	Thomas D. Twedt
(Not admitted in DC)	Christina S. Wadyka
Frances A. Peale	Seth M. Warner
Suzanne M. Perry	E. Adam Webb (Resident, Atlanta, Georgia Office)
Lisa M. Pfenninger	
(Not admitted in DC)	Karen M. Wheeler
Karen A. Post	(Not admitted in DC)
Timothy A. Power	Jill M. Wood (Resident, Atlanta, Georgia Office)
Leslie S. Price (Resident, Atlanta, Georgia Office)	
	Jessica Yoo
J. Duane Pugh Jr.	(Not admitted in DC)

SENIOR COUNSEL
Daniel W. Toohey

OF COUNSEL

Fayette B. Dow (1881-1962)	Steve J. Davis (Resident, Atlanta, Georgia Office)
Gaylen D. Kemp (Resident, Atlanta, Georgia Office)	
	Thomas J. Schoenbaum (Resident, Atlanta, Georgia Office)
Horace L. Lohnes (1897-1954)	
Fred W. Albertson	

For full biographical listings, see the Martindale-Hubbell Law Directory

* DRINKER BIDDLE & REATH (AV)

901 15th Street, N.W., Suite 900, 20005
Telephone: 202-842-8800
Fax: 202-842-8465.
Cable Address: "Debemac"
Philadelphia, Pennsylvania Office: Philadelphia National Bank Building, 1345 Chestnut Street.
Telephone: 215-988-2700.
Fax: 215-988-2757.
Cable Address: "Debemac."
Princeton, New Jersey Office: Suite 400, 47 Hulfish Street.
Telephone: 609-921-6336.
Fax: 609-921-2265.
Berwyn, Pennsylvania Office: Suite 300, 1000 Westlakes Drive.
Telephone: 610-993-2200.
Fax: 610-993-8585.
Lawrenceville, New Jersey Office: Princeton Pike Corporate Center, 1009 Lenox Drive, Building 4.
Telephone: 609-895-1600.
Telecopier: 609-895-1329.

RESIDENT PARTNERS

Joe D. Edge	Philip J. Mause
Michael L. Gassmann	James A. Meyers
Alan J. Joaquin	John W. Pettit
(Not admitted in DC)	Michael J. Remington
Joseph F. Johnston, Jr.	Richard M. Singer
Joaquin A. Marquez	Robert A. Skitol

OF COUNSEL

John P. Bankson, Jr.	Elizabeth Toni Guarino

RESIDENT ASSOCIATES

Richard J. Arsenault	George Galt
Mark F. Dever	(Not admitted in DC)
(Not admitted in DC)	Kevin M. Gross
Whitney Ellenby	Deborah M. Levy
(Not admitted in DC)	Elizabeth A. Marshall

Tina M. Pidgeon

For full biographical listings, see the Martindale-Hubbell Law Directory

DUNCAN & ALLEN (AV)

1575 Eye Street, N.W., 20005-1105
Telephone: 202-289-8400
Facsimile: 202-289-8450
Email: ENERGY@DUNCAN.ALLEN.COM

MEMBERS OF FIRM

C. Emerson Duncan, II	Gregg D. Ottinger
Donald R. Allen	John P. Williams

John P. Coyle

For full biographical listings, see the Martindale-Hubbell Law Directory

DWIGHT, ROYALL, HARRIS, KOEGEL & CASKEY

(See Rogers & Wells)

Washington—Continued

* DYKEMA GOSSETT PLLC (AV)

Franklin Square, Suite 300 West, 1300 I Street, N.W., 20005-3306
Telephone: 202-522-8600
Fax: 202-522-8669
Email: 2084153@mcimail.com
Ann Arbor, Michigan Office: 315 East Eisenhower Parkway, Suite 100, 48108-3306.
Telephone: 313-747-7660.
Fax: 313-747-7696.
Bloomfield Hills, Michigan Office: 1577 North Woodward Avenue, Suite 300, 48304-2820.
Telephone: 810-540-0700.
Fax: 810-540-0763.
Chicago, Illinois Office: 55 East Monroe Street, Suite 3250, 60603-5709.
Telephone: 312-551-4900.
Fax: 312-551-4919.
Detroit, Michigan Office: 400 Renaissance Center, 48243-1668.
Telephone: 313-568-6800.
Fax: 313-568-6594.
Grand Rapids, Michigan Office: 200 Oldtown Riverfront Building, 248 Louis Campau Promenade, N.W. 49503-2667.
Telephone: 616-776-7500.
Fax: 616-776-7573.
Lansing, Michigan Office: 800 Michigan National Tower, 48933-1707.
Telephone: 517-374-9100.
Fax: 517-374-9191.

RESIDENT MEMBERS

Edward A. Groobert	Howard E. O'Leary, Jr.
J. Timothy Hobbs	Fred L. Woodworth
D. Biard MacGuineas	(Member in Charge)
Bruce A. McDonald	Stephen H. Zimmerman
	(Not admitted in DC)

OF COUNSEL

Charles R. Bernardini	William H. Carroll
(Not admitted in DC)	

RESIDENT ASSOCIATES

Judy Parker Jenkins	Christopher Kelly

For full biographical listings, see the Martindale-Hubbell Law Directory

* ECKERT SEAMANS CHERIN & MELLOTT (AV)

Suite 600, 2100 Pennsylvania Avenue, N.W., 20037
Telephone: 202-659-6600
Telex: 62030761
Facsimile: 202-659-6699
Pittsburgh, Pennsylvania Office: 42nd Floor, 600 Grant Street.
Telephone: 412-566-6000.
Telex: 866172.
Facsimile: 412-566-6099.
Harrisburg, Pennsylvania Office: One South Market Square Building, 213 Market Street.
Telephone: 717-237-6000.
Facsimile: 717-237-6019.
Allentown, Pennsylvania Office: Sovereign Building, 609 Hamilton Mall.
Telephone: 610-432-3000.
Facsimile: 610-432-8827.
Philadelphia, Pennsylvania Office: 1700 Market Street, Suite 3232.
Telephone: 215-575-6000.
Telex: 845226.
Facsimile: 215-575-6015.
Boston, Massachusetts Office: One International Place, 18th Floor.
Telephone: 617-342-6800.
Facsimile: 617-342-6899.
Fort Lauderdale, Florida Office: Las Olas Center, 8th Floor, 450 East Las Olas Boulevard.
Telephone: 954-523-0400.
Facsimile: 954-523-7002.
Boca Raton, Florida Office: The Plaza, Suite 902, 5355 Town Center Road.
Telephone: 561-347-5100.
Facsimile: 561-347-5151.
Miami, Florida Office: Barnett Tower, 18th Floor, 701 Brickell Avenue.
Telephone: 305-373-9100.
Facsimile: 305-372-9400.
Tallahassee, Florida Office: Hospitality Square, Third Floor, 200 West College Avenue.
Telephone: 904-222-2515.
Facsimile: 904-222-3452.

MEMBERS OF FIRM

Anthony A. Anderson	Edward J. Gill, Jr.
Keith L. Baker	Edward R. Noonan
C. Jonathan Benner	Jane Sutter Starke
Jerry W. Cox	George J. Wallace
	G. Kent Woodman

SPECIAL COUNSEL

Sean T. Connaughton	R. Lawrence Coughlin, Jr.
	Leonard L. Fleisig

(See Next Column)

RESIDENT ASSOCIATES

Darin R. Bartram	Timi E. Nickerson
Ross A. Keene	(Not admitted in DC)
	Jeffrey E. Weinstein

For full biographical listings, see the Martindale-Hubbell Law Directory

KENNETH R. FEINBERG & ASSOCIATES (AV)

1120 20th Street, N.W. Suite 740 South, 20036
Telephone: 202-371-1110
Fax: 202-962-9290
New York, N.Y. Office: 780 3rd Avenue, Suite 2202.
Telephone: 212-527-9600.
Fax: 212-527-9611.

ASSOCIATES

Deborah E. Greenspan	Peter H. Woodin
Michael K. Rozen	(Not admitted in DC)
(Not admitted in DC)	M. Catherine Faint

OF COUNSEL

Jacqueline E. Zins

For full biographical listings, see the Martindale-Hubbell Law Directory

FISHER WAYLAND COOPER LEADER & ZARAGOZA L.L.P (AV)

A Registered Limited Liability Partnership
Suite 400, 2001 Pennsylvania Avenue, N.W., 20006-1851
Telephone: 202-659-3494
Facsimile: 202-296-6518
Email: fwclz@fwclz.com *URL:* http://www.fwclz.com

Ben S. Fisher (1890-1954)	David D. Oxenford
Charles V. Wayland (1910-1980)	Barry H. Gottfried
Ben C. Fisher	Bruce D. Jacobs
Martin R. Leader	Eliot J. Greenwald
Richard R. Zaragoza	Carroll John Yung
Clifford M. Harrington	Glenn S. Richards
Joel R. Kaswell	Barrie Debra Berman
Kathryn R. Schmeltzer	Francisco R. Montero
Douglas Woloshin	Robert C. Fisher
	Scott R. Flick

OF COUNSEL

Grover C. Cooper	John Q. Hearne

ASSOCIATES

Gregory L. Masters	Brooks B. Gracie III
(Not admitted in DC)	(Not admitted in DC)
Lauren Lynch Flick	Colette M. Capretz
Kevin M. Walsh	Jason S. Roberts
(Not admitted in DC)	(Not admitted in DC)
Miles S. Mason	Heidi Atassi Gaffney
Robert L. Galbreath	(Not admitted in DC)
(Not admitted in DC)	Stephen J. Berman
Dawn M. Sciarrino	(Not admitted in DC)
(Not admitted in DC)	Veronica D. McLaughlin
Karen C. Rindner	Stephanie Blessey Lilley
	Jaqualin Friend Peterson

For full biographical listings, see the Martindale-Hubbell Law Directory

* FOLEY, HOAG & ELIOT LLP (AV)

1615 L Street, N.W., 20036
Telephone: 202-775-0600
Telecopier: 202-857-0140
URL: http://www.fhe.com
Boston, Massachusetts Office: One Post Office Square.
Telephone: 617-832-1000. Cable Address "Foleyhoag".
Telex: 94-0693.
Telecopier: 617-832-7000.

MEMBERS OF FIRM

Paul E. Tsongas	James T. Montgomery, Jr.
(Not admitted in DC)	(Resident)
Dennis R. Kanin	Ellyn R. Weiss (Resident
John L. Burke, Jr.	Administrative Partner)
	Alan I. Baron

COUNSEL

Stephanie Cutler (Resident)	Peter R. Ginsberg
	Gregory J. Glover (Resident)

ASSOCIATES

Donald W. Muirhead	Jocelyn M. Sturdivant
(Not admitted in DC)	

For full biographical listings, see the Martindale-Hubbell Law Directory

Washington—Continued

∗ FOLEY & LARDNER (AV)

Washington Harbour, Suite 500, 3000 K Street, N.W., 20007-5109
Telephone: 202-672-5300
Facsimile: 202-672-5399
Telex: 904136 (FoleyLard Wash)
Milwaukee, Wisconsin Office: Firstar Center, 777 East Wisconsin Avenue.
Telephone: 414-271-2400.
Telex: 26-819 (Foley Lard Mil).
Facsimile: 414-297-4900.
Madison, Wisconsin Office: Verex Plaza, 150 East Gilman Street, P.O. Box 1497.
Telephone: 608-257-5035.
Telex: 262051 (F L Madison).
Facsimile: 608-258-4258.
Chicago, Illinois Office: Suite 3300, One IBM Plaza, 330 N. Wabash Avenue.
Telephone: 312-755-1900.
Facsimile: 312-755-1925.
Annapolis, Maryland Office: Suite 102, 175 Admiral Cochrane Drive.
Telephone: 301-266-8077.
Telex: 899149 (Oldtownpat).
Facsimile: 301-266-8664.
Jacksonville, Florida Office: The Greenleaf Building, 200 Laura Street, P.O. Box 240.
Telephone: 904-359-2000.
Facsimile: 904-359-8700.
Orlando, Florida Office: Suite 1800, 111 North Orange Avenue, P.O. Box 2193.
Telephone: 407-423-7656.
Telex: 441781 (HQ ORL).
Facsimile: 407-648-1743.
Tallahassee, Florida Office: Suite 300, 123 South Calhoun Street, P.O. Box 508.
Telephone: 904-222-6100.
Facsimile: 904-224-0496.
Tampa, Florida Office: Suite 2700, One Hundred N. Tampa Street, P.O. Box 3391.
Telephones: 813-229-2300; Pinellas County: 813-442-3296.
Facsimile: 813-221-4210. 813-446-9641.
Facsimile: 813-229-6282.
West Palm Beach, Florida Office: Suite 200, Phillips Point East Tower, 777 South Flagler Drive.
Telephone: 561-655-5050.
Facsimile: 561-655-6925.
Brussels, Belgium Office: Avenue Louise, 283.
Telephone: 32-2-646-2777.
Facsimile: 32-2-646-7574.
Foley Lardner Weissburg & Aronson Office Locations:
Los Angeles, California Office: 2049 Century Park East, Suite 3200.
Telephone: 310-277-2223.
Fax: 310-557-8475.
Sacramento, California Office: 770 L Street, Suite 1050.
Telephone: 916-443-8005.
Fax: 916-443-2240.
San Diego, California Office: 402 West Broadway, 23rd Floor.
Telephone: 619-234-6655.
Fax: 619-234-3510.
San Francisco, California Office: One Maritime Plaza, Sixth Floor.
Telephone: 415-434-4484.
Fax: 415-434-4507.

RESIDENT PARTNERS

Stephen A. Bent	David A. Sacks
James N. Bierman	Colin G. Sandercock
David A. Blumenthal	Jacqueline Marie Saue
Robert A. Burka	Bernhard D. Saxe
Steven B. Chameides	(Not admitted in DC)
Paul E. Cooney	Charles F. Schill
William T. Ellis	Richard L. Schwaab
John J. Feldhaus	(Not admitted in DC)
(Not admitted in DC)	Arthur Schwartz
Wendy L. Fields	Michael O. Spivey
Howard W. Fogt, Jr.	Charles J. Steele
Donald D. Jeffery	Jay N. Varon
Jack L. Lahr	J. Mark Waxman (Not admitted
Eugene M. Lee	in DC; Resident also at Foley
Peter C. Linzmeyer	Lardner Weissburg &
Peter G. Mack	Aronson, Los Angeles,
Lisa S. Mankofsky	California Office)
Brian J. McNamara	Samuel H. Weissbard
Sybil Meloy	Kenneth B. Winer
Paul R. Monsees	Samuel J. Winer
George E. Quillin	
(Not admitted in DC)	

RETIRED PARTNERS
Edwin Jason Dryer
OF COUNSEL

Melvin Blecher	Barbara Ann McDowell
	(Not admitted in DC)

(See Next Column)

SPECIAL COUNSEL

Lisa A. Smith	Yoichiro Yamaguchi
(Not admitted in DC)	(Not admitted in DC)
Harold C. Wegner	
(Not admitted in DC)	

RESIDENT ASSOCIATES

Phillip John Articola	Melinda F. Levitt
Todd J. Burns	Stephen B. Maebius
(Not admitted in DC)	Marvin A. Motsenbocker
Beth A. Burrous	(Not admitted in DC)
Stephen Donovan	Allison George Newbold
(Not admitted in DC)	Cynthia K. Nicholson
Patrick A. Doody	Richard C. Peet
David E. Dreifke	Don J. Pelto
Janell Mayo Duncan	Cameron C. Powell
Joseph D. Edmondson, Jr.	(Not admitted in DC)
Lloyd N. Fantroy	Alan D. Rutenberg
Patricia D. Granados	Keith M. Schwartz (Resident)
John P. Isacson, Jr.	Paul E. Steiner
Mary Cynthia Atchley Jester	(Not admitted in DC)
Phillip B. C. Jones	Samuel B. Sterrett, Jr.
Michael D. Kaminski	Lawrence M. Sung
Mary Michelle Kile	John P. Veschi
Johnny A. Kumar	(Not admitted in DC)
David W. Laub	Scott A. Westfahl
(Not admitted in DC)	Marcus P. Williams
Glenn Law	David Warren Woodward
	Gary M. Zinkgraf

For full biographical listings, see the Martindale-Hubbell Law Directory

---

FREEDMAN, LEVY, KROLL & SIMONDS (AV)

Suite 825, 1050 Connecticut Avenue, N.W., 20036-5366
Telephone: 202-457-5100
Cable Address: "Attorneys"
Telecopier: 202-457-5151
Email: flks@flks.com *URL:* http://www.flks.com/home/flks

MEMBERS OF FIRM

Walter Freedman	Marc B. Dorfman
Peter E. Panarites	John H. Chettle
Gary O. Cohen	Karen M. Wardzinski
Jay W. Freedman	Lawrence G. McBride
Arthur H. Bill	Emil Hirsch
Thomas C. Lauerman	Thomas L. James
Richard G. Stoll	David P. Novello
Stephen N. Shulman	Wayne M. Zell
	Richard T. Choi

OF COUNSEL

Arnold Levy	Milton P. Kroll
	Jerome H. Simonds

SPECIAL TAX COUNSEL
Norman C. Bensley (Not admitted in DC)

ASSOCIATES

Serena P. Wiltshire	Bruce A. Rosenblum
Patrick J. Kearney	David Seth Sanders
Philip Lawrence DeCamara, III	(Not admitted in DC)

For full biographical listings, see the Martindale-Hubbell Law Directory

---

FREER, McGARRY, BODANSKY & RUBIN, A PROFESSIONAL CORPORATION (AV)

Suite 600, 1000 Thomas Jefferson Street, N.W., 20007
Telephone: 202-965-6565
Fax: 202-965-4839

Patrick H. Allen	Robert L. Ruben
Robert L. Bodansky	Steven K. Rubin
Lois R. Finkelstein	Mark L. Shaffer
Robert E. Freer, Jr.	John F. Sherlock, III
Michael S. Levy	Richard P. Stanton
Thomas G. McGarry	(Not admitted in DC)

OF COUNSEL
Stephen N. Gell

Louis M. Aronson	Stephen M. Bellotti
Jocelyn B. Barone	Laurie Curry Daugherty
(Not admitted in DC)	

For full biographical listings, see the Martindale-Hubbell Law Directory

Washington—Continued

* FRIED, FRANK, HARRIS, SHRIVER & JACOBSON (AV)

A Partnership including Professional Corporations
Suite 800, 1001 Pennsylvania Avenue, N.W., 20004-2505
Telephone: 202-639-7000
Cable Address: "Steric Washington"
Telex: 892406
Telecopy Rapifax: 202-639-7008
Zap Mail: 202-338-0110
Email: postmaster@ffhsj.com
New York, New York Office: One New York Plaza.
Telephone: 212-859-8000.
Cable Address: "Steric New York." W.U. Int.
Telex: 620223. W.U. Int.
Telex: 662119. W.U. Domestic: 128173.
Telecopier: 212-859-4000 (Dex 6200).
Los Angeles, California Office: 725 South Figueroa Street.
Telephone: 213- 689-5800.
London, England Office: 4 Chiswell Street, London EC1Y 4UP.
Telephone: 011-44-171-972-9600.
Fax: 011-44-171-972-9602.
Paris, France Office: 7, Rue Royale, 75008.
Telephone: (+331) 40-17-04-04.
Fax: (+331) 40-17-08-30.

WASHINGTON, D.C. PARTNERS

David L. Ansell	Jay R. Kraemer
T. J. Anthony, Jr.	Kenneth S. Kramer (P.C.)
David E. Birenbaum	Robert H. Ledig
John T. Boese	Daniel E. Loeb
Diane E. Burkley	James J. McCullough
John W. Chierichella	Deneen J. Melander
Peter V. Z. Cobb	Carleton K. Montgomery
(Not admitted in DC)	Matt T. Morley
Joel R. Feidelman (P.C.)	Lynda Troutman O'Sullivan
Stephen I. Glover	Harvey L. Pitt
Jack B. Gordon	Elliot E. Polebaum
Karl A. Groskaufmanis	Richard A. Sauber
David B. Hardison	James H. Schropp
Thomas S. Harman	Richard A. Steinwurtzel
Dixie Lynn Johnson	William H. Taft, IV
Robert E. Juceam	Andrew P. Varney
(Not admitted in DC)	Michael L. Waldman
Alan S. Kaden	Thomas P. Vartanian

Louis D. Victorino

OF COUNSEL

Milton Eisenberg (P.C.)	Marcus A. Rowden
Martin D. Ginsburg (P.C.)	Sargent Shriver
Max M. Kampelman	Daniel M. Singer

ASSOCIATES

Jonathan S. Aronie	Douglas R.M. King
Alisa Babitz	Yan Liu
Lawrence R. Bard	Jay D. Majors
Douglas W. Baruch	Kimberly L. Marsh
Bruce J. Casino	R. Patrick Murphy
Anthony C. Cianciotti	Elton F. Norman
Arlene R. Dick	(Not admitted in DC)
(Not admitted in DC)	Monica L. Parry
Mark J. Dorsey	(Not admitted in DC)
Evan Jay Falchuk	Anne B. Perry
Dawn E. Faris	Douglas E. Perry
(Not admitted in DC)	John D. Petro
David L. Fenimore	Catherine Evans Pollack
Robert M. Fisher	(Not admitted in DC)
Cynthia M. Fornelli	Michael J. Rivera
Michele E. Foster	Pamela A. Roth
Lisa Ann Fuller	Lawrence E. Ruggiero
Janet G. Gamer	Jeremy D. Sacks
Raymond C. Garrigan	Carol A. Shubinski
(Not admitted in DC)	(Not admitted in DC)
Karen T. Grisez	M. Gilbey Strub
Shannon L. Haralson	C. Anthony Trambley
Matthew P. Haskins	Vasiliki B. Tsaganos
(Not admitted in DC)	Doretha M. VanSlyke
Erik J. Heipt	Nancy R. Wagner
(Not admitted in DC)	(Not admitted in DC)
Consuelo Justine Hitchcock	James McKay Weitzel, Jr.
Lanae Holbrook	Robert C. Westerfeldt
J. Todd Hutchins	Edward Brewster Whittemore
(Not admitted in DC)	(Not admitted in DC)
Jonathan M. Jacobs	David B. Wiseman
Kathryn M. Keating	(Not admitted in DC)
(Not admitted in DC)	Anthony S. Yoo
James S. Kennell	(Not admitted in DC)

For full biographical listings, see the Martindale-Hubbell Law Directory

FRIEDLANDER, MISLER, FRIEDLANDER, SLOAN & HERZ (AV)

Suite 700, 1101 Seventeenth Street, N.W., 20036
Telephone: 202-872-0800
Cable Address: "FMSHLAW"
Telex: 64273
URL: http://www.dclawfirm.com

MEMBERS OF FIRM

Stephen H. Friedlander	Morris Kletzkin
Leonard A. Sloan	Jeffrey W. Ochsman
Gerald Herz	Jerome Ostrov

Jana Kay Guggenheim

ASSOCIATES

Philippa T. Gasnier	Mark D. Crawford
Robert J. Strayhorne	Glenn W. D. Golding
Alan Dean Sundburg	Roberto L. Veloso

Todd S. Sapiro

OF COUNSEL

Robert E. Greenberg

SPECIAL COUNSEL

Judith A. Hoggan

RETIRED

Jack L. Friedlander	Albert D. Misler

For full biographical listings, see the Martindale-Hubbell Law Directory

---

* GRAHAM & JAMES LLP (AV)

Suite 700, 2000 M Street, N.W., 20036
Telephone: 202-463-0800
Telex: 90-4103 Chalgray Wsh
Telecopier: 202-463-0823
Email: jsnyder@gj.com URL: http://www.gj.com
Other offices located in: San Francisco, Los Angeles, Newport Beach, Palo Alto, Sacramento and Fresno, California; Seattle, Washington; New York, New York; Milan, Italy; Beijing, China; Tokyo, Japan; London, England; Dusseldorf, Germany.
Associated Offices: Deacons Graham & James, Hong Kong, Sydney, Melbourne, Brisbane, Perth and Canberra, Australia.
Affiliated Offices: Deacons Graham & James, Hanoi and Ho Chi Minh City, Vietnam; Taipei, Taiwan, Jakarta, Indonesia; and Bangkok, Thailand; Dewi Soeharto & Rekan, Jakarta, Indonesia; Graham & James in affiliation with Taylor Joynson Garrett, London, England, Bucharest, Romania and Brussels, Belgium; Haarmann, Hemmelrath & Partner, Berlin, Munich, Leipzig, Frankfurt and Dusseldorf, Germany and Prague, Czech Republic; Mishare M. Al-Ghazali & Partners, Kuwait; Law Firm of Salah Al-Hejailan, Jeddah and Riyadah, Saudi Arabia; Gallastegui & Lozano, S.C., Mexico City, Mexico.

MEMBERS OF FIRM

Richard K. Bank	A. Wayne Lalle, Jr.
J. Michael Cavanaugh	N. David Palmeter
Michael P. Daniels	Yoshihiro Saito
Grace Parke Fremlin	Christopher "Kip" Schwartz
Yasuhiro Hagihara	Jeffrey L. Snyder
Eliot J. Halperin	Pheng Theng Tan
Paul J. Kennedy	Ronald I. Tisch

Lawrence R. Walders

OF COUNSEL

Stuart H. Anolik	Carroll E. Dubuc
(Not admitted in DC)	

RESIDENT ASSOCIATES

Stefano Agostini	Patrick A. Klingman
Joel D. Bonfiglio	Rebekah Martin Liu
Andrea Fekkes Dynes	C. Dennis Southard, IV
Susan B. Gerson	Richard S. Toikka
Frances J. Henderson	Randi S. Turner

For full biographical listings, see the Martindale-Hubbell Law Directory

---

* HALE AND DORR (AV)

A Partnership including Professional Corporations
1455 Pennsylvania Avenue, N.W., 20004
Telephone: 202-942-8400
Cable Address: "Hafis Wsh"
Telecopier: 202-942-8484
Boston, Massachusetts Office: 60 State Street.
Telephone: 617-526-6000.
Cable Address: "Hafis."
Telex: 94-0472.
Telecopier: Domestic 617-526-5000; 617-742-9108.
Manchester, New Hampshire Office: 1155 Elm Street.
Telephone: 603-628-7400.
Telecopier: 603-627-3880.

MEMBERS OF FIRM

James L. Quarles III (Resident)	Jay P. Urwitz (Resident)
Allen H. Fox (Resident)	Jeffrey J. Davidson (Resident)
Paul G. Wallach (Resident)	William G. McElwain (Resident)
Geoffrey S. Stewart (Resident)	Gilbert B. Kaplan (Resident)
Steven S. Snider (Resident)	Kenneth H. Slade (Resident)
David Sylvester (Resident)	William F. Leahy (Resident)

(See Next Column)

HALE AND DORR, *Washington—Continued*

MEMBERS OF FIRM (Continued)

Brent B. Siler (Resident)	David A. Wilson (Resident)
Henry N. Wixon (Resident)	John C. Christie, Jr. (Resident)
Kenneth R. Meade (Resident)	Sean P. Sherman (Resident)
Paul W. Jameson (Resident)	Kathleen M. Weinstein (Resident)

RESIDENT ASSOCIATES

Wendy E. Anderson	Mark C. Kalpin
William C. Groscup	Barbara J. O'Connell (Not admitted in DC)
Barry J. Hurewitz	
Jane A. Kalinski (Not admitted in DC)	Cris R. Revaz
	John M. Ryan

Rusty Wilson

COUNSEL

Miriam R. Gamson	William F. Winslow

For full biographical listings, see the Martindale-Hubbell Law Directory

---

HOBBS, STRAUS, DEAN & WALKER (AV)

Suite 800, 1819 H Street, N.W., 20006
Telephone: 202-783-5100
Fax: 202-296-8834
Email: cwilliams@hsdwde.com
Portland, Oregon Office: 1001 S.W. Fifth Avenue, 13th Floor.
Telephone: 503-242-1745.
Fax: 503-242-1072.
Norman, Oklahoma Office: 216 E. Eufaula Street.
Telephone: 405-360-9425.
Fax: 405-360-9428.

MEMBERS OF FIRM

Charles A. Hobbs	Hans Walker, Jr.
Jerry C. Straus	Marsha Kostura Schmidt
S. Bobo Dean	Michael L. Roy
Frances L. Horn	Matthew S. Jaffe
Carol L. Barbero	Judith A. Shapiro

ASSOCIATES

Geoffrey D. Strommer (Not admitted in DC)	John P. Lowndes
	Robert J. Miller
William R. Norman, Jr.	(Not admitted in DC)

Joseph H. Webster

OF COUNSEL

Kaighn Smith, Jr. (Not admitted in DC)	Dean B. Suagee

LEGAL SUPPORT PERSONNEL

Karen J. Funk	Marie Osceola-Branch

For full biographical listings, see the Martindale-Hubbell Law Directory

---

HOGAN & HARTSON L.L.P. (AV)

Columbia Square, 555 13th Street, N.W., 20004-1109
Telephone: 202-637-5600
Telex: 89-2757
Cable Address: "Hogander Washington"
Fax: 202-637-5910
Email: HHINFO@DC4.HHLAW.COM
Brussels, Belgium Office: Avenue des Arts 41, 1040.
Telephone: (32.2) 505.09.11.
Fax: (32.2) 505.09.96.
Budapest, Hungary Office: Bank Center, Granite Tower, 9th Floor, 1944 Budapest, Hungary.
Telephone: (36-1) 302-9050.
Fax: (36-1) 302-9060.
London, England Office: 21 Garlick Hill, EC4V 2AU.
Telephone: (44 171) 815 1200.
Fax: (44 171) 329 0299.
Moscow, Russia Office: 33/2 Usacheva Street, Building 3, 119048.
Telephone: (7095) 245-5190. Int'l
Telephone: (7501-907-0451).
Fax: (7095) 245-5192.
Fax: (7501) 907-0462 (International).
Paris, France (Affiliated Office): Cariddi, Mee, Rué, Avocats Associés à la Cour de Paris, 12, rue de la Paix, 75002.
Telephone: (33-1) 42.61.57.71.
Fax: (33-1) 42.61.79.21.
Prague, Czech Republic Office: Opletalova 37, 110 00.
Telephone: (42-2) 2422-9009.
Fax: (42-2) 2421-5105.
Warsaw, Poland Office: Marszalkowska 6/6, 00-590.
Telephone: (48 22) 628 0201; Int'l (48) 3912 1413.
Fax: (48 22) 628 7787; Int'l (48) 3912 1511.
Baltimore, Maryland Office: 111 South Calvert Street, 16th Floor.
Telephone: 410-659-2700.
Fax: 410-539-6981.
Bethesda, Maryland Office: Two Democracy Center, Suite 720, 6903 Rockledge Drive.
Telephone: 301-564-5000.
Fax: 301-493-5169.

(See Next Column)

Colorado Springs, Colorado Office: Two North Cascade Avenue, Suite 1300.
Telephone: 719-448-5900.
Fax: 719-448-5922.
Denver, Colorado Office: One Tabor Center, Suite 1500, 1200 Seventeenth Street.
Telephone: 303-899-7300.
Fax: 303-899-7333.
McLean, Virginia Office: 8300 Greensboro Drive.
Telephone: 703-848-2600.
Fax: 703-448-7650.

MEMBERS OF FIRM

Frank J. Hogan (1877-1944)	Claud v. S. Eley (Resident, Brussels, Belgium Office)
Nelson T. Hartson (1887-1976)	E. Tazewell Ellett
Jonathan L. Abram	Robert J. Elliott
Gil A. Abramson (Resident, Baltimore, Maryland Office)	Frank J. Fahrenkopf, Jr.
Patricia Riley Ambrose	Kenneth W. Farber
Jeanne S. Archibald	Prentiss E. Feagles
Deborah Taylor Ashford	Douglas A. Fellman
Helen Clark Atkeson (Resident, Denver, Colorado Office)	P. Dustin Finney, Jr.
Steven E. Ballew (Resident, Warsaw, Poland Office)	Howard I. Flack
	John M. Gardner (Resident, Denver, Colorado Office)
James T. Banks	James A. Gede, Jr. (Resident, Baltimore, Maryland Office)
Michael D. Barnes	
George P. Barsness	Gerald E. Gilbert (Resident, McLean, Virginia Office)
Raymond J. Batla, Jr. (Prague, Czech Republic, London, England and Budapest, Hungary Offices)	Bruce W. Gilchrist
	Gardner F. Gillespie
George Beall (Resident, Baltimore, Maryland Office)	C. Michael Gilliland
	J. Warren Gorrell, Jr.
Richard K.A. Becker (Resident, McLean, Virginia Office)	Kevin G. Gralley (Resident, Baltimore, Maryland Office)
Joseph C. Bell (Also at Warsaw, Poland Office)	Benton R. Hammond
	Anthony S. Harrington
A. Lee Bentley, III	Joseph M. Hassett
Scott A. Blackmun (Resident, Colorado Springs, Colorado Office)	Kenneth J. Hautman (Resident, McLean, Virginia Office)
	Elizabeth Blossom Heffernan
Lisa Bonanno	David J. Hensler
David W. Bonser	Patrick F. Hofer
John W. Borkowski (Also practicing individually, New Orleans, Louisiana)	Steven P. Hollman
	Howard M. Holstein
	Janet Pitterle Holt
William J. Bowman	Craig A. Hoover
William A. Bradford, Jr.	Richard T. Horan, Jr. (Resident, McLean, Virginia Office)
Robert P. Brady	James A. Hourihan
Patricia A. Brannan	William Mike House
Rebecca B. Bronson (Resident, Moscow, Russia Office)	Eve N. Howard
	Irene E. Howie
Stanley J. Brown (Resident, Bethesda, Maryland Office)	Stephen J. Immelt (Resident, Baltimore, Maryland Office)
Thomas N. Bulleit, Jr.	Maciej Jamka (Resident, Warsaw, Poland Office)
David W. Burgett	
Raymond S. Calamaro	Robert M. Jeffers
Alan F. Cariddi (Resident, Paris, France)	Harry T. Jones, Jr.
	Jonathan S. Kahan
George U. Carneal	Robert H. Kapp
Robert B. Cave	Steven M. Kaufman
Michael L. Cheroutes (Not admitted in DC; Also at Denver, Colorado Office)	John C. Keeney, Jr.
	J. Clinton Kelly (Resident, Baltimore, Maryland Office)
Alphonso A. Christian, II	Nevin J. Kelly
Claudette M. Christian	Robert J. Kenney, Jr.
Ty Cobb (Also at Baltimore, Maryland Office)	David A. Kikel
	Andrew J. Kilcarr
Vincent H. Cohen	Carol Weld King
Michael D. Colglazier (Resident, Baltimore, Maryland Office)	David P. King (Resident, Baltimore, Maryland Office)
Joseph G. Connolly, Jr.	Duncan S. Klinedinst (Resident, McLean, Virginia Office)
Jonathan A. Constine	
John W. Cook (Resident, Colorado Springs, Colorado Office)	Edward L. Korwek
	Gary Jay Kushner
	Kevin J. Lanigan
Robert L. Corn-Revere	Mark J. Larson
Colin W. Craik (Resident, Prague, Czech Republic Office)	Philip C. Larson
	C. Stephen Lawrence
	Stephan E. Lawton
Dean W. Crowell (Paris, France and Moscow, Russia Offices)	Thomas B. Leary
	Lewis E. Leibowitz
Sara-Ann Determan	David G. Leitch
John F. Dienelt	Kevin J. Lipson
Edward C. Dolan	Timothy A. Lloyd
Mark D. Dopp	Walter G. Lohr, Jr. (Resident, Baltimore, Maryland Office)
Edward C. Duckers	
Robert B. Duncan (Also at McLean, Virginia Office)	Ellen R. Lokker
Richard E. Dunne, III (Resident, Baltimore, Maryland Office)	Daniel H. Maccoby (Resident, London, England Office)
	David B. H. Martin, Jr.
Isabel P. Dunst	Warren H. Maruyama
Alan L. Dye	John P. Mathis
	George W. Mayo, Jr.

(See Next Column)

HOGAN & HARTSON L.L.P.—*Continued*

MEMBERS OF FIRM (Continued)

Mark E. Mazo
Mark S. McConnell
Janet L. McDavid
Thomas L. McGovern III
James G. McMillan
Bruce C. Mee
(Resident, Paris, France)
George H. Mernick, III
Martin Michaelson
Kathleen M. Miko
Evan Miller
George W. Miller
H. Todd Miller
Randy E. Miller
Barbara F. Mishkin
Austin S. Mittler
Jean S. Moore
Dennis K. Moyer (Resident,
McLean, Virginia Office)
Kornelia Nagy-Koppany
(Resident, Budapest, Hungary
Office)
William L. Neff
Karol Lyn Newman
William D. Nussbaum
Gerald E. Oberst, Jr. (Resident,
Brussels, Belgium Office)
Maureen E. O'Bryon
Bob Glen Odle
Linda L. Oliver
Nancy Doerr O'Neil (Not
admitted in DC; Washington,
D.C. and Baltimore, Maryland
Offices)
Bruce E. Parmley
Bert R. Peña
E. Barrett Prettyman, Jr.
Michael A. Proett (London,
England and Moscow, Russia
Offices)
Patrick M. Raher
Terri Steinhaus Reiskin
William S. Reyner, Jr.
Leslie S. Ritts
John G. Roberts, Jr.
Richard S. Rodin
Paul G. Rogers
Peter A. Rohrbach
Peter J. Romeo
James J. Rosenhauer
Mace J. Rosenstein

Steven J. Routh
Fabrice Rué
(Resident, Paris, France)
David J. Saylor
William C. Schmidt
Jeffrey G. Schneider
David J. Scott (Resident,
Denver, Colorado Office)
James E. Showen
Howard S. Silver
Michael J. Silver (Resident,
Baltimore, Maryland Office)
Richard S. Silverman
Paul C. Skelly
Edward C. Sledge (Resident,
Baltimore, Maryland Office)
Walter A. Smith, Jr.
Maree F. Sneed
Allen R. Snyder
Clyde H. Sorrell, Jr. (Resident,
Bethesda, Maryland Office)
Jac K. Sperling (Resident,
Denver, Colorado Office)
Timothy Charles Stanceu
John S. Stanton
Stuart G. Stein
Steven B. Steinborn
Clifford D. Stromberg
Jan Tanzer (Resident, Prague,
Czech Republic Office)
Peter W. Tredick
Helen R. Trilling
Niki Frangos Tuttle (Resident,
Denver, Colorado Office)
Ralph S. Tyler (Resident,
Baltimore, Maryland Office)
Craig H. Ulman
Craig A. Umbaugh (Resident,
Denver, Colorado Office)
Ann Morgan Vickery
Eric Von Salzen
Robert J. Waldman
Donis G. Walker (Denver and
Colorado Springs, Colorado
Offices)
Richard L.A. Weiner
T. Clark Weymouth
Michael Cunningham Williams
Joel S. Winnik
Pamela G. Winthrop
Erik B. Wulff

Emily M. Yinger

COUNSEL

Lee E. Berner (Resident,
McLean, Virginia Office)
Marc H. Bozeman (Practicing
individually, Los Angeles,
California)
Pavel Bradac (Resident, Prague,
Czech Republic Office)
Nancy Andreas Clodfelter
(Resident, Denver, Colorado
Office)
Alexander A. Dubitsky
Jacquelyn E. Grillon
Susan E. Joseph
Lynn G. Kamarck
Bogudar Kordasiewicz
(Resident, Warsaw, Poland
Office)
Elizabeth J. Lentini (Denver,
Colorado Office and also
practicing individually,
Milwaukee, Wisconsin)

Scott R. Lilienthal
Laura E. Loeb
Dirk Lontings (Resident,
Brussels, Belgium Office)
Milan Lovíšek (Resident, Czech
Republic Office)
Philip D. Porter (Resident,
McLean, Virginia Office)
Gerard J. Prud'homme
Marissa G. Repp
Steven A. Robins (Resident,
Bethesda, Maryland Office)
Margaret E. Roggensack
Neil A. Simon
Lorraine Sostowski
Krzysztof Stefanowicz (Resident,
Warsaw, Poland Office)
Rose Ann C. Sullivan (Resident,
Colorado Springs, Colorado
Office)
Joseph H. Young (Resident,
Baltimore, Maryland Office)

OF COUNSEL

John P. Arness
Marvin J. Diamond
Dennis J. Lehr
Lee Loevinger

Sherwin J. Markman
Seymour S. Mintz
John J. Ross
Jerome N. Sonosky

Clayton K. Yeutter

ASSOCIATES

Roger P. Alford
Amy M. Allen
Donna Lady Alpi
Audrey J. Anderson
Merry C. Anderson

Jaime A. Areizaga-Soto
(Not admitted in DC)
Ana Cristina Arumi
(Not admitted in DC)

(See Next Column)

ASSOCIATES (Continued)

Robert L. Asher (London,
England and Moscow, Russia
Offices)
Rose Marie L. Audette
Rita Bársony (Resident,
Budapest, Hungary Office)
H. Christopher Bartolomucci
(Not admitted in DC)
Sydney B. Bath
Pascale I. Bissainthe
Suzanne M. Bonnet (Resident,
Denver, Colorado Office)
Krystna M. Boron
Donna A. Boswell
Kathryn Webb Bradley
(Resident, Denver, Colorado
Office)
Adam Braff
(Not admitted in DC)
Karen-Ann Broe (Resident,
Bethesda, Maryland Office)
Donald C. Brown Jr.
D. Lea Browning
Andrea M. Bruce
Brooke Bumpers
Paul A. Burkett
(Not admitted in DC)
Irene Florence Chang
(Not admitted in DC)
James C. Chen
Katherine Y.K. Cheung
Janet S. Chung
(Not admitted in DC)
Jessica C. Clark
(Not admitted in DC)
Laurie A. Clarke
Jacqueline P. Cleary
Keefe B. Clemons (Resident,
Baltimore, Maryland Office)
N. Thomas Connally, III
(Resident, McLean, Virginia
Office)
Maryanne Courtney
Tia Cudahy
Jenifer J. Curhan
(Not admitted in DC)
Elizabeth Gordon Dellenbaugh
Edward S. Desmarais, Jr.
Scott M. Deutchman
Kyle D. Dixon
(Not admitted in DC)
Daniel M. Donahue
Kristen A. Donoghue
(Not admitted in DC)
James H. Doyle
David R. Dunn (Resident,
Baltimore, Maryland Office)
S. Paige Eldridge
(Not admitted in DC)
Cori Flam
(Not admitted in DC)
William P. Flanagan
Christopher Foster
(Not admitted in DC)
Jody M. Foster
Jonathan S. Franklin
Amy Bowerman Freed
(Resident, Baltimore,
Maryland Office)
Brooke E. Frewing (Resident,
McLean, Virginia Office)
Deborah Schwager Froling
Aleksander Galos (Resident,
Warsaw, Poland Office)
Anthony L. Gardner (Brussels,
Belgium and Paris, France
Offices)
Gregory G. Garre
John F. Gaul
(Not admitted in DC)
Jeffrey S. George (Resident,
Colorado Springs, Colorado
Office)
Victoria W. Girard
Dean C. Graham
Catherine R. Guttman
(Not admitted in DC)
David S. Haddock, II (Resident,
McLean, Virginia Office)
Martin J. Hahn
Gregory W. Hair
(Not admitted in DC)
Gwyneth E. Hambley

David F. Hannan (Resident,
Baltimore, Maryland Office)
Shannon Thee Hanson
(Resident, Baltimore,
Maryland Office)
Karen M. Hardwick
Katherine Marie Harman-Stokes
(Not admitted in DC)
Michele Sasse Harrington
Steven H. Hartmann
(Not admitted in DC)
Karis A. Hastings
Melinda Reid Hatton
Christopher P. Healey
James G. Higham
(Not admitted in DC)
Linda A. Hildreth (Resident,
McLean, Virginia Office)
Janice Marchiafava Hogan
(Not admitted in DC)
Jana Hrstková (Resident,
Prague, Czech Republic
Office)
Kathryn R. Hu (Resident,
Baltimore, Maryland Office)
Stefan Jaworski (Resident,
Warsaw, Poland Office)
Sten A. Jensen
Kathleen C. Jones (Resident,
Baltimore, Maryland Office)
Melissa R. Jones
Kathryn L. Jorden
(Not admitted in DC)
Stephen L. Kabler (Resident,
Denver, Colorado Office)
Margaret E. Kane
Lawrence D. Kaplan
Robert W. Karwowski
(Resident, Warsaw, Poland
Office)
Nancy J. Kellner
Amy Folsom Kett (Resident,
McLean, Virginia Office)
Michael L. Kidney
Christopher L. Killion
Anne S. Kim
(Not admitted in DC)
Sarah L. Kinnick (Resident,
Denver, Colorado Office)
Dana L. Klapper (Resident,
Denver, Colorado Office)
Julia F. Kogan
(Not admitted in DC)
Tamás I. Kovács (Resident,
Budapest, Hungary Office)
Robert Krasnodebski (Resident,
Warsaw, Poland Office)
Joan H. Krause
Michele A. Kulerman
S. Gregg Kunzi
(Not admitted in DC)
Guido Lamal (Resident,
Brussels, Belgium Office)
Mark L. Landis
(Not admitted in DC)
Helene P. Lasker
Mitchell J. Lazris
Wendy A. Learmont
Joanne L. Leasure
F. William LeBeau
(Not admitted in DC)
C. Vincent Leon-Guerrero
(Resident, McLean, Virginia
Office)
John R. Lilyestrom
(Not admitted in DC)
David L. Littleton
Margaret C. Liu
Eric H. Loeb
(Not admitted in DC)
Jeffrey Alan Lowe
L. Weatherly Lowe
Karin Luftmanová (Resident,
Prague, Czech Republic
Office)
Paul D. Manca
Carmel Martin
(Not admitted in DC)
Thene M. Martin (Resident,
Baltimore, Maryland Office)
Helen P. McClure
Scott D. McClure

(See Next Column)

HOGAN & HARTSON L.L.P., *Washington—Continued*

ASSOCIATES (Continued)

Tracy L. McFerrin
(Not admitted in DC)
James H. McGrath, IV
(Resident, McLean, Virginia Office)
Mona Meeker (Resident, McLean, Virginia Office)
Craig B. Mendelsohn, M.D.
Kathy Marlo Miljanic
Jeremy B. Miller
Sheryl Rosensky Miller
Paul A. Minorini
William L. Monts, III
James J. Moore
Steven F. Morris
Steven A. Museles
Lech Najbauer (Resident, Warsaw, Poland Office)
Susan S. Namkung (Resident, McLean, Virginia Office)
Lakshmi Natarajan
Douglas R. M. Nazarian (Resident, Baltimore, Maryland Office)
J. Patrick Nevins
(Not admitted in DC)
David Newmann
Edward B. Parks, II
(Not admitted in DC)
Alane A. Peragallo (Resident, McLean, Virginia Office)
M. Elizabeth Peters
Douglas S. Phillips
Catherine L. Pinkerton
Clara M. Poffenberger
(Not admitted in DC)
Lisa L. Poole
Gwendolyn A. Powell
Sharis Arnold Pozen
Robert N. Rabecs
Rosemary H. Ratcliff
Jonathan T. Rees
Scott H. Reisch (Resident, Denver, Colorado Office)
Thomas E. Repke (Resident, McLean, Virginia Office)
Patrick J. Reynolds (Resident, Baltimore, Maryland Office)
Margaret T. Rhinelander
(Not admitted in DC)
Beth L. Roberts
Stephanie Robinson
Katherine P. Rosefsky (Resident, McLean, Virginia Office)
Susan M. Rotatori
Emily Beth Rubin
(Not admitted in DC)
James P. Ruggeri
Richard T. Saas
Joanna A. Sadowska (Resident, Warsaw, Poland Office)
Chase J. Sanders
Stephen M. Sargent
(Not admitted in DC)
Todd D. Schafer (Resident, Moscow, Russia Office)

Christopher A. Schindler
(Not admitted in DC)
Frédérique Schlumberger
(Resident, Paris, France)
Julie Mathews Schuetze
Michelle M. Shanahan
W. Ming Shao
(Not admitted in DC)
Jeffrey K. Shapiro
Scott G. Silverstein
David W. Smail
Margaret U. Song
Robert L. Spencer
Jolanta Sterbenz
Lowell R. Stern
Agnieszka Suchecka-Tarnacka
(Resident, Warsaw, Poland Office)
Molly E. Sullivan
Andrzej Sutkowski (Resident, Warsaw, Poland Office)
Marta I. Tanenhaus
Sharon L. Tasman (Resident, McLean, Virginia Office)
Farinaz S. Tehrani
Sergei V. Terentiev (Resident, Moscow, Russia Office)
Patricia S. Thompson
(Not admitted in DC)
Sonia Gustafson Thomsen
Andrew C. Topping (Resident, Baltimore, Maryland Office)
James K. Trefil
Pamela R. Trimble
(Not admitted in DC)
Albert W. Turnbull
Carol A. Umhoefer (Resident, Paris, France Office)
Stephen G. Vaskov
Katrien Vorlat (Resident, Brussels, Belgium Office)
Phyllis V. Wan (Resident, Denver, Colorado Office)
Edith F. Webster (Resident, Baltimore, Maryland Office)
Robert A. Welp
(Not admitted in DC)
Glenn P. Wicks
Edward C. Wilson, Jr.
Ronald J. Wiltsie, II (Resident, McLean, Virginia Office)
David A. Winter
Robert E. Witwer (Resident, Denver, Colorado Office)
Christopher S. Yoo
(Not admitted in DC)
Mitchell E. Zamoff
Artur Zawadowski (Resident, Warsaw, Poland Office)
Elizabeth (Elzbieta) M. Zechenter
Stephen J. Zempolich
Allison K. Zidlicky
Petra Žikovska (Resident, Prague, Czech Republic Office)

For full biographical listings, see the Martindale-Hubbell Law Directory

HOLLAND & KNIGHT LLP (AV)

A Partnership including Professional Corporations
2100 Pennsylvania Avenue, N.W., 20037
Telephone: 202-955-3000
Fax: 202-955-5564
Email: hklaw.com *URL:* http://www.hklaw.com
Fort Lauderdale, Florida Office: One East Broward Boulevard, Suite 1300.
Telephone: 954-525-1000.
Fax: 954-463-2030.
Jacksonville, Florida Office: 50 N. Laura Street, Suite 3900.
Telephone: 904-353-2000.
Fax: 904-358-1872.
Lakeland, Florida Office: 92 Lake Wire Drive.
Telephone: 941-682-1161.
Fax: 941-688-1186.
Miami, Florida Office: 701 Brickell Avenue, 30th Floor.
Telephone: 305-374-8500.
Fax: 305-787-7799.
Orlando, Florida Office: 200 S. Orange Avenue, Suite 2600.
Telephone: 407-425-8500.
Fax: 407-244-5288.

(See Next Column)

St. Petersburg, Florida Office: One Progress Plaza, Suite 1600.
Telephone: 813-896-7171.
Fax: 813-822-8048.
Tallahassee, Florida Office: 315 Calhoun Street, Suite 600.
Telephone: 904-224-7000.
Fax: 904-224-8832.
Tampa, Florida Office: 400 North Ashley, Suite 2300.
Telephone: 813-227-8500.
Fax: 813-229-0134.
West Palm Beach, Florida Office: 625 N. Flagler Drive, Suite 700.
Telephone: 561-833-2000.
Fax: 561-650-8399.
Atlanta, Georgia Office: One Atlantic Center, 1201 West Peachtree Street, N.E., Suite 2000.
Telephone: 404-817-8500.
Fax: 404-881-0470.

WASHINGTON, D.C. MEMBERS AND ASSOCIATES

James E. Akers
David H. Baker
Steven K. Berry
(Not admitted in DC)
Timothy J. Bloomfield
Stephen A. Bogorad
David W. Briggs
Henry J. Brothers II
John A. Buchman
Harold R. Bucholtz
William B. Canfield, III
Mark D. Colley
George A. Dalley
Ross W. Dembling
William J. Dempster
Steven A. Diaz
G. Richard Dunnells
Richard O. Duvall
Stuart S. Dye
Amy L. Edwards
J. Edward Fowler
(Not admitted in DC)
Alvin J. Geske
Robert E. Glenn, IV
Steven D. Gordon
T. Wayne Gray
Dennis M. Horn
Gina Schaar Howard
Edward W. Hummers, Jr.
David S. Kahn
Alan S. Kerxton
Paul J. Kiernan
Richard E. Lear

Jerry Levine
Michael L. Martinez
Dorn C. McGrath III
David P. Metzger
Maurice J. Montaldi
Richard Lee Moorhouse
Alberto J. Mora
S. Scott Morrison
William J. Mutryn
Christopher A. Myers
La Fonte Nesbitt
Stephen D. Niles
Keith A. Onsdorff
(Not admitted in DC)
Stephen J. Powell
Florence Weatherly Prioleau
Robert L. Rhodes, Jr.
Christopher L. Rissetto
Marvin Rosenberg
Michael J. Ruane
Alban Salaman
Stephen Brett Shapiro
Richard P. Sills
David C. Silver
Judy G. Sinkin
Chesterfield Smith
Mitchell H. Stabbe
Andrew W. Stephenson
Scott Andrew Sterling
Janet R. Studley
Charles Welch Tiedemann
David A. Vaughan
Stephen J. Weiss

Lawrence J. Wolk

Robert Bergen
(Not admitted in DC)
Melinda Burrows
Lynn Estes Calkins
Stephanie Childs
(Not admitted in DC)
Keith Clausen
(Not admitted in DC)
Jennifer Crowe
Laura A. Eilers
(Not admitted in DC)
Philip Tucker Evans
Laura E. Gasser
Richard M. Gold
Jonathan A. Greenberg
Robin Belton Hayes
Edward V. Hickey, III
Craig A. Holman
Julie Chung Kim
(Not admitted in DC)
Ernesto A. Lanza

Patricia Y. Lee
George T. Magee
Marc E. Miller
(Not admitted in DC)
Karis Lynn North
(Not admitted in DC)
Ronald A. Oleynik
Suzanne Parmet
Frank K. Peterson
Scott M. Pritchett
Joseph W. Rasnic
Lori R. Shapiro
(Not admitted in DC)
Theodore S. Silva, Jr.
Theodore Washington Small, Jr.
Jennifer M. Smith
Gloria B. Solomon
Leslie A. Spitalney
(Not admitted in DC)
Bradley D. Wine
Mary F. Withum

OF COUNSEL

Richard S. Weinstein (Not admitted in DC)

For full biographical listings, see the Martindale-Hubbell Law Directory

HOWREY & SIMON (AV)

1299 Pennsylvania Avenue, N.W., 20004-2402
Telephone: 202-783-0800
Fax: 202-383-6610
Los Angeles, California Office: Suite 1400, 550 South Hope Street, 90071-2604.
Telephone: 213-892-1800.
Fax: 213-892-2300.
Menlo Park, California Office: 301 Ravenswood Avenue, 94025.
Telephone: 415-463-8100.
Fax: 415-463-8400.

COUNSEL

William Simon   David C. Murchison
Harold F. Baker

(See Next Column)

HOWREY & SIMON—*Continued*

MEMBERS OF FIRM

Robert G. Abrams	Thomas A. Isaacson
Scott Arnold	Raymond A. Jacobsen, Jr.
Jeffrey I. Auerbach	Marcia Press Kaplan
Richard E. Ayres	Joel D. Kaufman
Gregory L. Baker	Anthony F. King
Darren B. Bernhard	Richard H. Kjeldgaard
George D. Billinson	Roger A. Klein
John Bodner, Jr.	Lisa I. Latorre
Ray S. Bolze	Joseph P. Lavelle
Marguerite Smith Boyd	Ezra C. Levine
Timothy E. Boyle	Mark I. Levy
John DeQ. Briggs, III	Christopher H. Marraro
Robert J. Brookhiser, Jr.	Rosemary H. McEnery
John F. Bruce	Katherine D. McManus
Robert M. Bruskin	Richard S. Meyer
Patricia G. Butler	Helen Katherine Michael
John G. Calender	Peter E. Moll
Allen Cannon III	Harold D. Murry, Jr.
Matthew J. Clark	John W. Nields, Jr.
Richard T. Colman	Gary H. Nunes
Basil C. Culyba	William R. O'Brien
Lee P. Curtis	John C. Peirce
James F. Davis	Eberhard W. Pfaller, Jr.
David C. Eddy	Paul Plaia, Jr.
W. Neil Eggleston	Keith E. Pugh, Jr.
Jeffrey N. Eisenstein	Richard A. Ripley
(Not admitted in DC)	William A. Roberts, III
Charles J. Engel, III	Jon Randall Roellke
Margaret H. Fitzsimmons	Robert F. Ruyak
Scott E. Flick	Lisa J. Saks
Joel M. Freed	Ralph J. Savarese
John G. Froemming	Mark C. Schechter
Kenneth A. Gallo	Marc G. Schildkraut
Jerrold J. Ganzfried	Claude F. Scott, Jr.
Sherry W. Gilbert	Thomas J. Scott, Jr.
Cecilia H. Gonzalez	Terrence C. Sheehy
David B. Graham	Herbert C. Shelley
Robert L. Green, Jr.	Harvey G. Sherzer
Alan M. Grimaldi	Robert H. Shulman
Edward Han	C. Scott Talbot
Stuart H. Harris	Richard E. Wallace, Jr.
Philip H. Hecht	William E. Wallace, III
John E. Heintz	William L. Webber
Edward P. Henneberry	Mark D. Wegener
Roxann E. Henry	A. Duncan Whitaker
Michael A. Hertzberg	Lois G. Williams
Thomas N. Heyer	Alan M. Wiseman
Robert H. Huey	Alan R. Yuspeh
Michael J. Hurley	Carmine R. Zarlenga

Margaret M. Zwisler

OF COUNSEL

J. Eric André	David R. Francis

SPECIAL COUNSEL

Juliana M. Cofrancesco	Gregg A. Hand
Barbara A. Friedman	John W. Kampman

INTERNATIONAL TRADE COUNSEL

Alice Alexandra Kipel

GOVERNMENT CONTRACTS COUNSEL

Lucy Eliasof Gies

RESEARCH AND INFORMATION SERVICES COUNSEL

Kerry L. Adams

ASSOCIATES

F. Alexander Amrein	Richard P. Castiglia, Jr.
Wendy M. Anderson	(Not admitted in DC)
Michele Arington	Jerone C. Cecelic
Timothy K. Armstrong	Hollis T. Chen
Maura Henry Barbour	Kelly A. Clement
Melvin Lee Barnes, Jr.	Richard B. Clifford, Jr.
G. Hunter Bates	Michael Paul Austern Cohen
(Not admitted in DC)	Gregory J. Commins, Jr.
Alicia J. Batts	Peter C. Condron
Leiv H. Blad, Jr.	Deborah L. Connor
John W. Bohn	Kieran M. Corcoran
William M. Bosch	Kellie A. Cosgrove
Karen F. Boyd	Michael G. Cowie
(Not admitted in DC)	Martin F. Cunniff
Daniel E. Brannen, Jr.	Daniel N. Daisak
Kenneth W. Brothers	Elisa A. D'Andrea
Jeffrey D. Brown	(Not admitted in DC)
David P. Burns	Brian A. Darst
James M. Burns	Mindy G. Davis
Celine T. Callahan	Lara A. Degenhart
Cono A. Carrano	Diana L. Dietrich
Matthew E. Carswell	Marlin Dohlman
(Not admitted in DC)	Jon B. Dubrow

(See Next Column)

ASSOCIATES (Continued)

Steven C. Dubuc	Christopher N. Olsen
(Not admitted in DC)	Joseph A. Ostoyich
Thomas M. Dunham	Hae-Chan Park
Jeremy W. Eisenberg	(Not admitted in DC)
Patrick D. Farrington	Geoffrey C. Pemble
(Not admitted in DC)	(Not admitted in DC)
Alan M. Fisch	Terry M. Petrie
(Not admitted in DC)	(Not admitted in DC)
Therese K. Francese	Dianne S. Pickersgill
Michele Van Patten Frank	Fabrizio F.R. Rasetti
(Not admitted in DC)	H. Jonathan Redway
Peder A. Garske	Thomas A. Reed
Steven N. Gersten	Bert C. Reiser
Thomas E. Gilbertsen	Moira T. Roberts
Robert L. Grabarek, Jr.	Scott L. Robertson
Kathleen M. Graber	(Not admitted in DC)
Charles E. Graf	Howard T. Rosenblatt
Douglas S. Grandstaff	John J. Rosenthal
Jonathan G. Graves	Matthew J. Schlesinger
Jennifer M. Hall	Edward B. Schwartz
William F. Hughes	Richard L. Schwartzbard
Robert P. Jacobs	Timothy L. Scott
Asheesh J. Jain	(Not admitted in DC)
Pamela S. Kane	Craig P. Seebald
Andrew T. Kerr	Laura S. Shores
Gilbert S. Keteltas	S. Lloyd Smith
Jason C. Klein	(Not admitted in DC)
James G. Kress	Jon A. Soderberg
Dawn K. Laske	Michael J. Songer
Elizabeth J. Leatherbarrow	(Not admitted in DC)
(Not admitted in DC)	Rachel Lisa Strong
Jeffrey M. Lenser	Marcia L. Stuart
Nancy C. Libin	Terry L. Sullivan
Charles A. Loughlin	(Not admitted in DC)
Karen Louise Manos	Anne Talbot
Keith R. Marino	Andrew E. Thomas
David R. Marsh	Gary Thompson
(Not admitted in DC)	Tamra L. Toussaint
Elizabeth B. McCallum	Thomas J. Trendl
James J. McGuire	ToQuyen T. Truong
Scott S. Megregian	Richard J. Veltman
Joseph A. Micallef	(Not admitted in DC)
Victor J. Miller	David S. Wachen
Richard D. Milone, Jr.	Brian D. Wallach
David M. Morris	Joseph J. Weissman
Harriet Mountcastle-Walsh	(Not admitted in DC)
Kirstin Ames Mueller	Evan Jeffrey Werbel
(Not admitted in DC)	Ellen S. Winter
P. Todd Mullins	Diane E. Wolf
Karen L. Nicastro	(Not admitted in DC)
Dimitri J. Nionakis	Matthew M. Wolf
Rodney J. Nydam	(Not admitted in DC)
Wendy S. Oatis	Thomas G. Woolston
Matthew J. O'Connor	Paul N. Zolfagari

For full biographical listings, see the Martindale-Hubbell Law Directory

---

★ HUGHES HUBBARD & REED LLP (AV)

1300 I Street, N.W., Suite 900 West, 20005-3306
Telephone: 202-408-3600
Telex: 89-2674
Telecopier: 202-408-3636
New York, New York Office: One Battery Park Plaza, 10004.
Telephone: 212-837-6000.
Telex: 427120.
Telecopier: 212-422-4726.
Los Angeles, California Office: 350 S. Grand Avenue, Suite 3600, 90071-3442.
Telephone: 213-613-2800.
Telecopier: 213-613-2950.
Miami, Florida Office: 201 South Biscayne Boulevard, Suite 2500, 33131-4332.
Telephone: 305-358-1666.
Fax: 305-371-8759.
Telex: 518785.
Paris, France Office: 47, Avenue Georges Mandel, 75116.
Telephone: 33 (0)1 44 05 80 00.
Telex: 645440.
Telecopier: 33 (0)1 45 53 15 04.

RESIDENT PARTNERS

Lawrence F. Bates	Robert P. Reznick
Dennis S. Klein	Kathleen M. Russo
John J. Mandler	William R. Stein

John M. Townsend

SPECIAL COUNSEL

Kevin M. Crotty	Mary Clare Fitzgerald
(Not admitted in DC)	(Not admitted in DC)
Alan G. Kashdan	Daniel Wolf

For full biographical listings, see the Martindale-Hubbell Law Directory

Washington—Continued

JACKSON & CAMPBELL, P.C. (AV)

South Tower, One Lafayette Centre, 1120-20th Street, N.W., 20036
Telephone: 202-457-1600
Telecopier: 202-457-1678
Email: JCLAWFIRM@AOL.COM
Rockville, Maryland Office: Suite 225, 200 A Monroe Street.
Telephone: 301-340-0450.
Baltimore, Maryland Office: 111 S. Calvert Street, Suite 2700.
Telephone: 410-385-5343.
Vienna, Virginia Office: 8300 Boone Boulevard, Suite 500.
Telephone: 703-522-1330.

Peter F. Axelrad	Robert N. Kelly
James E. Brammer	Richard S. Kuhl
John J. Brennan, III	Peter Lipresti
Richard W. Bryan	Warren C. Lutz
James E. Cervenak	Nicholas S. McConnell
Douglas W. Charnas	Michael J. McManus
David H. Cox	M. Elizabeth Medaglia
Richard J. DeFeo, Jr.	Donald N. Memmer
Timothy R. Dingilian	James R. Michal
Benjamin W. Dulany	Christine A. Nykiel
Arthur C. Elgin, Jr.	Kenneth Wells Parkinson
Patricia D. Gurne	Mary Lynn Reed
Christopher B. Hanback	James P. Schaller
Vernon W. Johnson, III	Alan R. Swendiman

SENIOR COUNSEL

Arthur D. Burger	Kathleen Kenny
	(Not admitted in DC)

Adam S. Caldwell	Joanna M. Pedas
Robert Clayton Cooper	Marc A. Peritz
Elisa A. Eisenberg	(Not admitted in DC)
Renee L. Giachino	Tonia Jones Powell
Mark A. Goodin	Robert E. Rider, Jr.
Thomas F. Gristina	Marci I. Rose
(Not admitted in DC)	E. Deren Rothenberger
Mary Anne Walker Hilliard	Kenneth E. Ryan
Maureen P. Kerrigan	Richard L. Schwartz
Gina S. Love	Judith A. Selby
John J. Matteo	Donald L. Uttrich
Douglas C. McAllister	John M. Vassiliades
Thomas P. McMahon	Peter A. von Mehren
(Not admitted in DC)	Liliana E. Ward
Scott Alton Mills	(Not admitted in DC)

For full biographical listings, see the Martindale-Hubbell Law Directory

JACKSON & KELLY (AV)

2401 Pennsylvania Avenue, N.W., Suite 400, 20037
Telephone: 202-973-0200
Fax: 202-973-0232
Charleston, West Virginia Office: 1600 Laidley Tower, P.O. Box 553.
Telephone: 304-340-1000.
Fax: 304-340-1130.
Martinsburg, West Virginia Office: 300 Foxcroft Avenue, P.O. Box 1068.
Telephone: 304-263-8800.
Fax: 304-263-7110.
Morgantown, West Virginia Office: 6000 Hampton Center, P.O. Box 619.
Telephone: 304-599-3000.
Fax: 304-285-2040.
New Martinsville, West Virginia Office: 256 Russell Avenue, P.O. Box 68.
Telephone: 304-455-1751.
Fax: 304-455-6314.
Charles Town, West Virginia Office: 700 East Washington Street, P.O. Box 983.
Telephone: 304-728-6088.
Fax: 304-728-6029.
Parkersburg, West Virginia Office: 412 Market Street, Suite 202, P.O. Box 1144.
Telephone: 304-424-3490.
Fax: 304-424-3499.
Fairmont, West Virginia Office: 1000 Technology Drive, Suite 1310.
Telephone: 304-368-2000.
Fax: 304-368-2020.
Lexington, Kentucky Office: 175 East Main Street, Suite 500, P.O. Box 2150.
Telephone: 606-255-9500.
Fax: 606-281-6478.
Denver, Colorado Office: Suite 2710, 1660 Lincoln Street.
Telephone: 303-837-0003.
Fax: 303-837-9688.

MEMBERS OF FIRM

Thad S. Huffman	G. Lindsay Simmons
(Administrative Manager)	L. Poe Leggette
John K. McDonald	

ASSOCIATES

James Zissler	Nancy L. Pell

(See Next Column)

OF COUNSEL

Louis J. Ferrara	Bruce A. Tassan
(Not admitted in DC)	

LEGAL SUPPORT PERSONNEL

Christina D. Larsen

For full biographical listings, see the Martindale-Hubbell Law Directory

✳ JONES, DAY, REAVIS & POGUE (AV)

Metropolitan Square, 1450 G Street, N.W., 20005-2088
Telephone: 202-879-3939
Cable Address: "Attorneys Washington"
Telex: W.U. (Domestic) 89-2410 ATTORNEYS WASH (International) 64363 ATTORNEYS WASH
Telecopier: 202-737-2832
In Atlanta, Georgia: 3500 One Peachtree Center, 303 Peachtree Street, N.E.
Telephone: 404-521-3939.
Cable Address: "Attorneys Atlanta".
Telex: 54-2711.
Telecopier: 404-581-8330.
In Brussels, Belgium: Avenue Louise 480, 7th Floor, B-1050 Brussels.
Telephone: 32-2-645-14-11.
Telecopier: 32-2-645-14-45.
In Chicago, Illinois: 77 West Wacker.
Telephone: 312-782-3939.
Telecopier: 312-782-8585.
In Cleveland, Ohio: North Point, 901 Lakeside Avenue.
Telephone: 216-586-3939.
Cable Address: "Attorneys Cleveland."
Telex: 980389.
Telecopier: 216-579-0212.
In Columbus, Ohio: 1900 Huntington Center.
Telephone: 614-469-3939.
Cable Address: "Attorneys Columbus."
Telecopier: 614-461-4198.
In Dallas, Texas: 2300 Trammell Crow Center, 2001 Ross Avenue.
Telephone: 214-220-3939.
Cable Address: "Attorneys Dallas."
Telex: 730852.
Telecopier: 214-969-5100.
In Frankfurt, Germany: Triton Haus, Bockenheimer Landstrasse 42, 60323 Frankfurt am Main.
Telephone: 49-69-9726-3939.
Telecopier: 49-69-9726-3993.
In Geneva, Switzerland: 20, rue de Candolle.
Telephone: 41-22-320-2339.
Telecopier: 41-22-320-1232.
In Hong Kong: 29th Floor, Entertainment Building, 30 Queen's Road Central.
Telephone: 852-2526-6895.
Telecopier: 852-2868-5871.
In Irvine, California: 2603 Main Street, Suite 900 .
Telephone: 714-851-3939.
Telex: 194911 Lawyers LSA.
Telecopier: 714-553-7539.
In London, England: One Mount Street.
Telephone: 44-71-493-9361.
Cable Address: "Surgoe London WI."
Telecopier: 44-71-493-9666.
In Los Angeles, California: 555 West Fifth Street, Suite 4600.
Telephone: 213-489-3939.
Telex: 181439 UD.
Telecopier: 213-243-2539.
In New Delhi, India: Pathak & Associates, 13th Floor, Dr. Gopal Das Bhaven, 28 Barakhamba Road.
Telephone: 91-11-373-8793.
Telecopier: 91-11-335-3761.
In New York, New York: 599 Lexington Avenue.
Telephone: 212-326-3939.
Cable Address: "JONESDAY NEWYORK."
Telex: 237013 JDRP UR.
Telecopier: 212-755-7306.
In Paris, France: 62, rue du Faubourg Saint-Honore.
Telephone: 33-1-44-71-3939.
Cable Address: "Surgoe Paris."
Telex: 290156 Surgoe.
Telecopier: 33-1-49-24-0471.
In Pittsburgh, Pennsylvania: 500 Grant Street, 31st Floor.
Telephone: 412-391-3939.
Cable Address: "Attorneys Pittsburgh".
Telecopier: 412-394-7959.
In Riyadh, Saudi Arabia: Law Offices of Saud M.A. Shawwaf, P.O. Box 22166.
Telephone: (966-1) 462-8866.
Telex: 401831 SAUCON SJ.
Telecopier: (966-1) 462-9001.
In Taipai, Taiwan: 8th Floor, 2 Tun Hwa South Road, Section 2.
Telephone: (886-2) 704-6808.
Telecopier: (886-2) 704-6791.

(See Next Column)

JONES, DAY, REAVIS & POGUE—*Continued*

In Tokyo, Japan: Toranomon MT Building, 4th Floor, 10-3, Toranomon 3-Chome, Minato-Ku, Tokyo 105, Japan.
Telephone: 81-3-3433-3939.
Telecopier: 81-3-5401-2725.

MEMBERS OF FIRM IN WASHINGTON, D.C.

Joseph S. Iannucci	David C. Roseman
Michael Bradfield	Lester W. Droller
Timothy B. Dyk	Raymond J. Wiacek
James T. O'Hara	Stephen J. Brogan
Frieda K. Wallison	Timothy J. Finn
J. Lawrence Manning, Jr.	Stephen C. Jones
Jonathan C. Rose	Gregory M. Luce
Sigmund T. Weiner	Toby G. Singer
James A. Wilderotter	Teresa A. Brooks
Robert F. McDermott, Jr.	Kathryn M. Fenton
Joe Sims	Peter F. Garvin, III
James J. Graham	Kevin D. McDonald
C. Thomas Long	Kenneth J. Ayres
Mark K. Sisitsky	Charles A. James
Junius C. McElveen, Jr.	Robert H. Klonoff
Paul S. Ryerson	Mary Ellen Powers
Tom D. Smith	Steven A. Teitelbaum
Joseph M. David, Jr.	Peter J. Biersteker
(Not admitted in DC)	Susan Zywien Haller
Clark Evans Downs	Carolyn Y. Thompson
Willis J. Goldsmith	Christopher F. Dugan
Phillip A. Proger	Patricia A. Dunn
Thomas F. Cullen, Jr.	Kevin D. Cramer
George T. Manning	Glen D. Nager
Robert S. Waters	Adrian Wager-Zito
Richard D. Avil, Jr.	Beth Heifetz
Donald B. Ayer	Barbara McDowell
Lawrence L. Lamade	William V. O'Reilly
John C. Roebuck	James D. Wareham

OF COUNSEL

Herbert J. Hansell	William E. Swope
(Not admitted in DC)	William J. Schilling
Peter E. Heyward	

SENIOR ATTORNEYS

David A. Copus	Jerome J. Zaucha
Robert C. Jones	Stephen J. Goodman

ASSOCIATES

Melissa T. Scanlon	Blaney Harper
Adel B.A. Al-Ali (Not admitted	(Not admitted in DC)
in the United States)	Andrew S. Reilly
Heidi Hughes Bumpers	Michael R. Shumaker
Kay Albaugh Hooker	Peter J. Wang
Mary L. Hale	Jonathan Berman
Charles V. Stewart	Richard J. Caplan
Julia M. Broas	Karie L. Delshad-Nik
David M. Matuszewski	Abhi-Shék Jain
Kathleen Marie McChesney	Mandy Jones
James E. Anklam	Gregory G. Katsas
Elliot D. Eder	William K. Kelso
Michael P. Gurdak	Marcia Y. Lucas
David E. Miller	Sarah Dryden Mackey
Gregory M. Shumaker	Sharon K. Mollman
Kevin J. McIntyre	Mary-Helen Perry
Candace A. Ridgway	Paul R. Reichert
Laura Sruggs Douglas	(Not admitted in DC)
James E. Gauch	Gary P. Zanfagna
Keith W. Holman	Lynn A. Airasian
R. Todd Johnson	(Not admitted in DC)
Anthony P. Lalla	Gretchen E. Crews
Steven J. Mintz	Thomas Molnar Fisher
Edward K.M. Bilich	(Not admitted in DC)
Gregory A. Castanias	Lisa Mangan Flicker
Denise A. Fee	Erica D. Foster
Edwin L. Fountain	(Not admitted in DC)
Eric Grant	Harry I. Johnson III
Daniel H. Bromberg	Michael L. Kolis
Dennis D. Dillon	Michael J. Kresslein
(Not admitted in DC)	Jason F. Leif
Janet A. Hendrick	(Not admitted in DC)
Stephen J. Jorden	Peter J. Love
Robin L. Juni	Kevin C. Maclay
Martin V. Kirkwood	Stefanie F. Roemer
Darryl R. Marsch	Martin S. Rowley
Elizabeth A. McLaughlin	Carol M. Stapleton
(Not admitted in DC)	Catherine M. Stavrakis
Stephen M. Springer	Brooks M. Beard
Jesse A. Witten	(Not admitted in DC)
Lynne A. Wurzburg	Maureen M. Carr
Geoffrey K. Beach	(Not admitted in DC)
Thomas M. Beck	Kenneth B. Driver
Thaddeus J. Burns	(Not admitted in DC)
Karen A. Doswell	Garrett B.M. Duarte
Joseph A. Goldman	(Not admitted in DC)
(Not admitted in DC)	Suzanne M. FitzGerald
Alice M. Goldwire	(Not admitted in DC)

(See Next Column)

ASSOCIATES (Continued)

Thomas C. Goldstein	John B. Nalbandian
(Not admitted in DC)	(Not admitted in DC)
Jacqueline M. Holmes	Bevin M.B. Newman
Jeffrey T. Hsu	Clinton R. Pinyan
(Not admitted in DC)	(Not admitted in DC)
Michael S. McFalls	Jodi B. Scherl
(Not admitted in DC)	Lydia P.A. Turnipseed
	(Not admitted in DC)

SENIOR STAFF ATTORNEYS

John P. McGrane, Jr.	Patrick L. Hubbard

For full biographical listings, see the Martindale-Hubbell Law Directory

---

✱ JONES, WALDO, HOLBROOK & McDONOUGH, A PROFESSIONAL CORPORATION (AV)

Suite 900, 2300 M Street, N.W., 20037
Telephone: 202-296-5950
Telecopier: 202-293-2509
Salt Lake City, Utah Office: 1500 First Interstate Plaza, 170 South Main Street.
Telephone: 801-521-3200.
Telecopier: 801-328-0537.
St. George, Utah Office: The Tabernacle Tower Building, 249 East Tabernacle.
Telephone: 801-628-1627.
Telecopier: 801-628-5225.

Barry D. Wood	Kay Allan Morrell
	(Not admitted in DC)

Mark A. Brinton (Not admitted in DC)

For full biographical listings, see the Martindale-Hubbell Law Directory

---

✱ KAYE, SCHOLER, FIERMAN, HAYS & HANDLER, LLP (AV)

A New York Limited Liability Partnership
McPherson Building, 901 Fifteenth Street, N.W., Suite 1100, 20005-2327
Telephone: 202-682-3500
Facsimile: 202-682-3580
New York, N.Y.: 425 Park Avenue, 10022-3598.
Telephone: 212-836-8000.
Telex: 234860 KAY UR.
Facsimile: 212-836-8689.
Los Angeles, California: 1999 Avenue of the Stars, Suite 1600, 90067-6048.
Telephone: 310-788-1000.
Facsimile: 310-788-1200.
Hong Kong: 9 Queen Road Centre, 18th Floor.
Telephone: 852-28458989.
Facsimile: 852-28453682; 2389.

RESIDENT PARTNERS

Terrence B. Adamson	Michael P. House
David O. Bickart	William A. Isaacson
G. Christopher Griner	Jonathan D. Schiller
Ronald K. Henry	Jason L. Shrinsky
Randall L. Speck	

SPECIAL COUNSEL

William D. Eberle (P.A.)	Abraham A. Ribicoff
(Not admitted in DC)	Steven L. Schwarcz
	(Not admitted in DC)

COUNSEL

Sylvia M. Becker	Irving Gastfreund
Christopher R. Brewster	R. Will Planert
Bruce Alan Eisen	John W. Schryber
James M. Weitzman	

RESIDENT ASSOCIATES

John G. Bickerman	Allan Gary Moskowitz
Ross D. Cooper	Raymond Paretzky
Farhad Jalinous	Mark A. Riordan
John R. Miles	William Todd Thomas

For full biographical listings, see the Martindale-Hubbell Law Directory

---

✱ KECK, MAHIN & CATE (AV)

A Partnership including Professional Corporations
555 12th Street, N.W. 6th Floor, 20004
Telephone: 202-637-3601
Telecopier: 202-347-0140
Chicago, Illinois Office: 77 West Wacker Drive, Suite 4900.
Telephone: 312-634-7700.
Fax: 312-634-5000.
Peoria, Illinois Office: 401 Main Street, Suite 1600.
Telephone: 309-673-1681.
Telecopier: 309-673-1690.
New York, N.Y. Office: 100 Maiden Lane, Suite 1600.
Telephone: 212-504-5630.
Telecopier: 212-504-5631.

(See Next Column)

KECK, MAHIN & CATE, *Washington—Continued*

MEMBERS OF FIRM AND ASSOCIATES

Donald O. Clark	Matthew F. Kadish
(Not admitted in DC)	George William Lewis
John M. Craig	(Not admitted in DC)
Richard R. Diefendorf	Ruth N. Morduch
(Not admitted in DC)	Philip L. O'Neill (P.C.)
Martin Fleit	Carlos M. Recio (P.C.)
Robin W. Grover	Norman H. Singer (P.C.)
Yoon Suk Ham	Paul H. Lamboley (P.C.)
(Not admitted in DC)	(Not admitted in DC)
Stanley S. Jutkowitz	Carl E. Zwisler III

For full biographical listings, see the Martindale-Hubbell Law Directory

---

* KILPATRICK & CODY, L.L.P. (AV)

Suite 800, 700 13th Street, N.W., 20005
Telephone: 202-508-5800
Telephone Copier: 202-508-5858
Atlanta, Georgia Office: Suite 2800, 1100 Peachtree Street.
Telephone: 404-815-6500. Telephone Copier: 404-815-6555.
Telex: 54-2307.
Augusta, Georgia Office: Suite 1400, First Union Bank Building, P.O. Box 2043, 30903.
Telephone: 706-724-2622.
Telecopier: 706-722-0219.
Brussels, Belgium Office: Avenue Louise 65, BTE 3, 1050 Brussels.
Telephone: (32) (2) 533-03-00.
Telecopier: (32) (2) 534-86-38.
London, England Office: 68 Pall Mall, London SW1Y 5ES, England.
Telephone: (44) (71) 321 0477.
Telecopier: (44) (71) 930 9733.

MEMBERS OF FIRM

Thomas K. Bick	C. Randall Nuckolls
Kurt E. Blase	Ronald L. Raider
Ronald A. Feuerstein	Steven J. Sacher
J. Vance Hughes	Frederick H. von Unwerth
Elliott H. Levitas	Martha Jo Wagner
Neil I. Levy	Mark D. Wincek

COUNSEL

David P. Phippen	William L. Sollee, Jr.

ASSOCIATES

George C. Beck	Devon Lee Miller
Wilburn L. Chesser	Emmett H. Miller
Vicki Arroyo Cochran	Richard T. Peterson
(Not admitted in DC)	(Not admitted in DC)
Michael P. Fortkort	David Pickle
Kenneth J. Markowitz	Dean W. Rutley
Charles T. Simmons	

For full biographical listings, see the Martindale-Hubbell Law Directory

---

* KIRLIN, CAMPBELL & KEATING (AV)

2nd Floor, 1 Farragut Square South, 888 Sixteenth Street, N.W., 20006
Telephone: 202-639-8000
Telecopier: 202-835-8238
Other Offices Located in: New York, N.Y., Long Beach, California, Stamford, Connecticut, Caldwell, New Jersey and Ft. Lauderdale, Fl.

RESIDENT OF COUNSEL

Gerald A. Malia	Russell T. Weil

For full biographical listings, see the Martindale-Hubbell Law Directory

---

* KUTAK ROCK (AV)

A Partnership including Professional Corporations
Suite 1000, 1101 Connecticut Avenue, N.W., 20036-4374
Telephone: 202-828-2400
Fax: 202-828-2488
URL: http://www.kutakrock.com
Atlanta, Georgia Office: Suite 2100, 225 Peachtree Street, NE, 30303-1731.
Telephone: 404-222-4600.
Facsimile: 404-222-4654.
Denver, Colorado Office: Suite 2900, 717 Seventeenth Street, 80202-3329.
Telephone: 303-297-2400.
Facsimile: 303-292-7799.
Kansas City, Missouri Office: United Missouri Bank Building, Third Floor, 9201 Ward Parkway.
Telephone: 816-361-3363.
Telecopier: 816-361-8397.
Little Rock, Arkansas Office: Suite 1770, 124 West Capitol Avenue, 72201-3719.
Telephone: 501-376-9208.
Facsimile: 501-375-3749.
New York, New York Office: 767 Third Avenue, 10017-2023.
Telephone: 212-752-0800.
Facsimile: 212-752-2281.

(See Next Column)

Oklahoma City, Oklahoma Office: Suite 475, 6305 Waterford Boulevard, 73118-1116.
Telephone: 405-848-2475.
Facsimile: 405-842-5748.
Omaha, Nebraska Office: The Omaha Building, 1650 Farnam Street, 68102-2186.
Telephone: 402-346-6000.
Facsimile: 402-346-1148.
Phoenix, Arizona Office: 16th Floor, 3300 North Central Avenue, 85012-2516.
Telephone: 602-285-1700.
Facsimile: 602-285-1868.
Pittsburgh, Pennsylvania Office: 1214 Frick Building, 437 Grant Street, 15219-6002.
Telephone: 412-261-6720.
Facsimile: 412-261-6717.

MEMBERS OF FIRM

W. Kimball Griffith	George R. Schlossberg
Joseph A. Ingrisano	Alan D. Strasser
Mitchell J. Bragin	Margo BeVier Stern
Allen S. Rugg	Patrick F. Brown
Robert L. Magielnicki	Alicia A. Terry
Gilbert W. Boyce	

OF COUNSEL

Barry P. Steinberg	Edward R. Venit

ASSOCIATES

Jill Ann Byrne	Amy E. Campbell
Jeffrey S. Ballard	(Not admitted in DC)
Bruce M. Serchuk	Deana L. Timberlake
Adam Augustine Carter	(Not admitted in DC)
Jennifer L. Peper	Stephen R. Smith
	(Not admitted in DC)

For full biographical listings, see the Martindale-Hubbell Law Directory

---

LEFTWICH & DOUGLAS, P.L.L.C. (AV)

Suite 600, 1401 New York Avenue., N.W., 20005
Telephone: 202-434-9100
Facsimile: 202-783-3420

MEMBERS OF FIRM

Frederick A. Douglas	Michael M. Hicks
James R. Murphy	Natalie O. Ludaway
Nicholas S. Penn	

ASSOCIATES

Curtis A. Boykin	Julie Ann Kaminski
Thomas D. Bridenbaugh	Melissa Blake Mannino
Leanne Cusumano	Rebecca Lynn Taylor
	(Not admitted in DC)

OF COUNSEL

Willie L. Leftwich

For full biographical listings, see the Martindale-Hubbell Law Directory

---

MARKS & MURASE L.L.P. (AV)

Suite 750, 2001 L Street, N.W., 20036-4910
Telephone: 202-955-4900
FAX: (202) 955-4933; 955-4932
New York, New York Office: 399 Park Avenue.
Telephone: 212-318-7700.
Los Angeles, California Office: Suite 1570, The Wells Fargo Center, 333 South Grand Avenue.
Telephone: 213-620-9690.

MEMBERS OF FIRM

Yoshihide Ito	Ramon P. Marks
(Not admitted in DC)	(Not admitted in DC)
Ronald P. Kananen	Neil E. McDonell
Richard Linn	(Not admitted in DC)
Roger L. Selfe	

OF COUNSEL

Matthew J. Marks

ASSOCIATES

Jeffrey L. Thompson

For full biographical listings, see the Martindale-Hubbell Law Directory

---

* MAYER, BROWN & PLATT (AV)

2000 Pennsylvania Avenue, N.W., 20006-1882
Telephone: (202) 463-2000
Facsimile: (202) 861-0473
Telex: 892603
Cable: LE MAYDC
URL: http://www.mayerbrown.com
Chicago, Illinois Office: 190 South LaSalle Street, 60603-3441.
Telephone: (312) 782-0600.
Facsimile: (312) 701-7711.
Telex: 190404.
Cable: LEMAY.

(See Next Column)

MAYER, BROWN & PLATT—*Continued*

Berlin, Germany Office: Spreeufer 5, 10178.
Telephone: 011-49-30-247-3800.
Facsimile: 011-49-30-247-38044.
Brussels, Belgium Office: Square de Meeûs 19/20, Bte. 4, 1050.
Telephone: 011-32-2-512-9878.
Facsimile: 011-32-2-511-3305.
Houston, Texas Office: 700 Louisiana Street, Suite 3600, 77002-2730.
Telephone: (713) 221-1651.
Facsimile: (713) 224-6410.
Telex: 775809.
Cable: LEMAYHOU.
London, England Office: 162 Queen Victoria Street, EC4V 4DB.
Telephone: 011-44-171-248-1465.
Facsimile: 011-44-171-329-4465.
Telex: 8811095.
Cable: LEMAYLDN.
Los Angeles, California Office: 350 South Grand Avenue, 25th Floor, 90071-1503.
Telephone: (213) 229-9500.
Facsimile: (213) 625-0248.
Telex: 188089.
Cable: LEMAYLA.
New York, New York Office: 1675 Broadway, 10019-5820.
Telephone: (212) 506-2500.
Facsimile: (212) 262-1910.
Telex: 701842.
Cable: LEMAYEN.
Representative Offices:
Almaty, Republic of Kazakhstan: 162 Tulebaev Street #32.
Telephone: 011-7-3272-636388.
Facsimile: 011-7-3272-507828.
Bishkek, Kyrgyz Republic: Suite 405, Prospekt Manasa 55, 720001.
Telephone: 011-7-3312-222970.
Facsimile: 011-7-3312-620980.
Köln, Germany: An Lyskirchen 14, 50676.
Telephone: 011-49-221-921-5210.
Facsimile: 011-49-221-921-5214.
Tashkent, Republic of Uzbekistan: 5th Floor, 1 Turab Tula Street, 700003.
Telephone: 011-7-3712-891179.
Facsimile: 011-7-3712-891178.
Mexico City, Mexico, D.F., Independent Mexico Correspondent: Jáuregui, Navarrete, Nader y Rojas, S.C. Abogados, Paseo de la Reforma 199, Pisos 15, 16 y 17, 06500, Mexico.
Telephone: 011 -525-591-16-55.
Facsimile: 011-525-535-80-62, 011-525-703-22-47.
Cable: JANANE.

PARTNERS

Diane E. Ambler	Erika Z. Jones
Robert E. Bloch	Simeon M. Kriesberg
David I. Bloom	Kathryn A. Kusske
Kim Marie Kozaczek Boylan	Philip Allen Lacovara
Charles Chu	Jerry L. Oppenheimer
Robert P. Davis	Carolyn P. Osolinik
Kerry Lynn Edwards	Stuart P. Pergament
Roy T. Englert, Jr.	Andrew J. Pincus
Richard J. Favretto	Lawrence S. Robbins
Marc Gary	Mark W. Ryan
Kenneth S. Geller	John P. Schmitz
Mark H. Gitenstein	Brian W. Smith
Lloyd S. Guerci	Adrian L. Steel, Jr.
Werner J. Hein	Robert H. Swart
(Not admitted in DC)	Evan M. Tager
Charles M. Horn	Charles S. Triplett

SENIOR COUNSEL
David B. Finnegan

SPECIAL COUNSEL
Charles Rothfeld

COUNSEL

Carol J. Bilzi	Richard K. Matta
C. Cabell Chinnis, Jr.	Amy L. Nathan
Mary A. Cole	Scott P. Perlman

Gregory S. Walden

ASSOCIATES

Robert L. Bronston	Andrew J. Morris
(Not admitted in DC)	Wendy Lefkoe Morris
Terence F. Browne	Sean P. Moylan
H. Thomas Byron, III	Kathryn Horton O'Brien
Blake M. Cornish	Kelley E. O'Brien
David C. Crane	(Not admitted in DC)
Thomas DiLenge	Gary Orseck
Donald M. Falk	C. Dirk Peterson
Julian P. Gehman	Jeffrey Alan Rackow
Myles R. Hansen	Laurie R. Rubenstein
David A. Hyman	Curtis W. Schuhmacher
Timothy E. Keehan	Adam C. Sloane
Kim D. Larsen	John J. Sullivan
Luke P. Levasseur	

(See Next Column)

ASSOCIATES (Continued)

Lily Fu Swenson	Alan E. Untereiner
(Not admitted in DC)	Gary A. Winters
	David H. Zielke

For full biographical listings, see the Martindale-Hubbell Law Directory

---

* McCUTCHEN, DOYLE, BROWN & ENERSEN (AV)

The Evening Star Building, Suite 800, 1101 Pennsylvania Avenue, N.W., 20004-2514
Telephone: 202-628-4900
Facsimile: 202-628-4912
Email: postmaster@mdbe.com
San Francisco, California Office: Three Embarcadero Center, 94111-4066.
Telephone: 415-393-2000.
Facsimile: 415-393-2286 (GI, II, III).
Telex: 340817 MACPAG SFO.
Los Angeles, California Office: 355 South Grand Avenue, Suite 4400, 90071-1560.
Telephone: 213-680-6400.
Facsimile: 213-680-6499.
San Jose, California Office: Market Post Tower, Suite 1500, 55 South Market Street, 95113-2327.
Telephone: 408-947-8400.
Facsimile: 408-947-4750.
Telex: 910 250 2931 MACPAG SJ.
Walnut Creek, California Office: 1331 North California Boulevard, Post Office Box V, 94596-4502.
Telephone: 510-937-8000.
Facsimile: 510-975-5390.
Palo Alto, California Office: One Embarcadero Place, 2100 Geng Road, 94303-0913.
Telephone: 415-846-4000.
Fax: 415-846-4086.
Taipei, Taiwan Republic of China Office: International Trade Building, Tenth Floor, 333 Keelung Road, Section 1, 110.
Telephone: 886-2-723-5000.
Facsimile: 886-2-757-6070.
Affiliated Offices in: Bangkok, Thailand; Beijing, China; Shanghai, China.

MEMBERS OF FIRM

David R. Andrews	Barry J. Cutler
Michael A. Brown	George J. Weiner
Patrick O. Cavanaugh	Michael C. White
Cynthia A. Coe	(Not admitted in DC)
Philip T. Cummings	
(Not admitted in DC)	

OF COUNSEL

Margaret A. Freeston	Elizabeth A. Pierce

ASSOCIATE
Julia A. Oas (Not admitted in DC)

For full biographical listings, see the Martindale-Hubbell Law Directory

---

* McGUIRE, WOODS, BATTLE & BOOTHE, L.L.P. (AV)

The Army and Navy Club Building, 1627 Eye Street, N.W., 20006-4007
Telephone: 202-857-1700
Fax: 202-857-1737
URL: http://www.mwbb.com
Alexandria, Virginia Office: Transpotomac Plaza, Suite 1000, 1199 North Fairfax Street, 22314-1437.
Telephone: 703-739-6200.
Fax: 703-739-6270.
Baltimore, Maryland Office: The Blaustein Building, One North Charles Street, 21201-3793.
Telephone: 410-659-4400.
Fax: 410-659-4599.
Charlottesville, Virginia Office: Court Square Building, P.O. Box 1288, 22902-1288.
Telephone: 804-977-2500.
Fax: 804-980-2222.
Jacksonville, Florida Office: Barnett Center, Suite 2750, 50 North Laura Street, 32202-3635.
Telephone: 904-798-3200.
Fax: 904-798-3207.
McLean, (Tysons Corner) Virginia Office: 8280 Greensboro Drive, Suite 900, Tysons Corner, 22102-3892.
Telephone: 703-712-5000.
Fax: 703-712-5050.
Norfolk, Virginia Office: World Trade Center, Suite 9000, 101 West Main Street, 23510-1655.
Telephone: 757-640-3700.
Fax: 757-640-3701.
Richmond, Virginia Office: One James Center, 901 East Cary Street, 23219-4030.
Telephone: 804-775-1000.
Fax: 804-775-1061.
Brussels, Belgium Office: 250 Avenue Louise, Bte. 64, 1050.
Telephone: (32 2) 629 42 11.
Fax: (32 2) 629 42 22.
Zürich, Switzerland Office: Bahnhofstrasse 3, 8022.
Telephone: (41 1) 225 20 00.
Fax: (41 1) 225 20 20.

(See Next Column)

McGuire, Woods, Battle & Boothe L.L.P., *Washington—Continued*

MEMBERS OF FIRM

James E. Ballowe, Jr.	Clifford R. Oviatt, Jr.
James D. Bridgeman	David H. Pankey
Thomas E. Cabaniss	Charlotte Rothenberg Rosen
(Not admitted in DC)	Larry D. Sharp
K. Stewart Evans, Jr.	Robert S. Smith
(Not admitted in DC)	(Not admitted in DC)
Larry B. Grimes	George J. Terwilliger III
Mary S. Head	Wallace L. Timmeny
Steven D. Kittrell	Sharon K. Tucker
Michael H. Levin	(Not admitted in DC)
Thomas J. McGonigle	Edward E. Zughaib

ASSOCIATES

Vincent J. Badolato	R. Lisa Mojiri-Azad
Kelly M. Boehringer	Amy R. Moschella
(Not admitted in DC)	(Not admitted in DC)
Amyli A. Cabiling	Susan Morley Olson
Neal J. Cabral	Erica S. Palim
Laura A. Colombell	David M. Young
Michael P. McGovern	(Not admitted in DC)
(Not admitted in DC)	

For full biographical listings, see the Martindale-Hubbell Law Directory

---

✱ McKenna & Cuneo, L.L.P. (AV)

1900 K Street, N.W., 20006
Telephone: 202-496-7500
Telecopier: 202-496-7756
URL: http://www.mckennacuneo.com
Los Angeles, California Office: 444 South Flower Street.
Telephone: 213-688-1000.
San Francisco, California Office: One Market, Steuart Street Tower, Twenty-Seventh Floor.
Telephone: 415-267-4000.
Denver, Colorado Office: 370 Seventeenth Street, Suite 4800.
Telephone: 303-634-4000.
San Diego, California Office: Symphony Towers, Suite 3200, 750B Street.
Telephone: 619-595-5400.
Dallas, Texas Office: 5700 Bank One Center, 1717 Main Street.
Telephone: 214-746-5700.
Brussels, Belgium Office: 56, rue des Colonies, Box 14, B-1000.
Telephone: 011-322-278-1211.

Ashley Sellers (1902-1977)   Gilbert A. Cuneo (1913-1978)

MEMBERS OF FIRM

Wilsie H. Adams, Jr.	Peter L. Gray
Jeffrey P. Altman	Allen B. Green
Tami Lyn Azorsky	Jacqueline A. Henson
Raymond B. Biagini	E. Sanderson Hoe
Lawrence J. Bogard	Michael T. Janik
Alexander J. Brittin	Daniel G. Jarcho
Alan C. Brown	Daniel E. Johnson
J. Keith Burt	Geoffrey T. Keating
John C. Chambers, Jr.	Frederic M. Levy
David A. Churchill	Robert A. Matthews
John D. Conner	Victoria A. McEneney
(Partner Emeritus)	Matthew J. McGrath
John D. Conner, Jr.	Douglas B. Mishkin
Del Stiltner Dameron	Charles A. O'Connor, III
Janice Davis	Patrick K. O'Keefe
C. Stanley Dees	Jacob B. Pankowski
Joseph F. Dennin	Thomas C. Papson
Kevin C. Dwyer	Larry R. Pilot
Lawrence S. Ebner	Raymond S. E. Pushkar
Lawrence M. Farrell	Andrew M. Reidy
Michael L. Fayad	Gary H. Sampliner
Richard A. Feinstein	Michael G. Scheininger
Peter Buck Feller	Catherine J. Serafin
Herbert L. Fenster	Carol A. Smoots
D. Michael Fitzhugh	Donald R. Stone
T. Mark Flanagan, Jr.	Michael K. Tomenga
Richard A. Flye	Kenneth W. Weinstein
Ruth S. Flynn	Gary L. Yingling
Charles E. Yonkers	

RESIDENT OF COUNSEL

Bruce J. Brennan	Kellie L. Newton
Cara S. Jablon	(Not admitted in DC)

RESIDENT ASSOCIATES

Paul D. Ackerman	Christopher C. Bouquet
Michael E. Anderson	Thomas F. Burke
Ray M. Aragon	Malaika D. Carter
Philip H. M. Beauregard	(Not admitted in DC)
Ann M. Begley	Robert L. Carter, Jr.
(Not admitted in DC)	Hilda Kay Cross
Andrew E. Bej	Rebecca L. Dandeker
Michelle Birnbaum	John A. Detzner
John A. Bonello	Jonathan L. Diesenhaus
Michael Boucher	Alison L. Doyle

(See Next Column)

RESIDENT ASSOCIATES (Continued)

Diane Estaire Flyer	Thomas S. McConville
Ian T. Graham	Jeffrey A. Miller
Larry J. Gusman	Michael R. Neilson
(Not admitted in DC)	William T. O'Brien
Kurt J. Hamrock	Suzan Onel
Jeffrey P. Hildebrant	Paul E. Pompeo
Michael H. Hinckle	Francis E. Purcell, Jr.
(Not admitted in DC)	Margaret C. Rhodes
Michael A. Hopkins	Stephen E. Ruscus
Gregory T. Jaeger	Alyssa T. Senzel
Kathleen D. Jaeger	Frederick F. Shaheen
Jamon A. Jarvis	Mark D. Shonkwiler
Donald O. Johnson	Todd A. Suko
Thomas B. Johnston	(Not admitted in DC)
Daryle A. Jordan	Edward L. Tabakin
David Kasanow	Cathleen Gillen Tierney
Joanne M. Kelly	Richard C. Wall
(Not admitted in DC)	Grail Peyton Walsh
Laura Frick Laemmle	Clarissa L. Weiant
(Not admitted in DC)	(Not admitted in DC)
Lisa A. Lavelle	Kimberly Heshima White
Chris S. Leason	(Not admitted in DC)
Joyce Y. Lim	Scott B. Whittier
Joanne E. Loercher	David B. Witherspoon
Gregory J. Madden	John P. Wunderli
David E. Maranville	Joanne L. Zimolzak

For full biographical listings, see the Martindale-Hubbell Law Directory

---

✱ Milbank, Tweed, Hadley & McCloy (AV)

Suite 1100, 1825 Eye Street, N.W., 20006
Telephone: 202-835-7500
Fax: 202-835-7586 ABA/net: MilbankDC
URL: http://www.milbank.com
New York, New York Offices: 1 Chase Manhattan Plaza, 10005.
Telephone: 212-530-5000.
Fax: 212-530-5219. ABA/net: MilbankNY. MCI Mail: MilbankTweed.
Midtown Office: 50 Rockefeller Plaza, 10020.
Telephone: 212-530-5800;
Fax: 212-530-0158.
Los Angeles, California Office: 601 South Figueroa Street, 90017.
Telephone: 213-892-4000.
Fax: 213-629-5063. ABA/net: MilbankLA.
Tokyo, Japan Office: Nippon Press Center Building, 2-1, Uchisaiwai-cho 2-chome, Chiyoda-ku, Tokyo 100.
Telephone: 011-813-3504-1050.
Fax: 011-81-3-3595-2790, 011-81-3-3502-5192.
London, England Office: Dashwood House, 69 Old Broad Street, London, EC2M 1QS.
Telephone: 011-44-171-448-3000.
Fax: 011-44-171-448-3029.
Hong Kong: 3007 Alexandra House, 16 Chater Road.
Telephone: 011-852-2971-4888.
Fax: 011-852-2840-0792, 011-852-2854-9046. ABA/net: MilbankHK.
Singapore Office: 14-02 Caltex House, 30 Raffles Place, 048622.
Telephone: 011-65-534-1700.
Fax: 011-65-534-2733. ABA/net: EDNANG.
Moscow, Russia Office: 24/27 Sadovaya-Samotyochnya, Moscow, 103051.
Telephone: 011-7-501-258-5015.
Fax: 011-7-501-258-5014.
Jakarta, Indonesia Correspondent Office: Makarim & Taira S., 17th Floor, Summitmas Tower, Jl, Jend. Sudirman 61, Jakarta.
Telephone: 011-62-21-252-1272 or 2460.
Fax: 011-62-21-252-2750 or 2751.

RESIDENT PARTNERS

Glenn S. Gerstell	John E. Shockey
Mark A. Kantor	Richard C. Tufaro
Gregory Evers May	William H. Webster

RETIRED PARTNER

Elliot L. Richardson

RESIDENT OF COUNSEL

Thomas J. Gallagher, Jr.	Robert F. Lawrence

RESIDENT ASSOCIATES

Ross D. Agre	Kathryn E. Hoff-Patrinos
Lisa M. Boykin	Julie M. Jacobs
(Not admitted in DC)	Dean A. Manson
Helen F. Choi	Elizabeth A. Poyck
Hillary S. DeNigro	Fred W. Reinke
Liane L. Heggy	Walter L. Stone
Melissa R. Hodgman	
(Not admitted in DC)	

For full biographical listings, see the Martindale-Hubbell Law Directory

---

Miller & Chevalier, Chartered (AV)

Established 1920
655 Fifteenth Street, N.W., Suite 900, 20005-5701
Telephone: 202-626-5800
Fax: 202-628-0858
Email: inquiries@milchev.com

(See Next Column)

MILLER & CHEVALIER CHARTERED—*Continued*

Grant D. Aldonas	Clarence T. Kipps, Jr.
James B. Altman	Emmett B. Lewis
J. Bradford Anwyll	Robert E. Liles, II
Ronald D. Aucutt	Lucinda A. Low
Dennis P. Bedell	Marcia Gunnell Madsen
James A. Bensfield	John B. Magee
Stuart E. Benson	Thomas W. Mahoney, Jr.
Leonard Bickwit, Jr.	Phillip L. Mann
John Mourer Bixler	William M. McGlone
Kathryn Bucher	Craig D. Miller
Michael D. Campbell	Robert Netherland Miller
Jay L. Carlson	(1879-1968)
Stuart Chevalier (1879-1956)	Robert L. Moore, II
Donald B. Craven	Anne E. Moran
Catherine L. Creech	Homer E. Moyer, Jr.
David B. Cubeta	Philip S. Neal
Catherine Curtiss	John Stephan Nolan
Terry Bancroft Dowd	C. Frederick Oliphant III
F. Scott Farmer	Jean A. Pawlow
A. John Gabig	Scott E. Pickens
Hal I. Gann	Catherine Tift Porter
Lawrence B. Gibbs	John Lloyd Rice
Gerald Goldman	Frederick H. Robinson
Alan I. Horowitz	Anthony F. Shelley
Robert K. Huffman	Mary Lou Soller
Catherine Veihmeyer Hughes	Richard C. Stark
Thomas D. Johnston	Patricia J. Sweeney
Robert A. Katcher	James P. Tuite
Kevin L. Kenworthy	F. Brook Voght

Alexander Zakupowsky, Jr.

OF COUNSEL

Charles T. Akre	David W. Richmond

Numa L. Smith, Jr.

Jessica C. Abrahams	George A. Hani
Josephine I. Aiello	Maureen Henry
(Not admitted in DC)	Peter B. Hutt II
Alvaro I. Anillo	Carol Ann Johnson
Kathryn Cameron Atkinson	(Not admitted in DC)
Michael E. Baillif	Paul F. Kirgis
Angela J. Barbee	Carol E. Lockwood
Andrea K. Bjorklund	James R. Lovelace
David B. Blair	Susan A. Maloney
Hartman E. Blanchard, Jr.	Peter B. Miller
Matthew J. Borger	Frances B. Morgan
(Not admitted in DC)	Lisa T. Murphy
Ross W. Branstetter	Holly A. Stuck Porter
Gregory M. Brown	(Not admitted in DC)
Kathleen B. Costello	Lisa M. Robinson
Rhonda Nesmith Crichlow	(Not admitted in DC)
John E. Davis	Amy L. Rothstein
David F. Dowd	Michael L. Schultz
Rocco V. Femia	(Not admitted in DC)
(Not admitted in DC)	Robert T. Smith
Laura G. Ferguson	(Not admitted in DC)
Marc J. Gerson	Heidi A. Sorensen
Stephanie Pontzer Gilson	Gary R. Vogel
Jeffrey A. Green	Claire S. Wellington
Cameron S. Hamrick	Benjamin D. M. Wood

Michael W. Wright

For full biographical listings, see the Martindale-Hubbell Law Directory

✱ MINTZ, LEVIN, COHN, FERRIS, GLOVSKY AND POPEO, P.C. (AV)

701 Pennsylvania Avenue, N.W., Suite 900, 20004-2608
Telephone: 202-434-7300
FAX: 202-434-7400
Internet: Each Attorney's Internet Address takes the following form: first inital, last name @mintz.com (e.g., rmintz@mintz.com)
Boston, Massachusetts Office: One Financial Center.
Telephone: 617-542-6000.
Cable Address: "Colemin."
Telex: 94-0198.

Francis X. Meaney	Rebecca L. Jackson
Charles D. Ferris	Charles Alan Samuels
William C. Brashares	Howard J. Symons
Frank W. Lloyd	David R. Ford
Thomas M. Antone, IV	Donna Nussinow Lampert
Bruce D. Sokler	James A. Kirkland
Alvin J. Lorman	Cherie R. Kiser

Christopher J. Harvie	Jonathan S. Wolin
(Not admitted in DC)	J. Stephen Zielezienski
William A. Davis	Robert N. Falk
Sara F. Seidman	Russell C. Merbeth
Christopher A. Holt	Dwayne O. Leslie

(See Next Column)

Deena Godshall Roth	Joanne S. Hovis
Michael B. Bressman	(Not admitted in DC)
James J. Valentino	Fernando R. Laguarda
Anthony E. Varona	Janell P. Fonsworth
Tara M. Corvo	(Not admitted in DC)
Gregory R. Firehock	Jennifer A. Purvis
	(Not admitted in DC)

For full biographical listings, see the Martindale-Hubbell Law Directory

TIMOTHY D. NAEGELE & ASSOCIATES (AV)

Suite 300, 1250 24th Street, N.W., 20037
Telephone: 202-466-7500
Facsimile: 202-466-3079 or 466-2888
Email: naegelewdc@aol.com *URL:* http://www.naegele.com
Los Angeles, California Office: Suite 2430, 1900 Avenue of the Stars, 90067.
Telephone: 310-557-2300.
Facsimile: 310-457-4014. Internet Web Site: http://www.naegele.com.
Internet E-mail: naegelewdc@aol.com.

ASSOCIATE

Ashley Gauthier (Not admitted in DC)

LEGAL SUPPORT PERSONNEL

LAW CLERKS

Robert C. Kersey	Kurt D. Naegele
(Not admitted in DC)	Darren H. Lubetzky

For full biographical listings, see the Martindale-Hubbell Law Directory

✱ O'CONNOR & HANNAN (AV)

Suite 800, 1919 Pennsylvania Avenue, N.W., 20006-3483
Telephone: 202-887-1400
Telecopy: 202-466-2198
Minneapolis, Minnesota Office: 700 Baker Building, 706 South Second Avenue.
Telephone: 612-343-1200.
Telecopy: 612-343-1256.

MEMBERS OF FIRM

Patrick J. O'Connor	James W. Symington
Edward W. Brooke	Donald R. Dinan
Thomas H. Quinn	Michael Colopy
David R. Melincoff	Thomas J. Corcoran
Hope S. Foster	Robert M. Adler
Patrick E. O'Donnell	Peter M. Kazon
F. Gordon Lee	Christina W. Fleps
George J. Mannina, Jr.	Timothy W. Jenkins
John J. McDermott	Gary C. Adler

John M. Himmelberg

Craig A. Koenigs

OF COUNSEL

Joseph H. Blatchford	William W. Nickerson
E. William Crotty	Audrey P. Rasmussen
David L. Hill	H. George Schweitzer
Charles R. McCarthy, Jr.	Thomas J. Schneider

Moshe Schuldinger

For full biographical listings, see the Martindale-Hubbell Law Directory

PATTON BOGGS, L.L.P. (AV)

2550 M Street, N.W., 20037-1350
Telephone: 202-457-6000
Telecopier: 202-457-6315
Baltimore, Maryland Office: Suite 1100, 250 W. Pratt Street, 21201.
Telephone: 410-659-5600.
Facsimile: 410-659-0621.
Dallas, Texas Office: 2626 Cole Avenue, Suite 700, 75204.
Telephone: 214-871-2141.
Facsimile: 214-871-2688.
Denver, Colorado Office: Suite 1975, 1660 Lincoln Street, 80264.
Telephone: 303-830-1776.
Facsimile: 303-894-9239.
Greensboro, North Carolina Office: 500 NCNB Building, 101 West Friendly Avenue, P.O. Drawer 20004, 27401.
Telephone: 910-273-1733.
Facsimile: 910-272-9254.
Research Triangle Park, North Carolina Office: P.O. Box 12596, 27709.
Telephone: 919-941-6838.
Fax: 919-941-6840.
Seattle, Washington Office: Suite 1400, 1000 Second Avenue, 98104.
Telephone: 206-382-0200.
Facsimile: 206-382-0363.

MEMBERS OF FIRM

James R. Patton, Jr.	J. Gordon Arbuckle (Resident,
George Blow (Retired)	Denver, Colorado Office)
Joseph L. Brand	William C. Foster
Thomas Hale Boggs, Jr.	David C. Todd
Timothy J. May	Richard Alan Earle
Elliot H. Cole	Robert H. Koehler

(See Next Column)

PATTON BOGGS L.L.P., *Washington—Continued*

MEMBERS OF FIRM (Continued)

David B. Robinson	W. Caffey Norman III
John H. Vogel	Paul A. J. Wilson
Allan Abbot Tuttle	Mary Elizabeth Bosco
John L. Oberdorfer	Read Kemp McCaffrey
Lanny J. Davis	Lansing B. Lee, III
Timothy A. Vanderver, Jr.	Mark A. Heller
Middleton A. Martin	Ross E. Eichberg
Garret G. Rasmussen	Gerald J. S. Laporte
James B. Christian, Jr.	Geoffrey G. Davis
David E. Dunn, III	Charles H. Camp
Ronald S. Liebman	Ray M. O'Hara
J. Kirk Wade	James R. Stuart, III
Stuart M. Pape	Martha M. Kendrick
Steven M. Schneebaum	Kenneth A. Grigg, Jr.
Cliff Massa III	Michael A. Curto
Shaoul Aslan	James A. Reeder
Donald V. Moorehead	Philip S. Kaplan
Frank R. Samolis	Daniel E. Waltz
Don A. Allen	John F. Fithian
George M. Borababy	Louise Nicholson Howe
Jeffrey T. Smith	Herbert W. Hecht, II
Katharine R. Boyce	Timothy B. Mills
George J. Schutzer	Benjamin L. Ginsberg
Scott N. Stone	William D. Ford
Michael D. Esch	Henry Chajet
John F. Jonas	Mark N. Savit
C. Allen Foster (Resident at Greensboro, North Carolina Office)	Robert S. Brams
	David J. Farber
	Daniel A. Kracov
Duane Alan Siler	Roger S. Ballentine
Russell V. Randle	Benjamin G. Chew
Jean Veeder MacHarg	Robert C. Jones
Dean M. Dilley	Richard M. Stolbach
John C. Martin	Paul C. Besozzi
Deborah M. Lodge	Stephen Diaz Gavin
Mitchell R. Berger	J. Jeffrey Craven
Donald H. Pearlman	Joseph E. Schmitz
Daniel H. Margolis	Penelope S. Farthing
Jeffrey L. Turner	Byron F. Marchant
Charles E. Talisman	James A. Hughes, Jr.

ASSOCIATES

Robert K. Taylor	Kyle Winston Parker
Benjamin O. Tayloe, Jr.	(Not admitted in DC)
Clayton Lee Hough	John Spitaleri Shaw
Brett S. Krantz	(Not admitted in DC)
Edward J. Newberry	Allen A. Flood, Jr.
Michael N. Druckman	(Not admitted in DC)
Denise A. Vanison	Jeffrey L. Ross
Curtis L. Culberson	David J. Bloch
Jamal Laurence El-Hindi	Jocelyn Aqua
G. Kendrick Macdowell	(Not admitted in DC)
Michael J. Schaengold	David A. Colodny
Timothy A. Diemand	Philip A. Bangert
Jeannie Yim	(Not admitted in DC)
Robert P. Ritger	Bess Johnson Michael
Laura C. Tayloe	Jennifer A Wiegleb
Elizabeth E. Tsakonas	(Not admitted in DC)
William E. Slade	Kenneth L. Le Bon
Fiti Alesana Sunia	(Not admitted in DC)
Ruth Lauren Ramsey	Adele L. Abrams
James F. Green	(Not admitted in DC)
Aubrey A. Rothrock, III	Makan Delrahim
John F. Cobau	(Not admitted in DC)
Thomas A. Duckenfield, III	Norah Virginia Dabney
Christy Gherlein Slade	Janet Fitzpatrick
John J. Deschauer, Jr.	Douglas C. Proxmire
Lynn T. Burleson	(Not admitted in DC)
(Not admitted in DC)	Harold H. Kim
Caroline F. May	(Not admitted in DC)
Carlos A. Solé, III	Christina Maria Erickson
Lawrence Duncan, III	(Not admitted in DC)
Andrew J. Lorentz	Jon Paul Morris
Julie A. Barrie	(Not admitted in DC)
Jeanne M. Liedtka	Stephen H. Sherman
Daniel R. Addison	Bradford E. Biegon
Thomas C. Downs	(Not admitted in DC)
Darryl D. Nirenberg	Mary P. Rouvelas
Eric A. Kuwana	(Not admitted in DC)
Donald F. McGahn	David W. Miller
Michael T. Wood	(Not admitted in DC)
(Not admitted in DC)	Rodney A. Grandon

OF COUNSEL

John C. Camp	Michelle D. Bernard
Nancy A. Murray	Lawrence H. Brinker

LEGAL SUPPORT PERSONNEL

TRANSPORTATION POLICY CONSULTANT

Carolina L. Mederos

ECONOMIST

David G. Raboy

(See Next Column)

ECONOMICS ASSOCIATE

Teri L. Simpson

LEGISLATIVE AFFAIRS SPECIALIST

John F. Kelly, Jr.

SENIOR HEALTH POLICY ADVISOR

JoAnn V. Willis

CONSULTANT

Rinaldo Petrignani

PUBLIC SERVICE COUNSEL

Melanie K. Gerber

PUBLIC POLICY SPECIALIST

Michael A. Brown

For full biographical listings, see the Martindale-Hubbell Law Directory

---

✱ PAUL, HASTINGS, JANOFSKY & WALKER LLP (AV)

A Limited Liability Partnership including Professional Corporations
Tenth Floor, 1299 Pennsylvania Avenue, N.W., 20004-2400
Telephone: 202-508-9500
Fax: 202-508-9700
Email: info@PHJW.com *URL:* http://www.phjw.com
Los Angeles, California Office: Twenty-Third Floor, 555 South Flower Street.
Telephone: 213-683-6000.
Orange County, California Office: Seventeenth Floor, 695 Town Center Drive, Costa Mesa.
Telephone: 714-668-6200.
Atlanta, Georgia Office: 24th Floor, 600 Peachtree Street, N.E.
Telephone: 404-815-2400.
Santa Monica, California Office: Fifth Floor, 1299 Ocean Avenue.
Telephone: 310-319-3300.
Stamford, Connecticut Office: Ninth Floor, 1055 Washington Boulevard.
Telephone: 203-961-7400.
New York, New York Office: 31st Floor, 399 Park Avenue.
Telephone: 212-318-6000.
Tokyo, Japan Office: Ark Mori Building, 30th Floor, 12-32 Akasaka, P.O. Box 577, 1-Chome, Minato-Ku.
Telephone: (03) 3586-4711.

MEMBERS OF FIRM

E. Lawrence Barcella, Jr.	Judith Richards Hope
Barbara Berish Brown	John Griffith Johnson, Jr.
R. Bruce Dickson	Thomas R. Lamia
E. Donald Elliott	G. Hamilton Loeb
Ralph B. Everett	Carl W. Northrop
Zachary D. Fasman	Charles A. Patrizia
John J. Gallagher	Paul L. Perito
Jon A. Geier	Bruce D. Ryan
Lawrence J. Hass	William A. Schmidt
	Michael A. Wiegard

OF COUNSEL

Edwin I. Colodny	Robert E. Pokusa
William D. DeGrandis	William Thomas Reeder, Jr.
Gage Randolph Johnson	Charles A. Shanor
Thomas J. Knapp	Margaret H. Spurlin
Neal D. Mollen	Patrick J. Whittle
Robert S. Plotkin	Kenneth M. Willner
	Gerald H. Yamada

ASSOCIATES

David M. Abbey	Alan B. Horowitz
Kirby D. Behre	E. Ashton Johnston
Sheryl J. Brown-Norman	George R. A. Jones
(Not admitted in DC)	Sarah M. McWilliams
David D. Burns	Jay A. Morrison
Dianne C. Carraway	Dena T. Sacco
(Not admitted in DC)	Nancy E. Shallow
Michelle Weisberg Cohen	Joshua H. Sternoff
Christine M. Crowe	(Not admitted in DC)
Behnam Dayanim	Randall M. Stone
Jewell L. Esposito	Erin M. Sweeney
Wendell M. Faria	Timothy J. Wellman
Scott M. Flicker	Annita M. Whichard
Intra L. Germanis	(Not admitted in DC)
	Jenny C. Wu

For full biographical listings, see the Martindale-Hubbell Law Directory

---

✱ PAUL, WEISS, RIFKIND, WHARTON & GARRISON (AV)

1615 L Street, N.W. Suite 1300, 20036-5694
Telephone: 202-223-7300
TDD 202-223-7490
Telex: WUI 666-843
Facsimile: 202-223-7420
Cable Address: "Longsight, New York"
New York, N.Y. Office: 1285 Avenue of the Americas, 10019-6064.
Telephones: 212-373-3000, TDD 212-373-2000.
Cable Address: "Longsight, New York".
Telex: WUI 666-843.
Facsimile: 212-757-3990.

(See Next Column)

PAUL, WEISS, RIFKIND, WHARTON & GARRISON—*Continued*

Paris, France Office: 62, rue du Faubourg Saint-Honoré, 75008.
Telephone: (33-1) 53.43.14.14.
Cable Address: "Longsight Paris".
Telex: 203178F.
Facsimile: (33-1) 53.43.00.23.
Tokyo, Japan Office: Fokoku Seimei Building, 2-2 Uchisaiwaicho 2-chome, Chiyoda-ku, Tokyo 100, Japan.
Telephone: (81-3) 3597-8101.
Facsimile: (81-3) 3597-8120.
Beijing, People's Republic of China Office: Suite 1910, Scitech Tower, 22 Jianguomenwai Dajie, 100004.
Telephones: (86-10) 65123628-30, (86-10) 65122288X.1910-12.
Telex: 210169 PWRWG CN.
Facsimile: 011 (86-10) 65123631.
Hong Kong Office: 13th Floor, Hong Kong Club Building, 3A Chater Road, Central Hong Kong.
Telephone: (011-852) 2536-9933.
Facsimile: 011 (852) 2536-9622.

RESIDENT PARTNERS

Terence J. Fortune	Warren B. Rudman
Robert E. Montgomery, Jr.	Phillip L. Spector
Lionel H. Olmer	Stuart G. Steingold

COUNSEL

A. Leon Higginbotham, Jr.

COMMUNICATIONS COUNSEL

Jeffrey H. Olson

INTERNATIONAL TRADE COUNSEL

Richard S. Elliott	Soon-Yub Samuel Kwon

RESIDENT ASSOCIATES

Swati Agrawal	Erik C. Luchs
(Not admitted in DC)	(Not admitted in DC)
Patrick S. Campbell	Robert P. Parker
(Not admitted in DC)	Susan E. Ryan
Diane C. Gaylor	Dale M. Sarro
Carl W. Hampe	(Not admitted in DC)
Norman J. Harrison	David J. Weiler
Barbara A. Yellen	

For full biographical listings, see the Martindale-Hubbell Law Directory

PEPPER, HAMILTON & SCHEETZ (AV)

1300 Nineteenth Street, N.W., 20036-1685
Telephone: 202-828-1200
Telecopy: 202-828-1665
Philadelphia, Pennsylvania Office: 3000 Two Logan Square, Eighteenth and Arch Streets, 19103-2799.
Telephone: 215-981-4000.
Fax: 215-981-4750.
Detroit, Michigan Office: 100 Renaissance Center, 36th Floor, 48243-1157.
Telephone: 313-259-7110.
Fax: 313-259-7926.
New York, New York Office: 450 Lexington Avenue, Suite 1600, 10017-3904.
Telephone: 212-878-3800.
Fax: 212-878-3835.
Wilmington, Delaware Office: 1201 Market Street, Suite 1600, P.O. Box 1709, 19899-1709.
Telephone: 302-777-6500.
Fax: 302-656-8865.
Pittsburgh, Pennsylvania Office: One Mellon Bank Center, 50th Floor, 500 Grant Street, 15219-2502.
Telephone: 412-454-5000.
Fax: 412-281-0717.
Harrisburg, Pennsylvania Office: 200 One Keystone Plaza, North Front and Market Streets, P.O. Box 1181, 17108-1181.
Telephone: 717-255-1155.
Fax: 717-238-0575.
Berwyn, Pennsylvania Office: 1235 Westlakes Drive, Suite 400, 19312-2401.
Telephone: 610-640-7800.
Fax: 610-640-7835.
Cherry Hill, New Jersey Office: LibertyView Building, Suite 500, 457 Haddonfield Road, 08002-2002.
Telephone: 609-317-9530.
Fax: 609-317-9238.
London, England Office: 9 Haywards Place, EC1R 0EE.
Telephone: 011-44-171-628-1122.
Fax: 011-44-171-628-6010.
Moscow, Russia Office: 19-27 Grokholsky Pereulok, 129010.
Telephone: 011-7-095-280-4493.
Fax: 011-7-095-280-5518.

PARTNERS

Michael B. Staebler (Not admitted in DC; Managing Partner, Washington, D.C. Office)	Jonathan D. Cahn
	Alfred W. Cortese, Jr.
	Elliot J. Feldman
	John B. Huffaker
Donald H. Green (Deputy Managing Partner, Washington, D.C. Office)	George A. Lehner
	Edward H. Lieberman
	Marc D. Machlin
Arthur B. Axelson	Edward A. McCullough

(See Next Column)

David J. McPherson	Sheldon L. Schreiberg
John Will Ongman	Gary S. Smuckler
Daniel I. Prywes	Stephen M. Truitt
Frank M. Rapoport	William J. Walsh
David A. Wormser	

OF COUNSEL

Larisa A. Afanasyeva	Otto J. Hetzel
(Not admitted in DC)	Lizbeth R. Levinson
Kathleen L. Blaner	William B. Simons
Christopher L. Davis	(Not admitted in DC)
(Not admitted in DC)	John A. Westberg
John F. DePodesta	
(Not admitted in DC)	

ASSOCIATES

JoAnna J. Barnes	John M. Flannery
June Blanchard Brown	H. David Kotz
John J. Burke	Michelle J. Morris
Charles H. Carpenter	Elizabeth Delgado Rodriguez
Gregory Scott Carter	Michael F. Wasserman
Gregory C. Dorris	James C. Wilson
Marvin W. Ehrlich	
(Not admitted in DC)	

For full biographical listings, see the Martindale-Hubbell Law Directory

✱ PERKINS COIE (AV)

A Law Partnership including Professional Corporations
Strategic Alliance with Russell & DuMoulin
607 Fourteenth Street, N.W., 20005
Telephone: 202-628-6600
Facsimile: 202-434-1690
Telex: 44-0277 PCSO
Seattle, Washington Office: 1201 Third Avenue, 40th Floor.
Telephone: 206-583-8888.
Facsimile: 206-583-8500.
Cable Address: "Perkins Seattle."
Telex: 32-0319 PERKINS SEA.
Anchorage, Alaska Office: 1029 West Third Avenue, Suite 300.
Telephone: 907-279-8561.
Facsimile: 907-276-3108.
Telex: 32-0319 PERKINS SEA.
Los Angeles, California Office: Ninth Floor, 1999 Avenue of the Stars.
Telephone: 310-788-9900.
Telex: 32-0319 PERKINS SEA.
Facsimile: 310-788-3399.
Olympia, Washington Office: 1110 Capital Way South, Suite 405.
Telephone: 360-956-3300.
Facsimile: 360-956-1208.
Portland, Oregon Office: 1211 Southwest Fifth Avenue, Suite 1500.
Telephone: 503-727-2000.
Facsimile: 503-727-2222.
Telex: 32-0319 PERKINS SEA.
Bellevue, Washington Office: Suite 1800, One Bellevue Center, 411 - 108th Avenue N.E.
Telephone: 206-453-6980.
Facsimile: 206-453-7350.
Telex: 32-0319 PERKINS SEA.
Spokane, Washington Office: North 221 Wall Street, Suite 600.
Telephone: 509-624-2212.
Facsimile: 509-458-3399.
Telex: 32-0319 PERKINS SEA.
Taipei, Taiwan Office: 8/F, TFIT Tower, 85 Jen Ai Road, Sec. 4.
Telephone: 886-2-778-1177.
Facsimile: 886-2-777-9898.
Hong Kong Office: 23rd Floor, Asia Pacific Finance Tower, Citibank Plaza, 3 Garden Road.
Telephone: 852-2878-1177.
Facsimile: 852-2524-9988.
London, England Office: St. Michael's Road, 1 George Yard, EC3V 9DH.
Telephone: 171-369-9966.
Facsimile: 171-369-9968.
Canada: Strategic Alliance with Russell & Dumoulin, 1700-1075 West Georgia Street, Vancouver, B.C. V6E 3G2.
Telephone: 604-631-3131.

RESIDENT MEMBERS

Robert F. Bauer	Kerry B. Long
Donald C. Baur	Guy R. Martin
Judith L. Corley	James R. Moore
Robert L. Deitz	Nancy W. Newkirk
John M. Devaney	Barry J. Reingold
Donald J. Friedman	Leonard E. Santos
Mary Rose Hughes	Benjamin S. Sharp
John P. Hume	Thomas V. Vakerics
Martin P. Willard	

OF COUNSEL

Thomas L. Adams, Jr.	Jeffrey G. Miller
Ellen L. Weintraub	

(See Next Column)

PERKINS COIE, *Washington—Continued*

RESIDENT ASSOCIATES

Karen Donovan	Sherri Braden Sampson
Marc E. Elias	(Not admitted in DC)
Andrew E. Falk	B. Holly Schadler
Barry I. Medintz	Mark T. Wasden
Kara M. Sacilotto	Sloane Anders Wildman

For full biographical listings, see the Martindale-Hubbell Law Directory

PIERSON SEMMES AND BEMIS (AV)

Canal Square, 1054 31st Street, N.W., 20007
Telephone: 202-333-4000
Telex: 248528 PSF UR;
Telecopier: 202-965-0100

MEMBERS OF FIRM

W. DeVier Pierson	William C. Lieblich
David H. Semmes	David J. Hill
Douglas Knox Bemis, Jr.	David F. B. Smith
Peter J. Levin	Paul Ryberg, Jr.
Mark E. Greenwold	Thomas S. Warrick
	Gerard A. Clark

ASSOCIATES

Clinton E. Cameron	Charles A. Jones
Tamara R. Gelboin	David A. Harrington
Conrad J. Jacoby	(Not admitted in DC)

For full biographical listings, see the Martindale-Hubbell Law Directory

* PILLSBURY MADISON & SUTRO LLP (AV)

1100 New York Avenue, N.W., Ninth Floor, 20005
Telephone: 202-861-3000
Fax: 202-822-0944
Email: pillsburylaw.com
Costa Mesa, California Office: Plaza Tower, 600 Anton Boulevard, Suite 1100, 92626.
Telephone: 714-436-6800.
Fax: 714-662-6999.
Los Angeles, California Office: Citicorp Plaza, 725 South Figueroa, Suite 1200, 90017.
Telephone: 213-488-7100.
Fax: 213-629-1033.
New York, New York Office: 520 Madison Avenue, 40th Floor, 10022.
Telephone: 212-328-4810.
Fax: 212-328-4824.
Silicon Valley Office, Menlo Park Location: 2700 Sand Hill Road, Menlo Park, 94025.
Telephone: 415-233-4500.
Fax: 415-233-4545.
Sacramento, California Office: 400 Capitol Mall, Suite 1700, 95814.
Telephone: 916-329-4700.
Fax: 916-441-3583.
San Diego, California Office: 101 West Broadway, Suite 1800, 92101.
Telephone: 619-234-5000.
Fax: 619-236-1995.
San Francisco, California Office: 235 Montgomery Street, 94104.
Telephone: 415-983-1000.
Fax: 415-983-1200.
Silicon Valley Office, San Jose Location: Ten Almaden Boulevard, San Jose, 95113.
Telephone: 408-947-4000.
Fax: 408-287-8341.
Hong Kong Office: 6/F Asia Pacific Finance Tower, Citibank Plaza, 3 Garden Road, Central.
Telephone: 011-852-2509-7100.
Fax: 011-852-2509-7188.
Tokyo, Japan Office: Pillsbury Madison & Sutro, Gaikokuho Jimu Bengoshi Jimusho, 5th Floor, Samon Eleven Building, 3-1, Samon-cho, Shinjuku-ku, Tokyo 160 Japan.
Telephone: 800-729-9830; 011-813-3354-3531.
Fax: 011-813-3354-3534.

Arlon V. Cushman (1892-1950)	William Michael Cushman
John J. Darby (1920-1950)	(1925-1964)

MEMBERS OF FIRM

James B. Atkin	Robert A. Gutkin
James D. Berquist	(Not admitted in DC)
Donald J. Bird	Lawrence Harbin
David W. Brinkman	David E. Hopmann
Susan Tucker Brown	(Not admitted in DC)
Ken M. Brown	David A. Jakopin
Terry Calvani	Kevin E. Joyce
(Not admitted in DC)	Richard L. Kirkpatrick
Kendrew H. Colton	Sheldon H. Klein
Chris Comuntzis	Timothy J. Klima
Lynn E. Eccleston	Gearry Lloyd Knight, Jr.
G. Paul Edgell	Paul N. Kokulis
David J. Evans	Dale S. Lazar
Stephen C. Glazier	Michelle N. Lester
Peter W. Gowdey	Raymond F. Lippitt

(See Next Column)

MEMBERS OF FIRM (Continued)

Carl G. Love	W. Jeffrey Schmidt
Edgar H. Martin	Jeffrey A. Simenauer
Paul F. McQuade	George M. Sirilla
Keith J. Mendelson	Jay B. Stephens
Robert A. Molan	Raymond L. Sweigart
John P. Moran	W. Warren Taltavull III
Mark G. Paulson	Thomas D. Terry
(Not admitted in DC)	(Not admitted in DC)
Glenn J. Perry	Benjamin M. Vandegrift
Edward M. Prince	William K. West, Jr.
	Paul E. White, Jr.

OF COUNSEL

Howard D. Doescher	Jacqueline Pace (Resident)
Sally D. Garr	Thomas G. Wiseman
Lawrence A. Hymo	(Not admitted in DC)

SENIOR COUNSEL

Theresa G. Fenelon

ASSOCIATES

William P. Atkins	David M. Haug
Holly E. Blewer	Adam R. Hess
Jack S. Barufka	Ann S. Hobbs
Brian J. Beatus	Kurt W. Lockwood
William H. Bollman	(Not admitted in DC)
Gregory P. Brummett	Timothy F. Loomis
(Not admitted in DC)	(Not admitted in DC)
Marlana Kathryn Chapin	James A. Meade
Michael A. Conley	Jeffrey Scott Melcher
(Not admitted in DC)	Anthony L. Miele
Michael R. Dzwonczyk	(Not admitted in DC)
Belinda Elvan Garrett	Christopher P. Murphy
(Not admitted in DC)	B.J. Sadoff
Jonathan Gentin	(Not admitted in DC)
Barry P. Golob	Edward J. Stemberger
John C. Gorecki	David S. Taylor
(Not admitted in DC)	Richard Wydeven
Michael W. Haas	Patricia R. Zeigler

For full biographical listings, see the Martindale-Hubbell Law Directory

* PIPER & MARBURY L.L.P. (AV)

1200 Nineteenth Street, N.W., 20036-2430
Telephone: 202-861-3900
FAX: 202-223-2085
Email: lawfirm@pipermar.com *URL:* http://www.pipermar.com
Baltimore, Maryland Office: Charles Center South, 36 South Charles Street, 21201-3018.
Telephone: 410-539-2530.
FAX: 410-539-0489.
Easton, Maryland Office: 117 Bay Street, 21601-2703.
Telephone: 410-820-4460.
FAX: 410-820-4463.
New York, N.Y. Office: 1251 Avenue of the Americas, 10020-1104.
Telephone: 212-835-6000.
FAX: 212-835-6001.
Philadelphia, Pennsylvania Office: 3400 Two Logan Square, 18th & Arch Streets, 19103-2762.
Telephone: 215-656-3300.
FAX: 215-656-3301.
Cherry Hill, New Jersey Office: 220 Lake Drive East, Suite 105, 08002.
Telephone: 609-982-7035.
FAX: 609-982-8379.

MEMBERS OF FIRM

Nathan B. Feinstein	Alan C. Porter
David V. Anthony	I. Scott Bass
Lewis A. Noonberg	(Not admitted in DC)
Sheldon Krantz	William D. Blakely
Robert W. Ogren	Michael F. Brockmeyer
Toni K. Allen	(Not admitted in DC)
Thomas H. Truitt	Stephen L. Owen
William R. Weissman	Joyce J. Gorman
Carl L. Vacketta	David B. Dempsey (P.C.)
Edwin M. Martin, Jr.	Jay Gary Finkelstein
Philip L. Cohan	Cynthia J. Morris
Steven K. Yablonski	David H. Bamberger
J. Brian Molloy	David Clarke, Jr.
Ronald L. Plesser	James M. Brogan
E. Leslie Hoffman, III	(Not admitted in DC)
(Not admitted in DC)	Anthony H. Rickert
Gregory A. Smith	James P. Rathvon
Mark J. Tauber	Douglas H. Green
Anthony L. Young	Nora E. Garrote
Randall B. Lowe	Steven J. Mandell
Thomas C. Wheeler	Donna Lee Yesner
Francis X. Markey	Stanley R. Soya
Jeffrey F. Liss	Theodore D. Segal
Larry D. Harris	Benjamin S. Boyd
Stephen R. Mysliwiec	Richard P. Rector
Daniel J. Carrigan	
(Not admitted in DC)	

(See Next Column)

PIPER & MARBURY L.L.P.—*Continued*

OF COUNSEL

Emilio W. Cividanes   Christopher J. Clay
Joseph K. Wiener   Julie Ronder Domike

SENIOR ATTORNEY

Richard C. Walters

RESIDENT ASSOCIATES

Richard J. Vacura   Mark J. O'Connor
James B. Reach   Brian D. Henderson
Carolyn M. Bamberger   (Not admitted in DC)
Mitchell S. Marder   Julie Arthur Garcia
  (Not admitted in DC)   Mary Ita Snyder
Barbara Rowland   (Not admitted in DC)
John L. Moore, Jr.   Daniel M. Horrigan
John E. Benedict   Elizabeth R. Dewey
Diana Pennington   (Not admitted in DC)
Leonard L. Gordon   Amy Davidson Bryant
  (Not admitted in DC)   Malcolm D. Woolf
Mary E. Gately   Holly Emrick Svetz
Timothy P. Branigan   Keara M. O'Donnell
Kevin P. Mullen   (Not admitted in DC)
Christine Stark   Daniel Warren Pugh
Norman L. Rave, Jr.   Chandra Emery
Nancy A. Spangler   (Not admitted in DC)
Kecia Boney   Carol A. Kelley
  (Not admitted in DC)   (Not admitted in DC)
Jane Kwok Ping Tam   Carol Guy-Jackson
  (Not admitted in DC)   (Not admitted in DC)
Eric B. Kantor   Heather E. Gange
James J. Halpert   (Not admitted in DC)
Merrill Philips   Laura S. Roecklein
Kimberly E. Wolod   Mary C. Ragsdale
Marianne Mancino Thiede (Not admitted in DC)
Timothy M. Cramer   Victoria Alexandra Schlesinger
Carla G. Pennington-Cross (Not admitted in DC)
Jennifer A. White   Kimberly Ann Crowder
                     (Not admitted in DC)

For full biographical listings, see the Martindale-Hubbell Law Directory

---

✲ POPHAM, HAIK, SCHNOBRICH & KAUFMAN, LTD. (AV)

Metropolitan Square Building, Suite 800, 1450 G Street, N.W., 20005
Telephone: 202-824-8000
Telefax: 202-824-8199
URL: http://www.popham.com
Minneapolis, Minnesota Office: Piper Jaffray Tower, Suite 3300, 222 South Ninth Street.
Telephone: 612-333-4800.
Telefax: 612-334-8888.
Denver, Colorado Office: One Tabor Center, Suite 2400, 1200 Seventeenth Street.
Telephone: 303-893-1200.
Telefax: 303-893-2194.
Miami, Florida Office: NationsBank Tower at International Place, 100 S.E. Second Street.
Telephone: 305-530-0050.
Telefax: 305-530-0055.

Donald A. Farmer Jr.   Stephen P. Murphy
Paul A. Koches   Susan A. Aaron
James P. Gallatin Jr.   George M. Foote
Harold J. Engel   Frederick P. Waite
B. Parker Livingston Jr.   Bassam N. Ibrahim
David C. Gryce   Patrick Haiping Hu
                     (Not admitted in DC)

Sandra K. Scholar   William O. Trousdell
Mark Brian Wychulis   (Not admitted in DC)
Mark G. Seifert   Kimberly Young
Holly M. Ford   (Not admitted in DC)
  (Not admitted in DC)   Denise Cheung
Peter J. Riebling   (Not admitted in DC)

OF COUNSEL

Patrick D. Doyle (Not admitted in the United States)

SPECIAL COUNSEL

Brian P. O'Shaughnessy

For full biographical listings, see the Martindale-Hubbell Law Directory

---

✲ PORTER, WRIGHT, MORRIS & ARTHUR (AV)

1233 20th Street, N.W., 20036-2395
Telephone: 202-778-3000; (800-456-7962)
Fax: 202-778-3063
Email: dca@porterwright.com
Columbus, Ohio Office: 41 South High Street, 43215-6194.
Telephones: 614-227-2000; (800-533-2794).
Fax: 614-227-2100. Internet: cmh@porterwright.com.
Dayton, Ohio Office: One Dayton Centre, One South Main Street, 45402.
Telephones: 513-228-2411; (800-533-4434).
Fax: 513-449-6820. Internet: day@porterwright. com.

(See Next Column)

Cincinnati, Ohio Office: 250 E. Fifth Street, 45202-4199.
Telephones: 513-381-4700; (800-582-5813).
Fax: 513-421-0991. Internet: cvg@porterwright.com.
Cleveland, Ohio Office: 925 Euclid Avenue, 44115-1483.
Telephones: 216-443-9000; (800-824-1980).
Fax: 216-443-9011. Internet: cle@porterwright.com.
Naples, Florida Office: 4501 Tamiami Trail North, 33940-3013.
Telephones: 941-263-8898; (800-876-7962).
Fax: 941-436-2990. Internet: apf@porterwright.com.

MEMBERS OF FIRM

Michael G. Dowd   Judd L. Kessler
E. Jay Finkel   Mark L. Lezell
Leslie Alan Glick   Ronald S. Perlman
Thomas O. Gorman   Robert E. Steinberg

RESIDENT ASSOCIATES

William P. McGrath, Jr.   Brian K. O'Bleness
                     (Not admitted in DC)

RESIDENT OF COUNSEL

Barbara A. Duncombe   William G. Porter, Jr.
Bart S. Fisher   James C. Stearns
James R. Hagerty   Donald P. Young
Frederick P. Hink   John Hardin Young

For full biographical listings, see the Martindale-Hubbell Law Directory

---

✲ POWELL, GOLDSTEIN, FRAZER & MURPHY (AV)

6th Floor, 1001 Pennsylvania Avenue, N.W., 20004
Telephone: 202-347-0066
Fax: 202-624-7222
Atlanta, Georgia Office: Sixteenth Floor, 191 Peachtree Street, N.E., 30303.
Telephone: 404-572-6600.
Telex: 542864.
Telecopier: 404-572-6999.
Cable Address: Pgfm.

RESIDENT MEMBERS

Elliott B. Adler   Harry Huge
J. Gail Bancroft   John J. Knapp
Richard M. Belanger   Stuart S. Kurlander
Jerome A. Breed   Simon Lazarus, III
Anne B. Camper   Niall P. Meagher
Michael H. Chanin   Alan K. Parver
William C. Crenshaw   Daniel M. Price
Keith A. Dunsmore   Charles H. Roistacher
  (Not admitted in DC)   Peter W. Segal
Neil R. Ellis   Lawrence B. Simons
Michael E. Fine   Peter O. Suchman
Anthony S. Freedman   Michael A. Taylor
Larry S. Gage   Robert Torresen, Jr.
Ronald S. Gart   William H.E. von Oehsen
David C. Hammond   Celeste M. Wasielewski
           Florence A. Wood

RESIDENT ASSOCIATES

Lee Ann Alexander   Lauren H. Kravetz
K. Sabrina Austin   Sheryl Krongold
Ralph J. Caccia   Anne M. Lewis
Carla Calobrisi   (Not admitted in DC)
Jill C. Chessen   Susan M. Mathews
William Gerald Driggers Richard A. Medway
Barbara D.A. Eyman   Julian S. Myers
Todd J. Friedbacher   Steven K. Stranne
Elizabeth Cole Hafner   David Sullivan
Robin Heimann-McGhee (Not admitted in DC)
Brett G. Kappel   Susan J. Thomas
         Colin W. Uckert

FOREIGN COUNSEL

Stanimir A. Alexandrov

OF COUNSEL

Brenda A. Jacobs   Florence R. Keenan
Susan P. Strommer

For full biographical listings, see the Martindale-Hubbell Law Directory

---

✲ PROSKAUER ROSE GOETZ & MENDELSOHN LLP (AV)

1233 Twentieth Street, N.W. Suite 800, 20036
Telephone: 202-416-6800
FAX: 202-416-6899
Email: info@proskauer.com *URL:* http://www.proskauer.com
New York, New York Office: 1585 Broadway.
Telephone: 212-969-3000.
Los Angeles, California Office: 2121 Avenue of the Stars, Suite 2700.
Telephone: 310-557-2900.
Boca Raton, Florida Office: One Boca Place, Suite 340 West, 2255 Glades Road.
Telephone: 407-241-7400.
Clifton, New Jersey Office: 1373 Broad Street, P.O. Box 4444.
Telephone: 201-779-6300.
Paris, France Office: Proskauer Rose Goetz & Mendelsohn, 9 rue Le Tasse.
Telephone: (33-1) 44 30 25 30.

(See Next Column)

PROSKAUER ROSE GOETZ & MENDELSOHN LLP, *Washington—Continued*

MEMBERS OF FIRM

Jon A. Baumgarten	Warren L. Dennis
Mark J. Biros	Malcolm J. Harkins, III
Arnold I. Burns	Ian K. Portnoy
Joseph E. Casson	Richard H. Rowe

Christopher Wolf

WASHINGTON, D.C.
SPECIAL COUNSEL

Thomas H. Brock	Mary E. Pivec
Bradley L. Kelly	(Not admitted in DC)

Eric J. Schwartz

WASHINGTON, D.C. ASSOCIATES

Margaret J. Babb	Richard A. Hearn
Christine D. Bachman	James P. Holloway
Donald L. Bell, II	Dorothy M. Ingalls
Richard S. Binstein	Karen E. Miller
Sarah T. Chasson	Paul M. Morris
Steven B. Fabrizio	Laura J. Oberbroeckling
Alec W. Farr	Matthew J. Oppenheim
Cecilia Fex	Cheralyn E. Schessler
Lloyd D. Fiorini	Pamela Beth Small

Susan A. Turner

For full biographical listings, see the Martindale-Hubbell Law Directory

LOUIS RABIL (AV)

Suite 901, 1825 K Street, N.W., 20006
Telephone: 202-466-4944
Fax: 202-223-3260
Email: lrabil@aol.com

For full biographical listings, see the Martindale-Hubbell Law Directory

* REED SMITH SHAW & McCLAY (AV)

Suite 1100 - East Tower, 1301 K Street, N.W., 20005-3317
Telephone: 202-414-9200
FAX: 202-414-9299
Email: rssm@rssm.com *URL:* http://www.rssm.com
Pittsburgh, Pennsylvania Office: 435 Sixth Avenue, 15219-1886.
Telephone: 412-288-3131.
FAX: 412-288-3063.
Philadelphia, Pennsylvania Office: 2500 One Liberty Place, 19103-7301.
Telephone: 215-851-8100.
FAX: 215-851-1420.
Harrisburg, Pennsylvania Office: 213 Market Street, 17101-2132.
Telephone: 717-234-5988.
FAX: 717-236-3777.
McLean, Virginia Office: Suite 1100, 8251 Greensboro Drive, 22102-3844.
Telephone: 703-734-4600.
FAX: 703-734-4699.
Princeton, New Jersey Office: 136 Main Street, Suite 250, 08540-5799.
Telephone: 609-987-0050.
FAX: 609-951-0824.
New York, N.Y. Office: 375 Park Avenue, Suite 301, 10152.
Telephone: 212-521-5400.
FAX: 212-521-5450.
Newark, New Jersey Office: One Gateway Center, 07102-5311.
Telephone: 201-622-1600.
Fax: 201-622-4747.

MEMBERS OF FIRM

Robert J. Aamoth	Nancy A. Luque
Kevin R. Barry	Michael C. Lynch
William O. Bittman	Kathleen H. McGuan
A. Scott Bolden	Donald J. Myers
Elizabeth B. Carder	Peter D. O'Connell
Bernard J. Casey	Joseph A. Rieser, Jr.
George R. Clark	Marnie K. Sarver
Carol Colborn	Gordon B. Schatz
Francis P. Dicello	Marc J. Scheineson
Robert A. Emmett	Delbert D. Smith
David C. Evans	Douglas K. Spaulding
Thomas C. Fox	Frederic T. Spindel
Virginia D. Green	Judith St. Ledger-Roty
Benjamin J. Griffin	Eugene Tillman
Joel M. Hamme	Harry H. Weil
Gordon W. Hatheway, Jr.	(Not admitted in DC)
(Also at New York, N.Y.)	M. Stephanie Wickouski
James K. Kearney	John M. Wood

COUNSEL

John A. Beck	Stefan M. Lopatkiewicz
Mary E. Buckles	William Morris
Vincent C. Burke III	Phillips S. Peter
Jonathan E. Canis	(Not admitted in DC)
James J. Freeman	J. Laurent Scharff
William A. Geoghegan	Ann E. Schmitt
Robert J. Hill	Jing Wang (Not admitted in
Brian A. Johnson	United States)

William H. Willcox

(See Next Column)

ASSOCIATES

Brigitte L. Adams	David Ober
Bhavana S. Boggs	Linda Lewis Rhodes
(Not admitted in DC)	Michael B. Richman
Deborah J. Dwight	Pamela Kauffman Riley
Jay L. Halpern	(Not admitted in DC)
Annemarie Scanlon Harthun	Mary E. Riordan
Julie E. Kass	James V. Schuster
(Not admitted in DC)	(Not admitted in DC)
Kathleen A. Kirby	Tamara V. Scoville
Wendy I. Kirchick	(Not admitted in DC)
(Not admitted in DC)	Enrico C. Soriano
Helen G. Kirsch	(Not admitted in DC)
Mark B. Langdon	Marla P. Spindel
Lisa L. Leibow	Daniel K. Steen
(Not admitted in DC)	David N. Tanenbaum
Paul G. Madison	(Not admitted in DC)
Robert M. Marino	Eric S. Tower
Joseph W. Metro	(Not admitted in DC)
David A. Mustone	David J. Winker
Nancy E. Nunan	(Not admitted in DC)

For full biographical listings, see the Martindale-Hubbell Law Directory

* REID & PRIEST LLP (AV)

Market Square, 701 Pennsylvania Ave., N.W., 20004-2625
Telephone: 202-508-4000
Facsimile: 202-508-4321
New York City Office: 40 West 57th Street, 10019-4097.
Telephone: 212-603-2000.
Fax: 212-603-2001.

Howard A. Cooper	Phillip G. Lookadoo
Deborah A. DeMasi	Allen S. Melser
Mark Fox Evens	Stephan M. Minikes
Lee M. Goodwin	James K. Mitchell
Jonathan W. Gottlieb	Judith D. O'Neill
Robert T. Hall, III	Courtney M. Price
Patricia M. Healy	Mark J. Riedy
Nathaniel A. Humphries	John R. Schaefgen, Jr.
David E. Jacobson	Carole Stern
William A. Kirk, Jr.	Kenneth B. Weiner
Richard J. Leidl	(Not admitted in DC)

Michael J. Zimmer

RESIDENT SENIOR COUNSEL

Richard M. Merriman

OF COUNSEL

Raymond F. Dacek	Vincent D. Salvatore, Jr.
David A. Gantz	(Not admitted in DC)
Michael D. Hornstein	Rachael E. Schwartz
Joanne C. Rutkowski (Not	
admitted in DC; Washington,	
D.C. Office)	

RESIDENT ASSOCIATES

Samir S. Desai	Brian J. McManus
(Not admitted in DC)	Timothy M. Murphy
Raymond C. Glenny	Frank S. Rosenberg
Janet Hernandez	(Not admitted in DC)
(Not admitted in DC)	Angana R. Shah
H. Rosemary Jeronimides	(Not admitted in DC)
(Not admitted in DC)	Linda J. Shapiro
Jennifer L. Karas	Becky L. Troutman
(Not admitted in DC)	(Not admitted in DC)
Alan Lescht	Allison S. Yamamoto
	(Not admitted in DC)

SPECIALISTS AND ADVISORS

Barry I. Berkoff	Donald Scheier
Nancy Gosin	William C. Weeden

For full biographical listings, see the Martindale-Hubbell Law Directory

* ROGERS & WELLS (AV)

607 Fourteenth Street, N.W., 20005-2018
Telephone: 202-434-0700
Facsimile: 202-434-0800
New York, New York Office: 200 Park Avenue, New York, N.Y. 10166-0153.
Telephone: 212-878-8000.
Facsimile: 212-878-8375. *Email:* email@rw.com.
Telex: 234493 RKWUR.
Los Angeles, California Office: 444 South Flower Street, Los Angeles, California 90071-2901.
Telephone: 213-689-2900.
Facsimile: 213-689-2999.
Paris, France Office: 47 Avenue Hoche, 75008 Paris, France.
Telephone: 33-1-44-09-46-00.
Facsimile: 33-1-42-67-50-81.
Telex: 651617 EURLAW.

(See Next Column)

ROGERS & WELLS—*Continued*

London, England Office: 40 Basinghall Street, London EC2V 5DE, England.
Telephone: 44-171-628-0101.
Facsimile: 44-171-628-6111.
Frankfurt, Germany Office: Westendstrasse 16-22, 60325 Frankfurt/Main, Federal Republic of Germany.
Telephone: 49-69-97-14-78-0.
Facsimile: 49-69-97-14-78-33.
Hong Kong Office: One Exchange Square, 8 Connaught Place, Central, Hong Kong.
Telephone: 852-2844-3500.
Facsimile: 852-2844-3555.

SENIOR PARTNER
William P. Rogers

PARTNERS

Kevin J. Arquit	Ira D. Hammerman
John H. C. Barron, Jr.	John Paul Ketels
Roger A. Clark	Steven A. Newborn
Roberto Dañino	William Silverman
Anthony F. Essaye	Ryan Trainer
Brandon J. Fields	Dale C. Turza

SENIOR COUNSEL
Eugene T. Rossides

COUNSEL AND OF COUNSEL

James C. Egan, Jr.	Thomas R. Petty
Douglas J. Heffner	Carrie A. Simon
James M. Lynch	Samuel A. Stern
Laura A. Wilkinson	

CONSULTANTS

Barbara J. Covell	Virginia L. Snider

ASSOCIATES

Kenneth H. Abbe	Donald E. Griffith
Jorge E. Alers	(Not admitted in DC)
Tracy E. Ballard	T. Douglas Hollowell
Amy E. Beargie	Denise Manning-Cabrol
Christopher T. Bruneau	(Not admitted in DC)
(Not admitted in DC)	Prakash H. Mehta
Henry Wolfgang Carter	Katherine Wells Meighan
Stephen J. Claeys	Cristina M. Mendoza
Shannon R. Clark	Michael J. Metzger
(Not admitted in DC)	Jennifer J. Mink
Richard Cohn	(Not admitted in DC)
(Not admitted in DC)	Maribeth Petrizzi
Charles M. Cole	Matthew J. Reilly
David D. DiBari	(Not admitted in DC)
Jennifer M. Drogula	Anthony J. Renzi, Jr.
Nancy Figg Duessel	Augusto Repetto
Paul S. Dwyer Jr.	(Not admitted in DC)
John J. Field	Andrew K. Rosa
(Not admitted in DC)	E. Pepper van Noppen
Kirsten A. Wolfe	

For full biographical listings, see the Martindale-Hubbell Law Directory

---

ROPES & GRAY (AV)

One Franklin Square, 1301 K Street, NW, Suite 800 East, 20005-3333
Telephone: 202-626-3900
Telecopy: 202-626-3961
Email: postmaster@ropesgray.com
Boston, Massachusetts Office: One International Place.
Telephone: 617-951-7000.
Fax: 617-951-7050.
Providence, Rhode Island Office: 30 Kennedy Plaza.
Telephone: 401-455-4400.
Fax: 401-455-4401.

RESIDENT MEMBERS

Thomas M. Susman	Russell A. Gaudreau, Jr.
Martin E. Lybecker	Samuel J. Buffone
Colburn T. Cherney	J. Daniel Berry
David O. Stewart	Alan G. Priest
Peter M. Brody	

COUNSEL
Mark A. Greenwood

RESIDENT ASSOCIATES

Thomas B. Smith	Brian L. Murray, Jr.
Dina L. Michels	(Not admitted in DC)
Ellen Page DelSole	Brian S. Chilton
James M. Lichtman	Cynthia M. Monaco
Maryellen M. Lundquist	(Not admitted in DC)
Françoise M. Haan	J. Steven Baughman
Mary C. Hennessey	

For full biographical listings, see the Martindale-Hubbell Law Directory

---

* ROSENMAN & COLIN LLP (AV)

1300 19th Street, N.W., 20036
Telephone: 202-463-4640
Facsimile: (202) 429-0046
New York, N.Y. Office: 575 Madison Avenue, 10022.
Telephone: 212-940-8800. *Facsimiles:* (212) 940-8776; (212) 935-0679.
Website: http://www.rosenman.com.
New Jersey Office: Suite 2600, 1 Gateway Center, Newark, New Jersey 07102-5397.
Telephone: 201-645-0572.
Facsimile: 201-645-0573.

RESIDENT PARTNERS

Howard J. Braun	Richard A. Gross
	Marybeth Sorady

COUNSEL
Lionel E. Pashkoff

SPECIAL COUNSEL

Theodore A. Howard	Jerold L. Jacobs
Richard A. Ifft	Sandra L. Spalletta

RESIDENT ASSOCIATES

Michael Dean Gaffney	Shelley Sadowsky
Lisa B. Lapinski	(Not admitted in DC)
Diane L. Mooney	J. Mark Young
Paul G. Roche	(Not admitted in DC)

For full biographical listings, see the Martindale-Hubbell Law Directory

---

ROYALL KOEGEL & WELLS

(See Rogers & Wells, New York, New York)

---

* SCHIFF HARDIN & WAITE (AV)

A Partnership including Professional Corporations
Founded 1864
1101 Connecticut Avenue, N.W., 20036
Telephone: 202-778-6400
Facsimile: 202-778-6460
Chicago, Illinois Office: 7200 Sears Tower, 60606.
Telephone: 312-876-1000.
Facsimile: 312-258-5600.
TWX: 910-221-2463.
New York, New York Office: 150 East 52nd Street, Suite 2900, 10022.
Telephone: 212-753-5000.
Facsimile: 212-753-5044.
Peoria, Illinois Office: 300 Hamilton Boulevard, Suite 100, 61602.
Telephone: 309-673-2800.
Facsimile: 309-673-2801.
Merrillville, Indiana Office: 8585 Broadway, Suite 842, 46410.
Telephone: 219-738-3820.
Facsimile: 219-738-3826.

RESIDENT PARTNERS

Edward J. Finn	Andrew M. Klein
Barbara K. Heffernan	Gearold L. Knowles
Drexel D. Journey	Shaheda Sultan

RESIDENT OF COUNSEL

John W. Glendening, Jr.	Edwin S. Rockefeller
Catherine A. Jacobson	John S. Schmid

RESIDENT ASSOCIATES

Debra Ann Palmer	M. Thompson Rattray

For full biographical listings, see the Martindale-Hubbell Law Directory

---

* SEWARD & KISSEL (AV)

(Smith & Martin 1890)
1200 G Street, N.W. Suite 350, 20005
Telephone: 202-737-8833
Cable Address: "Sewkis New York"
Telex: 23-9046; 62-0982
Facsimile: 202-737-5184
New York, New York Office: One Battery Park Plaza.
Telephone: 212-574-1200.
Facsimile: 212-480-8421.
Budapest, Hungary Representative Office: 64 Andrássy út, 1062 Budapest, Hungary.
Telephone: 361-312-7654.
Facsimile: 361-312-7682.

RESIDENT PARTNERS

Anthony C. J. Nuland	Paul T. Clark

RESIDENT COUNSEL

Keith H. Ellis	Francis S. Rath

SENIOR ATTORNEYS
Elizabeth Warner

(See Next Column)

SEWARD & KISSEL, *Washington—Continued*

RESIDENT ASSOCIATES

Kevin M. Broadwater	Frederick H. Sherley
Alison M. Fuller	(Not admitted in DC)

For full biographical listings, see the Martindale-Hubbell Law Directory

SHEA & GARDNER (AV)

1800 Massachusetts Avenue, N.W., 20036
Telephone: 202-828-2000
Cable Address: "Sandg"
Telex: 89-2399
Telecopier: 202-828-2195

MEMBERS OF FIRM

Francis M. Shea (1905-1989)	David B. Cook
Warner W. Gardner	Stephen J. Hadley
Lawrence J. Latto	William R. Galeota
Richard T. Conway	Patrick M. Hanlon
Robert T. Basseches	Timothy K. Shuba
Benjamin W. Boley	James R. Bird
Ralph J. Moore, Jr.	Michael S. Giannotto
Martin J. Flynn	Jeffrey C. Martin
Stephen J. Pollak	William R. Hanlon
David Booth Beers	Elizabeth Runyan Geise
Anthony A. Lapham	Collette C. Goodman
Richard M. Sharp	Julie M. Edmond
John D. Aldock	Laura S. Wertheimer
William S. Moore	Richard M. Wyner
John Townsend Rich	Thomas J. Mikula
James R. Bieke	Eugenia Langan
I. Michael Greenberger	Nancy B. Stone
R. James Woolsey	Christopher E. Palmer
Frederick C. Schafrick	Mark S. Raffman

OF COUNSEL

William H. Dempsey	Barbara L. Kirschten

ASSOCIATES

Eric C. Jeffrey	Erika K. Singer
Robert B. Wasserman	(Not admitted in DC)
Bernice M. Blair	David Allen Graff
Anne R. Bowden	(Not admitted in DC)
Cynthia Gurnee Pugh	A. Christopher Bryant
Dana J. Martin	(Not admitted in DC)
John Bradford Wiegmann	Christopher A. Ford
Michael K. Isenman	(Not admitted in DC)
Valerie Ellen Ross	Donald J. Munro
David J. Katz	(Not admitted in DC)
Celestine Richards McConville	Elizabeth A. Robischon
Kim Dettelbach	(Not admitted in DC)
Amy Horton	Howard R. Rubin
Susan L. Pacholski	(Not admitted in DC)
James R. Bramson	Jodi L. Short
Heather H. Anderson	(Not admitted in DC)
(Not admitted in DC)	Howard R. Sklamberg
Reena N. Glazer	(Not admitted in DC)

For full biographical listings, see the Martindale-Hubbell Law Directory

SHEARMAN & STERLING (AV)

801 Pennsylvania Avenue, N.W., 9th Floor, 20004-2604
Telephone: (202) 508-8000
Fax: (202) 508-8100
New York, N.Y. Office: 599 Lexington Avenue, New York, New York 10022-6069 and Citicorp Center, 153 East 53rd Street, New York, New York 10022-4676.
Telephone: (212) 848-4000.
Telex: 667290 Num Lau.
Fax: 599 Lexington Avenue: (212) 848-7179. Citicorp Center: (212) 848-5252.
Abu Dhabi, United Arab Emirates Office: P.O. Box 2948.
Telephone: (971-2) 324477.
Fax: (971-2) 774533.
Beijing, People's Republic of China Office: Suite #2205, Capital Mansion, No. 6, Xin Yuan Nan Lu. Chao Yang District, Beijing, 100004.
Telephone: (86-10)6465-4574.
Fax: (86-10) 6465-4578.
Budapest, Hungary Office: Szerb utca 17-19, 1056 Budapest.
Telephone: (36-1) 266-3522.
Fax: (36-1) 266-3523.
Düsseldorf, Federal Republic of Germany Office: Couvenstrasse 8 40211 Düsseldorf.
Telephone: (49 211) 178 88-0.
Fax: (49 211) 178 88-88.
Telex: 8588294 NYLO.
Frankfurt, Federal Republic of Germany Office: Bockenheimer Landstrasse 55, 60325 Frankfurt am Main.
Telephone: (49-69) 97107-0.
Fax: (49-69) 97107-100.
Hong Kong Office: Standard Chartered Bank Building, 4 Des Voeux Road, Central.
Telephone: (852) 2978-8000.
Fax: (852) 2978-8099.

(See Next Column)

London, England Office: 199 Bishopsgate, London EC2M 3TY.
Telephone: (44-171) 920-9000.
Fax: (44-171) 920-9020.
Los Angeles, California Office: 777 South Figueroa Street, 34th Floor, 90017-5418.
Telephone: (213) 239-0300.
Fax: (213) 239-0381, 614-0936.
Paris, France Office: 114 avenue des Champs-Elysées, 75008.
Telephone: (33-1) 53-89-7000.
Fax: (33-1) 53-89-7070.
Telex: 282964 ROYALE.
San Francisco, California Office: 555 California Street, 94104-1522.
Telephone: (415) 616-1100.
Fax: (415) 616-1199.
Singapore Office: 80 Raffles Place #16-21, UOB Plaza 2. Singapore 048624. Telephone (65) 230-3800.
Fax: (65) 230-3899.
Tokyo, Japan Office: Shearman & Sterling (Grant Finlayson Gaikokuho-Jimu-Bengoshi Jimusho), Fukoku Seimei Building, 5th Fl. 2-2-2, Uchisaiwaicho, Chiyoda-ku, Tokyo 100, Japan.
Telephone: (81 3) 5251-1601.
Fax: (81 3) 5251-1602.
Toronto, Ontario, Canada Office: Commerce Court West, Suite 4405, P.O. Box 247, M5L 1E8.
Telephone: (416) 360-8484.
Fax: (416) 360-2958.

RESIDENT PARTNERS

Thomas S. Martin	Stephen James Marzen
(Managing Partner)	Linda C. Quinn
Robert A. Bergquist	(Not admitted in DC)
Robert E. Dineen, Jr.	Steven C. Sunshine
(Not admitted in DC)	(Not admitted in DC)
Jonathan L. Greenblatt	Thomas B. Wilner
Jeffrey M. Winton	

OF COUNSEL

Edward Bransilver	Robert E. Herzstein

For full biographical listings, see the Martindale-Hubbell Law Directory

SHERMAN, MEEHAN, CURTIN & AIN, A PROFESSIONAL CORPORATION (AV)

Suite 600, 1900 M Street, NW, 20036-3565
Telephone: 202-530-3300
Facsimile: 202-530-4411
Email: info@smcalaw.com

Peter R. Sherman	David Bradford Law
Thomas P. Meehan	Randell C. Ogg
Michael F. Curtin	Faith D. Dornbrand
Sanford K. Ain	Mark S. Carlin
Lee H. Spence	Claudia Anne Pott
David Barmak	Sam H. Roberson
Thomas E. Dunigan	Charles B. Day
Douglas E. Fierberg	

OF COUNSEL

John O. Fox

Laurence E. Salans	Kala Shah
Lauren E. Shea	Charles A. Zdebski
Matthew P. Maloney	Albert S. Mazloom III
Jeffrey C. Weinstock	Theresa M. Miles

For full biographical listings, see the Martindale-Hubbell Law Directory

* SIDLEY & AUSTIN (AV)

A Partnership including Professional Corporations
1722 Eye Street, N.W., 20006
Telephone: 202-736-8000
Telecopier: 202-736-8711
Chicago, Illinois Office: One First National Plaza 60603.
Telephone: 312-853-7000.
Telecopier: 312-853-7036.
Los Angeles, California Office: 555 W. 5th Street, 40th Flr., 90013-1010.
Telephone: 213-896-6000.
Telecopier: 213-896-6600.
New York, New York Office: 875 Third Avenue 10022.
Telephone: 212-906-2000.
Telecopier: 212-906-2021.
Dallas, Texas Office: 4500 Renaissance Tower, 1201 Elm Street 75270.
Telephone: 214-939-4500.
Telecopier: 214-939-4600.
London, England Office: Royal Exchange, EC3V 3LE.
Telephone: 011-44-171-360-3600.
Telecopier: 011-44-171-626-9737.
Tokyo, Japan Office: Taisho Seimei Hibiya Building, 7th Floor, 9-1, Yura Kucho, 1 Chome, Chiyoda-ku, 100.
Telephone: 011-81-3-3218-5900.
Facsimile: 011-81-3-3218-5922.

(See Next Column)

SIDLEY & AUSTIN—*Continued*

Singapore Office: UIC Building, 32nd Floor, Suite 3207, 5 Shenton Way, Singapore 0106.
Telephone: 011-65-224-5000.
Telecopier: 011-65-224-0530.

RESIDENT PARTNERS

Christopher L. Bell	Jaye "Janet Marie" Letson
James F. Bendernagel, Jr.	David M. Levy
Jeffrey S. Berlin	David J. Lewis
Frederic G. Berner, Jr.	Angus Macbeth
Richard D. Bernstein	Lorrie M. Marcil
Samuel B. Boxerman	David Michael Miles
(Not admitted in DC)	Lawrence A. Miller
David T. Buente, Jr.	G. Paul Moates
C. John Buresh	Michael A. Nemeroff
Ann E. Bushmiller	Francis J. O'Toole
Robert J. Conlan, Jr.	Carter G. Phillips
(Not admitted in DC)	Vincent F. Prada
Daniel M. Davidson	P. David Richardson, II
William S. Eckland	Melvin Rishe
Eugene R. Elrod	Constance A. Sadler
Ronald S. Flagg	Gene C. Schaerr
Alan C. Geolot	Mark D. Schneider
Thomas C. Green	Langley R. Shook
Joseph R. Guerra	Howard J. Stanislawski
Samuel I. Gutter	David Teitelbaum
Mark E. Haddad	Joseph B. Tompkins, Jr.
Kevin Hawley	Thomas P. Van Wazer
Stephen S. Hill	R. Clark Wadlow
Mark D. Hopson	Michael D. Warden
James Alan Huizinga	Marc D. Wassermann
Terence M. Hynes	(Not admitted in DC)
George W. Jones, Jr.	R. Merinda Wilson
Peter D. Keisler	Elroy H. Wolff
Richard D. Klingler	Thomas H. Yancey

COUNSEL

Natalie H. Diana	Mark E. Martin
Myles E. Flint	Gary P. Quigley
(Not admitted in DC)	Charlotte Uram
Stephen B. Lyons	John F. Wester

Richard E. Young

STAFF ATTORNEY
Susan White Haag

RESIDENT ASSOCIATES

Ann K. Adams	Christine A. Liverzani
Ann M. Ball	Christopher P. Lu
Margaret S. Bass	Teresa L. McGhie
Clinton F. Beckner	Tracy M. McGowan
Bradford A. Berenson	Daniel Meron
John M. Casanova	Robert C. Nissen
(Not admitted in DC)	(Not admitted in DC)
James L. Connaughton	Rosalind M. Parker
Denise W. DeFranco	Tamara R. Parker
Thomas G. Echikson	Joseph C. Port, Jr.
Krista L. Edwards	Linda S. Portasik
Jeffrey P. Ehrlich	Theodore R. Posner
Doris S. Finnerman	(Not admitted in DC)
Nina B. Finston	Tamara L. Preiss
Nathan A. Forrester	Michael J. Raphael
(Not admitted in DC)	Nathan C. Sheers
Jacqueline Gerson	Michael L. Shore
Marisa A. Gomez	(Not admitted in DC)
Jeffrey T. Green	Andra J. Shuster
Karin L. Green	Donald H. Smith
(Not admitted in DC)	Stephen F. Smith
Mark P. Guerrera	(Not admitted in DC)
Paul A. Hemmersbaugh	Margaret F. Spring
Dennis D. Hirsch	Julia E. Sullivan
(Not admitted in DC)	Kathryn B. Thomson
Adam D. Hirsh	David B. Toscano
Michael J. Hunseder	(Not admitted in DC)
(Not admitted in DC)	Frank R. Volpe
Kurt H. Jacobs	(Not admitted in DC)
Paul E. Kalb	Claudia A. Von-Pervieux
Richard L. Larach	Christopher G. Woodward
Joan L. Larsen	James P. Young
David L. Lawson	Paul J. Zidlicky

For full biographical listings, see the Martindale-Hubbell Law Directory

---

✳ SKADDEN, ARPS, SLATE, MEAGHER & FLOM LLP (AV)

1440 New York Avenue, N.W., 20005
Telephone: 202-371-7000
Fax: 202-393-5760
Firm/Affiliate Offices:
New York, New York: 919 Third Avenue, 10022.
Telephone: 212-735-3000.
Fax: 212-735-2000; 212-735-2001.
Telex: 645899 Skarslaw.

(See Next Column)

Boston, Massachusetts: One Beacon Street, 02108.
Telephone: 617-573-4800.
Fax: 617-573-4822.
Wilmington, Delaware: Skadden, Arps, Slate, Meagher & Flom (Delaware), One Rodney Square, P.O. Box 636, 19899.
Telephone: 302-651-3000.
Fax: 302-651-3001.
Los Angeles, California: 300 South Grand Avenue, 90071.
Telephone: 213-687-5000.
Fax: 213-687-5600.
Chicago, Illinois: Skadden, Arps, Slate, Meagher & Flom (Illinois), 333 West Wacker Drive, 60606.
Telephone: 312-407-0700.
Fax: 312-407-0411.
San Francisco, California: Four Embarcadero Center, 94111.
Telephone: 415-984-6400.
Fax: 415-984-2698.
Houston, Texas: 1600 Smith Street, Suite 4460, 77002.
Telephone: 713-655-5100.
Fax: 713-655-5181.
Newark, New Jersey: Skadden, Arps, Slate, Meagher & Flom (New Jersey), One Newark Center, 07102.
Telephone: 201-639-6800.
Fax: 201-639-6858.
Tokyo, Japan: Skadden, Arps, Slate, Meagher & Flom (International), 403, ABS Building, 2-4-16 Kudan Minami, Chiyoda-ku, Tokyo 102.
Telephone: 81-3-3221-9738.
Fax: 81-3-3221-9753.
London, England: 25 Bucklersbury EC4N 8DA.
Telephone: 011-44-171-248-9929.
Fax: 011-44-171-489-8533.
Hong Kong: Skadden, Arps, Slate, Meagher & Flom (International), 30/F Peregrine Tower, Lippo Centre, 89 Queensway, Central.
Telephone: 011-852-2820-0700.
Fax: 011-852-2820-0727.
Sydney, New South Wales, 2000, Australia: Skadden, Arps, Slate, Meagher & Flom (International), Level 26-State Bank Centre, 52 Martin Place.
Telephone: 011-61-2-9224-6000.
Fax: 011-61-2-9224-6044.
Toronto, Ontario: Skadden, Arps, Slate, Meagher & Flom (International), Suite 1820, North Tower, P.O. Box 189, Royal Bank Plaza, M5J 2J4.
Telephone: 416-777-4700.
Fax: 416-777-4747.
Paris, France: 105 rue du Faubourg Saint-Honoré, 75008.
Telephone: 011-33-1-40-75-44-44.
Fax: 011-33-1-49-53-09-99.
Brussels, Belgium: Skadden, Arps, Slate, Meagher & Flom (International), 523 avenue Louise, Box 30, 1050.
Telephone: 011-32-2-648-7666.
Fax: 011-32-2-640-3032.
Frankfurt, am Main, Germany: Skadden, Arps, Slate, Meagher & Flom (International), MesseTurm, 27th Floor, 60308.
Telephone: 011-49-69-9757-3000.
Fax: 011-49-69-9757-3050.
Beijing, China: Skadden, Arps, Slate, Meagher & Flom (International), East Wing Office, Level 4, China World Trade Center, No. 1, Jian Guo Men Wai Avenue, 100004.
Telephone: 011-86-10-6505-5511.
Fax: 011-86-10-6505-5522.
Prague, Czech Republic: Skadden, Arps, Slate, Meagher & Flom (International), Husova 5, 110 00, Prague 1.
Telephone: 011-42-2-2424-8526.
Fax: 011-42-2-2424-8566.
Moscow, Russia: Pleteshkovsky Pereulok 3/2, 107005.
Telephone: 011-7-501-940-2304.
Fax: 011-7-501-940-2511.
Singapore, Singapore: Skadden, Arps, Slate, Meagher & Flom (International), 9 Temasek Boulevard, Suite 29-01, Suntec City Tower Two, Singapore, 038989.
Telephone: 011-65-434-2900.
Fax: 011-65-434-2988.

PARTNERS

Neal S. McCoy	Robert S. Bennett
John M. Nannes	Janet L. Goetz
Lynn R. Coleman	Alan Kriegel
Leslie J. Goldman	Jeanine L. Matte
Douglas G. Robinson	Pamela F. Olson
C. Benjamin Crisman, Jr.	Carl S. Rauh
Michael P. Rogan	John J. Mangan
Thomas R. Graham	William S. Scherman
Robert E. Lighthizer	Antoinette Cook Bush
Fred T. Goldberg, Jr.	Albert H. Turkus
Stephen W. Hamilton	Kenneth Berlin
William J. Sweet, Jr.	Mitchell S. Ettinger
Enid L. Veron	Kenneth A. Gross
Erica A. Ward	James V. Alpi
Glenn J. Berger	C. Kevin Barnette
Clifford M. Naeve	Jay L. Birnbaum
Martin Klepper	Andrew L. Sandler
Paul W. Oosterhuis	Mary Lou Steptoe
Richard L. Brusca	(Not admitted in DC)
Marcia R. Nirenstein	John C. Quale

(See Next Column)

SKADDEN, ARPS, SLATE, MEAGHER & FLOM LLP, *Washington—Continued*

SPECIAL COUNSEL

Robert B. Greenbaum   Kenneth Kraus
Edward D. Ross, Jr.

COUNSEL

John A. Amodeo	Edward J. Meehan
June Broadstone	Brian C. Mohr
Roseann M. Cutrone	D. Scott Nance
Mark C. Del Bianco	Stephen J. Narkin
Mona E. Ehlenberger	Saul M. Pilchen
John N. Estes, III	Leonard M. Rawicz
Matthew W. S. Estes	Amy R. Sabrin
Jerry L. Jackson	Donald L. Toker, Jr.

Nancy A. Wodka

OF COUNSEL

Philip McBride Johnson   Rodney O. Thorson
Martin Hoffmann

ASSOCIATES

Veronica A. Angulo	Rebecca J. Levenson
Christos T. Antoniou	(Not admitted in DC)
Bonnie J. Austin	James A. Losey
Nancy D. Baird	Ellen L. Lyons
Sue C. Bak	Gary A. MacDonald
Kurt W. Bilas	Marc Stukhart Martin
Jessie M. Brooks	Heidi L. Mason
Eric Clayton Broyles	August J. Matteis
(Not admitted in DC)	(Not admitted in DC)
Lance T. Brasher	Melissa C. McCann
Jeffry A. Brueggeman	(Not admitted in DC)
Ingo F. Burghardt	Stacie E. McGinn
(Not admitted in DC)	Nancy J. McGlynn
Judith A. Center	Timothy J. Moran
Paul J. Crispino	(Not admitted in DC)
David A. Domansky	Linda G. Morrison
Henry C. Eisenberg	Nancy K. Oliver
Kathleen A. Foudy	(Not admitted in DC)
James A. Frazer	Davidson M. Pattiz
Neil M. Freeman	(Not admitted in DC)
Don Joaquin Frost, Jr.	Catherine Kane Ronis
Clifford R. Gross	Nancy G. Rubin
Robert L. Harris	Peter B. Saba
Catharine A. Hartzenbusch	Frank C. Shaw
Christine L. Herrell	Faryar Shirzad
Richard A. Hindman	Kenneth K. Shiu
Babak Hoghooghi	Pankaj K. Sinha
(Not admitted in DC)	Matthew A. Stevens
Yana S. Hudson	James L. Tanner, Jr.
(Not admitted in DC)	Mayling Tom
Scot B. Hutchins	David J. Waksman
Chad S. Johnson	Jennifer K. Walter
(Not admitted in DC)	Troy S. Watkinson

Rhoda L. Weeks

For full biographical listings, see the Martindale-Hubbell Law Directory

SONNENSCHEIN NATH & ROSENTHAL (AV)

1301 K Street, N.W. Suite 600 East Tower, 20005
Telephone: 202-408-6400
Fax: 202-408-6399
Chicago, Illinois Office: Suite 8000 Sears Tower, 233 South Wacker Drive.
Telephone: 312-876-8000.
Cable Address: "Sonberk".
Telex: 25-3526.
Facsimile: 312-876-7934.
New York, N.Y. Office: 1221 Avenue of the Americas, 24th Floor.
Telephone: 212-768-6700.
Facsimile: 212-391-1247.
San Francisco, California Office: 685 Market Street, 10th Floor.
Telephone: 415-882-5000.
Facsimile: 415-543-5472.
Los Angeles, California Office: 601 South Figueroa Street, Suite 1500.
Telephone: 213-623-9300.
Facsimile: 213-623-9924.
St. Louis, Missouri Office: One Metropolitan Square, Suite 3000.
Telephone: 314-241-1800.
Facsimile: 314-259-5959.
Kansas City, Missouri Office: Suite 1100, 4520 Main Street, 64111.
Telephone: 816-932-4400.
Facsimile: 816-531-7545.
London, England Office: Sonnenscheins, Royex House, Aldermanbury Square, EC2V 7HR.
Telephone: 0171-600-2222.
Facsimile: 0171-600-2221.

RESIDENT PARTNERS

Amy L. Bess	Fred L. Levy
Carol Elder Bruce	Michael R. Maryn
Todd R. Eskelsen	Roger W. Patrick
Elizabeth A. Ferrell	Caryl A. Potter, III
John S. Hahn	Douglas E. Rosenthal
Stuart E. Hunt	Kirk R. Ruthenberg

(See Next Column)

RESIDENT PARTNERS (Continued)

Michael A. Schlanger	William E. Sudow
Ronald E. Stauffer	Jerome P. Weiss
	(Deceased, 1934-1996)

OF COUNSEL

Donald P. Arnavas

RESIDENT ASSOCIATES

Thomas B. Burnside	Catherine M. Myers
(Not admitted in DC)	Kenneth J. Pfaehler
John J. Calkins	(Not admitted in DC)
Maria Sileno DeLoughry	Gregory Y. Porter
Monica Shah Desai	(Not admitted in DC)
Jonathan J. Fisher	Jill I. Prater
(Not admitted in DC)	(Not admitted in DC)
Robert L. Foose, II	Daniel N. Segal
Catherine B. Gardner	Daniel J. Shonkwiler
(Not admitted in DC)	(Not admitted in DC)
Joseph P. Hornyak	Anoop G. Shroff
Gordon D. Klepper	(Not admitted in DC)
Lisa A. MacVittie	David J. Tess
Drew W. Marrocco	Frederick S. Young

For full biographical listings, see the Martindale-Hubbell Law Directory

SQUIRE, SANDERS & DEMPSEY (AV)

1201 Pennsylvania Avenue, N.W., P.O. Box 407, 20044-0407
Telephone: 202-626-6600
Fax: 202-626-6780
Cleveland, Ohio Office: 4900 Key Tower, 127 Public Square.
Telephone: 216-479-8500. *Fax's:* 216-479-8780, 216-479-8781, 216-479-8777, 216-479-8787, 216-479-8795, 216-479-8793, 216-479-8776, 216-479-8788.
Columbus, Ohio Office: 1300 Huntington Center, 41 South High Street, Columbus, Ohio 43215.
Telephone: 614-365-2700.
Fax: 614-365-2499.
Jacksonville, Florida Office: One Enterprise Center, Suite 2100, 225 Water Street.
Telephone: 904-353-1264.
Fax: 904-356-2986.
Miami, Florida Office: 201 South Biscayne Boulevard, Suite 2900 Miami Center.
Telephone: 305-577-8700.
Fax: 305-358-1425.
New York, New York Office: 350 Park Avenue, 15th Floor.
Telephone: 212-872-9800.
Fax: 212-872-9815.
Phoenix, Arizona Office: Two Renaissance Square, 40 North Central Avenue, Suite 2700.
Telephone: 602-528-4000.
Fax: 602-253-8129.
Brussels, Belgium Office: Avenue Louise, 165, Box 15, 1050 Brussels, Belgium.
Telephone: 011-32-2-648-1717.
TLX: 61961.
Cable: "Coxsquire".
Rapifax: 011-322-648-1064.
Prague, Czech Republic Office: Vaclavske Namesti 57, 11000 PRAHA 1, Czech Republic.
Telephone: 011-42-2-216-62111.
Fax: 011-42-2-216-62222.
Bratislava, Slovakia Office: Zochova 5, 811 03 Bratislava, Slovak Republic.
Telephone: 011-42-7-531-7611.
Fax: 011-42-7-580-2212.
Budapest, Hungary Office: Deak Ferenc Ut. 10, Office 304, H-1052 Budapest V., Hungary.
Telephones: 011-36-1-226-2024.
Fax: 011-36-1-226-2025.
London, England Office: 4th Floor, Royex House, Aldermanbury Square, London EC2V 7HR.
Telephone: 011-44-171-830-0055.
Fax: 011-44-171-830-0056.
Kiev, Ukraine Office: Vul. Prorizna 9, KV 20, Kiev 252030, Ukraine.
Telephone: 011-380-44-244-3452.
Fax: 011-380-44-228-4938.
Moscow, Russian Federation Office: 28 Pokrovka Street, No. 4-4A, Moscow 103062, Russian Federation.
Telephone: 7-503-956-3750.
Fax: 7-503-956-3635.

MEMBERS OF FIRM

Timothy W. Bergin	Joseph P. Markoski (Resident,
Samuel H. Black	London, England Office)
Alan L. Briggs	Herbert E. Marks
Donald T. Bucklin	Michael H. Mobbs (Resident
James V. Dick	Member, Moscow, Russian
Edward A. Geltman	Federation Office)
Edward J. Hawkins	James P. Murphy
John C. Henry, Jr.	Robert D. Papkin
Sherman E. Katz	Barry A. Pupkin
Scott T. Kragie	Edward W. Sauer
Henry W. Lavine	Marshall Sanford Sinick

(See Next Column)

SQUIRE, SANDERS & DEMPSEY—*Continued*

MEMBERS OF FIRM (Continued)

Ritchie T. Thomas	Glenn M. Young

RESIDENT OF COUNSEL

Patricia P. Bailey	Richard B. Lavine (Retired)
Ann R. Brashear	Thomas J. Quigley (Retired)
Elizabeth Glass Geltman	Judith Jurin Semo
Charles A. Vanik (Retired)	

ASSOCIATES

Marc Berejka	Wm. Smith Greig
Amy L Brown	(Not admitted in DC)
(Not admitted in DC)	Adam D. Krinsky
John A. Burlingame	(Not admitted in DC)
(Not admitted in DC)	Brian J. McHugh
Andrew W. Cohen	(Not admitted in DC)
Colleen A. Conry	Jonathan Jacob Nadler
Keith E. Dobbins	Mark D. Poindexter
Charles F. Donley II	Thomas E. Skilton
James M. Fink	Donald J. Snyder
(Not admitted in DC)	James P. Wehner
Stephanie A. Goldfine	(Not admitted in DC)
(Not admitted in DC)	

For full biographical listings, see the Martindale-Hubbell Law Directory

---

STEPTOE & JOHNSON LLP (AV)

1330 Connecticut Avenue, N.W., 20036
Telephone: 202-429-3000
Cable Address: "Stepjohn"
Telex: 89-2503
Telecopier: 202-429-3902
Email: wbatterton@steptoe.com *URL:* http://www.steptoe.com
Phoenix, Arizona Office: Two Renaissance Square, 40 N. Central Avenue, Suite 2400, 85004.
Telephone: 602-257-5200.
Moscow, Russia Office: Steptoe & Johnson International AOZT. 25 Tsvetnoy Boulevard, Building 3 Moscow, Russia 103051.
Telephone: 011-7-501-258-5250.
Fax: 011-7-501-258-5251.
Almaty, Kazakhstan Office: Steptoe & Johnson Company Almaty. 84 Gogol Street, Suite 213, 480083.
Telephones: (3272) 50-11-25, (3272) 32-25-39.

MEMBERS

Louis A. Johnson (1891-1966)	Arthur L. Bailey
Calvin H. Cobb, Jr.	Bruce E. Meyerson
Monroe Leigh	(Phoenix, Arizona Office)
Richard P. Taylor	Edmund W. Burke
John E. Nolan	Morgan D. Hodgson
Robert D. Wallick	Douglas G. Green
Laurence A. Short	Frederick S. Frei
James P. Holden	Ellen d'Alelio
Betty Jo Christian	Mark F. Horning
Robert E. Jordan III	Christopher T. Lutz
Matthew J. Zinn	Samuel T. Perkins
Robert E. McLaughlin	James B. Vasile
Sarah C. Carey	Ellen M. McNamara
Martin D. Schneiderman	Paul J. Ondrasik, Jr.
Richard O. Cunningham	Thomas C. Collier, Jr.
David L. Roll	Richard K. Willard
Richard H. Porter	Reid H. Weingarten
Sheldon E. Hochberg	Stewart A. Baker
Lawrence A. Katz	Charles G. Cole
(Phoenix, Arizona Office)	Susan H. Serling
Kenneth I. Jonson	Francis J. Burke, Jr.
Theodore E. Rhodes	(Phoenix, Arizona Office)
J. A. Bouknight, Jr.	William L. Martin II
James G. Derouin	Filiberto Agusti
(Phoenix, Arizona Office)	Thomas P. Barletta
Ronald S. Cooper	Timothy M. Walsh
Daniel J. Plaine	Peter L. Wellington
Terence P. Quinn	Olin L. Wethington
Roger E. Warin	Stephen A. Fennell
John R. Labovitz	Seth Goldberg
F. Michael Kail	Samuel M. Sipe, Jr.
Mark J. Silverman	Maureen O'Keefe Ward
William Karas	Barry J. Dale
John T. Collins	(Phoenix, Arizona Office)
Steven H. Brose	Gary A. Morgans
Robert W. Fleishman	J. William Koegel, Jr.
Howard H. Stahl	Steven Reed
W. George Grandison	Daniel C. Sauls

(See Next Column)

MEMBERS (Continued)

David J. Bodney	Steven J. Ross
(Phoenix, Arizona Office)	Jane I. Ryan
David B. Raskin	Carol A. Rhees
Blake D. Rubin	Jerald S. Howe Jr.
Walter H. White, Jr.	Robert T. Novick
(Moscow, Russia Office)	Virginia L. White-Mahaffey
Melanie F. Nussdorf	David H. Coburn
Philip L. Malet	Kevin M. Keyes
Antonia B. Ianniello	Anthony J. LaRocca
Edward J. Krauland	Alfred M. Mamlet
J. Walker Johnson	Arthur Randolph Bregman
Erik L. Kitchen	Steven K. Davidson
Floyd P. Bienstock	Harry Lee
(Phoenix, Arizona Office)	Mark A. Moran
Gary J. Rinkerman	David A. Selden
Stephen L. Sulzer	(Phoenix, Arizona Office)
George Ian Brandon	Thomas M. Barba
(Phoenix, Arizona Office)	William T. Hassler
John D. Graubert	Linda S. Stein
Scott H. Katzman	Gregory M. Giammittorio

Richard L. Roberts

OF COUNSEL

Laidler B. Mackall	Scott A. Harman
Richard A. Whiting	Joseph E. Stubbs
William K. Condrell	Edward J. Twomey
Cecil J. Olmstead	Errol R. Patterson
Richard Diamond	Ellen Kohn
Stanley Smilack	Mark J. Hulkower
Kenneth D. Ludwig	James B. Moorhead
Edward R. Mackiewicz	Stuart T. F. Huang
Anita G. Fox	Matthew D. Lerner
Sara Beth Watson	Tatiana K. Kovaleva
Carol A. Mitchell	(Moscow, Russia Office)

ASSOCIATES

Michael Hall Abbey	Dima Sami Hakura
Sergei Alimirzoev	Susan Harthill
(Moscow, Russia Office)	Sara E. Hauptfuehrer
Gulzhan S. Altinbajeva	David Heffernan
(Almaty Office)	(Not admitted in DC)
Kristin L. Amerling	Michael D. Hintze
(Not admitted in DC)	(Not admitted in DC)
Steven J. Barber	Helen Hiser
Benjamin R. Barnett	Frederick J. Horne
Kenneth R. Barr	Paul R. Hurst
(Not admitted in DC)	(Not admitted in DC)
Gracia M. Berg	John L. Jacobus
Eric Berger	Leo J. Jennings
Jennifer J. Berthiaume	Kevin M. Judiscak
(Not admitted in DC)	(Phoenix, Arizona Office)
Olga Bezrukova	Cathie A. Jurgensmeyer
(Moscow, Russia Office)	(Not admitted in DC)
Lisa Morganstern Bickel	Barbara K. Kagan
(Phoenix, Arizona Office)	Mindy A. Kaiden
David S. Biderman	J. Patrick Kennedy
Merritt R. Blakeslee	Jennifer L. Key
K. Lee Blalack, II	Mark G. Kisicki
Kent D. Bressie	(Phoenix, Arizona Office)
Elizabeth A. Schallop Call	Rebecca E. Kozloff
(Phoenix, Arizona Office)	(Phoenix, Arizona Office)
Tracey D. Chambers	William W. Kunze
Marina T. Charles	Miguel S. Lawson
Carolyn Doozan Clayton	Brian J. Leske
Shannen W. Coffin	Marvin H. Lett
Bennett Evan Cooper	Faye D. Levin
(Phoenix, Arizona Office)	Sidney P. Levinson
Gail B. Cooperman	Peter Lichtenbaum
(Not admitted in DC)	Mwanajuma P. Lugogo
Julia Court	Andrea R. Macintosh
Alan R. Davis	Kenneth H. Mack
(Phoenix, Arizona Office)	(Almaty Office)
Brian A. Davis	Saville A. Mallach (Not
R. Michael Dunnigan	Admitted in the United
(Phoenix, Arizona Office)	States)
Eric C. Emerson	Matthew Der Manuelian
Andrea C. Evans	(Moscow, Russia Office)
Kenneth P. Ewing	Pantelis Michalopoulos
James S. Felt	(Not admitted in DC)
Michelle Alison Fishburne	Kenneth L. Miller
John Flyger	Deborah A. Morris
Emily R. Froimson	Evan Anne O'Neill
(Phoenix, Arizona Office)	Tatiana Orlovskaya
Jeffrey Gans	(Moscow, Russia Office)
Caroline Gaudet	Stavros Papastavrou (Not
(Not admitted in DC)	admitted in the United States)
Michael B. Gerdes	Raymond E. Patricco
(Phoenix, Arizona Office)	(Not admitted in DC)
Catherine M. Giovannoni	Chaka M. Patterson
Lisa L. Glow	(Not admitted in DC)
(Phoenix, Arizona Office)	Marc A. Paul
Monica L. Goebel	Mary Woodson (Molly) Poag
(Phoenix, Arizona Office)	L. Matthew Quigley
Eric C. Grimm	(Not admitted in DC)

(See Next Column)

STEPTOE & JOHNSON LLP, *Washington—Continued*

ASSOCIATES (Continued)

Jennifer M. Quinn	Andrew J. Sweet
(Not admitted in DC)	(Phoenix, Arizona Office)
T. Robert Rehm, Jr.	Jerome T. Tao
Nancy A. Root	(Not admitted in DC)
(Not admitted in DC)	Cynthia L. Taub
Ronald Rothstein	Steven B. Teplinsky
Thomas J. Samuelian	Kathryn E. Underwood
Mary Margaret Scharf	(Phoenix, Arizona Office)
M. Jean Schlesinger	George C. Vitelli
Colleen Sechrest	David M. Wack
Eric G. Serron	Andrew Walker
(Not admitted in DC)	Tracy Lorenz Wareing
Kenneth J. Sheehan	(Phoenix, Arizona Office)
Maury D. Shenk	Brent Weingardt
Stephanie L. Siegel	Andrew J. Weinstein
Barbara Sloan	Melissa M. Weiss
Yekaterina V. Sorokina	Steven D. Wheeless
(Moscow, Russia Office)	(Phoenix, Arizona Office)
David A. Stein	Lisa M. Zarlenga
Pamela Strauss	(Not admitted in DC)
Peter B. Swann	Tracy Zorpette
(Phoenix, Arizona Office)	

LEGAL SUPPORT PERSONNEL

Christopher Cripps	Anne Phillips
(Moscow Office)	

For full biographical listings, see the Martindale-Hubbell Law Directory

---

STEWART AND STEWART (AV)

Suite 200, 2100 M Street, N.W., 20037-1207
Telephone: 202-785-4185
Telecopier: 202-466-1286; 466-1287; 466-1288
Email: general@stewartlaw.com

MEMBERS OF FIRM

Terence P. Stewart	Charles A. St. Charles
James R. Cannon, Jr.	William A. Fennell
Wesley K. Caine	Jimmie V. Reyna

Geert De Prest

FOUNDER AND SENIOR PARTNER EMERITUS

Eugene L. Stewart

ASSOCIATES

Patrick John McDonough	Mara M. Burr
(Not admitted in DC)	(Not admitted in DC)
Amy S. Dwyer	Roberta K. Maixner
Andrew G. Stephens	(Not admitted in DC)
(Not admitted in DC)	

COUNSEL

Bernard Spinoit (Not admitted in the United States)

OF COUNSEL

Lane Steven Hurewitz	Edwin A. Kilburn
David J. Branson	(Not admitted in DC)

For full biographical listings, see the Martindale-Hubbell Law Directory

---

＊ STROOCK & STROOCK & LAVAN (AV)

1150 Seventeenth Street, N.W. Suite 600, 20036-4652
Telephone: 202-452-9250
Telecopier: (202) 293-2293
New York, N.Y. Office: (as of 1/24/97) 180 Maiden Lane, New York, N.Y., 10038.
Telephone: 212-806-5400.
Telecopiers: (212) 806-5919; (212) 806-6006; (212) 806-6086; (212) 425-9509; (212) 806-6176.
New York Conference Center: 767 Third Avenue, New York, N.Y., 10017-2023.
Telephones: 212-806-5767; 5768; 5769; 5770.
Telecopier: (212) 421-6234.
Boston, Massachusetts Office: 100 Federal Street, 02110.
Telephone: 617-482-6800.
Fax: 617-330-511.
Budapest, Hungary Office: East-West Business Center, Rákóczi ut 1-3, H 1088.
Telephone: 011-361- 266-9520 or 011-361-266-7770.
Telecopier: 011-361-266-9279.
Los Angeles, California Office: Suite 1800, 2029 Century Park East, 90067-3086.
Telephone: 310-556-5800.
Telecopier: (310) 556-5959.
Miami, Florida Office: 200 South Biscayne Boulevard, Suite 3300, First Union Financial Center, 33131-2385.
Telephone: 305-358-9900.
Telecopiers: (305) 789-9302; (305) 372-3727.

RESIDENT PARTNERS

Richard K. Eaton	George G. Lorinczi
Walter Pozen	

(See Next Column)

Matthew H. McCarthy

For full biographical listings, see the Martindale-Hubbell Law Directory

---

＊ SULLIVAN & CROMWELL (AV)

1701 Pennsylvania Avenue, N.W., 20006-5805
Telephone: 202-956-7500
Telecopier: 202-293-6330
New York City Offices: 125 Broad Street, 10004-2498.
Telephone: 212-558-4000.
Telex: 62694.
Telecopier: 212-558-3588; 212-558-3792.
Los Angeles, California Office: 444 South Flower Street, 90071-2901.
Telephone: 213-955-8000.
Telecopier: 213-683-0457.
Paris Office: 8, Place Vendôme, 75001 Paris, France.
Telephone: (011)(331)4450-6000.
Telex: 240654.
Telecopier: (011)(331)4450-6060.
London Office: St. Olave's House, 9a Ironmonger Lane, London EC2V 8EY, England.
Telephone: (011)(44171)710-6500.
Telecopier: (011)(44171)710-6565.
Melbourne, Office: 101 Collins Street, Melbourne, Victoria 3000, Australia.
Telephone: (011)(613)9654-1500.
Telecopier: (011)(613)9654-2422.
Tokyo Office: Sullivan & Cromwell (Gaikokuho Jimu Bengoshi Jimusho), Akai Law Offices (Registered Associated Offices), Tokio Kaijo Building Shinkan, 2-1, Marunouchi 1-chome, Chiyoda-ku, Tokyo 100, Japan.
Telephone: (011)(813)3213-6140.
Telecopier: (011)(813)3213-6470.
Hong Kong Office: 28th Floor, Nine Queen's Road, Central, Hong Kong.
Telephone: (011)(852)2826-8688.
Telecopier: (011)(852)2522-2280.
Frankfurt Office: Oberlindau 54-56, 60323 Frankfurt am Main, Germany.
Telephone: (011)(4969)7191-260.
Telecopier: (011)(4969)7191-2610.

PARTNERS IN WASHINGTON, D.C.

Edwin D. Williamson	Robert H. Craft, Jr.
H. Rodgin Cohen	Margaret K. Pfeiffer
(Not admitted in DC)	Daryl A. Libow

Dennis C. Sullivan

OF COUNSEL IN WASHINGTON, D.C.

Janet Thiele Geldzahler	Douglas Mark McCall

SPECIAL COUNSEL IN WASHINGTON, D.C.

William J. Brown	Jeffrey W. Jacobs

ASSOCIATES IN WASHINGTON, D.C.

Catherine M. Clarkin	Paul J. McElroy
(Not admitted in DC)	Mary C. Moynihan
Walter J. Clayton, III	(Not admitted in DC)
Daniel G. Dufner, Jr.	Jack O'Kelley, III
(Not admitted in DC)	Kathryn E. Rorer
Jose Ignacio Fernandez	Samantha Evans Ross
Gregory Harrington	Richard H. Sauer
(Not admitted in DC)	Brett G. Scharffs
Bernard A. Joseph	(Not admitted in DC)
Thomas R. Leuba	Timothy E. Sheil

Anna Maria Kuzmik Walker

For full biographical listings, see the Martindale-Hubbell Law Directory

---

＊ THOMPSON COBURN (AV)

Suite 900, 700-14th Street, N.W., 20005-2010
Telephone: 202-508-1000
Telecopier: 202-508-1010
St. Louis, Missouri Office: One Mercantile Center.
Telephone: 314-552-6000.
Telecopier: 314-552-7000.
Belleville, Illinois Office: 525 West Main Street.
Telephone: 618-277-4700; 314-271-1800.
Telecopier: 618-236-3434.
St. Charles, Missouri Office: 200 North Third Street.
Telephone: 314-946-7717.
Telecopier: 314-946-4938.
Houston, Texas Office: 2400 NationsBank Center, 700 Louisiana.
Telephone: 713-225-3800.
Telecopier: 713-225-3828.

MEMBERS OF FIRM

Murray J. Belman	Barbara B. Powell
Milton D. Andrews	Edward J. Sheppard, IV
Michael A. Greenspan	Gerald D. Stoltz
John V. Austin	Marjorie F. Krumholz

ASSOCIATES

Catherine M. Beresovski	Adam H. Gordon
Jacqueline T. Colclough	Randall K. Hulme

Representative Clients: Cold Finished Steel Bar Institute; Comerica, Inc. (Michigan); Fleet Financial Corp. (Rhode Island); Kidder Peabody & Co., Incorporated; Manildra Milling Co.; Riso, Inc.; Shell Bermuda (Overseas)

(See Next Column)

THOMPSON COBURN—*Continued*

Limited; Tecumseh Products Co.; Union Carbide Corp.; United Jersey Banks (New Jersey).

For full biographical listings, see the Martindale-Hubbell Law Directory

TUTTLE, TAYLOR & HERON (AV)

1025 Thomas Jefferson Street, N.W., 20007-5201
Telephone: 202-342-1300
Facsimile: 202-342-5880
Los Angeles, California Office: Tuttle & Taylor, A Law Corporation, 355 South Grand Avenue, 40th Floor, 90071-3102.
Telephone: 213-683-0600.
Facsimile: 213-683-0225.
Sacramento, California Office: Tuttle & Taylor, A Law Corporation, 1521 I Street, 95814-2016.
Telephone: 916-441-2249.
Facsimile: 916-441-2910.

OF COUNSEL

Julian B. Heron, Jr.   Phillip L. Fraas

For full biographical listings, see the Martindale-Hubbell Law Directory

* VENABLE ATTORNEYS AT LAW VENABLE, BAETJER, HOWARD & CIVILETTI, LLP (AV)

A Partnership including Professional Corporations
Suite 1000, 1201 New York Avenue, N.W., 20005
Telephone: 202-962-4800
Fax: 202-962-8300
Baltimore, Maryland Office: Venable, Baetjer and Howard LLP, 1800 Mercantile Bank & Trust Building, 2 Hopkins Plaza.
Telephone: 410-244-7400.
McLean, Virginia Office: Venable, Baetjer and Howard LLP, Suite 400, 2010 Corporate Ridge.
Telephone: 703-760-1600.
Rockville, Maryland Office: Venable, Baetjer and Howard LLP, Suite 500, One Church Street, P. O. Box 1906.
Telephone: 301-217-5600.
Towson, Maryland Office: Venable, Baetjer and Howard LLP, 210 Allegheny Avenue, P. O. Box 5517.
Telephone: 410-494-6200.

MEMBERS OF FIRM

Benjamin R. Civiletti (P.C.) (Also at Baltimore and Towson, Maryland Offices)
Anthony M. Carey (Not admitted in DC; Also at Baltimore, Maryland Office)
Neal D. Borden (Not admitted in DC; Also at Baltimore, Maryland Office)
Thomas J. Kenney, Jr. (P.C.) (Not admitted in DC; Also at Baltimore, Maryland Office)
Jan K. Guben (Not admitted in DC; Also at Baltimore, Maryland Office)
Ian D. Volner
Thomas J. Madden
Ronald R. Glancz
David J. Levenson
Dennis J. Whittlesey
Douglas D. Connah, Jr. (P.C.) (Also at Baltimore, Maryland Office)
Joe A. Shull
Kenneth C. Bass, III (Also at McLean, Virginia Office)
John G. Milliken (Also at McLean, Virginia Office)
Joseph G. Block
Edward F. Glynn, Jr.
Robert G. Ames (Also at Baltimore, Maryland Office)
Thomas B. Hudson (Also at Baltimore, Maryland Office)
Michael Schatzow (Also at Baltimore, Maryland Office)
John F. Cooney
Bryson L. Cook (P.C.) (Not admitted in DC; Also at Baltimore, Maryland Office)
N. Frank Wiggins
James K. Archibald (Also at Baltimore, Maryland Office)

Judson W. Starr (Also at Baltimore and Towson, Maryland Offices)
James R. Myers
Ernest M. Stern
Jeffrey D. Knowles
Jeffrey A. Dunn (Also at Baltimore, Maryland Office)
George F. Pappas (Also at Baltimore, Maryland Office)
William D. Coston
Kenneth S. Slaughter
James L. Shea (Not admitted in DC; also at Baltimore, Maryland Office)
Maurice Baskin
John J. Pavlick, Jr.
Amy Berman Jackson
William D. Quarles (Also at Towson, Maryland Office)
Donald R. Hartman
Jeffrey L. Ihnen
Robert Charles Hill
James A. Dunbar (Also at Baltimore, Maryland Office)
Thomas J. Kelly, Jr.
Geoffrey M. Levitt
Robert J. Bolger, Jr. (Not admitted in DC; Also at Baltimore, Maryland Office)
Anita J. Finkelstein
Bruce H. Jurist (Also at Baltimore, Maryland Office)
Herbert G. Smith, II
Patrick J. Stewart (Also at Baltimore, Maryland Office)
John M. Gurley
James R. Burdett (Not admitted in DC)
Gary M. Hnath
Geoffrey R. Garinther (Not admitted in DC; Also at Baltimore, Maryland Office)

(See Next Column)

OF COUNSEL

Frank Horton
Richard H. Mays (Not admitted in DC; Also at McLean, Virginia Office)
Thomas J. Cooper

Kenneth G. Hurwitz (Also at Baltimore, Maryland Office)
Jerome S. Gabig, Jr.
Gary D. Hailey
Charles R. Marvin, Jr.

Barbara L. Waite

ASSOCIATES

David S. Berman
Gregory S. Braker
Pamela W. Carmody (Not admitted in DC; Also at Baltimore, Maryland Office)
Wallace E. Christner (Also at Baltimore, Maryland Office)
Carla Draluck Craft
Donald P. Creston
James Nicholas Czaban (Not admitted in DC)
David S. Darland
Paul A. Debolt (Not admitted in DC)
John P. Fielding (Also at McLean, Virginia Office)
David W. Goewey
John C. Hardwick, Jr. (Not admitted in DC)
Andrew R. Herrup
Houtan Khalili-Esfahani (Not admitted in DC)

Kevin Michael Kordziel
Fernand A. Lavallee
Edward Brendan Magrab
Valerie K. Mann
Vicki Margolis (Also at Baltimore, Maryland Office)
Matthew J. McConkey (Not admitted in DC)
Nuala McConnell (Not admitted in DC)
Heather L. McDowell
Lindsay Beardsworth Meyer
Juliana Schulte O'Reilly
Andrea S. Paterson
Lawrence C. Renbaum
Carl H. Settlemyer, III (Not admitted in DC)
Melissa Landau Steinman
Karen D. Woodard
Maureen Donahue Yuffee
Scott A. Zebrak (Not admitted in DC)

For full biographical listings, see the Martindale-Hubbell Law Directory

VERNER, LIIPFERT, BERNHARD, McPHERSON AND HAND, CHARTERED (AV)

901 15th Street, N.W., 20005-2301
Telephone: 202-371-6000
Cable Address: "Verlip"
Telex: 1561792 VERLIP UT
Fax: 202-371-6279
Email: verner.com
McLean, Virginia Office: Sixth Floor, 8280 Greensboro Drive, 22102.
Telephone: 703-749-6000.
Fax: 703-749-6027.
Houston, Texas Office: 2600 Texas Commerce Tower, 600 Travis, 77002.
Telephone: 713-237-9034.
Fax: 713-237-1216.
Honolulu, Hawaii Office: Hawaii Times Building, 928 Nuuanu Avenue, Suite 400, 96817.
Telephone: 808-566-0999.
Fax: 808-566-0995.
Austin, Texas Office: Suite 1440 San Jacinto Center, 98 San Jacinto Boulevard, 78701.
Telephone: 512-703-6000.
Fax: 512-703-6003.

Douglas Ochs Adler
Lloyd M. Bentsen (Resident, Houston, Texas Office)
Berl Bernhard
Graham Kerin Blair (Resident, Houston, Texas Office)
James J. Blanchard (Not admitted in DC)
Amy Laura Bondurant
Roy G. Bowman
R. Stuart Broom
Steven A. Buxbaum (Resident, Houston, Texas Office)
Douglas J. Colton
Brendan D. Cook (Resident, Houston, Texas Office)
Lawrence N. Cooper
Hopewell H. Darneille, III
Andrew D. Eskin
William C. Evans
Anne M. Ferazzi (Resident, Houston, Texas Office)
J. Cathy Fogel
Harold I. Freilich
Andrea Jill Grant
Lloyd N. Hand
James F. Hibey
Jane Hickie (Not admitted in DC)
Patrick L. Hughes (Resident, Houston, Texas Office)
Jared H. Jossem (Resident, Honolulu, Hawaii Office)
Thomas J. Keller
Gary J. Klein

Erwin G. Krasnow
Kyung S. Lee (Resident, Houston, Texas Office)
Lawrence E. Levinson (Not admitted in DC)
Don Charles Lewis
Lawrence Z. Lorber
Joseph L. Manson, III
Harry McPherson
John P. Melko (Resident, Houston, Texas Office)
Martin Mendelsohn
John A. Merrigan
James F. Miller
Brian A. Mizoguchi
Ronald B. Natalie
Paul E. Nordstrom
Glen L. Ortman
Lenard M. Parkins (Resident, Houston, Texas Office)
Russell E. Pommer
Neil T. Proto
Sherry A. Quirk
Barry D. Rhoads (Not admitted in DC)
Michael J. Roberts
William F. Roeder, Jr.
Lawrence R. Sidman
Keith D. Spickelmier (Resident, Houston, Texas Office)
Frederick J. Tansill
Susan O'Hearn Temkin
James M. Verner (Emeritus)
Clinton A. Vince

(See Next Column)

VERNER, LIIPFERT, BERNHARD, McPHERSON AND HAND CHARTERED, *Washington—Continued*

John D. Waihee, III (Resident, Honolulu, Hawaii Office)	Bernhardt K. Wruble
Buel White	William A. Zeitler
	John H. Zentay

SPECIAL COUNSEL
George J. Mitchell

SENIOR ATTORNEY
JoAnn Lippman (Resident, Houston, Texas Office)

SENIOR COUNSEL
Alvaro Cifuentes de Castro (Not admitted in DC)

OF COUNSEL

Howell E. Begle, Jr.	Frederick J. McConville
Michael D. Berg	Francis X. Mellon
David M. Davenport	Mikol S. B. Neilson
Philip R. Hochberg	Renton L. K. Nip (Resident, Honolulu, Hawaii Office)
James Allen Hoffman	Nancy A. Nord
James K. Jackson	Nell Payne
David B. Jacobsohn	Richard H. Saltsman
Bruce A. Kimble (Resident, McLean, Virginia Office)	Gene Schleppenbach
J. Robert Kirk	Julian L. Shepard
Stanley W. Legro	Laurie Sullivan (Not admitted in DC)

SENIOR ADVISOR
Ann W. Richards

Gregg S. Avitabile	Lori A. Hood (Resident, Houston, Texas Office)
Hever M. Bascon, Jr. (Not admitted in DC)	Lisa K. Hsiao
Matthew C. Bernstein	Lisa S. Jensen
Susan G. Blumenthal	David Jesulaitis (Resident, Houston, Texas Office)
Douglas C. Boggs (Not admitted in DC)	Steven R. Johnson
David A. Brakebill (Resident, Houston, Texas Office)	Kenric D. Kattner (Resident, Houston, Texas Office)
John B. Britton	Jane M. Lyons
Gary E. Bunce (Resident, McLean, Virginia Office)	Neil H. MacBride
Paula W. Chong (Resident, Honolulu, Hawaii Office)	Daniel C. Manatt (Not admitted in DC)
Montina M. Cole	Stephanie L. Marn (Resident, Honolulu, Hawaii Office)
Glenna England Crews	John R. Mietus, Jr.
Kathleen M. Cronin	William H. Minor
J. Elizabeth Dame (Resident, McLean, Virginia Office)	Trey A. Monsour (Resident, Houston, Texas Office)
Sherry Lane Deaver (Resident, Houston, Texas Office)	Joel D. Newton
Andrea Renee Dillman (Resident, Houston, Texas Office)	Sang Y. Paek (Not admitted in DC)
Christine F. Ericson	Tamara Schiebel Rickman (Resident, McLean, Virginia Office)
Frances G. Faigenblat	Sue Santa
Leo R. Fitzsimon (Not admitted in DC)	William R. Sherman
Henry Flores (Resident, Houston, Texas Office)	Kathy D. Smith
Amy L. Freeman	John H. Sterne, Jr. (Not admitted in DC)
Marla Grossman (Not admitted in DC)	Deborah A. Swanstrom
Lynn E. Haaland (Not admitted in DC)	Mary A. Van Cleve (Not admitted in DC)
Douglas W. Hall	Linda M. Weinberg
Alan N. Hernandez (Not admitted in DC)	Eric T. Werner
	Gretchen M. White
	Whitney J. Williams

LEGAL SUPPORT PERSONNEL

Suzanne D. Cartwright (Director of Legislative Affairs)	Rosemary B. Freeman (Legislative Consultant)
Denis J. Dwyer (Director of Legislative and Federal Affairs)	Nancy A. Sheliga (Legislative Consultant)
	Kevin Stoltzfus (Manager of Legislative Affairs)

For full biographical listings, see the Martindale-Hubbell Law Directory

---

* VINSON & ELKINS L.L.P. (AV)

A Registered Limited Liability Partnership
The Willard Office Building, 1455 Pennsylvania Avenue, N.W., 20004-1008
Telephone: 202-639-6500
Fax: 202-639-6604
Houston, Texas Office: 2300 First City Tower, 1001 Fannin.
Telephone: 713-758-2222.
Fax: 713-758-2346.
Austin, Texas Office: One American Center, Suite 2700, 600 Congress Avenue.
Telephone: 512-495-8400.
Fax: 512-495-8612.

(See Next Column)

Dallas, Texas Office: 3700 Trammell Crow Center, 2001 Ross Avenue.
Telephone: 214-220-7700.
Fax: 214-220-7716.
London Office: 47 Charles Street, Berkeley Square, London, W1X 7PB, England.
Telephone: (441-171) 491-7236.
Fax: (44-171) 499-5320.
Moscow, Russia Office: 16 Ulitsa Spiridonovka, Second Floor, 103001 Moscow, Russia.
Telephone: (70-95) 956-1995.
Telecopy: (70-95) 956-1996.
Singapore Office: 16 Collyer Quay, #33-01 Hitachi Tower, 049318.
Telephone: (65) 536-8300.
Fax: (65) 536-8311.

RESIDENT PARTNERS

Charles L. Almond	Ky P. Ewing, Jr.
Michael A. Andrews (Not admitted in DC)	Kevin A. Gaynor
David T. Andril	Michael J. Henke
Robert A. Armitage	Neil W. Imus
Alden L. Atkins	Theodore W. Kassinger
Page I. Austin (Not admitted in DC)	Gary M. Kotara
Dennis M. Barry	Cathy A. Lewis
Gary E. Block	Hugh M. McIntosh
C. Michael Buxton	Larry A. Oday
John E. Chapoton	Mark R. Spivak
David B. Cohen	John D. Taurman
Thomas Crichton, IV	Charles D. Tetrault
	Mark H. Tuohey, III
	Christine L. Vaughn

Adam Wenner

RESIDENT OF COUNSEL

Thomas R. Bartman	Robert A. Mazer
Patricia G. Bridwell	Carin J. Sigel
Dennis A. Klejna	Samuel B. Sterrett
William E. Lawler, III	Thomas A. Stout, Jr.

Paul L. Yde

RESIDENT ASSOCIATES

John H. Barquin (Not admitted in DC)	Bruce E. Kosub (Not admitted in DC)
J. Barclay Collins, III	Greta L.H. Lichtenbaum
Robert H. Cox	Holley Thomas Lutz
Christopher L. Crosswhite	Craig D. Margolis (Not admitted in DC)
John S. Decker	Philip A. Nickles (Not admitted in DC)
Debra J. Duncan	Cary D. Pugh
Mary E. Edmondson	David H. Robbins
Benjamin Erulkar	Michael A. Sanzo
John M. Faust	Albert D. Shuldiner
Jeffrey W. Ferguson	Heidi J. Stock
Tegan M. Flynn	Jerome A. Swindell (Not admitted in DC)
Glenn S. Greene	Anita Rutkowski Wilson
George C. Hopkins	Jonathan M. Zeitler
Joseph E. Hunsader (Not admitted in DC)	
Tara Isa Koslov	

For full biographical listings, see the Martindale-Hubbell Law Directory

---

* VORYS, SATER, SEYMOUR AND PEASE (AV)

Suite 1111, 1828 L Street, N.W., 20036-5104
Telephone: 202-467-8800
Telex: 440693
Telecopier: 202-467-8900
Email: vssp@dgsys.com *URL:* http://www.vssp.com
Columbus, Ohio Office: 52 East Gay Street, P.O. Box 1008, 43216-1008.
Telephone: 614-464-6400.
Telex: 241348.
Telecopier: 614-464-6350.
Cable Address: "Vorysater".
Cleveland, Ohio Office: 2100 One Cleveland Center, 1375 East Ninth Street, 44114-1724.
Telephone: 216-479-6100.
Telecopier: 216-479-6060.
Cincinnati, Ohio Office: Suite 2100, 221 East Fourth Street, P.O. Box 0236, 45201-0236.
Telephone: 513-723-4000.
Telecopier: 513-723-4056.

RESIDENT MEMBERS

Thomas R. Boland	Ellen A. Efros
Randal C. Teague	Warren W. Glick
John W. Wilmer, Jr.	James K. Alford

RESIDENT ASSOCIATES

Stephen H. Brown (Not admitted in DC)	George W. Swenson, Jr.
Timothy N. McGarey	Thomas B. Magee
Robert A. Hager	Steven R. Becker
	Susan R. Athari

OF COUNSEL

Pamela A. Bresnahan	Geoffrey S. Mitchell
Cory M. Amron	Mark J. Palchick

For full biographical listings, see the Martindale-Hubbell Law Directory

Washington—Continued

WATT, TIEDER & HOFFAR, L.L.P. (AV)

601 Pennsylvania Avenue, N.W., Suite 900, 20004
Telephone: 202-462-4697
Telecopier: 703-893-8029
McLean Virginia Office: 7929 Westpark Drive, Suite 400,
Telephone: 703-749-1000.
Telecopier: 703-893-8029.
Irvine California Office: 3 Park Plaza, Suite 1530.
Telephone: 714-852-6700.

MEMBERS OF FIRM

John B. Tieder, Jr.	Robert K. Cox
	David C. Romm

For full biographical listings, see the Martindale-Hubbell Law Directory

WHITE & CASE (AV)

601 Thirteenth Street, NW, Suite 600 South, 20005-3807
Telephone: 202-626-3600
Telex: 4069 562 4069 MCI UW
Facsimile: 202-639-9355
New York, New York:
Telephone: 212-819-8200.
Facsimile: 212-354-8113.
Los Angeles, California:
Telephone: 213-620-7700.
Facsimile: 213-687-0758; 213-617-2205; 213-617-0376.
Miami, Florida:
Telephone: 305-371-2700.
Facsimile: 305-358-5744; 305-358-5745.
Brussels, Belgium:
Telephone: (32-2) 647-05-89.
Facsimile: (32-2) 647-16-75.
Budapest, Hungary:
Telephone: (36-1) 269-0550.
Facsimile: (36-1) 269-1199.
Helsinki, Finland:
Telephone: (358-9) 631-100.
Facsimile: (358-9) 179-477.
Istanbul, Turkey:
Telephone: (90-212) 275-75-33; (90-212) 275-68-98.
Facsimile: (90-212) 275-75-43.
Ankara, Turkey:
Telephone: (90-312) 446-2180.
Facsimile: (90-312) 446-9871.
London, England:
Telephone: (44-171) 726-6361.
Facsimile: (44-171) 726-4314; (44-171) 726-8558.
Moscow, Russia:
Telephone: (7-095) 961-2112. Satelite
Telephone: (7-501) 961-2112.
Facsimile: (7-095) 961-2121. Satelite
Facsimile: (7-501) 961-2121.
Paris, France:
Telephone: (33) 01-42-60-34-05.
Facsimile: (33) 01-42-60-82-46.
Prague, Czech Republic:
Telephone: (42-2) 2481-1796.
Facsimile: (42-2) 232-5522; (42-2) 232-5585.
Stockholm, Sweden:
Telephone: (46-8) 679-80-30.
Facsimile: (46-8) 611-21-22.
Warsaw, Poland:
Telephone: (48-22) 625-33-33; (48-22) 622-67-67; (43-89) 12-19-06.
Facsimile: (48-22) 628-22-28.
Almaty, Kazakhstan:
Telephone: (7-3272) 50-74-91/2; (7-3272) 50-78-71.
Facsimile: (7-3272) 50-74-93.
Tashkent, Republic of Uzbekistan:
Telephone: (7-3712) 32-00-59; (7-3712) 32-01-49. Satellite
Telephone: (7-3712) 40-61-18; (7-3712) 40-61-24; (7-3712) 40-61-32.
Facsimile: (7-3712) 40-61-81.
Bangkok, Thailand: White & Case (Thailand) Limited.
Telephone: (662) 236-6154/7.
Facsimile: (662) 237-6771.
Bombay, India: Liaison Office, (91-22) 282-6300/01/02/03.
Facsimile: (91-22) 282-6305.
Hanoi, Vietnam: Representative Office,
Telephone: (84-4) 822-7575.
Facsimile: (84-4) 822-7297.
Hong Kong:
Telephone: (852) 2822-8700.
Facsimile: (852) 2845-9070.
Singapore, Republic of Singapore:
Telephone: (65) 225-6000.
Facsimile: (65) 225-6009.
Tokyo, Japan: Law Office of Tetsuya Morimoto,
Telephone: (81-3) 3239-4300.
Facsimile: (81-3) 3239-4330.
Jeddah, Saudi Arabia: Law Office of Hassan Mahassni,
Telephone: (966-2) 665-4353.
Facsimile: (966-2) 669-2996.

(See Next Column)

Riyadh, Saudi Arabia: Law Office of Hassan Mahassni,
Telephone: (966-1) 464-4006; (966-1) 462-1626.
Facsimile: (966-1) 465-1348.
Johannesburg, Republic of South Africa:
Telephone: 27 (11) 333-1584.
Facsimile: 27 (11) 333-0310.
Mexico City, Mexico:
Telephone: (52-5) 540-9600; (52-5) 520-4770.
Facsimile: (52-5) 520-4656; (52-5) 520-7262; (52-5) 520-1271; (52-5) 540-9698; (52-5) 540-9699.
Jakarta, Indonesia Office:
Telephone: (62-21) 250-5187; (62-21) 250-5188; (62-21) 250-5189.
Facsimile: (62-21) 250-5184.

PARTNERS

Charles N. Brower	David P. Houlihan
Linda E. Carlisle	Carolyn B. Lamm
William J. Clinton	Carmen D. Legato
Christopher F. Corr	Barry N. Machlin
Christopher M. Curran	William P. McClure
Bruce N. Davis	J. Roger Mentz
Victor J. DeSantis	Gregory J. Ossi
Alan M. Dunn	Robert D. Paul
J. Mark Gidley	Gregory J. Spak
William D. Hawkins III	Walter J. Spak

OF COUNSEL

David W. Hunt

ASSOCIATES

Glen S. Bernstein	Ellen M. Jakovic
Peter D. Bernstein	Kevin C. Jones
David E. Bond	Richard G. King
(Not admitted in DC)	Geoffrey B. Lanning
Vincent Bowen	(Not admitted in DC)
Jay S. Brown	Adams Chi-Peng Lee
(Not admitted in DC)	Lynda K. Marshall
Richard J. Burke	J. Russell McGranahan
Daniel S. Chen	(Not admitted in DC)
(Not admitted in DC)	Ellen S. Moore
Anna-Marie Christello-Roop	(Not admitted in DC)
Lisa A. Cottle	John W. Owczarski
John D. Donaldson	George L. Paul
(Not admitted in DC)	Edmund W. Sim
J. Brady Dugan	Anne D. Smith
(Not admitted in DC)	Abby Cohen Smutny
John G. Gleacher	Eric P. Spooner
(Not admitted in DC)	David R. Stepp
Robert G. Gosselink	Kurt C. Swainston
(Not admitted in DC)	Osamu Umejima
Wendy C. Hannan	Francis A. Vasquez, Jr.
William C. Holland	Kristina Zissis
Lisa L. Hubbard	(Not admitted in DC)

For full biographical listings, see the Martindale-Hubbell Law Directory

★ WHITEFORD, TAYLOR & PRESTON L.L.P. (AV)

1025 Connecticut Avenue, N.W., 20036-5405
Telephone: 202-659-6800
Fax: 202-331-0573
Email: 2019267@mcimail.com *URL:* http://www.wtplaw.com
Baltimore, Maryland Office: 7 Saint Paul Street.
Telephone: 410-347-8700.
Fax: 410-752-7092.
Towson, Maryland Office: 210 West Pennsylvania Avenue.
Telephone: 410-832-2000.
Fax: 410-832-2015.
Columbia, Maryland Office: 10440 Little Patuxent Parkway.
Telephone: 410-884-0700.
Fax: 410-884-0719.
Alexandria, Virginia Office: 1317 King Street.
Telephone: 703-836-5742.
Fax: 703-836-0265.

PARTNERS

Arthur P. Rogers	Kenneth J. Ingram
Glenn R. Bonard	Joseph D. Douglass
	John J. Hathway

OF COUNSEL

C. William Tayler	Lee A. Satterfield

RESIDENT ASSOCIATES

Andrew J. Terrell	Julianne Erin Dymowski
Mary Gillen Fenske	Brendan P. Bunn
	Denise E. Jackson

For full biographical listings, see the Martindale-Hubbell Law Directory

WILEY, REIN & FIELDING (AV)

1776 K Street, N.W., 20006-2304
Telephone: 202-429-7000
Facsimile: 202-429-7207

(See Next Column)

WILEY, REIN & FIELDING, *Washington—Continued*

MEMBERS OF FIRM

Richard E. Wiley	David E. Hilliard
Bert W. Rein	Trevor Potter
Fred F. Fielding	Hugh Latimer
Thomas W. Brunner	John B. Reynolds, III
James H. Wallace, Jr.	James T. Bruce, III
Charles Owen Verrill, Jr.	John A. Hodges
Rand L. Allen	William B. Baker
Andrew S. Krulwich	Katherine M. Holden
R. Michael Senkowski	Daniel E. Troy
Lawrence W. Secrest, III	Samuel D. Walker
Thomas W. Queen	Dag Wilkinson
Jan Witold Baran	Jerry V. Haines
Bruce L. McDonald	Alan H. Price
John B. Wyss	Peter D. Ross
Richard J. Bodorff	Arthur I. Cantor
Laura A. Foggan	Peter J. Klarfeld
Richard L. McConnell	Robert A. Smith
Walter J. Andrews	James C. Rubinger
Robert B. Bell	David S. Fortney
Matthew S. Simchak	(Not admitted in DC)
Carl R. Ramey	Donna Coleman Gregg
Stuart F. Carwile	Susan D. Sawtelle
Philip J. Davis	Richard H. Gordin
G. Philip Nowak	Marilyn E. Kerst
Bruce G. Joseph	John E. Barry
Thomas W. Kirby	Lon A. Berk
Jeffrey S. Linder	Paul F. Khoury
James R. W. Bayes	Carol A. Laham
Christopher D. Cerf	Joseph L. Ruby
Clifford M. Sloan	Eileen P. Bradner
John L. Bartlett	Kirk J. Nahra
Richard C. Lowery	Michael L. Sturm
Robert J. Butler	Frank Winston, Jr.
Robert L. Pettit	Russell D. Duncan
Jim Slattery	David R. Anderson
(Not admitted in DC)	Dominic T. Bodensteiner
Edwin O. Bailey	David L. Douglass
Keith S. Watson	David R. Hill
Michael Yourshaw	John R. Shane
Ida Wurczinger Draim	Nancy J. Victory

OF COUNSEL

Howard H. Bell	Kurt E. DeSoto
(Not admitted in DC)	Alison M. Duncan
William H. Berman	Carl R. Frank
Tyrone Brown	Gregory J. Vogt

ASSOCIATES

Karyn K. Ablin	Paul E. Janaskie
(Not admitted in DC)	Wayne D. Johnsen
Nancy M. Barnes	Robert E. Johnston
(Not admitted in DC)	Peter S. Jordan
Mary E. Borja	Treg A. Julander
John M. Burgett	Valerie E. Keller
Lauren A. Carbaugh	(Not admitted in DC)
Matthew A. Chavez	Cynthia L. Kendrick
Christine E. Connelly	Karen A. Kincaid
Jason P. Cronic	James R. Knox
Todd D. Daubert	(Not admitted in DC)
(Not admitted in DC)	Kenneth J. Krisko
Luis de la Torre	(Not admitted in DC)
Eric W. DeSilva	Gregory Lyons
Christine C. Drummond	Cherie L. Macauley
Elizabeth Ann Eastwood	(Not admitted in DC)
Terri A. Ecklebarger	Kevin J. Martin
(Not admitted in DC)	(Not admitted in DC)
Brook A. Edinger	Willis S. Martyn, III
(Not admitted in DC)	Bernard A. McDonough
Gregg L. Elias	William A. McGrath
Marisa Gallehr Faunce	Sean X. McKessy
Pamela J. Furman	Cara B. Moylan
Larry O. Natt Gantt, II	(Not admitted in DC)
(Not admitted in DC)	Mark H. Neblett
David J. Goldstone	Vipul N. Nishawala
(Not admitted in DC)	(Not admitted in DC)
Stephanie L. Goodman	Brian Nuterangelo
(Not admitted in DC)	Bruce A. Olcott
Edward J. Grass	Richard T. Pfohl
(Not admitted in DC)	Leslie A. Platt
Matthew B. Greiner	Stacy R. Robinson
Caitlin J. Halligan	Stephen J. Rosen
(Not admitted in DC)	James M. Ross
Rosemary C. Harold	(Not admitted in DC)
Phillip H. Harrington	Michael A. Rotker
Scott S. Harris	Jonathan M. Shaw
G. Michael Harvey	Roger C. Sherman
Dale E. Hausman	Jennifer A. Short
Allison R. Hayward	(Not admitted in DC)
Tanja E. Hens	William E. Smith
David J. Ignall	Todd M. Stansbury

(See Next Column)

ASSOCIATES (Continued)

Michael E. Toner	John C. Yang
Bryan N. Tramont	Suzanne Yelen
David A. Vogel	Christopher R. Yukins
Angela N. Watkins	Andrew P. Zappia
(Not admitted in DC)	(Not admitted in DC)
Andrew L. Wexton	
(Not admitted in DC)	

For full biographical listings, see the Martindale-Hubbell Law Directory

WILKES, ARTIS, HEDRICK & LANE, CHARTERED (AV)

Suite 1100, 1666 K Street, N.W., 20006-2897
Telephone: 202-457-7800
Cable Address: "Wilan, Washington, D.C."
Annapolis, Maryland Office: Suite 400, 47 State Circle.
Telephone: 410-263-7800.
Bethesda, Maryland Office: Suite 800, 3 Bethesda Metro Center.
Telephone: 301-654-7800.
Greenbelt, Maryland Office: Suite 410, 6305 Ivy Lane.
Telephone: 301-345-7700.
Fairfax, Virginia Office: Suite 600, 11320 Random Hills Road.
Telephone: 703-385-8000.
Waldorf, Maryland Office: Suite 101, 1 Post Office Road.
Telephone: 301-645-2464; 301-843-7610 (Metro).

James C. Wilkes (1899-1968)	Allen Jones, Jr.
James E. Artis (1907-1978)	Eric S. Kassoff (Resident,
David M. Bond	Bethesda, Maryland Office)
Stephen J. Braun (Resident,	Jonathan I. Kipnis (Resident,
Waldorf, Maryland Office)	Greenbelt, Maryland Office)
Charles A. Camalier, III	William Kominers (Resident,
Jerald S. Cohn	Bethesda, Maryland Office)
Christopher H. Collins	John D. Lane
James P. Downey (Resident,	J. Carter McKaig
Fairfax, Virginia Office)	Gerard P. Panaro
Maureen Ellen Dwyer	Robert X. Perry, Jr.
John T. Epting	Allison Carney Prince
Jonathan L. Farmer	John E. Prominski, Jr.
Nancy G. Fax (Resident,	Whayne S. Quin
Bethesda, Maryland Office)	Richard K. Reed (Resident,
Phil T. Feola	Greenbelt Maryland Office)
Stanley J. Fineman	Louis P. Robbins
David A. Fuss	David H. Saffern
Norman M. Glasgow	Kenneth L. Samuelson
Norman M. Glasgow, Jr.	Frank W. Stearns (Resident at
Larry A. Gordon (Resident,	Fairfax, Virginia Office)
Bethesda, Maryland Office)	Dana Brewington Stebbins
Robert L. Gorham	Lois J. Vermillion
Robert M. Gurss	Lorraine J. Webb (Resident,
Robert R. Harris (Resident,	Waldorf, Maryland Office)
Bethesda & Greenbelt,	Joseph B. Whitebread, Jr.
Maryland Offices)	Ramsey L. Woodworth

Matthew G. Ahrens (Resident,	Daniel G. Lloyd
Bethesda, Maryland Office)	Gail Prentiss Miller (Resident,
Ilene Baxt Campbell (Resident,	Fairfax, Virginia Office)
Fairfax, Virginia Office)	Matthew J. Murcko
Timothy Dugan (Resident,	(Not admitted in DC)
Bethesda, Maryland Office)	Mark S. Randall
Patricia Ann Harris (Resident,	Karin M. Ryan
Bethesda, Maryland Office)	Stuart A. Turow

For full biographical listings, see the Martindale-Hubbell Law Directory

WILLIAMS & CONNOLLY (AV)

725 Twelfth Street, N.W., 20005
Telephone: 202-434-5000

MEMBERS OF FIRM

Edward Bennett Williams	John J. Buckley, Jr.
(1920-1988)	Terrence O'Donnell
Paul R. Connolly (1922-1978)	Douglas R. Marvin
Vincent J. Fuller	John K. Villa
Raymond W. Bergan	Barry S. Simon
Jeremiah C. Collins	Kevin T. Baine
David Povich	Stephen L. Urbanczyk
Steven M. Umin	Philip J. Ward
John W. Vardaman	James A. Bruton, III
Paul Martin Wolff	Peter J. Kahn
J. Alan Galbraith	Lon S. Babby
John G. Kester	Michael S. Sundermeyer
William E. McDaniels	James T. Fuller, III
Brendan V. Sullivan, Jr.	David D. Aufhauser
Aubrey M. Daniel, III	Bruce R. Genderson
Richard M. Cooper	Carolyn H. Williams
Gerald A. Feffer	Frank Lane Heard III
Robert P. Watkins	Steven R. Kuney
Jerry L. Shulman	Gerson A. Zweifach
Lawrence Lucchino	Paul Mogin
Lewis H. Ferguson, III	Howard W. Gutman
Robert B. Barnett	Nancy F. Lesser
David E. Kendall	Richard S. Hoffman
Gregory B. Craig	Steven A. Steinbach

(See Next Column)

WILLIAMS & CONNOLLY—*Continued*

MEMBERS OF FIRM (Continued)

Mark S. Levinstein	David C. Kiernan
Mary Greer Clark	Lon E. Musslewhite
Daniel F. Katz	Robin E. Jacobsohn
Nicole K. Seligman	Charles A. Sweet
Robert M. Krasne	Heidi K. Hubbard
Kathleen L. Beggs	Glenn J. Pfadenhauer
William R. Murray, Jr.	George A. Borden
Eva Petko Esber	Robert J. Shaughnessy
Stephen D. Raber	Jonathan P. Graham

Allen P. Waxman

Eric M. Braun	Mark A. Smith
David S. Blatt	Michael K. Ross
Ari S. Zymelman	(Not admitted in DC)
Joseph D. Piorkowski, Jr.	Max Stier
Paul K. Dueffert	Angela S. Kim
Regina G. Maloney	J. Gordon Seymour
Dane H. Butswinkas	Matthew J. Herrington
Laurie S. Fulton	Suzanne H. Woods
Dennis M. Black	(Not admitted in DC)
Philip Andrew Sechler	Craig D. Singer
Martin C. Calhoun	Julie C. Hilden
Lynda Schuler	(Not admitted in DC)
Jacqueline E. Maitland Davies	Michael R. Pompeo
Donald R. Carlson	Tae-Sik Yoon
Robert M. Cary	Charles V. Ghoorah
Kevin M. Hodges	Kathleen H. Quimby
Eric A. Kuhl	Tiffany Berry West
S. Hollis M. Greenlaw	Susan L. Abbott
Paul A. Murphy	J. Andrew Keyes
David M. Zinn	Maria Laura Acebal
James P. A. Ryan	Dan S. Sokolov
John T. Parry	(Not admitted in DC)
Joseph G. Petrosinelli	Nicole Chapin Duke
Philip J. Deutch	Jonathan L. Marcus
Eric N. Lieberman	Thad A. Davis
Steven M. Farina	(Not admitted in DC)
Sharon L. Davis	Gilbert O. Greenman
Kevin Downey	(Not admitted in DC)
Paul B. Gaffney	Joanna L. Grossman
Thomas G. Hentoff	Oliver Garcia
Julie L. Ferguson	(Not admitted in DC)
Stuart G. Nash	Paul T. Hourihan
Emmet T. Flood	(Not admitted in DC)
Megan E. Hills	William J. Bachman
Marcie R. Ziegler	(Not admitted in DC)
Kenneth C. Smurzynski	Margaret A. Keeley
John E. Schmidtlein	(Not admitted in DC)
Jonathan Banks	Ann H. Rakestraw
Riyaz A. Kanji	(Not admitted in DC)
(Not admitted in DC)	

OF COUNSEL

Lyman G. Friedman	Charles D. Niemeier

For full biographical listings, see the Martindale-Hubbell Law Directory

---

* WILLKIE FARR & GALLAGHER (AV)

Three Lafayette Centre, 1155 21st Street, N.W., 20036-3384
Telephone: 202-328-8000
Fax: 202-887-8979
New York, N.Y. Office: One Citicorp Center, 153 East 53rd Street, 10022-4669.
Telephone: 212-821-8000.
Fax: 212-821-8111.
Paris, France Office: 21-23 rue de la Ville l'Evêque, 75008.
Telephone: 011-33-1-53-43-45-00.
Fax: 011-33-1-40-06-96-06.
London, England Office: 35 Wilson Street, EC2M 2SJ.
Telephone: 011-44-171-696-9060.
Fax: 011-44-171-417-9191.

RESIDENT MEMBERS

William H. Barringer	James P. Durling
Stephen R. Bell	Michael H. Hammer
Sue D. Blumenfeld	David P. Murray
Kevin B. Clark	Steven M. Oster
Brian Conboy	Kenneth J. Pierce
John P. Dean	Philip L. Verveer
Christopher A. Dunn	Theodore C. Whitehouse

RESIDENT COUNSEL

Noel Hemmendinger	Russell L. Smith

RESIDENT ASSOCIATES

Miriam A. Bishop	Lisa K. Coleman
Randy Branitsky	Carolyn W. Conkling
Francis M. Buono	Gregory K. Conway
A. Renée Callahan	Jennifer L. Desmond
(Not admitted in DC)	Jennifer A. Donaldson

(See Next Column)

RESIDENT ASSOCIATES (Continued)

Andrew D'Uva	William B. Lindsey
Brian Finley	John L. McGrew
Michael F. Finn	Edgar B. Miller
Nancy A. Fischer	George O. Nwanze
Katherine I. Funk	(Not admitted in DC)
Gunnar D. Halley	Michele R. Pistone
(Not admitted in DC)	Daniel L. Porter
Bradford T. Hammock	Gabriel R. Sanz-Rexach
(Not admitted in DC)	Conrad J. Smucker
Todd G. Hartman	Scott E. Stewart
Michael G. Jones	(Not admitted in DC)
Thomas Jones	Christopher S. Stokes
Bonni Fine Kaufman	Raymond F. Sullivan, Jr.
David R. King	Lyle B. Vander Schaaf
Angie W. Kronenberg	Jacqueline A. Weisman
(Not admitted in DC)	Lois G. Wye
Robert L. LaFrankie	Scott F. Young
Kara B. Leitner	(Not admitted in DC)
(Not admitted in DC)	

For full biographical listings, see the Martindale-Hubbell Law Directory

---

WILMER, CUTLER & PICKERING (AV)

2445 M Street, N.W., 20037-1420
Telephone: 202-663-6000
Fax: 202-663-6363
Email: Law@Wilmer.Com
Baltimore, Maryland Office: 100 Light Street, 21202.
Telephone: 410-986-2800.
Fax: 410-986-2828.
European Offices:
4 Carlton Gardens, London, SW1Y 5AA, England. Telephone: +44 (171) 872-1000.
Fax: +44 (171) 839-3537.
Rue de la Loi 15 Wetstraat, B-1040 Brussels, Belgium. Telephone: +32 (2) 285-4900.
Fax: +32 (2) 285-4949.
Friedrichstrasse 95, D-10117 Berlin, Germany. Telephone: +49 (30) 2022-6400.
Fax: +49 (30)2022-6500.

Richard H. Wilmer (1892-1976)

MEMBERS OF FIRM

Joel Rosenbloom	Andrew B. Weissman
Daniel K. Mayers	Lynn Bregman
Stephen H. Sachs	Stephen P. Doyle
Arthur F. Mathews	William R. Richardson, Jr.
James S. Campbell	George P. Stamas (Resident,
Dennis M. Flannery	Baltimore, Maryland Office)
Daniel Marcus	Harry J. Weiss
Jeffrey N. Shane	Brandon Becker
Louis R. Cohen	Russell J. Bruemmer
Michael R. Klein	Bruce E. Coolidge
F. David Lake, Jr.	Juanita A. Crowley
Paul J. Mode, Jr.	John Payton
Stephen F. Black	William J. Wilkins
C. Boyden Gray	Andrew N. Vollmer
Ronald J. Greene	Thomas W. White
Gary D. Wilson	Bruce M. Berman
C. Loring Jetton, Jr.	Thomas F. Connell
William T. Lake	Charles E. Davidow
James A. Rogers	Terrill A. Hyde
Michael L. Burack	Duane D. Morse
Michael S. Helfer	James S. Venit (Not admitted in
Neil J. King	DC; Resident, European
Dieter G. F. Lange (Resident,	Office, Brussels, Belgium)
European Office, London,	Dr. Andreas Weitbrecht
England)	(Resident, European Office,
Charles S. Levy	Brussels, Belgium)
Robert B. McCaw	Daniel H. Squire
Dr. Manfred Balz (Not admitted	W. Scott Blackmer
in the United States; Resident,	Gary B. Born (Resident,
European Office, Berlin,	European Office, London,
Germany)	England)
Richard W. Cass	Jeremy N. Rubenstein
Kenneth W. Gideon	John B. Watkins V (Resident,
William J. Kolasky, Jr.	Baltimore, Maryland Office)
Arthur L. Marriott (Resident,	Philip D. Anker
European Office, London,	Joseph K. Brenner
England)	Carol Clayton
A. Stephen Hut, Jr.	Thomas P. Olson
John Rounsaville, Jr.	Patrick J. Carome
Roger M. Witten	David P. Donovan
Robert C. Cassidy, Jr.	Paul A. von Hehn (Resident,
John D. Greenwald	European Office, Brussels,
(Not admitted in DC)	Belgium)
John H. Harwood II	Marc C. Hansen (Resident,
David M. Becker	European Office, Brussels,
Mary Carolyn Cox	Belgium)
Christopher R. Lipsett	Bryan Slone (Resident,
William J. Perlstein	Baltimore, Maryland Office)
Marianne K. Smythe	Stephen M. Cutler

(See Next Column)

WILMER, CUTLER & PICKERING, *Washington—Continued*

MEMBERS OF FIRM (Continued)

Andrew K. Parnell (Resident, European Office, London, England)	James R. Wrathall
	Yoon-Young Lee
	Gail C. Bernstein
Roger W. Yoerges	Susan P. Crawford
Laura B. Ahearn	Robert F. Hoyt
Mark D. Cahn	Steven F. Cherry
Eric R. Markus	Dr. Natalie Lübben (Resident, European Office, Berlin, Germany)
Eric J. Mogilnicki	
Robert B. Stack	

SENIOR COUNSEL

Lloyd N. Cutler	John H. Pickering

J. Roger Wollenberg

COUNSEL

Ezekiel G. Stoddard	Marc R. Cohen
Lester Nurick	Murray A. Indick
William A. Butler	R. Scott Kilgore
Leonard M. Shambon	Robert G. Bagnall
Patricia A. Sherman (Resident European Office, Brussels, Belgium)	Linda J. Miller
	Thomas J. Delaney
	Elizabeth Stevens Duane
John J. Kallaugher (Resident, European Office, London, England)	Mark A. Dewire (Resident, Baltimore, Maryland Office)
	Karen L. Barr
Marcia A. Wiss	Christian L. Duvernoy (Resident, European Office, Brussels, Belgium)
Carol H. Fishman	
Joseph E. Killory, Jr.	
Roger J. Patterson (Resident, Baltimore, Maryland Office)	Michael E. Herde
	Nancy L. Manzer

Ronald I. Meltzer

OF COUNSEL

Marshall Hornblower	Howard P. Willens
William R. Perlik	Max O. Truitt, Jr.
Robert P. Stranahan, Jr.	Timothy N. Black
Robert A. Hammond, III	Andrea Ann Timko

ASSOCIATES

Margaret L. Ackerley	Amy N. Kroll
James E. Anderson	Stavros J. Lambrinidis
Warren O. Asher	Robert H. Lantz
Brigida Benitez	Alyza D. Lewin
Karan Bhatia	Mark Stephen Lewis (Resident European Office London, England)
Dr. Matthias Bock (Resident, European Office London, England)	
	James W. Lowe
Anne D. Bolling	David A. Luigs (Not admitted in DC)
Katherine A. Bradley	
Anthony G. Brown	Craig Alford Masback
Kimble Charles Cannon (Not admitted in DC)	John Maull (Not admitted in DC)
	A. Kent Mayo
Gregorio B. Cater (Resident, Baltimore, Maryland Office)	Susan D. McAndrew
	Jane L. McClellan
David J. Charles	Michael A. McKenzie
Lynn R. Charytan	Charles Alan Mendels
Karen L. Cohen	Brian J. Menkes
Erik H. Corwin	Martin Menne (Resident, European Office, Berlin Germany)
Mary L. Coyne (Not admitted in DC)	
	Dr. Henning Mennenoeh (Resident, European Office, Berlin, Germany)
Stuart F. Delery	
Peggy Delinois	
Steven M. Dunne	Jonathan E. Meyer
Janet Durholz (Not admitted in DC)	Neil D. Midgley (Resident, European Office, London, England)
Daniel S. Ehrenberg	
Van W. Ellis	Kathleen M. Miller
Sara E. Emley	Thomas Mueller
Denise Esposito	Jean Paul M. Poitras (Resident, European Office Brussels, Belgium)
Gregory J. Ewald (Not admitted in DC)	
	Gordon Pearson
Jutta Von Falkenhausen (Resident, European Office, Berlin, Germany)	Suzanne G. Ramos (Not admitted in DC)
	Erika L. Robinson (Resident, Baltimore, Maryland Office)
Patrice Alexander Ficklin	
Steven P. Finizio	Alex E. Rogers
Joshua B. Fisher	Dominic David Roughton (Resident, European Office, London, England) (Not admitted in the United States)
Michael R. Fisher	
Jonathan J. Frankel	
Eric T. Frye	
Helen Anne Gaebler	Jacquelynn Ruff
Katherine H. Gibson	David Shub
Ankur J. Goel	Arnon D. Siegel
Leon B. Greenfield	Jeffrey P. Singdahlsen
Andrew M. Herman	John E. Smith (Not admitted in DC)
Camille D. Holmes	
Michael R. Holter (Resident, European Office, London, England)	David M. Sohn (Not admitted in DC)
	Laurie Michelle Stegman (Not admitted in DC)
Lawrence A. Kasten	
James P. Kelleher	
Ruth E. Kent	
Sara Needleman Kline	

(See Next Column)

ASSOCIATES (Continued)

Kara M. Stein	John A. Trenor (Not admitted in DC)
Ali M. Stoeppelwerth (Not admitted in DC)	
	Adam R. Waldman (Resident, Baltimore, Maryland Office)
Timothy E. Stumpff (Not admitted in DC)	
	Laura E. Walker
Edward P. Sullivan (Not admitted in DC)	Stuart M. Weiser
	David Albert Westbrook
Geoffrey Michael Taylor (Not admitted in the United States)	Deborah M. Wiggin (Not admitted in DC)
Nancy A. Heath Taylor	David M. Wohlstadter (Not admitted in DC)
David H. Topol	

Soo J. Yim

Robert S. McCormick (Not admitted in DC; Executive Director of the Firm)

For full biographical listings, see the Martindale-Hubbell Law Directory

✱ WINSTON & STRAWN (AV)

1400 L Street, N.W., 20005-3502
Telephone: 202-371-5700
Telex: 440574 INTLAW UI
Telecopier: 202-371-5950
Email: postmaster@winston.com
Chicago, Illinois Office: 35 West Wacker Drive, 60601.
Telephone: 315-558-5600.
Cable Address: "Winston Chicago."
Facsimile: 312-558-5700.
New York, N.Y. Office: 200 Park Avenue, 10166-4193.
Telephone: 212-294-6700.
Telecopier: 212-294-4700.
Cable Address: "Coledeitz, NYK."
Telex: (RCA) 232459.
Geneva, Switzerland Office: 43 Rue du Rhone, 1204.
Telephone: (4122) 7810506.
Fax: (4122) 7810361.
Paris, France Office: 6, rue du Cirque, 75008.
Telephone: (3314) 225-1055.
Fax: (3314) 225-0921.

MEMBERS OF FIRM

J. Michael McGarry, III	Norman R. Vander Clute
Nicholas S. Reynolds	M. Javade Chaudhri
Dean L. Overman	Benjamin P. Fishburne, III
Donald K. Dankner	Barry J. Hart
William J. Madden, Jr.	Steven M. Lucas
John P. Proctor	David W. Roderer
Edward F. Gerwin, Jr.	Charles L. Kinney
John R. Keys, Jr.	James R. Curtiss
Deborah C. Costlow	Sheldon L. Trubatch
Leonard W. Belter	Robert A. Mangrum
Richard C. Browne	William G. Miossi
Thomas M. Buchanan	James T. Pitts
Peter N. Hiebert	John Albert Whittaker, IV
Eric L. Hirschhorn	Timothy M. Broas
William K. Keane	Gordon Alan Coffee
Frederick J. Killion	Richard A. Hibey
John C. Kirtland	Christopher C. McIsaac
Joseph B. Knotts, Jr.	Eric W. Bloom
Michael R. Lemov	Perry D. Robinson
Malcolm H. Philips, Jr.	Michael L. Sibarium
Robert M. Rader	Thomas L. Mills
Daniel F. Stenger	Constantine G. Papavizas
Mark J. Wetterhahn	Jeffrey G. Berman
John E. Williams	Edmund D. Cooke, Jr.
David A. Repka	Peter M. Kirby
Peter Kryn Dykema	John Fehrenbach
Margaret A. Hill	William N. Hall
John A. Waits, II	William A. Anderson, II (Not admitted in DC)
James H. Burnley IV	
Beryl F. Anthony, Jr. (Not admitted in DC)	

OF COUNSEL

Robert M. Bor	Dennis M. Devaney
John H. More	Patrick L. Schmidt
Carl J. Peckinpaugh	John L. Napier

SENIOR ATTORNEYS

Anne W. Cottingham	William A. Horin

Chuncheng Lian

ASSOCIATES

John R. Ates	Alexandra R. Dapolito (Not admitted in DC)
Michael K. Atkinson	
Faton A. Bacaj	Jeanne M. Dennis
D. Randall Benn	Elizabeth J. Dillon (Not admitted in DC)
Robert A. Berger	
Cathy L. Burgess	Robert Linn Draper
Kenneth R. Button	F. Stanley Echols
Peter W. Colby	Felicia A. Emry (Not admitted in DC)
David F. Cutter (Not admitted in DC)	
	Joan B. Tucker Fife

(See Next Column)

WINSTON & STRAWN—*Continued*

ASSOCIATES (Continued)

Alan Gregg Fishel	Sandra L. Pearlman
Garry E. Garten	(Not admitted in DC)
(Not admitted in DC)	Thomas C. Poindexter
Marcia R. Gelman	Michael I. Raschid
Karen L. Grubber	Katherine A. Rutemiller
John F. Guyot	William B. Fenning Steinman
Robert E. Helfrich	Stacey J. Stern
(Not admitted in DC)	Frank J. Supik
Charles B. Klein	Kathryn M. Sutton
Andreas H. Leskovsek	Treg T. Tremont
Jay L. Levine	Daphine Trotter
(Not admitted in DC)	Monique M. Vasilchik
Eric J. Marcotte	Mary E. Wall
(Not admitted in DC)	(Not admitted in DC)
Donn C. Meindertsma	Raymond B. Wuslich
Francisco J. Pavia	

STAFF ATTORNEY
Pamela A. Rons

For full biographical listings, see the Martindale-Hubbell Law Directory

---

* WINTHROP, STIMSON, PUTNAM & ROBERTS (AV)

1133 Connecticut Avenue, N.W., 20036
Telephone: 202-775-9800
Telex: WINSTIM DC 316229
Telefax: 202-833-8491
New York, N.Y. Office: One Battery Park Plaza, 10004.
Telephone: 212-858-1000.
Fax: 212-858-1500.
Stamford, Connecticut Office: Financial Centre, 695 East Main Street, P.O. Box 6760, 06904-6760.
Telephone: 203-348-2300.
Fax: 203-965-8226.
Palm Beach, Florida Office: 125 Worth Avenue, 33480.
Telephone: 407-655-7297.
Fax: 407-833-6726.
London, England Office: 2 Throgmorton Avenue, London EC2N 2DL, England.
Telephone: 011-44171-628-4931.
Fax: 011-44171-638-0443.
Brussels, Belgium Office: Rue Du Taciturne 42, B-1040 Brussels, Belgium.
Telephone: 011-322-230-1392.
Fax: 011-322-230-9288.
Tokyo, Japan Office: 608 Atagoyama Bengoshi Building 6-7, Atago 1-chome, Minato-ku, Tokyo 105 Japan.
Telephone: 011-813-3437-9740.
Fax: 011-813-3437-9261.
Hong Kong Office: 2505 Asia Pacific Finance Tower, Citibank Plaza, 3 Garden Road, Central.
Telephone: 011-852-2530-3400.
Fax: 011-852-2530-3355.

RESIDENT PARTNERS

Isaac D. Benkin	Gerald D. Morgan, Jr.
Donald A. Carr	Mary Ann Walker
John E. Gillick	Christopher R. Wall
	Roger D. Wiegley

COUNSEL

Robert Reed Gray	Aileen Meyer
Marvin T. Griff	C. Christopher Parlin
Louis H. Kurrelmeyer	Kenneth P. Quinn
	(Not admitted in DC)

RESIDENT ASSOCIATES

David S. Christy, Jr.	Michael J. Levitin
David A. Crichlow	Mark A. Monborne
Thomas M. deButts	Joshua I. Romanow
William H. Espinosa	Stanley R. Scheiner
James L. Gallagher	Franceska O. Schroeder
(Not admitted in DC)	Paul W. Terry
Neil L. Levy	William L. Thomas

For full biographical listings, see the Martindale-Hubbell Law Directory

---

FLORIDA

AVENTURA, Dade Co.

BUCHANAN INGERSOLL, PROFESSIONAL CORPORATION (AV(T))

One Turnberry Place, 19495 Biscayne Boulevard, Suite 606, 33180
Telephone: 305-933-5600
Telecopier: 305-933-2350
URL: http://www.bipc.com
Pittsburgh, Pennsylvania Office: One Oxford Centre, 301 Grant Street, 20th Floor.
Telephone: 412-562-8800.

(See Next Column)

Philadelphia, Pennsylvania Office: Two Logan Square, Twelfth Floor, 18th & Arch Streets.
Telephone: 215-665-8700.
Harrisburg, Pennsylvania Office: 30 North Third Street.
Telephone: 717-237-4800.
Miami, Florida Office: NationsBank Tower, 100 S.E. Second Street.
Telephone: 305-347-4080.
Tampa, Florida Office: Suite 2500, 401 East Jackson Street.
Telephone: 813-222-8180.
Princeton, New Jersey Office: Buchanan Ingersoll, A Partnership, College Centre, 500 College Road East.
Telephone: 609-987-6800.
Lexington, Kentucky Office: Suite 600, PNC Bank Plaza, 200 West Vine Street.
Telephone: 606-225-5333.
Buffalo, New York Office: 1100 Main Place Tower, 350 Main Street.
Telephone: 716-854-4100.
Fax: 816-854-4227.

Joshua L. Dubin	Mark J. Neuberger

SENIOR ATTORNEYS
Ralph B. Bekkevold

Todd A. Bancroft	Randi S. Rothfield
Kevin Carmichael	Richard N. Schermer
Jeffrey M. Goodz	Rebecca S. Trinkler

For full biographical listings, see the Martindale-Hubbell Law Directory

---

BARTOW,* Polk Co.

FROST, O'TOOLE & SAUNDERS, P.A. (AV)

395 South Central Avenue, P.O. Box 2188, 33830
Telephone: 941-533-0314; 800-533-0967
Telecopier: 941-533-8985

John W. Frost, II	Robert A. Carr
Neal L. O'Toole	Robert H. Van Hart
Thomas C. Saunders	John Marc Tamayo
Richard E. "Rick" Dantzler	Mark A. Sessums
	Robert J. Aranda

Reference: Community National Bank, Bartow.

For full biographical listings, see the Martindale-Hubbell Law Directory

---

LANE, TROHN, CLARKE, BERTRAND, VREELAND & JACOBSEN, P.A. (AV)

150 East Davidson Street, P.O. Box 1578, 33830-1578
Telephone: 941-533-0866
Telecopier: 941-533-7255
Lakeland, Florida Office: One Lake Morton Drive. 38802.
Telephone: 941-284-2200.
Fax: 941-688-0310.

C. A. Boswell	Donald H. Wilson, Jr.
Wofford Hampton Stidham	Jonathan Stidham
Dabney L. Conner	Steven L. Selph

Approved Attorneys for: Attorneys' Title Insurance Fund.

For full biographical listings, see the Martindale-Hubbell Law Directory

---

BOCA RATON, Palm Beach Co.

BROAD AND CASSEL (AV)

A Partnership including Professional Associations
Corporate Centre at Boca Raton, Suite 300, 7777 Glades Road, 33434
Telephone: 561-483-7000
Telecopier: 561-483-7321
Fort Lauderdale, Florida Office: Suite 1130, Broward Financial Centre, 500 E. Broward Boulevard, 33394.
Telephone: 954-764-7060.
Miami, Florida Office: Miami Center, 201 South Biscayne Boulevard, Suite 3000, 33131.
Telephone: 305-373-9400.
Orlando, Florida Office: Barnett Bank Center, 390 N. Orange Avenue, Suite 1100, 32801.
Telephone: 407-839-4200.
Stuart, Florida Office: 900 East Ocean Boulevard, Suite 126, 33994.
Telephone: 561-283-3000.
Tallahassee, Florida Office: 215 South Monroe Street, Suite 400, 32302.
Telephone: 904-681-6810.
Tampa, Florida Office: 100 North Tampa, Suite 3500, 33602.
Telephone: 813-225-3020.
West Palm Beach, Florida Office: The Reflections Office Centre, 400 Australian Avenue, South, Fifth Floor, 33401.
Telephone: 561-832-3300.

PARTNERS

Jeffrey A. Deutch (P.A.)	Arvin J. Jaffe (P.A.)
Richard B. MacFarland (P.A.)	James J. Wheeler (P.A.)
	Amy S. Schlosser (P.A.)

(See Next Column)

BROAD AND CASSEL, *Boca Raton—Continued*

ASSOCIATES

David J. Powers　　　　　　　　　Edgar A. Benes

Carl S. Rosen

OF COUNSEL

Kenneth Edelman　　　　　　　　Jodi B. Laurence

For full biographical listings, see the Martindale-Hubbell Law Directory

OSBORNE, OSBORNE & deCLAIRE, P.A. (AV)

Suite 100 Via Mizner Financial Plaza, 798 South Federal Highway, P.O. Drawer 40, 33429-9974
Telephone: 561-395-1000
Fax: 561-368-6930

Ray C. Osborne　　　　　　　　　George F. deClaire
R. Brady Osborne, Jr.　　　　　　Ellen R. Itzler

Linda L. Snelling

Approved Attorneys for: First Union National Bank of Florida, N.A.; Sun-Bank/South Florida, N.A.; Northern Trust Bank of Florida. NationsBank of Florida, N.A.

For full biographical listings, see the Martindale-Hubbell Law Directory

PROSKAUER ROSE GOETZ & MENDELSOHN LLP (AV)

One Boca Place, Suite 340 West, 2255 Glades Road, 33431
Telephone: 407-241-7400 Toll Free, Elsewhere in Florida 800-432-7746
FAX: 407-241-7145
Email: info@proskauer.com *URL:* http://www.proskauer.com
New York, N.Y. Office: 1585 Broadway.
Telephone: 212-969-3000.
Washington, D.C. Office: 1233 Twentieth Street, N.W., Suite 800.
Telephone: 202-416-6800.
Los Angeles, California Office: 2121 Avenue of the Stars, Suite 2700.
Telephone: 310-557-2900.
Clifton, New Jersey Office: 1373 Broad Street, P.O. Box 4444.
Telephone: 201-779-6300.
Paris, France Office: Proskauer Rose Goetz & Mendelsohn, 9 rue Le Tasse.
Telephone: (33-1) 44 30 25 30.

MEMBERS OF FIRM

Jay S. Blumenkopf　　　　　　　Albert W. Gortz
Howard K. Coates, Jr.　　　　　Allan H. Weitzman
Joseph Erdman　　　　　　　　Christopher C. Wheeler

ASSOCIATES

Stephanie Dest Alexander　　　　Henry E. Lichtenberger
　(Not admitted in FL)　　　　　Kristina B. Pett
Dean M. Conway　　　　　　　　George A. Pincus
Jonathan M. Fordin　　　　　　Kenneth Strick
Brenda A. Friedman　　　　　　Donald "Rocky" E. Thompson,
Paul J. Geller　　　　　　　　　　II
David J. George　　　　　　　　Michael R. Tricarico
Stuart T. Kapp　　　　　　　　Matthew H. Triggs
　　　　　Gregory D. Whitworth

For full biographical listings, see the Martindale-Hubbell Law Directory

---

*BONIFAY,** Holmes Co. — (Refer to De Funiak Springs)

*BRADENTON,** Manatee Co.

GRIMES GOEBEL GRIMES HAWKINS & GLADFELTER, P.A. (AV)

The Professional Building, 1023 Manatee Avenue West, P.O. Box 1550, 34206
Telephone: 941-748-0151
Fax: 941-748-0158

William C. Grimes　　　　　　Leslie Horton Gladfelter
Caleb J. Grimes　　　　　　　William S. Galvano
John D. Hawkins　　　　　　　Douglas A. Peebles

Counsel for: Schroeder Manatee Inc. (Agriculture and Land Development); Pursley, Inc., (Horticulture, Retail and Land Development); Lombardo & Skipper, Inc. (Civil Engineers); CCI Environmental Services, Inc. (Environmental Consultants); Creekwood Investors, Ltd.; Old Hyde Park Village Center, Ltd.; First Federal Savings & Loan Association of Florida.
Approved Attorneys for: Lawyers Title Insurance Corp.; Chicago Title Insurance Co.; Attorneys Title Insurance Fund.

For full biographical listings, see the Martindale-Hubbell Law Directory

---

*BRONSON,** Levy Co. — (Refer to Gainesville)

*BUSHNELL,** Sumter Co. — (Refer to Ormond Beach)

*CHIPLEY,** Washington Co. — (Refer to Panama City)

---

*CLEARWATER,** Pinellas Co.

* indicates certain Bar Register subscribers whose principal office is located elsewhere in the state and who have arranged for representation as a part of the state capital listings that follow

JOHNSON, BLAKELY, POPE, BOKOR, RUPPEL & BURNS, P.A. (AV)

911 Chestnut Street, P.O. Box 1368, 34617
Telephone: 813-461-1818
Telecopier: 813-441-8617
Tampa, Florida Office: 100 N. Tampa Street, Suite 1800. P.O. Box 1100.
Telephone: 813-225-2500.
Telecopier: 813-223-7118.

E. D. Armstrong III　　　　　Roger A. Larson
John T. Blakely　　　　　　　John R. Lawson, Jr.
Bruce H. Bokor　　　　　　　Michael C. Markham
Guy M. Burns　　　　　　　　David J. Ottinger
Michael T. Cronin　　　　　　F. Wallace Pope, Jr.
Elizabeth J. Daniels　　　　　Darryl R. Richards
Lisa B. Dodge　　　　　　　　Dennis G. Ruppel
Marion Hale　　　　　　　　John A. Schaefer
Scott C. Ilgenfritz　　　　　Philip M. Shasteen
Frank R. Jakes　　　　　　　Charles M. Tatelbaum
Timothy A. Johnson, Jr.　　　Joan M. Vecchioli
　　　　　Julius J. Zschau

Bruce W. Barnes　　　　　　Michael G. Little
　(Resident at Tampa)　　　Stephanie T. Marquardt
Duane A. Daiker　　　　　　Charles A. Samarkos
James W. Humann　　　　　Anthony P. Zinge
Sharon E. Krick　　　　　　　(Resident at Tampa)

For full biographical listings, see the Martindale-Hubbell Law Directory

KWALL & SHOWERS, P.A. (AV)

133 North Fort Harrison Avenue, 34615
Telephone: 813-441-4947
Telecopier: 813-447-3158
Email: Kwall133@MSN.com

Louis Kwall　　　　　　　　Gregory K. Showers

For full biographical listings, see the Martindale-Hubbell Law Directory

* MACFARLANE FERGUSON & McMULLEN (AV)

Professional Association
AmSouth Bank Building, Suite 800, 400 Cleveland Street, P.O. Box 1669, 34617
Telephone: 813-441-8966
Fax: 813-442-8470
Tampa, Florida Office: 2300 Park Tower, 400 North Tampa Street. 33601.
Telephone: 813-273-4200.
Fax: 813-273-4396.

John Tweed McMullen　　　　R. Nathan Hightower
　(1913-1996)　　　　　　　Joshua Magidson
Harry S. Cline　　　　　　　Emil C. Marquardt, Jr.
Stephen O. Cole　　　　　　James A. Martin, Jr.
D. Scott Douglas　　　　　　Thomas C. Nash, II
　　　　　J. Paul Raymond

John Matthew Marquardt　　Nancy S. Paikoff
　　　　　Bryan J. Stanley

Representative Clients: BellSouth Telecommunications, Inc.; Capital City Bank Group, Inc.; CSX Transportation, Inc.; Lykes Bros. Inc. and Subsidiary Companies; Morton Plant Hospital; National Medical Enterprises, Inc.; Peoples Gas System, Inc.; Sprint Corp./United Telephone; Tampa Electric Co.; The Procter & Gamble Co.

For full biographical listings, see the Martindale-Hubbell Law Directory

---

COCOA, Brevard Co.

WESTMAN & LINTZ (AV)

1970 Michigan Avenue, Building F, 32922
Telephone: 407-690-1970
Facsimile: 407-690-2349

(See Next Column)

WESTMAN & LINTZ—*Continued*

Robert T. Westman   Lester C. Lintz

Representative Clients: Watson Paving, Inc.; Clontz Construction, Inc.; Circles of Care, Inc.; Harvey's Indian River Groves, Inc.; Goodson Paving, Inc.; BRPH Architects/Engineers, Inc.; Miorelli Engineering, Inc.; Southern Comfort Builders, Inc.; CMH Parks, Inc.

CORAL GABLES, Dade Co.

RICHARD H. HUNT & ASSOCIATES A PROFESSIONAL ASSOCIATION (AV)

2801 Ponce de Leon Boulevard Ninth Floor, 33134
Telephone: 305-569-9671
Telecopier: 305-445-7728
Email: huntmia@ix.netcom.com

Richard H. Hunt

Robert Scott Williams
SENIOR COUNSEL
George J. Baya (1900-1995)

For full biographical listings, see the Martindale-Hubbell Law Directory

WALTON LANTAFF SCHROEDER & CARSON (AV)

A Partnership including Professional Associations
Suite 1101 Gables International Plaza, 2655 Le Jeune Road, 33134
Telephone: 305-379-6411
Telecopier: 305-446-9206
Miami, Florida Office: One Biscayne Tower, 25th Floor, 2 South Biscayne Boulevard.
Telephone: 305-379-6411.
Telecopier: 305-577-3875.
West Palm Beach, Florida Office: United National Bank Tower, Suite 800, 1645 Palm Beach Lakes Boulevard.
Telephone: 407-689-6700.
Telecopier: 407-689-2647.
Fort Lauderdale, Florida Office: Third Floor, Blackstone Building, 707 Southeast Third Avenue.
Telephone: 305-463-8456.
Telecopier: 305-763-6294.

RESIDENT PARTNERS
Charles P. Sacher (P.A.)   Nicholas E. Christin (P.A.)
Gregory T. Martini
RESIDENT OF COUNSEL
Martin E. Segal (P.A.)   Robert B. Cole
RESIDENT ASSOCIATES
Charles S. Sacher   Stuart J. Haft

For full biographical listings, see the Martindale-Hubbell Law Directory

---

DANIA, Broward Co. — (Refer to Fort Lauderdale)

DAYTONA BEACH, Volusia Co.

FINK & SWEET (AV)

149 East International Speedway Boulevard, P.O. Box 265386, 32126
Telephone: 904-252-7653
Fax: 904-238-3604

Wesley A. Fink   Jeffrey C. Sweet

Representative Clients: SunTrust Bank of East Central Florida.
Approved Attorneys for: Attorneys' Title Insurance Fund; Commonwealth Land Title Insurance Co.; Chicago Title Insurance Co.
Reference: SunTrust Bank of East Central Florida.

For full biographical listings, see the Martindale-Hubbell Law Directory

LANDIS, GRAHAM, FRENCH, HUSFELD, SHERMAN & FORD, P.A. (AV)

Formerly Hull, Landis, Graham & French
543 South Ridgewood Avenue, 32114
Telephone: 904-252-4717
Fax: 904-253-7352
De Land, Florida Office: 145 East Rich Avenue, P.O. Box 48.
Telephone: 904-734-3451.
Deltona, Florida Office: 204 Medical Arts Center, 1555 Saxon Boulevard.
Telephone: 407-574-1461.
Fax: 407-574-0242.

Erskine W. Landis (1900-1967)   Richard S. Graham
John L. Graham (1905-1978)   William E. Sherman
Thorwald J. Husfeld (1926-1995)   Sam N. Masters
OF COUNSEL
J. Compton French

Counsel for: Barnett Bank of Volusia County; State Farm Mutual Automobile Insurance Co.; West Volusia Hospital Authority; Central Florida Fern Cooperative, Inc.; General Motors Corp.; South Florida Natural Gas Co.;

(See Next Column)

Florida Public Utilities Co.; Volusia County Industrial Development Authority; Florida United Methodist Children's Home: Volusia County Educational Facilities Authority.

For full biographical listings, see the Martindale-Hubbell Law Directory

---

DEERFIELD BEACH, Broward Co.

PATTERSON & HARMON, P.A. (AV)

665 S.E. 10th Street, 33441
Telephone: 954-421-7700
Fax: 954-421-7956

George A. Patterson   Blake M. Harmon

Representative Clients: Butler Properties, Ltd.; Powerline Development, Inc.; Rivertown Apartments, Inc.; Rivertown Manor Condominium Association; Stainless, Inc.; Reliance Enterprises; Ransco Development, Inc.
Approved Attorneys for: Attorneys' Title Insurance Fund; Chicago Title Insurance Co.
Reference: Barnett Bank of Broward County, N.A.

For full biographical listings, see the Martindale-Hubbell Law Directory

---

DE FUNIAK SPRINGS, Walton Co.

ANGUS G. ANDREWS (AV)

694 Baldwin Avenue, P.O. Box 112, 32435
Telephone: 904-892-2181
FAX: 904-892-5383

Representative Clients: Walton County School District; DeFuniak Springs Housing Authority; Gulf Power Co.; Coca-Cola Bottling Co.; Walton County Sheriff's Department; CSX Railroad Co.; Chautauqua Vinyards and Winery, Inc.; 4-Mile Village Property Owners Assoc.; Walton County Fair Assoc.

DE LAND, Volusia Co.

LANDIS, GRAHAM, FRENCH, HUSFELD, SHERMAN & FORD, P.A. (AV)

Formerly Hull, Landis, Graham & French
145 East Rich Avenue, P.O. Box 48, 32721-0048
Telephone: 904-734-3451
Fax: 904-736-1350
Daytona Beach, Florida Office: 543 South Ridgewood Avenue, 32114.
Telephone: 904-252-4717.
Deltona, Florida Office: 204 Medical Arts Center, 1555 Saxon Boulevard.
Telephone: 407-574-1461.
Fax: 407-574-0242.

Erskine W. Landis (1900-1967)   Joe G. Dykes, Jr.
John L. Graham (1905-1978)   Frank A. Ford, Jr.
Thorwald J. Husfeld (1926-1995)   Sam N. Masters
William E. Sherman   (Daytona Beach Office)
Richard S. Graham   Philip L. Partridge
  (Daytona Beach Office)   Edwin Channing Coolidge, Jr.
William A. Ottinger   Kent A. Showalter, III
  (Deltona Office)
OF COUNSEL
J. Compton French   Frank A. Ford, Sr.
  (Daytona Beach Office)

Counsel for: Barnett Bank of Volusia County; State Farm Mutual Automobile Insurance Co.; West Volusia Hospital Authority; Central Florida Fern Cooperative, Inc.; General Motors Corp.; South Florida Natural Gas Co.; Florida Public Utilities Co.; Volusia County Industrial Development Authority; Florida United Methodist Children's Home; Volusia County Educational Facilities Authority.

For full biographical listings, see the Martindale-Hubbell Law Directory

---

DELRAY BEACH, Palm Beach Co.

SIMON & SCHMIDT (AV)

100 N.E. Fifth Avenue, P.O. Box 2020, 33447
Telephone: 561-278-2601
Fax: 561-265-0286

MEMBERS OF FIRM
Ernest G. Simon   David W. Schmidt

Reference: Sun Bank/South Florida, N.A.

For full biographical listings, see the Martindale-Hubbell Law Directory

---

DELTONA, Volusia Co.

LANDIS, GRAHAM, FRENCH, HUSFELD, SHERMAN & FORD, P.A. (AV)

204 Medical Arts Center, 1555 Saxon Boulevard, 32725
Telephone: 407-574-1461
Fax: 407-574-0242
Daytona Beach, Florida Office: 543 South Ridgewood Avenue, 32114.
Telephone: 904-252-4717.

(See Next Column)

LANDIS, GRAHAM, FRENCH, HUSFELD, SHERMAN & FORD P.A., Deltona—Continued

De Land, Florida Office: 145 East Rich Avenue, P.O. Box 48.
Telephone: 904-734-3451.

Erskine W. Landis (1900-1967)   Thorwald J. Husfeld (1926-1995)
John L. Graham (1905-1978)   William A. Ottinger

Counsel for: Barnett Bank of Volusia County; State Farm Mutual Automobile Insurance Co.; West Volusia Hospital Authority; Central Florida Fern Cooperative, Inc.; General Motors Corp.; South Florida Natural Gas Co.; Florida Public Utilities Co.; Volusia County Industrial Development Authority; Florida United Methodist Children's Home; Volusia County Educational Facilities Authority.

For full biographical listings, see the Martindale-Hubbell Law Directory

---

FERNANDINA BEACH,* Nassau Co. — (Refer to Jacksonville)

FORT LAUDERDALE,* Broward Co.

BERRYHILL & WILLIAMS, P.A. (AV)

3000 North Federal Highway, Building 2 South, P.O. Box 24266, 33307
Telephone: 954-563-7143
FAX: 954-563-7208

Thomas O. Berryhill (1908-1978)   Martin F. Avery, Jr. (Retired)
O. Edgar Williams, Jr.

Local Counsel for: Bridgestone/Firestone, Inc.
Approved Attorneys for: Attorneys' Title Insurance Fund.
Reference: First Union National Bank of Florida.

For full biographical listings, see the Martindale-Hubbell Law Directory

WILLIAM E. BLYLER (AV)

1901 West Cypress Creek Road, Suite 415, 33309
Telephone: 954-351-7500

BRINKLEY, McNERNEY, MORGAN, SOLOMON & TATUM, LLP (AV)

Suite 1800, New River Center, 200 East Las Olas Boulevard, P.O. Box 522, 33301-2209
Telephone: Broward: 954-522-2200
Facsimile: 954-522-9123

MEMBERS OF FIRM

W. Michael Brinkley   Thomas R. Tatum
Michael J. McNerney   Stephen L. Ziegler
Philip J. Morgan   Kenneth E. Keechl
Harris K. Solomon   Donald J. Lunny, Jr.
Roberta G. Stanley

ASSOCIATES

Christopher M. Trapani   Thomas J. Ansbro
Kenneth J. Joyce   David F. Hanley
John A. Walker

OF COUNSEL

Amy R. Reeck

Approved Attorneys for: Attorneys' Title Insurance Fund; Chicago Title Insurance Co.; First American Title Insurance Co.

For full biographical listings, see the Martindale-Hubbell Law Directory

BROAD AND CASSEL (AV)

A Partnership including Professional Associations
Suite 1130, Broward Financial Centre, 500 E. Broward Boulevard, 33394
Telephone: 954-764-7060
Telecopier: 954-761-8135
Boca Raton, Florida Office: Corporate Centre at Boca Raton, Suite 300, 7777 Glades Road, 33434.
Telephone: 561-483-7000.
Miami, Florida Office: Miami Center, 201 South Biscayne Boulevard, Suite 3000, 33131.
Telephone: 305-373-9400.
Orlando, Florida Office: Barnett Bank Center, 390 N. Orange Avenue, Suite 1100, 32801.
Telephone: 407-839-4200.
Stuart, Florida Office: 900 East Ocean Boulevard, Suite 126, 33994.
Telephone: 561-283-3000.
Tallahassee, Florida Office: 215 South Monroe Street, Suite 400, 32302.
Telephone: 904-681-6810.
Tampa, Florida Office: 100 North Tampa, Suite 3500, 33602.
Telephone: 813-225-3020.
West Palm Beach, Florida Office: The Reflections Office Centre, 400 Australian Avenue, South, Fifth Floor, 33401.
Telephone: 561-832-3300.

RESIDENT PARTNERS

Martin R. Press (P.A.)   Andrew Cotzin (P.A.)
Gabriel L. Imperato (P.A.)   Lenore Schiller (P.A.)
Anne Novick Branan (P.A.)

(See Next Column)

RESIDENT ASSOCIATES

Barbara Carey del Castillo   Lester J. Perling
Michael Manthei   Jennifer A. Steward
Steve L. Waserstein   Luann M. Dominguez

For full biographical listings, see the Martindale-Hubbell Law Directory

CLARK & SCHOLNIK (AV)

A Partnership of Professional Associations
Coastal Tower, 2400 East Commercial Boulevard, Suite 820, 33308
Telephone: 954-776-3800; 954-771-4790
Telecopier: 954-776-3825

MEMBERS OF FIRM

Thomas M. Clark (P.A.)   Louis N. Scholnik (P.A.)

For full biographical listings, see the Martindale-Hubbell Law Directory

CONRAD, SCHERER & JENNE (AV)

A Partnership of Professional Associations
Eighth Floor, 633 South Federal Highway, P.O. Box 14723, 33302
Telephone: 954-462-5500
Facsimile: 954-463-9244
Miami, Florida Office: International Place. 100 Southeast 2nd Street. Suite 2800. 33131.
Telephone: 305-856-9920.
Facsimile: 305-374-4408.

MEMBERS OF FIRM

William R. Scherer, Jr., (P.A.)   William V. Carcioppolo (P.A.)
Kenneth C. Jenne, II (P.A.)   James M. Eckhart (P.A.)
Gary S. Genovese (P.A.)   Lynn Futch Cooney (P.A.)

OF COUNSEL

Rex Conrad   Paul R. Larkin, Jr.

ASSOCIATES

Linda Rae Spaulding   Willie Earl Hall
Kimberly A. Kisslan   Derick J. Roulhac
Reid A. Cocalis   William R. Scherer, III
Albert L. Frevola, Jr.   Vanessa A. Reynolds

Local Counsel for: American Home Assurance Group; Caterpillar Tractor Co.; Division of Risk Management, State of Florida; Florida East Coast Railway; Fort Motor Co.; Liberty Mutual Insurance Co.; Ryder Truck Lines; Unigard Insurance Group.
Approved Attorneys for: Attorneys' Title Insurance Fund.
Reference: Barnett Bank of Fort Lauderdale.

For full biographical listings, see the Martindale-Hubbell Law Directory

DOUMAR, CURTIS, CROSS, LAYSTROM & PERLOFF (AV)

A Partnership of Professional Corporations
1177 Southeast Third Avenue, 33316
Telephone: 954-525-3441
Fax: 954-525-3423
Direct Miami Line: 305-945-3172

MEMBERS OF FIRM

Raymond A. Doumar (P.C.)   E. Scott Allsworth (P.C.)
Charles L. Curtis (P.C.)   John D. Voigt (P.C.)
William S. Cross (P.C.)   Jeffrey S. Wachs (P.C.)
C. William Laystrom, Jr. (P.C.)   Mark E. Allsworth
John W. Perloff (P.C.)   Stuart J. Mac Iver

Representative Clients: Albertson's, Inc.; Robinson-Humphrey/American Express; Deutsch-Ireland Properties; Massey-Yardley Chrysler Plymouth, Inc.; Waste Management, Inc.; Planned Development Corp.; Toys-R-Us Inc.; Lumbermans Mutual Casualty Co.; Melvin Simon and Associates.

For full biographical listings, see the Martindale-Hubbell Law Directory

ESLER, PETRIE & LINDIE, P.A. (AV)

Suite 300 The Advocate Building, 315 S.E. Seventh Street, 33301
Telephone: 954-764-5400
FAX: 954-764-5408

Gary A. Esler   C. Daniel Petrie, Jr.
Beth G. Lindie

Representative Clients: The Chubb Group of Insurance Cos.; Fireman's Fund Insurance Co.; State of Florida-Department of Risk Management; Marriott Corp.; Gregson Furniture Industries, Inc.; Winsloew, Inc.; Richfield Hotel Management, Inc.; Mobile America Insurance Group, Inc.; Colonial Penn Insurance Co.
Reference: Capital Bank.

For full biographical listings, see the Martindale-Hubbell Law Directory

Fort Lauderdale—Continued

LAW OFFICES GOLDBERG, YOUNG & GRAVENHORST, P.A. (AV)

1630 North Federal Highway, P.O. Box 23800, 33307
Telephone: 954-564-8000
Telecopier: 954-564-0015
Boca Raton, Florida Office: The Plaza, Suite 303, 5355 Town Center Road.
Telephone: 561-395-1449.
North Palm Beach, Florida Office: Squires Building, Suite 113, 721 U.S. Highway One.
Telephone: 561-842-1986.

Paul Young	Jonathan S. Marcus
Lawrence H. Goldberg	Marvin A. Kirsner (Resident)
Paul S. Gravenhorst	Stephen N. Lipton

Kimberly Lynn Barbar	Suzanne W. Schwartz
Susan K. Connor	Marilyn K. Summitt
Daniel A. Jacobson	Frank A. Utset

Approved Attorneys for: Chicago Title Insurance Co.; Attorney's Title Insurance Fund; First American Title Insurance Co.; Commonwealth Land Title Insurance Cos.; American Pioneer Title Insurance Co.

For full biographical listings, see the Martindale-Hubbell Law Directory

HEINRICH GORDON HARGROVE WEIHE & JAMES, P.A. (AV)

500 East Broward Boulevard, Suite 1000, 33394-3092
Telephone: 954-527-2800
Facsimile: 954-524-9481
Email: heinrich-gordon.com
Palm Beach, Florida Office: 140 Royal Palm Way, Suite 206.
Telephone: 561-832-7600.
Facsimile: 561-833-0805.

Elicia D. Blackwell	Gordon James, III
Mark R. Boyd	Scott A. Markowitz
William Kent Brown	Moises Melendez
Linwood Cabot	Jeffrey A. O'Keefe
Sidney C. Calloway	Christine M. Peirano
Wendy Lynn Furman	Steven L. Redman
(Not admitted in FL)	Valerie Shea
Cathy Jo Goodwin	Gilbert E. Theissen
Richard G. Gordon	Rodney Earl Walton
John R. Hargrove	Kenneth W. Waterway
Eugene L. Heinrich	Bruce A. Weihe

OF COUNSEL
Hugh L. Carey (Not admitted in FL)

For full biographical listings, see the Martindale-Hubbell Law Directory

HOLLAND & KNIGHT LLP (AV)

A Partnership including Professional Corporations
One East Broward Boulevard, Suite 1300, 33301-4811
Telephone: 954-525-1000
Fax: 954-463-2030
Mailing Address: P.O. Box 14070, 33302-4070,
Email: hklaw.com *URL:* http://www.hklaw.com
Jacksonville, Florida Office: 50 N. Laura Street, Suite 3900.
Telephone: 904-353-2000.
Fax: 904-358-1872.
Lakeland, Florida Office: 92 Lake Wire Drive.
Telephone: 941-682-1161.
Fax: 941-688-1186.
Miami, Florida Office: 701 Brickell Avenue, 30th Floor.
Telephone: 305-374-8500.
Fax: 305-787-7799.
Orlando, Florida Office: 200 S. Orange Avenue, Suite 2600.
Telephone: 407-425-8500.
Fax: 407-244-5288.
St. Petersburg, Florida Office: One Progress Plaza, Suite 1600.
Telephone: 813-896-7171.
Fax: 813-822-8048.
Tallahassee, Florida Office: 315 Calhoun Street, Suite 600.
Telephone: 904-224-7000.
Fax: 904-224-8832.
Tampa, Florida Office: 400 North Ashley, Suite 2300.
Telephone: 813-227-8500.
Fax: 813-229-0134.
West Palm Beach, Florida Office: 625 N. Flagler Drive, Suite 700.
Telephone: 561-833-2000.
Fax: 561-650-8399.
Washington, D.C. Office: 2100 Pennsylvania Avenue, N.W.
Telephone: 202-955-3000.
Fax: 202-955-5564.
Atlanta, Georgia Office: 1201 West Peachtree Street, N.E., Suite 2000.
Telephone: 404-817-8500.
Fax: 404-881-0470.

(See Next Column)

FORT LAUDERDALE MEMBERS AND ASSOCIATES

Martin J. Alexander	Gerald L. Knight
Kathryn Klein Anderson	Judith Epstein Kreitzer
Constance R. Barnhart	Marie Lefere
Donn A. Beloff	Peter J. Manso
Curtis R. Cowan	(Not admitted in FL)
Susan F. Delegal	Theresa Wright McLaughlin
Diane A. DePoy	Stephen B. Moss
Irwin J. Fayne	James M. Norman
Robert E. Ferris, Jr.	Donald S. Showalter
Brian Foremny	Steven Sonberg
Joel K. Gustafson	Jon K. Stage
Lori R. Hartglass	Roma W. Theus, II
Thomas L. Kautz	Douglas A. Walker
	(Not admitted in FL)

Rodney H. Bell	Janna Peters Lhota
Teresita Garcia	Robbin Newman
Adam J. Hodkin	Robin S. Rosenbaum
Brian K. Hole	D. Ronald Surbey
Heather C. Keith	Philip E. Ward

Arnold M. Zipper

For full biographical listings, see the Martindale-Hubbell Law Directory

KRUPNICK CAMPBELL MALONE ROSELLI BUSER SLAMA & HANCOCK, P.A. (AV)

700 Southeast 3rd Avenue, 33316
Telephone: 954-763-8181
Fax: 954-763-8292

Jon E. Krupnick	Thomas E. Buser
Walter G. Campbell, Jr.	Joseph J. Slama
Kevin A. Malone	Kelly D. Hancock
Richard J. Roselli	Lisa A. McNelis

Louis R. Battista	Carol J. Healy
Ivan F. Cabrera	Elaine P. Krupnick
Robert D. Erben	Scott S. Liberman
Kelley Badger Gelb	Cinthia M. Manzano

Robert J. McKee

OF COUNSEL

Ben J. Weaver	Dianne Jay Weaver

Reference: Nations Bank.

For full biographical listings, see the Martindale-Hubbell Law Directory

LEONARD & MORRISON (AV)

Tenth Floor, 4875 North Federal Highway, P.O. Box 11025, 33339
Telephone: 954-776-3600
Fax: 954-776-3609

MEMBERS OF FIRM

William F. Leonard	Richard W. Morrison

C. Glenn Leonard

OF COUNSEL

William Robert Leonard

General Counsel for: Coral Ridge Golf Course, Inc.; Gill Hotels Co.; Sheraton Yankee Clipper Hotel; Royal Petroleum, Inc.
Representative Client: Plimpton Trusts.
Reference: Intercontinental Bank.

For full biographical listings, see the Martindale-Hubbell Law Directory

KENNETH R. MIKOS, P.A. (AV)

2780 East Oakland Park Boulevard, 33306
Telephone: 954-566-7200
Facsimile: 954-566-1568

Kenneth R. Mikos

Douglas F. Hoffman

Special Counsel to: Fort Lauderdale Civil Service Board.

For full biographical listings, see the Martindale-Hubbell Law Directory

MORGAN, CARRATT AND O'CONNOR, P.A. (AV)

Suite 500, 2601 East Oakland Park Boulevard, 33306
Telephone: 954-565-0501

Charles R. Morgan (Retired)	Terrence P. O'Connor
Harry G. Carratt	Michael E. O'Connor
Francis D. O'Connor	Gus H. Carratt

Approved Attorneys for: Attorneys' Title Insurance Fund.
Reference: First Union National Bank of Florida, Coral Ridge Branch.

For full biographical listings, see the Martindale-Hubbell Law Directory

Fort Lauderdale—Continued

PETERS, ROBERTSON, LAX, PARSONS, WELCHER, MOWERS & PASSARO, P.A. (AV)

Suite 600, 600 South Andrews Avenue, 34945
Telephone: 954-761-8999
Fax: 954-761-8990
Miami, Florida Office: Suite 600, Ingraham Building, 25 Southeast 2nd Avenue.
Telephone: 305-374-3103.
Fax: 305-377-9805.
Fort Myers, Florida Office: Key West Professional Centre, 1342 Colonial Boulevard, Suite 45.
Telephone: 941-936-1129.
Fax: 941-936-4036.
West Palm Beach, Florida Office: Galleria International Building, 301 Clematis Street, Suite 203.
Telephone: 407-832-9698.
Fax: 407-832-8355.

Geralyn M. Passaro

Steven Charles Simon

Representative Clients: Auto-Owners Insurance Co.; Dade County School Board; Employers Reinsurance Group; Gallagher Bassett Insurance Service; Maryland Casualty Co.

For full biographical listings, see the Martindale-Hubbell Law Directory

RUDEN, McCLOSKY, SMITH, SCHUSTER & RUSSELL, P.A. (AV)

200 East Broward Boulevard, P.O. Box 1900, 33302
Telephone: 954-764-6660
Telecopier: 954-764-4996
Email: info@ruden.com
Miami, Florida Office: Suite 1900 Barnett Tower, 701 Brickell Avenue.
Telephone: 305-789-2700.
Tallahassee, Florida Office: Suite 815, 215 South Monroe Street.
Telephone: 904-681-9027.
Naples, Florida Office: Suite 210, 5811 Pelican Bay Boulevard.
Telephone: 941-566-1221.
Sarasota, Florida Office: Suite 600, 1549 Ringling Boulevard.
Telephone: 941-365-0140.
St. Petersburg, Florida Office: Suite 1700, 150 Second Avenue North, P.O. Box 14034.
Telephone: 813-895-1971.
Tampa, Florida Office: Suite 2120, 100 North Tampa.
Telephone: 813-221-8027.

Lance H. Baker	Dennis D. Mele
Jeffrey H. Beck	Robert H. Miltenberger, II
David K. Blattner	Susan Patrey Motley
Thomas R. Bolf	Kevin J. O'Grady
Anibal Jose Cortina	David F. Parish
Michele Kane Cummings	John H. Pelzer
John L. Farquhar	Terrence Russell
Scott J. Fuerst	Bonnie S. Satterfield
Denise J. Ganz	Carl Schuster
Melinda S. Gentile	John L. Shiekman
W. Wyndham Geyer, Jr.	Peter D. Slavis
Bruce A. Goodman	Glenn N. Smith
Bruce D. Goorland	Barry E. Somerstein
Mark F. Grant	Mark K. Somerstein
Thomas O. Katz	Edwin J. Stacker
Michael H. Krul	Glen A. Stankee
Barry A. Mandelkorn	Elliot M. Stern
Scott H. Margol	John T. Winburn
Donald C. McClosky	Donald C. Works, III
Brian S. McHugh	David A. Zulian

Nathan A. Adams, IV	Bryan S. Greenberg
David T. Adonailo	Andrew M. Gross
Richard A. Aronsky	John R. Keller
Jeffrey A. Baskies	Beth-Ann Ellenberg Krimsky
Jerry Peter Brodsky	Robert B. Lochrie, III
Michael K. Chernick	Bruce E. Loren
Howard D. Cohen	Christine Q. McLeod
Michael A. Cohn	Bonnie L. Miskel
Corey Collins	Joseph Livio Parisi
Mitchell E. Cook	Maria L. Periharos
Michael E. Coviello	Paul B. Ranis
Teri L. Di Giulian	Ricardo A. Reyes
Joseph T. Ducanis Jr.	Jennifer J. Robinson
Daniella Friedman	Marlo Powell-Robinson
Thomas K. Gallagher	Shari J. Ronkin
Steven M. Gerson	Manuel R. Valcarcel, IV
Allyson DeLanie Goodwin	Jeffrey A. Weissman

Andrew D. Zaron

OF COUNSEL

Bruno L. Di Giulian	Sherman A. Katz
Samuel S. Fields	Robert G. Schrader

James F. Valenti, Jr.

(See Next Column)

SPECIAL COUNSEL
Mortyn K. Zietz (Not admitted in FL)

For full biographical listings, see the Martindale-Hubbell Law Directory

SHELDON J. SCHLESINGER, P.A. (AV)

1212 Southeast Third Avenue, 33335
Telephone: 954-467-8800

Sheldon J. Schlesinger	Robert W. Kelley
Scott P. Schlesinger	Sara C. Lindsey

For full biographical listings, see the Martindale-Hubbell Law Directory

WALTON LANTAFF SCHROEDER & CARSON (AV)

A Partnership including Professional Associations
Blackstone Building, Third Floor, 707 Southeast Third Avenue, P.O. Box 14309, 33302
Telephone: 954-463-8456
Telecopier: 954-763-6294
Miami, Florida Office: One Biscayne Tower, 25th Floor, 2 South Biscayne Boulevard.
Telephone: 305-379-6411.
Telecopier: 305-577-3875.
West Palm Beach, Florida Office: United National Bank Tower, Suite 800, 1645 Palm Beach Lakes Boulevard.
Telephone: 407-689-6700.
Telecopier: 407-689-2647.
Coral Gables, Florida Office: Suite 1101, Gables International Plaza, 2655 Le Jeune Road.
Telephone: 305-379-6411.
Telecopier: 305-446-9206.

RESIDENT PARTNERS

Stephen W. Bazinsky	Beth J. Leahy
Jonathan J. Davis	Deborah Poore Knight
Gregory J. Willis	Richard G. Rosenblum

Michael W. Baker

RESIDENT ASSOCIATES
Frank J. Taddeo

For full biographical listings, see the Martindale-Hubbell Law Directory

FORT MYERS,* Lee Co.

GOLDBERG, GOLDSTEIN & BUCKLEY, P.A. (AV)

1515 Broadway, P.O. Box 2366, 33901-2366
Telephone: 941-334-1146
Fax: 941-334-3039
Naples, Florida Office: 2150 Goodlette Road, Suite 105, Parkway Financial Center, 34102.
Telephone: 941-262-4888.
Fax: 941-262-8716.
Port Charlotte, Florida Office: Emerald Square, Suite 1, 2852 Tamiami Trail, 33952.
Telephone: 941-624-2393.
Fax: 941-624-2155.
Cape Coral, Florida Office: 1603 Hancock Bridge Parkway, 33990.
Telephone: 941-574-5575.
Fax: 941-574-9213.
Lehigh Acres, Florida Office: 1458 Lee Boulevard, Lee Boulevard Shopping Center, 33936.
Telephone: 941-368-6101.
Fax: 941-368-2461.
South Fort Myers, Florida Office: Horizon Plaza, 16050 South Tamiami Trail, Suite 101, 33908.
Telephone: 941-433-6777.
Fax: 941-433-0578.
Bonita Springs, Florida Office: 3431 Bonita Beach Road, Suite 208, 34134.
Telephone: 941-495-0003.
Fax: 941-495-0564.

Ray Goldstein	George J. Mitar
Stephen W. Buckley	Michael J. Ciccarone
Harvey B. Goldberg	Jay Cooper
John B. Cechman	Jonathan D. Conant
J. Jeffrey Rice	Raymond L. Racila
Richard Lee Purtz	Luis E. Insignares
Martin G. Arnowitz	Scot D. Goldberg

Approved Attorneys for: Attorneys' Title Insurance Fund.

For full biographical listings, see the Martindale-Hubbell Law Directory

HENDERSON, FRANKLIN, STARNES & HOLT, PROFESSIONAL ASSOCIATION (AV)

1715 Monroe Street, P.O. Box 280, 33902-0280
Telephone: 941-334-4121
Telecopier: 941-332-4494

(See Next Column)

HENDERSON, FRANKLIN, STARNES & HOLT PROFESSIONAL ASSOCIATION—
Continued

Albert M. Frierson	Douglas B. Szabo
Ernest H. Hatch, Jr.	Charles J. Basinait
Stephen L. Helgemo	Randal H. Thomas
Ronald W. Smalley	Robert C. Shearman
John A. Noland	Andrew L. Ringers, Jr.
William N. Horowitz	John F. Potanovic, Jr.
Gerald W. Pierce	Thomas H. Gunderson
J. Terrence Porter	David K. Fowler
Michael J. Corso	Paula F. Kelley
Vicki L. Sproat	Timothy J. Jesaitis
Denis H. Noah	Jeffrey D. Kottkamp
John W. Lewis	J. Eric Stiffler
Craig Ferrante	Bridget A. Mast
James L. Nulman	Theresa M. Kolish
Harold N. Hume, Jr.	Tricia A. Krinek
Bruce M. Stanley	J. Tom Smoot III
Daniel W. Sheppard	Thomas P. Clark
Russell P. Schropp	Janet C. Bernstein
Chad J. Motes	Michael S. Gross
Guy E. Whitesman	Mary G. Jack
Steven G. Koeppel	Cora Cisneros Molloy

Representative Clients: Aetna Property & Casualty Group; CIGNA Group; CSX Transportation, Inc.; Fireman's Fund Insurance Cos.; Barnett Bank of Lee County, N.A.; Northern Trust Bank of Florida, N.A.; The Hartford Insurance Group; Travelers Group; United Telephone Company of Florida.

For full biographical listings, see the Martindale-Hubbell Law Directory

---

LAW OFFICES OF LLOYD G. HENDRY, P.A. (AV)

Society First Federal Center, 2201 Second Street, Suite 502, P.O. Box 1509, 33902
Telephone: 941-332-7123
Fax: 941-332-5147

Lloyd G. Hendry	Mary Hendry Sonne
Harry O. Hendry	

For full biographical listings, see the Martindale-Hubbell Law Directory

---

PETERS, ROBERTSON, LAX, PARSONS, WELCHER, MOWERS & PASSARO, P.A. (AV)

Key West Professional Centre, 1342 Colonial Boulevard, Suite 7, 33907
Telephone: 941-936-1129
Fax: 941-936-4036
Miami, Florida Office: Suite 600, Ingraham Building, 25 Southeast 2nd Avenue.
Telephone: 305-374-3103.
Fax: 305-377-9805.
Fort Lauderdale, Florida Office: Suite 600, 600 South Andrews Avenue.
Telephone: 954-761-8999.
Fax: 954-761-8990.
West Palm Beach, Florida Office: Galleria International Building, 301 Clematis Street, Suite 203.
Telephone: 407-832-9698.
Fax: 407-832-8355.

Steven B. Sundook

Representative Clients: Auto-Owners Insurance Co.; Dade County School Board; Employers Reinsurance Group; Gallagher Bassett Insurance Service; Maryland Casualty Co.

For full biographical listings, see the Martindale-Hubbell Law Directory

---

SHEPPARD, BRETT, STEWART & HERSCH, P.A. (AV)

(Formerly Sheppard & Woolslair)
2121 West First Street, P.O. Drawer 400, 33902
Telephone: 941-334-1141
Fax: 941-334-3965

W. A. Sheppard (1898-1971)	Jay Andrew Brett
John K. Woolslair (1908-1968)	John F. Stewart
Craig R. Hersch	

OF COUNSEL
John Woolslair Sheppard

D. Hugh Kinsey, Jr.

Approved Attorneys for: Attorneys' Title Insurance Fund; Chicago Title Insurance Co.

For full biographical listings, see the Martindale-Hubbell Law Directory

---

SMOOT ADAMS EDWARDS & GREEN, P.A. (AV)

One University Park Suite 600, 12800 University Drive, P.O. Box 60259, 33906-6259
Telephone: 941-489-1776
(800) 226-1777 (in Florida)
Fax: 941-489-2444
Email: 71600.2745@compuserve.com

J. Tom Smoot, Jr.	Bruce D. Green
Hal Adams	Steven I. Winer
Franklyn A. (Chip) Johnson	Mark R. Komray
(1947-1991)	Clayton W. Crevasse
Charles B. Edwards	M. Brian Cheffer

Robert S. Forman	C. Berk Edwards, Jr.
Kathleen W. McBride	Melville G. Brinson, III
Lowell Schoenfeld	Samuel J. Hagan, IV.

For full biographical listings, see the Martindale-Hubbell Law Directory

---

FORT PIERCE,* St. Lucie Co.

BRENNAN, HAYSKAR, JEFFERSON, WALKER & SCHWERER, PROFESSIONAL ASSOCIATION (AV)

515-519 South Indian River Drive, P.O. Box 3779, 34948-3779
Telephone: 561-461-2310
Fax: 561-468-6580

John T. Brennan	Bradford L. Jefferson
Thad H. Carlton (1906-1965)	Robert V. Schwerer
Stephen G. Hayskar	James T. Walker

Frederick D. Stalls	Garrison M. Dundas
	Steven R. McCain

Representative Clients: Allstate Insurance Co.; Auto Owners Insurance Co.; Canal Insurance Co.; City of Fort Pierce; City of Stuart; First Union National Bank; First National Bank & Trust Co. of the Treasure Coast; Florida Farm Bureau Insurance Group; Kemper Insurance Group.

For full biographical listings, see the Martindale-Hubbell Law Directory

---

FORT WALTON BEACH, Okaloosa Co.

SMITH, GRIMSLEY, BAUMAN, PINKERTON, PETERMANN, SAXER & WELLS (AV)

A Partnership of Professional Associations
25 Walter Martin Avenue, P.O. Box 2379, 32549
Telephone: 904-243-8194
Telecopier: 904-664-5728

MEMBERS OF FIRM

Walter J. Smith (P.A.)	Drew S. Pinkerton (P.A.)
James W. Grimsley (P.A.)	Richard P. Petermann (P.A.)
Steven B. Bauman (P.A.)	Christopher P. Saxer (P.A.)
Kelvin Clyde Wells (P.A.)	

Representative Clients: First City Bank of Fort Walton; Regions Bank; First Alabama Bank; Vanguard Bank; Eglin BMW-Mazda; Preston Hood Chevrolet; Noland Co.; Abbott Realty Services.

For full biographical listings, see the Martindale-Hubbell Law Directory

---

GREEN COVE SPRINGS,* Clay Co. — (Refer to Jacksonville)

HOLLYWOOD, Broward Co.

ELLIS, SPENCER AND BUTLER (AV)

Emerald Hills Executive Plaza I, 4601 Sheridan Street, Suite 505, 33021
Telephone: Broward: 954-986-2291
Dade Line: 305-947-0620
Facsimile: 954-986-2778
Email: esb@esblaw.com

MEMBERS OF FIRM

Robert B. Butler	Robert Paul Keeley
W. Tinsley Ellis	Jonathan E. Brody
William S. Spencer	Chapman L. Smith, Jr.
Mark F. Butler	Charles S. Kyriazos
John C. Primeau	

OF COUNSEL
Sherwood Spencer (Retired)

General Counsel for: American Bank of Hollywood.
Representative Clients: American Bank of Hollywood; Bank of North America; Banaszak Concrete Corp.; Peakload, Inc. of America; Doby Building Supply, Inc.; Michael Swerdlow Companies; Construction Management Services, Inc.

For full biographical listings, see the Martindale-Hubbell Law Directory

Hollywood—Continued

MILLER, SCHWARTZ AND MILLER, P.A. (AV)

4040 Sheridan Street, 33021
Telephone: Hollywood: 954-962-2000
Miami: 625-3630
Telefax: 954-961-2124
954-962-3963

Joseph L. Schwartz	A. Matthew Miller
James Fox Miller	Robert M. Schwartz
	Charles Fox Miller

Approved Attorneys for: Attorneys' Title Insurance Fund.
Reference: First Union National Bank of Florida, Hollywood, Florida.

For full biographical listings, see the Martindale-Hubbell Law Directory

JACKSONVILLE,* Duval Co.

CORBIN, DICKINSON, DUVALL & KITCHEN (AV)

121 West Forsyth Street, Suite 1000, P.O. Box 41566, 32203
Telephone: 904-356-8073
Telecopier: 904-358-2319

MEMBERS OF FIRM

Peter Reed Corbin	John E. Duvall
John F. Dickinson	F. Damon Kitchen

ASSOCIATES

Richard L. Ruth	Kimberly A. Cannon

For full biographical listings, see the Martindale-Hubbell Law Directory

FANNIN, TYLER & HAMILTON, P.A. (AV)

Park Pointe, Suite D, 4741 Atlantic Boulevard, 32207-2127
Telephone: 904-398-9999
Facsimile: 904-398-0806

John F. Fannin	H. Tyrone Tyler
	J. Clark Hamilton, Jr.

Laura Fannin Jacqmein

For full biographical listings, see the Martindale-Hubbell Law Directory

FOLEY & LARDNER (AV)

The Greenleaf Building, 200 Laura Street, P.O. Box 240, 32201-0240
Telephone: 904-359-2000
Facsimile: 904-359-8700
Milwaukee, Wisconsin Office: Firstar Center, 777 East Wisconsin Avenue.
Telephone: 414-271-2400.
Telex: 26-819 (Foley Lard Mil).
Facsimile: 414-297-4900.
Madison, Wisconsin Office: Verex Plaza, 150 East Gilman Street, P.O. Box 1497.
Telephone: 608-257-5035.
Telex: 262051 (F L Madison).
Facsimile: 608-258-4258.
Chicago, Illinois Office: Suite 3300, One IBM Plaza, 330 N. Wabash Avenue.
Telephone: 312-755-1900.
Facsimile: 312-755-1925.
Washington, D.C. Office: Washington Harbour, Suite 500, 3000 K Street, N.W.
Telephone: 202-672-5300.
Telex: 904136 (Foley Lard Wsh).
Facsimile: 202-672-5399.
Annapolis, Maryland Office: Suite 102, 175 Admiral Cochrane Drive.
Telephone: 301-266-8077.
Telex: 899149 (Oldtownpat).
Facsimile: 301-266-8664.
Orlando, Florida Office: Suite 1800, 111 North Orange Avenue, P.O. Box 2193.
Telephone: 407-423-7656.
Telex: 441781 (HQ ORL).
Facsimile: 407-648-1743.
Tallahassee, Florida Office: Suite 300, 123 South Calhoun Street, P.O. Box 508.
Telephone: 904-222-6100.
Facsimile: 904-224-0496.
Tampa, Florida Office: Suite 2700, One Hundred N. Tampa Street, P.O. Box 3391.
Telephones: 813-229-2300; Pinellas County: 813-442-3296.
Facsimile: 813-221-4210. Pinellas County: 813-446-9641.
Facsimile: 813-229-6282.
West Palm Beach, Florida Office: Suite 200, Phillips Point East Tower, 777 South Flagler Drive.
Telephone: 407-655-5050.
Facsimile: 407-655-6925.
Brussels, Belgium Office: Avenue Louise, 283.
Telephone: 32-2-346-2777.
Facsimile: 32-2-646-7574.

(See Next Column)

Foley Lardner Weissburg & Aronson Office Locations:
Los Angeles, California Office: 2049 Century Park East, Suite 3200.
Telephone: 310-277-2223.
Fax: 310-557-8475.
Sacramento, California Office: 770 L Street, Suite 1050.
Telephone: 916-443-8005.
Fax: 916-443-2240.
San Diego California Office: 402 West Broadway, 23rd Floor.
Telephone: 619-234-6655.
Fax: 619-234-3510.
San Francisco, California Office: One Maritime Plaza, Sixth Floor.
Telephone: 415-434-4484.
Fax: 415-434-4507.

PARTNERS

John W. Caven, Jr.	Emerson M. Lotzia
Allan P. Clark	Jean M. Mangu
Charles E. Commander, III	E. Robert Meek
Gardner F. Davis	Sybil Meloy
Guy O. Farmer II	Luther F. Sadler, Jr.
Charles V. Hedrick	John T. Sefton
Linda Yayoi Kelso	John A. Tucker
William D. King	John M. Welch, Jr.
Chauncey W. Lever, Jr.	Steven A. Werber

OF COUNSEL

Jack H. Chambers	Paul C. Vance
Christopher H. Smith	
(Not admitted in FL)	

RETIRED PARTNERS

Thomas B. Slade, III

RESIDENT ASSOCIATES

Laura Henry Allen	Gary Ray Driver, Jr.
Charles B. Bennett	Melissa O. Hanson
Robert S. Bernstein	Richard W. Hawthorne
Jonathan D. Boggs	Chanley T. Howell
(Not admitted in FL)	Kevin E. Hyde
Tracy S. Carlin	Beth Joseph
John P. Cole	Kevin P. Leasure
David C. Cook	Matthew Stuart McAfee
Leah G. Cooper	Jeffrey M. McFarland
	Scott D. Richburg

For full biographical listings, see the Martindale-Hubbell Law Directory

GABEL & HAIR (AV)

76 South Laura Street, Suite 1600, 32202-3421
Telephone: 904-353-7329
Fax: 904-358-1637
Email: lawoffcs@gabelhair.com

MEMBERS OF FIRM

George D. Gabel, Jr.	Sheldon Boney Forte
Mattox S. Hair	Timothy J. Conner
Joel B. Toomey	Suzanne Meyer Judas
Robert M. Dees	Karen Harris Williams

ASSOCIATES

Michael L. Berry, Jr.	Karl B. Hanson, III
Robert Blaine Birthisel	Brooks Charles Rathet

Scott M. Loftin (1878-1953)	Harold B. Wahl (1907-1993)

Representative Clients: Florida Publishing Co. (Florida Times-Union); Florida Hotel-Motel Self Insurers Fund; Southern Bell Telephone & Telegraph Co.; Florida East Coast Railway Co.; WTLV Channel 12 TV; The Steamship Mutual Underwriting Association, Ltd.; The Standard Steamship Owners Protection & Indemnity Association, Ltd.; The Japan Ship Owners Mutual Protection & Indemnity Association; Liverpool & London Steamship Protection & Indemnity Association; Exxon Corp.

For full biographical listings, see the Martindale-Hubbell Law Directory

HOLLAND & KNIGHT LLP (AV)

A Partnership including Professional Corporations
50 N. Laura Street, Suite 3900, 32202
Telephone: 904-353-2000
Fax: 904-358-1872
Mailing Address: P.O. Box 52687, 32201
Email: hklaw.com *URL:* http://www.hklaw.com
Fort Lauderdale, Florida Office: One East Broward Boulevard, Suite 1300.
Telephone: 954-525-1000.
Fax: 954-463-2030.
Lakeland, Florida Office: 92 Lake Wire Drive.
Telephone: 941-682-1161.
Fax: 941-688-1186.
Miami, Florida Office: 701 Brickell Avenue, 30th Floor.
Telephone: 305-374-8500.
Fax: 305-787-7799.
Orlando, Florida Office: 200 S. Orange Avenue, Suite 2600.
Telephone: 407-425-8500.
Fax: 407-244-5288.

(See Next Column)

HOLLAND & KNIGHT LLP—*Continued*

St. Petersburg, Florida Office: One Progress Plaza, Suite 1600.
Telephone: 813-896-7171.
Fax: 813-822-8048.
Tallahassee, Florida Office: 315 Calhoun Street, Suite 600.
Telephone: 904-224-7000.
Fax: 904-224-8832.
Tampa, Florida Office: 400 North Ashley, Suite 2300.
Telephone: 813-227-8500.
Fax: 813-229-0134.
West Palm Beach Office: 625 N. Flagler Drive, Suite 700.
Telephone: 561-833-2000.
Fax: 561-650-8399.
Washington, D.C. Office: 2100 Pennsylvania Avenue, N.W.
Telephone: 202-955-3000.
Fax: 202-955-5564.
Atlanta, Georgia Office: 1201 West Peachtree Street, N.E., Suite 2000.
Telephone: 404-817-8500.
Fax: 404-881-0470.

JACKSONVILLE MEMBERS AND ASSOCIATES

Mark G. Alexander	Deborah A. Knauer
Charles W. Arnold, Jr.	Sharon Strayer Learch
Robert J. Beckham	Frederick J. Lotterhos, III
L. Kinder Cannon, III	Dominic C. MacKenzie
Valerie C. Chritton	Scott D. Makar
Hume F. Coleman	John M. McNatt, Jr.
Raymond Ehrlich	John J. Mikals
Robert R. Feagin, III	George E. Schulz, Jr.
Charlene Francis	Leonard A. Selber
Christopher J. Greene	M. Kami Smith
Lawrence J. Hamilton II	Donald W. Wallis
Linda Connor Kane	Alan M. Weiss

Martha McMahon Wirtz

Crystal J. Adkins	Todd C. Johnson
Thomas E. Bishop	Adam J. Kohl
Michael L Buckner	Frank A. Lonegro
Christopher G. Commander	Chad S. Roberts
Raye Curry	Ann R. Shorstein
Margaret Widman Dees	Gregory Williamson

COUNSEL

J. Shepard Bryan, Jr.	Philip Selber

For full biographical listings, see the Martindale-Hubbell Law Directory

MARKS, GRAY, CONROY & GIBBS, P.A. (AV)

Suite 800, 1200 Riverplace Boulevard, 32207
Telephone: 904-398-0900
Telecopier: 904-399-8440
Mailing Address: P.O. Box 447, 32201
Email: marksgra@gate.net

Richard P. Marks (1876-1942)	William M. Corley
Francis Michael Holt (1884-1946)	Jeptha F. Barbour
	Linda Cobb Ingham
James A. Yates (1885-1960)	Susan Smith Erdelyi
Sam R. Marks (1885-1973)	Robert E. Broach
Harry T. Gray (1890-1975)	Alan K. Ragan
Francis P. Conroy (1912-1991)	Daniel A. Nicholas
Delbridge L. Gibbs (1917-1992)	Stephen B. Gallagher
James C. Rinaman, Jr.	Milo Scott Thomas
H. Franklin Perritt, Jr.	Gregory A. Lawrence
Victor M. Halbach, Jr.	Edward Keenan Cottrell
Gerald W. Weedon	Leigh A. Studdard
Nicholas V. Pulignano, Jr.	James A. Hoener

OF COUNSEL
Randal C. Fairbanks

Representative Clients: Alamo Rent-A-Car, Inc.; American International Group; American President Lines, Ltd.; American Savings of Florida; Amerisure Insurance Group; Anesthesiologists' Professional Assurance Trust; Associated Aviation Underwriters; Barnett Bank, Inc.; Baxter Healthcare Corp.; Clorox Company.

For full biographical listings, see the Martindale-Hubbell Law Directory

MARTIN, ADE, BIRCHFIELD & MICKLER, P.A. (AV)

One Independent Drive Suite 3000, Post Office Box 59, 32201
Telephone: 904-354-2050
Fax: 904-354-5842

James L. Ade	Sharon Roberts Henderson
Lynda R. Aycock	Barbara Christie Johnston
W. O. Birchfield	Ralph H. Martin
Timothy A. Burleigh	Robert O. Mickler
Charles L. Cranford	John D. Milton, Jr.
Stephen H. Durant	Daniel B. Nunn, Jr.
T. William Glocker	Scott G. Schildberg
Stephen D. Halker	Gary Wilkinson

(See Next Column)

Phillip A. Delmont	Wilhelmina F. Kightlinger
Michael E. Goodbread, Jr.	Myra Loughran

Representative Clients: Continental Cablevision, Inc. (CATV); Deerwood/-Gate Lands; General Waterworks Corp.; Wilma South Corp.; First Union National Bank of Florida; Mac Papers, Inc.; Tree of Life, Inc.; United Water Florida, Inc.

For full biographical listings, see the Martindale-Hubbell Law Directory

McGUIRE, WOODS, BATTLE & BOOTHE (AV)

Barnett Center, Suite 2750, 50 North Laura Street, 32202-3635
Telephone: 904-798-3200
Fax: 904-798-3207
URL: http://www.mwbb.com
Alexandria, Virginia Office: McGuire, Woods, Battle & Boothe, L.L.P., Transpotomac Plaza, Suite 1000, 1199 North Fairfax Street, 22314-1437.
Telephone: 703-739-6200.
Fax: 703-739-6270.
Baltimore, Maryland Office: McGuire, Woods, Battle & Boothe, L.L.P., The Blaustein Building, One North Charles Street, 21201-3793.
Telephone: 410-659-4400.
Fax: 410-659-4599.
Charlottesville, Virginia Office: McGuire, Woods, Battle & Boothe, L.L.P., Court Square Building, P.O. Box 1288, 22902-1288.
Telephone: 804-977-2500.
Fax: 804-980-2222.
McLean, (Tysons Corner) Virginia Office: McGuire, Woods, Battle & Boothe, L.L.P., 8280 Greensboro Drive, Suite 900, Tysons Corner, 22102-3892.
Telephone: 703-712-5000.
Fax: 703-712-5050.
Norfolk, Virginia Office: McGuire, Woods, Battle & Booth, L.L.P., World Trade Center, Suite 9000, 101 West Main Street, 23510-1655.
Telephone: 757-640-3700.
Fax: 757-640-3701.
Richmond, Virginia Office: McGuire, Woods, Battle & Boothe, L.L.P., One James Center, 901 East Cary Street, 23219-4030.
Telephone: 804-775-1000.
Fax: 804-775-1061.
Washington, D.C. Office: McGuire, Woods, Battle & Boothe, L.L.P., The Army and Navy Club Building, 1627 Eye Street, N.W., 20006-4007.
Telephone: 202-857-1700.
Fax: 202-857-1737.
Brussels, Belgium Office: McGuire, Woods, Battle & Boothe, L.L.P., 250 Avenue Louise, Bte. 64, 1050.
Telephone: (32 2) 629 42 11.
Fax: (32 2) 629 42 22.
Zürich, Switzerland Office: McGuire, Woods, Battle & Boothe, L.L.P., Bahnhofstrasse 3, 8022.
Telephone: (41 1) 225 20 00.
Fax: (41 1) 225 20 20.

MEMBERS OF FIRM

Donald D. Anderson	Randal H. Drew
Scott S. Cairns	Nathan D. Goldman
Michael F. Dawes	Gresham R. Stoneburner

ASSOCIATES

Michael A. Abel	Marcia Morales Howard
Gwen Hutcheson Griggs	Keith D. Munson

For full biographical listings, see the Martindale-Hubbell Law Directory

MOSELEY, WARREN, PRICHARD & PARRISH, P.A. (AV)

501 West Bay Street, 32202
Telephone: 904-356-1306
Cable Address: "Ragland"
Telex: 5-6374
Telecopier: 904-354-0194

Reuben Ragland (1882-1954)	Joseph W. Prichard, Jr.
Louis Kurz (1891-1965)	Robert B. Parrish
E. Dale Joyner (1943-1993)	Andrew J. Knight II
James F. Moseley	Richard K. Jones
Robert E. Warren	James F. Moseley, Jr.

Phillip A. Buhler	Stanley M. Weston
Melanie E. Shepherd	Kimberly Held Israel
Victor J. Zambetti	Tracy A. Chesser
Mathew G. Nasrallah	Ivan A. Colao

OF COUNSEL

James E. Williams	Neil C. Taylor

Counsel for: CSX Transportation; Britannia Steam Ship Insurance Assn., Ltd.; The West of England Protection & Indemnity Assn. (Luxembourg); Crowley American Transport Services, Inc.; Howard Johnson Co.; United Kingdom Mutual Steamship Assurance Assn., Ltd. (Bermuda); General Food Corp.; The London Steam-Ship Owners' Mutual Insurance Assn., Ltd.

For full biographical listings, see the Martindale-Hubbell Law Directory

Jacksonville—Continued

SMITH HULSEY & BUSEY (AV)

1800 First Union National Bank Tower, 225 Water Street, P.O. Box
53315, 32201-3315
Telephone: 904-359-7700
Facsimile: 904-359-7708; 353-9908

Lloyd Smith (1915-1987)
MEMBERS OF FIRM

Dennis L. Blackburn	E. Owen McCuller, Jr.
Stephen D. Busey	James H. Post
Douglas D. Chunn	Bryan L. Putnal
Earl E. Googe, Jr.	E. Lanny Russell
Jeanne E. Helton	Joel Settembrini, Jr.
Cynthia C. Jackson	Tim E. Sleeth
G. Preston Keyes	John R. Smith, Jr.
William E. Kuntz	James J. Taylor, Jr.
M. Richard Lewis, Jr.	Timothy W. Volpe
John F. MacLennan	Waddell A. Wallace, III
Raymond R. Magley	Harry M. Wilson, III

Michael M. Bajalia	R. Leanne McKnight
James A. Bolling, Jr.	Mary E. McManus
E. Lanier Drew	Jeanne M. Miller
Diana Salama Farhat	Stephen D. Moore, Jr.
Martin A. Fitzpatrick	Howard J. Smith
Michael R. Freed	Steven G. Spears
Lee G. Kellison	Melissa Smith Turra
Lauren P. Langham	Herschel T. Vinyard, Jr
Marjorie Conner Makar	Leslie A. Wickes
Bradley R. Markey	Karl A. Zillgitt

OF COUNSEL

Mark Hulsey	John E. Thrasher

Representative Clients: Baptist/St. Vincent's Health System, Inc.; Browning-
Ferris Industries, Inc.; Champion Realty Corp. (Florida); First Union National Bank of Florida; Florida Rock Industries, Inc.; PGA Tour, Inc.;
KPMG Peat Marwick; The Regency Group, Inc.; The Ritz-Carlton Hotel
Co.; University of Florida.

For full biographical listings, see the Martindale-Hubbell Law Directory

SQUIRE, SANDERS & DEMPSEY (AV)

One Enterprise Center Suite 2100, 225 Water Street, 32202-4424
Telephone: 904-353-1264
Fax: 904-356-2986
Cleveland, Ohio Office: 4900 Key Tower, 127 Public Square, Cleveland,
Ohio 44114-1304.
Telephone: 216-479-8500. *Fax's:* 216-479-8780, 216-479-8781,
216-479-8787, 216-479-8795, 216-479-8793, 216-479-8776, 216-479-4877.
Columbus, Ohio Offices: 1300 Huntington Center, 41 South High Street,
Columbus, Ohio 43215-6150.
Telephone: 614-365-2700.
Fax: 614-365-2499.
Miami, Florida Office: 201 South Biscayne Boulevard, Suite 2900 Miami
Center, Miami, Florida 33131-4330.
Telephone: 305-577-8700.
Fax: 305-358-1425.
New York, New York Office: 350 Park Avenue, 15th Floor, New York,
New York 10022-4232.
Telephone: 212-872-9800.
Fax: 212-872-9815.
Phoenix, Arizona Office: Two Renaissance Square, 40 North Central
Avenue, Suite 2700, Phoenix, Arizona 85004-4441.
Telephone: 602-528-4000.
Fax: 602-253-8129.
Washington, D.C. Office: 1201 Pennsylvania Avenue, N.W., P.O. Box 407,
Washington, D.C. 20044-0407.
Telephone: 202-626-6600.
Fax: 202-626-6780.
London, England Office: 4th Floor, Royex House, Aldermanbury Square,
London EC2V 7HR.
Telephone: 011-44-171-830-0055.
Fax: 011-44-171-830-0056.
Brussels, Belgium Office: Avenue Louise, 165-Box 15, 1050 Brussels,
Belgium.
Telephone: 011-32-2-648-1717.
Fax: 011-32-2-648-1064.
Prague, Czech Republic Office: Vaclavske Namesti 57, 11000 PRAHA 1,
Czech Republic.
Telephone: 011-42-2-216-62111.
Fax: 011-42-2-216-62222.
Bratislava, Slovakia Office: Zochova 5, 811 03 Bratislava, Slovak Republic.
Telephone: 011-42-7-531-7611.
Fax: 011-42-7-580-2212.
Budapest, Hungary Office: Deak Ferenc Ut. 10, Office 304,H-1052
Budapest V., Hungary.
Telephones: 011-361-226-2024; 011-361-226-5038.
Fax: 011-361-226-2025.
Kiev, Ukraine Office: vul. Prorizna 9, KV 20, Kiev 252035, Ukraine.
Telephone: 011-380-44-244-3452.
Fax: 011-380-44-228-4938.

(See Next Column)

Moscow, Russian Federation Office: 28 Pokrovka Street, No. 4-4A,
Moscow 103062, Russian Federation.
Telephone: 7-503-956-3750.
Fax: 7-503-956-3635.

RESIDENT MEMBERS

Peter L. Dame	Robert O. Freeman
Judson Freeman, Jr.	John L. McWilliams, III

RESIDENT ASSOCIATES
Alexandra M. MacLennan

For full biographical listings, see the Martindale-Hubbell Law Directory

---

JASPER, * Hamilton Co. — (Refer to Madison)

KEY BISCAYNE, Dade Co.

ROBERTS & SALAZAR, L.L.P. (AV)

The Professionals' Building of Key Biscayne, 50 West Mashta
Drive, 33149
Telephone: 305-361-1383
Fax: 305-361-0385

Norman T. Roberts	Lisette Pie Salazar

OF COUNSEL
Marc A. Kuperman

Reference: Key Biscayne Bank and Trust Co.

For full biographical listings, see the Martindale-Hubbell Law Directory

---

KISSIMMEE, * Osceola Co.

TROUTMAN, WILLIAMS, IRVIN, GREEN & HELMS, PROFESSIONAL ASSOCIATION (AV)

Suite 206, 120 Broadway, 34741
Telephone: 407-933-8834
Telefax: 407-933-8253
Toll Free: 1-800-486-5149
Winter Park, Florida Office: 311 West Fairbanks Avenue, 32789.
Telephone: 407-647-2277.
Telefax: 407-628-2986.

Russell Troutman	Jack E. Bowen

LAKE CITY, * Columbia Co.

BRANNON, BROWN, HALEY, ROBINSON & BULLOCK, P.A. (AV)

10 North Columbia Street, P.O. Box 1029, 32056
Telephone: 904-752-3213
Fax: 904-755-4524

W. Brantley Brannon	Thomas W. Brown
(1907-1985)	Bruce W. Robinson
Clarence E. Brown	Stephen C. Bullock
William J. Haley	Robert E. Case, Jr.

Jaime Austrich

Counsel for: Aero Corp.; Barnett Bank of North Central Florida; Florida
Farm Bureau Insurance Co.; Florida Power & Light Co.; Home Insurance
Co.; Maryland Casualty Co.; Suwannee River Water Management District;
Travelers Insurance Co.; Packaging Corporation of America.

For full biographical listings, see the Martindale-Hubbell Law Directory

---

DARBY, PEELE, BOWDOIN & PAYNE (AV)

A Partnership including Professional Associations
327 North Hernando Street, P.O. Drawer 1707, 32056
Telephone: 904-752-4120
Fax: 904-755-4569

Herbert F. Darby (P.A.)	M. Blair Payne
S. Austin Peele (P.A.)	Thomas J. Kennon, III
W. Roderick Bowdoin (P.A.)	Teresa Byrd Morgan

Representative Clients: City of Jasper; City of Lake City; First Federal Savings Bank of Florida; General Motors Acceptance Corp.; NationsBank N.A.
(South); Town of White Springs; Rayonier, Inc.

For full biographical listings, see the Martindale-Hubbell Law Directory

---

LAKELAND, Polk Co.

HAHN, McCLURG, WATSON, GRIFFITH & BUSH, P.A. (AV)

101 South Florida Avenue, P.O. Box 38, 33802
Telephone: 941-688-7747
Telecopier: 941-683-4582

James P. Hahn	Stephen C. Watson
E.V. McClurg	John R. Griffith

Philip H. Bush

General Counsel: Peoples Bank of Lakeland; First Federal of Florida; Publix
Super Markets, Inc.
Approved Attorneys For: Attorneys' Title Insurance Fund; American Title
Insurance Co.; Title & Trust Company of Florida; Federal Land Bank of
Columbia, Columbia, S.C.

(See Next Column)

HAHN, McCLURG, WATSON, GRIFFITH & BUSH P.A.—*Continued*

Reference: Peoples Bank of Lakeland.

For full biographical listings, see the Martindale-Hubbell Law Directory

HARRIS, MIDYETTE, GEARY & DARBY, P.A. (AV)

2012 South Florida Avenue, P.O. Box 2451, 33806-2451
Telephone: 941-683-7567
FAX: 941-688-8099

Christy F. Harris (Mr.)	Joseph A. Geary
William M. Midyette, III	Ben H. Darby, Jr.

Eduardo F. Morrell	Louise D. Wilkinson
	Diane E. Hill

Approved Attorneys for: Attorneys' Title Insurance Fund.
References: Barnett Bank of Polk County; Watkins Motor Lines, Inc.; Linder Industrial Machinery Company; Tampa Armature Works, Inc.; Carter, Belcourt & Atkinson, C.P.A.'s.

For full biographical listings, see the Martindale-Hubbell Law Directory

HOLLAND & KNIGHT LLP (AV)

A Partnership including Professional Corporations
92 Lake Wire Drive, 33801
Telephone: 941-682-1161
Fax: 941-688-1186
Mailing Address: P.O. Box 32092, 33802
Email: hklaw.com *URL:* http://www.hklaw.com
Fort Lauderdale, Florida Office: One East Broward Boulevard, Suite 1300.
Telephone: 954-525-1000.
Fax: 954-463-2030.
Jacksonville, Florida Office: 50 N. Laura Street, Suite 3900.
Telephone: 904-353-2000.
Fax: 904-358-1872.
Miami, Florida Office: 701 Brickell Avenue, 30th Floor.
Telephone: 305-374-8500.
Fax: 305-787-7799.
Orlando, Florida Office: 200 S. Orange Avenue, Suite 600.
Telephone: 407-425-8500.
Fax: 407-244-5288.
St. Petersburg, Florida Office: One Progress Plaza, Suite 1600.
Telephone: 813-896-7171.
Fax: 813-822-8048.
Tallahassee, Florida Office: 315 Calhoun Street, Suite 600.
Telephone: 904-224-7000.
Fax: 904-224-8832.
Tampa, Florida Office: 400 North Ashley, Suite 2300.
Telephone: 813-227-8500.
Fax: 813-229-0134.
West Palm Beach, Florida Office: 625 N. Flagler Drive, Suite 700.
Telephone: 561-833-2000.
Fax: 561-650-8399.
Washington, D.C. Office: 2100 Pennsylvania Avenue, N.W.
Telephone: 202-955-3000.
Fax: 202-955-5564.
Atlanta, Georgia Office: 1201 West Peachtree Street, N.E., Suite 2000.
Telephone: 404-817-8500.
Fax: 404-881-0470.

LAKELAND MEMBERS AND ASSOCIATES

Thomas R. Bayless	C. Parkhill Mays, Jr.
Charles E. Bentley	Henry M. Morgan, Jr.
Randall C. Clement	Robert P. Murray
William S. Dufoe	Michael P. Sampson
William O. E. Henry	Harry M. Sawyer, Jr.
D. Burke Kibler, III	Richard B. Stephens, Jr.
Henry M. Kittleson	Richard L. Stockton
Edward F. Koren	Edward W. Vogel, III

Jeffrey E. Appel	Walter E. Engle, III
Barbara Willman Davis	Claude M. Harden, III
	Sandra Graham Sheets

For full biographical listings, see the Martindale-Hubbell Law Directory

LANE, TROHN, CLARKE, BERTRAND, VREELAND & JACOBSEN, P.A. (AV)

One Lake Morton Drive, P.O. Box 3, 33802-0003
Telephone: 941-284-2200
Telecopier: 941-688-0310
Bartow, Florida Office: 150 East Davidson Street. 33803.
Telephone: 941-533-0866.

A. H. Lane (Retired)	Christopher M. Fear
Robert L. Trohn	Gary S. Rabin
Thomas L. Clarke, Jr.	Robert M. Brush
Robert J. Bertrand	Kingswood Sprott, Jr.
John K. Vreeland	John A. Attaway, Jr.
Donald G. Jacobsen	Hank B. Campbell

(See Next Column)

Judith J. Flanders	Robert G. Stokes
Patrick J. Murphy	Mark N. Miller
Mitchell D. Franks	Jonathan B. Trohn
Janet M. Stuart	Edwin A. Scales, III

Christine M. Casingal	Stephen B. French

Counsel for: Ewell Industries, Inc.
Local Counsel for: Auto Owners Insurance Co.; Liberty Mutual Insurance Co.; St. Paul Fire & Marine Insurance Cos.; U.S. Fidelity & Guaranty Co.; State Farm Insurance Cos.
Approved Attorneys for: Attorneys' Title Insurance Fund; Chicago Title Insurance Co.

For full biographical listings, see the Martindale-Hubbell Law Directory

MARTIN & MARTIN, P.A. (AV)

200 Lake Morton Drive, 33801
Telephone: 941-688-7611
Telefax: 941-688-7329

E. Snow Martin	E. Snow Martin, Jr.
	Michael D. Martin

For full biographical listings, see the Martindale-Hubbell Law Directory

PETERSON & MYERS, P.A. (AV)

100 East Main Street, P.O. Box 24628, 33802-4628
Telephone: 941-683-6511; 676-6934
Telecopier: 941-682-8031
Lake Wales, Florida Office: 130 East Central Avenue, P.O. Box 1079.
Telephones: 941-676-7611; 683-8942.
Winter Haven, Florida Office: Suite 300, 141 5th Street, N.W., P.O. Drawer 7608.
Telephone: 941-294-3360.

Philip O. Allen	Peter J. Munson
Jack P. Brandon	Corneal B. Myers
Beach A Brooks, Jr.	Cornelius B. Myers, III
Kristen Marie Buzzanca	E. Blake Paul
J. Davis Connor	Robert E. Puterbaugh
Michael S. Craig	Abel A. Putnam
Roy A. Craig, Jr.	Thomas B. Putnam, Jr.
Jacob C. Dykxhoorn	Deborah A. Ruster
Dennis P. Johnson	Stephen R. Senn
Kevin C. Knowlton	Andrea Teves Smith
Douglas A. Lockwood, III	Keith H. Wadsworth
M. Craig Massey	Kerry M. Wilson

General Counsel for: Barnett Bank of Polk County.
Representative Clients: Mutual Wholesale Co.; Barnett Banks, Inc.; Ben Hill Griffin, Inc.; Alcoma Association, Inc.
Approved Attorneys for: Equitable Life Assurance Society of the United States; Federal Land Bank, Columbia, South Carolina; Attorneys' Title Insurance Fund.

For full biographical listings, see the Martindale-Hubbell Law Directory

LAKE MARY, Seminole Co. — (Refer to Longwood)

LAKE PLACID, Highlands Co.

SWAINE, HARRIS, SHEEHAN & McCLURE, P.A. (AV)

212 Interlake Boulevard, P.O. Box 548, 33852
Telephone: 941-465-2811
Fax: 941-465-6999
Email: lplaw@ct.net
Sebring, Florida Office: 425 South Commerce Avenue.
Telephone: 813-385-1549.
Fax: 813-471-0008. E-Mail: shsmlaw@ct.net.

J. Michael Swaine	John K. McClure
Bert J. Harris, III	J. Timothy Sheehan

	William J. Nielander

Representative Clients: Barnett Bank of Highlands County; Lykes Bros., Inc; City of Sebring; City of Lake Placid; Lakeshore Mall.
Approved Attorneys for: Attorneys' Title Insurance Corp.

For full biographical listings, see the Martindale-Hubbell Law Directory

LAKE WALES, Polk Co.

PETERSON & MYERS, P.A. (AV)

130 East Central Avenue, P.O. Box 1079, 33853
Telephone: 941-676-7611; 683-8942
Telecopier: 941-676-0643
Lakeland, Florida Office: 100 East Main Street, P.O. Box 24628.
Telephones: 941-683-6511; 676-6934.
Winter Haven, Florida Office: Suite 300, 141 5th Street, N.W., P.O. Drawer 7608.
Telephone: 941-294-3360.

(See Next Column)

PETERSON & MYERS P.A., *Lake Wales—Continued*

Philip O. Allen	Peter J. Munson
Jack P. Brandon	Corneal B. Myers
Beach A Brooks, Jr.	Cornelius B. Myers, III
Kristen Marie Buzzanca	E. Blake Paul
J. Davis Connor	Robert E. Puterbaugh
Michael S. Craig	Abel A. Putnam
Roy A. Craig, Jr.	Thomas B. Putnam, Jr.
Jacob C. Dykxhoorn	Deborah A. Ruster
Dennis P. Johnson	Stephen R. Senn
Kevin C. Knowlton	Andrea Teves Smith
Douglas A. Lockwood, III	Keith H. Wadsworth
M. Craig Massey	Kerry M. Wilson

General Counsel for: Barnett Bank of Polk County.
Representative Clients: Mutual Wholesale Co.; Barnett Banks, Inc.; Ben Hill Griffin, Inc.; Alcoma Association, Inc.
Approved Attorneys for: Equitable Life Assurance Society of the United States; Federal Land Bank, Columbia, South Carolina; Attorneys' Title Insurance Fund.

For full biographical listings, see the Martindale-Hubbell Law Directory

---

LEESBURG, Lake Co.

AUSTIN & PEPPERMAN (AV)

Suite C 1321 West Citizens Boulevard, P.O. Drawer 490200, 34749-0200
Telephone: 352-728-1020
Fax: 352-728-0595

Robert E. Austin, Jr.	Carla R. Pepperman

Representative Clients: Allstate Insurance Co.; American Excess Insurance Co.; American Re-Insurance Co.; Florida Rock Industries, Inc.; Goodyear Tire & Rubber Co.; Great American Insurance Co.

For full biographical listings, see the Martindale-Hubbell Law Directory

---

LIVE OAK,* Suwannee Co. — (Refer to Lake City)

MADISON,* Madison Co.

DAVIS, BROWNING & SCHNITKER (AV)

901 West Base Street, P.O. Drawer 652, 32340
Telephone: 904-973-4186
Fax: 904-973-8564

MEMBERS OF FIRM

W. T. Davis (1901-1988)	Edwin B. Browning, Jr.
	Clay A. Schnitker

ASSOCIATES

George T. Reeves

General Counsel for: Bank of Madison County; First Federal Bank; City of Madison; County of Madison; Town of Greenville.
Representative Clients: District School Board for Madison County; District School Board for Lafayette County; Quitman Federal Savings & Loan Association of Quitman, Georgia; First Union National Bank.

For full biographical listings, see the Martindale-Hubbell Law Directory

---

MARIANNA,* Jackson Co. — (Refer to Panama City)

MELBOURNE, Brevard Co.

KRASNY AND DETTMER (AV)

A Partnership of Professional Associations
780 South Apollo Boulevard, P.O. Box 428, 32902-0428
Telephone: 407-723-5646
Telecopier: 407-768-1147

Myron S. (Mike) Krasny (P.A.)	Dale A. Dettmer (P.A.)

Scott Krasny

Representative Client: Huntington National Bank of Florida.

For full biographical listings, see the Martindale-Hubbell Law Directory

---

NANCE, CACCIATORE, SISSERSON, DURYEA AND HAMILTON (AV)

525 North Harbor City Boulevard, 32935
Telephone: 407-254-8416
Fax: 407-259-8243

MEMBERS OF FIRM

James H. Nance	John N. Hamilton
Sammy Cacciatore	Charles G. Barger, Jr.
Ronald G. Duryea	James N. Nance

OF COUNSEL

James A. Sisserson

Reference: First Union Bank.

For full biographical listings, see the Martindale-Hubbell Law Directory

---

MIAMI,* Dade Co.

ADAMS & ADAMS (AV)

5th Floor, Concord Building, 66 West Flagler Street, 33130
Telephone: 305-371-3333
Broward: 954-728-8770
Telecopier: 305-372-3987

Richard B. Adams (1926-1983)	Richard B. Adams, Jr.
	R. Wade Adams

ASSOCIATES

Mai-Ling E. Castillo	Anthony P. Strasius
	Bryant Esquenazi

For full biographical listings, see the Martindale-Hubbell Law Directory

---

ANGONES, HUNTER, McCLURE, LYNCH & WILLIAMS, P.A. (AV)

Ninth Floor-Concord Building, 66 West Flagler Street, 33130
Telephone: 305-371-5000
Fort Lauderdale: 954-728-9112
FAX: 305-371-3948

Frank R. Angones	Christopher J. Lynch
Steven Kent Hunter	Stewart D. Williams
John McClure	B. Scott Hunter
	Leopoldo Garcia, Jr.

Thomas W. Paradise	Kara D. Phinney
Donna Joy Hunter	C. David Durkee
Lourdes Alfonsin Ruiz	Carlton A. Bober
	Surama Suarez

Insurance Clients: Allstate Insurance Co.; Prudential Property & Casualty Insurance Co.; Travelers Insurance Co.; Rollins Hudig Hall Healthcare Risk, Inc.

For full biographical listings, see the Martindale-Hubbell Law Directory

---

BAKER & McKENZIE (AV)

Barnett Tower, Suite 1600 701 Brickell Avenue, 33131-2827
Telephone: (305) 789-8900
Intn'l. Dialing: (1-305) 789-8900
Facsimile: (1-305) 789-8953
Associated Offices of Baker & McKenzie in: Almaty, Amsterdam, Bangkok, Barcelona, Beijing, Berlin, Bogotá, Brasília, Brussels, Budapest, Buenos Aires, Cairo, Caracas, Chicago, Dallas, Frankfurt, Geneva, Hanoi, Ho Chi Minh City, Hong Kong, Juárez, Kiev, Lausanne, London, Madrid, Manila, Melbourne, México City, Milan, Monterrey, Moscow, Münich, New York, Palo Alto, Paris, Prague, Rio de Janeiro, Riyadh, Rome, St. Petersburg, San Diego, San Francisco, Santiago, São Paulo, Singapore, Stockholm, Sydney, Taipei, Tijuana, Tokyo, Toronto, Valencia, Warsaw, Washington, D.C. and Zürich.
Correspondent Law Firm: Hadiputranto, Hadinoto & Partners, Jakarta.

MEMBERS OF FIRM

Donald J. Hayden	Robert F. Hudson, Jr.
(Not admitted in FL)	Noel H. Nation
	Eugene A. Rostov

LOCAL PARTNERS

James H. Barrett	Phillip M. Hudson, III
Kenneth F. Claussen	Charles Lea Hume
Nicholas J. DeNovio	Richard J. Ovelmen
	Jonathan H. (Jason) Warner

OF COUNSEL

Martin I. Kalish

COUNSEL

Landon K. Clayman	Anthony J. O'Donnell, Jr.

ASSOCIATES

C. Coleman G. Edmunds	Michael H. Hoffman
David R. Garcia	(Not admitted in FL)
	R. Allen Naudé

For full biographical listings, see the Martindale-Hubbell Law Directory

---

BIERMAN, SHOHAT, LOEWY, PERRY & KLEIN, PROFESSIONAL ASSOCIATION (AV)

Penthouse Two, 800 Brickell Avenue, 33131-2944
Telephone: 305-358-7000
Facsimile: 305-358-4010
Email: BSLPK@AOL.COM

Donald I. Bierman	Pamela I. Perry
Edward R. Shohat	Theodore Klein
Ira N. Loewy	Maria Beguiristain Shohat

Reference: United National Bank of Miami.

For full biographical listings, see the Martindale-Hubbell Law Directory

Miami—Continued

BROAD AND CASSEL (AV)

A Partnership including Professional Associations
Miami Center, 201 South Biscayne Boulevard, Suite 3000, 33131
Telephone: 305-373-9400
Telecopier: 305-373-9443
Boca Raton, Florida Office: Corporate Centre at Boca Raton, Suite 300, 7777 Glades Road, 33434.
Telephone: 561-483-7000.
Fort Lauderdale, Florida Office: Suite 1130, Broward Financial Centre, 500 E. Broward Boulevard, 33394.
Telephone: 954-764-7060.
Orlando, Florida Office: Barnett Bank Center, 390 N. Orange Avenue, Suite 1100, 32801.
Telephone: 407-839-4200.
Stuart, Florida Office: 900 East Ocean Boulevard, Suite 126, 33994.
Telephone: 561-283-3000.
Tallahassee, Florida Office: 215 South Monroe Street, Suite 400, 32302.
Telephone: 904-681-6810.
Tampa, Florida Office: 100 North Tampa, Suite 3500, 33602.
Telephone: 813-225-3020.
West Palm Beach, Florida Office: The Reflections Office Center, 400 Australian Avenue, South, Fifth Floor, 33401.
Telephone: 561-832-3300.

MEMBERS OF FIRM

Murray D. Shear (P.A.)	Jose I. Rojas (P.A.)
Mike Segal (P.A.)	Jose A. Santos, Jr., (P.A.)
(Managing Partner)	Nina S. Gordon (P.A.)
Marwin S. Cassel (P.A.)	A. Jeffry Robinson (P.A.)
Michael A. Dribin (P.A.)	Dale S. Bergman (P.A.)
William C. Phillippi (P.A.)	Dawn Lankford Bowling (P.A.)
Alan S. Lederman (P.A.)	Kathleen L. Deutsch (P.A.)
Virginia Easley Johnson (P.A.)	Michael Paul Bennett (P.A.)

ASSOCIATES

Paul Aiello	Linda C. Frazier
Michael P. Nido, Jr.	Rose M. Parish-Ramón
Gary Edward Lehman	Rodger L. Hochman
Tamara Carmichael	Kelly P. Campolo

Carlos O. Fernandez

OF COUNSEL

Shepard Broad	Norman Broad
Alvin Cassel	James S. Cassel

Counsel for: Bank of Central Florida.
Local Counsel for: Barnett Banks, Inc.; Republic National Bank.

For full biographical listings, see the Martindale-Hubbell Law Directory

COLSON, HICKS, EIDSON, COLSON & MATTHEWS (AV)

Floor 47 First Union Financial Center, 200 South Biscayne Boulevard, 33131-2351
Telephone: 305-373-5400

MEMBERS OF FIRM

Bill Colson	Tony Korvick
William M. Hicks	Enid Duany Mendoza
Mike Eidson	Newton P. Porter
Dean C. Colson	Julie Braman Kane
Joseph M. Matthews	Robb D. Steinberg

Brian Scott Yablonski

Reference: Northern Trust Bank of Florida.

For full biographical listings, see the Martindale-Hubbell Law Directory

THOMAS L. DAVID, P.A. (AV)

8th Floor, 1428 Brickell Avenue, 33131
Telephone: 305-371-6600
FAX: 305-371-5511

Thomas L. David

Reference: Citibank (Florida) N.A.

For full biographical listings, see the Martindale-Hubbell Law Directory

ENGELS, PERTNOY, SOLOWSKY & ALLEN, P.A. (AV)

International Place, 100 Southeast 2nd Street, 21st Floor, 33131
Telephone: 305-371-2223
Fax: 305-373-2073

Martin Engels	Jay Solowsky
Sidney M. Pertnoy	Richard Lewis Allen

Steven H. Brotman	Leah Lariviere
Alfred I. Hopkins	Suzanne Holland Youmans
Lori Jean Johnson	Stephen A. Marino, Jr.

For full biographical listings, see the Martindale-Hubbell Law Directory

GREENBERG, TRAURIG, HOFFMAN, LIPOFF, ROSEN & QUENTEL, P.A. (AV)

1221 Brickell Avenue, 33131
Telephone: 305-579-0500
Telex: 80-3124
Facsimile: 305-579-0717
Email: info@gtlaw.com
Fort Lauderdale, Florida Office: 515 East Las Olas Boulevard.
Telephone: 954-765-0500.
Facsimile: 954-765-1477.
West Palm Beach, Florida Office: 777 South Flagler Drive.
Telephone: 561-650-7900.
Facsimile: 561-655-6222.
Orlando, Florida Office: 111 North Orange Avenue.
Telephone: 407-420-1000.
Facsimile: 407-420-5909.
Tallahassee, Florida Office: 101 East College Avenue.
Telephone: 904-222-6891.
Facsimile: 904-681-0207.
New York, N.Y. Office: Citicorp Center, 153 East 53rd Street.
Telephone: 212-801-9200.
Facsimile: 212-223-7161.
Washington, D.C. Office: 1300 Connecticut Avenue, N.W.
Telephone: 202-331-3100.
Facsimile: 202-331-3101.

Fernando C. Alonso	Steven J. Kravitz
Cesar L. Alvarez	Steven A. Landy
Charles M. Auslander	Steven B. Lapidus
Kerri L. Barsh	Nancy B. Lash
Hilarie Bass	Oscar Levin
Norman J. Benford	Carlos E. Loumiet
Paul Berkowitz	Juan P. Loumiet
Mark D. Bloom	Bruce E. Macdonough
Burt Bruton	Pedro A. Martin
Sue McCourt Cobb	Roberto Martinez
Miguel De Grandy	Pedro J. Martinez-Fraga
Alan T. Dimond	Joel D. Maser
Lucia A. Dougherty	Juan J. Mayol, Jr.
Samuel J. Dubbin	Rebecca R. Orand
William B. Eck	Marshall R. Pasternack
Arthur J. England, Jr.	Albert D. Quentel
Gary M. Epstein	C. Ryan Reetz
Jorge L. Freeland	Raquel A. Rodriguez
Robert C. Gang	Marvin S. Rosen
Richard G. Garrett	Ronald M. Rosengarten
Bruce H. Giles-Klein	David L. Ross
Richard J. Giusto	Gary A. Saul
Lawrence Godofsky	Elliot H. Scherker
Steven E. Goldman	Mark P. Schnapp
Joseph Gary Goldstein	Clifford A. Schulman
Matthew B. Gorson	H. Allan Shore
Dianne Greenberg	Marlene K. Silverman
Robert L. Grossman	Holly R. Skolnick
Kenneth C. Hoffman	Charles E. Stiver, Jr.
Larry J. Hoffman	Joel L. Stocker
Osmond C. Howe, Jr.	Robert H. Traurig
Andrew Hulsh	Fern S. Watts
Martin Kalb	Howard W. Whitaker
David S. Kenin	Jerrold A. Wish
Shepard King	Timothy D. Wolfe

Diana S.C. Zeydel

V. Dawn Beighey	Craig T. McClung
Juan Carlos Campos	Bradley L. Mirkin
John G. Crabtree	(Not admitted in FL)
Brooke M. Deratany	Anna G. Oestereicher
Bert Diaz	Maury R. Olicker
Stacey Pastel Dougan	Jeffrey M. Oshinsky
Candace R. Duff	(Not admitted in FL)
Robert H. Fernandez	Prasan A. Pandite
Carl A. Fornaris	(Not admitted in FL)
Ricardo L. Fraga	Adrienne Friesner Pardo
Robin F. Frydman	Sylvia Sohn Penneys
Paige A. Harper	Roberto R. Pupo
Michael W. Hein	Daniel E. Reed
Steven M. Helfman	Andrés Rivero
Joseph M. Hernandez	Michael J. Rogal
John B. Hutton, III	Eric D. Rosenberg
Alison Marie Igoe	Mark A. Salky
Alan S. Krischer	Justin J. Sayfie
Gustavo J. Lamelas	Steven H. Scheichet
Linda E. Larrea	(Not admitted in FL)
Jeremy P. Leathe	Julie M. Schwartz
Moshe M. Lehrfield	Paul A. Shelowitz
Susan B. Leibowitz	Katherine E. Sidaway
James P. S. Leshaw	Lori A. Sochin
Frederic L. Levenson	Stacey L. Swaye
Fernando Margarit	Fredric P. Taubman
Joseph A. Marinello	Jeffrey S. Tenen
(Not admitted in FL)	N.J. Terris (Not admitted in FL)
Inés Marrero-Priegues	Merrill A. Ulmer
Enrique J. Martin	Javier L. Vazquez

(See Next Column)

GREENBERG, TRAURIG, HOFFMAN, LIPOFF, ROSEN & QUENTEL P.A.,
Miami—Continued

Brian J. Walsh	Laura R. Weinfeld
Elise D. Weakley	David E. Wells
Gary D. Weinfeld	William S. Wilson
	Linda G. Worton

OF COUNSEL

Patricia Menendez Cambo	Ambler H. Moss, Jr.
Paulo Cesar Miranda (Not	Joe N. Unger
admitted in United States)	Marc M. Watson
	Julie A. S. Williamson

LEGAL SUPPORT PERSONNEL

Linda Will	Terry Allen Seale,
(Director of Libraries)	Associate Librarian
Alfred Holmes	
(Technical Research Specialist)	

Representative Clients: American Express; Blockbuster Entertainment Corporation; Capital Bancorp; Delta Airlines; E. I. Dupont de Nemours, Inc.; MacAndrews and Forbes; Prudential Securities, Inc.; Sunglass Hut International, Inc.; Travelers Life Insurance Co. (The); Viacom International, Inc.

For full biographical listings, see the Martindale-Hubbell Law Directory

---

HADDAD, JOSEPHS, JACK, GAEBE & MARKARIAN (AV)

1493 Sunset Drive (Coral Gables), P.O. Box 345118, 33114
Telephone: Dade County: 305-666-6006
Telecopier: 305-662-9931
URL: http://www.haddadjosephs.com

MEMBERS OF FIRM

Gil Haddad	Lewis N. Jack, Jr.
Michael R. Josephs	John S. Gaebe
	David K. Markarian

ASSOCIATES

Elisabeth M. Allen	Lauren M. Ilvento
Helen Leen Miranda	Clifford A. Wolff
	John William Gautier

Representative Clients: U-Haul Corporation; ITT Sheraton; Zurich-American Insurance Company; Republic Claims Service Company; Southern Fire Insurance Adjusters.

For full biographical listings, see the Martindale-Hubbell Law Directory

---

HARDY & BISSETT, P.A. (AV)

501 Northeast First Avenue, 33132
Telephone: 305-358-6200
Broward: 954-462-6377
Fax: 305-577-8230
Email: 102132.403@compuserve.com
Boca Raton, Florida Office: 2201 Corporate Boulevard, N.W., Suite 205.
Telephone: 407-998-9202.
Telecopier: 407-998-9693.

G. Jack Hardy	G. William Bissett

Howard K. Cherna	H. Dane Mottlau
Lee Philip Teichner	Jana Marie Yaw

Representative Clients: International Paper Co.; Masonite Corp.; Bridgestone/Firestone Inc.; American International Underwriters; American International Group, Inc.; Crown Equipment Corp.; The Coleman Co., Inc.; Brown & Williamson; Black & Decker (U.S.), Inc.; S-B Power Tool Company.

For full biographical listings, see the Martindale-Hubbell Law Directory

---

HICKS, ANDERSON & BLUM, P.A. (AV)

Twenty Fourth Floor, 100 North Biscayne Boulevard, 33132
Telephone: 305-374-8171
Fax: 305-372-8038

Mark Hicks	Bambi G. Blum
Ralph O. Anderson	Jean Kneale

Gary A. Magnarini	Cindy L. Ebenfeld
Alyssa M. Campbell	Ila J. Klion
	Dinah S. Stein

OF COUNSEL

James E. Tribble	Roger L. Blackburn

For full biographical listings, see the Martindale-Hubbell Law Directory

---

HIGH, STACK, LAZENBY, PALAHACH & DEL AMO (AV)

A Partnership including Professional Associations
3929 Ponce de Leon Boulevard (Coral Gables), 33134
Telephone: 305-443-3329
Fax: 305-443-0850
Melbourne, Florida Office: High, Stack, Lazenby, Palahach, Maxwell & Morgan, 525 Strawbridge Avenue.
Telephone: 407-725-5525.
FAX: 407-984-2411.

MEMBERS OF FIRM

Robert King High (1924-1967)	George W. Maxwell, III
Charles R. Stack (P.A.)	(Resident at Melbourne
Robert A. Lazenby (P.A.)	Office)
Michael Palahach, III, (P.A.)	Clay D. Morgan (Resident at
Carlos C. del Amo	Melbourne Office)

ASSOCIATES

Jack L. Platt

OF COUNSEL

Alvin S. Cawn	Fernando M. Palacios
Christopher Mark Rundle	Reed C. Cary

For full biographical listings, see the Martindale-Hubbell Law Directory

---

HOLLAND & KNIGHT LLP (AV)

A Partnership including Professional Corporations
701 Brickell Avenue, 30th Floor, 33131
Telephone: 305-374-8500
Fax: 305-789-7799
Mailing Address: P.O. Box 015441, 33101
Email: hklaw.com *URL:* http://www.hklaw.com
Fort Lauderdale, Florida Office: One East Broward Boulevard, Suite 1300.
Telephone: 954-525-1000.
Fax: 954-463-2030.
Jacksonville, Florida Office: 50 N. Laura Street, Suite 3900.
Telephone: 904-353-2000.
Fax: 904-358-1872.
Lakeland, Florida Office: 92 Lake Wire Drive.
Telephone: 941-682-1161.
Fax: 941-688-1186.
Orlando, Florida Office: 200 S. Orange Avenue, Suite 2600.
Telephone: 407-425-8500.
Fax: 407-244-5288.
St. Petersburg, Florida Office: One Progress Plaza, Suite 1600.
Telephone: 813-896-7171.
Fax: 813-822-8048.
Tallahassee, Florida Office: 315 Calhoun Street, Suite 600.
Telephone: 904-224-7000.
Fax: 904-224-8832.
Tampa, Florida Office: 400 North Ashley, Suite 2300.
Telephone: 813-227-8500.
Fax: 813-229-0134.
West Palm Beach, Florida Office: 625 N. Flagler Drive, Suite 700.
Telephone: 561-833-2000.
Fax: 561-650-8399.
Washington, D.C. Office: 2100 Pennsylvania Avenue, N.W.
Telephone: 202-955-3000.
Fax: 202-955-5564.
Atlanta, Georgia Office: 1201 West Peachtree Street, N.E., Suite 2000.
Telephone: 404-817-8500.
Fax: 404-881-0470.

MIAMI MEMBERS AND ASSOCIATES

Ronald Albert, Jr.	John F. Halula
Kathryn Klein Anderson	William F. Hamilton
Susan H. Aprill	Jorge L. Hernandez-Toraño
Alcides I. Ávila	Stuart K. Hoffman
Gregory A. Baldwin	Marilyn J. Holifield
Christopher Noel Bellows	Bernard Jacobson
Rachel Blechman	Daniel Jacobson
William R. Bloom	Judith M. Korchin
Sanford L. Bohrer	Lee F. Lasris
John Campbell	Barbara Ehrich Locke
Mirta (Mikki) Canton	Amelia Rea Maguire
Jose A. Casal	George Mencio, Jr.
Matthew P. Coglianese	Michael T. Moore
Bruce Jay Colan	Tracy Nichols
J. Thomas Cookson	James M. Porter
J. Raul Cosio	Peter Prieto
George Crimarco	Craig V. Rasile
Douglas F. Darbut	Constance M. Ridder
Donald K. Duffy	Wilfredo A. Rodriguez
Juan C. Enjamio	José E. Sirvén
R. Thomas Farrar	Chesterfield Smith
Dante B. Fascell	Robert H. Smith
Martin Fine	Marty Steinberg
Robert J. Friedman	William S. Stevens, III
Daniel Gelber	Bruce Stone
W. Reeder Glass	Lynn C. Washington
James S. Groh	Andrew H. Weinstein
Steven H. Hagen	James D. Wing
	D. Farrington Yates

(See Next Column)

HOLLAND & KNIGHT LLP—Continued

Michelle Austin
Jeffrey Bast
Louise McAlpin Brais
Jose E. Cil
L. Frank Cordero
Samuel A. Danon
Kelly-Ann Gibbs
Olga Maria Gomez
Alex M. Gonzalez
Dalia Mercedes Gonzalez
Patricia M. Hernandez
D. Bruce Hoffman
Lucinda A. Hofmann
Valerie L. Hummel
 (Not admitted in FL)
Adolfo E. Jimenez
Robert J. Kuntz, Jr.
Robert K. Levenson

Sharon R. Liebman
Thomas H. Loffredo
Kelly A. Martin
Walfrido J. Martinez
Judith M. Mercier
Duccio Mortillaro
Bernard Pastor
Leon N. Patricios
Shawn R. Pringle
Vivian M. Rodriguez
Peter E. Salomon
Vanessa P. Sciarra
Lenore C. Smith
Stephen S. Stallings
Margarita Barreto Tercilla
Laurie A. Thompson
Lori K. Weems
Jeffrey A. Weissman

COUNSEL

Daniel S. Pearson   Roderick N. Petrey

For full biographical listings, see the Martindale-Hubbell Law Directory

HOWARD, BRAWNER & STONE (AV)

Suite 210 Grove Professional Building, 2950 S.W. 27th Avenue, 33133
Telephone: 305-448-2131
Telefax: 305-448-3184

MEMBERS OF FIRM

Philip L. Brawner   Richard J. Stone

ASSOCIATE

Kevin I. Schwartz

Reference: Coconut Grove Bank.

For full biographical listings, see the Martindale-Hubbell Law Directory

HUGHES HUBBARD & REED LLP (AV)

201 South Biscayne Boulevard Suite 2500, 33131-4332
Telephone: 305-358-1666
Fax: 305-371-8759
Telex: 518785
New York, New York Office: One Battery Park Plaza, 10004. Telephone 212-837-6000.
Cable Address: "Hughreed, New York."
Telex: 427120.
Telecopier: 212-422-4726.
Los Angeles, California Office: 350 S. Grand Street, Suite 3600, 90071-3442.
Telephone: 213-613-2800.
Telecopier: 213-613-2950.
Washington, D.C. Office: 1300 I Street, N.W., Suite 900 West, 20005.
Telephone: 202-408-3600.
Telex: 89-2674.
Telecopier: 202-408-3636.
Paris, France Office: 47, Avenue Georges Mandel, 75116.
Telephone: 33.10.44.05.8000.
Cable Address: "Hughreed, Paris."
Telex: 611986.
Telecopier: 33.01.45.53.1504.

RESIDENT PARTNERS

Robert Goldfarb
Timothy J. McCarthy
 (Not admitted in FL)

John E. Pearson
Herschel E. Sparks, Jr.
Nicolas Swerdloff

William A. Weber

OF COUNSEL

Antonio R. Zamora

SPECIAL COUNSEL

Eric D. Rapkin

For full biographical listings, see the Martindale-Hubbell Law Directory

KEITH, MACK, LEWIS, COHEN & LUMPKIN (AV)

First Union Financial Center, Twentieth Floor, 200 South Biscayne Boulevard, 33131-2310
Telephone: 305-358-7605
Fax: 305-358-4755
Email: PREVAIL@KEITHMACK.COM

MEMBERS OF FIRM

Edgar Lewis
Robert A. Cohen
R. Hugh Lumpkin
Gregg S. Ahrens

Jan Carson Cheezem
Loren S. Granoff
Jack S. Lewis
Alan Rosenthal

Norman S. Segall

(See Next Column)

ASSOCIATES

Michael J. Hogsten
Felix M. Lasarte
Dawn Marshall
Mercedes Padin

Michele S. Primeau
Cynthia Ramos
Jack R. Reiter
Karl J. Schumer

Jeffrey P. Shapiro

OF COUNSEL

Seymour D. Keith   James L. Mack

Representative Clients: CitiBank, F.S.B.; Attorneys Title Insurance Fund, Inc.; Barnett Bank, N.A.
Approved Counsel: First American Title Insurance Co.; Attorneys Title Insurance Fund, Inc.; Commonwealth Title Insurance Co.
Reference: CitiBank, F.S.B.

For full biographical listings, see the Martindale-Hubbell Law Directory

KELLY, BLACK, BLACK, BYRNE & BEASLEY, PROFESSIONAL ASSOCIATION (AV)

1400 Alfred I. du Pont Building, 169 East Flagler Street, 33131
Telephone: 305-358-5700
Fax: 305-358-7269

Hugo L. Black, Jr.
Robert Carleton Byrne

Joseph W. Beasley
Bonnie J. Losak-Jimenez

Nancy Hagan Henry

Representative Clients: Credit Suisse; Multi-Media Entertainment, Inc.; Japan Development Co.; Israel Discount Bank; EquityLine Securities, Inc.; Bacardi Imports, Inc.; City of Miami Beach Employees Retirement Trust; Pueblo International Inc.; Gumenick Properties Inc.
Reference: United National Bank.

For full biographical listings, see the Martindale-Hubbell Law Directory

KENNY NACHWALTER SEYMOUR ARNOLD CRITCHLOW & SPECTOR, PROFESSIONAL ASSOCIATION (AV)

1100 Miami Center, 201 South Biscayne Boulevard, 33131-4327
Telephone: 305-373-1000
Facsimile: 305-372-1861
ABA/net: 18338
Email: 7502552@MCIMAIL.COM
Rogersville, Tennessee Office: 107 East Main Street, Suite 301, 37857-3347.
Telephone: 423-272-5300.
Facsimile: 423-272-4961.

James J. Kenny
Michael Nachwalter
Thomas H. Seymour
Richard Alan Arnold
Richard H. Critchlow
Brian F. Spector

Kevin J. Murray
William J. Blechman
Harry R. Schafer
Deborah Sampieri Corbishley
David H. Lichter
Scott E. Perwin

Jeffrey T. Foreman
Lauren C. Ravkind
Katherine Clark Silverglate
Amanda M. McGovern

Paul C. Huck, Jr.
Tara Mary Higgins
Robert D.W. Landon, III
Miriam Lefkowitz

Representative Clients: Albertson's, Inc.; American Bankers Insurance Group; Cartier, Inc.; Ethan Allen, Inc.; Federated Department Stores, Inc.; The Florida Bar; GTE Directories Corp.; Siemens Credit Corp.; GTE Florida; Columbia HCA.

For full biographical listings, see the Martindale-Hubbell Law Directory

KUTNER, RUBINOFF, BUSH & LERNER (AV)

501 N.E. 1st Avenue, 33132
Telephone: 305-358-6200; Broward: 954-462-6377
Fax: 305-577-8230

MEMBERS OF FIRM

Arno Kutner
Edward G. Rubinoff

Kenneth J. Bush
Susan Scrivani Lerner

For full biographical listings, see the Martindale-Hubbell Law Directory

LEESFIELD, LEIGHTON & RUBIO, P.A. (AV)

2350 South Dixie Highway, 33133
Telephone: 305-854-4900/1-800-836-6400 (toll free)
Fax: 305-854-8266
Email: LEESFIELD@AOL.COM
Key West, Florida Office: 615 1/2 Whitehead Street.
Telephone: 305-296-1342.
Fax: 305-294-1793.

Ira H. Leesfield   John Elliott Leighton

Maria L. Rubio

George G. Mahfood   Steven R. Kozlowski

For full biographical listings, see the Martindale-Hubbell Law Directory

Miami—Continued

LAW OFFICE OF WILLIAM P. MCCAUGHAN (AV)

Suite 2803 World Trade Center, 80 S.W. Eighth Street, 33130
Telephone: 305-577-0058
Fax: 305-372-0526

For full biographical listings, see the Martindale-Hubbell Law Directory

MURAI, WALD, BIONDO & MORENO, P.A. (AV)

9th Floor Ingraham Building, 25 Southeast 2nd Avenue, 33131
Telephone: 305-358-5900
Fax: 305-358-9490

Rene V. Murai	Gerald J. Biondo
Gerald B. Wald	M. Cristina Moreno
William E. Davis	

Cristina Echarte Brochin	Lynette Ebeoglu McGuinness
Mary Leslie Smith	

Reference: Republic National Bank of Miami.

For full biographical listings, see the Martindale-Hubbell Law Directory

PATTERSON & SWEENY (AV)

A Partnership of Professional Associations
Suite 2450, Courthouse Tower, 44 West Flagler Street, 33130
Telephone: 305-350-9000
Fax: 305-372-3940

John H. Patterson (P.A.)	John H. Patterson, Jr. (P.A.)
James H. Sweeny, III (P.A.)	

OF COUNSEL

Cynthia Byrne Hall	Mark V. Silverio

For full biographical listings, see the Martindale-Hubbell Law Directory

PETERS, ROBERTSON, LAX, PARSONS, WELCHER, MOWERS & PASSARO, P.A. (AV)

Suite 600, Ingraham Building, 25 Southeast 2nd Avenue, 33131-1691
Telephone: 305-374-3103
Fax: 305-377-9805
Fort Lauderdale, Florida Office: Suite 600, 600 South Andrews Avenue.
Telephone: 954-761-8999.
Fax: 954-761-8990.
Fort Myers, Florida Office: Key West Professional Centre, 1342 Colonial Boulevard, Suite 45.
Telephone: 941-936-1129.
Fax: 941-936-4036.
West Palm Beach, Florida Office: Galleria International Building, 301 Clematis Street, Suite 203.
Telephone: 407-832-9698.
Fax: 407-832-8355.

Michael H. Lax	Roger G. Welcher
Neil P. Robertson	Jeffrey A. Mowers
John R. W. Parsons	Geralyn M. Passaro (Resident at Fort Lauderdale Office)

OF COUNSEL
Jackson L. Peters

Lawrence E. Margolis	Timothy J. Moffatt
Steven B. Sundook (Resident at Fort Myers Office)	Steven Charles Simon (Resident at Fort Lauderdale Office)
Jeanette G. Edwards	Walter H. Djokic (Resident at West Palm Beach Office)

Representative Clients: Auto-Owners Insurance Co.; Dade County School Board; Employers Reinsurance Group; Gallagher Bassett Insurance Service; Maryland Casualty Co.

For full biographical listings, see the Martindale-Hubbell Law Directory

PODHURST, ORSECK, JOSEFSBERG, EATON, MEADOW, OLIN & PERWIN, P.A. (AV)

Suite 800 City National Bank Building, 25 West Flagler
Street, 33130-1780
Telephone: 305-358-2800; Fort Lauderdale: 954-463-4346
Fax: 305-358-2382
Email: 76666.2340@COMPUSERVE.COM *URL:*
http://www.turbosales.com/"sfbj/podhurst.html

Aaron Podhurst	Michael S. Olin
Robert Orseck (1934-1978)	Joel S. Perwin
Robert C. Josefsberg	Steven C. Marks
Joel D. Eaton	Victor M. Diaz, Jr.
Barry L. Meadow	Katherine W. Ezell

Karen Podhurst Dern	Xavier Martínez

(See Next Column)

OF COUNSEL
Walter H. Beckham, Jr.

References: City National Bank of Miami; United National Bank of Miami.

For full biographical listings, see the Martindale-Hubbell Law Directory

RICHMAN, GREER, WEIL, BRUMBAUGH, MIRABITO & CHRISTENSEN, P.A. (AV)

Miami Center, Tenth Floor, 201 South Biscayne Boulevard, 33131
Telephone: 305-373-4000
Fax: 305-373-4099
West Palm Beach, Florida Office: Phillips Point East. Suite 1100. 777 South Flagler Drive. 33401.
Telephone: 407-803-3500.
Fax: 407-820-1608.

Gerald F. Richman	Gary S. Betensky
Alan G. Greer	Diane Wagner Katzen
Kenneth J. Weil	Manuel A. Garcia-Linares
John M. Brumbaugh	Carroll J. Kelly
Andrew J. Mirabito	Mark Anthony Romance
Bruce A. Christensen	Steven M. Brady
Charles H. Johnson	Lawrence Hugh Kunin
M. Margaret Haley	

Kenneth L. Dobkin	Christine R. Roberts

OF COUNSEL

Robert L. Floyd	Ray H. Pearson
Jeffrey D. Fisher	

Representative Clients: Shriners Hospitals for Crippled Children; Motorola, Inc.; Minnesota Mining and Manufacturing Co.; South Florida Hotel and Motel Assn.; The Lubrizol Corp.; Republic of Panama; Hallmark.

For full biographical listings, see the Martindale-Hubbell Law Directory

RUMBERGER, KIRK & CALDWELL, PROFESSIONAL ASSOCIATION (AV)

One Biscayne Tower, 2 South Biscayne Boulevard, Suite 3100, 33131
Telephone: 305-358-5577
Fax: 305-371-7580
URL: http://www.rumberger.com
Orlando, Florida Office: Signature Plaza, Suite 300, 201 South Orange Avenue, (32801), P.O. Box 1873, 32802.
Telephone: 407-872-7300.
Fax: 407-841-2133.
Tallahassee, Florida Office: 106 East College Avenue, Suite 700, (32301), P.O. Box 10507, 32302.
Telephone: 904-222-6550.
Fax: 940-222-8783.
Tampa, Florida Office: 100 North Tampa Street, Suite 2000, (33602), P.O. Box 3390, 33601.
Telephone: 813-223-4253.
Fax: 813-221-4752.

M. Stephen Smith	Holly Kelly Ennis
John Bond Atkinson	Joshua D. Lerner
Robert J. Rudock	Douglas E. Ede
Scott M. Sarason	Henry Salas
Lori Anne Brown	

Donald E. Fucik	Gustavo D. Lage
Mark E. Grimes	Daniel T. Doyle
Stuart L. Cohen	Lee S. Miller
Anthony J. Petrillo	Joseph M. Maus

Representative Clients: Automotive and other Manufacturers: General Motors Corp.; Nissan Motor Corporation in U.S.A.; Toyota Motor Sales, U.S.A., Inc. Insurance: Royal Insurance Co. Products Liability: Bombardier, Inc.; Outboard Marine Corp.

For full biographical listings, see the Martindale-Hubbell Law Directory

SAMS & MARTIN, P.A. (AV)

The Atrium, Suite 200, 1500 San Remo Avenue (Coral Gables), 33146
Telephone: 305-666-3181
Fax: 305-666-5867
Miami Lakes, Florida Office: Sams, Spier & Hollon, 7975 Northwest 154th Street, 33016.
Telephone: 305-362-6222.
Fax: 305-362-0111.

Murray Sams, Jr.	Timothy M. Martin

Joseph I. Lipsky	Arthur B. Stark, P.A.
Lisa Fialkow Levine	

For full biographical listings, see the Martindale-Hubbell Law Directory

Miami—Continued

SCHANTZ, SCHATZMAN & AARONSON, P.A. (AV)

Suite 1050 First Union Financial Center, 200 South Biscayne Boulevard, 33131
Telephone: 305-371-3100
Fax: 305-371-2024

Lawrence M. Schantz   Geoffrey S. Aaronson
Robert A. Schatzman   Carmen A. Accordino
         Alan Dagen

Allison R. Day   Joshua N. Bennett
Alan J. Perlman   Irving Shimoff
      Barry P. Gruher
OF COUNSEL
Mel Lamelas

For full biographical listings, see the Martindale-Hubbell Law Directory

---

SHUTTS & BOWEN (AV)

A Partnership including Professional Associations
1500 Miami Center, 201 South Biscayne Boulevard, 33131
Telephone: 305-358-6300
Telefax: 305-381-9982
URL: HTTP://WWW.LAWWORLD.COM/SHUTTS/
Orlando, Florida Office: 20 North Orange Avenue, Suite 1000.
Telephone: 407-423-3200.
Fax: 407-425-8316.
West Palm Beach, Florida Office: One Clearlake Centre, 250 Australian Avenue, Suite 500.
Telephone: 561-835-8500.
Fax: 561-650-8530.
Amsterdam, The Netherlands Office: Shutts & Bowen, B.V., Europa Boulevard 59, 1083 AD, Amsterdam.
Telephone: (31 20) 661-0969.
Fax: (31 20) 642-1475.
London, England Office: 43 Grosvenor Street, London W1X 9PG.
Telephone: 441-71-493-4840.
Telefax: 441-71-493-4299.

MEMBERS OF FIRM

Frank B. Shutts (1870-1947)   Richard M. Leslie (P.A.)
Crate D. Bowen (1871-1959)   Maxine Master Long
Gary M. Bagliebter   Don A. Lynn (P.A.)
Arnold L. Berman (Resident at   Lee D. Mackson
    West Palm Beach Office)   Antonio Martinez, Jr., (P.A.)
Joseph D. Bolton   David B. McCrea (P.A.)
Bowman Brown (P.A.)   Joseph F. McSorley (Resident at
Andrew M. Brumby   West Palm Beach Office)
    (Resident at Orlando Office)   John E. Meagher
Judith A. Burke   Arthur J. Menor (Resident at
Sheila M. Cesarano   West Palm Beach Office)
Gary J. Cohen   C. Richard Morgan
Jonathan Cohen   Timothy J. Murphy
Kevin D. Cowan   Phillip G. Newcomm (P.A.)
Luis A. de Armas   Louis Nostro
Jean-Charles Dibbs   Harold E. Patricoff Jr.
James F. Durham, II   Geoffrey Randall
James A. Farrell (Resident at   Margaret A. Rolando
    West Palm Beach Office)   Allan M. Rubin
Charles Robinson Fawsett (P.A.)   Raul J. Salas
Robert G. Fracasso, Jr.   Robert A. Savill
Robert A. Freyer   (Resident at Orlando Office)
    (Resident at Orlando Office)   John C. Shawde
Roger Friedbauer   Alfred G. Smith, II
David A. Gart (Resident at   William F. Smith
    West Palm Beach Office)   Robert C. Sommerville (P.A.)
Andrew L. Gordon   (Resident; West Palm Beach
Michael L. Gore   Office)
    (Resident at Orlando Office)   Xavier L. Suarez
Michael J. Grindstaff (P.A.)   Robert A. Wainger
    (Resident at Orlando Office)   Joseph Donald Wasil
Robert E. Gunn (P.A.)   Robert Wexler (Resident at
    (Resident at West Palm Beach   West Palm Beach Office)
    Office)   John B. White (P.A.)
Edmund T. Henry, III   James G. Willard
Mary Ruth Houston   (Resident at Orlando Office)
    (Resident at Orlando Office)   Scott G. Williams (Resident at
William N. Jacobs   West Palm Beach Office)
Rod Jones   Kenneth W. Wright
    (Resident at Orlando Office)   (Resident at Orlando Office)
John Thomas Kolinski   Robert T. Wright, Jr.

ASSOCIATES

Suzanne M. Amaducci   Jonathan D. Gerber (Resident at
    (Resident at Orlando Office)   West Palm Beach Office)
Maria J. Beguiristain   Robert B. Goldman (Resident at
Christopher W. Boyett   West Palm Beach Office)
Thomas P. Callan   David S. Goldstein
    (Resident at Orlando Office)   Joseph M. Goldstein
Gregory L. Denes   René J. González-Llorens
Terry B. Fein   Bradley S. Gould
Emilio Fernandez

(See Next Column)

ASSOCIATES (Continued)

Meredith A. Harper   Patrick M. Muldowney
    (Resident at Orlando Office)   (Resident at Orlando Office)
Marc J. Jason   Michelle R. North (Resident at
    (Resident at Orlando Office)   West Palm Beach Office)
Brian M. Jones   Aileen Ortega
    (Resident, Orlando Office)   Dario A. Perez
Jeffrey M. Landau   Joey Schlosberg
Lourdes B. Martinez-Esquivel   Geoffrey L. Travis
William G. Mc Cullough   Bryan S. Wells

OF COUNSEL

Jordan Bittel (P.A.)   Alexander Penelas
John S. Chowning (P.A.)   Stephen L. Perrone (P.A.)
John R. Day (P.A.)   Preston L. Prevatt
Stephen J. Gray (Resident,   Rosemarie N. Sanderson Schade
    London, England Office)   (P.A.) (Resident at
Marshall J. Langer (P.A.)   Amsterdam, The
    (Resident, London, England   Netherlands)
    Office)

CONSULTING ATTORNEY

Patrick L. Murray (Not admitted in the United States)

Representative Clients: Southern Bell Telephone Co.; General Electric Co.; Equitable Life Assurance Society of the U.S.; New England Mutual Life Insurance Co.; New York Life Insurance Co.

For full biographical listings, see the Martindale-Hubbell Law Directory

---

SIMMONS, HART & SHEEHE (AV)

A Partnership of Professional Associations
One Biscayne Tower, 2 South Biscayne Boulevard, Suite 1684, 33131
Telephone: 305-379-3515
Fax: 305-379-5404
Ocala, Florida Office: 125 Northeast First Avenue, Suite 1.
Telephone: 904-732-8121.
Fax: 904-368-2183.

Bryce W. Ackerman   Karl V. Hart
Daniel A. Amat   Phillip J. Sheehe
John B. Fuller   Young J. Simmons
Steven H. Gray   Jeffrey Skates
Timothy D. Haines   Marty Smith
      Louis V. Vendittelli

For full biographical listings, see the Martindale-Hubbell Law Directory

---

SPENCER AND KLEIN, PROFESSIONAL ASSOCIATION (AV)

Suite 1901, 801 Brickell Avenue, 33131
Telephone: 305-374-7700
Telecopier: 305-374-4890

Thomas R. Spencer, Jr.   Brent D. Klein

Paul D. Breitner   Cynthia A. Jacobs
Steven W. Simon   Richard C. Lorenzo
      David M. Tarlow
OF COUNSEL
Lawrence E. Major (P.A.)

Representative Clients: Aerocar Aviation, Inc.; America Publishing Group; American Association of Physicians and Surgeons; Coldwell Banker; Editorial Televisa; Grupo Anaya, S.A.; Independent Living Care, Inc.; Managed Care of America, Inc.; New Times, Inc.; Winn-Dixie Stores.

For full biographical listings, see the Martindale-Hubbell Law Directory

---

SQUIRE, SANDERS & DEMPSEY (AV)

201 South Biscayne Boulevard, Suite 2900 Miami Center, 33131-4330
Telephone: 305-577-8700
Fax: 305-358-1425
Cleveland, Ohio Office: 4900 Key Tower, 127 Public Square, Cleveland, Ohio 44114-1304.
Telephone: 216-479-8500. *Fax's:* 216-479-8780, 216-479-8781, 216-479-8787, 216-479-8795, 216-479-8793, 216-479-8776, 216-479-8788.
Columbus, Ohio Offices: 1300 Huntington Center, 41 South High Street, Columbus, Ohio 43215-6150.
Telephone: 614-365-2700.
Fax: 614-365-2499.
Jacksonville, Florida Office: One Enterprise Center, Suite 2100, 225 Water Street, Jacksonville, Florida 32202-4424.
Telephone: 904-353-1264.
Fax: 904-356-2986.
New York, New York Office: 350 Park Avenue, 15th Floor, New York, New York 10022-4232.
Telephone: 212-872-9800.
Fax: 212-872-9815.
Phoenix, Arizona Office: Two Renaissance Square, 40 North Central Avenue, Suite 2700, Phoenix, Arizona 85004-4441.
Telephone: 602-528-4000.
Fax: 602-253-8129.

(See Next Column)

SQUIRE, SANDERS & DEMPSEY, *Miami—Continued*

Washington, D.C. Office: 1201 Pennsylvania Avenue, N.W., P.O. Box 407, Washington, D.C. 20044-0407.
Telephone: 202-626-6600.
Fax: 202-626-6780.
London, England Office: 4th Floor, Royex House, Aldermanbury Square, London EC2V 7HR.
Telephone: 011-44-171-830-0055.
Fax: 011-44-171-830-0056.
Brussels, Belgium Office: Avenue Louise, 165-Box 15, 1050 Brussels, Belgium.
Telephone: 011-32-2-648-1717.
Fax: 011-32-2-648-1064.
Prague, Czech Republic Office: Vaclavska Namesti 57, 11000 PRAHA 1, Czech Republic.
Telephone: 011-42-2-216-62111.
Fax: 011-42-2-216-62222.
Bratislava, Slovakia Office: Zochova 5, 811-03 Bratislava, Slovak Republic.
Telephone: 011-42-7-531-7611.
Fax: 011-42-7-580-2212.
Budapest, Hungary Office: Deak Ferenc Ut. 10, Office 304, H-1052 Budapest V., Hungary.
Telephone: 011-36-1-226-2024.
Fax: 011-361-226-2025.
Kiev, Ukraine Office: vul. Prorizna 9, KV 20, Kiev 252030, Ukraine.
Telephone: 011-380-44-244-3452.
Fax: 011-380-44-228-4938.
Moscow, Russian Federation Office: 28 Pokrovka Street, No. 4-4A, Moscow 103062, Russian Federation.
Telephone: 7-503-956-3750.
Fax: 7-503-956-3635.

RESIDENT MEMBERS

Albert A. del Castillo Kenneth M. Myers
Luis Reiter

For full biographical listings, see the Martindale-Hubbell Law Directory

STEEL HECTOR & DAVIS LLP (AV)

A Registered Limited Liability Partnership
200 South Biscayne Boulevard, 33131-2398
Telephone: 305-577-7000
Telecopier: 305-577-7001
URL: http://www.steelhector.com
Key West, Florida Office: 330 Whitehead Street, Suite 250.
Telephone: 305-292-7272.
Telecopier: 305-292-7271.
Tallahassee, Florida Office, Suite 601, 215 South Monroe. *Telephone:* 904-222-2300.
Telecopier: 904-222-8410.
West Palm Beach, Florida Office: 1900 Phillips Point West.
Telephone: 407-650-7200.
Telecopier: 407-655-1509.
Caracas, Venezuela Office: Torre Europa, Nivel Oficinas #7-8, Avenida Francisco De Miranda, Caracas 1060.
Telephone: 582-951-4105.
Fax: 582-951-4106.
London, England Office: City Tower, Level 4, 40 Basinghall Street, London, U.K. EC2V 5DE.
Telephone: 44-171-382-9676.
Fax: 44-171-628-7710.

MEMBERS OF FIRM

William C. Steel (1916-1983)	Norman Davis
Darrey A. Davis (1910-1986)	Sonia de Cruz
Ron A. Adams (P.A.)	John W. Devine (P.A.)
Patricia Del Pino Arias	Ruben Diaz, Jr., (P.A.)
José I. Astigarraga	Jorge Diaz-Silveira (P.A.)
Thomas H. Barkdull, III, (P.A.) (Resident at West Palm Beach Office)	Zena Manes Dickstein (P.A.)
	Elizabeth J. du Fresne (P.A.)
	Thomas V. Eagan (P.A.)
Carlos A. Batlle (P.A.)	Mike F. Egan (Resident at West Palm Beach Office)
Lawrence P. Bemis (P.A.)	
Michael E. Botos (Resident at West Palm Beach Office)	D. Scott Elliott (P.A.) (Resident at West Palm Beach Office)
Brian R. Brattebo (Resident at West Palm Beach Office)	Joanne B. Erde (P.A.)
	Ellen Ann Feinberg (P.A.)
Mike S. Buckner (P.A.) (Resident at West Palm Beach Office)	Brian J. Felcoski (P.A.)
	Troy D. Ferguson
	Harry J. Friedman (P.A.)
John T. Butler	Gerry S. Gibson (P.A.) (Resident at West Palm Beach Office)
Mark R. Cheskin (P.A.)	
Matthew M. Childs (P.A.) (Resident at Tallahassee Office)	Harvey A. Goldman
	Daniel E. Gonzalez (P.A.)
Joseph C. Coates, III (Resident at West Palm Beach Office)	Denise Ann Gordon (Resident at West Palm Beach Office)
Barry G. Craig	James M. Grippando (P.A.)
Clay Craig	Charles A. Guyton (Resident at Tallahassee Office)
Denise Brody Crockett (P.A.)	
Maria T. Currier (P.A.)	George R. Harper (P.A.)
Alvin Bruce Davis	Alice G. Hector (P.A.)
Edward H. Davis, Jr. (P.A.)	Louis J. Hector
Gary Scott Davis (P.A.)	William K. Hill (P.A.)

(See Next Column)

MEMBERS OF FIRM (Continued)

Edward J. Hopkins (Resident at West Palm Beach Office)	Joseph W. Pallot (P.A.)
	Rebekah J. Poston
Thomas R. Julin	L. Martin Reeder, Jr. (Resident at West Palm Beach Office)
Thomas M. Karr (P.A.)	
Bradford D. Kaufman (P.A.) (Resident at West Palm Beach Office)	Mark T. Reeves (P.A.)
	Robert M. Rhodes (Resident at Tallahassee Office)
Patricia M. Kennedy (P.A.)	Traci H. Rollins (P.A.) (Resident at West Palm Beach Office)
William B. Killian	
Joseph P. Klock, Jr.	
Peter M. Kramer (P.A.)	Ira N. Rosner (P.A.)
Jeffrey L. Kravetz (P.A.)	Cathy Miller Sellers (Resident at Tallahassee Office)
Michael A. Laing (P.A.)	
Burton A. Landy (P.A.)	Sherwin P. Simmons (P.A.)
John W. Little, III (P.A.) (Resident at West Palm Beach Office)	Cristina M. Simon (Resident at West Palm Beach Office)
	John Edward Smith
David M. Lindsey	Jose F. Valdivia, III (P.A.)
Patricia Elaine Lowry (Resident at West Palm Beach Office)	John G. Van Laningham (P.A.) (Resident at West Palm Beach Office)
Bruce A. McAllister	
Thomas R. McGuigan (P.A.)	Jim Watt (P.A.) (Resident at West Palm Beach Office)
James M. Meyer (P.A.) (Resident, Caracas, Venezuela)	
	Abigail C. Watts-FitzGerald (P.A.)
Donald M. Middlebrooks	
James E. Morgan, III, (P.A.)	Victoria L. Weber (Resident at Tallahassee Office)
Guy E. Motzer (P.A.)	
Jeffrey I. Mullens (P.A.) (Resident at West Palm Beach Office)	Diane Noller Wells (P.A.)
	Thomas R. Woolsey (P.A.) (Resident at West Palm Beach Office)
Janet T. Munn	
Lewis F. Murphy (P.A.)	Miguel A. Zaldívar, Jr.
Thomas G. O'Brien III (Resident at West Palm Beach Office)	

ASSOCIATES

David Aronberg	Barbara Bolton Litten
Lisa R. Askowitz	David J. Maher
Jeffrey S. Bartel	Margarita M. Martinez
Donna E. Blanton (Resident at Tallahassee Office)	Ryon M. McCabe
	Edward M. Mullins
Sarah Becket Clasby	John B.T. Murray, Jr. (Resident at West Palm Beach Office)
Elisha L. Cohen	
Anne Tennant Cooney (Resident at West Palm Beach Office)	Mahesh H. Nanwani
	Christine A. Noworyta
Michael J. Corbera	F. David Olazabal
Glenn L. Criser (Resident at West Palm Beach Office)	Edward J. Pfister
	Matthew R. Piepenburg
Joseph F. Dearing	William Hoffman Pincus (Resident at West Palm Beach Office)
Ricardo J. Dopico	
Anne Marie Estevez	
Michelle A. Fongyee	Kim A. Prine (Resident at West Palm Beach Office)
Helen R. Franco (Resident at West Palm Beach Office)	
	Lornette A. Reynolds
Heather L. Gatley	Mark B. Roberts (Resident, West Palm Beach Office)
Patrick J. Goggins	
Gregory S. Grossman	L. Kirk Rogers
Lance A. Harke	Joel B. Ronkin
Belinda Ann Hatzenbuhler	Staci Schatzman
Marc Jason Heimowitz	Shanker Singham
Brian L. Heller	Jonathan Sjostrom (Resident at Tallahassee Office)
Reed Herrero	
Frank R. Jimenez	Jennifer Y. Sun
Beatriz Llorens Koltis	Edwin G. Torres
Lisa A. Landy	W. Kent Walker
Wendy S. Leavitt	Denise Wallace
William F. Lee	Nanette O'Donnell Wernstrom
Michael P. Levinson	Vikki Lynn Wulf (Resident at West Palm Beach)
Alvin F. Lindsay III	

OF COUNSEL

Wilson Smith (P.A.) Amy Lehman

Henry W. Wiggin

LEGAL SUPPORT PERSONNEL

James B. Krog

Representative Clients: FPL Group, Inc.; John Hancock Mutual Life Insurance Co.

For full biographical listings, see the Martindale-Hubbell Law Directory

STROOCK & STROOCK & LAVAN (AV)

200 South Biscayne Boulevard Suite 3300, First Union Financial Center, 33131-2385
Telephone: 305-358-9900
Telecopier: (305) 789-9302
New York, N.Y. Office: (as of 1/24/97) 180 Maiden Lane, New York, N.Y., 10038.
Telephone: 212-806-5400.
Telecopiers: (212) 806-5919; (212) 806-6006; (212) 806-6086; (212) 425-9509; (212) 806-6176.

(See Next Column)

STROOCK & STROOCK & LAVAN—*Continued*

New York Conference Center: 767 Third Avenue, New York, N.Y., 10017-2023.
Telephones: 212-806-5767; 5768; 5769; 5770.
Telecopier: (212) 421-6234.
Boston, Massachusetts Office: 100 Federal Street, 02110.
Telephone: 617-482-6800.
Fax: 617-330-5111.
Budapest, Hungary Office: East-West Business Center, Rákóczi ut 1-3, H-1088.
Telephone: 011-361-266-9520 or 011-361-266-7770.
Telecopier: 011-361-9279.
Los Angeles, California Office: Suite 1800, 2029 Century Park East, 90067-3086.
Telephone: 310-556-5800.
Telecopier: (310) 556-5959.
Washington, D.C. Office: 1150 Seventeenth Street, N.W., Suite 600, 20036-4652.
Telephone: 202-452-9250.
Telecopier: (202) 293-2293.

RESIDENT PARTNERS

Scott L. Baena	David C. Pollack
Michael Basile	Arnold D. Shevin
Robert K. Jordan	Paul Steven Singerman
Daniel Lampert	Robert W. Turken

RETIRED PARTNER

Robert L. Shevin	Charles R. Taine

COUNSEL

Richard S. Savitt

SPECIAL COUNSEL

Mindy A. Mora	Robert M. Siegel
	Carey A. Stiss

Kathleen M.P. Baker	Jonathan E. Minsker
M. St. John Daugherty	Jeff C. Schneider
Manuel A. Fernandez	Richard B. Simring
Claudia F. Haines	Steven J. Solomon
Ilyse Wrubel Homer	Steven M. Stoll
	Thomas E. Truske

For full biographical listings, see the Martindale-Hubbell Law Directory

THOMSON MURARO RAZOOK & HART, P.A. (AV)

17th Floor, One Southeast Third Avenue, 33131
Telephone: 305-350-7200
Telecopier: 305-374-1005

Parker Davidson Thomson	Jeffrey Watkin
Robert E. Muraro	Carol A. Licko
Richard J. Razook	Steven W. Davis
Brian A. Hart	Dennis M. Campbell
Sarah L. Schweitzer	Timothy J. Norris

OF COUNSEL

Robert N. Rothberg (Not admitted in FL)

PRACTICE ADVISOR

Elliott Manning

Eric L. Rosenberg	Gregg H. Metzger
	R. Amy Blum

Representative Clients: Bacardi; Community Television Foundation of South Florida, Inc.; Florida Jai-Alai; State of Florida; United States Sugar Corporation; Miami Columbus, Inc.; The Exotic Gardens, Inc.; Bank Audi; Ideon Group, Inc.; Florida Medical Services; Florida Institute of Health.

For full biographical listings, see the Martindale-Hubbell Law Directory

THORNTON, DAVIS & MURRAY, P.A. (AV)

World Trade Center, 80 Southwest Eighth Street Suite 2900, 33130
Telephone: 305-446-2646
Fax: 305-441-2374
Email: tdm@gate.net

John M. Murray	Frederick J. Fein
Barry L. Davis	Ana Maria Marin
J. Thompson Thornton	David P. Herman

Jeffrey F. D. Bogert	Harold E. Rambo, Jr.
Mark D. Bohm	Scott D. Rembold
Ury Fischer	Mario M. Ruiz
Holly S. Harvey	Steven E. Wallach
Kathleen M. O'Connor	Rebecca B. Watford

For full biographical listings, see the Martindale-Hubbell Law Directory

TRALINS AND ASSOCIATES, P.A. (AV)

Suite 3310 2 South Biscayne Boulevard, 33131
Telephone: 305-374-3300
Telefax: 305-374-4933

(See Next Column)

Myles J. Tralins

Mitchell R. Katz	Rachel S. Cohen

For full biographical listings, see the Martindale-Hubbell Law Directory

WALTON LANTAFF SCHROEDER & CARSON (AV)

A Partnership including Professional Associations
One Biscayne Tower, 25th Floor, 2 South Biscayne Boulevard, 33131
Telephone: 305-379-6411
Telecopier: 305-577-3875
West Palm Beach, Florida Office: United National Bank Tower, Suite 800, 1645 Palm Beach Lakes Boulevard.
Telephone: 407-689-6700.
Telecopier: 407-689-2647.
Fort Lauderdale, Florida Office: Blackstone Building, Third Floor, 707 Southeast Third Avenue.
Telephone: 305-463-8456.
Telecopier: 305-763-6294.
Coral Gables, Florida Office: Suite 1101, Gables International Plaza, 2655 Le Jeune Road.
Telephone: 305-379-6411.
Telecopier: 305-446-9206.

MEMBERS OF FIRM

Miller Walton (1901-1987)	Roberta J. Karp
William C. Lantaff (1913-1970)	(West Palm Beach Office)
Laurence A. Schroeder	John G. White, III
(1907-1995)	(West Palm Beach Office)
Charles P. Sacher (P.A.)	G. Bartram Billbrough, Jr.
(Coral Gables Office)	Robert J. Strunin
Michael R. Jenks (P.A.)	Deborah Poore Knight
David K. Tharp	(Ft. Lauderdale Office)
Wayne T. Gill (P.A.)	Richard G. Rosenblum
(West Palm Beach Office)	(Ft. Lauderdale Office)
Nicholas E. Christin (P.A.)	Henry Suarez
(Coral Gables Office)	David M. McDonald
Richard P. Cole (P.A.)	Michael W. Baker
Stephen W. Bazinsky	(Ft. Lauderdale Office)
(Ft. Lauderdale Office)	Robert L. Teitler
Charles Brown Mirman (P.A.)	Gregory T. Martini
Jonathan J. Davis	(Coral Gables Office)
(Ft. Lauderdale Office)	Robert M. Donlon
Bernard I. Probst	(West Palm Beach Office)
Lawrence D. Smith, Jr.	Geoffrey B. Marks
John P. Joy	Allison B. Chittem Harnett
John W. McLuskey	Juliean Lynn Rice-Charouhis
Gregory J. Willis	Gene P. Kissane
(Ft. Lauderdale Office)	Amy L. Smith
Beth J. Leahy	(West Palm Beach Office)
(Ft. Lauderdale Office)	

OF COUNSEL

Samuel O. Carson	Robert B. Cole
William J. Gray	(Coral Gables Office)
Martin E. Segal (P.A.)	
(Coral Gables Office)	

ASSOCIATES

Paul S. Martin	Joseph P. Cinney
Frank J. Taddeo	Rhett P. Dove, III
(Ft. Lauderdale Office)	Kenneth L. Valentini
Gregory William Coleman	Russell A. Dohan
(West Palm Beach Office)	Steven E. Foor
Scott Allan Cole	(West Palm Beach Office)
William G. Hersman	Ellen S. Malasky
Lawrence D. King	(West Palm Beach Office)
Charles S. Sacher	Warren Brown
(Coral Gables Office)	Charlie Martinez
George W. Bush, Jr.	Daniel A. Shapiro
(West Palm Beach Office)	Gregg R. Margre
Kurt A. Wyland	(West Palm Beach Office)
(West Palm Beach Office)	Steven C. Sessa
Nancy C. Valcarce	(West Palm Beach Office)
Kip O. Lassner	Stuart J. Haft
David S. Tadros	(Coral Gables Office)
(West Palm Beach Office)	

For full biographical listings, see the Martindale-Hubbell Law Directory

WELBAUM, GUERNSEY, HINGSTON, GREENLEAF & GREGORY, L.L.P. (AV)

Penthouse Suite, 901 Ponce de Leon Boulevard (Coral Gables), 33134-3009
Telephone: 305-441-8900
Fax: 305-441-2255

MEMBERS OF FIRM

R. Earl Welbaum	Robert A. Hingston
Dan B. Guernsey	W. Frank Greenleaf
	John H. Gregory

ASSOCIATES

Michael Yates	Mark D. Greenwell

(See Next Column)

WELBAUM, GUERNSEY, HINGSTON, GREENLEAF & GREGORY L.L.P., *Miami—Continued*

OF COUNSEL

Alice E. Warwick　　　　　　　René Sacasas

For full biographical listings, see the Martindale-Hubbell Law Directory

ZACK, SPARBER, KOSNITZKY, SPRATT & BROOKS, P.A. (AV)

International Place, 100 Southeast Second Street, Suite 2800, 33131-2144
Telephone: 305-539-8400
Facsimile: 305-539-1307

Stephen N. Zack	Bertha Claire Lee
Byron L. Sparber	Mitchell W. Mandler
Michael Kosnitzky	Deborah R. Mayo
William J. Spratt, Jr.	Nancy E. McCarthy
Gary S. Brooks	H. Stephen Rash
Jennifer G. Altman	Roland Sanchez-Medina, Jr.
Marc H. Auerbach	Ralph Shalom
Orion Gray Callison, III	Heileen Sosa
Alan G. Geffin	Henri I. Spiegel
Jorge A. Gonzalez	William Henry Stafford
Debra Weiss Goodstone	Jay A. Steinman
Louise T. Jeroslow	Thomas O. Wells

OF COUNSEL

Kimarie R. Stratos

For full biographical listings, see the Martindale-Hubbell Law Directory

---

MIAMI BEACH, Dade Co.

THERREL BAISDEN & MEYER WEISS (AV)

Suite 500, 1111 Lincoln Road Mall, 33139
Telephone: 305-672-1921
Telecopier: 305-674-0807

MEMBERS OF FIRM

Catchings Therrel (1890-1971)	Nicholas M. Daniels
Fred R. Baisden (1903-1971)	Ellen Rose
Baron De Hirsch Meyer (1899-1974)	Leo Rose, Jr.
	Fred R. Stanton
Milton Weiss (1913-1980)	Richard A. Wood

ASSOCIATES

Seth E. Ellis　　　　　　　Jonathan Feuerman
Peter M. Lopez

OF COUNSEL

David Darlow

General Counsel: Chase Federal Bank; Jefferson National Bank Trust Department; American Equity Site Developers.
Counsel for: City Planned Communities Corp.; Anthony Abraham Chevrolet.

For full biographical listings, see the Martindale-Hubbell Law Directory

---

MILTON,* Santa Rosa Co.

JOHNSON, GREEN, MILLER & GIBSON, P.A. (AV)

6850 Caroline Street, P.O. Box 605, 32572-0605
Telephone: 904-623-3841
Fax: 904-623-3555

T. Sol Johnson	Johnny L. Miller, Jr.
Paul R. Green	Michael Gibson

Representative Client: School Board of Santa Rosa County.

For full biographical listings, see the Martindale-Hubbell Law Directory

---

MONTICELLO,* Jefferson Co. — (Refer to Tallahassee)

NAPLES,* Collier Co.

CATALANO, FISHER, GREGORY & SULLIVAN, CHARTERED (AV)

Northern Trust Building, Suite 404, 4001 Tamiami Trail North, 33940
Telephone: 941-262-8000
Telecopier: 941-262-4372

Anthony J. Catalano	C. Neil Gregory
A. Alston Fisher, Jr.	John L. Sullivan, Jr.

For full biographical listings, see the Martindale-Hubbell Law Directory

JAMES W. ELKINS, P.A. (AV)

Suite 303 The Fairway Building, 1000 Tamiami Trail North, 33940
Telephone: 941-263-0910
Fax: 941-263-6091

James W. Elkins

Approved Attorney for: Attorneys Title Insurance Fund.

For full biographical listings, see the Martindale-Hubbell Law Directory

---

PORTER, WRIGHT, MORRIS & ARTHUR (AV)

4501 Tamiami Trail North, 33940-3013
Telephone: 941-263-8898; (800-876-7962)
FAX: 941-436-2990
Email: apf@porterwright.com
Columbus, Ohio Office: 41 South High Street, 43215-6194.
Telephones: 614-227-2000; (800-533-2794).
Fax: 614-227-2100. Internet: cmh@porterwright.com.
Dayton, Ohio Office: One Dayton Centre, One South Main Street, 45402-2028.
Telephones: 513-228-2411; (800-533-4434).
Fax: 513-449-6820. Internet: day@porterwright.com.
Cincinnati, Ohio Office: 250 E. Fifth Street, 45202-4199.
Telephones: 513-381-4700; (800-582-5813).
Fax: 513-421-0991. Internet: cvg@porterwright.com.
Cleveland, Ohio Office: 925 Euclid Avenue, 44115-1483.
Telephones: 216-443-9000; (800-824-1980).
Fax: 216-443-9011. Internet: cle@porterwright.com.
Washington, D.C. Office: 1233 20th Street, N.W., 20036-2395.
Telephones: 202-778-3000; (800-456-7962).
Fax: 202-778-3063. Internet: dca@porterwright.com.

MEMBERS OF FIRM

Robert M. Buckel (Resident)	Gary K. Wilson (Resident)
W. Jeffrey Cecil (Resident)	Harry L. Henning
Mary Beth Moser Clary	Richard M. Markus
Jeffrey S. Kannensohn	Ronald S. Perlman
James E. Willis (Resident)	Dixon F. Miller

OF COUNSEL

John D. Gast

RESIDENT ASSOCIATES

Margaret Castellana	J. Gary Shirk
Georgia A. Hiller	Stuart A. Thompson

For full biographical listings, see the Martindale-Hubbell Law Directory

---

QUARLES & BRADY (AV)

Barnett Center, 4501 Tamiami Trail North Suite 300, 33940-3060
Telephone: 941-262-5959
Fax: 941-434-4999
Milwaukee, Wisconsin Office: 411 East Wisconsin Avenue, 53202-4497.
Telephone: 414-277-5000.
Fax: 414-271-3552.
Madison, Wisconsin Office: Firstar Plaza, One South Pinckney Street, P.O. Box 2113, 53701-2113.
Telephone: 608-251-5000.
Fax: 608-251-9166.
West Palm Beach, Florida Office: 222 Lakeview Avenue, 4th Floor, 33401.
Telephone: 561-653-5000.
Fax: 561-653-5333.
Phoenix, Arizona Office: One Camelback Building, One East Camelback Road, Suite 400, 85012-1649.
Telephone: 602-230-5500.
Fax: 602-230-5598.

PARTNERS

Thomas E. Maloney	Robert E. Doyle, Jr.
F. Joseph McMackin, III	Leo J. Salvatori
Timothy G. Hains	Kimberly Leach Johnson

ASSOCIATES

Joseph D. Zaks	Kevin A. Denti
John D. Humphreville	Samara S. Holland
Louis D. D'Agostino	Mark Hubert Muller
James T. Demarest	

BUSINESS MANAGEMENT SUPPORT PERSONNEL

Jill M. Miller (Florida Administrator)

LEGAL ASSISTANTS

Susan L. Ahlborn	Tianna Costin

For full biographical listings, see the Martindale-Hubbell Law Directory

---

OCALA,* Marion Co.

AYRES, CLUSTER, CURRY, McCALL & BRIGGS, P.A. (AV)

21 Northeast First Avenue, P.O. Box 1148, 34478
Telephone: 352-351-2222
Telecopier: 352-351-0312

Willard Ayres (1910-1988)	Douglas H. Oswald
Edwin C. Cluster	James E. Collins
Landis V. Curry, Jr.	Scott Allan Frick
Wayne C. McCall	Jeffrey L. Sauey
Randy R. Briggs	Steven W. Wingo
C. Jeanne Bassett	

Counsel For: SunTrust Bank, North Central Florida; Castro Realty Corp.; Ocala Manufacturing Company (Not Inc.); Kinsman Stud Farm; Mockingbird Farm; Ocala Stud Farm; Live Oak Farm.
Local Counsel For: On Top of the World; AMREP Corp.; Avatar. Corporation of America.

For full biographical listings, see the Martindale-Hubbell Law Directory

Ocala—Continued

SAVAGE, KRIM & SIMONS, P.A. (AV)

121 N.W. Third Street, 34475-6695
Telephone: 352-732-8944
Fax: 352-867-0504

Charles A. Savage (1898-1994)   Frederick J. Krim
Gary C. Simons

Timothy S. Babiarz
OF COUNSEL
Richard T. Jones

Approved Attorneys for: Attorneys' Title Insurance Fund, Inc.; Federal Land Bank, Columbia, S. C.
References: Ocala National Bank; First Union National Bank of Florida; Barnett Bank of Marion County, N.A.; SunTrust Bank, North Central Florida.

For full biographical listings, see the Martindale-Hubbell Law Directory

SIMMONS, HART & SHEEHE (AV)

A Partnership of Professional Associations
125 Northeast First Avenue, Suite 1, P.O. Box 3310, 34478-3310
Telephone: 352-732-8121
Fax: 352-368-2183
Miami, Florida Office: One Biscayne Tower, Suite 1684, 2 South Biscayne Boulevard, 33131.
Telephone: 305-379-3515.
Fax: 305-379-5404.

Bryce W. Ackerman   Karl V. Hart
Daniel A. Amat   Young J. Simmons
John B. Fuller   Phillip J. Sheehe
Steven H. Gray   Jeffrey Skates
Timothy D. Haines   Marty Smith
Louis V. Vendittelli

Representative Clients: Keeneland Association, Inc.; CSX Railroad; Double Diamond Farm; California Federal Bank.

For full biographical listings, see the Martindale-Hubbell Law Directory

---

ORLANDO,* Orange Co.

ADAMS, HILL, REIS, ADAMS, HALL & SCHIEFFELIN (AV)

1417 East Concord Street, 32803
Telephone: 407-896-0425
Fax: 407-896-9236

MEMBERS OF FIRM
George E. Adams   Janet W. Adams
G. Bruce Hill   Larry D. Hall
Gregory F. Reis   Thomas L. Schieffelin, Jr.
ASSOCIATES
William W. Large   William H. Olney
Matthew P. Bartolomei Richard Coaxum, Jr
Christopher E. Butler

Representative Clients: Everglades Regional Medical Center; The Florida Hospital Trust Fund; The Florida Hospital Excess Trust Fund; Florida Hospital Workers Compensation/Self Insurance Trust Fund; Bartow Memorial Hospital; Bay Medical Center; Brooksville Regional Hospital; Cape Canaveral Hospital; Cape Coral Hospital; Desoto Memorial Hospital.

For full biographical listings, see the Martindale-Hubbell Law Directory

ADAMS & SPEARS, P.A. (AV)

940 Highland Avenue, P.O. Box 3627, 32802
Telephone: 407-422-8116
Fax: 407-648-1044
Email: 74767.2745@compuserve.com

Richard H. Adams, Jr.   Richard D. Connor, Jr.
Douglas C. Spears   Deborah B. Ansbro

Peter C. Vilmos   Elizabeth A. Baker
Joyce R. Adams
OF COUNSEL
Ley H. Smith

General Counsel for: Lochaven Federal Savings & Loan; Independence Mortgage Corporation of America.
Representative Clients: Ensign Property Group, Inc.; Deere Credit Services.

For full biographical listings, see the Martindale-Hubbell Law Directory

BAKER & HOSTETLER (AV)

SunBank Center, Suite 2300, 200 South Orange Avenue, 32802-3432
Telephone: 407-649-4000
In Cleveland, Ohio: 3200 National City Center, 1900 East Ninth Street.
Telephone: 216-621-0200.

(See Next Column)

In Columbus, Ohio: Capitol Square, Suite 2100, 65 East State Street.
Telephone: 614-228-1541.
In Denver, Colorado: 303 East 17th Avenue, Suite 1100.
Telephone: 303-861-0600.
In Houston, Texas: 1000 Louisiana, Suite 2000.
Telephone: 713-751-1600.
In Long Beach, California: 300 Oceangate, Suite 620.
Telephone: 310-432-2827.
In Los Angeles, California: 600 Wilshire Boulevard.
Telephone: 213-624-2400.
In Washington, D.C.: Washington Square, Suite 1100, 1050 Connecticut Avenue, N.W., Suite 1100.
Telephone: 202-861-1500.
In College Park, Maryland: 9658 Baltimore Boulevard, Suite 206.
Telephone: 301-441-2781.
In Alexandria, Virginia: 437 North Lee Street.
Telephone: 703-549-1294.
In San Francisco, California: One Sansome Street, Suite 2000.
Telephone: 415-951-4705.

MEMBERS OF FIRM IN ORLANDO, FLORIDA
G. Thomas Ball (Managing Partner-Orlando Office)
PARTNERS

Stephen E. Cook   Jerry R. Linscott
Thomas R. deRosa   John Melicharek, Jr.
  (Not admitted in FL)   Frank M. Mock
Denis L. Durkin   Rosemary O'Shea
James V. Etscorn   Hector A. Perez
John W. Foster, Sr.   Joel H. Sharp, Jr.
Richard T. Fulton   Lynn E. Wagner
Kurt P. Gruber   Robert J. Webb
Todd M. Hoepker   David S. Wood
Kenneth C. Wright

ASSOCIATES

Odiator Arugu   Joanne Braddock Lambert
Daniel Bachrach   Mark S. Lieblich
Lea A. Banks   Andrew T. Marcus
Elise L. Bloom   Richard D. Robinson
Jacqueline Bozzuto   Mark D. Scheinblum
Lynn E. Burnsed   (Not admitted in FL)
Jeffrey E. Decker   Dani D. Smith
Mary E. Fitzgibbons   Richard A. Solomon
Christopher N. Fountas   I. William Spivey, II
Joshua M. Glazov   Robert W. Thielhelm, Jr.
William C. Guthrie   Harkley R. Thornton
George F. Indest III   Rana Tiwari
Jeffery Q. Jonasen   Karen Whitehead

OF COUNSEL
Laurie J. Levin
RETIRED PARTNER
V. Keith Young

For full biographical listings, see the Martindale-Hubbell Law Directory

BROAD AND CASSEL (AV)

A Partnership including Professional Associations
Barnett Bank Center, 390 N. Orange Avenue, Suite 1100, 32801
Telephone: 407-839-4200
Telecopier: 407-425-8377
Boca Raton, Florida Office: Corporate Centre at Boca Raton, Suite 300, 7777 Glades Road, 33434.
Telephone: 561-483-7000.
Fort Lauderdale, Florida Office: Suite 1130, Broward Financial Centre, 500 E. Broward Boulevard, 33394.
Telephone: 954-764-7060.
Miami, Florida Office: Miami Center, 201 South Biscayne Boulevard, Suite 3000, 33131.
Telephone: 305-373-9400.
Stuart, Florida Office: 900 East Ocean Boulevard, Suite 126, 33994.
Telephone: 561-283-3000.
Tallahassee, Florida Office: 215 South Monroe Street, Suite 400, 32302.
Telephone: 904-681-6810.
Tampa, Florida Office: 100 North Tampa, Suite 3500, 33602.
Telephone: 813-225-3020.
West Palm Beach, Florida Office: The Reflections Office Center, Fifth Floor, 400 Australian Avenue, South, 33401.
Telephone: 561-832-3300.

RESIDENT PARTNERS
C. Ken Bishop (P.A.)   Robert T. Rosen (P.A.)
Robert D. Gatton (P.A.)   Randal M. Alligood (P.A.)
C. David Brown, II, (P.A.) Andrew B. Thomas (P.A.)
F. Vernon Bennett   Jack R. Elliott (P.A.)
Anthony W. Palma (P.A.)   Deborah H. Johnson (P.A.)
James E. Slater (P.A.)   Richard N. Milian (P.A.)
Marshall S. Harris (P.A.)

(See Next Column)

BROAD AND CASSEL, *Orlando—Continued*

RESIDENT ASSOCIATES

Roy S. Kobert	Robert F. Mallett
C. Christopher Killer	Jane B. Palmier
Douglas E. Starcher	Leigh Ann Murvin
Elisabeth E.Q. Scholes	T. Kevin Taylor
Keith F. White	David F. Leon
Robert Alfert, Jr.	Howard M. Robinson
Andrea J. Fowler	

OF COUNSEL

William M. Rowland, Jr. (P.A.)	Wanda L. Brown
I. Burton Spraker	Alan M. Gerlach, Jr.

General Counsel for: Bank of Central Florida; Trammell Crow Residential; CED, Inc.; Quality Factory Outlet Centers; Orlando-Orange County Expressway Authority; Orange County School Board.

Approved Attorneys for: Attorneys' Title Insurance Fund; Chicago Title Insurance Co.; Commonwealth Land Title Insurance Co.; Ticor Title Insurance Co.

For full biographical listings, see the Martindale-Hubbell Law Directory

CARLTON, FIELDS, WARD, EMMANUEL, SMITH & CUTLER, P.A. (AV)

Suite 1600 Citrus Center, 255 South Orange Avenue (32801-3488), P.O. Box 1171, 32801-1171
Telephone: 407-849-0300
Telecopier: (407) 648-9099
Pensacola, Florida Office: Harbourview Building, 4th Floor, 25 West Cedar Street, 32501-5974, P.O. Box 12426, 32582-2426.
Telephone: 904-434-0142.
St. Petersburg, Florida Office: Barnett Tower, Suite 2300, One Progress Plaza, 200 Central Avenue, 33701-4352, P.O. Box 2861, 33731-2861.
Telephone: 813-821-7000.
Tallahassee, Florida Office: 215 South Monroe Street, Suite 500, 32301-1866, P.O. Drawer 190, 32301-4352.
Telephone: 904-224-1585.
Tampa, Florida Office: One Harbour Place, 777 South Harbour Island Boulevard, 33602-5799, P.O. Box 3239, 33601-3239.
Telephone: 813-223-7000.
West Palm Beach, Florida Office: Esperanté, 222 Lakeview Avenue, Suite 1400, 33401-6149, P.O. Box 150, 33402-0150.
Telephone: 407-659-7070.

Lawrence M. Watson, Jr.	Jeffry R. Jontz
Roger D. Schwenke	Vernon Swartsel
George Barford	Laurel E. Lockett
Laurence E. Kinsolving	Daniel C. Johnson
Robert L. Young	Michael D. Williams
William D. Palmer	Thomas H. Justice III
Thomas D. Scanlon	Philip A. Diamond
Charles J. Cacciabeve	Alton L. Lightsey

OF COUNSEL

Davisson F. Dunlap	James A. Urban

Vivian P. Cocotas	Cindy L. Rodgers
Thomas P. Wert	Charlotte L. Warren

For full biographical listings, see the Martindale-Hubbell Law Directory

EUBANKS, HILYARD, RUMBLEY, MEIER & LENGAUER, A PROFESSIONAL ASSOCIATION (AV)

Suite 1700 - Gateway Center The Travelers Building, 1000 Legion Place, P.O. Box 4973, 32802-4973
Telephone: 407-425-4251
Telecopier: 407-841-8431

Ernest H. Eubanks	Bruce R. Bogan
Rodney G. Ross (1934-1982)	Melissa Arony
Sutton G. Hilyard, Jr.	Bobby G. Palmer, Jr.
G. Yates Rumbley	Edward L. Fagan
George A. Meier, III	Douglas G. Carey
Steven F. Lengauer	Virginia S. Williams
Jeffrey G. Slater	Wiley A. Rariden
Robert E. Bonner	Melinda G. Baum
Craig L. Brams	Perry W. Doran, II
Alexander Muszynski, III	Josh L. Poe
Bryan K. McMinn	

Representative Clients: Chubb & Son; Gallagher-Bassett Insurance Service; Kemper Group; Liberty Mutual Insurance Co.; Orange County, Florida/-City of Orlando; Reliance Insurance Cos.; United Technologies Corp.; Walt Disney World Co.; Zurich Insurance Co.

For full biographical listings, see the Martindale-Hubbell Law Directory

FOLEY & LARDNER (AV)

Suite 1800, 111 North Orange Avenue, P.O. Box 2193, 32802-2193
Telephone: 407-423-7656
Telex: 441781 (HQ ORL)
Facsimile: 407-648-1743
Milwaukee, Wisconsin Office: Firstar Center, 777 East Wisconsin Avenue.
Telephone: 414-271-2400.
Telex: 26-819 (Foley Lard Mil).
Facsimile: 414-297-4900.
Madison, Wisconsin Office: Verex Plaza, 150 East Gilman Street, P.O. Box 1497.
Telephone: 608-257-5035.
Telex: 262051 (F L Madison).
Facsimile: 608-258-4258.
Chicago, Illinois Office: Suite 3300, One IBM Plaza, 330 N. Wabash Avenue.
Telephone: 312-755-1900.
Facsimile: 312-755-1925.
Washington, D.C. Office: Washington Harbour, Suite 500, 3000 K Street, N.W.
Telephone: 202-672-5300.
Telex: 904136 (Foley Lard Wsh).
Facsimile: 202-672-5399.
Annapolis, Maryland Office: Suite 102, 175 Admiral Cochrane Drive.
Telephone: 301-266-8077.
Telex: 899149 (Oldtownpat).
Facsimile: 301-266-8664.
Jacksonville, Florida Office: The Greenleaf Building, 200 Laura Street, P.O. Box 240.
Telephone: 904-359-2000.
Facsimile: 904-359-8700.
Tallahassee, Florida Office: Suite 300, 123 South Calhoun Street, P.O. Box 508.
Telephone: 904-222-6100.
Facsimile: 904-224-0496.
Tampa, Florida Office: Suite 2700, One Hundred N. Tampa Street, P.O. Box 3391.
Telephones: 813-229-2300; Pinellas County: 813-442-3296.
Facsimile: 813-221-4210
West Palm Beach, Florida Office: Suite 200, Phillips Point East Tower, 777 South Flagler Drive.
Telephone: 407-655-5050.
Facsimile: 407-655-6925.
Brussels, Belgium Office: Avenue Louise, 283.
Telephone: 32-2-646-2777.
Facsimile: 32-2-646-7574.
Foley Lardner Weissburg & Aronson Office Locations:
Los Angeles, California Office: 2049 Century Park East, Suite 3200.
Telephone: 310-277-2223.
Fax: 310-557-8475.
Sacramento, California Office: 770 L Street, Suite 1050.
Telephone: 916-443-8005.
Fax: 916-443-2240.
San Diego, California Office: 402 West Broadway, 23rd Floor.
Telephone: 619-234-6655.
Fax: 619-234-3510.
San Francisco, California Office: One Maritime Plaza, Sixth Floor.
Telephone: 415-434-4484.
Fax: 415-434-4507.

RESIDENT PARTNERS

J. Gordon Arkin	Kathleen L. Maloney
Edmund T. Baxa, Jr.	Thomas K. Maurer
Terence J. Delahunty, Jr.	K. Rodney May
Richard A. DuRose	Sybil Meloy
Mark C. Extein	Christopher D. Rolle
James S. Grodin	Paul E. Rosenthal
Richard A. Heinle	John A. Sanders
Keith James Hesse	Ronald M. Schirtzer
John P. Horan	Christi L. Underwood
Michael A. Hornreich	Jon M. Wilson
R. Duke Woodson	

RETIRED PARTNERS

Norman F. Burke	Francis V. Gay
Egerton K. van den Berg	

RESIDENT ASSOCIATES

Bradley K. Alley	John S. Lord, Jr.
Anita L. Barber	Karen A. Lorenzen
Kelly M. Braun	Lucy Johnson Mangan
Jennifer S. Brown	Michele A. Matrick
Scott M. Clements	Lili C. Metcalf
W. Bruce DelValle	Daniel T. O'Keefe
Mary A. Doty	Jason A. Rosenthal
Martha H. Formella	Marian Wossum Schlow
Kevin D. Fowler	(Resident)
Michael Gay	Arthur D. Sims, II
John R. Hamilton	J. Walter Spiva
Deborah Lifshey	Barry L. Williams
(Not admitted in FL)	(Not admitted in FL)

General Counsel for: The Greater Orlando Aviation Authority.
Attorneys for: United Parcel Service of America, Inc.; Citrus Central, Inc.

For full biographical listings, see the Martindale-Hubbell Law Directory

Orlando—Continued

GURNEY & HANDLEY, P.A. (AV)

225 East Robinson Street, Suite 450, 32801
Telephone: 407-843-9500
Facsimile: 407-649-4941
Email: 74011.2161@compuserve.com

Leon H. Handley	Robert S. Green
Richard W. Lassiter	W. Marvin Hardy, III
John L. Sewell	Ronald L. Harrop
David W. Roquemore, Jr.	Francis E. Pierce, III

Peter N. Smith

David Brian Falstad	Michael V. Barszcz
J. Brian Baird	Steven H. Preston

Paul D. Rang

Representative Clients: Atlanta Casualty Company; Beneficial Mortgage Corp.; California Federal Bank, FSB; Government Employees Insurance Co.; Huntington National Bank of Florida; John Hancock Mutual Life Insurance Co.; Meritor Credit Corp.; Orlando Utilities Commission; Phoenix Home Life Mutual Insurance Co.; University of Florida.

For full biographical listings, see the Martindale-Hubbell Law Directory

HOLLAND & KNIGHT LLP (AV)

A Partnership including Professional Corporations
200 S. Orange Avenue, Suite 2600, 32801
Telephone: 407-425-8500
Fax: 407-244-5288
Mailing Address: P.O. Box 1526, 32802
Email: hklaw.com *URL:* http://www.hklaw.com
Fort Lauderdale, Florida Office: One East Broward Boulevard, Suite 1300.
Telephone: 954-525-1000.
Fax: 954-463-2030.
Jacksonville, Florida Office: 50 N. Laura Street, Suite 3900.
Telephone: 904-353-2000.
Fax: 904-358-1872.
Lakeland, Florida Office: 92 Lake Wire Drive.
Telephone: 941-682-1161.
Fax: 941-688-1186.
Miami, Florida Office: 701 Brickell Avenue, 30th Floor.
Telephone: 305-374-8500.
Fax: 305-787-7799.
St. Petersburg, Florida Office: One Progress Plaza, Suite 1600.
Telephone: 813-896-7171.
Fax: 813-822-8048.
Tallahassee, Florida Office: 315 Calhoun Street, Suite 600.
Telephone: 904-224-7000.
Fax: 904-224-8832.
Tampa, Florida Office: 400 North Ashley, Suite 2300.
Telephone: 813-227-8500.
Fax: 813-229-0134.
West Palm Beach, Florida Office: 625 N. Flagler Drive, Suite 700.
Telephone: 561-833-2000.
Fax: 561-650-8399.
Washington, D.C. Office: 2100 Pennsylvania Avenue, N.W.
Telephone: 202-955-3000.
Fax: 202-955-5564.
Atlanta, Georgia Office: 1201 West Peachtree Street, N.E., Suite 2000.
Telephone: 404-817-8500.
Fax: 404-881-0470.

ORLANDO MEMBERS AND ASSOCIATES

Thomas Boroughs	C. Parkhill Mays, Jr.
Mark J. Buhler	Brian A. McDowell
David E. Cardwell	Howell W. Melton, Jr.
Louis T. M. Conti	Leslie King O'Neal
Raymond Ehrlich	Robin Uricchio O'Quinn
James L. Fly	James A. Park, III
Catherine R. Henin-Clark	Steven R. Schooley
William O. E. Henry	James L. Simon
J. Fraser Himes	Roger W. Sims
Phyllis A. Hood	Lee Stuart Smith

Richard L. Stockton

Michael W. Andrew, Jr.	Gregory J. Johansen
Cynthia J. Brennan	Kevin P. Kelly
Mary Beth Cantrell	Thomas M. McAleavey
Robert J. Capko	Jennifer Herndon McRae
Christopher B. Clark	Rory C. Ryan
John R. Dierking	Stacey E. Young

OF COUNSEL
Richard L. Fletcher, Jr.

For full biographical listings, see the Martindale-Hubbell Law Directory

MATHEWS RAILEY DeCUBELLIS & GOODWIN, P.A. (AV)

Suite 801 Citrus Center, 255 South Orange Avenue, P.O. Box 4976, 32802-4976
Telephone: 407-872-2200
Telecopier: 407-423-1038

Lawrence G. Mathews, Jr.	Frank M. Bedell
David C. Goodwin	Mary M. Wills
Lilburn R. Railey, III	Jennifer S. Eden
Daniel L. DeCubellis	Mark L. Van Valkenburgh

OF COUNSEL
Lynn Walker Wright

LEGAL SUPPORT PERSONNEL

Carol D. Methven	Georgette Freid
W. Rogers Turner, Jr.	(Firm Administrator)

Representative Clients: Centex-Great Southwest Corp.; Design Professional Insurance Corp.; Florida Lawyers Mutual Insurance Corp.; International Game Technology, Inc.; Jennings Environmental Services, Inc.; Mader Southeast, Inc.; McDonald's Corporation; Orange County; PGA Tour, Inc.; SunTrust Bank, Inc.

For full biographical listings, see the Martindale-Hubbell Law Directory

RUMBERGER, KIRK & CALDWELL, PROFESSIONAL ASSOCIATION (AV)

Signature Plaza, Suite 300, 201 South Orange Avenue (32801), P.O. Box 1873, 32802
Telephone: 407-872-7300
Fax: 407-841-2133; 407-841-7710
URL: http://www.rumberger.com
Miami, Florida Office: One Biscayne Tower. 2 South Biscayne Boulevard, Suite 3100, 33131.
Telephone: 305-358-5577.
Fax: 305-371-7580.
Tallahassee, Florida Office: 106 East College Avenue, Suite 700, (32301), P.O. Box 10507, 32302.
Telephone: 904-222-6550.
Fax: 904-222-8783.
Tampa, Florida Office: 100 North Tampa Street, Suite 2000, (33602), P.O. Box 3390, 33601.
Telephone: 813-223-4253.
Fax: 813-221-4752.

E. Thom Rumberger	Francis H. Sheppard
William L. Kirk, Jr.	Douglas B. Brown
Lori Jean Caldwell	David C. Schwartz
J. Scott Kirk	Ernest H. Eubanks, Jr.
Michael R. Levin	Darryl L. Gavin
Clifford L. Adams	David B. Shelton
Wendy Vomacka	Daniel J. Gerber
Craig P. Niedenthal	Jeffrey S. Weiss

G. Mark Thompson	John W. Dill
Charles P. Mitchell	Richard A. Keller
Suzanne M. Barto Hill	Hayden R. Dempsey
Christopher T. Hill	Frank T. Allen
Lori M. M. Huckabee	Michael D. Crosbie
Sharon J. Duncan	Henry N. Didier, Jr.

Christa M. Cowart

Representative Clients: Automotive and other Manufacturers: General Motors Corp.; Mazda Motor of America Inc.; Nissan Motor Corp. in U.S.A.; Toyota Motor Sales, U.S.A., Inc. General: Allstate Insurance Co.; Royal Insurance Co. Aviation: AIG Aviation, Inc. Professional Liability: American International Group.

For full biographical listings, see the Martindale-Hubbell Law Directory

SANDERS, McEWAN, MARTINEZ, LUFF & DUKES, P.A. (AV)

108 East Central Boulevard, P.O. Box 753, 32801
Telephone: 407-423-8571
FAX: 407-423-8637
Email: smmld2@aol.com
Email: smmld@aol.com

Warren B. Parks (1879-1949)	Rafael E. "Ralph" Martinez
Wilson Sanders (1911-1981)	H. David Luff
O. Beverley McEwan (1913-1995)	Thomas E. Dukes, III
John S. McEwan, II	William E. Ruffier
	Pierre Seacord

Jeffrey Scott Badgley

Stephanie Ann Cunningham	Tyler S. McClay

Representative Clients: Auto Owners Insurance Co.; Bankers and Shippers Insurance Company of New York; Bridgestone/Firestone, Inc.; City Cab of Orlando, Inc.; CNA Insurance Company; Dependable Protective Mutual; Florida Physicians Insurance Co.; Gulf Atlantic Insurance Co.; Marine Office of America; M.C.I. Telecommunications Corporation.

For full biographical listings, see the Martindale-Hubbell Law Directory

Orlando—Continued

SHUTTS & BOWEN (AV)

A Partnership including Professional Associations
20 North Orange Avenue, Suite 1000, P.O. Box 2064, 32801
Telephone: 407-423-3200
Telefax: 407-425-8316
URL: HTTP://WWW.LAWWORLD.COM/SHUTTS/
Miami, Florida Office: 1500 Miami Center, 201 South Biscayne Boulevard.
Telephone: 305-358-6300.
Cable Address: "Shuttsbo."
Telefax: 305-381-9982.
West Palm Beach, Florida Office: One Clearlake Centre, 250 Australian
Avenue, Suite 500.
Telephone: 561-835-8500.
Fax: 561-650-8530.
Amsterdam, The Netherlands Office: Shutts & Bowen, B.V., Europa
Boulevard 59, 1083 AD, Amsterdam.
Telephone: (31 20) 661-0969.
Fax: (31 20) 642-1475.
London, England Office: 43 Grosvenor Street, London W1X 9PG.
Telephone: 441-71-493-4840.
Telefax: 441-71-493-4299.

MEMBERS OF FIRM

Andrew M. Brumby (Resident)	Mary Ruth Houston
Charles Robinson Fawsett (P.A.)	Rod Jones (Resident)
Robert A. Freyer (Resident)	Robert A. Savill (Resident)
Michael L. Gore (Resident)	James G. Willard (Resident)
Michael J. Grindstaff (P.A.)	Kenneth W. Wright (Resident)

RESIDENT ASSOCIATES

Suzanne M. Amaducci	Marc J. Jason
Thomas P. Callan	Brian M. Jones
Meredith A. Harper	Patrick M. Muldowney

For full biographical listings, see the Martindale-Hubbell Law Directory

CRAIG B. WARD, P.A. (AV)

Suite 501, 105 East Robinson Street, 32801
Telephone: 407-839-0222
Fax: 407-839-0577

Craig B. Ward
OF COUNSEL
Charles D. Miner

Representative Clients: Gladco, Inc. (American Gladiators); Lake of the
Woods Homeowners Association, Inc.; Metro One, Inc. (Real Estate); National Ambulance Builders, Inc.; Poole Construction Co., Inc.; Power Concrete Products Co.; Richard Sibley Associates, Inc. (Advertising); Scientific-Atlanta, Inc.
Approved Agent for: First American Title Insurance Co.; Attorneys' Title
Insurance Fund.

For full biographical listings, see the Martindale-Hubbell Law Directory

WINDERWEEDLE, HAINES, WARD & WOODMAN, P.A. (AV)

Barnett Bank Center, 390 North Orange Avenue, P.O. Box
1391, 32802-1391
Telephone: 407-423-4246
Telecopier: 407-423-7014
Winter Park, Florida Office: Barnett Bank Building 250 Park Avenue,
South, P.O. Box 880.
Telephone: 407-423-4246.
Telecopier: 407-645-3728.

Harold A. Ward, III	Thomas A. Simser, Jr.
Victor E. Woodman	Robert P. Major
William A. Walker II	James Edward Cheek, III
Joseph Penn Carolan, III	J. Jeffrey Deery
Allison L. Warren	

General Counsel: RoTech Medical Corp.
Counsel for: Barnett Bank of Central Florida, N.A.; Dialysis Laboratories
Management, Inc.; United Southern Bank.
Representative Clients: United American Bank; Georgia-Pacific Corp.; USX
Corp.

For full biographical listings, see the Martindale-Hubbell Law Directory

ZIMMERMAN, SHUFFIELD, KISER & SUTCLIFFE, P.A. (AV)

Landmark Center One, Suite 600, 315 East Robinson Street, P.O. Box
3000, 32802
Telephone: 407-425-7010
Telecopier: 407-425-2747

Bernard J. Zimmerman	Robert L. Dietz
W. Charles Shuffield	Stephen B. Hatcher
Wendell J. Kiser	Robert W. Peacock, Jr.
Roland A. Sutcliffe Jr.	Clement L. Hyland
Robert E. Mansbach, Jr.	J. Timothy Schulte
Pamela Lynn Foels	
OF COUNSEL	
Gerard J. Turner	

(See Next Column)

Melissa Dubina Kaplan	Kevin G. Malchow
Eric P. Gibbs	Thomas Warren Sculco
Joseph C. L. Wettach	Kevin L. Lienard
Edward C. Duncan, III	Daniel R. Murphy
Charles H. Leo	Michael C. Tyson
Vivian M. Reeves	Lori A. Walsingham Smith
Kraig N. Johnson	Scot G. Nimmo
Gene E. Crick, Jr.	Lynne R. Wilson
Charles B. Costar III	Lori A. Newsome
Joanne Marie Toner	

LEGAL SUPPORT PERSONNEL
PARALEGALS

Jeanne Ann Roper	Shannon E. Brooks
L. Darlene Riley	

For full biographical listings, see the Martindale-Hubbell Law Directory

---

PALATKA,* Putnam Co. — (Refer to St. Augustine)

PALM BEACH, Palm Beach Co.

CALDWELL & PACETTI (AV)

324 Royal Palm Way, P.O. Box 2775, 33480-2775
Telephone: 561-655-0620
Fax: 561-655-3775

MEMBERS OF FIRM

Manley P. Caldwell (1901-1971)	Charles F. Schoech
Madison F. Pacetti (1914-1994)	Elizabeth S. (Betsy) Burden
Manley P. Caldwell, Jr.	William E. Corley, III
Kenneth W. Edwards	Nicole Julianne Monsees
Mary M. Viator	John A. Weig

OF COUNSEL
Arthur E. Barrow (Retired)

Representative Clients: Shawano Drainage District; Acme Improvement District; Northern Palm Beach County Improvement District; Indian Trail Water Control District; Siemens Information Systems; Town Of Hypoluxo; Everglades Agricultural Area Environmental Protection District; Town of Lake
Clarke Shores.

For full biographical listings, see the Martindale-Hubbell Law Directory

MURPHY, REID, PILOTTE, ORD & AUSTIN (AV)

A Partnership of Professional Associations
Suite 100, 340 Royal Palm Way, 33480
Telephone: 561-655-4060
Facsimile: 561-832-5436
Vero Beach, Florida Office: Plantation Plaza, 6606-20th Street, P.O.
Drawer M.
Telephone: 561-567-6480.
Facsimile: 561-562-0220.

Eugene W. Murphy Jr. (P.A.)	George P. Ord (P.A.)
Frank T. Pilotte (P.A.)	Keith C. Austin, Jr. (P.A.)
OF COUNSEL	
Philip H. Reid, Jr.	

For full biographical listings, see the Martindale-Hubbell Law Directory

ROZELLE AND CALL (AV)

223 Sunset Avenue, Suite 200, P.O. Box 229, 33480
Telephone: 407-655-8585
Fax: 407-655-8663

MEMBERS OF FIRM

Douglas D. Rozelle, Jr.	John S. Call, Jr.

ASSOCIATES
Marc P. Barmat

Representative Clients: Wal-Mart Stores, Inc.; Motors Insurance Corp.;
American Contractors Insurance Group, Inc.; Continental Loss Adjusting
Co.; The Equitable Life Assurance Society; Connecticut General Life Insurance Co.; Safeco Insurance Co.; Phar-Mor of Florida, Inc.; World Wide Insurance Group; Chrysler Insurance Co.; United Service Automobile Association.

For full biographical listings, see the Martindale-Hubbell Law Directory

WINTHROP, STIMSON, PUTNAM & ROBERTS (AV)

125 Worth Avenue, 33480
Telephone: 407-655-7297
Telefax: 407-833-6726
New York, N.Y. Office: One Battery Park Plaza, 10004.
Telephone: 212-858-1000.
Fax: 212-858-1500.
Stamford, Connecticut Office: Financial Centre, 695 East Main Street, P.O.
Box 6760, 06904-6760.
Telephone: 203-348-2300.
Fax: 203-965-8226.

(See Next Column)

WINTHROP, STIMSON, PUTNAM & ROBERTS—*Continued*

Washington, D.C. Office: 1133 Connecticut Avenue, N.W., 20036.
Telephone: 202-775-9800.
Fax: 202-833-8491.
London, England Office: 2 Throgmorton Avenue, London, EC2N 2DL, England.
Telephone: 011-44171-628-4931.
Fax: 011-44171-638-0443.
Brussels, Belgium Office: Rue Du Taciturne 42, 1040 Brussels, Belgium.
Telephone: 011-322-230-1392.
Fax: 011-322-230-9288.
Tokyo, Japan Office: 608 Atagoyama Bengoshi Building 6-7, Atago 1-chome, Minato-ku, Tokyo 105 Japan.
Telephone: 011-813-3437-9740.
Fax: 011-813-3437-9261.
Hong Kong Office: 2505 Asia Pacific Finance Tower, Citibank Plaza, 3 Garden Road, Central.
Telephone: 011-852-2530-3400.
Fax: 011-852-2530-3355.

MEMBERS OF FIRM

Philip G. Hull   Michael V. Sterlacci

COUNSEL

John C. Dotterrer

SENIOR COUNSEL

Howard J. Falcon, Jr.   Douglas F. Williamson, Jr.

RESIDENT ASSOCIATES

George D. Karibjanian   Guy Rabideau

For full biographical listings, see the Martindale-Hubbell Law Directory

---

PALM BEACH GARDENS, Palm Beach Co.

SCOTT, ROYCE, HARRIS, BRYAN, BARRA & JORGENSEN, PROFESSIONAL ASSOCIATION (AV)

4400 PGA Boulevard, Suite 800, 33410
Telephone: 561-624-3900
Fax: 561-624-3533

Robert Claude Scott (1925-1982)   John M. Jorgensen
Raymond W. Royce   Richard K. Barra
J. Richard Harris   Barry B. Byrd
John L. Bryan, Jr.   Donna A. Nadeau
                        Kevin M. Wagner

LEGAL SUPPORT PERSONNEL

Cherisse C. Roy

Representative Clients: First Union National Bank of Florida, N.A.; John D. & Catherine T. MacArthur Foundation; The Realtors Association of the Palm Beaches, Inc.; Lost Tree Village; Jupiter Hills; Art Moran Pontiac, Inc.; Northern Trust Bank of Florida, N.A.; U.S. Trust Company of Florida; Chicago Title Insurance Co.

For full biographical listings, see the Martindale-Hubbell Law Directory

---

PANAMA CITY,* Bay Co.

BRYANT AND HIGBY, CHARTERED (AV)

833 Harrison Avenue, P.O. Drawer 860, 32402-0860
Telephone: 904-763-1787
Fax: 904-785-1533

Lynn C. Higby (1938-1992)   Rowlett W. Bryant
                Clifford C. Higby

Cecilia D. Redding

Representative Clients: Florida First Federal Savings Bank; City of Panama City, Florida; Panama City Port Authority; Corrections Corporation of America; Fireman's Fund Insurance Company.

For full biographical listings, see the Martindale-Hubbell Law Directory

---

RICHARD SMOAK (AV)

103 West 5th Street, P.O. Box 1006, 32402-1006
Telephone: 904-747-1900
Fax: 904-747-1910

Representative Clients: Panama City - Bay County Airport & Industrial District; Continental Insurance Co.; Florida Physicians Insurance Co.; Bay Bank & Trust Co.; Mutual of Omaha Insurance Co.; Ranger Insurance Co.; St. Paul Fire & Marine Insurance Co.; Stone Container Corporation; Atlanta & St. Andrews Bay Railway Co.

For full biographical listings, see the Martindale-Hubbell Law Directory

---

PENSACOLA,* Escambia Co.

BEGGS & LANE (AV)

Seventh Floor, Blount Building, 3 West Garden Street, P.O. Box 12950, 32576-2950
Telephone: 904-432-2451
Telecopier: 904-469-3330

(See Next Column)

MEMBERS OF FIRM

E. Dixie Beggs (Retired)   J. Nixon Daniel, III
Bert H. Lane (1917-1981)   G. Edison Holland, Jr.
Robert P. Gaines   Ralph A. Peterson
W. Spencer Mitchem   Gary B. Leuchtman
James M. Weber   John P. Daniel
Robert L. Crongeyer   Jeffrey A. Stone
John F. Windham   James S. Campbell

ASSOCIATES

Russell F. Van Sickle   Gary W. Huston
Russell A. Badders   Mary Jane Thies
David J. Barberie   James J. Crongeyer, Jr.

For full biographical listings, see the Martindale-Hubbell Law Directory

---

CARLTON, FIELDS, WARD, EMMANUEL, SMITH & CUTLER, P.A. (AV)

Harbourview Building, 4th Floor, 25 West Cedar Street (32501-5974), P.O. Box 12426, 32582-2426
Telephone: 904-434-0142
Telecopier: (904) 434-5366
Orlando, Florida Office: Suite 1600 Citrus Center, 255 South Orange Avenue, 32801-3488, P.O. Box 1171, 32802-1171.
Telephone: 407-849-0300.
St. Petersburg, Florida Office: Barnett Tower, Suite 2300, One Progress Plaza, 200 Central Avenue, 33701-4352, P.O. Box 2861, 33731-2861.
Telephone: 813-821-7000.
Tallahassee, Florida Office: 215 South Monroe Street, Suite 500, 32302-0190, P.O. Drawer 190, 32301-4352.
Telephone: 904-224-1585.
Tampa, Florida Office: One Harbour Place, 777 South Harbour Island Boulevard, 33602-5799, P.O. Box 3239, 33601-3239.
Telephone: 813-223-7000.
West Palm Beach, Florida Office: Esperanté, 222 Lakeview Avenue, Suite 1400, 33401-6149, P.O. Box 150, 33402-0150.
Telephone: 407-659-7070.

Wright Moulton   George Barford
Miles Davis   Laurel E. Lockett
Roger D. Schwenke   Stephen L. Walker
Jacob D. Varn   Bill B. McEachern, Jr.
                  Sally C. Bussell

Carol A. Ruebsamen   Elizabeth J. Partington

For full biographical listings, see the Martindale-Hubbell Law Directory

---

SHELL, FLEMING, DAVIS & MENGE, P.A. (AV)

Ninth Floor Seville Tower, P.O. Box 1831, 32598
Telephone: 904-434-2411
Fax: 904-435-1074

Thurston A. Shell   Charles L. Hoffman, Jr.
Fletcher Fleming   Stephen B. Shell
Rollin D. Davis, Jr.   Maureen Duignan
M. J. Menge   Jan Shackelford
Danny L. Kepner   Paul W. Groom II
                John B. Trawick

For full biographical listings, see the Martindale-Hubbell Law Directory

---

SMITH, SAUER & DeMARIA (AV)

510 East Zaragoza, P.O. Box 12446, 32501
Telephone: 904-434-2761
Fax: 904-438-8860
Email: 76666.3265@COMPUSERVE.COM

G. Thomas Smith   Jeffrey T. Sauer
              Kathleen K. DeMaria

OF COUNSEL

Carlton M. Johnson, Jr.

Representative Clients: Exxon Corp.; Amerada Hess; EastGroup Properties; American General.

For full biographical listings, see the Martindale-Hubbell Law Directory

---

PERRY,* Taylor Co. — (Refer to Madison)

POMPANO BEACH, Broward Co.

JOHN L. KORTHALS (AV)

1401 East Atlantic Boulevard, 33060
Telephone: 954-783-2999
FAX: 954-783-9832

For full biographical listings, see the Martindale-Hubbell Law Directory

PORT CHARLOTTE, Charlotte Co.

WILKINS, FROHLICH, JONES, HEVIA, RUSSELL & SUTTER, P.A. (AV)

18501 Murdock Circle, Suite 601, 33948
Telephone: 941-625-0700
Telecopier: 941-625-9540

Gary L. Wilkins	Jesus M. Hevia
W. Cort Frohlich	W. Kevin Russell
Phillip J. Jones	Brian O. Sutter
Melissa Green Jones	Louise O. Hanaoka

Victor G. Santiago

For full biographical listings, see the Martindale-Hubbell Law Directory

PORT ST. LUCIE, St. Lucie Co. — (Refer to Fort Pierce)

*PUNTA GORDA,** Charlotte Co.

WOTITZKY, WOTITZKY, MIZELL & ROSS, P.A. (AV)

223 Taylor Street, 33950
Telephone: 941-639-2171
Telecopier: 941-639-8617

John B. Mizell	Edward L. Wotitzky
Warren R. Ross	Hal F. Wotitzky

OF COUNSEL

Frank Wotitzky	Leo Wotitzky

Jason B. Goldman

Representative Client: Punta Gorda Corp.
Approved Attorneys for: Attorneys' Title Insurance Fund, Orlando, Florida; Chicago Title Insurance Co.

For full biographical listings, see the Martindale-Hubbell Law Directory

*QUINCY,** Gadsden Co.

LINES, HINSON AND LINES (AV)

121 North Madison Street, P.O. Box 550, 32353-0550
Telephone: 904-875-1300
Telecopier: 904-875-1350

MEMBERS OF FIRM

William D. Lines (1914-1992)	Alexander L. Hinson

Blucher B. Lines

Representative Clients: Talquin Electric Cooperative, Inc.; The Quincy State Bank; Quincy Telephone Co.; Georgia Pacific Corp.; Capital City Bank.

For full biographical listings, see the Martindale-Hubbell Law Directory

*ST. AUGUSTINE,** St. Johns Co.

UPCHURCH, BAILEY & UPCHURCH, P.A. (AV)

780 North Ponce de Leon Boulevard, P.O. Drawer 3007, 32085-3007
Telephone: 904-829-9066
Facsimile: 904-825-4862

John D. Bailey, Jr.	Tracy W. Upchurch
Frank D. Upchurch, III	Katherine Gaertner Jones

Michael A. Siragusa

OF COUNSEL

Frank D. Upchurch, Sr.	Frank D. Upchurch, Jr.
(1894-1987)	Hamilton D. Upchurch

Representative Clients: Aero Sport, Inc.; American Culinary Federation, Inc.; Barnett Bank, N.A. Penney Retirement Community, Inc.; St. Augustine Alligator Farm, Inc.; St. Augustine-St. Johns County Board of Realtors, Inc.
General Counsel: Flagler College; Flagler Hospital, Inc.; Prosperity Bank of St. Augustine; St. Johns County School Board.

For full biographical listings, see the Martindale-Hubbell Law Directory

ST. PETERSBURG, Pinellas Co.

ALLEN & MALLER, P.A. (AV)

4508 Central Avenue, 33711
Telephone: 813-321-3273
Fax: 813-323-2789

John T. Allen, Jr.	Karen E. Maller

Nicholas C. Glover	Bryan K. McLachlan

Representative Clients: G.J. Apple, Inc.; Federation of Mobile Home Owners; West Coast Regional Water Authority in Pipeline Litigation; Southern Plazas Med.
Special Counsel for: Pinellas County.
Reference: Rutland's Bank, Seminole, FL.

For full biographical listings, see the Martindale-Hubbell Law Directory

CARLTON, FIELDS, WARD, EMMANUEL, SMITH & CUTLER, P.A. (AV)

Barnett Tower, Suite 2300 One Progress Plaza, 200 Central Avenue (33701-4352), P.O. Box 2861, 33731-2861
Telephone: 813-821-7000
Fax: 813-822-3768
Orlando, Florida Office: Suite 1600, Citrus Center, 255 South Orange Avenue, 32801-3488, P.O. Box 1171, 32802-1171.
Telephone: 407-849-0300.
Pensacola, Florida Office: Harbourview Building, 4th Floor, 25 West Cedar Street, 32501-5974, P.O. Box 12426, 32582-2426.
Telephone: 904-434-0142.
Tallahassee, Florida Office: 215 South Monroe Street, Suite 500, 32301-1866, P.O. Drawer 190, 32301-4352.
Telephone: 904-224-1585.
Tampa, Florida Office: One Harbour Place, 777 South Harbour Island Boulevard, 33602-5799, P.O. Box 3239, 33601-3239.
Telephone: 813-223-7000.
West Palm Beach, Florida Office: Esperanté, 222 Lakeview Avenue, Suite 1400, 33401-6149, P.O. Box 150, 33402-0150.
Telephone: 407-659-7070.

Sylvia H. Walbolt	Steven C. Dupré
Alan C. Sundberg	Joel B. Giles
David G. Mulock	Lee H. Rightmyer
Gary L. Sasso	David R. Punzak
Jacob D. Varn	J. Michael Walls

OF COUNSEL

Roy G. Harrell, Jr.	John P. Higgins

Susan L. Landy	Amy E. Lettelleir
Randall J. Love	Jill H. Bowman

Maureen A. Godwin

For full biographical listings, see the Martindale-Hubbell Law Directory

HOLLAND & KNIGHT LLP (AV)

A Partnership including Professional Corporations
One Progress Plaza, Suite 1600, 33701-3845
Telephone: 813-896-7171
Fax: 813-822-8048
Mailing Address: P.O. Box 3542, 33731-3542
Email: hklaw.com *URL:* http://www.hklaw.com
Fort Lauderdale, Florida Office: One East Broward Boulevard, Suite 1300.
Telephone: 954-525-1000.
Fax: 954-463-2030.
Jacksonville, Florida Office: 50 N. Laura Street, Suite 3900.
Telephone: 904-353-2000.
Fax: 904-358-1872.
Lakeland, Florida Office: 92 Lake Wire Drive.
Telephone: 941-682-1161.
Fax: 941-688-1186.
Miami, Florida Office: 701 Brickell Avenue, 30th Floor.
Telephone: 305-374-8500.
Fax: 305-787-7799.
Orlando, Florida Office: 200 S. Orange Avenue, Suite 2600.
Telephone: 407-425-8500.
Fax: 407-244-5288.
Tallahassee, Florida Office: 315 Calhoun Street, Suite 600.
Telephone: 904-224-7000.
Fax: 904-224-8832.
Tampa, Florida Office: 400 N. Ashley.
Telephone: 813-227-8500.
Fax: 813-229-0134.
West Palm Beach, Florida Office: 625 N. Flagler Drive, Suite 700.
Telephone: 561-833-2000.
Fax: 561-650-8399.
Washington, D.C. Office: 2100 Pennsylvania Avenue, N.W.
Telephone: 202-955-3000.
Fax: 202-955-5564.
Atlanta, Georgia Office: 1201 West Peachtree Street, N.E., Suite 2000.
Telephone: 404-817-8500.
Fax: 404-881-0470.

William H. Bartlett	Ellen Neil Kalmbacher
Allan B. Davis	S. Curtis Kiser
Gerald D. Davis	William R. Lane, Jr.
Joseph W. Fleece	G. Dennis Lynn, Jr.
Joseph W. Fleece, III	Bruce Marger
William L. Johnson	R. Donald Mastry
Douglas S. Jones	Robert L. Paver

Charles W. Ross

Stephen C. Chumbris	Michael D. D. Geldart
Homer Duvall, III	Michael J. Loparco

Doreen Stone Young

For full biographical listings, see the Martindale-Hubbell Law Directory

SANFORD, * Seminole Co.

STENSTROM, McINTOSH, COLBERT, WHIGHAM & SIMMONS, P.A. (AV)

Suite 22 Sun Bank-Downtown, P.O. Box 4848, 32772-4848
Telephone: 407-322-2171
Fax: 407-330-2379
Email: stenstrom.com

Thomas E. Whigham	Franklin C. Whigham
(1952-1988)	Clayton D. Simmons
Douglas Stenstrom (Retired)	Robert K. McIntosh
William L. Colbert	Donna L. Surratt-McIntosh

William E. Reischmann, Jr.

Catherine D. Reischmann	James J. Partlow

Edgar J. Hedrick, III

OF COUNSEL

Kenneth W. McIntosh	S. Kirby Moncrief

Representative Clients: City of Sanford; City of Oviedo; City of Casselberry; Seminole Community College; City of Lake Mary; Sanford Housing Authority; City of DeBary; Seminole Soccer Club, Inc.; Tuskawilla Homeowners' Association; South Seminole-North Orange Wastewater Transmission Authority.

For full biographical listings, see the Martindale-Hubbell Law Directory

---

SARASOTA, * Sarasota Co.

BOWMAN, GEORGE, SCHEB, TOALE & MARSHALL, P.A. (AV)

22 South Tuttle Avenue, Suite 3, 34237
Telephone: 941-366-5510
FAX: 941-951-0839
Other Sarasota, Florida Office: 1605 Main Street, Suite 705, 34236.
Telephone: 941-366-3290.
Fax: 941-957-4890.

John F. Burket (1875-1947)	Eugene O. George
John F. Burket, Jr. (1915-1984)	Robert P. Scheb
V. Morris Smith (1921-1996)	James E. Toale
David G. Bowman, Sr.	Thomas K. Marshall

David G. Bowman, Jr.

OF COUNSEL

James J. Drymon	I. W. Whitesell, Jr.

Reference: SouthTrust Bank.

For full biographical listings, see the Martindale-Hubbell Law Directory

---

DICKINSON & GIBBONS, P.A. (AV)

1750 Ringling Boulevard, P.O. Box 3979, 34230
Telephone: 941-366-4680
FAX: 941-953-3136

Francis C. Dart (1902-1972)	Stephen G. Brannan
G. Hunter Gibbons	Deborah J. Blue
Ward E. Dahlgren	Jeffrey D. Peairs
Lewis F. Collins, Jr.	Douglas R. Wight
Gary H. Larsen	Stephen R. Kanzer
Camden T. French	David S. Preston
Ralph L. Marchbank, Jr.	Michael P. Murphy
A. James Rolfes	Evan N. Berlin
Burwell J. Jones	Adam Brum
Richard R. Garland	Kelly Selinsky

OF COUNSEL

Patrick H. Dickinson

LEGAL SUPPORT PERSONNEL

Christine C. Menzel	Karin M. Maple
Patricia L. Hunter	(Legal Assistant)
Janet E. Gadoury	Carol A. Owsianka
(Certified Legal Assistant)	(Legal Assistant)
Johanna H. Whitmire (Paralegal)	Susanne B. Bailey
Heather C. Schultz	(Legal Assistant)
(Legal Assistant)	

Representative Clients: Ford Motor Co.; Florida Power & Light Co.; Squibb Corp.
Insurance Clients: Liberty Mutual Insurance Co.; Allstate Insurance Co.; Nationwide Insurance Group; Ohio Casualty Insurance Co.; United States Fidelity & Guaranty Co.; State Farm Insurance Company.

For full biographical listings, see the Martindale-Hubbell Law Directory

---

NELSON ● HESSE (AV)

2070 Ringling Boulevard, P.O. Box 2524, 34230
Telephone: 941-366-7550
Fax: 941-955-3708

(See Next Column)

MEMBERS OF FIRM

Richard E. Nelson	Omer S. Causey
Ronald Alexander Cyril	William A. Dooley
(1938-1988)	Michael S. Drews
Richard L. Smith	Frederick J. Elbrecht
F. Steven Herb	Gary W. Peal

ASSOCIATES

Philip Sypula	J. Neal Mobley

Stephen M. Walker

General Counsel for: Enterprise National Bank; Dooley Mack Construction Co.
Representative Clients: Wellcraft Marine; Attorneys Title Insurance Fund; Travelers Insurance; SMH Radiology, Inc.; The Carlton Ranch, Inc.
References: Southtrust Bank; Enterprise National Bank.

For full biographical listings, see the Martindale-Hubbell Law Directory

---

WILLIAMS, PARKER, HARRISON, DIETZ & GETZEN, PROFESSIONAL ASSOCIATION (AV)

200 South Orange Avenue, 34236-6749
Telephone: 941-366-4800
Telecopier: 941-366-5109
Mailing Address: P.O. Box 3258, Sarasota, Florida, 34230-3258
Email: wphdg.law@netsrg.com *URL:*
http://www.sarasota-online.com/williamspa-w

J.J. Williams, Jr. (1886-1968)	Frank Strelec
W. Davis Parker (1920-1982)	Terri Salt Costa
William T. Harrison, Jr.	David A. Wallace
George A. Dietz	Mark A. Schwartz
Monte K. Marshall	Ric Gregoria
James L. Ritchey	Elvin W. Phillips
William G. Lambrecht	Jeffrey A. Grebe
John T. Berteau	John L. Moore
John V. Cannon, III	Morgan R. Bentley
Charles D. Bailey, Jr.	Susan A. Barrett
J. Michael Hartenstine	Carol Ann Kalish
Michele Boardman Grimes	Linda R. Getzen
James L. Turner	Kimberly J. Page
William M. Seider	Phillip D. Eck
Elizabeth C. Marshall	J. Hugh Middlebrooks
Robert W. Benjamin	Robert A. Warram

OF COUNSEL

William E. Getzen	Frazer F. Hilder

Hugh McPheeters, Jr.

LEGAL SUPPORT PERSONNEL

Mark Loveridge (Land Planner)

General Counsel for: Sarasota County Public Hospital Board; Sarasota-Manatee Airport Authority; Taylor Woodrow Homes Ltd.; FCCI Mutual Insurance Co.
Local Counsel for: NationsBank of Florida; Barnett Bank of Southwest Florida; Northern Trust Bank of Florida; SunTrust Bank, Gulfcoast.

For full biographical listings, see the Martindale-Hubbell Law Directory

---

SEBRING, * Highlands Co.

SWAINE, HARRIS, SHEEHAN & McCLURE, P.A. (AV)

425 South Commerce Avenue, 33870
Telephone: 941-385-1549
Fax: 941-471-0008
Email: shsmlaw@ct.net
Lake Placid, Florida Office: 212 Interlake Boulevard, P.O. Box 548.
Telephone: 813-465-2811.
Fax: 813-465-6999. E-Mail: lplaw@ct.net.

J. Michael Swaine	John K. McClure
Bert J. Harris, III	J. Timothy Sheehan

William J. Nielander

Representative Clients: Barnett Bank of Highlands County; Lykes Bros., Inc.; City of Sebring; City of Lake Placid; Lakeshore Mall.
Approved Attorneys for: Attorneys' Title Insurance Fund.

For full biographical listings, see the Martindale-Hubbell Law Directory

---

STARKE, * Bradford Co. — (Refer to Gainesville)

STUART, * Martin Co.

BROAD AND CASSEL (AV)

A Partnership including Professional Associations
900 East Ocean Boulevard, Suite 126, 33994
Telephone: 561-283-3000; 221-1861
Telecopier: 561-283-9622
Boca Raton, Florida Office: Corporate Centre at Boca Raton, Suite 300, 7777 Glades Road, 33434.
Telephone: 561-483-7000.
Fort Lauderdale, Florida Office: Suite 1130, Broward Financial Centre, 500 E. Broward Boulevard, 33394.
Telephone: 954-764-7060.

(See Next Column)

BROAD AND CASSEL, *Stuart—Continued*

Miami, Florida Office: Miami Center, 201 South Biscayne, Suite 3000, 33131.
Telephone: 305-373-9400.
Orlando, Florida Office: Barnett Bank Center, 390 North Orange Avenue, Suite 1100, 32801.
Telephone: 407-839-4200.
Tallahassee, Florida Office: 215 South Monroe Street, Suite 400, 32302.
Telephone: 904-681-6810.
Tampa, Florida Office: 100 North Tampa, Suite 3500, 33602.
Telephone: 813-225-3020.
West Palm Beach, Florida Office: The Reflections Office Center, Fifth Floor, 400 Australian Avenue, South, 33401.
Telephone: 561-832-3300.

PARTNERS

Patricia Lebow (P.A.)　　　　　Clifford I. Hertz (P.A.)
(Managing Partner)

ASSOCIATES

Jeffrey J. Suter　　　　　Andrew A. Reich

For full biographical listings, see the Martindale-Hubbell Law Directory

MOYLE, FLANIGAN, KATZ, KOLINS, RAYMOND & SHEEHAN, P.A. (AV)

900 South Federal Highway, 1st Floor, P.O. Box 658, 34995
Telephone: 561-288-1144
Facsimile: 561-288-1499
Palm Beach Gardens, Florida Office: 2401 P.G.A. Boulevard, Building C - Suite 120.
Telephone: 561-625-6480.
Facsimile: 561-625-5979.
Tallahassee, Florida Office: 210 South Monroe Street.
Telephone: 904-681-3828.
Facsimile: 904-681-8788.
West Palm Beach, Florida Office: 625 North Flagler Drive, 9th Floor.
Telephone: 561-659-7500.
Facsimile: 561-659-1789.

Linda R. McCann

For full biographical listings, see the Martindale-Hubbell Law Directory

---

TALLAHASSEE, * Leon Co.

* indicates certain Bar Register subscribers whose principal office is located elsewhere in the state and who have arranged for representation as a part of the state capital listings that follow

AUSLEY & McMULLEN, P.A. (AV)

Washington Square Building, 227 South Calhoun Street, P.O. Box 391, 32302
Telephone: 904-224-9115
Fax: 904-222-7560

John K. Aurell	Kenneth R. Hart
DuBose Ausley	David J. Hull
Margaret B. Ausley	Deborah Stephens Minnis
James D. Beasley	Carolyn D. Olive
John R. Beranek	R. Stan Peeler
C. Graham Carothers	Robert A. Pierce
Kevin J. Carroll	M. Julian Proctor, Jr.
Robert N. Clarke, Jr.	H. Palmer Proctor
J. Marshall Conrad	Steven P. Seymoe
Timothy B. Elliott	William M. Smith
Stephen C. Emmanuel	James Harold Thompson
John P. Fons	J. Jeffry Wahlen
Van P. Geeker	Emily S. Waugh
Michael J. Glazer	C. Gary Williams
	Lee L. Willis

Michael P. Bruyere　　　　　Stephanie Williams Redfearn

LEGAL SUPPORT PERSONNEL

GOVERNMENTAL LIAISON

Stephen D. Dyal

ADMINISTRATOR

Ronald C. Callen

Representative Clients: BellSouth Telecommunications, Inc.; Capital City Bank Group, Inc.; CSX Transportation, Inc.; Tenet Healthcare Corporation; Sprint Corp./United Telephone; Tampa Electric Co.

For full biographical listings, see the Martindale-Hubbell Law Directory

BROAD AND CASSEL (AV)

A Partnership including Professional Associations
215 South Monroe Street, Suite 400, P.O. Box 11300, 32301
Telephone: 904-681-6810
Telecopier: 904-681-9792
Boca Raton, Florida Office: Corporate Centre at Boca Raton, Suite 300, 7777 Glades Road, 33434.
Telephone: 561-483-7000.
Fort Lauderdale, Florida Office: Suite 1130, Broward Financial Centre, 500 E. Broward Boulevard, 33394.
Telephone: 954-764-7060.
Miami, Florida Office: Miami Center, 201 South Biscayne Boulevard, Suite 3000, 33131.
Telephone: 305-373-9400.
Orlando, Florida Office: Barnett Bank Center, 390 N. Orange Avenue, Suite 1100, 32801.
Telephone: 407-839-4200.
Stuart, Florida Office: 900 East Ocean Boulevard, Suite 126, 33994.
Telephone: 561-283-3000.
Tampa, Florida Office: 100 North Tampa, Suite 3500, 33602.
Telephone: 813-225-3020.
West Palm Beach, Florida Office: The Reflections Office Centre, 400 Australian Avenue, South, Fifth Floor, 33401.
Telephone: 561-832-3300.

PARTNERS

M. Stephen Turner (P.A.)	Charles S. Stratton (P.A.)
Ralph C. Datillio	David K. Miller (P.A.)
Douglas L. Mannheimer (P.A.)	Kelly Overstreet Johnson (P.A.)
	Mark D. Tucker

ASSOCIATES

Jay Adams　　　　　Michael R. Kercher
　　　　　David Allen Roberts

CONTRACT COUNSEL

Donna H. Stinson　　　　　R. Davis Thomas, Jr.
　　　　　　　　　　(Not admitted in FL)

For full biographical listings, see the Martindale-Hubbell Law Directory

---

* CARLTON, FIELDS, WARD, EMMANUEL, SMITH & CUTLER, P.A. (AV)

215 South Monroe Street, Suite 500 (32301-4352), P.O. Drawer 190, 32302-0190
Telephone: 904-224-1585
Telecopier: (904) 222-0398
Orlando, Florida Office: Suite 1600 Citrus Center, 255 South Orange Avenue, 32801-3488, P.O. Box 1171, 32802-1171.
Telephone: 407-849-0300.
Pensacola, Florida Office: Harbourview Building, 4th Floor, 25 West Cedar Street, 32501-5974, P. O. Box 12426, 32582-2426.
Telephone: 904-434-0142.
St. Petersburg, Florida Office: Barnett Tower, Suite 2300, One Progress Plaza, 200 Lakeview Avenue, 33701-4352, P.O. Box 2861, 33731-2861.
Telephone: 813-821-7000.
Tampa, Florida Office: One Harbour Place, 777 South Harbour Island Boulevard, 33602-5799, P.O. Box 3239, 33601-3239.
Telephone: 813-223-7000.
West Palm Beach, Florida Office: Esperanté, 222 Lakeview Avenue, Suite 1400, 33401-6149, P.O. Box 150, 33402-0150.
Telephone: 407-659-7070.

Alan C. Sundberg	Nancy G. Linnan
Jacob D. Varn	W. Douglas Hall
George Barford	F. Townsend Hawkes
Robert W. Pass	Martha Harrell Chumbler

OF COUNSEL

J. Robert McClure, Jr.

Richard T. Donelan, Jr.　　　　　Michael Patrick Donaldson

For full biographical listings, see the Martindale-Hubbell Law Directory

ERVIN, VARN, JACOBS AND ERVIN (AV)

305 South Gadsden Street, P.O. Drawer 1170, 32302
Telephone: 904-224-9135
Telecopier: 904-222-9164
Email: EVJE@NETTALLY.COM

MEMBERS OF FIRM

Thomas M. Ervin, Jr.	Melissa Fletcher Allaman
C. Everett Boyd, Jr.	Robert M. Ervin Jr.
	J. Stanley Chapman

ASSOCIATE

David R. Westcott

COUNSEL CONSULTANT

Robert M. Ervin

OF COUNSEL

Wilfred C. Varn	Richard W. Ervin
Joseph C. Jacobs	Marilyn K. Morris
	Pamela K. Frazier

(See Next Column)

ERVIN, VARN, JACOBS AND ERVIN—*Continued*

Representative Clients: Florida Association of Broadcasters; E. I. duPont de Nemours & Co., Inc.; Florida Credit Union League; Atlantic Richfield Co.; Wells Fargo Ag Credit Corp.; American Acceptance Corp.; Coastal Petroleum Co.; General Motors Corp.; Goodyear Tire and Rubber Co.; The Grand Union Co.

For full biographical listings, see the Martindale-Hubbell Law Directory

---

✱ FOLEY & LARDNER (AV)

Suite 300, 123 South Calhoun Street, P.O. Box 508, 32302-0508
Telephone: 904-222-6100
Facsimile: 904-224-0496
Milwaukee, Wisconsin Office: Firstar Center, 777 East Wisconsin Avenue.
Telephone: 414-271-2400.
Telex: 26-819 (Foley Lard Mil).
Facsimile: 414-297-4900.
Madison, Wisconsin Office: Verex Plaza, 150 East Gilman Street, P.O. Box 1497.
Telephone: 608-257-5035.
Telex: 262051 (F L Madison).
Facsimile: 608-258-4258.
Chicago, Illinois Office: Suite 3300, One IBM Plaza, 330 N. Wabash Avenue.
Telephone: 312-755-1900.
Facsimile: 312-755-1925.
Washington, D.C. Office: Washington Harbour, Suite 500, 3000 K Street, N.W.
Telephone: 202-672-5300.
Telex: 904136 (Foley Lard Wsh).
Facsimile: 202-672-5399.
Annapolis, Maryland Office: Suite 102, 175 Admiral Cochrane Drive.
Telephone: 301-266-8077.
Telex: 899149 (Oldtownpat).
Facsimile: 301-266-8664.
Jacksonville, Florida Office: The Greenleaf Building, 200 Laura Street, P.O. Box 240.
Telephone: 904-359-2000.
Facsimile: 904-359-8700.
Orlando, Florida Office: Suite 1800, 111 North Orange Avenue, P.O. Box 2193.
Telephone: 407-423-7656.
Telex: 441781 (HQ ORL).
Facsimile: 407-648-1743.
Tampa, Florida Office: Suite 2700, One Hundred N. Tampa Street, P.O. Box 3391.
Telephones: 813-229-2300; Pinellas County: 813-442-3296.
Facsimile: 813-221-4210.
West Palm Beach, Florida Office: Suite 200, Phillips Point East Tower, 777 South Flagler Drive.
Telephone: 561-655-5050.
Facsimile: 561-655-6925.
Brussels, Belgium Office: Avenue Louise, 283.
Telephone: 32-2-646-2777.
Facsimile: 32-2-646-7574.
Foley Lardner Weissburg & Aronson Office Locations:
Los Angeles, California Office: 2049 Century Park East, Suite 3200.
Telephone: 310-277-2223.
Fax: 310-557-8475.
Sacramento, California Office: 770 L Street, Suite 1050.
Telephone: 916-443-8005.
Fax: 916-443-2240.
San Diego, California Office: 402 West Broadway, 23rd Floor.
Telephone: 619-234-6655.
Fax: 619-234-3510.
San Francisco, California Office: One Maritime Plaza, Sixth Floor.
Telephone: 415-434-4484.
Fax: 415-434-4507.

RESIDENT PARTNER
Kevin G. Fitzgerald
RESIDENT OF COUNSEL
Joseph W. Jacobs

For full biographical listings, see the Martindale-Hubbell Law Directory

---

HENRY, BUCHANAN, HUDSON, SUBER & WILLIAMS, P.A. (AV)

117 South Gadsden Street P.O. Drawer 1049, 32302
Telephone: 904-222-2920
Telecopier: 904-224-0034

Bryan W. Henry (1925-1986)	Jesse F. Suber
John D. Buchanan, Jr.	Harriet W. Williams
Edwin R. Hudson	J. Steven Carter

Laura Beth Faragasso
GOVERNMENTAL CONSULTANT
Curt Blair

Reference: Barnett Bank of Tallahassee, Inc.

For full biographical listings, see the Martindale-Hubbell Law Directory

---

HOLLAND & KNIGHT LLP (AV)

A Partnership including Professional Corporations
315 Calhoun Street, Suite 600, 32301
Telephone: 904-224-7000
Fax: 904-224-8832
Mailing Address: P.O. Drawer 810, 32302
Email: hklaw.com *URL:* http://www.hklaw.com
Fort Lauderdale, Florida Office: One East Broward Boulevard, Suite 1300.
Telephone: 954-525-1000.
Fax: 954-463-2030.
Jacksonville, Florida Office: 50 N. Laura Street, Suite 3900.
Telephone: 904-353-2000.
Fax: 904-358-1872.
Lakeland, Florida Office: 92 Lake Wire Drive.
Telephone: 941-682-1161.
Fax: 941-688-1186.
Miami, Florida Office: 701 Brickell Avenue, 30th Floor.
Telephone: 305-374-8500.
Fax: 305-787-7799.
Orlando, Florida Office: 200 S. Orange Avenue, Suite 2600.
Telephone: 407-425-8500.
Fax: 407-244-5288.
St. Petersburg, Florida Office: One Progress Plaza, Suite 1600.
Telephone: 813-896-7171.
Fax: 813-822-8048.
Tampa, Florida Office: 400 North Ashley, Suite 2300.
Telephone: 813-227-8500.
Fax: 813-229-0134.
West Palm Beach, Florida Office: 625 N. Flagler Drive, Suite 700.
Telephone: 561-833-2000.
Fax: 561-650-8399.
Washington, D.C. Office: 2100 Pennsylvania Avenue, N.W.
Telephone: 202-922-3000.
Fax: 202-955-5564.
Atlanta, Georgia Office: 1201 West Peachtree Street, N.E., Suite 2000.
Telephone: 404-817-8500.
Fax: 404-881-0470.

TALLAHASSEE MEMBERS AND ASSOCIATES

Martha W. Barnett	S. Curtis Kiser
Elizabeth Bevington	David Bruce May, Jr.
Hume F. Coleman	R. Bruce McKibben, Jr.
Lawrence N. Curtin	Morris H. Miller
James Mann Ervin, Jr.	Samuel J. Morley
Robert R. Feagin, III	Lawrence E. Sellers, Jr.
Stephen F. Hanlon	Lawrence P. Stevenson
Mark E. Holcomb	William D. Townsend
Thomas J. Jones	Susan L. Turner

Steven J. Uhlfelder

Shannon B. Hartsfield	Susan L. Stephens
Cheridah V. Renuart	Karen D. Walker

Nina M. Zollo

For full biographical listings, see the Martindale-Hubbell Law Directory

---

HOPPING GREEN SAMS & SMITH, PROFESSIONAL ASSOCIATION (AV)

123 South Calhoun Street, P.O. Box 6526, 32314
Telephone: 904-222-7500
Fax: 904-224-8551

James S. Alves	Wade L. Hopping
Brian H. Bibeau	Frank E. Matthews
Kathleen L. Blizzard	Richard D. Melson
Elizabeth C. Bowman	David L. Powell
Richard S. Brightman	William D. Preston
Peter C. Cunningham	Carolyn S. Raepple
Ralph A. DeMeo	Douglas S. Roberts
Thomas M. DeRose	Gary P. Sams
William H. Green	Robert P. Smith

Cheryl G. Stuart

Gary K. Hunter, Jr.	Karen Peterson
Jonathan T. Johnson	Michael P. Petrovich
Robert A. Manning	R. Scott Ruth
Angela R. Morrison	W. Steve Sykes
Gary V. Perko	T. Kent Wetherell, II

OF COUNSEL
W. Robert Fokes

Representative Clients: Atlantic Gulf Communities; Dunes and Viera East Community Development Districts; Florida Electric Power Coordinating Group; Florida Power & Light Co.; MCI Telecommunications; Seminole Electric Co.; Sugar Cane Growers Cooperative of Florida; UPS; Waste Management, Inc.; Wheelabrator.

For full biographical listings, see the Martindale-Hubbell Law Directory

Tallahassee—Continued

* MOYLE, FLANIGAN, KATZ, KOLINS, RAYMOND & SHEEHAN, P.A. (AV)

210 South Monroe Street, 32301
Telephone: 904-681-3828
Facsimile: 904-681-8788
Palm Beach Gardens, Florida Office: 2401 P.G.A. Boulevard, Building C - Suite 120.
Telephone: 561-625-6480.
Facsimile: 561-625-5979.
Stuart, Florida Office: 900 South Federal Highway, 1st Floor.
Telephone: 561-288-1144.
Facsimile: 561-288-1499.
West Palm Beach, Florida Office: 625 North Flagler Drive, 9th Floor.
Telephone: 561-659-7500.
Facsimile: 561-659-1789.

Jon C. Moyle　　　　　　　Jon C. Moyle, Jr. (Resident)
　　　　　Thomas A. Sheehan, III

For full biographical listings, see the Martindale-Hubbell Law Directory

PENNINGTON, CULPEPPER, MOORE, WILKINSON, DUNBAR & DUNLAP, P.A. (AV)

215 South Monroe - 2nd Floor, 32301
Telephone: 904-222-3533
FAX: 904-222-2126
Email: Phlaw@Supernet.net

Bram D. E. Canter	John C. Pelham, Jr.
Robert Cintron, Jr.	Carl R. Pennington, Jr.
Robert S. Cohen	C. Edwin Rude, Jr.
Bruce Culpepper	Gary A. Shipman
Peter M. Dunbar	Cynthia S. Tunnicliff
Davisson F. Dunlap, Jr.	William E. Whitney
Martha J. Edenfield	Ben H. Wilkinson
Edgar M. Moore	Cathi C. Wilkinson

Barbara D. Auger	E. Murray Moore, Jr.
John Timothy Leadbeater	Jeffery A. Scott

OF COUNSEL

R. Stuart Huff (P.A.)	Scott Maddox
Christopher W. Kanaga	Herbert Forrester Clark
(Not admitted in FL)	(Not admitted in FL)
Douglas S. Lyons	William VanDercreek
	(Not admitted in FL)

SPECIAL CONSULTANTS

Randy Miller　　　　　　　David L. Swafford

Representative Clients: Time-Warner Communications; NationsBank of Florida, N.A.; First South Bank; Florida Association of Property Appraisers; Associated Industries of Florida; State of Florida, Department of Insurance; Tallahassee Memorial Regional Medical Center; Florida Radiological Society; National Association of Public Insurance Adjusters; Borg-Warner Protective Service.

For full biographical listings, see the Martindale-Hubbell Law Directory

* RUMBERGER, KIRK & CALDWELL, PROFESSIONAL ASSOCIATION (AV)

106 East College Avenue, Suite 700 (32301), P.O. Box 10507, 32302
Telephone: 904-222-6550
Fax: 904-222-8783
URL: http://www.rumberger.com
Orlando, Florida Office: Signature Plaza, Suite 300, 201 South Orange Avenue, (32801), P.O. Box 1873, 32802.
Telephone: 407-872-7300.
Fax: 407-841-2133.
Miami, Florida Office: One Biscayne Tower. 2 South Biscayne Boulevard, Suite 3100, 33131.
Telephone: 305-358-5577.
Fax: 305-371-7580.
Tampa, Florida Office: 100 North Tampa Street, Suite 2000, (33602), P.O. Box 3390, 33601.
Telephone: 813-223-4253.
Fax: 813-221-4752.

George N. Meros, Jr.　　　　　Robert L. Hessman

Michael E. Riley	Mary W. Chaisson
Lisa M. Appelo	William L. Sundberg

Representative Clients: Aviation: Aviation Underwriting Specialists. Automotive: General Motors Corp.; Mazda Motor of America, Inc.; Nissan Motor Corp. in U.S.A.; Toyota Motor Sales, U.S.A. Commercial: Metropolitan Life Insurance Co. General: Allstate Insurance Co.; Royal Insurance Co. Professional Liability: American International Group; COREGIS.

For full biographical listings, see the Martindale-Hubbell Law Directory

---

TAMPA, * Hillsborough Co.

ALLEN, DELL, FRANK & TRINKLE, P.A. (AV)

1240 Barnett Plaza, 101 East Kennedy Boulevard, P.O. Box 2111, 33601
Telephone: 813-223-5351
Telecopier: 813-229-6682

Ralph C. Dell	Robert A. Mora
Stewart C. Eggert	Benjamin G. Morris
Gary M. Witters	A. Christopher Kasten, II
Joseph G. Heyck, Jr.	Richard A. Harrison
Michael N. Brown	James S. Eggert
Marian P. McCulloch	Carlos A. Rodriguez
Steven F. Thompson	

Representative Clients: Tampa International Airport; Bank of Tampa; Florida Citrus Processors Assn.; The Coca Cola Co., Foods Division; Montgomery Elevator Co.; Seminole Electric Cooperative Inc.; Hillsborough County Hospital Authority; Tampa General Healthcare; Tampa Greyhound Track.

For full biographical listings, see the Martindale-Hubbell Law Directory

ALPERT, BARKER & CALCUTT, P.A. (AV)

First Union Center, Suite 2000, 100 South Ashley Drive (33602), P.O. Box 3270, 33601-3270
Telephone: 813-223-4131
Fax: 813-228-9612

Jonathan L. Alpert　　　　　　Chris A. Barker
　　　　　Patrick B. Calcutt

R. Christopher Rodems	William J. Cook
Gregory Joseph Blackburn	Emma Sleeth Hemness
David D. Ferrentino	Scott J. Flint
David A. Kessler	

Representative Clients: AABCO Mortgage & Investments, Inc.; Abbey/Foster, Inc.; Alexander & Alexander, Inc.; American International Group; American Risk Management Corp.; Atlantic Mutual Companies; The Clorox Co.; Colonia Insurance Co.; The Dow Chemical Co.; Gates McDonald and Company.

For full biographical listings, see the Martindale-Hubbell Law Directory

BROAD AND CASSEL (AV)

A Partnership including Professional Associations
100 North Tampa, Suite 3500, 33602
Telephone: 813-225-3020
Fax: 813-225-3039
Boca Raton, Florida Office: Corporate Centre at Boca Raton, Suite 300, 7777 Glades Road, 33434.
Telephone: 561-483-7000.
Fort Lauderdale, Florida Office: Suite 1130, Broward Financial Centre, 500 E. Broward Boulevard, 33394.
Telephone: 954-764-7060.
Miami, Florida Office: Miami Center, 201 South Biscayne Boulevard, Suite 3000, 33131.
Telephone: 305-373-9400.
Orlando, Florida Office: Barnett Bank Center, 390 N. Orange Avenue, Suite 1100, 32801.
Telephone: 407-839-4200.
Stuart, Florida Office: 900 E. Ocean Boulevard, Suite 126, 33994.
Telephone: 561-283-3000.
Tallahassee, Florida Office: 215 South Monroe Street, Suite 400, 32302.
Telephone: 904-681-6810.
West Palm Beach, Florida Office: The Reflections Office Center, Fifth Floor, 400 Australian Avenue, South, 33401.
Telephone: 561-832-3300.

RESIDENT PARTNERS

Theodore C. Taub (P.A.)　　　　Peter M. Cardillo (P.A.)
　　　　Robert E. Johnson (P.A.)

RESIDENT ASSOCIATES

Jonathan J. Ellis　　　　　　Katherine Castor

For full biographical listings, see the Martindale-Hubbell Law Directory

BUCHANAN INGERSOLL, PROFESSIONAL CORPORATION (AV Ⓣ)

Suite 2500, 401 East Jackson Street, 33602
Telephone: 813-222-8180
Telecopier: 813-222-8189
URL: http://www.bipc.com
Pittsburgh, Pennsylvania Office: One Oxford Centre, 301 Grant Street, 20th Floor.
Telephone: 412-562-8800.
Philadelphia, Pennsylvania Office: Two Logan Square, Twelfth Floor, 18th & Arch Streets.
Telephone: 215-665-8700.
Harrisburg, Pennsylvania Office: 30 North Third Street.
Telephone: 717-237-4800.
Aventura, Florida Office: 19495 Biscayne Boulevard, Suite 606.
Telephone: 305-933-5600.

(See Next Column)

BUCHANAN INGERSOLL PROFESSIONAL CORPORATION—*Continued*

Miami, Florida Office: NationsBank Tower, 100 S.E. Second Street.
Telephone: 305-347-4080.
Princeton, New Jersey Office: Buchanan Ingersoll, A Partnership, College Centre, 500 College Road East.
Telephone: 609-987-6800.
Lexington, Kentucky Office: Suite 600, PNC Bank Plaza, 200 West Vine Street.
Telephone: 606-225-5333.
Buffalo, New York Office: 1100 Main Place Tower, 350 Main Street.
Telephone: 716-854-4100.
Fax: 716-854-4227.

James J. Kennedy III
SENIOR ATTORNEYS
Mary Ann Lochner

Deborah L. Appel	Linda L. Fleming
Amy Lewis Bergen	Dale S. Webber

For full biographical listings, see the Martindale-Hubbell Law Directory

CARLTON, FIELDS, WARD, EMMANUEL, SMITH & CUTLER, P.A. (AV)

One Harbour Place, 777 South Harbour Island Boulevard (33602-5799), P.O. Box 3239, 33601-3239
Telephone: 813-223-7000
Telex: Carfield 52-2520
Telecopier: (813) 229-4133
Orlando, Florida Office: Suite 1600, Citrus Center, 255 South Orange Avenue, 32801-3488, P.O. Box 1171, 32802-1171.
Telephone: 407-849-0300.
Pensacola, Florida Office: Harbourview Building, 4th Floor, 25 West Cedar Street, 32501-5974, P.O. Box 12426, 32582-2426.
Telephone: 904-434-0142.
St. Petersburg, Florida Office: Barnett Tower, Suite 2300, One Progress Plaza, 200 Central Avenue, 33701-4352, P.O. Box 2861, 33731-2861.
Telephone: 813-821-7000.
Tallahassee, Florida Office: 215 South Monroe Street, Suite 500, 32301-4352, P.O Drawer 1900, 32302-0190.
Telephone: 904-224-1585.
West Palm Beach, Florida Office: Esperanté, 222 Lakeview Avenue, Suite 1400, 33401-6149, P.O. Box 150, 33402-0150.
Telephone: 407-659-7070.

Giddings E. Mabry (1877-1968)	Kenneth E. Graves
O. K. Reaves (1877-1970)	Chris S. Coutroulis
Doyle E. Carlton (1887-1972)	John W. Boult
Marvin Green (1904-1986)	Paul C. Davis
D. Wallace Fields (1910-1991)	Mark A. Brown
Michel G. Emmanuel (1918-1992)	Robert A. Soriano
	Robert L. Ciotti
David E. Ward (1909-1995)	Edward W. Gerecke
Wm. Reece Smith, Jr.	Robert M. Quinn
Edward I. Cutler	Gary L. Sasso
A. Broaddus Livingston	Donald R. Schmidt
Leonard H. Gilbert	Wallace B. Anderson, Jr.
Peter J. Winders	David P. Burke
William F. McGowan, Jr.	Edgel C. Lester, Jr.
Sylvia H. Walbolt	Nancy J. Faggianelli
David G. Mulock	Michael J. Nolan, II
Roger D. Schwenke	Luis Prats
Robert R. Vawter, Jr.	Richard B. Campbell
Laurence E. Kinsolving	James R. Wiley
Ruth Barnes Himes	Paula McDonald Rhodes
Robert W. Pass	J. Kevin Carey
Michael F. Nuechterlein	Laurel E. Lockett
George Barford	Richard A. Denmon
J. Bert Grandoff	Jeanette M. Flores
Steven L. Sparkman	Marylin E. Culp
Nathaniel L. Doliner	Michael J. Virgadamo
John P. McAdams	Mary Stenson Scriven
Gwynne A. Young	John J. Lamoureux
Thomas A. Snow	George J. Meyer
Donald E. Hemke	W. Patrick Ayers
D. Hywel Leonard	Morris C. Massey

Paul J. Ullom
OF COUNSEL

James W. Ault	Joseph B. Cofer

Arthur W. Fisher, III

Stephen D. Marlowe	Wm. Cary Wright
Gina Kress Grimes	Robert S. Freedman
Lavinia James Vaughn	David Matthew Allen
Sandra G. Porter	Ronald J. Tenpas
E. Kelly Bittick, Jr.	Kevin Jon Napper
Luis Alvarez, Jr.	Edward Kuchinski
Cathleen G. Bell	Joseph V. McNabb
Suzanne M. Elinger	Stephanie J. Young
Kathleen S. McLeroy	Victor D. Berg

(See Next Column)

Thomas P. Barber	Sheryl Seckel
Andrew Clifford Greenberg	John H. Zacharia
Thaxter A. Cooper	Hardy L. Roberts, III
Lorien Smith Johnson	Eric S. Adams
Kevin Hamilton Sutton	Robert Scott Collins
Kaiwen Tseng	Youndy C. Cook
Aimee Kemker Elson	Sharon P. Greenaway

Stephen M. Reams

For full biographical listings, see the Martindale-Hubbell Law Directory

CUNNINGHAM LAW GROUP, P.A. (AV)

100 Ashley Drive, South, Suite 100, 33602
Telephone: 813-228-0505
Telefax: 813-229-7982

Anthony W. Cunningham	James D. Clark
Donald G. Greiwe	Dana Solin Kanfer

For full biographical listings, see the Martindale-Hubbell Law Directory

FOLEY & LARDNER (AV)

Suite 2700, One Hundred N. Tampa Street, P.O. Box 3391, 33601-3391
Telephone: 813-229-2300;
Pinellas County: 813-442-3296
Facsimile: 813-221-4210
Milwaukee, Wisconsin Office: Firstar Center, 777 East Wisconsin Avenue.
Telephone: 414-271-2400.
Telex: 26-819 (Foley Lard Mil).
Facsimile: 414-297-4900.
Madison, Wisconsin Office: Verex Plaza, 150 East Gilman Street, P.O. Box 1497.
Telephone: 608-257-5035.
Telex: 262051 (F L Madison).
Facsimile: 608-258-4258.
Chicago, Illinois Office: Suite 3300, One IBM Plaza, 330 N. Wabash Avenue.
Telephone: 312-755-1900.
Facsimile: 312-755-1925.
Washington, D.C. Office: Washington Harbour, Suite 500, 3000 K Street, N.W.
Telephone: 202-672-5300.
Telex: 904136 (Foley Lard Wsh).
Facsimile: 202-672-5399.
Annapolis, Maryland Office: Suite 102, 175 Admiral Cochrane Drive.
Telephone: 301-266-8077.
Telex: 899149 (Oldtownpat).
Facsimile: 301-266-8664.
Jacksonville, Florida Office: The Greenleaf Building, 200 Laura Street, P.O. Box 240.
Telephone: 904-359-2000.
Facsimile: 904-359-8700.
Orlando, Florida Office: Suite 1800, 111 North Orange Avenue, P.O. Box 2193.
Telephone: 407-423-7656.
Telex: 441781 (HQ ORL).
Facsimile: 407-648-1743.
Tallahassee, Florida Office: Suite 300, 123 South Calhoun Street, P.O. Box 508.
Telephone: 904-222-6100.
Facsimile: 904-224-0496.
West Palm Beach, Florida Office: Suite 200, Phillips Point East Tower, 777 South Flagler Drive.
Telephone: 561-655-5050.
Facsimile: 561-655-6925.
Brussels, Belgium Office: Avenue Louise, 283.
Telephone: 32-2-646-2777.
Facsimile: 32-2-646-7574.
Foley Lardner Weissburg & Aronson Office Locations:
Los Angeles, California Office: 2049 Century Park East, Suite 3200.
Telephone: 310-277-2223.
Fax: 310-557-8475.
Sacramento, California Office: 770 L Street, Suite 1050.
Telephone: 916-443-8005.
Fax: 916-443-2240.
San Diego, California Office: 402 West Broadway, 23rd Floor.
Telephone: 619-234-6655.
Fax: 619-234-3510.
San Francisco, California Office: One Maritime Plaza, Sixth Floor.
Telephone: 415-434-4484.
Fax: 415-434-4507.

PARTNERS

Kenneth A. Beytin	David M. Rieth
Daniel N. Burton	David L. Robbins
Stephen A. Crane	Stanley A. Tarkow
James M. Landis	Martin A. Traber
Sybil Meloy	(Not admitted in FL)

Mark J. Wolfson
OF COUNSEL

Russell T. Alba	Lewis H. Hill, III

RETIRED PARTNERS
William J. Kiernan, Jr.

(See Next Column)

FOLEY & LARDNER, *Tampa—Continued*

RESIDENT ASSOCIATES

Charles "B.B." Abbott, II	Monta Michelle King
Matthew R. Costa	Gary D. Koch
Larry J. Davis, Jr.	Richard Thomas Petitt
Vitauts M. Gulbis	Terri Gillis Tucker
Scott D. Irwin	Anne J. Williams

Donald Alan Workman

For full biographical listings, see the Martindale-Hubbell Law Directory

GIBBONS, SMITH, COHN & ARNETT, A PROFESSIONAL ASSOCIATION (AV)

3321 Henderson Boulevard, P.O. Box 2177, 33601
Telephone: 813-877-9222
Fax: 813-877-9290
Email: GSCA@TFCTPA.com

Arthur S. Gibbons (1908-1986)	Patricia Arnett
Gary A. Gibbons	John R. Bello, Jr.
Kirk M. Gibbons	Larry M. Segall
Armin H. Smith, Jr.	Rod B. Neuman
Roy W. Cohn	Elizabeth A. Pereira

Patti W. Woodruff

For full biographical listings, see the Martindale-Hubbell Law Directory

HOLLAND & KNIGHT LLP (AV)

A Partnership including Professional Corporations
400 North Ashley, Suite 2300, 33602
Telephone: 813-227-8500
Fax: 813-229-0134
Mailing Address: P.O. Box 1288, 33601-1288
Email: hklaw.com *URL:* http://www.hklaw.com
Atlanta, Georgia Office: 1201 W. Peachtree Street, N.E., Suite 2000.
Telephone: 404-817-8500.
Fax: 404-881-0470.
Fort Lauderdale, Florida Office: One East Broward Boulevard, Suite 1300.
Telephone: 954-525-1000.
Fax: 954-463-2030.
Jacksonville, Florida Office: 50 N. Laura Street, Suite 3900.
Telephone: 904-353-2000.
Fax: 904-358-1872.
Lakeland, Florida Office: 92 Lake Wire Drive.
Telephone: 941-682-1161.
Fax: 941-688-1186.
Miami, Florida Office: 701 Brickell Avenue, 30th Floor.
Telephone: 305-374-8500.
Fax: 305-787-7799.
Orlando, Florida Office: 200 S. Orange Avenue, Suite 2600.
Telephone: 407-425-8500.
Fax: 407-244-5288.
St. Petersburg, Florida Office: One Progress Plaza, Suite 1600.
Telephone: 813-896-7171.
Fax: 813-822-8048.
Tallahassee, Florida Office: 315 Calhoun Street, Suite 600.
Telephone: 904-224-7000.
Fax: 904-224-8832.
West Palm Beach, Florida Office: 625 N. Flagler Drive, Suite 700.
Telephone: 561-833-2000.
Fax: 561-650-8399.
Washington, D.C. Office: 2100 Pennsylvania Avenue, N.W.
Telephone: 202-955-5550.
Fax: 202-955-5564.

TAMPA MEMBERS AND ASSOCIATES

A. Brian Albritton	John Arthur Jones
Rod Anderson	D. Burke Kibler, III
Robert J. Asti	Edward F. Koren
Chester E. Bacheller	William R. Lane, Jr.
Anderson L. Baldy III	Steven M. Larimore
Bernard A. Barton, Jr.	Jack A. Levine
Stacy D. Blank	Byrne Litschgi
Richard M. Blau	Carol J. LoCicero
David S. Bralow	Bill McBride (Managing Partner)
Karl J. Brandes (Executive Partner, Tampa Office)	Jack S. Newsome
	Paul E. Parrish
Steven L. Brannock	Thomas J. Patka
Warren M. Cason	Stephen J. Powell
William B. deMeza, Jr.	Bruce H. Roberson
Richard D. Eckhard	Frederick M. Rothenberg
John Germany	Frederick S. Schrils
Frederick J. Grady	James H. Shimberg, Jr.
Robert J. Grammig	David R. Singleton
Mark E. Grantham	Patrick W. Skelton
Gregory P. Hansel	Brian C. Sparks
G. Calvin Hayes	Charles L. Stutts
J. Fraser Himes	Gregg Darrow Thomas
George B. Howell, III	Robert H. Waltuch
Michael L. Jamieson	Julia Sullivan Waters
Douglas S. Jones	Douglas A. Wright

Barbara M. Yadley

(See Next Column)

R. Gregory Bailey	Toni L. Kemmerle
Laura Barber Belflower	Bradford D. Kimbro
C. Matthew Burns	James B. Lake
Michael L. Chapman	Dennis M. McClelland
Francis M. Curran	Susan Tillotson Mills
Kimberly Lee Franklin	Marni M. Morgan
Michael S. Goetz	John D. Mullen
Benjamin R. Hanan	Todd A. Nelson
Shane Hart	John E. Phillips
Christine A. Hearn	Samuel P. Queirolo
Elizabeth Belsom Johnson	Kimberly A. Stott

Carolyn T. Woods

OF COUNSEL

Charles M. Elson (Not admitted in FL)

For full biographical listings, see the Martindale-Hubbell Law Directory

HONIGMAN MILLER SCHWARTZ AND COHN (AV)

A Partnership including Professional Associations
2700 SunTrust Financial Centre, 401 E. Jackson Street, 33602-5226
Telephone: 813-221-6600
Telecopier: 813-223-4410
URL: http://law.honigman.com
West Palm Beach, Florida Office: Suite 800 Esperante Building, 222 Lakeview Avenue, 33401-6112.
Telephone: 561-838-4500.
Detroit, Michigan Office: 2290 First National Building, 48226.
Telephone: 313-256-7800.
Lansing, Michigan Office: 222 North Washington Square, Suite 400, 48933-1800.
Telephone: 517-484-8282.

MEMBERS

Robert W. Boos (P.A.)	Gregory G. Jones (P.A.)
Michael G. Cooke (P.A.)	Maria Maistrellis (P.A.)
Harry Christopher Goplerud (P.A.)	Barbara R. Pankau (P.A.)
	James B. Soble (P.A.)

John W. Voelpel

ASSOCIATES

Kevin M. Gilhool	Donald A. Mihokovich

Susan M. Salvatore

Representative Clients: SunTrust Bank, Tampa Bay; The Sembler Company; The Prudential Insurance Company of America; Raymond James & Assoc.; Whirlpool Corporation; Wilma South Management Corp.
Approved Attorneys for: Commonwealth Land Title Insurance Co.; First American Title Insurance Co.; Chicago Title Insurance Co.; Lawyers Title Insurance Co.

For full biographical listings, see the Martindale-Hubbell Law Directory

JOHNSON, BLAKELY, POPE, BOKOR, RUPPEL & BURNS, P.A. (AV)

100 North Tampa Street Suite 1800, P.O. Box 1100, 33601
Telephone: 813-225-2500
Telecopier: 813-223-7118
Clearwater, Florida Office: 911 Chestnut Street, P.O. Box 1368.
Telephone: 813-461-1818.
Telecopier: 813-441-8617.

John T. Blakely	Timothy A. Johnson, Jr.
Bruce H. Bokor	John R. Lawson, Jr.
Guy M. Burns	Michael C. Markham
Lisa B. Dodge	F. Wallace Pope, Jr.
Scott C. Ilgenfritz	Dennis G. Ruppel
Frank R. Jakes	Philip M. Shasteen

Charles M. Tatelbaum

Bruce W. Barnes	James W. Humann

Anthony P. Zinge

For full biographical listings, see the Martindale-Hubbell Law Directory

LAU, LANE, PIEPER, CONLEY & McCREADIE, P.A. (AV)

Suite 1700, 100 South Ashley, P.O. Box 838, 33601
Telephone: 813-229-2121
Telecopier: 813-228-7710
Port Canaveral, Florida Office: 405 Atlantis Road, Suite F.
Telephone: 407-799-3400.
Telecopier: 407-868-1025.

James V. Lau	Timothy C. Conley
Charles C. Lane	David W. McCreadie
Nathaniel G. W. Pieper	Annette Horan
Mary A. Lau	David F. Pope

Gregory P. Durham

For full biographical listings, see the Martindale-Hubbell Law Directory

Tampa—Continued

MACFARLANE FERGUSON & McMULLEN (AV)

Professional Association
2300 Park Tower, 400 North Tampa Street, P.O. Box 1531, 33601
Telephone: 813-273-4200
Fax: 813-273-4396
Clearwater, Florida Office: AmSouth Bank, Suite 800, 400 Cleveland Street, 34615.
Telephone: 813-441-8966.
Fax: 813-442-8470.

Howard P. Macfarlane (1888-1967)	Edward J. Kohrs
Chester H. Ferguson (1908-1983)	Andrew K. Macfarlane
David W. Adams	Ellen M. Macfarlane
John C. Bierley	Ted R. Manry, III
David M. Boggs	Carter B. McCain
Andrew Melton Brown	Mark E. McLaughlin
Robert W. Clark	Thomas B. Mimms, Jr.
Robert G. Cochran	John H. Mueller
Cody F. Davis	Vincent L. Nuccio, Jr.
W. Penn Dawson, III	Harold D. Oehler
James Craig Delesie, Sr.	Stephen L. Pankau
E. John Dinkel, III	Charles W. Pittman
Brian D. Forbes	Stephen H. Reynolds
Matthew J. Foster	Bruce M. Rodgers
Susan W. Fox	Gordon J. Schiff
Janet E. Goldberg	Stephen H. Sears
James W. Goodwin, II	T. Terrell Sessums
David J. Kadyk	Nathan B. Simpson
D. James Kadyk	H. Vance Smith
T. Paine Kelly, Jr.	William B. Taylor, IV
David C. G. Kerr	Stella Ferguson Thayer
	Claude H. Tison, Jr.
	Ansley Watson, Jr.

Denise L. Andersen	Walter Mathews, IV
Edward M. Copeland, IV	David M. Nicholson
Scott C. Davis	Dale J. Rickert
J. Craig Delesie, Jr.	Catherine R. Robinson
Sandra L. Fanning	James M. Robinson, IV
Patrick T. Lennon	Carolyn House Stewart

Staci R. Ward

Representative Clients: Beneficial Corporations; Checkers Drive-In Restaurants, Inc.; CNA Insurance Companies; Danka Industries, Inc.; The Edward J. De Bartolo Corporation; Lykes Bros. Inc. and subsidiary Companies; Morton Plant Hospital; Peoples Gas System, Inc.; Tampa Bay Downs, Inc.; Westinghouse Electric Corporation.

For full biographical listings, see the Martindale-Hubbell Law Directory

RUMBERGER, KIRK & CALDWELL, PROFESSIONAL ASSOCIATION (AV)

100 North Tampa Street, Suite 2000 (33602), P.O. Box 3390, 33601
Telephone: 813-223-4253
Fax: 813-221-4752
URL: http://www.rumberger.com
Miami, Florida Office: One Biscayne Tower, 2 South Biscayne Boulevard, Suite 3100, 33131.
Telephone: 305-358-5577.
Fax: 305-371-7580.
Orlando, Florida Office: Signature Plaza, Suite 300, 201 South Orange Avenue, (32801), P.O. Box 1873, 32802.
Telephone: 407-872-7300.
Fax: 407-841-2133.
Tallahassee, Florida Office: 106 East College Avenue, Suite 700, (32301), P.O. Box 10507, 32302.
Telephone: 904-222-6550.
Fax: 904-222-8783.

J. Richard Caldwell, Jr.	Susan Droppleman Duff

Ronald D. Darrigo	Bradley A. Kustin
Robert L. Blank	Kari A. Metzger

Angelina M. Grimes

Representative Clients: Automotive and other Manufacturers: General Motors Corp.; Mazda Motors of America, Inc.; Nissan Motor Corp. in U.S.A.; Toyota Motor Sales, U.S.A., Inc. General: Allstate Insurance Co.; Royal Insurance Co. Professional Liability: American International Group.

For full biographical listings, see the Martindale-Hubbell Law Directory

SHACKLEFORD, FARRIOR, STALLINGS & EVANS, PROFESSIONAL ASSOCIATION (AV)

Suite 1400, 501 East Kennedy Boulevard, P.O. Box 3324, 33601
Telephone: 813-273-5000
Cable Address: Intrepid, Tampa
Fax: 813-273-5145
Email: sfse@aol.com

(See Next Column)

R. W. Shackleford (1890-1964)	William A. Gillen, Jr.
T. M. Shackleford, Jr. (1884-1973)	Donald A. Gifford
J. Rex Farrior (1896-1993)	Joseph W. Clark
Warren Frazier (1935-1996)	Richard M. Zabak
Thomas C. MacDonald, Jr.	Peter J. Kelly
David G. Hanlon	James B. Murphy, Jr.
John I. Van Voris	David C. Banker
Lucius M. Dyal, Jr.	Joseph F. Kinman, Jr.
Stephen F. Myers	Daniel F. Molony
	Debra Ann Schrils

John A. Anthony

H. Hamilton Rice, III	Rebecca H. Steele
Jonathan S. Gilbert	Lorna A. McGeorge
Robert W. Bleakley	Neill R. Kahle
Brian P. Hall	David Tetrick, Jr.

Donna D. Bolin Wysong
OF COUNSEL
Norman Stallings

Representative Clients: Jim Walter Corporation; Eckerd Corporation; Merrill, Lynch, Pierce, Fennar & Smith, Inc.; Dow Chemical Company; Montgomery Ward & Co.; University of Florida; Tampa Sports Authority; Aetna Casualty & Surety Company; The Equitable Life Assurance Society of New York; John Hancock Mutual Life Insurance Company.

For full biographical listings, see the Martindale-Hubbell Law Directory

SHEAR, NEWMAN, HAHN AND ROSENKRANZ, P.A. (AV)

Suite 1000, 201 East Kennedy Boulevard, 33602
Telephone: 813-228-8530
FAX: 813-221-9122

L. David Shear	Glenn M. Burton
Jerry L. Newman	Roland J. Lamb
William E. Hahn	Bruce Douglas Lamb
Stanley W. Rosenkranz	Jeffrey Drew Butt
James R. Freeman	Mark J. Ragusa
Rodney W. Morgan	Kelly Jo Schmedt

Marilyn Drivas Sandborn	Mildred D. Beam-Rucker
Scott P. Distasio	Joseph F. Diaco, Jr.
Thomas M. Hoeler	Elizabeth (Betsey) Taylor Herd
Christopher J. Schulte	Timothy M. Cerio
Kimberly D. Holladay	Mindy Paige Brostoff
Debra L. Boje	Carl A. Goldman

OF COUNSEL

Daniel J. Gibby	Leonard L. Kleinman

References: NationsBank; First National Bank.

For full biographical listings, see the Martindale-Hubbell Law Directory

TRENAM, KEMKER, SCHARF, BARKIN, FRYE, O'NEILL & MULLIS, PROFESSIONAL ASSOCIATION (AV)

2700 Barnett Plaza, 101 East Kennedy Boulevard, P.O. Box 1102, 33602
Telephone: 813-223-7474
FAX: 813-229-6553
Telex: 6502251910 MCI
ABA/net 1574
St. Petersburg, Florida Office: 2100 Barnett Tower, One Progress Plaza.
Telephone: 813-898-7474.
Fax: 813-821-0407.

John J. Trenam (1912-1978)	Mary H. Quinlan
Harry Kemker (1930-1984)	David R. Brittain
Marvin E. Barkin	George E. Nader
William C. Frye	Edward C. LaRose
Albert C. O'Neill, Jr.	Roberta A. Colton
Harold W. Mullis, Jr.	Roberta Casper Watson
William Knight Zewadski	J. Alan Asendorf
Richard M. Leisner	John Daniel Goldsmith
Keith E. Rounsaville	Karen E. Lewis
Richard H. Sollner	John E. Johnson
Robert H. Buesing	D. Michael O'Leary
William G. Scott, III	Richard M. Hanchett
Stanley H. Eleff	Lansing C. Scriven
Gary I. Teblum	J. Cary Ross, Jr.
Nelson D. Blank	Marie Tomassi
John Sebastian Vento	Michael K. Green
Don B. Weinbren	Thomas D. Aitken

Elizabeth Pascale Francis	Charles M. Harris, Jr.
Wendolyn S. Busch	Laura E. Prather
Peter R. Wallace (St. Petersburg Office)	Richard J. McIntyre
H. Wayne Porter	Curran K. Porto
Dinita L. James	Randall C. McGeorge
Robert G. Stern	Paulee A. Coughlin
Nelson T. Castellano	Vincent B. Lynch
William H. Harrell, Jr.	John Panzarella
	Stephen Tabano

(See Next Column)

TRENAM, KEMKER, SCHARF, BARKIN, FRYE, O'NEILL & MULLIS
PROFESSIONAL ASSOCIATION, *Tampa—Continued*

Susanna M. Kramer	Rachelle L. DesVaux
(Not admitted in FL)	(Not admitted in FL)

Kelley C. Howard

OF COUNSEL

Leslie D. Scharf	James V. Carideo

For full biographical listings, see the Martindale-Hubbell Law Directory

ZINOBER & McCREA, P.A. (AV)

First of America Plaza, 201 East Kennedy Boulevard Suite 850, P.O. Box 1378, 33602
Telephone: 813-224-9004
Telecopier: 813-223-4881
Email: ZMLAW@aol.com

Peter W. Zinober	Richard C. McCrea, Jr.

Edwin J. Turanchik	Cynthia L. May
Frank E. Brown	Scott T. Silverman
Charles A. Powell, IV	Malanie J. LaFond
Jacqueline Ley Brown	Danielle R. May
Nancy A. Roslow	M. Sean Moyles

LEGAL SUPPORT PERSONNEL

Debra A. Douglas (Administrator)

For full biographical listings, see the Martindale-Hubbell Law Directory

---

TITUSVILLE,* Brevard Co.

SEVERS, STADLER & HARRIS, P.A. (AV)

509 Palm Avenue, P.O. Box 669, 32781-0669
Telephone: 407-267-1711; 407-632-2129
Fax: 407-632-2192

Dwight W. Severs	Richard E. Stadler

John M. Harris

Jan L. Miron

OF COUNSEL

John M. Starling

Representative Clients: City of Titusville; Brevard County Clerk of Court; The Goldfield Corp.; Sun Bank, N.A.; Town of Melbourne Village, AmSouth Bank.
Approved Attorneys for: Attorneys' Title Insurance Fund; Commonwealth Land Title Insurance Co.

For full biographical listings, see the Martindale-Hubbell Law Directory

---

VERO BEACH,* Indian River Co.

COLLINS, BROWN, CALDWELL, BARKETT, ROSSWAY, GARAVAGLIA & MOORE, CHARTERED (AV)

756 Beachland Boulevard, P.O. Box 3686, 32964
Telephone: 561-231-4343
FAX: 561-234-5213

George G. Collins, Jr.	Bradley W. Rossway
Calvin B. Brown	Michael J. Garavaglia
William W. Caldwell	John E. Moore, III
Bruce D. Barkett	Lisa N. Thompson

Reference: First Union Bank of Indian River County, Vero Beach, Florida.

For full biographical listings, see the Martindale-Hubbell Law Directory

---

GOULD, COOKSEY, FENNELL, O'NEILL & MARINE, PROFESSIONAL ASSOCIATION (AV)

979 Beachland Boulevard, 32963
Telephone: 561-231-1100
Fax: 561-231-2020

John R. Gould (1921-1988)	Darrell Fennell
Byron T. Cooksey	Eugene J. O'Neill

Christopher H. Marine

David M. Carter	Todd W. Fennell

Counsel for: Barnett Bank of Indian River County; Indian River National Bank; Citrus Bank, N.A.
Approved Attorneys for: Attorneys' Title Insurance Fund; Commonwealth Land Title Insurance Company; Lawyers Title Insurance Corp.; Federal Land Bank of Columbia.
Local Counsel for: Los Angeles Dodgers, Inc.

For full biographical listings, see the Martindale-Hubbell Law Directory

---

MOSS, HENDERSON, BLANTON, KOVAL & LANIER, P.A. (AV)

817 Beachland Boulevard, P.O. Box 3406, 32964-3406
Telephone: 561-231-1900
Fax: 561-231-4387

George H. Moss, II	Thomas A. Koval
Steve L. Henderson	Clinton W. Lanier
Robin A. Blanton	Fred L. Kretschmer, Jr.

Lisa D. Harpring

Lewis W. Murphy, Jr.	Kelly Cambron
Judith Goodman Hill	Lawrence Y. Leonard

David F. Mancini

OF COUNSEL

Charles E. Garris	Ford J. Fegert

Everett J. Van Gaasbeck

Representative Clients: Aetna Life & Casualty; Alcoa Florida, Inc.; Florida Power & Light Co.; Insurance Company of North America; Liberty Mutual Insurance Co.; Sears, Roebuck & Co.; Sugar Cane Growers Cooperative of Florida; Norfolk Southern Corporation/North American Van Lines, Inc.

For full biographical listings, see the Martindale-Hubbell Law Directory

---

SMITH & SMITH (AV)

Citrus Financial Center, Suite 301, 1717 Indian River Boulevard, 32960
Telephone: 561-567-4351
Fax: 561-567-4298

MEMBERS OF FIRM

Sherman N. Smith, Jr.	Sherman N. Smith, III

ASSOCIATE

Anthony T. Golden

References: Citrus Bank, N.A.; Northern Trust Bank of Vero Beach.

For full biographical listings, see the Martindale-Hubbell Law Directory

---

WEST PALM BEACH,* Palm Beach Co.

BROAD AND CASSEL (AV)

A Partnership including Professional Associations
The Reflections Office Centre, 400 Australian Avenue, South, Fifth Floor, 33401
Telephone: 561-832-3300
Telecopier: 561-655-1109
Boca Raton, Florida Office: Corporate Centre at Boca Raton, Suite 300, 7777 Glades Road, 33434.
Telephone: 561-483-7000.
Fort Lauderdale, Florida Office: Suite 1130, Broward Financial Centre, 500 E. Broward Boulevard, 33394.
Telephone: 954-764-7060.
Miami, Florida Office: Miami Center, 201 South Biscayne Boulevard, Suite 3000, 33131.
Telephone: 305-373-9400.
Orlando, Florida Office: Barnett Bank Center, 390 N. Orange Avenue, Suite 1100, 32801.
Telephone: 407-839-4200.
Stuart, Florida Office: 900 East Ocean Boulevard, Suite 126, 33994.
Telephone: 561-283-3000.
Tallahassee, Florida Office: 215 South Monroe Street, Suite 400, 32302.
Telephone: 904-681-6810.
Tampa, Florida Office: 100 North Tampa, Suite 3500, 33602.
Telephone: 813-225-3020.

PARTNERS

Patricia Lebow (P.A.)	Andrew D. Rafkin
(Managing Partner)	Jeffrey F. Gordon
Clifford I. Hertz (P.A.)	Steven Ellison

Ronald M. Gaché(P.A.)

ASSOCIATES

Joyce L. Elden	Peter M. Bernhardt
Jeffrey J. Suter	Debra B. Potter
Richard M. Benrubi	Tyrone L. Lufman

OF COUNSEL

William P. Burns	Kenneth Edelman

Jodi B. Laurence

For full biographical listings, see the Martindale-Hubbell Law Directory

---

CARLTON, FIELDS, WARD, EMMANUEL, SMITH & CUTLER, P.A. (AV)

Esperanté, 222 Lakeview Avenue, Suite 1400 (33401-6149), P.O. Box 150, 33402-0150
Telephone: 407-659-7070
Fax: 407-659-7368
Orlando, Florida Office: Suite 1600, Citrus Center, 255 South Orange Avenue, 32801-3488, P.O. Box 1171, 32802-1171.
Telephone: 407-849-0300.
Pensacola, Florida Office: Harbourview Building, 4th Floor, 25 West Cedar Street, 32501-5974, P.O. Box 12426, 32582-2426.
Telephone: 904-434-0142.

(See Next Column)

CARLTON, FIELDS, WARD, EMMANUEL, SMITH & CUTLER P.A.—*Continued*

St. Petersburg, Florida Office: Barnett Tower, Suite 2300, One Progress Plaza, 200 Central Avenue, 33701-4352, P.O. Box 2861, 33731-2861.
Telephone: 813-821-7000.
Tallahassee, Florida Office: 215 South Monroe Street, Suite 500, 32301-1866, P.O. Drawer 190, 32301-4352.
Telephone: 904-224-1585.
Tampa, Florida Office: One Harbour Place, 777 South Harbour Island Boulevard, 33602-5799, P.O. Box 3239, 33601-3239.
Telephone: 813-223-7000.

Gary M. Brandenburg	Stephen J. Krigbaum
Thomas A. Hanson	John R. Hart
Robert N. Gilbert	M. Richard Sapir
Michael S. Tammaro	Lynda J. Harris
Jacob D. Varn	Diana Lewis

Joseph Ianno, Jr.

OF COUNSEL

Thomas J. Schwartz

Kathleen Gilmore Kozinski	Mimi K. McAndrews
Michael J. Compagno	Donald Tobyn De Young

Henry S. Wulf

Patrick J. Rooney, Jr.

For full biographical listings, see the Martindale-Hubbell Law Directory

---

FOLEY & LARDNER (AV)

Suite 200, Phillips Point East Tower, 777 South Flagler Drive, 33401-6163
Telephone: 561-655-5050
Facsimile: 561-655-6925
Milwaukee, Wisconsin Office: Firstar Center, 777 East Wisconsin Avenue.
Telephone: 414-271-2400.
Telex: 26-819 (Foley Lard Mil).
Facsimile: 414-297-4900.
Madison, Wisconsin Office: Verex Plaza, 150 East Gilman Street, P.O. Box 1497.
Telephone: 608-257-5035.
Telex: 262051 (F L Madison).
Facsimile: 608-258-4258.
Chicago, Illinois Office: Suite 3300, One IBM Plaza, 330 N. Wabash Avenue.
Telephone: 312-755-1900.
Facsimile: 312-755-1925.
Washington, D.C. Office: Washington Harbour, Suite 500, 3000 K Street, N.W.,
Telephone: 202-672-5300.
Telex: 904136 (Foley Lard Wsh).
Facsimile: 202-672-5399.
Annapolis, Maryland Office: Suite 102, 175 Admiral Cochrane Drive.
Telephone: 301-266-8077.
Telex: 899149 (Oldtownpat).
Facsimile: 301-266-8664.
Jacksonville, Florida Office: The Greenleaf Building, 200 Laura Street, P.O. Box 240.
Telephone: 904-359-2000.
Facsimile: 904-359-8700.
Orlando, Florida Office: Suite 1800, 111 North Orange Avenue, P.O. Box 2193.
Telephone: 407-423-7656.
Telex: 441781 (HQ ORL).
Facsimile: 407-648-1743.
Tallahassee, Florida Office: Suite 300, 123 South Calhoun Street, P.O. Box 508.
Telephone: 904-222-6100.
Facsimile: 904-224-0496.
Tampa, Florida Office: Suite 2700, One Hundred N. Tampa Street, P.O. Box 3391.
Telephones: 813-229-2300; Pinellas County: 813-442-3296.
Facsimile: 813-221-4210.
Brussels, Belgium Office: Avenue Louise, 283.
Telephone: 32-2-646-2777.
Facsimile: 32-2-646-7574.
Foley Lardner Weissburg & Aronson Office Locations:
Los Angeles, California Office: 2049 Century Park East, Suite 3200.
Telephone: 310-277-2223.
Fax: 310-557-8475.
Sacramento, California Office: 770 L Street, Suite 1050.
Telephone: 916-443-8005.
Fax: 916-443-2240.
San Diego, California: 402 West Broadway, 23rd Floor.
Telephone: 619-234-6655.
Fax: 619-234-3510.
San Francisco, California Office: One Maritime Plaza, Sixth Floor.
Telephone: 415-434-4484.
Fax: 415-434-4507.

(See Next Column)

PARTNERS

Sybil Meloy	Jack A. Porter
Thomas F. Munro, II	Amy S. Rubin
Todd B. Pfister	William P. Sklar

RESIDENT ASSOCIATES

Claudia Saenz Amlie	Marilyn A. Moore
Richard S. Davis	Michael S. Popok

Alan C. Sheppard, Jr.

For full biographical listings, see the Martindale-Hubbell Law Directory

---

GUNSTER, YOAKLEY, VALDES-FAULI & STEWART, PROFESSIONAL ASSOCIATION (AV)

Phillips Point, Suite 500 East, 777 South Flagler Drive, 33401-6194
Telephone: 561-655-1980
Fax: 561-655-5677
Email: mmitrione@gunster.com *URL:* http://www.gunster.com
Miami, Florida Office: Suite 3400, One Biscayne Tower, 2 South Biscayne Boulevard.
Telephone: 305-376-6000.
Fax: 305-376-6010.
Fort Lauderdale, Florida Office: Broward Financial Centre, Suite 1400, 500 East Broward Boulevard.
Telephone: 954-462-2000.
Fax: 954-523-1722.
Palm Beach, Florida Office: 151 Royal Palm Way.
Telephone: 561-833-1970.
Fax: 561-650-0655.
Stuart, Florida Office: Suite 200, 800 S.E. Monterey Commons Boulevard.
Telephone: 561-288-1980.
Fax: 561-288-0610.
Vero Beach, Florida Office: Suite 301, 3055 Cardinal Drive.
Telephone: 561-234-1040.
Fax: 561-234-1518.
Tallahassee, Florida Office: 515 North Adams Street.
Telephone: 904-222-6660.
Fax: 904-222-1002.

John Kenneth Williamson (1892-1964)	Joseph F. Gunster (1894-1979)
	David S. Yoakley (1917-1994)

Jerry E. Aron	Daniel A. Hanley
David R. Atkinson, Jr.	Kenneth M. Hart
Bernard R. Baker, III	Richard D. Holt
Kenneth S. Beall, Jr.	Thomas P. Hunt
James B. Bertles	Garrison duP. Lickle
Donald J. Beuttenmuller, Jr.	Michael V. Mitrione
James R. Brindell	L. Louis Mrachek
Paul W. A. Courtnell, Jr.	Stephen C. Page
Lewis F. Crippen	Hugh W. Perry
G. Joseph Curley	Michael G. Platner
Leigh E. Dunston	Robert T. Scott
C. Craig Eller	Jeffrey A. Stoops

Peter Van Andel

Jack J. Aiello	Gordon R. Leech
Laurie B. Aiello	Patricia A. Leonard
Juan C. Antúnez	Kimberly Krumholtz Lunsford
Gregory K. Bader	Michelle Oms
David G. Bates	J. Coleman Prewitt, Jr.
G. Brian Butler	Alan Benjamin Rose
Ernest A. Cox, III	Brian C. Schneider
Lawrence J. Diamond	Gregor J. Schwinghammer
Jennifer Lynn Dolce	Neil H. Seidman
Karen M. Fingar-Kahane	(Not admitted in FL)
Roy E. Fitzgerald	Michael D. Simon
Robert M. Graham	Jeffrey M. Taylor
Pamela Kristen Kay	Kathy J. Tayon
Kurt E. Lee	Stephen G. Vogelsang

Alexandra M. Woodfield

OF COUNSEL

Bette Kester Conrad	A. Obie Stewart
Juan Lopez Palmer	John C. Rau

Seymour S. Sussman

Counsel for: City Savings Bank; Professional Golfers Association of America; Sun Bank/South Florida, N/A.

For full biographical listings, see the Martindale-Hubbell Law Directory

---

HOLLAND & KNIGHT LLP (AV)

A Partnership including Professional Corporations
625 N. Flagler Drive Suite 700, 33401
Telephone: 561-833-2000
Fax: 561-650-8399
Mailing Address: P.O. Box 3208, 33402
Email: hklaw.com *URL:* http://www.hklaw.com
Fort Lauderdale, Florida Office: One East Broward Boulevard, Suite 1300.
Telephone: 954-525-1000.
Fax: 954-463-2030.

(See Next Column)

HOLLAND & KNIGHT LLP, *West Palm Beach—Continued*

Jacksonville, Florida Office: 50 N. Laura Street, Suite 3900.
Telephone: 904-353-2000.
Fax: 904-358-1872.
Lakeland, Florida Office: 92 Lake Wire Drive.
Telephone: 941-682-1161.
Fax: 941-688-1186.
Miami, Florida Office: 701 Brickell Avenue, 30th Floor.
Telephone: 305-374-8500.
Fax: 305-787-7799.
Orlando, Florida Office: 200 S. Orange Avenue, Suite 2600.
Telephone: 407-425-8500.
Fax: 407-244-5288.
St. Petersburg, Florida Office: One Progress Plaza, Suite 1600.
Telephone: 813-896-7171.
Fax: 813-822-8048.
Tallahassee, Florida Office: 315 Calhoun Street, Suite 600.
Telephone: 904-224-7000.
Fax: 904-224-8832.
Washington, D.C. Office: 2100 Pennsylvania Avenue, N.W.
Telephone: 202-955-3000.
Fax: 202-955-5564.
Atlanta, Georgia Office: 1201 West Peachtree Street, N.E., Suite 2000.
Telephone: 404-817-8500.
Fax: 404-881-0470.

MEMBERS AND ASSOCIATES

Martin J. Alexander	William D. McEachern
Michael S. Greene	Scott B. Newman
Hank Jackson	David L. Perry, Jr.
Charles W. Littell	David J. White

Eunice Tall Baros	William P. Gray, III
Jennifer Shasha Brooker	William P. Heller
Rosanne M. Duane	Elizabeth D. Stone

OF COUNSEL

Richard L. Abedon	Richard S. Weinstein

For full biographical listings, see the Martindale-Hubbell Law Directory

HONIGMAN MILLER SCHWARTZ AND COHN (AV)

A Partnership including Professional Associations
Suite 800 Esperante Building, 222 Lakeview Avenue, 33401-6112
Telephone: 561-838-4500
Telecopier: 561-832-3036; 832-2645
URL: http://law.honigman.com
Tampa, Florida Office: 2700 SunTrust Financial Centre, 401 E. Jackson Street, 33602-5226.
Telephone: 813-221-6600.
Detroit, Michigan Office: 2290 First National Building, 48226.
Telephone: 313-256-7800.
Lansing, Michigan Office: 222 North Washington Square, Suite 400, 48933-1800.
Telephone: 517-484-8282.

MEMBERS

Carla L. Brown (P.A.)	Steven R. Parson (P.A.)
Ronald S. Kochman (P.A.)	Neil W. Platock (P.A.)
Mark Nussbaum (P.A.)	Marvin S. Rosen (P.A.)
	E. Lee Worsham (P.A.)

ASSOCIATE

Jose O. Diaz

General Counsel for: Forbes-Cohen Properties (The Garden Mall); Multivest Real Estate, Inc.; Pulte Corporation.
Representative Clients: Ford Motor Co.; Rite Aid Corporation; The Taubman Company, Inc.; The Travelers Insurance Company.

For full biographical listings, see the Martindale-Hubbell Law Directory

JONES, FOSTER, JOHNSTON & STUBBS, P.A. (AV)

Flagler Center Tower, 505 South Flagler Drive, Suite 1100, P.O. Box 3475, 33402-3475
Telephone: 561-659-3000
Fax: 561-832-1454

Sidney A. Stubbs	Peter A. Sachs
John Blair McCracken	Michael T. Kranz
John C. Randolph	John S. Trimper
Herbert Adams Weaver, Jr.	Mark B. Kleinfeld
Larry B. Alexander	Scott Gardner Hawkins
Thornton M. Henry	Steven J. Rothman
Margaret L. Cooper	Rebecca G. Doane
D. Culver Smith, III	Carl Angeloff (P.A.)
Allen R. Tomlinson	H. Michael Easley
Peter S. Holton	Joyce A. Conway

Christopher S. Duke	Edward Diaz
Scott L. McMullen	David Pratt
M. Tracey Biagiotti	Brian K. Waxman
Clay C. Brooker	David E. Dreyer
	(Not admitted in FL)

(See Next Column)

Counsel for: U.S. Trust Co.; NationsBank of Florida, N.A.; Island National Bank; Bankers Trust Company of Florida; Sun Bank/South Florida, N.A.; General Motors Acceptance Corp.

For full biographical listings, see the Martindale-Hubbell Law Directory

ROBERT S. LEVY, P.A. (AV)

Suite 502, The Forum, 1655 Palm Beach Lakes Boulevard, 33401
Telephone: 561-686-6080
Fax: 561-686-6085

Robert S. Levy

Reference: First Union National Bank of Florida.

For full biographical listings, see the Martindale-Hubbell Law Directory

MOYLE, FLANIGAN, KATZ, KOLINS, RAYMOND & SHEEHAN, P.A. (AV)

625 North Flagler Drive 9th Floor, P.O. Box 3888, 33402
Telephone: 561-659-7500
Facsimile: 561-659-1789
Palm Beach Gardens, Florida Office: 2401 P.G.A. Boulevard, Building C - Suite 120.
Telephone: 561-625-6480.
Facsimile: 561-625-5979.
Stuart, Florida Office: 900 South Federal Highway, 1st Floor.
Telephone: 561-288-1144.
Facsimile: 561-288-1499.
Tallahassee, Florida Office: 210 South Monroe Street.
Telephone: 904-681-3828.
Facsimile: 904-681-8788.

Peter L. Breton	Jon C. Moyle
John R. Eubanks	Jon C. Moyle, Jr.
John F. Flanigan	(Resident, Tallahassee Office)
Myra Gendel	Mark E. Raymond
Martin V. Katz	Thomas A. Sheehan, III
Ronald K. Kolins	Marta M. Suarez-Murias
Paul Andrew Krasker	Wilton L. White
Linda R. McCann	
(Resident, Stuart Office)	

OF COUNSEL

William J. Payne

For full biographical listings, see the Martindale-Hubbell Law Directory

PETERS, ROBERTSON, LAX, PARSONS, WELCHER, MOWERS & PASSARO, P.A. (AV)

Galleria International Building, 301 Clematis Street, Suite 203, 33401-4381
Telephone: 407-832-9698
Fax: 407-832-8355
Miami, Florida Office: Suite 600, Ingraham Building, 25 Southeast 2nd Avenue.
Telephone: 305-374-3103.
Fax: 305-377-9805.
Fort Lauderdale, Florida Office: Suite 600, 600 South Andrews Avenue.
Telephone: 954-761-8999.
Fax: 954-761-8990.
Fort Myers, Florida Office: Key West Professional Centre, 1342 Colonial Boulevard, Suite 45.
Telephone: 941-936-1129.
Fax: 941-936-4036.

Walter H. Djokic

Representative Clients: Auto-Owners Insurance Co.; Dade County School Board; Employers Reinsurance Group; Gallagher Bassett Insurance Service; Maryland Casualty Co.

For full biographical listings, see the Martindale-Hubbell Law Directory

QUARLES & BRADY (AV)

222 Lakeview Avenue, 4th Floor, 33401
Telephone: 561-653-5000
Fax: 561-653-5333
Milwaukee, Wisconsin Office: 411 East Wisconsin Avenue, 53202-4497.
Telephone: 414-277-5000.
Fax: 414-271-3552.
Madison, Wisconsin Office: Firstar Plaza, One South Pinckney Street, P.O. Box 2113, 53701-2113.
Telephone: 608-251-5000.
Fax: 608-251-9166.
Naples, Florida Office: Barnett Center, 4501 Tamiami Trail North, Suite 300, 33940-3060.
Telephone: 941-262-5959.
Fax: 941-434-4999.
Phoenix, Arizona Office: One Camelback Building, One East Camelback Road, Suite 400, 85012-1649.
Telephone: 602-230-5500.
Fax: 602-230-5598.

(See Next Column)

QUARLES & BRADY—*Continued*

PARTNERS

John S. Sammond	David L. Petersen
James A. McSwigan	Ned R. Nashban
J. Rodman Steele, Jr.	Paul M. Platte
	Gregory A. Nelson

ASSOCIATES

Nancy Berz Colman	Robert J. Sacco
Joseph W. Bain	Elizabeth A. Dougherty

BUSINESS MANAGEMENT SUPPORT PERSONNEL

Jill M. Miller (Florida Administrator)

LEGAL ASSISTANTS

Susan D. Bober	Conni Hager
Jacquelyn Brookings	Susan A. Hess
Carol Cavallerano	Lisa H. Paden

For full biographical listings, see the Martindale-Hubbell Law Directory

---

DONALD J. SASSER, P.A. (AV)

1800 Australian Avenue, South, Suite 203, P.O. Box 2907, 33402
Telephone: 561-689-4378
Fax: 561-689-4652

Donald J. Sasser

Jorge M. Cestero	Thomas J. Sasser

Reference: First Union National Bank of Florida.

For full biographical listings, see the Martindale-Hubbell Law Directory

---

SEARCY DENNEY SCAROLA BARNHART & SHIPLEY, PROFESSIONAL ASSOCIATION (AV)

2139 Palm Beach Lakes Boulevard, P.O. Drawer 3626, 33402-3626
Telephone: 407-686-6300
800-780-8607
800-220-7006 (Spanish)
Fax: 407-478-0754

Christian D. Searcy, Sr.	Lawrence J. Block, Jr.
Earl L. Denney, Jr.	C. Calvin Warriner, III
John Scarola	William A. Norton
F. Gregory Barnhart	David J. Sales
John A. Shipley	Christopher K. Speed
David K. Kelley, Jr.	William B. King

Karen E. Terry	T. Michael Kennedy
Katherine Ann Martinez	Todd S. Stewart
	Laurie J. Briggs

LEGAL SUPPORT PERSONNEL

Deane L. Cady (Paralegal/Investigator)	J. Peter Love (Paralegal/Investigator)
James E. Cook (Paralegal/Investigator)	Marjorie A. Morgan (Paralegal)
Emilio Diamantis (Paralegal/Investigator)	William H. Seabold (Paralegal/Investigator)
David W. Gilmore (Paralegal/Investigator)	Kathleen Simon (Paralegal)
Thaddeus E. Kulesa (Paralegal/Investigator)	Steve M. Smith (Paralegal/Investigator)
	Judson Whitehorn (Paralegal/Investigator)

For full biographical listings, see the Martindale-Hubbell Law Directory

---

SHUTTS & BOWEN (AV)

A Partnership including Professional Associations
One Clearlake Centre, 250 Australian Avenue Suite 500, 33401
Telephone: 561-835-8500
Fax: 561-650-8530
URL: HTTP://WWW.LAWWORLD.COM/SHUTTS/
Miami, Florida Office: 1500 Miami Center, 201 South Biscayne Boulevard.
Telephone: 305-358-6300.
Cable Address: "Shuttsbo."
Telefax: 305-381-9982.
Orlando, Florida Office: 20 North Orange Avenue, Suite 1000.
Telephone: 407-423-3200.
Fax: 407-425-8316.
Amsterdam, The Netherlands Office: Shutts & Bowen, B.V., Europa Boulevard 59, 1083 AD, Amsterdam.
Telephone: (31 20) 661-0969.
Fax: (31 20) 642-1475.
London, England Office: 43 Grosvenor Street, London W1X 9PG.
Telephone: 441-71-493-4840.
Telefax: 441-71-493-4299.

(See Next Column)

MEMBERS OF FIRM

Arnold L. Berman (Resident)	Joseph F. McSorley (Resident)
James A. Farrell	Arthur J. Menor (Resident)
Charles Robinson Fawsett (P.A.)	Robert C. Sommerville (P.A.)
David A. Gart	Robert Wexler
Robert E. Gunn (P.A.) (Resident)	John B. White (P.A.)
	Scott G. Williams (Resident)

RESIDENT ASSOCIATES

Jonathan D. Gerber	Robert B. Goldman
	Michelle R. North

OF COUNSEL

John R. Day (P.A.)

For full biographical listings, see the Martindale-Hubbell Law Directory

---

WALTON LANTAFF SCHROEDER & CARSON (AV)

A Partnership including Professional Associations
United National Bank Tower, Suite 800, 1645 Palm Beach Lakes Boulevard, P.O. Box 2966, 33401
Telephone: 407-689-6700
Telecopier: 407-689-2647
Miami, Florida Office: One Biscayne Tower, 25th Floor, 2 South Biscayne Boulevard.
Telephone: 305-379-6411.
Telecopier: 305-577-3875.
Fort Lauderdale, Florida Office: Third Floor, Blackstone Building, 707 Southeast Third Avenue.
Telephone: 305-463-8456.
Telecopier: 305-763-6294.
Coral Gables, Florida Office: Suite 1101, Gables International Plaza, 2655 Le Jeune Road.
Telephone: 305-379-6411.
Telecopier: 305-446-9206.

RESIDENT PARTNERS

Wayne T. Gill (P.A.)	John G. White, III
Roberta J. Karp	Amy L. Smith

RESIDENT ASSOCIATES

Robert M. Donlon	David S. Tadros
Gregory William Coleman	Steven E. Foor
George W. Bush, Jr.	Ellen S. Malasky
Kurt A. Wyland	Gregg R. Margre
	Steven C. Sessa

For full biographical listings, see the Martindale-Hubbell Law Directory

---

WINTER HAVEN, Polk Co.

CRITTENDEN & CRITTENDEN, P.A. (AV)

103 Avenue A., N.W., P.O. Drawer 152, 33882-0152
Telephone: 941-293-2161
Fax: 941-299-3207

H. C. Crittenden (1898-1969)	Robert R. Crittenden

LEGAL SUPPORT PERSONNEL

Peggy L. Thompson	Freida G. Hart

Counsel for: City of Lake Alfred, Florida; 400 and 402 Avenue K Prof. Partnerships; Town of Dundee; Town of Lake Hamilton.
Approved Attorney for: Lawyers Title Insurance Corp.; Federal Land Bank of Columbia, South Carolina; Attorneys' Title Insurance Fund.

PETERSON & MYERS, P.A. (AV)

Suite 300, 141 5th Street N.W., P.O. Drawer 7608, 33883-7608
Telephone: 941-294-3360
Lake Wales, Florida Office: 130 East Central Avenue, P.O. Box 1079.
Telephones: 941-676-7611; 683-8942.
Lakeland, Florida Office: 100 East Main Street, P.O. Box 24628.
Telephones: 941-683-6511; 676-6934.

Philip O. Allen	Peter J. Munson
Jack P. Brandon	Corneal B. Myers
Beach A Brooks, Jr.	Cornelius B. Myers, III
Kristen Marie Buzzanca	E. Blake Paul
J. Davis Connor	Robert E. Puterbaugh
Michael S. Craig	Abel A. Putnam
Roy A. Craig, Jr.	Thomas B. Putnam, Jr.
Jacob C. Dykxhoorn	Deborah A. Ruster
Dennis P. Johnson	Stephen R. Senn
Kevin C. Knowlton	Andrea Teves Smith
Douglas A. Lockwood, III	Keith H. Wadsworth
M. Craig Massey	Kerry M. Wilson

General Counsel for: Barnett Bank of Polk County.
Representative Clients: Mutual Wholesale Co.; Barnett Banks, Inc.; Ben Hill Griffin, Inc.; Alcoma Association, Inc.
Approved Attorneys for: Equitable Life Assurance Society of the United States; Federal Land Bank, Columbia, South Carolina; Attorneys' Title Insurance Fund.

For full biographical listings, see the Martindale-Hubbell Law Directory

WINTER PARK, Orange Co.

TROUTMAN, WILLIAMS, IRVIN, GREEN & HELMS, PROFESSIONAL ASSOCIATION (AV)

311 West Fairbanks Avenue, 32789
Telephone: 407-647-2277
Telefax: 407-628-2986
Toll Free: 1-800-486-5149
Kissimmee, Florida Office: Suite 206, 120 Broadway, 34741.
Telephone: 407-933-8834.
FAX: 407-933-8253.

Russell Troutman	Roger D. Helms
Joseph H. Williams	Jack E. Bowen
Paul B. Irvin	Joseph J. Polich, Jr.
Robert F. Green	Kim Michael Cullen
Joseph C. Perzan	

For full biographical listings, see the Martindale-Hubbell Law Directory

WINDERWEEDLE, HAINES, WARD & WOODMAN, P.A. (AV)

Barnett Bank Building, 250 Park Avenue, South, P.O. Box 880, 32790-0880
Telephone: 407-423-4246
Telecopier: 407-645-3728
Orlando, Florida Office: Barnett Bank Center, 390 North Orange Avenue, P.O. Box 1391.
Telephone: 407-423-4246.
Telecopier: 407-423-7014.

W. E. Winderweedle (1906-1979)	Gregory L. Holzhauer
Webber B. Haines (1906-1995)	Dykes C. Everett
Harold A. Ward, III	John H. Dyer, Jr.
Victor E. Woodman	William H. Robbinson, Jr.
John D. Haines	W. Graham White
William A. Walker II	Paula P. Lightsey
C. Brent McCaghren	Nancy S. Freeman
Randolph J. Rush	Brian W. Bennett
	(Not admitted in FL)

General Counsel for: Winter Park Health Foundation; City of Winter Park; RoTech Medical Corp.; Schwartz Electro-Optics, Inc.
Counsel for: Barnett Bank of Central Florida, N.A.; Florida Conference of the United Church of Christ, Inc.
Representative Clients: Georgia Pacific Corp.; USX Corp.

For full biographical listings, see the Martindale-Hubbell Law Directory

WINTER SPRINGS, Seminole Co. — (Refer to Longwood)

GEORGIA

ABBEVILLE,* Wilcox Co. — (Refer to Eastman)

ALMA,* Bacon Co. — (Refer to Douglas)

AMERICUS,* Sumter Co.

ELLIS, EASTERLIN, PEAGLER, GATEWOOD, HARPER & SKIPPER, P.C., A PROFESSIONAL CORPORATION (AV)

410 West Lamar Street, P.O. Box 488, 31709
Telephone: 912-924-9316
Fax: 912-924-6248

George R. Ellis, Sr. (1905-1988)	James C. Gatewood
George R. Ellis, Jr.	John V. Harper
Benjamin F. Easterlin, IV	James M. Skipper, Jr.
George M. Peagler, Jr.	Russ F. Barnes
William H. Dudley	

For full biographical listings, see the Martindale-Hubbell Law Directory

ASHBURN,* Turner Co. — (Refer to Tifton)

ATHENS,* Clarke Co.

BLASINGAME, BURCH, GARRARD, BRYANT & ASHLEY, P.C. (AV)

440 College Avenue North, P.O. Box 832, 30603
Telephone: 706-354-4000
Telecopier: 706-353-0673
Greensboro, Georgia Office: 122 N. Main Street, P.O. Box 67, 30642.
Telephone: 706-453-7139.
Fax: 706-453-7842.

J. Ralph Beaird	Andrew J. Hill, III
Gary B. Blasingame	Michael A. Morris
E. Davison Burch	Thomas H. Rogers, Jr.
Henry G. Garrard, III	William D. Harvard
Everett Clay Bryant	Rikard L. Bridges
W. Seaborn Ashley, Jr.	Ivan A. Gustafson

(See Next Column)

M. Steven Heath	David S. Thomson
Richard W. Schmidt	Christopher G. Conley
Milton F. Eisenberg	Lloyd N. Bell
Stephen E.B. Smith	Kim T. Stephens
J. Branson Parker	Amy Lou Reynolds
J. David Felt, Jr.	C. Kathryn Hackney
Kathleen M. Timmons	

Representative Clients: NationsBank of Georgia, N.A.; Georgia Power Co.; Georgia Natural Gas Co.; Pittsburgh Corning Corp.; Downtown Athens Development Authority; Georgia National Bank; Fowler Products Co., Inc.; St. Paul Fire & Marine Insurance Co.; Athens Newspapers, Inc.; First Commerce Bancorp, Inc.

For full biographical listings, see the Martindale-Hubbell Law Directory

McLEOD, BENTON, BEGNAUD & MARSHALL (AV)

8th Floor, NationsBank Building, P.O. Box 8108, 30603
Telephone: 706-549-9400
Fax: 706-549-9406

MEMBERS OF FIRM

Larry V. McLeod	Malcolm C. McArthur
Terrell W. Benton, Jr.	William C. Berryman, Jr.
Jeanette S. Scott	Daniel C. Haygood
Darrel Begnaud	Hilary N. Shuford
Andrew H. Marshall	Richard L. Brittain
Michael C. Pruett	

OF COUNSEL

Robert E. Gibson

Counsel for: NationsBank; Athens First Bank & Trust Company; Georgia Power Company; CSX Transportation, Inc.; St. Mary's Hospital; Benson's Inc.; Oconee County School District; Walton County School District; Clarke County School District.

For full biographical listings, see the Martindale-Hubbell Law Directory

ATLANTA,* Fulton Co.

ALEMBIK, FINE & CALLNER, P.A. (AV)

Marquis One Tower, Fourth Floor, 245 Peachtree Center Avenue, N.E., 30303
Telephone: 404-688-8800
Telecopier: 404-420-7191

Michael D. Alembik (1936-1993)	Ronald T. Gold
Lowell S. Fine	G. Michael Banick
Bruce W. Callner	Mark E. Bergeson
Kathy L. Portnoy	Russell P. Love

Z. Ileana Martinez	Janet Lichiello Franchi
Susan M. Lieppe	Heidi Koch Martin
Bruce R. Steinfeld	Janet Caroline Moja
John H. Zwald	

For full biographical listings, see the Martindale-Hubbell Law Directory

ALSTON & BIRD (AV)

A Partnership including Professional Corporations
One Atlantic Center, 1201 West Peachtree Street, 30309-3424
Telephone: 404-881-7000
Telecopier: 404-881-7777
Cable Address: AMGRAM GA
Telex: 54-2996
Easylink: 62985848
Washington, D.C. Office: 601 Pennsylvania Ave., N.W., North Building, Suite 250 20004.
Telephone: 202-508-3300.
Telecopier: 202-508-3333.

MEMBERS OF FIRM

G. Conley Ingram	Joe T. Taylor
Frazer Durrett, Jr.	Bernard L. Greer, Jr.
Ralph Williams, Jr.	William C. Humphreys, Jr.
L. Clifford Adams, Jr.	James S. Stokes
Walter W. Mitchell	Dow N. Kirkpatrick II
Michael A. Doyle	H. Sadler Poe
Alexander E. Wilson III	W. Terence Walsh
Ronald L. Reid	Philip C. Cook
Neil Williams	Robert C. Lower
John K. Train III	James F. Nellis, Jr.
B. Harvey Hill, Jr.	Timothy S. Perry
Robert G. Edge	Peter M. Wright
Rawson Foreman	Gerald W. Bowling
C. David Butler	Robert H. Buckler
Joseph V. Myers, Jr.	Arnold L. Feinstein
R. Neal Batson	Peter Kontio
F. Dean Copeland	Robert D. McCallum, Jr.
Sidney J. Nurkin	Jack S. Schroder, Jr.
Alexander W. Patterson	T. Michael Tennant
Oscar N. Persons	Benjamin T. White
Benjamin F. Johnson III	Michael R. Davis

(See Next Column)

ALSTON & BIRD—*Continued*

MEMBERS OF FIRM (Continued)

Kevin E. Grady	Albert E. Bender, Jr.
Jack H. Senterfitt	Richard T. Fulton
William H. Avery	Mary C. Gill
Peter Q. Bassett	William H. Hughes, Jr.
Judson Graves	Karol V. Mason
Forrest W. Hunter	Timothy J. Pakenham
Jonathan W. Lowe	Michael T. Petrik
Patrick M. Norton	Donna Potts Bergeson
Helene Z. Cohen	Bryan E. Davis
Peter M. Degnan	Richard W. Grice
Lee A. DeHihns III	Michael P. Kenny
Jay D. Bennett	Gerald L. Mize, Jr.
J. William Boone	Timothy J. Peaden
John L. Coalson, Jr.	Robert P. Riordan
Steven M. Collins	John E. Stephenson, Jr.
John L. Douglas	R. Gregory Brophy
Anne S. Rampacek	Clare H. Draper IV
Frank G. Smith III	R. Steve Ensor
John C. Weitnauer	Rebecca McLemore Lamberth
J. Vaughan Curtis	Stephen A. Opler
Christopher Glenn Sawyer	Laura Lewis Owens
Glenn R. Thomson	Craig R. Pett
Nill V. Toulme	Randall L. Allen
Pinney L. Allen	Robert O. Ball, III
James S. Hutchinson	David E. Brown, Jr.
Ralph F. MacDonald III	Dennis J. Connolly
R. Wayne Thorpe	Todd R. David
Jeffrey A. Allred	Elizabeth A. Gilley
John A. Buchman	Richard R. Hays
(Not admitted in GA)	H. Douglas Hinson
M. Hill Jeffries	William R. Klapp, Jr.
John I. Spangler III	William R. Mitchelson Jr.
Roger D. Taylor	Jennifer Brown Moore
(Not admitted in GA)	Mark C. Rusche
Laura Glover Thatcher	Marci P. Schmerler
Frank M. Conner III	Della Wager Wells
Martin J. Elgison	James J. Wolfson
Terence J. Greene	Robert L. Crewdson
Ira H. Parker	Paul M. Cushing
John C. Sawyer	Susan B. Devitt
Grant T. Stein	Joel J. Hughey
Gregory C. Braden	Sam K. Kaywood, Jr.
Charles A. Brake, Jr.	Teri T. McMahon
Patrick J. Flinn	Steven L. Pottle
H. Stephen Harris, Jr.	Michelle A. Williams
George M. Maxwell, Jr.	Douglas E. Cloud
Robert J. Middleton, Jr.	Beth K. Toberman
Theodore E. G. Pound	Charles H. Morgan
Bernard Taylor	Robert D. Mowrey

SENIOR COUNSEL
Pierre Howard

OF COUNSEL

Henry J. Miller	Sidney O. Smith, Jr.
Arthur Howell	Robert L. Foreman, Jr.
Eugene T. Branch	Richard A. Allison

ASSOCIATES

Kimberly A. Ackourey	Jo C. Dearing
Kristen D. Adams	Scott D. Dickinson
John M. Albright	John P. Donaldson
Craig D. Apolinsky	Johan Droogmans
Douglas S. Arnold	Brian D. Edwards
R. Brandon Asbill	Kathleen Capano Farley
Leslie Scott Askins	Lisa J. Farmer
Lori G. Baer	James G. Farris, Jr.
Julia L. Bassett	Sandra L. Fitzgerald
David A. Benoit	Christopher D. Ford
Stephen P. Berke	John P. Fry
(Not admitted in GA)	Anna W. Gaston
Elizabeth Bertschi	A. McCampbell Gibson
Jennifer B. Block	David S. Givelber
Rick D. Blumen	Andrea Goodrich
Christina K. Braisted	John H. Goselin, II
Lonnie T. Brown, Jr.	James C. Grant
Hilary E. Buckley	Randall D. Grayson
John E. Burgess	Ernest LaMont Greer
Angela T. Burnette	James W. Hagan
B. Davis Butler	Warren R. Hall, Jr.
W. Thomas Carter III	Mary Kathryn Hallman
Lisa H. Cassilly	Robb E. Hellwig
Kathryn M. Cole	Michelle M. Henkel
(Not admitted in GA)	John S. Hetzel
Alston D. Correll III	John R. Hickman
Ward Council	W. Hunter Holliday
Cynthia L. Counts	Lori P. Hughes
Christopher A. Crain	Susan E. Hurd
Robert B. Cunningham	Ginabeth B. Hutchison
Kristen K. Darnell	Clifton M. Iler
Frederick C. Dawkins	Kevin M. Ingham
Cari K. Dawson	Karen J. Jacobs

(See Next Column)

ASSOCIATES (Continued)

Kendall Taylor Jones	Laura Lea Putney
John A. Jordak, Jr.	Shruthi G. Reddy
James M. Jordan III	(Not admitted in GA)
William H. Jordan	Daniel L. Rikard
James M. Kapenstein	Kimberly Dyslin Rountree
(Not admitted in GA)	Lori L. Pruitt Rowland
Lisa M. Katz	William W. Sapp
Daniel A. Kent	Theodore J. Sawicki
W. Wayt King, Jr.	Debra K. Scott
Elise Kirban	Douglas G. Scribner
(Not admitted in GA)	Margaret A. Sheehan
Jason Klitenic	Candace N. Smith
Kimberly A. Knight	H. Suzanne Smith
Aldo L. LaFiandra	Richard A. Snow
Matthew W. Levin	Joseph P. L. Snyder
Cynthia A. Little	Robyn Ice Sosebee
Gretchen D. Locy	K. David Steele
Annette T. Lord	Philip R. Stein
Timothy Mann, Jr.	Michael L. Stevens
R. Lindsay Marshall	David J. Stewart
David M. Maxwell	Jeffrey W. Stump
Beth McRae Mayfield	Debra A. R. Sydnor
Meredith E. Mays	Jonathan H. Talcott
Michael R. McAlevey	(Not admitted in GA)
Kristine N. McAlister	Thomas F. Tallmadge, Jr.
Mark F. McElreath	Teresa D. Thebaut
Robin Lynn McGrath	Lisa A. Vash
Scott A. McLaren	Daniel R. Weede
J. Alan McNabb	Paul F. Wellborn III
Kristen P. Mersereau	Timothy G. Werner
Randolph A. Moore III	Valarie C. Williams
Leigh A. Morrissey	Robert M. Williamson
Ben E. Muraskin	(Not admitted in GA)
Peter C. November	Susan J. Wilson
Paul J. Nozick	Terri E. Wilson
Felipe M. Nunez	(Not admitted in GA)
Nicole Fletcher O'Connor	M. Russell Wofford, Jr.
Nils H. Okeson	(Not admitted in GA)
William S. Ortwein	Amy R. Wolverton
Brian B. Pastor	Robert Y. Wood III
William T. Plybon	Susan L. Wright

COUNSEL

Michael D. Kaufman	J. Kennard Neal
Leon Adams, Jr.	Eileen M. G. Scofield
Lawrie E. Demorest	Janet E. Witt
Steven D. Collier	Glenda G. Bugg
Gary E. McClanahan	Douglas B. Chappell
Homer Lee Walker	

For full biographical listings, see the Martindale-Hubbell Law Directory

---

ALTMAN, KRITZER & LEVICK, P.C. (AV)
Powers Ferry Landing, Suite 224, 6400 Powers Ferry Road, N.W., 30339
Telephone: 770-955-3555
Fax: 770-952-7821, 955-2866, 955-0038, 955-3697
New York, N.Y. Office: 730 Fifth Avenue, Suite 1805, 10019.
Telephone: 212-489-3745.
Fax: 212-489-3729.
Schaumburg, Illinois Affiliate: Altman, Kritzer & Levick, Ltd., Suite 700, 1101 Perimeter Drive, 60173.
Telephone: 847-240-0340.
Fax: 847-240-0344.

Allen D. Altman	Frank Slover
Craig H. Kritzer	Kenneth A. Shapiro
Mark J. Levick	Steven A. Pepper
D. Charles Houk	George A. Mattingly
Charles L. Wood	W. Daniel Hicks, Jr.
Ephraim Spielman	Susan E. Stoffer
Emily Sanford Bair	Robert D. Simons
Benno G. Rothschild, Jr.	Peter M. Hartman
Theodore H. Sandler	Duane D. Sitar

OF COUNSEL

Richard P. Rubenoff	John E. Taylor
William R. Ham	John H. Lewis
James R. Harland, Jr.	Steven J. Roberts

Debra M. Thompson	Pennington Gilbert Kamm
Lori E. Kilberg	Laurence B. Appel
Richard W. Probert	Karen M. Edwards
Andrew R. Bauman	Martin Friedgood
Lawrence H. Freiman	Theodore I. Blum
Jeremy D. Cohen	Laura M. Andrew
Craig P. Colburn, Jr.	Sheridan B. Johnson
Thomas D. White	Joel L. Silverman
Christian D. Shields	Susan M. Gordon

LEGAL SUPPORT PERSONNEL
Cynthia A. Groszkiewicz

Representative Clients: The Home Depot, Inc.; Atlantic Southeast Airlines, Inc.; Ingles Markets, Inc.; Pacesetter Steel Service, Inc.; Sears, Roebuck and Co.

(See Next Column)

ALTMAN, KRITZER & LEVICK P.C., *Atlanta—Continued*

For full biographical listings, see the Martindale-Hubbell Law Directory

FRANCIS M. BIRD, JR. (AV)

100 Galleria Parkway, N.W. Suite 1540, 30339
Telephone: 770-951-4720
Fax: 770-951-4723

For full biographical listings, see the Martindale-Hubbell Law Directory

CARTER & ANSLEY (AV)

Suite 1000 One Ninety One Peachtree Tower, 191 Peachtree
Street, 30303-1747
Telephone: 404-658-9220
Fax: 404-658-9726
Email: firm@carteransley.com

MEMBERS OF FIRM

Shepard Bryan (1871-1970)	Robert A. Barnaby, II
W. Colquitt Carter (1904-1988)	Thomas E. Magill
Ben Kingree, III	Robert O. McCloud, Jr.
Tommy T. Holland	Christopher N. Shuman
H. Sanders Carter, Jr.	Elizabeth J. Bondurant
A. T. Sorrells	Michael A. Coval

OF COUNSEL

Bonneau Ansley

ASSOCIATES

Rebecca J. Schmidt	Kenton J. Coppage
Keith L. Lindsay	Allison Mary Burns
Burke B. Johnson	Mary K. Pickard

Patrick C. DiCarlo

For full biographical listings, see the Martindale-Hubbell Law Directory

CHOREY, TAYLOR & FEIL, A PROFESSIONAL CORPORATION (AV)

Suite 1700, The Lenox Building, 3399 Peachtree Road, N.E., 30326
Telephone: 404-841-3200
Facsimile: 404-841-3221

Thomas V. Chorey, Jr.	Susan Shivers Fink
John L. Taylor, Jr.	Celeste McCollough
Eric D. Ranney	Matthew L. Hess
Otto F. Feil III	David A. Flanigan, Jr.

Jeffery T. Coleman	Lisa Fivars Harper

C. David Lumsden

OF COUNSEL

Zack D. Cravey, Jr.	Charles V. Gerkin, Jr.

For full biographical listings, see the Martindale-Hubbell Law Directory

DAVIS, MATTHEWS & QUIGLEY, P.C. (AV)

Fourteenth Floor, Lenox Towers II, 3400 Peachtree Road, 30326
Telephone: 404-261-3900
Telecopier: 404-261-0159
Email: dmq@interserv.com

Baxter L. Davis	Melvin L. Drake, Jr.
William M. Matthews	Richard W. Schiffman, Jr.
Ron L. Quigley	Frank A. DeVincent
J. Michael Harrison	Elizabeth Green Lindsey

Chason Lash Harrison, Jr.	Ted Matthew Scartz
Sylvia A. Martin	Bradley Jay Denson

Approved Attorneys for: Lawyers Title Insurance Corp.

For full biographical listings, see the Martindale-Hubbell Law Directory

DREW ECKL & FARNHAM (AV)

880 West Peachtree Street, P.O. Box 7600, 30357
Telephone: 404-885-1400
Facsimile: 404-876-0992
Email: drew@igc.apc.org

MEMBERS OF FIRM

W. Wray Eckl	T. Bart Gary
Clayton H. Farnham	Kenneth A. Hindman
Arthur H. Glaser	Paul W. Burke
James M. Poe	Daniel C. Kniffen
John A. Ferguson, Jr.	John C. Bruffey, Jr.
Theodore Freeman	Benton J. Mathis, Jr.
John P. Reale	John G. Blackmon, Jr.
Stevan A. Miller	Gary R. Hurst
H. Michael Bagley	Dennis M. Hall
Hall F. McKinley III	J. William Haley
G. Randall Moody	Ann Bishop Byars
B. Holland Pritchard	Stephen W. Mooney

(See Next Column)

ASSOCIATES

Nicole D. Tifverman	Patricia R. Stevens
L. Lee Bennett, Jr.	C. Lawrence Meyer
Katherine D. Dixon	Philip G. Pompilio
William T. Mitchell	Robert J. Moye III
J. Robb Cruser	Sean W. Conley
Philip Wade Savrin	Mary Anne Ackourey
Lucian Gillis, Jr.	Beverly Powell Sisk
Peter H. Schmidt, II	Marion M. Handley
April Rich	Stuart B. Bagley
Maureen M. Middleton	Thomas L. Walker
Robert L. Welch	James P. Anderson
Suzanne VonHarten Sanders	Kathryn Blythe Offer
Leigh Lawson Reeves	Donald M. McManus, Jr.
Bruce A. Taylor, Jr.	Peter B. Barlow
Douglas M. Baker	Nancy L. Pasterz
David R. Bergquist	Gregory G. Schultz
Charles L. Norton, Jr.	Christopher R. Stovall
Nancy F. Rigby	Charles E. Symington, Jr.
Douglas G. Smith, Jr.	Kristian Knochel
Terrence T. Rock	(Not admitted in GA)
Phillip Comer Griffeth	Lewis P. Perling
Marian S. Singer	Scott P. Archer
Steven D. Prelutsky	(Not admitted in GA)
Julianne L. Swilley	Fred L. Hubbs Jr.
B. Greg Cline	W. Gregory Pope

Jennifer E. Moore

SENIOR ATTORNEY

Richard Metzger

OF COUNSEL

Charles L. Drew	Anne M. Landrum
	Christopher E. Parker

Representative Clients: American International Adjustment Co.; C.W. Matthews Contracting Co., Inc.; CIGNA; Cooper Tire & Rubber Co.; Ford Motor Company; Frito-Lay, Inc.; General Motors Corporation; John H. Harland Company; National Service Industries, Inc.

For full biographical listings, see the Martindale-Hubbell Law Directory

FAIN, MAJOR & WILEY, P.C. (AV)

The Hurt Building, 50 Hurt Plaza, Suite 300, 30303
Telephone: 404-688-6633
Telecopier: 404-420-1544

Gene A. Major	Thomas E. Brennan
Charles A. Wiley, Jr.	John K. Miles, Jr.
	Darryl G. Haynes

Brian Alligood	Robert G. Mikell
Derek A. Mendicino	C. Todd Van Dyke
Kim Monroe Jackson	Debra C. Chew

Tracy M. Culver

OF COUNSEL

Donald M. Fain

Representative Clients: Allstate Insurance Co.; Budget Rent-A-Car; Arkansas Best Corp.; Chrysler Insurance Co.; Georgia Farm Bureau Mutual Insurance Co.; Hertz Corp.; Universal Underwriters Insurance Co.; Westfield Insurance co.; Winn-Dixie Stores, Inc.

For full biographical listings, see the Martindale-Hubbell Law Directory

GAMBRELL & STOLZ, L.L.P. (AV)

Suite 4300, One Peachtree Center, 303 Peachtree Street, 30308
Telephone: 404-577-6000
FAX: 404-221-6501
Email: lawfirm@gambrell.com
Northpark Office: Suite 1230, Northpark 400 Tower, 1000 Abernathy
Road, N.E., Atlanta, 30328.
Telephone: 404-577-6000.
FAX: 404-589-3400.

David H. Gambrell	William C. Tinsley, II
Irwin W. Stolz, Jr.	Henry B. Levi
Bryan M. Cavan	Leo J. Fogarty
Jon Lee Andersen	Linda A. Klein
James R. McGuone	Gary A. Barnes
Nedom A. Haley	Nancy E. Gordon
Robert G. Brazier	Michael M. Smith
Tobin N. Watt	Andrew H. Prussack
George M. Bobo	Verley J. Spivey

Alvin T. Wong

ASSOCIATES

Seaton D. Purdom	Sophia L. Herbert-Peterson
Charles N. Bowen	Ronald C. Melcher
James A. Nystrom	Vipanj B. Patel
Anna Marie Bacon-Tinsley Che	Michelle Kenyon

For full biographical listings, see the Martindale-Hubbell Law Directory

Atlanta—Continued

GLASS, McCULLOUGH, SHERRILL & HARROLD (AV)

1409 Peachtree Street, N.E., 30309
Telephone: 404-885-1500
Telecopier: 404-892-1801
Buckhead Office: Monarch Plaza, 3414 Peachtree Road, N.E., Suite 450, Atlanta, Georgia, 30326-1162.
Telephone: 404-885-1500.
Telecopier: 404-231-1978.
Washington, D.C. Office: 1150 17th Street, N.W., Suite 605. Washington, D.C., 20036.
Telephone: 202-785-8118.
Telecopier: 202-785-0128.
Knoxville, Tennessee Office: 606 West Main Avenue, Suite 205, P.O. Box 2543. Knoxville, Tennessee, 37901-2543.
Telephone: 423-971-5418.
Telecopier: 423-971-1706.

MEMBERS OF FIRM

Peter B. Glass	Ross P. Kendall
Kenneth R. McCullough	James W. King
John A. Sherrill	Paul P. Mattingly
Thomas J. Harrold, Jr.	George L. Murphy, Jr.
Gregory Bartko	Lori Ann Olejniczak
Jeffrey C. Baxter	Chester G. Rosenberg
Mark A. Block	Jerry A. Shaifer
William D. Brunstad	R. Phillip Shinall, III
T. Kennerly Carroll, Jr.	W. Clayton Sparrow, Jr.
Geoffrey H. Cederholm	John M. Stuckey, Jr.
William F. Clark	Bradley J. Taylor
Gardner G. Courson	Elizabeth S. Tonkin (Resident,
Luther C. Curtis	Knoxville, Tennessee Office)
William A. DuPre, IV	Robert M. Trusty
Allen W. Groves	Bradley E. Wahl
C. Walker Ingraham	Laura H. Walter (Not admitted
Ugo F. Ippolito	in GA; Resident, Washington,
James H. Kaminer, Jr.	D.C. Office)

Robert E. Wilson

OF COUNSEL

Glee A. Triplett	S. Andrew McKay

TAX COUNSEL

William M. Joseph

ASSOCIATES

Terence G. Clark	Jamie G. Miller
Patrick J. Clarke	Vincent J. Miraglia (Resident,
Michael David Crisp	Washington, D.C. Office)
Bryan A. Downs	Joseph V. Myers, III
L. Neill Edwards	Donna J. Nance
Jana L. Evans	Shannon L. Nagle
D. Lynn Holliday	(Not admitted in GA)
G. Wilson Horde, III	Christina Sungyoon Pak
(Not admitted in GA)	Robert T. Quackenboss
Keven K. Kenison	(Not admitted in GA)
Betsy Birns McCall	Richard D. Sanders
Margaret A. McCue	R. Bailey Teague
(Not admitted in GA)	

For full biographical listings, see the Martindale-Hubbell Law Directory

GOLDNER, SOMMERS, SCRUDDER & BASS (AV)

900 Circle 75 Parkway Suite 850, 30339
Telephone: 770-612-9200
Facsimile: 770-612-9201

Stephen L. Goldner	Glenn S. Bass
Susan V. Sommers	C. G. Jester, Jr.
Henry E. Scrudder, Jr.	Alfred A. Quillian, Jr.

Sandra G. Chase

Linda Jacobsen Pollock	Tammy Spivack Skinner
Benjamin David Ladner	Tiffany T. Norman
Marci R. Weston	R. Keith Whitesides
William W. Horlock, Jr.	Jane Carol Taylor

For full biographical listings, see the Martindale-Hubbell Law Directory

HAWKINS & PARNELL (AV)

4000 SunTrust Plaza, 303 Peachtree Street, N.E., 30308-3243
Telephone: 404-614-7400
Fax: 404-614-7500
Email: 73541.1626@compuserve.com

MEMBERS OF FIRM

Paul M. Hawkins	Frank C. Bedinger, III
J. Bruce Welch	Julia Bennett Jagger
Albert H. Parnell	Stephen M. Lore
A. Timothy Jones	William H. Major, III
Alan F. Herman	Edward M. Newsom
Howell Hollis, III	T. Ryan Mock, Jr.
Michael J. Goldman	Lawrence J. Myers
H. Lane Young, II	Jack N. Sibley
Joseph R. Cullens	Warner S. Fox

(See Next Column)

MEMBERS OF FIRM (Continued)

Robert U. Wright	Ollie M. Harton
Thomas F. Wamsley, Jr.	Kimberly Houston Ridley
Michael E. Hutchins	Barry S. Noeltner

Kenan G. Loomis

OF COUNSEL

J. R. Cullens

ASSOCIATES

Kevin J. Bahr	Stephen M. Brooks
Edwin L. Hall, Jr.	Allen L. Broughton
Roger M. Goode	Thomas G. Tidwell
Robert Rache Elarbee	Kristine Berry Morain
Charles R. Beans	Kristen K. Duggan
Dennis J. Manganiello	Michael A. Mills
Peter R. York	Jennifer A. Grandoff
Cullen Christie Wilkerson, Jr.	Debra E. LeVorse
Allen W. Nelson	Debra L. Dewar
Christine Lupo Mast	Jeb T. Branham
Blanche Rose Miller	Anita Wallace Thomas
Edward C. Henderson, Jr.	Andrew A. Davenport

For full biographical listings, see the Martindale-Hubbell Law Directory

THE HISHON FIRM, LLC (AV)

999 Peachtree Street N.E. Suite 1900, 30309
Telephone: 404-817-7791
Fax: 404-817-2486

Robert H. Hishon

Nancy R. Daspit

For full biographical listings, see the Martindale-Hubbell Law Directory

HOLT, NEY, ZATCOFF & WASSERMAN (AV)

A Partnership including Professional Corporations
100 Galleria Parkway, Suite 600, 30339
Telephone: 770-956-9600
Facsimile Number: 770-956-1490

MEMBERS OF FIRM

Robert G. Holt (P.C.)	Charles D. Vaughn
James M. Ney (P.C.)	Stephen C. Greenberg
Sanford H. Zatcoff (P.C.)	Richard P. Vornholt
Michael G. Wasserman (P.C.)	Barbara J. Schneider
J. Scott Jacobson	Brian P. Cain

David S. O'Quinn

ASSOCIATES

Jay Frank Castle	Thomas K. Anderson

Representative Clients: Champion Healthcare Corporation; Citibank, N.A.; Cummins South, Inc.; First American Title Insurance Co.; First National Bank of Chicago; First Union National Bank of Georgia; Gables Residential Trust; The University Financing Foundation, Inc.; NationsBank, N.A. (South); Safety-Kleen Corp.

For full biographical listings, see the Martindale-Hubbell Law Directory

JOHNSON & WARD (AV)

2100 The Equitable Building, 100 Peachtree Street N.W., 30303-1962
Telephone: 404-524-5626
Facsimile: 404-524-1769

OF COUNSEL

Inslee M. Johnson	D. Lake Rumsey, Jr.

Cullen M. Ward (1921-1979)

MEMBERS OF FIRM

William C. Lanham	Baxter P. Jones
Clark H. McGehee	William D. deGolian
John C. Dabney, Jr.	Bruce A. Maxwell

For full biographical listings, see the Martindale-Hubbell Law Directory

JONES, DAY, REAVIS & POGUE (AV)

3500 One Peachtree Center, 303 Peachtree Street, N.E., 30308-3242
Telephone: 404-521-3939
Cable Address: "Attorneys Atlanta"
Telex: 54-2711
Telecopier: 404-581-8330
In Brussels, Belgium: Avenue Louise 480, 7th Floor, B-1050 Brussels.
Telephone: 32-2-645-14-11.
Telecopier: 32-2-645-14-45.
In Chicago, Illinois: 77 West Wacker.
Telephone: 312-782-3939.
Telecopier: 312-782-8585.
In Cleveland, Ohio: North Point. 901 Lakeside Avenue.
Telephone: 216-586-3939.
Cable Address: "Attorneys Cleveland".
Telex: 980389.
Telecopier: 216-579-0212.

(See Next Column)

JONES, DAY, REAVIS & POGUE, *Atlanta—Continued*

In Columbus, Ohio: 1900 Huntington Center.
Telephone: 614-469-3939.
Cable Address: "Attorneys Columbus".
Telecopier: 614-461-4198.
In Dallas, Texas: 2300 Trammell Crow Center, 2001 Ross Avenue.
Telephone: 214-220-3939.
Cable Address: "Attorneys Dallas."
Telex: 730852.
Telecopier: 214-969-5100.
In Frankfurt, Germany: Triton Haus, Bockenheimer Landstrasse 42, 60323 Frankfurt am Main.
Telephone: 49-69-9726-3939.
Telecopier: 49-69-9726-3993.
In Geneva, Switzerland: 20, rue de Candolle.
Telephone: 41-22-320-2339.
Telecopier: 41-22-320-1232.
In Hong Kong: 29th Floor, Entertainment Building, 30 Queen's Road Central.
Telephone: 852-2526-6895.
Telecopier: 852-2868-5871 or 852-2868-5699.
In Irvine, California: 2603 Main Street, Suite 900.
Telephone: 714-851-3939.
Telex: 194911 Lawyers LSA.
Telecopier: 714-553-7539.
In London, England: One Mount Street.
Telephone: 44-71-493-9361.
Cable Address: "Surgoe London WI."
Telecopier: 44-71-493-9666.
In Los Angeles, California: 555 West Fifth Street, Suite 4600.
Telephone: 213-489-3939.
Telex: 181439 UD.
Telecopier: 213-243-2539.
In New Delhi, India: Pathak & Associates, 9th Floor, Dr. Gopal Das Bhaven, 28 Barakhamba Road.
Telephone: 91-11-331-9719.
Telecopier: 91-11-331-7802.
In New York, New York: 599 Lexington Avenue.
Telephone: 212-326-3939.
Cable Address: "JONESDAY NEWYORK."
Telex: 237013 JDRP UR.
Telecopier: 212-755-7306.
In Paris, France: 62, rue du Faubourg Saint-Honore.
Telephone: 33-1-44-71-3939.
Cable Address: "Surgoe Paris."
Telex: 290156 Surgoe.
Telecopier: 33-1-49-24-0471.
In Pittsburgh, Pennsylvania: 500 Grant Street, 31st Floor.
Telephone: 412-391-3939.
Cable Address: "Attorneys Pittsburgh".
Telecopier: 412-394-7959.
In Riyadh, Saudi Arabia: Law Offices of Saud M.A. Shawwaf, P.O. Box 22166.
Telephone: (966-1) 462-8866.
Telex: 401831 SAUCON SJ.
Telecopier: (966-1) 462-9001.
In Taipei, Taiwan: 8th Floor, 2 Tun Hwa South Road, Section 2.
Telephone: (886-2) 704-6808.
Telecopier: (886-2) 704-6791.
In Tokyo, Japan: Toranomon MT Building, 4th Floor, 10-3, Toranomon 3-Chome, Minato-ku, Tokyo 105, Japan.
Telephone: 81-3-3433-3939.
Telecopier: 81-3-5401-2725.
In Washington, D.C.: Metropolitan Square, 1450 G Street, N.W.
Telephone: 202-879-3939.
Cable Address: "Attorneys Washington."
Telex: 89-2410 ATTORNEYS WASH.
Telecopier: 202-737-2832.

MEMBERS OF FIRM IN ATLANTA

Robert W. Smith	James R. Johnson
Girard E. Boudreau, Jr.	John E. Zamer
Russell S. Grove, Jr.	Dan T. Carter
Christopher L. Carson	Scott A. Specht
W. Lyman Dillon	R. Dal Burton
Alvis E. Campbell	William B. B. Smith
William S. Paddock	Lisa Anne Stater
John M. Edwards, Jr.	R. Matthew Martin
Dorothy Yates Kirkley	Lizanne Thomas
James H. Landon	Deborah A. Sudbury
David J. Bailey	Gregory Russell Hanthorn
R. Mason Cargill	Rory D. Lyons
Milford B. Hatcher, Jr.	Ralph R. Morrison
Richard M. Kirby	Stephanie E. Parker
G. Lee Garrett, Jr.	Matthew J. Toddy
Paul Burke O'Hearn	(Not admitted in GA)
Barry J. Stein	Michael Joseph McConnell

OF COUNSEL

L. Travis Brannon, Jr.	James F. McEvoy
Dom H. Wyant	W. Rhett Tanner
	Ruth H. Gershon

(See Next Column)

SENIOR ATTORNEY

L. Trammell Newton, Jr.	Stephen B. Schrock
Arthur G. Kent	Aasia Mustakeem

ASSOCIATES

Sherie Shortridge Holmes	Sara M. Allswede
David P. Baum	(Not admitted in GA)
Sidney R. Brown	Mark R. Bridwell
William Baxter Rowland	Gregory M. Cole
David M. Monde	Curtis L. Doster
Edgar C. Snow, Jr.	Michelle A. Hickerson
Elaine Rogers Walsh	John H. Killeen
Wade R. Wright	Wendy Y. Normandin
Elizabeth Bolton Davis	Jennifer L. Radner
Mark L. Hanson	(Not admitted in GA)
Robert N. Johnson	Lisa M. Braxton
Paul S. Greco	Sara B. King
(Not admitted in GA)	L. Christine Lawson
Janine Cone Metcalf	Page A. Pate
Brad A. Baldwin	Sterling A. Spainhour, Jr.
Diane G. Pulley	Alison Cline Earles
Rayne Rasty	Kenneth C. Gibson
(Not admitted in GA)	Jeana Girard
John H. Williamson	Jeffrey L. Jefferson
Kelly R. Caffarelli	Erika Blum Johnson
J. Olen Earl	Megan A. Kelly
Kevin A. Hendricks	Theresia M. Moser
Donna C. Peavler	Eric S. Ogrey
(Not admitted in GA)	Deborah L. O'Neal-Johnson
Kim Purcell Pike	William N. Smith
John F. Simon	Jonathan A.K. Truelove
Douglas M. Towns	Susan C. Cox

For full biographical listings, see the Martindale-Hubbell Law Directory

KAUFMAN, CHAIKEN, RICKERTSEN, KREVOLIN, MILLER & HORST, A PROFESSIONAL CORPORATION (AV)

400 Perimeter Center Terrace, N.E., Suite 720, 30346-1234
Telephone: 770-390-9200
Facsimile: 770-395-6720
Email: rkaufm03@counsel.com

Robert J. Kaufman	Douglas P. Krevolin
Fredric Chaiken	Craig D. Miller
Donald L. Rickertsen	Jeffrey D. Horst

Michael G. Regas, II

OF COUNSEL

Walter E. Gomel	Ronald J. Davis

References: Gulf States Mortgage Co., Inc.; Dyer & Dyer Volvo, Inc.; Trust Company Bank; Wachovia Bank of Georgia.

For full biographical listings, see the Martindale-Hubbell Law Directory

KILPATRICK & CODY LLP (AV)

Suite 2800, 1100 Peachtree Street, 30309-4530
Telephone: 404-815-6500
Telephone Copier: 404-815-6555
Telex: 54-2307
Washington, D.C. Office: Suite 800, 700 13th Street, N.W., 20005.
Telephone: 202-508-5800. Telephone Copier: 202-508-5858.
Brussels, Belgium Office: Avenue Louise 65, BTE 3, 1050 Brussels.
Telephone: (32) (2) 533-03-00.
Telecopier: (32) (2) 534-86-38.
London, England Office: 68 Pall Mall, London, SW1Y 5ES, England.
Telephone: (44) (71) 321 0477.
Telecopier: (44) (71) 930 9733.
Augusta, Georgia Office: Suite 1400 First Union Bank Building, P.O. Box 2043, 30903. Telephone (706) 724-2622. Telecopier (706) 722-0219.

Alexander Stephens Clay	D. Lurton Massee, Jr.
(1905-1945)	(1936-1993)
Welborn B. Cody (1899-1976)	Devereaux F. McClatchey
William B. Gunter (1919-1986)	(1906-1993)
Harold Hirsch (1881-1939)	Louis Regenstein (1912-1994)
Martin E. Kilpatrick	Ernest P. Rogers (1903-1985)
(1905-1980)	Marion Smith (1884-1947)

Albert C. Tate, Jr. (1938-1983)

OF COUNSEL

Harry S. Baxter	George B. Haley
A. Gus Cleveland	Thomas C. Shelton

MEMBERS OF FIRM

Harold E. Abrams	Joseph M. Beck
Luis A. Aguilar	Michael D. Bednarek
Duane C. Aldrich	(Not admitted in GA)
Miles J. Alexander	Neal S. Berinhout
G. William Austin, III	Thomas K. Bick
Thomas William Baker	(Washington, D.C. Office)
Robert E. Banta	W. Stanley Blackburn
Rupert M. Barkoff	Kurt E. Blase
Sally Cotter Baxter	(Washington, D.C. Office)

(See Next Column)

KILPATRICK & CODY—*Continued*

MEMBERS OF FIRM (Continued)

William H. Boice
Richard R. Boisseau
R. Alexander Bransford, Jr.
William H. Brewster
William A. Burnham
Christopher P. Bussert
Susan A. Cahoon
Tim Carssow
Raymond G. Chadwick, Jr.
  (Augusta Office)
Richard R. Cheatham
Thomas H. Christopher
Gregory K. Cinnamon
Ted H. Clarkson
  (Augusta Office)
A. Stephens Clay
Evelyn H. Coats
James H. Coil III
Jerome F. Connell, Jr.
A. Kimbrough Davis
Jefferson Davis, Jr.
Roderick C. Dennehy, Jr.
W. Randy Eaddy
James L. Ewing, IV
Ronald A. Feuerstein
  (Washington, D.C. Office)
Candace L. Fowler
Lynn E. Fowler
Thompson H. Gooding, Jr.
F. Sheffield Hale
Thomas C. Harney
Frederick K. Heller, Jr.
  (Resident, Brussels, Belgium
  Office)
Dale Curtis Hogue, Sr.
  (Not admitted in GA)
Richard A. Horder
Stephen E. Hudson
J. Vance Hughes
Walter E. Johnson
Hilary P. Jordan
Jane E. Jordan
James R. Kanner
M. Andrew Kauss
Edward A. Kazmarek
Mark P. Kelly
Edmund M. Kneisel
Wyck A. Knox, Jr.
  (Augusta Office)
Larry D. Ledbetter
Colvin T. Leonard, III
Elliott H. Levitas
Neil I. Levy
  (Washington, D.C. Office)
Laurel J. Lucey
Alfred S. Lurey
Melinda A. Marbes

George T. Marcou
  (Not admitted in GA)
Suzanne G. Mason
Kent E. Mast
Gregg E. McDougal
  (Augusta Office)
Mara McRae
Dennis S. Meir
John M. Mitnick
C. Ray Mullins
C. Randall Nuckolls
Keith T. Ott (Resident, London,
  England Office)
Reinaldo Pascual
Matthew H. Patton
Alan R. Perry, Jr.
Barry Phillips
Joel B. Piassick
Judith A. Powell
John S. Pratt
Diane L. Prucino
Ronald L. Raider
  (Washington, D.C. Office)
Marc K. Ritzmann
Duncan A. Roush
Dean W. Russell
Steven J. Sacher
  (Washington, D.C. Office)
Gary K. Saidman
Brian Leonard Schleicher
Caroline W. Spangenberg
Ann Marie Stack
David A. Stockton
Jerre B. Swann
G. Paris Sykes, Jr.
Earle R. Taylor, III
G. Kimbrough Taylor, Jr.
Virginia S. Taylor
R. Scott Tewes
Martin R. Tilson, Jr.
Michael H. Trotter
Timothy N. Tucker
R. Slaton Tuggle, III
Michael W. Tyler
Jeffrey A. Van Detta
J. William Veatch, III
William J. Vesely, Jr.
Frederick H. von Unwerth
Martha Jo Wagner
  (Washington, D.C. Office)
J. Henry Walker, IV
Joe D. Whitley
Mark D. Wincek
  (Washington, D.C. Office)
David M. Zacks
Dennis L. Zakas
Deborah B. Zink

COUNSEL

Jan Meadows Davidson
Scott M. Dayan
Joycelyn L. Fleming
David P. Phippen
  (Washington, D.C. Office)

Pascale Rahman
  (Brussels, Belgium Office)
William L. Sollee, Jr.
  (Washington, D.C. Office)
Kathryn B. Solley

SENIOR ATTORNEY

Charles M. Rice

ASSOCIATES

Steven I. Addlestone
Amy Weinstein Adelman
Pervez Akhtar
  (London, England Office)
David K. Anderson
W. Christopher Arbery
William B. Barkley
George C. Beck
  (Washington, D.C. Office)
Craig E. Bertschi
James F. Bogan, III
Michael E. Brooks
Joel D. Bush, II
S. Kendall Butterworth
Wilburn L. Chesser
  (Washington, D.C. Office)
Richard Cicchillo, Jr.
Richard A. Clegg
  (Not admitted in GA)
James A. Coblin
Vicki Arroyo Cochran
  (Washington, D.C. Office)

Elizabeth H. Cohen
Elizabeth P. Cowie
Jackson E. Cox, II
  (Augusta Office)
Lexie L. Craven
Cecil L. Davis, Jr.
Theodore H. Davis, Jr.
Matt Dillard
Donald C. Evans, Jr.
Neil D. Falis
Michael P. Fortkort
  (Washington, D.C. Office)
J. Griffin Foster
William H. Fussell
Nancy G. Gilreath
Phyllis F. Granade
Bruce D. Gray
  (Not admitted in GA)
Daniel W. Hamilton
  (Augusta, Office)
Josephine M. Hammack
  (Washington, D.C. Office)

(See Next Column)

ASSOCIATES (Continued)

Richard B. Hankins
Ralph H. Harrison, III
Susan L. Hearne
Michael K. Heilbronner
Cesar E. Hernandez
Barry S. Herrin
Randolph H. Houchins
Ciannat M. Howett
Wei Hu
Joseph H. Huff
  (Augusta, Georgia Office)
Edward C. Konieczny
Phoebe A. Kornfeld
  (London, England Office)
Michael F. Labbee
  (Not admitted in GA)
Paul Vincent Lalli
Michael Dean Langford
W. Scott Laseter
Judith M. Levy
Mary Balent Long
William F. Long
Christopher B. Lyman
Stephanie K. Maffett
Kenneth J. Markowitz
  (Washington, D.C. Office)
Kevin M. McMahon
Todd C. Meyers
David G. Michell
Sonya W. Middleton
Devon Lee Miller
  (Washington, D.C. Office)
Emmett H. Miller
  (Washington, D.C. Office)
Mila A. Ostin
Mark A. Palmer
  (Not admitted in GA)
Richard T. Peterson (Resident,
  Washington, D.C. Office)

Daniel F. Piar
David Pickle
  (Washington, D.C. Office)
Newton G. Quantz, III
Derek P. Richman
Peter D. Roberts
Robert A. Rosenbloum
Michael B. Rubenstein
Dean W. Rutley
  (Washington, D.C. Office)
Jennifer S. Schumacher
Edwin S. Schwartz
R. Perry Sentell, III
  (Augusta Office)
Nagendra Setty
Lori J. Shapiro
Charles T. Simmons
  (Washington, D.C. Office)
Jeffrey T. Skinner
W. Craig Smith
  (Augusta, Georgia Office)
Trent B. Speckhals
James D. Steinberg
Mitchell G. Stockwell
Whit F. Stolz
Clark G. Sullivan
Geoffrey L. Sutcliffe
Jeffrey J. Toney
James A. Trigg
  (Not admitted in GA)
Ivo Vissenberg
Jill Warner
Ashley B. Watson
Mitchell G. Weatherly
Susan Plath Winston
Lisa G. Youngblood
Cheryl Knowles Zalesky

For full biographical listings, see the Martindale-Hubbell Law Directory

KUTAK ROCK (AV)

A Partnership including Professional Corporations
4400 Georgia-Pacific Center, 133 Peachtree Street, N.E., 30303-1808
Telephone: 404-222-4600
Fax: 404-222-4654
URL: http://www.kutakrock.com
Denver, Colorado Office: Suite 2900, 717 Seventeenth Street, 80202-3329.
Telephone: 303-297-2400.
Facsimile: 303-292-7799.
Little Rock, Arkansas Office: Suite 1770, 124 West Capitol Avenue,
72201-3719.
Telephone: 501-376-9208.
Facsimile: 501-375-3749.
Kansas City, Missouri Office: United Missouri Bank Building, Third Floor,
9201 Ward Parkway.
Telephone: 816-361-3363.
Telecopier: 816-361-8397.
New York, New York Office: 767 Third Avenue, 10017-2023.
Telephone: 212-752-0800.
Facsimile: 212-752-2281.
Oklahoma City, Oklahoma Office: Suite 475, 6305 Waterford Boulevard,
73118-1116.
Telephone: 405-848-2475.
Facsimile: 405-842-5748.
Omaha, Nebraska Office: The Omaha Building, 1650 Farnam Street,
68102-2186.
Telephone: 402-346-6000.
Facsimile: 402-346-1148.
Phoenix, Arizona Office: Suite 650, 3636 North Central Avenue,
85012-2516.
Telephone: 602-285-1700.
Facsimile: 602-285-1868.
Pittsburgh, Pennsylvania Office: 1214 Frick Building, 437 Grant Street,
15219-6002.
Telephone: 412-261-6720.
Facsimile: 412-261-6717.
Washington, D.C. Office: Suite 1000, 1101 Connecticut Avenue, NW,
20036-4374.
Telephone: 202-828-2400.
Facsimile: 202-828-2488.

MEMBERS OF FIRM

Lawrence L. Thompson
Michael K. Wolensky
Edward M. Ford
David L. Amsden
Robert G. Brunton
  (Not admitted in GA)

David A. Nix
Paul M. Smith
Gregory R. Crochet
Michael A. Kazamias

OF COUNSEL

Edwin L. Sterne   Thomas R. Todd, Jr.

(See Next Column)

KUTAK ROCK, *Atlanta—Continued*

ASSOCIATES

Sarah E. Day	Nanette L. Wesley
Angela G. Miele	Patricia G. Woods
David J. Gellen	Ginger K. Patton-Schmitt

For full biographical listings, see the Martindale-Hubbell Law Directory

LIPSHUTZ, GREENBLATT & KING (AV)

2300 Harris Tower-Peachtree Center, 233 Peachtree Street, N.E., 30303
Telephone: 404-688-2300
Fax: 404-588-0648

MEMBERS OF FIRM

Robert J. Lipshutz	Edward L. Greenblatt
	Randall M. Lipshutz

OF COUNSEL

William R. King	Tito Mazzetta
	James V. Zito

ASSOCIATES

Paula B. Smith	Timothy L. S. Sitz

For full biographical listings, see the Martindale-Hubbell Law Directory

LONG ALDRIDGE & NORMAN, LLP (AV)

A Limited Liability Partnership including Professional Corporations
One Peachtree Center, Suite 5300, 303 Peachtree Street, 30308
Telephone: 404-527-4000
Telecopier: 404-527-4198
Washington, D.C. Office: Suite 600, 701 Pennsylvania Avenue, N.W., 20004.
Telephone: 202-624-1200.
FAX: 202-624-1298.

MEMBERS OF FIRM

John G. Aldridge	Clay C. Long
Evan Appel	J. Allen Maines
David L. Balser	Gary W. Marsh
Douglas L. Beresford (Resident, Washington, D.C. Office)	Patrick M. McGeehan
Barbara A. Blackford	Barbara A. McIntyre
Phillip A. Bradley	Carl W. Mullis, III
Bruce P. Brown	Laura Fink Nix
David M. Calhoun	Albert G. Norman, Jr.
Stephen L. Camp	W. Gregory Null
Clyde E. Click	Leonard A. Silverstein
George (Buddy) Darden	Jacolyn A. Simmons (Resident, Washington, D.C. Office)
L. Craig Dowdy	Edgar H. Sims, Jr. (P.C.)
Deborah S. Ebel	Jesse J. Spikes
William L. Floyd	William F. Stevens
Gordon D. Giffin	John T. Stough, Jr. (Resident, Washington, D.C. Office)
Jeffrey K. Haidet	Patricia E. Tate
Thomas D. Hall	John E. Theberge (Resident, Washington, D.C. Office)
Robert D. Hancock, Jr.	James J. Thomas II
John E. Holtzinger, Jr. (Resident, Washington, D.C. Office)	William F. Timmons
R. William Ide III	Russell A. Tolley
David M. Ivey	Thomas R. B. Wardell
J. James Johnson	John L. Watkins
Margaret M. Joslin	Jack H. Watson, Jr. (Resident, Washington, D.C. Office)
Mark S. Kaufman	Terry R. Weiss
Paul H. Keck (Resident, Washington, D.C. Office)	Robert I. White (Resident, Washington, D.C. Office)
C. Edward Kuntz	Bruce H. Wynn
Mark S. Lange	
	Charles T. Zink

SENIOR COUNSEL

F. T. Davis, Jr., (P.C.)	W. Stell Huie

ASSOCIATES

Claire Alison Addlestone (Not admitted in GA)	Eric Charles Lang
Barry J. Armstrong	Robert J. LaPorta
Susan Rappa Bain	H. Franklin Layson
James L. Barkin	Ann-Marie M. McGaughey
Sheila Shuster Baye	Melinda McNally
R. Daniel Beale	Kyle Michel (Resident, Washington, D.C. Office)
Wayne N. Bradley	Charles J. Middleton (Not admitted in GA)
James D. Comerford	Paula Rafferty Miller
Robert E. DeWitt	Mindy S. Planer
Kevin M. Downey (Resident, Washington, D.C. Office)	Melanie McGee Platt
Tania Louise Dyson	Kenneth B. Pollock
Lynn Gavin	Thadd A. Prisco (Resident, Washington, D.C. Office)
Sharon M. Glenn	William E. Rice
Janet Eifert Haury	Russell J. Rogers
George F. Hobday, Jr. (Resident, Washington, D.C. Office)	Douglas D. Selph
	Johnathan H. Short
Virginia Ann Johnson	Lawrence A. Slovensky
Sherri L. Kimmell	Janice Nathanson Smith

(See Next Column)

ASSOCIATES (Continued)

Steven Paul Smith	J. Michael Wiggins
Briggs L. Tobin	Richard R. Willis
Charles D. Weiss	John F. Woodham
	Angelyn M. Wright

OF COUNSEL

William J. Carney	Matthew A. Towery
James W. Culbreth	Gerald D. Walling
J. Michell Philpott	Nancy A. White (Resident, Washington, D.C. Office)

Representative Clients: American Business Products, Inc.; Atlanta Gas Light Co.; The Cable Television Association of Georgia; Coca-Cola Enterprises, Inc.; Law Companies Group, Inc.; Murex Corp.; President Baking Company, Inc.

For full biographical listings, see the Martindale-Hubbell Law Directory

LONG, WEINBERG, ANSLEY AND WHEELER (AV)

A Partnership including Professional Corporations
999 Peachtree Street, N.E. Suite 2700, 30309
Telephone: 404-876-2700
Facsimile: 404-875-9433
Email: firm@lwaw.com

MEMBERS OF FIRM

Thomas J. Long (1898-1965)	Alan L. Newman
Palmer H. Ansley (1927-1991)	Marvin A. Devlin
Ben L. Weinberg, Jr., (P.C.)	Earl W. Gunn
Sidney F. Wheeler	C. Bradford Marsh
J. Kenneth Moorman	Arnold E. Gardner
John M. Hudgins, IV, (P.C.)	Lance D. Lourie
Robert G. Tanner	Milton B. Satcher, III
Joseph W. Watkins	David A. Sapp
James H. Fisher, II	Stephen H. Sparwath
M. Diane Owens	Kathryn S. Whitlock
Robert D. Roll	Mark E. Robinson
Kenneth Marc Barré, Jr.	Frederick N. Sager, Jr.
	Patricia M. Peters

ASSOCIATES

Quinton S. Seay	Dennis J. Webb, Jr.
Charles K. Reed	George A. Koenig
Sharon B. Austin	Griffith J. Winthrop, III
Carol P. Michel	Anandhi S. Rajan
John K. Train, IV	Christopher J. Graddock
Johnathan T. Krawcheck	Alan M. Maxwell
John C. Bonnie	Bonny H. Richardson
Emily J. Brantley	Stephen R. Chance
Paul L. Weisbecker	Pamela C. Corley
J. Calhoun Harris, Jr.	F. Faison Middleton, IV
Michele L. Davis	Kari A. Mercer
	Nancy E. Green

OF COUNSEL

Meade Burns

Representative Clients: Aetna Casualty & Surety Corp.; Chrysler Motors Corp.; Emory University; Dow Corning Corp.; Ford Motor Co.; Freuhauf Trailer Corp.; Merck; Otis Elevator Co.; St. Paul Fire & Marine Insurance Co.; Toyota Motor Sales U.S.A., Inc.

For full biographical listings, see the Martindale-Hubbell Law Directory

LORD, BISSELL & BROOK (AV)

One Atlantic Center, 1201 West Peachtree Street, N.W., Suite 3700, 30309
Telephone: 404-870-4600
Telecopy: 404-872-5547
Chicago, Illinois Office: Suites 2600-3600 Harris Bank Building, 115 South LaSalle Street, 60603.
Telephone: 312-443-0700.
Telecopy: 312-443-0570.
Cable Address: "Lowirco."
Telex: 25-0336.
Los Angeles, California Office: 300 South Grand Avenue, 90071-3200.
Telephone: 213-485-1500.
Telecopy: 213-485-1200.
Telex: 18-1135.
Rockford, Illinois Office: 120 West State Street, Suite 200, 61101.
Telephone: 815-963-8050.

RESIDENT PARTNERS

Michael J. Athans	J. Robert Persons
David G. Greene	Walton N. Smith
David M. Leonard	Thomas J. Strueber
	Richard M. Watson

RESIDENT ASSOCIATES

Andrea M. Brucoli	Terry R. Howell
Donald J. Chenevert	Brad Stewart Kalter
Steven R. Daniels	Kevin A. Maxim
Jeffrey R. Darby	Robert E. McLaughlin
Andrew R. Diamond	Prescott L. Nottingham
Paul L. Fields, Jr.	Corliss L. Worford
Gregory A. Gunter	James H. Wynn

(See Next Column)

LORD, BISSELL & BROOK—*Continued*

OF COUNSEL
Marsha Kellman Klevickis

For full biographical listings, see the Martindale-Hubbell Law Directory

MACEY, WILENSKY, COHEN, WITTNER & KESSLER, LLP (AV)

285 Peachtree Center Avenue, Suite 600, 30303-1229
Telephone: 404-584-1200
Telecopier: 404-681-4355
Other Atlanta, Georgia Office: 5784 Lake Forrest Drive, Suite 214, 30328.

MEMBERS OF FIRM

Morris W. Macey	Neil C. Gordon
Frank B. Wilensky	Susan L. Howick
H. William Cohen	M. Todd Westfall
Sheldon R. Wittner (1943-1988)	James R. Sacca
Richard P. Kessler, Jr.	David B. Kurzweil

ASSOCIATES

Shayna M. (Salomon) Steinfeld	Rachel Anderson Snider
Robert A. Winter	Barbara Ellis-Monro
Pamela Gronauer Hill	Ronald Alan Weiner
Richard C. Litwin	

For full biographical listings, see the Martindale-Hubbell Law Directory

PAUL, HASTINGS, JANOFSKY & WALKER LLP (AV)

A Limited Liability Partnership including Professional Corporations
Firm Established in 1951; Office in 1980.
24th Floor, 600 Peachtree Street, N.E., 30308-2222
Telephone: 404-815-2400
Fax: 404-815-2424
Email: info@PHJW.com
Los Angeles, California Office: Twenty-Third Floor 555 South Flower Street.
Telephone: 213-683-6000.
Orange County, California Office: Seventeenth Floor, 695 Town Center Drive, Costa Mesa.
Telephone: 714-668-6200.
Washington, D.C. Office: Tenth Floor, 1299 Pennsylvania Avenue, N.W.
Telephone: 202-508-9500.
Santa Monica, California Office: Fifth Floor, 1299 Ocean Avenue.
Telephone: 310-319-3300.
Stamford, Connecticut Office: Ninth Floor, 1055 Washington Boulevard.
Telephone: 203-961-7400.
New York, New York Office: 31st Floor, 399 Park Avenue.
Telephone: 212-318-6000.
Tokyo, Japan Office: Ark Mori Building, 30th Floor, 12-32 Akasaka, P.O. Box 577, 1-Chome, Minato-Ku.
Telephone: (03) 3586-4711.

MEMBERS OF FIRM

Richard M. Asbill	William B. Hill, Jr.
R. Lawrence Ashe, Jr., (P.C.)	Weyman T. Johnson, Jr.
Jesse H. Austin, III	Philip J. Marzetti
Keith W. Berglund	Chris D. Molen
Daryl R. Buffenstein	Julian D. Nealy
Thomas G. Burch, Jr.	John G. Parker
Ronald T. Coleman, Jr.	W. Andrew Scott
Kevin Conboy	Charles T. Sharbaugh
Paul J. Connell	Wayne H. Shortridge
James H. Cox	John H. Steed
William E. Eason, Jr.	C. Geoffrey Weirich

OF COUNSEL

Leslie A. Dent	Robert C. Moot, Jr.
Deborah A. Marlowe	Craig K. Pendergrast
	Charles A. Shanor

ASSOCIATES

Tracey T. Barbaree	Melinda L. Moseley
Stephanie A. Bohm	John J. Neely, III
Deborah M. Bradley (Not admitted in GA)	Elizabeth Hardy Noe
	Maureen E. O'Neill
Christine E. Cahill	Susan M. Pavlin
A. Craig Cleland	Tracy S. Plott
Kathleen O. Currey	Nancy E. Rafuse
Cindy J.K. Davis	Lynne H. Rambo
Michael W. Dubus (Not admitted in GA)	Kelly A. Regal
	T. Robert Reid
Susan Langley Elliott	Mathew Anthony Schuh
William P. Ewing	Joseph C. Sharp
David E. Gevertz	Naomi Weyand Smith
James R. Glenister	E. Gary Spitko
Susan E. Himmer	Brian D. Sullivan (Not admitted in GA)
Edward S. Johnson, Jr.	
Karen E. Jorik (Not admitted in GA)	Kristen K. Swartz
	Eric Jon Taylor
Janet L. Kishbaugh	Michael T. Voytek (Not admitted in GA)
Kelly D. Ludwick	
James W. Maxson	Stanley F. Wasowski

(See Next Column)

ASSOCIATES (Continued)

L. Kent Webb	Crystal L. Williams (Not admitted in GA)
Elise M. Whitaker	
Jonathan B. Wilson	

For full biographical listings, see the Martindale-Hubbell Law Directory

POPE, McGLAMRY, KILPATRICK & MORRISON (AV)

A Partnership including Professional Corporations
83 Walton Street, N.W., P.O. Box 1733, 30303
Telephone: 404-523-7706;
Phenix City, Alabama: 334-298-7354
Columbus, Georgia Office: 318 11th Street, 2nd Floor, P.O. Box 2128, 31902-2128.
Telephone: 706-324-0050.

MEMBERS OF FIRM

C. Neal Pope (P.C.)	R. Timothy Morrison
Max R. McGlamry (P.C.) (Resident, Columbus, Georgia Office)	Michael L. McGlamry
	Earle F. Lasseter
	William Usher Norwood, III
Paul V. Kilpatrick, Jr. (Resident, Columbus, Georgia Office)	William J. Cornwell
	Jay F. Hirsch
Wade H. Tomlinson, III	

RESIDENT ASSOCIATES

C. Elizabeth Pope

Reference: Columbus Bank & Trust Co.

For full biographical listings, see the Martindale-Hubbell Law Directory

POWELL, GOLDSTEIN, FRAZER & MURPHY (AV)

A Partnership including a Professional Corporation
191 Peachtree Street, N.E., Sixteenth Floor, 30303
Telephone: 404-572-6600
Telex: 542864
Telecopier: 404-572-6999
Cable Address: "Pgfm"
Washington, D.C. Office: Sixth Floor, 1001 Pennsylvania Avenue, N.W., 20004.
Telephone: 202-347-0066.

MEMBERS OF FIRM

John Dozier Little (1871-1934)	V. Scott Killingsworth
Arthur Gray Powell (1873-1951)	William L. Kinzer
Max F. Goldstein (1886-1973)	Kathryn L. Knudson
Burket Dean Murphy (1894-1981)	Jay J. Levin
	Robert C. Lewinson
Edward E. Dorsey (1920-1981)	William Joseph Linkous, Jr.
James N. Frazer (1903-1985)	Frank Love, Jr.
J. Winston Huff (1920-1996)	John T. Marshall
Eric W. Anderson	James J. McAlpin, Jr.
Gavin S. Appleby	Frank S. McGaughey, III
Richard L. Arenburg	Thomas R. McNeill
David M. Armitage	Richard H. Miller
David R. Aufdenspring	Richard C. Mitchell
David S. Baker	Walter G. Moeling, IV
Eric P. Berezin	Charles Eugene Murphy, Jr.
Jerry B. Blackstock	Lesly Gaynor Murray
Larry I. Bogart	David C. Nicholson
Mary Williams Bondurant	E. Penn Nicholson
Armin G. Brecher	John R. Parks
Janine Brown	Robert W. Patrick
Gregory M. Chait	William M. Ragland, Jr.
Paul F. Concannon	James C. Rawls
Frank A. Crisafi	Thomas S. Richey
William V. Custer, IV	Kim H. Roeder
Dean S. Daskal	David G. Ross
V. Robert Denham, Jr.	Joan Boilen Sasine
Gabriel Dumitrescu	Steven G. Schaffer
Marilyn M. Fish	William B. Shearer, Jr., P.C.
Elliott Goldstein	Jonathan R. Shils
Douglas S. Gosden	E. A. Simpson, Jr.
C. Scott Greene	Scott D. Smith
John M. Gross	W. Scott Sorrels
Wilbur Gordon Hamlin, Jr.	G. William Speer
John W. Harbin	Ronald D. Stallings
Robert R. Harlin	William J. Thompson
Hilary Harp	Robert M. Travis
James W. Hawkins	Rex R. Veal
Lewis C. Horne, Jr.	James A. Walker, Jr.
John H. Horne	G. Patrick Watson
Randall L. Hughes	Karen Wildau
LeeAnn Jones	Gregory H. Worthy
Jeffrey W. Kelley	John F. Wymer, III

ASSOCIATES

Michele L. Battle	Gil Y Burstiner
Thomas J. Biafore	Kathlynn Lea Butler
John R. Bielema, Jr.	Christen Civiletto Carey
Linda G. Birchall	Farah K. Carter
Anthony R. Boggs	Norma Lydia Casal
Cindy A. Brazell	W. Scott Creasman
William Bard Brockman	James A. Dudukovich

(See Next Column)

POWELL, GOLDSTEIN, FRAZER & MURPHY, *Atlanta—Continued*

ASSOCIATES (Continued)

Christopher P. Galanek	Samuel M. Matchett
Richard Ellett Green	Charlene L. McGinty
Carrie Ann Hanlon	Ephraim L. Michael
Kimberly C. Harris	Jona J. Miller
(Not admitted in GA)	Robin G. Moore
Matthew P. Holley	Robin Catherine Murray-Gill
Glenn E. Johnson	Patton
Joann Gallagher Jones	Linda C. Odom
Todd E. Jones	Eliot William Robinson
Pilar Gretchen Keagy	Laura L. Seidel
Leslie S. Kehoe	(Not admitted in GA)
Cynthia D. Kennedy	Raymond P. Sheley
Katherine M. Koops	Rebecca L. Sigmund
Charles H. Kuck	Debra L. Skal
Deborah Fleischer Kurzweil	Sara Kay Sledge
Anne Maher LaMastra	Lynn Murrell Sumlin
Beth Lanier	Marc A. Taylor
Marlo Orlin Leach	Michael Thompson
Mark A. Loeffler	Matthew J. Troy
Stacey C. Loftus	Nicole Jennings Wade
Kathryn A. Lumpkin	James K. Wagner, Jr.
Wendolyn Ward Markham	Sheridan M. Watson
Lisa J. Marks	Denise M. Wilson
Shawn Martin	(Not admitted in GA)
Adrienne E. Marting	Kristen Yadlosky

COUNSEL

Wendy L. Hagenau	Riccarda Heising
Carol D. Newman	

For full biographical listings, see the Martindale-Hubbell Law Directory

---

ROGERS & HARDIN (AV)

2700 International Tower, Peachtree Center, 229 Peachtree Street, N.E., 30303
Telephone: 404-522-4700
Telex: 54-2335
Facsimile: 404-525-2224
Email: LD+ARH%2005857@mcimail.com

MEMBERS OF FIRM

John J. Almond	Phillip S. McKinney
Miriam J. Dent	Robert A. Parker, Jr.
Steven E. Fox	Tony G. Powers
Edward J. Hardin	C. B. Rogers
Hunter R. Hughes, III	Michael Rosenzweig
Dan F. Laney, III	Peter W. Schneider
Stephen R. Leeds	Richard H. Sinkfield
Alan C. Leet	Paul W. Stivers

COUNSEL

David D. Willoughby

SENIOR ATTORNEYS

James W. Beverage	Laura H. Robison

ASSOCIATES

Kevin E. Broyles	Brett A. Rogers
Lisa Bodenstein Golan	Julie R. Schwartz
Amy S. Haney	Benjamin A. Stone
Terry L. Houser	David G. Thunhorst
Robert C. Hussle	William T. Watts, Jr.
Daniel McGinnis	Jeffrey W. Willis
Cynthia M. Montgomery	Daniel Dragomir Zegura
(Not admitted in GA)	

For full biographical listings, see the Martindale-Hubbell Law Directory

---

SMITH, GAMBRELL & RUSSELL (AV)

A Partnership including Professional Corporations
Suite 3100, Promenade II, 1230 Peachtree Street, N.E., 30309-3592
Telephone: 404-815-3500
Telecopy: 404-815-3509
Other Atlanta Office: Atlanta Financial Center, East Tower, 3343 Peachtree Road, N.E., Suite 1800.
Telephone: 404-264-2620.
Telecopier: 404-264-2652.

Alexander W. Smith (1861-1925)	I. T. Cohen (1908-1984)
Alexander W. Smith (1886-1964)	E. Smythe Gambrell (1896-1986)

MEMBERS OF FIRM

James H. Bratton, Jr.	John D. Saunders
David A. Handley	James H. Morgan, Jr.
Robert I. Paller (P.C.)	Thomas W. Rhodes
David J. Harris (P.C.)	Rawson C. Gordon
Robert P. Forrestal	Harry L. Hickson (P.C.)
(Not admitted in GA)	Arthur Jay Schwartz
Robert W. Beynart	Ira Genberg
Howard E. Turner	J. Rodgers Lunsford III
Hillyer McD. Young	Andrew C. Shovers
John A. Blackmon (P.C.)	Leland G. Cook (P.C.)
David M. Brown	William L. Meyer
Prentiss Q. Yancey, Jr.	Bruce I. Crabtree III

(See Next Column)

MEMBERS OF FIRM (Continued)

Robert C. Schwartz	Joyce B. Klemmer
Michael S. Haber	Richard G. Greenstein
Rex M. Lamb, III	John C. Ethridge, Jr.
Carlile M. Chambers	Peter M. Pearl
John P. Bailey	Mark G. Pottorff
David W. Santi	Sharon C. Duvall
John G. Despriet	David C. Newman
Ronald E. Barab	Edward H. Wasmuth, Jr.
William W. Maycock	John H. Spillman
James P. Monacell	Georges A. Hoffmann
William B. Wood	William S. Rogers, Jr.
Stephen E. O'Day	M. Timothy Elder
Stanley G. Brading, Jr.	Eric H. Mandus
W. Thomas King	Stefan-M. Tiessen
Stephen M. Forte	Robert T. Molinet
Bruce W. Moorhead, Jr.	Matthew S. Coles
E. Kendrick Smith	Paul G. Durdaller
Helen T. Ferraro	Herbert M. Hanegan
Hans-Michael Kraus	John T. Vian
Ronald W. Wells	Thomas M. Barton

OF COUNSEL

William W. Griffin	William Robert Mellen
Ben Kohler, Jr.	Harold L. Russell
Alexander W. Smith	

COUNSEL

Kenneth A. Cutshaw	Kristen Lewis Grice

ASSOCIATES

Marcia McCrory Ernst	David W. Quillian
Mark W. Kinzer	Mark C. de St. Aubin
Marlon F. Starr	Paul S. Lee
Robert Preston Brown	Deana K. Pruitt
Simone von Werden Kraus	Jason S. Bell
Bruce D. Cohen	Michael P. Kornheiser
L. Brett Lockwood	Keely Schneider-Truog
Glen P. Brock, III	Greta L. Thomasson
S. David McLean, Jr.	Paula C. Davis
John R. Schneider	Catherine M. Hilton
Dana M. Richens	Christopher W. Haffke
Sharon K. Kacmarcik	Michelle R. Craig
Dennis O. Doherty	Edward Davison Burch, Jr.
Patricia B. Eastwood	Catherine F. Boone
Hongli Ma	Rainey Lee Astin
Mary Maclean Doolan	John B. Shannon
Elizabeth G. Lowry	Michael W. King

For full biographical listings, see the Martindale-Hubbell Law Directory

---

SUTHERLAND, ASBILL & BRENNAN, L.L.P. (AV)

999 Peachtree Street, N.E., 30309-3996
Telephone: 404-853-8000
Facsimile: 404-853-8806
Email: postmaster@sablaw.com
Washington, D.C. Office: 1275 Pennsylvania Avenue, N.W., 20004-2404.
Telephone: 202-383-0100.
New York, N.Y. Office: 600 Madison Avenue, 11th Floor, 10022-1615.
Telephone: 212-605-6400.
Austin, Texas Office: 111 Congress Avenue, 23rd Floor, 78701-4079.
Telephone: 512-469-3350.

MEMBERS OF THE FIRM IN ATLANTA, GEORGIA

William A. Sutherland (1896-1987)	Mac Asbill, Sr. (1893-1992)
Alfred G. Adams, Jr.	Joseph B. Brennan (1903-1991)
F. Louise Adams	Barrett K. Hawks
Peter J. Anderson	Walter Hellerstein
William D. Barwick	(Not admitted in GA)
John W. Bonds, Jr.	James L. Henderson, III
William H. Bradley	Thomas C. Herman
Thomas M. Byrne	Charles D. Hurt, Jr.
John A. Chandler	J. Patton Hyman, III
Reginald J. Clark	Thomas B. Hyman, Jr.
George L. Cohen	James Bruce Jordan
Katherine Meyers Cohen	Edward W. Kallal, Jr.
N. Jerold Cohen	Mark D. Kaufman
Thomas A. Cox	Bennett Lexon Kight
Patricia Bayer Cunningham	Cada T. Kilgore, III
Peter H. Dean	Charles T. Lester, Jr.
Carey P. DeDeyn	Alfred A. Lindseth
B. Knox Dobbins	James R. McGibbon
Michael J. Egan	Daniel R. McKeithen
Eric R. Fenichel	John H. Mobley, II
J. D. Fleming, Jr.	Richard G. Murphy, Jr.
John H. Fleming	Judith A. O'Brien
Peter A. Fozzard	James A. Orr
Stephen F. Gertzman	William R. Patterson
James P. Groton	James R. Paulk, Jr.
C. Christopher Hagy	M. Celeste Pickron
H. Edward Hales, Jr.	Randall D. Quintrell
Victor P. Haley	Richard L. Robbins
William M. Hames	Haynes R. Roberts
James K. Hasson, Jr.	Teresa Wynn Roseborough
	Herbert J. Short, Jr.

(See Next Column)

SUTHERLAND, ASBILL & BRENNAN—*Continued*

MEMBERS OF THE FIRM
IN ATLANTA, GEORGIA (Continued)

George Anthony Smith	Mark D. Wasserman
Elizabeth Vranicar Tanis	Larry J. White
Randolph W. Thrower	James H. Wilson, Jr.
C. Christopher Trower	Walter H. Wingfield

COUNSEL OF THE FIRM
IN ATLANTA, GEORGIA

Elizabeth W. Boswell	Charles M. Flickinger
Edmund B. Burke	Patricia Anne Gorham
Louise B. Duffy	Alan J. Lowenthal
Donald M. Etheridge, Jr.	S. Lawrence Polk
(Not admitted in GA)	S. Perry Thomas, Jr.
William R. Wildman	

For full biographical listings, see the Martindale-Hubbell Law Directory

---

TROUTMAN SANDERS LLP (AV)

A Partnership including Professional Corporations
5200 NationsBank Plaza, 600 Peachtree Street, N.E., 30308-2216
Telephone: 404-885-3000
Fax: 404-885-3900
Other Atlanta Offices at: 999 Peachtree Street, Suite 750, 30309.
Telephone: 404-885-3651,
Facsimile: 404-885-3652.
Washington, D.C. Office: 601 Pennsylvania Avenue, N.W., North Building, Suite 640, 20004.
Telephone: 202-274-2950.
Facsimile: 202-274-2994.

MEMBERS OF FIRM

Dan MacDougald (1883-1953)	Donald W. Janney
Henry B. Troutman (1886-1978)	Kevin C. Greene
Robert S. Sams (1905-1969)	William N. Withrow, Jr.
William H. Schroder (1914-1970)	Richard H. Brody
R. J. Reynolds, Jr. (1902-1973)	Thomas E. Mattimoe
Jack P. Ashmore, Jr.	Arthur H. Domby
(1930-1976)	Hugh M. Davenport
Allen E. Lockerman (1906-1977)	Richard A. Hartnig
Carl E. Sanders	Patricia Ann Wilson
Joseph R. White, Jr.	Winifred D. Simpson
Robert L. Pennington	Mark Lee Elliott
Trammell E. Vickery	William B. Marianes
Richard A. Newton, P.C.	Bryan B. Lavine
Milton A. Carlton, Jr., P.C.	Jeffrey F. Hetsko
John D. McLanahan	Joel S. Goldman
Norman L. Underwood	John H. Johnson, Jr.
James E. Joiner, P.C.	Douglas D. Salyers
Dale M. Schwartz	M. Stuart Sutherland
John J. Dalton, P.C.	Hazen H. Dempster
Harvey A. Rosenzweig	Mark J. Newman
Robert W. Grout, P.C.	Kenneth R. Russell, Jr.
Ezra H. Cohen	Robert P. Williams, II
James L. Smith, III	David F. Golden
Stanley H. Hackett, P.C.	Mark S. VanderBroek
J. Dexter Edge, Jr., P.C.	Stephen W. Riddell
James C. Fleming, P.C.	Christopher S. Miller
James W. Addison	John Lamberski
Wayne R. Vason	Roger S. Reigner, Jr.
Robert H. Forry, P.C.	Robert C. Marshall
W. Randall Tye	DeWitt R. Rogers
J. Kirk Quillian	Alexander P. Woollcott
John W. Griffin	Scott A. Farrow
Robert d. Fortson	Charles F. Palmer
Daniel S. Reinhardt	Kaye Woodard Burwell
Alan E. Lubel	James A. Clark
Douglas L. Miller	James A. Lamberth
Robert W. Webb, Jr.	Michael V. Coleman
John W. Moore	William B. Conway, Jr.
Alan E. Serby	(Resident, Washington, D.C.
Ralph H. Greil	Office)
June Ann Sanders	R. Thomas Amis (Resident,
John R. Molm (Resident,	Washington, D.C. Office)
Washington, D.C. Office)	Larry E. Gramlich
Herbert D. Shellhouse	Walter E. Jospin
Robert D. Strauss	Daniel T. Falstad
John C. Beane	Steven J. Whitehead
Thomas J. Hartland, Jr.	Elizabeth Brannen Chandler
John T. W. Mercer	Maureen Theresa Callahan
Mary Grace Diehl	Hollister (Holly) Anne Hill
Robert P. Edwards, Jr.	James H. Keaten
N. Karen Deming	Richard Keck

ASSOCIATES

Joseph S. Asher	Allen Buckley
Joy Elizabeth Barbour	Thomas E. Campbell
(Not admitted in GA)	Lesley G. Carroll
Wendy Kestin Barkin	J. Michael Childers
Teresa B. Bass	Margaret L. Claiborne
Lisa Mihalick Beale	Elizabeth Clark-Morrison
Mark L. Booz	Channing H. Cline
John M. Bowler	Sean J. Coleman

(See Next Column)

ASSOCIATES (Continued)

John T. Cooper	Willie J. Lovett, Jr.
Joan B. Cravey	Michael A. Lueder
M. Travis DeHaven	Andrew F. MacDonald
M. Pilar Diaz	William P. Marsan (Resident,
Lora L. Donoghue	Washington, D.C. Office)
William M. Droze	Daniel R. McClure
Tracy G. Edmundson	(Not admitted in GA)
Lisa S. Edwards	Rosemarie McConnell
Douglas E. Ernst	C. LeeAnn McCurry
Terry P. Finnerty	David M. Menditto
Colin F. Flannery	(Not admitted in GA)
David B. Foshee	Stephanie J. Millet
Scott M. Frank	Craig S. Mordock
Michele R. Gelb	William A. Mullins (Resident,
Ashley Z. Hager	Washington, D.C. Office)
Douglas A. Henderson	Kathryn V. Nelson
Sharon N. Hill	Joyce M. Nuszbaum
Michael D. Hobbs, Jr.	Thomas L. Penland, Jr.
Frances M. Hong	Brian D. Poe
Allison Boyce Hudson	Randall R. Rainer
Scott A. Hudson	Earnest Redwine Jr.
Lorie Maring Hutchins	James K. Reed
Benjamin Lee Israel (Resident,	Matthew F. Roberts
Washington, D.C. Office)	Marc H. Salm
Robert M. Jackson	Christine N. Schneider
(Not admitted in GA)	Wendelin White Silliman
Robert E. James, II	John S. Snelling
Donna B. Johnson	Karen M. Stein
Michael E. Johnson	Eric A. Szweda
Roland M. Juarez	Karen G. Thompson
(Not admitted in GA)	Richard E. Thompson II
Kevin A. Kakareka	Stephanie E, Tillman
Robert W. Kamerschen	Melissa H. Trimble
Gwen R. Kaminsky	E. Fitzgerald Veira
Jennifer Katze	David C. Vigilante
Brett W. King (Resident,	Anthony C. Walsh
Washington, D.C. Office)	T. Clayton Walts
Laura H. Kriteman	James I. Warren, III
Amy Stutz Lettes	Susan Payor Wilkerson
Michael G. Leveille	A. Michelle Willis
Stephen E. Lewis	Martin M. Wilson
A. William Loeffler	Angela M. Woo
	Jianyi Zhang

OF COUNSEL

Edwin I. Hatch	Carl I. Gable, Jr., (P.C.)
(Not admitted in GA)	Harry V. Lamon, Jr., (P.C.)
Harold G. Clarke	Daniel H. Neely
Kevin C. Fitzgerald (Resident,	Ronald R. Ross (Resident,
Washington, D.C. Office)	Washington, D.C. Office)

For full biographical listings, see the Martindale-Hubbell Law Directory

---

WILSON, STRICKLAND & BENSON, P.C. (AV)

1100 One Midtown Plaza, 1360 Peachtree Street, N.E., 30309
Telephone: 404-870-1800
Telecopier: 404-870-1808

Warner R. Wilson, Jr.	N. Sandy Epstein
Frank B. Strickland	Daniel I. MacIntyre
Earl B. Benson, Jr.	Mary M. Brockington
R. Milton Crouch	L. Lou Allen

OF COUNSEL

John C. Pennington	Robert G. Wellon

COUNSEL

Craig N. Goodrich

Anne W. Lewis	Sara L. Doyle
Samuel T. Brannan	Carolyn A. Seabolt
F. Robert Slotkin, Jr.	John K. Rezac
	Christopher J. Moyen

For full biographical listings, see the Martindale-Hubbell Law Directory

---

AUGUSTA, * Richmond Co.

BURNSIDE, WALL, DANIEL, ELLISON & REVELL (AV)

A Partnership including Professional Corporations
454 Greene Street, P.O. Box 2125, 30903
Telephone: 706-722-0768
Fax: 706-722-5984

MEMBERS OF FIRM

Robert C. Daniel, Jr.	James B. Wall (P.C.)
(1943-1993)	James W. Ellison
Thomas R. Burnside, Jr. (P.C.)	Harry D. Revell
	Thomas R. Burnside, III

(See Next Column)

BURNSIDE, WALL, DANIEL, ELLISON & REVELL, *Augusta—Continued*

ASSOCIATE
Lori S. D'Alessio

Representative Clients: Augusta-Richmond County Commission-Council; National Science Center Foundation, Inc.; CSRA Regional Development Center; City of Harlem, Georgia; Liquid Carbonic Corp.; Southern Machine & Tool Co.; Jefferson EMC; Southeastern Equipment Co.; SECO Aviation, Inc.; SECO Parts & Equipment, Inc.

For full biographical listings, see the Martindale-Hubbell Law Directory

CAPERS, DUNBAR, SANDERS & BRUCKNER (AV)

Fifteenth Floor, First Union Bank Building, 30901-1454
Telephone: 706-722-7542
Telecopier: 706-724-7776

MEMBERS OF FIRM

John D. Capers	E. Frederick Sanders
Paul H. Dunbar, III	Ziva P. Bruckner

ASSOCIATES
Carl P. Dowling

For full biographical listings, see the Martindale-Hubbell Law Directory

DYE, TUCKER, EVERITT, WHEALE & LONG, A PROFESSIONAL ASSOCIATION (AV)

453 Greene Street, P.O. Box 2426, 30903
Telephone: 706-722-0771
Fax: 706-722-7028

A. Rowland Dye	Duncan D. Wheale
Thomas W. Tucker	John B. Long
A. Zachry Everitt	Benjamin H. Brewton
Troy A. Lanier	

OF COUNSEL
A. Montague Miller

Representative Clients: State Farm Insurance Cos.; The Travelers Insurance Co.; Georgia Power Co.; Wachovia National Bank (Augusta Division); Chubb Group; Montgomery Ward; Augusta Board of Realtors; Ryder Truck Rental, Inc.; Canal Insurance Company; St. Paul Fire and Marine Insurance Company.

For full biographical listings, see the Martindale-Hubbell Law Directory

FLETCHER, HARLEY & FLETCHER (AV)

429 Walker Street, P.O. Box 2084, 30903-2084
Telephone: 706-724-0558
Fax: 706-724-4730

MEMBERS OF FIRM

Leonard O. Fletcher, Jr.	C. Thompson Harley
W. Lawrence Fletcher	

For full biographical listings, see the Martindale-Hubbell Law Directory

FULCHER, HAGLER, REED, HANKS & HARPER (AV)

A Partnership including Professional Corporations
520 Greene Street, P.O. Box 1477, 30903-1477
Telephone: 706-724-0171
Telecopier: 706-724-4573

MEMBERS OF FIRM

William M. Fulcher (1902-1993)	Michael B. Hagler (P.C.)
Gould B. Hagler (Retired)	James W. Purcell (P.C.)
William C. Reed (Retired)	J. Arthur Davison (P.C.)
David H. Hanks (P.C.)	Mark C. Wilby (P.C.)
John I. Harper (P.C.)	Ronald C. Griffeth
Robert C. Hagler (P.C.)	N. Staten Bitting, Jr. (P.C.)
David P. Dekle (P.C.)	

ASSOCIATES

Scott W. Kelly	Elizabeth A. McLeod
Cynthia A. Gray	Barry A. Fleming

General Counsel for: GIW Industries, Inc.
Division Counsel for: CSX Transportation; Textron, Inc. (E-Z Go Car Division).
Counsel for: NationsBank; Georgia Natural Gas Co. (a division of Atlanta Gas Light Co.); Champion International Corp.; Aetna Life and Casualty; Liberty Mutual Insurance Company; St. Paul Fire & Marine Insurance Co.; Kimberly Clark Corporation.

For full biographical listings, see the Martindale-Hubbell Law Directory

HULL, TOWILL, NORMAN & BARRETT, A PROFESSIONAL CORPORATION (AV)

Seventh Floor, Trust Company Bank Building, P.O. Box 1564, 30903-1564
Telephone: 706-722-4481
Fax: 706-722-9779

(See Next Column)

James M. Hull (1885-1975)	Douglas D. Batchelor, Jr.
George B. Barrett (1894-1942)	David E. Hudson
Julian J. Willingham (1887-1963)	Neal W. Dickert
John Bell Towill (1907-1991)	John W. Gibson
Robert C. Norman	William F. Hammond
(Retired, 1991)	Mark S. Burgreen
W. Hale Barrett	George R. Hall
Lawton Jordan, Jr.	James B. Ellington
Patrick J. Rice	F. Michael Taylor

Robert A. Mullins	Michael S. Carlson
William J. Keogh, III	Ralph Emerson Hanna, III
Edward J. Tarver	Susan D. Barrett
J. Noel Schweers, III	Timothy E. Moses

Counsel for: Sun Trust Bank Augusta, N.A.; Georgia Federal Bank, FSB, Augusta Division; Southeastern Newspapers Corp.; Georgia Power Co.; Southern Bell Telephone & Telegraph Co.; St. Joseph Hospital, Augusta, Georgia, Inc.; Norfolk Southern Corp.; Merry Land & Investment Co., Inc.; Housing Authority of the City of Augusta; Georgia Press Association.

For full biographical listings, see the Martindale-Hubbell Law Directory

KILPATRICK & CODY (AV)

Suite 1400, First Union Bank Building, P.O. Box 2043, 30903
Telephone: 706-724-2622
Telephone Copier: 706-722-0219
Atlanta, Georgia Office: Suite 2800, 1100 Peachtree Street.
Telephone: 404-815-6500.
Telecopier: 404-815-6555.
Washington, D.C. Office: Suite 800, 700 13th Street, N.W., 20005.
Telephone: 202-508-5800. *Telephone Copier:* 202-508-5858.
Brussels, Belgium Office: Avenue Louise 65, BTE 3, 1050 Brussels.
Telephone: (32) (2) 533-03-00.
Telecopier: (32) (2) 534-86-38.
London, England Office: 68 Pall Mall, London, SW1Y 5ES, England.
Telephone: (44) (71) 321 0477.
Telecopier: (44) (71) 930 9733.

MEMBERS OF FIRM

Raymond G. Chadwick, Jr.	Wyck A. Knox, Jr.
Ted H. Clarkson	Gregg E. McDougal

ASSOCIATES

Jackson E. Cox, II	Joseph H. Huff
Daniel W. Hamilton	R. Perry Sentell, III
W. Craig Smith	

Representative Clients: University Health Services, Inc.; National Cardiovascular Network, Inc.; Atlanta Cardiology, P.C.; First Union National Bank of Georgia; A.A. Friedman Co.; Blanchard & Calhoun Real Estate Co., Inc.; Boardman Petroleum, Inc.; Castleberry's Food Co., Inc.; DSM Chemicals North America, Inc.; Westinghouse Savannah River Company.

For full biographical listings, see the Martindale-Hubbell Law Directory

PLUNKETT & PLUNKETT, P.C. (AV)

Suite 502 Trust Company Bank Building, 801 Broad Street, 30901
Telephone: 706-722-4111
Fax: 706-722-4817

Paul K. Plunkett	James T. Plunkett

For full biographical listings, see the Martindale-Hubbell Law Directory

SURRETT & COLEMAN, P.A. (AV)

901 Suntrust Bank Building, P.O. Box 1497, 30903
Telephone: 706-722-3301
Telecopier: 706-722-3318

Carl J. Surrett	Edward J. Coleman, III

Representative Clients: Sears, Roebuck & Co.; American Home Assurance Co.; Great Southwest Fire Insurance Co.; Duke Buick, Inc.; American Southern Insurance Co.; Scottsdale Insurance Co.; Providence Washington Insurance Co.; Nautilus Insurance Co.

For full biographical listings, see the Martindale-Hubbell Law Directory

THOMPSON & SMITH, P.C. (AV)

2909-A Professional Parkway, 30907
Telephone: 706-855-5600
Telecopier: 706-855-7020

James M. Thompson	Larry I. Smith

For full biographical listings, see the Martindale-Hubbell Law Directory

WARLICK, TRITT & STEBBINS (AV)

15th Floor, First Union Bank Building, 30901
Telephone: 706-722-7543
Fax: 706-722-1822
Columbia County Office: 119 Davis Road, Martinez, Georgia 30907.
Telephone: 706-860-7595.
Fax: 706-860-7597.

(See Next Column)

WARLICK, TRITT & STEBBINS—*Continued*

MEMBERS OF FIRM

William Byrd Warlick   Charles C. Stebbins, III
Roy D. Tritt   E. L. Clark Speese
(Resident, Martinez Office)

ASSOCIATES

D. Scott Broyles   C. Gregory Bryan
Robert C. Threlkeld

OF COUNSEL

Richard E. Miley

For full biographical listings, see the Martindale-Hubbell Law Directory

---

*BARNESVILLE,** Lamar Co. — (Refer to Forsyth)

---

*BLACKSHEAR,** Pierce Co. — (Refer to Waycross)

---

*BRUNSWICK,** Glynn Co.

LAW OFFICES OF JAMES A. BISHOP (AV)

Suite 401, First Federal Plaza, P.O. Box 1396, 31521-1396
Telephone: 912-264-2390
Fax: 912-264-5859

For full biographical listings, see the Martindale-Hubbell Law Directory

---

FENDIG, MCLEMORE, TAYLOR, WHITWORTH & DURHAM, P.C. (AV)

Suite 200 Suntrust Bank Building, P.O. Box 1996, 31521
Telephone: 912-264-4126
Telecopier: 912-264-0591

Albert Fendig, Jr.   Philip R. Taylor
Gilbert C. McLemore, Jr.   David T. Whitworth
James B. Durham

Donna L. Crossland   Beth M. Duncan

Counsel for: Suntrust Bank of S.E. Georgia, N.A.; First Federal Savings Bank; Sea Island Property Owners Assn.; Calsilite Manufacturing Co.; Continental Insurance Cos.; Crum & Forster; MIM Insurance Companies, Inc.; The Hertz Corp.; Insurance Company of North America; United States Fidelity & Guaranty Co.

For full biographical listings, see the Martindale-Hubbell Law Directory

---

GILBERT, HARRELL, GILBERT, SUMERFORD & MARTIN, P.C. (AV)

Suite 200 First Federal Plaza, 31521
Telephone: 912-265-6700
Fax: 912-264-3917

Wallace E. Harrell   Jameson L. Gregg
James B. Gilbert, Jr.   Wallace E. Harrell, III
Rees M. Sumerford   Charles G. Spalding
M. Fleming Martin, III   Lisa Godbey
Monroe Lynn Frey, III   Mark D. Johnson

J. Benedict Hartman

OF COUNSEL

James B. Gilbert   Joseph A. Whittle
H. Hall Ware, III

Attorneys for: Sea Island Co.; American National Bank; Georgia-Pacific Corp.; Atlanta Gas Light Co.; Sea Harvest Packing Co.; Zurich General Accident & Liability Insurance Co.; Lumbermens Mutual Casualty Co.; BMW of North America.
Assistant Division Counsel for: Southern Railway Co.
Counsel for: Hercules Inc.

For full biographical listings, see the Martindale-Hubbell Law Directory

---

ROUNTREE & SOUTHER (AV)

A Partnership including a Professional Corporation
708 G Street, P.O. Box 1414, 31521
Telephone: 912-264-6606
FAX: 912-264-6649

MEMBERS OF FIRM

George M. Rountree (P.C.)   R. Michael Souther

Representative Clients: General Motors Acceptance Corp.; C&S/Sovran Credit; Sears, Roebuck & Co.; Greentree Financial Corp.; First Federal Savings Bank of Brunswick; Murray Logging Co.

For full biographical listings, see the Martindale-Hubbell Law Directory

---

WHELCHEL, BROWN, READDICK & BUMGARTNER (AV)

5 Glynn Avenue, P.O. Box 220, 31521-0220
Telephone: 912-264-8544
Telecopier: 912-264-9667

(See Next Column)

MEMBERS OF FIRM

J. Thomas Whelchel   Terry L. Readdick
Richard A. Brown, Jr.   John E. Bumgartner
B. Kaye Katz

ASSOCIATES

G. Todd Carter   Raleigh W. Rollins, Jr.
Richard K. Strickland   Bradley J. Watkins

Representative Clients: Georgia Power Co.; Sears, Roebuck & Co.; Allstate Insurance Co.; Commercial Union Insurance Co.; Georgia Farm Bureau Mutual Insurance Co.; Government Employees Insurance Co.; Nationwide Insurance Co.; State Farm Insurance Cos.; Wausau Insurance Cos.

For full biographical listings, see the Martindale-Hubbell Law Directory

---

*BUCHANAN,** Haralson Co. — (Refer to Cedartown)

---

*BUENA VISTA,** Marion Co. — (Refer to Columbus)

BUFORD, Gwinnett Co.

CHANDLER AND BRITT (AV)

4350 South Lee Street, P.O. Box 1749, 30518
Telephone: 770-271-2991
Fax: 770-271-2986

MEMBERS OF FIRM

Richard B. Chandler, Jr.   Gregory D. Jay
Walt M. Britt   W. Wade Beavers

For full biographical listings, see the Martindale-Hubbell Law Directory

---

GIBSON DEAN II, P.C. (AV)

109 Main Street, P.O. Box 939, 30518
Telephone: 770-945-4976
Fax: 770-945-0234

Gibson Dean II

Reference: Peoples Bank & Trust.

For full biographical listings, see the Martindale-Hubbell Law Directory

---

*BUTLER,** Taylor Co. — (Refer to Macon)

---

*CAIRO,** Grady Co. — (Refer to Thomasville)

---

*CALHOUN,** Gordon Co.

CHANCE & MADDOX (AV)

204 North Wall Street, P.O. Box 577, 30703-0577
Telephone: 706-629-4407
Fax: 706-625-2488

MEMBERS OF FIRM

Ronald F. Chance (1908-1995)   J. C. Maddox
Tommy Lee Maddox

Representative Clients: Bowater, Inc.; Basic Materials, Inc.; Willcan, Inc.
Approved Attorneys for: Lawyers Title Insurance Corp. (Policy Issuing Agent); Farmers Home Administration; The Federal Land Bank of Columbia; Astro Dye Works, Inc.; Superior Manufactor Group; Atlanta Gas Light Co.; Georgia Power Company.

For full biographical listings, see the Martindale-Hubbell Law Directory

---

*CAMILLA,** Mitchell Co.

FRANK C. VANN (AV)

47 East Oakland Avenue, P.O. Box 387, 31730
Telephone: 912-336-8231
Fax: 912-336-8542

ASSOCIATE

Gregory A. Clark

Representative Clients: Baker County Bank; Mitchell County Board of Education; McNair Farms; Pinecliff Gin, Inc.; Mitchell County Farm Service, Inc.; Cagle Foods JV, L.L.C.

For full biographical listings, see the Martindale-Hubbell Law Directory

---

*CANTON,** Cherokee Co. — (Refer to Jasper)

---

*CARROLLTON,** Carroll Co.

TISINGER, TISINGER, VANCE & GREER, A PROFESSIONAL CORPORATION (AV)

100 Wagon Yard Plaza, P.O. Box 2069, 30117
Telephone: 770-834-4467
Fax: 770-834-5426

David H. Tisinger   G. Gregory Shadrix
Richard G. Tisinger, Sr.   Douglas C. Vassy
J. Thomas Vance   Phillip D. Wilkins
Thomas E. Greer   Stacey L. Blackmon
Kevin B. Buice   Steven T. Minor
C. David Mecklin, Jr.   Brian L. Howell

(See Next Column)

TISINGER, TISINGER, VANCE & GREER A PROFESSIONAL CORPORATION, *Carrollton—Continued*

Glenn M. Jarrell	Richard G. Tisinger, Jr.
David F. Miceli	John A. Harris
	Edith Freeman Rooks

Representative Clients: Atlanta Casualty Company; Carroll County Board of Education; Carrollton Federal Bank-FSB; City of Bowdon; City of Villa Rica; Georgia Farm Bureau Mutual Insurance Company; St. Paul Fire and Marine Insurance Company; Southwire Company; State Farm Mutual Automobile Insurance Company; Tanner Medical Center, Inc.

For full biographical listings, see the Martindale-Hubbell Law Directory

---

CARTERSVILLE,* Bartow Co.

AKIN & TATE, L.L.C. (AV)

11 West Public Square, P.O. Box 878, 30120
Telephone: 770-382-0780 and 770-386-4346
Facsimile: 770-386-1452

Warren Akin	Wm. Morgan Akin
	S. Lester Tate, III

Representative Clients: Georgia Power Co.; Bartow County Bank; Lumbermens Mutual Casualty Co.; Bartow Mutual Insurance Co.; Dan River Mills, Inc.; Phillips Fibers Corp. (Division of Phillips Petroleum Corp.); Nationwide Insurance Co.; Grange Mutual; First Brands Corporation.

For full biographical listings, see the Martindale-Hubbell Law Directory

---

JENKINS & NELSON, P.C. (AV)

15 South Public Square, 30120
Telephone: 770-387-1373
Fax: 770-387-2396

Frank E. Jenkins, III	G. Carey Nelson, P.C.

Kirk R. Fjelstul	Peter R. Olson
	Robert W. Lamb

For full biographical listings, see the Martindale-Hubbell Law Directory

---

CEDARTOWN,* Polk Co.

MUNDY & GAMMAGE, P.C. (AV)

216 Main Street, P.O. Box 930, 30125-0930
Telephone: 706-748-3870
Fax: 706-748-2489
Rome, Georgia Office: The Carnegie Building, 607 Broad Street.
Telephone: 706-290-5180.

Emil Lamar Gammage, Jr.	Miles L. Gammage
William D. Sparks	John S. Husser
(Mrs.) Gerry E. Holmes	B. Jean Crane
George E. Mundy	Kelly A. Benedict

For full biographical listings, see the Martindale-Hubbell Law Directory

---

YORK, McRAE & YORK (AV)

York Building, 117 E. Woodland Street, P.O. Box 246, 30125
Telephone: 770-748-3780
Fax: 770-748-1175

MEMBERS OF FIRM

Glenn T. York, Jr.	Michael D. McRae
	Michael H. York, Sr.

ASSOCIATES

Robert T. Monroe

Local Counsel for: Bowater North American Corp.
Representative Clients: First Federal Bank of Northwest Georgia; Polk School District; City of Cedartown; Cedartown-Polk County Hospital Authority; Cedartown Industrial Development Corp.; Rockmart Development Authority.

For full biographical listings, see the Martindale-Hubbell Law Directory

---

CHATSWORTH,* Murray Co. — (Refer to Dalton)

COCHRAN,* Bleckley Co. — (Refer to Eastman)

COLUMBUS,* Muscogee Co.

DAVIDSON, CALHOUN, MILLER & BUEHLER, P.C. (AV)

The Joseph House, 828 Broadway, P.O. Box 2828, 31902-2828
Telephone: 706-327-2552
Telecopier: 706-323-5838

J. Quentin Davidson, Jr.	David A. Buehler
Marcus B. Calhoun, Jr.	H. Owen Lee
Charles W. Miller	Jeffrey H. Kight

For full biographical listings, see the Martindale-Hubbell Law Directory

---

HATCHER, STUBBS, LAND, HOLLIS & ROTHSCHILD (AV)

A Limited Liability Partnership
Suite 500 The Corporate Center, 233 12th Street, P.O. Box 2707, 31902-2707
Telephone: 706-324-0201
Telecopier: 706-322-7747

MEMBERS OF FIRM

A. Edward Smith (1902-1962)	Charles T. Staples
S. B. Hatcher (1887-1968)	James E. Humes, II
J. Madden Hatcher (1897-1975)	Joseph L. Waldrep
Howell Hollis (1919-1991)	Robert C. Martin, Jr.
Aaron J. Land (1911-Retired)	George W. Mize, Jr.
Albert W. Stubbs	John M. Tanzine, III
Alan F. Rothschild	John McKay Sheftall
William B. Hardegree	Alan F. Rothschild, Jr.
Morton A. Harris	William C. Pound
J. Barrington Vaught	Mote W. Andrews III

ASSOCIATES

C. Morris Mullin	Teri Yancey Callahan
Theodore Darryl (Ted) Morgan	Gregory S. Ellington
	W. Fray McCormick

General Counsel for: SunTrust Bank, West Georgia, N.A.; TOM'S Foods Inc.; Muscogee County Board of Education; Kinnett Dairies, Inc.; St. Francis Hospital, Inc.; Georgia Crown Distributing Co.; The Jordan Company.
Local Counsel for: State Farm Insurance Cos.; AFLAC, Inc.; MAG Mutual Insurance Co.

For full biographical listings, see the Martindale-Hubbell Law Directory

---

POPE, McGLAMRY, KILPATRICK & MORRISON (AV)

A Partnership including Professional Corporations
318 11th Street, 2nd Floor, P.O. Box 2128, 31902-2128
Telephone: 706-324-0050;
Phenix City, Alabama: 334-298-7354
Atlanta, Georgia Office: 83 Walton Street, N.W., P.O. Box 1733, 30303.
Telephone: 404-523-7706.

MEMBERS OF FIRM

C. Neal Pope (P.C.)	Michael L. McGlamry
Max R. McGlamry (P.C.)	Earle F. Lasseter
(Resident)	William Usher Norwood, III
Paul V. Kilpatrick, Jr.	(Resident, Atlanta Office)
(Resident)	William J. Cornwell
R. Timothy Morrison	Jay F. Hirsch
	Wade H. Tomlinson, III

RESIDENT ASSOCIATES

Joan S. Redmond	Teresa Pike Majors
	Matthew N. Pope

Reference: Columbus Bank & Trust Co.

For full biographical listings, see the Martindale-Hubbell Law Directory

---

ROTHSCHILD & MORGAN (AV)

1030 First Avenue, P.O. Box 2788, 31902-2788
Telephone: 706-324-4167
FAX: 706-324-1969

MEMBERS OF FIRM

Martelle Layfield, Jr.	Jerome M. Rothschild
(1937-1989)	W. Donald Morgan, Jr.

ASSOCIATES

Neal J. Callahan

Reference: Columbus Bank and Trust Company.

For full biographical listings, see the Martindale-Hubbell Law Directory

---

COMMERCE, Jackson Co.

GREGORY M. PERRY (AV)

1774 North Broad Street, P.O. Box 299, 30529
Telephone: 706-335-3500
Fax: 706-335-5299

Representative Clients: Community Bank & Trust.
Local Counsel for: J.M. Huber Corp.

For full biographical listings, see the Martindale-Hubbell Law Directory

---

CONYERS,* Rockdale Co.

TALLEY & SHARP, P.C. (AV)

883 Commerce Drive, Suite 2B, P.O. Box 457, 30207
Telephone: 770-483-1431
Fax: 770-483-4912

Robert E. Talley	Janice Chandler Sharp

Daniel S. Digby

(See Next Column)

TALLEY & SHARP P.C.—*Continued*

LEGAL SUPPORT PERSONNEL
Kimberly A. Rowe

Attorneys for: City of Conyers; Trust Company Bank; Snapping Shoals Electric Membership Corp.; Housing Authority of Conyers, Georgia; Rockdale Hospital, Inc.

For full biographical listings, see the Martindale-Hubbell Law Directory

---

CORDELE,* Crisp Co.

DAVIS, GREGORY, CHRISTY & FOREHAND (AV)

708 East Sixteenth Avenue, P.O. Drawer 5230, 31010
Telephone: 912-273-7150
Fax: 912-273-7578
Vienna, Georgia Office: 104 West Union Street, P.O. Box 397.
Telephone: 912-268-4125.
Telecopier: 912-268-6373.

MEMBERS OF FIRM

Hardy Gregory, Jr.   John N. Davis
Gary C. Christy   David A. Forehand, Jr.

ASSOCIATES
Preyesh Kantilal Maniklal

OF COUNSEL
T. Hoyt Davis, Jr.

For full biographical listings, see the Martindale-Hubbell Law Directory

---

COVINGTON,* Newton Co. — (Refer to Monroe)

DAHLONEGA,* Lumpkin Co. — (Refer to Gainesville)

DALTON,* Whitfield Co.

MINOR, BELL & NEAL, P.C. (AV)

202 West Waugh Street, P.O. Box 2666, 30722-2666
Telephone: 706-226-2666
Telecopier: 706-278-3569

John T. Minor, III   William F. Jourdain
William W. Bell, Jr.   Harvard H. Kranzlein, Jr.
John P. Neal, III   Michael J. Tuck
John T. Minor, IV   Robert D. Jenkins
Stephen B. Farrow   Robert G. McCurry
                M. Shane Lovingood

For full biographical listings, see the Martindale-Hubbell Law Directory

MITCHELL & MITCHELL, P.C. (AV)

101 North Thornton Avenue, 30720
Telephone: 706-278-2040
Fax: 706-278-3040

D. Wright Mitchell (1895-1970)   James H. Bisson, III
Douglas W. Mitchell   Terry L. Miller
  (1921-1984)   Susan Williams Bisson
Erwin Mitchell   William J. Kimsey
Neil Wester   G. Gargandi Vaughn

Counsel for: The City of Dalton, Georgia; Conquest Carpet Mills, Inc.
Local Counsel for: Bituminous Casualty Corp.; CSX Corp.; NationsBank of Dalton, Georgia.
Reference: Nations Bank of Dalton, Georgia.

For full biographical listings, see the Martindale-Hubbell Law Directory

---

DAWSON,* Terrell Co. — (Refer to Albany)

DECATUR,* De Kalb Co.

DAVIS & DAVIS (AV)

921 Wachovia Bank Building, 30030
Telephone: 404-373-2531

Jefferson James Davis   Patricia Kunze Davis

Reference: Wachovia Bank of Atlanta.

For full biographical listings, see the Martindale-Hubbell Law Directory

HYATT & HYATT, P.C. (AV)

Suite 201, Trust Building, 545 North McDonough Street, 30030
Telephone: 404-378-3635
Fax: 404-377-8304

Charles H. Hyatt (1924-1995)   John M. Hyatt

For full biographical listings, see the Martindale-Hubbell Law Directory

---

KIDD & WITCHER (AV)

A Professional Association, Not a Partnership
118 East Trinity Place, 30030
Telephone: 404-373-1626
Facsimile: 404-378-0152

R. Hopkins Kidd   William G. Witcher, Jr.
          Thomas M. Witcher

For full biographical listings, see the Martindale-Hubbell Law Directory

SIMMONS, WARREN, SZCZECKO & McFEE, PROFESSIONAL ASSOCIATION (AV)

315 West Ponce de Leon Avenue, Suite 850, 30030
Telephone: 404-378-1711
Fax: 404-377-6101

M. T. Simmons, Jr.   Joseph Szczecko
Wesley B. Warren, Jr.   William C. McFee, Jr.

Representative Clients: David Hocker & Associates (Shopping Center Development); Julian LeCraw & Company (Real Estate); Intown Suites, Inc.; Preferred Lodging Systems, Inc.; Royal Oldsmobile.; Cotter & Co.; Atlanta Neurosurgical Associates, P.A.; Troncalli Motors, Inc.

For full biographical listings, see the Martindale-Hubbell Law Directory

---

DONALSONVILLE,* Seminole Co. — (Refer to Bainbridge)

DORAVILLE, De Kalb Co.

CHESNUT & LIVINGSTON, P.C. (AV)

6485 Peachtree Industrial Boulevard, 30360
Telephone: 770-458-7606
Fax: 770-457-6082

J. David Chesnut   Richard F. Livingston, Jr.
          Tom Pye

Christopher M. Kunkel   Charles A. Krawczyk
          Angela Hsu

For full biographical listings, see the Martindale-Hubbell Law Directory

JOE W. GERSTEIN, P.C. (AV)

6485 Peachtree Industrial Boulevard, 30360
Telephone: 770-458-7606
Fax: 770-457-6082

Joe W. Gerstein

For full biographical listings, see the Martindale-Hubbell Law Directory

---

DOUGLAS,* Coffee Co.

COTTINGHAM & PORTER, P.C. (AV)

319 East Ashley Street, P.O. Box 798, 31534-0798
Telephone: 912-384-1616
Fax: 912-384-1775

Sidney L. Cottingham   Robert L. Porter, Jr.
          William L. Thompson

Representative Clients: Brooks Auto Parts, Inc.; Coats & Clark, Inc.; Coffee County Bank; Coffee County Board of Education; Coffee County Hospital Authority; Douglas-Coffee County Industrial Authority; First National Bank of Coffee County, N.A.; Fletcher Oil Co., Inc.; Golden Poultry Company, Inc.; Joseph Campbell Co.

For full biographical listings, see the Martindale-Hubbell Law Directory

PRESTON & PRESTON, P.C. (AV)

220 East Ward Street, P.O. Box 71, 31533
Telephone: 912-384-4700
Fax: 912-384-5839

Montgomery L. Preston   Robert H. Preston
  (1910-1991)

Edward L. Bagwell, III

Attorneys for: Georgia Power Co.; Joseph R. Campbell Co.; SunTrust Company Bank, South Georgia, N.A. (Douglas Office); Lott Builders Supply Co.; Allstate Insurance Co.; Wal-Mart Stores, Inc.; Woodmen of the World Life Insurance Society; Atlantic Coast Federal Credit Union.
Issuing Agents for: Lawyers Title Insurance Corp.; First American Title Insurance Co.

For full biographical listings, see the Martindale-Hubbell Law Directory

---

EASTMAN,* Dodge Co.

HARRISON & WALL (AV)

202 Norman Avenue, P.O. Box 0967, 31023
Telephone: 912-374-4346

(See Next Column)

HARRISON & WALL, *Eastman—Continued*
MEMBERS OF FIRM
Milton Harrison　　　　　　　　　　Sarah F. Wall

Attorneys for: City of Eastman; City of Chester.
Approved Attorneys for: Lawyers Title Insurance Corp.; Ticor Title Insurance Co.; Kansas City Title Insurance Co.; Federal Land Bank of Columbia, S.C.; Central Georgia Federal Land Bank; Georgia Development Authority.

For full biographical listings, see the Martindale-Hubbell Law Directory

---

SMITH & HARRINGTON (AV)

505 Anson Avenue, P.O. Drawer 130, 31023
Telephone: 912-374-3488
Fax: 912-374-6317
Email: paliden@accucomm.net
MEMBERS OF FIRM
Will Ed Smith (1906-1990)　　　　Wilton D. Harrington
John P. Harrington

For full biographical listings, see the Martindale-Hubbell Law Directory

---

EATONTON, Putnam Co. — (Refer to Monticello)

ELBERTON, Elbert Co.

HEARD, LEVERETT, PHELPS, WEAVER & CAMPBELL (AV)

25 Thomas Street, P.O. Drawer 399, 30635
Telephone: 706-283-2651
Fax: 706-283-2670

Robert M. Heard　　　　　　　　　R. Chris Phelps
E. Freeman Leverett　　　　　　　　Cynthia G. Weaver
　　　　　　Richard D. Campbell

　　　　　　Robert F. Leverett

General Counsel for: Granite City Bank; Coggins Granite, Inc.
Counsel for: Georgia School Boards Assn.; Georgia Telephone Assn.; Elbert County Board of Education; City of Elberton; Fibers & Fabrics of Georgia, Inc.; Pennsylvania Granite Corp.
Approved Attorneys for: Chicago Title Co.; Minnesota Title Co.; South Carolina Title Co.

For full biographical listings, see the Martindale-Hubbell Law Directory

---

SMITH & HODGES (AV)

5 Thomas Street, P.O. Box 520, 30635
Telephone: 706-283-5543
Fax: 706-283-6968
MEMBERS OF FIRM
Truett Smith　　　　　　　　　　　Thomas L. Hodges, III

Attorneys for: First National Bank in Elberton; Elberton Furniture Co.; Elberton-Elbert County Hospital Authority.

For full biographical listings, see the Martindale-Hubbell Law Directory

---

ELLAVILLE, Schley Co. — (Refer to Albany)

FAYETTEVILLE, Fayette Co. — (Refer to Griffin)

FORSYTH, Monroe Co.

HAYGOOD, LYNCH, HARRIS & MELTON (AV)

87 North Lee Street, P.O. Box 657, 31029-2120
Telephone: 912-994-5171
Fax: 912-994-4588
Monticello, Georgia Office: 315 Forsyth Street, 31064.
Telephone: 706-468-8846.
MEMBERS OF FIRM
Charles B. Haygood, Jr.　　　　　Robert L. Harris
Larry Persons Lynch　　　　　　　C. Robert Melton

For full biographical listings, see the Martindale-Hubbell Law Directory

---

FORT VALLEY, Peach Co. — (Refer to Perry)

GAINESVILLE, Hall Co.

HARBEN & HARTLEY (AV)

539 Green Street, P.O. Box 2975, 30503
Telephone: 770-534-7341
Fax: 770-532-0399
MEMBERS OF FIRM
Sam S. Harben, Jr.　　　　　　　Martha McMasters Pearson
Phillip L. Hartley　　　　　　　　Emily Bagwell Harben
LEGAL SUPPORT PERSONNEL
Barbara J. Smith　　　　　　　　　Lisa A. Rosetti

For full biographical listings, see the Martindale-Hubbell Law Directory

---

HULSEY, OLIVER & MAHAR (AV)

200 E.E. Butler Parkway, P.O. Box 1457, 30503
Telephone: 770-532-6312
Fax: 770-531-9230
MEMBERS OF FIRM
E. D. Kenyon (1890-1981)　　　　R. David Syfan
Julius M. Hulsey　　　　　　　　　Jane A. Range
Samuel L. Oliver　　　　　　　　　Joseph D. Cooley, III
James E. Mahar, Jr.　　　　　　　Thomas L. Fitzgerald
　　　　　　Thomas D. Calkins
ASSOCIATES
B. Chan Caudell　　　　　　　　　Abbott S. Hayes, Jr.

Counsel for: Hall County, Georgia; Gainesville Bank & Trust; Lake Lanier Islands Development Authority; Ralston Purina Co.; Continental Grain Co.; Gold Kist, Inc.; Wayne Poultry, Inc.; Crystal Farms, Inc.; Wilheit Packaging Materials, Co.; United Cities Gas Co.

For full biographical listings, see the Martindale-Hubbell Law Directory

---

SMITH, GILLIAM AND WILLIAMS (AV)

200 Old Coca-Cola Building, 301 Green Street, N.W., P.O. Box 1098, 30503
Telephone: 770-536-3381
Fax: 770-531-1481
MEMBERS OF FIRM
R. Wilson Smith, Jr. (1906-1983)　Jerry A. Williams
John H. Smith　　　　　　　　　　Kelly Anne Miles
Steven P. Gilliam　　　　　　　　　Bradley J. Patten
ASSOCIATES
M. Tyler Smith　　　　　　　　　　Scott Arthur Ball

General Counsel for: Gainesville Industrial Electric Co.; Georgia Mutual Insurance, a Stock Company; L & R Farms; H. Wilson Manufacturing Co.; Goforth Electrical Supply; North Georgia Petroleum Co.; Gibbs Management Group, Inc.

For full biographical listings, see the Martindale-Hubbell Law Directory

---

STEWART, MELVIN & FROST (AV)

Hunt Tower, Suite 600, 200 Main Street, P.O. Box 3280, 30503
Telephone: 770-536-0101
Fax: 770-532-2171; 532-5071
MEMBERS OF FIRM
J. Douglas Stewart　　　　　　　J. Kenneth Nix
W. Woodrow Stewart　　　　　　T. Treadwell Syfan
John M. Melvin　　　　　　　　　G. Allen Broxton
Frank W. Armstrong　　　　　　　Steven A. Cornelison
William H. Blalock, Jr.　　　　　D. Thomas LeFevre
J. Randall Frost　　　　　　　　　J. C. Highsmith, Jr.
　　　　　　Mark W. Alexander
OF COUNSEL
Nancy L. Richardson

Representative Clients: The First National Bank of Gainesville; Gainesville & Hall County Development Authority; Georgia Chair Co.; Cargill, Inc.; McKibbon Bros., Inc.; ConAgra Poultry Company; Nationwide Insurance Cos.; The Travelers Cos.

For full biographical listings, see the Martindale-Hubbell Law Directory

---

WHELCHEL & DUNLAP (AV)

(Successors to Dunlap & Dunlap; NL Whelchel, Dunlap & Gignilliat)
405 Washington Street, N.E., P.O. Box 1, 30501
Telephone: 770-532-7211
Telecopier: 770-532-7361
MEMBERS OF FIRM
Edgar B. Dunlap (1892-1955)　　John A. Gram
William P. Whelchel (1895-1975)　Edgar B. Dunlap, II
William A. Bagwell　　　　　　　Thomas M. Cole
Wright Willingham　　　　　　　Thomas S. Bishop
William L. Rogers, Jr.　　　　　　Madeline S. Wirt
ASSOCIATES
Charles N. Kelley, Jr.　　　　　　Gregg Mitchel Porter
Carolina Den Brok-Perez　　　　Jason S. Rooks
OF COUNSEL
James A. Dunlap

General Counsel for: SunTrust Bank Northeast Georgia; Housing Authority of City of Gainesville; The Citizens Bank of Gainesville; Northeast Georgia Medical Center, Inc.
Counsel for: Georgia Power Co.; Milliken & Co.; Johnson & Johnson; Atlanta Gas Light Co.; CSX Transportation Inc.; CIGNA Property and Casualty Cos.

For full biographical listings, see the Martindale-Hubbell Law Directory

---

GREENSBORO, Greene Co. — (Refer to Madison)

GREENVILLE, Meriwether Co. — (Refer to La Grange)

GRIFFIN, Spalding Co.

CUMMING, CUMMING & ESARY (AV)

322 South Sixth Street, P.O. Box 577, 30224
Telephone: 770-227-3746
Fax: 770-227-3891

MEMBERS OF FIRM

D. R. Cumming (1888-1970)   W. Barron Cumming
Joseph R. Cumming (1906-1990)   Sidney R. Esary

Counsel for: First National Bank of Griffin; United Bank of Griffin; Rushton Cotton Mills.
Approved Attorneys for: Lawyers Title Insurance Corp.; Chicago Title Insurance Co.; Stewart Title Company.

For full biographical listings, see the Martindale-Hubbell Law Directory

---

ROBERT H. SMALLEY, JR. PROFESSIONAL CORPORATION (AV)

115 North Sixth Street, P.O. Box 907, 30224
Telephone: 770-228-2125
Telecopier: 770-228-5018

Robert H. Smalley, Jr.   Thomas E. Baynham, III

Representative Clients: The Bank Holding Company; The Bank of Spalding County; First Community Bank of Henry County; Griffin Spalding County Development Authority; Masada Communications, Ltd. (CATV); Union Camp Corp. (Local Counsel).

For full biographical listings, see the Martindale-Hubbell Law Directory

HARTWELL, Hart Co.

GORDON LAW FIRM (AV)

Gordon Building, P.O. Box 870, 30643
Telephone: 706-376-5418
FAX: 706-376-5416
Email: wgordon@counsel.com

Walter James Gordon

Eleanor Patat Cotton   Kimberly A. Wilkerson
LEGAL SUPPORT PERSONNEL
Flo W. Brown

References: NationsBank of Georgia, N.A.; The Bank of Hartwell; Athens First Bank & Trust Company.

For full biographical listings, see the Martindale-Hubbell Law Directory

HAWKINSVILLE, Pulaski Co. — (Refer to Perry)

HAZLEHURST, Jeff Davis Co. — (Refer to Eastman)

HINESVILLE, Liberty Co.

JONES, OSTEEN, JONES & ARNOLD (AV)

206 East Court Street, P.O. Box 800, 31313
Telephone: 912-876-0111
Cable Address: "JOJA"
Fax: 912-368-2979

MEMBERS OF FIRM

Charles M. Jones   Billy N. Jones
J. Noel Osteen   Jeffery L. Arnold
ASSOCIATES
G. Brinson Williams, Jr.   Mark W. Nickerson
Linnie L. Darden, III   L. Kelly Davis

General Counsel for: The Hinesville Bank; The Coastal Bank; Coastal Utilities, Inc.; Coastal Electric Membership Corp.; Liberty County Hospital Authority; Hinesville Area Board of Realtors; Liberty County Industrial Authority; Liberty County, Georgia; City of Riceboro.

For full biographical listings, see the Martindale-Hubbell Law Directory

JEFFERSON, Jackson Co. — (Refer to Athens)

JESUP, Wayne Co.

HOWARD, CARSWELL & BENNETT, P.C. (AV)

Lawyers Building, 145 North Brunswick Street, P.O. Box 543, 31598-0543
Telephone: 912-427-4268

Joseph H. Thomas (1909-1984)   Kenneth R. Carswell
Hubert H. Howard   R. Violet Bennett

Representative Clients: Graward General Companies; Independent Fire Insurance Companies; Georgia Insurers Insolvency Pool; The Seibels Bruce Insurance Company; Cigna; Rayonier, Inc.; Georgia Power Co.; Southern Trust Insurance Co.; Cotton States Insurance Co.; Lawyers Title Insurance Corp.;

For full biographical listings, see the Martindale-Hubbell Law Directory

JONESBORO, Clayton Co.

DRIEBE & DRIEBE, P.C. (AV)

6 Courthouse Way, P.O. Box 975, 30237
Telephone: 770-478-8894
Fax: 770-478-9606
Atlanta, Georgia Office: 152 Nassau Street, N.W.
Telephone: 404-524-0606.

Charles J. Driebe   Charles J. Driebe, Jr.

Approved Attorneys for: First American Title Insurance Co.; Attorney's Title Guaranty Fund.
Representative Clients: Henry County Airport, Inc.; Clayton News/Daily; Atlanta Beach Sports & Entertainment Park, Inc.; Los Toribios Mexican Restaurants, Inc.

For full biographical listings, see the Martindale-Hubbell Law Directory

---

OLIVER, DUCKWORTH, SPARGER & WINKLE, P.C. (AV)

146 McDonough Street, P.O. Box 37, 30236
Telephone: 770-478-8883
Fax: 770-473-0872

G. Robert Oliver   Kevin W. Sparger
              David P. Winkle

Kathy Brown Valencia
OF COUNSEL
William H. Duckworth, Jr.

Local Counsel for: Department of Transportation, State of Georgia.
Representative Clients: Clayton County Hospital Authority; Clayton County Water Authority; Clayton State College Foundation, Inc.; Clayton County Development Authority; Low Temp Industries, Inc.; Medical Association of Georgia Mutual Insurance Co.

For full biographical listings, see the Martindale-Hubbell Law Directory

LA FAYETTE, Walker Co.

WATSON & DANA (AV)

Corner Duke and Withers Streets, P.O. Box 1496, 30728
Telephone: 706-638-5225
Fax: 706-638-8070

MEMBERS OF FIRM
Dennis D. Watson   Joseph F. Dana
ASSOCIATES
David D. Gottlieb

Representative Clients: Bank of Dade, Trenton, Georgia; Walker County, Georgia; Synthetic Industries, Inc.; The Hospital Authority of Walker, Dade and Catoosa Counties; Cuna Mutual Insurance Group; Georgia Farm Bureau Mutual Insurance Company; MMI Companies, Inc.; National Union Fire Insurance Company; Nationwide Mutual Insurance Company; Preferred Risk Mutual Insurance Company.

For full biographical listings, see the Martindale-Hubbell Law Directory

---

THE WOMACK LAW FIRM (AV)

109 East Patton Avenue, P.O. Box 549, 30728
Telephone: 706-638-2234
FAX: 706-638-3173

MEMBERS OF FIRM
Ronald R. Womack
ASSOCIATES
John T. Siess

Counsel for: City of LaFayette; Housing Authority of the City of LaFayette; Walker County Board of Education; City of Trenton; State of Georgia Department of Transportation; Radix Broadcasting, Inc.

For full biographical listings, see the Martindale-Hubbell Law Directory

LA GRANGE, Troup Co.

DUNCAN, THOMASSON & ACREE (AV)

18 North LaFayette Square, P.O. Box 1168, 30241
Telephone: 706-882-7731
FAX: 706-845-1717

MEMBERS OF FIRM
Thurman E. Duncan   James T. Thomasson, Jr.
              Marc E. Acree

General Counsel for: Mountville Mills, Inc.; Daniel Realty & Insurance Co., Inc.; Commercial Bank and Trust Company of Troup County; Radiology Associates of West Georgia, P.C.; Woodbury Business Forms, Inc.
Approved Attorneys for: Lawyers Title Insurance Corp.; Chicago Title Insurance Co.

For full biographical listings, see the Martindale-Hubbell Law Directory

La Grange—Continued

LEWIS, TAYLOR & TODD, P.C. (AV)

304 Church Street, 30241
Telephone: 706-882-2501
Fax: 706-882-4905

George E. Sims, Jr. (1917-1967)	John M. Taylor
James R. Lewis	Jeffrey M. Todd
	Alex L. Dixon

Counsel for: Callaway Foundation, Inc.; Nations Bank; The City of La Grange; West Georgia Medical Center; Troup County Board of Education; Harris County Board of Education.
Local Counsel for: State Farm Mutual Automobile Insurance Co.; Liberty Mutual Insurance Co.
Approved Attorneys for: Ticor Title Insurance Co.; Lawyers Title Insurance Corp.

For full biographical listings, see the Martindale-Hubbell Law Directory

---

LAWRENCEVILLE, * Gwinnett Co.

ANDERSEN, DAVIDSON & TATE, P.C. (AV)

324 West Pike Street, Suite 200, P.O. Box 2000, 30246-2000
Telephone: 770-822-0900
Telecopier: 770-822-9680

Thomas J. Andersen	Thomas T. Tate
Gerald Davidson, Jr.	Jeffrey R. Mahaffey
	William M. Ray, II

Kathleen B. Guy	Tracey D. Mason
Jonathan D. Crumly	Michael J. Hay

OF COUNSEL

Ethel D. Andersen	R. Bradley Carr

References: Sun Trust Bank; The Bank of Gwinnett County; Chicago Title Insurance Co.; Title Insurance Company of Minnesota.

For full biographical listings, see the Martindale-Hubbell Law Directory

---

THOMPSON & SWEENY, P.C. (AV)

690 Longleaf Drive, P.O. Drawer 1250, 30246
Telephone: 770-963-1997
Telecopier: 770-822-2913

Virgil Lee Thompson, Jr.	Melanie D. Williams
Victoria Sweeny	Paul E. Andrew
	Jorgia C. Northrup

Representative Clients: Gwinnett County Board of Education; City of Auburn, Georgia; City of Sugar Hill, Georgia; City of Duluth, Georgia; City of Grayson, Georgia; Downtown Development Authority of Lawrenceville, Georgia; Hayes, James & Associates, Inc.

For full biographical listings, see the Martindale-Hubbell Law Directory

---

WEBB, TANNER & POWELL (AV)

Suite 300 Gwinnett Federal Building, 750 South Perry Street, P.O. Box 27, 30246
Telephone: 770-962-8545; 963-3423
Fax: 770-963-3424

MEMBERS OF FIRM

Jones Webb	Anthony O. L. Powell
William G. Tanner	Ralph L. Taylor, III
	Andrew R. Mertz

ASSOCIATES

Robert Jackson Wilson	A. Louise Tanner
Steven A. Pickens	Kevin T. Caiaccio

Attorneys for: Brand Banking Co.; City of Lawrenceville, Ga.; Water and Sewer Authority of Gwinnett County; West Georgia Farm Credit, ACA; Georgia Power Co.; Lawyers Title Insurance Corp.; Young Harris College, Young Harris, Georgia; Chicago Title Insurance Co.; International Safety Instruments.

For full biographical listings, see the Martindale-Hubbell Law Directory

---

LOUISVILLE, * Jefferson Co.

ABBOT, MURPHY AND HARVEY, P.C. (AV)

190 East 7th Street, P.O. Box 31, 30434
Telephone: 912-625-7281
Facsimile: 912-625-8200

W. Wright Abbot (1892-1969)	John R. Murphy, III
James C. Abbot	Fred K. Harvey, Jr.

B. Michael Arrington

Representative Clients: First National Bank & Trust Co., Louisville, Georgia; City of Louisville; J. M. Huber Corp.; Jefferson E.M.C.; Town of Bartow; Bank of Wadley; Forstmann and Company, Inc.; Fulghum Industries, Inc.; Hospital Authority of Jefferson County.

(See Next Column)

For full biographical listings, see the Martindale-Hubbell Law Directory

LYONS, * Toombs Co. — (Refer to Metter)

MACON, * Bibb Co.

ANDERSON, WALKER & REICHERT, P.C. (AV)

Suite 404 SunTrust Bank Building, P.O. Box 6497, 31208-6497
Telephone: 912-743-8651
Telecopier: 912-743-9636

R. Lanier Anderson (1871-1959)	Thomas L. Bass
R. Lanier Anderson, Jr. (1899-1984)	Albert P. Reichert, Jr.
Charles W. Walker (1905-1984)	John D. Reeves
Mallory C. Atkinson, Jr. (1939-1990)	Eugene S. Hatcher
Albert P. Reichert	Robert A. B. Reichert
	Susan S. Cole
	Jonathan A. Alderman
	Brown W. Dennis, Jr.

Charles E. Cox, Jr.	Travis M. Trimble
Ramsey T. Way, Jr.	Samuel G. Alderman, III
	Laura H. Wanamaker

Representative Clients: Riverwood International USA, Inc.; Hospital Corporation of America; Pepsi-Cola Bottling Company of Macon; Radiology Associates of Macon, P.C.; Thiele Kaolin Company; SunTrust Bank of Middle Georgia, N.A.
General Insurance Clients: Liberty Mutual Insurance Co.; Alexis, Inc.

For full biographical listings, see the Martindale-Hubbell Law Directory

---

CHAMBLESS, HIGDON & CARSON (AV)

Suite 200 Ambrose Baber Building, 577 Walnut Street, P.O. Box 246, 31298-5399
Telephone: 912-745-1181
Telecopier: 912-746-9479

MEMBERS OF FIRM

Joseph H. Davis	Thomas F. Richardson
Joseph H. Chambless	Mary Mendel Katz
David B. Higdon	Emmitte H. Griggs
James F. Carson, Jr.	Marc T. Treadwell

ASSOCIATES

Kim H. Stroup	Jon Christopher Wolfe
	James D. Tolliver

LEGAL SUPPORT PERSONNEL

Angie Horton	Erie Reed

Local Counsel for: Atlanta Gas Light Co.; First Union National Bank of Georgia; Security National Bank.

For full biographical listings, see the Martindale-Hubbell Law Directory

---

HALL, BLOCH, GARLAND & MEYER (AV)

1500 Charter Medical Building, P.O. Box 5088, 31213-3199
Telephone: 912-745-1625
Telecopier: 912-741-8822

MEMBERS OF FIRM

J. E. Hall (1876-1945)	Benjamin M. Garland
Charles J. Bloch (1893-1974)	J. Patrick Meyer, Jr.
Ellsworth Hall, Jr. (1908-1984)	J. Steven Stewart
J. René Hawkins (1924-1971)	J. Burton Wilkerson, Jr.
Ellsworth Hall, III	Duncan D. Walker, III
F. Kennedy Hall	Mark E. Toth

ASSOCIATES

John Flanders Kennedy	Todd C. Brooks
	Kimberly Cofer Harris

F. Kennedy Hall, Division Counsel (Georgia): Norfolk Southern Railway Company.
Counsel for: Wachovia Bank of Georgia, N.A.; Helena Chemical Corp.; Bell-South Mobility, Inc.; Fickling & Walker Asset and Property Management, Inc.; Navistar International Corporation.

For full biographical listings, see the Martindale-Hubbell Law Directory

---

HARRIS & JAMES (AV)

600 First Liberty Bank Tower, 201 Second Street, P.O. Box 4866, 31208-4866
Telephone: 912-745-9661
Telecopier: 912-745-9824

MEMBERS OF FIRM

John B. Harris, Jr.	John Burke Harris, III
John E. James	William C. Harris
	Kathryn Weigand Gerhardt

ASSOCIATES

Lisa Neill-Beckmann	Charles E. Johnson, III

(See Next Column)

HARRIS & JAMES—*Continued*

OF COUNSEL
Sarah Stevenson Harris

Representative Clients: Dry Branch Kaolin Co.; Georgia Department of Transportation; Jefferson-Pilot Life Insurance Co.; Public Service Telephone Co.; Riverside Cemetery; Hart's Mortuary; Macon Orthopedic & Hand Center, P.A.; Rivoli Orthopedic Assn., P.A.; Southeastern Store Owners Assn.; G C Quality Lubricants, Inc.

For full biographical listings, see the Martindale-Hubbell Law Directory

JONES, CORK & MILLER (AV)

435 Second Street, Fifth Floor, P.O. Box 6437, 31201-2724
Telephone: 912-745-2821
Telecopier: 912-743-9609
Email: lawyer@jonescork.com

MEMBERS OF FIRM

C. Baxter Jones (1895-1968)	Thomas C. Alexander
Charles M. Cork (1908-1982)	C. Ashley Royal
Charles M. Cork, Jr.	Robert C. Norman, Jr.
Carr G. Dodson	Jerry A. Lumley
Timothy K. Adams	John T. Mitchell, Jr.
John C. Cork	W. Carter Bates III
H. Jerome Strickland	Timothy Harden, III
Hubert C. Lovein, Jr.	Howard J. Strickland, Jr.
W. Warren Plowden, Jr.	Cater C. Thompson
Rufus D. Sams, III	Thomas W. Joyce
Thomas C. James, III	Brandon A. Oren
Steve L. Wilson	W. Kerry Howell

ASSOCIATES

David A. Pope	Scott W. Spivey
William T. Prescott	Sharon Hurt Reeves

Alan G. Snipes

OF COUNSEL

Wallace Miller, Jr.	John W. Smith

General Counsel for: The Bibb Co.; Sun Trust Bank Middle Georgia, N.A.; First Liberty Bank; Wesleyan College; Bibb County Board of Education.
Division Counsel for: Georgia Power Co.
Represent Locally: Southern Bell Telephone & Telegraph Co.; Allstate Insurance Co.; The City of Macon; St. Paul Fire & Marine Insurance Co.

For full biographical listings, see the Martindale-Hubbell Law Directory

O'NEAL, BROWN & SIZEMORE, A PROFESSIONAL CORPORATION (AV)

Suite 1001, American Federal Building, 544 Mulberry Street, 31201
Telephone: 912-742-8981
Telecopier: 912-743-5035
Atlanta, Georgia Office: Suite 2600, One Atlanta Plaza, 950 East Paces Ferry Road, N.E.
Telephone: 404-237-6701.
Telecopier: 404-233-1267.

H. T. O'Neal, Jr. (1924-1983)   Manley F. Brown
Lamar W. Sizemore, Jr.

John C. Clark
OF COUNSEL
James M. Wootan

For full biographical listings, see the Martindale-Hubbell Law Directory

SELL & MELTON (AV)

A Partnership including a Professional Corporation
14th Floor, Charter Medical Building, P.O. Box 229, 31297-2899
Telephone: 912-746-8521
Telecopier: 912-745-6426

Andrew W. McKenna (1918-1981)	Joseph W. Popper, Jr.
E. S. Sell, Jr.	Doye E. Green
John D. Comer	Edward S. Sell, III
Buckner F. Melton	John A. Draughon
Mitchel P. House, Jr.	R. (Chix) Miller
	Russell M. Boston (P.C.)

Brian J. Passante

ASSOCIATES

Jeffrey B. Hanson	David M. Cusson
Robert D. McCullers	John E. Payne
Michelle W. Johnson	W. Baxley Chew

LEGAL SUPPORT PERSONNEL
Linda Luck

General Counsel for: Macon Telegraph Publishing Co. (The Macon Telegraph); Macon-Bibb County Hospital Authority; County of Bibb; County of Twiggs; Smith & Sons Foods, Inc. (S & S Cafeterias); Macon Bibb County Industrial Authority; Burgess Pigment Co.

For full biographical listings, see the Martindale-Hubbell Law Directory

---

MADISON,* Morgan Co.

LAMBERT & ROFFMAN (AV)

126 East Washington Street, P.O. Box 169, 30650
Telephone: 706-342-3566
Telecopier: 706-342-9683

MEMBERS OF FIRM

E. R. Lambert	Allan R. Roffman

ASSOCIATES

M. Joseph Reitman, Jr.	Mark W. Dauenhauer

Representative Clients: Corporate: Walton Electric Membership Corp.; Wellington-Puritan, Inc.; Bank of Madison. Local Governments: Morgan County Board of Commissioners; City of Madison; City of Social Circle; Walton County Water and Sewage Authority.
Local Counsel: SunTrust Bank, Northeast Georgia, N.A.; Evergreen Timberlands Corp.

For full biographical listings, see the Martindale-Hubbell Law Directory

---

MARIETTA,* Cobb Co.

AWTREY AND PARKER, P.C. (AV)

211 Roswell Street, P.O. Box 997, 30061
Telephone: 770-424-8000
Fax: 770-424-1594

L. M. Awtrey, Jr. (1915-1986)	Donald A. Mangerie (1924-1988)
George L. Dozier, Jr.	Barbara H. Martin
Harvey D. Harkness	A. Sidney Parker
Mike Harrison	Robert B. Silliman

General Counsel for: Kennesaw Finance Co.; Cobb Electric Membership Corporation; Development Authority of Cobb County.
Local Counsel for: Coats & Clark; Bell South Mobility; Lockheed-Georgia Corp.; Post Properties, Inc.; CSX Transportation, Inc.

For full biographical listings, see the Martindale-Hubbell Law Directory

CUSTER & HILL, P.C. (AV)

241 Washington Avenue, P.O. Box 1224, 30061
Telephone: 770-429-8300
Fax: 770-429-8338

Lawrence B. Custer	Douglas A. Hill

Danna Lambert Wolfe
Reference: First Union National Bank.

For full biographical listings, see the Martindale-Hubbell Law Directory

DOWNEY & CLEVELAND (AV)

288 Washington Avenue, 30060
Telephone: 770-422-3233
Fax: 770-423-4199

OF COUNSEL
Lynn A. Downey
MEMBERS OF FIRM

Robert H. Cleveland (1940-1989)	Y. Kevin Williams
	Russell B. Davis
Joseph C. Parker	G. Lee Welborn
	Rodney S. Shockley

ASSOCIATES

W. Curtis Anderson	Todd E. Hatcher
Scott D. Clay	Richard A. Griggs
	Tara M. Waller

Representative Clients: Allstate Insurance Co.; St. Paul Insurance Cos.; Georgia Farm Bureau Mutual Insurance Co.; State Farm Insurance Cos.; Cotton States Mutual Insurance Co.; Colonial Insurance Co. of California; Progressive Insurance Company; Auto Owners Insurance Company; Deep South Surplus, Inc.; Ed Voyles Oldsmobile, Honda and Chrysler-Plymouth.

For full biographical listings, see the Martindale-Hubbell Law Directory

---

MCDONOUGH,* Henry Co.

SMITH, WELCH, STUDDARD & BRITTAIN (AV)

200 The Commerce Building, 235 Keys Ferry Street, P.O. Box 31, 30253
Telephone: 770-957-3937
Fax: 770-957-9165
Stockbridge, Georgia Office: 1231-A Eagle's Landing Parkway.
Telephone: 770-389-4864.
Fax: 770-389-5157.

MEMBERS OF FIRM

Ernest M. Smith (1911-1992)	Ben W. Studdard, III
A. J. Welch, Jr.	J. Mark Brittain
	(Resident, Stockbridge Office)

(See Next Column)

SMITH, WELCH, STUDDARD & BRITTAIN, *McDonough*—Continued

ASSOCIATES

Patrick D. Jaugstetter	Shawn Marie Story
E. Gilmore Maxwell	Arthur Scully Barbee

Representative Clients: Alliance Corp.; Atlanta Motor Speedway, Inc.; Bellamy-Strickland Chevrolet, Inc.; Ceramic and Metal Coatings Corp.; City of Hampton; City of Locust Grove; City of Stockbridge.

For full biographical listings, see the Martindale-Hubbell Law Directory

---

METTER,* Candler Co.

JONES AND SMITH, P.C. (AV)

21 North Kennedy Street, P.O. Box 296, 30439
Telephone: 912-685-5763
Telecopier: 912-685-4902

Bobby Jones	Julian B. Smith, Jr.

David N. Nelson	Troy Marsh

Representative Clients: Metter Banking Co.; Wallace Business Forms, Inc.; Cal-Maine Foods, Inc.; Franklin Chevrolet; Federal Land Bank; Georgia Farm Bureau Mutual Insurance Co., Inc.; The Travelers Insurance Co.; Nationwide Insurance Co.; Candler County Board of Commissioners; Hospital Authority of Candler County.

MILLEDGEVILLE,* Baldwin Co. — (Refer to Macon)

MILLEN,* Jenkins Co. — (Refer to Augusta)

MONROE,* Walton Co. — (Refer to Decatur)

MONTICELLO,* Jasper Co.

HAYGOOD, LYNCH, HARRIS & MELTON (AV)

315 Forsyth Street, 31064
Telephone: 706-468-8846
Forsyth, Georgia Office: 87 North Lee Street, 31029.
Telephone: 912-994-5171.
Fax: 912-994-4588.

Larry Persons Lynch

Representative Clients: Monroe County Industrial Development Authority; Fairfield Financial; Bank South, Jasper County, N.A.; Georgia Timberlands, Inc.
Local Counsel for: Atlanta Gas Light Co.; Bowater Southern Paper Corp.; Liberty Savings Bank.

For full biographical listings, see the Martindale-Hubbell Law Directory

---

MOULTRIE,* Colquitt Co.

MOORE, TYNDALL AND CASTELLOW (AV)

A Partnership of Professional Corporations
317 South Main Street, P.O. Box 190, 31776
Telephone: 912-985-1213
Fax: 912-890-1314

L. L. Moore (1880-1962)	David R. Tyndall (P.C.)
R. Lamar Moore (P.C.)	Lester M. Castellow (P.C.)

Representative Clients: Mobley Plant Company; Colquitt Electric Membership Corp.; Colquitt Ag Services, Inc.; Rich Oil Co.; Moultrie Farm Center; Destiny Industries, Inc.; Moultrie Manufacturing Co.
Local Counsel: The Equitable Life Assurance Society of the United States; Chubb & Son, Inc.

For full biographical listings, see the Martindale-Hubbell Law Directory

---

WHELCHEL, WHELCHEL & CARLTON (AV)

26 Second Avenue, S.W., P.O. Box 768, 31768
Telephone: 912-985-1590
Fax: 912-985-0946

MEMBERS OF FIRM

Hoyt H. Whelchel (1893-1960)	James C. Whelchel
Hoyt H. Whelchel, Jr.	John M. Carlton, Jr.

Representative Clients: Holman Supply Co.; United States Fidelity & Guaranty Co.; Great American Indemnity Co.; City of Moultrie; The St. Paul Cos.; Colquitt County Board of Education; Universal Underwriters Group; Riverside Manufacturing Company; Hospital Authority of Colquitt County.

For full biographical listings, see the Martindale-Hubbell Law Directory

---

NASHVILLE,* Berrien Co. — (Refer to Moultrie)

NEWNAN,* Coweta Co.

GLOVER & DAVIS, P.A. (AV)

10 Brown Street, P.O. Box 1038, 30264
Telephone: 770-253-4330
Fax: 770-251-7152
Peachtree City, Georgia Office: Suite 130, 200 Westpark Drive.
Telephone: 770-487-5834.
Fax: 770-487-3492.

J. Littleton Glover	W. Robert Hancock, Jr.
Welborn B. Davis, Jr.	(Resident, Peachtree Office)
(1922-1974)	Asa M. Powell, Jr.
J. Littleton Glover, Jr.	Jerry Ann Conner
Alan W. Jackson	Mark E. Dacy (Resident,
Randy E. Connell	Peachtree City Office)

Representative Clients: Newnan Savings Bank; Pike Transfer Co.; Batson-Cook Company, General Corporate and Construction Divisions; Coweta County, Georgia; Heard County, Georgia; Putnam-Greene Financial Corporation.
Local Counsel for: International Latex Corp.; First Union National Bank of Georgia; Wear Georgia; Farm Credit, ACA.

For full biographical listings, see the Martindale-Hubbell Law Directory

---

ROSENZWEIG, JONES & MacNABB, P.C. (AV)

32 South Court Square, P.O. Box 220, 30264
Telephone: 770-253-3282
Fax: 770-251-7262

George C. Rosenzweig	Sidney Pope Jones, Jr.
Joseph P. MacNabb	

Charles C. Witcher	Douglas L. Dreyer
Jonathan W. Hickman	

Approved Attorneys for: Lawyers Title Insurance Corp.; Chicago Title Insurance Co.

For full biographical listings, see the Martindale-Hubbell Law Directory

---

SANDERS, HAUGEN & SEARS, P.C. (AV)

11 Perry Street, P.O. Box 1177, 30263
Telephone: 770-253-3880
Fax: 770-254-0093

Walter D. Sanders (1909-1989)	C. Bradford Sears, Jr.
Willis G. Haugen	Walter S. Haugen

Attorneys for: Southern Railway System; Georgia Power Co.; City of Newnan; The Bibb Co.; Southern Bell Telephone Co.; Brown Steel Contractors.

For full biographical listings, see the Martindale-Hubbell Law Directory

---

WOOD, ODOM AND EDGE, P.A. (AV)

15 Jefferson Street, P.O. Drawer 1608, 30264
Telephone: 770-253-9885; 1-800-346-5357
Fax: 770-253-9896
Atlanta Telephone: 404-577-9024
Sharpsburg, Georgia Office: 3091 East Highway 34.
Telephone: 404-251-7266.
Telecopier: 404-251-7266.

Gus L. Wood	H. Parnell Odom
Arthur B. Edge, IV	

Jacquelyn L. Kneidel

LEGAL SUPPORT PERSONNEL

Laura MacBean

For full biographical listings, see the Martindale-Hubbell Law Directory

---

NORCROSS, Gwinnett Co.

GIBSON, DEAL AND FLETCHER, P.C. (AV)

Spalding Exchange, 3953 Holcomb Bridge Road, Suite 200, 30092
Telephone: 770-263-7200
Telecopier: 770-449-5395

John W. Gibson	James B. Deal
William A. Fletcher, Jr.	

References: Bank South, N.A.; First Gwinnett Bank.

For full biographical listings, see the Martindale-Hubbell Law Directory

---

THOMPSON, O'BRIEN, KEMP & NASUTI, P.C. (AV)

4845 Jimmy Carter Boulevard, 30093-3641
Telephone: 770-925-0111
Fax: 770-925-8597

(See Next Column)

THOMPSON, O'BRIEN, KEMP & NASUTI P.C.—*Continued*

R. Michael Thompson	John J. McCloskey
J. Patrick O'Brien	Paul J. Petras
Donna N. Kemp	Paul J. Morochnik
Albert F. Nasuti	Jill I. Seligman
Betty H. Morris	Kelly A. Carmody

Scott B. Riddle

OF COUNSEL

Scott L. Dix	Baylor B. Banks

For full biographical listings, see the Martindale-Hubbell Law Directory

WALLACE & DE MAYO, P.C. (AV)

6356 Corley Road, 30071-1704
Telephone: 707-446-9996
Fax: 707-368-8331

Richard T. De Mayo	Douglas W. Wallace

Paul J. Gallo

For full biographical listings, see the Martindale-Hubbell Law Directory

OCILLA,* Irwin Co.

WALTERS, DAVIS & PUJADAS, P.C. (AV)

South Cherry Street, P.O. Box 247, 31774
Telephone: 912-468-7472; 468-9433
Fax: 912-468-9022

W. Emory Walters	Thomas E. Pujadas
J. Harvey Davis	C. Vinson Walters, II

LEGAL SUPPORT PERSONNEL

Larry P. Harper

Attorneys for: Irwin County Board of Education; First State Bank of Ocilla; Irwin County; Wilcox County.
Local Counsel for: Georgia Farm Bureau Mutual Insurance Co.
Approved Attorneys for: Kaiser Aluminum & Chemical Sales, Inc.; Lawyers Title Insurance Corp.; Ticor Title Insurance Co.; Farmers Home Administration; Federal Land Bank of Columbia.

For full biographical listings, see the Martindale-Hubbell Law Directory

PERRY,* Houston Co.

DANIEL, LAWSON, TUGGLE & JERLES (AV)

912 Main Street, P.O. Box 89, 31069
Telephone: 912-987-2622
Fax: 912-987-7037

Hubert A. Aultman (1920-1977)

OF COUNSEL

David P. Hulbert

MEMBERS OF FIRM

Tom W. Daniel	Robert T. Tuggle, III
Hugh Lawson, Jr.	William R. Jerles, Jr.

Representative Clients: Flint Electric Membership Corp.; Houston County Board of Education; Tri-County Electric Membership Corp.; Agricultural Investment Management Corp.; The Bank of Perry.
Approved Attorneys for: Lawyers Title Insurance Corp.; Chicago Title Insurance Co.; Ticor Title Insurance Co.; Federal Land Bank of Columbia; Farmers Home Administration.

For full biographical listings, see the Martindale-Hubbell Law Directory

WALKER, HULBERT, GRAY & BYRD (AV)

909 Ball Street, P.O. Box 1234, 31069
Telephone: 912-987-1415
Fax: 912-987-1077

MEMBERS OF FIRM

Larry Walker	Michael G. Gray
David G. Walker	Charles W. Byrd
David P. Hulbert, Jr.	John D. Christy

ASSOCIATES

S. E. Moody, III

Representative Clients: City of Perry; City of Reynolds; Houston County Hospital Authority; Crossroads Bank of Georgia; World Acceptance Corporation; NavCom Defense Electronics, Inc.; Brown and Williamson Tobacco Corp.; E.C.I.; Embeco; Constitution States.

For full biographical listings, see the Martindale-Hubbell Law Directory

QUITMAN,* Brooks Co. — (Refer to Valdosta)

REIDSVILLE,* Tattnall Co. — (Refer to Metter)

RINGGOLD,* Catoosa Co. — (Refer to Dalton)

ROME,* Floyd Co.

BRINSON, ASKEW, BERRY, SEIGLER, RICHARDSON & DAVIS (AV)

A Partnership including Professional Corporations
Omberg House, 615 West First Street, P.O. Box 5513, 30162-5513
Telephone: 706-291-8853;
Atlanta: 404-521-0908
Telecopier: 706-234-3574

MEMBERS OF FIRM

Robert M. Brinson (P.C.)	Hendrick L. Cromartie, III
C. King Askew (P.C.)	Wright W. Smith
Robert L. Berry	Mark M. J. Webb
Joseph M. Seigler, Jr.	Joseph B. Atkins
Thomas D. Richardson	I. Stewart Duggan, Jr.
J. Anderson Davis	James Daniel Blitch

Representative Clients: City of Rome; Georgia Power Co.; General Electric Company; News Publishing Company (Rome News Tribune); Redmond Regional Medical Center; Oglethorpe Power Corp.; Suhner Manufacturing, Inc.; The Federal Land Bank of Columbia; AmSouth Bank of Georgia; United States Fidelity & Guaranty Co.

For full biographical listings, see the Martindale-Hubbell Law Directory

SHAW, MADDOX, GRAHAM, MONK & BOLING (AV)

SunTrust Company Bank Building, P.O. Box 29, 30162-0029
Telephone: 706-291-6223
Telecopier: 706-291-7429

MEMBERS OF FIRM

Charles C. Shaw	David F. Guldenschuh
James D. Maddox	Daniel M. Roper
John M. Graham, III	Jule W. Peek, Jr.
C. Wade Monk	Virginia B. Harman
William H. Boling, Jr.	Scott M. Smith
Jo H. Stegall, III	Thomas H. Manning

ASSOCIATES

D. David Tomlin	Mather D. Graham

OF COUNSEL

Oscar M. Smith

Representative Clients: SunTrust Bank of Northwest Georgia; Inland-Rome Inc.; Norfolk Southern Railway Co.; Aetna Casualty & Surety Co.; American Mutual Liability Insurance; Commercial Union Insurance Cos.; Hartford Accident & Indemnity Co.; St. Paul Insurance Cos.; Zurich-American Insurance Co.

For full biographical listings, see the Martindale-Hubbell Law Directory

ROSSVILLE, Walker Co.

HARRISS, HARTMAN, AARON, WHARTON, BOYD & SECORD, P.C. (AV)

200 McFarland Building, P.O. Drawer 220, 30741
Telephone: 706-861-0203

Robert J. Harriss	Robert A. Wharton, Jr.
James M. Aaron, Jr.	William G. Boyd

James A. Secord

Richard S. Taliaferro

For full biographical listings, see the Martindale-Hubbell Law Directory

SANDERSVILLE,* Washington Co. — (Refer to Louisville)

SAVANNAH,* Chatham Co.

BOUHAN, WILLIAMS & LEVY LLP (AV)

The Armstrong House, 447 Bull Street, P.O. Box 2139, 31402-2139
Telephone: 912-236-2491
Fax: 912-233-0811

MEMBERS OF FIRM

John J. Bouhan (1886-1971)	B. H. Levy, Jr.
B. H. Levy (1912-1988)	John G. Lientz
Frank W. Seiler	M. Tyus Butler, Jr.
Walter C. Hartridge	M. Brice Ladson
Edgar Pomeroy Williams	Roy E. Paul
Edwin D. Robb, Jr.	Joseph A. Mulherin, III
Leamon R. Holliday, III	Wilbur D. Owens, III
Lawrence Michael Donovan, Jr.	Peter D. Muller

OF COUNSEL

George W. Williams	John Michael Brennan
Alan S. Gaynor	Samuel A. Cann

ASSOCIATES

Melanie L. Marks	Timothy H. Edwards
Carlton E. Joyce	John David Lange
Jane L. Peeples	D. Michael Conner

(See Next Column)

BOUHAN, WILLIAMS & LEVY LLP, *Savannah—Continued*

General Counsel for: Savannah Electric and Power Co.; Wachovia Bank of Georgia, N.A.; Southeastern Maritime Co.; Solomons Co.; Fiduciary Services Corp.; Peeples Industry, Inc.; Board of Education of the City of Savannah and County of Chatham; The Branigar Organization, Inc.

For full biographical listings, see the Martindale-Hubbell Law Directory

BRANNEN, SEARCY & SMITH (AV)

22 East Thirty-Fourth Street, P.O. Box 8002, 31412
Telephone: 912-234-8875
Fax: 912-232-1792

Perry Brannen (1903-1984)	David R. Smith
Frank P. Brannen	Daniel C. Cohen
William N. Searcy	Wayne L. Durden

OF COUNSEL
William T. Daniel, Jr.

ASSOCIATES

Robert L. Jenkins	Margaret G. Culclasure
Bernard F. Kistler, Jr.	(Not admitted in GA)

Counsel for: Continental Insurance Co.

For full biographical listings, see the Martindale-Hubbell Law Directory

CHAMLEE, DUBUS & SIPPLE (AV)

Suite 301 Cluskey Building, 127 Abercorn Street, P.O. Box 9523, 31412
Telephone: 912-232-3311
Cable Address: "Floodtide"
Telecopier: 912-232-3253

MEMBERS OF FIRM

George H. Chamlee	Gustave R. Dubus, III
	David F. Sipple

For full biographical listings, see the Martindale-Hubbell Law Directory

ELLIS, PAINTER, RATTERREE & BART LLP (AV)

2 East Bryan Street, Tenth Floor, P.O. Box 9946, 31412
Telephone: 912-233-9700
Fax: 912-233-2281

J. Wiley Ellis	Randall K. Bart
Paul W. Painter, Jr.	Christopher E. Klein
R. Clay Ratterree	David W. Adams

OF COUNSEL
Robert A. Mason

Sarah Brown Akins	Tracy Cullen O'Connell
James K. Austin	Robert Mercer
	Paul Douglas Meyer

Representative Clients: Colonial Oil Industries, Inc.; Strachan Shipping Co.; Morris Newspaper Corp.; Green Tree Acceptance; Ford Motor Credit Co.; The Savannah Bank; Palmer & Cay, Inc.; Southern Motors of Savannah, Inc.; CIGNA Insurance Cos.; Commercial Union Insurance Cos.

For full biographical listings, see the Martindale-Hubbell Law Directory

HUNTER, MACLEAN, EXLEY & DUNN, P.C. (AV)

200 East St. Julian Street, P.O. Box 9848, 31412
Telephone: 912-236-0261
Cable Address: "Ancan"
Telecopier: 912-236-4936
Telex: 54-6483
Atlanta, Georgia Office: The Peachtree, 1355 Peachtree Street, N.E., Suite 1050.
Telephone: 404-876-3611.
Fax: 404-870-2025.

Malcolm R. Maclean	Anne Cote Marscher
John B. Miller	J. Reid Williamson, III
William M. Exley, Jr.	Marvin A. Fentress
Henry M. Dunn, Jr.	Edith H. Holloman
John M. Tatum	Glen M. Darbyshire
John M. Hewson, III	William E. Dillard, III
Arnold C. Young	R. Jason D'Cruz
M. Lane Morrison	Christopher Weis Phillips
W. Brooks Stillwell, III	David M. Hirsberg
F. Saunders Aldridge, III	Robert Alvin Lewallen, Jr.
Robert S. Glenn, Jr.	Kirby Clarice Gould
Lee C. Mundell	Darrin L. McCullough
Andrew H. Ernst	Ronnie D. Talley
Roland B. Williams	Nancy Patrick Nutting
Don L. Waters	Thomas Mills Fleming
Leonard J. Panzitta	George M. Earle
Dorothea Summerell Costrini	Steven J. Arsenault
Jonathan D. Sprague	Caroline Louise Osborne
Harold B. Yellin	Sarah H. Lamar
Wade W. Herring, II	Steven I. Loew

(See Next Column)

Michael Jonas Thomerson	Triece Gignilliat Ziblut
Edward O. Henneman	Timothy N. Toler
Thomas Sean Cullen	(Atlanta Office)
David M. Pernini	Daniel J. Mohan
Michael D. Robl	(Atlanta Office)
Frank S. Macgill	Jan M. Hunter (Atlanta Office)
Robert E. Spears, Jr.	Ward S. Bondurant
	(Atlanta Office)

OF COUNSEL
Nell C. Pillard

Representative Clients: Great Dane Trailers, Inc.; Fort Howard Corp.; West of England; Atlantic Wood Industries, Inc.; Home Insurance Co.; Savannah Foods & Industries, Inc.

For full biographical listings, see the Martindale-Hubbell Law Directory

INGLESBY, FALLIGANT, HORNE, COURINGTON & NASH, A PROFESSIONAL CORPORATION (AV)

17 West McDonough Street, P.O. Box 1368, 31402-1368
Telephone: 912-232-7000
Telecopier: 912-232-7300

Sam P. Inglesby, Jr.	Dorothy W. Courington, II
J. Daniel Falligant	Thomas A. Nash, Jr.
Kathleen Horne	Dolly Chisholm

Amy Lee Copeland	James F. Shehane, IV

Representative Clients: NationsBank of Georgia, N.A.; Gulfstream Aerospace Corp.; Rotary Corp.; Atlanta Gas Light Co.; Ford Motor Credit Co.; Independent Insurance Agents of Savannah, Inc.; Savannah Christian Preparatory School; Savannah Mall; Continental Grain.

For full biographical listings, see the Martindale-Hubbell Law Directory

---

SPARTA, * Hancock Co. — (Refer to Thomson)

STATESBORO, * Bulloch Co.

ALLEN & CLASSENS (AV)

30 North Main Street, P.O. Box 478, 30458
Telephone: 912-764-6221
FAX: 912-764-2724

MEMBERS OF FIRM

Francis W. Allen	Michael J. Classens

Attorneys for: Sea Island Bank.
Approved Attorneys for: Lawyers Title Insurance Corp.; Farmers Home Administration.

For full biographical listings, see the Martindale-Hubbell Law Directory

---

SWAINSBORO, * Emanuel Co.

SHEPHERD, GARY & McWHORTER (AV)

SSG Building, 104 East Moring Street, Drawer 99, 30401
Telephone: 912-237-7551

MEMBERS OF FIRM

Felix C. Williams (1899-1972)	Loren Gary, II
George L. Smith, II (1912-1973)	William H. McWhorter, Jr.
Sidney B. Shepherd	Millard B. Shepherd, Jr.

Representative Clients: Cities of Swainsboro, Adrian, Garfield and Nunez; The Citizens Bank of Swainsboro; Rayonier Inc.; Farm Bureau Insurance Co.
Approved Attorneys for: Lawyers Title Insurance Corp.; Ticor Title Insurance Co.; Title Insurance Company of Minnesota; Chicago Title Insurance Co.; Auto Parts & Supply.

For full biographical listings, see the Martindale-Hubbell Law Directory

---

SYLVANIA, * Screven Co. — (Refer to Metter)

SYLVESTER, * Worth Co. — (Refer to Albany)

TALBOTTON, * Talbot Co. — (Refer to Columbus)

TALLAPOOSA, Haralson Co. — (Refer to Carrollton)

THOMASTON, * Upson Co.

ADAMS, BARFIELD, DUNAWAY & HANKINSON (AV)

Atwater Building, Drawer 671, 30286
Telephone: 706-647-5466
Fax: 706-647-6434

MEMBERS OF FIRM

Dickson Adams (1919-1975)	Tommy R. Hankinson
Ronald Barfield	Catherine Barfield
David B. Dunaway	Ben J. Miller, Jr.

General Counsel for: City of Thomason; Thomaston Federal Savings Bank; Upson County Hospital Authority.
Representative Clients: Thomaston Mills, Inc.; Cincinnati Insurance Co.; City of Thomaston; West Georgia Farm Credit Service, ACA.
Approved Attorneys for: Lawyers Title Insurance Corp.; Chicago Title Insurance Co.

(See Next Column)

ADAMS, BARFIELD, DUNAWAY & HANKINSON—*Continued*

For full biographical listings, see the Martindale-Hubbell Law Directory

*THOMASVILLE,** Thomas Co.

ALEXANDER & VANN (AV)

218 East Jackson Street, P.O. Box 1479, 31799
Telephone: 912-226-2565
Fax: 912-228-0444

MEMBERS OF FIRM

Thomas H. Vann, Jr.	William C. Sanders
Charles H. Watt, III	David E. Wilder
John T. Holt	George R. Lilly, II

James H. Smith

Allen E. Lockerman, IV

Counsel for: Commercial Bank; Davis Water & Waste Industries, Inc.; Archbold Medical Center.
District Counsel for: CSX Transportation Inc.
Local Counsel for: State Farm Mutual Automobile Insurance Co.; Insurance Company of North America; Auto-Owners Insurance Co.

For full biographical listings, see the Martindale-Hubbell Law Directory

*THOMSON,** McDuffie Co.

KNOX AND SWAN (AV)

Knox Building, P.O. Box 539, 30824
Telephone: 706-595-1841
Fax: 706-595-2404

MEMBERS OF FIRM

Robert E. Knox (1916-1994)	Robert E. Knox, Jr.

W. Bryant Swan, Jr.

Representative Clients: Allied Bank of Georgia; First Savings Bank; Kingsley Mill Corp.; Hardware Mutual Casualty Co.; General Accident & Assurance Corp.; Employers Mutual of Wausau; Hartford Accident & Indemnity Co.; Sentry Insurance Group; Hoover Treated Wood Products Co.

For full biographical listings, see the Martindale-Hubbell Law Directory

*TIFTON,** Tift Co.

SIMS, FLEMING & SPURLIN, P.C. (AV)

823 Love Avenue, P.O. Box 1165, 31793
Telephone: 912-386-0964
Fax: 912-386-1452

John S. Sims, Jr.	John C. Spurlin
Carlton A. Fleming, Jr.	James M. Walker, III

R. David Bryan

Representative Clients: First Community Bank of Tifton; Trust Company Bank; Thomson Newspapers, Inc. (The Tifton Gazette); South Georgia Farm Credit Service; Griffin Truck Lines; State Farm Mutual Automobile Insurance Co.; State Farm Fire and Casualty Insurance Co.; Home Insurance Cos.; Georgia Casualty & Surety Co.; Nationwide Insurance Co.

For full biographical listings, see the Martindale-Hubbell Law Directory

*TOCCOA,** Stephens Co.

McCLURE, RAMSAY & DICKERSON (AV)

400 Falls Road, P.O. Drawer 1408, 30577
Telephone: 706-886-3178
Fax: 706-886-1150

MEMBERS OF FIRM

Clyde M. McClure (1892-1976)	John A. Dickerson
George B. Ramsay, Jr.	Allan R. Ramsay

Marlin R. Escoe

ASSOCIATES

Alice D. Hayes	Elizabeth Felton Moore

Luther H. Beck, Jr.

OF COUNSEL

Knox Bynum

Counsel for: Coats and Clark, Inc.; Stephens Federal Savings & Loan Assn.; St. Paul Insurance Cos.; State Farm Insurance Cos.; Cotton States Insurance Cos.; City of Toccoa; Citizens Bank; Habersham Plantation Corp.; Patterson Pump Co; Georgia Farm Bureau Insurance Companies.

For full biographical listings, see the Martindale-Hubbell Law Directory

*VALDOSTA,** Lowndes Co.

BARHAM, DOVER, BENNETT, MILLER, SHERWOOD & STONE (AV)

701 North Patterson Street, P.O. Box 729, 31603-0729
Telephone: 912-242-0314
Fax: 912-242-6495

(See Next Column)

Edwin G. Barham (1935-1992)	Willis L. Miller, III
John R. Bennett	J. Carol Sherwood, Jr.
J. Michael Dover	Wilton E. Stone, Jr.

Patricia McCorvey Karras	William W. Broadfoot, III

Representative Clients: First State Bank & Trust Co.; Liberty Savings Bank; Borg-Warner Acceptance Corp.; National Mortgage Co.; Locoga Federal Credit Union; Valdosta Teachers Federal Credit Union; W WSHF Radio; South Georgia Medical Center; Bell South; Credit Bureau of Valdosta, Inc.

For full biographical listings, see the Martindale-Hubbell Law Directory

ELLIOTT & BLACKBURN (AV)

First Liberty Bank Building, 509 North Patterson Street Suite 201, P.O. Box 579, 31603-0579
Telephone: 912-247-0800
912-242-3333
Telecopier: 912-242-0696

W. Gus Elliott	Walter G. Elliott, II
Oris D. Blackburn, Jr.	James L. Elliott

Representative Clients: Hospital Authority of Valdosta and Lowndes County d/b/a South Georgia Medical Center; Lowndes County; The Valdosta Daily Times; Bell South Telecommunications, Inc.; Sears, Roebuck & Company; Levi Strauss & Co.; John Deere & Co.; E. I. DuPont de Nemours & Company; BP Exploration & Oil, Inc.; National Indemnity Company.

For full biographical listings, see the Martindale-Hubbell Law Directory

TILLMAN, McTIER, COLEMAN, TALLEY, NEWBERN & KURRIE (AV)

910 North Patterson Street, P.O. Box 5437, 31603-5437
Telephone: 912-242-7562
Fax: 912-333-0885

MEMBERS OF FIRM

Henry T. Brice (1925-1976)	Thompson Kurrie, Jr.
B. Lamar Tillman (1912-1990)	Richard L. Coleman
John T. McTier	Edward F. Preston
Wade H. Coleman	William E. Holland
George T. Talley	R. Clay Powell
C. George Newbern	Gregory T. Talley

Attorneys for: NationsBank; Georgia Power Co.; Liberty Mutual Insurance Co.; USF&G Co.; Georgia Casualty & Surety Co.; Valdosta-Lowndes County Industrial Authority; City of Valdosta; American Turpentine Farmers Assn.

For full biographical listings, see the Martindale-Hubbell Law Directory

*VIENNA,** Dooly Co.

DAVIS, GREGORY, CHRISTY & FOREHAND (AV)

104 West Union Street, P.O. Box 397, 31092
Telephone: 912-268-4125
Telecopier: 912-268-6373
Cordele, Georgia Office: 708 East Sixteenth Avenue, P.O. Drawer 5230.
Telephone: 912-273-7150.
Fax: 912-273-7578.

MEMBERS OF FIRM

Hardy Gregory, Jr.	John N. Davis
Gary C. Christy	David A. Forehand, Jr.

Preyesh Kantilal Maniklal

OF COUNSEL

T. Hoyt Davis, Jr.

For full biographical listings, see the Martindale-Hubbell Law Directory

WARNER ROBINS, Houston Co.

ROY N. COWART, P.C. (AV)

1555 Watson Boulevard, P.O. Box 818, 31099
Telephone: 912-922-8515
FAX: 912-922-3184

Roy N. Cowart

Representative Clients: Park Newspapers of Georgia, Inc.; Shaheen Office Supply, Inc.; C.L. Williams Insurance Agency; Maria H. Bartlett, M.D.; Surgical Associates, P.C.; Robert A. Carter, M.D., P.C.; Golden Key Realty, Inc.; Stalnaker Plastics, Inc.

For full biographical listings, see the Martindale-Hubbell Law Directory

*WASHINGTON,** Wilkes Co. — (Refer to Athens)

*WAYNESBORO,** Burke Co. — (Refer to Augusta)

*WRIGHTSVILLE,** Johnson Co. — (Refer to Metter)

*ZEBULON,** Pike Co. — (Refer to Griffin)

HAWAII

HILO, * Hawaii Co.

CARLSMITH BALL WICHMAN CASE & ICHIKI (AV)

A Partnership including Law Corporations
121 Waianuenue Avenue, P.O. Box 686, 96721-0686
Telephone: 808-935-6644
Cable Address: "Carlsmith-Hilo"
Telecopier: 808-935-7975
Honolulu, Hawaii Office: Suite 2200, Pacific Tower, 1001 Bishop Street.
P.O. Box 656.
Telephone: 808-523-2500.
Kapolei, Hawaii Office: Kapolei Building, Suite 318, 1001 Kamokila
Boulevard.
Telephone: 808-523-2500.
Wailuku, Maui, Hawaii Office: One Main Plaza, Suite 400, 2200 Main
Street, P.O. Box 1086.
Telephone: 808-242-4535.
Kailua-Kona, Hawaii Office: Second Floor, Bank of Hawaii Annex
Building, P.O. Box 1720.
Telephone: 808-329-6464.
Agana, Guam Office: 4th Floor, Bank of Hawaii Building, P.O. Box BF.
Telephone: 671-472-6813.
Saipan, Commonwealth of the Northern Mariana Islands Office: Carlsmith
Building, Capitol Hill, P.O. Box 5241.
Telephone: (011) 670-322-3455.
Los Angeles, California Office: 555 South Flower Street, 25th Floor.
Telephone: 213-955-1200.
Washington, D.C. Office: 700 14th Street, N.W., 9th Floor.
Telephone: 202-508-1025.
Mexico City, Mexico Office: Monte Pelvoux 111, Piso 1, Col. Lomas de
Chapultepec, 11000 Mexico, D.F.
Telephone: (011-52-5) 520-8514.
Fax: (011-52-5) 540-1545.
*Mexico, D.F. Office of Carlsmith Ball Garcia Cacho y Asociados, S.C.
(Authorized to practice Mexican Law):* Monte Pelvoux 111, Piso 1, Col.
Lomas de Chapultepec, 11000, Mexico, D.F.
Telephone: (011-52-5) 520-8514.
Fax: (011-52-5) 540-1545.

MEMBER OF FIRM
Steven S. C. Lim

RESIDENT ASSOCIATES

Sherrill A. Atwood	Peter K. Kubota

For full biographical listings, see the Martindale-Hubbell Law Directory

HONOLULU, * Honolulu Co.

ALSTON, HUNT, FLOYD & ING ATTORNEYS AT LAW, A LAW CORPORATION (AV)

18th Floor Pacific Tower, 1001 Bishop Street, P.O. Box 2281, 96804
Telephone: 808-524-1800
Telecopier: 808-524-4591

Paul D. Alston	Bruce S. Noborikawa
William S. Hunt	Sharon A. Merkle
Shelby Anne Floyd	Everett S. Kaneshige
Louise K. Y. Ing	David A. Nakashima
Ellen Godbey Carson	Neil F. Hulbert

Mei Nakamoto	Marilyn Chung Ushijima
Peter C. Hsieh	Susan Jameson
Mary Martin	Joseph P. Viola
Jade Lynne Holck	Richard A. Yanagi
	Bradford L. Tannen

OF COUNSEL

Bruce H. Wakuzawa	Robert A. Marks

Representative Clients: Kaiser Aluminum and Chemical Co.; Federal Deposit Insurance Corp.; Kaiser Foundation Health Plan, Inc.; Chicago Title Insurance Co.; Amfac, Inc.

For full biographical listings, see the Martindale-Hubbell Law Directory

AYABE, CHONG, NISHIMOTO, SIA & NAKAMURA (AV)

A Partnership including a Professional Corporation
Pauahi Tower, Suite 2500, 1001 Bishop Street, 96813
Telephone: 808-537-6119
Telecopier: 808-526-3491

MEMBERS OF FIRM

Sidney K. Ayabe (P.C.)	Calvin E. Young
Robert A. Chong	Diane W. Wong
John S. Nishimoto	Rodney S. Nishida
Richard F. Nakamura	Patricia T. Fujii
Jeffrey H. K. Sia	Rhonda A. Nishimura
Kenneth T. Goya	Gail M. Kang
Francis M. Nakamoto	Ann H. Aratani

(See Next Column)

Philip S. Uesato	Virgil B. Prieto
Ronald M. Shigekane	J. Thomas Weber
Robin R. Horner	Robert Y. Nakamoto
Stephen G. Dyer	Robert A. Mash
Steven L. Goto	Gary S. Miyamoto

Representative Clients: Travelers Insurance Co.; St. Paul Fire and Marine Insurance Co.; The Employers Group of Insurance Companies; TIG Insurance Co.; Pacific Insurance Co.; Hartford Accident and Indemnity Co.; Continental Casualty Co.; CNA Insurance Co.

For full biographical listings, see the Martindale-Hubbell Law Directory

BURKE, SAKAI, McPHEETERS, BORDNER, IWANAGA & ESTES ATTORNEYS AT LAW, A LAW CORPORATION (AV)

3100 Mauka Tower, Grosvenor Center, 737 Bishop Street, 96813-3222
Telephone: 808-523-9833
Telecopier: 808-528-1656

Edmund Burke	Mary L. Lucasse
Wayne M. Sakai	David A. Gruebner
Howard F. McPheeters	Madalyn Purcell
William A. Bordner	Nadine L. Nakamura
Michiro Iwanaga	Judy Y. Chung
James T. Estes, Jr.	Allegra Hyte
Carlton W. T. Chun	Patricia C. Aburano
Kunio Kuwabe	Jan M. Tamura
Leta H. Price	John N.K. Burke

Representative Clients: Argonaut Insurance Co.; CIGNA; Design Professionals Insurance Co.; The Doctor's Company; General Star Indemnity; Longs Drug Store, Inc., California; Medical Insurance Exchange of California; Queens Medical Center; Straub Clinic & Hospital, Inc.; The Travelers Insurance Cos.

For full biographical listings, see the Martindale-Hubbell Law Directory

CADES SCHUTTE FLEMING & WRIGHT (AV)

Formerly Smith, Wild, Beebe & Cades
1000 Bishop Street, P.O. Box 939, 96808
Telephone: 808-521-9200
Telecopier: 808-531-8738
Email: cades@cades.com
Affiliated Law Firm: Udom-Prok Associates Law Offices, 105/36 Tharinee Mansion, Borom Raj Chananee Road Bangkoknoi, Bangkok, Thailand, 10700.
Telephone: 011 662 435-4146.
Kailua-Kona, Hawaii Office: Hualalai Center, Suite B-303, 75-170 Hualalai Road.
Telephone: 808-329-5811.
Telecopier: 808-326-1175.

MEMBERS OF FIRM

Robert B. Bunn	Vito Galati
E. Gunner Schull	Cary S. Matsushige
Donald E. Scearce	David Schulmeister
Richard A. Hicks	Milton M. Yasunaga
Roger H. Epstein	Susan Oki Mollway
Jeffrey S. Portnoy	Gino L. Gabrio
Bernice Littman	Colin O. Miwa
Nicholas C. Dreher	Martin E. Hsia
Mark A. Hazlett	Peter W. Olson
Philip J. Leas	Stewart J. Martin
David C. Larsen	Rhonda L. Griswold
Larry T. Takumi	Gail M. Tamashiro
William A. Cardwell	Grace Nihei Kido
C. Michael Hare	Donna Y. L. Leong
Richard R. Clifton	David F.E. Banks
Roy A. Vitousek, III	Dennis J. Gaughan
(Resident, Kona Office)	Patricia J. McHenry
Nelson N. S. Chun	K. James Steiner, Jr.
Darryl H. W. Johnston	Eric N. Roose

ASSOCIATES

Jeffrey D. Watts	Dean T. Yamamoto
Laurie A. Kuribayashi	Alan K. Hyde
James H. Ashford	Kelly G. LaPorte
Michele M. Sunahara	Johnnel L. Nakamura
Cynthia M. Johiro	Marc E. Rousseau
Dennis W. Chong Kee	Maria B. Mazzeo
Carlito P. Caliboso	Alexander Woody
Catherine A. Carey	Christopher I.L. Parsons
Daniel H. Devaney IV	Kenneth C. May
Karen Wong	Christopher T. Harrison
Michael H. Shikuma	Sarah O. Wang
Patrick W. Hanifin	Lynn H. Higashi
Eric S.T. Young	(Resident, Kona Office)
Mitchell C. Sockett	Kimberly O'Neill Jackson
Theodore D.C. Young	(Resident, Kona Office)

(See Next Column)

CADES SCHUTTE FLEMING & WRIGHT—*Continued*

Arthur G. Smith (1882-1966)	C. Frederick Schutte (1921-1988)
Urban Earl Wild (1891-1952)	Milton Cades (1903-1992)
Eugene H. Beebe (1889-1966)	A. Singleton Cagle (1923-1994)
Charles A. Gregory (1902-1972)	Edward deL. Boyle (1942-1994)
Douglas E. Prior (1936-1995)	

OF COUNSEL

J. Russell Cades	Harold S. Wright
William L. Fleming	James S. Campbell
William M. Swope	

Counsel for: First Hawaiian Bank; Alexander & Baldwin, Inc.; Theo. H. Davies & Co., Ltd.; C. Brewer & Company, Ltd.; Bank of America, FSB; The Bank of Tokyo, Ltd.; Haseko (Hawaii), Inc.; The Industrial Bank of Japan, Ltd.

For full biographical listings, see the Martindale-Hubbell Law Directory

CARLSMITH BALL WICHMAN CASE & ICHIKI (AV)

A Partnership including Law Corporations
Suite 2200, Pacific Tower, 1001 Bishop Street, P.O. Box 656, 96809-3402
Telephone: 808-523-2500
Cable Address: "CWCMI"
Telecopier: 808-523-0842
Telex: 723-8770 CWCMI HR
Kapolei, Hawaii Office: Kapolei Building, Suite 318, 1001 Kamokila Boulevard.
Telephone: 808-523-2500.
Wailuku, Maui Hawaii Office: One Main Plaza, Suite 400, 2200 Main Street, P.O. Box 1086.
Telephone: 808-242-4535.
Kailua-Kona, Hawaii Office: Second Floor, Bank of Hawaii Annex Building, P.O. Box 1720.
Telephone: 808-329-6464.
Hilo, Hawaii Office: 121 Waianuenue Avenue, P.O. Box 686.
Telephone: 808-935-6644.
Agana, Guam Office: 4th Floor, Bank of Hawaii Building, P.O. Box BF.
Telephone: 671-472-6813.
Saipan, Commonwealth of the Northern Mariana Islands Office: Carlsmith Building, Capitol Hill, P.O. Box 5241.
Telephone: (011) 670-322-3455.
Los Angeles, California Office: 555 South Flower Street, 25th Floor.
Telephone: 213-955-1200.
Washington, D.C. Office: 700 14th Street, N.W., 9th Floor.
Telephone: 202-508-1025.
Mexico City, Mexico Office: Monte Pelvous 111, Piso 1, Col. Lomas de Chapultepec 11000, Mexico, D.F.
Telephone: (011-52-5) 520-8514.
Fax: (011-52-5) 540-1545.
Mexico, D.F. Office of Carlsmith Ball Garcia Cacho y Asociados, S.C. (Authorized to practice Mexican Law): Monte Pelvoux 111, Piso 1, Col. Lomas de Chapultepec, 11000 Mexico, D.F.
Telephone: (011-52-5) 520-8514.
Fax: (011-52-5) 540-1545.

MEMBERS OF FIRM

William E. Atwater, III	Paul Mullin Ganley (A Law Corporation)
Annie Kun Baker (Partner, Resident at Los Angeles, California Office)	Alfonso García Cacho (Resident, Mexico Office)
Joseph A. Ball (Resident at Los Angeles, California Office)	Gary G. Grimmer
Roger B. Baymiller (Resident at Los Angeles, California Office)	George G. Grubb (A Law Corporation)
Nancy M. Beckner (Resident at Los Angeles, California Office)	Jonathan R. Hodes (Resident at Los Angeles, California Office)
Daniel A. Bent	David T. W. Huang
John F. Biehl (Resident at Saipan Office)	Andy M. Ichiki
James W. Boyle	Michelle C. Imata
Stephen L. Bradford (Resident at Los Angeles, California Office)	Philip D. Isaac (Resident at Agana, Guam Office)
Donn W. Carlsmith (A Law Corporation)	Eric A. James (Resident at Kapolei, Hawaii Office)
Edward E. Case	Robert N. Katayuma
James H. Case (A Law Corporation)	John C. Khil
Grant Y. M. Chun (Resident at Maui Office)	Karl K. Kobayashi
Mary Jane Connell	Nenad Krek
Ruth D. Davis (Resident at Agana, Guam Office)	Robert F. Kull (Resident at Los Angeles, California Office)
Patricia Devlin	David Patrick Ledger
Albert H. Ebright (Resident at Los Angeles, California Office)	Tom C. Leuteneker (Resident at Maui Office)
Steven M. Egesdal	Steven S. C. Lim (Resident, Hilo, Hawaii Office)
Anna M. Elento-Sneed	Tim Lui-Kwan
Terrence A. Everett (Resident at Los Angeles, California Office)	B. Martin Luna (Resident at Maui Office)
Anne Price Fortney (Resident at Washington, D.C. Office)	John P. Manaut
	Matthew M. Matsunaga
	John R. McDonough (Resident at Los Angeles, California Office)

(See Next Column)

Garry W. Morse (Resident at Agana, Guam Office)	Jonathan L. Smoller (Resident at Los Angeles, California Office)
Randolph G. Muhlestein (Resident at Los Angeles, California Office)	James L. Starshak
Joseph D. Mullender, Jr. (Resident at Los Angeles, California Office)	Robert Edward Strand
	Renee L. Stransky (Resident at Washington, D.C. Office)
Mark K. Murakami (Resident at Kapolei, Hawaii Office)	Gerald A. Sumida (A Law Corporation)
Steven M. Nagata	Thomas R. Sylvester
Craig G. Nakamura (Resident at Maui Office)	Lance F. Taniguchi
David R. Nevitt (Resident at Saipan Office)	Allan Edward Tebbetts (Resident at Los Angeles, California Office)
Lawrence S. Okinaga (A Law Corporation)	Robert D. Triantos (Resident at Kailua-Kona Office)
David S. Olson (Resident at Los Angeles, California Office)	Paul M. Ueoka (Resident at Maui Office)
John D. Osborn (Resident at Saipan Office)	J. Thomas Van Winkle (A Law Corporation)
James M. Polish (Resident at Los Angeles, California Office)	Charles R. Wichman
Sylvester V. Quitiquit (Resident at Kona, Hawaii Office)	Donald C. Williams (Resident, Los Angeles, California)
Dean H. Robb	William C. Williams, Jr. (Resident at Agana, Guam Office)
Tom E. Roesser	David W. K. Wong
John E. Rogers (Resident, Mexico, D.F., Mexico Office)	Jon T. Yamamura
Meredith M. Sayre (Resident at Agana, Guam Office)	Duane H. Zobrist (Resident at Los Angeles, California Office)
Marcia K. Schultz (Resident at Saipan Office)	Adrián Zubikarai Arriola (Resident, Mexico Office)

ASSOCIATES

Kristen S. Armstrong (Resident, Agana, Guam Office)	Kathryn-Jean T. Kanemori
Sherrill A. Atwood (Resident at Hilo Office)	Richard J Kiefer
Lisanne M. Butterfield (Resident, Agana, Guam Office)	Peter K. Kubota (Resident at Hilo, Hawaii Office)
	Katherine G. Leonard
Mark W. Eliashof	Patricia Racicot Manso (Resident, Mexico, D.F., Mexico Office)
Randall H. Endo (Resident at Maui Office)	Kevin E. Moore (Resident at Saipan Office)
Peter N. Greenfeld (Resident, Los Angeles Office)	Nathan T. Natori
Joanne L. Grimes (Resident, Agana, Guam Office)	Ian L. Sandison
	Juliana C. Sandvold (Resident at Saipan Office)
Charles M. Heaukulani (Resident at Kailua-Kona Office)	Sinforoso M. Tolentino (Resident at Agana, Guam Office)
Lahela Hekekia	Ann Luotto Wolf (Resident at Los Angeles, California Office)
William W. Huckins	
Allen R. Wolff	

OF COUNSEL

Herbert G. Baerwitz (Resident at Los Angeles, California Office)	Tom K. Houston (Resident at Los Angeles, California Office)
Roger P. Crouthamel (Resident at Agana, Guam Office)	Herman T. F. Lum (Resident, Honolulu, Hawaii Office)
Leigh-Wai Doo (Resident at Honolulu, Hawaii Office)	Aaron Schildhaus (Resident at Washington, D.C. Office)
Dagmar V. Halamka (Resident at Los Angeles, California Office)	Terry E. Thomason
	Robert R. Thornton (Resident at Los Angeles, California Office)

For full biographical listings, see the Martindale-Hubbell Law Directory

CHAR SAKAMOTO ISHII & LUM (AV)

Suite 850, 841 Bishop Street, 96813
Telephone: 808-522-5133
Facsimile: 808-522-5144

MEMBERS OF FIRM

Vernon F. L. Char	David M. K. Lum
Steven Ching	Charles E. McKay
Elizabeth Ann Ishii	Ronald R. Sakamoto

OF COUNSEL

Michael K. Tanigawa

Lana Proctor Banbury	Jacqueline H. Furuta
Earl M. Ching	Carolyn E. Hayashi
Carolyn M. Oshiro	

For full biographical listings, see the Martindale-Hubbell Law Directory

CHUN, KERR, DODD, BEAMAN & WONG (AV)

Suite 900, 745 Fort Street Mall, 96813
Telephone: 808-528-8200
Telecopier: 808-536-5869

(See Next Column)

CHUN, KERR, DODD, BEAMAN & WONG, *Honolulu—Continued*

MEMBERS OF FIRM

Edward Y. C. Chun	Danton S. Wong
George L. T. Kerr	Leroy E. Colombe
William H. Dodd	Trudy Burns Stone
Andrew V. Beaman	Kyong-Su Im

ASSOCIATES

Curtis L. Sano	Andrew R. Bunn

Tracy D. Tanaka

References: Bank of Hawaii; First Hawaiian Bank.

For full biographical listings, see the Martindale-Hubbell Law Directory

---

DAMON KEY BOCKEN LEONG KUPCHAK ATTORNEYS AT LAW, A LAW CORPORATION (AV)

1600 Pauahi Tower, 1001 Bishop Street, 96813-3480
Telephone: 808-531-8031
Facsimile: 808-533-2242

R. Charles Bocken	Gregory W. Kugle
Jennifer Z. Brooks	Kenneth R. Kupchak
Clinton K. L. Ching	Denis C. H. Leong
C. F. Damon, Jr.	David P. McCauley
Gerhard Frohlich	James C. McWhinnie
Cindy A. Goodness	Jeanine S. Ogawa
Diane Deskins Hastert	Anna H. Oshiro
Charles W. Key	Douglas C. Smith
Christine A. Kubota	Alan Van Etten

Michael A. Yoshida

OF COUNSEL

Erik D. Eike	X. Ben Tao

Robert H. Thomas

Representative Clients: American Express Travel Related Services Company, Inc.; AIG Aviation Inc.; BHP Petroleum American, Hawaii, Inc.; C. Brewer & Company, Ltd.; Odakyu Electric Co., Ltd. Fletcher Pacific Construction Co., Ltd.; The Travelers Companies; Kintetsu International Express; Microsoft Corporation; The Sumitomo Bank Limited. Ltd.

For full biographical listings, see the Martindale-Hubbell Law Directory

---

FUJIYAMA, DUFFY & FUJIYAMA ATTORNEYS AT LAW, A LAW CORPORATION (AV)

2700 Pauahi Tower, Bishop Square, 1001 Bishop Street, 96813
Telephone: 808-536-0802
Telecopier: 808-536-5117

Wallace S. Fujiyama (1925-1994)	Rodney M. Fujiyama
James E. Duffy, Jr.	Archie T. Ikehara

Leslie E. Kobayashi

Ward F. N. Fujimoto	Lee T. Nakamura
Gregg M. Ushiroda	Lisa-Ann L. Kimura
Reese R. Nakamura	Rew K. Ikazaki
Danielle Noel Degele-Mathews (Not admitted in HI)	

Representative Clients: Hartford Accident & Indemnity Co.; Maryland Casualty Co.; New England Mutual Life Insurance Co.; Duty Free Shoppers, Ltd.; West Beach Estates (Ko Olina Resort).

For full biographical listings, see the Martindale-Hubbell Law Directory

---

GOODSILL ANDERSON QUINN & STIFEL (AV)

Alii Place, Suite 1800, 1099 Alakea Street, P.O. Box 3196, 96801-3196
Telephone: 808-547-5600
FAX: 808-547-5880
Email: info@goodsill.com *URL:* http://www.goodsill.com/
Kailua-Kona Office: 75-170 Hualalai Professional Complex, Suite D-216, P.O. Box 2639.
Telephone: 808-329-7731.
FAX: 808-326-2384.

MEMBERS OF FIRM

Martin Anderson	Lisa Woods Munger
Hugh Shearer	Ernest J. T. Loo
Conrad M. Weiser	Bruce L. Lamon
David J. Dezzani	Peter T. Kashiwa
Ronald H. W. Lum	Russell S. Kato
David J. Reber	Lant A. Johnson
John R. Lacy	Vincent A. Piekarski
Raymond Shigeo Iwamoto	Mark B. Desmarais
Thomas W. Williams, Jr.	Linda Zichittella Leong
Michael A. Shea	Scott G. Leong
William S. Miller	Leighton J. H. S. Yuen
Jacqueline L. S. Earle	Corlis J. Chang
Kenneth A. Ross (Resident, Kailua-Kona Office)	Carl J. Schlack, Jr.
	Barbara A. Petrus
Lani L. Ewart	Robert J. Hackman
Randall K. Steverson	Cynthia M. Nojima
Patricia Y. Lee	Miki Okumura
Gary M. Slovin	Mark F. Ito

(See Next Column)

MEMBERS OF FIRM (Continued)

Wayne H. Muraoka	Gail Otsuka Ayabe
Audrey E. J. Ng	Dale Edward F.T. Zane
Donna A. Tanoue	LindaLee K. Farm
Gregory R. Kim	Margaret Jenkins Leong
Richard K. Mirikitani	Carol Ann Eblen
Alan S. Fujimoto	Craig I. Nakanishi
Walter C. Davison	P. Roy Catalani
David W. Sherman	Jeffrey Scott Piper
Gregg J. Kinkley	Roy John Tjioe
Raymond K. Okada	Lynne T. Toyofuku

COUNSEL

Randall W. Roth	A. Richard Philpott
E. Laurence Gay	Alan W. C. Ma

ASSOCIATES

Kurt K. Kawafuchi	Natalie S. Hiu
Kellie M. N. Sekiya	Russell K. Kaupu
Judy Y. Lee	Elizabeth B. Croom (Resident, Kailua-Kona Office)
Elizabeth A. Strance (Resident, Kailua-Kona Office)	Lisa A. Bail
Lennes N. Omuro	Mia Y. Teruya
Lisa T. Redell	Donna H. Kalama
Derek R. Kobayashi (Resident, Kailua-Kona Office)	Carolyn K. Gugelyk
	Douglas A. Codiga
Mary A. Renfer	Vincent J. Chow
Thomas L. Benedict	Lisa S. Ho Wong
Peter Y. Kikuta	Normand R. Lezy
Trisha M. Kimura	Richard H. S. Sing
Karen Lynn Scarborough Stanitz	Michael S. Joaquin
Edmund K. Saffery	Eric A. Elkind

Meredith A. Burns

OF COUNSEL

Marshall M. Goodsill	Genro Kashiwa
William F. Quinn	Robert G. Hite

Robert F. Hirano

Representative Clients: Aetna Life and Casualty; Argonaut Insurance Co.; Fireman's Fund Insurance Co.; The Home Insurance; Industrial Indemnity Co.; MEDMARC; State Farm Insurance Co.; Tokio Marine Management Inc.; Transamerica Insurance Co.; United States Aviation Underwriters Incorporated.

For full biographical listings, see the Martindale-Hubbell Law Directory

---

HAMILTON, GIBSON, NICKELSEN, RUSH & MOORE

(See Rush Moore Craven Sutton Morry & Beh)

KOBAYASHI, SUGITA & GODA (AV)

A Partnership including Professional Corporations
8th Floor, Hawaii Tower, 745 Fort Street, 96813
Telephone: 808-539-8700
Telecopier: 808-539-8799
Telex: 6502396585 MCI
MCI Mail: 23 96585
ABA/Net: ABA2281

MEMBERS OF FIRM

Bert T. Kobayashi, Jr., (Atty. at Law, A Law Corp.)	Wendell H. Fuji (Atty. at Law, A Law Corp.)
Kenneth Y. Sugita (Atty. at Law, A Law Corp.)	Robert K. Ichikawa (Atty. at Law, A Law Corp.)
Alan M. Goda (Atty. at Law, A Law Corp.)	Janeen-Ann A. Olds (Atty. At Law, A Law Corp.)
Dale W. Lee (Atty. at Law, A Law Corp.)	Clifford K. Higa (Atty. At Law, A Law Corp.)
Lex R. Smith (Atty. at Law, A Law Corp.)	Charles W. Gall (Atty. At Law, A Law Corp.)
Byron C. Feldman, II (Atty. at Law, A Law Corp.)	John F. Lezak (Atty. at Law, A Law Corp.)
David L. Monroy (Atty. at Law, A Law Corp.)	Larry L. Myers (Atty. at Law, A Law Corp.)

ASSOCIATES

Alan K. Maeda	Lisa W. Cataldo
Wintehn K. T. Park	Nathan H. Yoshimoto
Burt T. Lau	Jennifer M.L. Chock
Rod S. Aoki	Brian T. Nakanishi
Ernest H. Nomura	Jonathan A. Kobayashi
Joseph N. Kiyose	Bruce A. Nakamura
John A. Kodachi	Gary K. Nakata
Christopher T. Kobayashi	Ruth K. Oh

OF COUNSEL

Bert T. Kobayashi, Sr.

Reference: First Hawaiian Bank.

For full biographical listings, see the Martindale-Hubbell Law Directory

Honolulu—Continued

LYONS, BRANDT, COOK & HIRAMATSU (AV)

841 Bishop Street, Suite 1800, 96813
Telephone: 808-524-7030
Facsimile: 808-533-3011
Email: lbch@hits.net

MEMBERS OF FIRM

Samuel A. B. Lyons	Bradford F. K. Bliss
George W. Brandt	Steven Y. Otaguro
Thomas E. Cook	Stefan M. Reinke
Beverly Lynne K. Hiramatsu	Paul R. Grable
Jeffrey A. Griswold	Edquon Lee
Jill A. Fukunaga	

For full biographical listings, see the Martindale-Hubbell Law Directory

McCORRISTON MIHO MILLER MUKAI (AV)

Five Waterfront Plaza, 4th Floor, 500 Ala Moana Boulevard, 96813
Telephone: 808-529-7300
Facsimile: 808-524-8293
Cable: Attorneys, Honolulu
Mailing Address: P.O. Box 2800, Honolulu, Hawaii, 96803-2800
Hilo, Hawaii Office: 56 Waianuenue Avenue, Suite 217, 96720.
Telephone: 808-935-6537.
Facsimile: 808-935-3398.

PARTNERS

William C. McCorriston	Michael J. O'Malley
Jon T. Miho	Eric T. Kawatani
Clifford J. Miller	Randall K. Schmitt
Franklin K. Mukai	Keith K. Suzuka
Stanley Y. Mukai	John Y. Yamano
Donald K. O. Wong	R. John Seibert
D. Scott MacKinnon	Michael Rosenthal
Kenneth B. Marcus	Sharon H. Nishi
Kenneth G. K. Hoo	Thomas E. Bush
Patrick K. Lau	David J. Minkin
Mark J. Bennett	Randall F. Sakumoto
Nadine Y. Ando	Lisa M. Ginoza
Richard B. Miller	Andrew W. Char
David N. Kuriyama	Alexander R. Jampel

OF COUNSEL
Robert E. Warner

COUNSEL

Brian T. Hirai	Charles E. Pear, Jr.

ASSOCIATES

Kimberly Rae McCorkle	Joel D. Kam
Peter J. Hamasaki	Douglas K. Ushijima
Darren Patrick Conley	Shulammite Kim
Carrie K. Okinaga	David R. Harada-Stone
Christopher J. Cole	Dean J. Myatt
Stacey M. Robinson	

Representative Clients: Phillip Morris USA; Hawaii Dental Service; Mandarin Oriental Hotel Group; Sports Shinko Co., Ltd.; Boyd Gaming Corporation; Gallo Winery; Deloitte & Touche; Pacific Basin Economic Council.

For full biographical listings, see the Martindale-Hubbell Law Directory

PAUL, JOHNSON, PARK & NILES ATTORNEYS AT LAW, A LAW CORPORATION (AV)

Suite 1300 Pacific Tower, 1001 Bishop Street, P.O. Box 4438, 96812-4438
Telephone: 808-524-1212
Telecopier: 808-528-1654
Cable Address: "Pacificlaw"
Wailuku, Maui, Hawaii Office: 203 H.G.E.A. Building, 2145 Kaohu Street, P.O. Box 870. 96793-0870.
Telephone: 808-242-6644.
Fax: 808-244-9775.

James T. Paul	Sheryl L. Nicholson
David Arthur Johnson	Robyn B. Chun
Corey Y. S. Park	Judy A. Tanaka

Keith Y. Amemiya	Toni G. Bissen

OF COUNSEL
Sheila L. Y. Sakashita

For full biographical listings, see the Martindale-Hubbell Law Directory

REID, RICHARDS & MIYAGI (AV)

A Partnership including Professional Corporations
Pauahi Tower, Suite 1200, 1001 Bishop Street, 96813-3498
Telephone: 808-524-2466
Fax: 808-524-2556

(See Next Column)

MEMBERS OF FIRM

Carleton B. Reid (A Law Corporation)	Melvyn M. Miyagi (A Law Corporation)
Robert P. Richards (A Law Corporation)	Ralph J. O'Neill
	Katharine M. Nohr

James V. Myhre	Tamara M. Gerrard
Roy F. Epstein	John E. Drotz
Michele-Lynn E. Luke	Deborah Chen
L. Darlene Mitchell	Jennifer Ellen Reid
Marie A. Sheldon	Celia A. Urion
Michael H. Tsuchida	Irene C. Sun
Duane R. Miyashiro	

For full biographical listings, see the Martindale-Hubbell Law Directory

RUSH MOORE CRAVEN SUTTON MORRY & BEH (AV)

20th Floor, Hawaii Tower Amfac Center, 745 Fort Street, 96813-3862
Telephone: 808-521-0400
Facsimile: 808-521-0597
Cable Address: "Lawyers Honolulu"
Wailuku, Maui, Hawaii Office: One Main Plaza, Suite 650, 2200 Main Street.
Telephone: 808-244-3332.
Facsimile: 808-244-5322.

MEMBERS OF FIRM

Marshall B. Henshaw (1889-1970)	Stephen K. C. Mau (A Law Corporation)
William R. Loomis (1939-1980)	Earl T. Sato
Don C. Hamilton (1914-1984)	J. Stephen Street
Harold W. Nickelsen (1924-1985)	Jennifer M. Yusi
Frank D. Gibson, Jr. (1920-1990)	David Shibata
Harold W. Conroy (Retired)	Carol Y. Asai-Sato
Dwight M. Rush (Retired)	Susan Tius
Willson C. Moore, Jr. (Retired)	Cheryl A. Nakamura
Anthony B. Craven (Retired)	Irene A. Anzai
Richard C. Sutton, Jr.	Patricia Mathias NaPier
G. Richard Morry	Donald Carl Machado, Jr.
Walter Beh, II	Ray P. Wimberley (Resident at Maui Office)
Edward M. Sanpei	Tracy G. Chinen
	Daniel J. Berman
Douglas A. Crosier	

ASSOCIATES

Lisa K. Strandtman	Lance Scott Au
Caroline S. Otani	Denise P. Balanay
Jeffrey C. Johnson	Linda N. Monden (Resident at Wailuku Office)
Ann Kiele Watanabe	
Paul M. Iguchi	

Representative Clients: Bank of Hawaii; Pioneer Federal Savings Bank; Hyatt Corporation; Kamehameha Schools/Bernice Pauahi Bishop Estate; Government Employees Insurance Co.; Underwriters at Lloyds.

For full biographical listings, see the Martindale-Hubbell Law Directory

TORKILDSON, KATZ, FONSECA, JAFFE, MOORE & HETHERINGTON ATTORNEYS AT LAW, A LAW CORPORATION (AV)

Amfac Building, 15th Floor, 700 Bishop Street, 96813-4187
Telephone: 808-523-6000
Cable Address: "Counsel"
Telex: RCA 723-8185
Telecopier: 808-523-6001
Hilo, Hawaii Office: 100 Pauahi Street, Suite 206.
Telephone: 808-961-0406.
Telecopier: 808-935-6725.

Ernest C. Moore, Jr. (1913-1972)	Ronald I. Heller
Raymond M. Torkildson	Wilson M. N. Loo
Robert S. Katz	Steven B. Jacobson
Roger W. Fonseca	Sabrina R. Toma
Edward A. Jaffe	Perry W. Confalone
Ernest C. Moore, III	Oren T. Chikamoto
J. George Hetherington	Phillip A. Li
Terrence M. Lee	A. Scott Leithead (Resident, Hilo Office)
Richard M. Rand	Wayne S. Yoshigai
Jeffrey S. Harris	Steven L. F. Ho
Craig K. Hirai	Matt A. Tsukazaki
Gregory M. Sato	Steven V. Torkildson
John L. Knorek	

OF COUNSEL

Newton J. Chu (Resident, Hilo Office)	David Waters

Stephanie Anne Chin	Kelly Ann Patch
Timothy A. Walker	Clayton A. Kamida
Roman F. Amaguin, Jr.	

For full biographical listings, see the Martindale-Hubbell Law Directory

Honolulu—Continued

WATANABE, ING & KAWASHIMA (AV)

A Partnership including Professional Corporations
Hawaii Tower, 5th & 6th Floors, 745 Fort Street, 96813
Telephone: 808-544-8300
Facsimile: 808-544-8399

MEMBERS OF FIRM

Jeffrey N. Watanabe (Atty. at Law, A Law Corp.)	Lyle Y. Harada (Atty. at Law, A Law Corp.)
James Kawashima (Atty. at Law, A Law Corp.)	Michael A. Lorusso (Atty. at Law, A Law Corp.)
J. Douglas Ing (Atty. at Law, A Law Corp.)	Pamela J. Larson (Atty. At Law, A Law Corp.)
Wray H. Kondo (Atty. at Law, A Law Corp.)	William H. Gilardy, Jr. (Atty. At Law, A Law Corp.)
John T. Komeiji (Atty. at Law, A Law Corp.)	John R. Aube (Atty. at Law, A Law Corp.)
Ronald Y. K. Leong (Atty. at Law, A Law Corp.)	Jan M.L.Y. Amii (Atty. at Law, A Law Corp.)
Robert T. Takamatsu (Atty. at Law, A Law Corp.)	Edward B. Rogin (Atty. at Law, A Law Corp.)
Cynthia Winegar (Atty. at Law, A Law Corp.)	Seth M. Reiss
Randall Y. Yamamoto (Atty. at Law, A Law Corp.)	Curtis C. Kim

ASSOCIATES

Donna Y. Kanemaru	Michael C. Bird
George B. Apter	Brian Y. Hiyane
Marcus B. Sierra	Dennis J. Hwang
Lani Narikiyo	Teri Y. Kondo
Peter L. Fritz	Jeff N. Miyashiro
LLoyd S. Yoshioka	John Seiichi Sasaki
Beth K. Fujimoto	Gregory Y.P. Tom
Patsy H. Kirio	Eri Kashiwabara
Kevin H. Oda	Jonathan W. Y. Lai

Lester M. H. Goo

OF COUNSEL
George R. Ariyoshi

ASIA PACIFIC CONSULTANT
Victor Hao Li (Not admitted in HI)

LEGAL SUPPORT PERSONNEL
GOVERNMENT AFFAIRS ADVISOR
Millicent M. Y. H. Kim

References: First Hawaiian Bank; American Savings Bank.

For full biographical listings, see the Martindale-Hubbell Law Directory

MICHAEL J. Y. WONG (AV)

2222 Central Pacific Plaza, 220 South King Street, 96813
Telephone: 808-536-1855
Fax: 808-536-1857

ASSOCIATES
R. Malia Taum

For full biographical listings, see the Martindale-Hubbell Law Directory

KAHULUI, Maui Co.

MANCINI, ROWLAND & WELCH (AV)

A Partnership including Law Corporations
Formerly Case & Lynch of Miami, Florida.
The Kahului Building, 33 Lono Avenue, Suite 470, 96732-1681
Telephone: 808-871-8351
Facsimile: 808-871-0732

Paul R. Mancini (A Law Corporation)	Thomas D. Welch, Jr.
Robert E. Rowland (A Law Corporation)	Caroline Peters Egli
	R. Clay Sutherland
	Matthew V. Pietsch

OF COUNSEL
Robert A. Richardson

For full biographical listings, see the Martindale-Hubbell Law Directory

KAILUA-KONA, Hawaii Co.

CADES SCHUTTE FLEMING & WRIGHT (AV)

Hualalai Center, Suite B-303, 75-170 Hualalai Road, 96740
Telephone: 808-329-5811
Telecopier: 808-326-1175
Email: cades@cades.com
Honolulu, Hawaii Office: 1000 Bishop Street, P. O. Box 939.
Telephone: 808-521-9200.
Affiliated Law Firm: Udom-Prok Associates Law Offices, 105/36 Tharinee Mansion, Bormo Raj Chananee Road Bangkoknoi, Bangkok, Thailand, 10700.
Telephone: 011 662 435-4146.

(See Next Column)

RESIDENT PARTNER
Roy A. Vitousek, III
RESIDENT ASSOCIATES
Lynn H. Higashi   Kimberly O'Neill Jackson

For full biographical listings, see the Martindale-Hubbell Law Directory

CARLSMITH BALL WICHMAN CASE & ICHIKI (AV)

A Partnership including Law Corporations
Second Floor, Bank of Hawaii Annex Building, P.O. Box 1720, 96745-1720
Telephone: 808-329-6464
Telecopier: 808-329-9450
Honolulu, Hawaii Office: Suite 2200, Pacific Tower, 1001 Bishop Street. P.O. Box 656.
Telephone: 808-523-2500.
Kapolei, Hawaii Office: Kapolei Building, Suite 318, 1001 Kamokila Boulevard.
Telephone: 808-523-2500.
Wailuku, Maui, Hawaii Office: One Main Plaza, Suite 400, 2200 Main Street, P.O. Box 1086.
Telephone: 808-242-4535.
Hilo, Hawaii Office: 121 Waianuenue Avenue, P.O. Box 686.
Telephone: 808-935-6644.
Agana, Guam Office: 4th Floor, Bank of Hawaii Building, P.O. Box BF.
Telephone: 671-472-6813.
Saipan, Commonwealth of the Northern Mariana Islands Office: Carlsmith Building, Capitol Hill, P.O. Box 5241.
Telephone: (011) 670-322-3455.
Los Angeles, California Office: 555 South Flower Street, 25th Floor.
Telephone: 213-955-1200.
Washington, D.C. Office: 700 14th Street, N.W., 9th Floor.
Telephone: 202-508-1025.
Mexico City, Mexico Office: Monte Pelvoux 111, Piso 1, Col. Lomas de Chapultepec, 11000 Mexico, D.F.
Telephone: (011-52-5) 520-8514.
Fax: (011-52-5) 540-1545.
Mexico, D.F. Office of Carlsmith Ball Garcia Cacho y Asociados, S.C. (Authorized to practice Mexican Law): Monte Pelvoux 111, Piso 1, Col. Lomas de Chapultepec, 11000, Mexico, D.F.
Telephone: (011-52-5) 520-8514.
Fax: (011-52-5) 540-1545.

RESIDENT PARTNERS
Sylvester V. Quitiquit   Robert D. Triantos
RESIDENT ASSOCIATES
Charles M. Heaukulani

For full biographical listings, see the Martindale-Hubbell Law Directory

GOODSILL ANDERSON QUINN & STIFEL (AV)

75-170 Hualalai Professional Complex, Suite D-216, P.O. Box 2639, 96745
Telephone: 808-329-7731
FAX: 808-326-2384
Email: info@goodsill.com *URL:* http://www.goodsill.com/
Honolulu, Hawaii Office: Alii Place, Suite 1800, 1099 Alakea Street, P.O. Box 3196.
Telephone: 808-547-5600.
FAX: 808-547-5880.

RESIDENT MEMBERS
Kenneth A. Ross
RESIDENT ASSOCIATES
Elizabeth A. Strance   Derek R. Kobayashi
Elizabeth B. Croom

For full biographical listings, see the Martindale-Hubbell Law Directory

WAILUKU,* Maui Co.

CARLSMITH BALL WICHMAN CASE & ICHIKI (AV)

A Partnership including Law Corporations
One Main Plaza, Suite 400, 2200 Main Street, P.O. Box 1086, 96793-2225
Telephone: 808-242-4535
Telecopier: 808-244-4974
Honolulu, Hawaii Office: Suite 2200, Pacific Tower, 1001 Bishop Street. P.O. Box 656.
Telephone: 808-523-2500.
Kapolei, Hawaii Office: Kapolei Building, Suite 318, 1001 Kamokila Boulevard.
Telephone: 808-523-2500.
Kailua-Kona, Hawaii Office: Second Floor, Bank of Hawaii Annex Building, P.O. Box 1720.
Telephone: 808-329-6464.
Hilo, Hawaii Office: 121 Waianuenue Avenue, P.O. Box 686.
Telephone: 808-935-6644.
Agana, Guam Office: 4th Floor, Bank of Hawaii Building, P.O. Box BF.
Telephone: 671-472-6813.
Saipan, Commonwealth of the Northern Mariana Islands Office: Carlsmith Building, Capitol Hill, P.O. Box 5241.
Telephone: (011) 670-322-3455.

(See Next Column)

CARLSMITH BALL WICHMAN CASE & ICHIKI—Continued

Los Angeles, California Office: 555 South Flower Street, 25th Floor.
Telephone: 213-955-1200.
Washington, D.C. Office: 700 14th Street, N.W., 9th Floor.
Telephone: 202-508-1025.
Mexico City, Mexico Office: Monte Pelvoux 111, Piso 1, Col. Lomas de
Chapultepec, 11000 Mexico, D.F.
Telephone: (011-52-5) 520-8514.
Fax: (011-52-5) 540-1545.
Mexico, D.F. Office of Carlsmith Ball Garcia Cacho y Asociados, S.C.
(Authorized to practice Mexican Law): Monte Pelvoux 111, Piso 1, Col.
Lomas de Chapultepec, 11000 Mexico, D.F.
Telephone: (011-52-5) 540-8514.
Fax: (011-52-5) 540-1545.

RESIDENT PARTNERS

Grant Y. M. Chun	B. Martin Luna
Tom C. Leuteneker	Craig G. Nakamura

Paul M. Ueoka

ASSOCIATE

Randall H. Endo

For full biographical listings, see the Martindale-Hubbell Law Directory

PAUL, JOHNSON, PARKS & NILES ATTORNEYS AT LAW, A LAW CORPORATION (AV)

203 H.G.E.A. Building, 2145 Kaohu Street, P.O. Box 870, 96793-0870
Telephone: 808-242-6644
Fax: 808-244-9775
Honolulu, Hawaii Office: Suite 1300 Pacific Tower, 1001 Bishop Street,
P.O. Box 4438. 96812-4438.
Telephone: 808-524-1212.
Telecopier: 808-528-1654.

Dennis James Niles	William M. McKeon

Carla M. Nakata

For full biographical listings, see the Martindale-Hubbell Law Directory

IDAHO

AMERICAN FALLS,* Power Co. — (Refer to Pocatello)

BLACKFOOT,* Bingham Co. — (Refer to Pocatello)

BOISE,* Ada Co.

CANTRILL, SKINNER, SULLIVAN & KING (AV)

1423 Tyrell Lane, P.O. Box 359, 83701
Telephone: 208-344-8035
Fax: 208-345-7212

MEMBERS OF FIRM

David W. Cantrill	John L. King
Gardner W. Skinner, Jr.	Robert D. Lewis
Willis E. Sullivan, III	Frank P. Kotyk

ASSOCIATES

Tyra H. Stubbs	Clinton O. Casey

LEGAL SUPPORT PERSONNEL

Garianne Erwin

Representative Clients: Safeco Insurance Companies; Prudential Property and
Casualty Insurance Co.; State Insurance Fund; Farmers Insurance Co.; Jordan-Wilcomb Company; Nature Conservancy; Independent School District
of Boise City; Hartford Insurance Group.
Reference: Key Bank.

For full biographical listings, see the Martindale-Hubbell Law Directory

COSHO, HUMPHREY, GREENER & WELSH, P.A. (AV)

The Carnegie Building, 815 West Washington, 83702
Telephone: 208-344-7811
Fax: 208-338-3290
Email: tgwalker@micron.net

Louis H. Cosho	Stanley W. Welsh
Howard D. Humphrey	Fredric V. Shoemaker
Jack S. Gjording	Christopher C. Burke
Richard H. Greener	Joseph M. Meier

David M. Penny

Nancy Jo Hopkins Garrett	Steven B. Price
Tore Beal Gwartney	Chris Kronberg
Phil E. De Angeli	Thomas G. Walker, Jr.

Daniel Loras Glynn

Representative Clients: Reliance Insurance Co.; United Pacific Insurance Co.;
Mobil Oil Corp.; Micron Technology, Inc.; J. R. Simplot Co.; American
States Insurance Co.; Oregon Automobile Insurance Co; North Pacific Insurance Co.

(See Next Column)

For full biographical listings, see the Martindale-Hubbell Law Directory

EBERLE, BERLIN, KADING, TURNBOW & McKLVEEN, CHARTERED (AV)

Capitol Park Plaza, 300 North Sixth Street, P.O. Box 1368, 83701
Telephone: 208-344-8535
Facsimile: 208-344-8542

J. Louis Eberle (1890-1964)	Joseph H. Uberuaga, II
T.H. Eberle (1922-1977)	Robert L. Berlin
R.B. Kading, Jr.	Scott D. Hess
R.M. Turnbow	Bradley G. Andrews
William J. McKlveen	William A. Fuhrman
Warren Eugene Jones	Richard K. Lierz
Mark S. Geston	Neil D. McFeeley
Thomas R. Linville	Stephen A. Bradbury
Richard A. Riley	Kimbell D. Gourley

Steven E. Alkire

Ann K. Shepard	Stanley J. Tharp
Derrick J. O'Neill	Samuel A. Diddle

Sarah E. Scott

OF COUNSEL

James L. Berlin	Gary C. Randall

General Counsel: Key Bank of Idaho; Key Trust Company of the West; Key
Mortgage Funding; Diamond Sports.
Representative Clients: Key Bank of Idaho; U.S. West Communications; Cessna Aircraft Co.

For full biographical listings, see the Martindale-Hubbell Law Directory

ELAM & BURKE, A PROFESSIONAL ASSOCIATION (AV)

Key Financial Center, 702 West Idaho Street, P.O. Box 1539, 83701
Telephone: 208-343-5454
Telecopier: 208-384-5844
Email: eblaw@elamburke.com

Laurel E. Elam (1888-1974)	William G. Dryden
Carl A. Burke (1898-1961)	Peter C. K. Marshall
Carl P. Burke	Mary S. Hobson
M. Allyn Dingel, Jr.	Trudy Hanson Fouser
John Magel	Scott L. Campbell
David B. Lincoln	Bobbi Killian Dominick
James D. LaRue	William J. Batt
Randall A. Peterman	Jeffery J. Ventrella
Ryan P. Armbruster	James A. Ford
Melville W. Fisher, II	Jeffrey A. Thomson

Harry M. Lane, Jr.

J. Ray Durtschi	Sandra L. Clapp
Bradlee R. Frazer	Rebecca A. Broadbent
Jeffrey W. Pusch	Victoria C. Yu

Representative Clients: Morrison-Knudsen, Inc; Texas Instruments, Inc.;
Prudential Securities, Inc.; Pechiney Corp.; U.S. Bancorp; U.S. West Communications; State Farm Insurance Cos.; Sinclair Oil Co. d/b/a/ Sun Valley
Co.; Farmers Insurance Group; Thompson Creek Mining Co.

For full biographical listings, see the Martindale-Hubbell Law Directory

EVANS, KEANE LLP (AV)

Suite 200, 1101 West River Street, P.O. Box 959, 83701-0959
Telephone: 208-384-1800
Facsimile: 208-345-3514
Email: EKIDALAW@MICRON.NET
Kellogg, Idaho Office: 111 Main Street, P.O. Box 659.
Telephone: 208-784-1105.

MEMBERS OF FIRM

Rex Blackburn	Robert A. Anderson
Bruce C. Jones	Jed W. Manwaring
Barton L. Kline	James D. Hovren
William A. McCurdy	David W. Gratton

OF COUNSEL

Blaine F. Evans

K. Heidi Gudgell	Joyce Hettenbach
Thomas B. Humphrey	Michael P. Stefanic II
Jon M. Bauman	Paul J. Augustine
Kara Lee Barton	David V. Nielsen

Patrick E. Mahoney

KELLOGG OFFICE

James P. Keane (1925-1988)	Charles L. A. Cox
Fred M. Gibler	Justin W. Julian

(See Next Column)

Evans, Keane LLP, *Boise—Continued*

John O. Cossel

Representative Clients: American Cyanamid Co.; Chrysler Corp.; Coeur d'Alene Mines Corp.; Crum & Forster; Ford Motor Co.; Hecla Mining Co.; Idaho Power Co.; State Farm Mutual Automobile Insurance Co.; Sunshine Mining and Refining Company; U.S. Bank of Idaho, N.A.

For full biographical listings, see the Martindale-Hubbell Law Directory

JAMES R. GILLESPIE, P.A. (AV)

512 West Bannock, P.O. Box 2337, 83701
Telephone: 208-344-8400
Fax: 208-344-7100

James R. Gillespie

For full biographical listings, see the Martindale-Hubbell Law Directory

GREEN LAW OFFICES (AV)

P.O. Box 2597, 83701-2597
Telephone: 208-342-8915
Fax: 208-342-2718
Email: cumergreen@aol.com

Cumer L. Green
ASSOCIATES
Debra A. Silk
OF COUNSEL
Patti Powell
LEGAL SUPPORT PERSONNEL
Gary W. Shaw (Chief, Legal Support Group)

Representative Client: Idaho School Boards Association, Inc.; Potlatch Corporation; Bell Helmets, Inc.; R.C. Bigelow, Inc.; Fleetwood Enterprises, Inc.; United Airlines; Peter Schott's; Pacific Crown Timber; Croman Corp.; IDA-West Energy Co.

For full biographical listings, see the Martindale-Hubbell Law Directory

HOPKINS, RODEN, CROCKETT, HANSEN & HOOPES (AV)

802 West Bannock, Suite 900, P.O. Box 2110, 83701-2110
Telephone: 208-336-7930
Fax: 208-336-9154
Email: roden@micron.net
Idaho Falls, Idaho Office: 428 Park Avenue, P.O. Box 51219, 83405-1219.
Telephone: 208-523-4445.
Fax: 208-523-4474.

MEMBERS OF FIRM
William C. Roden

John R. Rowe	William E. Dean

Representative Clients: Wells Fargo Bank; The Nature Conservancy of Idaho; Micron Technology, Inc.; Hewlett Packard Co.; U.S. West Communications; Anheuser-Busch Companies, Inc.; Wal-Mart, Inc.; Eastern Idaho Economic Development Council, Inc.; Mutual of Enumclaw; Wausau Insurance Cos.

For full biographical listings, see the Martindale-Hubbell Law Directory

LYNCH & ASSOCIATES, P.L.L.C. (AV)

West One Plaza, 101 S. Capitol Boulevard, Suite 1601, P.O. Box 739, 83701
Telephone: 208-331-5088
Fax: 208-331-0088

James B. Lynch

Penny L. Dykas	Mary L. McDougal
Katherine M. Lynch	

For full biographical listings, see the Martindale-Hubbell Law Directory

MARTIN, CHAPMAN, SCHILD & LASSAW, CHARTERED (AV)

216 West Jefferson Street, P.O. Box 2898, 83701
Telephone: 208-343-6485
Fax: 208-343-9819
Sun Valley, Idaho Office: P.O. Box 744.
Telephone: 208-788-2876.
Fax: 208-788-2818.
Twin Falls, Idaho Office: 834 Falls Avenue, Suite 1020A.
Telephone: 208-734-9629.

John S. Chapman	Raymond D. Schild
J. F. Martin (1893-1967)	Donald A. Lassaw
C. Ben Martin (1921-1995)	Joseph John Alegria II
Thomas R. Henry	

References: West One Bank, Idaho, N.A. (formerly Idaho First National Bank); First Security Bank of Idaho, N.A.

(See Next Column)

For full biographical listings, see the Martindale-Hubbell Law Directory

MOFFATT, THOMAS, BARRETT, ROCK & FIELDS, CHARTERED (AV)

101 South Capitol Boulevard, P.O. Box 829, 83702
Telephone: 208-345-2000
FAX: 208-385-5384
Email: info@moffatt.com
Idaho Falls Office: 525 Park Avenue, Suite 2D, P.O. Box 1367, 83403.
Telephone: 208-522-6700.
FAX: 208-522-5111.
Pocatello, Idaho Office: 845 West Center, Suite C, P.O. Box 4941, 83201.
Telephone: 208-233-2001.

Willis C. Moffatt (1907-1980)	Stephen R. Thomas
Eugene C. Thomas	Jon S. Gorski
John W. Barrett	Gary T. Dance (Resident, Idaho
R. B. Rock	Falls and Pocatello Offices)
Richard C. Fields	Gerald T. Husch
Robert E. Bakes	Kirk R. Helvie
Paul S. Street	Thomas C. Morris
Larry C. Hunter	Michael E. Thomas
Glenna M. Christensen	James C. deGlee
Mark S. Prusynski	Patricia M. Olsson
Morgan W. Richards, Jr.	Mark A. Ellison
Michael G. McPeek	Patrick J. Kole

Stephen J. Olson	Bradley J. Williams
Andrew P. Doman	James L. Martin
David S. Jensen	Kelly Greene McConnell
Allen K. Davis	Michael B. Harrington
	(Not admitted in ID)

Representative Clients: BMC West Corporation; Chevron, U.S.A.; First Security Bank of Idaho, N.A.; General Motors Corp.; Idaho Potato Commission; Intermountain Gas Co.; John Alden Life Insurance Co.; Micron Technology, Inc.; Royal Insurance Cos.; St. Luke's Regional Medical Center & Mountain States Tumor Institute.

For full biographical listings, see the Martindale-Hubbell Law Directory

MOORE, BASKIN & PARKER (AV)

Washington Federal Plaza, 1001 West Idaho Street, Suite 400, P.O. Box 6756, 83707
Telephone: 208-336-6900
Facsimile: 208-336-7031

MEMBERS OF FIRM
Michael W. Moore	Thomas P. Baskin, III
	Paige Alan Parker

OF COUNSEL
Joseph M. Imhoff, Jr.

Representative Clients: Aetna Casualty & Surety, Co.; Capitol Indemnity Co.; Clarendon Insurance Co.; Crawford & Co.; Empire Fire & Marine Insurance Co.; Fireman's Fund Insurance Cos.; Idaho Counties Reciprocal Management Program; Idaho State Insurance Fund; Insurance Company of the West; Protective Insurance Co.

For full biographical listings, see the Martindale-Hubbell Law Directory

---

BONNERS FERRY, * Boundary Co. — (Refer to Coeur d'Alene)

BURLEY, * Cassia Co. — (Refer to Rupert)

CHALLIS, * Custer Co. — (Refer to Idaho Falls)

EMMETT, * Gem Co. — (Refer to Caldwell)

GOODING, * Gooding Co. — (Refer to Twin Falls)

HAILEY, * Blaine Co. — (Refer to Ketchum)

IDAHO FALLS, * Bonneville Co.

HOPKINS, RODEN, CROCKETT, HANSEN & HOOPES (AV)

428 Park Avenue, P.O. Box 51219, 83405-1219
Telephone: 208-523-4445
Fax: 208-523-4474
Email: hrchh@srv.net
Boise, Idaho Office: 802 West Bannock, Suite 900, P.O. Box 2110, 83701-2110.
Telephone: 208-336-7930.
Fax: 208-336-9154.

MEMBERS OF FIRM
Seward H. French, III	D. Fredrick Hoopes
(1941-1984)	Lary S. Larson
Ted C. Springer (1943-1984)	Paul B. Rippel
C. Timothy Hopkins	Teresa L. Sturm
William C. Roden	Steven K. Brown
Gregory L. Crockett	David H. Shipman
John D. Hansen	Katherine S. Moriarty

(See Next Column)

HOPKINS, RODEN, CROCKETT, HANSEN & HOOPES—*Continued*

John R. Rowe	William E. Dean
Reed E. Andrus	Mark Pannell
Curtis Reed Smith	(Not admitted in ID)

Steve Richards

REGISTERED PATENT AGENT

Robert A. deGroot

Representative Clients: Wells Fargo Bank; The Nature Conservancy of Idaho; Micron Technology, Inc.; Hewlett Packard Co.; U.S. West Communications; Anheuser-Busch Companies, Inc.; Wal-Mart, Inc.; Eastern Idaho Economic Development Council, Inc.; Mutual of Enumclaw; Wausau Insurance Cos.

For full biographical listings, see the Martindale-Hubbell Law Directory

PETERSEN, MOSS, OLSEN, CARR, ESKELSON & HALL (AV)

485 E Street, 83401
Telephone: 208-523-4650
FAX: 208-524-3391

MEMBERS OF FIRM

Dennis M. Olsen (1930-1985)	Wm. Charles Carr
George C. Petersen, Jr.	Scott P. Eskelson
Reed L. Moss	Stephen D. Hall

Representative Client: State Farm Insurance Cos.

For full biographical listings, see the Martindale-Hubbell Law Directory

ST. CLAIR, DALLING & MEACHAM (AV)

A Partnership including Professional Corporations
The Earl Building, 501 Park Avenue, P.O. Box 50050, 83405
Telephone: 208-522-2350
Fax: 208-524-6342

Clency St. Clair (1871-1957)	Dean Dalling (Chartered)
Robert W. St. Clair (1907-1989)	Gregory P. Meacham
William R. Dalling (Chartered)	(Chartered)

Karl R. Decker (Chartered)

Representative Clients: First Security Bank of Idaho, N.A.; Safeco Insurance Co.; Farmers Insurance Group; Kemper Insurance Cos.; Intermountain Health Care; TransAmerica Insurance Co.; Royal Insurance Co.; Eastern Idaho Regional Medical Center; Pacific Power & Light Co.; Merrill Lynch.

For full biographical listings, see the Martindale-Hubbell Law Directory

JEROME, * Jerome Co. — (Refer to Twin Falls)

KELLOGG, Shoshone Co.

EVANS, KEANE LLP (AV)

111 Main Street, P.O. Box 659, 83837
Telephone: 208-784-1105
Facsimile: 208-783-7601
Boise, Idaho Office: Suite 200, 1101 West River Street, P.O. Box 959.
Telephone: 208-384-1800

James P. Keane (1925-1988)	Charles L. A. Cox
Fred M. Gibler	Justin W. Julian

John O. Cossel

Representative Clients: American Cyanamid Co.; AMOCO; Coeur d'Alene Mines Corp.; Ford Motor Co.; Hecla Mining Co.; Idaho Power Co.; Insurance Company of North America; Sunshine Mining and Refining Co.; Volkswagen of America.

For full biographical listings, see the Martindale-Hubbell Law Directory

MALAD CITY, * Oneida Co. — (Refer to Pocatello)

MOSCOW, * Latah Co. — (Refer to Lewiston)

MOUNTAIN HOME, * Elmore Co. — (Refer to Boise)

NAMPA, Canyon Co. — (Refer to Caldwell)

PAYETTE, * Payette Co. — (Refer to Caldwell)

POCATELLO, * Bannock Co.

JONES, CHARTERED (AV)

415 South Arthur Avenue, P.O. Box 967, 83204-0967
Telephone: 208-232-5911
FAX: 208-232-5962

Lamont Jones	Thomas J. Holmes
Jack H. Robison	Jesse C. Robison

Representative Clients: First Security Bank of Idaho; Idaho Power Co.; American Land Title Company; City of Pocatello; Pocatello Regional Medical Center; Crossland Credit Corp.; North Pacific Insurance; Houston General Insurance; United States Fidelity & Guaranty Co.
Reference: First Security Bank of Idaho, N.A.

For full biographical listings, see the Martindale-Hubbell Law Directory

MERRILL & MERRILL, CHARTERED (AV)

Key Bank Building, P.O. Box 991, 83204
Telephone: 208-232-2286
Fax: 208-232-2499

A. L. Merrill (1886-1961)	D. Russell Wight
R. D. Merrill (1893-1972)	Thomas W. Clark
Wesley F. Merrill	David C. Nye
Dave R. Gallafent	Kent L. Hawkins
Stephen S. Dunn	Thomas J. Lyons

Representative Clients: Key Bank of Idaho; Phillips Petroleum Co.; The Travelers Insurance Co.; Aetna Casualty & Surety Co.; Hartford Accident & Indemnity Co.; Equitable Life Assurance Society; Utah Power & Light Co.; Pacific Corp.; Portneuf-Marsh Valley Canal Co.; Farm Bureau Mutual Insurance Co. of Idaho.

For full biographical listings, see the Martindale-Hubbell Law Directory

RACINE, OLSON, NYE, COOPER & BUDGE, CHARTERED (AV)

Center Plaza, Corner First & Center, P.O. Box 1391, 83204
Telephone: 208-232-6101
FAX: 208-232-6109

Louis F. Racine, Jr.	John R. Goodell
William D. Olson	John B. Ingelstrom
W. Marcus W. Nye	Daniel C. Green
Gary L. Cooper	Reed W. Larsen
Randall C. Budge	Brent O. Roche
John A. Bailey, Jr.	Kirk Hadley

Fred J. Lewis	David E. Alexander
Mitchell W. Brown	James P. Price
Eric S. Hunn	Lisa M. Christon

Representative Clients: Allstate Insurance Co.; Farmers Insurance Group of Cos.; Idaho Irrigation Pumpers Assn.; Monsanto Co.; North Pacific Insurance Co.; Safeco Insurance Co.; West One Bank.

For full biographical listings, see the Martindale-Hubbell Law Directory

SERVICE, GASSER & KERL (AV)

2043 East Center Street, P.O. Box 6009, 83205-6009
Telephone: 208-232-4471
Fax: 208-232-1808

MEMBERS OF FIRM

Archie W. Service	Steven V. Richert
Ron Kerl	James A. Spinner

Kay M. Christensen

OF COUNSEL

Clark Gasser

LEGAL SUPPORT PERSONNEL

LEGAL ASSISTANT

Darcy Taylor

Representative Clients: Key Bank of Idaho; Allied Insurance Group; Union Pacific Railroad Co.; Farm Credit Bank of Spokane; KHD Deutz of America Corp.; Interstate Production Credit Association; D.L. Evans Bank; Cowboy Oil Cos.
References: Key Bank of Idaho; First Security Bank of Idaho.

For full biographical listings, see the Martindale-Hubbell Law Directory

WARD, MAGUIRE & BYBEE (AV)

353 East Lander, P.O. Box 4758, 83205-4758
Telephone: 208-232-5167
FAX: 208-232-5181

MEMBERS OF FIRM

Martin R. Ward	David H. Maguire
	D. Kirk Bybee

ASSOCIATES

Kent V. Reynolds	David R. Kress

Representative Clients: Farmers Insurance Group (Truck Exchange); The American Insurance Group; Unigard Insurance Group; Hartford Mutual Insurance Co.; Transport Indemnity Co.; Aetna Insurance Co.

For full biographical listings, see the Martindale-Hubbell Law Directory

PRESTON, * Franklin Co. — (Refer to Pocatello)

REXBURG, * Madison Co.

RIGBY, THATCHER, ANDRUS, RIGBY, KAM & MOELLER, CHARTERED (AV)

25 North Second East, P.O. Box 250, 83440
Telephone: 208-356-3633
Fax: 208-356-0768
Email: rexlaw@srv.net

(See Next Column)

RIGBY, THATCHER, ANDRUS, RIGBY, KAM & MOELLER CHARTERED,
Rexburg—Continued

Ray W. Rigby	Jerry R. Rigby
Gordon S. Thatcher	Michael S. Kam
G. Rich Andrus	Gregory W. Moeller

Attorneys for: North Fork Reservoir Co.; Class "A" School Districts 321 & 322; Fall River, Raft River and Lost River Electric Cooperatives; Ultimate Director, Inc.; Madison Cooperative Association, Inc.; W.R. Henderson Construction, Inc.; Committee of Nine of Water District 01.
Representative Clients: Taylor Chevrolet Co.; Madison Cooperative Assn., Inc.; Valley Bank (Headquarter Office).

For full biographical listings, see the Martindale-Hubbell Law Directory

---

RIGBY,* Jefferson Co. — (Refer to Rexburg)

ST. ANTHONY,* Fremont Co. — (Refer to Rexburg)

SHOSHONE,* Lincoln Co. — (Refer to Ketchum)

TWIN FALLS,* Twin Falls Co.

COLEMAN, RITCHIE & ROBERTSON (AV)

156 2nd Avenue West, P.O. Box 525, 83303-0525
Telephone: 208-734-1224
Fax: 208-734-3983

MEMBERS OF FIRM

John R. Coleman	John S. Ritchie
	Thomas M. Robertson

Representative Clients: First Federal Savings Bank of Twin Falls and Branches in Rupert, Burley, Ketchum & Buhl, Idaho; West One Bank, Idaho, Trust Department, Twin Falls, Idaho; Canal Insurance Co.
References: West One Bank, Idaho, Twin Falls, Idaho; First Security Bank of Idaho, (Twin Falls Office); First Federal Savings Bank of Twin Falls.

For full biographical listings, see the Martindale-Hubbell Law Directory

---

WALLACE,* Shoshone Co. — (Refer to Kellogg)

WEISER,* Washington Co. — (Refer to Caldwell)

ILLINOIS

ALBION,* Edwards Co. — (Refer to Carmi)

ASHLAND, Cass Co. — (Refer to Beardstown)

AURORA, Kane Co.

MICKEY, WILSON, WEILER & RENZI, P.C. (AV)

2111 Plum Street, 2nd Floor, P.O. Box 787, 60507-0787
Telephone: 708-801-9699
FAX: 708-801-9715
Email: Mickeyww@aol.com

Gary K. Mickey	Bernard K. Weiler
Peter K. Wilson, Jr.	Constance Burnett Renzi
	Steven A. Andersson

Colleen G. Thomas

For full biographical listings, see the Martindale-Hubbell Law Directory

MURPHY, HUPP, FOOTE, MIELKE AND KINNALLY (AV)

North Island Center, P.O. Box 5030, 60507
Telephone: 708-844-0056
FAX: 708-844-1905

MEMBERS OF FIRM

William C. Murphy	Patrick M. Kinnally
Robert B. Hupp	Paul G. Krentz
Robert M. Foote	Joseph C. Loran
Craig S. Mielke	Gerald K. Hodge

Timothy D. O'Neil
OF COUNSEL
Robert T. Olson

Representative Clients: American Telephone & Telegraph Co.; Fox Valley Park District; Lyon Metal Products; Kane County Forest Preserve District; Hollywood Casino; Employers Mutual Insurance Co.; Forty-Eight Insulations, Inc.; UNR Asbestos Disease Trust; Richards-Wilcox Co.; National Bank & Trust Company of Syracuse.

For full biographical listings, see the Martindale-Hubbell Law Directory

(See Next Column)

BATAVIA, Kane Co.

DRENDEL, TATNALL, HOFFMAN & McCRACKEN, A PROFESSIONAL CORPORATION (AV)

201 Houston Street, Suite 300, P.O. Box 1808, 60510-6808
Telephone: 708-406-5440
FAX: 708-406-6179

Gilbert X. Drendel, Jr.	Thomas J. Hoffman
Susan B. Tatnall	Kevin G. Drendel
	Charles V. Muscarello

LEGAL SUPPORT PERSONNEL
Sheila Persinger (Legal Assistant)

Reference: Old Second National Bank of Aurora, Aurora, Illinois.

For full biographical listings, see the Martindale-Hubbell Law Directory

---

BELLEVILLE,* St. Clair Co.

DONOVAN, ROSE, NESTER, SZEWCZYK & JOLEY, P.C. (AV)

8 East Washington Street, 62220
Telephone: 618-235-2020
Telecopier: 618-235-9632

Dennis E. Rose	Edward J. Szewczyk
Michael J. Nester	Charles L. Joley

Kenneth M. Nussbaumer	Robert John Bassett
Georgiann Oliver	Kristine McGee Mack
	James T. Scott

LEGAL SUPPORT PERSONNEL
PARALEGAL

Margaret M. Branum	Tracy D. Richter
	Carol S. Clark

Representative Clients: State Farm Mutual Auto & Life Co.; Travelers Insurance Co.; Liberty Mutual Insurance Co.; Government Employees Insurance Co.; Great American Insurance Co.; Aetna Casualty & Surety Co.; Royal Globe Insurance Co.; Illinois Founders Insurance Co.; INA (Insurance Company of North America).

For full biographical listings, see the Martindale-Hubbell Law Directory

DUNHAM, BOMAN & LESKERA (AV)

208 North High Street, 62220
Telephone: 618-235-7222
Telecopier: 618-397-2285
East St. Louis, Illinois Office: 520 First Illinois Bank Building.
Telephone: 618-271-0535.
Telecopier: 618-271-2800.
Collinsville, Illinois Office: 300 West Clay Street.
Telephone: 618-344-7734.
Telecopier: 618-344-3853.

John W. Leskera	Russell K. Scott
William L. Berry	Robert D. Francis
Eric C. Young	John L. Bitzer

Attorneys For: Collinsville School District #10; Hanover Insurance Co.; Hartford Insurance Group; Home Indemnity Co.; State Farm Insurance Cos.; Transamerica Insurance Group; The Travelers Indemnity Co.; Wausau Insurance Cos.; Nationwide Insurance Co.; Atlantic Mutual Insurance Co..

For full biographical listings, see the Martindale-Hubbell Law Directory

GUNDLACH, LEE, EGGMANN, BOYLE & ROESSLER (AV)

5000 West Main Street, P.O. Box 23560, 62226-0560
Telephone: 618-277-9000; East St. Louis: 271-8000
Telecopier: 618-277-4594
St. Louis, Mo.
St. Louis, Missouri Office: 1010 Market Street, Suite 1640.
Telephone: 314-231-2084.
Telecopier: 314-231-1960.

PARTNERS

Norman J. Gundlach	Richard M. Roessler
Carl W. Lee	Kenneth L. Halvachs
Richard E. Boyle	Thomas R. Peters
	Charles J. Swartwout

ASSOCIATES

Karen E. Mason	Mary G. Sullivan
Robert D. Andrekanic	Terence M. Patton
Curtis Ray Picou	Mark R. Kurz

OF COUNSEL
Roger M. Fitz-Gerald

District Counsel for: CSX Transportation.
Division Counsel for: Norfolk-Southern Corp.
Attorneys for: Illinois Central Railroad; Illinois Power Co.; Metropolitan, Prudential, Equitable, John Hancock, Northwestern Mutual and General American Life Insurance Cos.

For full biographical listings, see the Martindale-Hubbell Law Directory

Belleville—Continued

NEVILLE, RICHARDS, DEFRANCO & WULLER (AV)

5 Park Place, 62221
Telephone: 618-277-0900
Facsimile: 618-277-0970

MEMBERS OF FIRM

James E. Neville	James E. DeFranco
Timothy S. Richards	Robert G. Wuller, Jr.

ASSOCIATES

Shari M. Brunton	Ellen M. Edmonds
Richard Thomas Roustio	

For full biographical listings, see the Martindale-Hubbell Law Directory

THOMPSON COBURN (AV)

525 West Main Street, 62220
Telephone: 618-277-4700; 314-271-1800
Telecopier: 618-236-3434
St. Louis, Missouri Office: One Mercantile Center.
Telephone: 314-552-6000.
Telecopier: 314-552-7000.
St. Charles, Missouri Office: 200 North Third Street.
Telephone: 314-946-7717.
Telecopier: 314-946-4938.
Washington, D.C. Office: 700 14th Street, N.W., Suite 900.
Telephone: 202-508-1000.
Telecopier: 202-508-1010.
Houston, Texas Office: 2400 NationsBank Center, 700 Louisiana.
Telephone: 713-225-3800.
Telecopier: 713-225-3828.

MEMBERS OF FIRM

Joseph R. Lowery	Mark Sableman
W. Thomas Coghill, Jr.	Charles M. Poplstein
Michael D. O'Keefe	Edward S. Bott, Jr.
Thomas W. Alvey, Jr.	Harry W. Wellford, Jr.
Karl D. Dexheimer	Myron A. Hanna
David F. Yates	Bradley A. Winters
Garrett C. Reuter	Mark J. Stegman
Raymond L. Massey	Edward A. Cohen
Gary Mayes	Nicholas J. Lamb
Thomas F. Hennessy, III	Francis X. Buckley, Jr.
William A. Schmitt	Kurt E. Reitz
Robert H. Brownlee	Kurt S. Schroeder
Thomas R. Jayne	James J. Murphy
Mary M. Bonacorsi	David A. Stratmann
Allen D. Allred	Roman P. Wuller
Dan H. Ball	Mark S. Schuver
William R. Bay	Conny Davinroy Beatty
	Joseph C. Orlet

OF COUNSEL

Robert L. Broderick	James R. Parham

ASSOCIATES

D. Kimberly Brown	Crystal M. Kennedy
Kelly M. Brown	Cherie K. Harpole Macdonald
James H. Ferrick, III	Melissa L. Mitchell
David S. Corwin	Eric R. Riess
Ellen F. Cruickshank	Deborah J. Volmert
Mary Sue Juen	T. Bradford Waltrip

Representative Clients: First Illinois Bank; General Motors Corp.; Harcros Pigments, Inc.; Illinois-American Water Co.; Magna Group, Inc.; Marsh Co.; Memorial Hospital of Belleville; Norfolk Southern Corp.; Peabody Coal Co.; Union Electric Co.

For full biographical listings, see the Martindale-Hubbell Law Directory

BELVIDERE, Boone Co. — (Refer to Rockford)

BENTON, Franklin Co.

HART AND HART (AV)

602 West Public Square, P.O. Box 937, 62812-0937
Telephone: 618-435-8123
Telecopier: 618-435-2962

William H. Hart (1862-1941)	Richard O. Hart
William W. Hart (1894-1968)	Murphy C. Hart
Marion M. Hart (1896-1964)	A. Courtney Cox
William W. Hart, Jr. (1925-1996)	Pamela Sue Lacey

Representative Clients: Boatmen's Bank; State Bank of Whittington; Magna Bank of Southern Illinois; Benton Park District; Benton Public Library District; HHL Financial Services; St. Mary's Hospital (Centralia); Credit Bureau Systems, Inc.

For full biographical listings, see the Martindale-Hubbell Law Directory

BLOOMINGTON, McLean Co.

DUNN, HUNDMAN, STANCZAK & WILLARD (AV)

1001 North Main Street, 61701
Telephone: 309-828-6241
FAX: 309-828-8321
Email: dunnlaw@aol.com

MEMBERS OF FIRM

Richard F. Dunn (1888-1963)	Mark T. Dunn
William T. Hundman	David L. Stanczak
	Donald A. Willard

ASSOCIATES

Douglas J. Hundman

OF COUNSEL

Louis F. Ulbrich	Richard T. Dunn

Representative Clients: Northeastern Illinois University; Governors State University; Western Illinois University; Chicago State University; First Federal Savings & Loan Association of Bloomington; Illinois Wesleyan University; Metropolitan Life Insurance Co., Agricultural Investments and Commercial Investments; Commerce Bank; Heartland Bank; Bluestem National Bank.

For full biographical listings, see the Martindale-Hubbell Law Directory

HARTWEG, MUELLER, TURNER, DRAZEWSKI & WOOD, P.C. (AV)

207 West Jefferson Street, Suite 400, P.O. Box 397, 61701-0397
Telephone: 309-827-0044
Telecopier: 309-829-0328

Darrell L. Hartweg	Ralph T. Turner
William A. Mueller, Jr.	Scott D. Drazewski
	George C Wood

Michael J. Robak

OF COUNSEL

John R. Luedtke

Reference: Magna Bank of McLean County.

For full biographical listings, see the Martindale-Hubbell Law Directory

CAIRO, Alexander Co. — (Refer to Marion)

CAMBRIDGE, Henry Co.

TELLEEN, BRAENDLE, HORBERG & SMITH, P.C. (AV)

124 West Exchange Street, P.O. Box 179, 61238
Telephone: 309-937-3339
Fax: 309-937-2830

Leonard E. Telleen (1877-1966)	James T. Braendle
Kenneth L. Telleen (Retired)	Kurt J. Horberg
Leonard W. Telleen (1911-1994)	Scott M. Smith

Reference: Peoples Bank of Cambridge.

For full biographical listings, see the Martindale-Hubbell Law Directory

CARBONDALE, Jackson Co.

FEIRICH/MAGER/GREEN/RYAN (AV)

2001 West Main Street, P.O. Box 1570, 62903-1570
Telephone: 618-529-3000
Telecopier: 618-529-3008

MEMBERS OF FIRM

T. Richard Mager	Michael F. Dahlen
Richard A. Green	Kevin L. Mechler
Mary Lou Rouhandeh	Rebecca Whittington
John C. Ryan	John S. Rendleman, III
	Pieter Noble Schmidt

ASSOCIATES

Edward Renshaw	Steve Erdely
Jeffrey Berkbigler	Kara L. Jones
	Gary B. Nelson

OF COUNSEL

John K. Feirich	John C. Feirich

Representative Clients: Country Mutual Insurance Co.; Sentry Insurance Co.; Great Central Insurance Co.; Consolidation Coal Co.; Heitman Properties, Ltd.; Southern Illinois Hospital Services; Mariah Boats, Inc.; Downstate National Banks.

For full biographical listings, see the Martindale-Hubbell Law Directory

CARLINVILLE, Macoupin Co.

PHELPS, KASTEN, RUYLE & BURNS (AV)

130 East Main Street, 62626
Telephone: 217-854-3283
FAX: 217-854-9527
Email: pkrb@cnmnet.com

MEMBERS OF FIRM

Edward R. Phelps (1904-1985)   Carl E. Kasten
John W. Russell ((Retired)   Nancy L. Ruyle
                Thomas P. Burns
ASSOCIATES
Byron J. Sims

Representative Clients: Carlinville National Bank; Blackburn University; Area Diesel Service, Inc.; Farmers and Merchants Bank; H & H Construction Services, Inc.

For full biographical listings, see the Martindale-Hubbell Law Directory

---

CARLYLE, Clinton Co. — (Refer to Centralia)

CARROLLTON, Greene Co. — (Refer to Carlinville)

CARTHAGE, Hancock Co.

HARTZELL, GLIDDEN, TUCKER AND HARTZELL (AV)

Williams Building, P.O. Box 70, 62321
Telephone: 217-357-3121
FAX: 217-357-2027
Macomb, Illinois Office: Old Bailey House, 100 South Campbell Street.
Telephone: 309-833-3121.

MEMBERS OF FIRM

Homer H. Williams (1894-1965)   John R. Glidden
Franklin M. Hartzell   Stanley L. Tucker
                Thomas F. Hartzell

Counsel for: Marine Trust Company of Carthage; Bowen State Bank; Pioneer Lumber Co.;
Local Counsel for: State Farm Mutual Insurance Co.; The Prudential Insurance Company of America; American States Insurance Co.

For full biographical listings, see the Martindale-Hubbell Law Directory

---

CHAMPAIGN, Champaign Co.

FLYNN, PALMER & TAGUE (AV)

402 West Church Street, P.O. Box 1517, 61824-1517
Telephone: 217-352-5181
Telecopier: 217-352-7964

MEMBERS OF FIRM

Leonard T. Flynn   Michael J. Tague
Charles L. Palmer   Richard P. Klaus
ASSOCIATES
James D. Green

Representative Clients: Bituminous Insurance Co.; Home Insurance Co.; Standard Mutual Insurance Co.; Universal Underwriters Co.; BankChampaign N.A.; Champaign National Bank; Champion Federal Savings and Loan; First Federal Savings and Loan of Champaign; Champaign Asphalt Co.; Champaign Board of Education.

For full biographical listings, see the Martindale-Hubbell Law Directory

LAW OFFICES OF LAWRENCE E. JOHNSON AND ASSOCIATES, P.C. (AV)

Jefferson Building, 202 West Hill Street, P.O. Box 1127, 61824-1127
Telephone: 217-352-3634
Fax: 217-356-7000

Lawrence E. Johnson   Catherine H. Barbercheck

James W. Dieker   Glenn Muller
Frederick W. Irion   Reid J. Rozen
                Ruby E. Williams

For full biographical listings, see the Martindale-Hubbell Law Directory

MEYER, CAPEL, HIRSCHFELD, MUNCY, JAHN & ALDEEN, P.C. (AV)

306 West Church Street, P.O. Box 6750, 61826-6750
Telephone: 217-352-1800
Telecopier: 217-352-1083
*Email:*attorneys@meyercapel.com *URL:* http://www.meyercapel.com
Urbana, Illinois Office: 300 West Main Street.
Telephone: 217-328-5520.

James L. Capel, Jr. (1933-1991)   Donald R. Aldeen
John C. Hirschfeld   John H. Elder
Dennis K. Muncy   David B. Sholem
Francis J. Jahn   Mark D. Lipton

(See Next Column)

Tracy J. Nugent   Patrick T. Fitzgerald
Richard T. West   Todd J. Black
Rusty W. Freeland   Mark P. Miller
Lorna K. Geiler   Joseph Dwyer Murphy

Neil R. Rafferty   Patricia L. Gruber
James M. Mullady   William B. Moore
Adam B. Hirschfeld   Rochelle A. Funderburg
            Evan D. Coobs
OF COUNSEL
August C. Meyer, Jr.   Richard J. Winkel, Jr.

Representative Clients: Bank of Illinois in Champaign; Bell Foods, Inc.; Champaign News-Gazette; Christie Clinic; Federal Deposit Insurance Corp.; Illini Cablevision, Inc.; Kuck & Associates, Inc.; Midwest Television, Inc.; Parkland College.

For full biographical listings, see the Martindale-Hubbell Law Directory

---

RAWLES, O'BYRNE, STANKO & KEPLEY, P.C. (AV)

501 West Church Street, P.O. Box 800, 61824-0800
Telephone: 217-352-7661
Telecopier: 217-352-2169

Donald M. Reno (1906-1987)   Edward H. Rawles
J. Michael O'Byrne   Stephen M. O'Byrne
Vance I. Kepley (Retired)   Glenn A. Stanko
            Brett A. Kepley

Timothy S. Jefferson
LEGAL SUPPORT PERSONNEL
Rose M. Lanter   Karen B. Judd (Legal Assistant)
(Legal Assistant)

Local Counsel for: Bank One of Champaign, Urbana; Covenant Medical Center; Gibson Community Hospital; Frances Nelson Health Center; University of Illinois; Pekin Insurance Company; Union Insurance Group; New Hampshire Insurance Group; Construction Industry Welfare Fund of Central Illinois; Terra International Inc.

For full biographical listings, see the Martindale-Hubbell Law Directory

THOMAS, MAMER & HAUGHEY (AV)

Fifth Floor, First of America Bank Building, 30 Main Street, 61820-3629
Telephone: 217-351-1500
Telecopier: 217-355-0087
Mailing Address: P.O. Box 560, Champaign, Illinois, 61824-0560

James G. Thomas (1901-1990)
MEMBERS OF FIRM
Stuart M. Mamer   Craig J. Causeman
Roger E. Haughey   Michael R. Cornyn
Lott H. Thomas   Richard R. Harden
William J. Brinkmann   Robert A. Hoffman
Howard W. Small   Dan M. Slack
David A. Bailie   David E. Krchak
            Bruce E. Warren
ASSOCIATES
Linda L. Laugges   John M. Sturmanis
            Bianca I. Truitt

Representative Clients: First of America Bank Illinois, N.A.; Board of Trustees of the University of Illinois; Illinois Provident Trust; Prudential Insurance Company of America; Thompson Lumber Co.; The Carle Foundation; The Carle Foundation Hospital; Aetna Life and Casualty Co.; St. Paul Insurance Co.

For full biographical listings, see the Martindale-Hubbell Law Directory

---

CHICAGO, Cook Co.

ALTHEIMER & GRAY (AV)

Suite 4000, 10 South Wacker Drive, 60606
Telephone: 312-715-4000
Fax: 312-715-4800
Telex: RCA 297102 A G UR
Warsaw, Poland Office: ul. Nowogrodzka 50, 00-950 Warsaw.
Telephones: 011-48-39-12-1338; 22-629-8357.
Fax: 011-48-22-628-3640.
Prague, Czech Republic Office: Platnerska 4, 110 00 Prague 1.
Telephone: 42-2 2481-2782.
Fax: 42-2 2481-0125.
Kiev, Ukraine Office: Suite 510, 42/4 Pushkinska Street, 252004. Kiev.
Telephone: 38-044-230-2534, Within Kiev: 246-5056.
Fax: 38-044-230-2535. Fax within Kiev: 246-5057.
Bratislava, Slovakia Office: Nam. SNP 15, 81006 Bratislava.
Telephone: 011-42-7-361-566.
Fax: 011-42-7-367-960.
Istanbul, Turkey Office: Tesvikiye Cad. 107, Tesvikiye Palas 7, Tesvikiye 80200 Istanbul, Turkey.
Telephone: 011-90-212-227-6750.
Fax: 011-90-212-227-6759.

(See Next Column)

ALTHEIMER & GRAY—Continued

Shanghai, Peoples Republic of China Office: Shanghai Union Building 100
Yan An Road Shanghai 200002.

Marlene R. Abrams	Mark Thomas Kindelin
Rolando R. Acosta	Ian S. Kopelman
Cathleen Hainer Albrecht	George Kovac
Alan J. Altheimer	Jeffrey T. Kraus
Mark H. Berens	Steve Lawrence
Anthony Bergamino, Jr.	Carol S. Lepman
Robert I. Berger	Richard F. Levy (P.C.)
Myles D. (Mush) Berman	Myron Lieberman
Paul P. Biebel, Jr.	Peter H. Lieberman
Bruce A. Bonjour	Corey E. Light
Robert P. Bramnik	Melvin K. Lippe
Scott A. Bremer	Theodore J. Low
Laurence R. Bronska	John E. Lowe
Robert E. Browne	C. Vincent Maloney
John J. Buttita	Jeremy D. Margolis
James E. Carroll	Erwin Mayer
Gery J. Chico	Thomas C. McDonough
Melanie Rovner Cohen	F. John McGinnis
Alexandra R. Cole	Edward E. McNally
George I. Cowell	John W. Morrison
Kenneth M. Crane	Paul K. Morton
James R. Cruger	Barry B. Nekritz
Susan J. Daley	S. Michael Peck
Paul M. Daugerdas	Daniel M. Pierce
Jeffrey P. De Jong	Anita J. Ponder
Laurence B. Dobkin	John F. Prusiecki
Stephen M. Dorfman	David B. Ritter
David L. Fargo	David C. Roston
Faye B. Feinstein	Robert J. Rubin
Kenneth R. Gaines	Terry M. Schlade
John F. Gibbons	Robert L. Schlossberg
Françoise Gilbert	David W. Schoenberg
Donald A. Gillies	Benjamin D. Schwartz
Norman M. Gold	Audrey E. Selin
Louis B. Goldman	Kenneth C. Shepro
Phillip Gordon	Mindy Wolin Sherman
James S. Gray	Jeffrey Norman Smith
Milton H. Gray	Judy Ludwig Smith
Martha Mahan Haines	Gary L. Specks
Roger B. Harris	John C. Stiefel
Wm. Bruce Hoff, Jr.	Julie A. Swanson
Robert M. Horwitch	Angelo F. Tiesi
Peter M. Howard	Jeffrey S. Torf
Robert A. Janoski	William F. Tueting
Jaroslawa Zelinsky Johnson	Darren B. Watts
David V. Kahn	Edward E. Wicks
Robert M. Kalec	Roger Wilen
Nancy L. Kasko	Donna M. Zak

RETIRED PARTNERS

Jacob Logan Fox	Samuel T. Lawton, Jr.
Lionel G. Gross	Sherwin J. Stone

Joseph J. Strasburger

ASSOCIATES

Rita M. Alliss	Janet M. Kyte
Michael H. Altman	David H. Latham
Robert M. Andalman	Lori A. Lenard
Susan D. Appel	Luis F. Machado
Sean W. Bezark	Susan J. Magar
Serge Biberman	M.E. Majeske
Robert E. Blacher	Daniel G.M. Marre
Andrew F. Bohutinsky	Douglas P. Martin
Curtis R. Calvert	Jane B. McCullough
Richard M. Carbonara	Andrew W. McCune
Benjamin L. Chu	Nadia A. Nagib
Christopher Combest	Dianne Marie Onichimowski
Thomas M. Connolly	(Not admitted in IL)
Ted A. Donner	Stephen R. Otis
Michael M. Eidelman	Jeanine M. Pisoni
Bradley M. Falk	Sherilyn Peace
Barry Fischer	Richard J. Rabbitt
Mark R. Galis	(Not admitted in IL)
Joseph P. Gattuso	Lisa A. Ronga
Judith A. Gold	Steven M. Saraisky
M. Christine Graff	Valerie Schultz
Andrew R. Greene	Dana S. Sherman
Kendy M. Hess	(Not admitted in IL)
Judson Cary Hite	Jon L. Stein
Gary R. Jarosik	Daniel N. Tucker
Miranda B. Jones	William E. Turner, II
Deborah K. Johns	Charles A. Valente
Renee F. Kessel	Joseph R. Vallort
David S. Klevatt	J. Eric Wise
Erika L. Kruse	Marjorie J. Zessar

(See Next Column)

COUNSEL

Charles F. Adler, Jr.	Philip L. Pomerance
Jules Dashow	Richard A. Prince
David J. Lester	Don H. Reuben
G. Douglas McMahon	Jack M. Siegel

For full biographical listings, see the Martindale-Hubbell Law Directory

ARONBERG GOLDGEHN DAVIS & GARMISA (AV)

Suite 3000 One IBM Plaza, 60611
Telephone: 312-828-9600
Telecopier: 312-828-9635

MEMBERS OF FIRM

Ronald J. Aronberg	James S. Jarvis
Christopher J. Bannon	Young Kim
Melvin A. Blum	Nathan H. Lichtenstein
Deborah G. Cole	Marc W. O'Brien
Steven P. Davis	Ned S. Robertson
William J. Garmisa	David H. Sachs
Mitchell S. Goldgehn	James A. Smith
Gene H. Hansen	Robert N. Sodikoff

Andrew S. Williams

OF COUNSEL

Charles E. Zeitlin

ASSOCIATES

Lisa J. Brodsky	Carol A. Martin
Jacqueline Shim Bryant	Susan H. Mendelsohn
John A. DiSalvo	John M. Riccione
Howard J. Fishman	William J. Serritella, Jr.
James J. Hickey	William C. Wilder

Dawn C. Wrona

For full biographical listings, see the Martindale-Hubbell Law Directory

BAKER & MCKENZIE (AV)

One Prudential Plaza, 130 East Randolph Drive, 60601
Telephone: (312) 861-8000
Intn'l. Dialing: (1-312) 861-8000
Facsimiles: (1-312) 861-2898; 861-2899; 861-2900;
861-8080 (Operator)
Associated Offices of Baker & McKenzie in: Almaty, Amsterdam, Bangkok,
Barcelona, Beijing, Berlin, Bogotá, Brasília, Brussels, Budapest, Buenos
Aires, Cairo, Caracas, Dallas, Frankfurt, Geneva, Hanoi, Ho Chi Minh
City, Hong Kong, Juárez, Kiev, Lausanne, London, Madrid, Manila,
Melbourne, México City, Miami, Milan, Monterrey, Moscow, New York,
Palo Alto, Paris, Prague, Rio de Janeiro, Riyadh, Rome, St. Petersburg,
San Diego, San Francisco, Santiago, São Paulo, Singapore, Stockholm,
Sydney, Taipei, Tijuana, Tokyo, Toronto, Valencia, Warsaw, Washington,
D.C. and Zürich.
Correspondent Law Firm: Hadiputranto, Hadinoto & Partners, Jakarta.

MEMBERS OF FIRM

Robert H. Aland	Neal A. Klegerman
Vincent M. Aquilino	Robert C. Knuepfer, Jr.
Russell Baker (1901-1979)	Karen A. Kuenster
James G. Barnes	Eric M. Lasry
Jack D. Beem	Gregg D. Lemein
Peter J. H. Bentley	Charles B. Lewis
Robert L. Berner, Jr.	William Joseph Linklater
Leslie A. Bertagnolli	Gerald L. Maatman, Jr.
Neal J. Block	Sebastiao de Souza Mattos Neto
Andrew J. Boling	Maura Ann McBreen
Michael L. Coleman	Paul McCarthy
John J. Conroy, Jr.	William S. McDowell, Jr.
Robert J. Cunningham	John C. McKenzie (1913-1962)
Robert E. Deignan	Michael S. Mensik
John W. Dondanville	Marcel J. Molins
Thomas A. Doyle	Peter J. Mone
Edwin R. Dunn	John E. Morrow
David W. Ellis	Thomas R. Nelson
John C. Filosa	Mark A. Oates
Richard M. Franklin	James M. O'Brien
Gary W. Fresen	Michael P. O'Brien
Robert J. Gareis	Daniel J. O'Connor
Michael J. Garvey	Michael A. Pollard
David P. Hackett	William Lynch Schaller
Thomas M. Haderlein	Dieter A. Schmitz
Donald J. Hayden	Premjit Singh
Frederick E. Henry	Paul D. Slocomb
J. Patrick Herald	Barbara C. Spudis
James T. Hitch, III	Philip F. Suse
Douglas Hoffman	Preston M. Torbert
Akira Ito	Michael J. Wagner
Jerome W. Jakubik	Friedrich J. Weinkopf
Thomas E. Johnson	Philip J. Zadeik
Sidney M. Kaplan	Jia Zhao
Mark L. Karasik	Edward J. Zulkey

(See Next Column)

BAKER & McKENZIE, *Chicago—Continued*

LOCAL PARTNERS

Lynn S. Baker	Francisco Miguel Noyola
Lisa Sopata Brogan	Vincent S. Oleszkiewicz
Steven D. Conlon	David I. Roche
Thomas W. Cushing	Brian C. Shea
Pablo A. Garcia-Moreno	Peter K. Trzyna
Lawrence F. Haas	(Not admitted in IL)
Pamela J. Mills	David A. Waimon
Patrick T. Navin	Michael J. Wynne

SENIOR COUNSEL

David S. Ruder

ASSOCIATES

Jonathan Adams R.	Sarah K. Long
(Not admitted in IL)	Todd O. Maiden
Patrick J. Ahern	Victor M. Marroquin
Matthew G. Allison	John D. Martin
Ellenore Angelidis	Stephanie L. Matthews
Regina F. Atkins	John M. McGarry
Gerald K. Bolkema	Mary Jo Naples Miller
Thomas W. Bottomlee	Elizabeth A. Mitchell
Barrie L. Brejcha	Betsy Stelle Morgan
Susan Miller Butera	Michael L. Morkin
Michael J. Castellino	John M. Murphy
Martin R. Castro	D. Tyler Nurnberg
David J. Davis	Ronald L. Ohren
Jennifer N. DeLisle	Nam H. Paik
Patrick D. Dolan	Oren S. Penn
(Not admitted in IL)	Joseph J. Quigley
Hugo Dubovoy (Not admitted	Joan M. Richman
in United States)	Suzanne M. Russell
Hillary A. Ebach	Paul E. Schick
Sarah E. Fandell	Maureen R. Smith
Cristina M. Ladeira Ferreira	Philip S. Stamatakos
Tamara L. Frantzen	Anthony G. Stamato
Rafael Gómez-Cabrera	James Lee Stetson
Amy Dickman Gray	Mark C. Swords
Maria G. Gutierrez	Thomas J. Vega-Byrnes
Brent A. Hannafan	Reynaldo Vizcarra Méndez (Not
Sam F. Zolondek Haviland	admitted in United States)
Yoong-Neung Kee	Joseph V. Walker
Alan L. Kennard	Julie C. H. Walsh
Samuel G. Kramer	Luis Carlos Watanabe (Not
Ingrid L. Lenhardt	admitted in United States)
(Not admitted in IL)	Jonathan M. Wilson
Elizabeth E. Lewis	David Wix
William M. Link	Richard M. Wolfson
Kevin J. Loechl	Brian K. Wydajewski

For full biographical listings, see the Martindale-Hubbell Law Directory

---

BELL, BOYD & LLOYD (AV)

Three First National Plaza Suite 3300, 70 West Madison Street, 60602
Telephone: 312-372-1121
FAX: 312-372-2098
Email: bbl@bbl.com
Washington, D.C. Office: 1615 L Street, N.W.
Telephone: 202-466-6300.
FAX: 202-463-0678.

MEMBERS OF FIRM

Jeffrey B. Aaronson	Lawrence M. Gavin
Michael J. Abernathy	Durward J. (James) Gehring
Gregory R. Andre	Carol A. Genis
Cameron S. Avery	Joseph V. Giffin
D. Daniel Barr	Victor E. Grimm
William L. Barr, Jr.	D. Scott Hargadon
Brian A. Bates	Warren C. Haskin
Paul M. Bauch	(Managing Partner)
Nancy E. Bertoglio	Thomas Z. Hayward, Jr.
Robert J. Best	Frank K. Heap
John H. Bitner	James P. Hemmer
Jeffrey A. Blevins	Francis J. Higgins
John C. Blew	Thomas C. Homburger
Christopher A. Bloom	Robert T. Johnson, Jr.
William G. Brown	Thomas F. Joyce
Terrence E. Budny	Tamra S. Kempf
William R. Carney	Maureen Ward Kirby
David D. Cleary	Jeffrey R. Ladd
Dale E. Colling	Daniel Lawler
James W. Collins	Alice S. Lonoff
Randy J. Curato	Lawrence M. Mages
James P. Daley	Patrick J. Maloney
Lee A. Daniels	Brian E. Martin
William F. Dolan	John T. McCarthy
Raymond H. Drymalski	Brigid M. McGrath
Steven E. Ducommun	D. Mark McMillan
Lawrence C. Eppley	Scott M. Mendel
Nicholas J. Etten	Rebecca C. Meriwether
James F. X. Fahy	Paul T. Metzger
Sanford R. Gail	John P. (Pete) Morrison
Stanley J. Garber	John R. Myers

(See Next Column)

MEMBERS OF FIRM (Continued)

Margery Newman	Alan M. Serwer
David M. Novak	Richard L. Sevcik
Michael K. Ohm	Peter M. Sfikas
Janet D. Olsen	Robert V. Shannon
Stephen J. O'Neil	Stuart A. Shanus
Matthew K. Phillips	Thomas C. Shields
Daniel J. Pope	Stanley P. Sklar
William S. Price	Cornelius J. Tanis
Kenneth E. Rechtoris	Edwin C. Thomas, III
James A. Romanyak	Larry L. Thompson
John W. Rotunno	Anita Medina Tyson
Peter G. Rush	John J. Verscaj
David M. Saltiel	John Craig Walker
Gregory J. Schroedter	Neal H. Weinfield
John P. Scotellaro	Donald S. Weiss
Michael Sennett	Cheryl Weissman

Robert L. Wiesenthal

OF COUNSEL

Stanton H. Berlin	Keith D. Schulz
Alan R. Brodie	Allen R. Smart
Richard L. Curry	John C. York
R. James Gormley	Laird Bell (1910-1965)
William N. Haddad	Darrell S. Boyd (1919-1971)
William B. Hanley	Glen A. Lloyd (1931-1975)
Rollin C. Huggins, Jr.	William G. Burns (1907-1988)
John T. Loughlin	J. William Hayton (1926-1994)
Charles T. Martin	Daniel P. Ward (1918-1995)
James T. Rhind	Jack M. Whitney, II (1922-1995)

ASSOCIATES

Philip P. Adler	Josh M. Leavitt
Andrew R. Andreasik	Kevin J. McCarthy
Mark D. Bauer	Margaret A. McGreal
Michelle D, Bowers	Carrie C. McNally
Randy A. Bridgeman	Kathleen M. Meyers-Grabemann
Robert Raymond Brown	Maricel M. Mojares
J. David Brymesser	Robert M. Moye
Thomas R. Carey	Sandra K. Newman
Hector Brian Centeno	Amy L. Ostrander
Douglas M. Chalmers	Carolyn S. Palk
Daniel C. Cole	Kenneth A. Peterson, Jr.
Micaela M. Daly	Matthew A. Phillips
Erik F. Dyhrkopp	Carla Rogers Redmond
Kathryn A. Finn	Edwin J. Reisinger
Marc D. Fisher	Ari J. Rosenthal
Brian T. Gardner	David Alan Schneider
(Not admitted in IL)	Ellen M. Sfikas
Edward M. Graham	Melissa Anne Siebert
Sana Hakim	Heather C. Steinmeyer
Paul W. Hartzel	Ernest W. Torain, Jr.
Joanne L. Hyman	James P. Tutaj
Kathryn D. Ingraham	Paul J. Walsen
Sarah K. Johnson	Dawn M. Weber
James Wm. Joseph	Stephen H. Wenc
Bryan E. Keyt	Stacy H. Winick

For full biographical listings, see the Martindale-Hubbell Law Directory

---

BRINKS HOFER GILSON & LIONE, A PROFESSIONAL CORPORATION (AV)

NBC Tower, 455 North Cityfront Plaza Drive, Suite 3600, 60611-5599
Telephone: 312-321-4200
Cable Address: "Judicature Chicago"
Telex: 254300
Facsimile: 312-321-4299
Email: brinkshofer.com
Toledo, Ohio Office: 1130 Edison Plaza.
Telephone: 419-244-6578.
Telex: 140342.
Facsimile: 419-244-8862.
Indianapolis, Indiana Office: One Indiana Square, Suite 2425.
Telephone: 317-636-0886.
Telex: 469632.
Facsimile: 317-634-6701. E-mail: 75471.352@compuserve.com.
Detroit, Michigan Office: 600 Renaissance Center, Suite 1400.
Telephone: 313-259-4118.
Facsimile: 313-259-4119.
Arlington, Virginia Office: Crystal Plaza One, 2001 S. Clark Street, Suite 208.
Telephone: 703-415-0303.
Telex: 140994.
Facsimile: 703-415-0304.

Henry L. Brinks	Jack C. Berenzweig
Roy E. Hofer	Jerold A. Jacover
Richard G. Lione	John J. Pavlak
Jerome Gilson	Gary M. Ropski
James B. Blanchard	William A. Webb
Robert L. Harmon	Joel W. Benson
Melvin F. Jager	John K. Lucas
David A. Anderson	Raymond W. Green

(See Next Column)

BRINKS HOFER GILSON & LIONE A PROFESSIONAL CORPORATION—Continued

Cynthia A. Homan
James R. Sobieraj
Richard A. Kaplan
Allan J. Sternstein
Steven P. Shurtz
Michael H. Baniak
Jeffery M. Duncan
Jeffery A. Handelman
Harold V. Johnson
John R. Crossan
Rodney A. Daniel

Glen P. Belvis
Doris Loew
Thomas J. Filarski
Robert W. Stevenson
William H. Frankel
Gustavo Siller, Jr.
Maxwell J. Petersen
Frank J. Kozak
James P. Naughton
Timothy Q. Delaney
Bradley G. Lane

Ralph J. Gabric

G. Peter Nichols
Natalie D. Kadievitch
Frank C. Nicholas
Jonathan E. Retsky
Michael E. Milz
Dominic P. Zanfardino
Katherine L. Tabor
Robert S. Mallin
William F. Prendergast
John C. Freeman
Jeffrey A. Pine
Curt J. Whitenack
Michael D. Gannon
Mary Vainisi Rogers
Michael P. Chu
Christopher M. Cavan
Colleen Connors Butler
Meredith L. Martin
Kent E. Genin
Craig A. Summerfield
Philip A. Jones

Marc V. Richards
Tracey R. Thomas
L. Ann Fitzgerald
Nanette M. Norton
Laura Beth Miller
Scott E. Rogers
(Not admitted in IL)
James M. McCarthy
Lalita P. Williams
George I. Lee
John J. Letts
Andrew D. Stover
Chen Wang
Thomas E. Wettermann
Frank Z. Yang
Stephanie S. Conis
Enrique Perez
Laura Darien Nammo
Sean M. Sullivan
Donna Shine Hennessy
Julie Lynne Kernwein

COUNSEL

F. David AuBuchon
William J. Cook
Barbara A. Larsen
(Not admitted in IL)

Alice O. Martin
E. Leonard Rubin
Mary M. Squyres

OF COUNSEL

Merrill N. Johnson (Not admitted in IL)

TOLEDO OFFICE

Vincent L. Barker, Jr.
(Managing Partner, Toledo
and Detroit Offices)

David D. Murray

Christina L. Brown
Larry Robert Meenan

David A. Spenard
Carlos M. Herrera

Peter J. Rashid

INDIANAPOLIS OFFICE

David H. Badger (Managing
Partner, Indianapolis Office)

Gerald H. Glanzman
Daniel L. Boots

Marshall E. Rosenberg

DETROIT OFFICE

Vincent L. Barker, Jr. (Managing Partner, Toledo and Detroit
Offices)

Peter J. Rashid

For full biographical listings, see the Martindale-Hubbell Law Directory

CASSIDAY, SCHADE & GLOOR (AV)

Suite 1200, 333 West Wacker Drive, 60606-1289
Telephone: 312-641-3100
Fax: 312-444-1669
Email: 210-8675@mcimail.com
Waukegan, Illinois Office: 415 Washington Street, Suite 214.
Telephone: 847-249-0700.
Wheaton, Illinois Office: 2100 Manchester Road, Suite 615.
Telephone: 630-682-9800.

MEMBERS OF FIRM

Timothy J. Ashe
Richard A. Barrett, Jr. (Resident
Partner, Wheaton, Illinois
Office)
Peter G. Bell
Marc F. Benjoya (Resident
Partner, Waukegan, Illinois
Office)
Thomas P. Boylan
Robert S. Burtker
Joseph A. Camarra
John D. Cassiday
Susan E. Seiwert Conner
Michael J. Cucco

John R. Davis (Resident
Partner, Waukegan, Illinois
Office)
Mary K. Finley
James A. Foster
Philip J. Fowler
William J. Furey
Joseph A. Giannelli
D. Patterson Gloor
Jean M. Golden
John D. Hackett
Michael J. Hennig
Brian J. Hickey
Richard C. Huettel

(See Next Column)

MEMBERS OF FIRM (Continued)

David A. Johnson
Jennifer Ann Keller
James W. Kopriva
Michael J. Morrissey
Constance R. O'Neill
Martha A. Pagliari
Anne R. Rempe

Bradford D. Roth
Rudolf G. Schade, Jr.
Gregory E. Schiller
John N. Seibel
A. Jeffrey Seidman
Brian C. Sundheim
Julie A. Teuscher

Bruce M. Wall

ASSOCIATES

James D. Ahern
Michele C. Anderson
Todd Alan Andrews
Neville M. Bilimoria
Karen M. Borg
Mark M. Brennan
Scott J. Brown
Byrdie Brownridge-Douglas
David R. Buetow
John K. DeVine
Daniel P. Duffy (Resident,
Wheaton, Illinois Office)
Diane C. Filipski
Kurtis G. Fouts
Theresa M. Freeman (Resident,
Waukegan, Illinois Office)
Catherine L. Garvey
Corey H. Grauer (Resident,
Waukegan, Illinois Office)
Vanessa Walker Hampton
Denise G. Hoeflich (Resident,
Waukegan, Illinois Office)
Patricia J. Hogan
Evan Hughes
Susan M. Hyser

Donald F. Ivansek
Julia A. Kelleher
Stephen M. Kightlinger
Michael S. Komoll
Andrew J. Kovarik
Sandra E. Kupelian
Deborah A. Martin-Sheridan
Kathleen M. McCabe
Richard A. Paulus
Brian Poust
Carolyn Quinn
Kimberly L. Robinson
Jeffrey R. Sandler
Amy F. Schwemer
Therese S. Seeley (Resident,
Wheaton, Illinois Office)
Daniel R. Shaffer
Michael Murphy Tannen
Steven P. Taub (Resident,
Waukegan, Illinois Office)
David C. Van Dyke
Lisa E. Wegrzyn
David A. Wilford
Nicholas C. York
Sally Jo Zimmerman

A list of Representative Clients will be made available upon request.

For full biographical listings, see the Martindale-Hubbell Law Directory

CHAPMAN AND CUTLER (AV)

111 West Monroe Street, 60603
Telephone: 312-845-3000
Fax: 312-701-2361
Salt Lake City, Utah Office: Suite 800, Key Bank Tower, 50 South Main
Street.
Telephone: 801-533-0066.
Fax: 801-533-9595.
Phoenix, Arizona Office: Suite 1100, One Renaissance Square, 2 North
Central Avenue.
Telephone: 602-256-4060.
Fax: 602-256-4099.

Ann Acker
Bruce D. Agin
Leah F. Arner
David T. B. Audley
Daniel J. Bacastow
Andrea G. Bacon
Michael P. Barrett
David S. Barritt
Walter P. Begley
Michael T. Benz
Jeffrey D. Berry
Deborah Thomas Boye
Lee A. Boye
James M. Breen
Edwin S. Brown
Jeffrey A. Burger
James C. Burr (Resident, Salt
Lake City Office)
George D. Buzard, III
Timothy J. Carey
Theodore S. Chapman
(1877-1943)
David J. Cholst
Debra S. Clark
Steven L. Clark
Rafael L. Cook
William E. Corbin, Jr.
Richard A. Cosgrove
David S. Crossett
Patricia M. Curtner
Henry E. Cutler (1879-1959)
Robert P. Davis
William R. DeHaan
(Resident, Phoenix Office)
John M. Dixon
Larry Elkins
Eric F. Fess
J. Richard Fisher, Jr.
C. Robert Foltz
Marc P. Franson

Steven G. Frost
Lynda K. Given
Wendy A. Grossman
Steven G. Hastings
Charles S. Hughes
Charles L. Jarik
James E. Jenz
Daniel L. Johnson
Charles A. Kelly
Richard F. Klein
Mark J. Kneedy
Jonathan A. Koff
Paul C. Kosin
Kelly K. Kost
Daniel J. Kucera
Harry P. Lamberson
Darrell R. Larsen, Jr.
Edward L. Lembitz, Jr.
Matthew R. Lewin
William M. Libit
Frederick V. Lochbihler
Robert E. Lockner
James E. Luebchow
Paul R. Madden
(Resident, Phoenix Office)
Elizabeth L. Majers
Richard A. Makarski
Neil R. Mann
Michael G. McGee
Timothy V. McGree
Terry A. McIlroy
David B. McMullen
Timothy P. Mohan
Thomas J. Morgan
(Resident, Phoenix Office)
Robert C. Nash
James P. O'Brien
Terence T. O'Meara
Robert W. Ollis, Jr.

(See Next Column)

CHAPMAN AND CUTLER, *Chicago—Continued*

John S. Overdorff (Resident, Phoenix Office)	James R. Theiss, Jr.
Stacy K. Pike	Kenneth R. M. Thompson
James R. Richardson	M. John Trofa
Ronald E. Rokosz	John L. Tuohy
Anthony R. Rosso	Kenneth J. Vaughan
Aron H. Routman	Terrence M. Walsh
David S. Schaffer, Jr.	John A. Ward
Richard J. Scott (Resident, Salt Lake City Office)	Daniel W. Weil
Edward V. Sommer	David G. Williams
James E. Spiotto	Karl T. Williams
George P. Sullivan, Jr.	Steven N. Wohl
	Richard A. Wohlleber
	Steven N. Zaris

Scott R. Anderson	Kristi A. Maher
Maria T. Aretakis	Sean T. Maloney
Daniel W. Baker	Simon C. J. Maple
Erin P. Bartholomy	Steven C. Mason (Not admitted in IL)
James E. Basta	Carol McAlpine
Stephen R. Boatwright (Resident, Phoenix Office)	Jane E. Nagle
Matthew C. Boba	James R. Nelson
James M. Broeking	Kyle E. Nenninger
Jon Michael Brown, Jr.	Brigitte T. Nuss
Nancy A. Burke	Lisa A. Olsen
Judy Smith Capobres	Thomas G. Park
Peter A. Clark	Edward J. Pelican
Stathy Darcy	Gary R. Polega
Liza G. Diaz	Thomas M. Quirk
David A. Ebroon	Dianne E. Rist
Lisa M. Engel	Eric M. Roberson
Daniel J. Favero	Susan E. Rollins
Kelly A. Fetzer	Christina L. Sciabica
Felice Foundos	Susan Shallenberger
August J. Francis	Todd N. Sheldon
Brian D. Free	Suzanne L. Shier
Basil V. Godellas	Timothy W. Smith
Stephanie L. Grauerholz	Frederick M. Snow
Paul K. Haberkamp	Mark A. Sternberg
Ronald J. Hacker	David J. Stevens (Resident, Salt Lake City Office)
John C. Hitt, Jr.	Ross D. Taylor
R. William Hunter	Tedd T. Termunde
Marie I. Jordan	Dawn M. Timan
Kevin P. Kalinich	Franklin H. Top III
Karla L. Kambic	Christopher J. Townsend
Julia S. Kemp	Robert G. Tucker
Barbara C. Klabacha	Demetria E. Vong-Spillan
Gregory A. Klamrzynski	Christopher F. Walrath
Colleen A. Kushner	Rodney G. Wendt (Resident, Salt Lake City Office)
Mark E. Laughman	Anthony D. Yager
Mark T. Lee (Resident, Phoenix Office)	Marie-Anne Zabrocki
Michael C. Lee	Jamie L. Zelvin
David A. Lullo	

OF COUNSEL

Peter V. Fazio	F. B. Hubachek, Jr.

For full biographical listings, see the Martindale-Hubbell Law Directory

CLAUSEN MILLER P.C. (AV)

10 South La Salle Street, 60603-1098
Telephone: 312-855-1010
Telecopier: 312-606-7777
Email: clientservices@clausen.com
Wheaton, Illinois Office: 2100 Manchester Road, Suite 1700, 60187-2402.
Telephone: 630-668-9100.
Telecopier: 630-668-9169.
European Affiliated Law Firm: Clausen Miller Europe GIE, La Giraudière Larroze & Associés, 58, Rue de Monceau, 75008 Paris, France.
Telephone: 33.1.44.95.25.25.
Telecopier: 33.1.44.95.25.00.
Telex: 649 622 F
and: 53, Avenue des Arts, 1040 Brussels, Belgium.
Telephone: 32.2.511.44.66.
Telecopier: 32.2.514.56.62.
New York, N.Y. Office: One Chase Manhattan Plaza, 10005.
Telephone: 212-805-3900.
Telecopier: 212-805-3939.
Newark, New Jersey Office: One Gateway Center, Suite 2600, 07102-5397.
Telephone: 201-645-0564.
Telecopier: 201-622-3423.
Troy, Michigan Office: 3155 West Big Beaver Road, 48084-3007.
Telephone: 810-816-0500.
Telecopier: 810-816-1011.

Craig M. Antas	Paul Bozych
Jeffrey J. Asperger	John F. Brennan
Ivar R. Azeris	Richard A. Buchanan
James S. Barber	Kevin P. Caraher
Diane M. Baron	Richard C. Clark

(See Next Column)

Michael W. Duffy (Managing Partner, Troy, Michigan Office)	Steven N. Novosad
George C. Ellison	William J. Oberts
James T. Ferrini	Mary C. O'Connor
Michael L. Foran	Margaret J. Orbon
David R. Ganfield II	Edward J. Ozog
Robert E. Gilmartin III	Douglas J. Palandech
Michael R. Grimm, Sr.	Matthew S. Ponzi
John T. Groark	Robert L. Reifenberg
Fredric J. Grossman	Thomas H. Ryerson (Resident, Wheaton Office)
William J. Hacker	Dominick W. Savaiano
Celeste A. Hill	Stephen J. Schlegel
James M. Hoey	Frank L. Schneider
Richard G. Howser	Gilbert J. Schroeder
John M. Hynes	Martin C. Sener
Edward M. Kay	Thomas J. Skeffington (Resident, New York, N.Y. and Newark, N.J. Offices)
Lisa Marco Kouba	
Tyler Jay Lory	Gregory S. Smith (Resident, Principal, New York Office)
Stephen D. Marcus	
Randall I. Marmor	Mary F. Stafford
Joyce M. Maxberry	Richard Wm Strawbridge
John B. McCabe	James R. Swinehart
Thomas A. McDonald	Harry L. Wilson
Richard L. Murphy	Kevin J. Young
James O. Nolan	Jeffrey R. Zehe
Frances T. Norek	George A. Zelcs

OF COUNSEL

William Michael Long

Nick Alexander (Resident, Wheaton Office)	Brenda Dunton McNamara
Kurt D. Baer	Kevin K. McQuillan
Robert T. Boylan	Maura Lutz Morgan
Patrick L. Breen	Bruce N. Moss (Resident, Troy, Michigan Office)
Keith E. Butler	Melissa A. Murphy-Petros
David M. Cabreré	Vincent S. Nadile (Resident, New York, N.Y. Office)
Meg Calk	
Susan Condon	Mary Blake Nasenbenny
Brian G. Cunningham	Erik W. Nielsen
John E. DeLascio	Christina J. Norton
Robert N. Dunn	Sonia V. Odarczenko
Margaret Hupp Fahey	Maureen A. O'Neill
Paul T. Falk	Thomas B. Orlando
Joseph T. Fernim	Benjamin E. Patterson
Dennis D. Fitzpatrick	Mark D. Paulson
Steven J. Fried (Resident, New York, N.Y. Office)	Amy Rich Paulus
	Dean A. Pelletier
Lyse M. Garant (Resident, New York, N.Y. Office)	Maryann Peronti (New York, N.Y. and Newark, New Jersey Offices)
James B. Glennon	
Mary Lu Hahn	Paul A. Peters
David M. Heilmann	William P. Pistorius
Harvey R. Herman	Bruce A. Radke
Timothy A. Hickey	John C. Raith
Daniel R. Hoyt	Dean S. Rauchwerger
Joseph J. Janatka	Paul Scott Ritchie
Cole S. Kain	Charles J. Rocco
Richard M. Kaplan	Mark J. Seplak
Kimbley A. Kearney	Susan M. Severtson
Paul D. Kerpan	Deborah L. Sheward (Resident, New York, N.Y. Office)
James J. Knibbs	
Melinda S. Kollross	M. David Short
Ilene M. Korey	James F. Smith
Richard H. Lehman	Marta A. Stein
John Limotte (Resident, New York, N.Y. Office)	Robert A. Stern (Resident, New York, N.Y. Office)
Bianca M. Loftus	Jerome C. Studer, Jr.
John J. Malm	Imelda R. Terrazino
Dirk Marschhausen (Resident, New York, N.Y. Office)	Michael L. Vittori
	Sava Alexander Vojcanin
James P. Marsh (Resident, Wheaton Office)	Debra B. Walker
	Dale F. Weigand
John C. Matson	Mark E. Wilson
Michael H. McColl	Michael E. Zidek (Resident, Wheaton Office)

References: The First National Bank of Chicago; La Salle National Bank.

For full biographical listings, see the Martindale-Hubbell Law Directory

DALEIDEN, THOMPSON & TREMAINE, LTD. (AV)

333 North Michigan Avenue Suite 2800, 60601-3901
Telephone: 312-899-1044
Fax: 312-899-0878

Norbert A. Daleiden	David F. Thompson
	Arthur J. Tremaine

For full biographical listings, see the Martindale-Hubbell Law Directory

Chicago—Continued

DICKINSON, WRIGHT, MOON, VAN DUSEN & FREEMAN (AV)

225 West Washington, Suite 400, 60606-3418
Telephone: 312-220-0300
Facsimile: 312-220-0021
Detroit, Michigan Office: 500 Woodward Avenue, Suite 4000.
Telephone: 313-223-3500.
Facsimile: 313-223-3598.
Bloomfield Hills, Michigan Office: 525 North Woodward Avenue, Suite 2000.
Telephone: 810-433-7200.
Facsimile: 810-433-7274.
Grand Rapids, Michigan Office: 200 Ottawa Avenue, N.W., Suite 900.
Telephone: 616-458-1300.
Facsimile: 616-458-6753.
Lansing, Michigan Office: Suite 200, 215 South Washington Square.
Telephone: 517-371-1730.
Facsimile: 517-371-2939.
Washington, D.C. Office: Suite 800, 1901 L Street, N.W.
Telephone: 202-659-1559.
Facsimile: 02-659-1559.

PARTNERS

Daniel F. Gosch	Robert P. Hurlbert
Ronald B. Grais	Carl D. Liggio, Sr.
Martin L. Greenberg	(Not admitted in IL)
Stephen S. Herseth	Creighton R. Meland, Jr.
Edgar C. Howbert	Michael S. Poulos
(Not admitted in IL)	Daniel James Sheridan
Jon Robert Steiger	

RESIDENT OF COUNSEL

Allan G. Sweig

RESIDENT ASSOCIATES

Sean D. Major	Louis Theros
Wendy Lee Toolin	

For full biographical listings, see the Martindale-Hubbell Law Directory

FOLEY & LARDNER (AV)

Suite 3300, One IBM Plaza, 330 N. Wabash Avenue, 60611-3608
Telephone: 312-755-1900
Facsimile: 312-755-1925
Milwaukee, Wisconsin Office: Firstar Center, 777 East Wisconsin Avenue.
Telephone: 414-271-2400.
Telex: 26-819 (Foley Lard Mil).
Facsimile: 414-297-4900.
Madison, Wisconsin Office: Verex Plaza, 150 East Gilman Street, P.O. Box 1497.
Telephone: 608-257-5035.
Facsimile: 608-258-4258.
Washington, D.C. Office: Washington Harbour, Suite 500, 3000 K Street, N.W.
Telephone: 202-672-5300.
Telex: 904136 (Foley Lard Wsh.).
Facsimile: 202-672-5399.
Annapolis, Maryland Office: Suite 102, 175 Admiral Cochrane Drive.
Telephone: 301-266-8077.
Telex: 899149 (Oldtownpat).
Facsimile: 301-266-8664.
Jacksonville, Florida Office: The Greenleaf Building, 200 Laura Street, P.O. Box 240.
Telephone: 904-359-2000.
Facsimile: 904-359-8700.
Orlando, Florida Office: Suite 1800, 111 North Orange Avenue, P.O. Box 2193.
Telephone: 407-423-7656.
Telex: 441781 (HQ ORL).
Facsimile: 407-648-1743.
Tallahassee, Florida Office: Suite 300, 123 South Calhoun Street, P.O. Box 508.
Telephone: 904-222-6100.
Facsimile: 904-224-0496.
Tampa, Florida Offices: Suite 2700, One Hundred N. Tampa Street, P.O. Box 3391.
Telephones: 813-229-2300; Pinellas County: 813-442-3296.
Facsimile: 813-221-4210.
West Palm Beach, Florida Office: Suite 200, Phillips Point East Tower, 777 South Flagler Drive.
Telephone: 407-655-5050.
Facsimile: 407-655-6925.
Brussels, Belgium Office: Avenue Louise, 283.
Telephone: 32-2-646-2777.
Facsimile: 32-2-646-7574.
Los Angeles, California Office: Foley Lardner Weissburg & Aronson, 2049 Century Park East, Suite 3200.
Telephone: 310-277-2223.
Fax: 310-557-8475.
Sacramento, California Office: Foley Lardner Weissburg & Aronson, 770 L Street, Suite 1050.
Telephone: 916-443-8005.
Fax: 916-443-2240.

(See Next Column)

San Diego, California Office: Foley Lardner Weissburg & Aronson, 402 West Broadway, 23rd Floor.
Telephone: 619-234-6655.
Fax: 619-234-3510.
San Francisco, California Office: Foley Lardner Weissburg & Aronson, One Maritime Plaza, Sixth Floor.
Telephone: 415-434-4484.
Fax: 415-434-4507.

PARTNERS

Evelyn C. Arkebauer	Chris J. Mollet
Salvatore A. Barbatano	Gerald J. Neal
Sharon R. Barner	Robert E. Neiman
Wesley N. Becker	Nehad S. Othman
Francis A. Citera	Jefferson Perkins
James D. Dasso	Richard J. Phelan
Scott E. Early	Mark L. Prager
Frederick L. Feldkamp	Randall S. Rapp
Joan M. Kubalanza	Hoken S. Seki
John D. Lien	Steven B. Silverman
J. Craig Long	George T. Simon
David S. Lott	Stephen M. Slavin
Edwin D. Mason	James R. Vogler
David M. Matteson	James A. Winkler
Malcolm McCaleb, Jr.	Robert J. Zimmerman

OF COUNSEL

Jay Jung Heum Kim	Frank J. McGarr
Kai Allen Nebel	

ASSOCIATES

Bradley S. Block	E. Anthony Lauerman III
Kevin J. Clancy	Nancy A. Needlman
Marilyn P. Dunn	Jeffery S. Norman
Jeanne Marie Gills	Randall L. Oyler
Charles R. Haywood	Janet E. Raycraft
Dianne L. Hicklen	David T. Rusoff
Dean M. Jeske	Becky B. Serafini
Bryan T. D. Jung	Michael J. Small
Carolyn E. Knecht	Jill Andrews Sprague
Thomas P. Krebs	Todd A. Strother
John R. Landis	Randi S. Valerious
(Not admitted in IL)	Jay O. Wright

For full biographical listings, see the Martindale-Hubbell Law Directory

GARDNER, CARTON & DOUGLAS (AV)

Quaker Tower, Suite 3400, 321 North Clark Street, 60610-4795
Telephone: 312-644-3000
Telex: 25-3628
Telecopier: 312-644-3381
Email : postmaster@gcd.com
Email: gcdlawchgo@gcd.com
Washington, D.C. Office: Suite 900, East Tower, 1301 K Street, N.W. 20005-3317.
Telephone: 202-408-7100.
Facsimile: 202-289-1504.

MEMBERS OF FIRM

Peter H. Merlin	W. David Braun
Gordon Lang, Jr.	W. Edward Webb
Joe A. Sutherland	Debra J. Schnebel
Dale Park, Jr.	Richard J. Kissel
George C. McKann	Roy M. Harsch
John T. Cusack	Susan M. Franzetti
L. Edward Bryant, Jr.	Crystal Pruess Bush
Paul H. Dykstra	Eileen Strang
Dewey B. Crawford	Nancy M. Borders
Robert J. Wilczek	Karen S. Lyons
Thomas Campbell	Michael P. Padden
Dennis J. Carlin	Frederick L. White
Richard L. Menson	Michael Duffy
Gordon B. Nash, Jr.	Deborah H. Bornstein
Geoffrey B. Shields	Ralph E. De Jong
William H. Roach, Jr.	Alex W. Zabrosky
David L. Hanson	Charles L. Byrum
Charles A. Freeman	Robert H. Skilton, III
Peter D. Clarke	Lee R. Cunningham
Donna S. Wetzler	Sherrie Travis
Quin R. Frazer	Richard W. Young
David L. Wolfe	Michael J. Hayes
Michael J. Koenigsknecht	Kathleen Mulligan
Stephen M. Gatlin	Warren von Credo Baker
James D. Parsons	Terence J. Cloney
Priscilla A. Walter	James D. McDonough
Glenn E. Ferencz	David A. Rubenstein
Glenn W. Reed	William J. Barrett
Michael E. Barry	Lawrence Fisher
David G. Strom	Patrick S. Coffey
Steven B. Kite	Robert A. Cosentino
Thomas E. Lanctot	Gary W. Howell
Edward Spacapan, Jr.	David N. Kay
Mark E. Furlane	Helen J. McSweeney
Bernadette Muller Broccolo	Peter J. Meyer
Michael W. Peregrine	Luis A. Berrones
Stephen P. Bedell	Wendy Freyer

(See Next Column)

GARDNER, CARTON & DOUGLAS, *Chicago—Continued*
MEMBERS OF FIRM (Continued)

Edwin A. Getz	Gary W. Garner
Adele A. Waller	D. Louis Glaser II
Henry deVos Lawrie, Jr.	Robert J. Joseph
Timothy R. Casey	Alan S. King
Karin Jagel Flynn	William J. Peltin
Derick C. Marsh	John A. Simon
Bart Thomas Murphy	John W. Watson, III
Michael D. Rosenbaum	Robert L. Capizzi
Irwin J. Saltz	Todd S. Parkhurst
Roxane C. Busey	Edward F. Dobbins, Jr.

Edward J. Tabaczyk

MEMBERS OF FIRM - WASHINGTON, D.C.

Francis E. Fletcher, Jr.	Rodney H. Glover
M. Scott Johnson	Ballard Jamieson, Jr.
E. Michael Flanagan	James Kevin Wholey
Peter H. Wyckoff	L. Stephen Quatannens
John E. Fiorini, III	Ronald L. Lord
Grier C. Raclin	James M. Jorling
Edward P. Taptich	Christopher L. White
W. N. Harrell Smith, IV	Thomas J. Dougherty, Jr.
Donna K. Thiel	T. J. Sullivan
David C. Main	Henry A. Gardner (1883-1968)
Patrick C. Rock	Alfred T. Carton (1884-1968)
Russell H. Fox	James H. Douglas, Jr.
	(1899-1988)

OF COUNSEL

Tom Arthur	William L. Morrison
John F. Beggan	John K. Notz, Jr.
Laurence A. Carton	Gordon H. Smith
Robert A. Gardner, Jr.	Morrison Waud
James J. McClure, Jr.	James A. Velde

COUNSEL

Joseph J. Bogdan	Maureen A. Miller
Edgar F. Heizer, III	Paul E. Schaafsma

COUNSEL - WASHINGTON, D.C.

James K. Edmundson	Kathleen M. Nilles

Rita M. Grant

ASSOCIATES

Simon B. Anolick	Mark A. Latham
Susan W. Ausman	Kimberly Ann Lingenfelter
Earl J. Barnes, II	Thaddeus J. Malik
Gail J. Berritt	Joan M. McCarthy
Mary S. Bosch	Timothy G. McDermott
Jennifer R. Breuer	Daniel D. McDevitt
Samuel T. Brkich	S. Patrick McKey
Daniel T. Brown	Alfonso McMillian, Jr.
Natalie M. Cadavid	Tracey L. Mihelic
Darren S. Cahr	James Sinclair Montague
Troy M. Calkins	Matthew S. Moran
Mary Devlin Capizzi	Katherine A. Nankervis
Devin Rainey Cuyler	Ganesh Natarajan
Mary Beth Cyze	Deena S. Newlander
John J. D'Attomo	Jeffrey S. O'Dwyer
Antonio DeBlasio	Michael D. Oettinger
Mary E. Dicig	Mildred V. Palmer
Mary M. Donners	Lewis T. Putman, Jr.
Ann M. Donohue	William John Quinlan
Christine E. Edwards	John T. Roache, Jr.
William M. Ejzak	Kimberly K. Rubel
William P. Farrell, Jr.	Cynthia A. Rybak
Monica A. Fennell	Roberta M. Saielli
Dr. Andre R. Fiebig	Arthur M. Scheller, III
Rodrigo D. Floro, Jr.	Mary E. Shannon
Michael T. Foley	Elizabeth C. Sheil
John P. Goebel	Nicole M. Smith
Linda A. Green	Wallace Cyril Solberg
Joseph H. Greenberg	Leslie A. Sowle
Terry M. Hackett	Michael J. Staab
Noreen A. Healy	Richard I. Stamm
Brian R. Hedlund	Timothy J. Stanton
Carol M. Hines	Andrea Stulgies-Clauss
Timothy A. Johnson	Kenneth Michael Sullivan
Ira M. Kalina	Douglas B. Swill
Alice E. Keane	Stacy L. Thomas
Sally Doubet King	Linn M. Visscher
Nancy Laethem	Susan M. Wagner
Frances P. LaFleur	Mary G. Wilson

ASSOCIATES - WASHINGTON, D.C.

Neela Agarwalla	George N. Grammas
Attison L. Barnes, III	Laurie A. Holmes
Marie Christine Berliner	Susan H. R. Jones
Venel D. Brown	Mary Lou Licwinko
Lauren Schaefer Drake	Diane E. McConkey
Eran N. Gasko	Robert J. Mueller

(See Next Column)

ASSOCIATES - WASHINGTON, D.C. (Continued)

Jocelyn R. Roy	Lisa M. Sotir
Robert A. Schwinger	Anne Murray Stamper
Gregory J. Wellins	

For full biographical listings, see the Martindale-Hubbell Law Directory

HINSHAW & CULBERTSON (AV)

A Partnership including Professional Corporations
222 North La Salle Street, Suite 300, 60601-1081
Telephone: 312-704-3000
Telex: 880-248
Telefax: 312-704-3001
Appleton, Wisconsin Office: 100 W. Lawrence Street.
Telephone: 414-738-7550.
Belleville, Illinois Office: 521 W. Main Street, Suite 300.
Telephone: 618-277-2400.
Bloomington, Illinois Office: 2205 E. Empire, Suite B.
Telephone: 309-662-6997.
Brookfield, Wisconsin Office: 175 N. Patrick Boulevard, Suite 115.
Telephone: 414-792-9150.
Champaign, Illinois Office: 1802 Fox Drive.
Telephone: 217-352-1400.
Fort Lauderdale, Florida Office: First Union Center, Suite 1310, 200 East Broward Boulevard.
Telephone: 954-467-7900.
Jacksonville, Florida Office: Jacksonville Center, 76 S. Laura, Suite 1702.
Telephone: 904-359-9620.
Joliet, Illinois Office: 57 N. Ottawa Street, Suite 314.
Telephone: 815-726-5910.
Lisle, Illinois Office: 4343 Commerce Court, Suite 415.
Telephone: 630-505-0010.
Miami, Florida Office: 200 S. Biscayne Boulevard, Suite 800.
Telephone: 305-358-7747.
Milwaukee, Wisconsin Office: 100 E. Wisconsin Avenue, Suite 2600.
Telephone: 414-276-6464.
Peoria, Illinois Office: 456 Fulton Street, Suite 298.
Telephone: 309-674-1025.
Rockford, Illinois Office: 220 E. State Street.
Telephone: 815-963-8488.
St. Louis, Missouri Office: 1010 Market Street.
Telephone: 314-421-6168 and 314-241-2600.
Springfield, Illinois Office: 400 S. Ninth Street, Suite 200.
Telephone: 217-528-7375.
Tampa, Florida Office: 100 S. Ashley, Suite 830.
Telephone: 813-276-1662.
Waukegan, Illinois Office: 415 W. Washington Street, Suite 202.
Telephone: 847-244-0551.

MEMBERS OF FIRM

Daniel J. Biederman	Daniel W. McGrath
Dan L. Boho	Gary E. Medler
Gregory B. Bolduc	Mark C. Metzger
Richard S. Borland	Lawrence R. Moelmann
Roy M. Bossen	Douglas H. Momeyer
Thomas L. Browne	Caroline A. Mondschean
Kevin W. Bruning	Peter C. Morse
Kevin Joseph Burke	Adria East Mossing
Thomas M. Burnham	Donald L. Mrozek
Julian C. Campbell, Jr.	Robert E. Nora
Bruce L. Carmen	Robert E. Nord
Shawn P. Clifford	Joseph J. O'Connell (P.C.)
William J. Connelly	Mark R. Olander
Clare E. Connor	Donald J. O'Meara (P.C.)
David R. Creagh	Dean E. Parker
Stanley J. Davidson	Patricia J. Prange
Katherine Smith Dedrick	Carol Proctor
John W. Dubbs, III	Edward G. Proctor
Carlton D. Fisher	Steven M. Puiszis
Thomas F. Ging	Michael J. Regan
Karen R. Goodman	Marcos Reilly
D. Kendall Griffith (P.C.)	Edward J. Rolwes
Edmund Gronkiewicz	Daniel K. Ryan
Thomas M. Hamilton	David M. Schultz
James Harbert	John L. Senica
Thomas B. Hart, Jr.	Kevin R. Sido
Susan M. Hickman	Laurie A. Siwek
James M. Hofert	George W. Spellmire, Jr.
William J. Holloway (P.C.)	Peter D. Sullivan
Charles A. Hornewer	Timothy M. Sullivan
G. William Hubbard II	Alan H. Swanson
Stephen D. Hurst	Stephen R. Swofford
Fritz K. Huszagh	Paula Fuller Tobin
E. Michael Kelly	Jerome R. Vainisi
Michael J. Leech	Joshua G. Vincent
David H. Levitt	Peter A. Walsh
Nancy G. Lischer	Todd M. Young
Tom H. Luetkemeyer	Joseph J. Hinshaw (1934-1973)
Stephen A. Malato	James G. Culbertson
Stephen H. Malato	(1934-1969)
Thomas S. Malciauskas	John M. Moelmann (1934-1974)
Paul C. Marengo	Thomas J. Weithers (1953-1982)
Terrence P. McAvoy	Ward Dunphy (1961-1979)
Thomas P. McGarry	Dennis J. Horan (1963-1988)

(See Next Column)

HINSHAW & CULBERTSON—*Continued*

ASSOCIATES

Joseph W. Balesteri	Kevin J. Kuhn
Christine Marie Biebel	Philip Reed Kujawa
Steven R. Bonanno	Maureen R. Lennon
Matthew G. Burke	Craig T. Liljestrand
Lisa M. Burman	Benjamin Tao-Lueh Lo
Susan D. Burns	Lauren A. Lundin
John M. Byrne	Monica F. MacNamara
Peter Herbert Carlson	Lisa L. Marre
Thomas J. Clark	Newton C. Marshall, II
Paul J. Clementi	Kathleen D. Mathewson
Richard M. Craig	Francis P. Morrissey
Kent J. Cummings	Renee J. Mortimer
Michael J. Denker	Michael S. Nardulli
David S. Eikenmeyer	Christine L. Olson
Lyndon M. Flosi	Suzanne Liv Page
John M. Foley	Lindsay A. Parkhurst
Alicia E. Fuentes	Richard B. Polony
JuliAnn Y. Geldner	Shoshan E. Reddington
Philip L. Goldberg	David J. Richards
Ilene S. Grant	Michael N. Ripani
Michael J. Hanahan	Vincent A. Sanchez
Julie A. Harms	V. Mishaune Sawyer
Michael T. Hepburn	Alicia Collias Schneider
Mary J. Hess	Timothy G. Shelton
Linda K. Horras	Steve C. Silvey
Kurt L. Hudson	Robert H. Smeltzer
Kristin E. Hutson	Kristine M. Sorenson
Richard Juarez	Robert H. Summers, Jr.
Larry C. Jurgens	Michael J. Torchalski

Patrick D. White

COUNSEL

Robert E. Ellis	George S. Hoban
Jerome A. Frazel, Jr.	Robert L. Kealy
Perry L. Fuller	John L. Kirkland
Ronald S. Ghilardi	James Tod Miles
Oliver W. Gregory, Jr.	Rudolph Miller
William P. Grogan	Paul L. Pawlowski (P.C.)
Leonel I. Hatch, Jr.	Karl M. Tippit

Representative Clients: Aetna Life & Casualty Co.; Allstate Insurance Co.; Argonaut Insurance Co.; Continental Insurance; Farmers Insurance Group; Fireman's Fund American; Hartford Insurance Group; Maryland Casualty Co.; Unigard Security; U.S. Fidelity & Guaranty Co.

For full biographical listings, see the Martindale-Hubbell Law Directory

---

HOPKINS & SUTTER (AV)

A Partnership including Professional Corporations
Three First National Plaza, 60602
Telephone: 312-558-6600
Cable Address: "Hopsut"
Telex: 206231
Fax: 312-558-6538
Email: postmaster@hopsut.com *URL:* http://www.hopsut.com
Washington, D.C. Office: 888 Sixteenth Street, N.W.
Telephone: 202-835-8000.
Cable Address: "Hamel".
Telex: 440374 "TALY-UI".
TWX: 710-822-1913.
Fax: 202-775-1648; 202-835-8136; 202-833-9185.
Detroit, Michigan Office: 1333 Brewery Park Boulevard, Suite 101.
Telephone: 313-396-6600.
Fax: 313-396-6117.

MEMBERS OF FIRM

Garland H. Allen	Paul F. Hanzlik
Bryan S. Anderson	Patrick M. Hardiman
Matthew J. Botica (P.C.)	F. Thomas Hecht
Marc S. Brenner	Patrick A. Heffernan
Richard Bromley	James R. Hellige
John T. Brooks	Wm. Carlisle Herbert
Thomas Buranosky	Neal Heriaud
Antony S. Burt	Scott J. Heyman
Patricia S. Cain	Van E. Holkeboer
R. Lee Christie	Glen H. Kanwit
Michael N. Conway	Christopher N. Knight
Mark Crane (P.C.)	Laurie A. Levin
Thomas M. Dethlefs	Burton H. Litwin
Scott A. Drane	Jeremiah Marsh (P.C.)
Laura L. Droegemueller	Mary Kay McCalla Martire
Lawrence M. Dubin (P.C.)	John W. McCaffrey
Michael F. Duhl	William J. McKenna, Jr.
Bennett L. Epstein	William G. McMaster, Jr.
Jay Erens	S. Kay McNab
Michael A. Ficaro	J. Alexander Meleney
Marilyn D. Franson	Claudette P. Miller
John N. Gavin (P.C.)	Joel L. Miller
Stanford J. Goldblatt	Kenneth W. Miller
Lynn H. Goldschmidt	Michael P. Morrison
George R. Goodman	David L. Morrow
David B. Goroff	Emily Koenig Neuberger

(See Next Column)

MEMBERS OF FIRM (Continued)

Richard S. Nikchevich	John L. Rogers, III
Marie C. Oldham	Michael Schneiderman
Wayne F. Osoba	John L. Snyder
James D. Ossyra	Michael B. Solow
Joe Ourth	Lawrence B. Swibel
Cordell J. Overgaard (P.C.)	Sam Vinson
John B. Palmer, III	Walter S. Weinberg
Robert W. Patterson (P.C.)	William C. Weinsheimer
Michael E. Phenner (P.C.)	Mark S. Weisberg
John J. Powers	Michael H. Woolever (P.C.)
John P. Ratnaswamy	John F. Zabriskie
William E. Rattner	Christopher W. Zibart
E. Glenn Rippie	Albert L. Hopkins (1908-1978)

Harry B. Sutter (1919-1957)

SENIOR COUNSEL

Thomas R. Mulroy (1905-1989)   Frederic W. Hickman (P.C.)

OF COUNSEL

William C. Childs	John C. Walker (P.C.)
Ralph E. Davis	Anderson A. Owen (1899-1983)
William P. Sutter (P.C.)	William A. Cromartie
C. Ives Waldo, Jr.	(1919-1985)

Charles W. Davis (1916-1987)

COUNSEL

Jay A. Steinberg

ASSOCIATES

Bradford J. Axel	Mark A. McDermott
Jennifer M. Baratta	Patrick J. Morris
William T. Casey	Mary C. O'Neil
Bruce W. Doughty	Julie Gage Palmer
Robert C. Feldmeier	George N. Panagakis
Tamar S. P. Genin	Kathleen R. Pasulka
Diane Gianos	Andrew S. Potts
Raymond T. Goetz	Bradley E. Riley
Jane H. Gorham	James F. Roberts
Robert R. Hall, Jr.	Jude M. Sullivan
Steven J. Holler	Thomas E. Sweeney
Ross E. Kimbarovsky	Deborah H. Telman
Winston K.C. Lam	Rebecca D. Ward
Jennifer A. Linderoth	Tracy D. Williams

Mark L. Winget

STAFF ATTORNEYS

Richard M. Fogel

For full biographical listings, see the Martindale-Hubbell Law Directory

---

JENNER & BLOCK (AV)

A Partnership including Professional Corporations
One IBM Plaza, 60611
Telephone: 312-222-9350
FAX: 312-527-0484
Telex: 270469
TWX: 9102215409
Cable Address: "Jenblock"
Washington, D.C. Office: 601 Thirteenth Street, N.W., Twelfth Floor.
Telephone: 202-639-6000.
FAX: 202-639-6066.
Cable Address: "Jenblock."
Lake Forest, Illinois Office: One Westminster Place.
Telephone: 847-295-9200.
FAX: 847-295-7810.

CHAIRMAN OF THE FIRM

Jerold S. Solovy

MEMBERS OF FIRM

Joel J. Africk	Richard A. Campbell
Gary W. Ballesteros	Susan M. Carlson (Resident,
Alex V. Barbour	Lake Forest, Illinois Office)
Howard R. Barron (Ltd.)	Neil E. Cass
Benjamin Beiler	Donald R. Cassling
James D. Benak	Nicholas D. Chabraja
Steven N. Berk (Resident,	Timothy J. Chorvat
Washington, D.C. Office)	Jeffrey D. Colman
Joseph G. Bisceglia	Cecelia M. Comito
Samuel W. Block (1911-1970)	Ada S. Cooper
Larry D. Blust	Joseph P. Covington (Resident,
Keith F. Bode (Ltd.)	Washington, D.C. Office)
David C. Bohan	Craig R. Culbertson
Richard C. Bollow	David W. DeBruin (Resident,
Darryl M. Bradford	Washington, D.C. Office)
David J. Bradford	Natalia Delgado
Ross B. Bricker	Christopher C. Dickinson
John H. Broadley (Resident,	Kenneth R. Dolin
Washington, D.C. Office)	Timothy R. Donovan
Michael T. Brody	Joseph E. Doyle
Patricia A. Bronte	Henry C. Eickelberg
Richard M. Brown	Jeffrey L. Elegant
Thomas C. Buchele	Bruce J. Ennis, Jr. (Resident,
Jerry J. Burgdoerfer	Washington, D.C. Office)
Robert L. Byman	Anthony C. Epstein (Resident,
Ray Worthy Campbell	Washington, D.C. Office)

(See Next Column)

JENNER & BLOCK, *Chicago—Continued*

MEMBERS OF FIRM (Continued)

Jerome L. Epstein (Resident, Washington, D. C. Office)
William H. Farley, Jr.
James H. Feldman
Nicole Finitzo (Resident, Lake Forest, Illinois Office)
Bill S. Forcade
Richard T. Franch
Peter B. Freeman
Ira S. Friedrich
Gregory S. Gallopoulos
Paul G. Gebhard
Frances Gecker
Jay S. Geller
Jefferson C. Glassie (Resident, Washington, D.C. Office)
Paula Cozzi Goedert
J. Cunyon Gordon
Robert L. Graham
Richard J. Gray
E. Lynn Grayson
David M. Greenwald
David K. Haase
Joan M. Hall (Ltd.)
David A. Handzo (Resident, Washington, D.C. Office)
Donald R. Harris (Ltd.)
Kenneth L. Harris
Barry A. Hartstein
William J. Haynes II (Resident, Washington, D.C. Office)
William D. Heinz
W. Richard Helms
Norman M. Hirsch
Russell J. Hoover
Donald S. Horvath
Jerald A. Jacobs (Resident, Washington, D.C. Office)
Albert E. Jenner, Jr. (1907-1988)
Richard C. Johnson (Resident, Washington, D.C. Office)
Alan R. Johnston
Horace W. Jordan, Jr. (Resident, Lake Forest, Illinois Office)
Rodney D. Joslin
Chester T. Kamin
Ann M. Kappler (Resident, Washington, D.C. Office)
Laura A. Kaster
Carter H. Klein
C. John Koch
Ellen R. Kordik
Kenneth A. Kroot
Brock R. Landry (Resident, Washington, D.C. Office)
Leslie H. Lepow (Resident, Washington, D.C. Office)
Barry Levenstam
Charles E. Levin
Katherine J. Levy (Resident, Lake Forest, Illinois Office)
Susan C. Levy
Edward J. Lewis, II
Christopher D. Liguori
Teri A. Lindquist
Linda L. Listrom
Alexander Lourie
Bradford P. Lyerla
Daniel Lynch
James M. Lynch
Shelley Malinowski
Michael Z. Margolies
Robert T. Markowski
Ronald L. Marmer
Arthur Mead Martin
Craig C. Martin
Terri L. Mascherin
John H. Mathias, Jr.
J. Kevin McCall
Charles J. McCarthy (Ltd.)
Thomas J. McCarthy
Mark J. McGuire (Resident, Washington, D.C. Office)
James A. McKenna
Thomas K. McQueen
Louis Milicich
Nory Miller (Resident, Washington, D.C. Office)
John B. Morris, Jr. (Resident, Washington, D.C. Office)

Thomas R. Mulroy, Jr.
Daniel R. Murray
Carl S. Nadler (Resident, Washington, D.C. Office)
David M. Neff
Barry S. Neuman (Resident, Washington, D.C. Office)
Matthew M. Neumeier
Joel T. Pelz
Randolph M. Perkins (Resident, Lake Forest, Illinois Office)
Ronald R. Peterson
Patrick J. Phillips
Kit A. Pierson (Resident, Washington, D.C. Office)
Susan R. Podolsky (Resident, Washington, D.C. Office)
Mark D. Pollack
Robert M. Portman (Resident, Washington, D.C. Office)
Rebecca L. Raftery
Ronald Ian Reicin
Raymond T. Reott
Donald I. Resnick
Craig A. Roeder
Carey S. Rosemarin
Brent N. Rushforth (Resident, Washington, D.C. Office)
James D. Ryndak
Sidney G. Saltz
David P. Sanders
David A. Savner
Gregory J. Scandaglia
Lawrence S. Schaner
Stephanie A. Scharf
Sidney I. Schenkier
Stanley A. Schlitter
Marshall John Schmitt
William L. Scogland
Donald P. Seberger (Resident, Lake Forest, Illinois Office)
Glenn K. Seidenfeld
Jeffrey T. Shaw
John D. Shugrue
Gabrielle Sigel
John B. Simon
Charles Sklarsky
D. Joe Smith (Resident, Washington, D.C. Office)
Paul M. Smith (Resident, Washington, D.C. Office)
Robert R. Stauffer
Catherine L. Steege
Barbara S. Steiner
Richard P. Steinken
Philip A. Stoffregen
Brent D. Stratton
Russ M. Strobel
Thomas P. Sullivan (Ltd.)
Steven M. Surdell
Mark K. Suri
Howard S. Suskin
Theodore R. Tetzlaff
James L. Thompson
C. Steven Tomashefsky
Philip W. Tone
Anton R. Valukas
Richard L. Verkler (Ltd.) (Resident, Lake Forest, Illinois Office)
Donald B. Verrilli, Jr. (Resident, Washington, D.C. Office)
William A. Von Hoene, Jr.
James A. Vroman
Michael S. Walsh
Ronald L. Wanke
Maryann A. Waryjas
Catherine P. Wassberg
C. David Watson
Eric H. Weimers
Diana C. White
Bruce G. Wilson
Francis J. Wirtz
Larry M. Wolfson
Robert Alan Wynbrandt
David B. Yelin
Robert P. Zapinski
J. Jeffrey Zimmerman

(See Next Column)

ASSOCIATES

Cathryn E. Albrecht
Thomas D. Amrine (Resident, Washington, D.C. Office)
J. Mark Appleberry
Ruth A. Bahe-Jachna
Jeralyn H. Baran
D. Scott Barash (Resident, Washington, D.C. Office)
Jacqueline C. Bares
Royce R. Bedward
Debbie L. Berman
Joshua G. Berman
Mitchell N. Berman (Resident, Washington, D.C. Office)
Brian W. Bilcer
Andrew Byerly Birge
Steven P. Blonder
M. Katherine Boychuk
Celiza P. Bragança
Kara Novaco Brockmeyer
Jennifer A. Burke
Stephen J. Campo (Resident, Lake Forest, Illinois Office)
Brian C. Cannon
Julia M. Carpenter (Resident, Washington, D.C. Office)
Ronald N. Carroll (Resident, Washington, D.C. Office)
Michael G. Cartier
Kelly A. Cassidy
Caroline K. Cheng
Theresa Chmara (Resident, Washington, D.C. Office)
Joseph E. Chontos (Resident, Washington, D.C. Office)
Deirdre E. Connell
Michael R. Conway, Jr.
Jacob I. Corré
John F. Cox
Melissa Crawford
Maureen F. Del Duca (Resident, Washington, D.C. Office)
Robert L. Denby
Andrea M. Despotes
Sean H. Donahue (Resident, Washington, D.C. Office)
Cynthia A. Drew
Ted Eidukas
Kristina M. Entner
David Feinberg
Sara L. Fiedler
Teri L. Firmiss
Joseph D. Frank
Michael S. Freeman
Gabriel A. Fuentes
Marc A. Goldman (Resident, Washington, D.C. Office)
Arthur Gollwitzer, III (Resident, Lake Forest, Illinois Office)
Michelle B. Goodman (Resident, Washington, D.C. Office)
Judith A. Grimmer
Valerie Grissom
Kelly A. Hackett
John J. Hamill
Brent D. Hanfling
Lois McKenna Henry (Resident, Washington, D.C. Office)
Reginald J. Hill
Sam Hirsch (Resident, Washington, D.C. Office)
Janice A. Hornaday
Douglas H. Hsiao (Resident, Washington, D.C. Office)
Daniel J. Hurtado
Douglas H. Jackson
Andrew M. Jacobs
Andrew A. Jacobson
David Jimenez-Ekman
Clark C. Johnson
Andrew K. Katsoudas
Jodie L. Kelley (Resident, Washington, D.C. Office)
Michael E. Kernan
Christine Kessler
Brent E. Kidwell
Estella Christie Kiser
Tamara S. Klein
Norbert B. Knapke, II
Jeffrey A. Koppy
David M. Kroeger

Kevin J. Landy (Resident, Washington, D.C. Office)
Roy L. LaParl
Vincent E. Lazar
Charles B. Leuin
Mark W. Lewis
Richard T. LiPuma
Gretchen M. Livingston
Scott T. Longman
Gregory P. Magarian (Resident, Washington, D.C. Office)
Edward F. Malone
Thomas A. Marrinson
Brian J. Masternak
Deanne E. Maynard (Resident, Washington, D.C. Office)
Andrew J. McLaughlin (Resident, Washington, D.C. Office)
John P. McMorrow
Stephen Merwise
Gary M. Miller
Samuel S. Miller
Brian K. Murphy
Martha E. Neil
J. Paul Oetken (Resident, Washington, D.C. Office)
Thomas S. O'Neill
Stephen E. Paffrath
Stephen A. K. Palmer
Dean N. Panos
Patrick L. Patras
Thomas J. Perrelli (Resident, Washington, D.C. Office)
Christine A. Picker
Hilda Harris Piell
Jeff S. Pitzer
Anthony C. Porcelli
R. Douglas Rees
Matthew J. Renaud
Stuart M. Rennert (Resident, Washington, D.C. Office)
Jeffrey L. Richman
Christina M. Riewer
Ilene S. Rineberg
Paul L. Rodriguez
Susan S. Rodriguez
Jodi K. Rosen
Dan A. Rosenbaum
Scott V. Rozmus
Mary Ruffolo (Resident, Lake Forest, Illinois Office)
William J. Ryan
Eric A. Sacks
Annemarie Schuller
Mark L. Schulman
Scott T. Schutte
David A. Schwartz
David L. Schwartz
Susan Lee K. Seah (Not admitted in IL)
Bridget Shahan (Resident, Washington, D.C. Office)
Christine Cohan Silverglade
Jodi Ann Simala
Steven M. Siros
Rochelle Price Slater
Daniel W. Smith
James B. Sowerby
Andrew M. Spangler
Bruce Spiva (Resident, Washington, D.C. Office)
Avidan J. Stern
Katherine J. Strandburg
Jerry L. Switzer, Jr.
Eric Taylor
Aylice M. Toohey
Terrence J. Truax
Jason C. Turner
Gregory C. Vamos
Marc Van Allen
Quentin D. Vaughan
Charlotte L. Wager
John F. Ward, Jr.
Benjamin C. Weinberg
Steven M. Wernikoff
Thomas M. Wilde
Eric J. Wilson
Daniel J. Winters
Stephen L. Wood
Andrew Zahaykevich

(See Next Column)

JENNER & BLOCK—*Continued*

OF COUNSEL

Gerhard E. Seidel (Resident, Lake Forest, Illinois Office)

LEGAL CONSULTANT ON THE LAWS OF CHINA

Ge Liu (Not admitted in United States)

For full biographical listings, see the Martindale-Hubbell Law Directory

JONES, DAY, REAVIS & POGUE (AV)

77 West Wacker, 60601-1692
Telephone: 312-782-3939
Telecopier: 312-782-8585
In Atlanta, Georgia: 3500 One Peachtree Center, 303 Peachtree Street, N.E.
Telephone: 404-521-3939.
Cable Address: "Attorneys Atlanta".
Telex: 54-2711.
Telecopier: 404-581-8330.
In Brussels, Belgium: Avenue Louise 480, 7th Floor, B-1050 Brussels.
Telephone: 32-2-645-14-11.
Telecopier: 32-2-645-14-45.
In Cleveland, Ohio: North Point, 901 Lakeside Avenue.
Telephone: 216-586-3939.
Cable Address: "Attorneys Cleveland."
Telex: 980389.
Telecopier: 216-579-0212.
In Columbus, Ohio: 1900 Huntington Center.
Telephone: 614-469-3939.
Cable Address: "Attorneys Columbus."
Telecopier: 614-461-4198.
In Dallas, Texas: 2300 Trammell Crow Center, 2001 Ross Avenue.
Telephone: 214-220-3939.
Cable Address: "Attorneys Dallas."
Telex: 730852.
Telecopier: 214-969-5100.
In Frankfurt, Germany: Triton Haus, Bockenheimer Landstrasse 42, 60323 Frankfurt am Main.
Telephone: 49-69-9726-3939.
Telecopier: 49-69-9726-3993.
In Geneva, Switzerland: 20, rue de Candolle.
Telephone: 41-22-320-2339.
Telecopier: 41-22-320-1232.
In Hong Kong: 29th Floor, Entertainment Building, 30 Queen's Road Central.
Telephone: 852-2526-6895.
Telecopier: 852-2868-5871 or 852-2868-5699.
In Irvine, California: 2603 Main Street, Suite 900.
Telephone: 714-851-3939.
Telex: 194911 Lawyers LSA.
Telecopier: 714-553-7539.
In London, England: One Mount Street.
Telephone: 44-71-493-9361.
Cable Address: "Surgoe London WI."
Telecopier: 44-71-493-9666.
In Los Angeles, California: 555 West Fifth Street, Suite 4600.
Telephone: 213-489-3939.
Telex: 181439 UD.
Telecopier: 213-243-2539.
In New Delhi, India: Pathak & Associates, 9th Floor, Dr. Gopal Das Bhaven, 28 Barakhamba Road.
Telephone: 91-11-331-9719.
Telecopier: 91-11-331-7802.
In New York, New York: 599 Lexington Avenue.
Telephone: 212-326-3939.
Cable Address: "JONESDAY NEWYORK."
Telex: 237013 JDRP UR.
Telecopier: 212-755-7306.
In Paris, France: 62, rue du Faubourg Saint-Honore.
Telephone: 33-1-44-71-3939.
Cable Address: "Surgoe Paris."
Telex: 290156 Surgoe.
Telecopier: 33-1-49-24-0471.
In Pittsburgh, Pennsylvania: 500 Grant Street, 31st Floor.
Telephone: 412-391-3939.
Cable Address: "Attorneys Pittsburgh."
Telecopier: 412-394-7959.
In Riyadh, Saudi Arabia: Law Offices of Saud M.A. Shawwaf, P.O. Box 22166.
Telephone: (966-1) 462-8866.
Telex: 401831 SAUCON SJ.
Telecopier: (966-1) 462-9001.
In Taipei, Taiwan: 8th Floor, 2 Tun Hwa South Road, Section 2.
Telephone: (886-2) 704-6808.
Telecopier: (886-2) 704-6791.
In Tokyo, Japan: Toranomon MT Building, 4th Floor, 10-3, Toranomon 3-Chome, Minato-ku, Tokyo 105, Japan.
Telephone: 81-3-3433-3939.
Telecopier: 81-3-5401-2725.

(See Next Column)

In Washington, D.C.: Metropolitan Square, 1450 G Street, N.W.
Telephone: 202-879-3939.
Cable Address: "Attorneys Washington."
Telex: 89-2410 ATTORNEYS WASH.
Telecopier: 202-737-2832.

MEMBERS OF FIRM IN CHICAGO

David J. Rosso	David S. Kurtz
Dan B. Miller	Harold C. Sutter
Ronald S. Rizzo	James R. Daly
(Not admitted in IL)	Lee Ann Russo
Robert A. Yolles	S. Louise Rankin
Ronald A. Sandler	Lester J. Savit
Douglas H. Walter	Michael F. Dolan
Dennis R. Homerin	Elizabeth Clough Kitslaar
Robert H. Baker	Vicki A. O'Meara
Thomas F. Gardner	David L. Witcoff
William P. Ritchie	Susan Elliott
Lynn Leland Coe	June K. Ghezzi
Paul W. Schroeder	Thomas P. McNulty
John P. C. Duncan	Christopher W. Flynn
Daniel E. Reidy	Robert J. Graves
David L. Carden	Irene Savanis
Gary T. Johnson	Robert C. Lee
Michael J. Mitchell	James A. White
James C. Hagy	Stephanie Balcerzak Graves
Boyd J. Springer	Charles T. Wehland

OF COUNSEL

Theodore R. Scott	Christian T. Jones
Clarence J. Fleming	William S. McKay, Jr.
James B. Raden	William J. Harmon
	Karl B. Anderson

SENIOR ATTORNEYS

John B. Carothers III	Russell L. McIlwain
	Linda A. Heban

ASSOCIATES

Sandra Byster Weiss	Tina M. Tabacchi
Nancy MacKimm	Jayant W. Tambe
Susan I. Matejcak	Steven A. Wright
Karen Kazel Poulos	Jill A. Centella
Steven M. Taibl	David J. Chorzempa
Joni L. Andrioff	Kathleen M. Curran
Jeffrey Wiley Linstrom	Douglas I. Lewis
Timothy J. Melton	Vik Puri
Richard K. Tomei	Brian L. Sedlak
Robert C. Micheletto	Michael B. Willian
Mary Jo Quinn	Kathleen L. Brennan De Jesus
Carol A. Ahern	Elizabeth Fletcher Brown
John F. Bibby, Jr.	Sujata T. Dayal
Julie O. Ehrlich	James M. Hall
John L. Clancy	Stephen E. Hall
(Not admitted in IL)	Julie A. Herzog
Jane K. Murphy	Mark P. Rotatori
Kathleen M. Boege	Robert J. Zeitler
James C. Dunlop	Anne C. Auten
Peter Nels Larson	Thomas D. Brooks
Benjamin L. Nortman	Elizabeth M. Georges
Timothy R. Pohl	Taras A. Gracey
Arlene Boxerman Rosenberg	Gregory D. Isbell
Grace L. Shaff	David J. Kates
Richard E. Aderman	Anastasia Katinas
Michael B. Gardiner	John A. Marlott
Michael J. Gray	Michel Vanesse
Laurie F. Humphrey	Edward B. Winslow
	Michael A. Witt

For full biographical listings, see the Martindale-Hubbell Law Directory

KATTEN MUCHIN & ZAVIS (AV)

A Partnership including Professional Corporations
525 West Monroe Street, Suite 1600, 60661-3693
Telephone: 312-902-5200
Telecopier: 312-902-1061
Irvine, California Office: Two Park Plaza, Suite 800.
Telephone: 714-263-3500.
Telecopier: 714-263-3533.
Los Angeles, California Office: 1999 Avenue of the Stars, Suite 1400.
Telephone: 310-788-4400.
Telecopier: 310-788-4471.
New York, New York Office: 40 Broad Street, Suite 2000.
Telephone: 212-612-9500.
Telecopier: 212-425-0266.
Washington, D.C. Office: 1025 Thomas Jefferson Street, N.W., East Lobby, Suite 700.
Telephone: 202-625-3500.
Telecopier: 202-298-7570.

CHICAGO, ILLINOIS OFFICE
MEMBERS OF FIRM

Cynthia Photos Abbott	Kevin L. Barney
Robert D. Aicher	Steven L. Bashwiner (P.C.)
Steven F. Banghart	Jonathan K. Baum
Sheldon I. Banoff (P.C.)	Howard L. Bernstein

(See Next Column)

KATTEN MUCHIN & ZAVIS, *Chicago—Continued*
CHICAGO, ILLINOIS OFFICE
MEMBERS OF FIRM (Continued)

Alan M. Berry (P.C.)	Antony J. McShane
Ronald S. Betman	David M. Meister (1946-1991)
Victor H. Bezman (P.C.)	Michael L. Molinaro
Jeffrey H. Brodsky	Timothy J. Moore
David A. Bronner (P.C.)	Allan B. Muchin (P.C.)
Edwin E. Brooks	Arthur B. Muir (P.C.)
Matthew S. Brown	Kathleen M. Murphy
David J. Bryant	James C. Murray, Jr.
Denise S. Burn	Steven V. Napolitano
James A. Burns, Jr.	Stephen M. Neumer
Michael R. Callahan	Terry E. Newman (P.C.)
Linda L. Cashmore	Wesley G. Nissen
Joel G. Chefitz	J. Phillip O'Brien
Barry A. Comin	Steven R. Olson
Adam C. Cooper	Michael L. Owen
David R. Dlugie	Russell N. Pallesen
William M. Doyle, Jr.	Arthur E. Pape (P.C.)
John J. Durso	Keith D. Pascus
Donald E. Egan (P.C.)	Timothy J. Patenode
Leonard A. Ferber	Jeffrey R. Patt
Laurel L. Fleming	Melvin E. Pearl (P.C.)
Renée M. Friedman	Gerald M. Penner (P.C.)
Gerald H. Galler (1934-1987)	Daniel J. Perlman
James M. Gecker	Peter Petrakis
William M. Gerek	Gregory P. L. Pierce
Mark D. Gerstein	George Pitt
Michael P. Goldman	Patricia J. Pokorski
Stuart E. Grass	Donna J. Pugh
Bryan J. Green	Jaye Quadrozzi
Lewis Greenbaum	Nancy J. Rich
Stuart N. Greenberger	Howard M. Richard (P.C.)
(1932-1986)	Saul E. Rudo
Russell E. Greenblatt (P.C.)	Barnett P. Ruttenberg (P.C.)
Arthur W. Hahn	Simonetti Samuels
James E. Hanlon, Jr.	David K. Schmitt
Jonathan W. Harris	Susan B. Schneider
Arnold S. Harrison (P.C.)	David B. Schulman (P.C.)
Kirk T. Hartley	Marshall T. Scott
Michael O. Hartz	Robert F. Seely
Robin Heiss	Richard M. Seligman (P.C.)
David S. Heller	Russell B. Selman
Ted S. Helwig	Vincent A. F. Sergi (P.C.)
Mary Ellen Hennessy	Steven A. Shapiro (P.C.)
Janet Goelz Hoffman	David R. Shevitz (P.C.)
Samuel B. Isaacson	Stuart P. Shulruff
Maurice Jacobs	Perry J. Shwachman
Kenneth M. Jacobson	Harvey M. Silets
Melvin L. Katten (P.C.)	Ross O. Silverman
Fred R. Kaufmann, Jr.	Ann Marie Sink
William H. Knopp	Earl B. Slavitt (P.C.)
Marla J. Kreindler	Robert Y. Sperling (P.C.)
William R. Kucera (1944-1989)	Robert M. Star
Patrick J. Lamb	Bonita L. Stone
Howard S. Lanznar	Marcia W. Sullivan (P.C.)
Jeffery Larry	Ira J. Swidler
Laurence H. Lenz, Jr.	Mark K. Thomas
David M. Lesser	Clay A. Tillack
Lawrence D. Levin	James D. Van De Graaff
Stephen D. Libowsky	Milton S. Wakschlag
Seth R. Madorsky	Jerry B. Wallack
Reid A. Mandel	Richard W. Waller (P.C.)
Floyd A. Mandell (P.C.)	Herbert S. Wander (P.C.)
James L. Marvin	Lee Ann Watson (P.C.)
Jeff J. Marwil	Elizabeth Fleming Weber
Nina B. Matis (P.C.)	John R. Weiss
William E. Mattingly (P.C.)	Kenneth R. Wylie
Thomas J. McFadden	Michael Wm. Zavis (P.C.)
Daniel J. McNamara	Sheldon T. Zenner

Mark S. Zolno
ASSOCIATES

Kristin J. Achterhof	Jeffrey G. Close
James Craig Anderson	Richard C. Cohan Jr.
Josef S. Athanas	Jonathan I. Cope
Nicole Nehama Auerbach	Tanya L. Curtis
Elizabeth R. Bacon Ehlers	William W. Davis
Jennifer A. Barrett	Leslie Dawn Dent
Eric M. Bayne	David B. Desser
(Not admitted in IL)	Karetha A. Dodd
Elizabeth S. Berghoff	Juliette G. Duara
Sean M. Berkowitz	Jacqueline Riley Dunn
Steven M. Bierig	Marguerite M. Elias
Andrew A. Block	Nancy Fallon-Houle
Emily J. Blum	Joel H. Feldman
Gregory W. Bowman	Teme T. Feldman
Robert J. Brantman	David A. Fisher
Noelle C. Brennan	Wendy Fleishman
Deane B. Brown	Joseph P. Franzetta
Dawn M. Canty	Raymond C. Fricke
Unah Choi	Ferdinand J. Gallo III
Edward X. Clinton, Jr.	Richard E. Ginsberg

(See Next Column)

ASSOCIATES (Continued)

Steven D. Ginsburg	Doreen A. Meinck
Tara A. Goff	(Not admitted in IL)
Susan L. Goldenberg	Todd R. Mendel
Scott Goldstein	Troy D. Merriman
Todd D. Golub	Linda L. Miller
David A. Handler	Kurt J. H. Mueller
Patricia M. Hanson	Craig E. Nelson
Megan Hardiman	Robert K. Niewijk
James D. Harrington	Lisa M. Noller
Charles Harris	Vickie L. Norman
Paul A. Haskins	David T. Novick
Kyle R. Hauberg	Laura A. O'Connell
Julie L. Helenbrook	Judy B. Oppenheim
Erica Tina Helfer	Andrew E. Packer
Amy A. Hijjawi	Catherine Patton
Kathleen L. Hobbins	Maureen Dolan Pearson
James Wellington Hutchison	Ellen P. Pesch
Marlene J. Igel	Matthew J. Petersen
Michael A. Jacobson	Michael M. Philipp
Mark L. Johnson	Michael J. Pinsel
Terry Horwitz Kass	Paul V. Possinger
David J. Kaufman	Jaime N. Rhum
Jacob J. Kaufman	Brian F. Richards
T.K. Khan	Geoffrey A. Richards
Thomas J. Kiser	Michael E. Roll
Adam R. Klein	Mary-Beth Chadwick Roselle
Kenneth M. Kliebard	Karen A. Ruzic
Matthew E. Krichbaum	Angela M. Sanchez
Julie A. Kunetka	Adam H. Schecter
Stewart T. Kusper	Harry J. Secaras
Terrence M. LaBant	Scott A. Semenek
Sharron Clark Lamoreaux	Jeffrey Allan Sepesi
Christine P. Le	Thomas B. Shapira
Deborah E. Lebold	Orrin S. Shifrin
Jeffrey Jay Levin	Paul G. Silver
Stephen J. Levy	Nina Momtazee Sitzer
Janet A. Lindeman	Peter J. Slate
Lisa K. Liou	Andrew D. Small
Tammy C. Lowe	W. Douglas Sprague III
John J. Lydon	Phyllis B. Sumner
Joan E. Maloney	Shereen Taylor
Richard S. Marks	Sally L. Venverloh
Laura Keidan Martin	Anthony L. Wanger
John R. McElyea	Peter R. Wilson
Lori L. Meehan	James M. Witz
Adam M. Meek	Timothy R. Wons
Vesper Mei	Mark D. Wood
Thomas J. Meier	Edward J. Zabrocki III
	(Not admitted in IL)

OF COUNSEL

Cary S. Glenner	Rex A. Guest

Lizabeth F. Horn

LOS ANGELES, CALIFORNIA
MEMBERS OF FIRM

James K. Baer	Angel Gomez, III
Kathryn A. Ballsun	Katherine E. Goodman
David M. Bass	Leslie R. Karp
Kent S. Beyer	Valerie E. Kincaid
Kenneth L. Block	Howard P. King (June 19,
Marsha A. Boysaw	1945-December 25, 1993)
John J. Chung	Thomas J. Leanse
Steve Cochran	Thomas S. Mahr
Craig D. Crockwell	Zia F. Modabber
Alan D. Croll	Stephen F. Moeller
Richard F. Davis (P.C.)	Daniel P. Pelliccioni (P.C.)
Michele M. Desoer	Stuart M. Richter
Robert T. Flick	Charles M. Stern
Allan B. Goldman	Gail Migdal Title
Robert D. Goldschein	Joel R. Weiner

IRVINE, CALIFORNIA
MEMBERS OF FIRM

Frederick H. Kranz	Thomas S. Mahr

Stuart M. Richter

NEW YORK, NEW YORK
MEMBERS OF FIRM

Linda B. Hirschson	John N. Romans

WASHINGTON, D.C.
MEMBERS OF FIRM

Gary P. Blitz	Jane A. Kanter
Joan E. Boros	Christopher S. Petito
Michael H. Cook	Carol R. Van Cleef

For full biographical listings, see the Martindale-Hubbell Law Directory

Chicago—Continued

KECK, MAHIN & CATE (AV)

A Partnership including Professional Corporations
77 West Wacker Drive Suite 4900, 60601-1693
Telephone: 312-634-7700
Cable Address: "Hamscott"
Telex: 25-3411
Fax: 312-634-5000
Washington, D.C. Office: 555 12th St., N.W., 6th Floor.
Telephone: 202-637-3601.
Telecopier: 202-347-0140.
Peoria, Illinois Office: 401 Main Street, Suite 1600.
Telephone: 309-673-1681.
Telecopier: 309-673-1690.
New York, N.Y. Office: 100 Maiden Lane, Suite 1600.
Telephone: 212-504-5630.
Telecopier: 212-504-5631.

MEMBERS OF FIRM AND ASSOCIATES

Stephen L. Agin (P.C.)	Robin R. Lunn (P.C.)
Nicholas J. Anjanos	David S. Martin
Robert Edward Arroyo (P.C.)	Warren J. Marwedel (P.C.)
James W. Ashley, Jr. (P.C.)	John A. McDonald (P.C.)
John R. F. Baer (P.C.)	Donald J. McNeil (P.C.)
R. Clay Bennett (P.C.)	Patrick J. McNerney
Debra Rae Bernard	Thomas J. McNulty (P.C.)
Keith J. Braskich (P.C.)	David R. Melton (P.C.)
(Resident, Peoria, Illinois	Aimee L. Merriman
Office)	Dennis Minichello (P.C.)
William H. Campbell (P.C.)	Anita T. Molano (P.C.)
(Resident, Peoria, Illinois	Ruth N. Morduch (Resident,
Office)	Washington, D.C. Office)
Michele R. Chaffee	Donald G. Mulack (P.C.)
Donald O. Clark (Resident,	Stanley C. Nardoni
Washington, D.C. Office)	Catherine A. T. Nelson
John M. Craig (Resident,	Dennis M. O'Dea (P.C.)
Washington, D.C. Office)	(Resident, New York, N.Y.
Amy H. Curtner	Office)
Steven E. Cyranoski	Michael C. O'Neil
Kendall W. Daines (Resident,	Philip L. O'Neill (P.C.)
Peoria, Illinois Office)	(Resident, Washington, D.C.
Roy G. Davis, P.C. (Resident,	Office)
Peoria, Illinois Office)	Julia H. Perkins
Richard R. Diefendorf	David J. Poirier
(Resident, Washington, D.C.	Dennis J. Powers
Office)	Robert W. Pratt
Michelle V. Dohra	Carlos M. Recio (P.C.)
Michael J. Dolesh (P.C.)	(Resident, Washington, D.C.
Jacqueline D. Dubin	Office)
Shari L. Friedman	Tracy Donner Reckmeyer
Kerry A. Garvey	Clarence Owen Redman (Ltd.,
Sheila R. Gibbs-Cunningham	P.C.)
Clarke Gillespie, III	Robert L. Reeb
Larry S. Goldberg (P.C.)	Richard L. Reinish (P.C.)
Linda Vernon Goldberg	J. Reed Roesler (P.C.) (Resident,
Robin W. Grover (Resident,	Peoria, Illinois Office)
Washington, D.C. Office)	Douglass F. Rohrman (P.C.)
Yoon Suk Ham (Resident,	Steven C. Roper
Washington, D.C. Office)	Robert A. Roth
Marianne Craigmile Holzhall	Carla J. Rozycki (P.C.)
Michael J. Hughes	Cary Brian Samowitz (Resident,
Minard E. Hulse, Jr.	New York, N.Y. Office)
William C. Ives (P.C.)	Robert J. Schneider (P.C.)
Janet L. Jannusch (Resident,	David M. Seghetti
Peoria, Illinois Office)	Larry Selander (P.C.)
John A. Jeffries (P.C.)	Norman H. Singer (P.C.)
Linda Urbanik Johnson	(Resident, Washington, D.C.
Laura K. Jortberg	Office)
Stanley S. Jutkowitz (Resident,	Monica L. Thompson (P.C.)
Washington, D.C. Office)	Bedell A. Tippins (P.C.)
Sheldon Karon (P.C.)	John B. Truskowski (P.C.)
Matthew F. Kadish (Resident,	Roy M. Van Cleave (P.C.)
Washington, D.C. Office)	Robert J. Vechiola
Kathleen Hechinger Kane	John S. Vishneski III
Michael L. Kenaga	Wesley S. Walton (P.C.)
Terence P. Kennedy	Dorothy Voss Ward
John A. Klages	Jeffrey J. Ward
Deborah L. Kuhn	Jeffrey B. Whitt
George William Lewis (Resident,	Dennis M. Wilson (P.C.)
Washington, D.C. Office)	Lawrence A. Wojcik (P.C.)
Roger L. Longtin (P.C.)	Richard K. Wray (P.C.)
Janet Otsuka Love (P.C.)	Norma W. Zeitler
David G. Lubben (Resident,	Howard P. Zweig (P.C.)
Peoria, Illinois Office)	

OF COUNSEL

F. Willis Caruso	Bruce R. Johnson
Michael K. Cavanaugh (P.C.)	Thomas W. Johnston
Peter M. Davis	James S. Laing
Ronald L. Engel	Paul H. Lamboley (P.C.)
Michael D. Goodman	(Resident, Washington, D.C.
Robert M. Grossman	Office)

(See Next Column)

OF COUNSEL (Continued)

James T. Otis	John Yonco
James M. Wetzel	Carl E. Zwisler III (Resident,
	Washington, D.C. Office)

For full biographical listings, see the Martindale-Hubbell Law Directory

---

LORD, BISSELL & BROOK (AV)

Suites 2600-3600 Harris Bank Building, 115 South La Salle Street, 60603
Telephone: 312-443-0700
Telecopy: 312-443-0570
Cable Address: "Lowirco"
Telex: 25-0336
Los Angeles, California Office: 300 South Grand Avenue, 90071-3200.
Telephone: 213-485-1500.
Telecopy: 213-485-1200.
Telex: 18-1135.
Atlanta, Georgia Office: One Atlantic Center, 1201 West Peachtree Street, N.W., Suite 3700, 30309.
Telephone: 404-870-4600.
Telecopy: 404-872-5547.
Rockford, Illinois Office: 120 West State Street, Suite 200, 61101.
Telephone: 815-963-8050.

MEMBERS OF FIRM

John Solon Lord (1881-1979)	Wallye Muzette Hill
Cushman Brewer Bissell	Thomas W. Jenkins
(1900-1987)	Diane I. Jennings
Herbert C. Brook (1910-1990)	Richard F. Johnson
Charles A. Adamek	William J. Kelty, III
(Resident, Los Angeles Office)	David L. Kendall
David J. Adams	Celeste M. King
Steven H. Adelman	Robert A. Knuti
David M. Agnew	Karen J. Kowal
John T. Anderson	Jeffrey S. Kravitz
Margaret M. Anderson	(Resident, Los Angeles Office)
William C. Anderson, III	Mark A. Kreger
Simon H. Aronson	Forrest B. Lammiman
Stephen C. Ascher	Paul H. LaRue, Jr.
Michael J. Athans	L. Anthony Lehr
(Resident, Atlanta Office)	David M. Leonard
Robert B. Austin	(Resident, Atlanta Office)
Gail M. Baev	Harvey S. Lichterman
(Resident, Los Angeles Office)	Gary L. Lockwood
Carey S. Barney	Timothy M. Maggio
M. Elizabeth Bennett	Lawrence A. Manson (P.C.)
Kirk A. Borchardt	Kay W. McCurdy
George L. Burgett	David C. McLauchlan
Thomas J. Burke, Jr.	R. R. McMahan
Chad M. Castro	Dale T. Miller
John S. Chapman	Hugh L. Moore
Marilee Clausing	Thomas J. Murnighan
C. Guerry Collins	Stephen M. Murray
(Resident, Los Angeles Office)	John N. Oest
Michael P. Comiskey	Keith D. Parr
R. Dean Conlin	Judy Platt Perlman
Robert P. Conlon	J. Robert Persons
Joseph E. Coughlin	(Resident, Atlanta Office)
Charles L. Crouch, III	Robert J. Pugliese
(Resident, Los Angeles Office)	Robert D. Rasor
Michael Davis	David R. Reed
Thomas W. Dempsey	Louis E. Rosen
Nick J. DiGiovanni	Daniel I. Schlessinger
Kirk W. Dillard	David R. Schmidt
Williams P. Dorr	Rudolf H. Schroeter
R. Bruce Duffield	(Resident, Los Angeles Office)
James R. Dwyer	Michael Schuette
David P. Faulkner	David L. Skelding
(Resident, Rockford Office)	David J. Slawkowski
Edward C. Fitzpatrick	Walter T. Slezak
Kurt W. Florian, Jr.	Walton N. Smith
Patricia J. Foltz	(Resident, Atlanta Office)
Bruce W. Foudree	Rowe W. Snider
Don W. Fowler	Lyle Wayne Sparks
Lawrence M. Friedman	Jeffry S. Spears
Roger R. Fross	(Resident, Rockford Office)
Mark R. Goodman	Maynerd I. Steinberg
Lawrence A. Gray	Thomas J. Strueber
David G. Greene	(Resident, Atlanta Office)
(Resident, Atlanta Office)	Catalina J. Sugayan
Hugh C. Griffin	Gerald O. Sweeney, Jr.
John C. Gurley	Jane H. Veldman
John B. Haarlow	Eugene H. Wachtel
Randall A. Hack	Ann Marie Walsh
David C. Hall	Thomas C. Walsh
Leisa J. Hamm	Richard M. Watson
Laurence A. Hansen	(Resident, Atlanta Office)
Louis S. Harrison	William T. Weaver
Michael R. Hassan	Frederic W. Weber
David F. Hauge	Gary W. Westerberg
(Resident, Los Angeles Office)	Richard L. Wexler
Richard A. Hemmings	Mark D. Wilcox

(See Next Column)

LORD, BISSELL & BROOK, *Chicago—Continued*
MEMBERS OF FIRM (Continued)
Keith G. Wileman
(Resident, Los Angeles Office)
Daniel J. Zollner

John M. Wulfers
Mary Jane Yardley

OF COUNSEL
Glen R. Bernfield
Paul C. Blume, Sr.
Marguerite L. Brown
(Resident, Los Angeles Office)
Dennis J. Fox
David M. Gooder
Thomas J. Healey
Bobbe Hirsh
Harold L. Jacobson
Stephen P. Kenney

Clark C. King, Jr.
Marsha Kellman Klevickis
(Resident, Atlanta Office)
Janice E. Linn
Richard E. Mueller
John K. O'Connor
John S. Shapira
John G. Smith
Forrest L. Tozer
James R. Wimmer

Canella Gekas Woyar

ASSOCIATES
Fred L. Alvarez
Robert P. Arnold
Robert A. Badgley
Hugh S. Balsam
Patricia J. Barker
Jon Biasetti
Kathleen M. Bickelhaupt
William P. Bila
Brenda Adams Bissett
(Resident, Los Angeles Office)
Gregory W. Black
Philip A. Bock
Cynthia L. Bordelon
Jospeh J. Borders
Timothy W. Brink
Jacqueline C. Brown
(Resident, Los Angeles Office)
Andrea M. Brucoli
(Resident Atlanta Office)
Cara E. Brusca
Alfred L. Buchanan
John D. Buchanan
(Resident, Los Angeles Office)
Michael T. Burnett
Stephanie A. Burris
Mary Ellen Busch
Terrence P. Canade
Cynthia J. Cappello
Christopher K. Carpenter
Donald J. Chenevert
(Resident, Atlanta Office)
Joyce F. Clough
Brian C. Coffey
Stephen L. Cope
(Resident, Los Angeles Office)
Daniel A. Cotter
Thomas D. Cunningham
Kelly J. Cummings
Steven R. Daniels
(Resident Atlanta Office)
Jeffrey R. Darby
(Resident, Atlanta Office)
Stephanie Elizabeth Deaner
(Resident, Los Angeles Office)
Andrew R. Diamond
(Resident, Atlanta Office)
Michael T. Donovan
Charissa Dorian
(Resident, Los Angeles Office)
Franklin T. Dunn
(Resident, Los Angeles Office)
Daniel W. Eck
Charles A. Egner
(Resident, Rockford Office)
William D. Ellison
Mark Scott Fall
(Resident, Los Angeles Office)
Paul L. Fields, Jr.
(Resident, Atlanta Office)
Ann Kettelson Ford
Albert E. Fowerbaugh, Jr.
Cynthia M. Frey
(Resident, Los Angeles Office)
Matthew T. Furton
Michael J. Gaertner
Brian T. Garelli
Edward P. Gibbons
Laura J. Ginett
Laura S. Golden
Jannis E. Goodnow
Gregory A. Gunter
(Resident, Atlanta Office)

Michael P. Hannigan
Colleen M. Hennessy
Sarah J. Hewitt
Joseph A. Hinkhouse
John M. Hochhausler
(Resident, Los Angeles Office)
Terry R. Howell
(Resident, Atlanta Office)
John E. Hrebec
John M. Hughes
Thomas P. Hyatte
Lisa A. Jensen
Christine M. Johnson
Susan P. Jordan
Brad Stewart Kalter
(Resident, Atlanta Office)
Amy Hoagland Kane
Laura A. Kane
Cynthia A. Kaufman
Jennifer A. Kenedy
Heather E. Kern
Camille N. Khodadad
Barbara J. Klass
(Resident, Los Angeles Office)
Jacqueline Redin Klein
(Resident, Los Angeles Office)
Scott A. Kogen
Charles R. Krikorian
Susan K. Laing
LouCinda Laughlin
(Resident, Los Angeles Office)
Lizbeth J. Lemke
Ronald M. Lepinskas
John S. Lindemann
Jeri Rouse Looney
(Resident, Los Angeles Office)
George D. Lozano
(Resident, Los Angeles Office)
Rita E. Luce
Mark J. Lura
Samuel A. Mandarino
Donald J. Manikas
Paul F. Matousek
Kevin A. Maxim
(Resident, Atlanta Office)
C. Kevin McCabe
Susan Magee McColgan
Richard O. McDermott
Molly C. McGinnis
John J. McGuirk
Kevin P. McJessy
Patrick John Mc Laughlin
Robert E. McLaughlin
(Resident, Atlanta Office)
Jan M. Michaels
Paul J. Molino
John S. Monical
Kathryn G. Montgomery
John W. Moss
James E. Nelson
Jeffrey J. Neuenschwander
William D. Nolen
Prescott L. Nottingham
(Resident, Atlanta Office)
Eric B. Noyes
Jennifer A. O'Malley
Christopher C. Osborne
Debra A. Osmond
Scott Richard Ostericher
Jason A. Parson
Margaret M. Pasulka
John M. Phelan

(See Next Column)

ASSOCIATES (Continued)
Dov. J. Pinchot
Mitchell J. Popham
(Resident, Los Angeles Office)
Michael E. Prangle
J. Brett Pritchard
Matthew W. Rappleye
John Carter Rich
Robert B. Robinson
Victoria A. Rohner
Leslie J. Rosen
Eric P. Schoonveld
Steven Schulwolf
Michael J. Scotti III
Amy E. Shappert
(Resident, Rockford Office)
Anthony B. Sherman
Linda J. Simon
Christine J. Siwik
Monica S. Smyth
Karen A. Soomekh
(Resident, Los Angeles Office)
Anne M. Stalder

Cynthia M. Storer
Richard P. Stowell
Denean K. Sturino
Jennifer L. Sucher
Robert E. Sweeney, Jr.
Ann Caroline Taylor
Terri L. Thomas
Michael P. Trier
Anne Kelly Turner
Todd M. Van Baren
Peter C. Van den Dool
Damon N. Vocke
David E. Walker
Sarah Marion Weil
John T. Williams
Anthony F. Witteman
(Resident, Los Angeles Office)
Corliss L. Worford
(Resident, Atlanta Office)
Kathryn C. Wyatt
James H. Wynn
(Resident, Atlanta Office)

Michael Yetnikoff

For full biographical listings, see the Martindale-Hubbell Law Directory

MANDEL, LIPTON AND STEVENSON LIMITED (AV)
Suite 2900, 120 North La Salle Street, 60602
Telephone: 312-236-7080
Facsimile: 312-236-0781

Richard L. Mandel
Alfred R. Lipton
Leonard M. Malkin
R. Peter Carey
Henry A. Waller
Kathleen Roseborough

Richard A. Lifshitz
Terry Yale Feiertag
Kathleen Hogan Morrison
Uve R. Jerzy
Carolyn E. Winter
Audrey L. Gaynor

Andrés J. Gallegos

Megan Kennedy Riordan
(Not admitted in IL)

OF COUNSEL
Nicholas Stevenson

Mark R. Ordower

LEGAL SUPPORT PERSONNEL
Jacqueline Steffens (Paralegal)

References: Northern Trust Co.; American National Bank of Chicago.

For full biographical listings, see the Martindale-Hubbell Law Directory

MAYER, BROWN & PLATT (AV)
190 South La Salle Street, 60603-3441
Telephone: (312) 782-0600
Facsimile: (312) 701-7711
Telex: 190404
Cable: LEMAY
URL: http://www.mayerbrown.com
Berlin, Germany Office: Spreeufer 5, 10178.
Telephone: 011-49-30-247-3800.
Facsimile: 011-49-30-247-38044.
Brussels, Belgium Office: Square de Meeûs 19/20, Bte. 4, 1050.
Telephone: 011-32-2-512-9878. Facsimile : 011-32-2-511-3305.
Telex: 20768 MBPBRU B.
Houston, Texas Office: 700 Louisiana Street, Suite 3600, 77002-2730.
Telephone: (713) 221-1651.
Facsimile: (713) 224-6410.
Telex: 775809.
Cable: LEMAYHOU.
London, England Office: 162 Queen Victoria Street, EC4V 4DB.
Telephone: 011-44-171-248-1465.
Facsimile: 011-44-171-329-4465.
Telex: 8811095.
Cable: LEMAYLDN.
Los Angeles, California Office: 350 South Grand Avenue, 25th Floor, 90071-1503.
Telephone: (213) 229-9500.
Facsimile: (213) 625-0248.
Telex: 188089.
Cable: LEMAYLA.
New York, New York Office: 1675 Broadway, 10019-5820.
Telephone: (212) 506-2500.
Facsimile: (212) 262-1910.
Telex: 701842.
Cable: LEMAYEN.
Washington, D.C. Office: 2000 Pennsylvania Avenue, N.W., 20006-1882.
Telephone: (202) 463-2000.
Facsimile: (202) 861-0473.
Telex: 892603.
Cable: LEMAYDC.
Representative Offices:
Almaty, Republic of Kazakhstan: 162 Tulebaev Street #32.
Telephone: 011-7-3272-636388.
Facsimile: 011-7-3272-507828.

(See Next Column)

MAYER, BROWN & PLATT—*Continued*

Bishkek, Kyrgyz Republic: Suite 405, Prospekt Manasa 55, 720001.
Telephone: 011-7-3312-222970.
Facsimile: 011-7-3312-620980.
Köln, Germany: An Lyskirchen 14, 50676.
Telephone: 011-49-221-921-5210.
Facsimile: 011-49-221-921-5214.
Tashkent, Republic of Uzbekistan: 5th Floor, 1 Turab Tula Street, 700003.
Telephone: 011-7-3712-891179.
Facsimile: 011-7-3712-891178.
Mexico City, Mexico, D.F., Independent Mexico Correspondent: Jáuregui, Navarrete, Nader y Rojas, S.C. Abogados, Paseo de la Reforma 199, Pisos 15, 16 y 17, 06500, Mexico.
Telephone: 011-525-591-16-55.
Facsimile: 011-525-535-80-62, 011-525-703-22-47.
Cable: JANANE.

MEMBERS OF FIRM

David F. Abbott
Lee N. Abrams
Diane E. Ambler
  (Washington, D.C. Office)
J. Trent Anderson
Percy L. Angelo
Franklin P. Auwarter
Robert C. Baptista, Jr.
Robert N. Barnard
Gregory L. Barton
Teresa A. Beaudet (Los Angeles, California Office)
Robert M. Berger
John C. Berghoff, Jr.
Nicole V.F. Bergman Fong
  (New York, N.Y. Office)
Barbara Bertok
Edward S. Best
Eric C. Bettelheim
  (London, England Office)
Barry P. Biggar
  (New York, N.Y. Office)
Christian F. Binnig
Timothy S. Bishop
Robert E. Bloch
  (Washington, D.C. Office)
David I. Bloom
  (Washington, D.C. Office)
Fern C. Bomchill
Kim Marie Boylan
  (Washington, D.C. Office)
Richard S. Brennan
Robert I. Bressman
  (New York, N.Y. Office)
Joan Edmonds Brophy
Richard F. Broude
  (New York, N.Y. Office)
Caroline Brower
Mary Rose Brusewitz
  (New York, N.Y. Office)
Michael A. Campbell
James B. Carlson
  (New York, N.Y. Office)
John M. Carroll
Jean S. Chan
  (New York, N.Y. Office)
Charles Chu
  (Washington, D.C. Office)
Diane Citron
  (Not admitted in IL)
Paul B. Clemenceau
  (Houston, Texas Office)
Barbara E. Cohen
Richard A. Cole
  (London, England Office)
Ian R. Coles
  (London, England Office)
Joseph P. Collins
Vincent J. Connelly
George W. Craven
Robert E. Curley
David S. Curry
William M. Daley
Peter V. Darrow
  (New York, N.Y. Office)
Robert P. Davis
  (Washington, D.C. Office)
Scott J. Davis
Laura A. DeFelice
  (New York, N.Y. Office)
Debora de Hoyos
William E. Deitrick
Julian C. D'Esposito, Jr.
Douglas A. Doetsch
Jerome F. Donohoe

David K. Duffee
  (New York, N.Y. Office)
Thomas C. Durham
Thomas M. Durkin
Louis P. Eatman (Los Angeles, California Office)
Kerry Lynn Edwards
  (Washington, D.C. Office)
Russell R. Eggert
Timothy B. Ellwood
  (Houston, Texas Office)
Roy T. Englert, Jr.
  (Washington, D.C. Office)
Tyrone C. Fahner
Richard J. Favretto
  (Washington, D.C. Office)
Michael R. Feagley
Robert F. Finke
L. Bruce Fischer (Los Angeles, California Office)
Robert V. Fitzsimmons
Delilah B. Flaum
Mary C. Fontaine
J. Paul Forrester
Andrew L. Frey
  (New York, N.Y. Office)
Dennis G. Friedman
Marc Gary
  (Washington, D.C. Office)
Barry Gassman
  (New York, N.Y. Office)
John J. Gearen
Kenneth S. Geller
  (Washington, D.C. Office)
Bettina Getz
Steven R. Gilford
Michael J. Gill
Mark H. Gitenstein
  (Washington, D.C. Office)
Ronald B. Given
James W. Gladden, Jr.
Joseph R. Goeke
Marcia E. Goodman
Jeffrey I. Gordon
Robert E. Gordon
William A. Gordon
Maureen J. Gorman
A. Duncan Gray, Jr.
  (Houston, Texas Office)
Lloyd S. Guerci
  (Washington, D.C. Office)
Frederic L. Hahn
John F. Halbleib
S. Alan Hamburger
  (Brussels, Belgium Office)
Marshall E. Hanbury
  (Not admitted in IL)
Kevin P. Hawken
Werner J. Hein
  (Washington, D.C. Office)
Robert A. Helman
Leo Herzel
Vincent E. Hillery
Catherine W. Hoeg
  (Houston, Texas Office)
Debra B. Hoffman
James D. Holzhauer
Thomas R. Hood
  (New York, N.Y. Office)
Charles M. Horn
  (Washington, D.C. Office)
Carrie Kiger Huff
Robert F. Hugi
Harley Hutchins
Ronald A. Jacks

(See Next Column)

Caryn L. Jacobs
John A. Janicik
Thomas N. Jersild
Erika Z. Jones
  (Washington, D.C. Office)
Roger J. Jones
James J. Junewicz
Ivan P. Kane
Harold L. Kaplan
Wayne S. Kaplan
Alvin Charles Katz
M. Marvin Katz
  (Houston, Texas Office)
Robert A. Kelman
Michael F. Kerr (Los Angeles, California Office)
Stanton A. Kessler
Nabil L. Khodadad
  (London, England Office)
Thomas S. Kiriakos
James E. Knox
William H. Knull, III
  (Houston, Texas Office)
Kenneth E. Kohler (Los Angeles, California Office)
Jason H. P. Kravitt
Simeon M. Kriesberg
  (Washington, D.C. Office)
Robert J. Kriss
Herbert W. Krueger
Kathryn A. Kusske
  (Washington, D.C. Office)
Philip Allen Lacovara
  (Washington, D.C. and New York Offices)
Duke R. Ligon
  (New York, N.Y. Office)
Stuart M. Litwin
Theodore A. Livingston, Jr.
Wayne R. Luepker
George A. Luscombe, II
Christine Lutgens
Daniel W. Luther
George W. Madison
  (New York, N.Y. Office)
Cary J. Malkin
John D. Marshall
Alan J. Martin
Andrew Mattei
  (New York, N.Y. Office)
Stephen J. Mattson
Frank D. Mayer, Jr.
Terri A. Mazur
Hugh R. McCombs
Howard M. McCue, III
James J. McGuire
  (New York, N.Y. Office)
T. Mark McLaughlin
Thomas B. McNeill
Jonathan C. Medow
Richard S. Millard
Jay Parry Monge
  (New York, N.Y. Office)
Deborah Alfred Monson
Donna Evensen Morgan
John E. Muench
J. Thomas Mullen
David Narefsky
Alec G. Nedelman (Los Angeles, California Office)
Brian E. Newhouse (Los Angeles, California Office)
C. Mark Nicolaides
  (Berlin, Germany Office)
Michael E. Niebruegge
  (Houston, Texas Office)
Philip J. Niehoff
Harvey Nixon
Frank P. Nocco
  (New York, N.Y. Office)
Lennine Occhino
Michele L. Odorizzi
Anna M. O'Meara
Jerry L. Oppenheimer
  (Washington, D.C. Office)
Joseph B. Organ
Carolyn P. Osolinik
  (Washington, D.C. Office)
Danuta Bembenista Panich
Stanley J. Parzen
George A. Pecoulas
Stuart P. Pergament
  (Washington, D.C. Office)

Denis Petkovic
  (London, England Office)
Andrew J. Pincus
  (Washington, D.C. Office)
Douglas A. Poe
George A. Ranney, Jr.
Mitchell D. Raup
Elizabeth A. Raymond
Phillip S. Reed
N. Neville Reid
Laura D. Richman
Michael P. Richman
  (New York, N.Y. Office)
M. Ellen Robb (Los Angeles, California Office)
Lawrence S. Robbins
  (Washington, D.C. Office)
Howard J. Roin
Matthew A. Rooney
Michael F. Rosenblum
Martin G. Rosenstein
Kenneth M. Rosenzweig
Paul J. N. Roy
Stuart M. Rozen
Deborah Schavey Ruff
George Ruhlen
  (Houston, Texas Office)
Donald W. Rupert
Mark W. Ryan
  (Washington, D.C. Office)
John R. Sagan
Alan N. Salpeter
Julia R. Sarron
William A. Schmalzl
John P. Schmitz (Not admitted in IL; Washington, D.C. and Berlin, Germany Offices)
Edward J. Schneidman
Joseph U. Schorer
James C. Schroeder
David A. Schuette
James A. Serritella
Stephen M. Shapiro
Kevin L. Shaw (Los Angeles, California Office)
Richard W. Shepro
Timothy C. Sherck
Brian W. Smith
  (Washington, D.C. Office)
Lawrence K. Snider
Neil M. Soltman (Los Angeles, California Office)
Robert A. Southern (Los Angeles, California Office)
David M. Spector
James S. Stanhaus
Adrian L. Steel, Jr.
  (Washington, D.C. Office)
J. Robert Stoll
Jeffrey M. Strauss
Robert H. Swart
  (Washington, D.C. Office)
Evan M. Tager
  (Washington, D.C. Office)
James E. Tancula
  (Houston, Texas Office)
Paul W. Theiss
Frederick B. Thomas
S. Raymond Tillett
William C. Tompsett
John M. Touhy
Charles S. Triplett
  (Washington, D.C. Office)
Watson B. Tucker
George J. Tzanetopoulos
Mark R. Uhrynuk
  (London, England Office)
Barry Alan Van Dyke
Terry Otero Vilardo
  (Houston, Texas Office)
Thomas M. Vitale
  (New York, N.Y. Office)
James R. Walther (Los Angeles, California Office)
Robert J. Ward
  (New York, N.Y. Office)
Michael O. Warnecke
Don L. Weaver (Los Angeles, California Office)
Priscilla P. Weaver
Seth J. Weinberger
Barry A. White
Joel V. Williamson

(See Next Column)

MAYER, BROWN & PLATT, *Chicago—Continued*

MEMBERS OF FIRM (Continued)

Richard S. Williamson
Douglas L. Wisner
  (New York, N.Y. Office)
Mark S. Wojciechowski
  (New York, N.Y. Office)

Steven Wolowitz
  (New York, N.Y. Office)
Herbert L. Zarov
Michael I. Zinder
  (New York, N.Y. Office)

SENIOR COUNSEL

Roger W. Barrett
Stuart Bernstein
Albert I. Edelman
  (New York, N.Y. Office)
David B. Finnegan
  (Washington, D.C. Office)

Patrick W. O'Brien
Justin A. Stanley
Edmund A. Stephan
Robert L. Stern

SPECIAL CONSULTANT

Michael W. McConnell (Not admitted in IL)

SPECIAL COUNSEL

Charles Rothfeld
  (Washington, D.C. Office)

David B. Weinberg
John Shepard Wiley, Jr. (Los
  Angeles, California Office)

COUNSEL

James R. Barry
Carol J. Bilzi
  (Washington, D.C. Office)
Steven E. Brummel
  (Brussels, Belgium Office)
Patricia B. Carlson
C. Cabell Chinnis, Jr.
  (Washington, D.C. Office)
Marla Chernof Cohen
Mary A. Cole
  (Washington, D.C. Office)
Richard C. Cummings, Jr.
Ronald R. Dietrich
Gary D. Friedman
  (New York, N.Y. Office)
Patricia V. Gentry
James C. Geoly
Graham C. Grady
Marian C. Haney
Thomas C. Havens
  (New York, New York Office)
John R. Hewitt
  (New York, N.Y. Office)
Diane M. Huff
John Chafer Huff
Gary A. Isaac
Dean Alan Isaacs
Warren L. Jervey
  (New York, N. Y. Office)
Nancy S. Kornick

Beth R. Kramer
  (New York, N. Y. Office)
Susan J. Launi
  (Brussels, Belgium Office)
Michele G. Magner
Philip H. Martin
Richard K. Matta
  (Washington, D.C. Office)
Kevin C. McDonald
Lillian Miller
Robert L. Morgan
  (Houston, Texas Office)
Donald C. Morris
Christopher P. Murphy (Los
  Angeles, California Office)
Amy L. Nathan
  (Washington, D.C. Office)
Rex A. Palmer
Scott P. Perlman
  (Washington, D.C. Office)
Diane J. Romza-Kutz
Cecilia A. Roth
Patricia F. Sharkey
Richard A. Speer
  (Not admitted in IL)
Michael L. Tucker
Jeffrey A. Usow
Gregory S. Walden
  (Washington, D.C. Office)
Neil A. Wasserstrom
  (Houston, Texas Office)

ASSOCIATES

Daniel Acosta
Nelson Kyunam Ahn
  (New York, N.Y. Office)
Douglas A. Albritton
Niyazbek B. Aldasheu
  (Houston, Texas Office)
Marwan Al-Turki
  (London, England Office)
Bradley J. Andreozzi
  (New York, N.Y. Office)
James A. Andrus
  (Houston, Texas Office)
Irina Aronov
  (London, England Office)
Andrei A. Baev (Los Angeles,
  California Office)
Lesa A. Barkowsky
  (New York, N.Y. Office)
Angela Barnes
Mary R. Barry
Audrey I. Bender
  (New York, New York Office)
Joanne E. Benisch
  (New York, N.Y. Office)
Michael E. Bieniek
Sara A. Biro
Richard L. Bjelde
  (Berlin, Germany Office)
Edward B. Black
  (London, England Office)
Michael T. Blair
Howard Alan Blaustein
  (New York, N.Y. Office)
Stephen D. Bohrer
  (New York, New York Office)

David C. Bolstad (Los Angeles,
  California Office)
Francis R. Bradley, III
  (Houston, Texas Office)
Jacqueline R. Brady (Los
  Angeles, California Office)
Addison D. Braendel
Philip O. Brandes
  (New York, N.Y. Office)
Matthew P. Brennan
  (New York, N.Y. Office)
Susan Brice
Patricia K. Brito
  (Houston, Texas Office)
Robert L. Bronston
  (Washington, D.C. Office)
Terence F. Browne
  (Washington, D.C. Office)
Ellen M. Bublick
Deborah H. Buttell
H. Thomas Byron, III
  (Washington, D.C. Office)
Kimberlee S. Cagle
  (Houston, Texas Office)
Timothy P. Callahan
Michelle A. Carey
  (New York, N.Y. Office)
David A. Carpenter
J. Russell Carr
Shant H. Chalian
  (New York, N.Y. Office)
Paul Chandler
Christopher D. Chen (Los
  Angeles, California Office)

(See Next Column)

ASSOCIATES (Continued)

Barbara A. Clark
  (Houston, Texas Office)
Jonathan Cleveland
G. Marcus Cole
Victoria R. Collado
Martin J. Collins
  (New York, N.Y. Office)
Rita N. Conroy
Blake M. Cornish
  (Washington, D.C. Office)
Jeanette L. Cotting
  (New York, N.Y. Office)
J. Tyson Covey
David C. Crane
  (Washington, D.C. Office)
Paul M. Crimmins
Kristen W. Crosby
John A. Curseaden
  (New York, N.Y. Office)
June E. Daniel
Raniero D'Aversa, Jr.
  (New York, N.Y. Office)
Diana L. Davis
  (Houston, Texas Office)
Sheila D'Cruz
John J. Dedyo
  (New York, N.Y. Office)
Daniel J. Delaney
Keith B. DeLeon
  (New York, N.Y. Office)
Lynn E. Delzell
Sharon L. De Vault
Thomas DiLenge
  (Washington, D.C. Office)
Thomas W. Dimond
Boise A. Ding (Los Angeles,
  California Office)
Courtney A. Dinsmore
  (New York, N.Y. Office)
Kelly J. Doherty
Peter J. Donoghue
Brian G. Donovan
Lisa M. Dooley
Angela K. Dorn
Robert M. Dow, Jr.
Eric S. Dreiband
Kira E. Druyan
Alyssa A. Dudkowski
Ralph P. Dudziak
Daniel Dumezich
Jack Edelbrock
Thomas P. Egan
Scott J. Eisen
Rebecca S. Eisner
Gayle L. Elsner
Donald M. Falk
  (Washington, D.C. Office)
Gary Feinerman
Sonia R. Ferguson
  (Houston, Texas Office)
Henry Einar Fink (Los Angeles,
  California Office)
Patricia A. Flaming
Robert M. Fogler
Kyle K. Fox
Douglas B. Frank (Los Angeles,
  California Office)
Ron D. Franklin
  (New York, N.Y. Office)
Fritz E. Freidinger
Kristin Frey
Jeffrey B. Frishman
Brian P. Gallagher
Vinny B. Ganga
  (London, England Office)
Kathy Woeber Gardner
Julian P. Gehman
  (Washington, D.C. Office)
Bruce L. Gelman
Robert H. George
  (Houston, Texas Office)
Matthew R. Gochberg
Jennifer B. Gold
  (New York, New York Office)
Kenneth A. Goldberg
David M. Goldman
  (New York, N.Y. Office)
Jeffrey A. Goldman
  (Not admitted in IL)
Jill R. Goodman
Ronald P. Gould
Glenn Graff

Anthony G. Graham (Los
  Angeles, California Office)
David W. Grawemeyer
Christopher Greene
  (New York, N.Y. Office)
Richard Greta (Los Angeles,
  California Office)
Lorie S. Griffen (Los Angeles,
  California Office)
Terri T. Griffiths
  (Houston, Texas Office)
Salvatore Guerrera
  (New York, N.Y. Office)
Sandra M. Gutierrez
  (New York, N.Y. Office)
Karen Hagnell
Janet L. Hall
Keith C. Hannigan
Myles R. Hansen
  (Washington, D.C. Office)
Gayle C. Hanz
  (Houston, Texas Office)
Donald F. Harmon
Robert G. Harvey
  (New York, N.Y. Office)
Ronald G. Hayden
Sara M. Hazelwood
  (New York, N.Y. Office)
Michael L. Hermsen
Daniel G. Hildebrand
David M. Hillman
  (New York, N.Y. Office)
Carol A. Hitselberger
Carole E. Howard
  (Houston, Texas Office)
Bart W. Huffman
  (Houston, Texas Office)
Daniel J. Hulseberg
David A. Hyman
  (Washington, D.C. Office)
Doug E. Ibendahl
Nikolay Y. Isaakov
  (Houston, Texas Office)
Tarek Ismail
Valerie-Leila Jaber
  (New York, N.Y. Office)
William J. Jackson
  (Houston, Texas Office)
Jerome J.M.F. Jauffret (Los
  Angeles, California Office)
Catherine C. Jenkins
  (New York, N.Y. Office)
Daniel T. Jenks
Paul A. Jorissen
Gulnara A. Kalikova
  (Houston, Texas Office)
Timothy E. Keehan
  (Washington, D.C. Office)
Charles S. Kelley
  (Houston, Texas Office)
Terry D. Kernell
  (Houston, Texas Office)
Thomas Kittle-Kamp
Marc L. Klyman
Anne Marie Konopack
Mary E. Kruit
Paul J. Kunkel
Dennis G. LaGory
Ronald M. Lambert
Chris D. Landgraff
Kim D. Larsen
  (Washington, D.C. Office)
Bennett W. Lasko
Benjamin W. Lau
  (New York, N.Y. Office)
Micholas A. Laveris
  (New York, N.Y. Office)
John F. Lawlor
Jeffrey E. Leeb
Kim A. Leffert
Stacey N. Lefont
  (New York, N.Y. Office)
Mary B. Lemuth
  (Houston, Texas Office)
Luke P. Levasseur
  (Washington, D.C. Office)
Fredrick S. Levin (Los Angeles,
  California Office)
Bruce H. Levine (Los Angeles,
  California Office)
William A. Levy
Jin Li (New York, N.Y. Office)

(See Next Column)

MAYER, BROWN & PLATT—*Continued*

ASSOCIATES (Continued)

James T. Lidbury
Erik J. Lillya
Jeri Lindahl-Garcia
Nicholas W. Lobenthal
  (New York, N.Y. Office)
Joan L. Long
Robert M. Lyons
  (London, England Office)
Reyna E. Marder
  (New York, N.Y. Office)
Marjorie M. Margolies
Jonathan L. Marks
Andrew S. Marovitz
Joseph M. Martin
Marlaine J. McVisk
Anthony P. Mechcatie
  (New York, N.Y. Office)
Demetrios G. Metropoulos
David E. Metz
Joyce L. Meyer
Paul Meyer
Tracy C. Missett
  (New York, N.Y. Office)
Bruce A. Mitchell
Antonio Molestina
  (New York, N.Y. Office)
Warren Mondscheim
Susan J. Moran
Allen D. Moreland
  (New York, N.Y. Office)
Andrew J. Morris
  (Washington, D.C. Office)
Wendy Lefkoe Morris
  (Washington, D.C. Office)
Richard T. Morrison
Joseph F. Morrissey
  (London, England Office)
Louis P. Moritz
Sean P. Moylan
  (Washington, D.C. Office)
Michael P. Murphy
John Nadolenco (Los Angeles,
  California Office)
Lucia Nale
Amy E. Newman
Jason Neumark
Joanna C. Nicholas
Limor Nissan
  (New York, N.Y. Office)
Kenneth E. Noble
Keith F. Oberkfell
Kathryn Horton O'Brien
  (Washington, D.C. Office)
Kelley E. O'Brien
  (Washington, D.C. Office)
Ger P. O'Donnell
A. Ken Okamoto (Los Angeles,
  California Office)
Gary Orseck
  (Washington, D.C. Office)
Rosaria Vivo Owen
Keith A. Palzer
  (New York, N.Y. Office)
Un Kyung Park
Jim P. Patti
Susan K. Pavlica
  (Houston, Texas Office)
Ross Pazzol
Mark W. Pearson
  (New York, N.Y. Office)
Daniel Penn
  (London, England Office)
Brad L. Peterson
C. Dirk Peterson
  (Washington, D.C. Office)
Vytas A. Petrulis
  (Houston, Texas Office)
Antonio N. Piccirillo
  (New York, N.Y. Office)
Jeffrey S. Piell
Wendy L. Pollack
  (New York, N.Y. Office)
Matthew A. Posthuma
Ashish S. Prasad
Maria M. Rabassa (Los Angeles,
  California Office)
Edward R. Rabe, Jr.
Jeffrey Alan Rackow
  (Washington, D.C. Office)

Victor Rampertab
  (New York, N.Y. Office)
Michael D. Rechtin, Jr.
Charles F. Regan, Jr.
Thomas S. Reif
Craig E. Reimer
Gary W. Reinbold
Andrew L. Reisman
Clisson S. Rexford
Mary Beth Rhoden (Los
  Angeles, California Office)
Robert S. Rigg
Daniel L. Ring
Erich G. Rhynhart
Michael P. Rissman
Gerardo Rivera
  (New York, N.Y. Office)
Carol S. Rivers
Walter M. Rogers
Julie A. Rosen
Frederic Rosenberg
  (New York, N.Y. Office)
Leonard X Rosenberg
Marc E. Rosenthal
Allison Young Ross
  (New York, N.Y. Office)
Laurie R. Rubenstein
  (Washington, D.C. Office)
Javier H. Rubinstein
Gail C. Saracco
Jeffrey W. Sarles
Stefan H. Sarles
  (London, England Office)
Jared Schenk
Nina E. Scholtz (Los Angeles,
  California Office)
Curtis W. Schuhmacher
  (Washington, D.C. Office)
Peter Schultz
Lynn A. Shapiro
Ronald M. Shoss
  (Houston, Texas Office)
Robert S. Shwarts
  (New York, N.Y. Office)
Richard Jay Silverstein
Jonathan E. Singer
Natalie E. Sivakoff
  (London, England Office)
Adam C. Sloane
  (Washington, D.C. Office)
Michael Sloyer
  (New York, N.Y. Office)
Diane Green Smith
Kerry T. Smith
Jennifer L. Sokol (Los Angeles,
  California Office)
Richard A. Spehr
  (New York, N.Y. Office)
Marc F. Sperber
Mary Ann Spiegel
Richard P. Spinelli
  (New York, N.Y. Office)
James M. Spira
Joseph A. Starkman
Marina M. Stephens
  (Houston, Texas Office)
Jeffrey Stern
  (New York, N.Y. Office)
Jeffrey W. Stewart
Scott M. Stewart
Glen F. Strong
John J. Sullivan
  (Washington, D.C. Office)
Michael T. Sullivan
David L. Sun
Lily Fu Swenson
  (Washington, D.C. Office)
Ying Hsein Tan
  (London, England Office)
Wayne L. Tang
Elaine M. Taussig
Mark R. Taylor
Mark R. Ter Molen
Carl J. Thomas (Los Angeles,
  California Office)
Michael J. Tobak, III
Oliver Ott Trumbo, III
  (New York, N.Y. Office)

ASSOCIATES (Continued)

(See Next Column)

Timothy J. Tyler
  (Houston, Texas Office)
Euchung Ung
  (New York, N.Y. Office)
Alan E. Untereiner
  (Washington, D.C. Office)
Lane W. Vanderslice
Stephen Van Dolsen
Robert G. Vanecko
John Voorhees
Alexander V. Voronin
Hoang Quan Vu
  (Houston, Texas Office)
Kathleen Walsh
  (New York, N.Y. Office)
Tracy Goad Walter
Guy G. Ward
Richard E. Weber, III
Lyman C. Welch
David M. Well
Thomas C. Wexler
  (London, England Office)
Lawrence E. White

Janet R. Widmaier
Anthony S. Wiedwiewcki
  (Houston, Texas Office)
Edward H. Williams
Kimberly S. Winick (Los
  Angeles, California Office)
Gary A. Winters
  (Washington, D.C. Office)
Lynne Helfand Wolfberg
Craig A. Woods
Nigel A. Wright
  (London, England Office)
Veronica L. Young
David C. Zeilstra
Leigh F. Zeising
Donald P. Zeithaml, Jr.
Michael T. Zeller
Scott M. Zemser
  (New York, N.Y. Office)
Richard G. Ziegler
David H. Zielke
  (Washington, D.C. Office)
Mary Lou Zwick

For full biographical listings, see the Martindale-Hubbell Law Directory

MAYER, FRIEDLICH, SPIESS, TIERNEY, BROWN & PLATT

(See Mayer, Brown & Platt)

McBRIDE BAKER & COLES (AV)

500 West Madison Street 40th Floor, 60661
Telephone: 312-715-5700
Cable Address: "Chilaw"
Telex: 270258
Telecopier: 312-993-9350
Email: lastname@mbc.com *URL:* http://www.mbc.com
Oakbrook Terrace, Illinois Office: Suite 1000, One Mid America Plaza,
60181-4710.
Telephone: 630-954-2100.
Telecopier: 630-954-2112.

MEMBERS OF FIRM

David Ackerman
Henry S. Allen, Jr.
Thomas P. Arden
Steven B. Bashaw
Michael J. Boland
Malcolm H. Brooks
Martin J. Campanella
William J. Cooney
John J. Cresto
Paul D. Frenz
Anthony L. Frink
Andrew R. Gelman
Geoffrey G. Gilbert
Lola Miranda Hale
Kenneth A. Jenero
Francis L. Keldermans
Thomas J. Kinasz
Evan M. Kjellenberg
Patrick W. Kocian
Clifton A. Lake
Richard S. Lauter
Steven R. Lifson

David S. Mann
Elias N. Matsakis
Richard F. Nelson
Carolyn O'Connor
Morgan J. Ordman
Elizabeth S. Perdue
Robert W. Queeney
Richard A. Redmond
G. Gale Roberson, Jr.
Anne Hamblin Schiave
Robert C. Schnitz
Robert I. Schwimmer
David Shayne
Thomas J. Smedinghoff
Mark A. Spognardi
Mark J. Steger
William M. Stevens
Steven B. Varick
Thomas P. Ward
Michael L. Weissman
Richard R. Winter
Joseph S. Wright, Jr.

Larry M. Zanger

SENIOR COUNSEL

Lawrence A. Coles, Jr.

OF COUNSEL

Robert O. Case

N. A. Jim Giambalvo

Thomas R. Leavens

ASSOCIATES

Naomi R. Angel
Andrew R. Basile
Adam E. Berman
Ruth Hill Bro
Marc L. Fogelberg
Edward J. Hannon
Jerald Holisky
Eric E. Mennel
Joseph S. Messer
Laura Newton

Lorijean G. Oei
Sarah E. Pace
Stacey L. Prange
Antonia Sexton Pritchard
George Michael Sanders
Paul R. Simons
Thomas R. Stilp
Peter J. Strand
Jonathan E. Strouse
Douglas C. Taylor

Jeffrey M. Teske

For full biographical listings, see the Martindale-Hubbell Law Directory

McFADDEN & DILLON, A PROFESSIONAL CORPORATION (AV)

135 South La Salle Street, Suite 2110, 60603
Telephone: 312-201-8300
Facsimile: 312-201-0535

(See Next Column)

MCFADDEN & DILLON A PROFESSIONAL CORPORATION, *Chicago—Continued*

Roger J. McFadden   Thomas J. Dillon

Tyrrel J. Penn

For full biographical listings, see the Martindale-Hubbell Law Directory

MILLER, SHAKMAN, HAMILTON, KURTZON & SCHLIFKE (AV)

Suite 1100, 208 South La Salle Street, 60604
Telephone: 312-263-3700
FAX: 312-263-3270

MEMBERS OF FIRM

Neil H. Adelman	Diane F. Klotnia
Marc O. Beem	Michael S. Kurtzon
Stephen J. Bisgeier	Scott M. Lapins
Geraldine Soat Brown	Edward W. Malstrom
Derek L. Cottier	Barry A. Miller
Edward W. Feldman	Ronald S. Miller
Arthur W. Friedman	Bernard A. Schlifke
Ruth Goldman	Mark A. Segal
R. Dickey Hamilton	Michael L. Shakman

OF COUNSEL

Morton John Barnard	David J. Krupp
Theodore Berger	Maurice Rosenfield
Norman Geis	Stanton Schuman

ASSOCIATES

Julie H. Friedman	Thomas M. Staunton
Sharon Zaban Letchinger	David A. O'Toole

For full biographical listings, see the Martindale-Hubbell Law Directory

PETERSON & ROSS (AV)

200 East Randolph Drive, Suite 7300, 60601-6969
Telephone: 312-861-1400
Telecopy: 312-565-0832
New York, N.Y. Office: 33 Whitehall Street, 27th Floor, 10004.
Telephone: 212-820-7700.
Los Angeles, California Office: 333 South Grand Avenue, Suite 1600, 90071-1520.
Telephone: 213-625-3500.
Springfield, Illinois Office: 600 South Second Street, Suite 400, 62704.
Telephone: 217-525-0700.
Morristown, New Jersey Office: 55 Madison Avenue, Suite 200, 07960.
Telephone: 201-993-9668.
Austin, Texas Office: 101 East Ninth Street, Suite 1000, 78701.
Telephone: 512-472-5587.

MEMBERS OF FIRM

Walter Henry Eckert (1923-1944)	Regina K. McCabe
	William A. Chittenden, III
Walter W. Ross, Jr. (1934-1972)	Anne Fiedler
Abe R. Peterson (1923-1983)	John E. Black, Jr.
Owen Rall (1933-1985)	Christopher J. Graham
Theodore A. Boundas	Larry A. Hoellwarth
Norbert J. Wegerzyn	Roderick T. Dunne
Daniel B. Hales	Priscilla A. May
Joseph J. Hasman	Donald A. Murday
J. Richard Childers	David T. Burrowes
Terry M. Cosgrove	Brian A. Frankl
John M. Duczynski	Donald B. Leventhal
Bonnie G. Lederman	Michael J. Rosen
Daniel A. Engel	Cecilia M. Clarke
John K. Silk	Theodore J. May
Walter M. Piecewicz	R. Nathan Randall
Geoffrey L. Isaac	William P. Rector
Charles D. Thomas	Dirk E. Ehlers
John T. Evrard	Sean Patrick MacCarthy
David J. Novotny	Marie L. Nienhuis
Robert L. Suomala	Clinton J. Wesolik

Peter F. Lovato, III

OF COUNSEL

Robert G. Schloerb	Lawrence X. Pusateri
J. Robert Geiman	Robert S. Milnikel

Theodore Joseph Tsoumas

ASSOCIATES

Anthony L. Abboud	David W. Groundwater
Esther S. Barron	Donna Haddad
Elena T. Becker	Gary A. Hood
Kathleen A. Brosnan	Marc A. Horwitz
Rene Robertson Campe	Ellen Duffy Jenkins
Jennifer L. Carow	Georgia L. Joyce
Patrick K. Cary	Tracy K. Jurusik
Janice L. Cleary	David L. Koury
Dennis B. Condon	Daniel S. Lambert
Carrie E. Cope	Francis Losurdo
Elizabeth Gwynn Dobie	Kent Maynard, Jr.
Calita L. Elston	Edmund S. McAlister
Lee Ann S. Galowich	Arthur J. McColgan, II
Jeannine M. Glavas	Ross I. Molho

(See Next Column)

ASSOCIATES (Continued)

William M. Monat	David F. Schmidt
Andrew J. Palmer	Julie Stern
S. Ana Perich	Douglas J. Varga
Lowndes C. Quinlan	Adam R. Walker
Raana C. Rafiullah	Michael P. Warnick

Suzane L. Woollums

RESIDENT PARTNERS AT SPRINGFIELD, ILLINOIS OFFICE

Zack Stamp	Kirk H. Petersen

RESIDENT PARTNER AT LOS ANGELES, CALIFORNIA OFFICE

Vivian Rigdon Bloomberg

RESIDENT PARTNERS AT MORRISTOWN, NEW JERSEY OFFICE

Valerie K. Bollheimer	Kenneth D. Merin

RESIDENT PARTNERS AT NEW YORK, N.Y. OFFICE

James A. Skarzynski	John S. Diaconis
Kevin T. Salter	Alexis J. Rogoski
John V. Coulter, Jr.	T. David Ackerman

RESIDENT OF COUNSEL AT AUSTIN, TEXAS OFFICE

James L. Nelson

RESIDENT ASSOCIATES AT LOS ANGELES, CALIFORNIA OFFICE

Gina M. Brown	David T. Gluck

Brett P. Wakino

RESIDENT ASSOCIATES AT SPRINGFIELD, ILLINOIS

Kevin J. McFadden

RESIDENT ASSOCIATES AT NEW YORK, N.Y. OFFICE

Charles M. Dickson Jr.	John J. Richardson
Ivan J. Dolowich	David I. Schonbrun
John J. McGreevy	Evan Shapiro
John C. Minett	Christopher F. Smith

Karen L. Stuttman

For full biographical listings, see the Martindale-Hubbell Law Directory

ROOKS, PITTS AND POUST (AV)

10 South Wacker Drive, Suite 2300, 60606
Telephone: 312-876-1700
Fax: 312-876-1155
Wheaton, Illinois Office: 201 Naperville Road.
Telephone: 708-690-8500.
Facsimile: 708-690-8553.
Joliet, Illinois Office: 111 North Ottawa Street.
Telephone: 815-727-4511.
Facsimile: 815-727-1586.
Winnetka, Illinois Office: 560 Green Bay Road.
Telephone: 847-441-5615.
Fax: 847-441-9367.

MEMBERS OF FIRM

Jay A. Lipe	Geoffrey A. Bryce
Ray F. Drexler	Lee T. Hettinger
Alan S. Ganz	Richard J. Kavanagh
Jerome N. Groark	Marc A. Primack
Arthur I. Gould	Marc D. Ginsberg
Robert J. Baron	Michael Gahan
Stephen E. Sward	Terrence M. Burns
David R. Abell	Mark W. Weisbard
John J. Blasi	Robert R. Gorbold
James H. Ihrke	George J. Vosicky
Thomas B. Cassidy	David J. Bressler
Wayne F. Plaza	Michael F. Sexton
Terrence E. Kiwala	Mark S. Anderson
George N. Gilkerson, Jr.	Thomas R. Hill
Terrence J. Madden	Patricia Cari Nowak
John J. Mangan	Janet A. Stiven
Frank C. Rowland	Mitchell E. Jones
Fred R. McMorris	Chris E. Limperis
James D. Grumley	Richard W. Schumacher
Ian M. Sherman	Charles A. Le Moine
Jeffrey M. Dalebroux	J. Barrett Long
Michael C. Borders	Karen Wilson Howard

Joan D. Lindauer

Russell A. Adkins	Gerald T. Karr
Harry N. Arger	Bryan Kopman
Diane P. Bartus	John Lipinsky
Richard Capra	Nick Marsico
Edward P. Dismukes	James W. McConkey
Glennon P. Dolan	Paul A. Michalik
Elizabeth E. Durbin	David L. Miller
Kerry L. Garvis	Michelle Mrozek
Gwen M. Geraghty	Daniel M. Noland
Pamela Davis Gorcowski	Thomas R. Osterberger
Christopher G. Guldberg	James L. Reed, Jr.
Maureen J. Hanlon	Frederick F. Richards, III
Scott M. Hardek	Kristan M. Ropers
Ellen D. Holzman	Nicole A. Roth
Carolyn J. Jones	Michael R. Stiff

COUNSEL

John G. Poust	Eugene H. Ruark

(See Next Column)

ROOKS, PITTS AND POUST—*Continued*

OF COUNSEL

Henry L. Pitts	D. Glenn Ofsthun
William W. Fullagar	Daniel P. Socha
Timothy J. Groark	John P. Hanna
Stuart C. Kroesch (Resident Of	H. Sam Onoda
Counsel, Joliet, Illinois Office)	James L. Donnelly

For full biographical listings, see the Martindale-Hubbell Law Directory

ROSENTHAL AND SCHANFIELD, PROFESSIONAL CORPORATION (AV)

46th Floor, 55 East Monroe Street, 60603
Telephone: 312-236-5622
Telecopier: 312-236-7274

David M. Alin	Henry M. Morris
Joseph A. Baldi	Gerald B. Mullin
Scott E. Becker	Joseph R. Podlewski, Jr.
Francis A. Beninati	Donald A. Robinson
Elizabeth C. Berg	Lester Rosen
Martin K. Blonder	Robert O. Rosenman
Marvin Cohn	William P. Rosenthal
James M. Dash	Leonard Schanfield (1921-1990)
I. Walter Deitch	Barry E. Semer
Drew Eugene Farkas	Mark L. Shapiro
Jay Russell Goldberg	Suzanne M. Soltan
David A. Golin	Charles R. Staley
David E. Gordon	Blooma Stark
William H. Kelly, Jr.	Ronald K. Szopa
Stephen P. Kikoler	Michael Viner
Richard F. Lee	Sheri E. Warsh
Ira M. Levin	Mary Prus Wasik
Joel C. Levin	Stanley R. Weinberger
Mark S. Lieberman	David L. Weinstein
Howard L. Mocerf	Thomas M. White

Edward J. Wong, III

OF COUNSEL

Alex Elson	Richard E. Friedman

For full biographical listings, see the Martindale-Hubbell Law Directory

ROSS & HARDIES (AV)

A Partnership including Professional Corporations
Suite 2500, 150 North Michigan Avenue, 60601
Telephone: 312-558-1000
Cable Address: "Daidin"
TWX: 910-221-1154
Telecopier: 312-750-8600
New York, N.Y. Office: 65 East 55th Street, 10022.
Telephone: 212-421-5555.
Telecopier: 212-421-5682.
Washington, D.C. Office: 888 - 16th Street, N.W., 20006.
Telephone: 202-296-8600.
Telecopier: 202-296-8791.
Somerset, New Jersey Office: 580 Howard Avenue, 08873.
Telephone: 908-563-2700.
Telecopier: 908-563-2777.

MEMBERS OF FIRM

CHICAGO, ILLINOIS OFFICE

William P. O'Keefe (1929-1979)	Charles M. Chadd
Clarence H. Ross (1950-1981)	C. Frederick LeBaron, Jr.
Richard F. Babcock (1957-1993)	Donald C. Pasulka
Melvin A. Hardies (1950-1994)	Jonathan G. Bunge *
Keith I. Parsons (1965-1996)	Richard T. Greenberg
David N. McBride	Michael C. Cook
William J. Winger *	Steven R. Smith
David F. Sterling	David L. Hartsell
Robert J. Pristave *	James J. Casey
Duane A. Feurer	Larry R. Goldstein
Richard J. Rappaport	Leslie D. Locke
Robert E. Wangard	Susan Grob Lichtenfeld
Michael H. King *	Monica A. Carroll
James K. Toohey	Elizabeth West Speidel
William D. Serritella	Mark N. Woyar
Richard E. Lieberman	Bernard Roccanova
Robert W. Kleinman	Susan M. Mongillo
Keith Philip Schoeneberger	Daniel P. Hogan
Paul A. Lutter	Robert T. Zielinski
Lawrence R. Samuels	Jeffrey E. Rogers
James T. Harrington	T. Stephen Dyer
Barbara Baran	Jacquelyn F. Kidder
Carol Berlin Manzoni	Patrick E. Brady
James B. Riley, Jr.	Alison Cornell Blair Laing
Louis W. Levit *	Arnold E. Grant
Richard J. Mason *	Jon K. Stromsta
Robert M. Fishman	Kurt H. Feuer
Raymond T. Murphy	Peter J. Valeta
Scott Hodes	Raymond H. Groble III
Gary L. Starkman	Ira P. Goldberg
Timothy C. Klenk	David L. Rieser

(See Next Column)

MEMBERS OF FIRM
CHICAGO, ILLINOIS OFFICE (Continued)

Elizabeth L. Corey	Janice K. Hamblin
Sean M. Sullivan	Brian A. Sher
Anne M. Beckert	Andrew D. Crain
Keith A. Dorman	Gail Chaney Kalinich
Patricia K. Smoots	Kimberly Ann Warnke
Steven M. Taber	Robert W. Glantz
Jules I. Crystal	Scott Becker
Neal A. Crowley	Debra L. Duzinskas
Jeffrey A. Berman	Darryl R. Davidson

NEW YORK, NEW YORK OFFICE

Joseph S. Kaplan	Michael J. Di Mattia
John B. Pellegrini	John M. Wyser-Pratte
Helen Davis Chaitman	Marshall Beil
Yvette Harmon	Robert S. Blaustein
Kenneth Zuckerbrot	Philip L. Guarino
Kevin T. Collins	Shari L. Pine
J. Joseph Bainton	Seth Goodchild
Richard A. Wilsker	Simon D. Cices

Alexander H. Schwartz

WASHINGTON, D.C. OFFICE

Myles J. Ambrose	Charles W. Petty, Jr.
Raymond J. Kimball	James A. Stenger
John A. Howell	Robert M. Disch
John R. Fornaciari	Evelyn M. Suarez
Stephen R. Ross	Jeffrey S. Neeley

SOMERSET, NEW JERSEY OFFICE

Helen Davis Chaitman

OF COUNSEL

CHICAGO, ILLINOIS OFFICE

Joann Tansey Angarola	Bruce J. McWhirter
Karl Berolzheimer	Walker Winter

Maurice P. Wolk

OF COUNSEL

NEW YORK, NEW YORK OFFICE

Leonard Rovins

OF COUNSEL

SOMERSET, N.J. OFFICE

George B. Gelman

ASSOCIATES

Colleen Elizabeth Baime	Stephen B. Mead
Scott S. Becvar	Mary Margaret Moore
Mary Clare Bonaccorsi	Helmer J. Nelson
Jerome K. Bowman	Olufemi F. Nicol
Elizabeth M. Bradshaw	Alice G. Owings
John M. Callahan	Jacqueline Rosenberg Peltz
Scott P. Downing	Michael R. Phillips
Thomas D. Drescher	David A. Piech
Jeffrey S. Dunlap	Christian M. Poland
Kelly J. B. Elvin	Mari Yamamoto Regnier
Kara M. Friedman	Sharon P. Riley
Lisa Allen Golant	Beth A. Sansiper
David S. Guin	Edward W. Schwartz
Darren J. Hunter	Brian L. Shaw
Kimberly J. Kannensohn	Leonora L. Shaw
Kathryn M. Kemp	Joanne A. Smet
Evan Marc Kraus	George J. Spathis
Emily H. Liebers	Kari J. Sperstad
Susan Febles Lifvendahl	Joel H. Spitz
Laura A. Lindner	Anne T. Stinneford
Mary Therese Link	Philip N. Storm
Amy B. Manning	Thomas D. Titsworth, Jr.
Ginger G. Mayer	Charles W. Wesselhoft
John P. McCabe	Neil G. Wolf
Lisa Iskalis McCarthy	Jay A. Yalowitz

Paul C. Ziebert

NEW YORK, NEW YORK OFFICE

Jose Anibal Baez	John J. Lee
Stephenie Leigh Brown	John G. McCarthy
Laura D. Castner	Thomas F. McInerney, III
Russell A. Divak	Theresa K. Nick
Carol A. Dunning	Kathryn C. Spann
Virginia J. Harnisch	Michael Yuri Sukhman
Donald S. Krueger	Catherine M. Vaczy

WASHINGTON, D.C. OFFICE

Amy L. Brett	Peter A. Martin
Susan E. Cosentino	John J. Vecchione

SOMERSET, NEW JERSEY OFFICE

David Michael Fabian	Kate T. Gallagher

Cynthia A. Lock

*Professional Corporation

For full biographical listings, see the Martindale-Hubbell Law Directory

Chicago—Continued

ROTHSCHILD, BARRY & MYERS (AV)

A Partnership including Professional Corporations
Suite 3900, 55 West Monroe Street, 60603-5012
Telephone: 312-372-2345
FAX: 312-372-2350

MEMBERS OF FIRM

Edward I. Rothschild (P.C.)	Roger J. Guerin
Norman J. Barry (P.C.)	Michael J. Wall
William G. Myers (P.C.)	Daniel Cummings
Melvin I. Mishkin	Christopher G. Walsh, Jr.
John J. Coffey, III	Kenneth P. Taube
Joseph P. Della Maria, Jr.	Jonathan E. Rothschild

Alan S. Madans

ASSOCIATES

Mary T. Meegan	Kevin J. Moore
John G. Dalton	Robin J. Korman-Powers

For full biographical listings, see the Martindale-Hubbell Law Directory

RUDNICK & WOLFE (AV)

A Partnership including Professional Corporations
203 North La Salle Street, Suite 1800, 60601-1293
Telephone: 312-368-4000
Telecopier: 312-236-7516
Telex: 754347
Tampa, Florida Office: 101 East Kennedy Boulevard, Suite 2000.
Telephone: 813-229-2111.
Telecopier: 813-229-1447.
Washington, D.C. Office: Rudnick, Wolfe, Epstien & Zeidman: 1201 New York Avenue, N.W., Penthouse, 20005-3919.
Telephone: 202-712-7200.
Telecopier: 202-712-7222.
Baltimore, Maryland Office: 111 South Calvert Street, Suite 2700, 21202.
Telephone: 410-385-0400.
Telecopier: 410-385-5201.

PARTNERS

Stanley J. Adelman	Sandra Y. Kellman
Ross J. Altman	Mary K. Krigbaum
James L. Beard	Michael P. Kuppersmith
Mark A. Berkoff	Stephen A. Landsman
Mark I. Bogart	Elaine Rappaport Lev
Thomas J. Boodell, Jr.	Peter A. Levy
Michael G. Brennan	Steven L. Loren
Hal M. Brown	Bruce D. Loring
Peter C. B. Bynoe	Gerald B. Lurie
William J. Campbell, Jr.	David G. Lynch
John Chen	John R. Mannix, Jr.
Fredric A. Cohen	Jerome Marks
Louis S. Cohen	Philip V. Martino
Janet B. Cory	James T. Mayer
Merle Teitelbaum Cowin	Adrianne C. Mazura
John T. J. Cusack	Carol A. McErlean
Gregory R. A. Dahlgren	Charles R. McKirdy
Byron S. Delman	Keith W. Medansky
Charles L. Edwards	David E. Mendelsohn
Michael H. Elam	Ralph R. Mickelson
Mark I. Feldman	Lee I. Miller
Lawrence J. Fey	Nicholas R. Minear
Sue Ann Fishbein	David N. Missner
Michael B. Fischer	Portia Owen Morrison
Paul E. Fisher	John R. Mussman
Bruce A. Fox	Mark P. Naughton, Jr.
Harold W. Francke	Theodore J. Novak (P.C.)
Elizabeth H. Friedgut	Sandra L. Oberkfell
J. Kevin Garvey	Jeffrey N. Owen
Deborah L. Gersh	George T. Plumb
Mark A. Gershon	Harold B. Pomerantz
Thomas F. Geselbracht	Mark A. Rabinowitz
Allen J. Ginsburg (P.C.)	J. Timothy Ramsey
David Glickstein	William L. Rawson
Edward S. Goldman	David L. Reifman
Michael R. Goldman	Lawrence A. Robins (P.C.)
Robert H. Goldman	Peter B. Ross
Stephen M. Gordon	Harry L. Rudnick (1936-1973)
Shepard Gould	Lewis G. Rudnick
Ross Green	Paul D. Rudnick
George L. Grumley	Renee M. Schoenberg
Errol R. Halperin	Stephen W. Schwab
John W. Harbst	Theodore A. Shapero
Kenneth Hartmann	Benjamin P. Shapiro
Stuart Hershman	Joseph W. Sheyka
John H. Heuberger	Donald A. Shindler
Paul Homer (P.C.)	David B. Sickle
Richard S. Homer	Seymour F. Simon
Gregory W. Hummel	Gary Mark Sircus
Richard S. Huszagh	Michael L. Sklar
Leroy G. Inskeep	Perry J. Snyderman
Howard E. Kane	Morton M. Steinberg
David J. Kayner	Sandra J. Wall

(See Next Column)

Robert I. Wertheimer	Theodore I. Yi
Dennis E. Wieczorek	Mark D. Yura
Dorian R. Williams	Miles J. Zaremski

William A. Zolla

ASSOCIATES

Jeffrey S. Arnold	Scott Lefelar
Bradley P. Balson	Christina King Loundy
Michael L. Ben-Isvy	Anna Kristin Marks
Adam Berkoff	Christina L. Martini
John D. Burke	Paul B. McCarthy
John G. Caruso	Sally J. McDonald
Rachel A. Contreni	Jill K. Miller
Mary Jane DeWeese	Alison M. Mitchell
Brian K. Doyle	Lisa Laney Moorehead
Mary Kay Gara Dreyfus	Michael J. Moran
Janice L. Duban	Douglas T. Moring
Wayne H. Elowe	Bruce C. Nelson
Mary A. Francis	Kristi Nelson
Elise A. Gibson	Kathleen L. Nooney
Deborah Gordon	David W. Norton
Elizabeth A. Graber	Michael G. Redstone
David V. Hall	Bradley V. Ritter
Peter G. Hallam	James D. Roberts
Karen K. Harris	Suzanne Robinson
Gary L. Hermanson	Elizabeth Rowntree
Robert G. Hertel, Jr.	William A. Rudnick
Holly Hirst	Lisa I. Sandlow
Matt Husami	M. Gretchen Silver
Scott E. Jordan	Heather Labadot Smedstad
Laura A. Josephson	Carol A. Sobczak
Richard Klawiter	Samuel B. Stempel
Jill Clark Laarman	Robert J. Weiss

Mark R. Williams

STAFF ATTORNEY

Jonathan A. Cohen

OF COUNSEL

Elizabeth H. Belkin	Laura Gerard Hassan
Randall J. Gingiss	John Zhengdong Huang
Reynaldo Preston Glover	Julius Y. Yacker

Merwin S. Rosenberg

For full biographical listings, see the Martindale-Hubbell Law Directory

SACHNOFF & WEAVER, LTD. (AV)

30 South Wacker Drive, Suite 2900, 60606
Telephone: 312-207-1000
Telecopier: 312-207-6400
Email: swltd@aol.com

Frank D. Ballantine	William A. O'Connor
Jack L. Block	Arnold A. Pagniucci
Craig T. Boggs	Jonathan S. Quinn
Barry S. Cain	Michael D. Richman
Gary S. Caplan	Brian D. Roche
Paul D. Carman	Lance R. Rodgers
Stuart J. Chanen	James A. Rolfes
Charles E. Dobrusin	Barry S. Rosen
Stewart Dolin	Carolyn Hope Rosenberg
William E. Doran	Harry B. Rosenberg
Candace J. Fabri	Ellis B. Rosenzweig
Joel S. Feldman	Lowell E. Sachnoff
Michael K. Fridkin	Joel R. Schaider
Roselyn L. Friedman	Howard Schickler
Matthew T. Gensburg	Bradley S. Schmarak
Jeffrey T. Gilbert	Charles P. Schulman
Neil Greenbaum	Jeffrey A. Schumacher
David A. Grossberg	Marshall Seeder
Misty S. Gruber	Clifford J. Shapiro
Seth M. Hemming	Jerold N. Siegan
Austin L. Hirsch	Duane F. Sigelko
Cynthia Jared	Richard G. Smolev
Marc Kieselstein	Sheldon L. Solow
Jeffrey L. London	Abraham J. Stern
Michael A. LoVallo	J. Samuel Tenenbaum
John D. Malarkey	Edward V. Walsh, III
Frances Meehan	William N. Weaver, Jr.
Joel M. Neuman	Sarah R. Wolff
Douglas R. Newkirk	Edward J. Wong, Jr. (On Leave)

Eugene F. Zelek, Jr.

J. Todd Arkebauer	Michael M. Kaplan
Christine M. Bodewes	Lisa J. Krasberg
Felice M. Bressler	Lisa M. Madigan
Sharon M. Buccino	Kerry A. Miller
Mary N. Cameli	John W. Moynihan
Valerie N. Childers	Robert H. Nathan
Charles A. Demirjian	Bina Sanghavi
Arthur D. Gunther	Lyn M. Schollett
Andrew Hartman	Susan D. Snyder
Darryl P. Jacobs	Ann M. Spillane
Jonathan T. Kamin	Tracy L. Treger

(See Next Column)

SACHNOFF & WEAVER LTD.—*Continued*

OF COUNSEL

Jules G. Cogan	Lewis Manilow
Nathan H Dardick	Leonard Jay Schrager
Ilene Dobrow Davidson	Ernest D. Simon
Judith Rea Heck	Joseph Stein
Richard C. Jones	Marvin A. Tenenbaum

For full biographical listings, see the Martindale-Hubbell Law Directory

SCHIFF HARDIN & WAITE (AV)

A Partnership including Professional Corporations
Founded 1864
7200 Sears Tower, 60606
Telephone: 312-876-1000; *Facsimile:* 312-258-5600.
Cable Address: Dallschiff. TWX: 910-221-2463.
Wash., D.C., New York, N.Y., Peoria, Ill. & Merrillville, IN.
Washington, D.C. Office: 1101 Connecticut Avenue, N.W.
Telephone: 202-778-6400.
Facsimile: 202-778-6460.
New York, New York Office: 150 East 52nd Street, Suite 2900.
Telephone: 212-753-5000.
Facsimile: 212-753-5044.
Peoria, Illinois Office: 300 Hamilton Boulevard, Suite 100.
Telephone: 309-673-2800.
Facsimile: 309-673-2801.
Merrillville, Indiana Office: 8585 Broadway, Suite 842.
Telephone: 219-738-3820.
Facsimile: 219-738-3826.

MEMBERS OF FIRM

Max Pam (1904-1925)	C. Richard Johnson
Harry B. Hurd (1904-1943)	Janet M. Johnson
Alexander F. Reichmann (1905-1948)	James M. Kane
	Andrew A. Kling
Andrew J. Dallstream (1927-1962)	Brian D. Kluever
	Aphrodite Kokolis
Sydney K. Schiff (1924-1973)	Aaron J. Kramer
Oscar D. Stern (1911-1973)	Joseph J. Krasovec, III
Louis S. Hardin (1925-1979)	Donald J. Kreger
Querin P. Dorschel (1939-1979)	Ruth E. Krugly
Lester G. Britton (1924-1983)	Ty D. Laurie
Thomas W. Abendroth	Eric L. Lohrenz
John F. Adams	Shirley M. Lukitsch
Barry S. Alberts	Joseph R. Lundy
Thomas L. Aldrich	Thomas P. Luning
David F. Allen (P.C.)	Paul M. Lurie
Bennett P. Applegate	Owen E. MacBride
Bruce Jay Baker	Neal A. Mancoff
Katharine L. Bensen	Wayne A. McCoy
Jill B. Berkeley	James R. McDaniel
Scott Bieber	W. Donald McSweeney (P.C.)
Lawrence Block (P.C.)	Michael S. Melbinger
Michael L. Brody	Michael L. Meyer
Harmon A. Brown	Robert J. Minkus
James E. Brown	Paula J. Morency
Mark W. Burns	Gary L. Mowder (P.C.)
Kevin J. Byrne	William H. Navin
Robert D. Campbell	Paul B. O'Flaherty (P.C.)
Joseph A. Cancila, Jr.	Joseph J. O'Hara, Jr.
James A. Clark	Roger Pascal
Carter C. Culver	Charles H.R. Peters
Heidi Dalenberg	Guenther M. Philipp (P.C.)
Stephanie H. Denby	Scott E. Pickens
Paul E. Dengel	Robert R. Pluth, Jr.
W. Brinkley Dickerson, Jr.	Carol R. Prygrosky
Erica L. Dolgin	Thomas B. Quinn
Patricia Dondanville	Robert John Regan
Stephen J. Dragich	Paul K. Rhoads
Joseph J. Duffy	Mitchell S. Rieger
Marci A. Eisenstein	Robert H. Riley
Catherine Masters Epstein	Burton R. Rissman (P.C.)
Kevin D. Evans	Kenneth M. Roberts
Peter V. Fazio, Jr.	Gabriel M. Rodriguez
J. Mark Fisher	Keith Shay (P.C.)
Charles D. Fox, IV	Mark D. Snider
Steven D. Friedland	Frederick J. Sperling
Mark C. Friedlander	Linda K. Stevens
Eugene J. Geekie, Jr.	Thomas Thorne-Thomsen
Patricia N. Gillman	Patricia J. Thompson
Stuart L. Goodman	Scott C. Tomassi
Stuart I. Graff	Darren M. R. Van Puymbrouck
Walter C. Greenough	James M. Van Vliet, Jr.
William M. Hannay	John J. Voortman (P.C.)
Frederick L. Hartmann, Jr.	Lisa A. Weiland
Barbara E. Hermansen	Bruce P. Weisenthal
Carrie Jankauer Hightman	Warren P. Wenzloff
David R. Hodgman	Linda Jeffries Wight
Allan Horwich	Robert B. Wilcox, Jr.
Richard J. Hoskins	Ronald Wilder
Lawrence H. Jacobson	Jay Williams

(See Next Column)

Helen T. Wilson	Mark C. Zaander
James B. Wilson (P.C.)	Sheldon A. Zabel
Christopher J. Zinski	

OF COUNSEL

Dean C. Cameron	Lael F. Johnson
Milton H. Cohen	Robert A. Monk
John T. Hayes	Norman Waite
John J. Waldron	

ASSOCIATES

Julia E. Allen	Mark J. Kosminskas
Janet Angstadt	Rosemary Krimbel
Lawrence C. Bachman	John F. Lapham
Lauralyn G. Bengel	Monica B. Lasky
David C. Blickenstaff	Lisa C. Leib
Chris L. Bollinger	J. Timothy Leslie
Stephen J. Bonebrake	Neil Lloyd
Daniel S. Brennan	Michael D. Lurie
Derrick L. Brent	Stephen Y. Ma
Lisa A. Brown	John C. Martin
David P. Buckley, Jr.	William E. Meyer, Jr.
Jeffrey J. Bushofsky	Jane Ellen Montgomery
Michael N. Delgass	Michael K. Moyers
Matthew J. Fischer	Thomas J. Pauloski
James P. Gaughan	Andrew C. Porter
W. Robert Gold	Lori Ann Prokes
Paul Edwin Greenwalt, III	Larry Rivkin
Alana L. Helverson	Lauren G. Robinson
Sondra A. Hemeryck	Lynn E. Rzonca
Andrea L. Horne	Jennifer L. Sachs
Ilan Huberman	Heather Chase Sawyer
Lesa Marie Ingraham	Christopher B. Schneider
David Jacobs	Daniel J. Schwartz
Jason W. Joseph	Adam C. Smedstad
Myriam Benhamou Kaplan	Debra L. Stetter
Michael L. Kayman	Michael F. Tomasek
James G. Keane	Victoria Karen Van Meter
Paula M. Ketcham	Mary A.M. Walters
Debra Ann Kleban	Glenn Weinstein
Kevin L. Kolton	Daniel E. White
Lisa Winger	

RESIDENT PARTNERS
WASHINGTON, D.C. OFFICE

Edward J. Finn	Andrew M. Klein
Barbara K. Heffernan	Gearold L. Knowles
Drexel D. Journey	Shaheda Sultan

RESIDENT OF COUNSEL

John W. Glendening, Jr.	Edwin S. Rockefeller
Catherine A. Jacobson	John S. Schmid

RESIDENT ASSOCIATES

Debra Ann Palmer	M. Thompson Rattray

RESIDENT PARTNERS
NEW YORK, NEW YORK OFFICE

Roy M. Adams	John C. Novogrod
Glenn Kurlander	Paul A. Scrudato

RESIDENT ASSOCIATE

Ivan Taback

RESIDENT PARTNERS
PEORIA, ILLINOIS OFFICE

Theodore L. Eissfeldt	David G. Kabbes

RESIDENT ASSOCIATE

Jason A. Zellers

RESIDENT PARTNER
MERRILLVILLE, INDIANA OFFICE

Peter L. Hatton

For full biographical listings, see the Martindale-Hubbell Law Directory

SCHWARTZBERG, BARNETT & COHEN (AV)

55 West Monroe Street, 2400 Xerox Centre, 60603-5040
Telephone: 312-726-3555
Fax: 312-726-6299
Cable Address: "Justice"
Email: sb&c@twty.chi.il.us

MEMBERS OF FIRM

Ralph M. Schwartzberg (1939-1975)	Mark T. Barnett (1939-1970)
	Hugh J. Schwartzberg
Benjamin H. Cohen	

OF COUNSEL

Eugene P. Thomas Jr.

For full biographical listings, see the Martindale-Hubbell Law Directory

Chicago—Continued

SEYFARTH, SHAW, FAIRWEATHER & GERALDSON (AV)

55 E. Monroe Street, Suite 4200, 60603-5803
Telephone: 312-346-8000
Facsimile: 312-269-8869
Cable Address: "Interlex"
International Telex: 25222
Email: mailbox@seyfarth.com *URL:* http://www.seyfarth.com
Washington, D.C. Office: 815 Connecticut Avenue, N.W.
Telephone: 202-463-2400.
Facsimile: 202-828-5393.
Los Angeles, California Office: 2029 Century Park East.
Telephone: 310-277-7200.
Facsimile: 310-201-5219.
New York, N.Y. Office: 900 Third Avenue, 16th Floor.
Telephone: 212-715-9000.
Facsimile: 212-752-3116.
San Francisco, California Office: Suite 2900, 101 California Street.
Telephone: 415-397-2823.
Facsimile: 415-397-8549.
Sacramento, California Office: 400 Capitol Mall, Suite 2350.
Telephone: 916-558-4828.
Facsimile: 916-558-4839.
Houston, Texas Office: 700 Louisiana Street, Suite 3900.
Telephone: 713-225-2300.
Facsimile: 713-225-2340.
Atlanta, Georgia Office: One Atlantic Center, 1201 West Peachtree Street, Suite 3260.
Brussels, Belgium Office: Avenue Louise 500, Box 8.
Telephone: (32) (2) 647. 60. 25.
Fax: (32) (2) 640. 70. 71.
Affiliated Law Firm:
Matray, Matray et Hallet, 34/24, Boulevard Frère-Orban, 4000, Liege, Belgium. *Telephone:* (32) (41) 52 70 68.
Telex: macoha 42330.
Telecopier: (32) (41) 52 08 57.

MEMBERS OF FIRM

John H. Anderson	Walter P. Loomis (Retired)
James Baird	Barbara K. Lundergan
Edward W. Bergmann	Richard M. Lyon (Retired)
Rody P. Biggert	Robert E. Maciorowski
Daniel M. Blouin	Marcia Andersen Mahoney
Michael E. Blount	Condon A. McGlothlen
Jerome F. Buch	Ellen E. McLaughlin
James A. Burstein	Robert J. Mignin
Philip V. Carter (Retired)	Philip A. Miscimarra
Mark A. Casciari	John T. Murray
Rose Marie J. Chidichimo	Camille A. Olson
Brent I. Clark	Jeryl Olson
R. Theodore Clark, Jr.	John J. O'Malley
John L. Collins	James P. Osick
Theodore E. Cornell III	Richard D. Ostrow
Douglas A. Darch	Robert J. Paley
Thomas G. Dent	Gus A. Paloian
Lawrence C. DiNardo	Thomas H. Peckham
Paul F. Donahue	Andrew H. Perellis
William J. Fairbanks	Thomas J. Piskorski
Owen Fairweather (1913-1987)	J. Stephen Poor
Brenda Hofman Feis	Gloria M. Portela
Fredric H. Fischer	John W. Powers
Deborah A. Folloni (Not admitted in IL; Resident)	Keith A. Reed
	Burton X. Rosenberg
Joan E. Gale	Jeffrey K. Ross
Raymond I. Geraldson (Retired)	David J. Rowland
Timothy F. Haley	Michael J. Rybicki
Valerie J. Hoffman	Jeremy P. Sackmann
William N. Howard	David A. Saunders
Charles C. Jackson	John S. Schauer
Eugene Jacobs	Ray J. Schoonhoven (Retired)
Jeffrey Jahns	James A. Schraidt
Carl E. Johnson	William P. Schurgin
Robert H. Joyce (Retired)	Kathleen R. Schwappach
Frederick M. Kaplan	Henry E. Seyfarth (1908-1991)
Gary S. Kaplan	Lee C. Shaw (Retired)
Joel H. Kaplan	Jeremy P. Sherman
Edward J. Karlin	Gerald D. Skoning
Jeffrey C. Kauffman	Robert J. Smith, Jr.
Raymond J. Kelly, Jr.	David S. Stone
Alvin L. Kruse	Elizabeth Pfeiler Strand
Andrew R. Laidlaw	Robert B. Ulrich
Richard B. Lapp	Alan L. Unikel
Dixie L. Laswell	Carson P. Veach
Christopher A. Lause	Alexander S. Vesselinovitch
Bart A. Lazar	Daniel J. Voelker
Howard L. Levine	Stanley A. Walton, III
Michael R. Levinson	Michael A. Warner
Mark A. Lies, II	Robert F. Weber
Ronald L. Lipinski	David M. Weiner
Bradford L. Livingston	John T. Weise (Retired)
Robert C. Long	Harold C. Wheeler

(See Next Column)

MEMBERS OF FIRM (Continued)

Debra A. Winiarski	Joseph E. Wyse (Retired)
Peter C. Woodford	Richard Demarest Yant
Sandra P. Zemm	

OF COUNSEL

Eric E. Boyd	Thomas D. Lupo
Frank L. Butler	Edward B. Miller
Philip L. Comella	Eugene L. Resnick
Fay Hartog	James C. Shanley
David B. Love	Kimberly A. Sipes-Early
Mark H. Sokolsky	

ASSOCIATES

Sari M. Alamuddin	Patricia Jeanne Hill
Andrew M. Altschul	Robert L. Jackson III
David S. Baffa	James D. Jorgensen
Douglas J. Bank	Tilden Katz
Patrice P. Barnard	Robert A. Kearney
Michelle T. Barrett	Deborah A. Kop
Douglas G. Beck	Ronald J. Kramer
Janice L. Block	Kenneth R. Landis, Jr.
Paul R. Brockmeyer	Jill Leka
Anthony B. Byergo	Patricia L. Mehler
Yvette Caizzi	Kristin Edell Michaels
Scott A. Carlson	Peter C. Miller
Kelli L. Christenson	Cynthia C. Mooney
William A. Cirignani	Kathleen Dillon Narko
Jeffrey E. Crane	Christopher E. Paetsch
James L. Curtis	Kathleen Paravola
Alan S. Dalinka	Gerald L. Pauling, II
Pamela A. Davidson	Jonathan A. Pearl
Paul S. Drizner	Stephanie L. Perl
William F. Dugan	Allegra R. Rich
Marcy S. Edwards	Joshua R. Rich
Drew M. Emmel	Suzanne E. Ritzler
William J. Factor	Valeria C. St. Vicina
Noah Finkel	Edward J. Santiago
Robert P. Flanagan	Marya Savich
Ana M. Flynn	Kenneth D. Schwartz
Beth R. French	Anna M. Scruggs
Susan F. Gallagher	Robert Sell
Eric W. Gallender	Dawn E. Sellstrom
Laura Roberts Garger	Bryan W. Sill
Jay A. Gitles	Susannah A. Smetana
Jody A. Gleason	Frederick T. Smith
Katharine E. Goldberg	Theodore C. Stamatakos
Hallie Goldman	Staci A. Stobart
Eric J. Gorman	Ethan E. Trull
Steven Louis Hamann	Joseph S. Turner
Amy Hartman	Daniel J. Ugaste
Janet C. Hershman	Alicia E. Wiltz
James M. Wyman	

For full biographical listings, see the Martindale-Hubbell Law Directory

SIDLEY & AUSTIN (AV)

A Partnership including Professional Corporations
One First National Plaza, 60603
Telephone: 312-853-7000
Telecopier: 312-853-7036
Los Angeles, California Office: 555 W. Fifth Street, 40th Flr., 90013-1010.
Telephone: 213-896-6000.
Telecopier: 213-896-6600.
New York, New York Office: 875 Third Avenue. 10022.
Telephone: 212-906-2000.
Telecopier: 212-906-2021.
Washington, D.C. Office: 1722 Eye Street, N.W., 20006.
Telephone: 202-736-8000.
Telecopier: 202-736-8711.
London, England Office: Royal Exchange, EC3V 3LE.
Telephone: 011-44-171-360-3600.
Telecopier: 011-44-171-626-9737.
Tokyo, Japan Office: Taisho Seimei Hibiya Building, 7th Floor, 9-1, Yurakucho, 1 Chome, Chiyoda-Ku, 100.
Telephone: 011-81-3-3218-5900.
Facsimile: 011-81-3-3218-5922.
Singapore Office: 36 Robinson Road, #18-01 City House, Singapore 0106.
Telephone: 011-65-224-5000.
Telecopier: 011-65-224-0530.

MEMBERS OF FIRM
CHICAGO, ILLINOIS OFFICE

Hugh A. Abrams	Lory A. Barsdate
Anthony J. Aiello	Susan T. Bart
Thomas W. Albrecht	Sara Elizabeth Bartlett
Geraldine M. Alexis	Frank V. Battle, Jr.
Julie O'Donnell Allen	William H. Baumgartner, Jr.
Gerald A. Ambrose	Larry D. Berning
Gerald L. Angst	H. Bruce Bernstein
Virginia L. Aronson	Stephan V. Beyer
Frederic J. Artwick	Alan P. Bielawski
Richard W. Astle	Jack R. Bierig
Larry A. Barden	Frank L. Bixby *
J. Robert Barr	Kevin F. Blatchford

(See Next Column)

SIDLEY & AUSTIN—*Continued*

MEMBERS OF FIRM
CHICAGO, ILLINOIS OFFICE (Continued)

Mark B. Blocker	Prentice H. Marshall, Jr.
John R. Box	R. Eden Martin
David J. Boyd	Henry L. Mason III
Thomas P. Brown	Elizabeth K. McCloy
Willis R. Buck, Jr.	John M. McDonough
James N. Cahan	John P. McGarrity
Stephen C. Carlson	Robert D. McLean
Walter C. Carlson	Thomas M. McMahon
David W. Carpenter	Michael I. Miller
Patrick S. Casey	Paul D. Monson
Thomas K. Cauley, Jr.	Scott J. Moore
Richard A. Cederoth	Thomas H. Morsch *
Linton J. Childs	Jodie L. Nedeau
James E. Clark	Joseph H. Nesler
Michael A. Clark	Mary C. Niehaus
Richard G. Clemens	William J. Nissen
Thomas A. Cole	Lawrence J. Nyhan
James F. Conlan	Richard J. O'Brien, Jr.
William F. Conlon	John M. O'Hare
Philip J. Crihfield	Richard F. O'Malley, Jr.
Michael W. Davis	Bridget R. O'Neill
William S. DeCarlo	Robert M. Olian
James C. Dechene	Dennis V. Osimitz
Wilbur C. Delp, Jr. *	Jules M. Perlberg *
Beth J. Dickstein	David T. Pritikin
J. Douglas Donenfeld	Imad I. Qasim
Charles W. Douglas	Richard D. Raskin
Maja Campbell Eaton	Marc E. Raven
Joseph S. Ehrman *	Anne E. Rea
Nathan P. Eimer	Sarah J. Read
David J. Engel	Thomas D. Rein
Robert A. Ferencz	Albert Ritchie
Bradford L. Ferguson	Kathleen L. Roach
William O. Fifield	Thomas A. Roberts
D. Cameron Findlay	Martin F. Robinson
Stephen P. Fitzell	Jeffrey S. Rothstein
Mary Patricia Flood	Priscilla E. Ryan
Robert P. Freeman	Thomas F. Ryan
Todd D. Freer	John J. Sabl
Gregory H. Furda	David R. Sawyier
John M. George, Jr.	David M. Schiffman
Brian J. Gold	Michael Schlesinger
Michael L. Gold	J. Andrew Schlickman
William C. Golden	Eugene A. Schoon
Andrew L. Goldstein	Charles E. Schrank
Sara J. Gourley	Andrew H. Shaw
David F. Graham	Stewart R. Shepherd
Jon M. Gregg	Michael S. Sigal
Jo Lynn Haley	John P. Simon
Pamela R. Hanebutt	Mary Jacobs Skinner
James A. Hardgrove	Lee M. Smolen
Holly A. Harrison	Sharp Sorensen
Joseph H. Harrison, Jr.	David M. Stahl
Janet E. Henderson	Debra J. Stanek
James W. Hitzeman	Jeffrey C. Steen
Kevin J. Hochberg	Philip P. Steptoe III
Michael G. Hron	Gary B. Stern
Lawrence H. Hunt, Jr.	David R. Stewart
DeVerille A. Huston	James R. Stinehart
Rick L. Jett	James R. Stinson
David B. Johnson	Susan A. Stone
Linzey D. Jones, Jr.	Sheila A. Sundvall
Richard B. Kapnick	Steven Sutherland
Timothy E. Kapshandy	Thomas E. Swaney
Jim L. Kaput	Michael J. Sweeney
Gerard D. Kelly	Dale E. Thomas
Gina B. Kennedy	Stephen P. Thomas
William D. Kerr	Jeffrey R. Tone
Sharon L. King	John W. Treece
Michael J. Kinn	Constantine L. Trela, Jr.
Lawrence I. Kipperman	Sherry S. Treston
Andrew G. Klevorn	Howard J. Trienens *
Shalom L. Kohn	Frank B. Vanker
Kiplund R. Kolkmeier	R. Todd Vieregg *
Jeffrey G. Kraft	Deirdre M. von Moltke
Bryan Krakauer	Roger A. Vree
Laurence D. Lasky	James F. Warchall
Laura L. Leonard	Melville W. Washburn
John G. Levi	Robert R. Watson
William F. Lloyd	Lyman W. Welch
James R. Looman	James S. Whitehead
Frederick C. Lowinger	Douglas H. Williams
Robert J. Maganuco	Latham Williams
Robert A. Malstrom	Clyde F. Willian
James L. Marovitz	Robert R. Wootton

Jay H. Zimbler

(See Next Column)

LOS ANGELES, CALIFORNIA OFFICE

Amy L. Applebaum	Richard W. Havel
Philip M. Battaglia	Marc I. Hayutin
David W. Burhenn	Michael C. Kelley
Gary J. Cohen	Moshe J. Kupietzky
Ronald C. Cohen	Perry L. Landsberg
Stephen G. Contopulos	Kenneth H. Levin
M. Scott Cooper	George M. Means
George Deukmejian	Theodore N. Miller
Lori Huff Dillman	Sally Schultz Neely
Edward D. Eddy III	Edwin L. Norris
Bradley H. Ellis	Peter I. Ostroff
Robert Fabrikant	Thomas E. Patterson
Howard D. Gest	Richard T. Peters
Richard J. Grad	Linda S. Peterson
Johnny D. Griggs	Judith M. Praitis
Larry G. Gutterridge	Howard J. Rubinroit *
Jennifer C. Hagle	Joel G. Samuels
Kent A. Halkett	Sherwin L. Samuels
Adam M. Handler	Ronie M. Schmelz
Thomas P. Hanrahan	D. William Wagner
James M. Harris	Michael D. Wright

WASHINGTON, D.C. OFFICE

Christopher L. Bell	Richard D. Klingler
Judith Hippler Bello	Jaye "Janet Marie" Letson
James F. Bendernagel Jr.	David M. Levy
Jeffrey S. Berlin	David J. Lewis
Frederic G. Berner, Jr.	Angus Macbeth
Richard D. Bernstein	Lorrie M. Marcil
Samuel B. Boxerman	David Michael Miles
David T. Buente, Jr.	Lawrence A. Miller
C. John Buresh	G. Paul Moates
Ann E. Bushmiller	Michael A. Nemeroff
Robert J. Conlan, Jr.	Francis J. O'Toole
Daniel M. Davidson	Carter G. Phillips
William S. Eckland	Vincent F. Prada
Eugene R. Elrod	P. David Richardson, II
Ronald S. Flagg	Melvin Rishe
Alan C. Geolot	Constance A. Sadler
Thomas C. Green	Gene C. Schaerr
Joseph R. Guerra	Mark D. Schneider
Samuel I. Gutter	Langley R. Shook
Mark E. Haddad	Howard J. Stanislawski
Kevin Hawley	David Teitelbaum
Stephen S. Hill	Joseph B. Tompkins, Jr.
Alan F. Holmer	Thomas P. Van Wazer
Mark D. Hopson	R. Clark Wadlow
James Alan Huizinga	Michael D. Warden
Terence M. Hynes	Marc D. Wassermann
George W. Jones, Jr.	R. Merinda Wilson
Peter D. Keisler	Elroy H. Wolff

Thomas H. Yancey

NEW YORK, NEW YORK OFFICE

James G. Archer	Thomas E. Pitts, Jr.
James D. Arden	Myles C. Pollin
Steven M. Bierman	Andrew C. Quale, Jr.
Shelley C. Chapman	David Alan Richards
Kelley A. Cornish	David L. Ridl
Maureen M. Crough	Paul K. Risko
Daniel S. Dokos	Irving L. Rotter
Scott M. Freeman	Elizabeth M. Sacksteder
Daniel A. Gerard	Robert H. Scarborough
Robert L. Golub	Michael J. Schmidtberger
Robert W. Hirth	L. Gilles Sion
John G. Hutchinson	Lee M. Stein
James D. Johnson	J. Ronald Trost
David M. Katz	Alan M. Unger
Daniel G. Kelly, Jr.	Alan S. Weil
Ralph E. Lerner	Paul R. Wysocki
Mir Mahboob Mahmood	Michael H. Yanowitch

LONDON, ENGLAND OFFICE

Gillian M. Andrews	Robert M. Plehn
Jane Borrows	Drew Scott
John Edwards	Sarah J. Smith
Graham A. Penn	Howard J. Waterman

TOKYO, JAPAN OFFICE

Shuichi Suzuki

COUNSEL
CHICAGO, ILLINOIS OFFICE

Mary A. Carragher	Lisa A. Hausten
James J. Carroll	John A. Heller
Robert E. Cronin	David R. Hill
Katherine J. D'Amaro	Loren E. Juhl
Robert A. Downing *	Edward P. Kenney
Carol A. Doyle	James W. Kissel
Arlene C. Erlebacher	Roger F. Lewis
Neil Flanagin *	Thomas W. Merrill
Robert R. Frei	Maurice J. Miller
Douglas F. Fuson	Newton N. Minow *
Alan Gabbay	Randal C. Picker
Donald J. Gralen *	William P. Richmond *

(See Next Column)

SIDLEY & AUSTIN, *Chicago—Continued*

COUNSEL
CHICAGO, ILLINOIS OFFICE (Continued)

William M. Sneed	R. Quincy White *
H. Blair White *	John C. Williams *

WASHINGTON, D.C. OFFICE

Natalie H. Diana	Gary P. Quigley
Myles E. Flint	Charlotte Uram
Stephen B. Lyons	John F. Wester
Mark E. Martin	Richard E. Young

NEW YORK, NEW YORK OFFICE

Richard A. Stanley	Barbara A. Vrancik
Richard B. Stewart	Henry R. Zheng

LOS ANGELES, CALIFORNIA OFFICE

James F. Donlan	Richard Schauer
Stuart L. Kadison	Yee-Yoong Yong

ASSOCIATES
CHICAGO, ILLINOIS OFFICE

Suresh T. Advani	Sarah R. Lyke
Frank Arado	Eric S. Mattson
Mary Beth Bailey	M. Kathleen McGowan
Jon A. Ballis	Patrick T. McNeil
Sandip K. Beri	Christopher J. Menting
Michael D. Bess	Carol C. Metcalfe
James B. Biery	Lisa S. Meyer
Jennifer L. Billingsley	Eugene L. Miller
Tracy Birmingham	Katie A. Moertl
Matthew C. Blickensderfer	Kathleen M. Mulligan
Jeanne B. Bowman	George L. Mullin
Stephanie N. Buettell	Joe C. Mullin
Michael V. Casaburi	I. Jack Nahmod
Jeffrey B. Charkow	Jason G. New
David R. Charles	Kristin A. Nichols
Paul L. Choi	Karen P. O'Neill
Theodore T. Chung	Fouad S. Onbargi
Mark D. Chutkow	(Not admitted in IL)
Lisa M. Cipriano	Darin V. Osmond
Denise M. Clark	Kathe A. Pate
Dennis M. Coghlan	Gordon P. Paulson
Thomas Conklin, Jr.	Leah Eisen Pazol
Alexandria J. Cravens	Kathleen Henry Pender
Eva S. Daniel	R. René Pengra
Susan M. Davies	Anastasia M. Polek
(Not admitted in IL)	John M. Rafkin
Tracy D. Daw	Sheri Rakowski
Jeffrey H. Dean	Rollin A. Ransom
William G. Dickett	Lisa J. Reategui
James W. Ducayet	Christopher A. Riley
Karen O. Dunlop	Ellen S. Robbins
Robert E. Easton	Richard E. Robbins
Steven J. Ellison	Beth J. Rosner
Brian J. Fahrney	Kim K. W. Rucker
Christopher R. Falk	Alfred N. Sacha
Thomas S. Finke	Scott E. Saef
Lynn D. Fleisher	Theodore R. Scarborough
Lisa D. Freeman	Karen M. Schellin
Gary D. Gerstman	Bryan A. Schneider
David C. Giardina	Joseph Schohl
Eric J. Glover	(Not admitted in IL)
Asheesh Goel	John T. Shapiro
David A. Goldberg	Hille von Rosenvinge Sheppard
Alan L. Goldman	Evelyn E. Shockley
Michael A. Gordon	Amanda Short
Christine H. Grahl	David J. Siegel
Mark I. Greenberg	Woon-Wah Siu
Craig A. Griffith	Joan E. Slavin
Karen L. Hale	Michael S. Smith
Susan V. Harris	Scott C. Solberg
John M. Heyde	James B. Speta
Cynthia A. Hickey	Stanley B. Stallworth
(Not admitted in IL)	Stephanie D. Stapleton
Arthur F. Hickok	Robert B. Stutz
Linda T. Ieleja	Eric H. Sussman
Stefanie Irwin	Paul A. Svoboda
Pran Jha	Byron F. Taylor
Matthew E. Johnson	James E. Taylor
Steven F. Katz	Nancy A. Temple
Mark L. Kaufmann	Thomas M. Thesing
Tamar B. Kelber	Sondra J. Thorson
Timothy J. Kenesey	Paul E. Veith
Colleen M. Kenney	William C. Way
Jordan A. Klein	Susan A. Weber
George C. Kokkines	David S. Weinberg
Brandon D. Lawniczak	James D. Weiss
Christine A. Leahy	Evan B. Westerfield
Sonja L. Lengnick	Marian E. Whiteman
Kirby H. Lewis	Marjorie Golis Wilde
Robert J. Lewis	Teresa Wilton
Mary H. Lindsay	Heidi Pfannkuch Windsor
Jon I. Loevy	David W. Wirt
Jonathan D. Lotsoff	Neil Wyland

(See Next Column)

ASSOCIATES
CHICAGO, ILLINOIS OFFICE (Continued)

Steven W. Young	Bruce M. Zessar
David J. Zampa	Sharon Sobczak Zuiker

STAFF ATTORNEYS
CHICAGO, ILLINOIS OFFICE

Kirsten Carlson	Mitchell Mick
Corlene Cathcart	Leanne Ebert Murphy
Nancy K. DuCharme	Timothy G. Payne
Kathryn Baugh Hofman	James W. Ritt
Murray L. Lyon	Steven Zoric

*Denotes a lawyer employed by a Professional Corporation which is a member of the Firm.

For full biographical listings, see the Martindale-Hubbell Law Directory

---

SONNENSCHEIN NATH & ROSENTHAL (AV)

Suite 8000 Sears Tower, 233 South Wacker Drive, 60606
Telephone: 312-876-8000
Cable Address: "Sonberk"
Telex: 25-3526
Telecopier: 312-876-7934
New York, N.Y. Office: 1221 Avenue of the Americas, 24th Floor.
Telephone: 212-768-6700.
Facsimile: 212-391-1247.
Washington, D.C. Office: 1301 K Street, N.W., Suite 600 East Tower.
Telephone: 202-408-6400.
Fax: 202-408-6399.
San Francisco, California Office: 685 Market Street, 10th Floor.
Telephone: 415-882-5000.
Facsimile: 415-543-5472.
Los Angeles, California Office: 601 South Figueroa Street, Suite 1500.
Telephone: 213-623-9300.
Facsimile: 213-623-9924.
St. Louis, Missouri Office: One Metropolitan Square, Suite 3000.
Telephone: 314-241-1800.
Facsimile: 314-259-5959.
Kansas City, Missouri Office: Suite 1100, 4520 Main Street, 64111.
Telephone: 816-932-4400.
Facsimile: 816-531-7545.
London, England Office: Sonnenscheins, Royex House, Aldermanbury Square, EC2V 7HR.
Telephone: 01710600-2222.
Facsimile: 0171-600-2221.

Edward Sonnenschein (1881-1935)	Hugo Sonnenschein (1883-1956)

MEMBERS OF FIRM

Neal I. Aizenstein
David Albenda (Not admitted in IL; Resident, New York, N.Y. Office)
Fredric P. Andes
Stuart Altschuler
Swanson W. Angle (Not admitted in IL; Resident, St. Louis, Missouri Office)
Reid L. Ashinoff (Not admitted in IL; Resident, New York, N.Y. Office)
Pamela Baker
Michael A. Bamberger (Not admitted in IL; Resident, New York, N.Y. Office)
William T. Barker
Michael A. Barnes (Not admitted in IL; Resident, San Francisco, California Office)
Michael H. Barr (Not admitted in IL; Resident, New York, N.Y. Office)
Wayne M. Barsky (Not admitted in IL; Resident, St. Louis, Missouri Office)
Michael J. Bayard (Resident, Los Angeles, California Office)
Carol Anne Been
Susan M. Benton-Powers
Dennis N. Berman (Resident, New York, N.Y. Office)
Frank C. Bernard
Amy L. Bess (Resident, Washington, D.C. Office)
Alan B. Bornstein (Not admitted in IL; Resident, St. Louis, Missouri Office)
Peter E. M. Borrowdale (Resident, London, England Office)
Roger T. Brice
Carol Elder Bruce (Not admitted in IL; Resident, Washington, D.C. Office)

Ernest P. Burger (Not admitted in IL; Resident, Los Angeles, California Office)
Charles R. Campbell, Jr. (Not admitted in IL; Resident, Los Angeles, California Office)
Leo J. Carlin (Deceased, 1988)
Lorie A. Chaiten
John Collen
Sherman P. Corwin
Robert E. Curry, Jr. (Resident, New York, N.Y. Office)
Steven R. Davidson
J. Ross Docksey
Jeffrey L. Dorman
Robin M. Edwards (Not admitted in IL; Resident, San Francisco, California Office)
Kevin J. Egan
Todd R. Eskelsen (Resident, Washington, D.C. Office)
Phyllis A. Ewer
James B. Fadim
Robert M. Farquharson (Deceased, 1987)
Richard L. Fenton
James R. Ferguson
Elizabeth A. Ferrell (Not admitted in IL; Resident, Washington, D.C. Office)
Samuel Fifer
Sheldon I. Fink
Amy H. Fisher (Not admitted in IL; Resident, New York, N.Y. Office)
Abraham Fishman
Karen H. Flax
Martin J. Foley (Not admitted in IL; Resident, Los Angeles, California Office)
Jeffrey C. Fort
Gary J. Fox
Matthew C. Fragner (Not admitted in IL; Resident, Los Angeles, California Office)

(See Next Column)

SONNENSCHEIN NATH & ROSENTHAL—*Continued*

MEMBERS OF FIRM (Continued)

Steven H. Frankel (Resident, San Francisco, California Office)
Louis S. Freeman
Linda E. Friedman (Not admitted in IL; Resident, New York, N.Y. Office)
Michael M. Froy
Lori L. Gaddis (Resident, St. Louis, Missouri Office)
David D. Gatchell (Resident, Kansas City, Missouri Office)
Brent Matthew Giddens (Not admitted in IL; Resident, Los Angeles, California Office)
Alan S. Gilbert
Paul E. B. Glad (Not admitted in IL; Resident, San Francisco, California Office)
Robert N. Grant
David M. Greenbaum (Not admitted in IL; Resident, New York, N.Y. Office)
John I. Grossbart
Peter J. Gurfein (Resident, Los Angeles, California Office)
Philip A. Haber (Resident, New York, N.Y. Office)
Douglas David Hacking (Resident, London, England Office)
Frank H. Hackmann (Resident, St. Louis, Missouri Office)
Elliott J. Hahn (Resident, Los Angeles, California Office)
John S. Hahn (Not admitted in IL; Resident, Washington, D.C. Office)
Wayne R. Hannah, Jr.
Mark T. Hansen (Not admitted in IL; Resident, Los Angeles, California Office)
Linda Chaplik Harris
Richard Harris (Deceased, 1986)
Blake L. Harrop
James A. Heeter (Resident, Kansas City, Missouri Office)
Roger K. Heidenreich (Resident, St. Louis, Missouri Office)
Jan P. Helder, Jr. (Resident, Kansas City, Missouri Office)
Marc B. Heller (Resident, New York, N.Y. Office)
Carl B. Hillemann III (Resident, St. Louis, Missouri Office)
Sue L. Himmelrich (Not admitted in IL; Resident, Los Angeles, California Office)
Harold C. Hirshman
Kenneth H. Hoch
Thomas Holden (Not admitted in IL; Resident, San Francisco, California Office)
Mitchell L. Hollins
Oliver L. Holmes (Not admitted in IL; Resident, San Francisco, California Office)
Donald P. Horwitz
Stuart E. Hunt (Not admitted in IL; Resident, Washington, D.C. Office)
Benjamin B. Iselin (Resident, New York, N.Y., Office)
David C. Jacobson
Fruman Jacobson
Marian S. Jacobson
Robert C. Johnson
Mark P. Johnson (Resident, Kansas City, Missouri Office)
Gayle M. Jones (Not admitted in IL; Resident, San Francisco, California Office)
Robert T. Joseph
Gregory S. Karawan (Not admitted in IL; Resident, New York, N.Y. Office)
Michelle Stark Kaufman (Resident, Kansas City, Missouri Office)
Louis C. Keiler

Ronald D. Kent (Not admitted in IL; Resident, Los Angeles, California Office)
H. Sinclair Kerr, Jr. (Not admitted in IL; Resident, San Francisco, California Office)
Christopher Q. King
Robert H. King, Jr.
Leslie A. Klein
James A. Klenk
Kenneth G. Kolmin
Karen Beth Ksander
Frederic S. Lane
David A. Lapins
John J. Lawlor
Mark R. Lehrer (Not admitted in IL; Resident, New York, N.Y. Office)
Edward L. Lembitz (1926-1993)
Jeffrey Lennard
Marc Levenstein
William G. Levi (Resident, Kansas City, Missouri Office)
Fred L. Levy (Not admitted in IL; Resident, Washington, D.C. Office)
Steven M. Levy
Julius Lewis
Mark J. Linderman (Not admitted in IL; Resident, San Francisco, California Office)
Scott A. Lindquist
Richard M. Lipton
R. Michael Lowenbaum (Not admitted in IL; Resident, St. Louis, Missouri Office)
Donald G. Lubin
David W. Maher
Barry S. Maram
Richard L. Marcus
Michael R. Maryn (Not admitted in IL; Resident, Washington, D.C. Office)
Sandra R. McCandless (Resident, San Francisco, California Office)
Jacques K. Meguire
Mark F. Mehlman
Michael W. Melendez (Not admitted in IL; Resident, San Francisco, California Office)
Cynthia L. Mellema (Not admitted in IL; Resident, San Francisco, California Office)
Robert F. Messerly
Paul J. Miller
Robert B. Millner
James L. Moeller (Resident, Kansas City, Missouri Office)
Patrick G. Moran
William C. Morison-Knox (Not admitted in IL; Resident, San Francisco, California Office)
Lisa Reilly Nadler
Bernard Nath
Marlene D. Nations
Dustin E. Neumark
Dennis Nathan Newman
Charles F. Newlin
Bernard J. Nussbaum
Philip A. O'Connell, Jr. (Resident, San Francisco, California Office)
Mary Denise O'Connor
Eric A. Oesterle
Thomas G. Opferman
Sanford M. Pastroff
Lee T. Paterson (Not admitted in IL; Resident, Los Angeles, California Office)
Roger W. Patrick (Not admitted in IL; Resident, Washington, D.C. Office)
Sidney M. Perlstadt
Laura R. Petroff (Resident, Los Angeles, California Office)
Earl E. Pollock
Alan M. Posner

MEMBERS OF FIRM (Continued)

(See Next Column)

Caryl A. Potter, III (Not admitted in IL; Resident, Washington, D.C. Office)
Duane C. Quaini
Charles A. Redd (Resident, St. Louis, Missouri Office)
Susan K. Reiter
C. Harker Rhodes, Jr.
Robert E. Richards
Andria K. Richey (Not admitted in IL; Resident, Los Angeles, California Office)
Michael W. Ring (Not admitted in IL; Resident, Los Angeles, California Office)
Michael D. Rosenthal
Samuel R. Rosenthal (1899-1994)
Edwin A. Rothschild (1910-1994)
Stephen H. Rovak (Resident, St. Louis, Missouri Office)
Timothy C. Russell (Not admitted in IL; Resident, Washington, D.C. Office)
Kirk R. Ruthenberg (Resident, Washington, D.C. Office)
Ivor E. Samson (Resident, San Francisco, California Office)
Charles D. Satinover
David L. Schiavone
Eric M. Schiller
Donald M. Schindel
Michael A. Schlanger (Not admitted in IL; Resident, Washington, D.C. Office)
Arnold P. Schuster (Not admitted in IL; Resident, San Francisco, California Office)
Peter von Schwartz de Megyesi (Resident, London, England Office)
Robert F. Scoular (Not admitted in IL; Resident, Los Angeles, California Office)
Norbert M. Seifert (Not admitted in IL; Resident, Los Angeles, California Office)
Gary Senner
J. A. Shafran (Not admitted in IL; Resident, Los Angeles, California Office)
Harold D. Shapiro
Gerald J. Sherman
Alan H. Silberman
Arthur J. Simon
Mark C. Simon

Roger C. Siske
Peter A. Smalbach (Resident, San Francisco, California Office)
Jane S. Smith (Resident, St. Louis, Missouri Office)
Charles Spiegel (Not admitted in IL; Resident, San Francisco, California Office)
Ronald E. Stauffer (Not admitted in IL; Resident, Washington, D.C. Office)
Thomas M. Stephens
Ellyn J. Steuer (Not admitted in IL; Resident, New York, N.Y. Office)
Errol L. Stone
Leslie Chambers Strohm (Resident, St. Louis, Missouri Office)
William E. Sudow (Resident, Washington, D.C. Office)
Daniel R. Swett
Eileen Bannon Trost
Scott Turow
Thomas K. Vandiver (Resident, St. Louis, Missouri Office)
Jacqueline M. Vidmar
Donna J. Vobornik
Susan M. Walker (Not admitted in IL; Resident, Los Angeles, California Office)
William M. Walsh (Resident, St. Louis, Missouri Office)
Everett S. Ward
Andrew L. Weil
Margo Weinstein
Jerome P. Weiss (1934-1996)
Linda D. White
James G. Wiehl (Not admitted in IL; Resident, St. Louis, Missouri Office)
Michael S. Wien (Not admitted in IL; Resident, New York, N.Y. Office)
John Leland Williams (Not admitted in IL; Resident, San Francisco, California Office)
Rebecca L. Williams
Daniel R. Wofsey (Resident, St. Louis, Missouri Office)
Jerome T. Wolf (Resident, Kansas City, Missouri Office)
Curtis E. Woods (Resident, Kansas City, Missouri Office)
Nicholas C. Yost (Resident, San Francisco, California Office)

OF COUNSEL

Jon K. Adams (Not admitted in IL; Resident, San Francisco, California Office)
Jean Allard
Donald P. Arnavas (Resident, Washington, D.C. Office)
Wayne H. Davis (Resident, New York, N.Y. Office)
Arnold B. Kanter
Brian N. Kaufman (Not admitted in IL; Resident, Kansas City, Missouri Office)
Rachel M. Lipschutz (Not admitted in IL; Resident, New York, N.Y. Office)

Neal R. Marder (Resident, Los Angeles, California Office)
Karen E. Milner (Resident, St. Louis, Missouri Office)
Robert B. Murphy (Resident, Washington, D.C. Office)
Jonathan Piper
Marshall S. Shapo
Charles M. Yablon (Not admitted in IL; Resident, New York, N.Y. Office)
Henry S. Zangwill (Resident, Los Angeles, California Office)

ASSOCIATES

Terence M. Abad (Resident, San Francisco, California Office)
Gwendolyn S. Andrey
Ronald S. Bell
Camille E. Bennett
Cheryl Dyer Berg (Resident, San Francisco, California Office)
Kirsten K. Bergin
Jana Cohen Blackman
Susan E. Bloch (Resident, San Francisco, California Office)
Betsy J. Braack
Julie A. Bregande (Resident, St. Louis, Missouri Office)
Debra M. Buhring
Thomas B. Burnside (Resident, Washington, D.C. Office)

William F. Burton (Not admitted in IL; Resident, Washington, D.C. Office)
Jeffry Butler (Resident, Los Angeles, California Office)
Jill Thompson Calian
Adam Scott Calisoff
John J. Calkins (Resident, Washington, D.C. Office)
Georgina Calvert-Lee (Not admitted in IL)
Anthony Capobianco (Resident, Los Angeles, California Office)
Clarissa Cerda
Somnath Chatterjee (Resident, San Francisco, California Office)

(See Next Column)

SONNENSCHEIN NATH & ROSENTHAL, *Chicago—Continued*

ASSOCIATES (Continued)

Nargis Choudhry (Resident, Los Angeles, California Office)
Richard J. Clyne
Karen E. Compton (Resident, San Francisco, California Office)
Patricia M. Cosgrove
Stephen J. Curran (Not admitted in IL; Resident, Los Angeles, California Office)
Margaret A. Daley
Susan Kay Daniel (Resident, St. Louis, Missouri Office)
Andrew L. DaSilva (Resident, New York, N.Y. Office)
Sally L. Davis
Valerie P. Debler (Resident, New York, New York Office)
Eric R. Decator
Maria Sileno DeLoughry (Resident, Washington, D.C. Office)
Monica Shah Desai (Resident, Washington, D.C. Office)
Kathleen T. Deveau
Mark L. Dosier
Kenneth Drake (Not admitted in IL; Resident, New York, New York Office)
Deborah F. Dubin (Resident, San Francisco, California Office)
Thomas E. Duley (Resident, San Francisco, California Office)
Terri Marie Esparza (Resident, San Francisco, California Office)
Weston A. Edwards (Resident, Los Angeles, California Office)
Timothy L. Elliott (Resident, St. Louis, Missouri Office)
Cynthia A. Faur
Caryn L. Finkle
Jonathan J. Fisher (Resident, Washington, D.C. Office)
Gerald E. Fradin
Gary A. Francesconi (Resident, St. Louis, Missouri Office)
Ann Ferguson Frolik
Margaret E. Gilk (Resident, Kansas City, Missouri Office)
Kenneth J. Gladish
Bryce P. Goeking (Not admitted in IL; Resident, San Francisco, California Office)
Jonathan F. Golding (Resident, Los Angeles, California Office)
Joshua D. Goldman
J. Timothy Gorman (Resident, St. Louis, Missouri Office)
Lisa R. Green (Resident, New York, N.Y. Office)
Steven Mark Greenbaum
Jonathan M. Griffiths (Resident, London, England Office)
Rosemary L.L. Gullikson
Scott L. Hammel
Mark L. Hanover
Brett J. Hart
Sandra D. Hauser (Not admitted in IL; Resident, New York, N.Y. Office)
James L. Heideman (Resident, San Francisco, California Office)
Michael A. Heller
Charles W. Hokanson (Resident, Los Angeles, California Office)
Joseph P. Hornyak (Not admitted in IL; Resident, Washington, D.C. Office)
LaShonda A. Hunt
Elissa L. Isaacs
Jeffrey S. Isaacs (Resident, New York, N.Y. Office)
Robert J. Isaacson (Resident, St. Louis, Missouri Office)
Bryan C. Jackson (Resident, Los Angeles, California Office)

Margaret A. Jacobs (Resident, New York, N.Y. Office)
John Grayson Johnson
Scott L. Jones (Not admitted in IL; Resident, Los Angeles, California Office)
Stephanie D. Jones
Edward J. Jordanich (Resident, New York, N.Y. Office)
David J. Kaplan (Resident, New York, N.Y. Office)
Matthew I. Kaplan (Resident, Los Angeles, California Office)
Steven R. Karl (Resident, St. Louis, Missouri Office)
Kenji Kawahigashi (Resident, Los Angeles, California Office)
Wendy J. Keith
Helen B. Kim (Resident, New York, N.Y. Office)
Namyon Kim (Resident, Los Angeles, California Office)
Jessie A. Kohler (Resident, Los Angeles, California Office)
John C. Koski
Timothy J. Kuester (Resident, Kansas City, Missouri Office)
Linda P. Kurtos
Thomas A. Labuda, Jr.
Mary Kay Lacey (Not admitted in IL; Resident, San Francisco, California Office)
David S. Ladwig (Resident, Kansas City, Missouri Office)
David C. Layden
Paul A. Leboffe (Not admitted in IL; Resident, San Francisco, California Office)
Pauline Ng Lee (Resident, Los Angeles, California Office)
J. Bradley Leitch (Not admitted in IL; Resident, Kansas City, Missouri Office)
Bruce H. Leshine (Resident, New York, N.Y. Office)
David E. Lieberman
Matthew F. Lintner (Resident, San Francisco, California Office)
Andrew R. Livingston (Not admitted in IL; Resident, San Francisco, California Office)
Michael R. Lufrano
Lisa A. MacVittie (Not admitted in IL; Resident, Washington, D.C. Office)
Rhonda V. Magee (Not admitted in IL; Resident, San Francisco, California Office)
Urooj Mahmud
Donna L. Marks
Drew W. Marrocco (Resident, Washington, D.C. Office)
Lisa M. Martens
Christopher Martin (Resident, London, England Office)
J. Robert Maxwell (Resident, San Francisco, California Office)
Jane Wells May
Michael D. McCullough
Sean McEneaney (Resident, San Francisco, California Office)
Debra McGuire (Resident, Washington, D.C. Office)
James K. McMurray (Resident, Kansas City, Missouri Office)
Diane M. Mellett (Resident, London, England Office)
Timothy M. Metzger
Gary Meyerhoff (Resident, New York, N.Y. Office)
Mary L. Mills
Kirk M. Minckler
Jane M. Moul (Resident, St. Louis, Missouri Office)
Stacey L. Murphy (Resident, St. Louis, Missouri Office)

ASSOCIATES (Continued)

(See Next Column)

Catherine M. Myers (Resident, Washington, D.C. Office)
Gregory R. Naron
Stephen J. O'Brien (Resident, St. Louis, Missouri Office)
Randall T. Oettle (Resident, St. Louis, Missouri Office)
Gregory M. Otto (Resident, St. Louis, Missouri Office)
Terrence R. Pace (Resident, Los Angeles, California Office)
Mark W. Page
Michael E. Pappas (Not admitted in IL; Resident, Los Angeles, California Office)
S. Jonathan Passman (Resident, London, England Office)
Dorothy P. Patton (Resident, New York, N.Y. Office)
Kenneth J. Pfaehler (Not admitted in IL; Resident, Washington, D.C. Office)
Marcie J. Pickard
Jerrie House Plegge (Resident, St. Louis, Missouri Office)
Andrew Eliot Porter (Resident, New York, N.Y. Office)
G. David Porter (Not admitted in IL; Resident, Kansas City, Missouri Office)
Erika K. Powers
Jill I. Prater (Resident, Washington, D.C. Office)
Timothy J. Prosser (Resident, St. Louis, Missouri Office)
Teresa Dale Pupillo (Resident, St. Louis, Missouri Office)
Anuja G. Purohit (Resident, San Francisco, California Office)
David T. Rankin (Resident, St. Louis, Missouri Office)
Susan H. Rider
Carlos Guillermo Rizowy
Jeffrey M. Rose (Resident, New York, N.Y. Office)
Hilary A. Ross (Resident, London, England Office)
Phillip A. Rothermich (Resident, St. Louis, Missouri Office)
Abigail L. Rudoff
W. Michael Ryan
Stephen Douglas Sayre
Carole Schecter
Leonora M. Schloss (Not admitted in IL; Resident, Los Angeles, California Office)
Tamara Seyler-James (Resident, Kansas City, Missouri Office)
Daniel J. Shonkwiler (Resident, Washington, D.C. Office)
Anoop G. Shroff (Resident, Washington, D.C. Office)
Felicia L. Silber (Not admitted in IL; Resident, Washington, D.C. Office)
David Simantob (Resident, Los Angeles, California Office)
Barbara Lee Smith
Gregory L. Smith (Resident, San Francisco, California Office)

Steven R. Smith (Resident, Los Angeles, California Office)
T. Mark Smith (Not admitted in IL; Resident, Los Angeles, California Office)
Christopher P. Sonderby (Resident, San Francisco, California Office)
Diane Sovereign (Resident, Los Angeles, California Office)
Faith H. Spencer
David J. Stagman
David M. Staker (Resident, Kansas City, Missouri Office)
Todd M. Stennes
Craig A. Sterling (Resident, San Francisco, California Office)
Brian R. St. James (Resident, St. Louis, Missouri Office)
Lisa N. Sweet
Jonathan D. Taft
Scott B. Tandy
David J. Tess (Resident, Washington, D.C. Office)
John T. Thomas (Resident, Kansas City, Missouri Office)
Pamela L. Thompson (Resident, New York, N.Y. Office)
Kenda Tomes
David W. Tufts (Resident, Los Angeles, California Office)
Kelly B. Valen (Resident, San Francisco, California Office)
Catherine A. Van Horn
Maralee Buttery Vezie (Resident, New York, N.Y. Office)
Alexandra von Ferstel (Not admitted in IL; Resident, New York, N.Y. Office)
John E. Walker (Resident, Los Angeles, California Office)
Lori Anne Ward (Not admitted in IL)
Anne Nicholson Weber
Aron G. Weber (Resident, New York, N.Y. Office)
Robert B. Weil
Wendy S. Weingart (Not admitted in IL; Resident, New York, N.Y. Office)
Patricia S. Williams (Resident, St. Louis, Missouri Office)
Bradd L. Williamson
Thomas A. Wilson
Benjamin E. Wolff III
Debra B. Yale
Paula M. Yost (Not admitted in IL; Resident, San Francisco, California Office)
Frederick S. Young (Resident, Washington, D.C. Office)
Lauren M. Yu (Resident, Los Angeles, California Office)
Consuelo A. Zermeno (Resident, Los Angeles, California Office)
Lisa R. Zornberg (Not admitted in IL; Resident, New York, N.Y. Office)

For full biographical listings, see the Martindale-Hubbell Law Directory

TAYLOR, MILLER, SPROWL, HOFFNAGLE & MERLETTI (AV)

33 North La Salle Street, Suite 2222, 60602-2691
Telephone: 312-782-6070
Fax: 312-782-6081

Orville Taylor (1885-1969)
John S. Miller (1888-1965)
James J. Hoffnagle
Roger A. Merletti

Ralph W. F. Lustgarten
Richard W. Oloffson
Frank C. Stevens
Roger LeRoy

OF COUNSEL

Charles R. Sprowl

ASSOCIATES

John R. Adams
Jack Bruce Batten
Karrieann M. Couture
Timothy Couture

Hugh J. Doyle
Daniel K. Fritz
Katherine M. Mulroy
Robert W. Rohm

For full biographical listings, see the Martindale-Hubbell Law Directory

Chicago—Continued

VEDDER, PRICE, KAUFMAN & KAMMHOLZ (AV)

A Partnership including Vedder, Price, Kaufman & Kammholz, P.C.
222 North La Salle Street, 60601-1003
Telephone: 312-609-7500
Fax: 312-609-5005
New York, New York Office: Vedder, Price, Kaufman, Kammholz & Day,
805 Third Avenue.
Telephone: 212-407-7700.

MEMBERS OF FIRM

Beverly B. Vedder (1887-1955)	Richard H. Levy
William F. Price (1909-1973)	E. Wayne Robinson
Charles R. Kaufman (1908-1990)	Douglas J. Polk
Theophil C. Kammholz	Richard F. Zehnle
(1909-1992)	John T. McEnroe
Stanley B. Block	James M. Kane
James S. Petrie	Margaret A. Arnold
George P. Blake	John R. Obiala
Frank G. Reeder	Cathy G. O'Kelly
Michael G. Beemer	Gregory G. Wrobel
Richard H. Schnadig	James A. Spizzo
John Jacoby	Benjamin J. Baker (1954-1995)
Paul F. Gleeson	Pearl A. Zager
Charles H. Wiggins, Jr.	Douglas J. Lipke
Theodore J. Tierney	Guy E. Snyder
Michael E. Reed	Edward C. Jepson, Jr.
Richard H. Sanders	Dalius F. Vasys
Charles F. Custer	Norman B. Julius
Michael L. Igoe, Jr.	Bruce R. Alper
Richard L. Williams III	Thomas P. Desmond
Allan E. Lapidus	Douglas M. Hambleton
Robert J. Stucker	Daniel T. Sherlock
Thomas L. O'Brien	Igor Potym
Richard C. Robin	Jonathan H. Bogaard
Robert J. Moran	John M. Wolff, Jr.
Robert J. Washlow	Edward A. Cohen
David E. Bennett	Jennifer R. Evans
Donald W. Jenkins	Daniel C. McKay, II
Daniel O'Rourke	Carol L. Browne
William F. Walsh	Diane M. Kehl
Richard A. Zachar	Dean N. Gerber
Nina Gidden Stillman	Janet M. Hedrick
Christine M. Rhode	David A. Sturms
Paul F. Russell	Anne M. Murphy
Lawrence L. Summers	Drew J. Scott
Thomas G. Abram	Joseph A. Strubbe
Michael G. Cleveland	Thomas E. Schnur
Lawrence J. Casazza	Karen L. Pszanka-Layng
Thomas A. Baker	Thomas P. Cimino, Jr.
Rene A. Torrado, Jr.	Randall Marc Lending
John J. Jacobsen, Jr.	Philip L. Mowery
David L. Doyle	Michael A. Nemeroff
Ludwig E. Kolman	Patricia J. Moore
Charles B. Wolf	Steven J. Gray
Michael W. Sculnick	Timothy W. O'Donnell

ASSOCIATES

Andrew M. Gardner	Alice Estill Burke
Lynne A. Gochanour	(Not admitted in IL)
Thomas G. Hancuch	Thomas R. Dee
Catherine A. Lemmer	Mark G. Malven
Jeffrey C. Davis	Paula K. DeAngelo
Lane R. Moyer	Ann M. Schlaffman
Edward M. McElroy	Shawn S. Magee
Carla Rendina Owen	Melissa J. Krasnow
Geoffrey R. Kass	Dahlia M. Ronen
Robert J. Patton	Barry J. Shulock
Marianne W. Culver	Valerie Depies Harper
Deborah A. Carroll	James V. Garvey
James A. Arpaia	Matthew T. O'Connor
Wayne S. Karbal	Patrick J. Bruks
Dena Economou	Ilana S. Kahan
Daniel J. Weissburg	David B.H. Williams
William J. Bettman	William E. Bailey
Michael P. Nicolai	Kelly A. Starr
Nancy M. Gerrity	Christine S. Davik-Galbraith
Jeffrey T. Veber	Yusuf Haroon Safdari
Dana Simaitis Armagno	Theresa M. Peyton
James E. Bayles, Jr.	Mary C. Waghorne
Brian C. Bendig	Tara H. Kwon

OF COUNSEL IN CHICAGO

Brainerd Chapman	Paul H. LaRue
Bernard J. Echlin	John J. Cassidy, Jr.

William L. Conaghan

PARTNERS AT NEW YORK CITY

Virgil B. Day	Denise L. Blau
John C. Grosz	John H. Eickemeyer
Dan L. Goldwasser	Neal I. Korval
Alan M. Koral	Ronald Scheinberg
Donald A. Wassall	Alfrado D. Donelson

(See Next Column)

ASSOCIATES AT NEW YORK CITY

Michael J. Crisafulli	Inge H.E. Jonckheer Maki
Jonathan A. Wexler	Boris B. Thomas
Neil A. Capobianco	Taryn V. Shelton

Renee L. Starr

OF COUNSEL AT NEW YORK CITY

Edward J. Walsh, Jr.	Edward F. Campbell, Jr.

Patricia Anne Lind

For full biographical listings, see the Martindale-Hubbell Law Directory

WILDMAN, HARROLD, ALLEN & DIXON (AV)

225 West Wacker Drive, 30th Floor, 60606-1229
Telephone: 312-201-2000
Cable Address: "Whad"
Fax: 312-201-2555
URL: http://www.whad.com
Aurora, Illinois Office: 1851 W. Galena Boulevard, Suite 210.
Telephone: 630-892-7021.
Fax: 630-892-7158.
Waukegan, Illinois Office: 404 West Water, P. O. Box 890.
Telephone: 847-623-0700.
Fax: 847-244-5273.
Lisle, Illinois Office: 4300 Commerce Court.
Telephone: 630-955-0555.
New York, New York Office: Wildman, Harrold, Allen, Dixon & Smith.
The International Building, 45 Rockefeller Plaza, Suite 353.
Telephone: 212-632-3850.
Fax: 212-632-3858.
Toronto, Ontario affiliated Office: Keel Cottrelle. 36 Toronto Street, Ninth
Floor, Suite 920.
Telephone: 416-367-2900.
Telefax: 416-367-2791.
Telex: 062-18660.
Mississauga, Ontario affiliated Office: Keel Cottrelle. 100 Matatson
Avenue East, Suite 104.
Telephone: 416-890-7700.
Fax: 416-890-8006.

MEMBERS OF FIRM

Thomas D. Allen	Anne Giddings Kimball
Benjamin P. Alschuler	Steven L. Larson
(Aurora Office)	(Waukegan Office)
John J. Arado	Dean J. Leffelman (Lisle Office)
Richard C. Bartelt	Brian W. Lewis
Michael R. Blankshain	Thomas M. Lynch
Bruce L. Boruszak	Joseph F. Madonia
Cal R. Burnton	Charles R. Mandly, Jr.
Douglas R. Carlson	Thomas I. Matyas
Paul S. Chervin	Michael L. McCluggage
(Waukegan Office)	Mark J. McCombs
James A. Christman	Donald R. McGarrah
Dana S. Connell	John E. McGovern, Jr.
John W. Costello	Sheldon P. Migdal
Barbara A. Cronin	Mark P. Miller
Thomas W. Daggett	James R. Morrin
Steven E. Danekas	Kathryn A. Mrkonich
Stewart S. Dixon	Richard D. Murphy Jr.
Michael Dockterman	Robert W. Newman
James P. Dorr	Timothy G. Nickels
Thomas P. Duffy	James T. Nyeste
John L. Eisel	Sarah L. Olson
Jerald P. Esrick	Richard C. Palmer
Roger G. Fein	David F. Pardys
Ira C. Feldman	(Waukegan Office)
James D. Fiffer	David J. Parsons
Donald E. Figliulo	Douglas L. Prochnow
David J. Fischer	Alan B. Roth
Donald Flayton	Fred E. Schulz
Craig Steven Fochler	Robert L. Shuftan
Kathy Pinkstaff Fox	Donald J. Simantz
John E. Frey	(Resident, Aurora Office)
Peter H. Fritts	Lisa S. Simmons
Richard P. Glovka	Thomas H. Snyder
Jeffrey P. Gray	Linda E. Spring
Charles J. Griffin, Jr.	(Waukegan Office)
Robert E. Haley	Sanford M. Stein
Robert E. Hamilton	R. John Street
Bernard Harrold	Robert A. Strelecky
H. Roderic Heard	(Lisle Office)
Ronald M. Hem (Aurora Office)	Richard B. Thies
Helaine Wachs Heydemann	Peter A. Tomaras
Mark W. Hianik	Thomas J. Verticchio
Anthony G. Hopp	Louis P. Vitullo
Keith C. Hult	James B. Vogts
Richard C. Johnson	Craig M. White
(Lisle Office)	Max Wildman
David A. Kanter	Dale G. Wills
Robert E. Kehoe, Jr.	John A. Ybarra

(See Next Column)

WILDMAN, HARROLD, ALLEN & DIXON, *Chicago—Continued*

COUNSEL

Howard Arvey	Robert M. Gunn
Marshall L. Burman	Lee B. McClain
Diane G. Elder	George W. Overton

Edwin A. Wahlen

Jody A. Ballmer	Michael J. Lotus
Kathryn S. Bedward	Susan Wiles
Deborah L. Bencik	Patricia Lynn McCarthy
John T. Benz	Jeffrey A. McIntyre
Eric P. Berlin	Jeffrey E. Michel
Stacey V. Bowers	Jill S. Miller
Leland H. Chait	Stephanie B. Miller
Bruce M. Chanen	Vania Montero
David J. Chroust (Lisle Office)	W. Scott Nehs
Richard L. Creech	Martha D. Owens
Jill A. Cuba	Barbara M. Prohaska
Maria F. Di Lorenzo	(Lisle Office)
Leo P. Dombrowski	Kevin B. Reid
Vilia M. Drazdys	John A. Roberts
Jeffrey W. Eich	Beth S. Rubin
Lawrence W. Falbe	Rohit Sahgal
Wendy L. Fink	Elizabeth A. Sanders
John Alden Fritchey IV	Jeannine Y. Sano
Nancy J. Fuller	Frederick L. Schwartz
Shanthi V. Gaur	Patricia A. Scott
Michael A. Glackin	Bradley F. Simon
Adam J. Glazer	David M. Simon
Louise M. Goodwin	Andrew E. Skopp
Kenneth M. Gorenberg	Ada Skyles
Dara J. Greenwald	Paul A. Slager
Scott Z. Hochfelder	Lauren S. Tashma
Richard M. Hoffman	John A. Terselic
James C. James, III	(Waukegan Office)
(Aurora Office)	Jeanne Walker
Elaine T. Karacic	Jennifer K. Walter
Elizabeth Keiley	Joleen S. Willis
Steven H. Klein	Adam C. Wit
Padmavati G. Klejwa	Robin L. Wolkoff
Christopher Kovach	Jonathan W. Young

For full biographical listings, see the Martindale-Hubbell Law Directory

---

WILLIAMS AND MONTGOMERY, LTD. (AV)

20 North Wacker Drive Suite 2100, 60606
Telephone: 312-443-3200
Facsimile: 312-443-1323
Email: WILLMONT@ATTMAIL.COM
Waukegan, Illinois Office: 33 North County Street.
Telephone: 847-360-1220.
Wheaton, Illinois Office: 310 S. County Farm Road.
Telephone: 708-690-3200.
Joliet, Illinois Office: 81 North Chicago Avenue.
Telephone: 815-727-2653.
Miami, Florida Office: Clarke, Silverglate, Williams and Montgomery, 100 North Biscayne Boulevard.
Telephone: 305-377-0700.
Facsimile: 305-377-3001.

Lloyd E. Williams, Jr.	Kevin Campbell
C. Barry Montgomery	David P. Boyd
Barry L. Kroll	Rodney E. VanAusdal
Thomas H. Neuckranz	Lori E. Iwan
Anthony P. Katauskas	Lawrence K. Rynning
David E. Morgans	Jeffrey H. Lipe
Craig A. Tomassi	Bruce W. Lyon
Nunzio C. Radogno	Thomas F. Cameli
Anthony J. Kiselis	Michael D. Huber
Edward J. Murphy	Lawrence A. Szymanski
Alton C. Haynes	Gregory J. Bird
James K. Horstman	Perry W. Hoag
Patrick F. Klunder	Hall Adams, III
David E. Stevenson	Mary Anne Sliwinski
Michael R. La Barge	Thomas J. Pontikis

Mark R. Misiorowski

OF COUNSEL

Manya A. Pastalan Grant

Brigid E. Kennedy	Brian J. Hunt
Peter J. Szatkowski	Bradley C. Nahrstadt
Douglas A. Miller	Karen M. Talty
Stephen W. Heil	Edward O. Pacer
Edward R. Moor	Gregory W. Beihl
J. Calvin Downing, III	Douglas W. Lohmar, Jr.
David E. Neumeister	John J. Duffy
Mark D. Brent	Peggy A. Edwards
Shimon B. Kahan	James L. Kopecky
Mark E. Winters	Channing K. Blair

(See Next Column)

Daniel F. D'Attomo	Alison M. Duffy
James P. Johnston	Kathleen Kelliher Mone
Michael J. Cunningham	Stacey A. Feeley
Jeannine S. Gilleran	Leslie T. Johnson
Deborah J. Spector	Brian P. O'Neill
Jeffrey A. Brauer	Kelly J. Pattison
Daniel J. Neppl	Summer E. Stevens
Jason D. Altman	James R. Studnicka
Evelyn Tsamtsouris Anthony	Henry G. Burnett
Anthony M. Pinto	Daniel H. Fogel
R. Kevin Belt	Laura A. Smith
Todd E. Carlson	Terrie L. Culver

For full biographical listings, see the Martindale-Hubbell Law Directory

WILSON & McILVAINE (AV)

500 West Madison, Suite 3700, 60661-2511
Telephone: 312-715-5000
Telecopier: 312-715-5155

PARTNERS

C. John Anderson	Sarah M. Linsley
Walter W. Bell	Thomas J. Magill
Cynthia A. Bergmann	Daniel C. McKay
Richard P. Blessen	Kendall R. Meyer
Thomas E. Chomicz	Dennis J. O'Hara
Michael F. Csar	Dwight B. Palmer, Jr.
Thomas G. Draths	Thomas A. Polachek
Marie K. Eitrheim	John J. Quinlisk
Robert F. Forrer	Janice E. Rodgers
James J. Gatziolis	Peter A. Sarasek
Timothy S. Harris	Quinton F. Seamons
Douglas R. Hoffman	Stephanie B. Shellenback
Richard L. Horn	Leonard S. Shifflett
Jerry D. Jones	Alexander Terras
Joseph M. Kehoe	John P. Vail
Gary H. Kline	Brian J. Wanca

ASSOCIATES

David B. Altman	Margaret M. Lloyd
Patrick J. Bitterman	Kathleen M. Myalls
Sara E. Elder	Alison L. Paul
Susan M. Hughes	Anne S. Quinn
Charles A. Lande	Todd A. Rowden
Heather A. Libbey	Kurt T. Temple

Mark A. Trager

OF COUNSEL

Kent Chandler, Jr.	Vernon T. Squires

For full biographical listings, see the Martindale-Hubbell Law Directory

WINSTON & STRAWN (AV)

35 West Wacker Drive, 60601
Telephone: 312-558-5600
Cable Address: "Winston Chicago"
Facsimile: 312-558-5700
Email: postmaster@winston.com *URL:*
http://www.lcp.com/The-Legal-List/LawFirms/7.260.html
Washington, D.C. Office: 1400 L Street, N.W., 20005-3502.
Telephone: 202-371-5700.
Telecopier: 202-371-5950.
Telex: 440574 INTLAW UI.
New York, N.Y. Office: 200 Park Avenue, 10166-4193.
Telephone: 212-294-6700.
Telecopier: 212-294-4700.
Cable Address: "Coledeitz, NYK".
Telex: (RCA) 232459.
Geneva, Switzerland Office: 43 Rue du Rhone, 1204.
Telephone: (4122) 7810506.
Fax: (4122) 7810361.
Paris, France Office: 6, rue du Cirque, 75008.
Telephone: (3314) 225-1055.
Fax: (3314) 225-0921.

Frederick H. Winston	Frederick S. Winston
(1853-1886)	(1878-1909)

Silas Hardy Strawn
(1891-1946)

MEMBERS OF FIRM

George B. Christensen	Albert Milstein
(Semi-Retired)	Kurt L. Schultz
Calvin P. Sawyier	James L. Fletcher
Thomas A. Reynolds, Jr.	Paul H. Hensel, Hiring Partner,
Edward L. Foote	Chief Administrative Partner
Bruce L. Bower	Columbus R. Gangemi, Jr.
Robert B. Golding (1923-1992)	Christopher D. Murtaugh
Richard J. Brennan	Robert F. Denvir
M. Finley Maxson	Hurd Baruch
Norman Waite, Jr.	Gary A. Goodman
Robert G. Lane	John R. Keys, Jr.
John W. Stack	(Washington, D.C. Office)
Stephen C. Bruner	Gregory S. Murray
Terry M. Grimm	James M. Neis
Dean L. Overman	Michael V. Hasten
(Washington, D.C. Office)	Susan E. Cremin
Scott M. Feldman	Robert W. Ericson
Duane M. Kelley	(New York, N.Y. Office)

(See Next Column)

WINSTON & STRAWN—*Continued*

MEMBERS OF FIRM (Continued)

Neil E. Holmen
Gerald C. Peterson
Kimball R. Anderson
David G. Crumbaugh
Jerome W. Pope
Thomas A. Reynolds, III
Robert F. Wall
Dan K. Webb
Wayne D. Boberg
Mark G. Henning
Gregory J. Malovance
Scott J. Szala
Clive M. Topol
Charles E. Stahl
James H. Russell
Thomas P. Fitzgerald
Deborah Gage Haude
Timothy J. Rivelli
Stephen C. Schulte
Edward F. Gerwin, Jr.
　(Washington, D.C. Office)
Jim L. Blanco
F. Ellen Duff
W. Kirk Grimm
Terry John Malik
Bruce A. Toth
Robert W. Tarun
James W. Doran
Arnold G. Gough, Jr.
Dennis J. Kelly
R. Mark McCareins
William J. Ralph
Stephen P. Durchslag
Edward L. Levine
　(New York, N.Y. Office)
Richard B. Teiman
　(New York, N.Y. Office)
Anthony J. D'Auria
　(New York, N.Y. Office)
Edward N. Meyer
　(New York, N.Y. Office)
Jonathan Goldstein
　(New York, N.Y. Office)
Joseph A. DiBenedetto
　(New York, N.Y. Office)
Jeffrey H. Elkin
　(New York, N.Y. Office)
Michael Hirschfeld
　(New York, N.Y. Office)
Howard Seife
　(New York, N.Y. Office)
Robert Scott Edmonds
　(New York, N.Y. Office)
James J. Terry
　(New York, N.Y. Office)
Susan Berkwitt-Malefakis
　(New York, N.Y. Office)
Joseph A. Walsh, Jr.
　(New York, N.Y. Office)
Steven F. Molo
Michael G. Robinson
Timothy J. Rooney
Mark M. Heatwole
Deborah C. Costlow
　(Washington, D.C. Office)
Paul B. Abramson
　(New York, N.Y. Office)
Kenneth C. H. Willig
　(New York, N.Y. Office)
Robert S. Fischler
　(New York, N.Y. Office)
John C. Phelan
　(New York, N.Y. Office)
Richard S. Talesnick
　(New York, N.Y. Office)
Leonard W. Belter
　(Washington, D.C. Office)
Richard C. Browne
　(Washington, D.C. Office)
Thomas M. Buchanan
　(Washington, D.C. Office)
Donald K. Dankner
　(Washington, D.C. Office)
Peter N. Hiebert
　(Washington, D.C. Office)
Eric L. Hirschhorn
　(Washington, D.C. Office)
William K. Keane
　(Washington, D.C. Office)
Frederick J. Killion
　(Washington, D.C. Office)

John C. Kirtland
　(Washington, D.C. Office)
Joseph B. Knotts, Jr.
　(Washington, D.C. Office)
Michael R. Lemov
　(Washington, D.C. Office)
William J. Madden, Jr.
　(Washington, D.C. Office)
J. Michael McGarry, III
　(Washington, D.C. Office)
Malcolm H. Philips, Jr.
　(Washington, D.C. Office)
John P. Proctor
　(Washington, D.C. Office)
Robert M. Rader
　(Washington, D.C. Office)
Nicholas S. Reynolds
　(Washington, D.C. Office)
Daniel F. Stenger
　(Washington, D.C. Office)
Mark J. Wetterhahn
　(Washington, D.C. Office)
John E. Williams
　(Washington, D.C. Office)
Howard M. Pearl
Lawrence R. Desideri
Herbert J. Deitz (1908-1992)
Thomas J. Quigley
　(New York, N.Y. Office)
David A. Repka
　(Washington, D.C. Office)
Norman Newman
　(New York, N.Y. Office)
Anthony F. LoFrisco
　(New York, N.Y. Office)
James R. Thompson, Jr.
　(New York, N.Y. Office)
Ronald G. Caso
　(New York, N.Y. Office)
Thomas R. Bearrows
Thomas F. Blakemore
Thomas J. Frederick
George C. Lombardi
Rex L. Sessions
Peter Kryn Dykema
　(Washington, D.C. Office)
Margaret A. Hill
　(Washington, D.C. Office)
John A. Waits, II
　(Washington, D.C. Office)
James H. Burnley IV
　(Washington, D.C. Office)
Beryl F. Anthony, Jr.
　(Washington, D.C. Office)
Christine L. Albright
Norman R. Vander Clute
　(Washington, D.C. Office)
Marc S. Palay
　(Geneva, Switzerland Office)
M. Javade Chaudhri
　(Washington, D.C. Office)
Benjamin P. Fishburne, III
　(Washington, D.C. Office)
Barry J. Hart
　(Washington, D.C. Office)
Steven M. Lucas
　(Washington, D.C. Office)
David W. Roderer
　(Washington, D.C. Office)
Jane DiRenzo Pigott
Charles L. Kinney
　(Washington, D.C. Office)
James R. Curtiss
　(Washington, D.C. Office)
Charles C. Adams, Jr.
　(Geneva, Switzerland Office)
Nicolas C. Ulmer
　(Geneva, Switzerland Office)
Julie A. Bauer
Charles B. Boehrer
Deborah K. Boling
Terrence R. Brady
Steven J. Gavin
John L. MacCarthy
Peter C. McCabe, III
William G. Miossi
　(Washington, D.C. Office)
Louis J. Weber III
Sheldon L. Trubatch
　(Washington, D.C. Office)
Bruce Baker

MEMBERS OF FIRM (Continued)

(See Next Column)

Timothy J. O'Brien
John C. Lorentzen
James M. Reum
Robert A. Mangrum
　(Washington, D.C. Office)
William D. Brewer
　(New York, N.Y. Office)
James D. Burton
Christina Karcher Corsiglia
W. Gordon Dobie
Patrick O. Doyle
Gemia McDearmon Jonscher
Kenneth T. Kristl
Andrew J. McDonough
Richard E. Morgan
Michael L. Mulhern
Richard W. Pearse
Helen D. Shapiro
Charles P. Sheets
Loren A. Weil
Kevin E. White
Andrea L. Flink
　(New York, N.Y. Office)
Alex C. Lengyel
　(New York, N.Y. Office)
Marc C. Lewis
　(New York, N.Y. Office)
Derek G. P. Mackenzie
　(New York, N.Y. Office)
Lori J. Van Auken
　(New York, N.Y. Office)
James T. Pitts
　(Washington, D.C. Office)
John Albert Whittaker, IV
　(Washington, D.C. Office)
William P. Perkins
　(New York, N.Y. Office)
Susan Schenkel-Savitt
　(New York, N.Y. Office)
Gordon Alan Coffee
　(Washington, D.C. Office)
R. Kenneth MacCallum
　(New York, N.Y. Office)
Gary H. Glaser
　(New York, N.Y. Office)
Patrick F. Murray
　(Paris, France Office)
Timothy M. Broas
　(Washington, D.C. Office)
Leland E. Hutchinson
M. David Galainena
William A. Carmell
　(New York, N.Y. Office)
Robert J. Nobile
　(New York, N.Y. Office)

Matthias A. Lydon
Mark L. Rotert
Richard A. Hibey
　(Washington, D.C. Office)
Christopher C. McIsaac
　(Washington, D.C. Office)
Eric W. Bloom
　(Washington, D.C. Office)
Mark A. Chudzinski
Oscar A. David
Anthony DiSarro
　(New York, N.Y. Office)
Daniel G. Dolan
William J. Fellerhoff
Gregory M. Garger
John B. Griffith
Brian S. Hart
Eleni Skoulikas Kouimelis
R. Cabell Morris, Jr.
Jennifer T. Nijman
Andrew W. Ratts
Perry D. Robinson
　(Washington, D.C. Office)
Michael L. Sibarium
　(Washington, D.C. Office)
Thomas V. Skinner
Thomas J. Wiegand
N. Theodore Zink, Jr.
Daniel C. Bird, Jr.
Sol Vincent
　(Paris, France Office)
Thomas J. Gormley
　(New York, N.Y. Office)
Thomas L. Mills
　(Washington, D.C. Office)
Constantine G. Papavizas
　(Washington, D.C. Office)
Jeffrey G. Berman
　(Washington, D.C. Office)
Robert C. Miller
　(New York, N.Y. Office)
Alan B. Howard
　(New York, N.Y. Office)
Evelyn J. Lehman
　(New York, N.Y. Office)
Edmund D. Cooke, Jr.
　(Washington, D.C. Office)
Peter M. Kirby
　(Washington, D.C. Office)
John Fehrenbach
　(Washington, D.C. Office)
William N. Hall
　(Washington, D.C. Office)
Younghee J. Ottley
Robert Everett Bostrom
　(New York, N.Y. Office)

OF COUNSEL

Robert M. Bor
　(Washington, D.C. Office)
John H. More
　(Washington, D.C. Office)
Frank D. Kenney (Retired)
James L. Perkins
Carl J. Peckinpaugh
　(Washington, D.C. Office)
Mary Hutchings Reed

Dennis M. Devaney
　(Washington, D.C. Office)
Jerome H. Gerson
Patrick L. Schmidt
　(Washington, D.C. Office)
John L. Napier
　(Washington, D.C. Office)
Ivan O. Kline
　(New York, N.Y. Office)

SENIOR ATTORNEYS

Lee M. Rubenstein
Timothy J. Oxley
Anne W. Cottingham
　(Washington, D.C. Office)
Jane E. Croes
　(New York, N.Y. Office)
E. King Poor
Barry L. Salkin
　(New York, N.Y. Office)

Darrell Widen
William A. Horin
　(Washington, D.C. Office)
Suzanne S. Greene
Paul J. Collins
　(New York, N.Y. Office)
Chuncheng Lian
　(Washington, D.C. Office)

ASSOCIATES

Mary M. Anderson
Glenn Allen Andreas, III
Dirk W. Andringa
Derek G. Barella
Robert L. Beranek
Matthew F. Bergmann
Brian T. Black
Bruce R. Braun
Jeffrey A. Brown
Kimberly J. Brown
Gregory J. Bynan
Melissa A. Campbell
Christopher S. Canning
Nancy L. Carey
John P. Carreon

John W. Christopher
Gabriela F. Cleveland
Jared Ryckoff Cloud
Frith C. Crandall
Timothy S. Crisp
Jack Crowe
Ken Cunningham
　(Not admitted in IL)
Timothy J. Dable
Thomas J. Daemen
　(Not admitted in IL)
Stephen V. D'Amore
Jennifer J. Demmon
Damon DiCastri
John M. Dickman

(See Next Column)

WINSTON & STRAWN, *Chicago—Continued*

ASSOCIATES (Continued)

Peter F. Donati	Laurie M. Miller
Michael T. Donovan	Brian M. Montgomery
David J. Doyle	John E. Mooney
George M. Doyle	Kevin J. Narko
Susan W. Drewke	Brian E. Neuffer
Dane Drobny	Jennifer McCracken New
Paul A. Duffy	Christopher M. Nolan
Todd J. Ehlman	Ronald J. Nye
Dena A. Epstein	Timothy P. O'Connor
Kevin D. Finger	Peter L. O'Reilly
Karen A. Foster	Michael D. Paley
Daniel P. Fowler	Raymond Perkins
(Not admitted in IL)	Peter W. Poulos
Margaret R. Gibbs	Kenneth P. Purcell
Patrick F. Gordon	Karen Caraher Quirk
Bradley C. Graveline	Reed W. Ramsay
John R. Grier	Michael P. Roche
Douglas P. Hardy	B. Ballard Rogers
(Not admitted in IL)	Elizabeth A. Russell-Simpler
Page Elizabeth Hartzell	Anita M. Sarafa-Williams
Kyle L. Harvey	John M. Schloerb
Linda J. Haynes	Helaine A. Scholnick
Brendan P. Head	Gay R. Schreiber
Brian L. Heidelberger	Joy Sellstrom
Diana Juliet Hsu	Colleen T. Shaughnessy
Patrick D. Hughes	Michelle L. Sieger
James F. Hurst	(Not admitted in IL)
E. Nkonye Iwerebon	Gregory K. Smith
Ronald H. Jacobson	Thomas Anthony Smith
Catherine Wozniak Joyce	Vanessa L. Smith
Peter J. Kocoras	Julie L. Soloway
David E. Koropp	Thomas W. Soseman
Adam S. Kosh	Joseph A. Spiegler
Brian J. Kozlowski	Michael J. Stepek
Stephen J. Legatzke	Kathleen Ann Swien
Jean Lin	Cheryl R. Tama
Alan V. Lindquist	Lauren D. W. Tatar
Marie A. Lona	Joseph James Torres
Roger S. Lucas	John J. Tully, Jr.
Gregory J. Lynch	Ricardo E. Ugarte
Alexis MacDowall	Jennifer A. Walker
Susan L. Mahoney	John N. Walker
Donald F. McLellan	Brant C. Weidner
Carolyn F. McNiven	Edward G. Zaknoen
Samuel Mendenhall	(Not admitted in IL)
Hal B. Merck	Joseph J. Zaknoen
Robert L. Michels	Susan McCaffery Zoeller

STAFF ATTORNEY

Stephen N. Sher

For full biographical listings, see the Martindale-Hubbell Law Directory

---

COLUMBIA, Monroe Co.

CROWDER & SCOGGINS, LTD. (AV)

121 West Legion Avenue, P.O. Box 167, 62236
Telephone: 618-281-7111
Fax: 618-281-7115

Floyd E. Crowder	Alan G. Pirtle
Mark C. Scoggins	Timothy A. Gutknecht
Mark S. Rohr	Elizabeth Ann Blackston

Counsel for: First Bank, Columbia; Columbia Quarry Co.; Luhr Bros., Inc.; Monroe County Title Co.; Chicago Title Co.; Illinois Excavators, Inc.; Rogers Redi-Mix, Inc.; Tower Rock Stone Co.; Gateway FS, Inc.

For full biographical listings, see the Martindale-Hubbell Law Directory

---

CRYSTAL LAKE, McHenry Co.

MILITELLO, ZANCK & COEN, P.C. (AV)

40 Brink Street, 60014
Telephone: 815-459-8800
FAX: 815-459-8429

James G. Militello	Patrick D. Coen
Thomas C. Zanck	James L. Wright

Mark S. Saladin	James G. Militello, III
Michael L. Orndahl	Barbara H. Switzer
	Michael K. Strachan

OF COUNSEL

Michael A. Ungvarsky, Jr.

References: Home State Bank of Crystal Lake; First National Bank of Crystal Lake; McHenry State Bank; Amcore Bank N.A., Woodstock.

For full biographical listings, see the Martindale-Hubbell Law Directory

---

ZUKOWSKI, ROGERS, FLOOD & McARDLE (AV)

50 Virginia Street, 60014
Telephone: 815-459-2050
Facsimile: 815-459-9057
Chicago, Illinois Office: 100 South Wacker Drive, Suite 1502.
Telephone: 312-407-7700.
Facsimile: 312-332-1901.

PARTNERS

H. David Rogers	David W. McArdle
Richard G. Flood	Jeannine A. Thoms
	Stuart D. Gordon

ASSOCIATES

William P. Stanton	Michael J. Chmiel
Melissa J. Cooney	Maureen T. Murphy
Kelly A. Cahill	E. Regan Shepley
Michael J. Smoron	Stuart M. Nagel
	Kevin J. O'Brien

OF COUNSEL

Timothy J. Curran	Francis S. Lorenz

For full biographical listings, see the Martindale-Hubbell Law Directory

---

DANVILLE,* Vermilion Co.

GUNN & HICKMAN, P.C. (AV)

220 North Vermilion Street, P.O. Box 706, 61832
Telephone: 217-446-0880
Fax: 217-442-3901

R.R. Bookwalter (1885-1951)	Horace E. Gunn
Walter T. Gunn (1879-1956)	William R. Kesler
I. Ray Carter (1891-1960)	John B. Jenkins
Robert Z. Hickman (1907-1994)	James L. Brougher
	Fred L. Hubbard

Counsel for: First Midwest Bank/Danville; Valmont Inc.; Hartford Accident & Indemnity Co.; Nacco Materials Handling Group, Inc.; Insurance Company of North America; Commercial Union Assurance Cos.; Ranger Insurance Co.; Iroquois Federal Savings & Loan Assn.; AgriBank, FCB; Westfield Insurance Companies.

For full biographical listings, see the Martindale-Hubbell Law Directory

---

HUTTON, LAURY, HESSER, LIETZ & WILCOX (AV)

16 West Madison Street, P.O. Box 1128, 61832
Telephone: 217-446-9436
FAX: 217-446-9462

MEMBERS OF FIRM

Jackson R. Hutton (1914-1991)	Gary D. Hesser
Everett L. Laury	Gregory G. Lietz
Austin W. Buchanan	Roy G. Wilcox
(1928-1973)	

Representative Clients: General Motors Corp.; Metropolitan Life Insurance Co.; The Equitable Life Assurance Society of the U.S.; Illinois State Medical Insurance Services, Inc.; Pekin Insurance Co.; St. Paul Fire and Marine Insurance Co.; Employers Reinsurance Corp.; Hertz Corp.

For full biographical listings, see the Martindale-Hubbell Law Directory

---

DECATUR,* Macon Co.

ERICKSON, DAVIS, MURPHY, JOHNSON, GRIFFITH & WALSH, LTD. (AV)

225 South Main Street, P.O. Box 25138, 62525-5138
Telephone: 217-428-0948
Fax: 217-428-0996

Wayne E. Armstrong	Evan H. Johnson
(1916-1977)	Thomas E. Griffith
Frederick P. Erickson	Michael A. Walsh
Garry E. Davis	Christopher K. Bradley
W. Scott Murphy	Bradley T. Paisley

Representative Clients: A.E. Staley Manufacturing Company; Archer Daniels Midland Company; Cincinnati Insurance Company; Country Mutual Insurance Company; General Casualty Insurance Companies; Illinois Power Company; Illinois State Medical Insurance Exchange; Millikin University; Reliance Insurance Company; Western States Insurance Company.

For full biographical listings, see the Martindale-Hubbell Law Directory

---

KEHART, SHAFTER, HUGHES & WEBBER, P.C. (AV)

500 First of America Center, P.O. Box 871, 62525-0871
Telephone: 217-428-4689
Telecopier: 217-422-7950

Michael J. Kehart	James E. Peckert
A. James Shafter	Gregory Q. Hill
Charles C. Hughes	Deanne F. Jones
Albert G. Webber IV	Michelle K. Robinson
Mark D. Gibson	Kevin L. Kehoe

(See Next Column)

KEHART, SHAFTER, HUGHES & WEBBER P.C.—*Continued*

OF COUNSEL

Albert G. Webber III   T. G. Bolen

Representative Clients: Archer-Daniels-Midland Co.; A.E. Staley Manufacturing Co.; Mueller Co.; Illinois Power Co.; Aetna Casualty & Surety Co.; Illinois State Medical Insurance Services; Wagner Castings Co.; Decatur Newspapers Inc. - Decatur Herald & Review; Lincoln Diagnostics; Hickory Point Bank & Trust.

For full biographical listings, see the Martindale-Hubbell Law Directory

---

SAMUELS, MILLER, SCHROEDER, JACKSON & SLY (AV)

406 First of America Center, P.O. Box 1400, 62525
Telephone: 217-429-4325
Telecopier: 217-425-6313
Arthur, Illinois Office: 131 B South Vine Street.
Telephone: 217-543-3403.

MEMBERS OF FIRM

Charles Chambers Le Forgee (1888-1951)	John E. Fick
Thomas Walter Samuels (1914-1989)	Guy E. Williams
	John S. Cobb
Carl R. Miller (1930-1986)	Mark E. Jackson
E. Wayne Schroeder (Retired)	Keith W. Casteel
William M. Rice (Retired)	Darrell A. Woolums
Jerald E. Jackson	John E. Sanner
James W. Alling	Edward Q. Costa
	James T. Jackson

ASSOCIATES

Rhonda Richards Heinz   Kristen E. Fligel

OF COUNSEL

Thomas S. Sly   Nicholas J. Neiers

Representative Clients: Illinois Power Company; Norfolk Southern Corporation; Decatur Memorial Hospital; Millikin University; St. Paul Insurance Co.; Kemper Group; Gallagher-Bassett.

For full biographical listings, see the Martindale-Hubbell Law Directory

---

DE KALB, De Kalb Co.

BOYLE, CORDES & BROWN (AV)

363 East Lincoln Highway, 60115
Telephone: 815-756-6328
Fax: 815-756-8842

MEMBERS OF FIRM

Gary W. Cordes   Charles G. Brown

OF COUNSEL

John G. Boyle

Representative Clients: DeKalb Park District; First of America Bank-DeKalb; City of DeKalb.
References: First of America Bank-DeKalb; First National Bank in DeKalb.

For full biographical listings, see the Martindale-Hubbell Law Directory

---

EAST ST. LOUIS, St. Clair Co.

CARR, KOREIN, TILLERY, KUNIN, MONTROY & GLASS (AV)

412 Missouri Avenue, 62201
Telephone: 618-274-0434
Telecopier: 618-274-8369
St. Louis, Missouri Office: 701 Market Street, Suite 300.
Telephone: 314-241-4844.
Telecopier: 314-241-3525.
Belleville, Illinois Office: 5520 West Main.
Telephone: 618-277-1180.

MEMBERS OF FIRM

Rex Carr	Joel A. Kunin
Sandor Korein	Gerald L. Montroy
Stephen M. Tillery	Mark Glass

ASSOCIATES

Mark M. Silvermintz	Christine J. Moody
Martin L. Perron	Steven A. Katz (Resident, St.
Staci M. Yandle	Louis, Missouri Office)
Steven M. Wallace	Michael H. Korein
Michael B. Marker	Richard P. Paletta
Ferne P. Wolf	(Not admitted in IL)
Mark A. Brueggemann	Timothy S. Wiltsie
Robert L. King	Roger F. Wilson

OF COUNSEL

Lawrence Alan Waldman   Katherine J. Tillery

References: Union Bank; First National Bank.

For full biographical listings, see the Martindale-Hubbell Law Directory

---

DUNHAM, BOMAN & LESKERA (AV)

520 First Illinois Bank Building, 327 Missouri Avenue, 62201
Telephone: 618-271-0535
Telecopier: 618-271-2800
Belleville, Illinois Office: 208 North High Street.
Telephone: 618-235-7222.
Telecopier: 618-397-2285.
Collinsville, Illinois Office: 300 West Clay Street.
Telephone: 618-344-7734.
Telecopier: 618-344-3853.

M.F. Oehmke (1887-1963)   Wm. C. Dunham (1893-1975)
Howard Boman (1917-1985)

MEMBERS OF FIRM

John W. Leskera	Russell K. Scott
William L. Berry	Robert D. Francis
Eric C. Young	John L. Bitzer

Attorneys For: Collinsville School District #10; Hanover Insurance Co.;; Hartford Insurance Group; Home Indemnity Co.; State Farm Insurance Cos.; Transamerica Insurance Group; The Travelers Indemnity Co.; Wausau Insurance Cos.; Nationwide Insurance Co.; Atlantic Mutual Insurance Co..

For full biographical listings, see the Martindale-Hubbell Law Directory

---

*EDWARDSVILLE,** Madison Co.

BURROUGHS, HEPLER, BROOM, MacDONALD & HEBRANK (AV)

Two Mark Twain Plaza, Suite 300, 103 West Vandalia Street, P.O. Box 510, 62025-0510
Telephone: 618-656-0184
Telecopier: 618-656-1364
Email: firm@ilmolaw.com

MEMBERS OF FIRM

George D. Burroughs (1873-1977)	G. Gordon Burroughs (Of Counsel)
William G. Burroughs (1872-1952)	Larry E. Hepler
	Gordon R. Broom
Mallory L. Burroughs (1884-1965)	Theodore J. MacDonald, Jr.
	Jeffrey S. Hebrank
Jesse L. Simpson (1884-1973)	Gary E. True
David L. Simpson (Retired)	Paul W. Johnson
William J. Knapp	

ASSOCIATES

Lisa K. Franke	Daniel W. Farroll
Jack H. Humes, Jr.	David J. Gerber
Melissa Griggs	Donald J. Ohl
L. David Green	D. Scott Rendleman
J. Todd Hayes	Gary A. Meadows
J. Robert Edmonds	T. Scott Stewart

Representative Clients: Ameritech; Travelers Insurance Co.; Fireman's Fund-American Insurance Group; CILCO; Employers Union Insurance Co.; The Hartford; Illinois Power Co.; W.R. Grace; Mark Twain Bank; Prairie Farms.

For full biographical listings, see the Martindale-Hubbell Law Directory

---

*EFFINGHAM,** Effingham Co. — (Refer to Vandalia)

ELGIN, Cook & Kane Cos.

ARIANO, ANDERSON, BAZOS, HARDY & CASTILLO (AV)

A Partnership of Professional Corporations
474 Summit Street, 60120
Telephone: 847-695-2400
Telecopy: 847-695-8397
Other Elgin Office: 1250 Larkin Avenue, Suite 100.
Telephone: 847-742-8800.
Fax: 847-742-9777
Huntley, Illinois Office: 10604 North Vine Street, 60142.
Telephone: 847-669-5020.

Frank V. Ariano	William F. Castillo
Allen M. Anderson	Gary M. Vanek
Peter C. Bazos	Daniel A. Weiler
Ralph C. Hardy	Brett E. Anderson

Chadwick I. Buttell   Scott Richmond

For full biographical listings, see the Martindale-Hubbell Law Directory

---

ELIZABETH, Jo Daviess Co. — (Refer to Galena)

---

*EUREKA,** Woodford Co. — (Refer to Peoria)

FAIRBURY, Livingston Co. — (Refer to Watseka)

---

*FAIRFIELD,** Wayne Co. — (Refer to Mount Vernon)

FLORA, Clay Co. — (Refer to Mount Vernon)

GALESBURG,* Knox Co.

BARASH & STOERZBACH, P.C. (AV)

139 South Cherry Street, P.O. Box 1328, 61402-1328
Telephone: 309-341-6000
Telecopier: 309-343-7500
Email: lawfirm@misslink.net

Burrel Barash (1906-1993)	Paul L. Mangieri
Robert C. Stoerzbach	John W. Robertson
Barry M. Barash	Pamela Wilcox
Dwayne I. Morrison	John R. Rehn
Daniel B. Stoerzbach	Daniel S. Alcorn

Representative Clients: Allstate Insurance Co.; American States; City of Knoxville, Illinois; Community School District No. 208 R.O.W.V.A.; Country Mutual Insurance Co.; Economy Fire & Casualty Co.; Farmers and Mechanics Bank; Galesburg Clinic; Hartford Insurance Co.; Ken Co.

For full biographical listings, see the Martindale-Hubbell Law Directory

HATTERY, SIMPSON & WEST (AV)

Suite 402 Hill Arcade, 61401
Telephone: 309-343-6152
Telecopier: 309-343-5103
Monmouth, Illinois Office: 1025 East Broadway.
Telephone: 309-734-3150.
Telefax: 309-734-7043.
Roseville, Illinois Office: 130 North Main Street.
Telephone: 309-426-2176.
Telefax: 309-426-2177.

MEMBERS OF FIRM

John J. Hattery	Timothy E. Sullivan
Roger L. Williamson	Carol Masden Simpson
S. David Simpson	George M. Hennenfent
Thomas G. West	(Resident at Roseville Office)
Ronald D. Stombaugh (Resident at Monmouth Office)	

For full biographical listings, see the Martindale-Hubbell Law Directory

KAVANAGH, SCULLY, SUDOW, WHITE & FREDERICK, P.C.

(See Peoria)

MUSTAIN LINDSTROM & HENSON (AV)

1865 North Henderson Street, Suite 11B, 61401
Telephone: 309-344-5252
Telecopier: 309-344-3939

MEMBERS OF FIRM

Douglas D. Mustain	Ronald Henson
Robert Lindstrom	Christopher Henson
Carl E. Hawkinson	

References: The Farmers and Mechanics Bank; Norwest Bank Illinois, N.A.; First Bank; First Financial Bank; Farmers State Bank of Western Illinois; McGladrey and Pullen.

For full biographical listings, see the Martindale-Hubbell Law Directory

GALVA, Henry Co.

EVERETT & LUYMES, P.C. (AV)

P.O. Box 165, 61434
Telephone: 309-932-2001
Fax: 309-932-3151

Reynolds M. Everett (1907-1989)	James B. Young (1914-1982)
	Reynolds M. Everett, Jr.
Keith A. Luymes	

Representative Clients: Norwest Bank N.A., Galva Branch; E.W. Houghton Lumber Co.; Dixline Co., Inc.; Gateway Coop; The Swedish Consultant General; Central Soya Co., Inc.; Wyffels Hybrids, Inc.; Galva, Bishop Hill and Clover Township Fire Districts; Woodhull Cooperative Grain Co.

For full biographical listings, see the Martindale-Hubbell Law Directory

GENESEO, Henry Co. — (Refer to Cambridge)

GENEVA,* Kane Co.

SMITH, LANDMEIER & SKAAR, P.C. (AV)

15 North Second Street, 60134
Telephone: 708-232-2880
Fax: 708-232-2889

Howard E. Smith, Jr.	Allen L. Landmeier
James D. Skaar	

Brian W. Baugh	Vincent J. Elders

References: Firstar Bank, Geneva, N.A., Geneva, Illinois; State Bank of Geneva, Geneva, Illinois.

(See Next Column)

For full biographical listings, see the Martindale-Hubbell Law Directory

GOLCONDA,* Pope Co. — (Refer to Harrisburg)

GRANITE CITY, Madison Co.

LUEDERS, ROBERTSON & KONZEN (AV)

1939 Delmar Avenue, 62040
Telephone: 618-876-8500
Telecopier: 618-876-4534
Danville, Illinois Office: 809 1/2 North Gilbert.
Telephone: 217-443-0304.
Fax: 217-443-0375.

MEMBERS OF FIRM

Wesley Lueders (1896-1957)	R. Eric Robertson
Randall Robertson	Edward C. Fitzhenry, Jr.
Leo H. Konzen	Brian E. Konzen
Paul G. Foran	

Representative Clients: Central Banc System, Inc. (Trust Division); Granite City Div., National Steel Corp.; A.O. Smith Corp.; The Nestle Co.; Olin Corp.; Archers-Daniels-Midland Co.; Illinois Industrial Energy Consumers (IIEC) including General Motors Corp.

For full biographical listings, see the Martindale-Hubbell Law Directory

GREENVILLE,* Bond Co. — (Refer to Hillsboro)

HARDIN,* Calhoun Co. — (Refer to Carrollton)

HARRISBURG,* Saline Co.

JELLIFFE, FERRELL & MORRIS (AV)

108 East Walnut Street, 62946
Telephone: 618-253-7153; 253-7647
Telecopier: 618-252-1843

OF COUNSEL

Charles R. Jelliffe

MEMBERS OF FIRM

DeWitt Twente (1904-1976)	Donald V. Ferrell
Walden E. Morris	

ASSOCIATES

Michal Doerge	Thomas J. Foster

Representative Clients: Auto-Owners Insurance; Country Cos; Metropolitan Life Insurance; Ohio Casualty Group; Standard Mutual Insurance Co.; State Farm Cos.; Redland Insurance Co.; Aetna Casualty & Surety Co.; Kerr-McGee Coal Corp.; Sahara Coal Co.

For full biographical listings, see the Martindale-Hubbell Law Directory

HARVARD, McHenry Co.

ELMAN & EHARDT, LTD. (AV)

205 East Front Street, 60033-2900
Telephone: 815-943-4051
Fax: 815-934-4086

William Elman

Reference: First State Bank of Harvard, Harvard, Illinois.

For full biographical listings, see the Martindale-Hubbell Law Directory

HAVANA,* Mason Co. — (Refer to Beardstown)

HENNEPIN,* Putnam Co.

BOYLE, GOLDSMITH & BOLIN (AV)

227 East Court Street, 61327
Telephone: 815-925-7393

MEMBERS OF FIRM

Walter Durley Boyle	Roger C. Bolin
Linn C. Goldsmith	James A. Mack

References: Farmers State Bank, McNabb, Illinois; The Putnam County Bank, Hennepin, Illinois.

For full biographical listings, see the Martindale-Hubbell Law Directory

HENRY, Marshall Co. — (Refer to Princeton)

HIGHLAND PARK, Lake Co.

PASQUESI, CENGEL AND PASQUESI, P.C. (AV)

460 Central Avenue, 60035
Telephone: 847-432-4300
Fax: 847-432-8392
Email: pasquesi-cengel@msn.com

Theodore A. Pasquesi	Thomas A. Cengel
Thomas A. Pasquesi	

For full biographical listings, see the Martindale-Hubbell Law Directory

HILLSBORO,* Montgomery Co. — (Refer to Vandalia)

JACKSONVILLE, * Morgan Co.

BELLATTI, FAY, BELLATTI & BEARD (AV)

333 West State Street, P.O. Box 696, 62651
Telephone: 217-245-7111
Fax: 217-245-2832
Office also at Ashland, Illinois. Telephone: 217-476-3318.

OF COUNSEL

William L. Fay	John E. Bellatti

MEMBERS OF FIRM

Walter R. Bellatti	Timothy E. Ruppel
Daniel J. Beard	Thomas L. Veith
	Jeffrey L. Soltermann

General Counsel for: Elliott State Bank; Bound to stay Bound Banks, Inc..
District Counsel for: Illinois Power Company; Norfolk Southern Railroad.
Representative Clients: Mobil Chemical Co.; Equitable Life Assurance Society; Prudential Insurance Co.; Allstate Insurance Co.; Travelers Insurance Co.; Corepak Packaging, Inc.

For full biographical listings, see the Martindale-Hubbell Law Directory

RAMMELKAMP, BRADNEY, DAHMAN, KUSTER, KEATON, FRITSCHE & LINDSAY, P.C. (AV)

232 West State Street, P.O. Box 489, 62651
Telephone: 217-245-6177
Fax: 217-243-7322
Email: ramlkamp@netjax.com

L.O. Vaught (1865-1955)	Larry D. Kuster
Carl E. Robinson (1886-1964)	Forrest G. Keaton
Orville N. Foreman (1904-1972)	Barbara Fritsche
Albert W. Hall (1912-1986)	Nancy Lindsay
Theodore C. Rammelkamp	Maria M. Gonzalez
(Retired)	Richard R. Freeman
Marc Dahman	H. Allen Yow

Brian L. Stocker

OF COUNSEL

Robert E. Bradney

Representative Clients: Country Mutual Insurance Co.; State Farm Mutual Auto Insurance Co.; American States Insurance; Pekin Insurance Co.; USF & G; Oscar Mayer Co., Inc.; Pleasant Plains State Bank.

For full biographical listings, see the Martindale-Hubbell Law Directory

JERSEYVILLE, * Jersey Co. — (Refer to Carrollton)

JOLIET, * Will Co.

HERSCHBACH, TRACY, JOHNSON, BERTANI & WILSON (AV)

Two Rialto Square, 116 North Chicago Street, Sixth Floor, 60432
Telephone: 815-723-8500
Fax: 815-727-4846

Wayne R. Johnson	David J. Silverman
Thomas R. Wilson	Roger D. Rickmon
Richard H. Teas	John S. Gallo
George F. Mahoney, III	George M. Ferreti
Raymond E. Meader	Richard E. Vogel
A. Michael Wojtak	Kerry Anne Weber
Kenneth A. Carlson	Scherrill W. Weichbrodt
	(1930-1993)

OF COUNSEL

Donald J. Tracy	Louis R. Bertani
	John L. O'Brien

RETIRED PARTNER

Walter O. Herschbach

General Counsel for: First National Bank of Joliet; First National Bancorp.
Representative Clients: Chicago Title Insurance Co.; Vulcan Materials Company; Dow Chemical, U.S.A.; Marathon Oil Co.; Waste Management, Inc.; The Copley Press, Inc.; Citizens Utilities Co.; Empress River Casino Corporation.

For full biographical listings, see the Martindale-Hubbell Law Directory

MCKEOWN, FITZGERALD, ZOLLNER, BUCK, HUTCHISON & RUTTLE (AV)

2455 Glenwood Avenue, 60435
Telephone: 815-729-4800
Fax: 815-729-4711
Frankfort, Illinois Office: 28 Kansas Street.
Telephone: 815-469-2176.
FAX: 815-469-0295.

MEMBERS OF FIRM

Charles J. McKeown	Max E. Zollner
(1908-1985)	Douglas P. Hutchison
Paul O. McKeown (1913-1982)	David L. Ruttle
Richard T. Buck (1936-1992)	Theodore J. Jarz
Joseph C. Fitzgerald	Douglas J. McKeown

(See Next Column)

MEMBERS OF FIRM (Continued)

Timothy J. Rathbun	Michael R. Lucas
James B. Harvey	Christopher N. Wise
Kenneth A. Grey	Gary S. Mueller

ASSOCIATES

Frank S. Cservenyak, Jr.	Kurt J. Keller
Arthur J. Wilhelmi	Kelly Kathleen James

OF COUNSEL

George E. Sangmeister	Stewart C. Hutchison

Representative Clients: Caterpillar Tractor Co.; First National Bank of Lockport; Homart Development Co.; First Midwest Bank, N.A.; Silver Cross Hospital; Joliet Township High School District; Villages of: Plainfield and Mokena; Southwest Agency for Risk Management; Joliet Junior College Foundation; Health Service Systems, Inc.

For full biographical listings, see the Martindale-Hubbell Law Directory

SPESIA, AYERS, ARDAUGH & WUNDERLICH (AV)

Two Rialto Square, 116 North Chicago Street, Suite 200, 60431
Telephone: 815-726-4311
Fax: 815-726-6828

MEMBERS OF FIRM

Douglas F. Spesia	John R. Ardaugh
E. Kent Ayers	Gary L. Wunderlich
	Dinah Lennon Archambeault

ASSOCIATES

John C. Roth	John M. Spesia
	Christian G. Spesia

OF COUNSEL

Ralph C. Murphy	Kenneth E. Timm
	Arthur T. Lennon (1923-1988)

Counsel For: Commonwealth Edison Co.; Illinois Bell Telephone Co.; Country Mutual Insurance Co.; Northern Illinois Gas Co.; Metropolitan Life Insurance Co.; Indiana Consolidated Insurance Cos.; A.N.R. Pipeline Co.; Amoco Chemical Corp.; Village of New Lenox; Peoples Gas Light & Coke Company.

For full biographical listings, see the Martindale-Hubbell Law Directory

KANKAKEE, * Kankakee Co.

ACKMAN, MAREK, BOYD AND WOODRUFF, LTD. (AV)

Suite 400, One Dearborn Square, 60901
Telephone: 815-933-6681
Fax: 815-933-9985
Watseka, Illinois Office: 200 East Walnut Street.
Telephone: 815-432-5215.
Fax: 815-432-3186.
Manteno, Illinois Office: 10 North Locust Street.
Telephone: 815-468-7751.

Richard L. Ackman	Robert W. Boyd
J. Dennis Marek	Deborah A. Woodruff

James A. Devine	John J. Boyd
	(Also at Manteno Office)

Representative Clients: American States Insurance Co.; Auto Owners Insurance Co.; Consumers Illinois Water Co.; Country Mutual Insurance Co.; Farmers Insurance Group; Martin Boyer Co. Inc.; Medical Protective Co.; Economy Fire & Casualty Co.; Union Ins. Co.

For full biographical listings, see the Martindale-Hubbell Law Directory

BLANKE, NORDEN, BARMANN, KRAMER & BOHLEN, P.C. (AV)

Suite 502, 200 East Court Street, P.O. Box 1787, 60901
Telephone: 815-939-1133
Fax: 815-939-0994

Armen R. Blanke (Deceased)	Glen R. Barmann
Paul F. Blanke (Retired)	Christopher W. Bohlen
Dennis A. Norden	Michael D. Kramer

For full biographical listings, see the Martindale-Hubbell Law Directory

KEWANEE, Henry Co. — (Refer to Cambridge)

LACON, * Marshall Co. — (Refer to Hennepin)

LA SALLE, La Salle Co.

HERBOLSHEIMER, LANNON, HENSON, DUNCAN AND REAGAN, P.C. (AV)

State Bank Building, Suite 400, 654 First Street, P.O. Box 539, 61301
Telephone: 815-223-0111
FAX: 815-223-5829
Ottawa, Illinois Office: First Federal Savings Bank Building, 633 LaSalle Street, Suite 409.
Telephone: 815-434-1400.

(See Next Column)

HERBOLSHEIMER, LANNON, HENSON, DUNCAN AND REAGAN P.C., *La Salle— Continued*

George L. Herbolsheimer	John S. Duncan, III
(1911-1992)	Michael T. Reagan
R. James Lannon, Jr.	(Resident, Ottawa Office)
T. Donald Henson	Douglas A. Gift

Gary R. Eiten

Karen C. Eiten	Jill W. Klein
Michael C. Jansz	Murl Tod Melton
(Resident, Ottawa Office)	Lawrence M. Kaschak

Attorneys for: Aetna Insurance Group; St. Paul Fire and Marine Insurance Co.; State Farm Insurance Co.; La Salle State Bank; The Daily News Tribune Company, La Salle; Eureka Savings Bank; Illinois Valley Community Hospital; Community Hospital of Ottawa; Commonwealth Edison, Co.; United States Fidelity & Guaranty, Co.

For full biographical listings, see the Martindale-Hubbell Law Directory

---

LEWISTOWN, * Fulton Co. — (Refer to Macomb)

LINCOLN, * Logan Co.

WOODS & BATES (AV)

306 Clinton Street, 62656
Telephone: 217-735-1234
Fax: 217-735-1236

MEMBERS OF FIRM
William B. Bates

OF COUNSEL

Robert J. Woods (Retired)	William C. Bates, Jr. (Retired)

Representative Clients: Illico Incorporated; The Abraham Lincoln Memorial Hospital; Christian Homes, Inc.; Lincoln Firemen's Pension Fund.

For full biographical listings, see the Martindale-Hubbell Law Directory

---

LITCHFIELD, Montgomery Co. — (Refer to Vandalia)

LOUISVILLE, * Clay Co. — (Refer to Mount Vernon)

MACOMB, * McDonough Co.

FLACK, McRAVEN & STEPHENS (AV)

32 West Side Courthouse Square, 61455
Telephone: 309-837-5000
Fax: 309-836-2335

MEMBERS OF FIRM

J. Dixson McRaven	Bruce J. Biagini
Charles Haynes Flack	James Patrick Murphy
Richard D. Stephens	Joseph W. McRaven
Lawrence J. Kwacala	A. Anthony Ashenhurst

Representative Clients: Union National Bank of Macomb; Citizens National Bank of Macomb; Western States Insurance Co.; Horace Mann Mutual Insurance Co.; United States Fidelity & Guaranty; NTN-Bower; Cooper Industries; McDonough District Hospital; Macomb Public Building Commission; First Federal Bank.

For full biographical listings, see the Martindale-Hubbell Law Directory

---

MARENGO, McHenry Co.

POLLOCK, MEYERS, EICKSTEADT & WEECH, LTD. (AV)

Harris Bank/Marengo, 100 West Washington Street, 60152
Telephone: 815-568-8071
FAX: 815-568-0003

Norman J. Pollock	Richard W. Eicksteadt
Harvey A. Meyers	Charles P. Weech

LEGAL SUPPORT PERSONNEL

Carolyn I. Haverly	Mary L. Gatto

Representative Clients: Harris Bank/Marengo; The State Bank of Woodstock; Woodstone Co.; Marengo Steel Co.; Marengo Disposal Co.; Key Development Co.; Agrinetics, Inc.; Compost Enterprises; McGill Metal Products Co.

For full biographical listings, see the Martindale-Hubbell Law Directory

---

MARION, * Williamson Co.

MITCHELL & MITCHELL (AV)

404 North Monroe, P.O. Box 488, 62959-2328
Telephone: 618-993-2134
Telecopier: 618-993-8702

J. C. Mitchell	Bruce W. Mitchell

Michelle M. Schafer

Representative Clients: St. Paul Fire & Casualty Insurance Company; Illinois State Medical Insurance Exchange; Liberty Mutual Insurance Company; Shelter Insurance Company; Corporate Services, Inc.; Wal-Mart Stores, Inc.;

(See Next Column)

Atlantic Mutual Insurance Company; Farmer's Insurance Exchange; United States Fidelity and Guarantee Company.

For full biographical listings, see the Martindale-Hubbell Law Directory

---

WINTERS, BREWSTER, CROSBY & PATCHETT (AV)

111 West Main, P.O. Box 700, 62959
Telephone: 618-997-5611
Fax: 618-997-6522

MEMBERS OF FIRM

Charles D. Winters (1917-1992)	Thomas F. Crosby, III
John S. Brewster	John R. (Randy) Patchett

ASSOCIATES

Andrea Lynn McNeill	Rick Wayne Aeilts

For full biographical listings, see the Martindale-Hubbell Law Directory

---

MARSHALL, * Clark Co. — (Refer to Paris)

MATTOON, Coles Co.

CRAIG & CRAIG (AV)

1807 Broadway, P.O. Box 689, 61938-0689
Telephone: 217-234-6481
Telecopier: 217-234-6486
Mount Vernon, Illinois Office: 227 1/2 South 9th Street.
Telephone: 618-244-7511.

MEMBERS OF FIRM

Craig Van Meter (1895-1981)	Stephen L. Corn
Fred H. Kelly (1894-1971)	Richard Charles Hayden
Robert M. Werden (1908-1969)	Robert G. Grierson
George N. Gilkerson	Gregory C. Ray
(1911-1985)	Paul R. Lynch (Resident, Mount
John H. Armstrong	Vernon Office)
John P. Ewart	Kenneth F. Werts (Resident,
Richard F. Record, Jr.	Mount Vernon Office)

John L. Barger

ASSOCIATES

Joshua N. Rosen (Resident,	Theresa M. Thomson
Mount Vernon Office)	Kristine M. Tuttle
Kathleen M. Stockwell	Henry P. Villani (Resident,
	Mount Vernon Office)

OF COUNSEL
Jack E. Horsley

Counsel for: Monterey Coal Co., a Division of Exxon Coal USA, Inc.; Marathon Oil Co.; Illinois Central R.R. Co.; Okaw Building & Loan Assn., Mattoon, Illinois; The Medical Protective Insurance Co.; Consolidated Communications, Inc.; Lloyds Underwriters at London; Hartford Insurance Co.; Coles Together, a Not-For-Profit Corp.; Coles Building Corporation.

For full biographical listings, see the Martindale-Hubbell Law Directory

---

HELLER, HOLMES & ASSOCIATES, P.C. (AV)

1101 Broadway, P.O. Box 889, 61938-0889
Telephone: 217-235-2700
FAX: 217-235-0743
Email: kent@advant.com

Harlan Heller	Brent D. Holmes

H. Kent Heller

Teresa K. Righter	David Stevens

Fred Johnson

Representative Clients: Quantum Chemical Co.; First National Bank of Effingham.
References: First National Bank, Mattoon, Ill.; Central National Bank of Mattoon.

For full biographical listings, see the Martindale-Hubbell Law Directory

---

MCLEANSBORO, * Hamilton Co. — (Refer to Mount Vernon)

METROPOLIS, * Massac Co. — (Refer to Marion)

MOLINE, Rock Island Co. — (Refer to Rock Island)

MONMOUTH, * Warren Co.

BEAL, PRATT AND PRATT (AV)

57 Southeast Public Square, P.O. Box 200, 61462-0200
Telephone: 309-734-3193
Telecopier: 309-734-7279

MEMBERS OF FIRM

Edward B. Love (1906-1972)	Channing L. Pratt
Marion L. Beal	Jane Hartley Pratt

Representative Clients: State Farm Mutual Insurance Co.; Western States Insurance; Wolverine Insurance; Aetna Life and Casualty; General Casualty Company of Wisconsin; Hawkeye Security Insurance; CNA Insurance.

For full biographical listings, see the Martindale-Hubbell Law Directory

MONTICELLO, Piatt Co. — (Refer to Champaign)

MORRISON, Whiteside Co.

LUDENS, POTTER & BURCH (AV)

409 North Cherry, P.O. Box 360, 61270-0360
Telephone: 815-772-2161
Telecopier: 815-772-7440
Email: ludenspb@essex1.com

MEMBERS OF FIRM

Lawrence A. Ludens (1912-1990)   William A. Burch
Robert H. Potter   Thomas J. Potter
                Stanley B. Steines

Representative Clients: Smith Trust & Savings Bank, Morrison, Illinois; Fulton State Bank, Fulton, Illinois; Farmers State Bank, Chadwick and Mount Carroll; First Illinois National Bank, Savanna, Ill.; Country Mutual Insurance Co.; Fulton Flood Control District, Fulton, Illinois; Farmers Savings Bank, Preston, Iowa; Miles Savings Bank, Miles, Iowa; Iowa Mutual Insurance Company.

For full biographical listings, see the Martindale-Hubbell Law Directory

MORTON, Tazewell Co. — (Refer to Peoria)

MOUND CITY, Pulaski Co. — (Refer to Marion)

MOUNT STERLING, Brown Co. — (Refer to Quincy)

MOUNT VERNON, Jefferson Co.

CAMPBELL, BLACK, CARNINE & HEDIN, P.C. (AV)

P.O. Drawer C, 62864
Telephone: 618-242-3310
Fax: 618-242-3735
Email: cbch@midwest.net *URL:* http://www.cbch.com

David A. Campbell   Carl L. Favreau
Terry R. Black   Howard W. Campbell
Roy L. Carnine   (1911-1980)
Craig R. Hedin   John E. Jacobsen (1922-1985)
Mark J. Ballard   Glenn E. Moore (1911-1991)
Jerome E. McDonald   David E. Furnall (1905-1993)

Fred R. Mann   Brian E. Leach

Representative Clients: Kerr-McGee Coal Corp.; Good Samaritan Hospital; Country Mutual Insurance Co.; Southern Illinois Stone Co; Rend Lake Conservancy District; Consolidation Coal Co.; Illinois State Medical Insurance Services; State Farm Automobile Insurance Co.; John Hancock Mutual Life Insurance Co.

For full biographical listings, see the Martindale-Hubbell Law Directory

HOWARD, LEGGANS, PIERCY & HOWARD (AV)

1008 Main, P.O. Drawer U, 62864
Telephone: 618-242-6594
Fax: 618-244-7197

MEMBERS OF FIRM

George W. Howard, Jr.   David R. Leggans
  (1907-1994)   David L. Piercy
G. W. Howard, III   Jeffrey G. Howard

Representative Clients: Boatmen's Bank of South Central Illinois; First State Bank of Dix; Tri-County Electric Cooperative; Hamilton County Telephone Co-op., City of Mt. Vernon; Mt. Vernon Township; Texico State Bank.

For full biographical listings, see the Martindale-Hubbell Law Directory

MITCHELL, NEUBAUER, SHAW & HANSON, P.C. (AV)

123 South 10th Street, Mercantile Bank Building, 6th Floor, P.O. Box 1088, 62864
Telephone: 618-242-0705
Telecopier: 618-242-4820

A. Ben Mitchell   Robert E. Shaw
Timothy R. Neubauer   Leslie James Hanson

Curtis W. Martin   T. David Purcell
Michael D. McHaney   David K. Overstreet

Attorneys For: Mercantile Bank of Mt. Vernon; Mt. Vernon Grade School District #80; Stewart Brothers Oil Producers; Illinois Super Foods, Inc.; Mt. Vernon Airport Authority; Henne Excavating & Construction.; J. M. Behimer Enterprises; Crossroads Community Hospital; Marion Ford-Mercury, Inc.

For full biographical listings, see the Martindale-Hubbell Law Directory

NAPERVILLE, Du Page Co.

NADELHOFFER, KUHN, MITCHELL, MOSS, SALOGA & LECHOWICZ, P.C. (AV)

111 East Jefferson Avenue, P.O. Box 359, 60566
Telephone: 630-355-1700
FAX: 630-355-0458

Daniel L. Kuhn   Jonathan Y. Moss
Paul M. Mitchell   James E. Saloga
              Alan E. Lechowicz

Robert I. Mork   Todd J. Schneider
Annette Kraus Corrigan   Jacqueline A. Koth

OF COUNSEL
Carleton Nadelhoffer

For full biographical listings, see the Martindale-Hubbell Law Directory

NEWTON, Jasper Co. — (Refer to Lawrenceville)

OAKBROOK TERRACE, Du Page Co.

GALLAGHER & JOSLYN (AV)

One Lincoln Centre, Suite 300, 60181
Telephone: 630-916-2600
FAX: 630-916-2606

MEMBERS OF FIRM

Gerard B. Gallagher   Barry E. Garley
David L. Joslyn   Susan B. Shelton
L. Judson Todhunter   Ira E. Sussman

OF COUNSEL

Peter A. Bauer   Laurie A. Silvestri
Leonard S. DeFranco   Daniel G. McNamara

For full biographical listings, see the Martindale-Hubbell Law Directory

OLNEY, Richland Co. — (Refer to Lawrenceville)

OQUAWKA, Henderson Co. — (Refer to Monmouth)

OREGON, Ogle Co.

WILLIAMS & McCARTHY, A PROFESSIONAL CORPORATION (AV)

607 Washington Street, P.O. Box 339, 61061
Telephone: 815-732-2101
Fax: 815-732-2289
Rockford, Illinois Office: 321 West State Street, P.O. Box 219.
Telephone: 815-987-8900.
Fax: 815-968-0019. ABANET: ABA 5519.

Kim D. Krahenbuhl   Wendy S. Howarter
Clayton L. Lindsey   Kari A. Vanderzyl

Representative Clients: Anderson Industries, Inc.; Liberty Mutual Insurance Co.; Atwood Industries, Inc.; The Travelers; American Mutual Insurance Co.; Rockford Memorial Hospital; Chrysler Corp.

For full biographical listings, see the Martindale-Hubbell Law Directory

OTTAWA, La Salle Co.

HUPP, LANUTI, IRION & MARTIN, P.C. (AV)

227 West Madison, P.O. Box 768, 61350
Telephone: 815-433-3111
Fax: 815-433-9109

Joseph E. Lanuti   George C. Hupp, Jr.
Paul V. Martin   Richard L. Burton

Michelle Hutson
OF COUNSEL
George C. Hupp

Representative Clients: Country Mutual Insurance Co.; State Farm Mutual Automobile Insurance Co.; State Farm Fire & Casualty Co.; Economy Fire and Casualty Co.; Employee Mutual Casualty Co.; Sentry Insurance Co.; United Fire and Casualty Co.; Allstate Insurance Co.; Millers Mutual Insurance Assn.; Continental Casualty Co.

For full biographical listings, see the Martindale-Hubbell Law Directory

MYERS, DAUGHERITY, BERRY & O'CONOR, LTD. (AV)

130 East Madison Street, 61350
Telephone: 815-434-6206
Fax: 815-434-6203
Email: mdboc@TheRamp.net
Streator, Illinois Office: 7 North Point Drive.
Telephone: 815-672-3116.
Fax: 815-672-0738.

(See Next Column)

MYERS, DAUGHERITY, BERRY & O'CONOR LTD., *Ottawa—Continued*

John A. Berry (1912-1986)	Eugene P. Daugherity
Stephen C. Myers	Richard J. Berry
	Andrew J. O'Conor

Sheryl H. Kuzma

Representative Clients: Auto Owners Insurance, Co.; Union Bank; First National Bank of Ottawa, Illinois; Union Bancorp Inc.; First State Bank; United States Fidelity & Guaranty Co.; St. Mary's Hospital; General Casualty Insurance, Co.

For full biographical listings, see the Martindale-Hubbell Law Directory

---

PEORIA, * Peoria Co.

CASSIDY & MUELLER (AV)

1510 First Financial Plaza, 61602
Telephone: 309-676-0591
FAX: 309-676-8036

MEMBERS OF FIRM

John E. Cassidy (1896-1984)	John E. Cassidy, III
John E. Cassidy, Jr.	Timothy J. Cassidy
David B. Mueller	Timothy J. Newlin

ASSOCIATES

Andrew D. Cassidy	Christopher F. Cassidy

Representative Clients: Aetna Casualty & Surety Co.; Atchison, Topeka & Santa Fe Railroad Co.; Continental Oil Company; E.I. DuPont-DeNemours & Company; Hartford Accident & Indemnity Company; Illinois-American Water Company; John P. Pearl & Associates, Ltd.; Liberty Mutual Insurance Co.; Occidental Petroleum Company; Warner-Lambert Company.

For full biographical listings, see the Martindale-Hubbell Law Directory

---

HOWARD & HOWARD ATTORNEYS, P.C. (AV)

The Creve Coeur Building, Suite 200, 321 Liberty Street, 61602-1403
Telephone: 309-672-1483
Telecopier: 309-672-1568
Kalamazoo, Michigan Office: The Kalamazoo Building, Suite 400, 107
West Michigan Avenue.
Telephone: 616-382-1483.
Telecopier: 616-382-1568.
Bloomfield Hills, Michigan Office: The Pinehurst Office Center, Suite 101,
1400 North Woodward Avenue.
Telephone: 810-645-1483.
Telecopier: 810-645-1568.
Lansing, Michigan Office: Suite 500, The Phoenix Building, 222
Washington Square, North.
Telephone: 517-485-1483.
Telecopier: 517-485-1568.
Tampa, Florida Office: First of America Plaza, Suite 2000, 201 East
Kennedy Boulevard.
Telephone: 813-229-1483.
Telecopier: 813-229-1568.

Jon S. Faletto	Timothy J. Howard
Stephen C. Ferlmann	Diana M. Jagiella
Joseph B. Hemker	Leonard W. Sachs
Frederick G. Hoffman	Jeffrey G. Sorenson
	Sandra M. Traicoff

Representative Clients: First of America Bank Corp.; Deere & Co.; Marion Memorial Hospital; W.R. Grace & Co.; Greater Peoria Airport Authority; Central Illinois Light Co.; Chrysler Corporation; City of Peoria; Lonza Chemical Co.; Environmental Science & Engineering, Inc.

For full biographical listings, see the Martindale-Hubbell Law Directory

---

JOHNSON, BUNCE & NOBLE, P.C. (AV)

Formerly Swain, Johnson & Gard
411 Hamilton Boulevard, Suite 1900, 61602
Telephone: 309-673-0741
Facsimile: 309-673-0751

Mishael O. Gard (Retired 1992)	Kent A. Noble
Arber Johnson (1915-1982)	Frederick A. Johnson
William M. Ahlenius	Ronald B. Schertz
James H. Bunce	James P. Johnson

Michael A. Hall	Michelle Mosby-Scott

OF COUNSEL

Frederick D. Johnson	Beth J. Fitch
	Mark D. Howard

Representative Clients: LaSalle Bank, F.S.B.; The Greater Peoria Sanitary District.

For full biographical listings, see the Martindale-Hubbell Law Directory

---

KAVANAGH, SCULLY, SUDOW, WHITE & FREDERICK, P.C. (AV)

301 S.W. Adams Street, Suite 700, 61602
Telephone: 309-676-1381
FAX: 309-676-0324
East Peoria, Illinois Office: 111 West Washington Street, Suite 206B.
Telephone: 309-694-3707.
Fax: 309-676-0324.

Jay T. Hunter (1873-1953)	David J. Walvoord
Eugene Davis McLaughlin	Charles G. Roth
(1894-1958)	David J. Dubicki
Richard J. Kavanagh	Phillip B. Lenzini
(1894-1963)	Karen M. Stumpe
J. Chase Scully, Jr. (1907-1969)	Brian D. Mooty
William McDowell Frederick	Douglas S. Slayton
(1907-1991)	James W. Springer
Joseph Z. Sudow	Gary E. Schmidt
Richard C. Kavanagh	Mark W. Marlott
Julian E. Cannell	David A. Koperski

OF COUNSEL

Eugene L. White	Julian B. Venezky
	Donald G. Beste

Counsel for: First of America Bank - Illinois, N.A.; AgriBank, FCB; Construction Equipment Federal Credit Union; Travelers Insurance Co.; Phoenix Mutual Life Insurance Co.; United States Fidelity & Guaranty Co.; Equitable Life Assurance Society of the U.S.; Board of Education of the City of Peoria School District, 150; Anderson State Bank.

For full biographical listings, see the Martindale-Hubbell Law Directory

---

KINGERY, DURREE, WAKEMAN & RYAN, ASSOC. (AV)

915 Commerce Bank Building, 61602
Telephone: 309-676-3612
FAX: 309-676-1329

Arthur R. Kingery	Christopher P. Ryan
Edward R. Durree	Craig J. Reiser
Steven A. Wakeman	Philip M. O'Donnell
	James P. Lawson

Reference: Commerce Bank of Peoria.

For full biographical listings, see the Martindale-Hubbell Law Directory

---

QUINN, JOHNSTON, HENDERSON & PRETORIUS, CHARTERED (AV)

(Formerly McConnell, Kennedy, Quinn & Johnston)
227 N. E. Jefferson Street, 61602
Telephone: 309-674-1133
Telecopier: 309-674-6503
Springfield, Illinois Office: Three North, Old State Capitol Plaza, 62701.
Telephone: 217-753-1133.

Lowell R. McConnell	Stephen P. Kelly
(1911-1971)	(Resident, Springfield Office)
Golden A. McConnell	Thomas L. Perkins
(1914-1974)	Laurie M. Judd
Joseph A. Leimkuehler	Stanley L. Morris
(1931-1974)	(Resident, Springfield Office)
Thomas B. Kennedy, Sr.	James Andrew Borland
(1912-1988)	(Resident, Springfield Office)
W. Thomas Johnston	Julie A. Ward
R. Michael Henderson	David Blair Collins
Murvel Pretorius, Jr.	John F. Kamin
Bradley W. Dunham	Jeanne Wysocki Ballor
Robert H. Jennetten	Scott R. Paulsen
Charles D. Knell	Michael J. Holt
Gregory A. Cerulo	Matthew B. Smith
Paul P. Gilfillan	James Michael Kelly
John P. Fleming	Laura M. Donahue
Mary W. McDade	Mark A. Haney
	Alexander C. Giftos

OF COUNSEL

Richard E. Quinn	William C. Nicol
	John C. Newell, Jr.

Representative Clients: Allstate Insurance Co.; American International Group; Bituminous Insurance Co.; General Motors; Illinois State Medical Insurance Services, Inc.; Pekin Insurance; Peoria Journal Star, Inc.; St. Paul Insurance Co.

For full biographical listings, see the Martindale-Hubbell Law Directory

Peoria—*Continued*

SCHIFF HARDIN & WAITE (AV)

A Partnership including Professional Corporations
Founded 1864
300 Hamilton Boulevard, Suite 100, 61602
Telephone: 309-673-2800
Facsimile: 309-673-2801
Chicago, Illinois Office: 7200 Sears Tower, 60606.
Telephone: 312-876-1000.
Facsimile: 312-258-5600.
TWX: 910-221-2463.
Washington, D.C. Office: 1101 Connecticut Avenue, N.W., 20036.
Telephone: 202-778-6400.
Facsimile: 202-778-6460.
New York, New York Office: 150 East 52nd Street, Suite 2900, 10022.
Telephone: 212-753-5000.
Facsimile: 212-753-5044.
Merrillville, Indiana Office: 8585 Broadway, Suite 842, 46410.
Telephone: 219-738-3820.
Facsimile: 219-738-3826.

RESIDENT PARTNERS

Theodore L. Eissfeldt   David G. Kabbes

RESIDENT ASSOCIATES

Jason A. Zellers

For full biographical listings, see the Martindale-Hubbell Law Directory

---

ROBERT C. STRODEL, LTD. (AV)

927 Commerce Bank Building, 61602
Telephone: 309-676-4500
Fax: 309-676-4566

Robert C. Strodel

For full biographical listings, see the Martindale-Hubbell Law Directory

---

SUTKOWSKI & WASHKUHN LTD. (AV)

124 Southwest Adams Street, Suite 560, 61602
Telephone: 309-673-4500
Facsimile: 309-673-2195

Edward F. Sutkowski   Dean B. Rhoads
Wilson C. Washkuhn   Robert H. Rhode

Steven P. Oates   M. Christine Keithley

Representative Clients: RLI Corp.; Bielfeldt & Company; DMI, Inc.; Laidlaw Corp.; David J. Vaughn Investments, Inc.; Good's Furniture House, Inc.; Excel Foundry & Machine, Inc.; Creative Products of Rossville, Inc.; Otto Baum & Sons, Inc.; Associated Anesthesiologists, S.C.

For full biographical listings, see the Martindale-Hubbell Law Directory

---

SWAIN, HARTSHORN & SCOTT (AV)

411 Hamilton Boulevard, Suite 1806, 61602-1104
Telephone: 309-637-1700; Toll Free (USA): 800-728-1806
Fax: 309-637-1708
URL: http://www.peorialaw.com

MEMBERS OF FIRM

Tim Swain   Donald M. Hartshorn
Robert W. Scott, Jr.

OF COUNSEL

Timothy W. Swain

For full biographical listings, see the Martindale-Hubbell Law Directory

---

WESTERVELT, JOHNSON, NICOLL & KELLER (AV)

14th Floor, First Financial Plaza, 411 Hamilton Boulevard, 61602
Telephone: 309-671-3550
FAX: 309-671-3588

MEMBERS OF FIRM

Frank T. Miller (1873-1948)   Thomas M. Hayes
O. P. Westervelt (1887-1970)   Thomas G. Harvel
Eugene R. Johnson (1899-1981)   Roger E. Holzgrafe
David A. Nicoll (1913-1993)   Daniel L. Johns
Homer W. Keller   Kevin D. Schneider
Robert D. Jackson   James R. Morrison
Wayne L. Hanold   L. Lee Smith
Ross E. Canterbury   Thomas W. O'Neal
James D. Broadway   Charles Couri

ASSOCIATES

Thomas A. McConnaughay   Bradly M. Butler
Barbara Kay Stille   Joseph J. Bembenek
J. Phillip Krajewski   Joseph B. VanFleet
Timothy S. Flaherty   Alan L. Hellman

(See Next Column)

COUNSEL

Seth M. Dabney   Arthur G. Greenberg

Representative Clients: Allstate Ins. Cos.; ASARCO, Inc.; Caterpillar Inc.; The Firestone Tire & Rubber Co.; John Deere Co.; The Methodist Medical Center of Illinois; Metropolitan Life Insurance Co.; Peoria and Pekin Union Ry. Co.; Sears, Roebuck and Co.; State Farm Insurance Cos.

For full biographical listings, see the Martindale-Hubbell Law Directory

---

PETERSBURG,* Menard Co. — (Refer to Springfield)

QUINCY,* Adams Co.

SCHMIEDESKAMP, ROBERTSON, NEU & MITCHELL (AV)

525 Jersey, P.O. Box 1069, 62306
Telephone: 217-223-3030
Telecopier: 217-223-1005

MEMBERS OF FIRM

Carl G. Schmiedeskamp   William M. McCleery, Jr.
  (1898-1987)   Ted M. Niemann
John T. Robertson (1916-1995)   Gena J. Awerkamp
Theodore Grant House   Brett K. Gorman
  (1930-1980)   John G. Stevenson, Jr.
Richard B. Neu   (Not admitted in IL)
Delmer R. Mitchell, Jr.   Harold B. Oakley
Dennis W. Gorman   Michael A. Bickhaus
William G. Keller, Jr.   Curtis T. Lovelace

Representative Clients: Mercantile Trust & Savings Bank; Moorman Manufacturing Co.; Travelers Insurance Co.; Hartford Accident & Indemnity Co.; Aetna Casualty & Surety Co.; Knapheide Mfg. Co.; Harris Corp.; Bituminous Casualty Corp.; Quincy Compressor Division of Colt Industries, Inc.

For full biographical listings, see the Martindale-Hubbell Law Directory

---

SCHOLZ, LOOS, PALMER, SIEBERS & DUESTERHAUS (AV)

625 Vermont Street, 62301
Telephone: 217-223-3444; 217-222-7620
FAX: 217-223-3450

MEMBERS OF FIRM

Richard F. Scholz, Sr.   James L. Palmer
  (1901-1975)   Steven E. Siebers
Delbert Loos (1909-1993)   Joseph A. Duesterhaus
Charles A. Scholz   Christopher G. Scholz

Representative Clients: Heintz Electric Co.; Sunset Home; Quincy Notre Dame Foundation; First Bankers Trust Company, N.A.; Merchants Wholesale, Inc.; Quincy Newspapers, Inc.
Local Counsel: Firemen's Fund Insurance; Niemann Foods Inc.

For full biographical listings, see the Martindale-Hubbell Law Directory

---

ROBINSON,* Crawford Co. — (Refer to Lawrenceville)

ROCHELLE, Ogle Co.

FEARER, NYE, AHLBERG & CHADWICK (AV)

420 Fourth Avenue, P.O. Box 117, 61068
Telephone: 815-562-2156
Fax: 815-562-2158
Oregon, Illinois Office: 209 South Fifth Street, P.O. Box 256, 61061.
Telephone: 815-732-6113.
Fax: 815-732-3193.

MEMBERS OF FIRM

Philip H. Nye, Jr.   James G. Ahlberg
Robert T. Chadwick

Represent: Del Monte Corp.; John Hancock Mutual Life Insurance Co.; Rochelle Savings and Loan Assoc.; Kishwaukee College; Kemper Insurance Group; First National Bank & Trust Co. of Rochelle.

For full biographical listings, see the Martindale-Hubbell Law Directory

---

ROCKFORD,* Winnebago Co.

HOLMSTROM & KENNEDY, P.C. (AV)

800 North Church Street, P.O. Box 589, 61105
Telephone: 815-962-7071
Fax: 815-962-7181

John Holmstrom, Jr.   Bradley T. Koch
Richard D. Gaines   Gregory P. Guth
Norman E. Lindstedt   Kim M. Casey
Philip R. Frankfort   Roberta L. Holzwarth
Donald L. Moore   Michael J. Schappert

Michael Jon Shalbrack

Bryan G. Selander   Alexander J. Mezny
Eugene G. Doherty   Lisa A. Leitter

Representative Clients: First Financial Bank; Lawyers Title Insurance Corp. (Rockford Title Co.); CNA Insurance; Northern Illinois Gas Co.; Nylint Corp.; Swedish American Health System; Premier Financial Services, Inc.;

(See Next Column)

HOLMSTROM & KENNEDY P.C., *Rockford—Continued*

St. Paul Fire & Marine Insurance Co.; Illinois State Medical Inter-Insurance Exchange; Illinois Central Gulf Railroad.

For full biographical listings, see the Martindale-Hubbell Law Directory

LORD, BISSELL & BROOK (AV)

120 West State Street, Suite 200, 61101
Telephone: 815-963-8050
Chicago, Illinois Office: Suites 2600-3600 Harris Bank Building, 115 South LaSalle Street, 60603.
Telephone: 312-443-0700.
Telecopy: 312-443-0570.
Cable Address: "Lowirco."
Telex: 25-0336.
Los Angeles, California Office: 300 South Grand Avenue, 90071-3200.
Telephone: 213-485-1500.
Telecopy: 213-485-1200.
Telex: 18-1135.
Atlanta, Georgia Office: One Atlantic Center, 1201 West Peachtree Street, N.W., Suite 3700, 30309.
Telephone: 404-870-4600.
Telecopy: 404-872-5547.

RESIDENT PARTNERS

David P. Faulkner | Jeffry S. Spears

RESIDENT ASSOCIATES

Charles A. Egner | Amy E. Shappert

For full biographical listings, see the Martindale-Hubbell Law Directory

WILLIAMS & McCARTHY, A PROFESSIONAL CORPORATION (AV)

321 West State Street, P.O. Box 219, 61105-0219
Telephone: 815-987-8900
Fax: 815-968-0019
URL: http://www.wilmac.com
Oregon, Illinois Office: 607 Washington Street. P.O. Box 339.
Telephone: 815-732-2101.
Fax: 815-732-2289.

John R. Kinley	Scott C. Sullivan
Elmer C. Rudy	Carol N. Bailey
Thomas S. Johnson (President, Williams & McCarthy)	Jane E. Durgom-Powers
	James P. Devine
Edward R. Telling, III	J. Mark Doherty
Russell D. Anderson	John J. Holevas
John E. Pfau	Timothy J. Rollins
Richard A. Berman	Clayton L. Lindsey (Resident Partner, Oregon, Illinois Office)
John W. Rosenbloom	
John L. Shepherd	
Terry D. Anderson	Stephen E. Balogh
Kim D. Krahenbuhl (Resident Partner, Oregon, Illinois Office)	Robert E. Luedke
	Marc C. Gravino
	Thomas P. Sandquist

Carl A. Ecklund	Ronald A. Barch
Wendy S. Howarter (Resident, Oregon, Illinois Office)	Troy E. Haggestad
	Kari A. Vanderzyl (Resident, Oregon, Illinois Office)

OF COUNSEL

John C. McCarthy

Representative Clients: Aircraft Gear Corp.; Anderson Industries, Inc.; Gallagher Bassett Insurance Co.; Liberty Mutual Insurance Co.; Atwood Industries, Inc.; The Travelers; American Mutual Insurance Co.; Rockford Health Systems; Chrysler Corp.; USF&G, West Bend.

For full biographical listings, see the Martindale-Hubbell Law Directory

ROCK ISLAND, * Rock Island Co.

KATZ, McHARD, BALCH, LEFSTEIN & FIEWEGER, P.C. (AV)

200 Plaza Office Building, 1705 Second Avenue, P.O. Box 3250, 61204-3250
Telephone: 309-788-5661
Facsimile: 309-788-5688

Isador I. Katz (1905-1996)	Samuel S. McHard
Bruce L. Balch	Dale G. Haake
Stuart R. Lefstein	Linda E. Frischmeyer
Martin H. Katz	Philip E. Koenig
Peter C. Fieweger	Brian S. Nelson
Frank R. Edwards	Stephen T. Fieweger
Robert T. Park	John F. Doak

Lori R. Lefstein	Jonathan J. Heiple

Attorneys for: Augustana College; O'Rourke Bros., Inc.; International Limousines, Ltd.; Reynolds State Bank.
Local Attorneys for: Aetna Casualty & Surety Co.; Maryland Casualty Co.; Liberty Mutual Insurance Co.; CIGNA Cos.; Country Mutual Insurance Co.; Cincinnati Insurance Co.

(See Next Column)

For full biographical listings, see the Martindale-Hubbell Law Directory

LANE & WATERMAN (AV)

500 Rock Island Bank Building, 61201
Telephone: 309-786-1600
Fax: 309-786-1794
Davenport, Iowa Office: 220 North Main Street, Suite 600.
Telephone: 319-324-3246.
Fax: 319-324-1616.

Robert A. Van Vooren	Peter J. Benson
Charles E. Miller	Constance A. Schriver
Dana M. Craig	John D. Telleen
Robert V. P. Waterman, Jr.	Richard A. Davidson

ASSOCIATES

Mary Woodburn Patch

For full biographical listings, see the Martindale-Hubbell Law Directory

WESSELS, STOJAN & STEPHENS P.C. (AV)

423 Seventeenth Street, Suite 101, P.O. Box 4300, 61204-4300
Telephone: 309-794-9400
Telecopier: 309-794-9386
Waterloo, Iowa Office: Suite 2, 227 East San Marnan Drive.
Telephone: 319-232-5904.
Fax: 319-232-7181.

Pete M. Wessels	B. Douglas Stephens
Clark J. Stojan	Mark A. Tarnow
Joel K. Heriford	

Caroline K. Bawden

OF COUNSEL

Henry G. Borden (Retired)

Representative Clients: First of America Bank-Quad Cities, N.A.; First National Bank of Moline.

RUSHVILLE, * Schuyler Co. — (Refer to Beardstown)

SALEM, * Marion Co. — (Refer to Centralia)

SHAWNEETOWN, * Gallatin Co. — (Refer to Harrisburg)

SHEFFIELD, Bureau Co. — (Refer to Mattoon)

SHELBYVILLE, * Shelby Co. — (Refer to Mattoon)

SPRINGFIELD, * Sangamon Co.

BROWN, HAY & STEPHENS (AV)

700 First National Bank Building, P.O. Box 2459, 62701-1489
Telephone: 217-544-8491
Fax: 217-544-9609

MEMBERS OF FIRM

Harvey B. Stephens	William F. Trapp
Edward J. Cunningham	Paul Bown
Robert M. Magill	Almon A. Manson, Jr.
Norman P. Jones	Dwight H. O'Keefe, III
Robert A. Stuart, Jr.	Donald R. Tracy
J. Patrick Joyce, Jr.	Emmet A. Fairfield
Eric L. Grenzebach	Denise M. Druhot
Jeffery M. Wilday	Harvey M. Stephens

COUNSEL

Ben L. DeBoice	Simon L. Friedman

ASSOCIATES

Elizabeth W. Anderson	James W. Bruner
Andrew T. Pribe	Lorilea Burkette
John Edward Childress	Frank I. Choi

General Counsel for: FirstBank of Illinois Co.; The First National Bank of Central Illinois; U.S. Electric Co.; Littler Trust Estate; Memorial Medical Center; Dot Foods, Inc.
Local Counsel for: Consolidation Coal Co.; Panhandle Eastern Pipe Line Co.; AMICA Mutual Insurance Co.

For full biographical listings, see the Martindale-Hubbell Law Directory

GIFFIN, WINNING, COHEN & BODEWES, P.C. (AV)

1 West Old State Capitol Plaza, Suite 600 Myers Building, P.O. Box 2117, 62705
Telephone: 217-525-1571
Facsimile: 217-525-1710
Email: jswartzn@counsel.com

(See Next Column)

GIFFIN, WINNING, COHEN & BODEWES P.C.—*Continued*

D. Logan Giffin (1890-1980)
Montgomery S. Winning (1892-1966)
C. Terry Lindner (1903-1987)
Alfred F. Newkirk (1904-1980)
James M. Winning (Retired)

Robert S. Cohen
Herman G. Bodewes
John L. Swartz
Carol Hansen Posegate
R. Mark Mifflin
Thomas P. Schanzle-Haskins, III

Gregory K. Harris

Arthur B. Cornell, Jr,
David A. Herman

Michael Joseph Mannion
Jane N. Denes

Stephan J. Roth

Representative Clients: Illinois State University; Magna Bank of Central Illinois, N.A.; Grinnell Mutual Reinsurance Co.; Illinois League of Financial Institutions; Southern Illinois University School of Medicine; Central Illinois Builders of A.G.C.; Great Central Insurance Cos.

For full biographical listings, see the Martindale-Hubbell Law Directory

GRAHAM AND GRAHAM (AV)

1201 South Eighth Street, 62703
Telephone: 217-523-4569

MEMBERS OF FIRM

James M. Graham (1851-1945)
James J. Graham (1880-1965)
Hugh J. Graham (1877-1972)

Hugh J. Graham, Jr. (1910-1994)
Hugh J. Graham, III

ASSOCIATES

Richard J. Wilderson
Nancy Eckert Martin

Dean W. Jackson
Bradley E. Huff

Counsel for: Hospital Sisters Health System.
Representative Clients: Chicago and Illinois Midland Railway; SPCSL Railway; St. Anthony's Memorial Hospital, Effingham; St. Mary's Hospital, Decatur; St. John's Hospital, Springfield.

For full biographical listings, see the Martindale-Hubbell Law Directory

HECKENKAMP, SIMHAUSER, WARD & ZERKLE (AV)

700 East Adams, Suite 202, P.O. Box 2378, 62705
Telephone: 217-528-5627
Fax: 217-528-2097
Email: hswz700@aol.com

Robert G. Heckenkamp
Walter J. Simhauser

William F. Fuiten (1946-1977)
Steven Carl Ward

James K. Zerkle

PARALEGALS

Gae A. Kelly

Julie Enlow

Representative Clients: The Travelers Insurance Co.; Springfield Fire & Casualty Insurance Co.; Charles E. Robbins, Real Estate and Development; Burwell Oil Services, Inc.; Petersburg Plumbing and Heating Co.,; Wareco, Inc.; First Financial Insurance Co.
Reference: Magna Bank of Illinois, Springfield.

For full biographical listings, see the Martindale-Hubbell Law Directory

LOEWENSTEIN, HAGEN, OEHLERT AND SMITH, P.C. (AV)

1204 South Fourth Street, 62703
Telephone: 217-525-1199
Telecopier: 217-522-6047

Ralph H. Loewenstein
Henry C. Hagen

Allen J. Oehlert
Gary L. Smith

For full biographical listings, see the Martindale-Hubbell Law Directory

MOHAN, ALEWELT, PRILLAMAN & ADAMI (AV)

First of America Center, Suite 325, 1 North Old Capitol Plaza, 62701-1323
Telephone: 217-528-2517
Telecopier: 217-528-2553
Email: fprillam@counsel.com.

MEMBERS

Edward J. Alewelt
Fred C. Prillaman

Paul E. Adami
Cheryl Stickel Neal

Stephen F. Hedinger

OF COUNSEL

James T. Mohan

ASSOCIATES

Becky S. McCray

Patrick D. Shaw

Joel A. Benoit

For full biographical listings, see the Martindale-Hubbell Law Directory

SORLING, NORTHRUP, HANNA, CULLEN AND COCHRAN, LTD. (AV)

Formerly Sorling, Catron and Hardin
800 Illinois Building, 607 East Adams Street, P.O. Box 5131, 62705
Telephone: 217-544-1144
Telecopier: 217-522-3173

Carl A. Sorling (1896-1991)
B. Lacey Catron, Jr. (1912-1959)
John H. Hardin (1909-1978)
George William Cullen (1917-1986)
Thomas L. Cochran (1916-1994)
Patrick V. Reilly
William S. Hanley
R. Gerald Barris
Stephen A. Tagge
Michael A. Myers
Carl Clark Germann

Gary A. Brown
Stephen R. Kaufmann
Frederick B. Hoffmann
William R. Enlow
Craig S. Burkhardt
Michael C. Connelly
Scott C. Helmholz
John A. Kauerauf
James M. Morphew
Stephen J. Bochenek
David A. Rolf
Stephen P. Horvat, Jr.

Margaret (Peggy) J. Ryan
Mark K. Cullen
Thomas H. Wilson
Todd Michael Turner

Charles J. Northrup
R. Lee Allen, Jr.
Paul D. Durbin
Michael T. Kokal

Elizabeth A. Urbance

OF COUNSEL

Charles H. Northrup

Philip E. Hanna

William B. Bates

Counsel for: Central Illinois Public Service Company; Bank One Springfield; Doctors Hospital, Springfield, Ill; Illini Dairy Queen, Inc.; Springfield Airport Authority.
Representative Clients: Monsanto Agricultural Products Co.; Franklin Life Insurance Co.; WICS-TV, Inc.

For full biographical listings, see the Martindale-Hubbell Law Directory

---

STREATOR, La Salle Co.

MYERS, DAUGHERITY, BERRY & O'CONOR, LTD. (AV)

7 Northpoint Drive, 61364
Telephone: 815-672-3116
Fax: 815-672-0738
Ottawa, Illinois Office: 130 East Madison Street.
Telephone: 815-434-6206.

John A. Berry (1912-1986)
Stephen C. Myers

Eugene P. Daugherity
Richard J. Berry

Andrew J. O'Conor

For full biographical listings, see the Martindale-Hubbell Law Directory

---

SULLIVAN,* Moultrie Co.

MCLAUGHLIN AND FLORINI, LTD. (AV)

16 South Washington Street, P.O. Box 233, 61951
Telephone: 217-728-7325
Fax: 217-728-8122

Joseph L. McLaughlin (1884-1963)

James M. McLaughlin
Joseph V. Florini

Representative Clients: Scott State Bank, Bethany, Ill.; Shank Road Oil & Culvert Co., Mattoon, Ill.; State Bank of Arthur, Ill.; First Mid-Illinois Bank & Trust.

For full biographical listings, see the Martindale-Hubbell Law Directory

---

TOLEDO,* Cumberland Co. — (Refer to Mattoon)

TUSCOLA,* Douglas Co.

RAYMOND LEE, JR. (AV)

Route 36 at Ohio Street, 61953
Telephone: 217-253-5414
Fax: 217-253-2320

Representative Clients: Furnished upon request.
References: First Federal Bank, Tuscola, Illinois; Tuscola National Bank, Tuscola, Illinois.

For full biographical listings, see the Martindale-Hubbell Law Directory

---

URBANA,* Champaign Co.

PHEBUS, WINKELMANN, WONG & BRAMFELD (AV)

136 West Main Street, P.O. Box 1008, 61801
Telephone: 217-337-1400
Telecopier: 217-337-1607

Darius E. Phebus
Wendell G. Winkelmann

Joseph W. Phebus
Betsy Pendleton Wong

John F. Bramfeld

(See Next Column)

PHEBUS, WINKELMANN, WONG & BRAMFELD, *Urbana—Continued*

　　　Thorpe Facer　　　　　　　　　Nancy J. Glidden
　　　　　　　　　Thomas F. Koester

Representative Clients: Busey Bank; Illinois Central Railroad Co.; Consolidated Rail Corp.; National Railroad Passenger Corp.; Peoples Gas Light and Coke Co.; National Gas Pipeline Company of America; International Brotherhood of Electrical Workers Local Union 601; Plumbers and Steamfitters Local Union 149; Urbana Park District.

For full biographical listings, see the Martindale-Hubbell Law Directory

---

WEBBER & THIES, P.C. (AV)

202 Lincoln Square, P.O. Box 189, 61803-0189
Telephone: 217-367-1126
FAX: 217-367-3752

Charles M. Webber (1903-1991)	David C. Thies
Richard L. Thies	Holten D. Summers
Craig R. Webber	Daniel P. Wurl
Carl M. Webber	John E. Thies

　Alan R. Singleton　　　　　　Phillip R. Van Ness
　　　　　　　Tammy Koester Parks

For full biographical listings, see the Martindale-Hubbell Law Directory

---

VANDALIA,* Fayette Co.

BURNSIDE DEES JOHNSTON & CHOISSER (AV)

First National Bank Building, 62471
Telephone: 618-283-3260
Fax: 618-283-2851

MEMBERS OF FIRM

J. G. Burnside (1873-1969)	Joe Dees
Robert G. Burnside	Jack B. Johnston
	Dale F. Choisser

General Counsel for: First National Bank; The First State Bank of St. Peter; State Bank of Farina; South-Central Regional Planning And Development Commission; S&S Urethane, Inc.
Local Counsel for: Pekin Insurance Co.

For full biographical listings, see the Martindale-Hubbell Law Directory

---

VIENNA,* Johnson Co. — (Refer to Harrisburg)

WATERLOO,* Monroe Co. — (Refer to Belleville)

WATSEKA,* Iroquois Co.

ACKMAN, MAREK, BOYD AND WOODRUFF, LTD. (AV)

200 East Walnut Street, 60970
Telephone: 815-432-5215
Fax: 815-432-3186
Kankakee, Illinois Office: Suite 400, One Dearborn Square.
Telephone: 815-933-6681.
Fax: 815-933-9985.
Manteno, Illinois Office: 10 North Locust Street.
Telephone: 815-468-7751

　J. Dennis Marek　　　　　　　Robert W. Boyd

　　　　　　　James A. Devine

Representative Clients: American States Insurance Co.; Consumers Illinois Water Co.; Country Mutual Insurance Co.; Farmers Insurance Group; Martin Boyer Co. Inc.; Medical Protective Co.; Union Insurance Co.

For full biographical listings, see the Martindale-Hubbell Law Directory

---

RAZZANO & KINZER (AV)

115 East Walnut Street, P.O. Box 300, 60970
Telephone: 815-432-2100; 432-4987
Piper City, Illinois Office: 12 West Peoria Street.
Telephone: 815-686-2243.
Clifton, Illinois Office: 1st National Bank Building.
Telephone: 815-694-2939.

MEMBERS OF FIRM

Wallace J. Bell (1903-1980)	A. William Razzano
Kenneth A. Smith (1909-1971)	James B. Kinzer, III

OF COUNSEL
　　　　　　Robert L. Dannehl

Representative Clients: First Trust & Savings Bank of Watseka, IL; Iroquois Memorial Hospital, Watseka, IL; Meier Oil Company; Manito Transit Co.; First National Bank of Clifton, IL; Bankers Life Co.; John Hancock Life Insurance Co.; Prudential Insurance Co.; United State Fidelity and Guaranty Co.; American States Insurance Co.

For full biographical listings, see the Martindale-Hubbell Law Directory

---

SUNDERLAND, MURPHY, SPENN AND JOHNSON (AV)

130 West Cherry Street, 60970
Telephone: 815-432-3936
Fax: 815-432-3112
Milford, Illinois Office: Corner of Axtel & Lyle Streets.
Telephone: 815-889-4928.
Danforth, Illinois Office: 100 South Front Street.
Telephone: 815-269-2744.
Cissna Park, Illinois Office: 102 North Second.
Telephone: 815-457-2136.

MEMBERS OF FIRM

Louis B. Sunderland	Theodore R. Spenn
Patrick J. Murphy	Kay Lawfer Johnson

　　　　　　Kevin H. Luebchow

Representative Clients: Central Bank, Ashkum, Illinois; Cissna Park State Bank; Citizens State Bank of Milford; Farmers State Bank of Danforth; Iroquois Title Co.; Iroquois Farmers State Bank; Iroquois Federal Savings and Loan Assn.; Milford Building & Loan Assn.; Watseka Farmers Grain Co.

For full biographical listings, see the Martindale-Hubbell Law Directory

---

WAUKEGAN,* Lake Co.

DIVER, GRACH, QUADE & MASINI (AV)

First Federal Savings and Loan Building, 111 North County Street, 60085
Telephone: 847-662-8611
FAX: 847-662-2960

MEMBERS OF FIRM

Clarence W. Diver (1883-1962)	David R. Quade
Thomas W. Diver	Robert J. Masini
Brian S. Grach	Sarah P. Lessman

　Heidi J. Aavang　　　　　　Donna-Jo Rodden Vorderstrasse
　　　　　Paula Vincich Randall

OF COUNSEL
　　　　　　David L. Hazan

A list of Representative Clients will be furnished upon request.
Reference: First Midwest Bank of Waukegan.

For full biographical listings, see the Martindale-Hubbell Law Directory

---

WHEATON,* Du Page Co.

CLAUSEN MILLER P.C. (AV)

Suite 1700, 2100 Manchester Road, 60187-2402
Telephone: 630-668-9100
Telecopier: 630-668-9169
Chicago, Illinois Office: 10 South La Salle Street, 60603-1098.
Telephone: 312-855-1010.
Telecopier: 312-606-7777. Internet E-Mail: clientservices@clausen.com.
European Affiliated Law Firm: Clausen Miller Europe GIE, LaGiraudière Larroze & Associés, 58, Rue de Monceau, 75008 Paris, France.
Telephone: 33.1.44.95.25.25.
Telecopier: 33.1.44.95.25.00.
Telex: 649 622 F
and: 53, Avenue des Artes, 1040 Brussels, Belgium.
Telephone: 32.2.511.44.66.
Telecopier: 32.2.514.56.62.
New York, N.Y. Office: One Chase Manhattan Plaza, 10005.
Telephone: 212-805-3900.
Telecopier: 212-805-3939.
Newark, New Jersey Office: One Gateway Center, Suite 2600, 07102-5397.
Telephone: 201-645-0564.
Telecopier: 201-622-3423.
Troy, Michigan Office: 3155 West Big Beaver Road, 48084-3007.
Telephone: 810-816-0500.
Telecopier: 810-816-1011.

　　　　　　Thomas H. Ryerson

　Nick Alexander　　　　　　　James P. Marsh
　　　　　　Michael E. Zidek

References: The First National Bank of Chicago; La Salle National Bank.

For full biographical listings, see the Martindale-Hubbell Law Directory

---

DONOVAN & ROBERTS, P.C. (AV)

104 East Roosevelt Road, Suite 202, P.O. Box 417, 60189-0417
Telephone: 630-668-4211
Fax: 630-668-2076

　Keith E. Roberts, Sr.　　　　　Keith E. (Chuck) Roberts, Jr.
　　　　　　James J. Konetski

(See Next Column)

DONOVAN & ROBERTS P.C.—*Continued*

Marie F. Leach	Robert M. Skutt
Mark J. Lyons	Robert J. Lentz
Andrew L. Dryjanski	Rosemarie Calandra

For full biographical listings, see the Martindale-Hubbell Law Directory

---

PICCIONE, KEELEY & ASSOCIATES, LTD. (AV)

County Farm Professional Park, 122 South County Farm
　Road, 60187-4523
Telephone: 630-653-8000
Telefax: 630-653-8029

John J. Piccione	Lynn R. Conrad
Patrick C. Keeley	Alison S. Franklin
Mark W. Tader	Thomas A. Jackson

For full biographical listings, see the Martindale-Hubbell Law Directory

---

RATHJE, WOODWARD, DYER & BURT (AV)

300 East Roosevelt Road, P.O. Box 786, 60189
Telephone: 708-668-8500
Fax: 708-668-9218

MEMBERS OF FIRM

Henry J. Burt, Jr.	Gary L. Taylor
R. Terence Kalina	John F. Garrow
Henry S. Stillwell, III	Reese J. Peck
	Tracy D. Kasson

ASSOCIATES

Daniel C. McCabe	Craig R. Belford
Rebecca S. Kahn	Mark W. Daniel

OF COUNSEL
Peter A. Zamis

Attorneys for: NBD Wheaton Bank.
Local Attorneys for: State Farm Insurance Co.; Amoco; Brinker International; Citizens Utilities; Commonwealth Edison Co.; Liberty Mutual Insurance Co.; McDonald's Corporation; The Ryland Group; Target Stores, Inc.

For full biographical listings, see the Martindale-Hubbell Law Directory

---

WINCHESTER, * Scott Co. — (Refer to Jacksonville)

WOODSTOCK, * McHenry Co.

CALDWELL, BERNER & CALDWELL (AV)

100 1/2 Cass Street, P.O. Box 1289, 60098
Telephone: 815-338-3300
Fax: 815-338-0015

MEMBERS OF FIRM

William I. Caldwell (1908-1971)	Michael T. Caldwell
James E. Berner	William I. Caldwell, Jr.
	Jeffrey A. Rouhandeh

Representative Clients: Amcore Bank N.A., Woodstock; Allstate Insurance Co.; American States Insurance Co.; Capitol Indemnity Corp.; Maryland Casualty Co.; Kemper Insurance Group; Northwestern National Insurance Group; C.N.A. Group; Universal Underwriters Insurance Co.; American Home Group.

For full biographical listings, see the Martindale-Hubbell Law Directory

---

KELL, NUELLE & LOIZZO (AV)

121 East Calhoun Street, 60098
Telephone: 815-338-4511
FAX: 815-338-0002

MEMBERS OF FIRM

Vette E. Kell	Thomas F. Loizzo
Thomas D. Nuelle	John Larry Phillips
	Gerald P. Lenzen

Representative Clients: General Casualty Companies; ITT Hartford; Home Insurance Co.; State Farm Mutual Automobile Insurance Co.; The Travelers Insurance Co.; Ohio Casualty Insurance Co.; Ohio Farmers Insurance Co.; Kemper Insurance Group; American Family Insurance Co.
Reference: State Bank of Woodstock.

For full biographical listings, see the Martindale-Hubbell Law Directory

---

YORKVILLE, * Kendall Co. — (Refer to Joliet)

INDIANA

ALBION, * Noble Co. — (Refer to Kendallville)

ANGOLA, * Steuben Co. — (Refer to Kendallville)

(See Next Column)

BATESVILLE, Ripley & Franklin Cos.

EATON & ROMWEBER (AV)

13 East George Street, 47006
Telephone: 812-934-5735
Fax: 812-934-6041
Versailles, Indiana Office: 123 South Main Street. P.O. Box 275.
Telephone 812-689-5111.
Fax: 812-689-5165.

MEMBERS OF FIRM

Larry L. Eaton	Anthony A. Romweber

ASSOCIATES
Evelina Coker Brown

For full biographical listings, see the Martindale-Hubbell Law Directory

---

BEDFORD, * Lawrence Co.

STEELE, STEELE, McSOLEY & McSOLEY (AV)

Bank One Building, Suite One, 1602 I Street, 47421
Telephone: 812-279-3513
Fax: 812-275-3504

MEMBERS OF FIRM

Ruel W. Steele (1908-1992)	Brent E. Steele
Byron W. Steele	Patrick S. McSoley
	Darlene Steele McSoley

Representative Clients: Bank One, Bloomington, NA, Bedford Branch; The First National Bank of Mitchell; The Times Mail (newspaper); Ralph Rogers & Co., Inc.; Indiana Bell Telephone Co.; Texas Gas Transmission Corporation; U.S. Gypsum Company.

For full biographical listings, see the Martindale-Hubbell Law Directory

---

BERNE, Adams Co. — (Refer to Fort Wayne)

BLOOMFIELD, * Greene Co. — (Refer to Bloomington)

BLOOMINGTON, * Monroe Co.

BUNGER & ROBERTSON (AV)

226 South College Square, P.O. Box 910, 47402-0910
Telephone: 812-332-9295
Fax: 812-331-8808

MEMBERS OF FIRM

Len E. Bunger, Jr. (1921-1993)	Joseph D. O'Connor III
Don M. Robertson	James L. Whitlatch
Thomas Bunger	Samuel R. Ardery

ASSOCIATES

Margaret M. Frisbie	William J. Beggs
	John W. Richards

Representative Clients: Aetna Insurance Companies; Bloomington Hospital; Commercial Union Group; Indiana Insurance Co.; Liberty Mutual Insurance; Medical Protective Co.; Monroe County Community School Corp.; Professional Golf Car, Inc.; Prudential Insurance Company of America; State Farm Automobile Insurance Co.

For full biographical listings, see the Martindale-Hubbell Law Directory

---

BLUFFTON, * Wells Co. — (Refer to Fort Wayne)

BOONVILLE, * Warrick Co. — (Refer to Evansville)

BREMEN, Marshall Co.

KIZER & NEU (AV)

1406 West Plymouth Street, P.O. Box 158, 46506
Telephone: 219-546-2626
FAX: 219-546-2608
Plymouth, Indiana Office: 319 West Jefferson Street. P.O. Box 158.
Telephone: 219-936-2169.
FAX: 219-936-2642.

James H. Neu (1917-1991)	Mark E. Wagner

Counsel for: The First State Bank, Bourbon, Indiana; Bremen Castings, Inc.; Bornemann Products, Inc.; Universal Bearings, Inc., all of Bremen, Indiana.

For full biographical listings, see the Martindale-Hubbell Law Directory

---

BROWNSTOWN, * Jackson Co. — (Refer to Seymour)

CANNELTON, * Perry Co. — (Refer to Tell City)

CARMEL, Hamilton Co.

CAMPBELL KYLE PROFFITT (AV)

Suite 400, 650 East Carmel Drive, 46032
Telephone: 317-846-6514
FAX: 317-843-8097
Noblesville, Indiana Office: 198 South Ninth Street, P.O. Box 2020.
Telephone: 317-773-2090.
Fax: 317-776-5051.

(See Next Column)

CAMPBELL KYLE PROFFITT, *Carmel—Continued*

MEMBERS OF FIRM

John D. Proffitt (Resident)　　　William E. Wendling, Jr.
Robert F. Campbell (Resident)　　　(Resident)
Deborah L. Farmer (Resident)　　　Anne Hensley Poindexter
　　　　　　　　　　　　　　　(Resident)

ASSOCIATES

Todd L. Ruetz (Resident)　　　Melissa A. Clark (Resident)

Representative Clients: Bridgewater/Firestone, Inc.; Vernon Insurance Cos.; Carmel Clay Schools; Clay Township Regional Waste District.

For full biographical listings, see the Martindale-Hubbell Law Directory

---

CHESTERTON, Porter Co.

HARRIS, WELSH & LUKMANN (AV)

107 Broadway, 46304
Telephone: 219-926-2114
Fax: 219-926-1503

MEMBERS OF FIRM

Michael C. Harris　　　Robert A. Welsh
L. Charles Lukmann, III

ASSOCIATES

Matthew R. Kaczmarek

Representative Clients: Northern Indiana Commuter Transportation District; Duneland School Corp.; Town of Burns Harbor, Indiana; Town of Pines; Town of Chesterton; Paulson Oil Co.; Steel & Machinery Transport, Inc.; Lake Erie Land Corps.; Porter Memorial Hospital; NBD Bank, NA.

For full biographical listings, see the Martindale-Hubbell Law Directory

---

CLARKSVILLE, Clark Co.

MAYER, VOGT, SMITH & PALMQUIST (AV)

501 Eastern Boulevard, 47129
Telephone: 812-288-1235
Louisville, Kentucky: 502-584-5800
Fax: 812-288-1240

MEMBERS OF FIRM

John M. Mayer (1913-1986)　　　Samuel H. Vogt, Jr.
Louis G. Mayer (1918-1991)　　　William E. Smith, III
John M. Mayer, Jr.　　　Steven K. Palmquist
　　　　　Cara Wells Stigger

ASSOCIATES

Susan Wagner Hynes　　　Kerstin Ann Schuhmann

Representative Clients: First Savings Bank, FSB; PNC Bank Indiana, Inc. *Approved Attorneys for:* Commonwealth Land Title Insurance Co.; Ticor Title Insurance Company; Old Republic National Title Insurance Company. *References:* First Savings Bank, FSB; PNC Bank Indiana, Inc.

For full biographical listings, see the Martindale-Hubbell Law Directory

---

CLINTON, Vermillion Co. — (Refer to Brazil)

COLUMBUS,* Bartholomew Co.

SHARPNACK, BIGLEY, DAVID & RUMPLE (AV)

321 Washington Street, P.O. Box 310, 47202-0310
Telephone: 812-372-1553
Fax: 812-372-1567

MEMBERS OF FIRM

Julian Sharpnack (1879-1968)　　　John R. Rumple
Lew G. Sharpnack (1905-1968)　　　Timothy J. Vrana
Thomas C. Bigley (1912-1978)　　　John A. Stroh
Maurice A. David (Retired)　　　Jeffrey S. Washburn
Thomas C. Bigley, Jr.　　　Joan Tupin Crites

Representative Clients: Irwin Union Bank and Trust Co.; PSI Energy, Inc.; State Farm Mutual Insurance Cos.; American States Insurance Co.; Home News Enterprises; Centra Federal Credit Union; Richards Elevator, Inc.; GRE Insurance Group; Indiana Farmers Insurance; Glick Farms, Inc.

For full biographical listings, see the Martindale-Hubbell Law Directory

---

CONNERSVILLE,* Fayette Co. — (Refer to Rushville)

CRAWFORDSVILLE,* Montgomery Co.

BERRY, CAPPER, DONALDSON & TULLEY (AV)

131 North Green Street, P.O. Box 429, 47933
Telephone: 317-362-7340
Fax: 317-362-5023

Andrew N. Foley (1909-1963)　　　Richard G. Tulley
John R. Berry (1907-1986)　　　John S. Capper, IV
　　　　　S. Bryan Donaldson

Representative Clients: Elston Bank & Trust Co.; R. R. Donnelley & Sons Co. (Crawfordsville Division); Linden State Bank; City of Crawfordsville, Ind.

For full biographical listings, see the Martindale-Hubbell Law Directory

---

HENTHORN, HARRIS AND TAYLOR, P.C. (AV)

122 East Main Street, P.O. Box 645, 47933
Telephone: 317-362-4440
Facsimile: 317-362-4521

Robert B. Harding (1908-1977)　　　C. Rex Henthorn
Carl F. Henthorn (Retired)　　　J. Lamont Harris
　　　　　Daniel L. Taylor

Stuart K. Weliever

Representative Clients: Sommer Metalcraft Corp.; U.S.F. & G. Co.; Indiana Insurance Co.; Bank One, Crawfordsville, N.A.; Farm Credit Services; Montgomery Savings Association; USA Life One Insurance Co. of Indiana; Heartland Co-Op, Inc.; Layne & Myers Grain Co., Inc.; Crawfordsville Journal-Review.

For full biographical listings, see the Martindale-Hubbell Law Directory

---

WERNLE, RISTINE & AYERS, L.P.C. (AV)

414 Ben Hur Building, 47933
Telephone: 317-362-2640
FAX: 317-362-8796

OF COUNSEL

Robert F. Wernle　　　Richard O. Ristine

MEMBERS OF FIRM

James E. Ayers　　　Gregory H. Miller

ASSOCIATES

Elizabeth A. Justice　　　Christopher V. Redmaster
　　　　　John K. Baird

LEGAL SUPPORT PERSONNEL

PARALEGAL

Louisa I. Blaich

Representative Clients: Wabash College; Lincoln Federal Savings Bank; Tri-County Bank and Trust Co.; Ameritech, Inc.; Banjo Corporation; North Montgomery Community School Corp.; Thrifty Wholesale Supply Inc.; United States Fidelity & Guaranty Co.; Ohio Casualty Co.

For full biographical listings, see the Martindale-Hubbell Law Directory

---

DANVILLE,* Hendricks Co.

HINKLE GIBBS & GUNDLACH (AV)

35 West Marion Street, 46122
Telephone: 317-745-5441
Fax: 317-745-0490
Avon, Indiana Office: 8499 East U.S. 36.
Telephone: 317-272-2677.
Fax: 317-272-5266.

MEMBERS OF FIRM

Ansel R. Pollard (1884-1971)　　　Kevin J. Hinkle
R. Steven Keck (Retired)　　　J. Gordon Gibbs, Jr.
Harlan H. Hinkle　　　Philip L. Gundlach

Representative Clients: Hendricks Community Hospital; Town of Lizton; The North Salem State Bank; Hendricks County Bank and Trust Co.; Plainfield Chrysler-Plymouth, Inc.; Kiefer & Associates, Inc.; ERA Preston Realtors; Dayton Enterprises, Inc.
References: Hendricks County Bank and Trust Co.; The North Salem State Bank.

For full biographical listings, see the Martindale-Hubbell Law Directory

---

ELKHART, Elkhart Co.

CHESTER, PFAFF & BROTHERSON (AV)

317 West Franklin Street, P.O. Box 507, 46515-0507
Telephone: 219-294-5421
Fax: 219-522-1476

MEMBERS OF FIRM

Robert A. Pfaff　　　Edward J. Chester
　　　　　Glenn E. Killoren

OF COUNSEL

Willard H. Chester　　　James R. Brotherson

ASSOCIATES

Robert C. Whippo　　　Craig A. Carpenter

LEGAL SUPPORT PERSONNEL

Wanda S. Wyrick (Paralegal)　　　Laura L. Ezzell (Paralegal)

For full biographical listings, see the Martindale-Hubbell Law Directory

---

ENGLISH,* Crawford Co. — (Refer to Tell City)

EVANSVILLE,* Vanderburgh Co.

BAMBERGER, FOREMAN, OSWALD AND HAHN (AV)

7th Floor Hulman Building, P.O. Box 657, 47704-0657
Telephone: 812-425-1591
Fax: 812-421-4936

(See Next Column)

BAMBERGER, FOREMAN, OSWALD AND HAHN—*Continued*

OF COUNSEL

William P. Foreman   Charles E. Oswald, Jr.

Jeffrey R. Kinney

MEMBERS OF FIRM

Frederick P. Bamberger	Fred S. White
(1903-1983)	R. Thomas Bodkin
Robert H. Hahn	Terry G. Farmer
George A. Porch	Roderick W. Clutter, Jr.
Robert M. Becker	Michele S. Bryant

David D. Bell

ASSOCIATES

J. Herbert Davis	M. Beth Burger
Marjorie A. Meeks	Charles A. Compton
Jason Lueking	S. Brent Almon
Catherine A. Nestrick	Laura A. Scott
Christopher Lee	Lori A. Yarbor

Sean M. Georges

Representative Clients: Aetna Life and Casualty Group; AT&T; CNB Bancshares Inc.; Dow Chemical Co.; Medical Protective Ins. Co.; Southern Indiana Gas and Electric Company; St. Mary's Medical Center of Evansville, Inc.; State Farm Mutual Automobile Ins. Co.; Travelers Ins. Co.; Welborn Clinic/HMO.

For full biographical listings, see the Martindale-Hubbell Law Directory

BOWERS, HARRISON, KENT & MILLER, LLP (AV)

25 N.W. Riverside Drive, P.O. Box 1287, 47706-1287
Telephone: 812-426-1231
Fax: 812-464-3676

MEMBERS OF FIRM

F. Wesley Bowers	Paul J. Wallace
Joseph H. Harrison	David E. Gray
David V. Miller	Gregory A. Kahre
Paul E. Black	Timothy J. Hubert
Gary R. Case	James P. Casey
Arthur D. Rutkowski	Thomas A. Massey
George C. Barnett, Jr.	Greg A. Granger
Terry Noffsinger	Joseph H. Harrison, Jr.

Lawrence L. Grimes

ASSOCIATES

Cedric Hustace	Elizabeth Healy Campbell
Christopher E. Carl	Douglas K. Briody
Michelle Agostino Cox	Holly H. Wilhelmus
Sara Harrison Zeidler	J. Edward Wicht

Paul Bernard Greif

OF COUNSEL

Addison M. Beavers   K. Wayne Kent

William G. Greif

Division Counsel in Indiana for: Southern Railway Co.
Representative Clients: Permanent Federal Savings Bank; Citizens Realty & Insurance, Inc.

For full biographical listings, see the Martindale-Hubbell Law Directory

KAHN, DEES, DONOVAN & KAHN (AV)

P.O. Box 3646, 47735-3646
Telephone: 812-423-3183
Fax: 812-423-3841
Email: evvlaw@k2d2.com

MEMBERS OF FIRM

Isidor Kahn (1887-1963)	Jon D. Goldman
Robert Kahn (Retired)	Brian P. Williams
Arthur R. Donovan (Retired)	G. Michael Schopmeyer
Alan N. Shovers	David L. Clark
Thomas O. Magan	John E. Hegeman
Larry R. Downs	Jeffrey K. Helfrich
Robert H. Brown	Jeffrey W. Ahlers

ASSOCIATES

Marjorie J. Scharpf	Mark L. Boos
Richard O. Hawley, Jr.	Mark A. McAnulty
Kent A. Brasseale, II	Mark W. Clark
Martha J. Posey	Allison K. Comstock

OF COUNSEL

Harry P. Dees   Marilyn R. Ratliff

Counsel for: Deaconess Hospital, Inc.; Keller Crescent Co., Inc.; Guardian Automotive Trim, Inc.; Atlas Van Lines, Inc.; Daughters of Charity of St. Vincent de Paul of Indiana, Inc.; Siemens Electromechanical Components, Inc.; Cresline Plastic Pipe Co., Inc.; Orion Electric (American) Inc.; University of Southern Indiana; Toyota Motor Corporate Services of North America, Inc.

For full biographical listings, see the Martindale-Hubbell Law Directory

KIGHTLINGER & GRAY (AV)

One Riverfront Place, Suite 210, 20 N.W. First Street, 47708
Telephone: 812-464-9508
Telecopier: 812-464-9511
Indianapolis, Indiana Office: Market Square Center, Suite 660, 151 North Delaware Street, 46204.
Telephone: 317-638-4521.
Telecopier: 317-636-5917.
New Albany, Indiana Office: Pinnacle Centre, Suite 200, 3317 Grant Line Road, P.O. Box 6727, 47151.
Telephone: 812-949-2300.
Telecopier: 812-949-8556.

RESIDENT PARTNERS

Brent R. Weil   David R. Sauvey

Jill Reifinger Marcrum

RESIDENT ASSOCIATES

Timothy A. Klingler	Jeffrey R. Walker
Dirck H. Stahl	Daniel A. Barfield

Representative Clients: American Family Mutual Insurance Co.; American International Group; American States; Associated Aviation Underwriters; Black & Decker (U.S., Inc.); Government Employees Insurance Co.; Mack Trucks, Inc.; Reliance Insurance Group.
Reference: INB National Bank.

For full biographical listings, see the Martindale-Hubbell Law Directory

STATHAM, JOHNSON & McCRAY (AV)

215 North West Martin Luther King Jr. Boulevard, P.O. Box 3567, 47734-3567
Telephone: 812-425-5223
Facsimile: 812-421-4238

MEMBERS OF FIRM

Herman L. McCray (1905-1984)	Thomas J. Kimpel
D. Bailey Merrill (1912-1993)	Donald J. Fuchs
William E. Statham	Gerald F. Allega
R. Eugene Johnson	Douglas V. Jessen
Michael McCray	Keith E. Rounder

ASSOCIATES

Thomas P. Norton	Brent Alan Raibley
Susan M. Swick	Bryan S. Rudisill

Neil Byron Chapman

Representative Clients: The Citizens National Bank of Evansville; Fidelity Federal Bancorp; First Indiana Bank; NBD Banking, N.A.; University of Evansville; Welborn Memorial Baptist Hospital; ALCOA; Cincinnati Insurance Company; Pennsylvania Hospital Insurance Co.; St. Paul Insurance Cos.

For full biographical listings, see the Martindale-Hubbell Law Directory

WRIGHT, EVANS AND DALY (AV)

425 Main Street, 47708
Telephone: 812-424-3300
Fax: 812-421-5588

MEMBERS OF FIRM

Claude B. Lynn (Retired)	Gerald H. Evans
Donald R. Wright	R. Lawrence Daly

Christopher L. Lucas

Representative Clients: Browning-Ferris Industries of Indiana, Inc.; Castle Contracting Co., Inc.; Computing Solutions, Inc.; Happy China Trading Corporation; Manpower Incorporated of Evansville; Need-A-Nurse, Inc.; Mills-Wallace and Associates, Inc. Design Professionals; Servicemaster of Evansville, Inc.; Siemers Glass Company, Inc.; Southwestern Indiana Mental Health Center, Inc.

For full biographical listings, see the Martindale-Hubbell Law Directory

FORT WAYNE,* Allen Co.

BAKER & DANIELS (AV)

111 East Wayne Street, Suite 800, 46802
Telephone: 219-424-8000
FAX: (219) 460-1700
Indianapolis, Indiana Office: 300 North Meridian Street.
Telephone: 317-237-0300.
South Bend, Indiana Office: First Bank Building, 205 West Jefferson Boulevard.
Telephone: 219-234-4149.
Elkhart, Indiana Office: 301 B South Main Street, Suite 307.
Telephone: 219-296-6000.
Washington, D.C. Office: 1701 K Street, N.W. Suite 400.
Telephone: 202-785-1565.

MEMBERS OF FIRM

F. B. Shoaff (1877-1961)	John F. Hoffman
John D. Shoaff (1908-1982)	Joseph W. Kimmell, II
Maclyn T. Parker	Anthony Niewyk
Martin A. Weissert	David A. Scott
George T. Dodd	Lawrence E. Shine
Robert T. Hoover	N. Reed Silliman
Thomas M. Shoaff	John R. Burns, III

(See Next Column)

BAKER & DANIELS, *Fort Wayne—Continued*

MEMBERS OF FIRM (Continued)

Steven H. Hazelrigg	Timothy J. Haffner
Steven L. Jackson	David P. Irmscher
Richard H. Blaich	Albert J. Dahm
Michael L. James	Douglas Dormire Powers
Jon A. Bomberger	Kevin R. Erdman
	Jeanne E. Longsworth

ASSOCIATES

Maria C. Campo	M. Randall Spencer
Jeffrey O. Davidson	Debra L. Schroeder
(Not admitted in IN)	Anthony M. Zirille
David B. Kagan	Kevin T. Duncan
(Not admitted in IN)	Amee R. McKim
Robert D. Moreland	Lisa M. Dillman
Jeffrey A. Townsend	David J. Kuker
Holly Demarest Warshauer	Paul P. Kiel
Gary D. Johnson	Brian C. Pauls
	Ginger L. Ringenberg

Representative Clients: Central Soya Co., Inc.; Essex Group, Inc.; ITT Corp.; Lincoln National Corp.; Lutheran Hospital of Indiana; Norwest Bank, Indiana, NA; Tokheim Corp.; Shambaugh & Son, Inc.; General Motors Corp.; Eli Lilly and Co.

For full biographical listings, see the Martindale-Hubbell Law Directory

BARRETT & McNAGNY (AV)

215 East Berry Street, P.O. Box 2263, 46801-2263
Telephone: 219-423-9551
Telecopier: 219-423-8924

MEMBERS OF FIRM

James M. Barrett (1852-1929)	Patrick G. Michaels
Ted S. Miller	Thomas M. Fink
Phil M. McNagny (1886-1969)	Richard E. Fox
Otto E. Grant, Jr. (1914-1969)	Gary J. Rickner
James M. Barrett, Jr.	John D. Walda
(1895-1979)	James P. Fenton
Byron F. Novitsky (1909-1988)	John P. Martin
J. A. Bruggeman (1906-1996)	Alan VerPlanck
Mentor Kraus (Retired)	Dennis C. Becker
J. Michael O'Hara	Thomas P. Yoder
Howard L. Chapman	Thomas M. Kimbrough
Paul S. Steigmeyer	Ronald J. Ehinger
John M. Clifton, Jr.	Stephen L. Chapman
Robert S. Walters	Thomas A. Herr
John F. Lyons	Thomas J. Markle
N. Thomas Horton, II	Michael P. O'Hara
Richard D. Robinson	Thomas M. Niezer
	Anthony M. Stites

ASSOCIATES

Renee R. Neeld	Kevin K. Fitzharris
David R. Steiner	Cathleen M. Shrader
	Anne E. Simerman

OF COUNSEL

William F. McNagny	James M. Barrett, III

Counsel for: Aetna Group; B.F. Goodrich Co.; Consolidated Rail Corp.; Franklin Electric Co., Inc.; Fort Wayne National Bank; Hartford Group; Northern Indiana Public Service Co.; OmniSource Corp.; Phelps Dodge Magnet Wire Corp.; Union Federal Savings Bank of Indianapolis.

For full biographical listings, see the Martindale-Hubbell Law Directory

BECKMAN, LAWSON, SANDLER, SNYDER & FEDEROFF (AV)

800 Standard Federal Plaza, 46802
Telephone: 219-422-0800
Facsimile: 219-420-1013
Syracuse, Indiana Office: 200 West Main Street.
Telephone: 219-457-5727.
Facsimile: 219-457-2056.

MEMBERS OF FIRM

Jack W. Lawson	William L. Sweet, Jr.
Frank J. Gray	John H. Brandt
Howard B. Sandler	Jeffrey L. Gage
Stephen R. Snyder	Thomas J. Goeglein
James A. Federoff	Jon A. Bragalone
	Brian J. T'Kindt

ASSOCIATES

Douglas R. Adelsperger	David D. Cornwell
Travis S. Friend	Craig R. Patterson
Jack C. Birch	Edward J. Ormsby
Robert L. Nicholson	Daniel B. Starr
W. Randall Kammeyer	Laurie A. Singh

OF COUNSEL

Frederick A. Beckman	Neil F. Sandler
	Douglas E. Miller

Reference: NBD, N.A.

For full biographical listings, see the Martindale-Hubbell Law Directory

BEERS, MALLERS, BACKS & SALIN (AV)

110 West Berry Street, Suite 1100, 46802
Telephone: 219-426-9706
Fax: 219-420-1314
LaGrange, Indiana Office: 108 West Michigan Street.
Telephone: 219-463-4949.
FAX: 219-463-2789.

MEMBERS OF FIRM

E. Ross Adair (1907-1983)	Robert Owen Vegeler
Ramon S. Perry (1913-1980)	G. William Fishering
Thomas E. Ruzzo (1942-1985)	Richard E. Beers
James F. Dumas (1911-1992)	Peter G. Mallers
George P. Mallers (1928-1994)	R. Scott Perry, Jr.
Orvas E. Beers	James P. Posey
Vincent J. Backs	John W. Bowers
Stephen W. Adair	Kurt Russell Bachman
	Stacey L. Katz

ASSOCIATES

Roy F. Kiplinger	Heidi Bieberich Adair
Kevin P. Bruns	Charles R. Shedlak

OF COUNSEL

James W. Jackson	Kenneth W. Maxfield

Representative Client: Farmers Mutual Insurance Company of Noble Co.

For full biographical listings, see the Martindale-Hubbell Law Directory

HELMKE, BEAMS, BOYER & WAGNER (AV)

300 Metro Building, Berry & Harrison Streets, 46802-2242
Telephone: 219-422-7422
Telecopier: 219-422-6764

MEMBERS OF FIRM

Walter E. Helmke (1901-1976)	Robert A. Wagner
Walter P. Helmke	J. Timothy McCaulay
R. David Boyer	Daniel J. Borgmann
	Trina Glusenkamp Gould

OF COUNSEL

Glen J. Beams	John G. Reiber

Representative Clients: Aalco Distributing Co., Inc.; Brotherhood Mutual Insurance Co.; Fremont Community Schools; Teco, Inc.; Air-O-Mat, Inc.; Leo Distributors, Inc.; The City of Fort Wayne, Indiana; Foellinger Foundation, Inc.

For full biographical listings, see the Martindale-Hubbell Law Directory

STANLEY A. LEVINE (AV)

Fort Wayne National Bank Building, Suite 2008, 110 West Berry Street, 46802
Telephone: 219-422-7431
Facsimile: 219-422-7433

For full biographical listings, see the Martindale-Hubbell Law Directory

ROTHBERG & LOGAN (AV)

(Formerly, Rothberg, Gallmeyer, Fruechtenicht & Logan)
2100 Fort Wayne National Bank Building, 110 West Berry Street, P.O. Box 11647, 46859-1647
Telephone: 219-422-9454
Telefax: 219-422-1622

MEMBERS OF FIRM

Sol Rothberg (1910-1993)	F. L. Dennis Logan
Thomas A. Gallmeyer	Scott T. Niemann
(1922-1981)	David R. Smelko
George E. Fruechtenicht	Dennis F. Dykhuizen
(1925-1996)	Catherine C. Ediger
Thomas D. Logan	Anne Carney
Martin T. Fletcher, Sr.	Gregory Martin Cole
	Michael T. Deam

ASSOCIATES

James A. Butz	J. Rickard Donovan
Brian L. Nehrig	N. Jean Schendel
Daniel G. McNamara	Samuel J. Talarico, Jr.

OF COUNSEL

John H. Heiney	Loren K. Allison

Counsel for: Parkview Memorial Hospital; Cameron Memorial Community Hospital; Norwest Bank Indiana, N.A.; NBD Bank, N.A.; Parkview Health System; Azar's, Incorporated; Fort Wayne-Allen County Airport Authority; Fort Wayne Public Transportation Corporation; Avis Industrial Corp.; Farm Credit Services of Mid-America, ASA; Slater Fort Wayne Federal Credit Union.

For full biographical listings, see the Martindale-Hubbell Law Directory

Fort Wayne—Continued

SHAMBAUGH, KAST, BECK & WILLIAMS (AV)

600 Standard Federal Plaza, 46802-2405
Telephone: 219-423-1430
Fax: 219-422-9038

MEMBERS OF FIRM

Willard Shambaugh (1897-1976)	Daniel E. Serban
Michael H. Kast	John B. Powell
Stephen J. Williams	Timothy L. Claxton
Edward E. Beck	James D. Streit

Counsel for: Hagerman Construction Corp.; Rogers Markets, Inc.; K & H Realty Corp.; Olive B. Cole Foundation; M. E. Raker Foundation, Inc.; Associates Financial Services Co., of Indiana, Inc.; Professional Federal Credit Union; Fort Wayne Education Association; American Ambassador Casualty Company; CBT Credit Services, Inc.

For full biographical listings, see the Martindale-Hubbell Law Directory

FOWLER,* Benton Co.

BARCE & RYAN (AV)

103 North Jackson Avenue, P.O. Box 252, 47944-0252
Telephone: 317-884-0383
Fax: 317-884-0445
Kentland, Indiana Office: 301 East Graham Street, P.O. Box 338, 47951-0338.
Telephone: 219-474-5158.
Fax: 219-474-6610.

MEMBER OF FIRM

John W. Barce	J. Edward Barce (Resident)

For full biographical listings, see the Martindale-Hubbell Law Directory

WEIST & KEPNER (AV)

Weist Building, P.O. Box 101, 47944
Telephone: 317-884-1840
Fax: Available Upon Request

William B. Weist	Rex W. Kepner

References: Fowler State Bank, Fowler, Indiana; Farmers and Merchants Bank, Boswell, Indiana.

For full biographical listings, see the Martindale-Hubbell Law Directory

FRANKLIN,* Johnson Co.

LA GRANGE, FREDBECK & DEPPE (AV)

Nine East Court, 46131
Telephone: 317-736-5138
Fax: 317-736-8268

Richard L. La Grange (Retired)
MEMBERS OF FIRM

Melvin N. Fredbeck	Brian J. Deppe
Eric W. Fredbeck	

Representative Clients: Clark-Pleasant Community School Corp.; Central Nine Vocational-Technical School; Johnson Memorial Hospital; Syndicate Theatres, Inc.; Town of Bargersville; Indiana Masonic Home; Hensley Township; Nineveh Township; Clark Township; Annual Reports, Inc.; Franklin United Methodist Home.

For full biographical listings, see the Martindale-Hubbell Law Directory

GARY, Lake Co.

STULTS, STULTS, FORSZT & PAWLOWSKI, A PROFESSIONAL ASSOCIATION (AV)

3637 Grant Street, P.O. Box 15050, 46409-5050
Telephone: 219-887-7000
Fax: 219-884-1179

Fred M. Stults, Jr.	Robert P. Forszt
Frederick M. Stults, III	David R. Pawlowski

Representative Clients: American Road Insurance Co.; Employers Casualty Co.; Indiana Insurance Co.; SAFECO Insurance Co.

For full biographical listings, see the Martindale-Hubbell Law Directory

GOSHEN,* Elkhart Co.

YODER, AINLAY, ULMER & BUCKINGHAM (AV)

130 North Main Street, P.O. Box 575, 46527-0575
Telephone: 219-533-1171
Telecopier: 219-534-4174
Email: yaub@thelocalnet.com

(See Next Column)

MEMBERS OF FIRM

George L. Pepple (1907-1963)	R. Gordon Lord
John D. Ulmer	Craig M. Buche
George E. Buckingham	Michael F. DeBoni
Gregory A. Hartzler	Alan L. Weldy
B. Douglas Hayes	

ASSOCIATES

Cassidy C. Fritz	Denise C. Davis
Mark A. Matthes	Bodie J. Stegelmann
David E. Swihart	

OF COUNSEL

Frank E. Yoder	Charles W. Ainlay

Counsel for: CTB, Inc.; Elkhart County Farm Bureau Credit Union; Elkhart County Government; First State Bank of Middlebury; Goshen College; Goshen General Hospital; Goshen Rubber Co.; HomeCrest Corporation; State Farm Insurance Cos.; Town of Middlebury, IN.

For full biographical listings, see the Martindale-Hubbell Law Directory

HAMMOND, Lake Co.

GALVIN, GALVIN & LEENEY (AV)

5231 Hohman Avenue, 46320
Telephone: 219-933-0380
Fax: 219-933-0471

MEMBERS OF FIRM

Edmond J. Leeney (1897-1978)	Carl N. Carpenter
Timothy P. Galvin, Sr. (1894-1993)	John E. Chevigny
	Timothy P. Galvin, Jr.
Francis J. Galvin, Sr. (1902-1995)	Patrick J. Galvin
	W. Patrick Downes

William G. Crabtree II	Julie A. Rosenwinkel
John H. Lloyd, IV	Amy Galvin Grogan

Attorneys for: Mercantile National Bank of Indiana; Citizens Financial Services, F.S.B.; State Farm Insurance Co.; Auto Owners Insurance Co.; CIGNA; Armco, Inc.; St. Margaret Mercy Healthcare Centers, Inc.; St. Anthony Hospital and Health Centers (Michigan City); Calumet Council, Inc., Boy Scouts of America; Chicago Title Insurance Company; Security Federal Bank, F.S.B.; First National Bank of Illinois; Home State Bank, N.A. (Crystal Lake, Il); Ford Motor Credit Company.

For full biographical listings, see the Martindale-Hubbell Law Directory

McHIE, MYERS, McHIE & ENSLEN (AV)

53 Muenich Court, 46320
Telephone: 219-931-1707
Telecopier: 219-932-2417

MEMBERS OF FIRM

G. Edward McHie	James E. McHie
Charles A. Myers	Charles Endicott Enslen
Carol M. Green	

Representative Clients: USX Corporation; Ronwal Transportation, Inc.; Hammond Redevelopment Commission; Hammond Economic Development Commission; Raytrans, Inc.; La Salle Steel Co.; Emro Marketing Co., A Division of Marathon Oil; Combined Transport Systems, Inc.

For full biographical listings, see the Martindale-Hubbell Law Directory

HARTFORD CITY,* Blackford Co. — (Refer to Marion)

INDIANAPOLIS,* Marion Co.

BAKER & DANIELS (AV)

300 North Meridian Street, 46204
Telephone: 317-237-0300
FAX: 317-237-1000
Fort Wayne, Indiana Office: 111 East Wayne Street, Suite 800.
Telephone: 219-424-8000.
South Bend, Indiana Office: First Bank Building, 205 West Jefferson Boulevard.
Telephone: 219-234-4149.
Elkhart, Indiana Office: 301 B South Main Street, Suite 307,
Telephone: 219-296-6000.
Washington, D.C. Office: 1701 K Street, N.W., Suite 400.
Telephone: 202-785-1565.

Albert Baker (1874-1942)	Edward Daniels (1877-1918)
Joseph Daniels (1914-1972)	

MEMBERS OF FIRM

Robert L. Jessup	Wendell R. Tucker
William F. Landers	Stephen A. Claffey
Michael R. Maine	David R. Hamer
Norman P. Rowe	Norman G. Tabler, Jr.
Terrill D. Albright	H. Patrick Callahan
Fred E. Schlegel	Rory O'Bryan
James A. Aschleman	Stephen H. Paul
Duejean Garrett	Charles T. Richardson
Phillip E. Bainbridge	Michael J. Huston
Jerry R. Jenkins	Lewis D. Beckwith

(See Next Column)

BAKER & DANIELS, *Indianapolis—Continued*

MEMBERS OF FIRM (Continued)

Donald P. Bennett	Jay Jaffe
Thomas G. Stayton	Alan L. McLaughlin
James M. Carr	Gayle L. Skolnik
James H. Ham, III	Brent D. Taylor
Mary Katherine Lisher	Anne Slaughter Andrew
Theodore J. Esping	Hudnall A. Pfeiffer
Brian K. Burke	Jeffrey M. Stautz
Daniel F. Evans, Jr.	Joseph H. Yeager, Jr.
Robert W. Elzer	Richard T. Freije, Jr.
John W. Purcell	G. Frederick Glass
Thomas A. Vogtner	Thomas A. Pitman
David C. Worrell	Byron K. Mason
Francina A. Dlouhy	Daniel L. Boeglin
John T. Neighbours	James W. Clark
Roberta Sabin Recker	Ronald D. Gifford
Gregory J. Utken	Karl P. Haas
David W. Miller	Jill Harris Tanner
J. Daniel Ogren	Mitzi Harris Martin
David Lawther Johnson	Joseph M. Scimia
Tibor D. Klopfer	Richard C. Starkey
George W. Somers	Robert S. Wynne
Lawrence A. Steward	Mary Booth Miller Stanley
David K. Herzog	John A. Gardner
Christopher G. Scanlon	Todd Murray Nierman
John B. Swarbrick, Jr.	Bradley Merrill Thompson
John R. Schaibley, III	Kevin M. Toner
Robert Kirk Stanley	J. Jeffrey Brown
Rebecca A. Richardson	Gregory N. Dale
Irene T. Adamczyk	David A. Given
Ben W. Blanton	John Joseph Tanner

COUNSEL

Byron P. Hollett	J. B. King
John D. Cochran	Henry B. Blackwell, II
Dan R. Winchell	Merrill S. Thompson
Joseph B. Carney	Arthur R. Whale
Thomas M. Lofton	Virgil L. Beeler

R. Matthew Neff

ASSOCIATES

Robert M. Bond	Amy E. Kosnoff
Debra L. Hinshaw	Carl R. Pebworth
Nancy J. Futterknecht	MaryAnn Schlegel Ruegger
Shaun Healy O'Brien	Ji-Qing Liu
Mark C. Sausser	Edward J. Prein
Sharon A. Hilmes	Mark J. Sifferlen
Wendy Wright Ponader	Thomas D. Bunton
Thomas C. Froehle Jr.	Nicole Jones Cail
Brant O. Gardner	Janet Madden Charles
Scott D. Himsel	Julie Manning Magid
Scott M. Kosnoff	Elizabeth A. Roberge
Cynthia Pearson Purvis	Kent A. Rollison
Andrew Z. Soshnick	Michael R. Watters
Brian S. Fennerty	Patrick S. Cross
Gregory J. Seketa	Charles A. Grandy
Mark E. Wright	Jennifer L. Brajkovich
Nancy G. Tinsley	Kerry Lynne Jones
Ellen E. Boshkoff	Jan Michelsen
Kevin P. Griffith	Brenda Hacker Osborne
Paul Lowell Haines	David P. Scharf
Michael J. MacLean	Pamela G. Schneeman
Leslie S. Rogers	Elizabeth Kelley Cierzniak
Mark A. Voigtmann	Paige N. Tobias-Button
Stephen L. Foutty	Christine J. Graffis

Joseph E. Miller, Jr.

FORT WAYNE OFFICE
MEMBERS OF FIRM

Maclyn T. Parker	John R. Burns, III
Martin A. Weissert	Steven H. Hazelrigg
George T. Dodd	Steven L. Jackson
Robert T. Hoover	Robert H. Blaich
Thomas M. Shoaff	Michael L. James
John F. Hoffman	Jon A. Bomberger
Joseph W. Kimmell, II	Timothy J. Haffner
Anthony Niewyk	David P. Irmscher
David A. Scott	Albert J. Dahm
Lawrence E. Shine	Douglas Dormire Powers
N. Reed Silliman	Kevin R. Erdman

Jeanne E. Longsworth

ASSOCIATES

Maria C. Campo	M. Randall Spencer
Jeffrey O. Davidson	Debra L. Schroeder
(Not admitted in IN)	Anthony M. Zirille
David B. Kagan	Kevin T. Duncan
(Not admitted in IN)	Amee R. McKim
Robert D. Moreland	Lisa M. Dillman
Jeffrey A. Townsend	David J. Kuker
Holly Demarest Warshauer	Paul P. Kiel
Gary D. Johnson	Brian C. Pauls

Ginger L. Ringenberg

(See Next Column)

SOUTH BEND, INDIANA OFFICE
MEMBERS OF FIRM

James D. Hall	James M. Matthews
Thomas J. Brunner, Jr.	Peter G. Trybula
Richard L. Hill	Paul J. Peralta

OF COUNSEL

Paul D. Borghesani	Ken C. Decker

ASSOCIATES

Daniel G. Areaux	David C. Read
D. Lucetta Pope	Lawrence R. Williams, II
Randolph R. Rompola	Kari A. Gallagher
Robert A. Wade	Edward A. Sullivan, III
Amy Lawrence Mader	Robert D. Null

ELKHART, INDIANA OFFICE
MEMBERS OF FIRM

Kennard R. Weaver	Peter G. Trybula

OF COUNSEL

Paul D. Borghesani	Eileen A. McAssey Groves

ASSOCIATES

Daniel G. Areaux	David C. Read
M. Angella Castille	Debra L. Schroeder

WASHINGTON, D.C. OFFICE
MEMBER OF FIRM

Frank S. Swain

LEGAL SUPPORT PERSONNEL

Eugene Valanzano　(Land Use Consultant)

Representative Clients: Anthem Insurance Companies, Inc.; AT&T Corp.; Bank One, Indianapolis, N.A.; Borg-Warner Corp.; City of Indianapolis; Cummins Engine Co.; Eli Lilly and Co.; General Motors Corp.; Indianapolis Public Schools; United Airlines.

For full biographical listings, see the Martindale-Hubbell Law Directory

---

BARNES & THORNBURG (AV)

1313 Merchants Bank Building, 11 South Meridian Street, 46204
Telephone: 317-638-1313
FAX: 317-231-7433; 317-231-7452
URL: http://www.btlaw.com
Fort Wayne, Indiana Office: Suite 600, One Summit Square, 46802.
Telephone: 219-423-9440.
FAX: 219-424-8316.
South Bend, Indiana Office: 600 First Source Bank Center, 100 North Michigan, 46601-1632.
Telephone: 219-233-1171.
FAX: 219-237-1125.
Elkhart, Indiana Office: 121 West Franklin Street, Suite 200, 46516.
Telephone: 219-293-0681.
FAX: 219-296-2535.
Chicago, Illinois Office: 200 West Madison Street, Suite 2610, 60606.
Telephone: 312-357-1313.
FAX: 312-759-5646.
Washington, D.C. Office: 1401 Eye Street, N.W., Suite 500, 20005.
Telephone: 202-289-1313.
FAX: 202-289-1330.

Earl B. Barnes (1881-1966)
MEMBERS OF FIRM

Richard E. Deer	Michael P. Lucas
Jack H. Rogers	John M. Kyle, III
Robert H. Reynolds	Michael K. McCrory
D. Reed Scism	Anne N. DePrez
Robert P. Johnstone	Robert D. MacGill
Tom Charles Huston	Robert T. Grand
Daniel H. FitzGibbon	Alan A. Levin
Stephen Kendall Smith	Kenneth H. Inskeep
Michael R. Fruehwald	Alan K. Mills
Edward O. DeLaney	Douglas J. Heckler
Donald E. Knebel	Timothy J. Riffle
Wayne C. Kreuscher	Steven W. Thornton
Kristin G. Fruehwald	Howard E. Kochell
Daniel W. McGill	Kenneth J. Yerkes
Kent E. Agness	Neal W. Steinbart
Michael R. Conner	David R. Warshauer
Claudia V. Swhier	Lynn C. Tyler
Catherine L. Bridge	Eric R. Moy
Larry J. Stroble	Jan M. Carroll
Michael Rosiello	Marcie R. Horowitz
Peter J. Rusthoven	Bruce D. Donaldson
Stephen W. Lee	Michael G. Paton
Stanley C. Fickle	Anne C. McGown
David M. Powlen	James M. Gutting

OF COUNSEL

Thomas M. Scanlon	Robert E. Highfield
Jerry P. Belknap	James A. McDermott
Louis A. Highmark	Shirley A. Shideler
John W. Houghton	Charles E. Bruess
Lester M. Ponder	Edward A. Keirn
William E. Roberts	Guinn P. Doyle
Henry C. Ryder	Margaret Best Burlingame

(See Next Column)

BARNES & THORNBURG—*Continued*

OF COUNSEL (Continued)

Dean T. Barnhard	Briane M. House
Mariana Richmond	Dwight D. Lueck
Frank McCloskey	Joseph E. Loftus

Michiharu Homma

ASSOCIATES

John R. Maley	Barbara J. Meier
Teresa E. Morton	Steven R. Schultz
Anthony C. Sullivan	Peter A. Morse, Jr.
Joseph C. Chapelle	Victoria A. Gorczyca
Andrew J. Detherage	Samantha M. Williams
Terry W. Dawson	John T. Bailey
Stephanie Perry Ganser	Edward Sean Griggs
Nicholas K. Kile	Nicholas E. Mathioudakis
William D. Hammel	Blake J. Burgan
Joseph G. Eaton	Christine K. Jacobson
Jeffery J. Qualkinbush	Todd G. Vare
Donald E. Williams	Deborah S. Baker
Stephen W. Kellams	Martín Montes
Louis G. Martine	William E. Padgett
Richard J. Hall	R. Trevor Carter
Bart A. Karwath	Brian L. Burdick
Michael A. Moffatt	Kevin E. Slaughter
Karen L. Kovalsky	Derek D. Murphy
(Not admitted in IN)	George A. Dremonas

INTELLECTUAL PROPERTY DEPARTMENT

MEMBERS OF FIRM

William R. Coffey	Richard D. Conard
Jerry E. Hyland	Steven R. Lammert

Richard A. Rezek

OF COUNSEL

Everet F. Smith	Nancy J. Harrison

ASSOCIATES

Timothy E. Niednagel	John Paul Breen
Barry D. Blount	Jill L. Werling

William A. Morrison

Representative Clients: Ameritech; Boehringer Mannheim Corporation; DowElanco; Eli Lilly and Company; Hillenbrand Industries; Indianapolis Newspapers, Inc.; The Lincoln National Life Insurance Company; Purdue Research Foundation; Simon Property Group; Toyota Motor Corporation.

For full biographical listings, see the Martindale-Hubbell Law Directory

---

BOSE MCKINNEY & EVANS (AV)

2700 First Indiana Plaza, 135 North Pennsylvania Street, 46204
Telephone: 317-684-5000
Facsimile: 317-684-5173
Indianapolis North Office: Suite 1201, 8888 Keystone Crossing, 46240.
Telephone: 317-574-3700.
Facsimile: 317-574-3716.

MEMBERS OF FIRM

William M. Evans (1923-1991)	George E. Purdy
Robert H. McKinney (Retired)	Keith E. White
John W. Wynne (Retired)	L. Parvin Price
Lewis C. Bose	David L. Swider
Wayne C. Ponader	James C. Carlino
James P. Seidensticker, Jr.	R. J. McConnell
Robert P. Kassing	C. Joseph Russell
G. Pearson Smith, Jr.	Jon M. Bailey
David A. Butcher	Elizabeth Theobald Young
Philip A. Nicely	Michael A. Trentadue
Theodore J. Nowacki	Karl R. Sturbaum
Kendall C. Crook	Robert B. Clemens
Ronald E. Elberger	Kathleen G. Lucas
David L. Wills	Roderick H. Morgan
Charles E. Rubright	Dwight L. Miller
Daniel C. Emerson	V. Samuel Laurin III
Jean S. Blackwell	E. Victor Indiano
Alan W. Becker	James E. Carlberg
Daniel B. Seitz	George Thomas Patton, Jr.
David A. Travelstead	Debra Linn Burns
Stephen E. Arthur	Gary L. Chapman
Margaret Bannon Miller	Robert K. Johnson
Ronald M. Soskin	James A. Coles

Donald M. Meyer

ASSOCIATES

Natalie J. Stucky	William C. Ahrbecker
Tammy K. Haney	Mary Beth Plummer
J. Scott Enright	Jane A. Phillips
Susan E. Traynor	Cathy Elliott
Karen Glasser Sharp	Amy Rankin Kennelly
Lisa C. McKinney	J. Christopher Janak
Alan S. Townsend	J. Gregory Shelley
Scott A. Weathers	Jeffrey M. Reed
Daniel P. McInerny	Jeffrey A. Hokanson
Robert C. Sproule	Stephanie Franco Holtzlander

Andrew M. McNeil

(See Next Column)

OF COUNSEL

Peter Lynn Goerges	Arthur W. DePrez

LEGAL SUPPORT PERSONNEL

Steven B. Granner (Zoning Consultant)

Representative Clients: Association of Indiana Life Insurance Cos.; Duke Realty Investments, Inc.; Emmis Broadcasting Corp.; First Indiana Bank; Indianapolis Colts, Inc.; Indiana League of Savings Institutions, Inc.; Prudential Life Insurance Co.; Metropolitan Life Insurance Co.; USX Corp.

For full biographical listings, see the Martindale-Hubbell Law Directory

---

BRATTAIN & MINNIX (AV)

151 North Delaware Street Suite 760, 46204
Telephone: 317-231-1750
Facsimile: 317-231-1760

Bruce D. Brattain	Larry A. Minnix

Linda Klain

For full biographical listings, see the Martindale-Hubbell Law Directory

---

DANN PECAR NEWMAN & KLEIMAN, PROFESSIONAL CORPORATION (AV)

Suite 2300, One American Square Box 82008, 46282
Telephone: 317-632-3232; Indiana: 800-622-4799
Telecopy: 317-632-2962

Theodore R. Dann (1907-1993)	Walter E. Wolf, Jr.
Joel Yonover (1932-1995)	Barry E. Beldin
Philip D. Pecar	Robert D. Swhier, Jr.
Norman R. Newman	James P. Moloy
David H. Kleiman	Robert J. Schuckit
Jon B. Abels	Andrew A. Kleiman
Melvin R. Daniel	Michael J. Gabovitch
Lawrence F. Dorocke	Steven M. Pecar
Jeffrey A. Abrams	Benjamin A. Pecar
James H. Schwarz	Richard O. Kissel, II
Robert A. Rose	Joseph D. Calderon

OF COUNSEL

Linda E. Cantor	Anthony J. Rose

Ellen C. Siakotos	Angela L. Mansfield
Stacy L. Hill	Martha M. K. Baird

Karin L. Veatch

Attorneys for: Indianapolis Machinery Co., Inc.; Melvin Simon & Associates, Inc.; Pacers Basketball Corp.; Universal Fire & Casualty Co., Inc.; Bank One, Indianapolis, NA; INB National Bank; Nachi Technology, Inc.; Pharmaceutical Corporation of America; Logo 7, Inc.

For full biographical listings, see the Martindale-Hubbell Law Directory

---

HACKMAN MCCLARNON HULETT & CRACRAFT (AV)

2400 One Indiana Square, 46204
Telephone: 317-636-5401
Facsimile: 317-686-3288
Email: hmhc@indy.net

MEMBERS OF FIRM

Marvin L. Hackman	Timothy K. Ryan
Robert S. Hulett	Philip B. McKiernan
Michael B. Cracraft	Vicki L. Anderson

ASSOCIATES

Thomas A. Dickey	Marci A. Reddick

OF COUNSEL

James R. McClarnon	John D. Cochran, Jr.

Mark S. Alderfer

Representative Clients: Ameritech Indiana; AT&T Technologies, Inc.; Citizens Gas & Coke Utility; F. C. Tucker Co., Inc.; Texas Eastern Products Pipeline Co.; Indiana Municipal Power Agency; I.V.C. Industrial Coatings, Inc.; McGraw-Hill Broadcasting Co., Inc.; NBD Bank, N.A.; State Farm Mutual Automobile Insurance Company.

For full biographical listings, see the Martindale-Hubbell Law Directory

---

HALL, RENDER, KILLIAN, HEATH & LYMAN, PROFESSIONAL CORPORATION (AV)

Suite 2000, One American Square Box 82064, 46282
Telephone: 317-633-4884
Fax: 317-633-4878
Email: hrkhl@hrkhl.com
Indianapolis North Office: Suite 820, 8402 Harcourt Road, 46260.
Telephone: 317-871-6222.
Fax: 317-338-3946.
Louisville, Kentucky Office: Providian Center, Suite 1530, 400 West Market Street, 40202.
Telephone: 502-568-1890.
Fax: 502-568-4878.

(See Next Column)

HALL, RENDER, KILLIAN, HEATH & LYMAN PROFESSIONAL CORPORATION, *Indianapolis—Continued*

William S. Hall	R. Thomas Carter (Not
John C. Render	admitted in IN; Resident,
Rex P. Killian	Louisville, Kentucky Office)
R. Terry Heath	Maureen O'Brien Griffin
Stephen W. Lyman	Robert A. Hicks
L. Richard Gohman	Kevin P. Speer
Jeffrey Peek	Jeffrey W. Short
Clifford A. Beyler	Gregory W. Moore
Joseph R. Impicciche	John C. Meade
Timothy C. Lawson	Clifton E. Johnson
Douglas P. Long	Martha B. Wentworth
William H. Thompson	Richard W. McMinn
Timothy W. Kennedy	Todd J. Selby
Steven H. Pratt	Gregg M. Wallander
N. Kent Smith	James B. Hogan
Mary C. Gaughan	Donald R. Russell
Fred J. Bachmann	D. David Freeman

David M. Leonard

Gregory P. Kult	William D. Roberts (Not
René Remek Savarise (Resident,	admitted in IN; Resident,
Louisville, Kentucky Office)	Louisville, Kentucky Office)
Michael Keith Pruitt	Keith D. Barber
John J. Andris, Jr. (Not	A. Courtney Guild, Jr. (Not
admitted in IN; Resident,	admitted in IN; Resident,
Louisville, Kentucky Office)	Louisville, Kentucky Office)
Pamela J. Jones	Samuel H. DeShazer (Not
Brantley H. Wright	admitted in IN; Resident,
James R. Willey	Louisville, Kentucky Office)
Christopher L. Riegler	Gerald L. Stovall (Not admitted
Jon F. Spadorcia	in IN; Resident, Louisville,
	Kentucky Office)

For full biographical listings, see the Martindale-Hubbell Law Directory

ICE MILLER DONADIO & RYAN (AV)

One American Square Box 82001, 46282-0002
Telephone: 317-236-2100
Fax: 317-236-2219
Email: leel@imdr.com *URL:* http://www.imdr.com
South Bend, Indiana Office: 211 West Washington Street, Suite 2420.
Telephone: 219-234-7933.
Fax: 219-234-7965. Internet E-mail: leel@imdr.com. Web Site Address: http://www.imdr.com.

MEMBERS OF FIRM

James V. Donadio	Jeffrey O. Lewis
Alan H. Lobley	John F. Prescott, Jr.
Jim A. O'Neal	Phillip L. Bayt
Donald G. Sutherland	Fred R. Biesecker
Leland B. Cross, Jr.	Thomas K. Downs
Leonard J. Betley	Mary Nold Larimore
Evan E. Steger	E. Van Olson
Berkley W. Duck	Lisa Stone Sciscoe
William R. Riggs	Marc W. Sciscoe
Ralph A. Cohen	Richard A. Smikle
Jack R. Snyder	John R. Thornburgh
Charles E. Wilson	Mary Beth Braitman
Arthur P. Kalleres	Brenda S. Horn
Bruce A. Polizotto	Gregory L. Pemberton
Jay G. Taylor	L. Alan Whaley
G. Daniel Kelley, Jr.	Robert B. Bush
Gordon D. Wishard	Bonnie L. Gallivan
S. R. Born	John T. Murphy
David M. Mattingly	Richard J. Thrapp
James D. Kemper	Zeff A. Weiss
Martin J. Klaper	Stephen J. Hackman
James R. Fisher	Steven K. Humke
Richard E. Parker	Debra Hanley Miller
John P. Ryan	Todd W. Ponder
Cory Brundage	Michael A. Wukmer
Harry L. Gonso	Lucy A. Emison
Terry A. M. Mumford	Michael J. Lewinski
Michael H. Boldt	Melissa Proffitt Reese
David J. Mallon, Jr.	Mark J. Richards
Thomas H. Ristine	Elizabeth A. Smith
Phillip R. Scaletta, III	Thomas W. Peterson
Barton T. Sprunger	Patricia A. Zelmer
Susan B. Tabler	Paul B. Overhauser
James L. Petersen	Lacy M. Johnson
James S. Cunning	Michael D. Marine
Gary J. Dankert	Henry A. Efroymson
Philip C. Genetos	Terri Ann Czajka
Byron L. Myers	Donald M. Snemis
James A. Shanahan	Dale E. Stackhouse
Michael A. Blickman	Daniel S. Corsaro
Philip A. Whistler	Michael A. Wilkins
Marcus B. Chandler	Sherry A. Fabina-Abney
Joseph E. DeGroff	Jane Neuhauser Herndon

(See Next Column)

SENIOR COUNSEL

Timothy W. Sullivan	Gene E. Wilkins
	Mark S. Moore

OF COUNSEL

William P. Diener	Kathleen K. Shortridge
Bradley L. Williams	Susan B. Rivas
Nancy Menard Riddle	Diana L. Wann
James B. Burroughs	Daniel E. Fisher
Karen L. Arland	Kelly Bauman Pitcher
Karen Ann P. Lloyd	Peggy J. Naile
Thomas C. Smith	Bruce W. Longbottom
Mark D. Grant	Catherine R. Reese

STAFF ATTORNEYS

Sandra K. Bickel	Mikio Nishizu
Dana G. Meier	Raymond J. Schoettle
John W. Rowings	Edward P. Steegmann
Suzanne S. Crouch	Michele Johnson Calderon
	Nathan B. Maudlin

RETIRED PARTNERS

Donald F. Elliott, Jr.	Alan T. Nolan
Kenneth Foster	Edward J. Ohleyer
George B. Gavit	Robert D. Risch
John A. Grayson	Geoffrey Segar
Robert D. McCord	Jerome M. Strauss
Merle H. Miller	James S. Telfer

ASSOCIATES

Joseph E. Whitsett, Jr.	Craig C. Burke
Kristin L. Altice	Kelly A. Evans
Kevin C. Woodhouse	Sarah K. Funke
Robert A. Anderson	Allan S. Katz
James Scott Fanzini	Gareth W. Kuhl
Laure V. Flaniken	Brendan J. McKeough
Kevin R. Knight	Harold C. Moore
Dominic F. Polizzotto	George A. Norwood
Brian G. Steinkamp	Tara L. Schulstad
Terrence J. Keusch	Rebecca J. Seamands
Michael J. Melliere	Christopher S. Sears
John J. Morse	Tracy J. (Vacek) Galbraith
Judy Starobin Okenfuss	Margaret R. Bernardin
Michael E. Schrader	Paul N. Alp
Stephanie Alden Smithey	David O. Barrett
Michael L. Tooley	Lynn M. Gagel
Kathleen S. Kiefer	Gina M. Giacone
Curtis W. McCauley	John M. Hakes
Dean T. Burger	James V. Hetzel
Laura B. Daghe	(Not admitted in IN)
Jodie L. Miner	Pamela V. Keller
Thomas E. Mixdorf	Angela R. Lang
Heather K. Olinger	Amy Corsaro Merritt
Antje C. Petersen	Kirstin Pace Salzman
Adam Arceneaux	Gretchen W. Snelling
Paul H. Sinclair	Michael A. Swift
Ann L. Theobald	Ponce D. Tidwell, Jr.
Anita M. Hodgson	Cindy M. Lott
Melissa R. Garrard	Melissa S. York
Doreen J. Gridley	Stanley W. Crosley
Jared L. Burden	(Not admitted in IN)

LEGAL SUPPORT PERSONNEL

Karen L. Stein-Ferguson	John W. Barker, Jr.
	(Not admitted in IN)

Counsel for: American United Life Insurance Co.; Chrysler Corp.; Ford Motor Company; General Electric Company; Indiana Bankers Assn.

For full biographical listings, see the Martindale-Hubbell Law Directory

JOHNSON, SMITH, PENCE, DENSBORN, WRIGHT & HEATH (AV)

One Indiana Square Suite 1800, 46204
Telephone: 317-634-9777
Telecopier: 317-636-9061

MEMBERS OF FIRM

John F. Joyce (1948-1994)	John R. Hammond, III
James T. Smith (1941-1995)	G. Ronald Heath
Wayne O Adams, III	Robert B. Hebert
Robert M. Baker, III	David J. Hensel
Thomas A. Barnard	John David Hoover
David G. Blachly	Andrew W. Hull
David J. Carr	Dennis A. Johnson
Sean Michael Clapp	Richard L. Johnson
Peter D. Cleveland	Michael J. Kaye
Jeffrey S. Cohen	John R. Kirkwood
James T. Crawford, Jr.	Padric K. J. O'Brien
David R. Day	Mark A. Palmer
Donald K. Densborn	Linda L. Pence
Thomas N. Eckerle	David Williams Russell
Mark W. Ford	David E. Wright

Sally Franklin Zweig

(See Next Column)

JOHNSON, SMITH, PENCE, DENSBORN, WRIGHT & HEATH—*Continued*

ASSOCIATES

Kelly R. Norris (1953-1989)	Patricia L. Marshall
Robert C. Wolf (1949-1993)	Stefany L. Mitlak
Carolyn H. Andretti	Alice McKenzie Morical
Maureen F. Barnard	Bradley C. Morris
Robert T. Buday	Steven J. Moss
Thomas G. Burroughs	Steven F. Pockrass
Anthony Scott Chinn	Michael D. Ramsey
Gretchen L. Doninger	David D. Robinson
Charles M. Freeland	Ronald G. Sentman
Jane Ann Himsel	David A. Tucker

OF COUNSEL

Earl Auberry (1923-1989)	David W. Givens
Larry A. Conrad (1935-1990)	William T. Lawrence
Laura S. Cohen	Lawrence W. Schmits
John K. Smeltzer	

For full biographical listings, see the Martindale-Hubbell Law Directory

KIGHTLINGER & GRAY (AV)

Market Square Center, Suite 660, 151 North Delaware Street, 46204
Telephone: 317-638-4521
Telecopier: 317-636-5917
Evansville, Indiana Office: One Riverfront Place, Suite 210, 20 N.W. First Street, 47708.
Telephone: 812-464-9508.
Telecopier: 812-464-9511.
New Albany, Indiana Office: Pinnacle Centre, Suite 200, 3317 Grant Line Road, P.O. Box 6727, 46151.
Telephone: 812-949-2300.
Telecopier: 812-949-8556.

MEMBERS OF FIRM

Robert J. Wampler	James W. Roehrdanz
Donald L. Dawson	Samuel A. Day
Peter G. Tamulonis	(Resident, New Albany Office)
Richard A. Young	Thomas B. Blackwell
J. Randall Aikman	Peter A. Velde
Michael E. Brown	Thomas J. Jarzyniecki, Jr.
Mark D. Gerth	Jeffrey A. Doty
Steven E. Springer	Thomas E. Wheeler II
Joan Fullam Irick	Rodney L. Scott
Richard T. Mullineaux	(Resident, New Albany Office)
(Resident, New Albany Office)	S. Michael Woodard
Robert M. Kelso	David R. Sauvey
Brent R. Weil	(Resident, Evansville Office)
(Resident, Evansville Office)	Jill Reifinger Marcrum
Philip Linnemeier	(Resident, Evansville Office)
John B. Drummy	Van T. Willis
	(Resident, New Albany Office)

OF COUNSEL

Mark William Gray	Roger H. Schmelzer

ASSOCIATES

Mary M. Nord	Diane E. Bluhm
(Resident, New Albany Office)	(Resident, New Albany Office)
William L. O'Connor	David R. Schanker
Scott L. Tyler	Candace L. Sage
(Resident, New Albany Office)	Robert J. Smith
Laura E. Moenning	Marti E. Thurman
Paul F. Lottes	(Resident, New Albany Office)
Christopher C. Hagenow	Jeffrey R. Walker
Eric D. Johnson	(Resident, Evansville Office)
Timothy A. Klingler	Daniel A. Barfield
(Resident, Evansville Office)	(Resident, Evansville Office)
Dirck H. Stahl	Pfenne P. Cantrell
(Resident, Evansville Office)	Marcia A. Mahony
Lowell T. Woods, Jr.	James B. Doyle
Gregory M. Reger	
(Resident, New Albany Office)	

Representative Clients: American Family Mutual Insurance Co.; American International Group; American States; Associated Aviation Underwriters; Black & Decker (U.S., Inc.); Government Employees Insurance Co.; Mack Trucks, Inc.; Reliance Insurance Group.
Reference: INB National Bank.

For full biographical listings, see the Martindale-Hubbell Law Directory

LEWIS & KAPPES, PROFESSIONAL CORPORATION (AV)

Suite 1700 One American Square, P.O. Box 82053, 46282
Telephone: 317-639-1210
Telecopier: 317-639-4882

Ted B. Lewis (1919-1991)	Thomas R. Ruge
Philip S. Kappes	C. Duane O'Neal
David W. Gray	Brett James Miller
John F. Wickes, Jr.	Richard T. Trettin
Gary P. Price	Todd A. Richardson
Steven L. Tuchman	Bette J. Dodd

(See Next Column)

Rhonda L. Kuchik	Pamela H. Sherwood
Peter S. French	Brian Andrew Statz
Donna H. Dubisky	

OF COUNSEL

Samuel A. Fuller	Kevin W. Dogan
Leslie Duvall	

For full biographical listings, see the Martindale-Hubbell Law Directory

LOCKE REYNOLDS BOYD & WEISELL (AV)

1000 Capital Center South, 201 North Illinois Street, 46204
Telephone: 317-237-3800
Telecopier: 317-237-3900

Theodore L. Locke (1891-1981)	Michael T. Bindner
Hugh E. Reynolds (1900-1968)	Michael J. Schneider
Emerson Boyd (1914-1986)	Kim F. Ebert
Hugh E. Reynolds, Jr.	David Elliott Jose
Lloyd H. Milliken, Jr.	Terrence L. Brookie
James S. Haramy	Richard A. Huser
William V. Hutchens	Jeffrey B. Bailey
James J. McGrath	Paul G. Reis
David S. Allen	Thomas J. Campbell
David M. Haskett	Diane Parsons Emswiller
Michael A. Bergin	Burton M. Harris
David T. Kasper	Howard R. Cohen
Stephen J. Dutton	Charles B. Baldwin
Steven J. Strawbridge	Andrew James Richardson
Thomas L. Davis	Thomas W. Farlow
Robert A. Fanning	Karl M. Koons, III
Randall R. Riggs	Julia F. Crowe
Alan S. Brown	James Dimos
Michael D. Moriarty	Kristen K. Rollison
Glenn T. Troyer	Thomas R. Schultz
Paul S. Mannweiler	Todd J. Kaiser
Mark J. Roberts	Jeffrey R. Gaither
Kevin Charles Murray	Eric A. Riegner
Julia Blackwell Gelinas	Kevin C. Schiferl
Ariane Schallwig Johnson	

Craig A. Wood	Jerrilyn Powers Ramsey
Jeffrey S. Dible	Katherine Coble Dassow
Stephen L. Vaughan	Kathleen A. Hash
Deanna A. Dean-Webster	Mary Margaret Ruth Feldhake
David S. Klinestiver	Nelson D. Alexander
Peter H. Pogue	Curt W. Hidde
John H. Daerr	Thomas E. Deer
John K. McDavid	Salim A. Hasan
Lisa Drees Tobin	Sandra Boyd Williams
Robert W. Wright	Donald B. Kite, Sr.
Kenneth B. Siepman	Thomas F. Bedsole
Jon M. Pinnick	Stephanie L. Valadez
Joyce A. Dietz	James D. Shircliff
Jeffrey J. Mortier	David Alexander Sorensen
Nicholas C. Pappas	Brian L. McDermott
Mary A. Schopper	Derek S. Burrell
Susan E. Cline	Dean R. Brackenridge
Bruce J. Alvarado	Etta M. Biloon

OF COUNSEL

William B. Weisell	Robert C. Riddell
William H. Vobach	Rodney E. Corson

Counsel for: Honda North America Motor Co., Inc.; CNA Insurance Cos.; General Motors Corp.; Montgomery Ward & Co., Inc.; I.D.S./American Express, Inc.; Kroger Co.; NBD Bank, N.A.; Navistar International Transportation Corp.; PEPSICO, Inc.; Resort Condominiums International, Inc.

For full biographical listings, see the Martindale-Hubbell Law Directory

ROCAP, WITCHGER & THRELKELD (AV)

One Indiana Square, Suite 2300, 46204
Telephone: 317-639-6281
FAX: 317-637-9056

James E. Rocap, Sr. (1881-1969)	John T. Rocap (1909-1980)
Keith C. Reese (1920-1993)	

MEMBERS OF FIRM

James E. Rocap, Jr.	Richard A. Rocap
James D. Witchger	Thomas Todd Reynolds
W. Brent Threlkeld	Robert S. O'Dell

ASSOCIATES

Nancy G. Curless	Mark A. Payne
Robert A. Durham	Kandice L. Kilkelly
Jeffrey V. Crabill	Dionne M. Carroll

OF COUNSEL

Joseph F. Quill

Counsel for: Phillips Petroleum Co.; State Farm Mutual Auto Insurance Co.; Cessna Finance Corp.; American Family Insurance Group; The Travelers Insurance Co.

(See Next Column)

ROCAP, WITCHGER & THRELKELD, *Indianapolis—Continued*

For full biographical listings, see the Martindale-Hubbell Law Directory

SOMMER & BARNARD, ATTORNEYS AT LAW, PC (AV)

4000 Bank One Tower, 111 Monument Circle, 46204-5140
Telephone: 317-630-4000
FAX: 317-236-9802
North Office: 8900 Keystone Crossing, Suite 1046, Indianapolis, Indiana, 46240-2134.
Telephone: 317-630-4000.
FAX: 317-844-4780.

James K. Sommer	Michael C. Terrell
William C. Barnard	Marlene Reich
James E. Hughes	Richard C. Richmond, III
Edward W. Harris, III	Julianne S. Lis-Milam
Frederick M. King	Steven C. Shockley
Jerald I. Ancel	Dan G. Sterner
James A. Strain	Erick D. Ponader
Eric R. Johnson	Lawrence A. Vanore
Gordon L. Pittenger	Donald C. Biggs
Frank J. Deveau	Debra McVicker Lynch
John E. Taylor	Gayle A. Reindl

Edwin J. Broecker	Scott R. Alexander
Thomas R. DeVoe	Dan L. O'Korn
Mary T. Doherty	Charles R. O'Keefe, Jr.
Scott E. Herbst	Lanae M. Harden

OF COUNSEL

Jerry Williams	Charles E. Valliere
Robert R. Clark	Ann Carr Mackey
Philip L. McCool	Verl L. Myers
Robert B. Bennett, Jr.	

Representative Clients: Comerica Bank; Excel Industries; Federal Express; Kimball International; Monsanto; Renault Automation; TRW, Inc.

For full biographical listings, see the Martindale-Hubbell Law Directory

STARK DONINGER & SMITH (AV)

Suite 700, 50 South Meridian Street, 46204
Telephone: 317-638-2400
Fax: 317-633-6618; 633-6619

MEMBERS OF FIRM

John C. Stark	Patricia Seasor Bailey
Bruce E. Smith	Brian J. Tuohy
John W. Van Buskirk	Mark A. Bailey
Richard W. Dyar	Lewis E. Willis, Jr.

ASSOCIATES

Thomas A. Brodnik	Richard B. Kaufman
Neil E. Lucas	Patrick J. Dietrick

COUNSEL

Clarence H. Doninger	Robert D. Maas
Gregory S. Fehribach	William K. Byrum

Reference: Huntington National Bank of Indiana; National Bank of Indianapolis.

For full biographical listings, see the Martindale-Hubbell Law Directory

WOODEN & McLAUGHLIN (AV)

1600 Capital Center South, 201 North Illinois Street, 46204
Telephone: 317-639-6151
Fax: 317-639-6444

MEMBERS OF FIRM

William P. Wooden	Dale W. Eikenberry
Robert L. McLaughlin	Andrew C. Charnstrom
Michael C. Cook	Daniel D. Trachtman
Ronald G. Salatich	Julie L. Michaelis
Thomas W. Dinwiddie	Thomas M. Hanahan
John D. Nell	Mary L. Titsworth
Douglas B. King	Kent M. Broach

ASSOCIATES

Jeffrey L. McKean	Michael Rabinowitch
Holly Hapak Betz	E. Joseph Kremp, III
Caroline Lingelbach Young	Joseph R. Alberts
Kurt A. Webber	John W. Hamilton
	(Not admitted in IN)

OF COUNSEL

Thomas D. Titsworth	Katherine L. Shelby

Representative Clients: AT&T; Amoco Oil Co.; Cook Group; Eaton & Lauth Development Co.; Exxon Corp.; Hospital Corporation of America; Merrell Dow Pharmaceutical, Inc.; Monroe Guaranty Insurance Company; Peabody Coal Company; Playtex Family Products, Inc.

For full biographical listings, see the Martindale-Hubbell Law Directory

---

JASONVILLE, Greene Co.

ROWE & HAWKINS (AV)

103 West Main Street, 47438
Telephone: 812-665-2268
Fax: 812-665-2817

John S. Rowe	Jeff R. Hawkins

For full biographical listings, see the Martindale-Hubbell Law Directory

---

JEFFERSONVILLE,* Clark Co.

SMITH, BARTLETT, HEEKE, CARPENTER & LEWIS (AV)

Holzbog House, 209 East Chestnut Street, P.O. Box 98, 47131-0098
Telephone: 812-282-7736
FAX: 812-284-8388

MEMBERS OF FIRM

Wilmer T. Fox (1881-1946)	Rick E. Bartlett
Charles C. Fox (1912-1975)	Sandra L. Heeke
Ernest W. Smith	Cheryl A. Carpenter
Sandra Winnett Lewis	

ASSOCIATES

Pamela K. Thompson	Mary E. Fondrisi

Representative Clients: NBD Bank, N.A.; Liberty Mutual Insurance Co.; Geo. Pfau's Sons Co., Inc.; American Family Insurance; PSI Energy; American States Insurance Co.

For full biographical listings, see the Martindale-Hubbell Law Directory

---

KENTLAND,* Newton Co.

BARCE & RYAN (AV)

301 East Graham Street, P.O. Box 338, 47951-0338
Telephone: 219-474-5158
Fax: 219-474-6610
Fowler, Indiana Office: 103 North Jackson Avenue, P.O. Box 252, 47944-0252.
Telephone: 317-884-0383.
Fax: 317-884-0445.

MEMBERS OF FIRM

John W. Barce	J. Edward Barce
R. Steven Ryan	(Resident at Fowler Office)
Judson Gregory Barce	

Representative Clients: USX Corporation; Metropolitan Life Insurance Company; Goodland State Bank; State Bank of Oxford; DeMotte State Bank; Newton County Stone; Northern Indiana Public Service Company; DeMeter, Inc; Town of Boswell; Town of Brook.

For full biographical listings, see the Martindale-Hubbell Law Directory

---

KOKOMO,* Howard Co.

FELL, McGARVEY, TRAURING & WILSON (AV)

515 West Sycamore Street, P.O. Box 958, 46903-0958
Telephone: 317-457-9321
Telecopier: 317-452-0882

MEMBERS OF FIRM

John E. Fell, Jr.	Thomas J. Trauring
Eugene J. McGarvey, Jr.	Alan D. Wilson

Representative Clients: Big R Stores; Cellular One of Kokomo, Inc.; First National Bank, Kokomo; Haynes International, Inc.; Hospital Authority of the City of Kokomo; Kokomo City Hall Building Corp.; PPG Industries, Inc.; Star Building Supply, Inc.; Mervis Industries, Inc.; Taylor Community School Corp.

For full biographical listings, see the Martindale-Hubbell Law Directory

---

LAFAYETTE,* Tippecanoe Co.

BALL, EGGLESTON, BUMBLEBURG & McBRIDE (AV)

810 Bank One Building, P.O. Box 1535, 47902
Telephone: 317-742-9046
Fax: 317-742-1966

Cable G. Ball (1904-1981)	Warren N. Eggleston
Owen Crook (1908-1977)	(1923-1991)

MEMBERS OF FIRM

Joseph T. Bumbleburg	Jeffrey J. Newell
John K. McBride	James T. Hodson
Jack L. Walkey	Brian Wade Walker
Michael J. Stapleton	Cheryl M. Knodle
Randy J. Williams	

General Counsel for: The Lafayette Union Railway Co.; Bank One, Lafayette, N.A.
Representative Clients: Farmers Insurance Group; General Accident Fire & Life Assurance Corp.; City of Lafayette Board of Parks and Recreation; West Lafayette Community School Corp.; Travelers Insurance Co.; Trustees, West Lafayette Public Library.

(See Next Column)

BALL, EGGLESTON, BUMBLEBURG & MCBRIDE—*Continued*

For full biographical listings, see the Martindale-Hubbell Law Directory

BENNETT, BOEHNING, POYNTER & CLARY (AV)

6th Floor, Lafayette Bank & Trust Building, 133 North Fourth Street,
P.O. Box 469, 47902-0469
Telephone: 317-742-9066
Telecopier: 317-742-7641

MEMBERS OF FIRM

William K. Bennett	Brent E Clary
Richard A. Boehning	Roger Wm. Bennett
Robert E. Poynter	Christine A. DeSanctis

ASSOCIATES

Marianne M. Owen	Andrew S. Gutwein
James A. Gothard	Stuart P. Boehning

General Counsel for: West Lafayette Regional Sewer District; Fred Gutwein
Son's Inc.; Industrial Plating, Inc.; Pizza King, Inc.; Lafayette Bank and
Trust Company; Journal and Courier.
Area and County Counsel for: ALCOA; Landis & Gyr; Banc One.
Approved Title Attorneys for: Lawyers Title Insurance Co.

For full biographical listings, see the Martindale-Hubbell Law Directory

MAYFIELD AND BROOKS (AV)

322 Main Street, P.O. Box 650, 47902
Telephone: 317-423-5454
FAX: 317-742-8666

MEMBERS OF FIRM

Ambrose R. Mayfield	Thomas L. Brooks
(1907-1980)	

ASSOCIATES

Phillip J. Scaletta, Jr.	Thomas L. Brooks, Jr.

Representative Clients: DeFouw Chevrolet, Inc.; Kendrick Buick-Cadillac,
Inc.; Lafayette Real Estate Marketing Corp.; Smith Office Equipment, Inc.;
American Vending Corp.; Sun Industries, Inc.; National Attorneys' Title
Insurance Fund, Inc.
Reference: NBD Bank, N.A.

PEARLMAN AND CHOSNEK, P.C. (AV)

316 Ferry Street, P.O. Box 708, 47902-0708
Telephone: 317-742-9081
Fax: 317-742-4379

Louis Pearlman, Jr. (1930-1992)	Edward Chosnek

David W. Haniford	Christopher Paul Hopson
	Michael A. Morrissey

Representative Clients: Tippecanoe Memory Gardens, Inc.; Industrial Federal
Credit Union; Farmers and Merchants Bank, Boswell, Indiana; Biggs Pump
& Supply, Inc; Brummett Elec. Co. Inc.; Klooz Plumbing, Inc.; Gene B.
Glick Mgmt. Co; Chauncey Hill Mall; Von Tobel Lumber & Hardware; Pur-
due Employees Federal Credit Union.
Reference: NBD Bank, N.W.

For full biographical listings, see the Martindale-Hubbell Law Directory

STUART & BRANIGIN (AV)

The Life Building, 300 Main Street, Suite 800, 47902
Telephone: 317-423-1561
Telecopier: 317-742-8175

MEMBERS OF FIRM

Allison Ellsworth Stuart	Stephen R. Pennell
(1886-1950)	Anthony S. Benton
Roger D. Branigin (1902-1975)	Erik D. Spykman
Russell H. Hart	William E. Emerick
Roger D. Branigin, Jr.	John C. Duffey
Thomas L. Ryan	Mark E. DeYoung
James V. McGlone	Thomas B. Parent
Carl W. Kloepfer	Laura L. Bowker
Thomas R. McCully	Kevin D. Nicoson
Larry R. Fisher	Susan K. Roberts
Nina B. Kirkpatrick	John M. Stuckey
Mark Lillianfeld	Deborah B. Trice

COUNSEL

John F. Bodle

ASSOCIATES

Brent W. Huber	David A. Starkweather
William P. Kealey	Geoffrey Blazi
	A. James Chareq

General Counsel for: The Lafayette Life Insurance Co.; INB National Bank,
N.W.; Lafayette Home Hospital, Inc.
State Counsel for: Norfolk & Western Railway Co.
Mr. Ryan is Counsel to: The Trustees of Purdue University.
Representative Clients: Aluminum Company of America; Liberty Mutual
Insurance Group.

(See Next Column)

For full biographical listings, see the Martindale-Hubbell Law Directory

LAGRANGE,* LaGrange Co. — (Refer to Elkhart)

LA PORTE,* La Porte Co.

NEWBY, LEWIS, KAMINSKI & JONES (AV)

916 Lincoln Way, 46350
Telephone: 219-362-1577
Direct Line Michigan City: 219-879-6300
Fax: 219-362-2106
Mailing Address: P.O. Box 1816, La Porte, Indiana, 46352-1816

MEMBERS OF FIRM

John E. Newby (1916-1990)	Edward L. Volk
Daniel E. Lewis, Jr.	Mark L. Phillips
Gene M. Jones	Martin W. Kus
John W. Newby	Marsha Schatz Volk
Perry F. Stump, Jr.	Mark A. Lienhoop
	James W. Kaminski

ASSOCIATES

William S. Kaminski	Christine A. Sulewski
	David P. Jones

SENIOR COUNSEL

Leon R. Kaminski

OF COUNSEL

Daniel E. Lewis

Counsel for: U. S. F. & G. Co.; State Farm Mutual Insurance Co.; Auto
Owners Insurance Co.; Liberty Mutual Insurance Co.; Sullair Corp.; La
Porte Community School Corp.; United Farm Bureau Mutual Insurance Co.;
Physicians Insurance of Indiana; La Porte Hospital, Inc.; Norwest Bank.

For full biographical listings, see the Martindale-Hubbell Law Directory

LOGANSPORT,* Cass Co.

MILLER, TOLBERT, MUEHLHAUSEN, MUEHLHAUSEN & GROFF, P.C. (AV)

216 Fourth Street Caller Box: 7010, 46947-7010
Telephone: 219-722-4343
FAX: 219-722-1936

Glenn L. Miller (1902-1992)	John C. Muehlhausen
George R. Wildman (1932-1994)	James K. Muehlhausen
Frank E. Tolbert	R. Tod Groff

John S. Damm

Counsel for: Area Five Council on Aging; ASCO Oil Company; Careage of
Logansport, Inc.; Carter Concrete Block, Inc.; Hartford Insurance Co.; J&P
Stores, Inc.; Logansport Memorial Hospital; Meridian Insurance Co.; Mo-
torists Mutual Insurance Co.; Ohio Casualty Insurance Co.

For full biographical listings, see the Martindale-Hubbell Law Directory

MADISON,* Jefferson Co.

COOPER, COX & BARLOW (AV)

201 East Main Street, 47250-3493
Telephone: 812-273-4440
FAX: 812-273-2329

MEMBERS OF FIRM

Charles W. Cooper	Joe E. Cox
	Robert L. Barlow, II

Representative Clients: Indiana Gas Co.; PSI Energy, Inc.; Madison Bank &
Trust Co.; Farmers Bank of Milton; United Farum Bureau Mutual Ins. Co.;
Hanover College; Hartford Insurance.

For full biographical listings, see the Martindale-Hubbell Law Directory

MARION,* Grant Co.

KILEY, KILEY, HARKER, MICHAEL & CERTAIN (AV)

300 West Third Street, P.O. Box 899, 46952-0899
Telephone: 317-664-9041
Fax: 317-664-8119

MEMBERS OF FIRM

Robert Ralph Batton	David L. Kiley, Sr.
(1890-1963)	Michael J. Kiley
Albert L. Harker (1904-1965)	Albert C. Harker
Albert Bonner Brown	Thomas W. Michael
(1911-1981)	Harry J. Certain

ASSOCIATE

Therese McCullough Pryor

Counsel for: Bank One, Marion, N.A.; Liniger Co., Inc.; Atlas Foundry Co.
Local Counsel for: GenCorp.; CPC Group; General Motors; Indiana Michi-
gan Power Co./AEP; Indiana Bell Telephone Co.; Foster-Forbes, Division of
American National Can Corp.

For full biographical listings, see the Martindale-Hubbell Law Directory

MARTINSVILLE, Morgan Co.

WEHRLE & SMITH, P.C. (AV)

359 East Morgan Street, P.O. Box 1452, 46151
Telephone: 317-342-7148
FAX: 317-342-0739

William H. Wehrle   Phillip R. Smith

F. Daniel Gettelfinger

For full biographical listings, see the Martindale-Hubbell Law Directory

MERRILLVILLE, Lake Co.

BURKE, MURPHY, COSTANZA & CUPPY (AV)

Suite 600 8585 Broadway, 46410-7064
Telephone: 219-769-1313
Telecopier: 219-769-6806
East Chicago, Indiana Office: First National Bank Building. 720 West Chicago Avenue.
Telephone: 219-397-2401.
Telecopier: 219-397-0508.
Valparaiso, Indiana Office: 15 North Franklin Street, Suite 200.
Telephone: 219-531-0134.
Telecopier: 219-531-0507.
Palm Harbor, Florida Office: Suite 280, 33920 U.S. Highway 19 North.
Telephone: 813-787-7799.
Telecopier: 813-787-7237.

MEMBERS OF FIRM

Edward L. Burke	Lambert C. Genetos
Lester F. Murphy (Resident,	George W. Carberry
East Chicago, Indiana and	David K. Ranich
Palm Harbor, Florida Offices)	Kathryn D. Schmidt
Joseph E. Costanza	David Cerven
Frederick M. Cuppy	Demetri J. Retson
Gerald K. Hrebec	Elizabeth P. Moenning
Andrew J. Kopko	Lily M. Schaefer

ASSOCIATES

Paula E. Neff	Kevin E. Steele
Todd A. Etzler	Philip C. Spahn
Stacia L. Yoon	Patrick P. Devine

OF COUNSEL

Gregory R. Lyman

Representative Clients: NBD Bank, N.A.; Centier Bank; Whiteco Industries; Lehigh Portland Cement Company; Continental Machine & Engineering Co., Inc.; Gary Steel Products Corp.; Superior Construction Co., Inc.; Federal National Mortgage Association; Morrison Construction Co.; St. Catherine Hospital of East Chicago, Indiana; Travelers/Aetna Casualty Corporation.

For full biographical listings, see the Martindale-Hubbell Law Directory

HODGES & DAVIS, P.C. (AV)

8700 Broadway, 46410
Telephone: 219-641-8700
Fax: 219-641-8710
Portage, Indiana Office: 6082 Lute Road. P.O. Box 1037.
Telephone: 219-762-9129.
Fax: 219-762-2826.

William F. Hodges (1877-1954)	Earle F. Hites
Claude V. Ridgely (1881-1963)	R. Lawrence Steele
Thomas M. Hodges (1906-1969)	Gregory A. Sobkowski
Herschel B. Davis (1901-1990)	Bonnie C. Coleman
Gilbert Gruenberg (1902-1989)	Jill M. Madajczyk
Bruce E. Sayers (1939-1990)	Laura B. Frost
Clyde D. Compton	David H. Kreider
William B. Davis	Robert G. Vann

OF COUNSEL

Edward J. Hussey

Representative Clients: The Methodist Hospitals, Inc.; City of Portage, Indiana; Jewel Cos., Inc.; Osco Drug, Inc.; Porter County Plan Commission.

For full biographical listings, see the Martindale-Hubbell Law Directory

HOEPPNER WAGNER AND EVANS (AV)

Twin Towers, Suite 606 South, 1000 East 80th Place, 46410
Telephone: 219-769-6552; 800-263-1466 (IN,IL)
Fax: 219-738-2349
Valparaiso, Indiana Office: 103 East Lincolnway, P.O. Box 2357, 46384-2357.
Telephone: 219-464-4961; 800-879-2246 (IN,IL).
Fax: 219-465-0603.

RESIDENT MEMBERS

John E. Hughes   F. Joseph Jaskowiak
Richard A. Browne

RESIDENT ASSOCIATES

J. Brian Hittinger   Jack A. Kramer

(See Next Column)

RESIDENT OF COUNSEL

Jim B. Brown

For full biographical listings, see the Martindale-Hubbell Law Directory

LUCAS, HOLCOMB & MEDREA (AV)

300 East 90th Drive, 46410
Telephone: 219-769-3561
Fax: 219-756-7409

MEMBERS OF FIRM

James A. Holcomb	Nick Katich
John O. Stiles	Mary Linda Casey
Daniel A. Medrea	Mark S. Lucas
Robert F. Peters	Karen L. Hughes
Stephen R. Place	David E. Woodward
Joseph M. Skozen	

ASSOCIATES

David A. Buls   Norman L. Burggraf

OF COUNSEL

Robert A. Lucas

Representative Clients: Bank One, Merrillville, N. A.; U. S. F. & G. Co.; Montgomery Ward Co.; Calumet Securities Corp. (Mortgage Bankers); Munster Medical Research Foundation, Inc. (Operating "The Community Hospital"); Hammond Clinic.

For full biographical listings, see the Martindale-Hubbell Law Directory

SPANGLER, JENNINGS & DOUGHERTY, P.C. (AV)

8396 Mississippi Street, 46410-6398
Telephone: 219-769-2323
Facsimile: 219-769-5007
Valparaiso, Indiana Office: 150 Lincolnway, Suite 3001.
Telephone: 219-462-6151.
FAX: 219-477-4935.

Ronald T. Spangler	David J. Hanson
Harry J. Jennings	Robert P. Kennedy
Patrick J. Dougherty	Allen B. Zaremba
(Valparaiso Office)	James T. McNiece
Duane V. Stoner (1923-1982)	Daniel A. Gioia
Samuel J. Furlin	James D. McQuillan
Richard A. Mayer	David L. Abel, II
Jay A. Charon	Harold G. Hagberg
John P. McQuillan	Lawrence A. Kalina
Samuel J. Bernardi, Jr.	Robert P. Stoner
(Valparaiso Office)	(Valparaiso Office)
Jon F. Schmoll	Gregory J. Tonner
Robert D. Hawk	Kathleen M. Maicher
Joseph E. McDonald	Paul B. Poracky
Peter G. Koransky	Robert D. Brown

Robert J. Dignam	Carl A. Greci
David R. Phillips	James M. Portelli
Kristin A. Mulholland	Thomas F. Shea
Anthony F. Tavitas	P. Stephen Fardy
Lloyd P. Mullen	Kelly E. O'Malley
Kisti Good Risse	John B. Bentz
Mark D. Geheb	Edward W. Hearn
Greg A. Bouwer	(Valparaiso Office)
Ginamarie Gaudio-Graves	Robert D. Hawk, Jr.
Victor H. Prasco	Gary T. Bell
Ricardo A. Hall	

OF COUNSEL

Clarence Borns

Representative Clients: Allstate Insurance Cos.; Bank One, Merriville, N.A.; First National Bank of Valparaiso; Ford Motor Credit Co.; Inland Steel Co.; Munster Calumet Shopping Center; School Town of Munster; St. Paul Insurance Cos.; State Farm Cos.; Volkswagen of America.

For full biographical listings, see the Martindale-Hubbell Law Directory

MICHIGAN CITY, La Porte Co.

SWEENEY, DABAGIA, DONOGHUE, THORNE, JANES & PAGOS (AV)

709 Franklin Square, P.O. Box 769, 46360
Telephone: 219-879-5321
Fax: 219-879-2942

MEMBERS OF FIRM

Clarence T. Sweeney (1899-1980)	Jeffrey L. Thorne
John H. Sweeney	William Janes
Lee W. Dabagia	Donald W. Pagos
Patrick E. Donoghue	Thais A. Bronner

References: First Citizens Bank, N.A.

For full biographical listings, see the Martindale-Hubbell Law Directory

MISHAWAKA, St. Joseph Co.

SCHINDLER AND OLSON (AV)

122 South Mill Street, P.O. Box 100, 46544
Telephone: 219-259-5461
Fax: 219-259-5462

OF COUNSEL
John W. Schindler (1884-1971)   John W. Schindler, Jr.
MEMBER OF FIRM
James J. Olson

Representative Clients: Penn-Harris-Madison School Corp.; School City of Mishawaka.
Reference: 1st Source Bank of Mishawaka.

For full biographical listings, see the Martindale-Hubbell Law Directory

---

*MONTICELLO,** White Co. — (Refer to Delphi)

*MUNCIE,** Delaware Co.

CANNON & BRUNS (AV)

119 North High Street, 47305
Telephone: 317-289-2161
FAX: 317-289-2162

MEMBERS OF FIRM
Thomas A. Cannon   William G. Bruns
Thomas A. Cannon, Jr.

References: First Merchants Bank, Muncie; American National Bank and Trust Company of Muncie.

For full biographical listings, see the Martindale-Hubbell Law Directory

---

MUNSTER, Lake Co.

LAW OFFICES OF EUGENE M. FEINGOLD (AV)

625 Ridge Road, Suite A, 46321
Telephone: 219-836-8800
Fax: 219-836-8944

ASSOCIATES
Steven P. Kennedy

For full biographical listings, see the Martindale-Hubbell Law Directory

---

LAW OFFICES OF TIMOTHY F. KELLY (AV)

Suite 2A, 9250 Columbia Avenue, 46321
Telephone: 219-836-4062
Telecopier: 219-836-0167
Email: 76325.1505@Compuserve.Com
MEMBERS OF FIRM
Timothy F. Kelly   Karl K. Vanzo
ASSOCIATES
Harvey Karlovac   Steven J. Sersic
LEGAL SUPPORT PERSONNEL
LEGAL ASSISTANTS
Kristen Cook Faso   Kathleen E. Peek

For full biographical listings, see the Martindale-Hubbell Law Directory

---

*NASHVILLE,** Brown Co. — (Refer to Bloomington)

*NEW ALBANY,** Floyd Co.

KIGHTLINGER & GRAY (AV)

Pinnacle Centre, Suite 200, 3317 Grant Line Road, P.O. Box 6727, 46151
Telephone: 812-949-2300
Telecopier: 812-949-8556
Indianapolis, Indiana Office: Market Square Center, Suite 660, 151 North Delaware Street, 46204.
Telephone: 317-638-4521.
Telecopier: 317-636-5917.
Evansville, Indiana Office: One Riverfront Place, Suite 210, 20 N.W. First Street, 47708.
Telephone: 812-464-9508.
Telecopier: 812-464-9511.

RESIDENT PARTNERS
Richard T. Mullineaux   Rodney L. Scott
Samuel A. Day   Van T. Willis
RESIDENT ASSOCIATES
Mary M. Nord   Gregory M. Reger
Scott L. Tyler   Diane E. Bluhm
Marti E. Thurman

Representative Clients: American Family Mutual Insurance Co.; American International Group; American States; Associated Aviation Underwriters; Black & Decker (U.S., Inc.); Government Employees Insurance Co.; Mack Trucks, Inc.; Reliance Insurance Group.
Reference: INB National Bank.

For full biographical listings, see the Martindale-Hubbell Law Directory

---

MATTOX & MATTOX (AV)

Suite 420 Elsby Building, P.O. Box 1203, 47151-1203
Telephone: 812-944-8005
Facsimile: 812-944-2255
Email: mattox@ntr.net
MEMBERS OF FIRM
Richard L. Mattox   S. Frank Mattox
ASSOCIATES
Linda A. Mattox   Derrick H. Wilson
Karen R. Goodwell

Representative Clients: AAOMS National Insurance; Cablelink, Inc.; Floyd Memorial Hospital; John Deere Co.; Kimball International, Inc.; The Medical Protective Co.; Papa Johns Intl., Inc.; PHICO Insurance Co.; Physicians Group, Inc.; Robinson Nugent, Inc.

For full biographical listings, see the Martindale-Hubbell Law Directory

---

WYATT, TARRANT & COMBS (AV)

(Formerly Orbison, O'Connor, MacGregor & Mattox)
The Elsby Building, 117 East Spring Street, 47150
Telephone: 812-945-3561
Telecopier: 812-949-2524
URL: http://www.wyattfirm.com
Louisville, Kentucky Office: Citizens Plaza.
Telephone: 502-589-5235.
Telecopier: 502-589-0309.
Lexington, Kentucky Office: 1700 Lexington Financial Center.
Telephone: 606-233-2012.
Telecopier: 606-259-0649.
Frankfort, Kentucky Office: The Taylor-Scott Building, 311 West Main Street, P.O. Box 495.
Telephone: 502-223-2104.
Telecopier: 502-227-7681.
Nashville, Tennessee Office: 1500 Nashville City Center, 511 Union Street.
Telephone: 615-244-0020.
Telecopier: 615-256-1726.
Music Row, Nashville Office: 29 Music Square East.
Telephone: 615-255-6161.
Telecopier: 615-254-4490.
Memphis, Tennessee Office: Crescent Center, Suite 650, 6075 Poplar Avenue.
Telephone: 901-537-1000.
Telecopier: 901-537-1010.
Hendersonville, Tennessee Office: 313 E. Main Street, Suite 1.
Telephone: 615-822-8822.
Telecopier: 615-824-4684.

MEMBERS OF FIRM
Telford B. Orbison (1901-1990)   Thomas W. Sinex
Charles E. MacGregor   J. Spencer Harmon
James E. Bourne   Richard A. Bierly
Janet K. Martin
ASSOCIATES
Larry R. Church   John W. Woodard, Jr.
OF COUNSEL
Richard C. O'Connor

Representative Clients: Allstate Insurance Co.; Amoco Oil Co.; Ford Motor Credit Corp.; Green Banner Publications, Inc.; Gettelfinger Popcorn Co., Inc.; Joe Huber Farms, Inc.; Indiana Bell Telephone Co.; Province of Our Lady of Consolation, Inc.; Public Service Indiana; United Farm Bureau Mutual Insurance Co.

For full biographical listings, see the Martindale-Hubbell Law Directory

---

NEW HAVEN, Allen Co. — (Refer to Ft. Wayne)

*NEWPORT,** Vermillion Co. — (Refer to Brazil)

*NOBLESVILLE,** Hamilton Co.

CAMPBELL KYLE PROFFITT (AV)

198 South Ninth Street, P.O. Box 2020, 46060-2020
Telephone: 317-773-2090
FAX: 317-776-5051
Carmel, Indiana Office: Suite 400, 650 East Carmel Drive.
Telephone: 317-846-6514.
Fax: 317-843-8097.

MEMBERS OF FIRM
Frank S. Campbell (1880-1964)   Jeffrey S. Nickloy
Frank W. Campbell (1916-1991)   Deborah L. Farmer
John M. Kyle   (Resident, Carmel Office)
John D. Proffitt   William E. Wendling, Jr.
   (Resident, Carmel Office)   (Resident, Carmel Office)
Robert F. Campbell   Anne Hensley Poindexter
   (Resident, Carmel Office)   (Resident, Carmel Office)
Andrew M. Barker

(See Next Column)

CAMPBELL KYLE PROFFITT, *Noblesville—Continued*

ASSOCIATES

Todd L. Ruetz
(Resident, Carmel Office)

Melissa A. Clark
(Resident, Carmel Office)

Matthew S. Love

Representative Clients: Bridgestone/Firestone Inc.; Mobil Oil Corp.; PSI Energy, Inc.

For full biographical listings, see the Martindale-Hubbell Law Directory

---

CHURCH, CHURCH, HITTLE & ANTRIM (AV)

938 Conner Street, P.O. Box 10, 46060-0010
Telephone: 317-773-2190
Telecopier: 317-773-5320
Email: cchadoug@msn.com

MEMBERS OF FIRM

Douglas D. Church	Bruce M. Bittner
Jack G. Hittle	Brian J. Zaiger
J. Michael Antrim	David Joseph Barker
Martin E. Risacher	Leslie Craig Henderzahs

OF COUNSEL

Manson E. Church

Representative Clients: Noblesville Schools; Westfield-Washington Schools; Indiana School Finance Corp.; Community Bank; Metrobank; Towns of Westfield, Fishers; Reynolds Farm Equipment Co.; Weihe Engineering; Historic Railroad Multijurisdictional Port Authority.

For full biographical listings, see the Martindale-Hubbell Law Directory

---

NORTH VERNON, Jennings Co.

McCONNELL AND FINNERTY (AV)

38 North 5th Street, P.O. Box 90, 47265
Telephone: 812-346-5201
FAX: 812-346-8470

MEMBERS OF FIRM

Ira B. Hamilton (1899-1982)	Harold H. McConnell
Corinne R. Finnerty	

ASSOCIATES

Alan L. Marshall	Jack A. Kugler

Representative Clients: Union Bank & Trust Co.; Farm Bureau Mutual Insurance Co.; Home Federal Savings Bank; Lees Inns of America, Inc.; Rose Acre Farms, Inc.; Pekin Insurance; Lee's Ready Mix & Trucking, Inc.

For full biographical listings, see the Martindale-Hubbell Law Directory

---

PAOLI,* Orange Co.

TUCKER AND TUCKER (AV)

188 South Court Street, 47454
Telephone: 812-723-2313
Fax: 812-723-3789

James C. Tucker

Counsel for: Orange County Bank; Citizens Bank, Orleans; Springs Valley Bank and Trust Co.; Bank of Mitchell, Paoli; Town of West Baden Springs; The Orleans Community Schools; The Springs Valley Community Schools; Paoli Community Schools; West Washington School Corporation; Reynolds, Inc.

For full biographical listings, see the Martindale-Hubbell Law Directory

---

PETERSBURG,* Pike Co. — (Refer to Vincennes)

PLYMOUTH,* Marshall Co.

KIZER & NEU (AV)

319 West Jefferson Street, P.O. Box 158, 46563
Telephone: 219-936-2169
FAX: 219-936-2642
Bremen, Indiana Office: 1406 West Plymouth Street, P.O. Box 158.
Telephone: 219-546-2626.
FAX: 219-546-2608.

MEMBERS OF FIRM

Marshall F. Kizer (1907-1988)	Jere L. Humphrey
James H. Neu (1917-1991)	Mark E. Wagner
Richard F. Joyce	(Resident at Bremen)
Harold L. Wyland	Ronald D. Gifford
James N. Clevenger	

Counsel for: The First State Bank, Bourbon, Indiana; 1st Source Bank of Marshall County; Prudential Insurance Company of America; Bremen Castings, Inc.; Bornemann Products, Inc.; Universal Bearings, Inc., all of Bremen, Indiana; Society Bank, South Bend, Indiana; 4th District Farm Credit Services.

For full biographical listings, see the Martindale-Hubbell Law Directory

---

PORTAGE, Porter Co.

HODGES & DAVIS, P.C. (AV)

6082 Lute Road, P.O. Box 1037, 46368
Telephone: 219-762-9129
Fax: 219-762-2826
Merrillville, Indiana Office: 8700 Broadway.
Telephone: 219-641-8700.
Fax: 219-641-8710.

Clyde D. Compton	R. Lawrence Steele
Earle F. Hites	Gregory A. Sobkowski
Bonnie C. Coleman	

Representative Clients: The Methodist Hospitals, Inc.; City of Portage, Indiana; Jewel Cos., Inc.; Osco Drug, Inc.; Porter County Plan Commission.

For full biographical listings, see the Martindale-Hubbell Law Directory

---

PORTLAND,* Jay Co. — (Refer to Fort Wayne)

PRINCETON,* Gibson Co.

HALL, PARTENHEIMER & KINKLE (AV)

219 North Hart Street, P.O. Box 313, 47670
Telephone: 812-386-0050
FAX: 812-385-2575

MEMBERS OF FIRM

Verner P. Partenheimer	J. Robert Kinkle
R. Scott Partenheimer	

Representative Clients: Interlake Inc.; Gibson County Bank; Old Ben Coal Co.
Approved Attorneys for: Lawyers Title Insurance; Ticor Title Insurance.

For full biographical listings, see the Martindale-Hubbell Law Directory

---

RISING SUN,* Ohio Co. — (Refer to Lawrenceburg)

ROCHESTER,* Fulton Co. — (Refer to Plymouth)

ROCKVILLE,* Parke Co. — (Refer to Terre Haute)

RUSHVILLE,* Rush Co.

EARNEST, FOSTER, EDER, LEVI & NORTHAM (AV)

114 West Third Street, P.O. Box 430, 46173
Telephone: 317-932-4118
Fax: 317-932-4486

Kenneth L. Earnest (1916-1995)

OF COUNSEL

James S. Foster

MEMBERS OF FIRM

Robert J. Eder	Richard K. Levi
David E. Northam	

Representative Clients: Rush County REMC; First Federal Savings and Loan Association of Rushville; Rush Memorial Hospital; Farm Bureau Insurance Co.; Farmers State Bank; The Sampler, Inc.; Ticor Title Insurance Co.

For full biographical listings, see the Martindale-Hubbell Law Directory

---

SALEM,* Washington Co.

MEAD, MEAD & THOMPSON (AV)

Mead Building, 108 East Market, P.O. Box 468, 47167-0468
Telephone: 812-883-4693
Fax: 812-883-2207
Email: JWMEAD@Blueriver.Net

MEMBERS OF FIRM

Walter G. Mead (1879-1976)	John W. Mead
Willis C. Mead (1914-1992)	Trent Thompson

ASSOCIATES

Mark D. Clark

A List of References will be furnished upon Request.

For full biographical listings, see the Martindale-Hubbell Law Directory

---

SHELBYVILLE,* Shelby Co.

ADAMS & CRAMER (AV)

33 West Washington Street, 46176
Telephone: 317-398-6626
Fax: 317-392-1962
Email: lawza@shelbynet.net

Ralph Adams (1901-1986)

MEMBERS OF FIRM

Fred V. Cramer	Robert W. Adams

(See Next Column)

ADAMS & CRAMER—*Continued*

ASSOCIATES

David A. Mack

Counsel for: Mickey's T-Mart; Town of Morristown, Indiana; Southwestern Consolidated Schools; Brewer Design Services; Fiddler's Three.

For full biographical listings, see the Martindale-Hubbell Law Directory

SHOALS,* Martin Co. — (Refer to Jasper)

SOUTH BEND,* St. Joseph Co.

BAKER & DANIELS (AV)

First Bank Building, 205 West Jefferson Boulevard, 46601
Telephone: 219-234-4149
Fax: 219-239-1900
Indianapolis, Indiana Office: 300 North Meridian Street.
Telephone: 317-237-0300.
Fort Wayne, Indiana Office: 111 East Wayne Street, Suite 800.
Telephone: 219-424-8000.
Elkhart, Indiana Office: 301 B South Main Street, Suite 307.
Telephone: 219-296-6000.
Washington, D.C. Office: 1701 K Street, N.W., Suite 400.
Telephone: 202-785-1565.

MEMBERS OF FIRM

James D. Hall	James M. Matthews
Thomas J. Brunner, Jr.	Peter G. Trybula
Richard L. Hill	Paul J. Peralta

OF COUNSEL

Paul D. Borghesani	Ken C. Decker

ASSOCIATES

Daniel G. Areaux	David C. Read
D. Lucetta Pope	Lawrence R. Williams, II
Randolph R. Rompola	(Resident)
(Resident)	Kari A. Gallagher (Resident)
Robert A. Wade	Edward A. Sullivan, III
Amy Lawrence Mader	(Resident)
(Resident)	Robert D. Null

Representative Clients: City of South Bend; 1st Source Bank; Jack-Post Corp.; Society Corp.; South Bend Drug Co.; WSBT, Inc.; General Motors Corp.; Eli Lilly and Company; Borg-Warner Corporation.

For full biographical listings, see the Martindale-Hubbell Law Directory

EDWARD N. KALAMAROS & ASSOCIATES PROFESSIONAL CORPORATION (AV)

129 North Michigan Avenue, P.O. Box 4156, 46634
Telephone: 219-232-4801
Telecopier: 219-232-9736

Edward N. Kalamaros	Philip E. Kalamaros
Timothy J. Walsh	Sally P. Norton
Thomas F. Cohen	Kevin W. Kearney
Joseph M. Forte	Peter J. Bagiackas
Robert Deane Woods	David A. Wemhoff
Patrick J. Hinkle	Eric G. Ciesielski

Representative Clients: South Bend Medical Foundation, Inc.; Powell Tool Supply, Inc.; Cooper Industries/Anco Division; Orthopedic & Sports Medicine Center of Northern Indiana, Inc.; Edward J. DeBartolo Corporation; University Park Mall; Marriott Corporation; Employers Reinsurance Corporation; Orion Group.

For full biographical listings, see the Martindale-Hubbell Law Directory

ROWE, ROWE & MAHER (AV)

Suite 900 Keybank Building, 46601
Telephone: 219-233-8200
Fax: 219-234-5987

R. Kent Rowe	R. Kent Rowe, III
Timothy J. Maher	

ASSOCIATES

Gregory J. Haines	Steven D. Groth
Lee Korzan	Marie Anne Hendrie

For full biographical listings, see the Martindale-Hubbell Law Directory

SPENCER,* Owen Co.

CHARLES W. EDWARDS (AV)

64 East Market Street, P.O. Box 108, 47460
Telephone: 812-829-2209
FAX: 812-829-2200
Email: cedwards@bluemarble.net

Approved Attorney for: Ticor Title Insurance Co.
Reference: Owen Community Bank.

For full biographical listings, see the Martindale-Hubbell Law Directory

SULLIVAN,* Sullivan Co. — (Refer to Terre Haute)

TERRE HAUTE,* Vigo Co.

COX, ZWERNER, GAMBILL & SULLIVAN (AV)

511 Wabash Avenue, P.O. Box 1625, 47808-1625
Telephone: 812-232-6003
Fax: 812-232-6567

MEMBERS OF FIRM

Ernest J. Zwerner (1918-1980)	David W. Sullivan
Benjamin G. Cox (1915-1988)	Robert L. Gowdy
Gilbert W. Gambill, Jr.	Louis F. Britton
James E. Sullivan	Carroll D. Smeltzer
Benjamin G. Cox, Jr.	Jeffry A. Lind

ASSOCIATES

Ronald E. Jumps

OF COUNSEL

Robert D. Hepburn

Counsel for: Terre Haute First National Bank; Farmers Insurance Group; Indiana-American Water Co.; Indiana State University; Merchants National Bank of Terre Haute; Rose-Hulman Institute of Technology; Tribune-Star Publishing Co., Inc.; Weston Paper & Manufacturing Co.

For full biographical listings, see the Martindale-Hubbell Law Directory

WILKINSON, GOELLER, MODESITT, WILKINSON & DRUMMY (AV)

333 Ohio Street, P.O. Box 800, 47808-0800
Telephone: 812-232-4311
Fax: 812-235-5107

MEMBERS OF FIRM

Myrl O. Wilkinson	John C. Wall
David H. Goeller	William M. Olah
Raymond H. Modesitt	Craig M. McKee
B. Curtis Wilkinson	Scott M. Kyrouac
William W. Drummy	Jeffrey A. Boyll
Kelvin L. Roots	David P. Friedrich

ASSOCIATES

Anthony R. Jost

Representative Corporate Clients: Merchants National Bank; Old National Trust Company; Old National Bank; CSX, Inc.; General Housewares Corp.; MAB Paints; Chicago Title Insurance Co.; Union Hospital; Associated Physicians and Surgeons Clinic, LLC.; PSI Energy, Inc.

For full biographical listings, see the Martindale-Hubbell Law Directory

TIPTON,* Tipton Co. — (Refer to Kokomo)

VALPARAISO,* Porter Co.

BLACHLY, TABOR, BOZIK & HARTMAN (AV)

Suite 401 Indiana Federal Building, 46383
Telephone: 219-464-1041
Fax: 219-464-0927

MEMBERS OF FIRM

Quentin A. Blachly	David L. Hollenbeck
Glenn J. Tabor	David L. DeBoer
James S. Bozik	Thomas F. Macke
Duane W. Hartman	Randall J. Zromkoski
Richard J. Rupcich	

ASSOCIATES

Roger A. Weitgenant	Craig R. Van Schouwen
Margaret Marie Loitz	

Reference: First National Bank.

For full biographical listings, see the Martindale-Hubbell Law Directory

DOUGLAS, ALEXA, KOEPPEN & HURLEY (AV)

14 Indiana Avenue, P.O. Box 209, 46384-0209
Telephone: 219-462-2126
Fax: 219-477-4408

MEMBERS OF FIRM

Herbert K. Douglas	R. Bradley Koeppen
William E. Alexa	Brian J. Hurley
Mark A. Gland	

OF COUNSEL

George W. Douglas

Attorneys for: Urschel Laboratories, Inc.; Northern Indiana Public Service Co.; Park District, City of Valparaiso; Emerson Electric.

For full biographical listings, see the Martindale-Hubbell Law Directory

Valparaiso—Continued

HOEPPNER WAGNER AND EVANS (AV)

103 East Lincolnway, P.O. Box 2357, 46384-2357
Telephone: 219-464-4961; 800-879-2246 (IN,IL)
Fax: 219-465-0603
Merrillville, Indiana Office: Twin Towers, Suite 606 South, 1000 East 80th Place, 46410.
Telephone: 219-769-6552; 800-263-1466. (IN,IL,).
Fax: 219-738-2349.

RETIRED
Delmar R. Hoeppner

MEMBERS OF FIRM

William H. Wagner	Ronald P. Kuker
Larry G. Evans	Richard A. Browne
William F. Satterlee, III	(Resident, Merrillville Office)
Gordon A. Etzler	F. Joseph Jaskowiak
John E. Hughes	(Resident, Merrillville Office)
(Resident, Merrillville Office)	Richard M. Davis
Morris A. Sunkel	Mark E. Schmidtke
James A. Cheslek	Todd A. Leeth
James L. Jorgensen	Michael P. Blaize

ASSOCIATES

Jonathan R. Hanson	Jeffrey W. Clymer
J. Brian Hittinger	Michael B. Miller
(Resident, Merrillville Office)	Jack A. Kramer
Lauren K. Kroeger	(Resident, Merrillville Office)

OF COUNSEL
Jim B. Brown (Resident, Merrillville Office)

Attorneys for: Bethlehem Steel Corp.; Chester, Inc.; Hunt-Wesson Foods, Inc.; NBD Bank, N.A.; Owens-Corning Fiberglas Corp.; Valparaiso University; State Farm Insurance; Allstate Insurance Co.; Indiana Federal Bank for Savings.

For full biographical listings, see the Martindale-Hubbell Law Directory

SPANGLER, JENNINGS & DOUGHERTY, P.C. (AV)

150 Lincolnway, Suite 3001, 46303
Telephone: 219-462-6151
FAX: 219-477-4935
Merrillville, Indiana Office: 8396 Mississippi Street.
Telephone: 219-769-2323.

RESIDENT PERSONNEL

Patrick J. Dougherty	Samuel J. Bernardi, Jr.
Duane V. Stoner (1923-1982)	Robert P. Stoner

Edward W. Hearn

Reference: First National Bank of Valparaiso.

For full biographical listings, see the Martindale-Hubbell Law Directory

VERSAILLES,* Ripley Co.

EATON & ROMWEBER (AV)

123 South Main Street, P.O. Box 275, 47042
Telephone: 812-689-5111
Fax: 812-689-5165
Batesville, Indiana Office: 13 East George Street. Telephone 812-934-5735. *Fax:* 812-934-6041.

MEMBERS OF FIRM

Larry L. Eaton	Anthony A. Romweber

ASSOCIATES

W. Gregory Coy	Eric E. Wright
	(Not admitted in IN)

For full biographical listings, see the Martindale-Hubbell Law Directory

VINCENNES,* Knox Co.

EMISON, DOOLITTLE, KOLB & ROELLGEN (AV)

Eighth & Busseron Streets, P.O. Box 215, 47591
Telephone: 812-882-2280
FAX: 812-885-2308
Email: emison@ns.kensco.net

MEMBERS OF FIRM

Rabb Emison	Jeffrey B. Kolb
Robert P. Doolittle, Jr.	J. David Roellgen

Clients Include: Security Bank & Trust Co.; Sun-Commercial Newspaper; Amoco Pipeline; Tenneco Energy; United Farm Bureau Mutual Insurance Co.

For full biographical listings, see the Martindale-Hubbell Law Directory

WABASH,* Wabash Co. — (Refer to Huntington)

WILLIAMSPORT,* Warren Co. — (Refer to Covington)

WINAMAC,* Pulaski Co. — (Refer to Logansport)

WINCHESTER,* Randolph Co. — (Refer to Richmond)

IOWA

ADEL,* Dallas Co. — (Refer to Dallas Center)

ALBIA,* Monroe Co. — (Refer to Ottumwa)

ALGONA,* Kossuth Co. — (Refer to Ft. Dodge)

AMES, Story Co.

SMITH, SHARP, BENSON, JAHN & FEILMEYER (AV)

618 Douglas, P.O. Box 270, 50010-0270
Telephone: 515-239-5000
Fax: 515-239-5010

MEMBERS OF FIRM

John E. Nutty (Retired)	David W. Benson
Donald L. Smith	Lawrence E. Jahn
Dale E. Sharp	Franklin J. Feilmeyer
Victoria A. Westenfield	

References: First National Bank, Ames, Iowa; Brenton Savings Bank, FSB.

For full biographical listings, see the Martindale-Hubbell Law Directory

ANAMOSA,* Jones Co. — (Refer to Cedar Rapids)

AUDUBON,* Audubon Co. — (Refer to Atlantic)

BEDFORD,* Taylor Co. — (Refer to Mt. Ayr)

BETTENDORF, Scott Co.

WELLS, GALLAGHER, ROEDER & MILLAGE (AV)

(Not a Partnership)
1989 Spruce Hills Drive, 52722
Telephone: 319-355-5303
Fax: 319-359-7711

Robert D. Wells (1904-1990)	Michael L. Roeder
Robert H. Gallagher	David A. Millage

Robert S. Gallagher

Representative Clients: Blue Grass Savings Bank; Farmers Savings Bank; Le Clair State Bank; Adams Door Co., Inc.; Engelbrecht Farms, Inc.; Brus Farms, Inc.; General Diesel, Inc.; Oertel Sheetmetal Co.; Rich Metal Co.; Eldridge Lumber Co., Inc.

For full biographical listings, see the Martindale-Hubbell Law Directory

BLOOMFIELD,* Davis Co. — (Refer to Ottumwa)

BURLINGTON,* Des Moines Co. — (Refer to Fort Madison)

CEDAR RAPIDS,* Linn Co.

LYNCH, DALLAS, SMITH & HARMAN, P.C. (AV)

526 Second Avenue SE, P.O. Box 2457, 52406-2457
Telephone: 319-365-9101
Facsimile: 319-365-9512

Charles J. Lynch (1905-1983)	Gerald Lyell Fatka
William M. Dallas (1905-1981)	Scott E. McLeod
Ralph V. Harman (Retired)	Robert R. Rush
Donald E. Smith	Wilford H. Stone
Donald G. Ribble	Sean W. McPartland
H. Edward Beatty	Matthew J. Nagle

Elizabeth D. Jacobi	Thomas D. Wolle
Susan H. Sibert	

Representative Clients: American States Insurance Co.; Blue Cross and Blue Shield of Iowa; Deere & Co.; Rockwell International Corp.; State Farm Insurance Cos.; The Travelers Insurance Cos.

For full biographical listings, see the Martindale-Hubbell Law Directory

SHUTTLEWORTH & INGERSOLL, P.C. (AV)

500 Firstar Bank Building, P.O. Box 2107, 52406-2107
Telephone: 319-365-9461
Fax: 319-365-8443
Email: si-law@inav.net

Thomas M. Collins	Glenn L. Johnson
James C. Nemmers	Thomas P. Peffer
Michael O. McDermott	Kevin H. Collins
John M. Bickel	William P. Prowell
Robert D. Houghton	Diane Kutzko
Richard S. Fry	Mark L. Zaiger
Richard C. Garberson	Douglas R. Oelschlaeger
Gary J. Streit	Constance M. Alt

(See Next Column)

SHUTTLEWORTH & INGERSOLL P.C.—*Continued*

Carroll J. Reasoner	William S. Hochstetler
Steven J. Pace	Kurt L. Kratovil
	LeeAnn M. Ferry

Christine L. McLaughlin	Douglas K. Burrell
William H. Courter	Kevin J. Caster
Dean D. Carrington	Theresa C. Davis
Nancy J. Penner	David T. Hayes

OF COUNSEL

W. R. Shuttleworth

COUNSEL

Joan Lipsky   Ann F. Hammond

Representative Clients: Amana Society; Archer-Daniels-Midland Co.; Cargill, Inc.; Cryovac, Inc., a Division of W. R. Grace & Co.; Firstar Bank Cedar Rapids, N.A.; General Mills, Inc.; General Motors Corp.; MCI; PMX Industries, Inc.; Rockwell International - Graphic Systems Division.

For full biographical listings, see the Martindale-Hubbell Law Directory

---

CENTERVILLE,* Appanoose Co. — (Refer to Ottumwa)

CHARITON,* Lucas Co. — (Refer to Knoxville)

CHARLES CITY,* Floyd Co.

EGGERT, ERB, O'DONOHOE, FRYE AND VON AH, P.L.C. (AV)

701 Blunt Parkway, P.O. Box 399, 50616
Telephone: 515-228-3727
Fax: 515-228-6524

Robert J. Eggert	Judith Mack O'Donohoe
James A. Erb	William M. Frye
	Lance W. Von Ah

Local Counsel for: Citizens National Bank; Family Community Credit Union.
Representative Clients: Dr. Mayfield Laboratories, Inc.; Allied Construction Co.; Farner-Hewitt; Greene Limestone Co.; Chautauqua Guest Homes.
Reference: Citizens National Bank.

For full biographical listings, see the Martindale-Hubbell Law Directory

---

CHEROKEE,* Cherokee Co.

HERRICK, ARY, COOK, COOK, COOK & COOK (AV)

209 West Willow Street, P.O. Box 209, 51012
Telephone: 712-225-5175
FAX: 712-225-5178

MEMBERS OF FIRM

William K. Herrick (1878-1944)	John H. Cook, Jr.
Lester C. Ary (1893-1962)	Richard Ary Cook
John Howard Cook	William D. Cook

Attorneys for: Cherokee State Bank; Cherokee Community School District; Lundell Construction Co., Inc.; Tiel Sanford Memorial Fund; Simonsen Mill Inc.; Sioux Valley Memorial Hospital; Obeco Inc.; Christensen Brothers Concrete; Cherokee Community Credit Union; First Trust and Savings Bank of Aurelia.

For full biographical listings, see the Martindale-Hubbell Law Directory

---

SAYRE & WITTGRAF (AV)

223 Pine Street, P.O. Box 535, 51012
Telephone: 712-225-6481
FAX: 712-225-5300

MEMBERS OF FIRM

Lew McDonald (1884-1963)	George W. Wittgraf
David L. Sayre	Daniel A. Meloy

Representative Clients: Central Trust and Savings Bank, Cherokee, Iowa; Wilson Foods Corp.; Grundman-Hicks Construction Co., Inc.; C-M-L Telephone Cooperative Association of Meriden, Iowa; Jesse's Fine Meats, Inc.; Beck Ranch Inc.; Continental Western Insurance Co.; United Fire and Casualty Co.

For full biographical listings, see the Martindale-Hubbell Law Directory

---

CLARINDA,* Page Co.

TURNER, JONES & BITTING (AV)

301 East Main Street, P.O. Box 231, 51632
Telephone: 712-542-2151
FAX: 712-542-2031

MEMBERS OF FIRM

Clinton H. Turner (1909-1969)	Paul W. Jones
Sanford A. Turner	Ronny M. Bitting

Representative Clients: Citizens State Bank, Clarinda, Iowa; City of Clarinda; Cities of Coin, Braddyville, Shambaugh, Blanchard and Northboro, Iowa; Lisle Corp., Clarinda, Iowa; Page County Federal Savings; Oxley Farms, Inc.
References: Citizens State Bank; Page County State Bank of Clarinda, Iowa.

For full biographical listings, see the Martindale-Hubbell Law Directory

---

CLARION,* Wright Co. — (Refer to Hampton)

CLINTON,* Clinton Co. — (Refer to Maquoketa)

COLUMBUS JUNCTION, Louisa Co. — (Refer to Muscatine)

CORNING,* Adams Co. — (Refer to Clarinda)

CORYDON,* Wayne Co. — (Refer to Mt. Ayr)

COUNCIL BLUFFS,* Pottawattamie Co.

PETERS LAW FIRM, P.C. (AV)

233 Pearl Street, P.O. Box 1078, 51502-1078
Telephone: 712-328-3157
FAX: 712-328-9092

James A. Campbell	Scott H. Peters
Dennis Leu	John M. McHale
Dennis M. Gray	Jacob J. Peters
James A. Thomas	Leo P. Martin
Lyle W. Ditmars	Scott J. Rogers
	Jon E. Heisterkamp

Edean Murray	Matthew G. Woods

RETIRED

John M. Peters

Representative Clients: Bluffs Run Casino; Mercantile Bank, Council Bluffs, IA; Grinnell Mutual Reinsurance Co.; Iowa West Racing Association; Rockwell International; Shelter Insurance; State Farm Insurance; Kemper Group; The Pillsbury Co.; The Cities of Crescent, Glenwood, Treynor, McClelland, Underwood.

For full biographical listings, see the Martindale-Hubbell Law Directory

---

REILLY, PETERSEN & HANNAN, P.L.C. (AV)

215 South Main Street, P.O. Box 1016, 51502-1016
Telephone: 712-328-1575
Fax: 712-328-1562

C. R. Hannan	Michael G. Reilly
	Deborah L. Petersen

References: FirsTier; Firstar Bank of Council Bluffs.

For full biographical listings, see the Martindale-Hubbell Law Directory

---

STUART, TINLEY, PETERS, THORN & HUGHES (AV)

Northwestern Bell Building, 310 West Kanesville Boulevard, Second Floor, P.O. Box 398, 51502-0398
Telephone: 712-322-4033
Fax: 712-322-6243

MEMBERS OF FIRM

James E. Thorn	Oscar E. Johnson (1901-1993)
William R. Hughes, Jr.	Robert M. Stuart (1914-1986)
Gary R. Faust	Jack W. Peters (1931-1993)
Kristopher K. Madsen	Emmet Tinley (Retired)

ASSOCIATES

Richard D. Crowl, Jr.

Representative Clients: Chicago, Burlington Northern Railroad Co.; Firstar Bank Iowa, N.A.; Fireman's Fund-American; Hartford Insurance Group; St. Paul Fire & Marine Group; Liberty Mutual Insurance Company; State Farm Insurance Companies.

For full biographical listings, see the Martindale-Hubbell Law Directory

---

TELPNER, PETERSON, SMITH & RUESCH (AV)

25 Main Place, Suite 200, P.O. Box 248, 51502-0248
Telephone: 712-325-9000
Fax: 712-328-1946

MEMBERS OF FIRM

Richard W. Peterson	Charles L. Smith
	Jack E. Ruesch

ASSOCIATES

Walter P. Thomas

OF COUNSEL

Maynard S. Telpner

Reference: Firstar Bank, Council Bluffs, Iowa.

For full biographical listings, see the Martindale-Hubbell Law Directory

---

CRESCO,* Howard Co.

ELWOOD, O'DONOHOE, O'CONNOR & STOCHL (AV)

217 North Elm Street, P.O. Box 377, 52136
Telephone: 319-547-3321
Fax: 319-547-3189
New Hampton, Iowa Office: 101 North Locust Avenue, P.O. Box 310.
Telephone: 515-394-5943.
Fax: 515-394-5945.

(See Next Column)

ELWOOD, O'DONOHOE, O'CONNOR & STOCHL, *Cresco—Continued*

MEMBERS OF FIRM

Henry L. Elwood	Christopher F. O'Donohoe
	Richard D. Stochl

ASSOCIATES

Darin Neely	Joseph Patrick Braun

OF COUNSEL

James D. O'Connor	James E. O'Donohoe

Representative Clients: Grinnell Mutual Reinsurance Co.; Security State Bank, New Hampton, Iowa; United Fire & Casualty Insurance Co.; Board of Trustees, New Hampton Municipal Light Plant; Citizens National Bank, New Hampton, Iowa; Farmers Cooperative, New Hampton, Iowa; Cresco Union Savings Bank, Cresco, Iowa; Boatmen's Bank, Cresco, Iowa; Featherlite Mfg., Inc.; Decorah State Bank, Protivin, Iowa.

---

*CRESTON,** Union Co. — (Refer to Mt. Ayr)

DALLAS CENTER, Dallas Co.

McDONALD, BROWN & FAGEN (AV)

502-15th Street, P.O. Box 250, 50063
Telephone: 515-992-3728
Fax: 515-992-3971
Email: DALCTLAW@Interramp.com

John C. McDonald	Ralph R. Brown
	Charles H. Fagen

ASSOCIATES

Duane P. Hagerty

Representative Clients: Brenton State Bank; Dallas Mutual Insurance Co.; City of Dallas Center; City of Granger; Dallas Center-Grimes Community School District; Spurgeon Manor, Inc.; Synhorst & Schraad, Inc.; Direct Connect, Inc.

---

*DAVENPORT,** Scott Co.

CARLIN, HELLSTROM & BITTNER (AV)

A Partnership including Professional Corporations
1000 Firstar Center, 52801
Telephone: 319-328-3333
Fax: 319-328-3352

John A. Hellstrom (1921-1992)	Michael J. Motto
John J. Carlin (Retired, 1993)	Michael K. Bush
R. Richard Bittner (P.C.)	Jeffrey S. Bittner
Robert D. Lambert (P.C.)	James D. Hoffman

ASSOCIATES

William J. Bush	James T. Carlin
	Sara Schroeder

Representative Clients: Mercantile Bank, FSB; Firstar Bank Iowa; Lawyers Title Insurance Co.; Iowa Mutual Insurance Co.; Palmer Communications, Inc.; Palmer College Foundation; Allied Mutual Insurance Co.; Farm & City Insurance Co.; Pekin Insurance Co.; The Connelly Group, L.P.

For full biographical listings, see the Martindale-Hubbell Law Directory

---

HENINGER AND HENINGER, PROFESSIONAL CORPORATION (AV)

Suite 501, 101 West Second Street, 52801
Telephone: 319-324-0418
Fax: 319-324-5808

Ralph U. Heninger (1908-1993)	Ralph H. Heninger
	Ralph W. Heninger

Representative Clients: Jumer's Rock Island Casino; Northwest Bank & Trust; Wyffels Hybrids, Inc.

For full biographical listings, see the Martindale-Hubbell Law Directory

---

LANE & WATERMAN (AV)

220 North Main Street, Suite 600, 52801
Telephone: 319-324-3246
Fax: 319-324-1616
Rock Island, Illinois Office: 500 Rock Island Bank Building.
Telephone: 309-786-1600.
Fax: 309-786-1794.

MEMBERS OF FIRM

Joe R. Lane (1902-1931)	Dana M. Craig
Charles M. Waterman	Terry M. Giebelstein
(1902-1924)	Rand S. Wonio
Robert V. P. Waterman	Curtis E. Beason
Robert A. Van Vooren	Robert V. P. Waterman, Jr.
Thomas N. Kamp	Peter J. Benson
William C. Davidson	Constance A. Schriver
C. Dana Waterman, III	R. Scott Van Vooren
Charles E. Miller	Thomas D. Waterman
Thomas J. Shields	John D. Telleen
James A. Mezvinsky	Richard A. Davidson
David A. Dettmann	Carole J. Anderson

(See Next Column)

MEMBERS OF FIRM (Continued)

Michael P. Byrne	Maria Mihalakis Waterman
Edmund H. Carroll, Jr.	John D. DeDoncker
	Jeffrey W. Paul

ASSOCIATES

Amy H. Snyder	Cameron A. Davidson
Mary Woodburn Patch	Judith L. Herrmann
Tracy L. Polaschek	Monique C. Gorsline
R. Clay Thompson	Jed E. Brokaw
Rachel R. Watkins Schoenig	Robert Blake McMonagle
Theodore F. Olt, III	(Not admitted in IA)

OF COUNSEL

Donald H. Sitz

Representative Clients: MidAmerican Energy Co.; Lee Enterprises, Inc.; Iowa-American Water Co.; Aluminum Company of America; ANR Pipeline Co.; Hartford Insurance Group; Aetna Life and Casualty Co.; Genesis Health System; Davenport Community School District; Commercial Union Insurance Co.

For full biographical listings, see the Martindale-Hubbell Law Directory

---

NOYES & GOSMA, L.L.P. (AV)

400 North Main Street, Suite 106, 52801
Telephone: 319-322-8223
Fax: 319-322-8234

MEMBERS OF FIRM

Michael L. Noyes	John S. Gosma

ASSOCIATES

Marie R. Rolling-Tarbox

OF COUNSEL

Clay LeGrand	Charles G. Rehling

Reference: Quad City Bank and Trust Company.

For full biographical listings, see the Martindale-Hubbell Law Directory

---

*DECORAH,** Winneshiek Co.

MILLER, PEARSON, GLOE, BURNS, BEATTY & COWIE, P.C. (AV)

301 West Broadway, 52101
Telephone: 319-382-4226
Fax: 319-382-3783

Frank R. Miller (1915-1977)	James Burns
Donald H. Gloe	Marion L. Beatty
	Robert J. Cowie, Jr.

OF COUNSEL

Floyd S. Pearson

Counsel for: Luther College; Decorah Community School District; Winneshiek County Memorial Hospital; Community First State Bank.
Local Counsel for: Iowa Mutual Insurance Cos.; Employers Mutual Liability Insurance Co. of Wisconsin; Continental Casualty Co.; Employers Mutual Casualty Co.; Grinnell Mutual Insurance Co.; Allied Mutual Insurance Co.

For full biographical listings, see the Martindale-Hubbell Law Directory

---

*DENISON,** Crawford Co. — (Refer to Carroll)

*DES MOINES,** Polk Co.

AHLERS, COONEY, DORWEILER, HAYNIE, SMITH & ALLBEE, P.C. (AV)

100 Court Avenue, Suite 600, 50309-2231
Telephone: 515-243-7611
Fax: 515-243-2149
Email: 72741.2443@compuserve.com

Philip J. Dorweiler	Randall H. Stefani
Kenneth H. Haynie	Elizabeth Gregg Kennedy
H. Richard Smith	Wade R. Hauser III
Robert G. Allbee	William J. Noth
John F. McKinney, Jr.	David M. Swinton
L. W. Rosebrook	Linda L. Kniep
Richard G. Santi	John D. Hintze
Edgar H. Bittle	Peter L. J. Pashler
Ronald L. Sutphin	Ivan T. Webber
Terry L. Monson	Serge H. Garrison
Lance A. Coppock	Jane B. McAllister
David H. Luginbill	R. Mark Cory
Mark W. Beerman	Ronald L. Peeler
Edward W. Remsburg	Andrew J. Bracken
	Steven L. Serck

OF COUNSEL

Paul F. Ahlers	James Evans Cooney

(See Next Column)

AHLERS, COONEY, DORWEILER, HAYNIE, SMITH & ALLBEE P.C.—*Continued*

Michael J. Eason
Carole A. Tillotson
Garth D Adams

Debra Townsend Lind
Steven Michael Nadel
Paul D. Burns

For full biographical listings, see the Martindale-Hubbell Law Directory

BELIN LAMSON McCORMICK ZUMBACH FLYNN, A PROFESSIONAL CORPORATION (AV)

2000 Financial Center, 50309
Telephone: 515-243-7100
Telecopier: 515-282-7615

David W. Belin
Jeffrey E. Lamson
Mark McCormick
Steven E. Zumbach
Thomas L. Flynn
Roger T. Stetson
Jon L. Staudt
Richard W. Lozier, Jr.
James V. Sarcone, Jr.
James R. Swanger
Jeffrey A. Krausman
Jeremy C. Sharpe
John T. Seitz
Robert A. Mullen

David L. Charles
William D. Bartine, II
Quentin R. Boyken
Charles F. Becker
Mark E. Weinhardt
Eric W. Burmeister
Dennis P. Ogden
Edward M. Mansfield
Margaret C. Callahan
Robert D. Sharp
John M. Bouslog
Michael R. Reck
David K. Basler
Eric R. Tausner

Danielle Marie Shelton

OF COUNSEL

Sue Luettjohann Seitz   Gerard D. Neugent

For full biographical listings, see the Martindale-Hubbell Law Directory

BROWN, WINICK, GRAVES, GROSS, BASKERVILLE, SCHOENEBAUM AND WALKER, P.L.C. (AV)

Suite 1100, Two Ruan Center, 601 Locust Street, 50309
Telephone: 515-242-2400
Fax: 515-283-0231
Pella, Iowa Office: 706 Washington Street, 50219.
Telephone: 515-628-4513.
Fax: 515-628-8494.

John G. Fletcher
Marvin Winick
Richard W. Baskerville
Bruce Graves
Steven C. Schoenebaum
E. Ralph Walker
Harold N. Schneebeck
Richard K. Updegraff
Paul D. Hietbrink
William C. Brown
Jill Thompson Hansen

James H. Gilliam
Charles J. Kalinoski
David J. Darrell
Margaret M. Chaplinsky
Douglas E. Gross
John D. Hunter
Robert D. Andeweg
Stuart I. Feldstein
Alice Eastman Helle
James T. Deiotte
Daniel L. Stockdale

Thomas D. Johnson

Barbara Brooker Burnett   Sean P. Moore
Christopher R. Sackett

OF COUNSEL

Walter R. Brown

For full biographical listings, see the Martindale-Hubbell Law Directory

CONNOLLY, O'MALLEY, LILLIS, HANSEN & OLSON, L.L.P. (AV)

820 Liberty Building, 6th & Grand Avenue, 50309
Telephone: 515-243-8157
Fax: 515-243-3919

MEMBERS OF FIRM

William J. Lillis
Russell J. Hansen
Michael W. O'Malley
Eugene E. Olson

Peter S. Cannon
Streetar Cameron
Douglas A. Fulton
Daniel L. Manning

Christopher R. Pose

OF COUNSEL

John Connolly, III

A list of Representative Clients will be furnished upon request.
References will be furnished upon request.

For full biographical listings, see the Martindale-Hubbell Law Directory

DAVIS, BROWN, KOEHN, SHORS & ROBERTS, P.C. (AV)

(Formerly Davis, Hockenberg, Wine, Brown, Koehn & Shors, P.C.)
The Financial Center, 666 Walnut Street, Suite 2500, 50309-3993
Telephone: 515-288-2500
Cable: Davis Law
Facsimile: 515-243-0654
Affiliated London, England Office: Vizards, Solicitors, 42 Bedford Row.
London WC1R 4JL England.
Telephone: 071-405-6302.
Facsimile: 071-405-6248.

A. Arthur Davis
Donald J. Brown
William J. Koehn
John D. Shors
Stephen W. Roberts
William R. King
Robert F. Holz, Jr.
Dennis D. Jerde
Robert A. Gamble
Michael G. Kulik
Richard E. Ramsay
F. Richard Thornton
Thomas E. Salsbery
Frank J. Carroll
Bruce I. Campbell
Jonathan C. Wilson
Patricia A. Shoff
Steven L. Nelson
David B. VanSickel
Gene R. La Suer
Deborah M. Tharnish

Brian L. Wirt
Kent A. Herink
Robert J. Douglas, Jr.
Nicholas H. Roby
Mark D. Walz
Gary M. Myers
Stanley J. Thompson
David A. Tank
David M. Erickson
Lori Torgerson Chesser
Jo Ellen Whitney
Becky S. Knutson
Julie Johnson McLean
David D. Nelson
Beverly Evans Grenier
  (Not admitted in IA)
M. Daniel Waters
Christopher P. Jannes
Brian J. Laurenzo
Sharon K. Malheiro
Kris Holub Smith

Sally A. Reavely

William A. Boatwright
Scott M. Brennan
Michael C. Gilchrist
James R. Foley
Jeanie Kunkle Vaudt

Debra Rectenbaugh-Pettit
Denise R. Claton
Matthew E. Laughlin
Mark L. Stember
Judith R. "Lynn" Boes

OF COUNSEL

Neal E. Smith
Donald A. Wine
A. J. Greffenius

C. Carleton Frederici
William D. Thomas
David W. Dunn

Jean McNeil Dunn

For full biographical listings, see the Martindale-Hubbell Law Directory

DICKINSON, MACKAMAN, TYLER & HAGEN, P.C. (AV)

Suite 1600 Hub Tower, 699 Walnut Street, 50309-3986
Telephone: 515-244-2600
Telecopier: 515-246-4550

L. J. Dickinson (1873-1968)
L. Call Dickinson (1905-1974)
Helen C. Adams
Susanna M. Albaugh
Brent R. Appel
Kimberley K. Baer
Barbara G. Barrett
Joseph A. Cacciatore
Bret A. Dublinske
Jeanine M. Freeman
Craig F. Graziano
Howard O. Hagen
J. Russell Hixson
Paul E. Horvath
F. Richard Lyford
David J. Lynch
John R. Mackaman

Richard A. Malm
James W. O'Brien
Arthur F. Owens
Rebecca Boyd Parrott
Jeffrey T. Ramsey
David M. Repp
David R. Rhein
  (Not admitted in IA)
Robert C. Rouwenhorst
Russell L. Samson
David S. Steward
Philip E. Stoffregen
Jon P. Sullivan
Celeste L. Tito
Paul R. Tyler
John K. Vernon
J. Marc Ward

Linda S. Weindruch

Representative Clients: Board of Water Works Trustees, Des Moines, Iowa; Merchants Bonding Co. (Mutual); Norwest Bank, N.A.; Adventure Lands of America; American Insurance Association; Associated Builders and Contractors of Iowa; Blue Cross and Blue Shield of Iowa; Budget Marketing, Inc.; Burlington Northern Railroad Co.; Central Iowa KFC.

For full biographical listings, see the Martindale-Hubbell Law Directory

DUNCAN, GREEN, BROWN, LANGENESS & ECKLEY, A PROFESSIONAL CORPORATION (AV)

380 Capital Square, 400 Locust Street, 50309-2331
Telephone: 515-288-6440
Fax: 515-288-6448

Hearst R. (Randy) Duncan, Jr.
Brent B. (Chris) Green
Gregory R. Brown

James B. Langeness
Stephen R. Eckley
Randolph Mathieson (Matt) Duncan

(See Next Column)

DUNCAN, GREEN, BROWN, LANGENESS & ECKLEY A PROFESSIONAL CORPORATION, *Des Moines—Continued*

Mariclare Thinnes Culver   Scott P. Duncan
Emily McAllister

Representative Clients: American Republic Insurance Co.; Charles Gabus Ford, Inc.; Fruehauf Trailer Corp.; Bridgestone/Firestone, Inc.; The Coleman Co.; The Goodyear Co.; City of Des Moines; Federated Rural Electric Insurance Cooperative; Heller Financial, Inc.; Coca Cola Corp.

For full biographical listings, see the Martindale-Hubbell Law Directory

---

FINLEY, ALT, SMITH, SCHARNBERG, MAY & CRAIG, P.C. (AV)

604 Locust Street, Fourth Floor Equitable Building, 50309
Telephone: 515-288-0145
Telecopier: 515-288-2724

Hubert C. Jones (1913-1974)	Lorraine J. May
Robert G. Riley (1916-1992)	David C. Craig
Thomas A. Finley	John D. (Jack) Hilmes
Jerry P. Alt	R. Todd Gaffney
Glenn L. Smith	V. Glenn Goodwin, Jr.
Steven K. Scharnberg	Dawn R. Siebert

Pamela J. Prager   Kerry A. Finley
Daniel E. Kelly

Representative Clients: Aetna Casualty & Surety Co.; Aetna Life Insurance Co.; ALAS; American Society of Composers, Authors and Publishers; Equitable Life Assurance Society of the U.S.; Federated Insurance Co.; Meredith Corp.
Iowa Attorneys for: Midwest Medical Insurance Co.
District Attorneys for: Norfolk & Southern Railroad; Soo Line Railroad Company.

For full biographical listings, see the Martindale-Hubbell Law Directory

---

GREFE & SIDNEY, P.L.C. (AV)

2222 Grand Avenue, P.O. Box 10434, 50306
Telephone: 515-245-4300
Fax: 515-245-4452
Email: GRANDFIRM@AOL.COM

Rolland E. Grefe	Robert C. Thomson
Ross H. Sidney	Craig S. Shannon
Thomas W. Carpenter	John Werner
Henry A. Harmon	Patrick J. McNulty
Claude H. Freeman	Mark W. Thomas
Stephen D. Hardy	Guy R. Cook
Mary E. Kiener	

Andrew D. Hall	Debra L. Scorpiniti
Stephanie L. Glenn	Marcy A. O'Brien
Mark A. Schultheis	Kristin L. Bohlken

Representative Clients: Adventurelands of America; Caseys General Stores, Inc.; Cincinnati Insurance Companies; Easter Enterprises, Inc.; Freeman Decorating Co.; Liberty Mutual Insurance Co.; Otis Elevator; Pella Corp.; State Farm Mutual Insurance Company; United States Fidelity and Guaranty Co.

For full biographical listings, see the Martindale-Hubbell Law Directory

---

HANSEN, McCLINTOCK & RILEY (AV)

Eighth Floor - Fleming Building, 218 Sixth Avenue, 50309
Telephone: 515-244-2141
Fax: 515-244-2931

MEMBERS OF FIRM

Haemer Wheatcraft (1904-1983)	Chester C. Woodburn, III
J. Rudolph Hansen (1904-1995)	William D. Scherle
John A. McClintock	David L. Brown
Ronald A. Riley	John E. Swanson

ASSOCIATES
James M. Ballard

Representative Clients: The St. Paul Companies; Bituminous Insurance Companies; Northwestern National Insurance Co.; The Travelers Insurance Companies; United States Aviation Insurance Group; American International Companies; Iowa Credit Union League; The McAninch Corp.; R. J. Reynolds Tobacco Co.; Brown Bros., Inc. Electrical Contractors.

For full biographical listings, see the Martindale-Hubbell Law Directory

---

HERRICK, LANGDON & LANGDON (AV)

1800 Financial Center, Seventh and Walnut, 50309
Telephone: 515-282-8150
Telecopier: 515-282-8226

(See Next Column)

MEMBERS OF FIRM

Allan A. Herrick (1896-1989)	William R. Clark, Jr.
Herschel G. Langdon	Richard N. Winders
Richard G. Langdon	Richard A. Steffen
Kermit B. Anderson	

ASSOCIATES
Michael B. O'Meara

Representative Clients: Norwest Bank Iowa, N.A.; Hy-Vee Food Stores, Inc.; MAPCO Inc.; The Principal Financial Group; Farmers Mutual Hail Insurance Co. of Iowa; Mercedes Benz of North America; West Bank.

For full biographical listings, see the Martindale-Hubbell Law Directory

---

PATTERSON, LORENTZEN, DUFFIELD, TIMMONS, IRISH, BECKER & ORDWAY, L.L.P. (AV)

729 Insurance Exchange Building, 50309
Telephone: 515-283-2147
Fax: 515-283-1002

MEMBERS OF FIRM

G. O. Patterson (1914-1982)	Gregory J. Wilson
James A. Lorentzen	Jeffrey A. Boehlert
Theodore T. Duffield	Douglas A. Haag
William E. Timmons (Retired)	Charles E. Cutler
Roy M. Irish	Michael D. Huppert
F. H. Becker (Retired)	Martin C. Sprock
Gary D. Ordway	William A. Wickett
Robin L. Hermann	Frederick M. Haskins
Harry Perkins, III	Jeffrey A. Baker
Michael F. Lacey, Jr.	Janice M. Herfkens

ASSOCIATES

Coreen K. Bezdicek	Patrick V. Waldron
Michael S Jones	

Representative Clients: Allied Mutual Insurance Company; CNA Insurance Company; Chubb Insurance Group; Continental Western Insurance Co.; Farmers Insurance Group; Farmland Insurance Company; Grinnell Mutual Reinsurance Company; Hawkeye Security Insurance Company; Iowa Insurance Institute, St. Paul Fire & Marine Insurance Company.

For full biographical listings, see the Martindale-Hubbell Law Directory

---

THE ROSENBERG LAW FIRM (AV)

1010 Insurance Exchange Building, 505 Fifth Avenue, 50309
Telephone: 515-243-7600

MEMBERS OF FIRM

Raymond Rosenberg	Brent D. Rosenberg
Dean A. Stowers	Carole L. Hunt

Reference: Firstar Bank, Des Moines, Iowa.

For full biographical listings, see the Martindale-Hubbell Law Directory

---

SHEARER, TEMPLER & PINGEL, A PROFESSIONAL CORPORATION (AV)

Suite 437 3737 Woodland Avenue (West Des Moines), P.O. Box 1991, 50309
Telephone: 515-225-3737
Fax: 515-225-9510

Ronni F. Begleiter	G. Brian Pingel
Thomas M. Cunningham	Leon R. Shearer
Michael A. Dee	Brenton D. Soderstrum
Joel H. Dorman	Thomas S. Stewart
Becky S. Goettsch	Jeffrey D. Stone
Jeffrey L. Goodman	David G. Stork
Lawrence L. Marcucci	John A. Templer, Jr.
John R. Perkins	Brett J. Trout

OF COUNSEL
Greg A. Naylor

For full biographical listings, see the Martindale-Hubbell Law Directory

---

SULLIVAN & WARD, P.C. (AV)

801 Grand, Suite 3500, 50309-2719
Telephone: 515-244-3500
Telecopier: 515-244-3599

John T. Ward	Robert M. Holliday
Harlan (Bud) Hockenberg	Mark Landa
Michael P. Joynt	John V. Donnelly
Louis R. Hockenberg	Donald L. Carr, II
Richard R. Chabot	Dennis L. Puckett
James G. Sawtelle	

Amy Laurel Christensen   Jill Mataya Corry
Jason D. Walke

Representative Clients: Iowa Association of Electric Cooperatives; Central Iowa Power Cooperative; Prudential Insurance Company of America; National Rural Utilities Cooperative Finance Corp.; Norwest Bank Des Moines, N.A.; First Union Mortgage Corp.; Travelers Insurance Co.; Siegwerk, Inc.

(See Next Column)

SULLIVAN & WARD P.C.—*Continued*

For full biographical listings, see the Martindale-Hubbell Law Directory

WASKER, DORR, WIMMER & MARCOUILLER, P.C. (AV)

801 Grand Avenue, Suite 3100, 50309-8036
Telephone: 515-283-1801
Facsimile: 515-283-1802

Charles F. Wasker | William J. Wimmer
Fred L. Dorr | D. Mark Marcouiller
Robert A. Sims

Matthew D. Kern
OF COUNSEL
Russell H. Laird

For full biographical listings, see the Martindale-Hubbell Law Directory

WHITFIELD & EDDY, P.L.C. (AV)

317 6th Avenue, Suite 1200 Locust at 6th, 50309-4110
Telephone: 515-288-6041
Fax: 515-246-1474

A. Roger Witke | Kevin M. Reynolds
Gary Gately | Thomas H. Burke
Timothy J. Walker | Thomas Henderson
David L. Phipps | George H. Frampton
Benjamin B. Ullem | Megan Manning Antenucci
Robert L. Fanter | Wendy L. Carlson
Bernard L. Spaeth, Jr. | Thomas S. Reavely
Rod Kubat | Gary A. Norton
William L. Fairbank | Mark V. Hanson
Robert G. Bridges | Maureen Roach Tobin
Jaki K. Samuelson | Jeffrey William Courter
August B. Landis

Richard J. Kirschman | Jason M. Casini
John F. Fatino | Rosco A. Ries
J. Campbell Helton
OF COUNSEL
John C. Eddy | Dean Dutton
Harley A. Whitfield | Richard Buenneke

General Counsel for: American Life and Casualty Co.; Hawkeye-Security Insurance Co.; Iowa Funeral Directors Assn.; The Statesman Group, Inc.; United Security Insurance Co.
Representative Clients: Brenton National Bank, N.A.; Crum & Forster Commercial Insurance; Decker Truck Line, Inc.; General Motors Co.

For full biographical listings, see the Martindale-Hubbell Law Directory

DE WITT, Clinton Co. — (Refer to Maquoketa)

*DUBUQUE,** Dubuque Co.

KANE, NORBY & REDDICK, P.C. (AV)

2477 J.F. Kennedy Road, Suite 102, 52002
Telephone: 319-582-7980
Fax: 319-582-5312
Email: knrpc@mwci.net

Brian J. Kane | Gary K. Norby
Les V. Reddick

D. Flint Drake | Michael J. Gau

For full biographical listings, see the Martindale-Hubbell Law Directory

O'CONNOR & THOMAS, P.C. (AV)

700 Locust Street, Suite 200, CyCare Plaza, 52001-6874
Telephone: 319-557-8400
Telecopier: 319-556-1867

Robert M. Bertsch | Chad C. Leitch
John C. O'Connor | Richard K. Whitty
Brendan T. Quann | Stephen C. Krumpe
A. John Arenz | Todd L. Stevenson

Brenda Stine-Reiher | James E. Goodman, Jr.
Davin C. Curtiss

Representative Clients: Interstate Power Co.; American Trust & Savings Bank; Hawkeye Bank of Dubuque; The Archdiocese of Dubuque; A.Y. McDonald Industries, Inc.; Hartford Accident & Indemnity Co.

For full biographical listings, see the Martindale-Hubbell Law Directory

*ELDORA,** Hardin Co.

WILSON & CRAIG, PROFESSIONAL CORPORATION (AV)

1305 Twelfth Street, P.O. Box 431, 50627-0431
Telephone: 515-858-5475
Fax: 515-858-3157
Hubbard, Iowa Office: 213 East Maple.
Telephone: 515-864-3338. Tuesday and Thursday A.M. only.

Donald C. Wilson | Patrick J. Craig
Mitchel T. Behr

Representative Clients: Hardin County Savings Bank, Eldora, Iowa; Security State Bank, Hubbard, Iowa; Cities of Hubbard and Union, Iowa; Harold H. Luiken & Sons, Inc., Steamboat Rock, Iowa; Dodger Industries, Inc., Eldora, Iowa; Whink Products Co., Eldora, Iowa; Heart of Iowa Telephone Cooperative, Union, Iowa.

*ELKADER,** Clayton Co. — (Refer to Waukon)

*EMMETSBURG,** Palo Alto Co. — (Refer to Algona)

*ESTHERVILLE,** Emmet Co.

FITZGIBBONS BROTHERS (AV)

A Partnership including a Professional Corporation
108 North 7th Street, P.O. Box 496, 51334
Telephone: 712-362-7215
Fax: 712-362-3526

MEMBERS OF FIRM
Leo E. Fitzgibbons | Harold W. White (P.C.)
Francis Fitzgibbons | Ned A. Stockdale
Joseph L. Fitzgibbons | David A. Lester

For full biographical listings, see the Martindale-Hubbell Law Directory

*FAIRFIELD,** Jefferson Co. — (Refer to Ottumwa)

*FOREST CITY,** Winnebago Co. — (Refer to Mason City)

*FORT DODGE,** Webster Co.

JOHNSON, ERB, BICE, KRAMER, GOOD & MULHOLLAND, P.C. (AV)

600 Boston Centre, P.O. Box 1396, 50501-1396
Telephone: 515-573-2181
Fax: 515-573-2548
Gowrie, Iowa Office: 1103 Market Street.
Telephone: 515-352-3111.
Fax: 515-352-3113.

Arthur H. Johnson | William J. Good
Dean P. Erb (Gowrie Office) | Neven J. Mulholland
Thomas J. Bice | Stuart J. Cochrane
James L. Kramer | Eric J. Eide

Susan L. Ahlers | Paul B. Ahlers
OF COUNSEL
Wilbur J. Latham

District Counsel for: Iowa-Illinois Gas & Electric Co.
Representative Clients: Cigna Property & Casualty Co.; Farmland Mutual Insurance Co. New Cooperative, Inc.; Trinity Regional Hospital; Boatmen's Bank of Fort Dodge; First American Bank Group, Ltd.; First Federal Savings Bank.

For full biographical listings, see the Martindale-Hubbell Law Directory

*GARNER,** Hancock Co. — (Refer to Algona)

*GLENWOOD,** Mills Co. — (Refer to Council Bluffs)

*GREENFIELD,** Adair Co. — (Refer to Winterset)

GRINNELL, Poweshiek Co.

BIERMAN & BIERMAN, P.C. (AV)

920 Main Street, P.O. Box 713, 50112
Telephone: 515-236-6128
Pella, Iowa Office: 702 Liberty Street, 50219.
Telephone: 515-628-3283.

John F. (Rick) Bierman, III | Terri A. Beukelman
OF COUNSEL
John F. Bierman

General Counsel for: Grinnell State Bank; Grinnell College; Miracle Recreation Equipment Co.

For full biographical listings, see the Martindale-Hubbell Law Directory

GRUNDY CENTER, * Grundy Co.

KLIEBENSTEIN, HERONIMUS & SCHMIDT (AV)

630 G Avenue, Box 308, 50638
Telephone: 319-824-6951
Fax: 319-824-6953

Don Kliebenstein   Thomas J. Heronimus
Kirby D. Schmidt
ASSOCIATE
Bradley J. Harris

Counsel for: Grundy National Bank, Grundy Center; Grundy Center Community School District; Kruger Seed Co.; Beaman Cooperative Co.; M.D. Meyer Seeds, Inc.
Local Counsel for: The Travelers Insurance Co. (Farm Mortgage Loan Department); Western Dressing, Inc.; R.S. Bacon Veneer Co.; Mutual Benefit Life Insurance Co. (Farm Mortgage Loan Department); Norwesco Contract Manufacturing.

For full biographical listings, see the Martindale-Hubbell Law Directory

---

GUTHRIE CENTER, * Guthrie Co. — (Refer to Perry)

HAMPTON, * Franklin Co.

HOBSON, CADY & CADY (AV)

9 First Street S.W., 50441
Telephone: 515-456-2555
Fax: 515-456-3315

MEMBERS OF FIRM
A. J. Hobson (1903-1972)   G. Arthur Cady
G. A. Cady, III

General Counsel for: Ag Services of America, Inc.
A list of Representative Clients will be furnished upon request.
References: First National Bank of Hampton; Liberty Bank & Trust.

For full biographical listings, see the Martindale-Hubbell Law Directory

---

HUBBARD, Hardin Co. — (Refer to Eldora)

HUMBOLDT, Humboldt Co. — (Refer to Fort Dodge)

IDA GROVE, * Ida Co. — (Refer to Cherokee)

INDEPENDENCE, * Buchanan Co. — (Refer to Waterloo)

IOWA CITY, * Johnson Co.

MEARDON, SUEPPEL, DOWNER & HAYES P.L.C. (AV)

122 South Linn Street, 52240
Telephone: 319-338-9222
Fax: 319-338-7250

William L. Meardon	Thomas D. Hobart
William F. Sueppel	Margaret T. Lainson
Robert N. Downer	Douglas D. Ruppert
James P. Hayes	Paul J. McAndrew, Jr.
James D. McCarragher	Timothy J. Krumm
Mark T. Hamer	William J. Sueppel

Charles A. Meardon   Steven A. Michalek

Representative Clients: United Technologies-Automotive; Perpetual Savings Bank; Economy Advertising Company; Metro Pavers, Inc.; League of Iowa Municipalities; Hills Bank and Trust Co.; J.M. Swank Co.; City of Muscatine; McComas-Lacina Construction Co., Inc.; Diamond Dave's Taco Company, Inc.

For full biographical listings, see the Martindale-Hubbell Law Directory

---

IOWA FALLS, Hardin Co.

WHITESELL & BICKNESE (AV)

Law House, 410 Washington Avenue, P.O. Box 336, 50126
Telephone: 515-648-4646
FAX: 515-648-3283

John P. Whitesell   Jennifer A. Bicknese

General Counsel for: Ellsworth College Trustees; PBW Broadcasting Corp. (KIFG, AM-FM); Jonathan, Ltd.; Ellsworth College Dormitories, Inc.; Competitive Capital Resources, Inc.; River Hills Financial Services, Inc.; R. L. Fridley Theatres, Inc.; RAAN, Inc. (Russian-American Agricultural Network); Paramount Management Group.

For full biographical listings, see the Martindale-Hubbell Law Directory

---

JEFFERSON, * Greene Co. — (Refer to Carroll)

KEOSAUQUA, * Van Buren Co. — (Refer to Ottumwa)

LENOX, Taylor Co. — (Refer to Mt. Ayr)

LEON, * Decatur Co. — (Refer to Mt. Ayr)

LOGAN, * Harrison Co. — (Refer to Harlan)

MANCHESTER, * Delaware Co. — (Refer to Dubuque)

MAPLETON, Monona Co. — (Refer to Sioux City)

MARSHALLTOWN, * Marshall Co.

CARTWRIGHT, DRUKER & RYDEN (AV)

112 West Church Street, P.O. Box 496, 50158
Telephone: 515-752-5467
Fax: 515-752-4370

MEMBERS OF FIRM

H. G. Cartwright (1902-1982)	John F. Veldey
Rex J. Ryden	Joel T. S. Greer
John B. Grier	Sharon Soorholtz Greer

Merrill C. Swartz
OF COUNSEL
Harry Druker

Representative Clients: Fisher Controls International Inc.; Mercantile Bank; Marshalltown Savings Bank, FSB; Travelers Insurance Co.; Lennox Industries Inc.; State Farm Mutual Insurance Co., Bloomington, Ill.; Farm Bureau Mutual Insurance Co.; Allied Group; Employers Group.

For full biographical listings, see the Martindale-Hubbell Law Directory

HARRISON, BRENNECKE, MOORE, SMAHA & McKIBBEN (AV)

302 Masonic Temple Building, P.O. Box 618, 50158
Telephone: 515-752-4271
Fax: 515-752-5266

MEMBERS OF FIRM

G. A. Mote (1874-1965)	Leslie E. Smaha
Arley J. Wilson (1913-1982)	Larry D. McKibben
Roger E. Harrison	James L. Goodman
Allen E. Brennecke	William J. Lorenz
James R. Moore	James C. Ellefson

Douglas W. Beals
ASSOCIATES
Michael R. Horn
OF COUNSEL
William L. Welp

Representative Clients: Farmers Savings Bank; Beaman, Iowa; Brenner Trust; Ottilie Farms, Inc.; Arbie Mineral Feed Co.; Cooper Farms, Inc.

For full biographical listings, see the Martindale-Hubbell Law Directory

JOHNSON, SUDENGA, LATHAM, PEGLOW & O'HARE (AV)

118 East Main Street, P.O. Box 1180, 50158-1180
Telephone: 515-752-8800
Telecopier: 515-752-8095

MEMBERS OF FIRM

Craig L. Johnson	W. J. Latham, Jr.
George W. Sudenga	Paul C. Peglow

Kevin M. O'Hare

Representative Clients: Economy Fire & Casualty Co.; John Hancock Mutual Life Insurance Co.; The Hartford Insurance Group; Plaza Family Dental Services; R. D. Stewart, Inc.; United Fire & Casualty Co.; United States Fidelity & Guaranty Co.; Horace Mann Insurance Company; Milwaukee Insurance; Pekin Insurance Company.

MASON CITY, * Cerro Gordo Co.

BROWN, KINSEY & FUNKHOUSER (AV)

214 North Adams, P.O. Box 679, 50402-0679
Telephone: 515-423-6223
Fax: 515-423-9995

MEMBERS OF FIRM

David E. Funkhouser	Scott D. Brown
Robert S. Kinsey, III	Kyndra Walton

ASSOCIATE
John P. Lander

Representative Clients: Allstate Insurance Co.; The St. Paul Companies; Continental Western Ins. Co.; Home Ins. Co.

For full biographical listings, see the Martindale-Hubbell Law Directory

WINSTON & BYRNE, LAWYERS, A PROFESSIONAL CORPORATION (AV)

119 Second Street, N.W., 50401
Telephone: 515-423-1913
Fax: 515-423-8998

Harold R. Winston   Michael G. Byrne

Representative Clients: Woodharbor Molding & Millworks, Inc.; Winkleman Farms, Inc.; Sparboe Iowa Corporation; Schmidt Family Farms, Inc.; First Citizen's National Bank of Mason City; Norwest Bank Iowa, N.A.

For full biographical listings, see the Martindale-Hubbell Law Directory

MONTEZUMA, Poweshiek Co. — (Refer to Newton)

MT. PLEASANT, Henry Co. — (Refer to Washington)

NASHUA, Chickasaw Co. — (Refer to Charles City)

NEVADA, Story Co.

CAHILL LAW OFFICES (AV)

1015 Fifth Street, 50201
Telephone: 515-382-6571
Fax: 515-382-4338

MEMBERS OF FIRM

Donald L. Nelson (1922-1984)   Thomas J. Cahill
Joseph R. Cahill

General Counsel for: Nevada National Bank.
Representative Clients: Colo Telephone Co.; Allied Group; Iowa Mutual Insurance Co.

For full biographical listings, see the Martindale-Hubbell Law Directory

NEW HAMPTON, Chickasaw Co.

ELWOOD, O'DONOHOE, O'CONNOR & STOCHL (AV)

101 North Locust Avenue, P.O. Box 310, 50659
Telephone: 515-394-5943
Fax: 515-394-5945
Cresco, Iowa Office: 217 North Elm Street. P.O. Box 377.
Telephone: 319-547-3321.
Fax: 319-547-3189.

MEMBERS OF FIRM

Henry L. Elwood   Christopher F. O'Donohoe
Richard D. Stochl

ASSOCIATES

Darin Neely   Joseph Patrick Braun

OF COUNSEL

James D. O'Connor   James E. O'Donohoe

Representative Clients: Grinnell Mutual Reinsurance Co.; Security State Bank, New Hampton, Iowa; United Fire & Casualty Insurance Co.; Board of Trustees, New Hampton Municipal Light Plant; Citizens National Bank, New Hampton, Iowa; Farmers Cooperative, New Hampton, Iowa; Cresco Union Savings Bank, Cresco, Iowa; Boatmen's Bank, Cresco, Iowa; Featherlite Mfg., Inc.; Decorah State Bank, Protivin, Iowa.

NEWTON, Jasper Co.

BRIERLY LAW OFFICE (AV)

211 First Avenue West, 50208
Telephone: 515-792-4160
Fax: 515-792-2410
Grinnell, Iowa Office: 717 Fifth Avenue.
Telephone: 515-236-8622.
Affiliated with Dale A. Lamb, Attorney at Law.
Sully, Iowa Office: 618 4th Street.
Telephone: 515-594-4420.

MEMBERS OF FIRM

Laurence L. Brierly (1903-1984)   Dennis F. Chalupa
Ennis McCall (1912-1987)   Bradley McCall
Lewis M. Girdner   Mark A. Otto

ASSOCIATES

John H. Terpstra   DuWayne J. Dalen
Lois J. Vroom

Representative Clients: Thombert, Inc. (Plastics); Edwards Publications, Inc.; Pyramid, Inc.; Mid-Iowa Savings Bank, FSB; Pleasantville State Bank; J. H. McKlveen and Co.; Midwest Manufacturing Co.; City of Mitchellville.

For full biographical listings, see the Martindale-Hubbell Law Directory

DIEHL CLAYTON & JACOBSEN (AV)

309 First Avenue West, 50208
Telephone: 515-792-6121
Fax: 515-792-4384

MEMBERS OF FIRM

H.C. Korf (1876-1936)   James W. Cleverley (1925-1989)
E.O. Korf (1889-1949)   Benjamin C. Clayton
J.N. Diehl (1913-1984)   Michael K. Jacobsen

Representative Clients: First State Bank, Lynnville, Iowa; Iowa Southern Utilities Co.; Economy Fire & Casualty Co.; Travelers Insurance Co.; Newton Clinic; Exchange State Bank, Mingo and Collins, Iowa; City of Lynnville, Iowa; City of Lambs Grove, Iowa.

For full biographical listings, see the Martindale-Hubbell Law Directory

NORTHWOOD, Worth Co. — (Refer to Mason City)

ORANGE CITY, Sioux Co. — (Refer to Le Mars)

OSAGE, Mitchell Co. — (Refer to Charles City)

OSCEOLA, Clarke Co. — (Refer to Indianola)

OTTUMWA, Wapello Co.

JOHNSON, HESTER, WALTER & HARRISON, L.L.P. (AV)

111 West Second Street, P.O. Box 716, 52501-0716
Telephone: 515-684-5481
Telecopier: 515-684-5487

MEMBERS OF FIRM

David J. Hester   Thomas M. Walter
Gayla R. Harrison

ASSOCIATES

Robert E. Breckenridge, II

OF COUNSEL

Walter F. Johnson

Representative Clients: Firstar Bank Ottumwa; Deere and Co.; Lee Enterprises Inc.; Liberty Mutual Insurance Co.; John Deere Ottumwa Works.

For full biographical listings, see the Martindale-Hubbell Law Directory

KIPLE, KIPLE, DENEFE, BEAVER & GARDNER (AV)

104 South Court Street, P.O. Box 493, 52501
Telephone: 515-683-1626
Fax: 515-683-3597

MEMBERS OF FIRM

James L. Kiple   J. Terrence Denefe
Charles M. Kiple   Jerome M. Beaver
Steven Gardner

General Counsel for: Firstar Bank Ottumwa; Winger Contracting Co.; Ideal Ready-Mix Co., Inc.; Wapello Rural Water Association, Inc.; Norris Asphalt Paving Co; J & J Steel, Inc.
Representative Clients: Crawford & Company; Farm Bureau Mutual Insurance Co.

For full biographical listings, see the Martindale-Hubbell Law Directory

PERRY, Dallas Co.

WILLIS & SACKETT (AV)

1212 Second Street, P.O. Box 310, 50220
Telephone: 515-465-5331
Telecopier: 515-465-5333

MEMBERS OF FIRM

Blake Willis (1892-1961)   Ned Willis
George H. Sackett (1900-1983)   G. Robert Sackett

Counsel for: Perry State Bank; City of Perry; Perry Community Schools.
Local Counsel: Farm Credit Bank of Omaha.

POCAHONTAS, Pocahontas Co. — (Refer to Rockwell City)

RED OAK, Montgomery Co. — (Refer to Clarinda)

ROCK RAPIDS, Lyon Co. — (Refer to Spirit Lake)

SAC CITY, Sac Co. — (Refer to Rockwell City)

SIBLEY, Osceola Co. — (Refer to Rock Rapids)

SIDNEY, Fremont Co. — (Refer to Hamburg)

SIGOURNEY, Keokuk Co. — (Refer to Ottumwa)

SIOUX CITY, Woodbury Co.

BERENSTEIN, MOORE, MOSER, BERENSTEIN & HEFFERNAN (AV)

300 Commerce Building, P.O. Box 3207, 51102
Telephone: 712-252-0020
Fax: 712-252-0656

MEMBERS OF FIRM

Marvin S. Berenstein   Craig S. Berenstein
Dan A. Moore   Maureen Brown Heffernan
Cynthia C. Moser   Richard H. Moeller
Jeffrey A. Johnson

ASSOCIATES

Greg Lawrence Berenstein   Douglas B. Hodgson
Mitchell A. Herigstad   Karen J. Epp
Scott J. Snyder   Louis S. Goldberg (1897-1984)

Representative Clients: Aalfs Manufacturing, Inc.; Boatmen's Bank; Beef Products, Inc.; Briar Cliff College; Canal Capital Corp.- Sioux City Stockyards; Firstar Bank Iowa, N.A.; Metropolitan Life Insurance Co.; Sioux Tools, Inc.- Snap-On-Tools; Marian Health Center, a division of Mercy Health Services; Wells Dairy & Blue Bunny Ice Cream.

For full biographical listings, see the Martindale-Hubbell Law Directory

Sioux City—Continued

GILES AND GILES (AV)

322 Frances Building, 505 Fifth Street, 51101
Telephone: 712-252-4458
FAX: 712-252-3400
Crofton, Nebraska Office: P. O. Box 88.
Telephone: 402-388-4215.

MEMBERS OF FIRM

W. Jefferson Giles, III   William J. Giles, IV

ASSOCIATES

Gregory Gifford Giles (On Leave)

Representative Clients: Security National Bank, Firstar Bank, Boatmen's Bank, all in Sioux City, Iowa; Live Stock State Bank, Yankton, SD.

For full biographical listings, see the Martindale-Hubbell Law Directory

HEIDMAN, REDMOND, FREDREGILL, PATTERSON, SCHATZ & PLAZA, L.L.P. (AV)

A Registered Limited Liability Partnership including Professional Corporations
701 Pierce Street, Suite 200, P.O. Box 3086, 51102
Telephone: 712-255-8838
Fax: 712-258-6714

MEMBERS OF FIRM

Marvin F. Heidman	Lance D. Ehmcke
James W. Redmond	Margaret M. Prahl
Alan E. Fredregill (P.C.)	John D. Ackerman
Charles T. Patterson	Gregg E. Williams
Kenneth C. Schatz (P.C.)	Judith A. Higgs
Thomas M. Plaza	John C. Gray
Daniel D. Dykstra	Daniel B. Shuck

Rita C. Grimm

ASSOCIATES

Ryan K. Crayne	Patrick L. Sealey
Charles E. Trullinger	John W. Gleysteen (Retired)
Edward C. Poulsen	Robert R. Eidsmoe (Retired)
Sabra K Craig	Jacob C. Gleysteen (1883-1943)

H. Clifford Harper (1891-1959)

Representative Clients: Aetna Casualty & Surety Co.; Irving F. Jensen Co., Inc.; Marian Health Center; Medical Protective Co.; John Morrell & Co.; Pig Improvement Co.; State Farm Mutual Insurance Co.; Terra International, Inc.; The Security National Bank of Sioux City; Wal-Mart Stores, Inc.

For full biographical listings, see the Martindale-Hubbell Law Directory

MARKS & MADSEN (AV)

Suite 303, United Federal Plaza Building, P.O. Box 3226, 51102
Telephone: 712-258-1200
Fax: 712-258-2012

MEMBERS OF FIRM

Bernard B. Marks   George F. Madsen

Representative Clients: Briar Cliff College; The Equitable Life Assurance Society of the U.S.; First Federal Savings Bank of Siouxland; First National Bank in Le Mars; Hirschbach Motor Lines, Inc.; Sioux City Brick and Tile Co.; The Security National Bank of Sioux City, Iowa; Siouxland Oncology-Hematology Associates; Valley Bank & Trust, Mapleton, Iowa; Western Iowa Tech. Community College.

For full biographical listings, see the Martindale-Hubbell Law Directory

MAYNE & MAYNE (AV)

400 Pioneer Bank Building, 701 Pierce Street, P.O. Box 5049, 51102-5049
Telephone: 712-252-3220
Fax: 712-252-1535

MEMBERS OF FIRM

Wiley Mayne   John D. Mayne
Robert J. Pierson

ASSOCIATE

Monte G. Richards (Not admitted in IA)

Representative Clients: American Telephone & Telegraph Co.; Amoco Oil Company; Central United Life Insurance Company; Century 21-Marketplace; Credit Bureau of Sioux City; Ford Motor Credit Company; Intensive Medical Services of Siouxland, P.C.; Metz Baking Company; Shell Chemical Company; U.S. West Communications Company.

For full biographical listings, see the Martindale-Hubbell Law Directory

RAWLINGS, NIELAND, PROBASCO, KILLINGER, ELLWANGER, JACOBS & MOHRHAUSER (AV)

522 Fourth Street, Suite 300, 51101
Telephone: 712-277-2373
FAX: 712-277-3304

James W. Kindig (1879-1950)   Lowell C. Kindig (1913-1992)
Robert E. Beebe (1913-1988)

(See Next Column)

MEMBERS OF FIRM

William J. Rawlings	Sam S. Killinger
Maurice B. Nieland	Michael W. Ellwanger
Gene A. Probasco	Michael P. Jacobs

Jeffrey R. Mohrhauser

ASSOCIATES

Jeffrey D. Garreans   Rebecca A. Nelson

Representative Clients: Arnold Motor Supply; Chesterman Co.; CNA Insurance Co.; Farmers Savings Bank, Remsen, Iowa; Farm Bureau Insurance Co.; Maryland Casualty Co.; Norwest Bank Iowa, National Association; NWIP, Inc.; St. Paul Fire and Marine Insurance Co.; United Fire and Casualty Co.

For full biographical listings, see the Martindale-Hubbell Law Directory

SHULL, COSGROVE, HELLIGE & LUNDBERG (AV)

700 Frances Building, 505 Fifth Street, P.O. Box 1828, 51102
Telephone: 712-255-4444
Telecopier: 712-255-4465

MEMBERS OF FIRM

James M. Cosgrove	Robert F. Meis
Michael R. Hellige	Scott A. Hindman
Paul D. Lundberg	James W. Radig

ASSOCIATES

Leif D. Erickson   Michael J. Frey
Stephen E. Doohen

RETIRED

D. Carlton Shull

Representative Clients: Burlington Northern Inc.; Employers Mutual Cos.; Ford Motor Co.; The Hartford; Liberty Mutual Insurance Co.; Prince Manufacturing Corp.; Sioux City Journal; The Travelers; Western Iowa Tech Community College.

For full biographical listings, see the Martindale-Hubbell Law Directory

---

SPENCER, * Clay Co. — (Refer to Spirit Lake)

SPIRIT LAKE, * Dickinson Co.

NAREY, CHOZEN AND SAUNDERS (AV)

Narey Building, 832 Lake Street, P.O. Box E, 51360-0605
Telephone: 712-336-3410
Fax: 712-336-0668

MEMBERS OF FIRM

Harry E. Narey (1885-1962)   Michael J. Chozen
Peter B. Narey   Lonnie B. Saunders

Representative Clients: First Bank and Trust, Spirit Lake, Iowa; Iowa Electric Light and Power Co., Spirit Lake, Iowa; State Bank of Terril, Terril, Iowa; State Bank, Spirit Lake, Iowa; Smith-Lumber, Inc.; Dickinson County Savings Bank; City of Okoboji; United Fire and Casualty Co.; Home Insurance Co.; City of Orleans.

For full biographical listings, see the Martindale-Hubbell Law Directory

---

STORM LAKE, * Buena Vista Co. — (Refer to Cherokee)

TIPTON, * Cedar Co. — (Refer to Iowa City)

TOLEDO, * Tama Co. — (Refer to Marshalltown)

VICTOR, Iowa Co. — (Refer to Marengo)

VINTON, * Benton Co. — (Refer to Cedar Rapids)

WAPELLO, * Louisa Co. — (Refer to Muscatine)

WATERLOO, * Black Hawk Co.

BEECHER, RATHERT, ROBERTS, FIELD, WALKER & MORRIS, P.C. (AV)

Suite 300 Court Square Building, 620 Lafayette Street, P.O. Box 178, 50704
Telephone: 319-234-1766
Telecopier: 319-234-1225

W. L. Beecher (1891-1976)	John R. Walker, Jr.
W. Louis Beecher	Richard R. Morris
John W. Rathert	Theresa E. Hoffman
Jay P. Roberts	Carter J. Stevens
Hugh M. Field	Eric W. Johnson

General Counsel for: American Black Hawk Broadcasting Co.
Representative Clients: Deere & Company; Chubb/Pacific Indemnity Group; The Equitable Life Assurance Society of the United States; Homeland Bank, N.A.

For full biographical listings, see the Martindale-Hubbell Law Directory

DUTTON, BRAUN, STAACK, HELLMAN & IVERSEN, P.L.C. (AV)

3151 Brockway Road, P.O. Box 810, 50704
Telephone: 319-234-4471
Fax: 319-234-8029

(See Next Column)

DUTTON, BRAUN, STAACK, HELLMAN & IVERSEN P.L.C.—*Continued*

David J. Dutton	Cheryl L. Weber
Robert W. Braun	Steven K. Daniels
Thomas L. Staack	Bruce L. Braley
James R. Hellman	John J. Hines
Gary D. Iversen	James F. Kalkhoff
Michael A. Mc Enroe	James Scott Bayne

Kevin D. Ahrenholz	Carolyn A. Rafferty

Chad A. Swanson

Representative Clients: Kemper Insurance Group; Grinnell Mutual Reinsurance Co.; Reliance National Insurance Co.; CNA Insurance Cos.; The Travers Insurance Co.; Hawkeye Community College; Crossroads Ford, Ltd.; Black Hawk County Solid Waste Management Commission; Iowa Community Credit Union; Allen Memorial Hospital.

For full biographical listings, see the Martindale-Hubbell Law Directory

SWISHER & COHRT, P.L.C. (AV)

528 West Fourth Street, P.O. Box 1200, 50704
Telephone: 319-232-6555
FAX: 319-232-4835

Benjamin F. Swisher (1878-1959)	J. Douglas Oberman
L. J. Cohrt (1898-1974)	Stephen J. Powell
Charles F. Swisher (1919-1986)	Jim D. DeKoster
Jeffrey J. Greenwood	Samuel C. Anderson
(1953-1995)	Robert C. Griffin
Eldon R. McCann	Kevin R. Rogers
Steven A. Weidner	Beth E. Hansen
Larry J. Cohrt	Mark F. Conway

Natalie Williams Burris

Firm is Counsel for: Koehring Corp.; Clay Equipment; Chamberlain Manufacturing Co.; Waterloo Courier.
Local Counsel for: Allied Group; John Deere Insurance; Liberty Mutual Insurance Co.

For full biographical listings, see the Martindale-Hubbell Law Directory

WAUKON,* Allamakee Co.

JACOBSON, BRISTOL, GARRETT & SWARTZ (AV)

Jacobson-Bristol Building, 25 First Avenue, N.W., P.O. Box 49, 52172
Telephone: 319-568-3439
Fax: 319-568-3210

MEMBERS OF FIRM

Arthur H. Jacobson (1910-1986)	James A. Garrett
James D. Bristol	Jeffrey L. Swartz
James E. Thomson	
(Retired, 1992)	

Representative Clients: Farmers & Merchants Savings Bank, Waukon, Iowa; Allied Group; Grinnell Mutual Reinsurance Co.; United Fire & Casualty Co.

For full biographical listings, see the Martindale-Hubbell Law Directory

WEBSTER CITY,* Hamilton Co. — (Refer to Fort Dodge)

WEST UNION,* Fayette Co. — (Refer to Waukon)

WILLIAMSBURG, Iowa Co. — (Refer to Marengo)

KANSAS

ABILENE,* Dickinson Co. — (Refer to Salina)

ALMA,* Wabaunsee Co. — (Refer to Manhattan)

ARKANSAS CITY, Cowley Co. — (Refer to Winfield)

ASHLAND,* Clark Co. — (Refer to Dodge City)

ATCHISON,* Atchison Co. — (Refer to Leavenworth)

ATWOOD,* Rawlins Co. — (Refer to Oberlin)

BELLEVILLE,* Republic Co. — (Refer to Concordia)

BURLINGTON,* Coffey Co. — (Refer to Emporia)

CHANUTE, Neosho Co.

HENSHALL, PENNINGTON & BRAKE (AV)

Lower Level Suite New Bank of Commerce Building, 101 West Main Street, P.O. Box 667, 66720
Telephone: 316-431-2600
Fax: 316-431-1505

(See Next Column)

Charles E. Henshall (1916-1982)	Robert Pennington
David S. Brake	

Representative Clients: Lancer Oil, Inc.; Fireman's Fund American Insurance Companies; Church Mutual Insurance Co.; Shelter Insurance Cos.; Farmers Casualty Cos.; Mid-Continent Casualty Co.; City of Chanute; Neosho Memorial Regional Medical Center.

CIMARRON,* Gray Co. — (Refer to Dodge City)

CLAY CENTER,* Clay Co. — (Refer to Junction City)

COLBY,* Thomas Co. — (Refer to Goodland)

COLDWATER,* Comanche Co. — (Refer to Pratt)

CONCORDIA,* Cloud Co. — (Refer to Salina)

COUNCIL GROVE,* Morris Co. — (Refer to Emporia)

DODGE CITY,* Ford Co.

FOULSTON & SIEFKIN L.L.P. (AV)

810 Frontview, P.O. Box 1147, 67801
Telephone: 316-227-8126
Fax: 316-227-8451
Wichita, Kansas Office: 100 North Broadway, 700 Fourth Financial Center, 67202.
Telephone: 316-267-6371.
FAX: 316-267-6345.
Topeka, Kansas Office: 1515 Bank IV Tower, 534 Kansas Avenue, 66603.
Telephone: 913-233-3600.
FAX: 913-233-1610.
Member: Lex Mundi, A Global Association of 126 Independent Firms.

MEMBERS OF FIRM

William P. Trenkle, Jr.	R. Douglas Reagan
David J. Rebein	D. Shane Bangerter

ASSOCIATES

Tamara L. Davis	Kenton T. Gleason

For full biographical listings, see the Martindale-Hubbell Law Directory

WILLIAMS, STROBEL, MALONE, MASON & RALPH, P.A. (AV)

Second Floor, Bank IV Building, P.O. Box 39, 67801
Telephone: 316-225-4168
FAX: 316-225-7261

Carl Van Riper (1879-1950)	Terry J. Malone
C. W. Hughes (1910-1960)	Ronald C. Mason
James A. Williams (Retired)	Bradley C. Ralph
Ken W. Strobel	Alisa A. Nickel

Representative Clients: Roto-Mix, Inc.; Hartford Accident & Indemnity Co.; Travelers Insurance Co.; Farmers State Bank, Bucklin; Dodge City Board of Education; City of Dodge City; West Plains Regional Medical Complex; Farmers Ins. Group; Monfort, Inc.; Shelter, Ins.

For full biographical listings, see the Martindale-Hubbell Law Directory

EL DORADO,* Butler Co. — (Refer to Eureka)

ELLSWORTH,* Ellsworth Co. — (Refer to Salina)

EMPORIA,* Lyon Co.

ATHERTON & ATHERTON (AV)

527 Commercial, Suite 304, P.O. Box 624, 66801
Telephone: 316-342-1277; 342-1278
FAX: 316-342-2343

MEMBERS OF FIRM

John G. Atherton	Stephen J. Atherton

Representative Clients: Bank IV, N.A., Emporia, Kansas; Great West Casualty Co. American States Insurance Cos.; Manufacturers and Wholesalers Indemnity Co.; American Casualty Cos.; Universal Underwriters Insurance Co.; Travelers Insurance Co.; Maryland Casualty Co.; Shelter Insurance Companies; American Family Insurance.

For full biographical listings, see the Martindale-Hubbell Law Directory

FORT SCOTT,* Bourbon Co.

SHORT, GENTRY & BISHOP, P.A. (AV)

Suite 100 Security Professional Center, Fourth and Judson, 66701
Telephone: 316-223-0530
Facsimile: 316-223-6956

Forrest E. Short	Charles H. Gentry
Patrick S. Bishop	

Counsel for: Bruce Marble & Granite Co., Inc.; Key Industries, Inc.; KMDO Broadcasting, Inc.; Bourbon County Consolidated Rural Water District #2; KVCY; National Indemnity Co.; Chicago Title Insurance Co.; Tri State Insurance Co.

For full biographical listings, see the Martindale-Hubbell Law Directory

FREDONIA, * Wilson Co. — (Refer to Chanute)

GARNETT, * Anderson Co.

STEVEN B. DOERING (AV)

111 East Fourth Street, P.O. Box 345, 66032
Telephone: 913-448-5493
FAX: 913-448-5458

Reference: Kansas State Bank.

For full biographical listings, see the Martindale-Hubbell Law Directory

GIRARD, * Crawford Co. — (Refer to Pittsburg)

GREAT BEND, * Barton Co.

CONNER & OPIE (AV)

Suite 102, 2015 Forest Avenue, Drawer E, 67530
Telephone: 316-793-5455
Fax: 316-793-5456

Samuel Maher (1849-1918)	Elrick C. Cole (1856-1937)
Theodore Cole (1852-1890)	William Osmond (1853-1947)
	T.B. Kelly (1889-1965)

MEMBERS OF FIRM

Fred L. Conner	Glenn E. Opie

General Counsel for: Straub Oilfield Services Inc-Case/International; Tretbar Farms.
Local Counsel for: Atchison, Topeka & Santa Fe Railway Co.; Continental Oil Co.; Texaco, Inc.; The Prudential Insurance Co. of America; Natural Gas Pipeline Company of America; General Motors Corp.; Coachman Industries; John Hancock Mutual Life Insurance Company.

For full biographical listings, see the Martindale-Hubbell Law Directory

HAYS, * Ellis Co.

DREILING, BIEKER & HOFFMAN (AV)

111 West 13th Street, P.O. Box 579, 67601
Telephone: 913-625-3537
FAX: 913-625-8129

MEMBERS OF FIRM

Norbert R. Dreiling	Dennis L. Bieker
	Donald F. Hoffman

ASSOCIATES

Melvin J. Sauer, Jr.	Robert E. Diehl

General Counsel: Dreiling Oil Company, Hays, Kansas; Golden Belt Bank, FSA, Ellis, Kansas; Midland Marketing, Inc., Hays, Kansas; St. John's Rest Home, Victoria & Hays, Kansas.
Representative Clients: Farm Bureau Mutual Insurance Company of Kansas; Midwest Energy of Hays, Kansas.

For full biographical listings, see the Martindale-Hubbell Law Directory

HIAWATHA, * Brown Co. — (Refer to Troy)

HOWARD, * Elk Co. — (Refer to Eureka)

HOXIE, * Sheridan Co. — (Refer to Oberlin)

HUGOTON, * Stevens Co. — (Refer to Liberal)

HUTCHINSON, * Reno Co.

GILLILAND & HAYES, P.A. A PROFESSIONAL CORPORATION (AV)

335 N. Washington, Suite 260, P.O. Box 2977, 67504-2977
Telephone: 316-662-0537
Facsimile: 316-669-9426
Wichita, Kansas Office: The Orpheum Centre, Suite 300, 200 North Broadway, P.O. Box 49406.
Telephone: 316-262-2266.
Facsimile: 316-263-2202.
Kansas City, Missouri Office: 1234 Penntower, 3100 Broadway.
Telephone: 816-753-3100.
Facsimile: 816-753-2271.

Robert J. Gilliland	Bradley D. Dillon
John F. Hayes	Gerald L. Green
James R. Gilliland	David N. Zimmerman (Not
John S. Schmidt	admitted in KS; Resident,
Bruce B. Waugh (Not admitted	Kansas City, Missouri Office)
in KS; Resident, Kansas City,	Carol Zuschek Smith (Resident,
Missouri Office)	Kansas City, Missouri Office)
Michael R. O'Neal	Kathleen A. Hardee (Resident,
	Kansas City, Missouri Office)

(See Next Column)

C. J. Wahrman, III (Resident,	Cinda L. Norberg
Kansas City, Missouri Office)	Laura A. Hederstedt
Matthew L. Bretz	Lisa M. Ward
Kendall R. Cunningham	Kimberly Breda Bushek
(Resident, Wichita Office)	(Resident, Kansas City,
	Missouri Office)

Representative Clients: Central Bank and Trust Co.; Dillon Cos., Inc.; AT&SF Railway Co.; Farm Bureau Mutual Insurance Co.; Hartford Insurance Cos.; Hutchinson Clinic, P.A.; Hutchinson Hospital Corp.; Southwestern Bell Telephone Co.; Stuckey Lumber & Supply, Inc.

For full biographical listings, see the Martindale-Hubbell Law Directory

MARTINDELL, SWEARER & SHAFFER (AV)

811 East Thirtieth Street, P.O. Box 1907, 67504-1907
Telephone: 316-662-3331
Fax: 316-662-9978
Kingman, Kansas Office: 120 East A Avenue, P.O. Box 415.
Telephone: 316-532-5158,
Fax: 316-532-2303.

MEMBERS OF FIRM

Robert C. Martindell	Charles D. Lee
John H. Shaffer	Francis E. Meisenheimer
William B. Swearer	(Resident, Kingman, Kansas
Elwin F. Cabbage	Office)
Jerry L. Ricksecker	John B. Swearer
Gerald E. Hertach	Jess W. Arbuckle

SPECIAL COUNSEL

John E. Caton

Representative Clients: Hutchinson Community College; Charles E. Carey Foundation, Inc.; Lowen Corporation; J.H. Shears Sons, Inc. (Contractors); Hutchinson Industrial District #1; Kansas Oxygen, Inc.

For full biographical listings, see the Martindale-Hubbell Law Directory

REYNOLDS, FORKER, BERKLEY, SUTER, ROSE & DOWER (AV)

Suite 200, 129 West 2nd Avenue, P.O. Box 1868, 67504-1868
Telephone: 316-663-7131
Fax: 316-669-0714

MEMBERS OF FIRM

Roy C. Davis (1890-1959)	John T. Suter
Robert Y. Jones (1912-1963)	Trish Rose
H. Newlin Reynolds	Thomas A. Dower
Dan W. Forker, Jr.	Raymond F. Berkley
	Michael C. Robinson

For full biographical listings, see the Martindale-Hubbell Law Directory

INDEPENDENCE, * Montgomery Co. — (Refer to Coffeyville)

IOLA, * Allen Co.

TALKINGTON & CLARK, L.L.P. (AV)

20 North Washington Avenue, P.O. Box 725, 66749
Telephone: 316-365-5125
FAX: 316-365-8066

MEMBERS OF FIRM

J. D. (Dave) Conderman	Robert V. Talkington
(1915-1978)	David A. Clark
	Kristen B. Patty Clark

Representative Clients: State Farm Mutual Insurance Co.; Medical Protective Co.; Allen County Hospital.

For full biographical listings, see the Martindale-Hubbell Law Directory

JETMORE, * Hodgeman Co. — (Refer to Dodge City)

JOHNSON, * Stanton Co. — (Refer to Garden City)

JUNCTION CITY, * Geary Co.

HARPER, HORNBAKER, ALTENHOFEN & OPAT, CHARTERED (AV)

715 North Washington Street, P.O. Box 168, 66441
Telephone: 913-762-2100
Fax: 913-762-2291

Howard W. Harper (1912-1988)	Charles W. Harper, II
Lee Hornbaker	Craig Altenhofen
Steven Hornbaker	Steven L. Opat

Representative Clients: First State Bank; City of Grandview Plaza; Commercial Union Insurance Co.; Dodson Group; State Farm Insurance Cos.; Reliance Insurance Co.; Employers Mutual; U.S.F.&G.
Approved Attorneys for: Chicago Title & Trust; Columbian Title & Trust.

For full biographical listings, see the Martindale-Hubbell Law Directory

Junction City—Continued

WEARY, DAVIS, HENRY, STRUEBING & TROUP (AV)

819 North Washington Street, P.O. Box 187, 66441
Telephone: 913-762-2210
Telefax: 913-238-3880

MEMBERS OF FIRM

Ulysses S. Weary (1885-1977)	Steven R. Struebing
Robert K. Weary	David P. Troup
Victor A. Davis, Jr.	Blair S. Jones
Keith R. Henry	Wendy L. Kaus

Representative Clients: Central National Bank; Unified School District #475; First State Bank of Junction City; Mid-America & Kansas CATV Assns. Local Counsel for: Sprint-United Telephone Company of Kansas; Continental Grain, Inc.; Wal-Mart Stores, Inc.; Douglas Cable Communications.

For full biographical listings, see the Martindale-Hubbell Law Directory

KANSAS CITY,* Wyandotte Co.

BODDINGTON & BROWN, CHTD. (AV)

Suite 100 Security Bank Building, Minnesota Avenue at 7th Street, 66101
Telephone: 913-371-1272
FAX: 913-371-5726

N. Jack Brown	Joseph R. Ebbert
Kenneth E. Holm	D. Scott Brown
Leo L. Logan	Stephen P. Doherty
David W. Hauber	Deborah Diaz Hodes

OF COUNSEL

Michael E. Callen	Albert M. Ross (Retired)
Edward M. Boddington, Jr. (Retired)	

For full biographical listings, see the Martindale-Hubbell Law Directory

HOLBROOK, HEAVEN & FAY, P.A. (AV)

757 Armstrong, P.O. Box 171927, 66117
Telephone: 913-342-2500
Fax: 913-342-0603
Merriam, Kansas Office: 6700 Antioch Street.
Telephone: 913-677-1717.
Fax: 913-677-0403.

Reid F. Holbrook	Kurt S. Brack
Lewis A. Heaven, Jr. (Resident, Merriam Office)	(Resident Merriam Office)
Ted F. Fay, Jr. (Resident, Merriam Office)	Sally A. Howard
	Brent G. Wright
Thomas E. Osborn	Henry F. Sonday, Jr.
Robert L. Kennedy	Joy D. Hays
Janet M. Simpson	(Resident Merriam Office)
John D. Tongier (Resident, Merriam Office)	Douglas G. Peterson
	Christopher T. Brumbaugh (Not admitted in KS; Resident Merriam Office)
Thomas M. Sutherland	
Thomas S. Busch (Resident, Merriam Office)	Daniel W. Peters
	Lynaia M. Holsapple

OF COUNSEL

Darrel E. Johnson (Resident, Merriam Office)

For full biographical listings, see the Martindale-Hubbell Law Directory

McANANY, VAN CLEAVE & PHILLIPS, P.A. (AV)

Fourth Floor, 707 Minnesota Avenue, P.O. Box 171300, 66117
Telephone: 913-371-3838
Facsimile: 913-371-4722
Lenexa, Kansas Office: Suite 200, 11900 West 87th Street Parkway.
Telephone: 913-888-9000.
Facsimile: 913-888-7049.
Kansas City, Missouri Office: Suite 304, 819 Walnut Street.
Telephone: 816-556-9417.

Edwin S. McAnany (1871-1954)	Wade A. Dorothy
Thomas M. Van Cleave (1887-1961)	(Resident, Lenexa Office)
	Robert F. Rowe, Jr.
Willard L. Phillips (1905-1989)	(Resident, Lenexa Office)
James R. Goheen (1942-1994)	Lawrence D. Greenbaum
John J. Jurcyk, Jr.	John David Jurcyk
Robert D. Benham	(Resident, Lenexa Office)
Clifford T. Mueller (Resident, Lenexa Office)	Douglas M. Greenwald
	Daniel F. Church
David M. Druten	Anton C. Andersen
Daniel B. Denk	Rosemary Podrebarac Case
Charles A. Getto	Joseph W. Hemberger
William P. Coates, Jr. (Resident, Lenexa Office)	Gregory D. Worth (Resident, Lenexa Office)
Frederick J. Greenbaum	Deryl William Wynn
Nancy S. Anstaett (Resident, Lenexa Office)	Rex Wayne Henoch (Resident, Lenexa Office)
Jeanne Gorman Rau	

(See Next Column)

Clifford K. Stubbs (Resident, Lenexa Office)	Joseph F. Reardon
	Carl A. Gallagher
Henry E. Couchman, Jr.	William A. Wolff
Eric Thomas Lanham	(Resident, Lenexa Office)
Gregory P. Goheen	Elizabeth A. Boldt
Paul K. Thoma	(Resident, Lenexa Office)
Stephen A. McManus	Dana D. Arth
Byron A. Bowles	(Resident, Lenexa Office)

OF COUNSEL

Thomas M. Van Cleave, Jr. (Resident, Lenexa Office)	Frank D. Menghini

Reference: Guaranty Bank and Trust Co.

For full biographical listings, see the Martindale-Hubbell Law Directory

KINGMAN,* Kingman Co. — (Refer to Pratt)

KINSLEY,* Edwards Co. — (Refer to Dodge City)

LA CROSSE,* Rush Co. — (Refer to Hays)

LARNED,* Pawnee Co. — (Refer to Great Bend)

LAWRENCE,* Douglas Co.

ALLEN, COOLEY & ALLEN (AV)

201 Mercantile Bank Tower, 900 Massachusetts, 66044-2868
Telephone: 913-843-0222
Fax: 913-843-0254

MEMBERS OF FIRM

Milton P. Allen, Sr. (1914-1988)	Milton P. Allen, Jr.
Gerald L. Cooley	John M. Cooley

ASSOCIATES

Michelle Ann Davis	Randall F. Larkin

Representative Clients: LRM Industries, Inc.; Shelter Insurance Cos.; National Casualty Insurance Co.; Coregis Insurance Company; Fireman's Fund Insurance Co.; B.A. Green Construction Co.; Westheffer Co., Inc.; The World Co., Inc.; Sunflower Cable TV; City of Lawrence.

For full biographical listings, see the Martindale-Hubbell Law Directory

BARBER, EMERSON, SPRINGER, ZINN & MURRAY, L.C. (AV)

1211 Massachusetts Street, P.O. Box 667, 66044
Telephone: 913-843-6600
Fax: 913-843-8405
Email: beszm@aol.com

John A. Emerson	Thomas V. Murray
Byron E. Springer	Calvin J. Karlin
Richard L. Zinn	Jane M. Eldredge
Mark A. Andersen	Charles F. Blaser
William N. Fleming	Cheryl L. Jackson

COUNSEL

Richard A. Barber	Martin B. Dickinson, Jr.
	Glee S. Smith, Jr.

Representative Clients: Mercantile Bank of Lawrence; University National Bank of Lawrence; Douglas County Bank; FMC Corp.; Mine Safety Appliances Co.; Equitable Life Assurance Society of the U.S.; The Travelers Insurance Co.; American Family Insurance Co.

For full biographical listings, see the Martindale-Hubbell Law Directory

LENEXA, Johnson Co.

McANANY, VAN CLEAVE & PHILLIPS, P.A. (AV)

Suite 200, 11900 West 87th Street Parkway, 66215
Telephone: 913-888-9000
Facsimile: 913-888-7049
Kansas City, Kansas Office: Fourth Floor, 707 Minnesota Avenue, P.O. Box 171300.
Telephone: 913-371-3838.
Facsimile: 913-371-4722.
Kansas City, Missouri Office: Suite 304, 819 Walnut Street.
Telephone: 816-556-9417.

RESIDENT ATTORNEYS

Clifford T. Mueller	Gregory D. Worth
William P. Coates, Jr.	Rex Wayne Henoch
Nancy S. Anstaett	Clifford K. Stubbs
Wade A. Dorothy	William A. Wolff
Robert F. Rowe, Jr.	Elizabeth A. Boldt
John David Jurcyk	Dana D. Arth

OF COUNSEL

Thomas M. Van Cleave, Jr.	Frank D. Menghini

Reference: Guaranty Bank and Trust Co.

For full biographical listings, see the Martindale-Hubbell Law Directory

LYNDON,* Osage Co. — (Refer to Ottawa)

LYONS,* Rice Co. — (Refer to McPherson)

*MANKATO,** Jewell Co. — (Refer to Beloit)

*MARION,** Marion Co. — (Refer to McPherson)

*MARYSVILLE,** Marshall Co.

GALLOWAY, WIEGERS & HEENEY (AV)

1114 Broadway, P.O. Box 468, 66508
Telephone: 913-562-2375
Fax: 913-562-5348

MEMBERS OF FIRM

Robert F. Galloway (1918-1986)	Richard D. Heeney
Edward F. Wiegers	Charles Thomas Kier
	Kim W. Cudney

Representative Clients: Citizens State Bank and Exchange National Bank, Maryville, Kansas; Landoll Corp; Bremen Farmers Mutual Insurance Co.; State Bank of Axtell; State Bank of Blue Rapids; Farm Credit Bank of Wichita.

*MCPHERSON,** McPherson Co.

BREMYER & WISE, P.A. (AV)

The Bremyer Building, 120 W. Kansas Avenue, P.O. Box 1146, 67460
Telephone: 316-241-0554
Telefax: 316-241-7692
Email: bwlaw@midusa.net

Robert W. Wise	Randee Koger
Brett A. Reber	Jill Bremyer-Archer
Casey R. Law	David N. Harger
	Jeffrey A. Houston

OF COUNSEL

John K. Bremyer	Jay K. Bremyer

For full biographical listings, see the Martindale-Hubbell Law Directory

*MEADE,** Meade Co. — (Refer to Dodge City)

*NEWTON,** Harvey Co. — (Refer to Wichita)

*NORTON,** Norton Co. — (Refer to Oberlin)

*OAKLEY,** Logan Co. — (Refer to Goodland)

*OSBORNE,** Osborne Co. — (Refer to Beloit)

*OSKALOOSA,** Jefferson Co. — (Refer to Valley Falls)

*OSWEGO,** Labette Co. — (Refer to Parsons)

OVERLAND PARK, Johnson Co.

PAYNE & JONES, CHARTERED (AV)

Commerce Terrace, College Boulevard at King 11000 King, P.O. Box 25625, 66225
Telephone: 913-469-4100
Fax: 913-469-8182

Howard E. Payne (1901-1976)	Stephen D. McGiffert
W. C. Jones (1908-1970)	Mark S. Gunnison
Robert P. Anderson	James J. Cramer
Keith Martin	Donald R. Whitney
H. Thomas Payne	David R. Smith
John H. Johntz, Jr.	Jon W. Gilchrist
Edward M. Boyle	Michael W. Lucansky
Barry W. McCormick	Michael B. Lowe
Thomas K. Jones	Julie A. N. Sample
David K. Martin	Dirk L. Hubbard
Jodde Olsen Lanning	Steven L. Passer
Thomas L. Griswold	J. Tyler Peters
Susan S. Baker	Scott M. Adam
Chris W. Henry	Scott C. Long
Kip A. Kubin	Roger Hadley Templin
	Robert E. James

Representative Clients: First Federal Savings & Loan Association of Olathe, Kansas; Aetna Casualty & Surety Co.; Commercial Union Insurance Cos.; Farmers Insurance Group; The Hartford Insurance Group; United States Fidelity & Guaranty Co.; CNA Insurance Co.

For full biographical listings, see the Martindale-Hubbell Law Directory

SHUGHART THOMSON & KILROY, A PROFESSIONAL CORPORATION (AV)

Suite 1100, 32 Corporate Woods, 9225 Indian Creek Parkway, 66210
Telephone: 913-451-3355
Email: Solutions@STKLAW.COM *URL:* http://www.stklaw.com
Kansas City, Missouri Office: Twelve Wyandotte Plaza, 120 West 12th Street.
Telephone: 816-421-3355.

(See Next Column)

KANSAS OFFICE ATTORNEYS

William V. North	Robert B. Keim
Steven D. Ruse	Gregory L. Musil
James P. O'Hara	Donald A. Culp
Anthony F. Rupp	Rebecca L. Warren
	Andrew M. DeMarea

For full biographical listings, see the Martindale-Hubbell Law Directory

WALLACE, SAUNDERS, AUSTIN, BROWN & ENOCHS, CHARTERED (AV)

10111 West 87th Street, P.O. Box 12290, 66282-2290
Telephone: 913-888-1000
Fax: 913-888-1065
Email: info@op.wsabe.com *URL:* http://www.wsabe.com
Wichita, Kansas Office: 600 Epic Center, 301 North Main Street, 67202-4806.
Telephone: 316-269-2100.
Fax: 316-269-2479.
Springfield, Missouri Office: 1201 Hammons Tower, 901 East St. Louis Street, 65806-2505.
Telephone: 417-866-2300.
Fax: 417-866-2444.
Kansas City, Missouri Office: 2405 Grand Boulevard, Suite 500, 64108.
Telephone: 913-888-1000.
Fax: 913-888-1065.

Frank Saunders, Jr.	Kevin L. Bennett
Barton Brown	Gary R. Terrill
Richmond M. Enochs	M. Duane Coyle
James G. Butler, Jr.	(Resident, Wichita Office)
James O. Schwinn	Timothy G. Lutz
Richard T. Merker	Mark V. Bodine
Jerome V. Bales	Norman I. Reichel, Jr.
H. Wayne Powers	Leonard R. Frischer
Rod L. Richardson	Bradley S. Russell
Paul Hasty, Jr.	Kirby A. Vernon
Barry E. Warren	(Resident, Wichita Office)
Sally H. Harris	Douglas C. Hobbs
Mark W. McKinzie	(Resident, Wichita Office)
Michael P. Oliver	Patrick E. McGrath
James L. Sanders	Robert A. Mintz
Rudolf H. Beese	D'Ambra Howard
Michael J. Dutton	J. Philip Davidson
Thomas D. Billam	(Resident, Wichita Office)

OF COUNSEL

Stephen H. Snead (Resident, Springfield, Missouri Office)	Timothy J. Finnerty (Resident, Wichita Office)
Barry D. Martin	Larry J. Austin (Retired)
	Kenneth B. Wallace (1912-1982)

D. Steven Marsh (Resident, Wichita Office)	Brian C. Behrens
	Scott R. Flucke
Karl Kuckelman	John V. Dwyer
John M. Ross	(Resident, Wichita Office)
Eric A. Van Beber	Mary Angela Lasagna
Patrick F. Hulla	(Not admitted in KS)
Michael D. Streit	C.J. Moeller (Resident,
(Resident, Wichita Office)	Springfield, Missouri Office)
Kurt W. Ratzlaff	Donald J. Fritschie
(Resident, Wichita Office)	C. Todd Navrat
Kristin J. Blomquist	Steven D. Harris
(Resident, Wichita Office)	Casey O. Housley
Derrick A. Pearce	John R. Weist
Chad K. Gillam	Kevin L. Fritz
Arlen L. Tanner	(Not admitted in KS)
Sue E. Yoakum	Thomas E. Patterson
Christopher John McCurdy	(Resident, Wichita Office)
(Resident, Wichita Office)	Tristram E. Felix
Sean T. McGrevey	(Resident, Wichita Office)

For full biographical listings, see the Martindale-Hubbell Law Directory

PARSONS, Labette Co.

DEARTH, MARKHAM & JACK, CHARTERED (AV)

1712 Broadway, P.O. Box 1034, 67357
Telephone: 316-421-1970; 421-3650
Fax: 316-421-8846

Glenn Jones (1911-1985)	David K. Markham
Richard C. Dearth	Jeffry L. Jack

OF COUNSEL

John B. Markham

Representative Clients: First National Bank and Trust Co.; Commercial Bank; Day & Zimmerman International, Inc.; Liberty Mutual Insurance Co.; American States Insurance Co.; Federated Insurance Co.

For full biographical listings, see the Martindale-Hubbell Law Directory

*PHILLIPSBURG,** Phillips Co. — (Refer to Oberlin)

PRAIRIE VILLAGE, Johnson Co.

BENNETT, LYTLE, WETZLER, MARTIN & PISHNY, L.C. (AV)

Suite 300 Greenview Place, 5000 West 95th Street, P.O. Box 8030, 66208
Telephone: 913-642-7300
Fax: 913-642-0520

Robert F. Bennett	James R. Orr
Robert F. Lytle	Andrew F. Sears
Charles E. Wetzler	Janice S. Martin
P. Stephen Martin	Patrick D. Gaston
Lyle D. Pishny	David J. Adkins
Richard S. Wetzler	Mark C. Owens
Bruce F. Landeck	Patricia A. Bennett

Nathan M. Sutton   David C. Wetzler
OF COUNSEL
Peter A. Martin, P.C.

For full biographical listings, see the Martindale-Hubbell Law Directory

PRATT, * Pratt Co.

HAMPTON & HAMPTON (AV)

Professional Building, 113 East Third, Drawer H, 67124-1108
Telephone: 316-672-5533
Fax: 316-672-6713

MEMBERS OF FIRM
B.V. Hampton (1914-1995)   Bill V. Hampton, Jr.

General Counsel for: First National Bank in Pratt; Pratt Community College/Area Vocational School; M-C Company; Unified School District 438; Pratt Ag Aviation, Inc.

For full biographical listings, see the Martindale-Hubbell Law Directory

RUSSELL, * Russell Co. — (Refer to Hays)

ST. FRANCIS, * Cheyenne Co. — (Refer to Goodland)

ST. JOHN, * Stafford Co.

SHIELDS LAW OFFICE, P.A. (AV)

106 East Third Street, P.O. Box 427, 67576
Telephone: 316-549-3212
Fax: 316-549-3268

Emerson H. Shields
Representative Client: First National Bank & Trust of St. John.

SALINA, * Saline Co.

CLARK, MIZE & LINVILLE, CHARTERED (AV)

129 South Eighth, P.O. Box 380, 67402-0380
Telephone: 913-823-6325
Fax: 913-823-1868

James P. Mize (1910-1988)	Lawton M. Nuss
L. O. Bengtson	Mickey W. Mosier
Peter L. Peterson	Paula J. Wright
John W. Mize	Eric N. Anderson
Greg A. Bengtson	Donald G. Reinsch

J. Jay Lang
OF COUNSEL
C. L. Clark (Retired)   Aubrey G. Linville (Retired)

Representative Clients: Salina Regional Health Center, Inc.; Coldwell-Banker, Antrim, Piper, Wenger Realtors, Inc.; Crestwood, Inc.; Kansas Wesleyan University; Premier Pneumatics; City of Salina; Sunflower Bank, N.A.; Tony's Pizza Service; Unified School District 305; Wilson & Company, Engineers & Architects.

For full biographical listings, see the Martindale-Hubbell Law Directory

HAMPTON, ROYCE, ENGLEMAN & NELSON (AV)

Ninth Floor United Building, 67401
Telephone: 913-827-7251
Fax: 913-827-2815

Howard Engleman (Retired)
MEMBERS OF FIRM

C. Stanley Nelson	David D. Moshier
Jack N. Stewart	J. Stan Sexton
W. Dean Owens	David R. Klaassen
N. Royce Nelson	Debra Egli James
Sidney A. Reitz	Jeffrey E. King

Terry Criss
SPECIAL COUNSEL
Clarence L. King, Jr.

(See Next Column)

ASSOCIATES
John Andrew O'Leary   Brian Wilson Wood

Representative Clients: Blue Beacon International, Inc.; First Bank Kansas; First National Bank of Beloit; Great Plains Manufacturing, Inc.; Kansas Grain & Feed Assn.; Morrison Enterprises; St. Francis Academy, Inc.; Salina Journal, Inc.; Salina Supply Co.; Sellers Tractor Co., Inc.

For full biographical listings, see the Martindale-Hubbell Law Directory

SCOTT CITY, * Scott Co. — (Refer to Garden City)

SEDAN, * Chautauqua Co. — (Refer to Coffeyville)

SENECA, * Nemaha Co. — (Refer to Marysville)

SHARON SPRINGS, * Wallace Co. — (Refer to Goodland)

SMITH CENTER, * Smith Co. — (Refer to Beloit)

STERLING, Rice Co. — (Refer to Hutchinson)

STOCKTON, * Rooks Co. — (Refer to Hays)

SYRACUSE, * Hamilton Co. — (Refer to Garden City)

TOPEKA, * Shawnee Co.

BENNETT & DILLON, L.L.P. (AV)

1605 Southwest 37th Street, 66611
Telephone: 913-267-5063
Fax: 913-267-2652

MEMBERS OF FIRM
Mark L. Bennett, Jr.   Wilburn Dillon, Jr.
Ann L. Hoover

Jeffrey D. Jackson

References: Commerce Bank and Trust; Columbian National Bank and Trust; Silver Lake State Bank.

For full biographical listings, see the Martindale-Hubbell Law Directory

COSGROVE, WEBB & OMAN (AV)

1100 Bank IV Tower, One Townsite Plaza, 66603
Telephone: 913-235-9511
Fax: 913-235-2082

MEMBERS OF FIRM

M. F. Cosgrove (1889-1961)	James D. Waugh (1922-1994)
Robert L. Webb (1890-1975)	Donald J. Horttor
Ralph W. Oman (1897-1984)	Edward L. Bailey
Philip E. Buzick (1918-1970)	Robert L. Baer
William B. McElhenny (1920-1976)	Charles T. Engel
	Carol B. Bonebrake

ASSOCIATES
Susan L. Mauch   John T. Houston
OF COUNSEL
Donald E. Jensen

For full biographical listings, see the Martindale-Hubbell Law Directory

DAVIS, UNREIN, HUMMER & BUCK, L.L.P. (AV)

100 East Ninth Street, Third Floor, P.O. Box 3575, 66601-3575
Telephone: 913-354-1100
Fax: 913-354-1113

MEMBERS OF FIRM

Byron M. Gray (1901-1986)	J. Franklin Hummer
Maurice D. Freidberg (1902-1965)	Mark A. Buck
	James B. Biggs
Charles L. Davis, Jr. (1921-1992)	Christopher M. Rohrer
	Brenda L. Head
Michael J. Unrein	Eric I. Unrein

OF COUNSEL
Gary D. McCallister

Representative Clients: Adams Business Forms; Bettis Asphalt Co., Inc.; Blue Cross & Blue Shield of Kansas; Cooper Tire & Rubber Co.; Famous Brands; J.M. Bauersfeld; Jostens, Inc.; Kansas Association of Realtors; McElroys, Inc.; McPherson Contractors.

For full biographical listings, see the Martindale-Hubbell Law Directory

FISHER, PATTERSON, SAYLER & SMITH, L.L.P. (AV)

534 South Kansas Avenue, Suite 400, P.O. Box 949, 66601
Telephone: 913-232-7761
Fax: 913-232-6604
Overland Park, Kansas Office: 11050 Roe Avenue, Suite 210, 66211.
Telephone: 913-339-6757.
Fax: 913-339-6187.

(See Next Column)

941A

FISHER, PATTERSON, SAYLER & SMITH L.L.P., *Topeka—Continued*

MEMBERS OF FIRM

Donald Patterson	Steve R. Fabert
Edwin Dudley Smith (Resident, Overland Park Office)	Ronald J. Laskowski
Larry G. Pepperdine	Michael K. Seck (Resident, Overland Park Office)
James P. Nordstrom	David P. Madden (Resident, Overland Park Office)
Justice B. King	
J. Steven Pigg	Steven K. Johnson

ASSOCIATES

Kristine A. Larscheid	Billy E. Newman
Patrick G. Reavey (Resident, Overland Park Office)	David R. Cooper

OF COUNSEL
David H. Fisher

RETIRED
Charles Keith Sayler (Retired)

Representative Clients: Gage Shopping Center, Inc.; Fireman's Fund-American Insurance Cos.; United States Fidelity and Guaranty Co.; The Procter & Gamble Company; American Cyanamid Company; Commercial Union Insurance Companies; National Casualty/Scottsdale Insurance Co.; The Hartford; Berkshire Hathaway Companies.

For full biographical listings, see the Martindale-Hubbell Law Directory

GOODELL, STRATTON, EDMONDS & PALMER, L.L.P. (AV)

515 South Kansas Avenue, 66603-3999
Telephone: 913-233-0593
Telecopier: 913-233-8870
Email: GSEP@CJNETWORKS.COM

MEMBERS OF FIRM

Gerald L. Goodell	Patrick M. Salsbury
Wayne T. Stratton	Michael W. Merriam
Arthur E. Palmer	John H. Stauffer, Jr.
H. Philip Elwood	Les E. Diehl
Harold S. Youngentob	David E. Bruns
Gerald J. Letourneau	N. Larry Bork
Charles R. Hay	John D. Ensley
	Catherine M. Walberg

OF COUNSEL

Robert E. Edmonds (Retired)	John A. Bausch
Robert A. McClure	Richard W. Holmes

ASSOCIATES

Steve A Schwarm	Penny R. Moylan
	Anne M. Kindling

SPECIAL COUNSEL

Joseph E. McKinney	Marta Fisher Linenberger
	Curtis J. Waugh

Counsel for: Columbian National Title Insurance Co.; Stauffer Communications, Inc.; Central Regional Dental Testing Service, Inc.; Heartland Community Bankers Association; The Menninger Foundation; Topeka Chamber of Commerce; Washburn University of Topeka; Reser's Fine Foods; ConAgra; Monfort, Inc.

For full biographical listings, see the Martindale-Hubbell Law Directory

PORTER, FAIRCHILD, WACHTER & HANEY, P.A. (AV)

Suite 1000, Bank IV Tower, 534 South Kansas Avenue, P.O. Box 1833, 66601-1833
Telephone: 913-235-2200
Facsimile: 913-235-8950

Ronald W. Fairchild	John H. Wachter
Thomas D. Haney	

OF COUNSEL
James W. Porter

James P. Kenner

For full biographical listings, see the Martindale-Hubbell Law Directory

WRIGHT, HENSON, SOMERS, SEBELIUS, CLARK & BAKER, LLP (AV)

Commerce Bank Building, 100 Southeast Ninth Street, 2nd Floor, P.O. Box 3555, 66601-3555
Telephone: 913-232-2200
FAX: 913-232-3344

MEMBERS OF FIRM

Thomas E. Wright	K. Gary Sebelius
Charles N. Henson	Bruce J. Clark
Dale L. Somers	Anne Lamborn Baker
	Evelyn Zabel Wilson

(See Next Column)

ASSOCIATES

Theron L. Sims	Michael M. Walker
	Donald Sutsu Lee

For full biographical listings, see the Martindale-Hubbell Law Directory

TRIBUNE,* Greeley Co. — (Refer to Garden City)

VALLEY FALLS, Jefferson Co.

LOWRY & JOHNSON (AV)

323 Broadway Avenue, P.O. Box 10, 66088
Telephone: 913-945-3281
Facsimile: 913-945-6255

MEMBERS OF FIRM

Gordon K. Lowry	Stuart S. Lowry

OF COUNSEL
Lauren M. Lowry

Attorneys for: Kendall State Bank, Valley Falls, Kansas; Leavenworth-Jefferson Electric Cooperative, Inc.; Unified School District #338, Valley Falls, Kansas; Delaware Watershed Joint District #10; Cities of Nortonville and Valley Falls, Kansas; Kaw Valley Electric Cooperative, Topeka, Kansas. *General Counsel for:* Kansas Electric Co-operatives, Inc.

For full biographical listings, see the Martindale-Hubbell Law Directory

WA KEENEY,* Trego Co. — (Refer to Hays)

WASHINGTON,* Washington Co. — (Refer to Marysville)

WICHITA,* Sedgwick Co.

DEPEW AND GILLEN, L.L.C. (AV)

151 North Main, Suite 700, 67202-1408
Telephone: 316-265-9621
Facsimile: 316-265-3819
Email: d-g@southwind.net

Spencer L. Depew	David W. Nickel
Dennis L. Gillen	Nicholas S. Daily
Randall K. Rathbun	David E. Rogers
Jack Scott McInteer	Charles C. Steincamp

For full biographical listings, see the Martindale-Hubbell Law Directory

FOULSTON & SIEFKIN L.L.P. (AV)

700 Fourth Financial Center, 67202
Telephone: 316-267-6371
Facsimile: 316-267-6345
Topeka, Kansas Office: 1515 Bank IV Tower, 534 Kansas Avenue, 66603.
Telephone: 913-233-3600.
Fax: 913-233-1610.
Dodge City, Kansas Office: 810 Frontview, P.O. Box 1147, 67801.
Telephone: 316-227-8126.
Fax: 316-227-8451.
Member: Lex Mundi, A Global Association of 126 Independent Firms.

MEMBERS OF FIRM

Robert L. Howard	Wyatt M. Wright
Charles J. Woodin	Jim H. Goering
Mikel L. Stout	Wyatt A. Hoch
Benjamin C. Langel	Amy S. Lemley
Phillip S. Frick	James P. Rankin
Stanley G. Andeel	(Resident, Topeka Office)
Frederick L. Haag	Douglas L. Hanisch
Richard D. Ewy	Douglas L. Stanley
Darrell L. Warta	J. Steven Massoni
Harvey R. Sorensen	Timothy B. Mustaine
James M. Armstrong	Jeffery A. Jordan
Mary Kathleen Babcock	Trisha A. Thelen
Charles P. Efflandt	William R. Wood, II
James D. Oliver	Eric F. Melgren
Gary L. Ayers	Kevin J. Arnel
Gloria G. Farha Flentje	Craig W. West
Larry G. Rapp	Carol A. Beier
R. Douglas Reagan	William P. Trenkle, Jr.
(Resident, Dodge City Office)	(Resident, Dodge City Office)
Jay F. Fowler	David J. Rebein
Stephen M. Kerwick	(Resident, Dodge City Office)
Gary E. Knight	Eric K. Kuhn
Christopher M. Hurst	Jay M. Rector
Vaughn Burkholder	Stewart T. Weaver
Terry C. Cupps	Thomas W. Young

SPECIAL COUNSEL

Nancy M. Clifton	David M. Traster
Gaye B. Tibbets	John C. Peck
James L. Grimes, Jr.	Robert A. Fox
(Resident, Topeka Office)	(Resident, Topeka Office)

OF COUNSEL

Richard C. Harris	Gerald Sawatzky

(See Next Column)

FOULSTON & SIEFKIN L.L.P.—*Continued*

ASSOCIATES

Mark A. Biberstein	Holly A. Dyer
Boyd A. Byers	Martha Aaron Ross
Jeffrey P. DeGraffenreid	Todd N. Tedesco

Representative Clients: Fourth Financial Corp. (Bank IV Kansas); The Boeing Company; The Coleman Co.; Koch Industries, Inc.; Pizza Hut, Inc.; State Farm Mutual Insurance Co.; Shelter Insurance Company; Atlantic Richfield Co.; The Sisters of St. Joseph of Wichita; The Wichita Clinic.

For full biographical listings, see the Martindale-Hubbell Law Directory

GOTT, YOUNG & BOGLE, P.A.

(See Young, Bogle, McCausland, Wells & Clark)

HERSHBERGER, PATTERSON, JONES & ROTH, L.C. (AV)

600 Hardage Center, 100 South Main, 67202-3779
Telephone: 316-263-7583
Fax: 316-263-7595

A. W. Hershberger (1897-1976)	J. Michael Kennalley
J. B. Patterson (1895-1957)	John A. Vetter
Richard Jones (1914-1988)	Edward L. Keeley
Jerome E. Jones	Bryce A. Abbott
Robert J. Roth	David J. Morgan
William R. Smith	Ken W. Dannenberg

Tracy A. Applegate

T. Lynn Ward	Gary K. Albin

OF COUNSEL

H. E. Jones	John L. Kratzer, Jr.

Counsel for: First National Bank in Wichita; Anadarko Petroleum Corporation; Chinese Industries; Mobil Oil Corp.; CNA Insurance; Royal Exchange Group; Central National Insurance Group; Transamerica Insurance Group; Northwestern National Insurance Group.

For full biographical listings, see the Martindale-Hubbell Law Directory

KAHRS, NELSON, FANNING, HITE & KELLOGG, L.L.P. (AV)

Suite 630, 200 West Douglas Street, 67202-3089
Telephone: 316-265-7761
Telecopier: 316-267-7803

MEMBERS OF FIRM

William A. Kahrs (1904-1989)	Arthur S. Chalmers
Robert H. Nelson (1904-1977)	Marc A. Powell
Darrell D. Kellogg (1931-1992)	Kim R. Martens
Richard C. Hite	Linda S. Parks
Richard L. Honeyman	Forrest James Robinson, Jr.
Larry A. Withers	Don D. Gribble, II
Gary A. Winfrey	John G. Pike
Clark R. Nelson	Vince P. Wheeler
Steven D. Gough	Alan R. Pfaff
Scott J. Gunderson	Dennis V. Lacey
Randy Troutt	Donald N. Peterson, II

ASSOCIATES

Todd M. Connell	Jeffrey R. Emerson
J. Scott Pohl	Lisa Adrian McPherson

Mary E. Giovanni

OF COUNSEL

H. W. Fanning	Robert Hall

Representative Clients: Advance Chemical Dist., Inc.; Learjet Corp.; Hahner, Foreman & Harness, Contractors; New York Life Ins. Co.; United States Fidelity & Guaranty Co; General Motors Corp.; St. Paul Ins. Cos.; Ruffin Hotel Corp.; Central Detroit Diesel Allison, Inc.

For full biographical listings, see the Martindale-Hubbell Law Directory

KLENDA, MITCHELL, AUSTERMAN & ZUERCHER, L.L.C. (AV)

1600 Epic Center, 301 North Main Street, 67202-4888
Telephone: 316-267-0331
Telecopier: 316-267-0333

L. D. Klenda	Jeffrey D. Peier
Alexander B. Mitchell, II	Ron Dean Beal
Gary M. Austerman	Scott A. Eads
Michael R. Biggs	Mark J. Lazzo
Alan D. Herman	John B. Gilliam
John V. Wachtel	Gregory B. Klenda
J. Michael Morris	Christopher A. McElgunn
David D. Broomfield	Robert (Rocky) D. Wiechman, Jr.

Geoffrey B. Amend	Mary T. Malicoat
Jennifer L. Grier	Daniel C. Schulte
Deborah L. Mahoney	Todd E. Shadid

(See Next Column)

OF COUNSEL

Vincent L. Bogart	Ronald M. Gott
Patricia J. Coffey	Bruce W. Zuercher

Representative Clients: Bombardier Capital Inc.; Kansas Newman College; National Cooperative Refinery Assn.; New York Bagel Enterprises, Inc.; Petroleum, Inc.; Play by Play Toys & Novelties, Inc.; THORN Americas, Inc. d/b/a Rent-A-Center of America, Inc.; Sterling House Corporation.
Franchise Client: ALCF, Inc. (Association of Little Caesars Franchisees); Olsten Staffing Service Franchisees.

For full biographical listings, see the Martindale-Hubbell Law Directory

MARTIN, PRINGLE, OLIVER, WALLACE & SWARTZ, L.L.P. (AV)

300 Page Court, 220 West Douglas Street, 67202-3194
Telephone: 316-265-9311
Telefax: 316-265-2955
Overland Park, Kansas Office: 6900 College Blvd., Suite 940.
Telephone: 913-491-5500.
Fax: 913-491-3341.

Robert Martin	Jeff C. Spahn, Jr.
William L. Oliver, Jr.	Jeff Kennedy
Paul B. Swartz	Terry L. Mann
Dwight D Wallace	Terry J. Torline
Larry B. Spikes	Stuart M. Kowalski
Martin W. Bauer	Brian S. Burris
David S. Wooding	Ann T. Rider
George C. Bruce	Michael G. Jones
Terry L. Malone	Richard K. Thompson

Kathryn Gardner	Brent A. Mitchell
Ellen Tracy	Roger E. McClellan

Jana V. Richards

OF COUNSEL

Orval J. Kaufman

LEGAL SUPPORT PERSONNEL

Patricia A. Gorham

General Counsel for: Travel Air Insurance Co., Ltd.; Mull Drilling Co.; Litigation Counsel for: Raytheon Aircraft Co.;
Representative Clients: K N Energy, Inc.; Multimedia Cablevision, Inc.; Peoples Natural Gas Co.; Commerce Bank; United Beechcraft, Inc.; Rose America.

For full biographical listings, see the Martindale-Hubbell Law Directory

MORRIS, LAING, EVANS, BROCK & KENNEDY, CHARTERED (AV)

Fourth Floor, 200 West Douglas, 67202-3084
Telephone: 316-262-2671
Fax: 316-262-6226; 262-5991
Topeka, Kansas Office: 800 S.W. Jackson, Suite 914, 66612-2214.
Telephone: 913-232-2662.
Fax: 913-232-9983.

Lester L. Morris (1901-1966)	Robert W. Coykendall
Verne M. Laing (Retired)	Robert K. Anderson
Ferd E. Evans, Jr. (1919-1991)	Susan R. Schrag
Robert B. Morton (Retired)	Robert E. Nugent
Ralph R. Brock	Michael Lennen
Joseph W. Kennedy	Karl R. Swartz
Robert I. Guenthner	Roger L. Theis
David C. Adams	Jana Deines Abbott
Ken M. Peterson	Richard F. Hayse
Richard D. Greene	(Resident, Topeka Office)
A. J. Schwartz, Jr.	Thomas R. Docking
Donald E. Schrag	Diane S. Worth
William B. Sorensen, Jr.	Tim J. Moore
Dennis M. Feeney	Bruce A. Ney
Jeffery L. Carmichael	Janet Huck Ward

References: The Emprise Banks of Kansas; Mercantile Bank of Topeka; Southwest National Bank; Twin Lakes National Bank.

For full biographical listings, see the Martindale-Hubbell Law Directory

TRIPLETT, WOOLF & GARRETSON, L.L.P. (AV)

Suite 800 Centre City Plaza, 151 North Main, 67202-1409
Telephone: 316-265-5700
Telecopy: 316-265-6165

MEMBERS OF FIRM

Thomas C. Triplett	Ron H. Harnden
John P. Woolf	Lee Thompson
Thomas P. Garretson	Eric S. Strickler
James A. Walker	Tad Patton
Timothy E. McKee	Bradley A. Stout
Theron E. Fry	Rachael K. Pirner
Eric B. Metz	Jeffrey D. Leonard

(See Next Column)

TRIPLETT, WOOLF & GARRETSON L.L.P., *Wichita—Continued*
ASSOCIATES
Nancy J. Strouse   Jeffery C. Dahlgren
Jeffrey E. Goering

Representative Clients: Anheuser-Busch Companies, Inc.; Brite Voice Systems, Inc.; Coleman Company, Inc.; Colorado Interstate Gas Co.; Dow Chemical Co.; Friends University; KPMG Peat Marwick; National Plastics Color, Inc.; Travelers Insurance Co.; Willis Corroon of Kansas, Inc.

For full biographical listings, see the Martindale-Hubbell Law Directory

YOUNG, BOGLE, McCAUSLAND, WELLS & CLARK, P.A. (AV)

106 West Douglas, Suite 923, 67202
Telephone: 316-265-7841
Facsimile: 316-265-3956

Glenn D. Young, Jr.   William A. Wells
Jerry D. Bogle   Kenneth M. Clark
Paul S. McCausland   Patrick C. Blanchard
Mark R. Maloney
OF COUNSEL
Orlin L. Wagner

Representative Clients: Bridgestone/Firestone Inc.; Deere & Co.; Citibank; Metropolitan Life Insurance Co.; Equitable Life Assurance Society of the United States; New York Life Insurance Co.

For full biographical listings, see the Martindale-Hubbell Law Directory

---

WINFIELD, * Cowley Co.

HERLOCKER, ROBERTS & ST. PETER, P.A. (AV)

115 East Ninth Avenue, P.O. Box 754, 67156
Telephone: 316-221-4600
FAX: 316-221-7504

Charles W. Roberts (1867-1941)   Kay Roberts
Lloyd S. Roberts (1900-1968)   Thomas D. Herlocker
Harry O. Janicke (1902-1978)   J. Dennis Herlocker
John A. Herlocker (1911-1984)   Nicholas M. St. Peter

Representative Clients: Risk Counselors, Inc.; Sidwell Charitable Trust; H. L. Snyder Memorial Research Foundation; Cover-rite Construction Services, Inc.; Winfield Medical Arts, P.A.; Sumner Regional Medical Center.

YATES CENTER, * Woodson Co. — (Refer to Chanute)

KENTUCKY

ALBANY, * Clinton Co. — (Refer to Glasgow)

ASHLAND, Boyd Co.

MARTIN, PICKLESIMER, JUSTICE & VINCENT (AV)

431 Sixteenth Street, P.O. Box 2528, 41105-2528
Telephone: 606-329-8338
Fax: 606-325-8199

Richard W. Martin   David Justice
Max D. Picklesimer   John F. Vincent
ASSOCIATES
Thomas Wade Lavender, II   Brian Leslie Hewlett

Representative Clients: City of Ashland; FIVCO Area Development District; Boyd County Sanitation District No. 2; Mid-America Distributors, Inc.
Insurance Counsel for: State Farm Mutual Automobile Insurance Co.; State Farm Fire and Casualty Co.; Aetna Casualty Insurance Co.; Grange Mutual Insurance Co.; Great American Insurance Co.

For full biographical listings, see the Martindale-Hubbell Law Directory

---

BARBOURVILLE, * Knox Co. — (Refer to Middlesboro)

BARDWELL, * Carlisle Co. — (Refer to Mayfield)

BEATTYVILLE, * Lee Co. — (Refer to Richmond)

BENTON, * Marshall Co. — (Refer to Murray)

BOWLING GREEN, * Warren Co.

BELL, ORR, AYERS & MOORE, P.S.C. (AV)

1010 College Street, P.O. Box 738, 42102-0738
Telephone: 502-781-8111
Telecopier: 502-781-9027

Chas. R. Bell (1891-1976)   Kevin C. Brooks
Joe B. Orr (1914-1987)   Timothy L. Mauldin
Reginald L. Ayers   Barton D. Darrell
Ray B. Buckberry, Jr.   Timothy L. Edelen
Quinten B. Marquette   Douglas W. Gott
George E. Strickler, Jr.   David T. Sparks
Stacey Johnson Hughes

(See Next Column)

General Counsel for: First American National Bank of Kentucky; Farm Credit Services of Mid-America, ACA.; Houchens Industries, Inc. (Food Markets and Shopping Centers); Warren County Board of Education; Bowling Green Municipal Utilities.
Representative Clients: Chicago Title Insurance Co.; Commonwealth Land Title Insurance Co.; Kentucky Farm Bureau Mutual Insurance Co.; Martin Automotive Group; Home Insurance Group.

For full biographical listings, see the Martindale-Hubbell Law Directory

BRODERICK, THORNTON & PIERCE (AV)

921 College Street, Phoenix Place, P.O. Box 1137, 42102-1137
Telephone: 502-782-6700
Facsimile: 502-782-3110

David F. Broderick   Steven O. Thornton
Darell R. Pierce
ASSOCIATES
Pamela Carolyn Bratcher   Kenneth P. O'Brien
B. Alan Simpson   Ann Toni Kereiakes
Julie F. Applegate

Representative Clients: Allstate Insurance Co.; National City Bank; American States Insurance Co.; Capital Enterprise Insurance; Fireman's Fund Insurance Co.; Imperial Casualty & Indemnity; Indiana Lumbermen's Mutual Insurance; Kentucky Medical Insurance Co.; Scotty's Contracting & Stone, Inc.; St. Paul Insurance Co.

For full biographical listings, see the Martindale-Hubbell Law Directory

COLE, MOORE & BAKER (AV)

921 College Street-Phoenix Place, P.O. Box 10240, 42102-7240
Telephone: 502-782-6666
FAX: 502-782-8666

MEMBERS OF FIRM
John David Cole   Frank Hampton Moore, Jr.
Matthew J. Baker
ASSOCIATES
Dov Moore   John David Cole, Jr.
C. Terrell Miller   Stefan R. Hughes
OF COUNSEL
Frank R. Goad

Counsel for: Western Kentucky Cola-Cola Bottling Co.; Clark Distributing Co., Inc.; Scotty's Contracting & Stone Co.
Local Counsel for: General Electric Co.; Bucyrus-Erie Company; Wal-Mart Stores, Inc.; Kroger/Country Oven.
Representative Insurance Clients: Liberty Mutual Insurance Co.; Travelers Insurance Co.; Wausau Insurance Co.

For full biographical listings, see the Martindale-Hubbell Law Directory

ENGLISH, LUCAS, PRIEST & OWSLEY (AV)

1101 College Street, P.O. Box 770, 42102-0770
Telephone: 502-781-6500
Telecopier: 502-782-7782
Email: inquiry@elpo.com

MEMBERS OF FIRM
Charles E. English   Murry A. Raines
James H. Lucas   Kurt W. Maier
Whayne C. Priest, Jr.   Charles E. English, Jr.
Michael A. Owsley   Wade T. Markham, II
Keith M. Carwell   D. Gaines Penn
ASSOCIATES
Robert A. Young   Marc Allen Lovell
Vance Cook   Regina Abrams
W. Cravens Priest, III   Jason P. Wright
Elizabeth J. McKinney

For full biographical listings, see the Martindale-Hubbell Law Directory

HARLIN & PARKER, P.S.C. (AV)

519 East Tenth Street, P.O. Box 390, 42102-0390
Telephone: 502-842-5611
Telefax: 502-842-2607

William Jerry Parker   Scott Charles Marks
James David Bryant   Mark D. Alcott
Jerry A. Burns   Michael Kirby Smith
OF COUNSEL
Maxey B. Harlin   Jo T. Orendorf

Insurance Clients: American Hardware Mutual Insurance Co.; CNA Insurance Companies; Government Employees Insurance Co.; American International Group.
Railroad and Utilities Clients: District Attorneys for BellSouth Telecommunications, Inc.; CSX Transportation, Inc.
Local Counsel for: General Motors Corp.; Ford Motor Co.; Chrysler Corp.

For full biographical listings, see the Martindale-Hubbell Law Directory

Bowling Green—Continued

KERRICK, GRISE & STIVERS (AV)

1025 State Street, P.O. Box 9547, 42102-9547
Telephone: 502-782-8160
Fax: 502-782-5856
Elizabethtown, Kentucky Office: 2935 Dolphin Drive, Suite 102.
Telephone: 502-769-5788.
Fax: 502-737-9285.

MEMBERS OF FIRM

Thomas N. Kerrick	Gregory N. Stivers
John R. Grise	H. Brent Brennenstuhl

ASSOCIATES

Lanna Martin Kilgore	Shawn Rosso Alcott
Laura M. Hagan (Resident, Elizabethtown Office)	Jason B. Bell

Representative Clients: Dollar General Corp.; Columbia Greenview Regional Hospital; Hospital Corporation of America; Hardin Memorial Hospital; Monarch Environmental, Inc.; Mid-South Management Group, Inc.; Trans Financial Bank; TKR Cable.

For full biographical listings, see the Martindale-Hubbell Law Directory

MILLIKEN LAW FIRM (AV)

426 East Main Street, P.O. Box 1640, 42102-1640
Telephone: 502-843-0800
Fax: 502-842-1237

W. Currie Milliken	Wesley V. Milliken

Reference: Trans Financial Bank, Bowling Green, Kentucky.

For full biographical listings, see the Martindale-Hubbell Law Directory

---

BURKESVILLE, * Cumberland Co. — (Refer to Glasgow)

CADIZ, * Trigg Co. — (Refer to Hopkinsville)

CALHOUN, * McLean Co. — (Refer to Owensboro)

CAMPBELLSVILLE, * Taylor Co. — (Refer to Glasgow)

CARLISLE, * Nicholas Co. — (Refer to Lexington)

CLINTON, * Hickman Co. — (Refer to Mayfield)

COLUMBIA, * Adair Co. — (Refer to Glasgow)

CORBIN, Knox & Whitley Cos.

LEICK, HAMMONS AND BRITTAIN (AV)

First National Bank & Trust Company Building, P.O. Box 1388, 40702
Telephone: 606-528-5252; 528-2442
Fax: 606-528-2491

MEMBERS OF FIRM

Herman E. Leick	Robert P. Hammons
	Gary W. Brittain

LEGAL SUPPORT PERSONNEL

Flora M. McFadden

Counsel for: The First National Bank & Trust Company of Corbin; Pepsi-Cola Bottling Company of Corbin; Corbin Board of Education.

For full biographical listings, see the Martindale-Hubbell Law Directory

---

COVINGTON, Kenton Co.

ADAMS, BROOKING, STEPNER, WOLTERMANN & DUSING (AV)

421 Garrard Street, P.O. Box 861, 41012
Telephone: 606-291-7270
Fax: 606-291-7902
Florence, Kentucky Office: 8100 Burlington Pike, Suite 400, 41042.
Telephone: 606-371-6220.
Fax: 606-371-8341.

Charles S. Adams (1906-1971)	Michael M. Sketch
John R. S. Brooking	(Resident at Florence Office)
Donald L. Stepner	Dennis R. Williams
James G. Woltermann	(Resident at Florence Office)
(Resident at Florence Office)	James R. Kruer
Gerald F. Dusing	Jeffrey C. Mando
(Resident at Florence Office)	R. Jeffrey Schlosser

ASSOCIATES

Marc D. Dietz	Lori A. Schlarman
(Resident at Florence Office)	(Resident, Florence Office)
Gregory S. Shumate	Chandra S. Baldwin
John S. "Brook" Brooking	Robert D. Dilts (Not admitted
(Resident at Florence Office)	in KY; Resident, Florence
Stacey L. Graus	Office)
Paul J. Darpel	Paul A. Poe (Not admitted in
(Resident, Florence Office)	KY; Resident, Florence
	Office)

Representative Clients: Balluff, Inc., Wampler, Inc., Kisters, Inc., Krauss-Maffei, Inc., A group of German companies; State Automobile Mutual Insurance Co.; Chevron of California; Great American Insurance Co.; Grange

(See Next Column)

Mutual Insurance Co.; Meridian Mutual Insurance Co.; Fifth-Third Bank of Northern Ky.; Northern Kentucky University; ITT Hartford.

For full biographical listings, see the Martindale-Hubbell Law Directory

O'HARA, RUBERG, TAYLOR, SLOAN AND SERGENT (AV)

Suite 209 C, Thomas More Park, P.O. Box 17411, 41017-0411
Telephone: 606-331-2000
Fax: 606-578-3365

MEMBERS OF FIRM

John J. O'Hara	David B. Sloan
Robert E. Ruberg	Gary J. Sergent
Arnold S. Taylor	Michael K. Ruberg
Donald J. Ruberg	Michael O'Hara

ASSOCIATES

Suzanne Cassidy

Representative Clients: Cincinnati Bell; American Transportation Enterprises; Union Light, Heat & Power Co.; Crum & Forster; American States Insurance Co.; Ohio Casualty Co.; Monticello Insurance Co.; United States Aviation Underwriters, Inc.
Local Counsel for: Lloyds of London.

For full biographical listings, see the Martindale-Hubbell Law Directory

STRAUSS & TROY A LEGAL PROFESSIONAL ASSOCIATION (AV)

Suite 1400, 50 East Rivercenter Boulevard, 41011
Telephone: 513-621-8900; 513-621-2120
Telecopier: 513-629-9444
Cincinnati, Ohio Office: 2100 PNC Center, 201 East Fifth Street.
Telephone: 513-621-2120.
Telecopier: 513-241-8259.

Gordon H. Hood (Resident)	Martin C. Butler (Resident)
	Timothy B. Theissen (Resident)

Marshall K. Dosker (Resident)	Pete A. Smith (Resident)

OF COUNSEL

Samuel M. Allen (Resident)	Paul J. Theissen (Resident)

For full biographical listings, see the Martindale-Hubbell Law Directory

WARE, BRYSON, WEST & KUMMER (AV)

157 Barnwood Drive, 41017
Telephone: 606-341-0255
FAX: 606-341-1876

MEMBERS OF FIRM

Rodney S. Bryson	Greg D. Voss
Larry C. West	Robert B. Cetrulo
John R. Kummer	Susanne M. Cetrulo
Mark W. Howard	David W. Martin

ASSOCIATES

W. L. (Skip) Hammons, Jr.	Orie S. Ware (1882-1974)
James M. West	William O. Ware (1908-1961)
	James C. Ware (1913-1991)

Attorneys for: First National Bank of Northern Ky.; State Farm Insurance Co.; Reliance Insurance Group; Maryland Casualty Insurance Co.; Kemper Insurance Co.; Prudential Insurance Co.; State Farm Fire & Casualty Insurance Co.; Shelby Mutual Insurance Co.; Cincinnati Insurance Co.

For full biographical listings, see the Martindale-Hubbell Law Directory

---

CRESTVIEW HILLS, Kenton Co.

TAFT, STETTINIUS & HOLLISTER (AV)

Thomas More Centre Suite 400, 2670 Chancellor Drive, 41017-3491
Telephone: 606-331-2838; 513-381-2838
Facsimile: 513-381-6613
Cincinnati, Ohio Office: 1800 Star Bank Center, 425 Walnut Street.
Telephone: 513-381-2838.
Columbus, Ohio Office: Twelfth Floor, 21 East State Street.
Telephone: 614-221-2838.
Cleveland, Ohio Office: Sixth Floor, Bond Court Building, 1300 East Ninth Street.
Telephone: 216-241-2838.

RESIDENT MEMBERS

Richard D. Spoor	Donald M. Hemmer
	Robert B. Craig

RESIDENT ASSOCIATES

Robert A. Winter Jr.	Joseph A. Rectenwald
Timothy L. Coyle	John C. Middleton

Counsel for: Clarion Mfg. Corp.; The David J. Joseph Company; G & J Pepsi Cola Bottlers, Inc.; Gibson Greetings, Inc.; James Graham Brown Foundation; KFD Sales and Service, Inc.; Paul Hemmer Construction Co.

For full biographical listings, see the Martindale-Hubbell Law Directory

---

DIXON, * Webster Co. — (Refer to Madisonville)

EDMONTON, * Metcalfe Co. — (Refer to Glasgow)

ELIZABETHTOWN, * Hardin Co.

COLEMAN & STEVENS (AV)

(Formerly Reford H. Coleman and Associates)
2907 Ring Road, P.O. Box 4030, 42702-4030
Telephone: 502-737-0600
Fax: 502-737-0488

Reford H. Coleman   Michael L. Stevens
_____

Beth Ann Lochmiller   M. Brent Hall
Kelly Mark Easton

Representative Clients: American States Insurance Cos.; Coca-Cola Bottling
Co.; Federated Rural Elec. Insurance Co.; Firemans Fund Insurance Cos.;
General Motors Corp.; Indiana Insurance Co.; Kentucky Farm Bureau Mutual Insurance Corp.; Liberty Mutual Insurance Co.; Ohio Casualty Insurance Group; United Services Automobile Association (State Counsel).

For full biographical listings, see the Martindale-Hubbell Law Directory

COLLIER, ARNETT, QUICK & COLEMAN (AV)

128 West Dixie Avenue, P.O. Box 847, 42701
Telephone: 502-765-4112
Fax: 502-769-3081

MEMBERS OF FIRM

James M. Collier   Kim F. Quick
John L. Arnett   Jerry M. Coleman
          Deborah Lewis Shaw

Counsel for: City of Elizabethtown; PNC Bank; Elizabethtown Independent
School District.
Representative Clients: Nationwide Insurance Co.; Shelter Insurance Co.;
State Farm Insurance Co.; Government Employees Insurance Co.; Liberty
Mutual Insurance Co.; Kemper Insurance Group; Motorist Mutual Insur-
ance Co.

For full biographical listings, see the Martindale-Hubbell Law Directory

LEWIS & PRESTON (AV)

102 West Dixie Avenue, 42701
Telephone: 502-765-4106
Fax: 502-737-0443

MEMBERS OF FIRM

Paul M. Lewis   Dwight Preston

Approved Attorneys for: Commonwealth Land Title.
Reference: Cecilian Bank.
Agents for: First American Title Insurance; Midland First American.

ELKTON, * Todd Co. — (Refer to Russellville)

FALMOUTH, * Pendleton Co. — (Refer to Newport)

FLEMINGSBURG, * Fleming Co. — (Refer to Morehead)

FLORENCE, Boone Co.

ADAMS, BROOKING, STEPNER, WOLTERMANN & DUSING (AV)

8100 Burlington Pike, Suite 400, 41042-0576
Telephone: 606-371-6220
Fax: 606-371-8341
Covington, Kentucky Office: 421 Garrard Street.
Telephone: 606-291-7270.
Fax: 606-291-7902.

John R. S. Brooking   Gerald F. Dusing (Resident)
Donald L. Stepner   Michael M. Sketch (Resident)
James G. Woltermann   Dennis R. Williams (Resident)
    (Resident)   Jeffrey C. Mando

ASSOCIATES

Marc D. Dietz (Resident)   Paul J. Darpel
Gregory S. Shumate   Chandra S. Baldwin
John S. "Brook" Brooking   Robert D. Dilts
    (Resident)   (Not admitted in KY)
Lori A. Schlarman   Paul A. Poe (Not admitted in
Stacey L. Graus   KY; Resident, Florence
                                  Office)

Representative Clients: State Automobile Mutual Insurance Co.; Standard Oil
Co. (Ky.); Great American Insurance Co.; Grange Mutual Insurance Co.;
Meridian Mutual Insurance Co.; Fifth-Third Bank of Boone County; North-
ern Kentucky University.

For full biographical listings, see the Martindale-Hubbell Law Directory

FRANKFORT, * Franklin Co.

* indicates certain Bar Register subscribers whose principal office is
located elsewhere in the state and who have arranged for representation
as a part of the state capital listings that follow

* STITES & HARBISON (AV)

Formerly Stites, McElwain & Fowler and Harbison, Kessinger, Lisle &
Bush
421 West Main Street, 40601
Telephone: 502-223-3477
Louisville, Kentucky Office: 400 West Market Street, Suite 1800.
Telephone: 502-587-3400.
Lexington, Kentucky Office: 2300 Lexington Financial Center.
Telephone: 606-226-2300.
Jeffersonville, Indiana Office: 323 East Court Avenue.
Telephone: 812-282-7566.

MEMBERS OF FIRM

Ben B. Fowler (1916-1990)   Mark R. Overstreet
Bruce F. Clark   Judith A. Villines
_____

Timothy C. Kimmel (Frankfort   Jason P. Thomas
    and Louisville Offices)

Representative Clients: South Central Bell Telephone Co.; New York Life
Insurance Co.; Chrysler Financial Corp.

For full biographical listings, see the Martindale-Hubbell Law Directory

STOLL, KEENON & PARK, LLP (AV)

307 Washington Street, 40601
Telephone: 502-875-6220
Telecopier: 502-875-6235
Lexington, Kentucky Office: 201 E. Main Street, Suite 1000.
Telephone: 606-231-3000.
Telecopier: 606-253-1093; 606-253-1027.
Louisville, Kentucky Office: 400 West Market Street, Suite 2650, 40202.
Telephone: 502-568-9100.
Telecopier: 502-568-5700.

Robert W. Kellerman   R. Douglas Martin

Representative Clients: Kentucky State University; Kentucky Press Assn.;
Plantmix Asphalt Industry of Kentucky, Inc.; Kentucky Optometric Assn.;
Kentucky Podiatry Assn.; Frankfort Scrap Metal Co.; Lexington Scrap
Metal Co.; Lowes, Inc. (Retail Stores); Farmers Bank and Capital Trust Co.;
Kentucky Retirement Systems.

For full biographical listings, see the Martindale-Hubbell Law Directory

WYATT, TARRANT & COMBS (AV)

The Taylor-Scott Building, 311 West Main Street, 40602
Telephone: 502-223-2104
Telecopier: 502-227-7681
URL: http://www.wyattfirm.com
Louisville, Kentucky Office: Citizens Plaza.
Telephone: 502-589-5235.
Telecopier: 502-589-0309.
Lexington, Kentucky Office: 1700 Lexington Financial Center.
Telephone: 606-233-2012.
Telecopier: 606-259-0649.
New Albany, Indiana Office: The Elsby Building, 117 East Spring Street.
Telephone: 812-945-3561.
Telecopier: 812-949-2524.
Memphis, Tennessee Office: Crescent Center, Suite 650, 6075 Poplar
Avenue.
Telephone: 901-537-1000.
Telecopier: 901-537-1010.
Nashville, Tennessee Office: 1500 Nashville City Center, 511 Union Street.
Telephone: 615-244-0020.
Telecopier: 615-256-1726.
Music Row, Nashville Office: 29 Music Square East.
Telephone: 615-255-6161.
Telecopier: 615-254-4490.
Hendersonville, Tennessee Office: 313 E. Main Street, Suite 1.
Telephone: 615-822-8822.
Telecopier: 615-824-4684.

MEMBERS OF FIRM

George L. Seay, Jr.   Joseph J. Zaluski

ASSOCIATES

Lesly Ann Reisenfeld-Davis

Representative Clients: Arch Mineral Corp.; Centran Corp.; David J. Joseph
Co.; Goodyear; Huscoal, Inc.; Hillshire Farms & Kahn's; Kentucky Crite-
rion Coal; Nutone, Inc.; Sara Lee Corp.; Zeigler Coal Holding Co., Inc.

For full biographical listings, see the Martindale-Hubbell Law Directory

GEORGETOWN, * Scott Co.

E. DURWARD WELDON (AV)

217 East Main Street, 40324
Telephone: 502-863-1285

Approved Attorney for: Lawyers Title Insurance Corporation of Richmond, Virginia; Louisville Title Division of Commonwealth Land Title Insurance Co. (Binder Agent); The Equitable Life Assurance Society of the United States.

For full biographical listings, see the Martindale-Hubbell Law Directory

GLASGOW, * Barren Co.

GARMON & GOODMAN (AV)

139 North Public Square, P.O. Box 663, 42142-0663
Telephone: 502-651-8812
Telecopier: 502-651-8846

MEMBERS OF FIRM

Larry D. Garmon   Charles A. Goodman III

Representative Clients: United Farm Tools, Inc.; James N. Gray Construction Co., Inc.; Pedigo-Lessenberry Insurance Agency, Inc.; Manning Motor Express, Inc.; Commonwealth Relocation Services; Central Soya, Inc.; Chrysler Credit Corp.
Approved Attorneys for: Chicago Title Insurance Co.; Commonwealth Land Title Insurance Co. (Agent).
Reference: Trans Financial Bank, N.A., Glasgow, Ky.

For full biographical listings, see the Martindale-Hubbell Law Directory

HERBERT & HERBERT (AV)

135 North Public Square, P.O. Box 1000, 42141
Telephone: 502-651-9000
Fax: 502-651-3317
Email: h&hlaw@glasgow-ky.com

MEMBERS OF FIRM

H. Jefferson Herbert, Jr.   Betty Reece Herbert

Representative Clients: Alliance Corp. (Construction); Eaton Corp.; Pan-Osten, Inc.; Supreme Mills, Inc.; T.J. Samson Community Hospital.
Approved Attorneys for: Fireman's Fund Insurance Companies; Indiana Insurance Co.; Agway Insurance Co.; Travelers Insurance Co.
Reference: South Central Bank, Glasgow, Kentucky.

For full biographical listings, see the Martindale-Hubbell Law Directory

RICHARDSON, GARDNER & BARRICKMAN (AV)

117 East Washington Street, 42141
Telephone: 502-651-8884; 651-2116
Facsimile: 502-651-3662

MEMBERS OF FIRM

Bobby H. Richardson   Uhel O. Barrickman
Woodford L. Gardner, Jr.   T. Richard Alexander, II

Representative Clients: Tenneco, Inc.; Liberty Mutual Insurance Co.; Aetna Casualty & Surety Co.; CSX; State Automobile Mutual Insurance Co.; The Travelers Insurance Co.; U.S. Fidelity & Guaranty Co.; Kentucky Farm Bureau Insurance Co.
Counsel for: New Farmers National Bank of Glasgow.

For full biographical listings, see the Martindale-Hubbell Law Directory

GREENUP, * Greenup Co.

WARNOCK & WARNOCK (AV)

221 Main Street, P.O. Box 617, 41144
Telephone: 606-473-5381

Frank H. Warnock   Frank K. Warnock

GREENVILLE, * Muhlenberg Co. — (Refer to Madisonville)

HARDINSBURG, * Breckinridge Co. — (Refer to Owensboro)

HARLAN, * Harlan Co.

RICE & HENDRICKSON (AV)

398 Woodland Hills, P.O. Box 980, 40831
Telephone: 606-573-3955
Fax: 606-573-3956

MEMBERS OF FIRM

William A. Rice   H. Kent Hendrickson

Representative Clients: USX Corp.; Navistar International Transportation Corp.; Bituminous Casualty Corp.; Kentucky Utilities Co.; Aetna Casualty & Surety Co.; Nationwide Insurance; The Hartford Insurance Group; Arch Mineral Corp.

For full biographical listings, see the Martindale-Hubbell Law Directory

HARTFORD, * Ohio Co. — (Refer to Owensboro)

HAZARD, * Perry Co.

BARRET, HAYNES, MAY, CARTER AND ROARK, P.S.C. (AV)

113 Lovern Street, P.O. Box 1017, 41701
Telephone: 606-436-2165; 436-4824
Fax: 606-439-1450

Maxwell P. Barret (1918-1988)   Ralph D. Carter
Hoover Haynes (Retired)   J. L. Roark
Randall Scott May   William Engle, III

Denise Moore Davidson   Deborah Lewis Bailey
John W. Barron

Representative Clients: Citizens State Bank; Virginia Iron, Coal & Coke Co.; Blue Diamond Coal Co.; Kentucky Power Co.; Royal Globe Insurance Co.; Firemen's Fund; American Insurance Group; Old Republic Insurance Co.; Nationwide Insurance Co.; Kentucky Farm Bureau Mutual Insurance Co.

For full biographical listings, see the Martindale-Hubbell Law Directory

GULLETT & COMBS (AV)

109 Broadway, Second Floor, P.O. Box 1039, 41702-5039
Telephone: 606-439-1373
Fax: 606-439-4450
Email: pgullett@mis.net; rgcombs@mis.net

MEMBERS OF FIRM

Asa P. Gullett, III   Ronald G. Combs

ASSOCIATES

Teresa G. Combs Reed   Matthew Lawton Bowling

LEGAL SUPPORT PERSONNEL

Jacqueline E. Goodin   Jimmie Lynn Jones

Reference: Peoples Bank and Trust Co.

For full biographical listings, see the Martindale-Hubbell Law Directory

HENDERSON, * Henderson Co.

DEEP & WOMACK (AV)

790 Bob Posey Street, P.O. Box 50, 42420
Telephone: 502-827-2522
Fax: 502-826-2870
Louisville, Kentucky Office: 1228 Starks Building, 455 South Fourth Avenue. P.O. Box 70033, 40270-0033.
Telephone: 502-589-2530.
Fax: 502-589-9297.

MEMBERS OF FIRM

Charles David Deep   James G. Womack
Zack N. Womack   Toni Cline Renfro
                         (Resident, Louisville Office)

For full biographical listings, see the Martindale-Hubbell Law Directory

KING, DEEP AND BRANAMAN (AV)

127 North Main Street, P.O. Box 43, 42420
Telephone: 502-827-1852
FAX: 502-826-7729

MEMBERS OF FIRM

Leo King (1893-1982)   Harry L. Mathison, Jr.
William M. Deep (1920-1990)   W. Mitchell Deep, Jr.
William Branaman   H. Randall Redding
          Dorin E. Luck

ASSOCIATES

Leslie M. Newman   Greg L. Gager

Counsel for: Ohio Valley National Bank of Henderson; Fireman's Fund; Reynolds Metals Co.; Medical Protective Co.; Allstate Insurance Co.; Able Energy Co.; Western Casualty & Surety Co.; Commercial Casualty Insurance Co.; First Indiana Bank; Farm Credit Services.

For full biographical listings, see the Martindale-Hubbell Law Directory

SHEFFER ● HOFFMAN (AV)

300 First Street, 42420
Telephone: 502-826-3300
Telecopier: 502-827-5070
URL: http://www.kylaw.com
Bowling Green, Kentucky Office: Fountain Square, 911 College Street, Suite A.
Telephone: 502-793-9300.
Telecopier: 502-843-9399.
Louisville, Kentucky Office: National City Tower, Suite 1600, 101 South Fifth Street.
Telephone: 502-582-1600.
Owensboro, Kentucky Office: 101 East Second Street.
Telephone: 502-684-3700.
Telecopier: 502-684-3881.
Paducah, Kentucky Office: 333 Broadway, Suite 1001.
Telephone: 502-443-9401.
Telecopier: 502-443-3624.

(See Next Column)

SHEFFER ● HOFFMAN, *Henderson—Continued*

MEMBERS OF FIRM

Ronald G. Sheffer
(Resident, Owensboro Office)
John Stanley Hoffman
(Resident)
David H. Thomason (Resident)
Peter B. Lewis
(Resident, Owensboro Office)
Michael W. Alvey
(Resident, Owensboro Office)

James A. Sigler
(Resident, Paducah Office)
John A. Sheffer
(Resident, Owensboro Office)
Karen L. Wilson (Resident)
Dawn S. Kelsey (Resident)
Donna M. Sauer (Resident)

OF COUNSEL

Charles B. West (Resident)

For full biographical listings, see the Martindale-Hubbell Law Directory

---

HICKMAN, * Fulton Co. — (Refer to Murray)

HOPKINSVILLE, * Christian Co.

KEMP AND KEMP (AV)

608 South Main Street, P.O. Box 648, 42241
Telephone: 502-886-8272
Fax: 502-885-5207

MEMBERS OF FIRM

J. Daniel Kemp   Judy Hall Kemp

Counsel for: Pennyrile Rural Electric Cooperative Corp.; Southern States Cooperative.
Approved Attorneys for: Farm Credit Services; Commonwealth Land Title Insurance Co. (Agent).
References: NationsBank, Hopkinsville, Kentucky; First City Bank & Trust Co., Hopkinsville, Kentucky; United Southern Bank, Hopkinsville, Ky.

For full biographical listings, see the Martindale-Hubbell Law Directory

---

LAW OFFICE OF PAUL K. TURNER (AV)

521 Weber Street, P.O. Box 627, 42241-0627
Telephone: 502-886-9453
Telecopier: 502-886-7732

Counsel for: Kentucky Finance Co.; Kentucky New Era (Newspaper); Flynn Enterprises.
Representative Clients: Bethlehem Steel; Pillsbury, Inc.
Approved Attorneys for: Commonwealth Land Title Insurance Co.; Trans Financial Bank; Trigg County Farmers Bank; First City Bank and Trust Company.
References: Nations Bank of Kentucky; Trigg County Farmers Bank, Cadiz, Ky.; First City Bank & Trust Co., Hopkinsville, Kentucky; Trans Financial Bank, Bowling Green, Scottsville and Dawson Springs, Kentucky.

For full biographical listings, see the Martindale-Hubbell Law Directory

---

HORSE CAVE, Hart Co.

HENSLEY, DUNN, ROSS & HOWARD (AV)

Professional Arts Building, 207 E. Main Street, P.O. Box 350, 42749
Telephone: 502-786-2155
FAX: 502-786-2118

MEMBERS OF FIRM

Robert B. Hensley
Gregory Y. Dunn

Patrick A. Ross
James I. Howard

Representative Clients: Kentucky Farm Bureau Mutual Insurance Co.; Liberty Mutual Insurance Co.; Ohio Casualty Insurance Co.; United States Fidelity & Guaranty Co.; Home Insurance Co.; Caverna Memorial Hospital; Westfield Cos.; State Auto Mutual Insurance Co.; Kentucky Central Insurance Co.; CIGNA Insurance Co.

For full biographical listings, see the Martindale-Hubbell Law Directory

---

HYDEN, * Leslie Co. — (Refer to Hazard)

IRVINE, * Estill Co. — (Refer to Richmond)

JACKSON, * Breathitt Co. — (Refer to Hazard)

JAMESTOWN, * Russell Co. — (Refer to Somerset)

LA GRANGE, * Oldham Co. — (Refer to Frankfort)

LANCASTER, * Garrard Co. — (Refer to Danville)

LAWRENCEBURG, * Anderson Co. — (Refer to Versailles)

LEBANON, * Marion Co. — (Refer to Harrodsburg)

LEITCHFIELD, * Grayson Co. — (Refer to Elizabethtown)

LEXINGTON, * Fayette Co.

BOEHL STOPHER & GRAVES (AV)

444 West Second Street, 40508
Telephone: 606-252-6721
FAX: 606-253-1445
Louisville, Kentucky Office: Suite 2300, Providian Center, 400 West Market Street.
Telephone: 502-589-5980.
Fax: 502-561-9400.
Paducah, Kentucky Office: Suite 340 Executive Inn Riverfront, One Executive Boulevard.
Telephone: 502-442-4369.
Fax: 502-442-4689.
Prestonsburg, Kentucky Office: 105 West Court Street.
Telephone: 606-886-8004.
Fax: 606-886-9579.
New Albany, Indiana Office: Elsby East, Suite 204, 400 Pearl Street.
Telephone: 812-948-5053.
Fax: 812-948-9233.

RESIDENT PARTNERS

W. T. Adkins
Nolan Carter, Jr.
Gregory K. Jenkins
Ronald L. Green

Steven G. Kinkel
Kim Martin Wilkie
Guillermo A. Carlos
James B. Cooper

RESIDENT ASSOCIATES

Steven R. Armstrong
Michael J. Cox

Patrick J. Murphy, II
Brennen C. Ragone

Fredrick A. Bailey, Jr.

Counsel for: Ford Motor Co.; Texas Eastern Transmission Corp.; Coca-Cola Bottling Co.; National Collegiate Athletic Assn.; Hartford Accident and Indemnity Co.; Continental Insurance Group; St. Paul Fire & Marine Insurance Co.; Lloyds of London; Old Republic Insurance Co.

For full biographical listings, see the Martindale-Hubbell Law Directory

---

BROCK, BROCK & BAGBY (AV)

190 Market Street, P.O. Box 1630, 40592-1630
Telephone: 606-255-7000
Fax: 606-255-6198

MEMBERS OF FIRM

Walter L. Brock, Jr. (1918-1995)
Daniel N. Brock

Glen S. Bagby
J. Robert Lyons, Jr.

ASSOCIATES

Bruce A. Rector   Jane Hampton Herrick

LEGAL SUPPORT PERSONNEL
PARALEGALS

Pamela H. Brown   Freda Greer Grubbs

For full biographical listings, see the Martindale-Hubbell Law Directory

---

BUCHANAN INGERSOLL, PROFESSIONAL CORPORATION (AV)

Suite 600, PNC Bank Plaza, 200 West Vine Street, 40507
Telephone: 606-225-5333
Telecopier: 606-225-5334
Pittsburgh, Pennsylvania Office: One Oxford Centre, 301 Grant Street, 20th Floor.
Telephone: 412-562-8800.
Philadelphia, Pennsylvania Office: Two Logan Square, Twelfth Floor, 18th & Arch Streets.
Telephone: 215-665-8700.
Harrisburg, Pennsylvania Office: 30 North Third Street.
Telephone: 717-237-4800.
Tampa, Florida Office: 101 East Kennedy Boulevard, Suite 1030.
Telephone: 813-222-8180.
North Miami Beach, Florida Office: 19495 Biscayne Boulevard, Suite 606.
Telephone: 305-933-5600.
Miami, Florida Office: Nationsbank Tower, 100 S.E. Second Street.
Telephone: 305-347-4080.
Princeton, New Jersey Office: Buchanan Ingersoll, A Partnership, College Centre, 500 College Road East.
Telephone: 609-987-6800.
Buffalo, New York Office: 1100 Main Place Tower, 350 Main Street.
Telephone: 716-854-4100.
Fax: 716-854-4227.

John R. Leathers

Stephen G. Allen

For full biographical listings, see the Martindale-Hubbell Law Directory

---

FOWLER, MEASLE & BELL, L.L.P. (AV)

Kincaid Towers, 300 West Vine Street, Suite 650, 40507-1660
Telephone: 606-252-6700
Fax: 606-255-3735

(See Next Column)

FOWLER, MEASLE & BELL L.L.P.—*Continued*

MEMBERS OF FIRM

Dan E. Fowler (1908-1991)	E. Patrick Moores
Robert H. Measle (1920-1993)	James D. Ishmael, Jr.
Thomas P. Bell (1922-1986)	John E. Hinkel, Jr.
Darrell B. Hancock (1923-1988)	Robert S. Ryan
Grover C. Thompson, Jr.	T. Bruce Bell
(1911-1988)	Michael W. Troutman
Taft A. McKinstry	Elizabeth S. Feamster
Guy R. Colson	R. Craig Reinhardt

S. Dianne Blanford

ASSOCIATES

Susan S. Kennedy	Brendan M. Turney
Barry M. Miller	Michael E. Liska

Katherine J. Hornback

OF COUNSEL

Walter C. Cox, Jr.

Representative Clients: General Electric Co.; Kentucky Farm Bureau Mutual Ins. Co.; State Farm Ins. Co.; Allstate Ins. Co.; Progressive Casualty Ins. Co.; Bank One, Lexington, N.A.; Kentucky Medical Services; PNC Bank, Kentucky, Inc.

For full biographical listings, see the Martindale-Hubbell Law Directory

---

GERALDS, MOLONEY & JONES (AV)

259 West Short Street, 40507
Telephone: 606-255-7946

R. P. Moloney (1902-1963)	Billy W. Sherrow
Donald P. Moloney (1921-1972)	John P. Schrader
Richard P. Moloney (1929-1972)	E. Douglas Stephan
Oscar H. Geralds, Jr.	Robert L. Swisher
Michael R. Moloney	John G. Rice
Ernest H. Jones, II	Frances Geralds Rohlfing

Gail Luhn Pyle

Representative Clients: Allstate Insurance Co.; Nationwide Insurance Co.; State Farm Mutual Automobile Insurance Co.; State Farm Fire and Casualty Co.; Colonial Insurance Company of California.
Reference: Bank of the Bluegrass & Trust Co.

For full biographical listings, see the Martindale-Hubbell Law Directory

---

GESS MATTINGLY & ATCHISON, P.S.C. (AV)

201 West Short Street, 40507-1269
Telephone: 606-252-9000
Facsimile: 606-233-4269

William B. Gess (1906-1985)	Walter R. Morris, Jr.
John G. Atchison, Jr.	Robert E. Maclin, III
Charles G. Wylie	Linda W. Christian
Natalie S. Wilson	Jeffrey R. Walker
Carl Timothy Cone	Elizabeth S. Hughes
Joseph H. Miller	Christel Schrader Nash
William W. Allen	Stephen P. Stoltz
Guy M. Graves	Stephen W. Atwood

OF COUNSEL

Jack F. Mattingly	Leslie G. Phillips

William R. Hilliard, Jr.

Representative Clients: National City Bank; WLEX-TV, Inc.; Prudential Insurance Company of America; Central Kentucky Agricultural Credit Assn.; B.F. Saul Real Estate Investment Trust; American Hardware Mutual Insurance Co.; The Procter & Gamble Co.; University of Kentucky Federal Credit Union; Prudential Securities, Inc.; Thomas & King, Inc.

For full biographical listings, see the Martindale-Hubbell Law Directory

---

HARBISON, KESSINGER, LISLE & BUSH

(See Stites & Harbison)

JACKSON & KELLY (AV)

175 East Main Street, Suite 500, P.O. Box 2150, 40595
Telephone: 606-255-9500
Fax: 606-281-6478
Charleston, West Virginia Office: 1600 Laidley Tower, P.O. Box 553.
Telephone: 304-340-1000.
Fax: 304-340-1130.
Washington, D.C. Office: 2401 Pennsylvania Avenue, N.W., Suite 400.
Telephone: 202-973-0200.
Fax: 202-973-0232.
Denver, Colorado Office: Suite 2710, 1660 Lincoln Street.
Telephone: 303-837-0003.
Fax: 303-837-9688.
Martinsburg, West Virginia Office: 300 Foxcroft Avenue, P.O. Box 1068.
Telephone: 304-263-8800.
Fax: 304-263-7110.
Morgantown, West Virginia Office: 6000 Hampton Center, P.O. Box 619.
Telephone: 304-599-3000.
Fax: 304-285-2040.

(See Next Column)

New Martinsville, West Virginia Office: 256 Russell Avenue, P.O. Box 68.
Telephone: 304-455-1751.
Fax: 304-455-6314.
Charles Town, West Virginia Office: 700 East Washington Street, P.O. Box 983.
Telephone: 304-728-6088.
Fax: 304-728-6029.
Parkersburg, West Virginia Office: 800 Garfield Avenue, P.O. Box 718, 26102.
Telephone: 304-422-1419.
Fax: 304-422-1422.
Fairmont, West Virginia Office: 1000 Technology Drive, Suite 1310, 26554.
Telephone: 304-368-2000.
Fax: 304-368-2020.

MEMBERS OF FIRM

William K. Bodell II	Martin E. Hall
William A. Hoskins, III	Kevin M. McGuire
(Administrative Manager)	W. Rodes Brown
Jeffrey J. Yost	Natalie D. Brown
A. Stuart Bennett	Dean K. Hunt
William E. Doll, Jr.	Stanton L. Cave

ASSOCIATES

Jacqueline Syers Duncan	Clifton B. Clark
Timothy Ray Coleman	John W. Walters
Sannie Overly	Robert F. Duncan

OF COUNSEL

James L. Gay

LEGAL SUPPORT PERSONNEL

Deanna L. Luxbacher

Representative Clients: Bank One; Consol of Kentucky; Cyprus Amax Minerals Co.; Electric Fuels Corp.; GTE Mobilnet; Kentucky Association of Counties and the Kentucky Municipal League; Kentucky Medical Assn.; Lane's End Farm; St. Joseph Hospital; TECO Energy, Inc.

For full biographical listings, see the Martindale-Hubbell Law Directory

---

KINKEAD & COLLIER (AV)

201 West Vine Street, 40507
Telephone: 606-233-3550
Facsimile: 606-255-1965

MEMBERS OF THE FIRM

Shelby C. Kinkead, Jr.	Wayne F. Collier

For full biographical listings, see the Martindale-Hubbell Law Directory

---

LANDRUM & SHOUSE (AV)

106 West Vine Street, P.O. Box 951, 40588-0951
Telephone: 606-255-2424
Facsimile: 606-233-0308
Louisville, Kentucky Office: 400 West Market Street, Suite 1550, 40202.
Telephone: 502-589-7616.
Facsimile: 502-589-2119.

MEMBERS OF FIRM

John H. Burrus	Mark J. Hinkel
Thomas M. Cooper	Delores Hill Pregliasco
William C. Shouse	(Resident, Louisville Office)
Pierce W. Hamblin	John Garry McNeill
Mark L. Moseley	Jack E. Toliver
Leslie Patterson Vose	R. Kent Westberry
John R. Martin, Jr.	(Resident, Louisville Office)
(Resident, Louisville Office)	J. Denis Ogburn
Larry C. Deener	(Resident, Louisville Office)
Sandra Mendez Dawahare	Jane Durkin Samuel

Douglas L. Hoots

ASSOCIATES

Stephen D. Milner	Frank M. Jenkins, III
Stephen R. Chappell	Sheila P. Hiestand
Charles E. Christian	Cynthia K. Lowe
Dave Whalin	Melanie Lee Straw-Boone
(Resident, Louisville Office)	(Resident, Louisville Office)
Daniel E. Murner	Carolyn C. Zerga
Joy Anna Anderson	Billie Sue M. Woolley
Courtney T. Baxter	David L. Bole
(Resident, Louisville Office)	

OF COUNSEL

Weldon Shouse

District Attorneys: CSX Transportation, Inc.
Special Trial Counsel: Ford Motor Co. and Affiliates (Eastern Kentucky); Clark Equipment Co.
Representative Clients: The Continental Insurance Cos.; U.S. Insurance Group; U.S. Fidelity & Guaranty Co.; Ohio Casualty Insurance Co.; CIGNA; Royal Insurance Cos.

For full biographical listings, see the Martindale-Hubbell Law Directory

Lexington—Continued

MARTIN, OCKERMAN & BRABANT (AV)

200 North Upper Street, 40507
Telephone: 606-254-4401
Fax: 606-231-7367
Email: ockerman@counsel.com

MEMBERS OF FIRM

Hogan Yancey (1881-1960)   Thomas C. Brabant
William B. Martin (1895-1975)   Foster Ockerman, Jr.
          Madeleine T. Baugh

OF COUNSEL

Foster Ockerman

Counsel for: Lexington Federal Savings Bank; Good Samaritan Foundation, Inc.; Equity Property and Development Co.; Park Communications of KY (WTVQ); AAA Blue Grass/Kentucky; Turfland Mall.
Reference: Bank One, Lexington, N.A.

For full biographical listings, see the Martindale-Hubbell Law Directory

NEWBERRY, HARGROVE & RAMBICURE, P.S.C. (AV)

2800 Lexington Financial Center, 250 West Main Street, 40507-1743
Telephone: 606-231-3700
Facsimile: 606-259-1092
Email: 75501.1035@compuserve.com *URL:* http://www.maxweb.com/nhr
Nicholasville, Kentucky Office: Moynahan, Irvin, Smith, Newberry, Hargrove & Rambicure, 110 North Main Street.
Telephone: 606-887-1200.
Facsimile: 606-885-2307.
Washington, D.C. Office: 1211 Connecticut Avenue, N.W., Suite 300.
Telephone: 202-466-3700.
Fax: 202-466-2007.
Frankfort, Kentucky Office: 232 St. Clair, P.O. Box 782.
Telephone: 502-875-3700.
Fax: 502-223-5676.

James H. Newberry, Jr.   T. Renee Mussetter Montague
James E. Hargrove   Garry A. Perry
William C. Rambicure   David C. Trimble
Bernard T. Moynahan, Jr.   Phillip J. Shepherd
  (Resident, Nicholasville   (Resident, Frankfort Office)
  Office)   Vicki L. Brooks
David R. Irvin (Resident,   Sarah Charles Wright
  Nicholasville Office)   Twyla Scudder Trujillo
Bruce E. Smith (Resident,   (Resident, Frankfort Office)
  Nicholasville Office)   Richard A. Whitaker (Resident,
Forrest W. Ragsdale, III   Nicholasville Office)
Brian C. Gardner   Steven D. Phillips
David William Regan (Resident,   Susan C. Sears
  Washington, D.C. Office)   Michelle M. Ciccarelli
          Jeffrey J. Kuebler

OF COUNSEL

Stephen L. Miller

Representative Clients: Airdrie Stud, Inc.; Bank One Lexington, N.A.; Kentucky Medical Insurance Co.; Long John Silver's, Inc.; Racing Corporation of America; University of Kentucky; Underwriters at Lloyds, London.

For full biographical listings, see the Martindale-Hubbell Law Directory

JAMES R. ODELL, P.S.C. (AV)

171 North Upper Street, 40507
Telephone: 606-231-0210
FAX: 606-252-2917

James R. Odell   George D. Smith

For full biographical listings, see the Martindale-Hubbell Law Directory

ROBERTS & SMITH (AV)

167 West Main Street Suite 200, 40507
Telephone: 606-233-1104

MEMBERS OF FIRM

Larry S. Roberts   Kenneth W. Smith

For full biographical listings, see the Martindale-Hubbell Law Directory

STITES & HARBISON (AV)

Formerly Stites, McElwain & Fowler and Harbison, Kessinger, Lisle & Bush
2300 Lexington Financial Center, 40507
Telephone: 606-226-2300
Louisville, Kentucky Office: 400 West Market Street, Suite 1800.
Telephone: 502-587-3400.
Frankfort, Kentucky Office: 421 West Main Street.
Telephone: 502-223-3477.
Jeffersonville, Indiana Office: 323 East Court Avenue.
Telephone: 812-282-7566.

(See Next Column)

MEMBERS OF FIRM

James W. Stites (1897-1975)   Charles J. Lisle
Clinton M. Harbison   John M. Famularo
  (1886-1975)   Thomas E. Meng
Ben B. Fowler (1916-1990)   Walter R. Byrne, Jr.
Richard Bush, Jr. (1915-1991)   Janet A. Craig
Kent McElwain (1927-1992)   Gregory P. Parsons
Charles E. Palmer, Jr.   Kenneth R. Sagan
Sidney C. Kinkead, Jr.   Richard G. Griffith
George W. Mills   J. Clarke Keller
Steven L. Beshear   Laura D. Keller
Joe B. Campbell   James W. Taylor
Bruce M. Reynolds   Ashley W. Ward
Buckner Hinkle, Jr.   W. Bradford Boone
J. David Porter   Philip L. Hanrahan
Stephen M. Ruschell   Lynn C. Stidham
Robert M. Beck, Jr.   Cheryl Ulene Lewis

Andrew R. Jacobs   William T. Shier
Michele Whittington   Lisa M. Ramsey
William T. Gorton III   Rebecca B. Stephenson
Margaret M. Pisacano   Lloyd C. Chatfield II
Benjamin Lee Kessinger, III   Amanda L. Pope
Lissa Wathen   Jason P. Thomas
Don A. Pisacano   Jane Brannon
Anne E. Gorham   Jeffrey J. Chapuran
          Dustin C. McCoy

OF COUNSEL

Rufus Lisle   Nathan Elliott, Jr.
          Ralph F. Kessinger

COUNSEL

Ben L. Kessinger, Jr.   Thomas J. Stipanowich
Calvert T. Roszell   Elizabeth Lee Thompson

For full biographical listings, see the Martindale-Hubbell Law Directory

STOLL, KEENON & PARK, LLP (AV)

201 E. Main Street, Suite 1000, 40507-1380
Telephone: 606-231-3000
Telecopier: 606-253-1093; 606-253-1027
Frankfort, Kentucky Office: 307 Washington Street, 40601.
Telephone: 502-875-6220.
Telecopier: 502-875-6235.
Louisville, Kentucky Office: 400 West Market Street, Suite 2650, 40202-3377.
Telephone: 502-568-9100.
Telecopier: 502-568-5700.

MEMBERS OF FIRM

Wallace Muir (1878-1947)   Gary L. Stage
Richard C. Stoll (1876-1949)   Herbert A. Miller, Jr.
Rodman W. Keenon (1883-1966)   Gary W. Barr
William H. Townsend   Donald P. Wagner
  (1890-1964)   Douglas P. Romaine
James Park (1892-1970)   Frank L. Wilford
John L. Davis (1913-1970)   Harvie B. Wilkinson
Gladney Harville (1921-1978)   Robert W. Kellerman
Gayle A. Mohney (1906-1980)   Lizbeth Ann Tully
G. Lee Langston (1942-1983)   J. David Smith, Jr.
C. William Swinford (1921-1986)   Eileen M. O'Brien
Robert F. Houlihan   David C. Schwetschenau
Leslie W. Morris II   Anita M. Britton
Lindsey W. Ingram, Jr.   Rena Gardner Wiseman
William L. Montague   Denise Kirk Ash
Bennett Clark   Bonnie Hoskins
Spencer D. Noe   C. Joseph Beavin
William T. Bishop, III   Diane M. Carlton
Joseph M. Scott, Jr.   Larry A. Sykes
Richard C. Stephenson   P. Douglas Barr
Charles E. Shivel, Jr.   Perry M. Bentley
Robert M. Watt, III   Dan M. Rose
J. Peter Cassidy, Jr.   Gregory D. Pavey
Samuel D. Hinkle IV   J. Mel Camenisch, Jr.
R. David Lester   John W. Walters, Jr.
Robert F. Houlihan, Jr.   David E. Fleenor
William M. Lear, Jr.   Lea Pauley Goff

ASSOCIATES

Mary Beth Griffith   Melissa Anne Stewart
Laura Day DelCotto   Palmer G. Vance, II
Culver V. Halliday   Richard A. Nunnelley
James L. Thomerson   Roger W. Madden
R. Douglas Martin   William L. Montague, Jr.
James D. Allen   Charles R. Baesler, Jr.
Susan Beverly Jones   Steven B. Loy
Todd S. Page   Gregory L. Taylor
John Browning Park   T. Christopher Daniel
          Lindsey W. Ingram, III

Representative Clients: Bank One, Lexington, NA; Farmers Capital Bank Corp.; The Tokai Bank Ltd.; Link Belt Construction Equipment Co.; General Motors Corp.; International Business Machines Corp.; Ohbayashi Corp.;

(See Next Column)

STOLL, KEENON & PARK LLP—*Continued*

R. J. Reynolds Tobacco Co.; Rockwell International Corp.; Square D Co.; Jim Walter Homes, Inc.

For full biographical listings, see the Martindale-Hubbell Law Directory

WILSON, DeCAMP & TALBOTT, P.S.C. (AV)

155 East Main Street, Suite 200, 40507-1332
Telephone: 606-225-1191
Fax: 606-225-5176

Philip E. Wilson   Patterson A. DeCamp
Earl S. Wilson, Jr.   John S. Talbott, III

Representative Clients: All-Phase Electric Supply Co.; American International Group; America Resources Insurance Company, Inc.; AZUR US, Inc.; Bluegrass Famous Recipe Fried Chicken, Inc.; Campbell House Inn; Codeco, Inc.; d/b/a Papa John's Pizza; Commonwealth Land Title Insurance Company; Community Bank of Lexington Inc.

For full biographical listings, see the Martindale-Hubbell Law Directory

WYATT, TARRANT & COMBS (AV)

1700 Lexington Financial Center, 40507
Telephone: 606-233-2012
Telecopier: 606-259-0649
URL: http://www.wyattfirm.com
Louisville, Kentucky Office: Citizens Plaza.
Telephone: 502-589-5235.
Telecopier: 502-589-0309.
Frankfort, Kentucky Office: The Taylor-Scott Building, 311 West Main Street.
Telephone: 502-223-2104.
Telecopier: 502-227-7681.
New Albany, Indiana Office: The Elsby Building, 117 East Spring Street.
Telephone: 812-945-3561.
Telecopier: 812-949-2524.
Memphis, Tennessee Office: Crescent Center, Suite 650, 6075 Poplar Avenue.
Telephone: 901-537-1000.
Telecopier: 901-537-1010.
Nashville, Tennessee Office: 1500 Nashville City Center, 511 Union Street.
Telephone: 615-244-0020.
Telecopier: 615-256-1726.
Music Row, Nashville Office: 29 Music Square East.
Telephone: 615-255-6161.
Telecopier: 615-254-4490.
Hendersonville, Tennessee Office: 313 E. Main Street, Suite 1.
Telephone: 615-822-8822.
Telecopier: 615-824-4684.

MEMBERS OF FIRM

Bert T. Combs (1911-1991)   J. Mark Burton
William H. McCann   Paul J. Cox
Herbert D. Sledd   Chauncey S.R. Curtz
H. Foster Pettit   John R. Rhorer, Jr.
Richard C. Ward   Judge B. Wilson II
Stewart E. Conner   Bruce B. McElvein
James T. Hodge   Debra H. Dawahare
Joseph H. Terry   George J. Miller
Henry E. Kinser   David A. Smart
Jeff A. Woods   Solomon Lee Van Meter
Thomas J. Luber   Karen J. Greenwell
Bradford L. Cowgill   William B. Owsley
Barbara B. Edelman   Marco M. Rajkovich, Jr.
Mark T. MacDonald   John M. Williams

ASSOCIATES

Penny R. Warren   Mary G. Barfield
Gayle B. McGrath   Todd K. Childers
Jennifer Leigh Sapp   William Craig Robertson III
Janet M. Graham   Bruce R. Smith
Troy D. Reynolds   Pamela R. Goodwine
Charles D. Webb, Jr.   Eric S. Horstmeyer
Julie O'Daniel McClellan

COUNSEL

Edward T. Breathitt, Jr.   Richard E. Fitzpatrick
Jack G. Jones, Jr.

OF COUNSEL

C. Kilmer Combs

Representative Clients: Arch Mineral Corp.; Ashland Coal, Inc.; Baptist Healthcare System, Inc.; Berwind Corp.; Design Professional Insurance Co.; Fasig-Tipton Co., Inc.; GRW Engineers, Inc.; Kentucky Coal Assn.; Lexington-Fayette Urban County Government; PNC Bank, Kentucky, Inc.

For full biographical listings, see the Martindale-Hubbell Law Directory

---

*LIBERTY,** Casey Co. — (Refer to Danville)

---

*LONDON,** Laurel Co.

CRABTREE & GOFORTH (AV)

120 East Fourth Street, 40741-1414
Telephone: 606-878-8888
Fax: 606-878-8899

Wm. Gary Crabtree   Michael A. Goforth

Representative Clients: Nationwide Insurance Co.; National Casualty Insurance Co.; Scottsdale Insurance Co.; CIGNA Insurance Co.; Coronet Insurance Co.; Protective Insurance Co.; Grange Mutual Cos.; Midwestern Indemnity Insurance Co.; Western Insurance Co.

For full biographical listings, see the Martindale-Hubbell Law Directory

FARMER, FARMER, KELLEY AND BROWN (AV)

502 West Fifth Street, Drawer 490, 40743
Telephone: 606-878-7640
Fax: 606-878-2364
Lexington, Kentucky Office: 121 Prosperous Place, Suite 13 B, 40509-1834.
Telephone: 606: 263-2567.
Facsimile: 606: 263-2567.

MEMBERS OF FIRM

F. Preston Farmer   Michael P. Farmer
John F. Kelley, Jr.   Martha L. Brown

ASSOCIATES

Suzanne S. Farmer   Bradford L. Breeding
Jason E. Williams   Estill D. Banks, II

For full biographical listings, see the Martindale-Hubbell Law Directory

HAMM, MILBY & RIDINGS (AV)

120 North Main Street, 40741
Telephone: 606-864-4126
Fax: 606-878-8144

MEMBERS OF FIRM

Robert L. Milby   Marcia Milby Ridings
                  Kenneth H. Gilliam

James A. Ridings   Gregory A. Lay
              LaDonna Lynn Koebel

Representative Clients: Acceleration National; Aetna Life & Casualty Ins. Co.; All Risk Claims Service, Inc.; Allstate Insurance Co.; Alexis; American Automobile Mutual Ins.; American Bankers; American Hardware Ins. Co.

For full biographical listings, see the Martindale-Hubbell Law Directory

REECE & LANG, P.S.C. (AV)

London Bank & Trust Building, 400 South Main Street, P.O. Drawer 5087, 40745-5087
Telephone: 606-864-2263
Fax: 606-878-6426

A. Douglas Reece   Leona A. Power
Timothy J. Walker   Mary-Ann Smyth
                Gary W. Napier

Representative Clients: AT&T Capital Corporation; Buckhead Lodging Associates; First State Bank & Trust Company of Manchester; First Capital Bank; Head Sports, Inc.; Impac Hotel Group; London Bank & Trust Company; London Food Services, Inc.; Pro Trust Capital, Inc.; Ryan Sports Management, Inc.; Ryan Sports & Entertainment Marketing, L.P.

For full biographical listings, see the Martindale-Hubbell Law Directory

TAYLOR, KELLER & DUNAWAY (AV)

802 North Main Street, P.O. Box 905, 40743-0905
Telephone: 606-878-8844
Facsimile: 606-878-5547

Boyd F. Taylor   J. Warren Keller
            Bridget L. Dunaway

ASSOCIATES

Jason Richardson

OF COUNSEL

Pamela Adams Chesnut

LEGAL SUPPORT PERSONNEL

Berneda Baker (Paralegal)   Cynthia K. Taylor (Paralegal)

Representative Clients: Chubb Group; Coronet Insurance Group; ITT Hartford; Mutual of Omaha; American General Property Insurance Co.; State Farm Fire & Casualty; State Farm Mutual Automobile Insurance Co.
Local Counsel for: Multi Line Claims Mgmt.
References: The First National Bank; Cumberland Valley National Bank & Trust Company of London, Kentucky.

For full biographical listings, see the Martindale-Hubbell Law Directory

London—Continued

TOOMS & HOUSE (AV)

310 West Fifth Street, P.O. Box 520, 40743-0520
Telephone: 606-864-4145
FAX: 606-864-4279

MEMBERS OF FIRM

Murray L. Brown (1894-1980) R. William Tooms
Roy E. Tooms (1917-1986) Brian C. House

Representative Clients: State Auto Mutual Insurance Co.; Grange Mutual Casualty Co.; Kentucky Farm Bureau Mutual Insurance Co.

For full biographical listings, see the Martindale-Hubbell Law Directory

---

LOUISA,* Lawrence Co. — (Refer to Paintsville)

LOUISVILLE,* Jefferson Co.

BEALE & HUMPHREY, P.S.C. (AV)

1906 Kentucky Home Life Building, 40202
Telephone: 502-584-5246
FAX: 502-585-4301
Lexington, Kentucky Office: Suite 500, Merrill-Lynch Building, 100 East Vine Street.
Telephone: 606-233-1527.
Jeffersonville, Indiana Office: 521 East Seventh Street.
Telephone: 812-283-7672.

Robert J. Beale Herman L. Humphrey

OF COUNSEL
Sidney N. White

Representative Clients: Carolina Casualty Insurance Co.; Amerisure Cos.; Guaranty National Insurance Co.; Occidental Fire & Casualty Co.; Equity Mutual Insurance Co.; Casualty Reciprocal Exchange; U-Haul Co.; Yellow Freight Systems; Lumber Mutual; National American Insurance Co.

For full biographical listings, see the Martindale-Hubbell Law Directory

---

BENNETT, BOWMAN, TRIPLETT & VITTITOW (AV)

First Trust Centre, Suite 400 South, 200 South Fifth Street, 40202
Telephone: 502-583-5581
Fax: 502-583-9622
Owensboro, Kentucky Office: 209 West Second Street, P.O. Box 765.
Telephone: 502-683-5308.
Fax: 502-685-1797.

MEMBERS OF FIRM

John L. Bennett (1918-1988) Robert Vic Bowers, Jr.
James G. Bowman (Resident at Owensboro
Chester A. Vittitow, Jr. Office)
Douglas B. Taylor James P. Dilbeck, Jr.
Robert R. deGolian John W. Tullis (Resident at
  Owensboro Office)

OF COUNSEL
Henry A. Triplett

Representative Clients: State Farm Mutual Automobile Insurance Co.; State Farm Fire & Casualty Co.; State Farm Life Insurance Co.; Ohio Casualty Insurance Co.; West American Insurance Co.; Ohio Security Insurance Co.; American International Group; Meridian Mutual Insurance Co.; Prudential Insurance Co.; Ranger Insurance Co.

For full biographical listings, see the Martindale-Hubbell Law Directory

---

BOEHL STOPHER & GRAVES (AV)

Suite 2300 Providian Center, 400 West Market Street, 40202-3354
Telephone: 502-589-5980
FAX: 502-561-9400
Lexington, Kentucky Office: 444 West Second Street.
Telephone: 606-252-6721.
Fax: 606-253-1445.
Paducah, Kentucky Office: Suite 340 Executive Inn Riverfront, One Executive Boulevard.
Telephone: 502-442-4369.
Fax: 502-442-4689.
Prestonsburg, Kentucky Office: 105 West Court Street.
Telephone: 606-886-8004.
Fax: 606-886-9579.
New Albany, Indiana Office: Elsby East, Suite 204, 400 Pearl Street.
Telephone: 812-948-5053.
Fax: 812-948-9233.

OF COUNSEL

Joseph E. Stopher George R. Effinger
  (Resident at Paducah)

MEMBERS OF FIRM

Herbert F. Boehl (1894-1986) William M. Newman, Jr.
Arthur J. Deindoerfer (1949-1995)
(1907-1990) William O. Guethlein
Raymond O. Harmon Galen J. White, Jr.
(1918-1990) William P. Swain
James M. Graves (1912-1994) Larry L. Johnson

(See Next Column)

MEMBERS OF FIRM (Continued)

W. T. Adkins John P. Rall
(Resident at Lexington) (Resident at Paducah)
Edward H. Stopher Kim Martin Wilkie
Nolan Carter, Jr. (Resident at Lexington)
(Resident at Lexington) John Harlan Callis, III
Jefferson K. Streepey (Resident at Prestonsburg)
Wesley G. Gatlin Charles D. Walter
George R. Carter (Resident at Paducah)
Robert E. Stopher Janie C. McKenzie
Philip J. Reverman, Jr. (Resident at Prestonsburg)
Jonathan Freed Guillermo A. Carlos
(Resident at Paducah) (Resident at Lexington)
Peter J. Glauber William B. Orberson
Gregory K. Jenkins John F. Parker Jr.
(Resident at Lexington) Jeffrey L. Hansford (Resident at
Raymond G. Smith New Albany, Indiana)
Walter E. Harding Matthew Hunter Jones (Resident
Robert M. Brooks at New Albany, Indiana)
John W. Phillips James B. Cooper
Susan D. Phillips (Resident at Lexington)
Ronald L. Green Martin H. Kinney, Jr.
(Resident at Lexington) Bayard V. Collier
Richard L. Walter (Resident at Prestonsburg)
(Resident at Paducah) Teresa M. Groves
Douglas A. U'Sellis (Resident at Paducah)
Steven G. Kinkel J. Bradley Sanders (Resident at
(Resident at Lexington) New Albany, Indiana)

ASSOCIATES

Mary Ann Kiwala Steven R. Armstrong
Bradley R. Hume (Resident at Lexington)
Richard W. Edwards Melissa Moore Lewis
John B. Moore (Resident at Prestonsburg)
David T. Klapheke Patrick J. Murphy, II
Robert D. McClure (Resident at Lexington)
Michael J. Cox Brennen C. Ragone
(Resident at Lexington) (Resident at Lexington)
William J. Crowe Gretchen R. Nunn
Denise Basford Askin (Resident at Prestonsburg)
David Sean Ragland Fredrick A. Bailey, Jr.
Jenifer A. Tarter (Resident at Lexington)
Daniel S. Stratemeyer David P. Haick
(Resident at Paducah) Garrett M. Estep
Michael S. Maloney Terri E. Kirkpatrick
E. Michael Ooley (Resident at Thomas M. Edelen
New Albany, Indiana) Tammy C. Snyder
John C. Talbott C. Tom Anderson
Deron L. Johnson (Resident at Prestonsburg)
(Resident at Prestonburg) Donna Jo Jenkins (Resident at
  New Albany, Indiana)

Counsel for: Ford Motor Co.; Texas Eastern Transmission Corp.; Coca-Cola Bottling Co.; Hartford Accident and Indemnity Co.; Continental Insurance Group; St. Paul Fire & Marine Insurance Co.; Lloyds of London; Old Republic Insurance Co.

For full biographical listings, see the Martindale-Hubbell Law Directory

---

CONLIFFE, SANDMANN & SULLIVAN (AV)

621 West Main Street, 40202
Telephone: 502-587-7711
Telecopier: 502-587-7756
Other Louisville Office: 4169 Westport Road, Suite 111, 40207.
Telephone: 502-896-2966.
Jeffersonville, Indiana Office: 141 E. Spring Street, 47150.
Telephone: 812-949-7711.

Charles I. Sandmann (1936-1992)

MEMBERS OF FIRM

I. G. Spencer, Jr. Sally Hardin Lambert
Karl N. Victor, Jr. Edwin J. Lowry, Jr.
Michael E. Conliffe Olivia Morris Fuchs
Richard M. Sullivan James A. Babbitz
Sam Deeb Kenneth A. Bohnert
Jack R. Underwood, Jr. James T. Mitchell
E. Bruce Neikirk Wm. Dennis Sims
Victoria Ann Ogden Edward F. Busch
Robert A. Donald, III Richard B. Taylor

Edward Lee Lasley

OF COUNSEL

Allen P. Dodd, III Alan R. Miller

For full biographical listings, see the Martindale-Hubbell Law Directory

---

EWEN, HILLIARD & BUSH (AV)

The Starks Building Suite 1090, 455 S. 4th Street, 40202
Telephone: 502-584-1090
Fax: 502-584-4707

MEMBERS OF FIRM

Victor W. Ewen (1924-1989) Frank P. Hilliard
A. Campbell Ewen John M. Bush

(See Next Column)

EWEN, HILLIARD & BUSH—*Continued*
ASSOCIATES

Kevin P. Kinney	Mark McClure Sandmann
Robert J. Rosing	Robin Lynn Burnham

For full biographical listings, see the Martindale-Hubbell Law Directory

JOSEPH G. GLASS (AV)

Suite 200, 235 South Fifth Street, 40202
Telephone: 502-584-7288
FAX: 502-584-0208

For full biographical listings, see the Martindale-Hubbell Law Directory

HIRN DOHENY & HARPER (AV)

A Partnership including a Professional Service Corporation
2000 Meidinger Tower, 40202
Telephone: 502-585-2450
Telecopiers: 502-585-2207; 585-2529
MEMBERS OF FIRM

Marvin J. Hirn	Scott W. Brinkman
Frank P. Doheny, Jr.	John E. Selent
David W. Harper	B. Todd Thompson
	Michael A. Valenti

ASSOCIATES

Steven A. Edwards	Millicent A. Tanner
Mary R. Harville	Robert W. Adams
Beverly J. Glascock	Trevor L. Earl
Jeffrey A. Hamilton	(Not admitted in KY)
Michael Marvin Hirn	Audra J. Eckerle

OF COUNSEL

Thomas J. Flynn	Stuart J. Frankenthal

Representative Clients: Humana, Inc.; Louisville Gas and Electric Co; Brandenbury Telephone; Lantech, Inc.; Mid-America Bank of Louisville; Indiana United Bancorp.; National City Bank, Kentucky; PNC Bank; Columbia/HCA; J.J.B. Hilliard, W.L. Lyons, Inc.

For full biographical listings, see the Martindale-Hubbell Law Directory

LANDRUM & SHOUSE (AV)

400 West Market Street Suite 1550, 40202
Telephone: 502-589-7616
Facsimile: 502-589-2119
Lexington, Kentucky Office: 106 West Vine Street, P.O. Box 951.
Telephone: 606-255-2424.
Facsimile: 606-233-0308.
RESIDENT MEMBERS OF THE FIRM

John R. Martin, Jr.	R. Kent Westberry
Delores Hill Pregliasco	J. Denis Ogburn

RESIDENT ASSOCIATES

Dave Whalin	Courtney T. Baxter
	Melanie Lee Straw-Boone

For full biographical listings, see the Martindale-Hubbell Law Directory

MACKENZIE & PEDEN, P.S.C. (AV)

650 Starks Building, 455 South Fourth Avenue, 40202-2509
Telephone: 502-589-1110
Fax: 502-589-1117
Other Louisville, Kentucky Office: 8311 Shelbyville Road.
Telephone: 502-426-6688.
Fax: 502-425-0561.

William B. Peden (Retired)	James T. Lobb
Thomas G. Mooney (1939-1991)	Valerie T. Mayer (Resident)
Wm. A. MacKenzie (Resident)	Edward H. Bartenstein
John G. Crutchfield	Judith B. Hoge
Wayne J. Carroll	Sidney L. Hymson
James C. Hickey	Lee Ann Risner
B. Carlton Neat, III	Charles T. Baxter
Robert W. Dickey	John Patrick Hamm
William B. Bardenwerper (Resident)	

OF COUNSEL

Walker C. Cunningham, Jr.	Robert W. Riley (Resident)
Lawrence J. Phillips	Stephen A. Schwager

Representative Clients: Allstate Insurance Co.; American States Insurance Co.; The Fund Insurance Companies; State Automobile Mutual Insurance Co..

For full biographical listings, see the Martindale-Hubbell Law Directory

FRANK MASCAGNI, III (AV)

Suite 200, Second Floor, Morrissey Building, 304 West Liberty Street, 40202-3012
Telephone: 502-583-2831
Fax: 502-583-3701

Reference: PNC Bank, Ky.

For full biographical listings, see the Martindale-Hubbell Law Directory

MIDDLETON & REUTLINGER, P.S.C. (AV)

2500 Brown and Williamson Tower, 40202-3410
Telephone: 502-584-1135
Fax: 502-561-0442
New Albany, Indiana Office: 2623 Charlestown Road, 47150.
Telephone: 812-944-7215.

O. Grant Bruton	G. Kennedy Hall, Jr.
Kenneth S. Handmaker	James R. Higgins, Jr.
Ian Y. Henderson	Mark S. Fenzel
James N. Williams, Jr.	Kathiejane Oehler
Charles G. Middleton, III	Charles G. Lamb
Charles D. Greenwell	Thomas W. Frentz
Brooks Alexander	William Jay Hunter, Jr.
John W. Bilby	James E. Milliman
C. Kent Hatfield	David J. Kellerman
Timothy P. O'Mara	Kipley J. McNally
Stewart L. Prather	Julie A. Gregory
D. Randall Gibson	Edward L. Galloway

Margaret E. Thorp	Augustus S. Herbert
Amy B. Berge	Dana L. Lucas
David W. Carrithers	Thomas P. O'Brien III
James C. Eaves, Jr.	John F. Salazar
Dennis D. Murrell	Nancy J. Schook
	Clayton R. Hume

OF COUNSEL

Albert F. Reutlinger (Retired)	Henry Meigs, II
	J. Paul Keith, III

Counsel for: Chevron USA; Logan Aluminum, Inc.; Louisville Gas & Electric Co.; MCI Telecommunications Corp.; Metropolitan Life Insurance Co.; Kosmos Cement Co.; Porcelain Metal Corp.; The Home Insurance Co.; The Kroger Co.; Demars Haka Development, Inc.

For full biographical listings, see the Martindale-Hubbell Law Directory

J. BRUCE MILLER LAW GROUP (AV)

621 West Main Street, Third Floor, 40202
Telephone: 502-587-0900
Telecopier: 502-587-9008

J. Bruce Miller	Michael J. Kitchen
Norma C. Miller	Jeffrey A. Haeberlin
Anthony L. Schnell	Katherine K. Kitchen
Denis B. Fleming, Jr.	J. Daniel Farrell
	(Not admitted in KY)

Representative Clients: Advance Machinery Co., Inc.; Anson Machine Mfg. Co.; Biddinger Investment Capital Corp. (Indiana); Carneal Enterprises, Inc. (Kentucky/Florida); MPD Inc. (Owensboro, Kentucky); Motion Picture Association of America; Packaging Unlimited Group (Kentucky/North Carolina); Paducah Medical Supply, Inc. (Kentucky/Tennessee/Florida); Sun Group Broadcasting, Inc. (Indiana/Tennessee); Louisville Gas & Electric Co.

For full biographical listings, see the Martindale-Hubbell Law Directory

MORGAN & POTTINGER, P.S.C. (AV)

601 West Main Street, 40202
Telephone: 502-589-2780
Telecopier: 502-585-3498
Lexington, Kentucky Office: 133 West Short Street.
Telephone: 606-253-1900.
Telecopier: 606-255-2038.
New Albany, Indiana Office: 400 Pearl Street, Suite 100.
Telephone: 812-948-0008.
Telecopier: 812-944-6215.

Patrick E. Morgan	Scott T. Rickman
John T. McGarvey	(Resident, Lexington Office)
C. Edward Hastie	J. Jeffrey Cooke
(Resident, Lexington Office)	Ruthanne Q. Whitt
M. Deane Stewart	M. Thurman Senn
James I. Murray	Garret B. Hannegan (Resident,
(Resident, Lexington Office)	New Albany, Indiana Office)
Douglas Gene Sharp	Hal D. Friedman
John A. Majors	Keith D. Mull (Resident, New
Mark J. Sandlin	Albany, Indiana Office)
	Thomas A. Howley

SENIOR COUNSEL

David C. Pottinger
COUNSEL

Elmer E. Morgan

(See Next Column)

MORGAN & POTTINGER P.S.C., *Louisville—Continued*

COUNSEL TO FIRM
Thomas C. Fenton

For full biographical listings, see the Martindale-Hubbell Law Directory

---

OLDFATHER & MORRIS (AV)

1330 South Third Street, 40208
Telephone: 502-637-7200
Fax: 502-637-3999
Email: om@ntr.net

Ann B. Oldfather	James Barrett
Douglas H. Morris, II	Jennifer Jordan Hall

For full biographical listings, see the Martindale-Hubbell Law Directory

---

RUBIN HAYS & FOLEY (AV)

First Trust Centre 200 South Fifth Street, 40202
Telephone: 502-569-7550
Telecopier: 502-569-7555

MEMBERS OF FIRM

Wm. Carl Fust	Lisa Koch Bryant
Harry Lee Meyer	Sharon C. Hardy
David W. Gray	Charles S. Musson
Irvin D. Foley	W. Randall Jones
Joseph R. Gathright, Jr.	K. Gail Russell

ASSOCIATES

Christian L. Juckett	Courtney Lynn McCall

OF COUNSEL

James E. Fahey	Newman T. Guthrie

Representative Clients: J.C. Bradford & Co., Inc.; J.J.B. Hilliard, W.L. Lyons, Inc.; Huntington National Bank; Liberty National Bank and Trust Company; National City Bank; PNC Bank; Prudential Bache & Co., Inc.; Prudential Securities, Inc.; Society Bank; Stock Yards Bank and Trust Co.

For full biographical listings, see the Martindale-Hubbell Law Directory

---

SEILLER & HANDMAKER, LLP (AV)

2200 Meidinger Tower, 40202
Telephone: 502-584-7400
Telecopier: 502-583-2100
Paris, Kentucky Office: Seiller, Handmaker & Blevins, P.S.C., 1431 South Main Street.
Telephone: 606-987-3980.
Telecopier: 606-987-3982.
Cynthiana, Kentucky Office: Seiller, Handmaker & Blevins, P.S.C., 9 South Walnut.
Telephone: 606-234-2880.
New Albany, Indiana Office: 202 Pearl Street.
Telephone: 812-948-8307.
Telecopier: 812-948-8383.

Edward F. Seiller (1897-1990)

MEMBERS OF FIRM

Stuart Allen Handmaker	Maury D. Kommor
Bill V. Seiller	Cynthia Compton Stone
David M. Cantor	Glenn A. Cohen
Neil C. Bordy	Tomi Anne Blevins Pulliam
Kyle Anne Citrynell	(Paris and Cynthiana Offices)

ASSOCIATES

Pamela M. Greenwell	Donna F. Townsend
Michael C. Bratcher	Gregory A. Lindsey
John E. Brengle	Vicki L. Buba
Patrick R. Holland, II	Allen C. Platt III (Resident,
Edwin Jon Wolfe	New Albany, Indiana Office)

OF COUNSEL

Robert S. Frey

For full biographical listings, see the Martindale-Hubbell Law Directory

---

STITES & HARBISON (AV)

Formerly Stites, McElwain & Fowler and Harbison, Kessinger, Lisle & Bush
400 West Market Street, Suite 1800, 40202
Telephone: 502-587-3400
Frankfort, Kentucky Office: 421 West Main Street.
Telephone: 502-223-3477.
Lexington, Kentucky Office: 2300 Lexington Financial Center.
Telephone: 606-226-2300.
Jeffersonville, Indiana Office: 323 East Court Avenue.
Telephone: 812-282-7566.

MEMBERS OF FIRM

James W. Stites (1897-1975)	Richard Bush, Jr. (1915-1991)
Clinton M. Harbison	Kent McElwain (1927-1992)
(1886-1980)	Lively M. Wilson
S. Lloyd Cardwell (1909-1987)	Charles E. Palmer, Jr.
Ben B. Fowler (1916-1990)	(Lexington, Kentucky Office)

(See Next Column)

MEMBERS OF FIRM (Continued)

David C. Brown	Philip W. Collier
Sidney C. Kinkead, Jr.	C. Craig Bradley, Jr.
(Lexington, Kentucky Office)	Mark R. Overstreet
George W. Mills	(Frankfort, Kentucky Office)
(Lexington, Kentucky Office)	W. Patrick Stallard
C. Dant Kearns	John A. Bartlett
W. Robinson Beard	Robert M. Connolly
Ralston W. Steenrod	John L. Tate
Robert W. Lanum	Jefferey M. Yussman
(Jeffersonville, Indiana Office)	Joseph L. Hamilton
Alfred S. Joseph, III	Janet A. Craig
Steven L. Beshear	(Lexington, Kentucky Office)
(Lexington, Kentucky Office)	James C. Seiffert
Joe B. Campbell	Gregory P. Parsons
(Lexington, Kentucky Office)	(Lexington, Kentucky Office)
J. Bissell Roberts	Judith A. Villines
Bruce M. Reynolds	(Frankfort, Kentucky Office)
(Lexington, Kentucky Office)	Kenneth R. Sagan
Charles J. Cronan, IV	(Lexington, Kentucky Office)
T. Kennedy Helm, III	Richard G. Griffith
Buckner Hinkle, Jr.	(Lexington, Kentucky Office)
(Lexington, Kentucky Office)	Michael D. Risley
William H. Haden, Jr.	J. Clarke Keller
J. David Porter	(Lexington, Kentucky Office)
(Lexington, Kentucky Office)	Laura D. Keller
Stephen M. Ruschell	(Lexington, Kentucky Office)
(Lexington, Kentucky Office)	James W. Taylor
Cecile Anne Blau	(Lexington, Kentucky Office)
(Jeffersonville, Indiana Office)	Alex P. Herrington, Jr.
Robert M. Beck, Jr.	Byron N. Miller
(Lexington, Kentucky Office)	Richard A. Vance
Charles J. Lisle	Ashley W. Ward
(Lexington, Kentucky Office)	(Lexington, Kentucky Office)
Jamieson G. McPherson	Allen L. Morris
Bruce F. Clark	(Jeffersonville, Indiana Office)
(Frankfort, Kentucky Office)	W. Bradford Boone
William E. Hellmann	(Lexington, Kentucky Office)
James R. Williamson	Susan C. Reisner
John M. Famularo	Philip L. Hanrahan
(Lexington, Kentucky Office)	(Lexington, Kentucky Office)
Thomas E. Meng	Rebecca F. Schupbach
(Lexington, Kentucky Office)	Carol Dan Browning
Douglass C. E. Farnsley	Cynthia L. Coffee
Robert W. Griffith	Lynn C. Stidham
Walter R. Byrne, Jr.	(Lexington, Kentucky Office)
(Lexington, Kentucky Office)	Cheryl Ulene Lewis
W. Kennedy Simpson	(Lexington, Kentucky Office)

Brooks D. Kubik	Douglas B. Bates
Andrew R. Jacobs	(Jeffersonville, Indiana Office)
(Lexington, Kentucky Office)	Monique R. Hunt
Michele Whittington	Timothy C. Kimmel (Louisville
(Lexington, Kentucky Office)	and Frankfort Offices)
Shannon Antle Hamilton	Lisa M. Ramsey
Kathleen O. McKune	(Lexington, Kentucky Office)
William T. Gorton III	Rebecca B. Stephenson
(Lexington, Kentucky Office)	(Lexington, Kentucky Office)
Margaret M. Pisacano	James W. Proud
(Lexington, Kentucky Office)	Lloyd C. Chatfield II
Benjamin Lee Kessinger, III	(Lexington, Kentucky Office)
(Lexington, Kentucky Office)	Barry A. Hines
T. Morgan Ward, Jr.	Lori R. Hollis
Lissa Wathen	Michael I. Kanovitz
(Lexington, Kentucky Office)	Amanda L. Pope
Brian A. Cromer	(Lexington, Kentucky Office)
Martha J. Hasselbacher	Jason P. Thomas (Frankfort and
Erica L. Horn	Lexington, Kentucky Offices)
Don A. Pisacano	Jane Brannon
(Lexington, Kentucky Office)	(Lexington, Kentucky Office)
Catharine C. Young	Jeffrey J. Chapuran
W. Bryan Hudson	(Lexington, Kentucky Office)
Brenda J. Runner	Gregory L. Davis
Jacqueline K. Armstrong	Marjorie A. Farris
Anne E. Gorham	Dustin C. McCoy
(Lexington, Kentucky Office)	(Lexington, Kentucky Office)
William T. Shier	Nancy E. McElwain
(Lexington, Kentucky Office)	Jennifer L. Robinson
Catherine Murr Young	Angela L. Stinebruner
W. Thomas Halbleib, Jr.	Christine S. Talley
	(Jeffersonville, Indiana Office)

OF COUNSEL

Rufus Lisle	T. Kennedy Helm, Jr.
(Lexington, Kentucky Office)	Ralph F. Kessinger
Nathan Elliott, Jr.	(Lexington, Kentucky Office)
(Lexington, Kentucky Office)	James W. Stites, Jr.

(See Next Column)

STITES & HARBISON—Continued

COUNSEL

Ben L. Kessinger, Jr.
(Lexington, Kentucky Office)
Calvert T. Roszell
(Lexington, Kentucky Office)
Romano L. Mazzoli
Thomas J. Stipanowich
(Lexington, Kentucky Office)

John A. Johnson
Edward J. O'Meara
Elizabeth Lee Thompson
(Lexington, Kentucky Office)
Paul J. Houk
J. Scott Greene

Representative Clients: South Central Bell Telephone Co.; Glenmore Distilleries Co.; New York Life Insurance Co.; Chrysler Financial Corp.; ARCO Metals Co.; Aetna Life & Casualty Insurance Cos.; Illinois Central Railroad Co.

For full biographical listings, see the Martindale-Hubbell Law Directory

STITES, McELWAIN & FOWLER

(See Stites & Harbison)

STOLL, KEENON & PARK, LLP (AV)

400 West Market Street Suite 2650, 40202-3377
Telephone: 502-568-9100
Telecopier: 502-568-5700
Frankfort, Kentucky Office: 307 Washington Street.
Telephone: 502-875-6220.
Telecopier: 502-875-6235.
Lexington, Kentucky Office: 210 E. Main Street, Suite 1000, 40507-1380.
Telephone: 606-231-3000.
Telecopier: 606-253-1093; 606-253-1380.

MEMBERS OF FIRM

Samuel D. Hinkle, IV
Lea Pauley Goff

Robert W. Kellerman

ASSOCIATES

Culver V. Halliday

Gregory L. Taylor

For full biographical listings, see the Martindale-Hubbell Law Directory

TILFORD, DOBBINS, ALEXANDER, BUCKAWAY & BLACK (AV)

Suite 1400, One Riverfront Plaza, 40202
Telephone: 502-584-6137

MEMBERS OF FIRM

Charles W. Dobbins (1916-1992)
Henry J. Tilford (1880-1968)
George S. Wetherby (1905-1954)
Lawrence W. Wetherby (1908-1994)
John T. Metcalf (1890-1974)
Stuart E. Alexander
William A. Buckaway, Jr.

Charles W. Dobbins, Jr.
Terrell L. Black
Mark Wesley Dobbins
Stuart E. Alexander, III
John M. Nader
John A. Wilmes
Sandra F. Keene
Thomas J.B. Hurst

David Dwight Cobb, Jr.

OF COUNSEL

Randolph Noe

Carolyn K. Balleisen

LEGAL SUPPORT PERSONNEL

Jennifer Olvey

For full biographical listings, see the Martindale-Hubbell Law Directory

WOODWARD, HOBSON & FULTON (AV)

2500 National City Tower, 101 South Fifth Street, 40202
Telephone: 502-581-8000
Fax: 502-581-8111
Lexington, Kentucky Office: PNC Bank Plaza, 200 West Vine Street, Suite 500.
Telephone: 606-244-7100.
Telecopier: 606-244-7111.
New Albany, Indiana Office: 611 East Spring Street, P.O. Box 288.
Telephone: 812-941-1800.
Telecopier: 812-941-1855.

MEMBERS OF FIRM

Ernest Woodward (1877-1968)
Robert P. Hobson (1893-1966)
Will H. Fulton (1888-1953)
John P. Sandidge
Ernest Woodward II (1917-1990)
John A. Fulton (1919-1987)
Kenneth L. Anderson
William D. Grubbs
Lionel A. Hawse (Resident, Lexington, Kentucky Office)
Harry K. Herren
David R. Monohan
Will H. Fulton
Robert L. Hallenberg
Richard H. C. Clay

Thomas A. Hoy
Mary Jo Wetzel (Resident, New Albany, Indiana Office)
John F. Gleason
Gregory L. Smith
Gregory A. Bölzle
J. Michael Dalton
Elizabeth Ullmer Mendel
Michael A. Luvisi
Jann B. Logsdon
Arthur L. Williams
Linsey W. West (Resident, Lexington, Kentucky Office)
Ellen M. Hesen
David T. Schaefer

Patrick Michael

(See Next Column)

ASSOCIATES

Benjamin Cowgill, Jr. (Resident, Lexington, Kentucky Office)
Robert J. Schumacher
Christopher R. Fitzpatrick
Eric M. Jensen
D. Craig York
Donna King Perry
Kathryn A. Quesenberry
Sandra Tremper O'Brien
Christopher R. Cashen (Resident, Lexington, Kentucky Office)

L. Jay Gilbert
C. Dean Furman
Christy Lee Hendricks
D. Sean Nilsen
Jill F. Lowenbraun
Rebecca L. Didat
R. Brian Evans
Catherine S. Astorino
William A. Green, III (Resident, Lexington, Kentucky Office)
Daniel W. Blougouras
Lydia Plamp Brownlow

OF COUNSEL

Fielden Woodward

Robert C. Hobson

Representative Clients: American Home Insurance Co.; Brown-Forman Corp.; CARITAS Health Services, Inc.; CSX Transportation, Inc.; Fischer Packing Company; Ford Motor Co.; Nationwide Insurance Co., Inc.; Ralston Purina Co.; Toyota Motor Corp.; Wal-Mart Stores, Inc.

For full biographical listings, see the Martindale-Hubbell Law Directory

WYATT, TARRANT & COMBS (AV)

Citizens Plaza, 40202
Telephone: 502-589-5235
Telecopier: 502-589-0309
URL: http://www.wyattfirm.com
Lexington, Kentucky Office: 1700 Lexington Financial Center.
Telephone: 606-233-2012.
Telecopier: 606-259-0649.
Frankfort, Kentucky Office: The Taylor-Scott Building, 311 West Main Street.
Telephone: 502-223-2104.
Telecopier: 502-227-7681.
New Albany, Indiana Office: The Elsby Building, 117 East Spring Street,
Telephone: 812-945-3561.
Telecopier: 812-949-2524.
Memphis, Tennessee Office: Crescent Center, Suite 650, 6075 Poplar Avenue.
Telephone. 901-537-1000.
Telecopier: 901-537-1010.
Nashville, Tennessee Office: 1500 Nashville City Center, 511 Union Street.
Telephone: 615-244-0020.
Telecopier: 615-256-1726.
Music Row, Nashville Office: 29 Music Square East.
Telephone: 615-255-6161.
Telecopier: 615-254-4490.
Hendersonville, Tennessee Office: 313 E. Main Street, Suite 1.
Telephone: 615-822-8822.
Telecopier: 615-824-4684.

MEMBERS OF FIRM

Wilson W. Wyatt, Sr. (1905-1996)
John E. Tarrant (1898-1990)
Bert T. Combs (1911-1991)
Telford B. Orbison (1901-1990)
Stuart E. Lampe (1906-1994)
John S. Osborn, Jr.
Robert L. Maddox
Edgar A. Zingman
Gordon B. Davidson
Lawrence L. Jones, III
Richard W. Iler
Russell H. Riggs
Robert C. Ewald
A. Wallace Grafton, Jr.
Samuel G. Bridge, Jr.
H. Alexander Campbell
Stewart E. Conner
R. Lawrence Baird
J. Larry Cashen
Parker W. Duncan, Jr.
Robert I. Cusick
Edwin S. Hopson
Grover C. Potts, Jr.
John P. Reisz
Jon L. Fleischaker
K. Gregory Haynes
M. Stephen Pitt
Stephen D. Berger
Francis J. Mellen, Jr.
Martin P. Duffy
Walter M. Jones
Michael B. Vincenti
Mark C. Blackwell

Frank F. Chuppe, Jr.
Thomas J. Luber
Allison Joseph Maggiolo
Richard Northern
Merrill S. Schell
J. Michael Brown
Paul J. Cox
Kimberly K. Greene
G. Alexander Hamilton
Patrick W. Mattingly
Parker W. Eads
David W. Seewer
Virginia Hamilton Snell
Arthur Adams Rouse
Gordon B. Wright
Cynthia W. Young
Byron E. Leet
Mary Ann Main
Caryn F. Price
Leo F. Camp
J. Anthony Goebel
Robert A. Heath
William H. Hollander
Michael Keith Kirk
Holliday Hopkins Thacker
Joan Lloyd Cooper
Stephen R. Price, Sr.
Mark A. Robinson
Rita L. McDonald
Michelle Turner
Cornelius E. Coryell, II
Jeffrey E. Wallace
Carole Douglas Christian
Denise St. Clair Kaiser

Donald J. Kelly

ASSOCIATES

Jane C. Foushee
Jean W. Bird
Barbara Wetzel Gernert
Robert A. Hawkins

James W. Lee
Caroline Miller Oyler
Clara M. Passafiume
Franklin K. Jelsma

(See Next Column)

WYATT, TARRANT & COMBS, *Louisville—Continued*

ASSOCIATES (Continued)

Kevin P. Crooks
 (Not admitted in KY)
Cynthia Blevins Doll
Deborah H. Patterson
Steven L. Snyder
Michelle D. Wyrick
Mitzi D. Wyrick

Gregory S. Berman
Craig A. Hawley
Cheryl Forino Wahl
Sandra Hinojosa Hubbard
Daniel V. Klump
David E. Saffer
Travis J. Thayer

COUNSEL

Frank W. Burke, Sr.
Martin Rockwell

Kevin J. Hable
Norman W. Graham

Clinton J Elliott

Representative Clients: Alliant Health System, Inc.; Ashland Oil, Inc.; Churchill Downs, Inc.; E.I. du Pont de Nemours and Company; Ford Motor Co.; Gannett Co., Inc./The Courier-Journal & Louisville Times; General Electric Co.; Henry Vogt Machine Co.; PNC Bank Corp; United Catalysts, Inc.

For full biographical listings, see the Martindale-Hubbell Law Directory

---

MADISONVILLE,* Hopkins Co.

MITCHELL, JOINER, HARDESTY & LOWTHER (AV)

113 East Center Street, Drawer 659, 42431-0659
Telephone: 502-825-4455
Telefax: 502-825-9600

Thomas A. Mitchell
Richard M. Joiner

Randall L. Hardesty
Charles E. Lowther

For full biographical listings, see the Martindale-Hubbell Law Directory

---

MANCHESTER,* Clay Co.

LAW FIRM OF NEVILLE SMITH (AV)

110 Lawyer Street, P.O. Box 447, 40962
Telephone: 606-598-2113
Fax: 606-598-8029

MEMBERS OF FIRM

Chas. C. Smith (1903-1975)   Neville Smith
            Harold Rader

Counsel for: Greenleaf Trucking Co.; Shamrock Coal Co.; Red Bird Hospital; Clay County Board of Education; Mid South Electrics, Inc.; Elk River Resources, Inc.
Local Counsel for: Kentucky Farm Bureau Insurance Cos.
Approved Attorneys for: Louisville Title Division of Commonwealth Land Title Insurance Co.; Title Insurance Company of Minnesota.

For full biographical listings, see the Martindale-Hubbell Law Directory

---

MARION,* Crittenden Co. — (Refer to Madisonville)

MAYFIELD,* Graves Co.

NEELY & BRIEN (AV)

238 North Seventh Street, 42066
Telephone: 502-247-9333
Fax: 502-247-7143

MEMBERS OF FIRM

Sam Boyd Neely   James B. Brien, Jr.
            S. Boyd Neely, Jr.

ASSOCIATES

Robert C. Brown   R. Brent Vasseur

Representative Clients: Peoples First Bank & Trust Co.; General Tire Inc. Kentucky Farm Bureau Mutual Insurance Co.; Mayfield City Board of Education; State Auto Insurance Co.; Hospital Corporation of America.; Republic Bank & Trust Co.
Approved Attorneys for: Louisville Title Division of Commonwealth Land Title Insurance Co.; Lawyers Title Insurance Corp.; Ticor Title Insurance Co.; Chicago Title Ins. Co.

For full biographical listings, see the Martindale-Hubbell Law Directory

---

MAYSVILLE,* Mason Co.

FOX, WOOD & WOOD (AV)

Trans Financial Bank Building, 33 1/2 West Second Street, 41056
Telephone: 606-564-5585
Fax: 606-564-6734

MEMBERS OF FIRM

Andrew V. Fox (1905-1977)   Woodson T. Wood
Donald L. Wood   John F. Estill

OF COUNSEL

Katherine L. Wood

ASSOCIATES

Andrew W. Wood

Representative Clients: Louisville Title Division of Commonwealth Land Title Insurance Co.; Dravo Lime Company; Motorists Mutual Insurance Co.; State Farm Mutual Automobile Insurance Co.

(See Next Column)

Approved Attorneys for: Chicago Title Insurance Co.; Farmers Home Administration; Louisville Title Division of Commonwealth Land Title Insurance Co.; Farm Credit Services.

For full biographical listings, see the Martindale-Hubbell Law Directory

---

MONTICELLO,* Wayne Co. — (Refer to Somerset)

MORGANFIELD,* Union Co. — (Refer to Henderson)

MORGANTOWN,* Butler Co. — (Refer to Bowling Green)

MOUNT OLIVET,* Robertson Co. — (Refer to Lexington)

MOUNT STERLING,* Montgomery Co.

WHITE, PECK, CARRINGTON AND McDONALD, LLP (AV)

26 Broadway, P.O. Box 950, 40353
Telephone: 606-498-2872
Telecopier: 606-498-2877

MEMBERS OF FIRM

Lewis A. White
Alan B. Peck

Grover A. Carrington
Michelle "Shelly" R. McDonald

ASSOCIATES

Stephen E. Neal

Counsel for: Bob's Food Service, Inc; Kentucky Farm Bureau Insurance Cos.; Mt. Sterling Advocate; Montgomery & Traders Bank & Trust Co.; Commonwealth Bank F.S.B.; Owingsville Banking Co.; Po Folks, Inc.; McCormick Lumber Co.; Walker Construction Co.; Warren Builders, Inc.

For full biographical listings, see the Martindale-Hubbell Law Directory

---

MOUNT VERNON,* Rockcastle Co.

CLONTZ & COX (AV)

Courthouse, 205 Main Street, P.O. Box 1350, 40456
Telephone: 606-256-5111
Fax: 606-256-2036

MEMBERS OF FIRM

Carl R. Clontz   Jerry J. Cox
            John E. Clontz

Representative Clients: The Bank of Mt. Vernon; Citizens Bank, Brodhead, Kentucky; Kentucky Farm Bureau Mutual Insurance Co.; Louisville Title Division of Commonwealth Land Title Insurance Co.
Reference: The Bank of Mt. Vernon, Mt. Vernon, Kentucky.

For full biographical listings, see the Martindale-Hubbell Law Directory

---

MUNFORDVILLE,* Hart Co. — (Refer to Horse Cave)

MURRAY,* Calloway Co.

GREGORY, EASLEY, BLANKENSHIP AND COURTNEY (AV)

204 South Sixth Street, P.O. Box 230, 42071
Telephone: 502-753-2633
Fax: 502-753-1825

MEMBERS OF FIRM

Nat R. Hughes (1906-1981)   R. Sidney Easley
John A. Gregory, Jr.   C. Mark Blankenship
            Dennis J. Courtney

Representative Clients: Kentucky Farm Bureau Mutual Insurance Co.; State Farm Mutual Automobile Insurance; R. T. Vanderbilt Co.; Briggs and Stratton Corp.; State Auto Insurance; Meridian Insurance Co.; Peoples Bank of Murray; Murray State University Credit Union.

For full biographical listings, see the Martindale-Hubbell Law Directory

---

NICHOLASVILLE,* Jessamine Co. — (Refer to Lexington)

OWENSBORO,* Daviess Co.

BAMBERGER & ABSHIER (AV)

111 West 2nd Street, 42303-4113
Telephone: 502-926-4545
Fax: 502-684-0064

MEMBERS OF FIRM

Ronald J. Bamberger   Phillip G. Abshier

ASSOCIATES

Angela L. Wathen

For full biographical listings, see the Martindale-Hubbell Law Directory

---

KAMUF, YEWELL, PACE & CONDON (AV)

Great Financial Federal Building, 322 Frederica Street, 42301
Telephone: 502-685-3901
Fax: 502-926-2005

MEMBERS OF FIRM

Charles J. Kamuf   Patrick D. Pace
David L. Yewell   David C. Condon

(See Next Column)

KAMUF, YEWELL, PACE & CONDON—*Continued*

ASSOCIATES

John M. Mischel

Representative Clients: Owensboro Municipal Utilities Commission; Lincoln Service Corp.; Hancock County Planning Commission; Daviess County Board of Education; Barmet Aluminum Corp.; Owensboro Sewer Commission; TICOR Title Insurance Co.; Chicago Title Insurance Co.; Owensboro Riverport Authority; Housing Authority of Owensboro.

For full biographical listings, see the Martindale-Hubbell Law Directory

McCARROLL, NUNLEY & HARTZ (AV)

111 East Third Street, P.O. Box 925, 42302-0925
Telephone: 502-683-3535
FAX: 502-926-6056

MEMBERS OF FIRM

Clarence McCarroll (1916-1989)   Marvin P. Nunley
Max S. Hartz

ASSOCIATES

Victoria L. Yevincy

Representative Clients: Aetna Casualty & Surety Company; Allstate Insurance Company; American Hardware Mutual Insurance Company; American Motorists Insurance Company; Automobile Club Insurance Company; Celina Mutual Insurance Company; Chubb Group of Insurance Companies; CIGNA Insurance Companies; Citizens Insurance Company of America; CNA Insurance Company.

For full biographical listings, see the Martindale-Hubbell Law Directory

SHEFFER ● HOFFMAN (AV)

101 East Second Street, 42303
Telephone: 502-684-3700
Telecopier: 502-684-3881
URL: http://www.kylaw.com
Bowling Green, Kentucky Office: Fountain Square, 911 College Street, Suite A.
Telephone: 502-793-9300.
Telecopier: 502-843-9399.
Henderson, Kentucky Office: 300 First Street.
Telephone: 502-826-3300.
Telecopier: 502-827-5070.
Louisville, Kentucky Office: National City Tower, Suite 1600, 101 South Fifth Street.
Telephone: 502-582-1600.
Paducah, Kentucky Office: 333 Broadway, Suite 1001.
Telephone: 502-443-9401.
Telecopier: 502-443-3624.

MEMBERS OF FIRM

Ronald G. Sheffer	William R. Duty (Resident)
John Stanley Hoffman	Tina R. McFarland Jones (Not
(Resident, Henderson Office)	admitted in KY; Resident)
Thomas L. Osborne	James H. Ball
(Resident, Paducah Office)	(Resident, Louisville Office)
Mark R. Hutchinson (Resident)	Mark E. Pfeifer (Resident)
Peter B. Lewis (Resident)	John H. Henderson (Resident)
Michael W. Alvey (Resident)	Edwin A. Jones
John A. Sheffer (Resident)	Lisa A. Payne
Howard E. Frasier, Jr.	Kerry L. Sigler
(Resident, Bowling Green	Christopher C. Wischer
Office)	David L. Dalton
Karen L. Wilson	
(Resident, Henderson Office)	

For full biographical listings, see the Martindale-Hubbell Law Directory

PADUCAH,* McCracken Co.

BOEHL STOPHER & GRAVES (AV)

Suite 340 Executive Inn Riverfront, One Executive Boulevard, 42001
Telephone: 502-442-4369
FAX: 502-442-4689
Louisville, Kentucky Office: Providian Center, Suite 2300, 400 West Market Street.
Telephone: 502-589-5980.
Fax: 502-561-9400.
Lexington, Kentucky Office: 444 West Second Street.
Telephone: 606-252-6721.
Fax: 606-253-1445.
Prestonsburg, Kentucky Office: 105 West Court Street.
Telephone: 606-886-8004.
Fax: 606-886-9579.
New Albany, Indiana Office: Elsby East, Suite 204, 400 Pearl Street.
Telephone: 812-948-5053.
Fax: 812-948-9233.

RESIDENT OF COUNSEL

George R. Effinger

(See Next Column)

RESIDENT PARTNERS

Jonathan Freed	John P. Rall
Richard L. Walter	Charles D. Walter
Teresa M. Groves	

RESIDENT ASSOCIATE

Daniel S. Stratemeyer

Counsel for: Ford Motor Co.; Texas Eastern Transmission Corp.; Coca-Cola Bottling Co.; National Collegiate Athletic Assn.; Hartford Accident and Indemnity Co.; Continental Insurance Group; St. Paul Fire & Marine Insurance Co.; Lloyds of London; Old Republic Insurance Co.

For full biographical listings, see the Martindale-Hubbell Law Directory

DENTON & KEULER (AV)

Paducah Bank & Trust Company Building, 555 Jefferson Street, P.O. Box 929, 42001
Telephone: 502-443-8253
Fax: 502-442-6000
Email: dentonkeuler@delphi.com

MEMBERS OF FIRM

W. David Denton	William E. Pinkston
Thomas J. Keuler	Lisa Hayden Emmons
David L. Kelly	

ASSOCIATES

William Kevin Shannon	Theodore S. Hutchins
Glenn D. Denton	

OF COUNSEL

Samuel Carlick

LEGAL SUPPORT PERSONNEL

PARALEGALS

Janet S. Burnett CPS	Christianne Chittenden
Douglas W. Painter	

Approved Attorneys for: Louisville Title Division of Commonwealth Land Title Insurance Co.; National Mortgage Co.
Reference: The Paducah Bank & Trust Co.

For full biographical listings, see the Martindale-Hubbell Law Directory

HARDY, TERRELL, BOSWELL & SIMS (AV)

425 South 6th Street, P.O. Box 1265, 42001
Telephone: 502-442-9237
Fax: 502-442-9411

MEMBERS OF FIRM

Adrian H. Terrell (1904-1970)	Burke B. Terrell
James L. Hardy (1918-1993)	J. David Boswell
Georgia Mae Nelson Dunn	Van Sims
(1908-1995)	

ASSOCIATE

Brian R. Fleming

Local Counsel for: Energas Co.
Insurance Clients: Kemper Group; Indiana Insurance Cos.; State Automobile Insurance Co.; Farmers Insurance Group; American States Insurance Co.; Kentucky Hospital Trust Association; Farmland Insurance Co.; Scottsdale Insurance Co.; Canal Insurance Co.

For full biographical listings, see the Martindale-Hubbell Law Directory

SHEFFER ● HOFFMAN (AV)

333 Broadway, Suite 1001, 42001
Telephone: 502-443-9401
Telecopier: 502-443-3624
URL: http://www.kylaw.com
Bowling Green, Kentucky Office: Fountain Square, 911 College Street, Suite A.
Telephone: 502-793-9300.
Telecopier: 502-843-9399.
Henderson, Kentucky Office: 300 First Street.
Telephone: 502-826-3300.
Telecopier: 502-827-5070.
Louisville, Kentucky Office: National City Tower, Suite 1600, 101 South Fifth Street.
Telephone: 502-582-1600.
Owensboro, Kentucky Office: 101 East Second Street.
Telephone: 502-684-3700.
Telecopier: 502-684-3881.

MEMBERS OF FIRM

Ronald G. Sheffer	James A. Sigler (Resident)
(Resident, Owensboro Office)	David B. Wrinkle (Resident)
Thomas L. Osborne	C. Thomas Miller (Resident)
Linda H. Terrell (Resident)	

For full biographical listings, see the Martindale-Hubbell Law Directory

PAINTSVILLE,* Johnson Co.

WELLS, PORTER, SCHMITT & JONES (AV)

327 Main Street, 41240
Telephone: 606-789-3747; 789-3749; 789-3775
Fax: 606-789-3790

MEMBERS OF FIRM

Z. Wells (1890-1946)	John V. Porter, Jr.
R. L. Wells (1894-1953)	Michael J. Schmitt
J. K. Wells	Donald L. Jones
Sandra Spurgeon	

ASSOCIATES

Johnny L. Griffith	Kimberly E. Colley
Jon H. Johnson	Darrin W. Banks
Garland Arnett, Jr.	

LEGAL SUPPORT PERSONNEL

Melinda A. Johnson (Paralegal) Natalie B. Caudill (Paralegal)

Representative Clients: Columbia Gas Transmission Corp.; Columbia Gas of Kentucky; C. & O. Railway Co.; Ashland Oil, Inc.; Travelers Insurance Co.; United States Fidelity & Guaranty Co.; Fireman's Fund-American Insurance Co.

For full biographical listings, see the Martindale-Hubbell Law Directory

PARIS,* Bourbon Co. — (Refer to Lexington)

PIKEVILLE,* Pike Co.

BAIRD, BAIRD, BAIRD AND JONES, P.S.C. (AV)

415 Second Street, P.O. Box 351, 41502
Telephone: 606-437-6276
Fax: 606-437-6383

William J. Baird (1913-1987)	James B. Ratliff
William J. Baird, III	Russell H. Davis, Jr.
John H. Baird	Billy R. Shelton
Charles J. Baird	Sam A. Carter
Paul Edward Jones	Lois A. Kitts
Terri Smith Walters	Virginia Baird Gannon

Representative Clients: Pikeville National Bank & Trust Co.; LP Big Sandy Co., Massachusetts; Coal Operators & Associates; Norfolk & Southern Railway Co.; Maryland Casualty Co.; Royal Globe Insurance Co.; The St. Paul Cos.
Approved Attorneys for: Lawyers Title Insurance Corp.

For full biographical listings, see the Martindale-Hubbell Law Directory

STRATTON, MAY, HAYS & HOGG, PSC (AV)

232 Second Street Ward Building, P.O. Box 851, 41502
Telephone: 606-437-7300
Fax: 606-437-7569
Whitesburg, Kentucky Office: By-Pass Highway 15. 41858.
Telephone: 606-633-9922.

Henry D. Stratton (1925-1989)	Stephen L. Hogg
Marrs Allen May	H. Edward Maddox
John D. Hays	F. Byrd Hogg (Resident,
David C. Stratton	Whitesburg, Kentucky Office)

LEGAL SUPPORT PERSONNEL
PARALEGALS

Carol Rowe Potter	Rebecca Branham
(Real Estate Paralegal)	(Litigation Paralegal)

General Counsel for: Trans Financial Bank of Pikeville.
Representative Clients: Virginia Iron Coal & Coke Co.; Commercial Union Insurance Co.; The Travelers Insurance Co.; Universal Underwriters Insurance Co.; Bituminous Casualty Co.; Enterprise Coal Company; South Central Bell; Scottsdale Insurance Co.
Reference: Transfinancial Bank, Pikeville.

For full biographical listings, see the Martindale-Hubbell Law Directory

PRESTONSBURG,* Floyd Co.

COMBS AND ISAAC (AV)

99 North Lake Drive, P.O. Box 189, 41653
Telephone: 606-886-2391; 886-2392
Fax: 606-886-2776

MEMBERS OF FIRM

James A. Combs	Gregory A. Isaac

For full biographical listings, see the Martindale-Hubbell Law Directory

KAZEE, KINNER & CHAFIN (AV)

119 East Court Street, P.O. Box 700, 41653
Telephone: 606-886-2361; 886-2362
FAX: 606-886-9603
Email: dbkazee@pcc-uky.campus.mci.net
Paintsville, Kentucky Office: Family Federal Building, Suite 202, P.O. Box 1275.
Telephone: 606-789-3059.

MEMBERS OF FIRM

D. B. Kazee	P. Franklin Heaberlin
Mitchell D. Kinner	Robert J. Patton
John T. Chafin	William C. Mullins

Representative Clients: Island Creek Coal Co.; The Elk Horn Coal Corp.; First Commonwealth Bank; Old Republic Insurance Co.; Zurich American Insurance Co.; Maryland Casualty Co.; Bituminous Casualty Corp.; Mack Financial Corp.; Nationwide Insurance; Kentucky May Coal Co., Inc.

For full biographical listings, see the Martindale-Hubbell Law Directory

PRINCETON,* Caldwell Co. — (Refer to Madisonville)

RICHMOND,* Madison Co.

COY, GILBERT & GILBERT (AV)

212 North Second Street, 40475
Telephone: 606-623-3877
Fax: 606-624-5435

MEMBERS OF FIRM

Charles R. Coy	Jerry W. Gilbert
James T. Gilbert	Sandra A. Bolin
	Mark A. Shepherd

General Counsel: Peoples Bank and Trust Co. of Madison County.

For full biographical listings, see the Martindale-Hubbell Law Directory

SHUMATE, FLAHERTY & EUBANKS (AV)

Formerly Shumate, Shumate & Flaherty
225 West Irvine Street, P.O. Box 157, 40476-0157
Telephone: 606-623-3049
Fax: 606-623-6406

MEMBERS OF FIRM

Hunter M. Shumate (1893-1971)	Peter J. Flaherty (1920-1978)
Thomas D. Shumate (1906-1978)	Peter J. Flaherty III
	Michael F. Eubanks

General Counsel for: Peoples Rural Telephone Cooperative Corp., McKee, Ky.

For full biographical listings, see the Martindale-Hubbell Law Directory

SALYERSVILLE,* Magoffin Co. — (Refer to Paintsville)

SANDY HOOK,* Elliott Co. — (Refer to Paintsville)

SCOTTSVILLE,* Allen Co. — (Refer to Bowling Green)

SMITHLAND,* Livingston Co. — (Refer to Paducah)

SOMERSET,* Pulaski Co.

THE FIRM OF JOHN G. PRATHER (AV)

Prather Building, P.O. Box 616, 42502-0616
Telephone: 606-679-1626; 679-4838; 678-5604
FAX: 606-679-8204

MEMBERS OF FIRM

John G. Prather	John G. Prather, Jr.
	Winter R. Huff (Ms.)

Representative Clients: First & Farmers Bank of Somerset; Aetna Casualty & Surety Co.; Continental Group; Sentry-Dairyland Insurance; Employers Group; Hartford Accident & Indemnity; Kemper Insurance Co.; Underwriters Adjusting Co.; Pulaski County Water District #2; Security Insurance Group.

For full biographical listings, see the Martindale-Hubbell Law Directory

SPRINGFIELD,* Washington Co. — (Refer to Bardstown)

STANFORD,* Lincoln Co. — (Refer to Danville)

STANTON,* Powell Co. — (Refer to Mount Sterling)

TAYLORSVILLE,* Spencer Co. — (Refer to Bardstown)

TOMPKINSVILLE,* Monroe Co. — (Refer to Glasgow)

WARSAW,* Gallatin Co. — (Refer to Frankfort)

WHITESBURG,* Letcher Co. — (Refer to Pikeville)

WHITLEY CITY,* McCreary Co. — (Refer to Somerset)

WICKLIFFE,* Ballard Co. — (Refer to Mayfield)

WINCHESTER,* Clark Co. — (Refer to Lexington)

LOUISIANA

*ABBEVILLE,** Vermilion Parish — (Refer to New Iberia)

*ALEXANDRIA,** Rapides Parish

GOLD, WEEMS, BRUSER, SUES & RUNDELL, A PROFESSIONAL LAW CORPORATION (AV)

2001 MacArthur Drive, P.O. Box 6118, 71307-6118
Telephone: 318-445-6471
Telecopier: 318-445-6476

Leo Gold (1907-1987)	Thomas K. Brocato
George B. Hall (1924-1971)	James Ogden Middleton, II
Charles S. Weems, III	Randall L. Wilmore
Henry B. Bruser, III	Dorrell Jarrell Brister
Eugene J. Sues	Carolyn J. Smilie
Edward E. Rundell	Gregory B. Upton
Robert G. Nida	Randall M. Seeser
Dee Dodson Drell	J. Michael Chamblee
Sam N. Poole, Jr.	Charles D. Elliott
Peggy Dean St. John	J. Kendall Rathburn
Kenneth O. Ortego	J. Christopher Peters
Raymond L. Brown, Jr.	Christin D. Bordelon

Amanda Wood Barnett

OF COUNSEL

Camille F. Gravel

Representative Clients: Automated Prescription Systems, Inc.; Roy O. Martin Lumber Co., Inc.; Rapides Bank & Trust Company in Alexandria; Aetna Casualty Group; Allstate Insurance Co.; Texas Industries, Inc.; International Paper Company; Louisiana-Pacific Corporation.

For full biographical listings, see the Martindale-Hubbell Law Directory

PROVOSTY, SADLER & DELAUNAY (AV)

7th Through 10th Floors Hibernia National Bank Building, 934 Third Street, P.O. Drawer 1791, 71309-1791
Telephone: 318-445-3631
Telecopier: 318-445-9377

MEMBERS OF FIRM

LeDoux R. Provosty (1894-1980)	David P. Spence
Richard B. Sadler, Jr. (1912-1990)	Frederick B. Alexius
	Stephen D. Wheelis
LeDoux R. Provosty, Jr. (1930-1995)	David R. Sobel
	Ricky L. Sooter
William H. deLaunay, Jr.	Andrew E. Schaffer
Albin A. Provosty, III	Jeffrey A. Riggs
H. Brenner Sadler	Joseph J. Bailey
Ronald J. Fiorenza	H. Bradford Calvit
	John P. Doggett

ASSOCIATES

Catherine G. Brame	Bryan Scott Cowart
Gregory L. Jones	Richard B. Rozanski

John Ryland

Local Counsel for: Central Louisiana Electric Company Inc.; Prudential Insurance Company of America; Dresser Industries, Inc.; Missouri Pacific Railroad Co.; Louisiana Intrastate Gas Co.; Insurance Company of North America; American Indemnity Group; The Haliburton Cos.; E. I. DuPont DeNemours Co.; St. Francis Cabrini Hospital.

For full biographical listings, see the Martindale-Hubbell Law Directory

*AMITE,** Tangipahoa Parish — (Refer to Hammond)

*ARCADIA,** Bienville Parish — (Refer to Ruston)

*BASTROP,** Morehouse Parish — (Refer to Monroe)

*BATON ROUGE,** East Baton Rouge Parish

BREAZEALE, SACHSE & WILSON, L.L.P. (AV)

Twenty-Third Floor, One American Place, P.O. Box 3197, 70821-3197
Telephone: 504-387-4000
Fax: 504-387-5397
New Orleans, Louisiana Office: LL&E Tower, Suite 2400, 909 Poydras Street.
Telephone: 504-582-1170.
Fax: 504-584-5452.

MEMBERS OF FIRM

H. Payne Breazeale (1886-1990)	Van R. Mayhall, Jr.
Victor A. Sachse, Jr. (1903-1979)	Leonard R. Nachman, II
Maurice J. Wilson (1919-1990)	Claude F. Reynaud, Jr.
H. Payne Breazeale, Jr. (1920-1979)	John J. Cooper (Resident, New Orleans Office)
Victor A. Sachse, III	Murphy J. Foster, III
Gordon A. Pugh	David R. Cassidy
James E. Toups, Jr.	Robert T. Bowsher
Paul M. Hebert, Jr.	Christine Lipsey

(See Next Column)

MEMBERS OF FIRM (Continued)

David R. Kelly	John W. Barton, Jr.
Cecil J. Blache	Joseph E. Friend (Resident, New Orleans Office)
Robert L. Atkinson	
David M. Charlton	Frank S. Craig, III
Douglas K. Williams	Jude C. Bursavich
Stephen F. Chiccarelli	Gary L. Laborde (Resident, New Orleans Office)
Emile C. Rolfs, III	
John F. Whitney (Resident, New Orleans Office)	Jon C. Adcock
	Leo C. Hamilton
John E. Heinrich	Gayla M. Moncla
Richard D. Leibowitz	Steven B. Loeb
Michael R. Hubbell	James R. Chastain, Jr.

ASSOCIATES

J. Mark Robinson	Elizabeth Sherman Cox
Linda Perez Clark	Andrew J. Harrison, Jr.
Trenton J. Oubre	Matthew M. Courtman
Gwen Petit Harmon	Andrew T. McMains
Luis A. Leitzelar	Wendy E. Wiseman
Jerry L. Stovall, Jr.	Cullen J. Dupuy
Jeanne C. Comeaux	Avery Lea Griffin (Resident, New Orleans Office)
Michael A. Crawford	

Joseph P. Titone

Counsel for: Hibernia National Bank; South Central Bell Telephone Co.; Allied-Signal Corp.; Reynolds Metal Co.; Illinois Central Railroad Co.; The Continental Insurance Cos.; Fireman's Fund American Group; Chicago Bridge & Iron Co.; Montgomery Ward & Co.

For full biographical listings, see the Martindale-Hubbell Law Directory

FUNDERBURK & ANDREWS (AV)

329 St. Ferdinand Street, 70802
Telephone: 504-387-2200
Fax: 504-383-0142

MEMBERS OF FIRM

Robert C. Funderburk, Jr.	David T. Butler, Jr.
Arthur H. Andrews	Scott H. Frugé

For full biographical listings, see the Martindale-Hubbell Law Directory

GUGLIELMO, MARKS, SCHUTTE, TERHOEVE & LOVE (AV)

(A Registered Limited Liability Partnership)
320 Somerulos Street, P.O. Box 3177, 70821-3177
Telephone: 504-387-6966
Fax: 504-387-8338

Carey J. Guglielmo	Glen Scott Love
Paul Marks, Jr.	Dawn T. Trabeau-Mire
Charles A. Schutte, Jr.	Joseph W. Mengis
Henry G. Terhoeve	Kevin P. Landreneau

Representative Clients: City National Bank; Greyhound Corp.; The Travelers Insurance Co.; Chrysler Corp.; State Farm Insurance Co's.; Travelers/Aetna Insurance Group; Aetna Life & Casualty Co.

For full biographical listings, see the Martindale-Hubbell Law Directory

KANTROW, SPAHT, WEAVER & BLITZER, A PROFESSIONAL LAW CORPORATION (AV)

Suite 300, City Plaza, 445 North Boulevard, P.O. Box 2997, 70821-2997
Telephone: 504-383-4703
Fax: 504-343-0630; 343-0637

Byron R. Kantrow	Vincent P. Fornias
Carlos G. Spaht	David S. Rubin
Geraldine B. Weaver	Diane L. Crochet
Sidney M. Blitzer, Jr.	Richard F. Zimmerman, Jr.
Paul H. Spaht	Bob D. Tucker
Lee C. Kantrow	Martin E. Golden
John C. Miller	Joseph A. Schittone, Jr.

S. Layne Lee	Connell L. Archey
J. Michael Robinson, Jr.	Randal J. Robert

Representative Clients: CNA Insurance Cos.; Federal Deposit Insurance Corp.; Hartford Insurance Group; Air Products and Chemicals, Inc.; CF Industries, Inc.; AT&T; United Companies Financial Corp.

For full biographical listings, see the Martindale-Hubbell Law Directory

KEAN, MILLER, HAWTHORNE, D'ARMOND, McCOWAN & JARMAN, L.L.P. (AV)

22nd Floor, One American Place, P.O. Box 3513, 70821
Telephone: 504-387-0999
Fax: 504-388-9133
New Orleans, Louisiana Office: Energy Centre, Suite 1470, 1100 Poydras Street.
Telephone: 504-585-3050.
Fax: 504-585-3051.
Plaquemine, Louisiana Office: Suite 10, 23425 Railroad Avenue.
Telephone: 504-687-9845.
Fax: 504-382-3445.

(See Next Column)

KEAN, MILLER, HAWTHORNE, D'ARMOND, McCOWAN & JARMAN L.L.P.,
Baton Rouge—Continued

MEMBERS OF FIRM

R. Gordon Kean, Jr. (1919-1992)	James R. Lackie
	David K. Nelson
Ben R. Miller, Jr.	J. Carter Wilkinson
Robert A. Hawthorne, Jr.	Sandra L. Edwards
William R. D'Armond	Bradley C. Myers
Charles S. McCowan, Jr.	Melanie M. Hartmann
G. William Jarman	Linda Sarradet Akchin
Leonard L. Kilgore III	James P. Doré
Gary A. Bezet	Erich P. Rapp
Carey J. Messina	Charles L. Patin, Jr.
Michael C. Garrard	Mathile W. Abramson
Vance A. Gibbs	Cynthia M. Chemay
Isaac M. Gregorie, Jr.	Todd A. Rossi
Maureen N. Harbourt	Katherine W. King
G. Blane Clark, Jr.	Gregg R. Kronenberger
M. Dwayne Johnson	Charles S. McCowan III

Jay M. Jalenak, Jr.

Kelly Wilkinson	Robert E. Dille
Ray C. Dawson	Murray A. Greene
Belinda B. LeBlanc	Julie Parelman Silbert (Resident, New Orleans Office)
Linda G. Rodrigue	
Theresa R. Hagen	Carolyn S. Parmenter
Glenn M. Farnet	Stephen M. Robinson
Esteban Herrera, Jr.	John W. Adams
Susan Knight Carter (Resident, New Orleans Office)	Connor B. Eglin
	Alan J. Berteau
J. Randy Young	Jean Ann Tolleson
John F. Jakuback	Robert H. Abbott, III
Barrye Panepinto Miyagi	Dean Paul Cazenave
L. Victor Gregoire	Kevin C. Curry
Mark D. Mese	Gordon D. Polozola
Robert M. Hoyland	Lana D. Davis
Mark A. Marionneaux	Gregory M. Anding
Gary P. Graphia	Troy J. Charpentier

SPECIAL COUNSEL

Gerald Le Van

OF COUNSEL

Reilly L. Stonecipher

LEGAL SUPPORT PERSONNEL

Yuxian Wang

Representative Clients: DSM Copolymer, Inc., Baton Rouge, LA; Exxon Corporation, Baton Rouge, LA; Georgia-Pacific Corporation, Atlanta, GA; Hancock Bank of Louisiana, Baton Rouge, LA; Lamar Advertising Company, Baton Rouge, LA; Louisiana Municipal Risk Management Agency, Baton Rouge, LA; Piccadilly Cafeterias, Inc., Baton Rouge, LA; Premier Bank, National Association, Baton Rouge, LA; Transcontinental Gas Pipeline Company, Houston, TX.

For full biographical listings, see the Martindale-Hubbell Law Directory

PHELPS DUNBAR, L.L.P. (AV)

Suite 701, City National Bank Building, P.O. Box 4412, 70821-4412
Telephone: 504-346-0285
Telecopier: 504-381-9197
Email: info@phelps.com
New Orleans, Louisiana Office: Texaco Center, 400 Poydras Street.
Telephone 504-566-1311.
Telecopier: 504-568-9130; 504-568-9007.
Cable Address: "Howspencer."
Telex: 584125 WU.
Telex: 6821155 WUI.
Jackson, Mississippi Office: Suite 500, Mtel Centré, 200 South Lamar Street, P.O. Box 23066.
Telephone: 601-352-2300.
Telecopier: 601-360-9777.
Tupelo, Mississippi Office: Seventh Floor, One Mississippi Plaza, P.O. Box 1220.
Telephone: 601-842-7907.
Telecopier: 601-842-3873.
Houston, Texas Office: Suite 900, 3040 Post Oak Boulevard.
Telephone: 713-626-1386.
Telecopier: 713-626-1388.
London, England Office: Suite 731, Level 7, Lloyd's, 1 Lime Street, London EC3M 7DQ England.
Telephone: 011-44-171-929-4765.
Telecopier: 011-44-171-929-0046.
Telex: 987321.

OF COUNSEL

Frank S. Craig, Jr.

(See Next Column)

RESIDENT PARTNERS

H. Alston Johnson, III	Steven J. Levine
Michael D. Hunt	Allen D. Darden
Jennifer Bowers Zimmerman	Randy P. Roussel
F. Scott Kaiser	Jonathan C. Benda
Richard E. Matheny	Thomas H. Kiggans

Marshall M. Redmon

COUNSEL

J. Michael Cutshaw	E. Jane Sherman

Jane A. Robert

RESIDENT ASSOCIATES

Jane H. Barney	Tricia A. Martinez
Rebecca Bellows Crawford	Patrick O'Hara
Susan W. Furr	John Whitney Pesnell
Margaret (Amie) Kozan	Patrick Ragan Richard
Darrell J. Loup	Diane Fagan Robinson

Representative Clients: Blue Cross & Blue Shield of Mississippi; City National Bank of Baton Rouge; Hibernia National Bank; Louisiana Companies; Louisiana Lottery Corporation; Louisiana Workers' Compensation Corporation; Missouri Pacific Railroad Co.; OHM Corporation; The Travelers Insurance Company; Uniroyal Chemical Company.

For full biographical listings, see the Martindale-Hubbell Law Directory

POWERS, CLEGG & WILLARD (AV)

7967 Office Park Boulevard, P.O. Box 15948, 70895
Telephone: 504-928-1951
Telecopier: 504-929-9834

MEMBERS OF FIRM

John Dale Powers	Michael V. Clegg

William E. Willard

ASSOCIATES

Neil H. Mixon	Robert J. Daigre
Mary A. Cazes	Nicholas Soileau

General Counsel for: Audubon Insurance Co.
Louisiana Counsel for: Hancock Bank & Trust Co.; Hertz Corp.; Ciba-Geigy Corp.; Utica Mutual Insurance Co.

For full biographical listings, see the Martindale-Hubbell Law Directory

TAYLOR, PORTER, BROOKS & PHILLIPS (AV)

Bank One Centre, 8th Floor, 451 Florida Street, P.O. Box 2471, 70821
Telephone: 504-387-3221
Telecopier: 504-346-8049
New Orleans, Louisiana Office: Pan-American Life Center, 601 Poydras Street, Suite 2415.
Telephone: 504-524-1956.
Fax: 504-522-1810.

OF COUNSEL

Robert J. Vandaworker	Frank M. Coates, Jr.

MEMBERS OF FIRM

Benjamin Brown Taylor (1885-1959)	W. Arthur Abercrombie, Jr.
	Fredrick R. Tulley
Charles Vernon Porter (1885-1962)	Vernon P. Middleton
	James L. Ellis
Laurance Waddill Brooks (1900-1971)	John Michael Parker
	Nancy C. Dougherty
Benjamin Brown Taylor, Jr. (1913-1990)	Mary E. Tharp
	J. Ashley Moore
Frank W. Middleton, Jr. (1919-1993)	Edwin W. Fleshman
	Vicki M. Crochet
Charles Worsham Phillips (1911-1995)	Harry J. Philips, Jr.
	Lloyd J. Lunceford
Tom F. Phillips	Thomas R. Peak
John I. Moore	C. Michael Hart
William H. McClendon, III	John F. McDermott
William A. Norfolk	Brett P. Furr
William Shelby McKenzie	M. Lenore Feeney
John S. Campbell, Jr.	Marc S. Whitfield
Robert H. Hodges	John H. Runnels
John L. Glover	David J. Messina (Resident, New Orleans Office)
John R. Tharp	
W. Luther Wilson	Gregory E. Bodin
J. Clayton Johnson	James C. Carver
G. Michael Pharis	Margaret L. Tooke
Eugene R. Groves	Deborah E. Lamb
A. Michael Dufilho	T. MacDougall Womack

ASSOCIATES

Kathleen C. Mason	Robert W. Barton
David H. Hanchey	Preston J. Castille, Jr.
David M. Bienvenu, Jr.	Eleanor Owen Kerr
Paul J. Ory (Resident, New Orleans Office)	Courtney S. De Blieux
	John Stewart Tharp
David J. Shelby, II	John S. Campbell, III
Erick Y. Miyagi	John P. Murrill
Jayne L. Middleton	Bonnie J. Davis

Mary Dougherty Jackson

(See Next Column)

TAYLOR, PORTER, BROOKS & PHILLIPS—*Continued*

General Counsel for: Baton Rouge Broadcasting Co.; Baton Rouge Water Works Co.; Louisiana State University and A. and M. College; Louisiana Television Broadcasting Co.; Our Lady of the Lake Hospital, Inc.; Pennington Biomedical Research Foundation; The Newton Group.

For full biographical listings, see the Martindale-Hubbell Law Directory

---

BUNKIE, Avoyelles Parish — (Refer to Marksville)

CAMERON, * Cameron Parish — (Refer to Lake Charles)

CLINTON, * East Feliciana Parish — (Refer to Baton Rouge)

COLUMBIA, * Caldwell Parish — (Refer to Monroe)

COUSHATTA, * Red River Parish — (Refer to Natchitoches)

CROWLEY, * Acadia Parish

BAROUSSE & CRATON (AV)

211 North Parkerson Avenue, P.O. Drawer 1305, 70527-1305
Telephone: 318-785-1000
Facsimile: 318-788-3219

MEMBERS OF FIRM

Homer Ed Barousse, Jr.   John F. Craton

Representative Clients: First Bank, N.A. of Crowley and Lake Charles; Francis Drilling Fluids, Ltd.; Farm Credit Bank of Texas; First South Production Credit Association; J.I. Case Credit Corporation; Louisiana Sheriffs' Association; Broussard Rice Mill, Inc.; Mermentau River Harbor and Terminal District; Farm Service Agency.

For full biographical listings, see the Martindale-Hubbell Law Directory

---

DE RIDDER, * Beauregard Parish

HALL, LESTAGE & LANDRENEAU (AV)

205 Second Street, P.O. Box 880, 70634
Telephone: 318-463-8692
Fax: 318-463-2272

MEMBERS OF FIRM

William E. Hall, Jr.   David R. Lestage
H. O. Lestage, III   F. Steve Landreneau
             Brian S. Lestage

Representative Clients: Boise Cascade Corp.; City Savings & Trust Co.; Crosby Land Resources; Firemen's Fund-American Cos.; Great American Insurance Co.; The Hartford Insurance Group; Pacific Marine Insurance Co.; State Farm Mutual Automobile Insurance Co.; The Travelers Insurance Co.; United States Fidelity & Guaranty Co.

For full biographical listings, see the Martindale-Hubbell Law Directory

---

DONALDSONVILLE, * Ascension Parish — (Refer to Plaquemine)

FRANKLIN, * St. Mary Parish

AYCOCK, HORNE & COLEMAN (AV)

519 Main Street, P.O. Box 592, 70538
Telephone: 318-828-1880
Fax: 318-828-2232
Morgan City, Louisiana Office: 1304 Victor II Boulevard, P.O. Box 1700.
Telephone: 504-384-4523.

MEMBERS OF FIRM

Clarence C. Aycock (1916-1987)   James R. McClelland
John E. Coleman, Jr.   Andrew Reed

OF COUNSEL

Tom Lee Horne, Jr.

Representative Clients: St. Mary Bank & Trust Co.; M.c. Bank & Trust Co.; South Central Bell Telephone Co.; Cotten Land Corp.; Bayou Bouillon Corp.; Meritrust Federal Savings Bank; St. Mary Galvanizing Corp.

For full biographical listings, see the Martindale-Hubbell Law Directory

---

FRANKLINTON, * Washington Parish — (Refer to Bogalusa)

GRETNA, * Jefferson Parish — (Refer to New Orleans)

JENNINGS, * Jefferson Davis Parish — (Refer to Lake Charles)

JONESBORO, * Jackson Parish — (Refer to Ruston)

LAFAYETTE, * Lafayette Parish

DAVIDSON, MEAUX, SONNIER, McELLIGOTT & SWIFT (AV)

810 South Buchanan Street, P.O. Drawer 2908, 70502
Telephone: 318-237-1660
Fax: 318-237-3676

(See Next Column)

MEMBERS OF FIRM

James J. Davidson, Jr.   John E. McElligott, Jr.
 (1904-1990)   John G. Swift
V. Farley Sonnier (1942-1988)   Jeffrey A. Rhoades
Richard C. Meaux, Sr.   Philip A. Fontenot
James J. Davidson, III   Kyle L. Gideon
         Theodore G. Edwards, IV

ASSOCIATES

Jhan C. Boudreaux Beaullieu   Mark C. Andrus

OF COUNSEL

Jan Whitehead Swift

General Counsel: Southwest Louisiana Electric Membership Corp., Inc.; Macro Oil Co., Inc.; Dwight W. Andrus Insurance Agency; Lafayette Airport Commission.
Local Counsel: Southern Pacific Transportation Co.
Representative Clients: Highlands Insurance Co.; Wal-Mart Stores, Inc.; USAA.

For full biographical listings, see the Martindale-Hubbell Law Directory

LAWRENCE E. DONOHOE, JR. (AV)

First National Bank Tower, 600 Jefferson, Suite 1210, 70501
Telephone: 318-266-2170
Fax: 318-234-6644

For full biographical listings, see the Martindale-Hubbell Law Directory

HILL & BEYER, A PROFESSIONAL LAW CORPORATION (AV)

101 LaRue France, Suite 502, P.O. Box 53006, 70505-3006
Telephone: 318-232-9733
Fax: 1-318-237-2566

John K. Hill, Jr.   Eugene P. Matherne (1962-1996)
Bret C. Beyer   Robert B. Purser
David R. Rabalais   Erin J. Sherburne
          Marianna Broussard

For full biographical listings, see the Martindale-Hubbell Law Directory

HOLLIER & RINGUET, A PROFESSIONAL LAW CORPORATION (AV)

302 Rue France, Suite 201, P.O. Box 52647, 70505
Telephone: 318-232-0002
Fax: 318-232-3410
Jennings, Louisiana Office: 227 North Main Street, 70546.
Telephone: 318-824-2000.

William C. Hollier   James L. Daniels
Reginald J. Ringuet   William H. Collier

Representative Clients: Acadiana Medical Laboratories, LTD.; Allied Finance Company of Louisiana, Inc.; Carrollton Resources Corporation; Chevron U.S.A., Inc.; Dependable Insurance Company; Forest Oil Corp.; Goodrich Operating Company, Inc.; Ron Guidry Enterprises, Inc.; Gulf States Utilities Co.

For full biographical listings, see the Martindale-Hubbell Law Directory

RICHARD R. KENNEDY A PROFESSIONAL LAW CORPORATION (AV)

309 Polk Street, P.O. Box 3243, 70502-3243
Telephone: 318-232-1934
Fax: 318-232-9720
Email: kennedy@net-connect.net

Richard R. Kennedy

For full biographical listings, see the Martindale-Hubbell Law Directory

THE LABORDE LAW FIRM, L.L.C. (AV)

3861 Ambassador Caffery Parkway, Suite 602, 70503
Telephone: 318-981-5959; 1-800-LABORDE
Fax: 318-981-7291

Paulin J. Laborde, Jr.   David C. Laborde

For full biographical listings, see the Martindale-Hubbell Law Directory

LISKOW & LEWIS, A PROFESSIONAL LAW CORPORATION (AV)

822 Harding Street, P.O. Box 52008, 70505
Telephone: 318-232-7424
Telecopier: 318-267-2399
New Orleans, Louisiana Office: 50th Floor, One Shell Square.
Telephone: 504-581-7979.
Telecopier: 504-592-5108; 504-592-5109.

RESIDENT PERSONNEL

Cullen R. Liskow (1893-1971)   Joseph C. Giglio, Jr.
Austin W. Lewis (1910-1974)   Patrick W. Gray
Thomas D. Hardeman   Thomas M. McNamara
Lawrence P. Simon, Jr.   James N. Mansfield, III
George H. Robinson, Jr.   Billy J. Domingue

(See Next Column)

LISKOW & LEWIS A PROFESSIONAL LAW CORPORATION, *Lafayette—Continued*

RESIDENT PERSONNEL (Continued)

Charles B. Griffis, III	Mark A. Lowe
Richard W. Revels, Jr.	George Arceneaux III
Joseph P. Hebert	Carmen M. Rodriguez

OF COUNSEL

Robert T. Jorden	James L. Pelletier

Matt Jones

Representative Clients: Amerada Hess Corp.; Amoco Corporation; Bank One; BP America Inc.; Hibernia National Bank; Hunt Oil Company; Louisiana Public Service Commission; Mobil Oil Corp.; OXY U.S.A. Inc.; Union Oil Company of California; Union Pacific Resources Company.

For full biographical listings, see the Martindale-Hubbell Law Directory

---

ONEBANE, BERNARD, TORIAN, DIAZ, MCNAMARA & ABELL (AV)

Suite 600, Versailles Centre, 102 Versailles Boulevard, P.O. Box 3507, 70502
Telephone: 318-237-2660
Telecopier: 318-266-1232
Cable Address: "Ondob"
Telex: 311283
Email: info@onebane.com

Joseph Onebane (1917-1987)	Joseph L. Lemoine, Jr.
John G. Torian, II (1936-1991)	Mark L. Riley
James E. Diaz	Graham N. Smith
Timothy J. McNamara	Gordon T. Whitman
Edward C. Abell, Jr.	Gary P. Kraus
Lawrence L. Lewis, III	Richard J. Petre, Jr.
Robert M. Mahony	Thomas G. Smart
Daniel G. Fournerat	Roger E. Ishee
Douglas W. Truxillo	John W. Penny, Jr.
Randall C. Songy	John A. Keller
Michael G. Durand	Jennifer McDaniel Kleinpeter
Greg Guidry	Steven C. Lanza

Joel P. Babineaux	Charles M. Gordon, Jr.
Ted M. Anthony	Brent G. Sonnier
Carolyn Trahan Bertrand	John D. Brouillette
Alison M. Brumley	Cristie L. Gautreaux
Craig A. Davis	Elise Mayers Bouchner
Jesse D. Lambert	(Not admitted in LA)

Cary B. Bryson

Representative Clients: Commercial Union Insurance Co.; Enron Corp.; First National Bank of Lafayette; Flores & Rucks, Inc.; Highlands Insurance Co.; Marathon Oil Co.; Pizza Hut, Inc.; Schering-Plough Corp.; Tenneco, Inc.; Whitney National Bank.

For full biographical listings, see the Martindale-Hubbell Law Directory

---

ROY, BIVINS, JUDICE & HENKE, A PROFESSIONAL LAW CORPORATION (AV)

600 Jefferson Street, Suite 800, P.O. Drawer Z, 70502
Telephone: 318-233-7430
Telecopier: 318-233-8403

Harmon F. Roy	Kenneth M. Henke
John A. Bivins	W. Alan Lilley
Ronald J. Judice	Philip E. Roberts

Patrick M. Wartelle

Representative Clients: Employers Insurance of Wausau; Louisiana Medical Mutual Insurance Co.; Aetna Casualty & Surety; Zurich Insurance Co.; Our Lady of Lourdes Regional Medical Center, Inc.; St Paul Fire & Marine Insurance Co.; First Financial Insurance Co.; Great Lakes Chemical; OSCA; Olsten Services, Inc.

For full biographical listings, see the Martindale-Hubbell Law Directory

---

SALOOM & SALOOM (AV)

211 West Main Street, P.O. Drawer 2999, 70502-2999
Telephone: 318-234-0111
Fax: 318-232-4144
Email: kalsal@aol.com

Kaliste J. Saloom, Jr.	Kaliste J. Saloom III

Gregory J. Saloom

Representative Clients: Sears, Roebuck and Co.; Flowers Industries; Huval Bakery, Inc.; Weatherford U.S., Inc.; Veteran Administration, Property Management Division; U.S. Dept. of Justice Private Counsel (litigation/collection); People's Enterprises.
References: First National Bank of Lafayette, Louisiana; Premier Bank of Lafayette, Inc.; LBA Savings Bank, Lafayette, Louisiana.

For full biographical listings, see the Martindale-Hubbell Law Directory

---

LAKE CHARLES, * Calcasieu Parish

BAGGETT, MCCALL & BURGESS, A PROFESSIONAL LAW CORPORATION (AV)

3006 Country Club Road, P.O. Drawer 7820, 70606-7820
Telephone: 318-478-8888
Fax: 318-478-8946
Email: bmblf@mail.maas.net

William B. Baggett	Jeffrey T. Gaughan
Robert C. McCall	Erin McCall Alley
William B. Baggett, Jr.	Christopher C. McCall
Roger G. Burgess	Nancy Jo Dougherty
Wells T. Watson	(Not admitted in LA)

For full biographical listings, see the Martindale-Hubbell Law Directory

---

BERGSTEDT & MOUNT (AV)

Second Floor, Magnolia Life Building, P.O. Drawer 3004, 70602-3004
Telephone: 318-433-3004
Facsimile: 318-433-8080

MEMBERS OF FIRM

Thomas M. Bergstedt	Benjamin W. Mount

ASSOCIATES

Van C. Seneca	Gregory P. Marceaux

Billy E. Loftin, Jr.

OF COUNSEL

Charles S. Ware

Representative Clients: Armstrong World Industries; Ashland Oil Co.; CIGNA Property & Casualty Companies; Homequity; Lake Area Medical Center; Leach Company; Olin Corporation; Terra Corporation; Town of Iowa; R. D. Werner Company.

For full biographical listings, see the Martindale-Hubbell Law Directory

---

JONES, TÊTE, NOLEN, HANCHEY, SWIFT, SPEARS & FONTI, L.L.P. (AV)

First Federal Building, P.O. Box 910, 70602
Telephone: 318-439-8315
Telefax: 436-5606; 433-5536

MEMBERS OF FIRM

Sam H. Jones (1897-1978)	Kenneth R. Spears
William R. Tête	Edward J. Fonti
William M. Nolen	Charles N. Harper
James C. Hanchey	Gregory W. Belfour
Carl H. Hanchey	Robert J. Tête
William B. Swift	Yul D. Lorio

OF COUNSEL

John A. Patin	Edward D. Myrick

ASSOCIATE

Lilynn A. Cutrer

General Counsel for: First Federal Savings & Loan Association of Lake Charles; Beauregard Electric Cooperative, Inc.
Representative Clients: Atlantic Richfield Company; CITGO Petroleum Corp.; Conoco Inc.; MONTELL U.S.A., Inc.; ITT Hartford; Olin Corporation; OXY USA Inc.; Premier Bank, National Association; W.R. Grace & Co.

For full biographical listings, see the Martindale-Hubbell Law Directory

---

PLAUCHÉ SMITH & NIESET, A PROFESSIONAL LAW CORPORATION (AV)

1123 Pithon Street, P.O. Drawer 1705, 70602
Telephone: 318-436-0522
Facsimile: 318-436-9637

S. W. Plauché (1889-1952)	Jeffrey M. Cole
S. W. Plauché, Jr. (1915-1966)	Andrew R. Johnson, IV
A. Lane Plauché	Charles V. Musso, Jr.
Allen L. Smith, Jr.	Christopher P. Ieyoub
James R. Nieset	H. David Vaughan, II
Frank M. Walker, Jr.	Joseph R. Pousson, Jr.
Michael J. McNulty, III	Rebecca S. Young

Representative Clients: CIGNA; CNA Insurance Cos.; Commercial Union Insurance Cos.; Crum & Forster; General Motors Corp.; Reliance Insurance Cos.; Royal Insurance Group; State Farm; U.S. Insurance Group.

For full biographical listings, see the Martindale-Hubbell Law Directory

---

RAGGIO, CAPPEL, CHOZEN & BERNIARD (AV)

500 Magnolia Life Building, P.O. Box 820, 70601
Telephone: 318-436-9481
Fax: 318-436-9499

(See Next Column)

RAGGIO, CAPPEL, CHOZEN & BERNIARD—*Continued*

MEMBERS OF FIRM

Alvin O. King (1890-1958)	Richard A. Chozen
Thomas C. Hall (1919-1973)	Stephen A. Berniard, Jr.
Thomas L. Raggio (Retired)	Christopher M. Trahan
Richard B. Cappel	L. Paul Foreman
Frederick L. Cappel	Kevin J. Koenig

Counsel for: Aetna Casualty & Surety Co.; Allstate Insurance Co.; Hercules Incorporated; Liberty Mutual Insurance Co.; Southern Pacific Co.; United States Fidelity and Guaranty Co.; Crowley Maritime Corp.; General Motors Corp.; Sabine Towing & Transportation Co.; E. I. duPont de Nemours & Co., Inc.

For full biographical listings, see the Martindale-Hubbell Law Directory

---

SCOFIELD, GERARD, VERON, SINGLETARY & POHORELSKY, A PROFESSIONAL LAW CORPORATION (AV)

1114 Ryan Street, P.O. Drawer 3028, 70601
Telephone: 318-433-9436
Telefax: 318-436-0306

John B. Scofield	John R. Pohorelsky
Richard E. Gerard, Jr.	Scott J. Scofield
J. Michael Veron	Patrick D. Gallaugher, Jr.
C. Eston Singletary	Robert E. Landry
Russell J. Stutes, Jr.	

Representative Clients: Admiral Insurance Co.; Amoco Production Co.; Banc One; Browning-Ferris Industries, Inc.; Brown & Root Construction Co.; Cosmos Broadcasting Corp.; Dresser Industries, Inc.; Kansas City Southern Railway Co.; Mobil Oil Corp.; Phillips Petroleum Co.

For full biographical listings, see the Martindale-Hubbell Law Directory

---

STOCKWELL, SIEVERT, VICCELLIO, CLEMENTS & SHADDOCK, L.L.P. (AV)

One Lakeside Plaza, P.O. Box 2900, 70601
Telephone: 318-436-9491
Fax: 318-493-7210; 493-2709

MEMBERS OF FIRM

Oliver P. Stockwell (1907-1993)	Stephen C. Polito
Fred H. Sievert, Jr. (1923-1988)	Robert S. Dampf
Charles D. Viccellio	William B. Monk
Robert W. Clements	H. Alan McCall
William E. Shaddock	Brian L. Coody
Emmett C. Sole	Paul L. Veazey, Jr.
John Stanton Bradford	James Anthony Blanco
Andrew D. McGlathery, III	

OF COUNSEL

Thomas G. Henning	Randy J. Fuerst

ASSOCIATES

H. Aubrey White, III	John Ernest William Baay, II
Benjamin J. Guilbeau, Jr.	Lee W. Boyer
Susan Gay Viccellio	Allen J. Mitchell, Jr.

Representative Clients: The Continental Insurance Cos.; State Farm Insurance Cos.; PPG Industries, Inc.; Entergy Gulf States Inc.; Lakeside National Bank of Lake Charles; Lake Charles Memorial Hospital; Texaco, Inc.; St. Patrick Hospital of Lake Charles; Firestone-Bridgestone, Inc.; Reliance Insurance Co.

For full biographical listings, see the Martindale-Hubbell Law Directory

---

LEESVILLE,* Vernon Parish — (Refer to De Ridder)

MANDEVILLE, St. Tammany Parish

BAILEY & DWYER (AV)

600 Mariner's Plaza, Suite 607, 70448
Telephone: 504-674-1105
Fax: 504-674-1966
Metairie Area Telephone: 504-833-8241
Fax: 504-837-4534

MEMBERS OF FIRM

B. Ralph Bailey	Frederick H. N. Dwyer
Scott O. Gaspard	

For full biographical listings, see the Martindale-Hubbell Law Directory

---

MANSFIELD,* De Soto Parish — (Refer to Shreveport)

MARKSVILLE,* Avoyelles Parish

LABORDE & LAFARGUE (AV)

Laborde Building, 313 North Main Street, P.O. Box 277, 71351
Telephone: 318-253-7521
Facisimile: 318-253-7522

(See Next Column)

MEMBERS OF FIRM

Cliffe E. Laborde, Jr. (1913-1983)	Edwin L. Lafargue
	David E. Lafargue

General Counsel for: Tidewater, Inc.; Tidex, Inc.; Haas Investment Co., Inc.; Hamburg Mills; Guaranty Seed Co.
Representative Clients: Pan American Petroleum Corp.; Murphy Oil Corp.; Ocean Drilling & Exploration Co.; Hilliard Oil & Gas, Inc.

For full biographical listings, see the Martindale-Hubbell Law Directory

---

METAIRIE, Jefferson Parish

BERNARD, CASSISA & ELLIOTT, A PROFESSIONAL LAW CORPORATION (AV)

1615 Metairie Road, P.O. Box 55490, 70055-5490
Telephone: 504-834-2612
Telecopier: 504-838-9438
Email: bcande@communique.net
Oxford, Mississippi Office: P.O. Box 1138, 38655.
Telephone: 601-234-7236.
Fax: 601-234-7691.

Peter L. Bernard, Jr. (1920-1991)	Paul V. Cassisa, Jr.
Frank L. Micholet (1913-1972)	Howard B. Kaplan
Paul V. Cassisa, Sr.	William L. Brockman
Stephen N. Elliott	Robert A. Knight
Benjamin Franklin Davis, Jr.	Collins C. Rossi
Eugene M. McEachin, Jr.	Dawn M. Palmisano
Robert A. McMahon, Jr.	Ann M. Sico
Carl J. Giffin, Jr.	Mark W. Verret

Representative Clients: Royal Insurance Group; General Motors Corp.; Hartford Insurance Group; Nissan Motor Corp.; Honda North America, Inc.

For full biographical listings, see the Martindale-Hubbell Law Directory

---

HAILEY, McNAMARA, HALL, LARMANN & PAPALE, L.L.P. (AV)

A Partnership including Law Corporations
Suite 1400, One Galleria Boulevard, P.O. Box 8288, 70011
Telephone: 504-836-6500
Fax: 504-836-6565

MEMBERS OF FIRM

James W. Hailey, Jr., (P.L.C.)	Michael J. Vondenstein
Henry D. McNamara, Jr., (P.L.C.)	David K. Persons
W. Marvin Hall (P.L.C.)	Dominic J. Ovella
Antonio E. Papale, Jr., (P.L.C.)	C. Kelly Lightfoot
Laurence E. Larmann (P.L.C.)	John T. Culotta (P.L.C.)
Michael P. Mentz	John E. Unsworth, Jr.
Richard T. Simmons, Jr.,(P.L.C.)	Julie DiFulco Robles
	Claude A. Greco

ASSOCIATES

William R. Seay, Jr.	Barbara E. Bourdonnay
Cyril B. Burck, Jr.	Kathryn T. Wiedorn
Valerie T. Schexnayder	Joseph L. Spilman, III
W. Evan Plauche	Caroline D. Ibos
Kurt D. Engelhardt	Robert D. Ford
W. Glenn Burns	David C. Fawley
James W. Hailey, III	Sharon Yarasavich Piper
Ivan A. Orihuela	Lynnette Hall-Lewis
Frederic Theodore Le Clercq (Not admitted in LA)	

Representative Clients: Certain Underwriters at Lloyds of London; Diamond Offshore Drilling Inc.; First American Title Insurance Company; The Flintkote Co.; Litton Industries; Lockheed Martin Corporation; Rheem Manufacturing Co.; State Farm Fire & Casualty Co.; Textron, Inc; Travelers Companies.

For full biographical listings, see the Martindale-Hubbell Law Directory

---

MINDEN,* Webster Parish

KITCHENS, BENTON, KITCHENS & WARREN, A PROFESSIONAL LAW CORPORATION (AV)

420 Broadway, P.O. Box 740, 71055
Telephone: 318-377-5331
Fax: 318-377-5361

Graydon K. Kitchens, Sr. (1903-1988)	Paul E. Kitchens
John B. Benton, Jr.	William Rick Warren
	Graydon K. Kitchens, III
Graydon K. Kitchens, Jr.	

Representative Clients: State Farm Insurance Co.; Howard Lumber & Supply Co., Inc.; Minden Building & Loan Assn.; Mister Twister, Inc.; Minden Housing Authority.
Reference: Minden Bank & Trust Co.

For full biographical listings, see the Martindale-Hubbell Law Directory

MONROE,* Ouachita Parish

DAVENPORT, FILES & KELLY, L.L.P. (AV)

1509 Lamy Lane, P.O. Box 4787, 71211-4787
Telephone: 318-387-6453
FAX: 318-323-6533

Thos. W. Davenport (1909-1962)	Jack B. Files
Wm. G. Kelly, Jr.	Mike C. Sanders
Thomas W. Davenport, Jr.	Ramsey L. Ogg
	Michael J. Fontenot

M. Shane Craighead	W. David Hammett
	Carey B. Underwood

STAFF ATTORNEY
Stacy L. Guice

Representative Clients: CHUBB Group; Crum & Forster Group; GAINSCO County Mutual Insurance Company; Government Employees Insurance Company; Highlands Insurance Company; Trinity Universal Insurance Company; Zurich American Insurance Companies.

For full biographical listings, see the Martindale-Hubbell Law Directory

HAYES, HARKEY, SMITH & CASCIO, L.L.P. (AV)

2811 Kilpatrick Boulevard, P.O. Box 8032, 71211-8032
Telephone: 318-387-2422
FAX: 318-388-5809

Thomas M. Hayes, Jr.	Charles S. Smith
(1915-1994)	Thomas M. Hayes, III
Louis D. Smith	Bruce McKamy Mintz
Joseph D. Cascio, Jr.	C. Joseph Roberts, III
	John B. Saye

OF COUNSEL
Haynes L. Harkey, Jr.

Karen L. Hayes	Elizabeth D. Bogan
	Harry McClellan Moffett, IV

Representative Clients: Hanover Insurance Co.; Cigna, Inc.; CNA; St. Francis Medical Center, Inc.; St. Paul Insurance Group; Travelers Insurance Co.; Cooper Industries; Riverwood International Corp.

For full biographical listings, see the Martindale-Hubbell Law Directory

HUDSON, POTTS & BERNSTEIN (AV)

10th Floor, Premier Bank Building, 130 DeSiard Street, Drawer 3008, 71210
Telephone: 318-388-4400
Fax: 318-322-4194
Email: hpb@iamerica.net *URL:* http://www.cust.iamerica.net/hpb

MEMBERS OF FIRM

F.G. Hudson, Sr. (1875-1913)	Ben R. Hanchey
W. N. Potts (1875-1890)	James A. Rountree
Henry Bernstein, Sr. (1897-1931)	W. Craig Henry
John J. Potts (1894-1935)	Gordon L. James
F. G. Hudson, Jr. (1909-1958)	Robert M. Baldwin
Murray Hudson (1920-1971)	Charles W. Herold, III
Henry Bernstein, Jr. (1930-1978)	William T. McNew
B. Roy Liuzza (1958-1984)	Brady Dean King, II
Robert C. Downing (1952-1991)	Jay P. Adams
Jesse D. McDonald	Brian P. Bowes
Paul K. Kirkpatrick, Jr.	Jan Peter Christiansen

ASSOCIATES

Stephen Adam North	Mary A. Buffington

General Attorneys for: Missouri Pacific Railroad Co.
Attorneys for: Bank One, Louisiana, N.A.; Premier Bank, Monroe; General Motors; Allstate Insurance Co.; State Farm Fire & Casualty Co.; Hartford Insurance Group; Royal Globe Insurance Cos.; Dodson Insurance Group.

For full biographical listings, see the Martindale-Hubbell Law Directory

SNELLINGS, BREARD, SARTOR, INABNETT & TRASCHER (AV)

1503 North 19th Street, P.O. Box 2055, 71207-2055
Telephone: 318-387-8000
Fax: 318-387-8200
Email: sbsit@bayou.com *URL:* http://www.bayou.com/sbsit

MEMBERS OF FIRM

George M. Snellings, Jr.	L. Kent Breard, Jr.
(1910-1984)	Clara Moss Sartor
Daniel Ryan Sartor, Jr.	William Brooks Watson
Carrick R. Inabnett	David C. McMillin
Charles C. Trascher, III	Jon Keith Guice

ASSOCIATES
Wendy E W Giovingo

(See Next Column)

OF COUNSEL
Kent Breard

Representative Clients: Central Bank; Delta Air Lines, Inc.; Federal Deposit Insurance Co.; Glenwood Regional Medical Center; John Hancock Mutual Life Insurance Company; Kemper Insurance Group; Horace Mann Insurance Cos.

For full biographical listings, see the Martindale-Hubbell Law Directory

MORGAN CITY, St. Mary Parish

LIPPMAN, MAHFOUZ & MARTIN (AV)

Inglewood Mall, 1025 Victor II Boulevard, P.O. Box 2526, 70381
Telephone: 504-384-1833
Fax: 504-385-4632

MEMBERS OF FIRM

Alfred S. Lippman	Thomas L. Mahfouz
	Dale P. Martin

ASSOCIATES

Brian M. Tranchina	David M. Thorguson

For full biographical listings, see the Martindale-Hubbell Law Directory

NATCHITOCHES,* Natchitoches Parish

McCOY, HAWTHORNE, ROBERTS & BEGNAUD, LTD. A LAW CORPORATION (AV)

300 St. Denis Street, P.O. Box 1369, 71458-1369
Telephone: 318-352-6495
Telecopier: 318-352-9982

Kenneth D. McCoy, Jr.	Mark L. Roberts
Dee A. Hawthorne	Mark A. Begnaud

Gregory D. Friedman

Representative Clients: Central Bank; Farm Credit Bank of Texas; First Bank of Natchitoches (general counsel); First South PCA; Natchitoches Parish Port Commission; Northwestern State University of Louisiana; Red River Waterway District; Reserve Life Insurance Co.; Riverwood International Corp.

For full biographical listings, see the Martindale-Hubbell Law Directory

NEW IBERIA,* Iberia Parish

LANDRY & WATKINS (AV)

211 East Main Street, P.O. Box 12040, 70562-2040
Telephone: 318-364-7626, Lafayette: 318-234-5921
Telecopier: 318-367-2715

MEMBERS OF FIRM

Alfred Smith Landry	Edward P. Landry
	William A. Repaske

OF COUNSEL

Jacob S. Landry	Guyton H. Watkins

ASSOCIATES

Kreig A. Breaux	Charles Benjamin Landry
	Richard A. Spears

Representative Clients: Entex, a Division of NorAm Energy Corp.; Iberia Sugar Co-operative, Inc.; The Continental Insurance Co.; Hartford Accident & Indemnity Co.; Iberia Savings Bank; Liberty Mutual Insurance Co.; Premier Bank, N.A.

For full biographical listings, see the Martindale-Hubbell Law Directory

NEW ORLEANS,* Orleans Parish

ADAMS AND REESE (AV)

Attorneys and Counselors at Law
Registered Limited Liability Partnership
4500 One Shell Square, 70139
Telephone: 504-581-3234
Telefax: 504-566-0210
Email: info@arlaw.com *URL:* http://www.arlaw.com/
Baton Rouge, Louisiana Office: Bank One Centre, 19th Floor, North Tower, 451 Florida Street.
Telephone: 504-336-5200.
Telefax: 504-336-5220.
Mobile, Alabama Office: 4500 One St. Louis Centre.
Telephone: 334-433-3234.
Telefax: 334-438-7733.
Washington, D.C. Office: 601 Thirteenth Street, N.W., Suite 445 North.
Telephone: 202-737-3234.
Fax: 202-737-0264.
Houston, Texas Office: 1100 Louisiana, Suite 5100.
Telephone: 713-652-5151.
Fax: 713-652-5152.

(See Next Column)

ADAMS AND REESE—*Continued*

MEMBERS OF FIRM

St. Clair Adams, Jr. (1906-1963)	Edwin C. Laizer
W. Ford Reese (1917-1971)	Martin A. Stern
Henry B. Alsobrook, Jr.	Leslie A. Lanusse
Sam A. LeBlanc, III	J. Forrest Hinton
Thomas J. Wyllie	Harry M. Zimmerman, Jr.
Joel L. Borrello	Warren E. Byrd II (Resident,
James E. Blazek	Baton Rouge Office)
Lawrence L. McNamara	J. Wendell Clark (Resident,
Edward J. Rice, Jr.	Baton Rouge Office)
Robert A. Vosbein	Lisa D. Newman
Louis A. Wilson, Jr.	A. Kirk Gasperecz
Robert B. Nolan	L. Thomas Styron (Resident,
Michael G. Crow	Mobile, Alabama Office)
Robert J. Conrad, Jr.	Lyn A. Batastini
Robert E. Couhig, Jr.	(Resident, Mobile, Alabama)
Eddy M. Quijano (Resident,	T. Semmes Favrot
Baton Rouge Office)	Patricia B. McMurray (Resident,
Mark C. Surprenant	Baton Rouge Office)
Philip A. Franco	Deborah Cunningham Foshee
Mark J. Spansel	Mark W. Coffin (Resident,
E. L. Henry (Resident, Baton	Houston, Texas Office)
Rouge Office)	Jane C. Whitten
Donald T. W. Phelps (Resident,	Kathleen F. Drew
Baton Rouge Office)	Donna M. Borrello
E. L. McCafferty, III (Resident,	Margaret M. Joffe
Mobile, Alabama Office)	James G. Perdigao
Frank Grey Redditt, Jr.	Earl A. Bridges, Jr.
Joseph W. Looney	E. Paige Sensenbrenner
Victor H. Lott, Jr. (Resident,	Timothy W. Burgmeier
Mobile, Alabama Office)	(Resident, Baton Rouge
Albert S. Dittmann, Jr.	Office)
Paul G. Pastorek	Brooke Duncan III
Thomas G. O'Brien	Janis van Meerveld
Charles F. Gay, Jr.	Judith W. Giorlando
Rebecca A. Bush	Cristina Romig Wheat
John M. Duck	Edward H. Arnold, III
Philip O. Bergeron	Rodi W. Culotta
Richard B. Eason, II	Michael M. Duran
F. Lee Butler	Francis V. Liantonio, Jr.
(Resident, Houston, Texas)	Mark R. Beebe
Paul O. Dicharry	Alex E. Cosculluela (Resident,
Luis A. Perez	Houston, Texas Office)
Lynn M. Luker	Erin Hunter Patterson (Resident,
Mark S. Embree	Houston, Texas Office)
Richard A. Goins	Ann M. Halphen
Joseph P. Gordon, Jr.	Robert L. Rieger, Jr.
William B. Gaudet	(Resident Baton Rouge Office)
Daryl G. Dursum	William E. Pritchard, III
(Resident, Houston, Texas)	E. Gregg Barrios
Scott E. Delacroix	B. Troy Villa
Glen M. Pilie	Sean D. Moore
Deborah B. Rouen	Jeffrey W. Bennett
Robin B. Cheatham	Kenneth F. Tamplain, Jr.
Louis C. LaCour, Jr.	Charles J. Duhe, Jr. (Resident,
Donald C. Massey	Baton Rouge Office)
Richard O. Kingrea (Resident,	
Baton Rouge Office)	

ASSOCIATES

Edward M. Morris	James T. Rogers, III
Erin R. Danielson	Richard J. Kernion, Jr.
Roy A. Perrin, III	Gregory A. Grefer
Sharon R. Rodi	Ralph H. Wall
Tyson B. Shofstahl	Terri Lyn Carmichael
Laurie Briggs Young	Jeffrey E. Richardson
Lisa Lemaire Maher	Ronald J. Triche
Arthur F. Hickham, Jr.	Terrance F. Henderson
Michael N. Mire	Douglas H. Edwards
William J. Kelly, III	John F. Fletcher
	(Not admitted in LA)

OF COUNSEL

Robert J. Conrad	Karen Lewis Wilkins
Joseph H. Kavanaugh	Julian P. Brignac

Representative Clients: American International Group, Inc.; Mobil Oil Corp.; Shell Oil Co.; Underwriters at Lloyds of London; Reichhold Chemicals, Inc.; Rollins Environmental Services, Inc.; Oschner Medical Center; Merrell Dow Pharmaceuticals, Inc.; Louisiana Medical Mutual Insurance Co. (LAM-MICO); Reading & Bates Drilling Co.

For full biographical listings, see the Martindale-Hubbell Law Directory

---

ATES & ASSOCIATES, A PROFESSIONAL LAW CORPORATION (AV)

One Canal Place, Suite 2300, 365 Canal Street, 70130
Telephone: 504-561-6623
Telefax: 504-764-9686
Destrehan, Louisiana Office: 13726 River Road, Suite A, 70047.
Telephone: 504-764-9911.
Telefax: 504-764-9686.

(See Next Column)

J. Robert Ates

For full biographical listings, see the Martindale-Hubbell Law Directory

---

BREAZEALE, SACHSE & WILSON, L.L.P. (AV)

LL&E Tower, Suite 2400, 909 Poydras Street, 70112
Telephone: 504-584-5454
Fax: 504-584-5452
Baton Rouge, Louisiana Office: Twenty-Third Floor, One American Place, P.O. Box 3197.
Telephone: 504-387-4000.
Fax: 504-387-5397.

MEMBERS OF FIRM

Gordon A. Pugh	John F. Whitney (Resident)
Van R. Mayhall, Jr.	Joseph E. Friend (Resident)
John J. Cooper (Resident)	Gary L. Laborde (Resident)
Cecil J. Blache	Avery Lea Griffin (Resident)

For full biographical listings, see the Martindale-Hubbell Law Directory

---

CHAFFE, McCALL, PHILLIPS, TOLER & SARPY, L.L.P. (AV)

A Partnership including a Professional Law Corporation
2300 Energy Centre, 1100 Poydras Street, 70163-2300
Telephone: 504-585-7000
Telecopier: 504-585-7075
Cable Address: "Denegre"
Telex: (AT&T) 460122 CMPTS
Email: cmptsno%2049698@mcimail.com *URL:* http://www.chaffe.com/
Baton Rouge, Louisiana Office: 202 Two United Plaza, 8550 United Plaza Boulevard.
Telephone: 504-922-4300.
Fax: 504-922-4304.
Miami, Florida Office: 2600 Brickell Bay Office Tower, 1001 South Bayshore Drive, 33131.
Telephone: 305-377-3770.
Fax: 305-377-0080.
Caracas, Venezuela Office: Edificio Exa, Piso 10, Oficina PH-10, Avenida Venezuela entre Calles EL Retiro y Alameda, El Rosal.
Telephone: 011-582-953-4136.
Fax: 011-582-953-6518.

MEMBERS OF FIRM

John Lemuel Toler (1895-1985)	Jose S. Canseco
Leon Sarpy	E. Howell Crosby
Donald A. Lindquist	Keith Eric Gisleson
Robert B. Deane	Henry D. Salassi, Jr. (Resident
Peter A. Feringa, Jr.	Partner, Baton Rouge)
J. Dwight LeBlanc, Jr.	W. Anthony Toups, III
Charles L. Chassaignac	Douglas L. Grundmeyer
G. Phillip Shuler, III	J. Gregory Wyrick
James A. Barton, III	Charles P. Blanchard
Robert B. Fisher, Jr.	Robert B. Landry, III
Corinne Ann Morrison	Brent A. Talbot
James A. Babst	Betty F. Mullin
William F. Grace, Jr.	Merle F. Shoughrue
Robert S. Rooth	James C. Young
Harry R. Holladay	Andrew C. Partee, Jr.
Marc G. Shachat	Mark L. Gundlach
L. Havard Scott, III	Mary L. Meyer
Derek Anthony Walker	Robert L. Clayton
Jonathan C. McCall	Daphne P. McNutt
Andrew Rinker, Jr.	Scott A. Soule
Kathleen S. Plemer	L. Kenneth Krogstad (Resident
Daniel L. Daboval	Partner, Baton Rouge)
Thomas D. Forbes	Curtis J. Mase (Resident
Julie D. Livaudais	Partner, Miami, Florida
John F. Olinde	Office)
Carmelite M. Bertaut	Ronald L. Naquin
John H. Clegg	Paul E. Ramoni, Jr.
David R. Richardson	H. Evans Scobee (Resident
Dona J. Dew	Special Partner, Baton Rouge)
John C. Saunders, Jr.	

ASSOCIATES

Eric J. Simonson	Deborah Duplechin Harkins
Bernardo Bentata	Julie D. Savage
(Resident Associate, Caracas)	Virginia R. Quijada
Scott C. Barney	Kellye L. Walker
G. Wade Wootan	(Not admitted in LA)
Gina M. Venezia	Beverly D. Eisenstadt (Resident,
Desha D. Dardenne	Miami, Florida Office)
Simeon Bernard Reimonenq, Jr.	James D. Gassenheimer
Keith C. Armstrong (Resident	(Resident, Miami, Florida
Associate, Baton Rouge)	Office)
Daniel A. Tadros	Lisa R. Hecht-Cronstedt
Frederick W. Veters	(Resident, Miami, Florida
D. Scott Landry (Resident	Office)
Associate, Baton Rouge)	Christopher J. Bailey (Resident,
Michael W. Tifft	Miami, Florida Office)

(See Next Column)

CHAFFE, McCALL, PHILLIPS, TOLER & SARPY, L.L.P., *New Orleans—Continued*

OF COUNSEL

George W. Pigman, Jr.
Gordon O. Ewin

Paul A. Nalty
Nathaniel P. Phillips, Jr.

Representative Clients: CSX Transportation, Inc. (formerly, Louisville & Nashville Railroad Co.); Alerion Bank; Hibernia Corp.; The Allstate Insurance Co.; The Equitable Life Assurance Society of the United States; Liverpool and London Steamship Protection and Indemnity Assn. Ltd.; The West of England Steam Ship Owners Mutual Insurance Assn. (Luxembourg); Associated Builders and Contractors, Inc.; Resolution Trust Corp.; Brown & Williamson Tobacco Corp.

For full biographical listings, see the Martindale-Hubbell Law Directory

---

CHRISTOVICH AND KEARNEY, L.L.P. (AV)

Suite 2300 Pan American Life Center, 601 Poydras Street, 70130-6078
Telephone: 504-561-5700
Fax: 504-561-5743
Houston, Texas Office: 700 Louisiana, Suite 4550, 77002.
Telephone: 713-225-2255.
Fax: 713-225-1112.

MEMBERS OF FIRM

Alvin R. Christovich, Jr.
William K. Christovich
J. Walter Ward, Jr.
Lawrence J. Ernst
James F. Holmes
Robert E. Peyton
C. Edgar Cloutier
Charles W. Schmidt, III
Richard K. Christovich
Terry Christovich Gay
Paul G. Preston
Michael M. Christovich

E. Phelps Gay
Thomas C. Cowan
Geoffrey P. Snodgrass
J. Warren Gardner, Jr.
Kevin R. Tully
Lance R. Rydberg
Elizabeth S. Cordes
John K. Leach
Fred T. Hinrichs
Daniel A. Rees
Charles M. Lanier, Jr.
Lyon H. Garrison

Philip J. Borne

ASSOCIATES

Bennett A. Midlo
(Not admitted in LA)
J. Roslyn Lemmon
James A. Holmes
Scott P. Yount
Patricia Broussard Judice
Ellen B. Woody
Patrick W. Drouilhet

Robert D. Peyton
Kenan S. Rand, Jr.
Joseph E. Cullens, Jr.
Todd A. Riddle
(Not admitted in LA)
Steve C. Dollinger
(Not admitted in LA)
D. Scott Slawson

Representative Clients: Associated Aviation Underwriters; Brown & Root, Inc.; Chubb/Pacific Indemnity Group; Continental Insurance Company; Crawford & Co.; Crum & Forster; Highlands Insurance Company; Insurance Company of North America; Liberty Mutual Insurance Company; Southern Pacific Transportation Co.

For full biographical listings, see the Martindale-Hubbell Law Directory

---

DEUTSCH, KERRIGAN & STILES, L.L.P. (AV)

A Partnership including Professional Law Corporations
755 Magazine Street, 70130-3672
Telephone: 504-581-5141
Cable Address: "Dekest"
Telex: 584358
Telecopier: 504-566-1201
Email: dks@dksno.com *URL:* http://www.dksno.com
St. Tammany Parish Office: 550 Pontchartrain Drive, Suite 200, Slidell, LA. 70458.
Telephone: 504-639-0555.
Fax: 504-639-0550.

MEMBERS OF FIRM

Eberhard P. Deutsch
(1897-1980)
R. Emmett Kerrigan
(1902-1980)
Harry F. Stiles (1902-1953)
Frederick R. Bott (P.L.C.)
William W. Messersmith, III,
(P.L.C.)
Peter J. Butler
Charles F. Seemann, Jr., (P.L.C.)
Robert E. Kerrigan, Jr., (P.L.C.)
Bertrand M. Cass, Jr.
Raymon G. Jones (P.L.C.)
Francis J. Barry, Jr.
Victor E. Stilwell, Jr., (P.L.C.)
Allen F. Campbell
Matt J. Farley (P.L.C.)
Philip D. Lorio, III
G. Alex Weller
A. Wendel Stout, III
Daniel A. Smith
Terrence L. Brennan
Marc J. Yellin (P.L.C.)

Howard L. Murphy
Darrell K. Cherry (P.L.C.)
Richard B. Montgomery III
William E. Wright, Jr.
Nancy J. Marshall
James G. Wyly, III
Ellis B. Murov (P.L.C.)
Duris L. Holmes
Janet L. MacDonell
Joseph L. McReynolds
W. Lee Kohler
Theodore L. White
William C. Harrison, Jr.
Judy L. Burnthorn
Carl A. Butler
Susan Whittington Leidner
Peter J. Butler, Jr.
Gary B. Roth
Gene R. Smith
Barbara Malik Weller
Lisa C. Winter
Karen Wells Roby
Karyn J. Vigh

(See Next Column)

OF COUNSEL

Brunswick G. Deutsch (P.L.C.)
Marian Mayer Berkett
Ralph L. Kaskell, Jr.
Malcolm W. Monroe

Francis G. Weller (P.L.C.)
Bernard Marcus (P.L.C.)
David C. Treen
Charles K. Reasonover (P.L.C.)

ASSOCIATES

Reneé C. McGinty
Herman J. Gesser, III
Richard G. Passler

Victor J. Franckiewicz, Jr.
W. Christopher Beary
Charles F. Seemann III

Pamela W. Carter

LEGAL SUPPORT PERSONNEL

S. William Provensal, III

For full biographical listings, see the Martindale-Hubbell Law Directory

---

FAVRET, DEMAREST, RUSSO & LUTKEWITTE, A PROFESSIONAL LAW CORPORATION (AV)

Suite 1400, 1515 Poydras Building, 1515 Poydras Street, 70112
Telephone: 504-561-1006
Telecopier: 504-523-0699

Clarence F. Favret, Sr.
(1896-1988)
Marshall J. Favret
J. Paul Demarest

Anthony J. Russo
Thomas J. Lutkewitte
Clarence F. Favret, III
Peter S. Thriffiley

Angela C. Imbornone

Dean Joseph Favret

Reference: Hibernia National Bank.

For full biographical listings, see the Martindale-Hubbell Law Directory

---

RICHARD A. FRASER, III (AV)

530 Natchez Street, Suite 200, 70130
Telephone: 504-581-4726
Facsimile: 504-581-1190

OF COUNSEL

William R. Campbell, Jr.

For full biographical listings, see the Martindale-Hubbell Law Directory

---

WARREN A. GOLDSTEIN A PROFESSIONAL LAW CORPORATION (AV)

1515 Poydras Street, Suite 2350, 70112
Telephone: 504-581-7933
FAX: 504-595-3355

Warren A. Goldstein

For full biographical listings, see the Martindale-Hubbell Law Directory

---

GORDON, ARATA, McCOLLAM & DUPLANTIS, L.L.P. (AV)

A Partnership including Professional Law Corporations
Place St. Charles, Suite 4000, 201 St. Charles Avenue, 70170-4000
Telephone: 504-582-1111
Fax: 504-582-1121
Lafayette, Louisiana Office: 625 East Kaliste Saloom Road.
Telephone: 318-237-0132.
Fax: 318-237-3451.
Baton Rouge, Louisiana Office: 1420 One American Place.
Telephone: 504-381-9643.
Fax: 504-336-9763.

MEMBERS OF FIRM

John A. Gordon (A P.L.C.)
Blake G. Arata (A P.L.C.)
John M. McCollam (A P.L.C.)
Ewell E. Eagan, Jr., (A P.L.C.)
Guy E. Wall
Cynthia A. Nicholson
Cathy E. Chessin
William T. D'Zurilla
Paul E. Bullington

Steven W. Copley
James L. Weiss
Jason A. T. Jumonville
Marion D. Welborn Weinstock
Ernest E. Svenson
Martin E. Landrieu
A. Gregory Grimsal
Donna Phillips Currault
Scott A. O'Connor

ASSOCIATES

C. Peck Hayne Jr.
Elizabeth L. Gordon

Camille Bienvenu Poche
Marcy V. Massengale

Tina Crawford Santopadre

LAFAYETTE OFFICE

RESIDENT MEMBERS OF FIRM

B. J. Duplantis (A P.L.C.)
Benjamin B. Blanchet

William F. Bailey
James E. Slatten, III

Samuel E. Masur

RESIDENT ASSOCIATES

Denis C. Swords

(See Next Column)

GORDON, ARATA, McCollam & Duplantis L.L.P.—*Continued*
BATON ROUGE OFFICE
RESIDENT ASSOCIATES

Teanna West Neskora　　　　　　Daniel J. Shapiro

Representative Clients: Amoco Production Co.; McMoran Oil & Gas Co., Inc.; First National Bank of Commerce of New Orleans; Universal Health Services, Inc.; Cox Cable Communications, Inc.; W.R. Grace & Co.; Lorillard, Inc.; First City Bancorporation; Pan-American Life Insurance Co.

For full biographical listings, see the Martindale-Hubbell Law Directory

---

GUSTE, BARNETT & SHUSHAN, L.L.P. (AV)

Entergy Corporation Building, 25th Floor, 639 Loyola
Avenue, 70113-7103
Telephone: 504-529-4141
Telecopier: 504-561-0326

MEMBERS OF FIRM

Roy F. Guste　　　　　　　　Richard L. Weil
William M. Barnett　　　　　　Robert A. Barnett
William J. Guste, III　　　　　Joseph B. Landry
Sidney L. Shushan (P.C.)　　　Paul M. Lavelle
J. Harrison Henderson, III　　Claude A. Schlesinger

Gideon T. Stanton, III　　　　Jonathan M. Shushan
Rachel I. Becker　　　　　　　C. Marcy Unkauf

Representative Clients: National Tea Co.; Figgie International, Inc.; Volvo-GM Heavy Truck Corp.; Colony Insurance Co.; Cardinal Insurance Co.; Aetna Life & Casualty Insurance Co.; Winn Dixie Stores, Inc.; Cooper Tire Co.; Johnson Controls, Inc.; Medical Malpractice Protection Plan, Inc.

For full biographical listings, see the Martindale-Hubbell Law Directory

---

HEBERT, MOULEDOUX & BLAND, A PROFESSIONAL LAW CORPORATION (AV)

Pan-American Life Center, Suite 1650, 601 Poydras Street, 70130
Telephone: 504-525-3333
Cable Address: "HMBL"
Telex: 588-092;
Fax: 504-523-4224

Maurice C. Hebert, Jr.　　　　Alan Guy Brackett
André J. Mouledoux　　　　　David M. Flotte
Wilton E. Bland, III　　　　　C. William Emory
Georges M. Legrand　　　　　C. Michael Parks
Roch P. Poelman　　　　　　　Daniel J. Hoerner
　　　　　　John H. Musser, V

Representative Clients: Archer-Daniels Midland Company; Bisso Marine Company, Inc.; Carline Geismar Fleet, Inc.; Cooper/T. Smith Stevedoring Company, Inc.; Delta Queen Steamboat Co.; Diamond Offshore Drilling, Inc.; LOOP INC.; Marine Equipment Management Corporation; McDermott Incorporated; Olympic Marine Company.

For full biographical listings, see the Martindale-Hubbell Law Directory

---

HERMAN, HERMAN, KATZ & COTLAR, L.L.P. (AV)

A Partnership including Professional Law Corporations
Formerly Herman & Herman
820 O'Keefe Avenue, 70113
Telephone: 504-581-4892
Telecopier: 504-561-6024

Harry Herman (1914-1987)　　Morton H. Katz (A Professional
Russ M. Herman (A　　　　　　Law Corporation)
　Professional Law Corporation)　Sidney A. Cotlar (A Professional
Maury A. Herman (A　　　　　　Law Corporation)
　Professional Law Corporation)　Steven J. Lane
　　　　　　Leonard A. Davis

James C. Klick　　　　　　　　Steve Herman
　　　　　　Brian D. Katz

For full biographical listings, see the Martindale-Hubbell Law Directory

---

JONES, WALKER, WAECHTER, POITEVENT, CARRÈRE & DENÈGRE, L.L.P. (AV)

Place St. Charles, 201 St. Charles Avenue, 70170-5100
Telephone: 504-582-8000
Telecopiers: Xerox 7033, 504-582-8549,
504-582-8574, 504-582-8583
Email: marketing@jwlaw.com
Baton Rouge, Louisiana Office: Fifth Floor, Four United Plaza, 8555 United Plaza Boulevard, 70809-7000.
Telephone: 504-231-2000.
Telecopier: 504-231-2010.
Lafayette, Louisiana Office: 201 Rue Iberville, Suite 210, 70508-3281.
Telephone: 318-232-5353.
Telecopier: Xerox 7021, 318-232-5415.

(See Next Column)

Washington, D.C. Office: Republic Place, Suite 245, 1776 Eye Street, N.W., 20006-3700.
Telephone: 202-828-8363.
Telecopier: Xerox 7021, 202-828-6907.

MEMBERS OF FIRM

Joseph Merrick Jones　　　　　Alton E. Bayard, III (Resident,
　(1903-1963)　　　　　　　　　Baton Rouge Office)
J. Mort Walker, Jr. (1904-1983)　Robert T. Lemon, II
Arthur J. Waechter, Jr.　　　　H. Mark Adams
Edward B. Poitevent　　　　　Elizabeth Jones Futrell
Ernest A. Carrère, Jr.　　　　Michael A. Chernekoff
George Denègre　　　　　　　Richard J. Tyler
John V. Baus　　　　　　　　　William H. Hines
Robert B. Acomb, Jr.　　　　　W. Philip Clinton
Edward B. Benjamin, Jr.　　　William B. Masters
Patrick W. Browne, Jr.　　　　Thomas A. Casey, Jr.
Charles W. Lane, III　　　　　R. Lewis McHenry
John J. Weigel　　　　　　　　Curtis R. Hearn
Donald L. King　　　　　　　　Gary H. Miller
James Larkin Selman, II　　　Carl D. Rosenblum
John R. Peters, Jr.　　　　　　Covert J. Geary
Thomas C. Keller　　　　　　　Pauline F. Hardin
Donald O. Collins　　　　　　R. Christian Johnsen (Resident,
John C. Combe, Jr.　　　　　　　Washington, D.C. Office)
R. Henry Sarpy, Jr.　　　　　　Kenneth J. Najder
Robert M. Contois, Jr.　　　　Thomas K. Potter, III
Edward F. Martin　　　　　　　Jefferson R. Tillery
Carl C. Hanemann　　　　　　Patrick J. Veters
Raymond J. Salassi, Jr.　　　　John L. Duvieilh
Stewart E. Niles, Jr.　　　　　Richard D. Bertram
John D. Kitchen　　　　　　　Lisa Manget Buchanan
Janice M. Foster　　　　　　　Wayne G. Zeringue, Jr.
Harry S. Hardin, III　　　　　Robert L. Walsh
John J. Broders　　　　　　　Leon Gary, Jr. (Resident, Baton
Glenn G. Goodier　　　　　　　Rouge Office)
Robert R. Casey　　　　　　　Charles A. Landry (Resident,
Edward J. Koehl, Jr.　　　　　　Baton Rouge Office)
Thomas M. Nosewicz　　　　　Donald E. Bradford (Resident,
David F. Edwards　　　　　　　Baton Rouge Office)
L. Richards McMillan, II　　　Michael T. Perry (Resident,
Howard E. Sinor, Jr.　　　　　　Baton Rouge Office)
R. Patrick Vance　　　　　　　Robert W. Scheffy, Jr.
Charles E. Leche　　　　　　　　(Resident, Baton Rouge
John G. Gomila, Jr.　　　　　　Office)
Robert B. Bieck, Jr.　　　　　B. Michael Mauldin (Resident,
Samuel O. Buckley, III　　　　　Baton Rouge Office)
Rudolph R. Ramelli　　　　　J. Rodney Ryan, Jr. (Resident,
Madeleine Fischer　　　　　　　Baton Rouge Office)
David G. Radlauer　　　　　　Davis B. Allgood (Resident,
John C. Blackman (Resident,　　Baton Rouge Office)
　Baton Rouge Office)　　　　　Louis S. Quinn, Jr. (Resident,
J. Kelly Duncan　　　　　　　　Baton Rouge Office)
Stanhope B. Denègre　　　　　Fred L. Chevalier (Resident,
Edward H. Bergin　　　　　　　Baton Rouge Office)
Grady S. Hurley　　　　　　　John C. Reynolds
Edward Dirk Wegmann　　　　M. Richard Schroeder
William M. Backstrom, Jr.　　J. Marshall Page, III
Alex P. Trostorff　　　　　　　Thomas Y. Roberson, Jr.
James E. Wright, III　　　　　William J. Joyce
Joseph J. Lowenthal, Jr.　　　Susan K. Chambers
Margaret F. Murphy　　　　　Robin D. McGuire
　　　　　　　　　　　　　　　　(Resident, Lafayette Office)

SPECIAL COUNSEL

John Clark Boyce (Resident,　　Mark G. Otts
　Baton Rouge Office)　　　　　William H. Strait
Thomas A. Casey (Resident,　　　(Not admitted in LA)
　Baton Rouge Office)　　　　　James P. Jones
James M. Field (Resident, Baton　　(Not admitted in LA)
　Rouge Office)　　　　　　　　Steve E. Hicks (Resident, Baton
Edward L. Merrigan (Resident,　　Rouge Office)
　Washington, D.C. Office)　　　Brad J. Axelrod (Not admitted
N. Hunter Johnston (Resident,　　in LA; Resident, Baton Rouge
　Washington, D.C. Office)　　　Office)
Stanley A. Millan　　　　　　James P. Barry (Not admitted in
A. Justin Ourso III (Resident,　　LA; Resident, Baton Rouge
　Baton Rouge Office)　　　　　Office)

ASSOCIATES

Virginia W. Gundlach　　　　Mary Ellen Jordan
Judith V. Windhorst　　　　　Donna Thompson Mueller
Jeffry W. Gray (Resident, Baton　F. Rivers Lelong, Jr.
　Rouge Office)　　　　　　　　Dionne M. Rousseau
Michael C. Herbert (Resident,　Tracy R. Bishop
　Baton Rouge Office)　　　　　H. Hughes Grehan
Jennifer L. Anderson (Resident,　Patricia A. Bethancourt
　Baton Rouge Office)　　　　　Andrew R. Lee
John B. Dunlap, III (Resident,　Edward J. Briscoe
　Baton Rouge Office)　　　　　Louis S. Nunes III
William L. Schuette, Jr.　　　Katy W. Kimbell
　(Resident, Baton Rouge　　　Laura Leigh Blackston
　Office)　　　　　　　　　　　Richard C. Badeaux
Douglas N. Currault II　　　　Michelle A. Bourque
S. Michele Ray　　　　　　　　Timothy S. Cragin
Nan Roberts Eitel　　　　　　Elizabeth Slatten Healy

(See Next Column)

JONES, WALKER, WAECHTER, POITEVENT, CARRÈRE & DENÈGRE, L.L.P., *New Orleans—Continued*

ASSOCIATES (Continued)

Roderick K. West	Kevin R. Hansbro
Tracy Neel	Michele Whitesell Crosby
Scott A. Decker	(Resident, Baton Rouge
Bari L. Giordano	Office)
Jeffrey W. Nolan	Alida C. Hainkel
Amy M. Winters	Jennifer L. Hantel
Michelle M. O'Daniels	Stephen G. Charbonnet
Mary L. Hassinger	Richard T. Gallagher, Jr.
Stacey Wayne Goff	Keith M. Landry
Mark W. Mercante	Jonathan H. Sandoz
Michael T. Johnson	Charles L. Rice, Jr.

Representative Clients: Avondale Industries, Inc.; Century Telephone Enterprises, Inc.; Entergy Corp.; First Commerce Corp.; International Shipholding Corp.; Offshore Pipelines, Inc.; South Central Bell; Texaco, Inc.; Tidewater, Inc.; The Travelers Companies.

For full biographical listings, see the Martindale-Hubbell Law Directory

---

LEAKE & ANDERSSON, L.L.P. (AV)

1700 Energy Centre, 1100 Poydras Street, 70163-1701
Telephone: 504-585-7500
Telecopier: 504-585-7775
Email: LA1700@aol.com

MEMBERS OF FIRM

Robert E. Leake, Jr.	Kevin O'Bryon
W. Paul Andersson	George D. Fagan
Lawrence A. Mann	Donald E. McKay, Jr.
Marta-Ann Schnabel O'Bryon	Stanton E. Shuler, Jr.

ASSOCIATES

Guy D. Perrier	Louis P. Bonnaffons
J. Ronald Ward, Jr.	Ellen H. Heidingsfelder
	Mark J. Doherty

Representative Clients: Commercial Credit Services Corp.; First Financial Insurance Co.; Government Employees Insurance Co.; National Food Processors, Inc.; National Union Fire Insurance Co.; Nationwide Insurance Co.; Professional Construction Services, Inc.

For full biographical listings, see the Martindale-Hubbell Law Directory

---

LISKOW & LEWIS, A PROFESSIONAL LAW CORPORATION (AV)

50th Floor, One Shell Square, 70139
Telephone: 504-581-7979
Telecopier: 504-556-4108; 504-556-4109
Lafayette, Louisiana Office: 822 Harding Street, P.O. Box 52008.
Telephone: 318-232-7424.
Telecopier: 318-267-2399.

Cullen R. Liskow (1893-1971)	George Denegre, Jr.
Austin W. Lewis (1910-1974)	Don K. Haycraft
Gene W. Lafitte	Wm. Craig Wyman
Billy H. Hines	James A. Brown
John M. King	R. Keith Jarrett
Leon J. Reymond, Jr.	Cheryl V. Cunningham
J. Berry St. John, Jr.	Stevia M. Walther
Donald R. Abaunza	Robert S. Angelico
John M. Wilson	Robert L. Theriot
Frederick W. Bradley	Dena L. Olivier
S. Gene Fendler	Marie Breaux
George J. Domas	Jonathan A. Hunter
Marilyn C. Maloney	Thomas P. Diaz
Robert E. Holden	Mary S. Johnson
Joe B. Norman	Kathleen Friel Hobson
Lambert M. Laperouse	Shaun G. Clarke
Philip K. Jones, Jr.	Scott C. Seiler
William W. Pugh	Cheryl Mollere Kornick
Marguerite A. Noonan	Mark D. Latham
David W. Leefe	John C. Anjier
Wm. Blake Bennett	Guenton C. Slawson, Jr.

OF COUNSEL

Charles C. Gremillion

Shannon Skelton Holtzman	Karen Daniel Ancelet
Carol Welborn Reisman	Michael D. Rubenstein
Jill Thompson Losch	Peter C. Muller
David L. Reisman	Susan Tart
Patricia Campbell Smith	Kevin P. Horne
Julia M. Pearce	Steven P. Crowther
	Harold J. Flanagan

RESIDENT PERSONNEL AT LAFAYETTE OFFICE

Thomas D. Hardeman	Billy J. Domingue
Lawrence P. Simon, Jr.	Charles B. Griffis, III
George R. Robinson, Jr.	Richard W. Revels, Jr.
Joseph C. Giglio, Jr.	Joseph P. Hebert
Patrick W. Gray	Mark A. Lowe
Thomas M. McNamara	George Arceneaux III
James N. Mansfield, III	Carmen M. Rodriguez

(See Next Column)

OF COUNSEL

Robert T. Jorden	James L. Pelletier

Matt Jones

Representative Clients: Atlantic Richfield Co.; BASF Corp.; Federal Deposit Insurance Corporation; First National Bank of Commerce; Hibernia National Bank; Legg Mason Wood Walker; Mobil Oil Corporation; Pennzoil Company; Prudential Securities Inc.; Texaco, Inc.

For full biographical listings, see the Martindale-Hubbell Law Directory

---

LOWE, STEIN, HOFFMAN, ALLWEISS & HAUVER, L.L.P. (AV)

One Shell Square, 701 Poydras Street Suite 3600, 70139-3600
Telephone: 504-581-2450
Telecopier: 504-581-2461

MEMBERS OF FIRM

Robert C. Lowe	Terence L. Hauver
Mark S. Stein	Ellen Widen Kessler
Mitchell J. Hoffman	Max J. Cohen
Michael R. Allweiss	Suzette Marie Smith
	David M. Prados

Judith A. Kaufman	Charlton D. Hunley
Marynell L. Piglia	Barbara H. Weiss
Kermit L. Roux, III	Paula H. Lee

OF COUNSEL

Mark S. Goldstein	Alicia M. Bendana

For full biographical listings, see the Martindale-Hubbell Law Directory

---

McGLINCHEY STAFFORD LANG (AV)

A Professional Limited Liability Company
643 Magazine Street, 70130-3477
Telephone: 504-586-1200
Fax: (504) 596-2800
TDD: (504) 596-2728
Telex: 584327
Cable Address: "MACSTAC"
Mailing Address: P.O. Box 60643, New Orleans, Louisiana, 70160-0643
Email: @mcglinchey.com
Dallas, Texas Office: 2777 Stemmons Freeway, Suite 925, 75207-2401.
Telephone: 214-634-3939.
Fax: 214-634-3971.
Houston, Texas Office: 2727 Allen Parkway, Suite 1900, 77019.
Telephone: 713-520-1900.
Fax: 713-520-1025.
Baton Rouge, Louisiana Office: Ninth Floor, One American Place, 70825-0001.
Telephone: 504-383-9000.
Fax: 504-343-3076.
Little Rock, Arkansas Office: 425 West Capitol, Suite 3900, 72201-3442.
Telephone: 501-371-9999.
Fax: 501-371-0035.
Jackson, Mississippi Office: Suite 1200, Mtel Centre South, 200 Lamar Street, 39201.
Telephone: 601-960-8400.
Fax: 601-960-8406.
Fort Smith, Arkansas Office: Brunwick Place, 101 North 10th Street, Suite D, 72901-2763.
Telephone: 501-783-8200.
Fax: 501-783-8265.
Lake Providence, Louisiana Office: 405 Morgan Street, 71254-2691.
Telephone: 318-559-1200.
Fax: 318-559-0609.

Dermot S. McGlinchey	Marie A. Moore
(1933-1993)	Rudy J. Cerone
Graham Stafford (1940-1987)	Anthony Rollo
Samuel Lang (1909-1989)	Craig Lewis Caesar
Colvin G. Norwood, Jr., (P.C.)	Eve B. Masinter
David S. Willenzik (P.C.)	Stephen W. Rider
Frank Voelker, Jr., (P.C.)	Eric A. Shuman
B. Franklin Martin, III, (P.C.)	Kathleen Krail Charvet
E. Fredrick Preis, Jr.	Thomas P. McAlister
Henri Wolbrette, III, (P.C.)	Laura Hobson Brown
Leopold Z. Sher (P.C.)	Robin Spencer Palmisano
William V. Dalferes, Jr., (P.C.)	James M. Garner
Peter L. Hilbert, Jr., (P.C.)	Charles R. Penot, Jr.
Constance Charles Willems	Debra Fischman Cottrell
Steven I. Klein (P.C.)	Arthur H. Leith
Bennet Scott Koren	Stephen P. Beiser
James M. Fantaci	Joseph F. Clark, Jr.
Kathleen A. Manning	Mary Lynne Friedman
Kenneth A. Weiss	Lauren A. Welch
Elwood F. Cahill, Jr.	Michael J. de Blanc, Jr.
Donna Guinn Klein	Katherine Conklin
Michael M. Noonan	Kevin L. O'Dea
Richard P. Richter	Robert P. Thibeaux
J. Patrick Beauchamp	Darnell Bludworth

(See Next Column)

McGLINCHEY STAFFORD LANG—*Continued*

Mark N. Bodin	Julie A. Unangst
Richard A. Aguilar	Daniel T. Plunkett
Lisa E. Maurer	Neal J. Kling
Thomas A. Roberts	Erin Fury Parkinson
Mark N. Mallery	Joseph C. Mandarino
Anita T. Lechner	Elena A. Lovoy
Margaret G. Diamond	Jennifer L. Dodge
Susan S. Harper	Keith A. Kornman
Monica A. Frois	Lauren L. Zimmermann
Karen T. Holzenthal	Deborah A. Van Meter
Margaret Woolverton Triebes	Susan Weidner Sileo
Louis J. Lupin	Monica Levine Lacks
Martha M. Young	Eliska Marie Kopfler
Elizabeth P. Blitch	Darrel J. Papillion
Patrick J. O'Cain	David Ball
Stephanie Karen Payne	Lezley Ann Kuntz
Dorothy Sheridan Watkins	John O. Pieksen, Jr.

Deirdre C. McGlinchey

OF COUNSEL

Joe Giarrusso, Jr.	René Webb Pennington
Timothy B. Francis	(Not admitted in LA)

For full biographical listings, see the Martindale-Hubbell Law Directory

MILLING, BENSON, WOODWARD, HILLYER, PIERSON & MILLER, L.L.P. (AV)

A Partnership including Professional Law Corporations
Suite Twenty-Three Hundred, 909 Poydras Street, 70112-1017
Telephone: 504-569-7000
Cable Address: "Milling"
Telex: 58-4211
Telecopier: 504-569-7001
ABA net: 15656
MCI Mail: "Milling"
Lafayette, Louisiana Office: 101 La Rue France, Suite 200.
Telephone: 318-232-3929.
Telecopier: 318-233-4957.

MEMBERS OF FIRM

David J. Conroy (P.C.)	James K. Irvin (P.C.)
Guy C. Lyman, Jr., (P.C.)	Hilton S. Bell (P.C.)
Neal D. Hobson (P.C.)	Katherine Goldman (P.C.)
F. Frank Fontenot (P.C.)	John W. Colbert (P.C.)
William C. Gambel (P.C.)	Bruce R. Hoefer, Jr. (P.C.)
Charles A. Snyder (P.C.)	David N. Schell, Jr. (P.C.)
Richard A. Whann (P.C.)	Mary L. Grier Holmes (P.C.)
Emile A. Wagner, III, (P.C.)	Jean M. Sweeney (P.C.)
Charles D. Marshall, Jr. (P.C.)	Patrick J. Butler, Jr. (P.C.)

Robert T. Lorio (P.C.)

PARTNERS EMERITUS

M. Truman Woodward, Jr., (P.C.)	Haywood H. Hillyer, Jr., (P.C.)
	G. Henry Pierson, Jr., (P.C.)

Joseph B. Miller

OF COUNSEL

Wilson S. Shirley, Jr., (P.C.)

SPECIAL COUNSEL

Timothy T. Roniger	Peter M. Meisner

Roger C. Linde

ASSOCIATES

Mark P. Dauer	Benjamin O. Schupp
Jay Corenswet	J. Timothy Betbeze
Ann C. Dowling	F. Paul Simoneaux, III
Alanna S. Arnold	Lisa F. Talley

LAFAYETTE OFFICE
RESIDENT MEMBERS OF FIRM

Robert L. Cabes (P.C.)

SPECIAL COUNSEL

John E. Castle, Jr.	Randall C Loewen

RESIDENT ASSOCIATES

Karen T. Bordelon	Gregory M. Attrep

Counsel for: Arthur Andersen & Co.; Chevron U.S.A., Inc.; The Dow Chemical Co.; The Louisiana Land & Exploration Co.; McDermott International Inc.; Phillips Petroleum; Whitney National Bank.

For full biographical listings, see the Martindale-Hubbell Law Directory

MOSELEY & ASSOCIATES, A PROFESSIONAL LAW CORPORATION (AV)

866 Camp Street, 70130
Telephone: 504-523-5220
Fax: 504-523-5225

Rockne L. Moseley	Janet Mary Ahern

For full biographical listings, see the Martindale-Hubbell Law Directory

PHELPS DUNBAR, L.L.P. (AV)

Texaco Center, 400 Poydras Street, 70130-3245
Telephone: 504-566-1311
Telecopier: 504-568-9130, 504-568-9007
Cable Address: "Howspencer"
Telex: 584125 WU
Telex: 6821155 WUI
Email: info@phelps.com
Baton Rouge, Louisiana Office: Suite 701, City National Bank Building, P.O. Box 4412.
Telephone: 504-346-0285.
Telecopier: 504-381-9197.
Jackson, Mississippi Office: Suite 500, Mtel Centré, 200 South Lamar Street, P.O. Box 23066.
Telephone: 601-352-2300.
Telecopier: 601-360-9777.
Tupelo, Mississippi Office: Seventh Floor, One Mississippi Plaza, P.O. Box 1220.
Telephone: 601-842-7907.
Telecopier: 601-842-3873.
Houston, Texas Office: Suite 900, 3040 Post Oak Boulevard.
Telephone: 713-626-1386.
Telecopier: 713-626-1388.
London, England Office: Suite 731, Level 7, Lloyd's, 1 Lime Street, London EC3M 7DQ England.
Telephone: 011-44-171-929-4765.
Telecopier: 011-44-171-929-0046.
Telex: 987321.

OF COUNSEL

John W. Sims	J. Barbee Winston
Frank S. Craig, Jr. (Resident, Baton Rouge, Louisiana Office)	John G. Weinmann
	George W. Healy, III

MEMBERS OF FIRM

James Bradley Kemp, Jr.	Arthur F. Jernigan, Jr. (Not admitted in LA; Resident, Jackson, Mississippi Office)
Harry S. Redmon, Jr.	
Fred M. Bush, Jr. (Not admitted in LA; Jackson and Tupelo, Mississippi Offices)	Luther T. Munford (Not admitted in LA; Resident, Jackson, Mississippi Office)
James H. Roussel	
Philip deV. Claverie	Dan M. McDaniel, Jr. (Not admitted in LA; Resident, Jackson, Mississippi Office)
Robert U. Soniat	
Charles M. Steen	George M. Gilly
Harry Rosenberg	Christopher O. Davis
F. M. Bush, III (Not admitted in LA; Jackson and Tupelo, Mississippi Offices)	William H. Howard, III
	Robert W. Nuzum
Harvey D. Wagar, III	Gary E. Friedman (Not admitted in LA; Resident, Jackson, Mississippi Office)
H. Alston Johnson, III (Resident, Baton Rouge, Louisiana Office)	
	Robert P. McCleskey, Jr.
Walker W. (Bill) Jones, III (Not admitted in LA; Houston, Texas, Jackson, Mississippi and London, England Offices)	Shaun B. Rafferty
	Brent B. Barriere
	Michael B. Wallace (Not admitted in LA; Resident, Jackson, Mississippi Office)
Ross F. Bass, Jr. (Not admitted in LA; Resident, Jackson, Mississippi Office)	
	Bruce V. Schewe
E. Clifton Hodge, Jr. (Not admitted in LA; Also at Jackson and Tupelo, Mississippi Offices)	J. Clifton Hall III
	G. Bruce Parkerson
	Jean Magee Hogan (Not admitted in LA; Jackson and Tupelo, Mississippi Offices)
C. Delbert Hosemann, Jr. (Not admitted in LA; Resident, Jackson, Mississippi Office)	
	Julia Marie Adams (Not admitted in LA; Resident, Houston, Texas Office)
Alan C. Wolf	
Paul O. Miller, III (Not admitted in LA; Resident, Jackson, Mississippi Office)	Deborah A. Newman (Not admitted in LA; Resident, Houston, Texas Office)
	William D. Aaron, Jr.
Armin J. Moeller, Jr. (Resident, Jackson, Mississippi Office)	Glover A. Russell, Jr. (Not admitted in LA; Resident, Jackson, Mississippi Office)
Kent E. Westmoreland (Not admitted in LA)	
	Stephen P. Hall
Claude LeRoy Stuart, III (Not admitted in LA; Resident, Houston, Texas Office)	James A. Stuckey
	Stephen H. Leech, Jr. (Not admitted in LA; Resident, Jackson, Mississippi Office)
Roy C. Cheatwood	
Edward B. Poitevent, II	W. Thomas Siler, Jr. (Not admitted in LA; Jackson and Tupelo, Mississippi Offices)
Danny G. Shaw	
Reuben V. Anderson (Not admitted in LA; Resident, Jackson, Mississippi Office)	R. Pepper Crutcher, Jr. (Jackson and Tupelo, Mississippi Offices)
George B. Hall, Jr.	
Robert C. Clotworthy	Nancy Scott Degan
Richard N. Dicharry	Virginia Boulet
Frank W. Trapp (Not admitted in LA; Resident, Jackson, Mississippi Office)	Jennifer Bowers Zimmerman (Resident, Baton Rouge, Louisiana Office)
Michael D. Hunt (Resident, Baton Rouge, Louisiana Office)	John P. Sneed (Resident, Jackson, Mississippi Office)

(See Next Column)

Phelps Dunbar L.L.P., New Orleans—Continued

MEMBERS OF FIRM (Continued)

F. Scott Kaiser (Resident, Baton Rouge, Louisiana Office)
Richard E. Matheny (Resident, Baton Rouge, Louisiana Office)
Deborah Shelby Nichols (Not admitted in LA; Resident, Jackson, Mississippi Office)
Brian D. Wallace
M. Nan Alessandra
Dana E. Kelly (Not admitted in LA; Resident, Jackson, Mississippi Office)
William C. Brabec (Not admitted in LA; Resident, Jackson, Mississippi Office)
David M. Hunter
Steven J. Levine (Resident, Baton Rouge, Louisiana Office)
Allen D. Darden (Resident, Baton Rouge, Louisiana Office)
Mary Ellen Roy
William I. Gault, Jr. (Not admitted in LA; Resident, Jackson, Mississippi Office)
Susan Fahey Desmond (Not admitted in LA; Resident, Jackson, Mississippi Office)
Barbara L. Arras

Randy P. Roussel (Resident, Baton Rouge, Louisiana Office)
Charles D. Porter (Not admitted in LA; Resident, Jackson, Mississippi Office)
David P. Webb (Not admitted in LA; Resident, Jackson, Mississippi Office)
Sessions Ault Hootsell III
Mark C. Dodart
Jonathan C. Benda (Resident, Baton Rouge, Louisiana Office)
Paul L. Peyronnin
Thomas H. Kiggans (Resident, Baton Rouge, Louisiana Office)
Marshall M. Redmon
David P. Steiner
Joseph A. Ziemianski (Not admitted in LA; Houston, Texas and Jackson, Mississippi Offices)
Gerardo R. Barrios
David M. Thomas, II (Not admitted in LA; Resident, Jackson, Mississippi Office)
Dinetia M. Newman (Not admitted in LA; Jackson and Tupelo, Mississippi Offices)

COUNSEL

Edwin K. Legnon
Jane E. Armstrong
J. Michael Cutshaw (Resident, Baton Rouge, Louisiana Office)
Alissa J. Allison
E. Jane Sherman (Resident, Baton Rouge, Louisiana Office)
G. Kay L. Trapp (Not admitted in LA; Jackson and Tupelo, Mississippi Offices)
Linda Bounds Sherman (Not admitted in LA; Resident, Jackson, Mississippi Office)

Gregory D. Pirkle (Not admitted in LA; Jackson and Tupelo, Mississippi Offices)
Gary Meringer
Jane A. Robert
Matthew R. Muth (Not admitted in LA; Resident, Houston, Texas Office)
John V. Eskrigge (Not admitted in LA; Resident, Jackson, Mississippi Office)

ASSOCIATES

David A. Abramson
Neil C. Abramson
Lee R. Adler
Steven Johnson Allen (Resident, Jackson, Mississippi Office)
Maria Artime (Not admitted in LA; Resident, Houston, Texas Office)
Laura Ann Baity
Jane H. Barney (Resident, Baton Rouge, Louisiana Office)
Scott W. Bates (Not admitted in LA; Houston, Texas and Jackson, Mississippi Offices)
John B. Beard (Not admitted in LA; Resident, Jackson, Mississippi Office)
Thomas M. Beh
Sheryl Bey (Resident, Jackson, Mississippi Office)
Wendy T. Blanchard
Maurice E. Bostick
Kathryn Irine Brooks (Not admitted in LA; Resident, Houston, Texas Office)
Stratton Bull (Not admitted in LA; Resident, Jackson, Mississippi Office)
Evan T. Caffrey (Not admitted in LA; Resident, Houston, Texas Office)
Heather J. Camp (Not admitted in LA; Resident, Jackson, Mississippi Office)
Laura C. Capshaw (Not admitted in LA; Resident, Houston, Texas Office)
Rebecca Y. Cooper
Diane Hollenshead Copes
James W. Craig (Not admitted in LA; Resident, Jackson, Mississippi Office)

Rebecca Bellows Crawford (Resident, Baton Rouge, Louisiana Office)
Malinda York Crouch (Not admitted in LA; Resident, Houston, Texas Office)
Andrea E. Culler (Not admitted in LA)
John C. Cunningham (Not admitted in LA; Resident, Houston, Texas Office)
Daniel E. Davillier
Caroline McS. Dolan
Derrick A. Dyer (Not admitted in LA; Resident, Jackson, Mississippi Office)
Robert S. Eitel
Ken Fairly (Not admitted in LA; Resident, Jackson, Mississippi Office)
Tanza C. Farr (Not admitted in LA; Resident, Houston, Texas Office)
Tracey E. Flemings
Peter N. Freiberg
Susan W. Furr (Resident, Baton Rouge, Louisiana Office)
Kevin M. Grace
N. Eleanor Graham
Eric T. Hamer (Not admitted in LA; Resident, Jackson, Mississippi Office)
Lawrence J. Hand, Jr.
Flynn M. Jennings (Not admitted in LA)
Jeffrey Starks Johnson
David M. Korn
Margaret (Amie) Kozan (Resident, Baton Rouge, Louisiana Office)
M. David Kurtz
Kent A. Lambert

(See Next Column)

ASSOCIATES (Continued)

John B. Landry, Jr. (Not admitted in LA; Resident, Jackson, Mississippi Office)
Darrell J. Loup (Resident, Baton Rouge, Louisiana Office)
Patricia Ann Lynch
Tricia A. Martinez (Resident, Baton Rouge, Louisiana Office)
Stephanie G. McShane
Pamela G. Michiels
Karen Klaas Milhollin (Not admitted in LA; Resident, Houston, Texas Office)
Jeffrey S. Moore (Not admitted in LA; Jackson and Tupelo, Mississippi Offices)
Michele C. Mount
Wendy Russell Mullins (Not admitted in LA; Resident, Jackson, Mississippi Office)
Leah E. Nunn
Skye Henry O'Donnell
Patrick O'Hara (Resident, Baton Rouge, Louisiana Office)
Daniel T. Pancamo
A. Matt Pesnell (Not admitted in LA; Resident, Jackson, Mississippi Office)
John Whitney Pesnell (Resident, Baton Rouge, Louisiana Office)
George C. Plauché (Resident, Houston, Texas Office)
Chelye E. Prichard (Not admitted in LA; Resident, Jackson, Mississippi Office)
Stanley T. Proctor (Not admitted in LA; Resident, Houston, Texas Office)
Katherine Karam Quirk
Patrick Ragan Richard (Resident, Baton Rouge, Louisiana Office)
Vanessa A. Richelle

Todd C. Richter (Not admitted in LA; Resident, Jackson, Mississippi Office)
William J. Riviere
Diane Fagan Robinson (Resident, Baton Rouge, Louisiana Office)
John W. Robinson, III (Not admitted in LA; Resident, Jackson, Mississippi Office)
Daniel C. Rodgers
Mary Frances Lindquist Rosamond
James A. Rowell
J. Marie Rudd
C. Catherine Scallan (Not admitted in LA; Resident, Jackson, Mississippi Office)
John L. Schouest (Resident, Houston, Texas Office)
Andrew L. Schwarcz
Jay Russell Sever
Wendy Moore Shelton (Not admitted in LA; Resident, Jackson, Mississippi Office)
Stacy Singleton
John W. Sinnott
Jennifer Burrows Solis
Tania Tetlow
E. Russell Turner (Not admitted in LA; Resident, Jackson, Mississippi Office)
Sheila T. Walet
G. Benjamin Ward
Michael F. Weiner
Lara E. White
Ronald J. White
Rebecca L. Wiggins (Not admitted in LA; Resident, Jackson, Mississippi Office)
Stephen M. Wilson (Not admitted in LA; Jackson and Tupelo, Mississippi Offices)
Mark E. Young
Dawei Zhang

Representative Clients: The Britannia Steamship Insurance Assn., Ltd.; Central Louisiana Electric Company, Inc.; Hibernia National Bank; Hilton Hotels Corp.; Louisiana Gas Service Co., Inc.; Missouri Pacific Railroad Co.; North Mississippi Health Services, Inc. (and affiliated entities); The Travelers Insurance Company; Underwriters at Lloyd's, London; Uniroyal Chemical Company.

For full biographical listings, see the Martindale-Hubbell Law Directory

SESSIONS & FISHMAN, L.L.P. (AV)

A Registered Limited Liability Partnership including Professional Corporations
Place St. Charles, 201 St. Charles Avenue, 70170-3500
Telephone: 504-582-1500
Telex: 58364NLN
Fax: 504-582-1555

MEMBERS OF FIRM

Max Nathan, Jr. (P.C.)
Robert E. Winn
Owen A. Neff
L. K. Clement, Jr.
William M. Lucas, Jr.
Michael J. Molony, Jr. (P.C.)
Jack M. Alltmont
J. David Forsyth
James Ryan, III
M. Shael Herman
Peter S. Title
Carole Cukell Neff
Stephen R. Doody
Louis Leonard Galvis
Reuben I. Friedman

Sally A. Shushan
Camilo K. Salas, III
Dorothy S. Jacobs (P.C.)
Joy Goldberg Braun
Andrew A. Braun
Joyce M. Dombourian (P.C.)
Alan D. Ezkovich
John William Hite, III
Sharon Cormack Mize
David H. Bernstein
Edward J. Rivera
David P. Salley
Valerie Welz Jusselin
Raymond P. Ward
Michael A. Berenson

ASSOCIATES

Corinne B. Viso
Brian D. Roth

Glen E. Mercer
Maria N. Rabieh

Representative Clients: Air Products & Chemicals, Inc.; Bethlehem Steel Corp.; Brown & Williamson Tobacco Corporation, as successor by merger to The American Tobacco Co.; The Equitable Life Assurance Society of the United States; Holiday Inns, Inc.; J.C. Penney Co., Inc.; State Farm Insurance Cos.; United Services Automobile Assn.; Volkswagen of America, Inc.

For full biographical listings, see the Martindale-Hubbell Law Directory

New Orleans—Continued

STONE, PIGMAN, WALTHER, WITTMANN & HUTCHINSON, L.L.P. (AV)

A Partnership including Professional Corporations
546 Carondelet Street, 70130-3588
Telephone: 504-581-3200
Fax: 504-581-3361
E-mail: attorney initials @ stonepigman.com
Baton Rouge, Louisiana Office: City National Bank Building, 445 North Boulevard, Suite 640, Baton Rouge, Louisiana 70802.
Telephone: 504-379-7400.
Fax: 504-379-7410.

MEMBERS OF FIRM

Saul Stone	Noel J. Darce
Paul O. H. Pigman (P.C.)	C. Lawrence Orlansky (P.C.)
Ewell P. Walther, Jr.	Richard C. Stanley
(1932-1990)	Calvin P. Brasseaux (P.C.)
Phillip A. Wittmann	Michael R. Schneider (P.C.)
Campbell C. Hutchinson (P.C.)	Scott T. Whittaker
David L. Stone (P.C.)	Denise M. Pilié(P.C.)
William D. Treeby (P.C.)	Barry W. Ashe (P.C.)
Hirschel T. Abbott, Jr., (P.C.)	George C. Freeman, III
Michael R. Fontham (P.C.)	Joseph L. Caverly (P.C.)
Anthony M. DiLeo (P.C.)	Nelea A. Absher (P.C.)
Wayne J. Lee (P.C.)	Cecilia C. Woodley (P.C.)
Clinton W. Shinn (P.C.)	Marc D. Winsberg
James C. Gulotta, Jr., (P.C.)	Michael D. Landry
Paul L. Zimmering	Mary L. Dumestre (P.C.)
John M. Landis	Robert E. Harrington (P.C.)
Stephen H. Kupperman (P.C.)	Karen H. Freese (P.C.)
Stephen G. Bullock	Laurie A. Barcelona
Kyle D. Schonekas	John P. Cerise (P.C.)
Steven W. Usdin (P.C.)	Paul J. Masinter
Judy Y. Barrasso (P.C.)	Thomas M. Flanagan
Susan Gayle Talley (P.C.)	Dorothy Hudson Wimberly
Douglas D. Dodd	Rachel Wendt Wisdom

SPECIAL COUNSEL

Warren M. Faris	Richard E. Sarver

ASSOCIATES

Linda R. Gallagher	C. Joyce Hall
Angela J. Crowder	Anne V. Winter
Dane S. Ciolino	Suzanne M. Ciaccio
Lynda C. Friedmann	Bryan C. Reuter
Edwin H. Neill, III	Kelly Lanning Turner
Victoria M. de Lisle	Michael Q. Walshe, Jr.
John Michael Harlow	Michelle L. Chauvin
Stephanie D. Shuler	Russell L. Jaffe
Kelly McNeil Legier	Joelle Flannigan Evans
Deborah Pearce-Reggio	Keith B. Hall
John P. LeBlanc	H. Minor Pipes, III

For full biographical listings, see the Martindale-Hubbell Law Directory

WALTER J. SUTHON III (AV)

1010 Whitney Building, 228 St. Charles Avenue, 70130
Telephone: 504-524-0681
Fax: 504-524-0685
For full biographical listings, see the Martindale-Hubbell Law Directory

TERRIBERRY, CARROLL & YANCEY, L.L.P. (AV)

3100 Energy Centre, 1100 Poydras Street, 70163-3100
Telephone: 504-523-6451
Cable Address: "Terrib"
Telex: 6821224 (WUI)
Fax: 504-524-3257

MEMBERS OF FIRM

Benjamin W. Yancey	Hugh Ramsay Straub
(1906-1991)	David B. Lawton
Walter Carroll, Jr. (Retired)	Roger D. Allen
Maurie D. Yager	Janet Wessler Marshall
G. Edward Merritt	D. Kirk Boswell
James L. Schupp, Jr.	Gary A. Hemphill
John A. Bolles	Laurence R. De Buys, IV
Charles F. Lozes	Kevin J. LaVie
Robert J. Barbier	Stephen E. Mattesky

COUNSEL

Andrew T. Martinez	Cynthia Anne Wegmann

ASSOCIATES

Gerald M. Baca	Michael M. Butterworth
John A. Scialdone	

Representative Clients: Assuranceforeningen Gard; Assuranceforeningen Skuld; Certain Underwriters at Lloyd's; The London Steam-Ship Owners' Mutual Insurance Assn. Ltd.; Lykes Bros. Steamship Co., Inc.; New Orleans Steamship Assn.; Nordisk Skibsrederforening (Northern Shipowners Defence Club); Scandinavian Marine Claims Office, Inc.; Steamship Mutual Underwriting Assn. Ltd.; United Kingdom Mutual Steam Ship Assurance Assn. Ltd.

For full biographical listings, see the Martindale-Hubbell Law Directory

---

NEW ROADS, * Pointe Coupee Parish — (Refer to Baton Rouge)

OPELOUSAS, * St. Landry Parish

DUBUISSON AND DUBUISSON (AV)

345 South Court Street, P.O. Box 230, 70570
Telephone: 318-942-6506
Fax: 318-942-8774

MEMBERS OF FIRM

E. B. Dubuisson (1865-1943)	James G. Dubuisson
Edward Dubuisson (1902-1966)	Edward B. Dubuisson

Representative Clients: The Travelers Insurance Co.; Missouri Pacific Railroad Co.; South Central Bell Telephone & Telegraph Co.; Pennsylvania Manufacturers Association Insurance Co.; Millers Mutual Insurance Association of Illinois; Connecticut General Life Insurance Co.; American Home Assurance Co.; Shell Oil Co.
Local Attorneys for: St. Landry Bank & Trust Co. (General Counsel); Cabot Carbon Co.

For full biographical listings, see the Martindale-Hubbell Law Directory

---

PLAQUEMINE, * Iberville Parish

BORRON & DELAHAYE, A PROFESSIONAL LAW CORPORATION (AV)

58065 Meriam Street, P.O. Box 679, 70765-0679
Telephone: 504-687-3571; 343-3148
Fax: 504-687-9695

MEMBERS OF FIRM

Paul G. Borron (1874-1960)	Paul G. Borron, III
Charles Ory Dupont (1919-1976)	John L. Delahaye

Representative Clients: Iberville Building & Loan Assn.; American Sugar Cane League; Iberville Trust & Savings Bank; South Central Bell Telephone Co.; Citizens Bank & Trust Co.; Iberville Motors, Inc.; A. Wilbert's Sons Limited Partnership; Hebert Brothers Engineers; Surgical Associates of Baton Rouge, Inc.; First American Title Insurance Co.

For full biographical listings, see the Martindale-Hubbell Law Directory

---

PORT ALLEN, * West Baton Rouge Parish — (Refer to Plaquemine)

ST. MARTINVILLE, * St. Martin Parish — (Refer to New Iberia)

SHREVEPORT, * Caddo Parish

BARLOW AND HARDTNER L.C. (AV)

Tenth Floor, Louisiana Tower, 401 Edwards Street, 71101-3289
Telephone: 318-227-1131
Telecopier: 318-227-1141
Mailing Address: P.O. Box 8, Shreveport, Louisiana, 71161-0008

Ray A. Barlow (1931-1995)	David R. Taggart
Quintin T. Hardtner, III	Clair F. White
Malcolm S. Murchison	Stephen E. Ramey
Kay Cowden Medlin	Philip E. Downer, III
Joseph L. Shea, Jr.	Michael B. Donald
Jay A. Greenleaf	

OF COUNSEL

Cecil E. Ramey, Jr.	Paula Hazelrig Hickman

Gail Bowen McCulloch	Robert W. Kyle
Jonathan D. Baughman	

Representative Clients: NorAm Energy Corp. (formerly Arkla, Inc.); The Magale Foundation; Central and South West Corporation; Panhandle Eastern Corp.; Pennzoil Producing Co.; Ashland Oil, Inc.; The Daughters of the Cross; Southwestern Electric Power Company; The Centex Construction Group; General Electric Co.

For full biographical listings, see the Martindale-Hubbell Law Directory

---

BLANCHARD, WALKER, O'QUIN & ROBERTS, A PROFESSIONAL LAW CORPORATION (AV)

Fourteenth Floor, Premier Bank Tower, 400 Texas Street, P.O. Drawer 1126, 71101
Telephone: 318-221-6858
Fax: 318-227-2967
Email: 103002.2215@compuserve.com
Bossier City, Louisiana Office: 2285 Benton Road, Suite B-201.
Telephone: 318-742-9255.
Fax: 318-742-9210.

Gilbert L. Hetherwick	Lawrence L. Jones
Robert Roberts III	Reginald E. Cassibry
Neilson S. Jacobs	(Resident, Bossier City Office)
John T. Cox, Jr.	J. David Garrett
J. Edgerton Pierson, Jr., (P.C.)	Cecil W. Talley
W. Michael Adams	Lawrence W. Pettiette, Jr.
Wm. Timothy Allen, III	W. Deryl Medlin
Don Weir, Jr.	James C. McMichael, Jr.

(See Next Column)

BLANCHARD, WALKER, O'QUIN & ROBERTS A PROFESSIONAL LAW
CORPORATION, *Shreveport—Continued*

Robert W. Johnson	A. M. Stroud, III
L. David Cromwell	Robert A. Dunkelman
Michael E. Riddick	Leslie Idom Kalmbach
Edward Keith Carter	Joseph S. Woodley
Donald Armand, Jr.	Edwin H. Byrd, III
Paul M. Adkins	Peter J. Rotolo, III

Robin C. Norman

OF COUNSEL

Pike Hall, Jr.	Marlin Risinger, Jr.

Gregory W. Jones

For full biographical listings, see the Martindale-Hubbell Law Directory

MAYER, SMITH & ROBERTS, L.L.P. (AV)

1550 Creswell, 71101
Telephone: 318-222-2135, 222-2268
Fax: 318-222-6420
Email: (Attorney's First Name)@MSRLAW.COM

MEMBERS OF FIRM

Caldwell Roberts	David Butterfield
Walter O. Hunter, Jr.	Henry N. Bellamy
Mark A. Goodwin	John C. Turnage
Ben Marshall, Jr.	Paul R. Mayer, Jr.
Alexander S. Lyons	Steven E. Soileau
Kim Purdy Thomas	Deborah Shea Baukman

Caldwell Roberts, Jr.

ASSOCIATES

Frank K. Carroll	Dalton Roberts Ross

OF COUNSEL

Charles L. Mayer	Paul R. Mayer

Representative Clients: CNA Insurance Companies; Liberty Mutual Insurance Company; The St. Paul Companies; United States Fidelity and Guaranty Company; Schumpert Medical Center; Travelers Insurance Company; Great American Insurance Company; Insurance Corporation of America; Highlands Insurance Company.

For full biographical listings, see the Martindale-Hubbell Law Directory

PEATROSS, GREER & FRAZIER (AV)

504 Texas Street, Suite 404, P.O. Box 404, 71162-0404
Telephone: 318-222-0202
Fax: 318-226-1364

MEMBERS OF FIRM

Charles B. Peatross	L. Edwin Greer

John M. Frazier

ASSOCIATES

Kenneth Craig Smith, Jr.

For full biographical listings, see the Martindale-Hubbell Law Directory

SHUEY & SMITH (AV)

509 Market Street Ninth Floor, 71101
Telephone: 318-221-8671
FAX: 318-222-4320

MEMBERS OF FIRM

W. Gene Carlton (1935-1975)	I. Henry Smith, Jr.
John M. Shuey	John M. Shuey, Jr.

John D. Collinsworth

COUNSEL

Hugh M. Stephens

Representative Clients: Tri-State Realty Co.; Schlumberger Technology Corp.

For full biographical listings, see the Martindale-Hubbell Law Directory

SIMON, FITZGERALD, COOKE, REED & WELCH (AV)

Suite 200, 4700 Line Avenue, 71106
Telephone: 318-868-2600
Telecopier: 318-868-8966

MEMBERS OF FIRM

Fred Simon (1904-1993)	Paul M. Cooke
Archie M. Simon	Chatham H. Reed
Thomas P. Fitzgerald	Keith M. Welch
(1914-1993)	Kevin R. Molloy

A list of Representative Clients will be furnished upon request.

For full biographical listings, see the Martindale-Hubbell Law Directory

(See Next Column)

SMITHERMAN, LUNN, CHASTAIN & HILL, L.L.P. (AV)

A Limited Liability Partnership including Professional Corporations
Commercial National Bank Building, 333 Texas Street, Suite
717, 71101-3666
Telephone: 318-227-1990
FAX: 318-222-0482
Bossier City, Louisiana Office: Greenacres Office Park, 2285 Benton Road,
Suite A-200, 71111.
Telephone: 318-746-4250.

MEMBERS OF FIRM

James E. Smitherman (1882-1967)	Ofie T. Rubin (1947-1991)
James E. Smitherman, Jr. (1914-1978)	Stuart D. Lunn (P.L.C.)
	Merritt B. Chastain, Jr., (P.L.C.)
	W. James Hill, III, (P.L.C.)
David E. Smitherman (1897-1984)	Donald Lee Brice, Jr.

OF COUNSEL

John A. Richardson	Gerald Le Van

Attorneys For: Home Federal Savings & Loan Assn.; Pennzoil Co.; Atlas Processing Co.; Red River Corp.; Wray Ford, Inc.; Boise Cascade Corp.; National Association of Pipe Coating Applicators; Southern Erection Co., Inc.; Fairfield Property Management; Cross Country Management, Inc.

For full biographical listings, see the Martindale-Hubbell Law Directory

WILKINSON, CARMODY & GILLIAM (AV)

1700 Beck Building, 400 Travis Street, P.O. Box 1707, 71166
Telephone: 318-221-4196
Telecopier: 318-221-3705

MEMBERS OF FIRM

John D. Wilkinson (1867-1929)	Bobby S. Gilliam
William Scott Wilkinson (1895-1985)	Mark E. Gilliam
	Penny D. Sellers
Arthur R. Carmody, Jr.	Patrick F. Robinson

Michael J. Ryan

Representative Clients: Farmers Insurance Group; Home Federal Savings & Loan Association of Shreveport; The Kansas City Southern Railway Co.; KTAL-TV; Lincoln National Life Insurance Co.; Mobil Oil Co.; Schumpert Medical Center; Sears, Roebuck & Co.; Southern Pacific Transportation Co.; Southwestern Electric Power Co.

For full biographical listings, see the Martindale-Hubbell Law Directory

---

VILLE PLATTE, * Evangeline Parish — (Refer to Opelousas)

WINNFIELD, * Winn Parish

SIMMONS AND DERR (AV)

Simmons Building, Church Street, P.O. Box 525, 71483
Telephone: 318-628-3951

MEMBERS OF FIRM

Kermit M. Simmons	Jacque D. Derr

Reference: Bank of Winnfield & Trust Co.

For full biographical listings, see the Martindale-Hubbell Law Directory

WINNSBORO, * Franklin Parish — (Refer to Rayville)

MAINE

AUBURN, * Androscoggin Co.

LINNELL, CHOATE & WEBBER (AV)

83 Pleasant Street, P.O. Box 190, 04212-0190
Telephone: 207-784-4563
Telefax: 207-784-1981

OF COUNSEL

Paul A. Choate

MEMBERS OF FIRM

Frank W. Linnell (1908-1977)	Richard J. O'Brien
Curtis Webber	Michelle A. Small
John R. Linnell	John W. Conway
Jon S. Oxman	J. Gordon Scannell, Jr.

ASSOCIATES

Rebecca S. K. Webber

Local Counsel for: Travelers Insurance Co.; Worcester Insurance Co.
General Counsel for: Mechanics Savings Bank; Farm Credit of Southern Maine; Radio Stations WLAM, WKZS and WQSS (Camden); City of Auburn; Mechanic Falls Sanitary District.

For full biographical listings, see the Martindale-Hubbell Law Directory

Auburn—Continued

SKELTON, TAINTOR & ABBOTT, A PROFESSIONAL CORPORATION (AV)

95 Main Street, P.O. Box 3200, 04212-3200
Telephone: 207-784-3200
Fax: 207-784-3345
Rumford, Maine Office: 150 Congress Street.
Telephone: 207-364-4593.

Charles H. Abbott	Peter M. Garcia
Stephen P. Beale	Ronald P. Lebel
Jill A. Checkoway	Michael R. Poulin
John B. Cole	Norman J. Rattey
Bryan M. Dench	Frederick G. Taintor (Retired)
	Stephen B. Wade

Jonathan Doolittle	Jennifer F. Kreckel, Resident,
Douglas Grauel	Rumford, Maine Office)
	Harold N. Skelton

OF COUNSEL
William B. Skelton, II

General Counsel for: Androscoggin Savings Bank; Bates College; Central Maine Medical Center; Auburn Savings & Loan Association; Auburn Housing Authority; Maine School Administrative District No. 52; W. S. Libbey Co.; Lewiston Sun-Journal.

For full biographical listings, see the Martindale-Hubbell Law Directory

---

AUGUSTA, * Kennebec Co.

* indicates certain Bar Register subscribers whose principal office is located elsewhere in the state and who have arranged for representation as a part of the state capital listings that follow

BERNSTEIN, SHUR, SAWYER & NELSON, A PROFESSIONAL CORPORATION (AV)

146 Capitol Street, P.O. Box 5057, 04332-5057
Telephone: 207-623-1596
Telecopier: 207-626-0200
Portland, Maine Office: 100 Middle Street, P.O. Box 9729.
Telephone: 207-774-1200.
Telecopier: 207-774-1127.
Kennebunk, Maine Office: 62 Portland Road.
Telephone: 207-985-7152.
Telecopier: 207-985-3174.

Richard M. Schade	Lee K. Bragg
	Lester F. Wilkinson, Jr.

Representative Clients: University of Maine; Fleet Bank of Maine; Sebago, Inc.; First NH Banks, Inc.; Greater Portland Transit District.

For full biographical listings, see the Martindale-Hubbell Law Directory

DOYLE & NELSON (AV)

150 Capitol Street, 04330
Telephone: 207-622-6124
Telefax: 207-623-1358
Toll Free: 800-639-3165

MEMBERS OF FIRM
Jon R. Doyle	Craig H. Nelson

ASSOCIATES
Daniel P. Riley, Jr.	Andrew B. MacLean

Local Counsel for: Citicorp and its subsidiaries; R.J. Reynolds Tobacco Co.; British Consulate General.
Counsel for: Financial Institutions Service Corp.; Miles Memorial Hospital; Maine Medical Records Assn.; Citicorp Acceptance Corp.; Citicorp Homeowners, Inc.

For full biographical listings, see the Martindale-Hubbell Law Directory

* PIERCE ATWOOD (AV)

77 Winthrop Street, 04330
Telephone: 207-622-6311
Fax: 207-623-9367
Email: info@PierceAtwood.com
Portland, Maine Office: One Monument Square.
Telephone: 207-791-1100.
Fax: 207-791-1350.
Newburyport, Massachusetts Office: 6 Harris Street.
Telephone: 508-465-9599.
Fax: 508-465-9945.

MEMBERS OF FIRM
Warren E. Winslow, Jr.	Michael D. Seitzinger
Malcolm L. Lyons	John C. Nivison

ASSOCIATE
Daniel J. Stevens

For full biographical listings, see the Martindale-Hubbell Law Directory

* PRETI, FLAHERTY, BELIVEAU & PACHIOS (AV)

A Limited Liability Company
45 Memorial Circle, P.O. Box 1058, 04332-1058
Telephone: 207-623-55300
Telecopier: 207-623-2914
Portland, Maine Office: 443 Congress Street, P.O. Box 11410, 04104-7410.
Telephone: 207-791-3000.
Telecopier: 207-791-3111.

RESIDENT MEMBERS OF FIRM
Severin M. Beliveau	James C. Pitney, Jr.
Michael J. Gentile	Virginia E. Davis
Bruce C. Gerrity	Joseph G. Donahue
Anthony W. Buxton	Ann R. Robinson
	Stephen E. F. Langsdorf

RESIDENT OF COUNSEL
Charles F. Dingman	Mark B. LeDuc

RESIDENT ASSOCIATES
Deirdre M. O'Callaghan	Jodie S. Sullivan
	Gregg D. Bernstein

For full biographical listings, see the Martindale-Hubbell Law Directory

---

BANGOR, * Penobscot Co.

EATON, PEABODY, BRADFORD & VEAGUE, P.A. (AV)

Fleet Center-Exchange Street, P.O. Box 1210, 04402-1210
Telephone: 207-947-0111
Telecopier: 207-942-3040
Email: epbv@aol.com
Augusta, Maine Office: 2 Central Plaza.
Telephone: 207-622-3747.
Telecopier: 207-622-9732.
Blue Hill, Maine Office: One East Blue Hill Road.
Telephone: 207-374-2812.
Telecopier: 207-374-2548.
Brunswick, Maine Office: 167 Park Row.
Telephone: 207-729-1144.
Telecopier: 207-729-1140.
Camden, Maine Office: 7-9 Washington Street.
Telephone: 207-236-3325.
Telecopier: 207-236-8611.
Dover-Foxcroft, Maine Office: 30 East Main Street.
Telephone: 207-564-8378.
Telecopier: 207-564-7059.

George F. Eaton (1892-1956)	Michael B. Trainor
Malcolm E. Morrell, Jr.	John A. Cunningham
Thomas M. Brown	(Resident, Brunswick Office)
Edward D. Leonard, III	William B. Devoe
Calvin E. True	Karen A. Huber
Bernard J. Kubetz	P. Andrew Hamilton
Thomas C. Johnston	Terry W. Calderwood
Clarissa B. Edelston	(Resident, Camden Office)
Douglas M. Smith	Paul L. Gibbons
(Dover-Foxcroft and Augusta	(Resident, Camden Office)
Offices)	Laurie A. Dart
Daniel G. McKay	Judy A.S. Metcalf
Stephen G. Morrell	(Resident, Brunswick Office)
(Resident, Brunswick Office)	Jonathan B. Huntington
Glen L. Porter	(Resident, Dover-Foxcroft
Gordon H. S. Scott	Office)
(Resident, Augusta Office)	R. Lee Ivy
Clare Hudson Payne	Thad B. Zmistowski

OF COUNSEL
George F. Peabody	Dorrance Sexton, Jr.
Martin L. Wilk	(Resident, Blue Hill Office)
(Resident, Brunswick Office)	

Lorena R. Rush	Allison C. Lucy
Dorisann B. W. Wagner	Roger Lang Huber
(Resident, Augusta Office)	David W. Kesner
	Theodore R. Foss

A List of Representative Clients available upon request.

For full biographical listings, see the Martindale-Hubbell Law Directory

GROSS, MINSKY, MOGUL & SINGAL, P.A. (AV)

Key Plaza, 23 Water Street, P.O. Box 917, 04402-0917
Telephone: 207-942-4644
Telecopier: 207-942-3699
Email: gmm&s-law@atlsysnet.com *URL:*
http://www.atlsysnet.com/gmms

(See Next Column)

GROSS, MINSKY, MOGUL & SINGAL P.A., *Bangor—Continued*

Edward I. Gross (Retired)	George C. Schelling
Jules L. Mogul (1930-1994)	Edward W. Gould
Norman Minsky	Steven J. Mogul
George Z. Singal	James R. Wholly
Louis H. Kornreich	Daniel A. Pileggi
	Philip K. Clarke

Wayne P. Libhart (Retired)	James S. Nixon
Sandra L. Rothera	F. Todd Lowell

Representative Client: Dahl Chase Pathology Associates.
Local Counsel for: The St. Paul Insurance Cos.; Aetna Life & Casualty Co.; Imperial Casualty & Indemnity Co.

For full biographical listings, see the Martindale-Hubbell Law Directory

VAFIADES, BROUNTAS & KOMINSKY (AV)

Key Plaza, 23 Water Street, P.O. Box 919, 04402-0919
Telephone: 207-947-6915
Telecopier: 207-941-0863

MEMBERS OF FIRM

Susan R. Kominsky	Eugene C. Coughlin, III
Marvin H. Glazier	Lisa Cohen Lunn

ASSOCIATES

Terence M. Harrigan	James C. Munch, III
	Paul R. Brown

OF COUNSEL

Lewis V. Vafiades	Nicholas P. Brountas

For full biographical listings, see the Martindale-Hubbell Law Directory

BAR HARBOR, Hancock Co.

FENTON, CHAPMAN, FENTON, SMITH & KANE, P.A. (AV)

109 Main Street, P.O. Box B, 04609
Telephone: 207-288-3331
FAX: 207-288-9326

William Fenton	Chadbourn H. Smith
Douglas B. Chapman	Daniel H. Kane (1940-1995)
Nathaniel R. Fenton	Hancock Griffin, Jr. (1912-1980)

Margaret A. Timothy	Eric Lindquist

OF COUNSEL

Edwin R. Smith

Reference: Bar Harbor Banking and Trust Co.

For full biographical listings, see the Martindale-Hubbell Law Directory

BATH,* Sagadahoc Co.

CONLEY & HALEY (AV)

Thirty Front Street, 04530
Telephone: 207-443-5576
Telefax: 207-443-6665

J. Michael Conley	Laura M. O'Hanlon
Mark L. Haley	Tracey G. Burton
Brian L. Champion	Julie G. Martin

Representative Clients: Bath Iron Works Corp.; Central Maine Power Co.; Saco Defense, Inc.; Sugarloaf Mountain Corp.; Maine Public Service Company.
References: Key Bank of Maine; First Federal Savings & Loan Association of Bath; Brunswick Federal Savings.

For full biographical listings, see the Martindale-Hubbell Law Directory

BIDDEFORD, York Co.

JENSEN BAIRD GARDNER & HENRY (AV)

(Successor to Walker, Bradford & LaBrique)
419 Alfred Street, 04005
Telephone: 207-282-5107
Telecopier: 207-282-6301
Portland, Maine Office: Ten Free Street.
Telephone: 207-775-7271.
Telecopier: 207-775-7935.

OF COUNSEL

John D. Bradford

RESIDENT MEMBERS OF FIRM

David J. Jones	Ralph W. Austin
	Keith R. Jacques

RESIDENT ASSOCIATES

Milda A. Castner	Anne H. Jordan

Representative Clients: General Motors Acceptance Corp.; Sedgwick James; Owens Corning Fiberglas; IBM; Key Bank of Maine.

(See Next Column)

For full biographical listings, see the Martindale-Hubbell Law Directory

FORT FAIRFIELD, Aroostook Co. — (Refer to Presque Isle)

GARDINER, Kennebec Co. — (Refer to Augusta)

KENNEBUNK, York Co.

BERNSTEIN, SHUR, SAWYER & NELSON, A PROFESSIONAL CORPORATION (AV)

62 Portland Road, 04043
Telephone: 207-985-7152
Telecopier: 207-985-3174
Portland, Maine Office: 100 Middle Street, P.O. Box 9729.
Telephone: 207-774-1200.
Telecopier: 774-1127.
Augusta, Maine Office: 146 Capital Street, Box 5057.
Telephone: 207-623-1596.
Telecopier: 626-0200.

Durward W. Parkinson	C. Wesley Crowell
Catherine O'Connor	Karen B. Lovell

Christian L. Barner (Resident)

Representative Clients: University of Maine; Fleet Bank of Maine; Sebago, Inc.; First NH Banks, Inc.; Greater Portland Transit District.

For full biographical listings, see the Martindale-Hubbell Law Directory

REAGAN, ADAMS & CADIGAN (AV)

Eleven Main Street, P.O. Box 709, 04043
Telephone: 207-985-7181
Telecopier: 207-985-7003

MEMBERS OF FIRM

Thomas J. Reagan	Wayne T. Adams
	Paul W. Cadigan

Counsel for: Kennebunk Savings Bank.

For full biographical listings, see the Martindale-Hubbell Law Directory

SMITH ELLIOTT SMITH & GARMEY, P.A. (AV)

Route One South, 9 York Street, 04043
Telephone: 207-985-4464
Telefax: 207-985-3946
Saco, Maine Office: 199 Main Street, P.O. Box 1179.
Telephone: 207-282-1527.
Telefax: 207-283-4412. Sanford
Telephone: 207-324-1560. Portland
Telephone: 207-774-3199. Wells
Telephone: 207-646-0970.
Portland, Maine Office: 100 Commercial Street, Suite 304.
Telephone: 207-774-3199.
Telefax: 207-774-2235.

Daniel F. Driscoll

Representative Clients: Town of Waterboro, Maine; City of Biddeford; Saco and Biddeford Savings Institution; Ocean Communities Federal Credit Union.
Local Counsel for: East Guard Insurance Co.
Reference: Saco & Biddeford Savings Institution.

For full biographical listings, see the Martindale-Hubbell Law Directory

LEWISTON, Androscoggin Co.

BRANN & ISAACSON (AV)

184 Main Street, P.O. Box 3070, 04243-3070
Telephone: 207-786-3566
Telecopier: 207-783-9325
Email: JMTHO7A@Prodigy.COM

MEMBERS OF FIRM

Louis J. Brann (1876-1948)	Martin I. Eisenstein
Peter A. Isaacson (1895-1980)	Martha E. Greene
Irving Isaacson	David W. Bertoni
George S. Isaacson	Peter D. Lowe
Alfred C. Frawley, III	Benjamin W. Lund

ASSOCIATES

Daniel C. Stockford	David C. Pierson
Roy T. Pierce	Kevin R. Haley

Representative Clients: L.L. Bean, Inc.; Direct Marketing Assn.; Readers Digest Assn.; The Sharper Image; Bantam Doubleday Dell, Inc.; FMC Corporation; Livermore Falls Trust Co.; Dow Chemical Co.; United Egg Producers; Miller Hydro Group.

For full biographical listings, see the Martindale-Hubbell Law Directory

*MACHIAS,** Washington Co. — (Refer to Ellsworth)

PORTLAND, * Cumberland Co.

AMERLING & BURNS, A PROFESSIONAL ASSOCIATION (AV)

193 Middle Street, 04101
Telephone: 207-775-3581
Facsimile: 207-775-3814
Affiliated St. Croix Office: Coon & Sanford, P.O. Box 25918, Six
Chandlers's Wharf, Suite 202, 00824-0918.

W. John Amerling	Arnold C. Macdonald
George F. Burns	Mary DeLano
David P. Ray	Joanne F. Cole

A. Robert Ruesch

OF COUNSEL

Bruce M. Jervis

Representative Clients: H.E. Sargent, Inc. (construction); Merrill Trust; J.M.
Huber, Inc.; Jackson Laboratories; Hague International (engineering); Aetna
Life & Casualty Co.; The Hartford; Great American Insurance Co.; Wausau
Insurance Co.

For full biographical listings, see the Martindale-Hubbell Law Directory

---

BENNETT AND ASSOCIATES, P.A. (AV)

Suite 300, 121 Middle Street, P.O. Box 7799, 04112-7799
Telephone: 207-773-4775
Telecopier: 207-774-2366
Email: 104142.2363@compuserve.com

Herbert H. Bennett (1928-1992)	Frederick B. Finberg
Peter Bennett	Melinda J. Caterine
Jeffrey Bennett	Clare S. Benedict

Counsel for: Associated Grocers of New England; General Star Indemnity
Company; Coca Cola Bottling Company of Northern New England, Inc.;
Northern Utilities/Bay State Gas; Pratt & Whitney (Division of United
Technologies); Primerica Financial Services (The Travelers); Sprague Energy
(C.H. Sprague & Son); Perrier Group of America, Inc.; Lepage Bakeries, Inc.
(Country Kitchen); Texaco, Inc.

For full biographical listings, see the Martindale-Hubbell Law Directory

---

BERNSTEIN, SHUR, SAWYER & NELSON, A PROFESSIONAL CORPORATION (AV)

100 Middle Street, P.O. Box 9729, 04104-5029
Telephone: 207-774-1200
Telecopier: 207-774-1127 Telecommunications: 761-2974
Email: lawyers@mainelaw.com
Augusta, Maine Office: 146 Capitol Street, Box 5057, 04330.
Telephone: 207-623-1596.
Telecopier: 207-626-0200.
Kennebunk, Maine Office: 62 Portland Road, 04043.
Telephone: 207-985-7152.
Telecopier: 207-985-3174.

Leonard M. Nelson	Robert H. Stier, Jr.
William W. Willard	Robert J. Keach
Gregory A. Tselikis	James A. Houle
F. Paul Frinsko	Catherine A. Lee
Peter J. Rubin	Durward W. Parkinson
Alan R. Atkins	John L. Carpenter
Eric F. Saunders	Patrick J. Scully
Gordon F. Grimes	Anthony E. Perkins
Philip H. Gleason	Catherine O'Connor
Geoffrey H. Hole	(Resident, Kennebunk Office)
Mary L. Schendel	Joseph J. Hahn
John M. R. Paterson	Diane S. Lukac
Linda A. Monica	Nelson A. Toner
Charles E. Miller	David A. Soley
Richard M. Schade	Lester F. Wilkinson, Jr.
Lee K. Bragg	C. Wesley Crowell
John H. Montgomery, III	Kenneth W. Lehman
Christopher L. Vaniotis	Kate S. Debevoise
Nathan H. Smith	Patricia A. Peard

Karen B. Lovell

Neal F. Pratt	Eliza M. Cope Nolan
Robert J. Crawford	Susan Bernstein Driscoll
Christian L. Barner	Glenn Israel
Robert F. Macdonald, Jr.	Todd S. Holbrook
Kenneth L. Jordan, Jr.	Gayle H. Allen
Jaimie Paul Schwartz	William M. Welch
Mary Elizabeth Fougere	Janet E. Milley
Scott E. Schul	Todd C. Goffman
Christopher J. Devlin	James P. Puhala, III

Elizabeth F. Stout Morley

OF COUNSEL

Sumner Thurman Bernstein	Herbert H. Sawyer

Representative Clients: UNUM; Georgia-Pacific Corp.; University of Maine;
Fleet Bank of Maine; First NH Banks, Inc.; Sebago, Inc.; Greater Portland
Transit District; Pharmacia, Inc.; Rite Aid; Northwest Airlines.

For full biographical listings, see the Martindale-Hubbell Law Directory

DRUMMOND & DRUMMOND (AV)

One Monument Way, 04101
Telephone: 207-774-0317
Telefax: 207-761-4690
Email: info@ddlaw.com

MEMBERS OF FIRM

David N. Fisher, Jr.	Arthur A. Cerullo
Horace W. Horton	James B. Barns
John B. Emory	Robert C. Santomenna

ASSOCIATES

Andrew W. Sparks	Jennifer I. Richard
Alexandra E. Caulfield	Wadleigh B. Drummond
Paul E. Peck	(1885-1979)
Shawn R. Megathlin	Josiah H. Drummond
	(1914-1991)

Representative Clients: W. L. Blake & Co.; Keeley Construction Co., Inc.;
Maine Surgical Supply Co.; Olympia Sport Center, Inc.

For full biographical listings, see the Martindale-Hubbell Law Directory

---

JENSEN BAIRD GARDNER & HENRY (AV)

Ten Free Street, P.O. Box 4510, 04112
Telephone: 207-775-7271
Telecopier: 207-775-7935
York County Office: 419 Alfred Street, Biddeford, Maine.
Telephone: 207-282-5107.
Telecopier: 207-282-6301.

OF COUNSEL

Raymond E. Jensen	Merton G. Henry
M. Donald Gardner	John D. Bradford (Resident,
	York County Office)

MEMBERS OF FIRM

Kenneth Baird (1914-1987)	Ronald A. Epstein
N. B. Walker (1851-1935)	William H. Dale
Thomas B. Walker (1882-1968)	Joseph H. Groff III
Walter E. Webber	Peter W. Greenleaf
Kenneth M. Cole, III	F. Bruce Sleeper
Nicholas S. Nadzo	Deborah M. Mann
Frank H. Frye	Leslie E. Lowry, III
James E. Kaplan	Keith R. Jacques (Resident,
David J. Jones (Resident, York	York County Office)
County Office)	Patricia McDonough Dunn
Michael A. Nelson	Michael J. Quinlan
Ralph W. Austin (Resident,	Elizabeth T. High
York County Office)	James N. Katsiaficas

ASSOCIATES

Julianne Cloutier	Anne H. Jordan (Resident, York
Milda A. Castner (Resident,	County Office)
York County Office)	Barry P. Fernald
Emily A. Bloch	Sally J. Daggett

Susan C. Steiner

Representative Clients: General Motors Acceptance Corp.; Aetna Life & Casualty; Owens Corning Fiberglass; IBM.

For full biographical listings, see the Martindale-Hubbell Law Directory

---

McCANDLESS & HUNT (AV)

57 Exchange Street, 04101
Telephone: 207-772-4100
Telecopier: 207-772-1300

MEMBERS OF FIRM

Eileen M. L. Epstein	David E. Hunt
Elizabeth T. McCandless	

ASSOCIATE

Dennis J. O'Donovan

For full biographical listings, see the Martindale-Hubbell Law Directory

---

PERKINS, THOMPSON, HINCKLEY & KEDDY, P.A. (AV)

One Canal Plaza, P.O. Box 426, 04112-0426
Telephone: 207-774-2635

Thomas Schulten	Peggy L. McGehee
Bruce E. Leddy	Melissa Hanley Murphy
Owen W. Wells	John H. Rich III
Douglas S. Carr	John A. Ciraldo
Andrew A. Cadot	John A. Hobson
John R. Opperman	Helen I. Muther
Philip C. Hunt	Timothy P. Benoit
John S. Upton	Fred W. Bopp III

Craig N. Denekas	David B. McConnell
Mark P. Snow	Peter S. Carlisle
William J. Sheils	Paul D. Pietropaoli

For full biographical listings, see the Martindale-Hubbell Law Directory

Portland—Continued

PIERCE ATWOOD (AV)

One Monument Square, 04101
Telephone: 207-791-1100
Fax: 207-791-1350
Email: info@PierceAtwood.com
Augusta, Maine Office: 77 Winthrop Street.
Telephone: 207-622-6311.
Fax: 207-623-9367.
Newburyport, Massachusetts Office: 6 Harris Street.
Telephone: 508-465-9599.
Fax: 508-465-9945.

MEMBERS OF FIRM

Leonard A. Pierce (1885-1960)	Daniel M. Snow
Edward W. Atwood (1897-1977)	Richard P. Hackett
Jotham D. Pierce (1918-1990)	Michael R. Currie
Fred C. Scribner, Jr. (1908-1994)	William J. Kayatta, Jr.
Ralph I. Lancaster, Jr.	Thomas R. Doyle
Gerald M. Amero	Christopher E. Howard
Bruce A. Coggeshall	Dennis C. Keeler
S. Mason Pratt, Jr.	Philip F. W. Ahrens, III
Daniel E. Boxer	James R. Erwin, II
Jotham D. Pierce, Jr.	Kevin F. Gordon
Warren E. Winslow, Jr.	Jacob A. Manheimer
(Resident, Augusta Office)	Elaine S. Falender
Everett P. Ingalls	John C. Nivison
Malcolm L. Lyons	(Resident, Augusta Office)
(Resident, Augusta Office)	Kenneth Fairbanks Gray
James B. Zimpritch	John J. Aromando
James G. Good	David J. Champoux
John O'Leary	William H. Nichols
Peter W. Culley	Gloria A. Pinza
Jeffrey M. White	William E. Taylor
Louise K. Thomas	Catherine R. Connors
John W. Gulliver	David E. Barry
John D. Delahanty	Dixon P. Pike
Charles S. Einsiedler, Jr.	Sarah H. Beard
Peter H. Jacobs	Anthony R. Derosby
Michael D. Seitzinger	Barbara K. Wheaton
(Resident, Augusta Office)	

OF COUNSEL

Charles W. Allen	William C. Smith
Vincent L. McKusick	Jeremiah D. Newbury
Sigrid E. Tompkins	Margaret Coughlin LePage

ASSOCIATES

Daniel J. Stevens	Foster A. Stewart, Jr
(Resident, Augusta Office)	Allan M. Muir
Michael N. Ambler, Jr.	William L. Worden
Kate L. Geoffroy	Debra L. Brown
Matthew D. Manahan	Marcia A. Metcalf
Eric D. Altholz	Abigail M. Holman
Richard P. Olson	Fall Ferguson
Mary McQuillen	Christopher M. Dawe
Adam H. Steinman	Geraldine G. Sanchez
Deborah L. Shaw	Keith J. Cunningham
James M. Saffian	(Not admitted in ME)
David P. Littell	K. Douglas Erdmann
Jonathan A. Block	Helen L. Edmonds
Jared S. des Rosiers	(Not admitted in ME)

COUNSEL

Michael S. Wilson	Judith A. Fletcher Woodbury

For full biographical listings, see the Martindale-Hubbell Law Directory

PRETI, FLAHERTY, BELIVEAU & PACHIOS (AV)

A Limited Liability Company
443 Congress Street, P.O. Box 11410, 04104-7410
Telephone: 207-791-3000
Telecopier: 207-791-3111
Email: admin@pfbpnet.com
Augusta, Maine Office: 45 Memorial Circle, P.O. Box 1058, 04332-1058.
Telephone: 207-623-5300.
Telecopier: 207-623-2914.

John J. Flaherty (1929-1995)

MEMBERS OF FIRM

Severin M. Beliveau	Anthony W. Buxton
(Augusta Office)	(Augusta Office)
Harold C. Pachios	Jeffrey T. Edwards
Michael J. Gentile	Michael G. Messerschmidt
(Augusta Office)	Randall B. Weill
Keith A. Powers	James C. Pitney, Jr.
Christopher D. Nyhan	(Augusta Office)
Eric P. Stauffer	Evan M. Hansen
Jonathan S. Piper	Virginia E. Davis
Daniel Rapaport	(Augusta Office)
John P. Doyle, Jr.	Edward R. Benjamin, Jr.
Bruce C. Gerrity	Leonard M. Gulino
(Augusta Office)	Dennis C. Sbrega

(See Next Column)

MEMBERS OF FIRM (Continued)

Geoffrey K. Cummings	David B. Van Slyke
Estelle A. Lavoie	Ann R. Robinson
Susan E. LoGiudice	(Augusta Office)
Michael Kaplan	Stephen E. F. Langsdorf
Michael L. Sheehan	(Augusta Office)
Joseph G. Donahue	John P. McVeigh
(Augusta Office)	Elizabeth A. Olivier

OF COUNSEL

Robert F. Preti	Charles F. Dingman
Albert J. Beliveau, Jr.	(Augusta Office)
Robert W. Smith	Mark B. LeDuc (Augusta Office)
Jeanne T. Cohn-Connor	

ASSOCIATES

Nelson J. Larkins	Elizabeth J. Wyman
James E. Phipps	Jodie S. Sullivan
Deirdre M. O'Callaghan	(Augusta Office)
(Augusta Office)	John S. Rudd
Scott T. Rodgers	Anne Skopp
Kevin J. Beal	Jeffrey F. Carlisle
Penny St. Louis	Heriberto Erin Rodriguez
Timothy J. Bryant	Gregg D. Bernstein
	(Augusta Office)

Representative Clients: The St. Paul Companies; Key Bank of Maine; Maine Municipal Assn.; Guy Gannett Publishing Co.; Maine Turnpike Authority; American International Group; Southern Maine Medical Center; NRG Barriers, Inc.; Maine Automobile Dealers Assn.; Bangor Hydro-Electric Co.

For full biographical listings, see the Martindale-Hubbell Law Directory

SMITH ELLIOTT SMITH & GARMEY, P.A. (AV)

100 Commercial Street, Suite 304, 04101
Telephone: 207-774-3199
Telefax: 207-774-2235
Kennebunk, Maine Office: Route One South, 9 York Street.
Telephone: 207-985-4464.
Telefax: 207-985-3946.
Saco, Maine Office: 199 Main Street, P.O. Box 1179.
Telephone: 207-282-1527.
Telefax: 207-283-4412. Sanford
Telephone: 207-324-1560. Wells
Telephone: 207-646-0970.

Randall E. Smith	Richard P. Romeo
Terrence D. Garmey	Robert H. Furbish

Representative Clients: Town of Waterboro, Maine; City of Biddeford; Saco and Biddeford Savings Institution; Ocean Communities Federal Credit Union.
Local Counsel for: East Guard Insurance Co.
Reference: Saco & Biddeford Savings Institution.

For full biographical listings, see the Martindale-Hubbell Law Directory

TROUBH, HEISLER & PIAMPIANO, P.C. (AV)

511 Congress Street, P.O. Box 9711, 04104-5011
Telephone: 207-780-6789
Fax: 207-774-2339

William B. Troubh	Thomas E. Getchell
Edwin A. Heisler	Michael Richards
Robert J. Piampiano	William K. McKinley
Kevin M. Gillis	Daniel F. Gilligan
Michael P. Boyd	Paul S. Bulger

John G. Richardson	Linda L. Sears
Daniel R. Felkel	

For full biographical listings, see the Martindale-Hubbell Law Directory

VERRILL & DANA (AV)

One Portland Square, P.O. Box 586, 04112-0586
Telephone: 207-774-4000
Fax: 207-774-7499
Email: advice@verdan.com *URL:* http://www.verdan.com
Augusta, Maine Office: 45 Memorial Circle, P.O. Box 957.
Telephone: 207-623-3889.
Fax: 207-622-3117.
Kennebunk, Maine Office: Lafayette Center, P.O. Box 266.
Telephone: 207-985-7193.
Fax: 207-985-3957.
Washington, D.C. Office: 400 North Capitol Street, Suite 585.
Telephone: 202-624-9733.
Fax: 202-393-5218.

COUNSEL

Roger A. Putnam	John L. Sullivan
Robert B. Williamson, Jr.	Marianne McGettigan
Louis A. Wood	Suzanne E. Meeker
Carolyn S. Wollen	

(See Next Column)

VERRILL & DANA—*Continued*

MEMBERS OF FIRM

Peter B. Webster	Gregg H. Ginn
Charles R. Oestreicher	David E. Warren
Michael T. Healy	William C. Knowles
Christopher J. W. Coggeshall	Gene R. Libby (Resident
Robert B. Patterson, Jr.	Partner, Kennebunk Office)
Bruce W. Bergen (Resident	James C. Palmer
Partner, Kennebunk Office)	Mark K. Googins
Judith M. Coburn	David C. Boyer, Jr.
Christopher S. Neagle	Douglas P. Currier
David C. Hillman	Kimberly S. Couch
James T. Kilbreth, III	James A. McCormack
John D. Duncan	Alan D. MacEwan
Andrew M. Horton	Charles C. Soltan (Resident
William S. Harwood	Partner, Augusta Office)
William S. Wilson, Jr.	Robert E. Cleaves, IV
James G. Goggin	Lisa S. Boehm
Beth Dobson	Michael W. Macleod-Ball
Gregory S. Fryer	(Resident Partner, Kennebunk
Gregory L. Foster	Office)

Claudia D. Raessler

ASSOCIATES

Kevin G. Anderson	Janet P. Judge
Charles P. Bacall	Kurt E. Klebe
Seth W. Brewster	Raymond A. Pelletier, Jr.
Robert C. Brooks	Jacqueline W. Rider
Juliet T. Browne	William J. Ryan, Jr.
Anthony M. Calcagni	Anthony A. Trask (Resident
Susan J. Clark	Associate, Augusta Office)
Roger A. Clement, Jr.	Wayne E. Tumlin
James I. Cohen	(Not admitted in ME)
Michael J. Donlan (Resident	Thomas A. Welch (Resident
Associate, Kennebunk Office)	Associate, Kennebunk Office)
David L. Galgay, Jr.	Laurie A. Williamson

LEGAL SUPPORT PERSONNEL

David A. Nicklas

Counsel for: ASCAP; Bowdoin College; Fleet Bank; Hannaford Bros. Co.; Maine Blue Cross and Blue Shield; Maine Public Service Co.; Peoples Heritage Bank; Portland Water District.

For full biographical listings, see the Martindale-Hubbell Law Directory

---

PRESQUE ISLE, Aroostook Co.

PHILLIPS, OLORE & DUNLAVEY, P.A. (AV)

Key Bank Building, 480 Main Street, P.O. Box 1087, 04769
Telephone: 207-769-2361
Fax: 207-769-2381

Wendell L. Phillips (1913-1972)	David A. Dunlavey
Hugo A. Olore, Jr.	Brent A. York

Representative Clients: City of Presque Isle; Town of Mapleton; Town of Chapman, Town of Ashland; Maine School Administrative District #32; Maine Potato Growers, Inc.; Government Employees Insurance Co.
Approved Attorneys for: Chicago Title Insurance Co.; First American Title Insurance Co.; The Security Title Guarantee Company of Baltimore.

For full biographical listings, see the Martindale-Hubbell Law Directory

---

ROCKLAND,* Knox Co.

STROUT & PAYSON, P.A. (AV)

10 Masonic Street, P.O. Box 248, 04841-0248
Telephone: 207-594-8400
Fax: 207-594-2724

Arthur E. Strout	Esther R. Barnhart
Joseph B. Pellicani (1936-1988)	Carol Ann Lundquist
Robert J. Levine	Randal E. Watkinson

Elizabeth Biddle Jennings

OF COUNSEL

Curtis M. Payson	John Knight

Approved Attorneys for: First American Title Insurance Co.; Chicago Title Insurance Co.

For full biographical listings, see the Martindale-Hubbell Law Directory

---

SACO, York Co.

SMITH ELLIOTT SMITH & GARMEY, P.A. (AV)

199 Main Street, P.O. Box 1179, 04072
Telephone: 207-282-1527
Telefax: 207-283-4412
Sanford Telephone: 207-324-1560
Portland Telephone: 207-774-3199
Wells Telephone: 207-646-0970
Kennebunk, Maine Office: Route One South, 9 York Street.
Telephone: 207-985-4464.
Telefax: 207-985-3946.

(See Next Column)

Portland, Maine Office: 100 Commercial Street, Suite 304.
Telephone: 207-774-3199.
Telefax: 207-774-2235.

Charles W. Smith (1915-1983)	Richard P. Romeo
Randall E. Smith	Robert H. Furbish
Charles W. Smith, Jr.	William S. Kany
Terrence D. Garmey	John H. O'Neil, Jr.
Peter W. Schroeter	Harry B. Center, II

David S. Abramson

Daniel F. Driscoll	Deborah Shelles Cameron
Barbara J. Petitti	Larissa J. Pratt

OF COUNSEL

Roger S. Elliott

Representative Clients: City of Biddeford; Town of Waterboro, Maine; Saco and Biddeford Savings Institution; Ocean Communities Federal Credit Union.
Local Counsel for: East Guard Insurance Co.
Reference: Saco & Biddeford Savings Institution.

For full biographical listings, see the Martindale-Hubbell Law Directory

---

SANFORD, York Co. — (Refer to Biddeford)

SKOWHEGAN,* Somerset Co.

DONALD E. EAMES (AV)

65 Cross Street, P.O. Box 959, 04976-0959
Telephone: 207-474-8105; 474-2626
Telefax: 207-474-8106

Representative Clients: Farrin Bros. & Smith, Contractors; Towns of Madison, Bingham, Canaan, Palmyra, Solon, New Portland; Moose River Lumber Co., Inc.; Lowell & Co.; The Bray Agency; Skowhegan State Fair; Hight-Chevrolet Buick, Inc.; Cadle Company; Redington-Fairview General Hospital; Redington Medical Associates.

For full biographical listings, see the Martindale-Hubbell Law Directory

WRIGHT & MILLS, P.A. (AV)

218 Water Street, P.O. Box 9, 04976
Telephone: 207-474-3324
Telefax: 207-474-3609

Carl R. Wright	Paul P. Sumberg
S. Peter Mills	Janet T. Mills

Kenneth A. Lexier

Representative Clients: Design Professionals Insurance Co., New Jersey; Solon Manufacturing Co., Solon, Maine; Kleinschmidt Associates-Engineers, Pittsfield, Maine; Acheron Engineering, Newport, Maine; E.W. Littlefield-Contractors, Hartland, Maine; WBRC-Architects, Bangor, Maine; Town of Skowhegan; Town of Norridgewock.

For full biographical listings, see the Martindale-Hubbell Law Directory

---

VAN BUREN, Aroostook Co. — (Refer to Presque Isle)

WATERVILLE, Kennebec Co.

MARDEN, DUBORD, BERNIER & STEVENS (AV)

44 Elm Street, P.O. Box 708, 04903-0708
Telephone: 207-873-0186
Telefax: 207-873-2245

MEMBERS OF FIRM

Robert A. Marden	J. William Druary, Jr.
William P. Dubord	Robert M. Marden
Stephen F. Dubord	David E. Bernier
Alton C. Stevens	Paula F. Caughey

Daniel J. Bernier

Representative Clients: Peoples Heritage Savings Bank; Kennebec Federal Savings Bank; Dexter Shoe Co.; Cianbro Corp.; Associated Grocers of Maine, Inc.; Mid-Maine Medical Center.

For full biographical listings, see the Martindale-Hubbell Law Directory

---

WEEKS & HUTCHINS (AV)

Two Park Place, P.O. Box 417, 04903-0417
Telephone: 207-872-2783
Telefax: 207-872-5749
Email: Lawweeks@mint.net

Thomas N. Weeks (1895-1985)	Roger A. Welch (1930-1993)
Bradford H. Hutchins	
(1907-1992)	

OF COUNSEL

Miles P. Frye

MEMBERS OF FIRM

Timothy R. O'Donnell	Waldemar G. Buschmann

Jonathan G. Rogers

(See Next Column)

WEEKS & HUTCHINS, *Waterville—Continued*

ASSOCIATES

Cheryl Hotchkiss Fasse   Rhett Gerhardt Wieland

Representative Clients: Scott Paper Co.; Colby College; Nationwide Insurance Group; First American Title Insurance Co.; Lawyers Title Insurance Corp.; Kennebec Water District; Waterville Osteopathic Hospital.

For full biographical listings, see the Martindale-Hubbell Law Directory

---

WELLS, York Co. — (Refer to Kennebunk)

*WISCASSET,** Lincoln Co. — (Refer to Brunswick)

YORK, York Co.

STRATER & STRATER, P.A. (AV)

266 York Street, P.O. Box 69, 03909
Telephone: 207-363-2900
Telefax: 207-363-2902

David Strater   Nicholas S. Strater

Representative Clients: Kennebunk Savings Bank; York Sewer District.
Approved Attorneys for: National Attorneys Title Insurance Co.; Lawyers Title Insurance Corp.; American Title Insurance Co.; Chicago Title Insurance Co.; Commonwealth Land Title Insurance Co.
References: Kennebunk Savings Bank; York Sewer District.

For full biographical listings, see the Martindale-Hubbell Law Directory

---

MARYLAND

---

*ANNAPOLIS,** Anne Arundel Co.

COUNCIL, BARADEL, KOSMERL & NOLAN, P.A. (AV)

125 West Street, Fourth Floor, P.O. Box 2289, 21404-2289
Telephone: 410-268-6600
Baltimore: 410-269-6190
Washington, D.C.: 301-261-2247
FAX: 410-269-8409

Ronald E. Council   William F. Flood, III
Ronald A. Baradel   Kevin M. Schaeffer
Wayne T. Kosmerl   John Ralph Greiber, Jr.
James P. Nolan   Donna McCabe Schaeffer
     Frederick C. Sussman

John Naumann Strange   Edwin H. Staples, II
Susan T. Ford   Susan H. Stobbart

OF COUNSEL

George N. Manis   Nicholas Goldsborough

Representative Clients: Anne Arundel County; Annapolis Bank and Trust; Farmers National Bank; Bank of Maryland; State Farm Mutual Automobile Insurance Co.; Annapolis Yacht Club; Annapolis Yacht Sales, Inc.

For full biographical listings, see the Martindale-Hubbell Law Directory

---

FOLEY & LARDNER (AV)

Suite 102, 175 Admiral Cochrane Drive, 21401-7367
Telephone: 410-266-8077
Telex: 899149 (Oldtownpat)
Facsimile: 410-266-8664
Milwaukee, Wisconsin Office: Firstar Center, 777 East Wisconsin Avenue.
Telephone: 414-271-2400.
Telex: 26-819 (Foley Lard Mil).
Facsimile: 414-297-4900.
Madison, Wisconsin Office: Verex Plaza, 150 East Gilman Street, P.O. Box 1497.
Telephone: 608-257-5035.
Facsimile: 608-258-4258.
Chicago, Illinois Office: Suite 3300, One IBM Plaza, 330 N. Wabash Avenue.
Telephone: 312-755-1900.
Facsimile: 312-755-1925.
Washington, D.C. Office: Washington Harbour, Suite 500, 3000 K Street, N.W.
Telephone: 202-672-5300.
Telex: 904136 (Foley Lard Wsh.)
Facsimile: 202-672-5399.
Jacksonville, Florida Office: The Greenleaf Building, 200 Laura Street. P.O. Box 240.
Telephone: 904-359-2000.
Facsimile: 904-359-8700.
Orlando, Florida Office: Suite 1800, 111 North Orange Avenue, P.O. Box 2193.
Telephone: 407-423-7656.
Telex: 441781 (HQ ORL).
Facsimile: 407-648-1743.

(See Next Column)

Tallahassee, Florida Office: Suite 300, 123 South Calhoun Street, P.O. Box 508.
Telephone: 904-222-6100.
Facsimile: 904-224-0496.
Tampa, Florida Office: Suite 2700, One Hundred N. Tampa Street, P.O. Box 3391.
Telephones: 813-229-2300; Pinellas County: 813-442-3296.
Facsimile: 813-221-4210. County: 813-446-9641.
West Palm Beach, Florida Office: Suite 200, Phillips Point East Tower, 777 South Flagler Drive.
Telephone: 407-655-5050.
Facsimile: 407-655-6925.
Brussels, Belgium Office: Avenue Louise, 283.
Telephone: 32-2-646-2777.
Fax: 32-2-646-7574.
Los Angeles, California Office: Foley Lardner Weissburg & Aronson, 2049 Century Park East, Suite 3200.
Telephone: 310-277-2223.
Fax: 310-557-8475.
Sacramento, California Office: Foley Lardner Weissburg & Aronson, 770 L Street, Suite 1050.
Telephone: 916-443-8005.
Fax: 916-443-2240.
San Diego, California Office: Foley Lardner Weissburg & Aronson, 402 West Broadway, 23rd Floor.
Telephone: 619-234-6655.
Fax: 619-234-3510.
San Francisco, California Office: Foley Larder Weissburg & Aronson, One Maritime Plaza, Sixth Floor.
Telephone: 415-434-4484.
Fax: 415-434-4507.

PARTNERS

David A. Blumenthal   Brian J. McNamara
(Not admitted in MD)   Arthur Schwartz

ASSOCIATES

John P. Veschi

For full biographical listings, see the Martindale-Hubbell Law Directory

---

*BALTIMORE,** (Independent City)

ALLEN, JOHNSON, ALEXANDER & KARP, P.A. (AV)

Suite 1540, 100 East Pratt Street, 21202
Telephone: 410-727-5000
Fax: 410-727-0861
Washington, D.C. Office: 1707 L Street, N.W., Suite 1050.
Telephone: 202-828-4141.

John D. Alexander, Jr.   D'Ana E. Johnson (Resident,
Daniel Karp   Washington, D.C. Office)
     Yvette M. Bryant

OF COUNSEL

Donald C. Allen

Denise Ramsburg Stanley   James X. Crogan, Jr.
George B. Breen (Not admitted   Kevin Bock Karpinski
in MD; Resident, Washington,   Gregory James Dumark
D.C. Office)

Representative Clients: Scottsdale Insurance Co.; Nautilus Insurance Co.; Jefferson Insurance Co.; Liberty Mutual Insurance Co.; Avis Rent-A-Car; Otis Elevator Co.; Montgomery Elevator Co.; Admiral Insurance Co.; Local Government Insurance Trust; Lancer Insurance Co.

For full biographical listings, see the Martindale-Hubbell Law Directory

---

BLUM, YUMKAS, MAILMAN, GUTMAN & DENICK, P.A. (AV)

1200 Mercantile Bank & Trust Building, Two Hopkins Plaza, 21201
Telephone: 410-385-4000
FAX: 410-385-4070

Jacob Blum (1907-1994)   Joseph C. Kovars
Charles Yumkas   Richard F. Cohn
Lloyd S. Mailman   Christopher W. Nicholson
Edward J. Gutman   F. Thomas Rafferty, III
Bernard S. Denick   Leslie R. Stellman
Irving F. Cohn   Stuart M. Schabes
Max S. Stadfeld   Edmund J. O'Meally
Rochelle Stutman Eisenberg   Thomas A. Bowden
Anthony P. Palaigos   Tammy Cohen Drescher
Louis J. Kozlakowski   Kenneth W. Cobleigh
     Robert D. Waldman

Gail D. Allen   Louise Bailey Kelley
     Kathleen A. Coulahan

LEGAL SUPPORT PERSONNEL

Wanita Sowell (Paralegal)   Kay Kimbal (Paralegal)

For full biographical listings, see the Martindale-Hubbell Law Directory

Baltimore—Continued

GALLAGHER, MAY & BURGOYNE (AV)

100 St. Paul Street Second Floor, 21202
Telephone: 410-576-2000
FAX: 410-576-2005

MEMBERS OF FIRM

Frank X. Gallagher (Retired)   Michael P. May
Michael H. Burgoyne

OF COUNSEL

James E. Garland

For full biographical listings, see the Martindale-Hubbell Law Directory

GORDON, FEINBLATT, ROTHMAN, HOFFBERGER & HOLLANDER, LLC (AV)

The Garrett Building, 233 East Redwood Street, 21202
Telephone: 410-576-4000
Fax: 410-576-4246
Telex: 908041 BAL

Donald N. Rothman	George K. Reynolds, III
Edward E. Obstler	Carla Stone Witzel
Lewis A. Kann	Abba David Poliakoff
Zelig Robinson	Jay A. Shulman
Sander L. Wise	Barbara Holtz Levine
Allan J. Malester	Michael C. Powell
David H. Fishman	Thomas X. Glancy, Jr.
Thomas J. Doud, Jr.	Michael J. Jack
Lawrence S. Greenwald	Jerrold A. Thrope
Sheila K. Sachs	Neil J. Schechter
Herbert Goldman	Lynn B. Sassin
Robert E. Sharkey	Marjorie A. Corwin
Marc P. Blum	Matthew P. Mellin
Lester D. Bailey	J. Ronald Shiff
Lawrence D. Coppel	Elliott Cowan
Nancy E. Paige	Hillel Tendler
Robert W. Katz	Bradford W. Warbasse
D. Robert Enten	Carolyn Jacobs
Barry F. Rosen (Chairman)	Peter B. Rosenwald, II
Henry E. Schwartz	Ned T. Himmelrich
Timothy D. A. Chriss	Ava Lias-Booker
Robert C. Kellner	Sharon D. Credit

OF COUNSEL

David P. Gordon	LeRoy E. Hoffberger
Eugene M. Feinblatt	Evan Alevizatos Chriss
William Donald Schaefer	

COUNSEL

Frances O. Taylor   Barnett Q. Brooks

Claire A. Smearman	Edward N. Kane, Jr.
Susan A. Nachman	Robin J. Siegel
Caroline G. Ellis	Catherine A. Bledsoe
Seth M. Rotenberg	Cheryl Fridkin Kitt
Robin L. Wexler	Michael A. Refolo
Karen Nash-Goetz	Eric N. Stravitz
Karen M. Crabtree	Rebecca L. Dietz
Raymond S. Butler	Joshua E. Neiman
Bradley J. Swallow	Steven A. Cohen
(Not admitted in MD)	Dorothy C. Alevizatos
David W. Lease	Sigmund R. Kallins

For full biographical listings, see the Martindale-Hubbell Law Directory

KRAMON & GRAHAM, P.A. (AV)

Commerce Place, One South Street, Suite 2600, 21202-3201
Telephone: 410-752-6030
Facsimile: 410-539-1269

Andrew Jay Graham	Marilyn Hope Fisher
James M. Kramon	Max H. Lauten
Lee H. Ogburn	Kathleen A. Birrane
Jeffrey H. Scherr	Kevin F. Arthur
Nancy E. Gregor	Aron U. Raskas
James P. Ulwick	Geoffrey H. Genth
Philip M. Andrews	Karl J. Nelson
Gertrude C. Bartel	Virginia A. Stuelpnagel
Severn E.S. Miller	

Representative Clients: Allstate Insurance Co.; Georgia-Pacific Corp.; INA-PRO; Sacred Heart Hospital; Toll Brothers, Inc.

For full biographical listings, see the Martindale-Hubbell Law Directory

NEUBERGER, QUINN, GIELEN, RUBIN & GIBBER, P.A. (AV)

27th Floor, Commerce Place, One South Street, 21202
Telephone: 410-332-8550
Fax: 410-332-8594

(See Next Column)

Isaac M. Neuberger	Robert M. Ercole
Michael L. Quinn	Thomas M. Wood, IV
Price O. Gielen	Deborah Hunt Devan
Richard Rubin	Stanley J. Neuhauser
Allan J. Gibber	Cynthia L. Leppert
Stanford D. Hess	Richard A. Monfred
John J. Kuchno	

Nathan D. Adler	Howard S. Schwartz
Karen B. Zale	Jason C. Hess
Hugh M. Bernstein	Alison J. Julio
Craig T. Sharkey	

Representative Clients: AOKI Corp.; Equifax; Johns Hopkins Health System; Luskins, Inc.; Maryland State Teachers Association; Rite Aid Corp.; Super Rite Foods; TESSCO Technologies; UNC Incorporated; Struever Bros. Eccles & Rouse.

For full biographical listings, see the Martindale-Hubbell Law Directory

NILES, BARTON & WILMER (AV)

1400 Legg Mason Tower, 111 South Calvert Street, 21202-6185
Telephone: 410-783-6300
Cable Address: "Nilwo"
Telecopier: 410-783-6363

MEMBERS OF FIRM

A. Adgate Duer	John L. Wood
John Gill Wharton	Paul W. Grimm
Forrest F. Bramble, Jr.	Steven E. Leder
Patrick J. B. Donnelly	C. Laurence Jenkins, Jr.
Paul B. Lang	Matthew L. Kimball
Larry J. Albert	R. Wayne Pierce
V. Timothy Bambrick	Carl F. Ameringer
Robert F. Scholz	David D. Gilliss
Robert P. O'Brien	April Unhui Hogsten

OF COUNSEL

Carlyle Barton, Jr.

ASSOCIATES

Susan D. Baker	George E. Reede, Jr
Susan B. Austin	Mary Alice McNamara
John C. Wetzel	Jeffrey A. Wothers
Andrew L. Jiranek	Craig D. Roswell
Paul McDermott Finamore	Gina M. Harasti
Tracy A. Mays	Howard A. Wolf-Rodda
Kevin J. Willging	

For full biographical listings, see the Martindale-Hubbell Law Directory

PHILLIPS P. O'SHAUGHNESSY, P.A. (AV)

1102 Terrace Glen, 21210
Telephone: 410-532-0300
FAX: 410-532-2220

Phillips P. O'Shaughnessy   Robin Frazier Kandel

For full biographical listings, see the Martindale-Hubbell Law Directory

PIERSON, PIERSON & NOLAN (AV)

Suite 1600 Redwood Tower, 217 East Redwood Street, 21202
Telephone: 410-727-7733
FAX: 410-625-0253

MEMBERS OF FIRM

Leon H. A. Pierson (1901-1981)	W. Michel Pierson
Edward Pierson (1906-1990)	James J. Nolan, Jr.
Robert L. Pierson	

OF COUNSEL

David S. Sykes

For full biographical listings, see the Martindale-Hubbell Law Directory

PIPER & MARBURY L.L.P. (AV)

Charles Center South, 36 South Charles Street, 21201-3018
Telephone: 410-539-2530
FAX: 410-539-0489
Email: lawfirm@pipermar.com
Washington, D.C. Office: 1200 Nineteenth Street, N.W., 20036-2430.
Telephone: 202-861-3900.
FAX: 202-223-2085.
Easton, Maryland Office: 117 Bay Street, 21601-2703.
Telephone: 410-820-4460.
FAX: 410-820-4463.
New York, N.Y. Office: 1251 Avenue of the Americas, 10020-1104.
Telephone: 212-835-6000.
FAX: 212-835-6001.
Philadelphia, Pennsylvania Office: 3400 Two Logan Square, 18th & Arch Streets, 19103-2762.
Telephone: 215-656-3300.
FAX: 215-656-3301.

(See Next Column)

PIPER & MARBURY L.L.P., *Baltimore—Continued*

MEMBERS OF FIRM

George L. Russell, Jr.
Nathan B. Feinstein (Resident, Washington, D.C. Office)
David V. Anthony (Resident, Washington, D.C. Office)
Roger D. Redden
Shale D. Stiller
Leonard E. Cohen
Wilbert H. Sirota
L. P. Scriggins
Lewis A. Noonberg (Resident, Washington, D.C. Office)
Sheldon Krantz (Resident, Washington, D.C. Office)
Robinson Markel (Resident, New York, N.Y. Office)
Joseph G. Finnerty, Jr.
Donald E. Sharpe
Robert W. Ogren (Resident, Washington, D.C. Office)
Robert A. Meister (Resident, New York, N.Y. Office)
Henry Robbins Lord
Toni K. Allen (Resident, Washington, D.C. Office)
Thomas H. Truitt (Resident, Washington, D.C. Office)
Stuart A. Smith (Resident, New York Office)
Raymond A. Mantle (Resident, New York, N.Y. Office)
William R. Weissman (Resident, Washington, D.C. Office)
Carl L. Vacketta (Resident, Washington, D.C. Office)
Raymond F. Steckel (Resident, New York, N.Y. Office)
Donald P. McPherson, III
Edwin M. Martin, Jr. (Resident, Washington, D.C. Office)
James A. Guadiana (Resident, New York, N.Y. Office)
Michael A. Varet (Resident, New York, N.Y. Office)
Lawrence M. Katz
Philip L. Cohan (Resident, Washington, D.C. Office)
George A. Nilson
Broughton M. Earnest (Resident, Easton Office)
Steven K. Yablonski (Resident, Washington, D.C. Office)
John E. Kratz, Jr.
James J. Winn, Jr.
Russell H. Gardner
J. Brian Molloy (Resident, Washington, D.C. Office)
Ronald L. Plesser (Resident, Washington, D.C. Office)
Charles J. Raubicheck (Resident, New York, N.Y. Office)
Robert F. Fink (Resident, New York, N.Y. Office)
Steven D. Shattuck
Mark Pollak
Stanard T. Klinefelter
Michael Esher Yaggy
Jay I. Morstein
E. Leslie Hoffman, III (Resident, Washington, D.C. Office)
Gregory A. Smith (Resident, Washington, D.C. Office)
Jayne M. Kurzman (Resident, New York, N.Y. Office)
Jeffrey D. Herschman
Joseph H. Langhirt
Neil J. Dilloff
Mark J. Tauber (Resident, Washington, D.C. Office)
Anthony L. Young (Resident, Washington, D.C. Office)
Richard M. Kremen
Randall B. Lowe (Washington, D.C. and New York, N.Y. Office)
Thomas C. Wheeler (Resident, Washington, D.C. Office)
Michael Hirschberg (Resident, New York, N.Y. Office)

Francis B. Burch, Jr.
Deborah E. Jennings
George E. Rahn, Jr. (Resident, Philadelphia, Pennsylvania Office)
Francis X. Markey (Resident, Washington, D.C. Office)
Leo G. Kailas (Resident, New York, N.Y. Office)
James D. Kleiner (Resident, New York, N.Y. Office)
Earl S. Wellschlager
Richard C. Tilghman, Jr.
Jeffrey F. Liss (Resident, Washington, D.C. Office)
Larry D. Harris (Resident, Washington, D.C. Office)
Richard J. Hafets
Edward J. Levin
Stephen R. Mysliwiec (Resident, Washington, D.C. Office)
Daniel J. Carrigan (Resident, Washington, D.C. Office)
Alan C. Porter (Resident, Washington, D.C. Office)
I. Scott Bass
Alfred Ferrer III (Resident, New York, N.Y. Office)
William F. Kiniry, Jr. (Resident, Philadelphia, Pennsylvania Office)
David P. Langlois (Resident, New York, N.Y. Office)
Robert W. Smith, Jr.
Elizabeth Grieb
John P. Machen
Mark J. Friedman
Kenneth L. Thompson
William D. Blakely (Resident, Washington, D.C. Office)
Michael F. Brockmeyer
Stephen L. Owen
Joyce J. Gorman (Resident, Washington, D.C. Office)
Stanley McDermott, III (Resident, New York, N.Y. Office)
David B. Dempsey (P.C.) (Resident, Washington, D.C. Office)
Stewart K. Diana
Lee A. Sheller
John E. Griffith, Jr.
Jay Gary Finkelstein (Resident, Washington, D.C. Office)
Andrew L. Deutsch (Resident, New York, N.Y. Office)
Elizabeth A. McKennon
Sandra P. Gohn
Jonathan D. Smith
William L. Henn, Jr.
Henry D. Kahn
Paul A. Tiburzi
Joel A. Dewey
Robert J. Mathias
David S. Musgrave
Marianne Schmitt Hellauer
Mark Muedeking
Cynthia J. Morris (Resident, Washington, D.C. Office)
David H. Bamberger (Resident, Washington, D.C. Office)
David Clarke, Jr. (Resident, Washington, D.C. Office)
Paul D. Shelton
Charles P. Scheeler
Christopher E. O'Brien (Resident, New York Office)
James M. Brogan
Garry P. McCormack (Resident, New York, N.Y. Office)
Anthony H. Rickert (Resident, Washington, D.C. Office)
Kurt J. Fischer
James P. Rathvon (Resident, Washington, D.C. Office)
Wm. Roger Truitt
Douglas H. Green (Resident, Washington, D.C. Office)

MEMBERS OF FIRM (Continued)

(See Next Column)

Nora E. Garrote (Resident, Washington, D.C. Office)
Raymond G. Mullady, Jr.
Steven J. Mandell (Resident, Washington, D.C. Office)
Donna Lee Yesner (Resident, Washington, D.C. Office)
Stanley R. Soya (Resident, Washington, D.C. Office)
Ronald P. Schiller (Resident, Philadelphia, Pennsylvania Office)
Emmett F. McGee, Jr.
Sheila Mosmiller Vidmar

Paul Stanley Novak
Theodore D. Segal
Eric B. Miller
Kristin H. R. Franceschi
Benjamin S. Boyd (Resident, Washington, D.C. Office)
Eric Paltell
Jay G. Cohen
Richard P. Rector (Resident, Washington, D.C. Office)
David B. Buss (Resident, New York, N.Y. Office)
Joseph G. Finnerty, III (Resident, New York, N.Y. Office)

OF COUNSEL

Robert M. Goldman
Robert B. Watts
M. Peter Moser
William L. Reynolds
Robert N. McKay (Not admitted in MD)
Evelyn W. Pasquier
Cindy V. Schlaefer (Resident, New York, N.Y. Office)
Emilio W. Cividanes (Resident, Washington, D.C. Office)

Mitchell E. Radin (Resident, New York, N.Y. Office)
Joseph K. Wiener (Resident, Washington, D.C. Office)
Christopher J. Clay (Resident, Washington, D.C. Office)
Paul J. Pollock (Resident, New York, N.Y. Office)
Frank T. Gray

PARTNER EMERITUS

Andre W. Brewster
Charles T. Albert

Edward Owen Clarke, Jr.
Decatur H. Miller

RETIRED PARTNER

Franklin G. Allen

SENIOR ATTORNEY

Richard C. Walters (Resident, Washington, D.C. Office)

ASSOCIATES

Anthony J. Rosso
Laura E. Perry
Lynette M. Phillips (Resident, New York, N.Y. Office)
Ray L. Earnest (Resident, Easton Office)
H. Mark Stichel
Richard J. Vacura (Resident, Washington, D.C. Office)
Howard A. Fried (Resident, New York, N.Y. Office)
James B. Reach (Resident, Washington, D.C. Office)
Gina Monath Zawitoski
Michael S. Barranco
John F. Kaufman
Michael R. Hepworth (Resident, New York, N.Y. Office)
James J. Halpert (Resident, Washington, D.C. Office)
Mary L. Porter
Kathleen A. Ellis
Barbara C. Woods
Carolyn M. Bamberger (Resident, Washington, D.C. Office)
Len Matsunaga (Resident, New York, N.Y. Office)
Mitchell S. Marder (Resident, Washington, D.C. Office)
Barbara Rowland (Resident, Washington, D.C. Office)
John L. Moore, Jr. (Resident, Washington, D.C. Office)
Thomas E. D. Millspaugh
Cristin Carnell Lambros
Stephen M. Sharkey
Jane A. Wilson
Jill Cantor Nord
Thomas L. Totten
Glen K. Allen
Robert C. Douglas
Susan K. Datesman
Ann L. Lamdin
O. Daniel Ansa (Resident, Philadelphia, Pennsylvania Office)
John E. Benedict (Resident, Washington, D.C. Office)
Theodore L. Charnley
Leonard L. Gordon (Resident, Washington, D.C. Office)
Brigit A. McCann Macksey
Anthony L. Meagher

Stephen A. Riddick
Mary E. Gately (Resident, Washington, D.C. Office)
James D. Mathias
Timothy P. Branigan (Resident, Washington, D.C. Office)
Diane Crosson McEnroe (Resident, New York, N.Y. Office)
Susan C. Stolzer (Resident, New York, N.Y. Office)
JoAnn E. Levin
Kimi N. Murakami (Resident, New York, N.Y. Office)
Herbert D. Frerichs, Jr.
Kevin P. Mullen (Resident, Washington, D.C. Office)
Carol M. Fischer (Resident, New York, N.Y. Office)
Hope P. Krebs (Resident, New York, N.Y. Office)
Christine Stark (Resident, Washington, D.C. Office)
Susan S. Sands
Norman L. Rave, Jr. (Resident, Washington, D.C. Office)
Katrina C. Kamantauskas-Holder
Marta D. Harting
Tracey Gann Turner
Carville B. Collins
Joseph Kernen (Resident, Philadelphia, Pennsylvania Office)
Deborah P. Nason (Resident, Philadelphia, Pennsylvania Office)
Nancy A. Spangler (Resident, Washington, D.C. Office)
A. Christopher Young (Resident, Philadelphia, Pennsylvania Office)
Kecia Boney (Resident, Washington, D.C. Office)
Jane Kwok Ping Tam (Resident, Washington, D.C. Office)
J. Benjamin Unkle, Jr.
Charles Kevin Kobbe
Ann Burke Lloyd
Anne-Therese Bechamps
Pamela A. Long
Eric B. Kantor (Resident, Washington, D.C. Office)

(See Next Column)

PIPER & MARBURY L.L.P.—*Continued*

ASSOCIATES (Continued)

Ellen H. Klestzick (Resident, New York, N.Y. Office)
Peter M. Corrigan (Resident, New York, N.Y. Office)
Gerard D. St. Ours
Merrill Philips (Resident, Washington, D.C. Office)
Kimberly E. Wolod (Resident, Washington, D.C. Office)
Marianne Mancino Thiede (Resident, Washington, D.C. Office)
John Caleb Dougherty
Stephanie D. Pullen Brown
Jordan I. Bailowitz
Edward F. Maluf (Resident, New York, N.Y. Office)
Timothy M. Cramer (Resident, Washington, D.C. Office)
Christopher W. Wasson (Resident, Philadelphia, Pennsylvania Office)
Theresa M. Connolly
Eric S. Connuck (Resident, New York, N.Y. Office)
William J. Brennan, IV (Not admitted in MD)
Lawrence R. Seidman
Paul J. Day
Carla G. Pennington-Cross (Resident, Washington, D.C. Office)
Jennifer A. White (Resident, Washington, D.C. Office)
Scott V. Kamins
Mark J. O'Connor (Resident, Washington, D.C. Office)
Wm. David Chalk
Keith E. Smith (Resident, Philadelphia, Pennsylvania Office)
Brian D. Henderson (Resident, Washington, D.C. Office)
Julie Arthur Garcia (Resident, Washington, D.C. Office)
H. Bruce Dorsey
Sonya Kazazian Hannan
Nanci S. Redman (Resident, Washington, D.C. Office)
Mary Ita Snyder (Resident, Washington, D.C. Office)
Daniel M. Horrigan (Resident, Washington, D.C. Office)
F. Joseph Gormley
Richard J. Marks
Jonathan David Eisner
Elizabeth R. Dewey (Resident, Washington, D.C. Office)
Patricia A. Sumner
James M. Grosser (Not admitted in MD)
Amy Davidson Bryant (Resident, Washington, D.C. Office)
David L. Weinreb (Resident, Philadelphia, Pennsylvania Office)
Malcolm D. Woolf (Resident, Washington, D.C. Office)
Holly Emrick Svetz (Resident, Washington, D.C. Office)

Christina L. Nargolwala (Resident, New York, N.Y. Office)
Jaemin Park
Heather Anne Klink
Loren H. Brown (Resident, New York, N.Y. Office)
Chuong H. Pham (Not admitted in MD)
Eugene A. Arbaugh, Jr.
George Faulkner Ritchie, IV
Guy E. Flynn
Keara M. O'Donnell (Resident, Washington, D.C. Office)
Norma Sharara
Paula J. McGill
Beth A. Winograd
Daniel Warren Pugh (Resident, Washington, D.C. Office)
Quincy M. Crawford, III
Jeffrey E. Gordon
Catherine Stuart Magargee (Resident, Philadelphia, Pennsylvania Office)
Kimberly A. Williams
Rachel B. Mandell
Chandra Emery (Resident, Washington, D.C. Office)
Carol A. Kelley (Resident, Washington, D.C. Office)
Carol Guy-Jackson (Resident, Washington, D.C. Office)
Alycia M. Vivona (Resident, New York, N.Y. Office)
Robert Weiss (Resident, New York, N.Y. Office)
Stefanie J. Fogel (Resident, Philadelphia, Pennsylvania Office)
Melissa Anemajanis Halton
Matthew A. Nyman (Not admitted in MD)
Barbara Regan (Resident, Philadelphia, Pennsylvania Office)
Heather E. Gange (Resident, Washington, D.C. Office)
Anne M. Lindner (Not admitted in MD)
Edward A. Bibko (Resident, New York, N.Y. Office)
Brett Ingerman
Leeann Kelly-Judd
Courtney Lewis Wood
Richard Ufford
Natalie F. Zaidman
Mary C. Ragsdale (Resident, Washington, D.C. Office)
Victoria Alexandra Schlesinger (Resident, Washington, D.C. Office)
Marta Michel (Resident, New York, N.Y. Office)
Rebecca Stevens (Not admitted in MD)
Kimberly Ann Crowder (Not admitted in MD)
Tilghman Earle Price
Susan C. Chu (Resident, New York, N.Y. Office)

For full biographical listings, see the Martindale-Hubbell Law Directory

---

SEMMES, BOWEN & SEMMES, A PROFESSIONAL CORPORATION (AV)

250 West Pratt Street, 21201
Telephone: 410-539-5040
Facsimile: 410-539-5223
URL: http://www.semmes.com
Washington D.C. Office: Suite 900, 1025 Connecticut Avenue, N.W.
Telephone: 202-822-8250.
Towson, Maryland Office: Eleventh Floor, 401 Washington Avenue.
Telephone: 410-296-4400.
Hagerstown, Maryland Office: 265 Mill Street.
Telephone: 301-739-4558.
Salisbury, Maryland Office: Suite 202, 212 East Main Street.
Telephone: 410-548-1212.
Wilmington, Delaware Office: One Commerce Center, 1201 North Orange Street, Suite 719.
Telephone: 302-884-6729.

(See Next Column)

PRINCIPALS

John E. Semmes (1851-1925)
Jesse N. Bowen (1879-1938)
John E. Semmes, Jr. (1881-1967)
Franklin Goldstein
Cleaveland D. Miller
Robert P. Mittelman
Alan N. Gamse
J. Snowden Stanley, Jr.,
Robert E. Scott, Jr.
Richard T. Sampson
Rudolph L. Rose
Kevin M. O'Connell
Michael W. Prokopik
William J. Jackson (Resident, Towson, Maryland Office)
Daniel J. Moore (Resident, Towson, Maryland Office)
JoAnne Zawitoski
Thomas G. Hagerty (Resident, Washington, D.C. Office)
Richard W. Scheiner
Maxine Adler
Perry E. Darby
Scott D. Goetsch (Resident, Towson, Maryland Office)

James A. Johnson
Patti Gilman West
Robert T. Franklin
Stan M. Haynes
Robert W. Hesselbacher, Jr.
Gary L. Bohlke (Not admitted in MD)
William H. Kable
Joanne M. Dicus
Kristine Kappeler Howanski (Resident, Towson, Maryland Office)
Mark D. Laponsky
Michael K. Wyatt (Resident, Washington, D.C. Office)
Stephen S. McCloskey
John S. Nevin (Resident, Washington, D.C. Office)
Kevin M. Soper (Resident, Towson, Maryland Office)
Margaret Fonshell Ward (Resident, Towson, Maryland Office)

OF COUNSEL

Thomas E. Cinnamond
David R. Owen
James D. Peacock

COUNSEL

William C. Trimble, Jr.
William R. Dorsey, III

SENIOR ASSOCIATES

Brian A. Balenson
Lori L. Blair (Resident, Towson, Maryland Office)
Paul N. Farquharson
Joseph F. Giordano (Resident, Washington, D.C. Office)
Denise A. Greig
Eugene I. Kane, Jr. (Resident, Washington, D.C. Office)
Heather Holt Kraus

Kent Koji Matsumoto
Thomas V. McCarron
Joel D. Newport (Resident, Towson, Maryland Office)
Christopher W. Poverman
Jennifer S. Pressman
Robert E. Rockwell (Resident, Hagerstown, Maryland Office)
David Arthur Skomba
Jonathan R. Topazian

Anthony Jackson Zaccagnini

ASSOCIATES

Eric S. Belk
Suzzanne W. Decker
Joseph M. English, IV
Willis Gunther Ferlise (Resident, Towson, Maryland Office)
David V. Fontana
Carolyn Moses Frank (Resident, Towson, Maryland Office)
Richard A. Froehlinger, III
Lawrence G. Giambelluca
Jonathan S. Greene
Gina M. Householder (Resident, Hagerstown, Maryland Office)
Maija B. Jackson

Gary W. Kuc
Sue Lawless
Stuart M. Lesser
Sussan Lee Mahallati (Resident, Washington, D.C. Office)
Erin M. Masson
Jeffrey A. Regner
Carolyn E. Ryan
Peter B. Silvain, Jr. (Resident, Salisbury, Maryland Office)
Roberta C. Sinopole (Resident, Towson, Maryland Office)
Ronald J. Travers
Glen H. Tschirgi

Eric Joseph Velapoldi

250 WEST PRATT STREET
BALTIMORE, MARYLAND 21201

TELEPHONE: 410-576-4858

John A. Scaldara
B. Marvin Potler

Sharon L. Guida
Douglas H. Seitz

Donald J. Walsh

Representative Clients of Semmes, Bowen & Semmes: Bethlehem Steel Corp.; E.I. du Pont de Nemours & Co.; General Electric Co.; Liberty Mutual Insurance Co.; MBNA, Inc.; Metropolitan Life Insurance Co.

For full biographical listings, see the Martindale-Hubbell Law Directory

---

SOMMER & STEELE, L.L.C. (AV)

The B & O Building, Suite 930, Two North Charles Street, 21201
Telephone: 410-783-2790
Fax: 410-783-2797

Peter J. Sommer
Deborah Williams Steele

ASSOCIATE

Samuel Joseph Mangione

OF COUNSEL

J. Stephen Simms

For full biographical listings, see the Martindale-Hubbell Law Directory

Baltimore—Continued

VENABLE ATTORNEYS AT LAW VENABLE, BAETJER AND HOWARD, LLP (AV)

A Partnership including Professional Corporations
1800 Mercantile Bank & Trust Building, 2 Hopkins Plaza, 21201
Telephone: 410-244-7400
Email: INFO@Venable.win.net
Washington, D.C. Office: Venable, Baetjer, Howard & Civiletti LLP. Suite 1000, 1201 New York Avenue, N.W.
Telephone: 202-962-4800.
McLean, Virginia Office: Suite 400, 2010 Corporate Ridge.
Telephone: 703-760-1600.
Rockville, Maryland Office: Suite 500, One Church Street, P. O. Box 1906.
Telephone: 301-217-5600.
Towson, Maryland Office: 210 Allegheny Avenue, P. O. Box 5517.
Telephone: 410-494-6200.

MEMBERS OF FIRM

Richard M. Venable (1839-1910)
Edwin G. Baetjer (1868-1945)
Charles McH. Howard (1870-1942)
Jacques T. Schlenger (P.C.)
William J. McCarthy (P.C.)
Russell Ronald Reno, Jr. (P.C.)
Thomas P. Perkins, III (P.C.)
James A. Cole
Benjamin R. Civiletti (P.C.) (Also at Washington, D.C. and Towson, Maryland Offices)
John B. Howard (Resident, Towson, Maryland Office)
Anthony M. Carey (Also at Washington, D.C. Office)
David E. Belcher
George Cochran Doub (P.C.)
John Henry Lewin, Jr. (P.C.)
Stanley Mazaroff (P.C.)
Lee M. Miller (P.C.)
Neal D. Borden (Also at Washington, D.C. Office)
Robert A. Shelton
Thomas J. Kenney, Jr. (P.C.) (Also at Washington, D.C. Office)
Roger W. Titus (Resident, Rockville, Maryland Office)
Daniel O'C. Tracy, Jr. (Also at Rockville, Maryland Office)
Jan K. Guben (Also at Washington, D. C Office)
Ian D. Volner (Not admitted in MD; Resident, Washington, D.C. Office)
Thomas W. W. Haines (P.C.)
Thomas J. Madden (Not admitted in MD; Resident, Washington, D.C. Office)
William L. Walsh, Jr. (P.C.) (Not admitted in MD; Resident, McLean, Virginia Office)
Ronald R. Glancz (Not admitted in MD; Resident, Washington, D.C. Office)
David J. Levenson (Not admitted in MD; Resident, Washington, D.C. Office)
Dennis J. Whittlesey (Not admitted in MD; Resident, Washington, D.C. Office)
Douglas D. Connah, Jr. (P.C.) (Also at Washington, D.C. Office)
Robert G. Smith (P.C.)
James D. Wright (P.C.)
Joe A. Shull (Resident, Washington, D.C. Office)
Kenneth C. Bass, III (Not admitted in MD; Washington, D.C. and McLean, Virginia Offices)
John H. Zink, III (Resident, Towson, Maryland Office)
Lars E. Anderson (Not admitted in MD; Resident, McLean, Virginia Office)
John G. Milliken (Not admitted in MD; Washington, D.C. and McLean, Virginia Offices)
Bruce E. Titus (Resident, McLean, Virginia Office)

Paul F. Strain (P.C.)
Alexander I. Lewis, III (P.C.) (Also at Towson, Maryland Office)
William D. Dolan, III (P.C.) (Not admitted in MD; Resident, McLean, Virginia Office)
Paul T. Glasgow (Resident, Rockville, Maryland Office)
Joseph C. Wich, Jr. (Resident, Towson, Maryland Office)
Joseph G. Block (Not admitted in MD; Resident, Washington, D.C. Office)
Sondra Harans Block (Resident, Rockville, Maryland Office)
Jeffrey J. Radowich
Edward F. Glynn, Jr. (Resident, Washington, D.C. Office)
Craig E. Smith
Robert G. Ames (Also at Washington, D.C. Office)
Michael Schatzow (Also at Washington, D.C. Office)
Thomas B. Hudson (Also at Washington, D.C. Office)
John F. Cooney (Not admitted in MD; Resident, Washington, D.C. Office)
Bryson L. Cook (P.C.) (Also at Washington, D.C. Office)
Nell B. Strachan
Barbara E. Schlaff
David G. Lane (Resident, McLean, Virginia Office)
L. Paige Marvel
N. Frank Wiggins (Not admitted in MD; Resident, Washington, D.C. Office)
Richard L. Wasserman (P.C.)
G. Stewart Webb, Jr.
James K. Archibald (Also at Washington, D.C. Office)
George W. Johnston (P.C.)
Constance H. Baker
Judson W. Starr (Not admitted in MD; Also at Washington, D.C. and Towson, Maryland Offices)
James R. Myers (Not admitted in MD; Resident, Washington, D.C. Office)
Ernest M. Stern (Resident, Washington, D.C. Office)
Edward L. Wender (P.C.)
David M. Fleishman
Jana Howard Carey (P.C.)
Jeffrey D. Knowles (Not admitted in MD; Resident, Washington, D.C. Office)
Jeffrey A. Dunn (also at Washington, D.C. Office)
Mitchell Kolkin
George F. Pappas (Also at Washington, D.C. Office)
William D. Coston (Not admitted in MD; Resident, Washington, D.C. Office)
Kenneth S. Slaughter (Not admitted in MD; Resident, Washington, D.C. Office)
Peter P. Parvis
James L. Shea (Also at Washington, D.C. Office)

(See Next Column)

MEMBERS OF FIRM (Continued)

Jeffrey P. Ayres (P.C.)
Brigid E. Kenney
Elizabeth C. Honeywell
Ellen F. Dyke (Not admitted in MD; Resident, McLean, Virginia Office)
Maurice Baskin (Resident, Washington, D.C. Office)
John J. Pavlick, Jr. (Not admitted in MD; Resident, Washington, D. C. Office)
Amy Berman Jackson (Not admitted in MD; Resident, Washington, D.C. Office)
William D. Quarles (Also at Washington, D.C. and Towson, Maryland Offices)
C. Carey Deeley, Jr. (Also at Towson, Maryland Office)
Kathleen Gallogly Cox (Resident, Towson, Maryland Office)
Donald R. Hartman (Not admitted in MD; Resident, Washington, D.C. Office)
Christopher R. Mellott
W. Robert Zinkham
David Eugene Rice
Cynthia M. Hahn (Resident, Towson, Maryland Office)
Jeffrey L. Ihnen (Not admitted in MD; Resident, Washington, D. C. Office)
John L. Sullivan, III (Not admitted in MD; Resident, McLean, Virginia Office)
Robert Charles Hill (Not admitted in MD; Resident, Washington, D.C. Office)
M. King Hill, III (Resident, Towson, Maryland Office)
James A. Dunbar (Also at Washington, D.C. Office)
Elizabeth R. Hughes
Ronald W. Taylor
Robert L. Waldman
Robert A. Cook
Thomas J. Kelly, Jr. (Not admitted in MD; Resident, Washington, D. C. Office)
John A. Roberts (Also at Rockville, Maryland Office)
Aline C. Ryan

Geoffrey M. Levitt (Not admitted in MD; Resident, Washington, D.C. Office)
Robert A. Hoffman (Resident, Towson, Maryland Office)
Robert J. Bolger, Jr. (Also at Washington, D.C. Office)
Anita J. Finkelstein (Not admitted in MD; Resident, Washington, D.C. Office)
David J. Heubeck
J. Michael Brennan (Resident, Towson, Maryland Office)
James F. Worrall (Not admitted in MD; Resident, Washington, D.C. Office)
Bruce H. Jurist (Also at Washington, D.C. Office)
James V. Bitonti (Resident, McLean, Virginia Office)
Herbert G. Smith, II (Not admitted in MD; Resident, Washington, D.C. Office)
Patrick J. Stewart (Also at Washington, D.C. Office)
Ariel Vannier
John M. Gurley (Not admitted in MD; Resident, Washington, D.C. Office)
David C. Mancini (Not admitted in MD; Resident, McLean, Virginia Office)
James R. Burdett (Not admitted in MD; Resident, Washington, D.C. Office)
Gary M. Hnath (Resident, Washington, D.C. Office)
Kevin L. Shepherd
James E. Cumbie
Newton B. Fowler, III
Michael J. Baader
Davis V. R. Sherman
Mitchell Y. Mirviss
Geoffrey R. Garinther (Also at Washington, D.C. Office)
Thomas M. Lingan
Terri L. Turner
Michael W. Robinson (Resident, McLean, Virginia Office)
Jeffrey K. Gonya
Francis X. Gallagher, Jr. (Not admitted in MD)
Elizabeth Marzo Borinsky

Robert H. Geis, Jr.

OF COUNSEL

A. Samuel Cook (P.C.) (Resident, Towson, Maryland Office)
Arthur W. Machen, Jr. (P.C.)
Herbert R. O'Conor, Jr. (Resident, Towson, Maryland Office)
Robert M. Thomas (P.C.)
Robert R. Bair (P.C.)
Frank Horton (Not admitted in MD; Resident, Washington, D.C. Office)
Richard H. Mays (Not admitted in MD; Washington, D.C. and McLean, Virginia Offices)
David D. Downes (Resident, Towson, Maryland Office)
Emried D. Cole, Jr.
Judith A. Armold
Thomas J. Cooper (Not admitted in MD; Resident, Washington, D. C. Office)

Kenneth G. Hurwitz (Also at Washington, D.C. Office)
Jerome S. Gabig, Jr. (Not admitted in MD; Resident, Washington, D.C. Office)
Gary D. Hailey (Not admitted in MD; Resident, Washington, D.C. Office)
Charles R. Marvin, Jr. (Not admitted in MD; Resident, Washington, D.C. Office)
John A. Wilhelm (Not admitted in MD; Resident, McLean, Virginia Office)
Todd K. Snyder
Barbara L. Waite (Resident, Washington, D.C. Office)
Mary T. Flynn (Not admitted in MD; Resident, McLean, Virginia Office)

ASSOCIATES

Scharon L. Ball
Paul D. Barker, Jr.
Louis B. Barr
David S. Berman (Resident, Washington, D.C. Office)
Gregory S. Braker (Resident, Washington, D.C. Office)
Eric L. Bryant
Courtney G. Capute
Pamela W. Carmody (Also at Washington, D.C. Office)
Daniel William China

Wallace E. Christner (Also at Washington, D.C. Office)
Patrick L. Clancy (Resident, Rockville, Maryland Office)
Kevin B. Collins (Also at Rockville, Maryland Office)
Michael W. Conron
Patricia Gillis Cousins (Resident, Rockville, Maryland Office)
Carla Draluck Craft (Resident, Washington, D.C. Office)

(See Next Column)

VENABLE ATTORNEYS AT LAW VENABLE, BAETJER AND HOWARD, LLP—
Continued

ASSOCIATES (Continued)

Donald P. Creston (Not
admitted in MD; Resident,
Washington, D.C. Office)
Gregory A. Cross
Peter J. Curtin
(Not admitted in MD)
James Nicholas Czaban (Not
admitted in MD; Resident,
Washington, D.C. Office)
Marina Lolley Dame (Resident,
Towson, Maryland Office)
Sandra Howard Darby
David S. Darland (Not admitted
in MD; Resident, Washington,
D.C. Office)
Paul A. Debolt (Not admitted in
MD; Resident, Washington,
D.C. Office)
Wm. Craig Dubishar (Not
admitted in MD; Resident,
McLean, Virginia Office)
John P. Edgar
John P. Fielding (Not admitted
in MD; Washington, D.C. and
McLean, Virginia Offices)
Melissa K. Force (Resident,
Towson, Maryland Office)
Rochelle Block Fowler
David W. Goewey (Not
admitted in MD; Resident,
Washington, D.C. Office)
E. Anne Hamel
John C. Hardwick, Jr. (Resident,
Washington, D.C. Office)
Andrew R. Herrup (Resident,
Washington, D.C. Office)
David R. Hodnett (Not
admitted in MD; Resident,
McLean, Virginia Office)
J. Scott Hommer, III (Not
admitted in MD; Resident,
McLean, Virginia Office)
Frederick M. Hopkins
Todd J. Horn
Maria F. Howell
Mary-Dulany James (Resident,
Towson, Maryland Office)
Melissa E. Kearney (Resident,
McLean, Virginia Office)
Houtan Khalili-Esfahani (Not
admitted in MD; Resident,
Washington, D.C. Office)
Kevin Michael Kordziel
(Resident, Washington, D.C.
Office)
Michael S. Kosmas
Gregory L. Laubach (Resident,
Rockville, Maryland Office)
Fernand A. Lavallee (Not
admitted in MD; Resident,
Washington, D. C. Office)
Wingrove S. Lynton
Edward Brendan Magrab
(Resident, Washington, D.C.
Office)
Patricia A. Malone (Resident,
Towson, Maryland Office)
Mark Darius Robert Maneche
Valerie K. Mann (Not admitted
in MD; Resident, Washington,
D.C. Office)

Anne W. Marculewicz
Vicki Margolis (Also at
Washington, D.C. Office)
Christine M. McAnney (Not
admitted in MD; Resident,
McLean, Virginia Office)
John A. McCauley
Matthew J. McConkey (Not
admitted in MD; Resident,
Washington, D.C. Office)
Nuala McConnell (Resident,
Washington, D.C. Office)
Heather L. McDowell (Resident,
Washington, D.C. Office)
Lindsay Beardsworth Meyer
(Not admitted in MD;
Resident, Washington, D.C.
Office)
Keith A. Mong
Traci H. Mundy (Not admitted
in MD; Resident, McLean,
Virginia Office)
Brian J. O'Connor
(Not admitted in MD)
Juliana Schulte O'Reilly
(Resident, Washington, D.C.
Office)
Urvi N. Patel
Andrea S. Paterson (Resident,
Washington, D.C. Office)
Richard J. Peltz
John T. Prisbe
Lawrence C. Renbaum
(Resident, Washington, D.C.
Office)
Christina L. Romeres
Joel W. Ruderman (Resident,
Rockville, Maryland Office)
April J. Sands
Dino S. Sangiamo
John Peter Sarbanes
Myriam Judith Schmell
Joseph C. Schmelter
Larry Robert Seegull
Carl H. Settlemyer, III
(Resident, Washington, D.C.
Office)
Melissa Landau Steinman
(Resident, Washington, D.C.
Office)
Thomas H. Strong
Neal H. Strum
Linda Marotta Thomas
Brian R. Trumbauer
Christine J. Warren
Paul N. Wengert (Not admitted
in MD; Resident, McLean,
Virginia Office)
Elizabeth M.S. Whaling
Corie L. Williams (Resident,
Towson, Maryland Office)
Katherine D. Williams
(Resident, Towson, Maryland
Office)
Karen D. Woodard (Resident,
Washington, D.C. Office)
Ariana Jean Wright (Resident,
Rockville, Maryland Office)
Maureen Donahue Yuffee
(Resident, Washington, D.C.
Office)

Robin L. Zimelman

For full biographical listings, see the Martindale-Hubbell Law Directory

---

ROBIN PAGE WEST (AV)

110 St. Paul Street, Suite 301, 21202
Telephone: 410-244-0400
Fax: 410-244-0402
Email: robin.west.esq@counsel.com

For full biographical listings, see the Martindale-Hubbell Law Directory

---

WHITEFORD, TAYLOR & PRESTON L.L.P. (AV)

7 Saint Paul Street, 21202-1626
Telephone: 410-347-8700
Telex: 5101012334
Fax: 410-752-7092
Email: 2019267@mcimail.com *URL:* http://www.wtplaw.com
Towson, Maryland Office: 210 West Pennsylvania Avenue.
Telephone: 410-832-2000.
Fax: 410-832-2015.
Washington, D.C. Office: 1025 Connecticut Avenue, N.W.
Telephone: 202-659-6800.
Fax: 202-331-0573.
Columbia, Maryland Office: 10440 Little Patuxent Parkway.
Telephone: 410-884-0700.
Fax: 410-884-0719.
Alexandria, Virginia Office: 1317 King Street.
Telephone: 703-836-5742.
Fax: 703-836-0265.

MEMBERS OF FIRM

Paul F. Due (1896-1972)
Palmer R. Nickerson
(1898-1969)
W. Hamilton Whiteford
(1903-1992)
B. Conway Taylor, Jr.
(1918-1993)
Wilbur D. Preston, Jr.
Richard C. Whiteford
Daniel H. Honemann
Larry M. Wolf
Arthur P. Rogers (Resident
Washington, D.C. Office)
Louis G. Close, Jr.
Joseph K. Pokempner
Robert S. Hillman
Fenton L. Martin
William B. Whiteford
Robert M. Wright
B. Ford Davis
Ascanio S. Boccuti
(Resident Towson Office)
Thomas C. Beach, III
Glenn R. Bonard (Resident
Washington, D.C. Office)
Kenneth J. Ingram (Resident
Washington, D.C. Office)
John A. Hayden, III
(Resident Towson Office)
Richard J. Magid
Robert Sloan, III
Ward B. Coe, III
(Managing Partner)
Frederick Singley Koontz
M. Natalie McSherry
George J. Bachrach
Robert B. Curran
Stephen B. Caplis
Dale B. Garbutt
Paul W. Madden
Stephen F. Fruin
James R. Chason
(Resident Towson Office)
James F. Rosner
(Resident Towson Office)
James C. Holman
Herman B. Rosenthal
Joseph V. Truhe, Jr.
Deborah H. Diehl
Joseph D. Douglass (Resident
Washington, D.C. Office)

Harry S. Johnson
William F. Ryan, Jr.
Gerard P. Sunderland
Steven E. Bers
William M. Davidow, Jr.
George S. Lawler
(Resident Towson Office)
Thomas P. Kimmitt, Jr.
(Resident Towson Office)
Jeanne M. Phelan
Kevin C. McCormick
Gail M. Stern
John V. Church
Jonathan E. Claiborne
(Resident Towson Office)
Albert J. Mezzanotte, Jr.
(Towson and Columbia
Offices)
Douglas F. Murray
Deborah Sweet Byrnes
(Resident Towson Office)
Warren N. Weaver
Barbara Lee Ayres
(Resident Towson Office)
Carol A. Zuckerman
Paul M. Nussbaum
G. Scott Barhight
(Resident Towson Office)
Edward M. Buxbaum
(Resident Towson Office)
Kenneth Oestreicher
John P. Evans
Dana C. Petersen
Anne Talbot Brennan
(Resident Towson Office)
Philip B. Barnes
(Resident Towson Office)
John J. Hathway (Columbia,
Maryland and Washington,
D.C. Offices)
Frank S. Jones, Jr.
Colleen R. Cross
Gardner M. Duvall
Eric W. Cowan
Lisa A. Kershner
Peter D. Guattery
Natalie C. Magdeburger
(Resident Towson Office)
Joseph N. Schaller

OF COUNSEL

Roger A. Clapp
J. Royall Tippett, Jr.
Ernest C. Trimble
(Resident Towson Office)
George D. Solter
(Resident Towson Office)

Edward A. Johnston
(Resident Towson Office)
C. William Tayler (Resident
Washington, D.C. Office)
John H. Somerville
Lee A. Satterfield (Resident
Washington, D.C. Office)

ASSOCIATES

Adelina M. Welch
Michael W. Fucheck
D. Scott Freed
Judith C. Ensor
(Resident Towson Office)
Howard R. Feldman
Jonathan Z. May
Gary S. Posner
John F. Carlton
Joseph J. Mezzanotte

Andrew J. Terrell (Resident
Washington, D.C. Office)
Thurman W. Zollicoffer, Jr.
Robert F. Carney
Sandra Harlen Benzer
Eva H. Hill
Edwin G. Fee, Jr.
(Resident Towson Office)
J. Van Lear Dorsey
(Resident Towson Office)

(See Next Column)

WHITEFORD, TAYLOR & PRESTON L.L.P., *Baltimore—Continued*

ASSOCIATES (Continued)

Lisa Walker Justis	Mary Claire Chesshire
Martin T. Fletcher	Dwight W. Stone, II
Catherine Whitehurst Steiner	S. Keith Moulsdale
Padraic McSherry Morton	David K. Gildea
Mark C. Kopec	(Resident Towson Office)
Gail Donovan Chester	Pamela M. Conover
Christine K. McSherry	Julie D. Wright
(Resident Towson Office)	(Resident Towson Office)
Mary Gillen Fenske (Resident	Courtenay M. Labson
Washington, D.C. Office)	Carmina Pérez
Michael A. Stover	Denise E. Jackson (Resident
Julianne Erin Dymowski	Washington, D.C. Office)
(Resident Washington, D.C.	Kim Y. Johnson
Office)	Robert Dennis Earle
Elise R. Davison	Kevin P. McCann
Steven E. Tiller	Wendy A. Hartmann
(Resident Towson Office)	Eric R. Harlan
Brendan P. Bunn (Resident	Melissa L. Menkel
Washington, D.C. Office)	Bradley S. Hames
Thomas J. Whiteford	(Resident Towson Office)
(Resident Towson Office)	Stephen K. Gallagher

For full biographical listings, see the Martindale-Hubbell Law Directory

---

WRIGHT, CONSTABLE & SKEEN (AV)

250 West Pratt Street, 13th Floor, 21201-2423
Telephone: 410-539-5541
Telex: 710 234-2383 CALDAS
Fax: 301-659-1350
Elkton, Maryland Office: 138 East Main Street.
Telephone: 301-398-1844.

MEMBERS OF FIRM

Wm. Pepper Constable	Monte Fried
(1882-1976)	James W. Constable
John D. Wright (1903-1976)	David W. Skeen
George W. Constable (Retired)	John Philip Miller
Read A. McCaffrey	James D. Skeen
William A. Skeen (Retired)	Kenneth F. Davies
C. Gordon Haines	Stephen F. White
Thomas F. Comber, 3rd	Brian S. Goodman
(Resident, Elkton Office)	Frederick L. Kobb
John Brentnall Powell, Jr.	Paul F. Evelius
Michael J. Abromaitis	Lois A. Fenner McBride

ASSOCIATES

Mary Alice Smolarek	Tracey Dee King
Catherine H. Bellinger	Charles J. Morton, Jr.

COUNSEL

Francis N. Iglehart, Jr.	P. McEvoy Cromwell

Representative Clients: AAI Corp.; Conowingo Power Co.; Weyerhaeuser Co.; Baltimore's International Culinary College, Inc.; Commercial Credit Corp.; Noxell Corp.; Consolidated Rail Corp.; Murray Corp.; Atlantic Mutual Insurance Co.; Sea Containers, Ltd.

For full biographical listings, see the Martindale-Hubbell Law Directory

---

BETHESDA, Montgomery Co.

THOMAS P. BROWN, III (AV)

4948 St. Elmo Avenue, Suite 208, 20814
Telephone: 301-986-9100
Fax: 301-986-9103

For full biographical listings, see the Martindale-Hubbell Law Directory

---

BULMAN, DUNIE, BURKE & FELD, CHARTERED (AV)

7427 Arlington Road, 20814-5397
Telephone: 301-656-1177
Facsimile: 301-986-9719

Maurice R. Dunie	Alan S. Feld
Lawrence Z. Bulman	Barry M. Nudelman
John F. Burke	Mark W. Shupe
	Jonathan F. Keiler

Nancy Bradley Farren	Sidney M. Goldstein (Retired)
Joseph D. Bulman (Not	Arthur S. Feld (1919-1979)
admitted in MD; Retired)	

For full biographical listings, see the Martindale-Hubbell Law Directory

---

CARLIN, BRADSHAW, THOMAS & YEATMAN L.L.P. (AV)

4405 East-West Highway, Suite 603, 20814
Telephone: 301-656-3800
Fax: 301-656-6703

(See Next Column)

Francis E. Yeatman	F. Douglas Yeatman
C. Brian Carlin	J. Douglas Bradshaw (Retired)
Howard J. Thomas (Retired)	

OF COUNSEL

E. Austin Carlin	Timothy Guy Casey

References: Citizens Bank & Trust Company of Maryland; Equitable Federal Savings Bank; Crestar Bank.

For full biographical listings, see the Martindale-Hubbell Law Directory

---

PALEY, ROTHMAN, GOLDSTEIN, ROSENBERG & COOPER, CHARTERED (AV)

Seventh Floor, One Bethesda Center, 4800 Hampden Lane, 20814
Telephone: 301-656-7603
Telecopier: 301-654-7354
Email: prg@paleyrothman.com

Glenn M. Cooper	Hope Eastman
Victor J. Rosenberg	Dennis L. Sharp
Mark S. Goldstein	R. Thomas Hoffmann
Mark S. Rothman	Albert D. Pailet
Stephen H. Paley	Diane A. Fox
Paula A. Calimafde	Theodore P. Stein
Ronald A. Dweck	Jeffrey A. Kolender
Arthur H. Blitz	Wendelin I. Lipp
Robert H. Maclay	Robert B. Bowytz
Steven A. Widdes	Mark A. Binstock

Patricia M. Weaver	Brent M. Goldstein
Alan D. Eisler	Jeffrey D. Olster
David M. Rothenstein	Kathleen M. Dumais

SENIOR COUNSEL

Alan S. Mark	Daniel S. Koch

For full biographical listings, see the Martindale-Hubbell Law Directory

---

BLADENSBURG, Prince Georges Co. — (Refer to Hyattsville)

CENTREVILLE, * Queen Annes Co.

THOMPSON & THOMPSON (AV)

118 North Commerce Street, 21617
Telephone: 410-758-0877
Fax: 410-758-2305

James E. Thompson, Jr.	Jeffrey E. Thompson

References: The Centreville National Bank; The Security Title Guaranty Co.

For full biographical listings, see the Martindale-Hubbell Law Directory

---

COLLEGE PARK, Prince Georges Co.

WILLONER, CALABRESE & ROSEN, P.A. (AV)

4603 Calvert Road, 20740-3421
Telephone: 301-699-1400
Fax: 301-779-2213

Ronald A. Willoner	Steven Rosen
John F. Calabrese	Stephen F. Shea

Thomas J. Love

Reference: Allegiance Bank, N.A., Bethesda, Maryland.

For full biographical listings, see the Martindale-Hubbell Law Directory

---

CUMBERLAND, * Allegany Co. — (Refer to Hagerstown)

DENTON, * Caroline Co. — (Refer to Easton)

EASTON, * Talbot Co.

WHEELER, THOMPSON, PARKER & COUNTS (AV)

129 North Washington Street, P.O. Box 1209, 21601
Telephone: 410-822-1122
Fax: 410-822-3635

MEMBERS OF FIRM

Edward T. Miller (1895-1968)	Dorothy H. Thompson
Ernest M. Thompson	Willard C. Parker, II
(1921-1989)	Richard L. Counts, III
Charles E. Wheeler	Douglas A. Collison

ASSOCIATES

John Whitelaw Ong

OF COUNSEL

Donald H. Olson	Philip E. Nuttle, Jr.

Representative Clients: Nationwide Insurance Co.; Home Indemnity Co.; Chicago Title Insurance Company of Maryland; State Farm Mutual Insurance Co.; Chesapeake College; Habitat for Humanity of Talbot County; Talbot County Board of Education; Fuller Motor Sales, Inc.; St. Michaels Housing Authority.

(See Next Column)

WHEELER, THOMPSON, PARKER & COUNTS—*Continued*

Reference: Nationsbank, Easton Branch.

For full biographical listings, see the Martindale-Hubbell Law Directory

ELKTON, Cecil Co.

WRIGHT, CONSTABLE & SKEEN (AV)

138 East Main Street, 21921
Telephone: 301-398-1844
Baltimore, Maryland Office: 250 West Pratt Street, 13th Floor.
Telephone: 410-539-5541.
Fax: 410-659-1350.

MEMBERS OF FIRM

Wm. Pepper Constable (1882-1976)	Thomas F. Comber, 3rd (Resident)

Representative Clients: Delaware Trust Co.; Whirlpool Financial; B&G Automotive, Inc.

For full biographical listings, see the Martindale-Hubbell Law Directory

ELLICOTT CITY, Howard Co.

LLOYD, KANE, WIEDER & WILLIS, P.A. (AV)

3716 Court Place, 21043
Telephone: 410-461-9400
FAX: 410-750-8544

Thomas E. Lloyd	Malcolm B. Kane
John Willis	

OF COUNSEL

Robert E. Wieder

Local Counsel for: Baltimore Gas & Electric Co.; Federal Land Bank of Baltimore; Sandy Spring National Bank and Savings Institution; Commercial and Farmers Bank; Potomac Electric Power Co.

For full biographical listings, see the Martindale-Hubbell Law Directory

FREDERICK, Frederick Co.

MILLER, MILLER & CANBY, CHARTERED (AV)

129-13 West Patrick Street, 21701
Telephone: 301-696-1380
FAX: 301-696-1385
Rockville, Maryland Office: 200-B Monroe Street.
Telephone: 301-762-5212.
FAX: 301-762-6044.

Robert L. Burchett	Diane M. Poole
Bruce N. Dean (Resident)	

Representative Clients: Montgomery General Hospital, Inc.; Sandy Spring National Bank of Maryland.

For full biographical listings, see the Martindale-Hubbell Law Directory

OFFUTT, HORMAN, BURDETTE & FREY, P.A. (AV)

Offutt Building, 22 West Second Street, 21701
Telephone: 301-662-8248;
Hagerstown: 301-293-6032;
Montgomery Co., D.C./Va. line: 301-948-5633
Fax: 301-663-8968

W. Jerome Offutt	George T. Horman
Amos A. Holter	Charles Burton Frey
John N. Burdette	Chris May

Representative Clients: Donald B. Rice Tire Co., Inc.; Meadows Van and Storage Co.; Central Maryland Farm Credit, ACA; QUADS Trust Co.; Frederick Aviation, Inc.
Local Counsel: St. James Servicing Corp.; First National Bank of Maryland.
Co-Counsel for: Central Maryland Farm Credit, ACA.
Reference: Frederick Branch of First National Bank of Maryland.

For full biographical listings, see the Martindale-Hubbell Law Directory

GREENBELT, Prince Georges Co.

JOSEPH, GREENWALD AND LAAKE, P.A. (AV)

Capital Office Park, 6404 Ivy Lane, Suite 400, 20770
Telephone: 301-220-2200
Telecopier: 301-220-1214

Fred R. Joseph	John Shay Parker
Andrew E. Greenwald	Peggy Crespi Kaplan
Walter E. Laake, Jr.	Barbara J. Gorinson
Stephen A. Friedman	Timothy P. O'Brien
Burt M. Kahn	Michael V. Statham
Michael D. Jackley	Jay P. Holland
Steven M. Pavsner	Lisa S. Segel

(See Next Column)

Steven J. Gaba	Jerry D. Miller
Steven B. Vinick	David Samuel Coaxum
Timothy S. Mitchell	

For full biographical listings, see the Martindale-Hubbell Law Directory

STANLEY S. PICKETT (AV)

Suite 414 Capital Office Park, 6411 Ivy Lane, 20770
Telephone: 301-513-0613
Fax: 301-513-0618

Stanley Sinclair Pickett

ASSOCIATE

Gordon J. Brumback

LEGAL SUPPORT PERSONNEL

Stacy S. Pickett (Law Clerk)	Vivian W. Wolfe (Paralegal)

Representative Clients: B.F. Saul Co.; McDonald and Eudy Printers, Inc.; Condominium Management, Inc.; Long & Foster Realtors; Mitron Systems Corp.; Coldwell Banker; Glenanden Housing Authority; Koones & Montgomery, Inc.; Community Associations, Inc.

For full biographical listings, see the Martindale-Hubbell Law Directory

REICHELT, NUSSBAUM, LAPLACA & MILLER (AV)

The Maryland Trade Center, Suite 1000, 7500 Greenway Center Drive, P.O. Box 627, 20768-0627
Telephone: 301-474-9000
Fax: 301-345-0565

MEMBERS OF FIRM

Herbert W. Reichelt (1908-1993)	Sheldon L. Gnatt
Ronald M. Miller	Raymond G. LaPlaca
T. Summers Gwynn, III	Daniel A. LaPlaca
Gary Greenwald	Gail Borjeson Viens
Andrew W. Nussbaum	Roger C. Thomas

ASSOCIATES

Wanda G. Caporaletti

OF COUNSEL

Paul M. Nussbaum	Toni Evon Clarke

Representative Clients: Tower Federal Credit Union; Suburban Bank of Maryland.
Reference: NationsBank of Maryland, N.A.

For full biographical listings, see the Martindale-Hubbell Law Directory

LANDOVER, Prince Georges Co.

KRAUSER & TAUB, P.C. (AV)

9200 Basil Court, Suite 300, 20785-5309
Telephone: 301-925-4900
FAX: 301-925-9752

Peter B. Krauser	Lawrence N. Taub

Seth D. Goldberg

For full biographical listings, see the Martindale-Hubbell Law Directory

LANHAM, Prince Georges Co.

DeCARO, DORAN, SICILIANO, GALLAGHER, SONNTAG & DeBLASIS (AV)

4601 Forbes Boulevard Suite 200, P.O. Box 40, 20703-0040
Telephone: 301-306-4300
Telecopier: 301-306-4988
Alexandria, Virginia Office: 1800 Diagonal Road, Suite 300.
Telephone: 703-548-0044.
Telecopier: 703-209-8548.

MEMBERS OF FIRM

Alan R. Siciliano	Charles E. Gallagher, Jr.
Jeffrey R. DeCaro	Samuel J. DeBlasis, II
W. Scott Sonntag	Christopher R. Dunn
Thomas L. Doran	Michael A. DeSantis
Timothy E. Howie	

ASSOCIATES

Deborah Elizabeth Sanders Kane	D. Lynne Jenkins
Neil Joseph MacDonald	Anne Marie McGinley
Amy T. Roberts	James D. Cardea
Michele L. Smith	Stephen J. Williams
Leslie D. Oliveri	Douglas K. Allston, Jr
Solomon Martin Sterenberg	Julie H. Favetta
Christine L. Pecora	

For full biographical listings, see the Martindale-Hubbell Law Directory

McCARTHY, BACON & COSTELLO, L.L.P. (AV)

Washington Business Park, Suite 300, 4640 Forbes Boulevard, 20706-4323
Telephone: 301-306-1900
Fax: 301-306-1988
Email: mbc@erols.com *URL:* http://www.erols.com/mbc

(See Next Column)

McCarthy, Bacon & Costello L.L.P., *Lanham—Continued*

MEMBERS OF FIRM

Kevin J. McCarthy	Michael McGowan
Edward C. Bacon	Patricia M. Thornton
John F. X. Costello	Mark D. Palmer

Stan Derwin Brown

ASSOCIATES

John T. Bergin	Timothy Altemus
Michael O. Glynn, III	Heather Jean Kelly

OF COUNSEL

Charles E. Channing, Jr.

For full biographical listings, see the Martindale-Hubbell Law Directory

---

LA PLATA,* Charles Co.

THOMAS C. HAYDEN, JR., P.A. (AV)

105 La Grange Avenue, P.O. Box 1039, 20646
Telephone: 301-934-9531; 301-870-3477
Fax: 301-934-5473

Thomas C. Hayden, Jr.	H. A. Turner, IV

Thomas R. Simpson, Jr.

Representative Client: County First Bank.
Reference: County First Bank, La Plata, Maryland.

For full biographical listings, see the Martindale-Hubbell Law Directory

---

MUDD, MUDD & FITZGERALD, P.A. (AV)

106 St. Mary's Avenue, P.O. Box 310, 20646
Telephone: 301-934-9541
FAX: 301-934-8178

John F. Mudd (1907-1950)	Thomas F. Mudd
F. DeSales Mudd (1933-1972)	John F. Mudd

Stephen P. Fitzgerald

Richard A. Cooper	Robert M. Burke

Mary T. Rice

Local Counsel for: County First Bank (La Plata); Potomac Electric Power Co.; The Hartford Insurance Group; Maryland Bank & Trust Co.; Chicago Title Insurance Co.; Peninsula Title Insurance Co.; Colonial Farm Credit Agric. Credit Assn.
Counsel for: Interstate General Corporation; SMO, Inc.

For full biographical listings, see the Martindale-Hubbell Law Directory

---

LEXINGTON PARK, St. Marys Co.

KENNEY, LACER, SPARLING, DENSFORD AND REYNOLDS, P.A. (AV)

One Hundred Exploration, Suite 2030, 20653
Telephone: 301-863-7054
Fax: 301-863-7112
Leonardtown, Maryland Office: 24 Courthouse Drive.
Telephone: 301-475-8310.
Prince Frederick, Maryland Office: 65 Duke Street, 20678.
Telephone: 410-535-4405.

John H. T. Briscoe (1890-1981)	George R. Sparling
James A. Kenney, III	Edward Kim Reynolds
Alfred A. Lacer	Joseph R. Densford

Representative Clients: The Wildwood Group; St. Mary's Medical Arts, Inc.; Maryland Automobile Insurance Fund.
Approved Attorneys for: Chicago Title Company of Maryland; Lawyers Title Insurance Corporation of Richmond, Virginia.

For full biographical listings, see the Martindale-Hubbell Law Directory

---

OCEAN CITY, Worcester Co.

J. HARRISON PHILLIPS, III (AV)

115-72nd Street, 21842
Telephone: 410-524-1944
Fax: 410-524-9240

References: Home Bank, Ocean City; Calvin B. Taylor Bank, Berlin, Maryland.

For full biographical listings, see the Martindale-Hubbell Law Directory

---

PRINCESS ANNE,* Somerset Co. — (Refer to Salisbury)

RIVERDALE, Prince Georges Co.

MEYERS, BILLINGSLEY, RODBELL & ROSENBAUM, P.A. (AV)

Suite 400 Berkshire Building, 6801 Kenilworth Avenue, 20737-1385
Telephone: 301-699-5800
Fax: 301-779-5746

(See Next Column)

William V. Meyers	Michele LaRocca
Lance W. Billingsley	Frederick Stichnoth
Paul B. Rodbell	Bud Stephen Tayman
Robert H. Rosenbaum	Paul A. Turkheimer
Russell E. Warfel	M. Andree Green
Linda C. Carter	Gina Marie Smith
Joseph B. Chazen	Mindy Sue Kursban

Reference: First National Bank of Maryland.

For full biographical listings, see the Martindale-Hubbell Law Directory

---

ROCKVILLE,* Montgomery Co.

BRAULT, GRAHAM, SCOTT & BRAULT (AV)

101 South Washington Street, 20850
Telephone: 301-424-1060
Fax: 301-424-7991
Washington, D.C. Office: 1906 Sunderland Place, N.W.
Telephone: 202-785-1200.
FAX: 202-785-4301.
Arlington, Virginia Office: Suite 1201, 2300 North Clarendon Boulevard, Courthouse Plaza.
Telephone: 703-358-9200.

OF COUNSEL

Laurence T. Scott	Janet S. Zigler (Resident)

MEMBERS OF FIRM

Denver H. Graham (1922-1987)	Daniel L. Shea (Resident)
Albert E. Brault (Retired)	M. Kathleen Parker (Resident)
Albert D. Brault (Resident)	David G. Mulquin (Resident)
Leo A. Roth, Jr.	James M. Brault (Resident)
James S. Wilson (Resident)	Regina Ann Casey (Resident)
Ronald G. Guziak	Sanford A. Friedman

ASSOCIATES

Holly D. Shupert (Resident)	Joan F. Brault (Resident)
Rhonda Ann Hurwitz (Resident)	Joseph P. Morra (Resident)

Michael A. Carlo

Representative Clients: American Oil Co.; Crum & Forster Group; Fireman's Fund American Insurance Cos.; Kemper Group; Reliance Insurance Cos.; Safeco Group; Government Employees Insurance Co.; Medical Mutual Insurance Society of Maryland; Legal Mutual Liability Insurance Society of Maryland.

For full biographical listings, see the Martindale-Hubbell Law Directory

---

BROMBERG, ROSENTHAL & SIEGEL (AV)

110 North Washington Street Suite 405, 20850-2223
Telephone: 301-251-6200
FAX: 301-309-9436
Washington, D.C. Office: Suite 536, 1522 K Street, N.W.

MEMBERS OF FIRM

Gary Siegel	Barry J. Rosenthal

Jonathan R. Bromberg

ASSOCIATES

Kenneth S. Golden

Representative Clients: Agriculture Federal Credit Union; GEICOS Federal Credit Union; Dexall Biomedical Labs; Security, Inc.; N.R.L. Federal Credit Union.

For full biographical listings, see the Martindale-Hubbell Law Directory

---

CHEN, WALSH, TECLER & McCABE (AV)

Suite 300, 200-A Monroe Street, 20850
Telephone: 301-279-9500
FAX: 301-294-5195

MEMBERS OF FIRM

William James Chen, Jr.	Kenneth B. Tecler
John Burgess Walsh, Jr.	John F. McCabe, Jr.

For full biographical listings, see the Martindale-Hubbell Law Directory

---

McCARTHY, WILSON & ETHRIDGE (AV)

100 South Washington Street, 20850
Telephone: 301-762-7770
FAX: 301-762-0374

MEMBERS OF FIRM

Joseph S. McCarthy (1918-1983)	Paul H. Ethridge
Charles E. Wilson, Jr.	Thomas Patrick Ryan

Robert B. Hetherington

ASSOCIATES

D. Elizabeth Walker	Charles Elliot Wilson, III
Rocco C. Nunzio	Juli Martin Tweedy
Edward J. Brown	Jonathan R. Clark

Representative Clients: Allstate Insurance Co.; Erie Insurance Exchange; Horace Mann Insurance Co.; Leaseway Transportation System, Inc.; Lloyd's of London; Massachusetts Mutual Life Insurance Co; Sears Roebuck & Co.

For full biographical listings, see the Martindale-Hubbell Law Directory

Rockville—Continued

MILLER, MILLER & CANBY, CHARTERED (AV)

200-B Monroe Street, 20850
Telephone: 301-762-5212
FAX: 301-762-6044
Frederick, Maryland Office: 129-13 West Patrick Street.
Telephone: 301-696-1380.
FAX: 301-696-1385.

William M. Canby (1930-1994)	Lewis R. Schumann
Robert L. Burchett	Joel S. Kline
Patrick C. McKeever	Diane M. Poole
James L. Thompson	Joseph P. Suntum

OF COUNSEL
James R. Miller, Jr.

Ellen S. Walker	Suzanne Levant Rotbert
Susan W. Carter	Scott N. Alperin
Bruce N. Dean	Laurie Breslin Thomas
(Resident, Frederick Office)	

Representative Clients: Asbury Methodist Home Inc.; Sandy Spring National Bank of Maryland.

For full biographical listings, see the Martindale-Hubbell Law Directory

MILLER, STEINBERG & HESSLER (AV)

Suite 414, 414 Hungerford Drive, 20850
Telephone: 301-424-1180
Fax: 301-424-8459

MEMBERS OF FIRM

James Robert Miller	Harvey B. Steinberg
	Kevin G. Hessler

Reference: NationsBank, Rockville Branch.

For full biographical listings, see the Martindale-Hubbell Law Directory

THOMAS D. MURPHY (AV)

Suite 2 Adams Law Center, 31 Wood Lane, 20850
Telephone: 301-424-0400

ASSOCIATE
James A. Mood, Jr.

For full biographical listings, see the Martindale-Hubbell Law Directory

ROWAN & QUIRK (AV)

The Adams Law Center, 27 Wood Lane, 20850
Telephone: 301-762-4050
FAX: 301-762-9189

MEMBERS OF FIRM

William J. Rowan, III	Joseph M. Quirk

ASSOCIATES
John G. Nalls

For full biographical listings, see the Martindale-Hubbell Law Directory

SHULMAN, ROGERS, GANDAL, PORDY & ECKER, P.A. (AV)

Third Floor, 11921 Rockville Pike, 20852-2743
Telephone: 301-230-5200
Telecopier: 301-230-2891
Email: litigate@srgpe.com; realprop@srgpe.com
Email: business@srgpe.com
Washington, D.C. Office: 1100 New York Avenue, N.W. West Tower, Suite 500.
Telephone: 202-872-0400.

Lawrence A. Shulman	Robert B. Canter
Donald R. Rogers	Edward F. Schiff
Larry N. Gandal	Daniel S. Krakower
Karl L. Ecker	Kevin P. Kennedy
David A. Pordy	James P. Sullivan
David D. Freishtat	Alan B. Sternstein
Martin P. Schaffer	Nancy P. Regelin
Christopher C. Roberts	Samuel M. Spiritos
Jeffrey A. Shane	Richard J. Melnick
Edward M. Hanson, Jr.	Martin Levine
David M. Kochanski	Olivia S. Byrne
Walter A. Oleniewski	Ashley Joel Gardner
Lawrence L. Bell	James M. Hoffman
James M. Kefauver	Thomas L. Hanley
Rebecca Oshoway	(Not admitted in MD)

OF COUNSEL

Lawrence J. Eisenberg	Fred S. Sommer
Solomon L. Margolis	Harry K. Schwartz
	(Not admitted in MD)

(See Next Column)

Michael J. Froehlich	Douglas K. Hirsch
William C. Davis, III	Patrick M. Martyn
James A. Powers	Kim A. Viti
Elizabeth N. Shomaker	John J. McKenna, Jr.
Michael V. Nakamura	Manisha D. Kapani
Paul A. Bellegarde	Barry P. Miller
Gregory J. Rupert	(Not admitted in MD)
Sandra E. Brusca	Timothy C. Lynch
Jonathan M. Forster	Todd I. Steinberg

Reference: Maryland National Bank, Montgomery County Regional Office.

For full biographical listings, see the Martindale-Hubbell Law Directory

STEIN, SPERLING, BENNETT, DE JONG, DRISCOLL, GREENFEIG & METRO, P.A. (AV)

25 West Middle Lane, 20850
Telephone: 301-340-2020; 800-435-5230
Telecopier: 301-340-8217

Millard S. Bennett	Ann G. Jakabcin
David S. De Jong	A. Howard Metro
David C. Driscoll, Jr.	Jeffrey M. Schwaber
Jack A. Garson	Donald N. Sperling
Stuart S. Greenfeig	Paul T. Stein

James D. Dalrymple	Ann Marie M. Mehlert
Fred A. Balkin	Ava L. Healy
Jeffrey D. Goldstein	Holly R. Eaton
Darcy A. Shoop	Moia T. Gruber

For full biographical listings, see the Martindale-Hubbell Law Directory

VENABLE ATTORNEYS AT LAW VENABLE, BAETJER AND HOWARD, LLP (AV)

A Partnership including Professional Corporations
Suite 500, One Church Street, P.O. Box 1906, 20850-4129
Telephone: 301-217-5600
FAX: 301-217-5617
Baltimore, Maryland Office: 1800 Mercantile Bank & Trust Building, 2 Hopkins Plaza.
Telephone: 410-244-7400.
Washington, D.C. Office: Venable, Baetjer, Howard & Civiletti LLP, Suite 1000, 1201 New York Avenue, N.W.
Telephone: 202-962-4800.
McLean, Virginia Office: Suite 400, 2010 Corporate Ridge.
Telephone: 703-760-1600.
Towson, Maryland, Office: 210 Allegheny Avenue, P. O. Box 5517.
Telephone: 410-494-6200.

MEMBERS OF FIRM

Roger W. Titus	Paul T. Glasgow
Daniel O'C. Tracy, Jr. (Also at Baltimore, Maryland Office)	Sondra Harans Block
	John A. Roberts (Also at Baltimore, Maryland Office)

ASSOCIATES

Patrick L. Clancy	Patricia Gillis Cousins
Kevin B. Collins (Also at Baltimore, Maryland Office)	Gregory L. Laubach
	Joel W. Ruderman
Ariana Jean Wright	

For full biographical listings, see the Martindale-Hubbell Law Directory

SALISBURY,* Wicomico Co.

ANTHENELLI & OTWAY (AV)

108 The Plaza, P.O. Box 4096, 21801
Telephone: 410-749-3900
Fax: 410-749-8577

MEMBERS OF FIRM

James V. Anthenelli	James L. Otway

For full biographical listings, see the Martindale-Hubbell Law Directory

DUVALL & DUVALL, L.L.P. (AV)

108 East Market Street, P.O. Box 4077, 21803-4077
Telephone: 410-548-1010
Fax: 410-548-1045

MEMBERS OF FIRM

William G. Duvall	Richard M. Duvall

Reference: Nations Bank.

For full biographical listings, see the Martindale-Hubbell Law Directory

Salisbury—Continued

WEBB, BURNETT, JACKSON, CORNBROOKS, WILBER, VORHIS & DOUSE, LLP (AV)

115 Broad Street, P.O. Box 910, 21801
Telephone: 410-742-3176
Fax: 410-742-0438
Email: webnett@shore.intercom.net

MEMBERS OF FIRM

Frederick W. C. Webb (1889-1956)	W. Newton Jackson, 3rd
John W. T. Webb (1918-1990)	Ernest I. Cornbrooks, III
K. King Burnett	Paul D. Wilber
	David A. Vorhis
David B. Douse	

ASSOCIATES

Chris Schiller Mason

Counsel for: First National Bank of Maryland (Salisbury branch); K & L Microwave, Inc.; Peninsula General Hospital Medical Center.
Local Attorneys for: State Farm Insurance Cos.; Nationwide Insurance Cos.; Travelers Insurance Co.; United States Fidelity & Guaranty Co.; Aetna Casualty & Surety Co.; Insurance Company of North America.

For full biographical listings, see the Martindale-Hubbell Law Directory

SILVER SPRING, Montgomery Co.

GINGELL & JENKINS, P.C. (AV)

Suite 506 Wheaton Plaza South, 11160 Veirs Mill Road, 20902
Telephone: 301-949-0100
Telecopier: 301-949-0467

Robert A. Gingell	Donn K. Jenkins
C. Lawrence Holcomb	Sebastian G. Wright

Representative Clients: Air Flow Co. (Industrial Air Conditioning); Bethesda Realty Co.; Photo Science, Inc.
References: Sovran Bank; First National Bank of Maryland (Rockville, Maryland, Branch); Signet Bank Maryland.

For full biographical listings, see the Martindale-Hubbell Law Directory

LINOWES AND BLOCHER LLP (AV)

Suite 1000, 1010 Wayne Avenue, 20910
Telephone: 301-588-8580
Telecopier: 301-495-9044
TTY/TDD: 301-588-3380
Email: inbox@linowes-law.com
Washington, D.C. Office: Suite 302, 1150 17th Street, N.W.
Telephone: 202-293-8510.
Telecopier: 202-293-8513.
Greenbelt, Maryland Office: Suite 402, 6411 Ivy Lane.
Telephone: 301-982-3382.
Telecopier: 301-982-0595.
Annapolis, Maryland Office: 145 Main Street.
Telephone: 410-268-0881.
Telecopier: 301-261-2603.
Frederick, Maryland Office: Suite 102, 228 W. Patrick Street.
Telephone: 301-695-0244.
Telecopier: 301-663-6656.
Columbia, Maryland Office: Suite B215, 10015 Old Columbia Road.
Telephone: 410-312-5457.
Fax: 410-290-5285.
Centreville, Maryland Office: 118 West Water Street.
Telephone: 410-758-2300.
Telecopier: 410-758-4605.

MEMBERS OF FIRM

Joseph P. Blocher	John L. Hollingshead
John J. Carmody, Jr. (Not admitted in MD)	Andrew L. Isaacson
	Kenneth S. Kamlet
Walter S. B. Childs (Resident Partner, Annapolis, Maryland office)	Stephen Z. Kaufman
	Lawrence R. Liebesman
	Robert H. Metz
David M. Cohen	John R. Orrick, Jr.
Kathryn J. Dahl (Resident Partner, Annapolis, Maryland office)	Robert C. Park, Jr.
	Leslie Moore Romine (Resident Partner, Greenbelt, Maryland office)
C. Robert Dalrymple	
John J. Delaney	Barbara A. Sears
Stephen P. Elmendorf	Raymond B. Via, Jr.
Andrew M. Goldstein	James A. Vidmar, Jr.
Gerald W. Heller	Roger D. Winston
William M. Hoffman, Jr.	James B. Witkin
Richard M. Zeidman	

PARTNERS EMERITUS

Charles G. Dalrymple	R. Robert Linowes

OF COUNSEL

Gary Altman	Myles Hannan
David L. Cahoon	Joseph A. Stevens (Resident, Centreville, Maryland office)
Bradford F. Englander	

(See Next Column)

ASSOCIATES

Danielle C. Agee	Bruce C. Johnson
Todd D. Brown	Dorothy H. Moore (Not admitted in MD)
Abigale Bruce-Watson (Resident, Greenbelt, Maryland office)	David M. Plott (Resident, Annapolis, Maryland office)
Duane J. Desiderio (Not admitted in MD)	David W. Rowan
James E. Gilbert	Paul-Michael Sweeney
Douglas M. Irvin	Emily J. Vaias
Anthony E. Waller	

Representative Clients: Boston Properties; The First National Bank of Maryland; Foulger/Pratt Development, Inc.; Hechinger Company; Manufacturers Life Insurance Co.; National Geographic Society; Wal-Mart, Inc.

For full biographical listings, see the Martindale-Hubbell Law Directory

LIPSHULTZ AND HONE, CHARTERED (AV)

Suite 108 Montgomery Center, 8630 Fenton Street, 20910
Telephone: 301-587-8500
Fax: 301-495-9759
Washington, D.C. Office: Suite 200, 2000 L Street, N.W.
Telephone: 202-872-0909.

Leonard L. Lipshultz	Ronald G. DeWald
John Llewellyn Hone	Michael T. O'Bryant (Not admitted in MD)
Stanley L. Lipshultz	
Frank L. Lipshultz	Stephen S. Brown
James R. Schraf	
Victor I. Weiner	Suzanne L. Ingersoll
Christopher A. Conte	Kathleen Wynne
Mark Feinroth	Jason A. Pardo

For full biographical listings, see the Martindale-Hubbell Law Directory

WHEELER & KORPECK, LLP (AV)

Suite 700, 8601 Georgia Avenue, 20910
Telephone: 301-587-6200
Telecopier: 301-589-6324
Email: wandkllp@atlantech.net

MEMBERS OF FIRM

William B. Wheeler (Retired)	Robert L. Brownell
Jerome E. Korpeck	Mark W. Kugler
William T. Wheeler	Roger K. Bain
Robert L. Flynn, III	

ASSOCIATES

Nicholas M. Fobe

OF COUNSEL

Patrick F. Greaney

Representative Clients: NationsBank, N.A.; Potomac Investment Associates; IDB-IIC Federal Credit Union; F.O. Day Paving Company; Rocky Gorge Enterprises; LLC; CSX Realty, Inc.; The Tower Companies; Polinger Companies; Ticor/Chicago Title Insurance Company; Redland/Genstar, Inc.

For full biographical listings, see the Martindale-Hubbell Law Directory

TOWSON,* Baltimore Co.

HOWELL, GATELY, WHITNEY & CARTER, LLP (AV)

401 Washington Avenue, Twelfth Floor, 21204
Telephone: 410-583-8000
Fax: 410-583-8031

MEMBERS OF FIRM

H. Thomas Howell	Daniel W. Whitney
William F. Gately	David A. Carter
Benjamin R. Goertemiller	William R. Levasseur

ASSOCIATES

Una M. Perez	Kathleen D. Leslie
George D. Bogris	Gerard Wm. Wittstadt, Jr.
Laura A. Gregory	

For full biographical listings, see the Martindale-Hubbell Law Directory

KALINOSKI & RIORDAN, P.A. (AV)

102 West Pennsylvania Avenue, Suite 500, 21204-4575
Telephone: 410-494-4499
Facsimile: 410-494-4977
URL: http://www.krlaw.com

Robert D. Kalinoski	Eileen B. Riordan

For full biographical listings, see the Martindale-Hubbell Law Directory

NOLAN, PLUMHOFF & WILLIAMS, CHARTERED (AV)

Suite 700 Court Towers, 210 West Pennsylvania Avenue, 21204
Telephone: 410-823-7800
Fax: 410-296-2765

(See Next Column)

NOLAN, PLUMHOFF & WILLIAMS CHARTERED—*Continued*

James D. Nolan (Retired, 1980)	Robert L. Hanley, Jr.
J. Earle Plumhoff (1940-1988)	Robert S. Glushakow
Ralph E. Deitz (1918-1990)	Stephen M. Schenning
Newton A. Williams	Douglas L. Burgess
Thomas J. Renner	Robert E. Cahill, Jr.
William P. Englehart, Jr.	C. William Clark
Stephen J. Nolan	E. Bruce Jones

Stuart Alan Schadt

Representative Clients: Baltimore County, Maryland; Bituminous Insurance Companies; Board of Education of Anne Arundel County; Carolina Freight Carriers Corporation; Humane Society of Baltimore County, Inc.; Patapsco Federal Savings & Loan Association; Pulte Home Corporation; Royal Oak Federal Savings Bank, F.S.B.; Shelter Development Corporation; Summit Broadcasting Corporation.

For full biographical listings, see the Martindale-Hubbell Law Directory

ROYSTON, MUELLER, MCLEAN & REID, LLP (AV)

Suite 600, 102 West Pennsylvania Avenue, 21204
Telephone: 410-823-1800
Fax: 410-828-7859

MEMBERS OF FIRM

R. Taylor McLean	Keith R. Truffer
E. Harrison Stone	Robert S. Handzo
Thomas F. McDonough	Edward J. Gilliss
Laurel Paretta Evans	John W. Browning

ASSOCIATES

Christine J. Saverda	Aaron Joseph Velli

Laurence Anne Ruth

OF COUNSEL

Richard A. Reid	Charles F. Stein III
Eugene W. Cunningham, Jr.	H. Emslie Parks

Representative Clients: Bank of Baltimore; Baltimore County Revenue Authority; Bell Atlantic-MD; The Reuben H. Donnelley Corporation; Genstar Stone Products Co.; Mercantile-Safe Deposit and Trust Co.; Morrison Restaurants, Inc.; Rosedale Federal Savings and Loan Assn.; Royal Insurance Co.; The Williams Companies, Inc.

For full biographical listings, see the Martindale-Hubbell Law Directory

VENABLE ATTORNEYS AT LAW VENABLE, BAETJER AND HOWARD, LLP (AV)

A Partnership including Professional Corporations
210 Allegheny Avenue, P.O. Box 5517, 21204
Telephone: 410-494-6200
FAX: 410-821-0147
Baltimore, Maryland Office: 1800 Mercantile Bank & Trust Building, 2 Hopkins Plaza.
Telephone: 410-244-7400.
Washington, D.C. Office: Venable, Baetjer, Howard & Civiletti LLP, Suite 1000, 1201 New York Avenue, N.W.
Telephone: 202-962-4800.
McLean, Virginia Office: Suite 400, 2010 Corporate Ridge.
Telephone: 703-760-1600.
Rockville, Maryland Office: Suite 500, One Church Street, P. O. Box 1906.
Telephone: 301-217-5600.

PARTNERS

James D. C. Downes (1906-1979)	Judson W. Starr (Not admitted in MD; Also at Washington, D.C. and Baltimore, Maryland Offices)
James H. Cook (1918-1993)	
Benjamin R. Civiletti (P.C.) (Also at Washington, D.C. and Baltimore, Maryland Offices)	
	William D. Quarles (Also at Washington, D.C. Office)
John B. Howard	C. Carey Deeley, Jr. (Also at Baltimore, Maryland Office)
John H. Zink, III	
Alexander I. Lewis, III (P.C.) (Also at Baltimore, Maryland Office)	Kathleen Gallogly Cox
	Cynthia M. Hahn
	M. King Hill, III
	Robert A. Hoffman
Joseph C. Wich, Jr.	J. Michael Brennan

OF COUNSEL

A. Samuel Cook (P.C.)	Herbert R. O'Conor, Jr.

David D. Downes

ASSOCIATES

Marina Lolley Dame	Patricia A. Malone
Melissa K. Force	Corie L. Williams
Mary-Dulany James	Katherine D. Williams

For full biographical listings, see the Martindale-Hubbell Law Directory

WHITEFORD, TAYLOR & PRESTON L.L.P. (AV)

210 West Pennsylvania Avenue, 21204-4515
Telephone: 410-832-2000
Fax: 410-832-2015
Email: 2019267@mcimail.com *URL:* http://www.wtplaw.com
Baltimore, Maryland Office: 7 Saint Paul Street.
Telephone: 410-347-8700.
Telex: 5101012334.
Fax: 410-752-7092.
Washington, D.C. Office: 1025 Connecticut Avenue, N.W.
Telephone: 202-659-6800.
Fax: 202-331-0573.
Columbia, Maryland Office: 10440 Little Patuxent Parkway.
Telephone: 410-884-0700.
Fax: 410-884-0719.
Alexandria, Virginia Office: 1317 King Street.
Telephone: 703-836-5742.
Fax: 703-836-0265.

PARTNERS

Ascanio S. Boccuti	Albert J. Mezzanotte, Jr.
John A. Hayden, III	Deborah Sweet Byrnes
James R. Chason	Barbara Lee Ayres
James F. Rosner	G. Scott Barhight
George S. Lawler	Edward M. Buxbaum
Thomas P. Kimmitt, Jr.	Anne Talbot Brennan
Jonathan E. Claiborne	Philip B. Barnes

Natalie C. Magdeburger

OF COUNSEL

Ernest C. Trimble	George D. Solter

Edward A. Johnston

RESIDENT ASSOCIATES

Judith C. Ensor	Steven E. Tiller
Edwin G. Fee, Jr.	Thomas J. Whiteford
J. Van Lear Dorsey	David K. Gildea
Christine K. McSherry	Julie D. Wright

Bradley S. Hames

For full biographical listings, see the Martindale-Hubbell Law Directory

---

UPPER MARLBORO,* Prince Georges Co.

KNIGHT, MANZI, BRENNAN, SHAY AND HAM, A PROFESSIONAL ASSOCIATION (AV)

14440 Old Mill Road, 20772
Telephone: 301-952-0100
Annapolis/Baltimore: 410-792-3786
Fax: 301-952-0221
Crofton, Maryland Office: 2411 Crofton Lane, # 26.
Telephone: 301-261-0808.
Fax: 301-261-6945.
Mitchellville, Maryland Office: 12164 Central Avenue, Suite 228.
Telephone: 301-390-0577.
Fax: 301-390-8464.

William E. Knight	John F. Shay, Jr.
Robert A. Manzi	Richard J. Ham
William C. Brennan, Jr.	Martin J. Shuham

Monica M. Haley-Pierson	Norman D. Rivera
Daniel F. Lynch III	Robert L. Lombardo

OF COUNSEL

Stuart R. Hammett

For full biographical listings, see the Martindale-Hubbell Law Directory

MENG & UREY (AV)

14507 Main Street, P.O. Box 549, 20773
Telephone: 301-627-1600
FAX: 301-627-2838

George E. Meng	Laura L. Greeves
Paul K. Urey, III	Ellen A. Marth

LEGAL SUPPORT PERSONNEL

Margaret Urey (Paralegal)

Representative Clients: State Farm Mutual Automobile Insurance Co.; State Farm Fire & Casualty Co.; Americlaim Adjustment Corp.; Old Line National Bank.

For full biographical listings, see the Martindale-Hubbell Law Directory

---

WESTMINSTER,* Carroll Co.

DAVIS & MURPHY (AV)

237 East Main Street, 21157
Telephone: 410-848-5411
Baltimore: 410-876-2757
Fax: 410-876-9158
Mount Airy, Maryland Office: 1512 Ridgeside Drive. P.O. Box 380.
Telephone: 301-831-7272; 410-549-1010.
Fax: 301-831-0724.

(See Next Column)

DAVIS & MURPHY, *Westminster—Continued*

MEMBERS OF FIRM

James Willard Davis   Daniel Murphy

ASSOCIATES

Michael D. Zimmer   Andrew C. Stone

Representative Clients: Masonry Contractors, Inc.; Westminster Bank and Trust Co.; Woodhaven Building and Developers, Inc.; Koren Development Inc.

References: Carroll County Bank and Trust Co.; Union National Bank; Westminster Bank and Trust Co.; Chicago Title Insurance.

For full biographical listings, see the Martindale-Hubbell Law Directory

---

DULANY & LEAHY (AV)

127 East Main Street, P.O. Box 525, 21158-0525
Telephone: 410-848-3333; Baltimore Line: 410-876-2117
FAX: 410-876-0747

MEMBERS OF FIRM

William B. Dulany   J. Brooks Leahy

ASSOCIATES

Amber Dahlgreen Curtis   Kenneth M. Williams

Representative Clients: Carroll County Bank and Trust Co.; Lehigh Portland Cement Co.; Pizza Hut of Maryland, Inc.; McGregor Printing Corporation; Mutual Fire Insurance Company of Carroll County.
Reference: Carroll County Bank and Trust Co.

For full biographical listings, see the Martindale-Hubbell Law Directory

---

WALSH & FISHER, A PROFESSIONAL ASSOCIATION (AV)

179 East Main Street, 21157
Telephone: 410-848-9200; 876-2135
Telecopier: 410-848-9313

D. Eugene Walsh (1895-1980)   Charles O. Fisher, Jr.
Charles O. Fisher   David B. Weisgerber

Representative Clients: Genstar Stone Products Co., Conewago Contractors, Inc.; Westminster Bank and Trust Co.; Carroll County General Hospital, Inc.; Adams County National Bank.

For full biographical listings, see the Martindale-Hubbell Law Directory

---

MASSACHUSETTS

ADAMS, Berkshire Co. — (Refer to Pittsfield)

AMESBURY, Essex Co.

HAMEL, DESHAIES & GAGLIARDI (AV)

Five Market Square, P.O. Box 198, 01913-0398
Telephone: 508-388-3558
Telecopier: 508-388-0441

MEMBERS OF FIRM

Richard P. Hamel   Robert J. Deshaies
Paul J. Gagliardi

ASSOCIATES

H. Scott Haskell   Roger D. Turgeon
Peter R. Ayer, Jr.   John R. Woelfel

Representative Clients: Essex County Gas Co., Amesbury, MA; First and Ocean National Bank, Newburyport, MA.
Approved Attorneys for: Chicago Title Insurance; Old Republic Title Insurance Co.

For full biographical listings, see the Martindale-Hubbell Law Directory

---

AMHERST, Hampshire Co. — (Refer to Northampton)

ATTLEBORO, Bristol Co.

COOGAN, SMITH, BENNETT, McGAHAN, LORINCZ & JACOBI (AV)

144 Bank Street, P.O. Box 2320, 02703
Telephone: 508-222-0002
Telecopier: 508-222-9095

MEMBERS OF FIRM

Peirce B. Smith   Michael T. McGahan
James Jerome Coogan   John F. D. Jacobi, III
Paul F. Lorincz   Timothy J. McGahan
Edward Kieran Shanley

OF COUNSEL

Charles E. Bennett

For full biographical listings, see the Martindale-Hubbell Law Directory

(See Next Column)

---

*BOSTON,** Suffolk Co.

* indicates certain Bar Register subscribers whose principal office is located elsewhere in the state and who have arranged for representation as a part of the state capital listings that follow

BARRON & STADFELD, P.C. (AV)

Two Center Plaza, 02108
Telephone: 617-723-9800
Telecopier: 617-523-8359
Email: PUBLIC@BARRONSTAD.COM *URL:* HTTP://WWW.BARRONSTAD.COM
Hyannis, Massachusetts Office: 258 Winter Street.
Telephone: 617-778-6622.

Bernard A. Dwork   Julie Taylor Moran
Enid M. Starr   Mitchell J. Notis
Thomas V. Bennett   Robert J. Hoffer
Edward E. Kelly   Joseph G. Butler
Kevin F. Moloney   Denise L. Page
David P. Dwork   Rosemary Purtell
Dorothy M. Bickford

Alison L. Berman   Kevin P. Scanlon
Roger T. Manwaring   Julian F. Montero
Judith C. Knight   Kathleen M. Morrissey
Shawn P. O'Rourke   Edward J. Fallman

OF COUNSEL

Hertz N. Henkoff

For full biographical listings, see the Martindale-Hubbell Law Directory

---

BERNKOPF, GOODMAN & BASEMAN LLP (AV)

125 Summer Street, 02110-1621
Telephone: 617-790-3000
Telecopier: 617-790-3300

MEMBERS OF FIRM

Abraham K. Cohen (1891-1957)   James B. Fox
Max E. Bernkopf (1919-1967)   Peter B. McGlynn
Sylvan A. Goodman (1935-1981)   Sheryl C. Starr
Harris I. Baseman   Richard B. Michaud
Kenneth M. Goldberg   Lydia G. Chesnick
Alan J. Grace   Martin C. Pomeroy
Marvin N. Geller   Eric R. Allon
Neil R. Markson   David L. Doyle
Gary P. Lilienthal   Barry S. Fischer

ASSOCIATES

John B. Harkavy   James M. Godec
James D. Friedman   Edward W. Wayland
Gwen P. Weisberg   Sharona Eliahou
Bruce D. Levin   Francis C. Morrissey
Richard P. Bennett   Todd D. Goldberg

For full biographical listings, see the Martindale-Hubbell Law Directory

---

BINGHAM, DANA & GOULD LLP (AV)

150 Federal Street, 02110
Telephone: 617-951-8000
Telecopy: 617-951-8736
Email: info@bingham.com
Hartford, Connecticut Office: 100 Pearl Street.
Telephone: 203-244-3770.
Telecopy: 203-527-5188.
London, England Office: 39 Victoria Street, SWIH 0EE.
Telephone: 011-44-71-799-2646.
Telecopy: 011-44-71-799-2654.
Washington, D.C. Office: 1200 19th Street, N.W., Suite 400.
Telephone: 202-778-6150.
Telecopy: 202-778-6155.

MEMBERS OF FIRM

Donald-Bruce Abrams   Amy L. Kyle
John F. Adkins   Paul J. Lambert (Resident in
Jonathan M. Albano   Washington, D.C. Office)
David M. Astrove (Resident in   George P. Mair
   Washington, D.C. Office)   Colin S. Marshall
Cynthia Faye Barnett   S. Elaine McChesney
Robert A. J. Barry, Jr.   William A. McCormack, Jr.
Alan W. Beloff   Robert E. McDonnell
Wayne D. Bennett   Scott Carson Moriearty
William N. Berkowitz   Justin P. Morreale
Jonathan K. Bernstein   Guy B. Moss
David C. Boch   David J. Murphy
Jeremiah J. Bresnahan, Jr.   Michael P. O'Brien
John S. Brown   Mark Oland (Resident in
Marijane Benner Browne   Hartford, Connecticut Office)
Lea Anne Copenhefer   Victor J. Paci
Neal J. Curtin   Victor H. Polk, Jr.
John J. Curtin, Jr.   Gerald F. Rath
James S. Davis   Marc A. Reardon
Robert M. Dombroff (Resident   Marcia Robinson

(See Next Column)

BINGHAM, DANA & GOULD LLP—*Continued*

in Hartford, Connecticut
Office)
Louis J. Duval
M. Gordon Ehrlich
Frederick F. Eisenbiegler
David L. Engel
Randal A. Farrar
Sula R. Fiszman
Jody E. Forchheimer
Francis H. Fox
F. Mark Fucci (Resident in
Hartford, Connecticut Office)
Daniel L. Goldberg
Gordon B. Greer
Linda J. Groves
Steven W. Hansen
Richard M. Harter
Henry S. Healy
Douglas M. Henry
Joe H. Hicks
Thomas John Holton
Russell E. Isaia
Charles L. Janes
David O. Johanson
Roger P. Joseph
Brian Keeler
Gerald J. Kehoe (Resident in
London, England Office)
William D. Kirchick
John R. Kirk
Joseph L. Kociubes
Ben M. Krowicki (Resident in
Hartford, Connecticut Office)

Neal A. Rosen
Stuart D. Rosen (Resident in
Hartford, Connecticut Office)
Barry P. Rosenthal (Resident in
Washington, D.C. Office)
Vincent M. Sacchetti
Edward A. Saxe
James G. Scantling (Resident in
Hartford, Connecticut Office)
Peter D. Schellie (Resident in
Washington, D.C. Office)
Scott M. Schooley (Resident in
Hartford, Connecticut Office)
Norman J. Shachoy
Leslie H. Shapiro
Bruce C. Silvers (Resident in
Hartford, Connecticut Office)
Lawrence I. Silverstein
John R. Skelton
Edwin E. Smith
John R. Snyder
William G. Southard
James C. Stokes
John R. Utzschneider
Paul M. Vaughn
Julio E. Vega
Thomas H. Walsh, Jr.
Judy K. Weinstein (Resident in
Hartford, Connecticut Office)
Sabin Willett
Robert M. Wolf
Jay S. Zimmerman
(Managing Partner)

Peter F. Zupcofska

OF COUNSEL

Austin S. Ashley
Hugh J. Ault
Sumner H. Babcock
Kenneth W. Bergen
J. Patrick Dowdall
Joseph H. B. Edwards
Roger D. Feldman
Joseph Ford
Robert J. Hallisey
Burton M. Harris
Janice W. Howe
Joseph F. Hunt
Richard H. Johnson

Catherine E. LaMarr (Resident
in Hartford, Connecticut
Office)
Richard D. Leggat
Peter H. Levine (Resident in
Hartford, Connecticut Office)
William J. McNally
James F. Monahan
Francis S. Moulton, Jr.
James N. Rice
Mark E. Robinson
James P. Rowles
James M. White, Jr.

Mari Anne Wilson

ASSOCIATES

Rebecca Federman Alperin
Jonathan B. Alter (Resident in
Hartford, Connecticut Office)
Frank A. Appicelli (Resident in
Hartford, Connecticut Office)
Marion Giliberti Barish
Mark W. Batten
Charles S. Baugh
(Not admitted in MA)
James L. Black, Jr.
Adam J. Bookbinder
Robert M. Borden (Resident in
Hartford, Connecticut Office)
Johan Van't Hul Brigham
Robert A. Buhlman
Dianne S. Burden
Teresa Burke (Resident in
Washington, D.C. Office)
Denise Jefferson Casper
Denise E. Choquette
Gary C. Christelis
(Not admitted in MA)
Laura A. Clark
John P. Coakley
John J. Concannon, III
Joanne D. Conte
(Not admitted in MA)
Sherry L. Countryman
Brian J. S. Cullen
Paula G. Curry
Matthew J. Cushing
Julia Frost Davies
Kimberly Davis
Susan Walsh Davis
Loraine de Jong (Resident in
London, England Office)
Mary Kathryn DeNevi
Deidre A. Doherty
MaryEllen S. Dolan (Resident in
Washington, D.C. Office)
Alicia L. Downey

Marianne M. Downie (Resident
in Hartford, Connecticut
Office)
Judith G. Edington
Stephen H. Faberman
(Not admitted in MA)
Timothy J. Fallon
Burt M. Fealing
Richard M. Filosa
Gerard P. Finn (Resident in
Washington, D.C. Office)
John J. Finn
Susan L. Fornaro
(Not admitted in MA)
Matthew F. Furlong
Ira H. Gaberman
Gregory J. Getschman
Michael E. Gibney
Gerald B. Goldberg (Resident in
Hartford, Connecticut Office)
Christopher D. T. Guiffre
Allison R. Handel
Thomas J. Hennessey
Patricia J. Hill
Jennifer H. Hurford
Barry N. Hurwitz
Meerie M. Joung
Sandra E. Kahn
Scott H. Kapilian
Richelle S. Kennedy
James D. Leroux
Peter J. Mancusi
A. Scott Marra
James C. McGrath
T. Joseph McNabb, Jr.
Kirsten N. Mellor
Stephen M. Miklus
Sarah E. Mizner
Patricia M. Natale
Karen E. Nelson
Andrew P. O'Meara, III

(See Next Column)

ASSOCIATES (Continued)

Douglas E. Onsi
Daniel I. Papermaster (Resident
in Hartford, Connecticut
Office)
Maria M. Park
Martin J. Pasqualini
Joseph P. Pelican (Resident in
Washington, D.C. Office)
Kathleen M. Phelps
J. Michael Pickett (Resident in
Washington, D.C. Office)
Andrew H. Pinkowski (Resident
in Hartford, Connecticut
Office)
Julie Scallen Reed
Donald P. Richards
Paul M. Robertson
James Scott Rollins (Resident in
Hartford, Connecticut Office)
Peter D. Rosenthal
Andrew L. Rotenberg
Laurie F. Rubin
Darcy A. Ryding
Jonathan M. Sachs
Andrés E. Saldaña
T. Malcolm Sandilands
Melissa R. Sarke (Resident in
Washington, D.C. Office)
Daniel S. Savrin
Matthew D. Schnall

Jeannie G. Sears
Deborah G. Segal (Resident in
Washington, D.C. Office)
Toby R. Serkin
Jonathan G. Shapiro
David P. Sharrow
(Not admitted in MA)
James W. Shaughnessy (Resident
in Hartford, Connecticut
Office)
Ann M. Siczewicz (Resident in
Hartford, Connecticut Office)
Charles L. Solomont
Jeffrey P. Steele
E. Clothier Tepper
Katherine A. Thatcher
Melissa M. Thompson
Richard A. Toelke
Neil W. Townsend
Matthew J. Tuttle
Erica H. Weiss (Resident in
Washington, D.C. Office)
Ian M. de Buy Wenniger
(Resident in London, England
Office)
David Yamin
Jeffrey B. Zeman (Resident in
Hartford, Connecticut Office)
Ron S. Zollman
Shannon S. Zollo

LEGAL SUPPORT PERSONNEL

William A. Bachman

For full biographical listings, see the Martindale-Hubbell Law Directory

BLOOM & BUELL (AV)

1340 Soldiers Field Road, 02135-1020
Telephone: 617-254-4400
Telecopier: 617-254-7610
Email: bloombue@ix.netcom.com

MEMBERS OF FIRM

Laurence J. Bloom   Barbara Hayes Buell
William J. Davenport

ASSOCIATES

Marc J. Gervais   Richard M. Haley
Barry T. Putterman

OF COUNSEL

Victoria L. Polito

LEGAL SUPPORT PERSONNEL

Lisa F. Tuccinardi

For full biographical listings, see the Martindale-Hubbell Law Directory

BROWN & STADFELD (AV)

66 Long Wharf, 02110
Telephone: 617-720-4200
Fax: 617-720-0240
Email: brownsta@world.std.com

Harold Brown   L. Seth Stadfeld

L. Michael Hankes   Catherine M. Keenan
Linda J. Keogh   Susan J. Assad

For full biographical listings, see the Martindale-Hubbell Law Directory

BURNS & LEVINSON LLP (AV)

125 Summer Street, 02110-1624
Telephone: 617-345-3000
Telecopier: 617-345-3299
Email: firm@B-L.com
Rockland, Massachusetts Office: 1001 Hingham Street.
Telephone: 617-982-4100.
Telecopier: 617-982-4141.

MEMBERS OF FIRM

Lawrence M. Levinson
Thomas D. Burns
Robert W. Weinstein
William H. Clancy
Barry L. Solar
Howard D. Medwed
John A. Donovan, Jr.
Norman C. Spector
Charles Mark Furcolo
Martin B. Shulkin
Steven C. Goodwin
George E. Christodoulo
David J. Hatem
Traver Clinton Smith, Jr.

Melvin A. Warshaw
Paul E. Stanzler
Michael Weinberg
Susan M. Barnard
Stuart M. Van Tine
(Resident, Rockland Office)
Nancy R. Van Tine
(Resident, Rockland Office)
David E. Grossman
Frederick S. Paulsen
David P. Rosenblatt
Joel S. Freedman
Barbara S. Hamelburg
Michael Ross Gottfried

(See Next Column)

BURNS & LEVINSON LLP, *Boston—Continued*

MEMBERS OF FIRM (Continued)

Evelyn A. Haralampu	Jeffrey R. Martin
Dennis J. Kelly	Gary W. Smith
Mark J. Levinson	Richard L. Wulsin
Michael H. Goshko	Jay S. Gregory
Richard A. Savrann	Cheryl A. Waterhouse
Raymond E. Baxter	David S. Branch
Jeffrey D. Sternklar	Steven L. Charlip
Michael G. Tracy	Kevin J. Kenneally
Robert C. Rives, Jr.	Michael J. Meagher
Warren D. Hutchison	Mark M. Christopher
Dana C. Blakslee	Mark Ventola
Darrell Mook	Maria-Eugenia Recalde

Jeffrey L. Alitz

ASSOCIATES

Lawrence J. McNally, Jr.	Renee Inomata
Michael P. Giunta	Andrew J. McBreen
(Resident, Rockland Office)	Mary E. Basile
Michelle F. Rosenberg	Ann M. Connell
(Resident, Rockland Office)	Jane C. Gorham
Maura A. Greene	Lynn A. Labanca
Mark C. DiVincenzo	Edward W. Little, Jr.
Ann M. Donovan	Amy L. McDonald
Frank C. Muggia	Mobina F. Mohsin
Luigi Leo	Constantia T. Papanikolaou
Pamela G. Smith	Lyn M. Lustig
Joni K. Mackler	James K. Schwartz
William H. DiAdamo	Steven E. Pazar
Andrew P. Botti	Paul T. Muniz
Holly A. Ditchfield	Howard A. Brick
Beverly A. Kogut	Kara M. Gallagher
Ellen Causey Peckham	Laura M. Berg
Anthony J. Fitzpatrick	Patrick J. Cassidy

OF COUNSEL

Karl Greenman	David M. Thomas
Edmund J. O'Brien	Herbert M. Weiss
Warren E. Tolman	George N. Tobia, Jr.

Harry A. Pierce

For full biographical listings, see the Martindale-Hubbell Law Directory

---

CASNER & EDWARDS, LLP (AV)

1 Federal Street, 27th Floor, 02110-2003
Telephone: 617-426-5900
Telecopier: 617-426-8810

MEMBERS OF FIRM

Thomas D. Edwards (1931-1987)	Terrance J. Hamilton
Andrew J. Casner, Jr.	Robert S. Kutner
Walter H. Mayo, III	David J. Chavolla
Martin E. Greenblatt	Robert L. Ciociola
Charles M. Hamann	Stephen M. Perry
Robert A. Murphy	Gary L. Hoff
Robert E. Cowden, III	Anita W. Robboy
John H. Ashby	Robert M. Mendillo
Douglas K. Mansfield	Peter A. Caro
Andrew M. Higgins	Joan M. Griffin

ASSOCIATES

Gaynor D. Casner	Matthew T. Murphy
Donna Brewer MacKenna	Thomas J. Walsh
Gary L. Kemp	Cristina V. Coletta

For full biographical listings, see the Martindale-Hubbell Law Directory

---

CHAPLIN & CHAPLIN (AV)

One State Street, 02109
Telephone: 617-227-0272
Fax: 617-227-3396
Email: 105050.2366@compuserve.com
Orleans, Massachusetts Office: 203 South Orleans Road.
Telephone: 508-255-6300.
Fax: 508-255-3005.

Ansel B. Chaplin   Anne Kenney Chaplin

OF COUNSEL
Donald M. Solomon

For full biographical listings, see the Martindale-Hubbell Law Directory

---

CHERWIN, GLICKMAN & THEISE, LLP (AV)

A Limited Liability Partnership including Professional Corporations
One International Place, 02110-2622
Telephone: 617-330-1625
Fax: 617-330-1642

(See Next Column)

Stanley A. Glickman	Douglas L. Jones (P.C.)
(1937-1994)	David K. Wanger
Joel I. Cherwin (P.C.)	William O. Rizzo
Jay F. Theise	Stanley B. Kay
Marshall D. Stein	Lisa Lee Foster

For full biographical listings, see the Martindale-Hubbell Law Directory

---

CHOATE, HALL & STEWART (AV)

A Partnership including Professional Corporations
Exchange Place, 53 State Street, 02109-2891
Telephone: 617-248-5000
Cable Address: "Chohalste".
Telecopier: 617-248-4000
Telex: 49615860.
Email: info@choate.com *URL:* http://www.choate.com

MEMBERS OF FIRM

James B. Adelman	Edwin A. James (P.C.)
Pamela E. Berman (P.C.)	Christopher M. Jedrey (P.C.)
Allen M. Bornheimer (P.C.)	Mitchell H. Kaplan (P.C.)
Samuel D. Bruskin (P.C.)	Alicia M. Colarte Kelly (P.C.)
Robert M. Buchanan, Jr. (P.C.)	Larry C. Kenna (P.C.)
Lyman G. Bullard, Jr. (P.C.)	W. Brewster Lee (P.C.)
Mark D. Cahill (P.C.)	Kevin J. Lesinski (P.C.)
Karen L. Cartotto (P.C.)	Kevin P. Light (P.C.)
Jonathan Chiel (P.C.)	William A. Lowell (P.C.)
Stephen M. L. Cohen (P.C.)	Thomas F. Maffei (P.C.)
Sarah Chapin Columbia (P.C.)	Steven L. Manchel (P.C.)
John M. Cornish (P.C.)	James A. McDaniel (P.C.)
F. Davis Dassori (P.C.)	Arnold P. Messing (P.C.)
Roslyn G. Daum (P.C.)	Mark A. Michelson (P.C.)
David S. Davenport (P.C.)	Paul D. Moore (P.C.)
Brian A. Davis (P.C.)	John A. Nadas (P.C.)
Ailsa DePrada Deitemeyer (P.C.)	Andrew L. Nichols (P.C.)
Scott A. Faust (P.C.)	Joseph E. O'Leary (P.C.)
Stephen K. Fogg	Jeremiah T. O'Sullivan (P.C.)
Robert S. Frank, Jr. (P.C.)	Peter M. Palladino (P.C.)
Marion R. Fremont-Smith (P.C.)	Sam Pasternack (P.C.)
William P. Gelnaw, Jr. (P.C.)	Frank B. Porter, Jr. (P.C.)
Frank Giso III (P.C.)	Cameron Read (P.C.)
Charles L. Glerum (P.C.)	William C. Rogers (P.C.)
Laura C. Glynn (P.C.)	James Roosevelt, Jr. (P.C.)
Myra J. Green (P.C.)	A. Hugh Scott (P.C.)
Andrew C. Griesinger (P.C.)	Thomas E. Shirley (P.C.)
John R. Grumbacher (P.C.)	Jo Ann Shotwell (P.C.)
Jeffrey L. Heidt (P.C.)	M. James Shumaker (P.C.)
James C. Heigham (P.C.)	David F. Slottje (P.C.)
Weld S. Henshaw (P.C.)	John R. Walkey (P.C.)
Carla B. Herwitz (P.C.)	Michael Arthur Walsh (P.C.)
Edward F. Hines, Jr. (P.C.)	Willie J. Washington (P.C.)
Richard N. Hoehn (P.C.)	Thomas H. P. Whitney, Jr.
Robert V. Jahrling, III (P.C.)	(P.C.)

Eric W. Wodlinger (P.C.)

OF COUNSEL

Joseph T. Baerlein	Kathleen King Parker
Nathaniel T. Dexter	Laurence D. Pierce
Judith A. Johnson	David J. Powsner

Nora J. Schneider

ASSOCIATES

Oliver F. Ames, Jr.	Eric Bradford Hermanson
David A. Attisani	Helen E. Holden
David P. Bergers	Shawn S. Hoyt
Julie B. Brennan	David P. Hutchinson
Michael Henry Bunis	Anne Rickard Jackowitz
Dilia M. Caballero	Kurt A. James
Tina A. Campbell	Beth R. Jimenez
Christopher H.M. Carter	Michael G. Jones
Katherine A. Chaurette	Gregory C. Keating
David A. Cifrino	Kerry S. Kehoe
Karen M. Collari	Adine Y. Kernberg-Varah
Jeanne C. Conerly	Brian J. King
Christine A. Conley	Karen D. Lane
Nolly Elisabeth Corley	Jeffrey A. Levinson
Andrea L. Crowley	Marni Smilow Levitt
David B. Currie	Diana K. Lloyd
Paul G. Cushing	Cynthia Thomas MacLean
Joshua A. Engel	Richard J. Maloney
Bret A. S. Fausett	Thomas F. Maloney
Michael C. Fondo	Eric J. Marandett
David A. Forman	Sam A. Mawn-Mahlau
Evelyn Estes Fortier	Elizabeth M. McCarron
(Not admitted in MA)	William H. McCarthy, Jr.
Frank N. Gaeta	Nicholas J. Nesgos
Deborah Kantar Gardner	Raymond A. O'Brien
Nancy W. Geary	Liam T. O'Connell
Douglas R. Gooding	Rachel K. Pemstein
James W. Hackett, Jr.	Paul D. Popeo
H. Hamilton Hackney, III	Lisa Richards Rahilly
James P. Hawkins	Douglas D. Robinow

(See Next Column)

CHOATE, HALL & STEWART—*Continued*

ASSOCIATES (Continued)

Heidi A. Schiller
Larry W. Schwartz
  (Not admitted in MA)
Amy R. Segal
Jill E. Severino
James S. Shorris
Leigh Earls Slayne
Christine G. Solt
Melanie S. Sommer
Kenneth E. Steinfield

Thomas J. Swan, III
Thomas M. Tomlinson
John S. Tuohy
John F. Ventola
Sara A. Walker
Lisa Fishbone Wallack
Mark A. Walsh
Keith E. Wexelblatt
Alyssa S. Wiener
Stephanie M. Williams

Joseph H. Zwicker

For full biographical listings, see the Martindale-Hubbell Law Directory

CORNELL AND GOLLUB (AV)

75 Federal Street, 02110
Telephone: 617-482-8100
Telecopier: 617-482-3917

MEMBERS OF FIRM

Robert W. Cornell (1910-1988)
Karl L. Gollub (1934-1985)
David H. Sempert
Philip J. Foley

Peter M. Durney
Paul F. Lynch
Jane Treen Brand
Janet J. Bobit

ASSOCIATES

Hugh M. Coxe
Thomas A. Pursley
David W. McGough
Susan Donaldson Novins
Marie Chadeayne Chafe

Thomas H. Dolan
Eric B. Goldberg
Kelly L. Wilkins
James P. Kerr
Patricia A. Hartnett

For full biographical listings, see the Martindale-Hubbell Law Directory

CRAIG AND MACAULEY, PROFESSIONAL CORPORATION (AV)

Federal Reserve Plaza, 600 Atlantic Avenue, 02210
Telephone: 617-367-9500
Telecopier: 617-742-1788; 617-248-0886
Email: cmpc@ultranet.com

Charles C. Craig (1904-1996)
John C. Craig
William F. Macauley
David F. Hannon
Mary P. Brody

A. Van C. Lanckton
Richard E. Quinby
Stephen Wald
William R. Moorman, Jr.
John G. Snyder

Martin P. Desmery

OF COUNSEL

Donald W. Suchma

Joseph A. Brear, Jr.

Alan D. Hoch
Christopher J. Panos
Anthony D. Rizzotti

Christopher S. Dalton
Mark A. Dorff
Jill Huban

Janice O'Neill Fahey

For full biographical listings, see the Martindale-Hubbell Law Directory

CUDDY BIXBY (AV)

One Financial Center, 02111
Telephone: 617-348-3600
Telecopier: 617-348-3643
Wellesley, Massachusetts Office: 60 Walnut Street.
Telephone: 617-235-1034.

Francis X. Cuddy (Retired)
Wayne E. Hartwell
Brian D. Bixby
Anthony M. Ambriano
Paul G. Boylan

Robert S. Marcus
Steven J. Marullo
Robert J. O'Regan
William R. Moriarty
Kevin P. Sweeney

Gina M. Salzillo

For full biographical listings, see the Martindale-Hubbell Law Directory

CURLEY & CURLEY, P.C. (AV)

27 School Street, 02108
Telephone: 617-523-2990
Fax: 617-523-7602

Robert A. Curley
Robert A. Curley, Jr.
Eugene F. Nowell
David D. Dowd

Martin J. Rooney
Lisabeth A. Ryan-Kundert
Stephen J. Gill
Marjory D. Robertson

For full biographical listings, see the Martindale-Hubbell Law Directory

DAY, BERRY & HOWARD (AV)

Twenty First Floor, 260 Franklin Street, 02110
Telephone: 617-345-4600
Telecopier: 617-345-4745
Email: Postmaster@dbh.com
Hartford, Connecticut Office: CityPlace I.
Telephone: 860-275-0100.
Telecopier: 860-275-0343.
Stamford, Connecticut Office: One Canterbury Green.
Telephone: 203-977-7300.
Telecopier: 203-977-7301.

MEMBERS OF FIRM IN BOSTON

James L. Ackerman
Joseph W. Ambash
Glenn E. Brace
David B. Broughel
Lewis A. Burleigh
Daniel J. Carragher
Jeffrey A. Clopeck
Nancy M. Cullen
George L. Cushing

Lisa J. Damon
Charles Donelan
William A. Hunter
J. Charles Mokriski
Ross A. Pascal
William Shields
H. Lawrence Tafe III
Kenneth E. Werner
Cynthia J. Williams

ASSOCIATES OF FIRM IN BOSTON

Laurie C. Buck
Colin Hugh Buckley
Allan C. Cave, Jr.
Edward J. Goddard
Jonathan I. Handler
Bruce D. Hickey
Jocelyn Lee
Rina M. Mayman
Carol M. Merchasin
Kathleen S. Moore
Mary Theresa Moran
David Nersessian

Kenneth B. Newton
Faith B. Nirenstein
Nancy M. Reimer
Jeffrey B. Renton
Mark C. Rosenthal
Jeffrey M. Rosin
Karen E. Schneck
Jan M. Siok
Gerald M. Slater
Maura D. Sullivan
James E. Venable, Jr.
Mark C. Wilson

G. Perry Wu

OF COUNSEL

Richard C. Csaplar, Jr.

COUNSEL

Ellen Jo Levesque

Kenneth A. Reich

For full biographical listings, see the Martindale-Hubbell Law Directory

* DECHERT PRICE & RHOADS (AV)

Ten Post Office Square South, 02109-4603
Telephone: 617-728-7100
Telefax: 617-426-6567
Philadelphia, Pennsylvania: 4000 Bell Atlantic Tower, 1717 Arch Street, 19103-2793.
Telephone: 215-994-4000.
New York, New York: 477 Madison Avenue, 10022-5891.
Telephone: 212-326-3500.
Washington, D.C.: 1500 K Street, N. W., 20005-1208.
Telephone: 202-626-3300.
Harrisburg, Pennsylvania: Thirty North Third Street, 17101-1603.
Telephone: 717-237-2000.
Princeton, New Jersey: Princeton Pike Corporate Center, P.O. Box 5218, 08543-5218.
Telephone: 609-520-3200.
Hartford, Connecticut: 90 State House Square, 16103-3702.
Telephone: 860-524-3999.
London, England: 2 Serjeants' Inn, EC4Y 1LT.
Telephone: (0171) 583-5353. (Also see Titmuss Sainer Dechert).
Brussels, Belgium: 65 Avenue Louise, 1050.
Telephone: (02) 535-5411.
Paris, France: 151, Boulevard Haussmann, 75008.
Telephone: (33-1) 53 83 84 70.

RESIDENT PARTNERS

Adrienne M. Baker
Timothy C. Blank
Bernard J. Bonn III

Susan M. Camillo
Joseph R. Fleming
Sheldon A. Jones

Alan L. Lefkowitz

RESIDENT OF COUNSEL

James M. Storey

RESIDENT ASSOCIATES

Katherine T. Alen
Allison R. First
Terrie J. Hanna
Deborah W. Kirchwey

Caroline Pearson
Jason A. Tucker
David C. Virnelli
Elaine Wallace

For full biographical listings, see the Martindale-Hubbell Law Directory

ESDAILE, BARRETT & ESDAILE (AV)

75 Federal Street, 02110
Telephone: 617-482-0333
Fax: 617-426-2978
Email: Esdaile@AOL.COM

(See Next Column)

ESDAILE, BARRETT & ESDAILE, *Boston—Continued*

MEMBERS OF FIRM

J. Newton Esdaile	Norman I. Jacobs
Charles W. Barrett, Jr.	Michael E. Mone
James N. Esdaile, Jr.	Patricia L. Kelly

Robert J. Rutecki

ASSOCIATES

Shaun Spencer Forsyth	C. William Barrett
Rhonda Traver Maloney	Mary Moynihan Conneely
Steven J. Ryan	Jon M. Jacobs

Kathryn E. Hand

OF COUNSEL

Charles J. Murray

For full biographical listings, see the Martindale-Hubbell Law Directory

---

FERRITER, SCOBBO, SIKORA, SINGAL, CARUSO & RODOPHELE, P.C. (AV)

One Beacon Street, 02108
Telephone: 617-589-0700
Fax: 617-589-0701

Nicholas J. Scobbo, Jr.	Bruce A. Singal
Robert M. Granger	Robert P. Rodophele
Gerald J. Caruso	Ann Ryan-Small

Vincent L. DiCianni

Lauren E. Duca	Lynn Peterson Read

William C. Athanas

OF COUNSEL

Alan L. Kovacs	Richard E. Connolly

For full biographical listings, see the Martindale-Hubbell Law Directory

---

FOLEY, HOAG & ELIOT LLP (AV)

One Post Office Square, 02109
Telephone: 617-832-1000
Cable Address: "Foleyhoag"
Telex: 94-0693
Telecopier: 617-832-7000
Email: fhe@fhe.com *URL:* http://www.fhe.com
Washington, D.C. Office: 1615 L Street, N.W.
Telephone: 202-775-0600.
Telecopier: 202-857-0140.

MEMBERS OF FIRM

David L. Weltman	Marc K. Temin
Verne W. Vance, Jr.	Toni G. Wolfman
David B. Ellis	Jacob N. Polatin
David W. Walker	Steven W. Phillips
Mark F. Clark	Laurie Burt
John D. Patterson, Jr.	William B. Koffel
James K. Brown	Kevin J. Fitzgerald
Robert L. Birnbaum	David R. Pierson
William J. Cheeseman	Dean F. Hanley
Christian M. Hoffman	Stefanie D. Cantor
Michael B. Keating	Robert W. Sweet, Jr.
Adam Sonnenschein	Brandon F. White
Leonard Schneidman	David R. Geiger
Edward N. Gadsby, Jr.	Bruce A. Kinn
Peter B. Ellis	Robert S. Sanoff
Alan I. Baron	James A. Smith
(Not admitted in MA)	Wendy B. Jacobs
Paul E. Tsongas	Gary C. Crossen
John H. Henn	Richard Belin
Barry B. White	James T. Montgomery, Jr.
Arnold M. Zaff	(Resident at Washington,
Louis P. Georgantas	D.C. Office)
Philip Burling	Andrew Z. Schwartz
John M. Stevens, Jr.	Ellyn R. Weiss (Resident
Peter W. Coogan	Administrative Partner,
Sandra Shapiro	Washington, D.C. Office)
Paul V. Lyons	Arlene L. Bender
Kenneth L. Grinnell	Jonathan H. Hulbert
Deborah A. Willard	Mark L. Johnson
John L. Burke, Jr. (Resident,	Bruce R. Parker
Washington, D.C. Office)	David A. Broadwin
Charles J. Beard	Carol Hempfling Pratt
Deborah B. Breznay	Michael N. Glanz
Richard W. Benka	Nicholas C. Theodorou
Stanley B. Bernstein	Richard R. Schaul-Yoder
Arthur G. Telegen	Susan Barbieri Montgomery
Thomas M. S. Hemnes	Seth D. Jaffe
Stephen B. Deutsch	Douglas M. McGarrah
Donald R. Ware	David H. Feinberg
Peter M. Rosenblum	William R. Kolb
Dennis R. Kanin	Anthony D. Mirenda
Paul R. Murphy	Teresa A. Martland

Paul V. Kelly

(See Next Column)

H. Kenneth Fish

OF COUNSEL

John F. Bok

COUNSEL

Diane E. Bissonnette	Mary Beth Gentleman
Edward G. Black	Gregory J. Glover (Resident at
(Not admitted in MA)	Washington, D.C. Office)
Robert L. Cowdrey	Gloria Cordes Larson
Stephanie Cutler (Resident at	Toby B. Richard
Washington, D.C. Office)	Charles E. Weinstein

ASSOCIATES

Feriale Abdullah	Amy B. G. Katz
Michael A. Albert	Jonathan A. Keselenko
Andrew D. Beard	T. Maria Lam
Steven A. Bercu	Claire Laporte
Pamela B. Blatte	Kenneth S. Leonetti
Sayoko Blodgett-Ford	George N. Lester
Jonathan E. Book	Joseph P. Liu
Michael Parker Boudett	Audrey C. Mark
Richard M. Brunell	Gerald A. Mc Donough
Marcel A. Bryar	Laurie M. McTeague
James W. Bucking	Earl W. Mellott, II
Marie E. Burke	Paul Millhouser
Vincent J. Canzoneri	Gregory T. Moffatt
Brian D. Carlson	Thomas N. Molins
Peter M. Casey	Donald W. Muirhead
Charles H. Cella	Jeffrey B. Mullan
Christine Chang	Gerard P. O'Connor
Karen B. Cheyney	Alexander H. Pyle
Jeffrey D. Collins	Jeffrey L. Quillen
Monica E. Conyngham	(Not admitted in MA)
Dan Danielsen	Sarah Burgess Reed
Amy P. Dennin	Jeffrey L. Roelofs
John K. DiPaolo	Mark D. Rosen
Michael V. Dowd	Michael L. Rosen
Deborah Drosnin	John A. Shope
Kristina A. Engberg	Thomas E. Stoddard
Jonathan M. Ettinger	Jocelyn M. Sturdivant (Resident
Jeffrey S. Follett	at Washington, D.C. Office)
Evan Georgopoulos	James E. Tucker
J. David Gibbs	Katharina E. von der
Theodora E. Goss	Schulenburg
John D. Hancock	Michele A. Whitham
Lisa C. Hay	Sara Elizabeth Wylie
Vickie L. Henry	Xinhua (Howard) Zhang
(Not admitted in MA)	Colin J. Zick
Michael I. Joachim	Timothy D. Zick
Adam P. Kahn	(Not admitted in MA)

For full biographical listings, see the Martindale-Hubbell Law Directory

---

FRIEDMAN & ATHERTON (AV)

(Formerly Friedman, Atherton, King & Turner)
(Formerly Friedman, Atherton, Sisson & Kozol)
Exchange Place, 53 State Street, 02109-2803
Telephone: 617-227-5540
Telecopier: 617-523-1559

Lee M. Friedman (1895-1957)	Percy A. Atherton (1903-1940)

Frank L. Kozol (1927-1993)

OF COUNSEL

Frank H. Shapiro

MEMBERS OF FIRM

Joel A. Kozol	Matthew S. Kozol
Lee H. Kozol	Alan M. Spiro
William I. Cowin	David L. Kelston
Robert D. Kozol	Victor Bass
Richard M. Zinner	David M. Kozol

ASSOCIATES

Andrew D. Cummings	Penny Kozol
Christine P. Deshler	Olive E. Larson
Paula F. Donahue	David A. Rich
Eric J. Kozol	Marie C. Vaccarelli

Herbert Weinberg

COUNSEL

Paul S. Alpert	Debra Dyleski-Najjar
Thomas C. Bailey	Michael P. Morizio

For full biographical listings, see the Martindale-Hubbell Law Directory

---

GADSBY & HANNAH LLP (AV)

225 Franklin Street, 02110
Telephone: 617-345-7000
Telex: 6817512 GADHAN BSN
Telefax: 617-345-7050
Email: gadsby@ghlaw.com *URL:* http://www.ghlaw.com
Washington, D.C. Office: 1747 Pennsylvania Avenue, N.W.
Telephone: 202-429-9600.

(See Next Column)

GADSBY & HANNAH LLP—*Continued*

PARTNERS

Richard K. Allen	Leonard L. Lewin
Ronald G. Busconi	Wesley J. Marshall, Jr.
Wendell Robert Carr, Jr.	Stanley A. Martin
Harold J. Carroll	Diane M. McDermott
Paul E. Clifford	John M. McKelway, Jr.
Thomas G. Collins	James J. Myers
Allan R. Curhan	Mark E. Schreiber
Marianne Gilleran	Michael N. Sheetz
George F. Hailer	Kevin J. Toomey
Harry R. Hauser	Patrick C. Toomey
Peter S. Johnson	Robert A. Trevisani
Robert J. Kaler	Walter D. Wekstein
Cynthia B. Keliher	Burton Winnick
Daniel J. Kelly	William A. Zucker

OF COUNSEL

John B. Miller	Fleming O'Meara Norwood

ASSOCIATES

Peter J. Allen	Paul Marshall Harris
(Not admitted in MA)	Jill Rosen Hyde
Joseph A. Barra	Lawrence R. Katz
(Not admitted in MA)	Dennis C. Liu
Marjorie E. Boone	Susan J Matthew
Jeffrey P. Cleven	Hiram N. Pan
Peter M. Coppinger	David H. Ruttenberg
Michael B. Donahue	Ellen Borkum Scult
Leigh A. Gilligan	Steven M. Shishko
John R. Hallal	Risa G. Sorkin
Rosa C. Hallowell	Peter F. Trotter

David M. Watson

WASHINGTON, D.C. OFFICE
RESIDENT PARTNERS

Mary Ann Gilleece	Lawrence G. Meyer
Michael A. Hordell	(Not admitted in MA)
Paul F. Kilmer	James M. Spears
(Not admitted in MA)	(Not admitted in MA)
Carol L. B. Matthews	
(Not admitted in MA)	

RESIDENT ASSOCIATES

Thomas W. Brooke	Stephen J. Jeffries
(Not admitted in MA)	Thomas B. Pahl
Laura L. Hoffman	
(Not admitted in MA)	

For full biographical listings, see the Martindale-Hubbell Law Directory

---

GILMAN, MCLAUGHLIN & HANRAHAN (AV)

A Partnership including a Professional Corporation
Harbor Plaza, 470 Atlantic Avenue, 02210
Telephone: 617-482-1900
Cable Address: Gilmac

Walter H. McLaughlin, Sr. (1907-1994)

MEMBERS OF FIRM

Walter H. McLaughlin, Jr.	William F. York
Robert E. McLaughlin	Michael Eby
David G. Hanrahan	J. David Moran (P.C.)
John B. Shevlin, Jr.	David L. Klebanoff

COUNSEL

Arthur M. Gilman	Donna E. Cohen

ASSOCIATES

Leigh A. McLaughlin	Bernice McPhillips
Marla B. Kirk	Ross D. Ginsberg

Robert E. McLaughlin, Jr.

For full biographical listings, see the Martindale-Hubbell Law Directory

---

GOODWIN, PROCTER & HOAR LLP (AV)

A Partnership including Professional Corporations
Exchange Place, 02109-2881
Telephone: 617-570-1000
Telecopier: 617-523-1231
Washington, D.C. Office: 901 Fifteenth Street, N.W.
Telephone: 202-414-6160.
Telecopier: 202-789-1720.

MEMBERS OF FIRM

Robert E. Goodwin (1878-1971)	A. Jeffrey Dando (P.C.)
Joseph O. Procter (1880-1932)	Donald P. Quinn (P.C.)
Samuel Hoar (1877-1952)	George W. Butterworth, III
Robert B. Fraser (P.C.)	David P. Ries (P.C.)
Preston H. Saunders (P.C.)	Richard E. Floor (P.C.)
Marshall Simonds (P.C.)	Michael Steinberg (P.C.)
William B. King (P.C.)	Jerome H. Somers (P.C.)
Samuel L. Batchelder, Jr.	Shepard M. Remis (P.C.)
William H. Gorham (P.C.)	Steven J. Comen
Edward T. O'Dell (P.C.)	Jeremiah S. Buckley (Resident,
Joseph W. Haley (P.C.)	Washington D.C. Office)

(See Next Column)

Jon D. Schneider (P.C.)	Philip H. Newman
Robert C. Pomeroy (P.C.)	Alexander A. Randall
Stephen W. Carr (P.C.)	Kevin M. Dennis
Paul F. Ware, Jr., (P.C.)	John J. Egan III
Don M. Kennedy (P.C.)	Geoffrey R. T. Kenyon
Richard A. Soden	Gilbert G. Menna (P.C.)
Edward L. Glazer (P.C.)	Adam N. Weisenberg (P.C.)
William V. Buccella	Nancer Ballard
Raymond P. Boulanger (P.C.)	Wilfred J. Benoit, Jr.
Thomas J. Griffin, Jr.	Trudy A. Ernst (P.C.)
Paul F. McDonough, Jr.	Daniel Patrick Condon
Robert F. Houser (P.C.)	Robert M. Hale
Howard A. Cubell	Christopher T. Katucki (P.C.)
Kenneth A. Cohen (P.C.)	F. Dennis Saylor, IV
John J. Cleary (P.C.)	John C. Englander
Michael H. Glazer (P.C.)	Christopher B. Barker
Francis W. Dubreuil (P.C.)	Ettore A. Santucci (P.C.)
Anthony M. Feeherry	Gregory A. Bibler
F. Beirne Lovely, Jr., (P.C.)	R. Todd Cronan
Paul R. Gauron (P.C.)	Jeffrey D. Plunkett
James J. Dillon (P.C.)	Ann D. Dexter
John Kenneth Felter (P.C.)	H. David Henken
Lawrence R. Cahill (P.C.)	Joseph L. Johnson III
Lawrence E. Kaplan (P.C.)	Paul C. Nightingale
Martin R. Healy	Joseph M. Kolar (Resident,
David F. Dietz (P.C.)	Washington, D.C. Office)
Paul W. Lee (P.C.)	Cerise H. Lim-Epstein
Edward Matson Sibble, Jr.,	Matthew T. Giuliani
(P.C.)	Elizabeth McDermott
William P. Mayer	Minta E. Kay (P.C.)
Daniel M. Glosband (P.C.)	Ross D. Gillman
Henry C. Dinger (P.C.)	J. Anthony Downs
Stuart M. Cable	Steven M. Ellis
Susan Hall Mygatt	Jeffrey C. Hadden
Paul D. Schwartz (P.C.)	H. Neal Sandford
Diane L. Currier (P.C.)	Bradford J. Smith
Thomas P. Storer (P.C.)	Mark E. Tully
James W. Nagle	Keith D. Shugarman (Resident,
Lynne B. Barr	Washington, D.C. Office)
Michael J. Pappone (P.C.)	Thomas M. Hefferon
Paul E. Nemser	Margaret B. Crockett
Marian A. Tse	Kenneth J. Parsigian
Martin Carmichael III (P.C.)	David L. Ruediger
Raymond C. Zemlin (P.C.)	David W. Watson
Christopher P. Davis	Robert P. Whalen, Jr.
Jeffrey M. Snyder (Resident,	Eileen M. Herlihy
Washington, D.C. Office)	Deirdre A. Cunnane
Stephen D. Poss (P.C.)	Elizabeth Shea Fries
Laura C. Hodges Taylor (P.C.)	Thomas P. LaFrance
John R. LeClaire (P.C.)	Mary-Kathleen O'Connell
Regina M. Pisa (P.C.)	Kim M. Rubin
William H. Whitledge (P.C.)	Barbara Healy Smith
Richard A. Oetheimer	John B. Steele

Andrew C. Sucoff

SENIOR COUNSEL

Alan Dankner	John O. Newell

Kristina Hansen Wardwell

OF COUNSEL

Charles D. Post	Arthur L. Stevenson
Frederick J. Robbins (P.C.)	Donald B. Gould
William J. Pechilis (P.C.)	Samuel Hoar
Russell G. Simpson (P.C.)	Donald J. Evans (P.C.)

COUNSEL

Henry B. Shepard, Jr., (P.C.)	Evan Jones

Daniel J. Mullen

ASSOCIATES

Gordon H. Piper	James M. Broderick
Michael J. Litchman	Kathryn I. Murtagh
A. Lauren Carpenter	Loraine Parkinson
Theresa A. Cook	Mary M. Diggins
Nina Raginsky Mishkin	John G. Loughnane
Thomas J. Phillips	Brenda Ruel Sharton
Donna Stoehr Hanlon	Jeremy M. Sternberg
Anthony S. Fiotto	Peter T. Fariel
Jennifer Hilton Weiss	Edward M. Schulman
Stephen V. Loughlin	Gregory J. Lyons
Gerard A. Caron	Bruce I. Tribush
John B. Daukas	Jeffrey P. Naimon
Robert A. Freeman	(Washington, D.C. Office)
Susan Goodhue	Joseph A. Piacquad
(Not admitted in MA)	Douglas Alexander Batt
Mary A. Daly	Maura Griffith Moffatt
Patricia D. Popov	Daniel P. Karnovsky
Catherine W. Gill	Felix S. Riccio
Peter F. Neronha	David R. Zipps
David M. Barlow	Giles A. Birch
Alesia D. Selby	J. Todd Hahn
(Not admitted in MA)	Rebecca A. Lee
James J. Berriman	Jennifer Locke

(See Next Column)

GOODWIN, PROCTER & HOAR LLP, *Boston—Continued*

ASSOCIATES (Continued)

Robert G. Schwartz, Jr.	Donna M. Brown
Steven E. Skwara	Karen B. Clark
Ellen S. Winer	Gus P. Coldebella
Jennifer M. Bott	Margaret A. Crouse
Carla Folz Brigham	Howard W. Davis
Robert G. Kester	Anthony H. Dowling
Neil McLaughlin	Peter M. Green
Lizette M. Perez	John T. Haggerty
Andrew M. Cohen	Michael K. Harrington
John Hunt	Stephen C. Kolocotronis
(Not admitted in MA)	Charles N. LeRay
Susan Miles von Herrmann	Jamie C. Mann
Patricia A. Johansen	Paige H. Pease
Stephen G. Charkoudian	Jeffrey M. Sachs
James A. Matarese	Lisa M. Savage
Andrew F. Viles	Paul D. Tutun
Nuria del Pilar Rivera	Darin K. Vest
B. Dane Dudley	Lawrence T. Weiss
Scott F. Duggan	R. David Hosp
Domenic P. Gaeta	(Not admitted in MA)
Samuel L. Richardson	Michelle E. Jones
Robert J. Waeldner	Eugenia M. Carris
John H. Branson	Christopher T. Holding
Margo H.K. Tank (Resident,	Thomas J. LaFond
Washington, D.C. Office)	Philip G. Malek
Michael K. Murray	Thomas I. Benda
Michelle Raftery	Diane Boissonneault
Andrea C. Kramer	John A. Cecere
(Not admitted in MA)	Douglas E. Cornelius
Janet M. Dunlap	Delida A. Costin
Jennifer Merrigan Fay	Daniel P. Dain
Michael J. Kendall	Nancy H. Duff
Paula D. Leca	Tracy B. Fitzpatrick
Laura J. Moloney	Jackson B.R. Galloway
David L. Permut	Bradley A. Jacobson
Melissa L. Roy	Jillian B. Johnston
Jeffrey D. Scheman	Melinda J. Kent
Kevin F. Slayne	Eric G. Kevorkian
Andrew J. Weidhaas	Andrew R. Levin
U. Gwyn Williams	Graham N. Luce
Dori Chadbourne Gouin	Mark R. Mansoor
James W. McGarry	John Barry McDonald
(Not admitted in MA)	Daniel S. Medwed
Thomas E. Joaquin	Natalie J. Muecke
(Not admitted in MA)	Diane M. Musi
Ronald J. DiPrete	Dana Ng
Robert N. Driscoll	Michael J. O'Connor
John P. Feeney	David A. Pignato
James H. Hammons, Jr.	Helene H. Ra
Jonathan S. Klavens	Linda M. Ratnik
Dana L. McAlister	Claire K. Smith
Stephen R. Smerek	Charles H. Sturdy
Elizabeth Z. Stavisky	Reed Sussman
Mark A. Weiss	Joan E. Tagliareni
Laurie Ilene Gelb	Robert J. Toner
Christopher W. Thome	Oleg A. Vyadro
Elyse Diamond Moskowitz	Jeremy S. Westin
Dorothy W. Bisbee	Diana McKearney

For full biographical listings, see the Martindale-Hubbell Law Directory

GOULSTON & STORRS, A PROFESSIONAL CORPORATION (AV)

400 Atlantic Avenue, 02110-2206
Telephone: 617-482-1776
Fax: 617-574-4112

H. Edward Abelson	Jordan P. Krasnow
David M. Abromowitz	Raymond M. Kwasnick
Steven R. Astrove	Richard Langerman
Daniel R. Avery	Phillip G. Levy
Mark D. Balk	Darline M. Lewis
Thomas P. Bloch	Frank E. Litwin
J. Robert Casey	Julia C. Livingston
Harry S. Dannenberg	Deborah R. Lunder
Nancy Mammel Davids	Robert J. Mack
Robert C. Davis	Adrienne M. Markham
Jack A. Eiferman	Richard A. Marks
Matthew E. Epstein	Patricia McGovern
Lester J. Fagen	Patricia Ann Metzer (Miss)
Leonard H. Freiman	Anne H. Meyer
Martin A. Glazer	Michael J. Moran
Alan S. Goldberg	James F. O'Brien
Robert P. Goldman	Rudolph F. Pierce
Barry D. Green	Michael M. Robinson
Michael A. Hammer	Philip R. Rosenblatt
Michael J. Haroz	Alan W. Rottenberg
Philip A. Herman	Eli Rubenstein
William A. Horne	Daniel C. Sacco
Douglas M. Husid	Nancy B. Samiljan
Denis M. King	Thomas J. Sartory

(See Next Column)

Kitt Sawitsky	Marilyn L. Sticklor
Barbara E. Schmitt	Robert S. Towsner
Joel B. Sherman	John E. Twohig
Donald L. Shulman	Arthur S. Waldstein
Ronald B. Shwartz	James F. Wallack
Thomas G. Sitzmann	Robert A. Weiland
Marvin Sparrow	David S. Weiss
Harold Stahler	Hynrich W. Wieschhoff

Jeffrey S. Wolfson

P. Michael Baratta	Francis N. Mastroianni
Patricia A. Brennan	Maura McCaffery
Kathryn Lachelt Brown	William E. Moderi
Effie J. Chan	Lynne Alix Morrison
Peter D. Corbett	Kathleen R. Moynihan
Christopher A. Ditunno	(Not admitted in MA)
David W. Fanikos	Kathryn A. Murphy
Martin M. Fantozzi	Nicole Shurman Murray
Julie A Frohlich	Shannon King Nash
Jocelyn F. Gordon	(Not admitted in MA)
Janice S. Gross	Jeffrey P. Neterval
Rusha Tejani Heneghan	(Not admitted in MA)
Deborah S. Horwitz	Emily S. Nozick
Natalie A. Jackvony	Kevin P. O'Flaherty
(Not admitted in MA)	Eve Grace Penoyer
Vicki L. Kaufman	Daniel S. Rabinovitz
Michael J. Kelly	Albert Rocha
Meryl Kessler	Douglas B. Rosner
Suzanne L. King	Steven Schwartz
Connie L. Kolb	William M. Seuch
Lawrence M. Kraus	Joel Sklar
John D. Lawrence	Steven J. Snyder
Pamela M. Maloney	Gretchen Snyder Wesley
Paige A. Manning	B. Andrew Zelermyer

OF COUNSEL

William O. Flannery

Samuel Markell (1888-1992)	David H. Greenberg (1905-1988)
Herbert B. Ehrmann (1891-1970)	Thomas Kaplan (1916-1993)

Jay E. Orlin (1936-1993)

For full biographical listings, see the Martindale-Hubbell Law Directory

---

HALE AND DORR (AV)

A Partnership including Professional Corporations
60 State Street, 02109
Telephone: 617-526-6000
Cable Address: "Hafis."
Telex: 94-0472
Telecopier: Domestic 617-526-5000; 617-742-9108
Washington, D.C. Office: 1455 Pennsylvania Avenue, N.W.
Telephone: 202-942-8400.
Cable Address: "Hafis Wsh."
Telecopier: 202-942-8484.
Manchester, New Hampshire Office: 1155 Elm Street.
Telephone: 603-628-7400.
Telecopier: 603-627-3880.

RETIRED PARTNERS

James D. St. Clair (P.C.)	Herbert W. Vaughan

MEMBERS OF FIRM

John F. Cogan, Jr. (P.C.)	Robert W. Mahoney
Norman B. Asher	Richard V. Wiebusch (Resident,
Jerome P. Facher	Manchester, New Hampshire
James A. Brink	Office)
Paul P. Brountas	Joseph P. Barri
John D. Hamilton, Jr.	Paul P. Daley
Robert E. Fast	Richard J. Innis
Harold Hestnes	Linda K. Sherman
Ernest V. Klein	James L. Quarles III (Resident,
John K. P. Stone, III	Washington, D.C. Office)
S. Donald Gonson	Joel H. Sirkin
Martin S. Kaplan (P.C.)	Joan A. Lukey
Hugh R. Jones, Jr.	Robert D. Keefe
Philip D. Stevenson	Jeffrey B. Rudman
Alexander A. Bernhard (P.C.)	David E. Redlick
Vincent P. McCarthy (P.C.)	Edward Young
Louis H. Hamel, Jr.	John A. Burgess
James B. Lampert	William F. Lee
John W. Delaney	Roger M. Ritt
John C. Christie, Jr. (Resident,	Mark G. Borden
Washington, D.C. Office)	Neil H. Jacobs
John G. Fabiano	Michael L. Fay
C. Hall Swaim	Jay P. Urwitz (Resident,
John H. Morton	Washington, D.C. Office)
John M. Westcott, Jr.	Gilbert B. Kaplan (Resident,
Richard W. Giuliani	Washington, D.C. Office)
Stephen H. Oleskey	Richard A. Johnston
Richard L. Berkman	John J. Regan
Thomas E. Neely	James C. Burling
Robert Tuchmann	Andrew H. Cohn
Harry T. Daniels	William H. Schmidt

(See Next Column)

HALE AND DORR—*Continued*

MEMBERS OF FIRM (Continued)

Peter B. Tarr	David C. Phelan
Katharine E. Bachman	Andrea J. Robinson
Mark N. Polebaum	Jonathan D. Rosenfeld
Allen H. Fox (Resident, Washington, D.C. Office)	Wayne L. Stoner
William C. Benjamin	Henry N. Wixon (Resident, Washington, D.C. Office)
Steven D. Singer	David B. Bassett
David H. Erichsen	John H. Chory
Paul G. Wallach (Resident, Washington, D.C. Office)	James W. Prendergast
Robert D. Burke	Brenda J. Fingold
Joseph J. Christian	Jude A. Curtis
William R. O'Reilly, Jr.	James A. Perley, Jr.
John D. Sigel	Scott A. Roberts
Thomas N. O'Connor	Elizabeth M. Leonard
Steven S. Snider (Resident, Washington, D.C. Office)	Paul G. Igoe
Geoffrey S. Stewart (Resident, Washington, D.C. Office)	David Marder
	Mary Jo Johnson
Michelle D. Miller	Paul Jakubowski
Merriann M. Panarella	Susan M. Kincaid
Jay E. Bothwick	Gary P. Brady
Sarah Rothermel	David A. Wilson (Resident, Washington, D.C. Office)
Jeffrey N. Carp	
Philip P. Rossetti	Donald R. Steinberg
David Sylvester (Resident, Washington, D.C. Office)	Donald J. Williamson (Resident, Manchester, New Hampshire Office)
Jeffrey J. Davidson (Resident, Washington, D.C. Office)	Paul W. Jameson (Resident, Washington, D.C. Office)
Kenneth H. Slade	Charles P. Kindregan
Olivia A. O'Neill	Virginia H. Kingsley
Pamela J. Wilson	Thomas S. Ward
Jennifer C. Snyder	Brian E. Whiteley
Thomas L. Barrette, Jr.	Jonathan Wolfman
William G. McElwain (Resident, Washington, D.C. Office)	Daniel W. Halston
	Stuart M. Falber
John F. Batter III	Carol A. Hannigan
Karen F. Green	Elaine M. Hartnett
Melvin R. Shuman	Michael J. LaCascia
Michael R. Heyison	S. Tara Miller
Christopher J. Perry	N. Roland Savage
Michael J. Bevilacqua	Anthony A. Scibelli
Rekha D. Packer	Daniel P. Tighe
David A. Westenberg	Gabrielle R. Wolohojian
Patrick J. Rondeau	Mark P. Goshko
Peter J. Macdonald	Dimitri P. Racklin
Mark G. Matuschak	James F. Kurkowski
Robert C. Kirsch (Resident, Manchester, New Hampshire Office)	Mitchel Appelbaum
	Keith R. Barnett
	Michael G. Bongiorno
Stephen A. Jonas	James R. Burke
Wayne M. Kennard	Jorge L. Contreras, Jr.
Richard M. Tardiff	William S. Gehrke
Jeffrey A. Stein	Richard N. Kimball
Hollie L. Baker (Not admitted in MA)	Daniel W. McCarthy
	Michael J. Nathanson
Jeffrey A. Hermanson	W. Scott O'Connell (Resident, Manchester, New Hampshire Office)
Hal J. Leibowitz	
Paul V. Rogers	Heidi C. Paulson
A. Silvana Giner	Leonard A. Pierce
Christopher P. Harvey	Michael P. Scanlon
William F. Leahy (Resident, Washington, D.C. Office)	Sean P. Sherman (Resident, Washington, D.C. Office)
Susan W. Murley	Susan McWhan Tobin
Brent B. Siler (Resident, Washington, D.C. Office)	Eve Stolov Vaudo
	Cynthia D. Vreeland (Not admitted in MA)
A. William Caporizzo	
Kenneth R. Meade (Resident, Washington, D.C. Office)	Kathleen M. Weinstein (Resident, Washington, D.C. Office)
William H. Paine	

COUNSEL

Samuel S. Dennis, 3rd, (P.C.)	William F. Winslow (Resident, Washington, D.C. Office)
James Segel	
James F. Millea, Jr.	Wayne A. Keown
Peter A. Spaeth	Robyn B. Klinger
Kenneth A. Hoxsie	Alfred Server
Miriam R. Gamson (Resident, Washington, D.C. Office)	

ASSOCIATES

Wendy E. Anderson (Resident, Washington, D.C. Office)	Jamie N. Class
	Sean A. Côté
Michael D. Bain	Kristen Allman Denison (Not admitted in MA)
Jane A. Bell	
Jonathan C. Black	Anne G. Depew
Sean T. Boulger	Michael A. Diener
Ryan R. Brenneman	Marc F. Dupré
Kathleen F. Burke	Stephen M. Edwards (Not admitted in MA)
Nicholas Carter	
Finn M. W. Caspersen	Jane B. Eiselein
Robin Colombo Cecere	Rebecca L. Fine

(See Next Column)

(See Next Column)

ASSOCIATES (Continued)

Robert F. Fitzpatrick Jr.	Lisa J. Pirozzolo
Michael J. Gartland	Linda E. Podheiser
Peter L. Gray	Scott E. Pueschel
William C. Groscup (Resident, Washington, D.C. Office)	Jay G. Reilly
	Cris R. Revaz (Resident, Washington, D.C. Office)
John Theodore Gutkoski	
Marc N. Henschke	M. Kathryn Rickards
Joseph C. Hogan, III	Noah W. Riordan (Not admitted in MA)
Barry J. Hurewitz (Resident, Washington, D.C. Office)	
	Wendy Rae Rodano (Resident, Washington, D.C. Office)
Jane A. Kalinski (Resident, Washington, D.C. Office)	
	Julia A. Rossetti
Mark C. Kalpin (Resident, Washington, D.C. Office)	John M. Ryan (Resident, Washington, D.C. Office)
Karen Katz (Not admitted in MA)	Lisa A. Rydin
	Hillary A. Sale
Lance A. Kawesch	Laura E. Schneider
Kevin P. Lanouette	Mark Daniel Selwyn
Lloyd Lipsett	Sara J. Shanahan
Scott A. Lively	Jason Tate Sherwood
Gordon J. MacDonald	Tarrant L. Sibley
Christine A. Maglione	Rutledge A. Simmons
Susan Valente Marandett	Joseph L. Stanganelli
Glenn M. Martin (Resident, Manchester, New Hampshire Office)	Anne Marie Tanin
	Cynthia Tanner
	Wendell C. Taylor
Dominic E. Massa	Mary E. Tenn
Joseph E. Mullaney, III	J. Patrick Toher
James J. Nicklaus	Beth E. Turetsky
Barbara J. O'Connell (Resident, Washington, D.C. Office)	Christopher Umana
	Rusty Wilson (Resident, Washington, D.C. Office)
Lauren C. Panora	
	Mark R. Young

William A. Caldwell	David J. Shapiro
Carolyn P. Partan	Laurence D. Shind
	Patricia Anne Whalen

For full biographical listings, see the Martindale-Hubbell Law Directory

HEMENWAY & BARNES (AV)

60 State Street, 02109
Telephone: 617-227-7940
Fax: 617-227-0781

MEMBERS OF FIRM

Alfred Hemenway (1863-1927)	Michael J. Puzo
Charles B. Barnes (1893-1956)	Thomas L. Guidi
George H. Kidder	Edward Notis-McConarty
David H. Morse	Diane C. Tillotson
Roy A. Hammer	Stephen W. Kidder
Lawrence T. Perera	Susan Hughes Banning
John J. Madden	Frederic J. Marx
George T. Shaw	Deborah J. Hall
Timothy F. Fidgeon	Kurt F. Somerville
Ruth R. Budd	Teresa A. Belmonte
Michael B. Elefante	Brian C. Broderick

COUNSEL

Michael L. Leshin

ASSOCIATES

Ellen Cope-Flanagan	Miranda Pickells Gooding
Andrea H. Maislen	James P. Warner
Barbara Zicht Richmond	Alan H. Roth
Marsha K. Zierk	Brendan P. Doherty
Charles Fayerweather	Gary M. Bishop

OF COUNSEL

Guido R. Perera

For full biographical listings, see the Martindale-Hubbell Law Directory

HILL & BARLOW, A PROFESSIONAL CORPORATION (AV)

One International Place, 02110
Telephone: 617-428-3000
Telecopier: 617-428-3500

Arthur Dehon Hill (1869-1947)	Timothy J. Dacey, III
Robert Shaw Barlow (1869-1943)	Charles R. Dougherty
	Bruce E. Falby
Richard L. Alfred	William B. Forbush III
Charles C. Ames	John G. Gillis
R. Hale Andrews, Jr.	John A. D. Gilmore
Charles A. Baker III	Michael J. Goldberg
Peter E. Ball	Lisa C. Goodheart
Thomas H. Belknap	Michael S. Greco
Gregory P. Bialecki	Joseph D. Hinkle
Martha Born	David A. Hoffman
Thomas C. Chase	Peter Katz
Richard S. Chute	Richard L. Levine
Penny P. Cobey	Winifred I. Li
Frances Cohen	Terrence W. Mahoney

(See Next Column)

HILL & BARLOW A PROFESSIONAL CORPORATION, *Boston—Continued*

Neil V. McKittrick	John L. Sullivan
Wayne H. Miller	Elliot M. Surkin
W. Hugh M. Morton	David W. Tarbet
Christopher L. Noble	Daniel A. Taylor
Stephen M. Nolan	Andrea M. Teichman
Gregory D. Peterson	Dennis W. Townley
Richard W. Renehan	William A. Truslow
Richard D. Rudman	E. Randolph Tucker
Carl M. Sapers	John C. Vincent, Jr.
Miriam Vock Sheehan	Barbara Freedman Wand
Joseph D. Steinfield	Michael D. Weisman
Jonathan Strong	Richard M. Zielinski

SENIOR COUNSEL

Gael Mahony

OF COUNSEL

Kingsbury Browne, Jr.	James R. Repetti
Nancy D. Israel	Richard A. Wiley

ASSOCIATE OF COUNSEL

Diane diIanni

Valerie L. Andrews	Brian P. Lenihan
Sarah H. Arnholz	Jonathan C. Lipson
Jarrett Tomás Barrios	Thomas R. Marton
Robert A. Bertsche	Alexander W. Moore
Katharine S. Bolland	Brian P. Murphy
Joshua M. Davis	Robert J. O'Connor, Jr.
Susan C. Dawson	Michael J. Pineault
Nancy E. Dempze	Amy B. Rifkind
Joseph L. Faber	Ellen J. Rubin
Magda L. Fleckner	C. Dylan Sanders
Gail A. Goolkasian	Robert F. Schwartz
Matthew T. Henshon	Cornelia R. Tenney
David P. Horne	Danielle Y. Vanderzanden
Mark J. Johnston	Timothy Veeser
Renée M. Jones	Michael D. Vhay
Melissa Kurnit	Audrey K. Wang
Monica P. LaFond	James H. Wickersham
	Daniel C. Winston

For full biographical listings, see the Martindale-Hubbell Law Directory

HINCKLEY, ALLEN & SNYDER (AV)

(Formerly Hinckley, Allen, Tobin & Silverstein and Snyder, Tepper & Comen)
One Financial Center, 02111-2625
Telephone: 617-345-9000
Providence, Rhode Island Office: 1500 Fleet Center.
Telephone: 401-274-2000.

MEMBERS OF FIRM

Paula K. Andrews	Matthew T. Marcello, III
Richard C. Arrighi	(Not admitted in MA)
E. Jerome Batty	Frederick P. McClure
(Not admitted in MA)	Robert W. Millen
Jonathan Bell	(Not admitted in MA)
Joseph S. U. Bodoff	Toni Ann Motta
Leon C. Boghossian III	(Not admitted in MA)
Paul Bork	Elizabeth Murdock Myers
Stephen J. Carlotti	H. Peter Olsen
(Not admitted in MA)	(Not admitted in MA)
Sean O. Coffey	John J. Pendergast, III
(Not admitted in MA)	(Not admitted in MA)
Scott E. Cooper	Gerald J. Petros
Thomas Roberts Courage	Richard H. Pierce
Thomas S. Crane	Brian P. Richards
Joseph P. Curran	(Not admitted in MA)
(Not admitted in MA)	Jeremy Ritzenberg
Michael P. DeFanti	Ralph J. Rivkind
Kristin A. DeKuiper	David J. Rubin
Joseph M. Di Orio	(Not admitted in MA)
(Not admitted in MA)	Dennis M. Ryan
Eric F. Eisenberg	Charles E. Schaub, Jr.
Malcolm Farmer, III	Douglas F. Seaver
Margaret D. Farrell	Frank A. Segall
(Not admitted in MA)	Paul A. Silver
Noel M. Field, Jr.	Evan Slavitt
(Not admitted in MA)	Richard G. Small
Pasco Gasbarro Jr.	Herman Snyder
Bruce G. Goodman	Robert F. Sylvia
Alan P. Gottlieb	Richard J. Tetrault
Gerard R. Goulet	Edwin G. Torrance
William R. Grimm	(Not admitted in MA)
Paul A. Hedstrom	Howard E. Walker
Joel Lewin	(Not admitted in MA)
Doris Jami Licht	Richard D. Wayne
Sandra Matrone Mack	John R. Allen (Retired)
(Not admitted in MA)	Richard W. Billings (Retired)

(See Next Column)

MEMBERS OF FIRM (Continued)

Thomas J. Hogan (Retired)	Robert F. Pickard (Retired)
James A. Jackson (Retired)	Robert W. Shadd (Retired)
James E. Keeley (Retired)	Richard F. Staples (Retired)
	Edward M. Watson (Retired)

ASSOCIATES

Cecily Venable Banks	James M. Madden
(Not admitted in MA)	Kimberly B. Marroni
Jane B. Becker	Michael S. McSherry
Maureen K. Bogue	Leslie B. Muldowney
Alexandra K. Callam	Mary Powers Murray
Clifford R. Cohen	Christopher W. Nelson
Jane E. Cohen	(Not admitted in MA)
David Barry Connolly	Paul F. O'Donnell, III
Carol E. Didget	Elena B. Olson
Susan F. Donahue	Julianne Palumbo
Michelle A. Ruberto Fonseca	Laura A. Pisaturo
Hugh J. Gorman, III	(Not admitted in MA)
Kim Herman Goslant	Susan E. Raitt
Christopher D. Guerin	James O. Reavis
Gloria Maria Gutierrez	Steven A. Remsberg
Thomas P. Hagen	Mark Resnick
Richard L. E. Jocelyn	Patrick A. Rogers
(Not admitted in MA)	(Not admitted in MA)
Brenna B. Jordan	Kathleen A. Ryan
Kelley Jordan-Price	Craig Michael Scott
Sabrina Katherine Lanz	Melissa D. Smith
	Lawrence W. Vernaglia

OF COUNSEL

David D. Barricelli	Willard Krasnow
(Not admitted in MA)	Willard R. Pope
Anthony J. Buccitelli	Bentley Tobin
Jacques V. Hopkins	Joachim A. Weissfeld
(Not admitted in MA)	(Not admitted in MA)

For full biographical listings, see the Martindale-Hubbell Law Directory

HUTCHINS, WHEELER & DITTMAR, A PROFESSIONAL CORPORATION (AV)

101 Federal Street, 02110
Telephone: 617-951-6600

STOCKHOLDERS/MEMBERS

Katherine L. Babson, Jr.	Anthony J. Medaglia, Jr. (P.C.)
Mark N. Berman	James L. Messenger
Laura L. Carroll	Arthur S. Meyers, Jr.
John H. Clymer	Evelyn Venables Moreno
Donald D. Cooper	Richard S. Nicholson
David T. Dinwoodey	Mary Ellen O'Mara
James S. Dittmar	Steven M. Peck
Alan H. Einhorn	Sanford F. Remz
Jack H. Fainberg	Michael J. Riccio, Jr.
Francis J. Feeney, Jr.	Sander A. Rikleen
Carolyn Jacoby Gabbay	Charles W. Robins
Ronald Garmey	Regina Strazulla Rockefeller
Frederick H. Grein, Jr.	David S. Rosenthal
John J. Griffin, Jr.	Robert P. Sherman
William E. Halmkin	Adrienne Smith
Harry A. Hanson, III	Richard M. Stein
John D. Hughes	Joseph C. Tanski
Franklin C. Huntington, IV	Robert A. Thompson
Jonathan R. Karis	John C. Thomson
Deborah S. Kay	Richard L. Trembowicz
Robert L. Kirby, Jr.	Andrew M. Troop
James A. Kobe	James R. Westra
David A. Martland	James G. Wheeler
	Jeffrey S. Wieand

ASSOCIATES

Robert G. Bannish	Denise L. Kosineski
John W. Banse	David P. Kreisler
David M. Barbash	Joseph Listengart
(Not admitted in MA)	Wanda A. Luettgen
N. Melina Bell	David B. Mack
R. Hitz Burton	Virginia P. Maffei
Thomas M. Camp	Joseph C. Marrow
Sean A. Carter	Daniel McCarthy
Thomas M. Ciampa	Karen M. O'Toole
Terence D. Condren	Patrick J. O'toole, Jr.
Alan Jay Cooke	Lisa A. Paolillo
W. Brett Davis	Donald W. Parker
David Ross De Veau	Gregory A. Pastore
Mark William Eagle	Laura Pritzker Peck
Robert M. Finkel	Margaret A. Robbins
Marilyn French	Mark D. Robins
Marc G. Guggenheim	Todd Rodman
Geoffrey Hargreaves-Heald	Andrew S. Rogovin
Andrew J. Hayden	Erin Keleher Shea
Meredith A. Helmer	(Not admitted in MA)
John F. Hemenway	Jeffrey Michael Snider
Arthur A. Hundhausen	Jolie C. Spring
Gwenwyn M. Janett	Jill M.E. Sullivan
Gordon M. Jones, III	Craig M. Tateronis

(See Next Column)

HUTCHINS, WHEELER & DITTMAR A PROFESSIONAL CORPORATION—
Continued

ASSOCIATES (Continued)

John M. Timperio	Paul S. Veidenheimer
Susan T. Valente	Joel L. Weeks

OF COUNSEL

Ernest G. Angevine (P.C.)	Rainer M. Kohler (P.C.)
Michael J. Connolly	Nicholas U. Sommerfeld

For full biographical listings, see the Martindale-Hubbell Law Directory

---

KOPELMAN AND PAIGE, P.C. (AV)

Park Square Building, 31 St. James Avenue, 7th Floor, 02116
Telephone: 617-556-0007
Fax: 617-654-1735

Leonard Kopelman	Barbara J. Saint Andre
Donald G. Paige	Joel B. Bard
Elizabeth A. Lane	Everett Joseph Marder
Joyce F. Frank	Patrick J. Costello
John W. Giorgio	Joseph L. Tehan, Jr.

William Hewig, III	David J. Doneski
Theresa M. Dowdy	Sandra M. Charton
Deborah Eliason	Ilana Marie Quirk
Jeanne S. McKnight	Brian W. Riley
Judith Chanoux Cutler	John Joseph Kenney, Jr.
Anne-Marie M. Hyland	Mary L. Giorgio
Richard Bowen	Kathleen Elisabeth Connolly
Cheryl Ann Banks	Mary Jo Harris
Michele E. Randazzo	

For full biographical listings, see the Martindale-Hubbell Law Directory

---

ARTHUR F. LICATA, P.C. (AV)

Federal Reserve Plaza, 600 Atlantic Avenue, 02210
Telephone: 617-523-9977
Fax: 617-523-7443

Arthur F. Licata

For full biographical listings, see the Martindale-Hubbell Law Directory

---

LOONEY & GROSSMAN (AV)

A Partnership including Professional Corporations
101 Arch Street, 02110-1112
Telephone: 617-951-2800
Fax: 617-951-2819

Stewart F. Grossman (P.C.)	Bradley W. Snyder
Richard J. Grahn	Wesley S. Chused
Bertram E. Snyder	Melvin S. Hoffman (P.C.)
Robert Cushman Barber	Joseph H. Matzkin

SENIOR COUNSEL

William F. Looney, Jr.

OF COUNSEL

Paul D. McCarthy	Sherman H. Starr, Jr.

ASSOCIATES

Seth H. Salinger	Lisa Sternschuss
Erin M. Gilligan	Keir J. Beadling
Maria Galvagna	Lauren K. Heggestad Dillon
Adam J. Ruttenberg	

For full biographical listings, see the Martindale-Hubbell Law Directory

---

MARTIN, MAGNUSON, McCARTHY & KENNEY (AV)

101 Merrimac Street, 02114-4716
Telephone: 617-227-3240
Telecopier: 617-227-3346

MEMBERS OF FIRM

Ephraim Martin (1900-1988)	Joseph L. Doherty, Jr. *
Clement McCarthy (1921-1985)	Paul R. Keane *
Raymond J. Kenney, Jr. *	John P. Mulvey *
Charles P. Reidy, III *	Paul M. McTague *
Daniel J. Griffin, Jr. *	Carol A. Kelly *
Philip E. Murray, Jr. *	Gail L. Anderson *
Edward F. Mahoney *	

COUNSEL

Harold E. Magnuson	Edward F. Hennessey

Joan L. Atlas *	Teresa J. Farris *
Joseph B. Bertrand *	Mark A. Newcity *
Martha A. Driscoll *	Kevin C. Reidy *
Douglas A. Robertson *	Stephen M. O'Shea *
Mary T. Gibbons *	Michael A. Uhlarik
Lisa A. Furnald	

(See Next Column)

Representative Clients: Allstate Insurance Co.; American International Adjustment Co.; Browning - Ferris Industries, Inc.; Fireman's Fund Insurance Cos.; Medical Professional Mutual Insurance Co.; Multi Systems Agency LTD.; Risk Management Foundation; St. Paul Insurance Cos.; Wausau Insurance Cos.
Reference: Fleet Bank.
*Employees of The Professional Corporation of McCarthy, Kenney & Reidy.

For full biographical listings, see the Martindale-Hubbell Law Directory

---

MINTZ, LEVIN, COHN, FERRIS, GLOVSKY AND POPEO, P.C. (AV)

One Financial Center, 02111
Telephone: 617-542-6000
FAX: 617-542-2241
Internet: Each Attorney's Internet Address takes the following form: first initial last name @mintz.com (e.g., rmintz@mintz.com)
Washington, D.C. Office: 701 Pennsylvania Avenue, N.W. Suite 900.
Telephone: 202-434-7300.
Fax: 202-434-7400.

Richard G. Mintz	Howard J. Symons (Resident, Washington, D.C. Office)
Jerome Gotkin	
Francis X. Meaney	Stanley A. Twarog
Charles D. Ferris (Resident, Washington, D.C. Office)	Douglas A. Zingale
	Elizabeth B. Burnett
R. Robert Popeo	Charles E. Carey
Peter Van	(Not admitted in MA)
Sidney A. Slobodkin	David R. Ford (Resident, Washington, D.C. Office)
William C. Brashares (Resident, Washington, D.C. Office)	
	Jonathan L. Kravetz
Kenneth J. Novack	Craig H. Campbell
Stanford N. Goldman, Jr.	Ann-Ellen Marcus Hornidge
(Not admitted in MA)	Eve T. Horwitz
Frank W. Lloyd (Resident, Washington, D.C. Office)	Kenneth M. Bello
	Peter A. Biagetti
Peter M. Saparoff	Rachael Macindoe Dorr
Thomas J. Kelly	H. Joseph Hameline
Stephen M. Weiner	Stephen T. Langer
David A. Gilbert	Bruce F. Metge
Thomas R. Murtagh	Paul D. Wilson
Frederick J. Pittaro	Joseph G. Blute
Paul D. Bishop	Donna Nussinow Lampert (Resident, Washington, D.C. Office)
Irwin M. Heller	
Stephen M. Leonard	
Robert M. Gault	Mary Lee Moore
David H. Halpert	Paul J. Ricotta
Martha J. Koster	Jeffrey S. Robbins
Michael P. Last	Samuel M. Starr
Thomas M. Reardon	Leocadia Irine Zak
Jeffrey M. Wiesen	Lee H. Glickenhaus
Joel R. Bloom	Timothy J. Langella
Richard E. Mikels	David E. Lurie
Dennis I. Greene	R. Mark Chamberlin
Richard R. Kelly	(Not admitted in MA)
John K. Markey	John R. Pomerance
Christopher H. Milton	Steven P. Rosenthal
Thomas M. Antone, IV (Resident, Washington, D.C. Office)	Leonard Weiser-Varon
	Joshua Davis
	Peter F. Demuth
Gregory A. Sandomirsky	James A. Kirkland (Resident, Washington, D.C. Office)
Bruce D. Sokler (Resident, Washington, D.C. Office)	
	Elizabeth P. Knauss
Maxwell D. Solet	Henry A. Sullivan
Michael S. Gardener	Kim V. Marrkand
Alvin J. Lorman	William M. Hill
C. Stephen Parker, Jr.	William W. Kannel
Michael J. Lieberman	Tracy A. Miner
John R. Regier	Richard H. Moche
David G. Spackman	Rosemary M. Allen
Andrew R. Urban	Michael F. Connolly
Ellen L. Janos	Lewis J. Geffen
Stuart A. Offner	Cherie R. Kiser (Resident, Washington, D.C. Office)
Rebecca L. Jackson (Resident, Washington, D.C. Office)	
	Anne Bruno Tully
Cameron F. Kerry	Beth I. Z. Boland
Charles Alan Samuels (Resident, Washington, D.C. Office)	Carleasa A. Coates
	Richard A. Goldman
Patrick J. Sharkey	Jeffrey R. Porter

OF COUNSEL

Francis X. Bellotti

SPECIAL COUNSEL

Judith Lidsky	David S. Lintz
John C. Plotkin	Susan J. Cohen

John Paul Sullivan	William P. McDermott
Walter J. Gorski	Catherine S. Stamps
(Not admitted in MA)	Marie Lefton
Robert J. Ryan	Susan Englander Hislop
Marilyn Newman	Jo Frances Kaplan

(See Next Column)

MINTZ, LEVIN, COHN, FERRIS, GLOVSKY AND POPEO P.C., *Boston—Continued*

Jodi M. Landau
Peter M. Miller
Joanne A. Robbins
Constance D. Sprauer
Christopher J. Harvie (Resident, Washington, D.C. Office)
Andrew N. Nathanson
Kathleen C. Tulloh Brink
William A. Davis (Resident, Washington, D.C. Office)
Meryl J. Epstein
Judith Slovin Levenfeld
Susan P. Phillips
Sara F. Seidman (Resident, Washington, D.C. Office)
Noam Ayali (Not admitted in MA)
Elizabeth Kagan Cooper
Michael L. Fantozzi (Not admitted in MA)
Shari A. Levitan
Linda B. Port
Navjeet K. Bal
Joseph P. Crawford-Kelly
Donna M. Evans
Allen H. Forbes
Alan S. Gale
Mary-Laura Greely
Christopher A. Holt (Resident, Washington, D.C. Office)
Peter S. Lawrence
Richard Mirabito
John F. Sylvia
John A. Sym
Sally E. Williamson
Jonathan S. Wolin (Resident, Washington, D.C. Office)
J. Stephen Zielezienski (Resident, Washington, D.C. Office)
Julie E. Bahret
Joseph P. Curtin
Shepard Davidson
Gail Eagan
Robert N. Falk (Resident, Washington, D.C. Office)
Richard W. Furcolo
John W. Hawkins
Kevin M. McGinty
Russell C. Merbeth (Resident, Washington, D.C. Office)
Stephen T. Murray
M. Daria Niewenhous
Thomas C. Walsh
Marion K. Antonucci
Michael R. B. Balfe
Meghan B. Burke
Peter T. Butterfield
Maryann Civitello
Patrick T. Clendenen

Jeffrey A. Dretler
Susan M. Finegan
Allan M. Green
Judith I. Jacobs
Dwayne O. Leslie (Resident, Washington, D.C. Office)
Joseph P. Messina
Valerie B. Robin
Deena Godshall Roth (Resident, Washington, D.C. Office)
Michael B. Bressman (Resident, Washington, D.C. Office)
Elizabeth Brody Gluck
Joseph L. Demeo
Julie E. Korostoff
Andrew J. Merken
A. W. Phinney, III
Jennifer P. Sacon
James J. Valentino (Resident, Washington, D.C. Office)
Anthony E. Varona (Resident, Washington, D.C. Office)
Joan E. Cirillo
Tara M. Corvo (Resident, Washington, D.C. Office)
Gregory R. Firehock (Resident, Washington, D.C. Office)
Bernard K. Hooper (Not admitted in MA)
Kimberly H. Kelley
Thomas S. Moffatt
Seni M. Adio
Susan M. Basham
Sarah S. Cabot
Mark D. Flaherty
Michael J. Gill
William C. Hicks (Not admitted in MA)
Joanne S. Hovis (Resident, Washington, D.C. Office)
Fernando R. Laguarda (Resident, Washington, D.C. Office)
Peter J. Marathas, Jr. (Not admitted in MA)
John Miller
Nancy D. Prior
Darin P. Smith
Wendy Zazik
Janell P. Fonsworth (Resident, Washington, D.C. Office)
Scott C. Ford
Matthew S. Forsyth
Anthony D. George
Cristina D. Hernandez-Malaby
Benjamin L. Hincks
John P. Kelleher
Jennifer A. Purvis (Resident, Washington, D.C. Office)

Deborah A. Sughrue

For full biographical listings, see the Martindale-Hubbell Law Directory

NUTTER, MCCLENNEN & FISH, LLP (AV)

A Partnership including a Professional Corporation
One International Place, 02110-2699
Telephone: 617-439-2000
Telex: 94-0790
Facsimile: 617-973-9748
Hyannis, Massachusetts Office: Route 28, 1185 Falmouth Road, P.O. Box 1630.
Telephone: 508-790-5400.
Telecopier: 508-771-8079.

MEMBERS OF FIRM

Edward C. Mendler
Dana C. Coggins
John P. Driscoll, Jr.
Edward F. McHugh, Jr.
Charles B. Abbott
Duane S. Batista
Charles R. Parrott
Constantine Alexander
James W. Hackett
Augustus F. Wagner, Jr.
Gene A. Blumenreich
Michael E. Mooney
Andrew J. McElaney, Jr.
Daniel J. Gleason
William T. Sherry, Jr.
William H. Baker

Michael J. Bohnen
Louis J. Marett
Charles A. Rosebrock
Robert A. Fishman
Edward P. Leibensperger
Stephen M. Andress
Thomas P. Jalkut
Neil P. Motenko
Anne Smiley Rogers
Mary K. Ryan
David E. Watson
Gary D. Zanercik
Peter Nils Baylor
Sharon R. Burger
Patrick M. Butler
Paul R. Eklund

(See Next Column)

MEMBERS OF FIRM (Continued)

James H. Simon
Michael T. Cetrone
Arthur R Hofmann, Jr.
David R. Schmahmann
Nelson G. Apjohn
Peter R. Brown
Dianne Hobbs
Marianne Ajemian
Martin C. Pentz
Robert L. Ullmann

William C. Geary, III
Stephen J. Brake
Lisa Cameron Wood
Michael K. Krebs
James E. Dawson
Beth H. Mitchell
Deborah J. Manus
Diane Rosse
Richard P. Schwartz
Timothy M. Smith

OF COUNSEL

Leonard Kaplan
Irving J. Helman (P.C.)
Norman T. Byrnes
William H. MacCrellish, Jr.
Frederick D. Herberich

Nathan Newbury III
Bancroft R. Wheeler
John Larkin Thompson
Frances H. Miller
Susan Leonard Repetti

David S. Szabo

JUNIOR PARTNERS

David C. Henderson
Donald Robert Peck
Nancy A. McGuire
Michael L. Chinitz
Douglas G. Kott

Hugh A. O'Reilly
Lori Jean Polacheck
Joseph F. Shea
Julia Satti Cosentino
Suzanne L. Glassburn

ASSOCIATES

Allison W. Allen
Shira M. Bayme
Victoria L. Botvin
Joseph M. Centofanti
John Christopher
Glenn E. Deegan
Rachna K. Dhanda
Mark R. Dolins
Samuel E. Feigin
David L. Ferrera
John C. Fitzpatrick
Sheila M. Flaherty
Gary L. Gill-Austern
Alexander S. Glovsky
Daniel Ross Harris
Thomas P. Howard
Ronald M. Jacobs
Connie Lee

Daniel J. Mahoney
Timothy C. McFarland
Susan C. Murphy
Daniel P. Olohan
Jonathan Z. Pearlson
Suzanne M. Quill
Andrée M. Saulnier
Erik A. Schmidt
Cheray G. Shein
Daniel S. Shore
Mark C. Solakian
Carol Meyerdierks Tsao
Christa von der Luft
Robert D. Webb
Daniel A. Wentworth
Kenneth T. Willis
Richard M. Wong
Terry L. Wood

HYANNIS, MASSACHUSETTS OFFICE
PARTNERS

Augustus F. Wagner, Jr.   Patrick M. Butler

OF COUNSEL

Edward F. McLaughlin, Jr.

ASSOCIATES

Shari L. Lobe   Sarah M. Manning

For full biographical listings, see the Martindale-Hubbell Law Directory

PALMER & DODGE LLP (AV)

One Beacon Street, 02108
Telephone: 617-573-0100
Facsimile: 617-227-4420

MEMBERS OF FIRM

Moorfield Storey (1887-1929)
John L. Thorndike (1887-1920)
Bradley W. Palmer (1893-1946)
Robert G. Dodge (1910-1964)
F. Andrew Anderson
Neil P. Arkuss
F. Kingston Berlew
Michael R. Brown
Robert W. Buck
Acheson H. Callaghan, Jr.
Lawrence B. Cohen
Norman P. Cohen
Matthew C. Dallett
Jeanne P. Darcey
Jean M. DeLuca
Ralph C. Derbyshire
Charles E. DeWitt, Jr.
Robert Duggan
Andrew L. Eisenberg
Lynnette C. Fallon
Steven N. Farber
John G. Faria
Mark A. Fischer
Ruth E. Fitch
Karl P. Fryzel
Ralph D. Gants
Nathaniel S. Gardiner
Michael T. Gass
Laurie S. Gill
Leon J. Glazerman
Robert H. Hale
Laurie J. Hall

Richard Hiersteiner
Malcolm E. Hindin
Jeffrey F. Jones
Stanley Keller
Ronald H. Kessel
Jerry V. Klima
Michael J. Lacek
William L. Lahey
Daryl J. Lapp
Scott P. Lewis
Francis C. Lynch
Michael Lytton
Judith A. Malone
Maureen P. Manning
Eric F. Menoyo
Thomas W. Merrill
Raymond M. Murphy
Arthur B. Page
David R. Pokross, Jr.
John E. Rattigan, Jr.
David R. Rodgers
Richard S. Rosenstein
Walter J. St. Onge, III
Thomas G. Schnorr
Steven L. Schreckinger
Thane D. Scott
Thomas M. Spera
Craig E. Stewart
Henry G. Stewart
Jeffrey Swope
Peter S. Terris
James L. Terry

(See Next Column)

PALMER & DODGE LLP—*Continued*

MEMBERS OF FIRM (Continued)

John M. Thomas	John Taylor Williams
George Ticknor	William Williams II
Roger P. Vacco	Donald F. Winter
James M. Whalen	Peter Wirth
William T. Whelan	Tamara S. Wolfson
John L. Whitlock	R. Robert Woodburn, Jr.

Jackson W. Wright, Jr.

COUNSEL

Stephen J. Abarbanel	Kevin R. McNamara
Susanna C. Burgett	Kathryn Cochrane Murphy
David J. Corrsin	Alan S. Musgrave
Jay E. Gruber	Zick Rubin
Rhonda G. Hollander	Russell B. Swapp
Ann C. King	Pamela M. Veasy

Cassandra Warshowsky

ASSOCIATES

Alicia Afalonis	Joseph J. Laferrera
Mary Ellen Alessandro	Tracey L. McCain
John J. Aquino	Stephen C. McEvoy
Jeffrey B. Araten	Brenda M. Mercurio
James T. Barrett	(Not admitted in MA)
Marsha Phillips Beatrice	David G. Mitchell
Mark L. Belanger	Eileen F. Morrison
Grace M. Blea-Nuñez	Daniel J. Moynihan, III
Katherine Keeton Carter	(Not admitted in MA)
John J. Cheney, III	Susan Murphy
Elizabeth A. Claffey	Harvey Nosowitz
Suzanne V. Cocca	George E. Olson
Stephen L. Coco	Mary Clements Pajak
Dyann Delvecchio	Mary Pauli
Maureen A. Dodig	Kirsten C. Poler
Marc Dohan	Gerald E. Quirk
Ronald S. Eppen	Dawn Reddy
Eileen Smith Ewing	Anne Robbins
Eileen Finan	Suzette Rodriguez
Joan Garrity Flynn	Elaine M. Rogers
Susan V. Fried	Marc A. Rubenstein
Akiyo Fujii	Kenneth W. Salinger
Jordana B. Glasgow	Matthew P. Schaefer
Jane M. Guevremont	Elizabeth P. Seaman
Joseph F. Hardcastle	Richard B. Smith
Nancy T. Harrington	G. Thacher Storm
John J. Hitt	Joshua M. Thayer
John C. Kacoyannakis	Kerry J. Tomasevich
Laura Anne Kelly	James G. Topetzes
Paul M. Kinsella	Mary S. Tracy
E. Edward Klotzbier	Aaron C. von Staats

Janet M. Zipin

OF COUNSEL

Virginia Aldrich	James W. Perkins
Theodore Chase	John A. Perkins
Casimir de Rham, Jr.	David E. Rideout
Robert J. McGee	Mary G. Sullivan
Robert P. Moncreiff	John P. Weitzel

John M. Woolsey, Jr.

For full biographical listings, see the Martindale-Hubbell Law Directory

---

PEABODY & ARNOLD (AV)

A Partnership including Professional Corporations
50 Rowes Wharf, 02110-3342
Telephone: 617-951-2100
Telecopier: 617-951-2125
Providence, Rhode Island Office: One Citizens Plaza, Suite 840.
Telephone: 401-831-8330.
Fax: 401-831-8359.

MEMBERS OF FIRM

Francis Peabody (1899-1938)	Paul R. Devin
Edward K. Arnold (1899-1937)	John K. Dineen
Samuel H. Batchelder	Michael P. Duffy
(1909-1966)	David W. Fitts
Willard B. Luther (1909-1962)	Thomas Frisardi
Vincent M. Amoroso	R. Alan Fryer
Paul J. Ayoub	Robert T. Gill (P.C.)
Jonathan Bangs	Michael J. Glazerman
James H. Belanger	John R. Gowell, Jr. (Resident,
Michael F. Burke	Providence, Rhode Island
Donald S. Burnham	Office)
Philip H. Cahalin	Deborah S. Griffin
Kevin C. Cain	Ripley E. Hastings
Frederick E. Connelly, Jr.	David F. Hendren
John P. Connelly	Joseph D. S. Hinkley
William A. Cotter, Jr., (P.C.)	Elizabeth Z. Holmes
Jason M. Cotton	James A. P. Homans
Robert J. Coughlin	William E. Kelly
Philip M. Cronin	Susan Fay Kendall
Linda S. Dalby	John A. Kessler, Jr.
Amanda D. Darwin	Anil Khosla
Allen N. David	Maynard M. Kirpalani

(See Next Column)

MEMBERS OF FIRM (Continued)

Robert A. McCall	Peter M. Shapland
Andrew R. Menard	Molly Haynes Sherden
Robert W. Monaghan	Joseph M. Smick
Alexander H. Pratt, Jr.	Randolph L. Smith
Frank N. Ray (Resident,	Vincent M. Tentindo
Providence, Rhode Island	Donald E. Vaughan
Office)	Robert A. Vigoda
Douglas C. Reynolds	Edward E. Watts, III
Samuel S. Robinson	Harvey Weiner
George C. Rockas	Gregory L. White
E. Macey Russell	Rebecca J. Wilson
Suanne C. St. Charles	Thomas A. Wooters
Peter B. Seamans	Mark E. Young

Stephen Ziobrowski

OF COUNSEL

Dale A. Coggins	Kent A. Willever (Resident,
Paul C. Kelly	Providence, Rhode Island
	Office)

COUNSEL

John G. Brooks	Robert D. Power

ASSOCIATES

Glenn B. Asch	John T. Smolak
Barry D. Ramsdell	Elsie Bennett Kappler
Jennifer L. Lauro	Mark W. McCarthy
Adam Simms	Kathleen M. Colbert
Frank S. Hamblett	Kristin Garner
Christine Hasiotis	Matthew H. Herndon
Amelia M. Charamba	John P. Dougherty
John J. Canniff	Robin E. Folsom
Robert Payne Fox, Jr.	Rita D. Lu
Chantal M. Healey	William Vance Hoch
John J. O'Connor	William M. ("Mo") Cowan
Sandra P. Criss	Martin S. Ebel
Joanne T. Marchi	Scott D. Karchmer
Thomas C. Farrell	Ingrid Sorensen
William J. Dellea	Timothy J. Culver
Anna M. Magliocco-Chagnon	Moujan M. Walkow
Leonard Louis Spada	Laurie Golding Bazarian

Jane E. Kirk

For full biographical listings, see the Martindale-Hubbell Law Directory

---

RACKEMANN, SAWYER & BREWSTER, PROFESSIONAL CORPORATION (AV)

One Financial Center, 02111
Telephone: 617-542-2300
Telecopier: 617-542-7437

William B. Tyler	Janet M. Smith
Henry H. Thayer	Peter Friedenberg
Stephen Carr Anderson	Richard S. Novak
Albert M. Fortier, Jr.	J. David Leslie
Michael F. O'Connell	Sanford M. Matathia
Stuart T. Freeland	Richard J. Gallogly
Alan B. Rubenstein	James A. Wachta
James R. Shea, Jr.	Hanson S. Reynolds
Brian M. Hurley	Donald R. Pinto, Jr.

COUNSEL

Ronald S. Duby	Gordon M. Orloff
Lucy West Behymer	Eric A. Smith

OF COUNSEL

Albert B. Wolfe	George V. Anastas
August R. Meyer	Edward M. Condit
Richard H. Lovell	Alexander H. Spaulding

Margaret L. Hayes	Peter A. Alpert
Daniel J. Ossoff	Ellen M. Harrington
Melissa Langer Ellis	Lauren D. Armstrong
Daniel J. Bailey, III	Robert B. Foster
Michael S. Giaimo	Andrew H. Butler
Maura E. Murphy	Gayle E. Parlee
Mary L. Gallant	Elizabeth A. Gibbons

Melissa Fang

For full biographical listings, see the Martindale-Hubbell Law Directory

---

REARDON & REARDON (AV)

69 Beacon Street, 02108
Telephone: 617-248-6998
Fax: 617-248-0837
Worcester, Massachusetts Office: One Exchange Place.
Telephone: 508-754-1111.
Fax: 508-797-6176.

MEMBERS OF FIRM

James G. Reardon	Frank S. Puccio, Jr.

References: Mechanics National Bank; Worcester County National Bank; Bank of New England, Worcester.

For full biographical listings, see the Martindale-Hubbell Law Directory

Boston—Continued

ROCHE, CARENS & DeGIACOMO, A PROFESSIONAL CORPORATION (AV)

One Post Office Square, 02109
Telephone: 617-451-9300
Facsimile: 617-482-3868
Woburn, Massachusetts Office: 400 Unicorn Park Drive.
Telephone: 617-933-5505.
Braintree, Massachusetts Office: 51 Commercial Street.
Telephone: 617-356-4210.

Frederick W. Roche (1914-1971)	Joan P. Armstrong
James R. DeGiacomo	Tracie L. Longman
Robert J. Sherer	Jacqueline Holmes Haley
Michael T. Putziger	(Resident, Braintree Office)
Judith K. Wyman	Francis A. DiLuna
John C. Wyman	(Resident, Woburn Office)
Richard J. Saletta	Thomas S. Vangel
John W. Gahan, III	Janis M. Berry
Frank M. Capezzera	Cynthia H.N. Post
Loring A. Cook, III	Elizabeth B. Ornstein
John J. O'Connor, Jr.	David A. Kelly
Thomas K. Zebrowski	(Resident, Braintree Office)
Susan J. Baronoff	Nancy M. Harris
Johanna Smith	(Resident, Braintree Office)
Mary S. Parker	Timothy P. Cox
Anne Hanford Stossel	Christine Previtera
Mark G. DeGiacomo	Barbara J. Kroncke
Joseph R. Tarby III	Lisa M. Rico
(Resident, Woburn Office)	

OF COUNSEL

Thomas J. Carens	Joel Z. Eigerman
Daniel J. Johnedis	Newton H. Levee
Lynne Callahan DeGiacomo	Arthur A. Smith, Jr.

For full biographical listings, see the Martindale-Hubbell Law Directory

ROPES & GRAY (AV)

One International Place, 02110
Telephone: 617-951-7000
Fax: 617-951-7050
Email: postmaster@ropesgray.com
Washington, D.C. Office: One Franklin Square, 1301 K Street, NW, Suite 800 East.
Telephone: 202-626-3900.
Telecopy: 202-626-3961.
Providence, Rhode Island Office: 30 Kennedy Plaza.
Telephone: 401-455-4400.
Telecopy: 401-455-4401.

MEMBERS OF FIRM

Thomas L. P. O'Donnell	Robert K. Gad, III
George C. Caner, Jr.	Douglas N. Ellis, Jr.
Champe A. Fisher	Stephen P. Lindsay
John E. Beard	Steven J. Simons
Truman S. Casner	Susan R. Shapiro
John A. Ritsher	Mary E. Weber
John A. Pike	John H. Mason
Edward A. Benjamin	David L. Raish
Arthur G. Siler	Thomas M. Susman
Howard K. Fuguet	(Washington, D.C. Office)
C. Dean Dusseault	Roscoe Trimmier, Jr.
Peter MacDougall	William S. Eggeling (Providence,
David J. Blattner, Jr.	Rhode Island Office)
Charles P. Normandin	Lawrence D. Bragg, III
Henry L. Hall, Jr.	Virginia F. Coleman
Jerome M. Leonard	R. Hardin Matthews
Thomas G. Dignan, Jr.	John W. Gerstmayr
Fred R. Becker	Daniel T. Roble
Nicholas A. Grace	Steven T. Hoort
Paul B. Galvani	Kenneth W. Erickson
Nelson G. Ross	Harvey J. Wolkoff
Robert F. Hayes	Edward J. Joyce
William G. Meserve	Gregory E. Moore
Philip J. Smith	David M. Mandel
Francis X. Hanlon	Nancy E. Ator
Edward P. Lawrence	Christopher A. Klem
Richard P. Ward	Robert D. Guiod
G. Marshall Moriarty	Nancy R. Rice
William L. Patton	Jeffrey B. Storer
Ruth R. O'Brien	James L. Sigel
Ronald L. Groves	Martin E. Lybecker
Thomas W. Taylor	(Washington, D.C. Office)
Peter H. Dodson	Stephen E. Shay
Ronald B. Schram	(Not admitted in MA)
Carolyn M. Osteen	Susan A. Johnston
Russell A. Gaudreau, Jr.	Dwight W. Quayle
William F. McCarthy	Robert N. Shapiro
Robert L. Nutt	R. Bradford Malt
Stephen B. Perlman	Winthrop G. Minot
Francis L. Coolidge	Geoffrey B. Davis (Providence,
John C. Kane, Jr.	Rhode Island Office)

(See Next Column)

MEMBERS OF FIRM (Continued)

Colburn T. Cherney	John M. Loder
(Washington, D.C. Office)	Timothy W. Diggins
Joseph B. Kittredge, Jr.	John T. Montgomery
Thomas H. Hannigan, Jr.	Dennis M. Coleman (Providence,
Don S. DeAmicis	Rhode Island Office)
David O. Stewart	Alan G. Priest
(Washington, D.C. Office)	(Washington, D.C. Office)
Claire R. McGuire	Mark V. Nuccio
Thomas B. Draper	Rom P. Watson
David C. Chapin	Martin J. Newhouse
David B. Walek	Larry J. Rowe
Steven A. Wilcox	R. Newcomb Stillwell
Gregory D. Sheehan	Mark P. Szpak
John C. Bartenstein	Susan M. Galli
Douglas H. Meal	John O. Chesley, II
Eric M. Elfman	Anne Phillips Ogilby
Deborah J. Weiss	Hemmie Chang
Richard J. Lettieri	Michael K. Fee
Steven A. Kaufman	Peter M. Brody
John D. Donovan, Jr.	(Washington, D.C. Office)
Adelbert L. Spitzer	Joan McPhee (Providence,
David A. Fine	Rhode Island Office)
Brett A. Robbins	Peter N. Rosenberg
Jonathan M. Zorn	Daniel S. Evans
William A. Knowlton	David A. McKay
Keith F. Higgins	Lauren I. Norton
Alfred O. Rose	Martin Hall
Samuel J. Buffone	Lee Rubin-Collins
(Washington, D.C. Office)	Walter R. McCabe, III
J. Daniel Berry	Ann L. Milner
(Washington, D.C. Office)	Randall W. Bodner
Karen Kemper Henson	Robert B. Gordon

Ivor Cary Armistead III

COUNSEL

Daniel Steiner	Mark A. Greenwood
Samuel Frankenheim	(Washington, D.C. Office)
Daniel I. Halperin	Diane B. Patrick
(Washington, D.C. Office)	Clayton S. Marsh
Donald W. Glazer	(Not admitted in MA)
William W. Park	John E. McElhinney

ASSOCIATES

Arthur W. Hughes, III	James M. Lichtman
W. Thomas Moulton, Jr.	(Washington, D.C. Office)
Robert C. Macaulay, Jr.	Collin J. Beecroft
John Billings French	Karen A. Johnson
(Not admitted in MA)	Richard D. Batchelder, Jr.
Susan T. Nicholson	Peter L. Ebb
Joseph M. Eagan	Theodore M. Hess-Mahan
Richard A. Szczebak	James M. Wilton
Steven F. Scott	Bonnie B. Edwards
Laurie R. Wallach	James W. Matthews
Thomas B. Smith	Howard S. Glazer
(Washington, D.C. Office)	James R. Brown, Jr.
Bryan Chegwidden	Christopher Ceruolo
Christopher M. Leich	Colleen M. Granahan
John B. Ayer	Sarah G. Manchester
Michele M. Garvin	Amy A. Null
Brenda Sweeny Diana	Tisa K. Hughes
Patrick Diaz	Nancy E. Taggart
(Not admitted in MA)	Maryellen M. Lundquist
Dina L. Michels	(Washington, D.C. Office)
(Washington, D.C. Office)	James S. DeGraw
Stephen W. Bernstein	Michael J. Savitz
John R. Baraniak, Jr.	Françoise M. Haan
Jacqueline E. Camp	(Washington, D.C. Office)
Mark R. DiOrio	Dacia A. Clayton
Raj Marphatia	Cynthia M. Monaco
Marc J. Bloostein	(Washington, D.C. Office)
David A. Brown	Aaron Kenan Kann
Loretta R. Richard	(Washington, D.C. Office)
Alyson B. Gal	Brian L. Murray, Jr.
Jane D. Goldstein	(Washington, D.C. Office)
Timothy M. McCrystal	Michael S. Sher
Diana L. Cooper	Josephine M. Greaves
Lisa M. Ropple	Michael P. Allen
David P. Lucey	Debra Brown Allen
Kevin J. O'Connor	Brigid K. Hurley
Kyle S. Chase	Joann S. Nestor
Eric Jaeger	Jennifer N. Samsel
Thomas P. Smith	Joseph T. Turo, Jr.
Patrick O'Brien	Darlene C. Lynch
Joel F. Freedman	David R. Baron
Mary C. Hennessey	Margaret C. Curtin
(Washington, D.C. Office)	(Not admitted in MA)
Richard E. Manley	Luke T. Cadigan
Matthew M. Burke	Michael F. Sexton
Deborah J. Coleman	William S. Elias II
Ellen Page DelSole	Joshua S. Levy
(Washington, D.C. Office)	Madeleine C. Timin
James B. Haines	(Not admitted in MA)
Timothy J. Hinkle	

(See Next Column)

ROPES & GRAY—*Continued*

ASSOCIATES (Continued)

Christopher J. Austin	E. David Pemstein
(Not admitted in MA)	Robert A. Skinner
Emily Germain Shea	Alison M. Tschopp
Darca L. Boom	Anne K. Hayes
Brian S. Chilton	Laura S. Hundley
(Washington, D.C. Office)	Philip C. Koski
Tristan Pivacek	David C. Sullivan
(Not admitted in MA)	Terrence J. Murray
Edward J. Hudson	Laura J. McCollum
(Not admitted in MA)	Silvestre A. Fontes
John Jay Althoff	Heidi Goldstein Shepherd
Lee S. Feldman	Mythili Tharmaratnam
Ana M. Francisco	Christine Y. Chi
Suzanne M. Lambert	Douglas H. Hallward-Driemeier
Brian D. McCabe	John B. Livingston
Sean W. Mullaney	Ann R. Parker
Ellen Solomon-Gonzales	Jane E. Willis
Caroline R. Rogers	Michael S. D'Orsi
Nicole R. Hartje	Joan F. Meissner
Edward A. Broderick	Daniel J. Burke
Mary A. Beckman	Michele T. Perillo
Peter E. Schwartz	Jeremiah G. Garvey
Christopher T. Boes	Robert G. Jones
(Not admitted in MA)	Robert R. Leveille
David C. Kravitz	Jennifer S. Lobel-Schneider
Alexander Manganiello	Deven C. McGraw
Peter K. Levitt	Brian G. Murphy
J. Steven Baughman	Michael J. Stick
(Washington, D.C. Office)	Lisa M. White
Vivian E. Lee	Shari H. Wolkon
(Not admitted in MA)	R. Bryan Woodard
Kyle A. Bettigole	Daniel J. Harding
Kendrick Chow	Stacy Kirk Piccoli
Joshua T. Gaines	Bryan A. Supran
Julie Haggerty Jones	Jill K. Chasson
Thomas R. Hiller	Charles E. D. Thorland
David Kantaros	Dennis P. Gallagher

Alex J. Grant

OF COUNSEL

H. Brian Holland	Henry S. Streeter
Allen O. Eaton	Peter Leffingwell Albrecht
James B. Ames	Oscar W. Haussermann, Jr.
Warren E. Carley	Paul F. Perkins
Edward B. Hanify	John M. Harrington, Jr.
Francis H. Burr	Alfred W. Fuller
Andrew H. Cox	Joan D. Fuller
Wilson C. Piper	George H. Lewald
Ernest J. Sargeant	Richard W. Southgate
Douglas Mercer	George T. Finnegan
Harry K. Mansfield	A. Lane McGovern

W. Lincoln Boyden

For full biographical listings, see the Martindale-Hubbell Law Directory

---

SHERBURNE, POWERS & NEEDHAM, P.C. (AV)

One Beacon Street, 02108
Telephone: 617-523-2700
Fax: 617-523-6850
Email: @SHERBURNE.COM

William D. Weeks	Benjamin Volinski
John T. Collins	Mark Schonfeld
Allan J. Landau	James D. Smeallie
Stephen A. Hopkins	Paul Killeen
Alan I. Falk	Gordon P. Katz
C. Thomas Swaim	Joseph B. Darby, III
James Pollock	Richard M Yanofsky
William V. Tripp III	James E. McDermott
Stephen S. Young	Kenneth P. Brier
William F. Machen	Robert V. Lizza
W. Robert Allison	Miriam Goldstein Altman
Philip J. Notopoulos	John J. Monaghan
Richard J. Hindlian	Margaret J. Palladino
Paul E. Troy	Mark C. Michalowski
Harold W. Potter, Jr.	David Scott Sloan
Philip S. Lapatin	M. Chrysa Long
Pamela A. Duckworth	Lawrence D. Bradley

Miriam J. McKendall

Cynthia A. Brown	Christopher J. Trombetta
Cynthia M. Hern	Elise N. Zoli
Meredeth A. Beers	Amy J. Mastrobattista
Dianne R. Phillips	Leslie A. Sprinkle
Paul M. James	Douglas W. Clapp
Theodore F. Hanselman	Jeffrey A. Huebschmann
Joshua C. Krumholz	Tamara E. Goulston
Ieuan G. Mahony	Paul G. Lannon, Jr.
Jeffrey J. Nix	Nicholas J. Psyhogeos
(Not admitted in MA)	Edward J. Naughton
Kenneth L. Harvey	Kathaleen Kelly Cutone

(See Next Column)

Laurie A. Tribble	Deborah Paige Stone
Neil C. Higgins	Brian R. Popiel

COUNSEL

Haig Der Manuelian	Karl J. Hirshman
Mason M. Taber, Jr.	Dale R. Johnson

For full biographical listings, see the Martindale-Hubbell Law Directory

---

SHERIN AND LODGEN LLP (AV)

100 Summer Street, 02110
Telephone: 617-426-5720
Fax: 617-542-5186
Email: lawyers@sherin.com
Los Angeles, California Office: 11300 W. Olympic Boulevard, Suite 700.
Telephone: 310-914-7891.
Fax: 310-552-5327.

MEMBERS OF FIRM

Arthur L. Sherin (1946-1964)	Mark A. Nowak
George E. Lodgen (1946-1971)	Ronald W. Ruth
Morton B. Brown	Steven D. Eimert
George Waldstein	Barbara A. O'Donnell
John M. Reed	A. Neil Hartzell
Robert J. Muldoon, Jr.	Kenneth J. Mickiewicz
Alette E. Reed	Craig M. Brown
Edward M. Bloom	Andrew Royce
Thomas J. Raftery	Daniel O. Gaquin
Joshua M. Alper	Thomas A. Hippler
Gary M. Markoff	Rhonda B. Parker
Bryan G. Killian	John J. Slater III
David A. Guberman	Philip G. Boyle
Kenneth R. Berman	Nereyda Garcia
Frank J. Bailey	John C. La Liberte
Thomas P. Gorman	Christopher A. Kenney
Dorothy Nelson Stookey	C. Forbes Sargent III

ASSOCIATES

Karen Elise Berman	Michael S. Bloom
Margaret H. Leeson	Carolyn M. Barker
Robert M. Carney	Karen O'Malley
Mary Ellen McDonough	Susanne M. Walsh
Caroline Woodward	Susan S. Sampson

Anne Marie Dowd

OF COUNSEL

Michael S. Strauss	David M. Franek

LEGAL SUPPORT PERSONNEL

Marilyn J. Stewart (Executive Director)

For full biographical listings, see the Martindale-Hubbell Law Directory

---

SIMONDS, WINSLOW, WILLIS & ABBOTT, A PROFESSIONAL ASSOCIATION (AV)

50 Congress Street, 02109
Telephone: 617-367-4747
Fax: 617-227-1961

William S. Abbott	Robert Torrence Morrison
Marc A. Elfman	Hugh V. A. Starkey
Robert S. Gulick	Dudley H. Willis
Brenda G. Levy	John L. Worden III

Edward J. Wynne III

For full biographical listings, see the Martindale-Hubbell Law Directory

---

SMITH, DUGGAN & JOHNSON (AV)

Two Center Plaza, 02108-1801
Telephone: 617-248-1900
Fax: 617-248-9320

MEMBERS OF FIRM

Scott A. Smith	Paul W. Johnson
Christopher A. Duggan	Garrick F. Cole

OF COUNSEL

H. Reed Witherby	Thomas G. Cooper
Alan B. Sherr	John B. Savoca

ASSOCIATES

Mark B. Rees	Juliana deHaan Rice
Tamara Lee Ricciardone	Richard H. Mandel
Matthew J. Walko	Barbara E. Schultz

For full biographical listings, see the Martindale-Hubbell Law Directory

---

TAYLOR, DUANE, BARTON & GILMAN (AV)

75 Federal Street, 02110
Telephone: 617-654-8208
Fax: 617-482-5350
Providence, Rhode Island Office: The Wilcox Building, 42 Weybosset Street.
Telephone: 401-273-7171.
Fax: 401-273-2904.

(See Next Column)

TAYLOR, DUANE, BARTON & GILMAN, *Boston—Continued*

MEMBERS OF FIRM

Allan E. Taylor	John J. Barton
James J. Duane, III	Pamela Slater Gilman

ASSOCIATES

Edward D. Shoulkin	Gina Witalec Verdi
Jennifer Ellis Burke	Robert C. Shindell
Francis A. Connor, III	Craig R. Waksler
	David G. Bowman

For full biographical listings, see the Martindale-Hubbell Law Directory

TESTA, HURWITZ & THIBEAULT, LLP (AV)

High Street Tower, 125 High Street, 02110
Telephone: 617-248-7000
Telecopier: 617-248-7100
Email: postmaster@tht.com

MEMBERS OF FIRM

Donald L. Anglehart	Gordon H. Hayes Jr.
William B. Asher Jr.	John M. Hession
Steven M. Bauer	Joseph A. Hugg
Jason Berger	Stephen A. Hurwitz
David C. Berry	Jin-Kyung (Kay) Kim
Scott A. Birnbaum	Rufus C. King
Margaret W. Brill	Kevin T. Lamb
Mark H. Burnett	Mark J. Macenka
David J. Byer	Timothy C. Maguire
Paula A. Campbell	John A. Meltaus
Edmund C. Case	Edwin L. Miller Jr.
E. Michael Collins	James P. O'Hare
Henry W. Comstock Jr.	Robin A. Painter
Karen Faulds Copenhaver	Brian E. Pastuszenski
Leslie E. Davis	Edmund R. Pitcher
F. George Davitt	Howard S. Rosenblum
Linda DeRenzo	William J. Schnoor Jr.
Eric A. Deutsch	William B. Simmons Jr.
Douglas R. Ederle	Mark D. Smith
Daniel P. Finkelman	Andrew E. Taylor Jr.
Adam P. Forman	Richard J. Testa
David S. Godkin	George W. Thibeault
Dean C. Gordanier Jr.	John F. Welsh
	Lawrence S. Wittenberg

COUNSEL

Kimberly M. Collins	Anne G. Plimpton

ASSOCIATES

Alan J. Applebaum	Minnie P. Joung
Jocelyn M. Arel	(Not admitted in MA)
Kevin M. Barry	Kimberley J. Kaplan-Gross
Thomas A. Beaudoin	Victoria L. Karlson
Mark T. Bettencourt	Erin E. Karzmer
(Not admitted in MA)	Robin D. Kelley
Deborah Sager Birnbach	Edward J. Kelly
Kelli A. Birtwell	Heidi L. Kessner
Mitchell S. Bloom	Douglas J. Kline
Marie H. Bowen	Mary B. Kuusisto
Dean J. Breda	Roger A. Lane
Alfred L. Browne	John D. Lanza
Steven C. Browne	Kathryn L. Leach
Debra A. Buxbaum	Laurence E. Lewis
Joseph A. Capraro, Jr.	Amy M. Liss
Christine S. Chung	George W. Lloyd
Rebecca A. Connolly	Robin R. Longo
William J. Corcoran	Robert B. Lovett
John J. Cotter	Peter E. Markman
Elisa T. Deener-Agus	Arnold P. May
Robert C. DeLena	Terrance P. McGuire
James D. Doherty	Kevin M. McKenna
Deborah B. Dong	David M. McPherson
Marla Dubin	Stephen T. Mears
Lisa S. Dumaw	Carl E. Metzger
Lois Brommer Duquette	Thomas C. Meyers
Roy D. Edelstein	(Not admitted in MA)
Barbara M. Fagan	Steven M. Mills
Catherine E. Fazio	Christopher M. Mirabile
Robert N. Feldman	Michael J. Mitchell
Gillian M. Fenton	Lisel M. Mittelholzer
Kathy A. Fields	Jonathan M. Moulton
Richard D. Forrest	John M. Mutkoski
Edward D. Freedman	Malcolm B. Nicholls III
Inez H. Friedman	(Not admitted in MA)
Suanne M. Garnier	Susan J. Nock
Joseph T. Gentile Jr.	Helen E. O'Rourke
Jennifer M. Goddard	Prasan A. Pandite
Lawrence A. Gold	Deborah J. Peckham
Kenneth J. Gordon	Tracy A. Peterson
Pamela B. Greene	Harold Francis Pfister
Laura S. Harper	Mark D. Pomfret
Kristie P. Hathaway	Jennifer A. Post
Jordan D. Hershman	J. Gilbert Power
Sara Hinchey	(Not admitted in MA)
Michael D. Hochberg	William L. Prickett

(See Next Column)

ASSOCIATES (Continued)

Michael Racanelli	Walter H. Stowell III
Kurt Rauschenbach	Megan M. Stride
Nina L. Ross	Anne Stuart
Susan P. Ruch	David W. Tegeler
David M. Samuels	Joseph R. Torpy
Richard S. Sanders	Robert J. Tosti
Sarah W. Saunders	Thomas A. Turano
Christina R. Schaper	Michael J. Twomey
Mark C. Schueppert	Miguel J. Vega
Catherine G. Simmons	Christine C. Vito
Craig T. Smith	Sarah A. Wasserman
Robert S. Steinberg	Jean Weidemier
Christopher R. Stone	Stephen D. Whetstone
Heather M. Stone	Courtney Allison Wilson
	(Not admitted in MA)

LEGAL SUPPORT PERSONNEL
REGISTERED PATENT AGENTS
TECHNOLOGY SPECIALISTS

Duncan A. Greenhalgh	Gretchen A. Rice
Isabelle A.S. Blundell	Christopher W. Stamos
Michael H. Brodowski	Diana M. Steel
	Patrick Robert Henson Waller

For full biographical listings, see the Martindale-Hubbell Law Directory

WARNER & STACKPOLE LLP (AV)

75 State Street, 02109
Telephone: 617-951-9000
Telecopier: 617-951-9151
Email: w&s@warstack.com

Joseph B. Warner (1848-1923)	E. Barton Chapin (1885-1967)
Pierpont L. Stackpole	
(1875-1936)	

MEMBERS OF FIRM

Samuel Adams	Ralph T. Lepore, III
Timothy B. Bancroft	Howard A. Levine
Deborah E. Barnard	Keith C. Long
Paul C. Bauer	John J. McCarthy
Kenneth S. Boger	Willard G. McGraw, Jr.
Edward J. Brennan, Jr.	Stephen E. Moore
Judith G. Dein	Christopher E. Nolin
Michael DeMarco	Stephen L. Palmer
Henry T. Goldman	Elizabeth F. Potter
Michael A. Hickey	Stanley V. Ragalevsky
Robert W. Holmes, Jr.	Janice Kelley Rowan
Antoinette D. Hubbard	Gordon M. Stevenson, Jr.
John C. Hutchins	Walter G. Van Dorn
Ronald F. Kehoe	James G. Ward
Joseph J. Leghorn	Peter T. Wechsler
Michael A. Leon	Robert A. Whitney

ASSOCIATES

Christa A. Arcos	Mark G. Maher
James J. Arguin	Kevin M. Meuse
Kenneth R. Brown	Fannie Iselin Minot
Daniel M. Carroll	Anne T. Mitchell
Alida M. Coo	Jessica Ferrell Parker
Ellen Donahue	Jill M. Pechacek
Kristine E. George	David J. Powers
Dwayne M. Grannum	Jennifer S. Rako
Alexis Smith Hamdan	Daniel E. Rosenfeld
Elizabeth W. Ho	Michael E. Scott
Nancy J. Kriegel	Karen R. Sweeney
Christopher G. Lang	Patricia Yung Wong
	Kathleen B. Woodard

COUNSEL

Andrew C. Bailey	Jerold S. Kayden
	David W. Lewis, Jr.

OF COUNSEL

Melville Chapin	John Clarke Kane
Norman A. Hubley	Endicott Smith

For full biographical listings, see the Martindale-Hubbell Law Directory

WHITE, INKER, ARONSON, P.C. (AV)

One Washington Mall, 02108
Telephone: 617-367-7700
Telecopier: 617-523-5085

Monroe L. Inker	Laura J. Cervizzi
Martin L. Aronson	Kevin R. Connelly
John P. White, Jr.	Libby G. Fulgione, II
Leilah Anne Keamy	James D. Takacs
Ann E. Wagner	Patricia A. Kindregan
Frances M. Giordano	Martha W. Carroll
	Laura Davis Smith

For full biographical listings, see the Martindale-Hubbell Law Directory

Boston—Continued

WILLCOX, PIROZZOLO AND MCCARTHY, PROFESSIONAL CORPORATION (AV)

50 Federal Street, 02110
Telephone: 617-482-5470
Telecopier: 617-423-1572

Harold M. Willcox (1925-1975)   Jack R. Pirozzolo
Richard F. McCarthy

Richard L. Binder   Richard E. Bennett
Judith Seplowitz Ziss
OF COUNSEL
Richard P. Crowley

For full biographical listings, see the Martindale-Hubbell Law Directory

---

BRAINTREE, Norfolk Co.

LANE, LANE AND KELLY (AV)

836 Washington Street, P.O. Box 850270, 02185
Telephone: 617-848-0040
Fax: 617-380-4136

Myron N. Lane (1907-1972)   Richard B. Lane
Robert P. Kelly
ASSOCIATES
Evelyn V. Henry   Edward D. McDonald
Joseph M. Young

Representative Client: The Braintree Cooperative Bank; Boston Federal Savings Bank; Chase Manhattan Financial Services, Inc.; Co-operative Bank of Concord; First Federal Savings Bank of America; Mellon Bank; Salem Five Cents Savings Bank; Wellesley Co-operative Bank; Gale Associates, Inc.; Garaventa U.S.A. Inc.

For full biographical listings, see the Martindale-Hubbell Law Directory

---

CAMBRIDGE,* Middlesex Co.

GORMLEY & COLUCCI, P.C. (AV)

One Main Street, P.O. Box 965, 02142-0900
Telephone: 617-349-3750
Fax: 617-661-2576

George F. Gormley   John D. Colucci

For full biographical listings, see the Martindale-Hubbell Law Directory

---

WILLIAM M. O'BRIEN (AV)

Suite 216, 186 Alewife Brook Parkway, 02138
Telephone: 617-661-2600
Fax: 617-864-0654

For full biographical listings, see the Martindale-Hubbell Law Directory

---

COHASSET, Norfolk Co.

LAW OFFICES OF RICHARD A. HENDERSON (AV)

76 South Main Street, 02025
Telephone: 617-383-9000
Fax: 617-383-9005

Representative Clients: Bank of Boston; Shawmut Bank, N.A.; Pilgrim Cooperative Bank; The Cooperative Bank of Concord; Dunkin Donuts, Inc.
Approved Attorneys for: Chicago Title Insurance Co.; Old Republic Title Insurance Co.; Lafayette Title Insurance Co.; Lawyers Title Insurance Co.

For full biographical listings, see the Martindale-Hubbell Law Directory

---

CONCORD, Middlesex Co.

EDES & EDES, INC., A PROFESSIONAL CORPORATION (AV)

97 Lowell Road, P.O. Box 278, 01742
Telephone: 508-369-3209
Fax: 508-371-9809

Richmond T. Edes
Reference: Middlesex Savings Bank.

For full biographical listings, see the Martindale-Hubbell Law Directory

---

DEDHAM,* Norfolk Co.

GELERMAN, CASHMAN & DONAHUE (AV)

270 Bridge Street, 02026-1798
Telephone: 617-329-8300
Telecopier: 617-329-0387

MEMBERS OF FIRM
Michael C. Donahue   Gail M. Buschmann
Daniel F. Cashman   John M. Lovely
Richard A. Gelerman   Robert Nichols

(See Next Column)

OF COUNSEL
Richard A. Feigenbaum

For full biographical listings, see the Martindale-Hubbell Law Directory

---

*EDGARTOWN,** Dukes Co. — (Refer to Osterville)

FRAMINGHAM, Middlesex Co.

HARGRAVES, KARB, WILCOX & GALVANI (AV)

The Corporate Center, 550 Cochituate Road, P.O. Box 966, 01701
Telephone: 508-620-0140
Fax: 508-875-7728

MEMBERS OF FIRM
Paul V. Galvani   Mark R. Haranas
William H. Mayer   Robert P. Jachowicz
Dana L. Mason   Evans J. Carter
William M. Pezzoni   Jack Merrill, Jr.
OF COUNSEL
Francis P. Wilcox, Jr.   Arthur M. Mason
Victor H. Galvani   Brenda S. Steinberg
Edward J. Mahan   Arthur M. Pearlman

Counsel for: Framingham Cooperative Bank; Lind-Farquhar Co.; Strathmore Machine Toole Co.; Framingham Housing Authority.
Local Counsel for: General Motors Corp. (Framingham, Mass.); Bose Corp.; Consolidated Rail Corp.; Kens Foods, Inc.; Framingham Ford.

For full biographical listings, see the Martindale-Hubbell Law Directory

---

STEWART T. HERRICK & ASSOCIATES (AV)

Suite 303, 1661 Worcester Road, 01701
Telephone: 508-875-0021
FAX: 508-875-0029

ASSOCIATES
Lauren P. Smith

For full biographical listings, see the Martindale-Hubbell Law Directory

---

GLOUCESTER, Essex Co. — (Refer to Beverly)

HARWICH PORT, Barnstable Co. — (Refer to Truro)

HINGHAM, Plymouth Co.

GILLIS & ANGLEY (AV)

Suite 227, 160 Old Derby Street, 02043
Telephone: 617-749-2432
Telecopier: 617-740-0768

MEMBERS OF FIRM
Ralph J. Gillis   Edward T. Angley

For full biographical listings, see the Martindale-Hubbell Law Directory

---

HOLYOKE, Hampden Co.

CHARTIER, OGAN, BRADY, LUKAKIS, SHUTE & EMMA (AV)

850 Building, 850 High Street, 01040
Telephone: 413-536-1395
Fax: 413-532-9583
Chicopee, Massachusetts Office: 19 Broadway, Suite B.
Telephone: 413-594-2723.

MEMBERS OF FIRM
Jacob Ogan (1895-1990)   Michael J. Lukakis
Louis Y. Chartier (1912-1993)   Robert W. Shute
Jane M. Bartello (1950-1994)   Charles J. Emma
Peter F. Brady   Michael T. Sarnacki
ASSOCIATES
Nikki A. Lukakis   William E. Rooney
OF COUNSEL
Norman Ogan (Retired)

Representative Clients: Holyoke Credit Union; Trust Insurance Co.; Commercial Union Insurance Co.; Commonwealth Packaging Corp.; Marcus Printing Co.; Greater Holyoke-Chicopee Board of Realtors; Westfield Gas and Electric Department Management Guild; Western Massachusetts Girl Scout Council, Inc.; AM Marketing, Inc.

For full biographical listings, see the Martindale-Hubbell Law Directory

---

LYON, FERRITER & FITZPATRICK (AV)

Whitney Place, 14 Bobala Road, 01040
Telephone: 413-536-4236
Fax: 413-536-3773

MEMBERS OF FIRM
Clarke S. Lyon   James F. Donnelly
Maurice J. Ferriter   Peter C. Connor
William D. Fitzpatrick   John J. Ferriter
Charles P. Lavelle   Priscilla Fifield Chesky
ASSOCIATES
Robert C. Sacco   Deborah Desmarais Ferriter

(See Next Column)

LYON, FERRITER & FITZPATRICK, *Holyoke—Continued*

OF COUNSEL

William E. Begley

Representative Clients: Mount Holyoke College; Newspapers of New England, Inc.; Loomis House Retirement Community; Atlas Copco Compressors Inc.; Hazen Paper Company.

For full biographical listings, see the Martindale-Hubbell Law Directory

HYANNIS, Barnstable Co.

MURPHY AND MURPHY (AV)

243 South Street, P.O. Box M, 02601
Telephone: 508-775-3116
Telecopier: 508-775-3720

MEMBERS OF FIRM

Henry L. Murphy, Jr.　　　　J. Douglas Murphy

ASSOCIATES

G. Arthur Hyland, Jr.　　　Susan Merritt-Glenny

For full biographical listings, see the Martindale-Hubbell Law Directory

LAWRENCE, Essex Co. — (Refer to Andover)

LEOMINSTER, Worcester Co. — (Refer to Worcester)

LOWELL, Middlesex Co.

DONAHUE & DONAHUE ATTORNEYS, P.C. (AV)

21 George Street, 01852
Telephone: 508-458-6887
Fax: 508-458-3424

Daniel J. Donahue (1860-1939)	Peter V. Lawlor
Joseph P. Donahue (1889-1973)	Bradford P. Fortin
Charles A. Donahue (1891-1964)	Richard K. Donahue, Jr.
Richard K. Donahue	Andrea S. Barisano
Joseph P. Donahue, Jr.	Matthew C. Donahue
Joseph D. Regan	Richard E. Cavanaugh
Michael W. Gallagher	Kelly R. Spencer
	Alicia A. Donahue

Representative Clients: The Travelers Insurance Co.; L'Energia Cogeneration, Inc.; Black & Decker; Burger King Corp.; White Consolidated, Inc.

For full biographical listings, see the Martindale-Hubbell Law Directory

GOLDMAN & CURTIS (AV)

Lowell Place, 144 Merrimack Street, 01852
Telephone: 508-454-8804, 729-2625

MEMBERS OF FIRM

Frank Goldman (1890-1965)	James T. Curtis
Robert H. Goldman (1918-1991)	Cornelia C. Adams

Gregory T. Curtis	Carolyn L. Greenberg

OF COUNSEL

Efthemios J. Bentas	James T. Curtis, Jr.
	Matthew P. Demaras

For full biographical listings, see the Martindale-Hubbell Law Directory

MIDDLEBORO, Plymouth Co. — (Refer to Fall River)

NEW BEDFORD, Bristol Co.

PRESCOTT, BULLARD & McLEOD (AV)

558 Pleasant Street, 02470
Telephone: 508-999-1351; 999-2381
General Office: 508-999-1351
Title Office: 508-999-2381
Fax: 508-999-9433

MEMBERS OF FIRM

John M. Bullard (1921-1965)	Davis C. Howes
Raymond McLeod (1948-1978)	Richard C. Borges
Bryant Prescott (1929-1982)	Peter M. Nicholson
Oliver Prescott, Jr. (1927-1984)	John M. Janiak
	Michael A. Kehoe

ASSOCIATES

David A. French, Jr.　　　Richard C. Borges, Jr.

Representative Clients: Compass Bank for Savings; Citizens Bank of Massachusetts; Atlantic Refining Co.; National Bank of Fairhaven; BayBank Southeast, National Association; Ashley Ford Sales, Inc.
Approved Attorneys for: Lawyers Title Insurance Corp.; Chicago Title Insurance Co.; Commonwealth Land Title Insurance Co.

For full biographical listings, see the Martindale-Hubbell Law Directory

NEWBURYPORT, Essex Co. — (Refer to Lawrence)

NORTHAMPTON,* Hampshire Co.

ETHEREDGE & STEUER, P.C. (AV)

64 Gothic Street, 01060
Telephone: 413-584-1600
Fax: 413-585-8406
Email: 105215.3374@compuserve.com

Edward D. Etheredge　　　Shelley Steuer

For full biographical listings, see the Martindale-Hubbell Law Directory

GROWHOSKI, CALLAHAN & KUZMESKI (AV)

60 State Street, 01060-3099
Telephone: 413-584-1500
Fax: 413-584-1670

MEMBERS OF FIRM

John M. Callahan	Thomas M. Growhoski
	David C. Kuzmeski

ASSOCIATES

Elizabeth C. Mulcahy

For full biographical listings, see the Martindale-Hubbell Law Directory

ORLEANS, Barnstable Co.

CHAPLIN & CHAPLIN (AV)

203 South Orleans Road, 02652
Telephone: 508-255-6300
Fax: 508-255-3005
Boston, Massachusetts Office: One State Street.
Telephone: 617-227-0272.
Fax: 617-227-3396.

Ansel B. Chaplin

For full biographical listings, see the Martindale-Hubbell Law Directory

PITTSFIELD,* Berkshire Co.

CAMPOLI & CURLEY, A PROFESSIONAL CORPORATION (AV)

27 Willis Street, P.O. Box 1384, 01202
Telephone: 413-443-6485
Fax: 413-448-6233

Andrew T. Campoli	J. Peri Campoli
Thomas L. Campoli	Thomas J. Curley, Jr.

Thomas J. Hamel	Robert A. Monteleone, Jr.
	Paula Kahn-Almgren

References: First Agricultural Bank; City Savings Bank.

For full biographical listings, see the Martindale-Hubbell Law Directory

MARTIN & OLIVEIRA (AV)

100 North Street, Suite 301, 01201
Telephone: 413-443-6455
Fax: 413-445-5883

Ronald E. Oliveira	John J. Martin, Jr.
John J. Martin, Sr.	William E. Martin

ASSOCIATE

Dawn M. Rich

Representative Clients: Hospital Underwriters Insurance Co.; Lawyers Title Insurance Co.; Massachusetts Medical Professional Insurance Association; Pilgrim Insurance Co.; Plymouth Rock Assurance Co.; St. Paul Insurance Co.; Berkshire Gas Co.

For full biographical listings, see the Martindale-Hubbell Law Directory

SPRINGFIELD,* Hampden Co.

COOLEY, SHRAIR P.C. (AV)

5th Floor, 1380 Main Street, 01103
Telephone: 413-781-0750
Telecopier: 413-733-3042

David A. Shrair	Rona S. Fingold
Irving D. Labovitz	Peter W. Shrair
Robert L. Dambrov	Norman C. Michaels
Alan S. Dambrov	Mark A. NeJame
Alice E. Zaft	Mark D. Mason
	Daniel E. Bruso

Reference: BayBank; Fleet Bank.

For full biographical listings, see the Martindale-Hubbell Law Directory

Springfield—Continued

DOHERTY, WALLACE, PILLSBURY AND MURPHY, P.C. (AV)

19th Floor, One Monarch Place, 1414 Main Street, 01144
Telephone: 413-733-3111
Telecopier: 413-734-3910
Email: DWPM@DWPM.COM

Dudley B. Wallace (1900-1987)	L. Jeffrey Meehan
Louis W. Doherty (1898-1990)	David J. Martel
Robert E. Murphy	John James McCarthy
Paul S. Doherty	Joan Ho Bond
Samuel A. Marsella	William P. Hadley
Philip J. Callan, Jr.	Barry M. Ryan
Gary P. Shannon	Deborah A. Basile
Robert L. Leonard	Paul M. Maleck
A. Craig Brown	Claire L. Thompson

W. Garth Janes

Michael J. Rye	Kevin M. Walkowski
Michael K. Callan	William F. Sullivan, Jr.

Steven M. Coyle
OF COUNSEL

Frederick S. Pillsbury	Matthew J. Ryan, Jr.

Gregory A. Schmidt

Local Counsel for: Nationwide Mutual Insurance Co.; Liberty Mutual Insurance Co.; General Motors Corp.; Wausau Insurance Cos.; Royal Insurance; Metropolitan Property & Liability Insurance Co.
Representative Clients: Fontaine Bros.; F.L. Roberts and Company Inc.; Town of Longmeadow.

For full biographical listings, see the Martindale-Hubbell Law Directory

EGAN, FLANAGAN AND COHEN, P.C. (AV)

67 Market Street, P.O. Box 9035, 01102-9035
Telephone: 413-737-0260
Fax: 413-737-0121
Email: efc@ix.netcom.com

James F. Egan (1896-1986)	Maurice M. Cahillane
Edward T. Collins (1902-1995)	Charles W. Danis, Jr.
William C. Flanagan	John G. Bagley
Charles S. Cohen	Robert L. Quinn
Mary Egan Boland	Eileen Z. Sorrentino
John J. Egan	David G. Cohen
Theodore C. Brown	Kirsten A. Beske
Edward J. McDonough, Jr.	Joseph A. Pacella

OF COUNSEL
J. David Keaney

Counsel for: Mercy Hospital; Roman Catholic Diocese of Springfield; McKinstry, Incorporated.

For full biographical listings, see the Martindale-Hubbell Law Directory

PELLEGRINI & SEELEY, P.C. (AV)

1145 Main Street, 01103
Telephone: 413-785-5300
Fax: 413-731-0626

Gilbert W. Baron (1911-1987)	Donald W. Blakesley
Gerard L. Pellegrini	Phyllis P. Ryan
Earlon L. Seeley, Jr.	Paul F. Schneider

Steven D. Rose	Thomas Casartello
Michael J. Chieco	Patrick C. Gable
Charles R. Casartello, Jr.	John J. Dumphy

For full biographical listings, see the Martindale-Hubbell Law Directory

ROBINSON DONOVAN MADDEN & BARRY, P.C. (AV)

Suite 1600, BayBank Tower, 1500 Main Street, 01115
Telephone: 413-732-2301
Fax: 413-785-4658

Homans Robinson (1894-1973)	Milton J. Donovan (1906-1995)
Lawrence M. Sinclair (1942-1986)	

OF COUNSEL

John H. Madden, Jr.	Victor Rosenberg
Edward J. Barry	Richard S. Milstein

Gordon H. Wentworth	John C. Sikorski
James H. Tourtelotte	Nancy Frankel Pelletier
Charles K. Bergin, Jr.	Paul S. Weinberg
Ronald C. Kidd	Frederica H. McCarthy
Jeffrey W. Roberts	Matthew J. King
Jeffrey L. McCormick	Neva Kaufman Rohan
James F. Martin	Douglas F. Boyd
Robert P. Cunningham	James K. Bodurtha

Keith A. Minoff

(See Next Column)

E. Paul Amata	Kimberly Davis Crear
(Not admitted in MA)	John W. Davis
James D. Chadwell	Edmund J. Gorman
Susan L. Cooper	Patricia M. Rapinchuk

Jonathan P. Rice

Representative Clients: The First National Bank of Boston; United Cooperative Bank; Fleet Bank, N.A.; American Policyholders Insurance Co.; CNA; Commercial Union Insurance Co.; Hanover Insurance Group.

For full biographical listings, see the Martindale-Hubbell Law Directory

RYAN, MARTIN, COSTELLO, LEITER, STEIGER & CASS, P.C. (AV)

Suite 2500, BayBank Tower, 1500 Main Street, P.O. Box 15629, 01115-5629
Telephone: 413-739-6971
Fax: 413-739-1441

Charles V. Ryan	Henry M. Downey
Philip J. Ryan	Joan C. Steiger
Bradford R. Martin, Jr.	Timothy J. Ryan
Mary K. Downey Costello	William J. Cass
Bruce L. Leiter	Michael P. Ryan

For full biographical listings, see the Martindale-Hubbell Law Directory

---

WALTHAM, Middlesex Co.

HARNISH, JENNEY, MITCHELL AND RESH (AV)

564 Main Street, 02154
Telephone: 617-894-0000
Telecopier: 617-893-8357

MEMBERS OF FIRM

Francis E. Jenney	Robert C. Mann
David L. Mitchell	Margaret Manzon Skinner
Harvey J. Resh	Rhonda B. Fogel
Joseph Melone	Cynthia Spahl

For full biographical listings, see the Martindale-Hubbell Law Directory

---

WESTFIELD, Hampden Co. — (Refer to Springfield)

WORCESTER, * Worcester Co.

FLETCHER, TILTON & WHIPPLE, P.C. (AV)

370 Main Street, 01608
Telephone: 508-798-8621
Telecopier: 508-791-1201

Sumner B. Tilton (1904-1981)	Arthur H. Miller
Paris Fletcher (1903-1989)	(Not admitted in MA)
Robert J. Whipple	James M. Burgoyne
George Avery White	William D. Jalkut
Henry C. Horner	Patricia Finnegan Gates
John E. Hodgson	Mark L. Donahue
Sumner B. Tilton, Jr.	Stuart A. Hammer
Phillips S. Davis	Lucille B. Brennan
Robert R. Kimball	Kirk A. Carter
Douglas Q. Meystre	Dennis F. Gorman
Alexander E. Drapos	Brian J. Buckley
Warner S. Fletcher	Sheila Campbell Murphy
Robert F. Dore, Jr.	David J. Officer

Donna Toman Salvidio

For full biographical listings, see the Martindale-Hubbell Law Directory

GLICKMAN, SUGARMAN & KNEELAND (AV)

11 Harvard Street, P.O. Box 2917, 01613
Telephone: 508-756-6206
Fax: 508-831-0443

MEMBERS OF FIRM

Melvyn Glickman	David W. Sugarman

David J. Kneeland, Jr.
ASSOCIATES

Joe Boynton	Wayne M. LeBlanc

For full biographical listings, see the Martindale-Hubbell Law Directory

WILLIAM J. LeDOUX (AV)

446 Main Street, 01608
Telephone: 508-792-5448
Fax: 508-792-5449
Email: WILEDOUX@BILLYLEDOUX.COM

For full biographical listings, see the Martindale-Hubbell Law Directory

MacCARTHY, POJANI & HURLEY (AV)

Worcester Plaza, 446 Main Street, 01608
Telephone: 508-798-2480
Fax: 508-797-9561

(See Next Column)

MacCarthy, Pojani & Hurley, *Worcester—Continued*

Philip J. MacCarthy	Howard E. Stempler
Dennis Pojani	John Macuga, Jr.
John F. Hurley, Jr.	William J. Ritter

Representative Clients: Fleet Bank of Massachusetts, N.A.; Melville Corp.; Travelers Insurance Co.; Liberty Mutual Co.; Commerce Insurance Co.; Worcester Mutual Insurance Co.; Health Plans, Inc.; Marane Oil Corp.

For full biographical listings, see the Martindale-Hubbell Law Directory

---

McGUIRE & McGUIRE, P.C. (AV)

340 Main Street, Suite 910, 01608
Telephone: 508-754-3291
Fax: 508-752-0553

John K. McGuire (1952-1985)   Joseph E. McGuire
John K. McGuire, Jr.

Penelope A. Kathiwala	Paul Durkee
Christine Griggs Narcisse	Teresa Brooks
	John Pedone

For full biographical listings, see the Martindale-Hubbell Law Directory

---

MIRICK, O'CONNELL, DeMALLIE & LOUGEE (AV)

1700 Bank of Boston Tower, 100 Front Street, 01608-1477
Telephone: 508-799-0541
Fax: 508-752-7305
Email: modl@modl.com

MEMBERS OF FIRM

Robert J. Martin	Stephen J. Doyle
Bayard T. DeMallie	Karen E. Ludington
David L. Lougee	Richard C. Van Nostrand
Robert V. Deiana	Jeffrey L. Donaldson
John O. Mirick	Paul J. D'Onfro
Demitrios M. Moschos	Janet Wilson Moore
Robert P. Lombardi	Alden J. Bianchi
Edward C. Bassett, Jr.	David E. Surprenant
James C. Donnelly, Jr.	Peter J. Dawson
Andrew B. O'Donnell	Joseph M. Hamilton
Michael R. Mosher	John S. Chinian
Robert L. Hamer	William S. Rogers, Jr.
	Joseph H. Baldiga

OF COUNSEL

Laurence H. Lougee	Gardener G. DeMallie
	Richard W. Mirick

ASSOCIATES

Larry E. Salem	Sharon De Louchrey
Robert S. Heppe, Jr.	Margaret J. Hurley
Charles B. Straus, III	Elizabeth L. B. Greene
Pamela H. Sager	Glen M. Mair
Joan O. Vorster	Michael G. Donovan
Michele P. Rosano	Paul W. Carey
Robert J. Travers	Jeffrey E. Swaim
Richard N. Bradley	Paul C. Smith

References: The First National Bank of Boston, Worcester; Flagship Bank & Trust Co., Worcester; Fleet Bank of Massachusetts, Worcester.

For full biographical listings, see the Martindale-Hubbell Law Directory

---

MOUNTAIN, DEARBORN & WHITING (AV)

370 Main Street, 01608
Telephone: 508-756-2423
Fax: 508-755-6640

MEMBERS OF FIRM

Alfred N. Whiting (1920-1989)	Francis J. Russell
Thomas R. Mountain	Dale R. Harger
Richard W. Dearborn	Mark W. Bloom
Samuel R. DeSimone	Donald J. O'Neil
Henry W. Beth	Lawrence S. Delaney
	Ann K. Molloy

ASSOCIATES

Richard M. Freije

For full biographical listings, see the Martindale-Hubbell Law Directory

---

REARDON & REARDON (AV)

One Exchange Place, 01608
Telephone: 508-754-1111
Fax: 508-797-6176
Boston, Massachusetts Office: 69 Beacon Street.
Telephone: 617-248-6998.
Fax: 617-248-0837.

(See Next Column)

MEMBERS OF FIRM

James G. Reardon	Margaret Reardon Suuberg
Edward P. Reardon	James G. Reardon, Jr.
Frank S. Puccio, Jr.	Julie E. Reardon
Austin M. Joyce	Michael J. Akerson
James G. Haddad	Francis J. Duggan

References: Mechanics National Bank; Shawmut Worcester County Bank N.A.; Bank of New England, Worcester.

For full biographical listings, see the Martindale-Hubbell Law Directory

---

MICHIGAN

ADRIAN, Lenawee Co.

WALKER, WATTS, JACKSON & McFARLAND (AV)

160 North Winter Street, 49221
Telephone: 517-265-8138
Fax: 517-265-8286

MEMBERS OF FIRM

William H. Walker	Mark A. Jackson
Prosser M. Watts, Jr.	Michael McFarland

Attorneys for: Bank of Lenawee; Consumers Power Co.; Norfolk & Western Railway Co.; Citizens Gas Fuel Co.; Auto Owners Insurance Co.; Amerisure Co.; Blissfield Manufacturing Co.; Adrian College.

For full biographical listings, see the Martindale-Hubbell Law Directory

---

ALLEGAN, Allegan Co.

ORTON, TOOMAN, HALE, McKOWN AND KIEL, P.C. (AV)

Court House Square, North, Drawer 239, 49010
Telephone: 616-673-2136
Fax: 616-673-2898

Rex W. Orton (1914-1988)	Gregory D. Hale
Lester J. Tooman	Stephen B. McKown
	David F. Kiel

Representative Clients: Allegan Public Schools; Dorr Township; Allegan General Hospital; Allegan Medical Clinic, P.C.; Kalamazoo Ferry Co.; Allegan Foundation.

For full biographical listings, see the Martindale-Hubbell Law Directory

---

ALMA, Gratiot Co.

FORTINO, PLAXTON & MOSKAL (AV)

Warwick Professional Center, 175 Warwick Drive, P.O. Box 578, 48801
Telephone: 517-463-2101
Fax: 517-463-2104

MEMBERS OF FIRM

Charles M. Fortino	Anthony G. Costanzo

OF COUNSEL

Alfred J. Fortino	Kenneth D. Plaxton

RETIRED

John J. Moskal

Attorneys for: Farmers State Bank, Breckenridge; State Farm Mutual Insurance Co.; Auto Owners Insurance Co.; The Ohio Casualty Ins. Co.; Commercial Bank; Bear Truss and Components Co.; Alma Iron and Metal; Powell Fabrication & Mfg.; City of Alma.

For full biographical listings, see the Martindale-Hubbell Law Directory

---

ALPENA, Alpena Co. — (Refer to Petoskey)

ANN ARBOR, Washtenaw Co.

BOOTHMAN, HEBERT & ELLER, P.C. (AV)

300 N. Fifth Avenue, Suite 140, 48108
Telephone: 313-995-9050
Fax: 313-995-8966
Detroit, Michigan Office: Marquette Building, 243 West Congress, Suite 950.
Telephone: 313-964-0150.
Fax: 313-964-2226.

Richard C. Boothman (Resident)

For full biographical listings, see the Martindale-Hubbell Law Directory

Ann Arbor—Continued

Braun Kendrick Finkbeiner PLC (AV)

700 First National Building, 48104
Telephone: 313-995-4100
Telecopier: 313-995-4798
URL: http://www.bkf-law.com
Bay City, Michigan Office: 201 Phoenix Building, P.O. Box 2039.
Telephone: 517-895-8505.
Telecopier: 517-895-8437.
Saginaw, Michigan Office: 101 N. Washington, Suite 812.
Telephone: 517-753-3461.
Telecopier: 517-753-3951.

Barry M. Levine

Representative Clients: The Dow Chemical Co.; General Motors Corp.; Lobdell Emery Manufacturing Co.; Merrill, Lynch, Inc.; Saginaw General Hospital; Saginaw News; The Wickes Foundation.

For full biographical listings, see the Martindale-Hubbell Law Directory

Conlin, McKenney & Philbrick, P.C. (AV)

350 South Main Street Suite 400, 48104-2131
Telephone: 313-761-9000
Fax: 313-761-9001

Edward F. Conlin (1902-1953)	Robert M. Brimacombe
John W. Conlin (1904-1972)	James A. Schriemer
Albert J. Parker (1901-1970)	William M. Sweet
Chris L. McKenney	Elizabeth M. Petoskey
Karl R. Frankena	Bradley J. MeLampy
Allen J. Philbrick	Joseph W. Phillips
Phillip J. Bowen	Lori A. Buiteweg
Michael D. Highfield	Douglas G. McClure
Bruce N. Elliott	Thomas B. Bourque
Neil J. Juliar	Marjorie M. Dixon

Kenneth L. Spencer
OF COUNSEL
John W. Conlin

Representative Clients: Fingerle Lumber Co.; Ann Arbor Area Board of Realtors; Borders, Inc.; Auto-Owners Insurance Co.; Key Bank.
Approved Attorneys for: Nations Title Insurance Co.; Ticor Title Insurance Co.

For full biographical listings, see the Martindale-Hubbell Law Directory

Davis and Fajen, P.C. (AV)

Suite 400, 320 North Main Street, 48104
Telephone: 313-995-0066
Facsimile: 313-995-0184
West Michigan Office: Davis, Fajen & Miller. Harbourfront Place, 41 Washington Street, Suite 260, Grand Haven, MI, 49417.
Telephone: 616-846-9875.
Facsimile: 616-846-4920.

Peter A. Davis	James A. Fajen

Nelson P. Miller

Richard B. Bailey	Matthew J. Jurson

Reference: First of America Bank-Ann Arbor.

For full biographical listings, see the Martindale-Hubbell Law Directory

Dykema Gossett PLLC (AV)

315 East Eisenhower Parkway, Suite 100, 48108-3306
Telephone: 313-747-7660
Telex: 23-0121
Fax: 313-747-7696
Email: 2084153@mcimail.com
Bloomfield Hills, Michigan Office: 1577 North Woodward Avenue, Suite 300, 48304-2820.
Telephone: 810-540-0700.
Fax: 810-540-0763.
Chicago, Illinois Office: 55 East Monroe Street, Suite 3250, 60603-5709.
Telephone: 312-551-4900.
Fax: 312-551-4919.
Detroit, Michigan Office: 400 Renaissance Center, 48243-1668.
Telephone: 313-568-6800.
Fax: 313-568-6594.
Grand Rapids, Michigan Office: 200 Oldtown Riverfront Building, 248 Louis Campau Promenade, N.W., 49503-2668.
Telephone: 616-776-7500.
Fax: 616-776-7573.
Lansing, Michigan Office: 800 Michigan National Tower, 48933-1707.
Telephone: 517-374-9100.
Fax: 517-374-9191.
Washington, D.C. Office: Franklin Square, Suite 300 West, 1300 I Street, N.W.. 20005-3306.
Telephone: 202-522-8600.
Fax: 202-522-8669.

(See Next Column)

RESIDENT MEMBERS

James M. Cameron, Jr.	Raymond T. Huetteman, Jr.
Bruce G. Davis	Sharon M. Kelly
Bettye S. Elkins	Richard J. Landau
James P. Greene	Janet L. Neary
E. Edward Hood	Jack C. Radcliffe, Jr.
(Member in Charge)	Jonathan D. Rowe

Daniel J. Stephenson
RESIDENT ASSOCIATES

Laura M. Benitez	Kathleen A. Reed
Marie R. Deveney	Kasandra L. Richardson
Steven Marchese	Jeffrey N. Silveri
Andrew J. McGuinness	Bradley L. Smith

For full biographical listings, see the Martindale-Hubbell Law Directory

Garan, Lucow, Miller, Seward & Becker, P.C. (AV)

101 North Main Street, Suite 801, 48104-1400
Telephone: 313-930-5600
Fax: 313-930-0043
Detroit, Michigan Office: 1000 Woodbridge Place.
Telephone: 313-446-1530.
Fax: 313-259-0450.
Port Huron, Michigan Office: Port Huron Office Center, 511 Fort Street, Suite 505.
Telephone: 810-985-4400.
Fax: 810-985-4107.
Grand Blanc, Michigan Office: 8332 Office Park Drive.
Telephone: 810-695-3700.
Fax: 810-695-6488.
Troy, Michigan Office: 1111 West Long Lake Road, Suite 300.
Telephone: 810-641-7600.
Fax: 810-641-0222.
Mount Clemens, Michigan Office: Towne Square Development, 10 South Main Street, Suite 307.
Telephone: 810-954-3800:
Fax: 810-954-3803.
Grand Rapids, Michigan Office: Campau Square Plaza Building, 99 Monore Avenue N.W., Suite 102.
Telephone: 616-732-5330.
Fax: 616-732-5333.

Judith A. Moskus (Resident)

John W. Whitman (Resident)	John J. Koselka (Resident)

For full biographical listings, see the Martindale-Hubbell Law Directory

Hooper, Hathaway, Price, Beuche & Wallace (AV)

126 South Main Street, 48104
Telephone: 313-662-4426
Fax: 313-662-9559

Joseph C. Hooper (1899-1980)	Gregory A. Spaly
John R. Hathaway (Retired)	Robert W. Southard
Alan E. Price	William J. Stapleton
James R. Beuche	Bruce C. Conybeare, Jr.
Bruce T. Wallace	Anthony P. Patti
Charles W. Borgsdorf	Marcia J. Major
Mark R. Daane	Angela L. Jackson

OF COUNSEL

James A. Evashevski	Roderick K. Daane

Representative Clients: Chem-Trend, Inc.; Dundee Cement Co.; Ervin Industries, Inc.; First Martin Corp.; Group 243 Design, Inc.; Honeywell; Microwave Sensors, Inc.; Shearson Lehman Hutton; O'Neal Construction Co.; Pittsfield Products, Inc.

For full biographical listings, see the Martindale-Hubbell Law Directory

Miller, Canfield, Paddock and Stone, P.L.C. (AV)

A Professional Limited Liability Company
Founded in 1852 by Sidney Davy Miller
101 North Main Street, Seventh Floor, 48104-1400
Telephone: 313-663-2445
Fax: 313-747-7147
Detroit, Michigan Office: 150 West Jefferson, Suite 2500, 48226-4415.
Telephone: 313-963-6420.
Fax: 313-496-7500.
Cable Address: "Stem Detroit."
Bloomfield Hills, Michigan Office: Suite 100, Pinehurst Office Center, 1400 North Woodward, 48303-2014.
Telephone: 313-645-5000.
Fax: 313-645-1917.
Grand Rapids, Michigan Office: 1200 Campau Square Plaza, 99 Monroe, N.W., 49503-2639.
Telephone: 616-454-8656.
Fax: 616-776-6322.
Howell, Michigan Office: 121 South Barnard Street, Suite 4, 48843-2305.
Telephone: 517-546-7600.
Telecopier: 517-546-6974.

(See Next Column)

MILLER, CANFIELD, PADDOCK AND STONE P.L.C., *Ann Arbor—Continued*

Kalamazoo, Michigan Office: 444 West Michigan Avenue, 49007-3752.
Telephone: 616-381-7030.
Fax: 616-382-0244.
Lansing, Michigan Office: One Michigan Avenue, Suite 900, 48933-1609.
Telephone: 517-487-2070.
Fax: 517-374-6304.
Monroe, Michigan Office: The Executive Centre, 214 East Elm Avenue, 48161-2682.
Telephone: 313-243-2000.
Fax: 313-243-0901.
Washington, D.C. Office: 1225 Nineteenth Street, N.W., Suite 400. 20036.
Telephone: 202-429-5575; 785-0600.
Fax: 202-331-1118; 785-1234.
Pensacola, Florida Office: 25 West Cedar, 32501.
Telephone: 904-469-1088.
Fax: 904-432-0677.
St. Petersburg, Florida Office: 100 Second Avenue S., Suite 7045, 33701.
Telephone: 813-982-6000.
Fax: 813-892-6002.
New York, New York Office: Eleventh Floor, 135 East 57th Street, 10022-2087.
Telephone: 212-754-5400.
Fax: 212-754-5401.
Gdansk, Poland Office: Suite 322, Dom Technika Building, UI. Rajska 6, 80-850.
Telephone: 011-485-831-2808.
Fax: 011-485-831-4719.
Warsaw, Poland Office: UI. Marszalkowska 82, Suite 561, 00-517.
Telephone: 011-482-623-6457 and 6458.
Fax: 011-482-623-6459.

RESIDENT PRINCIPALS

Robert E. Gilbert	Timothy D. Sochocki
Orin D. Brustad	David A. French
Deborah W. Thompson	J. David Reck
Erik H. Serr	David N. Parsigian
Allyn D. Kantor	Charles A. Duerr, Jr.

Marta A. Manildi

OF COUNSEL

Edmond F. DeVine	John B. DeVine

William R. Kotila

SENIOR ATTORNEYS

Ronald D. Gardner	Douglas M. Kilbourne

RESIDENT ASSOCIATES

John O. Renken	Alice Censoplano
Diane Benedict Cabbell	Suzanne L. DeVine

Representative Firm Clients: Chrysler Corporation; Comerica, Incorporated; City of Detroit, Michigan; Detroit Tigers, Inc.; First of Michigan; Ford Motor Company; Ford Motor Credit Company; Great Lakes Bancorp; Henry Ford Hospital; INVETECH Company.

For full biographical listings, see the Martindale-Hubbell Law Directory

PEAR SPERLING EGGAN & MUSKOVITZ, P.C. (AV)

Domino's Farms, 24 Frank Lloyd Wright Drive, 48105
Telephone: 313-665-4441
Fax: 313-665-8788
Ypsilanti, Michigan Offices: 5 South Washington Street.
Telephone: 313-483-3626 and 2164 Bellevue at Washtenaw.
Telephone: 313-483-7177.

Edwin L. Pear	Joel F. Graziani
Lawrence W. Sperling	Paul R. Fransway
Andrew M. Eggan	Francyne Stacey
Melvin J. Muskovitz	Helen Conklin Vick
Thomas E. Daniels	Scott H. Mandel

David E. Kempner

Counsel for: Domino's Pizza, Inc.; Townsend and Bottum, Inc.; Cleary College; Victory Lane Quick Oil Change Inc.; Citizens Banking Corp.; Washtenaw News Co., Inc.; Ann Arbor Transportation Authority; Meadowbrook Insurance Group; Michigan Municipal Liability & Property Pool.
Approved Attorneys for: Lawyers Title Insurance Corp.

For full biographical listings, see the Martindale-Hubbell Law Directory

---

BAD AXE, * Huron Co. — (Refer to Port Huron)

BATTLE CREEK, Calhoun Co.

SULLIVAN, HAMILTON, SCHULZ, LETZRING, SIMONS, KRETER, TOTH & LEBEUF, P.C. (AV)

One West Michigan Avenue, 49017
Telephone: 616-965-3216
Fax: 616-965-2919

(See Next Column)

Maxwell B. Allen (1884-1942)	Bert W. Schulz
John M. Allen (1914-1985)	Kurt F. Letzring
Ronald H. Ryan (1901-1988)	Stephen L. Simons
Raymond R. Allen (1919-1996)	Mark E. Kreter
James M. Sullivan	Michael J. Toth

Ronald A. Lebeuf

OF COUNSEL

Robert P. Hamilton

General Counsel for: Michigan Woodwork and Specialties.
Local Counsel for: The Medical Protective Co.; Gannett, Inc.; Automobile Club of Michigan Insurance Group and Insurance Assn. (AAA); Michigan Physicians Mutual Liability Co.; State Farm Mutual Insurance Co.; Auto Owners Insurance Co.; Cincinnati Insurance Co.; Nationwide Insurance Co.

For full biographical listings, see the Martindale-Hubbell Law Directory

VARNUM, RIDDERING, SCHMIDT & HOWLETT LLP (AV)

A Limited Liability Partnership including Professional Corporations
4950 West Dickman Road, Suite B-1, 49015
Telephone: 616-962-7144
Email: varnum@vrsh.com
Grand Rapids, Michigan Office: Bridgewater Place, P.O. Box 352, 49501-0352.
Telephone: 616-336-6000; 800-262-0011.
Facsimile: 616-336-7000.
Telex: 1561593 VARN.
Lansing, Michigan Office: The Victor Center, Suite 810, 201 North Washington Square, 48933.
Telephone: 517-482-6237.
Facsimile: 517-482-6937.
Kalamazoo, Michigan Office: 350 East Michigan Avenue, 49007.
Telephone: 616-382-2300.
Facsimile: 616-382-2382.
Grand Haven, Michigan Office: 321 Washington Street, P.O. Box 288, 49417.
Telephone: 616-846-7100.
Facsimile: 616-846-7101.
Bingham Farms, Michigan Office: 31600 Telegraph Road, Suite 230, 48025.
Telephone: 810-594-7330.
Facsimile: 810-594-7331.

MEMBER OF FIRM

Carl E. Ver Beek

For full biographical listings, see the Martindale-Hubbell Law Directory

---

BAY CITY, * Bay Co.

BRAUN KENDRICK FINKBEINER PLC (AV)

201 Phoenix Building, P.O. Box 2039, 48708
Telephone: 517-895-8505
Telecopier: 517-895-8437
URL: http://www.bkf-law.com
Saginaw, Michigan Office: 101 N. Washington, Suite 812. 8th Floor Second National Bank Building.
Telephone: 517-753-3461.
Telecopier: 517-753-3951.
Ann Arbor, Michigan Office: 700 First National Building.
Telephone: 313-995-4100.
Telecopier: 313-995-4798.

Ralph J. Isackson	Gregory E. Meter
George F. Gronewold, Jr.	Daniel S. Opperman
Frank M. Quinn	Gregory T. Demers

Jeffrey C. Wilson

OF COUNSEL

Patrick D. Neering

Michael E. Wooley

Representative Clients: APV Chemical Machinery, Inc.; Bay Health Systems; Catholic Federal Credit Union; City of Saginaw; City of Vassar; City of Milwaukee; Corporate Service; Cox Cable.

For full biographical listings, see the Martindale-Hubbell Law Directory

SEWARD, TALLY & PIGGOTT, P.C. (AV)

1009 Washington Avenue, P.O. Box 795, 48707-0795
Telephone: 517-892-6551
Fax: 517-892-1568

B. J. Tally, Jr.	John M. Morosi
Webster C. Tally	Kenneth K. Wright
Mark J. Brissette	Lewis M. Seward

Barbara F. Livingston

(See Next Column)

SEWARD, TALLY & PIGGOTT P.C.—Continued

OF COUNSEL

John W. Grigg John W. Piggott

Representative Clients: Bay Medical Care Facility; Dunlop Pontiac; Euclid Tool & Machine; Williams Cheese Co.; General Housing Corp.; Bank of Alma; Commercial National Bank of Ithaca; Farmers State Bank; First of America Bank Michigan, N.A.

Reference: First of America Bank Michigan, N.A.

For full biographical listings, see the Martindale-Hubbell Law Directory

SMITH & BROOKER, P.C. (AV)

703 Washington Avenue, P.O. Box X-921, 48707-0921
Telephone: 517-892-2595
Fax: 517-893-5113
Saginaw, Michigan Office: The Gold Building, 4855 State Street, Suite 4.
Telephone: 517-799-1891.
Flint, Michigan Office: 1309 South Linden Road, Suite C, P.O. Box 315000.
Telephone: 810-733-0140.

Carl H. Smith (1898-1981)   James K. Brooker (1902-1973)

RESIDENT ATTORNEYS

Glenn F. Doyle   George B. Mullison
Richard C. Sheppard   Charles T. Hewitt

OF COUNSEL

Carl H. Smith, Jr.   Albert C. Hicks

Representative Clients: Allen Medical Building Co.; Charter Township of Hampton; CIGNA; Medical Protective Insurance Co.; Monitor Sugar Co.; Region VII Area Agency on Aging; State Farm Mutual Automobile Insurance Co.; Sterling Area Health Center; Medical Staff of Bay Medical Center; Secura Insurance.

For full biographical listings, see the Martindale-Hubbell Law Directory

BEULAH, * Benzie Co.

MURCHIE, CALCUTT & BOYNTON

(See Traverse City)

BIRMINGHAM, Oakland Co.

HYMAN AND LIPPITT, P.C. (AV)

185 Oakland Avenue, Suite 300, P.O. Box 1750, 48009
Telephone: 810-646-8292
Facsimile: 810-646-8375

J. Leonard Hyman   Kenneth F. Neuman
Norman L. Lippitt   Terry S. Givens
Douglas A. Hyman   Paul J. Fischer
Brian D. O'Keefe   John A. Sellers
H. Joel Newman   Robert H. Lippitt
Nazli G. Sater   Roger L. Myers
                David N. Morrell, Jr.

For full biographical listings, see the Martindale-Hubbell Law Directory

MILLER, CANFIELD, PADDOCK AND STONE, P.L.C.

(See Bloomfield Hills)

BLOOMFIELD HILLS, Oakland Co.

ADKISON NEED (AV)

1533 North Woodward Avenue, Suite 210, 48304
Telephone: 810-540-7400
Fax: 810-540-7401
Email: AdkisNeed@aol.com

MEMBERS OF FIRM

Phillip G. Adkison   Paul Green
Gregory K. Need   Kelly A. Allen
                Deborah M. Schneider
ASSOCIATES

Richard D. Kuhn, Jr.   Ann D. Christ
Kathryn N. Nichols   Laura B. Andoni

For full biographical listings, see the Martindale-Hubbell Law Directory

BUESSER, BUESSER, BLACK, LYNCH, FRYHOFF & GRAHAM, P.C. (AV)

505 North Woodward Avenue, Suite 1000, 48304
Telephone: 810-642-7880
Telecopier: 810-642-9319
Detroit, Michigan Office: Suite 1750, 100 Renaissance Center.
Telephone: 313-259-5220.

(See Next Column)

Frederick G. Buesser, Jr.   Michael J. Black
(1916-1993)   John L. Hopkins, Jr.
Charles E. Blank   L. James Wilson
William R. Buesser   Charles D. Brown
William O. Lynch   Maureen B. Connaughton
Timothy T. Fryhoff   Charles P. Barnes
Ronald F. Graham   Diane M. Buettner
                Ronald C. Paul

Representative Clients: Wayne County Medical Society; Frances P. Rhoades Memorial Foundation; Detroit Country Day School; Air-Way Manufacturing Co.; American States University Co.; Holiday Inns, Inc.; The Promus Companies Incorporated; Premo Pharmaceutical Co.; Citizens Insurance Co. of America; Michigan River Corp.

For full biographical listings, see the Martindale-Hubbell Law Directory

COLOMBO AND COLOMBO, P.C. (AV)

1500 Woodward Avenue, Suite 300, P.O. Box 2028, 48303-2028
Telephone: 810-645-9300
Facsimile: 810-645-5418

Louis J. Colombo   Lawrence F. Raniszeski
Louis J. Colombo, Jr.   Robert Y. Weller, II
(1911-1979)   Robert J. Lenihan, II
Frederick Colombo   Bernard P. Paige
Charles A. LeFevre   Michael J. O'Shaughnessy
John P. Hartwig   John B. Alfs

                Patrick J. Ennis
                OF COUNSEL
Russell E. Knister   David J. Wellman
Christine Kotenko Martin   James H. Hudnut
                Peter Leto (P.C.)
        LEGAL SUPPORT PERSONNEL
        Mary F. Galasso (Legal Administrator)

For full biographical listings, see the Martindale-Hubbell Law Directory

DICKINSON, WRIGHT, MOON, VAN DUSEN & FREEMAN (AV)

525 North Woodward Avenue, Suite 2000, 48304-2970
Telephone: 810-433-7200
Facsimile: 810-433-7274
Detroit, Michigan Office: 500 Woodward Avenue, Suite 4000.
Telephone: 313-223-3500.
Facsimile: 313-223-3598.
Grand Rapids, Michigan Office: 200 Ottawa Avenue, N.W., Suite 900.
Telephone: 616-458-1300.
Facsimile: 616-458-6753.
Lansing, Michigan Office: Suite 200, 215 South Washington Square.
Telephone: 517-371-1730.
Facsimile: 517-487-4700.
Washington, D.C. Office: Suite 800, 1901 L Street, N.W.
Telephone: 202-457-0160.
Facsimile: 202-659-1559.
Chicago, Illinois Office: 225 West Washington, Suite 400.
Telephone: 312-220-0300.
Facsimile: 312-220-0021.

PARTNERS

Johanna H. Armstrong   Mary Anne Kickham
David R. Bruegel   Robert A. LaBelle
Maureen H. Burke   Linda S. McAlpine
Robert E. Carr   Cynthia A. Moore
Charles F. Clippert   Zan M. Nicolli
Margaret A. Coughlin   John H. Norris
Roger H. Cummings   Edward H. Pappas
Stephen E. Dawson   Richard W. Paul
Joseph W. DeLave   Eric J. Pelton
Sherisse Eddy Fiorvento   Robert V. Peterson
Judith E. Gowing   Elizabeth M. Pezzetti
Deborah L. Grace   Ward Randol, Jr.
Henry M. Grix   Christopher L. Rizik
Elizabeth Phelps Hardy   Douglas D. Roche
Charles T. Harris   Larry J. Stringer
                Margaret Van Meter
                OF COUNSEL
Paul T. Fitzpatrick   Bethany E. Hawkins
(Not admitted in MI)   Douglas L. Mann
                Thomas D. McLennan
RESIDENT ASSOCIATES

Terrence A. Barr   Robert B. Hotchkiss
Julia Turner Baumhart   Kelli L. Kerbawy
Jeffrey J. Brown   Thomas H. Kosik
Cynthia L. Della Torre   Judith Fertel Layne
Julie T. Emerick   Ola B. Najar
Sara Anne Engle   John T. Panourgias
Peter G. Golden   Gregory J. Parry
Nanci J. Grant   Marian Keidan Seltzer
                Linda J. Truitt

For full biographical listings, see the Martindale-Hubbell Law Directory

Bloomfield Hills—Continued

DYKEMA GOSSETT PLLC (AV)

1577 North Woodward Avenue Suite 300, 48304-2820
Telephone: 810-540-0700
Telex: 23-0121
Fax: 810-540-0763
Email: 2084153@mcimail.com
Ann Arbor, Michigan Office: 315 East Eisenhower Parkway, Suite 100, 48108-3306.
Telephone: 313-747-7660.
Fax: 313-747-7696.
Chicago, Illinois Office: 55 East Monroe Street, Suite 3250, 60603-5709.
Telephone: 312-551-4900.
Fax: 312-551-4919.
Detroit, Michigan Office: 400 Renaissance Center, 48243-1668.
Telephone: 313-568-6800.
Fax: 313-568-6594.
Grand Rapids, Michigan Office: 200 Oldtown Riverfront Building, 248 Louis Campau Promenade, N.W., 49503-2668.
Telephone: 616-776-7500.
Fax: 616-776-7573.
Lansing, Michigan Office: 800 Michigan National Tower, 48933-1707.
Telephone: 517-374-9100.
Fax: 517-374-9191.
Washington, D.C. Office: Franklin Square, Suite 300 West, 1300 I Street, N.W., 20005-3306.
Telephone: 202-522-8600.
Fax: 202-522-8669.

RESIDENT MEMBERS

Maria B. Abrahamsen	Robert L. Kelly
Robert A. Berlow	Gregory M. Kopacz
Bowden V. Brown	Stuart D. Logan
B. Kingsley Buhl	Howard N. Luckoff
Robert L. Duty	D. Richard McDonald
Fred J. Fechheimer	William T. Myers
Dennis M. Gannan	James D. Obermanns
Barbara L. Goldman	Marilyn A. Peters
Alan M. Greene	Ronald L. Rose
Dennis M. Haffey	Mary Elizabeth Royce
(Member in Charge)	Charles R. Rutherford
Craig L. John	Rex E. Schlaybaugh, Jr.
Louis W. Kasischke	Thomas B. Spillane, Jr.

Mark H. Sutton

OF COUNSEL

Gerald R. Black	Donald E. Shely
	John J. Slavin

RESIDENT ASSOCIATES

Brendan J. Cahill	Gerald T. Lievois
Donald M. Crawford	Andrew W. Mayoras
Hugo A. Delevie	Kevin G. Mierzwa
Douglas J. Fryer	Karen R. Pifer
Kimberly A. Gough	John W. Rees
Joseph H. Hickey	Laurence D. Rich
Kevin M. Hinman	Catherine Kim Shierk

Michael Tucker

For full biographical listings, see the Martindale-Hubbell Law Directory

FEENEY KELLETT WIENNER & BUSH, PROFESSIONAL CORPORATION (AV)

950 North Hunter Boulevard, Second Floor, 48304-3927
Telephone: 810-258-1580
Fax: 810-258-0421

James P. Feeney	Cheryl A. Bush
S. Thomas Wienner	Deborah F. Collins
Peter M. Kellett	David N. Goltz

OF COUNSEL

Thomas J. Manganello

James J. Majernik	Seth D. Gould
G. Gregory Schuetz	Patrick G. Seyferth
Jeffrey A. Gallant	Mark A. Fisher

Bryan D. Cross

For full biographical listings, see the Martindale-Hubbell Law Directory

HOWARD & HOWARD ATTORNEYS, P.C. (AV)

The Pinehurst Office Center, Suite 101, 1400 North Woodward Avenue, 48304-2856
Telephone: 810-645-1483
Telecopier: 810-645-1568
Kalamazoo, Michigan Office: The Kalamazoo Building, Suite 400, 107 West Michigan Avenue.
Telephone: 616-382-1483.
Telecopier: 616-382-1568.

(See Next Column)

Lansing, Michigan Office: The Phoenix Building, Suite 500, 222 Washington Square, North.
Telephone: 517-485-1483.
Telecopier: 517-485-1568.
Peoria, Illinois Office: The Creve Coeur Building, Suite 200, 321 Liberty Street.
Telephone: 309-672-1483.
Telecopier: 309-672-1568.
Tampa, Florida Office: First of America Plaza, Suite 2000, 201 East Kennedy Boulevard.
Telephone: 813-229-1483.
Telecopier: 813-229-1568.

Gustaf R. Andreasen	Timothy E. Kraepel
Robin W. Asher	Howard A. Lax
William G. Asimakis, Jr.	D. Craig Martin
Daniel L. Baker	Patrick M. McCarthy
Antoinette Beuche	Harold W. Milton, Jr.
Tammy L. Brown	Robert D. Mollhagen
John E. Carlson	Theodore W. Olds III
Philip T. Carter	Susan E. Padley
Christopher A. Chekan	Gary A. Peters
Kevin M. Chudler	Dorene M. Price
William J. Clemens	Roshunda L. Price-Harper
Michael G. Cruse	Jeffrey G. Raphelson
Thomas R. Curran, Jr.	Brad A. Rayle
Chris T. Danikolas	Brian J. Renaud
Charles E. Dunn	Robert C. Rosselot
Sally Lee Foley	(Not admitted in MI)
Carol A. Friend	Robert L. Schwartz
David J. Gaskey	Raymond E. Scott
Roger M. Groves	Jon E. Shackelford
John G. Hayward	Todd M. Stenerson
William H. Honaker	Thomas J. Tallerico
Robert B. Johnston	Laura A. Talt
J. Michael Kemp	Donald F. Tucker
Daniel N. King	Melanie Mayo West
Jon H. Kingsepp	James C. Wickens
Steven C. Kohl	John E. Young

Marla Gottlieb Zwas

Representative Clients: First of America Bank Corporation; W.R. Grace & Co.; Chrysler Corp.; Indian Head Industries; Coopers & Lybrand; Champion International.

For full biographical listings, see the Martindale-Hubbell Law Directory

MEYER, KIRK, SNYDER & SAFFORD, PLLC (AV)

Suite 100, 100 West Long Lake Road, 48304
Telephone: 810-647-5111
Telecopier: 810-647-6079
Detroit, Michigan Office: 2500 Penobscot Building.
Telephone: 313-961-1261.

George H. Meyer	Ralph R. Safford
John M. Kirk	Patrick K. Rode
George E. Snyder	Donald H. Baker, Jr.

Christopher F. Clark	Boyd C. Farnam
	Debra S. Meier

OF COUNSEL

Mark R. Solomon

Representative Clients: Available Upon Request.

For full biographical listings, see the Martindale-Hubbell Law Directory

MILLER, CANFIELD, PADDOCK AND STONE, P.L.C. (AV)

A Professional Limited Liability Company
Founded in 1852 by Sidney Davy Miller
Suite 100 Pinehurst Office Center, 1400 North Woodward, P.O. Box 2014, 48303-2014
Telephone: 810-645-5000
Fax: 810-645-1917
Fax: 810-258-3036
Detroit, Michigan Office: 150 West Jefferson, Suite 2500, 48226-4415.
Telephone: 313-963-6420.
Fax: 313-496-7500.
Cable Address: "Stem Detroit."
Ann Arbor, Michigan Office: 101 North Main Street, 7th Floor, 48104-1400.
Telephone: 313-663-2445.
Fax: 313-747-7147.
Grand Rapids, Michigan Office: 1200 Campau Square Plaza, 99 Monroe, N.W., 49503-2639.
Telephone: 616-454-8656.
Fax: 616-776-6322.
Howell, Michigan Office: 121 South Barnard Street, Suite 4, 48843-2305.
Telephone: 517-546-7600.
Fax: 517-546-6974.
Kalamazoo, Michigan Office: 444 West Michigan Avenue, 49007-3752.
Telephone: 616-381-7030.
Fax: 616-382-0244.

(See Next Column)

MILLER, CANFIELD, PADDOCK AND STONE P.L.C.—*Continued*

Lansing, Michigan Office: One Michigan Avenue, Suite 900, 48933-1609.
Telephone: 517-487-2070.
Fax: 517-374-6304.
Monroe, Michigan Office: The Executive Centre, 214 East Elm Avenue,
48161-2682.
Telephone: 313-243-2000.
Fax: 313-243-0901.
Washington, D.C. Office: 1225 Nineteenth Street, N.W., Suite 400. 20036.
Telephone: 202-429-5575; 785-0600.
Fax: 202-331-1118; 785-1234.
Pensacola, Florida Office: 25 West Cedar, 32501.
Telephone: 904-469-1088.
Fax: 904-432-0677.
St. Petersburg, Florida Office: 100 Second Avenue S., Suite 7045, 33701.
Telephone: 813-982-6000.
Fax: 813-892-6002.
New York, New York Office: Eleventh Floor, 135 East 57th Street,
10022-2087.
Telephone: 212-754-5400.
Fax: 212-754-5401.
Gdansk, Poland Office: Suite 322, Dom Technika Building, UI. Rajska 6,
80-850.
Telephone: 011-485-831-2808.
Fax: 011-485-831-4719.
Warsaw, Poland Office: UI. Marszalkowska 82, Suite 561, 00-517.
Telephone: 011-482-623-6457 and 6458.
Fax: 011-482-623-6459.

RESIDENT PRINCIPALS

Lawrence A. King (P.C.)	John J. Collins, Jr.
John W. Gelder	Stephen G. Palms
John A. Thurber (P.C.)	Frank L. Andrews
John A. Marxer (P.C.)	J. Kevin Trimmer
Kenneth E. Konop	Thomas G. Appleman
Ronald H. Riback	Gregory V. Di Censo
James W. Williams	Brad B. Arbuckle

Ronald E. Hodess

RESIDENT OF COUNSEL

Henry R. Nolte, Jr.

RESIDENT ASSOCIATES

Dawn M. Schluter	Lisa D. Pick
Sally A. Hamby	Anna M. Maiuri

Representative Firm Clients: Chrysler Corporation; Comerica, Incorporated; City of Detroit, Michigan; Detroit Tigers, Inc.; First of Michigan; Ford Motor Company; Ford Motor Credit Company; Great Lakes Bancorp; Henry Ford Hospital; INVETECH Company.

For full biographical listings, see the Martindale-Hubbell Law Directory

---

CADILLAC,* Wexford Co.

MURCHIE, CALCUTT & BOYNTON

(See Traverse City)

CASSOPOLIS,* Cass Co. — (Refer to Niles)

CHARLEVOIX,* Charlevoix Co.

MURCHIE, CALCUTT & BOYNTON

(See Traverse City)

CHARLOTTE,* Eaton Co. — (Refer to Lansing)

CORUNNA,* Shiawassee Co. — (Refer to Flint)

DETROIT,* Wayne Co.

BODMAN, LONGLEY & DAHLING LLP (AV)

34th Floor 100 Renaissance Center, 48243
Telephone: 313-259-7777
Fax: 313-393-7579
Email: 2080194@mcimail.com
Troy, Michigan Office: Suite 2020, 755 West Big Beaver Road.
Telephone: 810-362-2110.
Fax: 810-244-0780.
Ann Arbor, Michigan Office: 110 Miller, Suite 300.
Telephone: 313-761-3780.
Fax: 313-930-2494.
Northern Michigan Office: 229 Court Street, P.O. Box 405, Cheboygan.
Telephone: 616-627-4351.
Fax: 616-627-2802.

MEMBERS OF FIRM

Henry E. Bodman (1874-1963)	Alfred C. Wortley, Jr.
Clifford B. Longley (1888-1954)	Michael B. Lewiston
Louis F. Dahling (1892-1992)	George D. Miller, Jr.
Pierre V. Heftler	Mark W. Griffin
Richard D. Rohr	(Ann Arbor Office)
Theodore Souris	Thomas A. Roach
Joseph A. Sullivan	(Ann Arbor Office)
Carson C. Grunewald	Kenneth R. Lango (Troy Office)
Walter O. Koch (Troy Office)	James T. Heimbuch

(See Next Column)

MEMBERS OF FIRM (Continued)

Herold McC. Deason	Harvey W. Berman
James A. Smith	(Ann Arbor Office)
James R. Buschmann	Barbara Bowman Bluford
George G. Kemsley	R. Craig Hupp
Joseph N. Brown	Lawrence P. Hanson
David M. Hempstead	(Northern Michigan Office)
Joseph J. Kochanek	Christopher J. Dine
Randolph S. Perry	(Troy Office)
James J. Walsh	Henry N. Carnaby (Troy Office)
David G. Chardavoyne	Jerold Lax (Ann Arbor Office)
David W. Hipp	Linda J. Throne
Robert G. Brower	(Northern Michigan Office)
Larry R. Shulman	Diane L. Akers
Charles N. Raimi	Ralph E. McDowell
Terrence B. Larkin (Troy Office)	Susan M. Kornfield
Thomas Van Dusen	(Ann Arbor Office)
(Troy Office)	Stephen I. Greenhalgh
Fredrick J. Dindoffer	Kathleen O'C. Hickey
Robert J. Diehl, Jr.	Patrick C. Cauley
John C. Cashen (Troy Office)	Dennis J. Levasseur
James C. Conboy, Jr.	David P. Larsen
(Northern Michigan Office)	Kay E. Malaney (Troy Office)
Lloyd C. Fell	Gail Pabarue Bennett
(Northern Michigan Office)	Gary D. Reeves (Troy Office)
F. Thomas Lewand	Barnett Jay Colvin
Michael A. Stack	David W. Barton
(Northern Michigan Office)	(Northern Michigan Office)
Kathleen A. Lieder	Sandra L. Sorini
(Northern Michigan Office)	(Ann Arbor Office)
Karen L. Piper	Stephen K. Postema
Martha Bedsole Goodloe	(Ann Arbor Office)
(Troy Office)	

COUNSEL

Robert A. Nitschke	Lewis A. Rockwell
John S. Dobson	
(Ann Arbor Office)	

ASSOCIATES

Bonnie S. Sherr	Andrew Z. Spilkin
Laurie A. Allen (Troy Office)	Sarah Heisler Gidley
Marc M. Bakst	Michael J. Laramie
Jodee Fishman Raines	David L. Kasper (Troy Office)
Nicholas P. Scavone, Jr.	Cortney E. Goldberg
Deanna L. Dixon	John G. Grzybek
W. Allen De Young	Amy J. Durant
(Northern Michigan Office)	(Cheboygan Office)
Mary A. Kosmalski	Andrew H. Curoe
Christian W. Fabian	(Not admitted in MI)
Jane Henderson Marshall	Courtland W. Anderson
Timothy R. Damschroder	(Ann Arbor Office)
(Ann Arbor Office)	Paul R. Bernard
David A. Shand	(Not admitted in MI)
(Ann Arbor Office)	John P. Hale
Laurie E. Phelan	James D. Lewis
Laura M. Napiewocki	(Ann Arbor Office)

REGULATORY CONSULTANT

Becky D. Kelly (Northern Michigan Office)

Representative Clients: Archdiocese of Detroit; Comerica Bank; The Detroit Lions, Inc.; Ford Estates; General Motors Corporation; Charles Stewart Mott Foundation; Norfolk Southern Corporation; Panhandle Eastern Corporation; State Farm Mutual Automobile Insurance Company.

For full biographical listings, see the Martindale-Hubbell Law Directory

---

BOOTHMAN, HEBERT & ELLER, P.C. (AV)

Marquette Building, 243 West Congress, Suite 950, 48226
Telephone: 313-964-0150
Fax: 313-964-2226
Ann Arbor, Michigan Office: 300 N. Fifth Avenue, Suite 140.
Telephone: 313-995-9050.
Fax: 313-995-8966.

Dale L. Hebert	Gary S. Eller
Richard C. Boothman	
(Resident, Ann Arbor Office)	

George D. Moustakas	Marta J. Hoffman
Roy A. Luttmann	Sharon E. Hollins

Joyce E. Taylor

OF COUNSEL

L. Stewart Hastings, Jr.	Kathryn A. Kerka

Representative Clients: University of Michigan; Michigan Physicians Mutual Liability Co.; Emergency Physicians Medical Group; Kaiser Permanente; Physicians Insurance Co. of Michigan.
Reference: Comerica Bank-Detroit.

For full biographical listings, see the Martindale-Hubbell Law Directory

Detroit—Continued

BRADY HATHAWAY, PROFESSIONAL CORPORATION (AV)

1330 Buhl Building, 48226-3602
Telephone: 313-965-3700
Telecopier: 313-965-2830

John F. Brady	Daniel J. Bretz
Thomas M. J. Hathaway	Liliana A. Ciccodicola
Thomas P. Brady	Connie M. Cessante

OF COUNSEL

James A. Hathaway	Ingrid K. Brey

Representative Clients: Beam Stream, Inc.; Bundy Tubing Company; Energy Conversion Devices, Inc.; Schering Corporation; Warner-Lambert; Wolverine Technologies; ABB Environmental Services; GMIS, Inc.; Marriott Corp.

For full biographical listings, see the Martindale-Hubbell Law Directory

BUTZEL LONG, A PROFESSIONAL CORPORATION (AV)

Suite 900, 150 West Jefferson, 48226
Telephone: 313-225-7000
Telecopier: 313-225-7080
Email: melnick @ butzel.com *URL:* http://www.butzel.com
Birmingham, Michigan Office: Suite 200, 32270 Telegraph Road.
Telephone: 810-258-1616.
Telecopier: 810-258-1439.
Lansing, Michigan Office: 118 West Ottawa Street.
Telephone: 517-372-6622.
Telecopier: 517-372-6672.
Ann Arbor, Michigan Office: Suite 300, 350 South Main Street.
Telephone: 313-995-3110.
Telecopier: 313-995-1777.
Grosse Pointe Farms, Michigan Office: Suite 260, 21 Kercheval.
Telephone: 313-886-5446.
Telecopier: 313-886-2114.

Leo M. Butzel (1874-1961)	Keefe A. Brooks
Thomas G. Long (1883-1973)	Justin G. Klimko
William M. Saxton	Michael D. Guzick
Harold A. Ruemenapp	(Birmingham)
Stephen A. Bromberg	James E. Wynne
(Birmingham)	Michael J. Lavoie
Morris Milmet (Birmingham)	Michael F. Golab (Birmingham)
Robert J. Battista	Edward M. Kalinka
Frank B. Vecchio (Birmingham)	(Birmingham)
Allan Nachman (Birmingham)	Gordon J. Walker (Birmingham)
William R. Ralls (Lansing)	James L. Hughes
Xhafer Orhan	Arthur Dudley II
George H. Zinn, Jr.	E. William S. Shipman
C. Peter Theut	Richard P. Saslow
William H. Dance	Gordon W. Didier (Birmingham)
John H. Dudley, Jr.	Dennis K. Egan
Richard E. Rassel	Bruce L. Sendek
Abba I. Friedman (Birmingham)	Terry O. Lang
Edward D. Gold (Birmingham)	Steven D. Weyhing (Lansing)
Robert B. Foster (Ann Arbor)	Lynne E. Deitch
Paul L. Triemstra (Birmingham)	Daniel B. Tukel
Jack D. Shumate (Birmingham)	Marissa W. Pollick (Ann Arbor)
Edward M. Kronk	Alan S. Levine (Birmingham)
Philip J. Kessler	Leonard M. Niehoff
Thomas E. Sizemore	(Ann Arbor)
Donald B. Miller	Carey A. DeWitt
John P. Hancock, Jr.	David H. Oermann
James E. Stewart	(Birmingham)
Frederick G. Buesser, III	James Y. Stewart (Birmingham)
(Birmingham)	Eric J. Flessland (Birmingham)
Leonard F. Charla	Lynn Abraham Sheehy
T. Gordon Scupholm II	Robert A. Boonin
(Birmingham)	Sheldon H. Klein
James C. Bruno	Andrea Roumell Dickson
David W. Sommerfeld	Melvin J. Hollowell, Jr.
(Birmingham and Grosse	J. Michael Huget (Ann Arbor)
Pointe Farms)	Anthony J. Saulino, Jr.
Thomas B. Radom	(Birmingham)
(Birmingham)	James S. Rosenfeld
David W. Berry (Birmingham)	Clara DeMatteis Mager
Carl Rashid, Jr.	Patrick A. Karbowski
D. Stewart Green (Birmingham)	(Birmingham)
Dennis B. Schultz	Ronald E. Reynolds
Mark T. Nelson	(Birmingham)
Daniel P. Malone	Kenneth H. Adamczyk
Jordan S. Schreier (Ann Arbor)	

COUNSEL

Oscar H. Feldman (Birmingham)	David F. DuMouchel

INTERNATIONAL PRACTICE ADVISOR

Akira Hara (Not admitted United States)

CONSULTING COUNSEL

Douglas G. Graham	John P. Williams
(Grosse Pointe Farms)	John B. Weaver

(See Next Column)

OF COUNSEL

George E. Brand, Jr.	John J. Kuhn
Sidney L. Cohn (Birmingham)	William A. Penner, Jr.
Darlene M. Domanik	Robin S. Phillips (Ann Arbor)
David M. Gaskin	Erwin S. Simon
(Grosse Pointe Farms)	Malcolm J. Sutherland

Katherine B. Albrecht	Lois Elizabeth Bingham
(Birmingham)	Sherri A. Krause
David K. Tillman	Robin K. Luce
Phillip C. Korovesis	Patricia E. Nessel (Birmingham)
Barbara T. Pichan	Barbara L. McQuade
Richard T. Hewlett	Laurie J. Michelson
Robert P. Perry (Birmingham)	Herbert C. Donovan
Nicholas J. Stasevich	Caridad Pastor-Klucens
Susan Klein Friedlaender	Timothy E. Galligan
(Birmingham)	Wendel Vincent Hall (Lansing)
James J. Urban (Lansing)	Joseph M. Rogowski, II
Leland R. Rosier (Lansing)	Priscilla J. Krebs
Daniel R. W. Rustmann	John C. Blattner (Ann Arbor)
Eugene H. Boyle, Jr.	Antoinette M. Pilzner
Debra Auerbach Clephane	Laurie Callahan Endsley
Timothy M. Labadie	James A. Gray, III
Paul S. Lewandowski	Tammy L. Hussin (Lansing)
Susan Hartmus Hiser	James P. Allen
Elizabeth A. DuMouchelle	Pamela A. Zauel (Ann Arbor)
Robert E. Norton II	James F. Gehrke
James J. Giszczak	Brett D. Pynnonen

Representative Clients: Bridgestone/Firestone, Inc.; Detroit Diesel Corp.; The Detroit News, Inc.; Kelly Services; Kelsey Hayes Co.; Merrill Lynch Pierce Fenner & Smith, Inc.; Stroh Brewery Co.; Takata Corp.; United Parcel Services of America, Inc.; The University of Michigan.

For full biographical listings, see the Martindale-Hubbell Law Directory

CLARK HILL P.L.C. (AV)

500 Woodward Avenue, Suite 3500, 48226
Telephone: 313-965-8300
Facsimile: 313-962-4348
Oakland County, Michigan Office: Third Floor, 255 South Woodward Avenue, Birmingham.
Telephone: 810-642-9692.
Facsimile: 810-642-2174.
Lansing, Michigan Office: Suite 600, 200 North Capitol Avenue.
Telephone: 517-484-4481.
Facsimile: 517-484-1246.
Minneapolis, Minnesota Office: Suite 1000, One Financial Plaza, 120 South Sixth Street.
Telephone: 612-332-0102.
Facsimile: 612-332-3225.
Kansas City, Missouri Office: Suite 1400, Bryant Building, 1102 Grand Avenue.
Telephone: 816-221-5578.
Facsimile: 816-221-0303.

David P. Wood	David H. Paruch (Resident,
Robert B. Webster (Resident,	Oakland County Office)
Oakland County Office)	Dennis G. Bonucchi
George N. Bashara, Jr.	Frank T. Mamat
Laurence M. Scoville, Jr.	Robert A. W. Strong
William B. Dunn	James E. Baiers
J. Walker Henry	Kevin S. Hendrick
Douglas J. Rasmussen	Charles H. Polzin (Resident,
Douglas H. West	Oakland County Office)
Hanley M. Gurwin (Resident,	William A. Moore
Oakland County Office)	Wendy L. Potts (Resident,
D. Kerry Crenshaw	Oakland County Office)
Timothy W. Mast (Resident,	Louis J. Porter
Oakland County Office)	(Resident, Lansing Office)
Timothy D. Wittlinger	Duane L. Tarnacki
(Resident, Oakland County	Daniel J. Scully, Jr.
Office)	Michael S. Khoury
Ralph H. Houghton, Jr.	Peter A. Jackson
David M. Hayes	Joseph A. Bonventre
Thomas F. Sweeney (Resident,	Timothy M. Koltun
Oakland County Office)	Michael G. Cumming
Robert G. Buydens	Michael J. Sullivan
J. Thomas Lenga	Rachelle G. Silberberg
Richard C. Marsh	Cynthia L.M. Johnson
John F. Burns	Daniel H. Minkus (Resident,
James E. Brenner	Oakland County Office)
Fred W. Batten	Kevin M. Bernys (Resident,
Roderick S. Coy	Oakland County Office)
(Resident, Lansing Office)	LaVern A. Pritchard
P. Robert Brown, Jr.	(Resident, Minneapolis Office)
Robert L. Weyhing, III	David M. Lawson (Resident,
David E. Nims, III	Oakland County Office)
Thomas S. Nowinski	Margaret Carroll Alli (Resident,
Richard C. Sanders	Oakland County Office)
Robert W. Morgan	John J. Hern, Jr.

(See Next Column)

CLARK HILL P.L.C.—*Continued*

Dorothy Hanigan Basmaji
(Resident, Oakland County
Office)
Charles G. Goedert (Resident,
Oakland County Office)
Paul E. Scheidemantel
J. Thomas MacFarlane
(Resident, Oakland County
Office)

Edward C. Hammond
John E. Berg
Andrea M. Kanski
Thomas M. Dixon
Judith Greenstone Miller
Edward J. Hood
Elizabeth Jolliffe Basten

COUNSEL
Charles M. Bayer

SENIOR ATTORNEYS

A. David Baumhart, III
(Resident, Oakland County
Office)

David A. Vorbeck
(Resident, Kansas City Office)
Mark W. McInerney

OF COUNSEL

John C. Donnelly
Leonard W. Smith
Martin C. Oetting

Lee B. Durham, Jr. (Resident,
Oakland County Office)
Dwight H. Vincent

Amy A. Stawski (Resident,
Oakland County Office)
Neysa L. Day
(Resident, Kansas City Office)
John M. Ketcham
Michael I. Conlon
Kevin H. Breck (Resident,
Oakland County Office)
Kay Rivest Butler
Patricia Bordman
Marsha Kay Nettles
Robin D. Ferriby
Kerry A. Anderson
Katrina I. Crawley
Bernard T. Lourim
David A. Breuch
Patrice Asimakis
Stewart A. Binke
(Resident, Lansing Office)
Mary Ray Brophy (Resident,
Oakland County Office)

Stephen J. Videto
(Resident, Lansing Office)
Mary C. Dirkes
Georgette Borrego Dulworth
Teresa J. Kimker
(Resident, Minneapolis Office)
Jennifer Crawford
M. Maureen McHugh
Jeffrey A. Schultz
John P. Hensien
Gerald E. Szpotek, Jr.
Michael F. Smith
Donald F. Berschback, II
Louise B. Sable
Kathleen M. Deegan
David Scott Mendelson
(Resident, Oakland County
Office)
Christopher A. McMican
Amy Malone
Joseph A. Ciucci

Margery Siegel Klausner

For full biographical listings, see the Martindale-Hubbell Law Directory

DICKINSON, WRIGHT, MOON, VAN DUSEN & FREEMAN (AV)

500 Woodward Avenue, Suite 4000, 48226-3425
Telephone: 313-223-3500
Facsimile: 313-223-3598
Bloomfield Hills, Michigan Office: 525 North Woodward Avenue, Suite
2000.
Telephone: 810-433-7200.
Facsimile: 810-433-7274.
Grand Rapids, Michigan Office: 200 Ottawa Avenue, N.W., Suite 900.
Telephone: 616-458-1300.
Facsimile: 616-458-6753.
Lansing, Michigan Office: Suite 200, 215 South Washington Square.
Telephone: 517-371-1730.
Facsimile: 517-487-4700.
Washington, D.C. Office: Suite 800, 1901 L Street, N.W.
Telephone: 202-457-0160.
Facsimile: 202-659-1559.
Chicago, Illinois Office: 225 West Washington, Suite 400.
Telephone: 312-220-0300.
Facsimile: 312-220-0021.

Selden S. Dickinson (1892-1964)
Edward P. Wright (1894-1962)

Richard C. Van Dusen
(1925-1991)

MEMBERS OF FIRM

Johanna H. Armstrong
(Bloomfield Hills Office)
George R. Ashford
William C. Bertrand, Jr.
(Lansing Office)
James W. Bliss (Lansing Office)
Richard M. Bolton
Andrew S. Boyce
Richard L. Braun, II
David R. Bruegel
(Bloomfield Hills Office)
William T. Burgess
Maureen H. Burke
(Bloomfield Hills Office)
Lawrence G. Campbell
James N. Candler, Jr.
Robert E. Carr
(Bloomfield Hills Office)
Stuart F. Cheney
(Grand Rapids Office)

Conrad J. Clark
(Washington, D.C. Office)
Charles F. Clippert
(Bloomfield Hills Office)
Margaret A. Coughlin
(Bloomfield Hills Office)
Roger H. Cummings
(Bloomfield Hills Office)
Michael S. Daar
Julia Donovan Darlow
Stephen E. Dawson
(Bloomfield Hills Office)
Joseph W. DeLave
(Bloomfield Hills Office)
David R. Deromedi
Terence M. Donnelly
Dwight D. Ebaugh
(Lansing Office)
Peter H. Ellsworth
(Lansing Office)

(See Next Column)

MEMBERS OF FIRM (Continued)

William E. Elwood
(Washington, D.C. Office)
Barbara Hughes Erard
John A. Everhardus
Joseph A. Fink (Lansing Office)
Sherisse Eddy Fiorvento
(Bloomfield Hills Office)
William J. Fisher, III
(Grand Rapids Office)
Richard A. Glaser
(Grand Rapids Office)
Daniel F. Gosch
(Chicago, Illinois Office)
Judith E. Gowing
(Bloomfield Hills Office)
Kirk E. Grable (Lansing Office)
Deborah L. Grace
(Bloomfield Hills Office)
Ronald B. Grais
(Chicago, Illinois Office)
Martin L. Greenberg
(Chicago, Illinois Office)
Henry M. Grix
(Bloomfield Hills Office)
K. Scott Hamilton
Michael C. Hammer
Thomas D. Hammerschmidt, Jr.
Craig W. Hammond
Verne C. Hampton, II
Elizabeth Phelps Hardy
(Bloomfield Hills Office)
Charles T. Harris
(Bloomfield Hills Office)
Stephen S. Herseth
(Chicago, Illinois Office)
Mark R. High
Steven H. Hilfinger
Edgar C. Howbert (Detroit,
Michigan and Chicago, Illinois
Offices)
Timothy H. Howlett
Robert P. Hurlbert
(Chicago, Illinois Office)
Maurice G. Jenkins
W. Anthony Jenkins
Jerry L. Johnson
Mary Elizabeth Kelly
Mary Anne Kickham
(Bloomfield Hills Office)
Thomas G. Kienbaum
Robert S. Krause
John A. Krsul, Jr.
Robert A. LaBelle
(Bloomfield Hills Office)
Kathleen A. Lang
John K. Lawrence
Patrick J. Ledwidge
Keith J. Lerminiaux
Carl D. Liggio, Sr.
(Chicago, Illinois Office)
Samuel D. Littlepage
(Washington, D.C. Office)
Joseph C. Marshall, III
Noel D. Massie
Linda S. McAlpine
(Bloomfield Hills Office)
Kenneth J. McIntyre
Russell A. McNair, Jr.
Thomas G. McNeill
Richard D McNulty
(Lansing Office)
Creighton R. Meland, Jr.
(Chicago, Illinois Office)
Richard J. Meyers
Cynthia A. Moore
(Bloomfield Hills Office)

Steven C. Nadeau
Sharon R. Newlon
Zan M. Nicolli
(Bloomfield Hills Office)
John H. Norris
(Bloomfield Hills Office)
James Gavan O'Connor
(Grand Rapids Office)
Theodore R. Opperwall
Dustin P. Ordway
(Grand Rapids Office)
Francis R. Ortiz
Edward H. Pappas
(Bloomfield Hills Office)
Richard W. Paul
(Bloomfield Hills Office)
Eric J. Pelton
(Bloomfield Hills Office)
Robert V. Peterson
(Bloomfield Hills Office)
Jeffrey M. Petrash
(Washington, D.C. Office)
Elizabeth M. Pezzetti
(Bloomfield Hills Office)
David E. Pierson
(Lansing Office)
Michael T. Platt
(Washington, D.C. Office)
James A. Plemmons
Michael S. Poulos
(Chicago, Illinois Office)
Robert W. Powell
Ward Randol, Jr.
(Bloomfield Hills Office)
Claudia Rast
Mark K. Riashi
Christopher L. Rizik
(Bloomfield Hills Office)
Douglas D. Roche
(Bloomfield Hills Office)
James A. Samborn
Jerome M. Schwartz
Susan J. Schwartz
(Chicago, Illinois Office)
John E. S. Scott
Peter S. Sheldon
(Lansing Office)
Daniel James Sheridan
(Chicago, Illinois Office)
Colleen M. Shevnock
William P. Shield, Jr.
Kester K. So (Lansing Office)
Herbert G. Sparrow, III
Jon Robert Steiger
(Chicago, Illinois Office)
Larry J. Stringer
(Bloomfield Hills Office)
Jeffery V. Stuckey
(Lansing Office)
John L. Teeples
(Grand Rapids Office)
Bruce C. Thelen
Margaret Van Meter
(Bloomfield Hills Office)
Michael Gary Vartanian
Richard A. Wendt
Richard A. Wilhelm
J. Bryan Williams
Rock A. Wood
(Grand Rapids Office)
Paul M. Wyzgoski
Thomas V. Yates
Cynthia M. York
Jennifer A. Zinn

CONSULTING PARTNERS

Fred W. Freeman
Ernest Getz
Charles R. Kinnaird

Charles R. Moon
W. Gerald Warren
Judson Werbelow
(Lansing Office)

OF COUNSEL

Marc A. Bergsman
(Washington, D.C. Office)
Geoffrey A. Fields
(Grand Rapids Office)
Paul T. Fitzpatrick
(Bloomfield Hills Office)
Michael F. Gadola
(Lansing Office)
David R. Haarz
(Washington, D.C. Office)

Bethany E. Hawkins
(Bloomfield Hills Office)
Douglas L. Mann
(Bloomfield Hills Office)
Thomas D. McLennan
(Bloomfield Hills Office)
Lucien N. Nedzi
(Washington, D.C. Office)
Allan G. Sweig
(Chicago, Illinois Office)

(See Next Column)

DICKINSON, WRIGHT, MOON, VAN DUSEN & FREEMAN, *Detroit—Continued*

OF COUNSEL (Continued)

Douglas J. Van Der Aa
(Grand Rapids Office)
Stephanie Karen Wade
(Washington, D.C. Office)

Philip F. Wood
(Grand Rapids Office)
John A. Ziegler, Jr.

ASSOCIATES

Terrence A. Barr
(Bloomfield Hills Office)
Julia Turner Baumhart
(Bloomfield Hills Office)
Edward R. Becker
(Lansing Office)
Harolyn D. Beverly
Rindala Beydoun
Robert F. Boesiger
Shari M. Borsini
Jeffrey J. Brown
(Bloomfield Hills Office)
Robert B. Brown
Bruce R. Byrd
Stephanie Dawkins Davis
Cynthia L. Della Torre
(Bloomfield Hills Office)
Mark Alan Densmore
Julie T. Emerick
(Bloomfield Hills Office)
Sara Anne Engle
(Bloomfield Hills Office)
Julia L. Ernst
Peter G. Golden
(Bloomfield Hills Office)
Nanci J. Grant
(Bloomfield Hills Office)
Erin E. Gravelyn
(Grand Rapids Office)
Jana L. Henkel-Benjamin
Robert B. Hotchkiss
(Bloomfield Hills Office)
Kyle M. H. Jones
Kelli L. Kerbawy
(Bloomfield Hills Office)
Thomas H. Kosik
(Bloomfield Hills Office)
Monica J. Labe
Judith Fertel Layne
(Bloomfield Hills Office)

Mi Young Lee
Barbara R. Lentz
Leslee M. Lewis
(Grand Rapids Office)
Lynne Olman Lourim
Edwin J. Lukas
Elizabeth Virginia Main
Sean D. Major
(Chicago, Illinois Office)
Amy E. Martin (Lansing Office)
Sarah A. McLaren
Gloria Kay Miller
Ola B. Najar
(Bloomfield Hills Office)
Kathryn Kraus Nunzio
(Grand Rapids Office)
Richard W. Paige
John T. Panourgias
(Bloomfield Hills Office)
Gregory J. Parry
(Bloomfield Hills Office)
Jeffery M. Peterson
Daniel D. Quick
Jeffrey S. Ruprich
Marian Keidan Seltzer
(Bloomfield Hills Office)
Kent L. Sevener
Paul L. Sharer
(Washington, D.C. Office)
Louis Theros
(Chicago, Illinois Office)
Michelle V. Thurber
Joseph P. Tocco
James M. Toner
Wendy Lee Toolin
(Chicago, Illinois Office)
Linda J. Truitt
(Bloomfield Hills Office)
Rhonda D. Welburn
Kathryn S. Wood

LEGAL SUPPORT PERSONNEL

CHIEF INFORMATION OFFICER
Michael W. Harnish

JAPANESE CLIENT SUPPORT
Yukiko Sato (Bloomfield Hills Office)

Representative Clients: FAUNUC Robotics North America, Inc.; Federal-Mogul Corp.; Florists' Transworld Delivery Assn.; Kmart Corp.; Kuhlman Corp.; Michigan Consolidated Gas Co.; NBD Bank.

For full biographical listings, see the Martindale-Hubbell Law Directory

---

DYKEMA GOSSETT PLLC (AV)

400 Renaissance Center, 48243-1668
Telephone: 313-568-6800
Cable Address: "Dyke-Detroit"
Telex: 23-0121
Fax: 313-568-6594
Email: 2084153@mcimail.com
Ann Arbor, Michigan Office: 315 East Eisenhower Parkway, Suite 100, 48108-3306.
Telephone: 313-747-7660.
Fax: 313-747-7696.
Bloomfield Hills, Michigan Office: 1577 North Woodward Avenue, Suite 300, 48304-2820.
Telephone: 810-540-0700.
Fax: 810-540-0763.
Chicago, Illinois Office: 55 East Monroe Street, Suite 3250, 60603-5709.
Telephone: 312-551-4900.
Fax: 312-551-4919.
Grand Rapids, Michigan Office: 200 Oldtown Riverfront Building, 248 Louis Campau Promenade, N.W., 49503-2668.
Telephone: 616-776-7500.
Fax: 616-776-7573.
Lansing, Michigan Office: 800 Michigan National Tower, 48933-1707.
Telephone: 517-374-9100.
Fax: 517-374-9191.
Washington, D.C. Office: Franklin Square, Suite 300 West, 1300 I Street, N.W., 20005-3306.
Telephone: 202-522-8600.
Fax: 202-522-8669.

(See Next Column)

MEMBERS OF FIRM

Maria B. Abrahamsen (Resident at Bloomfield Hills Office)
Ted T. Amsden
Susan Artinian
George W. Ash
Joseph C. Basta
Richard B. Baxter (Resident at Grand Rapids Office)
Robert A. Berlow (Resident at Bloomfield Hills Office)
J. Michael Bernard
William J. Brennan (Resident at Grand Rapids Office)
Bowden V. Brown (Resident at Bloomfield Hills Office)
B. Kingsley Buhl (Resident at Bloomfield Hills Office)
James M. Cameron, Jr. (Resident at Ann Arbor Office)
Timothy K. Carroll
James W. Collier
Laurence D. Connor
Michael P. Cooney
Bruce G. Davis (Resident at Ann Arbor Office)
Joseph F. Dillon
J. Terrance Dillon (Resident at Grand Rapids Office)
Alan R. Dominick (Resident at Lansing Office)
David E. Doran (Resident at Grand Rapids Office)
Robert L. Duty (Resident at Bloomfield Hills Office)
Bettye S. Elkins (Resident at Ann Arbor Office)
James M. Elsworth
John A. Entenman
Albert Ernst (Resident at Lansing Office)
Fred J. Fechheimer (Resident at Bloomfield Hills Office)
J. Kay Felt
John A. Ferroli (Resident at Grand Rapids Office)
William E. Fisher
Jane Forbes
Robert J. Franzinger
Martin Jay Galvin
Dennis M. Gannan (Resident at Bloomfield Hills Office)
Barbara L. Goldman (Resident at Bloomfield Hills Office)
Alan M. Greene (Resident at Bloomfield Hills Office)
James P. Greene (Resident at Ann Arbor Office)
Steven E. Grob
Edward A. Groobert (Not admitted in MI; Resident at Washington, D.C. Office)
Dennis M. Haffey (Member in Charge of Bloomfield Hills Office)
Mark E. Hauck
Patrick F. Hickey
J. Timothy Hobbs (Not admitted in MI; Resident at Washington, D.C. Office)
E. Edward Hood (Member in Charge of Ann Arbor Office)
Raymond T. Huetteman, Jr. (Resident at Ann Arbor Office)
Kathryn J. Humphrey
Margaret Adams Hunter
Mark D. Jacobs
Craig L. John (Resident at Bloomfield Hills Office)
Louis W. Kasischke (Resident at Bloomfield Hills Office)
Barbara A. Kaye
Robert L. Kelly (Resident at Bloomfield Hills Office)
Sharon M. Kelly (Resident at Ann Arbor Office)
Mary Steck Kershner
James P. Kiefer (Resident at Lansing Office)
Gregory M. Kopacz (Resident at Bloomfield Hills Office)
Susan Allene Kovach

Kathrin E. Kudner
Richard J. Landau (Resident at Ann Arbor Office)
Mark C. Larson
Michael A. Lesha
Kathleen McCree Lewis
Seth M. Lloyd
Stuart D. Logan (Resident at Bloomfield Hills Office)
Howard N. Luckoff (Resident at Bloomfield Hills Office)
D. Biard MacGuineas (Not admitted in MI; Resident at Washington, D.C. Office)
Stewart L. Mandell
Richard M. Matthews
Bonnie L. Mayfield
Jerome I. Maynard (Member in Charge of Chicago, Illinois Office)
Richard J. McClear
Debra M. McCulloch
Bruce A. McDonald (Not admitted in MI; Resident at Washington, D.C. Office)
D. Richard McDonald (Resident at Bloomfield Hills Office)
Thomas J. McGraw
Richard D. McLellan (Member in Charge of Lansing Office)
Patrick E. Mears (Resident at Grand Rapids Office)
Derek I. Meier
Fredrick M. Miller
Aleksandra A. Miziolek
Stephen S. Muhich (Resident at Grand Rapids Office)
William T. Myers (Resident at Bloomfield Hills Office)
Janet L. Neary (Resident at Ann Arbor Office)
Robert L. Nelson (Member in Charge of Grand Rapids Office)
James D. Obermanns (Resident at Bloomfield Hills Office)
Theodore H. Oldham
Howard E. O'Leary, Jr. (Resident at Washington, D.C. Office)
Judy A. O'Neill
Brian J. Page (Resident at Grand Rapids Office)
William J. Perrone (Resident at Lansing Office)
Marilyn A. Peters (Resident at Bloomfield Hills Office)
Cameron H. Piggott
Thomas W. B. Porter
Richard E. Rabbideau
Jack C. Radcliffe, Jr. (Resident at Ann Arbor Office)
Paul R. Rentenbach
Joseph A. Ritok, Jr.
Ronald L. Rose (Resident at Bloomfield Hills Office)
Jonathan D. Rowe (Resident at Ann Arbor Office)
Mary Elizabeth Royce (Resident at Bloomfield Hills Office)
Charles R. Rutherford (Resident at Bloomfield Hills Office)
Suzanne Sahakian
Ronald J. Santo
Rex E. Schlaybaugh, Jr. (Resident at Bloomfield Hills Office)
Lloyd A. Semple (Chairman of the Firm)
Lori M. Silsbury (Resident at Lansing Office)
Thomas B. Spillane, Jr. (Resident at Bloomfield Hills Office)
Wilfred A. Steiner, Jr.
Daniel J. Stephenson (Resident at Ann Arbor Office)
Mark H. Sutton (Resident at Bloomfield Hills Office)
Roger K. Timm
Paul H. Townsend, Jr.
David L. Tripp
Thomas Stephen Vaughn

(See Next Column)

DYKEMA GOSSETT PLLC—*Continued*

MEMBERS OF FIRM (Continued)

Stephen D. Winter
Fred L. Woodworth (Member in Charge of Washington, D.C. Office)
Daniel G. Wyllie

Donald S. Young
Stephen H. Zimmerman (Resident at Lansing and Washington, D.C. Offices)
Frank K. Zinn

OF COUNSEL

Charles R. Bernardini (Not admitted in MI; Resident at Washington, D.C. and Chicago, Illinois Offices)
Gerald R. Black (Resident at Bloomfield Hills Office)
James T. Blake
William H. Carroll (Not admitted in MI; Resident at Washington, D.C. Office)

Edward J. Chalfie (Not admitted in MI; Resident at Chicago, Illinois Office)
Eugene A. Gargaro, Jr.
Donald E. Shely (Resident at Bloomfield Hills Office)
John J. Slavin (Resident at Bloomfield Hills Office)

RETIRED PARTNERS

Earl R. Boonstra
James W. Draper

Edward C. Hanpeter
James D. Tracy

Paul R. Trigg, Jr.

Raymond K. Dykema (1889-1971)
Elroy O. Jones (1889-1973)

Renville Wheat (1893-1968)
James H. Spencer (1908-1970)
Nathan B. Goodnow (1906-1985)

ASSOCIATES

Joaquim Darrel Barros
Laura M. Benitez (Resident at Ann Arbor Office)
John F. Birmingham, Jr.
Thomas S. Bishoff
Kevin J. Bonner
Scott D. Broekstra (Resident at Grand Rapids Office)
Daniel J. Brondyk (Resident at Grand Rapids Office)
Michael J. Brown (Resident at Lansing Office)
James A. Bruinsma (Resident at Grand Rapids Office)
Brendan J. Cahill (Resident at Bloomfield Hills Office)
Sean M. Carty
Margaret A. Costello
Sandra Miller Cotter (Resident at Lansing Office)
Donald M. Crawford (Resident at Bloomfield Hills Office)
Hugo A. Delevie (Resident at Bloomfield Hills Office)
Mark E. Derwent (Resident at Grand Rapids Office)
Marie R. Deveney (Resident at Ann Arbor Office)
Dennis M. Doherty
Phyllis Donaldson-Adams
Elizabeth M. Donovan
Laura J. Eisele
Joseph K. Erhardt
Aren L. Fairchild
Ann D. Fillingham (Resident at Lansing Office)
Cheryl Anne Fletcher
Kiffi Y. Ford
Douglas J. Fryer (Resident at Bloomfield Hills Office)
Kevin P. Fularczyk
Grant P. Gilezan
Julia A. Goatley (Resident at Lansing Office)
Kimberly A. Gough (Resident at Bloomfield Hills Office)
Marguerite Marie Gritenas
David G. Hagens (Resident at Grand Rapids Office)
James F. Hermon
Joseph H. Hickey (Resident at Bloomfield Hills Office)
Kevin M. Hinman (Resident at Bloomfield Hills Office)
Robert M. Horwitz
Jennifer J. Howe (Resident at Chicago, Illinois Office)
Judy Parker Jenkins (Not admitted in MI; Resident at Washington, D.C. Office)
Zora E. Johnson

Christopher Kelly (Not admitted in MI; Resident at Washington, D.C. Office)
Nicole Yvette Lamb-Hale
Joanne R. Lax
William J. Lewandowski
Gerald T. Lievois (Resident at Bloomfield Hills Office)
Mary T. Malpass
Steven Marchese (Resident at Ann Arbor Office)
Bryan D. Marcus
Andrew W. Mayoras (Resident at Bloomfield Hills Office)
Andrew J. McGuinness (Resident at Ann Arbor Office)
Mark A. Metz
Kevin G. Mierzwa (Resident at Bloomfield Hills Office)
Ava K. Ortner
James C. Partridge
Geoffrey T. Pavlic
Mark W. Peters
Karen R. Pifer (Resident at Bloomfield Hills Office)
Dennis M. Pousak
Kathleen A. Reed (Resident at Ann Arbor Office)
John W. Rees (Resident at Bloomfield Hills Office)
Laurence D. Rich (Resident at Bloomfield Hills Office)
Kasandra L. Richardson (Resident at Ann Arbor Office)
Carol H. Rodriguez
Steven J. Rollins (Not admitted in MI; Resident at Chicago, Illinois Office)
Ann Marie Ronchetto
Nader J. Samii
Rosemary G. Schikora
William R. Schikora
Catherine Kim Shierk (Resident at Bloomfield Hills Office)
Todd J. Shoudy
Jeffrey N. Silveri (Resident at Ann Arbor Office)
Bradley L. Smith (Resident at Ann Arbor Office)
Robert E. Smith (Resident at Lansing Office)
Ronald J. Torbert
Michael Tucker (Resident at Bloomfield Hills Office)
Penny Brown Webster
Jill M. Wheaton
Marvin Douglas Wilder
Wendell Alan Wilk (Resident at Lansing Office)

(See Next Column)

ASSOCIATES (Continued)

Alethea Wilson
Leonard C. Wolfe (Resident at Lansing Office)
Nicholas G. Zotos

Sherrill D. Wolford
James Zavell
Kevin M. Zielke

For full biographical listings, see the Martindale-Hubbell Law Directory

---

FEIKENS, VANDER MALE, STEVENS, BELLAMY & GILCHRIST, P.C. (AV)

One Detroit Center Suite 3400, 500 Woodward Avenue, 48226-3406
Telephone: 313-962-5909
Fax: 313-962-3125
Email: FEIKENS@COUNSEL.COM

Robert E. Dice (1922-1983)
Jon Feikens
Jack E. Vander Male
Frederick B. Bellamy
Alan Gordon Gilchrist
L. Neal Kennedy
Bruce A. VandeVusse

Lee A. Stevens
William C. Hurley
Linda M. Galbraith
Michael S. Cafferty
Robert H. Feikens
Gerald W. Van Wyke
Roger L. Wolcott

Sharon McPhail

Richard G. Koefod
Joseph E. Kozely, Jr.
Jeffrey Feikens

Keith J. Soltis
Michael B. Barey
Renee T. VanderHagen

Michael P. Citrin

OF COUNSEL

Sam W. Thomas (P.C.)   Walter Vincent Bernard III

LEGAL SUPPORT PERSONNEL

PARALEGALS

Robert Westveer   Linda Barthlow

For full biographical listings, see the Martindale-Hubbell Law Directory

---

FILDEW HINKS, P.L.L.C. (AV)

3600 Penobscot Building, 645 Griswold Street, 48226-4291
Telephone: 313-961-9700
Telecopier: 313-961-0754

MEMBERS OF FIRM

Stanley L. Fildew (1896-1978)
Frank T. Hinks (1887-1974)
Richard E. Hinks (1916-1990)
John H. Fildew
Alan C. Miller
Charles D. Todd III

Randall S. Wangen
Mary Jane Ruffley
Robert D. Welchli
William P. Thorpe
Colleen A. Kramer
Stephen J. Pokoj

ASSOCIATES

Charles S. Kennedy, III   Walter B. Fisher, Jr.

References: First of America Bank-Detroit, N.A.; Comerica Bank-Detroit; National Bank of Detroit.

For full biographical listings, see the Martindale-Hubbell Law Directory

---

FOSTER, MEADOWS & BALLARD, P.C. (AV)

3200 Penobscot Building, 48226
Telephone: 313-961-3234
Cable Address: "Foster"
Telex: 23-5823
Facsimile: 313-961-6184

Sparkman D. Foster (1897-1967)
Charles R. Hrdlicka
Paul D. Galea

Richard A. Dietz
Robert H. Fortunate
Robert G. Lahiff

Camille A. Raffa-Dietz

Michael J. Liddane   Paul A. Kettunen

OF COUNSEL

John L. Foster   John F. Langs
John A. Mundell, Jr.

For full biographical listings, see the Martindale-Hubbell Law Directory

---

GARAN, LUCOW, MILLER, SEWARD & BECKER, P.C. (AV)

1000 Woodbridge Place, 48207-3192
Telephone: 313-446-1530
Fax: 313-259-0450
Email: glm@gnn.com
Grand Blanc, Michigan Office: 8332 Office Park Drive.
Telephone: 810-695-3700.
Fax: 810-695-6488.
Port Huron, Michigan Office: Port Huron Office Center, 511 Fort Street, Suite 505.
Telephone: 810-985-4400.
Fax: 810-985-4107.
Ann Arbor, Michigan Office: 101 North Main Street, Suite 801.
Telephone: 313-930-5600.
Fax: 313-930-0043.

(See Next Column)

GARAN, LUCOW, MILLER, SEWARD & BECKER P.C., *Detroit—Continued*

Troy, Michigan Office: 1111 West Long Lake Road, Suite 300.
Telephone: 810-641-7600.
Fax: 810-641-0222.
Mount Clemens, Michigan Office: Towne Square Development, 10 S. Main Street, Suite 307.
Telephone: 810-954-3800.
Fax: 810-954-3803.
Grand Rapids, Michigan Office: Campau Square Plaza Building, 99 Monroe Avenue N.W., Suite 102.
Telephone: 616-732-5330.
Fax: 616-732-5333.

Matthew A. Seward	Thomas W. Emery
Thomas F. Myers	Joseph Crystal
Dennis P. Partridge	Jon P. Desenberg
John E. McSorley	Boyd E. Chapin, Jr.
Lamont E. Buffington	Frederick B. Plumb
Thomas L. Misuraca	Mark C. Smiley
Rosalind Rochkind	James S. Goulding
James J. Hayes, Jr.	John J. Gillooly

Daniel S. Saylor	Steven E. Nurenberg
Peter B. Worden, Jr.	Anne K. Newcomer
Charlotte H. Johnson	Robert A. Obringer
David M. Shafer	Eun (Ellen) G. Ha
Lloyd G. Johnson	Stephen A. Coticchio
Robert D. Goldstein	Timothy J. Jordan
Michael J. Paolucci	Thomas M. Lenney
Michael J. DePolo	Lynn E. Geist
C. David Miller, II	Mark T. Rajt

OF COUNSEL

Daniel L. Garan	Beth A. Andrews
Milton Lucow	Nancy J. Bourget
Albert A. Miller	David L. Lattie
Roy E. Castetter	Meri Craver Borin

Counsel for: Allstate Insurance Co.; Sears, Roebuck & Co.; Liberty Mutual Insurance Co.; Continental Insurance Companies.

For full biographical listings, see the Martindale-Hubbell Law Directory

HONIGMAN MILLER SCHWARTZ AND COHN (AV)

A Partnership including Professional Corporations
2290 First National Building, 48226
Telephone: 313-256-7800
Telecopier: 313-962-0176
Telex: 235705
URL: http://law.honigman.com
Lansing, Michigan Office: Phoenix Building, 222 North Washington Square, Suite 400, 48933-1800.
Telephone: 517-484-8282.
West Palm Beach, Florida Office: Suite 800 Esperante Building, 222 Lakeview Avenue, 33401-6112.
Telephone: 561-838-4500.
Tampa, Florida Office: 2700 SunTrust Financial Centre, 401 E. Jackson Street, 33602-5226.
Telephone: 813-221-6600.

MEMBERS OF FIRM

Richard J. Aaron (Lansing, Michigan Office)	David A. Ettinger
Joel S. Adelman	Robert A. Fineman
Peter M. Alter	Herschel P. Fink
John E. Amerman	David Foltyn
Norman C. Ankers	Frederick J. Frank
Joseph T. Aoun	Michael J. Friedman
Frederick M. Baker, Jr. (Lansing, Michigan Office)	William F. Frey
	H. Alan Gocha
C. Leslie Banas	Kenneth C. Gold
Donald F. Baty, Jr.	Mark A. Goldsmith
Thomas J. Beale	Philip A. Grashoff, Jr.
Norman H. Beitner	Margaret E. Greene
Stanford P. Berenbaum	Gerald M. Griffith
Maurice S. Binkow	Norman D. Hawkins
Richard Bisio	Daniel G. Helton
Jonathan R. Borenstein	Raymond W. Henney
Jay E. Brant	Carl W. Herstein
Keith B. Braun	William O. Hochkammer
Richard J. Burstein	Steven G. Howell
Rebecca L. Burtless-Creps	Alan M. Hurvitz
Judy B. Calton	Robert A. Hykan
William M. Cassetta	Jeffrey A. Hyman
Sally J. Churchill	Norman Hyman
Carol A. Clark	Linn A. Hynds
Gerald S. Cook	Howard B. Iwrey
Roger Cook	Robert M. Jackson
Gregory J. DeMars	Sandra L. Jasinski (Lansing, Michigan Office)
Daniel J. Demlow (Lansing, Michigan Office)	John M. Kamins
Patrick T. Duerr	John S. Kane (Lansing, Michigan Office)
Christopher J. Dunsky	Edward F. Kickham
John H. Eggertsen	

(See Next Column)

MEMBERS OF FIRM (Continued)

Timothy Sawyer Knowlton (Lansing, Michigan Office)	Samina R. Schey
Kevin Kohls	Laurence J. Schiff
Jeffrey R. Kravitz	Edward R. Schonberg
Robert J. Krueger, Jr.	Alan E. Schwartz
Donald J. Kunz	Alan Stuart Schwartz
Mary Jo Larson	Benjamin O. Schwendener, Jr. (Lansing, Michigan Office)
Marguerite Munson Lentz	Mark Shaevsky
Denise J. Lewis	Michael B. Shapiro
Stuart M. Lockman	Sherill Siebert
Ronald S. Longhofer	John Sklar
Lawrence D. McLaughlin	Richard S. Soble
Mitchell R. Meisner	Samuel T. Stahl
A. David Mikesell	Mark A. Stern
Mark Morton (Lansing, Michigan Office)	Theodore B. Sylwestrzak
Cyril Moscow	Stuart H. Teger
Brian J. Negele	Sheryl L. Toby
Charles Nida	Sheldon S. Toll
James H. Novis	Brad M. Tomtishen
Joseph G. Nuyen, Jr.	Gary A. Trepod (Lansing, Michigan Office)
Nancy M. Omichinski	Grant R. Trigger
David K. Page	Alan M. Valade
Lisa M. Panepucci	(Lansing, Michigan Office)
Alex L. Parrish	Stephen Wasinger
John D. Pirich (Lansing, Michigan Office)	Robert B. Weiss
	Mark R. Werder
Joseph M. Polito	Randall P. Whately
Paul Revere, III	William C. Whitbeck (Lansing, Michigan Office)
Julie E. Robertson	
G. Scott Romney	William A. Wichers II
Linda S. Ross	Sheldon P. Winkelman
Chris E. Rossman	I. W. Winsten
J. Adam Rothstein	Jeffrey L. Woolstrum
Phyllis G. Rozof	Ruth E. Zimmerman (Lansing, Michigan Office)
Roberta R. Russ	
Jerome M. Salle	William J. Zousmer
William D. Sargent	Richard E. Zuckerman

ASSOCIATES

Jean-Vierre Adams	S. Lee Johnson
Ann L. Andrews (Lansing, Michigan Office)	Carey F. Kalmowitz
	Walter J. Kramarz
David E. Barnes	Dawn R. Kreysar
David A. Breach	Russell S. Linden
Michael J. Byrnes	Steven E. Mellen
James T. Carroll, III	Jill Mainster Menuck
Amy M. Colton	Lawrence J. Murphy
Cameron J. Evans	Andrew S. Rosenman
Gail A. Eynon	Tracy E. Silverman
J. Thomas Ferries	Denise K. Stellmach
Amy B. Folbe	Michelle Epstein Taigman
Andrew J. Gerdes (Lansing, Michigan Office)	Mary Ann Taylor (Detroit and Lansing, Michigan Offices)
William S. Hammond	Cynthia G. Thomas
Gregory D. Hanley	Barbara A. Van Zanten
Andrea Hansen (Lansing, Michigan Office)	Eugene V. Wade, Jr.
	Lisa M. Waits

Jennifer S. Zbytowski

OF COUNSEL

Milton J. Miller	William F. Ikard (Not admitted in MI)
Rodman N. Myers	Jason L. Honigman (1904-1990)
Asher Rabinowitz	Irwin I. Cohn (1896-1984)
Margaret Shannon	
James Popp (Not admitted in MI)	

RESIDENT IN WEST PALM BEACH, FLORIDA OFFICE

MEMBERS

Carla L. Brown (P.A.)	Steven R. Parson (P.A.)
Morris C. Brown (P.A.)	Neil W. Platock (P.A.)
Ronald S. Kochman (P.A.)	Marvin S. Rosen (P.A.)
Mark Nussbaum (P.A.)	Steven L. Schwarzberg (P.A.)

E. Lee Worsham (P.A.)

ASSOCIATE

Jose O. Diaz

RESIDENT IN TAMPA, FLORIDA OFFICE

MEMBERS

Robert W. Boos (P.A.)	Gregory G. Jones (P.A.)
Michael G. Cooke (P.A.)	Maria Maistrellis (P.A.)
Harry Christopher Goplerud (P.A.)	Barbara R. Pankau (P.A.)
	James B. Soble (P.A.)

John W. Voelpel

ASSOCIATES

Kevin M. Gilhool	Donald A. Mihokovich

Susan M. Salvatore

General Counsel for: Arbor Drugs Inc.; The Detroit Free Press; The Detroit Medical Center; Handleman Co.; Pulte Corporation; William C. Roney & Co.

(See Next Column)

HONIGMAN MILLER SCHWARTZ AND COHN—*Continued*

Local or Special Counsel for: American Society of Composers, Authors and Publishers (ASCAP); AutoAlliance International Inc. (formerly Mazda Motor Manufacturing (USA) Corporation); NBD Bank; The Taubman Company, Inc.

For full biographical listings, see the Martindale-Hubbell Law Directory

JAFFE, RAITT, HEUER & WEISS, PROFESSIONAL CORPORATION (AV)

One Woodward Avenue, Suite 2400, 48226
Telephone: 313-961-8380
Telecopier: 313-961-8358
Cable Address: "Jafsni"
Southfield, Michigan Office: Travelers Tower, Suite 1520.
Telephone: 313-961-8380.
Monroe, Michigan Office: 214 East Elm Avenue, Suite 208,
Telephone: 313-241-6470.
Telefacsimile: 313-241-3849.

Judith Lowitz Adler	James G. Petrangelo (Resident,
Gail A. Anderson	Monroe, Michigan Office)
Christopher A. Andreoff	Steven C. Powell
Julia Blakeslee	Victor F. Ptasznik
Robert S. Bolton	Mark K. Rabidoux
Alexander B. Bragdon	Cecil G. Raitt
Penny L. Carolan	David H. Raitt
R. Christopher Cataldo	Michael A. Rajt
Thomas E. Coughlin	Gerald F. Reinhart
Jeffrey L. Forman	Louis P. Rochkind
Wallace H. Glendening	Mark D. Rubenfire
Gary R. Glenn	Daniella Saltz
Joel S. Golden	Stephen G. Schafer
Robert J. Gordon	Linda C. Scheuerman
Larry K. Griffis	Brian G. Shannon
Howard B. Hill	Joseph J. Shannon
Jeffrey G. Heuer	Lawrence R. Shoffner
John A. Hohman, Jr. (Resident,	William E. Sider
Monroe, Michigan Office)	Arthur H. Siegal
Blair B. Hysni	Elliot A. Spoon
Lisa Biddinger Hysni	Peter Sugar
Ira J. Jaffe	George A. Sumnik
Robin H. Krueger	Susan M. Sutton
Mark P. Krysinski	Holli Hart Targan
Sharon J. LaDuke	Nancy L. Waldmann
Melanie LaFave	David D. Warner
Robert E. Lewis	Arthur A. Weiss
Susan S. Lichterman	Jeffrey D. Weisserman
Eric A. Linden	Jay L. Welford
Ralph R. Margulis	Cynthia A. White
Joel J. Morris	Thomas H. Williams
Lawrence C. Patrick, Jr.	Janet G. Witkowski
Richard A. Zussman	

Derek S. Adolf	Stephen S. Laplante
David P. Armstrong	Carla M. Mecoli Kamp
Susan Michelle Bakst	Joshua F. Opperer
Eric S. Bronstein	Jane Derse Quasarano
Linda M. Bruton	Thomas L. Shaevsky
Karen J. Craft	Jon A. Sherk
Lesley A. Gaber	Jordan H. Smith
Kerry Gross-Bondy (Resident,	Jeffrey M. Weiss
Monroe, Michigan Office)	Laith L. Yaldoo
Liam E. Hart	Wendy L Zabriskie
Donald A. Jordan	Lisa B. Zimmer

OF COUNSEL

David Griem	Carolyn Slasinski-Griem
Nathan L. Milstein	

Representative Clients: Michigan State Hospital Finance Auth.; The Stroh Brewery Co.; Unisys Corp.; Weiss Construction Co.

For full biographical listings, see the Martindale-Hubbell Law Directory

KELLER, THOMA, SCHWARZE, SCHWARZE, DuBAY & KATZ, P.C. (AV)

440 East Congress, 5th Floor, 48226
Telephone: 313-965-7610
Bloomfield Hills, Michigan Office: Suite 122, 100 West Long Lake Road.
Telephone: 810-642-5218.

Leonard A. Keller (1906-1970)	Gary P. King
Frederick B. Schwarze	Robert A. Lusk
Thomas H. Schwarze	Linda M. Foster
Dennis B. DuBay	Bruce M. Bagdady
James R. Miller	Carl F. Schwarze
Stewart J. Katz	George P. Butler, III
Anthony J. Heckemeyer	Brian A. Kreucher
Thomas L. Fleury	Kenneth C. Howell
Terrence J. Miglio	Mark C. Knoth

(See Next Column)

Patrice L. Baker	Martha A. Proctor
John J. Rabaut	Joseph R. Furton, Jr.
James Joseph Boutrous, II	

OF COUNSEL

Richard J. Thoma	Charles E. Keller

Counsel for: Livonia Public Schools; Ludington News Co., Inc.
Representative Clients: Borg-Warner Corp.; E & L Transport Co.; The Kroger Co.; Holnam, Inc.
Public Employer Clients: City of Farmington Hills; City of Flint; City of Grosse Pointe Woods; Saginaw Public Schools.

For full biographical listings, see the Martindale-Hubbell Law Directory

MEYER, KIRK, SNYDER & SAFFORD, PLLC (AV)

2500 Penobscot Building, 48226
Telephone: 313-961-1261
Fax: 810-647-6079
Bloomfield Hills, Michigan Office: Suite 100, 100 West Long Lake Road.
Telephone: 313-647-5111.
Telecopier: 313-647-6079.

George H. Meyer	Ralph R. Safford
John M. Kirk	Patrick K. Rode
George E. Snyder	Donald H. Baker, Jr.

Christopher F. Clark	Boyd C. Farnam
Debra S. Meier	

OF COUNSEL

Mark R. Solomon

Representative Clients: Available Upon Request.

For full biographical listings, see the Martindale-Hubbell Law Directory

MILLER, CANFIELD, PADDOCK AND STONE, P.L.C. (AV)

A Professional Limited Liability Company
Founded in 1852 by Sidney Davy Miller
150 West Jefferson, Suite 2500, 48226-4415
Telephone: 313-963-6420
Fax: 313-496-7500
Cable Address: "Stem Detroit"
Detroit, Michigan Office: 150 West Jefferson, Suite 2500, 48226-4415.
Telephone: 313-963-6420.
Fax: 313-496-7500.
Cable Address: "Stem Detroit."
Ann Arbor, Michigan Office: 101 North Main Street, 7th Floor, 48104-1400.
Telephone: 313-663-2445.
Fax: 313-747-7147.
Bloomfield Hills, Michigan Office: Suite 100, Pinehurst Office Center, 1400 North Woodward, 48303-2014.
Telephone: 313-645-5000.
Fax: 313-645-1917.
Grand Rapids, Michigan Office: 1200 Campau Square Plaza, 99 Monroe, N.W., 49503-2639.
Telephone: 616-454-8656.
Fax: 616-776-6322.
Howell, Michigan Office: 121 South Barnard Street, Suite 4, 48843-2305.
Telephone: 517-546-7600.
Telecopier: 517-546-6974.
Kalamazoo, Michigan Office: 444 West Michigan Avenue, 49007-3752.
Telephone: 616-381-7030.
Fax: 616-382-0244.
Lansing, Michigan Office: One Michigan Avenue, Suite 900, 48933-1609.
Telephone: 517-487-2070.
Fax: 517-374-6304.
Monroe, Michigan Office: The Executive Centre, 214 East Elm Avenue, 48161-2682.
Telephone: 313-243-2000.
Fax: 313-243-0901.
Washington, D.C. Office: 1225 Nineteenth Street, N.W., Suite 400. 20036.
Telephone: 202-429-5575; 785-0600.
Fax: 202-331-1118; 785-1234.
Pensacola, Florida Office: 25 West Cedar, 32501.
Telephone: 904-469-1088.
Fax: 904-432-0677.
St. Petersburg, Florida Office: 100 Second Avenue S., Suite 7045, 33701.
Telephone: 813-982-6000.
Fax: 813-892-6002.
New York, New York Office: Eleventh Floor, 135 East 57th Street, 10022-2087.
Telephone: 212-754-5400.
Fax: 212-754-5401.
Gdansk, Poland Office: Suite 322, Dom Technika Building, UI. Rajska 6, 80-850.
Telephone: 011-485-831-2808.
Fax: 011-485-831-4719.
Warsaw, Poland Office: UI. Marszalkowska 82, Suite 561, 00-517.
Telephone: 011-482-623-6457 and 6458.
Fax: 011-482-623-6459.

(See Next Column)

MILLER, CANFIELD, PADDOCK AND STONE P.L.C., *Detroit—Continued*

PRINCIPALS OF FIRM

Lawrence A. King (P.C.)
(Bloomfield Hills Office)
Robert E. Hammell
John W. Gelder
(Bloomfield Hills Office)
George E. Parker, III
Stevan Uzelac (P.C.)
Gilbert E. Gove
Robert S. Ketchum
Samuel J. McKim, III, (P.C.)
Rocque E. Lipford (P.C.)
(Monroe Office)
Joel L. Piell
Robert E. Gilbert
(Ann Arbor Office)
Eric V. Brown, Jr.
(Kalamazoo Office)
Bruce D. Birgbauer
John A. Thurber (P.C.)
(Bloomfield Hills Office)
Orin D. Brustad
Carl H. von Ende
Erik H. Serr (Ann Arbor Office)
Allyn D. Kantor
(Ann Arbor Office)
Charles E. Ritter
(Kalamazoo Office)
Thomas G. Parachini
John A. Campbell
(Kalamazoo Office)
David D. Joswick (P.C.)
Charles L. Burleigh, Jr.
John A. Marxer (P.C.)
(Bloomfield Hills Office)
Gregory L. Curtner
(New York, N.Y. Office)
Dennis R. Neiman
Kenneth E. Konop
(Bloomfield Hills Office)
Leonard D. Givens
W. Mack Faison
Joseph F. Galvin
Ronald H. Riback
(Bloomfield Hills Office)
James W. Williams
(Bloomfield Hills Office)
Thomas P. Hustoles
(Kalamazoo Office)
William J. Danhof
(Lansing Office)
Clarence L. Pozza, Jr.
Jerry T. Rupley
Michael W. Hartmann
Kent E. Shafer
James C. Foresman
John J. Collins, Jr.
(Bloomfield Hills Office)
John R. Cook
(Kalamazoo Office)
Thomas W. Linn
Stephen G. Palms
(Bloomfield Hills Office)
Jerome R. Watson
Frank L. Andrews (Detroit and
Bloomfield Hills Offices)
Donna J. Donati
Donald W. Keim
Larry J. Saylor
Mark E. Putney (Grand Rapids
Office Resident Director)
James G. Vantine, Jr.
(Kalamazoo Office)
Richard J. Seryak
Michael R. Atkins
(Lansing Office)
Leland D. Barringer
Timothy D. Sochocki
(Ann Arbor Office)
Thomas C. Phillips
(Lansing Office)
Christopher J. Dembowski
(Lansing Office)
Marjory G. Basile
Terrence M. Crawford
Michael J. Hodge
(Lansing Office)

J. Kevin Trimmer
(Bloomfield Hills Office)
Richard A. Gaffin
(Grand Rapids Office)
Kevin M. McCarthy
(Kalamazoo Office)
Ronald E. Baylor
(Kalamazoo Office)
Beverly Hall Burns
Charles S. Mishkind (Grand
Rapids, Lansing and
Kalamazoo Offices)
Stephen J. Ott
Amanda Van Dusen
Peter W. Waldmeir
Thomas G. Appleman
(Bloomfield Hills Office)
Thomas H. Van Dis
(Kalamazoo Office)
Walter Briggs Connolly, Jr.
Michael P. Coakley
Cynthia B. Faulhaber
(Lansing Office)
Jeffrey M. McHugh
Robert F. Rhoades
James E. Spurr
(Kalamazoo Office)
Gregory V. Di Censo
(Bloomfield Hills Office)
Brad B. Arbuckle
(Bloomfield Hills Office)
Mark T. Boonstra
Harold W. Bulger, Jr.
Michael G. Campbell
(Grand Rapids Office)
David A. French
(Ann Arbor Office)
Michael A. Limauro
Karen Ann McCoy
Kevin J. Moody (Lansing Office)
Steven M. Stankewicz
(Kalamazoo Office)
Robert E. Lee Wright
Michael A. Indenbaum
Alison B. Marshall
(Washington, D.C. Office)
J. David Reck (Ann Arbor and
Howell Offices)
Michael H. Traison
Jonathan S. Green
Le Roy L. Asher, Jr.
Vernon Bennett III (Grand
Rapids and Kalamazoo
Offices)
Douglas W. Crim
(Grand Rapids Office)
Pamela Chapman Enslen
(Kalamazoo Office)
Michael P. McGee
David N. Parsigian
(Ann Arbor Office)
Jay B. Rising (Lansing Office)
Deborah W. Thompson
Richard T. Urbis
Richard F. X. Urisko
Steven A. Roach
Richard A. Walawender
Brian J. Doren
Irene Bruce Hathaway
Michael A. Luberto, Jr.
Megan P. Norris
Lawrence M. Dudek
Charles A. Duerr, Jr.
(Ann Arbor Office)
Ronald E. Hodess
(Bloomfield Hills Office)
Donald J. Hutchinson
Marta A. Manildi
(Ann Arbor Office)
Kathryn L. Ossian
Don M. Schmidt
(Kalamazoo Office)
Kurt N. Sherwood
(Kalamazoo Office)

(See Next Column)

OF COUNSEL

William G. Butler
Eric V. Brown, Sr.
(Kalamazoo Office)
Edmond F. DeVine
(Ann Arbor Office)
James E. Tobin
John B. DeVine
(Ann Arbor Office)
Stratton S. Brown
Richard B. Gushée
Peter P. Thurber
Joseph F. Maycock, Jr.
Allen Schwartz
Richard A. Jones (P.C.)
David E. Hathaway
(Grand Rapids Office)
Gerard Thomas
(Kalamazoo Office)
George E. Bushnell, Jr.
Henry R. Nolte, Jr.
(Bloomfield Hills Office)
Lawrence D. Owen
(Lansing Office)
Anne H. Hiemstra

Richard I. Lott
(Pensacola, Florida Office)
Nicholas P. Miller
(Washington, D.C. Office)
Joseph Van Eaton
(Washington, D.C. Office)
Tillman L. Lay
(Washington, D.C. Office)
William R. Malone
(Washington, D.C. Office)
David K. McLeod
David L. Kaser (Principal)
Edward F. Langs
Steven E. Chester
(Resident, Lansing Office)
Raphael A. Monsanto
(Not admitted in MI)
Benita J. Rohm
(Not admitted in MI)
Geoffrey M. Chinn
(New York Office)
Richard I. Loebl
William R. Kotila
(Ann Arbor Office)

SENIOR ATTORNEYS

Leo P. Goddeyne
(Kalamazoo Office)
Ronald D. Gardner
(Ann Arbor Office)
Elise S. Levasseur
William B. Beach
Robert J. Sandler
Sherry Katz-Crank
(Lansing Office)
David J. Hasper
(Grand Rapids Office)
Susan E. Juroe
(Washington, D.C. Office)
Michael A. Alaimo
David A. Gatchell
(St. Petersburg Office)

John G. VanSlambrouck
(Kalamazoo Office)
Roselyn R. Parmenter
George D. Mesritz
Steven C. Kahn
(Washington, D.C. Office)
Frederick E. Ellrod III
(Washington, D.C. Office)
Douglas M. Kilbourne
(Ann Arbor Office)
Walter A. Payne, III
Stephen L. Elkins
(Grand Rapids Office)
Clifford T. Flood
(Lansing Office)

ASSOCIATES

Patricia D. Lott
(Pensacola Office)
Matthew C. Ames
(Washington, D.C. Office)
Ballard Jay Yelton III
(Kalamazoo Office)
Thomas R. Cox
Lori L. Purkey
(Kalamazoo Office)
Joanne B. Faycurry
Dawn M. Schluter
(Bloomfield Hills Office)
Robert J. Haddad
John H. Willems
James R. Lancaster, Jr.
(Lansing Office)
John O. Renken (Ann Arbor
and Washington, D.C. Offices)
J. Darrell Peterson
(Washington, D.C. Office)
Frederick A. Acomb
Joseph G. Sullivan
John C. Arndts
Brian S. Westenberg
Amy S. Davis
A. Michael Palizzi
Sally A. Hamby
(Bloomfield Hills Office)
Patrick F. McGow
Paul G. Machesky
Robert R. Lech
Lisa D. Pick
(Bloomfield Hills Office)
Michael C. Fayz
Anna M. Maiuri
(Bloomfield Hills Office)
Thomas D. Colis
Dean M. Altobelli
(Lansing Office)
Derek T. Montgomery
Diane Benedict Cabbell
(Ann Arbor Office)

Mark K. Schrupp
Terence A. Thomas
Kristin M. Neun
(Washington, D.C. Office)
Bradley C. White
(Grand Rapids Office)
Jeffrey D. Adelman
Loyal A. Eldridge, III
(Kalamazoo Office)
Kurt P. McCamman
(Kalamazoo Office)
Daniel H. Roberts
(Grand Rapids Office)
Scott R. Sikkenga
(Kalamazoo Office)
Erin Quinn Gery
(Washington, D.C. Office)
Karl N. Gellert
Julie S. Silberg
James B. Thelen
(Kalamazoo Office)
Yvonne R. Haddad
Anthony J. Mavrinac
John T. Stecco
(Grand Rapids Office)
Clara G. Dequick
Michael V. Camarota
(Grand Rapids Office)
Robbi L. Sackville
Alice Censoplano
(Ann Arbor Office)
Thomas A. Norton
Louis B. Reinwasser
(Lansing Office)
Suzanne L. DeVine
(Ann Arbor Office)
Karen M. Hassevoort
(Kalamazoo Office)
Susan I. Robbins
(New York Office)

Representative Firm Clients: Chrysler Corporation; Comerica, Incorporated; City of Detroit, Michigan; Detroit Tigers, Inc.; First of Michigan; Ford Motor Company; Ford Motor Credit Company; Great Lakes Bancorp; Henry Ford Hospital; INVETECH Company.

For full biographical listings, see the Martindale-Hubbell Law Directory

Detroit—Continued

PEPPER, HAMILTON & SCHEETZ (AV)

100 Renaissance Center, 36th Floor, 48243-1157
Telephone: 313-259-7110
Telecopy: 313-259-7926
Philadelphia, Pennsylvania Office: 3000 Two Logan Square, Eighteenth and Arch Streets, 19103-2799.
Telephone: 215-981-4000.
Fax: 215-981-4750.
Washington, D.C. Office: 1300 Nineteenth Street, N.W., 20036-1685.
Telephone: 202-828-1200.
Fax: 202-828-1665.
New York, New York Office: 450 Lexington Avenue, Suite 1600, 10017-3904.
Telephone: 212-878-3800.
Fax: 212-878-3835.
Wilmington, Delaware Office: 1201 Market Street, Suite 1600, P.O. Box 1709, 19899-1709.
Telephone: 302-777-6500.
Fax: 302-656-8865.
Pittsburgh, Pennsylvania Office: One Mellon Bank Center, 50th Floor, 500 Grant Street, 15219-2502.
Telephone: 412-454-5000.
Fax: 412-281-0717.
Harrisburg, Pennsylvania Office: 200 One Keystone Plaza, North Front and Market Streets, P.O. Box 1181, 17108-1181.
Telephone: 717-255-1155.
Fax: 717-238-0575.
Berwyn, Pennsylvania Office: 1235 Westlakes Drive, Suite 400, 19312-2401.
Telephone: 610-640-7800.
Fax: 610-640-7835.
Cherry Hill, New Jersey Office: Liberty View Building, Suite 500, 457 Haddonfield Road, 08002-2002.
Telephone: 609-317-9530.
Fax: 609-317-9238.
London, England Office: 9 Haywards Place, EC1R 0EE.
Telephone: 011-44-171-628-1122.
Fax: 011-44-171-628-6010.
Moscow, Russia Office: 19-27 Grokholsky Pereulok, 129010.
Telephone: 011-7-095-280-4493.
Fax: 011-7-095-280-5518.

PARTNERS

Abraham Singer (Managing Partner, Detroit Office)	Stuart E. Hertzberg
Joel D. Applebaum	Dennis S. Kayes
Hugh Douglas Camitta	Kay Standridge Kress
I. William Cohen	Robert C. Ludolph
Michael A. Fleming	Catherine C. Lynem
Scott L. Gorland	David L. Maurer
Lisa Sommers Gretchko	David Murphy
Richard D. Grow	Barbara Rom
Vicki R. Harding	Richard A. Rossman
	Michael B. Staebler
Thomas P. Wilczak	

OF COUNSEL

Mark E. Schlussel

ASSOCIATES

Rachel Grossman Baxter	AnnMarie Black Dahms
Judith E. Caliman	René M. L. Hansemann
Todd A. Caraway	Matthew J. Lund
Ciara M. Comerford	Stacey A. Mufson
Karl S. Dahlquist	Drew S. Norton
Marianne Lebeuf Wade	

For full biographical listings, see the Martindale-Hubbell Law Directory

---

RILEY AND ROUMELL, P.C. (AV)

7th Floor, Ford Building, 48226-3986
Telephone: 313-962-8255
Telefax: 313-962-2937

Wallace D. Riley	Amy E. Newberg
George T. Roumell, Jr.	Alfred John Eppens
William F. Dennis	Wilber M. Brucker III
Steven M. Zarowny	Allen J. Lippitt
Gregory T. Schultz	

OF COUNSEL

William D. Cohan	Emmet E. Tracy, Jr.

Representative Clients: First of Chicago NBD Corp.; Comerica Bank-Detroit; Federal National Mortgage Assn.; Federal Home Loan Mortgage Corp.; SCOR S.A.; Chas. Verheyden, Inc.; Detroit Board of Education; County of Wayne; City of Livonia.

For full biographical listings, see the Martindale-Hubbell Law Directory

SCHUREMAN, FRAKES, GLASS & WULFMEIER (AV)

440 East Congress, Fourth Floor, 48226
Telephone: 313-961-1500
Telecopier: 313-961-1087
Harbor Springs, Michigan Office: One Spring Street Sq., 49740.
Telephone: 616-526-1145.
Telecopier: 616-526-9343.

MEMBERS OF FIRM

Jeptha W. Schureman	LeRoy H. Wulfmeier, III
John C. Frakes, Jr.	Cheryl L. Chandler
Charles F. Glass	David M. Ottenwess

ASSOCIATES

Daniel J. Dulworth	John J. Moran
Paul A. Salyers	

Reference: Comerica.

For full biographical listings, see the Martindale-Hubbell Law Directory

---

TIMMIS & INMAN, L.L.P. (AV)

300 Talon Centre, 48207
Telephone: 313-396-4200
Telecopier: 313-396-4228

Michael T. Timmis	Henry J. Brennan, III
Robert E. Graziani	Mark W. Peyser
George A. Peck	Richard M. Miettinen
Charles W. Royer	Lisa R. Gorman
Richard L. Levin	Bradley J. Knickerbocker
George M. Malis	

Michael F. Wais	Patrick B. Carey
John P. Kanan	Erich J. D'Andrea
Shannon M. Nichols	

OF COUNSEL

Wayne C. Inman	William B. Fitzgerald
W. Clark Durant, III	

Representative Clients: Stylecraft Printing Co.; Stylerite Label Corp.; Retail Resources, Inc.; Deneb Robotics, Inc.; Applied Process, Inc.; Insilco Corp.; Variety Foods, Inc.; Certain Underwriters at Lloyds of London; Eastpointe Radiologists, P.C.; Talon Automotive Group L.L.C.

For full biographical listings, see the Martindale-Hubbell Law Directory

---

VANDEVEER GARZIA, PROFESSIONAL CORPORATION (AV)

Suite 1600, 333 West Fort Street, 48226
Telephone: 313-961-4880
Fax: 313-961-3822
Oakland County Office: 220 Park Street, Suite 300, Birmingham, Michigan.
Telephone: 810-645-0100.
Fax: 810-645-2430.
Macomb County Office: 50 Crocker Boulevard, Mount Clemens, Michigan.
Telephone: 810-468-4880.
Fax: 810-465-7159.
West Michigan Office: 1121 Ottawa Beach Road, Suite 140, Holland Michigan.
Telephone: 616-399-8600.
Fax: 616-786-9095.

Fred L. Vandeveer (1879-1972)	Ronald L. Cornell (Resident, Macomb County Office)
James E. Haggerty, Sr. (1900-1966)	Gary Alan Miller
Leroy G. Vandeveer (1902-1981)	William L. Kiriazis
Buelle A. Doelle (1902-1985)	Cynthia E. Merry
Thomas P. Rockwell	Daniel P. Steele
James A. Sullivan	Shelley K. Miller (Resident, Oakland County Office)
James E. Plastow, Jr.	Terrance P. Lynch
Michael M. Hathaway	
John J. Lynch, III (Resident, Oakland County Office)	Dennis B. Cotter
	Lynda Barbat Farnen
Thomas M. Peters	Bruce E. Pearce
James K. Thome	Hal O. Carroll
Paul C. Pfister	

David B. Timmis (Resident, Oakland County Office)	C. Edward Hildebrandt (Resident, Oakland County Office)
Nancy A. Hensley	
Dawn Twydell Gladhill	Donald C. Brownell
Michael T. Ryan	

Representative Clients: Aetna Casualty and Surety Co.; Bic Corp.; CNA Insurance Group; Travelers Insurance Co.; United States Aviation Underwriters; Goodyear Tire & Rubber Co.

For full biographical listings, see the Martindale-Hubbell Law Directory

EAST LANSING, Ingham Co.

FARHAT, STORY & KRAUS, P.C. (AV)

Beacon Place, 4572 South Hagadorn Road, Suite 3, 48823
Telephone: 517-351-3700
Fax: 517-332-4122
Email: rkraus@sojourn.com

Leo A. Farhat	Chris A. Bergstrom
James E. Burns (1925-1979)	Kitty L. Groh
Monte R. Story	Charles R. Toy
Richard C. Kraus	David M. Platt
Max R. Hoffman Jr.	Thomas L. Sparks

Lawrence P. Schweitzer	Daniel B. Morgan
Debra A. Geroux	Mary K. Robbins-Kralapp

Representative Clients: Big L. Corp.; Michigan Automotive Wholesalers Association.; Hartman-Fabco, Inc.; Lansing Electric Motors, Inc.; Mike Miller Lincoln Mercury; Edward Rose Realty, Inc.; Jackson National Life Insurance; Squires School and Commercial Sales; GTE Directory Services Corp.; Lansing School District.

For full biographical listings, see the Martindale-Hubbell Law Directory

SMITH HAUGHEY RICE & ROEGGE, P.C. (AV)

1301 North Hagadorn Road, 48823-2320
Telephone: 517-332-3030
Facsimile: 517-332-3468
Grand Rapids, Michigan Office: 200 Calder Plaza Building, 250 Monroe Avenue, N.W., 49503-2251.
Telephone: 616-774-8000.
Facsimile: 616-774-2461.
Traverse City, Michigan Office: 241 East State Street, P.O. Box 848, 49685-0848.
Telephone: 616-929-4878.
Facsimile: 616-929-4182.

Douglas G. Powe

Daniel N. Stephens	James R. Duby, Jr.
Veronica A. Marsich	

Representative Clients: Chevron; Cincinnati Insurance Co.; General Motors Corp.; Kemper Insurance Group; Michigan Hospital Assn.; Navistar International; St. Paul Insurance Cos.; Steelcase, Inc.; Sears Roebuck & Co.; Dow Elanco.

For full biographical listings, see the Martindale-Hubbell Law Directory

FARMINGTON HILLS, Oakland Co.

COUZENS, LANSKY, FEALK, ELLIS, ROEDER & LAZAR, P.C. (AV)

33533 West Twelve Mile Road, Suite 150, P.O. Box 9057, 48333-9057
Telephone: 810-489-8600
Telecopier: 810-489-4156

Sheldon A. Fealk	Lisa J. Walters
Jack S. Couzens, II	Stephen Scapelliti
Jerry M. Ellis	Donald A. Wagner
Donald M. Lansky	Michael P. Witzke
Bruce J. Lazar	Cyrus Raamin Kashef
Alan C. Roeder	Gregg A. Nathanson
Renard J. Kolasa	Mark S. Frankel
Kathryn Gilson Sussman	Lynette M. Sheldon
Jeffrey A. Levine	Roger E. Winkelman
Phillip L. Sternberg	David B. Deutsch
Marc L. Prey	Monica Demko Moons

Representative Clients: Provided upon request.
Reference: Comerica Bank-Southfield.

For full biographical listings, see the Martindale-Hubbell Law Directory

FLINT, * Genesee Co.

MacDONALD, FITZGERALD & MacDONALD, P.C. (AV)

200 McKinnon Building, 48502
Telephone: 810-232-3184; 234-2204
Fax: 810-232-9632

Robert J. MacDonald	John J. FitzGerald (1919-1995)
(1914-1987)	R. Duncan MacDonald
Timothy J. MacDonald	

References: Michigan National Bank; Genesee Merchants Bank & Trust Co.

For full biographical listings, see the Martindale-Hubbell Law Directory

SMITH & BROOKER, P.C. (AV)

1309 South Linden Road Suite C, P.O. Box 315000, 48532
Telephone: 810-733-0140
Fax: 810-733-6661
Bay City, Michigan Office: 703 Washington Avenue.
Telephone: 517-892-2595.
Saginaw, Michigan Office: The Gold Building, 4855 State Street, Suite 4.
Telephone: 517-799-1891.

RESIDENT ATTORNEYS

Thomas A. Connolly	Peter L. Diesel

OF COUNSEL

Carl H. Smith, Jr.	Albert C. Hicks

Representative Clients: CIGNA; Ford Motor Co.; State Farm Mutual Automobile Insurance Co.; State Farm Fire & Casualty; Employers Mutual Companies; Michigan Lawyers Mutual; Auto Owners Insurance; Michigan Municipal Risk Authority; Monumental General Insurance; Lake State Railway Co.

For full biographical listings, see the Martindale-Hubbell Law Directory

GRAND BLANC, Genesee Co.

GARAN, LUCOW, MILLER, SEWARD & BECKER, P.C. (AV)

8332 Office Park Drive, 48439
Telephone: 810-695-3700
Fax: 810-695-6488
Detroit, Michigan Office: 1000 Woodbridge Place.
Telephone: 313-446-1530.
Fax: 313-259-0450.
Port Huron, Michigan Office: Port Huron Office Center, 511 Fort Street, Suite 505.
Telephone: 810-985-4400.
Fax: 810-985-4187.
Ann Arbor, Michigan Office: 101 North Main Street, Suite 801.
Telephone: 313-930-5600.
Fax: 313-930-0043.
Troy, Michigan Office: 1111 West Long Lake Road, Suite 300.
Telephone: 810-641-7600.
Fax: 810-641-0222.
Mount Clemens, Michigan Office: Towne Square Development, 10 S. Main Street, Suite 307.
Telephone: 810-954-3800.
Fax: 810-954-3803.
Grand Rapids, Michigan Office: Campau Square Plaza Building, 99 Monroe Avenue N.W., Suite 102.
Telephone: 616-732-5330.
Fax: 616-732-5333.

Joseph Kochis (Resident)	William J. Brickley (Resident)

Kenneth V. Klaus (Resident)	Jeffrey B. Hollander (Resident)
Brian E. Etzel (Resident)	

For full biographical listings, see the Martindale-Hubbell Law Directory

GRAND RAPIDS, * Kent Co.

ALLABEN, MASSIE, VANDER WEYDEN & TIMMER (AV)

Suite 850, Commerce Building, 5 Lyon Street, N.W., 49503
Telephone: 616-774-2182
Fax: 616-774-0602

MEMBERS OF FIRM

Fred Roland Allaben	Keith A. Vander Weyden
(1901-1985)	John J. Timmer
Sam F. Massie, Jr.	Robert W. Bandeen

John R. Allaben

Representative Clients: Auto Club Insurance Assn.; American States Insurance Co.; Michigan Mutual Liability Co.; Fidelity & Casualty Company of New York; U.S. Aircraft Insurance Group; Security Mutual Casualty Co.; Nationwide Mutual Insurance Co.; Security Mutual Casualty Co.; Nationwide Mutual Insurance Co.; Union Insurance Co.

For full biographical listings, see the Martindale-Hubbell Law Directory

BORRE, PETERSON, FOWLER & REENS, P.C. (AV)

The Philo C. Fuller House, 44 Lafayette, N.E., P.O. Box 1767, 49501-1767
Telephone: 616-459-1971
Fax: 616-459-2393

Glen V. Borre	Frank H. Johnson
James B. Peterson	Mark D. Sevald
Ben A. Fowler	Harold E. Nelson
William C. Reens	William R. Vander Sluis
	William G. Krupar

References: Old Kent Bank; NBD Bank; FMB-First Michigan Bank - Grand Rapids.

For full biographical listings, see the Martindale-Hubbell Law Directory

Grand Rapids—Continued

CHOLETTE, PERKINS & BUCHANAN (AV)

900 Campau Square Plaza Building, 99 Monroe Avenue, N.W., 49503
Telephone: 616-774-2131
Fax: 616-774-7016

Paul E. Cholette (1897-1974)   William D. Buchanan
William A. Perkins (1905-1986)   (1909-1992)

MEMBERS OF FIRM

Calvin R. Danhof	Marc A. Kidder
Frederick W. Bleakley	Michael C. Mysliwiec
Reynolds A. Brander, Jr.	Evan L. MacFarlane
Edward Malinzak	John A. Quinn
Bruce M. Bieneman	Albert J. Engel, III
William J. Warren	Stephen C. Oldstrom
Donald C. Exelby	William E. McDonald, Jr.
Thomas H. Cypher	Mark E. Fatum
William A. Brengle	Richard K. Grover, Jr.
Alfred J. Parent	David J. DeGraw
Charles H. Worsfold	Martin W. Buschle
Michael P. McCasey	Miles J. Murphy, III

ASSOCIATES

Kenneth L. Block	Martha P. Forman
William J. Yob	Kathrine M. West
Robert E. Attmore	Ilse K. Masselink
John P. Lewis	

Counsel for: Aetna Casualty & Surety Co.; Argonaut Insurance Co.; Auto-Owners Insurance Co.; Employers Mutual; Liberty Mutual Insurance Co.; Sentry Group; State Farm Insurance; Eastern Aviation and Marine Underwriters; Home Insurance Co.; Nationwide Insurance.

For full biographical listings, see the Martindale-Hubbell Law Directory

DICKINSON, WRIGHT, MOON, VAN DUSEN & FREEMAN (AV)

200 Ottawa Avenue, N.W., Suite 900, 49503-2423
Telephone: 616-458-1300
Facsimile: 616-458-6753
Detroit, Michigan Office: 500 Woodward Avenue, Suite 4000.
Telephone: 313-223-3500.
Facsimile: 313-223-3598.
Bloomfield Hills, Michigan Office: 525 North Woodward Avenue, Suite 2000.
Telephone: 810-433-7200.
Facsimile: 810-433-7274.
Lansing, Michigan Office: Suite 200, 215 South Washington Square.
Telephone: 517-371-1730.
Facsimile: 517-487-4700.
Washington, D.C. Office: Suite 800, 1901 L Street, N.W.
Telephone: 202-457-0160.
Facsimile: 202-659-1559.
Chicago, Illinois Office: 225 West Washington, Suite 400.
Telephone: 312-220-0300.
Facsimile: 312-220-0021.

RESIDENT PARTNERS

Stuart F. Cheney	Dustin P. Ordway
William J. Fisher, III	John L. Teeples
Richard A. Glaser	Richard A. Wendt
James Gavan O'Connor	Rock A. Wood

OF COUNSEL

Geoffrey A. Fields   Douglas J. Van Der Aa
Philip F. Wood

RESIDENT ASSOCIATES

Erin E. Gravelyn   Leslee M. Lewis
Kathryn Kraus Nunzio

For full biographical listings, see the Martindale-Hubbell Law Directory

DYKEMA GOSSETT PLLC (AV)

200 Oldtown Riverfront Building, 248 Louis Campau Promenade, N.W., 49503-2668
Telephone: 616-776-7500
Telex: 23-0121
Fax: 616-776-7573
Email: 2084153@mcimail.com
Ann Arbor, Michigan Office: 315 East Eisenhower Parkway, Suite 100, 48108-3306.
Telephone: 313-747-7660.
Fax: 313-747-7696.
Bloomfield Hills, Michigan Office: 1577 North Woodward Avenue, Suite 300, 48304-2820.
Telephone: 810-540-0700.
Fax: 810-540-0763.
Chicago, Illinois Office: 55 East Monroe Street, Suite 3250, 60603-5709.
Telephone: 312-551-4900.
Fax: 312-551-4919.
Detroit, Michigan Office: 400 Renaissance Center, 48243-1668.
Telephone: 313-568-6800.
Fax: 313-568-6594.

(See Next Column)

Lansing, Michigan Office: 800 Michigan National Tower, 48933-1707.
Telephone: 517-374-9100.
Fax: 517-374-9191.
Washington, D.C. Office: Franklin Square, Suite 300 West, 1300 I Street, N.W., 20005-3306.
Telephone: 202-522-8600.
Fax: 202-522-8669.

RESIDENT MEMBERS

Richard B. Baxter	Patrick E. Mears
William J. Brennan	Stephen S. Muhich
J. Terrance Dillon	Robert L. Nelson
David E. Doran	(Member in Charge)
John A. Ferroli	Brian J. Page

RESIDENT ASSOCIATES

Scott D. Broekstra	James R. Bruinsma
Daniel J. Brondyk	Mark E. Derwent
David G. Hagens	

For full biographical listings, see the Martindale-Hubbell Law Directory

GRUEL, MILLS, NIMS AND PYLMAN (AV)

50 Monroe Place, Suite 700 West, 49503
Telephone: 616-235-5500
Fax: 616-235-5550

MEMBERS OF FIRM

Grant J. Gruel	Scott R. Melton
William F. Mills	Brion J. Brooks
J. Clarke Nims	Thomas R. Behm
Norman H. Pylman, II	J. Paul Janes

Representative Clients: Aquinas College; Bell Helmet Co.; Blodgett Memorial Medical Center; Butterworth Hospital; Chem Central, Inc.; Cook Pump Co.; Grove, Inc.; NBDC; Heim Corp.

For full biographical listings, see the Martindale-Hubbell Law Directory

LAW, WEATHERS & RICHARDSON, P.C. (AV)

Bridgewater Place, Suite 800, 333 Bridge Street, N.W., 49504
Telephone: 616-459-1171
Facsimile: 616-732-1740

OF COUNSEL

Niel A. Weathers (Retired)	Robert W. Richardson
Jerome Van H. Sluggett	Walter B. Freihofer
(Retired)	John R. Nichols
W. Fred Hunting, Jr.	

William R. Hineline	Kurt G. Yost
Robert P. Cooper	Anthony P. Gauthier
Alan C. Bennett	Clifford H. Bloom
James L. Wernstrom	Scott G. Smith
Stephen D. Turner	Douglas W. Van Essen
John P. Schneider	Ingrid A. Jensen
Christopher L. Edgar	Ellen S. Carmody
John M. Huff	James A. Ens
Kevin B. Krauss	Bruce A. Courtade
Robert A. Buchanan	Mary Jane Rhoades
John H. Gretzinger	Jeffrey J. Van Winkle
Henry G. Swain	Jeffrey VanHorne Sluggett

David W. Centner	Terry E. Tobias
Roger A. Swets	M. Bridget Gleason
James T. Polonczyk	Michael J. Roth
Ronald M. Stella	Brian S. Fleetham

Representative Clients: F.D.I.C.; Ford Motor Credit Co.; Herman Miller, Inc.; Kent County Aeronautics Board; Marriott Corp.; The Procter & Gamble Co.; Peerless Insurance Co.; Ryder Systems, Inc.

For full biographical listings, see the Martindale-Hubbell Law Directory

McSHANE & BOWIE, P.L.C. (AV)

1100 Campau Square Plaza, 99 Monroe Avenue, N.W., P.O. Box 360, 49501-0360
Telephone: 616-732-5000
Fax: 616-732-5099

OF COUNSEL

Jack M. Bowie (Retired)

MEMBERS OF FIRM

T. Gerald McShane (1902-1982)	Terry J. Mroz
David L. Smith	Dan M. Challa
William H. Bowie	John F. Shape
Keith P. Walker	Wayne P. Bryan

ASSOCIATES

Norman E. Jabin	Michael D. DeVries
Mark A. VandenBosch	Judy L. Walton

Representative Clients: Old Kent Bank; Amway Corp.; Hartger & Willard Mortgage Associates; Betten Dodge, Inc.; Randers Engineering, Inc.; BETA Design Group, Inc.; Wolverine Gas & Oil Co., Inc.; M. W. VanderVeen Co.

For full biographical listings, see the Martindale-Hubbell Law Directory

Grand Rapids—Continued

MILLER, CANFIELD, PADDOCK AND STONE, P.L.C. (AV)

A Professional Limited Liability Company
Founded in 1852 by Sidney Davy Miller
1200 Campau Square Plaza, 99 Monroe, N.W., P.O. Box 329, 49503-2639
Telephone: 616-454-8656
Fax: 616-776-6322
Detroit, Michigan Office: 150 West Jefferson, Suite 2500, 48226-4415.
Telephone: 313-963-6420.
Fax: 313-496-7500.
Cable Address: "Stem Detroit."
Ann Arbor, Michigan Office: 101 North Main Street, 7th Floor, 48104-1400.
Telephone: 313-663-2445.
Fax: 313-747-7147.
Bloomfield Hills, Michigan Office: Suite 100, Pinehurst Office Center, 1400 North Woodward, 48303-2014.
Telephone: 313-645-5000.
Fax: 313-645-1917.
Howell, Michigan Office: 121 South Barnard Street, Suite 4, 48843-2305.
Telephone: 517-546-7600.
Telecopier: 517-546-6974.
Kalamazoo, Michigan Office: 444 West Michigan Avenue, 49007-3752.
Telephone: 616-381-7030.
Fax: 616-382-0244.
Lansing, Michigan Office: One Michigan Avenue, Suite 900, 48933-1609.
Telephone: 517-487-2070.
Fax: 517-374-6304.
Monroe, Michigan Office: The Executive Centre, 214 East Elm Avenue, 48161-2682.
Telephone: 313-243-2000.
Fax: 313-243-0901.
Washington, D.C. Office: 1225 Nineteenth Street, N.W., Suite 400. 20036.
Telephone: 202-429-5575; 785-0600.
Fax: 202-331-1118; 785-1234.
Pensacola, Florida Office: 25 West Cedar 32501.
Telephone: 904-469-1088.
Fax: 904-432-0677.
St. Petersburg Florida Office: 100 Second Avenue S., Suite 7045, 33701.
Telephone: 813-982-6000.
Fax: 813-892-6002.
New York, New York Office: Eleventh Floor, 135 East 57th Street, 10022-2087.
Telephone: 212-754-5400.
Fax: 212-754-5401.
Gdansk, Poland Office: Suite 322, Dom Technika Building, UI. Rajska 6, 80-850.
Telephone: 011-485-831-2808.
Fax: 011-485-831-4719.
Warsaw, Poland Office: UI. Marszalkowska 82, Suite 561, 00-517.
Telephone: 011-482-623-6457 and 6458.
Fax: 011-482-623-6459.

PRINCIPALS OF FIRM

Mark E. Putney (Resident Director, Grand Rapids Office)
Richard A. Gaffin
Charles S. Mishkind (Detroit, Lansing and Kalamazoo Offices)
Michael G. Campbell
Robert E. Lee Wright
Vernon Bennett III
Douglas W. Crim

OF COUNSEL
David E. Hathaway

SENIOR ATTORNEYS
David J. Hasper
Stephen L. Elkins

ASSOCIATES
John C. Arndts
Bradley C. White
Daniel H. Roberts
John T. Stecco
Michael V. Camarota

Representative Firm Clients: Chrysler Corporation; Comerica, Incorporated; City of Detroit, Michigan; Detroit Tigers, Inc.; First of Michigan; Ford Motor Company; Ford Motor Credit Company; Great Lakes Bancorp; Henry Ford Hospital; INVETECH Company.

For full biographical listings, see the Martindale-Hubbell Law Directory

SMITH HAUGHEY RICE & ROEGGE, P.C. (AV)

200 Calder Plaza Building, 250 Monroe Avenue, N.W., 49503-2251
Telephone: 616-774-8000
Facsimile: 616-774-2461
East Lansing, Michigan Office: 1301 North Hagadorn Road, 48823-2320.
Telephone: 517-332-3030.
Facsimile: 517-332-3468.
Traverse City, Michigan Office: 241 East State Street, P.O. Box 848, 49685-0848.
Telephone: 616-929-4878.
Facsimile: 616-929-4182.

(See Next Column)

Clifford A. Mitts (1902-1962)
Laurence D. Smith (1913-1980)
Robert V.V. Rice (1899-1982)
Michael S. Barnes (1944-1989)
L. Roland Roegge
Thomas F. Blackwell
P. Laurence Mulvihill
Lawrence P. Mulligan
Thomas R. Tasker
Paul H. Reinhardt
Lance R. Mather
Charles F. Behler
John R. Sparks
Gary A. Rowe
William W. Jack, Jr.
William J. Hondorp
Thomas M. Weibel
James G. Black
E. Thomas Mc Carthy, Jr.
Glenn W. House, Jr.
Thomas R. Wurst
Craig R. Noland
Paul M. Oleniczak
Craig S. Neckers
Thomas E. Kent
Leonard M. Hickey
John C. O'Loughlin
Anthony J. Quarto
Bruce P. Rissi
John M. Kruis
Paul Van Oostenburg
Dale Ann Iverson
William R. Jewell
Jon D. Vander Ploeg
Patrick F. Geary
Terence J. Ackert
Brian J. Kilbane
Dan C. Porter
Phillip K. Mowers
Carol D. Carlson
Christopher R. Genther

Kay L. Griffith Hammond
Marilyn S. Nickell
Beth Suzanne Kromer
Robert M. Kruse
John B. Combs
Aileen M. Simet
Matthew L. Meyer
Elizabeth Roberts VerHey
Jennifer Jane Nasser
Ginny Kaye Mikita
Karl Werner Butterer, Jr.
Susan Soon Im
J. Joseph Rossi
Stacie R. Seitz
Dwight K. Hamilton

OF COUNSEL
A. B. Smith, Jr.
David O. Haughey
Susan Bradley Jakubowski
Thomas P. Scholler

Representative Clients: Chevron; Cincinnati Insurance Co.; General Motors Corp.; Kemper Insurance Group; Michigan Hospital Assn.; Navistar International; St. Paul Insurance Cos.; Steelcase, Inc.; Sears Roebuck & Co.; Dow Elanco.

For full biographical listings, see the Martindale-Hubbell Law Directory

VARNUM, RIDDERING, SCHMIDT & HOWLETT LLP (AV)

A Limited Liability Partnership including Professional Corporations
Bridgewater Place, P.O. Box 352, 49501-0352
Telephone: 616-336-6000
800-262-0011
Facsimile: 616-336-7000
Telex: 1561593 VARN
Email: varnum@vrsh.com
Lansing, Michigan Office: The Victor Center, Suite 810, 210 North Washington Square, 48933.
Telephone: 517-482-6237.
Facsimile: 517-482-6937.
Kalamazoo, Michigan Office: 350 East Michigan Avenue, 49007.
Telephone: 616-382-2300.
Facsimile: 616-382-2382.
Grand Haven, Michigan Office: 321 Washington Street, P.O. Box 288, 49417.
Telephone: 616-846-7100.
Facsimile: 616-846-7101.
Battle Creek, Michigan Office: 4950 West Dickman Road, Suite B-1, 49015.
Telephone: 616-962-7144.
Bingham Farms, Michigan Office: 31600 Telegraph Road, Suite 230, 48025.
Telephone: 810-594-7330.
Facsimile: 810-594- 7331.

MEMBERS OF FIRM

James N. DeBoer, Jr.
William K. Van't Hof
Hilary F. Snell
Peter Armstrong
Robert J. Eleveld
Kent J. Vana
Carl E. Ver Beek
Jon F. DeWitt
John C. Carlyle (Resident at Grand Haven Office)
Donald L. Johnson
Daniel C. Molhoek
Gary P. Skinner
Thomas T. Huff (Resident at Kalamazoo Office)
Timothy J. Curtin
John E. McGarry
Dirk Hoffius
J. Terry Moran
Thomas J. Mulder
Thomas J. Barnes
Robert D. Kullgren
Richard A. Kay
Larry J. Titley
Bruce A. Barnhart
Fredric A. Sytsma
Jack D. Sage
Jeffrey L. Schad
Thomas G. Demling
John W. Pestle
Robert P. Cooper
Frank G. Dunten, P.C.
Nyal D. Deems
Richard A. Hooker (Resident at Kalamazoo Office)
Randall W. Kraker
Peter A. Smit
Mark C. Hanisch
Marilyn A. Lankfer
Thomas L. Lockhart
Robert L. Diamond
Bruce G. Hudson (Resident at Lansing Office)
Bruce Goodman
Joseph J. Vogan
Eric J. Schneidewind (Resident at Lansing Office)
Teresa S. Decker

(See Next Column)

VARNUM, RIDDERING, SCHMIDT & HOWLETT LLP—*Continued*

MEMBERS OF FIRM (Continued)

Jeffrey R. Hughes	Timothy E. Eagle
Richard W. Butler, Jr.	David A. Rhem
Lawrence P. Burns	Donald P. Lawless
Matthew D. Zimmerman	Michael S. McElwee (Resident
William E. Rohn	at Kalamazoo Office)
John Patrick White	George B. Davis
Charles M. Denton II	Jacqueline D. Scott
Paul M. Kara	N. Stevenson Jennette III
Jeffrey D. Smith (Resident at	David E. Preston
Kalamazoo Office)	Jeffrey W. Beswick (Resident at
Mark L. Collins	Grand Haven Office)
Jonathan W. Anderson	Elizabeth Joy Fossel
Carl Oosterhouse, P.C.	Joel E. Bair
William J. Lawrence III	Joan E. Schleef
Gregory M. Palmer	Scott A. Huizenga
Susan M. Wyngaarden	Richard J. McKenna
Kaplin S. Jones, P.C.	Michael F. Kelly
Stephen P. Afendoulis	Kathleen P. Fochtman
David E. Khorey	Jeffrey J. Fraser
Michael G. Wooldridge	Richard D. Fries
Timothy J. Tornga	James R. Stadler
Perrin Rynders	Richard R. Symons
Mark S. Allard	Jeffery S. Crampton

Maureen Potter

OF COUNSEL

John L. Wierengo, Jr.	Eugene Alkema
F. William Hutchinson	Gordon B. Boozer
R. Stuart Hoffius	H. Edward Paul

COUNSEL

William J. Halliday, Jr.	H. Raymond Andrews, Jr.
Terrance R. Bacon	James R. Viventi
H. Lawrence Smith	(Resident at Lansing Office)
Peter Visserman	David L. Porteous
Fred M. Woodruff, Jr. (Resident	
at Bingham Farms Office)	

ASSOCIATES

Andrew J. Kok	Mary C. Bonnema
Patrick A. Miles, Jr.	Jon M. Bylsma
Eric J. Guerin (Resident at	Joseph B. Levan
Kalamazoo Office)	Dale R. Rietberg
Steven J. Morren	Mark M. Davis
Kevin Abraham Rynbrandt	Linda L. Bunge
Michael X. Hidalgo	Anthony R. Comden
Thomas G. Kyros	Beverly Holaday
Alfred L. Schubkegel, Jr.	(Resident at Lansing Office)
(Resident at Kalamazoo	Eric C. Fleetham
Office)	Richard B. Evans
Pamela J. Tyler	G. Thomas Williams, III

STAFF ATTORNEYS

Randall J. Groendyk	Marc Daneman

Elizabeth A. Jamieson

Counsel for: First Michigan Bank Corp.; Herman Miller, Inc.

For full biographical listings, see the Martindale-Hubbell Law Directory

---

WARDROP & WARDROP, P.C. (AV)

800 NBD Bank Building, 200 Ottawa Avenue N.W., 49503
Telephone: 616-459-1225
Fax: 616-459-7273

Robert F. Wardrop II	Thomas M. Wardrop

Mary Saur Cohn

For full biographical listings, see the Martindale-Hubbell Law Directory

---

WARNER NORCROSS & JUDD LLP (AV)

900 Old Kent Building, 111 Lyon Street, N.W., 49503-2489
Telephone: 616-752-2000
Fax: 616-752-2500
Muskegon, Michigan Office: 400 Terrace Plaza, P.O. Box 900.
Telephone: 616-727-2600.
Fax: 616-727-2699.
Holland, Michigan Office: Curtis Center, Suite 300, 170 College Avenue.
Telephone: 616-396-9800.
Fax: 616-396-3656.

OF COUNSEL

Lawson E. Becker	Harold F. Schumacher
Conrad A. Bradshaw	Charles C. Lundstrom

Thomas R. Winquist

MEMBERS OF FIRM

David A. Warner (1883-1966)	Leonard D. Verdier, Jr.
George S. Norcross (1889-1960)	(1915-1989)
Siegel W. Judd (1895-1982)	Thomas J. McNamara
Platt W. Dockery (1906-1974)	(1936-1989)
J. M. Neath, Jr. (1928-1974)	Phil R. Johnson (1908-1990)

(See Next Column)

MEMBERS OF FIRM (Continued)

George L. Whitfield	Blake W. Krueger
Wallson G. Knack	John G. Cameron, Jr.
Charles E. McCallum	John H. McKendry, Jr.
Jerome M. Smith	(Resident at Muskegon Office)
John D. Tully	Paul T. Sorensen
R. Malcolm Cumming	Carl W. Dufendach
William K. Holmes	Stephen C. Waterbury
Roger M. Clark	Rodney D. Martin
John H. Logie	Richard E. Cassard
Donald J. Veldman	Alex J. DeYonker
(Resident at Muskegon Office)	Charles E. Burpee
I. John Snider, II	John D. Dunn
(Resident at Muskegon Office)	William W. Hall
Jack B. Combs	Bruce C. Young
Joseph F. Martin	Shane B. Hansen
John R. Marquis	F. William McKee
(Resident at Holland Office)	Louis C. Rabaut
John H. Martin	Paul R. Jackson
(Resident at Muskegon Office)	(Resident at Muskegon Office)
James H. Breay	Douglas A. Dozeman
Ernest M. Sharpe	John V. Byl
Vernon P. Saper	Janet Percy Knaus
Hugh H. Makens	Kathleen M. Hanenburg
Joseph M. Sweeney	Tracy T. Larsen
Gordon R. Lewis	Sue O. Conway
Robert J. Chovanec	Steven R. Heacock
Peter L. Gustafson	Cameron S. DeLong
Roger H. Oetting	Jeffrey B. Power
J. A. Cragwall, Jr.	Scott D. Hubbard
Stephen R. Kretschman	Stephen B. Grow
W. Michael Van Haren	Richard L. Bouma
Richard A. Durell	Daniel R. Gravelyn
Michael L. Robinson	Robert J. Jonker
Eugene E. Smary	Devin S. Schindler
Douglas E. Wagner	Michael H. Schubert
Robert W. Sikkel (Muskegon	(Resident at Muskegon Office)
and Holland Offices)	Valerie Pierre Simmons
Thomas H. Thornhill	William C. Fulkerson
(Resident at Muskegon Office)	Anthony J. Kolenic, Jr.
Jeffrey O. Birkhold	James Moskal
Timothy Hillegonds	Mark K. Harder
	(Resident at Holland Office)

ASSOCIATES

Weldon H. Schwartz	Elizabeth M. Topliffe
Kenneth W. Vermeulen	Susan N. McFee
Mark E. Brouwer	Julie H. Sullivan
Jeffrey S. Battershall	Molly E. McFarlane
Jeffrey A. Ott	William P. Dani
Martha Walters Atwater	Andrew D. Hakken
Rodrick W. Lewis	Andrea J. Bernard
Kevin G. Dougherty	Lori L. Gibson
Melvin G. Moseley, Jr.	Mark T. Ostrowski
James J. Rabaut	Daniel B. Ruble
James P. Enright	Paul L. Winter
Timothy L. Horner	(Resident at Muskegon Office)
Richard D. Cornell, Jr.	Douglas W. Poland
(Resident at Muskegon Office)	Michael P. Lunt
R. Paul Guerre	Carin L. Ojala
Loren M. Andrulis	Daniel K. DeWitt
Karen J. Vanderwerff	Michael K. Molitor
Susan Gell Meyers	Melissa L. Collar
Judith W. Hooyenga (Resident)	Michael J. Puca
Gordon J. Toering	Robert Dubault
Frank E. Berrodin	(Resident at Muskegon Office)
Norbert F. Kugele	Tanya E. Buhk
Shaun M. Murphy	(Resident at Holland Office)
Kevin P. McDowell	James D. Zwiers
(Resident at Holland Office)	Edward J. Bardelli
Mark J. Wassink	Tashia L. Rivard
Dennis J. Donohue	Daniel P. Ettinger
Michael I. Kleaveland	James L. Scott II
(Resident at Muskegon Office)	Steven W. Clark

General Counsel for: Bissell Inc.; Blodgett Memorial Medical Center; Guardsman Products, Inc.; Haworth, Inc.; Kysor Industrial Corp.; Michigan Bankers Assn.; Old Kent Financial Corp.; Steelcase Inc.; Wolverine World Wide, Inc.

For full biographical listings, see the Martindale-Hubbell Law Directory

---

WHEELER UPHAM, A PROFESSIONAL CORPORATION (AV)

Second Floor, Trust Building, 40 Pearl Street, N.W., 49503-3001
Telephone: 616-459-7100
Fax: 616-459-6366

Gordon B. Wheeler (1904-1986)	William H. Heritage, Jr.
Buford A. Upham (Retired)	Kenneth E. Tiews
Robert H. Gillette	Jack L. Hoffman
Geoffrey L. Gillis	Janet C. Baxter
John M. Roels	Peter Kladder, III
Gary A. Maximiuk	James M. Shade
Timothy J. Orlebeke	Thomas A. Kuiper

(See Next Column)

WHEELER UPHAM A PROFESSIONAL CORPORATION, *Grand Rapids—Continued*

Counsel For: Prudential Ins. Co.; Metropolitan Life Ins. Co.; Travelers Ins. Co.; Farmers Ins. Group; Auto-Owners Ins. Co.; Independent Cooperative Milk Producers Assn.; Medtronic, Inc.; Navistar; Westdale Better Homes and Gardens; Gospel Films, Inc.

For full biographical listings, see the Martindale-Hubbell Law Directory

---

GROSSE POINTE, Wayne Co.

DOLD, SPATH & McKELVIE, P.C. (AV)

17190 Denver Avenue, P.O. Box 36786, 48236-0786
Telephone: 313-886-7500
Fax: 313-886-7505
Troy, Michigan Office: 5445 Corporate Drive, Suite 170.
Telephone: 810-952-5100.
Fax: 810-952-5138.

Douglas H. Dold (Resident)

Elisabeth Hessheimer Gregory

Representative Clients: Allpoints Warehousing Corp.; Conquest Construction Co.; Dearborn Capital Corp.; Dinverno Waste Disposal; Ford Motor Credit Co.; General Motors Corp.; New Bright Industries; Triad Financial, Inc.; U.S. Chemical Co.;

For full biographical listings, see the Martindale-Hubbell Law Directory

---

HART,* Oceana Co. — (Refer to Ludington)

HILLSDALE,* Hillsdale Co.

PARKER, HAYES & LOVINGER, P.C. (AV)

14-16 South Howell Street, P.O. Box 358, 49242
Telephone: 517-437-7210
Fax: 517-437-0260

James B. Parker　　　　　　　Lawrence L. Hayes, Jr.
　　　　　　John P. Lovinger

Representative Clients: Hillsdale County National Bank; Village of Jonesville; Ann Arbor Associates; Hillsdale & Branch Counties (Labor Counsel); Hillsdale College; Powell Petroleum Co.; Foulke Construction Co.; Bailey Mfg. Corp.; Somerset Township; Hillsdale Tool & Mfg. Co.

For full biographical listings, see the Martindale-Hubbell Law Directory

---

HOLLAND, Ottawa Co.

CUNNINGHAM DALMAN, P.C. (AV)

321 Settlers Road, P.O. Box 1767, 49422-1767
Telephone: 616-392-1821
Fax: 616-392-4769

Gordon H. Cunningham　　　　Kenneth B. Breese
Ronald L. Dalman　　　　　　Jeffrey K. Helder
Max R. Murphy　　　　　　　Ronald J. Vander Veen
James A. Bidol　　　　　　　David M. Zessin
Andrew J. Mulder　　　　　　Mark H. Zietlow
Joel G. Bouwens　　　　　　James W. Bouwens
　　　　　Randall S. Schipper

Susan E. Vroegop　　　　　　Melinda M. Abney
　　　　　　　OF COUNSEL
Vernon D. Ten Cate　　　　　Kenneth B. Peirce, Jr.

Representative Clients: FMB-First Michigan Bank; First of America Bank-Holland, N.A.; Ottawa Savings Bank; City of Holland; Auto Club Insurance Assn. (AAA); American States Insurance Co.; Holland Economic Development Corp.; Hope College; Western Theological Seminary.
Reference: FMB-First Michigan Bank.

For full biographical listings, see the Martindale-Hubbell Law Directory

---

WARNER NORCROSS & JUDD LLP (AV)

Curtis Center, Suite 300, 170 College Avenue, 49423-2920
Telephone: 616-396-9800
Fax: 616-396-3656
Grand Rapids, Michigan Office: 900 Old Kent Building, 111 Lyon Street, N.W.
Telephone: 616-752-2000.
Fax: 616-752-2500.
Muskegon, Michigan Office: 400 Terrace Plaza, P.O. Box 900.
Telephone: 616-727-2600.
Fax: 616-727-2699.

MEMBERS OF FIRM
John R. Marquis (Resident)　　　Robert W. Sikkel
　　　　Mark K. Harder (Resident)

(See Next Column)

ASSOCIATES
Kevin P. McDowell (Resident)　　Tanya E. Buhk (Resident)

General Counsel for: Atmosphere Processing, Inc.; Dew-El Corp.; Draw Form, Inc.; First of America Bank-Holland; Holland Community Hospital; Howard Miller Clock Co.; J.B. Laboratories, Inc.; Lamb, Inc.; Lumir Corp.; Manpower Temporary Services.

For full biographical listings, see the Martindale-Hubbell Law Directory

---

HOUGHTON,* Houghton Co.

VAIRO, MECHLIN, TOMASI, JOHNSON & MANCHESTER (AV)

400 East Houghton Avenue, 49931
Telephone: 906-482-0770
Fax: 906-482-2938
Calumet, Michigan Office: 200 5th Street.
Telephone: 906-337-0312.

MEMBERS OF FIRM
Gerald G. Vairo　　　　　　Paul J. Tomasi
David R. Mechlin　　　　　Frederick N. Johnson
Jeryl A. Manchester

Michael J. Mannisto

Representative Clients: Accident Fund Company; Auto Club Insurance Association; Auto Owners Insurance Co.; Citizens Insurance Company of America; Fireman's Fund Insurance Co.; First of America Bank; U.S.F.&G.; Michigan Technological University; South Range State Bank; Upper Peninsula Power Co.

For full biographical listings, see the Martindale-Hubbell Law Directory

---

IONIA,* Ionia Co. — (Refer to Grand Rapids)

IRA, St. Clair Co. — (Refer to Ishpeming)

IRON MOUNTAIN,* Dickinson Co. — (Refer to Ishpeming)

ITHACA,* Gratiot Co. — (Refer to Alma)

JACKSON,* Jackson Co.

BULLEN, MOILANEN, KLAASEN & SWAN, P.C. (AV)

402 South Brown Street, 49203
Telephone: 517-788-8500
Fax: 517-788-8507

Lawrence L. Bullen　　　　　Terry J. Klaasen
Philip M. Moilanen　　　　　David W. Swan

David H. Black, Jr.
OF COUNSEL
T. Harrison Stanton　　　　　Frank C. Painter (1905-1976)
J. Adrian Rosenburg
(1896-1983)

Counsel for: Comerica Bank-Jackson; C.N.A. Insurance Group; Employers of Wausau Insurance Co.
General Counsel for: Decker Manufacturing Corp., Albion; Weatherwax Investment Co.; Dawlen Corp.; Photo Marketing Association International.
Local Counsel for: Marathon Oil Co.; Sears Roebuck & Co.; Montgomery Ward.

For full biographical listings, see the Martindale-Hubbell Law Directory

---

KALAMAZOO,* Kalamazoo Co.

EARLY, LENNON, PETERS & CROCKER, P.C. (AV)

900 Comerica Building, 49007-4752
Telephone: 616-381-8844
Fax: 616-349-8525

George H. Lennon, III　　　　Gordon C. Miller
John T. Peters, Jr.　　　　　Blake D. Crocker
David G. Crocker　　　　　　Robert M. Taylor
Harold E. Fischer, Jr.　　　　Patrick D. Crocker
Lawrence M. Brenton　　　　Andrew J. Vorbrich
　　　　　Nicolette G. Hahn
　　　　　OF COUNSEL
Vincent T. Early　　　　　　C. H. Mullen
　　　　Thompson Bennett

Attorneys for: General Motors Corp.; Wal-Mart Stores; Borgess Medical Center; Aetna Insurance: Kemper Group; Medical Protective Co.; Zurich Insurance; AAA; Liberty Mutual; Home Insurance.

For full biographical listings, see the Martindale-Hubbell Law Directory

Kalamazoo—Continued

HOWARD & HOWARD ATTORNEYS, P.C. (AV)

The Kalamazoo Building, Suite 400, 107 West Michigan
   Avenue, 49007-3956
Telephone: 616-382-1483
Telecopier: 616-382-1568
Bloomfield Hills, Michigan Office: The Pinehurst Office Center, Suite 101,
1400 North Woodward Avenue.
Telephone: 810-645-1483.
Telecopier: 810-645-1568.
Lansing, Michigan Office: The Phoenix Building, Suite 500, 222
Washington Square North.
Telephone: 517-485-1483.
Telecopier: 517-485-1568.
Peoria, Illinois Office: The Creve Coeur Building, Suite 200, 321 Liberty
Street.
Telephone: 309-672-1483.
Telecopier: 309-672-1568.
Tampa, Florida Office: First of America Plaza, Suite 2000, 201 East
Kennedy Boulevard.
Telephone: 813-229-1483.
Telecopier: 813-229-1568.

John W. Allen	Bruce R. Grubb
Gerry Bartlett-McMahon	Joseph B. Hemker
Robert C. Beck	John C. Howard
Stephen D. Bigelow	J. Michael Kemp
Eric E. Breisach	Peter J. Livingston
Jeffrey P. Chalmers	D. Craig Martin
Michael L. Chojnowski	Lawrence J. Murphy
William A. Dornbos	David E. Riggs
James H. Geary	Shamra M. Van Wagoner

Myra L. Willis

Representative Clients: First of America Bank Corporation; Simpson Paper
Co.; Kellogg Co.; Stryker Corp.; Chrysler Corporation.

For full biographical listings, see the Martindale-Hubbell Law Directory

---

KREIS, ENDERLE, CALLANDER & HUDGINS, A PROFESSIONAL CORPORATION (AV)

One Moorsbridge, P.O. Box 4010, 49003-4010
Telephone: 616-324-3000
Telecopier: 616-324-3010
Email: kech@sapien.net *URL:* http://www.kech.com

Russell A. Kreis	Thomas G. King
Alan G. Enderle	Daniel P. McGlinn
Douglas L. Callander	Raymond C. Schultz
C. Reid Hudgins III	Jeffrey D. Swenarton
Robert B. Borsos	James C. Boerigter
Jeffrey C. O'Brien	John F. Koryto
Stephen J. Hessen	Janice Roark Peters
Jeffery S. Rubel	Matthew S. DePerno

For full biographical listings, see the Martindale-Hubbell Law Directory

---

LEWIS & ALLEN, P.C. (AV)

Old Kent Bank Building, Suite 800, 136 East Michigan
   Avenue, 49007-3946
Telephone: 616-388-7600
Fax: 616-349-3831

Dean S. Lewis	William A. Redmond
W. Fred Allen, Jr.	Stephen M. Denenfeld
Winfield J. Hollander	Gregory G. St. Arnauld
Bruce W. Martin	Anne McGregor Fries
Daniel L. Conklin	Thomas P. Lewis

Christopher T. Haenicke

LEGAL SUPPORT PERSONNEL

Dorothy B. Kelly

For full biographical listings, see the Martindale-Hubbell Law Directory

---

LILLY & LILLY, P.C. (AV)

505 South Park Street, 49007
Telephone: 616-381-7763
Fax: 616-344-6880

Charles M. Lilly (1903-1990)   Terrence J. Lilly

For full biographical listings, see the Martindale-Hubbell Law Directory

MILLER, CANFIELD, PADDOCK AND STONE, P.L.C. (AV)

A Professional Limited Liability Company
Founded in 1852 by Sidney Davy Miller
444 West Michigan Avenue, 49007-3752
Telephone: 616-381-7030
Fax: 616-382-0244
Detroit, Michigan Office: 150 West Jefferson, Suite 2500, 48226-4415.
Telephone: 313-963-6420.
Fax: 313-496-7500.
Cable Address: "Stem Detroit."
Ann Arbor, Michigan Office: 101 North Main Street, 7th Floor,
48104-1400.
Telephone: 313-663-2445.
Fax: 313-747-7147.
Bloomfield Hills, Michigan Office: Suite 100, Pinehurst Office Center, 1400
North Woodward, 48303-2014.
Telephone: 313-645-5000.
Fax: 313-645-1917.
Grand Rapids, Michigan Office: 1200 Campau Square Plaza, 99 Monroe,
N.W., 49503-2639.
Telephone: 616-454-8656.
Fax: 616-776-6322.
Howell, Michigan Office: 121 South Barnard Street, Suite 4, 48843-2305.
Telephone: 517-546-7600.
Telecopier: 517-546-6974.
Lansing, Michigan Office: One Michigan Avenue, Suite 900, 48933-1609.
Telephone: 517-487-2070.
Fax: 517-374-6304.
Monroe, Michigan Office: The Executive Centre, 214 East Elm Avenue,
48161-2682.
Telephone: 313-243-2000.
Fax: 313-243-0901.
Washington, D.C. Office: 1225 Nineteenth Street, N.W., Suite 400. 20036.
Telephone: 202-429-5575; 785-0600.
Fax: 202-331-1118; 785-1234.
Pensacola, Florida Office: 25 West Cedar, 32501.
Telephone: 904-469-1088.
Fax: 904-432-0677.
St. Petersburg, Florida Office: 100 Second Avenue S., Suite 7045, 33701.
Telephone: 813-982-6000.
Fax: 813-892-6002.
New York, New York Office: Eleventh Floor, 135 East 57th Street,
10022-2087.
Telephone: 212-754-5400.
Fax: 212-754-5401.
Gdansk, Poland Office: Suite 322, Dom Technika Building, UI. Rajska 6,
80-850.
Telephone: 011-485-831-2808.
Fax: 011-485-831-4719.
Warsaw, Poland Office: UI. Marszalkowska 82, Suite 561, 00-517.
Telephone: 011-482-623-6457 and 6458.
Fax: 011-482-623-6459.

PRINCIPALS OF FIRM

Eric V. Brown, Jr.	Thomas H. Van Dis
Charles E. Ritter	James E. Spurr
John A. Campbell	Steven M. Stankewicz
Thomas P. Hustoles	Vernon Bennett III
John R. Cook	Pamela Chapman Enslen
James G. Vantine, Jr.	Don M. Schmidt
Kevin M. McCarthy	Kurt N. Sherwood
Ronald E. Baylor	
Charles S. Mishkind (Grand Rapids, Detroit and Lansing Offices)	

OF COUNSEL

Eric V. Brown, Sr.	Gerard Thomas

SENIOR ATTORNEYS

Leo P. Goddeyne	John G. VanSlambrouck

ASSOCIATES

Ballard Jay Yelton, III	Kurt P. McCamman
Lori L. Purkey	Scott R. Sikkenga
Loyal A. Eldridge, III	James B. Thelen

Karen M. Hassevoort

Representative Firm Clients: Chrysler Corporation; Comerica, Incorporated;
City of Detroit, Michigan; Detroit Tigers, Inc.; First of Michigan; Ford Mo-
tor Company; Ford Motor Credit Company; Great Lakes Bancorp; Henry
Ford Hospital; INVETECH Company.

For full biographical listings, see the Martindale-Hubbell Law Directory

Kalamazoo—Continued

VARNUM, RIDDERING, SCHMIDT & HOWLETT LLP (AV)

A Limited Liability Partnership including Professional Corporations
350 East Michigan Avenue, 49007
Telephone: 616-382-2300
Facsimile: 616-382-2382
Email: varnum@vrsh.com
Grand Rapids, Michigan Office: Bridgewater Place, P.O. Box 352, 49501-0352.
Telephone: 616-336-6000; 800-262-0011.
Facsimile: 616-336-7000.
Telex: 1561593 VARN.
Lansing, Michigan Office: The Victor Center, Suite 810, 210 North Washington Square, 48933.
Telephone: 517-482-6237.
Facsimile: 517-482-6937.
Grand Haven, Michigan Office: 321 Washington Street, P.O. Box 288.
Telephone: 616-846-7100.
Facsimile: 616-846-7101.
Battle Creek, Michigan Office: 4950 West Dickman Road, Suite B-1, 49015.
Telephone: 616-962-7144.
Bingham Farms, Michigan Office: 31600 Telegraph Road, Suite 230, 48025.
Telephone: 810-594-7330. 810-594-7331.

MEMBERS OF FIRM

Thomas T. Huff (Resident)	Jeffrey D. Smith (Resident)
Richard A. Hooker (Resident)	Michael S. McElwee (Resident)
Richard D. Fries (Resident)	

COUNSEL
Peter Visserman

ASSOCIATES

Eric J. Guerin (Resident)	Alfred L. Schubkegel, Jr. (Resident)

Counsel For: AgriStor Credit Corp.; ASMO Manufacturing (Japan); Armstrong International; Arvco Container Corp.; Bond Supply Co.; Bowers Manufacturing Co.; Channel 41, Inc.; Comerica Bank-Kalamazoo; Getman Corp.; Michigan National Bank.

For full biographical listings, see the Martindale-Hubbell Law Directory

---

LANSING, Ingham Co.

* indicates certain Bar Register subscribers whose principal office is located elsewhere in the state and who have arranged for representation as a part of the state capital listings that follow

---

* DICKINSON, WRIGHT, MOON, VAN DUSEN & FREEMAN (AV)

Suite 200, 215 South Washington Square, 48933-1816
Telephone: 517-371-1730
Facsimile: 517-487-4700
Detroit, Michigan Office: 500 Woodward Avenue, Suite 4000.
Telephone: 313-223-3500.
Facsimile: 313-223-3598.
Bloomfield Hills, Michigan Office: 525 North Woodward Avenue, Suite 2000.
Telephone: 810-433-7200.
Facsimile: 810-433-7274.
Grand Rapids, Michigan Office: 200 Ottawa Avenue, N.W., Suite 900.
Telephone: 616-458-1300. Facsimile 616-458-6753.
Washington, D.C. Office: Suite 800, 1901 L Street, N.W.
Telephone: 202-457-0160.
Facsimile: 202-659-1559.
Chicago, Illinois Office: 225 West Washington, Suite 400.
Telephone: 312-220-0300.
Facsimile: 312-220-0021.

RESIDENT PARTNERS

William C. Bertrand, Jr.	Kirk E. Grable
James W. Bliss	Richard D McNulty
Dwight D. Ebaugh	David E. Pierson
Peter H. Ellsworth	Peter S. Sheldon
Joseph A. Fink	Kester K. So
Jeffery V. Stuckey	

OF COUNSEL
Michael F. Gadola

CONSULTING PARTNER
Judson Werbelow

RESIDENT ASSOCIATES

Edward R. Becker	Jeffrey E. Thompson
Amy E. Martin (Not admitted in MI)	

For full biographical listings, see the Martindale-Hubbell Law Directory

---

DUNNINGS & FRAWLEY, P.C. (AV)

Duncan Building, 530 South Pine Street, 48933-2299
Telephone: 517-487-8222
Fax: 517-487-2026
Email: conrights@voyager.net

Stuart J. Dunnings, Jr.	John J. Frawley

Stuart J. Dunnings, III	Steven D. Dunnings
Shauna L. Dunnings	

Representative Clients: Lansing Board of Education; Lansing Housing Commission; Ford Motor Co.
References: First of America; Michigan National Bank.

For full biographical listings, see the Martindale-Hubbell Law Directory

---

* DYKEMA GOSSETT PLLC (AV)

800 Michigan National Tower, 48933-1707
Telephone: 517-374-9100
Telex: 23-0121
Fax: 517-374-9191
Email: 2084153@mcimail.com
Ann Arbor, Michigan Office: 315 East Eisenhower Parkway, Suite 100, 49108-3306.
Telephone: 313-747-7660.
Fax: 313-747-7696.
Bloomfield Hills, Michigan Office: 1577 North Woodward Avenue, Suite 300, 48304-2820.
Telephone: 810-540-0700.
Fax: 810-540-0763.
Chicago, Illinois Office: 55 East Monroe Street, Suite 3250, 60603-5709.
Telephone: 312-551-4900.
Fax: 312-551-4919.
Detroit, Michigan Office: 400 Renaissance Center, 48243-1668.
Telephone: 313-568-6800.
Fax: 313-568-6594.
Grand Rapids, Michigan Office: 200 Oldtown Riverfront Building, 248 Louis Campau Promenade, N.W., 49503-2668.
Telephone: 616-776-7500.
Fax: 616-776-7573.
Washington, D.C. Office: Franklin Square, Suite 300 West, 1300 I Street, N.W., 20005-3306.
Telephone: 202-522-8600.
Fax: 202-522-8669.

RESIDENT MEMBERS

Alan R. Dominick	William J. Perrone
Albert Ernst	Lori M. Silsbury
James P. Kiefer	Stephen H. Zimmerman
Richard D. McLellan (Member in Charge)	

RESIDENT ASSOCIATES

Michael J. Brown	Julia A. Goatley
Sandra Miller Cotter	Robert E. Smith
Ann D. Fillingham	Wendell Alan Wilk
Leonard C. Wolfe	

For full biographical listings, see the Martindale-Hubbell Law Directory

---

FOSTER, SWIFT, COLLINS & SMITH, P.C. (AV)

313 South Washington Square, 48933-2193
Telephone: 517-371-8100
Telecopier: 517-371-8200
URL: http://www.fosterswift.com
Farmington Hills, Michigan Office: 32300 Northwestern Highway, Suite 230.
Telephone: 810-539-9900.
Fax: 810-851-7504.

Walter S. Foster (1877-1961)	David J. Houston
Richard B. Foster	Brian A. Kaser
Lawrence B. Lindemer	Steven L. Owen
Theodore W. Swift	Sherry A. Stein
John L. Collins	Brent A. Titus
Webb A. Smith	Stephen J. Lowney
Allan J. Claypool	Louis K. Nigg
Gary J. McRay	Glen A. Schmiege
Robert J. McCullen	Patricia A. Calore
Stephen I. Jurmu	Kevin T. McGraw
William K. Fahey	Michael J. Bommarito
Stephen O. Schultz	Deanna Swisher
William R. Schulz	Jean G. Schtokal
David H. Aldrich	Mark H. Canady
Scott A. Storey	Eric E. Doster
Charles A. Janssen	Michael W. Puerner
Charles E. Barbieri	Stephen J. Rhodes
James B. Jensen, Jr.	Matt G. Hrebec
Scott L. Mandel	James M. Alexander
Robert E. McFarland	Brian G. Goodenough
Kathryn M. Niemer	Melissa J. Jackson
James B. Croom	Steven H. Lasher
Michael D. Sanders	Nancy L. Kahn

(See Next Column)

FOSTER, SWIFT, COLLINS & SMITH P.C.—*Continued*

Mark J. Burzych	Todd A. Smith
Thomas R. Meagher	Matthew W. Collins
Douglas A. Mielock	Sheralee S. Hurwitz
Scott R. Forbush	Christopher A. Ballard
Peter R. Albertins	Rebecca S. Davies
Scott A. Chernich	Andrea J. Roe
Lisa E. Claypool	Jennifer M. Van Horn

R. Lance Boldrey

OF COUNSEL

John W. Ester	David VanderHaagen

Kenneth T. Brooks

LEGAL SUPPORT PERSONNEL

LEGAL ASSISTANTS

Laurie A. Awad	Michelle A. Payne
Sharon K. Carpenter	Jeanne M. Phillips
Sandra L. De Santis	Toni R. Rhodabeck
Victoria J.A. Dye	Lisa J. Silverthorn, CLA
Kelly A. LaGrave, CLA	Theresa G. Solberg
Anita R. Lindgren	Janice S. Underwood

Jaxine L. Wintjen, CLA

General Counsel for: First American Bank-Central; Story, Inc.; Michigan Milk Producers Assn.; Edward W. Sparrow Hospital; St. Lawrence Hospital; Demmer Corp.; Michigan Financial Corp.
Local Counsel for: Shell Oil Co.; Michigan-Mutual Insurance Co.; Century Telephone.

For full biographical listings, see the Martindale-Hubbell Law Directory

---

FRASER TREBILCOCK DAVIS & FOSTER, P.C. (AV)

1000 Michigan National Tower, 48933
Telephone: 517-482-5800
Fax: 517-482-0887

Joe C. Foster, Jr.	Ronald R. Sutton
Eugene Townsend (1926-1982)	Iris K. Socolofsky-Linder
Ronald R. Pentecost	Brett Jon Bean
Peter L. Dunlap	Richard C. Lowe
Everett R. Zack	Gary C. Rogers
Douglas J. Austin	Mark A. Bush
Robert W. Stocker, II	Michael H. Perry
Michael E. Cavanaugh	Brandon W. Zuk
John J. Loose	David D. Waddell
David E. S. Marvin	Thomas J. Waters
Stephen L. Burlingame	Mark R. Fox
C. Mark Hoover	Nancy L. Little
Darrell A. Lindman	Sharon A. Bruner

Michael C. Levine	Brian D. Herrington
Michael S. Ashton	David Brickey
Michael James Reilly	Marcy R. Meyer
Michelyn E. Pastuer	Wendy Mrazek Guilfoyle
Patrick K. Thornton	Graham K. Crabtree
Charyn K. Hain	Melinda A. Carlson

Kerry D. Hettinger

OF COUNSEL

Archie C. Fraser	James R. Davis
Everett R. Trebilcock	Donald A. Hines

Counsel for: Auto Club Insurance Assn. (ACIA); Auto Owners Insurance Co.; City of Mackinac Island; Federal Insurance Co.; Grand Trunk Railroad Co.; Prudential Insurance Company of America; State Farm Automobile Insurance Co.

For full biographical listings, see the Martindale-Hubbell Law Directory

---

✱ HONIGMAN MILLER SCHWARTZ AND COHN (AV)

A Partnership including Professional Corporations
222 North Washington Square, Suite 400, 48933-1800
Telephone: 517-484-8282
Telecopier: 517-484-8286
URL: http://law.honigman.com
Detroit, Michigan Office: 2290 First National Building, 48226.
Telephone: 313-256-7800.
West Palm Beach, Florida Office: Suite 800 Esperante Building, 222 Lakeview Avenue, 33401-6112.
Telephone: 561-838-4500.
Tampa, Florida Office: 2700 SunTrust Financial Centre, 401 E. Jackson Street, 33602-5226.
Telephone: 813-221-6600.

MEMBERS

Richard J. Aaron	Mark Morton
Frederick M. Baker, Jr.	John D. Pirich
Daniel J. Demlow	Benjamin O. Schwendener, Jr.
Sandra L. Jasinski	Gary A. Trepod
John S. Kane	Alan M. Valade
Timothy Sawyer Knowlton	William C. Whitbeck

Ruth E. Zimmerman

(See Next Column)

ASSOCIATES

Ann L. Andrews	Andrea Hansen
Andrew J. Gerdes	Mary Ann Taylor

General Counsel for: Dart Container Corp; Forbes-Cohen Properties (The Lansing Mall); Granger Land Development Co.; Michigan Hospital Association.
Legal or Special Counsel for: Champion International; Greater Detroit Resource Recovery Authority; First American Title Insurance Company of the Midwest; Michigan Gas Utilities, a division of UtiliCorp United, Inc.

For full biographical listings, see the Martindale-Hubbell Law Directory

---

HOWARD & HOWARD ATTORNEYS, P.C. (AV)

The Phoenix Building, Suite 500, 222 Washington Square, North, 48933-1817
Telephone: 517-485-1483
Telecopier: 517-485-1568
Kalamazoo, Michigan Office: The Kalamazoo Building, Suite 400, 107 West Michigan Avenue.
Telephone: 616-382-1483.
Telecopier: 616-382-1568.
Bloomfield Hills, Michigan Office: The Pinehurst Office Center, Suite 101, 1400 North Woodward Avenue.
Telephone: 810-645-1483.
Telecopier: 810-645-1568.
Peoria, Illinois Office: The Creve Coeur Building, Suite 200, 321 Liberty Street.
Telephone: 309-672-1483.
Telecopier: 309-672-1568.
Tampa, Florida Office: First of America Plaza, Suite 2000, 201 East Kennedy Boulevard.
Telephone: 813-229-1483.
Telecopier: 813-229-1568.

Todd D. Chamberlain	J. Michael Kemp
Christopher C. Cinnamon	James E. Lozier
David C. Coey	D. Craig Martin
Kim D. Crooks	C. Douglas Moran
Michele LaForest Halloran	Brad S. Rutledge
Patrick D. Hanes	Gina M. Torielli
Ellen M. Harvath	Donald F. Tucker

Patrick R. Van Tiflin

Representative Clients: First of America Bank Corporation; W.R. Grace & Co.; Chrysler Corp.; Deere & Company; CSX Transportation, Inc.
Local Counsel for: General Motors Corp.; American Cyanamid Co.

For full biographical listings, see the Martindale-Hubbell Law Directory

---

LOOMIS, EWERT, PARSLEY, DAVIS & GOTTING, P.C. (AV)

232 South Capitol Avenue, Suite 1000, 48933
Telephone: 517-482-2400
Facsimile: 517-482-0070

Plummer Snyder (1900-1974)	Michael G. Oliva
William D. Parsley	Jeffrey W. Bracken
Jack C. Davis (P.C.)	Catherine A. Jacobs
Karl L. Gotting (P.C.)	Ronald W. Bloomberg
David M. Lick	Michael H. Rhodes
Harvey J. Messing	Howard J. Soifer
James R. Neal	Jeffrey L. Green
Kenneth W. Beall	Gary L. Field

Sherri A. Wellman	Marc D. Matlock
Kelly K. Reed	Eldonna M. Ruddock
Jeffrey S. Theuer	Todd A. Svanda

OF COUNSEL

George W. Loomis (P.C.)	Quentin A. Ewert

Representative Clients: Altman Development Co.; Century Telephone Enterprises; Columbian Distribution, Inc.; Comerica Bank; Consumers Power Co.; The Douglas Company; Southeastern Michigan Gas Enterprises, Inc.; Wal-Mart Stores, Inc.; Wisconsin Electric Power Co.

For full biographical listings, see the Martindale-Hubbell Law Directory

---

MILLER, CANFIELD, PADDOCK AND STONE, P.L.C. (AV)

A Professional Limited Liability Company
Founded in 1852 by Sidney Davy Miller
Suite 900, One Michigan Avenue, 48933-1609
Telephone: 517-487-2070
Fax: 517-374-6304
Detroit, Michigan Office: 150 West Jefferson, Suite 2500, 48226-4415.
Telephone: 313-963-6420.
Fax: 313-496-7500.
Cable Address: "Stem Detroit."
Ann Arbor, Michigan Office: 101 North Main Street, 7th Floor, 48104-1400.
Telephone: 313-663-2445.
Fax: 313-747-7147.

(See Next Column)

MILLER, CANFIELD, PADDOCK AND STONE P.L.C., *Lansing—Continued*

Bloomfield Hills, Michigan Office: Suite 100, Pinehurst Office Center, 1400 North Woodward, 48303-2014.
Telephone: 313-645-5000.
Fax: 313-645-1917.
Grand Rapids, Michigan Office: 1200 Campau Square Plaza, 99 Monroe, N.W., 49503-2639.
Telephone: 616-454-8656.
Fax: 616-776-6322.
Howell, Michigan Office: 121 South Barnard Street, Suite 4, 48843-2305.
Telephone: 517-546-7600.
Telecopier: 517-546-6974.
Kalamazoo, Michigan Office: 444 West Michigan Avenue, 49007-3752.
Telephone: 616-381-7030.
Fax: 616-382-0244.
Monroe, Michigan Office: The Executive Centre, 214 East Elm Avenue, 48161-2682.
Telephone: 313-243-2000.
Fax: 313-243-0901.
Washington, D.C. Office: 1225 Nineteenth Street, N.W., Suite 400. 20036.
Telephone: 202-429-5575; 785-0600.
Fax: 202-331-1118; 785-1234.
Pensacola, Florida Office: 25 West Cedar, 32501.
Telephone: 904-469-1088.
Fax: 904-432-0677.
St. Petersburg Office: 100 Second Avenue S., Suite 7045, 33701.
Telephone: 813-982-6000.
Fax: 813-892-6002.
New York, New York Office: Eleventh Floor, 135 East 57th Street, 10022-2087.
Telephone: 212-754-5400.
Fax: 212-754-5401.
Gdansk, Poland Office: Suite 322, Dom Technika Building, UI. Rajska 6, 80-850.
Telephone: 011-485-831-2808.
Fax: 011-485-831-4719.
Warsaw, Poland Office: UI. Marszalkowska 82, Suite 561, 00-517.
Telephone: 011-482-623-6457 and 6458.
Fax: 011-482-623-6459.

PRINCIPALS OF FIRM

William J. Danhof (Resident)
Michael R. Atkins (Resident)
Thomas C. Phillips (Resident)
Christopher J. Dembowski (Resident)
Michael J. Hodge (Resident)
Cynthia B. Faulhaber (President)
Kevin J. Moody (Resident)
Jay B. Rising (Resident)

OF COUNSEL

Lawrence D. Owen (Resident)   Steven E. Chester

RESIDENT SENIOR ATTORNEY

Sherry Katz-Crank

SENIOR ATTORNEY

Clifford T. Flood

RESIDENT ASSOCIATES

James R. Lancaster, Jr.   Dean M. Altobelli
Louis B. Reinwasser

Representative Firm Clients: Chrysler Corporation; Comerica, Incorporated; City of Detroit, Michigan; Detroit Tigers, Inc.; First of Michigan; Ford Motor Company; Ford Motor Credit Company; Great Lakes Bancorp; Henry Ford Hospital; INVETECH Company.

For full biographical listings, see the Martindale-Hubbell Law Directory

SMITH HAUGHEY RICE & ROEGGE, P.C.

(See East Lansing)

TIMMER, JAMO & O'LEARY (AV)

521 Seymour Avenue, 48933
Telephone: 517-371-3500
Fax: 517-371-4514

MEMBERS OF FIRM

James A. Timmer   James S. O'Leary
James S. Jamo   Kathleen A. Lopilato

Representative Clients: Auto-Owners Insurance Co.; National Indemnity Insurance Co.; Travelers Insurance Co.; Ohio Farmers Insurance Co.; Bankers Life & Casualty Co.; Western Casualty & Surety Co.; Indiana Insurance Group; Western Surety Co.; Michigan Municipal League; Preston Trucking.

For full biographical listings, see the Martindale-Hubbell Law Directory

---

LAPEER, * Lapeer Co.

TAYLOR, BUTTERFIELD, RISEMAN, CLARK, HOWELL AND CHURCHILL, P.C. (AV)

407 Clay Street, 48446
Telephone: 810-664-5921
Fax: 810-664-0904

(See Next Column)

Robert L. Taylor (1909-1992)
Carl M. Riseman
Thomas K. Butterfield
Emory W. Clark
Gary W. Howell
David J. Churchill

Steven D. Jarvis   Erik J. Reinhardt
Ronald D. Elling

Representative Clients: Lapeer County Bank & Trust Co.; State Mutual Insurance Co.; Kirk Construction Co.; Lapeer County & City Economic Development Corp.; Lapeer Co. Abstract & Title Co.; Carl M. Schultz, Inc.; Lapeer Metal Products, Inc.; Capac State Bank; Southern Thumb Co-op, Inc.; Camtron Coatings Company.

For full biographical listings, see the Martindale-Hubbell Law Directory

---

LELAND, * Leelanau Co.

MURCHIE, CALCUTT & BOYNTON

(See Traverse City)

MANISTEE, * Manistee Co. — (Refer to Ludington)

MANISTIQUE, * Schoolcraft Co. — (Refer to Escanaba)

MARQUETTE, * Marquette Co.

KENDRICKS BORDEAU, P.C. (AV)

128 West Spring Street, 49855
Telephone: 906-226-2543
Fax: 906-226-2819

George T. Kendricks (1918-1991)
Robert M. Bordeau
Stephen F. Adamini
Ronald D. Keefe
William R. Smith
Dennis H. Girard
Kenneth J. Seavoy
D. Gregor MacGregor, III
Tami M. Seavoy
Michael J. Kolasa
Scott A. Wolfson

For full biographical listings, see the Martindale-Hubbell Law Directory

---

MARSHALL, * Calhoun Co. — (Refer to Battle Creek)

MENOMINEE, * Menominee Co. — (Refer to Escanaba)

MIDLAND, * Midland Co.

HANDLON, EASTMAN & DEWITT, P.C. (AV)

Suite 1100 Courthouse Square Building, 240 West Main Street, 48640
Telephone: 517-631-5490
Fax: 517-631-1777

Richard M. Handlon   David S. DeWitt
Tad J. Eastman   Michael J. Beale

Representative Clients: Comerica Bank-Midland Co.; Household Finance; Remax, Inc.; Stanford L.P. Gas, Inc.; Cherryview Development Corp.; Buckingham Computer Services, Inc.
References: Comerica Bank-Midland; Chemical Bank & Trust Co.

For full biographical listings, see the Martindale-Hubbell Law Directory

---

RIECKER, VAN DAM, BARKER, BLACK & ZUBER, P.C. (AV)

414 Townsend Street, P.O. Box 632, 48640
Telephone: 517-631-1025
Facsimile: 517-631-9880

John E. Riecker   Richard William Barker
Philip Van Dam   R. Drummond Black
Julie M. Zuber

General Counsel for: Herbert H. and Grace A. Dow Foundation; Harry A. and Margaret D. Towsley Foundation; Midland Center for the Arts; Dow-Howell-Gilmore Associates, Inc.
Counsel for: Comerica Bank N.A.; Mid Michigan Regional Health System; Wolverine Bank, F.B.S.; Northern Star Companies; Midland County Growth and Economic Development Corp.; Bresnan Communications, Inc.

For full biographical listings, see the Martindale-Hubbell Law Directory

---

MONROE, * Monroe Co.

JAFFE, RAITT, HEUER & WEISS, PROFESSIONAL CORPORATION (AV)

214 East Elm Avenue, Suite 208, 48161
Telephone: 313-241-6470
Telefacsimile: 313-241-3849
Detroit, Michigan Office: One Woodward Avenue, Suite 2400.
Telephone: 313-961-8380.
Telecopier: 313-961-8358.
Southfield, Michigan Office: Suite 1520, Travelers Tower.
Telephone: 313-961-8380.

Alexander B. Bragdon   James G. Petrangelo (Resident)
John A. Hohman, Jr. (Resident)   Lawrence R. Shoffner

(See Next Column)

JAFFE, RAITT, HEUER & WEISS PROFESSIONAL CORPORATION—*Continued*

Kerry Gross-Bondy (Resident)
Representative Clients: Berlin Township; Frenchtown Charter Township.

For full biographical listings, see the Martindale-Hubbell Law Directory

MILLER, CANFIELD, PADDOCK AND STONE, P.L.C. (AV)

A Professional Limited Liability Company
Founded in 1852 by Sidney Davy Miller
The Executive Centre, 214 East Elm Avenue, 48161-2682
Telephone: 313-243-2000
Fax: 313-243-0901
Detroit, Michigan Office: 150 West Jefferson, Suite 2500, 48226-4415.
Telephone: 313-963-6420.
Fax: 313-496-7500.
Cable Address: "Stem Detroit."
Ann Arbor, Michigan Office: 101 North Main Street, 7th Floor, 48104-1400.
Telephone: 313-663-2445.
Fax: 313-747-7147.
Bloomfield Hills, Michigan Office: Suite 100, Pinehurst Office Center, 1400 North Woodward, 48303-2014.
Telephone: 313-645-5000.
Fax: 313-645-1917.
Grand Rapids, Michigan Office: 1200 Campau Square Plaza, 99 Monroe, N.W., 49503-2639.
Telephone: 616-454-8656.
Fax: 616-776-6322.
Howell, Michigan Office: 121 South Barnard Street, Suite 4, 48843-2305.
Telephone: 517-546-7600.
Telecopier: 517-546-6974.
Kalamazoo, Michigan Office: 444 West Michigan Avenue, 49007-3752.
Telephone: 616-381-7030.
Fax: 616-382-0244.
Lansing, Michigan Office: One Michigan Avenue, Suite 900, 48933-1609.
Telephone: 517-487-2070.
Fax: 517-374-6304.
Washington, D.C. Office: 1225 Nineteenth Street, N.W., Suite 400. 20036.
Telephone: 202-429-5575; 785-0600.
Fax: 202-331-1118; 785-1234.
Pensacola, Florida Office: 25 West Cedar, 32501.
Telephone: 904-469-1088.
Fax: 904-432-0677.
St. Petersburg, Florida Office: 100 Second Avenue S., Suite 7045, 33701.
Telephone: 813-982-6000.
Fax: 813-892-6002.
Gdansk, Poland Office: Suite 322, Dom Technika Building, UI. Rajska 6, 80-850.
Telephone: 011-485-831-2808.
Fax: 011-485-831-4719.
Warsaw, Poland Office: UI. Marszalkowska 82, Suite 561, 00-517.
Telephone: 011-482-623-6457 and 6458.
Fax: 011-482-623-6459.

RESIDENT PRINCIPALS
Rocque E. Lipford (P.C.)

Representative Firm Clients: Chrysler Corporation; Comerica, Incorporated; City of Detroit, Michigan; Detroit Tigers, Inc.; First of Michigan; Ford Motor Company; Ford Motor Credit Company; Great Lakes Bancorp; Henry Ford Hospital; INVETECH Company.

For full biographical listings, see the Martindale-Hubbell Law Directory

READY, SULLIVAN & READY, L.L.P. (AV)

204 South Macomb Street, 48161
Telephone: 313-242-7600
Fax: 313-242-0366

MEMBERS OF FIRM

Thomas D. Ready	Durward L. Hutchinson
Michael L. Heller	John F. Ready

ASSOCIATES

Conly K. Crossley	Timothy F. Sheridan
Christina D. Hills	Frank L. Arnold

Representative Client: Motorists Insurance Cos.

For full biographical listings, see the Martindale-Hubbell Law Directory

MOUNT CLEMENS,* Macomb Co.

GARAN, LUCOW, MILLER, SEWARD & BECKER, P.C. (AV)

Towne Square Development, 10 S. Main Street Suite 307, 48043-2370
Telephone: 810-954-3800
Fax: 810-954-3803
Detroit, Michigan Office: 1000 Woodbridge Place.
Telephone: 313-446-1530.
Fax: 313-259-0450.
Grand Blanc, Michigan Office: 8332 Office Park Drive.
Telephone: 810-695-3700.
Fax: 810-695-6488.

(See Next Column)

Ann Arbor, Michigan Office: 101 North Main Street, Suite 801.
Telephone: 313-930-5600.
Fax: 313-930-0043.
Troy, Michigan Office: 1111 West Long Lake Road, Suite 300.
Telephone: 810-641-7600.
Fax: 810-641-0222.
Port Huron, Michigan Office: Port Huron Office Center, 511 Fort Street, Suite 505.
Telephone: 810-985-4400.
Fax: 810-985-4107.
Grand Rapids, Michigan Office: Campau Square Plaza Building, 99 Monroe Avenue N.W., Suite 102.
Telephone: 616-732-5330.
Fax: 616-732-5333.

Millard W. H. Becker, Jr.	Richard E. Eaton

Timothy E. O'Neill

For full biographical listings, see the Martindale-Hubbell Law Directory

VANDEVEER GARZIA, PROFESSIONAL CORPORATION (AV)

50 Crocker Boulevard, 48043
Telephone: 810-468-4880
Fax: 810-465-7159
Wayne County Office: Suite 1600, 333 West Fort Street, Detroit, Michigan.
Telephone: 313-961-4880.
Fax: 313-961-3822.
Oakland County Office: 220 Park Street, Suite 300, Birmingham, Michigan.
Telephone: 810-645-0100.
Fax: 810-645-2430.
West Michigan Office: 1121 Ottawa Beach Road, Suite 140, Holland, Michigan.
Telephone: 616-399-8600.
Fax: 616-786-9095.

RESIDENT PERSONNEL
Ronald L. Cornell

Representative Clients: Aetna Casualty and Surety Co.; Chubb Insurance; Farmers Insurance Group; Goodyear Tire & Rubber Co.; Transamerica Insurance Group.

For full biographical listings, see the Martindale-Hubbell Law Directory

MOUNT PLEASANT,* Isabella Co.

HALL AND LEWIS, P.C. (AV)

300 South University Avenue, 48858
Telephone: 517-773-0004
Fax: 517-772-1512

Thomas W. Hall, Jr.	John W. Lewis

Dennis J. Nurkiewicz, Jr.

Representative Clients: Blodgett Oil Co., Inc.; Clark's Manufactured Homes, Inc.; Curtice Lumber Co.; DeWitt Lumber Co.; The Embers, Inc.; Exploration Enterprises, Inc.; Family Home Health Care; Fast Environmental, Inc.; Isabella Community Credit Union; Midland Area Credit Union.

For full biographical listings, see the Martindale-Hubbell Law Directory

LYNCH, GALLAGHER, LYNCH & MARTINEAU, P.L.L.C. (AV)

555 North Main Street, P.O. Box 446, 48858
Telephone: 517-773-9961
Fax: 517-773-2107
Lansing, Michigan Office: 2400 Lake Lansing Road, Suite B.
Telephone: 517-485-0400.
Fax: 517-485-0402.

MEMBERS OF FIRM

Edward N. Lynch (1908-1984)	Paula K. Manis
Byron P. Gallagher	(Resident at Lansing Office)
John J. Lynch	Michael J. Hackett
Steven W. Martineau	Byron P. Gallagher, Jr.
Sue A. Jeffers	Nancy E. Gallagher
Jennifer M. Galloway	

OF COUNSEL
Richard J. Garcia

Representative Clients: Amoco Production, Co.; Liquid Transport, Inc.; Central Concrete Products; Central Michigan University; Northern Michigan Oil and Gas Corp.

For full biographical listings, see the Martindale-Hubbell Law Directory

MUNISING,* Alger Co. — (Refer to Marquette)

MUSKEGON,* Muskegon Co.

CULVER, KNOWLTON, EVEN & FRANKS (AV)

250 Terrace Plaza, P.O. Box 629, 49443
Telephone: 616-724-4320
Telecopier: 616-724-4330

MEMBERS OF FIRM

Fred C. Culver, Jr.	Eugene A. Franks
Michael M. Knowlton	David E. Waterstradt
Kevin B. Even	Jeanette M. Colella
Foster D. Potter	

Representative Clients: SPX Corp.; First of America Bank-West Michigan; Old Kent Bank of Grand Haven; Comerica Bank; East Shore Chemical Company; Muskegon County Association of Realtors; Midland Groceries.

For full biographical listings, see the Martindale-Hubbell Law Directory

LAGUE, NEWMAN & IRISH, A PROFESSIONAL CORPORATION (AV)

600 Terrace Plaza, P.O. Box 389, 49443
Telephone: 616-725-8148
Telecopier: 616-726-3404
Email: firm@lnilaw.com

Eric R. Fox	Kit McPheeters
Eric R. Gielow	David R. Munroe
Karen L. Kayes	William M. Newman
Richard C. Lague	Philip M. Stoffan
Chris Ann McGuigan	J. Scott Timmer
Alvin D. Treado	

LEGAL SUPPORT PERSONNEL
Rebecca A. McCroskey

General Counsel: Hackley Hospital & Medical Center; Kaydon Corp.; Cole's Quality Foods; Kurdziel Industries.
Local Counsel: SPX Corp.; Booth Newspapers Inc.; First of America Bank-West Michigan; Spring Manufacturers Institute, Inc.

For full biographical listings, see the Martindale-Hubbell Law Directory

WARNER NORCROSS & JUDD LLP (AV)

400 Terrace Plaza, P.O. Box 900, 49443-0900
Telephone: 616-727-2600
Fax: 616-727-2699
Grand Rapids, Michigan Office: 900 Old Kent Building, 111 Lyon Street, N.W.
Telephone: 616-752-2000.
Fax: 616-752-2500.
Holland, Michigan Office: Curtis Center, Suite 300, 170 College Avenue.
Telephone: 616-396-9800.
Fax: 616-396-3656.

MEMBERS OF FIRM

Donald J. Veldman (Resident)	Thomas H. Thornhill (Resident)
I. John Snider, II (Resident)	John H. McKendry, Jr.
John H. Martin (Resident)	(Resident)
Michael L. Robinson	Paul R. Jackson (Resident)
Robert W. Sikkel	Michael H. Schubert (Resident)

ASSOCIATES

Rodrick W. Lewis	Michael I. Kleaveland (Resident)
Richard D. Cornell, Jr.	Paul L. Winter (Resident)
(Resident)	Robert Dubault (Resident)

Representative Clients: Amstore Corp.; Andrie, Inc.; Bristol-Myers Squibb; Cannon-Muskegon Corp.; Comerica Bank; Cordova Chemical Co.; First Michigan Bank Corp.; First of America Bank - West Michigan; Fisher Steel and Supply Co.; Hastings Manufacturing Co.

For full biographical listings, see the Martindale-Hubbell Law Directory

NEWBERRY,* Luce Co. — (Refer to Marquette)

NILES, Berrien Co.

HADSELL, LANDGRAF & LYNCH (AV)

19 South 3rd Street, P.O. Box 610, 49120
Telephone: 616-683-6500
Fax: 616-683-0600

MEMBERS OF FIRM

Philip A. Hadsell, Jr.	Christopher J. Lynch
Robert L. Landgraf, Jr.	René J. VanSteelandt

ASSOCIATES
Mona Walsh Holland

Representative Clients: National Standard Co.; French Paper Co.; Simplicity Pattern Co.; Lawyers' Title Insurance Corp.; Fairplain Plaza Co.; City of Niles; City of Buchanan; American Electric Power Co.

For full biographical listings, see the Martindale-Hubbell Law Directory

OWOSSO, Shiawassee Co. — (Refer to Flint)

PAW PAW,* Van Buren Co. — (Refer to Kalamazoo)

PETOSKEY,* Emmet Co.

STROUP & TRESIDDER, P.C. (AV)

Pennsylvania Plaza, P.O. Box 809, 49770
Telephone: 616-347-3907
Fax: 616-347-2499

Nathaniel W. Stroup	Stephen J. Tresidder
	Joel D. Wurster

Representative Clients: NBD of Petoskey, N.A.; Hodgkiss & Douma, Inc.; Michigan Physicians Mutual Liability Co.; Public Schools of Petoskey, Michigan; Top O'Michigan Electric Co.; Emmet County Road Commission; Amerisure.

For full biographical listings, see the Martindale-Hubbell Law Directory

PONTIAC,* Oakland Co.

BOOTH PATTERSON, P.C. (AV)

1090 West Huron Street, 48328
Telephone: 810-681-1200
Fax: 810-681-1754

Douglas W. Booth (1918-1992)	David J. Lee
Calvin E. Patterson (1913-1987)	Allan T. Motzny
Parvin C. Lee, Jr.	Michael J. Hughes
J. Timothy Patterson	Michael D. Bishop
Eric S. Meier	

For full biographical listings, see the Martindale-Hubbell Law Directory

PORT HURON,* St. Clair Co.

FLETCHER DeGROW (AV)

522 Michigan Street, 48060-3893
Telephone: 810-987-8444
Facsimile: 810-987-8149

MEMBERS OF FIRM

Gary A. Fletcher	Dan L. DeGrow
	Mark G. Clark

ASSOCIATES

John D. Tomlinson	William L. Fealko, III

OF COUNSEL
Anthony M. Bonadio

Representative Clients: Fremont Mutual Insurance Co.; Westfield Insurance Co.; Michigan Municipal Risk Management Authority; City of Port Huron; City of Marysville; Port Huron Area School District; Marysville Public Schools; Wirtz Manufacturing Co.; Raymond Excavating; Relleum Real Estate Development Co.

For full biographical listings, see the Martindale-Hubbell Law Directory

GARAN, LUCOW, MILLER, SEWARD & BECKER, P.C. (AV)

Port Huron Office Center, 511 Fort Street, Suite 505, 48060-3922
Telephone: 810-985-4400
Fax: 810-985-4107
Detroit, Michigan Office: 1000 Woodbridge Place.
Telephone: 313-446-1530.
Fax: 313-259-0450.
Grand Blanc, Michigan Office: 8332 Office Park Drive.
Telephone: 810-695-3700.
Fax: 810-695-6488.
Ann Arbor, Michigan Office: 101 North Main Street, Suite 801.
Telephone: 313-930-5600.
Fax: 313-930-0043.
Troy, Michigan Office: 1111 West Long Lake Road, Suite 300.
Telephone: 810-641-7600.
Fax: 810-641-0222.
Mount Clemens, Michigan Office: Towne Square Development, 10 S. Main Street, Suite 307.
Telephone: 810-954-3800.
Fax: 810-954-3803.
Grand Rapids, Michigan Office: Campau Square Plaza Building, 99 Monroe Avenue N.W., Suite 102.
Telephone: 616-732-5330.
Fax: 616-732-5333.

John P. Seyfried (Resident)

Randolph J. Martinek	David J. Roe

For full biographical listings, see the Martindale-Hubbell Law Directory

REED CITY,* Osceola Co. — (Refer to Big Rapids)

SAGINAW, * Saginaw Co.

BRAUN KENDRICK FINKBEINER PLC (AV)

101 N. Washington Suite 812, 48607-1297
Telephone: 517-753-3461
Telecopier: 517-753-3951
URL: http://www.bkf-law.com
Bay City, Michigan Office: 201 Phoenix Building, P.O. Box 2039.
Telephone: 517-895-8505.
Telecopier: 517-895-8437.
Ann Arbor, Michigan Office: 700 First National Building.
Telephone: 313-995-4100.
Telecopier: 313-995-4798.

Hugo E. Braun (1894-1973)	Robert A. Kendrick
Russell A. Schafer (1906-1982)	Charles A. Gilfeather
James V. Finkbeiner	Thomas R. Luplow
Hugo E. Braun, Jr.	John A. Decker
Edward J. McArdle (1938-1989)	Michael J. Sauer
Thomas F James (1940-1990)	Timothy L Curtiss
C. Patrick Kaltenbach	Scott C. Strattard
Harold J. Blanchet, Jr.	Craig W. Horn
David L. Turner	Francis J. Keating
Kenneth W. Kable	Barry M. Levine
E. Louis Ognisanti	Brian F. Bauer
Bruce L. Dalrymple	Judith A. Lincoln

Irenna M. Garapetian	Jamie C. Hecht Nisidis
Brian S. Makaric	Frances Kay Courter
Glenn L. Fitkin	Ellen E. Crane

OF COUNSEL

Thomas M. Murphy   J. Richard Kendrick
          Morton E. Weldy

Representative Clients: The Dow Chemical Co.; General Motors Corp.; Lobdell Emery Manufacturing Co.; Merrill, Lynch, Inc.; Saginaw General Hospital; Saginaw News; The Wickes Foundation.

For full biographical listings, see the Martindale-Hubbell Law Directory

O'NEILL, WALLACE & DOYLE, P.C. (AV)

Suite 302 Four Flags Office Center, 300 St. Andrews Road, P.O. Box 1966, 48605
Telephone: 517-790-0960
Fax: 517-790-6902
Flint, Michigan Office: 2483 South Linden Road.
Telephone: 810-732-7079.
Fax: 810-732-5889.

Terence J. O'Neill	Thomas J. Doyle
David A. Wallace	Charles F. Filipiak

David Carbajal	John J. Danieleski, Jr.
James E. O'Neill, III	Norman J. Christopherson

Representative Clients: Home Insurance Co.; Great American Insurance Co.; Farmers Insurance Co.; Cincinnati Insurance Co.; Ohio Casualty Insurance Co.; Safeco Insurance Co.; Liberty Mutual Insurance Co.; CUNA Mutual Insurance.; Pioneer State Mutual Insurance Co.; Auto Owners Insurance Co.

For full biographical listings, see the Martindale-Hubbell Law Directory

SMITH & BROOKER, P.C. (AV)

The Gold Building, 4855 State Street, Suite 4, 48603
Telephone: 517-799-1891
Fax: 517-799-1145
Bay City, Michigan Office: 703 Washington Avenue.
Telephone: 517-892-2595.
Flint, Michigan Office: 1309 South Linden Road, Suite C, P.O. Box 315000.
Telephone: 810-733-0140.

RESIDENT ATTORNEYS

Francis B. Drinan   Michael J. Huffman

OF COUNSEL

Carl H. Smith, Jr.   Albert C. Hicks

Representative Clients: CIGNA; Citizens Insurance Co.; City of Saginaw; Saginaw Township Community Schools; State Farm Mutual Automobile Insurance Co.; CSX Transportation.

For full biographical listings, see the Martindale-Hubbell Law Directory

ST. IGNACE, * Mackinac Co.

BROWN AND BROWN (AV)

First National Bank Building, 49781
Telephone: 906-643-7800
Fax: 906-643-7157

MEMBERS OF FIRM

James J. Brown (1839-1920)	Prentiss M. Brown, Jr.
Prentiss M. Brown (1889-1973)	Charles M. Brown
James J. Brown (Retired)	Tom H. Evashevski

(See Next Column)

Counsel for: Union Terminal and Piers, Mackinac Island, Michigan; First National Bank, St. Ignace; Mackinac Island Carriage Tours; McGregor Oil Co.; City of St. Ignace.

For full biographical listings, see the Martindale-Hubbell Law Directory

ST. JOSEPH, * Berrien Co.

BUTZBAUGH & DEWANE, P.L.C. (AV)

Law and Title Building, 811 Ship Street, P.O. Box 27, 49085
Telephone: 616-983-0191
Fax: 616-983-5078
Email: b__d__law@parrett.net

MEMBERS OF FIRM

Alfred M. Butzbaugh	Randall L. Juergensen
John E. Dewane	Michael J. Roberts

OF COUNSEL

Lester E. Page   David Vander Ploeg
          James B. McQuillan

Representative Clients: SJS Federal Savings Bank; American Society of Agricultural Engineers; Whirlpool Corp.; Transamerica Insurance Group; Automobile Club Insurance Assn.; Imperial Printing Co.

For full biographical listings, see the Martindale-Hubbell Law Directory

FISHER LAW OFFICE (AV)

Law & Title Building, 811 Ship Street, P.O. Box 83, 49085-0083
Telephone: 616-983-5511
Telecopier: 616-893-5571

Vance A. Fisher

For full biographical listings, see the Martindale-Hubbell Law Directory

SPELMAN, SAUER & BURDICK, P.C. (AV)

414 Main Street, P.O. Box 378, 49085
Telephone: 616-983-0531
Telecopier: 616-983-1936

John H. Spelman	Jonathan B. Sauer
Carl R. Burdick	

Scott A. Dienes

Representative Clients: Sears, Roebuck & Co.; Foremost Insurance Co.; Whirlpool Corp.; The City of Watervliet; Southeast Berrien County Landfill Authority; Fremont Mutual Insurance Co.; North Pointe Insurance Co.; Mono-Ceramics, Inc.; Lincoln Charter Township; First Resource Federal Credit Union.

For full biographical listings, see the Martindale-Hubbell Law Directory

SAULT STE. MARIE, * Chippewa Co.

MOHER & CANNELLO, P.C. (AV)

150 Water Street, P.O. Box 538, 49783
Telephone: 906-632-3397
Fax: 906-632-0479
Newberry, Michigan Office: 200 East John.
Telephone: 906-293-3600.

Thomas G. Moher	Steven J. Cannello
Timothy S. Moher	

LEGAL SUPPORT PERSONNEL

Bridgette A. Moher

Representative Clients: City of Sault Ste. Marie, Michigan; FMB Sault Bank; Sault Ste. Marie Economic Development Corp.; State of Michigan; Michigan Department of Transportation; Tendercare Nursing Homes of Michigan; Chippewa County, Village of De Tour; Pickford Township.

For full biographical listings, see the Martindale-Hubbell Law Directory

SHELBY, Oceana Co. — (Refer to Muskegon)

SOUTHFIELD, Oakland Co.

JAFFE, RAITT, HEUER & WEISS, PROFESSIONAL CORPORATION (AV)

Travelers Tower, Suite 1520, 48076
Telephone: 313-961-8380
Detroit, Michigan Office: One Woodward Avenue, Suite 2400.
Telephone: 313-961-8380.
Telecopier: 313-961-8358.
Monroe, Michigan Office: 214 East Elm Avenue, Suite 208.
Telephone: 313-241-6470.
Telefacsimile: 313-241-3849.

Ira J. Jaffe

Representative Clients: Edgemere Enterprises; Frankel Associates; Somerset Inn & Apartments; Unisys Corp.

For full biographical listings, see the Martindale-Hubbell Law Directory

Southfield—Continued

MASON, STEINHARDT, JACOBS & PERLMAN, PROFESSIONAL CORPORATION (AV)

Suite 1500, 4000 Town Center, 48075-1415
Telephone: 810-358-2090
Fax: 810-358-3599

Gordon I. Ginsberg	Jerome P. Pesick
Irving I. Boigon	Robert G. Schuch (1943-1995)
Jack Schon	Richard A. Polk
Walter B. Mason, Jr.	Jay W. Tower
Frederick D. Steinhardt	Jonathan B. Frank
John E. Jacobs	Neil S. Silver
Michael B. Perlman	L. Jeffrey Zauberman

Diane Flagg Goldstein	H. Adam Cohen

David E. Nykanen

OF COUNSEL

Erwin B. Ellmann	Marvin C. Daitch
Randolph J. Friedman	John M. Roche

Representative Clients: Citibank, N.A.; City of Dearborn; DeMattia Development Co.; Forest City Enterprises; Michigan Wholesale Drug Assn.; Mortgage Bankers Association of Michigan; Nationwide Insurance Co.; City of Taylor; Union Labor Life Insurance Co.; Yellow Freight Systems, Inc.

For full biographical listings, see the Martindale-Hubbell Law Directory

SOMMERS, SCHWARTZ, SILVER & SCHWARTZ, P.C. (AV)

2000 Town Center, Suite 900, 48075
Telephone: 810-355-0300
Telecopier: 810-746-4001
Plymouth, Michigan Office: 747 South Main Street.
Telephone: 313-455-4250.

Stanley S. Schwartz	Daniel D. Swanson
Leonard B. Schwartz	Michael J. Cunningham
Lawrence Warren	Cecil F. Boyle, Jr.
Steven J. Schwartz	J. Lee Tilson
John F. Vos, III	James D. Ledbetter
Jeffrey N. Shillman	Patrick Burkett
Jeremy L. Winer	David A. Kotzian
David R. Getto	Matthew G. Curtis
Norman D. Tucker	Charles R. Ash, III
Robert H. Darling	Helen K. Joyner
Paul W. Hines	Robert J. Schwartz
Donald J. Gasiorek	John L. Runco
Patrick B. McCauley	Patricia A. Stamler
Justin C. Ravitz	Susanne Pryce
Kenneth V. Cockrel (1938-1988)	Lisa K. Pernick
Gary A. Taback	Joseph H. Bourgon
Allen J. Kovinsky	Tracy L. Allen
David L. Nelson	Sam G. Morgan
Robert G. Portnoy	Saulius K. Mikalonis
Joseph A. Golden	Andrew Kochanowski
William M. Brukoff	David J. Shea
Stephen N. Leuchtman	Murray C. Slomovitz
Richard D. Toth	Anne M. Schoepfle
Allen J. Wall	Carl B. Downing
Richard D. Fox	Gary D. Dodds
Frank Mafrice	Jabran G. Yasso
James J. Vlasic	Kenneth T. Watkins
Victor A. Coen	Gary E. Abeska
Richard L. Groffsky	David J Szymanski
David J. Winter	Craig E. Feringa
Joseph E. Grinnan	Lenora R. Roland
David M. Black	Scott C. Hess
B. A. Tyler	David F. Greco
Robert B. Sickels	Peter L. Schwartz

OF COUNSEL

Norman Samuel Sommers	H. Rollin Allen
Howard Silver	Charles S. Farmer
Paul Groffsky	Marvin R. Stempien
Donald R. Epstein	John F. Kelly

General Counsel for: City of Taylor; Foodland Distributors; C.A. Muer Corporation; Vlasic & Company; Nederlander Corporation; Midwest Health Centers, P.C.
Representative Clients: Crum & Forster Insurance Company; City of Pontiac; Michigan National Bank.

For full biographical listings, see the Martindale-Hubbell Law Directory

STANDISH, Arenac Co. — (Refer to Bay City)

STANTON, Montcalm Co.

MIEL MIEL & PERRY (AV)

125 West Main Street, P.O. Box 8, 48888
Telephone: 517-831-5208; 831-4727
Fax: 517-831-8854

(See Next Column)

OF COUNSEL
C. Homer Miel
MEMBERS OF FIRM

Charles H. Miel	C. Robert Perry

Counsel for: Chemical Bank Montcalm; Montcalm Community College; City of Stanton; Montcalm Title Co.; Townships of Belvidere, Maple Valley, Pine, Sidney; Village of McBride.

For full biographical listings, see the Martindale-Hubbell Law Directory

STERLING HEIGHTS, Macomb Co.

O'REILLY, RANCILIO, NITZ, ANDREWS & TURNBULL, P.C. (AV)

One Sterling Town Center, 12900 Hall Road, Suite 350, 48313-1151
Telephone: 810-726-1000
Fax: 810-726-1560

Paul J. O'Reilly	Bert T. Ross
Kenneth L. Rancilio	Michael J. Piatek
John A. Nitz	Pauline Stoey Baleda
Clark A. Andrews	Christopher P. Baker
Charles E. Turnbull	David B. Viar
Neil J. Lehto	Susan A. Rancilio
Craig S. Schoenherr, Sr.	Michael F. Goethals

Danon D. Goodrum

OF COUNSEL
Gary J. Collins

Representative Clients: ACE Finishing, Inc.; Central Building Co.; Century Telecommunications Services, Inc.; Chivas Products, Ltd.; City of Harper Woods; City of Sterling Heights; Delta Fuels, Inc.; DJR Development Co.; First of America Bank Michigan, N.A.; First Optometry Eye Care Centers, Inc.

For full biographical listings, see the Martindale-Hubbell Law Directory

STURGIS, St. Joseph Co.

DRESSER LAW OFFICE, P.C. (AV)

112 South Monroe Street, 49091
Telephone: 616-651-3281
Fax: 616-651-3261
Email: law@voyager.net

Raymond H. Dresser (1901-1968)	John R. Dresser
John E. Oster (1948-1981)	Robert P. Brothers
Raymond H. Dresser, Jr.	Walter H. Gilbert
	Patrick Joseph Haas, Jr.

LEGAL SUPPORT PERSONNEL
Mary G. Dresser (Legal Assistant)

Attorneys for: Freeman Manufacturing Co.; Burr Oak Tool and Gauge, Inc.; Citizens Bank; Michigan; Sturgis Federal Savings Bank; Midwest Tool & Cutlery, Co.

For full biographical listings, see the Martindale-Hubbell Law Directory

TAWAS CITY, Iosco Co.

LAW OFFICES OF MYLES AND TYLER (AV)

502 Lake Street, 48764-0518
Telephone: 517-362-4405
Telefax: 517-362-7840

Kenneth J. Myles	Ronald R. Tyler

For full biographical listings, see the Martindale-Hubbell Law Directory

THREE RIVERS, St. Joseph Co. — (Refer to Sturgis)

TRAVERSE CITY, Grand Traverse Co.

MURCHIE, CALCUTT & BOYNTON (AV)

109 East Front Street, Suite 300, 49684
Telephone: 616-947-7190
Fax: 616-947-4341

Robert B. Murchie (1894-1975)	William B. Calcutt
Harry Calcutt	Mark A. Burnheimer
Jack E. Boynton	Dawn M. Rogers

ASSOCIATE
Ralph J. Dilley (Not admitted in MI)

General Counsel for: Old Kent Bank-Grand Traverse; Northwestern Savings Bank & Trust; Central-State Bancorp; Traverse City Record Eagle; WPNB-7 & WTOM-4; Emergency Consultants, Inc.; National Guardian Risk Retention Group, Inc.; Farmers Mutual Insurance Co.; Environmental Solutions, Inc.
Local Counsel for: Consumers Power Co.

For full biographical listings, see the Martindale-Hubbell Law Directory

Traverse City—Continued

RUNNING, WISE, WILSON, FORD AND PHILLIPS, P.L.C. (AV)

326 State Street, P.O. Box 686, 49684
Telephone: 616-946-2700
Tele-Fax: 616-946-0857

Harry T. Running (Deceased)   William L. Wise (Retired)

MEMBERS OF FIRM

Patrick J. Wilson	James C. Adams
Richard W. Ford	Sandra P. Howard
Thomas J. Phillips	Kent E. Gerberding

ASSOCIATES

Shelley A. Kester   Bradley L. Putney

OF COUNSEL

J. Bruce Donaldson   Douglas J. Donaldson

Representative Clients: Peninsula Fruit Exchange; Oleson Food Stores; Munson Healthcare; Munson Medical Center; Grand Traverse County Road Commission; Townships of Peninsula, East Bay, Garfield, Almira, Homestead.

For full biographical listings, see the Martindale-Hubbell Law Directory

SMITH HAUGHEY RICE & ROEGGE, P.C. (AV)

241 East State Street, P.O. Box 848, 49685-0848
Telephone: 616-929-4878
Facsimile: 616-929-4182
Grand Rapids, Michigan Office: 200 Calder Plaza Building, 250 Monroe Avenue, N.W., 49503-2251.
Telephone: 616-774-8000.
Facsimile: 616-774-2461.
East Lansing, Michigan Office: 1301 North Hagadorn Road, 48823-2320.
Telephone: 517-332-3030.
Facsimile: 517-332-3468.

George Frederick Bearup	Charles B. Judson
Mark P. Bickel	Robert W. Tubbs
P. David Vinocur	Robert M. Faulkner
R. Jay Hardin	Thomas C. Kates

John R. Vander Veen	Jeffrey R. Wonacott
Mark D. Williams	Todd W. Millar
	Erin Eileen Gerrity

Representative Clients: Chevron; Cincinnati Insurance Co.; General Motors Corp.; Kemper Insurance Group; Michigan Hospital Assn.; Navistar International; St. Paul Insurance Cos.; Steelcase, Inc.; Sears Roebuck & Co.; Dow Elanco.

For full biographical listings, see the Martindale-Hubbell Law Directory

SMITH, JOHNSON & BRANDT, ATTORNEYS, P.C. (AV)

603 Bay Street, P.O. Box 705, 49685
Telephone: 616-946-0700
Fax: 616-946-1735
Lansing, Michigan Office: Suite 402, 116 West Ottawa Street.
Telephone: 517-482-5142.

Louis A. Smith	Donald A. Brandt
H. Wendell Johnson	Allen G. Anderson
	Edgar Roy III

Paul T. Jarboe	Joseph E. Quandt
Thomas A. Pezzetti	Timothy Paul Smith

OF COUNSEL
Barbara Ann Assendelft

Representative Clients: Alden State Bank; Empire National Bank of Traverse City; First of America Bank Michigan, N.A.; Garland; Grand Traverse Mall Limited Partnership; Green Tree Acceptance, Inc.; Lansing Automakers' Federal Credit Union; Michigan Automobile Dealers Association; Cherry Capital Oldsmobile Cadillac L.L.C.; Elmer's Crane and Dozer, Inc.

For full biographical listings, see the Martindale-Hubbell Law Directory

---

TROY, Oakland Co.

CAMPBELL, O'BRIEN & MISTELE, P.C. (AV)

850 Stephenson Highway Suite 410, 48083-1163
Telephone: 810-588-5800
Fax: 810-588-6669

Edwin G. O'Brien (1907-1983)	Arthur R. Spears, Jr.
Dale C. Campbell	Paul W. Loock
Henry E. Mistele	Robert J. Figa
	Curtis H. Mistele

References: First of America; Comerica Bank.

For full biographical listings, see the Martindale-Hubbell Law Directory

CHARTERS, HECK, O'DONNELL, PETRULIS & ZORZA, P.C. (AV)

100 West Big Beaver Road, Suite 660, 48084-5283
Telephone: 810-680-8811
Fax: 810-680-9960

John P. Charters	Margaret A. O'Donnell
Michael A. Heck	Donald L. Petrulis
	John L. Zorza, II

Allan R. Gurvitz   Eric Goldstein

For full biographical listings, see the Martindale-Hubbell Law Directory

DOLD, SPATH & McKELVIE, P.C. (AV)

5445 Corporate Drive, Suite 170, 48098
Telephone: 810-952-5100
Fax: 810-952-5138
Grosse Pointe, Michigan Office: 17190 Denver Avenue, P.O. Box 36786.
Telephone: 313-886-7500.
Fax: 313-886-7505.

Douglas H. Dold (Resident, Grosse Pointe, Michigan Office)	John M. Spath
	Charles L. McKelvie
	Frank M. DeLuca

Elisabeth Hessheimer Gregory	Julie C. Canner
Edward L. Ewald	Tony F. Di Ponio
	M. Ted Kiriazis

Representative Clients: Allpoints Warehousing Corp.; Conquest Construction Co.; Dearborn Capital Corp.; Dinverno Waste Disposal; Ford Motor Credit Co.; General Motors Corp.; New Bright Industries; Triad Financial, Inc.; U.S. Chemical Co.;

For full biographical listings, see the Martindale-Hubbell Law Directory

GARAN, LUCOW, MILLER, SEWARD & BECKER, P.C. (AV)

1111 West Long Lake Road, Suite 300, 48098-6333
Telephone: 810-641-7600
Fax: 810-641-0222
Detroit, Michigan Office: 10000 Woodbridge Place.
Telephone: 313-446-1530.
Fax: 313-259-0450.
Grand Blanc, Michigan Office: 8332 Office Park Drive.
Telephone: 810-695-3700.
Fax: 810-695-6488.
Port Huron, Michigan Office: Port Huron Office Center, 511 Fort Street, Suite 505.
Telephone: 810-985-4400.
Fax: 810-985-4107.
Ann Arbor, Michigan Office: 101 North Main Street, Suite 801.
Telephone: 313-930-5600.
Fax: 313-930-0043.
Mount Clemens, Michigan Office: Suite 307, Towne Square Development, 10 South Main Street.
Telephone: 810-954-3800.
Fax: 810-954-3803.
Grand Rapids, Michigan Office: Campau Square Plaza Building, 99 Monroe Avenue N.W., Suite 102.
Telephone: 616-732-5330.
Fax: 616-732-5333.

James L. Borin	James W. Heckman
Roger A. Smith	Edward M. Freeland
Mark Shreve	Steven A. Matta
	Ian C. Simpson

Susan M. Williams	Charles S. Hegarty
David J. Lankford	Douglas R. Kelly
	Michael D. Russell

Counsel for: Allstate Insurance Co.; Sears, Roebuck & Co.; Liberty Mutual Insurance Co.; Continental Insurance Companies.

For full biographical listings, see the Martindale-Hubbell Law Directory

AUSTIN HIRSCHHORN, P.C. (AV)

Suite 710 Columbia Center, 201 West Big Beaver Road, 48084-4152
Telephone: 810-680-1660
Fax: 810-680-1671

Austin Hirschhorn

For full biographical listings, see the Martindale-Hubbell Law Directory

MATHESON, PARR, SCHULER, EWALD & JOLLY, L.L.P. (AV)

2555 Crooks Road, Suite 200, 48084
Telephone: 810-643-7900
Telecopier: 810-643-0417

(See Next Column)

MATHESON, PARR, SCHULER, EWALD & JOLLY L.L.P., *Troy—Continued*
MEMBERS OF FIRM

George S. Dixon (1906-1973)	Robert D. Schuler
Albert D. Matheson (1912-1990)	Terence K. Jolly
Robert Alan Parr	James D. Osmer
Eugene C. Ewald	John A. Stevens

Marta D. Remeniuk

Representative Clients: National Automobile Transporters Labor Division; Brink's Inc.; Expertec, Inc.; Advance Technology, Inc.; Frito-Lay, Inc.
Reference: Comerica Bank.

For full biographical listings, see the Martindale-Hubbell Law Directory

POLING, McGAW & POLING, P.C. (AV)

Suite 275, 5435 Corporate Drive, 48098
Telephone: 810-641-0500
Telecopier: 810-641-0506

Benson T. Buck (1926-1989)	Richard B. Poling, Jr.
Richard B. Poling	Gregory C. Hamilton
D. Douglas McGaw	Veronica B. O'Haro

James R. Parker
OF COUNSEL
Ralph S. Moore

Representative Clients: County of Oakland; City of Troy; United States Fidelity & Guaranty Co.; Sentry Insurance Co.; Admiral Insurance; DeMaria Construction Co.; Leo Corporation; Aetna Casualty and Surety Co.; Concord Design; Pneumo-Abex.

For full biographical listings, see the Martindale-Hubbell Law Directory

---

YPSILANTI, Washtenaw Co.

PEAR SPERLING EGGAN & MUSKOVITZ, P.C. (AV)

5 South Washington Street, 48197
Telephone: 313-483-3626
Fax: 313-483-1107
Ann Arbor, Michigan Office: Domino's Farms, 24 Frank Lloyd Wright Drive.
Telephone: 313-665-4441
Other Ypsilanti, Michigan Office: 2164 Bellevue at Washtenaw.
Telephone: 313-483-7177.

Lawrence W. Sperling	Thomas E. Daniels
Andrew M. Eggan	Helen Conklin Vick

Counsel for: Domino's Pizza, Inc.; Citizens Banking Corp.; Townsend and Bottum, Inc.; The Credit Bureau of Ypsilanti; City of Ypsilanti (Labor Counsel); Michigan Municipal Worker's Compensation; Self-Insurance Fund.
Approved Attorneys for: Lawyers Title Insurance Corp.

For full biographical listings, see the Martindale-Hubbell Law Directory

---

GUAM

AGANA, Agana Dist.

CARLSMITH BALL WICHMAN CASE & ICHIKI

A Partnership including Law Corporations
4th Floor Bank of Hawaii Building, P.O. Box BF, 96910-5027
Telephone: 671-472-6813
Telex: 721-6445 CWCMI GM
Telecopier: 671-477-4375
Honolulu, Hawaii Office: Suite 2200, Pacific Tower, 1001 Bishop Street. P.O. Box 656.
Telephone: 808-523-2500.
Kapolei, Hawaii Office: Kapolei Building, Suite 318, 1001 Kamokila Boulevard.
Telephone: 808-523-2500.
Wailuku, Maui Hawaii Office: One Main Plaza, Suite 400, 2200 Main Street, P.O. Box 1086.
Telephone: 808-242-4535.
Kailua-Kona, Hawaii Office: Second Floor, Bank of Hawaii Annex Building, P.O. Box 1720.
Telephone: 808-329-6464.
Hilo, Hawaii Office: 121 Waianuenue Avenue, P.O. Box 686.
Telephone: 808-935-6644.
Saipan, Commonwealth of the Northern Mariana Islands Office: Carlsmith Building, Capitol Hill, P.O. Box 5241.
Telephone: (011) 670-322-3455.
Washington, D.C. Office: 700 14th Street, N.W., 9th Floor.
Telephone: 202-508-1025.
Mexico City, Mexico Office: Monte Pelvous 111, Piso 1, Col. Lomas de Chapultepec 11000, Mexico, D.F.
Telephone: (011-52-5) 520-8514.
Fax: (011-52-5) 540-1545.

(See Next Column)

Mexico, D.F. Office of Carlsmith Ball Garcia Cacho y Asociados, S.C. (Authorized to practice Mexican Law): Monte Pelvoux 111, Piso 1, Col. Lomas de Chapultepec, 11000 Mexico, D.F.
Telephone: (011-52-5) 520-8514.
Fax: (011-52-5) 540-1545.

MEMBERS OF FIRM

Ruth D. Davis	Garry W. Morse
Philip D. Isaac	Meredith M. Sayre

William C. Williams, Jr.
RESIDENT ASSOCIATES

Kristen S. Armstrong	Joanne L. Grimes
Lisanne M. Butterfield	Sinforoso M. Tolentino

OF COUNSEL
Roger P. Crouthamel

For full biographical listings, see the Martindale-Hubbell Law Directory

---

TIMOTHY A. STEWART

162 Archbishop Felixberto Camacho Flores Street, 96910
Telephone: 671-472-6978
Telecopier: 671-472-8782

Representative Agency Clients: American Bureau of Collections; National Association of Credit Management; Furst and Furst; United Mercantile Agencies; Financial Collection Agencies.
Representative Subrogation Clients: CIGNA/AFIA Cos.; AIG/AIU Cos.; Chung Kuo Insurance Co., Ltd.

For full biographical listings, see the Martindale-Hubbell Law Directory

HEALTH CARE LAW

ALABAMA

BIRMINGHAM, * Jefferson Co.

BERKOWITZ, LEFKOVITS, ISOM & KUSHNER, A PROFESSIONAL CORPORATION (AV)

1600 SouthTrust Tower, 420 North Twentieth Street, 35203
Telephone: 205-328-0480
Telecopier: 205-322-8007

Harold B. Kushner	A. Lee Martin, Jr.
B. G. Minisman, Jr.	Thomas O. Kolb
Walton E. Williams III	

Judy P. Hamer	Robin L. Tucker

Representative Clients: AlaTenn Resources, Inc.; AMI Brookwood Medical Centers; The Baptist Medical Centers; B.A.S.S., Inc.; Hanna Steel Co., Inc.; McDonald's Corp.; Parisian, Inc.; Outpatient Services East, Ltd.; Southeast Health Plan, Inc.

For Complete List of Firm Personnel, See General Section

For full biographical listings, see the Martindale-Hubbell Law Directory

BRADLEY, ARANT, ROSE & WHITE (AV)

2001 Park Place, Suite 1400, P.O. Box 830709, 35283-0709
Telephone: 205-521-8000
Facsimile: 205-252-0264
Facsimile (SouthTrust Tower Office): 205-251-9915
URL: http://www.BARW.COM
Huntsville, Alabama Office: 200 Clinton Avenue West, Suite 900, 35801.
Telephone: 205-517-5100.
Facsimile: 205-533-5069.

MEMBERS OF FIRM

John K. Molen	James S. Christie, Jr.
Lant B. Davis	Deane K. Corliss
Scott E. Ludwig	
(Resident, Huntsville Office)	

COUNSEL
Joan Crowder Ragsdale
ASSOCIATES

Richard L. Sharff, Jr.	David E. Roth

For Complete List of Firm Personnel, See General Section

For full biographical listings, see the Martindale-Hubbell Law Directory

HASKELL SLAUGHTER & YOUNG, L.L.C. (AV)

1200 AmSouth/Harbert Plaza, 1901 Sixth Avenue North, 35203
Telephone: 205-251-1000
Facsimile: 205-324-1133
Montgomery, Alabama Office: 305 South Lawrence Street, P.O. Box 4660.
36103-4660.
Telephone: 334-265-8573.
Facsimile: 334-264-7945.

William M. Slaughter	Mark Edward Ezell
E. Alston Ray	Ross N. Cohen

Representative Clients: Baxter Healthcare Corporation; The Bradford Group, Inc.; The Coalition for Employee Healthcare, Inc.; HEALTHSOUTH Corporation/HEALTHSOUTH Medical Centers; MedPartners, Inc.; Northeast Alabama Regional Medical Center; Pickens County (Alabama) Medical Center.

For Complete List of Firm Personnel, See General Section

For full biographical listings, see the Martindale-Hubbell Law Directory

PARSONS, LEE & JULIANO, P.C. (AV)

2200 AmSouth/Harbert Plaza, 1901 Sixth Avenue, North, P.O. Box 371088, 35237-1088
Telephone: 205-326-6600
Fax: 205-324-7097

Robert E. Parsons	David A. Lee
Jasper P. Juliano	John M. Bergquist
Marcus W. Lee	Paul J. DeMarco
Marda W. Sydnor	Deborah Ann Payne
Tracy Toussaint	

OF COUNSEL
Dorothy A. Powell

For full biographical listings, see the Martindale-Hubbell Law Directory

MOBILE, * Mobile Co.

JOHNSTONE, ADAMS, BAILEY, GORDON AND HARRIS, L.L.C. (AV)

Royal St. Francis Building, 104 St. Francis Street, P.O. Box 1988, 36633
Telephone: 334-432-7682
Facsimile: 334-432-2800
Telex: 782040

MEMBERS OF FIRM

E. Watson Smith	Gregory C. Buffalow
Wade B. Perry, Jr.	R. Gregory Watts

General Counsel for: First Alabama Bank, Mobile; Infirmary Health System/Mobile Infirmary Medical Center/Rotary Rehabilitation Hospital (Multi-Hospital System).
Counsel for: Oil and Gas: Exxon Corp. Business and Corporate: Bell South Telecommunications, Inc.; Aluminum Co. of America; Michelin North America, Inc.; Metropolitan Life Insurance Co.; The Travelers Insurance Cos. Marine: The West of England Ship Owners Mutual Protection and Indemnity Association (Luxembourg); The Standard Steamship Owners' Protection and Indemnity Association (Bermuda) Ltd.

For Complete List of Firm Personnel, See General Section

For full biographical listings, see the Martindale-Hubbell Law Directory

MONTGOMERY, * Montgomery Co.

BRANTLEY & WILKERSON, P.C. (AV)

405 South Hull Street, P.O. Box 830, 36101-0830
Telephone: 334-265-1500
Fax: 334-265-0319

Paul A. Brantley	Mark D. Wilkerson
Leah Snell Stephens	

Representative Clients: Alabama Board of Nursing (Hearing Officer); State Health Planning and Development Agency (Hearing Officer).
Reference: South Trust Bank, N.A.

For full biographical listings, see the Martindale-Hubbell Law Directory

ARIZONA

PHOENIX, * Maricopa Co.

ALLEN & PRICE, P.L.C. (AV)

2850 East Camelback Road, Suite 170, 85016-4380
Telephone: 602-381-0500
Fax: 602-381-8899
Email: price@aplaw.com
Email: allen@aplaw.com

Robert E. B. Allen	Charles S. Price

For full biographical listings, see the Martindale-Hubbell Law Directory

BONN, LUSCHER, PADDEN & WILKINS, CHARTERED (AV)

805 North Second Street, 85004
Telephone: 602-254-5557
Fax: 602-254-0656

Brian A. Luscher	Jeff C. Padden
Ronald A. Rice	

For full biographical listings, see the Martindale-Hubbell Law Directory

COPPERSMITH & GORDON P.L.C. (AV)

2633 East Indian School Road, Suite 300, 85016-6759
Telephone: 602-224-0999
Fax: 602-224-6020
Email: SAMnANDY@aol.com

Samuel G. Coppersmith	Andrew S. Gordon

OF COUNSEL
M. Joyce Geyser

Reference: Norwest Bank Arizona, N.A.

For full biographical listings, see the Martindale-Hubbell Law Directory

DOYLE, WINTHROP, OBERBILLIG & WEST, P.C. (AV)

2800 North Central Avenue Suite 1550, 85004
Telephone: 602-240-6711
Fax: 602-240-6951
Mailing Address: P.O. Box 10417, Phoenix, Arizona, 85064-0417

Lawrence F. Winthrop	Robert H. Oberbillig
William H. Doyle	John C. West

For full biographical listings, see the Martindale-Hubbell Law Directory

Phoenix—Continued

FENNEMORE CRAIG, A PROFESSIONAL CORPORATION (AV)

Two North Central, Suite 2200, 85004
Telephone: 602-257-8700
Fax: 602-257-8527
Scottsdale, Arizona Office: 6263 North Scottsdale Road, Suite 290, 85250.
Telephone: 602-257-5400.
Fax: 602-257-5409.
Tucson, Arizona Office: One South Church Avenue, Suite 1030, 85701.
Telephone: 520-791-6800.
Fax: 520-791-6820.

Michael Preston Green	Phillip F. Fargotstein
Jay S. Ruffner	Andrew M. Federhar
Timothy J. Burke	J. Barry Shelley

Theresa Dwyer	Jean Marie Sullivan

For Complete List of Firm Personnel, See General Section

For full biographical listings, see the Martindale-Hubbell Law Directory

GAMMAGE & BURNHAM, P.L.C. (AV)

One Renaissance Square, Two North Central Avenue, Suite 1800, 85004
Telephone: 602-256-0566
Fax: 602-256-4475

MEMBERS OF FIRM

Richard B. Burnham	Curtis A. Ullman
	Susan L. Watchman

Representative Clients: St. Joseph's Hospital; Samaritan Health System; St. Mary's Hospital & Health Center; Holy Cross Hospital & Health Center; John C. Lincoln Hospital & Health Center; Southwest Catholic Health Network Corp.; Yuma Regional Medical Center; St. Joseph's Hospital of Tucson.

For Complete List of Firm Personnel, See General Section

For full biographical listings, see the Martindale-Hubbell Law Directory

JENNINGS, STROUSS AND SALMON, P.L.C. (AV)

A Professional Limited Liability Company
One Renaissance Square, Two North Central, 85004-2393
Telephone: 602-262-5911
Fax: 602-253-3255

George C. Spilsbury	Joen M. Schaefer
Rita A. Meiser	Robert J. Werner

For Complete List of Firm Personnel, See General Section

For full biographical listings, see the Martindale-Hubbell Law Directory

LEWIS AND ROCA, LLP (AV)

A Limited Liability Partnership including a Professional Corporation
40 North Central Avenue, 85004-4429
Telephone: 602-262-5311
Fax: 602-262-5747
Email: mlp@lrlaw.com
Tucson, Arizona Office: One South Church Avenue, Suite 700, 86701-1620.
Telephone: 520-622-2090.
Fax: 520-622-3088. E-Mail: mlp@lrlaw.com.

MEMBERS OF FIRM

Merton E. Marks (P.C.)	Foster Robberson
Beth J. Schermer	David M. Bixby
Karen Carter Owens	J. Tyler Haahr

ASSOCIATES

Julie Mathis Nelson	Bruce E. Samuels

Representative Clients: Arizona Hospital Assn.; Blood Systems, Inc.; Mutual Insurance Company of Arizona; Phoenix Memorial Hospital; St. Joseph's; Samaritan Health System; Scottsdale Memorial Hospitals.

For Complete List of Firm Personnel, See General Section

For full biographical listings, see the Martindale-Hubbell Law Directory

MITTEN, GOODWIN & RAUP, A PROFESSIONAL CORPORATION (AV)

One Columbus Plaza, 3636 North Central, Suite 1200, 85012
Telephone: 602-650-2000
Fax: 602-264-7033
Email: mgr@starlink.com

Roger C. Mitten	Stephen C. Yost
Calvin L. Raup	Scott J. Hergenroether

Steven P. Kramer	Jeffery S. Slater
Sharon Elizabeth Ravenscroft	Gary Beren
	Jeffrey J. Campbell

For full biographical listings, see the Martindale-Hubbell Law Directory

O'CONNOR, CAVANAGH, ANDERSON, KILLINGSWORTH & BESHEARS, A PROFESSIONAL ASSOCIATION (AV)

One East Camelback Road, Suite 1100, 85012-1656
Telephone: 602-263-2400
FAX: 602-263-2900
Email: firminfo@arizlaw.com
Sun City, Arizona Office: 13250 North Del Webb Boulevard, Suite B, 85351.
Telephone: 602-263-2808.
FAX: 602-933-3100.
Tucson, Arizona Office: O'Connor Cavanagh Molloy Jones, 33 N. Stone, Suite 2100, 85701, P.O. Box 2268, 85702.
Telephone: 520-622-3531.
FAX: 520-624-2816.
Nogales, Arizona Office: 1891 North Mastick Way, 85621.
Telephone: 520-761-4215.
FAX: 520-761-3505.

Ralph E. Hunsaker	John B. Furman
George H. Mitchell	Stephen E. Richman
Harding B. Cure	David A. Van Engelhoven
Richard C. Smith	Paul J. Giancola
Philip C. Gerard	Lawrence J. Rosenfeld

Leigh A. Kaylor	Jonathan R. Feldman

Representative Clients: Samaritan Health Systems; MICA; St. Paul Insurance Co.; Podiatry Insurance Company of America; United Health Care; Medi-Max; Golden Rule Insurance Company.

For Complete List of Firm Personnel, See General Section

For full biographical listings, see the Martindale-Hubbell Law Directory

QUARLES & BRADY (AV)

One Camelback Building, One East Camelback Road, Suite 400, 85012-1649
Telephone: 602-230-5500
Fax: 602-230-5598
Milwaukee, Wisconsin Office: 411 East Wisconsin Avenue.
Telephone: 414-277-5000.
Fax: 414-271-3552.
Madison, Wisconsin Office: First Wisconsin Plaza, One South Pinckney Street, P.O. Box 2113.
Telephone: 608-251-5000.
Fax: 608-251-9166.
West Palm Beach, Florida Office: 222 Lakeview Ave., 4th Floor.
Telephone: 407-653-5000.
Fax: 407-653-5333.
Naples, Florida Office: Barnett Center, 4501 Tamiami Trail North, Suite 300.
Telephone: 813-262-5959.
Fax: 813-434-4999.

MEMBER OF THE FIRM

Judith M. Bailey

For Complete List of Firm Personnel, See General Section

For full biographical listings, see the Martindale-Hubbell Law Directory

SNELL & WILMER, L.L.P. (AV)

One Arizona Center, 85004-0001
Telephone: 602-382-6000
Fax: 602-382-6070
Tucson, Arizona Office: 1500 Norwest Tower, One South Church Avenue 85701-1612.
Telephone: 520-882-1200.
Fax: 520-884-1294.
Orange County Office: 1920 Main Street, Suite 1200, P.O. Box 57062, Irvine, California, 92619-7062.
Telephone: 714-253-2700.
Fax: 714-955-2507.
Salt Lake City, Utah Office: Broadway Centre, 111 East Broadway, Suite 900, 84111-1004.
Telephone: 801-237-1900.
Fax: 801-237-1950.

MEMBERS OF FIRM

Gerard Morales	Barry D. Halpern
Richard W. Sheffield	Terry Morris Roman
	Thea Foglietta Silverstein

OF COUNSEL

Edward Jacobson

Representative Clients: The Arizona Medical Assn.; The Maricopa County Medical Society; Mayo Clinic, Scottsdale; CIGNA Health Care of Arizona, Inc.; Mutual Insurance Company of Arizona; Lincoln Health Resources Corp.; Samaritan Health Services; Scottsdale Memorial Hospital.

For Complete List of Firm Personnel, See General Section

For full biographical listings, see the Martindale-Hubbell Law Directory

Phoenix—Continued

ULRICH, KESSLER & ANGER, P.C. (AV)

Suite 1000, 3030 North Central Avenue, 85012-2717
Telephone: 602-248-9465
Fax: 602-248-0165
Email: ukapc@aol.com

Paul G. Ulrich   Donn G. Kessler
William H. Anger

For full biographical listings, see the Martindale-Hubbell Law Directory

TUCSON, * Pima Co.

RAVEN, KIRSCHNER & NORELL, P.C. (AV)

Suite 1600, One South Church Avenue, 85701-1612
Telephone: 520-628-8700
Telefax: 520-798-5200

Andrew Oldland Norell   Mark B. Raven

Representative Clients: Continental Medical Systems, Inc.; El Paso Natural Gas Co.; Norwest Bank Arizona; El Rio-Santa Cruz Neighborhood Health Center, Inc.; Resolution Trust Corp.; Sierra Vista Community Hospital; Southern Arizona Rehabilitation Hospital; Northern Cochise Community Hospital.

For Complete List of Firm Personnel, See General Section

For full biographical listings, see the Martindale-Hubbell Law Directory

ARKANSAS

LITTLE ROCK, * Pulaski Co.

BARBER, McCASKILL, AMSLER, JONES & HALE, P.A. (AV)

2700 First Commercial Building, 400 West Capitol Avenue, 72201-3414
Telephone: 501-372-6175
Telecopier: 501-375-2802

Azro L. Barber (1885-1979)	Richard C. Kalkbrenner
Elbert A. Henry (1889-1966)	G. Spence Fricke
John B. Thurman (1912-1971)	Gail Ponder Gaines
Austin McCaskill, Sr.	Michael J. Emerson
Guy Amsler, Jr.	R. Kenny McCulloch
Glenn W. Jones	Tim A. Cheatham
Michael E. Hale	Joseph F. Kolb
John S. Cherry, Jr.	Scott Michael Strauss
Robert L. Henry, III	Derek J. Edwards
Micheal L. Alexander	Thomas E. Osment, Jr.
William H. Edwards, Jr.	Christopher Gomlicker

Attorneys for: Associated Aviation Underwriters; Canal Insurance Co.; Fireman's Fund Insurance Co.; General Motors Corp.; General Motors Acceptance Corp.; Hanover Insurance Co.; Home Insurance Co.; Royal Insurance; United States Fidelity & Guaranty Co.; Universal Underwriters Insurance Co.

For full biographical listings, see the Martindale-Hubbell Law Directory

CALIFORNIA

BEVERLY HILLS, Los Angeles Co.

HERZOG, FISHER & GRAYSON, A LAW CORPORATION (AV)

9460 Wilshire Boulevard Fifth Floor, 90212
Telephone: 310-278-4300
Fax: 310-278-5430

James P. Herzog   David R. Fisher
Michael A. Grayson

Pamela M. Rosenthal   Eric M. Rosin
OF COUNSEL
Todd I. Grayson

For full biographical listings, see the Martindale-Hubbell Law Directory

FRESNO, * Fresno Co.

DOWLING, AARON & KEELER, INCORPORATED (AV)

Suite 200, 6051 North Fresno Street, 93710
Telephone: 209-432-4500
Fax: 209-432-4590
Email: dowling-law.com

(See Next Column)

Michael D. Dowling   Richard M. Aaron
John C. Ganahl
Reference: Wells Fargo Bank (Main).

For Complete List of Firm Personnel, See General Section

For full biographical listings, see the Martindale-Hubbell Law Directory

KIMBLE, MacMICHAEL & UPTON, A PROFESSIONAL CORPORATION (AV)

Fig Garden Financial Center, 5260 North Palm Avenue, Suite 221, P.O. Box 9489, 93792-9489
Telephone: 209-435-5500
Telecopier: 209-435-1500
Email: kmu@primenet.com

Joseph C. Kimble (1910-1972)	Robert H. Scribner
Thomas A. MacMichael (1920-1990)	Michael E. Moss
Jon Wallace Upton	Mark D. Miller
Robert E. Bergin	Michael F. Tatham
Jeffrey G. Boswell	W. Richard Lee
Steven D. McGee	D. Tyler Tharpe
Robert E. Ward	Sylvia Halkousis Coyle
John P. Eleazarian	S. Brett Sutton
	Michael J. Jurkovich

Douglas V. Thornton	Susan King Hatmaker
Robert William Branch	Lawrence J. Salisbury
Donald J. Pool	Daniel R. Foster
Meredith E. Allen	

OF COUNSEL
Mary Ann Bluhm

For full biographical listings, see the Martindale-Hubbell Law Directory

SAGASER, HANSEN, FRANSON & JAMISON, A PROFESSIONAL CORPORATION (AV)

2445 Capitol Street, Second Floor, P.O. Box 1632, 93717-1632
Telephone: 209-233-4800
Fax: 209-233-9330

Eric K. Hansen (1952-1996)	Kimberly A. Gaab
Howard A. Sagaser	Patti L. Williams
Donald R. Franson, Jr.	K. Poncho Baker
Daniel O. Jamison	Kristi R. Culver
Nancy A. Maler	Catherine J. Cerna

For full biographical listings, see the Martindale-Hubbell Law Directory

STAMMER, McKNIGHT, BARNUM & BAILEY (AV)

2540 West Shaw Lane, Suite 110, P.O. Box 9789, 93794-9789
Telephone: 209-449-0571
Fax: 209-432-2619

W. H. Stammer (1891-1969)	Frank D. Maul
James K. Barnum (1918-1987)	Craig M. Mortensen
Dean A. Bailey (1924-1995)	Jerry D. Jones
Galen McKnight (1904-1991)	Michael P. Mallery
James N. Hays	M. Bruce Smith
Carey H. Johnson	Thomas J. Georgouses

ASSOCIATES

Steven R. Stoker	Bruce J. Berger
M. Jaqueline Yates	Celene M.E. Boggs

Representative Clients: Community Hospital of Central California; Memorial Hospital of Modesto; Madera Community Hospital; Valley Medical Center; Truck Insurance Exchange.
Reference: Bank of America National Trust & Savings Assn. (Fresno Main Office).

For full biographical listings, see the Martindale-Hubbell Law Directory

LOS ANGELES, * Los Angeles Co.

DEMETRIOU, DEL GUERCIO, SPRINGER & MOYER, LLP (AV)

801 South Grand Avenue, 10th Floor, 90017
Telephone: 213-624-8407
Telecopy: 213-624-0174
Email: ddsm@juno.com *URL:* http://www.ddsm.com

MEMBERS OF FIRM

Chris G. Demetriou (1915-1989)	Laurie E. Davis
Jeffrey Z. B. Springer	Gregory D. Trimarche
Craig A. Moyer	Karen McLaurin Chang
Angela Shanahan	Leslie M. Smario
Stephen A. Del Guercio	Andrew J. Bracker
Michael A. Francis	Kimberly E. Lewand
Regina Liudzius Cobb	Jennifer T. Taggart
	Robert P. Silverstein

(See Next Column)

DEMETRIOU, DEL GUERCIO, SPRINGER & MOYER LLP, *Los Angeles—Continued*

OF COUNSEL

Ronald J. Del Guercio　　　　Richard A. Del Guercio
James P. Del Guercio

Reference: Bank of America, L.A. Main Office, Los Angeles, Calif.

For full biographical listings, see the Martindale-Hubbell Law Directory

---

FOLEY LARDNER WEISSBURG & ARONSON (AV)

35th Floor, One Century Plaza, 2029 Century Park East (Century City), 90067-3021
Telephone: 310-277-2223
Facsimile: 310-557-8475
Sacramento, California Office: Suite 1050, 770 L Street.
Telephone: 916-443-8005.
Facsimile: 916-443-2240.
San Diego, California Office: 402 West Broadway, 23rd. Floor.
Telephone: 619-234-6655.
Facsimile: 619-234-3510.
San Francisco, California Office: One Maritime Plaza, 6th Floor.
Telephone: 415-434-4484.
Facsimile: 415-434-4507.

Robert A. Klein
Peter Aronson
Carl Weissburg
Richard A. Blacker
Mark S. Windisch
J. Mark Waxman
Carl H. Hitchner (Resident at San Francisco Office)
Robert D. Sevell
Richard F. Seiden
Gregory W. McClune (Resident at San Francisco Office)
George L. Root, Jr. (Resident at San Diego Office)
James R. Kalyvas
Michael G. McCarty (Resident, San Diego Office)
Richard M. Albert
Ralph B. Kostant
Laurence R. Arnold (Resident at San Francisco Office)
Anita D. Lee
Samuel F. Hoffman (Resident at San Diego Office)
Samuel H. Weissbard (Not admitted in CA)
Thomas L. Driscoll (Resident, San Francisco Office)
Jonathan M. Lindeke (Resident at San Francisco Office)
C. Darryl Cordero
Denise R. Rodriguez

Stephen W. Parrish (Resident at San Francisco Office)
R. Michael Scarano (Resident at San Diego Office)
David A. Blumenthal (Not admitted in CA; Resident also at Foley & Lardner, Washington, D.C. & Annapolis, Maryland Offices)
Lowell C. Brown
Gregory V. Moser (Resident at San Diego Office)
Robert E. Goldstein
Tami S. Smason
Lawrence C. Conn
Mark T. Schieble (Resident at San Francisco Office)
Robert C. Leventhal
Larry L. Marshall (Resident at San Diego Office)
Clare Richardson
Carol Isackson (Resident at San Diego Office)
Dorothy J. Stephens (Resident at Sacramento Office)
Paul Gustav Neumann (Resident at San Francisco Office)
Charles B. Oppenheim
James N. Godes
Ingeborg E. Penner (Resident at San Francisco Office)
Robyn A. Meinhardt

OF COUNSEL

Judith E. Solomon (Resident at San Diego Office)
Robert J. Enders
Mark E. Reagan (Resident at San Francisco Office)

Frederick Martin, Jr. (Resident at San Diego Office)
Mary K. Norvell (Resident at San Diego Office)
Jeffrey R. Bates

Adam B. Schiff

Shirley J. Paine
Howard W. Cohen
Jonathon E. Cohn
Steven J. Simerlein (Resident at San Diego Office)
Amy B. Hafey
Diane Ung
Christopher E. Love
Terri Wagner Cammarano
Leila Nourani
Karen S. Weinstein
Lorna D. Hennington
Braulio Montesino
Shana T. Torem
David A. Renas (Resident at San Diego Office)
Ioana Petrou (Resident at San Francisco Office)
T. Joshua Ritz
Sharon M. Kopman
Kimberly F. Applequist
Lynn R. Goodfellow (Resident, San Diego Office)
James D. Nguyen
Andrew M. Agtagma

John H. Douglas (Resident, San Francisco Office)
Margaret M. McCahill (Resident, San Diego Office)
David T. Morris (Resident, San Francisco Office)
Nathan D. Schmidt (Resident, Sacrament Office)
Paula C. Ohliger (Resident, San Francisco Office)
Michael J. Sieradzki (Resident, San Francisco, Office)
Lisa Goodwin Michael
René Bowser (Resident, San Francisco Office)
Jeffrey M. Pomerance
Charles R. Zubrzycki
Lisa A. Palombo
Daron L. Tooch
Julie Christine Ashby (Resident at San Diego Office)
Monica Gonzalez Brisbane (Resident at Sacramento Office)
Robert J. Wenbourne (Resident at Sacramento Office)

For full biographical listings, see the Martindale-Hubbell Law Directory

---

GALTON & HELM (AV)

500 South Grand Avenue, Suite 1200, 90071
Telephone: 213-629-8800
Telecopier: 213-629-0037
Palm Desert, California Office: 73-290 El Paseo, Suite 377.
Telephone: 619-776-5600.
Fax: 619-776-5602.

MEMBERS OF FIRM

Stephen H. Galton
Hugh H. Helm
Michael F. Bell

Daniel W. Maguire (Resident at Palm Desert)
David A. Lingenbrink

ASSOCIATES

Chris D. Olsen
Melissa M. Cowan
Edith Sanchez Shea

Joanna M. Eoff
Michael B. Bernacchi
Mark A. Riekhof (Resident, Glendale Office)

LEGAL SUPPORT PERSONNEL

Lana Banks (Paralegal)

Stephanie M. McCarthy (Paralegal)

For full biographical listings, see the Martindale-Hubbell Law Directory

---

HOOPER, LUNDY & BOOKMAN, INC. (AV)

Watt Plaza, Suite 1600, 1875 Century Park East, 90067-2517
Telephone: 310-551-8111
Telecopier: 310-551-8181

Robert W. Lundy, Jr.
Patric Hooper
Lloyd A. Bookman
W. Bradley Tully
John R. Hellow

Angela A. Mickelson
Laurence D. Getzoff
Jay N. Hartz
Byron J. Gross
David P. Henninger

Todd E. Swanson

Gina Reese
Jonathan P. Neustadter
Kenneth J. Carl
Julia Schollenberger
Thomas B. Croke IV

Michele Melden
Mark Jeffry Dicks
Salvatore A. Zoida
Kevin A. Corbett
Betty J. Levine

William A. Larkin

Representative Clients: Tenet Healthcare Corp.; Kaiser Foundation Health Plan; City of Hope National Medical Center; County of Los Angeles; Physicians and Surgeons Laboratories, Inc.; Queen of Angels/Hollywood Presbyterian Medical Center; Beach Cities Health District; Kauai Medical Group; Vista Health Plans.
Reference: City National Bank.

For full biographical listings, see the Martindale-Hubbell Law Directory

---

HORVITZ & LEVY (AV)

A Partnership including Professional Corporations
18th Floor, 15760 Ventura Boulevard (Encino), 91436
Telephone: 818-995-0800; 213-872-0802
FAX: 818-995-3157

Ellis J. Horvitz (A P.C.)
Barry R. Levy (A P.C.)
Peter Abrahams
David M. Axelrad
Frederic D. Cohen
S. Thomas Todd
David S. Ettinger

Daniel J. Gonzalez
Mitchell C. Tilner
Christina J. Imre
Lisa Perrochet
Stephen E. Norris
Sandra J. Smith
John A. Taylor, Jr.

Mary F. Dant
Ari R. Kleiman
Lisa R. Jaskol
Julie L. Woods
Holly R. Paul
H. Thomas Watson

Andrea M. Gauthier
Elizabeth Skorcz Anthony
Christine A. Pagac
Judith E. Gordon
Patricia Lofton
L. Rachel Lerman Helyar (Not admitted in CA)

OF COUNSEL

Jon B. Eisenberg

Representative Clients: California Medical Association; California Association of Hospitals and Health Systems; Truck Insurance Exchange; Cedars-Sinai Medical Center; Southern California Physicians Insurance Exchange; Truck Insurance Exchange; Physicians & Surgeons Division of Fremont Indemnity; NORCAL Mutual Insurance Company; Kaiser Foundation Health Plan, Inc.; CHD Insurance Services.

For full biographical listings, see the Martindale-Hubbell Law Directory

---

KONOWIECKI & RANK (AV)

A Partnership including a Professional Corporation
First Interstate World Center, 633 West 5th Street, Suite 3500, 90071-2007
Telephone: 213-229-0990
Telefax: 213-229-0992

(See Next Column)

KONOWIECKI & RANK—*Continued*

Peter C. Rank	Kevin B. Kroeker
Joseph S. Konowiecki	Peter Roan
Michael C. Foster	Peter R. Mason
Jon N. Manzanares	Denise E. Hanna

ASSOCIATES

Cynthia J. Billey	Phillip R. Maltin
Edna M. Chism	Scott J. Moore
Ronan Cohen	John A. Mueller
Rosa Kwon Easton	Leslie Overfelt
Robert C. Hayden	Catherine M. Polisoto

Harold C. Pope

LEGAL SUPPORT PERSONNEL

Curtis J. Bergeron

Representative Clients: PacifiCare Health Systems, Inc.; UniHealth America; Columbia General Life Insurance Co.; Santa Clarita Health Care Assoc.; College Health Enterprises; Granada Hills Community Hospital; Redlands Community Hospital; Bay Shores Medical Group.
Reference: Bank of America.

For full biographical listings, see the Martindale-Hubbell Law Directory

---

RUNQUIST & ASSOCIATES (AV)

10821 Huston Street (North Hollywood), 91601-4613
Telephone: 818-760-8986
Fax: 818-760-8314
Email: RUNQUIST@silicon.net

Lisa A. Runquist

Ingrid P. Mittermaier

OF COUNSEL

J. Diane Parrish

For full biographical listings, see the Martindale-Hubbell Law Directory

---

OAKLAND, Alameda Co.

HAIMS, JOHNSON, MACGOWAN & MCINERNEY (AV)

490 Grand Avenue, 94610
Telephone: 510-835-0500
Facsimile: 510-835-2833

MEMBERS OF FIRM

Arnold B. Haims	Randy M. Marmor
Gary R. Johnson	John K. Kirby
Clyde L. MacGowan	Robert J. Frassetto
Thomas McInerney	Caroline N. Valentino
Lawrence A. Baker	Dianne D. Peebles

ASSOCIATES

Joseph Y. Ahn	Anne M. Michaels
Edward D. Baldwin	Michelle Diane Perry
Marc P. Bouret	Edward C. Schroeder, Jr.

For full biographical listings, see the Martindale-Hubbell Law Directory

---

PEZZOLA & REINKE, A PROFESSIONAL CORPORATION (AV)

Suite 1300, Lake Merritt Plaza, 1999 Harrison Street, 94612
Telephone: 510-273-8750
Telecopier: 510-834-7440
San Francisco, California Office: 650 California Street, 32nd Floor, 94111.
Telephone: 415-989-9710.
Menlo Park, California Office: 3000 Sand Hill Road, Building 4, Suite 160, 94025.
Telephone: 415-854-8797.

Stephen P. Pezzola	Donald C. Reinke

Thomas A. Maier

Representative Clients: Primed Management Consulting; The Eye Care Network; Pacific Chiropractic Resources; California Medical Association; Health Business Development; Intracellular Diagnostics, Inc.; Radiation Oncology Center; Medlogic Global Corporation.

For full biographical listings, see the Martindale-Hubbell Law Directory

---

PASADENA, Los Angeles Co.

JAY D. CHRISTENSEN AND ASSOCIATES (AV)

225 South Lake, Ninth Floor, 91101
Telephone: 818-568-2900
Fax: 818-568-1566

Jay D. Christensen, P.C.

OF COUNSEL

Stephen G. Auer	Gail M. Betz

For full biographical listings, see the Martindale-Hubbell Law Directory

---

SACRAMENTO, Sacramento Co.

HUNTER RICHEY DI BENEDETTO & BREWER, LLP (AV)

A Limited Liability Partnership
Renaissance Tower, 801 K Street, 23rd Floor, 95814-3525
Telephone: 916-491-3000
Facsimile: 916-491-3080
Email: hrdb@hrdb.com *URL:* http://www.hrdb.com

MEMBERS OF FIRM

William S. Hunter	James F. Geary
Win R. Richey	Janet C. Eisenbeis
Florence L. Di Benedetto	Jeffery D. Harris
Roy E. Brewer	Stephen C. Ruehmann
Anne E. Ferguson	Ralph T. Ferguson
Judith J. Citko	Sharon K. Sandeen

Kathryn T. Papalia

LEGAL SUPPORT PERSONNEL

Lori J. Kelly (Paralegal)	Michele L. Nickell
Deborah M. Romero (Paralegal)	(Legal Assistant)
Linda Jane Hall	Dawn Krein (Legal Assistant)
(Legal Assistant)	Stephanie L. Neumann
Jennifer E. Mueller	(Legal Assistant)
(Legal Assistant)	

For full biographical listings, see the Martindale-Hubbell Law Directory

---

LIVINGSTON & MATTESICH, LAW CORPORATION (AV)

1201 K Street, Suite 1100, 95814
Telephone: 916-442-1111
Fax: 916-448-1709
Email: liv-matt@gvn.net

Gene Livingston	Carol Livingston
James M. Mattesich	Rebecca M. Ceniceros

Steven P. Belzer	Trisha M. McAlmond

Reference: Bank of California.

For full biographical listings, see the Martindale-Hubbell Law Directory

---

SAN BERNARDINO, San Bernardino Co.

KASSEL & KASSEL (AV)

A Group of Independent Law Offices
Suite 207, Wells Fargo Bank Building, 334 West Third Street, 92401
Telephone: 909-884-6455
Fax: 909-884-8032

Philip Kassel	Gregory H. Kassel

References: Wells Fargo Bank; Bank of America; Bank of San Bernardino.

For full biographical listings, see the Martindale-Hubbell Law Directory

---

SAN DIEGO, San Diego Co.

LINDLEY, LAZAR & SCALES, A PROFESSIONAL CORPORATION (AV)

One America Plaza, 600 West Broadway, Suite 1400, 92101-3302
Telephone: 619-234-9181
Fax: 619-234-8475
Email: 104413.1175@compuserve.com

Robert M. McLeod	Stephen F. Treadgold
William E. Johns	Kenneth C. Jones

Representative Clients: San Diego Hospital Association; San Diego Blood Bank; Donald N. Sharp Memorial Hospital; Sharp Cabrillo Hospital; Sharp Knollwood Convalescent Hospital; VNA Health Services of San Diego.

For Complete List of Firm Personnel, See General Section

For full biographical listings, see the Martindale-Hubbell Law Directory

---

SAN FRANCISCO, San Francisco Co.

LAW OFFICES OF RAYMOND N. STELLA ERLACH (AV)

4 Embarcadero Center, Seventeenth Floor, 94111
Telephone: 415-788-3322
FAX: 415-788-8613

Raymond N. Erlach

OF COUNSEL

Gregory J. Erlach	Stephen Peter U. Erlach

For full biographical listings, see the Martindale-Hubbell Law Directory

San Francisco—Continued

STUBBS, HITTIG & LEONE, A PROFESSIONAL CORPORATION (AV)

Fox Plaza, Suite 818, 1390 Market Street, 94102-5399
Telephone: 415-861-8200
Telecopier: 415-861-6700
Email: SHLSF@aol.com

Gregory E. Stubbs	Louis A. Leone
H. Christopher Hittig	Marina B. Pitts

For full biographical listings, see the Martindale-Hubbell Law Directory

---

SAN JOSE,* Santa Clara Co.

HINSHAW, WINKLER, DRAA, MARSH & STILL (AV)

152 North Third Street, Suite 300, P.O. Box 15030, 95115-0030
Telephone: 408-293-5959
Fax: 408-280-0966
Email: hinshaw-law.com

MEMBERS OF FIRM

Edward A. Hinshaw	Gerhard O. Winkler
Tyler G. Draa	Barry C. Marsh
Thomas E. Still	

ASSOCIATES

Lynne Thaxter Brown	Jennifer H. Still
Bradford J. Hinshaw	Megan A. Smith

For full biographical listings, see the Martindale-Hubbell Law Directory

---

SANTA ANA,* Orange Co.

McNEIL AND SUSSON, A PROFESSIONAL CORPORATION (AV)

2100 North Broadway, Suite 103, 92706-2624
Telephone: 714-835-1922
Facsimile: 714-835-2720

Joseph D. McNeil	Dana E. Susson

Kathryn Arnold	Edward A. Stumpp
James R. Parrett	

For full biographical listings, see the Martindale-Hubbell Law Directory

---

COLORADO

DENVER,* Denver Co.

HOLME ROBERTS & OWEN LLP (AV)

Suite 4100, 1700 Lincoln, 80203
Telephone: 303-861-7000
Telecopier: 303-866-0200
Email: hro@hro.com *URL:* http://www.hro.com
Boulder, Colorado Office: Suite 400, 1401 Pearl Street.
Telephone: 303-444-5955.
Telecopier: 303-444-1063.
Colorado Springs, Colorado Office: Suite 1300, 90 South Cascade Avenue.
Telephone: 719-473-3800.
Telecopier: 719-633-1518.
Salt Lake City, Utah Office: Suite 1100, 111 East Broadway.
Telephone: 801-521-5800.
Telecopier: 801-521-9639.
London, England Office: Mellier House, 26a Albemarle Street.
Telephone: 44-171-499-8776.
Telecopier: 44-171-499-7769.
Moscow, Russia Office: Kosmodamianskaya Nab. #52/1, Suite 9100, 113054.
Telephone: 7095-961-3000.
Telecopier: 7095-961-3001.
Kiev, Ukraine Office: Terestchenkovskaya #19, Suite 2, 252004.
Telephone: 380-44-224-1348.
Telecopier: 380-44-224-4986.

PARTNERS OF FIRM

Donald J. Hopkins	Thomas M. James
Richard L. Nagl	(Colorado Springs Office)
(Colorado Springs Office)	Susan E. Duffey Campbell
Nick Nimmo	(Colorado Springs Office)
Steve L. Gaines	John R. Wylie
(Colorado Springs Office)	(Colorado Springs Office)
Bruce F. Black	Mary Hurley Stuart
Mary L. Groves	Christopher Cipoletti
	(Colorado Springs Office)

OF COUNSEL

Richard L. Schrepferman

SPECIAL COUNSEL

Diane S. Barrett	Gary R. Thorup
Laurence B. James	(Salt Lake City Office)

(See Next Column)

SENIOR COUNSEL

Kathryn Stoker Worford

ASSOCIATES

Blaine J. Benard	Maria Mashenka Lundberg
(Salt Lake City Office)	Timothy G. Pfeifer
	(Colorado Springs Office)

For Complete List of Firm Personnel, See General Section

For full biographical listings, see the Martindale-Hubbell Law Directory

---

OTTEN, JOHNSON, ROBINSON, NEFF & RAGONETTI, P.C. (AV)

950 Seventeenth Street, 16th Floor, 80202
Telephone: 303-825-8400
Telecopier: 303-825-6525

William R. Neff	Karen L. Barsch

Representative Clients: Aetna Life Insurance Co.; The Broe Companies; Inc.; Colorado National Bank; Connecticut General Life Insurance Co.; First Nationwide Bank; Homart Development Co.; Land Title Guarantee Co.; Trizec Corporation Ltd.; U.S. West Communications, Inc.; The Western Sugar Co.

For Complete List of Firm Personnel, See General Section

For full biographical listings, see the Martindale-Hubbell Law Directory

---

CONNECTICUT

HARTFORD,* Hartford Co.

O'BRIEN, TANSKI, TANZER & YOUNG (AV)

CityPlace II, 06103
Telephone: 860-525-2700
Telefax: 860-247-7861

MEMBERS OF FIRM

Donald W. O'Brien	Roland F. Young, III
James M. Tanski	Robert E. Kiley
Lois B. Tanzer	Thomas O. Anderson
Nancy Phillips Maxwell	

OF COUNSEL

Hilary Fisher Nelson	Donna R. Zito

ASSOCIATES

Caroline Schnog	P. Jo Anne Burgh
Robert D. Silva	Jennifer L. Cox
Albert G. Danker, Jr.	Tanya Feliciano

References: Shawmut National Bank; New England Bank.

For full biographical listings, see the Martindale-Hubbell Law Directory

---

NEW HAVEN,* New Haven Co.

WIGGIN & DANA (AV)

One Century Tower, 06508-1832
Telephone: 203-498-4400
Telefax: 203-782-2889
Hartford, Connecticut Office: One CityPlace.
Telephone: 203-297-3700.
FAX: 203-525-9380.
Stamford, Connecticut Office: Three Stamford Plaza, 301 Tresser Boulevard.
Telephone: 203-363-7600.
Telefax: 203-363-7676.

MEMBERS OF FIRM

John Q. Tilson	Melinda A. Agsten
J. Michael Eisner	Jeanette Carpenter Schreiber
Maureen Weaver	

ASSOCIATES

John E. Buerkert, Jr.	Eric P. Neff
Julie Behm Carter	(Resident at Hartford)
Michelle Wilcox DeBarge	Susan M. Neilson
Merton G. Gollaher	Karen E. Overchuk
	(Resident at Hartford)

For Complete List of Firm Personnel, See General Section

For full biographical listings, see the Martindale-Hubbell Law Directory

---

STAMFORD, Fairfield Co.

ROSENBLUM & FILAN (AV Ⓣ)

One Landmark Square, 06901
Telephone: 203-358-9200
Fax: 203-969-6140
Email: JBR@counsel.com
White Plains, New York Office: 50 Main Street. 10606.
Telephone: 914-686-6100.
Fax: 914-686-6140.

(See Next Column)

ROSENBLUM & FILAN—*Continued*

New York, New York Office: 400 Madison Avenue. 10017.
Telephone: 212-888-8001.
Fax: 212-888-3331.

MEMBERS OF FIRM

Patrick J. Filan	James B. Rosenblum

James S. Newfield	Theodore J. Greene
Michelle L. Youtz	Christina M. Casagrande
Brian M. Rosen	JoAnn Provetto

For full biographical listings, see the Martindale-Hubbell Law Directory

---

DISTRICT OF COLUMBIA

WASHINGTON, D.C. Co.

* indicates certain Bar Register subscribers, in cities of comparable size and importance, who maintain an additional office in Washington, D.C. and who have arranged for representation as a part of the Washington, D.C. listings that follow

THE FALK LAW FIRM (AV)

A Professional Limited Company
Suite 260 One Westin Center, 2445 M Street, N.W., 20037
Telephone: 202-833-8700
Telecopier: 202-872-1725
Email: FalkLaw@erols.com

James H. Falk, Sr.	John M. Falk
James H. Falk, Jr.	Robert K. Tompkins

OF COUNSEL

Pierre E. Murphy	Elizabeth C. Collins

For full biographical listings, see the Martindale-Hubbell Law Directory

FELDESMAN, TUCKER, LEIFER, FIDELL & BANK (AV)

2001 L Street, N.W., Suite 300, 20036
Telephone: 202-466-8960
Telefax: 202-293-8103
Rockville, Maryland Office: One Church Street, Suite 800.
Telephone: 301-279-6770.
Arlington, Virginia Office: 2009 North 14th Street, Suite 610.
Telephone: 703-841-4245.

Margaret H. Long (1940-1990)

MEMBERS OF FIRM

James L. Feldesman	Pamela Borland Forbes
Marna Susan Tucker	Mary S. Pence
Jacqueline C. Leifer	Jonathan M. Dana
Eugene R. Fidell	Martha JP McQuade
Rita M. Bank	Roger A. Schwartz

Beth Goodman

ASSOCIATES

Tanya Ann Harvey	Bruce F. Hoffmeister
Michael B. Glomb	David P. Sheldon
Edward T. Waters	(Not admitted in DC)
Margaret J. McKinney	Robin Ann Clark
Lisa V. Terry	(Not admitted in DC)
(Not admitted in DC)	Nancy Joan Sardeson
Deborah Lynn Pollock	(Not admitted in DC)
Karen Burke	Garrett Lamont Lee
Kelly A. Sweeney	(Not admitted in DC)
(Not admitted in DC)	Nancy Evert

Maria-Cristina Fernandez

For full biographical listings, see the Martindale-Hubbell Law Directory

GROVE, JASKIEWICZ AND COBERT (AV)

Suite 400, 1730 M Street, N.W., 20036
Telephone: 202-296-2900
Telecopier: 202-296-1370
Baltimore, Maryland Office: The Park Plaza, 800 North Charles Street, Suite 400.
Telephone: 301-727-7010.

MEMBERS OF FIRM

William J. Grove (1914-1988)	Joseph Michael Roberts
Ronald N. Cobert	Andrew M. Danas
Edward J. Kiley	Andrew M. Whitman
Robert L. Cope	(Not admitted in DC)

OF COUNSEL

Leonard A. Jaskiewicz	Lawrence E. Dubé, Jr.
James F. Flint	James K. Jeanblanc

Edmund M. Jaskiewicz

For full biographical listings, see the Martindale-Hubbell Law Directory

MICHAELS, WISHNER & BONNER, P.C. (AV)

Suite 900, 1140 Connecticut Avenue, N.W., 20036
Telephone: 202-223-5000
Telecopier: 202-857-0634
Email: mwb@mwblegal.com

Walter J. Bonner	Joel L. Michaels
John T. Brennan, Jr.	David W. O'Brien
Mark R. Eaton	Michael R. Pollard
David Florin	Christine Clements Rinn
Thomas A. Guidoboni	Robert L. Roth
Arthur N. Lerner	Barbara H. Ryland
Stephen W. McVearry	Kathleen M. Stratton
Scott Meza	Mark J. Wishner

James F.C. Worrall

Margit H. Nahra	Beth M. Kramer
Robert S. Canterman	(Not admitted in DC)
Thomas R. Hoffman	Jessica S. Schaffer
(Not admitted in DC)	

OF COUNSEL

Ralph Werner

For full biographical listings, see the Martindale-Hubbell Law Directory

POWERS, PYLES, SUTTER & VERVILLE, P.C. (AV)

Third Floor, 1275 Pennsylvania Avenue, N.W., 20004
Telephone: 202-466-6550; 296-9243
Fax: 202-785-1756
Email: ppsv@ppsv.com *URL:* http://www.ppsv.com

Galen D. Powers	Mark R. Fitzgerald
James C. Pyles	Thomas K. Hyatt
Ronald N. Sutter	Robert J. Saner, II
Richard E. Verville	Stanley A. Freeman
Mary Susan Philp	Barbara E. Straub

David C. Beck

Peter W. Thomas	Suzanne Seftel
Christopher L. Keough	Deena M. Umbarger
Joel M. Rudnick	(Not admitted in DC)
(Not admitted in DC)	Daniel H. Orenstein
	(Not admitted in DC)

OF COUNSEL

Jenny Ann Brody	Donald W. Aaronson
Rebecca L. Burke	Joe R. G. Fulcher

Douglas Benson Tesdahl

LEGAL SUPPORT PERSONNEL

Marina Weiss

For full biographical listings, see the Martindale-Hubbell Law Directory

SCHMELTZER, APTAKER & SHEPARD, P.C. (AV)

The Watergate, Suite 1000, 2600 Virginia Avenue, N.W., 20037-1905
Telephone: 202-333-8800
Cable Address: "Ship"
Telex: 440517
Facsimile: 202-342-3434
Email: sas@saslaw.com *URL:* http://www.saspc.com
Los Angeles, California Office: 1999 Avenue of the Stars, Twenty-Seventh Floor, 90067-4095.
Telephone: 310-557-2966.
FAX: 310-286-6610.

Frank H. Case III

Wayne T. Ault

COUNSEL

Denise Bonn	Martin Jay Gaynes

For full biographical listings, see the Martindale-Hubbell Law Directory

* VENABLE ATTORNEYS AT LAW VENABLE, BAETJER, HOWARD & CIVILETTI, LLP (AV)

A Partnership including Professional Corporations
Suite 1000, 1201 New York Avenue, N.W., 20005
Telephone: 202-962-4800
Fax: 202-962-8300
Baltimore, Maryland Office: Venable, Baetjer and Howard LLP, 1800 Mercantile Bank & Trust Building, 2 Hopkins Plaza.
Telephone: 410-244-7400.
McLean, Virginia Office: Venable, Baetjer and Howard LLP, Suite 400, 2010 Corporate Ridge.
Telephone: 703-760-1600.
Rockville, Maryland Office: Venable, Baetjer and Howard LLP, Suite 500, One Church Street, P. O. Box 1906.
Telephone: 301-217-5600.

(See Next Column)

VENABLE ATTORNEYS AT LAW VENABLE, BAETJER, HOWARD & CIVILETTI, LLP, *Washington—Continued*

Towson, Maryland Office: Venable, Baetjer and Howard LLP, 210 Allegheny Avenue, P. O. Box 5517.
Telephone: 410-494-6200.

MEMBERS OF FIRM

Benjamin R. Civiletti (P.C.) (Also at Baltimore and Towson, Maryland Offices)
Thomas J. Kenney, Jr. (P.C.) (Not admitted in DC; Also at Baltimore, Maryland Office)
Kenneth C. Bass, III (Also at McLean, Virginia Office)
Robert G. Ames (Also at Baltimore, Maryland Office)
James K. Archibald (Also at Baltimore, Maryland Office)
Jeffrey A. Dunn (Also at Baltimore, Maryland Office)

George F. Pappas (Also at Baltimore, Maryland Office)
Kenneth S. Slaughter
James L. Shea (Not admitted in DC; also at Baltimore, Maryland Office)
Amy Berman Jackson
William D. Quarles (Also at Towson, Maryland Office)
James A. Dunbar (Also at Baltimore, Maryland Office)
Geoffrey R. Garinther (Not admitted in DC; Also at Baltimore, Maryland Office)

ASSOCIATE
David W. Goewey

For Complete List of Firm Personnel, See General Section

For full biographical listings, see the Martindale-Hubbell Law Directory

FLORIDA

JACKSONVILLE,* Duval Co.

SMITH HULSEY & BUSEY (AV)

1800 First Union National Bank Tower, 225 Water Street, P.O. Box 53315, 32201-3315
Telephone: 904-359-7700
Facsimile: 904-359-7708; 353-9908

Lloyd Smith (1915-1987)
MEMBERS OF FIRM

Dennis L. Blackburn
Stephen D. Busey
Douglas D. Chunn
Earl E. Googe, Jr.
Jeanne E. Helton
Cynthia C. Jackson
G. Preston Keyes
William E. Kuntz
M. Richard Lewis, Jr.
John F. MacLennan
Raymond R. Magley

E. Owen McCuller, Jr.
James H. Post
Bryan L. Putnal
E. Lanny Russell
Joel Settembrini, Jr.
Tim E. Sleeth
John R. Smith, Jr.
James J. Taylor, Jr.
Timothy W. Volpe
Waddell A. Wallace, III
Harry M. Wilson, III

Michael M. Bajalia
James A. Bolling, Jr.
E. Lanier Drew
Diana Salama Farhat
Martin A. Fitzpatrick
Michael R. Freed
Lee G. Kellison
Lauren P. Langham
Marjorie Conner Makar
Bradley R. Markey

R. Leanne McKnight
Mary E. McManus
Jeanne M. Miller
Stephen D. Moore, Jr.
Howard J. Smith
Steven G. Spears
Melissa Smith Turra
Herschel T. Vinyard, Jr
Leslie A. Wickes
Karl A. Zillgitt

OF COUNSEL
Mark Hulsey
John E. Thrasher

Representative Clients: Baptist/St. Vincent's Health System, Inc.; Browning-Ferris Industries, Inc.; Champion Realty Corp. (Florida); First Union National Bank of Florida; Florida Rock Industries, Inc.; PGA Tour, Inc.; KPMG Peat Marwick; The Regency Group, Inc.; The Ritz-Carlton Hotel Co.; University of Florida.

For full biographical listings, see the Martindale-Hubbell Law Directory

MIAMI,* Dade Co.

ZACK, SPARBER, KOSNITZKY, SPRATT & BROOKS, P.A. (AV)

International Place, 100 Southeast Second Street, Suite 2800, 33131-2144
Telephone: 305-539-8400
Facsimile: 305-539-1307

Michael Kosnitzky
William J. Spratt, Jr.

Marc H. Auerbach
Louise T. Jeroslow

OF COUNSEL
Kimarie R. Stratos

For Complete List of Firm Personnel, See General Section

For full biographical listings, see the Martindale-Hubbell Law Directory

ORLANDO,* Orange Co.

ADAMS, HILL, REIS, ADAMS, HALL & SCHIEFFELIN (AV)

1417 East Concord Street, 32803
Telephone: 407-896-0425
Fax: 407-896-9236

MEMBERS OF FIRM

George E. Adams
G. Bruce Hill
Gregory F. Reis

Janet W. Adams
Larry D. Hall
Thomas L. Schieffelin, Jr.

ASSOCIATES

William W. Large
Matthew P. Bartolomei

William H. Olney
Richard Coaxum, Jr

Christopher E. Butler

Representative Clients: Everglades Regional Medical Center; The Florida Hospital Trust Fund; The Florida Hospital Excess Trust Fund; Florida Hospital Workers Compensation/Self Insurance Trust Fund; Bartow Memorial Hospital; Bay Medical Center; Brooksville Regional Hospital; Cape Canaveral Hospital; Cape Coral Hospital; Desoto Memorial Hospital.

For full biographical listings, see the Martindale-Hubbell Law Directory

BOBO, SPICER, CIOTOLI, FULFORD, BOCCHINO, DEBEVOISE & LE CLAINCHE, P.A. (AV)

Landmark Center One, Suite 510, 315 East Robinson Street, 32801-1949
Telephone: 407-849-1060
Fax: 407-843-4751
West Palm Beach, Florida Office: Esperante, Sixth Floor, 222 Lakeview Avenue, 33401.
Telephone: 407-684-6600.
FAX: 407-684-3828.

John W. Bocchino
D. Andrew DeBevoise
Patti A. Haber

Gregorio A. Francis
Ingrid A. de Graaff
Thomas W. Poulton

For full biographical listings, see the Martindale-Hubbell Law Directory

SARASOTA,* Sarasota Co.

WILLIAMS, PARKER, HARRISON, DIETZ & GETZEN, PROFESSIONAL ASSOCIATION (AV)

200 South Orange Avenue, 34236-6749
Telephone: 941-366-4800
Telecopier: 941-366-5109
Mailing Address: P.O. Box 3258, Sarasota, Florida, 34230-3258
Email: wphdg.law@netsrg.com *URL:* http://www.sarasota-online.com/williamspa-w

J.J. Williams, Jr. (1886-1968)
W. Davis Parker (1920-1982)
William T. Harrison, Jr.
George A. Dietz
Monte K. Marshall
James L. Ritchey
William G. Lambrecht
John T. Berteau
John V. Cannon, III
Charles D. Bailey, Jr.
J. Michael Hartenstine
Michele Boardman Grimes
James L. Turner
William M. Seider
Elizabeth C. Marshall
Robert W. Benjamin

Frank Strelec
Terri Salt Costa
David A. Wallace
Mark A. Schwartz
Ric Gregoria
Elvin W. Phillips
Jeffrey A. Grebe
John L. Moore
Morgan R. Bentley
Susan A. Barrett
Carol Ann Kalish
Linda R. Getzen
Kimberly J. Page
Phillip D. Eck
J. Hugh Middlebrooks
Robert A. Warram

OF COUNSEL
William E. Getzen
Frazer F. Hilder
Hugh McPheeters, Jr.

LEGAL SUPPORT PERSONNEL
Mark Loveridge (Land Planner)

General Counsel for: Sarasota County Public Hospital Board; Sarasota-Manatee Airport Authority; Taylor Woodrow Homes Ltd.; FCCI Mutual Insurance Co.
Local Counsel for: NationsBank of Florida; Barnett Bank of Southwest Florida; Northern Trust Bank of Florida; SunTrust Bank, Gulfcoast.

For full biographical listings, see the Martindale-Hubbell Law Directory

TALLAHASSEE,* Leon Co.

McFARLAIN, WILEY, CASSEDY & JONES, PROFESSIONAL ASSOCIATION (AV)

215 South Monroe Street, Suite 600, P.O. Box 2174, 32316-2174
Telephone: 904-222-2107
Telecopier: 904-222-8475

(See Next Column)

MCFARLAIN, WILEY, CASSEDY & JONES PROFESSIONAL ASSOCIATION—
Continued

Richard C. McFarlain	Charles A. Stampelos
William B. Wiley	Linda McMullen
Marshall R. Cassedy	H. Darrell White, Jr.
Douglas P. Jones	Christopher Barkas

Harold R. Mardenborough, Jr.	Rogelio J. Fontela
Robert A. McNeely	Patrick John McGinley

For full biographical listings, see the Martindale-Hubbell Law Directory

RADEY MCARTHUR & FREHN (AV)

101 South Monroe Street, 32301
Telephone: 904-681-7766
Fax: 904-681-0160
Email: Radeylaw@aol.com

John Radey   Elizabeth Waas McArthur
            Jeffrey L. Frehn

Representative Clients: Columbia/HCA Healthcare Corp.; Columbia Tallahassee Community Hospital; Tampa General Hospital; Columbia Medical Center-Sanford; Columbia Lawnwood Regional Medical Center.

For full biographical listings, see the Martindale-Hubbell Law Directory

ROSE, SUNDSTROM & BENTLEY (AV)

A Partnership including Professional Associations
2548 Blairstone Pines Drive, P.O. Box 1567, 32302-1567
Telephone: 904-877-6555
Telecopier: 904-656-4029

MEMBERS OF FIRM

Chris H. Bentley (P.A.)	Diane D. Tremor (P.A.)
Steven T. Mindlin (P.A.)	John L. Wharton

Representative Clients: Arbor Health Care Co.; Columbia/HCA Health Care Corp.; Shands Hospital.
Reference: Barnett Bank, Tallahassee.

For full biographical listings, see the Martindale-Hubbell Law Directory

TAMPA,* Hillsborough Co.

BUCHANAN INGERSOLL, PROFESSIONAL CORPORATION (AVⓉ)

Suite 2500, 401 East Jackson Street, 33602
Telephone: 813-222-8180
Telecopier: 813-222-8189
URL: http://www.bipc.com
Pittsburgh, Pennsylvania Office: One Oxford Centre, 301 Grant Street, 20th Floor.
Telephone: 412-562-8800.
Philadelphia, Pennsylvania Office: Two Logan Square, Twelfth Floor, 18th & Arch Streets.
Telephone: 215-665-8700.
Harrisburg, Pennsylvania Office: 30 North Third Street.
Telephone: 717-237-4800.
Aventura, Florida Office: 19495 Biscayne Boulevard, Suite 606.
Telephone: 305-933-5600.
Miami, Florida Office: NationsBank Tower, 100 S.E. Second Street.
Telephone: 305-347-4080.
Princeton, New Jersey Office: Buchanan Ingersoll, A Partnership, College Centre, 500 College Road East.
Telephone: 609-987-6800.
Lexington, Kentucky Office: Suite 600, PNC Bank Plaza, 200 West Vine Street.
Telephone: 606-225-5333.
Buffalo, New York Office: 1100 Main Place Tower, 350 Main Street.
Telephone: 716-854-4100.
Fax: 716-854-4227.

James J. Kennedy III

For Complete List of Firm Personnel, See General Section

For full biographical listings, see the Martindale-Hubbell Law Directory

SHEAR, NEWMAN, HAHN AND ROSENKRANZ, P.A. (AV)

Suite 1000, 201 East Kennedy Boulevard, 33602
Telephone: 813-228-8530
FAX: 813-221-9122

L. David Shear	Glenn M. Burton
Jerry L. Newman	Roland J. Lamb
William E. Hahn	Bruce Douglas Lamb
Stanley W. Rosenkranz	Jeffrey Drew Butt
James R. Freeman	Mark J. Ragusa
Rodney W. Morgan	Kelly Jo Schmedt

(See Next Column)

Marilyn Drivas Sandborn	Mildred D. Beam-Rucker
Scott P. Distasio	Joseph F. Diaco, Jr.
Thomas M. Hoeler	Elizabeth (Betsey) Taylor Herd
Christopher J. Schulte	Timothy M. Cerio
Kimberly D. Holladay	Mindy Paige Brostoff
Debra L. Boje	Carl A. Goldman

OF COUNSEL

Daniel J. Gibby   Leonard L. Kleinman

References: NationsBank; First National Bank.

For full biographical listings, see the Martindale-Hubbell Law Directory

SHOFI, SMITH, HENNEN & GRAMOVOT, P.A. (AV)

One North Dale Mabry, Suite 800, P.O. Box 10430, 33679-0430
Telephone: 813-876-7796
FAX: 813-876-0509

John D. Shofi	Larry I. Gramovot
John S. Smith	Sandra L. Peacock
William E. Hennen	Matthew R. Danahy
James E. Bogos	

Jon A. McAuliffe	Rochelle L. Lefler
Frank Clark	Kenneth S. Takacs, Jr.

Reference: City Bank of Tampa.

For full biographical listings, see the Martindale-Hubbell Law Directory

VERO BEACH,* Indian River Co.

STEWART & NALL, P.A. (AV)

3355 Ocean Drive, P.O. Box 3345, 32964-3345
Telephone: 561-231-3500
FAX: 561-231-9876

William J. Stewart	Cynthia L. Cambron
Robert C. Nall	Edith E. Collins
Troy B. Hafner	

Representative Clients: Indian River Memorial Hospital, Inc.; Florida Eye Institute; Indian River Hospital Foundation, Inc.; Indian River Health Services Corp.; Indian River Cardiac Rehab. Lab., Inc.; Health Systems of Indian River, Inc.

For full biographical listings, see the Martindale-Hubbell Law Directory

WEST PALM BEACH,* Palm Beach Co.

BOBO, SPICER, CIOTOLI, FULFORD, BOCCHINO, DEBEVOISE & LE CLAINCHE, P.A. (AV)

Esperante, Sixth Floor, 222 Lakeview Avenue, 33401
Telephone: 407-684-6600
Fax: 407-684-3828
Orlando, Florida Office: Landmark Center One, Suite 510, 315 East Robinson Street, 32801-1949.
Telephone: 407-849-1060.
Fax: 407-843-4751.

A. Russell Bobo	D. Andrew DeBevoise
David W. Spicer	(Resident, Orlando Office)
Eugene L. Ciotoli	Stephan A. Le Clainche
Jeffrey C. Fulford	Patti A. Haber
John W. Bocchino	(Resident, Orlando Office)
(Resident, Orlando Office)	Joseph A. Osborne

Mark Alan Glassman	Casey D. Shomo
Michael S. Smith	Armando T. Lauritano
Neil A. Deleon	Ingrid A. de Graaff
Gregorio A. Francis	(Resident, Orlando Office)
(Resident, Orlando Office)	Thomas W. Poulton
Michael D. Burt	(Resident, Orlando Office)

For full biographical listings, see the Martindale-Hubbell Law Directory

WINTER PARK, Orange Co.

KENNETH E. BROOTEN, JR. CHARTERED (AV)

631 West Fairbanks Avenue, 32789
Telephone: 407-645-4447
Fax: 407-628-2220

Kenneth E. Brooten, Jr.

For full biographical listings, see the Martindale-Hubbell Law Directory

GEORGIA

ATHENS,* Clarke Co.

McLEOD, BENTON, BEGNAUD & MARSHALL (AV)

8th Floor, NationsBank Building, P.O. Box 8108, 30603
Telephone: 706-549-9400
Fax: 706-549-9406

MEMBERS OF FIRM

Larry V. McLeod	Malcolm C. McArthur
Terrell W. Benton, Jr.	William C. Berryman, Jr.
Jeanette S. Scott	Daniel C. Haygood
Darrel Begnaud	Hilary N. Shuford
Andrew H. Marshall	Richard L. Brittain

Michael C. Pruett

OF COUNSEL

Robert E. Gibson

Counsel for: NationsBank; Athens First Bank & Trust Company; Georgia Power Company; CSX Transportation, Inc.; St. Mary's Hospital; Benson's Inc.; Oconee County School District; Walton County School District; Clarke County School District.

For full biographical listings, see the Martindale-Hubbell Law Directory

ATLANTA,* Fulton Co.

ALSTON & BIRD (AV)

A Partnership including Professional Corporations
One Atlantic Center, 1201 West Peachtree Street, 30309-3424
Telephone: 404-881-7000
Telecopier: 404-881-7777
Cable Address: AMGRAM GA
Telex: 54-2996
Easylink: 62985848
Washington, D.C. Office: 601 Pennsylvania Ave., N.W., North Building, Suite 250 20004.
Telephone: 202-508-3300.
Telecopier: 202-508-3333.

MEMBERS OF FIRM

G. Conley Ingram	J. Vaughan Curtis
Ronald L. Reid	Theodore E. G. Pound
Dow N. Kirkpatrick II	Bernard Taylor
Robert C. Lower	Donna Potts Bergeson
Peter M. Wright	R. Gregory Brophy
Robert D. McCallum, Jr.	Laura Lewis Owens
Jack S. Schroder, Jr.	Richard R. Hays
Kevin E. Grady	Susan B. Devitt
Judson Graves	Steven L. Pottle
Jonathan W. Lowe	Michelle A. Williams

ASSOCIATES

Kimberly A. Ackourey	James C. Grant
Kristen D. Adams	Clifton M. Iler
Craig D. Apolinsky	Karen J. Jacobs
Lori G. Baer	Daniel A. Kent
Elizabeth Bertschi	Kimberly A. Knight
Jennifer B. Block	Annette T. Lord
Lonnie T. Brown, Jr.	Nils H. Okeson
Hilary E. Buckley	William T. Plybon
Angela T. Burnette	Shruthi G. Reddy
B. Davis Butler	(Not admitted in GA)
Cynthia L. Counts	H. Suzanne Smith
Frederick C. Dawkins	Richard A. Snow
John P. Donaldson	Debra A. R. Sydnor
David S. Givelber	Paul F. Wellborn III

COUNSEL

Lawrie E. Demorest	Gary E. McClanahan

Representative Clients: ActaMed Corp.; Coram Healthcare; First Physician Care; Medifax, Inc.; The Emory Clinic, Inc.; PhyCor, Inc.; Kaiser Permanente; Georgia Hospital Assoc.; Surgical Health Corp.; VHA of Georgia.

For Complete List of Firm Personnel, See General Section

For full biographical listings, see the Martindale-Hubbell Law Directory

GOLDNER, SOMMERS, SCRUDDER & BASS (AV)

900 Circle 75 Parkway Suite 850, 30339
Telephone: 770-612-9200
Facsimile: 770-612-9201

Stephen L. Goldner	Susan V. Sommers

For Complete List of Firm Personnel, See General Section

For full biographical listings, see the Martindale-Hubbell Law Directory

HOLT, NEY, ZATCOFF & WASSERMAN (AV)

A Partnership including Professional Corporations
100 Galleria Parkway, Suite 600, 30339
Telephone: 770-956-9600
Facsimile Number: 770-956-1490

MEMBER OF FIRM

Michael G. Wasserman (P.C.)

Representative Clients: Champion Healthcare Corporation; Pathology Institute of Middle Georgia, P.C.

For Complete List of Firm Personnel, See General Section

For full biographical listings, see the Martindale-Hubbell Law Directory

KILPATRICK & CODY LLP (AV)

Suite 2800, 1100 Peachtree Street, 30309-4530
Telephone: 404-815-6500
Telephone Copier: 404-815-6555
Telex: 54-2307
Washington, D.C. Office: Suite 800, 700 13th Street, N.W., 20005.
Telephone: 202-508-5800. *Telephone Copier:* 202-508-5858.
Brussels, Belgium Office: Avenue Louise 65, BTE 3, 1050 Brussels.
Telephone: (32) (2) 533-03-00.
Telecopier: (32) (2) 534-86-38.
London, England Office: 68 Pall Mall, London, SW1Y 5ES, England.
Telephone: (44) (71) 321 0477.
Telecopier: (44) (71) 930 9733.
Augusta, Georgia Office: Suite 1400 First Union Bank Building, P.O. Box 2043, 30903. Telephone (706) 724-2622. Telecopier (706) 722-0219.

MEMBERS OF FIRM

Thomas William Baker	Michael H. Trotter
Jane E. Jordan	Frederick H. von Unwerth
James R. Kanner	David M. Zacks
Wyck A. Knox, Jr.	Deborah B. Zink
(Augusta Office)	

ASSOCIATES

William B. Barkley	Sonya W. Middleton
Phyllis F. Granade	W. Craig Smith
Barry S. Herrin	(Augusta, Georgia Office)
Joseph H. Huff	
(Augusta, Georgia Office)	

For Complete List of Firm Personnel, See General Section

For full biographical listings, see the Martindale-Hubbell Law Directory

LONG ALDRIDGE & NORMAN, LLP (AV)

A Limited Liability Partnership including Professional Corporations
One Peachtree Center, Suite 5300, 303 Peachtree Street, 30308
Telephone: 404-527-4000
Telecopier: 404-527-4198
Washington, D.C. Office: Suite 600, 701 Pennsylvania Avenue, N.W., 20004.
Telephone: 202-624-1200.
FAX: 202-624-1298.

MEMBERS OF FIRM

Barbara L. Blackford	Edgar H. Sims, Jr. (P.C.)
R. William Ide III	Jesse J. Spikes
J. James Johnson	John E. Theberge (Resident,
Mark S. Lange	Washington, D.C. Office)

ASSOCIATES

James D. Comerford	Robert E. DeWitt
	Briggs L. Tobin

For Complete List of Firm Personnel, See General Section

For full biographical listings, see the Martindale-Hubbell Law Directory

PARKER, HUDSON, RAINER & DOBBS (AV)

1500 Marquis Two Tower, 285 Peachtree Center Avenue, N.E., 30303
Telephone: 404-523-5300
FAX: 404-522-8409
Tallahassee, Florida Office: The Perkins House, 118 North Gadsden Street, 32301.
Telephone: 904-681-0191.
FAX: 904-681-9493.

MEMBERS OF FIRM

John H. Parker, Jr.	Jonathan L. Rue
Paul L. Hudson, Jr.	David G. Cleveland
Robert A. Weiss (Not admitted	Theodore N. McDowell, Jr.
in GA; Resident, Tallahassee,	Leo E. Reichert
Florida Office)	

For full biographical listings, see the Martindale-Hubbell Law Directory

PIERCE & YOUNG (AV)

Building 1700, 2255 Cumberland Parkway Northwest, 30339-4575
Telephone: 770-435-0500
Telecopier: 770-435-0362

(See Next Column)

PIERCE & YOUNG—*Continued*

MEMBERS OF FIRM

J. Wayne Pierce   Richard M. Young

ASSOCIATE

Christy A. Dunkelberger

For full biographical listings, see the Martindale-Hubbell Law Directory

SUMNER & ANDERSON (AV)

A Limited Liability Company
Suite 700, The Hurt Building, 50 Hurt Plaza, 30303
Telephone: 404-588-9000
Fax: 404-525-1116
Orlando, Florida Office: 940 Highland Avenue, 32802.
Telephone: 407-841-3000.
Fax: 407-841-0022.
Beaufort, South Carolina Office: 1001 Bay Street, Suite 102, 29902.
Telephone: 803-986-1000.
Fax: 803-986-1002.

MEMBERS OF FIRM

William E. Sumner   Steven E. Harbour
Stephen J. Anderson   David A. Webster

ASSOCIATES

Gerald Kirk Domescik   Anne S. Douds (Resident,
Kathleen M. Fischer   Beaufort, South Carolina)
Everrette V. Snotherly, III   Elizabeth A. Green (Resident,
Jerry P. Doyle   Orlando, Florida Office)

For full biographical listings, see the Martindale-Hubbell Law Directory

SUTHERLAND, ASBILL & BRENNAN, L.L.P. (AV)

999 Peachtree Street, N.E., 30309-3996
Telephone: 404-853-8000
Facsimile: 404-853-8806
Email: postmaster@sablaw.com
Washington, D.C. Office: 1275 Pennsylvania Avenue, N.W., 20004-2404.
Telephone: 202-383-0100.
New York, N.Y. Office: 600 Madison Avenue, 11th Floor, 10022-1615.
Telephone: 212-605-6400.
Austin, Texas Office: 111 Congress Avenue, 23rd Floor, 78701-4079.
Telephone: 512-469-3350.

Katherine Meyers Cohen   James R. McGibbon
James K. Hasson, Jr.   Richard L. Robbins

COUNSEL OF THE FIRM
IN ATLANTA, GEORGIA

Donald M. Etheridge, Jr. (Not admitted in GA)

For Complete List of Firm Personnel, See General Section

For full biographical listings, see the Martindale-Hubbell Law Directory

AUGUSTA,* Richmond Co.

PAINE, McELREATH & HYDER, P.C. (AV)

301 Wheeler Executive Center, 3540 Wheeler Road, 30909
Telephone: 706-738-9710
Telecopier: 706-738-9761

Travers W. Paine, III   Benjamin F. McElreath
James D. Hyder, Jr.

For full biographical listings, see the Martindale-Hubbell Law Directory

CARROLLTON,* Carroll Co.

TISINGER, TISINGER, VANCE & GREER, A PROFESSIONAL CORPORATION (AV)

100 Wagon Yard Plaza, P.O. Box 2069, 30117
Telephone: 770-834-4467
Fax: 770-834-5426

J. Thomas Vance   Steven T. Minor

Representative Clients: Tanner Medical Center, Inc.; Carroll City-County Hospital Authority; Heard County Hospital Authority.

For Complete List of Firm Personnel, See General Section

For full biographical listings, see the Martindale-Hubbell Law Directory

COLUMBUS,* Muscogee Co.

ROTHSCHILD & MORGAN (AV)

1030 First Avenue, P.O. Box 2788, 31902-2788
Telephone: 706-324-4167
FAX: 706-324-1969

MEMBERS OF FIRM

Martelle Layfield, Jr.   Jerome M. Rothschild
(1937-1989)   W. Donald Morgan, Jr.

(See Next Column)

ASSOCIATE

Neal J. Callahan

Reference: Columbus Bank and Trust Company.

For full biographical listings, see the Martindale-Hubbell Law Directory

MACON,* Bibb Co.

SELL & MELTON (AV)

A Partnership including a Professional Corporation
14th Floor, Charter Medical Building, P.O. Box 229, 31297-2899
Telephone: 912-746-8521
Telecopier: 912-745-6426

John D. Comer

ASSOCIATES

Jeffrey B. Hanson   Michelle W. Johnson

General Counsel for: Macon Telegraph Publishing Co. (The Macon Telegraph); Macon-Bibb County Hospital Authority; County of Bibb; County of Twiggs; Smith & Sons Foods, Inc. (S & S Cafeterias); Macon Bibb County Industrial Authority; Burgess Pigment Co.

For Complete List of Firm Personnel, See General Section

For full biographical listings, see the Martindale-Hubbell Law Directory

NORCROSS, Gwinnett Co.

PHEARS & MOLDOVAN (AV)

A Partnership of Professional Corporations
4725 Peachtree Corners Circle Suite 375, 30092
Telephone: 770-446-2116
Telecopier: 770-263-6715

MEMBERS OF FIRM

H. Wayne Phears (P.C.)   Victor L. Moldovan (P.C.)

Richard E. Harris   Wendy A. Jacobs

For full biographical listings, see the Martindale-Hubbell Law Directory

SAVANNAH,* Chatham Co.

SILVERS, SIMPSON & CREASY, P.C. (AV)

Suite 102, AmeriBank Plaza, 7393 Hodgson Memorial Drive, 31406
Telephone: 912-925-7200
Facsimile: 912-925-0100

Mark M. Silvers, Jr.   K. Russell Simpson
                              Neil A. Creasy

Representative Clients: Coastal Dialysis and Medical Clinic, Inc.; Physicians' Health Care Services, Ltd.; South Coast Medical Group, P.C.; Savannah Hematology-Oncology Associates, P.C.; Georgia Ear Institute Physicians; Pediatric Associates of Savannah, P.C.

For full biographical listings, see the Martindale-Hubbell Law Directory

HAWAII

HONOLULU,* Honolulu Co.

DWYER IMANAKA SCHRAFF KUDO MEYER & FUJIMOTO ATTORNEYS AT LAW, A LAW CORPORATION (AV)

1800 Pioneer Plaza, 900 Fort Street Mall, 96813
Telephone: 808-524-8000
Telecopier: 808-526-1419
Mailing Address: P.O. Box 2727, 96803
Email: hawaiilaw@dwyer-imanaka.com *URL:*
http://www.dwyer-imanaka.com

John R. Dwyer, Jr.   William G. Meyer, III
Mitchell A. Imanaka   Wesley M. Fujimoto
Paul A. Schraff   Ronald Van Grant
Benjamin A. Kudo (Atty. at   Jon M. H. Pang
  Law, A Law Corp.)   Blake W. Bushnell
                  Adelbert Green

Richard T. Asato, Jr.   Jeffery S. Werbelow
Scott W. Settle   Lori Ann K. Koseki
Darcie S. Yoshinaga   Troy T. Fukuhara
Lawrence I. Kawasaki   Katy Y. Chen
Stacy E. Uehara   Naomi S. Uyeno
Kris N. Nakagawa   Roger B. McKeague

OF COUNSEL

Randall Y. Iwase   R. Brian Tsujimura

For full biographical listings, see the Martindale-Hubbell Law Directory

Honolulu—Continued

ROBBINS & RHODES ATTORNEYS AT LAW, A LAW CORPORATION (AV)

Suite 2200 Davies Pacific Center, 841 Bishop Street, 96813
Telephone: 808-524-2355
Fax: 808-526-0290

Kenneth S. Robbins   Vincent A. Rhodes
Shinken Naitoh

Representative Clients: Farmers Insurance Group; Hawaii Association of Physicians for Indemnification (HAPI); Hawaii Psychological Association; John Burns School of Medicine Residency Program; Kapiolani Health Care Systems, Inc.; Kona Hospital; Maui Memorial Hospital; North Hawaii Community Hospital; State of Hawaii; Wilcox Memorial Hospital.

For full biographical listings, see the Martindale-Hubbell Law Directory

IDAHO

BOISE,* Ada Co.

MOFFATT, THOMAS, BARRETT, ROCK & FIELDS, CHARTERED (AV)

101 South Capitol Boulevard, P.O. Box 829, 83702
Telephone: 208-345-2000
FAX: 208-385-5384
Email: info@moffatt.com
Idaho Falls Office: 525 Park Avenue, Suite 2D, P.O. Box 1367, 83403.
Telephone: 208-522-6700.
FAX: 208-522-5111.
Pocatello, Idaho Office: 845 West Center, Suite C, P.O. Box 4941, 83201.
Telephone: 208-233-2001.

Eugene C. Thomas   Richard C. Fields
Morgan W. Richards, Jr.

Representative Clients: BMC West Corporation; Chevron, U.S.A.; First Security Bank of Idaho, N.A.; General Motors Corp.; Idaho Potato Commission; Intermountain Gas Co.; John Alden Life Insurance Co.; Micron Technology, Inc.; Royal Insurance Cos.; St. Luke's Regional Medical Center & Mountain States Tumor Institute.

For Complete List of Firm Personnel, See General Section

For full biographical listings, see the Martindale-Hubbell Law Directory

POCATELLO,* Bannock Co.

MERRILL & MERRILL, CHARTERED (AV)

Key Bank Building, P.O. Box 991, 83204
Telephone: 208-232-2286
Fax: 208-232-2499

D. Russell Wight

Representative Clients: Bannock Regional Medical Center.

For Complete List of Firm Personnel, See General Section

For full biographical listings, see the Martindale-Hubbell Law Directory

ILLINOIS

CHICAGO,* Cook Co.

BELL, BOYD & LLOYD (AV)

Three First National Plaza Suite 3300, 70 West Madison Street, 60602
Telephone: 312-372-1121
FAX: 312-372-2098
Email: bbl@bbl.com
Washington, D.C. Office: 1615 L Street, N.W.
Telephone: 202-466-6300.
FAX: 202-463-0678.

MEMBERS OF FIRM

Lee A. Daniels	Richard L. Sevcik
Raymond H. Drymalski	Peter M. Sfikas
Tamra S. Kempf	Thomas C. Shields
Jeffrey R. Ladd	Cheryl Weissman

For Complete List of Firm Personnel, See General Section

For full biographical listings, see the Martindale-Hubbell Law Directory

THE ELDEN LAW FIRM (AV)

150 North Michigan Avenue, 30th Floor, 60601-7567
Telephone: 312-781-3600
Fax: 312-781-3601

(See Next Column)

Douglas L. Elden	Robbin C. Elden

OF COUNSEL

Charles M. Jacobs	Susan Weagly

For full biographical listings, see the Martindale-Hubbell Law Directory

FORAN & SCHULTZ (AV)

Suite 3000, 30 North La Salle Street, 60602
Telephone: 312-368-8330
Fax: 312-580-2600

MEMBER OF FIRM
Brooke R. Whitted
ASSOCIATES

Mitchell S. Chaban	Jessica Dickstein

For full biographical listings, see the Martindale-Hubbell Law Directory

GESSLER, HUGHES & SOCOL, LTD. (AV)

Three First National Plaza, Suite 2200, 60602
Telephone: 312-580-0100
Telecopy: 312-580-1994

Mark S. Dym	Terence J. Moran
George W. Gessler	Mark D. Olson
John K. Hughes	Matthew J. Piers
William P. Jones	David J. Pritchard
Peter M. Katsaros	Kalman D. Resnick
Mark A. LaRose	Frederick S. Rhine
Kimberley Marsh	Jonathan A. Rothstein

Donna Kaner Socol

Benjamin P. Beringer	Alex W. Miller
Darilyn W. Bock	Belkis Cervantes Muldoon
Gary Chodorow	Jonathan D. Rosenblum
Anjali Dayal	Marci S. Sperling
Ruth M. Dunning	Dana H. Sukenik
Adam D. Ingber	J. Eric Vander Arend
Michael J. Klein	Maria L. Vertuno
Laura C. Liu	Mark B. Weiner

Charles H. Wintersteen
OF COUNSEL

James T. Derico, Jr.	Darius S. Francescatti, M.D.
	Susan R. Gzesh

For full biographical listings, see the Martindale-Hubbell Law Directory

TERRELL J. ISSELHARD AND ASSOCIATES, LTD. PROFESSIONAL CORPORATION (AV)

Suite 3000, Thirtieth Floor, 200 North La Salle Street, 60601-1083
Telephone: 312-372-5225
Fax: 312-704-4959

Terrell J. Isselhard

David T. Pence

For full biographical listings, see the Martindale-Hubbell Law Directory

SCHWARTZBERG, BARNETT & COHEN (AV)

55 West Monroe Street, 2400 Xerox Centre, 60603-5040
Telephone: 312-726-3555
Fax: 312-726-6299
Cable Address: "Justice"
Email: sb&c@twty.chi.il.us

MEMBERS OF FIRM

Ralph M. Schwartzberg (1939-1975)	Mark T. Barnett (1939-1970)
	Hugh J. Schwartzberg
Benjamin H. Cohen	

OF COUNSEL
Eugene P. Thomas Jr.

For full biographical listings, see the Martindale-Hubbell Law Directory

WILDMAN, HARROLD, ALLEN & DIXON (AV)

225 West Wacker Drive, 30th Floor, 60606-1229
Telephone: 312-201-2000
Cable Address: "Whad"
Fax: 312-201-2555
URL: http://www.whad.com
Aurora, Illinois Office: 1851 W. Galena Boulevard, Suite 210.
Telephone: 630-892-7021.
Fax: 630-892-7158.
Waukegan, Illinois Office: 404 West Water, P. O. Box 890.
Telephone: 847-623-0700.
Fax: 847-244-5273.
Lisle, Illinois Office: 4300 Commerce Court.
Telephone: 630-955-0555.

(See Next Column)

WILDMAN, HARROLD, ALLEN & DIXON—Continued

New York, New York Office: Wildman, Harrold, Allen, Dixon & Smith.
The International Building, 45 Rockefeller Plaza, Suite 353.
Telephone: 212-632-3850.
Fax: 212-632-3858.
Toronto, Ontario affiliated Office: Keel Cottrelle. 36 Toronto Street, Ninth
Floor, Suite 920.
Telephone: 416-367-2900.
Telefax: 416-367-2791.
Telex: 062-18660.
Mississauga, Ontario affiliated Office: Keel Cottrelle. 100 Matatson
Avenue East, Suite 104.
Telephone: 416-890-7700.
Fax: 416-890-8006.

MEMBERS OF FIRM

Douglas R. Carlson	Helaine Wachs Heydemann
James A. Christman	David F. Pardys
Jerald P. Esrick	(Waukegan Office)

John A. Roberts

For Complete List of Firm Personnel, See General Section

For full biographical listings, see the Martindale-Hubbell Law Directory

EVANSTON, Cook Co.

ATKINSON & ATKINSON (AV)

1603 Orrington Avenue, Suite 2080, 60201
Telephone: 708-864-0070
Facsimile: 708-864-0588

MEMBERS OF FIRM

John F. Atkinson	Dale J. Atkinson

ASSOCIATE

David C. Thollander

A list of Representative Clients will be furnished upon request.

For full biographical listings, see the Martindale-Hubbell Law Directory

KANKAKEE,* Kankakee Co.

BLANKE, NORDEN, BARMANN, KRAMER & BOHLEN, P.C. (AV)

Suite 502, 200 East Court Street, P.O. Box 1787, 60901
Telephone: 815-939-1133
Fax: 815-939-0994

Armen R. Blanke (Deceased)	Glen R. Barmann
Paul F. Blanke (Retired)	Christopher W. Bohlen
Dennis A. Norden	Michael D. Kramer

For full biographical listings, see the Martindale-Hubbell Law Directory

INDIANA

BLOOMINGTON,* Monroe Co.

BUNGER & ROBERTSON (AV)

226 South College Square, P.O. Box 910, 47402-0910
Telephone: 812-332-9295
Fax: 812-331-8808

MEMBERS OF FIRM

Joseph D. O'Connor III	James L. Whitlatch

ASSOCIATE

William J. Beggs

Representative Clients: Bloomington Hospital, Inc.; Bloomington Convalescent Center; Nurse Call Plus; Hospice of Bloomington; Phico Insurance, Co.; Medical Protective Insurance Co.; Children's Organ Transplant Association.

For Complete List of Firm Personnel, See General Section

For full biographical listings, see the Martindale-Hubbell Law Directory

EVANSVILLE,* Vanderburgh Co.

BAMBERGER, FOREMAN, OSWALD AND HAHN (AV)

7th Floor Hulman Building, P.O. Box 657, 47704-0657
Telephone: 812-425-1591
Fax: 812-421-4936

MEMBERS OF FIRM

Robert H. Hahn	R. Thomas Bodkin
Fred S. White	Michele S. Bryant

ASSOCIATE

Catherine A. Nestrick

Representative Clients: AT&T; Dow Chemical Co.; Medical Protective Insurance Co.; St. Mary's Medical Center of Evansville, Inc.; Evansville International Medicine Associates; The Heart Group.

(See Next Column)

For Complete List of Firm Personnel, See General Section

For full biographical listings, see the Martindale-Hubbell Law Directory

FINE & HATFIELD (AV)

520 N.W. Second Street, P.O. Box 779, 47705-0779
Telephone: 812-425-3592
Telecopier: 812-421-4269
Email: Fine@Fine-Hatfield.com *URL:* http://www.Fine-Hatfield.com

MEMBER OF FIRM

Thomas R. Fitzsimmons

A List of Representative Clients Furnished Upon Request.

For full biographical listings, see the Martindale-Hubbell Law Directory

KAHN, DEES, DONOVAN & KAHN (AV)

P.O. Box 3646, 47735-3646
Telephone: 812-423-3183
Fax: 812-423-3841
Email: evvlaw@k2d2.com

MEMBERS OF FIRM

Alan N. Shovers	G. Michael Schopmeyer
Thomas O. Magan	John E. Hegeman
Larry R. Downs	Jeffrey K. Helfrich

ASSOCIATES

Kent A. Brasseale, II	Mark L. Boos

Counsel for: Deaconess Hospital, Inc.; Wabash General Hospital; Welborn Baptist Hospital; The Rehabilitation Center; Healthsouth Tri-State Rehabilitation Hospital.

For Complete List of Firm Personnel, See General Section

For full biographical listings, see the Martindale-Hubbell Law Directory

ZIEMER, STAYMAN, WEITZEL & SHOULDERS (AV)

(Formerly Early, Arnold & Ziemer)
One Riverfront Place, 20 N.W. First Street 9th Floor, P.O. Box 916, 47706-0916
Telephone: 812-424-7575
Telecopier: 812-421-5089

MEMBERS OF FIRM

Ted C. Ziemer, Jr.	Gregory G. Meyer
Patrick A. Shoulders	Rebecca T. Kasha

ASSOCIATES

Gary K. Price	Robert L. Burkart

Reference: Old National Bank in Evansville.

For full biographical listings, see the Martindale-Hubbell Law Directory

HAMMOND, Lake Co.

GALVIN, GALVIN & LEENEY (AV)

5231 Hohman Avenue, 46320
Telephone: 219-933-0380
Fax: 219-933-0471

MEMBERS OF FIRM

Edmond J. Leeney (1897-1978)	Carl N. Carpenter
Timothy P. Galvin, Sr. (1894-1993)	John E. Chevigny
	Timothy P. Galvin, Jr.
Francis J. Galvin, Sr. (1902-1995)	Patrick J. Galvin
	W. Patrick Downes

William G. Crabtree II	Julie A. Rosenwinkel
John H. Lloyd, IV	Amy Galvin Grogan

Attorneys for: CIGNA; St. Margaret Mercy Healthcare Centers, Inc.; St. Anthony Hospital and Health Centers (Michigan City); St. Elizabeth Hospital (LaFayette, IN).

For full biographical listings, see the Martindale-Hubbell Law Directory

INDIANAPOLIS,* Marion Co.

HALL, RENDER, KILLIAN, HEATH & LYMAN, PROFESSIONAL CORPORATION (AV)

Suite 2000, One American Square Box 82064, 46282
Telephone: 317-633-4884
Fax: 317-633-4878
Email: hrkhl@hrkhl.com
Indianapolis North Office: Suite 820, 8402 Harcourt Road, 46260.
Telephone: 317-871-6222.
Fax: 317-338-3946.
Louisville, Kentucky Office: Providian Center, Suite 1530, 400 West Market Street, 40202.
Telephone: 502-568-1890.
Fax: 502-568-4878.

(See Next Column)

HALL, RENDER, KILLIAN, HEATH & LYMAN PROFESSIONAL CORPORATION, *Indianapolis—Continued*

William S. Hall	R. Thomas Carter (Not
John C. Render	admitted in IN; Resident,
Rex P. Killian	Louisville, Kentucky Office)
R. Terry Heath	Maureen O'Brien Griffin
Stephen W. Lyman	Robert A. Hicks
L. Richard Gohman	Kevin P. Speer
Jeffrey Peek	Jeffrey W. Short
Clifford A. Beyler	Gregory W. Moore
Joseph R. Impicciche	John C. Meade
Timothy C. Lawson	Clifton E. Johnson
Douglas P. Long	Martha B. Wentworth
William H. Thompson	Richard W. McMinn
Timothy W. Kennedy	Todd J. Selby
Steven H. Pratt	Gregg M. Wallander
N. Kent Smith	James B. Hogan
Mary C. Gaughan	Donald R. Russell
Fred J. Bachmann	D. David Freeman

David M. Leonard

Gregory P. Kult	William D. Roberts (Not
René Remek Savarise (Resident,	admitted in IN; Resident,
Louisville, Kentucky Office)	Louisville, Kentucky Office)
Michael Keith Pruitt	Keith D. Barber
John J. Andris, Jr. (Not	A. Courtney Guild, Jr. (Not
admitted in IN; Resident,	admitted in IN; Resident,
Louisville, Kentucky Office)	Louisville, Kentucky Office)
Pamela J. Jones	Samuel H. DeShazer (Not
Brantley H. Wright	admitted in IN; Resident,
James R. Willey	Louisville, Kentucky Office)
Christopher L. Riegler	Gerald L. Stovall (Not admitted
Jon F. Spadorcia	in IN; Resident, Louisville,
	Kentucky Office)

Representative Clients: St. Vincent Hospital and Health Care Center, Inc.; Indiana Hospital & Healthcare Association; Indiana University Medical Center; St. Joseph Medical Center of Fort Wayne; Methodist Hospitals-Gary, Indiana; Memorial Hospital of South Bend; Good Samaritan Hospital.

For full biographical listings, see the Martindale-Hubbell Law Directory

ICE MILLER DONADIO & RYAN (AV)

One American Square Box 82001, 46282-0002
Telephone: 317-236-2100
Fax: 317-236-2219
Email: leel@imdr.com *URL:* http://www.imdr.com
South Bend, Indiana Office: 211 West Washington Street, Suite 2420.
Telephone: 219-234-7933.
Fax: 219-234-7965. Internet E-mail: leel@imdr.com. Web Site Address: http://www.imdr.com.

MEMBERS OF FIRM

Leland B. Cross, Jr.	Michael A. Blickman
Leonard J. Betley	Mary Nold Larimore
Ralph A. Cohen	Brenda S. Horn
James D. Kemper	Gregory L. Pemberton
Harry L. Gonso	L. Alan Whaley
David J. Mallon, Jr.	Bonnie L. Gallivan

Sherry A. Fabina-Abney

OF COUNSEL

Nancy Menard Riddle	Susan B. Rivas
Karen Ann P. Lloyd	Kelly Bauman Pitcher

STAFF ATTORNEY

Michele Johnson Calderon

RETIRED PARTNER

Geoffrey Segar

ASSOCIATES

Kevin C. Woodhouse	Paul H. Sinclair
Laure V. Flaniken	Ann L. Theobald
Kevin R. Knight	Anita M. Hodgson
Michael J. Melliere	Christopher S. Sears

Ponce D. Tidwell, Jr.

For Complete List of Firm Personnel, See General Section

For full biographical listings, see the Martindale-Hubbell Law Directory

JOHNSON, SMITH, PENCE, DENSBORN, WRIGHT & HEATH (AV)

One Indiana Square Suite 1800, 46204
Telephone: 317-634-9777
Telecopier: 317-636-9061

MEMBERS OF FIRM

Thomas A. Barnard	Andrew W. Hull
David G. Blachly	John R. Kirkwood
David J. Carr	Padric K. J. O'Brien
Sean Michael Clapp	Mark A. Palmer
Donald K. Densborn	Linda L. Pence
David J. Hensel	David E. Wright
John David Hoover	Sally Franklin Zweig

(See Next Column)

ASSOCIATES

Maureen F. Barnard	Patricia L. Marshall
Jane Ann Himsel	Steven J. Moss

OF COUNSEL

Lawrence W. Schmits

For Complete List of Firm Personnel, See General Section

For full biographical listings, see the Martindale-Hubbell Law Directory

LOCKE REYNOLDS BOYD & WEISELL (AV)

1000 Capital Center South, 201 North Illinois Street, 46204
Telephone: 317-237-3800
Telecopier: 317-237-3900

Glenn T. Troyer	David Elliott Jose
Michael T. Bindner	Thomas W. Farlow

Peter H. Pogue

Representative Clients: Carmel Health Care Management, Inc.; Caylor-Nickel, P.C.; Evergreen Healthcare, Ltd.; G.U. Surgeons of Indiana, Inc.; Madison County Imaging, P.C.; Memorial Hospital of Michigan City; St. Francis Hospital Center; Tri-County Community Mental Health Center; Columbia/HCA (The Women's Hospital-Indianapolis).

For Complete List of Firm Personnel, See General Section

For full biographical listings, see the Martindale-Hubbell Law Directory

McNAMAR, FEARNOW & McSHARAR, P.C. (AV)

Bank One Center Tower, 111 Monument Circle, Suite 4500, 46204-5145
Telephone: 317-630-4500
Fax: 317-630-4501
Email: dmcnamara40@aol.com

David F. McNamar	Alastair J. Warr
Randall R. Fearnow	John H. Sharpe
Janet A. McSharar	Paul (Rick) Rauch, III

For full biographical listings, see the Martindale-Hubbell Law Directory

LAFAYETTE,* Tippecanoe Co.

STUART & BRANIGIN (AV)

The Life Building, 300 Main Street, Suite 800, 47902
Telephone: 317-423-1561
Telecopier: 317-742-8175

MEMBERS OF FIRM

Thomas R. McCully	Larry R. Fisher

Nina B. Kirkpatrick

Representative Client: Wabash Valley Hospital, Inc.

For Complete List of Firm Personnel, See General Section

For full biographical listings, see the Martindale-Hubbell Law Directory

MERRILLVILLE, Lake Co.

HODGES & DAVIS, P.C. (AV)

8700 Broadway, 46410
Telephone: 219-641-8700
Fax: 219-641-8710
Portage, Indiana Office: 6082 Lute Road. P.O. Box 1037.
Telephone: 219-762-9129.
Fax: 219-762-2826.

Clyde D. Compton	Bonnie C. Coleman
William B. Davis	Jill M. Madajczyk
Earle F. Hites	Laura B. Frost
R. Lawrence Steele	David H. Kreider
Gregory A. Sobkowski	Robert G. Vann

OF COUNSEL

Edward J. Hussey

Representative Clients: The Methodist Hospitals, Inc.; Lincolnshire Health Center; The Lutheran Retirement Home of Northwest Indiana; Geminus Corp.; Visiting Nurse Association of Northwest Indiana, Inc.; Visiting Nurse Association of Porter County, Indiana, Inc.

For Complete List of Firm Personnel, See General Section

For full biographical listings, see the Martindale-Hubbell Law Directory

PORTAGE, Porter Co.

HODGES & DAVIS, P.C. (AV)

6082 Lute Road, P.O. Box 1037, 46368
Telephone: 219-762-9129
Fax: 219-762-2826
Merrillville, Indiana Office: 8700 Broadway.
Telephone: 219-641-8700.
Fax: 219-641-8710.

(See Next Column)

HODGES & DAVIS P.C.—*Continued*

Clyde D. Compton	R. Lawrence Steele
Earle F. Hites	Gregory A. Sobkowski
Bonnie C. Coleman	

Representative Clients: The Methodist Hospitals, Inc.; Lincolnshire Health Center; The Lutheran Retirement Home of Northwest, Indiana; Geminus Corp.; Visiting Nurse Association of Northwest Indiana, Inc.; Visiting Nurse Association of Porter County, Indiana, Inc.

For full biographical listings, see the Martindale-Hubbell Law Directory

SOUTH BEND, * St. Joseph Co.

JONES, OBENCHAIN, FORD, PANKOW, LEWIS & WOODS (AV)

1800 Valley American Bank Building, P.O. Box 4577, 46634
Telephone: 219-233-1194
Fax: 233-8957; 233-9675

Vitus G. Jones (1879-1951)	Roland Obenchain (Retired)
Roland Obenchain (1890-1961)	Milton A. Johnson (Retired)
Francis Jones (1907-1988)	James H. Pankow (Retired)

MEMBERS OF FIRM

Thomas F. Lewis, Jr.	Robert M. Edwards, Jr.
Timothy W. Woods	John B. Ford
John R. Obenchain	Mark J. Phillipoff
Robert W. Mysliwiec	John W. Van Laere

ASSOCIATES

Edward P. Benchik	Robert S. Sanderson
Thomas F. Lewis, III	

OF COUNSEL

G. Burt Ford

Representative Clients: Saint Joseph's Medical Center; Holy Cross Health Systems; Healthwin Hospital; St. Joseph's Care Group.

For full biographical listings, see the Martindale-Hubbell Law Directory

TERRE HAUTE, * Vigo Co.

WILKINSON, GOELLER, MODESITT, WILKINSON & DRUMMY (AV)

333 Ohio Street, P.O. Box 800, 47808-0800
Telephone: 812-232-4311
Fax: 812-235-5107

MEMBERS OF FIRM

Myrl O. Wilkinson	John C. Wall
B. Curtis Wilkinson	Craig M. McKee

Representative Corporate Clients: Union Hospital; Associated Physicians and Surgeons Clinic, LCC;

For Complete List of Firm Personnel, See General Section

For full biographical listings, see the Martindale-Hubbell Law Directory

IOWA

DES MOINES, * Polk Co.

FINLEY, ALT, SMITH, SCHARNBERG, MAY & CRAIG, P.C. (AV)

604 Locust Street, Fourth Floor Equitable Building, 50309
Telephone: 515-288-0145
Telecopier: 515-288-2724

Thomas A. Finley	Lorraine J. May
David C. Craig	

Representative Clients: Aetna Casualty & Surety Co.; Aetna Life Insurance Co.; ALAS; American Society of Composers, Authors and Publishers; Equitable Life Assurance Society of the U.S.; Federated Insurance Co.; Meredith Corp.; Catholic Health Corp.
Iowa Attorneys for: Midwest Medical Insurance Co.

For Complete List of Firm Personnel, See General Section

For full biographical listings, see the Martindale-Hubbell Law Directory

KANSAS

OLATHE, * Johnson Co.

HACKLER, HINKLE & HACKLER, CHARTERED (AV)

201 North Cherry, P.O. Box 1, 66051-0001
Telephone: 913-764-8000
Fax: 913-764-3609

(See Next Column)

Eugene T. Hackler	Amy E. Hackler
Ronald G. Hinkle	
Mark J. Eichholz	Edwin D. Smith, V

For full biographical listings, see the Martindale-Hubbell Law Directory

TOPEKA, * Shawnee Co.

GOODELL, STRATTON, EDMONDS & PALMER, L.L.P. (AV)

515 South Kansas Avenue, 66603-3999
Telephone: 913-233-0593
Telecopier: 913-233-8870
Email: GSEP@CJNETWORKS.COM

MEMBERS OF FIRM

Gerald L. Goodell	Harold S. Youngentob
Wayne T. Stratton	Charles R. Hay
Arthur E. Palmer	Les E. Diehl
H. Philip Elwood	David E. Bruns
Catherine M. Walberg	

ASSOCIATE

Steve A Schwarm

SPECIAL COUNSEL

Marta Fisher Linenberger	Curtis J. Waugh

Counsel for: The Menninger Foundation; Stormont-Vail Regional Health Center; St. Paul Fire & Marine Insurance Co.; Kansas Hospital Association; Heartland Health; Kansas Medical Society; Columbia HCA, Overland Park, Kansas; Pratt Regional Medical Center; Great Plains Health Alliance; Shawnee County Mental Health Center.

For Complete List of Firm Personnel, See General Section

For full biographical listings, see the Martindale-Hubbell Law Directory

WICHITA, * Sedgwick Co.

FOULSTON & SIEFKIN L.L.P. (AV)

700 Fourth Financial Center, 67202
Telephone: 316-267-6371
Facsimile: 316-267-6345
Topeka, Kansas Office: 1515 Bank IV Tower, 534 Kansas Avenue, 66603.
Telephone: 913-233-3600.
Fax: 913-233-1610.
Dodge City, Kansas Office: 810 Frontview, P.O. Box 1147, 67801.
Telephone: 316-227-8126.
Fax: 316-227-8451.
Member: Lex Mundi, A Global Association of 126 Independent Firms.

MEMBERS OF FIRM

Stanley G. Andeel	Gary E. Knight

For Complete List of Firm Personnel, See General Section

For full biographical listings, see the Martindale-Hubbell Law Directory

KENTUCKY

BOWLING GREEN, * Warren Co.

KERRICK, GRISE & STIVERS (AV)

1025 State Street, P.O. Box 9547, 42102-9547
Telephone: 502-782-8160
Fax: 502-782-5856
Elizabethtown, Kentucky Office: 2935 Dolphin Drive, Suite 102.
Telephone: 502-769-5788.
Fax: 502-737-9285.

MEMBERS OF FIRM

Thomas N. Kerrick	Gregory N. Stivers
John R. Grise	H. Brent Brennenstuhl

ASSOCIATES

Lanna Martin Kilgore	Shawn Rosso Alcott
Laura M. Hagan (Resident, Elizabethtown Office)	Jason B. Bell

Representative Clients: Columbia Greenview Regional Hospital; Riverdell Hospital; Hospital Corporation of America; Russell County Hospital; Wayne County Hospital; Hardin Memorial Hospital; Kentucky Hospital Association Trust.

For full biographical listings, see the Martindale-Hubbell Law Directory

CRESTVIEW HILLS, Kenton Co.

THE LAW OFFICE OF JOHN C. GILLILAND, II (AV)

Chancellor Commons/Thomas More Centre, 2670 Chancellor Drive, Suite 290, 41017
Telephone: 606-344-8515
Fax: 606-344-8516

(See Next Column)

THE LAW OFFICE OF JOHN C. GILLILAND, II, *Crestview Hills—Continued*

Elizabeth A. Zink-Pearson   Sarah Mortensen Patton

For full biographical listings, see the Martindale-Hubbell Law Directory

LEXINGTON,* Fayette Co.

PIPER, WELLMAN & BOWERS (AV)

200 North Upper Street, 40507
Telephone: 606-231-1012
Fax: 606-231-7367
Email: pwb200@uky.campus.mci.net

MEMBERS OF FIRM

George C. Piper   Dean T. Wellman
Barbara J. Bowers

ASSOCIATE

Johann F. Herklotz

Representative Clients: Kentucky Hospital Association Trust; Woodford Hospital; Garrard Memorial Hospital; Century American Insurance Co.; Guaranty National Insurance Co.; Hillhaven Corp.; Sisters of Charity of Nazareth Health System, Inc. d/b/a/ St. Josephs Hospital; Kentucky River Medical Center; The Reciprocal Alliance.

For full biographical listings, see the Martindale-Hubbell Law Directory

STOLL, KEENON & PARK, LLP (AV)

201 E. Main Street, Suite 1000, 40507-1380
Telephone: 606-231-3000
Telecopier: 606-253-1093; 606-253-1027
Frankfort, Kentucky Office: 307 Washington Street, 40601.
Telephone: 502-875-6220.
Telecopier: 502-875-6235.
Louisville, Kentucky Office: 400 West Market Street, Suite 2650, 40202-3377.
Telephone: 502-568-9100.
Telecopier: 502-568-5700.

MEMBERS OF FIRM

J. Peter Cassidy, Jr.   William M. Lear, Jr.
Samuel D. Hinkle IV   Gary L. Stage
R. David Lester   J. David Smith, Jr.
Dan M. Rose

Representative Clients: Kentucky Medical Services Foundation, Inc.; Louden & Co., Inc.; Louisville Pathology Foundation, Inc.; Medical Rehabilitation Centers, Inc.; Pathology & Cytology Laboratories, Inc.; Sisters of Charity of Nazareth Health Corp.; University Pathologists, P.S.C.; Women's Care Center, PLLC.

For Complete List of Firm Personnel, See General Section

For full biographical listings, see the Martindale-Hubbell Law Directory

LOUISVILLE,* Jefferson Co.

WOODWARD, HOBSON & FULTON (AV)

2500 National City Tower, 101 South Fifth Street, 40202
Telephone: 502-581-8000
Fax: 502-581-8111
Lexington, Kentucky Office: PNC Bank Plaza, 200 West Vine Street, Suite 500.
Telephone: 606-244-7100.
Telecopier: 606-244-7111.
New Albany, Indiana Office: 611 East Spring Street, P.O. Box 288.
Telephone: 812-941-1800.
Telecopier: 812-941-1855.

MEMBERS OF FIRM

David R. Monohan   Mary Jo Wetzel (Resident, New
Thomas A. Hoy   Albany, Indiana Office)
Jann B. Logsdon

ASSOCIATE

Rebecca L. Didat

Representative Clients: Sisters of Charity of Nazareth Health System, Inc.; CARITAS Health Services, Inc.; Marymount Medical Center, Inc.

For Complete List of Firm Personnel, See General Section

For full biographical listings, see the Martindale-Hubbell Law Directory

LOUISIANA

BATON ROUGE,* East Baton Rouge Parish

WATSON, BLANCHE, WILSON & POSNER (AV)

505 North Boulevard, P.O. Drawer 2995, 70821-2995
Telephone: 504-387-5511
Fax: 504-387-5972

(See Next Column)

Robert L. Roland   Michael M. Remson
Peter T. Dazzio   P. Chauvin Wilkinson, Jr.
Felix R. Weill   Randall L. Champagne
William E. Scott, III   René J. Pfefferle

ASSOCIATE

P. Scott Jolly

Representative Clients: Baton Rouge General Medical Center; General Health System, Inc.; Louisiana Hospital Association Trust Fund; Woman's Hospital Foundation.

For full biographical listings, see the Martindale-Hubbell Law Directory

MONROE,* Ouachita Parish

McLEOD VERLANDER (AV)

A Partnership including Professional Law Corporations
1900 North 18th Street, Suite 610, P.O. Box 2270, 71207-2270
Telephone: 318-325-7000
Telecopier: 318-324-0580
Email: mvlaw@iamerica.net

MEMBERS OF FIRM

Robert P. McLeod (P.L.C.)   Rick W. Duplissey
David E. Verlander, III (P.L.C.)   Pamela G. Nathan
Laurie J. Burkett

Representative Clients: Columbia North Monroe Hospital; Columbia Health Systems; The Orthopaedic Clinic of Monroe, Inc.; Louisiana Medical Mutual Insurance Co.; Extracorporeal Technologies, Inc.; Daig Corporation.

For full biographical listings, see the Martindale-Hubbell Law Directory

NEW ORLEANS,* Orleans Parish

BOGGS, LOEHN & RODRIGUE (AV)

A Partnership including Law Corporations
Suite 1800 Lykes Center, 300 Poydras Street, 70130-3597
Telephone: 504-523-7090
Fax: 504-581-6822

Charles A. Boggs (A Law   Edward A. Rodrigue, Jr., (A
     Corporation)   Law Corporation)
Thomas E. Loehn (A Law   Robert I. Baudouin
     Corporation)   Jedd S. Malish

Reference: First National Bank of Commerce, New Orleans, La.

For full biographical listings, see the Martindale-Hubbell Law Directory

BROOK, PIZZA & VAN LOON, L.L.P. (AV)

400 Poydras Street, Suite 2500, 70130
Telephone: 504-566-0600
Telecopier: 504-595-8715
Email: lawfirm@bpvl.com
Slidell, Louisiana Office: 1400 A Gause Boulevard.
Telephone: 504-641-9468.
Telecopier: 504-643-7631.
Baton Rouge, Louisiana Office: 9100 Bluebonnet Centre Boulevard, Suite 402.
Telephone: 504-291-7300.
Telecopier: 504-291-4524.

Jack Pierce Brook   Normand F. Pizza
Ernest N. Morial (1929-1989)   Jan T. Van Loon
Richard Ernest Santora

David M. Latham   Christopher J. Shenfield
David Shaw   Douglas R. Kinler
Stephanie B. LaBorde (Resident, Baton Rouge Office)

SPECIAL COUNSEL

Betty Jean George Ray   Mark D. Hudak
(Resident, Baton Rouge Office)

OF COUNSEL

Nyda Brook Zelenka   Carlina Davila L. Shenfield (not
Herschel C. Adcock   admitted in the United States)

For full biographical listings, see the Martindale-Hubbell Law Directory

MAINE

BANGOR,* Penobscot Co.

Eaton, Peabody, Bradford & Veague, P.A. (AV)

Fleet Center-Exchange Street, P.O. Box 1210, 04402-1210
Telephone: 207-947-0111
Telecopier: 207-942-3040
Email: epbv@aol.com
Augusta, Maine Office: 2 Central Plaza.
Telephone: 207-622-3747.
Telecopier: 207-622-9732.
Blue Hill, Maine Office: One East Blue Hill Road.
Telephone: 207-374-2812.
Telecopier: 207-374-2548.
Brunswick, Maine Office: 167 Park Row.
Telephone: 207-729-1144.
Telecopier: 207-729-1140.
Camden, Maine Office: 7-9 Washington Street.
Telephone: 207-236-3325.
Telecopier: 207-236-8611.
Dover-Foxcroft, Maine Office: 30 East Main Street.
Telephone: 207-564-8378.
Telecopier: 207-564-7059.

Malcolm E. Morrell, Jr.   Daniel G. McKay

A List of Representative Clients available upon request.

For Complete List of Firm Personnel, See General Section

For full biographical listings, see the Martindale-Hubbell Law Directory

PORTLAND,* Cumberland Co.

Friedman & Babcock (AV)

Suite 400, Six City Center, P.O. Box 4726, 04112-4726
Telephone: 207-761-0900
Telecopier: 207-761-0186

MEMBERS OF FIRM

Harold J. Friedman   Thomas A. Cox
Ernest J. Babcock   Karen Frink Wolf
Martha C. Gaythwaite   Jennifer S. Begel
Laurence H. Leavitt

ASSOCIATES

Theodore H. Irwin, Jr.   Elizabeth A. Germani
Lee H. Bals   Jonathan Marc Dunitz
Michelle Allott   Darren Blaine Riggle
Arthur J. Lamothe   Tracy D. Hill
Bruce W. Hepler

For full biographical listings, see the Martindale-Hubbell Law Directory

Kozak, Gayer & Brodek, P.A. (AV)

75 Market Street, 04101
Telephone: 207-756-7750
Fax: 207-756-7754
Augusta, Maine, Office: 168 Capitol Street.
Telephone: 207-621-4390.
Fax: 207-621-4394.
Bangor, Maine Office: 15 Columbia Street.
Telephone: 207-990-4800.
Fax: 207-990-4804.

Joseph M. Kozak   Benjamin P. Townsend
Gordon K. Gayer   Michael A. Duddy
Gregory A. Brodek   Barbara G. Shaw

For full biographical listings, see the Martindale-Hubbell Law Directory

Preti, Flaherty, Beliveau & Pachios (AV)

A Limited Liability Company
443 Congress Street, P.O. Box 11410, 04104-7410
Telephone: 207-791-3000
Telecopier: 207-791-3111
Email: admin@pfbpnet.com
Augusta, Maine Office: 45 Memorial Circle, P.O. Box 1058, 04332-1058.
Telephone: 207-623-5300.
Telecopier: 207-623-2914.

MEMBERS OF FIRM

Christopher D. Nyhan   John P. Doyle, Jr.
Eric P. Stauffer   Michael G. Messerschmidt
Susan E. LoGiudice

OF COUNSEL

Charles F. Dingman (Augusta Office)

ASSOCIATE

James E. Phipps

Representative Clients: Jackson Brook Institute; Mid-Maine Medical Center; Eastern Maine Medical Center; Southern Maine Medical Center; Franklin Memorial Hospital; Maine Hospital Assn.; Stephens Memorial Hospital;

(See Next Column)

Rumford Community Hospital; Mt. Desert Island Hospital; Maine Health Care Assn.

For Complete List of Firm Personnel, See General Section

For full biographical listings, see the Martindale-Hubbell Law Directory

Verrill & Dana (AV)

One Portland Square, P.O. Box 586, 04112-0586
Telephone: 207-774-4000
Fax: 207-774-7499
Email: advice@verdan.com *URL:* http://www.verdan.com
Augusta, Maine Office: 45 Memorial Circle, P.O. Box 957.
Telephone: 207-623-3889.
Fax: 207-622-3117.
Kennebunk, Maine Office: Lafayette Center, P.O. Box 266.
Telephone: 207-985-7193.
Fax: 207-985-3957.
Washington, D.C. Office: 400 North Capitol Street, Suite 585.
Telephone: 202-624-9733.
Fax: 202-393-5218.

MEMBERS OF FIRM

David C. Hillman   Beth Dobson
Claudia D. Raessler

For Complete List of Firm Personnel, See General Section

For full biographical listings, see the Martindale-Hubbell Law Directory

SOUTH PORTLAND, Cumberland Co.

Van Meer & Belanger, P.A. (AV)

25 Long Creek Drive, 04106
Telephone: 207-871-7500
Fax: 207-871-7505

Thomas J. Van Meer   D. Kelley Young
Norman R. Belanger   Richard N. Bryant

Betts J. Gorsky

For full biographical listings, see the Martindale-Hubbell Law Directory

MARYLAND

BALTIMORE,* (Independent City)

Gallagher, Evelius & Jones (AV)

Park Charles Suite 400, 218 North Charles Street, 21201
Telephone: 410-727-7702
Telecopier: 410-837-3079

MEMBERS OF FIRM

Francis X. Gallagher   Linda H. Jones
  (1928-1972)   Jack C. Tranter
C. Edward Jones (Retired)   Christopher J. Fritz
John C. Evelius   David E. Raderman
Richard O. Berndt   Peter E. Keith
Thomas N. Biddison, Jr.   Nita L. Schultz
Robert R. Kern, Jr.   Michael W. Skojec
Saul E. Gilstein   Kathryn Kelley Hoskins
Thomas B. Lewis   Mark P. Keener
Bonnie Abrams Travieso   Kevin J. Davidson
Stephen A. Goldberg   Eileen M. Lunga
Lori A. Nicolle

ASSOCIATES

Kenneth S. Gross   Matthew W. Oakey
Thomas C. Dame   Paula B. Grant
Mary Catherine Collins Gaver   Rebecca A. Weaver
Julie Ellen Squire   Michael J. Henigan
David W. Kinkopf

LEGAL ASSISTANTS

Patricia C. Quayle   Iris T. H. Heath
Jeanmarie McGlynn   Cheryl J. Reinke

Representative Clients: Roman Catholic Archdiocese of Baltimore; Bozzuto & Associates, Inc.; The Enterprise Foundation; Mercy Medical Center, Inc.; First National Bank of Maryland.

For full biographical listings, see the Martindale-Hubbell Law Directory

Venable Attorneys at Law Venable, Baetjer and Howard, LLP (AV)

A Partnership including Professional Corporations
1800 Mercantile Bank & Trust Building, 2 Hopkins Plaza, 21201
Telephone: 410-244-7400
Email: INFO@Venable.win.net
Washington, D.C. Office: Venable, Baetjer, Howard & Civiletti LLP. Suite 1000, 1201 New York Avenue, N.W.
Telephone: 202-962-4800.

(See Next Column)

VENABLE ATTORNEYS AT LAW VENABLE, BAETJER AND HOWARD, LLP, Baltimore—Continued

McLean, Virginia Office: Suite 400, 2010 Corporate Ridge.
Telephone: 703-760-1600.
Rockville, Maryland Office: Suite 500, One Church Street, P. O. Box 1906.
Telephone: 301-217-5600.
Towson, Maryland Office: 210 Allegheny Avenue, P. O. Box 5517.
Telephone: 410-494-6200.

MEMBERS OF FIRM

Benjamin R. Civiletti (P.C.) (Also at Washington, D.C. and Towson, Maryland Offices)
Robert A. Shelton
Thomas J. Kenney, Jr. (P.C.) (Also at Washington, D.C. Office)
Kenneth C. Bass, III (Not admitted in MD; Washington, D.C. and McLean, Virginia Offices)
Paul F. Strain (P.C.)
William D. Dolan, III (P.C.) (Not admitted in MD; Resident, McLean, Virginia Office)
Joseph C. Wich, Jr. (Resident, Towson, Maryland Office)
Robert G. Ames (Also at Washington, D.C. Office)
Nell B. Strachan
Barbara E. Schlaff
L. Paige Marvel
G. Stewart Webb, Jr.
James K. Archibald (Also at Washington, D.C. Office)
George W. Johnston (P.C.)
Constance H. Baker
Edward L. Wender (P.C.)
David M. Fleishman
Jana Howard Carey (P.C.)

Jeffrey A. Dunn (also at Washington, D.C. Office)
George F. Pappas (Also at Washington, D.C. Office)
Kenneth S. Slaughter (Not admitted in MD; Resident, Washington, D.C. Office)
Peter P. Parvis
James L. Shea (Also at Washington, D.C. Office)
Amy Berman Jackson (Not admitted in MD; Resident, Washington, D.C. Office)
William D. Quarles (Also at Washington, D.C. and Towson, Maryland Offices)
Kathleen Gallogly Cox (Resident, Towson, Maryland Office)
W. Robert Zinkham
M. King Hill, III (Resident, Towson, Maryland Office)
James A. Dunbar (Also at Washington, D.C. Office)
Robert L. Waldman
David J. Heubeck
Davis V. R. Sherman
Geoffrey R. Garinther (Also at Washington, D.C. Office)
Terri L. Turner
Michael W. Robinson (Resident, McLean, Virginia Office)

OF COUNSEL

A. Samuel Cook (P.C.) (Resident, Towson, Maryland Office)

Herbert R. O'Conor, Jr. (Resident, Towson, Maryland Office)

ASSOCIATES

David W. Goewey (Not admitted in MD; Resident, Washington, D.C. Office)
Todd J. Horn

Vicki Margolis (Also at Washington, D.C. Office)
John T. Prisbe
John Peter Sarbanes

For Complete List of Firm Personnel, See General Section

For full biographical listings, see the Martindale-Hubbell Law Directory

---

EASTON, * Talbot Co.

THOMAS T. ALSPACH (AV)

295 Bay Street, Suite One, P.O. Box 1358, 21601
Telephone: 410-822-9100
Fax: 410-822-2550

For full biographical listings, see the Martindale-Hubbell Law Directory

---

MASSACHUSETTS

BOSTON, * Suffolk Co.

BLOOM & BUELL (AV)

1340 Soldiers Field Road, 02135-1020
Telephone: 617-254-4400
Telecopier: 617-254-7610
Email: bloombue@ix.netcom.com

MEMBERS OF FIRM

Laurence J. Bloom
Barbara Hayes Buell
William J. Davenport

ASSOCIATES

Marc J. Gervais
Richard M. Haley
Barry T. Putterman

OF COUNSEL

Victoria L. Polito

LEGAL SUPPORT PERSONNEL

Lisa F. Tuccinardi

For full biographical listings, see the Martindale-Hubbell Law Directory

PEABODY & ARNOLD (AV)

A Partnership including Professional Corporations
50 Rowes Wharf, 02110-3342
Telephone: 617-951-2100
Telecopier: 617-951-2125
Providence, Rhode Island Office: One Citizens Plaza, Suite 840.
Telephone: 401-831-8330.
Fax: 401-831-8359.

MEMBERS OF FIRM

James H. Belanger
Donald S. Burnham

David F. Hendren
Andrew R. Menard

For Complete List of Firm Personnel, See General Section

For full biographical listings, see the Martindale-Hubbell Law Directory

---

PITTSFIELD, * Berkshire Co.

CAIN, HIBBARD, MYERS & COOK, A PROFESSIONAL CORPORATION (AV)

66 West Street, 01201
Telephone: 413-443-4771
Telecopier: 413-443-7694
Great Barrington, Massachusetts Office: 309 Main Street, 01230.
Telephone: 413-528-4771.
Fax: 413-528-5553.

C. Jeffrey Cook
John F. Rogers

William B. Roberts
Steven Taylor Smith

Nancy A. Lyon

Representative Clients: Fairview Extended Care Services, Inc.; Williamstown Medical Associates, P.C.; Berkshire Health Systems, Inc.; Berkshire Medical Center, Inc.; Berkshire Physicians & Surgeons, P.C.
Local Counsel for: General Electric Co.; Boston Symphony Orchestra; State-wide Funding Corporation.

For full biographical listings, see the Martindale-Hubbell Law Directory

---

SPRINGFIELD, * Hampden Co.

ANNINO, DRAPER & MOORE, P.C. (AV)

Suite 1818 BayBank Tower, 1500 Main Street, P.O. Box 15428, 01115
Telephone: 413-732-6400
Fax: 413-732-3339
Westfield, Massachusetts Office: 52 Court Street.
Telephone: 413-562-9829.

Calvin W. Annino, Jr.
Mark E. Draper

Louis S. Moore
Michael R. Siddall

For full biographical listings, see the Martindale-Hubbell Law Directory

---

MICHIGAN

BINGHAM FARMS, Oakland Co.

SMALL, TOTH, BALDRIDGE & VAN BELKUM, P.C. (AV)

30100 Telegraph Road Suite 250, 48025-4516
Telephone: 810-647-9595
Facsimile: 810-647-9599

Richard L. Small
John M. Toth

David M. Baldridge
Thomas G. Van Belkum

Keith P. Felty

Representative Clients: The Medical Protective Co.; Michigan Physicians Mutual Liability Insurance Co.; Physicians Insurance Company of Michigan; Michigan Society of Oral and Maxillofacial Surgeons; Michigan Association of Orthodontists; Michigan Association of Endodontists; AAMOS National; California Association of Oral and Maxillofacial Surgeons; Oakwood United Hospitals; The Detroit Medical Center Affiliated Hospitals.

For full biographical listings, see the Martindale-Hubbell Law Directory

---

BIRMINGHAM, Oakland Co.

GOREN & GOREN, P.C. (AV)

Suite 470, 30400 Telegraph Road, 48025
Telephone: 810-540-3100

(See Next Column)

GOREN & GOREN P.C.—Continued

Robert Goren   Steven E. Goren

Reference: Michigan National Bank-Oakland.

BLOOMFIELD HILLS, Oakland Co.

DAVID D. PATTON & ASSOCIATES, P.C. (AV)

100 Bloomfield Hills Parkway, Suite 110, 48304
Telephone: 810-258-6020
Fax: 810-258-6052
Email: Litigation@Aol.Com

David D. Patton

Ellen Bartman Jannette   Patricia C. White
David H. Patton (1912-1993)

For full biographical listings, see the Martindale-Hubbell Law Directory

PORTNOY, PIDGEON & ROTH, P.C. (AV)

3883 Telegraph, Suite 103, 48302
Telephone: 810-647-4242
Fax: 810-647-8251
Email: DWINNIE103@AOL.COM

Bernard N. Portnoy   Marc S. Berlin
James M. Pidgeon   Berton K. May
Robert P. Roth   Sheila Connor-Heath
            Charles A. Harrison III

Representative Clients: North Oakland Medical Center, Pontiac General Hospital Division; Hurly Medical Center, Flint, Michigan; McLaren Regional Medical Center, Flint, Michigan; William Beaumont Hospital, Royal Oak, Michigan; Detroit Osteopathic Hospital; Horizon Health Systems; Bi-County Community Hospital; Riverside Osteopathic; Lapeer Regional Hospital; OUM Group.

For full biographical listings, see the Martindale-Hubbell Law Directory

DETROIT,* Wayne Co.

BODMAN, LONGLEY & DAHLING LLP (AV)

34th Floor 100 Renaissance Center, 48243
Telephone: 313-259-7777
Fax: 313-393-7579
Email: 2080194@mcimail.com
Troy, Michigan Office: Suite 2020, 755 West Big Beaver Road.
Telephone: 810-362-2110.
Fax: 810-244-0780.
Ann Arbor, Michigan Office: 110 Miller, Suite 300.
Telephone: 313-761-3780.
Fax: 313-930-2494.
Northern Michigan Office: 229 Court Street, P.O. Box 405, Cheboygan.
Telephone: 616-627-4351.
Fax: 616-627-2802.

MEMBERS OF FIRM

Mark W. Griffin   Karen L. Piper
 (Ann Arbor Office)   Barbara Bowman Bluford
Randolph S. Perry   Lawrence P. Hanson
Charles N. Raimi   (Northern Michigan Office)
Lloyd C. Fell   Kay E. Malaney (Troy Office)
 (Northern Michigan Office)   Gail Pabarue Bennett
F. Thomas Lewand   Sandra L. Sorini
Kathleen A. Lieder   (Ann Arbor Office)
 (Northern Michigan Office)

ASSOCIATES

Jodee Fishman Raines   Deanna L. Dixon
            Laura M. Napiewocki

For Representative Client List, See General Section

For Complete List of Firm Personnel, See General Section

For full biographical listings, see the Martindale-Hubbell Law Directory

BUTZEL LONG, A PROFESSIONAL CORPORATION (AV)

Suite 900, 150 West Jefferson, 48226
Telephone: 313-225-7000
Telecopier: 313-225-7080
Email: melnick@butzel.com *URL:* http://www.butzel.com
Birmingham, Michigan Office: Suite 200, 32270 Telegraph Road.
Telephone: 810-258-1616.
Telecopier: 810-258-1439.
Lansing, Michigan Office: 118 West Ottawa Street.
Telephone: 517-372-6622.
Telecopier: 517-372-6672.
Ann Arbor, Michigan Office: Suite 300, 350 South Main Street.
Telephone: 313-995-3110.
Telecopier: 313-995-1777.
Grosse Pointe Farms, Michigan Office: Suite 260, 21 Kercheval.
Telephone: 313-886-5446.
Telecopier: 313-886-2114.

(See Next Column)

Philip J. Kessler   James L. Hughes
John P. Hancock, Jr.   E. William S. Shipman
D. Stewart Green (Birmingham)   Carey A. DeWitt
Keefe A. Brooks   Andrea Roumell Dickson
Gordon J. Walker (Birmingham)   Clara DeMatteis Mager
        Jordan S. Schreier (Ann Arbor)

Representative Clients: Blue Care Network; Blue Cross and Blue Shield of Michigan; Chelsea Community Hospital; Memorial Health Care; Mercy Health Services; Mt. Clemens General Hospital; Sinai Hospital; University of Michigan; William Beaumont Hospital.

For Complete List of Firm Personnel, See General Section

For full biographical listings, see the Martindale-Hubbell Law Directory

DYKEMA GOSSETT PLLC (AV)

400 Renaissance Center, 48243-1668
Telephone: 313-568-6800
Cable Address: "Dyke-Detroit"
Telex: 23-0121
Fax: 313-568-6594
Email: 2084153@mcimail.com
Ann Arbor, Michigan Office: 315 East Eisenhower Parkway, Suite 100, 48108-3306.
Telephone: 313-747-7660.
Fax: 313-747-7696.
Bloomfield Hills, Michigan Office: 1577 North Woodward Avenue, Suite 300, 48304-2820.
Telephone: 810-540-0700.
Fax: 810-540-0763.
Chicago, Illinois Office: 55 East Monroe Street, Suite 3250, 60603-5709.
Telephone: 312-551-4900.
Fax: 312-551-4919.
Grand Rapids, Michigan Office: 200 Oldtown Riverfront Building, 248 Louis Campau Promenade, N.W., 49503-2668.
Telephone: 616-776-7500.
Fax: 616-776-7573.
Lansing, Michigan Office: 800 Michigan National Tower, 48933-1707.
Telephone: 517-374-9100.
Fax: 517-374-9191.
Washington, D.C. Office: Franklin Square, Suite 300 West, 1300 I Street, N.W., 20005-3306.
Telephone: 202-522-8600.
Fax: 202-522-8669.

MEMBERS OF FIRM

Maria B. Abrahamsen (Resident   Jane Forbes
 at Bloomfield Hills Office)   Kathrin E. Kudner
Bettye S. Elkins (Resident at   Seth M. Lloyd
 Ann Arbor Office)   Thomas J. McGraw
J. Kay Felt   Lloyd A. Semple
                                  (Chairman of the Firm)

ASSOCIATES

Phyllis Donaldson-Adams   Kathleen A. Reed (Resident at
Joanne R. Lax   Ann Arbor Office)

For Complete List of Firm Personnel, See General Section

For full biographical listings, see the Martindale-Hubbell Law Directory

FEIKENS, VANDER MALE, STEVENS, BELLAMY & GILCHRIST, P.C. (AV)

One Detroit Center Suite 3400, 500 Woodward Avenue, 48226-3406
Telephone: 313-962-5909
Fax: 313-962-3125
Email: FEIKENS@COUNSEL.COM

Jack E. Vander Male   Frederick B. Bellamy
            L. Neal Kennedy

Richard G. Koefod   Jeffrey Feikens
Joseph E. Kozely, Jr.   Keith J. Soltis
            Michael B. Barey

For Complete List of Firm Personnel, See General Section

For full biographical listings, see the Martindale-Hubbell Law Directory

HONIGMAN MILLER SCHWARTZ AND COHN (AV)

A Partnership including Professional Corporations
2290 First National Building, 48226
Telephone: 313-256-7800
Telecopier: 313-962-0176
Telex: 235705
URL: http://law.honigman.com
Lansing, Michigan Office: Phoenix Building, 222 North Washington Square, Suite 400, 48933-1800.
Telephone: 517-484-8282.
West Palm Beach, Florida Office: Suite 800 Esperante Building, 222 Lakeview Avenue, 33401-6112.
Telephone: 561-838-4500.

(See Next Column)

HONIGMAN MILLER SCHWARTZ AND COHN, *Detroit—Continued*

Tampa, Florida Office: 2700 SunTrust Financial Centre, 401 E. Jackson Street, 33602-5226.
Telephone: 813-221-6600.

MEMBERS OF FIRM

Joseph T. Aoun	Stuart M. Lockman
William M. Cassetta	Joseph G. Nuyen, Jr.
Gerald M. Griffith	Julie E. Robertson
William O. Hochkammer	Linda S. Ross
Linn A. Hynds	Chris E. Rossman

ASSOCIATES

William S. Hammond	Dawn R. Kreysar
Carey F. Kalmowitz	Tracy E. Silverman

OF COUNSEL

Margaret Shannon

RESIDENT IN WEST PALM BEACH, FLORIDA OFFICE

MEMBER

Mark Nussbaum (P.A.)

ASSOCIATE

Jose O. Diaz

RESIDENT IN TAMPA, FLORIDA OFFICE

MEMBER

Barbara R. Pankau (P.A.)

Counsel to: CoreSource, Inc. (Northbrook, Illinois); The Detroit Medical Center (Detroit, MI); Mercy Health Services (Farmington Hills, MI); Intracoastal Health Systems (West Palm Beach, FL); Michigan Health and Hospital Association (Lansing, MI); Home Medical Equipment Association of Michigan (Lansing, MI); Florida Health Choice (Delray Beach, FL); SSM Health Care System (St. Louis, MO); Holy Cross Hospital (Ft. Lauderdale, FL); Medical Specialists of the Palm Beaches.

For Complete List of Firm Personnel, See General Section

For full biographical listings, see the Martindale-Hubbell Law Directory

---

JAFFE, RAITT, HEUER & WEISS, PROFESSIONAL CORPORATION (AV)

One Woodward Avenue, Suite 2400, 48226
Telephone: 313-961-8380
Telecopier: 313-961-8358
Cable Address: "Jafsni"
Southfield, Michigan Office: Travelers Tower, Suite 1520.
Telephone: 313-961-8380.
Monroe, Michigan Office: 214 East Elm Avenue, Suite 208,
Telephone: 313-241-6470.
Telefacsimile: 313-241-3849.

Alexander B. Bragdon	Linda C. Scheuerman
	Arthur A. Weiss

For Complete List of Firm Personnel, See General Section

For full biographical listings, see the Martindale-Hubbell Law Directory

---

LEWIS, CLAY & MUNDAY, A PROFESSIONAL CORPORATION (AV)

(Formerly Lewis, White & Clay, P.C.)
1300 First National Building, 660 Woodward Avenue, 48226-3531
Telephone: 313-961-2550
Troy, Michigan Office: Liberty Center, Suite 200. 100 West Big Beaver Road. 48084.
Telephone: 810-680-6702.
Fax: 810-680-6703.
Washington, D.C. Office: 1000 16th Street, N.W., Suite 401. 20036.
Telephone: 202-835-0616.
Fax: 202-833-3316.
Boston, Massachusetts Office: 10 Post Office Square.
Telephone: 617-422-8646.
Fax: 617-338-5693.

David Baker Lewis	Frank E. Barbee
Eric Lee Clay	Camille Stearns Miller
Reuben A. Munday	Michael T. Raymond
Ulysses Whittaker Boykin	Jacqueline H. Sellers
Carl F. Stafford	David N. Zacks
Helen Francine Strong	Thomas J. Guyer
	Blair A. Person

Karen Kendrick Brown (Resident, Washington, D.C. Office)	Hans J. Massaquoi, Jr.
	Nancy C. Borland
J. Taylor Teasdale	Tammy L. Terry
Wade Harper McCree	Lynn Westfall Gross
Tyrone A. Powell	Suzanne P. Pope
Susan D. Hoffman	Matthew R. Halpin
John J. Walsh	Donica Thomas Varner
Andrea L. Powell	Damon L. White
Althea Lynn Foster	(Not admitted in MI)
	Kathleen L. Royal

(See Next Column)

COUNSEL

Otis M. Smith (1922-1994)	G. Allen Bass (Resident, Boston, Massachusetts Office)
Herbert O. Reid, Sr. (1915-1991)	

Representative Clients: Omnicare Health Plan; Aetna Life & Casualty Co.; Chrysler Motors Corp.; Chrysler Financial Corp.; MCI Communications Corp.; City of Detroit; City of Detroit Building Authority; City of Detroit Downtown Development Authority; Consolidated Rail Corp. (Conrail); Equitable Life Assurance Society of the United States.

For full biographical listings, see the Martindale-Hubbell Law Directory

---

TIMMIS & INMAN, L.L.P. (AV)

300 Talon Centre, 48207
Telephone: 313-396-4200
Telecopier: 313-396-4228

George A. Peck	Richard L. Levin
Charles W. Royer	Richard M. Miettinen

OF COUNSEL

Wayne C. Inman	William B. Fitzgerald

Representative Client: Mt. Clemens General Hospital; Eastpointe Radiologists, P.C.

For Complete List of Firm Personnel, See General Section

For full biographical listings, see the Martindale-Hubbell Law Directory

---

EAST LANSING, Ingham Co.

FARHAT, STORY & KRAUS, P.C. (AV)

Beacon Place, 4572 South Hagadorn Road, Suite 3, 48823
Telephone: 517-351-3700
Fax: 517-332-4122
Email: rkraus@sojourn.com

Leo A. Farhat	Chris A. Bergstrom
James E. Burns (1925-1979)	Kitty L. Groh
Monte R. Story	Charles R. Toy
Richard C. Kraus	David M. Platt
Max R. Hoffman Jr.	Thomas L. Sparks

Lawrence P. Schweitzer	Daniel B. Morgan
Debra A. Geroux	Mary K. Robbins-Kralapp

Representative Clients: National Association of Rural Health Clinics; Cedar Springs Medical Clinic; Borgess Hospital; Michigan Association of Physician Assistants; Michigan Non-Profit Homes Association; Physical Therapy Associates; Pinconning Medical Care; Saginaw General Hospital; Muskegon General Hospital; Saratoga Community Hospital.

For full biographical listings, see the Martindale-Hubbell Law Directory

---

*GRAND RAPIDS,** Kent Co.

GRUEL, MILLS, NIMS AND PYLMAN (AV)

50 Monroe Place, Suite 700 West, 49503
Telephone: 616-235-5500
Fax: 616-235-5550

MEMBERS OF FIRM

Grant J. Gruel	Scott R. Melton
William F. Mills	Brion J. Brooks
J. Clarke Nims	Thomas R. Behm
Norman H. Pylman, II	J. Paul Janes

Representative Clients: Aquinas College; Bell Helmet Co.; Blodgett Memorial Medical Center; Butterworth Hospital; Chem Central, Inc.; Cook Pump Co.; Grove, Inc.; NBDC; Heim Corp.

For full biographical listings, see the Martindale-Hubbell Law Directory

---

WARNER NORCROSS & JUDD LLP (AV)

900 Old Kent Building, 111 Lyon Street, N.W., 49503-2489
Telephone: 616-752-2000
Fax: 616-752-2500
Muskegon, Michigan Office: 400 Terrace Plaza, P.O. Box 900.
Telephone: 616-727-2600.
Fax: 616-727-2699.
Holland, Michigan Office: Curtis Center, Suite 300, 170 College Avenue.
Telephone: 616-396-9800.
Fax: 616-396-3656.

MEMBERS OF FIRM

John H. Logie	Cameron S. DeLong
	Richard L. Bouma

ASSOCIATE

Susan Gell Meyers

Representative Clients: Blodgett Memorial Medical Center; Ferguson Healthcare System; Holland Communications.

For Complete List of Firm Personnel, See General Section

For full biographical listings, see the Martindale-Hubbell Law Directory

KALAMAZOO,* Kalamazoo Co.

KREIS, ENDERLE, CALLANDER & HUDGINS, A PROFESSIONAL CORPORATION (AV)

One Moorsbridge, P.O. Box 4010, 49003-4010
Telephone: 616-324-3000
Telecopier: 616-324-3010
Email: kech@sapien.net URL: http://www.kech.com

Russell A. Kreis	C. Reid Hudgins III
Alan G. Enderle	Daniel P. McGlinn

For Complete List of Firm Personnel, See General Section

For full biographical listings, see the Martindale-Hubbell Law Directory

LANSING, Ingham Co.

FOSTER, SWIFT, COLLINS & SMITH, P.C. (AV)

313 South Washington Square, 48933-2193
Telephone: 517-371-8100
Telecopier: 517-371-8200
URL: http://www.fosterswift.com
Farmington Hills, Michigan Office: 32300 Northwestern Highway, Suite 230.
Telephone: 810-539-9900.
Fax: 810-851-7504.

Gary J. McRay	Brian A. Kaser
Stephen I. Jurmu	Louis K. Nigg
James B. Jensen, Jr.	Jean G. Schtokal
	Eric E. Doster

General Counsel for: First American Bank-Central; Story, Inc.; Michigan Milk Producers Assn.; Edward W. Sparrow Hospital; St. Lawrence Hospital; Demmer Corp.; Michigan Financial Corp.
Local Counsel for: Shell Oil Co.; Michigan-Mutual Insurance Co.; Century Telephone.

For Complete List of Firm Personnel, See General Section

For full biographical listings, see the Martindale-Hubbell Law Directory

FRASER TREBILCOCK DAVIS & FOSTER, P.C. (AV)

1000 Michigan National Tower, 48933
Telephone: 517-482-5800
Fax: 517-482-0887

Peter L. Dunlap	Stephen L. Burlingame
Robert W. Stocker, II	Iris K. Socolofsky-Linder

Michael C. Levine

Counsel for: Beverly Enterprises; Health Management Services; Michigan Center Medical Center; Michigan Non-Profit Homes Association; Tendercare Corp.; The Nursing Home Group.

For Complete List of Firm Personnel, See General Section

For full biographical listings, see the Martindale-Hubbell Law Directory

MUSKEGON,* Muskegon Co.

LAGUE, NEWMAN & IRISH, A PROFESSIONAL CORPORATION (AV)

600 Terrace Plaza, P.O. Box 389, 49443
Telephone: 616-725-8148
Telecopier: 616-726-3404
Email: firm@lnilaw.com

Richard C. Lague	Chris Ann McGuigan
	Philip M. Stoffan

General Counsel: Hackley Hospital & Medical Center; Zeeland Community Hospital; Mecosta County General Hospital; Lakeland Regional Health Systems; Physician's Organization of West Michigan; Mid South Physicians Alliance; Mid South Health Plan; Kankakee Integrated Care Network.

For Complete List of Firm Personnel, See General Section

For full biographical listings, see the Martindale-Hubbell Law Directory

PORT HURON,* St. Clair Co.

FLETCHER DEGROW (AV)

522 Michigan Street, 48060-3893
Telephone: 810-987-8444
Facsimile: 810-987-8149

MEMBERS OF FIRM

Gary A. Fletcher	Dan L. DeGrow
	Mark G. Clark

ASSOCIATES

John D. Tomlinson	William L. Fealko, III

(See Next Column)

OF COUNSEL
Anthony M. Bonadio

Representative Clients: Port Huron Hospital; Purt Huron Eye Clinic; Fremont Mutual Insurance Co.; Westfield Insurance Co.; Michigan Municipal Risk Management Authority; City of Port Huron; City of Marysville; Port Huron Area School District; Marysville Public Schools.

For full biographical listings, see the Martindale-Hubbell Law Directory

SOUTHFIELD, Oakland Co.

FRIMET & ROGALSKI, P.C. (AV)

2000 Town Center, Suite 2700, 48075-1108
Telephone: 810-358-0080
Telecopier: 810-358-0449

Gilbert M. Frimet	Alan T. Rogalski
	John A. Michalsen (1955-1994)

OF COUNSEL

Bruce C. Blanton	Rubenstein Plotkin, Professional
Edward B. Meth	Corporation, , Southfield, Michigan

Representative Clients: Westland Convalescent Center; Northwood, Inc.; Basha Diagnostics, P.C.; Binson's Hospital Supplies, Inc.; Beaumont Physicians Group; Providence Medical Group; Macomb Anesthesia, P.C.; Family Home Care; Camelids of Delaware, Inc.; Downriver Mental Health Clinic, P.C.

For full biographical listings, see the Martindale-Hubbell Law Directory

SOMMERS, SCHWARTZ, SILVER & SCHWARTZ, P.C. (AV)

2000 Town Center, Suite 900, 48075
Telephone: 810-355-0300
Telecopier: 810-746-4001
Plymouth, Michigan Office: 747 South Main Street.
Telephone: 313-455-4250.

Steven J. Schwartz	James J. Vlasic

General Counsel for: City of Taylor; Foodland Distributors; C.A. Muer Corporation; Vlasic & Company; Nederlander Corporation; Midwest Health Centers, P.C.
Representative Clients: Crum & Forster Insurance Company; City of Pontiac; Michigan National Bank.

For Complete List of Firm Personnel, See General Section

For full biographical listings, see the Martindale-Hubbell Law Directory

TRAVERSE CITY,* Grand Traverse Co.

RUNNING, WISE, WILSON, FORD AND PHILLIPS, P.L.C. (AV)

326 State Street, P.O. Box 686, 49684
Telephone: 616-946-2700
Tele-Fax: 616-946-0857

Harry T. Running (Deceased)	William L. Wise (Retired)

MEMBERS OF FIRM

Patrick J. Wilson	James C. Adams
Richard W. Ford	Sandra P. Howard
Thomas J. Phillips	Kent E. Gerberding

ASSOCIATES

Shelley A. Kester	Bradley L. Putney

OF COUNSEL

J. Bruce Donaldson	Douglas J. Donaldson

Representative Clients: Munson Healthcare; Munson Medical Center; Traverse Community Hospital.
Local Counsel For: Auto-Owners Insurance Co.; John Hancock Mutual Life Insurance Co.; Amoco Production Co.; Paul Oliver Memorial Hospital.

For full biographical listings, see the Martindale-Hubbell Law Directory

TROY, Oakland Co.

BARLOW & LANGE, P.C. (AV)

3290 West Big Beaver Road Suite 310, 48084
Telephone: 810-649-3150
Facsimile: 810-649-3175

Thomas W. H. Barlow	Craig S. Schwartz
Craig W. Lange	Matthew S. Derby
Paul W. Coughenour	Gary S. Fealk

LEGAL SUPPORT PERSONNEL

Laura L. Russell

For full biographical listings, see the Martindale-Hubbell Law Directory

POLING, MCGAW & POLING, P.C. (AV)

Suite 275, 5435 Corporate Drive, 48098
Telephone: 810-641-0500
Telecopier: 810-641-0506

(See Next Column)

POLING, MCGAW & POLING P.C., *Troy—Continued*

Benson T. Buck (1926-1989)
Richard B. Poling
D. Douglas McGaw

Richard B. Poling, Jr.
Gregory C. Hamilton
Veronica B. O'Haro

James R. Parker

OF COUNSEL

Ralph S. Moore

Representative Clients: County of Oakland; City of Troy; United States Fidelity & Guaranty Co.; Sentry Insurance Co.; Admiral Insurance; DeMaria Construction Co.; Leo Corporation; Aetna Casualty and Surety Co.; Concord Design; Pneumo-Abex.

For full biographical listings, see the Martindale-Hubbell Law Directory

IMMIGRATION AND NATURALIZATION

ALABAMA

BIRMINGHAM, * Jefferson Co.

BRADLEY, ARANT, ROSE & WHITE (AV)

2001 Park Place, Suite 1400, P.O. Box 830709, 35283-0709
Telephone: 205-521-8000
Facsimile: 205-252-0264
Facsimile (SouthTrust Tower Office): 205-251-9915
URL: http://www.BARW.COM
Huntsville, Alabama Office: 200 Clinton Avenue West, Suite 900, 35801.
Telephone: 205-517-5100.
Facsimile: 205-533-5069.

MEMBER OF FIRM
G. Edward Cassady, III

For Complete List of Firm Personnel, See General Section

For full biographical listings, see the Martindale-Hubbell Law Directory

HUNTSVILLE, * Madison Co.

FOLEY, SMITH & MAHMOOD, P.C. (AV)

200 West Court Square, Suite 804, 35801
Telephone: 205-536-8877
800-680-LAWS (5297)
Fax: 205-536-0610
Email: JUNES@HIWAAY.NET

Robert Sellers Smith	Richard William Foley
Gulam Rafiqueuddin Mahmood	(Not admitted in AL)

For full biographical listings, see the Martindale-Hubbell Law Directory

ARIZONA

PHOENIX, * Maricopa Co.

VLASSIS & VLASSIS (AV)

1545 West Thomas Road, 85015
Telephone: 602-248-8811
Fax: 602-274-8983

George P. Vlassis	Elizabeth D. Vlassis

References: Bank One; Citibank.

For full biographical listings, see the Martindale-Hubbell Law Directory

CALIFORNIA

GLENDALE, Los Angeles Co.

BAKER, OLSON, LeCROY & DANIELIAN, A LAW CORPORATION (AV)

144 North Brand Boulevard, P.O. Box 29062, 91209-9062
Telephone: 818-502-5600
Facsimile: 818-241-2653

Sheldon S. Baker	Charles L. LeCroy, III
Eric Olson	Arsen Danielian

Michael S. Simon
OF COUNSEL
John J. Jacobson

For full biographical listings, see the Martindale-Hubbell Law Directory

IRVINE, Orange Co.

HIRSON WEXLER PERL & STARK, A PROFESSIONAL CORPORATION (AV)

Jamboree Center, One Park Plaza, Suite 950, 92614
Telephone: 714-251-8844
Fax: 714-251-1545
Email: immigration__law@msn.com *URL:* http://www.immig.com
Los Angeles, California Office: 6310 San Vicente Boulevard, Suite 415, 90048.
Telephone: 213-936-0200.
Fax: 213-936-4488. *E-Mail:* 73411.37@compuserve.com. *Web-Site:* http://www.immig.com.

(See Next Column)

San Diego, California Office: 4275 Executive Square, Suite 800, 92037.
Telephone: 619-452-5700.
Fax: 619-452-1911. *E-Mail:* hkps@immiglaw.com. *Web-Site:* http://www.immig.com.
Phoenix, Arizona Office: 3443 North Central Avenue, Suite 706, 85012.
Telephone: 602-266-4700.
Fax: 602-265-8108. *E-Mail:* 73344.21@compuserve.com. *Web-Site:* http://www.immig.com.
Dallas, Texas Office: Heritage Square Tower II, 7th Floor, 5001 L.B.J. Freeway, 75244.
Telephone: 214-991-7400.
Fax: 214-991-1501. *E-Mail:* hkps@immig-law.com. *Web-Site:* http://www.immig.com.

David Hirson	Joanne Trifilo Stark (Resident,
Mitchell L. Wexler	Phoenix, Arizona Office)
Gary B. Perl (Resident, San	
Diego, California and Dallas,	
Texas Offices)	

OF COUNSEL
Lance Kaplan

For full biographical listings, see the Martindale-Hubbell Law Directory

LOS ANGELES, * Los Angeles Co.

BONAPARTE & MIYAMOTO, A PROFESSIONAL LAW CORPORATION (AV)

11911 San Vicente Boulevard, Suite 355, 90049
Telephone: 310-471-3481
FAX: 310-471-1686
Email: 73344.441@Compuserve.com
Other Los Angeles Office: 919 South Grand Avenue, Suite 208E.
Telephone: 213-688-8872.
FAX: 213-688-8887.
Newport Beach, California Office: 5030 Campus Drive.
Telephone: 714-955-2012.
FAX: 714-833-1423.

Ronald H. Bonaparte	Lynn Miyamoto

Thomas E. Cummings

For full biographical listings, see the Martindale-Hubbell Law Directory

RALPH EHRENPREIS A PROFESSIONAL LAW CORPORATION (AV)

Suite 450, 1801 Century Park East, 90067
Telephone: 310-553-6600
Telefax: 310-553-2616
Cable Address: "Immlaw"

Ralph Ehrenpreis

Bernard J. Lurie

References: City National Bank (Beverly Hills Office, Beverly Hills, California); Great American Bank (Century City Office, Los Angeles, California).

For full biographical listings, see the Martindale-Hubbell Law Directory

AGGIE R. HOFFMAN (AV)

6300 Wilshire Boulevard, Suite 1560, 90048
Telephone: 213-655-0123
Fax: 213-655-3345

For full biographical listings, see the Martindale-Hubbell Law Directory

MARK A. IVENER A LAW CORPORATION (AV)

11601 Wilshire Boulevard, Suite 1430, 90025
Telephone: 310-477-3000
Fax: 310-477-2652
Email: mark@ivener.com *URL:* http://www.ilw.com/ivener
Canadian Associate Office: 1300-808 Nelson Street, Vancouver, British Columbia V6Z 2H2.
Telephone: 604-688-0558.
FAX: 604-685-8972.
Japanese Associate Office: 13th Floor Urbannet Otemachi Building, 2-2-2 Otemachi, Chiyoda-Ku, Tokyo 100, Japan.
Telephone: 813-3231-8888.
Fax: 813-3231-8881.

Mark A. Ivener

For full biographical listings, see the Martindale-Hubbell Law Directory

JOHN A. JOANNES A PROFESSIONAL CORPORATION (AV)

11911 San Vicente Boulevard Suite 375, 90049
Telephone: 310-440-4240
Facsimile: 310-471-2862
Email: jjoannespc@aol.com *URL:* http://www.primenet.com/~joannes/

John A. Joannes

(See Next Column)

JOHN A. JOANNES A PROFESSIONAL CORPORATION, *Los Angeles—Continued*

OF COUNSEL
Stephen L. Teller

For full biographical listings, see the Martindale-Hubbell Law Directory

OCHOA & SILLAS (AV)

444 South, Flower Street, 18th Floor, 90071
Telephone: 213-362-1400
Fax: 213-622-0162
Sacramento, California Office: Wells Fargo Center, 400 Capitol Mall, Suite 1850.
Telephone: 916-447-3383.
FAX: 916-447-3495.
Mexico City, Mexico Office: Bosques de Duraznos, No. 65-507-B, Bosques de Las Lomas, 11700 Mexico, D.F.
Telephone: 905-596-68-48.

MEMBERS OF FIRM
Ralph M. Ochoa   Herman Sillas
                 Jesse M. Jauregui

ASSOCIATES
Francisco Valles Lopez   Thomas J. Joy
Evan F. Hadnot   Mario Cordero

OF COUNSEL
Cochran & Lotkin, , Washington, D.C.

LEGAL SUPPORT PERSONNEL
Manuel Tejeda (Paralegal)   Jeanette M. Palma (Paralegal)
          Lori Lee Marino (Paralegal)

For full biographical listings, see the Martindale-Hubbell Law Directory

O'MELVENY & MYERS LLP (AV)

400 South Hope Street, 90071-2899
Telephone: 213-669-6000
Cable Address: "Moms"
Facsimile: 213-669-6407
Email: omminfo@omm.com
Century City, California Office: 1999 Avenue of the Stars, 90067-6035.
Telephone: 310-553-6700.
Facsimile: 310-246-6779.
Newport Beach, California Office: 610 Newport Center Drive, 92660-6429.
Telephone: 714-760-9600.
Cable Address: "Moms".
Facsimile: 714-669-6994.
San Francisco, California Office: Embarcadero Center West Tower, 275 Battery Street, 94111-3305.
Telephone: 415-984-8700.
Facsimile: 415-984-8701.
New York, New York Office: Citicorp Center, 153 East 53rd Street, 10022-4611.
Telephone: 212-326-2000.
Facsimile: 212-326-2061.
Washington, D.C. Office: 555 13th Street, N.W., 20004-1109.
Telephone: 202-383-5300.
Cable Address: "Moms".
Facsimile: 202-383-5414.
London, England Office: 10 Finsbury Square, London, EC2A 1LA.
Telephone: 0171-256-8451.
Facsimile: 0171-638-8205.
Tokyo, Japan Office: Sanbancho KB-6 Building, 6 Sanbancho, Chiyoda-ku, Tokyo 102, Japan.
Telephone: 03-3239-2900.
Facsimile: 03-3239-2432.
Hong Kong Office: Suite 1905, Peregrine Tower, Lippo Centre, 89 Queensway, Central, Hong Kong.
Telephone: 852-2523-8266.
Facsimile: 852-2522-1760.
Shanghai, Peoples Republic of China Office: Shanghai International Trade Centre, Suite 2011, 2200 Yan An Road West, Shanghai, 200335, PRC.
Telephone: 86-21-6219-5363.
Facsimile: 86-21-6275-4949.

PARTNER
Lowell C. Martindale, Jr. (Newport Beach Office)

For Complete List of Firm Personnel, See General Section

For full biographical listings, see the Martindale-Hubbell Law Directory

LAW OFFICES OF CARL SHUSTERMAN (AV)

One Wilshire Building, 624 South Grand Avenue, Suite 1608, 90017
Telephone: 213-623-4592
Fax: 213-623-3720
Email: visalaw@ix.netcom.com *URL:*
http://websites.earthlink.net/~visalaw

(See Next Column)

ASSOCIATES
Elahe Najfabadi   Claire H. Kim
          Ellen Ma Lee

For full biographical listings, see the Martindale-Hubbell Law Directory

BERNARD P. WOLFSDORF A PROFESSIONAL CORPORATION (AV)

17383 Sunset Boulevard, Suite 120 (Pacific Palisades), 90272
Telephone: 310-573-4242
FAX: 310-573-5093
Email: visalaw@wolfsdorf.com *URL:* http://ilw.com/wolfsdorf

Bernard P. Wolfsdorf

Michele A. Buchanan   Michael S. Greenbaum
C. Daniel Levy   (Not admitted in CA)
Stephen M. Dewar   Mitchell Berenson
  (Not admitted in CA)

For full biographical listings, see the Martindale-Hubbell Law Directory

---

PASADENA, Los Angeles Co.

MARGARET ANN REDMOND (AV)

Suite 726, 301 East Colorado Boulevard, 91101
Telephone: 818-584-9050
FAX: 818-584-6463
Email: 73411.230@compuserve.com

For full biographical listings, see the Martindale-Hubbell Law Directory

---

*SAN DIEGO,** San Diego Co.

KING & BALLOW (AV)

2700 Symphony Towers, 750 B Street, 92101
Telephone: 619-236-9401
Fax: 619-236-9437
URL: http://www.king-ballow.com
Nashville, Tennessee Office: 1200 Noel Place, 200 Fourth Avenue, North, 37219.
Telephone: 615-259-3456.
Fax: 615-254-7907.

MEMBERS OF FIRM
Frank S. King, Jr.   R. Eddie Wayland
  (Not admitted in CA)   (Not admitted in CA)
Robert L. Ballow   Paul H. Duvall (Resident)
  (Not admitted in CA)   Mark E. Hunt
Richard C. Lowe   (Not admitted in CA)
  (Not admitted in CA)   Lynn Siegel

ASSOCIATES
Leslie E. Lewis   Bruce C. Young

Representative Clients: Gen Probe, Inc., San Diego, California; Rohr Industries, Inc., Chula Vista, California; Solar Turbines, Inc., San Diego, California.

For full biographical listings, see the Martindale-Hubbell Law Directory

---

*SAN FRANCISCO,** San Francisco Co.

LAW OFFICES JACK I. KAISER (AV)

633 Battery Street, Sixth Floor, 94111
Telephone: 415-986-4444
Facsimile: 415-986-7224

For full biographical listings, see the Martindale-Hubbell Law Directory

---

STUDIO CITY, Los Angeles Co.

THE MILLER LAW OFFICES (AV)

12441 Ventura Boulevard, 91604
Telephone: 818-508-9005
Fax: 818-508-9458

Charles M. Miller   Terri Senesac Miller

John M. Levant

For full biographical listings, see the Martindale-Hubbell Law Directory

COLORADO

---

*DENVER,** Denver Co.

ALLOTT & MAKAR, A PROFESSIONAL CORPORATION (AV)

Suite 260, 2305 East Arapahoe Road (Littleton), 80122
Telephone: 303-797-8055
Fax: 303-797-6136
Email: 73032.64@compuserve.com

Ann Allott	L. Ari Weitzhandler
Margaret C. Makar	Daniel C. Horne

For full biographical listings, see the Martindale-Hubbell Law Directory

---

C. JAMES COOPER, JR. (AV)

12075 East 45th Avenue, Suite 315, 80239-3128
Telephone: 303-371-1822
Fax: 303-373-1822

References: First Interstate Bank of Denver; City Wide Bank of Denver.

For full biographical listings, see the Martindale-Hubbell Law Directory

---

ROBERT G. HEISERMAN, P.C. (AV)

Suite 2280, Bank Western Tower, 1675 Broadway, 80202
Telephone: 303-629-1065
Toll Free: 800-873-3302
Fax: 303-623-1710
Aspen, Colorado Office: 318 West Main Street.
Telephone: 970-925-2702.

Robert G. Heiserman

Barbara H. Lutes

Reference: Norwest Bank, Denver, N.A.

For full biographical listings, see the Martindale-Hubbell Law Directory

---

CONNECTICUT

WESTPORT, Fairfield Co.

WILLIAM L. SCHEFFLER & ASSOCIATES (AV(T))

P.O. Box 2773, 06880-0773
Telephone: 203-226-6600; 1-800-429-4480
Telecopier: 203-227-1873

For full biographical listings, see the Martindale-Hubbell Law Directory

---

DISTRICT OF COLUMBIA

WASHINGTON, D.C. Co.

CARLINER AND REMES, P.C. (AV)

Suite 903, 1700 K Street, N.W., 20006
Telephone: 202-223-0050
FAX: 202-223-0052

David Carliner	Robert A. Remes

Ladan Mirbagheri Smith	Jeffrey E. González-Pérez
Niloofar Assadnia	(Not admitted in DC)
(Not admitted in DC)	

For full biographical listings, see the Martindale-Hubbell Law Directory

COHN AND MARKS (AV)

Suite 600, 1333 New Hampshire Avenue, N.W., 20036
Telephone: 202-293-3860
Fax: 202-293-4827
URL: http://www.cohnmarks.com

MEMBERS OF FIRM

Joel H. Levy	Richard A. Helmick
Robert B. Jacobi	Wayne Coy, Jr.
Roy R. Russo	Mark L. Pelesh
Ronald A. Siegel	J. Brian De Boice
Lawrence N. Cohn	Edward N. Leavy

ASSOCIATES

Susan Valerie Sachs	Kevin M. Goldberg
John R. Przypszny	Michael A. McVicker
A. Sheba Chacko	(Not admitted in DC)

(See Next Column)

OF COUNSEL

Marcus Cohn	Stanley S. Neustadt
Leonard H. Marks	Stanley B. Cohen
	Richard M. Schmidt, Jr.

LEGAL SUPPORT PERSONNEL
SPECIALIST (NON-LAWYER)
Sharon H. Bob (Higher Education Specialist on Policy and
Regulation)

For full biographical listings, see the Martindale-Hubbell Law Directory

---

MAGGIO & KATTAR, P.C. (AV)

Eleven Dupont Circle, N.W., Suite 775, 20036
Telephone: 202-483-0053
FAX: 202-483-6801
Email: inquire@maggio-kattar.com *URL:* http://www.maggio-kattar.com

Michael Maggio

Alison J. Brown	Cora D. Tekach
(Not admitted in DC)	(Not admitted in DC)
Elizabeth A. Quinn	Atessa Chehrazi
(Not admitted in DC)	(Not admitted in DC)

For full biographical listings, see the Martindale-Hubbell Law Directory

---

NOTO & OSWALD, P.C. (AV)

1100 New York Avenue, N.W. West Tower-Suite 350, 20005-3934
Telephone: 202-408-1313
Fax: 202-326-5299

Mario T. Noto	Howard C.M. Hobbs
Robert L. Oswald	(Not admitted in DC)
Danielle L. C. Beach	Marina E. Grigoriev
(Not admitted in DC)	(Not admitted in DC)
Kieran R. McCormack	
(Not admitted in DC)	

For full biographical listings, see the Martindale-Hubbell Law Directory

---

PALMA R. YANNI (AV)

2612 P Street, N.W., 20007
Telephone: 202-338-1995
Fax: 202-338-1994
Email: 73411.103@compuserve.com

For full biographical listings, see the Martindale-Hubbell Law Directory

---

FLORIDA

---

*MIAMI,** Dade Co.

MICHAEL A. BANDER, P.A. (AV)

Rivergate Plaza, Suite 300, 444 Brickell Avenue, 33131
Telephone: Dade: 305-358-5800
Fax: 305-374-6593
Email: 73032.332@compuserve.com *URL:* http://ILW.COM/BANDER

Michael A. Bander

Tammy Fox-Isicoff	Antonia Canero-Davies

For full biographical listings, see the Martindale-Hubbell Law Directory

---

BRAUWERMAN & ASSOCIATES, P.A. (AV)

1000 Brickell Avenue, Suite 520, 33131
Telephone: 305-758-1234
Telecopier: 305-576-6251
Email: 73032.545@compuserve.com
Fort Lauderdale, Florida Office: Executive Pavilion, Suite 502, 300 N.W.
82 Avenue (Plantation).
Telephone: 954-527-1234.
Telecopier: 954-424-8935.

Jeffrey N. Brauwerman

Bradley O. June

For full biographical listings, see the Martindale-Hubbell Law Directory

---

RIFKIN AND WARREN LOLI, P.A. (AV)

1110 Brickell Avenue, Suite 210, 33131
Telephone: 305-371-2777
Facsimile: 305-375-9517

Larry S. Rifkin	Barbara Warren Loli

(See Next Column)

RIFKIN AND WARREN LOLI P.A., *Miami—Continued*

Maya Chatterjea   Cecilia M. Olavarria

For full biographical listings, see the Martindale-Hubbell Law Directory

LAW OFFICES OF MICHAEL SHANE, P.A. (AV)

19 West Flagler Street Suite 607, 33130
Telephone: 305-371-8777
Fax: 305-371-3726
Email: 73032.446@COMPUSERVE.COM

Michael Shane
LEGAL SUPPORT PERSONNEL
(Paralegal) Raquel Vega   (Paralegal) Rosa Fraga

For full biographical listings, see the Martindale-Hubbell Law Directory

WEISS & HERNANDEZ, P.A. (AV)

1401 Brickell Avenue, Suite 300, 33131-3502
Telephone: 305-358-1500
Facsimile: 305-358-1921
Palm Beach Gardens, Florida Office: 4360 Northlake Boulevard, Suite 106, 33420.
Telephone: 407-627-4700.
Fax: 407-368-9274.
Boca Raton, Florida Office: The Plaza-Suite 801, 5355 Town Center Road.
Telephone: 407-393-7400.
Telecopier: 407-368-9274.

Michael N. Weiss   Eugenio Hernandez

Damaris Y. Garcia   Luis A. Cordero
Rebeca F. Yaker

For full biographical listings, see the Martindale-Hubbell Law Directory

ORLANDO,* Orange Co.

MAGUIRE, VOORHIS & WELLS, P.A. (AV)

Two South Orange Avenue and, 200 South Orange Avenue, Suite 3000,
P.O. Box 633, 32802
Telephone: 407-244-1100
Telecopier: 407-423-8796
Email: mvw@mvw.com *URL:* http:// www.mvw.com
Melbourne, Florida Office: 1499 South Harbor City Boulevard, Suite 303.
Telephone: 407-951-1776.
Fax: 407-951-1849.
Tallahassee, Florida Office: 2804 Remington Green Circle, Suite 4.
Telephone 904-386-6060.
Fax: 904-385-8220.

A. Guy Neff

Representative Clients: Universal Studios Florida, Union Mortgage Corp. of Florida.

For full biographical listings, see the Martindale-Hubbell Law Directory

TAMPA,* Hillsborough Co.

RICHARD MANEY & ASSOCIATES, P.A. (AV)

Barnett Plaza, 101 East Kennedy Boulevard, Suite 3170, 33602-5152
Telephone: 813-221-1366
Fax: 813-223-5920

Richard Henry Maney

Jeffrey Lee Gordon   B. John Ovink

For full biographical listings, see the Martindale-Hubbell Law Directory

GEORGIA

ATLANTA,* Fulton Co.

ALSTON & BIRD (AV)

A Partnership including Professional Corporations
One Atlantic Center, 1201 West Peachtree Street, 30309-3424
Telephone: 404-881-7000
Telecopier: 404-881-7777
Cable Address: AMGRAM GA
Telex: 54-2996
Easylink: 62985848
Washington, D.C. Office: 601 Pennsylvania Ave., N.W., North Building, Suite 250 20004.
Telephone: 202-508-3300.
Telecopier: 202-508-3333.

(See Next Column)

MEMBER OF FIRM
Bernard L. Greer, Jr.
COUNSEL
Eileen M. G. Scofield

Representative Client: Suntory Water Group, Inc.

For Complete List of Firm Personnel, See General Section

For full biographical listings, see the Martindale-Hubbell Law Directory

GLASS, McCULLOUGH, SHERRILL & HARROLD (AV)

1409 Peachtree Street, N.E., 30309
Telephone: 404-885-1500
Telecopier: 404-892-1801
Buckhead Office: Monarch Plaza, 3414 Peachtree Road, N.E., Suite 450, Atlanta, Georgia, 30326-1162.
Telephone: 404-885-1500.
Telecopier: 404-231-1978.
Washington, D.C. Office: 1150 17th Street, N.W., Suite 605. Washington, D.C., 20036.
Telephone: 202-785-8118.
Telecopier: 202-785-0128.
Knoxville, Tennessee Office: 606 West Main Avenue, Suite 205, P.O. Box 2543. Knoxville, Tennessee, 37901-2543.
Telephone: 423-971-5418.
Telecopier: 423-971-1706.

MEMBER OF FIRM
James W. King
ASSOCIATE
Christina Sungyoon Pak

For Complete List of Firm Personnel, See General Section

For full biographical listings, see the Martindale-Hubbell Law Directory

KILPATRICK & CODY LLP (AV)

Suite 2800, 1100 Peachtree Street, 30309-4530
Telephone: 404-815-6500
Telephone Copier: 404-815-6555
Telex: 54-2307
Washington, D.C. Office: Suite 800, 700 13th Street, N.W., 20005.
Telephone: 202-508-5800. Telephone Copier: 202-508-5858.
Brussels, Belgium Office: Avenue Louise 65, BTE 3, 1050 Brussels.
Telephone: (32) (2) 533-03-00.
Telecopier: (32) (2) 534-86-38.
London, England Office: 68 Pall Mall, London, SW1Y 5ES, England.
Telephone: (44) (71) 321 0477.
Telecopier: (44) (71) 930 9733.
Augusta, Georgia Office: Suite 1400 First Union Bank Building, P.O. Box 2043, 30903. Telephone (706) 724-2622. Telecopier (706) 722-0219.

MEMBER OF FIRM
Robert E. Banta
COUNSEL
Joycelyn L. Fleming
ASSOCIATE
Peter D. Roberts

For Complete List of Firm Personnel, See General Section

For full biographical listings, see the Martindale-Hubbell Law Directory

LONG ALDRIDGE & NORMAN, LLP (AV)

A Limited Liability Partnership including Professional Corporations
One Peachtree Center, Suite 5300, 303 Peachtree Street, 30308
Telephone: 404-527-4000
Telecopier: 404-527-4198
Washington, D.C. Office: Suite 600, 701 Pennsylvania Avenue, N.W., 20004.
Telephone: 202-624-1200.
FAX: 202-624-1298.

MEMBER OF FIRM
Gordon D. Giffin
ASSOCIATE
James D. Comerford

For Complete List of Firm Personnel, See General Section

For full biographical listings, see the Martindale-Hubbell Law Directory

POWELL, GOLDSTEIN, FRAZER & MURPHY (AV)

A Partnership including a Professional Corporation
191 Peachtree Street, N.E., Sixteenth Floor, 30303
Telephone: 404-572-6600
Telex: 542864
Telecopier: 404-572-6999
Cable Address: "Pgfm"
Washington, D.C. Office: Sixth Floor, 1001 Pennsylvania Avenue, N.W., 20004.
Telephone: 202-347-0066.

(See Next Column)

POWELL, GOLDSTEIN, FRAZER & MURPHY—*Continued*

ASSOCIATES

Charles H. Kuck Rebecca L. Sigmund

Representative Clients: Nedlloyd Lines (USA), Inc.; CSR America, Inc.; Miescor (USA), Inc.; The Fuji Bank-Atlanta, Limited; Kubota Manufacturing Corporation of America, Inc.

For Complete List of Firm Personnel, See General Section

For full biographical listings, see the Martindale-Hubbell Law Directory

---

DAN E. WHITE (AV)

The Peachtree Building, 1355 Peachtree Street N.W., Suite 2000, 30309
Telephone: 404-892-3114
Fax: 404-892-3309

For full biographical listings, see the Martindale-Hubbell Law Directory

---

SAVANNAH, Chatham Co.

GANNAM & GNANN (AV)

130 West Bay Street, P.O. Box 10085, 31412
Telephone: 912-232-1192
Fax: 912-238-9917

MEMBERS OF FIRM

Michael J. Gannam J. Hamrick Gnann, Jr.
Joseph M. Gannam

For full biographical listings, see the Martindale-Hubbell Law Directory

---

HAWAII

HONOLULU, Honolulu Co.

LYNCH & FARMER (AV)

Suite 2500, Mauka Tower Grosvenor Center, 737 Bishop Street, 96813
Telephone: 808-528-0100
Facsimile: 808-528-4997

David C. Farmer Steven J. Kim
Paul A. Lynch

COUNSEL

Ronald T. Oldenberg William F. Thompson, III

OF COUNSEL

David W. Proudfoot

LEGAL SUPPORT PERSONNEL

Paul E. Strack Hee J. (Joyce) Chung

For full biographical listings, see the Martindale-Hubbell Law Directory

---

ILLINOIS

AURORA, Kane Co.

MURPHY, HUPP, FOOTE, MIELKE AND KINNALLY (AV)

North Island Center, P.O. Box 5030, 60507
Telephone: 708-844-0056
FAX: 708-844-1905

MEMBERS OF FIRM

Robert B. Hupp Patrick M. Kinnally

Representative Clients: American Telephone & Telegraph Co.; Fox Valley Park District; Lyon Metal Products; Kane County Forest Preserve District; Hollywood Casino; Employers Mutual Insurance Co.; Forty-Eight Insulations, Inc.; UNR Asbestos Disease Trust; Richards-Wilcox Co.; National Bank & Trust Company of Syracuse.

For Complete List of Firm Personnel, See General Section

For full biographical listings, see the Martindale-Hubbell Law Directory

---

CHICAGO, Cook Co.

GESSLER, HUGHES & SOCOL, LTD. (AV)

Three First National Plaza, Suite 2200, 60602
Telephone: 312-580-0100
Telecopy: 312-580-1994

(See Next Column)

Mark S. Dym Terence J. Moran
George W. Gessler Mark D. Olson
John K. Hughes Matthew J. Piers
William P. Jones David J. Pritchard
Peter M. Katsaros Kalman D. Resnick
Mark A. LaRose Frederick S. Rhine
Kimberley Marsh Jonathan A. Rothstein
Donna Kaner Socol

Benjamin P. Beringer Alex W. Miller
Darilyn W. Bock Belkis Cervantes Muldoon
Gary Chodorow Jonathan D. Rosenblum
Anjali Dayal Marci S. Sperling
Ruth M. Dunning Dana H. Sukenik
Adam D. Ingber J. Eric Vander Arend
Michael J. Klein Maria L. Vertuno
Laura C. Liu Mark B. Weiner
Charles H. Wintersteen

OF COUNSEL

James T. Derico, Jr. Darius S. Francescatti, M.D.
Susan R. Gzesh

For full biographical listings, see the Martindale-Hubbell Law Directory

---

MANDEL, LIPTON AND STEVENSON LIMITED (AV)

Suite 2900, 120 North La Salle Street, 60602
Telephone: 312-236-7080
Facsimile: 312-236-0781

Richard L. Mandel Richard A. Lifshitz
Alfred R. Lipton Terry Yale Feiertag
Leonard M. Malkin Kathleen Hogan Morrison
R. Peter Carey Uve R. Jerzy
Henry A. Waller Carolyn E. Winter
Kathleen Roseborough Audrey L. Gaynor

Andrés J. Gallegos Megan Kennedy Riordan
  (Not admitted in IL)

OF COUNSEL

Nicholas Stevenson Mark R. Ordower

LEGAL SUPPORT PERSONNEL

Jacqueline Steffens (Paralegal)

References: Northern Trust Co.; American National Bank of Chicago.

For full biographical listings, see the Martindale-Hubbell Law Directory

---

MINSKY, McCORMICK & HALLAGAN, P.C. (AV)

122 South Michigan Avenue, Suite 1800, 60603
Telephone: 312-427-6163
Telefax: 312-427-6513

Joseph Minsky (1925-1992) James E. Hallagan
Margaret H. McCormick Deborah J. Kartje
Carlina Tapia-Ruano

For full biographical listings, see the Martindale-Hubbell Law Directory

---

INDIANA

INDIANAPOLIS, Marion Co.

ICE MILLER DONADIO & RYAN (AV)

One American Square Box 82001, 46282-0002
Telephone: 317-236-2100
Fax: 317-236-2219
Email: leel@imdr.com *URL:* http://www.imdr.com
South Bend, Indiana Office: 211 West Washington Street, Suite 2420.
Telephone: 219-234-7933.
Fax: 219-234-7965. Internet E-mail: leel@imdr.com. Web Site Address:
http://www.imdr.com.

MEMBERS OF FIRM

Richard E. Parker Thomas H. Ristine
Dale E. Stackhouse

STAFF ATTORNEY

Mikio Nishizu

Representative Clients: Aisin Seiki; Butler University; Indiana Precision Technology; Norcote International; Ontario Corp; PK U.S.A.; Pac West Racing; St. Joseph's Hospital; Thomson Consumer Electronics; Wavetek Communications.

For Complete List of Firm Personnel, See General Section

For full biographical listings, see the Martindale-Hubbell Law Directory

KENTUCKY

BOWLING GREEN, * Warren Co.

ENGLISH, LUCAS, PRIEST & OWSLEY (AV)

1101 College Street, P.O. Box 770, 42102-0770
Telephone: 502-781-6500
Telecopier: 502-782-7782
Email: inquiry@elpo.com

MEMBERS OF FIRM

Charles E. English   Wade T. Markham, II
ASSOCIATE
Vance Cook

For Complete List of Firm Personnel, See General Section

For full biographical listings, see the Martindale-Hubbell Law Directory

---

LOUISVILLE, * Jefferson Co.

MOSLEY, CLARE & TOWNES (AV)

Fifth Floor, Hart Block Building, 730 West Main Street, 40202
Telephone: 502-583-7400
Telecopier: 502-589-4997

MEMBERS OF FIRM

Eugene L. Mosley   Larry C. Ethridge
Dennis M. Clare   Victor L. Baltzell, Jr.
W. Waverley Townes   William J. Nold
       Judith E. McDonald-Burkman
ASSOCIATES
E. Jeffrey Mosley   Eileen L. Minto

For full biographical listings, see the Martindale-Hubbell Law Directory

---

LOUISIANA

METAIRIE, Jefferson Parish

DAVID A. M. WARE & ASSOCIATES (AV)

Two Lakeway Center, 3850 North Causeway Boulevard, Suite 1555, 70002
Telephone: 504-830-5900
Toll Free: 1-800-537-0179
Local: (504) 830-5900
After hours: 504-893-3943
Telefax: 504-830-5909
Baton Rouge, Louisiana Office: Suite C, 11750 Bricksome Avenue.
Telephone: 504-292-9091.
Telefax: 504-296-5401.
Pensacola, Florida Office: 210 S. Palafox Place, 32501.
Telephone: 904-434-9094.
Fax: 904-434-6850.

Representative Clients: Ford, Bacon & Davis Engineers; Dover Elevator.

For full biographical listings, see the Martindale-Hubbell Law Directory

---

NEW ORLEANS, * Orleans Parish

MUROV & WARD, A PROFESSIONAL LAW CORPORATION (AV)

615 Baronne Street Suite 150, 70113
Telephone: 504-523-6100
Email: 73344.240@Compeerserve.com

Mark G. Murov   Rita K. Ward

Allyson C. Martin   Jeremy Scott Zollinger
     Lara J. Jensen

Reference: Whitney National Bank, New Orleans, La.

MAINE

PORTLAND, * Cumberland Co.

PIERCE ATWOOD (AV)

One Monument Square, 04101
Telephone: 207-791-1100
Fax: 207-791-1350
Email: info@PierceAtwood.com
Augusta, Maine Office: 77 Winthrop Street.
Telephone: 207-622-6311.
Fax: 207-623-9367.

(See Next Column)

Newburyport, Massachusetts Office: 6 Harris Street.
Telephone: 508-465-9599.
Fax: 508-465-9945.

MEMBERS OF FIRM

Charles S. Einsiedler, Jr.   Anthony R. Derosby

For Complete List of Firm Personnel, See General Section

For full biographical listings, see the Martindale-Hubbell Law Directory

---

MARYLAND

BALTIMORE, * (Independent City)

VENABLE ATTORNEYS AT LAW VENABLE, BAETJER AND HOWARD, LLP (AV)

A Partnership including Professional Corporations
1800 Mercantile Bank & Trust Building, 2 Hopkins Plaza, 21201
Telephone: 410-244-7400
Email: INFO@Venable.win.net
Washington, D.C. Office: Venable, Baetjer, Howard & Civiletti LLP. Suite 1000, 1201 New York Avenue, N.W.
Telephone: 202-962-4800.
McLean, Virginia Office: Suite 400, 2010 Corporate Ridge.
Telephone: 703-760-1600.
Rockville, Maryland Office: Suite 500, One Church Street, P. O. Box 1906.
Telephone: 301-217-5600.
Towson, Maryland Office: 210 Allegheny Avenue, P. O. Box 5517.
Telephone: 410-494-6200.

MEMBERS OF FIRM

Alexander I. Lewis, III (P.C.) (Also at Towson, Maryland Office)   Robert Charles Hill (Not admitted in MD; Resident, Washington, D.C. Office)
Jana Howard Carey (P.C.)   John M. Gurley (Not admitted in MD; Resident, Washington, D.C. Office)
Maurice Baskin (Resident, Washington, D.C. Office)

For Complete List of Firm Personnel, See General Section

For full biographical listings, see the Martindale-Hubbell Law Directory

---

MASSACHUSETTS

BOSTON, * Suffolk Co.

LAWRENCE D. BASTONE (AV)

85 Devonshire Street, 02109
Telephone: 617-BAS-TONE; 617-227-3535
Telecopier: 617-720-4927

For full biographical listings, see the Martindale-Hubbell Law Directory

---

PALMER & DODGE LLP (AV)

One Beacon Street, 02108
Telephone: 617-573-0100
Facsimile: 617-227-4420

MEMBER OF FIRM

F. Kingston Berlew
COUNSEL
Kevin R. McNamara   Alan S. Musgrave
      Russell B. Swapp

For Complete List of Firm Personnel, See General Section

For full biographical listings, see the Martindale-Hubbell Law Directory

---

MICHIGAN

BLOOMFIELD HILLS, Oakland Co.

HOWARD & HOWARD ATTORNEYS, P.C. (AV)

The Pinehurst Office Center, Suite 101, 1400 North Woodward Avenue, 48304-2856
Telephone: 810-645-1483
Telecopier: 810-645-1568
Kalamazoo, Michigan Office: The Kalamazoo Building, Suite 400, 107 West Michigan Avenue.
Telephone: 616-382-1483.
Telecopier: 616-382-1568.

(See Next Column)

HOWARD & HOWARD ATTORNEYS P.C.—*Continued*

Lansing, Michigan Office: The Phoenix Building, Suite 500, 222 Washington Square, North.
Telephone: 517-485-1483.
Telecopier: 517-485-1568.
Peoria, Illinois Office: The Creve Coeur Building, Suite 200, 321 Liberty Street.
Telephone: 309-672-1483.
Telecopier: 309-672-1568.
Tampa, Florida Office: First of America Plaza, Suite 2000, 201 East Kennedy Boulevard.
Telephone: 813-229-1483.
Telecopier: 813-229-1568.

Gustaf R. Andreasen   James C. Wickens

Representative Clients: For Representative Client list, see General Practice, Bloomfield Hills, MI.

For Complete List of Firm Personnel, See General Section

For full biographical listings, see the Martindale-Hubbell Law Directory

DETROIT,* Wayne Co.

BARRIS, SOTT, DENN & DRIKER, P.L.L.C. (AV)

211 West Fort Street, Fifteenth Floor, 48226-3281
Telephone: 313-965-9725
Telecopier: 313-965-2493
313-965-5398

Donald E. Barris	Robert E. Kass
Herbert Sott	Daniel M. Share
David L. Denn	Elaine Fieldman
Eugene Driker	Morley Witus
William G. Barris	John A. Libby
Sharon M. Woods	James S. Fontichiaro
Stephen E. Glazek	Daniel J. LaCombe

Robert E. Epstein
COUNSEL
Leon S. Cohan
OF COUNSEL
Stanley M. Weingarden

Dennis M. Barnes	Monique K. Cirelli
Matthew J. Boettcher	Laura Suzanne Laurence
Thomas F. Cavalier	Molly Giles
C. David Bargamian	Eric S. Rosenthal
Michael J. Reynolds	Claudia D. Orr
Elizabeth A. Carrie	Alicia Monique Nails

Representative Clients: American Construction, Inc.; Automotive Service Council of Michigan; Avis Rent A Car System, Inc.; Burton-Katzman Development Co.; Citation Clinical Laboratory, Ltd.; Consumers Power Co.; Cottage Health Services Corp.; County of Wayne, Michigan.

For full biographical listings, see the Martindale-Hubbell Law Directory

BRADY HATHAWAY, PROFESSIONAL CORPORATION (AV)

1330 Buhl Building, 48226-3602
Telephone: 313-965-3700
Telecopier: 313-965-2830

Thomas P. Brady
OF COUNSEL
Ingrid K. Brey

Representative Clients: Titan Insurance; Honey Baked Ham Co.; American Community Mutual Insurance Co.; Marriott Corp.; Village Green Management Co.

For Complete List of Firm Personnel, See General Section

For full biographical listings, see the Martindale-Hubbell Law Directory

BUTZEL LONG, A PROFESSIONAL CORPORATION (AV)

Suite 900, 150 West Jefferson, 48226
Telephone: 313-225-7000
Telecopier: 313-225-7080
Email: melnick@butzel.com *URL:* http://www.butzel.com
Birmingham, Michigan Office: Suite 200, 32270 Telegraph Road.
Telephone: 810-258-1616.
Telecopier: 810-258-1439.
Lansing, Michigan Office: 118 West Ottawa Street.
Telephone: 517-372-6622.
Telecopier: 517-372-6672.
Ann Arbor, Michigan Office: Suite 300, 350 South Main Street.
Telephone: 313-995-3110.
Telecopier: 313-995-1777.
Grosse Pointe Farms, Michigan Office: Suite 260, 21 Kercheval.
Telephone: 313-886-5446.
Telecopier: 313-886-2114.

(See Next Column)

William H. Dance	James C. Bruno
Clara DeMatteis Mager	

Nicholas J. Stasevich	Caridad Pastor-Klucens
Debra Auerbach Clephane	Priscilla J. Krebs

Representative Clients: ABB Robotics; William Beaumont Hospital; Detroit Diesel Corp.; Kajima International, Inc.; Kelly Services; Kelsey Hayes Co.; New Venture Gear; Rockwell International; Takata Corp.; The University of Michigan.

For Complete List of Firm Personnel, See General Section

For full biographical listings, see the Martindale-Hubbell Law Directory

CLARK HILL P.L.C. (AV)

500 Woodward Avenue, Suite 3500, 48226
Telephone: 313-965-8300
Facsimile: 313-962-4348
Oakland County, Michigan Office: Third Floor, 255 South Woodward Avenue, Birmingham.
Telephone: 810-642-9692.
Facsimile: 810-642-2174.
Lansing, Michigan Office: Suite 600, 200 North Capitol Avenue.
Telephone: 517-484-4481.
Facsimile: 517-484-1246.
Minneapolis, Minnesota Office: Suite 1000, One Financial Plaza, 120 South Sixth Street.
Telephone: 612-332-0102.
Facsimile: 612-332-3225.
Kansas City, Missouri Office: Suite 1400, Bryant Building, 1102 Grand Avenue.
Telephone: 816-221-5578.
Facsimile: 816-221-0303.

David H. Paruch (Resident, Oakland County Office)   Dorothy Hanigan Basmaji (Resident, Oakland County Office)

Representative Clients: The Budd Company; Detroit Center Tool, Inc.; Euclid-Hitachi Heavy Equipment, Inc.; Hayes Wheels International, Inc./Kelsey-Hayes Co.; Pontifical Institute for Foreign Missions (P.I.M.E.) Inc.; R.P. Scherer Corporation; UNISYS Corporation; Volvo Construction Equipment North America, Inc.; Zeidler-Roberts Partnership/Architects.

For Complete List of Firm Personnel, See General Section

For full biographical listings, see the Martindale-Hubbell Law Directory

ENGLISH & VAN HORNE, P.C. (AV)

4472 Penobscot Building, 48226
Telephone: 313-961-5100

John E. English   Pieter H. van Horne (Retired)
OF COUNSEL
Richard W. Pierce, P.C.

Reference: First of America Bank (Main Office Branch), Detroit.

For full biographical listings, see the Martindale-Hubbell Law Directory

FOSTER, MEADOWS & BALLARD, P.C. (AV)

3200 Penobscot Building, 48226
Telephone: 313-961-3234
Cable Address: "Foster"
Telex: 23-5823
Facsimile: 313-961-6184

Sparkman D. Foster (1897-1967)	Richard A. Dietz
Charles R. Hrdlicka	Robert H. Fortunate
Paul D. Galea	Robert G. Lahiff
	Camille A. Raffa-Dietz

Michael J. Liddane	Paul A. Kettunen
	OF COUNSEL
John L. Foster	John F. Langs
John A. Mundell, Jr.	

For full biographical listings, see the Martindale-Hubbell Law Directory

GRAND RAPIDS,* Kent Co.

WARNER NORCROSS & JUDD LLP (AV)

900 Old Kent Building, 111 Lyon Street, N.W., 49503-2489
Telephone: 616-752-2000
Fax: 616-752-2500
Muskegon, Michigan Office: 400 Terrace Plaza, P.O. Box 900.
Telephone: 616-727-2600.
Fax: 616-727-2699.
Holland, Michigan Office: Curtis Center, Suite 300, 170 College Avenue.
Telephone: 616-396-9800.
Fax: 616-396-3656.

(See Next Column)

WARNER NORCROSS & JUDD LLP, *Grand Rapids—Continued*

MEMBERS OF FIRM

Charles E. McCallum   Janet Percy Knaus

For Complete List of Firm Personnel, See General Section

For full biographical listings, see the Martindale-Hubbell Law Directory

---

*KALAMAZOO,** Kalamazoo Co.

KREIS, ENDERLE, CALLANDER & HUDGINS, A PROFESSIONAL CORPORATION (AV)

One Moorsbridge, P.O. Box 4010, 49003-4010
Telephone: 616-324-3000
Telecopier: 616-324-3010
Email: kech@sapien.net *URL:* http://www.kech.com

Douglas L. Callander   John F. Koryto

For Complete List of Firm Personnel, See General Section

For full biographical listings, see the Martindale-Hubbell Law Directory

---

LANSING, Ingham Co.

FOSTER, SWIFT, COLLINS & SMITH, P.C. (AV)

313 South Washington Square, 48933-2193
Telephone: 517-371-8100
Telecopier: 517-371-8200
URL: http://www.fosterswift.com
Farmington Hills, Michigan Office: 32300 Northwestern Highway, Suite 230.
Telephone: 810-539-9900.
Fax: 810-851-7504.

Gary J. McRay   Jean G. Schtokal

General Counsel for: First American Bank-Central; Story, Inc.; Michigan Milk Producers Assn.; Edward W. Sparrow Hospital; St. Lawrence Hospital; Demmer Corp.; Michigan Financial Corp.
Local Counsel for: Shell Oil Co.; Michigan-Mutual Insurance Co.; Century Telephone.

For Complete List of Firm Personnel, See General Section

For full biographical listings, see the Martindale-Hubbell Law Directory

INSURANCE DEFENSE

ALABAMA

ANDALUSIA,* Covington Co.

POWELL, PEEK & WEAVER (AV)

Court Square, P.O. Drawer 969, 36420
Telephone: 334-222-4103
Facsimile: 334-222-4105

MEMBERS OF FIRM

Abner R. Powell (1875-1940)   Abner R. Powell, III
Abner R. Powell, Jr.   John M. Peek
(1916-1987)   Gary L. Weaver

ASSOCIATE

Abner Riley Powell, IV

Representative Clients: State Farm Insurance Group; U.S.F. & G. Co.; CNA Insurance; ALFA, Auto Owners Insurance Co.; Georgia Farm Bureau; Southern Guaranty Co.

For full biographical listings, see the Martindale-Hubbell Law Directory

ATHENS,* Limestone Co.

PATTON, LATHAM, LEGGE & COLE (AV)

Professional Building, 315 West Market Street, P.O. Box 470, 35611
Telephone: 205-232-2010
Fax: 205-230-0610

MEMBERS OF FIRM

Roy B. Patton (1885-1954)   Byrd R. Latham
David U. Patton (Retired)   Winston V. Legge, Jr.
P. Michael Cole

Local Counsel for: Auto-Owners Insurance Co.; Avis; Blue Cross and Blue Shield of Alabama; CIGNA Insurance Cos.; Gold Kist, Inc.; State Farm Life Insurance Co.; State Farm Mutual Automobile Insurance Co.; Travelers Insurance Co.; United States Fidelity and Guaranty Co.; Wausau Insurance Company.

For full biographical listings, see the Martindale-Hubbell Law Directory

BIRMINGHAM,* Jefferson Co.

BRADLEY, ARANT, ROSE & WHITE (AV)

2001 Park Place, Suite 1400, P.O. Box 830709, 35283-0709
Telephone: 205-521-8000
Facsimile: 205-252-0264
Facsimile (SouthTrust Tower Office): 205-251-9915
URL: http://www.BARW.COM
Huntsville, Alabama Office: 200 Clinton Avenue West, Suite 900, 35801.
Telephone: 205-517-5100.
Facsimile: 205-533-5069.

MEMBERS OF FIRM

John H. Morrow   Joseph S. Bird, III
Hobart A. McWhorter, Jr.   John D. Watson, III
James W. Gewin   Michael R. Pennington
Brittin Turner Coleman   Philip J. Carroll III
Norman Jetmundsen, Jr.   James S. Christie, Jr.

COUNSEL

Scott M. Phelps

ASSOCIATE

Amy K. Myers

For Complete List of Firm Personnel, See General Section

For full biographical listings, see the Martindale-Hubbell Law Directory

HARRIS, CLECKLER, BERG & ROGERS, P.C. (AV)

Historic 2007 Building, 2007 Third Avenue North, 35203-2366
Telephone: 205-328-2366
Telecopier: 205-328-0013
Email: hcbr@bham.mindspring.com

Lyman H. Harris   Lonette Lamb Berg
Michael H. Cleckler   Susan Rogers

Matthew J. Dougherty   Jeffrey K. Hollis
Brock G. Murphy

For full biographical listings, see the Martindale-Hubbell Law Directory

JANECKY, NEWELL, POTTS, WELLS & WILSON, P.C. (AV)

Suite 3120, AmSouth-Harbert Plaza, 1901 Sixth Avenue North, 35203
Telephone: 205-252-4441
FAX: 205-252-0320
Mobile, Alabama Office: 3300 First National Bank Building, P.O. Box 2987.
Telephone: 205-432-8786.
FAX: 205-432-5900.
Pensacola, Florida Office: Suite 313, 25 West Cedar Street.
Telephone: 904-432-6066.

J. F. (Jack) Janecky   David M. Wilson

Michael J. Cohan   Nicholas Wyckoff Woodfield

For full biographical listings, see the Martindale-Hubbell Law Directory

LLOYD, SCHREIBER, GRAY AND GAINES, P.C. (AV)

Two Perimeter Park South Suite 100, 35243
Telephone: 205-967-8822
Telecopier: 205-967-2380

James S. Lloyd   Mark C. Peterson
Joseph Allen Schreiber   Gerald Alan Templeton
James C. Gray, III   Daniel S. Wolter
Ralph D. Gaines, III   Stephen Errol Whitehead

Kyle L. Kinney   Laura C. Nettles
Legrand H. Amberson, Jr.   Catherine L. Hogewood
Thomas J. Skinner, IV   Ashley T. Robinson
Stuart Yates Johnson

For full biographical listings, see the Martindale-Hubbell Law Directory

LONDON & YANCEY (AV)

1000 Park Place Tower, 2001 Park Place, 35203
Telephone: 205-251-2531
FAX: 205-251-8929

MEMBERS OF FIRM

Alex T. London (1847-1908)   Thomas R. Elliott, Jr.
John London (1848-1935)   Bert S. Nettles
George W. Yancey (1883-1962)   Richard W. Lewis

ASSOCIATES

Allen R. Trippeer, Jr.   Laura Ellison Proctor
Mark David Hess   Paige Elliott-Pinson
Lisa Wright Borden   F. Daniel Wood, Jr.
A. David Fawal   C. Dennis Hughes
Michael J. Velezis

OF COUNSEL

Robert W. Norris

Representative Clients: State of Alabama; Cincinnati Ins. Co.; Lloyd's of London; Blue Cross/Blue Shield; Attorney's Mutual of Alabama; State Farm; CIGNA; Royal Ins. Co. of America; Paul Revere Ins. Co.; Chubb Group.

For full biographical listings, see the Martindale-Hubbell Law Directory

PARSONS, LEE & JULIANO, P.C. (AV)

2200 AmSouth/Harbert Plaza, 1901 Sixth Avenue, North, P.O. Box 371088, 35237-1088
Telephone: 205-326-6600
Fax: 205-324-7097

Robert E. Parsons   David A. Lee
Jasper P. Juliano   John M. Bergquist
Marcus W. Lee   Paul J. DeMarco
Marda W. Sydnor   Deborah Ann Payne
Tracy Toussaint

OF COUNSEL

Dorothy A. Powell

For full biographical listings, see the Martindale-Hubbell Law Directory

PORTERFIELD, HARPER & MILLS, P.A. (AV)

22 Inverness Center Parkway, Suite 600, P.O. Box 530790, 35253-0790
Telephone: 205-980-5000
Fax: 205-980-5001

Jack B. Porterfield, Jr.   Philip F. Hutcheson
Larry W. Harper   H. C. "Trey" Ireland, III
William T. Mills, II   Keith J. Pflaum
William Dudley Motlow, Jr.   Michael L. Haggard

Stephen Douglas Christie   Don L. Hall
Timothy W. Knight   W. Perry Webb
Mark E. King   Stephen Christopher Still
Karen Walker Casey   Eric Daniel Hoaglund
Kristin Daniels Horn   Michael Robert Lunsford

Representative Clients: CIGNA; St. Paul Insurance Co.; The Travelers; Figge International; White Consolidated Industries; Terex Corp.; Wausau Insurance; Baptist Health Systems, Inc.; Bruno's, Inc.; Harley Davidson, Inc.

(See Next Column)

PORTERFIELD, HARPER & MILLS P.A., Birmingham—Continued

For full biographical listings, see the Martindale-Hubbell Law Directory

SMITH, SPIRES & PEDDY (AV)

650 Financial Center, 505 North Twentieth Street, 35203-2662
Telephone: 205-251-5885

Paul G. Smith	Michael B. Walls
Thomas S. Spires	Todd Hamilton
A. Joe Peddy	Scott M. Roberts

ASSOCIATES

Thomas Coleman, Jr.	Alan B. Lasseter
D. Gregory Dunagan	Reed R. Bates
David A. Hughes	

Representative Clients: Banker's & Shippers Insurance Co.; Alfa Insurance Co.; United States Fidelity & Guaranty Insurance Co.; R & D Trucking, Inc.; Racetrac Petroleum, Inc.; Transport South Inc.; Old Dominion Freight Line, Inc.; American States Insurance Co.; Trinity Industries, Inc.; Penn General.

For full biographical listings, see the Martindale-Hubbell Law Directory

SPAIN & GILLON, L.L.C. (AV)

The Zinszer Building, 2117 2nd Avenue North, 35203
Telephone: 205-328-4100
Telecopier: 205-324-8866

MEMBERS OF FIRM

H. Hobart Grooms, Jr.	Charles D. Stewart
Ollie L. Blan, Jr.	Thomas M. Eden, III
Eugene P. Stutts	Paul L. Sotherland
W. Gregory Smith	

General Counsel for: Liberty National Life Insurance Co.; Piggly Wiggly Alabama Distributing Co.; Alabama Insurance Guaranty Association; Alabama Life and Disability Insurance Guaranty Association; Alabama Insurance Underwriters Association.
Counsel for: The Minnesota Mutual Insurance Company of America; Government Employees Insurance Co.; Massachusetts Mutual Life Insurance Co.

For Complete List of Firm Personnel, See General Section

For full biographical listings, see the Martindale-Hubbell Law Directory

STARNES & ATCHISON (AV)

100 Brookwood Place, P.O. Box 598512, 35259-8512
Telephone: 205-868-6000
Telecopier: 205-868-6099

MEMBERS OF FIRM

W. Stancil Starnes	Carol A. Smith
W. Michael Atchison	E. Martin Bloom
William Anthony Davis, III	Michael K. Beard
L. Graves Stiff, III	Robert P. Mackenzie, III
Jeffrey E. Friedman	

ASSOCIATES

Steven T. McMeekin	Jeannie Bugg Walston
Joe L. Leak	P. Thomas Dazzio, Jr.

Representative Clients: Mutual Assurance, Inc.; CNA Insurance Co.; United States Fidelity & Guaranty Co.; Zurich Insurance Company; AIG Adjustment Aviation; Travelers Ins. Co.; Aetna Casualty & Surety Co.; Hartford Insurance Company; State Farm Mutual Auto Co.; American Medical International.

For full biographical listings, see the Martindale-Hubbell Law Directory

BREWTON,* Escambia Co.

OTTS, MOORE & JORDAN (AV)

401 Evergreen Avenue, P.O. Box 467, 36427
Telephone: 334-867-7724
Fax: 334-867-2624

MEMBERS OF FIRM

Lee M. Otts	John Thaddeus Moore
J. David Jordan	

Representative Clients: Container Corporation of America; First National Bank, Brewton; Southern Pine Electric Cooperative; Exxon Corp.; Mobil-GC Corp.; Pennzoil Exploration & Production Co.; Oryx Energy Co.; Auto-Owners Insurance Co.
Approved Attorneys for: Mississippi Valley Title Insurance Co.; First American Title Insurance Co.

CULLMAN,* Cullman Co.

ST. JOHN & ST. JOHN (AV)

108 Third Street South East, P.O. Drawer K, 35055
Telephone: 205-734-3542
Fax: 205-734-3544

(See Next Column)

MEMBERS OF FIRM

F. E. St. John (1874-1943)	Juliet G. St. John
Finis E. St. John (1909-1984)	Finis E. St. John, IV
Finis E. St. John, III	Gaynor L. St. John
(1933-1984)	Wells Rutland Turner, III

Attorneys for: U.S. Fidelity & Guaranty Co.; Golden-Rod Broilers, Inc.; Travelers Insurance Cos.; Liberty Mutual Insurance Cos.; ALFA Mutual Insurance Co.; First Federal Savings & Loan; The Atlanta Casualty Companies; Auto-Owners Insurance Co.

For full biographical listings, see the Martindale-Hubbell Law Directory

DECATUR,* Morgan Co.

EYSTER, KEY, TUBB, WEAVER & ROTH (AV)

Eyster Building, 402 East Moulton Street, S.E., P.O. Box 1607, 35602
Telephone: 205-353-6761
Fax: 205-353-6767

John C. Eyster (1863-1926)	Wm. B. Eyster (1921-1995)
Charles H. Eyster, Sr.	
(1888-1964)	

MEMBERS OF FIRM

John S. Key	Nicholas B. Roth
J. Glynn Tubb	J. Witty Allen
Laurence C. Weaver	William L. Middleton, III
James G. Adams, Jr.	

ASSOCIATES

Jenny L. Mcleroy	John R. Baggette, Jr.

General Counsel for: Alabama Farmers Cooperative.
Regional Counsel for: AmSouth Bank.
Local Counsel for: Allstate Insurance Co.; Liberty Mutual Insurance Co.; Maryland Casualty Co.; Saginaw Steering Gear Division, General Motors Corp.; State Farm Mutual Automobile Insurance Co.; The Travelers.

For full biographical listings, see the Martindale-Hubbell Law Directory

HARRIS, CADDELL & SHANKS, P.C. (AV)

214 Johnston Street, S.E., P.O. Box 2688, 35602-2688
Telephone: 205-340-8000
Telecopier: 205-340-8040

Julian Harris (1904-1994)	Thomas A. Caddell
Norman W. Harris (P.C.)	William E. Shinn, Jr.
(Retired)	Gary A. Phillips
Philip T. Shanks (Retired)	Dow M. Perry, Jr.
Charles L. Murphree (Retired)	Barnes F. Lovelace, Jr.
John A. Caddell (P.A.)	Arthur W. Orr
Robert H. Harris	J. Noel King
Jon H. Moores	Jeffrey S. Brown

Attorneys for: Acceptance Insurance Co.; Auto-Owners Insurance Co.; ALFA Insurance Cos.; American General Life & Accident Insurance Co.; Amerisure Ins. Co.; Canal Ins. Co.; Michigan Mutual Ins. Co.; Southern Guaranty Ins. Co.; U.S.F. & G. Co.; Utica Mutual Ins. Co.

For full biographical listings, see the Martindale-Hubbell Law Directory

DOTHAN,* Houston Co.

COBB & SHEALY, P.A. (AV)

206 North Lena Street, P.O. Box 6346, 36302
Telephone: 334-794-8526
Fax: 334-677-0030

Herman W. Cobb	Richard Elder Crum
Steadman S. Shealy, Jr.	James H. Pike
Raymond Todd Derrick	Joseph A. Morris
A. Gary Jones	

OF COUNSEL

Joey Hornsby

Representative Clients: Travelers Insurance; Nationwide Insurance; Auto-Owners Insurance; Employers Casualty of Texas; Safeco Insurance; Federated Insurance; Universal Underwriters; National Security Insurance; Great Central Insurance.
Approved Title Attorneys for: Lawyers Title Insurance Corp.

For full biographical listings, see the Martindale-Hubbell Law Directory

LEE & McINISH (AV)

238 West Main Street, P.O. Box 1665, 36302
Telephone: 334-792-4156
Facsimile: 334-794-8342

MEMBERS OF FIRM

W. L. Lee (1873-1944)	William C. Carn, III
Alto V. Lee, III (1915-1987)	Peter A. McInish
William L. Lee, III	Jerry M. White
Alan C. Livingston	William L. Lee, IV

(See Next Column)

LEE & McINISH—*Continued*

OF COUNSEL

H. Dwight McInish

Counsel for: Seaboard Coast Line Railroad Co.; Atlanta & St. Andrews Bay Railroad Co.; ALFA; U. S. F. & G. Co.; Maryland Casualty Co.; Continental Insurance Cos.; Royal-Globe Group; Slocomb National Bank; The Federal Land Bank of Jackson; GTE South.

For full biographical listings, see the Martindale-Hubbell Law Directory

---

ENTERPRISE, Coffee Co.

CASSADY, FULLER & MARSH (AV)

203 East Lee Avenue, P.O. Box 780, 36331
Telephone: 334-347-2626
Telecopier: 334-393-1396

MEMBERS OF FIRM

Joe C. Cassady	M. Dale Marsh
Kenneth T. Fuller	Joe C. Cassady, Jr.
	Mark E. Fuller

ASSOCIATES

R. Rainer Cotter, III	J.P. Sawyer

Representative Clients: First Alabama Bank; Enterprise Hospital Board; Sessions Co., Inc.; Allstate; State Farm Mutual Insurance Co.; Community Bank & Trust Co.; Conagra, Inc.
Approved Attorneys for: First American Title Insurance Co.

For full biographical listings, see the Martindale-Hubbell Law Directory

---

FLORENCE,* Lauderdale Co.

JONES & TROUSDALE (AV)

115 Helton Court, Suite B, P.O. Box 367, 35631-0367
Telephone: 205-767-0333
Telefax: 205-767-0331

MEMBERS OF FIRM

Robert E. Jones, III	Preston S. Trousdale, Jr.

A. DeLoach Stewart

For full biographical listings, see the Martindale-Hubbell Law Directory

---

KELLER AND PAINE (AV)

An Association of Professional Corporations
212 South Cedar Street, P.O. Box 933, 35631
Telephone: 205-764-5822
Fax: 205-767-6360

MEMBERS OF FIRM

Jesse A. Keller	Michael T. Paine
Peter L. Paine	(Not admitted in AL)

LEGAL SUPPORT PERSONNEL

Carmel Sizemore	Gayle Blake

Counsel for: The American Road Insurance Co.; Lambert Transfer Co.

For full biographical listings, see the Martindale-Hubbell Law Directory

---

O'BANNON & O'BANNON, LLC (AV)

402 South Pine Street, P.O. Box 1428, 35631
Telephone: 205-767-6731
Facsimile: 205-766-5390
Email: 102670.3357@compuserve.com

MEMBERS OF FIRM

A. Stewart O'Bannon, Jr.	Christopher E. Connolly
A. Stewart O'Bannon, III	Christopher A. Smith
	Heath F. Trousdale

For full biographical listings, see the Martindale-Hubbell Law Directory

---

FORT PAYNE,* De Kalb Co.

KELLETT & KELLETT, P.A. (AV)

106 Alabama Avenue, S.W., P.O. Box 715, 35967
Telephone: 205-845-4541

Joseph C. Kellett	Patricia C. Kellett

Attorneys for: V.I. Prewett & Son, Inc.; AmSouth Bank, N.A.; St. Paul Insurance Cos.; DeKalb-Cherokee Counties Gas District; Home Insurance Co.; Johnson Hosiery Mills, Inc.; Cherokee Hosiery Mills, Inc.; Alfa Mutual Insurance Co.

For full biographical listings, see the Martindale-Hubbell Law Directory

---

SCRUGGS, JORDAN, DODD & DODD, P.A. (AV)

207 Alabama Avenue, South, P.O. Box 1109, 35967
Telephone: 205-845-5932
Fax: 205-845-4325

(See Next Column)

William D. Scruggs, Jr.	David Dodd
Robert K. Jordan	E. Allen Dodd, Jr.

Representative Clients: State Farm Insurance Company; Allstate Insurance Co., Inc.; USF&G Insurance Co.; Nucor, Inc.; Ladd Engineering, Inc.; ALABAMA Band; First Federal Savings & Loan Association of Dekalb County; Fritz Structural Steel, Inc.; Williamson Oil Co., Inc.

For full biographical listings, see the Martindale-Hubbell Law Directory

---

GADSDEN,* Etowah Co.

DORTCH, WRIGHT & WRIGHT (AV)

239 College Street, P.O. Box 405, 35902
Telephone: 205-546-4616

MEMBERS OF FIRM

Walter R. Dortch (1847-1926)	William B. Dortch (1892-1983)
G. C. Allen (1872-1935)	Curtis Wright
	Curtis Wright, II

Attorneys for: St. Paul Insurance Cos.; Employers Insurance of Wausau; Mutual Assurance Society of Alabama; State Farm Insurance Cos.; Alabama Hospital Association Trust; Mutual Savings Life Insurance Co.; Lawyers Title Insurance Corp.; Nationwide Mutual Insurance Co.; Government Employees Insurance Co.; CSX Transportation Systems.

For full biographical listings, see the Martindale-Hubbell Law Directory

---

FORD AND ASSOCIATES, P.C. (AV)

The Lancaster Building, 645 Walnut Street, Suite 5, P.O. Box 388, 35902
Telephone: 205-546-5432
Fax: 205-546-5435

George P. Ford

Richard M. Blythe

Reference: AmSouth Bank, N.A.

For Complete List of Firm Personnel, See General Section

For full biographical listings, see the Martindale-Hubbell Law Directory

---

SIMMONS, BRUNSON AND SASSER, ATTORNEYS, P.A. (AV)

1411 Rainbow Drive, P.O. Box 1189, 35902
Telephone: 205-546-9206
Telecopier: 205-546-8091

Clarence Simmons, Jr.	Steve P. Brunson
	James T. Sasser

Rebecca A. Walker	Jeff George Underwood
Jeffrey A. Brown	Scott C. Lloyd
	(Not admitted in AL)

Attorneys for: Preferred Risk Mutual Insurance Co.; ALFA Mutual Insurance Co.; Royal Insurance Cos.
Approved Attorneys for: Lawyers Title Insurance Corp.; Mississippi Valley Title Insurance Co.

For full biographical listings, see the Martindale-Hubbell Law Directory

---

TORBERT & TORBERT, P.A. (AV)

1024 Forrest Avenue, 35901
Telephone: 205-547-7551
Fax: 205-547-7553

Jack W. Torbert	Jack W. Torbert, Jr.

References: South Trust Bank of Etowah County, N.A.; First Alabama Bank of Gadsden, N.A.

For full biographical listings, see the Martindale-Hubbell Law Directory

---

GUNTERSVILLE,* Marshall Co.

LUSK & LUSK (AV)

452 Gunter Avenue, P.O. Box 609, 35976
Telephone: 205-582-3248
Fax: 205-582-3215

MEMBERS OF FIRM

Marion F. Lusk (1896-1986)	Louis B. Lusk

Representative Clients: AmSouth Bank of Alabama, Guntersville; United States Fidelity & Guaranty Co.; The Travelers Insurance Co.; St. Paul Cos.; ALFA Mutual Insurance Cos.; Hartford Group; Liberty Mutual Insurance Co.; Allstate Insurance Co.; Home of New York Group.

For full biographical listings, see the Martindale-Hubbell Law Directory

---

HALEYVILLE, Winston Co.

LOWE, MOBLEY & LOWE (AV)

1210-21st Street, P.O. Box 576, 35565
Telephone: 205-486-5296
Fax: 205-486-4531

(See Next Column)

Lowe, Mobley & Lowe, *Haleyville—Continued*

MEMBERS OF FIRM

Walter Joe James, Jr. (1923-1990)

John W. Lowe

Jeffery A. Mobley

Jonathan B. Lowe

Representative Clients: Traders & Farmers Bank; Burdick-West Memorial Hospital.
Approved Attorneys for: Lawyers Title Insurance Corp.

For full biographical listings, see the Martindale-Hubbell Law Directory

HUNTSVILLE,* Madison Co.

BRADLEY, ARANT, ROSE & WHITE (AV)

200 Clinton Avenue West, Suite 900, 35801
Telephone: 205-517-5100
Facsimile: 205-533-5069
URL: http://www.BARW.COM
Birmingham, Alabama Office: 2001 Park Place, Suite 1400, P.O. Box 830709.
Telephone: 205-521-8000.
Facsimile: 205-251-8611, 251-8665, 252-0264. Facsimile (SouthTrust Tower Office): 205-251-9915.

RESIDENT PARTNERS

Gary C. Huckaby

Patrick H. Graves, Jr.

E. Cutter Hughes, Jr.

G. Rick Hall

Warne S. Heath

RESIDENT ASSOCIATES

Carolyn Reed Douglas

Kimberly A. Bessiere

For Complete List of Firm Personnel, See General Section

For full biographical listings, see the Martindale-Hubbell Law Directory

SPURRIER, RICE, WOOD & HALL (AV)

3226 Bob Wallace Avenue, 35805
Telephone: 205-533-5015
Fax: 205-536-0105

MEMBERS OF FIRM

Donald N. Spurrier

Robert V. Wood, Jr.

Benjamin R. Rice

Ruth Ann Hall

ASSOCIATES

Earl Thomas Forbes

Deborah S. Hensley

G. Douglas Benson

Jonathan B. Medlock

Representative Clients: Alabama Hospital Association Trust Fund; Alfa Insurance Co.; Allstate Insurance Co.; Atlanta Casualty; Auto-Owners Insurance Co.; Balboa Property & Casualty Co.; Bruno's; Casualty Indemnity Exchange; Chubb Group of Insurance Cos.; CIGNA Insurance Cos.

For full biographical listings, see the Martindale-Hubbell Law Directory

MOBILE,* Mobile Co.

ARMBRECHT, JACKSON, DeMOUY, CROWE, HOLMES & REEVES, L.L.C. (AV)

1300 AmSouth Center, P.O. Box 290, 36601
Telephone: 334-405-1300
Facsimile: 334-432-6843; 433-3821

MEMBERS OF FIRM

Rae M. Crowe

Edward A. Dean

Broox G. Holmes, Jr.

Reggie Copeland, Jr.

W. Boyd Reeves

Ray Morgan Thompson

Kirk C. Shaw

Robert J. Mullican

Norman E. Waldrop, Jr.

Wm. Steele Holman II

Grover E. Asmus II

Coleman F. Meador

Douglas L. Brown

James E. Robertson, Jr.

Donald C. Radcliff

Scott G. Brown

M. Kathleen Miller

Clifford C. Brady

Richard W. Franklin

ASSOCIATES

Stephen Russell Copeland

Rodney R. Cate

Representative Clients: American Surety Group (Regional Counsel); Burlington Northern Railroad Co. (District Counsel); Loyal American Life Insurance Co.; Kimberly Clark Corporation; Travelers Insurance Co.; Wausau Insurance Companies.

For Complete List of Firm Personnel, See General Section

For full biographical listings, see the Martindale-Hubbell Law Directory

BRISKMAN & BINION, P.C. (AV)

205 Church Street, P.O. Box 43, 36601
Telephone: 334-433-7600
Fax: 334-433-4485

(See Next Column)

Donald M. Briskman

Christ N. Coumanis

Mack B. Binion

Walter G. (Stoney) Chavers

A List of Representative Clients will be furnished upon request.
References: First Alabama Bank; AmSouth Bank, N.A.; Southtrust Bank of Mobile.

For full biographical listings, see the Martindale-Hubbell Law Directory

COLLINS, GALLOWAY & SMITH (AV)

3263 Cottage Hill Road, P.O. Box 16629, 36616-0629
Telephone: 334-476-4493
Fax: 334-479-5566

MEMBERS OF FIRM

Thomas M. Galloway

Lawrence M. Wettermark

Robert H. Smith

Robert M. Galloway

Thomas M. Galloway, Jr.

Mark J. Everest

ASSOCIATES

Theodore L. Greenspan

Andrew J. Rutens

General Counsel for: Mobile Greyhound Park.
Counsel for: Alfa Mutual Insurance Co.; American States Ins. Co.; Cigna Ins. Co.; County of Mobile.

For full biographical listings, see the Martindale-Hubbell Law Directory

GARDNER, MIDDLEBROOKS, FLEMING & HAMILTON, P.C. (AV)

64 North Royal Street P.O. Drawer 3103, 36652
Telephone: 334-433-8100
Telecopier: 334-433-8181

J. Cecil Gardner

Charles J. Fleming

Sherwood C. Middlebrooks, III

W. Michael Hamilton (Not admitted in AL)

John D. Gibbons

William H. Reece

Christopher E. Krafchak

Mary Elizabeth Olsen

The Continental Insurance Cos.; The Fidelity and Casualty Co. of N.Y.; Canal Insurance Co.; Safeway Insurance Company of Alabama; Honda Motor Co.; Toyota Motor Co., U.S.A.; Bay Equipment Co.; Lyon Properties, Inc.

For full biographical listings, see the Martindale-Hubbell Law Directory

HELMSING, LYONS, SIMS & LEACH, P.C. (AV)

The Laclede Building, 150 Government Street, P.O. Box 2767, 36652
Telephone: 334-432-5521
Telecopy: 334-432-0633

Larry U. Sims

Robert H. Rouse

Champ Lyons, Jr.

Charles H. Dodson, Jr.

Frederick G. Helmsing

Richard E. Davis

John N. Leach, Jr.

Joseph P. H. Babington

Warren C. Herlong, Jr.

John J. Crowley, Jr.

James B. Newman

Joseph D. Steadman

Todd S. Strohmeyer

John Townsend Dukes

William R. Lancaster

P. Bradley Murray

Robin Kilpatrick Fincher

Leslie T. Fields

For full biographical listings, see the Martindale-Hubbell Law Directory

INGE, TWITTY & DUFFY (AV)

1410 First Alabama Bank Building, 56 St. Joseph Street, P.O. Box 1109, 36633
Telephone: 334-433-3200
Facsimile: 334-433-3444

MEMBERS OF FIRM

James J. Duffy, Jr.

James J. Duffy, III

Francis H. Inge (1902-1959)

Thos. E. Twitty (1901-1975)

Richard H. Inge (1912-1980)

For full biographical listings, see the Martindale-Hubbell Law Directory

JANECKY, NEWELL, POTTS, WELLS & WILSON, P.C. (AV)

3300 First National Bank Building, P.O. Box 2987, 36652
Telephone: 334-432-8786
FAX: 334-432-5900
Birmingham, Alabama Office: Suite 3120, AmSouth-Harbert Plaza, 1901 Sixth Avenue North.
Telephone: 205-252-4441.
FAX: 205-252-0320.
Pensacola, Florida Office: Suite 313, 25 West Cedar Street.
Telephone: 904-432-6066.

J. F. (Jack) Janecky

David M. Wilson (Resident, Birmingham Office)

Mark A. Newell

Charles J. Potts

Susan Gunnells Smith

Judson W. Wells

Kevin F. Masterson

(See Next Column)

JANECKY, NEWELL, POTTS, WELLS & WILSON P.C.—*Continued*

Benjamin H. Albritton	Nicholas Wyckoff Woodfield
Michael J. Cohan	(Resident, Birmingham Office)
(Resident, Birmingham Office)	Julie L. Jenkins
Robert Scott Traweek (Resident,	(Not admitted in AL)
Pensacola, Florida Office)	

Representative Clients: Alexis, Inc.; Alabama Forest Products Self Insurance Fund/Association Self Insurers, Inc.; Association Self Insurers Services, Inc.; Alabama Home Builders Self Insurance Fund/Construction Claims Management; Auto-Owners Insurance Co.; Blue Cross and Blue Shield of Alabama; Canal Insurance Co.; Coregis Insurance Co.; Electric Mutual Insurance Co.; Fireman's Fund Insurance Cos.

For full biographical listings, see the Martindale-Hubbell Law Directory

JOHNSTONE, ADAMS, BAILEY, GORDON AND HARRIS, L.L.C. (AV)

Royal St. Francis Building, 104 St. Francis Street, P.O. Box 1988, 36633
Telephone: 334-432-7682
Facsimile: 334-432-2800
Telex: 782040

MEMBERS OF FIRM

Ben H. Harris, Jr.	I. David Cherniak
William H. Hardie, Jr.	David C. Hannan
Joseph M. Allen, Jr.	Wade B. Perry, Jr.
Celia J. Collins	

ASSOCIATES

Tracy P. Turner	Lawrence J. Seiter
W. Andrew Wing, II	

General Counsel for: First Alabama Bank, Mobile; Infirmary Health System/Mobile Infirmary Medical Center/Rotary Rehabilitation Hospital (Multi-Hospital System).
Counsel for: Oil and Gas: Exxon Corp. Business and Corporate: Bell South Telecommunications, Inc.; Aluminum Co. of America; Michelin North America, Inc.; Metropolitan Life Insurance Co.; The Travelers Insurance Cos. Marine: The West of England Ship Owners Mutual Protection and Indemnity Association (Luxembourg); The Standard Steamship Owners' Protection and Indemnity Association (Bermuda) Ltd.

For Complete List of Firm Personnel, See General Section

For full biographical listings, see the Martindale-Hubbell Law Directory

MONTGOMERY,* Montgomery Co.

BEERS, ANDERSON, JACKSON & SMITH, P.C. (AV)

250 Commerce Street, P.O. Box 1988, 36102
Telephone: 334-834-5311
Fax: 334-834-5362
Birmingham, Alabama Office: 2101 6th Avenue North, Suite 701, 35203.
Telephone: 205-254-1958.
Fax: 205-224-3802.

Michael B. Beers	Jeffrey W. Smith
James H. Anderson	Christopher J. Hughes
Micheal S. Jackson	David B. Chancellor
William F. Patty	

OF COUNSEL
D. Patrick Harris

For full biographical listings, see the Martindale-Hubbell Law Directory

BRANTLEY & WILKERSON, P.C. (AV)

405 South Hull Street, P.O. Box 830, 36101-0830
Telephone: 334-265-1500
Fax: 334-265-0319

Paul A. Brantley	Mark D. Wilkerson

Representative Clients: Associated Resources, Inc.; Construction Claims Management, Inc.; Federated Rural Electric Insurance Corp.; Southern Risk Services, Inc.
Reference: South Trust Bank, N.A.

For full biographical listings, see the Martindale-Hubbell Law Directory

GIDIERE & HINTON (AV)

904 Union Bank Building, 60 Commerce Street, 36104
Telephone: 334-834-9950

MEMBERS OF FIRM

Philip S. Gidiere, Jr.	Jack B. Hinton, Jr.
Steven K. Herndon	

Representative Client: The St. Paul Cos.

For full biographical listings, see the Martindale-Hubbell Law Directory

MELTON, ESPY, WILLIAMS & HAYES, P.C. (AV)

301 Adams Avenue, P.O. Drawer 5130, 36103-5130
Telephone: 334-263-6621
Telecopier: 334-263-7252

Oakley Melton, Jr.	James E. Williams
Joseph C. Espy, III	Armstead Lester Hayes III

For full biographical listings, see the Martindale-Hubbell Law Directory

MORROW, ROMINE & PEARSON, P.C. (AV)

122 South Hull Street, P.O. Box 4804, 36103-4804
Telephone: 334-262-7707
Fax: 334-262-7742

Roger S. Morrow	Wesley Romine
Joel H. Pearson	

Representative Clients: Auto Owner's Insurance Co.; Owner's Insurance Co.; Universal Underwriters Insurance Group; Ranger Insurance Co.; Universal Underwriters Life Insurance Co.; Universal Underwriters Service Corp.; Construction Materials Limited, Inc.; Ben Atkinson Motors, Inc.; American Liberty Insurance Co.; Health Services, Inc.

For full biographical listings, see the Martindale-Hubbell Law Directory

NIX, HOLTSFORD & VERCELLI, P.C. (AV)

300 A Water Street, Suite 300, P.O. Box 4128, 36103
Telephone: 334-262-2006
Fax: 334-834-3616

H. E. Nix, Jr.	Charles E. Vercelli, Jr.
Alex L. Holtsford, Jr.	Floyd R. Gilliland
T. Randall Lyons	

Marianne T. Cosse	Phil Collins
Steven A. Higgins	G. Gregory Locklier
David M. Anderson	David P. Stevens

Representative Clients: Auto-Owners Insurance Co.; Alfa Insurance Companies; Crum & Forster; Gay & Taylor; Kemper Group; Ranger Insurance Co.; State Farm Mutual Insurance Companies; United States Fidelity & Guaranty Co.; Wal-Mart Stores; Wausau Insurance Co.

For full biographical listings, see the Martindale-Hubbell Law Directory

WEBB & ELEY, P.C. (AV)

166 Commerce Street, Suite 300, P.O. Box 238, 36101-0238
Telephone: 334-262-1850
Fax: 334-262-1772

James W. Webb	Craig S. Dillard
Michael M. Eley	Daryl L. Masters
Kendrick E. Webb	Bart Harmon
Mary E. Pilcher	

William R. Chandler	Pamela P. Robinson
Frank E. Bankston, Jr.	Shawn Junkins
Kelly Gallops Davidson	Edward Cary Hixon

Representative Clients: American-Amicable Life Insurance Co.; Great American Insurance Co.; Independent Fire Insurance Co.; Connecticut Specialty Insurance Group; Valley Life and Casualty Co.; Lumbermen's Underwriting Alliance; Receivership Estate of Empire Life Insurance Company of America; First Union Mortgage Corp.; Association of County Commissions of Alabama; Woodmen of the World Life Insurance Society.

For full biographical listings, see the Martindale-Hubbell Law Directory

OPELIKA,* Lee Co.

WALKER, HILL, ADAMS, UMBACH, MEADOWS & WALTON (AV)

Walker Building, 205 South 9th Street, P.O. Box 2069, 36803
Telephone: 334-745-6466
Fax: 334-749-2800

MEMBERS OF FIRM

Jacob A. Walker (1889-1973)	Robert T. Meadows, III
Phillip E. Adams, Jr.	Will O. (Trip) Walton, III
Arnold W. Umbach, Jr.	Jacob A. Walker, III

ASSOCIATES

Russell K. Bush	Robbie A. Hyde

OF COUNSEL

Jacob Walker	Hoyt W. Hill

For full biographical listings, see the Martindale-Hubbell Law Directory

OZARK,* Dale Co.

STEAGALL & FILMORE, A PROFESSIONAL CORPORATION (AV)

315 South Union Avenue, P.O. Box 280, 36361
Telephone: 334-774-2501
Fax: 334-445-0848

(See Next Column)

Steagall & Filmore A Professional Corporation, *Ozark—Continued*

Henry B. Steagall, III	William H. Filmore

State Farm Insurance Cos.; Alfa Insurance Cos.; Intergon Insurance Co.; E&O Professionals; Stonewall Insurance Co.; VASA North Atlantic Insurance Co.; American Liberty Insurance Co.

For full biographical listings, see the Martindale-Hubbell Law Directory

---

PELL CITY, St. Clair Co.

BLAIR, HOLLADAY AND PARSONS (AV)

St. Clair Land Title Building, 1711 Cogswell Avenue, 35125
Telephone: 205-884-3440
Fax: 205-884-3442

MEMBERS OF FIRM

A. Dwight Blair	Hugh E. Holladay
Elizabeth S. Parsons	

Representative Clients: Colonial Bank; Metro Bank; Am South Bank; St. Clair Federal Savings Bank; State Farm Mutual Insurance Cos; ALFA Mutual Insurance Co.; Allstate Insurance Cos.; St. Paul Insurance Cos.; Auto Owners Insurance Co.; Reliance Insurance Cos.

For full biographical listings, see the Martindale-Hubbell Law Directory

---

RUSSELLVILLE,* Franklin Co.

FINE & McDOWELL (AV)

507 North Jackson, P.O. Box 818, 35653
Telephone: 205-332-1660
Fax: 205-332-0318

Joe Fine	Daniel G. McDowell

ASSOCIATES

Eddie Beason	John F. Pilati

Representative Clients: Citizens Bank & Savings Co. of Russellville; Citigroup; City of Phil Campbell; Russellville City Board of Education; Franklin County Board of Education; Mutual Savings Life Insurance Co.; State Farm Fire & Casualty Co.; State Farm Mutual Automobile Ins. Co.; Franklin County Board of Commissioners; Marshall Durbin Co.

For full biographical listings, see the Martindale-Hubbell Law Directory

---

TROY,* Pike Co.

CALHOUN, FAULK, WATKINS & CLOWER, L.L.C. (AV)

78 South Court Square, P.O. Box 489, 36081
Telephone: 334-566-7200
Fax: 334-566-7584

Richard F. Calhoun	William Keith Watkins
Joseph E. Faulk	James G. Clower (Retired)

Robert Curry Faircloth

Representative Clients: State Farm Mutual Automobile, Insurance Co.; Hartford Insurance Group; Contheki Insurance Cos.; Aetna Insurance Co.; Travelers Insurance Cos.; Allstate Insurance Co.; Liberty National Life Insurance Co.

For full biographical listings, see the Martindale-Hubbell Law Directory

---

TUSCALOOSA,* Tuscaloosa Co.

DAVIDSON, WIGGINS & CROWDER, P.C. (AV)

2625 Eighth Street, P.O. Box 1939, 35403
Telephone: 205-759-5771
Fax: 205-752-8259

M. McCoy Davidson	A. Courtney Crowder
G. Stephen Wiggins	David Ryan

OF COUNSEL

Hugh W. Roberts, Jr.

Brett Ross

Attorneys for: Canal Insurance Co.; Government Employees Insurance Co.; The Travelers Group; Auto-Owners Insurance Co.; Continental National American Group; Federated Insurance; Lynn Insurance Group; The Trinity Cos.; The PMA Group; Nationwide Ins. Co.; Colonial Ins. Co. of California.

For full biographical listings, see the Martindale-Hubbell Law Directory

PHELPS, JENKINS, GIBSON & FOWLER (AV)

1201 Greensboro Avenue, P.O. Box 020848, 35402-0848
Telephone: 205-345-5100
Fax: 205-758-4394
Fax: 205-391-6658

(See Next Column)

MEMBERS OF FIRM

Sam M. Phelps	Randolph M. Fowler
James J. Jenkins	Michael S. Burroughs
Johnson Russell Gibson, III	C. Barton Adcox
Farley A. Poellnitz	

ASSOCIATES

Karen C. Welborn	Stephen E. Snow
Sandra C. Guin	Thomas W. Davis
Lisa Paul Hodges	M. Kristi Wallace

LEGAL SUPPORT PERSONNEL

Alicia Suzanne Wilson	Ashley D. Sparks
Cathey Raye Hartline	Kimberly Susan Wright

Attorneys for: Aetna Insurance Co.; Allstate Insurance Co.; Carolina Casualty Insurance Co.; Continental Insurance Cos.; Fireman's Fund-American Insurance Cos.; Great American Insurance Co.; Hanover Insurance Co.

For full biographical listings, see the Martindale-Hubbell Law Directory

ZEANAH, HUST, SUMMERFORD, DAVIS & JONES, L.L.C. (AV)

Seventh Floor, AmSouth Bank Building, P.O. Box 1310, 35403
Telephone: 205-349-1383
Fax: 205-391-1319

MEMBERS OF FIRM

Olin W. Zeanah (1922-1987)	Kenneth D. Davis
Wilbor J. Hust, Jr.	Christopher H. Jones
E. Clark Summerford	Beverly A. Smith

OF COUNSEL

Marvin T. Ormond

Representative Clients: Alfa Insurance Cos.; Hartford Insurance Group; Home Insurance Co.; Nationwide Insurance Co.; Alabama Power Co.; Liberty Mutual Insurance Co.; The Uniroyal Goodrich Tire Co.

For full biographical listings, see the Martindale-Hubbell Law Directory

---

ALASKA

ANCHORAGE,* Third Judicial District

DELANEY, WILES, HAYES, GERETY & ELLIS, INC. (AV)

1007 West Third Avenue, Suite 400, 99501
Telephone: 907-279-3581
Fax: 907-277-1331

Daniel A. Gerety	James B. Friderici
Clay A. Young	Howard A. Lazar
William E. Moseley	Donald C. Thomas
Timothy J. Lamb	

Representative Clients: Continental Insurance Co.; Liberty Northwest; Maryland Insurance Group; Royal Globe Insurance Co.; The Doctors Company; Norcal Mutual Insurance Co.; HealthCare Indemnity Co.; Medical Insurance Exchange of California; Lutheran Health Systems; Great American Insurance Company.

For Complete List of Firm Personnel, See General Section

For full biographical listings, see the Martindale-Hubbell Law Directory

---

ARIZONA

FLAGSTAFF,* Coconino Co.

ASPEY, WATKINS & DIESEL, P.L.L.C. (AV)

123 North San Francisco, 3rd Floor, 86001
Telephone: 520-774-1478
Facsimile: 520-774-8404
Sedona, Arizona Office: 120 Soldier Pass Road.
Telephone: 520-282-5955.
Facsimile: 520-282-5962.
Page, Arizona Office: 904 North Navajo.
Telephone: 520-645-9694.
Cottonwood, Arizona Office: 2400 E. Highway 89A, Suite C.
Telephone: 520-639-1881.
Facsimile: 520-639-0272.

MEMBERS OF FIRM

Frederick M. Fritz Aspey	Donald H. Bayles, Jr.
Harold L. Watkins	Kaign N. Christy
Louis M. Diesel	John J. Dempsey
Bruce S. Griffen	Zachary J. Markham

James E. Ledbetter	Roger M. Baeurle
Whitney Cunningham	Amy E. Mabius
Pernell Whynn McGuire	Stephen A. Thompson
Joel E. Sannes	

(See Next Column)

ASPEY, WATKINS & DIESEL P.L.L.C.—*Continued*

LEGAL SUPPORT PERSONNEL

Karla H. Falls, CLAS
(Legal Assistant)
Rocky C. Nissen (Paralegal
Assistant, Sedona, Arizona
Office)
Deborah D. Roberts, CLA
(Legal Assistant)

Dominic M. Marino, Jr,
(Paralegal Assistant)
Carrie R. Flynn (Litigation
Paralegal, Cottonwood,
Arizona Office)

Representative Clients: Farmer's Insurance Company of Arizona; Pepsi-Cola Bottling Company of Northern Arizona; Bill Luke's Chrysler-Plymouth, Inc.; First American Title Insurance Company; Transnation Title Insurance Co.; Page Electric Utility; Comprehensive Access Health Plan, Inc.; Northern Arizona Healthcare Corporation.
Reference: First Interstate Bank-Arizona, N.A., Flagstaff, Arizona.

For full biographical listings, see the Martindale-Hubbell Law Directory

---

MANGUM, WALL, STOOPS & WARDEN, P.L.L.C. (AV)

222 East Birch Avenue, P.O. Box 10, 86002
Telephone: 520-779-6951
Fax: 520-773-1312

H. Karl Mangum (1908-1993)

OF COUNSEL

Douglas J. Wall   Robert W. Warden

MEMBERS OF FIRM

Daniel J. Stoops   Stephen K. Smith
A. Dean Pickett   Melinda L. Garrahan

ASSOCIATES

Deborah M. Fine   David L. Anderson
Michael H. Hinson

Representative Clients: Northern Arizona University; Flagstaff Unified School District; Museum of Northern Arizona; City of Sedona; Arizona School Board Association.
Local Counsel for: Bank of America-Arizona; Arizona Public Service; U.S.A.A.; State Farm Fire & Casualty Ins. Co.; Insurance Company of the West.

For Complete List of Firm Personnel, See General Section

For full biographical listings, see the Martindale-Hubbell Law Directory

---

*PHOENIX,** Maricopa Co.

BESS & DYSART, P.C. (AV)

7210 North 16th Street, 82020-5201
Telephone: 602-331-4600
Telecopier: 602-331-8600

Leon D. Bess   Timothy R. Hyland
Robert L. Dysart   William M. Demlong
Donald R. Kunz   Matthew D. Kleifield

Stephanie L. Chilton   Donald J. Sapala

For full biographical listings, see the Martindale-Hubbell Law Directory

---

BONNETT, FAIRBOURN, FRIEDMAN & BALINT, P.C. (AV)

4041 North Central Avenue Suite 1100, 85012
Telephone: 602-274-1100
Fax: 602-274-1199

William G. Fairbourn   Robert J. Spurlock
C. Kevin Dykstra

For full biographical listings, see the Martindale-Hubbell Law Directory

---

MICHAEL E. BRADFORD (AV)

4131 North 24th Street Building C Suite 201, 85016
Telephone: 602-955-0088
FAX: 602-955-6445

LEGAL SUPPORT PERSONNEL
Sandra M. Simcox
OF COUNSEL
Jerry Steele

For full biographical listings, see the Martindale-Hubbell Law Directory

---

BROENING, OBERG, WOODS, WILSON & CASS, P.C. (AV)

1122 East Jefferson Street, P.O. Box 20527, 85036
Telephone: 602-271-7700
Telecopier: 602-258-7785
Email: aznvlaw@indirect.com *URL:* http://www.azlvlaw.com
Las Vegas, Nevada Office: 3930 Howard Hughes Parkway, Suite 200, 89109.
Telephone: 702-893-3383.
Fax: 702-893-3789.

(See Next Column)

James R. Broening   Cynthia van R. Cheney
Terrence P. Woods   Gary A. Fadell
John W. Oberg   Douglas G. Shook
Donald Wilson, Jr.   Mary B. Wilson
V. Andrew Cass   Bruce M. Preston
Kenneth C. Miller   Robert M. Moore
Neal B. Thomas   James G. McElwee, Jr.
Wesley S. Loy   David S. Shughart, III
Michael M. Haran   Marilyn D. Cage
Jerry T. Collen   John P. Robertson, II
David S. Cohen

Clark V. Vellis   Bethanne Klopp-Bryant
(Resident, Las Vegas, Nevada)   (Resident, Las Vegas, Nevada)
Katherine M. Barrett   Jeffrey H. Ballin
(Resident, Las Vegas, Nevada)   (Resident, Las Vegas, Nevada)
Mark G. Henness   Arleen N. Kaizer
(Resident, Las Vegas, Nevada)   (Resident, Las Vegas, Nevada)
Riley A. Clayton   Hayley B. Chambers
(Resident, Las Vegas, Nevada)   (Resident, Las Vegas, Nevada)
James W. Howard, Jr.

OF COUNSEL

Kevin T. Ahern   Richard E. Chambliss
Donald J. Newman

Representative Clients: Chubb Group of Insurance Cos.; Farmers Insurance Group; Home Insurance Co.; Ohio Casualty Insurance Group; St. Paul Fire and Marine Insurance Companies.

For full biographical listings, see the Martindale-Hubbell Law Directory

---

BROWDER & KENNEY, P.C. (AV)

1202 East Missouri Avenue Suite 200, 85014
Telephone: 602-264-6666
FAX: 602-264-6968

Robert W. Browder   Edward A. Kenney

Representative Clients: National Crane Corp.; Wausau Insurance Cos.; Harnischfeger Corp.; New England Insurance Co.; Consolidated Aluminum Corp.; Century-National Insurance Co.; Worldwide Insurance Co.; Koehring Cranes & Excavators; Grove Worldwide.
Reference: Bank One.

For full biographical listings, see the Martindale-Hubbell Law Directory

---

BURCH & CRACCHIOLO, P.A. (AV)

702 East Osborn Road, Suite 200, 85014
Telephone: 602-274-7611
Fax: 602-234-0341
Mailing Address: P.O. Box 16882, Phoenix, AZ, 85011

Brian Kaven   F. Michael Carroll
Daniel R. Malinski

Theodore (Todd) Julian

Representative Clients: Bashas' Inc.; Farmers Insurance Group; U-Haul International, Inc.

For Complete List of Firm Personnel, See General Section

For full biographical listings, see the Martindale-Hubbell Law Directory

---

CHARLES T. CARSON (AV)

3200 North Central Avenue Suite 1130, 85012
Telephone: 602-230-8819
Fax: 602-230-1335

For full biographical listings, see the Martindale-Hubbell Law Directory

---

COHEN MCGOVERN SHORALL & STEVENS, P.C. (AV)

2828 North Central Avenue, Suite 1210, 85004-1022
Telephone: 602-230-5400
Fax: 602-230-5432

Larry J. Cohen   Thomas J. Shorall, Jr.
Thomas P. McGovern   Don C. Stevens, II

Penny Taylor Moore   Scott M. Zerlaut
Lisa K. Hudson   Leslie J. Cuevas
Lynn M. Allen

Representative Clients: Aetna; Atlantic Mutual; Allstate; Northbrook; Great American; Travelers; Transamerica; State of Arizona.

For full biographical listings, see the Martindale-Hubbell Law Directory

---

COPPLE, CHAMBERLIN & BOEHM, P.C. (AV)

Suite 300 The Brookstone, 2025 North Third Street, 85004
Telephone: 602-528-4700
Fax: 602-253-4909

(See Next Column)

COPPLE, CHAMBERLIN & BOEHM P.C., *Phoenix—Continued*

Steven D. Copple
Thomas J. Chamberlin
Scott E. Boehm
Robert S. Murphy

OF COUNSEL
Frederick O. Robertshaw

Representative Clients: Aetna Casualty & Surety Co.; Verco Manufacturing Co.

For full biographical listings, see the Martindale-Hubbell Law Directory

CRONIN & STANEWICH (AV)

One Columbus Plaza, 3636 North Central Avenue, Suite 560, 85012
Telephone: 602-222-4646
Fax: 602-222-4656

MEMBERS OF FIRM

Robert S. Cronin, Jr.
Robert B. Stanewich

For full biographical listings, see the Martindale-Hubbell Law Directory

DOHERTY & VENEZIA, A PROFESSIONAL CORPORATION (AV)

100 West Clarendon, Suite 1720, 85013
Telephone: 602-277-1585
Fax: 602-277-1182

Julie A. Doherty
Stephen M. Venezia

For full biographical listings, see the Martindale-Hubbell Law Directory

DOYLE, WINTHROP, OBERBILLIG & WEST, P.C. (AV)

2800 North Central Avenue Suite 1550, 85004
Telephone: 602-240-6711
Fax: 602-240-6951
Mailing Address: P.O. Box 10417, Phoenix, Arizona, 85064-0417

William H. Doyle
Angila L. Gallenstein

For full biographical listings, see the Martindale-Hubbell Law Directory

FENNEMORE CRAIG, A PROFESSIONAL CORPORATION (AV)

Two North Central, Suite 2200, 85004
Telephone: 602-257-8700
Fax: 602-257-8527
Scottsdale, Arizona Office: 6263 North Scottsdale Road, Suite 290, 85250.
Telephone: 602-257-5400.
Fax: 602-257-5409.
Tucson, Arizona Office: One South Church Avenue, Suite 1030, 85701.
Telephone: 520-791-6800.
Fax: 520-791-6820.

Kenneth J. Sherk
John D. Everroad
William L. Thorpe
Phillip F. Fargotstein
Kaye L. McCarthy
William T. Burghart
Andrew M. Federhar

Jean Marie Sullivan
Douglas C. Northup
Marc H. Lamber

For Complete List of Firm Personnel, See General Section

For full biographical listings, see the Martindale-Hubbell Law Directory

HARRIS & PALUMBO, A PROFESSIONAL CORPORATION (AV)

361 East Coronado, Suite 101, P.O. Box 13568, 85002-3568
Telephone: 602-271-9344
Fax: 602-252-2099

John David Harris
Kevin W. Keenan
Gene M. Cullan
Frank I. Powers
Shawn M. Cunningham

OF COUNSEL
Anthony J. Palumbo

For full biographical listings, see the Martindale-Hubbell Law Directory

HOLLOWAY ODEGARD & SWEENEY, P.C. (AV)

3101 North Central Avenue, Suite 1200, 85012
Telephone: 602-240-6670
Telefax: 602-240-6677

Paul W. Holloway
Sally A. Odegard
Kevin B. Sweeney
Ruth Franklin
Peter C. Kelly
Gil Shuga
Jacqueline D. Hoyt

OF COUNSEL
Joseph C. Dolan
Charles M. Callahan

For full biographical listings, see the Martindale-Hubbell Law Directory

JENNINGS, STROUSS AND SALMON, P.L.C. (AV)

A Professional Limited Liability Company
One Renaissance Square, Two North Central, 85004-2393
Telephone: 602-262-5911
Fax: 602-253-3255

T. Patrick Flood
W. Michael Flood
Gary L. Stuart
Barry E. Lewin
Jay A. Fradkin
H. Christian Bode
Jon D. Schneider
Michael J. O'Connor
Katherine M. Cooper
Charles D. Onofry

Jennifer M. Bligh
Kim D. Steinmetz
Cody M. Hall
Lisa A. Frey

For Complete List of Firm Personnel, See General Section

For full biographical listings, see the Martindale-Hubbell Law Directory

MARK & PEARLSTEIN, P.A. (AV)

Suite 150 The Brookstone, 2025 North Third Street, 85004
Telephone: 602-257-0200
Fax: 602-271-4711

Leonard J. Mark
Mr. Lynn M. Pearlstein

OF COUNSEL
Stephen G. Campbell

For full biographical listings, see the Martindale-Hubbell Law Directory

MICHAEL L. McALLISTER, LTD. (AV)

2025 North Third Street Suite 100, 85004
Telephone: 602-253-8840
Telefax: 602-253-5526

Michael L. McAllister

Representative Clients: Allianz Insurance Group; Arizona State Compensation Fund; Crum Forester Managers Group; Liberty Mutual Company; Willis/Corroon.

For full biographical listings, see the Martindale-Hubbell Law Directory

MITTEN, GOODWIN & RAUP, A PROFESSIONAL CORPORATION (AV)

One Columbus Plaza, 3636 North Central, Suite 1200, 85012
Telephone: 602-650-2000
Fax: 602-264-7033
Email: mgr@starlink.com

Roger C. Mitten
Brian M. Goodwin
Calvin L. Raup
Edward R. Glady, Jr.
Stephen C. Yost
Martin P. Clare
Scott J. Hergenroether

Steven P. Kramer
Sharon Elizabeth Ravenscroft
Jeffery S. Slater
Gary Beren
Jeffrey J. Campbell

OF COUNSEL
Richard M. Davis

For full biographical listings, see the Martindale-Hubbell Law Directory

MUCHMORE & WALLWORK, A PROFESSIONAL CORPORATION (AV)

2700 North Central Avenue, Suite 1225, 85004-1165
Telephone: 602-240-6699
Data: 602-240-6698
Facsimile: 602-240-6697
Email: muchwork@mmww.com *URL:* http://www.mmww.com

Charles J. Muchmore
Nicholas J. Wallwork

COUNSEL
Margaret M. Dean
Fredric D. Bellamy
Kathy E. Shimpock

Bridget S. Bade
(Senior Associate)
Carolina L. Carver
Margaret Benny Hurst

LEGAL SUPPORT PERSONNEL
Gloria A. Torres (Administrator and Senior Paralegal)
John A. Bennett (Litigation Support Manager)
Gale James (Finance Manager and Paralegal)

Representative Clients: AgrEvo USA Company; BHP Copper Inc.; City of Scottsdale; Cyprus Amax Minerals Company; General Electric Co.; Homes by Dave Brown, Inc.; National Indemnity Insurance Company; Standard Insurance Company; Washington Mills Electro Minerals Company.
Reference: M & I Thunderbird Bank.

For full biographical listings, see the Martindale-Hubbell Law Directory

Phoenix—Continued

O'CONNOR, CAVANAGH, ANDERSON, KILLINGSWORTH & BESHEARS, A PROFESSIONAL ASSOCIATION (AV)

One East Camelback Road, Suite 1100, 85012-1656
Telephone: 602-263-2400
FAX: 602-263-2900
Email: firminfo@arizlaw.com
Sun City, Arizona Office: 13250 North Del Webb Boulevard, Suite B, 85351.
Telephone: 602-263-2808.
FAX: 602-933-3100.
Tucson, Arizona Office: O'Connor Cavanagh Molloy Jones, 33 N. Stone, Suite 2100, 85701, P.O. Box 2268, 85702.
Telephone: 520-622-3531.
FAX: 520-624-2816.
Nogales, Arizona Office: 1891 North Mastick Way, 85621.
Telephone: 520-761-4215.
FAX: 520-761-3505.

Harry J. Cavanagh	Scott A. Salmon
Robert G. Beshears	David L. Kurtz
Ralph E. Hunsaker	Paul J. Giancola
George H. Mitchell	Pamela M. Overton
Richard J. Woods	Frank M. Fox
Carol N. Cure	Lisa M. Sommer
Lucas J. Narducci	

Robert L. Ehmann	R. Corey Hill
Troy B. Froderman	

Ashley D. Adams	Mark D. Dillon
Carla A. Wortley	Frank W. Moskowitz
Carl O. Wortley, III	Steven J. German
Eric A. Mark	

Representative Clients: State Farm; Liberty Mutual; The Home; The Hartford; CNA; TIG (formerly Transamerica); Reliance; Mutual Insurance Company of Arizona.

For Complete List of Firm Personnel, See General Section

For full biographical listings, see the Martindale-Hubbell Law Directory

PERRY, PIERSON & SILVER, P.L.C. (AV)

2901 North Central Avenue Suite 300, 85012
Telephone: 602-285-5165
Facsimile: 602-285-5100

Allan R. Perry	Timothy L. Pierson
Leon B. Silver	

For full biographical listings, see the Martindale-Hubbell Law Directory

PLATTNER VERDERAME, P.C. (AV)

333 East Osborn, Suite 315, 85012-2365
Telephone: 602-266-2002
Fax: 602-266-6908

Richard S. Plattner	Frank Verderame

Randall A. Hinsch	David A. Thomson
Laurence G. Tinsley, Jr.	

Representative Clients: Paradigm Insurance Company.

For full biographical listings, see the Martindale-Hubbell Law Directory

RAYMOND, GREER & SASSAMAN, P.C. (AV)

3003 North Central, Suite 1902, 85012
Telephone: 602-274-0500
Fax: 602-265-7560

Randy L. Sassaman	Leonard D. Greer
Michael J. Raymond	

OF COUNSEL

Mark J. Moryl

For full biographical listings, see the Martindale-Hubbell Law Directory

RENAUD, COOK & DRURY, P.A. (AV)

617 North 2nd Avenue, 85003
Telephone: 602-253-5101
Fax: 602-254-1448
Email: rcdlaw@rcdlaw.com
Scottsdale, Arizona Office: 6991 East Camelback Road, #D-103, 85251.
Telephone: 602-874-9000.
Fax: 602-874-9866.

J. Gordon Cook	James L. Blair
William W. Drury, Jr.	Steven G. Mesaros
Charles A. Struble	

(See Next Column)

W. Lloyd Benner	Charles S. Hover, III
Wade R. Causey	Diane Mihalsky
Richard N. Crenshaw	Tamara D. Nydell

For full biographical listings, see the Martindale-Hubbell Law Directory

RHEES & HOPKINS (AV)

100 West Clarendon Suite 710, 85013
Telephone: 602-263-6010
Fax: 602-263-6016

Michael L. Rhees	Stephen M. Hopkins
Richard B. Murphy	

For full biographical listings, see the Martindale-Hubbell Law Directory

RIDENOUR, SWENSON, CLEERE & EVANS, P.C. (AV)

40 North Central Avenue, Suite 1400, 85004
Telephone: 602-254-2143
Fax: 602-254-8670

Harold H. Swenson	Michael J. Frazelle
James W. Evans	John W. Storer, III
Robert R. Beltz	Joseph A. Kendhammer
Lloyd J. Andrews	Peter S. Spaw

Scott A. Holden	Roger W. Riviere
Lee P. Blake	

Representative Clients: State Farm Insurance Co.; Cincinnati Insurance Co.; Travelers Insurance Co.; American National Insurance Co.; Allstate Insurance Co.; Geico; TIG Insurance Co.; St. Paul Fire & Marine Insurance Co.; G.A.B. Business Systems; Economy Insurance Co.

For full biographical listings, see the Martindale-Hubbell Law Directory

ROBBINS & GREEN, A PROFESSIONAL ASSOCIATION (AV)

1800 Norwest Tower, 3300 North Central Avenue, 85012-9826
Telephone: 602-248-7600
Fax: 602-266-5369

Philip A. Robbins	William H. Sandweg III
Richard W. Abbuhl	Brian Imbornoni
Dwayne Ross	

For Complete List of Firm Personnel, See General Section

For full biographical listings, see the Martindale-Hubbell Law Directory

SHIMMEL, HILL, BISHOP & GRUENDER, P.C. (AV)

3700 North 24th Street, 85016
Telephone: 602-224-9500
Telecopier: 602-955-6176

Daniel F. Gruender	Scott J. Richardson

OF COUNSEL

Charles A. Finch

Representative Clients: AZ Property & Casualty Guaranty Fund; GAB Business Services; Liberty Mutual Insurance Co.; Rushmore National Life Insurance Co.; Prairie State Life Insurance Co.

For full biographical listings, see the Martindale-Hubbell Law Directory

LAW OFFICES OF RICHARD L. STROHM, P.C. (AV)

1136 East Campbell, 85014
Telephone: 602-279-6316
Mobile: 602-616-7094
Facsimile: 602-279-7102
Email: 102442.1444@compuserve.com

Richard L. Strohm

OF COUNSEL

Brad K. Keogh	Nedra J. Bates

LEGAL SUPPORT PERSONNEL

Mindy L. Raymond	Barbara A. Shore
(Legal Assistant)	(Nurse Paralegal)
Richard M. Knaeble	
(Licensed Private Investigator)	

Representative Clients: Alamo Car Rental Inc.; State of Arizona; BancPlus Mortgage Co; Maricopa County (Metropolitan Phoenix); Ryder Truck Rental; The Trammell Crow Companies; Barnett Bank.

For full biographical listings, see the Martindale-Hubbell Law Directory

STRUCKMEYER AND WILSON (AV)

910 East Osborn Road, 85014
Telephone: 602-248-9222
Fax: 602-263-0464

(See Next Column)

STRUCKMEYER AND WILSON, *Phoenix—Continued*

Donald R. Wilson	Fred C. Struckmeyer, Jr.
	(1912-1992)

ASSOCIATES

Charles E. Fleury	Stephen W. Tully
William G. Caravetta	Kent J. Hammond
John P. Kaites	Donald R. House

Representative Clients: American International Group; Commercial Union Cos.; Fireman's Fund American Insurance Cos.; Granite States Insurance Co.; Horace Mann Insurance Cos.; United States Fidelity and Guaranty Co.; Zurich Insurance Co.; Ohio Casualty; Jewelers Mutual Insurance; National Union Fire Insurance Co.

For full biographical listings, see the Martindale-Hubbell Law Directory

THOMAS & ELARDO, P.C. (AV)

2700 North Central Avenue, Suite 1500, 85004
Telephone: 602-274-8289
Fax: 602-285-4482

Benjamin C. Thomas	John A. Elardo

Mark Carl Brachtl	David C. Hauschild
Laura Rogers	Matthew J. Devlin
	Martin A. Bihn

Representative Clients: Alexsis Risk Management Services; Allied Group Ins.; Allstate Ins. Co.; American States Ins. Co.; Atlanta Casualty Ins. Co.; California Casualty Ins. Co.; CIGNA; CNA; Constitution State Management Co.; Continental Loss Adjustment Co.

For full biographical listings, see the Martindale-Hubbell Law Directory

TURLEY & SWAN, P.C. (AV)

The Brookstone Office Complex, 2025 North Third Street, Suite 350, 85004-1471
Telephone: 602-254-1444
Fax: 602-229-1936

Albert R. Vermeire (1947-1988)	Christopher J. Bork
Kent E. Turley	Christopher M. O'Donnell
Joseph B. Swan, Jr.	Elizabeth Savoini Fitch
	Thomas J. Howard

For full biographical listings, see the Martindale-Hubbell Law Directory

PRESCOTT, * Yavapai Co.

FAVOUR, MOORE & WILHELMSEN, A PROFESSIONAL ASSOCIATION (AV)

1580 Plaza West Drive, P.O. Box 1391, 86302
Telephone: 520-445-2444
Fax: 520-771-0450

John M. Favour	Mark M. Moore
	David K. Wilhelmsen

Representative Clients: Employers Mutual Co.; Lawyers Title Insurance Co.; Farmers Insurance Group; Equity General Insurance Co.; Central Life Assurance Co.; Equity Fire and Casualty Co.; Economy Fire & Casualty Co.

For full biographical listings, see the Martindale-Hubbell Law Directory

SCOTTSDALE, Maricopa Co.

GROSSMAN, O'GRADY & McGOLDRICK, P.C. (AV)

5040 East Shea Boulevard Suite 168, 85254
Telephone: 602-948-9424
Fax: 602-948-9425

Jill H. Grossman	Evan S. Goldstein
Paul J. McGoldrick	Keith B. Forsyth

Sanford K. Gerber

OF COUNSEL

Michael J. O'Grady

For full biographical listings, see the Martindale-Hubbell Law Directory

TUCSON, * Pima Co.

CHANDLER, TULLAR, UDALL & REDHAIR (AV)

1700 Bank of America Plaza, 33 North Stone Avenue, 85701
Telephone: 520-623-4353
Telefax: 520-792-3426

(See Next Column)

MEMBERS OF FIRM

Thomas Chandler	Dwight M. Whitley, Jr.
D. B. Udall	E. Hardy Smith
Jack Redhair	John J. Brady
Joe F. Tarver, Jr.	Christopher J. Smith
Steven Weatherspoon	Charles V. Harrington
Edwin M. Gaines, Jr.	Bruce G. MacDonald
	Christopher C. Browning

ASSOCIATES

Joel T. Ireland	Kurt Kroese
Mark Fredenberg	Sean C. Chapman
Mariann T. Shinoskie	Anne M. Fulton

Representative Clients: Arizona Electric Power Cooperative, Inc.; CNA Insurance; Farmers Insurance Exchange; Mutual Insurance Company of Arizona; The Travelers Insurance Co.; Transamerica Insurance Co.; Chubb Group of Insurance Co.; National Aviation Underwriters; St. Paul Insurance Co.; State Farm Mutual Insurance Cos.

For full biographical listings, see the Martindale-Hubbell Law Directory

DUFFIELD, MILLER, YOUNG, ADAMSON & ALFRED, P.C. (AV)

Suite 711, Transamerica Building, 177 North Church Avenue, 85701
Telephone: 520-792-1181
FAX: 520-792-2859
Green Valley, Arizona Office: 101-65 South La Canada, Green Valley Mall.
Telephone: 520-625-4404.
Fax: 520-625-4453.
La Paloma Office: La Paloma Corporate Center, 3573 East Sunrise Drive, Suite 115, Tucson, Arizona.
Telephone: 520-577-1135.
Fax: 520-577-1079.

Philip Hawley Smith	Thomas R. Althaus
Arthur H. Miller (1935-1995)	Richard Duffield
Larry R. Adamson	Eugene C. Gieseler
Samuel D. Alfred	K. Alexander Hobson
	Michael C. Young

LEGAL SUPPORT PERSONNEL

Cynthia Sargent Althaus	Joan Shelton, CLA
Mary Jane Arnesen	Christine M. Smith
Katrina Hillman	Barbara L. Steimle
Elizabeth Kohl-Sturgeon	Elaine Webb

Representative Clients: San Xavier Rock & Materials; Community Water Company of Green Valley.
Insurance Company Clientele: State Farm Mutual Insurance Cos.; Automobile Club Insurance Co.; Colonial Penn Insurance Co.; Metropolitan Property & Liability Insurance Co.; National Indemnity Ins. Co.

For full biographical listings, see the Martindale-Hubbell Law Directory

GOERING, ROBERTS, BERKMAN, RUBIN & BROGNA, P.C. (AV)

Suite 302, 1840 East River Road, 85718
Telephone: 520-577-9300
Fax: 520-577-0848

Scott Goering	David L. Berkman
Howard T. Roberts, Jr.	William L. Rubin
	Carmine A. Brogna

Christopher L. Enos

Representative Clients: Fireman's Fund Insurance; Safeco Insurance; Royal Insurance; Sentry Insurance; American International Group; Farmers Insurance; USAA; Country Companies; Cigna.
Reference: Bank One.

For full biographical listings, see the Martindale-Hubbell Law Directory

HAZLETT & WILKES (AV)

310 South Williams Boulevard, Suite 305, 85711
Telephone: 520-790-9663
Fax: 520-790-9616

MEMBERS OF FIRM

Carl E. Hazlett	James M. Wilkes

ASSOCIATE

Thomas M. Bayham

For full biographical listings, see the Martindale-Hubbell Law Directory

KIMBLE, GOTHREAU & NELSON, P.C. (AV)

5285 East Williams Circle, Suite 3500, 85711-7411
Telephone: 520-748-2440
Fax: 520-748-2469

Michael J. Gothreau (1943-1990)	David F. Toone
Darwin J. Nelson	Michelle T. Lopez
Daryl A. Audilett	Negatu Molla
Lawrence McDonough	Michael E. Medina
	Andrew J. Petersen

(See Next Column)

KIMBLE, GOTHREAU & NELSON P.C.—*Continued*
OF COUNSEL
William Kimble

Representative Clients: State of Arizona; General Motors Corp.; Procter & Gamble Co.; St. Paul Fire and Marine Insurance Co.; City of Tucson; Tucson Electric Power Co.; United States Fidelity & Guaranty Co.; Coriegis Co.; Allstate Insurance Co.

For full biographical listings, see the Martindale-Hubbell Law Directory

LESHER & LESHER, A PROFESSIONAL CORPORATION (AV)

3773 East Broadway, 85716
Telephone: 520-795-4800
Telefax: 520-325-7609

Stephen H. Lesher   Robert O. Lesher

Representative Clients: Associated Aviation Underwriters; Empire Fire and Marine Insurance Co.; Merck and Co., Inc.; Underwriters at Lloyd's, London.

For full biographical listings, see the Martindale-Hubbell Law Directory

O'CONNOR CAVANAGH MOLLOY JONES, A PROFESSIONAL ASSOCIATION (AV)

Suite 2100 33 N. Stone, P.O. Box 2268, 85702
Telephone: 520-622-3531
FAX: 520-624-2816
Email: firminfo@arizlaw.com
Phoenix, Arizona Office: O'Connor, Cavanagh, Anderson, Killingsworth & Beshears, One East Camelback Road, Suite 1100, 85012.
Telephone: 602-263-2400.
FAX: 602-263-2900.
Sun City, Arizona Office: O'Connor, Cavanagh, Anderson, Killingsworth & Beshears, 13250 North Del Webb Boulevard, Suite B, 85351.
Telephone: 602-263-2808.
FAX: 602-933-3100.
Nogales, Arizona Office: O'Connor, Cavanagh, Anderson, Killingsworth & Beshears, 1891 North Mastick Way, 85621.
Telephone: 520-761-4215.
FAX: 520-761-3505.

Peter Akmajian   Drue A. Morgan-Birch

Amy M. Samberg   James D. Campbell

Representative Clients: Three-Five Systems; Main Street & Main; ITT Cannon; Bank of America; The Dial Corp; The Hartford; Dow Corning Corp.; Charles Schwab & Co., Inc.

For Complete List of Firm Personnel, See General Section

For full biographical listings, see the Martindale-Hubbell Law Directory

RABINOVITZ & ASSOCIATES, P.C. (AV)

721 North 4th Avenue, P.O. Box 41600, 85717
Telephone: 520-624-5526
Toll Free: 1-800-365-0821
Fax: 520-622-3776

Bernard I. Rabinovitz

John D. Ellis
OF COUNSEL
Clark J. Sloan (Not admitted in AZ)
LEGAL SUPPORT PERSONNEL
Michael Nelson (Paralegal)   Lisa Busciglio (Paralegal)
Ruth Polizz

Representative Client: Firemans Fund Insurance Co.

For full biographical listings, see the Martindale-Hubbell Law Directory

*YUMA,** Yuma Co.

CLARK & CARTER (AV)

256 South Second Avenue, 85364
Telephone: 520-783-6233
Fax: 520-783-0533

MEMBERS OF FIRM
A. James Clark   Rick K. Carter
ASSOCIATE
Heather D. Burgess

For full biographical listings, see the Martindale-Hubbell Law Directory

ARKANSAS

*BATESVILLE,** Independence Co.

GREGG, HART & FARRIS (AV)

262 Boswell Street, P.O. Box 2496, 72501
Telephone: 501-793-7556
Fax: 501-793-6921

MEMBERS OF FIRM
John C. Gregg   Josephine Linker Hart
Phillip B. Farris

For full biographical listings, see the Martindale-Hubbell Law Directory

*BENTON,** Saline Co.

ELLIS LAW FIRM (AV)

126 North Main Street, P.O. Box 1259, 72015
Telephone: 501-776-3916; Little Rock: 375-5210
Fax: 501-776-2278
Email: ellislaw@aol.com
Email: 76403.507@compuserve.com

MEMBER OF FIRM
George D. Ellis
LEGAL SUPPORT PERSONNEL
Rhonda Beck Malone (Paralegal)

References: The Union Bank of Benton; Benton State Bank.

For full biographical listings, see the Martindale-Hubbell Law Directory

*BLYTHEVILLE,** Mississippi Co.

REID, BURGE, PREVALLET & COLEMAN (AV)

417 North Broadway, P.O. Box 107, 72316-0107
Telephone: 501-763-4586
Fax: 501-763-4642

MEMBERS OF FIRM
Max B. Reid (1895-1959)   Richard A. Reid
Dan M. Burge   Donald E. Prevallet
Robert Lynn Coleman

Counsel for: Farmers Bank and Trust Co.; Arkansas Power & Light Co.; Bush Canning Co.; Allstate Insurance Cos.; Farmers Insurance Group; Wausau Insurance Cos.; United States Fidelity & Guaranty Co.; State Farm Cos.; Hartford Group.

For full biographical listings, see the Martindale-Hubbell Law Directory

*FAYETTEVILLE,** Washington Co.

DAVIS, COX & WRIGHT, PLC (AV)

19 East Mountain Street, P.O. Drawer 1688, 72702-1688
Telephone: 501-521-7600
Fax: 501-521-7661

Sidney P. Davis, Jr.   William Jackson Butt, II
Walter B. Cox   Kelly P. Carithers
Tilden P. Wright, III   Tim E. Howell
Constance G. Clark   Don A. Taylor
                 Paul H. Taylor

John G. Trice   Mark W. Dossett
Laura J. Andress   David L. McCune

For full biographical listings, see the Martindale-Hubbell Law Directory

JONES, JONES & LUSHBAUGH, PLC (AV)

112 South East Street, 72701
Telephone: 501-443-4313, 443-2021
Fax: 501-575-0528
Email: gjones@intellinet.com

Lewis D. Jones   Gregory D. Jones
Bradley H. Lushbaugh

Representative Clients: Allstate Insurance Co.; The Home Insurance Co.; Horace Mann Insurance Co.; Miller's Mutual Fire Insurance Co.; The Firemen's Insurance Companies; Countrywide Insurance Group; AM Family Insurance Co.; Boatman's National Bank of Northwest Arkansas.
Approved Attorneys for: Lawyers Title Insurance Co.
Reference: Boatman's National Bank of Northwest Arkansas.

For full biographical listings, see the Martindale-Hubbell Law Directory

*FORREST CITY,** St. Francis Co.

BUTLER, HICKY & LONG (AV)

2216 North Washington Street, P.O. Box 989, 72335
Telephone: 501-633-4611
FAX: 501-633-6848

(See Next Column)

BUTLER, HICKY & LONG, *Forrest City—Continued*

MEMBERS OF FIRM

Philip Hicky	Fletcher Long, Jr.

ASSOCIATES

Gary J. Mitchusson	Rita Reed Harris

Representative Clients: First National Bank of Eastern Arkansas; Southern Farm Bureau Insurance Cos.; United States Aviation Underwriters Group; National Aviation Underwriters; Hartford Accident and Indemnity Co.; Peoples Implement Co.

For full biographical listings, see the Martindale-Hubbell Law Directory

---

FORT SMITH,* Sebastian Co.

HARDIN, DAWSON & TERRY (AV)

Suite 500, Superior Federal Tower, 5000 Rogers Avenue, P.O. Box 10127, 72917-0127
Telephone: 501-452-2200
FAX: 501-452-9097

MEMBERS OF FIRM

G. C. Hardin (1884-1964)	Robert M. Honea
P. H. Hardin	J. Leslie Evitts III
Robert T. Dawson	J. Rodney Mills
Rex M. Terry	Kirkman T. Dougherty
	J. Gregory Magness

Counsel for: Superior Federal Bank, FSB; The Kansas City Southern Railway Co.; KFSM-TV; Johnson & Johnson; ASARCO Inc.; Allstate Insurance Co.; Southern Farm Bureau Insurance Co.; CIGNA, General Accident; State Automobile Insurance Co.; Silvey Co.

For full biographical listings, see the Martindale-Hubbell Law Directory

---

JONES, JACKSON & MOLL, PLC (AV)

401 North Seventh Street, P.O. Box 2023, 72902
Telephone: 501-782-7203
Fax: 501-782-9460
Email: jjmlaw@aol.com

MEMBERS OF FIRM

Robert L. Jones, Jr.	Kendall B. Jones
Randolph C. Jackson	Mark A. Moll
	J. Scott Hardin

Insurance Counsel for: Farmers Insurance Group; State Farm Insurance Cos.; Maryland Insurance Cos.; Shelter Insurance Cos.; Travelers Insurance Co.; CNA Insurance Co.; Automobile Club Insurance Cos.
Counsel for: Merchants National Bank, Fort Smith, Arkansas; Beverly Enterprises, Inc.; Austin Powder Co.

For full biographical listings, see the Martindale-Hubbell Law Directory

---

SHAW, LEDBETTER, HORNBERGER, COGBILL & ARNOLD (AV)

South Seventh and Parker, P.O. Box 185, 72902-0185
Telephone: 501-782-7294
FAX: 501-782-1493

Bruce H. Shaw (1904-1990)	Richard B. Shaw (1927-1988)

MEMBERS OF FIRM

Charles R. Ledbetter	James A. Arnold, II
Robert E. Hornberger	Ronald D. Harrison
J. Michael Cogbill	E. Diane Graham
	R. Ray Fulmer, II

ASSOCIATE

Rebecca D. Hattabaugh

OF COUNSEL

J. Michael Shaw

Representative Clients: First National Bank of Fort Smith; Bank of Mansfield; Commercial Bank at Alma; Mid-South Dredging Co.
Local Attorneys for: Liberty Mutual Insurance Co.; St. Paul Insurance Cos.; Fireman's Fund Ins. Co.; American Physicians Insurance Exchange; CIGNA Ins. Co.; Canal Insurance Co.

For full biographical listings, see the Martindale-Hubbell Law Directory

---

JONESBORO,* Craighead Co.

BARRETT & DEACON (AV)

Union Planters Bank Building, 300 South Church Street, P.O. Box 1700, 72403
Telephone: 501-931-1700
FAX: 501-931-1800

MEMBERS OF FIRM

Joe C. Barrett (1897-1980)	David W. Cahoon
John C. Deacon	Ralph W. Waddell
J. Barry Deacon	Paul D. Waddell
	D. Price Marshall, Jr.

(See Next Column)

ASSOCIATES

James D. Bradbury	Kevin W. Cole
	Anita S. Perkins

For full biographical listings, see the Martindale-Hubbell Law Directory

---

PENIX, PENIX, LUSBY AND NIX (AV)

401 South Main Street, P.O. Box 1306, 72403-1306
Telephone: 501-932-7449
Fax: 501-933-7281

MEMBERS OF FIRM

Roy Penix (1891-1978)	Bill Penix
Marian F. Penix (1924-1991)	Richard A. Lusby
	J. Robin Nix, II

Representative Clients: American Policyholders Ins. Co.; CIGNA Cos.; Liberty Mutual Insurance Co.; Sentry and Dairyland Insurance Co.; American General Life & Accident.

For full biographical listings, see the Martindale-Hubbell Law Directory

---

SNELLGROVE, LASER, LANGLEY, LOVETT & CULPEPPER (AV)

Second Floor, 111 East Huntington, P.O. Box 1346, 72403-1346
Telephone: 501-932-8357
Fax: 501-932-5488

MEMBERS OF FIRM

G. D. Walker (1910-1989)	Glenn Lovett, Jr.
Frank Snellgrove, Jr.	Malcolm Culpepper
David N. Laser	D. Todd Williams
Stanley R. Langley	Michael E. Mullally
	P. Sanders Huckabee

Representative Clients: Union Planters Bank of Northeast Arkansas (formerly Mercantile Bank); First Bank of Arkansas; Travelers Insurance Co.; Aetna Insurance Co.; ITT Hartford Insurance Co.; Commercial Union Insurance Co.; CNA Insurance Group; State Farm Insurance Cos.; Columbia Mutual Insurance Co.; Bituminous Insurance Co.

For full biographical listings, see the Martindale-Hubbell Law Directory

---

WOMACK, LANDIS, PHELPS, MCNEILL & MCDANIEL, A PROFESSIONAL ASSOCIATION (AV)

Century Center, Washington at Madison, P.O. Box 3077, 72403
Telephone: 501-932-0900
Fax: 501-932-2553

Tom D. Womack	John V. Phelps
Carl David Landis	Paul D. McNeill
	Lucinda McDaniel

Brant Perkins	Jeffrey W. Puryear
Donald L. Parker II	Mark Alan Mayfield
	David Christopher Gardner

Representative Clients: Arkansas State University; Bank of Trumann; E.C. Barton & Co.; Kraft General Foods Corp.; Home Indemnity Company of N.Y.; St. Paul Insurance Cos.; Shelter Insurance Co.; United States Fidelity & Guaranty Co.

For full biographical listings, see the Martindale-Hubbell Law Directory

---

LITTLE ROCK,* Pulaski Co.

ALLEN LAW FIRM, A PROFESSIONAL CORPORATION (AV)

950 Centre Place, 212 Center Street, 72201
Telephone: 501-374-7100
Telecopier: 501-374-1611
Email: hwallen@cei.net

H. William Allen

Sandra E. Jackson

Representative Clients: Colonia Insurance Company; Shoney's, Inc.

For full biographical listings, see the Martindale-Hubbell Law Directory

---

ANDERSON & KILPATRICK (AV)

The First Commercial Building, 400 West Capitol Avenue, Suite 2640, 72201
Telephone: 501-372-1887
Fax: 501-372-7706
Email: ande@cei.net

MEMBERS OF FIRM

Overton S. Anderson, II	Aylmer Gene Williams
Joseph E. Kilpatrick, Jr.	Randy P. Murphy
Michael E. Aud	Mariam T. Hopkins

ASSOCIATES

Michael P. Vanderford	Penny Brown Wilbourn
	C. Timothy Spainhour

For full biographical listings, see the Martindale-Hubbell Law Directory

Little Rock—Continued

BARBER, McCASKILL, AMSLER, JONES & HALE, P.A. (AV)

2700 First Commercial Building, 400 West Capitol Avenue, 72201-3414
Telephone: 501-372-6175
Telecopier: 501-375-2802

Azro L. Barber (1885-1979)	Richard C. Kalkbrenner
Elbert A. Henry (1889-1966)	G. Spence Fricke
John B. Thurman (1912-1971)	Gail Ponder Gaines
Austin McCaskill, Sr.	Michael J. Emerson
Guy Amsler, Jr.	R. Kenny McCulloch
Glenn W. Jones	Tim A. Cheatham
Michael E. Hale	Joseph F. Kolb
John S. Cherry, Jr.	Scott Michael Strauss
Robert L. Henry, III	Derek J. Edwards
Micheal L. Alexander	Thomas E. Osment, Jr.
William H. Edwards, Jr.	Christopher Gomlicker

Attorneys for: Associated Aviation Underwriters; Canal Insurance Co.; Fireman's Fund Insurance Co.; General Motors Corp.; General Motors Acceptance Corp.; Hanover Insurance Co.; Home Insurance Co.; Royal Insurance; United States Fidelity & Guaranty Co.; Universal Underwriters Insurance Co.

For full biographical listings, see the Martindale-Hubbell Law Directory

FRIDAY, ELDREDGE & CLARK (AV)

A Partnership including Professional Associations
Formerly, Smith, Williams, Friday, Eldredge & Clark
2000 First Commercial Building, 400 West Capitol Avenue, 72201-3493
Telephone: 501-376-2011
Telecopier: 501-376-2147; 376-6369
Email: fecmh@fec.sprint.com

MEMBERS OF FIRM

William H. Sutton (P.A.)	William Mell Griffin III, (P.A.)
Frederick S. Ursery (P.A.)	Kevin A. Crass (P.A.)
John Dewey Watson (P.A.)	William A. Waddell, Jr., (P.A.)
J. Phillip Malcom (P.A.)	Scott J. Lancaster (P.A.)
James M. Simpson, Jr., (P.A.)	James C. Baker (P.A.)
Donald H. Bacon (P.A.)	Scott H. Tucker (P.A.)
Barry E. Coplin (P.A.)	Guy Alton Wade (P.A.)
Elizabeth Robben Murray (P.A.)	J. Michael Pickens (P.A.)
Laura Hensley Smith (P.A.)	Tonia P. Jones (P.A.)
David D. Wilson (P.A.)	

ASSOCIATES

Gregory D. Taylor	Betty J. Demory
Fran C. Hickman	Will Bond
Clifford W. Plunkett	

Counsel for: Union Pacific System; St. Paul Insurance Co.; Liberty Mutual Insurance Co.; Cigna Property & Casualty Co.; Arkansas Power & Light Co.; Dillard Department Stores, Inc.; First Commercial Corp.; Browning Arms Co.; Phillips Petroleum Co.; Aetna Casualty & Surety Co.

For Complete List of Firm Personnel, See General Section

For full biographical listings, see the Martindale-Hubbell Law Directory

HUCKABAY, MUNSON, ROWLETT & TILLEY, P.A. (AV)

First Commercial Building, Suite 1900, 400 West Capitol, 72201
Telephone: 501-374-6535
Fax: 501-374-5906

Mike Huckabay	John E. Moore
Bruce E. Munson	Tim Boone
Beverly A. Rowlett	Rick Runnells
James W. Tilley	Sarah Ann Presson
Edward T. Oglesby	

D. Michael Huckabay, Jr.	Elizabeth Fletcher Rogers
Carol Lockard Worley	Julia L. Busfield
Mark S. Breeding	Jane M. Yocum
Terry D. Dugger	

Representative Clients: Allstate Insurance Company; American International Group; Farmers Insurance Group; General Electric Company; Nationwide Insurance Company; Safeco Insurance Company; State Farm Mutual Automobile Insurance Company; State Farm Fire and Casualty Company; Tenet Healthcare Corp.; United States Fidelity and Guaranty Company.

For full biographical listings, see the Martindale-Hubbell Law Directory

LASER, WILSON, BUFFORD & WATTS, P.A. (AV)

101 S. Spring Street, Suite 300, 72201-2488
Telephone: 501-376-2981
Telecopier: 501-376-2417

(See Next Column)

Sam Laser	Walter A. Kendel, Jr.
Richard N. Watts	Brian A. Brown
Kevin J. Staten	Karen J. Hughes
Alfred F. Angulo, Jr.	Gena Gregory
David M. Donovan	Keith Martin McPherson
Thomas J. Diaz	

Representative Clients: Allstate Insurance Co.; American International Insurance Group; Continental Insurance Cos.; Farm Bureau Insurance Cos. (Casualty & Fire); Farmers Insurance Group; GAB Business Services, Inc.; St. Paul Insurance Cos.; Scottsdale Insurance Co.; State Farm Auto (Fire) Insurance Cos.

For Complete List of Firm Personnel, See General Section

For full biographical listings, see the Martindale-Hubbell Law Directory

ROSE LAW FIRM, A PROFESSIONAL ASSOCIATION (AV)

120 East Fourth Street, 72201
Telephone: 501-375-9131
Telecopy: 501-375-1309

Jerry C. Jones	Richard T. Donovan
David L. Williams	James H. Druff
James Hunter Birch	Amy Lee Stewart

COUNSEL
Phillip Carroll

Representative Clients: The Equitable Life Assurance Society of the United States; Bridgestone/Firestone, Inc.; CIGNA Companies; Georgia-Pacific Corp.; General Motors Corp.; John Hancock Mutual Life Insurance Co.; Kemper Insurance Group; New York Life Insurance Co.; The Prudential Insurance Company of America; USX Corp.

For Complete List of Firm Personnel, See General Section

For full biographical listings, see the Martindale-Hubbell Law Directory

SPRINGDALE, Washington Co.

ROY & LAMBERT (AV)

2706 South Dividend Drive, P.O. Drawer 7030, 72766-7030
Telephone: 501-756-8510
Fax: 501-756-8562

MEMBERS OF FIRM

James M. Roy, Jr.	Robert J. Lambert, Jr.

ASSOCIATES

Jerry L. Lovelace	Jon P. Robinson
Brian D. Wood	James H. Bingaman

OF COUNSEL
John D. Copeland

Representative Clients: State Farm Mutual Automobile Insurance Co.; State Farm Fire and Casualty Co.; Shelter Mutual Insurance Co.; Silvey Insurance Companies; Columbia Mutual Insurance Co.; State Volunteer Mutual Insurance Co.; Farmers Insurance Group; Springdale Bank & Trust; 4-State Poultry Supply, Inc.; Commerce Construction Co.

For full biographical listings, see the Martindale-Hubbell Law Directory

WEST MEMPHIS, Crittenden Co.

RIEVES & MAYTON (AV)

304 East Broadway, P.O. Box 1359, 72303
Telephone: 501-735-3420
Telecopier: 501-735-4678

MEMBERS OF FIRM

Elton A. Rieves, Jr. (1909-1984)	Michael R. Mayton
Elton A. Rieves, III	Elton A. Rieves, IV
Martin W. Bowen	

ASSOCIATES

William Terrell Smith, Jr.	David S. Wilson, III

For full biographical listings, see the Martindale-Hubbell Law Directory

CALIFORNIA

BAKERSFIELD,* Kern Co.

ROBINSON, PALMER & LOGAN (AV)

Suite 150, 3434 Truxtun Avenue, 93301
Telephone: 805-323-8277
Fax: 805-323-4205

MEMBERS OF FIRM

Oliver U. Robinson	William D. Palmer
Gary L. Logan	

(See Next Column)

ROBINSON, PALMER & LOGAN, *Bakersfield—Continued*

ASSOCIATES

Luke A. Foster   Marshall S. Fontes

For full biographical listings, see the Martindale-Hubbell Law Directory

BERKELEY, Alameda Co.

BURESH, KAPLAN, JANG, FELLER & AUSTIN (AV)

2298 Durant Avenue, 94704
Telephone: 510-548-7474
Fax: 510-548-7488

Scott Buresh   Steven K. Austin
Ann S. Kaplan   Gina Dashman Boer
Alan J. Jang   Peggy Chang
Fred M. Feller   Daniel L. Cook
                Noël Sidney Plummer

For full biographical listings, see the Martindale-Hubbell Law Directory

BEVERLY HILLS, Los Angeles Co.

HERZOG, FISHER & GRAYSON, A LAW CORPORATION (AV)

9460 Wilshire Boulevard Fifth Floor, 90212
Telephone: 310-278-4300
Fax: 310-278-5430

James P. Herzog   David R. Fisher
                Michael A. Grayson

Pamela M. Rosenthal   Eric M. Rosin
                OF COUNSEL
                Todd I. Grayson

For full biographical listings, see the Martindale-Hubbell Law Directory

WILNER, KLEIN & SIEGEL, A PROFESSIONAL CORPORATION (AV)

Suite 700, 9601 Wilshire Boulevard, 90210
Telephone: 213-272-8631; 310-550-4595
Facsimile: 213-272-4339
Brea, California Office: 3230 East Imperial Highway, Suite 309.
Telephone: 714-579-2600.
Facsimile: 714-579-2549.

Walter Klein   Wendy A. Goldberg
Samuel Wilner   Jodi Zucker Taksar
Leonard Siegel   Edward E. Wallace
Laura J. Snoke   Alan Goldberg
                Joseph R. Serpico

Gary S. Kessler   Patrick M. Malone
Marc H. Goldsmith   Nora J. Hite
Floyd W. Cranmore   Mitchell S. Brachman
Teri E. Lawson   Stephen Coopersmith
Edwin J. Howard   Neil M. Popowitz
Thomas M. Ware, II   Jeffrey W. Deane
Joshua B. Bereny   Steven J. Parker
James P. Dexheimer   (Resident, Brea Office)
Eric S. Blum   Darrell J. Mariz
  (Resident, Brea Office)

                OF COUNSEL
Allan E. Wilion, Inc.   Michael J. Grobaty
Richard B. Kott   (Resident, Brea Office)
  (Resident, Brea Office)

Reference: Mitsui Manufacturers Bank.

For full biographical listings, see the Martindale-Hubbell Law Directory

BURBANK, Los Angeles Co.

MARRONE ROBINSON FREDERICK & FOSTER, PROFESSIONAL CORPORATION (AV)

111 North First Street, Suite 300, 91502-1851
Telephone: 818-841-1144
Fax: 818-841-0746

Phillip R. Marrone   J. Alan Frederick
Jay Robinson   Thomas A. Foster
                Robert Boon

Dennis P. De Franzo   James Fitzgerald Robinson
Gary D. Ellington   John F. Schilling
Scot G. Sandoval   Katherine P. Shannon
Kathryn M. Loock   Karen B. Goldberg
Peter Y. Lee   Donald M. Stone
                Douglas Fee

Representative Clients: Collier-Keyworth Co.; Columbia Pictures Industries, Inc.; Fireman's Insurance of Washington, D.C.; Holiday Inn, Inc.; MCA; Inc.; National Continental Insurance Co.; Textron, Inc.

(See Next Column)

For full biographical listings, see the Martindale-Hubbell Law Directory

BURLINGAME, San Mateo Co.

WINTERS, KRUG & DELBON (AV)

345 Lorton Avenue, Suite 204, 94010-4116
Telephone: 415-579-1422
Fax: 415-579-1852

MEMBERS OF FIRM

William L. Nagle   David A. Delbon
John S. Krug   Cheryl A. Noll
Daniel W. Winters   Jerry E. Nastari
                David F. Zucca

Representative Clients: State Farm Mutual Automobile Insurance Co.; State Farm Fire & Casualty Co.; Fireman's Fund Insurance Cos.; Tokio Marine Management Co.; California State Automobile Assn.; Chubb Group of Insurance Cos.; Argonaut Insurance Co.; Aviation Office of America; Cities of: Burlingame, Half Moon Bay, South San Francisco and San Carlos; Towns of Hillsborough and Woodside.

For full biographical listings, see the Martindale-Hubbell Law Directory

CHICO, Butte Co.

CRAIG AND SHEPHERD (AV)

Suite 1, 1367 East Lassen Avenue, P.O. Box 658, 95927-0658
Telephone: 916-893-3700
Fax: 916-893-1579

MEMBERS OF FIRM

Maynard C. Craig   Michael T. Shepherd
                ASSOCIATES
Bruce S. Alpert   Richard L. Crabtree

For full biographical listings, see the Martindale-Hubbell Law Directory

COSTA MESA, Orange Co.

ELY, FRITZ & HOGAN (AV)

3100 Bristol Street #200, 92626
Telephone: 714-556-1480
Telecopier: 714-556-2863

MEMBERS OF FIRM

Thomas W. Ely   Michael G. Hogan
James H. Fritz   Jerome D. Rybarczyk

Charles A. Correia   Ronald F. Templer
                Allen D. MacNeil
                OF COUNSEL
                Gerald W. Mouzis

For full biographical listings, see the Martindale-Hubbell Law Directory

DANVILLE, Contra Costa Co.

CRADDICK, CANDLAND & CONTI, PROFESSIONAL CORPORATION (AV)

Danville-San Ramon Medical Center, 915 San Ramon Valley Boulevard, Suite 260, 94526-0810
Telephone: 510-838-1100
Fax: 510-743-0729

Marrs A. Craddick   Judy S. Craddick
D. Stuart Candland   Robert W. Hodges
Richard J. Conti   W. David Walker
                Robert W. Lamson

Phillip J. Maddux   Michael J. Garvin
Jean Louise Perry   Diane C. Miller
                Steven L. Brown, Jr.

For full biographical listings, see the Martindale-Hubbell Law Directory

EL SEGUNDO, Los Angeles Co.

McGARRY & LAUFENBERG (AV)

300 North Sepulveda Boulevard, Suite 2294, 90245
Telephone: 310-335-1780
Fax: 310-335-1790

MEMBERS OF FIRM

James J. McGarry   Jeffrey J. Laufenberg
                William Leamon Cummings
                ASSOCIATES
Daniel D. Laufenberg   John E. Zegel

For full biographical listings, see the Martindale-Hubbell Law Directory

ENCINO, Los Angeles Co.

SPILE & SIEGAL, LLP (AV)

Formerly, Krivis, Spile and Siegal, LLP
16501 Ventura Boulevard Suite 610, 91436
Telephone: 818-784-6899
Facsimile: 818-784-0176
Email: fsiegal@counsel.com

Steven D. Spile	Floyd J. Siegal

ASSOCIATES

Andrew L. Leff	Michael P West

OF COUNSEL

David I. Karp	Olga M. Moretti
Jeffrey L. Krivis	David M. Galanti
Richard R. Leuthold	

For full biographical listings, see the Martindale-Hubbell Law Directory

STAITMAN, SNYDER & TANNENBAUM (AV)

Suite 1401, 16633 Ventura Boulevard, 91436-1840
Telephone: 818-981-5300; 213-872-3530
FAX: 818-981-7104

Jack M. Staitman	Jack J. Tannenbaum
Bradley A. Snyder	David K. Dorenfeld

Rodger S. Greiner	Gerald P. Peters
Deborah K. Galer	

For full biographical listings, see the Martindale-Hubbell Law Directory

STONE & ROSENBLATT, A PROFESSIONAL CORPORATION (AV)

16133 Ventura Boulevard Suite 855, 91436
Telephone: 818-789-2232
Fax: 818-789-2269

Ira H. Rosenblatt	Gregory E. Stone

Camille Calvert	Richard S. McGuire
Adam J. Soibelman	

For full biographical listings, see the Martindale-Hubbell Law Directory

EUREKA, * Humboldt Co.

JANSSEN, MALLOY, MARCHI, NEEDHAM & MORRISON (AV)

730 Fifth Street, P.O. Drawer 1288, 95501
Telephone: 707-445-2071
Fax: 707-445-8305

MEMBERS OF FIRM

Clayton R. Janssen	Michael F. Malloy
Nicholas R. Marchi	Michael W. Morrison
W. Timothy Needham	

ASSOCIATE

Catherine M. Koshkin

Counsel for: Clinic Mutual Insurance Co.; TRW, Inc.; U.S. Bank; The Travelers Insurance Co.; General Hospital; Pacific Bell; Reichhold Chemicals, Inc.; Safeco Insurance Companies of America; Lawyers Mutual Insurance Co.

For full biographical listings, see the Martindale-Hubbell Law Directory

MITCHELL, BRISSO, DELANEY & VRIEZE (AV)

814 Seventh Street, P.O. Drawer 1008, 95502
Telephone: 707-443-5643
Fax: 707-444-9586

MEMBERS OF FIRM

Clifford B. Mitchell	Paul A. Brisso
Nancy K. Delaney	John M. Vrieze
C. Todd Endres	

ASSOCIATES

William F. Mitchell	Cherie L. Evans
Russell Scott Gans	

RETIRED PARTNER

Robert C. Dedekam

Representative Clients: California Automobile Assn.; State Farm; Allstate; Fireman's Fund; Hartford; Travelers; Wausau; Viking; Nationwide; Redwood Empire Municipal Insurance Fund.

For full biographical listings, see the Martindale-Hubbell Law Directory

FRESNO, * Fresno Co.

DOWLING, AARON & KEELER, INCORPORATED (AV)

Suite 200, 6051 North Fresno Street, 93710
Telephone: 209-432-4500
Fax: 209-432-4590
Email: dowling-law.com

Philip David Kopp	Francine Marie Kanne

Richard E. Heatter	James C. Sherwood

Reference: Wells Fargo Bank (Main).

For Complete List of Firm Personnel, See General Section

For full biographical listings, see the Martindale-Hubbell Law Directory

PARICHAN, RENBERG, CROSSMAN & HARVEY, LAW CORPORATION (AV)

Suite 130, 2350 West Shaw Avenue, P.O. Box 9950, 93794-0950
Telephone: 209-431-6300
Fax: 209-432-1018

Harold A. Parichan	Stephen T. Knudsen
Charles L. Renberg	Larry C. Gollmer
Richard C. Crossman	Robert G. Eliason
Ima Jean Harvey	Steven M. McQuillan

Deborah A. Coe	Karen L. Lynch
Maureen P. Holford	Michael L. Renberg

Reference: Bank of America, Commercial Banking Office, Fresno, California.

For full biographical listings, see the Martindale-Hubbell Law Directory

STAMMER, McKNIGHT, BARNUM & BAILEY (AV)

2540 West Shaw Lane, Suite 110, P.O. Box 9789, 93794-9789
Telephone: 209-449-0571
Fax: 209-432-2619

W. H. Stammer (1891-1969)	Frank D. Maul
James K. Barnum (1918-1987)	Craig M. Mortensen
Dean A. Bailey (1924-1995)	Jerry D. Jones
Galen McKnight (1904-1991)	Michael P. Mallery
James N. Hays	M. Bruce Smith
Carey H. Johnson	Thomas J. Georgouses

ASSOCIATES

Steven R. Stoker	Bruce J. Berger
M. Jaqueline Yates	Celene M.E. Boggs

Representative Clients: The Travelers Insurance Group; State Farm Insurance Cos.; Farmers Insurance Group; Grocers Insurance Company; Golden Eagle Insurance Company.
Reference: Bank of America Trust & Savings Assn. (Fresno Main Office).

For full biographical listings, see the Martindale-Hubbell Law Directory

GLENDALE, Los Angeles Co.

HAGENBAUGH & MURPHY (AV)

A Partnership including Professional Corporations
700 North Central Avenue, Suite 500, 91203
Telephone: 818-240-2600
Fax: 818-240-1253
Email: hmurphy@interserv.com *URL:* http://www.seamless.com/hm/
Orange County, California Office: 701 South Parker Street, Suite 8200, Orange.
Telephone: 714-835-5406.
Fax: 714-835-5949.
San Bernardino, California Office: 301 Vanderbilt Way, Suite 220.
Telephone: 909-884-5331.
FAX: 909-889-1250.

Van A. Hagenbaugh (1914-1980)	Daniel A. Leipold (Resident, Orange County Office)
Sigurd E. Murphy (1903-1976)	
William D. Stewart (A P.C.)	Craig D. Aronson
John J. Tary (A P.C.)	Paul G. Szumiak
Raymond R. Moore (A P.C.)	Robert F. Donohue (Resident, Orange County Office)
Neil R. Gunny (Resident, Orange County Office)	
Alan R. Zuckerman	Katharine L. Spaniac (Resident, San Bernardino Office)
David L. Winter	Alan H. Boon (Resident, Orange County Office)
Mary E. Porter	

Jamie B. Skebba

Raymond T. Gail (Resident, San Bernardino Office)	Steven M. Schuetze
Kirk G. Neiberger	Thomas J. Heatly
Meredith A. Musicant	Matthew R. Rungaitis
David M. Chute (Resident, Orange County Office)	Stephen Barry
Luanne Walsh	Julie M. DeRose
Rhonda L. Etzwiler	Randal A. Whitecotton (Resident, San Bernardino Office)

(See Next Column)

HAGENBAUGH & MURPHY, *Glendale—Continued*

Cathy L. Shipe (Resident, Orange County Office)	Melinda W. Ebelhar
Keri Lynn Bush	Kirk N. Sullivan
Michael A. Tonya	Gary P. Simonian
Laura C. McLennan	Mark Habeeb
Graciela L. Freixes	Howard J. Hirsch (Resident, Orange County Office)

Michelle Mann

Representative Clients: Farmers Insurance Group; Truck Insurance Exchange; Fire Insurance Exchange.

For full biographical listings, see the Martindale-Hubbell Law Directory

THOMAS & PRICE (AV)

535 North Brand Boulevard, 7th Floor, 91203
Telephone: 213-387-4800; 818-500-4800
FAX: 818-500-4822
Ventura, California Office: 1655 Mesa Verde Avenue, Suite 230.
Telephone: 805-642-6255.
Fax: 805-642-4580.

MEMBERS OF FIRM

Michael Thomas	Craig R. Donahue
Bonnie R. Louis	Maureen F. Thomas

ASSOCIATES

John P. DeGomez	Christian E. Sanne
Timothy A. Hodge	Benjimin M. Brees
Linda B. Hurevitz	Janet L. Keuper

Kevin M. McCormick

OF COUNSEL

Lawrence E. Price

For full biographical listings, see the Martindale-Hubbell Law Directory

IRVINE, Orange Co.

ANDRADE & MUZI (AV)

Marine National Bank Building, 18401 Von Karman, Suite 350, 92715
Telephone: 714-553-1951
Telecopier: 714-553-0655
San Diego, California Office: Tokia Bank Building, 3111 Camino Del Rio North, Suite 1100.
Telephone: 619-291-2481.

MEMBERS OF FIRM

Richard B. Andrade	Abilio Tavares, Jr.
Andrew C. Muzi	Samuel G. Broyles, Jr.
Ronald G. Holbert	Frank A. Satalino

OF COUNSEL

Kurt Kupferman

American International Cos.; American Home Assurance; Insurance Company of North America (INA); National Union Fire Insurance of Pittsburgh, PA.; Aetna Insurance Co.; Fremont Insurance Co.; Maryland Casualty; Commercial Union Insurance Co.; Superior National Insurance Co.; Lloyds of London.

For full biographical listings, see the Martindale-Hubbell Law Directory

GAUNTLETT & ASSOCIATES (AV)

18400 Von Karman, Suite 300, 92612
Telephone: 714-553-1010
Fax: 714-553-2050
Email: ugauntlett@aol.com

David A. Gauntlett

David A. Stall	Elizabeth A. Gillis (Not admitted in CA)
Leo E. Lundberg, Jr.	
Michael Danton Richardson	Mark H. Plager (Not admitted in CA)
William P. Warden	
Stanley H. Shure	Jeffrey S. Allison

OF COUNSEL

Gary L. Hinman	Jose Zorrilla, Jr.

For full biographical listings, see the Martindale-Hubbell Law Directory

MOWER, KOELLER, NEBEKER, CARLSON & HALUCK (AV)

108 Pacifica, P.O. Box 19799, 92713-9799
Telephone: 714-753-1229
Fax: 714-753-1413
San Bernardino, California Office: 412 West Hospitality Lane, Suite 300, 92408.
Telephone: 909-381-3334.
Fax: 909-889-2007.
San Diego, California Office: 225 Broadway, 21st Floor.
Telephone: 619-233-1600.
Fax: 619-236-0527.
Yuma, Arizona Office: 212 South 2nd Avenue, P.O. Bin 11791.
Telephone: 520-782-2531.
Fax: 520-782-5319.

(See Next Column)

MEMBERS OF FIRM

Jon R. Mower	Patrick A. Carreon
Keith D. Koeller	Lynn M. Bouslog
William L. Haluck	Edward W. Schmitt
Joseph J. Cullen	Ellen E. Hunter

Nancy J. Altman	Ferdinand M. Trampe
Mark D. Newcomb	James A. Burton
Terrence J. Giannone	Eric W. Smith

Steven G. Holett

For full biographical listings, see the Martindale-Hubbell Law Directory

PIVO & HALBREICH (AV)

1920 Main Street, Suite 800, 92714
Telephone: 714-253-2000

Kenneth R. Pivo	Douglas A. Amo
Eva S. Halbreich	Richard O. Schwartz

Mona Z. Hanna

ASSOCIATES

Charles A. Palmer	Michael A. Brodie
William J. Mall, III	Lance Gordon Greene
Kathleen E. Wilcox	Annie Glass Henshel
Timothy J. Lippert	Jennifer Batliner

Representative Clients: Physicians and Surgeons Underwriters Corp.; Fremont Indemnity; American Continental Insurance Co.; AKROS Medico Enterprises; Kaiser Foundation Healthplan, Inc.; Caronia Corp.; The Doctor's Co.; Harbor Regional Center; Developmental Disabilities Regional Center; South Central Los Angeles Regional Center.

For full biographical listings, see the Martindale-Hubbell Law Directory

WESIERSKI & ZUREK (AV)

Suite 1500, 5 Park Plaza, 92714
Telephone: 714-975-1000
Telecopier: 714-756-0517
Glendale, California Office: 800 North Brand Boulevard, Suite 250.
Telephone: 818-543-6100.
Telecopier: 818-543-6101.

PARTNERS

Christopher P. Wesierski	Terence P. Carney
Ronald Zurek (Resident, Glendale Office)	Thomas G. Wianecki
	Stephen M. Ziemann
Daniel J. Ford, Jr.	Mark E. Brubaker

ASSOCIATES

Christopher M. Fisher	Steven D. Turner
Mark J. Giannamore	Robert M. Binam
Paul J. Lipman	Diane E. Jacobs
David F. Mastan	Bruce V. Rorty

For full biographical listings, see the Martindale-Hubbell Law Directory

LA JOLLA, San Diego Co.

LAW OFFICES OF MAURILE C. TREMBLAY A PROFESSIONAL CORPORATION (AV)

4180 La Jolla Village Drive, Suite 210, 92037
Telephone: 619-558-3030
FAX: 619-558-2502

Maurile C. Tremblay	Mark D. Estle

For full biographical listings, see the Martindale-Hubbell Law Directory

LARKSPUR, Marin Co.

WEINBERG, HOFFMAN & CASEY (AV)

A Partnership including a Professional Corporation
900 Larkspur Landing Circle, Suite 155, 94939
Telephone: 415-461-9666
Fax: 415-461-9681

Ivan Weinberg	Joseph Hoffman

A. Michael Casey

OF COUNSEL

Mark Ropers

For full biographical listings, see the Martindale-Hubbell Law Directory

LONG BEACH, Los Angeles Co.

BENNETT & KISTNER (AV)

115 Pine Avenue, Suite 600, 90802-4446
Telephone: 310-435-6675
Fax: 310-437-8375

Charles J. Bennett	Wayne T. Kistner

Richard R. Bradbury

ASSOCIATE

Charles H. Smith

(See Next Column)

BENNETT & KISTNER—*Continued*

OF COUNSEL
Christopher Johns

Representative Clients: The Hertz Corp.; Mattel, Inc.; Di Salvo Trucking Co.; Long Beach Community Medical Center; Los Angeles County Metropolitan Transportation Authority; Long Beach Memorial Medical Center; Saddleback Memorial Medical Center; Utah Home Fire Insurance; P.C.H. Enterprise, Inc.
Reference: Ken Walker of Farmers & Merchants Bank, Long Beach, California.

FISHER & PORTER, A LAW CORPORATION (AV)

110 Pine Avenue, 11th Floor, P.O. Box 22686, 90801-5686
Telephone: 310-435-5626
Telex: 284549 FPKLAW UR
Fax: 310-432-5399

Gerald M. Fisher   Therese G. Groff
David S. Porter   Michael W. Lodwick
George P. Hassapis

OF COUNSEL
Stephen C. Klausen   Stephen Chace Bass
Anthony P. Lombardo

Vicki L. Hassman   Michael J. McLaughlin
Linda A. Mancini   Sandra L. Gryder
Kenneth F. Mattfeld

For full biographical listings, see the Martindale-Hubbell Law Directory

---

FLYNN, DELICH & WISE (AV)

One World Trade Center, Suite 1800, 90831-1800
Telephone: 310-435-2626
Fax: 310-437-7555
San Francisco, California Office: Suite 1750, 580 California Street.
Telephone: 415-693-5566.
Fax: 415-693-0410.

Erich P. Wise   Nicholas S. Politis

Representative Clients: American Hawaii Cruises; Holland America Line; Through Transport Mutual Insurance Association, Ltd.; The Britannia Steam Ship Insurance Association Limited; The Steamship Mutual Underwriting Association (Bermuda) Ltd.; General Steamship Corp., Ltd.; Commodore Cruise Line, Ltd.; Interocean Steamship Corporation; Sea-Land Service, Inc.; Hatteras Yachts.

For full biographical listings, see the Martindale-Hubbell Law Directory

---

FORD, WALKER, HAGGERTY & BEHAR, PROFESSIONAL LAW CORPORATION (AV)

One World Trade Center, Twenty Seventh Floor, 90831
Telephone: 310-983-2500
Telecopier: 310-983-2555

G. Richard Ford   Donna Rogers Kirby
Timothy L. Walker   Tina Ivankovic Mangarpan
William C. Haggerty   Susan D. Berger
Jeffrey S. Behar   Joseph A. Heath
Mark Steven Hennings   Robert J. Chavez
J. Michael McClure

Arthur W. Schultz   Theodore A. Clapp
Jon T. Moseley   Stanley L. Scarlett
Maxine J. Lebowitz   Scott A. Ritsema
Timothy P. McDonald   Michael Guy Martin
K. Michele Williams   Colleen A. Strong
Stephen Ward Moore   Thomas L. Gourde
James D. Savage   Patrick J. Stark
Todd D. Pearl   Shayne L. Wulterin
Patrick J. Gibbs   Charles D. Jarrell
James O. Miller   Charles J. Schmitt
David Huchel   Kyle A. Ostergrad
Robert Reisinger   Todd L. Kessler

OF COUNSEL
Theodore P. Shield, P.L.C.

For full biographical listings, see the Martindale-Hubbell Law Directory

---

MOORE, RUTTER & EVANS (AV)

A Partnership including a Professional Corporation
555 East Ocean Boulevard, Suite 500, 90802-5090
Telephone: 310-494-6667; 435-4499
Facsimile: 310-495-4229
Huntington Beach, California Office: 2100 Main Street, Suite 280, 92648.
Telephone: 714-374-3333.

RESIDENT PARTNERS
Neal Moore   Mark D. Rutter
William D. Evans (P.C.)

(See Next Column)

OF COUNSEL
Michael J. Emling

For full biographical listings, see the Martindale-Hubbell Law Directory

---

WISE, WIEZOREK, TIMMONS & WISE, A PROFESSIONAL CORPORATION (AV)

3700 Santa Fe Avenue, Suite 300, P.O. Box 2190, 90810
Telephone: 310-834-5028
Fax: 310-834-8018
Redding, California Office: 443 Redcliff Drive, Suite 230.
Telephone: 916-221-7632.
Fax: 916-221-8832.

George E. Wise   Richard P. Dieffenbach
Duane H. Timmons   Steven C. Rice
Anthony F. Wiezorek   Stephen M. Smith
Susan E. Anderson Wise   Thomas J. Yocis
Albert F. Padley, III   James M. Cox
Michael J. Pearce   Mathew J. Vande Wydeven
Mark C. Allen, III   Tae J. Im

For full biographical listings, see the Martindale-Hubbell Law Directory

---

LOS ANGELES, * Los Angeles Co.

ALLEN, RHODES, SOBELSOHN & JOHNSON, LLP (AV)

10866 Wilshire Boulevard, Suite 200, 90024
Telephone: 310-475-0875; 213-879-9660
Santa Barbara, California Office: 125 East De La Guerra, 2nd Floor.
Telephone: 805-965-5236.

MEMBERS OF FIRM
Bernard Sobelsohn   Michael E. Johnson (Resident, Santa Barbara Office)

OF COUNSEL
David B. Allen   J. Richard Rhodes

Reference: Wells Fargo Bank.

For full biographical listings, see the Martindale-Hubbell Law Directory

---

ANDERSON, ABLON, LEWIS & GALE, LLP (AV)

Suite 2000 Equitable Plaza Building, 3435 Wilshire Boulevard, 90010
Telephone: 213-388-3385
Telecopier: 213-388-8432
Thousand Oaks, California Office: 220-H Briarwood Building, 299 West Hillcrest Drive, 91360.
Telephone: 805-373-5273.
Fax: 805-495-1456.

MEMBERS OF FIRM
Robert E. Lewis   Jerald E. Gale
Harris D. Bass

ASSOCIATES
Farhad Kazemzadeh   Candace Connart Bleifer
Robert David Schwartz

OF COUNSEL
Charles R. Anderson (Retired)   Herman Ablon (Retired)

Representative Clients: Maremont Corp.; Chansler & Lyon Co., Inc.
Reference: Bank of America (Wilshire Center Branch).

For full biographical listings, see the Martindale-Hubbell Law Directory

---

BACON & MILLS, LLP (AV)

800 Wilshire Boulevard, Suite 950, 90017
Telephone: 213-486-6500
Fax: 213-486-6552
West Covina, California Office: 100 North Barranca Street, 11th Floor.
Telephone: 818-915-6555.
Fax: 818-915-8855.

Robert Parker Mills   James W. Colfer
Robert L. Bacon   Carl Andrew Botterud
Theodore E. Bacon (Resident at Adam J. Gerard
West Covina Office)   Howard S. Hou

For full biographical listings, see the Martindale-Hubbell Law Directory

---

BARTON, KLUGMAN & OETTING (AV)

A Partnership including Professional Corporations
37th Floor, 333 South Grand Avenue, 90071-1599
Telephone: 213-621-4000
Telecopier: 213-625-1832
Newport Beach Office: Suite 700, 4400 MacArthur Boulevard, P.O. Box 2350, 92660.
Telephone: 714-752-7551.
Telecopier: 714-752-0288.

COUNSEL TO FIRM
Robert M. Barton *   Robert H. Klugman *
Richard F. Oetting *

(See Next Column)

BARTON, KLUGMAN & OETTING, *Los Angeles—Continued*

MEMBERS OF FIRM

David F. Morgan *	David J. Cartano *
William D. Herz *	Martin J. Spear
Charles J. Schufreider *	Tod V. Beebe *
Robert Louis Fisher *	Ronald R. St. John
Gilbert D. Jensen *	Mark A. Newton *

Margot I. McLeay

ASSOCIATES

Barbara W. G. Crowley	Reiko L. Furuta

Jaleen Nelson

References: The Bank of California (Southern California Headquarters); Wells Fargo Bank, N.A. (Wells Fargo Center, Los Angeles).
*Denotes a lawyer whose Professional Corporation is a member of the partnership or is Counsel to the Firm

For full biographical listings, see the Martindale-Hubbell Law Directory

BELCHER, HENZIE & BIEGENZAHN, A PROFESSIONAL CORPORATION (AV)

333 South Hope Street, Suite 3650, 90071-1479
Telephone: 213-624-8293
Telecopier: 213-895-6082

Frank B. Belcher (1891-1979)	E. Lee Horton
David Bernard (1931-1978)	William T. DelHagen
John S. Curtis	Julia Azrael

Jeffrey L. Horwith	James C. Hildebrand
Georgette Renata Herget	Robert S. Cooper
David L. Bonar	Wun-ee Chelsea Chen
Raymond E. Hane, III	John Erin McOsker

Mary E. Gram

OF COUNSEL

George M. Henzie	Leo J. Biegenzahn

James M. Derr

Reference: Bank of America (Los Angeles Main Office).

For full biographical listings, see the Martindale-Hubbell Law Directory

BLACK COMPEAN HALL & LENNEMAN (AV)

One Wilshire, Suite 1000 624 South Grand Avenue, 90017
Telephone: 213-629-9500
FAX: 213-629-4868
Email: bchl@earthlink.net

MEMBERS OF FIRM

Robert H. Black	Frederick G. Hall
Michael D. Compean	Annette J. Lenneman

ASSOCIATES

William J. Light	Margie Castillo
Vicente Valencia, Jr.	Lara Michelle Brya

Meredith A. Czapla

Reference: Sterling Bank.

For full biographical listings, see the Martindale-Hubbell Law Directory

BOOTH, MITCHEL & STRANGE (AV)

30th Floor-Equitable Plaza, 3435 Wilshire Boulevard, 90010-2050
Telephone: 213-738-0100
Fax: 213-380-3308
Costa Mesa, California Office: 3080 Bristol Street, Suite 550.
Telephone: 714-641-0217.
Fax: 714-957-0411.
San Diego, California Office: 550 West "C" Street. Suite 1560.
Telephone: 619-238-7620.
Fax: 619-238-7625.

MEMBERS OF FIRM

Bates Booth (1903-1967)	Marla Lamedman Kelley
Norman R. Willian (1917-1968)	(Resident, Costa Mesa Office)
Michael D. Kellogg (1949-1996)	Kevin K. Callahan
William F. Rummler	Robert F. Keehn
Michael T. Lowe	Paul R. Howell
(Resident, Costa Mesa Office)	Craig E. Guenther
Joseph A. Burrow	(Resident, Costa Mesa Office)
Seth W. Whitaker	David L. Hughes
Walter B. Hill, Jr.	(Resident, Costa Mesa Office)
(Resident, Costa Mesa Office)	Daniel M. Crowley
Robert H. Briggs	Steven M. Mitchel
(Resident, Costa Mesa Office)	Robert C. Niesley
David R. Kipper	James G. Stanley
	(Resident, Costa Mesa Office)

OF COUNSEL

George C. Mitchel	Owen W. Strange

(See Next Column)

ASSOCIATES

John J. Arens	Cory J. King
Richard W. Davis	Michelle M. La Mar
James A. Holl, III	Christopher C. Lewi
Robert W. Huston	Clinton Davis Robison
Thomas T. Johnson	Robert H. Shaffer, Jr.

RESIDENT ASSOCIATES COSTA MESA OFFICE

Elizabeth Currin Bonn	Scott S. Mizen
Stacie L. Brandt	Sean T. Osborn
David F. McPherson	Laila Morcos Santana

RESIDENT ASSOCIATES SAN DIEGO OFFICE

Derek J. Emge	Robert F. Tyson, Jr.

Representative Clients: Southern California Gas Co.; Southern Counties Title Insurance Co.

For full biographical listings, see the Martindale-Hubbell Law Directory

BOTTUM & FELITON, A PROFESSIONAL CORPORATION (AV)

Suite 1500, South Tower, 3200 Wilshire Boulevard, 90010
Telephone: 213-487-0402
Fax: 213-386-9803
San Diego, California Office: Suite 400 Emerald Plaza, 402 West Broadway.
Telephone: 619-595-4857.
Fax: 619-595-4863.

John R. Feliton, Jr.	Steve Johnson
Robert A. Wooten, Jr.	Mark A. Oertel

Alexander F. Giovanniello

Kenneth C. Feldman	Julie A. Covell
Jerry Garcia	Karl R. Loureiro
Paul K. Schrieffer	Sean T. Hamada
Scott A. Hampton	Gary F. Werner
Gregg S. Garfinkel	Victor I. King
Brian E. Cooper	Andrea J. Lang

Linwood Warren, Jr.

For full biographical listings, see the Martindale-Hubbell Law Directory

BUCHALTER, NEMER, FIELDS & YOUNGER, A PROFESSIONAL CORPORATION (AV)

24th Floor, 601 South Figueroa Street, 90017
Telephone: 213-891-0700
Fax: 213-896-0400
Email: buchalter@earthlink.net *URL:* http://www.buchalter.com
New York, New York Office: 15th Floor, 605 Third Avenue.
Telephone: 212-490-8600.
Fax: 212-490-6022.
San Francisco, California Office: 29th Floor, 333 Market Street.
Telephone: 415-227-0900.
Fax: 415-227-0770.
Newport Beach, California Office: Suite 1450, 620 Newport Center Drive.
Telephone: 714-760-1121.
Fax: 714-720-0182.

Murray M. Fields	Philip J. Wolman
Richard Jay Goldstein	Mark A. Bonenfant
Michael L. Wachtell	David S. Kyman
Robert C. Colton	Jeffrey S. Wruble
Jay R. Ziegler	Pamela Kohlman Webster
Michael J. Cereseto	Matthew W. Kavanaugh
Bernard E. Le Sage	Robert J. Davidson

Bernard D. Bollinger, Jr.

OF COUNSEL

Stuart D. Buchalter	Geoffrey Forsythe Bogeaus
	Holly J. Fujie

Glenn L. Savard

References: City National Bank; Wells Fargo Bank; Metrobank.

For Complete List of Firm Personnel, See General Section

For full biographical listings, see the Martindale-Hubbell Law Directory

CHAPMAN & GLUCKSMAN, A PROFESSIONAL CORPORATION (AV)

11900 West Olympic Boulevard, Suite 800, 90064-0704
Telephone: 310-207-7722
Facsimile: 310-207-6550

Richard H. Glucksman	Wendy M. Housman
Arthur J. Chapman	James C. Earle
Randall J. Dean	Craig A. Roeb

(See Next Column)

CHAPMAN & GLUCKSMAN A PROFESSIONAL CORPORATION—*Continued*

Thomas L. Halliwell
Dominic J. Fote
Christopher R. Kent
Andrew B. Cohn
Jeffrey A. Cohen
Glenn T. Barger

Christine L. Vanderbilt
Gregory Sabo
Rita Mongoven Miller
Todd M. Mobley
D. Scott Dodd
Jon A. Turigliatto

Karen S. Danto

OF COUNSEL

Thomas J. Pabst

Reference: First Professional Bank, Santa Monica.

For full biographical listings, see the Martindale-Hubbell Law Directory

CLARK & TREVITHICK, A PROFESSIONAL CORPORATION (AV)

800 Wilshire Boulevard, 12th Floor, 90017
Telephone: 213-629-5700
Telecopier: 213-624-9441
San Francisco, California Office: 456 Montgomery Street, 20th Floor.
Telephone: 415-288-6520.
Fax: 415-398-2820.

Philip W. Bartenetti
Dolores Cordell
Vincent Tricarico

Leonard Brazil
Arturo Santana Jr.
Kerry T. Ryan

References: Wells Fargo Bank (Los Angeles Main Office); National Bank of California.

For Complete List of Firm Personnel, See General Section

For full biographical listings, see the Martindale-Hubbell Law Directory

DAAR & NEWMAN, PROFESSIONAL CORPORATION (AV)

Suite 2500, 865 South Figueroa Street, 90017-2567
Telephone: 213-892-0999
FAX: 213-892-1066

David Daar
Michael R. Newman

Jeffery J. Daar
Marsha McLean-Utley

Michael J. White

OF COUNSEL

Rodney W. Loeb

William F. White, Jr.

Samuel T. Rees

LEGAL SUPPORT PERSONNEL

Joe A. Morton

Frank E. Raab

Representative Clients: Allianz Insurance Co.; American Income Life Insurance Co.; American Life and Casualty Insurance Co.; Balboa Insurance Co.; California Casualty Insurance Co.; National Benefit Life Insurance Co.; Capital Life Insurance Co.; Charter National Life; Columbian Mutual Life; Connecticut Mutual Life Insurance Co.

For full biographical listings, see the Martindale-Hubbell Law Directory

DANIELS, BARATTA & FINE (AV)

A Partnership including a Professional Corporation
1801 Century Park East, 9th Floor, 90067
Telephone: 310-556-7900
Telecopier: 310-556-2807
Bakersfield, California Office: 5201 California Avenue, Suite 400.
Telephone: 805-335-7788.
Telecopier: 805-324-3660.

MEMBERS OF FIRM

John P. Daniels (Inc.)
James M. Baratta
Paul R. Fine
Nathan B. Hoffman

Mary Hulett
Michael B. Geibel
James I. Montgomery, Jr.
Lance D. Orloff

Mark R. Israel

ASSOCIATES

Ilene Wendy Kurtzman
Janet Sacks
Michael N. Schonbuch
Scott M. Leavitt
Michelle R. Press
Scott Ashford Brooks
Craig A. Laidig
Robin A. Webb
Craig S. Momita

Spencer A. Schneider
Angelo A. Du Plantier, III
Leslie E. Wright, III.
Erin B. Hallissy
Kena B. Chin
Dean Bengston
Peter Anders Nyquist
Jeannie Masse
Lori Chotiner

Maureen M. Michail

OF COUNSEL

Timothy J. Hughes

Drew T. Hanker

Mark A. Vega

For full biographical listings, see the Martindale-Hubbell Law Directory

DAVIS & FOX (AV)

1901 Avenue of the Stars, Suite 400, 90067
Telephone: 310-286-2915
Fax: 310-286-2916

MEMBERS OF FIRM

Calvin E. Davis

Steven A. Fox

ASSOCIATES

Brian Aronson

Amy L. Freisleben

Susan R. Peck

OF COUNSEL

Herbert D. Meyers

For full biographical listings, see the Martindale-Hubbell Law Directory

DIDAK & JACK (AV)

11755 Wilshire Boulevard, 15th Floor, 90025
Telephone: 310-473-7173
Fax: 310-312-1077

MEMBERS OF FIRM

Mark F. Didak

Travis R. Jack

For full biographical listings, see the Martindale-Hubbell Law Directory

FONDA, GARRARD, HILBERMAN & DAVIS, A PROFESSIONAL CORPORATION (AV)

1888 Century Park East, 21st Floor, 90067
Telephone: 310-553-1121
FAX: 310-553-4232

Donald A. Garrard
Peter M. Fonda

Joe W. Hilberman
Steven D. Davis

Patrick W. Mayer

Gloria Kurman Apt
Diane M. Daly
Tracy T. Davis

Laurie DeYoung
Thomas E. Donahue
Frederick James

David M. Samuels

Representative Clients: Utica Mutual Insurance Co.; Truck Ins. Exchange; Twentieth Century Ins.; Allstate Ins. Co.; Regents of California; State Farm Ins. Co.
Reference: Sanwa Bank of California (Los Angeles Headquarters Corporate Office).

For full biographical listings, see the Martindale-Hubbell Law Directory

GALTON & HELM (AV)

500 South Grand Avenue, Suite 1200, 90071
Telephone: 213-629-8800
Telecopier: 213-629-0037
Palm Desert, California Office: 73-290 El Paseo, Suite 377.
Telephone: 619-776-5600.
Fax: 619-776-5602.

MEMBERS OF FIRM

Stephen H. Galton
Hugh H. Helm
Michael F. Bell

Daniel W. Maguire
(Resident at Palm Desert)
David A. Lingenbrink

ASSOCIATES

Chris D. Olsen
Melissa M. Cowan
Edith Sanchez Shea

Joanna M. Eoff
Michael B. Bernacchi
Mark A. Riekhof
(Resident, Glendale Office)

LEGAL SUPPORT PERSONNEL

Lana Banks (Paralegal)

Stephanie M. McCarthy
(Paralegal)

For full biographical listings, see the Martindale-Hubbell Law Directory

HAWKINS, SCHNABEL, LINDAHL & BECK (AV)

660 South Figueroa Street, Suite 1500, 90017
Telephone: 213-488-3900
Telecopier: 213-486-9883
Email: 102175.3573@compuserve.com

MEMBERS OF FIRM

Roger E. Hawkins
Laurence H. Schnabel
George M. Lindahl

Jon P. Kardassakis
William E. Keitel
R. Timothy Stone

For full biographical listings, see the Martindale-Hubbell Law Directory

HONN & SECOF (AV)

510 West Sixth Street, Suite 910, 90014-1310
Telephone: 213-629-3900
Telecopier: 213-624-5362

Richard A. Honn

Howard S. Secof

(See Next Column)

HONN & SECOF, *Los Angeles—Continued*

ASSOCIATE
Wayne T. Kasai

Reference: Wells Fargo Bank.

For full biographical listings, see the Martindale-Hubbell Law Directory

HORNBERGER & CRISWELL (AV)

444 South Flower, 31st Floor, 90071
Telephone: 213-488-1655
Facsimile: 213-488-1255
Email: kbranch0@counsel.com

MEMBERS OF FIRM
Nicholas W. Hornberger	Ann M. Ghazarians
Leslie E. Criswell	Michael A. Brewer
	Scott Alan Freedman

ASSOCIATES
Marlin E. Howes	James M. Slominski
Christopher T. Olsen	Michael C. Denlinger
Scott B. Cloud	Gayle L. Eskridge

OF COUNSEL
David E. Bower	William P. Driscoll

For full biographical listings, see the Martindale-Hubbell Law Directory

HORVITZ & LEVY (AV)

A Partnership including Professional Corporations
18th Floor, 15760 Ventura Boulevard (Encino), 91436
Telephone: 818-995-0800; 213-872-0802
FAX: 818-995-3157

Ellis J. Horvitz (A P.C.)	Daniel J. Gonzalez
Barry R. Levy (A P.C.)	Mitchell C. Tilner
Peter Abrahams	Christina J. Imre
David M. Axelrad	Lisa Perrochet
Frederic D. Cohen	Stephen E. Norris
S. Thomas Todd	Sandra J. Smith
David S. Ettinger	John A. Taylor, Jr.

Mary F. Dant	Andrea M. Gauthier
Ari R. Kleiman	Elizabeth Skorcz Anthony
Lisa R. Jaskol	Christine A. Pagac
Julie L. Woods	Judith E. Gordon
Holly R. Paul	Patricia Lofton
H. Thomas Watson	L. Rachel Lerman Helyar
	(Not admitted in CA)

OF COUNSEL
Jon B. Eisenberg

Representative Clients: State Farm Insurance Company; Farmers Insurance Group of Companies; AIG Risk Management; CNA Insurance; Home Insurance Company; Allstate Insurance Company; Transamerica Insurance Company; California Insurance Guarantee Association; 20th Century Insurance Company.

For full biographical listings, see the Martindale-Hubbell Law Directory

INGLIS, LEDBETTER & GOWER (AV)

500 South Grand Avenue, 18th Floor, 90071-2612
Telephone: 213-627-6800
Facsimile: 213-622-2857

MEMBERS OF FIRM
Michael K. Inglis	Richard G. Ritchie
Steven K. Ledbetter	Gregory H. Gocke
Richard S. Gower	John E. Hope

ASSOCIATES
Timothy E. Kearns	James W. Holchin
	Nancy B. Gonzalez

LEGAL SUPPORT PERSONNEL
Kevin Watkins

Representative Clients: Barnes-Dyer; Brehm Communications, Inc.; Inter-Insurance Exchange of the Automobile Club of Southern California; Presto Food Products, Inc.; Prudential Property and Casualty Insurance Co.; Safariland Ltd., Inc.; Cecil Saydah Co.

For full biographical listings, see the Martindale-Hubbell Law Directory

JONES, DAY, REAVIS & POGUE (AV)

555 West Fifth Street Suite 4600, 90013-1025
Telephone: 213-489-3939
Telex: 181439 UD
Telecopier: 213-243-2539
In Irvine, California: 2603 Main Street, Suite 900.
Telephone: 714-851-3939.
Telex: 194911 Lawyers LSA.
Telecopier: 714-553-7539.

(See Next Column)

In Atlanta, Georgia: 3500 One Peachtree Center, 303 Peachtree Street, N.E.
Telephone: 404-521-3939.
Cable Address: "Attorneys Atlanta".
Telex: 54-2711.
Telecopier: 404-581-8330.
In Brussels, Belgium: Avenue Louise 480, 7th Floor, B-1050 Brussels.
Telephone: 32-2-645-14-11.
Telecopier: 32-2-645-14-45.
In Chicago, Illinois: 77 West Wacker.
Telephone: 312-782-3939.
Telecopier: 312-782-8585.
In Cleveland, Ohio: North Point, 901 Lakeside Avenue.
Telephone: 216-586-3939.
Cable Address: "Attorneys Cleveland."
Telex: 980389.
Telecopier: 216-579-0212.
In Columbus, Ohio: 1900 Huntington Center.
Telephone: 614-469-3939.
Cable Address: "Attorneys Columbus."
Telecopier: 614-461-4198.
In Dallas, Texas: 2300 Trammell Crow Center, 2001 Ross Avenue.
Telephone: 214-220-3939.
Cable Address: "Attorneys Dallas."
Telex: 730852.
Telecopier: 214-969-5100.
In Frankfurt, Germany: Triton Haus, Bockenheimer Landstrasse 42, 60323 Frankfurt am Main.
Telephone: 49-69-9726-3939.
Telecopier: 49-69-9726-3993.
In Geneva, Switzerland: 20, rue de Candolle.
Telephone: 41-22-320-2339.
Telecopier: 41-22-320-1232.
In Hong Kong: 29th Floor, Entertainment Building, 30 Queen's Road Central.
Telephone: 852-2526-6895.
Telecopier: 852-2868-5871.
In London England: Bucklersbury House, 3 Queen Victoria Street.
Telephone: 44-171-236-3939.
Telecopier: 44-171-236-1113.
In New Delhi, India: Pathak & Associates, 13th Floor, Dr. Gopal Das Bhaven, 28 Barakhamba Road.
Telephone: 91-11-373-8793.
Telecopier: 91-11-335-3761.
In New York, New York: 599 Lexington Avenue.
Telephone: 212-326-3939.
Cable Address: "JONESDAY NEWYORK."
Telex: 237013 JDRP UR.
Telecopier: 212-755-7306.
In Paris, France: 62, rue du Faubourg Saint-Honore.
Telephone: 33-1-44-71-3939.
Telex: 290156 Surgoe.
Telecopier: 33-1-49-24-0471.
In Pittsburgh, Pennsylvania: 500 Grant Street, 31st Floor.
Telephone: 412-391-3939.
Cable Address: "Attorneys Pittsburgh".
Telecopier: 412-394-7959.
In Riyadh, Saudi Arabia: The International Law Firm, Sulaymaniyah Center, Tahlia Street, P.O. Box 22166.
Telephone: (966-1) 462-8866.
Telecopier: (966-1) 462-9001.
In Taipei, Taiwan: 8th Floor, 2 Tun Hwa South Road, Section 2.
Telephone: (886-2) 704-6808.
Telecopier: (886-2) 704-6791.
In Tokyo, Japan: Toranomon MT Building, 4th Floor, 10-3, Toranomon 3-Chome, Minato-ku, Tokyo 105, Japan.
Telephone: 81-3-3433-3939.
Telecopier: 81-3-5401-2725.
In Washington, D.C.: Metropolitan Square, 1450 G Street, N.W.
Telephone: 202-879-3939.
Cable Address: "Attorneys Washington."
Telex: 89-2410 ATTORNEYS WASH.
Telecopier: 202-737-2832.

MEMBER OF FIRM IN LOS ANGELES
Lester O. Brown

For Complete List of Firm Personnel, See General Section

For full biographical listings, see the Martindale-Hubbell Law Directory

KERN, STREETER & GONZALEZ (AV)

601 West 5th Street, Suite 1100, 90071
Telephone: 213-629-8100
Facsimile: 213-627-8765

MEMBERS OF FIRM
René J. Kern, Jr.	John W. Streeter
	Michael D. Gonzalez

(See Next Column)

KERN, STREETER & GONZALEZ—*Continued*

ASSOCIATES

Tina L. Gentile   Angela J. Armitage
Claudia T. Beightol   Christina L. Young

Representative Clients: Farmers Insurance Group; The Home Insurance Co.; 20th Century Insurance Group; United States Fidelity and Guaranty Co.; St. Paul Fire & Marine Insurance Co.; TM Claims Service, Inc.

For full biographical listings, see the Martindale-Hubbell Law Directory

---

KOSLOV & MEDLEN (AV)

30141 Agoura Road, Suite 200, 91301-4334
Telephone: 818-597-9996
FAX: 818-597-8848

MEMBERS OF FIRM

John Koslov   William P. Medlen

ASSOCIATE

Sabrina Simmons-Brill

For full biographical listings, see the Martindale-Hubbell Law Directory

---

McKAY, BYRNE & GRAHAM (AV)

3250 Wilshire Boulevard, Suite 603, 90010
Telephone: 213-386-6900
Fax: 213-381-1762

John P. McKay   Barry Hassenberg
Michael A. Byrne   Mark G. Cunningham
Robert L. Graham   Paul A. de Lorimier

Jeffrey Cabot Myers   Michael L. Fox

OF COUNSEL

Gail D. Solo (A Professional Corporation)

For full biographical listings, see the Martindale-Hubbell Law Directory

---

MEYERS, BIANCHI & McCONNELL, A PROFESSIONAL CORPORATION (AV)

11859 Wilshire Boulevard, Fourth Floor, 90025-6601
Telephone: 310-312-0772
Cable Address: "Trialaw"
Facsimile: 310-312-0656
New York, New York Office: 400 Madison Avenue.
Telephone: 212-509-1663.
Facsimile: 212-269-5927.

Jeffrey G. Meyers   Martin E. Pulverman
John W. McConnell III   Elizabeth A. Kooyman

Patrick D. Bingham   James M. Fowler
Frederick S. Reisz   Carol J. Knoblow
Elizabeth S. Agmon   Heidi M. Yoshioka

OF COUNSEL

James S. Bianchi   Carole D. Bos
Harris Zeitzew   (Not admitted in CA)
Andrew Feldman
   (Not admitted in CA)

Reference: Bank of America (Century City Branch).

For full biographical listings, see the Martindale-Hubbell Law Directory

---

MILLARD, PILCHOWSKI, HOLWEGER & CHILD, P.C. (AV)

A Partnership including Professional Corporations
12th Floor, 655 South Hope Street, 90017-3211
Telephone: 213-627-3113
Fax: 213-623-9237
Email: mphc@loop.com

L. Raymond Millard (P.C.)   Marie Polizzi Holweger
Thomas S. Pilchowski (P.C.)   Bradford T. Child

Bradley P. Childers   Jeniffer A. Wilder
Elizabeth T. Fitzgerald   Russell W. Schatz, Jr.

For full biographical listings, see the Martindale-Hubbell Law Directory

---

NEUMEYER & BOYD, LLP (AV)

2029 Century Park East, Suite 1100, 90067
Telephone: 310-553-9393
Fax: 310-553-8437

MEMBERS OF FIRM

Richard A. Neumeyer   Lydia E. Hachmeister
Carol Boyd   Steven A. Freeman

(See Next Column)

ASSOCIATES

Katherine Tatikian   Daniel F. Sanchez
Susie J. Kater   Stuart L. Brody
                 Reid L. Denham

For full biographical listings, see the Martindale-Hubbell Law Directory

---

OCHOA & SILLAS (AV)

444 South, Flower Street, 18th Floor, 90071
Telephone: 213-362-1400
Fax: 213-622-0162
Sacramento, California Office: Wells Fargo Center, 400 Capitol Mall, Suite 1850.
Telephone: 916-447-3383.
FAX: 916-447-3495.
Mexico City, Mexico Office: Bosques de Duraznos, No. 65-507-B, Bosques de Las Lomas, 11700 Mexico, D.F.
Telephone: 905-596-68-48.

MEMBERS OF FIRM

Ralph M. Ochoa   Jesse M. Jauregui
Herman Sillas   Jacqueline Rich Moore

ASSOCIATES

Jack T. Molodanof   Carlos Hilario
Tomás R. Lopez   Evan F. Hadnot
Rita A. Reyes   Thomas J. Joy
                 Mario Cordero

OF COUNSEL

Cochran & Lotkin, , Washington, D.C.

LEGAL SUPPORT PERSONNEL

Manuel Tejeda (Paralegal)   Jeanette M. Palma (Paralegal)
                 Lori Lee Marino (Paralegal)

For full biographical listings, see the Martindale-Hubbell Law Directory

---

O'MELVENY & MYERS LLP (AV)

400 South Hope Street, 90071-2899
Telephone: 213-669-6000
Cable Address: "Moms"
Facsimile: 213-669-6407
Email: omminfo@omm.com
Century City, California Office: 1999 Avenue of the Stars, 90067-6035.
Telephone: 310-553-6700.
Facsimile: 310-246-6779.
Newport Beach, California Office: 610 Newport Center Drive, 92660-6429.
Telephone: 714-760-9600.
Cable Address: "Moms".
Facsimile: 714-669-6994.
San Francisco, California Office: Embarcadero Center West Tower, 275 Battery Street, 94111-3305.
Telephone: 415-984-8700.
Facsimile: 415-984-8701.
New York, New York Office: Citicorp Center, 153 East 53rd Street, 10022-4611.
Telephone: 212-326-2000.
Facsimile: 212-326-2061.
Washington, D.C. Office: 555 13th Street, N.W., 20004-1109.
Telephone: 202-383-5300.
Cable Address: "Moms".
Facsimile: 202-383-5414.
London, England Office: 10 Finsbury Square, London, EC2A 1LA.
Telephone: 0171-256-8451.
Facsimile: 0171-638-8205.
Tokyo, Japan Office: Sanbancho KB-6 Building, 6 Sanbancho, Chiyoda-ku, Tokyo 102, Japan.
Telephone: 03-3239-2900.
Facsimile: 03-3239-2432.
Hong Kong Office: Suite 1905, Peregrine Tower, Lippo Centre, 89 Queensway, Central, Hong Kong.
Telephone: 852-2523-8266.
Facsimile: 852-2522-1760.
Shanghai, Peoples Republic of China Office: Shanghai International Trade Centre, Suite 2011, 2200 Yan An Road West, Shanghai, 200335, PRC.
Telephone: 86-21-6219-5363.
Facsimile: 86-21-6275-4949.

PARTNER

Richard B. Goetz

For Complete List of Firm Personnel, See General Section

For full biographical listings, see the Martindale-Hubbell Law Directory

---

OSTROVE, KRANTZ & OSTROVE, A PROFESSIONAL CORPORATION (AV)

(Successor To: Ostrove and Lancer, A Professional Corporation; David Ostrove, A Professional Corporation)
5757 Wilshire Boulevard, Suite 535, 90036-3600
Telephone: 213-939-3400
Fax: 213-939-3500
Email: OSTROVE@AOL.COM

(See Next Column)

OSTROVE, KRANTZ & OSTROVE A PROFESSIONAL CORPORATION, *Los Angeles—Continued*

David Ostrove   David S. Krantz
          Kenneth E. Ostrove

Reference: First Business Bank.

For full biographical listings, see the Martindale-Hubbell Law Directory

---

PARSONS AND DESTIAN (AV)

1055 Wilshire Boulevard, Suite 1750, 90017
Telephone: 213-975-0064
Telecopier: 213-975-1172
Email: dparsla@gnn.com
London, England Office: Guild House, 36-38 Fenchurch Street. EC3M 3DQ.
Telephone: 071-929-5252.
Telecopier: 071-283-4466.
Telex: 914561.

MEMBERS OF FIRM

David W. Parsons   Tony Destian

OF COUNSEL

G. David Rubin

For full biographical listings, see the Martindale-Hubbell Law Directory

---

PRESTHOLT, KLEEGER, FIDONE & VILLASENOR (AV)

Suite 1600, 1055 West 7th Street, 90017
Telephone: 213-895-4811
FAX: 213-895-4817
San Francisco, California Office: 989 Market Street, 6th Floor.
Telephone: 415-267-6362.
Fax: 415-267-6275.

MEMBERS OF FIRM

David A. Prestholt	Lisa L. Loveridge
Kenneth S. Kleeger	Archie Chin
Gary P. Fidone	Robert J. Scott, Jr.
Lisa A. Villasenor	Avigal Horrow
Brian D. Holmberg	Jamie Ann Louie
Willi H. Siepmann	Robert S. Putnam
David Crawford, III	Arnie E. Goldstein
	Brian J. Finn

For full biographical listings, see the Martindale-Hubbell Law Directory

---

RADCLIFF, FRANDSEN & DONGELL (AV)

40th Floor, 777 South Figueroa Street, 90017
Telephone: 213-614-1990
Facsimile: 213-489-9263
San Francisco, California Office: 88 Kearny Street, Suite 1475.
Telephone: 415-399-8393.
Facsimile: 415-989-5465.
Rome, Italy Office: Via Tacito, 7.
Telephone: (39) 06-323-5588.
Facsimile: (39) 06-324-3392.

MEMBERS OF FIRM

Jules G. Radcliff, Jr.   Russell Mackay Frandsen
       Richard A. Dongell

OF COUNSEL

Tal Clifton Finney

ASSOCIATES

Francis P. Aspessi	Jeffrey C. Mayes
Ruben A. Castellon	Marisa A. Moret
William W. Funderburk, Jr.	Daniel E. Park
Jeffrey A. Gagliardi	Scott D. Pinsky
David K. Lee	Eric H. Saiki
Maria Anna Mancini	Steve R. Segura
	Glenn M. White

For full biographical listings, see the Martindale-Hubbell Law Directory

---

GERALD G. REPPETTO (AV)

Equitable Building, 3435 Wilshire Boulevard, Suite 640, 90010
Telephone: 213-388-4320
FAX: 213-383-1231

For full biographical listings, see the Martindale-Hubbell Law Directory

---

ROBIE & MATTHAI, A PROFESSIONAL CORPORATION (AV)

Biltmore Tower, 500 South Grand, Suite 1500, 90071
Telephone: 213-624-3062
Fax: 213-624-2563

James R. Robie	Kyle Kveton
Edith R. Matthai	Maria Louise Cousineau
Michael J. O'Neill	Pamela E. Dunn

(See Next Column)

Craig W. Brunet	Karen R. Palmersheim
Kim W. Sellars	Brian D. Huben
Teresa J. Friederichs	Wendy L. Schneider
Bernadine J. Stolar	Natalie A. Kouyoumdjian
Claudia Sokol	Gabrielle M. Jackson

Representative Clients: State Farm Fire & Casualty Co.; The Travelers; Fireman's Fund Ins. Co.; Lawyers Mutual Ins. Co.; Carrier Corp.
Reference: First Professional Bank.

For full biographical listings, see the Martindale-Hubbell Law Directory

---

SCHELL & DELAMER, LLP (AV)

A Partnership including Professional Corporations
865 South Figueroa Street Suite 2750, 90017
Telephone: 213-622-8181
Fax: 213-627-5252
Thousand Oaks, California Office: 100 East Thousand Oaks Boulevard, Suite 142.
Telephone: 805-496-9533.
Fax: 805-496-3424.

Gerald F. H. Delamer (1892-1955)	Garrin James Shaw (Professional Corporation)
Walter O. Schell (1895-1981)	Robert S. Hamrick (Professional Corporation)
Roland R. Kaspar (Professional Corporation)	Jeffrey F. Briskin
Katherine B. Pene	

ASSOCIATES

Candace E. Ahrens Kallberg	John J. Latzanich, II. (Resident at Thousand Oaks Office)
Denise A. Nardi	Lori M. Levine
Randy A. Berg	Sylvia Havens
Kenneth S. Markson	Roman Y. Nykolyshyn
Joseph P. Sepikas	
Gregory J. Amantia (Resident at Thousand Oaks Office)	

Representative Clients: Hartford Insurance Group; Liberty Mutual Group; Travelers Insurance Co.
References: Los Angeles: First Interstate Bank; Merrill-Lynch.

For full biographical listings, see the Martindale-Hubbell Law Directory

---

SELMAN ● BREITMAN (AV)

11766 Wilshire Boulevard, Sixth Floor, 90025-6538
Telephone: 310-445-0800
Fax: 310-473-2525
San Diego, California Office: Emerald Plaza, 402 W. Broadway, Suite 400.
Telephone: 619-595-4880.
Facsimile: 619-595-4890.
San Francisco, California Office: Citicorp Center, One Sansome Street, Suite 1900.
Telephone: 415-951-4646.
Fax: 415-951-4676.

MEMBERS OF FIRM

Neil H. Selman	Elaine K. Fresch
Craig R. Breitman	Nicholas Banko
Robert A. Steller (Partner, San Diego Office)	Brad D. Bleichner
Alan B. Yuter	David L. Jones
Nancy W. Shokohi	Mark L. Jubelt
Jeffrey C. Segal	Monica Cruz Thornton
A. Scott Goldberg	David T. Bamberger
	Sterling Tao (Partner, San Francisco Office)

Lynette Klawon	James B. Kamanski
Ramon Z. Bacerdo (Resident, San Francisco Office)	Michael L. Mengoli
John S. Knowlton	Rita H. Issagholian
Murray M. Sinclair	Sarah F. Burke (Resident, San Diego Office)
Jeffrey A. Simmons	Darcy D. Jorgensen
Mark S. Gruskin	Linda S. Wendell (Resident, San Francisco Office)
Anthony L. Cione	
Christopher J. Harrington	Jeffrey S. Bolender
Sheryl W. Leichenger	Jeffrey T. Briggs
Theresa Ann Loss	Marcie A. Keenan
Jerry C. Popovich	Lisa M. Dyson (Resident, San Francisco Office)
Lisa Hannah Kahn	
David H. Oken	Aimee Y. Wong
Katy A. Nelson	Grace Horoupian
Jan Long Pocaterra	Kathleen T. Deeley
Kim Karelis	Christopher A. Petrovic
Asim K. Desai	Kimberly D. Allario (Resident, San Diego Office)
Pauline A. New	
Dianne M. Costales	Wendy Wen Yun Chang
Eldon S. Edson	Jack M. Zakariaie

OF COUNSEL

Thomas A. Leary (Of Counsel, San Diego Office)

Reference: City National Bank (Beverly Hills Branch).

For full biographical listings, see the Martindale-Hubbell Law Directory

Los Angeles—Continued

STEVENS, KRAMER, AVERBUCK & HARRIS, A PROFESSIONAL CORPORATION (AV)

1990 South Bundy Drive, Suite 340, 90025
Telephone: 310-442-8435
Fax: 310-442-8441
Irvine, California Office: 18400 Von Karman Avenue, Suite 615, 92612.
Telephone: 714-253-9553.
Fax: 714-253-9643.

Carl R. Stevens	Clayton C. Averbuck
Jeffrey S. Kramer	Charles L. Harris (Resident Partner, Irvine Office)

Angela M. Rossi	Lydia R. Bouzaglou
Craig H. Marcus	(Resident, Irvine Office)
Valerie McSwain	John R. Marking
(Resident Irvine Office)	(Resident, Irvine Office)
Christopher J. Nevis	Robert A. Fisher, II
Lee E. Burrows	(Resident, Irvine Office)
(Resident, Irvine Office)	Jeanne E. Pepper
Monica A. Blut	(Resident, Irvine Office)
Angie Y. Yoon	Ada Berman
Carrie Ann Moffett	Marissa R. Arrache

For full biographical listings, see the Martindale-Hubbell Law Directory

STOCKWELL, HARRIS, WIDOM & WOOLVERTON, A PROFESSIONAL CORPORATION (AV)

6222 Wilshire Boulevard, Sixth Floor, P.O. Box 48917, 90048-0917
Telephone: 213-935-6669; 818-784-6222; 310-277-6669
Fax: 213-935-0198
Santa Ana, California Office: Suite 500, 1551 N. Tustin Avenue, P.O. Box 11979.
Telephone: 714-479-1180.
Fax: 714-479-1190.
Ventura, California Office: 2021 Sperry Avenue, Suite 46.
Telephone: 805-654-8994; 213-617-7290.
Fax: 805-654-1546.
San Bernardino, California Office: Suite 303, 215 North "D" Street.
Telephone: 909-381-5553.
Fax: 909-384-9981.
San Diego, California Office: Suite 400, 402 West Broadway.
Telephone: 619-235-6054.
Fax: 619-231-0129.
Grover Beach, California Office: Suite 307, 200 South 13th Street.
Telephone: 805-473-0720.
Fax: 805-473-0635.

Steven I. Harris	Lawrence S. Mendelsohn
(Managing Attorney)	Edwin H. McKnight, Jr.
Patricia A. Olive	(Resident, Santa Ana Office)
David L. Slucter (Resident, San Bernardino Office)	Steven A. Meline (Resident, Santa Ana Office)
Richard M. Widom	Ted L. Hirschberger
(Managing Attorney)	Theodore G. Schneider, Jr.
Jeffrey T. Landres	(Resident, San Bernardino
(Resident, Ventura Office)	Office)
Linda S. Freeman (Santa Ana and San Diego Offices)	Lawrence B. Madans
	Lester D. Marshall
Michael L. Terry (Resident, Grover Beach Office)	John R. Payne
	George Woolverton
William M. Carero	James C. Shipley
Brian R. Horan	(Resident, Ventura Office)
David F. Grant	Jeffrey Eugene Lowe
(Resident, Santa Office Office)	(Resident, Santa Ana Office)
Edward S. Muehl (Santa Ana and San Diego Offices)	

For full biographical listings, see the Martindale-Hubbell Law Directory

VEATCH, CARLSON, GROGAN & NELSON (AV)

A Partnership including a Professional Corporation
3926 Wilshire Boulevard, 90010
Telephone: 213-381-2861
Telefax: 213-383-6370

MEMBERS OF FIRM

James C. Galloway, Jr. (A Professional Corporation)	Gordon F. Sausser
	Thomas M. Phillips
Anthony D. Seine	Amy W. Lyons
Mark A. Weinstein	Michael Eric Wasserman
John A. Peterson	Michael A. Kramer

ASSOCIATES

Hollis O. Dyer	Dawn M. Costello
Mark M. Rudy	Daniel R. Brown
D. Michael Bush	Stephen D. Enerle
André S. Goodchild	John J. Nolan, III
Kevin L. Henderson	Steven W. Sedach
Gilbert A. Garcia	Joan E. Hewitt
William G. Lieb	Joanne M. Andrew

(See Next Column)

OF COUNSEL

David J. Aisenson (Judge Retired)	Lyn A. Woodward

For full biographical listings, see the Martindale-Hubbell Law Directory

MODESTO,* Stanislaus Co.

BRUNN & FLYNN, A PROFESSIONAL CORPORATION (AV)

928 12th Street, P.O. Box 3366, 95353
Telephone: 209-521-2133
Fax: 209-521-7584
Email: brunnfly@ix.netcom.com

Charles K. Brunn	Gerald E. Brunn
Timothy T. Flynn	Roger S. Matzkind

Michael G. Donovan	Andrew N. Eshoo

Representative Clients: ACWA-Joint Powers Insurance Authority; Andreini & Company Insurance; Basic Resources, Inc.; CIGNA Insurance Cos.; City of Merced; City of Turlock; CNA Insurance Cos.; Colonial Insurance Co.; County of Mariposa; County of Merced.

For full biographical listings, see the Martindale-Hubbell Law Directory

CARDOZO & CARDOZO (AV)

1101 Sylvan Avenue, #B-4, 95350
Telephone: 209-571-3600
FAX: 209-571-1553

MEMBERS OF FIRM

A. A. Cardozo, Jr.	Richard A. Cardozo

LEGAL SUPPORT PERSONNEL

Patricia Bowers

For full biographical listings, see the Martindale-Hubbell Law Directory

MONTEREY, Monterey Co.

HARRAY, MASUDA & LINKER (AV)

80 Garden Court, Suite 260, 93940
Telephone: 408-373-3101
Fax: 408-373-6712

Richard K. Harray	Michael P. Masuda
	Stan L. Linker

Representative Clients: Travelers/Aetna; The Doctors' Company/CHIC; Program Beta; CNA; DPIC; Sequoia Insurance Co.; Midstate Ins. Co.; County of Monterey; Cities of Monterey, Pacific Grove & Seaside.

For full biographical listings, see the Martindale-Hubbell Law Directory

NEWPORT BEACH, Orange Co.

KELEGIAN & THOMAS (AV)

4685 MacArthur Court, Suite 400, 92660
Telephone: 714-553-1200
Fax: 714-553-1013
Email: KelThomLaw@aol.com

Mark A. Kelegian	James P. Habel
Michael Paul Thomas	Jeri E. Tabback
Joseph P. Gallo	Dean H. McVay
Bruce A. Thomason	Erik R. Musurlian
Steven M. Hepps	William N. Villard

For full biographical listings, see the Martindale-Hubbell Law Directory

OAKLAND,* Alameda Co.

BENNETT, SAMUELSEN, REYNOLDS AND ALLARD, A PROFESSIONAL CORPORATION (AV)

1951 Webster Street, Suite 200, 94612
Telephone: 510-444-7688; 510-987-8001
Fax: 510-444-5849

Bryant M. Bennett (Retired)	Richard L. Reynolds
David J. Samuelsen	Anthony J. Allard
	John G. Cowperthwaite

Roger Blake Hohnsbeen	Frederick W. Gatt
Don Henry Schaefer	Rodney Ian Headington
Thomas S. Gelini	Candace Smith-Dabney

Representative Clients: Allstate Insurance Co.; California State Automobile Assn.; The Continental Insurance Cos.; County of Alameda.

For full biographical listings, see the Martindale-Hubbell Law Directory

HAIMS, JOHNSON, MACGOWAN & MCINERNEY (AV)

490 Grand Avenue, 94610
Telephone: 510-835-0500
Facsimile: 510-835-2833

(See Next Column)

HAIMS, JOHNSON, MACGOWAN & McINERNEY, *Oakland—Continued*

MEMBERS OF FIRM

Arnold B. Haims	Randy M. Marmor
Gary R. Johnson	John K. Kirby
Clyde L. MacGowan	Robert J. Frassetto
Thomas McInerney	Caroline N. Valentino
Lawrence A. Baker	Dianne D. Peebles

ASSOCIATES

Joseph Y. Ahn	Anne M. Michaels
Edward D. Baldwin	Michelle Diane Perry
Marc P. Bouret	Edward C. Schroeder, Jr.

For full biographical listings, see the Martindale-Hubbell Law Directory

HARDIN, COOK, LOPER, ENGEL & BERGEZ (AV)

1999 Harrison Street, 18th Floor, 94612-3541
Telephone: 510-444-3131
Telecopier: 510-839-7940

MEMBERS OF FIRM

Raymond J. Bergez	Matthew S. Conant
Ralph A. Lombardi	Chris P. Lavdiotis
Willard L. Alloway	Robert D. Eassa
Gennaro A. Filice, III	Peter O. Glaessner
Bruce P. Loper	Nicholas D. Kayhan
Bruce E. McLeod	John A. De Pasquale
Eugene Brown, Jr.	Peter A. Strotz

Amber L. Kelly	Amee A. Mikacich
Elsa M. Baldwin	Timothy J. McCaffery
Marshall A. Johnson	Stephen J. Valen
Diane R. Stanton	Troy D. McMahan
Jennifer M. Walker	GayLynn Renee Kirn
Margaret L. Kotzebue	Richard V. Normington III
Jonathan M. Cohen	

Representative Clients: Firemans Fund Insurance Cos.; City of Piedmont; The Dow Chemical Co.; Nissan Motor Corp.; Subaru of America; Weyerhauser Co.; Bay Area Rapid Transit District; Diamond Shamrock; Home Indemnity Co.; Rhone-Poulenc.

For Complete List of Firm Personnel, See General Section

For full biographical listings, see the Martindale-Hubbell Law Directory

RANKIN, SPROAT, MIRES, TRAPANI & REISER, A PROFESSIONAL CORPORATION (AV)

Suite 1616, 1800 Harrison Street, 94612
Telephone: 510-465-3922
Fax: 510-452-3006
Email: rankin@best.com *URL:* http://www.rankinlaw.com

Joseph F. Rankin (-1977)	Geoffrey A. Mires
Patrick T. Rankin (1943-1990)	Thomas A. Trapani
Ronald G. Sproat	Michael J. Reiser

David T. Shuey	Eugene G. Ashley
G. Trent Morrow	Kevin R. Mintz
Maribel Delgado Osborne	

LEGAL SUPPORT PERSONNEL

Jennifer L. Rankin (Administrator)	Sue Perata (Medical Paralegal)
Betty E. Evans (Nurse Paralegal)	Trish J. Fuzesy (Paralegal)
	Sally J. Attia (Medical Paralegal)

Reference: Union Bank.

For full biographical listings, see the Martindale-Hubbell Law Directory

RYAN, ANDRADA & LIFTER, A PROFESSIONAL CORPORATION (AV)

Tenth Floor, Kaiser Center Building, 300 Lakeside Drive, Suite 1045, 94612-3536
Telephone: 510-763-6510
Fax: 510-763-3921

Joseph D. Ryan, Jr.	Charles E. Kallgren
J. Randall Andrada	Rhonda D. Shelton
Jill J. Lifter	Lora Vail French
Jolie Krakauer	Vikki L. Barron
Glenn Gould	Bruce A. McIntosh
Michael J. Daley	Michael J. Thomas
Laura E. Ozak	

Representative Clients: Alameda Contra Costa County Transit District; CNA Insurance Companies; Truck Insurance Exchange; Liberty Mutual Insurance Group; Safeway Stores, Inc.

For full biographical listings, see the Martindale-Hubbell Law Directory

---

ORANGE, Orange Co.

HOLLINS, SCHECHTER & FEINSTEIN, A PROFESSIONAL CORPORATION (AV)

12th Floor, 505 South Main Street, P.O. Box 11021, 92856
Telephone: 714-558-9119
Fax: 714-558-9091
San Diego, California Office: 12526 High Bluff Drive, Suite 300, 92130.
Telephone: 619-792-3502.
Moreno Valley, California Office: 22690 Cactus Avenue, Suite 240, 92553.
Telephone: 909-247-2903.
Palm Springs, California Office: 1111 Tahquitz Canyon Way, Suite 121, 92262.
Telephone: 619-416-0288.

Andrew S. Hollins	Kenneth E. Gertz
Bruce Lee Schechter	Jack H. Snyder
Thomas M. Condas	Kenneth C. Jones
Thomas L. Hyatt	

Bryan R. Bush	Meka Moore
Mary Ann Schiller	Eric M. Schiffer
Joy L. Krikorian	Tanja Darrow-Means
Robert M. DeNichilo	Dao-Mary Do
Elliott J. Block	Jodie P. Filkins
Wendy Aline Mitchell	Richard T. Collins

OF COUNSEL

Marc J. Feinstein

Representative Clients: Acceptance Risk Managers; Admiral Insurance Co.; American Drug Store, Inc.; American States Insurance Co.; Colonial Penn Insurance Co.; Commercial Union Insurance Cos.; Farmers Insurance Group; Home Base d.b.a. Waban; Hull & Co., Inc.; Investors Insurance Group.

For full biographical listings, see the Martindale-Hubbell Law Directory

---

MARLIN & SALTZMAN, A PROFESSIONAL LAW CORPORATION (AV)

701 South Parker Street, Suite 8800, 92868-4720
Telephone: 714-541-1066
Fax: 714-542-4184
Woodland Hills, California Office: Westhills Plaza, 20700 Ventura Boulevard, Suite 227, 91364.
Telephone: 818-702-0600.
Fax: 818-702-6555.
San Diego, California Office: 750 "B" Street Suite 1925.
Telephone: 619-235-0600.
Fax: 619-235-0675.
Oakland, California Office: 1999 Harrison Street, Suite 990.
Telephone: 510-208-9400.
Fax: 510-208-9410.

Louis M. Marlin	Stanley D. Saltzman

Kathy Carter	Craig Pynes
Christy L. Conner	Katy M. Gronowski
Lynne A. Pearson	John Hollingshead
Toni L. Kern	Jeffrey R. Vincent
Scott A. Marriott	Marilynn J. Winters
William C. Gibson	Daniel J. Yauger
Alan S. Lazar	Thomas F. Hozduk (Resident, Woodland Hills Office)

For full biographical listings, see the Martindale-Hubbell Law Directory

---

OXNARD, Ventura Co.

LAWLER, BONHAM & WALSH (AV)

300 Esplanade Drive, Suite, 1900, P.O. Box 5527, 93031
Telephone: 805-485-8921
MCI Fax: 805-485-3766
Email: LBW@INTERNETMCI.COM

MEMBERS OF FIRM

Byron J. Lawler	Henry J. Walsh
Terrence J. Bonham	Carol A. Woo
Korman Dorsey Ellis	

ASSOCIATES

Richard A Shimmel	Maureen M. Houska

For full biographical listings, see the Martindale-Hubbell Law Directory

LAW OFFICES OF ALAN E. WISOTSKY (AV)

1000 Town Center Drive Suite 200, 93030
Telephone: 805-278-0920
Fax: 805-278-0289

(See Next Column)

LAW OFFICES OF ALAN E. WISOTSKY—*Continued*

ASSOCIATES

Brian P. Keighron　　　　　　　Jeffrey B. Held
　　　　　　Philip Erickson

For full biographical listings, see the Martindale-Hubbell Law Directory

---

PASADENA, Los Angeles Co.

BURNS, AMMIRATO, PALUMBO, MILAM & BARONIAN, A PROFESSIONAL LAW CORPORATION (AV)

65 North Raymond Avenue, 2nd Floor, 91103-3919
Telephone: 818-796-5053; 213-258-8282
Fax: 818-792-3078
Long Beach, California Office: One World Trade Center, Suite 1200.
Telephone: 310-436-8338; 714-952-1047.
Fax: 310-432-6049.

Michael A. Burns　　　　　　　Bruce Palumbo
Vincent A. Ammirato,　　　　　Jeffrey L. Milam
　Resident, Long Bch　　　　　Robert H. Baronian

Normand A. Ayotte　　　　　　Michael P. Vicencia,
Colleen Clark　　　　　　　　　Resident, LOng Bch
Valerie Julien-Peto　　　　　　Michael E. Wenzel,
Susan E. Luhring　　　　　　　Resident, Long Bch
Grace C. Mori,
　Resident, Long Bch

Reference: First Los Angeles Bank.

For full biographical listings, see the Martindale-Hubbell Law Directory

---

CAIRNS, DOYLE, LANS, NICHOLAS & SONI, A LAW CORPORATION (AV)

Ninth Floor, 225 South Lake Avenue, 91101
Telephone: 818-683-3111
Telecopier: 818-683-4999

John D. Cairns　　　　　　　　Stephen M. Lans
John C. Doyle　　　　　　　　　Francisco J. Nicholas
　　　　Rohini Soni (1956-1994)

Representative Clients: Allstate Insurance Companies; Burger King Corp.; California Insurance Guarantee Assn.; California United Bank; CIGNA Insurance Companies; City of Pasadena; Cumis Insurance Society, Inc.; Employer's Mutual Insurance Companies; State Farm Insurance Companies; Tokio Marine Insurance.

For full biographical listings, see the Martindale-Hubbell Law Directory

---

COLLINS, COLLINS, MUIR & TRAVER (AV)

Successor to Collins & Collins
Suite 300, 265 North Euclid, 91101
Telephone: 818-793-1163
FAX: 818-793-5982
Newport Beach, California Office: 333 Bayside Drive, 92660.
Telephone: 714-723-6284.
Fax: 714-723-7701.

MEMBERS OF FIRM

James E. Collins (1910-1987)　　Robert J. Traver
John J. Collins　　　　　　　　Frank J. D'Oro
Samuel J. Muir　　　　　　　　Brian K. Stewart

ASSOCIATES

Paul L. Rupard　　　　　　　　Christine E. Drage
Robert H. Stellwagen, Jr.　　　Peter L. Stacy
Tomas A. Guterres　　　　　　Stephen W. Olson

For full biographical listings, see the Martindale-Hubbell Law Directory

---

FREEBURG, JUDY & NETTELS (AV)

600 South Lake Avenue, 91106
Telephone: 818-585-4150
FAX: 818-585-0718
Santa Ana, California Office: Xerox Centre. 1851 East First Street, Suite 120. 92705-4017.
Telephone: 714-569-0950.
Facsimile: 714-569-0955.

Steven J. Freeburg　　　　　　J. Lawrence Judy
　　　　Charles F. Nettels

ASSOCIATES

Ingall W. Bull, Jr.　　　　　　Holly A. McNulty
Richard B. Castle　　　　　　　Karen S. Freeburg
Cynthia B. Schaldenbrand　　　Jennifer D. Helsel
　(Resident, Santa Ana Office)　William R. Francis
Robert S. Brody　　　　　　　Fred W. Brandt
　　　　Carla Crochet

For full biographical listings, see the Martindale-Hubbell Law Directory

---

KOLTS AND NAWA (AV)

The Walnut Plaza, Suite 195, 215 North Marengo Avenue, 91101
Telephone: 818-584-6968
FAX: 818-584-5718

MEMBERS OF FIRM

Raymond G. Kolts　　　　　　Gary C. Nawa

ASSOCIATES

Lynn M. Johnson　　　　　　　Francis T. Kalinski, II
Linda M. Toutant　　　　　　　Diane L. Darvey
　　　Michael A. J. Nangano

OF COUNSEL

Kathlene Landgraf Kolts

For full biographical listings, see the Martindale-Hubbell Law Directory

---

OVERLANDER, LEWIS & RUSSELL (AV)

65 North Raymond Avenue, Suite 210, 91103
Telephone: 818-304-0500
Fax: 818-304-9750

Thomas F. Overlander　　　　　Edwin A. Lewis
　　　Richard L. Russell, Jr.

Craig J. Miller　　　　　　　　Sherri Lynette Woods

For full biographical listings, see the Martindale-Hubbell Law Directory

---

*REDDING,** Shasta Co.

HALKIDES & MORGAN, A PROFESSIONAL CORPORATION (AV)

833 Mistletoe Lane, P.O. Drawer 492170, 96049-2170
Telephone: 916-221-8150
Fax: 916-221-7963
Email: gdh@halkides-morgan.com *URL:* http://www.halkides-morgan.com

G. Dennis Halkides　　　　　　William D. Ayres
Arthur L. Morgan, Jr.　　　　　John P. Kelley
　　　Mary Catherine Pearl

Representative Clients: Anheuser-Busch, Inc.; Cessna Aircraft Co.; County of Shasta; Gallagher Bassett Insurance Service; Great American Insurance Co.; Northern California Schools Insurance Group; Novastar International; Simpson Timber Co.; Standard Oil Company of California; The Times-Mirror Co.

For full biographical listings, see the Martindale-Hubbell Law Directory

---

MAIRE, MANSELL & BEASLEY, A LAW CORPORATION (AV)

2851 Park Marina Drive Suite 300, P.O. Drawer 994607, 96099-4607
Telephone: 916-246-6050
Fax: 916-246-6060
Email: MAIREMB@AOL.COM

Wayne H. Maire　　　　　　　Linda M. Carpenter
Patrick R. Beasley　　　　　　David S. Perrine
Adam M. Pressman　　　　　　Cynthia L. Cooper
　　　　Eric R. Maire

For full biographical listings, see the Martindale-Hubbell Law Directory

---

DOUGLAS H. NEWLAN (AV)

434 Redcliff Drive, Suite B, P.O. Box 491736, 96049-1736
Telephone: 916-221-0184
Fax: 916-221-8744

For full biographical listings, see the Martindale-Hubbell Law Directory

---

REDONDO BEACH, Los Angeles Co.

LAW OFFICES OF ARTHUR W. FRANCIS, JR. A PROFESSIONAL CORPORATION (AV)

2522 Artesia Boulevard, 90278
Telephone: 310-316-1988
Fax: 310-318-5894

Arthur W. Francis, Jr.

OF COUNSEL

Terry Chevillat

For full biographical listings, see the Martindale-Hubbell Law Directory

---

*REDWOOD CITY,** San Mateo Co.

BRANSON, FITZGERALD & HOWARD A PROFESSIONAL CORPORATION (AV)

Suite 400, 643 Bair Island Road, 94063
Telephone: 415-365-7710
Fax: 415-364-LAWS

(See Next Column)

BRANSON, FITZGERALD & HOWARD A PROFESSIONAL CORPORATION, *Redwood City—Continued*

Thomas A. Branson	Harry A. Griffith, III
Dermot J. FitzGerald	Carol P. Smith
Joseph C. Howard, Jr.	David S. Secrest
Fred R. Brinkop	Judith Friederici
Henry D. Rome	Shawn M. Ridley
Kristi L. Curtis	John R. Campo
Glenn D. Martin	John H. Podesta
David L. Strong	Sondra E. Kirwan

Elizabeth J. Von Emster

OF COUNSEL

Dwight S. Haldan

Reference: Union Bank.

For full biographical listings, see the Martindale-Hubbell Law Directory

LOW, BALL & LYNCH, A PROFESSIONAL CORPORATION (AV)

10 Twin Dolphin, Suite B-500, 94065
Telephone: 415-591-8822
Fax: 415-591-8884
San Francisco, California Office: 601 California Street, Suite 2100, 94108.
Telephone: 415-981-6630.
Monterey, California Office: 10 Ragsdale Drive, Suite 175, 93940.
Telephone: 408-655-8822.

Raymond Coates	David L. Blinn
Chester G. Moore, III	Janet Kulig
James D. Miller	Thomas E. Mulvihill
William H. Holsinger	Jennifer Elizabeth Acheson

John R. Baumann	Joseph M. Fenech

Michael E. Sandgren

For full biographical listings, see the Martindale-Hubbell Law Directory

OWEN & MELBYE, A PROFESSIONAL CORPORATION (AV)

700 Jefferson Street, 94063
Telephone: 415-364-6500
Fax: 415-365-7036
Tahoe City, California Office: P.O. Box 1524.
Telephone: 916-546-2473.

William H. Owen	Edmund M. Scott
Richard B. Melbye	Pamela J. Helmer
Norman J. Roger	John S. Posthauer

Paul R. Mangiantini

Albert P. Blake, Jr.	Conor A. Meyers
Dawn M. Patterson	Mary P. Derner

Representative Clients: Aetna Cravens Dargan Co.; Avco Lycoming; Beech Aircraft Corp.; California Casualty Indemnity Exchange; K & K Claims Service; Kemper Insurance Cos.; Mutual Service Insurance Co.; State Farm Mutual Insurance Cos.; Underwriters at Lloyds; United States Aviation Insurance Group.

For full biographical listings, see the Martindale-Hubbell Law Directory

SACRAMENTO,* Sacramento Co.

CAULFIELD, DAVIES & DONAHUE (AV)

3500 American River Drive, Suite 100, 95864
Telephone: 916-487-7700
Fairfield, California Office: Fairfield West Plaza, 1455 Oliver Road, Suite 130.
Telephone: 707-426-0223.

MEMBERS OF FIRM

Richard Hyland Caulfield	James R. Donahue
Robert E. Davies	Bruce E. Leonard

ASSOCIATES

David N. Tedesco	Jennifer Gittisriboongul
Matthew Paul Donahue	John T. Stralen
Brian C. Haydon	David D. Poland

Shannon Spellacy

For full biographical listings, see the Martindale-Hubbell Law Directory

DIEPENBROCK & COSTA (AV)

455 University Avenue, Suite 300, 95825
Telephone: 916-565-6222
Fax: 916-565-6220

MEMBERS OF FIRM

Anthony C. Diepenbrock	Daniel P. Costa

(See Next Column)

ASSOCIATES

John P. Cotter	Jeanne M. Carroll

Representative Clients: American Nuclear Insurer; Caldwell International; Central States of Omaha; Century Surety Co.; CIGNA; Citation; Colonial Penn; Connecticut Speciality Insurance Co.; Federated Mutual; Fleming & Hall.

For full biographical listings, see the Martindale-Hubbell Law Directory

HANSEN, BOYD, CULHANE & WATSON (AV)

A Partnership including Professional Corporations
Central City Centre, 1331 Twenty-First Street, 95814
Telephone: 916-444-2550
Telecopier: 916-444-2358

Hartley T. Hansen (Inc.)	Lawrence R. Watson
Kevin R. Culhane (Inc.)	John J. Rueda
David E. Boyd	James J. Banks

Lorraine M. Pavlovich

OF COUNSEL

Betsy S. Kimball

Thomas L. Riordan	Pamela B. Hooley
James O. Moses	Roger R. Billings

For full biographical listings, see the Martindale-Hubbell Law Directory

HARDY ERICH BROWN & WILSON, A PROFESSIONAL CORPORATION (AV)

1000 G Street, 95814
Telephone: 916-449-3800
Fax: 916-449-3888
Mailing Address: P.O. Box 13530, Sacramento, California, 95853-4530

John Quincy Brown, Jr.	Bruce E. Salenko
Anthony D. Osmundson	Daniel J. Coyle
Thomas C. Richards	Brian H. Charter
L. Thomas Wagner	Larry Caldwell
David L. Perrault	Richard L. Alley
John Quincy Brown, III	Glenda N. Reager
David S. Worthington	Whitney A. Davis
L. Kent Wyatt	John C. Miller, Jr.

Michael J. Nelson

OF COUNSEL

Cavan Hardy	William A. Wilson
Norwood R. Erich	Richard M. Cunha

Linda Wilson Bloom	Jay A. Resendez
Sara A. Clark	Kelly F. Watson

Kristine E. Balough

Representative Clients: AIG Aviation, Inc.; The Chubb Insurance Company; Fireman's Fund Insurance Company; Grange Insurance Association; The Infinity Group; Insurance Company of the West; Royal Insurance Company; Travelers Insurance Company; Twentieth Century Insurance Company.

For full biographical listings, see the Martindale-Hubbell Law Directory

JOHNSON, SCHACHTER & COLLINS, A PROFESSIONAL CORPORATION (AV)

701 University Avenue, Suite 150, 95825
Telephone: 916-921-5800
Telecopier: 916-921-0247
Email: 102514.3714@COMPUSERVE.COM

Robert H. Johnson	Alesa M. Schachter

Kim H. Collins

George W. Holt	Carrie G. Pratt
Timothy P. Dailey	R. James Miller

OF COUNSEL

Ford R. Smith	Carolyn M. Wood

Susanne M. Shelley

Representative Clients: Fireman's Fund Insurance Cos.; GAB Business Services; Jonsson Communications Corp.; McClatchy Newspapers and Broadcasting; State Farm Fire & Casualty Co.; State Farm Mutual Automobile Insurance Co.
Reference: Business & Professional Bank, Sacramento.

For full biographical listings, see the Martindale-Hubbell Law Directory

KEITGES, BANGLE & OWENSBY, A PROFESSIONAL LAW CORPORATION (AV)

2150 River Plaza Drive, Suite 205, 95833
Telephone: 916-568-3400
Fax: 916-568-3404
Fairfield, California Office: 1261 Travis Boulevard, Suite 270. 94533.
Telephone: 707-422-1301.
Fax: 707-427-6677.

(See Next Column)

KEITGES, BANGLE & OWENSBY A PROFESSIONAL LAW CORPORATION—
Continued

Cyril A. Keitges, Jr.	Tracy Owensby
Raymond Bangle, III	Jill H. Latchaw

For full biographical listings, see the Martindale-Hubbell Law Directory

LEWIS & BACON, A PROFESSIONAL CORPORATION (AV)

Ramona Hotel Office Building, 1001 Sixth Street, Suite 203, 95814
Telephone: 916-444-7340
Fax: 916-444-7411

Steven A. Lewis	Kenneth E. Bacon

Sharon B. Futerman	Heidi S. Cordeiro

For full biographical listings, see the Martindale-Hubbell Law Directory

MASON & THOMAS (AV)

2151 River Plaza Drive, Suite 100, P.O. Box 868, 95812-0868
Telephone: 916-567-8211
Fax: 916-567-8212

MEMBERS OF FIRM

Stephen A. Mason	Bradley S. Thomas

ASSOCIATES

Douglas W. Brown	Kevin L. Elder
Robert G. Kruse	Michele Raley
David S. Yost	David T. Ludington
Patrick J. Hehir	Timothy T. Wright
Anastasia Baskerville	

For full biographical listings, see the Martindale-Hubbell Law Directory

MATHENY POIDMORE LINKERT & SEARS (AV)

3638 American River Drive, P.O. Box 13711, 95853-4711
Telephone: 916-978-3434
Fax: 916-978-3430
Email: mpls1@netcom.com

MEMBERS OF FIRM

Henry G. Matheny (1933-1984)	James C. Damir
Anthony J. Poidmore	Michael A. Bishop
Douglas A. Sears	Ernest A. Long
Richard S. Linkert	Joann Georgallis
Kent M. Luckey	

ASSOCIATES

Matthew C. Jaime	Cathy A. Reynolds
Robert B. Berrigan	Eric R. Wiesel
Stephen J. Nardine	Reed R. Johnson
Ronald E. Enabnit	Danielle M. Guard
Andrea M. Croak	

LEGAL SUPPORT PERSONNEL

PARALEGALS

Karen D. Fisher	Lynell Rae Steed
Fran Studer	Jennifer Bachman
Debbie Sue Miller	

For full biographical listings, see the Martindale-Hubbell Law Directory

McDONALD, SAELTZER, MORRIS, CREEGGAN & WADDOCK (AV)

555 Capitol Mall, Suite 700, 95814
Telephone: 916-444-5706
Fax: 916-444-8529

MEMBERS OF FIRM

Eugene W. Saeltzer	Richard C. Creeggan
William O. Morris	Thomas P. Waddock
Gregory R. Madsen	

ASSOCIATES

Hank G. Greenblatt	Andrea Rae Austin
Jon S. Allin	S. Maylee Singer
Scott W. DePeel	Jay Steven Linden
Denise C. Standridge	Kenneth M. Goulart
Matthew P. Maniscalco	

OF COUNSEL

Douglas B. McDonald

Reference: Wells Fargo Bank.

For full biographical listings, see the Martindale-Hubbell Law Directory

NAGELEY, MEREDITH & RAMSEY, INC. (AV)

8001 Folsom Boulevard, Suite 200, P.O. Box 276270, 95827-6270
Telephone: 916-386-8282
Fax: 916-386-8952

Sam R. Nageley	Gregory A. Meredith
Joe Ramsey	

(See Next Column)

Drew M. Johnson	Carole Sharples
Craig S. MacGlashan	L. Alan Warwick
Michael B. O'Harra	Janet M. Meredith
Lawrence N. Hensley	Debbie J. Vorous
James C. Keowen	

OF COUNSEL

Andrea M. Miller

For full biographical listings, see the Martindale-Hubbell Law Directory

SCHUERING ZIMMERMAN & SCULLY, LLP (AV)

400 University Avenue, 95825
Telephone: 916-567-0400
Fax: 916-568-0400

MEMBERS OF FIRM

Steven T. Scully (1948-1994)	Lawrence S. Giardina
Leo H. Schuering, Jr.	Anthony D. Lauria
Robert H. Zimmerman	Keith D. Chidlaw
Thomas J. Doyle	John J. Sillis

Regina A. Favors	Donna W. Low
Raymond R. Gates	Dominique A. Pollara
Christian Koster	Theodore D. Poppinga
Scott A. Linn	John P. Rhode
Douglas L. Smith	

For full biographical listings, see the Martindale-Hubbell Law Directory

SAN BERNARDINO,* San Bernardino Co.

WILSON, BORROR, DUNN & DAVIS (AV)

Suite 307, The Bank of California Building, 255 North D Street, 92401
Telephone: 909-884-8855
Fax: 909-884-5161

MEMBERS OF FIRM

Fred A. Wilson (1886-1973)	James R. Dunn
Wm. H. Wilson (1915-1981)	Thomas M. Davis
Keith D. Davis	

ASSOCIATES

Timothy P. Prince	Sarah L. Overton

OF COUNSEL

Caywood J. Borror

Representative Clients: Travelers Insurance Co.; Rockwell International; Westinghouse Air Brake Co.; Goodyear Tire and Rubber Co.; Home Insurance Co.; Cities of: Redlands, Chino, Colton, San Bernardino and Upland; The Canadian Insurance Co.

For full biographical listings, see the Martindale-Hubbell Law Directory

SAN DIEGO,* San Diego Co.

BELSKY & ASSOCIATES (AV)

610 West Ash Street, Suite 700, 92101
Telephone: 619-232-8300
Fax: 619-338-0066

Daniel S. Belsky

Gabriel M. Benrubi	Cynthia Brack McGrew
Lisa L. Hillan	Timothy J. Tatro
Vincent J. Iuliano	Peter A. Zamoyski

References: Centre For Health Care Medical Associates; The Doctor's Company; Grossmont Bank; Graybill Medical Group, Inc.; Kaiser Foundation HealthPlan, Inc.; Norcal Mutual Insurance Co.; Sharp Mission Park Medical Group; Sharp Rees-Stealy Medical Group; Southern California Physician Insurance Exchange; Unifirst.

For full biographical listings, see the Martindale-Hubbell Law Directory

CHAPIN, FLEMING & WINET, A PROFESSIONAL CORPORATION (AV)

Library, 501 West Broadway, 15th Floor, 92101
Telephone: 619-232-4261
Telefax: 619-232-4840
Email: cfwlaw@adnc.com *URL:* http://www.sandiego-online.com/cfwlaw
Vista, California Office: 410 South Melrose Drive, Suite 101.
Telephone: 619-758-4261.
Telefax: 619-758-6420.
Los Angeles, California Office: 12121 Wilshire Boulevard, Suite 401.
Telephone: 310-826-0133.
Telefax: 310-207-4236.
Palm Springs, California Office: 225 North El Cielo Road, Suite 470.
Telephone: 619-416-1400.
Telefax: 619-416-1405.

(See Next Column)

CHAPIN, FLEMING & WINET A PROFESSIONAL CORPORATION, *San Diego—Continued*

Victor M. Barr, Jr.	Traci Lynn Kuchta
Craig H. Bell	Dana Marie Lawson
(Resident, Los Angeles Office)	(Resident, Los Angeles Office)
Darryn L. Berner	Jeffrey J. Leist
Kelli Jean Brooks	(Resident, Los Angeles Office)
Michael S. Burke	Tonya L. Morgan
David H. Bushnell	(Resident, Los Angeles Office)
(Resident, Los Angeles Office)	David A. Myers
Richard D. Carter	(Resident, Los Angeles Office)
(Resident, Los Angeles Office)	Brenda J. Pannell
Dean G. Chandler	(Resident, Los Angeles Office)
(Resident, Vista Office)	Kennett L. Patrick
Edward D. Chapin	(Resident, Vista Office)
Victoria Chen	Thomas V. Perea
George Chuang	(Resident, Los Angeles Office)
(Resident, Los Angeles Office)	Roger L. Popeney
Amber L. Eck	Maria C. Roberts
Robert Ehrenreich	Lawrence W. Shea, II
(Resident, Los Angeles Office)	Douglas J. Simpson
Scott K. Endsley	Spencer C. Skeen
George E. Fleming	(Resident, Los Angeles Office)
Antonio Gastelum (Not	Howard Smith
admitted in United States)	(Resident, Los Angeles Office)
Shirley A. Gauvin	Patricia L. Sullivan
Katherine M. Green	Gregory S. Tavill
Terence L. Greene	Frank L. Tobin
Gregory Kevin Hansen	Grace I. Wang
Howard L. Hoffenberg	(Resident, Los Angeles Office)
(Resident, Los Angeles Office)	Peter C. Ward
Patrick M. Howe	Jeffrey A. Weaver (Resident,
Aaron H. Katz	Palm Springs Office)
Elizabeth J. Koumas	Randall L. Winet
	(Resident, Vista Office)

OF COUNSEL

George F. Braun	Irwin Waldman (A P.C.)
Arthur D. Rutledge	(Resident, Los Angeles Office)
(Resident, Los Angeles Office)	James Michael Zimmerman
Jeffrey C. Stodel	
(Resident, Los Angeles Office)	

For full biographical listings, see the Martindale-Hubbell Law Directory

---

FERRIS & BRITTON, A PROFESSIONAL CORPORATION (AV)

1600 First National Bank Center, 401 West A Street, 92101
Telephone: 619-233-3131
Fax: 619-232-9316

Christopher Q. Britton	Steven J. Pynes
	Michael R. Weinstein

Representative Clients: Allstate Insurance Co.; Aetna Insurance Co.; Maryland Casualty Co.

For Complete List of Firm Personnel, See General Section

For full biographical listings, see the Martindale-Hubbell Law Directory

---

LAW OFFICES OF STEVEN R. HAASIS (AV)

First National Bank Building, 401 West "A" Street, 14th Floor, 92101-3509
Telephone: 619-236-9933
Fax: 619-236-8961

ASSOCIATE
Nelson J. Goodin

For full biographical listings, see the Martindale-Hubbell Law Directory

---

LAW OFFICES OF ROBERT S. KILBORNE IV (AV)

First National Bank Building, 401 West "A' Street, Suite 1850, 92101
Telephone: 619-237-1047
Fax: 619-237-1096

ASSOCIATE
David Arbogast
OF COUNSEL
Russell B. Wagner

For full biographical listings, see the Martindale-Hubbell Law Directory

---

LUCE, FORWARD, HAMILTON & SCRIPPS LLP (AV)

A Partnership including Professional Corporations
600 West Broadway, Suite 2600, 92101
Telephone: 619-236-1414
Fax: 619-232-8311
URL: http://www.luce.com
La Jolla, California Office: 4275 Executive Square, Suite 800, 92037.
Telephone: 619-535-2639.
Fax: 619-453-2812.

(See Next Column)

Los Angeles, California Office: 777 South Figueroa, Suite 3600, 90017.
Telephone: 213-892-4992.
Fax: 213-892-7731.
San Francisco, California Office: 100 Bush Street, 20th Floor, 94104.
Telephone: 415-395-7900.
Fax: 415-395-7949.
New York, N.Y. Office: Citicorp Center, 153 East 53rd Street, 26th Floor, 10022.
Telephone: 212-754-1414.
Fax: 212-644-9727.
Chicago, Illinois Office: 180 North La Salle Street, Suite 1125, 60601.
Telephone: 312-641-0580.
Fax: 312-641-0380.

MEMBERS OF FIRM

Scott W. Sonne	Cathy L. Croshaw (Resident,
(Managing Partner)	San Francisco Office)
Mark W. Hansen	Jeffrey L. Fillerup (Resident,
Peter H. Klee	San Francisco Office)
R. Randal Crispen	Kimball Ann Lane (Resident,
Mitchell L. Lathrop (Resident,	New York, N.Y. Office)
New York, N.Y. Office)	Craig R. Brown (Resident, New
Kathy P. Waring	York, N.Y. Office)
John L. Riedl	Daniel I. Simon
Rex Heeseman	(Resident, Los Angeles Office)
(Resident, Los Angeles Office)	Debra A. Chong (Resident, San
James E. Fitzgerald	Francisco Office)
(Resident, Los Angeles Office)	Nancy J. Gleason (Resident,
Andrew J. Waxler	Chicago, Illinois Office)
(Resident, Los Angeles Office)	Robin Craig-Olson (Resident,
	San Francisco Office)

SPECIAL COUNSEL

Harvey T. Elam (Resident, San	Philip J. McGuire (Resident,
Francisco Office)	Chicago, Illinois Office)

ASSOCIATES

Marc J. Feldman	Bridget Klein Moorhead
Valerie R. Cardenas	Laura L. Jackson (Resident, San
Roger D. Brown	Francisco Office)
Sonia S. Waisman	Christine M. Megna (Resident,
Nancy L. Beattie	New York, N.Y. Office)
Armin R. Callo	Sean C. Sheely (Resident, New
Roger S. Sampson (Resident,	York, N.Y. Office)
San Francisco Office)	Cathie A. Childs
James A. Goniea (Resident, San	Ronald D. Getchey
Francisco Office)	Christina Bull Arndt
Patricia Dee-Bilka (Resident,	(Resident, Los Angeles Office)
New York, N.Y. Office)	Matthew C. Elstein
Joseph F. Bermudez (Resident,	(Resident, Los Angeles Office)
New York, N.Y. Office)	Eric Todd Jorgensen
Huhnsik Chung (Resident, New	(Resident, Los Angeles Office)
York, N.Y. Office)	Greg R Groeneveld
Frances J. Phillips (Resident,	(Resident, Los Angeles Office)
New York, N.Y. Office)	Blaze D. Waleski (Resident,
Richard J. Fabian (Resident,	New York, N.Y. Office)
New York, N.Y. Office)	Gregory H. King
Julie B. Pollack (Resident, New	(Resident, Los Angeles Office)
York, N.Y. Office)	Deborah A. Primps (Resident,
Lourdes M. Slater (Resident,	New York, N.Y. Office)
New York, N.Y. Office)	Patrick J. McGuire (Resident,
Lisa J. Greene (Resident, New	Chicago, Illinois Office)
York, N.Y. Office)	Robert C. Thurston (Resident,
	Chicago, Illinois Office)

For Complete List of Firm Personnel, See General Section

For full biographical listings, see the Martindale-Hubbell Law Directory

---

NEIL, DYMOTT, PERKINS, BROWN & FRANK, A PROFESSIONAL CORPORATION (AV)

1010 Second Avenue, Suite 2500, 92101-4959
Telephone: 619-238-1712
Fax: 619-238-1562

Michael I. Neil	David G. Brown
Thomas M. Dymott	Robert W. Frank
Roger G. Perkins	Gina L. Lacagnina
	Robert W. Harrison

Reference: Scripps Bank.

For full biographical listings, see the Martindale-Hubbell Law Directory

---

SPARBER, FERGUSON, PONDER & RYAN, A PROFESSIONAL LAW CORPORATION (AV)

Imperial Bank Building, 701 "B" Street, Tenth Floor, 92101-8103
Telephone: 619-239-3600
Facsimile: 619-239-5601

Richard E. Sparber	Greg J. Ryan
James P. Ferguson	Richard J. Annen
John E. Ponder	Daniel F. Morrin
	Gary B. Rudolph

(See Next Column)

SPARBER, FERGUSON, PONDER & RYAN A PROFESSIONAL LAW
CORPORATION—*Continued*

Todd R. Gabriel	William P. Fennell
Carol R. McGinnis	James E. Highsmith

OF COUNSEL
Mark P. Mandell
LEGAL SUPPORT PERSONNEL
LEGAL ADMINISTRATOR
Beverly K. Driscoll

For full biographical listings, see the Martindale-Hubbell Law Directory

WINGERT, GREBING, ANELLO & BRUBAKER (AV)

A Partnership including Professional Corporations
One America Plaza, Seventh Floor, 600 West Broadway, 92101-3370
Telephone: 619-232-8151
Facsimile: 619-232-4665
Email: wgab@wgab.com
Las Vegas, Nevada Office: Ryan, Marks and Johnson, 317 South Sixth
Street, 89101.
Telephone: 702-471-7270.
Facsimile: 702-471-1245.

MEMBERS OF FIRM

John R. Wingert (A Professional Corporation)	James Goodwin
	Shawn D. Morris
Charles R. Grebing (A Professional Corporation)	Robert M. Caietti
	Eileen Mulligan Marks (Resident, Las Vegas, Nevada Office)
Michael M. Anello (A Professional Corporation)	
Alan K. Brubaker (A Professional Corporation)	Christopher W. Todd
	Robert L. Johnson (Resident, Las Vegas, Nevada Office)
Norman A. Ryan (Resident, Las Vegas, Nevada Office)	Robert M. Juskie

John S. Addams
ASSOCIATES

Julie E. Saake	James J. Brown, Jr.
Michael Sullivan	Craig Gross
Carolyn P. Gallinghouse	Stephen C. Grebing
Kimberly I. Cary	Brian P. Worthington
Terie M. Theis	Melanie A. Jubelirer
James P. Broder (Resident, Las Vegas, Nevada Office)	Kimberly A. Davis
	Michael W. Vivoli

OF COUNSEL
William L. Todd, Jr.

Representative Clients: California Casualty Insurance Co.; Farmers Insurance
Group; The Ohio Casualty Group; United Services Automobile Assn.;
United States Fidelity & Guaranty Co.

For full biographical listings, see the Martindale-Hubbell Law Directory

---

SAN FRANCISCO,* San Francisco Co.

BISHOP, BARRY, HOWE, HANEY & RYDER, A PROFESSIONAL CORPORATION (AV)

Embarcadero Center West, 12th Floor, 275 Battery Street, 94111-3333
Telephone: 415-421-8550
FAX: 415-362-4730

Ross R. Ryder (1940-1989)	Thomas O. Haran
Nelson C. Barry	Rebecca B. Aherne
Drayton F. Howe, Jr.	Michael W. Bolechowski
Jeffrey N. Haney	Mark C. Raskoff

Patricia S. Lakner

William R. Brown	Stacey A. Kuch
J. Scott Wood	Marco R. Sumarriva
Mitchell J. Alward	Curtis A. Canfield
Lawrence S. Molton	Gregory R. de la Peña
Susan Knell Bumbalo	Paul Andrew Herp
Brook Bernard Bond	Rebecca E. Thomson
Marisa D'Amico	Jane E. Carey

OF COUNSEL
Woodrow W. Denney

Reference: The Redwood Bank.

For full biographical listings, see the Martindale-Hubbell Law Directory

BOUGHEY, GARVIE & BUSHNER (AV)

One Post Street, Suite 2400, 94104-5228
Telephone: 415-398-4500
Fax: 415-398-2455
Email: 73410.1133@compuserve.com
Honolulu, Hawaii Office: Seven Waterfront Plaza, 500 Alla Moana
Boulevard, Suite 400, 96813.
Telephone: 808-599-8856.
Fax: 800-585-9332. Fax out of U.S.A.: 510-472-6569.

(See Next Column)

MEMBERS OF FIRM

James D. Boughey	Ronald S. Bushner
Robert C. Garvie	Eileen R. Ridley

Donald A. Velez, Jr.	George H. Keller
Ginger M. English	Larry E. Wollert, II

For full biographical listings, see the Martindale-Hubbell Law Directory

FISHER & HURST, LLP (AV)

353 Sacramento Street, 94111
Telephone: 415-956-8000
Facsimile: 415-398-1182
Email: Fisher@ix.netcom.com

Harold J. Chase (1921-1973)	Geoffrey A. Beaty
James T. Hurst (1933-1983)	Arthur Schwartz
Charles Negley	Robert Berg
Robert N. Schiff	Lori A. Sebransky
Steven L. Sumnick	Laura Hamilton Smith

Beverly M. Ma
OF COUNSEL
Peter W. Fisher
ASSOCIATES

David A. Firestone	Heidi L. Burch
David G. Valdez	Suzanne Solomon

For full biographical listings, see the Martindale-Hubbell Law Directory

FLYNN, DELICH & WISE (AV)

Suite 1750, 580 California Street, 94104
Telephone: 415-693-5566
Fax: 415-693-0410
Long Beach, California Office: 1 World Trade Center, Suite 1800.
Telephone: 310-435-2626.
Fax: 310-437-7555.

John Allen Flynn	Sam D. Delich
	James B. Nebel

Representative Clients: American Hawaii Cruises; Holland America Line;
Through Transport Mutual Insurance Association, Ltd.; The Britannia
Steam Ship Insurance Association Limited; The Steamship Mutual Underwriting Association (Bermuda) Ltd.; General Steamship Corp., Ltd.; Commodore Cruise Line, Ltd.; Interocean Steamship Corporation; Sea-Land Service, Inc.; Hatteras Yachts.

For full biographical listings, see the Martindale-Hubbell Law Directory

GUDMUNDSON, SIGGINS, STONE & SKINNER (AV)

One Embarcadero Center, Suite 1350, 94111
Telephone: 415-391-4200
FAX: 415-989-4739

MEMBERS OF FIRM

Richard J. Siggins	Jeffrey A. Skinner
Harold A. Stone	Francis M. McKeown

ASSOCIATES

Mark A. Hagopian	Dale T. Boutiette
	James S. McPherson

OF COUNSEL
W. W. Gudmundson

For full biographical listings, see the Martindale-Hubbell Law Directory

HARDIMAN, OLSON & CARROLL, A LAW PARTNERSHIP (AV)

160 Pine Street, Suite 700, 94111
Telephone: 415-248-3930
Fax: 415-248-3933
Torrance, California Office: Union Bank Tower, 21515 Hawthorne
Boulevard, Suite 590, 90503.
Telephone: 310-792-5200.
Fax: 310-792-5202.

Michael F. Hardiman

For full biographical listings, see the Martindale-Hubbell Law Directory

IMAI, TADLOCK & KEENEY (AV)

180 Montgomery Street, Suite 1000, 94104
Telephone: 415-989-8687
Fax: 415-989-7640

Bruce Imai	Robert C. Keeney
Terry G. Tadlock	Theodore T. Cordery

Judith L. Alex	Joan E. Marquardt
Jeffrey C. Tung	Janet M. Heckmann
Brian H. Buddell	Kimberly A. Harrell

For full biographical listings, see the Martindale-Hubbell Law Directory

San Francisco—Continued

LAWRENCE E. KERN A LAW CORPORATION (AV)

Sutter Plaza, Suite 600, 1388 Sutter Street, 94109
Telephone: 415-474-1900
Fax: 415-474-0302

Lawrence E. Kern	Philip A. Segal
John A. Noda	Reuben B. Jacobson
Joseph M. Devine	Judith S. McAulay
Michael G. Thomas	

Representative Clients: California State Automobile Assn.; Farmers Insurance Group; Yellow Cab Co.; State Farm; Atlantic Mutual Insurance Co.; Valley Insurance Co.; Mercury Insurance Group.

For full biographical listings, see the Martindale-Hubbell Law Directory

KINDER, WUERFEL & CHOLAKIAN, A PROFESSIONAL CORPORATION (AV)

555 Montgomery Street, Ninth Floor, 94111
Telephone: 415-398-1551; 800-992-5990
FAX: 415-398-3301
URL: www.kwcapc.com
Santa Rosa, California Office: 2300 Northpoint Parkway.
Telephones: 707-522-8020; 800-992-5990.
FAX: 707-522-8022.
Costa Mesa, California Office: Avenue of the Arts.
Telephone: 714-825-3590; 800-992-5990.

H. Stuart Kinder	Kevin K. Cholakian
Mark D. Wuerfel	Julian J. Pardini
	(Resident, Santa Rosa Office)

SPECIAL COUNSEL

Mark A. Koop	Nan R. Hooven
	Paul B. Justi

Robert E. Belshaw	Peter R. Harris
David H. Bennett	(Resident, Santa Rosa Office)
Dean C. Burnick	Kathleen M. Hurly
Cheryl Castrogiovanni	Timothy S. Kirk
Douglas M. Chapman	Bryan A. McBurney
Christopher J. Connell	Steven J. Plas
(Resident, Santa Rosa Office)	Anthony O. Ricucci
Michael J. Estep	Charlene P. Rosack
James M. Gentile	Scott A. Slomiak
Garth A. Gersten	Michael A. Topp
Victor G. Greene	Harold A. Weston

LEGAL SUPPORT PERSONNEL

Gary T. Hall, Legal Administrator

For full biographical listings, see the Martindale-Hubbell Law Directory

LEACH, McGREEVY & BAUTISTA (AV)

1735 Pacific Avenue, 94109
Telephone: 415-775-4455
Telefax: 415-775-7435
Southern California Office: 13643 Fifth Street, Chino, CA. 91710.
Telephone: 909-590-2224.

Theodore Tamba (1900-1973)	Teresa A. Cunningham
John T. Harmon (1928-1993)	J. Curtis Cox
David G. Leach	Robert W. Shinnick
Richard E. McGreevy	Philip T. Kilduff
A. Marquez Bautista	Paul David Katerndahl

ASSOCIATE

John C. Connolly

OF COUNSEL

Roger G. Eliassen	Lloyd F. Postel

For full biographical listings, see the Martindale-Hubbell Law Directory

McGLYNN, McLORG & RITCHIE (AV)

Bayside Plaza, 177 Steuart Street, Suite 200, 94105
Telephone: 415-543-9000
Fax: 415-543-8300
Sacramento, California Office: 980 Ninth Street, 19th Floor, 95814.
Telephone: 916-446-6979.
Facsimile: 916-444-0826.

MEMBERS OF FIRM

John P. McGlynn	Daniel J. Meagher, Jr.
Vincent B. McLorg	Dane T. Jones
James R. Ritchie	Robyn Schanzenbach
Susan L. Penney	Wallace M. Tice
Karen E. Kirby	

ASSOCIATES

Michele A. Perussina	Andrew A. Vandeveld
Michael C. Scanlon, Jr.	Cynthia L. Leahy
Allison K. West	Sandra A. Milligan

For full biographical listings, see the Martindale-Hubbell Law Directory

MURPHY, PEARSON, BRADLEY & FEENEY, A PROFESSIONAL CORPORATION (AV)

88 Kearny Street, 11th Floor, 94108
Telephone: 415-788-1900
Telecopier: 415-393-8087
Sacramento, California Office: Suite 200, 3600 American River Drive, 95864.
Telephone: 916-483-6074.
Telecopier: 916-483-6088.

James A. Murphy	William S. Kronenberg
Gregory A. Bastian	
(Resident, Sacramento Office)	

For Complete List of Firm Personnel, See General Section

For full biographical listings, see the Martindale-Hubbell Law Directory

SARRAIL, LYNCH & HALL (AV)

44 Montgomery Street, 34th Floor, 94104
Telephone: 415-398-2404
Fax: 415-391-9076

Stephen W. Hall (1955-1993)	James A. Sarrail
Linda J. Lynch	

Michael J. Ruggles	Susan A. Byron
David Y. Wong	Ernest D. Faitos
Jonathan S. Larsen	Brian D. Harrison
Sheila M. Salomon	

OF COUNSEL

Jack A. Pollatsek

LEGAL SUPPORT PERSONNEL

Cynthia R. Benzerara

For full biographical listings, see the Martindale-Hubbell Law Directory

SCADDEN, HAMILTON & RYAN (AV)

580 California Street, Suite 1400, 94104
Telephone: 415-362-5116
Facsimile: 415-362-4214

James G. Scadden	Robert J. Ryan
Robert P. Hamilton	James P. Cunningham

James F. Hetherington	Eileen Santana Wright
Charles O. Thompson	Vincent C. Milani

LEGAL SUPPORT PERSONNEL

Laurie C. Meyer

For full biographical listings, see the Martindale-Hubbell Law Directory

STUBBS, HITTIG & LEONE, A PROFESSIONAL CORPORATION (AV)

Fox Plaza, Suite 818, 1390 Market Street, 94102-5399
Telephone: 415-861-8200
Telecopier: 415-861-6700
Email: SHLSF@aol.com

Gregory E. Stubbs	Louis A. Leone
H. Christopher Hittig	Marina B. Pitts

For full biographical listings, see the Martindale-Hubbell Law Directory

THORNTON, TAYLOR, DOWNS, BECKER, TOLSON & DOHERTY (AV)

A Partnership including Professional Corporations
16th Floor, 505 Sansome Street, 94111
Telephone: 415-421-8890
Fax: 415-421-0688

MEMBERS OF FIRM

H.A. Thornton (1887-1953)	Pamela Wilson Levin
Evans M. Taylor (1903-1991)	Clarke B. Holland
Otto F. Becker	Jonathan H. Erb
Greg S. Tolson (P.C.)	Phillip F. Shinn
Francis X. Doherty (P.C.)	Patrick J. Bailey
Mary M. Drinan	

ASSOCIATES

Stephen F. Henry	Stephan L. Eberle
Brendan J. Fogarty	Stephan T. Pastis
David B. A. Demo	Celia W. Lee
Sandra E. Stone	Andrew J. Brown
Fiel D. Tigno	Andrean L. Kalemis

OF COUNSEL

Jerome F. Downs

For full biographical listings, see the Martindale-Hubbell Law Directory

San Francisco—Continued

VOGL & MEREDITH (AV)

456 Montgomery Street, 20th Floor, 94104
Telephone: 415-398-0200
Facsimile: 415-398-2820

Samuel E. Meredith	Jean N. Yeh
David R. Vogl	Janet Brayer
John P. Walovich	Thomas S. Clifton

Jill M. Thayer	Mark Ginalski
	Nicole L. Meredith

For full biographical listings, see the Martindale-Hubbell Law Directory

SAN JOSE,* Santa Clara Co.

CAMPBELL, WARBURTON, FITZSIMMONS, SMITH, MENDELL & PASTORE, A PROFESSIONAL CORPORATION (AV)

111 West St. John Street, Suite 440, P.O. Box 1867, 95113
Telephone: 408-295-7701
Fax: 408-295-1423

John R. Fitzsimmons, Jr.	Ralph E. Mendell
C. Michael Smith	Nicholas Pastore
	J. Michael Fitzsimmons

William R. Colucci	Carolyn M. Rose

Representative Corporate Clients: Helene Curtis, Inc.; Viking Freight System, Inc.
Representative Insurance Clients: California State Automobile Assn.; Farmers Insurance Group; Travelers Insurance Co.; Westfield Insurance Cos.; Michelin Tire Corp. (Self Insured).

For Complete List of Firm Personnel, See General Section

For full biographical listings, see the Martindale-Hubbell Law Directory

COLLINS & SCHLOTHAUER (AV)

An Association of Attorneys including a Professional Corporation
60 South Market Street, Suite 1100, 95113-2369
Telephone: 408-298-5161
Fax: 408-297-5766
Affiliated Los Angeles, California Office: Schlothauer, Collins & Macaluso, 11661 San Vicente Boulevard, Suite 303.
Telephone: 310-820-8606.
Fax: 310-820-7057.

Mark Scott Collins (Inc.)	Linda L. Duiven
David N. Poll	Jovita Prestoza

OF COUNSEL

Thomas L. Schlothauer	Todd E. Macaluso

Representative Clients: Unigard Insurance; Farmers Insurance Co.; Fire Insurance Exchange; National American Insurance Co.; ABAG (Association of Bay Area Governmental Entities).

For full biographical listings, see the Martindale-Hubbell Law Directory

HINSHAW, WINKLER, DRAA, MARSH & STILL (AV)

152 North Third Street, Suite 300, P.O. Box 15030, 95115-0030
Telephone: 408-293-5959
Fax: 408-280-0966
Email: hinshaw-law.com

MEMBERS OF FIRM

Edward A. Hinshaw	Gerhard O. Winkler
Tyler G. Draa	Barry C. Marsh
	Thomas E. Still

ASSOCIATES

Lynne Thaxter Brown	Jennifer H. Still
Bradford J. Hinshaw	Megan A. Smith

For full biographical listings, see the Martindale-Hubbell Law Directory

ROBINSON & WOOD, INC. (AV)

227 North First Street, 95113
Telephone: 408-298-7120
Fax: 408-298-0477
Email: rw@r-winc.com

Archie S. Robinson	Jonathan L. Lee
Weldon S. Wood	Jon B. Zimmerman
Thomas R. Fellows	Mark B. Schellerup
David S. Henningsen	Andrew W. Olsson
Hugh F. Lennon	Erica R. Yew
Jesse F. Ruiz	Arthur J. Casey
Christian B. Nielsen	Joseph C. Balestrieri

(See Next Column)

John L. Winchester, III	Wendy Woolpert
Chadney C. Ankele	Ann A. Nguyen
Robert A. Nakamae	Kenneth I. Schumaker
Rebecca L. Moon	Anne C. Bailey
Wendy E. Flockhart	Stephen D. Bays

For full biographical listings, see the Martindale-Hubbell Law Directory

VAN LOUCKS & HANLEY (AV)

160 West Santa Clara Street, Suite 1050, 95113
Telephone: 408-494-0400
Fax: 408-494-0404

Geoffrey Van Loucks	Anthony L. Hanley

Michael K. Budra

Reference: San Jose National Bank.

For full biographical listings, see the Martindale-Hubbell Law Directory

SAN MATEO, San Mateo Co.

McDOWALL, COTTER, DUNN, VALE & BRACCO, A PROFESSIONAL CORPORATION (AV)

2070 Pioneer Court, P.O. Box 937, 94403
Telephone: 415-572-7933
Fax: 415-572-0834
Palo Alto, California Office: 425 Sherman Avenue, Suite 100.
Telephone: 408-244-8755; *Other Areas:* 415-326-8410.
Fax: 415-326-3911.

William D. McDowall	Robert D. Vale
Bernard T. Cotter	Michael A. Bracco
Thomas G. Dunn	David S Rosenbaum
	Richard M. Kelly

Representative Clients: State Farm Mutual Automobile Insurance Co.; State Farm Fire & Casualty Co.; California State Automobile Assn.; Insurance Company of the West; Allegiance Insurance Co.; Argonaut Insurance Cos.

For full biographical listings, see the Martindale-Hubbell Law Directory

SAN RAFAEL,* Marin Co.

PLASTIRAS & FORSBLAD (AV)

24 Professional Center Parkway, Suite 150, 94903
Telephone: 415-472-8100
Fax: 415-472-8110
Email: plastir@ix.netcom.com

Basil Plastiras	David R. Forsblad

Martin Anderson	Michael P. Terrizzi

For full biographical listings, see the Martindale-Hubbell Law Directory

SANTA ANA,* Orange Co.

BEAM, BROBECK & WEST (AV)

600 West Santa Ana Boulevard, Suite 1000, 92701
Telephone: 714-558-3944
Fax: 714-568-0129

MEMBERS OF FIRM

Byron J. Beam	Kirk H. Nakamura
David J. Brobeck, Jr.	Robert H. McMillan
John E. West	Daniel R. Sullivan

ASSOCIATES

Betsey J. Jeffery	Donald S. Zalewski
Charles W. Matheis, Jr.	Geralyn L. Skapik
Robert C. Hastie	David R. Rosenberg
Gregory L. Rippetoe	Louise M. Douville
Jennifer J. Miller	Kermit D. Marsh

Representative Clients: Aetna Insurance Co.; American General Life Insurance Co.; American Hospital Supply; Carl Warren & Co.; Casualty Insurance Co.; City of Anaheim; City of Fullerton; City of Newport Beach; Empire Insurance Cos.; Physicians Interindemnity.

For full biographical listings, see the Martindale-Hubbell Law Directory

CASSIDY, WARNER, THURBER & LANE, A PROFESSIONAL CORPORATION (AV)

600 West Santa Ana Boulevard, Suite 700, 92701
Telephone: 714-835-9431
Fax: 714-835-5264

Alvin M. Cassidy	David K. Thurber
B. Kent Warner	Timothy X. Lane
	Bruce A. Winstead

(See Next Column)

CASSIDY, WARNER, THURBER & LANE A PROFESSIONAL CORPORATION, *Santa Ana—Continued*

Lloyd W. Felver   David C. Olson
Glen A. Stebens

For full biographical listings, see the Martindale-Hubbell Law Directory

GARRETT & JENSEN (AV)

433 Civic Center Drive, West, P.O. Box 22002, 92702-2002
Telephone: 714-550-0100
Fax: 714-550-0471
Riverside, California Office: 3403 10th Street, Suite 700.
Telephone: 909-781-0222.

MEMBERS OF FIRM

Boyd F. Jensen, II   Mark S. Armijo
Betty Fracisco   Jennifer Malone
Douglas M. Borthwick

OF COUNSEL

Kenneth R. Garrett

Representative Clients: Allstate Insurance Co.; Automobile Club of Southern California; Fireman's Fund American Insurance Co.; Government Employees Insurance Co.

For full biographical listings, see the Martindale-Hubbell Law Directory

HAIGHT, BROWN & BONESTEEL (AV)

A Partnership including Professional Corporations
Suite 900, 5 Hutton Centre Drive, 92707
Telephone: 714-754-1100
Telecopier: 714-754-0826
Santa Monica, California Office: 1620 26th Street, Suite 4000 North, P.O. Box 680.
Telephone: 310-449-6000.
Telecopier: 310-829-5117.
Telex: 705837.
Riverside, California Office: 3750 University Avenue, Suite 650.
Telephone: 909-341-8300.
Fax: 909-341-8309.
San Francisco, California Office: 20 Sansome Street, Suite 300.
Telephone: 415-986-7700.
Fax: 415-986-6954.

RESIDENT MEMBERS

Bruce L. Cleeland   Jay T. Thompson

ASSOCIATES

Laura M. Knox (Resident)   Jeffrey S. Gerardo (Resident)

Counsel for: Orange County: Aetna Casualty and Surety Co.; Zurich-American Insurance Cos.; Industrial Indemnity Co.; Professional Liability Claims Managers; Maryland Casualty Insurance Co.; Royal Insurance Company of America.

For Complete List of Firm Personnel, See General Section

For full biographical listings, see the Martindale-Hubbell Law Directory

HOWARD, MOSS, LOVEDER, STRICKROTH & WALKER (AV)

A Partnership including Professional Corporations
2677 North Main Street, Suite 800, 92705-6631
Telephone: 714-542-6300
Telecopier: 714-542-6987
Riverside, California Office: 6700 Indiana Avenue, Suite 160.
Telephone: 909-341-8353.
Telecopier: 909-275-9637.

PARTNERS

Theodore R. Howard (A   Michael J. Strickroth
  Professional Corporation)   Robert A. Walker (Resident,
Robert J. Moss (A Professional   Riverside, California Office)
  Corporation)   Margaret M. Parker
James E. Loveder   Michael F. Moran

ASSOCIATES

Eugene Edward Keller II   James W. Daley
Mitchell L. Leverett   Brent C. Vian
  (Resident, Riverside Office) James J. Orland

For full biographical listings, see the Martindale-Hubbell Law Directory

LONG & WILLIAMSON, A PROFESSIONAL CORPORATION (AV)

5 Hutton Centre Drive, Suite 1000, 92707
Telephone: 714-668-1400
Fax: 714-668-1411
San Diego, California Office: 501 West Broadway, Suite 1600.
Telephone: 619-234-5400.
Fax: 619-235-9449.

Patrick A. Long   John S. Williamson

(See Next Column)

Thomas E. Martin   Mark B. Buehler
John A. Delis   Marc T.A. Fitch
              Anthony J. Dunne

Reference: Orange National Bank.

For full biographical listings, see the Martindale-Hubbell Law Directory

LAW OFFICES OF R. Q. SHUPE (AV)

A Partnership including a Professional Corporation
333 Civic Center Drive West, 92701
Telephone: 714-558-4898
Telecopier: 714-558-9060
San Diego, California Office: Shupe & Bayuk, 600 West Broadway, Suite 1400.
Telephone: 619-231-6252.
Fax: 619-231-6204.

R. Q. Shupe (A Professional   Christopher W. Bayuk
  Corporation)   (Resident, San Diego,
                                  California)

William D. Schuster   Clifford P. Connors
G. Peter Norregard   Julie Ellen Wyne
              Eric S. McIntosh

For full biographical listings, see the Martindale-Hubbell Law Directory

*SANTA BARBARA,** Santa Barbara Co.

ALLEN, RHODES, SOBELSOHN & JOHNSON, LLP (AV)

125 East De La Guerra, 2nd Floor, 93101
Telephone: 805-965-5236
Los Angeles, California Office: 10866 Wilshire Boulevard, Suite 200.
Telephone: 310-475-0875; 213-879-9660.

MEMBER OF FIRM

Michael E. Johnson

Reference: Wells Fargo Bank.

For full biographical listings, see the Martindale-Hubbell Law Directory

ARCHBALD & SPRAY (AV)

505 Bath Street, 93101
Telephone: 805-564-2070
Telecopier: 805-564-2081
Email: arch@silcom.com

MEMBERS OF FIRM

Malcolm Archbald (Retired)   Karen T. Burgett
Joseph L. Spray (1927-1985)   Edwin K. Loskamp
Kenneth L. Moes   Wm. Brennan Lynch
J. William McLafferty   Michael A. Colton
Douglas B. Large   Ann Gormican Anderson

SENIOR ATTORNEYS

Peri Maziarz   Katherine H. Bower

ASSOCIATE

Cheryl A. Shaw

OF COUNSEL

John W. Warnock

Representative Clients: Acclaim Administrators; Cigna; E&O Professionals; Lancer Insurance; Pioneer; Scottsdale Insurance Company; Shand Morahan & Company; Sutter Insurance; Utica Mutual Insurance; Zurich American Insurance.

For full biographical listings, see the Martindale-Hubbell Law Directory

KINKLE, RODIGER AND SPRIGGS, PROFESSIONAL CORPORATION (AV)

125 East De La Guerra Street, 93101-2239
Telephone: 805-966-4700
Fax: 805-966-4120
Los Angeles, California Office: 600 North Grand Avenue.
Telephone: 213-629-1261.
Fax: 213-629-8382.
Santa Ana, California Office: 837 North Ross Street.
Telephone: 714-835-9011.
Fax: 714-667-7806.
Riverside, California Office: 3333 14th Street.
Telephone: 909-683-2410; 800-235-2039.
Fax: 909-683-7759.
San Diego, California Office: Suite 900 Driver Insurance Center, 1620 Fifth Avenue, P.O. Box 127900.
Telephone: 619-233-4566.
Fax: 619-233-8554.

(See Next Column)

KINKLE, RODIGER AND SPRIGGS PROFESSIONAL CORPORATION—*Continued*

John V. Hager (Managing Attorney)	Joy L. Lim
	Jeffery D. Lim
Edwin C. Mann	Chad M. Slack
Donna D. Geck	

For full biographical listings, see the Martindale-Hubbell Law Directory

SANTA MONICA, Los Angeles Co.

HAIGHT, BROWN & BONESTEEL (AV)

A Partnership including Professional Corporations
1620 26th Street, Suite 4000 North, P.O. Box 680, 90404
Telephone: 310-449-6000
Telecopier: 310-829-5117
Telex: 705837
Santa Ana, California Office: Suite 900, 5 Hutton Centre Drive.
Telephone: 714-754-1100.
Telecopier: 714-754-0826.
Riverside, California Office: 3750 University Avenue, Suite 650.
Telephone: 909-341-8300.
Fax: 909-341-8309.
San Francisco, California Office: 201 Sansome Street, Suite 300.
Telephone: 415-986-7700.
Fax: 415-986-6954.

MEMBERS OF FIRM

Peter Q. Ezzell (A Professional Corporation)	Kevin R. Crisp
	Lee Marshall
William G. Baumgaertner (A Professional Corporation)	Steven E. Moyer
	Kenneth G. Anderson
Peter A. Dubrawski	William O. Martin, Jr.
J. R. Seashore	David C. McGovern

ASSOCIATES

Alicia E. Taylor	Michael J. Sipos
S. Christian Stouder	Michael H. Gottschlich

For Complete List of Firm Personnel, See General Section

For full biographical listings, see the Martindale-Hubbell Law Directory

KOHRS, FISKE & STEUR (AV)

3250 Ocean Park Boulevard, 90405
Telephone: 310-452-5524
Telecopier: 310-452-6115

MEMBERS OF FIRM

Conrad Kohrs	Chad M. Steur
J. Peter Fiske	Kim F. Cassulo

LEGAL SUPPORT PERSONNEL
Sarah Elizabeth Robbins

For full biographical listings, see the Martindale-Hubbell Law Directory

SANTA ROSA,* Sonoma Co.

THE LAW OFFICES OF CAMPBELL, ANDERSON, CASEY, SINK & JOHNSON A PROFESSIONAL CORPORATION (AV)

Suite 202, 3333 Mendocino Avenue, 95403
Telephone: 707-525-8200
Fax: 707-525-0435
Cloverdale, California Office: 112 West First Street.
Telephone: 707-894-3941.

Thomas A. Campbell	Michael J. Casey
William D. Anderson	Thomas Reed Sink
John E. Johnson	

Daniel Alan Dexter

For full biographical listings, see the Martindale-Hubbell Law Directory

STOCKTON,* San Joaquin Co.

MAYALL, HURLEY, KNUTSEN, SMITH & GREEN, A PROFESSIONAL CORPORATION (AV)

2453 Grand Canal Boulevard, Second Floor, 95207-8253
Telephone: 209-477-3833
Fax: 209-473-4818

Edwin Mayall (1907-1980)	William W. Hale
John J. Hurley (Retired)	Mark Stephen Adams
Clarence D. Knutsen	J. Anthony Abbott
Alan E. Smith	Peter J. Whipple
Dennis J. Green	Kristen M. Hegge
Vladimir F. Kozina	

(See Next Column)

William L. Anderson	William J. Gorham, III
Donald W. West	Matthew Christopher Felix
Robert E. Laubengayer	Joseph A. Salazar, Jr.
Mark E. Berry	Steven A. Malcoun
Lesley Solomon	

Representative Clients: Allstate Insurance Co.; California State Automobile Assn.; Fireman's Fund Insurance Co.; General Motors Corp.; Texaco, Inc; State Farm Mutual Insurance Cos.; Beck Development, Inc; HD Arnaiz, Ltd; Vito Transporation; The Alpine Group.

For full biographical listings, see the Martindale-Hubbell Law Directory

TARZANA, Los Angeles Co.

WASSERMAN, COMDEN & CASSELMAN L.L.P. (AV)

5567 Reseda Boulevard, Suite 330, P.O. Box 7033, 91357-7033
Telephone: 818-705-6800; 213-872-0995
Fax: 818-345-0162; 996-8266

MEMBERS OF FIRM

Steve K. Wasserman	Jay N. Rosenwald
Leonard J. Comden	Daniel E. Lewis
David B. Casselman	Crystal A. Zarpas
Clifford H. Pearson	Gary S. Soter
Rebecca J. Schroer	Catherine Stevenson Garcia
Glenn A. Brown, Jr.	

ASSOCIATES

Joel Fischman	Richard A. Brownstein
Jeffrey K. Jayson	Albert G. Turner, Jr.
Lloyd S. Mann	Kenneth M. Jones
J. Christopher Bennington	Sharon Zemel
Norman L. Pearl	L. Stephen Albright
Todd A. Chamberlain	John A. Raymond
Howard S. Blum	Michael E. Garner
Marina N. Vitek	

OF COUNSEL
Cecilia S. Wu

Representative Clients: Toplis & Harding; Appalachian Insurance; Lumbermens Mutual Insurance Co.; State Farm Fire and Casualty Co.; Factory Mutual Engineering; Cravens, Dargan & Co.; Lloyd's of London.

For full biographical listings, see the Martindale-Hubbell Law Directory

VENTURA,* Ventura Co.

ENGLE & BRIDE (AV)

353 San Jon Road, 93001
Telephone: 805-643-2200
Fax: 805-643-3062

MEMBERS OF FIRM

Benjamin J. Engle	Robert F. Bride

ASSOCIATES

Daniel J. Carobine	Gary M. Schumacher
Matthew P. Guasco	

For full biographical listings, see the Martindale-Hubbell Law Directory

HENDERSON, WOHLGEMUTH & BOHL, A PROFESSIONAL CORPORATION (AV)

1893 Knoll Drive, 93003-7388
Telephone: 805-654-1980
Telecopier: 805-654-8106
Woodland Hills, California Office: 20350 Ventura Boulevard, #230, 91364-2452.
Telephone: 818-592-0081.
Fax: 818-592-0654.

Joseph R. Henderson	Thomas M. Bohl
Steven H. Wohlgemuth (Resident, Woodland Hills, California Office)	

Matthew M. Haffner	James B. Cole
Andrew K. Whitman	Diane L. Goad (Resident, Woodland Hills, California Office)
Jeffrey N. Leader (Resident, Woodland Hills, California Office)	
	Anthony B. Nixon
Karen M. Harmeling (Resident, Woodland Hills, California Office)	Risa-Lee Miller

Representative Clients: Alexsis Risk Management; Allstate Insurance; American International Group; American States Insurance; Amerispec Home Inspection Service; Argonaut Insurance; California Insurance Guarantee Association; Carl Warren & Company; CHUBB Group; CIGNA Companies.

For full biographical listings, see the Martindale-Hubbell Law Directory

WALNUT CREEK, Contra Costa Co.

ANDERSON, GALLOWAY & LUCCHESE, A PROFESSIONAL CORPORATION (AV)

1676 North California Boulevard, Suite 500, 94596-4183
Telephone: 510-943-6383
Facsimile: 510-943-7542

Robert L. Anderson	Stephen J. Brooks
George Patrick Galloway	Joseph S. Picchi
David R. Lucchese	Coleen L. Welch
Martin J. Everson	Deborah C. Moritz-Farr
Thomas J. Donnelly	Marc G. Cowden
Ralph J. Smith	Erin Ruddy Sabey
James M. Nelson	Lea K. McMahan
Scott E. Murray	Michael E. Brewer
David A. Depolo	Sonja M. Dahl
Karen A. Sparks	Thomas J. Tarkoff

For full biographical listings, see the Martindale-Hubbell Law Directory

WESTLAKE VILLAGE, Ventura Co.

MICHAELIS, MONTANARI & JOHNSON, A PROFESSIONAL LAW CORPORATION (AV)

2829 Townsgate Road, Suite 150, 91361
Telephone: 805-371-4611
Fax: 805-371-4617

James I. Michaelis	Garry L. Montanari
James P. Johnson	Gary J. LaPook

Michael D. Pilla	Miriam Piwoz Goodman
Wesley S. Wenig	

For full biographical listings, see the Martindale-Hubbell Law Directory

WOODLAND HILLS, Los Angeles Co.

HENDERSON, WOHLGEMUTH & BOHL, A PROFESSIONAL CORPORATION (AV)

20350 Ventura Boulevard #230, 91364-2452
Telephone: 818-592-0081
Fax: 818-592-0654
Ventura, California Office: 1893 Knoll Drive. Telephone 805-654-1980.
Telecopier: 805-654-8106.

Joseph R. Henderson	Steven H. Wohlgemuth
Thomas M. Bohl	(Resident)

Jeffrey N. Leader (Resident)	Karen M. Harmeling (Resident)
Diane L. Goad (Resident)	

For full biographical listings, see the Martindale-Hubbell Law Directory

COLORADO

BOULDER, * Boulder Co.

MARTIN & MEHAFFY (AV)

1655 Walnut Street, P.O. Box 1260, 80302
Telephone: 303-442-3375
Fax: 303-444-8398
Email: mmllc@aol.com *URL:* http://www.planetnetwork.com/law/
MEMBERS OF FIRM

James G. Martin (Retired)	Joel C. Maguire
John R. Mehaffy	Jeffrey L. Skovron
Lawrence C. Rider	Matthew S. Humphrey
Donald James Humphrey	Jonathan L. Miller

OF COUNSEL
Richard A. Tharp

Approved Attorneys for: Attorneys Title Guaranty Fund, Inc.

For full biographical listings, see the Martindale-Hubbell Law Directory

COLORADO SPRINGS, * El Paso Co.

KANE & DONLEY, P.C. (AV)

90 South Cascade Avenue, Suite 830, 80903
Telephone: 719-471-1650
Fax: 719-471-1663
Mailing Address: P.O. Box 1119, Colorado Springs, CO, 80901

Jerry A. Donley	Mark H. Kane
	Jack E. Donley

William A. Palmer	Hayden W. Kane, II

(See Next Column)

OF COUNSEL
Hayden W. Kane

Representative Clients: American International Companies; Shelter Insurance Co.; Metropolitan Insurance Co.
Reference: Norwest Bank of Colorado Springs.

For full biographical listings, see the Martindale-Hubbell Law Directory

RETHERFORD, MULLEN, JOHNSON & BRUCE, L.L.C. (AV)

415 South Sahwatch, P.O. Box 1580, 80901
Telephone: 719-475-2014
Fax: 719-630-1267

MEMBERS OF FIRM

Jerry A. Retherford	Neil C. Bruce
J. Stephen Mullen	Patrick R. Salt
Anthony A. Johnson	J. Ronald Voss
Lori M. Moore	

ASSOCIATES

Amelia L. Klemme	Debra A. Long
M. James Zendejas	Patricia Richardson

OF COUNSEL

E. William Shaffer, Jr.	Carla M. Albers

Representative Clients: Allstate Insurance Company; American Continental Insurance Company; American National Property & Casualty Insurance Company; American States Insurance Company; COPIC Insurance; EMC Insurance Companies; Farmers Insurance Exchange; GEICO; Hawkeye-Security Insurance Company; ITT Hartford.

For full biographical listings, see the Martindale-Hubbell Law Directory

DENVER, * Denver Co.

ALEXANDER & CRABTREE, P.C. (AV)

216 16th Street, Suite 1300, 80202-5127
Telephone: 303-825-7307
Fax: 303-825-3202
Email: halexand@alexcrab.com *URL:* http://www.alexcrab.com

Hugh Alexander	C. Scott Crabtree

Stephen Fitzsimmons

For full biographical listings, see the Martindale-Hubbell Law Directory

BURG & ELDREDGE, P.C. (AV)

P.O. Box 370385, 80237
Telephone: 303-779-5595
Fax: 303-779-0527
Albuquerque, New Mexico Office: 201 Third Street N.W., Suite 1500.
Telephone: 505-242-7020.
Fax: 505-242-7247.

Michael S. Burg	R. Hunter Ellington
Peter W. Burg	Thomas W. Henderson
Scott J. Eldredge	Janet R. Spies
David P. Hersh	Tom Van Buskirk
David M. Houliston	Matthew R. Giacomini
Kerry N. Jardine	

Kieth Van Doren	Rosemary Orsini
Brendan O'Rourke Powers	Robb A. Nelson
Jack D. Robinson	Matthew David Bailis
Kirstin G. Lindberg	Christina C. Vigil (Resident,
Bradley W. Howard (Resident, Albuquerque, New Mexico Office)	Albuquerque, New Mexico)
	Holly S. Baer
Matthew S. McElhiney	James R. Brewster (Resident,
Christian C. Doherty (Resident, Albuquerque, New Mexico Office)	Albuquerque, New Mexico Office)
	Jonathon P. Brody
	Brett Myer Perry

OF COUNSEL
Dale J. Coplan

Representative Clients: Allied Group Insurance; Budget Rent-A-Car; CNA Insurance Companies; Continental Divide Insurance Co.; Crum & Forster Commercial Insurance Co.; Hartford Insurance Cos.; National Farmers Union Insurance; Progressive Insurance Co.; Royal Insurance; TIG Insurance Company.

For full biographical listings, see the Martindale-Hubbell Law Directory

GRUND & BRESLAU, P.C. (AV)

303 East Seventeenth Avenue, Suite 1030, 80203-1260
Telephone: 303-830-7770
Facsimile: 303-830-2313

John W. Grund	Della S. Nelson
Brad W. Breslau	Phillip Jeffrey Frazee

Representative Clients: Admiral Insurance Co.; Allstate Insurance Co.; Coca Cola Enterprises, Inc.; Custard Insurance Adjusters, Inc.; Essex Insurance Co.; Hawkeye Security Insurance Co.; Homestead Insurance Co.; Horace

(See Next Column)

GRUND & BRESLAU P.C.—*Continued*

Mann Insurance Co.; PAFCO General Insurance Co.; United States Fidelity & Guaranty Co.

For full biographical listings, see the Martindale-Hubbell Law Directory

HALABY CROSS LIECHTY & SCHLUTER (AV)

Suite 1400, 1873 South Bellaire Street, 80222
Telephone: 303-691-5300
Fax: 303-691-5307

Theodore S. Halaby	Robert M. Liechty
Jonathan A. Cross	Leslie L. Schluter

ASSOCIATES

Jon A. Halaby	R. Craig Hess
Heidi A. Harpowiski	

For full biographical listings, see the Martindale-Hubbell Law Directory

LONG & JAUDON, P.C. (AV)

The Bailey Mansion, 1600 Ogden Street, 80218-1414
Telephone: 303-832-1122
FAX: 303-832-1348

Lawrence A. Long (1908-1992)	Alan D. Avery
Joseph C. Jaudon, Jr.	Cecelia A. Fleischner
David B. Higgins	Walter N. Houghtaling
Frederick W. Long	Ellen Rubright Ivy
Gary B. Blum	Christine Anne Craigmile
Michael T. McConnell	Carla M. LaRosa
Stephen P. Hopkins	Sheri Lyn Hood
Robert M. Baldwin	Thomas C. Kearns, Jr.
Dennis Woodfin Brown	Margaret J. Walton
David H. Yun	

Representative Clients: Aetna Life & Casualty Company; The Doctors Company; Home Insurance Company; Baxter Healthcare; CNA.

For Complete List of Firm Personnel, See General Section

For full biographical listings, see the Martindale-Hubbell Law Directory

MARKUSSON, GREEN & JARVIS, P.C. (AV)

Suite 2300, 1050 Seventeenth Street, 80265
Telephone: 303-572-4200
Fax: 303-595-3780

James K. Green	H. Keith Jarvis
Dennis H. Markusson	

Thomas E. Napp	Jason L. Romero
Kimberly J. Kernan	
(Not admitted in CO)	

Representative Clients: CIGNA Cos.; Commercial Union Insurance Companies; Farmers Insurance Group; Medmarc; Ohio Casualty Group; Reliance Insurance Co.; Republic Insurance Co.; Traveler's Insurance Companies; United Pacific Insurance Co.; Utah Home Fire Insurance Co.

For full biographical listings, see the Martindale-Hubbell Law Directory

WELLS, ANDERSON & RACE, LLC (AV)

1700 Broadway, Suite 1850, 80290
Telephone: 303-830-1212
Fax: 303-830-0898

Mary A. Wells	Geoffrey S. Race
Sheryl L. Anderson	Suanne M. Dell

Gregory E. Sopkin

Representative Clients: Allied Group Insurance; American Eagle Group, Ins.; Chubb/Pacific Indemnity Group; Great American Insurance Cos.; Hartford Insurance Groups; American States Ins. Co.; Royal Insurance Co.; State Farm Fire and Casualty Co.; The St. Paul Insurance Cos.; United Fire and Casualty Co.

For full biographical listings, see the Martindale-Hubbell Law Directory

WHITE AND STEELE, PROFESSIONAL CORPORATION (AV)

1225 17th Street, Suite 2800, 80202
Telephone: 303-296-2828
Telecopier: 303-296-3131
Email: law@wsteele.com
Cheyenne, Wyoming Office: 1912 Capital Avenue, Suite 416, 82003.
Telephone: 307-778-4160.
Telecopier: 307-778-7041.

Lowell White (1897-1983)	James M. Dieterich
Walter A. Steele	Glendon L. Laird
R. Eric Peterson	John Lebsack
Stephen K. Gerdes	Stephen G. Sparr
Michael W. Anderson	John P. Craver

(See Next Column)

David J. Nowak	Thomas B. Quinn
Sandra L. Spencer	Michael J. Daugherty
John M. Palmeri	Ted A. Krumreich
Frederick W. Klann	William F. Campbell, Jr.
Richard M. Kaudy	Kurt A. Horton
Peter W. Rietz	Stewart J. Rourke
Robert R. Carlson	

Christopher P. Kenney	Kimberly A. Viergever
Robert H. Coate	J. Barton Maxwell
Michelle R. Magruder	Sherri L. Sweers
Monty L. Barnett	Shanise M. Black
Joseph R. King	Matthew W. Tills
Frank D. Sledge	Claire Diaz
Kristi Blumhardt	Charles W. Yett
Keith R. Olivera	Laura E. David Fuller

OF COUNSEL

Fred L. Witsell	Kevin W. Hecht

Colorado Tort Counsel for: Goodyear Tire and Rubber Co.; The Dow Chemical Co.; Celotex.
Insurance Clients: Allied Insurance Co.; CNA; Kemper Insurance Group; Massachusetts Mutual Life Insurance Co.; Underwriters at Lloyds; U.S.A.A.; Farmers Insurance Group.

For Complete List of Firm Personnel, See General Section

For full biographical listings, see the Martindale-Hubbell Law Directory

DURANGO,* La Plata Co.

McLACHLAN & GOLDMAN, LLC (AV)

850 1/2 Main Avenue, P.O. Box 2270, 81302-2270
Telephone: 970-259-8747
Facsimile: 970-259-8790
Email: LAWMCGLD@FRONTIER.NET

Michael E. McLachlan	Michael A. Goldman

Jeffery P. Robbins

For full biographical listings, see the Martindale-Hubbell Law Directory

CONNECTICUT

BRIDGEPORT,* Fairfield Co.

BAI, POLLOCK AND COYNE, P.C. (AV)

Park City Plaza, 10 Middle Street, P.O. Box 1978, 06604
Telephone: 203-366-7991
Fax: 203-366-4723
Email: bpc@snet.net

Arnold J. Bai (1931-1992)	Garie J. Mulcahey
Paul E. Pollock	Raymond J. Plouffe, Jr.
James E. Coyne	Philip F. von Kuhn
Jeffrey A. Blueweiss	Madonna A. Sacco
Michael S. Lynch	

David J. Robertson	Colleen D. Fries
Edward P. Brady III	Neal P. Rogan
Andrew S. Turret	Jacquelyn Conlon
Gaileen A. Kaufman	Janine M. Savarese
Kevin S. Coyne	Louis A. Annecchino
Kristin Beth Comstock	

For full biographical listings, see the Martindale-Hubbell Law Directory

COTTER, COTTER AND SOHON, P.C. (AV)

P.O. Box 5660 Bayview Station, 06610
Telephone: 203-335-3131
Fax: 203-874-1983
Milford, Connecticut Office: 500 Boston Post Road, 06460.
Telephone: 203-882-7143.
Fax: 203-874-1983.

D. Harold Cotter (1893-1961)	Ellen M. Costello
Thomas H. Cotter	Kevin M. Blake
John J. Cotter	Catherine A. Stewart
Kevin M. Tepas	Michael V. Vocalina
Daniel H. Cotter	James F Mullen
William L. Cotter	James P. Mooney
Catherine N. Anderson	Matthias J. DeAngelo

Representative Clients: Royal Globe Indemnity Co.; Covenant Group; United States Fidelity & Guaranty Co.; Commercial Union Insurance Co.; Transport Insurance Co.; Metropolitan Insurance Co.; CNA; Nationwide Insurance Co.; Employers of Wassau Insurance Co.; Peerless Insurance Co.

For full biographical listings, see the Martindale-Hubbell Law Directory

Bridgeport—Continued

WILLIAMS, COONEY & SHEEHY (AV)

One Lafayette Circle, 06604
Telephone: 203-331-0888
Telecopier: 203-331-0896

MEMBERS OF FIRM

Ronald D. Williams	Peter J. Dauk
Robert J. Cooney	Dion W. Moore
Edward Maum Sheehy	Ronald D. Williams, Jr.
Peter D. Clark	Francis A. Smith, Jr.
	(1951-1989)

Michael P. Bowler	Paul Sean Curtin
Michael Cuff Deakin	Suzannah Kim Nigro

Representative Clients: Aetna Life & Casualty Co.; Nationwide Insurance Co.; Connecticut Medical Insurance Co.; The Travelers; Utica Mutual Insurance Co.; Pennsylvania National Insurance; Podiatry Insurance Company of America; Preferred Physicians Mutual; Medical Liability Mutual Insurance Company; General Star Indemnity Company.

For full biographical listings, see the Martindale-Hubbell Law Directory

---

FAIRFIELD, Fairfield Co.

FRIEDMAN, MELLITZ & NEWMAN, P.C. (AV)

Successor to: Friedman & Friedman; Mellitz Krentzman & Newman
One Eliot Place, 06430
Telephone: 203-259-5300
Fax: 203-259-2996

Arthur D. Friedman	Joanne Patricia Sheehan
Noel R. Newman	Cheryl Ann Carolan
Steven A. Levy	Arthur Levy, Jr.

For full biographical listings, see the Martindale-Hubbell Law Directory

---

JONTOS & LOTTY (AV)

1212 Post Road, P.O. Box 218, 06430
Telephone: 203-259-7009
FAX: 203-254-7780

MEMBERS OF FIRM

Richard A. Jontos (1935-1995)	Robert W. Lotty
Kathryn J. Coassin	

For full biographical listings, see the Martindale-Hubbell Law Directory

---

HARTFORD,* Hartford Co.

GORDON, MUIR AND FOLEY (AV)

Hartford Square North, Ten Columbus Boulevard, 06106-5123
Telephone: 860-525-5361
Telecopier: 860-525-4849

MEMBERS OF FIRM

William S. Gordon, Jr.	William J. Gallitto
(1946-1956)	Gerald R. Swirsky
George Muir (1939-1976)	Robert J. O'Brien
Edward J. Foley (1955-1983)	Philip J. O'Connor
Peter C. Schwartz	Kenneth G. Williams
John J. Reid	Chester J. Bukowski
John H. Goodrich, Jr.	Mary Ann Santacroce
R. Bradley Wolfe	J. Lawrence Price
Jon Stephen Berk	Mary Anne Alicia Charron
James G. Kelly	

ASSOCIATES

Kevin F. Morin	Andrew J. Hern
Claudia A. Baio	Eileen McCarthy Geel
Patrick T. Treacy	Christopher L. Slack
Renee W. Dwyer	

OF COUNSEL

Stephen M. Riley

Reference: Fleet Bank.

For full biographical listings, see the Martindale-Hubbell Law Directory

---

HORTON, SHIELDS & CORMIER, P.C. (AV)

90 Gillett Street, 06105
Telephone: 860-522-8338
Email: kmurdo01@counsel.com

Wesley W. Horton	Susan M. Cormier
Robert M. Shields, Jr.	Kimberly A. Knox
Karen L. Murdoch	

John A. Reed	Kenneth J. Bartschi

For full biographical listings, see the Martindale-Hubbell Law Directory

---

HOWD & LUDORF (AV)

65 Wethersfield Avenue, 06114
Telephone: 860-249-1361
Telecopier: 860-543-7155
Email: handl@ix.netcom.com

MEMBERS OF FIRM

John R. Lilliendahl, III	Linda Gray MacDonald
John J. Bogdanski	John P. Majewski
Philip T. Newbury, Jr.	Kimberly B. McCarthy
Thomas R. Gerarde	Jane E. Hugo
Mark J. Claflin	Susan D. Giacalone
William F. Corrigan	Michael J. Rose
Christopher M. Vossler	David S. Monastersky
Mark Sheehan	

RETIRED

Edward S. Ludorf

Representative Clients: CIGNA; Reliance; Chrysler; Toyota; Harsco; Ladder Management; Baxter International; Black & Decker; Texaco; Windsor Insurance Co.

For full biographical listings, see the Martindale-Hubbell Law Directory

---

JACKSON, O'KEEFE AND PHELAN (AV)

36 Russ Street, 06106-1571
Telephone: 860-278-4040
Fax: 860-527-2500
West Hartford, Connecticut Office: 62 LaSalle Road.
Telephone: 860-521-7500.
Fax: 860-561-5399.
Bethlehem, Connecticut Office: 423 Munger Lane. Telephone/Fax: 203-266-5255.

MEMBERS OF FIRM

Jay W. Jackson	Michael E. Riley
Andrew J. O'Keefe	Peter K. O'Keefe
Denise Martino Phelan	Philip R. Dunn, Jr.
Matthew J. O'Keefe	Kathryn M. Cunningham
Joseph M. Busher, Jr.	

Representative Clients: Travelers Aetna Property Casualty Co.; ITT Hartford; Liberty Mutual Insurance Co.; Connecticut Medical Insurance Co.

For full biographical listings, see the Martindale-Hubbell Law Directory

---

KENNY, BRIMMER, MELLEY & MAHONEY (AV)

5 Grand Street, 06106
Telephone: 860-527-4226
FAX: 860-527-0214

Joseph P. Kenny (1920-1993)

MEMBERS OF FIRM

Leslie R. Brimmer	William J. Melley, III
Richard C. Mahoney	

ASSOCIATES

Anita M. Varunes	Beverly Johns
Dennis F. McCarthy	Edward J. Fitzgerald

Representative Clients: Allstate Insurance Co.; Peerless Insurance Co.; Berkshire Mutual Fire Insurance Co.; Dorchester Mutual Fire Insurance Co.; Abington Mutual Fire Insurance Co.

For full biographical listings, see the Martindale-Hubbell Law Directory

---

MOLLER, DiPENTIMA, PECK AND O'BRIEN, LLC (AV)

1010 Wethersfield Avenue, 06114
Telephone: 860-296-1010
Fax: 860-947-3236

William R. Moller	Michael Ruben Peck
Anthony F. DiPentima	John J. O'Brien, Jr.

For full biographical listings, see the Martindale-Hubbell Law Directory

---

O'BRIEN, TANSKI, TANZER & YOUNG (AV)

CityPlace II, 06103
Telephone: 860-525-2700
Telefax: 860-247-7861

MEMBERS OF FIRM

Donald W. O'Brien	Roland F. Young, III
James M. Tanski	Robert E. Kiley
Lois B. Tanzer	Thomas O. Anderson
Nancy Phillips Maxwell	

OF COUNSEL

Hilary Fisher Nelson	Donna R. Zito

ASSOCIATES

Caroline Schnog	P. Jo Anne Burgh
Robert D. Silva	Jennifer L. Cox
Albert G. Danker, Jr.	Tanya Feliciano

References: Shawmut National Bank; New England Bank.

For full biographical listings, see the Martindale-Hubbell Law Directory

Hartford—Continued

REGNIER, TAYLOR, CURRAN & EDDY (AV)

CityPlace, 06103-4402
Telephone: 860-249-9121
FAX: 860-527-4343

MEMBERS OF FIRM

J. Ronald Regnier (1906-1987)	Ralph G. Eddy
Robert F. Taylor (1930-1994)	Jack D. Miller
Edmund T. Curran	Lawrence L. Connelli

ASSOCIATES

A. Patrick Alcarez	Frederick M. O'Brien
Robert B. McLaughlin	Keith Mccabe
A. Alan Sheffy	Beth D. Griffin
Robert A. Byers	Douglas E. Gilmore
Jay F. Huntington	Peter J. Casey

Andrew W. Bray

Representative Clients: Atlantic Mutual Insurance Co.; Government Employees Insurance Co.; Hartford Accident & Indemnity Co.; Hartford Fire Insurance Co.; Pioneer Co-operative Fire; United Services Automobile Assn.; Vermont Mutual Insurance Co.

For full biographical listings, see the Martindale-Hubbell Law Directory

SKELLEY ROTTNER P.C. (AV)

P.O. Box 340890, 06134-0890
Telephone: 860-561-7077
Telecopier: 860-561-7088

Joseph F. Skelley, Jr.	Randall M. Hayes
(1927-1995)	Elizabeth M. Cristofaro
Joel J. Rottner	Kirby G. Huget
Susan L. Miller	Edward W. Gasser
James G. Geanuracos	Matthew Dallas Gordon

OF COUNSEL

Susan E. Malliet	Carl F. Yeich

Laura Ondrush	Alys Portman Smith
Robyn Sondak	Jonathan Kline

Sharon Shafer Spungen

References: Fleet Bank; Liberty Bank.

For full biographical listings, see the Martindale-Hubbell Law Directory

SOROKIN SOROKIN GROSS HYDE & WILLIAMS P.C. (AV)

One Corporate Center, 06103
Telephone: 860-525-6645
Fax: 860-522-1781
Simsbury, Connecticut Office: 730 Hopmeadow Street.
Telephone: 860-651-9348.
Rocky Hill, Connecticut Office: 2360 Main Street.
Telephone: 860-563-9305.
Fax: 860-529-6931.

John J. Bracken III	Jeffrey R. Martin
Clifford J. Grandjean	Richard C. Robinson

Jeffery P. Apuzzo

For Complete List of Firm Personnel, See General Section

For full biographical listings, see the Martindale-Hubbell Law Directory

NEW HAVEN,* New Haven Co.

PAUL A. SCHOLDER ATTORNEY AT LAW, P.C. (AV)

2 Whitney Avenue, P.O. Box 1722, 06507
Telephone: 203-777-7218
Fax: 203-772-2672
Email: PaulA.Scholder,P.C.102261.2673@CompuServe.com

Paul A. Scholder

John J. Morgan

References: Peoples Bank; Lafayette American Bank.

For full biographical listings, see the Martindale-Hubbell Law Directory

SHAY & SLOCUM (AV)

234 Church Street, P.O. Box 1921, 06509
Telephone: 203-772-3600
Fax: 203-787-4581

MEMBERS OF FIRM

Edward N. Shay	Shaun M. Slocum

Representative Clients: Hartford Accident and Indemnity Co.; United Services Automobile Association; Commercial Union Insurance Co.; Atlantic Mutual Insurance Co.; Northbrook Insurance Co.; Safeco Insurance Co.; Andover Insurance Co.; National Interstate Transportation Insurance Specialists; First Financial Insurance Co.; Burlington Insurance Group.

(See Next Column)

For full biographical listings, see the Martindale-Hubbell Law Directory

NORWICH,* New London Co.

BROWN, JACOBSON, TILLINGHAST, LAHAN & KING, P.C. (AV)

Uncas-Merchants National Bank Building, 22 Courthouse Square, 06360
Telephone: 860-889-3321
Fax: 860-886-0673

Milton L. Jacobson	Karl-Erik Sternlof
Vincent A. Laudone	Michael P. Carey
Wayne G. Tillinghast	Jeffrey R. Godley
P. Michael Lahan	Michael E. Kennedy
Michael E. Driscoll	Doreen A. West
David S. Williams	Elizabeth Conway
Michael A. Blanchard	John F. Duggan
John C. Wirzbicki	Gerald M. Smith, Jr.
Michael D. Colonese	Jeffrey F. Buebendorf

OF COUNSEL

Allyn L. Brown, Jr.	James J. Dutton, Jr.
Charles W. Jewett	Jackson T. King, Jr.

Representative Clients: Nationwide Insurance Co.; Aetna Casualty & Surety Co.; Chelsea-Groton Savings Bank; Norwich Community Development Corp.

For full biographical listings, see the Martindale-Hubbell Law Directory

DELAWARE

WILMINGTON,* New Castle Co.

WARREN B. BURT & ASSOCIATES (AV)

1700 Mellon Bank Center, 919 Market Street, 19801-3023
Telephone: 302-429-9430
Fax: 302-429-9427

ASSOCIATES

Richard D. Abrams	Michael F. Duggan

For full biographical listings, see the Martindale-Hubbell Law Directory

CASARINO, CHRISTMAN & SHALK (AV)

Suite 1220, 222 Delaware Avenue, P.O. Box 1276, 19899
Telephone: 302-594-4500
Telecopier: 302-594-4509

MEMBERS OF FIRM

Stephen P. Casarino	Beth H. Christman
Colin M. Shalk	Donald M. Ransom

Patricia L. Peterson

Kenneth M. Doss	Diane M. Willette
Patricia Bartley Schwartz	Stacey L. Cummings

For full biographical listings, see the Martindale-Hubbell Law Directory

PHILLIPS, GOLDMAN & SPENCE, P.A. (AV)

1200 North Broom Street, 19806
Telephone: 302-655-4200
Telecopier: 302-655-4210

John C. Phillips, Jr.	Robert S. Goldman

Stephen W. Spence

Robert F. Phillips	Steven K. Kortanek
Lisa Cresci McLaughlin	James P. Hall

For full biographical listings, see the Martindale-Hubbell Law Directory

PRICKETT, JONES, ELLIOTT, KRISTOL & SCHNEE (AV)

1310 King Street, P.O. Box 1328, 19899-1328
Telephone: 302-888-6500
Telecopier: 302-658-8111; 658-7257
Email: attorneys@prickett.com URL: http://www.prickett.com
Dover, Delaware Office: 26 The Green.
Telephone: 302-674-3841.
Kennett Square, Pennsylvania Office: 217 West State Street.
Telephone: 610-444-1573.

MEMBERS OF FIRM

Carl Schnee	Kevin M. Howard
Mason E. Turner, Jr.	(Resident at Dover Office)
Richard P. S. Hannum	Ralph K. ("Dirk") Durstein, III
David E. Brand	W. Wade W. Scott
Timothy A. Casey	Gary F. Traynor
Paul M. Lukoff	(Resident at Dover Office)

(See Next Column)

PRICKETT, JONES, ELLIOTT, KRISTOL & SCHNEE, *Wilmington—Continued*
ASSOCIATES
Chandlee Johnson Kuhn
J. Kate Stickles

Gretchen Ann Bender
Rebecca D. Batson
(Resident at Dover Office)

Representative Clients: Browning-Ferris Industries; Computer Associates International; Delmarva Power & Light; Nationwide.

For Complete List of Firm Personnel, See General Section

For full biographical listings, see the Martindale-Hubbell Law Directory

SMITH, KATZENSTEIN & FURLOW (AV)

The Corporate Plaza, 800 Delaware Avenue, P.O. Box 410, 19899
Telephone: 302-652-8400
Fax: 302-652-8405

MEMBERS OF FIRM
Robert J. Katzenstein
Susan L. Parker

Laurence V. Cronin
Brett D. Fallon

Kathleen M. Miller
COUNSEL
Charles E. Butler

For Complete List of Firm Personnel, See General Section

For full biographical listings, see the Martindale-Hubbell Law Directory

THEISEN, LANK, MULFORD & GOLDBERG, P.A. (AV)

Ninth Floor, One Commerce Center, P.O. Box 1470, 19899
Telephone: 302-656-7712
Fax: 302-655-0923
Email: Theisen@delcorp.com *URL:* http://www.delcorp.theisen.com

Aubrey B. Lank
John G. Mulford

Steven D. Goldberg
Michael J. Goodrick
David S. Lank

Richard L. Abbott
OF COUNSEL
Vincent A. Theisen (Retired)

References: Wilmington Trust Co.; PNC Bank.

For full biographical listings, see the Martindale-Hubbell Law Directory

TRZUSKOWSKI, KIPP, KELLEHER & PEARCE, P.A. (AV)

1020 North Bancroft Parkway, P.O. Box 429, 19899-0429
Telephone: 302-571-1782
Fax: 302-571-1638

Francis J. Trzuskowski
James F. Kipp
Daniel F. Kelleher

Robert K. Pearce
Edward F. Kafader
Francis J. Schanne

For full biographical listings, see the Martindale-Hubbell Law Directory

DISTRICT OF COLUMBIA

WASHINGTON, D.C. Co.

* indicates certain Bar Register subscribers, in cities of comparable size and importance, who maintain an additional office in Washington, D.C. and who have arranged for representation as a part of the Washington, D.C. listings that follow

ALLEN, JOHNSON, ALEXANDER & KARP, P.A. (AV)

1707 L Street, N.W., Suite 1050, 20036
Telephone: 202-828-4141
Fax: 202-429-8798
Baltimore, Maryland Office: Suite 1540, 100 East Pratt Street.
Telephone: 410-727-5000.

D'Ana E. Johnson

Representative Clients: Scottsdale Insurance Co.; Nautilus Insurance Co.; Jefferson Insurance Co.; Liberty Mutual Insurance Co.; Avis Rent-A-Car; Otis Elevator Co.; Montgomery Elevator Co.; Admiral Insurance Co.; Local Government Insurance Trust; Lancer Insurance Co.

For Complete List of Firm Personnel, See General Section

For full biographical listings, see the Martindale-Hubbell Law Directory

CARR GOODSON LEE & WARNER, A PROFESSIONAL CORPORATION (AV)

1301 K Street, N.W., Suite 400, East Tower, 20005-3300
Telephone: 202-310-5500
Telecopier: 202-310-5555
Email: info@cglw.com *URL:* http://www.cglw.com
Fairfax, Virginia Office: Tycon Towers, 8000 Towers Crescent Drive, Suite 1350, Vienna, Virginia, 22182.
Telephone: 703-691-8818.
Baltimore, Maryland Office: 201 North Charles St., 21201.
Telephone: 410-752-1570.
Rockville, Maryland Office: 31 Wood Lane, 20850.
Telephone: 301-424-7024.

Robert W. Goodson
James F. Lee, Jr.
Paul J. Maloney
Thomas L. McCally
Terrence M. McShane

Kevin M. Murphy
Walter J. Murphy, Jr.
Brian H. Rhatigan
Alexander D. Shoaibi
Jan E. Simonsen
James A. Welch

Janette M. Blee
(Not admitted in DC)
Teresa Grace Fay

Shadonna E. Hale
David H. Jacobs
(Not admitted in DC)
Clifton B. Welch

For Complete List of Firm Personnel, See General Section

For full biographical listings, see the Martindale-Hubbell Law Directory

CONDON & FORSYTH (AV)

1016 Sixteenth Street, N.W., 20036
Telephone: 202-289-0500
Telecopier: 202-289-4524
Email: 103345.1077@compuserve.com
New York, N.Y. Office: 1251 Avenue of the Americas.
Telephone: 212-921-5100.
Telex: 426978.
Telecopier: 212-575-3638; 212-575-1298; 212-719-3638.
Los Angeles, California Office: 1900 Avenue of the Stars.
Telephone: 310-557-2030.
Telecopier: 310-557-1299.

RESIDENT PARTNERS
Thomas J. Whalen

Timothy J. Lynes
COUNSEL
Evelyn D. Sahr
SENIOR ATTORNEY
David G. Schryver
RESIDENT ASSOCIATES
Thomas E. Healey

David F. Rifkind
(Not admitted in DC)

For full biographical listings, see the Martindale-Hubbell Law Directory

THE FALK LAW FIRM (AV)

A Professional Limited Company
Suite 260 One Westin Center, 2445 M Street, N.W., 20037
Telephone: 202-833-8700
Telecopier: 202-872-1725
Email: FalkLaw@erols.com

James H. Falk, Sr.
James H. Falk, Jr.

John M. Falk
Robert K. Tompkins
OF COUNSEL
Pierre E. Murphy

Elizabeth C. Collins

For full biographical listings, see the Martindale-Hubbell Law Directory

KENNETH R. FEINBERG & ASSOCIATES (AV)

1120 20th Street, N.W. Suite 740 South, 20036
Telephone: 202-371-1110
Fax: 202-962-9290
New York, N.Y. Office: 780 3rd Avenue, Suite 2202.
Telephone: 212-527-9600.
Fax: 212-527-9611.

ASSOCIATES
Deborah E. Greenspan
Michael K. Rozen
(Not admitted in DC)

Peter H. Woodin
(Not admitted in DC)
M. Catherine Faint
OF COUNSEL
Jacqueline E. Zins

For full biographical listings, see the Martindale-Hubbell Law Directory

Washington—Continued

JORDAN COYNE & SAVITS (AV)

1100 Connecticut Avenue, N.W., Suite 600, 20036
Telephone: 202-296-4747
Telecopier: 202-496-2800
Email: dansmith@washdc.mindspring.com
Rockville, Maryland Office: 33 Wood Lane.
Telephone: 301-424-4161.
Baltimore, Maryland Office: 400 E. Pratt Street.
Telephone: 410-625-5080.
Fairfax, Virginia Office: 10486 Armstrong Street.
Telephone: 703-246-0900.
Telecopier: 703-591-3673.
Leesburg, Virginia Office: 305 Harrison Street, S.E.
Telephones: 703-777-6084; 202-478-1895.
Telecopier: 703-771-6383. *E-Mail:* dansmith@washdc.mindspring.com.

ASSOCIATES

Sandra L. Brown
(Not admitted in DC)
Jennifer Ramey Helsel
(Not admitted in DC)

James John Bresnicky
(Not admitted in DC)

Representative Clients: Aetna Casualty & Surety Co.; American International Group; Budget Rent A Car System; Design Professionals Insurance Co.; Giant Food; Marriott Corp.; Minnesota Mining & Manufacturing; Risk Enterprises Management Ltd.; Scottsdale Insurance Co.; Washington Adventist Hospital.

For full biographical listings, see the Martindale-Hubbell Law Directory

MACLEAY, LYNCH, GREGG & LYNCH, P.C. (AV)

Suite 1150, 1629 K Street, N.W., 20006
Telephone: 202-785-0123
FAX: 202-393-3390

Donald Macleay (1908-1994)
Hugh Lynch, Jr. (1913-1994)
John C. Lynch

Bruce F. Robertson
Michael Maloney
Robert P. Lynch

Robert G. McGinley

Jack David Lapidus
OF COUNSEL
James C. Gregg

For full biographical listings, see the Martindale-Hubbell Law Directory

* VENABLE ATTORNEYS AT LAW VENABLE, BAETJER, HOWARD & CIVILETTI, LLP (AV)

A Partnership including Professional Corporations
Suite 1000, 1201 New York Avenue, N.W., 20005
Telephone: 202-962-4800
Fax: 202-962-8300
Baltimore, Maryland Office: Venable, Baetjer and Howard LLP, 1800 Mercantile Bank & Trust Building, 2 Hopkins Plaza.
Telephone: 410-244-7400.
McLean, Virginia Office: Venable, Baetjer and Howard LLP, Suite 400, 2010 Corporate Ridge.
Telephone: 703-760-1600.
Rockville, Maryland Office: Venable, Baetjer and Howard LLP, Suite 500, One Church Street, P. O. Box 1906.
Telephone: 301-217-5600.
Towson, Maryland Office: Venable, Baetjer and Howard LLP, 210 Allegheny Avenue, P. O. Box 5517.
Telephone: 410-494-6200.

MEMBERS OF FIRM

Benjamin R. Civiletti (P.C.)
(Also at Baltimore and
Towson, Maryland Offices)
Ronald R. Glancz
Douglas D. Connah, Jr. (P.C.)
(Also at Baltimore, Maryland
Office)
James K. Archibald (Also at
Baltimore, Maryland Office)

Jeffrey A. Dunn (Also at
Baltimore, Maryland Office)
George F. Pappas (Also at
Baltimore, Maryland Office)
James L. Shea (Not admitted in
DC; also at Baltimore,
Maryland Office)

For Complete List of Firm Personnel, See General Section

For full biographical listings, see the Martindale-Hubbell Law Directory

WILMER, CUTLER & PICKERING (AV)

2445 M Street, N.W., 20037-1420
Telephone: 202-663-6000
Fax: 202-663-6363
Email: Law@Wilmer.Com
Baltimore, Maryland Office: 100 Light Street, 21202.
Telephone: 410-986-2800.
Fax: 410-986-2828.
European Offices:
4 Carlton Gardens, London, SW1Y 5AA, England. Telephone: +44 (171) 872-1000.
Fax: +44 (171) 839-3537.

(See Next Column)

Rue de la Loi 15Wetstraat, B-1040 Brussels, Belgium. Telephone: +32 (2) 285-4900.
Fax: +32 (2) 285-4949.
Friedrichstrasse 95, D-10117 Berlin, Germany. Telephone: +49 (30) 2022-6400.
Fax: +49 (30)2022-6500.

MEMBERS OF FIRM

Dennis M. Flannery
A. Stephen Hut, Jr.
Lynn Bregman
John Payton
Thomas F. Connell

W. Scott Blackmer
Philip D. Anker
Joseph K. Brenner
David P. Donovan
Roger W. Yoerges

COUNSEL
Carol H. Fishman

For Complete List of Firm Personnel, See General Section

For full biographical listings, see the Martindale-Hubbell Law Directory

FLORIDA

AVENTURA, Dade Co.

BUCHANAN INGERSOLL, PROFESSIONAL CORPORATION (AV Ⓣ)

One Turnberry Place, 19495 Biscayne Boulevard, Suite 606, 33180
Telephone: 305-933-5600
Telecopier: 305-933-2350
URL: http://www.bipc.com
Pittsburgh, Pennsylvania Office: One Oxford Centre, 301 Grant Street, 20th Floor.
Telephone: 412-562-8800.
Philadelphia, Pennsylvania Office: Two Logan Square, Twelfth Floor, 18th & Arch Streets.
Telephone: 215-665-8700.
Harrisburg, Pennsylvania Office: 30 North Third Street.
Telephone: 717-237-4800.
Miami, Florida Office: NationsBank Tower, 100 S.E. Second Street.
Telephone: 305-347-4080.
Tampa, Florida Office: Suite 2500, 401 East Jackson Street.
Telephone: 813-222-8180.
Princeton, New Jersey Office: Buchanan Ingersoll, A Partnership, College Centre, 500 College Road East.
Telephone: 609-987-6800.
Lexington, Kentucky Office: Suite 600, PNC Bank Plaza, 200 West Vine Street.
Telephone: 606-225-5333.
Buffalo, New York Office: 1100 Main Place Tower, 350 Main Street.
Telephone: 716-854-4100.
Fax: 816-854-4227.

Joshua L. Dubin

Mark J. Neuberger

SENIOR ATTORNEY
Ralph B. Bekkevold

Todd A. Bancroft
Kevin Carmichael
Jeffrey M. Goodz

Randi S. Rothfield
Richard N. Schermer
Rebecca S. Trinkler

For full biographical listings, see the Martindale-Hubbell Law Directory

BOCA RATON, Palm Beach Co.

MICHAUD, BUSCHMANN, FOX, FERRARA & MITTELMARK, P.A. (AV)

33 Southeast 8th Street, 33432
Telephone: 561-392-0540
Fax: 561-392-0582
Email: Bocalaw@MBFFM.com

Scott H. Michaud
Paul Buschmann

Brian S. Fox
James T. Ferrara

Michael K. Mittelmark

Marc T. Millian

For full biographical listings, see the Martindale-Hubbell Law Directory

CORAL GABLES, Dade Co.

PARENTI, FALK & WAAS, P.A. (AV)

113 Almeria Avenue, 33134
Telephone: 305-447-6500
Fax: 305-447-1777

Michael J. Parenti, III
Glenn P. Falk
Norman M. Waas

Edward Hernandez
Armando Cortina
Gail Leverett Parenti

(See Next Column)

PARENTI, FALK & WAAS P.A., *Coral Gables—Continued*

Scott Solomon　　　　　　　　Michael Patrick Bonner
　　　　　Michael A. Sastre

For full biographical listings, see the Martindale-Hubbell Law Directory

---

DAYTONA BEACH, Volusia Co.

EUBANK, HASSELL & ASSOC., P.A. (AV)

Suite 301, 149 South Ridgewood Avenue, P.O. Box 2229, 32115-2229
Telephone: 904-238-1357
Telecopier: 904-258-7406

James O. Eubank, II　　　　　　F. Bradley Hassell

M. Jennifer Moorhead　　　　　　K. Judith Lane
Timothy A. Traster　　　　　　　Wiley S. Boston
Perette M. Lawrence　　　　　　C. Richard Penalta

For full biographical listings, see the Martindale-Hubbell Law Directory

SMITH, SCHODER & BOUCK, P.A. (AV)

605 South Ridgewood Avenue, 32014
Telephone: 904-255-0505
FAX: 904-252-4794
Other Daytona Beach Office: 214 Loomis Avenue.
Telephone: 904-255-6711.

James W. Smith　　　　　　　　Kim E. Bouck
C. Anthony Schoder, Jr.　　　　Todd Michael Cranshaw
　　　　　M. Kathleen Roddenberry

For full biographical listings, see the Martindale-Hubbell Law Directory

---

FORT LAUDERDALE,* Broward Co.

CONRAD, SCHERER & JENNE (AV)

A Partnership of Professional Associations
Eighth Floor, 633 South Federal Highway, P.O. Box 14723, 33302
Telephone: 954-462-5500
Facsimile: 954-463-9244
Miami, Florida Office: International Place. 100 Southeast 2nd Street. Suite 2800. 33131.
Telephone: 305-856-9920.
Facsimile: 305-374-4408.

MEMBERS OF FIRM

William R. Scherer, Jr., (P.A.)　　Gary S. Genovese (P.A.)
Kenneth C. Jenne, II (P.A.)　　　William V. Carcioppolo (P.A.)
　　　　Lynn Futch Cooney (P.A.)

OF COUNSEL
Rex Conrad

ASSOCIATES

Linda Rae Spaulding　　　　　　Reid A. Cocalis
Kimberly A. Kisslan　　　　　　Albert L. Frevola, Jr.

Local Counsel for: American Home Assurance Group; Caterpillar Tractor Co.; Division of Risk Management, State of Florida; Florida East Coast Railway; Fort Motor Co.; Liberty Mutual Insurance Co.; Ryder Truck Lines; Unigard Insurance Group.
Approved Attorneys for: Attorneys' Title Insurance Fund.
Reference: Barnett Bank of Fort Lauderdale.

For Complete List of Firm Personnel, See General Section

For full biographical listings, see the Martindale-Hubbell Law Directory

ENTIN & MARGULES, P.A. (AV)

200 East Broward Boulevard Suite 1210, 33301
Telephone: 954-761-7201
Dade: 305-935-0242
Fax: 954-767-8343

Alvin E. Entin　　　　　　　　Richard F. Della Fera
Leon R. Margules　　　　　　　Jacqueline Perczek

Mario Permuth (Not Admitted　　Richard Perlini
　in United States)

OF COUNSEL
Steven E. Goldman

For full biographical listings, see the Martindale-Hubbell Law Directory

ESLER, PETRIE & LINDIE, P.A. (AV)

Suite 300 The Advocate Building, 315 S.E. Seventh Street, 33301
Telephone: 954-764-5400
FAX: 954-764-5408

(See Next Column)

Gary A. Esler　　　　　　　　C. Daniel Petrie, Jr.
　　　　　Beth G. Lindie

Representative Clients: The Chubb Group of Insurance Cos.; Fireman's Fund Insurance Co.; Infinity Insurance Co.; Fortune Insurance Co.; State of Florida-Department of Risk Management; Crum and Forster Commercial Insurance Co.; Colonial Penn Insurance Co.; American Vehicle Insurance Co.
References: Capital Bank.

For full biographical listings, see the Martindale-Hubbell Law Directory

HALICZER, PETTIS & WHITE, P.A. (AV)

101 Northeast Third Avenue, Sixth Floor, 33301
Telephone: 954-523-9922
Fax: 954-522-2512
Orlando, Florida Office: NationsBank Building. Suite 1275. 111 North Orange Avenue. 32801.
Telephone: 407-841-9866.
Fax: 407-841-9915.

James S. Haliczer　　　　　　　Kenneth E. White
Eugene K. Pettis　　　　　　　Lorna E. Brown-Burton

Amy B. Talisman　　　　　　　Margaret A. Benenati
Dean A. Robertson　　　　　　Gina E. Caruso

For full biographical listings, see the Martindale-Hubbell Law Directory

KESSLER, MASSEY, CATRI, HOLTON & KESSLER, P.A. (AV)

110 Tower, Twentieth Floor, 110 Southeast Sixth Street, 33301
Telephone: 954-463-8593
Fax: 954-462-1303

Charles T. Kessler　　　　　　Paula C. Kessler
Albert P. Massey, III　　　　　Gregory G. Coican
Wesley L. Catri　　　　　　　Andrea L. Kessler
Raymond O. Holton, Jr.　　　　Edward D. Schuster

Gerard A. Tuzzio　　　　　　　Edwina V. Kessler

For full biographical listings, see the Martindale-Hubbell Law Directory

KUBICKI DRAPER (AV)

One East Broward Boulevard Suite 1600, 33301
Telephone: 954-768-0011
Fax: 954-768-0514
Miami, Florida Office: Penthouse City National Bank Building, 25 West Flagler Street, 33130.
Telephone: 305-374-1212.
Fax: 305-374-7846.
West Palm Beach, Florida Office: United National Bank Tower, Suite 1100, 1645 Palm Beach Lakes Boulevard, 33401.
Telephone: 561-640-0303.
Fax: 561-640-0524.

Robert J. Cousins　　　　　　Kenneth M. Oliver
Clifford Gorman　　　　　　　Jane Carlene Rankin
　　　　Robert N. Sechen

Earleen H. Cote　　　　　　　Lisa Schloss McMillan
Keith Emory Cunningham　　　Nicholas G. Milano
Jeff P. Cynamon　　　　　　　Jorge A. Peña
　　　　Harold A. Saul

For full biographical listings, see the Martindale-Hubbell Law Directory

PETERSON, BERNARD, VANDENBERG, ZEI, GEISLER & MARTIN (AV)

707 Southeast Third Avenue, P.O. Drawer 14126, 33302
Telephone: 954-763-3200
Fax: 954-728-9019
West Palm Beach, Florida Office: 1550 Southern Boulevard, Suite 300.
Telephone: 561-686-5005.
Fax: 561-471-5603.
Stuart, Florida Office: 2100 E. Ocean Boulevard, Suite 103.
Telephone: 561-286-9881.
Fort Myers, Florida Office: 2222 Second Street.
Telephone: 941-334-9100.
Key Largo, Florida Office: 164 North Bay Harbor Drive.
Telephone: 800-393-3901.

Eric A. Peterson　　　　　　　William Zei
　　　　William M. Martin

Michael A. Acker　　　　　　　Heather S. Rogers
Lewis A. Berns　　　　　　　Susan Y. Slaton
　　　　Andrew Y. Winston

OF COUNSEL
Leonard M. Bernard, Jr.

For full biographical listings, see the Martindale-Hubbell Law Directory

FORT MYERS, * Lee Co.

HENDERSON, FRANKLIN, STARNES & HOLT, PROFESSIONAL ASSOCIATION (AV)

1715 Monroe Street, P.O. Box 280, 33902-0280
Telephone: 941-334-4121
Telecopier: 941-332-4494

Albert M. Frierson	Daniel W. Sheppard
Stephen L. Helgemo	Chad J. Motes
John A. Noland	Steven G. Koeppel
Gerald W. Pierce	Douglas B. Szabo
J. Terrence Porter	Randal H. Thomas
Michael J. Corso	Robert C. Shearman
Vicki L. Sproat	Andrew L. Ringers, Jr.
John W. Lewis	John F. Potanovic, Jr.
Craig Ferrante	Paula F. Kelley
James L. Nulman	Timothy J. Jesaitis
Harold N. Hume, Jr.	Jeffrey D. Kottkamp
Bruce M. Stanley	J. Eric Stiffler

Mary G. Jack

Representative Clients: Aetna Property & Casualty Group; CIGNA Group; CSX Transportation, Inc.; Fireman's Fund Insurance Cos.; Barnett Bank of Lee County, N.A.; Northern Trust Bank of Florida, N.A.; The Hartford Insurance Group; Travelers Group; United Telephone Company of Florida.

For Complete List of Firm Personnel, See General Section

For full biographical listings, see the Martindale-Hubbell Law Directory

SMOOT ADAMS EDWARDS & GREEN, P.A. (AV)

One University Park Suite 600, 12800 University Drive, P.O. Box 60259, 33906-6259
Telephone: 941-489-1776
(800) 226-1777 (in Florida)
Fax: 941-489-2444
Email: 71600.2745@compuserve.com

J. Tom Smoot, Jr.	Bruce D. Green
Hal Adams	Steven I. Winer
Franklyn A. (Chip) Johnson	Mark R. Komray
(1947-1991)	Clayton W. Crevasse
Charles B. Edwards	M. Brian Cheffer

Robert S. Forman	C. Berk Edwards, Jr.
Kathleen W. McBride	Melville G. Brinson, III
Lowell Schoenfeld	Samuel J. Hagan, IV.

For full biographical listings, see the Martindale-Hubbell Law Directory

---

JACKSONVILLE, * Duval Co.

COKER, MYERS, SCHICKEL & SORENSON, P.A. (AV)

136 East Bay Street, P.O. Box 1860, 32201
Telephone: 904-356-6071
Fax: 904-353-2425

Howard C. Coker	R. Daniel Noey
M. Wayne Myers	Tonya Jo Wade
John J. Schickel	Ronald M. Owen
Charles A. Sorenson	John Moffitt Howell
Mark M. Green	Stephen M. Armstrong
Samuel H. Lanier	Corinne L. Heller
J. Thomas McKeel	Paul H. McLester
Wm. Earl Higginbotham	James H. Daniel

For full biographical listings, see the Martindale-Hubbell Law Directory

FANNIN, TYLER & HAMILTON, P.A. (AV)

Park Pointe, Suite D, 4741 Atlantic Boulevard, 32207-2127
Telephone: 904-398-9999
Facsimile: 904-398-0806

John F. Fannin	H. Tyrone Tyler

J. Clark Hamilton, Jr.

Laura Fannin Jacqmein

For full biographical listings, see the Martindale-Hubbell Law Directory

MOSELEY, WARREN, PRICHARD & PARRISH, P.A. (AV)

501 West Bay Street, 32202
Telephone: 904-356-1306
Cable Address: "Ragland"
Telex: 5-6374
Telecopier: 904-354-0194

(See Next Column)

Reuben Ragland (1882-1954)	Joseph W. Prichard, Jr.
Louis Kurz (1891-1965)	Robert B. Parrish
E. Dale Joyner (1943-1993)	Andrew J. Knight II
James F. Moseley	Richard K. Jones
Robert E. Warren	James F. Moseley, Jr.

Phillip A. Buhler	Stanley M. Weston
Melanie E. Shepherd	Kimberly Held Israel
Victor J. Zambetti	Tracy A. Chesser
Mathew G. Nasrallah	Ivan A. Colao

OF COUNSEL

James E. Williams	Neil C. Taylor

Counsel for: CSX Transportation; Britannia Steam Ship Insurance Assn., Ltd.; The West of England Protection & Indemnity Assn. (Luxembourg); Crowley American Transport Services, Inc.; Howard Johnson Co.; United Kingdom Mutual Steamship Assurance Assn., Ltd. (Bermuda); General Food Corp.; The London Steam-Ship Owners' Mutual Insurance Assn., Ltd.

For full biographical listings, see the Martindale-Hubbell Law Directory

TYGART AND SCHULER, P.A. (AV)

103 Barnett Regency Tower, 9550 Regency Square Boulevard, 32225-8164
Telephone: 904-721-0744
Facsimile: 904-721-5080

S. Thompson Tygart, Jr.	Carl Scott Schuler

Representative Client: Allstate Insurance Co.
Reference: Barnett Bank of Regency.

For full biographical listings, see the Martindale-Hubbell Law Directory

---

JUPITER, Palm Beach Co.

THOMAS J. SCHULTE, P.A. (AV)

Suite 500, 1001 North U.S. Highway One, 33477
Telephone: 561-746-8600
Fax: 561-744-0670

Thomas J. Schulte

Representative Clients: Firemens' Fund Insurance Co.; Liberty Mutual Insurance, Co.; CIGNA; Professional Risk Management Services, Inc.; Florida Physicians Insurance Trust; Investors Insurance Group; Catholic Diocese of Palm Beach; Gallagher & Bassett Services, Inc.; Anesthesiologists Professional Assurance Co.

For full biographical listings, see the Martindale-Hubbell Law Directory

---

LAKELAND, Polk Co.

CRAWFORD & RODDENBERY, P.A. (AV)

Second Floor Citrus & Chemical Bank Building, 6150 South Florida Avenue, P.O. Box 5947, 33807
Telephone: 941-644-8929
Fax: 941-647-5331

Sidney M. Crawford	Neil A. Roddenbery

Representative Clients: All Indemnity Co.; All State Insurance Co.; Allstate Property & Casualty Ins. Co.; Fleetwood Enterprises, Inc.; Florida Farm Bureau Ins. Cos.; Foremost Insurance Co.; American Federation Ins. Co.; Bliss-McKnight Management Corp. of Florida.

For full biographical listings, see the Martindale-Hubbell Law Directory

---

MIAMI, * Dade Co.

ANGONES, HUNTER, McCLURE, LYNCH & WILLIAMS, P.A. (AV)

Ninth Floor-Concord Building, 66 West Flagler Street, 33130
Telephone: 305-371-5000
Fort Lauderdale: 954-728-9112
FAX: 305-371-3948

Frank R. Angones	Christopher J. Lynch
Steven Kent Hunter	Stewart D. Williams
John McClure	B. Scott Hunter

Leopoldo Garcia, Jr.

Thomas W. Paradise	Lourdes Alfonsin Ruiz
Donna Joy Hunter	Kara D. Phinney

C. David Durkee

Insurance Clients: Allstate Insurance Co.; Prudential Property & Casualty Insurance Co.; Travelers Insurance Co.; Rollins Hudig Hall Healthcare Risk, Inc.

For Complete List of Firm Personnel, See General Section

For full biographical listings, see the Martindale-Hubbell Law Directory

ARMSTRONG & MEJER, P.A. (AV)

Suite 1111 Douglas Centre, 2600 Douglas Road (Coral Gables), 33134
Telephone: 305-444-3355
Fax: 305-442-4300

(See Next Column)

ARMSTRONG & MEJER P.A., *Miami—Continued*

Timothy J. Armstrong   Alvaro L. Mejer

M. Emelina Mejer-Kondla

Reference: First Union National Bank.

For full biographical listings, see the Martindale-Hubbell Law Directory

DANIELS, KASHTAN & FORNARIS, P.A. (AV)

241 Sevilla Avenue, Penthouse 2, 33134
Telephone: 305-448-7988
Telecopier: 305-448-7978

Richard G. Daniels   Martha D. Fornaris
Michael F. Kashtan   Angel Garcia
                    John E. Oramas

Albert Blair   David N. Gambach
Elizabeth M. Touma   Camille D. Riviere
Ana M. Latour   Katherine Lamas
                    Tracey A. Wright

Reference: Barnett Bank.

For full biographical listings, see the Martindale-Hubbell Law Directory

LAW OFFICES OF DAVID L. DEEHL (AV)

Suite 1575 Courthouse Tower, 44 West Flagler Street, 33130
Telephone: 305-358-9700
Telecopier: 305-358-4036
Email: DAVID@DEEHL.COM

ASSOCIATES
Susan Stanfill Carlson   Susan Guller
OF COUNSEL
                Michele K. Feinzig

For full biographical listings, see the Martindale-Hubbell Law Directory

JOHN S. FREUD, P.A. (AV)

Suite 300, Office In The Grove, 2699 South Bayshore Drive, 33133
Telephone: 305-859-2002
Fax: 305-854-2006

John S. Freud

Peter E. Abraham   Michael J. Schwartz

For full biographical listings, see the Martindale-Hubbell Law Directory

GEORGE, HARTZ, LUNDEEN, FLAGG & FULMER (AV)

4800 LeJeune Road (Coral Gables), 33146
Telephone: 305-662-4800
Fax: 305-667-8015
Fort Lauderdale, Florida Office: Suite 333 Justice Building East, 524 South Andrews Avenue, 33301.
Telephone: 954-462-1620.
Fax: 954-462-3629.
Fort Myers, Florida Office: Suite 402, Barnett Centre, 2000 Main Street, 33901.
Telephone: 941-337-7787.
Fax: 941-337-4303.
Tallahassee, Florida Office: Suite 900, Highpoint Center, 106 East College Avenue, 32302.
Telephone: 904-224-5252.
Fax: 904-222-3082.
West Palm Beach, Florida Office: Brandywine Centre 11, 560 Village Blvd., Suite 380, 33409.
Telephone: 561-478-8880.
Fax: 561-478-8838.
Orlando, Florida Office: 225 East Robinson Street, Suite 505, 32801.
Telephone: 407-843-4646.
Fax: 407-843-4264.

Charles K. George   Stanley V. Buky (Resident, West
Charles Michael Hartz   Palm Beach Office)
Mitchell L. Lundeen   Crane A. Johnstone (Resident,
Clinton D. Flagg   Fort Lauderdale Office)
Liana C. Silsby (Resident, Fort   Douglas W. Barnes (Resident,
  Lauderdale Office)   Fort Lauderdale Office)
C. Richard Fulmer, Jr.   Craig R. Stevens
  (Resident, Fort Lauderdale   (Resident at Ft. Myers Office)
  Office)   Lynne E. Denneler
A. Scott Lundeen   (Resident, Fort Myers Office)
David V. King (Resident, Fort
  Lauderdale Office)

(See Next Column)

ASSOCIATES

John R. Buchholz   Douglas Brent Steier
Maria A. Santoro   (Resident, Fort Myers Office)
  (Resident, Tallahassee Office)   Matthew S. Nelles (Resident,
Esther E. Galicia (Resident, Fort   Fort Lauderdale Office)
  Lauderdale Office)   Misty Merri Catherine Taylor
Matthew F. Minno   George A. Sarduy
  (Resident, Tallahassee Office)   Michael W. LeRoy (Resident,
Michael H. Imber (Resident,   Fort Lauderdale Office)
  West Palm Beach Office)   Jack R. Simmons (Resident,
Peter K. Spillis   Fort Lauderdale Office)
Loren Sonesen   R. David de Armas
Susan Bernhardt Rogers   (Resident, Orlando Office)
  (Resident at Ft. Lauderdale   Jennifer L. Bushey (Resident,
  Office)   West Palm Beach Office)
Timothy Dunbrack   Scott B. Albee
  (Resident, Orlando Office)   (Resident, Fort Myers Office)
Charles M.P. George   Darin J. Lentner (Resident, Fort
Frank Angione, Jr. (Resident,   Lauderdale Office)
  Fort Lauderdale Office)

For full biographical listings, see the Martindale-Hubbell Law Directory

HADDAD, JOSEPHS, JACK, GAEBE & MARKARIAN (AV)

1493 Sunset Drive (Coral Gables), P.O. Box 345118, 33114
Telephone: Dade County: 305-666-6006
Telecopier: 305-662-9931
URL: http://www.haddadjosephs.com

MEMBERS OF FIRM
Gil Haddad   Lewis N. Jack, Jr.
Michael R. Josephs   John S. Gaebe
                David K. Markarian
ASSOCIATES
Elisabeth M. Allen   Lauren M. Ilvento
Helen Leen Miranda   Clifford A. Wolff
                John William Gautier

Representative Clients: U-Haul Corporation; ITT Sheraton; Zurich-American Insurance Company; Republic Claims Service Company; Southern Fire Insurance Adjusters.

For full biographical listings, see the Martindale-Hubbell Law Directory

HAYDEN AND MILLIKEN, P.A. (AV)

Suite 63, 5915 Ponce de Leon Boulevard, 33146-2477
Telephone: 305-662-1523
Fax: 305-663-1358
Tampa, Florida Office: 615 De Leon Street 33606-2719.
Telephone: 813-251-1770.
Fax: 813-254-5436.

Reginald M. Hayden, Jr.   Timothy P. Shusta (Resident,
William Barry Milliken   Tampa, Florida Office)
William R. Boeringer   Michael J. Cappucio
                Thomas W. Snook

Matthew J. Valcourt   Patricia R. Spivey
  (Resident, Tampa Office)

Representative Clients: Regency Cruise Lines; Seaboard Marine, Ltd.; Tropical Shipping and Construction Co., Ltd.; Great American Insurance Co.; Marine Office of America Corp.; St. Paul Fire and Marine Insurance Co.; Britannia P & I; Newcastle P & I; Steamship Mutual; The Swedish Club.

For full biographical listings, see the Martindale-Hubbell Law Directory

KUBICKI DRAPER (AV)

Penthouse City National Bank Building, 25 West Flagler Street, 33130
Telephone: 305-374-1212
Fax: 305-374-7846
West Palm Beach, Florida Office: United National Bank Tower, Suite 1100, 1645 Palm Beach Lakes Boulevard, 33401.
Telephone: 561-640-0303.
Fax: 561-640-0524.
Fort Lauderdale, Florida Office: One East Broward Boulevard, Suite 1600, 33301.
Telephone: 954-768-0011.
Fax: 954-768-0514.

Gene Kubicki   Angela C. Flowers
Daniel Draper, Jr.   Joseph J. Kalbac, Jr.
Robert F. Bouchard   Elwood T. Lippincott, Jr.
Robert Baldwin Brown, III   Peter H. Murphy
                Robert N. Sechen

Caryn Bellus-Lewis   Anthony L. Pietrofesa
Roland A. Diaz   Antonio J. Rodriguez
Suzanne A. Dockerty   Elizabeth M. Rodriguez
Meg G. Kerr   Ronald L. Roth
Brad J. McCormick   Carol A. Scott
Dennis J. Murphy   Martin Van Haasteren
Charles Mustell   Charles Handel Watkins
David B. Pakula   Harold West

(See Next Column)

KUBICKI DRAPER—*Continued*

OF COUNSEL
Aubrey L. Talburt

For full biographical listings, see the Martindale-Hubbell Law Directory

ARTHUR C. MOLLER, P.A. (AV)

Aviation Avenue at South Bayshore Drive, 2601 South Bayshore Drive, Suite 700, 33133
Telephone: 305-854-4440
Facsimile: 305-854-3699

Arthur C. Moller, III

Mark A. Johnson   Carol Lynn Finklehoffe
Rogelio A. Zaldivar

Representative Clients: AIG Aviation; Phoenix Aviation Managers; The Generali; London Underwriters and Companies; Somerset; E Systems, Inc.; Loss Management Services; Continental Aviation Underwriters; Comnav; Reliance Insurance Companies.

For full biographical listings, see the Martindale-Hubbell Law Directory

PONZOLI, WASSENBERG & SPERKACZ, P.A. (AV)

302 Roland/Continental Plaza, 3250 Mary Street, 33133
Telephone: 305-442-1654
Fax: 305-567-0334

Ronald P. Ponzoli   Zorian Sperkacz
Richard L. Wassenberg   John P. Keller

Reference: City National Bank of Miami.

For full biographical listings, see the Martindale-Hubbell Law Directory

PYSZKA, DOUBERLEY, BLACKMON, LEVY & SAVOLA, P.A. (AV)

Fifth Floor, Grand Bay Plaza, 2665 South Bayshore Drive, 33133
Telephone: 305-858-6614

Gerard E. Pyszka   Phillip D. Blackmon, Jr.
William M. Douberley   Benjamin D. Levy
L.H. Steven Savola

Lisa Connor Cicero   Michael C. Foster
Cindy J. Mishcon   Eric D. Sachs
Lesa K. Kelley   Richard E. Leff

For full biographical listings, see the Martindale-Hubbell Law Directory

SPARKMAN, ROBB, NELSON, MASON & GINSBURG (AV)

Suite 1003 Biscayne Building, 19 West Flagler Street, 33130
Telephone: 305-374-0033
Broward: 954-522-0045
Fax: 305-539-0767
Fort Lauderdale, Florida Office: Suite 1210, 110 Tower, 110 S.E. Sixth Street.
Telephones: 305-463-3590; *Dade:* 305-945-4461.
West Palm Beach, Florida Office: 324 Datura Street, Suite 303. Telephone 407-659-6933.
Fax: 407-659-4328.

MEMBERS OF FIRM
James T. Sparkman   Donald Edward Mason
Michael A. Robb   Paul S. Ginsburg
Richard M. Nelson   Dan Kaufman
Valerie Kiffin Lewis
ASSOCIATE
John W. Reis

For full biographical listings, see the Martindale-Hubbell Law Directory

LELAND E. STANSELL, JR., P.A. (AV)

903 Biscayne Building, 19 West Flagler Street, 33130
Telephone: 305-374-5911
Fax: 305-374-5337

Leland E. Stansell, Jr.

Roberto M. Ureta

For full biographical listings, see the Martindale-Hubbell Law Directory

VALLE & CRAIG, P.A. (AV)

Suite 2520 World Trade Center, 80 Southwest Eighth Street, P.O. Box 113009, 33111-3009
Telephone: 305-373-2888; 1800-609-6151
Facsimile: 305-373-2889

Laurence F. Valle   Lawrance B. Craig, III
Timothy Maze Hartley

(See Next Column)

Frank J. Sioli, Jr.   Nicole F. Ehart
Michael J. Lynott

For full biographical listings, see the Martindale-Hubbell Law Directory

---

NAPLES,* Collier Co.

HARDT LAW OFFICES, P.A. (AV)

Suite 705 SunTrust Building, 801 Laurel Oak Drive, 34108
Telephone: 941-598-2900
Fax: 941-598-3785

Frederick R. Hardt

References: Northern Trust Bank of Florida/Naples, N.A.; U.S. Trust Company of Florida; Sun Bank/Naples, N.A.

For full biographical listings, see the Martindale-Hubbell Law Directory

---

NEW PORT RICHEY, Pasco Co.

ROBERTS, SOJKA & ASSOCIATES, P.A. (AV)

5841 Main Street, 34652
Telephone: 813-847-1103
West Palm Beach, Florida Office: Roberts & Sojka, P.A., 1675 Palm Beach Lakes Boulevard, Seventh Floor, P.O. Drawer 4178, 33402.
Telephone: 561-686-1800.
Fax: 561-686-1533.

Gary W. Roberts   Cindy A. Sojka

For full biographical listings, see the Martindale-Hubbell Law Directory

---

ORLANDO,* Orange Co.

ADAMS, HILL, REIS, ADAMS, HALL & SCHIEFFELIN (AV)

1417 East Concord Street, 32803
Telephone: 407-896-0425
Fax: 407-896-9236

MEMBERS OF FIRM
George E. Adams   Janet W. Adams
G. Bruce Hill   Larry D. Hall
Gregory F. Reis   Thomas L. Schieffelin, Jr.
ASSOCIATES
William W. Large   William H. Olney
Matthew P. Bartolomei   Richard Coaxum, Jr
Christopher E. Butler

Representative Clients: Everglades Regional Medical Center; The Florida Hospital Trust Fund; The Florida Hospital Excess Trust Fund; Florida Hospital Workers Compensation/Self Insurance Trust Fund; Bartow Memorial Hospital; Bay Medical Center; Brooksville Regional Hospital; Cape Canaveral Hospital; Cape Coral Hospital; Desoto Memorial Hospital.

For full biographical listings, see the Martindale-Hubbell Law Directory

CAMERON, MARRIOTT, WALSH, HODGES & COLEMAN, P.A. (AV)

15 West Church Street, 32801
Telephone: 407-841-5030
Fax: 407-843-1727
Daytona Beach, Florida Office: 432 South Beach Street.
Telephone: 904-257-1755.
Fax: 904-252-5601.
Ocala, Florida Office: 18 Northeast First Ave.
Telephone: 904-351-1119.
Fax: 904-351-0151.

A. Craig Cameron   E. Peyton Hodges
Frank Marriott, Jr.   Christopher C. Coleman
J. David Walsh (Resident,
   Daytona Beach Office)

James A. Chereskin (Resident,   Douglas J. LaPointe
   Daytona Beach Office)   Sheryl Simonetta Zust (Resident,
Patrick M. DeLong   Daytona Beach Office)
Kevin K. Chase   Louis D. Kaye

Representative Clients: Albertson's; AIG; All-State; Auto Owners; American Family Insurance Group; American Fire and Casualty Insurance Co.; AT&T; Automobile Club Insurance Co.; Avis; Black & Decker.

For full biographical listings, see the Martindale-Hubbell Law Directory

McDONOUGH, O'DELL, BEERS, WIELAND, WILLIAMS AND KRAKAR (AV)

19 East Central Boulevard, P.O. Drawer 1991, 32802
Telephone: 407-425-7577
Fax: 407-423-0234

(See Next Column)

MCDONOUGH, O'DELL, BEERS, WIELAND, WILLIAMS AND KRAKAR,
Orlando—Continued

John R. McDonough	Donald N. Williams
Donald L. O'Dell	Michael J. Krakar
David C. Beers	A. Scott Toney
William J. Wieland	Nicholas a. Shannin
	Douglas K. Gartenlaub

For full biographical listings, see the Martindale-Hubbell Law Directory

McGEE & POWERS, P.A. (AV)

201 East Pine Street, Suite 700, P.O. Box 3589, 32801
Telephone: 407-422-5742
Telecopy: 407-423-1377

Patrick A. McGee	Deborah S. Hernandez
James K. Powers	Brenda J. Newman
	Melissa Arnold McGee

For full biographical listings, see the Martindale-Hubbell Law Directory

O'NEILL, CHAPIN, MARKS, LIEBMAN, COOPER & CARR (AV)

A Partnership including Professional Associations
865 Eola Park Center, 200 East Robinson Street, 32801
Telephone: 407-425-2751
Telex: 407-423-1192

Bernard C. O'Neill, Jr. (P.A.)	John B. Liebman (P.A.)
Bruce E. Chapin (P.A.)	Mark O. Cooper (P.A.)
Robert O. Marks (P.A.)	George E. Carr (P.A.)

ASSOCIATE
Rod C. Lundy

Reference: First Union National Bank.

For full biographical listings, see the Martindale-Hubbell Law Directory

SHEPARD, FILBURN & GOODBLATT, P.A. (AV)

First Union Tower, Suite 1107, 20 North Orange Avenue, 32801
Telephone: 407-481-2020
Fax: 407-481-0208
Email: sf2law@aol.com

Clifford B. Shepard, III	Jenna R. Rinehart
Mark C. Filburn	Michael J. Kirwin
Amy E. Goodblatt	(Not admitted in FL)

Representative Clients: Cintas Corporation; Intercargo Insurance Company; Trade Insurance Services, Inc.; Integon General Insurance Company; Danella Construction Company; Adventist Health Systems, Inc.; Titan Indemnity Company; Hersh National Painting & Roofing Company; Sysco Food Services, Inc.; American Contractors Indemnity Company.

For full biographical listings, see the Martindale-Hubbell Law Directory

TARASKA, GROWER & KETCHAM, P.A. (AV)

390 North Orange Avenue, Suite 1900, P.O. Box 538065, 32853-8065
Telephone: 407-423-9545
Telefacsimile: 407-425-7104

Joseph M. Taraska	Launa K. Rutherford
Mason H. Grower, III	A. Scott Noecker
Walter A. Ketcham, Jr.	Michael C. Siboni
Hector A. Moré	Jeanelle G. Bronson
	Eric R. Eide

David B. Blessing	T. Lee Bodie
G. Franklin Bishop, III	Gregory W. Stoner
David W. Henry	Lori A. Wellbaum
Patrick H. Telan	Ian D. Forsyth
Gregory A. Fencik	Jack Erskine Holt, III
Benjamin W. Newman	Daniel A. Kiefer

For full biographical listings, see the Martindale-Hubbell Law Directory

---

PENSACOLA,* Escambia Co.

BELL, SCHUSTER & WHEELER, P.A. (AV)

119 West Garden Street, P.O. Box 12564, 32573-2564
Telephone: 904-438-1691
Fax: 904-438-3641

Robert D. Bell	Thomas E. Wheeler, Jr.
Charles A. Schuster	David W. Hiers

For full biographical listings, see the Martindale-Hubbell Law Directory

BRIDGERS, GILL & HOLMAN (AV)

121 Palafox Place, 32501
Telephone: 904-432-6484
Fax: 904-432-6383

(See Next Column)

MEMBERS OF FIRM

J. Dixon Bridgers, III	Stephen T. Holman
Jeffrey P. Gill	Tracey Scalfano Witt

For full biographical listings, see the Martindale-Hubbell Law Directory

JANECKY, NEWELL, POTTS, WELLS & WILSON, P.C. (AV)

25 West Cedar Street, Suite 313, 32501-5900
Telephone: 904-432-6066
Mobile, Alabama, Office: 3300 First National Bank Building, Post Office Box 2987.
Telephone: 205-432-8786.
Fax: 205-432-5900
Birmingham, Alabama Office: Suite 3120, AmSouth-Harbert Plaza, 1901 Sixth Avenue North, 35203.
Telephone: 205-252-4441.
Fax: 205-252-0320.

J. F. (Jack) Janecky	Mark A. Newell
	Kevin F. Masterson

Robert Scott Traweek (Resident, Pensacola, Florida Office)

Representative Clients: Alexis, Inc.; Associate Self Insurance Services, Inc.; Associated Group Services/Alabama Home Builders Self Insurers Fund; Auto-Owners Ins. Co.; Blue Cross and Blue Shield of Alabama; Canal Ins. Co.; Electric Mutual Ins. Co.; Fireman's Fund Ins. Cos.; Nationwide Ins. Co.; Principal Mutual Life Ins. Co.

For full biographical listings, see the Martindale-Hubbell Law Directory

B. RICHARD YOUNG, P.A. (AV)

309B South Palafox Place, 32501
Telephone: 904-432-2222
Fax: 904-432-1444

B. Richard Young

Penny L. Hendrix	Michael T. Bill

For full biographical listings, see the Martindale-Hubbell Law Directory

---

ROCKLEDGE, Brevard Co.

KANE, SINGER, PLANCK, DONOGHUE, CLARK & MIXSON, P.A. (AV)

1286 South Florida Avenue, Suite One, 32955
Telephone: 407-639-1340
Panafax: 407-631-3142
Orlando, Florida Office: 2816 East Robinson Avenue, Suite One.
Telephone: 407-898-9130. Pana
fax: 407-898-9164.

Thomas G. Kane	Richard C. Singer
	Gregory J. Donoghue

For full biographical listings, see the Martindale-Hubbell Law Directory

---

ST. PETERSBURG, Pinellas Co.

FOX, GROVE, ABBEY, ADAMS, BYELICK & KIERNAN (AV)

Eleventh Floor, 360 Central Avenue, 33701
Telephone: 813-821-2080
FAX: 813-822-3970
Tampa, Florida Office: 500 East Kennedy Boulevard, Suite 200.
Telephone: 813-223-7800.
Fox & Grove, Chartered Offices:
Chicago, Illinois Office: 311 South Wacker Drive, Suite 6200.
Telephone: 312-876-0500.
San Francisco, California Office: 240 Stockton Street, Suite 900.
Telephone: 415-956-1360.

OF COUNSEL
Kalvin M. Grove

MEMBERS OF FIRM

David J. Abbey	Michael K. Kiernan
Jeffrey M. Adams	Joseph P. Ludovici
Robert P. Byelick	V. Joseph Mueller
	Robert J. Lancaster

ASSOCIATES

Hillary H. Coleman	Samantha A. Brem
Heather C. Goodis	J. Marc Perez
Kimberly A. Staffa	Christopher D. Marone
	Jaime B. Eagan

Reference: First Union Bank.

For full biographical listings, see the Martindale-Hubbell Law Directory

SARASOTA, * Sarasota Co.

DICKINSON & GIBBONS, P.A. (AV)

1750 Ringling Boulevard, P.O. Box 3979, 34230
Telephone: 941-366-4680
FAX: 941-953-3136

Francis C. Dart (1902-1972)	Burwell J. Jones
G. Hunter Gibbons	Richard R. Garland
Ward E. Dahlgren	Stephen G. Brannan
Lewis F. Collins, Jr.	Deborah J. Blue
Gary H. Larsen	Jeffrey D. Peairs
Camden T. French	Douglas R. Wight
Ralph L. Marchbank, Jr.	Stephen R. Kanzer
A. James Rolfes	David S. Preston

OF COUNSEL
Patrick H. Dickinson
LEGAL SUPPORT PERSONNEL

Christine C. Menzel	Janet E. Gadoury
Patricia L. Hunter	(Certified Legal Assistant)

Representative Clients: Ford Motor Co.; Florida Power & Light Co.; Squibb Corp.
Insurance Clients: Liberty Mutual Insurance Co.; Allstate Insurance Co.; Nationwide Insurance Group; Ohio Casualty Insurance Co.; United States Fidelity & Guaranty Co.; State Farm Insurance Company.

For Complete List of Firm Personnel, See General Section

For full biographical listings, see the Martindale-Hubbell Law Directory

TALLAHASSEE, * Leon Co.

HENRY, BUCHANAN, HUDSON, SUBER & WILLIAMS, P.A. (AV)

117 South Gadsden Street P.O. Drawer 1049, 32302
Telephone: 904-222-2920
Telecopier: 904-224-0034

Bryan W. Henry (1925-1986)	Jesse F. Suber
John D. Buchanan, Jr.	Harriet W. Williams
Edwin R. Hudson	J. Steven Carter

Laura Beth Faragasso
GOVERNMENTAL CONSULTANT
Curt Blair

Reference: Barnett Bank of Tallahassee, Inc.

For full biographical listings, see the Martindale-Hubbell Law Directory

THE MANG LAW FIRM, P.A. (AV)

660 East Jefferson Street, P.O. Box 11127, 32302-3127
Telephone: 904-222-7710
Telecopier: 904-222-6019

Douglas A. Mang	Wendy Russell Wiener
Connie Jo Pecori	Robert E. Wolfe, JR.

For full biographical listings, see the Martindale-Hubbell Law Directory

McFARLAIN, WILEY, CASSEDY & JONES, PROFESSIONAL ASSOCIATION (AV)

215 South Monroe Street, Suite 600, P.O. Box 2174, 32316-2174
Telephone: 904-222-2107
Telecopier: 904-222-8475

Richard C. McFarlain	Charles A. Stampelos
William B. Wiley	Linda McMullen
Marshall R. Cassedy	H. Darrell White, Jr.
Douglas P. Jones	Christopher Barkas

Harold R. Mardenborough, Jr.	Rogelio J. Fontela
Robert A. McNeely	Patrick John McGinley

For full biographical listings, see the Martindale-Hubbell Law Directory

TAMPA, * Hillsborough Co.

ALPERT, BARKER & CALCUTT, P.A. (AV)

First Union Center, Suite 2000, 100 South Ashley Drive (33602), P.O. Box 3270, 33601-3270
Telephone: 813-223-4131
Fax: 813-228-9612

Jonathan L. Alpert	Chris A. Barker
Patrick B. Calcutt	

R. Christopher Rodems	William J. Cook
Gregory Joseph Blackburn	Emma Sleeth Hemness
David D. Ferrentino	Scott J. Flint
David A. Kessler	

Representative Clients: Alexander & Alexander, Inc.; American International Group; Colonia Insurance Co.; Hospital Underwriting Group; American International Group; Nationwide Insurance Co.; RLI Insurance Corp.; Scott

(See Next Column)

Wetzel Services; Skandia America Group; The Seibels Bruce Insurance Companies.

For full biographical listings, see the Martindale-Hubbell Law Directory

BARR, MURMAN, TONELLI, HERZFELD & RUBIN (AV)

Enterprise Plaza, Suite 901, 201 East Kennedy Boulevard, P.O. Box 172669, 33672-0669
Telephone: 813-223-3951
Fax: 813-229-2254

James A. Murman	Ellen H. Lorenzen
Michael A. Tonelli	John R. Dixon
Daniel H. Sleet	Michael A. Connolly
Ashley J. McCorvey	

OF COUNSEL
Billy R. Barr

Representative Client: CIGNA Insurance Co.

For full biographical listings, see the Martindale-Hubbell Law Directory

CARSON, GUEMMER & NICHOLSON (AV)

3002 West Kennedy Boulevard, 33609
Telephone: 813-875-1973
FAX: 813-875-2467

MEMBERS OF FIRM

Wallis M. Carson	Albert M. Guemmer
Gary W. Nicholson	

Representative Clients: American Security Insurance Co.; Cavalier Insurance Co.; Carolina Casualty Insurance Co.; Central Mutual Insurance Co.; Colonial Penn Insurance Co.; Farmers Insurance Exchange; New Hampshire Insurance Co.; South Carolina Insurance Co.; Southeastern Fidelity Insurance Co.; Standard Guaranty Insurance Co.

For full biographical listings, see the Martindale-Hubbell Law Directory

HAYDEN AND MILLIKEN, P.A. (AV)

615 de Leon Street, 33606-2719
Telephone: 813-251-1770
Fax: 813-254-5436
Miami, Florida Office: Suite 63, 5915 Ponce de Leon Boulevard.
Telephone: 305-662-1523.
Fax: 305-663-1358.

Reginald M. Hayden, Jr.	William Barry Milliken
Timothy P. Shusta (Resident)	

Matthew J. Valcourt

Representative Clients: Regency Cruise Lines; Seaboard Marine, Ltd.; Tropical Shipping and Construction Co., Ltd.; Great American Insurance Co.; Marine Office of America Corp.; St. Paul Fire and Marine Insurance Co.; Britannia P & I; Newcastle P & I; Steamship Mutual.
Reference: Dadeland Bank.

For full biographical listings, see the Martindale-Hubbell Law Directory

LAU, LANE, PIEPER, CONLEY & McCREADIE, P.A. (AV)

Suite 1700, 100 South Ashley, P.O. Box 838, 33601
Telephone: 813-229-2121
Telecopier: 813-228-7710
Port Canaveral, Florida Office: 405 Atlantis Road, Suite F.
Telephone: 407-799-3400.
Telecopier: 407-868-1025.

James V. Lau	Timothy C. Conley
Charles C. Lane	David W. McCreadie
Nathaniel G. W. Pieper	Annette Horan
Mary A. Lau	David F. Pope
Gregory P. Durham	

For full biographical listings, see the Martindale-Hubbell Law Directory

MITCHELL AND CARTER, PROFESSIONAL ASSOCIATION (AV)

501 East Kennedy Boulevard, Suite 1207, 33602
Telephone: 813-221-0811
FAX: 813-228-9770

Keith M. Carter	Daniel P. Mitchell
S. Allison Hicks	Alan F. Scharf

Representative Clients: Government Employees Insurance Co.; The Hanover Insurance Co.; Worldwide Insurance Co.; Southern Insurance Group; Durham Life Assurance Co.; Carolina Casualty Co.; Capital Enterprise Insurance Co.; Merastar Insurance Co.; Vanliner Insurance Co.

For full biographical listings, see the Martindale-Hubbell Law Directory

Tampa—Continued

RYWANT, ALVAREZ, JONES & RUSSO, PROFESSIONAL ASSOCIATION (AV)

Suite 500 Perry Paint & Glass Building, 109 North Brush Street, P.O. Box 3283, 33601
Telephone: 813-229-7007
Fax: 813-223-6544
Ocala, Florida Office: 3300 S.W. 34th Avenue, Suite 124C, 32674.
Telephone: 904-237-8810.
FAX: 904-237-2022.

Manuel J. Alvarez	Steven D. Lehner
Jill Diziel Emerson	Burke G. Lopez
Darrell D. Dirks	Kerry C. McGuinn, Jr.
Matthew D. Emerson	Andrew F. Russo
John A.C. Guyton, III	Michael S. Rywant
Gregory D. Jones	James R. Wilson

LEGAL SUPPORT PERSONNEL
Bradley Hugh Holt

Representative Clients: Peerless Insurance Co.; Gulf Insurance Group; Employers Casualty Co.; Landmark Insurance Co.

For full biographical listings, see the Martindale-Hubbell Law Directory

SANTOS & DUTTON, P.A. (AV)

One Harbour Place, Suite 950, 777 South Harbour Island Boulevard, 33602
Telephone: 813-229-1111
Fax: 813-229-3311

F. Robert Santos	Scott W. Dutton

Daniel J. Lynott	David G. Henry

Jeffrey S. Hunter

Representative Clients: American Vehicle Insurance; Capacity Insurance Co.; Erie Insurance Co.; Fortune Insurance Group; The Hanover Insurance Co.; The Travelers Insurance Co.; The Shelby Insurance Group; Usher Insurance Co.

For full biographical listings, see the Martindale-Hubbell Law Directory

SHEAR, NEWMAN, HAHN AND ROSENKRANZ, P.A. (AV)

Suite 1000, 201 East Kennedy Boulevard, 33602
Telephone: 813-228-8530
FAX: 813-221-9122

L. David Shear	Glenn M. Burton
Jerry L. Newman	Roland J. Lamb
William E. Hahn	Bruce Douglas Lamb
Stanley W. Rosenkranz	Jeffrey Drew Butt
James R. Freeman	Mark J. Ragusa
Rodney W. Morgan	Kelly Jo Schmedt

Marilyn Drivas Sandborn	Mildred D. Beam-Rucker
Scott P. Distasio	Joseph F. Diaco, Jr.
Thomas M. Hoeler	Elizabeth (Betsey) Taylor Herd
Christopher J. Schulte	Timothy M. Cerio
Kimberly D. Holladay	Mindy Paige Brostoff
Debra L. Boje	Carl A. Goldman

OF COUNSEL

Daniel J. Gibby	Leonard L. Kleinman

References: NationsBank; First National Bank.

For full biographical listings, see the Martindale-Hubbell Law Directory

SHOFI, SMITH, HENNEN & GRAMOVOT, P.A. (AV)

One North Dale Mabry, Suite 800, P.O. Box 10430, 33679-0430
Telephone: 813-876-7796
FAX: 813-876-0509

John D. Shofi	Larry I. Gramovot
John S. Smith	Sandra L. Peacock
William E. Hennen	Matthew R. Danahy

James E. Bogos

Jon A. McAuliffe	Rochelle L. Lefler
Frank Clark	Kenneth S. Takacs, Jr.

Reference: City Bank of Tampa.

For full biographical listings, see the Martindale-Hubbell Law Directory

STUART, STRICKLAND & CAGLIANONE, P.A. (AV)

605 South Boulevard, 33606
Telephone: 813-251-8081
Fax: 813-254-2459
Brooksville, Florida Office: 217 Howell Avenue.
Telephone: 904-796-6733.
Fax: 904-799-7506.

(See Next Column)

Stephen K. Stuart	Steven A. Strickland
Jeffrey A. Caglianone	

Francis Anthony Miller

Representative Clients: Allstate Insurance Co.; Purina Mills, Inc.; Auto Owners Insurance Co.; Metropolitan Insurance Co.; Firemens Fund Insurance Co.
Reference: City Bank of Tampa.

For full biographical listings, see the Martindale-Hubbell Law Directory

WOOD, CRIST & VALENTI, P.A. (AV)

One Tampa City Center Suite 1700, 33602-5187
Telephone: 813-229-6311
Fax: 813-225-2633

J. Emory Wood	Charles J. Crist, Jr.
	Lorraine A. Valenti

Stephen A. Barnes

Representative Clients: Casualty Indemnity Exchange; State Farm Fire & Casualty Co.; State Farm Mutual Automobile Insurance Co.; Southern Insurance Co.; Nationwide Insurance Co.; Coronet Insurance Co.; General Telephone Company of Florida; Apex Adjusting Co.; Unisource Insurance Co.

For full biographical listings, see the Martindale-Hubbell Law Directory

VERO BEACH,* Indian River Co.

MOSS, HENDERSON, BLANTON, KOVAL & LANIER, P.A. (AV)

817 Beachland Boulevard, P.O. Box 3406, 32964-3406
Telephone: 561-231-1900
Fax: 561-231-4387

George H. Moss, II	Thomas A. Koval
Steve L. Henderson	Clinton W. Lanier
Robin A. Blanton	Fred L. Kretschmer, Jr.
	Lisa D. Harpring

Lewis W. Murphy, Jr.	Kelly Cambron
Judith Goodman Hill	Lawrence Y. Leonard
	David F. Mancini

OF COUNSEL

Charles E. Garris	Ford J. Fegert
	Everett J. Van Gaasbeck

Representative Clients: Aetna Life & Casualty; Alcoa Florida, Inc.; Florida Power & Light Co.; Insurance Company of North America; Liberty Mutual Insurance Co.; Sears, Roebuck & Co.; Sugar Cane Growers Cooperative of Florida; Norfolk Southern Corporation/North American Van Lines, Inc.

For full biographical listings, see the Martindale-Hubbell Law Directory

WEST PALM BEACH,* Palm Beach Co.

ALAN C. ESPY, P.A. (AV)

Commerce Pointe, Suite 420, 1818 South Australian Avenue, 33409
Telephone: 561-478-4777
Fax: 561-478-0886

Alan C. Espy

Steven J. Cramer

For full biographical listings, see the Martindale-Hubbell Law Directory

KUBICKI DRAPER (AV)

United National Bank Tower, Suite 1100, 1645 Palm Beach Lakes Boulevard, 33401
Telephone: 561-640-0303
Fax: 561-640-0524
Miami, Florida Office: Penthouse City National Bank Building, 25 West Flagler Street, 33130.
Telephone: 305-374-1212.
Telecopier: 305-374-7846.
Fort Lauderdale, Florida Office: One East Broward Boulevard, Suite 1600, 33301.
Telephone: 954-768-0011.
Fax: 954-768-0514.

David Knight	Michael S. Smith
Stephen W. Schwed	Hubert S. McGinley

Laurie J. Adams	Rosemarie Gasparri
J. Bowen Brown	Joseph Brian Landy
F. Neal Colvin, Jr.	Matthew N. Posgay

For full biographical listings, see the Martindale-Hubbell Law Directory

West Palm Beach—Continued

PETERSON, BERNARD, VANDENBERG, ZEI, GEISLER & MARTIN (AV)

1550 Southern Boulevard, Suite 300, P.O. Drawer 15700, 33416
Telephone: 561-686-5005
Fax: 561-471-5603
Fort Lauderdale, Florida Office: 707 Southeast Third Avenue, Suite 500, P.O. Drawer 14126.
Telephone: 954-763-3200.
Fax: 954-728-9019.
Stuart, Florida Office: Suite 103, 2100 East Ocean Boulevard.
Telephone: 561-286-9881.
Fort Myers, Florida Office: 2222 Second Street, 33901.
Telephone: 941-334-9100.
Key Largo, Florida Office: 164 North Bay Harbor Drive, 33037.
Telephone: 800-393-3901.

PALM BEACH COUNTY OFFICE

Eric A. Peterson	Dennis A. Vandenberg
	Robert E. Geisler

Eugene H. Brandt	Edwin E. Mortell, III
Elizabeth J. Fedele	Elizabeth A. Metzger
Stephen K. Mergler	Diran V. Seropian
	Guy E. Quattlebaum

For full biographical listings, see the Martindale-Hubbell Law Directory

WIEDERHOLD, MOSES, BULFIN & RUBIN, P.A. (AV)

Northbridge Centre, Suite 800, 515 North Flagler Drive, P.O. Box 3918, 33401
Telephone: 407-659-2296;
Broward: 954-763-5630
FAX: 407-659-2865

John P. Wiederhold	John J. Bulfin
Robert D. Moses	Kenneth M. Rubin

Lawrence I. Bass	Kay Seeber Hoff
	Bruce R. Katzell

LEGAL SUPPORT PERSONNEL

Thomas M. Blinstrub

Reference: Barnett Bank of Palm Beach County.

For full biographical listings, see the Martindale-Hubbell Law Directory

GEORGIA

ALBANY, * Dougherty Co.

PERRY & WALTERS (AV)

409-411 North Jackson Street, P.O. Box 469, 31702-0469
Telephone: 912-432-7438; 432-7481
Telecopier: 912-436-1417
Other Albany, Georgia Office: 503 North Jackson Street, P.O. Box 445, 31702-0445.
Telephone: 912-432-9960.

MEMBERS OF FIRM

R. Edgar Campbell	Samuel Brown Lippitt, Jr.
Keith T. Dorough	R. Kelly Raulerson
Richard W. Fields	James E. Reynolds, Jr.
	Edgar B. Wilkin, Jr.

OF COUNSEL

H. H. Perry, Jr.	Jesse W. Walters

Division Counsel for: Seaboard Coast Line Railroad Co.
General Counsel for: First State Bank & Trust Co.; Carlton Co.; Bob's Candies, Inc.; Alcon Associates, Inc.; Albany-Dougherty County Hospital Authority.
Representative Clients: Merck & Co., Inc.; CNA Insurance; Chrysler Credit Corp.

For full biographical listings, see the Martindale-Hubbell Law Directory

AMERICUS, * Sumter Co.

ELLIS, EASTERLIN, PEAGLER, GATEWOOD, HARPER & SKIPPER, P.C., A PROFESSIONAL CORPORATION (AV)

410 West Lamar Street, P.O. Box 488, 31709
Telephone: 912-924-9316
Fax: 912-924-6248

(See Next Column)

George R. Ellis, Sr. (1905-1988)	James C. Gatewood
George R. Ellis, Jr.	John V. Harper
Benjamin F. Easterlin, IV	James M. Skipper, Jr.
George M. Peagler, Jr.	Russ F. Barnes
	William H. Dudley

For full biographical listings, see the Martindale-Hubbell Law Directory

ATHENS, * Clarke Co.

BLASINGAME, BURCH, GARRARD, BRYANT & ASHLEY, P.C. (AV)

440 College Avenue North, P.O. Box 832, 30603
Telephone: 706-354-4000
Telecopier: 706-353-0673
Greensboro, Georgia Office: 122 N. Main Street, P.O. Box 67, 30642.
Telephone: 706-453-7139.
Fax: 706-453-7842.

J. Ralph Beaird	Andrew J. Hill, III
Gary B. Blasingame	Michael A. Morris
E. Davison Burch	Thomas H. Rogers, Jr.
Henry G. Garrard, III	William D. Harvard
Everett Clay Bryant	Rikard L. Bridges
W. Seaborn Ashley, Jr.	Ivan A. Gustafson
M. Steven Heath	David S. Thomson

Richard W. Schmidt	Christopher G. Conley
Milton F. Eisenberg	Lloyd N. Bell
Stephen E.B. Smith	Kim T. Stephens
J. Branson Parker	Amy Lou Reynolds
J. David Felt, Jr.	C. Kathryn Hackney
	Kathleen M. Timmons

Representative Clients: NationsBank of Georgia, N.A.; Georgia Power Co.; Georgia Natural Gas Co.; Pittsburgh Corning Corp.; Downtown Athens Development Authority; Georgia National Bank; Fowler Products Co., Inc.; St. Paul Fire & Marine Insurance Co.; Athens Newspapers, Inc.; First Commerce Bancorp, Inc.

For full biographical listings, see the Martindale-Hubbell Law Directory

ATLANTA, * Fulton Co.

ALEMBIK, FINE & CALLNER, P.A. (AV)

Marquis One Tower, Fourth Floor, 245 Peachtree Center Avenue, N.E., 30303
Telephone: 404-688-8800
Telecopier: 404-420-7191

Michael D. Alembik (1936-1993)	Ronald T. Gold
Lowell S. Fine	G. Michael Banick
Bruce W. Callner	Mark E. Bergeson
Kathy L. Portnoy	Russell P. Love

Z. Ileana Martinez	Janet Lichiello Franchi
Susan M. Lieppe	Heidi Koch Martin
Bruce R. Steinfeld	Janet Caroline Moja
	John H. Zwald

For full biographical listings, see the Martindale-Hubbell Law Directory

BOVIS, KYLE & BURCH (AV)

A Partnership including Professional Corporations
Third Floor, 53 Perimeter Center East, 30346
Telephone: 770-391-9100
Telecopier: 770-668-0878

MEMBERS OF FIRM

John M. Bovis (P.C.)	W. Bruce Barrickman
Steven J. Kyle (P.C.)	Gregory R. Veal
John V. Burch (P.C.)	Charles M. McDaniel, Jr.
James E. Singer	Timothy J. Burson
	William S. Allred

ASSOCIATES

Charles M. Medlin	John H. Peavy Jr.
J.S. Scott Busby	Timothy A. Hickey, Jr.
Claude P. Czaja	J. Anthony Love

For full biographical listings, see the Martindale-Hubbell Law Directory

CRIM & BASSLER (AV)

100 Galleria Parkway, Suite 1510, 30339
Telephone: 770-956-1813
Fax: 770-955-5976

MEMBERS OF FIRM

Candler Crim, Jr.	Nikolai Makarenko, Jr.
Harry W. Bassler	Kimberly Leigh Schwartz
Thomas S. Bechtel	Mitchel S. Evans
Joseph M. Murphey	Terence D. Williams

ASSOCIATES

Kelly Amanda Lee	Michael O. Sheridan

(See Next Column)

CRIM & BASSLER, *Atlanta—Continued*

OF COUNSEL

William W. Horton

References: The Bank of the South; First Georgia Bank; Trust Company of Georgia.

For full biographical listings, see the Martindale-Hubbell Law Directory

DENNIS, CORRY, PORTER & GRAY (AV)

3300 One Atlanta Plaza, 950 East Paces Ferry Road, P.O. Box 18640, 30326
Telephone: 404-816-2800
Wats: 800-735-0838
Fax: 404-816-5656

MEMBERS OF FIRM

Robert E. Corry, Jr.	James S. Strawinski
R. Clay Porter	Grant B. Smith
William E. Gray, II	Frederick D. Evans, III

OF COUNSEL

Douglas Dennis

ASSOCIATES

Robert G. Ballard	Brian DeVoe Rogers
Matthew J. Jewell	Julia J. Yoffee
Pamela Jean Gray	Scott W. McMickle
J. Steven Fisher	Susan E. Cartwright
Thomas D. Trask	Christopher D. Pixley
Robert David Schoen	Raymond J. Kurey
Alison Roberts Solomon	Amber B. Shushan

Representative Clients: Schneider National, Inc.; Roadway Express, Inc.; Caliber System, Inc.

For full biographical listings, see the Martindale-Hubbell Law Directory

DREW ECKL & FARNHAM (AV)

880 West Peachtree Street, P.O. Box 7600, 30357
Telephone: 404-885-1400
Facsimile: 404-876-0992
Email: drew@igc.apc.org

MEMBERS OF FIRM

W. Wray Eckl	T. Bart Gary
Clayton H. Farnham	Kenneth A. Hindman
Arthur H. Glaser	Paul W. Burke
James M. Poe	Daniel C. Kniffen
John A. Ferguson, Jr.	John C. Bruffey, Jr.
Theodore Freeman	Benton J. Mathis, Jr.
John P. Reale	John G. Blackmon, Jr.
Stevan A. Miller	Gary R. Hurst
H. Michael Bagley	Dennis M. Hall
Hall F. McKinley III	J. William Haley
G. Randall Moody	Ann Bishop Byars
B. Holland Pritchard	Stephen W. Mooney

ASSOCIATES

Nicole D. Tifverman	Patricia R. Stevens
L. Lee Bennett, Jr.	C. Lawrence Meyer
Katherine D. Dixon	Philip G. Pompilio
William T. Mitchell	Robert J. Moye III
J. Robb Cruser	Sean W. Conley
Philip Wade Savrin	Mary Anne Ackourey
Lucian Gillis, Jr.	Beverly Powell Sisk
Peter H. Schmidt, II	Marion M. Handley
April Rich	Stuart B. Bagley
Maureen M. Middleton	Thomas L. Walker
Robert L. Welch	James P. Anderson
Suzanne VonHarten Sanders	Kathryn Blythe Offer
Leigh Lawson Reeves	Donald M. McManus, Jr.
Bruce A. Taylor, Jr.	Peter B. Barlow
Douglas M. Baker	Nancy L. Pasterz
David R. Bergquist	Gregory G. Schultz
Charles L. Norton, Jr.	Christopher R. Stovall
Nancy F. Rigby	Charles E. Symington, Jr.
Douglas G. Smith, Jr.	Kristian Knochel
Terrence T. Rock	(Not admitted in GA)
Phillip Comer Griffeth	Lewis P. Perling
Marian S. Singer	Scott P. Archer
Steven D. Prelutsky	(Not admitted in GA)
Julianne L. Swilley	Fred L. Hubbs Jr.
B. Greg Cline	W. Gregory Pope

Jennifer E. Moore

SENIOR ATTORNEY

Richard Metzger

OF COUNSEL

Charles L. Drew	Anne M. Landrum
Christopher E. Parker	

Representative Clients: Insurance Company of North America; Scottsdale Insurance Co.; American International Group; Hanover Insurance Company; C.N.A. Insurance Co.; Church Mutual Insurance Co.; Continental Loss Adjusting Services; TIG Insurance Company; United States Fidelity and Guaranty; CIGNA Companies.

(See Next Column)

For full biographical listings, see the Martindale-Hubbell Law Directory

ENGLAND & McKNIGHT (AV)

Suite 410 River Ridge, 9040 Roswell Road, 30350
Telephone: 770-641-6010
FAX: 770-641-6003

MEMBERS OF FIRM

J. Melvin England	Robert H. McKnight, Jr.

Reference: Nations Bank N.A.

For full biographical listings, see the Martindale-Hubbell Law Directory

FAIN, MAJOR & WILEY, P.C. (AV)

The Hurt Building, 50 Hurt Plaza, Suite 300, 30303
Telephone: 404-688-6633
Telecopier: 404-420-1544

Gene A. Major	Thomas E. Brennan
Charles A. Wiley, Jr.	John K. Miles, Jr.
Darryl G. Haynes	

Brian Alligood	Robert G. Mikell
Derek A. Mendicino	C. Todd Van Dyke
Kim Monroe Jackson	Debra C. Chew
Tracy M. Culver	

OF COUNSEL

Donald M. Fain

Representative Clients: Allstate Insurance Co.; Budget Rent-A-Car; Arkansas Best Corp.; Chrysler Insurance Co.; Georgia Farm Bureau Mutual Insurance Co.; Hertz Corp.; Universal Underwriters Insurance Co.; Westfield Insurance co.; Winn-Dixie Stores, Inc.

For full biographical listings, see the Martindale-Hubbell Law Directory

GOLDNER, SOMMERS, SCRUDDER & BASS (AV)

900 Circle 75 Parkway Suite 850, 30339
Telephone: 770-612-9200
Facsimile: 770-612-9201

Stephen L. Goldner	Glenn S. Bass
Susan V. Sommers	C. G. Jester, Jr.
Henry E. Scrudder, Jr.	Alfred A. Quillian, Jr.
Sandra G. Chase	

Linda Jacobsen Pollock	Tammy Spivack Skinner
Benjamin David Ladner	Tiffany T. Norman
Marci R. Weston	R. Keith Whitesides
William W. Horlock, Jr.	Jane Carol Taylor

For full biographical listings, see the Martindale-Hubbell Law Directory

GOODMAN, McGUFFEY, AUST & LINDSEY (AV)

2100 Tower Place, 3340 Peachtree Road, N.E., 30326-1084
Telephone: 404-264-1500
Fax: 404-264-1737

MEMBERS OF FIRM

William S. Goodman	Edward H. Lindsey, Jr.
C. Wade McGuffey, Jr.	Joe David Jackson
Judy Farrington Aust	William P. Claxton

ASSOCIATES

Leslie Stewart Sullivan	Kimberly Cronkright Raley
Kathryn A. Cater	James Bradley McClung
J. Matthew Maguire, Jr.	

For full biographical listings, see the Martindale-Hubbell Law Directory

HARMAN, OWEN, SAUNDERS & SWEENEY, A PROFESSIONAL CORPORATION (AV)

1900 Peachtree Center Tower, 230 Peachtree Street, N.W., 30303
Telephone: 404-688-2600
Telecopier: 404-525-4347

H. Andrew Owen	David C. Will
Frederick F. Saunders, Jr.	Charles J. Cole
Timothy J. Sweeney	Rolfe M. Martin
Perry A. Phillips	Merritt McGarrah Wofford
Michael W. McElroy	Aaron J. Aberson

For full biographical listings, see the Martindale-Hubbell Law Directory

THE MARTIN LAW FIRM, P.C. (AV)

6201 Powers Ferry Road, Suite 350, 30339-5407
Telephone: 770-612-1400
Telecopier: 770-612-1414

B. Morris Martin

For full biographical listings, see the Martindale-Hubbell Law Directory

Atlanta—Continued

MOZLEY, FINLAYSON & LOGGINS LLP (AV)

A Limited Liability Partnership
One Premier Plaza Suite 900, 5605 Glenridge Drive, 30342
Telephone: 404-256-0700
Telecopier: 404-250-9355

MEMBERS OF FIRM

J. Arthur Mozley	C. David Hailey
Robert M. Finlayson II	Richard D. Hall
Sewell K. Loggins	R. Ann Grier
William D. Harrison	Wayne D. Taylor
Eric D. Griffin, Jr.	Lawrence B. Domenico

ASSOCIATES

Edward C. Bresee, Jr.	J. Marcus Howard

For full biographical listings, see the Martindale-Hubbell Law Directory

PIERCE & YOUNG (AV)

Building 1700, 2255 Cumberland Parkway Northwest, 30339-4575
Telephone: 770-435-0500
Telecopier: 770-435-0362

MEMBERS OF FIRM

J. Wayne Pierce	Richard M. Young

ASSOCIATE

Christy A. Dunkelberger

For full biographical listings, see the Martindale-Hubbell Law Directory

SCHULTEN, WARD & TURNER (AV)

Suite 1100 The Hurt Building, 50 Hurt Plaza, 30303
Telephone: 404-688-6800
Fax: 404-688-6840

MEMBERS OF FIRM

Wm. Scott Schulten	Kevin L. Ward
	David L. Turner

ASSOCIATES

Lou Litchfield	Clay Morris Westbrook
Susan Kastan Murphey	Julie H. McGhee

OF COUNSEL

Donald W. Osborne

Reference: NationsBank of Georgia, N.A.

For full biographical listings, see the Martindale-Hubbell Law Directory

THOMAS, KENNEDY, SAMPSON & PATTERSON (AV)

55 Marietta Street, N.W., Suite 1600, 30303
Telephone: 404-688-4503
Telecopier: 404-681-2950

MEMBERS OF FIRM

John Loren Kennedy (1942-1994)	P. Andrew Patterson
Thomas G. Sampson	Myra H. Dixon
	Jeffrey E. Tompkins

ASSOCIATES

Rosalind T. Drakeford	Adam L. Smith
Melynee C. Leftridge	Thomas G. Sampson, II
La'Sean M. Zilton	Ceasar C. Mitchell, II.
R. E. Thomas, Jr. (1911-1996)	

LEGAL SUPPORT PERSONNEL

Gwendolyn C.H. Dixon	Yvonne Torrence
Elbetha (Beth) Martin	Priscilla Yolanda Kelly
Nancy Allen-Haskell	Lureece D. Lewis (Paralegal)

For full biographical listings, see the Martindale-Hubbell Law Directory

WADE & CAMPBELL, LLP (AV)

Cumberland Center II, 3100 Cumberland Circle, Suite 1500, 30339
Telephone: 770-850-5000
FAX: 770-850-5075
Email: wadecamp@mindspring.com

MEMBERS OF FIRM

Allison Wade	Douglas N. Campbell
	Michael S. Thwaites

ASSOCIATES

Nancy P. Parson	Steven W. Hardy
Edward H. Nicholson, Jr.	Steven H. Jackman
	Walter Hamberg, III

Representative Clients: Allstate Life Insurance Company; American International Life Assurance Company of New York; The Central National Life Insurance Company of Omaha, Nebraska; Cologne Life Reinsurance Company; Commercial Life Insurance Company; General American Life Insurance Company; Integrity Underwriters, LLC; The Murray Ohio Manufacturing Company; Primerica Life Insurance Company; United Insurance Company of America.

For full biographical listings, see the Martindale-Hubbell Law Directory

WEBB, CARLOCK, COPELAND, SEMLER & STAIR (AV)

A Partnership including Professional Corporations
2600 Marquis Two Tower, 285 Peachtree Center Avenue, P.O. Box 56887, 30343-0887
Telephone: 404-522-8220
Fax: 404-523-2345

MEMBERS OF FIRM

Dennis J. Webb (P.C.)	Wayne D. McGrew, III
Thomas S. Carlock (P.C.)	Douglas A. Wilde
Robert C. Semler (P.C.)	Frederick M. Valz, III
Wade K. Copeland (P.C.)	E. Alan Miller
Kent T. Stair (P.C.)	Johannes S. Kingma
Douglas W. Smith	Dennis G. Lovell, Jr.
David F. Root	Brian R. Neary
William E. Zschunke	Marvin D. Dikeman

ASSOCIATES

Robert W. Browning	Mary Katherine Smith
Philip P. Taylor	Leslie B. Zacks
David D. Cookson	Andrette Watson
Todd M. Yates	Gregg A. Landau
Adam L. Appel	James R. Doyle, II
R. Michael Ethridge	Lynn B. Olmert
Daniel J. Huff	Alissa H. Codel
Scott D. Huray	Kimberly L. Kilpatrick
Gregory H. Wheeler	Colleen P. O'Neill
Christopher A. Whitlock	Martin Enrique Valbuena
John W. Sandifer	Melissa C. Duffey
Craig A. Brookes	Matthew L. Hilt
	Michael J. Azzariti

For full biographical listings, see the Martindale-Hubbell Law Directory

WILSON, STRICKLAND & BENSON, P.C. (AV)

1100 One Midtown Plaza, 1360 Peachtree Street, N.E., 30309
Telephone: 404-870-1800
Telecopier: 404-870-1808

Earl B. Benson, Jr.	N. Sandy Epstein
	Mary M. Brockington

For Complete List of Firm Personnel, See General Section

For full biographical listings, see the Martindale-Hubbell Law Directory

---

AUGUSTA,* Richmond Co.

ALLGOOD, CHILDS, MEHRHOF AND MILLIANS, P.C. (AV)

615 Telfair Building, P.O. Box 1523, 30903
Telephone: 706-724-6526
Fax: 706-724-0043

T. Allen Childs, Jr.	Michael W. Millians
Richard R. Mehrhof, Jr.	Thomas F. Allgood, Jr.

OF COUNSEL

Thomas F. Allgood, Sr.

Representative Clients: Allstate Insurance Co.; Therman Ceramics.

For full biographical listings, see the Martindale-Hubbell Law Directory

CAPERS, DUNBAR, SANDERS & BRUCKNER (AV)

Fifteenth Floor, First Union Bank Building, 30901-1454
Telephone: 706-722-7542
Telecopier: 706-724-7776

MEMBERS OF FIRM

John D. Capers	E. Frederick Sanders
Paul H. Dunbar, III	Ziva P. Bruckner

ASSOCIATE

Carl P. Dowling

For full biographical listings, see the Martindale-Hubbell Law Directory

DYE, TUCKER, EVERITT, WHEALE & LONG, A PROFESSIONAL ASSOCIATION (AV)

453 Greene Street, P.O. Box 2426, 30903
Telephone: 706-722-0771
Fax: 706-722-7028

A. Rowland Dye	Duncan D. Wheale
Thomas W. Tucker	John B. Long
A. Zachry Everitt	Benjamin H. Brewton
	Troy A. Lanier

OF COUNSEL

A. Montague Miller

Representative Clients: State Farm Insurance Cos.; The Travelers Insurance Co.; Georgia Power Co.; Wachovia National Bank (Augusta Division); Chubb Group; Montgomery Ward; Augusta Board of Realtors; Ryder Truck Rental, Inc.; Canal Insurance Company; St. Paul Fire and Marine Insurance Company.

(See Next Column)

Dye, Tucker, Everitt, Wheale & Long A Professional Association, *Augusta—Continued*

For full biographical listings, see the Martindale-Hubbell Law Directory

FULCHER, HAGLER, REED, HANKS & HARPER (AV)

A Partnership including Professional Corporations
520 Greene Street, P.O. Box 1477, 30903-1477
Telephone: 706-724-0171
Telecopier: 706-724-4573

MEMBERS OF FIRM

William M. Fulcher (1902-1993)	Michael B. Hagler (P.C.)
Gould B. Hagler (Retired)	James W. Purcell (P.C.)
William C. Reed (Retired)	J. Arthur Davison (P.C.)
David H. Hanks (P.C.)	Mark C. Wilby (P.C.)
John I. Harper (P.C.)	Ronald C. Griffeth
Robert C. Hagler (P.C.)	N. Staten Bitting, Jr. (P.C.)

David P. Dekle (P.C.)

ASSOCIATES

Elizabeth A. McLeod	Barry A. Fleming

General Counsel for: GIW Industries, Inc.
Division Counsel for: CSX Transportation; Textron, Inc. (E-Z Go Car Division).
Counsel for: NationsBank; Georgia Natural Gas Co. (a division of Atlanta Gas Light Co.); Champion International Corp.; Aetna Life and Casualty; Liberty Mutual Insurance Company; St. Paul Fire & Marine Insurance Co.; Kimberly Clark Corporation.

For Complete List of Firm Personnel, See General Section

For full biographical listings, see the Martindale-Hubbell Law Directory

HULL, TOWILL, NORMAN & BARRETT, A PROFESSIONAL CORPORATION (AV)

Seventh Floor, Trust Company Bank Building, P.O. Box 1564, 30903-1564
Telephone: 706-722-4481
Fax: 706-722-9779

James M. Hull (1885-1975)	Douglas D. Batchelor, Jr.
George B. Barrett (1894-1942)	David E. Hudson
Julian J. Willingham (1887-1963)	Neal W. Dickert
John Bell Towill (1907-1991)	John W. Gibson
Robert C. Norman	William F. Hammond
(Retired, 1991)	Mark S. Burgreen
W. Hale Barrett	George R. Hall
Lawton Jordan, Jr.	James B. Ellington
Patrick J. Rice	F. Michael Taylor

Robert A. Mullins	Michael S. Carlson
William J. Keogh, III	Ralph Emerson Hanna, III
Edward J. Tarver	Susan D. Barrett
J. Noel Schweers, III	Timothy E. Moses

Counsel for: Sun Trust Bank Augusta, N.A.; Georgia Federal Bank, FSB, Augusta Division; Southeastern Newspapers Corp.; Georgia Power Co.; Southern Bell Telephone & Telegraph Co.; St. Joseph Hospital, Augusta, Georgia, Inc.; Norfolk Southern Corp.; Merry Land & Investment Co., Inc.; Housing Authority of the City of Augusta; Georgia Press Association.

For full biographical listings, see the Martindale-Hubbell Law Directory

WILEY S. OBENSHAIN, III, P.C. (AV)

511 Courthouse Lane, 30901
Telephone: 706-722-1789
Fax: 706-722-3934

Wiley S. Obenshain, III

For full biographical listings, see the Martindale-Hubbell Law Directory

SURRETT & COLEMAN, P.A. (AV)

901 Suntrust Bank Building, P.O. Box 1497, 30903
Telephone: 706-722-3301
Telecopier: 706-722-3318

Carl J. Surrett	Edward J. Coleman, III

Representative Clients: Sears, Roebuck & Co.; American Home Assurance Co.; Great Southwest Fire Insurance Co.; Duke Buick, Inc.; American Southern Insurance Co.; Scottsdale Insurance Co.; Providence Washington Insurance Co.; Nautilus Insurance Co.

For full biographical listings, see the Martindale-Hubbell Law Directory

THOMPSON & SMITH, P.C. (AV)

2909-A Professional Parkway, 30907
Telephone: 706-855-5600
Telecopier: 706-855-7020

(See Next Column)

James M. Thompson	Larry I. Smith

For full biographical listings, see the Martindale-Hubbell Law Directory

BRUNSWICK,* Glynn Co.

FENDIG, McLEMORE, TAYLOR, WHITWORTH & DURHAM, P.C. (AV)

Suite 200 Suntrust Bank Building, P.O. Box 1996, 31521
Telephone: 912-264-4126
Telecopier: 912-264-0591

Albert Fendig, Jr.	Philip R. Taylor
Gilbert C. McLemore, Jr.	David T. Whitworth

James B. Durham

Donna L. Crossland	Beth M. Duncan

Counsel for: Suntrust Bank of S.E. Georgia, N.A.; First Federal Savings Bank; Sea Island Property Owners Assn.; Calsilite Manufacturing Co.; Continental Insurance Cos.; Crum & Forster; MIM Insurance Companies, Inc.; The Hertz Corp.; Insurance Company of North America; United States Fidelity & Guaranty Co.

For full biographical listings, see the Martindale-Hubbell Law Directory

GILBERT, HARRELL, GILBERT, SUMERFORD & MARTIN, P.C. (AV)

Suite 200 First Federal Plaza, 31521
Telephone: 912-265-6700
Fax: 912-264-3917

Wallace E. Harrell	Jameson L. Gregg
James B. Gilbert, Jr.	Wallace E. Harrell, III
Rees M. Sumerford	Charles G. Spalding
M. Fleming Martin, III	Lisa Godbey
Monroe Lynn Frey, III	Mark D. Johnson

J. Benedict Hartman

OF COUNSEL

James B. Gilbert	Joseph A. Whittle

H. Hall Ware, III

Representative Clients: Zurich General Accident & Liability Insurance Co.; Lumbermen's Mutual Casualty Co.; The Travelers Insurance Co.; Liberty Mutual Insurance Co.; Metropolitan Life Insurance Co.; Jefferson Standard Life Insurance Co.; The Continental Insurance Co.; Home Indemnity Co.; Fidelity General Insurance Co.; American Mutual Liability Insurance Co.

For full biographical listings, see the Martindale-Hubbell Law Directory

JORDAN & O'DONNELL (AV)

1528 Ellis Street, P.O. Box 2115, 31521
Telephone: 912-262-9200
Fax: 912-262-0277

Randall A. Jordan	Rita C. Spalding
Christopher J. O'Donnell	Steven P. Bristol

Representative Clients: Norfolk Southern Corp.; National Foundation Life Insurance Co.; American Centennial Insurance Co.; Delta Life Insurance Co.; Cooper Industries, Inc.; McGraw-Edison Co.; Progressive Preferred Insurance Co.; Integrity Insurance Co.; AllState Insurance Co.; Occidental Fire & Casualty of North Carolina.

For full biographical listings, see the Martindale-Hubbell Law Directory

WHELCHEL, BROWN, READDICK & BUMGARTNER (AV)

5 Glynn Avenue, P.O. Box 220, 31521-0220
Telephone: 912-264-8544
Telecopier: 912-264-9667

MEMBERS OF FIRM

J. Thomas Whelchel	Terry L. Readdick
Richard A. Brown, Jr.	John E. Bumgartner

B. Kaye Katz

ASSOCIATES

G. Todd Carter	Raleigh W. Rollins, Jr.
Richard K. Strickland	Bradley J. Watkins

Representative Clients: Georgia Power Co.; Sears, Roebuck & Co.; Allstate Insurance Co.; Commercial Union Insurance Co.; Georgia Farm Bureau Mutual Insurance Co.; Government Employees Insurance Co.; Nationwide Insurance Co.; State Farm Insurance Cos.; Wausau Insurance Cos.

For full biographical listings, see the Martindale-Hubbell Law Directory

CARROLLTON,* Carroll Co.

TISINGER, TISINGER, VANCE & GREER, A PROFESSIONAL CORPORATION (AV)

100 Wagon Yard Plaza, P.O. Box 2069, 30117
Telephone: 770-834-4467
Fax: 770-834-5426

(See Next Column)

TISINGER, TISINGER, VANCE & GREER A PROFESSIONAL CORPORATION—
Continued

Thomas E. Greer	Glenn M. Jarrell
Kevin B. Buice	David F. Miceli
Douglas C. Vassy	Richard G. Tisinger, Jr.
Brian L. Howell	John A. Harris

Representative Clients: ALFA; Atlanta Casualty Company; Cincinnati Insurance Company; Cotton States Insurance Company; Federated Electric Insurance Company; Georgia Farm Bureau Mutual Insurance Company; Greater New York Mutual Insurance Co.; State Farm Mutual Automobile Insurance Company; State Farm Fire and Casualty Company.

For Complete List of Firm Personnel, See General Section

For full biographical listings, see the Martindale-Hubbell Law Directory

COLUMBUS,* Muscogee Co.

HATCHER, STUBBS, LAND, HOLLIS & ROTHSCHILD (AV)

A Limited Liability Partnership
Suite 500 The Corporate Center, 233 12th Street, P.O. Box 2707, 31902-2707
Telephone: 706-324-0201
Telecopier: 706-322-7747

MEMBERS OF FIRM

William B. Hardegree	Joseph L. Waldrep
James E. Humes, II	Robert C. Martin, Jr.

ASSOCIATES

C. Morris Mullin	Teri Yancey Callahan
Theodore Darryl (Ted) Morgan	Gregory S. Ellington

Division Counsel for: Georgia Power Co.
Assistant Division Counsel for: Norfolk Southern Corp.
Local Counsel for: State Farm Insurance Cos.; Liberty Mutual Insurance Co.; Home Insurance Co.; Kemper Insurance Co.; MAG Mutual Insurance Co.; Southern Guaranty Insurance Co.; Cigna Corp. (INA-Aetna); Fireman's Fund-American Insurance Cos.; Safeco Insurance Company.

For Complete List of Firm Personnel, See General Section

For full biographical listings, see the Martindale-Hubbell Law Directory

ROTHSCHILD & MORGAN (AV)

1030 First Avenue, P.O. Box 2788, 31902-2788
Telephone: 706-324-4167
FAX: 706-324-1969

MEMBERS OF FIRM

Jerome M. Rothschild	W. Donald Morgan, Jr.

ASSOCIATE
Neal J. Callahan

Reference: Columbus Bank and Trust Company.

For Complete List of Firm Personnel, See General Section

For full biographical listings, see the Martindale-Hubbell Law Directory

DALTON,* Whitfield Co.

KINNEY, KEMP, PICKELL, SPONCLER & JOINER (AV)

A Partnership including a Professional Corporation
225 W. King Street, P.O. Box 398, 30722-0398
Telephone: 706-278-5211
FAX: 706-275-6566

MEMBERS OF FIRM

R. Carter Pittman (1898-1972)	Horace Greely Joiner, Jr.
L. Hugh Kemp (P.C.)	Henry C. Tharpe, Jr.
Charles L. Pickell	F. Gregory Melton
Maurice M. Sponcler, Jr.	Richard W. Andrews
Timothy H. Allred	

ASSOCIATES

Mark D. Newberry	Robert Adam Cowan

OF COUNSEL
Hinton Eugene Kinney

General Counsel for: North Georgia Electric Membership Cooperative; Queen Carpet Corp.; Hardwick Bank & Trust Company.
Representative Clients: Allstate Insurance Co.; Liberty Mutual Insurance Co.; State Farm Mutual Automobile Insurance Co.; Norfolk Southern Railway Company; General Motors Corporation and Dalton Board of Education.

For full biographical listings, see the Martindale-Hubbell Law Directory

DECATUR,* De Kalb Co.

PARKERSON, SHELFER & GROFF (AV)

715 First Union Plaza of Decatur, 250 East Ponce de Leon Avenue, 30030-3490
Telephone: 404-377-8143
Telecopier: 404-373-6829

(See Next Column)

MEMBERS OF FIRM

William S. Shelfer (1900-1975)	William S. Shelfer, Jr.
I. J. Parkerson	David B. Groff

Reference: Nations Bank of Georgia.

For full biographical listings, see the Martindale-Hubbell Law Directory

GAINESVILLE,* Hall Co.

SMITH, GILLIAM AND WILLIAMS (AV)

200 Old Coca-Cola Building, 301 Green Street, N.W., P.O. Box 1098, 30503
Telephone: 770-536-3381
Fax: 770-531-1481

MEMBERS OF FIRM

R. Wilson Smith, Jr. (1906-1983)	Jerry A. Williams
John H. Smith	Kelly Anne Miles
Steven P. Gilliam	Bradley J. Patten

ASSOCIATES

M. Tyler Smith	Scott Arthur Ball

General Counsel for: Gainesville Industrial Electric Co.; Georgia Mutual Insurance, a Stock Company; L & R Farms; H. Wilson Manufacturing Co.; Goforth Electrical Supply; North Georgia Petroleum Co.; Gibbs Management Group, Inc.

For full biographical listings, see the Martindale-Hubbell Law Directory

JESUP,* Wayne Co.

HOWARD, CARSWELL & BENNETT, P.C. (AV)

Lawyers Building, 145 North Brunswick Street, P.O. Box 543, 31598-0543
Telephone: 912-427-4268

Joseph H. Thomas (1909-1984)	Kenneth R. Carswell
Hubert H. Howard	R. Violet Bennett

Representative Clients: Independent Fire Insurance Cos.; Georgia Insurers Insolvency Pool; The Seibels Bruce Insurance Co.; Southern Trust Insurance Co.; CIGNA Insurance Cos.; Southern Fidelity Insurance Co.; Great Central Insurance Co.; Kemper Insurance Co.; Cotton States Insurance Co.; Liberty Mutual Insurance Co.

For full biographical listings, see the Martindale-Hubbell Law Directory

MACON,* Bibb Co.

ANDERSON, WALKER & REICHERT, P.C. (AV)

Suite 404 SunTrust Bank Building, P.O. Box 6497, 31208-6497
Telephone: 912-743-8651
Telecopier: 912-743-9636

Albert P. Reichert	Eugene S. Hatcher
Thomas L. Bass	Robert A. B. Reichert
Albert P. Reichert, Jr.	Susan S. Cole
John D. Reeves	Jonathan A. Alderman
	Brown W. Dennis, Jr.

Charles E. Cox, Jr.	Travis M. Trimble
Ramsey T. Way, Jr.	Samuel G. Alderman, III
	Laura H. Wanamaker

Representative Clients: Riverwood International USA, Inc.; Hospital Corporation of America; Pepsi-Cola Bottling Company of Macon; Radiology Associates of Macon, P.C.; Thiele Kaolin Company; SunTrust Bank of Middle Georgia, N.A.
General Insurance Clients: Liberty Mutual Insurance Co.; Alexis, Inc.

For Complete List of Firm Personnel, See General Section

For full biographical listings, see the Martindale-Hubbell Law Directory

CHAMBLESS, HIGDON & CARSON (AV)

Suite 200 Ambrose Baber Building, 577 Walnut Street, P.O. Box 246, 31298-5399
Telephone: 912-745-1181
Telecopier: 912-746-9479

MEMBERS OF FIRM

Joseph H. Davis	Thomas F. Richardson
Joseph H. Chambless	Mary Mendel Katz
David B. Higdon	Emmitte H. Griggs
James F. Carson, Jr.	Marc T. Treadwell

ASSOCIATES

Kim H. Stroup	Jon Christopher Wolfe
James D. Tolliver	

LEGAL SUPPORT PERSONNEL

Angie Horton	Erie Reed

Local Counsel for: Atlanta Gas Light Co.; First Union National Bank of Georgia; Security National Bank.

For full biographical listings, see the Martindale-Hubbell Law Directory

Macon—Continued

HALL, BLOCH, GARLAND & MEYER (AV)

1500 Charter Medical Building, P.O. Box 5088, 31213-3199
Telephone: 912-745-1625
Telecopier: 912-741-8822

MEMBERS OF FIRM

F. Kennedy Hall
Benjamin M. Garland

J. Steven Stewart
Mark E. Toth

ASSOCIATES

John Flanders Kennedy
Todd C. Brooks

Representative Clients: Norfolk Southern Railway Company; Central of Georgia Railroad Company; Railway Claims Services, Inc.; United States Fidelity & Guaranty Company; Houston General Insurance Company; Rail Tex, Inc.; Georgia Central Railway Company.

For Complete List of Firm Personnel, See General Section

For full biographical listings, see the Martindale-Hubbell Law Directory

---

MARIETTA, Cobb Co.

DOWNEY & CLEVELAND (AV)

288 Washington Avenue, 30060
Telephone: 770-422-3233
Fax: 770-423-4199

OF COUNSEL

Lynn A. Downey

MEMBERS OF FIRM

Robert H. Cleveland
(1940-1989)
Joseph C. Parker

Y. Kevin Williams
Russell B. Davis
G. Lee Welborn

Rodney S. Shockley

ASSOCIATES

W. Curtis Anderson
Scott D. Clay

Todd E. Hatcher
Richard A. Griggs

Tara M. Waller

Representative Clients: Allstate Insurance Co.; St. Paul Insurance Cos.; Georgia Farm Bureau Mutual Insurance Co.; State Farm Insurance Cos.; Cotton States Mutual Insurance Co.; Colonial Insurance Co. of California; Progressive Insurance Company; Auto Owners Insurance Company; Deep South Surplus, Inc.; Ed Voyles Oldsmobile, Honda and Chrysler-Plymouth.

For full biographical listings, see the Martindale-Hubbell Law Directory

---

MOORE INGRAM JOHNSON & STEELE (AV)

A Limited Liability Company
192 Anderson Street, P.O. Box 3305, 30060
Telephone: 770-429-1499
Telecopier: 770-429-8631

MEMBERS OF FIRM

John H. Moore
William R. Johnson

Robert D. Ingram
G. Phillip Beggs

ASSOCIATES

Jeffrey A. Watkins
Robert E. Jones
Michelle S. Davenport

Kevin B. Carlock
Alexander T. Galloway, III
G. Andy Adamek

Scott Gregory Wagner

Representative Clients: Crawford & Co.; The PMA Group; Scottsdale Insurance Co.; Transamerica Specialty Insurance Co.; Great Central Insurance Company; Wausau Insurance Company; Georgia Oilman's Association; Associated Risk Services, Inc.; PCA Solutions, Inc.; Coca Cola Enterprises.

For full biographical listings, see the Martindale-Hubbell Law Directory

---

ROME, Floyd Co.

BRINSON, ASKEW, BERRY, SEIGLER, RICHARDSON & DAVIS (AV)

A Partnership including Professional Corporations
Omberg House, 615 West First Street, P.O. Box 5513, 30162-5513
Telephone: 706-291-8853;
Atlanta: 404-521-0908
Telecopier: 706-234-3574

MEMBERS OF FIRM

Robert M. Brinson (P.C.)
C. King Askew (P.C.)
Robert L. Berry
Joseph M. Seigler, Jr.
Thomas D. Richardson
J. Anderson Davis

Hendrick L. Cromartie, III
Wright W. Smith
Mark M. J. Webb
Joseph B. Atkins
I. Stewart Duggan, Jr.
James Daniel Blitch

Representative Clients: City of Rome; Georgia Power Co.; General Electric Company; News Publishing Company (Rome News Tribune); Redmond Regional Medical Center; Oglethorpe Power Corp.; Suhner Manufacturing, Inc.; The Federal Land Bank of Columbia; AmSouth Bank of Georgia; United States Fidelity & Guaranty Co.

For full biographical listings, see the Martindale-Hubbell Law Directory

---

SAVANNAH, Chatham Co.

BARROW, SIMS, MORROW, LEE & GARDNER, A PROFESSIONAL CORPORATION (AV)

111 West Congress Street, P.O. Box 8185, 31412
Telephone: 912-234-7215
Fax: 912-234-7119

Charles W. Barrow
R. Stephen Sims
Jordon D. Morrow

A. Mark Lee
James R. Gardner
Christine J. Bedingfield

OF COUNSEL

Jay D. Gardner

For full biographical listings, see the Martindale-Hubbell Law Directory

---

BRANNEN, SEARCY & SMITH (AV)

22 East Thirty-Fourth Street, P.O. Box 8002, 31412
Telephone: 912-234-8875
Fax: 912-232-1792

Perry Brannen (1903-1984)
Frank P. Brannen
William N. Searcy

David R. Smith
Daniel C. Cohen
Wayne L. Durden

OF COUNSEL

William T. Daniel, Jr.

ASSOCIATES

Robert L. Jenkins
Bernard F. Kistler, Jr.

Margaret G. Culclasure
(Not admitted in GA)

Counsel for: Continental Insurance Co.

For full biographical listings, see the Martindale-Hubbell Law Directory

---

KARSMAN, BROOKS & CALLAWAY, P.C. (AV)

301 West Congress Street, P.O. Box 9149, 31412
Telephone: 912-238-2750
Cable Address: "Karbro"
Telecopier: 912-238-2767

Stanley M. Karsman
Charles C. Brooks
Timothy F. Callaway, III
Stanley E. Harris, Jr.
James L. Drake, Jr.
Dana F. Braun

R. Krannert Riddle
Edward M. Hughes
Shari Sigman Miltiades
D. Campbell Bowman, Jr.
Timothy J. Haeussler
Tracie Grove Smith

For full biographical listings, see the Martindale-Hubbell Law Directory

---

KENT, WORSHAM & SMART (AV)

The Callen Trust Building, 42 East Bay Street, P.O. Box 9117, 31412
Telephone: 912-238-1500
FAX: 912-238-5515

MEMBERS OF FIRM

Martin Kent
Hugh M. Worsham, Jr.

Don Smart

LEGAL SUPPORT PERSONNEL

Linda Susan Phipps

References: The Coastal Bank of Georgia.

For full biographical listings, see the Martindale-Hubbell Law Directory

---

WOODALL AND MACKENZIE, P.C. (AV)

327 Tattnall Street, P.O. Box 10166, 31412
Telephone: 912-238-9999

John T. Woodall
Malcolm Mackenzie, III

Peter A. Giusti

Reference: Trust Company Bank.

For full biographical listings, see the Martindale-Hubbell Law Directory

---

STATESBORO, Bulloch Co.

BROWN & LIVINGSTON, P.C. (AV)

26 North Main Street, P.O. Box 1988, 30458
Telephone: 912-489-6900
Fax: 912-764-2251

Charles H. Brown
Becky Dasher Livingston

Jeff S. Akins

Local Counsel For: John Hancock Mutual Insurance Co.; Grinnell Corp.; Shuman Construction Co.; Georgia Farm Bureau Mutual Insurance Co.; First Bank of Coastal Georgia; Health Management Associates; Montgomery County Bank; Fickling & Walker.

For full biographical listings, see the Martindale-Hubbell Law Directory

SWAINSBORO,* Emanuel Co.

SHEPHERD, GARY & McWHORTER (AV)

SSG Building, 104 East Moring Street, Drawer 99, 30401
Telephone: 912-237-7551

MEMBERS OF FIRM

Felix C. Williams (1899-1972)	Loren Gary, II
George L. Smith, II (1912-1973)	William H. McWhorter, Jr.
Sidney B. Shepherd	Millard B. Shepherd, Jr.

Representative Clients: City of Swainsboro, Adrian, Garfield and Nunez; The Citizens Bank of Swainsboro; Rayonier, Inc.; Farm Bureau Insurance Co.; Yeomans Wood and Timer Co.

For full biographical listings, see the Martindale-Hubbell Law Directory

TOCCOA,* Stephens Co.

McCLURE, RAMSAY & DICKERSON (AV)

400 Falls Road, P.O. Drawer 1408, 30577
Telephone: 706-886-3178
Fax: 706-886-1150

MEMBERS OF FIRM

Clyde M. McClure (1892-1976)	John A. Dickerson
George B. Ramsay, Jr.	Allan R. Ramsay
	Marlin R. Escoe	

ASSOCIATES

Alice D. Hayes	Elizabeth Felton Moore
	Luther H. Beck, Jr.	

OF COUNSEL

Knox Bynum

Counsel for: Coats and Clark, Inc.; Stephens Federal Savings & Loan Assn.; St. Paul Insurance Cos.; State Farm Insurance Cos.; Cotton States Insurance Cos.; City of Toccoa; Citizens Bank; Habersham Plantation Corp.; Patterson Pump Co; Georgia Farm Bureau Insurance Companies.

For full biographical listings, see the Martindale-Hubbell Law Directory

VALDOSTA,* Lowndes Co.

CLYATT, CLYATT, WALLACE & DeVAUGHN, P.C. (AV)

410 North Valdosta Road, P.O. Box 5799, 31603
Telephone: 912-241-9091
Fax: 912-245-1635

Robert M. Clyatt	Russell Cotter Wallace
Melissa M. Clyatt	C. Elizabeth DeVaughn
	Joni B. Parker	

For full biographical listings, see the Martindale-Hubbell Law Directory

TILLMAN, McTIER, COLEMAN, TALLEY, NEWBERN & KURRIE (AV)

910 North Patterson Street, P.O. Box 5437, 31603-5437
Telephone: 912-242-7562
Fax: 912-333-0885

MEMBERS OF FIRM

Henry T. Brice (1925-1976)	Thompson Kurrie, Jr.
B. Lamar Tillman (1912-1990)	Richard L. Coleman
John T. McTier	Edward F. Preston
Wade H. Coleman	William E. Holland
George T. Talley	R. Clay Powell
C. George Newbern	Gregory T. Talley

Representative Clients: Liberty Mutual Insurance Co.; Metropolitan Insurance Co.; USF&G Co.; American Mutual Fire Insurance Co.; Safeco Insurance Co.; American Hardware Mutual Insurance Co.; Georgia Casualty & Surety Co.; Reserve Life Insurance Co.; Grange Mutual Casualty Co.; Commercial Union Insurance Cos.

For full biographical listings, see the Martindale-Hubbell Law Directory

YOUNG, THAGARD, HOFFMAN, SCOTT & SMITH (AV)

801 Northwood Park Drive, P.O. Box 820, 31601-0820
Telephone: 912-242-2520
FAX: 912-245-1635

OF COUNSEL

Cam U. Young

MEMBERS OF FIRM

F. Thomas Young	Daniel C. Hoffman
James B. Thagard	H. Pearce Scott
	J. Holder Smith, Jr.	

ASSOCIATE

Mae Elizabeth Clevand (Not admitted in GA)

Attorneys for: State Farm Insurance Cos.; INA/Aetna Insurance Co.; Travelers Insurance Co.; Maryland Casualty Insurance Co.; Allstate Insurance Co.; Fireman's Fund Insurance Cos.; Aetna Casualty & Surety Cos.; Auto-Owners Insurance Co.; Home Insurance Cos; Georgia Farm Bureau Mutual Insurance Co.

(See Next Column)

For full biographical listings, see the Martindale-Hubbell Law Directory

WAYCROSS,* Ware Co.

DILLARD, BOWER AND EAST (AV)

209 Tebeau Street, P.O. Box 898, 31501
Telephone: 912-285-2915
Fax: 912-285-2249

MEMBERS OF FIRM

Terry A. Dillard	Bryant H. Bower, Jr.
	Joseph E. East	

ASSOCIATES

Scott C. Crowley	Rebecca R. Crowley

Attorneys For: American International Adjustment Co.; Auto-Owners Insurance Co.; Chrysler Corp.; Farmers Insurance Group; Georgia Farm Bureau Mutual Insurance Co.; G.M.A.C.; Grange Mutual Insurance Co.; Guaranty National Insurance Co.; Hoffman La Roche.

For full biographical listings, see the Martindale-Hubbell Law Directory

---

HAWAII

HONOLULU,* Honolulu Co.

ALCANTARA & FRAME ATTORNEYS AT LAW, A LAW CORPORATION (AV)

Suite 1100 Pioneer Plaza, 900 Fort Street Mall, 96813
Telephone: 808-536-6922
Fax: 808-521-8898
Telex: 650-225-8816
WUI: 101-650 225-8816
MCI ID: 225-8816
San Diego, California: 402 West Broadway, Suite 400.
Telephone: 619-595-3175.
Fax: 619-595-3176.

Leonard F. Alcantara	Robert G. Frame
	Bryan Y. Y. Ho	

Joy Lee Cauble	Michael D. Formby
John O'Kane, Jr.	Eldon M. Ching
Evelyn J. Black	James W. Alcantara (Resident, San Diego, California)

Reference: City Bank, Honolulu.

For full biographical listings, see the Martindale-Hubbell Law Directory

GEORGE W. ASHFORD, JR. (AV)

2910 Pacific Tower, 1001 Bishop Street, 96813
Telephone: 808-528-0444
Telecopier: (808) 533-0761
Cable Address: Justlaw

Representative Clients: Lloyds of London; Baker Industries, Inc.; Burns International Security Services; Clark Equipment Co.; Great Lakes Chemical Corporation; California Union Insurance Co.; Great American Insurance Companies; Guaranty National Companies; Horace Mann Insurance Company; Marine Office of America Corp.

For full biographical listings, see the Martindale-Hubbell Law Directory

AYABE, CHONG, NISHIMOTO, SIA & NAKAMURA (AV)

A Partnership including a Professional Corporation
Pauahi Tower, Suite 2500, 1001 Bishop Street, 96813
Telephone: 808-537-6119
Telecopier: 808-526-3491

MEMBERS OF FIRM

Sidney K. Ayabe (P.C.)	Calvin E. Young
Robert A. Chong	Diane W. Wong
John S. Nishimoto	Rodney S. Nishida
Richard F. Nakamura	Patricia T. Fujii
Jeffrey H. K. Sia	Rhonda A. Nishimura
Kenneth T. Goya	Gail M. Kang
Francis M. Nakamoto	Ann H. Aratani

Philip S. Uesato	Virgil B. Prieto
Ronald M. Shigekane	J. Thomas Weber
Robin R. Horner	Robert Y. Nakamoto
Stephen G. Dyer	Robert A. Mash
Steven L. Goto	Gary S. Miyamoto

Representative Clients: Travelers Insurance Co.; St. Paul Fire and Marine Insurance Co.; The Employers Group of Insurance Companies; TIG Insurance Co.; Pacific Insurance Co.; Hartford Accident and Indemnity Co.; Continental Casualty Co.; CNA Insurance Co.; Wausau Insurance Co.

For full biographical listings, see the Martindale-Hubbell Law Directory

Honolulu—Continued

DWYER IMANAKA SCHRAFF KUDO MEYER & FUJIMOTO ATTORNEYS AT LAW, A LAW CORPORATION (AV)

1800 Pioneer Plaza, 900 Fort Street Mall, 96813
Telephone: 808-524-8000
Telecopier: 808-526-1419
Mailing Address: P.O. Box 2727, 96803
Email: hawaiilaw@dwyer-imanaka.com *URL:*
http://www.dwyer-imanaka.com

John R. Dwyer, Jr.	William G. Meyer, III
Mitchell A. Imanaka	Wesley M. Fujimoto
Paul A. Schraff	Ronald Van Grant
Benjamin A. Kudo (Atty. at Law, A Law Corp.)	Jon M. H. Pang
	Blake W. Bushnell

Adelbert Green

Richard T. Asato, Jr.	Jeffery S. Werbelow
Scott W. Settle	Lori Ann K. Koseki
Darcie S. Yoshinaga	Troy T. Fukuhara
Lawrence I. Kawasaki	Katy Y. Chen
Stacy E. Uehara	Naomi S. Uyeno
Kris N. Nakagawa	Roger B. McKeague

OF COUNSEL

Randall Y. Iwase	R. Brian Tsujimura

For full biographical listings, see the Martindale-Hubbell Law Directory

FUKUNAGA MATAYOSHI HERSHEY & CHING (AV)

A Partnership including a Law Corporation
City Center, Third Floor, 810 Richards Street, 96813
Telephone: 808-533-4300
Fax: 808-531-7585

PARTNERS

Kenneth K. Fukunaga	James H. Hershey
Jerold T. Matayoshi (A Law Corporation)	Wesley H. H. Ching
	Patricia Kehau Wall

ASSOCIATES

Lois H. Yamaguchi	Robert R. Sadaoka
	Lindai M. Dang

OF COUNSEL

Leighton K. Chong

Representative Clients: Employers Reinsurance Corporation; First Insurance Co. of Hawaii, Ltd.; General Accident Insurance; Hartford Insurance Group, Inc.; Pacific Insurance Co., Ltd.; Tokio Marine & Fire Insurance, Co., Ltd.; Wausau Underwriters Insurance Co.; Yasuda Fire & Marine.

For full biographical listings, see the Martindale-Hubbell Law Directory

GREELEY WALKER & KOWEN (AV)

A Partnership including a Law Corporation
Suite 1300 Pauahi Tower, 1001 Bishop Street, 96813
Telephone: 808-526-2211
Telecopier: 808-528-4690

MEMBERS OF FIRM

Burnham H. Greeley (A Law Corporation)	Susan P. Walker
	Richard J. Kowen

Janice T. Futa

ASSOCIATES

Frank P. Richardson	Kimberly Ann Greeley
	Andrew D. Smith

Representative Clients: Abbott Laboratories; The Boeing Company; E.I. du Pont deNemours and Company, Incorporated; General Motors Corporation; Japan Tobacco International Corporation; Maytag Corporation; Phillips Petroleum Company; Sears, Roebuck and Co.; Toyota Motor Corporation; United States Aviation Underwriters, Inc.

For full biographical listings, see the Martindale-Hubbell Law Directory

KESSNER DUCA UMEBAYASHI BAIN & MATSUNAGA ATTORNEYS AT LAW, A LAW CORPORATION (AV)

19th Floor, Central Pacific Plaza, 220 South King Street, 96813
Telephone: 808-536-1900
Telecopier: 808-529-7177
Telex: 723 8616 OPAC IIR

Robert C. Kessner	Elton John Bain
James N. Duca	Emma S. Matsunaga
Clyde S. Umebayashi	Muriel M. Taira

Beverly S. K. Tom	Melanie S. Ono
Jacqueline W.S. Amai	Darin P. Wright
Dawn Jordan	Cori Ann C. Yokota

For full biographical listings, see the Martindale-Hubbell Law Directory

McCORRISTON MIHO MILLER MUKAI (AV)

Five Waterfront Plaza, 4th Floor, 500 Ala Moana Boulevard, 96813
Telephone: 808-529-7300
Facsimile: 808-524-8293
Cable: Attorneys, Honolulu
Mailing Address: P.O. Box 2800, Honolulu, Hawaii, 96803-2800
Hilo, Hawaii Office: 56 Waianuenue Avenue, Suite 217, 96720.
Telephone: 808-935-6537.
Facsimile: 808-935-3398.

PARTNERS

William C. McCorriston	Randall K. Schmitt
Mark J. Bennett	John Y. Yamano
Nadine Y. Ando	R. John Seibert
Richard B. Miller	Thomas E. Bush

Lisa M. Ginoza

ASSOCIATES

Kimberly Rae McCorkle	Christopher J. Cole
Carrie K. Okinaga	Joel D. Kam

David R. Harada-Stone

Representative Clients: Allstate Insurance Company; State Farm Insurance; Scottsdale Insurance Company; American Insurance Group; Design Professional Insurance Company.

For Complete List of Firm Personnel, See General Section

For full biographical listings, see the Martindale-Hubbell Law Directory

REID, RICHARDS & MIYAGI (AV)

A Partnership including Professional Corporations
Pauahi Tower, Suite 1200, 1001 Bishop Street, 96813-3498
Telephone: 808-524-2466
Fax: 808-524-2556

MEMBERS OF FIRM

Carleton B. Reid (A Law Corporation)	Melvyn M. Miyagi (A Law Corporation)
Robert P. Richards (A Law Corporation)	Ralph J. O'Neill
	Katharine M. Nohr

James V. Myhre	Tamara M. Gerrard
Roy F. Epstein	John E. Drotz
Michele-Lynn E. Luke	Deborah Chen
L. Darlene Mitchell	Jennifer Ellen Reid
Marie A. Sheldon	Celia A. Urion
Michael H. Tsuchida	Irene C. Sun

Duane R. Miyashiro

For full biographical listings, see the Martindale-Hubbell Law Directory

ROBBINS & RHODES ATTORNEYS AT LAW, A LAW CORPORATION (AV)

Suite 2200 Davies Pacific Center, 841 Bishop Street, 96813
Telephone: 808-524-2355
Fax: 808-526-0290

Kenneth S. Robbins	Shinken Naitoh

Representative Clients: Aetna Casualty & Surety, Inc.; American Reinsurance Co.; CNA Insurance Co.; Employers Reinsurance Corp.; General Reinsurance Co.; Guaranty National Insurance Co.; Industrial Underwriters Insurance Co.; Mid American MGA, Inc.; Woodbridge Insurance Co.

For full biographical listings, see the Martindale-Hubbell Law Directory

TAM, O'CONNOR & HENDERSON ATTORNEYS AT LAW, A LAW CORPORATION (AV)

20th Floor, Central Pacific Plaza, 220 South King Street, 96813
Telephone: 808-545-3030
Fax: 808-523-8051
Fax: 808-537-6782

James K. Tam	Wayne K. T. Mau
Michael F. O'Connor	Lissa H. Andrews
Harvey E. Henderson, Jr.	Robert M. Yamauchi
William J. Nagle, III	Darryl M. Taira

Ashley K. Ikeda

Christopher Shea Goodwin	Stuart M. Kodish
Lisa Anne Gruebner	John S. Nitao
Wesley H. Ikeda	Nathan M. Osada

Representative Clients: Western Heritage Insurance Co.; American International Companies; Burlington Insurance Co.; Federal Insurance Co.; Chubb-/Pacific Indemnity Group; Alexander & Baldwin, Inc.; United States Services Automobile Assn.; First Federal Savings & Loan; Territorial Savings & Loan Assn.

For full biographical listings, see the Martindale-Hubbell Law Directory

Honolulu—Continued

WATANABE, ING & KAWASHIMA (AV)

A Partnership including Professional Corporations
Hawaii Tower, 5th & 6th Floors, 745 Fort Street, 96813
Telephone: 808-544-8300
Facsimile: 808-544-8399

MEMBERS OF FIRM

Jeffrey N. Watanabe (Atty. at Law, A Law Corp.)	Lyle Y. Harada (Atty. at Law, A Law Corp.)
James Kawashima (Atty. at Law, A Law Corp.)	Michael A. Lorusso (Atty. at Law, A Law Corp.)
J. Douglas Ing (Atty. at Law, A Law Corp.)	Pamela J. Larson (Atty. At Law, A Law Corp.)
Wray H. Kondo (Atty. at Law, A Law Corp.)	William H. Gilardy, Jr. (Atty. At Law, A Law Corp.)
John T. Komeiji (Atty. at Law, A Law Corp.)	John R. Aube (Atty. at Law, A Law Corp.)
Ronald Y. K. Leong (Atty. at Law, A Law Corp.)	Jan M.L.Y. Amii (Atty. at Law, A Law Corp.)
Robert T. Takamatsu (Atty. at Law, A Law Corp.)	Edward B. Rogin (Atty. at Law, A Law Corp.)
Cynthia Winegar (Atty. at Law, A Law Corp.)	Seth M. Reiss
Randall Y. Yamamoto (Atty. at Law, A Law Corp.)	Curtis C. Kim

ASSOCIATES

Donna Y. Kanemaru	Kevin H. Oda
George B. Apter	Michael C. Bird
Marcus B. Sierra	Brian Y. Hiyane
Lani Narikiyo	Dennis J. Hwang
Peter L. Fritz	Teri Y. Kondo
LLoyd S. Yoshioka	Jeff N. Miyashiro
Beth K. Fujimoto	John Seiichi Sasaki
Patsy H. Kirio	Gregory Y.P. Tom

OF COUNSEL

George R. Ariyoshi

ASIA PACIFIC CONSULTANT

Victor Hao Li (Not admitted in HI)

LEGAL SUPPORT PERSONNEL

GOVERNMENT AFFAIRS ADVISOR

Millicent M. Y. H. Kim

References: First Hawaiian Bank; American Savings Bank.

For Complete List of Firm Personnel, See General Section

For full biographical listings, see the Martindale-Hubbell Law Directory

IDAHO

BOISE,* Ada Co.

BOWEN, BRASSEY, GARDNER, WETHERELL & CRAWFORD (AV)

Jefferson Place, 350 North Ninth Street - Suite 400, P.O. Box 1009, 83701
Telephone: 208-344-7300
Facsimile: 208-344-7077

R. Daniel Bowen	Alan R. Gardner
Andrew C. Brassey	Robert T. Wetherell
	J. Nick Crawford

ASSOCIATES

Eric Stephen Bailey	Clayton Gill
Debra Young Irish	Michael J. Elia
	Peter W. Ware, Jr.

Representative Clients: Safeco Insurance Cos.; Industrial Indemnity Co.; Transamerica Insurance Group; Fireman's Fund Insurance Co.; Royal Insurance Co.; Lumbermans Mutual Insurance Co.; American Motorists Insurance Co.; Northwestern National Insurance Co.; Reliance Insurance Co.; Insurance Company of North America.

For full biographical listings, see the Martindale-Hubbell Law Directory

CANTRILL, SKINNER, SULLIVAN & KING (AV)

1423 Tyrell Lane, P.O. Box 359, 83701
Telephone: 208-344-8035
Fax: 208-345-7212

MEMBERS OF FIRM

David W. Cantrill	John L. King
Gardner W. Skinner, Jr.	Robert D. Lewis
Willis E. Sullivan, III	Frank P. Kotyk

ASSOCIATES

Tyra H. Stubbs	Clinton O. Casey

(See Next Column)

LEGAL SUPPORT PERSONNEL

Garianne Erwin

Representative Clients: Safeco Insurance Companies; Prudential Property and Casualty Insurance Co.; State Insurance Fund; Farmers Insurance Co.; Jordan-Wilcomb Company; Nature Conservancy; Independent School District of Boise City; Hartford Insurance Group.
Reference: Key Bank.

For full biographical listings, see the Martindale-Hubbell Law Directory

JAMES J. DAVIS (AV)

500 East Baybrook Court, Suite 105, P.O. Box 8126, 83707
Telephone: 208-336-3244
Facsimile: 208-336-3374

ASSOCIATE

Anna K. Fiedler	Thomas E. Dvorak

Representative Clients: Risk Enterprise Management Limited; National Casualty Insurance Co.; Scottsdale Insurance Co.; Idaho County Reciprocal Management Program; Boise City, Idaho; State of Idaho; Willis Corroon.

For full biographical listings, see the Martindale-Hubbell Law Directory

ELAM & BURKE, A PROFESSIONAL ASSOCIATION (AV)

Key Financial Center, 702 West Idaho Street, P.O. Box 1539, 83701
Telephone: 208-343-5454
Telecopier: 208-384-5844
Email: eblaw@elamburke.com

M. Allyn Dingel, Jr.	William G. Dryden
John Magel	Trudy Hanson Fouser
James D. LaRue	Jeffery J. Ventrella
	Jeffrey A. Thomson

J. Ray Durtschi	Rebecca A. Broadbent

Representative Clients: State Farm Insurance; United Heritage Mutual Life Insurance; Progressive Insurance Co.; Farmers Insurance; Employers Reinsurance Corp.; Prudential Insurance Company of America; Idaho State Insurance Fund; Ohio Casualty Insurance Companies; Wausau Insurance Co.; Lincoln National Life Insurance.

For Complete List of Firm Personnel, See General Section

For full biographical listings, see the Martindale-Hubbell Law Directory

HAMLIN & SASSER, P.A. (AV)

3100 S. Vista Avenue, Suite 200, 83705
Telephone: 208-344-8474
Fax: 208-344-8479
Email: hamsass@cyberhighway.net

Robert G. Hamlin	David Sasser
M. Michael Sasser	Patrick J. Inglis
	Roger J. Hales

Kirtlan G. Naylor	Lisa Bertoch
Kathryn T. Langfield	Mark A. Kubinski
Ronald D. Christian	Matthew R. Harrison
	Timothy D. Wilson

Representative Clients: Alcoa; Allstate Insurance Co.; American Agency Life Insurance Co.; American Family Life Insurance Co.; American Hardware Mutual Insurance Co.; Amex Life Assurance Co.; Attorney Liability Protection Society, Inc.; Beneficial Finance Co.; Boise Air Service; CNA Insurance Cos.

For full biographical listings, see the Martindale-Hubbell Law Directory

LYNCH & ASSOCIATES, P.L.L.C. (AV)

West One Plaza, 101 S. Capitol Boulevard, Suite 1601, P.O. Box 739, 83701
Telephone: 208-331-5088
Fax: 208-331-0088

James B. Lynch

Penny L. Dykas	Mary L. McDougal
	Katherine M. Lynch

For full biographical listings, see the Martindale-Hubbell Law Directory

MOORE, BASKIN & PARKER (AV)

Washington Federal Plaza, 1001 West Idaho Street, Suite 400, P.O. Box 6756, 83707
Telephone: 208-336-6900
Facsimile: 208-336-7031

MEMBERS OF FIRM

Michael W. Moore	Thomas P. Baskin, III
	Paige Alan Parker

(See Next Column)

MOORE, BASKIN & PARKER, *Boise—Continued*

OF COUNSEL

Joseph M. Imhoff, Jr.

Representative Clients: Aetna Casualty & Surety, Co.; Capitol Indemnity Co.; Clarendon Insurance Co.; Crawford & Co.; Empire Fire & Marine Insurance Co.; Fireman's Fund Insurance Cos.; Idaho Counties Reciprocal Management Program; Idaho State Insurance Fund; Insurance Company of the West; Protective Insurance Co.

For full biographical listings, see the Martindale-Hubbell Law Directory

---

POCATELLO,* Bannock Co.

MERRILL & MERRILL, CHARTERED (AV)

Key Bank Building, P.O. Box 991, 83204
Telephone: 208-232-2286
Fax: 208-232-2499

Wesley F. Merrill	D. Russell Wight
Stephen S. Dunn	David C. Nye
	Kent L. Hawkins

Representative Clients: Farm Bureau Mutual Insurance Co. of Idaho; Aetna Life & Casualty; St. Paul Insurance; The Travelers Insurance Co.

For Complete List of Firm Personnel, See General Section

For full biographical listings, see the Martindale-Hubbell Law Directory

---

ILLINOIS

AURORA, Kane Co.

MURPHY, HUPP, FOOTE, MIELKE AND KINNALLY (AV)

North Island Center, P.O. Box 5030, 60507
Telephone: 708-844-0056
FAX: 708-844-1905

MEMBERS OF FIRM

William C. Murphy	Patrick M. Kinnally
Robert B. Hupp	Paul G. Krentz
Robert M. Foote	Joseph C. Loran
Craig S. Mielke	Gerald K. Hodge

Timothy D. O'Neil

OF COUNSEL

Robert T. Olson

Representative Clients: American Telephone & Telegraph Co.; Fox Valley Park District; Lyon Metal Products; Kane County Forest Preserve District; Hollywood Casino; Employers Mutual Insurance Co.; Forty-Eight Insulations, Inc.; UNR Asbestos Disease Trust; Richards-Wilcox Co.; National Bank & Trust Company of Syracuse.

For full biographical listings, see the Martindale-Hubbell Law Directory

---

BELLEVILLE,* St. Clair Co.

CHURCHILL MCDONNELL & HATCH (AV)

10 East Washington Street, Suite 101, 62220
Telephone: 618-233-4525; 314-231-9961
Telecopier: 618-234-9826
St. Louis (Clayton), Missouri Office: Suite 1806, 7777 Bonhomme Avenue.
Telephone: 314-863-0220.

MEMBERS OF FIRM

Allen D. Churchill	Joseph B. McDonnell
	Mary Ann Hatch

ASSOCIATE

Paul J. Evans

Representative Clients: Cigna Insurance Co.; Agora Syndicate; ISBA Mutual Insurance Co.; Bridgestone/Firestone, Tire Sales Co.; The Travelers Insurance Co.; National Steel Corp., Granite City Steel Division; Coldwell Banker; Associated Physicians Insurance Co.; Combustion Engineering Company.
Reference: Magna Bank, N.A.

For full biographical listings, see the Martindale-Hubbell Law Directory

DONOVAN, ROSE, NESTER, SZEWCZYK & JOLEY, P.C. (AV)

8 East Washington Street, 62220
Telephone: 618-235-2020
Telecopier: 618-235-9632

Dennis E. Rose	Edward J. Szewczyk
Michael J. Nester	Charles L. Joley

(See Next Column)

Kenneth M. Nussbaumer	Georgiann Oliver

Representative Clients: State Farm Mutual Auto & Life Co.; Travelers Insurance Co.; Liberty Mutual Insurance Co.; Government Employees Insurance Co.; Great American Insurance Co.; Aetna Casualty & Surety Co.; Royal Globe Insurance Co.; Illinois Founders Insurance Co.; INA (Insurance Company of North America).

For Complete List of Firm Personnel, See General Section

For full biographical listings, see the Martindale-Hubbell Law Directory

---

DUNHAM, BOMAN & LESKERA (AV)

208 North High Street, 62220
Telephone: 618-235-7222
Telecopier: 618-397-2285
East St. Louis, Illinois Office: 520 First Illinois Bank Building.
Telephone: 618-271-0535.
Telecopier: 618-271-2800.
Collinsville, Illinois Office: 300 West Clay Street.
Telephone: 618-344-7734.
Telecopier: 618-344-3853.

John W. Leskera	Russell K. Scott
William L. Berry	Robert D. Francis
Eric C. Young	John L. Bitzer

Attorneys For: Collinsville School District #10; Hanover Insurance Co.;ct Hartford Insurance Group; Home Indemnity Co.; State Farm Insurance Cos.; Transamerica Insurance Group; The Travelers Indemnity Co.; Wausau Insurance Cos.; Nationwide Insurance Co.; Atlantic Mutual Insurance Co..

For full biographical listings, see the Martindale-Hubbell Law Directory

---

FREEARK, HARVEY, MENDILLO, DENNIS & WULLER, PROFESSIONAL CORPORATION (AV)

115 West Washington Street, P.O. Box 546, 62222
Telephone: 618-233-2686
Telecopier: 618-233-5677

Ray H. Freeark, Jr.	James R. Mendillo
Ted R. Harvey, Jr.	Ted W. Dennis
	Ransom P. Wuller

Jeffery A. Cain	Denise Rusnack
Michael P. Murphy	Anneliesa B. Fierstos

Representative Clients: American Federation of Teachers, Local 434, Belleville, Illinois and 743, Granite City, Illinois.
Local Counsel for: Illinois State Medical Inter-Insurance Exchange, Chicago, Illinois; Sentry Insurance Co., Stevens Point, Wisconsin; General Casualty Cos., Springfield, Illinois and Sun Prairie, Wisconsin; Allstate Insurance Co., St. Louis, Missouri and Arlington Heights, Illinois; St. Paul Fire & Marine Insurance Co.; Safeco Insurance Co., St. Louis, Missouri; Travelers Insurance Co.; Northbrook Insurance Co., Arlington Heights, Illinois; Employers Insurance of Wausau, River Forest, Illinois and St. Louis, Missouri.

For full biographical listings, see the Martindale-Hubbell Law Directory

---

NEVILLE, RICHARDS, DEFRANCO & WULLER (AV)

5 Park Place, 62221
Telephone: 618-277-0900
Facsimile: 618-277-0970

MEMBERS OF FIRM

James E. Neville	James E. DeFranco
Timothy S. Richards	Robert G. Wuller, Jr.

ASSOCIATES

Shari M. Brunton	Ellen M. Edmonds
	Richard Thomas Roustio

For full biographical listings, see the Martindale-Hubbell Law Directory

---

WALKER & WILLIAMS, PROFESSIONAL CORPORATION (AV)

4343 West Main Street, 62223
Telephone: 618-274-1000; 277-1000
Telecopier: 618-233-1637
Edwardsville, Illinois Office: 70 Edwardsville Professional Park.
Telephone: 618-656-9222.
St. Louis, Missouri Office: 906 Olive, Suite 1250.
Telephone: 314-241-2441.
Telecopier: 314-241-7240.

Ralph D. Walker (1906-1988)	Dale L. Bode
Wayne P. Williams (1904-1990)	James C. Cook
David B. Stutsman	Thomas E. Jones
John B. Gunn	Anthony L. Martin (Resident,
Donald J. Dahlmann	St. Louis, Missouri Office)
	Harlan A. Harla

Michael D. Clark	John E. Sabo
Paul P. Waller III	Leslie Offergeld
James R. Garrison	Elaine C. Fusco

(See Next Column)

WALKER & WILLIAMS PROFESSIONAL CORPORATION—*Continued*

Representative Clients: Allstate Insurance Co.; Alton and Southern Railway Co.; Consolidated Rail Corp.; CSX Transportation, Inc.; Farmers Insurance Group; Firemen's Fund American Insurance Cos.; Madison Mutual Insurance Co.; St. Louis Southwestern Railway Co.; Scottsdale Insurance Cos.; Union Pacific Railroad.

For full biographical listings, see the Martindale-Hubbell Law Directory

BOLINGBROOK, Will Co.

MOSS AND BLOOMBERG, LTD. (AV)

305 West Briarcliff Road, Suite 201, P.O. Box 1158, 60440-0858
Telephone: 630-759-0800
Telecopier: 630-759-8504

Barry L. Moss	Steven P. Bloomberg
George A. Marchetti	

David J. Freeman	Daniel C Shapiro
Norma J. Guess	Judson L. Strain

For full biographical listings, see the Martindale-Hubbell Law Directory

CARBONDALE, Jackson Co.

BRANDON & SCHMIDT (AV)

916 West Main Street, P.O. Box 3898, 62902-3898
Telephone: 618-549-0777
Telecopier: 618-457-4691

MEMBERS OF FIRM

Wm. Kent Brandon	Charles E. Schmidt

ASSOCIATES

Jeffrey A. Goffinet	Christy W. Solverson
Reona J. Jack	

Representative Clients: State Farm Mutual Automobile Insurance Co.; State Farm Fire & Casualty Co.; Milwaukee Insurance Co.; Pekin Insurance Co.; Grinnel Mutual Reinsurance Co.; Western Casualty & Surety Co. (The Western Insurance Cos.); Illinois State Medical Ins. Services; Associated Physicians Ins. Co.; Hartford Ins. Co.
Reference: First National Bank of Carbondale.

For full biographical listings, see the Martindale-Hubbell Law Directory

CENTRALIA, Marion Co.

WHAM & WHAM (AV)

212 E. Broadway, 62801
Telephone: 618-532-5621
Fax: 618-532-5055

Charles Wham (1887-1963)	John P. Wham (1902-1992)

MEMBERS OF FIRM

James B. Wham	Janie F. Smith
Richard A. Cary	Jennifer J. Price
	Daniel R. Price

OF COUNSEL

William B. Wham

Counsel for: State Farm Mutual Insurance Cos.; Country Mutual Insurance Cos.; Lloyds of London; Aetna Group; Economy Fire & Casualty Co.

For full biographical listings, see the Martindale-Hubbell Law Directory

CHAMPAIGN, Champaign Co.

THOMAS, MAMER & HAUGHEY (AV)

Fifth Floor, First of America Bank Building, 30 Main Street, 61820-3629
Telephone: 217-351-1500
Telecopier: 217-355-0087
Mailing Address: P.O. Box 560, Champaign, Illinois, 61824-0560

James G. Thomas (1901-1990)

MEMBERS OF FIRM

Stuart M. Mamer	Craig J. Causeman
Roger E. Haughey	Michael R. Cornyn
Lott H. Thomas	Richard R. Harden
William J. Brinkmann	Robert A. Hoffman
Howard W. Small	Dan M. Slack
David A. Bailie	David E. Krchak
	Bruce E. Warren

ASSOCIATES

Linda L. Laugges	John M. Sturmanis
	Bianca I. Truitt

Representative Clients: First of America Bank Illinois, N.A.; Board of Trustees of the University of Illinois; Illinois Provident Trust; Prudential Insurance Company of America; Thompson Lumber Co.; The Carle Foundation; The Carle Foundation Hospital; Aetna Life and Casualty Co.; St. Paul Insurance Co.

For full biographical listings, see the Martindale-Hubbell Law Directory

CHICAGO,* Cook Co.

ARONBERG GOLDGEHN DAVIS & GARMISA (AV)

Suite 3000 One IBM Plaza, 60611
Telephone: 312-828-9600
Telecopier: 312-828-9635

MEMBERS OF FIRM

Christopher J. Bannon	Gene H. Hansen
Mitchell S. Goldgehn	James A. Smith

ASSOCIATES

Lisa J. Brodsky	James J. Hickey
John A. DiSalvo	William J. Serritella, Jr.
Howard J. Fishman	William C. Wilder
	Dawn C. Wrona

For Complete List of Firm Personnel, See General Section

For full biographical listings, see the Martindale-Hubbell Law Directory

BATES MECKLER BULGER & TILSON (AV)

8200 Sears Tower, 233 South Wacker, 60606
Telephone: 312-474-7900
Facsimile: 312-474-7898
URL: http://www.bmbt.com

MEMBERS OF FIRM

Robert J. Bates, Jr.	Kathleen H. Jensen
Scott L. Carey	Mari Henry Leigh
Janet R. Davis	Mary F. Licari
Maria G. Enriquez	Michael M. Marick
Francis X. Grossi, Jr.	Bruce R. Meckler
Maryann C. Hayes	Steven D. Pearson
	Scott M. Seaman

ASSOCIATES

Anne L. Blume	Christopher E. Kentra
Dina L. Brantman	Charlene Kittredge
Catherine M. Crisham	Michael I. Leonard
Joseph E. Cwik	Felicia Lynn Gerber Perlman
John K. Daly	John R. Rapasky
(Not admitted in IL)	Brett G. Rawitz
Robin Edelstein	John E. Rodewald
Mary E. Gootjes	Mark G. Sheridan
Robert C. Heist	Frederick W. Stein
James H. Kallianis, Jr.	Monica T. Sullivan
	Timothy A. Wolfe

OF COUNSEL

Stanley V. Figura	Matthew M. Murphy
Joseph Frontino	Thomas J. O'Brien
Philip R. King	Brian J. Williams

For full biographical listings, see the Martindale-Hubbell Law Directory

BELGRADE AND O'DONNELL, A PROFESSIONAL CORPORATION (AV)

311 South Wacker Drive, Suite 2770, 60606
Telephone: 312-360-9500
Facsimile: 312-360-9550

Steven B. Belgrade	Kim Richard Kardas
John A. O'Donnell	Rachel A. Tindel
George M. Velcich	Daniel Donohue

For full biographical listings, see the Martindale-Hubbell Law Directory

BLATT, HAMMESFAHR & EATON (AV)

333 W. Wacker Drive, Suite 1900, 60606
Telephone: 312-357-1277
FAX: 312-357-0198
Email: BHE@BHELAW.COM *URL:* HTTP://WWW.BHELAW.COM

MEMBERS OF FIRM

Richard Lee Blatt	Lori S. Nugent
Larry R. Eaton	Peter M. Page
Bruce M. Engel	William F. Richardson
Brent J. Graber	Gregory G. Smith
Robert W. Hammesfahr	Leonard S. Surdyk
Gregory D. Hopp	Patrick T. Walsh
Joanne J. Matousek	Judith M. Wexler
	Scott W. Wright

ASSOCIATES

David W. Alberts	Jill Ann Kaplan
David Hollingshead Anderson	Andrea C. Kenealey
Christopher R. Barth	Elizabeth E. Kim
Julie S. Bender	Kathleen A. McQueeny
Kristin M. Buchholz	Stephen R. Meinertzhagen
Andrea L. Caplan	Hallie J. Miller
Susan J. Cheney	Ziyad I. Naccasha
Lisa A. Dunsky	Kevin J. Rielley
Mary E. Fechtig	Stephen J. Rosenfeld
S. William Grimes	Scott V. Scarpelli
Josh M. Kantrow	Dana L. Schmitt

(See Next Column)

BLATT, HAMMESFAHR & EATON, *Chicago—Continued*

ASSOCIATES (Continued)

Susan B. Shulman	Timothy L. Swabb
George Matthew Silvers	Matthew T. Walsh
Janet B. Stern	Laura R. Zaroski

OF COUNSEL
Shane V. Nugent

For full biographical listings, see the Martindale-Hubbell Law Directory

BRYDGES RISEBOROUGH PETERSON FRANKE AND MORRIS (AV)

A Partnership including Professional Corporations
28th Floor, 150 North Michigan Avenue, 60601
Telephone: 312-782-5042
FAX: 312-704-9107
Waukegan, Illinois Office: 110 North West Street.
Telephone: 847-249-0300.
FAX: 847-249-4755.
Phoenix, Arizona Office: 3030 North Central Avenue, Suite 408.
Telephone: 602-631-4400.
FAX: 602-631-4404.

MEMBERS OF FIRM

Louis W. Brydges, Sr.	Scott E. Nemanich
Allyn J. Franke	Reid S. Jacobson
George E. Riseborough (A Professional Corporation)	Donald M. Lonchar, Jr.
	Peter J. Nordigian
J. V. Schaffenegger (1914-1986)	Robert L. Snook
Ralph Miller (1922-1988)	Stacey L. Seneczko
Donald G. Peterson	Rebecca Sarah Larson
Thomas A. Morris, Jr., (A Professional Corporation)	Neal T. Goldstein
	Monica J. Conrad
Donald L. Sime	Gioconda (Jackie) V. Iannicelli
John H. Krackenberger	Jennifer M. Lundy
Jay Scott Nelson	Eleanor P. Cabreré
Michael A. Strom	Linda A. White
Louis W. Brydges, Jr.	William G. Berg
Leslie A. Peterson	John W. Dixon
Thomas K. Gerling	Thomas A. Kiepura

OF COUNSEL

Harry D. Strouse	Thomas J. Moran (1920-1995)
Jack L. Watson	

For full biographical listings, see the Martindale-Hubbell Law Directory

CRYSTAL, HEYTOW & WARNICK, P.C. (AV)

Suite 1850, 200 North La Salle Street, 60601
Telephone: 312-541-1700
Facsimile: 312-541-9798

Frederick H. Crystal	Jeffrey L. Warnick
Richard D. Heytow	William G. Lacy

Robin Kaplan	Renata Seward

For full biographical listings, see the Martindale-Hubbell Law Directory

DOWD & DOWD, LTD. (AV)

Suite 1000, 55 West Wacker Drive, 60601
Telephone: 312-704-4400
Telecopier: 312-704-4500

Joseph V. Dowd	Robert C. Yelton III
Michael E. Dowd	Patrick C. Dowd
Kenneth Gurber	Robert J. Golden
	Karen W. Worsek

S. Robert Depke	John M. McAndrews
Ryan J. Harrington	Edward W. McNabola
Jeffrey Edward Kehl	Martha A. Niles
Sarah A. Kennedy	Michael G. Patrizio
Richard B. Korn	Patrick J. Ruberry
Joseph J. Leonard	Anthony R. Rutkowski
Ronald J. Lukes	Jeffrey Scott Wrage

LEGAL SUPPORT PERSONNEL

Carol Barnes	Jill A. Weiseman

OF COUNSEL

Guenther Ahlf	John A. Garrity, III
	Joel S. Ostrow

For full biographical listings, see the Martindale-Hubbell Law Directory

EICH & FRANKLIN (AV)

Suite 1206, 22 West Monroe Street, 60603
Telephone: 312-263-0599
Fax: 312-263-6768

MEMBERS OF FIRM

Edwin W. Eich, Jr.	Charles R. Franklin

(See Next Column)

Noel B. Haberek, Jr.	Daniel J. Lachat
Harold Himelman	Thomas G. Grace

For full biographical listings, see the Martindale-Hubbell Law Directory

GAROFALO, HANSON, SCHREIBER & VANDLIK, CHARTERED (AV)

211 West Wacker Drive, 14th Floor, 60606-1217
Telephone: 312-670-2000
Facsimile: 312-419-1336

Joseph A. Garofalo	Robert G. Lammie
Alan V. Hanson	Bennett F. Hart
Scott T. Schreiber	Philip G. Brinckerhoff
Mark J. Vandlik	Gregory P. Sujack
David F. Buysse	Derek A. Storm
	Steven R. Scarlati, Jr.

Jonathan E. Barrish	Andrew L. Rane
Michael S. Purves	Kathleen M. Callahan
Kerrie A. Lethbridge	Kurt E. Hanson

For full biographical listings, see the Martindale-Hubbell Law Directory

GESSLER, HUGHES & SOCOL, LTD. (AV)

Three First National Plaza, Suite 2200, 60602
Telephone: 312-580-0100
Telecopy: 312-580-1994

Mark S. Dym	Terence J. Moran
George W. Gessler	Mark D. Olson
John K. Hughes	Matthew J. Piers
William P. Jones	David J. Pritchard
Peter M. Katsaros	Kalman D. Resnick
Mark A. LaRose	Frederick S. Rhine
Kimberley Marsh	Jonathan A. Rothstein
	Donna Kaner Socol

Benjamin P. Beringer	Alex W. Miller
Darilyn W. Bock	Belkis Cervantes Muldoon
Gary Chodorow	Jonathan D. Rosenblum
Anjali Dayal	Marci S. Sperling
Ruth M. Dunning	Dana H. Sukenik
Adam D. Ingber	J. Eric Vander Arend
Michael J. Klein	Maria L. Vertuno
Laura C. Liu	Mark B. Weiner
	Charles H. Wintersteen

OF COUNSEL

James T. Derico, Jr.	Darius S. Francescatti, M.D.
	Susan R. Gzesh

For full biographical listings, see the Martindale-Hubbell Law Directory

GLEASON AND McGUIRE (AV)

180 North La Salle Street, Suite 1125, 60601
Telephone: 312-641-0580
Fax: 312-641-0380
Email: gm@coveragelaw.com *URL:* http://wwwcoveragelaw.com

MEMBERS OF FIRM

Nancy J. Gleason	Philip J. McGuire

ASSOCIATES

Robert C. Thurston	Patrick J. McGuire

OF COUNSEL
Thea M. Pazen

For full biographical listings, see the Martindale-Hubbell Law Directory

GUNTY & McCARTHY (AV)

150 South Wacker Drive, Suite 1025, 60606
Telephone: 312-541-0022
Facsimile: 312-541-0033
St. Louis, Missouri Office: 1515 North Warson Road, Suite 137.
Telephone: 314-427-7262.
Facsimile: 314-427-7268.

Susan Gunty	James P. McCarthy

Stephen K. Milott	Kirk Austin
Paul D. Van Lysebettens	Karyn S. Glennon

For full biographical listings, see the Martindale-Hubbell Law Directory

HASKELL & PERRIN (AV)

200 West Adams, Suite 2600, 60606
Telephone: 312-781-9393
Fax: 312-781-9178

(See Next Column)

HASKELL & PERRIN—*Continued*

MEMBERS OF FIRM

James Kirk Perrin	Stephen Sonderby
John J. Lynch	Kevin W. Doherty
Mary Elizabeth Denefe	Edward J. Matushek, III
Jerome J. Duchowicz	Daniel P. Caswell
Michael J. Sehr	Mary Jo Greene
Marsha K. Ross	Teresa J. Rooney

Floyd A. Wisner

OF COUNSEL

Donald M. Haskell

ASSOCIATES

Mark T. Banovetz	Safia Kahn
Blair S. Barbour	Timothy W. Kelly
Jonathan E. Beck	Rein F. Krammer
Peter G. Bora	Daniel M. Latreille
Eileen King Bower	Robert J. Marshall
Robert W. Brunner	David A. Nilles
Thomas M. Crawford	William J. Perry
Patrick Christopher Cremin, Jr.	Nancy J. Robinson
Debra L. Denslaw	Joseph B. Royster
(Not admitted in IL)	Michelle B. Sage
Steven J. Fleischer	Christine A. Schmidt
Kathryn M. Frost	Douglas M. Sinars
Myrna B. Galang	Frank B. Slepicka
Dawn M. Gonzalez	Michael Sullivan
Elizabeth M. Handzel	Virginia M. Vermillion
Elizabeth Thorne Jozefowicz	Alan S. Zelkowitz

For full biographical listings, see the Martindale-Hubbell Law Directory

---

JOHNSON & BELL, LTD. (AV)

Suite 2200, 222 North La Salle Street, 60601
Telephone: 312-372-0770
Facsimile: 312-372-9818
Wheaton, Illinois Office: Suite 1640, 2100 Manchester Road.
Telephone: 630-510-0880.
Facsimile: 630-510-0939.

William V. Johnson	Edward D. D'Arcy, Jr.
John W. Bell	Michael P. Siavelis
Jack T. Riley, Jr.	William A. Geiser
Brian C. Fetzer	Thomas J. Koch
Thomas H. Fegan	Kevin G. Owens
Thomas W. Murphy	Dennis C. Cusack
Thomas J. Andrews	Emilio E. Machado
William G. Beatty	Charles P. Rantis
John A. Childers	Dean M. Athans
Robert L. Nora	Robert J. Comfort
Margaret A. Unger	Alan Jay Goldstein
Timothy J. McKay	Susan Marzec Hannigan
Howard Patrick Morris	Daniel C. Murray
Scott W. Hoyne	Thomas F. Poelking
James S. Stickles, Jr.	William S. Allen
Frederick S. Mueller	William K. McVisk
Joseph R. Marconi	Gary A. Grasso
Robert M. Burke	Glenn F. Fencl
Kurt C. Meihofer	Frances J. Skinner-Lewis
Debra A. DiMaggio	Joseph F. Spitzzeri
Cornelius J. Harrington, III	Joseph B. Carini, III
Michael B. Gunzburg	Kathryn K. Loft
Charles W. Planek	Paul A. Tanzillo

William J. Anaya	Brian T. Levin
Susan Choi Brennan	Bruce M. Lichtcsien
Jean Harris Brown	Steven E. Lieb
Frank S. Capuani	Richard P. Long
Gregory D. Conforti	Michael J. Lynch
Christopher M. Daddino	David M. Macksey
Maria S. Doughty	Robert R. McNamara
Patrick T. Garvey	Joseph J. McNerney
Laura B. Glaser	Peter A. Nicholson
Kevin J. Greenwood	Frank P. Nowicki
Sean J. Hardy	Richard C. Perna
Guy Halpern	Brendan S. Power
William O. Ivy, Jr.	Lynne M. Reardon
Mark D. Johnson	Marilyn McCabe Reidy
Matthew L. Johnson	Zachary S. Rudman
Robert Johnson	Joseph D. Ryan
Janet A. Kachoyeanos	Ann M. Smith
Mindy L. Kallus	Robert Spitkovsky, Jr.
Mary Kenney	Terry Takash
Andrea H. Kott	Kelly N. Warnick
Genevie F. Labuda	Steven F. Wittman
Elizabeth Olen Lazzara	Robert W. York

References available upon request.

For full biographical listings, see the Martindale-Hubbell Law Directory

---

JOHNSON, DROZDZIK, VAN DRISKA & ANDROS, LTD. A PROFESSIONAL CORPORATION (AV)

200 West Adams Street, Suite 1005, 60606
Telephone: 312-236-6006
FAX: 312-236-4731

Anita Senese-Johnson	George J. Andros
Ronald L. Drozdzik	Gail A. Galante
Rebecca Schneiderman	Jack M. Shanahan
(1940-1987)	Patrick D. Duffy
Terrance J. Van Driska	
(1932-1995)	

For full biographical listings, see the Martindale-Hubbell Law Directory

---

KAPLAN & BEGY (AV)

One First National Plaza 51st Floor, 60603
Telephone: 312-345-3000
Fax: 312-345-3119

MEMBERS OF FIRM

Fred C. Begy, III	Joseph A. Bosco
Larry S. Kaplan	Martin K. LaPointe
James D. Solon	Richard A. Walker
Robert C. von Ohlen, Jr.	Mitchell J. Kanaan

ASSOCIATES

John B. Austin	Michael J. Vint
Donald F. Brosnan	Maritoni Derecho Kane
(Not admitted in IL)	Adriana Gardella
J. Peter Martin	Michael J. Frazier
Neal J. Moglin	John T. Midgett
Jeffrey E. Margulis	Keith S. Yamaguchi
Kevin R. Davis	Rose Jagust
Patrick J. Keating	Thomas C. Sokol

Terrill Elise Pierce

For full biographical listings, see the Martindale-Hubbell Law Directory

---

KIESLER & BERMAN (AV)

Suite 1300, 188 West Randolph Street, 60601
Telephone: 312-332-2840
FAX: 312-332-4547
Email: info@thekillerbees.com
Wheaton Office: 2100 Manchester, Suite 504.
Telephone: 630-752-8247.
Fax: 630-752-9587.
Joliet Office: 57 West Jefferson Street.
Telephone: 815-723-2755.
Fax: 815-723-2763.
Waukegan Office: 216 Madison Street.
Telephone: 847-244-5805.
Fax: 847-244-3996.

MEMBERS OF FIRM

Marvin D. Berman	Dale L. Schlafer
Robert L. Kiesler	Edward L. Cooper
Clinton J. Feil	Lyle F. Koester
Alan P. Miller	Mark S. Vilimek
John R. Garofalo	Rory D. Cassidy
Stephen B. Frew	Patti Olson Deuel

David J. Kiesler

ASSOCIATES

Bradley D. Alexander	Cynthia A. Meister
Robert A. Barba	Peter R. Mennella
Donna D. Ciancio	Shannon Francis O'Shea
James V. Creen	Jeffrey S. Pavlovich
Daniel E. Falb	John J. Piegore
Mary E. Haeger	Paul N. Reidy
Shari J. Kalik	Michael G. Ryan
Hector Ledesma	Daniel J. Softcheck
Bryan W. Luce	Lisa A. Weiss
William P. McElligott	Jeanne M. Zeiger

SENIOR COUNSEL

Eugene S. Goldenson	Frank N. Rago

For full biographical listings, see the Martindale-Hubbell Law Directory

---

MACCABE & MCGUIRE (AV)

Suite 3333, 77 West Wacker Drive, 60601
Telephone: 312-357-2600
Fax: 312-357-0317
Email: MacMcLaw77@aol.com

MEMBERS OF FIRM

Edward H. MacCabe	Maureen A. McGuire

ASSOCIATES

Timothy J. Murphy	Margaret T. Conway
Diedre S. Dunn	John C. Hurley

Lori G. Gabriel

(See Next Column)

MacCabe & McGuire, *Chicago—Continued*

OF COUNSEL
Brian J. Mulhern

For full biographical listings, see the Martindale-Hubbell Law Directory

MERLO, KANOFSKY & BRINKMEIER, LTD. (AV)

208 South La Salle Street, Suite 950, 60604
Telephone: 312-553-5500
Facsimile: 312-553-1586

Michael J. Merlo	Alan J. Brinkmeier
Martin A. Kanofsky	Michael R. Gregg

Steven R. Apel	Anne M. O'Brien
Michael J. Gilmartin	Joseph R. Ramos
Donald G. Machalinski	Linda J. Schneider
Suzanne J. Massel	Perry M. Shorris
Mary K. McGahey	William M. Sweetnam

Sandra J. Weber

For full biographical listings, see the Martindale-Hubbell Law Directory

MORA & BAUGH, LTD. (AV)

55 West Monroe Street, Suite 600, 60603
Telephone: 312-759-1400
Facsimile: 312-759-0402
West Palm Beach, Florida Office: Mora, Baugh & Derrevere, 224 Datura Street, Suite 1102.
Telephone: 407-835-3753.
Facsimile: 407-835-9831.

Steven H. Mora	David A. Baugh

David R. Carlson

Ellen L. Flannigan
OF COUNSEL

Robert M. Greco	Frank W. Nagorka

For full biographical listings, see the Martindale-Hubbell Law Directory

SANCHEZ & DANIELS (AV)

Suite 500, 333 West Wacker Drive, 60606
Telephone: 312-641-1555
Fax: 312-641-3004
Wheaton, Illinois Office: 2100 Manchester Road, Suite 101.
Telephone: 708-871-6161.
Fax: 708-871-9771.
Boston, Massachusetts Office: Sanchez, Daniels & Fitch, 101 Federal Street, Suite 1934.
Telephone: 617-478-0547.
Fax: 617-478-0544.

MEMBERS OF FIRM

Manuel "Manny" Sanchez	Timothy V. Hoffman
John D. Daniels	Robert T. Varney
Lori S. Yokoyama	Franklin U. Valderrama

George L. Acosta

John J. Skawski	Vanessa L. Vargas
Lela D. Johnson	Marcelle R. Kott
Rebecca Morrissey	Yvette Rivas Diamond
Hugh C. O'Donnell	Stacey Sherr Michelon
Jane Solmor-Mordini	Julie F. Furer
Francine Stulac	Darryl Tom
Edward N. Robles	Susan K. Chae
Joseph P. Bonaccorsi	Edward M. Ordonez
Mark I. Fishbein	Paige Donaldson
Deborah L. Nico	Lesley A. Corey

For full biographical listings, see the Martindale-Hubbell Law Directory

SCARIANO, KULA, ELLCH AND HIMES, CHARTERED (AV)

Two Prudential Plaza 180 North Stetson Suite 3100, 60601-6224
Telephone: 312-565-3100
Facsimile: 312-565-0000
Chicago Heights, Illinois Office: 1450 Aberdeen.
Telephone: 708-755-1900.
Facsimile: 708-755-0000.

Anthony G. Scariano	Kathleen Field Orr
David P. Kula	John M. Izzo
Robert H. Ellch	Raymond A. Hauser
Alan T. Sraga	Kathleen Roche Hirsman
A. Lynn Himes	Joanne W. Schochat
Justino D. Petrarca	Anthony Ficarelli
Lawrence Jay Weiner	G. Robb Cooper

Daniel M. Boyle
OF COUNSEL

Max A. Bailey	John B. Kralovec

(See Next Column)

Patrick J. Broncato	Kelly A. Hayden
Rosanne Ciambrone	Todd K. Hayden
Jon G. Crawford	David A. Hemenway
Joel R. DeTella	Sarah E. Joyce
Teri E. Engler	Christopher L. Petrarca
Andrew C. Eulass	Shelia C. Riley

Janet L. Schwieters

For full biographical listings, see the Martindale-Hubbell Law Directory

STELLATO & SCHWARTZ, LTD. (AV)

120 North La Salle Street, 34th Floor, 60602
Telephone: 312-419-1011
Telecopier: 312-419-1012

Donald E. Stellato	Robert A. Muhr
Esther Joy Schwartz	James Bartlett

John W. Gilligan III

Steven Blair Borkan	Paul R. Walker-Bright
James Scott McMahon	Derek M. Barker
Nicholas J. Scarpelli	Joseph D. Gergeni
Ann Killian Perry	Thomas Krieger
Jennifer M. Ellin	John H. Silvestri
Michael P. Bregenzer	Cheryl L. Sepulveda

Elaine S. Vorberg

Representative Clients: American Drug Stores Company; Automobile Club of Michigan; Budget Rent A Car Corp.; The Fireman's Fund Insurance; First Mercury Syndicate; First Nonprofit Companies; Jewel Companies, Inc.; Kmart Corporation; Northland Insurance Co.; United Services Automobile Association.

For full biographical listings, see the Martindale-Hubbell Law Directory

STEVENSON, RUSIN AND FRIEDMAN, LTD. (AV)

Suite 1530 10 South Riverside Plaza, 60606
Telephone: 312-454-5110
Fax: 312-454-6166

OF COUNSEL

Douglas F. Stevenson	Larry J. Chilton
Michael E. Rusin	David William Porter
Stephen J. Friedman	Gregory G. Vacala
John A. Maciorowski	Jon Yambert
Kenneth N. Marshall	Daniel Arkin

Randall R. Stark

Jean Marie Calcagno	Scott A. Labow
Brad A. Carder	Sharon M. Peart
Paul A. Coghlan	Theodore James Powers
P. Bartley Durham	Mark P. Rusin
Daniel R. Egan	Kevin A. Shaw
Frederick Scott Glassman	James J. Zahour

For full biographical listings, see the Martindale-Hubbell Law Directory

SWANSON, MARTIN & BELL (AV)

One IBM Plaza, Suite 2900, 60611
Telephone: 312-321-9100
Fax: 312-321-0990
Wheaton, Illinois Office: 2100 Manchester Road, C-1420.
Telephone: 708-653-2266.
Fax: 708-653-2292.

MEMBERS OF FIRM

Lenard C. Swanson	Lawrence Helms
Kevin T. Martin	Joseph P. Switzer
Brian W. Bell	George F. Fitzpatrick, Jr.
Stanley V. Boychuck	David E. Kawala
Kay L. Schichtel	Bruce S. Terlep
David J. Cahill	(Resident, Wheaton Office)
(Resident, Wheaton Office)	Robert J. Meyer

ASSOCIATES

Kevin V. Boyle	A. Jay Koehler, III
Michael J. Hossack	Sheryl A. Pethers
Matthew D. Jacobson	Barbara N. Petrungaro
(Resident, Wheaton Office)	Aaron T. Shepley
Joseph P. Kincaid	André Martin Thapedi
Patricia S. Kocour	William Blake Weiler

OF COUNSEL

Edward T. Butt, Jr.	John C. Church

For full biographical listings, see the Martindale-Hubbell Law Directory

TAYLOR, MILLER, SPROWL, HOFFNAGLE & MERLETTI (AV)

33 North La Salle Street, Suite 2222, 60602-2691
Telephone: 312-782-6070
Fax: 312-782-6081

(See Next Column)

TAYLOR, MILLER, SPROWL, HOFFNAGLE & MERLETTI—*Continued*

Orville Taylor (1885-1969)	Ralph W. F. Lustgarten
John S. Miller (1888-1965)	Richard W. Oloffson
James J. Hoffnagle	Frank C. Stevens
Roger A. Merletti	Roger LeRoy

OF COUNSEL

Charles R. Sprowl

ASSOCIATES

John R. Adams	Hugh J. Doyle
Jack Bruce Batten	Daniel K. Fritz
Karrieann M. Couture	Katherine M. Mulroy
Timothy Couture	Robert W. Rohm

For full biographical listings, see the Martindale-Hubbell Law Directory

---

TRIBLER ORPETT PALMER & CRONE, A PROFESSIONAL CORPORATION (AV)

30 North La Salle Street, Suite 2200, 60602
Telephone: 312-201-6400
Fax: 312-201-6401
Schaumburg, Illinois Office: Suite 1260, 1450 East American Lane.
Telephone: 847-517-8400.
Fax: 847-517-8401.

Douglas C. Crone	H. Wesley Sunu
Steven R. McMannon	Willis R. Tribler
Michael J. Meyer	William J. Wall
Mitchell A. Orpett	(Not admitted in IL)
Thomas R. Palmer	
(Resident, Schaumburg Office)	

John W. Carver	Lisa O'Malley
Molly A. Griffin	Christopher J. Ondrula
David P. Hahn	Matthew B. Parker
Kyle J. Kirkham	Stanley D. Sterna
(Resident, Schaumburg Office)	Panos T. Topalis

OF COUNSEL

Daniel D. Drew	John W. Wardell
	(Resident, Schaumburg Office)

For full biographical listings, see the Martindale-Hubbell Law Directory

---

COLLINSVILLE, Madison Co.

DUNHAM, BOMAN & LESKERA (AV)

300 West Clay Street, 62234
Telephone: 618-344-7734
Telecopier: 618-344-3853
East St. Louis, Illinois Office: 520 First Illinois Bank Building.
Telephone: 618-271-0535.
Telecopier: 618-271-2800.
Belleville, Illinois Office: 208 North High Street.
Telephone: 618-397-2151.
Telecopier: 618-397-2285.

John W. Leskera	William L. Berry

For full biographical listings, see the Martindale-Hubbell Law Directory

---

DANVILLE,* Vermilion Co.

HUTTON, LAURY, HESSER, LIETZ & WILCOX (AV)

16 West Madison Street, P.O. Box 1128, 61832
Telephone: 217-446-9436
FAX: 217-446-9462

MEMBERS OF FIRM

Everett L. Laury	Gregory G. Lietz
Gary D. Hesser	Roy G. Wilcox

Representative Clients: Pekin Insurance; Prudential Insurance Company; Metropolitan Life Insurance Company; Illinois State Medical Insurance Services, Inc.; Associated Physicians Insurance Company; Employers Reinsurance Corp.; Northwestern National Insurance Company; St. Paul Insurance Companies; Clarendon National Insurance Company; General Motors Corporation.

For Complete List of Firm Personnel, See General Section

For full biographical listings, see the Martindale-Hubbell Law Directory

---

DECATUR,* Macon Co.

ERICKSON, DAVIS, MURPHY, JOHNSON, GRIFFITH & WALSH, LTD. (AV)

225 South Main Street, P.O. Box 25138, 62525-5138
Telephone: 217-428-0948
Fax: 217-428-0996

(See Next Column)

Garry E. Davis	Michael A. Walsh
Evan H. Johnson	Bradley T. Paisley

Representative Clients: A.E. Staley Manufacturing Company; Archer Daniels Midland Company; Cincinnati Insurance Company; Country Mutual Insurance Company; General Casualty Insurance Companies; Illinois Power Company; Illinois State Medical Insurance Exchange; Millikin University; Reliance Insurance Company; Western States Insurance Company.

For Complete List of Firm Personnel, See General Section

For full biographical listings, see the Martindale-Hubbell Law Directory

---

TIETZ & RICHARDSON (AV)

444 Millikin Court Building, P.O. Box 1664, 62525
Telephone: 217-425-1515
Telecopier: 217-425-4077

Christopher M. Tietz	Jeffrey D. Richardson

Representative Clients: Farmers Insurance Group; Standard Mutual Insurance Co.; Canal Insurance Co.; United Capitol Insurance Co.; National States Insurance Co.; Unigard Insurance Group; American Republic Insurance Co.

For full biographical listings, see the Martindale-Hubbell Law Directory

---

EDWARDSVILLE,* Madison Co.

HEYL, ROYSTER, VOELKER & ALLEN, PROFESSIONAL CORPORATION (AV)

Suite 100, Mark Twain Plaza II, 103 West Vandalia Street, P.O. Box 467, 62025
Telephone: 618-656-4646
Telecopier: 618-656-7940
Peoria, Illinois Office: Suite 600, Bank One Building, 124 S.W. Adams, 61602.
Telephone: 309-676-0400.
Telecopier: 309-676-3374.
Springfield, Illinois Office: Suite 575, First of America Center, P.O. Box 1687, 62705.
Telephone: 217-522-8822.
Telecopier: 217-523-3902.
Urbana, Illinois Office: Suite 300, 102 East Main Street, P.O. Box 129, 61801.
Telephone: 217-344-0060.
Telecopier: 217-344-9295.
Rockford, Illinois Office: Suite 1015, Talcott Building, P.O. Box 1288, 61105.
Telephone: 815-963-4454.
Telecopier: 815-963-0399.

RESIDENT PERSONNEL

Robert H. Shultz, Jr.	John A. Ess
	Kent L. Plotner

RESIDENT OF COUNSEL

Robert T. Bruegge	William J. Becker

Timothy D. Seifert	Joe Francis Grabowski V
Robert D. Rowland	James A. Telthorst
Christine M. Giacomini	William R. Miller
	Gerry A. Ess

For full biographical listings, see the Martindale-Hubbell Law Directory

---

REED, ARMSTRONG, GORMAN, COFFEY, GILBERT & MUDGE, PROFESSIONAL CORPORATION (AV)

One Mark Twain Plaza, Suite 300, P.O. Box 368, 62025
Telephone: 618-656-0257
Facsimile: 618-692-4416
Other Edwardsville Office: 125 North Buchanan, P.O. Box 247.
Telephone: 618-656-2244.
Fax: 618-658-1307.
Springfield, Illinois Office: One West Old State Capital Plaza, Suite 400, Myers Building.
Telephone: 217-525-1366.
Fax: 217-525-0986.

Harry C. Armstrong	Martin K. Morrissey
James E. Gorman	Charles C. Compton
Stephen C. Mudge	Kevin J. Babb

Michael J. Bedesky	Bryan L. Skelton
David Laurent	Michelle A. Kunin
	Ronald D. Robinson

Representative Clients: State Farm Insurance Cos.; Country Companies; Standard Mutual Casualty Co.; General Casualty Co. of Wisconsin; Lloyds of London; Hawkeye Security Insurance Co.; Shelter Insurance Companies; Pekin Insurance Cos.; American International Adjusting Co.; Employers Reinsurance Corp.

For full biographical listings, see the Martindale-Hubbell Law Directory

Edwardsville—Continued

THOMSON & BEHR (AV)

22 B Glen - Ed Professional Park, P.O. Box 538, 62025
Telephone: 618-692-0028
Telecopier: 618-692-0269

MEMBERS OF FIRM

Stephen W. Thomson   Richard J. Behr

Danya L. Johnson

For full biographical listings, see the Martindale-Hubbell Law Directory

WALKER & WILLIAMS, PROFESSIONAL CORPORATION (AV)

70 Edwardsville Professional Park, 62025
Telephone: 618-656-9222
Belleville, Illinois Office: 4343 West Main Street.
Telephones: 618-274-1000; 277-1000.
Telecopier: 618-233-1637.
St. Louis, Missouri Office: 906 Olive, Suite 1250.
Telephone: 314-241-2441.
Telecopier: 314-241-7240.

Dale L. Bode

For full biographical listings, see the Martindale-Hubbell Law Directory

GALESBURG,* Knox Co.

MUSTAIN LINDSTROM & HENSON (AV)

1865 North Henderson Street, Suite 11B, 61401
Telephone: 309-344-5252
Telecopier: 309-344-3939

MEMBERS OF FIRM

Douglas D. Mustain   Ronald Henson
Robert Lindstrom   Christopher Henson
                Carl E. Hawkinson

References: The Farmers and Mechanics Bank; Norwest Bank Illinois, N.A.; First Bank; First Financial Bank; Farmers State Bank of Western Illinois; McGladrey and Pullen.

For full biographical listings, see the Martindale-Hubbell Law Directory

HARRISBURG,* Saline Co.

JELLIFFE, FERRELL & MORRIS (AV)

108 East Walnut Street, 62946
Telephone: 618-253-7153; 253-7647
Telecopier: 618-252-1843

OF COUNSEL
Charles R. Jelliffe
MEMBERS OF FIRM
DeWitt Twente (1904-1976)   Donald V. Ferrell
                Walden E. Morris
ASSOCIATES
Michal Doerge   Thomas J. Foster

Representative Clients: Auto-Owners Insurance; Country Cos; Metropolitan Life Insurance; Ohio Casualty Group; Standard Mutual Insurance Co.; State Farm Cos.; Redland Insurance Co.; Aetna Casualty & Surety Co.; Kerr-McGee Coal Corp.; Sahara Coal Co.

For full biographical listings, see the Martindale-Hubbell Law Directory

JACKSONVILLE,* Morgan Co.

RAMMELKAMP, BRADNEY, DAHMAN, KUSTER, KEATON, FRITSCHE & LINDSAY, P.C. (AV)

232 West State Street, P.O. Box 489, 62651
Telephone: 217-245-6177
Fax: 217-243-7322
Email: ramlkamp@netjax.com

L.O. Vaught (1865-1955)   Larry D. Kuster
Carl E. Robinson (1886-1964)   Forrest G. Keaton
Orville N. Foreman (1904-1972)   Barbara Fritsche
Albert W. Hall (1912-1986)   Nancy Lindsay
Theodore C. Rammelkamp   Maria M. Gonzalez
  (Retired)   Richard R. Freeman
Marc Dahman   H. Allen Yow

Brian L. Stocker
OF COUNSEL
Robert E. Bradney

Representative Clients: State Farm Mutual Auto Insurance; State Farm Fire & Casualty; Shelter Insurance; Millers National Insurance; Grinnell Mutual Insurance; Auto-Owners Insurance; Milwaukee Insurance; Pekin Farmers Insurance Co.; New Hampshire Insurance Co.; Zurich Insurance Co.

For full biographical listings, see the Martindale-Hubbell Law Directory

KANKAKEE,* Kankakee Co.

ACKMAN, MAREK, BOYD AND WOODRUFF, LTD. (AV)

Suite 400, One Dearborn Square, 60901
Telephone: 815-933-6681
Fax: 815-933-9985
Watseka, Illinois Office: 200 East Walnut Street.
Telephone: 815-432-5215.
Fax: 815-432-3186.
Manteno, Illinois Office: 10 North Locust Street.
Telephone: 815-468-7751.

Richard L. Ackman   Robert W. Boyd
J. Dennis Marek   Deborah A. Woodruff

James A. Devine   John J. Boyd
                                  (Also at Manteno Office)

Representative Clients: American States Insurance Co.; Auto Owners Insurance Co.; Consumers Illinois Water Co.; Country Mutual Insurance Co.; Farmers Insurance Group; Martin Boyer Co. Inc.; Medical Protective Co.; Watseka First National Bank; Union Ins. Co.; Bituminous Ins. Co.

For full biographical listings, see the Martindale-Hubbell Law Directory

LA SALLE, La Salle Co.

HERBOLSHEIMER, LANNON, HENSON, DUNCAN AND REAGAN, P.C. (AV)

State Bank Building, Suite 400, 654 First Street, P.O. Box 539, 61301
Telephone: 815-223-0111
FAX: 815-223-5829
Ottawa, Illinois Office: First Federal Savings Bank Building, 633 LaSalle Street, Suite 409.
Telephone: 815-434-1400.

George L. Herbolsheimer   John S. Duncan, III
  (1911-1992)   Michael T. Reagan
R. James Lannon, Jr.   (Resident, Ottawa Office)
T. Donald Henson   Douglas A. Gift
                Gary R. Eiten

Karen C. Eiten   Jill W. Klein
Michael C. Jansz   Murl Tod Melton
  (Resident, Ottawa Office)   Lawrence M. Kaschak

Attorneys for: Aetna Insurance Group; St. Paul Fire and Marine Insurance Co.; State Farm Insurance Co.; The La Salle National Bank; La Salle State Bank; The Daily News Tribune Company, La Salle; Eureka Savings and Loan Assn.; Illinois Valley Community Hospital; Community Hospital of Ottawa; Commonwealth Edison, Co.

For full biographical listings, see the Martindale-Hubbell Law Directory

MARION,* Williamson Co.

MITCHELL & MITCHELL (AV)

404 North Monroe, P.O. Box 488, 62959-2328
Telephone: 618-993-2134
Telecopier: 618-993-8702

J. C. Mitchell   Bruce W. Mitchell

Michelle M. Schafer

Representative Clients: St. Paul Fire & Casualty Insurance Company; Liberty Mutual Insurance Company; Shelter Insurance Company; Claims Management, Inc.; Seaboard Underwriters; Kemper Insurance; Sentry Claims; Aetna; Walmart Stores, Inc.

For full biographical listings, see the Martindale-Hubbell Law Directory

MOUNT VERNON,* Jefferson Co.

CAMPBELL, BLACK, CARNINE & HEDIN, P.C. (AV)

P.O. Drawer C, 62864
Telephone: 618-242-3310
Fax: 618-242-3735
Email: cbch@midwest.net *URL:* http://www.cbch.com

David A. Campbell   Carl L. Favreau
Terry R. Black   Howard W. Campbell
Roy L. Carnine   (1911-1980)
Craig R. Hedin   John E. Jacobsen (1922-1985)
Mark J. Ballard   Glenn E. Moore (1911-1991)
Jerome E. McDonald   David E. Furnall (1905-1993)

Fred R. Mann   Brian E. Leach

Representative Clients: Kerr-McGee Coal Corp.; Good Samaritan Hospital; Country Mutual Insurance Co.; Southern Illinois Stone Co; Rend Lake Conservancy District; Consolidation Coal Co.; Illinois State Medical Insurance Services; State Farm Automobile Insurance Co.; John Hancock Mutual Life Insurance Co.

For full biographical listings, see the Martindale-Hubbell Law Directory

OAKBROOK TERRACE, Du Page Co.

GALLAGHER & JOSLYN (AV)

One Lincoln Centre, Suite 300, 60181
Telephone: 630-916-2600
FAX: 630-916-2606

MEMBERS OF FIRM

Gerard B. Gallagher
David L. Joslyn

Barry E. Garley
Ira E. Sussman

OF COUNSEL

Peter A. Bauer

Leonard S. DeFranco

For Complete List of Firm Personnel, See General Section

For full biographical listings, see the Martindale-Hubbell Law Directory

OTTAWA, La Salle Co.

HUPP, LANUTI, IRION & MARTIN, P.C. (AV)

227 West Madison, P.O. Box 768, 61350
Telephone: 815-433-3111
Fax: 815-433-9109

Joseph E. Lanuti
Paul V. Martin

George C. Hupp, Jr.
Richard L. Burton

Michelle Hutson

OF COUNSEL

George C. Hupp

Representative Clients: Country Mutual Insurance Co.; State Farm Mutual Automobile Insurance Co.; State Farm Fire & Casualty Co.; Economy Fire and Casualty Co.; Employee Mutual Casualty Co.; Sentry Insurance Co.; United Fire and Casualty Co.; Allstate Insurance Co.; Millers Mutual Insurance Assn.; Continental Casualty Co.

For full biographical listings, see the Martindale-Hubbell Law Directory

PEORIA, Peoria Co.

HEYL, ROYSTER, VOELKER & ALLEN, PROFESSIONAL CORPORATION (AV)

Suite 600, Bank One Building, 124 S.W. Adams, 61602
Telephone: 309-676-0400
Telecopier: 309-676-3374
Email: 75047.3416@COMPUSERVE.COM
Springfield, Illinois Office: Suite 575, First of America Center, P.O. Box 1687, 62705.
Telephone: 217-522-8822.
Telecopier: 217-523-3902.
Urbana, Illinois Office: Suite 300, 102 East Main Street, P.O. Box 129, 61801.
Telephone: 217-344-0060.
Telecopier: 217-344-9295.
Rockford, Illinois Office: Suite 1015, Talcott Building, P.O. Box 1288, 61105.
Telephone: 815-963-4454.
Telecopier: 815-963-0399.
Edwardsville, Illinois Office: Suite 100, Mark Twain Plaza II, 103 West Vandalia Street, P.O. Box 467, 62025.
Telephone: 618-656-4646.
Telecopier: 618-656-7940.

Clarence W. Heyl (1884-1968)
John H. Royster (1907-1985)
William J. Voelker, Jr. (1917-1993)
Lyle W. Allen (Of Counsel)
Richard N. Molchan (Of Counsel)
Gary M. Peplow
Duncan B. Cooper III
Robert V. Dewey, Jr.
Brent H. Gwillim
Rex K. Linder

Timothy L. Bertschy
Gary D. Nelson
David R. Sinn
Roger R. Clayton
Bradford B. Ingram
Nicholas J. Bertschy
Stephen J. Heine
Karen L. Kendall
William I. Covey
Christopher P. Larson
Craig S. Young
James M. Voelker

RESIDENT OF COUNSEL

John C. Mulgrew, Jr.

Stephen J. Thomas
Elizabeth Wiese Christensen
J. Kevin Wolfe
David A. Perkins
Joseph G. Feehan
Lisa A. LaConte
Matthew S. Hefflefinger

Brad A. Elward
Craig L. Unrath
James J. Manning
Cheryl G. Bluth
Mark D. Hansen
Henry Vicary, III
Patricia M. Gibson

For full biographical listings, see the Martindale-Hubbell Law Directory

QUINCY, Adams Co.

KEEFE, BRENNAN & BRENNAN (AV)

314 North Sixth Street, 62301
Telephone: 217-223-1555
Fax: 217-223-1570
Email: kbb@bcl.net *URL:* http://www.bcl.net/~kbb/

MEMBERS OF FIRM

James N. Keefe

Jerry L. Brennan
Babette L. Brennan

Representative Clients: State Farm Insurance Co.; Illinois State Medical Insurance; Grinnell Mutual; Lloyds of London; Transamerica Insurance Group; Fireman's Fund; AEtna; Sentry Insurance Co.; Iowa Mutual; Allied Insurance.

For full biographical listings, see the Martindale-Hubbell Law Directory

SCHMIEDESKAMP, ROBERTSON, NEU & MITCHELL (AV)

525 Jersey, P.O. Box 1069, 62306
Telephone: 217-223-3030
Telecopier: 217-223-1005

MEMBERS OF FIRM

Richard B. Neu
Delmer R. Mitchell, Jr.
Dennis W. Gorman
William G. Keller, Jr.
William M. McCleery, Jr.
Ted M. Niemann

Gena J. Awerkamp
Brett K. Gorman
John G. Stevenson, Jr. (Not admitted in IL)
Michael A. Bickhaus
Curtis T. Lovelace

Representative Clients: Mercantile Trust & Savings Bank; Moorman Manufacturing Co.; Travelers Insurance Co.; Hartford Accident & Indemnity Co.; Aetna Casualty & Surety Co.; Knapheide Mfg. Co.; Harris Corp.; Bituminous Casualty Corp.; Quincy Compressor Division of Colt Industries, Inc.

For Complete List of Firm Personnel, See General Section

For full biographical listings, see the Martindale-Hubbell Law Directory

ROCKFORD, Winnebago Co.

HEYL, ROYSTER, VOELKER & ALLEN, PROFESSIONAL CORPORATION (AV)

Suite 1015, Talcott Building, P.O. Box 1288, 61105
Telephone: 815-963-4454
Telecopier: 815-963-0399
Peoria, Illinois Office: Suite 600, Bank One Building, 124 S.W. Adams, 61602.
Telephone: 309-676-0400.
Telecopier: 309-676-3374.
Springfield, Illinois Office: Suite 575, First Of America Center, P.O. Box 1687, 62705.
Telephone: 217-522-8822.
Telecopier: 217-523-3902.
Urbana, Illinois Office: Suite 300, 102 East Main Street, P.O. Box 129, 61801.
Telephone: 217-344-0060.
Telecopier: 217-344-9295.
Edwardsville, Illinois Office: Suite 100, Mark Twain Plaza II, 103 West Vandalia Street, P.O. Box 467, 62025.
Telephone: 618-656-4646.
Telecopier: 618-656-7940.

RESIDENT PERSONNEL

Douglas J. Pomatto

Kevin J. Luther
Richard K. Hunsaker

Janet E. Lanpher
Mark J. McClenathan
Charles D. McCann
John D. Lanpher

Susan M. Witt
Gregory F. Coplan
Pamela J. King
John P. Kolb
Matthew S. Morrison

For full biographical listings, see the Martindale-Hubbell Law Directory

PICHA & SALISBURY (AV)

Edgebrook Court Building, 1639 North Alpine, Suite 300, 61107-1449
Telephone: 815-227-4300
FAX: 815-227-4330

MEMBERS OF FIRM

George J. Picha

Jeffrey L. Salisbury
Lloyd R. McCumber

ASSOCIATES

William A. Meister

Amy J. Szczepaniak

Representative Clients: General Casualty Companies; Liberty Mutual Insurance Group; Westfield Companies; Zurich-American Insurance Company.

For full biographical listings, see the Martindale-Hubbell Law Directory

SPRINGFIELD, Sangamon Co.

GIFFIN, WINNING, COHEN & BODEWES, P.C. (AV)

1 West Old State Capitol Plaza, Suite 600 Myers Building, P.O. Box 2117, 62705
Telephone: 217-525-1571
Facsimile: 217-525-1710
Email: jswartzn@counsel.com

Carol Hansen Posegate
R. Mark Mifflin

Thomas P. Schanzle-Haskins, III
Gregory K. Harris

Representative Clients: Illinois State University Board of Trustees; Allstate Insurance Co.; Grinnell Mutual Reinsurance Company; Horace Mann Insurance Company; Great Central Insurance Cos.; Transamerica Insurance Company; Associated Beer Distributors of Illinois Risk Management Association.

For Complete List of Firm Personnel, See General Section

For full biographical listings, see the Martindale-Hubbell Law Directory

HEYL, ROYSTER, VOELKER & ALLEN, PROFESSIONAL CORPORATION (AV)

Suite 575, First of America Center, P.O. Box 1687, 62705
Telephone: 217-522-8822
Telecopier: 217-523-3902
Peoria, Illinois Office: Suite 600, Bank One Building, 124 S.W. Adams, 61602.
Telephone: 309-676-0400.
Telecopier: 309-676-3374.
Urbana, Illinois Office: Suite 300, 102 East Main Street, P.O. Box 129, 61801.
Telephone: 217-344-0060.
Telecopier: 217-344-9295.
Rockford, Illinois Office: Suite 1015, Talcott Building, P.O. Box 1288, 61105.
Telephone: 815-963-4454.
Telecopier: 815-963-0399.
Edwardsville, Illinois Office: Suite 100, Mark Twain Plaza II, 103 West Vandalia Street, P.O. Box 467, 62025.
Telephone: 618-656-4646.
Telecopier: 618-656-7940.

RESIDENT PERSONNEL

Frederick P. Velde
Gary L. Borah
Gary S. Schwab
Adrian E. Harless

Francis J. Lynch
Scott D. Spooner
Daniel R. Simmons
Patrick J. Londrigan

RESIDENT OF COUNSEL
Roy O. Gulley

Daniel P. Schuering
Steven C. Rahn
Kurt M. Koepke

David V. White
John E. Kerley
Susan D. Hoffee-Hunt

John P. Leahy

For full biographical listings, see the Martindale-Hubbell Law Directory

URBANA, Champaign Co.

HEYL, ROYSTER, VOELKER & ALLEN, PROFESSIONAL CORPORATION (AV)

Suite 300, 102 East Main Street, P.O. Box 129, 61801
Telephone: 217-344-0060
Telecopier: 217-344-9295
Peoria, Illinois Office: Suite 600, Bank One Building, 124 S.W. Adams, 61602.
Telephone: 309-676-0400.
Telecopier: 309-676-3374.
Springfield, Illinois Office: Suite 575, First Of America Center, P.O. Box 1687, 62705.
Telephone: 217-522-8822.
Telecopier: 217-523-3902.
Rockford, Illinois Office: Suite 1015, Talcott Building, P.O. Box 1288, 61105.
Telephone: 815-963-4454.
Telecopier: 815-963-0399.
Edwardsville, Illinois Office: Suite 100, Mark Twain Plaza II, 103 West Vandalia Street, P.O. Box 467, 62025.
Telephone: 618-656-4646.
Telecopier: 618-656-7940.

RESIDENT PERSONNEL

James C. Kearns
Edward M. Wagner

Michael E. Raub
Bruce L. Bonds

John D. Flodstrom

RESIDENT OF COUNSEL
James W. Cox

(See Next Column)

Bradford J. Peterson
Elaine Massock

Fred K. Heinrich

For full biographical listings, see the Martindale-Hubbell Law Directory

WEBBER & THIES, P.C. (AV)

202 Lincoln Square, P.O. Box 189, 61803-0189
Telephone: 217-367-1126
FAX: 217-367-3752

Daniel P. Wurl

John E. Thies

For Complete List of Firm Personnel, See General Section

For full biographical listings, see the Martindale-Hubbell Law Directory

WAUKEGAN, Lake Co.

DIVER, GRACH, QUADE & MASINI (AV)

First Federal Savings and Loan Building, 111 North County Street, 60085
Telephone: 847-662-8611
FAX: 847-662-2960

MEMBERS OF FIRM

Clarence W. Diver (1883-1962)
Thomas W. Diver
Brian S. Grach

David R. Quade
Robert J. Masini
Sarah P. Lessman

Heidi J. Aavang

Donna-Jo Rodden Vorderstrasse

Paula Vincich Randall

OF COUNSEL
David L. Hazan

A list of Representative Clients will be furnished upon request.
Reference: First Midwest Bank of Waukegan.

For full biographical listings, see the Martindale-Hubbell Law Directory

WHEATON, Du Page Co.

SWANSON, MARTIN & BELL (AV)

2100 Manchester Road C-1420, 60187
Telephone: 708-653-2266
Fax: 708-653-2292
Chicago, Illinois Office: Suite 2900, One IBM Plaza.
Telephone: 312-321-9100.
Fax: 312-321-0990.

MEMBERS OF FIRM

Lenard C. Swanson

David J. Cahill (Resident)

Bruce S. Terlep

ASSOCIATE
Matthew D. Jacobson

For full biographical listings, see the Martindale-Hubbell Law Directory

INDIANA

BLOOMINGTON, Monroe Co.

BUNGER & ROBERTSON (AV)

226 South College Square, P.O. Box 910, 47402-0910
Telephone: 812-332-9295
Fax: 812-331-8808

MEMBERS OF FIRM

Don M. Robertson
Joseph D. O'Connor III

James L. Whitlatch
Samuel R. Ardery

ASSOCIATES

William J. Beggs

John W. Richards

Representative Clients: Aetna Insurance Companies; Bloomington Hospital; Commercial Union Group; Indiana Insurance Co.; Liberty Mutual Insurance; Medical Protective Co.; Monroe County Community School Corp.; Professional Golf Car, Inc.; Prudential Insurance Company of America; State Farm Automobile Insurance Co.

For Complete List of Firm Personnel, See General Section

For full biographical listings, see the Martindale-Hubbell Law Directory

KELLEY, BELCHER & BROWN, A PROFESSIONAL CORPORATION (AV)

301 West Seventh Street, P.O. Box 3250, 47402-3250
Telephone: 812-336-9963
Telecopier: 812-336-4588

William H. Kelley

Thomas J. Belcher

(See Next Column)

KELLEY, BELCHER & BROWN A PROFESSIONAL CORPORATION—*Continued*

Shannon L. Robinson   Darla Sue Brown
Jennifer A. Bauer

For full biographical listings, see the Martindale-Hubbell Law Directory

MILLER CARSON BOXBERGER & MURPHY (AV)

3100 John Hinkle Place, Suite 106, 47408
Telephone: 812-333-1225
Fax: 812-333-1925
Fort Wayne, Indiana Office: 1400 One Summit Square.
Telephone: 219-423-9411.
Telecopier: 219-423-4329.

Edward J. Liptak   Douglas A. Hoffman

Representative Corporate and Financial Clients: Advanced Machine & Tool Corporation; Ford Motor Credit Company; NBD Bank, N.A.; Wal-Mart Inc.
Representative Insurance Clients: Bliss-McKnight Group; Employer's Mutual Company; Employers Mutual of Wausau; General Accident Fire & Life Assurance Corp., LTD.

For full biographical listings, see the Martindale-Hubbell Law Directory

COLUMBUS,* Bartholomew Co.

SHARPNACK, BIGLEY, DAVID & RUMPLE (AV)

321 Washington Street, P.O. Box 310, 47202-0310
Telephone: 812-372-1553
Fax: 812-372-1567

MEMBERS OF FIRM

Thomas C. Bigley, Jr.   John A. Stroh
Timothy J. Vrana   Joan Tupin Crites

Representative Clients: State Farm Mutual Insurance Cos.; American States Insurance Co.; GRE Insurance Group; Indiana Farmers Insurance.

For Complete List of Firm Personnel, See General Section

For full biographical listings, see the Martindale-Hubbell Law Directory

EVANSVILLE,* Vanderburgh Co.

FINE & HATFIELD (AV)

520 N.W. Second Street, P.O. Box 779, 47705-0779
Telephone: 812-425-3592
Telecopier: 812-421-4269
Email: Fine@Fine-Hatfield.com *URL:* http://www.Fine-Hatfield.com

MEMBERS OF FIRM

Thomas H. Bryan   Patricia Kay Woodring
Danny E. Glass   William H. Mullis

ASSOCIATES

Debra S. McGowan   H. Linwood Shannon, III
Todd I. Glass

A List of Representative Clients Furnished Upon Request.

For full biographical listings, see the Martindale-Hubbell Law Directory

KAHN, DEES, DONOVAN & KAHN (AV)

P.O. Box 3646, 47735-3646
Telephone: 812-423-3183
Fax: 812-423-3841
Email: evvlaw@k2d2.com

MEMBERS OF FIRM

David L. Clark   Jeffrey W. Ahlers

ASSOCIATES

Richard O. Hawley, Jr.   Martha J. Posey
Mark W. Clark

Representative Clients: United States Fidelity & Guaranty Insurance Co.; United Farm Bureau Mutual of Indiana; Neare, Gibbs River Marine Underwriters; I.T.T. Hartford Insurance Co.; American Family Insurance Co.; CIGNA Insurance Co.; Fireman's Fund Insurance Co.; CNA Insurance Co.; Chubb Insurance.

For Complete List of Firm Personnel, See General Section

For full biographical listings, see the Martindale-Hubbell Law Directory

MATTINGLY, RUDOLPH, FINE & PORTER (AV)

221 N.W. Fifth Street, Second Floor, P.O. Box 1507, 47706
Telephone: 812-422-9444
Fax: 812-421-7459
Email: mrfp@evansville.net

MEMBERS OF FIRM

Ross E. Rudolph   James D. Johnson

(See Next Column)

ASSOCIATE

Jeffrey W. Henning

Reference: National City Bank of Evansville.

For full biographical listings, see the Martindale-Hubbell Law Directory

STATHAM, JOHNSON & MCCRAY (AV)

215 North West Martin Luther King Jr. Boulevard, P.O. Box 3567, 47734-3567
Telephone: 812-425-5223
Facsimile: 812-421-4238

MEMBERS OF FIRM

William E. Statham   Gerald F. Allega
Michael McCray   Douglas V. Jessen

ASSOCIATES

Brent Alan Raibley   Bryan S. Rudisill
Neil Byron Chapman

Representative Clients: American Family Insurance Group; American States Insurance; Hartford Insurance Group; Indiana Insurance Cos.; Medical Protective Insurance Co.; Ohio Casualty Group; Pennsylvania Hospital Insurance Co.; Monroe Guaranty Company; St. Paul Insurance Companies; Wausau Insurance Companies.

For Complete List of Firm Personnel, See General Section

For full biographical listings, see the Martindale-Hubbell Law Directory

WRIGHT, EVANS AND DALY (AV)

425 Main Street, 47708
Telephone: 812-424-3300
Fax: 812-421-5588

MEMBERS OF FIRM

Donald R. Wright   R. Lawrence Daly

Representative Clients: Allstate Insurance Company; Canal Insurance Company; Church Mutual Insurance Company; Home Insurance Companies; Liberty Mutual Insurance Company; Mutual of Omaha; Northbrook Property and Casualty Insurance Company; United Farm Bureau Mutual Insurance Company; Wausau Insurance Company; Westfield Insurance Companies of Indiana, Inc.

For Complete List of Firm Personnel, See General Section

For full biographical listings, see the Martindale-Hubbell Law Directory

FORT WAYNE,* Allen Co.

HUNT, SUEDHOFF, BORROR & EILBACHER (AV)

900 Courtside, 803 South Calhoun Street, P.O. Box 11489, 46858-1489
Telephone: 219-423-1311
Telecopier: 219-424-5396

RETIRED

Carl J. Suedhoff, Jr.

MEMBERS OF FIRM

Leigh L. Hunt (1899-1975)   Thomas W. Belleperche
William E. Borror (1932-1989)   Mark W. Baeverstad
Leonard E. Eilbacher   Michael D. Mustard
Robert E. Kabisch   Branch R. Lew
Arthur G. Surguine, Jr.   Carla J. Baird
Thomas C. Ewing   James J. Shea
Carolyn White Spengler   Scott L. Bunnell
Dane L. Tubergen

ASSOCIATES

Charles H. Bassford, IV   Daniel J. Palmer
Carolyn M. Trier   Brian L. England
Kathleen A. Kilar   Craig J. Bobay
W. Douglas Lemon

For full biographical listings, see the Martindale-Hubbell Law Directory

MILLER CARSON BOXBERGER & MURPHY (AV)

1400 One Summit Square, 46802-3137
Telephone: 219-423-9411
Telecopier: 219-423-4329
Bloomington, Indiana Office: 3100 John Hinkle Place, Suite 106.
Telephone: 812-333-1225.
Fax: 812-333-1925.

MEMBERS OF FIRM

Milford M. Miller, Jr.   Richard P. Samek
Philip L. Carson   Phillip A. Renz
Bruce O. Boxberger   Edward J. Liptak (Resident,
Edward L. Murphy, Jr.   Bloomington, Indiana Office)
Thomas W. Yoder   Robert T. Keen, Jr.
Charles R. Cogdell   Larry L. Barnard
John J. Wernet   Arthur E. Mandelbaum

(See Next Column)

MILLER CARSON BOXBERGER & MURPHY, *Fort Wayne—Continued*

ASSOCIATES

Diana Carol Bauer	Douglas A. Hoffman
James P. Buchholz	Karl J. Veracco
Timothy A. Manges	Timothy M. Pape
(Not admitted in IN)	

Representative Clients: Kelsey Hayes Wheels International, Inc.; Employers Mutual of Wausau Cos.; General Accident, Fire & Life Assurance Corp. Ltd.; Bliss McKnight Group; Wal-Mart, Inc.; Employers Mutual Cos.; Bituminous Insurance Cos.; Allstate Insurance; Crum & Foster Commercial Insurance; The Medical Protective Company.

For full biographical listings, see the Martindale-Hubbell Law Directory

---

GARY, Lake Co.

STULTS, STULTS, FORSZT & PAWLOWSKI, A PROFESSIONAL ASSOCIATION (AV)

3637 Grant Street, P.O. Box 15050, 46409-5050
Telephone: 219-887-7000
Fax: 219-884-1179

Fred M. Stults, Jr.	Robert P. Forszt
Frederick M. Stults, III	David R. Pawlowski

Representative Clients: American Road Insurance Co.; Employers Casualty Co.; Indiana Insurance Co.; SAFECO Insurance Co.

For full biographical listings, see the Martindale-Hubbell Law Directory

---

HAMMOND, Lake Co.

ABRAHAMSON, REED & ADLEY (AV)

200 Russell Street, 46320
Telephone: 219-937-1500
Fax: 219-937-3174

MEMBERS OF FIRM

Harold Abrahamson	Kenneth D. Reed
Michael C. Adley	

ASSOCIATES

Scott R. Bilse	Christopher R. Karsten

References: Calumet National Bank, Hammond; Mercantile National Bank, Hammond.

For full biographical listings, see the Martindale-Hubbell Law Directory

GALVIN, GALVIN & LEENEY (AV)

5231 Hohman Avenue, 46320
Telephone: 219-933-0380
Fax: 219-933-0471

MEMBERS OF FIRM

Edmond J. Leeney (1897-1978)	Carl N. Carpenter
Timothy P. Galvin, Sr.	John E. Chevigny
(1894-1993)	Timothy P. Galvin, Jr.
Francis J. Galvin, Sr.	Patrick J. Galvin
(1902-1995)	W. Patrick Downes

William G. Crabtree II	Julie A. Rosenwinkel
John H. Lloyd, IV	Amy Galvin Grogan

Attorneys For: State Farm Insurance Co.; Auto Owners Insurance Co.; CIGNA; St. Margaret Mercy Healthcare Centers, Inc.; St. Anthony Hospital and Health Centers (Michigan City); Pepsi-Cola General Bottlers, Inc.; Chicago Title Insurance Company; Ohio Casualty Company; American National Property and Casualty Co.; St. Elizabeth Hospital (LaFayette, IN).

For full biographical listings, see the Martindale-Hubbell Law Directory

FREDERICK H. LINK (AV)

5253 Hohman Avenue, 46320
Telephone: 219-933-1400

For full biographical listings, see the Martindale-Hubbell Law Directory

---

INDIANAPOLIS,* Marion Co.

ICE MILLER DONADIO & RYAN (AV)

One American Square Box 82001, 46282-0002
Telephone: 317-236-2100
Fax: 317-236-2219
Email: leel@imdr.com *URL:* http://www.imdr.com
South Bend, Indiana Office: 211 West Washington Street, Suite 2420.
Telephone: 219-234-7933.
Fax: 219-234-7965. Internet E-mail: leel@imdr.com. Web Site Address: http://www.imdr.com.

MEMBERS OF FIRM

James V. Donadio	David M. Mattingly
Jim A. O'Neal	James R. Fisher
Evan E. Steger	Cory Brundage
Ralph A. Cohen	David J. Mallon, Jr.
Arthur P. Kalleres	James L. Petersen

(See Next Column)

MEMBERS OF FIRM (Continued)

Gary J. Dankert	Michael D. Marine
John F. Prescott, Jr.	Terri Ann Czajka
Richard A. Smikle	Donald M. Snemis
Debra Hanley Miller	Michael A. Wilkins
Sherry A. Fabina-Abney	

OF COUNSEL

Kelly Bauman Pitcher

RETIRED PARTNER

Edward J. Ohleyer

ASSOCIATES

Kristin L. Altice	Thomas E. Mixdorf
Robert A. Anderson	Adam Arceneaux
James Scott Fanzini	Paul N. Alp
Laura B. Daghe	Cindy M. Lott
Jodie L. Miner	Melissa S. York

Representative Clients: Liberty Mutual Insurance; Northland Insurance Co.; National Indemnity Co.; Great West Casualty; St. Paul Fire & Marine Insurance; CNA Insurance Co.; Worldwide Insurance Co.; Employers Insurance of Wausau.

For Complete List of Firm Personnel, See General Section

For full biographical listings, see the Martindale-Hubbell Law Directory

JOHNSON, SMITH, PENCE, DENSBORN, WRIGHT & HEATH (AV)

One Indiana Square Suite 1800, 46204
Telephone: 317-634-9777
Telecopier: 317-636-9061

MEMBERS OF FIRM

Robert M. Baker, III	John David Hoover
Sean Michael Clapp	Andrew W. Hull
G. Ronald Heath	Mark A. Palmer
Linda L. Pence	

ASSOCIATES

Steven J. Moss	David A. Tucker

For Complete List of Firm Personnel, See General Section

For full biographical listings, see the Martindale-Hubbell Law Directory

LINDER & HOLLOWELL (AV)

615 Russell Avenue, P.O. Box 845, 46206-0845
Telephone: 317-637-3170
Fax: Available Upon Request

MEMBERS OF FIRM

Robert Hollowell (1899-1980)	Charles W. Linder, Jr.

ASSOCIATES

H. Andrew Sonneborn	Sharon L. Wright
Lewis J. Gregory	

For full biographical listings, see the Martindale-Hubbell Law Directory

LOCKE REYNOLDS BOYD & WEISELL (AV)

1000 Capital Center South, 201 North Illinois Street, 46204
Telephone: 317-237-3800
Telecopier: 317-237-3900

Hugh E. Reynolds, Jr.	Julia Blackwell Gelinas
Lloyd H. Milliken, Jr.	Richard A. Huser
William V. Hutchens	Thomas J. Campbell
David S. Allen	Diane Parsons Emswiller
David M. Haskett	Burton M. Harris
Michael A. Bergin	Thomas W. Farlow
David T. Kasper	Karl M. Koons, III
Steven J. Strawbridge	Julia F. Crowe
Thomas L. Davis	James Dimos
Robert A. Fanning	Kristen K. Rollison
Randall R. Riggs	Thomas R. Schultz
Alan S. Brown	Todd J. Kaiser
Mark J. Roberts	Eric A. Riegner
Kevin Charles Murray	Kevin C. Schiferl
Ariane Schallwig Johnson	

Stephen L. Vaughan	Jerrilyn Powers Ramsey
Peter H. Pogue	Katherine Coble Dassow
John H. Daerr	Mary Margaret Ruth Feldhake
John K. McDavid	Nelson D. Alexander
Robert W. Wright	Donald B. Kite, Sr.
Jeffrey J. Mortier	Thomas F. Bedsole
Nicholas C. Pappas	Stephanie L. Valadez
Mary A. Schopper	David Alexander Sorensen
Susan E. Cline	Derek S. Burrell
Dean R. Brackenridge	

OF COUNSEL

William H. Vobach	Robert C. Riddell

Representative Clients: Associated Aviation Underwriters; Center for Claims Resolution; Citizens Insurance Co. (The Hanover Group); CNA Insurance Cos.; The Hartford Insurance Co.; The Medical Protective Co.; Nationwide

(See Next Column)

LOCKE REYNOLDS BOYD & WEISELL—*Continued*

Insurance Co.; PHICO Insurance Co.; Royal Insurance Cos.; U.S.F. & G. Cos.

For Complete List of Firm Personnel, See General Section

For full biographical listings, see the Martindale-Hubbell Law Directory

---

MEILS, THOMPSON, DIETZ & CONGLETON (AV)

Suite 830, Two Market Square Center, 251 East Ohio Street, 46204
Telephone: 317-637-1383
Fax: 317-264-2573

MEMBERS OF FIRM

Rick D. Meils   R. Michael Congleton
                Scott A. Harkness

Representative Clients: Indiana Insurance Co.; Consolidated Insurance Cos.; Michigan Mutual Insurance Co.; American Family Insurance Co.; Northeastern Insurance Co.; Northland Insurance Co.; Capitol Amendnity; Acceptance Insurance Co.; Statesman Insurance Co.

For full biographical listings, see the Martindale-Hubbell Law Directory

---

OSBORN HINER LISHER & ORZESKE, P.C. (AV)

Suite 380, One Woodfield, 8330 Woodfield Crossing Boulevard, 46240
Telephone: 317-469-2100
Fax: 317-469-9011

John L. Lisher   Donald G. Orzeske

Donald K. Broad   Christopher Hamilton
OF COUNSEL
William M. Osborn   Edward A. Straith-Miller

For full biographical listings, see the Martindale-Hubbell Law Directory

---

ROCAP, WITCHGER & THRELKELD (AV)

One Indiana Square, Suite 2300, 46204
Telephone: 317-639-6281
FAX: 317-637-9056

James E. Rocap, Sr. (1881-1969)   John T. Rocap (1909-1980)
        Keith C. Reese (1920-1993)
MEMBERS OF FIRM
James E. Rocap, Jr.   Richard A. Rocap
James D. Witchger   Thomas Todd Reynolds
W. Brent Threlkeld   Robert S. O'Dell
ASSOCIATES
Nancy G. Curless   Mark A. Payne
Robert A. Durham   Kandice L. Kilkelly
Jeffrey V. Crabill   Dionne M. Carroll
OF COUNSEL
Joseph F. Quill

Representative Clients: Motorist Mutual Insurance Co.; American Family Insurance Group; The Travelers Insurance Co.; State Farm Fire and Casualty Insurance Co.; Reliance National Insurance Co.; Statesman Insurance Co.; USAA Insurance; State Farm Mutual Automobile Insurance Co.; Northwestern National Insurance Co.

For full biographical listings, see the Martindale-Hubbell Law Directory

---

STEPHENSON DALY MOROW AND KURNIK, P.C. (AV)

8710 North Meridian Street Suite 200, 46260-5307
Telephone: 317-844-3830
Fax: 317-573-4194

James S. Stephenson   William W. Kurnik
John P. Daly, Jr.   Richelle V. Cohen
Michael R. Morow   Caren Lynn Pollack

Ronald J. Semler   John T. Roy
G. Richard Potter   Tonya M. Aretz
Kirk A. Horn   Mark A. Holloway

Representative Clients: Governmental Interinsurance Exchange; Interstate Insurance Group; Crum & Forster Commercial Insurance; Industrial Indemnity Insurance; Imperial Casualty Co.; National Fire and Casualty Co.; Indiana Political Subdivision Risk Management Fund; Gallagher Bassett Services; Mt. Hawley Insurance Co.; Illinois Farmers Ins. Group.; Indiana Farmers Insurance Co.; Indiana Insurance Co.; JWF Specialty; St. Paul Fire & Marine Ins. Co.; Titan Indemnity Co.; VASA North Atlantic Ins. Co.

For full biographical listings, see the Martindale-Hubbell Law Directory

---

YARLING, ROBINSON, HAMMEL & LAMB (AV)

151 North Delaware, Suite 1535, P.O. Box 44128, 46204
Telephone: 317-262-8800
Fax: 317-262-3046

(See Next Column)

MEMBERS OF FIRM

Richard W. Yarling   Edgar H. Lamb
Charles F. Robinson, Jr.   Douglas E. Rogers
John W. Hammel   Mark S. Gray
Linda Y. Hammel   Matthew C. Robinson

Representative Clients: Allstate Insurance Co.; American Family Mutual Insurance Company; Chrysler Credit Corporation; Fleet Financenter; General Motors Acceptance Corporation; Household Finance Corporation; Monroe Guaranty Insurance Company; Northbrook Property & Casualty Company; Pafco General Insurance Company; Security Pacific Finance Corporation.

For full biographical listings, see the Martindale-Hubbell Law Directory

---

KOKOMO, * Howard Co.

FELL, McGARVEY, TRAURING & WILSON (AV)

515 West Sycamore Street, P.O. Box 958, 46903-0958
Telephone: 317-457-9321
Telecopier: 317-452-0882

MEMBERS OF FIRM

John E. Fell, Jr.   Thomas J. Trauring
Eugene J. McGarvey, Jr.   Alan D. Wilson

Representative Clients: Aetna Casualty & Surety Co.; American States Insurance Co.; Celina Insurance Co.; Fireman's Fund Insurance Co.; Indiana Farms Mutual Insurance Co.; Hartford Insurance Co.; Meridian Insurance Co.; National General Insurance Co.; State Automobile Insurance Co.

For full biographical listings, see the Martindale-Hubbell Law Directory

---

LAFAYETTE, * Tippecanoe Co.

BALL, EGGLESTON, BUMBLEBURG & McBRIDE (AV)

810 Bank One Building, P.O. Box 1535, 47902
Telephone: 317-742-9046
Fax: 317-742-1966

Cable G. Ball (1904-1981)   Warren N. Eggleston
Owen Crook (1908-1977)   (1923-1991)
MEMBERS OF FIRM
Joseph T. Bumbleburg   Jeffrey J. Newell
John K. McBride   James T. Hodson
Jack L. Walkey   Brian Wade Walker
Michael J. Stapleton   Cheryl M. Knodle
        Randy J. Williams

Representative Clients: Travelers Insurance Co.; Grain Dealers Mutual Insurance Co.; Indiana Farmers Insurance Group; Indiana Insurance Co.; American Family Insurance Co.

For full biographical listings, see the Martindale-Hubbell Law Directory

---

STUART & BRANIGIN (AV)

The Life Building, 300 Main Street, Suite 800, 47902
Telephone: 317-423-1561
Telecopier: 317-742-8175

MEMBERS OF FIRM

Allison Ellsworth Stuart   William E. Emerick
  (1886-1950)   John C. Duffey
Roger D. Branigin (1902-1975) Thomas B. Parent
Russell H. Hart   Laura L. Bowker
James V. McGlone   Kevin D. Nicoson
Larry R. Fisher   Susan K. Roberts
Stephen R. Pennell   John M. Stuckey
Anthony S. Benton   Deborah B. Trice
ASSOCIATE
Brent W. Huber

General Counsel for: The Lafayette Life Insurance Co.; INB National Bank, N.W.; Lafayette Home Hospital, Inc.
State Counsel for: Norfolk & Western Railway Co.
Mr. Ryan is Counsel to: The Trustees of Purdue University.
Representative Clients: Aluminum Company of America; Liberty Mutual Insurance Group.

For Complete List of Firm Personnel, See General Section

For full biographical listings, see the Martindale-Hubbell Law Directory

---

LA PORTE, * La Porte Co.

NEWBY, LEWIS, KAMINSKI & JONES (AV)

916 Lincoln Way, 46350
Telephone: 219-362-1577
Direct Line Michigan City: 219-879-6300
Fax: 219-362-2106
Mailing Address: P.O. Box 1816, La Porte, Indiana, 46352-1816

(See Next Column)

NEWBY, LEWIS, KAMINSKI & JONES, *La Porte—Continued*

MEMBERS OF FIRM

John E. Newby (1916-1990)	Edward L. Volk
Daniel E. Lewis, Jr.	Mark L. Phillips
Gene M. Jones	Martin W. Kus
John W. Newby	Marsha Schatz Volk
Perry F. Stump, Jr.	Mark A. Lienhoop
James W. Kaminski	

ASSOCIATES

William S. Kaminski	Christine A. Sulewski
David P. Jones	

SENIOR COUNSEL

Leon R. Kaminski

OF COUNSEL

Daniel E. Lewis

Counsel for: U. S. F. & G. Co.; State Farm Mutual Insurance Co.; Auto Owners Insurance Co.; La Porte Bank & Trust Co.; Liberty Mutual Insurance Co.; Sullair Corp.; La Porte Community School Corp.; United Farm Bureau Mutual Insurance Co.; Physicians Insurance of Indiana; Medical Protective Co.

For full biographical listings, see the Martindale-Hubbell Law Directory

---

MARION,* Grant Co.

KILEY, KILEY, HARKER, MICHAEL & CERTAIN (AV)

300 West Third Street, P.O. Box 899, 46952-0899
Telephone: 317-664-9041
Fax: 317-664-8119

MEMBERS OF FIRM

Robert Ralph Batton (1890-1963)	David L. Kiley, Sr.
Albert L. Harker (1904-1965)	Michael J. Kiley
Albert Bonner Brown (1911-1981)	Albert C. Harker
	Thomas W. Michael
	Harry J. Certain

ASSOCIATE

Therese McCullough Pryor

Counsel for: Bank One, Marion, N.A.; Liniger Co., Inc.; Atlas Foundry Co. *Local Counsel for:* GenCorp.; CPC Group; General Motors; Indiana Michigan Power Co./AEP; Indiana Bell Telephone Co.; Foster-Forbes, Division of American National Can Corp.

For full biographical listings, see the Martindale-Hubbell Law Directory

---

MERRILLVILLE, Lake Co.

BURKE, MURPHY, COSTANZA & CUPPY (AV)

Suite 600 8585 Broadway, 46410-7064
Telephone: 219-769-1313
Telecopier: 219-769-6806
East Chicago, Indiana Office: First National Bank Building. 720 West Chicago Avenue.
Telephone: 219-397-2401.
Telecopier: 219-397-0508.
Valparaiso, Indiana Office: 15 North Franklin Street, Suite 200.
Telephone: 219-531-0134.
Telecopier: 219-531-0507.
Palm Harbor, Florida Office: Suite 280, 33920 U.S. Highway 19 North.
Telephone: 813-787-7799.
Telecopier: 813-787-7237.

MEMBERS OF FIRM

Lester F. Murphy (Resident, East Chicago, Indiana and Palm Harbor, Florida Offices)	Frederick M. Cuppy
	David K. Ranich
	Kathryn D. Schmidt
David Cerven	

ASSOCIATE

Kevin E. Steele

OF COUNSEL

Gregory R. Lyman

Representative Clients: Aetna Casualty & Surety Co. (Regional Consultants); General Accident Ins.; Metropolitan Life Ins.; Preferred Risk Insurance Company; Melvin Simon & Associates.

For Complete List of Firm Personnel, See General Section

For full biographical listings, see the Martindale-Hubbell Law Directory

---

HOEPPNER WAGNER AND EVANS (AV)

Twin Towers, Suite 606 South, 1000 East 80th Place, 46410
Telephone: 219-769-6552; 800-263-1466 (IN,IL)
Fax: 219-738-2349
Valparaiso, Indiana Office: 103 East Lincolnway, P.O. Box 2357, 46384-2357.
Telephone: 219-464-4961; 800-879-2246 (IN,IL).
Fax: 219-465-0603.

(See Next Column)

RESIDENT MEMBERS

John E. Hughes	F. Joseph Jaskowiak

Representative Clients: State Farm Insurance; The Travelers Insurance Company; Continental Loss Adjusting Services; Auto Owners Insurance; Indiana Insurance; Allstate Insurance; General Accident Insurance; American Family Insurance; Protective Insurance; Heritage Mutual Insurance Company.

For Complete List of Firm Personnel, See General Section

For full biographical listings, see the Martindale-Hubbell Law Directory

---

SPANGLER, JENNINGS & DOUGHERTY, P.C. (AV)

8396 Mississippi Street, 46410-6398
Telephone: 219-769-2323
Facsimile: 219-769-5007
Valparaiso, Indiana Office: 150 Lincolnway, Suite 3001.
Telephone: 219-462-6151.
FAX: 219-477-4935.

Ronald T. Spangler	Robert P. Kennedy
Patrick J. Dougherty (Valparaiso Office)	James T. McNiece
Samuel J. Furlin	James D. McQuillan
John P. McQuillan	David L. Abel, II
Samuel J. Bernardi, Jr. (Valparaiso Office)	Robert P. Stoner (Valparaiso Office)
Jon F. Schmoll	Gregory J. Tonner
Robert D. Hawk	Kathleen M. Maicher
David J. Hanson	Paul B. Poracky
	Robert D. Brown

Robert J. Dignam	Kristin A. Mulholland
David R. Phillips	Kisti Good Risse

Representative Clients: Allstate Insurance Cos.; American International Group; American States Insurance Co.; Associates Financial Services Co. of Indiana; Bank One, Merriville, N.A.; Bank One Leasing; Beneficial Financial Co.; Boise Cascade Corp.; CNA Insurance; Chrysler Financial Corp.

For Complete List of Firm Personnel, See General Section

For full biographical listings, see the Martindale-Hubbell Law Directory

---

MUNSTER, Lake Co.

LAW OFFICES OF TIMOTHY F. KELLY (AV)

Suite 2A, 9250 Columbia Avenue, 46321
Telephone: 219-836-4062
Telecopier: 219-836-0167
Email: 76325.1505@Compuserve.Com

MEMBERS OF FIRM

Timothy F. Kelly	Karl K. Vanzo

ASSOCIATES

Harvey Karlovac	Steven J. Sersic

For Complete List of Firm Personnel, See General Section

For full biographical listings, see the Martindale-Hubbell Law Directory

---

SOUTH BEND,* St. Joseph Co.

DORAN BLACKMOND READY HAMILTON & WILLIAMS (AV)

1700 Valley American Bank Building, 211 W. Washington Street, 46601
Telephone: 219-288-1800
Fax: 219-236-4265

MEMBERS OF FIRM

M. Edward Doran (1895-1982)	David T. Ready
John E. Doran	John C. Hamilton
Don G. Blackmond	A. Howard Williams

ASSOCIATE

Don Gregory Blackmond

For full biographical listings, see the Martindale-Hubbell Law Directory

---

JONES, OBENCHAIN, FORD, PANKOW, LEWIS & WOODS (AV)

1800 Valley American Bank Building, P.O. Box 4577, 46634
Telephone: 219-233-1194
Fax: 233-8957; 233-9675

Vitus G. Jones (1879-1951)	Roland Obenchain (Retired)
Roland Obenchain (1890-1961)	Milton A. Johnson (Retired)
Francis Jones (1907-1988)	James H. Pankow (Retired)

MEMBERS OF FIRM

Thomas F. Lewis, Jr.	Robert M. Edwards, Jr.
Timothy W. Woods	John B. Ford
John R. Obenchain	Mark J. Phillipoff
Robert W. Mysliwiec	John W. Van Laere

ASSOCIATES

Edward P. Benchik	Robert S. Sanderson
Thomas F. Lewis, III	

(See Next Column)

JONES, OBENCHAIN, FORD, PANKOW, LEWIS & WOODS—*Continued*

OF COUNSEL

G. Burt Ford

Representative Clients: American Family Insurance Group; The Travelers; Ohio Casualty Group; Frankenmuth Mutual Insurance Co.; Motorists Insurance Co.; Farm Bureau of Michigan; GAB Business Services; Government Employees Insurance Co.; Transamerica Insurance; Progressive Health.

For full biographical listings, see the Martindale-Hubbell Law Directory

---

EDWARD N. KALAMAROS & ASSOCIATES PROFESSIONAL CORPORATION (AV)

129 North Michigan Avenue, P.O. Box 4156, 46634
Telephone: 219-232-4801
Telecopier: 219-232-9736

Edward N. Kalamaros	Philip E. Kalamaros
Timothy J. Walsh	Sally P. Norton
Thomas F. Cohen	Kevin W. Kearney
Joseph M. Forte	Peter J. Bagiackas
Robert Deane Woods	David A. Wemhoff
Patrick J. Hinkle	Eric G. Ciesielski

Representative Clients: Liberty Mutual Insurance Co.; Employers Mutual of Wausau; Fireman's Fund American Insurance Group; St. Paul Insurance Companies; U.S.F. & G.; Cincinnati Insurance Co.; Kemper Group; Continental Loss Adjusting Services, Inc.; Orion Group.

For full biographical listings, see the Martindale-Hubbell Law Directory

---

MAY, OBERFELL & LORBER (AV)

300 North Michigan Street, 46601
Telephone: 219-232-2031
Facsimile: 219-232-9789
Elkhart, Indiana Office: 307 South Main Street.
Telephone: 219-295-7281.
Facsimile: 219-295-7273.

MEMBERS OF FIRM

John J. Lorber	Wendell W. Walsh
	Joseph J. Jensen

Representative Clients: Keybank; Penn Central Corporation; Orbitron Industries, Inc.; ITT Hartford; ASA Corporation; Kemper Group; Metropolitan Life Insurance Co.; Nationwide Insurance Co.; Pennsylvania Hospital Insurance Co.; Physicians Insurance Co.; State Farm Fire and Casualty Co.; State Farm Mutual Automobile Insurance Co.

For full biographical listings, see the Martindale-Hubbell Law Directory

---

ROWE, ROWE & MAHER (AV)

Suite 900 Keybank Building, 46601
Telephone: 219-233-8200
Fax: 219-234-5987

R. Kent Rowe	R. Kent Rowe, III
	Timothy J. Maher

ASSOCIATES

Gregory J. Haines	Steven D. Groth
Lee Korzan	Marie Anne Hendrie

For full biographical listings, see the Martindale-Hubbell Law Directory

---

TERRE HAUTE,* Vigo Co.

COX, ZWERNER, GAMBILL & SULLIVAN (AV)

511 Wabash Avenue, P.O. Box 1625, 47808-1625
Telephone: 812-232-6003
Fax: 812-232-6567

MEMBERS OF FIRM

Ernest J. Zwerner (1918-1980)	David W. Sullivan
Benjamin G. Cox (1915-1988)	Robert L. Gowdy
Gilbert W. Gambill, Jr.	Louis F. Britton
James E. Sullivan	Carroll D. Smeltzer
Benjamin G. Cox, Jr.	Jeffry A. Lind

ASSOCIATE

Ronald E. Jumps

OF COUNSEL

Robert D. Hepburn

Counsel for: Terre Haute First National Bank; Farmers Insurance Group; Indiana-American Water Co.; Indiana State University; Merchants National Bank of Terre Haute; Rose-Hulman Institute of Technology; Tribune-Star Publishing Co., Inc.; Weston Paper & Manufacturing Co.; Equitable Life Assurance Society of U.S.; Federated Mutual Insurance Co.; Fireman's Fund; General Accident Group; Guaranty National Insurance; Milwaukee Mutual Insurance Co.; Ohio Casualty Insurance Co.; Hartford Insurance; The Travelers Co.; United Services Auto Assn.; Vernon Insurance Co.

For full biographical listings, see the Martindale-Hubbell Law Directory

---

SACOPULOS, JOHNSON, CARTER & SACOPULOS (AV)

31 South Seventh Street, 47807
Telephone: 812-238-2565
FAX: 812-238-1945

MEMBERS OF FIRM

Gus Sacopulos	Gregory S. Carter
R. Steven Johnson	Peter J. Sacopulos
	Michael J. Sacopulos

Representative Clients: Bituminous Casualty; Auto-Owners Insurance Co.; Indiana Insurance Co.; Victoria Ins. Co.; Cigna Insurance; American States Insurance Co.; CNA Insurance Co.; Physicians & Surgeons Insurance Co.; American Family Insurance Co.; WalMart Stores, Inc.

For full biographical listings, see the Martindale-Hubbell Law Directory

---

WILKINSON, GOELLER, MODESITT, WILKINSON & DRUMMY (AV)

333 Ohio Street, P.O. Box 800, 47808-0800
Telephone: 812-232-4311
Fax: 812-235-5107

MEMBERS OF FIRM

Myrl O. Wilkinson	John C. Wall
Raymond H. Modesitt	Craig M. McKee
B. Curtis Wilkinson	Scott M. Kyrouac
William W. Drummy	Jeffrey A. Boyll
	David P. Friedrich

Representative Clients: State Farm Mutual Automobile Insurance Co.; State Farm Fire & Casualty Co.; The Medical Protective Co.; Physicians Insurance Company of Indiana; Phico Insurance Co.; Indiana Insurance Cos.; Motorists Mutual Insurance Co.; United Farm Bureau Mutual Insurance Company; St. Paul Insurance Companies.

For Complete List of Firm Personnel, See General Section

For full biographical listings, see the Martindale-Hubbell Law Directory

---

VALPARAISO,* Porter Co.

HOEPPNER WAGNER AND EVANS (AV)

103 East Lincolnway, P.O. Box 2357, 46384-2357
Telephone: 219-464-4961; 800-879-2246 (IN,IL)
Fax: 219-465-0603
Merrillville, Indiana Office: Twin Towers, Suite 606 South, 1000 East 80th Place, 46410.
Telephone: 219-769-6552; 800-263-1466. (IN,IL,).
Fax: 219-738-2349.

MEMBERS OF FIRM

Larry G. Evans	F. Joseph Jaskowiak
William F. Satterlee, III	(Resident, Merrillville Office)
James A. Cheslek	Richard M. Davis
Ronald P. Kuker	Michael P. Blaize

ASSOCIATES

Jonathan R. Hanson	Jeffrey W. Clymer
Lauren K. Kroeger	Jack A. Kramer
	(Resident, Merrillville Office)

Representative Clients: State Farm Insurance; The Travelers Insurance Company; Continental Loss Adjusting Services; Auto Owners Insurance; Indiana Insurance; Allstate Insurance; General Accident Insurance; American Family Insurance; Protective Insurance; Heritage Mutual Insurance Company.

For Complete List of Firm Personnel, See General Section

For full biographical listings, see the Martindale-Hubbell Law Directory

---

VERSAILLES,* Ripley Co.

EATON & ROMWEBER (AV)

123 South Main Street, P.O. Box 275, 47042
Telephone: 812-689-5111
Fax: 812-689-5165
Batesville, Indiana Office: 13 East George Street. Telephone 812-934-5735.
Fax: 812-934-6041.

MEMBERS OF FIRM

Larry L. Eaton	Anthony A. Romweber

ASSOCIATES

W. Gregory Coy	Eric E. Wright
	(Not admitted in IN)

For full biographical listings, see the Martindale-Hubbell Law Directory

---

VINCENNES,* Knox Co.

EMISON, DOOLITTLE, KOLB & ROELLGEN (AV)

Eighth & Busseron Streets, P.O. Box 215, 47591
Telephone: 812-882-2280
FAX: 812-885-2308
Email: emison@ns.kensco.net

(See Next Column)

EMISON, DOOLITTLE, KOLB & ROELLGEN, *Vincennes—Continued*

MEMBERS OF FIRM

Rabb Emison	Jeffrey B. Kolb
Robert P. Doolittle, Jr.	J. David Roellgen

Clients Include: American Family Insurance, Co.; Cincinnati Insurance, Co.; Indiana Insurance, Co.; Ohio Casualty Insurance, Co.; United Farm Bureau Insurance, Co.; Sentry Insurance, Co.; GRE Insurance, Co.; Prudential Insurance, Co.

For full biographical listings, see the Martindale-Hubbell Law Directory

---

WARSAW,* Kosciusko Co.

ROCKHILL, PINNICK, PEQUIGNOT, HELM, LANDIS & RIGDON (AV)

105 East Main Street, 46580-2742
Telephone: 219-267-6116
Telecopier: 219-269-9264

MEMBERS OF FIRM

Brooks C. Pinnick	Vern K. Landis
Stanley E. Pequignot	Jay A. Rigdon
Richard K. Helm	Jamelyn E. Freeman

OF COUNSEL

Alvin T. Rockhill

Representative Clients: State Farm Insurance Cos.; United Farm Bureau Mutual Insurance Co.; Motorists Mutual Insurance Co.; American States Insurance.; Brotherhood Mutual Insurance.

For full biographical listings, see the Martindale-Hubbell Law Directory

---

IOWA

CEDAR RAPIDS,* Linn Co.

PICKENS, BARNES & ABERNATHY (AV)

Tenth Floor American Building, P.O. Box 74170, 52407-4170
Telephone: 319-366-7621
Fax: 319-366-3158

RETIRED

James F. Pickens

OF COUNSEL

Minor Barnes

MEMBERS OF FIRM

Terry J. Abernathy	Matthew G. Novak

ASSOCIATES

JoAnne M. Lilledahl	Cheryl M. Rosenberg

A list of Representative Clients furnished upon request.

For full biographical listings, see the Martindale-Hubbell Law Directory

SHUTTLEWORTH & INGERSOLL, P.C. (AV)

500 Firstar Bank Building, P.O. Box 2107, 52406-2107
Telephone: 319-365-9461
Fax: 319-365-8443
Email: si-law@inav.net

John M. Bickel	Thomas P. Peffer
Robert D. Houghton	Kevin H. Collins
Richard S. Fry	Diane Kutzko
Richard C. Garberson	Mark L. Zaiger
Steven J. Pace	Douglas R. Oelschlaeger
Glenn L. Johnson	Constance M. Alt
	Kurt L. Kratovil

Christine L. McLaughlin	William H. Courter

Representative Clients: Allied Insurance Group; Auto-Owners Insurance; CIGNA Companies; CNA Insurance Companies; Farmers Insurance Group; Farmland Mutual Insurance Company; Fireman's Fund Insurance Companies; General Casualty Company of Wisconsin; IMT Insurance Company.

For Complete List of Firm Personnel, See General Section

For full biographical listings, see the Martindale-Hubbell Law Directory

---

COUNCIL BLUFFS,* Pottawattamie Co.

SMITH PETERSON LAW FIRM (AV)

35 Main Place, Suite 300, P.O. Box 249, 51502
Telephone: 712-328-1833
Fax: 712-328-8320
Omaha, Nebraska Office: 9290 West Dodge Road, Suite 205.
Telephone: 402-397-8500.
Fax: 402-397-5519.

(See Next Column)

MEMBERS OF FIRM

Raymond A. Smith (1892-1977)	Lawrence J. Beckman
John LeRoy Peterson (1895-1969)	Gregory G. Barntsen
	W. Curtis Hewett
Harold T. Beckman	Steven H. Krohn
Robert J. Laubenthal	Randy R. Ewing
Richard A. Heininger	Joseph D. Thornton

ASSOCIATES

T. J. Pattermann	Paul M. Shotkoski
Daniel Fretheim	(Not admitted in IA)

Representative Clients: Redland Insurance Group; Iowa Western Community College; Farm Credit Bank of Omaha; Demma Fruit Co.; Peoples National Bank; Council Bluffs Board of Water Works Trustee.

For full biographical listings, see the Martindale-Hubbell Law Directory

---

DECORAH,* Winneshiek Co.

MILLER, PEARSON, GLOE, BURNS, BEATTY & COWIE, P.C. (AV)

301 West Broadway, 52101
Telephone: 319-382-4226
Fax: 319-382-3783

Frank R. Miller (1915-1977)	James Burns
Donald H. Gloe	Marion L. Beatty
	Robert J. Cowie, Jr.

OF COUNSEL

Floyd S. Pearson

Counsel for: Luther College; Decorah Community School District; Winneshiek County Memorial Hospital; Community First State Bank.
Local Counsel for: Iowa Mutual Insurance Cos.; Employers Mutual Liability Insurance Co. of Wisconsin; Continental Casualty Co.; Employers Mutual Casualty Co.; Grinnell Mutual Insurance Co.; Allied Mutual Insurance Co.

For full biographical listings, see the Martindale-Hubbell Law Directory

---

DES MOINES,* Polk Co.

FINLEY, ALT, SMITH, SCHARNBERG, MAY & CRAIG, P.C. (AV)

604 Locust Street, Fourth Floor Equitable Building, 50309
Telephone: 515-288-0145
Telecopier: 515-288-2724

Thomas A. Finley	Steven K. Scharnberg
Glenn L. Smith	Lorraine J. May
	John D. (Jack) Hilmes

Kerry A. Finley

Representative Clients: Aetna Casualty & Surety Co.; Aetna Life Insurance Co.; ALAS; American Society of Composers, Authors and Publishers; Equitable Life Assurance Society of the U.S.; Federated Insurance Co.; Meredith Corp.
Iowa Attorneys for: Midwest Medical Insurance Co.
District Attorneys for: Norfolk & Southern Railroad; Soo Line Railroad Company.

For Complete List of Firm Personnel, See General Section

For full biographical listings, see the Martindale-Hubbell Law Directory

GREFE & SIDNEY, P.L.C. (AV)

2222 Grand Avenue, P.O. Box 10434, 50306
Telephone: 515-245-4300
Fax: 515-245-4452
Email: GRANDFIRM@AOL.COM

Ross H. Sidney	John Werner
Henry A. Harmon	Patrick J. McNulty
Claude H. Freeman	Mark W. Thomas
Stephen D. Hardy	Guy R. Cook

Andrew D. Hall	Debra L. Scorpiniti
Stephanie L. Glenn	Marcy A. O'Brien
Mark A. Schultheis	Kristin L. Bohlken

Representative Clients: Adventurelands of America; Caseys General Stores, Inc.; Cincinnati Insurance Company; Crum and Forster; Employers Mutual Insurance; Liberty Mutual Insurance Co.; Montgomery Elevator; Otis Elevator; Reliance Insurance; State Farm Mutual Insurance Companies.

For Complete List of Firm Personnel, See General Section

For full biographical listings, see the Martindale-Hubbell Law Directory

HANSEN, McCLINTOCK & RILEY (AV)

Eighth Floor - Fleming Building, 218 Sixth Avenue, 50309
Telephone: 515-244-2141
Fax: 515-244-2931

(See Next Column)

HANSEN, MCCLINTOCK & RILEY—*Continued*

MEMBERS OF FIRM

Haemer Wheatcraft (1904-1983)	Chester C. Woodburn, III
J. Rudolph Hansen (1904-1995)	William D. Scherle
John A. McClintock	David L. Brown
Ronald A. Riley	John E. Swanson

ASSOCIATE

James M. Ballard

Representative Clients: The St. Paul Companies; Bituminous Insurance Companies; Northwestern National Insurance Co.; The Travelers Insurance Companies; United States Aviation Insurance Group; American International Companies; Iowa Credit Union League; The McAninch Corp.; R. J. Reynolds Tobacco Co.; Brown Bros., Inc. Electrical Contractors.

For full biographical listings, see the Martindale-Hubbell Law Directory

HERRICK, LANGDON & LANGDON (AV)

1800 Financial Center, Seventh and Walnut, 50309
Telephone: 515-282-8150
Telecopier: 515-282-8226

MEMBERS OF FIRM

Allan A. Herrick (1896-1989)	William R. Clark, Jr.
Herschel G. Langdon	Richard N. Winders
Richard G. Langdon	Richard A. Steffen

Kermit B. Anderson

ASSOCIATE

Michael B. O'Meara

Representative Clients: Coregis; Jefferson Insurance Group; ITT Hartford; CIGNA; Ohio Casualty Group; Union Insurance Group; Canal Insurance Co.; CNA Health Pro; Globe American Casualty Co.; Northbrook Property & Casualty Co.

For full biographical listings, see the Martindale-Hubbell Law Directory

HUBER, BOOK, CORTESE, HAPPE & BROWN, P.L.C. (AV)

500 Liberty Building, 50309-2421
Telephone: 515-243-4148
Fax: 515-243-5481

MEMBERS OF FIRM

James C. Huber	Joseph S. Cortese II
Richard G. Book	Joseph A. Happe

Terrence D. Brown

ASSOCIATES

Patrick D. Smith	Brian M. F. Kennedy

Deborah M. Stein

Representative Clients: Liberty Mutual Insurance Co.; Royal-Globe Group; Fireman's Fund American Insurance Companies; Continental Insurance Companies; Security Insurance Group; Home Insurance Co.; U.S. Insurance Group.
Reference: Boatmen's Bank.

For full biographical listings, see the Martindale-Hubbell Law Directory

PATTERSON, LORENTZEN, DUFFIELD, TIMMONS, IRISH, BECKER & ORDWAY, L.L.P. (AV)

729 Insurance Exchange Building, 50309
Telephone: 515-283-2147
Fax: 515-283-1002

MEMBERS OF FIRM

G. O. Patterson (1914-1982)	Gregory J. Wilson
James A. Lorentzen	Jeffrey A. Boehlert
Theodore T. Duffield	Douglas A. Haag
William E. Timmons (Retired)	Charles E. Cutler
Roy M. Irish	Michael D. Huppert
F. H. Becker (Retired)	Martin C. Sprock
Gary D. Ordway	William A. Wickett
Robin L. Hermann	Frederick M. Haskins
Harry Perkins, III	Jeffrey A. Baker
Michael F. Lacey, Jr.	Janice M. Herfkens

ASSOCIATES

Coreen K. Bezdicek	Patrick V. Waldron

Michael S Jones

Representative Clients: Allied Mutual Insurance Company; CNA Insurance Company; Chubb Insurance Group; Continental Western Insurance Co.; Farmers Insurance Group; Farmland Insurance Company; Grinnell Mutual Reinsurance Company; Hawkeye Security Insurance Company; Iowa Insurance Institute, St. Paul Fire & Marine Insurance Company.

For full biographical listings, see the Martindale-Hubbell Law Directory

PEDDICORD, WHARTON, THUNE AND SPENCER, A PROFESSIONAL CORPORATION (AV)

700 Des Moines Building, 405 Sixth Avenue, P.O. Box 9130, 50306-9130
Telephone: 515-243-2100
Fax: 515-243-2132
1-800-383-2100

(See Next Column)

Roland D. Peddicord	Stephen W. Spencer
John M. Wharton	Lee P. Hook
Paul C. Thune	Fred L. Morris

Joseph M. Barron	Michael S. Roling
Timothy W. Wegman	Steven T. Durick

For full biographical listings, see the Martindale-Hubbell Law Directory

WHITFIELD & EDDY, P.L.C. (AV)

317 6th Avenue, Suite 1200 Locust at 6th, 50309-4110
Telephone: 515-288-6041
Fax: 515-246-1474

A. Roger Witke	Kevin M. Reynolds
Timothy J. Walker	Thomas H. Burke
David L. Phipps	Thomas Henderson
Benjamin B. Ullem	George H. Frampton
Robert L. Fanter	Megan Manning Antenucci
Bernard L. Spaeth, Jr.	Wendy L. Carlson
Rod Kubat	Gary A. Norton
William L. Fairbank	Mark V. Hanson
Robert G. Bridges	Maureen Roach Tobin
Jaki K. Samuelson	Jeffrey William Courter

August B. Landis

Richard J. Kirschman	Jason M. Casini

OF COUNSEL

Dean Dutton

General Counsel for: American Life and Casualty Co.; Hawkeye; Security Insurance Co.; The Statesman Group, Inc.; United Security Insurance Co.
Representative Clients: Crum & Forster Commercial Insurance; National Insurance Assn.; Royal Insurance; Tudor Insurance.

For Complete List of Firm Personnel, See General Section

For full biographical listings, see the Martindale-Hubbell Law Directory

*HARLAN,** Shelby Co.

KOHORST LAW FIRM (AV)

602 Market Street Building, P.O. Box 722, 51537-0722
Telephone: 712-755-3156
Fax: 712-755-7404

Robert Kohorst	Kathleen Schomer Kohorst

ASSOCIATES

William T. Early	Steven Elza Goodlow

Representative Clients: Employers Mutual Insurance Companies of Des Moines, Iowa; Farm Service Co-op., Harlan, Iowa; Thermogas Co., Tulsa, Oklahoma; Mid-America Pipeline Company, Inc., Tulsa, Oklahoma; United Fire & Casualty Co.; Farmers Mutual Telephone Co., Harlan, Iowa.

For full biographical listings, see the Martindale-Hubbell Law Directory

*OSKALOOSA,** Mahaska Co.

POTHOVEN, BLOMGREN & STRAVERS (AV)

1201 High Avenue West, P.O. Box 1066, 52577
Telephone: 515-673-4438
Fax: 515-673-5177
Email: PBSLAW@KDSI.NET

MEMBERS OF FIRM

Marion H. Pothoven	James Q. Blomgren

Randall C. Stravers

ASSOCIATE

Julie Bond Fisher

For full biographical listings, see the Martindale-Hubbell Law Directory

*SIOUX CITY,** Woodbury Co.

HEIDMAN, REDMOND, FREDREGILL, PATTERSON, SCHATZ & PLAZA, L.L.P. (AV)

A Registered Limited Liability Partnership including Professional Corporations
701 Pierce Street, Suite 200, P.O. Box 3086, 51102
Telephone: 712-255-8838
Fax: 712-258-6714

MEMBERS OF FIRM

Marvin F. Heidman	Lance D. Ehmcke
James W. Redmond	Margaret M. Prahl
Alan E. Fredregill (P.C.)	John D. Ackerman
Charles T. Patterson	Gregg E. Williams
Kenneth C. Schatz (P.C.)	Judith A. Higgs
Thomas M. Plaza	John C. Gray
Daniel D. Dykstra	Daniel B. Shuck

Rita C. Grimm

(See Next Column)

HEIDMAN, REDMOND, FREDREGILL, PATTERSON, SCHATZ & PLAZA L.L.P.,
Sioux City—Continued

ASSOCIATES

Ryan K. Crayne	Patrick L. Sealey
Charles E. Trullinger	John W. Gleysteen (Retired)
Edward C. Poulsen	Robert R. Eidsmoe (Retired)
Sabra K Craig	Jacob C. Gleysteen (1883-1943)
H. Clifford Harper (1891-1959)	

Representative Clients: Aetna Casualty & Surety Co.; Irving F. Jensen Co., Inc.; Marian Health Center; Medical Protective Co.; John Morrell & Co.; Pig Improvement Co.; State Farm Mutual Insurance Co.; Terra International, Inc.; The Security National Bank of Sioux City; Wal-Mart Stores, Inc.

For full biographical listings, see the Martindale-Hubbell Law Directory

MAYNE & MAYNE (AV)

400 Pioneer Bank Building, 701 Pierce Street, P.O. Box 5049, 51102-5049
Telephone: 712-252-3220
Fax: 712-252-1535

MEMBERS OF FIRM

Wiley Mayne	John D. Mayne
Robert J. Pierson	

ASSOCIATE

Monte G. Richards (Not admitted in IA)

Representative Clients: American Home Insurance Co.; American Empire Insurance Company; Capitol Indemnity Company; Chubb Insurance; Design Professionals Financial Corp.; Fremont Indemnity Company; Heritage Insurance; Podiatry Insurance Company of America; Ranger Insurance; Utica Mutual Insurance Company.

For full biographical listings, see the Martindale-Hubbell Law Directory

---

*WATERLOO,** Black Hawk Co.

SWISHER & COHRT, P.L.C. (AV)

528 West Fourth Street, P.O. Box 1200, 50704
Telephone: 319-232-6555
FAX: 319-232-4835

Benjamin F. Swisher (1878-1959)	J. Douglas Oberman
L. J. Cohrt (1898-1974)	Stephen J. Powell
Charles F. Swisher (1919-1986)	Jim D. DeKoster
Jeffrey J. Greenwood (1953-1995)	Samuel C. Anderson
	Robert C. Griffin
Eldon R. McCann	Kevin R. Rogers
Steven A. Weidner	Beth E. Hansen
Larry J. Cohrt	Mark F. Conway

Natalie Williams Burris

Firm is Counsel for: Koehring Corp.; Clay Equipment; Chamberlain Manufacturing Co.; Waterloo Courier.
Local Counsel for: Allied Group; John Deere Insurance; Liberty Mutual Insurance Co.

For full biographical listings, see the Martindale-Hubbell Law Directory

---

KANSAS

*KANSAS CITY,** Wyandotte Co.

HOLBROOK, HEAVEN & FAY, P.A. (AV)

757 Armstrong, P.O. Box 171927, 66117
Telephone: 913-342-2500
Fax: 913-342-0603
Merriam, Kansas Office: 6700 Antioch Street.
Telephone: 913-677-1717.
Fax: 913-677-0403.

Reid F. Holbrook	Thomas M. Sutherland
Lewis A. Heaven, Jr. (Resident, Merriam Office)	Thomas S. Busch (Resident, Merriam Office)
Ted F. Fay, Jr. (Resident, Merriam Office)	Kurt S. Brack (Resident Merriam Office)
Thomas E. Osborn	Sally A. Howard
Robert L. Kennedy	Brent G. Wright
Janet M. Simpson	Daniel W. Peters
John D. Tongier (Resident, Merriam Office)	

For Complete List of Firm Personnel, See General Section

For full biographical listings, see the Martindale-Hubbell Law Directory

McANANY, VAN CLEAVE & PHILLIPS, P.A. (AV)

Fourth Floor, 707 Minnesota Avenue, P.O. Box 171300, 66117
Telephone: 913-371-3838
Facsimile: 913-371-4722
Lenexa, Kansas Office: Suite 200, 11900 West 87th Street Parkway.
Telephone: 913-888-9000.
Facsimile: 913-888-7049.
Kansas City, Missouri Office: Suite 304, 819 Walnut Street.
Telephone: 816-556-9417.

John J. Jurcyk, Jr.	William P. Coates, Jr. (Resident, Lenexa Office)
Robert D. Benham	
Clifford T. Mueller (Resident, Lenexa Office)	Douglas M. Greenwald

OF COUNSEL

Frank D. Menghini

Reference: Guaranty Bank and Trust Co.

For Complete List of Firm Personnel, See General Section

For full biographical listings, see the Martindale-Hubbell Law Directory

---

OVERLAND PARK, Johnson Co.

FISHER, PATTERSON, SAYLER & SMITH, L.L.P. (AV)

11050 Roe Avenue, Suite 210, 66211
Telephone: 913-339-6757
FAX: 913-339-6187
Topeka, Kansas Office: 534 South Kansas Avenue, Suite 400, P.O. Box 949, 66601.
Telephone: 913-232-7761.
Fax: 913-232-6604.

MEMBERS OF FIRM

Edwin Dudley Smith (Resident)	Michael K. Seck (Resident)
David P. Madden (Resident)	

ASSOCIATE

Patrick G. Reavey (Resident)

For full biographical listings, see the Martindale-Hubbell Law Directory

---

*TOPEKA,** Shawnee Co.

DAVIS, UNREIN, HUMMER & BUCK, L.L.P. (AV)

100 East Ninth Street, Third Floor, P.O. Box 3575, 66601-3575
Telephone: 913-354-1100
Fax: 913-354-1113

MEMBERS OF FIRM

Byron M. Gray (1901-1986)	J. Franklin Hummer
Maurice D. Freidberg (1902-1965)	Mark A. Buck
	James B. Biggs
Charles L. Davis, Jr. (1921-1992)	Christopher M. Rohrer
	Brenda L. Head
Michael J. Unrein	Eric I. Unrein

OF COUNSEL

Gary D. McCallister

Representative Clients: American Family Insurance Group; American Bankers Ins. Co.; General Casualty Company; Hawkeye Security Insurance Co.; Preferred Risk Insurance Co.; Silvey Insurance Co.; Union Insurance Co.; United Fire & Casualty Co.; Utica Mutual Insurance Co.; Wausau Insurance Co.

For full biographical listings, see the Martindale-Hubbell Law Directory

---

FISHER, PATTERSON, SAYLER & SMITH, L.L.P. (AV)

534 South Kansas Avenue, Suite 400, P.O. Box 949, 66601
Telephone: 913-232-7761
Fax: 913-232-6604
Overland Park, Kansas Office: 11050 Roe Avenue, Suite 210, 66211.
Telephone: 913-339-6757.
Fax: 913-339-6187.

MEMBERS OF FIRM

Donald Patterson	Steve R. Fabert
Edwin Dudley Smith (Resident, Overland Park Office)	Ronald J. Laskowski
Larry G. Pepperdine	Michael K. Seck (Resident, Overland Park Office)
James P. Nordstrom	David P. Madden (Resident, Overland Park Office)
Justice B. King	
J. Steven Pigg	Steven K. Johnson

ASSOCIATES

Kristine A. Larscheid	Billy E. Newman
Patrick G. Reavey (Resident, Overland Park Office)	David R. Cooper

OF COUNSEL

David H. Fisher

RETIRED

Charles Keith Sayler (Retired)

Representative Clients: Gage Shopping Center, Inc.; Fireman's Fund-American Insurance Cos.; United States Fidelity and Guaranty Co.; The Procter & Gamble Company; American Cyanamid Company; Commercial

(See Next Column)

FISHER, PATTERSON, SAYLER & SMITH L.L.P.—*Continued*

Union Insurance Companies; National Casualty/Scottsdale Insurance Co.; The Hartford; Berkshire Hathaway Companies.

For full biographical listings, see the Martindale-Hubbell Law Directory

GOODELL, STRATTON, EDMONDS & PALMER, L.L.P. (AV)

515 South Kansas Avenue, 66603-3999
Telephone: 913-233-0593
Telecopier: 913-233-8870
Email: GSEP@CJNETWORKS.COM

MEMBERS OF FIRM

Gerald L. Goodell	Michael W. Merriam
Wayne T. Stratton	John H. Stauffer, Jr.
Arthur E. Palmer	Les E. Diehl
Harold S. Youngentob	David E. Bruns
Charles R. Hay	N. Larry Bork
Patrick M. Salsbury	John D. Ensley

Catherine M. Walberg

OF COUNSEL

John A. Bausch

ASSOCIATE

Steve A Schwarm

SPECIAL COUNSEL

Marta Fisher Linenberger   Curtis J. Waugh

Counsel for: Farm Bureau Mutual Insurance Co.; Metropolitan Life Insurance Co.; St. Paul Fire & Marine Insurance Co.; American Home Life Insurance Co.; Allied Group Insurance; Farmers Insurance Group; Federated Insurance Company; PHICO Insurance Group; American Fidelity Insurance Co.; National Farmers Union Property and Casualty Co.

For Complete List of Firm Personnel, See General Section

For full biographical listings, see the Martindale-Hubbell Law Directory

WRIGHT, HENSON, SOMERS, SEBELIUS, CLARK & BAKER, LLP (AV)

Commerce Bank Building, 100 Southeast Ninth Street, 2nd Floor, P.O. Box 3555, 66601-3555
Telephone: 913-232-2200
FAX: 913-232-3344

MEMBERS OF FIRM

Thomas E. Wright	Anne Lamborn Baker
K. Gary Sebelius	Evelyn Zabel Wilson

ASSOCIATES

Michael M. Walker	Donald Sutsu Lee

For Complete List of Firm Personnel, See General Section

For full biographical listings, see the Martindale-Hubbell Law Directory

WICHITA,* Sedgwick Co.

DEPEW AND GILLEN, L.L.C. (AV)

151 North Main, Suite 700, 67202-1408
Telephone: 316-265-9621
Facsimile: 316-265-3819
Email: d-g@southwind.net

Spencer L. Depew	David W. Nickel
Dennis L. Gillen	Nicholas S. Daily
Randall K. Rathbun	David E. Rogers
Jack Scott McInteer	Charles C. Steincamp

For full biographical listings, see the Martindale-Hubbell Law Directory

FOULSTON & SIEFKIN L.L.P. (AV)

700 Fourth Financial Center, 67202
Telephone: 316-267-6371
Facsimile: 316-267-6345
Topeka, Kansas Office: 1515 Bank IV Tower, 534 Kansas Avenue, 66603.
Telephone: 913-233-3600.
Fax: 913-233-1610.
Dodge City, Kansas Office: 810 Frontview, P.O. Box 1147, 67801.
Telephone: 316-227-8126.
Fax: 316-227-8451.
Member: Lex Mundi, A Global Association of 126 Independent Firms.

MEMBERS OF FIRM

Frederick L. Haag	Stephen M. Kerwick
Darrell L. Warta	Vaughn Burkholder
Jay F. Fowler	Amy S. Lemley

Craig W. West

For Complete List of Firm Personnel, See General Section

For full biographical listings, see the Martindale-Hubbell Law Directory

HERSHBERGER, PATTERSON, JONES & ROTH, L.C. (AV)

600 Hardage Center, 100 South Main, 67202-3779
Telephone: 316-263-7583
Fax: 316-263-7595

William R. Smith	David J. Morgan
J. Michael Kennalley	Tracy A. Applegate

OF COUNSEL

H. E. Jones

Counsel for: First National Bank in Wichita; Anadarko Petroleum Corporation; Mobil Oil Corp.; CNA Insurance; Royal Exchange Group; Central National Insurance Group; Transamerica Insurance Group; Northwestern National Insurance Group; St. Paul Cos.

For Complete List of Firm Personnel, See General Section

For full biographical listings, see the Martindale-Hubbell Law Directory

JOHNSON & KENNEDY (AV)

River Park Place, 727 North Waco, Suite 585, 67203-3596
Telephone: 316-263-4921
Fax: 316-263-0045

MEMBERS OF FIRM

Douglas D. Johnson	David L. Dahl
E. Craig Kennedy	Barbara Scott Girard

OF COUNSEL

John Philip Kassebaum

Representative Clients: Vulcan Materials Co.; American Family Insurance Group.

For full biographical listings, see the Martindale-Hubbell Law Directory

KAHRS, NELSON, FANNING, HITE & KELLOGG, L.L.P. (AV)

Suite 630, 200 West Douglas Street, 67202-3089
Telephone: 316-265-7761
Telecopier: 316-267-7803

MEMBERS OF FIRM

Richard L. Honeyman	Marc A. Powell
Larry A. Withers	Kim R. Martens
Gary A. Winfrey	Forrest James Robinson, Jr.
Scott J. Gunderson	Don D. Gribble, II
Randy Troutt	Vince P. Wheeler
Arthur S. Chalmers	Alan R. Pfaff

Dennis V. Lacey

ASSOCIATES

Jeffrey R. Emerson	Lisa Adrian McPherson

Representative Clients: Attorneys Liability Protection Society; American States Ins. Co.; Chubb-Pacific Ins. Group; CNA; Farm Bureau Mutual Ins. Co.; Howe Associates, Inc.; Kansas Medical Mutual; Maryland Casualty Co.; The St. Paul Cos.; United States Fidelity and Guaranty.

For Complete List of Firm Personnel, See General Section

For full biographical listings, see the Martindale-Hubbell Law Directory

YOUNG, BOGLE, McCAUSLAND, WELLS & CLARK, P.A. (AV)

106 West Douglas, Suite 923, 67202
Telephone: 316-265-7841
Facsimile: 316-265-3956

Jerry D. Bogle	Kenneth M. Clark
Paul S. McCausland	Patrick C. Blanchard
William A. Wells	Mark R. Maloney

Representative Clients: Provident Life & Accident Insurance Co.; The Equitable Life Assurance Society of the United States; John Deere Insurance Co.; Metropolitan Life Ins. Co.; Horace Mann Ins. Co.; John Hancock Mutual Life Ins Co.; ITT Life Ins. Co.; Benefit Trust Life Ins. Co.; Home Life Insurance Co.; Minnesota Mutual Life Insurance Co.; Farmers Insurance Group.

For Complete List of Firm Personnel, See General Section

For full biographical listings, see the Martindale-Hubbell Law Directory

KENTUCKY

ASHLAND, Boyd Co.

MARTIN, PICKLESIMER, JUSTICE & VINCENT (AV)

431 Sixteenth Street, P.O. Box 2528, 41105-2528
Telephone: 606-329-8338
Fax: 606-325-8199

Richard W. Martin	David Justice
Max D. Picklesimer	John F. Vincent

(See Next Column)

MARTIN, PICKLESIMER, JUSTICE & VINCENT, *Ashland—Continued*

ASSOCIATES

Thomas Wade Lavender, II   Brian Leslie Hewlett

Representative Clients: City of Ashland; FIVCO Area Development District; Boyd County Sanitation District No. 2; Mid-America Distributors, Inc.
Insurance Counsel for: State Farm Mutual Automobile Insurance Co.; State Farm Fire and Casualty Co.; Aetna Casualty Insurance Co.; Grange Mutual Insurance Co.; Great American Insurance Co.

For full biographical listings, see the Martindale-Hubbell Law Directory

---

BOWLING GREEN,* Warren Co.

BRODERICK, THORNTON & PIERCE (AV)

921 College Street, Phoenix Place, P.O. Box 1137, 42102-1137
Telephone: 502-782-6700
Facsimile: 502-782-3110

David F. Broderick   Steven O. Thornton
                    Darell R. Pierce

ASSOCIATES

Pamela Carolyn Bratcher   B. Alan Simpson
                Kenneth P. O'Brien

Representative Clients: Allstate Insurance Co.; National City Bank; American States Insurance Co.; Capital Enterprise Insurance; Fireman's Fund Insurance Co.; Imperial Casualty & Indemnity; Indiana Lumbermen's Mutual Insurance; Kentucky Medical Insurance Co.; Scotty's Contracting & Stone, Inc.; St. Paul Insurance Co.

For Complete List of Firm Personnel, See General Section

For full biographical listings, see the Martindale-Hubbell Law Directory

---

HARLIN & PARKER, P.S.C. (AV)

519 East Tenth Street, P.O. Box 390, 42102-0390
Telephone: 502-842-5611
Telefax: 502-842-2607

William Jerry Parker   Scott Charles Marks
                Mark D. Alcott

Insurance Clients: American Hardware Mutual Insurance Co.; CNA; Government Employees Insurance Co.; AIG Insurance Cos.
Railroad and Utilities Clients: District Attorneys for BellSouth Telecommunications, Inc.
Local Counsel for: General Motors Corp.; Ford Motor Co.; Chrysler Corp.

For Complete List of Firm Personnel, See General Section

For full biographical listings, see the Martindale-Hubbell Law Directory

---

HIXSON, DOWNEY & TRAVELSTED (AV)

537 East Tenth Street, P.O. Box 3250, 42102-3250
Telephone: 502-782-3580
FAX: 502-782-6095

MEMBERS OF FIRM

Stephen L. Hixson   Steven D. Downey
                Penny Travelsted

ASSOCIATES

Joseph R. Kirwan   Benjamin D. Crocker

OF COUNSEL

William E. Allender

For full biographical listings, see the Martindale-Hubbell Law Directory

---

KERRICK, GRISE & STIVERS (AV)

1025 State Street, P.O. Box 9547, 42102-9547
Telephone: 502-782-8160
Fax: 502-782-5856
Elizabethtown, Kentucky Office: 2935 Dolphin Drive, Suite 102.
Telephone: 502-769-5788.
Fax: 502-737-9285.

MEMBERS OF FIRM

Thomas N. Kerrick   Gregory N. Stivers
John R. Grise   H. Brent Brennenstuhl

ASSOCIATES

Lanna Martin Kilgore   Shawn Rosso Alcott
Laura M. Hagan (Resident,   Jason B. Bell
  Elizabethtown Office)

Representative Clients: Hartford Insurance Group; Nationwide Insurance Co.; Cincinnati Insurance Co.; Firemans Fund Insurance Co.; Kentucky Hospital Association Trust; Kentucky Medical Insurance Company; Northland Insurance Cos.; Anthem Casualty Insurance Group; Kemper National Insurance Companies; Generali-U.S. Branch Insurance Company.

For full biographical listings, see the Martindale-Hubbell Law Directory

---

MILLIKEN LAW FIRM (AV)

426 East Main Street, P.O. Box 1640, 42102-1640
Telephone: 502-843-0800
Fax: 502-842-1237

W. Currie Milliken   Wesley V. Milliken

Reference: Trans Financial Bank, Bowling Green, Kentucky.

For full biographical listings, see the Martindale-Hubbell Law Directory

---

COVINGTON, Kenton Co.

ADAMS, BROOKING, STEPNER, WOLTERMANN & DUSING (AV)

421 Garrard Street, P.O. Box 861, 41012
Telephone: 606-291-7270
Fax: 606-291-7902
Florence, Kentucky Office: 8100 Burlington Pike, Suite 400, 41042.
Telephone: 606-371-6220.
Fax: 606-371-8341.

Donald L. Stepner   James R. Kruer
Gerald F. Dusing   Jeffrey C. Mando
(Resident at Florence Office)

ASSOCIATES

Stacey L. Graus   Chandra S. Baldwin

Representative Clients: Balluff, Inc., Wampler, Inc., Kisters, Inc., Krauss-Maffei, Inc., A group of German companies; State Automobile Mutual Insurance Co.; Chevron of California; Great American Insurance Co.; Grange Mutual Insurance Co.; Meridian Mutual Insurance Co.; Fifth-Third Bank of Northern Ky.; Northern Kentucky University; ITT Hartford.

For Complete List of Firm Personnel, See General Section

For full biographical listings, see the Martindale-Hubbell Law Directory

---

WARE, BRYSON, WEST & KUMMER (AV)

157 Barnwood Drive, 41017
Telephone: 606-341-0255
FAX: 606-341-1876

MEMBERS OF FIRM

Rodney S. Bryson   Greg D. Voss
Larry C. West   Robert B. Cetrulo
John R. Kummer   Susanne M. Cetrulo
Mark W. Howard   David W. Martin

ASSOCIATES

W. L. (Skip) Hammons, Jr.   Orie S. Ware (1882-1974)
James M. West   William O. Ware (1908-1961)
                James C. Ware (1913-1991)

Attorneys for: First National Bank of Northern Ky.; State Farm Insurance Co.; Reliance Insurance Group; Maryland Casualty Insurance Co.; Kemper Insurance Co.; Prudential Insurance Co.; State Farm Fire & Casualty Insurance Co.; Shelby Mutual Insurance Co.; Cincinnati Insurance Co.

For full biographical listings, see the Martindale-Hubbell Law Directory

---

DANVILLE,* Boyle Co.

SHEEHAN, BARNETT & HAYS, P.S.C. (AV)

114 South Fourth Street, P.O. Box 1517, 40423-1517
Telephone: 606-236-2641; 606-734-7552
FAX: 606-236-1483

James G. Sheehan, Jr.   Edward D. Hays
James William Barnett   Rebecca Lynn Rice

Representative Clients: Bank One; National City Bank; Great Financial Bank; Kentucky Farm Bureau Mutual Insurance Co.; Motorist Mutual Insurance Co.; R.R. Donnelley & Sons, Inc.; State Automobile Mutual Insurance Co.; City of Danville; Shelter Insurance Co.; Trim Masters, Inc.

For full biographical listings, see the Martindale-Hubbell Law Directory

---

ELIZABETHTOWN,* Hardin Co.

COLEMAN & STEVENS (AV)

(Formerly Reford H. Coleman and Associates)
2907 Ring Road, P.O. Box 4030, 42702-4030
Telephone: 502-737-0600
Fax: 502-737-0488

Reford H. Coleman   Michael L. Stevens

Beth Ann Lochmiller   M. Brent Hall
                Kelly Mark Easton

Representative Clients: American States Insurance Cos.; Coca-Cola Bottling Co.; Federated Rural Elec. Insurance Co.; Firemans Fund Insurance Cos.; General Motors Corp.; Indiana Insurance Co.; Kentucky Farm Bureau Mutual Insurance Corp.; Liberty Mutual Insurance Co.; Ohio Casualty Insurance Group; United Services Automobile Association (State Counsel).

For full biographical listings, see the Martindale-Hubbell Law Directory

Elizabethtown—Continued

COLLIER, ARNETT, QUICK & COLEMAN (AV)

128 West Dixie Avenue, P.O. Box 847, 42701
Telephone: 502-765-4112
Fax: 502-769-3081

MEMBERS OF FIRM

James M. Collier	Kim F. Quick
John L. Arnett	Jerry M. Coleman
Deborah Lewis Shaw	

Counsel for: City of Elizabethtown; PNC Bank; Elizabethtown Independent School District.
Representative Clients: Nationwide Insurance Co.; Shelter Insurance Co.; State Farm Insurance Co.; Government Employees Insurance Co.; Liberty Mutual Insurance Co.; Kemper Insurance Group; Motorist Mutual Insurance Co.

For full biographical listings, see the Martindale-Hubbell Law Directory

---

FLORENCE, Boone Co.

ADAMS, BROOKING, STEPNER, WOLTERMANN & DUSING (AV)

8100 Burlington Pike, Suite 400, 41042-0576
Telephone: 606-371-6220
Fax: 606-371-8341
Covington, Kentucky Office: 421 Garrard Street.
Telephone: 606-291-7270.
Fax: 606-291-7902.

Donald L. Stepner	Gerald F. Dusing (Resident)
Jeffrey C. Mando	

ASSOCIATE
Stacey L. Graus

Representative Clients: State Automobile Mutual Insurance Co.; Standard Oil Co. (Ky.); Great American Insurance Co.; Grange Mutual Insurance Co.; Meridian Mutual Insurance Co.; Fifth-Third Bank of Boone County; Northern Kentucky University.

For Complete List of Firm Personnel, See General Section

For full biographical listings, see the Martindale-Hubbell Law Directory

---

HARLAN,* Harlan Co.

HUFF LAW OFFICES (AV)

417 East Mound Street, Drawer 151, 40831
Telephone: 606-573-4466
Fax: 606-573-7078

Gayle G. Huff
ASSOCIATE
Antony L. Saragas

Representative Clients: Old Republic Insurance Co.; Underwriters Safety & Claims; Manalapan Mining Co.; R.B. Coal Co.; Eastover Mining Co., a division of Duke Power Co.

For full biographical listings, see the Martindale-Hubbell Law Directory

---

RICE & HENDRICKSON (AV)

398 Woodland Hills, P.O. Box 980, 40831
Telephone: 606-573-3955
Fax: 606-573-3956

MEMBERS OF FIRM

William A. Rice	H. Kent Hendrickson

Representative Clients: USX Corp.; Navistar International Transportation Corp.; Bituminous Casualty Corp.; Kentucky Utilities Co.; Aetna Casualty & Surety Co.; Nationwide Insurance; The Hartford Insurance Group; Arch Mineral Corp.

For full biographical listings, see the Martindale-Hubbell Law Directory

---

HENDERSON,* Henderson Co.

DEEP & WOMACK (AV)

790 Bob Posey Street, P.O. Box 50, 42420
Telephone: 502-827-2522
Fax: 502-826-2870
Louisville, Kentucky Office: 1228 Starks Building, 455 South Fourth Avenue. P.O. Box 70033, 40270-0033.
Telephone: 502-589-2530.
Fax: 502-589-9297.

MEMBERS OF FIRM

Charles David Deep	James G. Womack
Zack N. Womack	Toni Cline Renfro
	(Resident, Louisville Office)

For full biographical listings, see the Martindale-Hubbell Law Directory

---

KING, DEEP AND BRANAMAN (AV)

127 North Main Street, P.O. Box 43, 42420
Telephone: 502-827-1852
FAX: 502-826-7729

MEMBERS OF FIRM

Leo King (1893-1982)	Harry L. Mathison, Jr.
William M. Deep (1920-1990)	W. Mitchell Deep, Jr.
William Branaman	H. Randall Redding
	Dorin E. Luck

ASSOCIATES

Leslie M. Newman	Greg L. Gager

Counsel for: Allstate Insurance; MMI; Commercial Union Insurance; Farmland Insurance; Michigan Mutual Insurance Co.; Western Casualty & Surety Co.; State Auto Mutual Insurance Co.; Motorists Mutual Insurance Co.; American States Insurance Co.; Home Insurance Co.

For full biographical listings, see the Martindale-Hubbell Law Directory

---

LEXINGTON,* Fayette Co.

FOWLER, MEASLE & BELL, L.L.P. (AV)

Kincaid Towers, 300 West Vine Street, Suite 650, 40507-1660
Telephone: 606-252-6700
Fax: 606-255-3735

MEMBERS OF FIRM

Guy R. Colson	T. Bruce Bell
E. Patrick Moores	Elizabeth S. Feamster
James D. Ishmael, Jr.	R. Craig Reinhardt

ASSOCIATES

Susan S. Kennedy	Michael E. Liska
Barry M. Miller	Katherine J. Hornback

OF COUNSEL
Walter C. Cox, Jr.

Representative Clients: General Electric Co.; Kentucky Farm Bureau Mutual Ins. Co.; State Farm Ins. Co.; Allstate Ins. Co.; Progressive Casualty Ins. Co.; Bank One, Lexington, N.A.; Kentucky Medical Services; PNC Bank, Kentucky, Inc.

For Complete List of Firm Personnel, See General Section

For full biographical listings, see the Martindale-Hubbell Law Directory

---

GERALDS, MOLONEY & JONES (AV)

259 West Short Street, 40507
Telephone: 606-255-7946

R. P. Moloney (1902-1963)	Billy W. Sherrow
Donald P. Moloney (1921-1972)	John P. Schrader
Richard P. Moloney (1929-1972)	E. Douglas Stephan
Oscar H. Geralds, Jr.	Robert L. Swisher
Michael R. Moloney	John G. Rice
Ernest H. Jones, II	Frances Geralds Rohlfing
	Gail Luhn Pyle

Representative Clients: Allstate Insurance Co.; Nationwide Insurance Co.; State Farm Mutual Automobile Insurance Co.; State Farm Fire and Casualty Co.; Colonial Insurance Company of California.
Reference: Bank of the Bluegrass & Trust Co.

For full biographical listings, see the Martindale-Hubbell Law Directory

---

KINKEAD & COLLIER (AV)

201 West Vine Street, 40507
Telephone: 606-233-3550
Facsimile: 606-255-1965

MEMBERS OF THE FIRM

Shelby C. Kinkead, Jr.	Wayne F. Collier

For full biographical listings, see the Martindale-Hubbell Law Directory

---

LANDRUM & SHOUSE (AV)

106 West Vine Street, P.O. Box 951, 40588-0951
Telephone: 606-255-2424
Facsimile: 606-233-0308
Louisville, Kentucky Office: 400 West Market Street, Suite 1550, 40202.
Telephone: 502-589-7616.
Facsimile: 502-589-2119.

MEMBERS OF FIRM

John H. Burrus	Mark J. Hinkel
Thomas M. Cooper	Delores Hill Pregliasco
William C. Shouse	(Resident, Louisville Office)
Pierce W. Hamblin	John Garry McNeill
Mark L. Moseley	Jack E. Toliver
Leslie Patterson Vose	R. Kent Westberry
John R. Martin, Jr.	(Resident, Louisville Office)
(Resident, Louisville Office)	J. Denis Ogburn
Larry C. Deener	(Resident, Louisville Office)
Sandra Mendez Dawahare	Jane Durkin Samuel
	Douglas L. Hoots

(See Next Column)

LANDRUM & SHOUSE, *Lexington—Continued*

ASSOCIATES

Stephen D. Milner	Daniel E. Murner
Stephen R. Chappell	Courtney T. Baxter
Charles E. Christian	(Resident, Louisville Office)
Dave Whalin	Frank M. Jenkins, III
(Resident, Louisville Office)	

OF COUNSEL

Weldon Shouse

District Attorneys: CSX Transportation, Inc.
Special Trial Counsel: Ford Motor Co. and Affiliates (Eastern Kentucky); Clark Equipment Co.
Representative Clients: The Continental Insurance Cos.; U.S. Insurance Group; U.S. Fidelity & Guaranty Co.; Ohio Casualty Insurance Co.; CIGNA; Royal Insurance Cos.

For Complete List of Firm Personnel, See General Section

For full biographical listings, see the Martindale-Hubbell Law Directory

LYNN, FULKERSON AND NICHOLS (AV)

267 West Short Street, 40507
Telephone: 606-253-0523
Telefax: 606-254-2098

MEMBERS OF FIRM

Deddo G. Lynn	Calvin R. Fulkerson
Mark E. Nichols	

ASSOCIATES

Allen E. Grimes, III	Jo Alice Van Nagell
Janet L. Gawthrop	

OF COUNSEL

Edward R. Hays	Gordon W. Moss

Representative Clients: United States Fidelity & Guaranty Co.; The Travelers Insurance Co.

For full biographical listings, see the Martindale-Hubbell Law Directory

PIPER, WELLMAN & BOWERS (AV)

200 North Upper Street, 40507
Telephone: 606-231-1012
Fax: 606-231-7367
Email: pwb200@uky.campus.mci.net

MEMBERS OF FIRM

George C. Piper	Dean T. Wellman
Barbara J. Bowers	

ASSOCIATE

Johann F. Herklotz

Representative Clients: Kentucky Hospital Association Trust; Woodford Hospital; Garrard Memorial Hospital; Century American Insurance Co.; Guaranty National Insurance Co.; Hillhaven Corp.; Sisters of Charity of Nazareth Health System, Inc. d/b/a/ St. Josephs Hospital; Kentucky River Medical Center; The Reciprocal Alliance.

For full biographical listings, see the Martindale-Hubbell Law Directory

ROBERTS & SMITH (AV)

167 West Main Street Suite 200, 40507
Telephone: 606-233-1104

MEMBERS OF FIRM

Larry S. Roberts	Kenneth W. Smith

For full biographical listings, see the Martindale-Hubbell Law Directory

STOLL, KEENON & PARK, LLP (AV)

201 E. Main Street, Suite 1000, 40507-1380
Telephone: 606-231-3000
Telecopier: 606-253-1093; 606-253-1027
Frankfort, Kentucky Office: 307 Washington Street, 40601.
Telephone: 502-875-6220.
Telecopier: 502-875-6235.
Louisville, Kentucky Office: 400 West Market Street, Suite 2650, 40202-3377.
Telephone: 502-568-9100.
Telecopier: 502-568-5700.

MEMBERS OF FIRM

Leslie W. Morris II	Robert W. Kellerman
Spencer D. Noe	Eileen M. O'Brien
J. Peter Cassidy, Jr.	Perry M. Bentley

ASSOCIATES

James L. Thomerson	Todd S. Page
Palmer G. Vance, II	

Representative Clients: American International Group; CNA Insurance Co.; Commercial Union Insurance Co.; Employers Reinsurance Corp.; Fireman's Fund Insurance Co.; Government Employees Insurance Co.; Grange Mutual Casualty Co.; GRE; State Auto Mutual Insurance Co.; Westfield Cos.

(See Next Column)

For Complete List of Firm Personnel, See General Section

For full biographical listings, see the Martindale-Hubbell Law Directory

VIMONT & WILLS (AV)

Suite 300, 155 East Main Street, 40507-1317
Telephone: 606-252-2202
Telecopier: 606-259-2927

MEMBERS OF FIRM

Richard E. Vimont	Timothy C. Wills

ASSOCIATES

Barbara Booker Wills	J. Stan Lee

For full biographical listings, see the Martindale-Hubbell Law Directory

---

LONDON, Laurel Co.*

CRABTREE & GOFORTH (AV)

120 East Fourth Street, 40741-1414
Telephone: 606-878-8888
Fax: 606-878-8899

Wm. Gary Crabtree	Michael A. Goforth

Insurance Defense Clients: National Casualty Insurance Co.; Scottsdale Insurance Co.; Grange Mutual Cos.; Interstate National Insurance; Midwestern Indemnity Insurance.; Nationwide Insurance Co.; The Northbrook Co.; Preferred Risk Mutual; Midwestern Indemnity Insurance Co.; Western Insurance Cos.

For full biographical listings, see the Martindale-Hubbell Law Directory

FARMER, FARMER, KELLEY AND BROWN (AV)

502 West Fifth Street, Drawer 490, 40743
Telephone: 606-878-7640
Fax: 606-878-2364
Lexington, Kentucky Office: 121 Prosperous Place, Suite 13 B, 40509-1834.
Telephone: 606: 263-2567.
Facsimile: 606: 263-2567.

MEMBERS OF FIRM

F. Preston Farmer	Michael P. Farmer
John F. Kelley, Jr.	Martha L. Brown

ASSOCIATES

Suzanne S. Farmer	Bradford L. Breeding
Jason E. Williams	Estill D. Banks, II

Representative Clients: Bituminous Insurance Co.; State Farm Mutual Automobile Insurance Co.; State Farm Fire & Casualty Insurance; Walmart Stores; Geico; Kentucky National Insurance Co.; Century Claims; National Insurance Association; Shelter Insurance Co.; Crumb & Forester Underwriters Group.

For full biographical listings, see the Martindale-Hubbell Law Directory

HAMM, MILBY & RIDINGS (AV)

120 North Main Street, 40741
Telephone: 606-864-4126
Fax: 606-878-8144

MEMBERS OF FIRM

Robert L. Milby	Marcia Milby Ridings
	Kenneth H. Gilliam

James A. Ridings	Gregory A. Lay
	LaDonna Lynn Koebel

Representative Clients: Acceleration National; Aetna Life & Casualty Ins. Co.; All Risk Claims Service, Inc.; Allstate Insurance Co.; Alexis; American Automobile Mutual Ins.; American Bankers; American Hardware Ins. Co.; American Home Ins.; American Inter-Fidelity Exchange.

For full biographical listings, see the Martindale-Hubbell Law Directory

TAYLOR, KELLER & DUNAWAY (AV)

802 North Main Street, P.O. Box 905, 40743-0905
Telephone: 606-878-8844
Facsimile: 606-878-5547

Boyd F. Taylor	J. Warren Keller
	Bridget L. Dunaway

ASSOCIATE

Jason Richardson

OF COUNSEL

Pamela Adams Chesnut

LEGAL SUPPORT PERSONNEL

Berneda Baker (Paralegal)	Cynthia K. Taylor (Paralegal)

Representative Clients: Chubb Group; Coronet Insurance Group; ITT Hartford; Mutual of Omaha; American General Property Ins. Co.; State Farm Fire & Casualty; State Farm Mutual Automobile Insurance Co.; Lloyds of London; American Indemnity Group.

For full biographical listings, see the Martindale-Hubbell Law Directory

London—Continued

TOOMS & HOUSE (AV)

310 West Fifth Street, P.O. Box 520, 40743-0520
Telephone: 606-864-4145
FAX: 606-864-4279

MEMBERS OF FIRM

Murray L. Brown (1894-1980)   R. William Tooms
Roy E. Tooms (1917-1986)   Brian C. House

Representative Insurance Clients: State Auto Mutual Insurance Co.; Grange Mutual Casualty Co.; Kentucky Farm Bureau Mutual Insurance Co.; Canal Insurance Co.; Crawford Risk Management Services; Imperial Casualty Co.; National Union Fire Insurance Co.; Insbrok; Corporate Services, Inc.; Scottsdale Insurance Co.

For full biographical listings, see the Martindale-Hubbell Law Directory

---

LOUISVILLE,* Jefferson Co.

BENNETT, BOWMAN, TRIPLETT & VITTITOW (AV)

First Trust Centre, Suite 400 South, 200 South Fifth Street, 40202
Telephone: 502-583-5581
Fax: 502-583-9622
Owensboro, Kentucky Office: 209 West Second Street, P.O. Box 765.
Telephone: 502-683-5308.
Fax: 502-685-1797.

MEMBERS OF FIRM

John L. Bennett (1918-1988)   Robert Vic Bowers, Jr.
James G. Bowman   (Resident at Owensboro
Chester A. Vittitow, Jr.   Office)
Douglas B. Taylor   James P. Dilbeck, Jr.
Robert R. deGolian   John W. Tullis (Resident at
      Owensboro Office)

OF COUNSEL

Henry A. Triplett

Representative Clients: State Farm Mutual Automobile Insurance Co.; State Farm Fire & Casualty Co.; State Farm Life Insurance Co.; Ohio Casualty Insurance Co.; West American Insurance Co.; Ohio Security Insurance Co.; American International Group; Meridian Mutual Insurance Co.; Prudential Insurance Co.; Ranger Insurance Co.

For full biographical listings, see the Martindale-Hubbell Law Directory

---

EWEN, HILLIARD & BUSH (AV)

The Starks Building Suite 1090, 455 S. 4th Street, 40202
Telephone: 502-584-1090
Fax: 502-584-4707

MEMBERS OF FIRM

Victor W. Ewen (1924-1989)   Frank P. Hilliard
A. Campbell Ewen   John M. Bush

ASSOCIATES

Kevin P. Kinney   Mark McClure Sandmann
Robert J. Rosing   Robin Lynn Burnham

For full biographical listings, see the Martindale-Hubbell Law Directory

---

GOLDBERG & SIMPSON, P.S.C. (AV)

3000 National City Tower, 40202
Telephone: 502-589-4440
Telefax: 502-581-1344
Washington, D.C. Office: 1200 G Street, N.W. - Suite 800, 20005.
Telephone: 202-434-8968.
Telefax: 202-737-5822.

Fred M. Goldberg   William J. Hust, III
David B. Ratterman   (Not admitted in KY)
Jonathan D. Goldberg   Mary Alice Maple
James S. Goldberg   Emily L. Lawrence
Mitchell A. Charney   Douglas S. Haynes
Steven A. Goodman   Jan M. West
Edward L. Schoenbaechler   Charles H. Cassis
Cathy S. Pike   Robin Sylvester Craddock
Stephen E. Smith   John Joseph McLaughlin
Cynthia Buss Maddox   Leslie E. Huber
      Anthony J Elpers

OF COUNSEL

Ronald V. Simpson   Kenneth G. Lee (Not admitted
David A. Brill   in KY; Resident, Washington,
      D.C. Office)

Representative Clients: National City Bank; Liberty Mutual Insurance Co.; Jewish Hospital Healthcare Services, Inc.; Louisville & Jefferson County Board of Health; Providian Corp.

For full biographical listings, see the Martindale-Hubbell Law Directory

---

HUMMEL & COAN (AV)

Kentucky Home Life Building, The Seventeenth Floor, 239 South Fifth Street, 40202-3268
Telephone: 502-585-3084
Fax: 502-585-3548

OF COUNSEL

Washer Kaplan Rothschild Aberson & Miller

MEMBERS OF FIRM

Dennis J. Hummel   Marvin L. Coan

ASSOCIATE

David L. Sage II

Representative Clients: Georgia Pacific Corp.; Safeco Insurance Cos.; GRE Insurance Group; The Aetna Casualty & Surety Co.; Dr. Bizer's Vision World; Calvert Insurance Co.; Western Heritage Insurance Co.; Nobel Insurance Company.

For full biographical listings, see the Martindale-Hubbell Law Directory

---

LANDRUM & SHOUSE (AV)

400 West Market Street Suite 1550, 40202
Telephone: 502-589-7616
Facsimile: 502-589-2119
Lexington, Kentucky Office: 106 West Vine Street, P.O. Box 951.
Telephone: 606-255-2424.
Facsimile: 606-233-0308.

RESIDENT MEMBERS OF THE FIRM

John R. Martin, Jr.   R. Kent Westberry
Delores Hill Pregliasco   J. Denis Ogburn

RESIDENT ASSOCIATES

Dave Whalin   Courtney T. Baxter

For Complete List of Firm Personnel, See General Section

For full biographical listings, see the Martindale-Hubbell Law Directory

---

MACKENZIE & PEDEN, P.S.C. (AV)

650 Starks Building, 455 South Fourth Avenue, 40202-2509
Telephone: 502-589-1110
Fax: 502-589-1117
Other Louisville, Kentucky Office: 8311 Shelbyville Road.
Telephone: 502-426-6688.
Fax: 502-425-0561.

William B. Peden (Retired)   James T. Lobb
Thomas G. Mooney (1939-1991)   Valerie T. Mayer (Resident)
Wm. A. MacKenzie (Resident)   Edward H. Bartenstein
John G. Crutchfield   Judith B. Hoge
Wayne J. Carroll   Sidney L. Hymson
James C. Hickey   Lee Ann Risner
B. Carlton Neat, III   Charles T. Baxter
Robert W. Dickey   John Patrick Hamm
William B. Bardenwerper
   (Resident)

OF COUNSEL

Walker C. Cunningham, Jr.   Robert W. Riley (Resident)
Lawrence J. Phillips   Stephen A. Schwager

Representative Clients: Allstate Insurance Co.; American States Insurance Co.; The Fund Insurance Companies; State Automobile Mutual Insurance Co..

For full biographical listings, see the Martindale-Hubbell Law Directory

---

MIDDLETON & REUTLINGER, P.S.C. (AV)

2500 Brown and Williamson Tower, 40202-3410
Telephone: 502-584-1135
Fax: 502-561-0442
New Albany, Indiana Office: 2623 Charlestown Road, 47150.
Telephone: 812-944-7215.

O. Grant Bruton   D. Randall Gibson
Kenneth S. Handmaker   G. Kennedy Hall, Jr.
Charles G. Middleton, III   Mark S. Fenzel
Charles D. Greenwell   Kathiejane Oehler
John W. Bilby   William Jay Hunter, Jr.
Timothy P. O'Mara   James E. Milliman
Stewart L. Prather   David J. Kellerman
      Julie A. Gregory

Amy B. Berge   Augustus S. Herbert
Dennis D. Murrell   Dana L. Lucas

Counsel for: Chevron USA; Logan Aluminum, Inc.; Louisville Gas & Electric Co.; MCI Telecommunications Corp.; Metropolitan Life Insurance Co.; Kosmos Cement Co.; Porcelain Metal Corp.; The Home Insurance Co.; The Kroger Co.; Demars Haka Development, Inc.

For Complete List of Firm Personnel, See General Section

For full biographical listings, see the Martindale-Hubbell Law Directory

Louisville—Continued

O'BRYAN, BROWN & TONER (AV)

Suite 1500 Starks Building, 40202
Telephone: 502-585-4700
Fax: 502-585-4703
Email: OBTLAW@aol.com

MEMBERS OF FIRM

Donald K. Brown, Jr.	David Scott Strite
Christopher P. O'Bryan	Andrew N. Clooney
Gerald R. Toner	Cathleen Charters Palmer
John L. Dotson	Clay Edwards
Emily A. Hoffman	Eric A. Paine
James P. Grohmann	Beth H. McMasters

OF COUNSEL

Joseph C. O'Bryan

For full biographical listings, see the Martindale-Hubbell Law Directory

PEDLEY, ZIELKE & GORDINIER (AV)

1150 Starks Building, 455 South Fourth Avenue, 40202
Telephone: 502-589-4600
Fax: 502-584-0422

MEMBERS OF FIRM

Lawrence L. Pedley	William W. Stodghill
Laurence J. Zielke	P. Stephen Gordinier
John K. Gordinier	Schuyler J. Olt

Frank G. Simpson, III

OF COUNSEL

Caroline George Meena

ASSOCIATE

John H. Dwyer, Jr.

For full biographical listings, see the Martindale-Hubbell Law Directory

SEGAL AND SHANKS (AV)

327 Guthrie Green, 40202
Telephone: 502-583-3455
Fax: 502-583-3039
Jeffersonville, Indiana Office: 425 East 7th Street.
Telephone: 812-288-7107.

MEMBERS OF FIRM

Richard G. Segal	Perry Adanick
C. A. Dudley Shanks	Eileen M. Walsh
Fred Stair	Charles L. Koby

ASSOCIATES

Lisa M. Patrick	Russell D. Ford

For full biographical listings, see the Martindale-Hubbell Law Directory

TILFORD, DOBBINS, ALEXANDER, BUCKAWAY & BLACK (AV)

Suite 1400, One Riverfront Plaza, 40202
Telephone: 502-584-6137

MEMBERS OF FIRM

Charles W. Dobbins (1916-1992)	Charles W. Dobbins, Jr.
Henry J. Tilford (1880-1968)	Terrell L. Black
George S. Wetherby (1905-1954)	Mark Wesley Dobbins
Lawrence W. Wetherby (1908-1994)	Stuart E. Alexander, III
	John M. Nader
John T. Metcalf (1890-1974)	John A. Wilmes
Stuart E. Alexander	Sandra F. Keene
William A. Buckaway, Jr.	Thomas J.B. Hurst

David Dwight Cobb, Jr.

OF COUNSEL

Randolph Noe	Carolyn K. Balleisen

LEGAL SUPPORT PERSONNEL

Jennifer Olvey

For full biographical listings, see the Martindale-Hubbell Law Directory

WILLIAMS & WAGONER (AV)

101 Bullitt Lane, Oxmoor Place, 40222
Telephone: 502-429-5700
Fax: 502-429-5720
Lexington, Kentucky Office: Lexington Financial Center, 250 West Main Street, Suite 710.
Telephone: 606-252-3669.
Telecopier: 606-252-3487.

MEMBERS OF FIRM

Philip Williams	C. Thomas Hectus
James R. Wagoner	L. J. (Todd) Hollenbach, IV
W. Kenneth Nevitt	Dennis L. Mattingly
Carole M. Pearlman	Carla Foreman Dallas

(See Next Column)

ASSOCIATES

Robert M. Beal	R. Scott Summers
R. Thad Keal	(Resident, Lexington Office)
David Scott Dupps	Sun S. Choy
James M. Burd	Craig Louis Johnson
Robert A. Button, Jr.	Jeffrey T. Sampson
M. Kathryn Manis	J. Key Schoen
(Resident, Lexington Office)	Annette C. Karem
Mary E. Schaffner	Jane Rice Williams
George T. T. Kitchen III	(Resident, Lexington Office)

For full biographical listings, see the Martindale-Hubbell Law Directory

WOODWARD, HOBSON & FULTON (AV)

2500 National City Tower, 101 South Fifth Street, 40202
Telephone: 502-581-8000
Fax: 502-581-8111
Lexington, Kentucky Office: PNC Bank Plaza, 200 West Vine Street, Suite 500.
Telephone: 606-244-7100.
Telecopier: 606-244-7111.
New Albany, Indiana Office: 611 East Spring Street, P.O. Box 288.
Telephone: 812-941-1800.
Telecopier: 812-941-1855.

MEMBERS OF FIRM

Harry K. Herren	Gregory L. Smith
Richard H. C. Clay	Elizabeth Ullmer Mendel

ASSOCIATES

Benjamin Cowgill, Jr. (Resident, Lexington, Kentucky Office)	Jill F. Lowenbraun
	Rebecca L. Didat
Christy Lee Hendricks	R. Brian Evans

Catherine S. Astorino

Representative Clients: America Home Insurance Co.; Fireman's Fund Insurance Co.; Liberty Mutual Insurance Co.; Nationwide Insurance Co., Inc.; Prudential Property and Casualty Co.; Royal Insurance Co.; Underwriters at Lloyd's London; CNA Insurance Co.; CIGNA Corp.; American International Group.

For Complete List of Firm Personnel, See General Section

For full biographical listings, see the Martindale-Hubbell Law Directory

MOREHEAD,* Rowan Co.

DEHNER & ELLIS (AV)

206 East Main Street, 40351
Telephone: 606-783-1504
FAX: 606-784-2744

Truman L. Dehner	John J. Ellis

For full biographical listings, see the Martindale-Hubbell Law Directory

OWENSBORO,* Daviess Co.

WILSON, JOHNSON & PRESSER (AV)

418 West Third Street, 42301
Telephone: 502-926-1717
Fax: 502-926-1722

MEMBERS OF FIRM

R. Allen Wilson	E. Louis Johnson

Ronald L. Presser

For full biographical listings, see the Martindale-Hubbell Law Directory

PAINTSVILLE,* Johnson Co.

WELLS, PORTER, SCHMITT & JONES (AV)

327 Main Street, 41240
Telephone: 606-789-3747; 789-3749; 789-3775
Fax: 606-789-3790

MEMBERS OF FIRM

Michael J. Schmitt	Donald L. Jones

Sandra Spurgeon

ASSOCIATES

Kimberly E. Colley	Darrin W. Banks

LEGAL SUPPORT PERSONNEL

Melinda A. Johnson (Paralegal)	Natalie B. Caudill (Paralegal)

Representative Clients: Kentucky Farm Bureau; Allstate; Grange; CNA; Fireman's Fund; Northbrook; Continental Insurance; CIGNA; Ohio Casualty; Tennessee Farmers Insurance.

For Complete List of Firm Personnel, See General Section

For full biographical listings, see the Martindale-Hubbell Law Directory

PIKEVILLE,* Pike Co.

STRATTON, MAY, HAYS & HOGG, PSC (AV)

232 Second Street Ward Building, P.O. Box 851, 41502
Telephone: 606-437-7300
Fax: 606-437-7569
Whitesburg, Kentucky Office: By-Pass Highway 15. 41858.
Telephone: 606-633-9922.

Henry D. Stratton (1925-1989)	Stephen L. Hogg
Marrs Allen May	H. Edward Maddox
John D. Hays	F. Byrd Hogg (Resident,
David C. Stratton	Whitesburg, Kentucky Office)

LEGAL SUPPORT PERSONNEL
PARALEGALS

Carol Rowe Potter	Rebecca Branham
(Real Estate Paralegal)	(Litigation Paralegal)

Representative Clients: Commercial Union Insurance Co.; The Travelers Insurance Co.; Universal Underwriters Insurance Co.; Bituminous Casualty Co.; Kentucky National Insurance Co.; Scottsdale Insurance Co.; Massachusetts Mutual Insurance Co.; Farmland Insurance Co., MSI Insurance; Lawyers Title Insurance Corp.

For full biographical listings, see the Martindale-Hubbell Law Directory

PRESTONSBURG,* Floyd Co.

KAZEE, KINNER & CHAFIN (AV)

119 East Court Street, P.O. Box 700, 41653
Telephone: 606-886-2361; 886-2362
FAX: 606-886-9603
Email: dbkazee@pcc-uky.campus.mci.net
Paintsville, Kentucky Office: Family Federal Building, Suite 202, P.O. Box 1275.
Telephone: 606-789-3059.

MEMBERS OF FIRM

D. B. Kazee	P. Franklin Heaberlin
Mitchell D. Kinner	Robert J. Patton
John T. Chafin	William C. Mullins

Representative Clients: Maryland Casualty Co.; Old Republic Insurance Co.; St. Paul Insurance Cos.; Bituminous Casualty Corp.; Commercial Union Assurance Co.; Kentucky Central Insurance Cos.; Capital Enterprise Insurance Group; State Automobile Mutual Insurance Co.; Reliance Insurance Co.; Scottsdale Insurance Co.

For full biographical listings, see the Martindale-Hubbell Law Directory

SOMERSET,* Pulaski Co.

ADAMS & ADAMS (AV)

35 Public Square, P.O. Box 35, 42502-0035
Telephone: 606-679-6741; 678-4916
Fax: 606-679-3691

MEMBERS OF FIRM

Charles C. Adams	Norma B. Adams

ASSOCIATE

Jane Adams Venters

Counsel for: First and Farmers Bank of Somerset, Inc.; Aluminum Wheel Technology, Inc.
Representative Clients: Community Trust Bank, FSB; Aluminum Wheel Technology, Inc.; Food Fair Cos.; Kentucky Farm Bureau Mutual Insurance Cos.; Cumberland Valley Communications; Shamrock Coal Co.; Railum, Inc.; Hartco Flooring Co.

For full biographical listings, see the Martindale-Hubbell Law Directory

VANCEBURG,* Lewis Co.

STANLEY AND BERTRAM, P.S.C. (AV)

P.O. Box 40, 41179-0040
Telephone: 606-796-3024; 796-3025
Fax: 606-796-2113

Avery L. Stanley	Thomas M. Bertram, II
	Anita Esham Stanley

A list of Representative Clients will be furnished upon request.

For full biographical listings, see the Martindale-Hubbell Law Directory

LOUISIANA

ALEXANDRIA,* Rapides Parish

McLURE, PICKELS AND REICHMAN (AV)

901 Sixth Street, P.O. Box 1525, 71309-1525
Telephone: 318-445-5317
Fax: 318-442-3009

(See Next Column)

MEMBERS OF FIRM

Thomas C. McLure, Jr.	John G. McLure
(1915-1984)	John C. Pickels
James B. Reichman	

ASSOCIATES

Bonita K. Preuett	Ann E. Lowrey

Representative Clients: State Farm Mutual Automobile Insurance Company; USAA Group; State Farm Fire and Casualty Co.

For full biographical listings, see the Martindale-Hubbell Law Directory

BATON ROUGE,* East Baton Rouge Parish

BELL, COOPER & HYMAN, A PROFESSIONAL LAW CORPORATION (AV)

4734 Jamestown Avenue, P.O. Box 80177, 70898
Telephone: 504-927-0161
Fax: 504-927-6007

David S. Bell	Michael L. Hyman
Arthur R. Cooper	Janice M. Church
	Sandra Sheridan Rester

Reference: Union Planters Bank.

For full biographical listings, see the Martindale-Hubbell Law Directory

FUNDERBURK & ANDREWS (AV)

329 St. Ferdinand Street, 70802
Telephone: 504-387-2200
Fax: 504-383-0142

MEMBERS OF FIRM

Robert C. Funderburk, Jr.	David T. Butler, Jr.
Arthur H. Andrews	Scott H. Frugé

For full biographical listings, see the Martindale-Hubbell Law Directory

GUGLIELMO, MARKS, SCHUTTE, TERHOEVE & LOVE (AV)

(A Registered Limited Liability Partnership)
320 Somerulos Street, P.O. Box 3177, 70821-3177
Telephone: 504-387-6966
Fax: 504-387-8338

Carey J. Guglielmo	Glen Scott Love
Paul Marks, Jr.	Dawn T. Trabeau-Mire
Charles A. Schutte, Jr.	Joseph W. Mengis
Henry G. Terhoeve	Kevin P. Landreneau

Representative Clients: Liberty Mutual Insurance Co.; Commercial Union Insurance Co.; Louisiana Insurance Guarantee Association; State Farm Mutual Automobile Insurance Co.; Allstate Insurance Co.; Aetna Life & Casualty Co.; Prudential Property & Casualty Co.

For full biographical listings, see the Martindale-Hubbell Law Directory

LAW OFFICES OF ROBERT D. HOOVER, P.L.C. (AV)

533 Europe Street, P.O. Box 4248, 70821-4248
Telephone: 504-381-9386
Fax: 504-383-9147

Robert D. Hoover

For full biographical listings, see the Martindale-Hubbell Law Directory

KLEINPETER & KLEINPETER (AV)

1680 South Lobdell Avenue, Suite E, P.O. Box 66443, 70896
Telephone: 504-926-5093
Telecopier: 5048-926-5318

MEMBERS OF FIRM

Robert L. Kleinpeter	R. Loren Kleinpeter

Representative Clients: Argonaut Insurance Co.; American Indemnity Co.; Allstate Insurance Co.; Consolidated American Inc. Co.; South Carolina Insurance Co.; TransAmerica Insurance Group; St. Paul Fire & Marine Insurance Co.; Scottsdale Insurance Co.; Fireman's Fund Insurance Co.; Western Heritage Insurance Co.

For full biographical listings, see the Martindale-Hubbell Law Directory

LANE, FERTITTA, LANE, JANNEY & THOMAS (AV)

435 Louisiana Avenue, P.O. Box 3335, 70821
Telephone: 504-387-0241
Fax: 504-387-1238

MEMBERS OF FIRM

Horace C. Lane (1921-1989)	Thomas A. Lane
Frank A. Fertitta	William F. Janney
	Richard S. Thomas

ASSOCIATE

Margaret T. Lane

Representative Clients: State Farm Mutual Automobile Insurance Co.; State Farm Fire & Casualty Co.; United States Fidelity & Guaranty Co.; Aetna Casualty & Surety Co.; Employers Liability Assurance Corp., Ltd.; Allstate

(See Next Column)

LANE, FERTITTA, LANE, JANNEY & THOMAS, *Baton Rouge—Continued*

Insurance Co.; St. Paul Fire and Marine Insurance Co.; The Medical Protective Co.; Safeco Insurance Co. of America; Horace Mann Insurance Co.

For full biographical listings, see the Martindale-Hubbell Law Directory

NAVRATIL, HARDY & BOURGEOIS (AV)

445 North Boulevard, Suite 800, P.O. Box 3551, 70821-3551
Telephone: 504-379-7300
Fax: 504-379-7316

MEMBERS OF FIRM

Boris F. Navratil   David H. Hardy
André G. Bourgeois

ASSOCIATE

Alan P. McGlynn

OF COUNSEL

Robert L. Boese   Johnnie L. Matthews
George Sheram King

For full biographical listings, see the Martindale-Hubbell Law Directory

SEALE, SMITH, ZUBER & BARNETTE (AV)

Two United Plaza, Suite 200, 8550 United Plaza Boulevard, 70809
Telephone: 504-924-1600
Telecopier: 504-924-6100

Armbrust Gordon Seale (1913-1989)	Ronald A. Seale
Robert W. Smith (1922-1989)	Brent E. Kinchen
Donald S. Zuber	Charles K. Watts
Kenneth E. Barnette	Myron A. Walker, Jr.
William C. Kaufman III	Daniel A. Reed
John W. L. Swanner	William C. Rowe, Jr.
James H. Morgan III	Lawrence R. Anderson, Jr.
	Catherine S. Nobile

ASSOCIATES

Richard T. Reed   Anthony J. Russo, Jr.
Barbara G. Chatelain   Gregory D. Polozola

Representative Clients: Farmers Insurance Group; St. Paul Fire and Marine Insurance Company; United Services Automobile Association; General Motors Acceptance Corporation.
Reference: City National Bank, Baton Rouge, Louisiana.

For full biographical listings, see the Martindale-Hubbell Law Directory

SHOCKEY & ZIOBER, A PROFESSIONAL LAW CORPORATION (AV)

Suite 3-A, 5551 Corporate Boulevard, P.O. Box 80286, 70898-0286
Telephone: 504-929-8929
Telecopier: 504-928-7694

John David Ziober   William C. Shockey

Emily Phillips Ziober   Jennifer R. Treadway Morris
Douglas J. Cochran   James E. Moore, Jr.

For full biographical listings, see the Martindale-Hubbell Law Directory

O'NEAL WALSH & ASSOCIATES (AV)

501 Louisiana Avenue, 70802
Telephone: 504-383-8649
FAX: 504-344-1687
Mailing Address: P.O. Box 3157, Baton Rouge, Louisiana, 70821-3157

David M. Lefeve   Matthew W. Bailey
W. Paul Wilkins   J. Clayton Culotta
Joseph H. Garbarino

For full biographical listings, see the Martindale-Hubbell Law Directory

DE RIDDER,* Beauregard Parish

HALL, LESTAGE & LANDRENEAU (AV)

205 Second Street, P.O. Box 880, 70634
Telephone: 318-463-8692
Fax: 318-463-2272

MEMBERS OF FIRM

William E. Hall, Jr.   David R. Lestage
H. O. Lestage, III   F. Steve Landreneau
Brian S. Lestage

Representative Clients: Boise Cascade Corp.; City Savings & Trust Co.; Crosby Land Resources; Firemen's Fund-American Cos.; Great American Insurance Co.; The Hartford Insurance Group; Pacific Marine Insurance Co.; State Farm Mutual Automobile Insurance Co.; The Travelers Insurance Co.; United States Fidelity & Guaranty Co.

For full biographical listings, see the Martindale-Hubbell Law Directory

EUNICE, St. Landry Parish

I. JACKSON BURSON, JR. A PROFESSIONAL LAW CORPORATION (AV)

220 North Second Street, P.O. Box 985, 70535
Telephone: 318-457-1227
Fax: 318-457-8860

I. Jackson Burson, Jr.

For full biographical listings, see the Martindale-Hubbell Law Directory

HOUMA,* Terrebonne Parish

HENDERSON, HANEMANN & MORRIS, A PROFESSIONAL LAW CORPORATION (AV)

300 Lafayette Street, 70360
Telephone: 504-868-2081
New Orleans: 504-581-1434
Telecopier: 504-868-0080

Philip E. Henderson	Joseph A. Reilly, Jr.
Charles Hanemann	J. René Williams
Robert L. Morris (1940-1986)	Kevin J. Webb
J. Mark Graham	Barry J. Boudreaux

Representative Clients: Aetna Casualty & Surety Co.; Travelers Insurance Companies; Gray & Company, Inc.; Union Oil Company of California; Tenneco, Inc.; Minnesota Mining and Manufacturing Co.

For full biographical listings, see the Martindale-Hubbell Law Directory

McMAHON & McCOLLAM (AV)

628 Wood Street, P.O. Box 1548, 70361-1548
Telephone: 504-868-0104
Fax: 504-851-3069

MEMBERS OF FIRM

Philip J. McMahon   Edmund McCollam

ASSOCIATE

Carl T. Conrad

Representative Clients: Traveler's Insurance Co.; Shell Oil Co.; Gulf Oil Co.; Sooner Pipe and Supply Co.; Terrebonne Lumber and Concrete Co., Inc.; Burns Construction Co.; Perque Floor Covering, Inc.; Texaco, Inc.; Contran Realty Corp.; Tube-Alloy Corp.

For full biographical listings, see the Martindale-Hubbell Law Directory

LAFAYETTE,* Lafayette Parish

ALLEN & GOOCH (AV)

1015 St. John Street, P.O. Drawer 3768, 70502-3768
Telephone: 318-233-5056
Telecopier: 318-267-1343

MEMBERS OF FIRM

Joel E. Gooch	James H. Gibson
St. Paul Bourgeois, IV	Emile Joseph, Jr.
Arthur I. Robison	Neil G. Vincent
Randall K. Theunissen	Nora M. Stelly
Frank A. Flynn	Paul J. McMahon, III
Clay Morgan Allen	Michael E. Parker
William H. Parker, III	Blaise M. Sonnier
Raymond C. Jackson, III	Troy A. Broussard
John H. Hughes	Ben D. Davis
Charles M. Kreamer	

Approved Attorneys/Agents for: United General Title Insurance Co.; Lawyers Title Insurance Corp.
Representative Clients: Albertson's Inc.; Alcon Laboratories, Inc.; Alexis; Allstate Insurance Co.; American Continental Insurance Co.; American Excel Corp.; American Hardware Mutual Insurance Co.; American International Adjustment Co.

For full biographical listings, see the Martindale-Hubbell Law Directory

DAVIDSON, MEAUX, SONNIER, McELLIGOTT & SWIFT (AV)

810 South Buchanan Street, P.O. Drawer 2908, 70502
Telephone: 318-237-1660
Fax: 318-237-3676

MEMBERS OF FIRM

James J. Davidson, Jr. (1904-1990)	John E. McElligott, Jr.
V. Farley Sonnier (1942-1988)	John G. Swift
Richard C. Meaux, Sr.	Jeffrey A. Rhoades
James J. Davidson, III	Philip A. Fontenot
Theodore G. Edwards, IV	Kyle L. Gideon

ASSOCIATES

Jhan C. Boudreaux Beaullieu   Mark C. Andrus

General Counsel: Southwest Louisiana Electric Membership Corp., Inc.; Macro Oil Co., Inc.; Dwight W. Andrus Insurance Agency; Lafayette Airport Commission.

(See Next Column)

DAVIDSON, MEAUX, SONNIER, McELLIGOTT & SWIFT—*Continued*

Local Counsel: Southern Pacific Transportation Co.
Representative Clients: Highlands Insurance Co.; Wal-Mart Stores, Inc.; USAA.

For Complete List of Firm Personnel, See General Section

For full biographical listings, see the Martindale-Hubbell Law Directory

HILL & BEYER, A PROFESSIONAL LAW CORPORATION (AV)

101 LaRue France, Suite 502, P.O. Box 53006, 70505-3006
Telephone: 318-232-9733
Fax: 1-318-237-2566

John K. Hill, Jr.	Eugene P. Matherne (1962-1996)
Bret C. Beyer	Robert B. Purser
David R. Rabalais	Erin J. Sherburne
Marianna Broussard	

For full biographical listings, see the Martindale-Hubbell Law Directory

JEANSONNE & REMONDET, L.L.C. (AV)

200 West Congress Street, Suite 1100, P.O. Box 91530, 70509
Telephone: 318-237-4370
Facsimile: 318-235-2011

John A. Jeansonne, Jr.	Michael J. Remondet, Jr.

ASSOCIATES

G. Andrew Veazey	Lisa C. McCowen
George R. Knox	

LEGAL SUPPORT PERSONNEL

Theresa G. Fuselier (Paralegal)

For full biographical listings, see the Martindale-Hubbell Law Directory

JUDICE & ADLEY, A PROFESSIONAL LAW CORPORATION (AV)

926 Coolidge Boulevard, Drawer 51769, 70505
Telephone: 318-235-2405
Fax: 318-235-0965

Marc W. Judice	Katherine A. Pavy
Michael W. Adley	Deborah DeoGracias Trahan
James J. Hautot, Jr.	William Scott Judice

Representative Clients: American International Cos.; Chubb Group; Electric Mutual Insurance Co.; Evanston Insurance Co.; First Horizon Insurance Co.; First State Insurance Co.; General Electric Co.; The Hartford Group; Highlands Insurance Co.; Insurance Company of North America.

For full biographical listings, see the Martindale-Hubbell Law Directory

THE JUNEAU FIRM A PROFESSIONAL LAW CORPORATION (AV)

The Harding Center, 1018 Harding Street Suite 202, 70503
Telephone: 318-269-0052
Facsimile: 318-269-0061
Mailing Address: P.O. Drawer 51268, Lafayette, Louisiana, 70505-1268

Patrick A. Juneau	Barry L. Domingue
Michael J. Juneau	Thomas R. Juneau
Sue Nations	

For full biographical listings, see the Martindale-Hubbell Law Directory

LABORDE & NEUNER (AV)

A Partnership of Professional Corporations
One Petroleum Center, 1001 West Pinhook Road Suite 200, P.O. Drawer 52828, 70505-2828
Telephone: 318-237-7000
Telecopier: 318-233-9450

MEMBERS OF FIRM

C.E. Laborde, Jr. (1913-1983)	Louis Simon II (P.C.)
Cliffe E. Laborde III (P.C.)	Dean Anderson Cole (P.C.)
Frank X. Neuner, Jr. (P.C.)	Ben L. Mayeaux (P.C.)
James L. Pate (P.C.)	Susan Stagg Robinson (P.C.)
Robert E. Torian (P.C.)	

ASSOCIATES

James D. Hollier	Henry H. LeBas
Melissa L. Theriot	Kenneth W. Jones, Jr.

OF COUNSEL

C. Michael Hill	Edwin L. Lafargue

Representative Clients: Cargill, Inc.; Certain Underwriters at Lloyds; Chevron U.S.A., Inc.; Cigna/INA; CNA Insurance Companies; Dean Witter Reynolds, Inc.; Delmar Systems, Inc.; Diamond Offshore Drilling Co.; Employers Reinsurance Corp.; Executive Risk Consultants, Inc.

For full biographical listings, see the Martindale-Hubbell Law Directory

ONEBANE, BERNARD, TORIAN, DIAZ, McNAMARA & ABELL (AV)

Suite 600, Versailles Centre, 102 Versailles Boulevard, P.O. Box 3507, 70502
Telephone: 318-237-2660
Telecopier: 318-266-1232
Cable Address: "Ondob"
Telex: 311283
Email: info@onebane.com

Joseph Onebane (1917-1987)	Joseph L. Lemoine, Jr.
John G. Torian, II (1936-1991)	Mark L. Riley
James E. Diaz	Graham N. Smith
Timothy J. McNamara	Gordon T. Whitman
Edward C. Abell, Jr.	Gary P. Kraus
Lawrence L. Lewis, III	Richard J. Petre, Jr.
Robert M. Mahony	Thomas G. Smart
Daniel G. Fournerat	Roger E. Ishee
Douglas W. Truxillo	John W. Penny, Jr.
Randall C. Songy	John A. Keller
Michael G. Durand	Jennifer McDaniel Kleinpeter
Greg Guidry	Steven C. Lanza

Joel P. Babineaux	Charles M. Gordon, Jr.
Ted M. Anthony	Brent G. Sonnier
Carolyn Trahan Bertrand	John D. Brouillette
Alison M. Brumley	Cristie L. Gautreaux
Craig A. Davis	Elise Mayers Bouchner
Jesse D. Lambert	(Not admitted in LA)
Cary B. Bryson	

Representative Clients: Commercial Union Insurance Co.; Enron Corp.; First National Bank of Lafayette; Flores & Rucks, Inc.; Highlands Insurance Co.; Marathon Oil Co.; Pizza Hut, Inc.; Schering-Plough Corp.; Tenneco, Inc.; Whitney National Bank.

For full biographical listings, see the Martindale-Hubbell Law Directory

PREIS KRAFT & ROY, A PROFESSIONAL LAW CORPORATION (AV)

Suite 400, Versailles Centré, 102 Versailles Boulevard, P.O. Drawer 94-C, 70509
Telephone: 318-237-6062
Fax: 318-237-9129
New Orleans, Louisiana Office: Pan American Life Center, 601 Poydras Street, Suite 2582.
Telephone: 504-581-6062.
Fax: 504-581-4862.

Edwin G. Preis, Jr.	Charles A. Mouton
Ralph E. Kraft	Kay A. Theunissen
L. Lane Roy	Jennifer E. Beyer
Ward Lafleur	George D. Ernest, III
F. Douglas Gatz, Jr.	Richard J. Hymel

Christopher Shannon Hardy	Timothy W. Basden
Wesley Elmer	Earl F. Sundmaker, III
Marc C. Greco	Jennifer Smith Lee
G. Edward Williams, Jr.	Anita L. Wolverton
Macy M. Hamm	

Approved Counsel for: American Gulf Group; American International Group; American Oilfield Divers, Inc.; American P & I Club; American United Life Insurance Company; Association of Diving Contractors, Inc.; Assuranceforeningen Gard; Assuranceforeningen Skuld, Automation Communication Engineering Corporation; Cal Dive International, Inc.; CBI Industries, Inc.

For full biographical listings, see the Martindale-Hubbell Law Directory

VOORHIES & LABBÉ, A PROFESSIONAL LAW CORPORATION (AV)

Fourth Floor, Acadiana National Bank Building, 700 St. John Street, P.O. Box 3527, 70502
Telephone: 318-232-9700
Telecopier: 318-235-4943

Bennett J. Voorhies (1901-1970)	John C. Jones
Donald Labbé (1900-1966)	Robert M. Francez
D. Mark Bienvenu (1931-1991)	Robert M. Kallam
H. Edwin McGlasson, Jr.	Elizabeth L. Guglielmo
W. Gerald Gaudet	Samuel R. Aucoin
Richard D. Chappuis, Jr.	James Allen Lochridge, Jr.
William M. Bass	Mary McCrory Hamilton
Robert A. Lecky	Bradley Joseph Haight
John N. Chappuis	Simone Chachere Dupre
Robert L. Ellender	George J. Armbruster, III
Cyd Sheree Page	Bradley J. Schlotterer

OF COUNSEL

John W. Hutchison

Representative Clients: Adams & Porter Associates; Aetna Casualty & Surety Insurance Co.; AIG Aviation, Inc.; American Home Assurance Co.; AMICA Mutual Insurance Co.; Appalachian Insurance Co.; Audubon/AIG

(See Next Column)

VOORHIES & LABBÉ A PROFESSIONAL LAW CORPORATION, *Lafayette*—
Continued

Insurance Co.; Aviation Office of America; Bellefonte Insurance Co.; Chubb
Group of Insurance Co. Co.

For full biographical listings, see the Martindale-Hubbell Law Directory

LAKE CHARLES,* Calcasieu Parish

BERGSTEDT & MOUNT (AV)

Second Floor, Magnolia Life Building, P.O. Drawer 3004, 70602-3004
Telephone: 318-433-3004
Facsimile: 318-433-8080

MEMBERS OF FIRM

Thomas M. Bergstedt	Benjamin W. Mount

ASSOCIATES

Van C. Seneca	Gregory P. Marceaux
Billy E. Loftin, Jr.	

OF COUNSEL

Charles S. Ware

Representative Clients: Armstrong World Industries; Ashland Oil Co.;
CIGNA Property & Casualty Companies; Homequity; Lake Area Medical
Center; Leach Company; Olin Corporation; Terra Corporation; Town of
Iowa; R. D. Werner Company.

For full biographical listings, see the Martindale-Hubbell Law Directory

THE CARMOUCHE LAW FIRM A PROFESSIONAL CORPORATION (AV)

Bank One Tower, 901 Lakeshore Drive, Suite 900, P.O. Drawer
2001, 70601-5270
Telephone: 318-433-0355
Telecopier: 318-433-1274
Email: clf@carmouche.com

David R. Frohn	Scott J. Pias
Terry Thibodeaux	

Elizabeth B. Hollins	Robin A. Anderson

For full biographical listings, see the Martindale-Hubbell Law Directory

JONES, TÊTE, NOLEN, HANCHEY, SWIFT, SPEARS & FONTI, L.L.P. (AV)

First Federal Building, P.O. Box 910, 70602
Telephone: 318-439-8315
Telefax: 436-5606; 433-5536

MEMBERS OF FIRM

Sam H. Jones (1897-1978)	Kenneth R. Spears
William R. Tête	Edward J. Fonti
William M. Nolen	Charles N. Harper
James C. Hanchey	Gregory W. Belfour
Carl H. Hanchey	Robert J. Tête
William B. Swift	Yul D. Lorio

OF COUNSEL

John A. Patin	Edward D. Myrick

ASSOCIATE

Lilynn A. Cutrer

Representative Clients: CIGNA Property and Casualty Companies; ITT
Hartford; Life Insurance Company of the Southwest; State and County Mutual Fire Insurance Company; Federated Rural Electric Insurance Corp.

For full biographical listings, see the Martindale-Hubbell Law Directory

PLAUCHÉ SMITH & NIESET, A PROFESSIONAL LAW CORPORATION (AV)

1123 Pithon Street, P.O. Drawer 1705, 70602
Telephone: 318-436-0522
Facsimile: 318-436-9637

S. W. Plauché (1889-1952)	Jeffrey M. Cole
S. W. Plauché, Jr. (1915-1966)	Andrew R. Johnson, IV
A. Lane Plauché	Charles V. Musso, Jr.
Allen L. Smith, Jr.	Christopher P. Ieyoub
James R. Nieset	H. David Vaughan, II
Frank M. Walker, Jr.	Joseph R. Pousson, Jr.
Michael J. McNulty, III	Rebecca S. Young

Representative Clients: CIGNA; CNA Insurance Cos.; Commercial Union
Insurance Cos.; Crum & Forster; General Motors Corp.; Reliance Insurance
Cos.; Royal Insurance Group; State Farm; U.S. Insurance Group.

For full biographical listings, see the Martindale-Hubbell Law Directory

MANDEVILLE, St. Tammany Parish

BAILEY & DWYER (AV)

600 Mariner's Plaza, Suite 607, 70448
Telephone: 504-674-1105
Fax: 504-674-1966
Metairie Area Telephone: 504-833-8241
Fax: 504-837-4534

MEMBERS OF FIRM

B. Ralph Bailey	Frederick H. N. Dwyer
	Scott O. Gaspard

For full biographical listings, see the Martindale-Hubbell Law Directory

METAIRIE, Jefferson Parish

HAILEY, MCNAMARA, HALL, LARMANN & PAPALE, L.L.P. (AV)

A Partnership including Law Corporations
Suite 1400, One Galleria Boulevard, P.O. Box 8288, 70011
Telephone: 504-836-6500
Fax: 504-836-6565

MEMBERS OF FIRM

James W. Hailey, Jr., (P.L.C.)	Michael J. Vondenstein
Henry D. McNamara, Jr., (P.L.C.)	David K. Persons
W. Marvin Hall (P.L.C.)	Dominic J. Ovella
Antonio E. Papale, Jr., (P.L.C.)	C. Kelly Lightfoot
Laurence E. Larmann (P.L.C.)	John T. Culotta (P.L.C.)
Michael P. Mentz	John E. Unsworth, Jr.
Richard T. Simmons, Jr.,(P.L.C.)	Julie DiFulco Robles
	Claude A. Greco

ASSOCIATES

William R. Seay, Jr.	Barbara E. Bourdonnay
Cyril B. Burck, Jr.	Kathryn T. Wiedorn
Valerie T. Schexnayder	Joseph S. Spilman, III
W. Evan Plauche	Caroline D. Ibos
Kurt D. Engelhardt	Robert D. Ford
W. Glenn Burns	David C. Fawley
James W. Hailey, III	Sharon Yarasavich Piper
Ivan A. Orihuela	Lynnette Hall-Lewis
Frederic Theodore Le Clercq (Not admitted in LA)	

Representative Clients: Certain Underwriters at Lloyds of London; Diamond
Offshore Drilling Inc.; First American Title Insurance Company; The Flintkote Co.; Litton Industries; Lockheed Martin Corporation; Rheem Manufacturing Co.; State Farm Fire & Casualty Co.; Textron, Inc; Travelers Companies.

For full biographical listings, see the Martindale-Hubbell Law Directory

JUGE, NAPOLITANO, LEYVA & GUILBEAU (AV)

3838 North Causeway Boulevard Suite 2500, 70002-1767
Telephone: 504-831-7270
Fax: 504-831-7284
Baton Rouge Office: 9613 Interline Avenue, Suite C.
Telephone: 504-928-DFND.

Denis Paul Juge	Teresa C. Leyva
Jeffrey C. Napolitano	Joseph B. Guilbeau
	Thomas M. Ruli

Kelann Etta Larguier	Charles W. Farr
Frank Whiteley	Macr E. Devenport
Lawrence B. Frieman	Gerard J. Haddican, II
Mayra Leyva	Patrick J. Browne, Jr.

For full biographical listings, see the Martindale-Hubbell Law Directory

MONROE,* Ouachita Parish

DAVENPORT, FILES & KELLY, L.L.P. (AV)

1509 Lamy Lane, P.O. Box 4787, 71211-4787
Telephone: 318-387-6453
FAX: 318-323-6533

Thos. W. Davenport (1909-1962)	Jack B. Files
Wm. G. Kelly, Jr.	Mike C. Sanders
Thomas W. Davenport, Jr.	Ramsey L. Ogg
	Michael J. Fontenot

M. Shane Craighead	W. David Hammett
	Carey B. Underwood

STAFF ATTORNEY

Stacy L. Guice

Representative Clients: American International Group (AIG); Chubb Group;
Commercial Aviation; GAINSCO; GEICO; Highlands Ins. Co.; Scottsdale
Ins. Co.; Trinity Universal Ins. Co.; United States Aircraft Ins. Group; Zu-
rich-American Ins. Cos.

For full biographical listings, see the Martindale-Hubbell Law Directory

Monroe—Continued

HAYES, HARKEY, SMITH & CASCIO, L.L.P. (AV)

2811 Kilpatrick Boulevard, P.O. Box 8032, 71211-8032
Telephone: 318-387-2422
FAX: 318-388-5809

Thomas M. Hayes, Jr.	Charles S. Smith
(1915-1994)	Thomas M. Hayes, III
Louis D. Smith	Bruce McKamy Mintz
Joseph D. Cascio, Jr.	C. Joseph Roberts, III

John B. Saye

OF COUNSEL

Haynes L. Harkey, Jr.

Karen L. Hayes	Elizabeth D. Bogan

Harry McClellan Moffett, IV

Representative Clients: Employers Reinsurance Corporation; Hanover Insurance Co.; Cigna, Inc.; CNA; Home Insurance Co.; Ohio Casualty Insurance Cos.; State Farm Insurance Co.; St. Francis Medical Center, Inc.; St. Paul Insurance Group; Travelers Ins. Co.

For full biographical listings, see the Martindale-Hubbell Law Directory

HUDSON, POTTS & BERNSTEIN (AV)

10th Floor, Premier Bank Building, 130 DeSiard Street, Drawer 3008, 71210
Telephone: 318-388-4400
Fax: 318-322-4194
Email: hpb@iamerica.net *URL:* http://www.cust.iamerica.net/hpb

MEMBERS OF FIRM

F.G. Hudson, Sr. (1875-1913)	Ben R. Hanchey
W. N. Potts (1875-1890)	James A. Rountree
Henry Bernstein, Sr. (1897-1931)	W. Craig Henry
John J. Potts (1894-1935)	Gordon L. James
F. G. Hudson, Jr. (1909-1958)	Robert M. Baldwin
Murray Hudson (1920-1971)	Charles W. Herold, III
Henry Bernstein, Jr. (1930-1978)	William T. McNew
B. Roy Liuzza (1958-1984)	Brady Dean King, II
Robert C. Downing (1952-1991)	Jay P. Adams
Jesse D. McDonald	Brian P. Bowes
Paul K. Kirkpatrick, Jr.	Jan Peter Christiansen

ASSOCIATES

Stephen Adam North	Mary A. Buffington

General Attorneys for: Missouri Pacific Railroad Co.
Attorneys for: Bank One, Louisiana, N.A.; Premier Bank, Monroe; General Motors; Allstate Insurance Co.; State Farm Fire & Casualty Co.; Hartford Insurance Group; Royal Globe Insurance Cos.; Dodson Insurance Group.

For full biographical listings, see the Martindale-Hubbell Law Directory

---

NEW IBERIA, Iberia Parish

CAFFERY, OUBRE, DUGAS & CAMPBELL, L.L.P. (AV)

420 Iberia Street, P.O. Drawer 12410, 70562-2410
Telephone: 318-364-1816
Fax: 318-364-9822

MEMBERS OF FIRM

Patrick T. Caffery	Michael W. Campbell
Jerry A. Oubre	Charles C. Garrison
David R. Dugas	Michael M. Caffery

Michelle E. Oubre

For full biographical listings, see the Martindale-Hubbell Law Directory

LANDRY & WATKINS (AV)

211 East Main Street, P.O. Box 12040, 70562-2040
Telephone: 318-364-7626, Lafayette: 318-234-5921
Telecopier: 318-367-2715

MEMBERS OF FIRM

Alfred Smith Landry	Edward P. Landry

William A. Repaske

OF COUNSEL

Jacob S. Landry	Guyton H. Watkins

ASSOCIATES

Kreig A. Breaux	Charles Benjamin Landry

Richard A. Spears

Representative Clients: Entex, a Division of NorAm Energy Corp.; Iberia Sugar Co-operative, Inc.; The Continental Insurance Co.; Hartford Accident & Indemnity Co.; Iberia Savings Bank; Liberty Mutual Insurance Co.; Premier Bank, N.A.

For full biographical listings, see the Martindale-Hubbell Law Directory

---

NEW ORLEANS, Orleans Parish

ADAMS, JOHNSTON & ORECK, A PROFESSIONAL LAW CORPORATION (AV)

Suite 2490, Pan American Life Center, 601 Poydras Street, 70130
Telephone: 504-581-2606
Telecopier: 504-525-1488
Boulder, Colorado Office: Vectra Bank Building, 1919 14th Street, Suite 609.
Telephone: 303-444-2993.

Jesse R. Adams, Jr.	Anne Derbes Keller
Robert M. Johnston	Jesse R. Adams, III
Bruce J. Oreck (Resident,	Adam W. Chase (Resident,
Boulder, Colorado Office)	Boulder, Colorado Office)
D. Russell Holwadel	Shannon Howard-Duhon
Thomas S. Morse	Nicole Crighton (Resident,
	Boulder, Colorado Office)

Representative Clients: Allianz Insurance Company; Amana Refrigeration, Inc.; Americas Insurance Company; Associated Risk Services Inc.; Aviation Underwriting Specialists, Inc.; Beech Aircraft Corporation; Dresser Industries, Inc.; Employers National Insurance Corporation; Fairgrounds Corporation; Trinity Universal Ins. Companies.

For full biographical listings, see the Martindale-Hubbell Law Directory

BEST KOEPPEL, A PROFESSIONAL LAW CORPORATION (AV)

LL & E Tower, 909 Poydras Street Suite 2200, 70112
Telephone: 504-593-2400
Telecopier: 504-593-2401
Houston, Texas Office: Weslayan Tower, 24 Greenway Plaza, Suite 925, 77046.
Telephone: 713-622-9761.
Telecopier: 713-622-0448.

Laurence E. Best	André C. Gaudin
Peter S. Koeppel	R. Jeffrey Bridger
Steven K. Best (Resident,	Steven D. Naumann (Resident,
Houston, Texas Office)	Houston, Texas Office)

Don Paul Landry

LEGAL SUPPORT PERSONNEL

PARALEGAL

Rhonda A. Usey

Representative Clients: Lexington Insurance Co.; Hanover Insurance Co.; Rowan Companies, Inc.

For full biographical listings, see the Martindale-Hubbell Law Directory

BOGGS, LOEHN & RODRIGUE (AV)

A Partnership including Law Corporations
Suite 1800 Lykes Center, 300 Poydras Street, 70130-3597
Telephone: 504-523-7090
Fax: 504-581-6822

Charles A. Boggs (A Law	Edward A. Rodrigue, Jr., (A
Corporation)	Law Corporation)
Thomas E. Loehn (A Law	Robert I. Baudouin
Corporation)	Jedd S. Malish

Reference: First National Bank of Commerce, New Orleans, La.

For full biographical listings, see the Martindale-Hubbell Law Directory

CHRISTOVICH AND KEARNEY, L.L.P. (AV)

Suite 2300 Pan American Life Center, 601 Poydras Street, 70130-6078
Telephone: 504-561-5700
Fax: 504-561-5743
Houston, Texas Office: 700 Louisiana, Suite 4550, 77002.
Telephone: 713-225-2255.
Fax: 713-225-1112.

MEMBERS OF FIRM

Alvin R. Christovich, Jr.	E. Phelps Gay
William K. Christovich	Thomas C. Cowan
J. Walter Ward, Jr.	Geoffrey P. Snodgrass
Lawrence J. Ernst	J. Warren Gardner, Jr.
James F. Holmes	Kevin R. Tully
Robert E. Peyton	Lance R. Rydberg
C. Edgar Cloutier	Elizabeth S. Cordes
Charles W. Schmidt, III	John K. Leach
Richard K. Christovich	Fred T. Hinrichs
Terry Christovich Gay	Daniel A. Rees
Paul G. Preston	Charles M. Lanier, Jr.
Michael M. Christovich	Lyon H. Garrison

Philip J. Borne

ASSOCIATES

Bennett A. Midlo	Ellen B. Woody
(Not admitted in LA)	Patrick W. Drouilhet
J. Roslyn Lemmon	Robert D. Peyton
James A. Holmes	Kenan S. Rand, Jr.
Scott P. Yount	Joseph E. Cullens, Jr.
Patricia Broussard Judice	

(See Next Column)

CHRISTOVICH AND KEARNEY L.L.P., *New Orleans—Continued*

ASSOCIATES (Continued)

Todd A. Riddle   Steve C. Dollinger
(Not admitted in LA)   (Not admitted in LA)
D. Scott Slawson

Representative Clients: Associated Aviation Underwriters; Brown & Root, Inc.; Chubb/Pacific Indemnity Group; Continental Insurance Company; Crawford & Co.; Crum & Forster; Highlands Insurance Company; Insurance Company of North America; Liberty Mutual Insurance Company; Southern Pacific Transportation Co.

For full biographical listings, see the Martindale-Hubbell Law Directory

---

DEUTSCH, KERRIGAN & STILES, L.L.P. (AV)

A Partnership including Professional Law Corporations
755 Magazine Street, 70130-3672
Telephone: 504-581-5141
Cable Address: "Dekest"
Telex: 584358
Telecopier: 504-566-1201
Email: dks@dksno.com *URL:* http://www.dksno.com
St. Tammany Parish Office: 550 Pontchartrain Drive, Suite 200, Slidell, LA. 70458.
Telephone: 504-639-0555.
Fax: 504-639-0550

MEMBERS OF FIRM

Robert E. Kerrigan, Jr., (P.L.C.)   James G. Wyly, III
Raymon G. Jones (P.L.C.)   Theodore L. White
Philip D. Lorio, III   William C. Harrison, Jr.
Marc J. Yellin (P.L.C.)   Judy L. Burnthorn
Howard L. Murphy   Carl A. Butler
Darrell K. Cherry (P.L.C.)   Gary B. Roth
William E. Wright, Jr.   Barbara Malik Weller
Nancy J. Marshall   Lisa C. Winter
Karyn J. Vigh

OF COUNSEL

Francis G. Weller (P.L.C.)

ASSOCIATES

Victor J. Franckiewicz, Jr.   Pamela W. Carter

For Complete List of Firm Personnel, See General Section

For full biographical listings, see the Martindale-Hubbell Law Directory

---

FRILOT, PARTRIDGE, KOHNKE & CLEMENTS, L.C. (AV)

3600 Energy Centre, 1100 Poydras Street, 70163-3600
Telephone: 504-599-8000
Telecopier: 504-599-8100
Email: postmaster@fpkc.ccmail.compuserve.com *URL:* hhtp://www.fpkc.com

Sidney A. Backstrom   Douglas P. Matthews
C. William Belsom, Jr.   Stephanie Ann May
Francis H. Brown, III   Kenneth A. Mayeaux
James H. Brown, Jr.   Robert B. McNeal
George E. Cain, Jr.   Wayne K. McNeil
Michael T. Cali   Patrick J. McShane
Miles P. Clements   Joseph N. Mole
Andrew S. de Klerk   David A. Olson
George A. Frilot, III (A   Scott S. Partridge
   Professional Law Corp.)   Greg A. Pellegrini
Frederick T. Greschner, Jr.   Michael R. Phillips
John J. Hainkel, III   James F. Shuey
Edward F. Kohnke, IV   James R. Silverstein
Allen J. Krouse, III   Peter E. Sperling
J. Dwight LeBlanc, III   Patrick A. Talley (P.C.)

For full biographical listings, see the Martindale-Hubbell Law Directory

---

HABANS, BOLOGNA & CARRIERE, A PROFESSIONAL LAW CORPORATION (AV)

Suite 2323, 1515 Poydras Street, 70112
Telephone: 504-524-2323
Telex: 151514 HABA M UT
Telecopier: 504-522-7224
Cable Address: HABOL

Robert N. Habans, Jr.   John C. McNeese
William F. Bologna   Aimée Carriere
James D. Carriere   Dwight L. Acomb
Julien F. Jurgens

For full biographical listings, see the Martindale-Hubbell Law Directory

---

HAMMETT & BAUS (AV)

A Partnership of Professional Corporations
200 Carondelet Street Suite 1600, 70130-2922
Telephone: 504-569-0380
Fax: 504-569-0386
Email: hammett@accesscom.net

(See Next Column)

Donald A. Hammett, P.C.   David S. Daly
John V. Baus, Jr., P.C.   Jennifer Carter de Blanc

For full biographical listings, see the Martindale-Hubbell Law Directory

---

JOHNSON, JOHNSON, BARRIOS & YACOUBIAN, A PROFESSIONAL LAW CORPORATION (AV)

4900 One Shell Square, 70139-4901
Telephone: 504-528-3001
Facsimile: 504-528-3030

Ronald A. Johnson   Bettye A. Barrios
Edward S. Johnson   Alan J. Yacoubian

Salvador J. Pusateri   Cindy T. Matherne
Rene S. Paysse, Jr.   William K. Hawkins

Representative Clients: Adams & Porter International, Inc.; Alexander & Alexander, Inc.; Alliance Steel, Inc.; Amoco Corporation; Burnett & Company; Charter Group, Inc.; Community Associates, Inc.; Concord General Corporation; Continental Underwriters, Ltd.; Riscorp Risk Management Services LLC.

For full biographical listings, see the Martindale-Hubbell Law Directory

---

LEA, TYNAN & McGEHEE, P.L.C. (AV)

Southern Marine and Aviation Building, 610 Poydras Street Suite 500, 70130
Telephone: 504-523-4500
Fax: 504-525-7208

Arden J. Lea   Joseph P. Tynan
W. Clay McGehee

MEXICAN LEGAL ADVISOR

Ricardo Lan (Not admitted in the United States)

For full biographical listings, see the Martindale-Hubbell Law Directory

---

LEAKE & ANDERSSON, L.L.P. (AV)

1700 Energy Centre, 1100 Poydras Street, 70163-1701
Telephone: 504-585-7500
Telecopier: 504-585-7775
Email: LA1700@aol.com

MEMBERS OF FIRM

Robert E. Leake, Jr.   Kevin O'Bryon
W. Paul Andersson   George D. Fagan
Lawrence A. Mann   Donald E. McKay, Jr.
Marta-Ann Schnabel O'Bryon   Stanton E. Shuler, Jr.

ASSOCIATE

Guy D. Perrier

Representative Clients: GEICO; Preferred Risk Mutual Insurance Co.; Progressive Casualty Insurance Co.; National Union Fire Insurance Co.; Nationwide Insurance Co.; U.S. Fire Insurance Co.; First Financial Insurance Co.

For Complete List of Firm Personnel, See General Section

For full biographical listings, see the Martindale-Hubbell Law Directory

---

LOZES & CAMBRE (AV)

1010 Common Street, Suite 1550, 70112
Telephone: 504-581-4455
Fax: 504-587-9408

OF COUNSEL

Felicien P. Lozes

MEMBERS OF FIRM

David M. Cambre   Jeffery P. Lozes
Steven M. Lozes   Christopher Lozes

Representative Client: Merit Insurance Co.

For full biographical listings, see the Martindale-Hubbell Law Directory

---

MIDDLEBERG, RIDDLE & GIANNA (AV)

31st Floor, Place St. Charles, 201 St. Charles Avenue, 70170-3100
Telephone: 504-525-7200
Telecopier: 504-581-5983
Dallas, Texas Office: 2323 Bryan Street, Suite 1600.
Telephone: 214-220-6300;
Telecopier: 214-220-2785.
Austin, Texas Office: 1300 South Mopac Expressway, First Floor.
Telephone: 512-434-8334.

MEMBERS OF FIRM

Ira Joel Middleberg   Dominic J. Gianna
Michael Lee Riddle
  (Austin and Dallas, Texas)

(See Next Column)

MIDDLEBERG, RIDDLE & GIANNA—*Continued*

Paul J. Mirabile	Tina S. Clark
John D. Person	E. Ralph Lupin
Alan Dean Weinberger	A.J. Herbert, III
L. Marlene Quarles	Marshall J. Simien, Jr.
Ronald J. Vega	Wade P. Webster
Edward T. Suffern, Jr.	Brian G. Meissner
	Rebecca J. King

For full biographical listings, see the Martindale-Hubbell Law Directory

O'NEIL, EICHIN, MILLER, SAPORITO & HARRIS, A LAW CORPORATION (AV)

639 Loyola Avenue, Suite 2200, 70113
Telephone: 504-525-3200
Cable Address: ONEMILL NLN
Telex: ITT 460125
Answer Back: ONEMILL NLN
Facsimile: 504-529-7389 (Groups 1, 2 & 3)

William E. O'Neil	John F. Fay, Jr.
Earl S. Eichin, Jr.	Alfred J. Rufty
Machale A. Miller	Michael D. Sledge
Jerry L. Saporito	Brandt K. Enos
Rufus C. Harris, III	Gregory G. Barnett
I. Matthew Williamson	Iliaura Hands
Lindsay A. Larson, III	Spiro J. Verras

OF COUNSEL
Terry A. McCall

Representative Clients: Cargill, Inc.; St. Paul Fire & Marine Insurance Company; CIGNA Companies, (P & C Group); Reliance National Insurance Company; Marine Office of America; General Motors Corp.; Toyota Motor Sales, U.S.A., Inc.; Royal Insurance Group; Hartford Insurance Company; Quaker Oats Company, Inc.

For full biographical listings, see the Martindale-Hubbell Law Directory

PLAUCHÉ, MASELLI & LANDRY (AV)

Place St. Charles, Suite 4240, 201 St. Charles Avenue, 70170-4240
Telephone: 504-582-1142
Fax: 504-582-1172

MEMBERS OF FIRM

Andrew L. Plauché, Jr.	Joseph Maselli, Jr.
	Arthur W. Landry

ASSOCIATES

P. Bruin Hays, III	Robert E. Caraway, III
Tracey L. Rannals	Elizabeth Ashley Carter
	Thomas L. Hutchinson

Reference: First National Bank of Commerce.

For full biographical listings, see the Martindale-Hubbell Law Directory

PULASKI, GIEGER & LABORDE, L.L.C. (AV)

Suite 4800, One Shell Square, 701 Poydras Street, 70139
Telephone: 504-561-0400
Telecopier: 504-561-1011

Michael T. Pulaski (P.C.)	Leo R. McAloon, III
Ernest P. Gieger, Jr., (P.C.)	John P. Gonzalez
Kenneth H. Laborde (P.C.)	J. Jeffery Raborn
Robert W. Maxwell (P.C.)	Lance Blake Williams
Keith W. McDaniel (P.C.)	James E. Swinnen
Sharon D. Smith (P.C.)	Gina S. Montgomery
Gary G. Hebert	Mary Beth Meyer
	Julianne T. Echols

For full biographical listings, see the Martindale-Hubbell Law Directory

WAGNER, BAGOT & GLEASON (AV)

Suite 2660, Poydras Center, 650 Poydras Street, 70130-6105
Telephone: 504-525-2141
Telecopier: 504-523-1587
TWX: 5106017673
ELN: 62928850
"INCISIVE"

Thomas J. Wagner	Harvey G. Gleason
Michael H. Bagot, Jr.	Whitney L. Cole
	Eric D. Suben

For full biographical listings, see the Martindale-Hubbell Law Directory

WARD, NELSON & PELLETERI, L.L.C. (AV)

1539 Jackson Avenue, 6th Floor, 70130
Telephone: 504-561-5000
Fax: 504-588-1334
Covington, Louisiana Office: 616 East Boston Street.
Telephone: 504-898-0940.

(See Next Column)

MEMBERS OF FIRM

Joseph R. Ward, Jr.	Raymond A. Pelleteri, Jr.
Craig R. Nelson	Emery N. Voorhies
	Lisa A. Condrey

ASSOCIATES

Lynn H. Frank	Charles S. Green, Jr
	James Everet Brouillette

OF COUNSEL

Oris Creighton	Christina Papastavros Fay

Representative Clients: Associated Aviation Underwriters; Associated International Underwriters; Continental Insurance Co.; Fidelity & Casualty of New York; Fireman's Insurance of Newark; Gulf Ins. Co.; Prudential Property and Cas. Ins. Co.; RLI Insurance Group; State Farm Fire & Casualty Co.; State Farms Mutual Automobile Insurance Co.; Zurich American Group.

For full biographical listings, see the Martindale-Hubbell Law Directory

OPELOUSAS,* St. Landry Parish

DAUZAT, FALGOUST, CAVINESS & BIENVENU (AV)

510 South Court Street, P.O. Box 1450, 70571
Telephone: 318-942-5811
Fax: 318-948-9512

MEMBERS OF FIRM

Jimmy L. Dauzat	Peter F. Caviness
Jerry J. Falgoust	Steven J. Bienvenu

Representative Clients: State Farm Mutual Automobile Insurance Co.; The Travelers Insurance Co.; Farm Bureau Insurance Co's.; Audubon Insurance Co.; Kemper Insurance Group; United States Fidelity & Guaranty Co.; Louisiana Indemnity Co.; Louisiana Insurance Guaranty Assn.; Time Insurance Co.; Executive Fund Life Insurance Co.

For full biographical listings, see the Martindale-Hubbell Law Directory

SHREVEPORT,* Caddo Parish

BARLOW AND HARDTNER L.C. (AV)

Tenth Floor, Louisiana Tower, 401 Edwards Street, 71101-3289
Telephone: 318-227-1131
Telecopier: 318-227-1141
Mailing Address: P.O. Box 8, Shreveport, Louisiana, 71161-0008

Joseph L. Shea, Jr.	Michael B. Donald
	Jay A. Greenleaf

Representative Clients: Kelley Oil Corporation; NorAm Energy Corp. (formerly Arkla, Inc.); Central and South West Corporation; Panhandle Eastern Corp.; Providence Washington Insurance Co.; Pennzoil Producing Co.; Johnson Controls, Inc.; Ashland Oil, Inc.; Southwestern Electric Power Company.

For Complete List of Firm Personnel, See General Section

For full biographical listings, see the Martindale-Hubbell Law Directory

MAYER, SMITH & ROBERTS, L.L.P. (AV)

1550 Creswell, 71101
Telephone: 318-222-2135, 222-2268
Fax: 318-222-6420
Email: (Attorney's First Name)@MSRLAW.COM

MEMBERS OF FIRM

Caldwell Roberts	David Butterfield
Walter O. Hunter, Jr.	Henry N. Bellamy
Mark A. Goodwin	John C. Turnage
Ben Marshall, Jr.	Paul R. Mayer, Jr.
Alexander S. Lyons	Steven E. Soileau
Kim Purdy Thomas	Deborah Shea Baukman
	Caldwell Roberts, Jr.

ASSOCIATES

Frank K. Carroll	Dalton Roberts Ross

OF COUNSEL

Charles L. Mayer	Paul R. Mayer

Representative Clients: CNA Insurance Companies; Liberty Mutual Insurance Company; The St. Paul Companies; United States Fidelity and Guaranty Company; Schumpert Medical Center; Travelers Insurance Company; Great American Insurance Company; Insurance Corporation of America; Highlands Insurance Company.

For full biographical listings, see the Martindale-Hubbell Law Directory

WILKINSON, CARMODY & GILLIAM (AV)

1700 Beck Building, 400 Travis Street, P.O. Box 1707, 71166
Telephone: 318-221-4196
Telecopier: 318-221-3705

(See Next Column)

WILKINSON, CARMODY & GILLIAM, *Shreveport—Continued*

MEMBERS OF FIRM

John D. Wilkinson (1867-1929)	Bobby S. Gilliam
William Scott Wilkinson	Mark E. Gilliam
(1895-1985)	Penny D. Sellers
Arthur R. Carmody, Jr.	Patrick F. Robinson

Michael J. Ryan

Representative Clients: Farmers Insurance Group; Home Federal Savings & Loan Association of Shreveport; The Kansas City Southern Railway Co.; KTAL-TV; Lincoln National Life Insurance Co.; Mobil Oil Co.; Schumpert Medical Center; Sears, Roebuck & Co.; Southern Pacific Transportation Co.; Southwestern Electric Power Co.

For full biographical listings, see the Martindale-Hubbell Law Directory

---

MAINE

AUGUSTA,* Kennebec Co.

JOHNSON, WEBBERT & LAUBENSTEIN (AV)

160 Capitol Street, P.O. Box 29, 04332-0029
Telephone: 207-623-5110
Fax: 207-622-4160

Phillip E. Johnson	David G. Webbert

William H. Laubenstein, III

Representative Clients: Agway, Inc.; American Eagle Insurance Co.; AVEMCO; Central Maine Power Co.; The Doctors Company; ITT/Hartford; Loss Management Services, Inc.; Shand, Morahan & Co.; Union Water Power Company; USAIG.

For full biographical listings, see the Martindale-Hubbell Law Directory

---

BANGOR,* Penobscot Co.

EATON, PEABODY, BRADFORD & VEAGUE, P.A. (AV)

Fleet Center-Exchange Street, P.O. Box 1210, 04402-1210
Telephone: 207-947-0111
Telecopier: 207-942-3040
Email: epbv@aol.com
Augusta, Maine Office: 2 Central Plaza.
Telephone: 207-622-3747.
Telecopier: 207-622-9732.
Blue Hill, Maine Office: One East Blue Hill Road.
Telephone: 207-374-2812.
Telecopier: 207-374-2548.
Brunswick, Maine Office: 167 Park Row.
Telephone: 207-729-1144.
Telecopier: 207-729-1140.
Camden, Maine Office: 7-9 Washington Street.
Telephone: 207-236-3325.
Telecopier: 207-236-8611.
Dover-Foxcroft, Maine Office: 30 East Main Street.
Telephone: 207-564-8378.
Telecopier: 207-564-7059.

Bernard J. Kubetz	William B. Devoe
Douglas M. Smith	Judy A.S. Metcalf
(Dover-Foxcroft and Augusta	(Resident, Brunswick Office)
Offices)	Jonathan B. Huntington
Glen L. Porter	(Resident, Dover-Foxcroft
Gordon H. S. Scott	Office)
(Resident, Augusta Office)	

A List of Representative Clients available upon request.

For Complete List of Firm Personnel, See General Section

For full biographical listings, see the Martindale-Hubbell Law Directory

---

RUDMAN & WINCHELL (AV)

84 Harlow Street, P.O. Box 1401, 04402-1401
Telephone: 207-947-4501
Telecopy: 207-941-9715

MEMBERS OF FIRM

Abraham M. Rudman	Frank T. McGuire
(1896-1970)	Bruce C. Mallonee
Albert H. Winchell, Jr.	Paul H. Sighinolfi
(1924-1992)	William H. Hanson
Gerald E. Rudman	George Franklin Eaton, II
Phillip D. Buckley	Edith A. Richardson
Michael P. Friedman	Michael M. McAleer
Winfred A. Stevens	Brett D. Baber
Robert E. Sutcliffe	Barbara A. Cardone
Paul W. Chaiken	Robert E. Murray, Jr.
David C. King	Edmond J. Bearor
John W. McCarthy	Curtis E. Kimball

(See Next Column)

ASSOCIATES

Jane E. Skelton	Karen D. Kemble
Brent A. Singer	Leigh Stephens McCarthy

Counsel for: Penobscot Shoe Co.; Sherman Lumber Co.; Webber Oil Co.; Fleet Bank of Maine; Key Bank of Maine; McCain Foods, Inc.
Local Counsel for: Commercial Union Assurance Cos.; Hanover Insurance Company; Kemper Insurance Group; Liberty Mutual Insurance Co.

For full biographical listings, see the Martindale-Hubbell Law Directory

---

VAFIADES, BROUNTAS & KOMINSKY (AV)

Key Plaza, 23 Water Street, P.O. Box 919, 04402-0919
Telephone: 207-947-6915
Telecopier: 207-941-0863

MEMBER OF FIRM

Eugene C. Coughlin, III

ASSOCIATES

Terence M. Harrigan	James C. Munch, III

OF COUNSEL

Lewis V. Vafiades

Representative Clients: Allstate Insurance Company; Chubb Group; Greater New York Mutual Insurance Company; Metropolitan Property and Liability Insurance Company; National Grange Mutual Insurance Company.

For Complete List of Firm Personnel, See General Section

For full biographical listings, see the Martindale-Hubbell Law Directory

---

PORTLAND,* Cumberland Co.

AMERLING & BURNS, A PROFESSIONAL ASSOCIATION (AV)

193 Middle Street, 04101
Telephone: 207-775-3581
Facsimile: 207-775-3814
Affiliated St. Croix Office: Coon & Sanford, P.O. Box 25918, Six Chandlers's Wharf, Suite 202, 00824-0918.

W. John Amerling	Arnold C. Macdonald
George F. Burns	Mary DeLano
David P. Ray	Joanne F. Cole

A. Robert Ruesch

OF COUNSEL

Bruce M. Jervis

Aetna Life & Casualty Co.; The Harford; Great American Insurance Co.; Wausau Ins. Co.

For full biographical listings, see the Martindale-Hubbell Law Directory

---

BEALS & QUINN (AV)

77 Middle Street, 04101
Telephone: 207-774-2900
Fax: 207-774-2656
Email: BealsQuinn@aol.com

George W. Beals	Thomas J. Quinn

ASSOCIATES

Naomi Honeth	Elizabeth Lancaster Peoples

For full biographical listings, see the Martindale-Hubbell Law Directory

---

DOUGLAS, WHITING, DENHAM & ROGERS (AV)

103 Exchange Street, P.O. Box 7108, 04112
Telephone: 207-774-1486
Facsimile: 207-774-3147

MEMBERS OF FIRM

Martica S. Douglas	Elizabeth Ernst Hood
Stephen C. Whiting	James E. Fortin
Alison A. Denham	Robert M. Morris
Deborah Buccina Rogers	Sheilah R. McLaughlin

Representative Clients: Allstate Insurance Co.; Metropolitan Property and Casualty Insurance Co.; AMICA Mutual Insurance Co.; National Grange Mutual; Continental/CNA; General Accident Group; Sentry Insurance Co.'s; The Travelers ; Zurich-American Insurance Co.

For full biographical listings, see the Martindale-Hubbell Law Directory

---

FRIEDMAN & BABCOCK (AV)

Suite 400, Six City Center, P.O. Box 4726, 04112-4726
Telephone: 207-761-0900
Telecopier: 207-761-0186

MEMBERS OF FIRM

Harold J. Friedman	Thomas A. Cox
Ernest J. Babcock	Karen Frink Wolf
Martha C. Gaythwaite	Jennifer S. Begel

Laurence H. Leavitt

(See Next Column)

FRIEDMAN & BABCOCK—*Continued*

ASSOCIATES

Theodore H. Irwin, Jr.	Elizabeth A. Germani
Lee H. Bals	Jonathan Marc Dunitz
Michelle Allott	Darren Blaine Riggle
Arthur J. Lamothe	Tracy D. Hill

Bruce W. Hepler

For full biographical listings, see the Martindale-Hubbell Law Directory

---

MONAGHAN, LEAHY, HOCHADEL & LIBBY (AV)

95 Exchange Street, P.O. Box 7046, 04112-7046
Telephone: 207-774-3906
Facsimile: 207-774-3965

MEMBERS OF FIRM

Thomas F. Monaghan	Christopher C. Dinan
Thomas G. Leahy	Matthew J. Monaghan
Joseph M. Hochadel	Michael H. Hill
Kevin G. Libby	William R. Fisher

ASSOCIATES

Cornelia Fuchs Fisher	John J. Wall, III

Noah D. Wuesthoff

OF COUNSEL

William E. Saufley

Representative Client: Oxford Bank & Trust.
Reference: Maine National Bank.

For full biographical listings, see the Martindale-Hubbell Law Directory

---

PETRUCCELLI & MARTIN (AV)

50 Monument Square, P.O. Box 9733, 04104-5033
Telephone: 207-775-0200
Telecopier: 207-775-2360

MEMBERS OF FIRM

Gerald F. Petruccelli	Daniel W. Bates
Joel C. Martin	Michael K. Martin

James B. Haddow

ASSOCIATES

Linda C. Russell	Thomas C. Bradley

John Anderson

Representative Clients: Associated Aviation Underwriters; Bombardier, Inc.; Chicago Title Insurance Co.; Chubb Insurance Co.; Medical Mutual Insurance Company of Maine; Norfolk Dedham Mutual Insurance Co.; Northern Security Insurance Co.; Ticor Title Insurance Co.; Union Mutual Fire Insurance Co.; Vermont Mutual Insurance Co.

For full biographical listings, see the Martindale-Hubbell Law Directory

---

PIERCE ATWOOD (AV)

One Monument Square, 04101
Telephone: 207-791-1100
Fax: 207-791-1350
Email: info@PierceAtwood.com
Augusta, Maine Office: 77 Winthrop Street.
Telephone: 207-622-6311.
Fax: 207-623-9367.
Newburyport, Massachusetts Office: 6 Harris Street.
Telephone: 508-465-9599.
Fax: 508-465-9945.

MEMBERS OF FIRM

Ralph I. Lancaster, Jr.	Louise K. Thomas
Malcolm L. Lyons	Michael D. Seitzinger
(Resident, Augusta Office)	(Resident, Augusta Office)
Peter W. Culley	John J. Aromando

David E. Barry

ASSOCIATES

Daniel J. Stevens	Deborah L. Shaw
(Resident, Augusta Office)	Jared S. des Rosiers
Michael N. Ambler, Jr.	Debra L. Brown

COUNSEL

Michael S. Wilson

For Complete List of Firm Personnel, See General Section

For full biographical listings, see the Martindale-Hubbell Law Directory

---

PRETI, FLAHERTY, BELIVEAU & PACHIOS (AV)

A Limited Liability Company
443 Congress Street, P.O. Box 11410, 04104-7410
Telephone: 207-791-3000
Telecopier: 207-791-3111
Email: admin@pfbpnet.com
Augusta, Maine Office: 45 Memorial Circle, P.O. Box 1058, 04332-1058.
Telephone: 207-623-5300.
Telecopier: 207-623-2914.

(See Next Column)

MEMBERS OF FIRM

Severin M. Beliveau	Michael G. Messerschmidt
(Augusta Office)	Randall B. Weill
Keith A. Powers	Evan M. Hansen
Christopher D. Nyhan	Edward R. Benjamin, Jr.
Jonathan S. Piper	Geoffrey K. Cummings
Daniel Rapaport	Michael Kaplan
Bruce C. Gerrity	Stephen E. F. Langsdorf
(Augusta Office)	(Augusta Office)
Jeffrey T. Edwards	John P. McVeigh

Elizabeth A. Olivier

OF COUNSEL

Albert J. Beliveau, Jr.

ASSOCIATES

Nelson J. Larkins	Kevin J. Beal

Representative Clients: The St. Paul Companies; Maine Municipal Assn.; American International Group; MGA Insurance Services; Gallagher Bassett; Dunlap Corp.; Crawford and Co.; Maine Bonding Co.; The Travelers Insurance Co.; United States Fidelity and Guaranty Co.

For Complete List of Firm Personnel, See General Section

For full biographical listings, see the Martindale-Hubbell Law Directory

---

RICHARDSON, WHITMAN, LARGE & BADGER, A PROFESSIONAL CORPORATION (AV)

465 Congress Street, 04101-3528
Telephone: 207-774-7474
Telecopier: 207-774-1343
Email: Portland@rwlb.com *URL:* http://wwwrwlb.com
Bangor, Maine Office: 82 Columbia Street, P.O. Box 2429.
Telephone: 207-945-5900.
Telecopier: 207-945-0758.

Harrison L. Richardson	Elizabeth G. Stouder
John S. Whitman	Barri Bloom
Wendell G. Large	Ann M. Murray
Frederick J. Badger, Jr.	(Resident, Bangor Maine)
(Resident, Bangor Office)	

Frederick F. Costlow	Anne H. Cressey
(Resident, Bangor Office)	Thomas R. McKeon
John B. Lucy	Carol I. Eisenberg
(Resident, Bangor Office)	

For full biographical listings, see the Martindale-Hubbell Law Directory

---

THOMPSON & BOWIE (AV)

Three Canal Plaza, P.O. Box 4630, 04112
Telephone: 207-774-2500
Telecopier: 207-774-3591

MEMBERS OF FIRM

Roy E. Thompson, Jr.	Frank W. DeLong, III
James M. Bowie	Michael E. Saucier
Daniel R. Mawhinney	Mark V. Franco
Rebecca H. Farnum	Elizabeth Knox Peck
Glenn H. Robinson	Cathy S. Roberts

ASSOCIATE

Paul C. Catsos

Representative Clients: Aetna Casualty & Surety; CNA Insurance Co.; Chubb Group; CIGNA Property & Casualty Companies; Lexington Insurance Co.; Liberty Mutual Insurance Co.; Nationwide Mutual Insurance Co.; Prudential Insurance Co.; Travelers Insurance Co.; Continental Group.

For full biographical listings, see the Martindale-Hubbell Law Directory

---

WRIGHT, COON & CUNNINGHAM, P.A. (AV)

377 Fore Street, P.O. Box 7526, 04112
Telephone: 207-775-7722
Fax: 207-772-7045
Email: lexfori@lexfori.com

Steven F. Wright	John R. Coon

Gregory M. Cunningham

For full biographical listings, see the Martindale-Hubbell Law Directory

---

MARYLAND

---

*BALTIMORE,** (Independent City)

ALLEN, JOHNSON, ALEXANDER & KARP, P.A. (AV)

Suite 1540, 100 East Pratt Street, 21202
Telephone: 410-727-5000
Fax: 410-727-0861
Washington, D.C. Office: 1707 L Street, N.W., Suite 1050.
Telephone: 202-828-4141.

(See Next Column)

ALLEN, JOHNSON, ALEXANDER & KARP P.A., *Baltimore—Continued*

John D. Alexander, Jr.   D'Ana E. Johnson (Resident,
Daniel Karp   Washington, D.C. Office)

Yvette M. Bryant

OF COUNSEL

Donald C. Allen

Denise Ramsburg Stanley   James X. Crogan, Jr.
George B. Breen (Not admitted   Kevin Bock Karpinski
   in MD; Resident, Washington,   Gregory James Dumark
   D.C. Office)

Representative Clients: Scottsdale Insurance Co.; Nautilus Insurance Co.; Jefferson Insurance Co.; Liberty Mutual Insurance Co.; Avis Rent-A-Car; Otis Elevator Co.; Montgomery Elevator Co.; Admiral Insurance Co.; Local Government Insurance Trust; Lancer Insurance Co.

For full biographical listings, see the Martindale-Hubbell Law Directory

---

FERGUSON, SCHETELICH, HEFFERNAN & MURDOCK, P.A. (AV)

1300 NationsBank Center 1, 100 South Charles Street, 21201
Telephone: 410-837-2200
Fax: 410-837-1188
Email: fshm@ix.netcom

Robert L. Ferguson, Jr.   Christopher J. Heffernan
Thomas J. Schetelich   M. Brooke Murdock

Michael N. Russo, Jr.   Peter Joseph Basile
Jodi K. Ebersole   Ann D. Ware

For full biographical listings, see the Martindale-Hubbell Law Directory

---

FUNK & BOLTON, A PROFESSIONAL ASSOCIATION (AV)

USF&G Tower Building, Suite 900, 100 Light Street, 21202
Telephone: 410-659-7700
Facsimile: 410-659-7773
Email: FBLAW.COM

David M. Funk   Lindsey A. Rader
Bryan D. Bolton   Steven Jared Troy
Timothy E. Dixon   Derek B. Yarmis

OF COUNSEL

J. Frank Nayden   Bryson F. Popham
             Deborah R. Rivkin

For full biographical listings, see the Martindale-Hubbell Law Directory

---

GOODELL, DEVRIES, LEECH & GRAY, LLP (AV)

Suite 2000, One South Street, 21202
Telephone: 410-783-4000
Telecopy: 410-783-4040
Email: GDLG@GDLG.COM

MEMBERS OF FIRM

E. Charles Dann, Jr.   David W. Allen
             Linda S. Woolf

For full biographical listings, see the Martindale-Hubbell Law Directory

---

JORDAN COYNE & SAVITS (AV)

400 E. Pratt Street, 21202
Telephone: 410-625-5080
Washington, D.C. Office: 1100 Connecticut Avenue, N.W., Suite 600.
Telephone: 202-296-4747.
Telecopier: 202-496-2800.
Rockville, Maryland Office: 33 Wood Lane.
Telephone: 301-424-4161. 202-842-2587.
Fairfax, Virginia Office: 10486 Armstrong Street.
Telephone: 703-246-0900.
Telecopier: 703-591-3673.
Leesburg, Virginia Office: 305 Harrison Street, S.E.
Telephones: 703-777-6084; 202-478-1895.
Telecopier: 703-771-6383. E-Mail: dansmith@washdc.mindspring.com.

Joel M. Savits   D. Stephenson Schwinn
             David B. Stratton

Representative Clients: Aetna Casualty & Surety Co.; American International Group; Budget Rent A Car Systems; Design Professionals Insurance Co.; Giant Food; Marriott Corp.; Minnesota Mining & Manufacturing; Risk Enterprises Management Ltd.; Scottsdale Insurance Co.; Washington Adventist Hospital.

For full biographical listings, see the Martindale-Hubbell Law Directory

---

NEAD, HOFFMAN & KAREY (AV)

Suite 800 W.R. Grace Building, 10 East Baltimore Street, 21202
Telephone: 410-837-1828
FAX: 410-783-5078

(See Next Column)

MEMBERS OF FIRM

Robert K. Nead   Gilbert A. Hoffman
             Joseph N. Karey

Sandra B. Minton   Mark R. Brown

Representative Clients: State Farm Insurance; Horace Mann Insurance Cos.; Consolidated Freightways; Penn Mutual Insurance Co.; Lancer Insurance Co.; Carborundum Co.; Kennecott Industries.
Reference: NationsBank.

For full biographical listings, see the Martindale-Hubbell Law Directory

---

ROLLINS, SMALKIN, RICHARDS & MACKIE (AV)

401 North Charles Street, 21201
Telephone: 410-727-2443
Fax: 410-727-8390

MEMBERS OF FIRM

H. Beale Rollins (1898-1985)   John F. Linsenmeyer
Samuel S. Smalkin (1906-1982)   Thomas C. Gentner
T. Benjamin Weston (1913-1980)   Glenn W. Trimmer
Thomas G. Andrew (1910-1973)   Patrick G. Cullen
Edward C. Mackie   James P. O'Meara

             Dennis J. Sullivan

ASSOCIATES

Paul G. Donoghue   Donna Lynn Kolakowski-Hollen
Ralph E. Wilson III   Meg Bantley Whiteford
Kenneth G. Macleay   Anthony G. Lardieri

OF COUNSEL

Raymond A. Richards (Retired)   Hartman J. Miller

For full biographical listings, see the Martindale-Hubbell Law Directory

---

SIMMONS AND FIELDS, P.A. (AV)

200 Blaustein Building, One North Charles Street, 21201
Telephone: 410-539-0380

Robert L. Simmons   John Addison Howard
C. Russell Fields   Karen A. Besok
George W. Fanshaw, III   Marsha L. Krawitz
Hans J. Phillips   Gregory Sean Fanshaw

For full biographical listings, see the Martindale-Hubbell Law Directory

---

THIEBLOT, RYAN, MARTIN & MILLER, P.A. (AV)

4th Floor, The World Trade Center, 21202-3091
Telephone: 410-837-1140
Washington, D.C. Line: 202-628-8223
Fax: 410-837-3282
Towson, Maryland Office: Atlantic Federal Building. Suite 400. 100 West Road. 21204.
Telephone: 410-828-5900.

Robert J. Thieblot   Robert D. Harwick, Jr.
Anthony W. Ryan   Anne M. Hrehorovich
J. Edward Martin, Jr.   Donna Marie Raffaele
Bruce R. Miller   Hamilton Fisk Tyler
             Samuel S. Field III

Representative Clients: Allianz Underwriters Insurance Co.; Aviation Underwriting Specialists; Florists Insurance; General Accident Insurance Co.; Nautilus Insurance Co.; Scottsdale Insurance Co.; USF&G Company; TIG Insurance Company; Travelers Companies.

For full biographical listings, see the Martindale-Hubbell Law Directory

---

VENABLE ATTORNEYS AT LAW VENABLE, BAETJER AND HOWARD, LLP (AV)

A Partnership including Professional Corporations
1800 Mercantile Bank & Trust Building, 2 Hopkins Plaza, 21201
Telephone: 410-244-7400
Email: INFO@Venable.win.net
Washington, D.C. Office: Venable, Baetjer, Howard & Civiletti LLP. Suite 1000, 1201 New York Avenue, N.W.
Telephone: 202-962-4800.
McLean, Virginia Office: Suite 400, 2010 Corporate Ridge.
Telephone: 703-760-1600.
Rockville, Maryland Office: Suite 500, One Church Street, P. O. Box 1906.
Telephone: 301-217-5600.
Towson, Maryland Office: 210 Allegheny Avenue, P. O. Box 5517.
Telephone: 410-494-6200.

MEMBERS OF FIRM

Benjamin R. Civiletti (P.C.)   Ronald R. Glancz (Not
   (Also at Washington, D.C.   admitted in MD; Resident,
   and Towson, Maryland   Washington, D.C. Office)
   Offices)   Douglas D. Connah, Jr. (P.C.)
John Henry Lewin, Jr. (P.C.)   (Also at Washington, D.C.
Roger W. Titus (Resident,   Office)
   Rockville, Maryland Office)

(See Next Column)

VENABLE ATTORNEYS AT LAW VENABLE, BAETJER AND HOWARD, LLP—
Continued

MEMBERS OF FIRM (Continued)

John H. Zink, III (Resident, Towson, Maryland Office)

James L. Shea (Also at Washington, D.C. Office)

Bruce E. Titus (Resident, McLean, Virginia Office)

Jeffrey P. Ayres (P.C.)

William D. Dolan, III (P.C.) (Not admitted in MD; Resident, McLean, Virginia Office)

C. Carey Deeley, Jr. (Also at Towson, Maryland Office)

Kathleen Gallogly Cox (Resident, Towson, Maryland Office)

Paul T. Glasgow (Resident, Rockville, Maryland Office)

Christopher R. Mellott

Joseph C. Wich, Jr. (Resident, Towson, Maryland Office)

Cynthia M. Hahn (Resident, Towson, Maryland Office)

Nell B. Strachan

M. King Hill, III (Resident, Towson, Maryland Office)

James K. Archibald (Also at Washington, D.C. Office)

John A. Roberts (Also at Rockville, Maryland Office)

Jeffrey A. Dunn (also at Washington, D.C. Office)

David J. Heubeck

George F. Pappas (Also at Washington, D.C. Office)

Herbert G. Smith, II (Not admitted in MD; Resident, Washington, D.C. Office)

ASSOCIATES

Daniel William China

Christine M. McAnney (Not admitted in MD; Resident, McLean, Virginia Office)

Marina Lolley Dame (Resident, Towson, Maryland Office)

Mary-Dulany James (Resident, Towson, Maryland Office)

John A. McCauley

John T. Prisbe

Patricia A. Malone (Resident, Towson, Maryland Office)

Linda Marotta Thomas

For Complete List of Firm Personnel, See General Section

For full biographical listings, see the Martindale-Hubbell Law Directory

---

WARD, KERSHAW & MINTON, A PROFESSIONAL ASSOCIATION (AV)

113 West Monument Street, 21201
Telephone: 410-685-6700
Fax: 410-685-6704
Email: wkmfirm@aol.com

John T. Ward
Robert B. Kershaw
Thomas J. Minton

OF COUNSEL

Richard V. Falcon

For full biographical listings, see the Martindale-Hubbell Law Directory

---

YOUNG & VALKENET, L.L.C. (AV)

Suite 707 The Susquehanna Building, 29 West Susquehanna Avenue, 21204
Telephone: 410-583-2414
Telefax: 410-583-2418

Thomas G. Young, III
Thomas C. Valkenet
David Jude Carlin

For full biographical listings, see the Martindale-Hubbell Law Directory

---

LANHAM, Prince Georges Co.

DeCARO, DORAN, SICILIANO, GALLAGHER, SONNTAG & DeBLASIS (AV)

4601 Forbes Boulevard Suite 200, P.O. Box 40, 20703-0040
Telephone: 301-306-4300
Telecopier: 301-306-4988
Alexandria, Virginia Office: 1800 Diagonal Road, Suite 300.
Telephone: 703-548-0044.
Telecopier: 703-209-8548.

MEMBERS OF FIRM

Alan R. Siciliano
Charles E. Gallagher, Jr.

Jeffrey R. DeCaro
Samuel J. DeBlasis, II

W. Scott Sonntag
Christopher R. Dunn

Thomas L. Doran
Michael A. DeSantis

Timothy E. Howie

ASSOCIATES

Deborah Elizabeth Sanders Kane
D. Lynne Jenkins

Neil Joseph MacDonald
Anne Marie McGinley

Amy T. Roberts
James D. Cardea

Michele L. Smith
Stephen J. Williams

Leslie D. Oliveri
Douglas K. Allston, Jr

Solomon Martin Sterenberg
Julie H. Favetta

Christine L. Pecora

For full biographical listings, see the Martindale-Hubbell Law Directory

---

ROCKVILLE,* Montgomery Co.

ANDERSON & QUINN (AV)

The Adams Law Center, 25 Wood Lane, 20850

(See Next Column)

Telephone: 301-762-3303
FAX: 301-762-3776
Other Rockville Maryland Office: 110 North West St., Suite 501, 20850.
Telephone: 301-340-0800.

MEMBERS OF FIRM

Charles C. Collins (1900-1973)
Donald P. Maiberger

Robert E. Anderson (Not admitted in MD; Retired)
Robert P. Scanlon

James G. Healy

Francis X. Quinn
John A. Rego

ASSOCIATES

Alice Kelley Scanlon
Mary L. Fellin

Marnie E. Simon
Kelly Ann McInerney

Kerry Patricia Shanahan
Timothy J. Mulreany

Representative Clients: C & P Telephone; Commercial Union Insurance Cos.; Allstate Insurance Co.; State Farm Mutual Automobile Insurance Co.; Liberty Mutual Insurance Co.; Northbrook Insurance Cos.; Travelers Insurance Co.; National General Insurance Co.; American International Adjustment Co.; Marriott Corp.

For full biographical listings, see the Martindale-Hubbell Law Directory

---

ARMSTRONG, DONOHUE & CEPPOS, CHARTERED (AV)

Suite 101, 204 Monroe Street, 20850
Telephone: 301-251-0440
Telecopier: 301-279-5929

Larry A. Ceppos
H. Kenneth Armstrong

H. Patrick Donohue
Benjamin S. Vaughan

John C. Monahan

Oya S. Oner
Sharon A. Marcial

Pamela Barrow Kincheloe
J. Eric Rhoades

Richard S. Schrager
Garrett V. Williams

Andrew J. Marter

Representative Clients: Medical Mutual Liability Insurance Society of Maryland; Kaiser Permanente; Shady Grove Adventist Hospital; American Medical International, Inc.; Crum & Forster Commercial Insurance Cos.; Atlantic Mutual Insurance Co.; Nationwide Mutual Insurance Co.; Harleysville Mutual Insurance Co.; St. Paul Fire & Marine Insurance Co.; American Reliance Insurance Co.

For full biographical listings, see the Martindale-Hubbell Law Directory

---

BRAULT, GRAHAM, SCOTT & BRAULT (AV)

101 South Washington Street, 20850
Telephone: 301-424-1060
Fax: 301-424-7991
Washington, D.C. Office: 1906 Sunderland Place, N.W.
Telephone: 202-785-1200.
FAX: 202-785-4301.
Arlington, Virginia Office: Suite 1201, 2300 North Clarendon Boulevard, Courthouse Plaza.
Telephone: 703-358-9200.

OF COUNSEL

Laurence T. Scott
Janet S. Zigler (Resident)

MEMBERS OF FIRM

Denver H. Graham (1922-1987)
Daniel L. Shea (Resident)

Albert E. Brault (Retired)
M. Kathleen Parker (Resident)

Albert D. Brault (Resident)
David G. Mulquin (Resident)

Leo A. Roth, Jr.
James M. Brault (Resident)

James S. Wilson (Resident)
Regina Ann Casey (Resident)

Ronald G. Guziak
Sanford A. Friedman

ASSOCIATES

Holly D. Shupert (Resident)
Joan F. Brault (Resident)

Rhonda Ann Hurwitz (Resident)
Joseph P. Morra (Resident)

Michael A. Carlo

Representative Clients: American Oil Co.; Crum & Forster Group; Fireman's Fund American Insurance Cos.; Kemper Group; Reliance Insurance Cos.; Safeco Group; Government Employees Insurance Co.; Medical Mutual Insurance Society of Maryland; Legal Mutual Liability Insurance Society of Maryland.

For full biographical listings, see the Martindale-Hubbell Law Directory

---

JORDAN COYNE & SAVITS (AV)

33 Wood Lane, 20850-2228
Telephone: 301-424-4161
Washington, D.C. Office: 1100 Connecticut Avenue, N.W., Suite 600.
Telephone: 202-296-4747.
Telecopier: 202-496-2800.
Baltimore, Maryland Office: 400 E. Pratt Street.
Telephone: 410-625-5080.
Fairfax, Virginia Office: 10486 Armstrong Street.
Telephone: 703-246-0900.
Telecopier: 703-591-3673.
Leesburg, Virginia Office: 305 Harrison Street, S.E.
Telephones: 703-777-6084; 202-478-1895.
Telecopier: 703-771-6383. E-Mail: dansmith@washdc.mindspring.com

(See Next Column)

JORDAN COYNE & SAVITS, *Rockville—Continued*

Joel M. Savits　　　　　　　　D. Stephenson Schwinn
　　　　　　　David B. Stratton
ASSOCIATES

William Ward Nooter　　　　　Ellen Giblin Draper
Deborah Murrell Whelihan　　　Sandra L. Brown
Clifton Merritt Mount　　　　　Laura S. Roecklein
　　　　　James John Bresnicky

Representative Clients: Aetna Casualty & Surety Co.; American International Group; Budget Rent A Car Systems; Design Professionals Insurance Co.; Giant Food; Marriott Corp.; Minnesota Mining & Manufacturing; Risk Enterprises Management Ltd.; Scottsdale Insurance Co.; Washington Adventist Hospital.

For full biographical listings, see the Martindale-Hubbell Law Directory

---

SILVER SPRING, Montgomery Co.

LIPSHULTZ AND HONE, CHARTERED (AV)

Suite 108 Montgomery Center, 8630 Fenton Street, 20910
Telephone: 301-587-8500
Fax: 301-495-9759
Washington, D.C. Office: Suite 200, 2000 L Street, N.W.
Telephone: 202-872-0909.

Stanley L. Lipshultz　　　　　Stephen S. Brown
Michael T. O'Bryant
(Not admitted in MD)

　　　　　Victor I. Weiner
For Complete List of Firm Personnel, See General Section

For full biographical listings, see the Martindale-Hubbell Law Directory

---

TOWSON,* Baltimore Co.

HOWELL, GATELY, WHITNEY & CARTER, LLP (AV)

401 Washington Avenue, Twelfth Floor, 21204
Telephone: 410-583-8000
Fax: 410-583-8031

MEMBERS OF FIRM

H. Thomas Howell　　　　　Daniel W. Whitney
William F. Gately　　　　　David A. Carter
Benjamin R. Goertemiller　　William R. Levasseur

ASSOCIATES

Una M. Perez　　　　　　Kathleen D. Leslie
George D. Bogris　　　　Gerard Wm. Wittstadt, Jr.
　　　　　Laura A. Gregory

For full biographical listings, see the Martindale-Hubbell Law Directory

MUDD, HARRISON & BURCH (AV)

105 West Chesapeake Avenue, 300 Jefferson Building, 21204
Telephone: 410-828-1335
FAX: 410-828-1042

MEMBERS OF FIRM

John E. Mudd　　　　　　Douglas W. Biser
T. Rogers Harrison (1949-1995)　H. Patrick Stringer, Jr.
Richard C. Burch　　　　Andrew Janquitto

James R. Andersen　　　　Thomas Patrick Dwyer
OF COUNSEL
Delverne A. Dressel (Resident)　Wm. T. Russell, Jr.

Representative Clients: The Maryland Insurance Group; The Ohio Insurance Group; USAA Property & Casualty Insurance; Safeco Insurance Companies; Montgomery Mutual Insurance Co.; North American Specialty Insurance; Mutual Benefit Insurance Co.; Peninsula General Insurance Co.; Universal Underwriters Group; Kemper Insurance Cos.

For full biographical listings, see the Martindale-Hubbell Law Directory

ROSOLIO, SILVERMAN & KOTZ, P.A. (AV)

Suite 220 Nottingham Centre, 502 Washington Avenue, 21204
Telephone: 410-339-7100
Fax: 410-339-7107

Charles E. Rosolio　　　　Jeffrey M. Kotz
Steven D. Silverman　　　Deborah C. Dopkin
　　　　Douglas S. Curtis
OF COUNSEL
　　　　Stephen M. Ehudin

For full biographical listings, see the Martindale-Hubbell Law Directory

---

VENABLE ATTORNEYS AT LAW VENABLE, BAETJER AND HOWARD, LLP (AV)

A Partnership including Professional Corporations
210 Allegheny Avenue, P.O. Box 5517, 21204
Telephone: 410-494-6200
FAX: 410-821-0147
Baltimore, Maryland Office: 1800 Mercantile Bank & Trust Building, 2 Hopkins Plaza.
Telephone: 410-244-7400.
Washington, D.C. Office: Venable, Baetjer, Howard & Civiletti LLP, Suite 1000, 1201 New York Avenue, N.W.
Telephone: 202-962-4800.
McLean, Virginia Office: Suite 400, 2010 Corporate Ridge.
Telephone: 703-760-1600.
Rockville, Maryland Office: Suite 500, One Church Street, P. O. Box 1906.
Telephone: 301-217-5600.

PARTNERS

Benjamin R. Civiletti (P.C.)　　Joseph C. Wich, Jr.
(Also at Washington, D.C.　　C. Carey Deeley, Jr. (Also at
and Baltimore, Maryland　　　Baltimore, Maryland Office)
Offices)　　　　　　　　Kathleen Gallogly Cox
John H. Zink, III　　　　　Cynthia M. Hahn
　　　　　M. King Hill, III
ASSOCIATES
Marina Lolley Dame　　　　Mary-Dulany James
　　　　Patricia A. Malone

For Complete List of Firm Personnel, See General Section

For full biographical listings, see the Martindale-Hubbell Law Directory

---

UPPER MARLBORO,* Prince Georges Co.

MENG & UREY (AV)

14507 Main Street, P.O. Box 549, 20773
Telephone: 301-627-1600
FAX: 301-627-2838

George E. Meng　　　　　Laura L. Greeves
Paul K. Urey, III　　　　Ellen A. Marth
LEGAL SUPPORT PERSONNEL
　　　　Margaret Urey (Paralegal)

Representative Clients: State Farm Mutual Automobile Insurance Co.; State Farm Fire & Casualty Co.; Americlaim Adjustment Corp.; Old Line National Bank.

For full biographical listings, see the Martindale-Hubbell Law Directory

---

MASSACHUSETTS

BOSTON,* Suffolk Co.

BADGER, DOLAN, PARKER & COHEN (AV)

Formerly Badger, Sullivan, Kelley & Cole
2 Oliver Street, 02109
Telephone: 617-482-3030
Fax: 617-482-6919
Email: Badger@ma.ultranet.com

MEMBERS OF FIRM

Walter I. Badger (1885-1926)　George F. Parker, III
John J. Sullivan (1926-1979)　James B. Dolan, Jr.
David W. Kelley (1935-1986)　Lawrence J. Cohen
ASSOCIATES
Audrey LaRowe Nee　　　Paul J. Barresi
　　　　John J. Pentz
OF COUNSEL
Joseph E. Rendini　　　　G. Mitchell Eckel, III

For full biographical listings, see the Martindale-Hubbell Law Directory

BLOOM & BUELL (AV)

1340 Soldiers Field Road, 02135-1020
Telephone: 617-254-4400
Telecopier: 617-254-7610
Email: bloombue@ix.netcom.com

MEMBERS OF FIRM

Laurence J. Bloom　　　　Barbara Hayes Buell
　　　　William J. Davenport
ASSOCIATES
Marc J. Gervais　　　　　Richard M. Haley
　　　　Barry T. Putterman
OF COUNSEL
　　　　Victoria L. Polito

(See Next Column)

BLOOM & BUELL—*Continued*

LEGAL SUPPORT PERSONNEL

Lisa F. Tuccinardi

For full biographical listings, see the Martindale-Hubbell Law Directory

COGAVIN AND WAYSTACK (AV)

2 Center Plaza, 02108
Telephone: 617-742-3340
Telecopier: 617-723-7563

MEMBERS OF FIRM

John J. Cogavin	John P. Fitzgerald
Edward W. Waystack	Gerard A. Butler

Kevin J. McGinty

ASSOCIATES

David T. Donnelly	Audrey Lewchik Bradley
John J. Jarosak	Daniel S. McInnis
Thomas M. Franco	William P. Hurley
Mark A. Darling	Laura E. Iannetta
Owen Roe O'Neill	Thomas G. Leonard, Jr.

John A. Dolan

Representative Clients: Fireman's Fund Insurance Co.; The Andover Companies; The Hartford Insurance Co.; The Travelers Insurance Co.; Plymouth Rock Assurance Corporation; Metropolitan Insurance Co.; Maryland Casualty Insurance Co.; Chubb Insurance Company; National Grange Mutual Insurance Co.; Zurich-American Insurance Group.

For full biographical listings, see the Martindale-Hubbell Law Directory

CORNELL AND GOLLUB (AV)

75 Federal Street, 02110
Telephone: 617-482-8100
Telecopier: 617-482-3917

MEMBERS OF FIRM

Robert W. Cornell (1910-1988)	Peter M. Durney
Karl L. Gollub (1934-1985)	Paul F. Lynch
David H. Sempert	Jane Treen Brand
Philip J. Foley	Janet J. Bobit

ASSOCIATES

Hugh M. Coxe	Thomas H. Dolan
Thomas A. Pursley	Eric B. Goldberg
David W. McGough	Kelly L. Wilkins
Susan Donaldson Novins	James P. Kerr
Marie Chadeayne Chafe	Patricia A. Hartnett

For full biographical listings, see the Martindale-Hubbell Law Directory

CURLEY & CURLEY, P.C. (AV)

27 School Street, 02108
Telephone: 617-523-2990
Fax: 617-523-7602

Robert A. Curley	Martin J. Rooney
Robert A. Curley, Jr.	Lisabeth A. Ryan-Kundert
Eugene F. Nowell	Stephen J. Gill
David D. Dowd	Marjory D. Robertson

For full biographical listings, see the Martindale-Hubbell Law Directory

FINNEGAN, UNDERWOOD, RYAN & TIERNEY (AV)

20 Custom House Street Suite 550, 02110
Telephone: 617-345-0020
Fax: 617-345-0150

MEMBERS OF FIRM

David I. Finnegan	John G. Ryan
Richard J. Underwood	Philip T. Tierney

ASSOCIATES

Peter J. McCue	Kim Beringhause Peacock
Susan E. Ireland	Susan Underwood
Stimpson B. Hubbard	Susan Schramm

For full biographical listings, see the Martindale-Hubbell Law Directory

FINNERTY & FINNERTY (AV)

Suite 230, 21 Custom House Street, 02110
Telephone: 617-737-3770
Fax: 617-737-0684

MEMBERS OF FIRM

John F. Finnerty (1917-1994)	Gail E. Finnerty
John F. Finnerty, Jr.	Brian P. Finnerty

Reference: Fleet Bank.

For full biographical listings, see the Martindale-Hubbell Law Directory

GRIFFIN & GOULKA (AV)

Two Oliver Street, 02109
Telephone: 617-423-6677
Telecopier: 617-423-5755

(See Next Column)

MEMBERS OF FIRM

J. Kenneth Griffin	Joanne L. Goulka

Christopher S. Williams

ASSOCIATES

Monique H. Gerson	Sara E. McGrath
Robert P. La Hait	Clark W. Yudysky

For full biographical listings, see the Martindale-Hubbell Law Directory

KOPELMAN AND PAIGE, P.C. (AV)

Park Square Building, 31 St. James Avenue, 7th Floor, 02116
Telephone: 617-556-0007
Fax: 617-654-1735

Leonard Kopelman	John W. Giorgio
Donald G. Paige	Barbara J. Saint Andre
Elizabeth A. Lane	Joel B. Bard
Joyce F. Frank	Everett Joseph Marder

Patrick J. Costello

William Hewig, III

For Complete List of Firm Personnel, See General Section

For full biographical listings, see the Martindale-Hubbell Law Directory

MARTIN, MAGNUSON, McCARTHY & KENNEY (AV)

101 Merrimac Street, 02114-4716
Telephone: 617-227-3240
Telecopier: 617-227-3346

MEMBERS OF FIRM

Ephraim Martin (1900-1988)	Joseph L. Doherty, Jr. *
Clement McCarthy (1921-1985)	Paul R. Keane *
Raymond J. Kenney, Jr. *	John P. Mulvey *
Charles P. Reidy, III *	Paul M. McTague *
Daniel J. Griffin, Jr. *	Carol A. Kelly *
Philip E. Murray, Jr. *	Gail L. Anderson *

Edward F. Mahoney *

COUNSEL

Harold E. Magnuson	Edward F. Hennessey

Joan L. Atlas *	Teresa J. Farris *
Joseph B. Bertrand *	Mark A. Newcity *
Martha A. Driscoll *	Kevin C. Reidy *
Douglas A. Robertson *	Stephen M. O'Shea *
Mary T. Gibbons *	Michael A. Uhlarik

Lisa A. Furnald

Representative Clients: Allstate Insurance Co.; American International Adjustment Co.; Browning - Ferris Industries, Inc.; Fireman's Fund Insurance Cos.; Medical Professional Mutual Insurance Co.; Multi Systems Agency LTD.; Risk Management Foundation; St. Paul Insurance Cos.; Wausau Insurance Cos.
Reference: Fleet Bank.
*Employees of The Professional Corporation of McCarthy, Kenney & Reidy.

For full biographical listings, see the Martindale-Hubbell Law Directory

McCORMACK & EPSTEIN (AV)

One International Place, 02110
Telephone: 617-951-2929
Telecopier: 617-951-2672
New York, N.Y. Office: 330 Madison Avenue, Twenty Seventh Floor.
Telephone: 212-935-0881.

MEMBERS OF FIRM

Robert D. Epstein	Mark E. Cohen
Michael J. McCormack	Joseph H. Aronson

Brian C. Duffey	Amy M. Soisson
George X. Pucci	Stephen D. Rosenberg
Marc L. LaCasse	Mary-Elise Connolly

Kjersten Johnsen

Representative Clients: First State Insurance Co.; Crum & Forster Commercial Insurance; Liberty Mutual Insurance Co.; United States Fidelity & Guaranty Co.; Massachusetts Bay Transportation Authority; Technical Aid Corporation.

For full biographical listings, see the Martindale-Hubbell Law Directory

PALMER & DODGE LLP (AV)

One Beacon Street, 02108
Telephone: 617-573-0100
Facsimile: 617-227-4420

MEMBERS OF FIRM

Acheson H. Callaghan, Jr.	Steven L. Schreckinger
Michael T. Gass	Thane D. Scott
Michael J. Lacek	Craig E. Stewart
Scott P. Lewis	Jeffrey Swope

Tamara S. Wolfson

(See Next Column)

PALMER & DODGE LLP, Boston—Continued

COUNSEL

Stephen J. Abarbanel   Cassandra Warshowsky

For Complete List of Firm Personnel, See General Section

For full biographical listings, see the Martindale-Hubbell Law Directory

PEABODY & ARNOLD (AV)

A Partnership including Professional Corporations
50 Rowes Wharf, 02110-3342
Telephone: 617-951-2100
Telecopier: 617-951-2125
Providence, Rhode Island Office: One Citizens Plaza, Suite 840.
Telephone: 401-831-8330.
Fax: 401-831-8359.

MEMBERS OF FIRM

Vincent M. Amoroso	Elizabeth Z. Holmes
John P. Connelly	Maynard M. Kirpalani
William A. Cotter, Jr., (P.C.)	Robert A. McCall
Philip M. Cronin	Robert W. Monaghan
Allen N. David	Alexander H. Pratt, Jr.
Paul R. Devin	George C. Rockas
Michael P. Duffy	E. Macey Russell
Thomas Frisardi	Molly Haynes Sherden
R. Alan Fryer	Joseph M. Smick
Robert T. Gill (P.C.)	Randolph L. Smith
Deborah S. Griffin	Harvey Weiner

Rebecca J. Wilson

OF COUNSEL

Dale A. Coggins

ASSOCIATES

Barry D. Ramsdell	Elsie Bennett Kappler
Jennifer L. Lauro	Kathleen M. Colbert
Adam Simms	Kristin Garner
Christine Hasiotis	Robin E. Folsom
Chantal M. Healey	Rita D. Lu
Sandra P. Criss	William Vance Hoch
Thomas C. Farrell	William M. ("Mo") Cowan

Martin S. Ebel

For Complete List of Firm Personnel, See General Section

For full biographical listings, see the Martindale-Hubbell Law Directory

PETTINGELL & REGAN (AV)

85 Devonshire Street, 02109
Telephone: 617-723-0901
Fax: 617-723-0977

Richard H. Pettingell   Joseph A. Regan

ASSOCIATES

Robert E. Kiely	Paige L. Tobin
Brian J. Gunning	Malcolm Patrick Galvin, III

For full biographical listings, see the Martindale-Hubbell Law Directory

SHAPIRO & ASSOCIATES (AV)

One Beacon Street, 24th Floor, 02108
Telephone: 617-227-8100
Fax: 617-523-8100

Daniel B. Shapiro

ASSOCIATE

Bruce H. Norwell

Representative Clients: NLC Insurance Companies; Trust Insurance Co.; Liberty Mutual Insurance Co.

For full biographical listings, see the Martindale-Hubbell Law Directory

TAYLOR, DUANE, BARTON & GILMAN (AV)

75 Federal Street, 02110
Telephone: 617-654-8208
Fax: 617-482-5350
Providence, Rhode Island Office: The Wilcox Building, 42 Weybosset Street.
Telephone: 401-273-7171.
Fax: 401-273-2904.

MEMBERS OF FIRM

Allan E. Taylor	John J. Barton
James J. Duane, III	Pamela Slater Gilman

ASSOCIATES

Edward D. Shoulkin	Gina Witalec Verdi
Jennifer Ellis Burke	Robert C. Shindell
Francis A. Connor, III	Craig R. Waksler

David G. Bowman

For full biographical listings, see the Martindale-Hubbell Law Directory

WARNER & STACKPOLE LLP (AV)

75 State Street, 02109
Telephone: 617-951-9000
Telecopier: 617-951-9151
Email: w&s@warstack.com

MEMBERS OF FIRM

Michael DeMarco	Keith C. Long
Antoinette D. Hubbard	Janice Kelley Rowan
Ralph T. Lepore, III	Robert A. Whitney

ASSOCIATES

Alida M. Coo	Anne T. Mitchell
Kristine E. George	Daniel E. Rosenfeld
Nancy J. Kriegel	Karen R. Sweeney

OF COUNSEL

Norman A. Hubley

For Complete List of Firm Personnel, See General Section

For full biographical listings, see the Martindale-Hubbell Law Directory

---

BROCKTON, Plymouth Co.

VINCENT P. CAHALANE, P.C. (AV)

478 Torrey Street, 02401
Telephone: 508-588-1222
Fax: 508-584-4748

Vincent P. Cahalane	Julie A. Cahalane Cahill
Robert J. Zullas	John E. Cahill

Representative Clients: General Motors Co.; Quincy Mutual Fire Insurance Co.; American States Insurance Co.; Admiral Insurance Co.; United States Fidelity & Guaranty; Reliance Insurance Co.

For full biographical listings, see the Martindale-Hubbell Law Directory

MONE, D'AMBROSE & HANYEN, P.C. (AV)

529 Pearl Street, 02401
Telephone: 508-583-7010
Fax: 508-583-7062
Email: MDANDH@AOL.com

Francis D. Mone (1930-1962)	Brian J. Mone
William K. Mone (1949-1979)	Robert E. Langway, Jr.
James J. D'Ambrose	J. Gary Bennett
Clyde K. Hanyen, Jr.	Gerard J. Good

Jennifer R. Rossi

Representative Clients: Commercial Union Insurance Cos.; Southeastern Regional Vocational School Committee; Providence-Washington Insurance Co. *Reference:* Fleet Bank.

For full biographical listings, see the Martindale-Hubbell Law Directory

---

CAMBRIDGE,* Middlesex Co.

GORMLEY & COLUCCI, P.C. (AV)

One Main Street, P.O. Box 965, 02142-0900
Telephone: 617-349-3750
Fax: 617-661-2576

George F. Gormley   John D. Colucci

For full biographical listings, see the Martindale-Hubbell Law Directory

NEVILLE & KELLEY (AV)

Bulfinch Square, 43 Thorndike Street, 02141
Telephone: 617-876-7100
Fax: 617-225-0627

MEMBERS OF FIRM

Constance M. Neville   Paul R. Kelley

Sara Gens Birenbaum	June Harris
Patricia J. DiGiovanni	Kimberly D. Goodman
John L. Kerr	Nina E. Kallen

OF COUNSEL

Paul Michael Richardson

For full biographical listings, see the Martindale-Hubbell Law Directory

---

LOWELL, Middlesex Co.

DONAHUE & DONAHUE ATTORNEYS, P.C. (AV)

21 George Street, 01852
Telephone: 508-458-6887
Fax: 508-458-3424

(See Next Column)

DONAHUE & DONAHUE ATTORNEYS, P.C.—Continued

Daniel J. Donahue (1860-1939)	Peter V. Lawlor
Joseph P. Donahue (1889-1973)	Bradford P. Fortin
Charles A. Donahue (1891-1964)	Richard K. Donahue, Jr.
Richard K. Donahue	Andrea S. Barisano
Joseph P. Donahue, Jr.	Matthew C. Donahue
Joseph D. Regan	Richard E. Cavanaugh
Michael W. Gallagher	Kelly R. Spencer

Alicia A. Donahue

Representative Clients: The Travelers Insurance Co.; Jefferson Insurance; Monticello Insurance; Coregis Group; Rockwell International Corp.

For full biographical listings, see the Martindale-Hubbell Law Directory

---

NEW BEDFORD, Bristol Co.

MCLAUGHLIN & FOLAN, P.C. (AV)

401 County Street, P.O. Box 2095, 02741-2095
Telephone: 508-992-9800
Fax: 508-992-9730

David A. McLaughlin	John F. Folan
Mary Alice S. McLaughlin	Michael J. McGlone

John H. Solomito	John A. Leone

OF COUNSEL
Chris Byron

For full biographical listings, see the Martindale-Hubbell Law Directory

---

PITTSFIELD,* Berkshire Co.

CAMPOLI & CURLEY, A PROFESSIONAL CORPORATION (AV)

27 Willis Street, P.O. Box 1384, 01202
Telephone: 413-443-6485
Fax: 413-448-6233

Andrew T. Campoli	J. Peri Campoli
Thomas L. Campoli	Thomas J. Curley, Jr.

Thomas J. Hamel	Robert A. Monteleone, Jr.

Paula Kahn-Almgren

References: First Agricultural Bank; City Savings Bank.

For full biographical listings, see the Martindale-Hubbell Law Directory

---

SPRINGFIELD,* Hampden Co.

BROOKS, MULCAHY, SANBORN & WILLIAMS (AV)

14th Floor, One Monarch Place, 1414 Main Street, 01144
Telephone: 413-734-2156
Fax: 413-731-8924

MEMBERS OF FIRM

Clarence R. Brooks (1901-1970)	David W. Sanborn
Philip A. Brooks	H. Gregory Williams
Eugene J. Mulcahy	Ronald S. Smith

Lisa Brodeur-McGan

ASSOCIATE
Michael E. Mulcahy

Local Counsel for: Travelers Insurance Co.; Western World Insurance Co., Inc.; Greater New York Mutual Ins.; Cigna Healthplan of Massachusetts, Inc.; Northeast Utilities; Bay Colony Mobile Home Park Associates.
Counsel for: Bruschi Brothers, Inc.; W.J. Foss Co.

For full biographical listings, see the Martindale-Hubbell Law Directory

---

KELLY, PESSOLANO & WITHERS, P.C. (AV)

115 State Street, 01103
Telephone: 413-781-4700
Fax: 413-781-0471
Email: KPWPC@AOL.COM

George F. Kelly	Joseph P. Pessolano

Kevin D. Withers

Neil C. Darragh

For full biographical listings, see the Martindale-Hubbell Law Directory

---

MORIARTY, DONOGHUE & LEJA, P.C. (AV)

1331 Main Street, 01103
Telephone: 413-737-4319
Fax: 413-732-8767

James P. Moriarty (1878-1973)	Edward V. Leja
Thomas J. Donoghue	Patricia A. Barbalunga

(See Next Column)

Robert F. Connelly	John B. Stewart

Bernard J. Romani III

Local Counsel for: Insurance Company of North America; United Community Insurance Company; Transamerica Insurance Co.; Preferred Mutual Insurance Co.; Utica Mutual Insurance Co.; Spalding & Evenflo Cos. Inc.; St. Paul Insurance Co.; Cigna Insurance Co.; Ina Pro; Ford Motor Co.

For full biographical listings, see the Martindale-Hubbell Law Directory

---

ROBINSON DONOVAN MADDEN & BARRY, P.C. (AV)

Suite 1600, BayBank Tower, 1500 Main Street, 01115
Telephone: 413-732-2301
Fax: 413-785-4658

Homans Robinson (1894-1973)	Milton J. Donovan (1906-1995)
Lawrence M. Sinclair (1942-1986)	

OF COUNSEL

John H. Madden, Jr.	Victor Rosenberg
Edward J. Barry	Richard S. Milstein

Gordon H. Wentworth	John C. Sikorski
James H. Tourtelotte	Nancy Frankel Pelletier
Charles K. Bergin, Jr.	Paul S. Weinberg
Ronald C. Kidd	Frederica H. McCarthy
Jeffrey W. Roberts	Matthew J. King
Jeffrey L. McCormick	Neva Kaufman Rohan
James F. Martin	Douglas F. Boyd
Robert P. Cunningham	James K. Bodurtha

Keith A. Minoff

E. Paul Amata (Not admitted in MA)	Kimberly Davis Crear
	John W. Davis
James D. Chadwell	Edmund J. Gorman
Susan L. Cooper	Patricia M. Rapinchuk

Jonathan P. Rice

Representative Clients: The First National Bank of Boston; United Cooperative Bank; Fleet Bank, N.A.; American Policyholders Insurance Co.; CNA; Commercial Union Insurance Co.; Hanover Insurance Group.

For full biographical listings, see the Martindale-Hubbell Law Directory

---

WORCESTER,* Worcester Co.

FULLER, ROSENBERG, PALMER & BELIVEAU (AV)

14 Harvard Street, P.O. Box 764, 01613
Telephone: 508-755-5225
Telecopier: 508-757-1039

MEMBERS OF FIRM

Albert E. Fuller	Peter A. Palmer
Kenneth F. Rosenberg	Thomas W. Beliveau

ASSOCIATES

Robert W. Towle	Michael I. Mutter
Julie Bednarz Russell	Brian F. Welsh
Timothy O. Ribley	John J. Finn
Mark W. Murphy	James C. Crowley, Jr.
Lisa R. Bertonazzi	John P. Donohue
Mark C. Darling	James F. Gettens
William J. Mason	John Arthur Johnson
Antoinette J. Yitchinsky	Ann F. Scannell

For full biographical listings, see the Martindale-Hubbell Law Directory

---

HEALY & ROCHELEAU, P.C. (AV)

Denholm Building, 484 Main Street Suite 560, 01608
Telephone: 508-791-6287
Fax: 508-791-2652

J. Oscar Rocheleau (1906-1990)	David F. Hassett
Edward P. Healy	Gerard T. Donnelly

Anthony N. Tomasiello, Jr.	Sarah L. Brown
Janet E. Kaufman	Jennifer A. Whelan

Reference: Shawmut Worcester County Bank N.A.

For full biographical listings, see the Martindale-Hubbell Law Directory

---

MACCARTHY, POJANI & HURLEY (AV)

Worcester Plaza, 446 Main Street, 01608
Telephone: 508-798-2480
Fax: 508-797-9561

Philip J. MacCarthy	Howard E. Stempler
John F. Hurley, Jr.	William J. Ritter

Representative Clients: Fleet Bank of Massachusetts, N.A.; Melville Corp.; Travelers Insurance Co.; Liberty Mutual Co.; Commerce Insurance Co.; Worcester Mutual Insurance Co.; Health Plans, Inc.; Marane Oil Corp.

(See Next Column)

MacCARTHY, POJANI & HURLEY, *Worcester—Continued*

For Complete List of Firm Personnel, See General Section

For full biographical listings, see the Martindale-Hubbell Law Directory

MILTON, LAURENCE & DIXON (AV)

100 Front Street, Suite 825, 01608
Telephone: 508-791-6386
Fax: 508-799-4879

MEMBERS OF FIRM

Stanley B. Milton (1899-1992)	Karen A. Loughlin
Robert C. Milton (1932-1977)	Beth Anne Bagley
Gerard R. Laurence	Daniel M. Wrenn
Charles W. Dixon	William R. Trainor
Paul P. O'Connor	Karyn E. Polito

OF COUNSEL

John G. Preston

Representative Clients: Aetna Life and Casualty Co.; American Policyholders Insurance Co.; CIGNA; Chubb & Sons; Continental Insurance Co.; General Accident Group; Hanover Insurance Co.; Liberty Mutual Insurance Co.; Medical Malpractice Joint Underwriting Association of Massachusetts; St. Paul Tire and Marine Insurance Co.

For full biographical listings, see the Martindale-Hubbell Law Directory

MICHIGAN

ANN ARBOR,* Washtenaw Co.

BOOTHMAN, HEBERT & ELLER, P.C. (AV)

300 N. Fifth Avenue, Suite 140, 48108
Telephone: 313-995-9050
Fax: 313-995-8966
Detroit, Michigan Office: Marquette Building, 243 West Congress, Suite 950.
Telephone: 313-964-0150.
Fax: 313-964-2226.

Richard C. Boothman (Resident)

For full biographical listings, see the Martindale-Hubbell Law Directory

BRAUN KENDRICK FINKBEINER PLC (AV)

700 First National Building, 48104
Telephone: 313-995-4100
Telecopier: 313-995-4798
URL: http://www.bkf-law.com
Bay City, Michigan Office: 201 Phoenix Building, P.O. Box 2039.
Telephone: 517-895-8505.
Telecopier: 517-895-8437.
Saginaw, Michigan Office: 101 N. Washington, Suite 812.
Telephone: 517-753-3461.
Telecopier: 517-753-3951.

Barry M. Levine

Representative Clients: Farm Bureau Insurance Group; Firemans Fund American Insurance; Frankenmuth Mutual Insurance Co.; Fremont Mutual Insurance Co.; Great Lakes American Life Ins. Co.; Hartford Insurance Group; Hastings Mutual Insurance Co.; Kemper Insurance Group; Michigan Mutual Liability Co.; Mutual Benefit Life Ins. Co.

For full biographical listings, see the Martindale-Hubbell Law Directory

HURBIS & CLINTON (AV)

Fifth Floor, City Center Building, 48104
Telephone: 313-761-8358
Fax: 313-761-3134

Charles J. Hurbis	Mary F. Clinton
Robert Lipnik	Georgette E. David

Representative Clients: General Motors Corp.; ITT Hartford; Insurance Company of North America; The University of Michigan; North Oakland Medical Center; City of Pontiac; Sears Roebuck and Co.; Montgomery Ward and Co., Inc.; Sedjwick-James, Inc.

For full biographical listings, see the Martindale-Hubbell Law Directory

MILLER, CANFIELD, PADDOCK AND STONE, P.L.C. (AV)

A Professional Limited Liability Company
Founded in 1852 by Sidney Davy Miller
101 North Main Street, Seventh Floor, 48104-1400
Telephone: 313-663-2445
Fax: 313-747-7147
Detroit, Michigan Office: 150 West Jefferson, Suite 2500, 48226-4415.
Telephone: 313-963-6420.
Fax: 313-496-7500.
Cable Address: "Stem Detroit."
Bloomfield Hills, Michigan Office: Suite 100, Pinehurst Office Center, 1400 North Woodward, 48303-2014.
Telephone: 313-645-5000.
Fax: 313-645-1917.
Grand Rapids, Michigan Office: 1200 Campau Square Plaza, 99 Monroe, N.W., 49503-2639.
Telephone: 616-454-8656.
Fax: 616-776-6322.
Howell, Michigan Office: 121 South Barnard Street, Suite 4, 48843-2305.
Telephone: 517-546-7600.
Telecopier: 517-546-6974.
Kalamazoo, Michigan Office: 444 West Michigan Avenue, 49007-3752.
Telephone: 616-381-7030.
Fax: 616-382-0244.
Lansing, Michigan Office: One Michigan Avenue, Suite 900, 48933-1609.
Telephone: 517-487-2070.
Fax: 517-374-6304.
Monroe, Michigan Office: The Executive Centre, 214 East Elm Avenue, 48161-2682.
Telephone: 313-243-2000.
Fax: 313-243-0901.
Washington, D.C. Office: 1225 Nineteenth Street, N.W., Suite 400. 20036.
Telephone: 202-429-5575; 785-0600.
Fax: 202-331-1118; 785-1234.
Pensacola, Florida Office: 25 West Cedar, 32501.
Telephone: 904-469-1088.
Fax: 904-432-0677.
St. Petersburg, Florida Office: 100 Second Avenue S., Suite 7045, 33701.
Telephone: 813-982-6000.
Fax: 813-892-6002.
New York, New York Office: Eleventh Floor, 135 East 57th Street, 10022-2087.
Telephone: 212-754-5400.
Fax: 212-754-5401.
Gdansk, Poland Office: Suite 322, Dom Technika Building, UI. Rajska 6, 80-850.
Telephone: 011-485-831-2808.
Fax: 011-485-831-4719.
Warsaw, Poland Office: UI. Marszalkowska 82, Suite 561, 00-517.
Telephone: 011-482-623-6457 and 6458.
Fax: 011-482-623-6459.

RESIDENT PRINCIPALS

Robert E. Gilbert	David A. French
Allyn D. Kantor	Marta A. Manildi

Representative Firm Clients: Chrysler Corporation; Comerica, Incorporated; City of Detroit, Michigan; Detroit Tigers, Inc.; First of Michigan; Ford Motor Company; Ford Motor Credit Company; Great Lakes Bancorp; Henry Ford Hospital; INVETECH Company.

For Complete List of Firm Personnel, See General Section

For full biographical listings, see the Martindale-Hubbell Law Directory

---

BATTLE CREEK, Calhoun Co.

SULLIVAN, HAMILTON, SCHULZ, LETZRING, SIMONS, KRETER, TOTH & LEBEUF, P.C. (AV)

One West Michigan Avenue, 49017
Telephone: 616-965-3216
Fax: 616-965-2919

Maxwell B. Allen (1884-1942)	Bert W. Schulz
John M. Allen (1914-1985)	Kurt F. Letzring
Ronald H. Ryan (1901-1988)	Stephen L. Simons
Raymond R. Allen (1919-1996)	Mark E. Kreter
James M. Sullivan	Michael J. Toth

Ronald A. Lebeuf

OF COUNSEL

Robert P. Hamilton

General Counsel for: Michigan Woodwork and Specialties.
Local Counsel for: The Medical Protective Co.; Gannett, Inc.; Automobile Club of Michigan Insurance Group and Insurance Assn. (AAA); Michigan Physicians Mutual Liability Co.; State Farm Mutual Insurance Co.; Auto Owners Insurance Co.; Cincinnati Insurance Co.; Nationwide Insurance Co.

For full biographical listings, see the Martindale-Hubbell Law Directory

BINGHAM FARMS, Oakland Co.

SMALL, TOTH, BALDRIDGE & VAN BELKUM, P.C. (AV)

30100 Telegraph Road Suite 250, 48025-4516
Telephone: 810-647-9595
Facsimile: 810-647-9599

Richard L. Small	David M. Baldridge
John M. Toth	Thomas G. Van Belkum

Keith P. Felty

Representative Clients: Kemper Insurance Group; Mt. Vernon Insurance Co.; Allstate Insurance Co.; Anthem Insurance Co.; Lincoln Insurance Group; Philadelphia Insurance Cos.; Hastings Mutual Insurance Co.; General Star Management Co.; Lincoln Mutual Insurance Co.; CNA Insurance Group.

For full biographical listings, see the Martindale-Hubbell Law Directory

BIRMINGHAM, Oakland Co.

KELL & LYNCH, P.C. (AV)

300 East Maple Road, Suite 200, 48009
Telephone: 810-647-2333
Telefax: 810-647-2781

Michael V. Kell	Margaret A. Lynch

Jennifer T. Gilhool	Steven M. Ribiat
(Not admitted in MI)	

OF COUNSEL
M. Andrea Vaughn

Representative Clients: AlliedSignal, Inc.; AMP Inc.; Dow Corning Corp.; Hatteras Yachts; Lectron Products, Inc.; Metromedia Steakhouses, Inc.; Sybron Corp.; Michigan Consolidated Gas Co.; American Natural Resources.

For full biographical listings, see the Martindale-Hubbell Law Directory

LACEY & JONES (AV)

600 South Adams Road, Suite 300, 48009-6827
Telephone: 810-433-1414
Fax: 810-433-1241
Grand Rapids, Michigan Office: Suite 430, Ledyard Building, 125 Ottawa Avenue, N.W.
Telephone: 616-776-3641.
Fax: 616-776-3516.

Ralph B. Lacey (1885-1966)	Francis L. Sylvester (Retired)
William J. Jones (1908-1991)	Paul Van Hartesveldt (Retired)
Robert B. Lacey (1912-1976)	John A. Hilgendorf (Retired)

MEMBERS OF FIRM

Theodore A. Lughezzani	Dennis E. Zacharski
Steve N. Yardley	T. F. Felker, Jr.
John Hayes	Gerald M. Marcinkoski
Charles E. Mann	William A. Day
Larry P. Beidelman	Kathleen McNichol Behn
Bruce C. Roberts	Richard N. Lovernick
Lawrence G. Kozaruk	Peter M. Roggenbaum
David J. Duthie	
(Resident, Grand Rapids)	

ASSOCIATES

Michael T. Reinholm	Timothy D. Finegan
Johnnie B. Rambus	Robert H. Orlowski, Jr.
Sean J. Powers	J. Patrick O'Neill
Timothy M. McAree	Dawn M. Sutkiewicz
(Resident, Grand Rapids)	D. Michael McCann

OF COUNSEL

Thomas J. Sullivan	Robert L. Beardslee

William G. Sinn

Representative Clients: Alexsis, Inc.; Ameritech; Chrysler Corporation; CIGNA; Liberty Mutual Insurance Company; Meijer, Inc.; Metropolitan Prop. & Casualty; Michigan Hospital Association; Travelers Insurance Company.

For full biographical listings, see the Martindale-Hubbell Law Directory

BLOOMFIELD HILLS, Oakland Co.

FEDERLEIN & KERANEN, P.C. (AV)

6895 Telegraph Road, 48301
Telephone: 810-647-9653
Fax: 810-647-9683
Email: 102416.1133@COMPUSERVE.COM
Detroit, Michigan Office: 407 East Fort, Suite 350.
Telephone: 313-965-6090.

Walter J. Federlein	Thomas M. Keranen

(See Next Column)

Frederick F. Butters	Maria J. Bernard

Peter J. Cavanaugh

For full biographical listings, see the Martindale-Hubbell Law Directory

LEHMAN & VALENTINO, P.C. (AV)

1411 South Woodward Avenue, Suite 200, 48302
Telephone: 810-334-7787
Fax: 810-334-7202

Richard L. Lehman	Paul G. Valentino

Victor P. Valentino

OF COUNSEL
Patrick M. Cleary

Reference: NBD.

For full biographical listings, see the Martindale-Hubbell Law Directory

RICHARD A. PATTERSON, P.C. (AV)

6905 Telegraph Road Suite 215, 48301
Telephone: 810-647-6950
Facsimile: 810-645-0917

Richard A. Patterson

Representative Clients: Metropolitan Life; Ohio National Life; The Credit Life Insurance Company; Travelers Insurance Co.; Imperial Casualty and Indemnity.

For full biographical listings, see the Martindale-Hubbell Law Directory

DAVID D. PATTON & ASSOCIATES, P.C. (AV)

100 Bloomfield Hills Parkway, Suite 110, 48304
Telephone: 810-258-6020
Fax: 810-258-6052
Email: Litigation@Aol.Com

David D. Patton

Ellen Bartman Jannette	Patricia C. White

David H. Patton (1912-1993)

For full biographical listings, see the Martindale-Hubbell Law Directory

PORTNOY, PIDGEON & ROTH, P.C. (AV)

3883 Telegraph, Suite 103, 48302
Telephone: 810-647-4242
Fax: 810-647-8251
Email: DWINNIE103@AOL.COM

Bernard N. Portnoy	Marc S. Berlin
James M. Pidgeon	Berton K. May
Robert P. Roth	Sheila Connor-Heath

Charles A. Harrison III

Representative Clients: Continental Insurance Co.; Continental Health Care.

For full biographical listings, see the Martindale-Hubbell Law Directory

DETROIT, * Wayne Co.

BLAKE, KIRCHNER, SYMONDS, MACFARLANE, LARSON & SMITH, P.C. (AV)

1432 Buhl Building, 48226
Telephone: 313-961-7321
Fax: 313-961-5972

F. Peter Blake	Meria E. Larson
Arthur G. Kirchner	Richard P. Smith
Daniel C. Symonds	Kevin T. Kennedy
Bruce F. MacFarlane	Jane P. Garrett

Christopher G. Manolis

David B. Klein	Michael P. Donnelly

Kim Leslie Kretzschmar

Reference: Comerica Bank.

For full biographical listings, see the Martindale-Hubbell Law Directory

BOOTHMAN, HEBERT & ELLER, P.C. (AV)

Marquette Building, 243 West Congress, Suite 950, 48226
Telephone: 313-964-0150
Fax: 313-964-2226
Ann Arbor, Michigan Office: 300 N. Fifth Avenue, Suite 140.
Telephone: 313-995-9050.
Fax: 313-995-8966.

Dale L. Hebert	Gary S. Eller
Richard C. Boothman	
(Resident, Ann Arbor Office)	

(See Next Column)

BOOTHMAN, HEBERT & ELLER P.C., *Detroit—Continued*

George D. Moustakas	Marta J. Hoffman
Roy A. Luttmann	Sharon E. Hollins
	Joyce E. Taylor

OF COUNSEL

L. Stewart Hastings, Jr.	Kathryn A. Kerka

Representative Clients: University of Michigan; Michigan Physicians Mutual Liability Co.; Emergency Physicians Medical Group; Kaiser Permanente; Physicians Insurance Co. of Michigan.
Reference: Comerica Bank-Detroit.

For full biographical listings, see the Martindale-Hubbell Law Directory

EGGENBERGER, EGGENBERGER, McKINNEY, WEBER & HOFMEISTER, P.C. (AV)

42nd Floor Penobscot Building, 48226
Telephone: 313-961-9722

William J. Eggenberger	John P. McKinney
(1900-1984)	Stephen L. Weber
William D. Eggenberger	Paul D. Hofmeister
Robert E. Eggenberger	Thomas R. Paxton

Mary T. Humbert	James B. Eggenberger

Representative Clients: Central National Insurance of Omaha; Great Central Insurance Co.; Inland Mutual Insurance Co.; Midwest Mutual Insurance Co.; Motor Land Insurance Co.; Pioneer Mutual Casualty Co.; Preferred Risk Mutual Insurance Company of Des Moines Iowa; Puritan Insurance Co.; State Farm Fire and Casualty Co.; State Farm Mutual Automobile Insurance Co.

For full biographical listings, see the Martindale-Hubbell Law Directory

FEIKENS, VANDER MALE, STEVENS, BELLAMY & GILCHRIST, P.C. (AV)

One Detroit Center Suite 3400, 500 Woodward Avenue, 48226-3406
Telephone: 313-962-5909
Fax: 313-962-3125
Email: FEIKENS@COUNSEL.COM

Robert E. Dice (1922-1983)	Lee A. Stevens
Jon Feikens	William C. Hurley
Jack E. Vander Male	Linda M. Galbraith
Frederick B. Bellamy	Michael S. Cafferty
Alan Gordon Gilchrist	Robert H. Feikens
L. Neal Kennedy	Gerald W. Van Wyke
Bruce A. VandeVusse	Roger L. Wolcott
	Sharon McPhail

Richard G. Koefod	Keith J. Soltis
Joseph E. Kozely, Jr.	Michael B. Barey
Jeffrey Feikens	Renee T. VanderHagen
	Michael P. Citrin

OF COUNSEL

Sam W. Thomas (P.C.)	Walter Vincent Bernard III

LEGAL SUPPORT PERSONNEL

PARALEGALS

Robert Westveer	Linda Barthlow

For full biographical listings, see the Martindale-Hubbell Law Directory

FOSTER, MEADOWS & BALLARD, P.C. (AV)

3200 Penobscot Building, 48226
Telephone: 313-961-3234
Cable Address: "Foster"
Telex: 23-5823
Facsimile: 313-961-6184

Sparkman D. Foster (1897-1967)	Richard A. Dietz
Charles R. Hrdlicka	Robert H. Fortunate
Paul D. Galea	Robert G. Lahiff
	Camille A. Raffa-Dietz

Michael J. Liddane	Paul A. Kettunen

OF COUNSEL

John L. Foster	John F. Langs
	John A. Mundell, Jr.

Representative Clients: Alexander & Alexander; Frank B. Hall & Company of New York; Great American Insurance Co.; Marine Office of America; St. Paul Companies; Utica Mutual Insurance.

For full biographical listings, see the Martindale-Hubbell Law Directory

GARAN, LUCOW, MILLER, SEWARD & BECKER, P.C. (AV)

1000 Woodbridge Place, 48207-3192
Telephone: 313-446-1530
Fax: 313-259-0450
Email: glm@gnn.com
Grand Blanc, Michigan Office: 8332 Office Park Drive.
Telephone: 810-695-3700.
Fax: 810-695-6488.
Port Huron, Michigan Office: Port Huron Office Center, 511 Fort Street, Suite 505.
Telephone: 810-985-4400.
Fax: 810-985-4107.
Ann Arbor, Michigan Office: 101 North Main Street, Suite 801.
Telephone: 313-930-5600.
Fax: 313-930-0043.
Troy, Michigan Office: 1111 West Long Lake Road, Suite 300.
Telephone: 810-641-7600.
Fax: 810-641-0222.
Mount Clemens, Michigan Office: Towne Square Development, 10 S. Main Street, Suite 307.
Telephone: 810-954-3800.
Fax: 810-954-3803.
Grand Rapids, Michigan Office: Campau Square Plaza Building, 99 Monroe Avenue N.W., Suite 102.
Telephone: 616-732-5330.
Fax: 616-732-5333.

Matthew A. Seward	James J. Hayes, Jr.
Thomas F. Myers	Thomas W. Emery
Dennis P. Partridge	Joseph Crystal
John E. McSorley	Boyd E. Chapin, Jr.
Lamont E. Buffington	Frederick B. Plumb
Thomas L. Misuraca	Mark C. Smiley
Rosalind Rochkind	James S. Goulding
	John J. Gillooly

Daniel S. Saylor	Michael J. DePolo
Peter B. Worden, Jr.	C. David Miller, II
Charlotte H. Johnson	Anne K. Newcomer
David M. Shafer	Eun (Ellen) G. Ha
Lloyd G. Johnson	Timothy J. Jordan
Robert D. Goldstein	Lynn E. Geist
Michael J. Paolucci	Mark T. Rajt

OF COUNSEL

Daniel L. Garan	Beth A. Andrews
Milton Lucow	Nancy J. Bourget
Albert A. Miller	David L. Lattie
Roy E. Castetter	Meri Craver Borin

Counsel for: Allstate Insurance Co.; Sears, Roebuck & Co.; Liberty Mutual Insurance Co.; Continental Insurance Companies.

For Complete List of Firm Personnel, See General Section

For full biographical listings, see the Martindale-Hubbell Law Directory

HAYDUK, ANDREWS & HYPNAR, P.C. (AV)

1700 Buhl Building, 535 Griswold, 48226
Telephone: 313-962-4500
Fax: 313-964-6577

Mark S. Hayduk	Robin K. Andrews
	Mark A. Hypnar

Sean Angus McPhillips	Lynn E. Radke

Representative Clients: Farmers Insurance Group; Admiral Insurance Co.; American Modern Home Insurance; Western Heritage Insurance; Northpointe Insurance; Shelby Mutual Insurance; Scibal Ins. Co.; Vik Brothers Ins.; Investors Ins. Group.

For full biographical listings, see the Martindale-Hubbell Law Directory

KELLER, THOMA, SCHWARZE, SCHWARZE, DuBAY & KATZ, P.C. (AV)

440 East Congress, 5th Floor, 48226
Telephone: 313-965-7610
Bloomfield Hills, Michigan Office: Suite 122, 100 West Long Lake Road.
Telephone: 810-642-5218.

Leonard A. Keller (1906-1970)	Linda M. Foster
Frederick B. Schwarze	Bruce M. Bagdady
Thomas H. Schwarze	Carl F. Schwarze
Dennis B. DuBay	George P. Butler, III
James R. Miller	Brian A. Kreucher
Stewart J. Katz	Kenneth C. Howell
Anthony J. Heckemeyer	Mark C. Knoth
Thomas L. Fleury	Patrice L. Baker
Terrence J. Miglio	John J. Rabaut
Gary P. King	Martha A. Proctor
Robert A. Lusk	Joseph R. Furton, Jr.
	James Joseph Boutrous, II

(See Next Column)

KELLER, THOMA, SCHWARZE, SCHWARZE, DUBAY & KATZ P.C.—*Continued*

OF COUNSEL

Richard J. Thoma   Charles E. Keller

Counsel for: Livonia Public Schools; Ludington News Co., Inc.
Representative Clients: Borg-Warner Corp.; E & L Transport Co.; The Kroger Co.; Holnam, Inc.
Public Employer Clients: City of Farmington Hills; City of Flint; City of Grosse Pointe Woods; Saginaw Public Schools.

For full biographical listings, see the Martindale-Hubbell Law Directory

---

LUPO & KOCZKUR, P.C. (AV)

1000 First National Building, 48226
Telephone: 313-964-0110
Fax: 313-964-3711

Dane A. Lupo   Paul S. Koczkur

Peter Kennedy Moody   Alexander B. Jarowyj
OF COUNSEL
Hulen R. Simpson   Dehai Tao

Representative Clients: Anheuser-Busch, Inc.; United Artists; ITT; Olsten; Thermadyne Industries; National Beverage; CIGNA/Insurance Company of North America; Michigan Millers; Walt Disney World; Vic Tanny International.

For full biographical listings, see the Martindale-Hubbell Law Directory

---

MAGER, MERCER, SCOTT & ALBER, P.C. (AV)

500 Woodward Avenue Suite 3400, 48226
Telephone: 313-962-8212
Facsimile: 313-962-5413
Oakland County Office: Top of Troy Building, 755 West Big Beaver, Suite 1700, Troy, Michigan.
Telephone: 810-362-8212.
Facsimile: 810-362-6944.
Macomb County Office: 18285 Ten Mile Road, Suite 100, Roseville, Michigan.
Telephone: 810-771-1100.
Facsimile: 810-775-5170.

George J. Mager, Jr.

Representative Clients: American States Insurance Co.; CIGNA; Federal Insurance Co.; Reliance Insurance Co.; State Farm Insurance Co.; United Insurance Company of America.

For full biographical listings, see the Martindale-Hubbell Law Directory

---

MEGANCK & COTHORN, P.C. (AV)

Suite 950, 400 Renaissance Center, 48243-1509
Telephone: 313-259-6330
Fax: 313-259-7037

Allan G. Meganck   John A. Cothorn
Suzanne C. Stanczyk

Thomas Myers   William G. Oldford, Jr.
OF COUNSEL
David M. Thoms

Representative Clients: Ford Motor Company; Norton Co.; K-Mart Corp.; The Stanley Works; Textron; Figgie International; Phone-Poulenc Rorer Pharmaceuticals, Inc.; National Chiropractic Mutual Insurance Co.; Kellermeyer Building Services, Inc.; Tokio Marine Management Co.

For full biographical listings, see the Martindale-Hubbell Law Directory

---

MILLER, CANFIELD, PADDOCK AND STONE, P.L.C. (AV)

A Professional Limited Liability Company
Founded in 1852 by Sidney Davy Miller
150 West Jefferson, Suite 2500, 48226-4415
Telephone: 313-963-6420
Fax: 313-496-7500
Cable Address: "Stem Detroit"
Detroit, Michigan Office: 150 West Jefferson, Suite 2500, 48226-4415.
Telephone: 313-963-6420.
Fax: 313-496-7500.
Cable Address: "Stem Detroit."
Ann Arbor, Michigan Office: 101 North Main Street, 7th Floor, 48104-1400.
Telephone: 313-663-2445.
Fax: 313-747-7147.
Bloomfield Hills, Michigan Office: Suite 100, Pinehurst Office Center, 1400 North Woodward, 48303-2014.
Telephone: 313-645-5000.
Fax: 313-645-1917.

(See Next Column)

Grand Rapids, Michigan Office: 1200 Campau Square Plaza, 99 Monroe, N.W., 49503-2639.
Telephone: 616-454-8656.
Fax: 616-776-6322.
Howell, Michigan Office: 121 South Barnard Street, Suite 4, 48843-2305.
Telephone: 517-546-7600.
Telecopier: 517-546-6974.
Kalamazoo, Michigan Office: 444 West Michigan Avenue, 49007-3752.
Telephone: 616-381-7030.
Fax: 616-382-0244.
Lansing, Michigan Office: One Michigan Avenue, Suite 900, 48933-1609.
Telephone: 517-487-2070.
Fax: 517-374-6304.
Monroe, Michigan Office: The Executive Centre, 214 East Elm Avenue, 48161-2682.
Telephone: 313-243-2000.
Fax: 313-243-0901.
Washington, D.C. Office: 1225 Nineteenth Street, N.W., Suite 400. 20036.
Telephone: 202-429-5575; 785-0600.
Fax: 202-331-1118; 785-1234.
Pensacola, Florida Office: 25 West Cedar, 32501.
Telephone: 904-469-1088.
Fax: 904-432-0677.
St. Petersburg, Florida Office: 100 Second Avenue S., Suite 7045, 33701.
Telephone: 813-982-6000.
Fax: 813-892-6002.
New York, New York Office: Eleventh Floor, 135 East 57th Street, 10022-2087.
Telephone: 212-754-5400.
Fax: 212-754-5401.
Gdansk, Poland Office: Suite 322, Dom Technika Building, UI. Rajska 6, 80-850.
Telephone: 011-485-831-2808.
Fax: 011-485-831-4719.
Warsaw, Poland Office: UI. Marszalkowska 82, Suite 561, 00-517.
Telephone: 011-482-623-6457 and 6458.
Fax: 011-482-623-6459.

PRINCIPALS OF FIRM

Gilbert E. Gove	Stephen J. Ott
Carl H. von Ende	Michael P. Coakley
Allyn D. Kantor	James E. Spurr
(Ann Arbor Office)	(Kalamazoo Office)
Charles E. Ritter	Mark T. Boonstra
(Kalamazoo Office)	David A. French
Thomas G. Parachini	(Ann Arbor Office)
Gregory L. Curtner	Le Roy L. Asher, Jr.
(New York, N.Y. Office)	Pamela Chapman Enslen
W. Mack Faison	(Kalamazoo Office)
Joseph F. Galvin	Richard T. Urbis
Clarence L. Pozza, Jr.	Richard F. X. Urisko
Michael W. Hartmann	Steven A. Roach
Larry J. Saylor	Brian J. Doren
James G. Vantine, Jr.	Irene Bruce Hathaway
(Kalamazoo Office)	Lawrence M. Dudek
Leland D. Barringer	Marta A. Manildi
Marjory G. Basile	(Ann Arbor Office)

Kathryn L. Ossian
OF COUNSEL
George E. Bushnell, Jr.
ASSOCIATES

Ballard Jay Yelton III	Thomas R. Cox
(Kalamazoo Office)	Robert J. Haddad

Frederick A. Acomb

Representative Firm Clients: Chrysler Corporation; Comerica, Incorporated; City of Detroit, Michigan; Detroit Tigers, Inc.; First of Michigan; Ford Motor Company; Ford Motor Credit Company; Great Lakes Bancorp; Henry Ford Hospital; INVETECH Company.

For Complete List of Firm Personnel, See General Section

For full biographical listings, see the Martindale-Hubbell Law Directory

---

PATTERSON, PHIFER & PHILLIPS, P.C. (AV)

L. B. King Building, 1274 Library Street, Suite 500, 48226
Telephone: 313-964-2360

Michael D. Patterson   Randolph D. Phifer
Dwight W. Phillips

Joseph M. White   Eugene M. Holmes
Lisa A. Cylar

Representative Clients: Detroit Board of Education; Fireman's Fund Insurance Co.; General Motors Corp.; Home Federal Savings Bank; Liberty Mutual Insurance Co.; Metropolitan Life Insurance Co.; Michigan Basic Property Insurance Assn.; New York Life Insurance Co.; Wayne State University.
Reference: First of American Bank-Detroit, N.A.

For full biographical listings, see the Martindale-Hubbell Law Directory

Detroit—Continued

RUTLEDGE, MANION, RABAUT, TERRY & THOMAS, P.C. (AV)

2300 Buhl Building, 48226
Telephone: 313-965-6100
Telefax: 313-965-6558

Alvin A. Rutledge	Elmer L. Roller
Paul J. Manion	Anthony J. Calati
Vincent C. Rabaut, Jr.	Mary L. Dresbach
Christopher L. Terry	Lisa Sabon Anstess
David M. Thomas	Patrick D. Filbin
Michael A. Gunderson	David A. Brauer

Matthew A. Brauer

LEGAL SUPPORT PERSONNEL
PARALEGALS

Gloria A. Lambright	Laura A. Matheson

Doreen A. Honn

For full biographical listings, see the Martindale-Hubbell Law Directory

SCHUREMAN, FRAKES, GLASS & WULFMEIER (AV)

440 East Congress, Fourth Floor, 48226
Telephone: 313-961-1500
Telecopier: 313-961-1087
Harbor Springs, Michigan Office: One Spring Street Sq., 49740.
Telephone: 616-526-1145.
Telecopier: 616-526-9343.

MEMBERS OF FIRM

Jeptha W. Schureman	LeRoy H. Wulfmeier, III
John C. Frakes, Jr.	Cheryl L. Chandler
Charles F. Glass	David M. Ottenwess

ASSOCIATES

Daniel J. Dulworth	John J. Moran

Paul A. Salyers

Reference: Comerica.

For full biographical listings, see the Martindale-Hubbell Law Directory

TIMMIS & INMAN, L.L.P. (AV)

300 Talon Centre, 48207
Telephone: 313-396-4200
Telecopier: 313-396-4228

Robert E. Graziani	Mark W. Peyser

Bradley J. Knickerbocker

Erich J. D'Andrea

Representative Clients: Continental Insurance Company; Sentry Insurance Co.; Transamerica Insurance Group; Certain Underwriters at Lloyds of London; Regency Insurance Co.; Tangent Insurance Co.; Wausau Insurance Co.

For Complete List of Firm Personnel, See General Section

For full biographical listings, see the Martindale-Hubbell Law Directory

VANDEVEER GARZIA, PROFESSIONAL CORPORATION (AV)

Suite 1600, 333 West Fort Street, 48226
Telephone: 313-961-4880
Fax: 313-961-3822
Oakland County Office: 220 Park Street, Suite 300, Birmingham, Michigan.
Telephone: 810-645-0100.
Fax: 810-645-2430.
Macomb County Office: 50 Crocker Boulevard, Mount Clemens, Michigan.
Telephone: 810-468-4880.
Fax: 810-465-7159.
West Michigan Office: 1121 Ottawa Beach Road, Suite 140, Holland Michigan.
Telephone: 616-399-8600.
Fax: 616-786-9095.

Thomas P. Rockwell	Gary Alan Miller
James A. Sullivan	William L. Kiriazis
Michael M. Hathaway	Cynthia E. Merry
John J. Lynch, III (Resident, Oakland County Office)	Daniel P. Steele
	Shelley K. Miller (Resident, Oakland County Office)
Thomas M. Peters	
James K. Thome	Terrance P. Lynch
Ronald L. Cornell (Resident, Macomb County Office)	Dennis B. Cotter

Representative Clients: Aetna Casualty and Surety Co.; Bic Corp.; CNA Insurance Co.; Chubb Insurance; Farmers Insurance Group; Home Insurance Co.; Maryland Casualty Co.; Michigan Property & Casualty; Republic Franklin Insurance Co.; Sentry Insurance Co.; Travelers Insurance Co.; Transamerica Insurance Co.

For Complete List of Firm Personnel, See General Section

For full biographical listings, see the Martindale-Hubbell Law Directory

---

EAST LANSING, Ingham Co.

SMITH HAUGHEY RICE & ROEGGE, P.C. (AV)

1301 North Hagadorn Road, 48823-2320
Telephone: 517-332-3030
Facsimile: 517-332-3468
Grand Rapids, Michigan Office: 200 Calder Plaza Building, 250 Monroe Avenue, N.W., 49503-2251.
Telephone: 616-774-8000.
Facsimile: 616-774-2461.
Traverse City, Michigan Office: 241 East State Street, P.O. Box 848, 49685-0848.
Telephone: 616-929-4878.
Facsimile: 616-929-4182.

Douglas G. Powe

Daniel N. Stephens	James R. Duby, Jr.

Veronica A. Marsich

Representative Clients: Chevron; Cincinnati Insurance Co.; General Motors Corp.; Kemper Insurance Group; Michigan Hospital Assn.; Navistar International; St. Paul Insurance Cos.; Steelcase, Inc.; Sears Roebuck & Co.; Dow Elanco.

For full biographical listings, see the Martindale-Hubbell Law Directory

---

FARMINGTON HILLS, Oakland Co.

HALIW, SICILIANO AND MYCHALOWYCH (AV)

37000 Grand River, Suite 350, 48335
Telephone: 810-442-0510
Fax: 810-442-0518

MEMBERS OF FIRM

Andrew J. Haliw III	Nanette Lynn Korpi
Joseph A. Siciliano	Raymond L. Feul
Andrew W. Mychalowych	Frank E. Henke

For full biographical listings, see the Martindale-Hubbell Law Directory

JOHNSON, ROSATI, GALICA, LaBARGE, ASELTYNE, SUGAMELI & FIELD, P.C. (AV)

34405 W. Twelve Mile Road, Suite 200, 48331-5627
Telephone: 810-489-4100
Fax: 810-489-1726
Bay City, Michigan Office: 420 Shearer Building, 311 Center Avenue, 48708.
Telephone: 517-894-2600; 517-894-7191.
Fax: 517-894-7177.
Lansing, Michigan Office: 303 S. Waverly Road, 48917.
Telephone: 517-886-3800.
Fax: 517-886-9154.
St. Clair Shores, Michigan Office: 19900 E. 10 Mile Road, 48080.
Telephone: 313-777-3377.

Christopher J. Johnson	Laura Amtsbuechler
Carol A. Rosati	Marcia L. Howe
Kenneth G. Galica	Edward M. Olson
S. Randall Field	Daniel P. Dalton
Michael E. Rosati	Margaret T. Debler
Michael J. Sugameli	Marcelyn A. Stepanski
Kenneth A. Slusser	Andrey T. Tomkiw

Linda B. Taylor

Representative Clients: Michigan Municipal Risk Management Authority; Metropolitan Association for Improved School Legislation Risk Management Trust; Indiana Insurance Co.; County of Lapeer; County of Van Buren; County of Otsego; City of Romulus; City of Harper Woods; City of Hazel Park; Chirco Realty.

For full biographical listings, see the Martindale-Hubbell Law Directory

KAUFMAN AND PAYTON (AV)

200 Kaufman Financial Center, 30833 Northwestern Highway, 48334
Telephone: 810-626-5000
Telefacsimile: 810-626-2843
Grand Rapids, Michigan Office: 420 Trust Building.
Telephone: 616-459-4200.
Fax: 616-459-4929.
Traverse City, Michigan Office: 122 West State Street.
Telephone: 616-947-4050.
Fax: 616-947-7321.

Alan Jay Kaufman	Raymond I. Foley, II
Donald L. Payton	Jeffrey K. Van Hattum
Stephen R. Levine	Leo D. Neville
Ralph C. Chapa, Jr.	John Eric Franceschi

Tamera Lee Green

For full biographical listings, see the Martindale-Hubbell Law Directory

Farmington Hills—Continued

NEMIER, TOLARI, LANDRY, MAZZEO & JOHNSON, P.C. (AV)

37000 Grand River, Suite 300, 48335
Telephone: 810-476-6900
Fax: 810-476-6564

Craig L. Nemier	David B. Landry
Jeffrey L. Tolari	Rik Mazzeo
Mark R. Johnson	

Michelle E. Mathieu	Kathy Contos Nash
Christopher A. Todd	Douglas S. Loomer
Thomas S. McLeod	Gregory A. Light

OF COUNSEL

William R. Still	Terry E. Pietryga

LEGAL SUPPORT PERSONNEL

Veeder Ann Willey (Support Staff)

Representative Clients: Amerisure/Michigan Mutual Insurance Co.; Chubb Group of Insurance Cos.; Citizens Insurance Co.; Crum & Forster (U.S. Insurance Group); General Accident Insurance; State Farm Fire & Casualty; Nationwide; St. Paul Fire & Marine Insurance Co.; Westfield Insurance Cos.; PepsiCo.

For full biographical listings, see the Martindale-Hubbell Law Directory

---

FLINT,* Genesee Co.

LAW OFFICES OF PATRICK M. KIRBY A PROFESSIONAL CORPORATION (AV)

G1335 South Linden Road, Suite G, 48532
Telephone: 810-230-0833
Fax: 810-230-8222

Patrick M. Kirby

Todd O. Pope

Representative Clients: Brotherhood Mutual Insurance Co.; K & K Insurance Group.

For full biographical listings, see the Martindale-Hubbell Law Directory

---

GAYLORD,* Otsego Co.

BENSINGER, COTANT, MENKES & AARDEMA, P.C. (AV)

308 West Main Street, P.O. Box 1000, 49735
Telephone: 517-732-7536
Fax: 517-732-4922
Grand Rapids, Michigan Office: 983 Spaulding Avenue, S.E.
Telephone: 616-949-7963.
Fax: 616-949-5264.
Marquette, Michigan Office: 122 West Bluff.
Telephone: 906-225-1000.
Fax: 906-225-0818.

Richard G. Bensinger	James F. Pagels
James C. Cotant	Steven C. Byram
Michael E. Menkes	Michael J. Harrelson
Patrick J. Michaels	William M. Fury
Daniel Joseph Bebble	

Representative Clients: Accident Fund of Michigan; Auto-Owner Insurance Co.; Citizens/Hanover Insurance Co.; Farm Bureau Mutual Insurance Co.; Employers Reinsurance Co.; Lake State Mutual Insurance Co.; Michigan Hospital Association; Michigan Licensed Beverage Association; Physicians Insurance Co. of Michigan; State Farm Mutual Insurance Co.

For full biographical listings, see the Martindale-Hubbell Law Directory

---

GRAND RAPIDS,* Kent Co.

ALLABEN, MASSIE, VANDER WEYDEN & TIMMER (AV)

Suite 850, Commerce Building, 5 Lyon Street, N.W., 49503
Telephone: 616-774-2182
Fax: 616-774-0602

MEMBERS OF FIRM

Fred Roland Allaben	Keith A. Vander Weyden
(1901-1985)	John J. Timmer
Sam F. Massie, Jr.	Robert W. Bandeen

John R. Allaben

Representative Clients: American Syayes Insurance Co.; Michigan Mutual Liability Co.; National Union Insurance Cos.; Fidelity & Casualty Company of New York; U.S. Aircraft Insurance Group; Union Insurance Co.; The Continental Insurance Co.; Hanover Insurance Co.; Royal Globe Insurance Co.

For full biographical listings, see the Martindale-Hubbell Law Directory

---

BENSINGER, COTANT, MENKES & AARDEMA, P.C. (AV)

983 Spaulding Avenue, S.E., 49546
Telephone: 616-949-7963
Fax: 616-949-5264
Gaylord, Michigan Office: 308 West Main, P.O. Box 1000.
Telephone: 517-732-7536.
Fax: 517-732-4922.
Marquette, Michigan Office: 122 West Bluff.
Telephone: 906-225-1000.
Fax: 906-225-0818.

Robert Bryan Aardema	Brian W. Whitelaw
Kerr L. Moyer	Dale L. Arndt

Representative Clients: Allstate Insurance Co.; Physicians Insurance Co. of Michigan; State Farm Mutual Insurance Co.; Foremost Insurance Co.; Northern Mutual Insurance; Auto-Owners Insurance Co.; Insurance Equities Corp.; Osteopathic Mutual Insurance Co. Northbrook Insurance Co.; Michigan Hospital Association.

For full biographical listings, see the Martindale-Hubbell Law Directory

---

BOS & GLAZIER, P.L.C. (AV)

300 Ottawa N.W., Suite 800, 49503
Telephone: 616-458-6814
Fax: 616-458-0608
Email: BGLAZIOO@counsel.com

Carole D. Bos	Susan Wilson Keener
Bradley K. Glazier	Gwen E. Buday
Anne M. Frye	

For full biographical listings, see the Martindale-Hubbell Law Directory

---

BREMER, WADE, NELSON, LOHR & COREY, LLP (AV)

600 3 Mile Road, N.W., 49544-1601
Telephone: 616-784-4434
Fax: 616-784-7322

MEMBERS OF FIRM

William M. Bremer	Phillip J. Nelson
Michael D. Wade	James H. Lohr
Michael J. Corey	

ASSOCIATES

Barbara L. Olafsson	Olafur A. Olafsson

LEGAL SUPPORT PERSONNEL

Kathleen A. Fitzpatrick

Representative Clients: Auto Club Insurance Co.; Auto Owners Insurance Co.; Capitol Indemnity Corp.; Citizens Insurance Company of America; The Continental Insurance Cos.; Continental Loss Adjustment Services; Empire Fire & Marine Ins. Co.; Harco Insurance Co.; Medical Protective Co.; Meridian Mutual Insurance Co.; Ranger Insurance; Secura Insurance Co.

For full biographical listings, see the Martindale-Hubbell Law Directory

---

CHOLETTE, PERKINS & BUCHANAN (AV)

900 Campau Square Plaza Building, 99 Monroe Avenue, N.W., 49503
Telephone: 616-774-2131
Fax: 616-774-7016

MEMBERS OF FIRM

Calvin R. Danhof	Marc A. Kidder
Frederick W. Bleakley	Michael C. Mysliwiec
Reynolds A. Brander, Jr.	Evan L. MacFarlane
Edward Malinzak	John A. Quinn
Bruce M. Bieneman	Albert J. Engel, III
William J. Warren	Stephen C. Oldstrom
Donald C. Exelby	William E. McDonald, Jr.
Thomas H. Cypher	Mark E. Fatum
William A. Brengle	Richard K. Grover, Jr.
Alfred J. Parent	David J. DeGraw
Charles H. Worsfold	Martin W. Buschle
Michael P. McCasey	Miles J. Murphy, III

ASSOCIATES

Kenneth L. Block	Martha P. Forman
William J. Yob	Kathrine M. West
Robert E. Attmore	Ilse K. Masselink
John P. Lewis	

Counsel for: Aetna Casualty & Surety Co.; Argonaut Insurance Co.; Auto-Owners Insurance Co.; Employers Mutual; Liberty Mutual Insurance Co.; Sentry Group; State Farm Insurance; Eastern Aviation and Marine Underwriters; Home Insurance Co.; Nationwide Insurance.

For Complete List of Firm Personnel, See General Section

For full biographical listings, see the Martindale-Hubbell Law Directory

---

GRZANKA GRIT (AV)

2025 East Beltline, S.E., Suite 101, 49546
Telephone: 616-956-5559
Facsimile: 616-956-7546

(See Next Column)

GRZANKA GRIT, *Grand Rapids—Continued*

MEMBERS OF FIRM

Charles F. Grzanka　　　　　Constance J. Grzanka
Randall R. Grit

ASSOCIATES

Garrett J. Tenhave-Chapman　　　Christi L. Burda
Dennis P. Flynn

For full biographical listings, see the Martindale-Hubbell Law Directory

---

ROBERTS, BETZ & BLOSS, P.C. (AV)

555 Riverfront Plaza Building, 55 Campau, 49503
Telephone: 616-235-9955
Telecopier: 616-235-0404

Michael J. Roberts	Michael T. Small
Michael W. Betz	Ralph M. Reisinger
David J. Bloss	Henry S. Emrich
Gregory A. Block	Allan C. Vander Laan
George J. Quist	

For full biographical listings, see the Martindale-Hubbell Law Directory

---

SMITH HAUGHEY RICE & ROEGGE, P.C. (AV)

200 Calder Plaza Building, 250 Monroe Avenue, N.W., 49503-2251
Telephone: 616-774-8000
Facsimile: 616-774-2461
East Lansing, Michigan Office: 1301 North Hagadorn Road, 48823-2320.
Telephone: 517-332-3030.
Facsimile: 517-332-3468.
Traverse City, Michigan Office: 241 East State Street, P.O. Box 848, 49685-0848.
Telephone: 616-929-4878.
Facsimile: 616-929-4182.

Clifford A. Mitts (1902-1962)	Thomas R. Wurst
Laurence D. Smith (1913-1980)	Craig R. Noland
Robert V.V. Rice (1899-1982)	Paul M. Oleniczak
Michael S. Barnes (1944-1989)	Craig S. Neckers
L. Roland Roegge	Thomas E. Kent
Thomas F. Blackwell	Leonard M. Hickey
P. Laurence Mulvihill	John C. O'Loughlin
Lawrence P. Mulligan	Anthony J. Quarto
Thomas R. Tasker	Bruce P. Rissi
Paul H. Reinhardt	John M. Kruis
Lance R. Mather	Paul Van Oostenburg
Charles F. Behler	Dale Ann Iverson
John R. Sparks	William R. Jewell
Gary A. Rowe	Jon D. Vander Ploeg
William W. Jack, Jr.	Patrick F. Geary
William J. Hondorp	Terence J. Ackert
Thomas M. Weibel	Brian J. Kilbane
James G. Black	Dan C. Porter
E. Thomas Mc Carthy, Jr.	Phillip K. Mowers
Glenn W. House, Jr.	Carol D. Carlson
Christopher R. Genther	

Kay L. Griffith Hammond	Elizabeth Roberts VerHey
Marilyn S. Nickell	Jennifer Jane Nasser
Beth Suzanne Kromer	Ginny Kaye Mikita
Robert M. Kruse	Karl Werner Butterer, Jr.
John B. Combs	Susan Soon Im
Aileen M. Simet	J. Joseph Rossi
Matthew L. Meyer	Stacie R. Seitz
Dwight K. Hamilton	

OF COUNSEL

A. B. Smith, Jr.	Susan Bradley Jakubowski
David O. Haughey	Thomas P. Scholler

Representative Clients: Chevron; Cincinnati Insurance Co.; General Motors Corp.; Kemper Insurance Group; Michigan Hospital Assn.; Navistar International; St. Paul Insurance Cos.; Steelcase, Inc.

For full biographical listings, see the Martindale-Hubbell Law Directory

---

TOLLEY, VANDENBOSCH & WALTON, P.C. (AV)

5650 Foremost Drive, S.E., 49546
Telephone: 616-942-8090
Facsimile: 616-942-4677

Peter R. Tolley	David L. Harrison
Michael C. Walton	Richard J. Durden
Lawrence Korolewicz	Robert C. Greene
Todd R. Dickinson	Miles J. Postema
Paul L. Nelson	James K. Schepers
James B. Doezema	Susan Jasper Stein
Mark J. Colon	

Representative Clients: State Farm Insurance Co.; Sentry Insurance Co.; Fremont Mutual Insurance Co.; Phoenix Aviation; Admiral Insurance; Kemper Insurance; Northbrook Excess & Surplus Insurance Co.; St. Paul Companies; Aetna Insurance Co.; Chicago Title Insurance Co.

(See Next Column)

For full biographical listings, see the Martindale-Hubbell Law Directory

WHEELER UPHAM, A PROFESSIONAL CORPORATION (AV)

Second Floor, Trust Building, 40 Pearl Street, N.W., 49503-3001
Telephone: 616-459-7100
Fax: 616-459-6366

Gordon B. Wheeler (1904-1986)	William H. Heritage, Jr.
Buford A. Upham (Retired)	Kenneth E. Tiews
Robert H. Gillette	Jack L. Hoffman
Geoffrey L. Gillis	Janet C. Baxter
John M. Roels	Peter Kladder, III
Gary A. Maximiuk	James M. Shade
Timothy J. Orlebeke	Thomas A. Kuiper

Counsel For: Prudential Ins. Co.; Metropolitan Life Ins. Co.; Travelers Ins. Co.; Farmers Ins. Group; Auto-Owners Ins. Co.; Farm Bureau Ins. Co.; Countrywide Services; Cuprum S.A. de C.V.; American Premier Underwriters, Inc.; VIK Bros.

For full biographical listings, see the Martindale-Hubbell Law Directory

---

HILLSDALE,* Hillsdale Co.

LOREN, SHIRK & SNELL (AV)

91 South Broad (M.99), P.O. Box 246, 49242
Telephone: 517-439-1421
Fax: 517-439-9030

Lewis I. Loren	Kevin G. Shirk
	Michelle A. Snell

Representative Clients: Auto-Owners Insurance Co.; City of Litchfield; Hillsdale County Road Comm.; AAA of Michigan; City of Reading; Jefferson Township; City of Hillsdale; County National Bank; Hillsdale Board of Public Utilities.

For full biographical listings, see the Martindale-Hubbell Law Directory

---

HOLLAND, Ottawa Co.

CUNNINGHAM DALMAN, P.C. (AV)

321 Settlers Road, P.O. Box 1767, 49422-1767
Telephone: 616-392-1821
Fax: 616-392-4769

Gordon H. Cunningham	Kenneth B. Breese
Ronald L. Dalman	Jeffrey K. Helder
Max R. Murphy	Ronald J. Vander Veen
James A. Bidol	David M. Zessin
Andrew J. Mulder	Mark H. Zietlow
Joel G. Bouwens	James W. Bouwens
Randall S. Schipper	

Susan E. Vroegop	Melinda M. Abney

OF COUNSEL

Vernon D. Ten Cate	Kenneth B. Peirce, Jr.

Representative Clients: Auto Club Insurance Assn. (AAA); American States Insurance Co.; FMB-First Michigan Bank; First of America Bank - Holland, N.A.; Ottawa Savings Bank; City of Holland; Board of County Road Commissioners; Holland Economic Development Corp.

For full biographical listings, see the Martindale-Hubbell Law Directory

---

HOUGHTON,* Houghton Co.

VAIRO, MECHLIN, TOMASI, JOHNSON & MANCHESTER (AV)

400 East Houghton Avenue, 49931
Telephone: 906-482-0770
Fax: 906-482-2938
Calumet, Michigan Office: 200 5th Street.
Telephone: 906-337-0312.

MEMBERS OF FIRM

Gerald G. Vairo	Paul J. Tomasi
David R. Mechlin	Frederick N. Johnson
Jeryl A. Manchester	

Michael J. Mannisto

Representative Clients: U.S.F.& G., Insurance Companies; Aetna Life and Casualty Company; Auto Owners Insurance Company; Auto Club Insurance Assn.; Citizens Insurance Company of America; Wausau Insurance Companies; CNA Insurance Companies; Accident Fund Company; U.S.F.&G.

For full biographical listings, see the Martindale-Hubbell Law Directory

---

JACKSON,* Jackson Co.

BULLEN, MOILANEN, KLAASEN & SWAN, P.C. (AV)

402 South Brown Street, 49203
Telephone: 517-788-8500
Fax: 517-788-8507

(See Next Column)

BULLEN, MOILANEN, KLAASEN & SWAN P.C.—*Continued*

Lawrence L. Bullen	Terry J. Klaasen
Philip M. Moilanen	David W. Swan

David H. Black, Jr.

OF COUNSEL

T. Harrison Stanton	Frank C. Painter (1905-1976)
J. Adrian Rosenburg	
(1896-1983)	

Representative Clients: Midland National Insurance Co.; National Grange Insurance Co.; Nationwide Insurance Group; Employers of Wausau Insurance Co.; Gulf Insurance Group; Hartford Insurance; Hastings Mutual Insurance Co.; John Hancock Insurance Co.; Michigan Millers Mutual Insurance Co.; Vesta Insurance Group.

For full biographical listings, see the Martindale-Hubbell Law Directory

---

KALAMAZOO,* Kalamazoo Co.

DIETRICH, ZODY, HOWARD & VANDERROEST, P.C. (AV)

834 King Highway, Suite 110, 49001
Telephone: 616-344-9236
Fax: 616-344-0412

G. Philip Dietrich	James W. Smith
Richard J. Howard	James E. VanderRoest
	Philip W. Dietrich

OF COUNSEL

Brenda Wheeler Zody

Representative Clients: John Hancock Mutual Life Insurance Co.; Prudential Property and Casualty Insurance Co.; Southern Michigan Mutual Insurance Co.; Monroe Guaranty Insurance Co.; Nationwide Insurance Co.; Brotherhood Mutual Insurance Co.; United Casualty Insurance Co.

For full biographical listings, see the Martindale-Hubbell Law Directory

---

EARLY, LENNON, PETERS & CROCKER, P.C. (AV)

900 Comerica Building, 49007-4752
Telephone: 616-381-8844
Fax: 616-349-8525

John T. Peters, Jr.	Harold E. Fischer, Jr.

Attorneys for: General Motors Corp.; Wal-Mart Stores; Borgess Medical Center; Aetna Insurance; Kemper Group; Medical Protective Co.; Zurich Insurance; AAA; Liberty Mutual; Home Insurance.

For Complete List of Firm Personnel, See General Section

For full biographical listings, see the Martindale-Hubbell Law Directory

---

HOWARD & HOWARD ATTORNEYS, P.C. (AV)

The Kalamazoo Building, Suite 400, 107 West Michigan
Avenue, 49007-3956
Telephone: 616-382-1483
Telecopier: 616-382-1568
Bloomfield Hills, Michigan Office: The Pinehurst Office Center, Suite 101, 1400 North Woodward Avenue.
Telephone: 810-645-1483.
Telecopier: 810-645-1568.
Lansing, Michigan Office: The Phoenix Building, Suite 500, 222 Washington Square North.
Telephone: 517-485-1483.
Telecopier: 517-485-1568.
Peoria, Illinois Office: The Creve Coeur Building, Suite 200, 321 Liberty Street.
Telephone: 309-672-1483.
Telecopier: 309-672-1568.
Tampa, Florida Office: First of America Plaza, Suite 2000, 201 East Kennedy Boulevard.
Telephone: 813-229-1483.
Telecopier: 813-229-1568.

John W. Allen	James H. Geary
Robert C. Beck	Myra L. Willis

Representative Clients: For Representative Client list, see General Practice, Kalamazoo, MI.

For Complete List of Firm Personnel, See General Section

For full biographical listings, see the Martindale-Hubbell Law Directory

---

LILLY & LILLY, P.C. (AV)

505 South Park Street, 49007
Telephone: 616-381-7763
Fax: 616-344-6880

Charles M. Lilly (1903-1990)	Terrence J. Lilly

For full biographical listings, see the Martindale-Hubbell Law Directory

---

MILLER, CANFIELD, PADDOCK AND STONE, P.L.C. (AV)

A Professional Limited Liability Company
Founded in 1852 by Sidney Davy Miller
444 West Michigan Avenue, 49007-3752
Telephone: 616-381-7030
Fax: 616-382-0244
Detroit, Michigan Office: 150 West Jefferson, Suite 2500, 48226-4415.
Telephone: 313-963-6420.
Fax: 313-496-7500.
Cable Address: "Stem Detroit."
Ann Arbor, Michigan Office: 101 North Main Street, 7th Floor, 48104-1400.
Telephone: 313-663-2445.
Fax: 313-747-7147.
Bloomfield Hills, Michigan Office: Suite 100, Pinehurst Office Center, 1400 North Woodward, 48303-2014.
Telephone: 313-645-5000.
Fax: 313-645-1917.
Grand Rapids, Michigan Office: 1200 Campau Square Plaza, 99 Monroe, N.W., 49503-2639.
Telephone: 616-454-8656.
Fax: 616-776-6322.
Howell, Michigan Office: 121 South Barnard Street, Suite 4, 48843-2305.
Telephone: 517-546-7600.
Telecopier: 517-546-6974.
Lansing, Michigan Office: One Michigan Avenue, Suite 900, 48933-1609.
Telephone: 517-487-2070.
Fax: 517-374-6304.
Monroe, Michigan Office: The Executive Centre, 214 East Elm Avenue, 48161-2682.
Telephone: 313-243-2000.
Fax: 313-243-0901.
Washington, D.C. Office: 1225 Nineteenth Street, N.W., Suite 400. 20036.
Telephone: 202-429-5575; 785-0600.
Fax: 202-331-1118; 785-1234.
Pensacola, Florida Office: 25 West Cedar, 32501.
Telephone: 904-469-1088.
Fax: 904-432-0677.
St. Petersburg, Florida Office: 100 Second Avenue S., Suite 7045, 33701.
Telephone: 813-982-6000.
Fax: 813-892-6002.
New York, New York Office: Eleventh Floor, 135 East 57th Street, 10022-2087.
Telephone: 212-754-5400.
Fax: 212-754-5401.
Gdansk, Poland Office: Suite 322, Dom Technika Building, UI. Rajska 6, 80-850.
Telephone: 011-485-831-2808.
Fax: 011-485-831-4719.
Warsaw, Poland Office: UI. Marszalkowska 82, Suite 561, 00-517.
Telephone: 011-482-623-6457 and 6458.
Fax: 011-482-623-6459.

PRINCIPALS OF FIRM

Eric V. Brown, Jr.	Ronald E. Baylor
Charles E. Ritter	James E. Spurr
James G. Vantine, Jr.	Pamela Chapman Enslen

ASSOCIATES

Ballard Jay Yelton, III	Kurt P. McCamman
	Scott R. Sikkenga

Representative Firm Clients: Chrysler Corporation; Comerica, Incorporated; City of Detroit, Michigan; Detroit Tigers, Inc.; First of Michigan; Ford Motor Company; Ford Motor Credit Company; Great Lakes Bancorp; Henry Ford Hospital; INVETECH Company.

For Complete List of Firm Personnel, See General Section

For full biographical listings, see the Martindale-Hubbell Law Directory

---

RYAN, JAMIESON & MORRIS (AV)

121 West Cedar Street, 49007
Telephone: 616-382-5143
Fax: 616-382-1896

James D. Ryan	Daniel K. Jamieson
	Christopher D. Morris

ASSOCIATE

Ronald W. Ryan

Representative Clients: Auto-Owners Insurance Co.; Imperial Midwest Insurance Co.; Liberty Mutual Insurance Co.; Michigan Property and Casualty Guaranty Association.

For full biographical listings, see the Martindale-Hubbell Law Directory

LANSING, Ingham Co.

* indicates certain Bar Register subscribers whose principal office is located elsewhere in the state and who have arranged for representation as a part of the state capital listings that follow

FOSTER, SWIFT, COLLINS & SMITH, P.C. (AV)

313 South Washington Square, 48933-2193
Telephone: 517-371-8100
Telecopier: 517-371-8200
URL: http://www.fosterswift.com
Farmington Hills, Michigan Office: 32300 Northwestern Highway, Suite 230.
Telephone: 810-539-9900.
Fax: 810-851-7504.

John L. Collins	Scott L. Mandel
Webb A. Smith	Michael D. Sanders
William R. Schulz	Kevin T. McGraw
David H. Aldrich	Mark H. Canady
Scott A. Storey	Michael W. Puerner
Charles E. Barbieri	Matthew W. Collins

LEGAL SUPPORT PERSONNEL
LEGAL ASSISTANTS

Laurie A. Awad	Theresa G. Solberg

Representative Clients: Citizens Insurance Company of America; Michigan Blue Cross and Blue Shield; Michigan Mutual Insurance Co.; Transamerica Insurance Co.; Royal Globe Insurance Co.; Physician Insurance Company of Michigan; Michigan Physicians Mutual Insurance Co.; Meridian Mutual Insurance Company.

For Complete List of Firm Personnel, See General Section

For full biographical listings, see the Martindale-Hubbell Law Directory

FRASER TREBILCOCK DAVIS & FOSTER, P.C. (AV)

1000 Michigan National Tower, 48933
Telephone: 517-482-5800
Fax: 517-482-0887

Peter L. Dunlap	Brett Jon Bean
C. Mark Hoover	Gary C. Rogers
Ronald R. Sutton	Mark A. Bush

Patrick K. Thornton	Brian D. Herrington

Representative Clients: Auto Owners Insurance Co.; Federated Insurance Co.; Hartford Insurance Co.; Metropolitan Life Insurance Co.; Michigan Physicians Mutual Liability Co.; Physicians Insurance Company of Michigan; Prudential Insurance Company of America; State Farm Insurance Co.

For Complete List of Firm Personnel, See General Section

For full biographical listings, see the Martindale-Hubbell Law Directory

* HONIGMAN MILLER SCHWARTZ AND COHN (AV)

A Partnership including Professional Corporations
222 North Washington Square, Suite 400, 48933-1800
Telephone: 517-484-8282
Telecopier: 517-484-8286
URL: http://www.law.honigman.com
Detroit, Michigan Office: 2290 First National Building, 48226.
Telephone: 313-256-7800.
West Palm Beach, Florida Office: Suite 800 Esperante Building, 222 Lakeview Avenue, 33401-6112.
Telephone: 561-838-4500.
Tampa, Florida Office: 2700 SunTrust Financial Centre, 401 E. Jackson Street, 33602-5226.
Telephone: 813-221-6600.

MEMBERS

Frederick M. Baker, Jr.	John D. Pirich
Daniel J. Demlow	Benjamin O. Schwendener, Jr.
Sandra L. Jasinski	Gary A. Trepod
John S. Kane	Alan M. Valade
Timothy Sawyer Knowlton	William C. Whitbeck
Mark Morton	Ruth E. Zimmerman

ASSOCIATES

Ann L. Andrews	Andrew J. Gerdes

Representative Clients: Aon Corporation; Continental Insurance.

For Complete List of Firm Personnel, See General Section

For full biographical listings, see the Martindale-Hubbell Law Directory

HOWARD & HOWARD ATTORNEYS, P.C. (AV)

The Phoenix Building, Suite 500, 222 Washington Square, North, 48933-1817
Telephone: 517-485-1483
Telecopier: 517-485-1568
Kalamazoo, Michigan Office: The Kalamazoo Building, Suite 400, 107 West Michigan Avenue.
Telephone: 616-382-1483.
Telecopier: 616-382-1568.
Bloomfield Hills, Michigan Office: The Pinehurst Office Center, Suite 101, 1400 North Woodward Avenue.
Telephone: 810-645-1483.
Telecopier: 810-645-1568.
Peoria, Illinois Office: The Creve Coeur Building, Suite 200, 321 Liberty Street.
Telephone: 309-672-1483.
Telecopier: 309-672-1568.
Tampa, Florida Office: First of America Plaza, Suite 2000, 201 East Kennedy Boulevard.
Telephone: 813-229-1483.
Telecopier: 813-229-1568.

David C. Coey	James E. Lozier
	C. Douglas Moran

Representative Clients: For Representative Client list, see General Practice, Lansing, MI.

For Complete List of Firm Personnel, See General Section

For full biographical listings, see the Martindale-Hubbell Law Directory

RAYMOND JOSEPH (AV)

1602 Michigan National Tower, 48933
Telephone: 517-372-4410
Fax: 517-372-2137

OF COUNSEL

George R. Sidwell (1899-1983)	Michael Bowman
	Bruce C. Blanton

Representative Clients: Ashland Oil, Inc.; Complete Auto Transit, Inc.; Employers Insurance of Wausau; Evans Products Co.; Grain Dealers Mutl.; Harbor Insurance Co.; Interstate Motor Freight System; Lansing Symphony Assn., Inc.; Prudential LMI Insurance Co.

For full biographical listings, see the Martindale-Hubbell Law Directory

SMITH HAUGHEY RICE & ROEGGE, P.C.

(See East Lansing)

TIMMER, JAMO & O'LEARY (AV)

521 Seymour Avenue, 48933
Telephone: 517-371-3500
Fax: 517-371-4514

MEMBERS OF FIRM

James A. Timmer	James S. O'Leary
James S. Jamo	Kathleen A. Lopilato

Representative Clients: Auto Owners Insurance Co.; National Indemnity Insurance Co.; Pennsylvania Insurance Co.; Travelers Insurance Co.; Ohio Farmers Insurance Co.; Bankers Life & Casualty Co.; Western Casualty & Surety Co.; Indiana Insurance Co.; Western Surety Co.; United State Aviation Underwriters.

For full biographical listings, see the Martindale-Hubbell Law Directory

MARQUETTE, ***** Marquette Co.

BENSINGER, COTANT, MENKES & AARDEMA, P.C. (AV)

122 West Bluff, 49855
Telephone: 906-225-1000
Fax: 906-225-0818
Gaylord, Michigan Office: 308 West Main, P.O. Box 1000.
Telephone: 517-732-7536.
Fax: 517-732-4922.
Grand Rapids, Michigan Office: 983 Spaulding Avenue, S.E.
Telephone: 616-949-7963.
Fax: 616-949-5264.

Gregory A. Elzinga	Michael G. Summers (Resident)
William J. Maynard	Lynn A. Moon (Resident)
Glenn W. Smith	Roger W. Zappa (Resident)

Representative Clients: Allstate Insurance Co.; Auto-Owners Insurance Co.; Michigan Physicians Insurance Co.; Northern Mutual Insurance Co.; Federated Insurance Co.; Employers Reinsurance Co.; D & N Bank-FSB; Michigan Licensed Beverage Association; State Farm Insurance Co.; Farm Bureau Mutual Insurance Co.

For full biographical listings, see the Martindale-Hubbell Law Directory

SWANSON & DETTMANN (AV)

Marquette Professional Building, 148 West Washington Street, 49855
Telephone: 906-228-7355
Fax: 906-228-7357

(See Next Column)

SWANSON & DETTMANN—*Continued*

MEMBERS OF FIRM

Keith E. Swanson   Darrell R. Dettmann

Representative Clients: Kemper Insurance Cos.; USF&G Insurance Co.; SET-SEG, Inc.; Gallagher Bassett Insurance Service; North Pointe Insurance Co.; Auto Owners Insurance Co.; CoreSource, Inc.; USAA; Upper Peninsula Health Education Corp.; Travelers Insurance Co.
Reference: First of America Bank-Marquette, N.A.

For full biographical listings, see the Martindale-Hubbell Law Directory

MONROE,* Monroe Co.

BRAUNLICH, RUSSOW & BRAUNLICH, A PROFESSIONAL CORPORATION (AV)

111 South Macomb Street, 48161
Telephone: 313-241-8300
Fax: 313-241-7715

William J. Braunlich, Jr.   Thomas P. Russow
(1924-1992)   William H. Braunlich

Philip A. Costello   Marie C. Kennedy
Patricia M. Poupard   Susan J. Mehregan
Ann L. Nickel   Robert Wetzel
Michael G. Roehrig

LEGAL SUPPORT PERSONNEL

Ruth G. Flint

Representative Clients: State Farm Mutual Insurance Co.; Auto Club Insurance Assn.; Farm Bureau Insurance Co.; Home Mutual Insurance Co.; Cincinnati Insurance Co.; Board of Road Commissioners, Monroe County; Port of Monroe; Monroe County Community College; City of Luna Pier; City of Petersburg.

For full biographical listings, see the Martindale-Hubbell Law Directory

MOUNT CLEMENS,* Macomb Co.

WELCH, MACALPINE, BAHORSKI, BIEGLECKI & FARRELL, P.C. (AV)

71 North Avenue, 48043-5543
Telephone: 810-469-1111; 1-800-252-1654
Facsimile: 810-469-1609

Terry S. Welch   Thomas R. Bieglecki
Robert F. MacAlpine   Thaddeus M. Dombrowski
Timothy A. Bahorski   Marc P. Shaberman
John B. Farrell   Michael W. Sickles
Christopher R. Baratta

For full biographical listings, see the Martindale-Hubbell Law Directory

PETOSKEY,* Emmet Co.

STROUP & TRESIDDER, P.C. (AV)

Pennsylvania Plaza, P.O. Box 809, 49770
Telephone: 616-347-3907
Fax: 616-347-2499

Nathaniel W. Stroup   Stephen J. Tresidder
Joel D. Wurster

Representative Clients: NBD of Petoskey, N.A.; Hodgkiss & Douma, Inc.; Michigan Physicians Mutual Liability Co.; Public Schools of Petoskey, Michigan; Top O'Michigan Electric Co.; Emmet County Road Commission; Amerisure.

For full biographical listings, see the Martindale-Hubbell Law Directory

PLYMOUTH, Wayne Co.

DRAUGELIS & ASHTON, L.L.P. (AV)

843 Penniman Avenue, 48170-1690
Telephone: 313-453-4044
Clawson, Michigan Office: 380 North Main Street.
Telephone: 810-588-7704.

MEMBERS OF FIRM

Edward F. Draugelis   Lamberto DiStefano
John A. Ashton   David T. Rogers
Donald S. Scully   Joseph R. Conte
Richard T. Haynes   Steven O. Ashton

ASSOCIATES

Dawn E. Clancy   Anne K. Mayer
Timothy M. O'Connor   Sally S. Stauffer
Floyd C. Virant   Darlene M. Germaine
Taras P. Jarema   Joel B. Ashton
Deborah A. Tonelli   Donald E. Walker
Timothy M. McKercher   Kathryn R. Mccool

Representative Clients: State Farm Automobile Insurance Co.; State Farm Fire and Casualty Co.

For full biographical listings, see the Martindale-Hubbell Law Directory

PORTAGE, Kalamazoo Co.

SMITH, LAPARL, MEQUIO & KONING, P.C. (AV)

550 West Centre Avenue, 49024
Telephone: 616-323-0200
Facsimile: 616-323-3109

C. Giles Smith, Jr.   James D. Mequio
John R. LaParl, Jr.   James H. Koning

OF COUNSEL

John R. LaParl, Sr.

For full biographical listings, see the Martindale-Hubbell Law Directory

PORT HURON,* St. Clair Co.

FLETCHER DeGROW (AV)

522 Michigan Street, 48060-3893
Telephone: 810-987-8444
Facsimile: 810-987-8149

MEMBERS OF FIRM

Gary A. Fletcher   Mark G. Clark

ASSOCIATE

William L. Fealko, III

Representative Clients: Fremont Mutual Insurance Co.; Westfield Insurance Co.; Michigan Municipal Risk Management Authority; City of Port Huron; City of Marysville; Port Huron Area School District; Marysville Public Schools; Wirtz Manufacturing Co.; Raymond Excavating; Relleum Real Estate Development Co.

For Complete List of Firm Personnel, See General Section

For full biographical listings, see the Martindale-Hubbell Law Directory

ROYAL OAK, Oakland Co.

CARDELLI, SCHAEFER & MASON, P.C. (AV)

322 West Lincoln, 48067
Telephone: 810-544-1100
Toll Free 1-800-411-7774
Telecopier: 810-544-1191

Thomas G. Cardelli   William C. Schaefer
Laura D. Mason

Deborah A. Hebert   Tara Hanley Bratton
Mary Ann J. O'Neil   Diane T. Gorczyca
Lillian C. Pierce   Ronald E. Beier, II
John L. Weston

Representative Clients: Aetna Casualty & Surety Company; Allianz Insurance Company; Casualty Reciprocal Exchange; Cigna Companies; ITT Hartford Insurance; Indiana Insurance.

For full biographical listings, see the Martindale-Hubbell Law Directory

SAGINAW,* Saginaw Co.

BRAUN KENDRICK FINKBEINER PLC (AV)

101 N. Washington Suite 812, 48607-1297
Telephone: 517-753-3461
Telecopier: 517-753-3951
URL: http://www.bkf-law.com
Bay City, Michigan Office: 201 Phoenix Building, P.O. Box 2039.
Telephone: 517-895-8505.
Telecopier: 517-895-8437.
Ann Arbor, Michigan Office: 700 First National Building.
Telephone: 313-995-4100.
Telecopier: 313-995-4798.

Harold J. Blanchet, Jr.   Charles A. Gilfeather
E. Louis Ognisanti   Timothy L Curtiss
Bruce L. Dalrymple   Scott C. Strattard
Craig W. Horn

Brian S. Makaric

Representative Clients: Farm Bureau Insurance Group; Firemans Fund American Insurance; Frankenmuth Mutual Insurance Co.; Fremont Mutual Insurance Co.; Great Lakes American Life Ins. Co.; Hartford Insurance Group; Hastings Mutual Insurance Co.; Kemper Insurance Group; Michigan Mutual Liability Co.; Mutual Benefit Life Ins. Co.

For Complete List of Firm Personnel, See General Section

For full biographical listings, see the Martindale-Hubbell Law Directory

FORDNEY, DUST & PRINE (AV)

An Association of Professional Corporations
Suite 410 B Plaza North, 4800 Fashion Square Boulevard, P.O. Box 5289, 48603-0289
Telephone: 517-791-7060
Fax: 517-791-8009

(See Next Column)

FORDNEY, DUST & PRINE, *Saginaw—Continued*

MEMBERS OF FIRM

J. Michael Fordney	Andrew W. Prine
Tobin H. Dust	Matthew J. Coffey

For full biographical listings, see the Martindale-Hubbell Law Directory

O'NEILL, WALLACE & DOYLE, P.C. (AV)

Suite 302 Four Flags Office Center, 300 St. Andrews Road, P.O. Box 1966, 48605
Telephone: 517-790-0960
Fax: 517-790-6902
Flint, Michigan Office: 2483 South Linden Road.
Telephone: 810-732-7079.
Fax: 810-732-5889.

Terence J. O'Neill	Thomas J. Doyle
David A. Wallace	Charles F. Filipiak

David Carbajal	John J. Danieleski, Jr.
James E. O'Neill, III	Norman J. Christopherson

Representative Clients: Home Insurance Co.; Great American Insurance Co.; Farmers Insurance Co.; Cincinnati Insurance Co.; Ohio Casualty Insurance Co.; Safeco Insurance Co.; Liberty Mutual Insurance Co.; CUNA Mutual Insurance.; Pioneer State Mutual Insurance Co.; Auto Owners Insurance Co.

For full biographical listings, see the Martindale-Hubbell Law Directory

ST. CLAIR SHORES, Macomb Co.

SAURBIER, PARADISO & DAVIS, P.L.C. (AV)

Suite 402, 400 Maple Park Boulevard, 48081
Telephone: 810-447-3700
Fax: 810-447-3755
Email: SAURBIR@IBM.NET
Detroit, Office: 1028 Buhl Building.
Telephone: 313-965-2220.

Scott A. Saurbier	Anthony J. Paradiso
	Kevin L. Davis

ASSOCIATES

Joel A. Sanfield	Amy A. Baranski
Marc D. Saurbier	Jennifer A. Mazzuchi
David Steiger	Cheryl L. Ronk
John M. Perrin	Lawrence T Garcia
	Gwendolyn M. Cook Jones

For full biographical listings, see the Martindale-Hubbell Law Directory

ST. JOSEPH,* Berrien Co.

BUTZBAUGH & DEWANE, P.L.C. (AV)

Law and Title Building, 811 Ship Street, P.O. Box 27, 49085
Telephone: 616-983-0191
Fax: 616-983-5078
Email: b⊗d⊗law@parrett.net

MEMBERS OF FIRM

John E. Dewane	Randall L. Juergensen

Representative Clients: SJS Federal Savings Bank; American Society of Agricultural Engineers; Whirlpool Corp.; Transamerica Insurance Group; Automobile Club Insurance Assn.; Imperial Printing Co.

For Complete List of Firm Personnel, See General Section

For full biographical listings, see the Martindale-Hubbell Law Directory

SOUTHFIELD, Oakland Co.

COLLINS, EINHORN, FARRELL & ULANOFF, A PROFESSIONAL CORPORATION (AV)

4000 Town Center, Suite 909, 48075-1473
Telephone: 810-355-4141
Facsimile: 810-355-2277

Morton H. Collins	Dale J. McLellan
Brian D. Einhorn	Kenneth C. Merritt
Clayton F. Farrell	Noreen L. Slank
Stuart A. Ulanoff	Michael J. Sullivan
	Janice G. Hildenbrand

Gerald A. Pawlak	Deborah A. Lujan
Neil W. MacCallum	Barbara H. Goldman
Timothy Orlando	Shannon M. Kos
Theresa M. Asoklis	Kevin P. Moloughney
Karen C. Liddle	Susan P. Saltzman
Lisa L. Fadler	Laura A. Ruckle

For full biographical listings, see the Martindale-Hubbell Law Directory

HIGHLAND & ZANETTI (AV)

Suite 205, 24445 Northwestern Highway, 48075
Telephone: 810-352-9580

John N. Highland	J. R. Zanetti, Jr.
	R. Michael John

Duncan Hall Brown	Ronald D. Holton

For full biographical listings, see the Martindale-Hubbell Law Directory

O'LEARY, O'LEARY, JACOBS, MATTSON, PERRY & MASON, P.C. (AV)

26777 Central Park Boulevard, Suite 275, 48076
Telephone: 810-948-1000
Fax: 810-799-8265
Email: olearyjacobs@michbar.org

John Patrick O'Leary	C. Kenneth Perry, Jr.
Thomas M. O'Leary	Larry G. Mason
John P. Jacobs	D. Jennifer Andreou
Kenneth M. Mattson	Kevin P. Hanbury
	Alice A. Zetusky

For full biographical listings, see the Martindale-Hubbell Law Directory

PROVIZER, LICHTENSTEIN & PHILLIPS, P.C. (AV)

4000 Town Center, Suite 1800, 48075
Telephone: 810-352-9080
Facsimile: 810-352-1491

Harold M. Provizer	Constance S. Hall
Randall E. Phillips	Noel F. Beck
Marilyn A. Madorsky	William J. Selinsky
Deborah Molitz	Todd B. Denenberg
	Jason Milstone

Representative Clients: Jefferson Ins. Co.; Reliance National Ins. Co.; Blackmoor Group; Thomas Howell Group; Fleming & Hall.

For full biographical listings, see the Martindale-Hubbell Law Directory

SCHWARTZ & JALKANEN, P.C. (AV)

Suite 200, 24400 Northwestern Highway, 48075
Telephone: 810-352-2555
Facsimile: 810-352-5963

Melvin R. Schwartz	Arthur W. Jalkanen
	Karl Eric Hannum

Deborah L. Laura	Lori A. Barker

For full biographical listings, see the Martindale-Hubbell Law Directory

SOMMERS, SCHWARTZ, SILVER & SCHWARTZ, P.C. (AV)

2000 Town Center, Suite 900, 48075
Telephone: 810-355-0300
Telecopier: 810-746-4001
Plymouth, Michigan Office: 747 South Main Street.
Telephone: 313-455-4250.

Leonard B. Schwartz	Allen J. Wall
John F. Vos, III	Joseph E. Grinnan
Robert G. Portnoy	Lisa K. Pernick

Representative Clients: Crum & Forster Insurance Company; Great American Insurance Company; Royal Insurance Company; Michigan Mutual/Amerisure Insurance Company; Universal Underwriters Insurance Company; ESIS, Inc.; Corporate Service, Inc.

For Complete List of Firm Personnel, See General Section

For full biographical listings, see the Martindale-Hubbell Law Directory

SULLIVAN, WARD, BONE, TYLER & ASHER, P.C. (AV)

25800 Northwestern Highway, Suite 1000, 48075
Telephone: 810-746-0700
FAX: 810-746-2760
Traverse City, Michigan Office: 12935 S. West Bay Shore Drive, Suite 310, Lake States Building.
Telephone: 616-947-1335.
Grand Rapids, Michigan Office: 2025 East Beltline S.E., Suite 406.
Telephone: 616-940-4114.

Richard G. Ward	Renée S. Siegan
Richard A. Bone	John M. Simmerer
David M. Tyler	Eric D. Geller
Stanley G. Thayer	Dale Louis Gudenau
Lee C. Patton	Michelle A. Thomas
Gerard J. Andree	Sharon S. Almonrode
Alan S. Helmore	Robert E. Sullivan, Jr.
Scott D. Feringa	Colin H. John, Jr.
Thomas L. Auth, Jr.	Charles E. Randau
Kevin J. Gleeson	Michael J. Asher

(See Next Column)

SULLIVAN, WARD, BONE, TYLER & ASHER P.C.—*Continued*

Jeffery G. Powers	Thomas M. Slavin
Ronald S. Lederman	Donald K. Warwick
Sheri B. Cataldo	Randi P. Glanz
William J. Ewald	

Representative Clients: Allstate Insurance Co.; American International Group; American States Insurance Co.; The Great Atlantic & Pacific Tea Company; William Beaumont Hospital; Beech Aircraft; Bormans, Inc. dba/Farmer Jack Supermarkets; City of Detroit; CNA Insurance Companies; Continental Loss Adjusting Services.

For full biographical listings, see the Martindale-Hubbell Law Directory

---

TRAVERSE CITY,* Grand Traverse Co.

RUNNING, WISE, WILSON, FORD AND PHILLIPS, P.L.C. (AV)

326 State Street, P.O. Box 686, 49684
Telephone: 616-946-2700
Tele-Fax: 616-946-0857

Harry T. Running (Deceased)	William L. Wise (Retired)

MEMBERS OF FIRM

Patrick J. Wilson	James C. Adams
Richard W. Ford	Sandra P. Howard
Thomas J. Phillips	Kent E. Gerberding

ASSOCIATES

Shelley A. Kester	Bradley L. Putney

OF COUNSEL

J. Bruce Donaldson	Douglas J. Donaldson

Local Counsel For: Auto-Owners Insurance Co.; John Hancock Mutual Life Insurance Co.; Amoco Production Co.; Underwriters at Lloyds London; Bankers Multiple Line Insurance Co.; OCI Corp of Michigan; Traverse City Public Schools; America's Insurance Company.

For full biographical listings, see the Martindale-Hubbell Law Directory

---

SMITH HAUGHEY RICE & ROEGGE, P.C. (AV)

241 East State Street, P.O. Box 848, 49685-0848
Telephone: 616-929-4878
Facsimile: 616-929-4182
Grand Rapids, Michigan Office: 200 Calder Plaza Building, 250 Monroe Avenue, N.W., 49503-2251.
Telephone: 616-774-8000.
Facsimile: 616-774-2461.
East Lansing, Michigan Office: 1301 North Hagadorn Road, 48823-2320.
Telephone: 517-332-3030.
Facsimile: 517-332-3468.

George Frederick Bearup	Charles B. Judson
Mark P. Bickel	Robert W. Tubbs
P. David Vinocur	Robert M. Faulkner
R. Jay Hardin	Thomas C. Kates

John R. Vander Veen	Jeffrey R. Wonacott
Mark D. Williams	Todd W. Millar
Erin Eileen Gerrity	

Representative Clients: Chevron; Cincinnati Insurance Co.; General Motors Corp.; Kemper Insurance Group; Michigan Hospital Assn.; Navistar International; St. Paul Insurance Cos.; Steelcase, Inc.; Sears Roebuck & Co.; Dow Elanco.

For full biographical listings, see the Martindale-Hubbell Law Directory

---

ROBERT P. TREMP, P.C. (AV)

3939 M-72 East (Williamsburg), P.O. Box 3019, 49685-3019
Telephone: 616-938-2888
Telefax: 616-938-2988
Email: rptpc@traverse.com
Marquette, Michigan Office: 307 South Front Street, Suite 202.
Telephone: 906-228-8263.
Telefax: 906-228-5282.

Robert P. Tremp

LEGAL SUPPORT PERSONNEL

Paul Joseph Tremp (Private Investigator)

For full biographical listings, see the Martindale-Hubbell Law Directory

---

TROY, Oakland Co.

HOLAHAN, MALLOY, MAYBAUGH & MONNICH (AV)

Suite 100, 2690 Crooks Road, 48084-4700
Telephone: 810-362-4747
Fax: 810-362-4779
East Tawas, Michigan Office: 910 East Bay Street.
Telephone: 517-362-4747.
Fax: 517-362-7331.

(See Next Column)

MEMBERS OF FIRM

J. Michael Malloy, III	David L. Delie, Jr.
James D. Maybaugh	William J. Kliffel
John R. Monnich	Ingrid Rosvold Kliffel

OF COUNSEL

Thomas H. O'Connor	Maureen Holahan (Retired; Resident, East Tawas Office)

Representative Clients: Chubb Companies; American States Insurance Co.; Travelers Insurance; Employers Reinsurance; Hartford Insurance Company.

For full biographical listings, see the Martindale-Hubbell Law Directory

---

POLING, McGAW & POLING, P.C. (AV)

Suite 275, 5435 Corporate Drive, 48098
Telephone: 810-641-0500
Telecopier: 810-641-0506

Benson T. Buck (1926-1989)	Richard B. Poling, Jr.
Richard B. Poling	Gregory C. Hamilton
D. Douglas McGaw	Veronica B. O'Haro
James R. Parker	

OF COUNSEL

Ralph S. Moore

Representative Clients: County of Oakland; City of Troy; United States Fidelity & Guaranty Co.; Sentry Insurance Co.; Admiral Insurance; DeMaria Construction Co.; Leo Corporation; Aetna Casualty and Surety Co.; Concord Design; Pneumo-Abex.

For full biographical listings, see the Martindale-Hubbell Law Directory

---

REYNOLDS, BEEBY & MAGNUSON, P.C. (AV)

50 West Big Beaver Road Suite 400, 48084
Telephone: 810-740-9860
Fax: 810-740-9870
Detroit, Michigan Office: Ford Building, Suite 531.
Telephone: 313-961-2720.
Fax: 313-961-5930.

Gregory A. Reynolds	Kenneth M. Zorn
Arnold N. Magnuson, Jr.	Thomas G. Grubba
Frank K. Mandlebaum	

Elizabeth A. Fellows	Joseph J. Wright

Representative Clients: Employers Casualty Co.; Liberty Mutual Insurance Co.; Royal Insurance Corp.

For full biographical listings, see the Martindale-Hubbell Law Directory

---

SCHIER, DENEWETH & PARFITT, P.C. (AV)

888 West Big Beaver Road, Suite 610, 48084-4737
Telephone: 810-362-5600
Telecopier: 810-362-0073

Carl F. Schier	Timothy P. Dugan
Ronald A. Deneweth	Janette E. Frank
Chris Parfitt	Mark D. Sassak

OF COUNSEL

Edward A. Ryder

Reference: CNA Insurance Companies; Citizens Insurance Company; Fireman's Fund Insurance Co.; Michigan Property & Casualty Guaranty Company; North American Specialty Insurance; St. Paul Insurance Company; TIG Insurance Company; Travelers Indemnity Company; USF&G Insurance Company; Westfield Companies.

For full biographical listings, see the Martindale-Hubbell Law Directory

---

WEST BLOOMFIELD, Oakland Co.

CHEATHAM & ACKER, P.C. (AV)

5777 West Maple Road, Suite 130, P.O. Box 255002, 48325-5002
Telephone: 810-932-2000
Fax: 810-932-2008

Charles C. Cheatham	Lawrence J. Acker

Tracy A. Leahy	Mary E. Hollman
Christopher P. Jelinek	

COUNSEL

Lynn L. Lower

For full biographical listings, see the Martindale-Hubbell Law Directory

---

LAW OFFICES OF DAVID J. COOPER A PROFESSIONAL CORPORATION (AV)

5777 West Maple, Suite 130, P.O. Box 255002, 48325-5002
Telephone: 810-932-8582
Fax: 810-932-2166
Email: AXDEF@aol.com

(See Next Column)

Law Offices of David J. Cooper A Professional Corporation, *West Bloomfield—Continued*

David J. Cooper

For full biographical listings, see the Martindale-Hubbell Law Directory

Law Offices of Lee Estes (AV)

5777 West Maple Road, Suite 130, P.O. Box 255002, 48325-5002
Telephone: 810-855-0770
Facsimile: 810-932-2008
Email: LESTES@gnn.com

For full biographical listings, see the Martindale-Hubbell Law Directory

WEST BRANCH,* Ogemaw Co.

Jennings, Jennings & Macdonald, P.C. (AV)

152 North Fourth Street, P.O. Box 67, 48661
Telephone: 517-345-3344

William P. Jennings　　　　　　　　William P. Jennings, Jr.
Jon Robert Macdonald

Karen M. Macdonald

For full biographical listings, see the Martindale-Hubbell Law Directory

INTERNATIONAL BUSINESS LAW

ALABAMA

BIRMINGHAM, * Jefferson Co.

BRADLEY, ARANT, ROSE & WHITE (AV)

2001 Park Place, Suite 1400, P.O. Box 830709, 35283-0709
Telephone: 205-521-8000
Facsimile: 205-252-0264
Facsimile (SouthTrust Tower Office): 205-251-9915
URL: http://www.BARW.COM
Huntsville, Alabama Office: 200 Clinton Avenue West, Suite 900, 35801.
Telephone: 205-517-5100.
Facsimile: 205-533-5069.

MEMBERS OF FIRM

Thomas Neely Carruthers, Jr.	Andrew Robert Greene
Thad Gladden Long	G. Edward Cassady, III
A. H. Gaede, Jr.	John E. Hagefstration, Jr.
James Patrick Alexander	Virginia Calvert Patterson

ASSOCIATES

Douglas E. Eckert	Helena F. Tozzi

For Complete List of Firm Personnel, See General Section

For full biographical listings, see the Martindale-Hubbell Law Directory

HUNTSVILLE, * Madison Co.

FOLEY, SMITH & MAHMOOD, P.C. (AV)

200 West Court Square, Suite 804, 35801
Telephone: 205-536-8877
800-680-LAWS (5297)
Fax: 205-536-0610
Email: JUNES@HIWAAY.NET

Robert Sellers Smith	Richard William Foley
Gulam Rafiqueuddin Mahmood	(Not admitted in AL)

For full biographical listings, see the Martindale-Hubbell Law Directory

ARIZONA

NOGALES, * Santa Cruz Co.

O'CONNOR, CAVANAGH, ANDERSON, KILLINGSWORTH & BESHEARS, A PROFESSIONAL ASSOCIATION (AV)

1891 North Mastick Way, 85621
Telephone: 520-761-4215
FAX: 520-761-3505
Email: firminfo@arizlaw.com
Phoenix, Arizona Office: One East Camelback Road, Suite 1100, 85012.
Telephone: 602-263-2400.
FAX: 602-263-2900.
Tucson, Arizona Office: O'Connor Cavanagh Molloy Jones, 33 N. Stone, Suite 2100, 85701, P.O. Box 2268, 85702.
Telephone: 520-622-3531.
FAX: 520-624-2816.
Sun City, Arizona Office: 13250 North Del Webb Boulevard, Suite B, 85351.
Telephone: 602-263-2808.
FAX: 602-933-3100.

Hector G. Arana	Kimberly A. Howard Arana

Representative Clients: Omega Produce Co.; Frank's Distributing, Inc.; City of Nogales; Collectron of Ariz., Inc.; James K. Wilson Produce Co.; Agricola Bon, S. de R.L. de C.V.; Angel Demerutis E.; Rene Carrillo C.; Arturo Lomeli; Theojary Crisantes E.

For Complete List of Firm Personnel, See General Section

For full biographical listings, see the Martindale-Hubbell Law Directory

PHOENIX, * Maricopa Co.

MEYERS LAW FIRM (AV)

Suite 900, 2398 East Camelback Road, 85016
Telephone: 602-468-8900
Telecopier: 602-468-8910

Donald D. Meyers

(See Next Column)

Charles W. Lotzar	James F. Wees
Donald L. Meyers	Jason A. Donkersley

Reference: Bank of America, Arizona.

For full biographical listings, see the Martindale-Hubbell Law Directory

O'CONNOR, CAVANAGH, ANDERSON, KILLINGSWORTH & BESHEARS, A PROFESSIONAL ASSOCIATION (AV)

One East Camelback Road, Suite 1100, 85012-1656
Telephone: 602-263-2400
FAX: 602-263-2900
Email: firminfo@arizlaw.com
Sun City, Arizona Office: 13250 North Del Webb Boulevard, Suite B, 85351.
Telephone: 602-263-2808.
FAX: 602-933-3100.
Tucson, Arizona Office: O'Connor Cavanagh Molloy Jones, 33 N. Stone, Suite 2100, 85701, P.O. Box 2268, 85702.
Telephone: 520-622-3531.
FAX: 520-624-2816.
Nogales, Arizona Office: 1891 North Mastick Way, 85621.
Telephone: 520-761-4215.
FAX: 520-761-3505.

Gerald L. Jacobs	John B. Furman
	David L. Lansky

OF COUNSEL
Shoshana B. Tancer

Representative Clients: Rural/Metro Corp.; ITT Cannon; Cerprobe Corp.; Viasoft, Inc.

For Complete List of Firm Personnel, See General Section

For full biographical listings, see the Martindale-Hubbell Law Directory

QUARLES & BRADY (AV)

One Camelback Building, One East Camelback Road, Suite 400, 85012-1649
Telephone: 602-230-5500
Fax: 602-230-5598
Milwaukee, Wisconsin Office: 411 East Wisconsin Avenue.
Telephone: 414-277-5000.
Fax: 414-271-3552.
Madison, Wisconsin Office: First Wisconsin Plaza, One South Pinckney Street, P.O. Box 2113.
Telephone: 608-251-5000.
Fax: 608-251-9166.
West Palm Beach, Florida Office: 222 Lakeview Ave., 4th Floor.
Telephone: 407-653-5000.
Fax: 407-653-5333.
Naples, Florida Office: Barnett Center, 4501 Tamiami Trail North, Suite 300.
Telephone: 813-262-5959.
Fax: 813-434-4999.

MEMBERS OF THE FIRM

P. Robert Moya	David G. Beauchamp

For Complete List of Firm Personnel, See General Section

For full biographical listings, see the Martindale-Hubbell Law Directory

ARKANSAS

LITTLE ROCK, * Pulaski Co.

ROSE LAW FIRM, A PROFESSIONAL ASSOCIATION (AV)

120 East Fourth Street, 72201
Telephone: 501-375-9131
Telecopy: 501-375-1309

Herbert C. Rule, III	William H. Kennedy, III
W. Wilson Jones	Les R. Baledge
Allen W. Bird, II	Richard N. Massey
William E. Bishop	Amy Lee Stewart

COUNSEL
John A. Davis, III

Kathryn Bennett Perkins	Goodloe M. Partee
John P. Fletcher	Michael N. Shannon

Counsel for: Aluminum Company of America; Bridgestone/Firestone, Inc.; The Equitable Life Assurance Society of The United States; General Motors Corp.; The Prudential Insurance Company of America; Stephens Group Inc.; TCBY Enterprises, Inc.; Tyson Foods, Inc.

For Complete List of Firm Personnel, See General Section

For full biographical listings, see the Martindale-Hubbell Law Directory

CALIFORNIA

CLAREMONT, Los Angeles Co.

JOHN W. TULAC (AV)

401 Harvard Avenue, 91711
Telephone: 909-445-1100
Fax: 909-445-1104
Email: jwtulac@ix.netcom.com
Reference: Marine National Bank, Irvine.

For full biographical listings, see the Martindale-Hubbell Law Directory

---

IRVINE, Orange Co.

BROWN, PISTONE, HURLEY & VAN VLEAR, A PROFESSIONAL CORPORATION (AV)

Suite 900 AT&T Building, 8001 Irvine Center Drive, 92618-2921
Telephone: 714-727-0559
Fax: 714-727-0656
Email: BPHVLAW@AOL.COM
Phoenix, Arizona Office: 2999 North 44th Street, Suite 300.
Telephone: 602-968-2427.
Fax: 602-840-0794.
San Diego, California Office: 4350 La Jolla Village Drive, Suite 300.
Telephone: 619-546-4368.
Fax: 619-453-2839.
Sacramento, California Office: 980 Ninth Street, 16th Floor.
Telephone: 916-449-9541.
Fax: 916-446-7104.

Ernest C. Brown	Gregory F. Hurley
Thomas A. Pistone	John E. Van Vlear
Michael K. Wolder	

Francis T. Donohue, III	Sheila I. Patterson
Robert C. Schneider (Resident,	Michael R. Gandee
Phoenix, Arizona Office)	Julia E. Kress

OF COUNSEL

Robert G. Mahan	Brian A. Runkel
Stephen M. Wontrobski	(Not admitted in CA)

For full biographical listings, see the Martindale-Hubbell Law Directory

---

WATT, TIEDER & HOFFAR, L.L.P. (AV ⓣ)

3 Park Plaza, Suite 1530, 92714
Telephone: 714-852-6700
Telecopier: 714-261-0771
McLean Virginia Office: 7929 Westpark Drive, Suite 400,
Telephone: 703-749-1000.
Telecopier: 703-893-8029.
Washington, D.C. Office: 601 Pennsylvania Avenue, N.W. Suite 900,
Telephone: 202-462-4697.

MEMBERS OF FIRM

John B. Tieder, Jr.	Michael G. Long
(Not admitted in CA)	Christopher P. Pappas
Robert M. Fitzgerald	
(Not admitted in CA)	

ASSOCIATE
Gregory John Dukellis

For full biographical listings, see the Martindale-Hubbell Law Directory

---

LONG BEACH, Los Angeles Co.

FLYNN, DELICH & WISE (AV)

One World Trade Center, Suite 1800, 90831-1800
Telephone: 310-435-2626
Fax: 310-437-7555
San Francisco, California Office: Suite 1750, 580 California Street.
Telephone: 415-693-5566.
Fax: 415-693-0410.

Erich P. Wise	Nicholas S. Politis

Representative Clients: American Hawaii Cruises; Holland America Line; Through Transport Mutual Insurance Association, Ltd.; The Britannia Steam Ship Insurance Association Limited; The Steamship Mutual Underwriting Association (Bermuda) Ltd.; General Steamship Corp., Ltd.; Commodore Cruise Line, Ltd.; Interocean Steamship Corporation; Sea-Land Service, Inc.; Hatteras Yachts.

For full biographical listings, see the Martindale-Hubbell Law Directory

---

RUSSELL & MIRKOVICH (AV)

One World Trade Center, Suite 1450, 90831-1450
Telephone: 310-436-9911
FAX: 310-436-1897

(See Next Column)

Carlton E. Russell	Joseph N. Mirkovich

For full biographical listings, see the Martindale-Hubbell Law Directory

WILLIAMS WOOLLEY COGSWELL NAKAZAWA & RUSSELL (AV)

111 West Ocean Boulevard, Suite 2000, 90802-4614
Telephone: 310-495-6000
Telecopier: 310-435-1359; 310-435-6812
Telex: ITT: 4933872; WU: 984929
Email: wwlaw@msn.com
Rancho Santa Fe, California Office: P.O. Box 9120, 16236 San Dieguito Road, Building 3, Suite 3-15, 92067.
Telephone: 619-497-0284.
Fax: 619-759-9938.
Port Hueneme, California Office: 237 E. Hueneme Road, Suite A, 93041.
Telephone: 805-488-8560.
Fax: 805-488-7896.

MEMBERS OF FIRM

Reed M. Williams	Alan Nakazawa
David E. R. Woolley	Blake W. Larkin
Forrest R. Cogswell	Thomas A. Russell

ASSOCIATES

Todd A. Valdes	Thomas G. Walsh
	Richard J. Nikas

For full biographical listings, see the Martindale-Hubbell Law Directory

---

LOS ANGELES,* Los Angeles Co.

LAW OFFICES OF DAVID B. BLOOM A PROFESSIONAL CORPORATION (AV)

3325 Wilshire Boulevard, Ninth Floor, 90010
Telephone: 213-938-5248; 384-4088
Telecopier: 213-385-2009

David B. Bloom

Stephen S. Monroe (A	Susan Carole Jay
Professional Corporation)	Edward Idell
Raphael A. Rosemblat	Sandra Kamenir
James E. Adler	Steven Wayne Lazarus
Bonni S. Mantovani	Andrew Edward Briseno
Roy A. Levun	Harold C. Klaskin
Cherie S. Raidy	Shelley M. Gould
Jonathan Udell	Peter O. Israel

For full biographical listings, see the Martindale-Hubbell Law Directory

---

BRAND FARRAR DZIUBLA FREILICH & KOLSTAD, LLP (AV)

Counsellors at Law
515 South Flower Street, Suite 3500, 90071-2201
Telephone: 213-228-0288
Facsimile: 213-426-6222
Correspondent Offices: Hong Kong, Shanghai, Beijing, Guangzhou, Xiamen, Shenzhen, Ulaanbaatar, New York and San Francisco.

Michael A. Brand	Amy E. Freilich
David W. Farrar	Charles K. Kolstad
Robert W. Dziubla	Margaret G. Graf

OF COUNSEL

H. Bennett Arnberger	Julia Marie Shymansky
David C. Buxbaum	Yelena Yeruhim
Sherry L. Geyer	Norman A. Chernin
Manender M. Grewal (Not	Joan M. Marquardt
admitted in the United States)	

For full biographical listings, see the Martindale-Hubbell Law Directory

---

LAW OFFICES OF RICHARD I. FINE & ASSOCIATES A PROFESSIONAL CORPORATION (AV)

Suite 1000, 10100 Santa Monica Boulevard (Century City), 90067-4090
Telephone: 310-277-5833
Rapifax: 310-277-1543

Richard I. Fine

Sunny S. Huo	Genalin Y. Sulat

LEGAL SUPPORT PERSONNEL
Mary Benson (Senior Paralegal)

For full biographical listings, see the Martindale-Hubbell Law Directory

---

MATTHIAS & BERG LLP (AV)

Seventh Floor, 515 South Flower Street, 90071
Telephone: 213-895-4200
Telecopier: 213-895-4058

(See Next Column)

MATTHIAS & BERG LLP—*Continued*

Michael R. Matthias   Stuart R. Singer
Jeffrey P. Berg   Kenneth M. H. Hoff
Michael D. Berger

Representative Clients: Synagro Technologies, Inc.; Mexalit, S.A.; Maxitile, Inc.; Allstar Inns; Chatsworth Products, Inc.; International Meta Systems, Inc.; Residential Resources, Inc.; AVIC Group International, Inc.; AutoBitter Group, Inc. National Quality Care, Inc.; Greater China Corp.; HBO Ole. *Reference:* First Professional Bank.

For full biographical listings, see the Martindale-Hubbell Law Directory

O'MELVENY & MYERS LLP (AV)

400 South Hope Street, 90071-2899
Telephone: 213-669-6000
Cable Address: "Moms"
Facsimile: 213-669-6407
Email: omminfo@omm.com
Century City, California Office: 1999 Avenue of the Stars, 90067-6035.
Telephone: 310-553-6700.
Facsimile: 310-246-6779.
Newport Beach, California Office: 610 Newport Center Drive, 92660-6429.
Telephone: 714-760-9600.
Cable Address: "Moms".
Facsimile: 714-669-6994.
San Francisco, California Office: Embarcadero Center West Tower, 275 Battery Street, 94111-3305.
Telephone: 415-984-8700.
Facsimile: 415-984-8701.
New York, New York Office: Citicorp Center, 153 East 53rd Street, 10022-4611.
Telephone: 212-326-2000.
Facsimile: 212-326-2061.
Washington, D.C. Office: 555 13th Street, N.W., 20004-1109.
Telephone: 202-383-5300.
Cable Address: "Moms".
Facsimile: 202-383-5414.
London, England Office: 10 Finsbury Square, London, EC2A 1LA.
Telephone: 0171-256-8451.
Facsimile: 0171-638-8205.
Tokyo, Japan Office: Sanbancho KB-6 Building, 6 Sanbancho, Chiyoda-ku, Tokyo 102, Japan.
Telephone: 03-3239-2900.
Facsimile: 03-3239-2432.
Hong Kong Office: Suite 1905, Peregrine Tower, Lippo Centre, 89 Queensway, Central, Hong Kong.
Telephone: 852-2523-8266.
Facsimile: 852-2522-1760.
Shanghai, Peoples Republic of China Office: Shanghai International Trade Centre, Suite 2011, 2200 Yan An Road West, Shanghai, 200335, PRC.
Telephone: 86-21-6219-5363.
Facsimile: 86-21-6275-4949.

PARTNER
Greyson Lee Bryan

For Complete List of Firm Personnel, See General Section

For full biographical listings, see the Martindale-Hubbell Law Directory

ROBERT P. PALAZZO (AV)

3002 Midvale Avenue, Suite 209, 90034
Telephone: 310-474-5483
Fax: 310-474-6736
Inyo County Law Office: 230 South Main Street, Darwin, California 93522.
Telephone: 619-876-5941.

For full biographical listings, see the Martindale-Hubbell Law Directory

RADCLIFF, FRANDSEN & DONGELL (AV)

40th Floor, 777 South Figueroa Street, 90017
Telephone: 213-614-1990
Facsimile: 213-489-9263
San Francisco, California Office: 88 Kearny Street, Suite 1475.
Telephone: 415-399-8393.
Facsimile: 415-989-5465.
Rome, Italy Office: Via Tacito, 7.
Telephone: (39) 06-323-5588.
Facsimile: (39) 06-324-3392.

MEMBERS OF FIRM
Jules G. Radcliff, Jr.   Russell Mackay Frandsen
Richard A. Dongell
OF COUNSEL
Tal Clifton Finney

(See Next Column)

ASSOCIATES

Francis P. Aspessi   Jeffrey C. Mayes
Ruben A. Castellon   Marisa A. Moret
William W. Funderburk, Jr.   Daniel E. Park
Jeffrey A. Gagliardi   Scott D. Pinsky
David K. Lee   Eric H. Saiki
Maria Anna Mancini   Steve R. Segura
Glenn M. White

For full biographical listings, see the Martindale-Hubbell Law Directory

MODESTO, * Stanislaus Co.

RICHARD DOUGLAS BREW A PROFESSIONAL LAW CORPORATION (AV)

Suite 350 / Judge Frank C. Damrell Building, 1601 I Street, 95354-1110
Telephone: 209-572-3157
Telefax: 209-572-4641
Email: interleg.com

Richard Douglas Brew

For full biographical listings, see the Martindale-Hubbell Law Directory

NEWPORT BEACH, Orange Co.

ALVARADO, SMITH, VILLA & SANCHEZ, A PROFESSIONAL CORPORATION (AV)

Suite 800, 4695 MacArthur Court, P.O. Box 8677, 92658-8677
Telephone: 714-955-1433
Fax: 714-955-1704
URL: http://www.Alvarado-Smith.com
Los Angeles, California Office, 611 West Sixth Street, Suite 2650.
Telephone: 213-229-2554.
Fax: 213-617-8966.

Raymond G. Alvarado   John M. Sorich
   (Resident, Los Angeles Office)   Barbara L. Tang
Ruben A. Smith   Raúl F. Salinas
Maurice Sanchez   (Resident Los Angeles Office)
Fernando Villa
   (Resident, Los Angeles Office)

J. Michelle Hickey   Amy Toboco Dibb
   (Resident, Los Angeles Office)   Steven M. Lawrence
John B. Carmichael, III   (Resident, Los Angeles Office)
Frances Q. Jett   Robert W. Brown, Jr.
   (Resident, Los Angeles Office)   (Resident, Los Angeles Office)
Susan Bade Hull   Steven C. Yung
   (Resident, Los Angeles Office)   (Resident, Los Angeles Office)
Christopher M. Leo   Thomas A. Zeigler
Roger E. Borg

For full biographical listings, see the Martindale-Hubbell Law Directory

LAW OFFICES OF DON M. DRYSDALE (AV)

Suite 700, 610 Newport Center Drive, 92660-6442
Telephone: 714-760-9677
Fax: 714-760-9551
Email: 75722.164@compuserve.com

LEGAL SUPPORT PERSONNEL
Irene E. Reynolds   Tiffany L. Milby
Michelle K. Drysdale

For full biographical listings, see the Martindale-Hubbell Law Directory

FRANK B. MYERS (AV)

Suite 720, 4400 MacArthur Boulevard, 92660
Telephone: 714-752-2001
Facsimile: 714-955-3670

For full biographical listings, see the Martindale-Hubbell Law Directory

YOUNG & AMUNDSEN (AV)

620 Newport Center Drive, Suite 420, 92660
Telephone: 714-640-4400
Fax: 714-717-4862

MEMBERS OF FIRM
Steven R. Young   Roland J. Amundsen

For full biographical listings, see the Martindale-Hubbell Law Directory

SAN DIEGO, * San Diego Co.

LAW OFFICES OF CHARLES P. LEBEAU (AV)

Golden Triangle La Jolla Centre I Union Bank Building, Suite 1070, 4660 La Jolla Village Drive, 92122-4606
Telephone: 619-456-1100; 619-455-1100
Fax: 619-455-5024
URL: http://www.lebeaulaw.com/
Detroit, Michigan Office: 400 Renaissance Center, Suite 500.
Telephone: 313-396-1765; 800-897-5266.
Fax: 619-455-5024.

LEGAL SUPPORT PERSONNEL
Mary Pomerene   Brenda Barron
                    Rebecca Rocha

For full biographical listings, see the Martindale-Hubbell Law Directory

PAGE, POLIN & BUSCH, A PROFESSIONAL CORPORATION (AV)

350 West Ash Street, Suite 900, 92101-3436
Telephone: 619-231-1822
Fax: 619-231-1877
Fax: 619-231-1875
Email: pagepolin@pagepolin.com

Michael E. Busch   Richard W. Page
Kathleen A. Cashman-Kramer   Kenneth D. Polin
Richard L. Moskitis   Steven G. Rowles

Rod S. Fiori   Michael G. Rowles
Dorothy A. Johnson   (Not admitted in CA)
Jolene L. Parker   Barry M. Taira

For full biographical listings, see the Martindale-Hubbell Law Directory

SAN FRANCISCO, * San Francisco Co.

LAW OFFICES OF KEVIN W. FINCK (AV)

Two Embarcadero Center, Suite 1670, 94111
Telephone: 415-296-9100
Facsimile: 415-394-6446

Michael L. Dobrov
OF COUNSEL
Marla Raucher Osborn

For full biographical listings, see the Martindale-Hubbell Law Directory

FLYNN, DELICH & WISE (AV)

Suite 1750, 580 California Street, 94104
Telephone: 415-693-5566
Fax: 415-693-0410
Long Beach, California Office: 1 World Trade Center, Suite 1800.
Telephone: 310-435-2626.
Fax: 310-437-7555.

John Allen Flynn   Sam D. Delich
                    James B. Nebel

Representative Clients: American Hawaii Cruises; Holland America Line; Through Transport Mutual Insurance Association, Ltd.; The Britannia Steam Ship Insurance Association Limited; The Steamship Mutual Underwriting Association (Bermuda) Ltd.; General Steamship Corp., Ltd.; Commodore Cruise Line, Ltd.; Interocean Steamship Corporation; Sea-Land Service, Inc.; Hatteras Yachts.

For full biographical listings, see the Martindale-Hubbell Law Directory

STIMMEL, STIMMEL & SMITH, A PROFESSIONAL CORPORATION (AV)

100 Bush Street, Suite 850, 94104
Telephone: 415-392-2018
Fax: 415-392-2018

Norman S. Stimmel (1914-1991)   Lee D. Stimmel
                    Andrine K. Smith
                    OF COUNSEL
Linda S. Votaw   Jeffrey S. Rosen

For full biographical listings, see the Martindale-Hubbell Law Directory

VENTURA, * Ventura Co.

LASCHER & LASCHER, A PROFESSIONAL CORPORATION (AV)

605 Poli Street, P.O. Box 25540, 93002
Telephone: 805-648-3228
Fax: 805-643-7692
Email: lascher@isle.net

Edward L. Lascher (1928-1991)   Wendy Cole Lascher

(See Next Column)

Gabriele Mezger-Lashly
Reference: First National Bank of Ventura.

For full biographical listings, see the Martindale-Hubbell Law Directory

COLORADO

COLORADO SPRINGS, * El Paso Co.

FLYNN McKENNA WRIGHT & KARSH (AV)

limited liability company
Plaza of the Rockies 111 South Tejon, Suite 202, 80903
Telephone: 719-578-8444
Fax: 719-578-8836

James T. Flynn   Randolph M. Karsh
R. Tim McKenna   Brian T. Murphy
Bruce M. Wright   Michael C. Potarf

Representative Clients: Barrers, Siqueiros y Torres Landa, S.C. (Mexico City).

For full biographical listings, see the Martindale-Hubbell Law Directory

DENVER, * Denver Co.

HARRY L. ARKIN & ASSOCIATES, P.C. (AV)

Suite 2750 Lincoln Center, 1660 Lincoln Street, 80264
Telephone: 303-863-8400
Telefax: 303-832-4703
Email: harkin00@counsel.com
London, England Office: Verulam Chambers, Peer House, 8-14 Verulam Street, WCIX 8LZ.
Telephone: 071 813-2400.
Fax: 071 405-3870.

Harry L. Arkin

Sharon E. Smith
LEGAL SUPPORT PERSONNEL
Patricia A. Hanson

For full biographical listings, see the Martindale-Hubbell Law Directory

HOLME ROBERTS & OWEN LLP (AV)

Suite 4100, 1700 Lincoln, 80203
Telephone: 303-861-7000
Telecopier: 303-866-0200
Email: hro@hro.com *URL:* http://www.hro.com
Boulder, Colorado Office: Suite 400, 1401 Pearl Street.
Telephone: 303-444-5955.
Telecopier: 303-444-1063.
Colorado Springs, Colorado Office: Suite 1300, 90 South Cascade Avenue.
Telephone: 719-473-3800.
Telecopier: 719-633-1518.
Salt Lake City, Utah Office: Suite 1100, 111 East Broadway.
Telephone: 801-521-5800.
Telecopier: 801-521-9639.
London, England Office: Mellier House, 26a Albemarle Street.
Telephone: 44-171-499-8776.
Telecopier: 44-171-499-7769.
Moscow, Russia Office: Kosmodamianskaya Nab. #52/1, Suite 9100, 113054.
Telephone: 7095-961-3000.
Telecopier: 7095-961-3001.
Kiev, Ukraine Office: Terestchenkovskaya #19, Suite 2, 252004.
Telephone: 380-44-224-1348.
Telecopier: 380-44-224-4986.

PARTNERS OF FIRM
Frank Erisman   David B. Wilson
Charles A. Ramunno   Garth B. Jensen
Bruce R. Kohler (Co-Resident   Margaret B. McLean (Resident
  Managing Partner, London,   Managing Partner, Moscow,
  England Office)   Russia Office and Co-Resident
Judith L. L. Roberts   Managing Partner, London,
  (Co-Director, Moscow Office;   England Office)
  London Office)   Paul G. Thompson
Steven B. Richardson   Kevin P. Block (Managing
John F. Knoeckel   Partner, Kiev Office)
                    Mark M. Hrenya
                    OF COUNSEL
                    John P. Babb
                    SPECIAL COUNSEL
            Frank J Schuchat (Not admitted in CO)

(See Next Column)

HOLME ROBERTS & OWEN LLP—*Continued*

ASSOCIATES

Marat Ametov (Moscow Office)	Nikita O. Sergeyev
Christopher Boffey (Resident,	(Moscow, Russia Office)
Moscow, Russia Office)	Rashid Sharipov (Resident,
Valery Fedichin (Kiev Office)	Moscow, Russia Office)
Shuang Hu	Alexander Udovenko
Elena Kuryatnikova	(Moscow, Russia Office)
(Moscow, Russia Office)	Anna B. Veiksha (Kiev Office)
Neil F. O'Donnell	Masahiro Max Yoshimura
(Moscow Office)	

For Complete List of Firm Personnel, See General Section

For full biographical listings, see the Martindale-Hubbell Law Directory

---

SOLOMON PEARL BLUM & QUINN LLP (AV)

1700 Broadway, Suite 1820, 80290
Telephone: 303-832-6686
Fax: 303-832-6653
Email: SolPearl@aol.com
New York, New York Office: Woolworth Building, 37th Floor, 233
Broadway, 10007.
Charlotte Amalie, St. Thomas, Virgin Islands Affiliated Office: Grunet
Stout & Bruch, 24-25 Kongens Gade, P.O. Box 1030, 00804.
Telephone: 809-774-1320.
Fax: 809-774-7839.
Denver, Colorado Affiliated Office: Dufford & Brown, P.C., 1700
Broadway, Suite 1700, 80290.
Telephone: 303-861-8013.
Facsimile: 303-832-3804.

Robert A. Solomon	William L. Blum
Clifford R. Pearl	(Not admitted in CO)
	Thomas F. Quinn

For full biographical listings, see the Martindale-Hubbell Law Directory

---

WELBORN SULLIVAN MECK & TOOLEY, P.C. (AV)

1775 Sherman Street, Suite 1800, 80203-4318
Telephone: 303-830-2500
Facsimile: 303-832-2366
Email: wsmt.denver@mep-1.sprint.com
Republic of Kazakstan Branch Office: 480100 Almaty 38 Dostyk Prospect,
Suite 703.
Telephone: +7-3272 617-422; 616-509; 616-642.
Fax: +7-3272 615-840. *Email:* wsmt.welborn@mep-1.sprint.com.

John F. Welborn	Marla E. Valdez
John F. Meck	Karen Ostrander-Krug

Scott L. Sells

For Complete List of Firm Personnel, See General Section

For full biographical listings, see the Martindale-Hubbell Law Directory

---

DISTRICT OF COLUMBIA

WASHINGTON, D.C. Co.

* indicates certain Bar Register subscribers, in cities of comparable
size and importance, who maintain an additional office in
Washington, D.C. and who have arranged for representation as a
part of the Washington, D.C. listings that follow

BERLINER, CORCORAN & ROWE, L.L.P. (AV)

A Partnership including a Professional Corporation
1101 Seventeenth Street, N.W., 20036-4798
Telephone: 202-293-5555
FAX: 202-293-9035

MEMBERS OF FIRM

Thomas G. Corcoran, Jr.	Michael W. Beasley
Neal E. Krucoff	Clemens Kochinke
Henry M. Lloyd (P.C.)	John A. Ordway, Jr.
Wayne H. Rusch	John L. Simson

COUNSEL

Henry A. Berliner, Jr.	Peter Heidenberger
Rufus King	Lothar Griessbach

ASSOCIATES

Kathleen S. Rice	Jay A. Rosenthal

For full biographical listings, see the Martindale-Hubbell Law Directory

---

CAMERON & HORNBOSTEL, L.L.P. (AV)

Suite 700, 818 Connecticut Avenue, N.W., 20006
Telephone: 202-293-4690
Cable Address: "Continent"
Telecopier: 202-293-1877
Email: camhorn@ix.netcom.com
New York, N.Y. Office: 230 Park Avenue.
Telephone: 212-682-4902.
Cable Address: "Continents, New York".
Telecopier: 212-697-0946.

MEMBERS OF FIRM

Duncan H. Cameron	Alexander W. Sierck
Bertrand J. Delanney (Resident,	Frederick Simpich
New York, N.Y. Office)	Larry W. Thomas
Peter A. Hornbostel	Howard L. Vickery (Resident,
William K. Ince	New York, N.Y. Office)
Dennis James, Jr.	Bruce Zagaris

ASSOCIATES

Zoe J. Bercovitch (Resident,	Theodore R. Lazo
New York, N.Y. Office)	Michele C. Sherman
David M. Schwartz	

OF COUNSEL

Carolyn W. Davenport	Richard C. Katz
(Resident, New York, N.Y.	(Not admitted in DC)
Office)	Geoffrey H. Ward (Resident,
Stephen M. Wallenstein	New York, N.Y. Office)

For full biographical listings, see the Martindale-Hubbell Law Directory

---

DAHLGREN AND CLOSE (AV)

1000 Connecticut Avenue, N.W., Suite 204, 20036
Telephone: 202-659-1440
Fax: 202-659-5755
Cable Address: "Darclo"

MEMBERS OF FIRM

John O. Dahlgren (1913-1989)	David P. Close

OF COUNSEL

Joseph D. Crumlish

For full biographical listings, see the Martindale-Hubbell Law Directory

---

✱ KIRLIN, CAMPBELL & KEATING (AV)

2nd Floor, 1 Farragut Square South, 888 Sixteenth Street, N.W., 20006
Telephone: 202-639-8000
Telecopier: 202-835-8238
Other Offices Located in: New York, N.Y., Long Beach, California,
Stamford, Connecticut, Caldwell, New Jersey and Ft. Lauderdale, Fl.

RESIDENT OF COUNSEL

Gerald A. Malia	Russell T. Weil

For full biographical listings, see the Martindale-Hubbell Law Directory

---

MURPHY & WEBER (AV)

818 Connecticut Avenue, N.W., 20006
Telephone: 202-833-9211
Fax: 202-293-1877
Email: Murphywebr@aol.com
Associated Offices: Kiskalt, Dielmann & Schoenberger (Frankfurt) and
Fact Law Group (Helsinki & Washington).

MEMBERS OF FIRM

Terence Roche Murphy	Charles A. Weber

COUNSEL

Heinz J. Dielmann

For full biographical listings, see the Martindale-Hubbell Law Directory

---

REICHLER, MILTON & MEDEL (AV)

Suite 1200, 1747 Pennsylvania Avenue, N.W., 20006-4604
Telephone: 202-223-1200
Fax: 202-785-6687

Paul S. Reichler	Arthur V. Medel
Kathleen M. Milton	Janis H. Brennan

ASSOCIATES

Padideh Ala'i	Alima Joned
Melissa E. Crow	Daniel M. Malabonga
(Not admitted in DC)	(Not admitted in DC)

OF COUNSEL

T. Jay Barrymore	Traci Duvall Humes

For full biographical listings, see the Martindale-Hubbell Law Directory

Washington—Continued

SHAWN, MANN & NIEDERMAYER, L.L.P. (AV)

1850 M Street, N.W., Suite 280, 20036-5803
Telephone: 202-331-7900
Fax: 202-331-0726
Washington, D.C., Government Affairs Office: 499 S. Capitol Street, S.W.,
Suite 420.
Telephone: 202-842-3000.
Fax: 202-547-7161.
Los Angeles, California Office: 2029 Century Park East, Suite 1690.
Telephone: 310-553-8065.
Fax: 310-557-0729.
San Diego, California Office: 401 West "A" Street, Suite 1850.
Telephone: 619-236-0303.
Fax: 619-238-8181.
San Francisco, California Office: The Fox Plaza, 1390 Market Street, Suite
1204.
Telephone: 415-982-0150.
Fax: 415-522-0513.
Bloomington, Minnesota Office: 2090 West 98th Street.
Telephone: 612-881-6577.
Fax: 612-881-6894.

MEMBER OF FIRM
William H. Shawn

For full biographical listings, see the Martindale-Hubbell Law Directory

STEPTOE & JOHNSON LLP (AV)

1330 Connecticut Avenue, N.W., 20036
Telephone: 202-429-3000
Cable Address: "Stepjohn"
Telex: 89-2503
Telecopier: 202-429-3902
Email: wbatterton@steptoe.com *URL:* http://www.steptoe.com
Phoenix, Arizona Office: Two Renaissance Square, 40 N. Central Avenue,
Suite 2400, 85004.
Telephone: 602-257-5200.
Moscow, Russia Office: Steptoe & Johnson International AOZT. 25
Tsvetnoy Boulevard, Building 3 Moscow, Russia 103051.
Telephone: 011-7-501-258-5250.
Fax: 011-7-501-258-5251.
Almaty, Kazakhstan Office: Steptoe & Johnson Company Almaty. 84
Gogol Street, Suite 213, 480083.
Telephones: (3272) 50-11-25, (3272) 32-25-39.

MEMBERS

Monroe Leigh	Filiberto Agusti
Sarah C. Carey	Olin L. Wethington
Richard O. Cunningham	Walter H. White, Jr.
Sheldon E. Hochberg	(Moscow, Russia Office)
Daniel J. Plaine	Edward J. Krauland
William Karas	Robert T. Novick
Robert W. Fleishman	Anthony J. LaRocca
W. George Grandison	Arthur Randolph Bregman
Stewart A. Baker	Mark A. Moran

OF COUNSEL

Cecil J. Olmstead	Stanley Smilack
Richard Diamond	Carol A. Mitchell

For Complete List of Firm Personnel, See General Section

For full biographical listings, see the Martindale-Hubbell Law Directory

STEWART AND STEWART (AV)

Suite 200, 2100 M Street, N.W., 20037-1207
Telephone: 202-785-4185
Telecopier: 202-466-1286; 466-1287; 466-1288
Email: general@stewartlaw.com

MEMBERS OF FIRM

Terence P. Stewart	Charles A. St. Charles
James R. Cannon, Jr.	William A. Fennell
Wesley K. Caine	Jimmie V. Reyna

Geert De Prest

FOUNDER AND SENIOR PARTNER EMERITUS
Eugene L. Stewart

ASSOCIATES

Patrick John McDonough	Mara M. Burr
(Not admitted in DC)	(Not admitted in DC)
Amy S. Dwyer	Roberta K. Maixner
Andrew G. Stephens	(Not admitted in DC)
(Not admitted in DC)	

COUNSEL
Bernard Spinoit (Not admitted in the United States)

OF COUNSEL

Lane Steven Hurewitz	Edwin A. Kilburn
David J. Branson	(Not admitted in DC)

For full biographical listings, see the Martindale-Hubbell Law Directory

WATT, TIEDER & HOFFAR, L.L.P. (AV)

601 Pennsylvania Avenue, N.W., Suite 900, 20004
Telephone: 202-462-4697
Telecopier: 703-893-8029
McLean Virginia Office: 7929 Westpark Drive, Suite 400,
Telephone: 703-749-1000.
Telecopier: 703-893-8029.
Irvine California Office: 3 Park Plaza, Suite 1530.
Telephone: 714-852-6700.

MEMBERS OF FIRM

John B. Tieder, Jr.	Robert K. Cox
	David C. Romm

For full biographical listings, see the Martindale-Hubbell Law Directory

WIGMAN, COHEN, LEITNER & MYERS, A PROFESSIONAL CORPORATION (AV)

Intellectual Property and International Trade Attorneys
The Farragut Building 10th Floor, 900 17th Street, N.W., 20006
Telephone: 202-463-7700
Facsimile: 202-463-6915
Email: iplaw@laser.net

Herbert Cohen	Saul Leitner
Victor M. Wigman	Edward J. Farrell
George C. Myers, Jr.	Michael C. Greenbaum
(Not admitted in DC)	

Jan Christensen	Suzanne F. Gisler Metzler
Dorothy H. Patterson	(Not admitted in DC)
Michael D. White	Karl O. Neidert
Jonathan M. Cohen	(Not admitted in DC)
(Not admitted in DC)	Joseph G. Seeber

OF COUNSEL
Donald R. Greene

For full biographical listings, see the Martindale-Hubbell Law Directory

WILMER, CUTLER & PICKERING (AV)

2445 M Street, N.W., 20037-1420
Telephone: 202-663-6000
Fax: 202-663-6363
Email: Law@Wilmer.Com
Baltimore, Maryland Office: 100 Light Street, 21202.
Telephone: 410-986-2800.
Fax: 410-986-2828.
European Offices:
4 Carlton Gardens, London, SW1Y 5AA, England. Telephone: +44 (171)
872-1000.
Fax: +44 (171) 839-3537.
Rue de la Loi 15Wetstraat, B-1040 Brussels, Belgium. Telephone: +32 (2)
285-4900.
Fax: +32 (2) 285-4949.
Friedrichstrasse 95, D-10117 Berlin, Germany. Telephone: +49 (30)
2022-6400.
Fax: +49 (30)2022-6500.

MEMBERS OF FIRM

Daniel K. Mayers	Russell J. Bruemmer
James S. Campbell	William J. Wilkins
Jeffrey N. Shane	Andrew N. Vollmer
Louis R. Cohen	James S. Venit (Not admitted in
F. David Lake, Jr.	DC; Resident, European
Paul J. Mode, Jr.	Office, Brussels, Belgium)
C. Loring Jetton, Jr.	Dr. Andreas Weitbrecht
William T. Lake	(Resident, European Office,
Dieter G. F. Lange (Resident,	Brussels, Belgium)
European Office, London,	W. Scott Blackmer
England)	Gary B. Born (Resident,
Charles S. Levy	European Office, London,
Dr. Manfred Balz (Not admitted	England)
in the United States; Resident,	John B. Watkins V (Resident,
European Office, Berlin,	Baltimore, Maryland Office)
Germany)	Paul A. von Hehn (Resident,
Richard W. Cass	European Office, Brussels,
Kenneth W. Gideon	Belgium)
Arthur L. Marriott (Resident,	Marc C. Hansen (Resident,
European Office, London,	European Office, Brussels,
England)	Belgium)
Robert C. Cassidy, Jr.	Bryan Slone (Resident,
John D. Greenwald	Baltimore, Maryland Office)
(Not admitted in DC)	Andrew K. Parnell (Resident,
John H. Harwood II	European Office, London,
Stephen P. Doyle	England)
George P. Stamas (Resident,	
Baltimore, Maryland Office)	

SENIOR COUNSEL

Lloyd N. Cutler	John H. Pickering

(See Next Column)

WILMER, CUTLER & PICKERING—*Continued*

COUNSEL

Lester Nurick
Leonard M. Shambon
Patricia A. Sherman (Resident
European Office, Brussels,
Belgium)

John J. Kallaugher (Resident,
European Office, London,
England)

For Complete List of Firm Personnel, See General Section

For full biographical listings, see the Martindale-Hubbell Law Directory

FLORIDA

KISSIMMEE, * Osceola Co.

POHL & SHORT, P.A.

(See Winter Park)

MIAMI, * Dade Co.

BIERMAN, SHOHAT, LOEWY, PERRY & KLEIN, PROFESSIONAL ASSOCIATION (AV)

Penthouse Two, 800 Brickell Avenue, 33131-2944
Telephone: 305-358-7000
Facsimile: 305-358-4010
Email: BSLPK@AOL.COM

Donald I. Bierman
Edward R. Shohat
Ira N. Loewy

Pamela I. Perry
Theodore Klein
Maria Beguiristain Shohat

Reference: United National Bank of Miami.

For full biographical listings, see the Martindale-Hubbell Law Directory

MURAI, WALD, BIONDO & MORENO, P.A. (AV)

9th Floor Ingraham Building, 25 Southeast 2nd Avenue, 33131
Telephone: 305-358-5900
Fax: 305-358-9490

Rene V. Murai
Gerald B. Wald

Gerald J. Biondo
M. Cristina Moreno

William E. Davis

Cristina Echarte Brochin

Lynette Ebeoglu McGuinness

Mary Leslie Smith

Reference: Republic National Bank of Miami.

For full biographical listings, see the Martindale-Hubbell Law Directory

SIMMONS, HART & SHEEHE (AV)

A Partnership of Professional Associations
One Biscayne Tower, 2 South Biscayne Boulevard, Suite 1684, 33131
Telephone: 305-379-3515
Fax: 305-379-5404
Ocala, Florida Office: 125 Northeast First Avenue, Suite 1.
Telephone: 904-732-8121.
Fax: 904-368-2183.

Bryce W. Ackerman
Daniel A. Amat
John B. Fuller
Steven H. Gray
Timothy D. Haines

Karl V. Hart
Phillip J. Sheehe
Young J. Simmons
Jeffrey Skates
Marty Smith

Louis V. Vendittelli

For full biographical listings, see the Martindale-Hubbell Law Directory

SPENCER AND KLEIN, PROFESSIONAL ASSOCIATION (AV)

Suite 1901, 801 Brickell Avenue, 33131
Telephone: 305-374-7700
Telecopier: 305-374-4890

Thomas R. Spencer, Jr.

Brent D. Klein

Representative Clients: Aerocar Aviation, Inc.; America Publishing Group; American Association of Physicians and Surgeons; Coldwell Banker; Editorial Televisa; Grupo Anaya, S.A.; Independent Living Care, Inc.; Managed Care of America, Inc.; New Times, Inc.; Winn-Dixie Stores.

For Complete List of Firm Personnel, See General Section

For full biographical listings, see the Martindale-Hubbell Law Directory

NAPLES, * Collier Co.

EMERSON & EMERSON, P.A. (AV)

The Aragon Building, 385 Thirteenth Avenue South, 34201
Telephone: 941-261-5200
Telecopier: 941-261-5201

John W. Emerson

Ralph W. Emerson (1932-1989)

Representative Clients: Krehling Industries, Inc.; E-Squared; Chemical Technologys International, Inc.

For full biographical listings, see the Martindale-Hubbell Law Directory

OCALA, * Marion Co.

SIMMONS, HART & SHEEHE (AV)

A Partnership of Professional Associations
125 Northeast First Avenue, Suite 1, P.O. Box 3310, 34478-3310
Telephone: 352-732-8121
Fax: 352-368-2183
Miami, Florida Office: One Biscayne Tower, Suite 1684, 2 South Biscayne Boulevard, 33131.
Telephone: 305-379-3515.
Fax: 305-379-5404.

Bryce W. Ackerman
Daniel A. Amat
John B. Fuller
Steven H. Gray
Timothy D. Haines

Karl V. Hart
Young J. Simmons
Phillip J. Sheehe
Jeffrey Skates
Marty Smith

Louis V. Vendittelli

Representative Clients: Keeneland Association, Inc.; CSX Railroad; Double Diamond Farm; California Federal Bank.

For full biographical listings, see the Martindale-Hubbell Law Directory

ORLANDO, * Orange Co.

POHL & SHORT, P.A.

(See Winter Park)

SARASOTA, * Sarasota Co.

WILLIAMS, PARKER, HARRISON, DIETZ & GETZEN, PROFESSIONAL ASSOCIATION (AV)

200 South Orange Avenue, 34236-6749
Telephone: 941-366-4800
Telecopier: 941-366-5109
Mailing Address: P.O. Box 3258, Sarasota, Florida, 34230-3258
Email: wphdg.law@netsrg.com *URL:*
http://www.sarasota-online.com/williamspa-w

J.J. Williams, Jr. (1886-1968)
W. Davis Parker (1920-1982)
William T. Harrison, Jr.
George A. Dietz
Monte K. Marshall
James L. Ritchey
William G. Lambrecht
John T. Berteau
John V. Cannon, III
Charles D. Bailey, Jr.
J. Michael Hartenstine
Michele Boardman Grimes
James L. Turner
William M. Seider
Elizabeth C. Marshall
Robert W. Benjamin

Frank Strelec
Terri Salt Costa
David A. Wallace
Mark A. Schwartz
Ric Gregoria
Elvin W. Phillips
Jeffrey A. Grebe
John L. Moore
Morgan R. Bentley
Susan A. Barrett
Carol Ann Kalish
Linda R. Getzen
Kimberly J. Page
Phillip D. Eck
J. Hugh Middlebrooks
Robert A. Warram

OF COUNSEL

William E. Getzen

Frazer F. Hilder

Hugh McPheeters, Jr.

LEGAL SUPPORT PERSONNEL

Mark Loveridge (Land Planner)

General Counsel for: Sarasota County Public Hospital Board; Sarasota-Manatee Airport Authority; Taylor Woodrow Homes Ltd.; FCCI Mutual Insurance Co.
Local Counsel for: NationsBank of Florida; Barnett Bank of Southwest Florida; Northern Trust Bank of Florida; SunTrust Bank, Gulfcoast.

For full biographical listings, see the Martindale-Hubbell Law Directory

TAMPA, * Hillsborough Co.

SHARP & SMITH, P.A. (AV)

One Urban Centre, Suite 745, 4830 West Kennedy Boulevard, 33609
Telephone: 813-286-4199
FAX: 813-286-4197
Email: sharpsmith@earthlink.net

(See Next Column)

SHARP & SMITH P.A., *Tampa—Continued*

William M. Sharp, Sr.   Karen Rowley Smith
William T. Harrison, III

For full biographical listings, see the Martindale-Hubbell Law Directory

WEST PALM BEACH,* Palm Beach Co.

GEORGE C. J. MOORE (AV)

105 South Narcissus Avenue, Suite 812, 33401
Telephone: 561-833-9000
Telefax: 561-833-9990
Email: barrister@flinet.com
London, England Office: 10 King's Bench Walk, Temple, EC4 7EB.
Telephone: 0171-353-2501.
Grand Turk, West Indies Office: P.O. Box 163.
Telephone: 809-946-2089.

For full biographical listings, see the Martindale-Hubbell Law Directory

---

WINTER PARK, Orange Co.

POHL & SHORT, P.A. (AV)

280 West Canton Avenue, Suite 410, P.O. Box 3208, 32790
Telephone: 407-647-7645; 407-647-POHL
Telefax: 407-647-2314

Frank L. Pohl   C. Teresa de Arrigoitia
Houston E. Short   George A. Golder
Dwight I. Cool   Norma Stanley
James Everett Shepherd V   Mark W. Garrett
      John R. Simpson, Jr.

Representative Clients: American Pioneer Title Insurance Company; Institute of Internal Auditors, Inc.; Thompson Steel, Inc.; SunTrust, N.A.; The Bank of Winter Park; Bekins Moving and Storage Co., Inc.; Champion Boats, Inc.; KeyCom Telephone Systems, Inc.

For full biographical listings, see the Martindale-Hubbell Law Directory

---

GEORGIA

ATLANTA,* Fulton Co.

ALSTON & BIRD (AV)

A Partnership including Professional Corporations
One Atlantic Center, 1201 West Peachtree Street, 30309-3424
Telephone: 404-881-7000
Telecopier: 404-881-7777
Cable Address: AMGRAM GA
Telex: 54-2996
Easylink: 62985848
Washington, D.C. Office: 601 Pennsylvania Ave., N.W., North Building, Suite 250 20004.
Telephone: 202-508-3300.
Telecopier: 202-508-3333.

MEMBERS OF FIRM

Joe T. Taylor   Peter Kontio
Bernard L. Greer, Jr.   Patrick M. Norton
Timothy S. Perry   H. Stephen Harris, Jr.
     Sam K. Kaywood, Jr.

ASSOCIATES

Johan Droogmans   Gretchen D. Locy
     Felipe M. Nunez

COUNSEL

Eileen M. G. Scofield

Representative Clients: GTE Personal Communications Services, Riverwood International; Fortis, Inc.; Lithonia Lighting (NSI); Genuine Parts Company; Ritz-Carlton Hotels; Heidemij; Nakanishi; Whessoe; Farnell; Mitsui; Matsushita.

For Complete List of Firm Personnel, See General Section

For full biographical listings, see the Martindale-Hubbell Law Directory

---

GLASS, MCCULLOUGH, SHERRILL & HARROLD (AV)

1409 Peachtree Street, N.E., 30309
Telephone: 404-885-1500
Telecopier: 404-892-1801
Buckhead Office: Monarch Plaza, 3414 Peachtree Road, N.E., Suite 450, Atlanta, Georgia, 30326-1162.
Telephone: 404-885-1500.
Telecopier: 404-231-1978.
Washington, D.C. Office: 1150 17th Street, N.W., Suite 605. Washington, D.C., 20036.
Telephone: 202-785-8118.
Telecopier: 202-785-0128.

(See Next Column)

Knoxville, Tennessee Office: 606 West Main Avenue, Suite 205, P.O. Box 2543. Knoxville, Tennessee, 37901-2543.
Telephone: 423-971-5418.
Telecopier: 423-971-1706.

MEMBERS OF FIRM

Thomas J. Harrold, Jr.   Ross P. Kendall
Ugo F. Ippolito   James W. King
    W. Clayton Sparrow, Jr.

TAX COUNSEL

William M. Joseph

ASSOCIATES

L. Neill Edwards   Betsy Birns McCall
    Christina Sungyoon Pak

For Complete List of Firm Personnel, See General Section

For full biographical listings, see the Martindale-Hubbell Law Directory

---

HARKLEROAD & HERMANCE, A PROFESSIONAL CORPORATION (AV)

2500 Cain Tower-Peachtree Center, 229 Peachtree Street, N.E., 30303
Telephone: 404-588-9211
Telex II: 810-751-3228
Telecopier: 404-659-0860

Donald R. Harkleroad   James P. Hermance

For full biographical listings, see the Martindale-Hubbell Law Directory

---

KILPATRICK & CODY LLP (AV)

Suite 2800, 1100 Peachtree Street, 30309-4530
Telephone: 404-815-6500
Telephone Copier: 404-815-6555
Telex: 54-2307
Washington, D.C. Office: Suite 800, 700 13th Street, N.W., 20005.
Telephone: 202-508-5800. Telephone Copier: 202-508-5858.
Brussels, Belgium Office: Avenue Louise 65, BTE 3, 1050 Brussels.
Telephone: (32) (2) 533-03-00.
Telecopier: (32) (2) 534-86-38.
London, England Office: 68 Pall Mall, London, SW1Y 5ES, England.
Telephone: (44) (71) 321 0477.
Telecopier: (44) (71) 930 9733.
Augusta, Georgia Office: Suite 1400 First Union Bank Building, P.O. Box 2043, 30903. Telephone (706) 724-2622. Telecopier (706) 722-0219.

MEMBERS OF FIRM

Luis A. Aguilar   Keith T. Ott (Resident, London,
Gregory K. Cinnamon   England Office)
Frederick K. Heller, Jr.   Reinaldo Pascual
 (Resident, Brussels, Belgium Marc K. Ritzmann
 Office)   Gary K. Saidman
     G. Kimbrough Taylor, Jr.

COUNSEL

Pascale Rahman (Brussels, Belgium Office)

ASSOCIATES

Pervez Akhtar   Wei Hu
 (London, England Office) Mila A. Ostin
Donald C. Evans, Jr.   Ivo Vissenberg

For Complete List of Firm Personnel, See General Section

For full biographical listings, see the Martindale-Hubbell Law Directory

---

JAMES C. NOBLES, JR. (AV)

3085 One Atlantic Center, 1201 West Peachtree Street, N.W., 30309
Telephone: 404-875-3600
Telecopier: 404-875-1500

Reference: Trust Company Bank.

For full biographical listings, see the Martindale-Hubbell Law Directory

---

PIERCE & YOUNG (AV)

Building 1700, 2255 Cumberland Parkway Northwest, 30339-4575
Telephone: 770-435-0500
Telecopier: 770-435-0362

MEMBER OF FIRM

J. Wayne Pierce

For full biographical listings, see the Martindale-Hubbell Law Directory

HAWAII

HONOLULU, Honolulu Co.

LAW OFFICES OF DAVID F. DAY (AV)

Grosvenor Center Mauka Tower Suite 1788, 737 Bishop Street, 96813
Telephone: 808-531-8020
Fax: 808-521-0962
Email: ddayofc@lava.net

For full biographical listings, see the Martindale-Hubbell Law Directory

LAW OFFICES OF MANUEL D. GARCIA (AV)

Makai Tower, Grosvenor Center, Suite 2550, 733 Bishop Street, 96813
Telephone: 808-522-0755
Facsimile: 808-522-0760

For full biographical listings, see the Martindale-Hubbell Law Directory

McCORRISTON MIHO MILLER MUKAI (AV)

Five Waterfront Plaza, 4th Floor, 500 Ala Moana Boulevard, 96813
Telephone: 808-529-7300
Facsimile: 808-524-8293
Cable: Attorneys, Honolulu
Mailing Address: P.O. Box 2800, Honolulu, Hawaii, 96803-2800
Hilo, Hawaii Office: 56 Waianuenue Avenue, Suite 217, 96720.
Telephone: 808-935-6537.
Facsimile: 808-935-3398.

PARTNERS

Jon T. Miho	David N. Kuriyama
Clifford J. Miller	Eric T. Kawatani
Franklin K. Mukai	Keith K. Suzuka
Stanley Y. Mukai	Randall F. Sakumoto
D. Scott MacKinnon	Andrew W. Char
Kenneth B. Marcus	Alexander R. Jampel

COUNSEL
Charles E. Pear, Jr.

ASSOCIATES

Peter J. Hamasaki	Joel D. Kam
Darren Patrick Conley	Shulammite Kim
Dean J. Myatt	

Representative Clients: TSA International Limited; Niju-Ichi Corporation; Mainami Boeki Co., Ltd.; The Daiichi Housing Co., Ltd.; Japan Leasing Corporation; Long Term Credit Bank of Japan; Seven-Eleven Japan Co., Ltd.; New Oji Paper Co., Ltd.; Marubeni Corporation; Sports Shinko (Hawaii) Co., Ltd.

For Complete List of Firm Personnel, See General Section

For full biographical listings, see the Martindale-Hubbell Law Directory

STUBENBERG & DURRETT (AV)

1400 Pauahi Tower, 1001 Bishop Street, 96813
Telephone: 808-526-0892
Fax: 808-533-4399

James A. Stubenberg	Jonathan S. Durrett

Richard A. Kersenbrock, Jr.	Joseph L. Dwight, IV
Valerie J. Lam	Vivien Mia Weber

OF COUNSEL

Lorrie L. Stone	Russell W. Lousich
James P. Clarke	

For full biographical listings, see the Martindale-Hubbell Law Directory

ILLINOIS

CHICAGO, Cook Co.

ARTHUR FAKES, P.C.

(See Lombard)

PATTISHALL, McAULIFFE, NEWBURY, HILLIARD & GERALDSON (AV)

Suite 5000, 311 South Wacker Drive, 60606
Telephone: 312-554-8000
Facsimile: 312-554-8015
Washington, D.C. Office: 320 Watergate, Six Hundred, 20037.
Telephone: 202-338-1300.
Facsimile: 202-338-9349.

(See Next Column)

MEMBERS OF FIRM

Beverly W. Pattishall	Robert W. Sacoff
Jeremiah D. McAuliffe	Mark V. B. Partridge
Robert M. Newbury	Joseph N. Welch II
Benjamin S. Warren III	Mark H. Hellmann
(Resident Partner,	Jean Marie R. Pechette
Washington, D.C. Office)	Daniel D. Frohling
Raymond I. Geraldson, Jr.	John Thompson Brown
David Craig Hilliard	Mary E. Innis
Edward G. Wierzbicki	Douglas N. Masters

Brett A. August	Kevin T. Conroy
Jonathan S. Jennings	Mark F. Schultz
John Michael Murphy	Bradley L. Cohn
Maxine Lans Retsky	Susan D. Hanaway
Nancy L. Clarke	Victor F. DeFrancis

For full biographical listings, see the Martindale-Hubbell Law Directory

SIEGEL, MOSES, SCHOENSTADT & WEBSTER, P.C. (AV)

111 East Wacker Drive Suite 2800, 60601-4801
Telephone: 312-658-2000
Fax: 312-658-2022

Morton Siegel	Richard G. Schoenstadt
Michael A. Moses	James L. Webster
	Jennifer G. Hoff

For full biographical listings, see the Martindale-Hubbell Law Directory

LOMBARD, Du Page Co.

ARTHUR FAKES, P.C. (AV)

929 South Main Street, Suite 109, 60148
Telephone: 630-268-0600
Telecopier: 630-268-0642
Email: ARTFAKES@AOL.COM

Arthur Fakes

For full biographical listings, see the Martindale-Hubbell Law Directory

INDIANA

*INDIANAPOLIS,** Marion Co.

BAMBERGER & FEIBLEMAN (AV)

54 Monument Circle Suite 600, 46204-2947
Telephone: 317-639-5151
FAX: 317-269-2030

MEMBER OF FIRM
D. Robert Webster

Representative Clients: C.I.T. Corp.; FFI Corporation; Kipp Brothers, Inc.; BancPlus Mortgage Corp.; Hiway Parts, Inc.; NBD, Indiana; Tube Processing Corp.; Indiana Mortgage Corp.

For full biographical listings, see the Martindale-Hubbell Law Directory

KANSAS

*WICHITA,** Sedgwick Co.

FOULSTON & SIEFKIN L.L.P. (AV)

700 Fourth Financial Center, 67202
Telephone: 316-267-6371
Facsimile: 316-267-6345
Topeka, Kansas Office: 1515 Bank IV Tower, 534 Kansas Avenue, 66603.
Telephone: 913-233-3600.
Fax: 913-233-1610.
Dodge City, Kansas Office: 810 Frontview, P.O. Box 1147, 67801.
Telephone: 316-227-8126.
Fax: 316-227-8451.
Member: Lex Mundi, A Global Association of 126 Independent Firms.

MEMBERS OF FIRM

Benjamin C. Langel	Harvey R. Sorensen
	Larry G. Rapp

For Complete List of Firm Personnel, See General Section

For full biographical listings, see the Martindale-Hubbell Law Directory

LOUISIANA

NEW ORLEANS, Orleans Parish

GAINSBURGH, BENJAMIN, DAVID, MEUNIER, NORIEA & WARSHAUER (AV)

2800 Energy Centre, 1100 Poydras, 70163-2800
Telephone: 504-522-2304
Telecopier: 504-528-9973
Email: GAINSBEN@IAMERICA.NET

OF COUNSEL

Samuel C. Gainsburgh (P.L.C.)   Jack C. Benjamin (P.L.C.)

MEMBERS OF FIRM

Robert J. David	Irving J. Warshauer
George S. Meyer (1939-1977)	Stevan C. Dittman
Gerald E. Meunier	Madeleine M. Landrieu
Nick F. Noriea, Jr.	Darryl M. Phillips

ASSOCIATES

Michael G. Calogero   Jeffrey A. Mitchell

For full biographical listings, see the Martindale-Hubbell Law Directory

LEA, TYNAN & McGEHEE, P.L.C. (AV)

Southern Marine and Aviation Building, 610 Poydras Street Suite 500, 70130
Telephone: 504-523-4500
Fax: 504-525-7208

Arden J. Lea   Joseph P. Tynan
                W. Clay McGehee

MEXICAN LEGAL ADVISOR

Ricardo Lan (Not admitted in the United States)

For full biographical listings, see the Martindale-Hubbell Law Directory

WAGNER, BAGOT & GLEASON (AV)

Suite 2660, Poydras Center, 650 Poydras Street, 70130-6105
Telephone: 504-525-2141
Telecopier: 504-523-1587
TWX: 5106017673
ELN: 62928850
"INCISIVE"

Thomas J. Wagner	Harvey G. Gleason
Michael H. Bagot, Jr.	Whitney L. Cole
Eric D. Suben	

For full biographical listings, see the Martindale-Hubbell Law Directory

MAINE

BAR HARBOR, Hancock Co.

FENTON, CHAPMAN, FENTON, SMITH & KANE, P.A. (AV)

109 Main Street, P.O. Box B, 04609
Telephone: 207-288-3331
FAX: 207-288-9326

William Fenton	Chadbourn H. Smith
Douglas B. Chapman	Daniel H. Kane (1940-1995)
Nathaniel R. Fenton	Hancock Griffin, Jr. (1912-1980)

Margaret A. Timothy   Eric Lindquist

OF COUNSEL

Edwin R. Smith

Reference: Bar Harbor Banking and Trust Co.

For full biographical listings, see the Martindale-Hubbell Law Directory

MASSACHUSETTS

BOSTON, Suffolk Co.

ARESTY INTERNATIONAL LAW OFFICES (AV)

Bay 107, Union Wharf, 02109
Telephone: 617-367-8393
Fax: 617-742-6452

Jeffrey M. Aresty

ASSOCIATE

Andrew S. Breines

(See Next Column)

INTERNATIONAL LAW CONSULTANT
Yi-Fu (Eve) Sun

For full biographical listings, see the Martindale-Hubbell Law Directory

KOPELMAN AND PAIGE, P.C. (AV)

Park Square Building, 31 St. James Avenue, 7th Floor, 02116
Telephone: 617-556-0007
Fax: 617-654-1735

Leonard Kopelman

For Complete List of Firm Personnel, See General Section

For full biographical listings, see the Martindale-Hubbell Law Directory

PALMER & DODGE LLP (AV)

One Beacon Street, 02108
Telephone: 617-573-0100
Facsimile: 617-227-4420

MEMBERS OF FIRM

F. Andrew Anderson	Stanley Keller
F. Kingston Berlew	Michael Lytton
Robert Duggan	William T. Whelan
Karl P. Fryzel	John Taylor Williams

For Complete List of Firm Personnel, See General Section

For full biographical listings, see the Martindale-Hubbell Law Directory

PEABODY & ARNOLD (AV)

A Partnership including Professional Corporations
50 Rowes Wharf, 02110-3342
Telephone: 617-951-2100
Telecopier: 617-951-2125
Providence, Rhode Island Office: One Citizens Plaza, Suite 840.
Telephone: 401-831-8330.
Fax: 401-831-8359.

MEMBERS OF FIRM

Anil Khosla   Thomas A. Wooters

For Complete List of Firm Personnel, See General Section

For full biographical listings, see the Martindale-Hubbell Law Directory

NEWTON, Middlesex Co.

VACOVEC, MAYOTTE & SINGER (AV)

Two Newton Place, Suite 340, 255 Washington Street, 02158-1633
Telephone: 617-964-0500
Fax: 617-969-2002
Email: vacovec@aol.com

MEMBERS OF FIRM

Kenneth J. Vacovec	Paula N. Singer
Maureen C. Mayotte	Jeffrey M. Brown
Kenneth H. Light	

ASSOCIATES

Angela M. Cox   Arthur R. Kerr, II
            Sam J. Serbello

OF COUNSEL

Stephen P. Koster   John G. Ganick

For full biographical listings, see the Martindale-Hubbell Law Directory

MICHIGAN

ANN ARBOR, Washtenaw Co.

MILLER, CANFIELD, PADDOCK AND STONE, P.L.C. (AV)

A Professional Limited Liability Company
Founded in 1852 by Sidney Davy Miller
101 North Main Street, Seventh Floor, 48104-1400
Telephone: 313-663-2445
Fax: 313-747-7147
Detroit, Michigan Office: 150 West Jefferson, Suite 2500, 48226-4415.
Telephone: 313-963-6420.
Fax: 313-496-7500.
Cable Address: "Stem Detroit."
Bloomfield Hills, Michigan Office: Suite 100, Pinehurst Office Center, 1400 North Woodward, 48303-2014.
Telephone: 313-645-5000.
Fax: 313-645-1917.
Grand Rapids, Michigan Office: 1200 Campau Square Plaza, 99 Monroe, N.W., 49503-2639.
Telephone: 616-454-8656.
Fax: 616-776-6322.

(See Next Column)

MILLER, CANFIELD, PADDOCK AND STONE P.L.C.—*Continued*

Howell, Michigan Office: 121 South Barnard Street, Suite 4, 48843-2305.
Telephone: 517-546-7600.
Telecopier: 517-546-6974.
Kalamazoo, Michigan Office: 444 West Michigan Avenue, 49007-3752.
Telephone: 616-381-7030.
Fax: 616-382-0244.
Lansing, Michigan Office: One Michigan Avenue, Suite 900, 48933-1609.
Telephone: 517-487-2070.
Fax: 517-374-6304.
Monroe, Michigan Office: The Executive Centre, 214 East Elm Avenue, 48161-2682.
Telephone: 313-243-2000.
Fax: 313-243-0901.
Washington, D.C. Office: 1225 Nineteenth Street, N.W., Suite 400. 20036.
Telephone: 202-429-5575; 785-0600.
Fax: 202-331-1118; 785-1234.
Pensacola, Florida Office: 25 West Cedar, 32501.
Telephone: 904-469-1088.
Fax: 904-432-0677.
St. Petersburg, Florida Office: 100 Second Avenue S., Suite 7045, 33701.
Telephone: 813-982-6000.
Fax: 813-892-6002.
New York, New York Office: Eleventh Floor, 135 East 57th Street, 10022-2087.
Telephone: 212-754-5400.
Fax: 212-754-5401.
Gdansk, Poland Office: Suite 322, Dom Technika Building, UI. Rajska 6, 80-850.
Telephone: 011-485-831-2808.
Fax: 011-485-831-4719.
Warsaw, Poland Office: UI. Marszalkowska 82, Suite 561, 00-517.
Telephone: 011-482-623-6457 and 6458.
Fax: 011-482-623-6459.

RESIDENT PRINCIPALS

Erik H. Serr   J. David Reck

Representative Firm Clients: Chrysler Corporation; Comerica, Incorporated; City of Detroit, Michigan; Detroit Tigers, Inc.; First of Michigan; Ford Motor Company; Ford Motor Credit Company; Great Lakes Bancorp; Henry Ford Hospital; INVETECH Company.

For Complete List of Firm Personnel, See General Section

For full biographical listings, see the Martindale-Hubbell Law Directory

---

BLOOMFIELD HILLS, Oakland Co.

MILLER, CANFIELD, PADDOCK AND STONE, P.L.C. (AV)

A Professional Limited Liability Company
Founded in 1852 by Sidney Davy Miller
Suite 100 Pinehurst Office Center, 1400 North Woodward, P.O. Box 2014, 48303-2014
Telephone: 810-645-5000
Fax: 810-645-1917
Fax: 810-258-3036
Detroit, Michigan Office: 150 West Jefferson, Suite 2500, 48226-4415.
Telephone: 313-963-6420.
Fax: 313-496-7500.
Cable Address: "Stem Detroit."
Ann Arbor, Michigan Office: 101 North Main Street, 7th Floor, 48104-1400.
Telephone: 313-663-2445.
Fax: 313-747-7147.
Grand Rapids, Michigan Office: 1200 Campau Square Plaza, 99 Monroe, N.W., 49503-2639.
Telephone: 616-454-8656.
Fax: 616-776-6322.
Howell, Michigan Office: 121 South Barnard Street, Suite 4, 48843-2305.
Telephone: 517-546-7600.
Telecopier: 517-546-6974.
Kalamazoo, Michigan Office: 444 West Michigan Avenue, 49007-3752.
Telephone: 616-381-7030.
Fax: 616-382-0244.
Lansing, Michigan Office: One Michigan Avenue, Suite 900, 48933-1609.
Telephone: 517-487-2070.
Fax: 517-374-6304.
Monroe, Michigan Office: The Executive Centre, 214 East Elm Avenue, 48161-2682.
Telephone: 313-243-2000.
Fax: 313-243-0901.
Washington, D.C. Office: 1225 Nineteenth Street, N.W., Suite 400. 20036.
Telephone: 202-429-5575; 785-0600.
Fax: 202-331-1118; 785-1234.
Pensacola, Florida Office: 25 West Cedar, 32501.
Telephone: 904-469-1088.
Fax: 904-432-0677.
St. Petersburg, Florida Office: 100 Second Avenue S., Suite 7045, 33701.
Telephone: 813-982-6000.
Fax: 813-892-6002.

(See Next Column)

New York, New York Office: Eleventh Floor, 135 East 57th Street, 10022-2087.
Telephone: 212-754-5400.
Fax: 212-754-5401.
Gdansk, Poland Office: Suite 322, Dom Technika Building, UI. Rajska 6, 80-850.
Telephone: 011-485-831-2808.
Fax: 011-485-831-4719.
Warsaw, Poland Office: UI. Marszalkowska 82, Suite 561, 00-517.
Telephone: 011-482-623-6457 and 6458.
Fax: 011-482-623-6459.

RESIDENT PRINCIPALS

John A. Thurber (P.C.)   John A. Marxer (P.C.)

RESIDENT OF COUNSEL

Henry R. Nolte, Jr.

Representative Firm Clients: Chrysler Corporation; Comerica, Incorporated; City of Detroit, Michigan; Detroit Tigers, Inc.; First of Michigan; Ford Motor Company; Ford Motor Credit Company; Great Lakes Bancorp; Henry Ford Hospital; INVETECH Company.

For Complete List of Firm Personnel, See General Section

For full biographical listings, see the Martindale-Hubbell Law Directory

---

DETROIT,* Wayne Co.

DYKEMA GOSSETT PLLC (AV)

400 Renaissance Center, 48243-1668
Telephone: 313-568-6800
Cable Address: "Dyke-Detroit"
Telex: 23-0121
Fax: 313-568-6594
Email: 2084153@mcimail.com
Ann Arbor, Michigan Office: 315 East Eisenhower Parkway, Suite 100, 48108-3306.
Telephone: 313-747-7660.
Fax: 313-747-7696.
Bloomfield Hills, Michigan Office: 1577 North Woodward Avenue, Suite 300, 48304-2820.
Telephone: 810-540-0700.
Fax: 810-540-0763.
Chicago, Illinois Office: 55 East Monroe Street, Suite 3250, 60603-5709.
Telephone: 312-551-4900.
Fax: 312-551-4919.
Grand Rapids, Michigan Office: 200 Oldtown Riverfront Building, 248 Louis Campau Promenade, N.W., 49503-2668.
Telephone: 616-776-7500.
Fax: 616-776-7573.
Lansing, Michigan Office: 800 Michigan National Tower, 48933-1707.
Telephone: 517-374-9100.
Fax: 517-374-9191.
Washington, D.C. Office: Franklin Square, Suite 300 West, 1300 I Street, N.W., 20005-3306.
Telephone: 202-522-8600.
Fax: 202-522-8669.

MEMBERS OF FIRM

Ted T. Amsden	Bonnie L. Mayfield
George W. Ash	Jerome I. Maynard (Member in Charge of Chicago, Illinois Office)
J. Michael Bernard	
B. Kingsley Buhl (Resident at Bloomfield Hills Office)	
Bruce G. Davis (Resident at Ann Arbor Office)	Bruce A. McDonald (Not admitted in MI; Resident at Washington, D.C. Office)
Joseph F. Dillon	Richard D. McLellan (Member in Charge of Lansing Office)
Fred J. Fechheimer (Resident at Bloomfield Hills Office)	
Barbara L. Goldman (Resident at Bloomfield Hills Office)	Patrick E. Mears (Resident at Grand Rapids Office)
Steven E. Grob	Derek I. Meier
Gregory M. Kopacz (Resident at Bloomfield Hills Office)	Aleksandra A. Miziolek
	Judy A. O'Neill
	Paul R. Rentenbach
Richard M. Matthews	Thomas Stephen Vaughn

Stephen D. Winter

OF COUNSEL

Charles R. Bernardini (Not admitted in MI; Resident at Washington, D.C. and Chicago, Illinois Offices)	William H. Carroll (Not admitted in MI; Resident at Washington, D.C. Office)

ASSOCIATES

Margaret A. Costello	Rosemary G. Schikora
Marguerite Marie Gritenas	Jeffrey N. Silveri (Resident at Ann Arbor Office)
Dennis M. Pousak	

For Complete List of Firm Personnel, See General Section

For full biographical listings, see the Martindale-Hubbell Law Directory

Detroit—Continued

MILLER, CANFIELD, PADDOCK AND STONE, P.L.C. (AV)

A Professional Limited Liability Company
Founded in 1852 by Sidney Davy Miller
150 West Jefferson, Suite 2500, 48226-4415
Telephone: 313-963-6420
Fax: 313-496-7500
Cable Address: "Stem Detroit"
Detroit, Michigan Office: 150 West Jefferson, Suite 2500, 48226-4415.
Telephone: 313-963-6420.
Fax: 313-496-7500.
Cable Address: "Stem Detroit."
Ann Arbor, Michigan Office: 101 North Main Street, 7th Floor,
48104-1400.
Telephone: 313-663-2445.
Fax: 313-747-7147.
Bloomfield Hills, Michigan Office: Suite 100, Pinehurst Office Center, 1400
North Woodward, 48303-2014.
Telephone: 313-645-5000.
Fax: 313-645-1917.
Grand Rapids, Michigan Office: 1200 Campau Square Plaza, 99 Monroe,
N.W., 49503-2639.
Telephone: 616-454-8656.
Fax: 616-776-6322.
Howell, Michigan Office: 121 South Barnard Street, Suite 4, 48843-2305.
Telephone: 517-546-7600.
Telecopier: 517-546-6974.
Kalamazoo, Michigan Office: 444 West Michigan Avenue, 49007-3752.
Telephone: 616-381-7030.
Fax: 616-382-0244.
Lansing, Michigan Office: One Michigan Avenue, Suite 900, 48933-1609.
Telephone: 517-487-2070.
Fax: 517-374-6304.
Monroe, Michigan Office: The Executive Centre, 214 East Elm Avenue,
48161-2682.
Telephone: 313-243-2000.
Fax: 313-243-0901.
Washington, D.C. Office: 1225 Nineteenth Street, N.W., Suite 400. 20036.
Telephone: 202-429-5575; 785-0600.
Fax: 202-331-1118; 785-1234.
Pensacola, Florida Office: 25 West Cedar, 32501.
Telephone: 904-469-1088.
Fax: 904-432-0677.
St. Petersburg, Florida Office: 100 Second Avenue S., Suite 7045, 33701.
Telephone: 813-982-6000.
Fax: 813-892-6002.
New York, New York Office: Eleventh Floor, 135 East 57th Street,
10022-2087.
Telephone: 212-754-5400.
Fax: 212-754-5401.
Gdansk, Poland Office: Suite 322, Dom Technika Building, UI. Rajska 6,
80-850.
Telephone: 011-485-831-2808.
Fax: 011-485-831-4719.
Warsaw, Poland Office: UI. Marszalkowska 82, Suite 561, 00-517.
Telephone: 011-482-623-6457 and 6458.
Fax: 011-482-623-6459.

PRINCIPALS OF FIRM

Robert S. Ketchum	David D. Joswick (P.C.)
Rocque E. Lipford (P.C.)	John A. Marxer (P.C.)
(Monroe Office)	(Bloomfield Hills Office)
Eric V. Brown, Jr.	John J. Collins, Jr.
(Kalamazoo Office)	(Bloomfield Hills Office)
Bruce D. Birgbauer	Thomas G. Appleman
John A. Thurber (P.C.)	(Bloomfield Hills Office)
(Bloomfield Hills Office)	J. David Reck (Ann Arbor and
Erik H. Serr (Ann Arbor Office)	Howell Offices)

Richard A. Walawender

OF COUNSEL

Gerard Thomas	Henry R. Nolte, Jr.
(Kalamazoo Office)	(Bloomfield Hills Office)

SENIOR ATTORNEY
Elise S. Levasseur

Representative Firm Clients: Chrysler Corporation; Comerica, Incorporated;
City of Detroit, Michigan; Detroit Tigers, Inc.; First of Michigan; Ford Motor Company; Ford Motor Credit Company; Great Lakes Bancorp; Henry Ford Hospital; INVETECH Company.

For Complete List of Firm Personnel, See General Section

For full biographical listings, see the Martindale-Hubbell Law Directory

---

GRAND RAPIDS, * Kent Co.

MILLER, CANFIELD, PADDOCK AND STONE, P.L.C. (AV)

A Professional Limited Liability Company
Founded in 1852 by Sidney Davy Miller
1200 Campau Square Plaza, 99 Monroe, N.W., P.O. Box 329, 49503-2639
Telephone: 616-454-8656
Fax: 616-776-6322
Detroit, Michigan Office: 150 West Jefferson, Suite 2500, 48226-4415.
Telephone: 313-963-6420.
Fax: 313-496-7500.
Cable Address: "Stem Detroit."
Ann Arbor, Michigan Office: 101 North Main Street, 7th Floor,
48104-1400.
Telephone: 313-663-2445.
Fax: 313-747-7147.
Bloomfield Hills, Michigan Office: Suite 100, Pinehurst Office Center, 1400
North Woodward, 48303-2014.
Telephone: 313-645-5000.
Fax: 313-645-1917.
Howell, Michigan Office: 121 South Barnard Street, Suite 4, 48843-2305.
Telephone: 517-546-7600.
Telecopier: 517-546-6974.
Kalamazoo, Michigan Office: 444 West Michigan Avenue, 49007-3752.
Telephone: 616-381-7030.
Fax: 616-382-0244.
Lansing, Michigan Office: One Michigan Avenue, Suite 900, 48933-1609.
Telephone: 517-487-2070.
Fax: 517-374-6304.
Monroe, Michigan Office: The Executive Centre, 214 East Elm Avenue,
48161-2682.
Telephone: 313-243-2000.
Fax: 313-243-0901.
Washington, D.C. Office: 1225 Nineteenth Street, N.W., Suite 400. 20036.
Telephone: 202-429-5575; 785-0600.
Fax: 202-331-1118; 785-1234.
Pensacola, Florida Office: 25 West Cedar 32501.
Telephone: 904-469-1088.
Fax: 904-432-0677.
St. Petersburg Florida Office: 100 Second Avenue S., Suite 7045, 33701.
Telephone: 813-982-6000.
Fax: 813-892-6002.
New York, New York Office: Eleventh Floor, 135 East 57th Street,
10022-2087.
Telephone: 212-754-5400.
Fax: 212-754-5401.
Gdansk, Poland Office: Suite 322, Dom Technika Building, UI. Rajska 6,
80-850.
Telephone: 011-485-831-2808.
Fax: 011-485-831-4719.
Warsaw, Poland Office: UI. Marszalkowska 82, Suite 561, 00-517.
Telephone: 011-482-623-6457 and 6458.
Fax: 011-482-623-6459.

PRINCIPALS OF FIRM

Mark E. Putney (Resident	Michael G. Campbell
Director, Grand Rapids	Robert E. Lee Wright
Office)	Vernon Bennett III
Richard A. Gaffin	Douglas W. Crim
Charles S. Mishkind (Detroit,	
Lansing and Kalamazoo	
Offices)	

OF COUNSEL
David E. Hathaway

SENIOR ATTORNEYS

David J. Hasper	Stephen L. Elkins

ASSOCIATES

John C. Arndts	Daniel H. Roberts
Bradley C. White	John T. Stecco

Michael V. Camarota

Representative Firm Clients: Chrysler Corporation; Comerica, Incorporated;
City of Detroit, Michigan; Detroit Tigers, Inc.; First of Michigan; Ford Motor Company; Ford Motor Credit Company; Great Lakes Bancorp; Henry Ford Hospital; INVETECH Company.

For full biographical listings, see the Martindale-Hubbell Law Directory

---

PRICE, HENEVELD, COOPER, DEWITT & LITTON (AV)

695 Kenmoor, S.E., P.O. Box 2567, 49501
Telephone: 616-949-9610
Telecopier: 616-957-8196

MEMBERS OF FIRM

Peter P. Price (Retired)	Randall G. Litton
Lloyd A. Heneveld	James A. Mitchell
Richard C. Cooper	Harold W. Reick
William W. DeWitt	Carl S. Clark

Daniel L. Girdwood

(See Next Column)

PRICE, HENEVELD, COOPER, DeWITT & LITTON—*Continued*

ASSOCIATES

Douglas H. Siegel	Gunther J. Evanina
(Not admitted in MI)	Steven C. Wichmann
Barry C. Kane	Jay G. Durst
Terry S. Callaghan	(Not admitted in MI)

Representative Clients: Amway Corp.; Michigan State University; Dow Chemical Co.; Gerber Products Co.; Kysor Industrial Corp.; L. Perrigo Co.; Prince Corp.; Ralston Purina Co.; Steelcase, Inc.; Wolverine World Wide, Inc.

For full biographical listings, see the Martindale-Hubbell Law Directory

---

KALAMAZOO,* Kalamazoo Co.

MILLER, CANFIELD, PADDOCK AND STONE, P.L.C. (AV)

A Professional Limited Liability Company
Founded in 1852 by Sidney Davy Miller
444 West Michigan Avenue, 49007-3752
Telephone: 616-381-7030
Fax: 616-382-0244
Detroit, Michigan Office: 150 West Jefferson, Suite 2500, 48226-4415.
Telephone: 313-963-6420.
Fax: 313-496-7500.
Cable Address: "Stem Detroit."
Ann Arbor, Michigan Office: 101 North Main Street, 7th Floor, 48104-1400.
Telephone: 313-663-2445.
Fax: 313-747-7147.
Bloomfield Hills, Michigan Office: Suite 100, Pinehurst Office Center, 1400 North Woodward, 48303-2014.
Telephone: 313-645-5000.
Fax: 313-645-1917.
Grand Rapids, Michigan Office: 1200 Campau Square Plaza, 99 Monroe, N.W., 49503-2639.
Telephone: 616-454-8656.
Fax: 616-776-6322.
Howell, Michigan Office: 121 South Barnard Street, Suite 4, 48843-2305.
Telephone: 517-546-7600.
Telecopier: 517-546-6974.
Lansing, Michigan Office: One Michigan Avenue, Suite 900, 48933-1609.
Telephone: 517-487-2070.
Fax: 517-374-6304.
Monroe, Michigan Office: The Executive Centre, 214 East Elm Avenue, 48161-2682.
Telephone: 313-243-2000.
Fax: 313-243-0901.
Washington, D.C. Office: 1225 Nineteenth Street, N.W., Suite 400. 20036.
Telephone: 202-429-5575; 785-0600.
Fax: 202-331-1118; 785-1234.
Pensacola, Florida Office: 25 West Cedar, 32501.
Telephone: 904-469-1088.
Fax: 904-432-0677.
St. Petersburg, Florida Office: 100 Second Avenue S., Suite 7045, 33701.
Telephone: 813-982-6000.
Fax: 813-892-6002.
New York, New York Office: Eleventh Floor, 135 East 57th Street, 10022-2087.
Telephone: 212-754-5400.
Fax: 212-754-5401.
Gdansk, Poland Office: Suite 322, Dom Technika Building, UI. Rajska 6, 80-850.
Telephone: 011-485-831-2808.
Fax: 011-485-831-4719.
Warsaw, Poland Office: UI. Marszalkowska 82, Suite 561, 00-517.
Telephone: 011-482-623-6457 and 6458.
Fax: 011-482-623-6459.

PRINCIPALS OF FIRM
Eric V. Brown, Jr.
OF COUNSEL
Gerard Thomas

Representative Firm Clients: Chrysler Corporation; Comerica, Incorporated; City of Detroit, Michigan; Detroit Tigers, Inc.; First of Michigan; Ford Motor Company; Ford Motor Credit Company; Great Lakes Bancorp; Henry Ford Hospital; INVETECH Company.

For Complete List of Firm Personnel, See General Section

For full biographical listings, see the Martindale-Hubbell Law Directory

---

LANSING, Ingham Co.

FOSTER, SWIFT, COLLINS & SMITH, P.C. (AV)

313 South Washington Square, 48933-2193
Telephone: 517-371-8100
Telecopier: 517-371-8200
URL: http://www.fosterswift.com
Farmington Hills, Michigan Office: 32300 Northwestern Highway, Suite 230.
Telephone: 810-539-9900.
Fax: 810-851-7504.

Gary J. McRay	Jean G. Schtokal

General Counsel for: First American Bank-Central; Story, Inc.; Michigan Milk Producers Assn.; Edward W. Sparrow Hospital; St. Lawrence Hospital; Demmer Corp.; Michigan Financial Corp.
Local Counsel for: Shell Oil Co.; Michigan-Mutual Insurance Co.; Century Telephone.

For Complete List of Firm Personnel, See General Section

For full biographical listings, see the Martindale-Hubbell Law Directory

---

MONROE,* Monroe Co.

MILLER, CANFIELD, PADDOCK AND STONE, P.L.C. (AV)

A Professional Limited Liability Company
Founded in 1852 by Sidney Davy Miller
The Executive Centre, 214 East Elm Avenue, 48161-2682
Telephone: 313-243-2000.
Fax: 313-243-0901.
Detroit, Michigan Office: 150 West Jefferson, Suite 2500, 48226-4415.
Telephone: 313-963-6420.
Fax: 313-496-7500.
Cable Address: "Stem Detroit."
Ann Arbor, Michigan Office: 101 North Main Street, 7th Floor, 48104-1400.
Telephone: 313-663-2445.
Fax: 313-747-7147.
Bloomfield Hills, Michigan Office: Suite 100, Pinehurst Office Center, 1400 North Woodward, 48303-2014.
Telephone: 313-645-5000.
Fax: 313-645-1917.
Grand Rapids, Michigan Office: 1200 Campau Square Plaza, 99 Monroe, N.W., 49503-2639.
Telephone: 616-454-8656.
Fax: 616-776-6322.
Howell, Michigan Office: 121 South Barnard Street, Suite 4, 48843-2305.
Telephone: 517-546-7600.
Telecopier: 517-546-6974.
Kalamazoo, Michigan Office: 444 West Michigan Avenue, 49007-3752.
Telephone: 616-381-7030.
Fax: 616-382-0244.
Lansing, Michigan Office: One Michigan Avenue, Suite 900, 48933-1609.
Telephone: 517-487-2070.
Fax: 517-374-6304.
Washington, D.C. Office: 1225 Nineteenth Street, N.W., Suite 400. 20036.
Telephone: 202-429-5575; 785-0600.
Fax: 202-331-1118; 785-1234.
Pensacola, Florida Office: 25 West Cedar, 32501.
Telephone: 904-469-1088.
Fax: 904-432-0677.
St. Petersburg, Florida Office: 100 Second Avenue S., Suite 7045, 33701.
Telephone: 813-982-6000.
Fax: 813-892-6002.
Gdansk, Poland Office: Suite 322, Dom Technika Building, UI. Rajska 6, 80-850.
Telephone: 011-485-831-2808.
Fax: 011-485-831-4719.
Warsaw, Poland Office: UI. Marszalkowska 82, Suite 561, 00-517.
Telephone: 011-482-623-6457 and 6458.
Fax: 011-482-623-6459.

RESIDENT PRINCIPALS
Rocque E. Lipford (P.C.)

Representative Firm Clients: Chrysler Corporation; Comerica, Incorporated; City of Detroit, Michigan; Detroit Tigers, Inc.; First of Michigan; Ford Motor Company; Ford Motor Credit Company; Great Lakes Bancorp; Henry Ford Hospital; INVETECH Company.

For full biographical listings, see the Martindale-Hubbell Law Directory

INTERNATIONAL TRADE LAW

CALIFORNIA

CLAREMONT, Los Angeles Co.

JOHN W. TULAC (AV)

401 Harvard Avenue, 91711
Telephone: 909-445-1100
Fax: 909-445-1104
Email: jwtulac@ix.netcom.com

Reference: Marine National Bank, Irvine.

For full biographical listings, see the Martindale-Hubbell Law Directory

LOS ANGELES,* Los Angeles Co.

STANTON P. BELLAND, P.C. (AV)

10 Universal City Plaza, Suite 2000, 91608-7806
Telephone: 818-754-3770
Telecopier: 818-754-3780

Stanton P. Belland

For full biographical listings, see the Martindale-Hubbell Law Directory

BRAND FARRAR DZIUBLA FREILICH & KOLSTAD, LLP (AV)

Counsellors at Law
515 South Flower Street, Suite 3500, 90071-2201
Telephone: 213-228-0288
Facsimile: 213-426-6222
Correspondent Offices: Hong Kong, Shanghai, Beijing, Guangzhou, Xiamen, Shenzhen, Ulaanbaatar, New York and San Francisco.

Michael A. Brand	Amy E. Freilich
David W. Farrar	Charles K. Kolstad
Robert W. Dziubla	Margaret G. Graf

OF COUNSEL

H. Bennett Arnberger	Julia Marie Shymansky
David C. Buxbaum	Yelena Yeruhim
Sherry L. Geyer	Norman A. Chernin
Manender M. Grewal (Not admitted in the United States)	Joan M. Marquardt

For full biographical listings, see the Martindale-Hubbell Law Directory

STEIN SHOSTAK SHOSTAK & O'HARA, A PROFESSIONAL CORPORATION (AV)

515 South Figueroa Street, Suite 1200, 90071-3329
Telephone: 213-486-0010
Fax: 213-486-0011
Washington, D.C. Office: Suite 807, 1620 L Street, N.W.
Telephone: 202-223-6270.
Fax: 202-659-4237.
San Diego, California Office: 2675 Customhouse Court, Suite B.
Telephone: 619-661-6317.
Fax: 619-661-1448.

Philip Stein (1899-1955)	S. Richard Shostak
Marjorie M. Shostak	Joseph P. Cox
	Steven B. Zisser

OF COUNSEL
James F. O'Hara

For full biographical listings, see the Martindale-Hubbell Law Directory

OAKLAND,* Alameda Co.

HARVEY W. STEIN A PROFESSIONAL CORPORATION (AV)

Suite 600 Transpacific Centre, 1000 Broadway, 94607
Telephone: 510-763-6233
Fax: 510-832-1717

Harvey W. Stein

For full biographical listings, see the Martindale-Hubbell Law Directory

DISTRICT OF COLUMBIA

WASHINGTON, D.C. Co.

ADDUCI, MASTRIANI & SCHAUMBERG, L.L.P. (AV)

1140 Connecticut Avenue, N.W., Suite 250, 20036
Telephone: 202-467-6300
Telefax: 202-466-2006
Email: adduci.com

MEMBERS OF FIRM

V. James Adduci, II	James C. Lydon
Louis S. Mastriani	(Not in DC)
Tom M. Schaumberg	David A. Guth
Ronald J. Kubovcik	Katherine S. Nucci
Barbara A. Murphy	Larry L. Shatzer, II
Timothy Sullivan	Marcela B. Stras

Anri Suzuki	Peter B. Martine
Gregory C. Anthes	Michael L. Doane
	Martin R. Fischer

A list of Representative Clients and References will be furnished upon request.

For full biographical listings, see the Martindale-Hubbell Law Directory

SHARRETTS, PALEY, CARTER & BLAUVELT, P.C. (AV)

Suite 725, 1707 L Street, N.W., 20036
Telephone: 202-223-4433
Cable Address: "Customlex" Washington
Fax: 202-659-3904
Email: 102160.3466@compuserve.com *URL:* http://www.sharretts-paley.com
New York, N.Y. Office: 26th Floor, 67 Broad Street.
Telephone: 212-425-0055.

M. Barry Levy (Not admitted in DC)	Duncan A. Nixon (Not admitted in DC; Resident)
Gail T. Cumins (Not admitted in DC)	Beatrice A. Brickell (Resident)

For full biographical listings, see the Martindale-Hubbell Law Directory

FLORIDA

WINTER PARK, Orange Co.

KENNETH E. BROOTEN, JR. CHARTERED (AV)

631 West Fairbanks Avenue, 32789
Telephone: 407-645-4447
Fax: 407-628-2220

Kenneth E. Brooten, Jr.

For full biographical listings, see the Martindale-Hubbell Law Directory

INDIANA

INDIANAPOLIS,* Marion Co.

ICE MILLER DONADIO & RYAN (AV)

One American Square Box 82001, 46282-0002
Telephone: 317-236-2100
Fax: 317-236-2219
Email: leel@imdr.com *URL:* http://www.imdr.com
South Bend, Indiana Office: 211 West Washington Street, Suite 2420.
Telephone: 219-234-7933.
Fax: 219-234-7965. Internet E-mail: leel@imdr.com. Web Site Address: http://www.imdr.com.

MEMBERS OF FIRM

Donald G. Sutherland	Harry L. Gonso
Richard E. Parker	Dale E. Stackhouse

OF COUNSEL

Susan B. Rivas	Daniel E. Fisher

STAFF ATTORNEY
Mikio Nishizu

ASSOCIATE
Antje C. Petersen

Representative Clients: Avesta Sheffield; Biomet, Inc.; Reilly Industries, Inc.; INTAT Precision, Inc.; Delco Remy America, Inc.; Magnequench International, Inc.; Aisin USA Mfg., Inc.; Toyota Equipment Mfg. Inc. (Toyoda Automatic Loom Works, Ltd.); Perry Manufacturing, Inc.; Norcote International, Inc.; Resort Condominiums International, Inc.

(See Next Column)

ICE MILLER DONADIO & RYAN, *Indianapolis—Continued*

For Complete List of Firm Personnel, See General Section

For full biographical listings, see the Martindale-Hubbell Law Directory

---

MAINE

PORTLAND,* Cumberland Co.

PERKINS, THOMPSON, HINCKLEY & KEDDY, P.A. (AV)

One Canal Plaza, P.O. Box 426, 04112-0426
Telephone: 207-774-2635

Thomas Schulten	Peggy L. McGehee
Bruce E. Leddy	Melissa Hanley Murphy
Owen W. Wells	John H. Rich III
Douglas S. Carr	John A. Ciraldo
Andrew A. Cadot	John A. Hobson
John R. Opperman	Helen I. Muther
Philip C. Hunt	Timothy P. Benoit
John S. Upton	Fred W. Bopp III

Craig N. Denekas	David B. McConnell
Mark P. Snow	Peter S. Carlisle
William J. Sheils	Paul D. Pietropaoli

For full biographical listings, see the Martindale-Hubbell Law Directory

---

MICHIGAN

DETROIT,* Wayne Co.

BUTZEL LONG, A PROFESSIONAL CORPORATION (AV)

Suite 900, 150 West Jefferson, 48226
Telephone: 313-225-7000
Telecopier: 313-225-7080
Email: melnick@butzel.com *URL:* http://www.butzel.com
Birmingham, Michigan Office: Suite 200, 32270 Telegraph Road.
Telephone: 810-258-1616.
Telecopier: 810-258-1439.
Lansing, Michigan Office: 118 West Ottawa Street.
Telephone: 517-372-6622.
Telecopier: 517-372-6672.
Ann Arbor, Michigan Office: Suite 300, 350 South Main Street.
Telephone: 313-995-3110.
Telecopier: 313-995-1777.
Grosse Pointe Farms, Michigan Office: Suite 260, 21 Kercheval.
Telephone: 313-886-5446.
Telecopier: 313-886-2114.

Morris Milmet (Birmingham)	Daniel P. Malone
C. Peter Theut	Justin G. Klimko
William H. Dance	James L. Hughes
Richard E. Rassel	Arthur Dudley II
Edward M. Kronk	Gordon W. Didier (Birmingham)
James C. Bruno	Terry O. Lang
	Clara DeMatteis Mager

Nicholas J. Stasevich	Debra Auerbach Clephane
	Priscilla J. Krebs

Representative Clients: ABB Flexible Automation; American International Airways; Detroit International Bridge; Dynax Corp.; Gifu Seiki USA; Ingersoll-Rand Co.; McKechnie PLC; Motor Wheel Corp.; New Venture Gear; Ricardo Group PLC.

For Complete List of Firm Personnel, See General Section

For full biographical listings, see the Martindale-Hubbell Law Directory

LABOR AND EMPLOYMENT LAW

ALABAMA

BIRMINGHAM,* Jefferson Co.

BERKOWITZ, LEFKOVITS, ISOM & KUSHNER, A PROFESSIONAL CORPORATION (AV)

1600 SouthTrust Tower, 420 North Twentieth Street, 35203
Telephone: 205-328-0480
Telecopier: 205-322-8007

Frank S. James III   D. J. Simonetti
                    Wesley C. Redmond

Representative Clients: AlaTenn Resources, Inc.; B.A.S.S., Inc.; CLP Corporation (McDonald's Franchise); Daniel Corp.; Hanna Steel Co., Inc.; Jefferson Home Furniture, Inc.; Liberty Trouser Co., Inc.; Parisian, Inc.; Southern Pipe & Supply Co., Inc.; The Personnel Board of Jefferson County, Alabama.

For Complete List of Firm Personnel, See General Section

For full biographical listings, see the Martindale-Hubbell Law Directory

BRADLEY, ARANT, ROSE & WHITE (AV)

2001 Park Place, Suite 1400, P.O. Box 830709, 35283-0709
Telephone: 205-521-8000
Facsimile: 205-252-0264
Facsimile (SouthTrust Tower Office): 205-251-9915
URL: http://www.BARW.COM
Huntsville, Alabama Office: 200 Clinton Avenue West, Suite 900, 35801.
Telephone: 205-517-5100.
Facsimile: 205-533-5069.

MEMBERS OF FIRM

John James Coleman, Jr.   John William Hargrove
James Patrick Alexander   Forrest K. Covington
Robert K. Spotswood   James S. Christie, Jr.
James Walker May   Warne S. Heath
Jay D. St. Clair   (Resident, Huntsville Office)
                    Anne R. Yuengert
ASSOCIATES

Amy K. Myers   Kimberly A. Bessiere
Arnold W. Umbach, III   (Resident, Huntsville Office)
John W. Smith T   Abdul K. Kallon
James W. Davis   Kelly Hubbard Estes
T. Matthew Miller   Julie Scharfenberg Elmer
                    David M. Lawson

For Complete List of Firm Personnel, See General Section

For full biographical listings, see the Martindale-Hubbell Law Directory

BURR & FORMAN (AV)

3100 SouthTrust Tower, 420 North 20th Street, 35203
Telephone: 205-251-3000
Telecopier: 205-458-5100
Huntsville, Alabama Office: Suite 204, Regency Center, 400 Meridian Street.
Telephone: 205-551-0010.
Atlanta, Georgia Office: Suite 1800, One Georgia Center, 600 West Peachtree Street, 30308.
Telephone: 404-817-3536.
Facsimile: 404-817-3244.

MEMBERS OF FIRM

C. V. Stelzenmuller   T. Thomas Cottingham, III
J. Fredric Ingram   J. Patrick Logan
Mark Taliaferro, Jr.   F. A. Flowers, III
D. Frank Davis   Michael L. Lucas
                    Dent M. Morton
OF COUNSEL
                    Samuel H. Burr

For Complete List of Firm Personnel, See General Section

For full biographical listings, see the Martindale-Hubbell Law Directory

CONSTANGY, BROOKS & SMITH, LLC (AV)

Suite 1410 AmSouth/Harbert Plaza, 1901 Sixth Avenue North, 35203-2602
Telephone: 205-252-9321
Atlanta, Georgia Office: Suite 2400, 230 Peachtree Street, N.W.
Telephone: 404-525-8622.
Nashville, Tennessee Office: Suite 1080 Vanderbilt Plaza, 2100 West End Avenue.
Telephone: 615-321-5891.
Columbia, South Carolina Office: Suite 810 NationsBank Tower. 1301 Gervais Street,
Telephone: 803-256-3200.

(See Next Column)

Winston-Salem, North Carolina Office: Suite 300, 101 South Stratford Road.
Telephone: 910-721-1001, 704-344-1040 (Charlotte).
Arlington, Virginia Office: Suite 990, 13 North 17th Street.
Telephone: 703-527-0900.
Fax: 703-527-2605.

RESIDENT MEMBERS

J. Richard Walton   Richard O. Brown
Chris Mitchell   Carol Sue Nelson
RESIDENT ASSOCIATES

Thomas A. Davis   Michael D. Giles
Tammy L. Dobbs   Lisa Narrell-Mead

Representative Clients: Blockbuster Entertainment Corp.; Blue Cross/Blue Shield of Alabama; Consolidated Freightways, Inc.; Delta Woodside Industries; McDonald's; Merck & Co., Inc.; Philip-Morris Cos., Inc.; Phillips Van Heusen Corp.; Sara Lee Corp.; SunTrust.

For full biographical listings, see the Martindale-Hubbell Law Directory

COOPER, MITCH, CRAWFORD, KUYKENDALL & WHATLEY, L.L.C. (AV)

1100 Financial Center, 505 20th Street North, 35203-2605
Telephone: 205-328-9576
Telecopier: 205-328-9669

MEMBERS OF FIRM

Jerome A. Cooper   Frederick T. Kuykendall, III
William E. Mitch   Joe R. Whatley, Jr.
Thomas N. Crawford, Jr.   Glen M. Connor
                    Patricia Guthrie Fraley
ASSOCIATES

Candis A. McGowan   Maureen Kane Berg
Andrew C. Allen   Gerald B. Taylor, Jr.
William Z. Cullen   Peter H. Burke
Samuel H. Heldman   Charlene Cullen
Hilary E. Ball-Walker   William Todd Harvey
                    Richard Paul Rouco
OF COUNSEL

W. Braxton Schell, Jr.   Russell Jackson Drake

Counsel for: United Steelworkers of America, AFL-CIO; Birmingham Plumbers & Steamfitters Local Union No. 91 Pension Fund.
Reference: AMSouth Bank of Birmingham.

For full biographical listings, see the Martindale-Hubbell Law Directory

GORDON, SILBERMAN, WIGGINS & CHILDS, A PROFESSIONAL CORPORATION (AV)

1400 SouthTrust Tower, 420 North 20th Street, 35203
Telephone: 205-328-0640
Telecopier: 205-254-1500

Robert L. Wiggins, Jr.   Richard J. Ebbinghouse
Robert F. Childs, Jr.   Ann K. Wiggins
C. Michael Quinn   Samuel Fisher
James Mendelsohn   Ann C. Robertson

Elizabeth Evans Courtney   Gregory O. Wiggins
Byron R. Perkins   Lee Winston
Jon C. Goldfarb   Deborah A. Mattison
                    Rocco Calamusa, Jr.

For Complete List of Firm Personnel, See General Section

For full biographical listings, see the Martindale-Hubbell Law Directory

HASKELL SLAUGHTER & YOUNG, L.L.C. (AV)

1200 AmSouth/Harbert Plaza, 1901 Sixth Avenue North, 35203
Telephone: 205-251-1000
Facsimile: 205-324-1133
Montgomery, Alabama Office: 305 South Lawrence Street, P.O. Box 4660. 36103-4660.
Telephone: 334-265-8573.
Facsimile: 334-264-7945.

Frank M. Young, III   Ross N. Cohen
Stephen L. Poer   Richard H. Walston
Beverly P. Baker   Michael K. K. Choy

Paula B. Carroll   Georgia S. Roberson
                    Rebecca Higgins Hunt

Representative Clients: Baxter Healthcare Corporation; The Bradford Group, Inc.; The Coalition for Employee Healthcare, Inc.; The Equitable Life Assurance Society of the United States; Jefferson County Racing Association; Marshall Durbin Companies; Montgomery County, Alabama; Raytheon Aircraft Company; Ridout's-Brown-Service Inc.; Webster Industries, Inc.

For Complete List of Firm Personnel, See General Section

For full biographical listings, see the Martindale-Hubbell Law Directory

Birmingham—Continued

JOHNSTON, BARTON, PROCTOR & POWELL (AV)

2900 AmSouth/Harbert Plaza, 1901 Sixth Avenue North, 35203-2618
Telephone: 205-458-9400
Telecopier: 205-458-9500

MEMBERS OF FIRM

Harvey Deramus (1904-1970)	James C. Barton, Jr.
Alfred M. Naff (1923-1993)	Thomas E. Walker
Gilbert E. Johnston (1916-1994)	Anne P. Wheeler
G. Burns Proctor, Jr.	Barry V. Frederick
Sydney L. Lavender	Hollinger F. Barnard
Charles A. Powell, III	William D. Jones III
Jerome K. Lanning	David W. Proctor
Don B. Long, Jr.	Oscar M. Price III
Charles L. Robinson	W. Hill Sewell
J. William Rose, Jr.	Robert S. Vance, Jr.
Gilbert E. Johnston, Jr.	Richard J. Brockman
Ralph H. Smith II	Anthony A. Joseph

William G. Somerville, III

COUNSEL

Josh Mullins, Jr.	Paul E. Toppins

R. Marcus Givhan

OF COUNSEL

James C. Barton	Alfred Swedlaw

Alan W. Heldman

ASSOCIATES

William K. Hancock	Helen Kathryn Downs
James P. Pewitt	Jennifer Fox Swain
Scott Wells Ford	Spencer A. Kinderman
David M. Hunt	Scott R. McLaughlin
Lee M. Pope	Bradley C. Mayhew
John W. Sheffield	W. Jonathan Daniel
Haskins W. Jones	J. Vincent Edge
Russell L. Irby, III	Allison Powell

General Counsel for: Anderson News Co.; The Baptist Medical Centers; The Birmingham News Co.; Process Equipment, Inc.
Counsel for: BellSouth Services, Inc.; Continental Grain Co.; Times-Mirror Broadcasting (WVTM-TV, Channel 13).

For full biographical listings, see the Martindale-Hubbell Law Directory

LEHR MIDDLEBROOKS PRICE & PROCTOR, P.C. (AV)

2021 Third Avenue North, Suite 300, 35203
Telephone: 205-326-3002
Telecopier: 205-326-3008

Richard I. Lehr	Brent L. Crumpton
David J. Middlebrooks	Steven M. Stastny
Terry Price	Robert L. Beeman, II
R. David Proctor	Christopher S. Enloe
Albert L. Vreeland, II	(Not admitted in AL)

For full biographical listings, see the Martindale-Hubbell Law Directory

NAKAMURA & QUINN (AV)

Suite 300, Landmark Center, 2100 First Avenue North, 35203
Telephone: 205-323-8504
Telefax: 205-323-1102
TDD 1-800-548-2546

MEMBERS OF FIRM

Patrick K. Nakamura	Robert M. Weaver
John L. Quinn	Claudia H. Pearson

George N. Davies

ASSOCIATE

Graham L. Sisson, Jr.

For full biographical listings, see the Martindale-Hubbell Law Directory

SPAIN & GILLON, L.L.C. (AV)

The Zinszer Building, 2117 2nd Avenue North, 35203
Telephone: 205-328-4100
Telecopier: 205-324-8866

MEMBERS OF FIRM

Samuel H. Frazier	Alton B. Parker, Jr.

Thomas M. Eden, III

General Counsel for: Liberty National Life Insurance Co.; Piggly Wiggly Alabama Distributing Co.; Alabama Insurance Guaranty Association; Alabama Life and Disability Insurance Guaranty Association; Alabama Insurance Underwriters Association.
Counsel for: University of Alabama at Birmingham; Jefferson County Health Department; City of Birmingham.

For Complete List of Firm Personnel, See General Section

For full biographical listings, see the Martindale-Hubbell Law Directory

---

HUNTSVILLE, * Madison Co.

BRADLEY, ARANT, ROSE & WHITE (AV)

200 Clinton Avenue West, Suite 900, 35801
Telephone: 205-517-5100
Facsimile: 205-533-5069
URL: http://www.BARW.COM
Birmingham, Alabama Office: 2001 Park Place, Suite 1400, P.O. Box 830709.
Telephone: 205-521-8000.
Facsimile: 205-251-8611, 251-8665, 252-0264. Facsimile (SouthTrust Tower Office): 205-251-9915.

RESIDENT PARTNERS

E. Cutter Hughes, Jr.	Warne S. Heath

RESIDENT ASSOCIATES

Carolyn Reed Douglas	Kimberly A. Bessiere

For Complete List of Firm Personnel, See General Section

For full biographical listings, see the Martindale-Hubbell Law Directory

---

MOBILE, * Mobile Co.

ARMBRECHT, JACKSON, DEMOUY, CROWE, HOLMES & REEVES, L.L.C. (AV)

1300 AmSouth Center, P.O. Box 290, 36601
Telephone: 334-405-1300
Facsimile: 334-432-6843; 433-3821

MEMBERS OF FIRM

Broox G. Holmes, Jr.	David A. Bagwell
William B. Harvey	James Donald Hughes
Kirk C. Shaw	Broox G. Holmes

Representative Clients: Automation Technology International, Inc.; Loyal American Life Insurance Co.; WKRG-TV, Inc.; BP Oil Co.; Kimberly Clark Corporation; David Volkert & Assoc., Inc.; Southern Chemical Formulators, Inc.; University of South Alabama.

For Complete List of Firm Personnel, See General Section

For full biographical listings, see the Martindale-Hubbell Law Directory

GARDNER, MIDDLEBROOKS, FLEMING & HAMILTON, P.C. (AV)

64 North Royal Street P.O. Drawer 3103, 36652
Telephone: 334-433-8100
Telecopier: 334-433-8181

J. Cecil Gardner	Charles J. Fleming
Sherwood C. Middlebrooks, III	W. Michael Hamilton
	(Not admitted in AL)

John D. Gibbons	William H. Reece
Christopher E. Krafchak	Mary Elizabeth Olsen

Representative Clients: Alabama AFL-CIO; Southwest Alabama Labor Council, AFL-CIO; Greater Mobile Port Council, AFL-CIO; Mobile/Pensacola; Building Trades Council, AFL-C10; United Paperworkers International Union, AFL CIO, CLC; Oil, Chemical & Atomic Workers International Union, AFL-CIO; International Organization of Masters, Mates & Pilots, AFL-CIO; International Brotherhood of Boilermakers, AFL-CIO; International Alliance of Theatrical Stage Employees & Moving Picture Machine Operators, AFL-CIO.

For full biographical listings, see the Martindale-Hubbell Law Directory

JOHNSTONE, ADAMS, BAILEY, GORDON AND HARRIS, L.L.C. (AV)

Royal St. Francis Building, 104 St. Francis Street, P.O. Box 1988, 36633
Telephone: 334-432-7682
Facsimile: 334-432-2800
Telex: 782040

MEMBERS OF FIRM

Brock B. Gordon	Gregory C. Buffalow
Wade B. Perry, Jr.	Celia J. Collins

ASSOCIATE

Tracy P. Turner

Representative Clients: The Lerio Corp.; First Alabama Bank, Mobile; Infirmary Health System/Mobile Infirmary Medical Center/Rotary Rehabilitation Hospital (Multi-hospital system); Aluminum Company of America; Transportation Leasing Co.; Clark County Board of Education; Mobile Mental Health Center, Inc.

For Complete List of Firm Personnel, See General Section

For full biographical listings, see the Martindale-Hubbell Law Directory

LYONS, PIPES & COOK, P.C. (AV)

2 North Royal Street, P.O. Box 2727, 36652-2727
Telephone: 334-432-4481
Cable Address: "Lysea"
Telecopier: 334-433-1820

(See Next Column)

LYONS, PIPES & COOK P.C.—*Continued*

Wesley Pipes   W. David Johnson, Jr.

Representative Clients: Carriers Container Council, Inc.; Crawford & Company; Inchcape Shipping Services, Inc.; INSBROK; International Systems, Inc.; Jordan Industries, Inc.; Marriott Corporation; Massachusetts Mutual Life Insurance Co.; Spectacor Management Group; United States Fidelity & Guaranty.

For Complete List of Firm Personnel, See General Section

For full biographical listings, see the Martindale-Hubbell Law Directory

---

MONTGOMERY,* Montgomery Co.

HASKELL SLAUGHTER & YOUNG, L.L.C. (AV)

305 South Lawrence Street, P.O. Box 4660, 36103-4660
Telephone: 334-265-8573
Facsimile: 334-264-7945
Birmingham, Alabama Office: 1200 AmSouth/Harbert Plaza, 1901 Sixth Avenue North. 35203
Telephone: 205-251-1000.
Facsimile: 205-324-1133.

Thomas T. Gallion, III   Constance A. Caldwell

Representative Clients: Baxter Healthcare Corporation; The Bradford Group, Inc.; The Coalition for Employee Healthcare, Inc.; Jefferson County Racing Association; Manpower Temporary Services (Alabama); Marshall Durbin Companies; Montgomery County, Alabama; Ridout's-Brown-Service Inc.; Webster Industries, Inc.

For Complete List of Firm Personnel, See General Section

For full biographical listings, see the Martindale-Hubbell Law Directory

THOMAS, MEANS & GILLIS, P.C. (AV)

3121 Zelda Court, Drawer 5058, 36103-5058
Telephone: 334-270-1033
Fax: 334-260-9396
Birmingham, Alabama Office: 1100 Financial Center, 35203.
Telephone: 205-328-7915.
Fax: 205-328-9669.

Kenneth L. Thomas (Resident,   Tyrone C. Means
  Birmingham, Alabama Office)   Henry Lewis Gillis

J. Mark Englehart   Launice P. Sills
Cynthia W. Clinton   Anita L. Kelly
                  Milton J. Westry

For full biographical listings, see the Martindale-Hubbell Law Directory

VOLZ, PRESTWOOD & HANAN, P.C. (AV)

350 Adams Avenue, P.O. Box 1910, 36102-1910
Telephone: 334-264-6401
Fax: 334-834-4954

Charles H. Volz, Jr.   Charles H. Volz, III
Alvin T. Prestwood   Clinton Chadwell Carter
Ellis D. Hanan   Daniel Lewis Feinstein
           LEGAL SUPPORT PERSONNEL
                  Mark A.W. Turpen

For full biographical listings, see the Martindale-Hubbell Law Directory

---

ALASKA

ANCHORAGE,* Third Judicial District

OWENS & TURNER, A PROFESSIONAL CORPORATION (AV)

1500 West 33rd Avenue, Suite 200, 99503-3502
Telephone: 907-276-3963
Facsimile: 907-277-3695

Thomas P. Owens, Jr.   William F. Mede
Terrance A. Turner   Scott J. Nordstrand

Erin R. Brewer   Gregory S. Fisher
Patrick J McCabe   Kimberly K. Geariety
           LEGAL SUPPORT PERSONNEL
                  Susan M. Lamb

Representative Clients: AT&T Alascom; Alaska Housing Finance Corporation; Alaska Railroad Corporation; Arctic Slone Regional Corporation; BP Exploration (Alask) Inc.; Cook Inlet Region, Inc.; Municipality of Anchorage; Petro Star, Inc.; State of Alaska; University of Alaska.

For full biographical listings, see the Martindale-Hubbell Law Directory

---

ARIZONA

FLAGSTAFF,* Coconino Co.

HUFFORD, HORSTMAN, MCCULLOUGH & MONGINI, P.C. (AV)

323 North Leroux Street, P.O. Box B, 86002-0808
Telephone: 520-774-1453
Fax: 520-779-3621

C. Benson Hufford   Margaret A. McCullough
Patrice M. Horstman   Michael E.J. Mongini
                  Eve A. Parnell

                  Philip (Jay) McCarthy, Jr.
           LEGAL SUPPORT PERSONNEL
Doris Utzinger   Amy Klein (Legal Assistant)

Reference: First Interstate Bank of Arizona, N.A.

For full biographical listings, see the Martindale-Hubbell Law Directory

PHOENIX,* Maricopa Co.

BROWN & BAIN, A PROFESSIONAL ASSOCIATION (AV)

2901 North Central Avenue, P.O. Box 400, 85001-0400
Telephone: 602-351-8000
Telecopier: 602-351-8516
Palo Alto, California Affiliated Office: Brown & Bain, 1755 Embarcadero Road, Suite 200.
Telephone: 415-856-9411.
Telecopier: 415-856-6061.
Tucson, Arizona Affiliated Office: Brown & Bain, A Professional Association. One South Church Avenue, Nineteenth Floor, P.O. Box 2265.
Telephone: 602-798-7900
Telecopier: 602-798-7945.

Daniel C. Barr   Philip R. Higdon
Michael P. Berman   (Resident at Tucson Office)
Amy J. Gittler   Diane L. Madenci
Richard H. Harvey   (Resident at Tucson Office)
  (Resident at Palo Alto Office)   Sarah R. Simmons
                                        (Resident at Tucson Office)

For Complete List of Firm Personnel, See General Section

For full biographical listings, see the Martindale-Hubbell Law Directory

FENNEMORE CRAIG, A PROFESSIONAL CORPORATION (AV)

Two North Central, Suite 2200, 85004
Telephone: 602-257-8700
Fax: 602-257-8527
Scottsdale, Arizona Office: 6263 North Scottsdale Road, Suite 290, 85250.
Telephone: 602-257-5400.
Fax: 602-257-5409.
Tucson, Arizona Office: One South Church Avenue, Suite 1030, 85701.
Telephone: 520-791-6800.
Fax: 520-791-6820.

Donald R. Gilbert   Loral Deatherage
Ronald J. Stolkin   John J. Balitis, Jr.
                  Janice Procter-Murphy

James D. Burgess   Erin E. Flaharty

For Complete List of Firm Personnel, See General Section

For full biographical listings, see the Martindale-Hubbell Law Directory

JEROME L. FROIMSON (AV)

340 East Palm Lane, Suite 275, 85004
Telephone: 602-252-4990
Fax: 602-271-9308

For full biographical listings, see the Martindale-Hubbell Law Directory

DAVID F. GOMEZ A PROFESSIONAL CORPORATION (AV)

2525 East Camelback Road Suite 860, 85016
Telephone: 602-957-8686
Telecopier: 602-956-9854
Email: DFGPC@aol.com

                  David F. Gomez

                  Michael J. Petitti, Jr.

For full biographical listings, see the Martindale-Hubbell Law Directory

Phoenix—Continued

JENNINGS, STROUSS AND SALMON, P.L.C. (AV)

A Professional Limited Liability Company
One Renaissance Square, Two North Central, 85004-2393
Telephone: 602-262-5911
Fax: 602-253-3255

Gerald W. Alston	Glenn J. Carter
Rita A. Meiser	Ernest Calderon
Gary L. Lassen	John J. Egbert

Robert D. Haws

Gordon Lewis	Brad Denton
Tracye R. Grinnage	Gregory J. Stanton

For Complete List of Firm Personnel, See General Section

For full biographical listings, see the Martindale-Hubbell Law Directory

RODNEY G. JOHNSON, LTD. (AV)

7301 North 16th Street, Suite 103, 85020-5224
Telephone: 602-371-0087
Fax: 602-870-0296

Rodney G. Johnson

For full biographical listings, see the Martindale-Hubbell Law Directory

GUY DAVID KNOLLER, P.C. (AV)

1401 First Interstate Bank Tower, 3550 North Central Avenue, 85012
Telephone: 602-230-1099
Fax: 602-274-0103

Guy David Knoller

For full biographical listings, see the Martindale-Hubbell Law Directory

LEWIS AND ROCA, LLP (AV)

A Limited Liability Partnership including a Professional Corporation
40 North Central Avenue, 85004-4429
Telephone: 602-262-5311
Fax: 602-262-5747
Email: mlp@lrlaw.com
Tucson, Arizona Office: One South Church Avenue, Suite 700, 86701-1620.
Telephone: 520-622-2090.
Fax: 520-622-3088. E-Mail: mlp@lrlaw.com.

MEMBERS OF FIRM

Marty Harper	Richard S. Cohen
Barbara J. Muller	Allen R. Clarke
Steven J. Hulsman	Christopher J. Brelje
Jane E. Reddin	Thomas J. Kennedy

ASSOCIATES

Barbara Anstey Hoerner	Rebecca L. Story

Representative Clients: Arizona Public Service Co.; City of Phoenix; Gosnell Development Corp.; MCI Communications Corp.; Maricopa Community College District; Phoenix Memorial Hospital; Rockford Corp.; Skymall, Inc.; Southwest Risk Services; United Parcel Service, Inc.

For Complete List of Firm Personnel, See General Section

For full biographical listings, see the Martindale-Hubbell Law Directory

THE LAW OFFICES OF STANLEY LUBIN (AV)

2702 North Third Street Suite 3020, 85004
Telephone: 602-234-0008
Fax: 602-264-0676

ASSOCIATE
Nicholas J. Enoch

For full biographical listings, see the Martindale-Hubbell Law Directory

MITTEN, GOODWIN & RAUP, A PROFESSIONAL CORPORATION (AV)

One Columbus Plaza, 3636 North Central, Suite 1200, 85012
Telephone: 602-650-2000
Fax: 602-264-7033
Email: mgr@starlink.com

Brian M. Goodwin	Martin P. Clare

For full biographical listings, see the Martindale-Hubbell Law Directory

O'CONNOR, CAVANAGH, ANDERSON, KILLINGSWORTH & BESHEARS, A PROFESSIONAL ASSOCIATION (AV)

One East Camelback Road, Suite 1100, 85012-1656
Telephone: 602-263-2400
FAX: 602-263-2900
Email: firminfo@arizlaw.com
Sun City, Arizona Office: 13250 North Del Webb Boulevard, Suite B, 85351.
Telephone: 602-263-2808.
FAX: 602-933-3100.

(See Next Column)

Tucson, Arizona Office: O'Connor Cavanagh Molloy Jones, 33 N. Stone, Suite 2100, 85701, P.O. Box 2268, 85702.
Telephone: 520-622-3531.
FAX: 520-624-2816.
Nogales, Arizona Office: 1891 North Mastick Way, 85621.
Telephone: 520-761-4215.
FAX: 520-761-3505.

Lawrence J. Rosenfeld

David A. Kelly	Helen Rubenstein Holden

Jill E.C. Freret
OF COUNSEL
Shoshana B. Tancer

Representative Clients: American Fence Corp.; Carnation Dairy Co.; Glendale Union High School District; Smith's Food & Drug Centers, Inc.

For Complete List of Firm Personnel, See General Section

For full biographical listings, see the Martindale-Hubbell Law Directory

QUARLES & BRADY (AV)

One Camelback Building, One East Camelback Road, Suite 400, 85012-1649
Telephone: 602-230-5500
Fax: 602-230-5598
Milwaukee, Wisconsin Office: 411 East Wisconsin Avenue.
Telephone: 414-277-5000.
Fax: 414-271-3552.
Madison, Wisconsin Office: First Wisconsin Plaza, One South Pinckney Street, P.O. Box 2113.
Telephone: 608-251-5000.
Fax: 608-251-9166.
West Palm Beach, Florida Office: 222 Lakeview Ave., 4th Floor.
Telephone: 407-653-5000.
Fax: 407-653-5333.
Naples, Florida Office: Barnett Center, 4501 Tamiami Trail North, Suite 300.
Telephone: 813-262-5959.
Fax: 813-434-4999.

MEMBERS OF THE FIRM

Charles W. Herf	William M. Shattuck

Jon E. Pettibone
ASSOCIATES

Colleen A. Scherkenbach	Jennifer N. MacLennan
Jose L. Martinez	David T. Barton
Wendy L. Gerlach	Amy O'Melia-Endres

For Complete List of Firm Personnel, See General Section

For full biographical listings, see the Martindale-Hubbell Law Directory

SHIMMEL, HILL, BISHOP & GRUENDER, P.C. (AV)

3700 North 24th Street, 85016
Telephone: 602-224-9500
Telecopier: 602-955-6176

Daniel F. Gruender	Keith F. Overholt

Michael V. Perry

Representative Clients: Bashas' Stores; Black Mesa Pipeline Co.; Associated General Contractors of America; The Ashton Companies; First American Health Concepts, Inc.; Baker Bros.

For full biographical listings, see the Martindale-Hubbell Law Directory

SNELL & WILMER, L.L.P. (AV)

One Arizona Center, 85004-0001
Telephone: 602-382-6000
Fax: 602-382-6070
Tucson, Arizona Office: 1500 Norwest Tower, One South Church Avenue 85701-1612.
Telephone: 520-882-1200.
Fax: 520-884-1294.
Orange County Office: 1920 Main Street, Suite 1200, P.O. Box 57062, Irvine, California, 92619-7062.
Telephone: 714-253-2700.
Fax: 714-955-2507.
Salt Lake City, Utah Office: Broadway Centre, 111 East Broadway, Suite 900, 84111-1004.
Telephone: 801-237-1900.
Fax: 801-237-1950.

MEMBERS OF FIRM

Robert J. Deeny	William R. Hayden
Gerard Morales	Rebecca A. Winterscheidt

Charles P. Keller
SENIOR ATTORNEY
William P. Allen

Representative Clients: ABF Freight System, Inc.; Apollo Group, Inc.; Banc One Corporation; Brown & Root; Centex Corp.; Del Webb; Intel Corp.; Mayo Clinic; Remington Arms Company, Inc.; Service Corporation International.

(See Next Column)

SNELL & WILMER L.L.P.—*Continued*

For Complete List of Firm Personnel, See General Section

For full biographical listings, see the Martindale-Hubbell Law Directory

TUCSON, * Pima Co.

ERNEST ALLEN COHEN (AV)

6426 Calle de Los Seris, P.O. Box 37273, 85740
Telephone: 520-297-4100
Fax: 520-297-4105

Representative Clients: International Organization of Masters, Mates & Pilots, ILA, AFL-CIO; Lawyers Mediation Service Corp.; Coast Guard Legal Aid Counsel; Masters, Mates & Pilots Health & Benefit Plan; Co-Counsel, Officers Union of International Seamen.

For full biographical listings, see the Martindale-Hubbell Law Directory

FENNEMORE CRAIG, A PROFESSIONAL CORPORATION (AV)

Suite 1030, One South Church Avenue, 85701-1620
Telephone: 520-791-6800.
Fax: 520-791-6820.
Phoenix, Arizona Office: Two North Central Avenue, Suite 2200, 85004.
Telephone: 602-257-8700.
Fax: 602-257-8527.
Scottsdale, Arizona Office: 6263 North Scottsdale Road, Suite 290, 85250.
Telephone: 602-257-5400.
Fax: 602-257-5409.

Ronald J. Stolkin — Christopher P. Staring

For Complete List of Firm Personnel, See General Section

For full biographical listings, see the Martindale-Hubbell Law Directory

RAVEN, KIRSCHNER & NORELL, P.C. (AV)

Suite 1600, One South Church Avenue, 85701-1612
Telephone: 520-628-8700
Telefax: 520-798-5200

Donald T. Awerkamp — Barry Kirschner

Representative Clients: Continental Medical Systems, Inc.; El Paso Natural Gas Co.; Norwest Bank Arizona; El Rio-Santa Cruz Neighborhood Health Center, Inc.; Resolution Trust Corp.; Sierra Vista Community Hospital; Southern Arizona Rehabilitation Hospital; Northern Cochise Community Hospital.

For Complete List of Firm Personnel, See General Section

For full biographical listings, see the Martindale-Hubbell Law Directory

SNELL & WILMER, L.L.P. (AV)

1500 Norwest Tower, One South Church Avenue, 85701-1612
Telephone: 520-882-1200
Fax: 520-884-1294
Phoenix, Arizona Office: One Arizona Center, 85004-0001.
Telephone: 602-382-6000.
Fax: 602-382-6070.
Orange County Office: 1920 Main Street, Suite 1200, P.O. Box 57062, Irvine, California, 92619-7062.
Telephone: 714-253-2700
Fax: 714-955-2507.
Salt Lake City, Utah Office: Broadway Centre, 111 East Broadway, Suite 900, 84111- 1004.
Telephone: 801-237-1900.
Fax: 801-237-1950.

MEMBERS OF FIRM

John A. Robertson — Tibor Nagy, Jr.

Representative Clients: Apache Nitrogen Products, Inc.; Arizona Electric Power Cooperative, Inc.; ASARCO; Association of Universities for Research in Astronomy, Inc.; BHP Copper, Inc. (formerly Magna Copper Company); Insight Distribution Network, Inc.; Lockheed-Martin Corp.; McDonnell Douglas Helicopter Systems; State of Arizona; Transit Management of Tuscon, Inc.

For full biographical listings, see the Martindale-Hubbell Law Directory

ARKANSAS

CAMDEN, * Ouachita Co.

ALLEN P. ROBERTS, P.A. (AV)

119 Van Buren Street, NW, P.O. Box 280, 71701
Telephone: 501-836-5310
FAX: 501-836-9662

(See Next Column)

Allen P. Roberts

Representative Clients: International Paper Co.; Camden Fairview School District; The City of Camden; Byars Oil Co.; American Fuel Cell & Coated Fabrics Co.; Star City School District; Highland Resources, Inc.; Circle B Logging Co.; First National Bank, Magnolia, Arkansas.

For full biographical listings, see the Martindale-Hubbell Law Directory

LITTLE ROCK, * Pulaski Co.

FRIDAY, ELDREDGE & CLARK (AV)

A Partnership including Professional Associations
Formerly, Smith, Williams, Friday, Eldredge & Clark
2000 First Commercial Building, 400 West Capitol Avenue, 72201-3493
Telephone: 501-376-2011
Telecopier: 501-376-2147; 376-6369
Email: fecmh@fec.sprint.com

MEMBERS OF FIRM

James W. Moore — Walter A. Paulson, II, (P.A.)
Oscar E. Davis, Jr., (P.A.) — Christopher J. Heller (P.A.)
Michael Scott Moore (P.A.)

ASSOCIATES

Andrew T. Turner — Daniel Lee Herrington

COUNSEL

B. S. Clark

Counsel for: Union Pacific System; St. Paul Insurance Co.; Liberty Mutual Insurance Co.; Cigna Property & Casualty Co.; Arkansas Power & Light Co.; Dillard Department Stores, Inc.; First Commercial Corp.; Browning Arms Co.; Phillips Petroleum Co.; Aetna Casualty & Surety Co.

For Complete List of Firm Personnel, See General Section

For full biographical listings, see the Martindale-Hubbell Law Directory

HILBURN, CALHOON, HARPER, PRUNISKI & CALHOUN, LTD. (AV)

P.O. Box 1256, 72203-1256
Telephone: 501-372-0110
Fax: 501-372-2029
North Little Rock, Arkansas Office: Eighth Floor, Mercantile Bank Building, One Riverfront Place, P.O. Box 5551, 72119.
Telephone: 501-372-0110.
Fax: 501-372-2029.

David M. Fuqua — Phil Campbell
James M. McHaney, Jr. — Scott E. Daniel

Representative Clients: Mercantile Bank of Central Arkansas; Merrill Lynch Pierce Fenner & Smith, Inc.; Central Arkansas Risk Management Association; Smith Barney, Inc.; The Kroger Co.

For Complete List of Firm Personnel, See General Section

For full biographical listings, see the Martindale-Hubbell Law Directory

ROSE LAW FIRM, A PROFESSIONAL ASSOCIATION (AV)

120 East Fourth Street, 72201
Telephone: 501-375-9131
Telecopy: 501-375-1309

Tim Boe — James Hunter Birch
James M. Gary

Mark Alan Peoples

Representative Clients: Acxiom Corporation, ALCOA; Aromatique, Inc.; Harvest Foods; Georgia-Pacific Corporation; Merico, Inc., d/b/a Colonial Bakery; Pat Salmon & Sons, Inc.; Schering-Plough Corporation; Weyerhaeuser Company.

For Complete List of Firm Personnel, See General Section

For full biographical listings, see the Martindale-Hubbell Law Directory

WRIGHT, LINDSEY & JENNINGS (AV)

200 West Capitol Avenue, Suite 2200, 72201
Telephone: 501-371-0808
Fax: 501-376-9442
Email: tgraves@wlj.com *URL:* http://www.wlj.com/
Fayetteville, Arkansas Office: 101 West Mountain Street, Suite 206, 72701.
Telephone: 501-575-0808.
Fax: 501-575-0999.
Russellville, Arkansas Office: Suite E, 1110 West B Street.
Telephone: 501-968-7995.

John G. Lile — John D. Davis
Kathlyn Graves — William Stuart Jackson
Don S. McKinney

Representative Clients: United Parcel Service; Meyer's Bakery Inc.; Hudson Foods, Inc.; St. Joseph's Regional Health Center; Arkansas Electric Coop.; Boatmen's National Bank of Arkansas.

(See Next Column)

WRIGHT, LINDSEY & JENNINGS, *Little Rock—Continued*

For full biographical listings, see the Martindale-Hubbell Law Directory

PINE BLUFF, * Jefferson Co.

RAMSAY, BRIDGFORTH, HARRELSON & STARLING (AV)

11th Floor, Simmons First National Building, P.O. Drawer 8509, 71611
Telephone: 501-535-9000
FAX: 501-535-8544

MEMBER OF FIRM
Spencer F. Robinson

Representative Clients: Simmons First National Bank; Pine Bluff Sand & Gravel Co.; Stant, Inc.; McGeorge Contracting Co., Inc.; Television Station KATV.

For Complete List of Firm Personnel, See General Section

For full biographical listings, see the Martindale-Hubbell Law Directory

CALIFORNIA

BAKERSFIELD, * Kern Co.

KLEIN, WEGIS, DENATALE, GOLDNER & MUIR, LLP (AV)

A Partnership including Professional Corporations
(Formerly Di Giorgio, Davis, Klein, Wegis, Duggan & Friedman)
ARCO Tower, 4550 California Avenue, Second Floor, P.O. Box 11172, 93389-1172
Telephone: 805-395-1000
Telecopier: 805-326-0418
Email: kwdgm@kwdgm.com

MEMBERS OF FIRM
Anthony J. Klein (Inc.)   Jay L. Rosenlieb
ASSOCIATES
Barry E. Rosenberg   Jeffrey W. Noe

Representative Clients: Smith International, Inc.; Sandrini Brothers Company; Nahama & Weagant Energy Co.; EIU of California, Inc.; Kern County Hay Growers Association, Inc.

For Complete List of Firm Personnel, See General Section

For full biographical listings, see the Martindale-Hubbell Law Directory

BEVERLY HILLS, Los Angeles Co.

STONE & HILES (AV)

9440 Santa Monica Boulevard, Penthouse, 90210
Telephone: 310-274-8749
Telecopier: 310-550-0483
Email: stonehil@he.net *URL:* http://www.he.net/~stonehil

MEMBERS OF FIRM
Richard A. Stone   Russel D. Hiles
          Benjamin S. Cardozo
ASSOCIATES
Marc A. Legget   Angela D. Robledo
Doreen M. Mercado   David L. Schaffer
Margaret Monos   Heather L. Weakley
          Robert D. Stubblefield

For full biographical listings, see the Martindale-Hubbell Law Directory

SWERDLOW, FLORENCE & SANCHEZ, A LAW CORPORATION (AV)

Suite 828, 9401 Wilshire Boulevard, 90212
Telephone: 310-201-4700
Fax: 310-273-8680
Email: lucihamilton@compuserve.com

Seymour Swerdlow   Sandy K. Rathbun
Kenneth J. Florence   Rosario M. Tobias
Millicent N. Sanchez   Amy R. Pleatman

For full biographical listings, see the Martindale-Hubbell Law Directory

CAMARILLO, Ventura Co.

H. ROY JEPPSON A PROFESSIONAL CORPORATION (AV)

1100 Paseo Camarillo, 93010
Telephone: 805-482-3322
FAX: 805-482-6672
Email: roy@vcol.net

H. Roy Jeppson

(See Next Column)

Robyn F. Stalk

For full biographical listings, see the Martindale-Hubbell Law Directory

CLAREMONT, Los Angeles Co.

JOHN C. MCCARTHY (AV)

401 Harvard Avenue, 91711
Telephone: 909-621-4984
Telecopier: 909-621-5757

For full biographical listings, see the Martindale-Hubbell Law Directory

COSTA MESA, Orange Co.

RICKS & ANDERSON, A LAW CORPORATION (AV)

3200 Park Center Drive, Suite 1155, 92626-4413
Telephone: 714-966-9190

Cecil E. Ricks, Jr.   Annette L. Anderson

For full biographical listings, see the Martindale-Hubbell Law Directory

RUTAN & TUCKER, LLP (AV)

A Partnership including Professional Corporations
611 Anton Boulevard, Suite 1400, P.O. Box 1950, 92626
Telephone: 714-641-5100; 213-625-7586
Telecopier: 714-546-9035
Email: rutan&tucker@mcimail.com *URL:* http://www.rutan.com

MEMBERS OF FIRM
David C. Larsen (P.C.)   William W. Wynder
David J. Aleshire   Ernest W. Klatte III
James L. Morris   Jeffrey Wertheimer
          Lien Ski Harrison
ASSOCIATES
Carol Landis Demmler   Sandra J. Young
Richard K. Howell   Jennifer White-Sperling

For Complete List of Firm Personnel, See General Section

For full biographical listings, see the Martindale-Hubbell Law Directory

FRESNO, * Fresno Co.

JORY, PETERSON, WATKINS & SMITH (AV)

555 West Shaw, Suite C-1, P.O. Box 5394, 93755
Telephone: 209-225-6700
Telecopier: 209-225-3416

MEMBERS OF FIRM
Jay V. Jory   Michael Jens F. Smith
John E. Peterson   Marcia A. Ross
Cal B. Watkins, Jr.   William M. Woolman
ASSOCIATES
John J. Stander   Carla M. McCormack
Jeff W. Reisig   Matthew D. Ruyak

Reference: Valliwide Bank.

For full biographical listings, see the Martindale-Hubbell Law Directory

LANG, RICHERT & PATCH, A PROFESSIONAL CORPORATION (AV)

Fig Garden Financial Center, 5200 North Palm Avenue, 4th Floor, P.O. Box 40012, 93755
Telephone: 209-228-6700
Fax: 209-228-6727

Frank H. Lang   Victoria J. Salisch
William T. Richert (1937-1993)   Bradley A. Silva
Robert L. Patch, II   Charles Trudrung Taylor
Val W. Saldaña   Mark L. Creede
Douglas E. Noll   Peter N. Zeitler
Michael T. Hertz   Charles L. Doerksen

Laurie L. Quigley   Nabil E. Zumout
Douglas E. Griffin   Shawn H. Alikian
          Thomas E. Gauthier

References: Wells Fargo Bank (Fresno Main Office).

For full biographical listings, see the Martindale-Hubbell Law Directory

SAGASER, HANSEN, FRANSON & JAMISON, A PROFESSIONAL CORPORATION (AV)

2445 Capitol Street, Second Floor, P.O. Box 1632, 93717-1632
Telephone: 209-233-4800
Fax: 209-233-9330

(See Next Column)

SAGASER, HANSEN, FRANSON & JAMISON A PROFESSIONAL CORPORATION—
Continued

Eric K. Hansen (1952-1996)	Kimberly A. Gaab
Howard A. Sagaser	Patti L. Williams
Donald R. Franson, Jr.	K. Poncho Baker
Daniel O. Jamison	Kristi R. Culver
Nancy A. Maler	Catherine J. Cerna

For full biographical listings, see the Martindale-Hubbell Law Directory

FULLERTON, Orange Co.

ELENBAAS & SCHOEMAN (AV)

Suite 235, 1370 N. Brea Boulevard, 92635
Telephone: 714-871-7100
Fax: 714-871-7142

Thomas E. Elenbaas   Cara Hagan Schoeman

For full biographical listings, see the Martindale-Hubbell Law Directory

GLENDALE, Los Angeles Co.

OTT & HOROWITZ, A PROFESSIONAL CORPORATION (AV)

700 North Central Avenue, 8th Floor, Suite 850, 91203
Telephone: 818-242-3100
Fax: 818-242-3102
Email: ohlaw@aol.com

Thomas H. Ott   Craig A. Horowitz
Wayne D. Clayton

Steven H. Taylor   Janine R. Menhennet
Patrick Carey

Representative Clients: Alhambra Unified School District; Calif. Credit
Union League; Cuna Mutual Ins. Group; Hughes Aircraft Corp.; Lockheed
Federal Credit Union.

For full biographical listings, see the Martindale-Hubbell Law Directory

IRVINE, Orange Co.

ANDRADE & MUZI (AV)

Marine National Bank Building, 18401 Von Karman, Suite 350, 92715
Telephone: 714-553-1951
Telecopier: 714-553-0655
San Diego, California Office: Tokia Bank Building, 3111 Camino Del Rio
North, Suite 1100.
Telephone: 619-291-2481.

MEMBERS OF FIRM

Richard B. Andrade	Abilio Tavares, Jr.
Andrew C. Muzi	Samuel G. Broyles, Jr.
Ronald G. Holbert	Frank A. Satalino

OF COUNSEL
Kurt Kupferman

Representative Clients: Advanco Constructor's, Inc.; American Insurance
Company of North America; Fireman's Fund Insurance Co.; CIGNA Insur-
ance Co.; Gentosi Bros., Inc.; Griffith Co.; Steve Bubalo Construction Co.;
Sukut Construction, Inc.; U.S. Rentals, Inc.; Veco International, Inc.

For full biographical listings, see the Martindale-Hubbell Law Directory

GAUNTLETT & ASSOCIATES (AV)

18400 Von Karman, Suite 300, 92612
Telephone: 714-553-1010
Fax: 714-553-2050
Email: ugauntlett@aol.com

David A. Gauntlett

David A. Stall	Elizabeth A. Gillis
Leo E. Lundberg, Jr.	(Not admitted in CA)
Michael Danton Richardson	Mark H. Plager
William P. Warden	(Not admitted in CA)
Stanley H. Shure	Jeffrey S. Allison

OF COUNSEL
Gary L. Hinman   Jose Zorrilla, Jr.

For full biographical listings, see the Martindale-Hubbell Law Directory

SNELL & WILMER, L.L.P. (AV)

1920 Main Street, Suite 1200, 92614
Telephone: 714-253-2700
FAX: 714-955-2507
URL: http://www.swlaw.com
Phoenix, Arizona Office: One Arizona Center, 85004-0001.
Telephone: 602-382-6000.
Fax: 602-382-6070.

(See Next Column)

Tucson, Arizona Office: Norwest Tower, Suite 1500, One South Church
Avenue, 85701-1612.
Telephone: 520-882-1200.
Fax: 520-884-1294.
Salt Lake City, Utah Office: Broadway Centre, 111 East Broadway, Suite
900, 84111-1004.
Telephone: 801-237-1900.
Fax: 801-237-1950.

MEMBERS OF FIRM
Christy D. Joseph   William S. O'Hare, Jr.
(Resident)

For Complete List of Firm Personnel, See General Section

For full biographical listings, see the Martindale-Hubbell Law Directory

LAGUNA HILLS, Orange Co.

MICHELLE A. REINGLASS (AV)

Suite 170 23161 Millcreek Road, 92653
Telephone: 714-587-0460
FAX: 714-587-1004

ASSOCIATE
Michelle M. Lents

For full biographical listings, see the Martindale-Hubbell Law Directory

LONG BEACH, Los Angeles Co.

CAMERON, MADDEN, PEARLSON, GALE & SELLARS (AV)

One World Trade Center Suite 1600, 90831-1600
Telephone: 310-436-3888
Telecopier: 310-437-1967

MEMBERS OF THE FIRM

Timothy C. Cameron	Patrick T. Madden
Charles M. Gale	Paul R. Pearlson
James D. Sellars	

ASSOCIATE
Lillian D. Salinger

For full biographical listings, see the Martindale-Hubbell Law Directory

LOS ANGELES,* Los Angeles Co.

BAKER & HOSTETLER (AV)

600 Wilshire Boulevard, 90017-3212
Telephone: 213-624-2400
FAX: 213-975-1740
In Cleveland, Ohio: 3200 National City Center, 1900 East Ninth Street.
Telephone: 216-621-0200.
In Columbus, Ohio: Capitol Square, Suite 2100, 65 East State Street.
Telephone: 614-228-1541.
In Denver, Colorado: 303 East 17th Avenue, Suite 1100.
Telephone: 303-861-0600.
In Houston, Texas: 1000 Louisiana, Suite 2000.
Telephone: 713-236-0020.
In Long Beach, California: 300 Oceangate, Suite 620.
Telephone: 310-432-2827.
In Orlando, Florida: SunBank Center, Suite 2300, 200 South Orange
Avenue.
Telephone: 407-649-4000.
In Washington, D. C.: Washington Square, Suite 1100, 1050 Connecticut
Avenue, N. W.
Telephone: 202-861-1500.
In College Park, Maryland: 9658 Baltimore Boulevard, Suite 206.
Telephone: 301-441-2781.
In Alexandria, Virginia: 437 North Lee Street.
Telephone: 703-549-1294.
In San Francisco, California: One Sansome Street, Suite 2000.
Telephone: 415-951-4705.

PARTNERS
Michael M. Johnson   Teresa R. Tracy
ASSOCIATE
Keith A. Fink

For Complete List of Firm Personnel, See General Section

For full biographical listings, see the Martindale-Hubbell Law Directory

BERGMAN & WEDNER, INC. (AV)

Suite 900, 10880 Wilshire Boulevard, 90024
Telephone: 310-470-6110
Fax: Available on Request

Gregory M. Bergman	Robert M. Mason III
Gregory A. Wedner	Kristi Anne Sjoholm-Sierchio
Mark E. Fingerman	Keith A. Robinson
Alan Harvey Mittelman	John P. Dacey

John V. Tamborelli	Lisa S. Shukiar
Blithe Ann Smith	Daphne M. Humphreys
Suzanne Z. Shbaro	

(See Next Column)

BERGMAN & WEDNER INC., *Los Angeles—Continued*

OF COUNSEL

Lloyd A. Bergman (1923-1994)   Jacob A. Wedner

SPECIAL COUNSEL

Richard V. Godino

For full biographical listings, see the Martindale-Hubbell Law Directory

BOTTUM & FELITON, A PROFESSIONAL CORPORATION (AV)

Suite 1500, South Tower, 3200 Wilshire Boulevard, 90010
Telephone: 213-487-0402
Fax: 213-386-9803
San Diego, California Office: Suite 400 Emerald Plaza, 402 West Broadway.
Telephone: 619-595-4857.
Fax: 619-595-4863.

John R. Feliton, Jr.	Steve Johnson
Robert A. Wooten, Jr.	Mark A. Oertel
Alexander F. Giovanniello	

Paul K. Schrieffer	Brian E. Cooper
Scott A. Hampton	Karl R. Loureiro

For full biographical listings, see the Martindale-Hubbell Law Directory

BUCHALTER, NEMER, FIELDS & YOUNGER, A PROFESSIONAL CORPORATION (AV)

24th Floor, 601 South Figueroa Street, 90017
Telephone: 213-891-0700
Fax: 213-896-0400
Email: buchalter@earthlink.net *URL:* http://www.buchalter.com
New York, New York Office: 15th Floor, 605 Third Avenue.
Telephone: 212-490-8600.
Fax: 212-490-6022.
San Francisco, California Office: 29th Floor, 333 Market Street.
Telephone: 415-227-0900.
Fax: 415-227-0770.
Newport Beach, California Office: Suite 1450, 620 Newport Center Drive.
Telephone: 714-760-1121.
Fax: 714-720-0182.

Arthur Chinski	Keith B. Bardellini

References: City National Bank; Wells Fargo Bank; Metrobank.

For Complete List of Firm Personnel, See General Section

For full biographical listings, see the Martindale-Hubbell Law Directory

CLARK & TREVITHICK, A PROFESSIONAL CORPORATION (AV)

800 Wilshire Boulevard, 12th Floor, 90017
Telephone: 213-629-5700
Telecopier: 213-624-9441
San Francisco, California Office: 456 Montgomery Street, 20th Floor.
Telephone: 415-288-6520.
Fax: 415-398-2820.

Philip W. Bartenetti	Dolores Cordell

References: Wells Fargo Bank (Los Angeles Main Office); National Bank of California.

For Complete List of Firm Personnel, See General Section

For full biographical listings, see the Martindale-Hubbell Law Directory

FORD & HARRISON (AV)

333 South Grand Avenue Suite 3680, 90071
Telephone: 213-680-3410
FAX: 213-680-4161
Atlanta, Georgia Office: 600 Peachtree at the Circle Building, 1275 Peachtree Street, N.E., 30309.
Telephone: 404-888-3800.
Fax: 404-888-3863.
Miami, Florida Office: Alley and Alley/Ford & Harrison. 516 Ingraham Building, 25 S.E. 2nd Avenue, 33131.
Telephone: 305-379-3811.
Fax: 305-358-5933.
Tampa, Florida Office: Alley and Alley/Ford & Harrison. 205 Brush Street, P.O. Box 1427, 33601.
Telephone: 813-229-6481.
Fax: 813-223-7029.
Washington, D.C. Office: 1920 N Street, N.W., Suite 200, 20036.
Telephone: 202-463-6633.
Fax: 202-466-5705.

MEMBERS OF FIRM

Michael L. Lowry	Glen H. Mertens

(See Next Column)

ASSOCIATES

Maral Donoyan	Kari Haugen

Representative Clients: Coca-Cola Enterprises; Columbia/HCA Healthcare Corp.; Delta Air Lines, Inc.; Federal Express Corporation; Kellogg Company; LIN Television Corp.; Nestle USA, Inc.; Regional Airline Assn.

For full biographical listings, see the Martindale-Hubbell Law Directory

GARTNER & YOUNG, A PROFESSIONAL CORPORATION (AV)

1925 Century Park East, Suite 2050, 90067-2709
Telephone: 310-556-3576
Fax: 310-556-8459

Naomi Young	Lawrence J. Gartner

Christopher Adams Thorn	Jill Henson
Kimberly M. Talley	Angela J. Reddock
Jennifer L. Futch	Gregory P. Bright

For full biographical listings, see the Martindale-Hubbell Law Directory

GOLDSTEIN, KENNEDY & PETITO (AV)

Suite 1018, 1880 Century Park East (Century City), 90067
Telephone: 310-553-4746; 213-879-1401
Fax: 310-282-8070

Charles H. Goldstein	Gregory G. Kennedy
	Deborah Hanna Petito

Lauren A. Dean	Edward J. Gervin
	Frank A. Magnanimo

OF COUNSEL

Thomas A. Fournie

For full biographical listings, see the Martindale-Hubbell Law Directory

GRAY, YORK, DUFFY & RATTET (AV)

15760 Ventura Boulevard, 16th Floor (Encino), 91436
Telephone: 818-907-4000; 310-553-0445
FAX: 818-783-4551

MEMBERS OF FIRM

John J. Duffy	Arlene A. Colman
Gary S. Rattet	Louis A. Cappadona

ASSOCIATES

Amalia L. Taylor	John L. Barber
	Bridgett Esquibias

Reference: Marathon National Bank, Los Angeles, California.

For full biographical listings, see the Martindale-Hubbell Law Directory

HILL, FARRER & BURRILL LLP (AV)

A Limited Liability Partnership including Professional Corporations
35th Floor, Union Bank Square, 445 South Figueroa Street, 90071
Telephone: 213-620-0460
Fax: 213-624-4840

MEMBERS OF FIRM

Stanley E. Tobin (P.C.)	Jonathan M. Brandler (P.C.)
Kyle D. Brown (P.C.)	James A. Bowles (P.C.)
Stuart H. Young, Jr., (P.C.)	Ronald W. Novotny (P.C.)
James G. Johnson (P.C.)	Suzanne J. Holland
G. Cresswell Templeton III	

OF COUNSEL

Edwin H. Franzen (P.C.)

For Complete List of Firm Personnel, See General Section

For full biographical listings, see the Martindale-Hubbell Law Directory

HORNBERGER & CRISWELL (AV)

444 South Flower, 31st Floor, 90071
Telephone: 213-488-1655
Facsimile: 213-488-1255
Email: kbranch0@counsel.com

MEMBERS OF FIRM

Nicholas W. Hornberger	Ann M. Ghazarians
Leslie E. Criswell	Michael A. Brewer
	Scott Alan Freedman

ASSOCIATES

Marlin E. Howes	James M. Slominski
Christopher T. Olsen	Michael C. Denlinger
Scott B. Cloud	Gayle L. Eskridge

OF COUNSEL

David E. Bower	William P. Driscoll

For full biographical listings, see the Martindale-Hubbell Law Directory

Los Angeles—Continued

IVERSON, YOAKUM, PAPIANO & HATCH (AV)

One Wilshire Building, 27th Floor 624 South Grand Avenue, 90017
Telephone: 213-624-7444
Telecopier: 213 629-4563

Paul E. Iverson (1907-1975)   Frank B. Yoakum, Jr.
                                  (1906-1991)

MEMBERS OF FIRM

Neil Papiano   Arnold D. Larson
Patrick M. Mc Adam   John M. Garrick

ASSOCIATES

Douglas C. Pease   Mary P. Lightfoot
Andrew K. Doty   Mark Pearson
Melissa A. Immel   Frederick Brevard Hayes

OF COUNSEL
R. Noel Hatch

Representative Clients: Lockheed Corp.; International Paper; Bridgestone/-Firestone, Inc.
Reference: Security Pacific National Bank (Los Angeles Head Office).

For Complete List of Firm Personnel, See General Section

For full biographical listings, see the Martindale-Hubbell Law Directory

KNEE & MASON (AV)

A Partnership
Suite 2050, 2049 Century Park East, 90067
Telephone: 310-551-0909
Fax: 310-552-9818
Email: kmfirm@aol.com

MEMBERS OF FIRM

Howard M. Knee   Melanie C. Ross
Belle C. Mason   Lora Silverman
Gregory N. Karasik   Stephen M. Benardo
                Lisa G. Sherman

OF COUNSEL

Ted R. Huebner   Heather A. Lindquist

For full biographical listings, see the Martindale-Hubbell Law Directory

LOEB & LOEB LLP (AV)

A Limited Liability Partnership including Professional Corporations
Suite 1800, 1000 Wilshire Boulevard, 90017-2475
Telephone: 213-688-3400
Facsimile: 213-688-3460; 688-3461; 688-3462
Century City, California Office: Suite 2200, 10100 Santa Monica
Boulevard, Los Angeles, 90067-4164.
Telephone: 310-282-2000.
Facsimile: 310-282-2191; 282-2192.
New York, N.Y. Office: 345 Park Avenue, 10154-0037.
Telephone: 212-407-4000.
Facsimile: 212-407-4990.
Washington, D.C. Office: Suite 601, 2100 M Street N.W., 20037-1207.
Telephone: 202-223-5700.
Facsimile: 202-223-5704.
Nashville, Tennessee Office: 45 Music Square West, 37203-3205.
Telephone: 615-749-8300;
Facsimile: 615-749-8308.
Rome, Italy Office: Piazza Digione 1, 00197.
Telephone: 011-396-808-8456.
Facsimile: 011-396-808-8288.

MEMBERS OF FIRM

Fred B. Griffin   Raymond W. Thomas
Richard W. Kopenhefer   (Century City Office)
  (Century City Office)

ASSOCIATES

Marita T. Covarrubias   Arya Towfighi
  (Century City Office)   (Century City Office)
Richard J. Frey   Richard S. Zuniga
  (Century City Office)   (Century City Office)

For Complete List of Firm Personnel, See General Section

For full biographical listings, see the Martindale-Hubbell Law Directory

MITCHELL, SILBERBERG & KNUPP LLP (AV)

A Partnership including Professional Corporations
11377 West Olympic Boulevard, 90064
Telephone: 310-312-2000
Fax: 310-312-3100

MEMBERS OF FIRM

Steven M. Schneider (A   Lawrence A. Ginsberg (A
  Professional Corporation)   Professional Corporation)
Deborah P. Koeffler (A   Mark A. Wasserman (A
  Professional Corporation)   Professional Corporation)
William L. Cole (A Professional   Allen J. Gross (A Professional
  Corporation)   Corporation)

(See Next Column)

Lawrence A. Michaels (A   Larry C. Drapkin (A
  Professional Corporation)   Professional Corporation)

ASSOCIATES

Mary Courtney Burke   Tracy L. Thornburg
Brian S. Arbetter   Jennifer Lightman Wessels
Michelle Abend Bauman   Lee Anne Steinberg
Adam Levin   Stefano G. Moscato
                Suzanne M. Steinke

References: Wells Fargo Bank, N.A.; Merrill, Lynch.

For Complete List of Firm Personnel, See General Section

For full biographical listings, see the Martindale-Hubbell Law Directory

OCHOA & SILLAS (AV)

444 South, Flower Street, 18th Floor, 90071
Telephone: 213-362-1400
Fax: 213-622-0162
Sacramento, California Office: Wells Fargo Center, 400 Capitol Mall, Suite 1850.
Telephone: 916-447-3383.
FAX: 916-447-3495.
Mexico City, Mexico Office: Bosques de Duraznos, No. 65-507-B, Bosques de Las Lomas, 11700 Mexico, D.F.
Telephone: 905-596-68-48.

MEMBERS OF FIRM

Ralph M. Ochoa   Jesse M. Jauregui
Herman Sillas   Jacqueline Rich Moore

ASSOCIATES

Jack T. Molodanof   Carlos Hilario
Tomás R. Lopez   Joyce E. Earl
Rita A. Reyes   Christopher Gonzalez
                Evan F. Hadnot

OF COUNSEL

Cochran & Lotkin, , Washington, D.C.

LEGAL SUPPORT PERSONNEL

Manuel Tejeda (Paralegal)   Jeanette M. Palma (Paralegal)
                Lori Lee Marino (Paralegal)

For full biographical listings, see the Martindale-Hubbell Law Directory

O'MELVENY & MYERS LLP (AV)

400 South Hope Street, 90071-2899
Telephone: 213-669-6000
Cable Address: "Moms"
Facsimile: 213-669-6407
Email: omminfo@omm.com
Century City, California Office: 1999 Avenue of the Stars, 90067-6035.
Telephone: 310-553-6700.
Facsimile: 310-246-6779.
Newport Beach, California Office: 610 Newport Center Drive, 92660-6429.
Telephone: 714-760-9600.
Cable Address: "Moms".
Facsimile: 714-669-6994.
San Francisco, California Office: Embarcadero Center West Tower, 275 Battery Street, 94111-3305.
Telephone: 415-984-8700.
Facsimile: 415-984-8701.
New York, New York Office: Citicorp Center, 153 East 53rd Street, 10022-4611.
Telephone: 212-326-2000.
Facsimile: 212-326-2061.
Washington, D.C. Office: 555 13th Street, N.W., 20004-1109.
Telephone: 202-383-5300.
Cable Address: "Moms".
Facsimile: 202-383-5414.
London, England Office: 10 Finsbury Square, London, EC2A 1LA.
Telephone: 0171-256-8451.
Facsimile: 0171-638-8205.
Tokyo, Japan Office: Sanbancho KB-6 Building, 6 Sanbancho, Chiyoda-ku, Tokyo 102, Japan.
Telephone: 03-3239-2900.
Facsimile: 03-3239-2432.
Hong Kong Office: Suite 1905, Peregrine Tower, Lippo Centre, 89 Queensway, Central, Hong Kong.
Telephone: 852-2523-8266.
Facsimile: 852-2522-1760.
Shanghai, Peoples Republic of China Office: Shanghai International Trade Centre, Suite 2011, 2200 Yan An Road West, Shanghai, 200335, PRC.
Telephone: 86-21-6219-5363.
Facsimile: 86-21-6275-4949.

PARTNER

Gordon E. Krischer

For Complete List of Firm Personnel, See General Section

For full biographical listings, see the Martindale-Hubbell Law Directory

Los Angeles—Continued

POSNER & ROSEN, P.C. (AV)

3600 Wilshire Boulevard Suite 1800, 90010-2622
Telephone: 213-389-6050
Fax: 213-389-0663

Michael P. Posner	Howard Z. Rosen
Olivia A. Burgos	Laurence P. Posner

For full biographical listings, see the Martindale-Hubbell Law Directory

RADCLIFF, FRANDSEN & DONGELL (AV)

40th Floor, 777 South Figueroa Street, 90017
Telephone: 213-614-1990
Facsimile: 213-489-9263
San Francisco, California Office: 88 Kearny Street, Suite 1475.
Telephone: 415-399-8393.
Facsimile: 415-989-5465.
Rome, Italy Office: Via Tacito, 7.
Telephone: (39) 06-323-5588.
Facsimile: (39) 06-324-3392.

MEMBERS OF FIRM

Jules G. Radcliff, Jr.	Russell Mackay Frandsen
Richard A. Dongell	

OF COUNSEL

Tal Clifton Finney

ASSOCIATES

Francis P. Aspessi	Jeffrey C. Mayes
Ruben A. Castellon	Marisa A. Moret
William W. Funderburk, Jr.	Daniel E. Park
Jeffrey A. Gagliardi	Scott D. Pinsky
David K. Lee	Eric H. Saiki
Maria Anna Mancini	Steve R. Segura
Glenn M. White	

For full biographical listings, see the Martindale-Hubbell Law Directory

REXON, FREEDMAN, KLEPETAR & HAMBLETON, A PROFESSIONAL CORPORATION (AV)

12100 Wilshire Boulevard, Suite 730, 90025
Telephone: 310-826-8300
FAX: 310-826-0333

Brian L. Rexon	Ronald J. Klepetar
Jeffrey C. Freedman	Debby R. Hambleton
Wendy K. Genz	

Steven J. Prough	Stephanie J. Hart

Reference: Santa Monica Bank.

For full biographical listings, see the Martindale-Hubbell Law Directory

SCHWARTZ, STEINSAPIR, DOHRMANN & SOMMERS (AV)

6300 Wilshire Boulevard, Suite 2000, 90048
Telephone: 213-655-4700
Fax: 213-655-4488
Pittsburgh, Pennsylvania Office: 3600 One Oxford Centre.
Telephone: 412-456-2008.
Fax: 412-456-2020.

MEMBERS OF FIRM

Laurence D. Steinsapir	Margo A. Feinberg
Robert M. Dohrmann	Henry M. Willis
Richard D. Sommers	Dennis J. Murphy
Stuart Libicki	D. William Heine, Jr.
Michael R. Feinberg	Claude Cazzulino
Michael D. Four	Dolly M. Gee

ASSOCIATES

Brenda E. Sutton	Erika A. Zucker

For full biographical listings, see the Martindale-Hubbell Law Directory

SHEPPARD, MULLIN, RICHTER & HAMPTON LLP (AV)

A Limited Liability Partnership including Professional Corporations
Forty-Eighth Floor, 333 South Hope Street, 90071-1448
Telephone: 213-620-1780
Telecopier: 213-620-1398
Cable Address: "Sheplaw"
Email: info@smrh.com *URL:* http://www.smrh.com
Orange County, California Office: 650 Town Center Drive, 4th Floor, Costa Mesa.
Telephone: 714-513-5100.
Telecopier: 714-513-5130. Home Page Address: http://www.smrh.com.
San Francisco, California Office: Seventeenth Floor, Four Embarcadero Center.
Telephone: 415-434-9100.
Telecopier: 415-434-3947. Home Page Address: http://www.smrh.com.

(See Next Column)

San Diego, California Office: Nineteenth Floor, 501 West Broadway.
Telephone: 619-338-6500.
Telecopier: 619-234-3815. Home Page Address: http://www.smrh.com.

MEMBERS OF FIRM

Charles F. Barker	Douglas R. Hart
Dennis Childs (San Diego Office)	Richard L. Lotts *
	David A. Maddux *
John D. Collins * (San Diego Office)	Ryan D. McCortney
	Richard J. Simmons
Richard M. Freeman * (San Diego Office)	Ann Kane Smith
	Dianne Baquet Smith
Guy N. Halgren (San Diego Office)	William V. Whelan (San Diego Office)

*Professional Corporation

For full biographical listings, see the Martindale-Hubbell Law Directory

STOCKWELL, HARRIS, WIDOM & WOOLVERTON, A PROFESSIONAL CORPORATION (AV)

6222 Wilshire Boulevard, Sixth Floor, P.O. Box 48917, 90048-0917
Telephone: 213-935-6669; 818-784-6222; 310-277-6669
Fax: 213-935-0198
Santa Ana, California Office: Suite 500, 1551 N. Tustin Avenue, P.O. Box 11979.
Telephone: 714-479-1180.
Fax: 714-479-1190.
Ventura, California Office: 2021 Sperry Avenue, Suite 46.
Telephone: 805-654-8994; 213-617-7290.
Fax: 805-654-1546.
San Bernardino, California Office: Suite 303, 215 North "D" Street.
Telephone: 909-381-5553.
Fax: 909-384-9981.
San Diego, California Office: Suite 400, 402 West Broadway.
Telephone: 619-235-6054.
Fax: 619-231-0129.
Grover Beach, California Office: Suite 307, 200 South 13th Street.
Telephone: 805-473-0720.
Fax: 805-473-0635.

Steven I. Harris (Managing Attorney)	Lawrence S. Mendelsohn
Patricia A. Olive	Edwin H. McKnight, Jr. (Resident, Santa Ana Office)
David L. Slucter (Resident, San Bernardino Office)	Steven A. Meline (Resident, Santa Ana Office)
Richard M. Widom (Managing Attorney)	Ted L. Hirschberger
Jeffrey T. Landres (Resident, Ventura Office)	Theodore G. Schneider, Jr. (Resident, San Bernardino Office)
Linda S. Freeman (Santa Ana and San Diego Offices)	Lawrence B. Madans
Michael L. Terry (Resident, Grover Beach Office)	Lester D. Marshall
	John R. Payne
William M. Carero	George Woolverton
Brian R. Horan	James C. Shipley (Resident, Ventura Office)
David F. Grant (Resident, Santa Office Office)	Jeffrey Eugene Lowe (Resident, Santa Ana Office)
Edward S. Muehl (Santa Ana and San Diego Offices)	

For full biographical listings, see the Martindale-Hubbell Law Directory

---

MENLO PARK, San Mateo Co.

DYER & WHITE (AV)

Suite 200, 800 Oak Grove Avenue, 94025
Telephone: 415-325-7000
Fax: 415-325-3116

MEMBERS OF FIRM

Charles A. Dyer	Rand N. White

For full biographical listings, see the Martindale-Hubbell Law Directory

---

MODESTO,* Stanislaus Co.

CARDOZO & CARDOZO (AV)

1101 Sylvan Avenue, #B-4, 95350
Telephone: 209-571-3600
FAX: 209-571-1553

MEMBER OF FIRM

A. A. Cardozo, Jr.

LEGAL SUPPORT PERSONNEL

Patricia Bowers

For full biographical listings, see the Martindale-Hubbell Law Directory

NEWPORT BEACH, Orange Co.

FISHER & PHILLIPS (AV)

A Partnership including Professional Corporations and Associations
4675 MacArthur Court, Suite 550, 92660
Telephone: 714-851-2424
Telecopier: 714-851-0152
Atlanta, Georgia Office: 1500 Resurgens Plaza, 945 East Paces Ferry Road, N.E., 30326.
Telephone: 404-231-1400.
Telecopier: 404-240-4249.
Telex: 54-2331.
Fort Lauderdale, Florida Office: Suite 2300 NationsBank Tower, One Financial Plaza, 33394.
Telephone: 954-525-4800.
Telecopier: 954-525-8739.
Redwood City, California Office: Suite 345, Three Lagoon Drive, 94065.
Telephone: 415-592-6160.
Telecopier: 415-592-6385.
New Orleans, Louisiana Office: 3710 Place St. Charles, 201 St. Charles Avenue, 70170.
Telephone: 504-522-3303.
Telecopier: 504-529-3850.

RESIDENT MEMBERS

Robert J. Bekken	Karl R. Lindegren
James J. McDonald, Jr.	Robert V. Schnitz

RESIDENT ASSOCIATES

Georgia V. Ingram	Warren Lee Nelson
Robert Yonowitz	Anne M. Terra
John M. Polson	Christopher C. Hoffman
Lyne A. Richardson	Nancy E. McAllister
Cynthia Walker Lane	Michelle M. Casey
Jeffrey B. Freid	Christina T. Nguyen

Representative Clients: Behr Process Corp.; California Motor Car Dealers Assn.; Marie Callendar Pie Shops, Inc.; Motor Car Dealers Association of Orange County; New Car Dealers Association of San Diego; Textron, Inc.

For full biographical listings, see the Martindale-Hubbell Law Directory

---

McDERMOTT, WILL & EMERY (AV)

A Partnership including Professional Corporations
1301 Dove Street, Suite 500, 92660-2444
Telephone: 714-851-0633
Facsimile: 714-851-9348
URL: http://www.mwe.com
Chicago, Illinois Office: 227 West Monroe Street.
Telephone: 312-372-2000.
Facsimile: 312-984-7700.
Boston, Massachusetts Office: 75 State Street, Suite 1700.
Telephone: 617-345-5000.
Facsimile: 617-345-5077.
Miami, Florida Office: 201 South Biscayne Boulevard.
Telephone: 305-358-3500.
Facsimile: 305-347-6500.
Washington, D.C. Office: 1850 K Street, N.W.
Telephone: 202-887-8000.
Facsimile: 202-778-8087.
Los Angeles, California Office: 2049 Century Park East.
Telephone: 310-277-4110.
Facsimile: 310-277-4730.
New York, N.Y. Office: 50 Rockefeller Plaza.
Telephone: 212-547-5508.
Facsimile: 212-547-5444.
St. Petersburg, Russia Office: AOZT McDermott, Will & Emery, Griboyedova Canal 36, 191023 St. Petersburg, Russia.
Telephone: (7) (812) 310-52-44; 310-55-44; 310-59-44; 850-20-45.
Facsimile: (7) (812) 310-54-46; 325-84-50.
Vilnius, Lithuania Office: Smetonos 6, 2600 Vilnius, Lithuania.
Telephone: 370 2 61-43-08.
Facsimile: 370 2 22-79-55.

MEMBER OF FIRM
Peter D. Holbrook

For full biographical listings, see the Martindale-Hubbell Law Directory

---

OAKLAND, * Alameda Co.

ANTHONY & CARLSON (AV)

1999 Harrison Street, Suite 1750, 94612
Telephone: 510-835-8400
Fax: 510-835-5566

MEMBERS OF FIRM

Steven R. Anthony	Richard H. Carlson

ASSOCIATE
Barbara L. Vankoll

OF COUNSEL
Jane L. Trigero

For full biographical listings, see the Martindale-Hubbell Law Directory

---

CORBETT & KANE, A PROFESSIONAL CORPORATION (AV)

2000 Powell Street, Suite 1450 (Emeryville), 94608
Telephone: 510-547-2434
Fax: 510-658-5014
Email: attorney@cklaw.com *URL:* http://www.cklaw.com
San Francisco, California Office: Citicorp Center, One Sansome Street, Suite 1900.
Telephone: 415-956-4100.

Judith Droz Keyes	Tim J. Emert
Mary Maloney Roberts	Denise M. DeRose
Sharon J. Grodin	Ian P. Fellerman

For full biographical listings, see the Martindale-Hubbell Law Directory

---

GWILLIAM, IVARY, CHIOSSO, CAVALLI & BREWER, A PROFESSIONAL CORPORATION (AV)

1999 Harrison Street, Suite 1600, 94612-3528
Telephone: 510-832-5411
Fax: 510-832-1918
Mailing Address: P.O. Box 2079, 94604-2079
Email: Info@GICCB.com

J. Gary Gwilliam	James R. Chiosso
Eric H. Ivary	Steven R. Cavalli
	Steven J. Brewer

Marguerite E. Meade	Steven A. Reaves
	Molly Harrington

Reference: Civic Bank of Commerce, Oakland, California.

For full biographical listings, see the Martindale-Hubbell Law Directory .

VAN BLOIS, KNOWLES, SCHWARTZ & BASKIN (AV)

Suite 2245 Ordway Building, One Kaiser Plaza, 94612
Telephone: 510-444-1906
Contra Costa County 510-947-1055
Fax: 510-444-1294

MEMBERS OF FIRM

R. Lewis Van Blois	Ellen R. Schwartz
Thomas C. Knowles	Richard J. Baskin

OF COUNSEL
Charles E. Farnsworth

For full biographical listings, see the Martindale-Hubbell Law Directory

---

PALM SPRINGS, Riverside Co.

FITZGERALD & ASSOCIATES (AV)

3001 Tahquitz Canyon Way, Suite 105, 92262
Telephone: 619-325-5055
FAX: 619-327-9262

John E. FitzGerald, III

Morton Gollin

Representative Clients: Armtec Defense Products; Desert Hospital; Association of California Hospital Districts; Eldorado Country Club; Palm Springs Savings Bank; Denny's; Desert Sun; Stratamerica, Inc.; Fantasy Springs Casino; KPSI; KWXY; KNWZ; KFRG; Smoke Tree Ranch; Keystone, Inc.
Reference: Palm Desert National Bank.

For full biographical listings, see the Martindale-Hubbell Law Directory

---

PASADENA, Los Angeles Co.

FRANSCELL, STRICKLAND, ROBERTS & LAWRENCE, A PROFESSIONAL CORPORATION (AV)

Penthouse, 225 South Lake Avenue, 91101-3005
Telephone: 818-304-7830; 213-684-7830
Fax: 818-795-7460
Santa Ana, California Office: Suite 800, 401 Civic Center Drive West.
Telephone: 714-543-6511.
Fax: 714-543-6711.
Riverside, California Office: Suite 670, 3801 University Avenue.
Telephone: 909-686-1000.
Fax: 909-686-2565.

George J. Franscell	Scott D. MacLatchie
Tracy Strickland	S. Frank Harrell
(Resident, Santa Ana Office)	(Resident, Santa Ana Office)
Barbara E. Roberts	Donald C. McFarlane
(Resident, Riverside Office)	(Resident, Santa Ana Office)
David D. Lawrence	Libby Wong
Carol Ann Rohr	Cindy S. Lee

(See Next Column)

FRANSCELL, STRICKLAND, ROBERTS & LAWRENCE A PROFESSIONAL CORPORATION, *Pasadena—Continued*

　　Martin J. De Vries　　　　　　　Ann Marie Sanders
　　(Resident, Riverside Office)　　Priscilla F. Slocum
　　　　　　　Garth Matthew Drozin

For full biographical listings, see the Martindale-Hubbell Law Directory

OVERLANDER, LEWIS & RUSSELL (AV)

65 North Raymond Avenue, Suite 210, 91103
Telephone: 818-304-0500
Fax: 818-304-9750

　　Thomas F. Overlander　　　　Edwin A. Lewis
　　　　　　　Richard L. Russell, Jr.

　　Craig J. Miller　　　　　　Sherri Lynette Woods

For full biographical listings, see the Martindale-Hubbell Law Directory

LLOYD C. OWNBEY, JR. (AV)

180 South Lake Avenue, Suite 510, 91101-2683
Telephone: 818-440-5960
Fax: 818-585-9669

For full biographical listings, see the Martindale-Hubbell Law Directory

---

REDWOOD CITY,* San Mateo Co.

FISHER & PHILLIPS (AV)

A Partnership including Professional Corporations and Associations
Suite 345, Three Lagoon Drive, 94065
Telephone: 415-592-6160
Telecopier: 415-592-6385
Atlanta, Georgia Office: 1500 Resurgens Plaza, 945 East Paces Ferry Road, N.E., 30326.
Telephone: 404-231-1400.
Telecopier: 404-240-4249.
Telex: 54-2331.
Fort Lauderdale, Florida Office: Suite 2300 NationsBank Tower, One Financial Plaza, 33394.
Telephone: 954-525-4800.
Telecopier: 954-525-8739.
Newport Beach, California Office: 4675 MacArthur Court, Suite 550, 92660.
Telephone: 714-851-2424.
Telecopier: 714-851-0152.
New Orleans, Louisiana Office: 3710 Place St. Charles, 201 St. Charles Avenue, 70170.
Telephone: 504-522-3303.
Telecopier: 504-529-3850.

RESIDENT MEMBERS
Ned A. Fine　　　　　　　　John D. McLachlan
　　　　　Lynn D. Lieber
RESIDENT ASSOCIATES
Donald E. Cope　　　　　　Martha V. Howton
John Phillip Boggs　　　　　C. Trevor Skarda

Representative Clients: California Motor Car Dealers Assn.; Centex Cement; Consolidated Freightways, Inc.; The Limited; Nestle Beverage Co.; Waste Management of North America; Willamette Industries, Inc.; Zurn Nepco.

For full biographical listings, see the Martindale-Hubbell Law Directory

M. GERALD SCHWARTZBACH (AV)

601 Brewster Avenue, P.O. Box 3389, 94103
Telephone: 415-367-6811
Fax: 415-368-0367

For full biographical listings, see the Martindale-Hubbell Law Directory

---

SACRAMENTO,* Sacramento Co.

HARDY ERICH BROWN & WILSON, A PROFESSIONAL CORPORATION (AV)

1000 G Street, 95814
Telephone: 916-449-3800
Fax: 916-449-3888
Mailing Address: P.O. Box 13530, Sacramento, California, 95853-4530

　　David L. Perrault　　　　　Daniel J. Coyle
　　　　　Glenda N. Reager

　　Jay A. Resendez　　　　　Kelly F. Watson
　　　　　Kristine E. Balough

Representative Clients: American Promotional Events, Inc.; Crain Industries, Inc.; E-Z Communications; The Infinity Group; Kmart Corporation; National Education Corporation; Sacramento Baking Company; Sacramento Municipal Utility District; Swift Transportation; Tahoe City Public Utilities District.

For full biographical listings, see the Martindale-Hubbell Law Directory

---

LIVINGSTON & MATTESICH, LAW CORPORATION (AV)

1201 K Street, Suite 1100, 95814
Telephone: 916-442-1111
Fax: 916-448-1709
Email: liv-matt@gvn.net

　　Gene Livingston　　　　　Carol Livingston
　　James M. Mattesich　　　　Rebecca M. Ceniceros

　　Steven P. Belzer　　　　　Trisha M. McAlmond

Reference: Bank of California.

For full biographical listings, see the Martindale-Hubbell Law Directory

SCHACHTER, KRISTOFF, ORENSTEIN & BERKOWITZ, L.L.P. (AV)

980 9th Street, Suite 1760, 95814
Telephone: 916-442-3333
Telecopier: 916-442-2348
San Francisco, California Office: 505 Montgomery Street, 14th Floor.
Telephone: 415-391-3333.
Telecopier: 415-392-6589.
Menlo Park, California Office: 90 Middlefield Road, Suite 201.
Telephone: 415-473-1400.
Telecopier: 415-463-0346.

RESIDENT PARTNER
　　John D. Adkisson
RESIDENT ASSOCIATES
Gail Cecchettini Whaley　　　Drew R. Liebert

For full biographical listings, see the Martindale-Hubbell Law Directory

---

SAN DIEGO,* San Diego Co.

BARKER, THOMAS, McCOLLOCH & WALTERS, A PROFESSIONAL LAW CORPORATION (AV)

1455 Frazee Road, Suite 800, 92108
Telephone: 619-682-4040
Facsimile: 619-220-7056

　　Douglas H. Barker　　　　Michael D. Liuzzi
　　Anastasia E. Thomas　　　Jeffrey L. Mason
　　Michael T. McColloch　　　Jean Detmann Fisher
　　Elizabeth A. Walters　　　Joyce R. Dondanville
　　　　　Douglas V. Fettel

For full biographical listings, see the Martindale-Hubbell Law Directory

FERRIS & BRITTON, A PROFESSIONAL CORPORATION (AV)

1600 First National Bank Center, 401 West A Street, 92101
Telephone: 619-233-3131
Fax: 619-232-9316

　　Alfred G. Ferris　　　　　Steven J. Pynes
　　Christopher Q. Britton　　　Michael R. Weinstein

Representative Clients: Agouron Pharmaceuticals, Inc.; Coast Distributing Co.; Cox Communications, Inc.; Enterprise Rent-a-Car; Invitrogen Corporation; Par Broadcasting Co.; Peninsula Bank; Structural Bioinformatics, Inc.; Teleport Communications Group; Southwest Airlines.

For Complete List of Firm Personnel, See General Section

For full biographical listings, see the Martindale-Hubbell Law Directory

LUCE, FORWARD, HAMILTON & SCRIPPS LLP (AV)

A Partnership including Professional Corporations
600 West Broadway, Suite 2600, 92101
Telephone: 619-236-1414
Fax: 619-232-8311
URL: http://www.luce.com
La Jolla, California Office: 4275 Executive Square, Suite 800, 92037.
Telephone: 619-535-2639.
Fax: 619-453-2812.
Los Angeles, California Office: 777 South Figueroa, Suite 3600, 90017.
Telephone: 213-892-4992.
Fax: 213-892-7731.
San Francisco, California Office: 100 Bush Street, 20th Floor, 94104.
Telephone: 415-395-7900.
Fax: 415-395-7949.
New York, N.Y. Office: Citicorp Center, 153 East 53rd Street, 26th Floor, 10022.
Telephone: 212-754-1414.
Fax: 212-644-9727.
Chicago, Illinois Office: 180 North La Salle Street, Suite 1125, 60601.
Telephone: 312-641-0580.
Fax: 312-641-0380.

MEMBERS OF FIRM
　　George S. Howard, Jr.　　　Daniel N. Riesenberg
　　Craig A. Schloss　　　　　Kathryn A. Bernert
　　Robert A. Levy　　　　　　Mary L. Russell
　　　　　William T. Earley

(See Next Column)

LUCE, FORWARD, HAMILTON & SCRIPPS LLP—*Continued*

ASSOCIATES

Maria C. Heredia	Kelly Capen Douglas
Richard J. Bergstrom	Julie A. Vogelzang
Tami Johnson Penner	Leticia Olivarez Cadena

For Complete List of Firm Personnel, See General Section

For full biographical listings, see the Martindale-Hubbell Law Directory

OLINS, FOERSTER & HAYES (AV)

A Legal Liability Partnership including Professional Corporation
2214 Second Avenue, 92101
Telephone: 619-238-1601
Fax: 619-238-1613
Email: ofh@cts.com
Santa Ana, California Office: 1314 West Fifth Street, Suite C, 92703.
Telephone: 714-836-9777.
Fax: 714-954-1156.
Riverside, California Office: 4361 Latham Street, Suite 240, 92501.
Telephone: 909-683-2485.
Fax: 909-683-1064.

MEMBERS OF FIRM

Douglas F. Olins	Barrett J. Foerster (A P.C.)
Dennis J. Hayes	

ASSOCIATES

Laura H. Miller	Karen L. Cote
John C. Zucconi	(Resident, Riverside Office)
Barbara J. Ginsberg	
(Resident, Santa Ana Office)	

Representative Clients: United Food and Commercial Workers International Union, AFL-CIO; United Food and Commercial Workers, Locals 1036 and 588; American Federation of State, County and Municipal Employees, Local 127; American Postal Workers Union, California Area Local; American Postal Workers Union, San Diego Chapter; Association of Orange County Deputy Sheriffs; Sacramento County Deputy Sheriffs Assn.; Santa Ana Firemen's Benevolent Association; San Bernardino Public Employees Association.

For full biographical listings, see the Martindale-Hubbell Law Directory

STOKES & MURPHY (AV)

3131 Camino del Rio North Suite 320, 92108
Telephone: 619-285-8181
Fax: 619-285-8168
Atlanta, Georgia Office: 3593 Hemphill Street, P.O. Box 87468.
Telephone: 404-766-0076.
Fax: 404-766-8823.
Pittsburgh, Pennsylvania Office: Foster Plaza, 680 Andersen Drive.
Telephone: 412-937-3277.
Fax: 412-920-5751.

Robert L. Murphy

RESIDENT ASSOCIATES

Tricia D. Mading	Paul F. Sorrentino

For full biographical listings, see the Martindale-Hubbell Law Directory

SAN FRANCISCO,* San Francisco Co.

BIANCO & MURPHY (AV)

44 Montgomery Street, Suite 4010, 94104
Telephone: 415-362-3344
Telecopier: 415-986-5271
Email: LAWRLB@AOL.COM

MEMBERS OF FIRM

Robert L. Bianco	Stephen M. Murphy

ASSOCIATES

Joseph P. Meyers	Gregory O. Bianco
Christopher M. Windle	

For full biographical listings, see the Martindale-Hubbell Law Directory

BREON, O'DONNELL, MILLER, BROWN & DANNIS (AV)

19th Floor, Stevenson Place, 71 Stevenson Street, 94105
Telephone: 415-543-4111
Fax: 415-543-4384
Palos Verdes Estates, California Office: Suite 3A, 2550 Via Tejon, 90274.
Telephone: 310-373-6857.
FAX: 310-373-6808.
Salinas, California Office: Suite H120, 17842 Moro Road, Suite F120, 93907.
Telephone: 408-663-0470.

(See Next Column)

MEMBERS OF FIRM

Keith V. Breon	Emi R. Uyehara
Margaret E. O'Donnell	Bridget A. Flanagan
David G. Miller (Resident, Palos Verdes Estates Office)	Nancy B. Bourne
	Kathryn Luhe
Priscilla Brown	Marilyn J. Cleveland
Gregory J. Dannis	Laurie S. Juengert

Joan Birdt (Resident, Palos Verdes Estates Office)	Aaron Kaufmann
	SueAnn Salmon Evans
David A. Wolf	(Resident, Palos Verdes
Claudia L. Madrigal	Estates Office)
Peter W. Sturges	Janet L. Mueller (Resident,
Laurie E. Reynolds	Palos Verdes Estates Office)
Guy A. Bryant	Ivette Peña (Resident, Palos
Jane Mitchell Weston	Verdes Estates Office)

SPECIAL COUNSEL

Martha Buell Scott	Marilyn Kaplan

Representative Clients: Monterey Peninsula Unified School Dist.; Mt. Diablo Unified School Dist.; Palo Alto Unified School Dist.; Santa Cruz City Schools.

For full biographical listings, see the Martindale-Hubbell Law Directory

BRONSON, BRONSON & McKINNON LLP (AV)

A Partnership including Professional Corporations
505 Montgomery Street, 94111-2514
Telephone: 415-986-4200
Fax: 415-982-1394
Telex: 255921 KINBR UR
Email: moreinfo@bronson.com *URL:* http://www.bronson.com
Los Angeles, California Office: 444 South Flower Street, 24th Floor.
Telephone: 213-627-2000.
San Jose, California Office: 10 Almaden Boulevard, Suite 600.
Telephone: 408-293-0599.

MEMBERS OF FIRM

Lynn A. Bersch	Edwin L. Currey, Jr.
Patricia H. Cullison	Gilmore F. Diekmann, Jr.
	Robert William Tollen

RESIDENT ASSOCIATES

Erika C. Collins	Mary Bossart Halfpenny
	Debora A. Morrison

For Complete List of Firm Personnel, See General Section

For full biographical listings, see the Martindale-Hubbell Law Directory

CORBETT & KANE, A PROFESSIONAL CORPORATION (AV)

Citicorp Center, One Sansome Street, Suite 1900, 94104
Telephone: 415-956-4100
Email: attorney@cklaw.com *URL:* http://www.cklaw.com
Oakland, California Office: 2000 Powell Street, Suite 1450 (Emeryville).
Telephone: 510-547-2434;
Fax: 510-658-5014.

Judith Droz Keyes	Tim J. Emert
Mary Maloney Roberts	Denise M. DeRose
Sharon J. Grodin	Ian P. Fellerman

For full biographical listings, see the Martindale-Hubbell Law Directory

LAFAYETTE, KUMAGAI & CLARKE (AV)

100 Spear Street, Suite 400, 94105
Telephone: 415-357-4600
Facsimile: 415-357-4605

MEMBERS OF FIRM

Gary T. Lafayette	Kevin M. Clarke
	Susan T. Kumagai

ASSOCIATE

Valerie A. Andersen

For full biographical listings, see the Martindale-Hubbell Law Directory

LIEFF, CABRASER, HEIMANN & BERNSTEIN, LLP (AV)

Embarcadero Center West, 30th Floor, 275 Battery Street, 94111
Telephone: 415-956-1000
Telecopier: 415-956-1008
Email: mail@lchb.com

Robert L. Lieff	Michael F. Ram
Elizabeth J. Cabraser	Joseph R. Saveri
Richard M. Heimann	Donald C. Arbitblit
William Bernstein	Robert J. Nelson
William B. Hirsch	Jacqueline E. Mottek
James M. Finberg	Morris A. Ratner
Karen E. Karpen	Melanie M. Piech

(See Next Column)

LIEFF, CABRASER, HEIMANN & BERNSTEIN LLP, *San Francisco—Continued*

Richard L. Akel	Anthony K. Lee
Christine J. Anderson	Fabrice V. Nijhof
Kelly M. Dermody	Trina N. Parker
Eric B. Fastiff	Jonathan D. Selbin
Richard M. Franco	Mark N. Todzo

Heather A. Woodard

For full biographical listings, see the Martindale-Hubbell Law Directory

THE LUCAS LAW FIRM (AV)

Embarcadero West, Suite 1450, 275 Battery Street, 94111
Telephone: 415-434-3100
FAX: 415-434-0300

Kathleen M. Lucas

ASSOCIATE

Thomas E. Duckworth

For full biographical listings, see the Martindale-Hubbell Law Directory

MORGENSTEIN & JUBELIRER, LLP (AV)

A Partnership including a Professional Corporation
One Market Plaza, Spear Street Tower, 32nd Floor, 94105
Telephone: 415-896-0666
Fax: 415-896-5592
Email: jubelirer@aol.com

MEMBERS OF FIRM

Marvin D. Morgenstein (P.C.)	Rocky N. Unruh
Eliot S. Jubelirer	James L. McGinnis
Lee Ann Huntington	Charles W. LaGrave
Jean L. Bertrand	Wendi J. Berkowitz
Jeffrey R. Williams	John S. Worden
James R. Balich	Robert B. Mullen

OF COUNSEL
Laurie K. Anger

Lewis D. Barr	Natasha L. Golding
David H. Bromfield	Stephen M. Hankins
Michael "Cael" S. Davis	Simon E. Kisch
Roberta Nicol Dempster	John J. Petry

Bruce A. Wagman

For full biographical listings, see the Martindale-Hubbell Law Directory

ROGERS, JOSEPH, O'DONNELL & QUINN, A PROFESSIONAL CORPORATION (AV)

311 California Street, 94104
Telephone: 415-956-2828
Fax: 415-956-6457

Allan J. Joseph	Anna M. Rossi
Martin Quinn	Connie M. Teevan
Neil H. O'Donnell	Allen Samelson
Margot Wenger	Suzanne M. Mellard
Pamela Phillips	Neil H. Weinstein
Renée D. Wasserman	Patricia A. Meagher

Merri A. Baldwin

OF COUNSEL

Joseph W. Rogers	William Bennett Turner

Kyra A. Subbotin

David F. Innis	Ian K. Sweedler
Jennifer M. Kawamura	Matthew D. Levett
Sean M. SeLegue	E. Sean McLoughlin

Aaron P. Silberman

SPECIAL COUNSEL

Valerie Ackerman

For full biographical listings, see the Martindale-Hubbell Law Directory

ROSEN, BIEN & ASARO (AV)

Eighth Floor, 155 Montgomery Street, 94104
Telephone: 415-433-6830
Fax: 415-433-7104
Email: rba@rbalaw.com

Sanford Jay Rosen	Michael W. Bien

Andrea G. Asaro

Thomas Nolan	William H.D. Fernholz
Donna Petrine	Doris Y. Ng
M.J. Tony Paikeday	A. Marie Villafaña

For full biographical listings, see the Martindale-Hubbell Law Directory

SCHACHTER, KRISTOFF, ORENSTEIN & BERKOWITZ, L.L.P. (AV)

505 Montgomery Street, 14th Floor, 94111
Telephone: 415-391-3333
Telecopier: 415-392-6589
Sacramento, California Office: 980 9th Street, Suite 1760.
Telephone: 916-442-3333.
Telecopier: 916-442-2348.
Menlo Park, California Office: 90 Middlefield Road, Suite 201.
Telephone: 415-473-1400.
Telecopier: 415-463-0346.

MEMBERS OF FIRM

Victor Schachter	Gale Heuman Borden
Robert P. Kristoff	(Resident, Menlo Park Office)
Morton H. Orenstein	John F. Penrose
Alan R. Berkowitz	John D. Adkisson
Thomas E. Geidt	(Resident, Sacramento Office)
Ronald J. Souza	Christopher E. Cobey
Steven R. Blackburn	Daniel A. Briskin

ASSOCIATES

Allen M. Kato	Sharon Zezima
Lisa Bradley	Drew R. Liebert
Joseph D. Miller	(Resident, Sacramento Office)
Chandler A. Rand	Paul D. Warenski
Gail Cecchettini Whaley	Alia Samad-Salameh
(Resident, Sacramento Office)	Rochelle C. Holzman

For full biographical listings, see the Martindale-Hubbell Law Directory

SIGERMAN & WEGLEY (AV)

100 Bush Street Suite 2000, 94104
Telephone: 415-989-0715
Facsimile: 415-989-1639

Jon B. Sigerman	Reese W. Wegley

For full biographical listings, see the Martindale-Hubbell Law Directory

SAN JOSE,* Santa Clara Co.

BOHN, BENNION & NILAND (AV)

Fairmont Plaza, 50 West San Fernando Street Suite 1020, 95113
Telephone: 408-279-4222
Fax: 408-295-2222

MEMBERS OF FIRM

Robert H. Bohn	David J. Bennion

Edward L. Niland

ASSOCIATE
Robert H. Bohn, Jr.

OF COUNSEL
Jeffrey W. Rickard

For full biographical listings, see the Martindale-Hubbell Law Directory

McMANIS, FAULKNER & MORGAN (AV)

160 West Santa Clara Street, 10th Floor, 95113
Telephone: 408-279-8700
Fax: 408-279-3244; 408-279-0494
Email: mfm@mfmlaw.com

MEMBERS OF FIRM

James McManis	William Faulkner

Donelle Morgan

ASSOCIATES

Nora Rousso	Michael Reedy
Lisa Herrick	Douglas Watanabe

Kelly McHaffie

For full biographical listings, see the Martindale-Hubbell Law Directory

McPHARLIN, SPRINKLES & THOMAS, LLP (AV)

Ten Almaden Boulevard, Suite 1460, 95113
Telephone: 408-293-1900
Fax: 408-293-1999

MEMBERS OF FIRM

Linda Hendrix McPharlin	Mary Lee Malysz
Catherine C. Sprinkles	Paul M. Hogan
N. David Thomas	Paul S. Avilla

For full biographical listings, see the Martindale-Hubbell Law Directory

SAN MATEO, San Mateo Co.

QUADROS & JOHNSON (AV)

1400 Fashion Island Boulevard, Suite 800, 94404
Telephone: 415-377-4300
Telecopier: 415-573-1387

Katherine M. Quadros	Benjamin A. Johnson

SENIOR ASSOCIATE
Kenyon Mark Lee

(See Next Column)

QUADROS & JOHNSON—*Continued*
ASSOCIATES

Leslie A. Eberhardt   Michael D. Wood
OF COUNSEL
Arthur L. Hillman, Jr.

Representative Clients: Anning Johnson Co. (national gypsum board and asbestos abatement contractor); Bechtel Corporation; Blue Cross of California (major health benefits insurer); Browning-Ferris Industries, Inc. (national waste management company); Los Angeles County Metropolitan Transportation Authority; Mutual Savings & Loan; Pacific Gas and Electric Co.; Safeway, Inc.; Santa Clara County Transit District; Sasco Electric.

For full biographical listings, see the Martindale-Hubbell Law Directory

---

SAN RAFAEL, * Marin Co.

RAGGHIANTI • FREITAS • MONTOBBIO • WALLACE LLP (AV)

874 Fourth Street, Suite D, 94901
Telephone: 415-453-9433
Fax: 415-453-8269

Gary T. Ragghianti   J. Randolph Wallace
David P. Freitas   Patrick M. Macias
J. Mark Montobbio   Robert F. Epstein
John Ralph Thomas

For full biographical listings, see the Martindale-Hubbell Law Directory

---

SANTA ANA, * Orange Co.

FERRUZZO & FERRUZZO (AV)

A Partnership of Professional Corporations
2114 North Broadway, 92706
Telephone: 714-834-9322
Telecopier: 714-834-9358

MEMBERS OF FIRM

Thomas G. Ferruzzo (A   James K. Leese (A Professional
Professional Corporation)   Corporation)
James J. Ferruzzo (A
Professional Corporation)

ASSOCIATES

John R. Pelle   Maria Ann Newkirk
Dirk E. Petchul   Paul A. Madruga
Gregory J. Ferruzzo   Lisa L. Schultz
OF COUNSEL
M. Susan Watson

For full biographical listings, see the Martindale-Hubbell Law Directory

---

HORTON BARBARO & REILLY (AV)

A Partnership including Professional Corporations
Second Floor, 200 North Main Street, 92701
Telephone: 714-835-2122
Fax: 714-973-4892
Email: HBR@Hortonetal.com *URL:* http://www.Hortonetal.com

MEMBERS OF FIRM

Jay Cordell Horton (A   Geoffrey S. Gray
Professional Corporation)   John R. Hanna
Frank P. Barbaro (A   William O. Humphreys
Professional Corporation)   Karen L. Karavatos
Ned P. Reilly (A Professional John E. O'Brien, Jr.
Corporation)

ASSOCIATES

Malena R. LeClair   Timothy V. Kassouni
Robert J. Younger   Richard E. Donahoo

For full biographical listings, see the Martindale-Hubbell Law Directory

---

HERBERT A. MOSS (AV)

1851 East First Street, Suite 800, 92705
Telephone: 714-547-7712
Fax: 714-543-8406

For full biographical listings, see the Martindale-Hubbell Law Directory

---

SANTA BARBARA, * Santa Barbara Co.

ARCHBALD & SPRAY (AV)

505 Bath Street, 93101
Telephone: 805-564-2070
Telecopier: 805-564-2081
Email: arch@silcom.com

MEMBERS OF FIRM

Malcolm Archbald (Retired)   Karen T. Burgett
Joseph L. Spray (1927-1985)   Edwin K. Loskamp
Kenneth L. Moes   Wm. Brennan Lynch
J. William McLafferty   Michael A. Colton
Douglas B. Large   Ann Gormican Anderson

(See Next Column)

SENIOR ATTORNEYS

Peri Maziarz   Katherine H. Bower
ASSOCIATE
Cheryl A. Shaw
OF COUNSEL
John W. Warnock

Representative Clients: California Thrift & Loan; Exxon Corporation; Isla Vista Recreation & Park District; City of Lompoc; Mission Industries; Pleasant Travel Service, Inc.; Tandy Corporation; The Limited; Santa Barbara Metropolitan Transit District; Santa Barbara Regional Health Authority.

For full biographical listings, see the Martindale-Hubbell Law Directory

---

SANTA MONICA, Los Angeles Co.

FOGEL, FELDMAN, OSTROV, RINGLER & KLEVENS, A LAW CORPORATION (AV)

1620 26th Street, Suite 100 South, 90404-4040
Telephone: 310-453-6711
Fax: 310-828-2191

Daniel Fogel (1923-1991)   Joel N. Klevens
Lester G. Ostrov   Robert M. Turner
Larry R. Feldman   Jerome L. Ringler
Richard L. Rosett

Stephen D. Rothschild   Toni Martinson
Leighanne Lake   David Bricker
Thomas H. Peters   Mark S. Eisenberg
OF COUNSEL
Carol S. May

Reference: Republic Bank of California, Beverly Hills, California.

For full biographical listings, see the Martindale-Hubbell Law Directory

---

HAIGHT, BROWN & BONESTEEL (AV)

A Partnership including Professional Corporations
1620 26th Street, Suite 4000 North, P.O. Box 680, 90404
Telephone: 310-449-6000
Telecopier: 310-829-5117
Telex: 705837
Santa Ana, California Office: Suite 900, 5 Hutton Centre Drive.
Telephone: 714-754-1100.
Telecopier: 714-754-0826.
Riverside, California Office: 3750 University Avenue, Suite 650.
Telephone: 909-341-8300.
Fax: 909-341-8309.
San Francisco, California Office: 201 Sansome Street, Suite 300.
Telephone: 415-986-7700.
Fax: 415-986-6954.

MEMBERS OF FIRM

Harold Hansen Brown (A   George Christensen
Professional Corporation)   Neil G. McNiece

For Complete List of Firm Personnel, See General Section

For full biographical listings, see the Martindale-Hubbell Law Directory

---

SANTA ROSA, * Sonoma Co.

BELDEN, ABBEY, WEITZENBERG & KELLY, A PROFESSIONAL CORPORATION (AV)

1105 North Dutton Avenue, P.O. Box 1566, 95402
Telephone: 707-542-5050
Telecopier: 707-542-2589

Thomas P. Kelly, Jr.   Richard W. Abbey

Representative Clients: Exchange Bank of Santa Rosa; Westamerica Bank; North Bay Title Co.; Northwestern Title Security Co.; Geyser Peak Winery; Santa Rosa City School District; Sonoma National Bank; Arrowwood Vineyards & Winery; Arthur & DeVincenzi Concrete; Friedman Bros. Hardware, Inc.

For Complete List of Firm Personnel, See General Section

For full biographical listings, see the Martindale-Hubbell Law Directory

---

VENTURA, * Ventura Co.

FAIRFIELD, STRAUSS, URITZ & KINIGSTEIN, A PROFESSIONAL CORPORATION (AV)

290 Maple Court, Suite 200, 93003
Telephone: 805-644-7458
Fax: 805-644-4325
Email: mail@venturalaw.com *URL:* http://www.venturalaw.com

William D. Fairfield   Curt W. Uritz
Anthony R. Strauss   Terry Kinigstein

(See Next Column)

FAIRFIELD, STRAUSS, URITZ & KINIGSTEIN A PROFESSIONAL CORPORATION,
Ventura—Continued

Wilfred J. Freeman   Bruce P. Crary

For full biographical listings, see the Martindale-Hubbell Law Directory

TAYLOR MCCORD, A LAW CORPORATION (AV)

721 East Main Street, P.O. Box 1477, 93002
Telephone: 805-648-4700
Fax: 805-653-6124

Richard L. Taylor   Robert L. McCord, Jr.
    David L. Praver

Patrick Cherry   Susan D. Siple
    Rebbecca F. Calderwood
LEGAL SUPPORT PERSONNEL
PARALEGALS
Stephanie Gibson   Adele Rubino
    Diane Lovato

For full biographical listings, see the Martindale-Hubbell Law Directory

COLORADO

DENVER,* Denver Co.

DIXON AND SNOW, P.C. (AV)

425 South Cherry Street, Suite 1000, 80222
Telephone: 303-394-2200
FAX: 303-394-2340

Jerre W. Dixon   Rod W. Snow
    Steven Janiszewski

For full biographical listings, see the Martindale-Hubbell Law Directory

DUFFORD & BROWN, P.C. (AV)

1700 Broadway, Suite 1700, 80290-1701
Telephone: 303-861-8013
Facsimile: 303-832-3804
Affiliated Office: Solomon, Pearl, Blum & Quinn, L.L.P., New York, NY
and Denver, Colorado.

Thomas G. Brown   David W. Furgason
    Scott J. Mikulecky

Thomas E. J. Hazard
SPECIAL COUNSEL
Lawrence D. Stone

Representative Clients: CF&I Steel, L.P.; Reorganized CF&I Steel Corporation; Reorganized Colorado & Wyoming Railway Company; Colorado Permanente Medical Group, P.C.; Colorado Compensation Insurance Authority.

For Complete List of Firm Personnel, See General Section

For full biographical listings, see the Martindale-Hubbell Law Directory

GREGSON AND PIXLER, P.C. (AV)

1775 Mellon Financial Center, 1775 Sherman Street, 80203
Telephone: 303-861-2702
Fax: 303-861-2706

Ronald E. Gregson   Hugh S. Pixler

Bradley M. Knepper   Jennifer J. Gifford

For full biographical listings, see the Martindale-Hubbell Law Directory

LARRY F. HOBBS, P.C. (AV)

Colorado State Bank Building, 1600 Broadway, Suite 2375, 80202
Telephone: 303-861-2300
Telecopier: 303-861-2824

Larry F. Hobbs

For full biographical listings, see the Martindale-Hubbell Law Directory

HOLME ROBERTS & OWEN LLP (AV)

Suite 4100, 1700 Lincoln, 80203
Telephone: 303-861-7000
Telecopier: 303-866-0200
Email: hro@hro.com *URL:* http://www.hro.com
Boulder, Colorado Office: Suite 400, 1401 Pearl Street.
Telephone: 303-444-5955.
Telecopier: 303-444-1063.
Colorado Springs, Colorado Office: Suite 1300, 90 South Cascade Avenue.
Telephone: 719-473-3800.
Telecopier: 719-633-1518.
Salt Lake City, Utah Office: Suite 1100, 111 East Broadway.
Telephone: 801-521-5800.
Telecopier: 801-521-9639.
London, England Office: Mellier House, 26a Albemarle Street.
Telephone: 44-171-499-8776.
Telecopier: 44-171-499-7769.
Moscow, Russia Office: Kosmodamianskaya Nab. #52/1, Suite 9100, 113054.
Telephone: 7095-961-3000.
Telecopier: 7095-961-3001.
Kiev, Ukraine Office: Terestchenkovskaya #19, Suite 2, 252004.
Telephone: 380-44-224-1348.
Telecopier: 380-44-224-4986.

PARTNERS OF FIRM

David T. Mitzner   David B. Wilson
John R. Webb   Mary Hurley Stuart
Richard L. Nagl   Kevin P. Block (Managing
 (Colorado Springs Office) Partner, Kiev Office)
Carolyn E. Daniels   Edwin P. Aro
K. Preston Oade, Jr.   Steven C. Bednar
Katherine Jean Peck   (Salt Lake City Office)
Brent E. Rychener   Christopher Cipoletti
 (Colorado Springs Office) (Colorado Springs Office)
Susan E. Duffey Campbell
 (Colorado Springs Office)

SPECIAL COUNSEL
David H. Goldberg
ASSOCIATES

Daniel P. Maguire   Timothy G. Pfeifer
Deborah S. Menkins   (Colorado Springs Office)
 (Colorado Springs Office) Sharon A. Thomas
Felicity A. O'Herron   (Colorado Springs Office)

For Complete List of Firm Personnel, See General Section

For full biographical listings, see the Martindale-Hubbell Law Directory

LONG & JAUDON, P.C. (AV)

The Bailey Mansion, 1600 Ogden Street, 80218-1414
Telephone: 303-832-1122
FAX: 303-832-1348

James A. Dierker   Gary B. Blum
    Margaret J. Walton

Representative Clients: St. Joseph Hospital; King Soopers, Inc. (Dillon Companies, Inc.).

For Complete List of Firm Personnel, See General Section

For full biographical listings, see the Martindale-Hubbell Law Directory

LAW OFFICES OF JOHN W. MCKENDREE (AV)

Creswell Mansion, 1244 Grant Street, 80203
Telephone: 303-861-8906
Fax: 303-861-7773

John W. McKendree
ASSOCIATE
Elizabeth G. McKendree

Counsel For: Colorado-Wyoming Teamsters Construction Workers Local Union No. 13; United Brotherhood of Carpenters and Joiners of America Local 1583; International Federation of Petroleum and Chemical Workers; International Labor Relations Services, Inc.; Teamsters Local 13 Health and Welfare Trust Fund; Teamsters Local 13 Vacation Trust Fund; Colorado Centennial District Counsel of Carpenters; Boilermakers Lodge 101; Brakemans' Association of America; Boilermakers National Pension Trust.

For full biographical listings, see the Martindale-Hubbell Law Directory

TODD J. MCNAMARA, P.C. (AV)

1700 Lincoln Street, Suite 3850, 80203
Telephone: 303-830-7924
Fax: 303-830-2626

Todd J. McNamara

Margaret Brown Funk

For full biographical listings, see the Martindale-Hubbell Law Directory

Denver—Continued

OTTEN, JOHNSON, ROBINSON, NEFF & RAGONETTI, P.C. (AV)

950 Seventeenth Street, 16th Floor, 80202
Telephone: 303-825-8400
Telecopier: 303-825-6525

William F. Schoeberlein	P. Kathleen Lower
Lawrence W. Marquess	Todd A. Fredrickson
Edward P. Timmins	Darin Mackender
	Kathryn A. Plonsky

Representative Clients: Aetna Life Insurance Co.; The Broe Companies; Inc.; Colorado National Bank; Connecticut General Life Insurance Co.; First Nationwide Bank; Homart Development Co.; Land Title Guarantee Co.; Trizec Corporation Ltd.; U.S. West Communications, Inc.; The Western Sugar Co.

For Complete List of Firm Personnel, See General Section

For full biographical listings, see the Martindale-Hubbell Law Directory

---

SEMPLE & JACKSON, P.C. (AV)

The Chancery Building, Suite 1603, 1120 Lincoln Street, 80203
Telephone: 303-595-0941
Fax: 303-861-9608

Martin Semple	Michael H. Jackson
	Patrick B. Mooney

Representative Clients: Denver Public Schools; Adams County School District No. 50; City of Aurora; Denver Center for the Performing Arts; Intermountain Rural Electric Association; City of Thornton; Aspen Imaging International, Inc.; National Printing & Packaging Corp.; City of Englewood.

For full biographical listings, see the Martindale-Hubbell Law Directory

---

SHERMAN & HOWARD L.L.C. (AV)

Attorneys and Counselors at Law
633 Seventeenth Street, Suite 3000, 80202
Telephone: 303-297-2900
Telecopier: 303-298-0940
Colorado Springs, Colorado Office: Suite 1500, 90 South Cascade Avenue, 80903.
Telephone: 719-475-2440.
Las Vegas, Nevada Office: Swendseid & Stern a member in Sherman & Howard L.L.C., 317 Sixth Street, 89101.
Telephone: 702-387-6073.
Reno, Nevada Office: Swendseid & Stern, a member in Sherman & Howard L.L.C., 50 West Liberty Street, Suite 660, 89501.
Telephone: 702-323-1980.

James E. Hautzinger	Theodore A. Olsen
E. Lee Dale	Edmond F. Noel, Jr.
Charles W. Newcom	N. Dawn Webber
Raymond M. Deeny	(Colorado Springs Office)
(Colorado Springs Office)	Glenn H. Schlabs
W.V. Bernie Siebert	(Colorado Springs Office)
	Andrew W. Volin

Wayne W. Williams	Jennifer R. George
(Colorado Springs Office)	(Colorado Springs Office)
Donna K. McNamara	Paul J. McCue
Monica T. Langley	Heather Fox Vickles
Leslie A. Petri	Jennifer M. Mardosz

Representative Clients: AT&T Corp.; Newmont Gold Corp.; Rockwell International Corp.; Public Service Company of Colorado.

For Complete List of Firm Personnel, See General Section

For full biographical listings, see the Martindale-Hubbell Law Directory

---

STETTNER, MILLER AND COHN, P.C. (AV)

Lawrence Street Center, Suite 1000, 1380 Lawrence Street, 80204-2058
Telephone: 303-534-0273
Fax: 303-534-5036
Colorado Springs Office: The Woodmen Center. 1130 West Woodmen Road. 80910.
Telephone: 719-598-0590.

Kenneth R. Stettner	John S. Finn
Robert R. Miller	Bruce C. Anderson
Robert I. Cohn	William C. Berger
Katherine Ann Raabe	Shannon Way Roberts

Representative Clients: Associated General Contractors of Colorado, Building Chapter, Inc.; The Aetna Casualty and Surety Co.; Craig Hospital; McDonald's Corp; Hensel Phelps Construction Co.; Adams County School District No. 14; Federal Express Corp.; McLane Co., Inc.; Health One; Wal-Mart Stores, Inc.

For full biographical listings, see the Martindale-Hubbell Law Directory

---

GOLDEN, * Jefferson Co.

BRADLEY, CAMPBELL, CARNEY & MADSEN, PROFESSIONAL CORPORATION (AV)

1717 Washington Avenue, 80401-1994
Telephone: 303-278-3300
Fax: 303-278-3379
Email: firm@bccm.com

Earl K. Madsen	Russell Carparelli

Counsel for: Coors Brewing Co.; Coors Ceramics Co.; Evergreen National Bank, Evergreen, Colorado; Clear Creek National Bank, Georgetown, Colorado; ASARCO, Inc.; Morrison-Knudsen; Westinghouse Electric Corp.
Local Counsel for: Public Service Company of Colorado.
Reference: Colorado National Bank, Denver, Colorado.

For Complete List of Firm Personnel, See General Section

For full biographical listings, see the Martindale-Hubbell Law Directory

---

CONNECTICUT

HARTFORD, * Hartford Co.

KAINEN, STARR, GARFIELD, WRIGHT & ESCALERA, P.C. (AV)

55 Farmington Avenue, 06105
Telephone: 860-251-6686
FAX: 860-251-6687

Burton Kainen	Diana Garfield
Gary S. Starr	Susan M. Wright
	Miguel A. Escalera, Jr.

Sheldon D. Myers	Jennifer L. Dixon
Vaughan Finn	Michael Liam O'Connor

For full biographical listings, see the Martindale-Hubbell Law Directory

---

SHIPMAN & GOODWIN LLP (AV)

One American Row, 06103-2819
Telephone: 860-251-5000
Telecopier: 860-251-5099
Email: first initial last name @goodwin.com
Email: www@goodwin.com *URL:* http://shipman-goodwin.com
Lakeville, Connecticut Office: Porter Street.
Telephone: 203-435-2539.
Stamford, Connecticut Office: One Landmark Square.
Telephone: 203-324-8100.

MEMBERS OF FIRM

Paul W. Orth	Thomas B. Mooney
Brian Clemow	Saranne P. Murray
Brenda A. Eckert	Linda L. Yoder
	Richard A. Mills, Jr.

ASSOCIATES

Patrick J. McHale	Karen H. Simmonds
Susan C. Freedman	Natalie W. Welsh
Christine L. Chinni	Andrew J. Cohen
Kimberly A. Mango	Raymond M. Bernstein
Scott D. Macdonald	Henry J. Zaccardi
Gerald P. Stergio	Jennifer Brown Mailly

Representative Labor Clients: American Red Cross; Blue Cross & Blue Shield of Connecticut; City of Bristol; Institute of Living; Keeney Manufacturing Co.; Stamford Board of Education; City of Danbury; Trinity College; West Hartford Board of Education.

For Complete List of Firm Personnel, See General Section

For full biographical listings, see the Martindale-Hubbell Law Directory

---

SIEGEL, O'CONNOR, SCHIFF & ZANGARI, P.C. (AV)

150 Trumbull Street, 06103
Telephone: 860-727-8900
New Haven, Connecticut Office: 171 Orange Street, P.O. Drawer 906.
Telephone: 203-789-0001.

Hugh W. Cuthbertson (Resident, New Haven, Connecticut Office)	Peter A. Janus (Resident)
	Richard D. O'Connor (Resident)
Frederick L. Dorsey (Resident, New Haven, Connecticut Office)	Edward F. O'Donnell, Jr. (Resident)
	Robert J. Percy (Resident)
Glenn A. Duhl (Resident, New Haven, Connecticut Office)	Donald W. Strickland (Resident)

OF COUNSEL

Jay S. Siegel (Resident)

(See Next Column)

SIEGEL, O'CONNOR, SCHIFF & ZANGARI P.C., *Hartford—Continued*

Michael J. Eagen (Resident)	Dana Shaw MacKinnon
Christine E. Farrell (Resident)	(Resident)
Nicholas J. Grello, Jr. (Resident)	John M. Simon (Resident, New
George J. Kelly, Jr. (Resident)	Haven, Connecticut Office)
Richard F. Vitarelli (Resident)	

For full biographical listings, see the Martindale-Hubbell Law Directory

---

SOROKIN SOROKIN GROSS HYDE & WILLIAMS P.C. (AV)

One Corporate Center, 06103
Telephone: 860-525-6645
Fax: 860-522-1781
Simsbury, Connecticut Office: 730 Hopmeadow Street.
Telephone: 860-651-9348.
Rocky Hill, Connecticut Office: 2360 Main Street.
Telephone: 860-563-9305.
Fax: 860-529-6931.

Andrew C. Glassman	Richard C. Robinson

Sharon Kowal Freilich	Joshua A. Hawks-Ladds

For Complete List of Firm Personnel, See General Section

For full biographical listings, see the Martindale-Hubbell Law Directory

---

WILLIAM S. ZEMAN (AV)

Capitol Suites, 21 Oak Street, Suite 207, 06106
Telephone: 860-297-6505
Fax: 860-246-3727
Mailing Address: P.O. Box 270067, West Hartford, Connecticut,
06127-0067

For full biographical listings, see the Martindale-Hubbell Law Directory

---

NEW BRITAIN, *Hartford Co.*

EISENBERG, ANDERSON, MICHALIK & LYNCH (AV)

136 West Main Street, P.O. Box 2950, 06050-2950
Telephone: 860-229-4855; 225-8403
Fax: 860-223-4026
Email: KSLATERO@counsel.com
Email: ELYNCHOO@Counsel.com

Harold J. Eisenberg (1906-1995)

MEMBERS OF FIRM

Stephen J. Anderson	Charles W. Bauer
Robert A. Michalik	Dennis G. Ciccarillo
Edward T. Lynch, Jr.	Paul T. Czepiga
Carl R. Ficks, Jr.	

ASSOCIATES

Pamela Reardon Reynolds	Thomas A. Pavano
Bruce A. Zawodniak	Kenneth R. Slater, Jr.
JoAnn Centrilla-Silvia	Jeffrey F. Gostyla

Representative Clients: Apple Health Care; Berlin Steel Construction Co.; CIGNA; Connecticut Employees Union "Independent"; Fleet Bank, N.A.; ITT Sealectro; Magson Uniform Corp.; TILCON Connecticut Inc.

For full biographical listings, see the Martindale-Hubbell Law Directory

---

NEW HAVEN,* *New Haven Co.*

LYNCH, TRAUB, KEEFE AND ERRANTE, A PROFESSIONAL CORPORATION (AV)

52 Trumbull Street, P.O. Box 1612, 06506
Telephone: 203-787-0275
Fax: 203-782-0278
Email: ltke@snet.com *URL:* http://www.ltke.com

Stephen I. Traub	Donn A. Swift
Hugh F. Keefe	Charles E. Tiernan, III
Steven J. Errante	Robert W. Lynch
John J. Keefe, Jr.	Richard W. Lynch
John M. Walsh, Jr.	

Suzanne L. McAlpine	Lee Kennedy Tiernan
Christopher M. Licari	William F. Clark
Eric P. Smith	James A. Mongillo

OF COUNSEL
William C. Lynch

Local Counsel for: Transport Insurance Co., Dallas, Texas; American Trucking Associations; Roadway Express, Inc., Akron, Ohio; A.R.A. Philadelphia, Penn.; Consolidated Freightways, Menlo Park, California; Ogden Corp.; The Hauler Work.
Labor Counsel: Coca-Cola, U.S.A., Atlanta, Georgia (Private Truck Operation); The Dow Chemical Co.; Cincinnati Milacron.

For full biographical listings, see the Martindale-Hubbell Law Directory

---

ROSEN & DOLAN, P.C. (AV)

400 Orange Street, 06511
Telephone: 203-787-3513
Fax: 203-789-1605
Email: davidrosen@counsel.com
Email: spincus@counsel.com

David N. Rosen

Stephen M. Pincus

Reference: Peoples Bank.

For Complete List of Firm Personnel, See General Section

For full biographical listings, see the Martindale-Hubbell Law Directory

---

SIEGEL, O'CONNOR, SCHIFF & ZANGARI, P.C. (AV)

171 Orange Street P.O. Drawer 906, 06510
Telephone: 203-789-0001
Hartford, Connecticut Office: 150 Trumbull Street.
Telephone: 860-727-8900.

John W. Beck (Resident, Hartford, Connecticut Office)	Peter A. Janus (Resident, Hartford, Connecticut Office)
Gregory J. Bezz (Resident)	Richard D. O'Connor (Resident, Hartford, Connecticut Office)
Carole Williams Briggs (Resident, Hartford, Connecticut Office)	Edward F. O'Donnell, Jr. (Resident, Hartford, Connecticut Office)
Robert F. Cohn (Resident)	Robert J. Percy (Resident, Hartford, Connecticut Office)
Hugh W. Cuthbertson (Resident)	Donald W. Strickland (Resident, Hartford, Connecticut Office)
Frederick L. Dorsey (Resident)	Mario J. Zangari (Resident)
Glenn A. Duhl (Resident)	
Peter D. Hershman (Resident)	

Christine A. Barker (Resident)	Dana Shaw MacKinnon (Resident, Hartford, Connecticut Office)
David G. Call (Resident, Hartford, Connecticut Office)	
Michael J. Eagen (Resident, Hartford, Connecticut Office)	Oscar M. Parente (Resident)
	Andrew L. Rodman (Resident)
Christine E. Farrell (Resident, Hartford Connecticut Office)	John M. Simon (Resident)
	Howard A. Steinman (Resident, Hartford, Connecticut Office)
Nicholas J. Grello, Jr. (Resident, Hartford, Connecticut Office)	Richard F. Vitarelli (Resident, Hartford, Connecticut Office)
George J. Kelly, Jr. (Resident, Hartford, Connecticut Office)	

For full biographical listings, see the Martindale-Hubbell Law Directory

---

WIGGIN & DANA (AV)

One Century Tower, 06508-1832
Telephone: 203-498-4400
Telefax: 203-782-2889
Hartford, Connecticut Office: One CityPlace.
Telephone: 203-297-3700.
FAX: 203-525-9380.
Stamford, Connecticut Office: Three Stamford Plaza, 301 Tresser Boulevard.
Telephone: 203-363-7600.
Telefax: 203-363-7676.

MEMBERS OF FIRM

Peter J. Lefeber	Sherry L. Dominick
John G. Zandy	Penny Quinn Seaman
Karen L. Clute	

ASSOCIATES

Joan M. Allen	Marcia Kenny Keegan
Inez M. Diaz	(Resident at Hartford)
Stephen B. Harris (Resident at Hartford)	Lisa Dougherty Kenna
	Mumtaza Malaika Rahi
Claudia Damsky Heyman	Peter M. Wendzel
Bernard E. Jacques (Resident at Hartford)	

For Complete List of Firm Personnel, See General Section

For full biographical listings, see the Martindale-Hubbell Law Directory

---

NORWALK, *Fairfield Co.*

STEPHEN P. HORNER & ASSOCIATES (AV)

148 East Avenue, Suite 1N, 06851
Telephone: 203-857-5514
Facsimile: 203-857-5522

ASSOCIATES

Patricia C. Moran	Julia Griffin Murphy
Patricia B. Skelly	Steven V. Bielenda

For full biographical listings, see the Martindale-Hubbell Law Directory

STAMFORD, Fairfield Co.

CASPER & DE TOLEDO LLC (AV)

1111 Summer Street, 06905
Telephone: 203-325-8600
Fax: 203-323-5970

Stewart M. Casper	Victoria de Toledo
Renée Mayerson Cannella	Melissa Balaban

For full biographical listings, see the Martindale-Hubbell Law Directory

---

WATERBURY, New Haven Co.

SUMMA & RYAN, P.C. (AV)

19-21 Holmes Avenue, 06710
Telephone: 203-755-0390
Fax: 203-756-8746

Joseph B. Summa	Mary Jane Ryan
David A. Ryan, Jr.	

William A. Ryan

LEGAL SUPPORT PERSONNEL

Cheryl P. Macdonald	Elissa L. Velez

For full biographical listings, see the Martindale-Hubbell Law Directory

---

WESTPORT, Fairfield Co.

LEVETT, ROCKWOOD & SANDERS, PROFESSIONAL CORPORATION (AV)

33 Riverside Avenue, P.O. Box 5116, 06881
Telephone: 203-222-0885
Telecopier: 203-226-8025

David R. Levett	Sharon M. Schweitzer
John Sanders	Barbara A. Young
B. Lance Sauerteig	Steven M. Siegelaub
Madeleine F. Grossman	Marc J. Kurzman
James M. Barton	Suzanne B. Albani
Judy A. Rabkin	Peter H. Struzzi
Dorit Schutzengel Heimer	Edward B. Chansky
Cheryl L. Johnson	

OF COUNSEL

William O. Rockwood, Jr.

Robin K. Higgins	Ernest C. Mysogland
Patricia D. Weitzman	

Representative Clients: Bankers Trust Company; Cannondale Corp.; Caradon, Inc.; Electrolux Corporation; Exxon Chemical Corporation; HealthSouth Corp.; Heyman Properties; Hospital of Saint Raphael; Marketing Corporation of America; St. Vincent's Medical Center.

For full biographical listings, see the Martindale-Hubbell Law Directory

---

DELAWARE

*WILMINGTON,** New Castle Co.

SMITH, KATZENSTEIN & FURLOW (AV)

The Corporate Plaza, 800 Delaware Avenue, P.O. Box 410, 19899
Telephone: 302-652-8400
Fax: 302-652-8405

MEMBERS OF FIRM

Craig B. Smith	Susan L. Parker
Robert J. Katzenstein	Laurence V. Cronin
David A. Jenkins	Brett D. Fallon
Anne E. Bookout	Stephen M. Miller
Joanne M. Shalk	Kathleen M. Miller

COUNSEL

Charles E. Butler

OF COUNSEL

Clark W. Furlow

For full biographical listings, see the Martindale-Hubbell Law Directory

---

DISTRICT OF COLUMBIA

WASHINGTON, D.C. Co.

* indicates certain Bar Register subscribers, in cities of comparable size and importance, who maintain an additional office in Washington, D.C. and who have arranged for representation as a part of the Washington, D.C. listings that follow

BAKER & HOSTETLER (AV)

Washington Square, Suite 1100, 1050 Connecticut Avenue, N.W., 20036-5304
Telephone: 202-861-1500
In Cleveland, Ohio: 3200 National City Center, 1900 East Ninth Street.
Telephone: 216-621-0200.
In Columbus, Ohio: Capitol Square, Suite 2100, 65 East State Street.
Telephone: 614-228-1541.
In Denver, Colorado: 303 East 17th Avenue, Suite 1100.
Telephone: 303-861-0600.
In Houston, Texas: 1000 Louisiana, Suite 2000.
Telephone: 713-751-1600.
In Long Beach, California: 300 Oceangate, Suite 620.
Telephone: 310-432-2827.
In Los Angeles, California: 600 Wilshire Boulevard.
Telephone: 213-624-2400.
In Orlando, Florida: SunBank Center, Suite 2300, 200 South Orange Avenue.
Telephone: 305-841-1111.
In College Park, Maryland: 9658 Baltimore Boulevard, Suite 206.
Telephone: 301-441-2781.
In Alexandria, Virginia: 437 North Lee Street.
Telephone: 703-549-1294.
In San Francisco, California: One Sansome Street, Suite 2000.
Telephone: 415-951-4705.

PARTNERS

David Alistair Grant	Brian S. Harvey
Betty Southard Murphy	

ASSOCIATE

John S. Farrington (Not admitted in DC)

For Complete List of Firm Personnel, See General Section

For full biographical listings, see the Martindale-Hubbell Law Directory

---

LAW OFFICE OF BERT NEIL BISGYER (AV)

1025 Thomas Jefferson Street, N.W. Suite 525 East, 20037
Telephone: 202-338-2172
Telecopier: 202-338-2447

OF COUNSEL

Carl S. Silverman

For full biographical listings, see the Martindale-Hubbell Law Directory

---

COHEN, MILSTEIN, HAUSFELD & TOLL, P.L.L.C. (AV)

West Tower, Suite 500, 1100 New York Avenue, N.W., 20005-3964
Telephone: 202-408-4600
Facsimile: 202-408-4699

MEMBERS OF FIRM

Jerry S. Cohen (1925-1995)	Lisa M. Mezzetti
Herbert E. Milstein	Andrew N. Friedman
Michael D. Hausfeld	Richard S. Lewis
Steven J. Toll	Daniel S. Sommers
Ann C. Yahner	Daniel A. Small
	(Not admitted in DC)

ASSOCIATES

Gary E. Mason	Michael J. Flannery
Cyrus Mehri	Paul T. Gallagher
Sharon A. Snyder	Alexander E. Barnett
Mark S. Willis	Angeline G. Chen
(Not admitted in DC)	Victoria C. Arthaud
Lillian S. Hagen	(Not admitted in DC)

OF COUNSEL

Anthony Z. Roisman

For full biographical listings, see the Martindale-Hubbell Law Directory

---

CONDON & FORSYTH (AV)

1016 Sixteenth Street, N.W., 20036
Telephone: 202-289-0500
Telecopier: 202-289-4524
Email: 103345.1077@compuserve.com
New York, N.Y. Office: 1251 Avenue of the Americas.
Telephone: 212-921-5100.
Telex: 426978.
Telecopier: 212-575-3638; 212-575-1298; 212-719-3638.
Los Angeles, California Office: 1900 Avenue of the Stars.
Telephone: 310-557-2030.
Telecopier: 310-557-1299.

(See Next Column)

CONDON & FORSYTH, *Washington—Continued*

RESIDENT PARTNERS

Thomas J. Whalen   Timothy J. Lynes

COUNSEL

Evelyn D. Sahr

SENIOR ATTORNEY

David G. Schryver

RESIDENT ASSOCIATES

Thomas E. Healey   David F. Rifkind
                                    (Not admitted in DC)

For full biographical listings, see the Martindale-Hubbell Law Directory

CONNERTON & RAY (AV)

Fourth Floor, 1920 L Street, N.W., 20036-5004
Telephone: 202-466-6790
Telecopier: 202-659-3458

MEMBERS OF FIRM

Robert J. Connerton   Tèrese M. Connerton
James S. Ray   John McN. Broaddus
Phillis Payne   Daniel S. Kozma
     Michael Barrett

NON-ATTORNEY MEMBER

David L. Mallino

NON-ATTORNEY LEGISLATIVE DIRECTOR

Jack Curran

ASSOCIATE

Jennifer M. Roof

For full biographical listings, see the Martindale-Hubbell Law Directory

THE FALK LAW FIRM (AV)

A Professional Limited Company
Suite 260 One Westin Center, 2445 M Street, N.W., 20037
Telephone: 202-833-8700
Telecopier: 202-872-1725
Email: FalkLaw@erols.com

James H. Falk, Sr.   John M. Falk
James H. Falk, Jr.   Robert K. Tompkins

OF COUNSEL

Pierre E. Murphy   Elizabeth C. Collins

For full biographical listings, see the Martindale-Hubbell Law Directory

KENNETH R. FEINBERG & ASSOCIATES (AV)

1120 20th Street, N.W. Suite 740 South, 20036
Telephone: 202-371-1110
Fax: 202-962-9290
New York, N.Y. Office: 780 3rd Avenue, Suite 2202.
Telephone: 212-527-9600.
Fax: 212-527-9611.

ASSOCIATES

Deborah E. Greenspan   Peter H. Woodin
Michael K. Rozen   (Not admitted in DC)
   (Not admitted in DC)   M. Catherine Faint

OF COUNSEL

Jacqueline E. Zins

For full biographical listings, see the Martindale-Hubbell Law Directory

FRIEDLANDER, MISLER, FRIEDLANDER, SLOAN & HERZ (AV)

Suite 700, 1101 Seventeenth Street, N.W., 20036
Telephone: 202-872-0800
Cable Address: "FMSHLAW"
Telex: 64273
URL: http://www.dclawfirm.com

MEMBERS OF FIRM

Stephen H. Friedlander   Morris Kletzkin
Leonard A. Sloan   Jeffrey W. Ochsman
Gerald Herz   Jerome Ostrov
     Jana Kay Guggenheim

ASSOCIATES

Philippa T. Gasnier   Mark D. Crawford
Robert J. Strayhorne   Glenn W. D. Golding
Alan Dean Sundburg   Roberto L. Veloso
     Todd S. Sapiro

OF COUNSEL

Robert E. Greenberg

SPECIAL COUNSEL

Judith A. Hoggan

(See Next Column)

RETIRED

Jack L. Friedlander   Albert D. Misler

For full biographical listings, see the Martindale-Hubbell Law Directory

HIGHSAW, MAHONEY & CLARKE, P.C. (AV)

Suite 210, 1050 Seventeenth Street, N.W., 20036
Telephone: 202-296-8500
Fax: 202-296-7143

James L. Highsaw (1970-1992)   Donald F. Griffin
William G. Mahoney   Melissa B. Kirgis
John O'B. Clarke, Jr.   (Not admitted in DC)
Richard S. Edelman   Francisco J. Ruben
L. Pat Wynns   (Not admitted in DC)

For full biographical listings, see the Martindale-Hubbell Law Directory

* JONES, DAY, REAVIS & POGUE (AV)

Metropolitan Square, 1450 G Street, N.W., 20005-2088
Telephone: 202-879-3939
Cable Address: "Attorneys Washington"
Telex: W.U. (Domestic) 89-2410 ATTORNEYS WASH (International)
64363 ATTORNEYS WASH
Telecopier: 202-737-2832
In Atlanta, Georgia: 3500 One Peachtree Center, 303 Peachtree Street, N.E
.
Telephone: 404-521-3939.
Cable Address: "Attorneys Atlanta".
Telex: 54-2711.
Telecopier: 404-581-8330.
In Brussels, Belgium: Avenue Louise 480, 7th Floor, B-1050 Brussels.
Telephone: 32-2-645-14-11.
Telecopier: 32-2-645-14-45.
In Chicago, Illinois: 77 West Wacker.
Telephone: 312-782-3939.
Telecopier: 312-782-8585.
In Cleveland, Ohio: North Point, 901 Lakeside Avenue.
Telephone: 216-586-3939.
Cable Address: "Attorneys Cleveland."
Telex: 980389.
Telecopier: 216-579-0212.
In Columbus, Ohio: 1900 Huntington Center.
Telephone: 614-469-3939.
Cable Address: "Attorneys Columbus."
Telecopier: 614-461-4198.
In Dallas, Texas: 2300 Trammell Crow Center, 2001 Ross Avenue.
Telephone: 214-220-3939.
Cable Address: "Attorneys Dallas."
Telex: 730852.
Telecopier: 214-969-5100.
In Frankfurt, Germany: Triton Haus, Bockenheimer Landstrasse 42, 60323 Frankfurt am Main.
Telephone: 49-69-9726-3939.
Telecopier: 49-69-9726-3993.
In Geneva, Switzerland: 20, rue de Candolle.
Telephone: 41-22-320-2339.
Telecopier: 41-22-320-1232.
In Hong Kong: 29th Floor, Entertainment Building, 30 Queen's Road Central.
Telephone: 852-2526-6895.
Telecopier: 852-2868-5871.
In Irvine, California: 2603 Main Street, Suite 900 .
Telephone: 714-851-3939.
Telex: 194911 Lawyers LSA.
Telecopier: 714-553-7539.
In London, England: One Mount Street.
Telephone: 44-71-493-9361.
Cable Address: "Surgoe London WI."
Telecopier: 44-71-493-9666.
In Los Angeles, California: 555 West Fifth Street, Suite 4600.
Telephone: 213-489-3939.
Telex: 181439 UD.
Telecopier: 213-243-2539.
In New Delhi, India: Pathak & Associates, 13th Floor, Dr. Gopal Das Bhaven, 28 Barakhamba Road.
Telephone: 91-11-373-8793.
Telecopier: 91-11-335-3761.
In New York, New York: 599 Lexington Avenue.
Telephone: 212-326-3939.
Cable Address: "JONESDAY NEWYORK."
Telex: 237013 JDRP UR.
Telecopier: 212-755-7306.
In Paris, France: 62, rue du Faubourg Saint-Honore.
Telephone: 33-1-44-71-3939.
Cable Address: "Surgoe Paris."
Telex: 290156 Surgoe.
Telecopier: 33-1-49-24-0471.
In Pittsburgh, Pennsylvania: 500 Grant Street, 31st Floor.
Telephone: 412-391-3939.
Cable Address: "Attorneys Pittsburgh".
Telecopier: 412-394-7959.

(See Next Column)

JONES, DAY, REAVIS & POGUE—*Continued*

In Riyadh, Saudi Arabia: Law Offices of Saud M.A. Shawwaf, P.O. Box 22166.
Telephone: (966-1) 462-8866.
Telex: 401831 SAUCON SJ.
Telecopier: (966-1) 462-9001.
In Taipei, Taiwan: 8th Floor, 2 Tun Hwa South Road, Section 2.
Telephone: (886-2) 704-6808.
Telecopier: (886-2) 704-6791.
In Tokyo, Japan: Toranomon MT Building, 4th Floor, 10-3, Toranomon 3-Chome, Minato-Ku, Tokyo 105, Japan.
Telephone: 81-3-3433-3939.
Telecopier: 81-3-5401-2725.

MEMBER OF FIRM IN WASHINGTON, D.C.
Willis J. Goldsmith

SENIOR ATTORNEY
David A. Copus

For Complete List of Firm Personnel, See General Section

For full biographical listings, see the Martindale-Hubbell Law Directory

---

* McDERMOTT, WILL & EMERY (AV)

A Partnership including Professional Corporations
1850 K Street, N.W., 20006-2296
Telephone: 202-887-8000
Facsimile: 202-778-8087
URL: http://www.mwe.com
Chicago, Illinois Office: 227 West Monroe Street.
Telephone: 312-372-2000.
Facsimile: 312-984-7700.
Boston, Massachusetts Office: 75 State Street, Suite 1700.
Telephone: 617-345-5000.
Facsimile: 617-345-5077.
Miami, Florida Office: 201 South Biscayne Boulevard.
Telephone: 305-358-3500.
Facsimile: 305-347-6500.
Los Angeles, California Office: 2049 Century Park East.
Telephone: 310-277-4110.
Facsimile: 310-277-4730.
Newport Beach, California Office: 1301 Dove Street, Suite 500.
Telephone: 714-851-0633.
Facsimile: 714-851-9348.
New York, N.Y. Office: 50 Rockefeller Plaza.
Telephone: 212-547-5508.
Facsimile: 212-547-5444.
St. Petersburg, Russia Office: AOZT McDermott, Will & Emery, Griboyedova Canal 36, 191023, St. Petersburg, Russia.
Telephone: (7) (812) 310-52-44; 310-55-44; 310-59-44; 850-20-45.
Facsimile: (7) (812) 310-54-46; 325-84-50.
Vilnius, Lithuania Office: Smetonos 6, 2600 Vilnius, Lithuania.
Telephone: 370 2 61-43-08.
Facsimile: 370 2 22-79-55.

MEMBERS OF FIRM
Robert C. Gombar *	Melissa L. Peppe
Amy E. Hancock	Arthur G. Sapper
Stephen C. Yohay	

*Denotes a lawyer employed by a Professional Corporation which is a member of the Firm

For full biographical listings, see the Martindale-Hubbell Law Directory

---

McGUINESS & WILLIAMS (AV)

Suite 1200, 1015 Fifteenth Street, N.W., 20005
Telephone: 202-789-8600
Telecopier: 202-789-1708
Email: M&W@Mindspring.com
Northern Virginia Office: 12110 Sunset Hills Road, Reston, Virginia, 22090.
Telephone: 703-476-9009.

MEMBERS OF FIRM
Jeffrey C. McGuiness	Monte B. Lake
Jeffrey A. Norris	Robert E. Williams
Edward E. Potter	Ann Elizabeth Reesman
G. John Tysse	Salvador T. Perkins
Daniel V. Yager	

ASSOCIATES
Ellen Duffy McKay	Mary Chlopecki
	(Not admitted in DC)

OF COUNSEL
Lorence L Kessler	William N. LaForge
Lynnette Conway Jacquez	Sandra J. Boyd
Susan S. Nussbaum	

SENIOR ADVISOR
Steve Bartlett

(See Next Column)

CONSULTANTS
William F. Holmes	John C. Runyan
James S. Holt	Max Lyons
Kenneth L. Deavers	Anita U. Hattiangadi

For full biographical listings, see the Martindale-Hubbell Law Directory

---

O'DONOGHUE & O'DONOGHUE (AV)

4748 Wisconsin Avenue, N.W., 20016
Telephone: 202-362-0041
Telecopier: 202-362-2640
Philadelphia, Pennsylvania Office: 1056 Public Ledger Building, 150 South Independence Mall W.
Telephone: 215-629-4970.
Telecopier: 215-629-4996.

MEMBERS OF FIRM
Martin F. O'Donoghue (1903-1973)	Joseph P. Boyle (Resident, Philadelphia, Pennsylvania Office)
Patrick C. O'Donoghue (1930-1979)	Francis J. Martorana
Donald J. Capuano	Nicholas R. Femia
James R. O'Connell	Ellen O. Boardman
Robert Matisoff	Charles W. Gilligan
Joyce A. Mader	Louis P. Malone III
Sally M. Tedrow	Mary Capuano Feller
Brian A. Powers	John Leary
John L. Bohman	(Not admitted in DC)

ASSOCIATES
John R. Harney	Linda J. Tarlow
Gerard M. Waites (Not admitted in DC)	John M. McIntire
	Mark W. Kunst
Scott A. Cronin (Resident, Philadelphia, Pennsylvania Office)	Kenneth M. Johnson
	Benjamin N. Davis
R. Richard Hopp	(Not admitted in DC)
Marc D. Keffer	Linda Delivorias
	(Not admitted in DC)

OF COUNSEL
Phyllis C. Borzi

For full biographical listings, see the Martindale-Hubbell Law Directory

---

* OGLETREE, DEAKINS, NASH, SMOAK & STEWART, P.C. (AV)

Fifth Floor, 2400 N Street, N.W., 20037
Telephone: 202-887-0855
Facsimile: 202-887-0866
Atlanta, Georgia Office: 3800 One Atlantic Center, 1201 West Peachtree Street, N.W.
Telephone: 404-881-1300.
Houston, Texas Office: One Allen Center, 500 Dallas Street, Suite 3000.
Telephone: 713-655-0855.
Greenville, South Carolina Office: The Ogletree Building, 300 North Main Street, P.O. Box 2757.
Telephone: 864-271-1300.
Charleston, South Carolina Office: First Union Building, Suite 310, 177 Meeting Street, P.O. Box 1808.
Telephone: 803-853-1300.
Columbia, South Carolina Office: Palmetto Center, Suite 1820, 1426 Main Street, P.O. Box 11206.
Telephone: 803-252-1300.
Nashville, Tennessee Office: SunTrust Center, Suite 800, 424 Church Street.
Telephone: 615-254-1900.
Raleigh, North Carolina Office: Suite 511, 4101 Lake Boone Trail, P.O. Box 31608.
Telephone: 919-787-9700.
Albany, New York Office: 4th Floor, One Steuben Place.
Telephone: 518-434-1300.
Winston-Salem, North Carolina Office: 4400 Silas Creek Parkway, Suite 101.
Telephone: 910-765-0057.

Homer L. Deakins, Jr.	Jonathan R. Mook
Lewis Tyson Smoak	Joel A. Daniel
J. Hamilton Stewart, III	Robert T. Lee
Peter H. Kiefer	David Edward Jones
Marshall B. Babson	(Not admitted in DC)
Franklin H. Goldberger	Michael J. Murphy
Harold P. Coxson, Jr.	Erin Elizabeth Powell
Bernard P. Jeweler	Sue J. Henry

OF COUNSEL
Stanley R. Strauss	Todd M. Rubin
John A. Penello	
(Not admitted in DC)	

Representative Clients: CertainTeed Corp.; Chevron USA Products Co.; Deere & Co.; Eastman Chemical Company; Eastman Kodak Co.; Fluor Corporation; General Electric Co.; John Hancock Mutual Life Insurance Co.; Michelin Tire Corporation; Science Application International Corp.

For full biographical listings, see the Martindale-Hubbell Law Directory

Washington—Continued

* REED SMITH SHAW & MCCLAY (AV)

Suite 1100 - East Tower, 1301 K Street, N.W., 20005-3317
Telephone: 202-414-9200
FAX: 202-414-9299
Email: rssm@rssm.com *URL:* http://www.rssm.com
Pittsburgh, Pennsylvania Office: 435 Sixth Avenue, 15219-1886.
Telephone: 412-288-3131.
FAX: 412-288-3063.
Philadelphia, Pennsylvania Office: 2500 One Liberty Place, 19103-7301.
Telephone: 215-851-8100.
FAX: 215-851-1420.
Harrisburg, Pennsylvania Office: 213 Market Street, 17101-2132.
Telephone: 717-234-5988.
FAX: 717-236-3777.
McLean, Virginia Office: Suite 1100, 8251 Greensboro Drive, 22102-3844.
Telephone: 703-734-4600.
FAX: 703-734-4699.
Princeton, New Jersey Office: 136 Main Street, Suite 250, 08540-5799.
Telephone: 609-987-0050.
FAX: 609-951-0824.
New York, N.Y. Office: 375 Park Avenue, Suite 301, 10152.
Telephone: 212-521-5400.
FAX: 212-521-5450.
Newark, New Jersey Office: One Gateway Center, 07102-5311.
Telephone: 201-622-1600.
Fax: 201-622-4747.

MEMBER OF FIRM
Michael C. Lynch

For Complete List of Firm Personnel, See General Section

For full biographical listings, see the Martindale-Hubbell Law Directory

SANDERS, SCHNABEL, BRANDENBURG & ZIMMERMAN, P.C. (AV)

Suite 900, 900 Seventeenth Street, N.W., 20006
Telephone: 202-638-2241
Telecopier: 202-293-3419

John A. Sanders (Retired)	David Weingarten
Dan S. Brandenburg	Richard Landfield
Lawrence T. Zimmerman	William H. Bradford, Jr.

Paul O. Jolis

Cheryl Risley Hughes	Stacey A. Bradford

OF COUNSEL
Robert V. Schnabel

For full biographical listings, see the Martindale-Hubbell Law Directory

SCHMELTZER, APTAKER & SHEPARD, P.C. (AV)

The Watergate, Suite 1000, 2600 Virginia Avenue, N.W., 20037-1905
Telephone: 202-333-8800
Cable Address: "Ship"
Telex: 440517
Facsimile: 202-342-3434
Email: sas@saspc.com *URL:* http://www.saspc.com
Los Angeles, California Office: 1999 Avenue of the Stars, Twenty-Seventh Floor, 90067-4095.
Telephone: 310-557-2966.
FAX: 310-286-6610.

Ira M. Shepard	Robert L. Duston
Paul M. Heylman	Don A. Zimmerman
John A. McGuinn	Katherine Brewer
Gary L. Lieber	Scott Robins
Edward R. Levin	Henry A. Platt

Anessa Abrams (Not admitted in DC)

For full biographical listings, see the Martindale-Hubbell Law Directory

SHAW, BRANSFORD & O'ROURKE, A PROFESSIONAL CORPORATION (AV)

815 Connecticut Avenue, N.W., 20006
Telephone: 202-463-8400
Telecopier: 202-833-8082
Email: sbolaw@sbolaw.com *URL:* http://www.sbolaw.com/SBOLAW/

G. Jerry Shaw, Jr. *	Thomas J. O'Rourke
William L. Bransford	Diana J. Veilleux

Debra L. Roth	Alicia Anne Simolunas
Christopher M. Okay	Robert E. Gans
Susan Elizabeth Shaw	
(Not admitted in DC)	

*Professional Corporation

For full biographical listings, see the Martindale-Hubbell Law Directory

SLEVIN & HART, P.C. (AV)

1625 Massachusetts Avenue, N.W., Suite 450, 20036
Telephone: 202-797-8700
FAX: 202-234-8231

Barry S. Slevin	Fredrick M. Marx
Thomas J. Hart	Jeffrey S. Endick

Marc H. Rifkind

Lynn A. Bowers	Kirsten M. Pullin
(Not admitted in DC)	(Not admitted in DC)
Patricia W. S. Douglas	Elliot D. Raff
Sharon McNeilly Goodman	(Not admitted in DC)
Allison A. Madan	Felicia S. Pearlberg
	(Not admitted in DC)

For full biographical listings, see the Martindale-Hubbell Law Directory

THOMPSON AND HUTSON (AV)

Suite 900, 1317 F Street, N.W., 20004
Telephone: 202-783-1900
Fax: 202-783-5995
Greenville, South Carolina Office: 301 North Main Street, Suite 1700.
Telephone: 803-242-3200.
Fax: 803-233-7867. E-mail address: thlaw@mindspring.com

MEMBERS OF FIRM

Robert T. Thompson	Melvin R. Hutson

David L. Thompson (Resident)

For full biographical listings, see the Martindale-Hubbell Law Directory

* VENABLE ATTORNEYS AT LAW VENABLE, BAETJER, HOWARD & CIVILETTI, LLP (AV)

A Partnership including Professional Corporations
Suite 1000, 1201 New York Avenue, N.W., 20005
Telephone: 202-962-4800
Fax: 202-962-8300
Baltimore, Maryland Office: Venable, Baetjer and Howard LLP, 1800 Mercantile Bank & Trust Building, 2 Hopkins Plaza.
Telephone: 410-244-7400.
McLean, Virginia Office: Venable, Baetjer and Howard LLP, Suite 400, 2010 Corporate Ridge.
Telephone: 703-760-1600.
Rockville, Maryland Office: Venable, Baetjer and Howard LLP, Suite 500, One Church Street, P. O. Box 1906.
Telephone: 301-217-5600.
Towson, Maryland Office: Venable, Baetjer and Howard LLP, 210 Allegheny Avenue, P. O. Box 5517.
Telephone: 410-494-6200.

MEMBERS OF FIRM

Douglas D. Connah, Jr. (P.C.) (Also at Baltimore, Maryland Office)	George F. Pappas (Also at Baltimore, Maryland Office)
Kenneth C. Bass, III (Also at McLean, Virginia Office)	James L. Shea (Not admitted in DC; also at Baltimore, Maryland Office)
Joseph G. Block	Maurice Baskin
Robert G. Ames (Also at Baltimore, Maryland Office)	James A. Dunbar (Also at Baltimore, Maryland Office)
Jeffrey A. Dunn (Also at Baltimore, Maryland Office)	Patrick J. Stewart (Also at Baltimore, Maryland Office)

Gary M. Hnath

ASSOCIATES

David W. Goewey	Karen D. Woodard
John C. Hardwick, Jr. (Not admitted in DC)	

For Complete List of Firm Personnel, See General Section

For full biographical listings, see the Martindale-Hubbell Law Directory

VERNER, LIIPFERT, BERNHARD, MCPHERSON AND HAND, CHARTERED (AV)

901 15th Street, N.W., 20005-2301
Telephone: 202-371-6000
Cable Address: "Verlip"
Telex: 1561792 VERLIP UT
Fax: 202-371-6279
Email: verner.com
McLean, Virginia Office: Sixth Floor, 8280 Greensboro Drive, 22102.
Telephone: 703-749-6000.
Fax: 703-749-6027.
Houston, Texas Office: 2600 Texas Commerce Tower, 600 Travis, 77002.
Telephone: 713-237-9034.
Fax: 713-237-1216.
Honolulu, Hawaii Office: Hawaii Times Building, 928 Nuuanu Avenue, Suite 400, 96817.
Telephone: 808-566-0999.
Fax: 808-566-0995.

(See Next Column)

VERNER, LIIPFERT, BERNHARD, MCPHERSON AND HAND CHARTERED—
Continued

Austin, Texas Office: Suite 1440 San Jacinto Center, 98 San Jacinto
Boulevard, 78701.
Telephone: 512-703-6000.
Fax: 512-703-6003.

Lawrence Z. Lorber   Joseph L. Manson, III
          Ronald B. Natalie
          OF COUNSEL
          J. Robert Kirk

For Complete List of Firm Personnel, See General Section

For full biographical listings, see the Martindale-Hubbell Law Directory

---

FLORIDA

FORT LAUDERDALE, * Broward Co.

AMLONG & AMLONG, P.A. (AV)

Second Floor, 500 Northeast Fourth Street, 33301
Telephone: 954-462-1983
FAX: 954-523-3192

Karen Coolman Amlong   William R. Amlong

Robyn S. Hankins   Sheryl T. Simon
Walter W. Palmer   Lisa Beth Stern

For full biographical listings, see the Martindale-Hubbell Law Directory

FISHER & PHILLIPS (AV)

A Partnership including Professional Corporations and Associations
Suite 2300 NationsBank Tower, One Financial Plaza, 33394
Telephone: 954-525-4800
Telecopier: 954-525-8739
Atlanta, Georgia Office: 1500 Resurgens Plaza, 945 East Paces Ferry
Road, N.E., 30326.
Telephone: 404-231-1400.
Telecopier: 404-240-4249.
Telex: 54-2331.
Redwood City, California Office: Suite 345, Three Lagoon Drive, 94065.
Telephone: 415-592-6160.
Telecopier: 415-592-6385.
Newport Beach, California Office: 4675 MacArthur Court, Suite 550,
92660.
Telephone: 714-851-2424.
Telecopier: 714-851-0152.
New Orleans, Louisiana Office: 3710 Place St. Charles, 201 St. Charles
Avenue, 70170.
Telephone: 504-522-3303.
Telecopier: 504-529-3850.

RESIDENT MEMBERS
Charles S. Caulkins (P.A.)   James C. Polkinghorn
Christopher D. Robinson   Kenneth A. Knox
RESIDENT ASSOCIATES
David H. Spalter   Annalisa Martinez-Cooper
Suzanne K. Bogdan   Wendy J. Smith
          Ashley Howell Kaplan

Representative Clients: Boca Raton Resort & Club; Dean Foods/T.G. Lee
Foods, Inc.; Hyatt Corp.; Independent Life & Accident Insurance Co.;
Miller Brewing Co.; Textron, Inc.; The Prudential Insurance Company of
America; United States Sugar Corp./South Bay Growers.

For full biographical listings, see the Martindale-Hubbell Law Directory

TRIPP, SCOTT, CONKLIN & SMITH (AV)

28th Floor, 110 Tower, 110 S.E. 6th Street, P.O. Box 14245, 33301
Telephone: 954-525-7500
Telecopier: 954-761-8475

Norman D. Tripp   Timothy J. McDermott
James A. Scott   Kimberly A. Gilmour
Howard L. Conklin   Richard D. Heller
Dennis Dustin Smith   Gregory A. McLaughlin
Peter G. Herman   Steven C. Elkin
Garry W. Johnson   Drake M. Batchelder
          OF COUNSEL
Robert E. Huebner   Welcom H. Watson, Jr.
          ASSOCIATES
O. Mason Hurst, II   Heidi E. Davis
Matthew Zifrony   Jeffrey S. Wood
Grant J. Smith   Scott J. Jordan
William J. Gross   Jason A. Diamond
Paul Octavio Lopez   Christopher L. Smith
Daniel E. Taylor   Angelia Maria Baldwin

(See Next Column)

Representative Clients: Alamo Rent A Car, Inc.; Gehl Group, Inc.; Crab Pot
Restaurants; Certified Tours; Florida Heat Pump, Inc.; Precision Resource,
Fla. Division; Impra, Inc.

For full biographical listings, see the Martindale-Hubbell Law Directory

---

FORT MYERS, * Lee Co.

KUNKEL MILLER & HAMENT (AV)

Sun Bank Financial Center, Suite 416, 12730 New Brittany
Boulevard, 33907
Telephone: 941-278-1600
Telecopier: 941-278-9056
Sarasota, Florida Office: Southtrust Bank Plaza, Suite 882, 1800 Second
Street, 34236.
Telephone: 941-365-6006.
Fax: 941-365-6209.
Tampa, Florida Office: 15438 North Florida Avenue, Suite 106.
Telephone: 813-963-7736.
Telefax: 813-969-3639.

Daniel H. Kunkel   Michael R. Miller
          John M. Hament

Jody A. O'Konski   Michele M. Perri
          Linda G. Sasser

Representative Clients: Florida Health Care Assn.; Gold & Diamond Source;
New London, Connecticut Convalescent Center; Mid-Hudson, NY Cablevi-
sion; The Hillhaven Corp.; Bon Secours Hospital; Integrated Health Services,
Inc.; Florida Association of Professional Employer Organizations.

For full biographical listings, see the Martindale-Hubbell Law Directory

---

FORT PIERCE, * St. Lucie Co.

J. DAVID RICHESON & ASSOCIATES, P.A. (AV)

317 South 2nd Street, P.O. Box 4048, 34948
Telephone: 561-465-5111
FAX: 561-466-0378
West Palm Beach, Florida Office: Suite 900 Forum III Building, 1655
Palm Beach Lakes Boulevard, 33401.
Telephone: 561-689-6660.

J. David Richeson

Elizabeth Coke

For full biographical listings, see the Martindale-Hubbell Law Directory

---

JACKSONVILLE, * Duval Co.

COFFMAN, COLEMAN, ANDREWS & GROGAN, PROFESSIONAL ASSOCIATION (AV)

2065 Herschel Street, P.O. Box 40089, 32203
Telephone: 904-389-5161
Telecopier: 904-387-9340

Daniel R. Coffman, Jr.   Mary W. Jarrett
Patrick D. Coleman   Robert G. Riegel, Jr.
William H. Andrews   Marc M. Mayo
Michael K. Grogan   Joann M. Bricker
Eric J. Holshouser   Michael G. Prendergast
          Timothy B. Strong

Gregory D. Holland   Kyle J. Stroh
Heather A. Owen   Jeffrey P. Watson
Margaret W. Means   Jennifer Sue Yates
          Edward H. Trent

Representative Clients: American Home Products Corp.; Anheuser-Busch
Companies, Inc.; Atlantic Marine, Inc.; Baptist/St. Vincent's Health System;
Blue Cross and Blue Shield of Florida, Inc.; Winn-Dixie Stores, Inc.; Xerox
Corp.

For full biographical listings, see the Martindale-Hubbell Law Directory

---

CORBIN, DICKINSON, DUVALL & KITCHEN (AV)

121 West Forsyth Street, Suite 1000, P.O. Box 41566, 32203
Telephone: 904-356-8073
Telecopier: 904-358-2319

MEMBERS OF FIRM
Peter Reed Corbin   John E. Duvall
John F. Dickinson   F. Damon Kitchen
          ASSOCIATES
Richard L. Ruth   Kimberly A. Cannon

Representative Clients: Allied Signal Corp.; Carolina Freight Carriers Corp.;
Consolidated Freightways Corp.; The Haskell Co.; International Speedway
Corp.; Mobil Oil Corp.; Sears, Roebuck and Co.; State of Florida; University
of North Florida; Lanier Worldwide, Inc.

For full biographical listings, see the Martindale-Hubbell Law Directory

Jacksonville—Continued

HAYNSWORTH, BALDWIN, JOHNSON AND HARPER (AV)

Formerly Hamilton & Bowden
1506 Prudential Drive, P.O. Box 40593, 32203
Telephone: 904-396-3000
Facsimile: 904-396-9999
Tampa, Florida Office: 600 North Westshore Boulevard, Suite 200.
Telephone: 813-289-1247.
Macon, Georgia Office: 577 Mulberry Street, Suite 710, P.O. Box 1975.
Telephone: 912-746-0262.
Greenville, South Carolina Office: Haynsworth, Baldwin, Johnson &
Greaves, P.A., 918 South Pleasantburg Drive, P.O. Box 10888.
Telephone: 864-271-7410.
Columbia, South Carolina Office: Haynsworth, Baldwin, Johnson &
Greaves, P.A., 1201 Main Street, Suite 1230.
Telephone: 803-799-5858.
Raleigh, North Carolina Office: Haynsworth, Baldwin, Johnson & Greaves,
P.A., 3605 Glenwood Avenue, Suite 210, P.O. Box 10035.
Telephone: 919-782-3340.
Greensboro, North Carolina Office: Haynsworth, Baldwin, Johnson &
Greaves, P.A., 2709 Henry Street, P.O. Box 13310.
Telephone: 910-375-9737.
Charlotte, North Carolina Office: Haynsworth, Baldwin, Johnson &
Greaves, P.A., 400 West Trade Street.
Telephone: 704-342-2588.

MEMBERS OF FIRM

Knox L. Haynsworth, Jr.	G. Thomas Harper (Resident)
(Not admitted in FL)	Charles F. Henley, Jr. (Resident)
Kimberly T. Acuna (Resident)	Elizabeth A. Maas (Resident)

Representative Clients: Belk Department Stores; The Coca-Cola Company
Foods Division; Florida Mining & Materials, Inc.; Great Dane Trailers, Inc.;
Kmart Corp.; Lockheed Missiles and Space Company, Inc.; Stone Container
Corp.; Winn-Dixie Stores, Inc.

For full biographical listings, see the Martindale-Hubbell Law Directory

HEDRICK, DEWBERRY & REGAN, P.A. (AV)

50 North Laura Street, Suite 2225, 32202
Telephone: 904-356-1300
Fax: 904-356-8050

Michael J. Dewberry	Alexandra Krueger Hedrick
	Jeffrey C. Regan
Clinton Allen Wright, III	Evan G. Frayman

For full biographical listings, see the Martindale-Hubbell Law Directory

---

KISSIMMEE,* Osceola Co.

POHL & SHORT, P.A.

(See Winter Park)

MIAMI,* Dade Co.

ALLEY AND ALLEY/FORD & HARRISON (AV)

516 Ingraham Building, 25 S.E. 2nd Avenue, 33131
Telephone: 305-379-3811
Fax: 305-358-5933
Tampa, Florida Office: 205 Brush Street, P.O. Box 1427, 33601.
Telephone: 813-229-6481.
Fax: 813-223-7029.
Atlanta, Georgia Office: Ford & Harrison, 600 Peachtree at the Circle
Building, 1275 Peachtree Street, N.E., 30309.
Telephone: 404-888-3800.
Fax: 404-888-3863.
Los Angeles, California Office: Ford & Harrison, 333 South Grand
Avenue, Suite 3680, 90071.
Telephone: 213-680-3410.
Fax: 213-680-4161.
Washington, D.C. Office: Ford & Harrison, 1920 N Street, N.W., Suite
200, 20036.
Telephone: 202-463-6633.
Fax: 202-466-5705.

Granville M. Alley, Jr.	John-Edward Alley
(1929-1976)	Joseph Z. Fleming
	Edmund J. McKenna

Representative Clients: The Wackenhut Corporation and subsidiaries; Publix
Super Markets, Inc.; Braman Motors; Biltmore Securities; Sysco Corp.; Sky-
line Mobile Homes, Inc.; Associated Grocers of Florida; Baxter Healthcare
Corp. (Dade Div.); Edron Fixture Corp.

For full biographical listings, see the Martindale-Hubbell Law Directory

NEIL FLAXMAN PROFESSIONAL ASSOCIATION (AV)

550 Biltmore Way (Coral Gables), 33134
Telephone: 305-445-1388
Fax: 305-443-0279

(See Next Column)

Neil Flaxman

Maria E. Cespedes

For full biographical listings, see the Martindale-Hubbell Law Directory

McDERMOTT, WILL & EMERY (AV)

A Partnership including Professional Corporations
201 South Biscayne Boulevard, 33131-4336
Telephone: 305-358-3500
Facsimile: 305-347-6500
URL: http://www.mwe.com
Chicago, Illinois Office: 227 West Monroe Street.
Telephone: 312-372-2000.
Facsimile: 312-984-7700.
Boston, Massachusetts Office: 75 State Street, Suite 1700.
Telephone: 617-345-5000.
Facsimile: 617-345-5077.
Washington, D.C. Office: 1850 K Street, N.W.
Telephone: 202-887-8000.
Facsimile: 202-778-8087.
Los Angeles, California Office: 2049 Century Park East.
Telephone: 310-277-4110.
Facsimile: 310-277-4730.
Newport Beach, California Office: 1301 Dove Street, Suite 500.
Telephone: 714-851-0633.
Facsimile: 714-851-9348.
New York, N.Y. Office: 50 Rockefeller Plaza.
Telephone: 212-547-5508.
Facsimile: 212-547-5444.
St. Petersburg, Russia Office: AOZT McDermott, Will & Emery,
Griboyedova Canal 36, 191023 St. Petersburg, Russia.
Telephone: (7) (812) 310-52-44; 310-55-44; 310-59-44; 850-20-45.
Facsimile: (7) (812) 310-54-46; 325-84-50.
Vilnius, Lithuania Office: Smetonos 6, 2600 Vilnius, Lithuania.
Telephone: 370 2 61-43-08.
Facsimile: 370 2 22-79-55.

MEMBER OF FIRM

Steven E. Siff *

For full biographical listings, see the Martindale-Hubbell Law Directory

MULLER, MINTZ, KORNREICH, CALDWELL, CASEY, CROSLAND & BRAMNICK, P.A. (AV)

Suite 3600 First Union Financial Center, 200 South Biscayne
Boulevard, 33131
Telephone: 305-358-5500
Broward: 954-522-0393
Orlando, Florida Office: Suite 1525 Citrus Center, 255 South Orange
Avenue.
Telephone: 407-843-1400.

David V. Kornreich	Andrew K. Williams
Michael W. Casey, III	Donna M. DiChiara
James C. Crosland	Paul T. Ryder
James S. Bramnick	Frank H. Henry
Paul C. Heidmann	Richard D. Tuschman
Gordon D. Rogers	Teresa Adamson Herrmann
John D. Gronda	Kelly Cheary
Carmen S. Johnson	Neil F. McGuinness
Jeffrey E. Mandel	Ronnie S. Carter
Denise M. Heekin	Mary E. Lytle

Representative Clients: Florida Power & Light Co.; Universal Studios; Ameri-
can Telephone & Telegraph Co.; J.C. Penney Co.; Smith Barney; Sunbeam
Television Corp.; Associated of General Contractors; Calder Race Course;
Chase Federal Bank; Columbia Broadcasting Systems, Inc.

For full biographical listings, see the Martindale-Hubbell Law Directory

DONALD T. RYCE, P.A. (AV)

5151 Collins Avenue, Suite 1036 (Miami Beach), 33140
Telephone: 305-864-1211
Fax: 305-864-4161
Email: dryce000@COUNSEL.COM

Donald T. Ryce

Claudine Ryce (Not admitted in FL)

For full biographical listings, see the Martindale-Hubbell Law Directory

---

ORLANDO,* Orange Co.

BROWN & GREEN, P.A. (AV)

135 North Magnolia Avenue, P.O. Box 3108, 32802
Telephone: 407-425-7755
Fax: 407-422-7865

(See Next Column)

Brown & Green P.A.—*Continued*

James G. Brown	Joseph E. Blitch
Dorothy F. Green	M. Susan Sacco

For full biographical listings, see the Martindale-Hubbell Law Directory

FOLEY & LARDNER (AV)

Suite 1800, 111 North Orange Avenue, P.O. Box 2193, 32802-2193
Telephone: 407-423-7656
Telex: 441781 (HQ ORL)
Facsimile: 407-648-1743
Milwaukee, Wisconsin Office: Firstar Center, 777 East Wisconsin Avenue.
Telephone: 414-271-2400.
Telex: 26-819 (Foley Lard Mil).
Facsimile: 414-297-4900.
Madison, Wisconsin Office: Verex Plaza, 150 East Gilman Street, P.O. Box 1497.
Telephone: 608-257-5035.
Telex: 262051 (F L Madison).
Facsimile: 608-258-4258.
Chicago, Illinois Office: Suite 3300, One IBM Plaza, 330 N. Wabash Avenue.
Telephone: 312-755-1900.
Facsimile: 312-755-1925.
Washington, D.C. Office: Washington Harbour, Suite 500, 3000 K Street, N.W.
Telephone: 202-672-5300.
Telex: 904136 (Foley Lard Wsh).
Facsimile: 202-672-5399.
Annapolis, Maryland Office: Suite 102, 175 Admiral Cochrane Drive.
Telephone: 301-266-8077.
Telex: 899149 (Oldtownpat).
Facsimile: 301-266-8664.
Jacksonville, Florida Office: The Greenleaf Building, 200 Laura Street, P.O. Box 240.
Telephone: 904-359-2000.
Facsimile: 904-359-8700.
Tallahassee, Florida Office: Suite 300, 123 South Calhoun Street, P.O. Box 508.
Telephone: 904-222-6100.
Facsimile: 904-224-0496.
Tampa, Florida Office: Suite 2700, One Hundred N. Tampa Street, P.O. Box 3391.
Telephones: 813-229-2300; Pinellas County: 813-442-3296.
Facsimile: 813-221-4210
West Palm Beach, Florida Office: Suite 200, Phillips Point East Tower, 777 South Flagler Drive.
Telephone: 407-655-5050.
Facsimile: 407-655-6925.
Brussels, Belgium Office: Avenue Louise, 283.
Telephone: 32-2-646-2777.
Facsimile: 32-2-646-7574.
Foley Lardner Weissburg & Aronson Office Locations:
Los Angeles, California Office: 2049 Century Park East, Suite 3200.
Telephone: 310-277-2223.
Fax: 310-557-8475.
Sacramento, California Office: 770 L Street, Suite 1050.
Telephone: 916-443-8005.
Fax: 916-443-2240.
San Diego, California Office: 402 West Broadway, 23rd Floor.
Telephone: 619-234-6655.
Fax: 619-234-3510.
San Francisco, California Office: One Maritime Plaza, Sixth Floor.
Telephone: 415-434-4484.
Fax: 415-434-4507.

RETIRED PARTNER
Norman F. Burke

General Counsel for: The Greater Orlando Aviation Authority.
Attorneys for: United Parcel Service of America, Inc.; Citrus Central, Inc.

For Complete List of Firm Personnel, See General Section

For full biographical listings, see the Martindale-Hubbell Law Directory

GARWOOD, MCKENNA, MCKENNA & WOLF, P.A. (AV)

815 North Garland Avenue, P.O. Box 60, 32802
Telephone: 407-841-9496
1-800-941-9496
Telex: 407-841-0600
Other Orlando Office: 509 West Colonial Drive.
Cocoa, Florida Office: 200 Brevard Avenue.

Thomas C. Garwood, Jr.	Allen J. McKenna
Susan K. McKenna	Kay L. Wolf

John M. Finnigan	Kenneth Sydney Gluckman
Arthur R. Brown, Jr.	Elizabeth Hickman
Alfred Truesdell	Lori R. Benton

(See Next Column)

LEGAL SUPPORT PERSONNEL
PARALEGALS

Renea Rowe Radford	Rosalind S. McMullen
Eva L. Eaton	S. Cheray Stone
Susan Fowler DeZonia	Connie S. Smith
Linda L. Henry	Donna Jo Toney
	Tobi R. Loy

For full biographical listings, see the Martindale-Hubbell Law Directory

MORAN & SHAMS, P.A. (AV)

111 North Orange Avenue, Suite 1200, P.O. Box 472, 32802-0472
Telephone: 407-841-4141
Fax: 407-841-4148
Email: moran-shams@moran-shams.com

Thomas P. Moran	Robert W. Rasch
Kelly T. Blystone	Christopher C. Skambis
Brian J. Moran	James F. Kidd

Representative Clients: Adventist Health System Sunbelt Healthcare Corporation; China Group, Inc.; Cruises Only, Inc.; Florida Hospital; Gencor Industries Inc.; H.J. Heinz Co.; Kvaerner Tralfalger House Construction Co.; Medical Artificial Intelligence Inc.; Presbyterian Retirement Communities, Inc.; Vermont American Corporation.

For full biographical listings, see the Martindale-Hubbell Law Directory

MULLER, MINTZ, KORNREICH, CALDWELL, CASEY, CROSLAND & BRAMNICK, P.A. (AV)

Suite 1525 Citrus Center, 255 South Orange Avenue, 32801
Telephone: 407-843-1400
Miami, Florida Office: Suite 3600 First Union Financial Center, 200 South Biscayne Boulevard.
Telephone: 305-358-5500, Broward: 954-522-0393.

David V. Kornreich	Jeffrey E. Mandel
Michael W. Casey, III	Teresa Adamson Herrmann
James C. Crosland	Mary E. Lytle
James S. Bramnick	Benton N. Wood

Representative Clients: Florida Power & Light Co.; Universal Studios; American Telephone & Telegraph Co.; J.C. Penney Co.; Columbia Broadcasting Systems, Inc. (CBS Inc.); National Car Rental Systems, Inc.; Motorola, Inc.; Palm Beach County; Volusia County; South Miami Hospital.

For full biographical listings, see the Martindale-Hubbell Law Directory

POHL & SHORT, P.A.

(See Winter Park)

PORT RICHEY, Pasco Co.

THORNTON, TORRENCE & GONZALES, P.A. (AV)

6645 Ridge Road, 34668
Telephone: 813-845-6224
Telecopier: 813-845-7895

Ronald G. Thornton	Alfred W. Torrence, Jr.
Larry J. Gonzales	

Mark A. Goettel

For full biographical listings, see the Martindale-Hubbell Law Directory

---

SARASOTA, Sarasota Co.

KUNKEL MILLER & HAMENT (AV)

Southtrust Bank Plaza, Suite 882, 1800 Second Street, 34236
Telephone: 941-365-6006
Telecopier: 941-365-6209
Fort Myers, Florida Office: Sunbank Financial Center, Suite 400, 12730 New Brittany Boulevard.
Telephone: 813-278-1600.
Telecopier: 813-278-9056.
Tampa, Florida Office: 15438 North Florida Avenue, Suite 106.
Telephone: 813-963-7736.
Telefax: 813-969-3639.

MEMBERS OF FIRM

Daniel H. Kunkel	Michael R. Miller
John M. Hament	

Jody A. O'Konski	Michele M. Perri
Linda G. Sasser	

Representative Clients: S & E Contractors, Inc.; Asolo Center For The Performing Arts; Sun Coast Closures, Inc.; Sun Coast Media Group, Inc.; Manatee Memorial Hospital; Florida Aluminum and Steel Fabricators; Safetronics, Inc.; Sarasota University Club; Mote Marine Laboratory; First of Englewood.

For full biographical listings, see the Martindale-Hubbell Law Directory

TALLAHASSEE, Leon Co.

THE MANG LAW FIRM, P.A. (AV)

660 East Jefferson Street, P.O. Box 11127, 32302-3127
Telephone: 904-222-7710
Telecopier: 904-222-6019

Douglas A. Mang	Wendy Russell Wiener
Connie Jo Pecori	Robert E. Wolfe, JR.

For full biographical listings, see the Martindale-Hubbell Law Directory

TAMPA, Hillsborough Co.

ALLEY AND ALLEY/FORD & HARRISON (AV)

205 Brush Street, P.O. Box 1427, 33601
Telephone: 813-229-6481
Fax: 813-223-7029
Atlanta, Georgia Office: Ford & Harrison, 600 Peachtree at the Circle Building, 1275 Peachtree Street, N.E., 30309.
Telephone: 404-888-3800.
Fax: 404-888-3863.
Los Angeles, California Office: Ford & Harrison, 333 South Grand Avenue, Suite 3680, 90071.
Telephone: 213-680-3410.
Fax: 213-680-4161.
Miami, Florida Office: 516 Ingraham Building, 25 S.E. 2nd Avenue, 33131.
Telephone: 305-379-3811.
Fax: 305-358-5933.
Washington, D.C. Office: Ford & Harrison, 1920 N Street, N.W., Suite 200, 20036.
Telephone: 202-463-6633.
Fax: 202-466-5705.

Granville M. Alley, Jr.	Tony B. Griffin
(1929-1976)	James M. Craig
John-Edward Alley	David S. Shankman
Robert D. Hall, Jr.	Edmund J. McKenna

ASSOCIATES

Glen A. Bassett	David S. Harvey, Jr
Craig L. Berman	Tracey Karen Jaensch
Pedro P. Forment	Amy Wright Littrell
Collins Guyton	Jennifer M. Monrose
John A. Rine	

Representative Clients: Better Business Forms; Florida Southern College; Opus South Corp.; City of Panama City, Florida; Publix Super Markets, Inc.; Santa Fe Healthcare Systems; Skyline Mobile Homes, Inc.; Southwest Florida Water Management District; Payroll Transfers, Inc.; Val-Pak Direct Marketing System.

For full biographical listings, see the Martindale-Hubbell Law Directory

HAYNSWORTH, BALDWIN, JOHNSON AND HARPER (AV)

600 North Westshore Boulevard, Suite 200, 33609
Telephone: 813-289-1247
Facsimile: 813-289-6530
Jacksonville, Florida Office: 1506 Prudential Drive, P.O. Box 40593.
Telephone: 904-396-3000.
Macon, Georgia Office: 577 Mulberry Street, Suite 710, P.O. Box 1975.
Telephone: 912-746-0262.
Greenville, South Carolina Office: Haynsworth, Baldwin, Johnson & Greaves, P.A., 918 South Pleasantburg Drive, P.O. Box 10888.
Telephone: 864-271-7410.
Columbia, South Carolina Office: Haynsworth, Baldwin, Johnson & Greaves, P.A., 1201 Main Street, Suite 1230.
Telephone: 803-799-5858.
Raleigh, North Carolina Office: Haynsworth, Baldwin, Johnson & Greaves, P.A., 3605 Glenwood Avenue, Suite 210, P.O. Box 10035.
Telephone: 919-782-3340.
Greensboro, North Carolina Office: Haynsworth, Baldwin, Johnson & Greaves, P.A., 2709 Henry Street, P.O. Box 13310.
Telephone: 910-375-9737.
Charlotte, North Carolina Office: Haynsworth, Baldwin, Johnson & Greaves, P.A., 400 West Trade Street.
Telephone: 704-342-2588.

MEMBERS OF FIRM

Knox L. Haynsworth, Jr.	Bradley R. Johnson (Resident)
(Not admitted in FL)	Grant D. Petersen (Resident)
M. Kristen Allman (Resident)	

Donna M. Griffin (Resident)	Phillip B. Russell

Representative Clients: The Bank of Tampa; Golden Gem Growers, Inc.; Group Technologies Corporation; Indian River Memorial Hospital, Inc.; Kmart Corp.; J.C. Penney Company, Inc.; Pick Kwik Food Stores; Wellcraft Marine Corporation.

For full biographical listings, see the Martindale-Hubbell Law Directory

KUNKEL MILLER & HAMENT (AV)

Magdalene Center, Suite 106, 15438 North Florida Avenue, 33631
Telephone: 813-963-7736
Fax: 813-969-3639
Sarasota, Florida Office: Suite 882, 1800 Second Street.
Telephone: 813-365-6006.
Telecopier: 813-365-6209.
Fort Myers, Florida Office: Sunbank Financial Center, Suite 400, 12730 New Brittany Boulevard.
Telephone: 813-278-1600.
Telecopier: 813-278-9056.

Daniel H. Kunkel	Michael R. Miller
	John M. Hament

Jody A. O'Konski	Michele M. Perri
	Linda G. Sasser

Representative Clients: Gold & Diamond Source; New London, Connecticut Convalescent Center; Mid-Hudson, NY Cablevision; The Hillhaven Corp.; Bon Secours Hospital; Florida Association of Professional Employer Organizations; Integrated Health Services, Inc.

For full biographical listings, see the Martindale-Hubbell Law Directory

THOMPSON, SIZEMORE & GONZALEZ, PROFESSIONAL ASSOCIATION (AV)

Suite 200, 109 North Brush Street, 33601
Telephone: 813-273-0050
Fax: 813-273-0072

Harrison C. Thompson, Jr.	Gregory A. Hearing
(1925-1994)	Charles J. Thomas
William E. Sizemore	Arnold B. Corsmeier
Thomas M. Gonzalez	Kevin D. Johnson
Mark A. Hanley	John W. Bencivenga
Robin E. Greiwe	Kelly L. Soud

Representative Clients: Associated Builders & Contractors, Inc.; Campbell's National Car Rental; E-Systems, Inc.; Fish Memorial Hospital; Ford Motor Co.; General Telephone Company of Florida; Lockheed Missiles & Space Co.; Shands Teaching Hospital & Clinics; University of South Florida.

For full biographical listings, see the Martindale-Hubbell Law Directory

ZINOBER & McCREA, P.A. (AV)

First of America Plaza, 201 East Kennedy Boulevard Suite 850, P.O. Box 1378, 33602
Telephone: 813-224-9004
Telecopier: 813-223-4881
Email: ZMLAW@aol.com

Peter W. Zinober	Richard C. McCrea, Jr.

Edwin J. Turanchik	Cynthia L. May
Frank E. Brown	Scott T. Silverman
Charles A. Powell, IV	Malanie J. LaFond
Jacqueline Ley Brown	Danielle R. May
Nancy A. Roslow	M. Sean Moyles

LEGAL SUPPORT PERSONNEL
Debra A. Douglas (Administrator)

For full biographical listings, see the Martindale-Hubbell Law Directory

WEST PALM BEACH, Palm Beach Co.

QUARLES & BRADY (AV)

222 Lakeview Avenue, 4th Floor, 33401
Telephone: 561-653-5000
Fax: 561-653-5333
Milwaukee, Wisconsin Office: 411 East Wisconsin Avenue, 53202-4497.
Telephone: 414-277-5000.
Fax: 414-271-3552.
Madison, Wisconsin Office: Firstar Plaza, One South Pinckney Street, P.O. Box 2113, 53701-2113.
Telephone: 608-251-5000.
Fax: 608-251-9166.
Naples, Florida Office: Barnett Center, 4501 Tamiami Trail North, Suite 300, 33940-3060.
Telephone: 941-262-5959.
Fax: 941-434-4999.
Phoenix, Arizona Office: One Camelback Building, One East Camelback Road, Suite 400, 85012-1649.
Telephone: 602-230-5500.
Fax: 602-230-5598.

PARTNER
Paul M. Platte
ASSOCIATE
Elizabeth A. Dougherty

For Complete List of Firm Personnel, See General Section

For full biographical listings, see the Martindale-Hubbell Law Directory

West Palm Beach—Continued

J. DAVID RICHESON & ASSOCIATES, P.A. (AV)

Suite 900 Forum III Building, 1655 Palm Beach Lakes Boulevard, 33401
Telephone: 561-689-6660
Fort Pierce, Florida Office: 317 South 2nd Street, P.O. Box 4048, 34948.
Telephone: 561-465-5111.

J. David Richeson

Elizabeth Coke

For full biographical listings, see the Martindale-Hubbell Law Directory

WINTER PARK, Orange Co.

DEMPSEY & ASSOCIATES, P.A. (AV)

Suite 200, 1031 West Morse Boulevard, 32789
Telephone: 407-740-7778
Telecopier: 407-740-0911

Bernard H. Dempsey, Jr.   Michael C. Sasso

Frederick C. Barnes   Daniel N. Brodersen
                 Peter Francis Carr, Jr.

For full biographical listings, see the Martindale-Hubbell Law Directory

POHL & SHORT, P.A. (AV)

280 West Canton Avenue, Suite 410, P.O. Box 3208, 32790
Telephone: 407-647-7645; 407-647-POHL
Telefax: 407-647-2314

Frank L. Pohl	C. Teresa de Arrigoitia
Houston E. Short	George A. Golder
Dwight I. Cool	Norma Stanley
James Everett Shepherd V	Mark W. Garrett
John R. Simpson, Jr.	

Representative Clients: American Pioneer Title Insurance Company; Institute of Internal Auditors, Inc.; Thompson Steel, Inc.; SunTrust, N.A.; The Bank of Winter Park; Bekins Moving and Storage Co., Inc.; Champion Boats, Inc.; KeyCom Telephone Systems, Inc.

For full biographical listings, see the Martindale-Hubbell Law Directory

GEORGIA

ATLANTA,* Fulton Co.

ALSTON & BIRD (AV)

A Partnership including Professional Corporations
One Atlantic Center, 1201 West Peachtree Street, 30309-3424
Telephone: 404-881-7000
Telecopier: 404-881-7777
Cable Address: AMGRAM GA
Telex: 54-2996
Easylink: 62985848
Washington, D.C. Office: 601 Pennsylvania Ave., N.W., North Building, Suite 250 20004.
Telephone: 202-508-3300.
Telecopier: 202-508-3333.

MEMBERS OF FIRM

Alexander E. Wilson III	Robert P. Riordan
Robert H. Buckler	Clare H. Draper IV
Forrest W. Hunter	R. Steve Ensor
Anne S. Rampacek	Charles H. Morgan

ASSOCIATES

Brian D. Edwards	Kevin M. Ingham
Anna W. Gaston	Cynthia A. Little
Randall D. Grayson	R. Lindsay Marshall
Warren R. Hall, Jr.	Debra K. Scott

COUNSEL

Michael D. Kaufman   Eileen M. G. Scofield

Representative Clients: AFLAC, Inc.; Alumax; Atlantic Steel Industries, Inc.; Beers Construction Company; Georgia-Pacific Corporation; National Data Corporation; Printpack, Inc.; Primerica Financial Services, Inc.; The Ritz-Carlton Hotel Company; Waffle House, Inc.

For Complete List of Firm Personnel, See General Section

For full biographical listings, see the Martindale-Hubbell Law Directory

ARNOLD & ANDERSON (AV)

1200 Peachtree Center Cain Tower, 229 Peachtree Street, N.E., 30303
Telephone: 404-584-0200
Fax: 404-584-0845

(See Next Column)

MEMBERS OF FIRM

John M. Arnold	David H. Grigereit
John K. Anderson	Kevin P. Hishta
R. Bryan Struble, Jr.	

OF COUNSEL

James P. Swann, Jr.

Representative Clients: EBCO Manufacturing Co.; Flowers Industries, Inc.; Golf Host Resorts, Inc. d/b/a "Tamarron" Hilton Resort; Life Care Centers of America; MagneTek, Inc.; M.O.D.E., Inc.; Mother's Cake & Cookie Co.; My Bread Baking Co.; Petrie Retail, Inc.; President Baking Co., Inc.

For full biographical listings, see the Martindale-Hubbell Law Directory

CONSTANGY, BROOKS & SMITH, LLC (AV)

Suite 2400, 230 Peachtree Street, N.W., 30303-1557
Telephone: 404-525-8622
Birmingham, Alabama Office: Suite 1410 AmSouth/Harbert Plaza, 1901 Sixth Avenue North.
Telephone: 205-252-9321.
Nashville, Tennessee Office: Suite 1080 Vanderbilt Plaza, 2100 West End Avenue.
Telephone: 615-320-5200.
Columbia, South Carolina Office: Suite 810 NationsBank Tower, 1301 Gervais Street.
Telephone: 803-256-3200.
Winston-Salem, North Carolina Office: Suite 300, 101 South Stratford Road.
Telephone: 910-721-1001. Charlotte: 704-344-1040.
Arlington, Virginia Office: Suite 990, 13 North 17th Street.
Telephone: 703-527-0900.
Fax: 703-527-2605.

MEMBERS OF FIRM

Lovic A. Brooks, Jr.	Patrick R. Tyson
James F. Smith	(Not admitted in GA)
George B. Smith	William Keith Principe
Michael J. Shershin, Jr.	Neil H. Wasser
Herman L. Allison	R. Carl Cannon
Alan L. Rolnick	Steven S. Greene
Edward Katze	Mitchell S. Allen
Fred M. Richardson	Gregory W. Blount
Lee E. Boeke	Donald W. Benson
Townsell G. Marshall, Jr.	Frank B. Shuster
Daniel P. Murphy	Robert C. Lemert, Jr.
Rosemary C. Lumpkins	

ASSOCIATES

Michael L. Blumenthal	Timothy R. Newton
Mark A. Crawford	Mandi M. Norton
Karen A. Davis	Iván M. Viera
Timothy A. Davis	(Not admitted in GA)
Ruth L. Flemister	Nedra L. Wick
J. Michael Kettle	Timothy L. Williams
Wayne W. Wisong	

Representative Clients: Blockbuster Entertainment Corp.; Blue Cross/Blue Shield of Alabama; Consolidated Freightways, Inc.; McDonald's; Merck & Co., Inc.; Mohawk Carpet Corporation; Philip-Morris Cos., Inc.; Phillips Van Heusen Corp.; Sara Lee Corp.; SunTrust.

For full biographical listings, see the Martindale-Hubbell Law Directory

DREW ECKL & FARNHAM (AV)

880 West Peachtree Street, P.O. Box 7600, 30357
Telephone: 404-885-1400
Facsimile: 404-876-0992
Email: drew@igc.apc.org

MEMBERS OF FIRM

Theodore Freeman	Daniel C. Kniffen
B. Holland Pritchard	Benton J. Mathis, Jr.
Stephen W. Mooney	

ASSOCIATES

Peter H. Schmidt, II	Nancy F. Rigby
April Rich	Mary Anne Ackourey
Maureen M. Middleton	Stuart B. Bagley
Leigh Lawson Reeves	Jennifer E. Moore

OF COUNSEL

Christopher E. Parker

Representative Clients: Abrams Industries, Inc.; AGCO Corporation; C.W. Matthews Contracting Co., Inc.; Chicago Title & Trust Co.; Diamond Mills, Inc.; General Motors Corp.; Frito Lay, Inc.; Interstate Brands Corp.; John H. Harland Co.; National Services Industries, Inc.

For Complete List of Firm Personnel, See General Section

For full biographical listings, see the Martindale-Hubbell Law Directory

ELARBEE, THOMPSON & TRAPNELL (AV)

800 Peachtree-Cain Tower, 229 Peachtree Street, N.E., 30303
Telephone: 404-659-6700
Fax: 404-222-9718

(See Next Column)

ELARBEE, THOMPSON & TRAPNELL, *Atlanta—Continued*

MEMBERS OF FIRM

Fred W. Elarbee, Jr. (1925-1986)	Robert J. Martin, Jr.
Robert L. Thompson	Joseph M. Freeman
John R. Trapnell	Stanford G. Wilson
David M. Vaughan	Brent L. Wilson
John Lewis Sapp	Victor A. Cavanaugh
William M. Earnest	Nancy F. Reynolds
Charles K. Howard, Jr.	Sharon Parker Morgan
Walter O. Lambeth, Jr.	Mark D. Halverson
R. Read Gignilliat	

ASSOCIATES

Douglas H. Duerr	Kenneth N. Winkler
Victor J. Maya	Frederick L. Douglas
Jan M. Jacobson	Catherine M. Norman
William Drummond Deveney	Laura K. Johnson
Patrick L. Lail	Scott E. Atwood
Kelly Michael Hundley	(Not admitted in GA)
Stephanie E. Meyerson	

Representative Clients: Cox Communications, Inc.; Dunlop Tire Corp.; National Service Industries; Atlanta Gas Light Co.; Brown & Williamson Tobacco Corp.; Engelhard Corp.; Louisiana-Pacific Corp.; MCI Communications Corp.; Florida Power and Light Co.; Southwire Co.

For full biographical listings, see the Martindale-Hubbell Law Directory

---

FAIN, MAJOR & WILEY, P.C. (AV)

The Hurt Building, 50 Hurt Plaza, Suite 300, 30303
Telephone: 404-688-6633
Telecopier: 404-420-1544

Gene A. Major	Thomas E. Brennan
Charles A. Wiley, Jr.	Darryl G. Haynes

Brian Alligood	Derek A. Mendicino

OF COUNSEL
Donald M. Fain

Representative Clients: Allstate Insurance Co.; Budget Rent-A-Car; Arkansas Best Corp.; Chrysler Insurance Co.; Georgia Farm Bureau Mutual Insurance Co.; Hertz Corp.; Universal Underwriters Insurance Co.; Westfield Insurance co.; Winn-Dixie Stores, Inc.

For Complete List of Firm Personnel, See General Section

For full biographical listings, see the Martindale-Hubbell Law Directory

---

FISHER & PHILLIPS (AV)

A Partnership including Professional Corporations and Associations
1500 Resurgens Plaza, 945 East Paces Ferry Road, N.E., 30326
Telephone: 404-231-1400
Telecopier: 404-240-4249;
Telex: 54-2331
Fort Lauderdale, Florida Office: Suite 2300 NationsBank Tower, One Financial Plaza, 33394.
Telephone: 954-525-4800.
Telecopier: 954-525-8739.
Redwood City, California Office: Suite 345, Three Lagoon Drive, 94065.
Telephone: 415-592-6160.
Telecopier: 415-592-6385.
Newport Beach, California Office: 4675 MacArthur Court, Suite 550, 92660.
Telephone: 714-851-2424.
Telecopier: 714-851-0152.
New Orleans, Louisiana Office: 3710 Place St. Charles, 201 St. Charles Avenue, 70170.
Telephone: 504-522-3303.
Telecopier: 504-529-3850.

MEMBERS OF FIRM

I. Walter Fisher (1914-1994)	Ralph J. Zatzkis (Resident
Erle Phillips (P.C.)	Partner, New Orleans,
Robert J. Berghel (P.C.)	Louisiana Office)
Donald E. Wright (P.C.)	Charles S. Caulkins (P.A.)
Charles Kelso	(Resident Partner, Fort
Donald B. Harden (P.C.)	Lauderdale, Florida Office)
H. Victor Hansen (P.C.)	Robert J. Bekken (Resident
Robert W. Ashmore	Partner, Newport Beach,
John M. Capron	California Office)
James M. Walters (P.C.)	Ann Margaret Pointer
Claud L. McIver, III, (P.C.)	Michael S. Mitchell (Resident
Henry A. Huettner	Partner, New Orleans,
Ned A. Fine (Resident Partner,	Louisiana Office)
Redwood City, California	F. Kytle Frye, III
Office)	John E. Donovan
Griffin B. Bell, Jr.	John E. Thompson
William F. Kaspers (P.C.)	Thomas P. Rebel
Dean E. Rice (P.C.)	Benjamin B. Culp, Jr.
Reginald J. Bell	Ruth W. Woodling
Michael C. Towers	Douglas R. Sullenberger
Robert C. Christenson	Mairen C. Kelly

(See Next Column)

James D. Morgan (Resident Partner, New Orleans, Louisiana Office)	Robert P. Foster
	David R. Kresser
	David C. Whitlock
Sandra Mills Feingerts (Resident Partner, New Orleans, Louisiana Office)	Keith B. Romich
	Charles A. Hawkins
Roger K. Quillen	Andria Lure Ryan
John B. Gamble, Jr.	Cynthia L. Gleason
Walter J. Kruger, III	Kurt N. Peterson
John D. McLachlan (Resident Partner, Redwood City, California Office)	Karl R. Lindegren (Resident Partner, Newport Beach, California Office)
Burton F. Dodd	James C. Polkinghorn (Resident Partner, Fort Lauderdale, Florida Office)
Christopher D. Robinson (Resident Partner, Fort Lauderdale, Florida Office)	
	Kenneth A. Knox (Resident Partner, Fort Lauderdale, Florida Office)
Lawrence S. McGoldrick	
D. Albert Brannen	Robert V. Schnitz (Resident Partner, Newport Beach, California Office)
James J. McDonald, Jr. (Resident Partner, Newport Beach, California Office)	
	Lynn D. Lieber (Resident Partner, Redwood City, California Office)
Howard A. Mavity	

ASSOCIATES

David E. Duclos	Allison E. Thornton
Steven M. Bernstein	Warren Lee Nelson (Resident, Newport Beach, California Office)
Annette Marie Houck (Resident, Redwood City, California Office)	
	Susan Rinehart Ashcom
Joseph M. English	Howard B. Jackson
Georgia V. Ingram (Resident, Newport Beach, California Office)	John Phillip Boggs (Resident, Redwood City, California Office)
Stephen J. Roppolo (Resident, New Orleans, Louisiana Office)	Cheri Ann Masdea
	Bryan T. White
	Carlton C. Pilger
Robert Yonowitz (Resident, Newport Beach, California Office)	Anne M. Terra (Resident, Newport Beach, California Office)
Christine E. Howard	Ronald M. Broudy
Kenneth J. Barr	Sheldon W. Snipe
Michael D. Kabat	Christopher C. Hoffman (Resident, Newport Beach, California Office)
John M. Polson (Resident, Newport Beach, California Office)	
	John C. Glancy (Resident, Fort Lauderdale, Florida Office)
Gary E. Thomas	Leonard J. Hope
Ilene Weisbard Berman	Myrna A. Andresen (Resident, New Orleans, Louisiana Office)
Tillman Y. Coffey	
Timothy R. Maguire	
David H. Spalter (Resident, Fort Lauderdale, Florida Office)	Jeffrey A. Hannah
Robert A. Lippitt	W. Spencer Hamer (Resident, Newport Beach, California Office)
Myra K. Creighton	
Richard H. Kimberly, Jr.	
Suzanne K. Bogdan (Resident, Fort Lauderdale, Florida Office)	Courtney B. Hall (Resident, New Orleans, Louisiana Office)
Timothy H. Scott (Resident, New Orleans, Louisiana Office)	
	Joseph P. Shelton
C. R. Wright	Scott D. Piper
Donald E. Cope (Resident, Redwood City, California Office)	Eric K. Smith
	Tricia D. Martin
	Debbie A. Dickinson
Tracy L. Moon, Jr.	Martha V. Howton (Resident, Redwood City, California Office)
Kelly Lynn Kubes	
Jeffrey B. Freid (Resident, Newport Beach, California Office)	Allan L. Richards
	Daniel S. Fellner (Not admitted in GA)
Anderson B. Scott	Nancy E. Davis (Resident, Newport Beach, California Office)
Michelle C. Hamilton (Resident, New Orleans, Louisiana Office)	
	Judy L. Poag

Representative Clients: Airborne Express Corp.; Alaska International Industries, Inc.; Emory University; The Henley Group, Inc.; Miller Brewing Co.; The Prudential Insurance Company of America; United States Sugar Corp.; Yellow Freight System, Inc.

For full biographical listings, see the Martindale-Hubbell Law Directory

---

FORD & HARRISON (AV)

600 Peachtree at the Circle Building, 1275 Peachtree Street, N.E., 30309
Telephone: 404-888-3800
FAX: 404-888-3863
Los Angeles, California Office: 333 South Grand Avenue, Suite 3680, 90071.
Telephone: 213-680-3410.
Fax: 213-680-4161.
Miami, Florida Office: Alley and Alley/Ford & Harrison. 516 Ingraham Building, 25 S.E. 2nd Avenue, 33131.
Telephones: 305-373-0791; 305-371-6753.
Fax: 305-358-5933.

(See Next Column)

FORD & HARRISON—Continued

Tampa, Florida Office: Alley and Alley/Ford & Harrison. 205 Brush Street. P.O. Box 1427, 33601.
Telephone: 813-229-6481.
Fax: 813-223-7029.
Washington, D.C. Office: 1920 N Street, N.W., Suite 200, 20036.
Telephone: 202-463-6633.
Fax: 202-466-5705.

MEMBERS OF FIRM

Granville M. Alley, Jr. (1929-1976)	Thomas J. Kassin
William F. Ford (1936-1990)	Bennet D. Alsher
C. Lash Harrison	E. Scott Smith
John-Edward Alley (Not admitted in GA)	Glen H. Mertens (Resident, Los Angeles, California Office)
James C. Hoover	Jack B. Albanese
Joseph Z. Fleming (Resident, Miami, Florida Office)	Patricia G. Griffith
	Karin A. Verdon
Michael L. Lowry	F. Carter Tate
Ronald R. Kimzey	Peter F. Munger
Ronald C. Henson (Resident, Washington, D.C. Office)	William N. Hiers, Jr.
	Mallory E. Phillips, III
David C. Hagaman	Jon M. Gumbel
Michael H. Campbell	Robert E. Rigrish
Robert D. Hall, Jr. (Resident, Tampa, Florida Office)	Claude T. Sullivan
	Joshua M. Javits (Resident, Washington, D.C. Office)
D. Gerald Coker	John L. Monroe, Jr.
Paul David Jones	Frederick L. Warren, III
Jeffrey W. Bell	James M. Craig (Resident, Tampa, Florida Office)
Norman A. Quandt	
Tony B. Griffin (Resident, Tampa, Florida Office)	Chad A. Shultz
	Paul T. Ryan
Paula A. Hilburn	David S. Shankman (Resident, Tampa, Florida Office)

ASSOCIATES

Laura S. Bannon	Kari Haugen (Resident, Los Angeles, California Office)
Glen A. Bassett (Resident, Tampa, Florida Office)	Carolyn E. King
Craig L. Berman (Resident, Tampa, Florida Office)	Steven J. Lewengrub
	Ross E. Longood
Patricia Greene Butler	Andrew D. McClintock
Rebecca D. Cottingham	Edmund J. McKenna (Resident, Tampa, Florida Office)
Timothy L. Covington	
Caroline Wight Donaldson	Kevin J. Mencke
Maral Donoyan (Resident, Los Angeles, California Office)	Jeffrey D. Mokotoff (Not admitted in GA)
Marc J. Esposito	Jennifer M. Monrose (Resident, Tampa, Florida Office)
Ruth H. Fife	
Pedro P. Forment (Resident, Tampa, Florida Office)	M. Elizabeth Ortega
	Sarah B. Pierce
David N. Goldman	Karen L. Still
Leanne C. Groce	John R. Sumner, Jr
Collins Guyton (Resident, Tampa, Florida Office)	Nicole Marie Walthour (Not admitted in GA)
David Harvey (Resident, Tampa, Florida Office)	

OF COUNSEL

F. Carlton King, Jr.	Steven J. Ross
Glenn R. Bunting	William B. Paul

Representative Clients: Carrier Corporation; Columbia/HCA Healthcare Corp.; Delta Air Lines, Inc.; Federal Express Corporation; Kellogg Company; Knight Publishing Company; LIN Television Corp.; Nestle USA, Inc.; Publix Super Markets, Inc.; Regional Airline Assn.

For full biographical listings, see the Martindale-Hubbell Law Directory

---

IRVIN, STANFORD & KESSLER (AV)

One Buckhead Plaza, 3060 Peachtree Road, Suite 1050, 30305
Telephone: 404-364-2010
Fax: 404-364-2013

MEMBERS OF FIRM

Ann Hale-Smith	Gary R. Kessler
A. McArthur Irvin	Gregory S. Richters
Sandra Kaye	E. Ray Stanford, Jr.

Elizabeth Pettigrew West

For full biographical listings, see the Martindale-Hubbell Law Directory

---

JONES, DAY, REAVIS & POGUE (AV)

3500 One Peachtree Center, 303 Peachtree Street, N.E., 30308-3242
Telephone: 404-521-3939
Cable Address: "Attorneys Atlanta"
Telex: 54-2711
Telecopier: 404-581-8330
In Brussels, Belgium: Avenue Louise 480, 7th Floor, B-1050 Brussels.
Telephone: 32-2-645-14-11.
Telecopier: 32-2-645-14-45.
In Chicago, Illinois: 77 West Wacker.
Telephone: 312-782-3939.
Telecopier: 312-782-8585.

(See Next Column)

In Cleveland, Ohio: North Point. 901 Lakeside Avenue.
Telephone: 216-586-3939.
Cable Address: "Attorneys Cleveland".
Telex: 980389.
Telecopier: 216-579-0212.
In Columbus, Ohio: 1900 Huntington Center.
Telephone: 614-469-3939.
Cable Address: "Attorneys Columbus".
Telecopier: 614-461-4198.
In Dallas, Texas: 2300 Trammell Crow Center, 2001 Ross Avenue.
Telephone: 214-220-3939.
Cable Address: "Attorneys Dallas."
Telex: 730852.
Telecopier: 214-969-5100.
In Frankfurt, Germany: Triton Haus, Bockenheimer Landstrasse 42, 60323 Frankfurt am Main.
Telephone: 49-69-9726-3939.
Telecopier: 49-69-9726-3993.
In Geneva, Switzerland: 20, rue de Candolle.
Telephone: 41-22-320-2339.
Telecopier: 41-22-320-1232.
In Hong Kong: 29th Floor, Entertainment Building, 30 Queen's Road Central.
Telephone.
Telecopier: 852-2526-6895.
Telecopier: 852-2868-5871 or 852-2868-5699.
In Irvine, California: 2603 Main Street, Suite 900.
Telephone: 714-851-3939.
Telex: 194911 Lawyers LSA.
Telecopier: 714-553-7539.
In London, England: One Mount Street.
Telephone: 44-71-493-9361.
Cable Address: "Surgoe London WI."
Telecopier: 44-71-493-9666.
In Los Angeles, California: 555 West Fifth Street, Suite 4600.
Telephone: 213-489-3939.
Telex: 181439 UD.
Telecopier: 213-243-2539.
In New Delhi, India: Pathak & Associates, 9th Floor, Dr. Gopal Das Bhaven, 28 Barakhamba Road.
Telephone: 91-11-331-9719.
Telecopier: 91-11-331-7802.
In New York, New York: 599 Lexington Avenue.
Telephone: 212-326-3939.
Cable Address: "JONESDAY NEWYORK."
Telex: 237013 JDRP UR.
Telecopier: 212-755-7306.
In Paris, France: 62, rue du Faubourg Saint-Honore.
Telephone: 33-1-44-71-3939.
Cable Address: "Surgoe Paris."
Telex: 290156 Surgoe.
Telecopier: 33-1-49-24-0471.
In Pittsburgh, Pennsylvania: 500 Grant Street, 31st Floor.
Telephone: 412-391-3939.
Cable Address: "Attorneys Pittsburgh".
Telecopier: 412-394-7959.
In Riyadh, Saudi Arabia: Law Offices of Saud M.A. Shawwaf, P.O. Box 22166.
Telephone: (966-1) 462-8866.
Telex: 401831 SAUCON SJ.
Telecopier: (966-1) 462-9001.
In Taipei, Taiwan: 8th Floor, 2 Tun Hwa South Road, Section 2.
Telephone: (886-2) 704-6808.
Telecopier: (886-2) 704-6791.
In Tokyo, Japan: Toranomon MT Building, 4th Floor, 10-3, Toranomon 3-Chome, Minato-ku, Tokyo 105, Japan.
Telephone: 81-3-3433-3939.
Telecopier: 81-3-5401-2725.
In Washington, D.C.: Metropolitan Square, 1450 G Street, N.W.
Telephone: 202-879-3939.
Cable Address: "Attorneys Washington."
Telex: 89-2410 ATTORNEYS WASH.
Telecopier: 202-737-2832.

MEMBER OF FIRM IN ATLANTA

Deborah A. Sudbury

For Complete List of Firm Personnel, See General Section

For full biographical listings, see the Martindale-Hubbell Law Directory

---

KILPATRICK & CODY LLP (AV)

Suite 2800, 1100 Peachtree Street, 30309-4530
Telephone: 404-815-6500
Telephone Copier: 404-815-6555
Telex: 54-2307
Washington, D.C. Office: Suite 800, 700 13th Street, N.W., 20005.
Telephone: 202-508-5800. Telephone Copier: 202-508-5858.
Brussels, Belgium Office: Avenue Louise 65, BTE 3, 1050 Brussels.
Telephone: (32) (2) 533-03-00.
Telecopier: (32) (2) 534-86-38.
London, England Office: 68 Pall Mall, London, SW1Y 5ES, England.
Telephone: (44) (71) 321 0477.
Telecopier: (44) (71) 930 9733.
Augusta, Georgia Office: Suite 1400 First Union Bank Building, P.O. Box 2043, 30903. Telephone (706) 724-2622. Telecopier (706) 722-0219.

(See Next Column)

KILPATRICK & CODY, *Atlanta—Continued*

MEMBERS OF FIRM

Duane C. Aldrich	Walter E. Johnson
Robert E. Banta	Edmund M. Kneisel
Richard R. Boisseau	Diane L. Prucino
Thomas H. Christopher	G. Paris Sykes, Jr.
James H. Coil III	R. Slaton Tuggle, III

Jeffrey A. Van Detta

COUNSEL

David P. Phippen (Washington, D.C. Office)

SENIOR ATTORNEY

Charles M. Rice

ASSOCIATES

Amy Weinstein Adelman	Paul Vincent Lalli
W. Christopher Arbery	Daniel F. Piar
Richard B. Hankins	Lori J. Shapiro

Susan Plath Winston

For Complete List of Firm Personnel, See General Section

For full biographical listings, see the Martindale-Hubbell Law Directory

---

LONG ALDRIDGE & NORMAN, LLP (AV)

A Limited Liability Partnership including Professional Corporations
One Peachtree Center, Suite 5300, 303 Peachtree Street, 30308
Telephone: 404-527-4000
Telecopier: 404-527-4198
Washington, D.C. Office: Suite 600, 701 Pennsylvania Avenue, N.W., 20004.
Telephone: 202-624-1200.
FAX: 202-624-1298.

MEMBERS OF FIRM

Phillip A. Bradley	Deborah S. Ebel

ASSOCIATES

R. Daniel Beale	Sherri L. Kimmell

OF COUNSEL

J. Michell Philpott

For Complete List of Firm Personnel, See General Section

For full biographical listings, see the Martindale-Hubbell Law Directory

---

McKEE & BARGE (AV)

Suite 400, The Candler Building, 127 Peachtree Street, N.E., 30303
Telephone: 404-577-8300
Fax: 404-577-4902
Newnan, Georgia Office: 19 Spring Street, 30263.
Telephone: 404-577-8300.
Fax: 404-577-4902.

MEMBERS OF FIRM

Patrick W. McKee	Richmond Mason Barge

Christopher J. Ramig

ASSOCIATES

Richard H. Barbe	Susan J. Rickertsen

OF COUNSEL

James R. Marshall

For full biographical listings, see the Martindale-Hubbell Law Directory

---

OGLETREE, DEAKINS, NASH, SMOAK & STEWART, L.L.P. (AV)

3800 One Atlantic Center, 1201 West Peachtree Street, N.W., 30309
Telephone: 404-881-1300
Facsimile: 404-870-1732
Washington, D.C. Office: Fifth Floor, 2400 N Street, N.W.
Telephone: 202-887-0855.
Houston, Texas Office: Ogletree, Deakins, Nash, Smoak & Stewart, P.C., One Allen Center, 500 Dallas Street, Suite 3000.
Telephone: 713-655-0855.
Greenville, South Carolina Office: The Ogletree Building, 300 North Main Street, P.O. Box 2757.
Telephone: 864-271-1300.
Charleston, South Carolina Office: First Union Building, Suite 310, 177 Meeting Street, P.O. Box 1808.
Telephone: 803-853-1300.
Columbia, South Carolina Office: Palmetto Center, Suite 1820, 1426 Main Street, P.O. Box 11206.
Telephone: 803-252-1300.
Nashville, Tennessee Office: SunTrust Center, Suite 800, 424 Church Street.
Telephone: 615-254-1900.
Raleigh, North Carolina Office: 4101 Lake Boone Trail, Suite 511, P.O. Box 31608.
Telephone: 919-787-9700.
Albany, New York Office: 4th Floor, One Steuben Place.
Telephone: 518-434-1300.

(See Next Column)

MEMBERS OF FIRM

Homer L. Deakins, Jr.	Kristofer K. Strasser
Martha C. Perrin	Janet Quick Lewis
Wade V. Mallard, Jr.	Devin M. Ehrlich
M. Baker Wyche, III	Gregory J. Hare
Robert O. Sands	Mark L. Keenan
William A. Gray	Calvin Garner Sanford, Jr.
Margaret Hutchins Campbell	Kelly Jean Beard
Dara L. DeHaven	Dionysia L. Johnson
J. Stephen Shi	Gail E. Farb
William S. Myers	Jill W. Richburg
Charles E. Feuss	Andrea L. Bailey
David Edward Jones	L. Stanford Sherrill, Jr.
Jay Michael Barber	Lisa Robette Claxton
Phillip Lee Conner	Thomas E.D. Calender
C. Thomas Davis	E. Paige Simpkins

Representative Clients: Deere & Co.; Duke Power Co.; Eastman Chemical Co.; Flour Corporation; Mercedes Banz U.S. International, Inc.; Nissan Motor Manufacturing Corporation U.S.A.; R. J. Reynolds Tobacco Co.; Rockwell International; Textron Incorporated; Wachovia Corporation.

For full biographical listings, see the Martindale-Hubbell Law Directory

---

SCHULTEN, WARD & TURNER (AV)

Suite 1100 The Hurt Building, 50 Hurt Plaza, 30303
Telephone: 404-688-6800
Fax: 404-688-6840

MEMBERS OF FIRM

Wm. Scott Schulten	Kevin L. Ward

David L. Turner

ASSOCIATES

Lou Litchfield	Clay Morris Westbrook
Susan Kastan Murphey	Julie H. McGhee

OF COUNSEL

Donald W. Osborne

Reference: NationsBank of Georgia, N.A.

For full biographical listings, see the Martindale-Hubbell Law Directory

---

SHAPIRO, FUSSELL, WEDGE, SMOTHERMAN & MARTIN (AV)

One Midtown Plaza, Suite 1200, 1360 Peachtree Street, 30309-3214
Telephone: 404-870-2200
Facsimile: 404-870-2222

MEMBERS OF FIRM

J. Ben Shapiro, Jr.	Nicholas S. Papleacos
Ira J. Smotherman, Jr.	Seth Price
Herman L. Fussell	Michael P. Davis
Robert B. Wedge	David L. Tank
H. Fielder Martin	Cyrell E. Lynch
Ronald J. Garber	Scott I. Zucker

Daniel M. Jennings

ASSOCIATES

Connie H. Buffington	Katherine Lynn Freeman
Jason Allen Cooper	Mary L. Hahn

Wade H. Purcell

For full biographical listings, see the Martindale-Hubbell Law Directory

---

SMITH, CURRIE & HANCOCK (AV)

2600 Harris Tower-Peachtree Center, 233 Peachtree Street, N.E., 30303-1530
Telephone: 404-521-3800
Telecopier: 404-688-0671

MEMBERS OF FIRM

G. Maynard Smith (1907-1992).	Ronald G. Robey
Overton A. Currie	William E. Dorris
E. Reginald Hancock (Retired)	Brian G. Corgan
Luther P. House, Jr.	Charles W. Surasky
Glower W. Jones	Robert N. Godfrey
Robert B. Ansley, Jr.	John T. Flynn
George K. McPherson, Jr.	James F. Butler, III
Bert R. Oastler	Joseph C. Staak
James Allan Smith	Hubert J. Bell, Jr.
John G. Skinner	Philip E. Beck
J. Thomas Kilpatrick	Neal J. Sweeney
Aubrey L. Coleman, Jr.	Frederick L. Wright
Larry E. Forrester	James K. Bidgood, Jr.
Thomas E. Abernathy, IV	Randall F. Hafer
Philip L. Fortune	S. Gregory Joy
John C. Stout, Jr.	Fredric W. Stearns
Daniel M. Shea	Robert C. Chambers
Thomas J. Kelleher, Jr.	Karl Dix, Jr.
Frank E. Riggs, Jr.	William R. Poplin, Jr.

OF COUNSEL

James E. Stephenson	John E. Menechino, Jr.
Joseph Paul Henner	Marty N. Martenson

(See Next Column)

SMITH, CURRIE & HANCOCK—*Continued*

ASSOCIATES

Daniel F. DuPré	Ronald G. Polly, Jr.
Catherine M. Hobart	William L. Baggett, Jr.
George Papaioanou	R. Lee Mann, III
Christine M. MacIver	J. Cletus McGinty
Craig P. Siegenthaler	Steven C. Ellingson
Suzanne J. Mulliken	Veronica J. Cherniak
R. Randy Edwards	Kimmberly M. Bulkley
J. Chadwick Hatmaker	Scott C. Casey
Jennifer R. Williams	Kathryn B. Vargo

Labor Relations Clients: Echlin, Inc.; Genuine Parts Co. (NAPA); Proctor & Gamble Co.; First Union Corp.
Construction Clients: P.J. Dick, Inc.; Jacobs Engineering; Kitchell Contractors; Robertson-Ceco Corp.

For full biographical listings, see the Martindale-Hubbell Law Directory

STOKES LAZARUS & CARMICHAEL (AV)

80 Peachtree Park Drive, N.E., 30309-1320
Telephone: 404-352-1465
Fax: 404-352-8463

MEMBERS OF FIRM

Marion B. Stokes	William K. Carmichael
Wayne H. Lazarus	Michael J. Ernst

ASSOCIATES

Douglas L. Brooks	Gregory Mark Simpson
	Kevin R. Wolff

For full biographical listings, see the Martindale-Hubbell Law Directory

STOKES & MURPHY (AV)

Waterstone, Suite 350, 4751 Best Road, 30337
Telephone: 404-766-0076
Fax: 404-766-8823
San Diego, California Office: 3131 Camino del Rio North, Suite 320.
Telephone: 619-285-8181.
Fax: 619-285-8168
Pittsburgh, Pennsylvania Office: Foster Plaza, 680 Andersen Drive.
Telephone: 412-937-3277.
Fax: 412-920-5751.

Arch Y. Stokes	Margaret Mead Stokes
Robert L. Murphy	Karl M. Terrell
(Resident, San Diego Office)	John M. O'Donnell (Not
John R. Hunt	admitted in GA; Resident,
	Pittsburgh Office)

ASSOCIATES

Anne-Marie Mizel	Tricia D. Mading (Not admitted
(Not admitted in GA)	in GA; Resident, San Diego
Christopher T. Terrell	Office)
Carol A. Burkett Hawkins	Paul F. Sorrentino (Not
(Not admitted in GA)	admitted in GA; Resident,
	San Diego Office)

For full biographical listings, see the Martindale-Hubbell Law Directory

AUGUSTA,* Richmond Co.

STANLEY C. HOUSE (AV)

Suite 506 The Lamar Building, 753 Broad Street, P.O. Box 915, 30903-0915
Telephone: 706-722-3341
Fax: 706-722-0471
Email: schouse@counsel.com

Approved Attorney for: Lawyers Title Insurance Corp.
References: First Union Bank & Trust (Augusta); NationsBank (Augusta).

For full biographical listings, see the Martindale-Hubbell Law Directory

BRUNSWICK,* Glynn Co.

WHELCHEL, BROWN, READDICK & BUMGARTNER (AV)

5 Glynn Avenue, P.O. Box 220, 31521-0220
Telephone: 912-264-8544
Telecopier: 912-264-9667

MEMBERS OF FIRM

J. Thomas Whelchel	Terry L. Readdick
Richard A. Brown, Jr.	John E. Bumgartner
	B. Kaye Katz

ASSOCIATES

G. Todd Carter	Raleigh W. Rollins, Jr.
Richard K. Strickland	Bradley J. Watkins

Representative Clients: Georgia Power Co.; Sears, Roebuck & Co.; Allstate Insurance Co.; Commercial Union Insurance Co.; Georgia Farm Bureau Mutual Insurance Co.; Government Employees Insurance Co.; Nationwide Insurance Co.; State Farm Insurance Cos.; Wausau Insurance Cos.

For full biographical listings, see the Martindale-Hubbell Law Directory

GAINESVILLE,* Hall Co.

HARBEN & HARTLEY (AV)

539 Green Street, P.O. Box 2975, 30503
Telephone: 770-534-7341
Fax: 770-532-0399

MEMBERS OF FIRM

Sam S. Harben, Jr.	Martha McMasters Pearson
Phillip L. Hartley	Emily Bagwell Harben

LEGAL SUPPORT PERSONNEL

Barbara J. Smith	Lisa A. Rosetti

For full biographical listings, see the Martindale-Hubbell Law Directory

MACON,* Bibb Co.

HAYNSWORTH, BALDWIN, JOHNSON AND HARPER (AV)

577 Mulberry Street, Suite 710, P.O. Box 1975, 31202-1975
Telephone: 912-746-0262
Facsimile: 912-746-0797
Tampa, Florida Office: 600 North Westshore Boulevard, Suite 200.
Telephone: 813-289-1247.
Jacksonville, Florida Office: 1506 Prudential Drive, P.O. Box 40593.
Telephone: 904-396-3000.
Greenville, South Carolina Office: Haynsworth, Baldwin, Johnson & Greaves, P.A., 918 South Pleasantburg Drive, P.O. Box 10888.
Telephone: 864-271-7410.
Columbia, South Carolina Office: Haynsworth, Baldwin, Johnson & Greaves, P.A., 1201 Main Street, Suite 1230.
Telephone: 803-799-5858.
Raleigh, North Carolina Office: Haynsworth, Baldwin, Johnson & Greaves, P.A., 3605 Glenwood Avenue, Suite 210. P.O. Box 10035.
Telephone: 919-782-3340.
Greensboro, North Carolina Office: Haynsworth, Baldwin, Johnson & Greaves, P.A., 2709 Henry Street, P.O. Box 13310.
Telephone: 910-375-9737.
Charlotte, North Carolina Office: Haynsworth, Baldwin, Johnson & Greaves, P.A., 400 West Trade Street.
Telephone: 704-342-2588.

MEMBERS OF FIRM

Knox L. Haynsworth, Jr.	John G. Creech
(Not admitted in GA)	W. Melvin Haas, III (Resident)

Jeffery L. Thompson (Resident)	William M. Clifton, III
	(Resident)

OF COUNSEL

Edgar W. Ennis, Jr. (Resident)

Representative Clients: Boeing Georgia, Inc.; Fieldcrest Cannon, Inc.; General Mills; Georgia Employers Assn.; Gold Kist, Inc.; The Kroger Co.; McDonnell Douglas Corp.; Northrop Corp.; St. Joseph Hospital; Wm. Wrigley Jr. Co.

For full biographical listings, see the Martindale-Hubbell Law Directory

SAVANNAH,* Chatham Co.

FORBES & BOWMAN (AV)

Park South D-14, 7505 Waters Avenue, P.O. Box 13929, 31416-0929
Telephone: 912-352-1190
FAX: 912-352-1471

Morton G. Forbes	John A. Foster
Catherine M. Bowman	Doris E. Brannon
	Scot V. Pool

Representative Clients: AIG Claims Service; John S. James Co.; Second Harvest Food Bank; Town & Country Extermination Co., Inc.

For full biographical listings, see the Martindale-Hubbell Law Directory

HUNTER, MACLEAN, EXLEY & DUNN, P.C. (AV)

200 East St. Julian Street, P.O. Box 9848, 31412
Telephone: 912-236-0261
Cable Address: "Ancan"
Telecopier: 912-236-4936
Telex: 54-6483
Atlanta, Georgia Office: The Peachtree, 1355 Peachtree Street, N.E., Suite 1050.
Telephone: 404-876-3611.
Fax: 404-870-2025.

Malcolm R. Maclean	Wade W. Herring, II
	R. Jason D'Cruz

Representative Clients: Memorial Medical Center, Inc.; Jefferson-Pilot Life Insurance Co.; Operations Management, Inc.; Atlantic Wood Industries, Inc.; Bradley Plywood; Byrd Cookie Co.; Carson Products Co.; Friedman's, Inc.; Brasseler, U.S.A., Inc.; Domtar Gypsum.

For Complete List of Firm Personnel, See General Section

For full biographical listings, see the Martindale-Hubbell Law Directory

Savannah—Continued

KARSMAN, BROOKS & CALLAWAY, P.C. (AV)

301 West Congress Street, P.O. Box 9149, 31412
Telephone: 912-238-2750
Cable Address: "Karbro"
Telecopier: 912-238-2767

Stanley M. Karsman	R. Krannert Riddle
Charles C. Brooks	Edward M. Hughes
Timothy F. Callaway, III	Shari Sigman Miltiades
Stanley E. Harris, Jr.	D. Campbell Bowman, Jr.
James L. Drake, Jr.	Timothy J. Haeussler
Dana F. Braun	Tracie Grove Smith

For full biographical listings, see the Martindale-Hubbell Law Directory

---

HAWAII

HONOLULU,* Honolulu Co.

DWYER IMANAKA SCHRAFF KUDO MEYER & FUJIMOTO ATTORNEYS AT LAW, A LAW CORPORATION (AV)

1800 Pioneer Plaza, 900 Fort Street Mall, 96813
Telephone: 808-524-8000
Telecopier: 808-526-1419
Mailing Address: P.O. Box 2727, 96803
Email: hawaiilaw@dwyer-imanaka.com URL:
http://www.dwyer-imanaka.com

John R. Dwyer, Jr.	William G. Meyer, III
Mitchell A. Imanaka	Wesley M. Fujimoto
Paul A. Schraff	Ronald Van Grant
Benjamin A. Kudo (Atty. at	Jon M. H. Pang
Law, A Law Corp.)	Blake W. Bushnell

Adelbert Green

Richard T. Asato, Jr.	Jeffery S. Werbelow
Scott W. Settle	Lori Ann K. Koseki
Darcie S. Yoshinaga	Troy T. Fukuhara
Lawrence I. Kawasaki	Katy Y. Chen
Stacy E. Uehara	Naomi S. Uyeno
Kris N. Nakagawa	Roger B. McKeague

OF COUNSEL

Randall Y. Iwase	R. Brian Tsujimura

For full biographical listings, see the Martindale-Hubbell Law Directory

TORKILDSON, KATZ, FONSECA, JAFFE, MOORE & HETHERINGTON ATTORNEYS AT LAW, A LAW CORPORATION (AV)

Amfac Building, 15th Floor, 700 Bishop Street, 96813-4187
Telephone: 808-523-6000
Cable Address: "Counsel"
Telex: RCA 723-8185
Telecopier: 808-523-6001
Hilo, Hawaii Office: 100 Pauahi Street, Suite 206.
Telephone: 808-961-0406.
Telecopier: 808-935-6725.

Raymond M. Torkildson	Gregory M. Sato
Robert S. Katz	John L. Knorek
Ernest C. Moore, III	Sabrina R. Toma
Richard M. Rand	Perry W. Confalone
Jeffrey S. Harris	Wayne S. Yoshigai

Clayton A. Kamida	Roman F. Amaguin, Jr.

Representative Clients: Alexander & Baldwin, Inc.; Aloha Airlines, Inc.; Amfac, Inc.; Castle and Cooke, Inc.; Castle Medical Center; Theo H. Davies and Co., Ltd.; First Hawaiian Bank; General Motors Corp.; Council of Hawaii Hotels.

For Complete List of Firm Personnel, See General Section

For full biographical listings, see the Martindale-Hubbell Law Directory

---

IDAHO

BOISE,* Ada Co.

ELAM & BURKE, A PROFESSIONAL ASSOCIATION (AV)

Key Financial Center, 702 West Idaho Street, P.O. Box 1539, 83701
Telephone: 208-343-5454
Telecopier: 208-384-5844
Email: eblaw@elamburke.com

Ryan P. Armbruster	Bobbi Killian Dominick
Trudy Hanson Fouser	James A. Ford

Rebecca A. Broadbent

Representative Clients: Morrison-Knudsen, Inc.; U.S. West Communications; State Farm Insurance Cos.; Payless Drug Stores, Northwest; United Heritage Mutual Life Insurance Co.; Con-Agra, Inc.; J.R. Simplot Co.

For Complete List of Firm Personnel, See General Section

For full biographical listings, see the Martindale-Hubbell Law Directory

MOFFATT, THOMAS, BARRETT, ROCK & FIELDS, CHARTERED (AV)

101 South Capitol Boulevard, P.O. Box 829, 83702
Telephone: 208-345-2000
FAX: 208-385-5384
Email: info@moffatt.com
Idaho Falls Office: 525 Park Avenue, Suite 2D, P.O. Box 1367, 83403.
Telephone: 208-522-6700.
FAX: 208-522-5111.
Pocatello, Idaho Office: 845 West Center, Suite C, P.O. Box 4941, 83201.
Telephone: 208-233-2001.

Richard C. Fields	Patricia M. Olsson

Representative Clients: BMC West Corporation; Chevron, U.S.A.; First Security Bank of Idaho, N.A.; General Motors Corp.; Idaho Potato Commission; Intermountain Gas Co.; John Alden Life Insurance Co.; Micron Technology, Inc.; Royal Insurance Cos.; St. Luke's Regional Medical Center & Mountain States Tumor Institute.

For Complete List of Firm Personnel, See General Section

For full biographical listings, see the Martindale-Hubbell Law Directory

---

ILLINOIS

BELLEVILLE,* St. Clair Co.

THOMPSON COBURN (AV)

525 West Main Street, 62220
Telephone: 618-277-4700; 314-271-1800
Telecopier: 618-236-3434
St. Louis, Missouri Office: One Mercantile Center.
Telephone: 314-552-6000.
Telecopier: 314-552-7000.
St. Charles, Missouri Office: 200 North Third Street.
Telephone: 314-946-7717.
Telecopier: 314-946-4938.
Washington, D.C. Office: 700 14th Street, N.W., Suite 900.
Telephone: 202-508-1000.
Telecopier: 202-508-1010.
Houston, Texas Office: 2400 NationsBank Center, 700 Louisiana.
Telephone: 713-225-3800.
Telecopier: 713-225-3828.

MEMBERS OF FIRM

David F. Yates	Charles M. Poplstein

Harry W. Wellford, Jr.

OF COUNSEL

Robert L. Broderick

ASSOCIATE

Kelly M. Brown

Representative Clients: First Illinois Bank; Harcros Pigments, Inc.; Magna Group, Inc.; Memorial Hospital of Belleville; Monterey Coal Company, a division of Exxon Corporation; Norfolk Southern Corp. & affiliates; Peabody Coal Company; Zeigler Coal Company; City of Belleville.

For Complete List of Firm Personnel, See General Section

For full biographical listings, see the Martindale-Hubbell Law Directory

---

CHICAGO,* Cook Co.

ALBERT, BATES, WHITEHEAD & McGAUGH, P.C. (AV)

One South Wacker Drive, Suite 1990, 60606
Telephone: 312-357-6300
Fax: 312-357-6219

(See Next Column)

ALBERT, BATES, WHITEHEAD & McGAUGH P.C.—*Continued*

Jorge C. Albala	Laurie D. Jaffe
Charles G. Albert	Robert Kinchen
Peter H. Barrow	Raymond S. McGaugh
Fredrick H. Bates	Rory Dean Smith
Jerry D. Brown	Laura D. Ryan
Kathie M. Contois	Gregory C. Whitehead
	Allison L. Wood

For full biographical listings, see the Martindale-Hubbell Law Directory

BANTA, COX & HENNESSY (AV)

55 West Monroe Street, Suite 3500, 60603
Telephone: 312-236-0177
Fax: 312-236-5517

MEMBERS OF FIRM

Don A. Banta	J. Kevin Hennessy
	Anthony S. Graefe

Ann L. Crane	Mark Hansen
	Janice M. Rauen

For full biographical listings, see the Martindale-Hubbell Law Directory

BATES MECKLER BULGER & TILSON (AV)

8200 Sears Tower, 233 South Wacker, 60606
Telephone: 312-474-7900
Facsimile: 312-474-7898
URL: http://www.bmbt.com

MEMBERS OF FIRM

Brian W. Bulger	Paul R. Garry
J. Stuart Garbutt	Joseph E. Tilson

ASSOCIATES

Robin Edelstein	Brett G. Rawitz
Michael I. Leonard	Frederick W. Stein
Lisa A. Miller	Timothy A. Wolfe

OF COUNSEL

Brian J. Williams

For full biographical listings, see the Martindale-Hubbell Law Directory

BELL, BOYD & LLOYD (AV)

Three First National Plaza Suite 3300, 70 West Madison Street, 60602
Telephone: 312-372-1121
FAX: 312-372-2098
Email: bbl@bbl.com
Washington, D.C. Office: 1615 L Street, N.W.
Telephone: 202-466-6300.
FAX: 202-463-0678.

MEMBERS OF FIRM

Nancy E. Bertoglio	John P. (Pete) Morrison
Jeffrey A. Blevins	David M. Novak
James P. Daley	Gregory J. Schroedter
Stanley J. Garber	Edwin C. Thomas, III

OF COUNSEL

William B. Hanley

ASSOCIATES

Robert Raymond Brown	Joanne L. Hyman
Douglas M. Chalmers	David Alan Schneider
	Melissa Anne Siebert

For Complete List of Firm Personnel, See General Section

For full biographical listings, see the Martindale-Hubbell Law Directory

BERMAN & YOTIS, A PROFESSIONAL ASSOCIATION (AV)

(A Professional Association comprised of Professional Corporations)
Suite 2215, 100 North La Salle Street, 60602
Telephone: 312-726-0531
Fax: 312-726-4928

Michael H. Berman (P.C.)	William W. Yotis, III, (P.C.)

Joy C. Airaudi	Dean J. Papadakis
Eric D. Kaplan	Dean Gournis

OF COUNSEL

Karen C. Yotis

For full biographical listings, see the Martindale-Hubbell Law Directory

SUSAN BOGART (AV)

10 South La Salle Street, Suite 3505, 60603
Telephone: 312-726-9060
Fax: 312-726-9248

For full biographical listings, see the Martindale-Hubbell Law Directory

BRITTAIN SLEDZ MORRIS & SLOVAK, A PROFESSIONAL CORPORATION (AV)

500 Marquette Building, 140 South Dearborn, 60603
Telephone: 312-346-4515
Fax: 312-346-4523

E. Allan Kovar (1927-1987)	Ralph A. Morris
Max G. Brittain, Jr.	John J. Murphy, Jr.
James F. Hendricks, Jr.	Mary Aileen O'Callaghan
Gabriel J. Minc	Henry W. Sledz, Jr.
	Patricia Costello Slovak

Christine Greener	Jane M. McFetridge
John Joseph Lynch	Wendy L. Nutt

OF COUNSEL

Kearney W. Kilens	John B. Murnighan
Mary J. McNichols	P. Neill Petronella

For full biographical listings, see the Martindale-Hubbell Law Directory

CONNELLY, SHEEHAN & MORAN (AV)

350 North La Salle Street Suite 750, 60610
Telephone: 312-321-1969
Fax: 312-321-1968

MEMBERS OF FIRM

P. Kevin Connelly	Martin Harris
Jody Wilner Moran	Patrick V. Melfi
Michael J. Sheehan	James J. Oh

ASSOCIATES

Michael H. Cramer	David N. Michael
Rachel A. Hart	Julie Ann Sklaver
Anne E. Larson	Allison Zousmer Stein

Representative Clients: All Seasons Services, Inc.; American International Group, Inc.; Chicago Park District; J.C. Penney Company, Inc.; Mars, Inc.; Maryville Academy; National Automatic Merchandising Assn.; The Quaker Oats Co.; VWR Scientific; Woolworth Corp.

For full biographical listings, see the Martindale-Hubbell Law Directory

THE LAW OFFICES OF EDNA SELAN EPSTEIN (AV)

321 South Plymouth Court Suite 800, 60603
Telephone: 312-408-2750
FAX: 312-408-2760

Edna Selan Epstein

For full biographical listings, see the Martindale-Hubbell Law Directory

FOX & GROVE, CHARTERED (AV)

311 South Wacker Drive Suite 6200, 60606
Telephone: 312-876-0500
Telecopier: 312-362-0700
St. Petersburg, Florida Office: Fox, Grove, Abbey, Adams, Byelick & Kiernan, Eleventh Floor, 360 Central Avenue.
Telephone: 813-821-2080.
Tampa, Florida Office: Fox, Grove, Abbey, Adams, Byelick & Kiernan, 500 East Kennedy Boulevard, Suite 200.
Telephone: 813-223-7800.
San Francisco, California Office: 240 Stockton Street, Suite 900.
Telephone: 415-956-1360.

Shayle P. Fox	Marty Denis
Kalvin M. Grove	Steven L. Gillman
Lawrence M. Cohen	William Henry Barrett
S. Richard Pincus	Allison C. Blakley
Russell M. Kofoed	Jeffrey E. Beeson
Jeffrey S. Goldman	Robert M. Mintz
	Joel W. Rice

Mark T. Dabertin	Elisabeth E. Snyder
Tamra S. Domeyer	(Not admitted in IL)
Davi L. Hirsch	Todd D. Steenson
Joshua D. Holleb	Michael L. Sullivan
Daniel A. Kazlauski	Lynn Urkov Thorpe
Daniel R. Madock	Douglas M. Werman
Michael Paull	David Zatuchni

Labor Counsel for: National Association of Independent Insurers; Alliance of American Insurers; Great American Insurance Co.; CNA Financial Corp.; California Casualty Management.
Representative Labor Clients: Liberty Mutual Insurance Co.; Certified Grocers Midwest; Sears Logistics Services; National Wrecking Co.; GAB Business Services, Inc.

For full biographical listings, see the Martindale-Hubbell Law Directory

Chicago—Continued

FRANCZEK ● SULLIVAN ● MANN ● CREMENT ● HEIN ● RELIAS, P.C. (AV)

Suite 3400, 300 South Wacker Drive, 60606-6785
Telephone: 312-986-0300
FAX: 312-986-9192
URL: http://www.nlfpc.com

Anthony J. Crement	Paul A. Millichap
J. Todd Faulkner	David P. Radelet
James C. Franczek, Jr.	John A. Relias
Ronald J. Hein, Jr.	Michael I. Richardson
Lisa A. Lopatka	Charles P. Rose
Bruce C. Mackey	William R. Sullivan, Jr.
Robert E. Mann	Andrea R. Waintroob

James J. Zuehl

Sheila M. Brennan	John F. Kuenstler
Terrence T. Creamer	Mary Kinsella Lawler
Erika Dillon	Richard P. McArdle
Edward N. Druck	Alec Rubenstein
Michael Z. Green	Sally J. Scott
Pamela B. Hall	Patricia Trainor

Michael A. Warner, Jr.

OF COUNSEL

Wesley A. Wildman	Patricia J. Whitten

John L. Wren

LEGAL SUPPORT PERSONNEL

Caty E. Kearney

For full biographical listings, see the Martindale-Hubbell Law Directory

GESSLER, HUGHES & SOCOL, LTD. (AV)

Three First National Plaza, Suite 2200, 60602
Telephone: 312-580-0100
Telecopy: 312-580-1994

Mark S. Dym	Terence J. Moran
George W. Gessler	Mark D. Olson
John K. Hughes	Matthew J. Piers
William P. Jones	David J. Pritchard
Peter M. Katsaros	Kalman D. Resnick
Mark A. LaRose	Frederick S. Rhine
Kimberley Marsh	Jonathan A. Rothstein

Donna Kaner Socol

Benjamin P. Beringer	Alex W. Miller
Darilyn W. Bock	Belkis Cervantes Muldoon
Gary Chodorow	Jonathan D. Rosenblum
Anjali Dayal	Marci S. Sperling
Ruth M. Dunning	Dana H. Sukenik
Adam D. Ingber	J. Eric Vander Arend
Michael J. Klein	Maria L. Vertuno
Laura C. Liu	Mark B. Weiner

Charles H. Wintersteen

OF COUNSEL

James T. Derico, Jr.	Darius S. Francescatti, M.D.

Susan R. Gzesh

For full biographical listings, see the Martindale-Hubbell Law Directory

GREENE AND LETTS (AV)

30 North La Salle Street, Suite 1520, 60602
Telephone: 312-346-1100
Telefax: 312-346-4571

MEMBERS OF FIRM

Martin P. Greene	Eileen M. Letts

ASSOCIATES

Kellye A. Keyes	Terri J. Smith

Allen P. Walker

LEGAL SUPPORT PERSONNEL

Donna M. Cole

For full biographical listings, see the Martindale-Hubbell Law Directory

JONES, DAY, REAVIS & POGUE (AV)

77 West Wacker, 60601-1692
Telephone: 312-782-3939
Telecopier: 312-782-8585
In Atlanta, Georgia: 3500 One Peachtree Center, 303 Peachtree Street, N.E.
Telephone: 404-521-3939.
Cable Address: "Attorneys Atlanta".
Telex: 54-2711.
Telecopier: 404-581-8330.
In Brussels, Belgium: Avenue Louise 480, 7th Floor, B-1050 Brussels.
Telephone: 32-2-645-14-11.
Telecopier: 32-2-645-14-45.

(See Next Column)

In Cleveland, Ohio: North Point, 901 Lakeside Avenue.
Telephone: 216-586-3939.
Cable Address: "Attorneys Cleveland."
Telex: 980389.
Telecopier: 216-579-0212.
In Columbus, Ohio: 1900 Huntington Center.
Telephone: 614-469-3939.
Cable Address: "Attorneys Columbus."
Telecopier: 614-461-4198.
In Dallas, Texas: 2300 Trammell Crow Center, 2001 Ross Avenue.
Telephone: 214-220-3939.
Cable Address: "Attorneys Dallas."
Telex: 730852.
Telecopier: 214-969-5100.
In Frankfurt, Germany: Triton Haus, Bockenheimer Landstrasse 42, 60323 Frankfurt am Main.
Telephone: 49-69-9726-3939.
Telecopier: 49-69-9726-3993.
In Geneva, Switzerland: 20, rue de Candolle.
Telephone: 41-22-320-2339.
Telecopier: 41-22-320-1232.
In Hong Kong: 29th Floor, Entertainment Building, 30 Queen's Road Central.
Telephone: 852-2526-6895.
Telecopier: 852-2868-5871 or 852-2868-5699.
In Irvine, California: 2603 Main Street, Suite 900.
Telephone: 714-851-3939.
Telex: 194911 Lawyers LSA.
Telecopier: 714-553-7539.
In London, England: One Mount Street.
Telephone: 44-71-493-9361.
Cable Address: "Surgoe London WI."
Telecopier: 44-71-493-9666.
In Los Angeles, California: 555 West Fifth Street, Suite 4600.
Telephone: 213-489-3939.
Telex: 181439 UD.
Telecopier: 213-243-2539.
In New Delhi, India: Pathak & Associates, 9th Floor, Dr. Gopal Das Bhaven, 28 Barakhamba Road.
Telephone: 91-11-331-9719.
Telecopier: 91-11-331-7802.
In New York, New York: 599 Lexington Avenue.
Telephone: 212-326-3939.
Cable Address: "JONESDAY NEWYORK."
Telex: 237013 JDRP UR.
Telecopier: 212-755-7306.
In Paris, France: 62, rue du Faubourg Saint-Honore.
Telephone: 33-1-44-71-3939.
Cable Address: "Surgoe Paris."
Telex: 290156 Surgoe.
Telecopier: 33-1-49-24-0471.
In Pittsburgh, Pennsylvania: 500 Grant Street, 31st Floor.
Telephone: 412-391-3939.
Cable Address: "Attorneys Pittsburgh."
Telecopier: 412-394-7959.
In Riyadh, Saudi Arabia: Law Offices of Saud M.A. Shawwaf, P.O. Box 22166.
Telephone: (966-1) 462-8866.
Telex: 401831 SAUCON SJ.
Telecopier: (966-1) 462-9001.
In Taipei, Taiwan: 8th Floor, 2 Tun Hwa South Road, Section 2.
Telephone: (886-2) 704-6808.
Telecopier: (886-2) 704-6791.
In Tokyo, Japan: Toranomon MT Building, 4th Floor, 10-3, Toranomon 3-Chome, Minato-ku, Tokyo 105, Japan.
Telephone: 81-3-3433-3939.
Telecopier: 81-3-5401-2725.
In Washington, D.C.: Metropolitan Square, 1450 G Street, N.W.
Telephone: 202-879-3939.
Cable Address: "Attorneys Washington."
Telex: 89-2410 ATTORNEYS WASH.
Telecopier: 202-737-2832.

MEMBER OF FIRM IN CHICAGO

Dennis R. Homerin

For Complete List of Firm Personnel, See General Section

For full biographical listings, see the Martindale-Hubbell Law Directory

KAPLAN & BEGY (AV)

One First National Plaza 51st Floor, 60603
Telephone: 312-345-3000
Fax: 312-345-3119

MEMBERS OF FIRM

Fred C. Begy, III	Joseph A. Bosco
Larry S. Kaplan	Martin K. LaPointe
James D. Solon	Richard A. Walker
Robert C. von Ohlen, Jr.	Mitchell J. Kanaan

(See Next Column)

KAPLAN & BEGY—*Continued*

ASSOCIATES

John B. Austin	Michael J. Vint
Donald F. Brosnan	Maritoni Derecho Kane
(Not admitted in IL)	Adriana Gardella
J. Peter Martin	Michael J. Frazier
Neal J. Moglin	John T. Midgett
Jeffrey E. Margulis	Keith S. Yamaguchi
Kevin R. Davis	Rose Jagust
Patrick J. Keating	Thomas C. Sokol

Terrill Elise Pierce

For full biographical listings, see the Martindale-Hubbell Law Directory

LANER, MUCHIN, DOMBROW, BECKER, LEVIN AND TOMINBERG, LTD. (AV)

515 North State Street, Suite 2800, 60610
Telephone: 312-467-9800
Fax: 312-467-9479

Richard W. Laner	Joseph H. Yastrow
Lawrence F. Doppelt	Joseph M. Gagliardo
(1935-1979)	Robert H. Brown
Arthur B. Muchin	James J. Convery
Anthony E. Dombrow	Robert S. Letchinger
William L. Becker	Violet M. Clark
Alan M. Levin	James F. Vanek
Carl S. Tominberg	Jeffrey P. Carren
Mark L. Juster	Jane E. Shaffer
Gary Alan Wincek	Jill P. O'Brien
Michael Klupchak	Neil P. Stern

Thomas Vasiljevich

Robert T. Bernstein	Maureen A. Gorman
Thomas Bradley	Stefanie W. Kohen
Beth A. Clukey	Linda J. Lemel
Jeffrey S. Fowler	Clifford R. Perry, III
Scott A. Gore	Shavaun Adams-Taylor

OF COUNSEL

Isaiah S. Dorfman	Herman J. De Koven

Seymour Cohen

References: NBD Bank Chicago; Illinois; La Salle National Bank & Trust Co.

For full biographical listings, see the Martindale-Hubbell Law Directory

MATKOV, SALZMAN, MADOFF & GUNN (AV)

Suite 2900, 55 East Monroe Street, 60603-5709
Telephone: 312-332-0777
Telecopier: 312-332-6130

MEMBERS OF FIRM

George J. Matkov, Jr.	Jay G. Swardenski
James John Salzman	John N. Raudabaugh
Jeffrey L. Madoff	(Not admitted in IL)
Allan Gunn	Julia A. Martin
Larry G. Hall	Frank J. Saibert
Kenneth T. Lopatka	Steven L. Brenneman
Michael W. Duffee	Elliot H. Goldman

Deborah Lee Smith

ASSOCIATES

Mark J. Mahoney	Tammy D. McCutchen
Beth Elaine Koch	Karen J. Fellows
Christopher A. Johlie	Thomas M. Dugard
John D. Nelson	Jacqueline M. Damm
Lisa A. Wetzel	Jennifer L. Levi
Craig R. Thorstenson	Rachel B. Cowen
Kenneth F. Sparks	Susan A. Pipal
(Not admitted in IL)	Daniel B. Pasternak

For full biographical listings, see the Martindale-Hubbell Law Directory

McBRIDE BAKER & COLES (AV)

500 West Madison Street 40th Floor, 60661
Telephone: 312-715-5700
Cable Address: "Chilaw"
Telex: 270258
Telecopier: 312-993-9350
Email: lastname@mbc.com *URL:* http://www.mbc.com
Oakbrook Terrace, Illinois Office: Suite 1000, One Mid America Plaza, 60181-4710.
Telephone: 630-954-2100.
Telecopier: 630-954-2112.

MEMBERS OF FIRM

William J. Cooney	Richard F. Nelson
Kenneth A. Jenero	Mark A. Spognardi
Patrick W. Kocian	Mark J. Steger
Clifton A. Lake	William M. Stevens

Steven B. Varick

(See Next Column)

ASSOCIATES

Eric E. Mennel	George Michael Sanders

For Complete List of Firm Personnel, See General Section

For full biographical listings, see the Martindale-Hubbell Law Directory

McDERMOTT, WILL & EMERY (AV)

A Partnership including Professional Corporations
227 West Monroe Street, 60606-5096
Telephone: 312-372-2000
Facsimile: 312-984-7700
Boston, Massachusetts Office: 75 State Street, Suite 1700.
Telephone: 617-345-5000.
Facsimile: 617-345-5077.
Miami, Florida Office: 201 South Biscayne Boulevard.
Telephone: 305-358-3500.
Facsimile: 305-347-6500.
Washington, D.C. Office: 1850 K Street, N.W.
Telephone: 202-887-8000.
Facsimile: 202-778-8087.
Los Angeles, California Office: 2049 Century Park East.
Telephone: 310-277-4110.
Facsimile: 310-277-4730.
Newport Beach, California Office: 1301 Dove Street, Suite 500.
Telephone: 714-851-0633.
Facsimile: 714-851-9348.
New York, N.Y. Office: 1211 Avenue of the Americas.
Telephone: 212-768-5400.
Facsimile: 212-768-5444.
St. Petersburg, Russia Office: AOZT McDermott, Will & Emery, Griboyedova Canal 36, 191023 St. Petersburg, Russia.
Telephone: (7) (812) 310-52-44; 310-55-44; 310-59-44; 850-20-45.
Facsimile: (7) (812) 310-54-46; 325-84-50.
Vilnius, Lithuania Office: Smetonos 6, 2600 Vilnius, Lithuania.
Telephone: 370 2 61-43-08.
Facsimile: 370 2 22-79-55.

MEMBERS OF FIRM

Julie Badel	Howard L. Kastel *
Christine M. Drylie	Nancy G. Ross
Stephen D. Erf	Alan S. Rutkoff

Harry M. Sangerman *

*Denotes a lawyer employed by a Professional Corporation which is a member of the Firm.

For full biographical listings, see the Martindale-Hubbell Law Directory

McFADDEN & DILLON, A PROFESSIONAL CORPORATION (AV)

135 South La Salle Street, Suite 2110, 60603
Telephone: 312-201-8300
Facsimile: 312-201-0535

Roger J. McFadden	Thomas J. Dillon

Tyrrel J. Penn

For full biographical listings, see the Martindale-Hubbell Law Directory

MURPHY, SMITH & POLK, A PROFESSIONAL CORPORATION (AV)

Twenty-Fifth Floor, Two First National Plaza 20 South Clark Street, 60603-1891
Telephone: 312-558-1220
Telecopier: 807-3619
Email: msp@pg.net

Charles E. Murphy	Peter M. Kelly, II
Arthur B. Smith, Jr.	Richard L. Samson
Lee T. Polk	Carol A. Poplawski
Robert P. Casey	Dwight D. Pancottine
Michael T. Roumell	Daniel J. Ashley

Tracey L. Truesdale	Joseph E. Burke
Julia A. Donnelly	Charles R. Marcordes
Peter A. Steinmeyer	Sandra K. Carolina

OF COUNSEL

Karl W. Grabemann

For full biographical listings, see the Martindale-Hubbell Law Directory

SCARIANO, KULA, ELLCH AND HIMES, CHARTERED (AV)

Two Prudential Plaza 180 North Stetson Suite 3100, 60601-6224
Telephone: 312-565-3100
Facsimile: 312-565-0000
Chicago Heights, Illinois Office: 1450 Aberdeen.
Telephone: 708-755-1900.
Facsimile: 708-755-0000.

(See Next Column)

SCARIANO, KULA, ELLCH AND HIMES CHARTERED, *Chicago—Continued*

Anthony G. Scariano　　　　　Kathleen Field Orr
David P. Kula　　　　　　　　John M. Izzo
Robert H. Ellch　　　　　　　Raymond A. Hauser
Alan T. Sraga　　　　　　　　Kathleen Roche Hirsman
A. Lynn Himes　　　　　　　　Joanne W. Schochat
Justino D. Petrarca　　　　　Anthony Ficarelli
Lawrence Jay Weiner　　　　　G. Robb Cooper
　　　　　　　Daniel M. Boyle
　　　　　　　OF COUNSEL
Max A. Bailey　　　　　　　　John B. Kralovec

Patrick J. Broncato　　　　　Kelly A. Hayden
Rosanne Ciambrone　　　　　　Todd K. Hayden
Jon G. Crawford　　　　　　　David A. Hemenway
Joel R. DeTella　　　　　　　Sarah E. Joyce
Teri E. Engler　　　　　　　　Christopher L. Petrarca
Andrew C. Eulass　　　　　　　Shelia C. Riley
　　　　　　　Janet L. Schwieters

For full biographical listings, see the Martindale-Hubbell Law Directory

SMETANA & AVAKIAN (AV)

333 West Wacker Drive Suite 1015, 60606
Telephone: 312-357-0250
Facsimile: 312-357-0251
Washington, D.C. Office: 1919 Pennsylvania Avenue, N.W.
Telephone: 202-659-8087.
Facsimile: 703-321-7342.
North Springfield, Virginia Office: Suite 103, 5211 Port Royal Road.
Telephone: 703-321-9181.
Fax: 703-321-7342.

MEMBERS OF FIRM
Gerard C. Smetana　　　　　　Michael E. Avakian
　　　　　Robert J. Wittebort, Jr.
　　　　　OF COUNSEL
David E. Goodrich　　　　　　James V. Daffada
　　　　　Charmia Ylagan

For full biographical listings, see the Martindale-Hubbell Law Directory

SWANSON, MARTIN & BELL (AV)

One IBM Plaza, Suite 2900, 60611
Telephone: 312-321-9100
Fax: 312-321-0990
Wheaton, Illinois Office: 2100 Manchester Road, C-1420.
Telephone: 708-653-2266.
Fax: 708-653-2292.

MEMBER OF FIRM
Kevin T. Martin
ASSOCIATE
Barbara N. Petrungaro

For full biographical listings, see the Martindale-Hubbell Law Directory

VEDDER, PRICE, KAUFMAN & KAMMHOLZ (AV)

A Partnership including Vedder, Price, Kaufman & Kammholz, P.C.
222 North La Salle Street, 60601-1003
Telephone: 312-609-7500
Fax: 312-609-5005
New York, New York Office: Vedder, Price, Kaufman, Kammholz & Day,
805 Third Avenue.
Telephone: 212-407-7700.

MEMBERS OF FIRM
James S. Petrie　　　　　　　Michael G. Cleveland
George P. Blake　　　　　　　Lawrence J. Casazza
Richard H. Schnadig　　　　　Charles B. Wolf
John Jacoby　　　　　　　　　Michael W. Sculnick
Paul F. Gleeson　　　　　　　James A. Spizzo
Theodore J. Tierney　　　　　Edward C. Jepson, Jr.
Allan E. Lapidus　　　　　　　Bruce R. Alper
Richard C. Robin　　　　　　　Carol L. Browne
Nina Gidden Stillman　　　　　Janet M. Hedrick
Lawrence L. Summers　　　　　Randall Marc Lending
Thomas G. Abram　　　　　　　Philip L. Mowery
　　　　　　　ASSOCIATES
Thomas G. Hancuch　　　　　　Paula K. DeAngelo
Carla Rendina Owen　　　　　　Ann M. Schlaffman
Michael P. Nicolai　　　　　　Valerie Depies Harper
Nancy M. Gerrity　　　　　　　Kelly A. Starr
　　　　PARTNERS AT NEW YORK CITY
Virgil B. Day　　　　　　　　Alan M. Koral
John C. Grosz　　　　　　　　John H. Eickemeyer
　　　　　　Neal I. Korval

(See Next Column)

ASSOCIATES AT NEW YORK CITY
Jonathan A. Wexler　　　　　　Neil A. Capobianco

For Complete List of Firm Personnel, See General Section

For full biographical listings, see the Martindale-Hubbell Law Directory

WILDMAN, HARROLD, ALLEN & DIXON (AV)

225 West Wacker Drive, 30th Floor, 60606-1229
Telephone: 312-201-2000
Cable Address: "Whad"
Fax: 312-201-2555
URL: http://www.whad.com
Aurora, Illinois Office: 1851 W. Galena Boulevard, Suite 210.
Telephone: 630-892-7021.
Fax: 630-892-7158.
Waukegan, Illinois Office: 404 West Water, P. O. Box 890.
Telephone: 847-623-0700.
Fax: 847-244-5273.
Lisle, Illinois Office: 4300 Commerce Court.
Telephone: 630-955-0555.
New York, New York Office: Wildman, Harrold, Allen, Dixon & Smith.
The International Building, 45 Rockefeller Plaza, Suite 353.
Telephone: 212-632-3850.
Fax: 212-632-3858.
Toronto, Ontario affiliated Office: Keel Cottrelle. 36 Toronto Street, Ninth
Floor, Suite 920.
Telephone: 416-367-2900.
Telefax: 416-367-2791.
Telex: 062-18660.
Mississauga, Ontario affiliated Office: Keel Cottrelle. 100 Matatson
Avenue East, Suite 104.
Telephone: 416-890-7700.
Fax: 416-890-8006.

MEMBERS OF FIRM
Dana S. Connell　　　　　　　Anne Giddings Kimball
Barbara A. Cronin　　　　　　Kathryn A. Mrkonich
James D. Fiffer　　　　　　　David J. Parsons
Charles J. Griffin, Jr.　　　Fred E. Schulz
Keith C. Hult　　　　　　　　John A. Ybarra
　　　　　　　COUNSEL
　　　　　　Lee B. McClain

Jody A. Ballmer　　　　　　　Vania Montero
Richard L. Creech　　　　　　Rohit Sahgal
Shanthi V. Gaur　　　　　　　Frederick L. Schwartz
Jill S. Miller　　　　　　　　Patricia A. Scott
　　　　　　　Adam C. Wit

For Complete List of Firm Personnel, See General Section

For full biographical listings, see the Martindale-Hubbell Law Directory

WITWER, POLTROCK & GIAMPIETRO (AV)

Suite 2700, 125 South Wacker Drive, 60606
Telephone: 312-332-6000; 236-0606
FAX: 312-332-6008
Email: wpglawyr@mcs.net

MEMBERS OF FIRM
Samuel W. Witwer　　　　　　　Wayne B. Giampietro
Lawrence A. Poltrock　　　　　Brian M. Waldron
Samuel W. Witwer, Jr.　　　　Gregory N. Freerksen
　　　　　　Richard F. Sarna
　　　　　　　ASSOCIATES
James B. Dykehouse　　　　　　Michael J. Merrick
Arlene Y. Coleman-Romeo　　　Jennifer K. Poltrock
Sharon M. Goss　　　　　　　　James Patrick Popp
Donn P. LaHaie　　　　　　　　Gwendolyn D. Reeves
Thomas M. McCallister
　(Not admitted in IL)

For full biographical listings, see the Martindale-Hubbell Law Directory

GALESBURG,* Knox Co.

MUSTAIN LINDSTROM & HENSON (AV)

1865 North Henderson Street, Suite 11B, 61401
Telephone: 309-344-5252
Telecopier: 309-344-3939

MEMBERS OF FIRM
Douglas D. Mustain　　　　　　Ronald Henson
Robert Lindstrom　　　　　　　Christopher Henson
　　　　　Carl E. Hawkinson

References: The Farmers and Mechanics Bank; Norwest Bank Illinois, N.A.;
First Bank; First Financial Bank; Farmers State Bank of Western Illinois;
McGladrey and Pullen.

For full biographical listings, see the Martindale-Hubbell Law Directory

MATTOON, Coles Co.

CRAIG & CRAIG (AV)

1807 Broadway, P.O. Box 689, 61938-0689
Telephone: 217-234-6481
Telecopier: 217-234-6486
Mount Vernon, Illinois Office: 227 1/2 South 9th Street.
Telephone: 618-244-7511.

MEMBERS OF FIRM

Craig Van Meter (1895-1981)	Stephen L. Corn
Fred H. Kelly (1894-1971)	Richard Charles Hayden
Robert M. Werden (1908-1969)	Robert G. Grierson
George N. Gilkerson	Gregory C. Ray
(1911-1985)	Paul R. Lynch (Resident, Mount
John H. Armstrong	Vernon Office)
John P. Ewart	Kenneth F. Werts (Resident,
Richard F. Record, Jr.	Mount Vernon Office)

John L. Barger

ASSOCIATES

Joshua N. Rosen (Resident,	Theresa M. Thomson
Mount Vernon Office)	Kristine M. Tuttle
Kathleen M. Stockwell	Henry P. Villani (Resident,
	Mount Vernon Office)

OF COUNSEL

Jack E. Horsley

Counsel for: Monterey Coal Co., a Division of Exxon Coal USA, Inc.; Marathon Oil Co.; Illinois Central R.R. Co.; Okaw Building & Loan Assn., Mattoon, Illinois; The Medical Protective Insurance Co.; Consolidated Communications, Inc.; Lloyds Underwriters at London; Hartford Insurance Co.; Coles Together, a Not-For-Profit Corp.; Coles Building Corporation.

For full biographical listings, see the Martindale-Hubbell Law Directory

*PEORIA,** Peoria Co.

HOWARD & HOWARD ATTORNEYS, P.C. (AV)

The Creve Coeur Building, Suite 200, 321 Liberty Street, 61602-1403
Telephone: 309-672-1483
Telecopier: 309-672-1568
Kalamazoo, Michigan Office: The Kalamazoo Building, Suite 400, 107 West Michigan Avenue.
Telephone: 616-382-1483.
Telecopier: 616-382-1568.
Bloomfield Hills, Michigan Office: The Pinehurst Office Center, Suite 101, 1400 North Woodward Avenue.
Telephone: 810-645-1483.
Telecopier: 810-645-1568.
Lansing, Michigan Office: Suite 500, The Phoenix Building, 222 Washington Square, North.
Telephone: 517-485-1483.
Telecopier: 517-485-1568.
Tampa, Florida Office: First of America Plaza, Suite 2000, 201 East Kennedy Boulevard.
Telephone: 813-229-1483.
Telecopier: 813-229-1568.

Frederick G. Hoffman	Leonard W. Sachs

Representative Clients: For Representative Client list, see General Practice, Peoria, IL.

For Complete List of Firm Personnel, See General Section

For full biographical listings, see the Martindale-Hubbell Law Directory

KAVANAGH, SCULLY, SUDOW, WHITE & FREDERICK, P.C. (AV)

301 S.W. Adams Street, Suite 700, 61602
Telephone: 309-676-1381
FAX: 309-676-0324
East Peoria, Illinois Office: 111 West Washington Street, Suite 206B.
Telephone: 309-694-3707.
Fax: 309-676-0324.

Julian E. Cannell	James W. Springer
Charles G. Roth	Mark W. Marlott
Phillip B. Lenzini	David A. Koperski

Counsel for: First of America Bank - Illinois, N.A.; Travelers Insurance Co.; Phoenix Mutual Life Insurance Co.; Board of Education of the City of Peoria School District, 150; Anderson State Bank; Foster & Gallagher, Inc.; Champion Furnace Pipe Company; M.H. Equipment Corporation; Cohen Furniture Company; AgriBank FCB

For Complete List of Firm Personnel, See General Section

For full biographical listings, see the Martindale-Hubbell Law Directory

ST. CHARLES, Kane Co.

WESSELS & PAUTSCH, P.C. (AV)

Dunham Center, 2035 Foxfield Drive, 60174
Telephone: 630-377-1554
FAX: 630-377-1653
http://www.w-p.com/homepg.htm
Milwaukee, Wisconsin Office: Two Plaza East, 330 East Kilbourn Avenue, Suite 1475.
Telephone: 414-291-0600.
FAX: 414-291-0200.
Chicago, Illinois Office: Chicago Bar Association Building, 321 South Plymouth Court, Suite 900.
Telephone: 312-461-0500.
Fax: 312-461-0595.
Davenport, Iowa Office: Northwest Bank Building, 101 W. Second Street, Suite 405.
Telephone: 319-333-9102.
Fax: 319-333-9105.

Richard H. Wessels	Nancy E. Joerg
Earl P. Bailey	
(Not admitted in IL)	

Joseph R. Hlavin, Jr.	H. Allan Stark
Gregory H. Andrews	(Not admitted in IL)

Phillip B. Wilson

Representative Clients: Ace Hardware Corp.; Allied Van Lines, Inc.; Chicagoland Home Furnishings Assoc.; U.S. Precision Glass Co.; Edward Hines Lumber Co.; McCrory Stores; Patten Industries, Inc.; TSC Industries, Inc.

For full biographical listings, see the Martindale-Hubbell Law Directory

*SPRINGFIELD,** Sangamon Co.

LOEWENSTEIN, HAGEN, OEHLERT AND SMITH, P.C. (AV)

1204 South Fourth Street, 62703
Telephone: 217-525-1199
Telecopier: 217-522-6047

Ralph H. Loewenstein	Allen J. Oehlert
Henry C. Hagen	Gary L. Smith

For full biographical listings, see the Martindale-Hubbell Law Directory

*URBANA,** Champaign Co.

WEBBER & THIES, P.C. (AV)

202 Lincoln Square, P.O. Box 189, 61803-0189
Telephone: 217-367-1126
FAX: 217-367-3752

David C. Thies	John E. Thies

For Complete List of Firm Personnel, See General Section

For full biographical listings, see the Martindale-Hubbell Law Directory

INDIANA

ELKHART, Elkhart Co.

CHESTER, PFAFF & BROTHERSON (AV)

317 West Franklin Street, P.O. Box 507, 46515-0507
Telephone: 219-294-5421
Fax: 219-522-1476

MEMBER OF FIRM

Robert A. Pfaff

ASSOCIATE

Robert C. Whippo

For Complete List of Firm Personnel, See General Section

For full biographical listings, see the Martindale-Hubbell Law Directory

*EVANSVILLE,** Vanderburgh Co.

BERGER AND BERGER (AV)

313 Main Street, 47708-1485
Telephone: 812-425-8101;
Indiana Only: 800-622-3604;
Outside Indiana: 800-327-0182
Fax: 812-421-5909

MEMBERS OF FIRM

Sydney L. Berger (1917-1988)	Mark W. Rietman
Charles L. Berger	Robert J. Pigman
Sheila M. Corcoran	Andrew S. Ward

References: Citizens National Bank of Evansville; Old National Bank in Evansville.

(See Next Column)

BERGER AND BERGER, *Evansville—Continued*

For full biographical listings, see the Martindale-Hubbell Law Directory

---

BOWERS, HARRISON, KENT & MILLER, LLP (AV)

25 N.W. Riverside Drive, P.O. Box 1287, 47706-1287
Telephone: 812-426-1231
Fax: 812-464-3676

MEMBERS OF FIRM

Arthur D. Rutkowski   James P. Casey

Division Counsel in Indiana for: Southern Railway Co.
Representative Clients: Permanent Federal Savings Bank; Citizens Realty & Insurance, Inc.

For Complete List of Firm Personnel, See General Section

For full biographical listings, see the Martindale-Hubbell Law Directory

---

FINE & HATFIELD (AV)

520 N.W. Second Street, P.O. Box 779, 47705-0779
Telephone: 812-425-3592
Telecopier: 812-421-4269
Email: Fine@Fine-Hatfield.com *URL:* http://www.Fine-Hatfield.com

MEMBERS OF FIRM

Ronald R. Allen   Danny E. Glass

A List of Representative Clients Furnished Upon Request.

For full biographical listings, see the Martindale-Hubbell Law Directory

---

KAHN, DEES, DONOVAN & KAHN (AV)

P.O. Box 3646, 47735-3646
Telephone: 812-423-3183
Fax: 812-423-3841
Email: evvlaw@k2d2.com

MEMBERS OF FIRM

Arthur R. Donovan (Retired)   Larry R. Downs
Thomas O. Magan   Robert H. Brown
Jon D. Goldman

ASSOCIATE

Mark W. Clark

Representative Clients: University of Evansville; University of Southern Indiana; Welborn Hospital; Toyota Motor Manufacturing USA, Inc.; Lewis Bakeries, Inc.; Deaconess Hospital, Inc.; Guardian Automotive Trim, Inc.; Siemens Electromechanical Components, Inc.; Hella North America, Inc.; Champion Laboratories, Inc.

For Complete List of Firm Personnel, See General Section

For full biographical listings, see the Martindale-Hubbell Law Directory

---

ZIEMER, STAYMAN, WEITZEL & SHOULDERS (AV)

(Formerly Early, Arnold & Ziemer)
One Riverfront Place, 20 N.W. First Street 9th Floor, P.O. Box 916, 47706-0916
Telephone: 812-424-7575
Telecopier: 812-421-5089

MEMBERS OF FIRM

Patrick A. Shoulders   Wm. Michael Schiff
Rebecca T. Kasha

ASSOCIATES

Mary Lee Franke   David A. Guerrettaz

Reference: Old National Bank in Evansville.

For full biographical listings, see the Martindale-Hubbell Law Directory

---

FORT WAYNE,* Allen Co.

BECKMAN, LAWSON, SANDLER, SNYDER & FEDEROFF (AV)

800 Standard Federal Plaza, 46802
Telephone: 219-422-0800
Facsimile: 219-420-1013
Syracuse, Indiana Office: 200 West Main Street.
Telephone: 219-457-5727.
Facsimile: 219-457-2056.

MEMBERS OF FIRM

Jack W. Lawson   William L. Sweet, Jr.
Frank J. Gray   John H. Brandt
Howard B. Sandler   Jeffrey L. Gage
Stephen R. Snyder   Thomas J. Goeglein
James A. Federoff   Jon A. Bragalone
Brian J. T'Kindt

ASSOCIATES

Douglas R. Adelsperger   David D. Cornwell
Travis S. Friend   Craig R. Patterson
Jack C. Birch   Edward J. Ormsby
Robert L. Nicholson   Daniel B. Starr
W. Randall Kammeyer   Laurie A. Singh

(See Next Column)

OF COUNSEL

Frederick A. Beckman   Neil F. Sandler
Douglas E. Miller

Reference: NBD, N.A.

For full biographical listings, see the Martindale-Hubbell Law Directory

---

BEERS, MALLERS, BACKS & SALIN (AV)

110 West Berry Street, Suite 1100, 46802
Telephone: 219-426-9706
Fax: 219-420-1314
LaGrange, Indiana Office: 108 West Michigan Street.
Telephone: 219-463-4949.
FAX: 219-463-2789.

MEMBERS OF FIRM

E. Ross Adair (1907-1983)   Robert Owen Vegeler
Ramon S. Perry (1913-1980)   G. William Fishering
Thomas E. Ruzzo (1942-1985)   Richard E. Beers
James F. Dumas (1911-1992)   Peter G. Mallers
George P. Mallers (1928-1994)   R. Scott Perry, Jr.
Orvas E. Beers   James P. Posey
Vincent J. Backs   John W. Bowers
Stephen W. Adair   Kurt Russell Bachman
Stacey L. Katz

ASSOCIATES

Roy F. Kiplinger   Heidi Bieberich Adair
Kevin P. Bruns   Charles R. Shedlak

OF COUNSEL

James W. Jackson   Kenneth W. Maxfield

Representative Client: Farmers Mutual Insurance Company of Noble Co.

For full biographical listings, see the Martindale-Hubbell Law Directory

---

GALLUCCI, HOPKINS & THEISEN, P.C. (AV)

229 West Berry Street, Suite 400, P.O. Box 12663, 46864-2663
Telephone: 219-424-3800
Telecopier: 219-420-1260
Email: gallucci@ghtlaw.com

William T. Hopkins, Jr.   Mark S. Kittaka
John C. Theisen   Tonya S. Shea
John T. Menzie   Eric H. J. Stahlhut
M. Scott Hall   Jeffrey S. Schafer
Michael A. Scheer   Holly A. Brady
Thomas N. O'Malley   Karen A. Festa

For full biographical listings, see the Martindale-Hubbell Law Directory

---

INDIANAPOLIS,* Marion Co.

BAKER & DANIELS (AV)

300 North Meridian Street, 46204
Telephone: 317-237-0300
FAX: 317-237-1000
Fort Wayne, Indiana Office: 111 East Wayne Street, Suite 800.
Telephone: 219-424-8000.
South Bend, Indiana Office: First Bank Building, 205 West Jefferson Boulevard.
Telephone: 219-234-4149.
Elkhart, Indiana Office: 301 B South Main Street, Suite 307,
Telephone: 219-296-6000.
Washington, D.C. Office: 1701 K Street, N.W., Suite 400.
Telephone: 202-785-1565.

MEMBERS OF FIRM

Michael R. Maine   Gregory J. Utken
Wendell R. Tucker   David W. Miller
H. Patrick Callahan   Irene T. Adamczyk
John W. Purcell   Gayle L. Skolnik
John T. Neighbours   Hudnall A. Pfeiffer
Roberta Sabin Recker   Todd Murray Nierman
Gregory N. Dale

ASSOCIATES

Debra L. Hinshaw   Ji-Qing Liu
Nancy J. Futterknecht   Mark J. Sifferlen
Cynthia Pearson Purvis   Julie Manning Magid
Michael J. MacLean   Jan Michelsen

Representative Clients: Anthem Insurance Companies, Inc.; AT&T Corp.; Bank One, Indianapolis, N.A.; Borg-Warner Corp.; City of Indianapolis; Cummins Engine Co.; Eli Lilly and Co.; General Motors Corp.; Indianapolis Public Schools; United Airlines.

For Complete List of Firm Personnel, See General Section

For full biographical listings, see the Martindale-Hubbell Law Directory

Indianapolis—Continued

BOSE MCKINNEY & EVANS (AV)

2700 First Indiana Plaza, 135 North Pennsylvania Street, 46204
Telephone: 317-684-5000
Facsimile: 317-684-5173
Indianapolis North Office: Suite 1201, 8888 Keystone Crossing, 46240.
Telephone: 317-574-3700.
Facsimile: 317-574-3716.

MEMBERS OF FIRM

Charles R. Rubright	Keith E. White
Daniel C. Emerson	David L. Swider
Margaret Bannon Miller	Jon M. Bailey

ASSOCIATES

Susan E. Traynor	Karen Glasser Sharp

Representative Clients: Anacomp, Inc.; First Indiana Bank; United Parcel Service, Inc.; Metropolitan School District of Wayne Township Marion County, Indiana; Conseco, Inc.; Indianapolis Colts, Inc.; The Somerset Group, Inc.; The Quaker Oats Co.; National Football League; Cellular One Indianapolis.

For Complete List of Firm Personnel, See General Section

For full biographical listings, see the Martindale-Hubbell Law Directory

BUSCHMANN, CARR & SHANKS, PROFESSIONAL CORPORATION (AV)

1020 Market Tower, 10 West Market Street, 46204-2963
Telephone: 317-636-5511
Fax: 317-636-3661
Email: bcs@indy.net *URL:* http://www.buschmann.com/bcs/

John R. Carr, III	Stephen R. Buschmann
	John N. Shanks II

Representative Clients: Archer-Daniels Midland Co.; Ball Corp.; Industrial Valley Title Insurance; Creative Risk Management, Inc.; Deflecto Corporation; Glenfed Mortgage Corp.; Gates McDonald; Merchants National Bank & Trust Company of Muncie; Monumental Life Insurance Co.; National Council on Compensation Insurance.

For full biographical listings, see the Martindale-Hubbell Law Directory

ICE MILLER DONADIO & RYAN (AV)

One American Square Box 82001, 46282-0002
Telephone: 317-236-2100
Fax: 317-236-2219
Email: leel@imdr.com *URL:* http://www.imdr.com
South Bend, Indiana Office: 211 West Washington Street, Suite 2420.
Telephone: 219-234-7933.
Fax: 219-234-7965. Internet E-mail: leel@imdr.com. Web Site Address: http://www.imdr.com.

MEMBERS OF FIRM

Leland B. Cross, Jr.	Michael H. Boldt
William R. Riggs	Susan B. Tabler
S. R. Born	Byron L. Myers
Martin J. Klaper	Michael A. Blickman
Richard E. Parker	Robert B. Bush
Melissa Proffitt Reese	

STAFF ATTORNEY

Mikio Nishizu

RETIRED PARTNER

Alan T. Nolan

ASSOCIATES

Michael L. Tooley	Kelly A. Evans
Paul H. Sinclair	Pamela V. Keller

Counsel for: AMAX Coal Co.; Associated General Contractors of Indiana, Inc.; Citizens Gas and Coke Utility; Community Hospital, Indianapolis; Cummins Engine Company, Columbus; General Housewares Corp.; Terre Haute; Grote Industries, Inc., Madison; Indiana University; Ivy Tech State College.

For Complete List of Firm Personnel, See General Section

For full biographical listings, see the Martindale-Hubbell Law Directory

LOCKE REYNOLDS BOYD & WEISELL (AV)

1000 Capital Center South, 201 North Illinois Street, 46204
Telephone: 317-237-3800
Telecopier: 317-237-3900

James S. Haramy	Kim F. Ebert
Paul S. Mannweiler	Charles B. Baldwin
Michael T. Bindner	Julia F. Crowe
Ariane Schallwig Johnson	

Lisa Drees Tobin	Kathleen A. Hash
Kenneth B. Siepman	Thomas E. Deer
Brian L. McDermott	

(See Next Column)

Representative Clients: Ameritech Indiana; BMG Music; Indiana State University; Kraft General Foods; The Kroger Co.; Methodist Hospital of Indiana, Inc.; Miller Pipeline Corporation; Navistar International Transportation Corp.; Toyota Industrial Equipment Manufacturing, Inc.

For Complete List of Firm Personnel, See General Section

For full biographical listings, see the Martindale-Hubbell Law Directory

MCTURNAN & TURNER (AV)

2400 Market Tower, 10 West Market Street, 46204
Telephone: 317-464-8181
Telecopier: 317-464-8131

Lee B. McTurnan	Jacqueline Bowman Ponder
Wayne C. Turner	Steven M. Badger
Judy L. Woods	Matthew W. Foster
Matthew J. Salzman	

For full biographical listings, see the Martindale-Hubbell Law Directory

OWEN SHOUP TROLSON & KINZIE (AV)

Suite 3680 Bank One Tower, 111 Monument Circle, 46204-5136
Telephone: 317-267-3595
Fax: 317-267-3597

MEMBERS OF FIRM

Michael W. Owen	S. Douglas Trolson
Steven V. Shoup	Jan J. Kinzie

OF COUNSEL

Warren D. Krebs

Reference: National Bank of Indianapolis.

For full biographical listings, see the Martindale-Hubbell Law Directory

SOMMER & BARNARD, ATTORNEYS AT LAW, PC (AV)

4000 Bank One Tower, 111 Monument Circle, 46204-5140
Telephone: 317-630-4000
FAX: 317-236-9802
North Office: 8900 Keystone Crossing, Suite 1046, Indianapolis, Indiana, 46240-2134.
Telephone: 317-630-4000.
FAX: 317-844-4780.

Frederick M. King	Michael C. Terrell

Charles R. O'Keefe, Jr.

Representative Clients: Dow Chemical Co.; Farm Bureau Insurance Co.; Wabash National Corp.; Indiana Veneers Corp.; MCL Cafeterias; MPD, Inc.; Syndicate Sales, Inc.; Woods Wire Products, Inc.;

For Complete List of Firm Personnel, See General Section

For full biographical listings, see the Martindale-Hubbell Law Directory

---

*LAFAYETTE,** Tippecanoe Co.

STUART & BRANIGIN (AV)

The Life Building, 300 Main Street, Suite 800, 47902
Telephone: 317-423-1561
Telecopier: 317-742-8175

MEMBERS OF FIRM

Allison Ellsworth Stuart (1886-1950)	Stephen R. Pennell
Roger D. Branigin (1902-1975)	Anthony S. Benton
Russell H. Hart	Erik D. Spykman
Roger D. Branigin, Jr.	William E. Emerick
Thomas L. Ryan	John C. Duffey
James V. McGlone	Mark E. DeYoung
Carl W. Kloepfer	Thomas B. Parent
Thomas R. McCully	Laura L. Bowker
Larry R. Fisher	Kevin D. Nicoson
Nina B. Kirkpatrick	Susan K. Roberts
Mark Lillianfeld	John M. Stuckey
	Deborah B. Trice

COUNSEL

John F. Bodle

ASSOCIATES

Brent W. Huber	David A. Starkweather
William P. Kealey	Geoffrey Blazi
A. James Chareq	

General Counsel for: The Lafayette Life Insurance Co.; INB National Bank, N.W.; Lafayette Home Hospital, Inc.
State Counsel for: Norfolk & Western Railway Co.
Mr. Ryan is Counsel to: The Trustees of Purdue University.
Representative Clients: Aluminum Company of America; Liberty Mutual Insurance Group.

For full biographical listings, see the Martindale-Hubbell Law Directory

LA PORTE,* La Porte Co.

NEWBY, LEWIS, KAMINSKI & JONES (AV)

916 Lincoln Way, 46350
Telephone: 219-362-1577
Direct Line Michigan City: 219-879-6300
Fax: 219-362-2106
Mailing Address: P.O. Box 1816, La Porte, Indiana, 46352-1816

MEMBERS OF FIRM

John E. Newby (1916-1990)	Edward L. Volk
Daniel E. Lewis, Jr.	Mark L. Phillips
Gene M. Jones	Martin W. Kus
John W. Newby	Marsha Schatz Volk
Perry F. Stump, Jr.	Mark A. Lienhoop

James W. Kaminski

ASSOCIATES

William S. Kaminski	Christine A. Sulewski

David P. Jones

SENIOR COUNSEL

Leon R. Kaminski

OF COUNSEL

Daniel E. Lewis

Counsel for: U. S. F. & G. Co.; State Farm Mutual Insurance Co.; Auto Owners Insurance Co.; Liberty Mutual Insurance Co.; Sullair Corp.; La Porte Community School Corp.; United Farm Bureau Mutual Insurance Co.; Physicians Insurance of Indiana; La Porte Hospital, Inc.; Norwest Bank.

For full biographical listings, see the Martindale-Hubbell Law Directory

---

MARION,* Grant Co.

KILEY, KILEY, HARKER, MICHAEL & CERTAIN (AV)

300 West Third Street, P.O. Box 899, 46952-0899
Telephone: 317-664-9041
Fax: 317-664-8119

MEMBERS OF FIRM

Robert Ralph Batton (1890-1963)	David L. Kiley, Sr.
	Michael J. Kiley
Albert L. Harker (1904-1965)	Albert C. Harker
Albert Bonner Brown (1911-1981)	Thomas W. Michael
	Harry J. Certain

ASSOCIATE

Therese McCullough Pryor

Counsel for: Bank One, Marion, N.A.; Liniger Co., Inc.; Atlas Foundry Co.
Local Counsel for: GenCorp.; CPC Group; General Motors; Indiana Michigan Power Co./AEP; Indiana Bell Telephone Co.; Foster-Forbes, Division of American National Can Corp.

For full biographical listings, see the Martindale-Hubbell Law Directory

---

MERRILLVILLE, Lake Co.

BURKE, MURPHY, COSTANZA & CUPPY (AV)

Suite 600 8585 Broadway, 46410-7064
Telephone: 219-769-1313
Telecopier: 219-769-6806
East Chicago, Indiana Office: First National Bank Building. 720 West Chicago Avenue.
Telephone: 219-397-2401.
Telecopier: 219-397-0508.
Valparaiso, Indiana Office: 15 North Franklin Street, Suite 200.
Telephone: 219-531-0134.
Telecopier: 219-531-0507.
Palm Harbor, Florida Office: Suite 280, 33920 U.S. Highway 19 North.
Telephone: 813-787-7799.
Telecopier: 813-787-7237.

MEMBERS OF FIRM

Frederick M. Cuppy	Gerald K. Hrebec
Kathryn D. Schmidt	

ASSOCIATE

Kevin E. Steele

OF COUNSEL

Gregory R. Lyman

Representative Clients: Whiteco Industries; Continental Machine & Engineering Co., Inc.; Gary Steel Products Corp.; Superior Construction Co., Inc.; Federal National Mortgage Association; Morrison Construction Co.; St. Catherine Hospital of East Chicago, Indiana.

For Complete List of Firm Personnel, See General Section

For full biographical listings, see the Martindale-Hubbell Law Directory

---

HOEPPNER WAGNER AND EVANS (AV)

Twin Towers, Suite 606 South, 1000 East 80th Place, 46410
Telephone: 219-769-6552; 800-263-1466 (IN,IL)
Fax: 219-738-2349
Valparaiso, Indiana Office: 103 East Lincolnway, P.O. Box 2357, 46384-2357.
Telephone: 219-464-4961; 800-879-2246 (IN,IL).
Fax: 219-465-0603.

RESIDENT MEMBERS

John E. Hughes	F. Joseph Jaskowiak

Representative Clients: Bethlehem Steel Corporation; National Steel Corporation; Valparaiso University; Powdertech Industries.

For Complete List of Firm Personnel, See General Section

For full biographical listings, see the Martindale-Hubbell Law Directory

---

MUNSTER, Lake Co.

LAW OFFICES OF TIMOTHY F. KELLY (AV)

Suite 2A, 9250 Columbia Avenue, 46321
Telephone: 219-836-4062
Telecopier: 219-836-0167
Email: 76325.1505@Compuserve.Com

MEMBERS OF FIRM

Timothy F. Kelly	Karl K. Vanzo

ASSOCIATES

Harvey Karlovac	Steven J. Sersic

For Complete List of Firm Personnel, See General Section

For full biographical listings, see the Martindale-Hubbell Law Directory

---

SOUTH BEND,* St. Joseph Co.

JONES, OBENCHAIN, FORD, PANKOW, LEWIS & WOODS (AV)

1800 Valley American Bank Building, P.O. Box 4577, 46634
Telephone: 219-233-1194
Fax: 233-8957; 233-9675

Vitus G. Jones (1879-1951)	Roland Obenchain (Retired)
Roland Obenchain (1890-1961)	Milton A. Johnson (Retired)
Francis Jones (1907-1988)	James H. Pankow (Retired)

MEMBERS OF FIRM

Thomas F. Lewis, Jr.	Robert M. Edwards, Jr.
Timothy W. Woods	John B. Ford
John R. Obenchain	Mark J. Phillipoff
Robert W. Mysliwiec	John W. Van Laere

ASSOCIATES

Edward P. Benchik	Robert S. Sanderson

Thomas F. Lewis, III

OF COUNSEL

G. Burt Ford

Attorneys For: Koontz-Wagner Electric Co.; South Bend Controls; McDaniel Fire Systems; Network Field Services; Miles Inc.; Kuert Concrete, Inc.

For full biographical listings, see the Martindale-Hubbell Law Directory

---

VALPARAISO,* Porter Co.

HOEPPNER WAGNER AND EVANS (AV)

103 East Lincolnway, P.O. Box 2357, 46384-2357
Telephone: 219-464-4961; 800-879-2246 (IN,IL)
Fax: 219-465-0603
Merrillville, Indiana Office: Twin Towers, Suite 606 South, 1000 East 80th Place, 46410.
Telephone: 219-769-6552; 800-263-1466. (IN,IL,).
Fax: 219-738-2349.

MEMBERS OF FIRM

Larry G. Evans	James L. Jorgensen
William F. Satterlee, III	Ronald P. Kuker
Gordon A. Etzler	F. Joseph Jaskowiak
James A. Cheslek	(Resident, Merrillville Office)

Mark E. Schmidtke

ASSOCIATES

Jonathan R. Hanson	Jack A. Kramer
Lauren K. Kroeger	(Resident, Merrillville Office)

Representative Clients: Bethlehem Steel Corporation; National Steel Corporation; Valparaiso University; Powdertech Industries; Ugimag.

For Complete List of Firm Personnel, See General Section

For full biographical listings, see the Martindale-Hubbell Law Directory

IOWA

CEDAR RAPIDS,* Linn Co.

SHUTTLEWORTH & INGERSOLL, P.C. (AV)

500 Firstar Bank Building, P.O. Box 2107, 52406-2107
Telephone: 319-365-9461
Fax: 319-365-8443
Email: si-law@inav.net

Glenn L. Johnson   Mark L. Zaiger
                     Constance M. Alt

Representative Clients: Amana Society; Archer-Daniels-Midland Co.; Cargill, Inc.; Cryovac, Inc., a Division of W. R. Grace & Co.; Firstar Bank Cedar Rapids, N.A.; General Mills, Inc.; MCI; PMX Industries, Inc.; Rockwell International - Graphic Systems Division.

For Complete List of Firm Personnel, See General Section

For full biographical listings, see the Martindale-Hubbell Law Directory

COUNCIL BLUFFS,* Pottawattamie Co.

SMITH PETERSON LAW FIRM (AV)

35 Main Place, Suite 300, P.O. Box 249, 51502
Telephone: 712-328-1833
Fax: 712-328-8320
Omaha, Nebraska Office: 9290 West Dodge Road, Suite 205.
Telephone: 402-397-8500.
Fax: 402-397-5519.

MEMBERS OF FIRM

Raymond A. Smith (1892-1977)   Lawrence J. Beckman
John LeRoy Peterson   Gregory G. Barntsen
  (1895-1969)   W. Curtis Hewett
Harold T. Beckman   Steven H. Krohn
Robert J. Laubenthal   Randy R. Ewing
Richard A. Heininger   Joseph D. Thornton

ASSOCIATES

T. J. Pattermann   Paul M. Shotkoski
Daniel Fretheim   (Not admitted in IA)

Representative Clients: Redland Insurance Group; Iowa Western Community College; Farm Credit Bank of Omaha; Demma Fruit Co.; Peoples National Bank; Council Bluffs Board of Water Works Trustee.

For full biographical listings, see the Martindale-Hubbell Law Directory

DES MOINES,* Polk Co.

DICKINSON, MACKAMAN, TYLER & HAGEN, P.C. (AV)

Suite 1600 Hub Tower, 699 Walnut Street, 50309-3986
Telephone: 515-244-2600
Telecopier: 515-246-4550

Helen C. Adams   Rebecca Boyd Parrott
Brent R. Appel   Russell L. Samson
Kimberley K. Baer   David S. Steward
Joseph A. Cacciatore   John K. Vernon

Representative Clients: Adventure Lands of America; Budget Marketing Inc.; Central Tractor Farm & Country, Inc.; Dahl's Food Markets; Central Iowa KFC; Montfort, Inc.; Des Moines Board of Water Works Trustees.

For Complete List of Firm Personnel, See General Section

For full biographical listings, see the Martindale-Hubbell Law Directory

FINLEY, ALT, SMITH, SCHARNBERG, MAY & CRAIG, P.C. (AV)

604 Locust Street, Fourth Floor Equitable Building, 50309
Telephone: 515-288-0145
Telecopier: 515-288-2724

Lorraine J. May   Dawn R. Siebert

Pamela J. Prager

Representative Clients: Aetna Casualty & Surety Co.; Aetna Life Insurance Co.; ALAS; American Society of Composers, Authors and Publishers; Equitable Life Assurance Society of the U.S.; Federated Insurance Co.; Meredith Corp.
Iowa Attorneys for: Midwest Medical Insurance Co.
District Attorneys for: Norfolk & Southern Railroad; Soo Line Railroad Company.

For Complete List of Firm Personnel, See General Section

For full biographical listings, see the Martindale-Hubbell Law Directory

SHEARER, TEMPLER & PINGEL, A PROFESSIONAL CORPORATION (AV)

Suite 437 3737 Woodland Avenue (West Des Moines), P.O. Box 1991, 50309
Telephone: 515-225-3737
Fax: 515-225-9510

(See Next Column)

Thomas M. Cunningham   Leon R. Shearer
Becky S. Goettsch   Brenton D. Soderstrum
                     OF COUNSEL
                     Greg A. Naylor

For Complete List of Firm Personnel, See General Section

For full biographical listings, see the Martindale-Hubbell Law Directory

SIOUX CITY,* Woodbury Co.

SMITH & McELWAIN (AV)

505 Fifth, Suite 530, P.O. Box 1194, 51101
Telephone: 712-255-8094

MEMBERS OF FIRM

Harry H. Smith   MacDonald Smith
              Dennis M. McElwain

Representative Clients: Iowa Federation of Labor; Iowa State Building & Construction Trades Council; Bakers' Pension Fund; Iowa State Educational Assn.
Reference: Norwest Bank, N.A.

For full biographical listings, see the Martindale-Hubbell Law Directory

WATERLOO,* Black Hawk Co.

SWISHER & COHRT, P.L.C. (AV)

528 West Fourth Street, P.O. Box 1200, 50704
Telephone: 319-232-6555
FAX: 319-232-4835

Benjamin F. Swisher (1878-1959)   J. Douglas Oberman
L. J. Cohrt (1898-1974)   Stephen J. Powell
Charles F. Swisher (1919-1986)   Jim D. DeKoster
Jeffrey J. Greenwood   Samuel C. Anderson
  (1953-1995)   Robert C. Griffin
Eldon R. McCann   Kevin R. Rogers
Steven A. Weidner   Beth E. Hansen
Larry J. Cohrt   Mark F. Conway

Natalie Williams Burris

Firm is Counsel for: Koehring Corp.; Clay Equipment; Chamberlain Manufacturing Co.; Waterloo Courier.
Local Counsel for: Allied Group; John Deere Insurance; Liberty Mutual Insurance Co.

For full biographical listings, see the Martindale-Hubbell Law Directory

KANSAS

OVERLAND PARK, Johnson Co.

FISHER, PATTERSON, SAYLER & SMITH, L.L.P. (AV)

11050 Roe Avenue, Suite 210, 66211
Telephone: 913-339-6757
FAX: 913-339-6187
Topeka, Kansas Office: 534 South Kansas Avenue, Suite 400, P.O. Box 949, 66601.
Telephone: 913-232-7761.
Fax: 913-232-6604.

MEMBERS OF FIRM

Edwin Dudley Smith (Resident)   Michael K. Seck (Resident)
              David P. Madden (Resident)
ASSOCIATE
              Patrick G. Reavey (Resident)

For full biographical listings, see the Martindale-Hubbell Law Directory

TOPEKA,* Shawnee Co.

FISHER, PATTERSON, SAYLER & SMITH, L.L.P. (AV)

534 South Kansas Avenue, Suite 400, P.O. Box 949, 66601
Telephone: 913-232-7761
Fax: 913-232-6604
Overland Park, Kansas Office: 11050 Roe Avenue, Suite 210, 66211.
Telephone: 913-339-6757.
Fax: 913-339-6187.

MEMBERS OF FIRM

Donald Patterson   Steve R. Fabert
Edwin Dudley Smith (Resident,   Ronald J. Laskowski
  Overland Park Office)   Michael K. Seck (Resident,
Larry G. Pepperdine   Overland Park Office)
James P. Nordstrom   David P. Madden (Resident,
Justice B. King   Overland Park Office)
J. Steven Pigg   Steven K. Johnson

(See Next Column)

FISHER, PATTERSON, SAYLER & SMITH L.L.P., *Topeka—Continued*

ASSOCIATES

Kristine A. Larscheid
Patrick G. Reavey (Resident, Overland Park Office)
Billy E. Newman
David R. Cooper

OF COUNSEL

David H. Fisher

RETIRED

Charles Keith Sayler (Retired)

Representative Clients: Gage Shopping Center, Inc.; Fireman's Fund-American Insurance Cos.; United States Fidelity and Guaranty Co.; The Procter & Gamble Company; American Cyanamid Company; Commercial Union Insurance Companies; National Casualty/Scottsdale Insurance Co.; The Hartford; Berkshire Hathaway Companies.

For full biographical listings, see the Martindale-Hubbell Law Directory

GOODELL, STRATTON, EDMONDS & PALMER, L.L.P. (AV)

515 South Kansas Avenue, 66603-3999
Telephone: 913-233-0593
Telecopier: 913-233-8870
Email: GSEP@CJNETWORKS.COM

MEMBERS OF FIRM

Arthur E. Palmer
Harold S. Youngentob
Charles R. Hay
John D. Ensley
Michael W. Merriam
John H. Stauffer, Jr.
Les E. Diehl

SPECIAL COUNSEL

Marta Fisher Linenberger

Counsel for: Columbian National Title Insurance Co.; The Menninger Foundation; Kansas Medical Society; Kansas Hospital Association; Washburn University; Topeka Metropolitan Transit Authority; Hills Pet Nutrition, Inc.; City of Topeka; American Investors Life Ins. Co.; Stormont-Vail Regional Health Center.

For Complete List of Firm Personnel, See General Section

For full biographical listings, see the Martindale-Hubbell Law Directory

WRIGHT, HENSON, SOMERS, SEBELIUS, CLARK & BAKER, LLP (AV)

Commerce Bank Building, 100 Southeast Ninth Street, 2nd Floor, P.O. Box 3555, 66601-3555
Telephone: 913-232-2200
FAX: 913-232-3344

MEMBER OF FIRM

K. Gary Sebelius

ASSOCIATE

Michael M. Walker

Representative Client: Western Resources, Inc.; KPL/Gas Service Company; St. Francis Hospital and Medical Center; Adams Business Forms; The May Department Stores, Inc.; Payless ShoeSource, Inc.; IBP, Inc,

For Complete List of Firm Personnel, See General Section

For full biographical listings, see the Martindale-Hubbell Law Directory

WICHITA,* Sedgwick Co.

FOULSTON & SIEFKIN L.L.P. (AV)

700 Fourth Financial Center, 67202
Telephone: 316-267-6371
Facsimile: 316-267-6345
Topeka, Kansas Office: 1515 Bank IV Tower, 534 Kansas Avenue, 66603.
Telephone: 913-233-3600.
Fax: 913-233-1610.
Dodge City, Kansas Office: 810 Frontview, P.O. Box 1147, 67801.
Telephone: 316-227-8126.
Fax: 316-227-8451.
Member: Lex Mundi, A Global Association of 126 Independent Firms.

MEMBERS OF FIRM

Mary Kathleen Babcock
Gloria G. Farha Flentje
Douglas L. Stanley
J. Steven Massoni

For Complete List of Firm Personnel, See General Section

For full biographical listings, see the Martindale-Hubbell Law Directory

MARTIN, CHURCHILL, OVERMAN, HILL & COLE, CHARTERED (AV)

500 North Market Street, 67214
Telephone: 316-263-3200
Telecopier: 316-263-6298

(See Next Column)

W. Stanley Churchill
Robert D. Overman
Donald E. Hill
Charles E. Cole, Jr.
Ross A. Hollander
Jeffrey B. Hurt
Paul C. Herr

RETIRED

Marvin J. Martin

Kasey Alan Rogg   Gregory D. Ballew

Representative Clients: Labor Relations: Koch Industries, Inc.; Southwest Petro-Chem., (Division of Witco Corp.); Wescon Products Co. (Division of Latshaw Enterprises).

For full biographical listings, see the Martindale-Hubbell Law Directory

KENTUCKY

BOWLING GREEN,* Warren Co.

ENGLISH, LUCAS, PRIEST & OWSLEY (AV)

1101 College Street, P.O. Box 770, 42102-0770
Telephone: 502-781-6500
Telecopier: 502-782-7782
Email: inquiry@elpo.com

MEMBERS OF FIRM

James H. Lucas
Michael A. Owsley
D. Gaines Penn

ASSOCIATE

Regina Abrams

For Complete List of Firm Personnel, See General Section

For full biographical listings, see the Martindale-Hubbell Law Directory

KERRICK, GRISE & STIVERS (AV)

1025 State Street, P.O. Box 9547, 42102-9547
Telephone: 502-782-8160
Fax: 502-782-5856
Elizabethtown, Kentucky Office: 2935 Dolphin Drive, Suite 102.
Telephone: 502-769-5788.
Fax: 502-737-9285.

MEMBERS OF FIRM

Thomas N. Kerrick
John R. Grise
Gregory N. Stivers
H. Brent Brennenstuhl

ASSOCIATES

Lanna Martin Kilgore
Laura M. Hagan (Resident, Elizabethtown Office)
Shawn Rosso Alcott
Jason B. Bell

Representative Clients: Dollar General Corp.; Columbia Greenview Regional Hospital; Hospital Corporation of America; Hardin Memorial Hospital; Monarch Environmental, Inc.; Mid-South Management Group, Inc.; Trans Financial Bank; TKR Cable.

For full biographical listings, see the Martindale-Hubbell Law Directory

CRESTVIEW HILLS, Kenton Co.

THE LAW OFFICE OF JOHN C. GILLILAND, II (AV)

Chancellor Commons/Thomas More Centre, 2670 Chancellor Drive, Suite 290, 41017
Telephone: 606-344-8515
Fax: 606-344-8516

Elizabeth A. Zink-Pearson   Sarah Mortensen Patton

For full biographical listings, see the Martindale-Hubbell Law Directory

HARLAN,* Harlan Co.

HUFF LAW OFFICES (AV)

417 East Mound Street, Drawer 151, 40831
Telephone: 606-573-4466
Fax: 606-573-7078

Gayle G. Huff

ASSOCIATE

Antony L. Saragas

Representative Clients: Old Republic Insurance Co.; Underwriters Safety & Claims; Manalapan Mining Co.; R.B. Coal Co.; Eastover Mining Co., a division of Duke Power Co.

For full biographical listings, see the Martindale-Hubbell Law Directory

Harlan—Continued

RICE & HENDRICKSON (AV)

398 Woodland Hills, P.O. Box 980, 40831
Telephone: 606-573-3955
Fax: 606-573-3956

MEMBERS OF FIRM

William A. Rice   H. Kent Hendrickson

Representative Clients: USX Corp.; Navistar International Transportation Corp.; Bituminous Casualty Corp.; Kentucky Utilities Co.; Aetna Casualty & Surety Co.; Nationwide Insurance; The Hartford Insurance Group; Arch Mineral Corp.

For full biographical listings, see the Martindale-Hubbell Law Directory

LEXINGTON,* Fayette Co.

GESS MATTINGLY & ATCHISON, P.S.C. (AV)

201 West Short Street, 40507-1269
Telephone: 606-252-9000
Facsimile: 606-233-4269

William B. Gess (1906-1985)	Walter R. Morris, Jr.
John G. Atchison, Jr.	Robert E. Maclin, III
Charles G. Wylie	Linda W. Christian
Natalie S. Wilson	Jeffrey R. Walker
Carl Timothy Cone	Elizabeth S. Hughes
Joseph H. Miller	Christel Schrader Nash
William W. Allen	Stephen P. Stoltz
Guy M. Graves	Stephen W. Atwood

OF COUNSEL

Jack F. Mattingly   Leslie G. Phillips
William R. Hilliard, Jr.

Representative Clients: National City Bank; WLEX-TV, Inc.; Prudential Insurance Company of America; Central Kentucky Agricultural Credit Assn.; B.F. Saul Real Estate Investment Trust; American Hardware Mutual Insurance Co.; The Procter & Gamble Co.; University of Kentucky Federal Credit Union; Prudential Securities, Inc.; Thomas & King, Inc.

For full biographical listings, see the Martindale-Hubbell Law Directory

LANDRUM & SHOUSE (AV)

106 West Vine Street, P.O. Box 951, 40588-0951
Telephone: 606-255-2424
Facsimile: 606-233-0308
Louisville, Kentucky Office: 400 West Market Street, Suite 1550, 40202.
Telephone: 502-589-7616.
Facsimile: 502-589-2119.

MEMBERS OF FIRM

Mark L. Moseley   Leslie Patterson Vose
Sandra Mendez Dawahare

District Attorneys: CSX Transportation, Inc.
Special Trial Counsel: Ford Motor Co. and Affiliates (Eastern Kentucky); Clark Equipment Co.
Representative Clients: The Continental Insurance Cos.; U.S. Insurance Group; U.S. Fidelity & Guaranty Co.; Ohio Casualty Insurance Co.; CIGNA; Royal Insurance Cos.

For Complete List of Firm Personnel, See General Section

For full biographical listings, see the Martindale-Hubbell Law Directory

STOLL, KEENON & PARK, LLP (AV)

201 E. Main Street, Suite 1000, 40507-1380
Telephone: 606-231-3000
Telecopier: 606-253-1093; 606-253-1027
Frankfort, Kentucky Office: 307 Washington Street, 40601.
Telephone: 502-875-6220.
Telecopier: 502-875-6235.
Louisville, Kentucky Office: 400 West Market Street, Suite 2650, 40202-3377.
Telephone: 502-568-9100.
Telecopier: 502-568-5700.

MEMBERS OF FIRM

Robert F. Houlihan	Donald P. Wagner
Richard C. Stephenson	C. Joseph Beavin
Robert F. Houlihan, Jr.	Larry A. Sykes
	P. Douglas Barr

ASSOCIATES

Mary Beth Griffith	James D. Allen
James L. Thomerson	Charles R. Baesler, Jr.

Representative Clients: Consolidated Freightways, Inc.; IBM Corp.; Johnson Controls, Inc.; Kentucky Utilities Co.; Lexmark International, Inc.; OSRAM Sylvania, Inc.; Parker Hannifin Corp.; Square D Co.; The Trane Co.; Transylvania University

For Complete List of Firm Personnel, See General Section

For full biographical listings, see the Martindale-Hubbell Law Directory

VIMONT & WILLS (AV)

Suite 300, 155 East Main Street, 40507-1317
Telephone: 606-252-2202
Telecopier: 606-259-2927

MEMBER OF FIRM

Timothy C. Wills

ASSOCIATE

Barbara Booker Wills

For full biographical listings, see the Martindale-Hubbell Law Directory

LOUISVILLE,* Jefferson Co.

GREENEBAUM DOLL & McDONALD PLLC (AV)

3300 National City Tower, 40202
Telephone: 502-589-4200
Fax: 502-587-3695
Lexington, Kentucky Office: 1400 Vine Center Tower.
Telephone: 606-231-8500.
Fax: 606-255-2742.
Covington, Kentucky Office: 50 East River Center Boulevard, P.O. Box 2050.
Telephone: 606-655-4200.
Fax: 606-655-4239.
Cincinnati, Ohio Office: 832 Main Street.
Telephone: 513-421-8087.
Fax: 513-421-8089.

Richard S. Cleary	Philip C. Eschels
Margaret E. Keane	Jeffrey A. Savarise
	Thomas J. Birchfield

ASSOCIATES

Brent R. Baughman	Luann Devine
Elizabeth W. Lykins	(Not admitted in KY)

Representative Clients: Andalex Resources, Inc.; Ashland Oil, Inc.; Boise Cascade Corp.; Commonwealth Aluminum Corp.; Johnson Controls, Inc.; National Tobacco Co., L.P.; North American Philips Corp.; Shoney's, Inc.; Toyota Motor Manufacturing, U.S.A., Inc.; University of Louisville.

For full biographical listings, see the Martindale-Hubbell Law Directory

RICH & D'AMBROSIO, P.S.C. (AV)

Sterling Place Business Park, 3044 Breckenridge Lane Suite 103, 40220
Telephone: 502-493-0503
Fax: 502-493-0504

Ivan H. Rich, Jr.   Joseph G. D'Ambrosio
Kathleen Archer

For full biographical listings, see the Martindale-Hubbell Law Directory

SEILLER & HANDMAKER, LLP (AV)

2200 Meidinger Tower, 40202
Telephone: 502-584-7400
Telecopier: 502-583-2100
Paris, Kentucky Office: Seiller, Handmaker & Blevins, P.S.C., 1431 South Main Street.
Telephone: 606-987-3980.
Telecopier: 606-987-3982.
Cynthiana, Kentucky Office: Seiller, Handmaker & Blevins, P.S.C., 9 South Walnut.
Telephone: 606-234-2880.
New Albany, Indiana Office: 202 Pearl Street.
Telephone: 812-948-8307.
Telecopier: 812-948-8383.

Edward F. Seiller (1897-1990)

MEMBERS OF FIRM

Stuart Allen Handmaker	Maury D. Kommor
Bill V. Seiller	Cynthia Compton Stone
David M. Cantor	Glenn A. Cohen
Neil C. Bordy	Tomi Anne Blevins Pulliam
Kyle Anne Citrynell	(Paris and Cynthiana Offices)

ASSOCIATES

Pamela M. Greenwell	Donna F. Townsend
Michael C. Bratcher	Gregory A. Lindsey
John E. Brengle	Vicki L. Buba
Patrick R. Holland, II	Allen C. Platt III (Resident,
Edwin Jon Wolfe	New Albany, Indiana Office)

OF COUNSEL

Robert S. Frey

For full biographical listings, see the Martindale-Hubbell Law Directory

SMITH AND SMITH (AV)

400 North, First Trust Centre, 200 South Fifth Street, 40202-3204
Telephone: 502-587-0761
Fax: 502-589-5345

(See Next Column)

SMITH AND SMITH, *Louisville—Continued*

James U. Smith, Jr. (1914-1977)	Andrew J. Russell
S. Russell Smith (1921-1973)	S. Russell Smith, Jr.
Joseph A. Worthington	W. Kevin Smith
James U. Smith, III	John O. Sheller
Candice Laurine Bogie	

Representative Clients: Associated Builders and Contractors, Inc.; Blount, Inc.; Hall Contracting Corp.; Henry Vogt Machine Co.; Highlands Regional Medical Center; The Rogers Group; Whayne Supply Co.; W.R. Grace & Co.

For full biographical listings, see the Martindale-Hubbell Law Directory

WOODWARD, HOBSON & FULTON (AV)

2500 National City Tower, 101 South Fifth Street, 40202
Telephone: 502-581-8000
Fax: 502-581-8111
Lexington, Kentucky Office: PNC Bank Plaza, 200 West Vine Street, Suite 500.
Telephone: 606-244-7100.
Telecopier: 606-244-7111.
New Albany, Indiana Office: 611 East Spring Street, P.O. Box 288.
Telephone: 812-941-1800.
Telecopier: 812-941-1855.

MEMBERS OF FIRM
Michael A. Luvisi	Ellen M. Hesen

ASSOCIATES
Robert J. Schumacher	D. Sean Nilsen
Donna King Perry	R. Brian Evans
Kathryn A. Quesenberry	Catherine S. Astorino

Representative Clients: Brown-Forman Corp.; CSX Transportation; Fischer Packing Company; Res-Care, Inc.; Providian Corporation; Bank One; Louisville Water Co.; CARITAS Health Services, Inc.; Wal-Mart Stores, Inc.; A. O. Smith Corp.

For Complete List of Firm Personnel, See General Section

For full biographical listings, see the Martindale-Hubbell Law Directory

LOUISIANA

BATON ROUGE, * East Baton Rouge Parish

BREAZEALE, SACHSE & WILSON, L.L.P. (AV)

Twenty-Third Floor, One American Place, P.O. Box 3197, 70821-3197
Telephone: 504-387-4000
Fax: 504-387-5397
New Orleans, Louisiana Office: LL&E Tower, Suite 2400, 909 Poydras Street.
Telephone: 504-582-1170.
Fax: 504-584-5452.

MEMBERS OF FIRM
Gordon A. Pugh	Murphy J. Foster, III
Leo C. Hamilton	

ASSOCIATES
Jerry L. Stovall, Jr.	Matthew M. Courtman

Counsel for: Hibernia National Bank; South Central Bell Telephone Co.; Allied-Signal Corp.; Reynolds Metal Co.; Illinois Central Railroad Co.; The Continental Insurance Cos.; Fireman's Fund American Group; Chicago Bridge & Iron Co.; Montgomery Ward & Co.

For Complete List of Firm Personnel, See General Section

For full biographical listings, see the Martindale-Hubbell Law Directory

KEAN, MILLER, HAWTHORNE, D'ARMOND, McCOWAN & JARMAN, L.L.P. (AV)

22nd Floor, One American Place, P.O. Box 3513, 70821
Telephone: 504-387-0999
Fax: 504-388-9133
New Orleans, Louisiana Office: Energy Centre, Suite 1470, 1100 Poydras Street.
Telephone: 504-585-3050.
Fax: 504-585-3051.
Plaquemine, Louisiana Office: Suite 10, 23425 Railroad Avenue.
Telephone: 504-687-9845.
Fax: 504-382-3445.

MEMBERS OF FIRM
William R. D'Armond	Melanie M. Hartmann
Michael C. Garrard	Cynthia M. Chemay
Gregg R. Kronenberger	

(See Next Column)

Theresa R. Hagen	Carolyn S. Parmenter

Representative Clients: Anco Industries, Inc., Baton Rouge, LA; BASF Corporation, Parsippany, NJ; Cajun Electric Power Co-op., Baton Rouge, LA; City of Baton Rouge/Parish of East Baton Rouge; DSM Copolymer, Inc., Baton Rouge, LA; Georgia Gulf Corporation, Atlanta, GA; The Lamar Advertising Co., Baton Rouge, LA; Piccadilly Cafeterias, Inc., Baton Rouge, LA; Turner Industries, Ltd., Baton Rouge, LA; Vulcan Materials Company, Geismar, LA.

For Complete List of Firm Personnel, See General Section

For full biographical listings, see the Martindale-Hubbell Law Directory

LAFAYETTE, * Lafayette Parish

HILL & BEYER, A PROFESSIONAL LAW CORPORATION (AV)

101 LaRue France, Suite 502, P.O. Box 53006, 70505-3006
Telephone: 318-232-9733
Fax: 318-237-2566

John K. Hill, Jr.	Eugene P. Matherne (1962-1996)
Bret C. Beyer	Robert B. Purser
David R. Rabalais	Erin J. Sherburne
Marianna Broussard	

For full biographical listings, see the Martindale-Hubbell Law Directory

LAKE CHARLES, * Calcasieu Parish

JONES, TÊTE, NOLEN, HANCHEY, SWIFT, SPEARS & FONTI, L.L.P. (AV)

First Federal Building, P.O. Box 910, 70602
Telephone: 318-439-8315
Telefax: 436-5606; 433-5536

MEMBERS OF FIRM
Sam H. Jones (1897-1978)	Kenneth R. Spears
William R. Tête	Edward J. Fonti
William M. Nolen	Charles N. Harper
James C. Hanchey	Gregory W. Belfour
Carl H. Hanchey	Robert J. Tête
William B. Swift	Yul D. Lorio

OF COUNSEL
John A. Patin	Edward D. Myrick

ASSOCIATE
Lilynn A. Cutrer

General Counsel for: First Federal Savings & Loan Association of Lake Charles; Beauregard Electric Cooperative, Inc.
Representative Clients: Atlantic Richfield Company; CITGO Petroleum Corp.; Conoco Inc.; MONTELL, U.S.A., Inc.; ITT Hartford; Olin Corporation; OXY USA Inc.; Premier Bank, National Association; W.R. Grace & Co.; Dresser Industries, Inc.

For full biographical listings, see the Martindale-Hubbell Law Directory

METAIRIE, Jefferson Parish

JUGE, NAPOLITANO, LEYVA & GUILBEAU (AV)

3838 North Causeway Boulevard Suite 2500, 70002-1767
Telephone: 504-831-7270
Fax: 504-831-7284
Baton Rouge Office: 9613 Interline Avenue, Suite C.
Telephone: 504-928-DFND.

Denis Paul Juge	Teresa C. Leyva
Jeffrey C. Napolitano	Joseph B. Guilbeau
Thomas M. Ruli	

Kelann Etta Larguier	Charles W. Farr
Frank Whiteley	Macr E. Devenport
Lawrence B. Frieman	Gerard J. Haddican, II
Mayra Leyva	Patrick J. Browne, Jr.

For full biographical listings, see the Martindale-Hubbell Law Directory

NEW ORLEANS, * Orleans Parish

CHAFFE, McCALL, PHILLIPS, TOLER & SARPY, L.L.P. (AV)

A Partnership including a Professional Law Corporation
2300 Energy Centre, 1100 Poydras Street, 70163-2300
Telephone: 504-585-7000
Telecopier: 504-585-7075
Cable Address: "Denegre"
Telex: (AT&T) 460122 CMPTS
Email: cmptsno%2049698@mcimail.com *URL:* http://www.chaffe.com/
Baton Rouge, Louisiana Office: 202 Two United Plaza, 8550 United Plaza Boulevard.
Telephone: 504-922-4300.
Fax: 504-922-4304.

(See Next Column)

CHAFFE, McCALL, PHILLIPS, TOLER & SARPY, L.L.P.—*Continued*

Miami, Florida Office: 2600 Brickell Bay Office Tower, 1001 South Bayshore Drive, 33131.
Telephone: 305-377-3770.
Fax: 305-377-0080.
Caracas, Venezuela Office: Edificio Exa, Piso 10, Oficina PH-10, Avenida Venezuela entre Calles EL Retiro y Alameda, El Rosal.
Telephone: 011-582-953-4136.
Fax: 011-582-953-6518.

MEMBERS OF FIRM

G. Phillip Shuler, III	Dona J. Dew
Julie D. Livaudais	Robert B. Landry, III
	Andrew C. Partee, Jr.

ASSOCIATES

Desha D. Dardenne	Julie D. Savage
D. Scott Landry (Resident Associate, Baton Rouge)	

Representative Clients: Associated Builders and Contractors, Inc.; Dillard Department Stores, Inc.; Hills Bros. Coffee Co.; Marriott Corporation; Roadway Express, Inc.; Seventh Ward General Hospital; Schwrgmann Giant Super Markets, Inc.; Tulane University; Tulane University Hospital and Clinic.

For Complete List of Firm Personnel, See General Section

For full biographical listings, see the Martindale-Hubbell Law Directory

---

DEUTSCH, KERRIGAN & STILES, L.L.P. (AV)

A Partnership including Professional Law Corporations
755 Magazine Street, 70130-3672
Telephone: 504-581-5141
Cable Address: "Dekest"
Telex: 584358
Telecopier: 504-566-1201
Email: dks@dksno.com *URL:* http://www.dksno.com
St. Tammany Parish Office: 550 Pontchartrain Drive, Suite 200, Slidell, LA. 70458.
Telephone: 504-639-0555.
Fax: 504-639-0550

MEMBERS OF FIRM

Ellis B. Murov (P.L.C.)	Judy L. Burnthorn
	Carl A. Butler

OF COUNSEL

Bernard Marcus (P.L.C.)	Charles K. Reasonover (P.L.C.)

ASSOCIATE

Charles F. Seemann III

For Complete List of Firm Personnel, See General Section

For full biographical listings, see the Martindale-Hubbell Law Directory

---

McCALLA, THOMPSON, PYBURN, HYMOWITZ & SHAPIRO (AV)

A Limited Liability Partnership including Professional Corporations
Suite 2800, Poydras Center, 650 Poydras Street, 70130
Telephone: 504-524-2499
Fax: 504-523-8679

MEMBERS OF FIRM

Christopher P. Charlton (1956-1993)	Keith M. Pyburn, Jr., (P.C.)
Robert K. McCalla (P.C.)	Steven Hymowitz (P.C.)
Horace A. Thompson, III, (P.C.)	Howard Shapiro (P.C.)
	Stefanie Band Allweiss

ASSOCIATES

Heather G. Magier	Megan Shemwell-Nash
Taryn S. Southon	Joan Marie Canny
Steven R. Cupp	Edward F. Harold
Anne H. Breaux	Robert Rachal
James M. McGrew	David P. Bendana
	James W. Ouzts, Jr.

For full biographical listings, see the Martindale-Hubbell Law Directory

---

PHELPS DUNBAR, L.L.P. (AV)

Texaco Center, 400 Poydras Street, 70130-3245
Telephone: 504-566-1311
Telecopier: 504-568-9130, 504-568-9007
Cable Address: "Howspencer"
Telex: 584125 WU
Telex: 6821155 WUI
Email: info@phelps.com
Baton Rouge, Louisiana Office: Suite 701, City National Bank Building, P.O. Box 4412.
Telephone: 504-346-0285.
Telecopier: 504-381-9197.
Jackson, Mississippi Office: Suite 500, Mtel Centré, 200 South Lamar Street, P.O. Box 23066.
Telephone: 601-352-2300.
Telecopier: 601-360-9777.

(See Next Column)

Tupelo, Mississippi Office: Seventh Floor, One Mississippi Plaza, P.O. Box 1220.
Telephone: 601-842-7907.
Telecopier: 601-842-3873.
Houston, Texas Office: Suite 900, 3040 Post Oak Boulevard.
Telephone: 713-626-1386.
Telecopier: 713-626-1388.
London, England Office: Suite 731, Level 7, Lloyd's, 1 Lime Street, London EC3M 7DQ England.
Telephone: 011-44-171-929-4765.
Telecopier: 011-44-171-929-0046.
Telex: 987321.

MEMBERS OF FIRM

Paul O. Miller, III (Not admitted in LA; Resident, Jackson, Mississippi Office)	M. Nan Alessandra
Armin J. Moeller, Jr. (Resident, Jackson, Mississippi Office)	William I. Gault, Jr. (Not admitted in LA; Resident, Jackson, Mississippi Office)
Gary E. Friedman (Not admitted in LA; Resident, Jackson, Mississippi Office)	Susan Fahey Desmond (Not admitted in LA; Resident, Jackson, Mississippi Office)
William D. Aaron, Jr.	Thomas H. Kiggans (Resident, Baton Rouge, Louisiana Office)
W. Thomas Siler, Jr. (Not admitted in LA; Jackson and Tupelo, Mississippi Offices)	David M. Thomas, II (Not admitted in LA; Resident, Jackson, Mississippi Office)
R. Pepper Crutcher, Jr. (Jackson and Tupelo, Mississippi Offices)	

COUNSEL

Jane E. Armstrong

ASSOCIATES

Steven Johnson Allen (Resident, Jackson, Mississippi Office)	Chelye E. Prichard (Not admitted in LA; Resident, Jackson, Mississippi Office)
Ken Fairly (Not admitted in LA; Resident, Jackson, Mississippi Office)	C. Catherine Scallan (Not admitted in LA; Resident, Jackson, Mississippi Office)
Susan W. Furr (Resident, Baton Rouge, Louisiana Office)	Wendy Moore Shelton (Not admitted in LA; Resident, Jackson, Mississippi Office)
N. Eleanor Graham	
David M. Korn	
Tricia A. Martinez (Resident, Baton Rouge, Louisiana Office)	E. Russell Turner (Not admitted in LA; Resident, Jackson, Mississippi Office)
Skye Henry O'Donnell	Michael F. Weiner
A. Matt Pesnell (Not admitted in LA; Resident, Jackson, Mississippi Office)	

Representative Clients: Dow Chemical USA; General Motors Corporation; Laitram Corporation; Louisiana Lottery Corporation; Mississippi Municipal Liability Plan; Philip Morris Incorporated; Pulitzer Broadcasting Corp.; SmithKline Beecham Clinical Laboratories; Textron, Inc.; Union Pacific Railroad Company.

For Complete List of Firm Personnel, See General Section

For full biographical listings, see the Martindale-Hubbell Law Directory

---

WAGNER, BAGOT & GLEASON (AV)

Suite 2660, Poydras Center, 650 Poydras Street, 70130-6105
Telephone: 504-525-2141
Telecopier: 504-523-1587
TWX: 5106017673
ELN: 62928850
"INCISIVE"

Thomas J. Wagner	Harvey G. Gleason
Michael H. Bagot, Jr.	Whitney L. Cole
	Eric D. Suben

For full biographical listings, see the Martindale-Hubbell Law Directory

---

SHREVEPORT,* Caddo Parish

WILKINSON, CARMODY & GILLIAM (AV)

1700 Beck Building, 400 Travis Street, P.O. Box 1707, 71166
Telephone: 318-221-4196
Telecopier: 318-221-3705

MEMBERS OF FIRM

John D. Wilkinson (1867-1929)	Bobby S. Gilliam
William Scott Wilkinson (1895-1985)	Mark E. Gilliam
Arthur R. Carmody, Jr.	Penny D. Sellers
	Patrick F. Robinson
	Michael J. Ryan

Representative Clients: Farmers Insurance Group; Home Federal Savings & Loan Association of Shreveport; The Kansas City Southern Railway Co.; KTAL-TV; Lincoln National Life Insurance Co.; Mobil Oil Co.; Schumpert Medical Center; Sears, Roebuck & Co.; Southern Pacific Transportation Co.; Southwestern Electric Power Co.

For full biographical listings, see the Martindale-Hubbell Law Directory

MAINE

AUGUSTA, * Kennebec Co.

JOHNSON, WEBBERT & LAUBENSTEIN (AV)

160 Capitol Street, P.O. Box 29, 04332-0029
Telephone: 207-623-5110
Fax: 207-622-4160

Phillip E. Johnson	David G. Webbert
William H. Laubenstein, III	

Representative Clients: Agway, Inc.; AVEMCO; Central Maine Power Co.; The Doctors Company; ITT/Hartford; Loss Management Services, Inc.; Shand, Morahan & Co.; Union Water Power Company.

For full biographical listings, see the Martindale-Hubbell Law Directory

---

BANGOR, * Penobscot Co.

EATON, PEABODY, BRADFORD & VEAGUE, P.A. (AV)

Fleet Center-Exchange Street, P.O. Box 1210, 04402-1210
Telephone: 207-947-0111
Telecopier: 207-942-3040
Email: epbv@aol.com
Augusta, Maine Office: 2 Central Plaza.
Telephone: 207-622-3747.
Telecopier: 207-622-9732.
Blue Hill, Maine Office: One East Blue Hill Road.
Telephone: 207-374-2812.
Telecopier: 207-374-2548.
Brunswick, Maine Office: 167 Park Row.
Telephone: 207-729-1144.
Telecopier: 207-729-1140.
Camden, Maine Office: 7-9 Washington Street.
Telephone: 207-236-3325.
Telecopier: 207-236-8611.
Dover-Foxcroft, Maine Office: 30 East Main Street.
Telephone: 207-564-8378.
Telecopier: 207-564-7059.

Malcolm E. Morrell, Jr.	Thomas C. Johnston
Clare Hudson Payne	

A List of Representative Clients available upon request.

For Complete List of Firm Personnel, See General Section

For full biographical listings, see the Martindale-Hubbell Law Directory

---

RUDMAN & WINCHELL (AV)

84 Harlow Street, P.O. Box 1401, 04402-1401
Telephone: 207-947-4501
Telecopy: 207-941-9715

MEMBERS OF FIRM

Abraham M. Rudman	Frank T. McGuire
(1896-1970)	Bruce C. Mallonee
Albert H. Winchell, Jr.	Paul H. Sighinolfi
(1924-1992)	William H. Hanson
Gerald E. Rudman	George Franklin Eaton, II
Phillip D. Buckley	Edith A. Richardson
Michael P. Friedman	Michael M. McAleer
Winfred A. Stevens	Brett D. Baber
Robert E. Sutcliffe	Barbara A. Cardone
Paul W. Chaiken	Robert E. Murray, Jr.
David C. King	Edmond J. Bearor
John W. McCarthy	Curtis E. Kimball

ASSOCIATES

Jane E. Skelton	Karen D. Kemble
Brent A. Singer	Leigh Stephens McCarthy

Counsel for: Penobscot Shoe Co.; Sherman Lumber Co.; Webber Oil Co.; Fleet Bank of Maine; Key Bank of Maine; McCain Foods, Inc.
Local Counsel for: Commercial Union Assurance Cos.; Hanover Insurance Company; Kemper Insurance Group; Liberty Mutual Insurance Co.

For full biographical listings, see the Martindale-Hubbell Law Directory

---

BATH, * Sagadahoc Co.

CONLEY & HALEY (AV)

Thirty Front Street, 04530
Telephone: 207-443-5576
Telefax: 207-443-6665

Mark L. Haley	Laura M. O'Hanlon
Tracey G. Burton	

Representative Clients: Bath Iron Works Corporation; Central Maine Power Company; Saco Defense, Inc.; Sugarloaf Mountain Corporation.
References: Key Bank of Maine; First Federal Savings & Loan Association of Bath; Brunswick Federal Savings.

(See Next Column)

For Complete List of Firm Personnel, See General Section

For full biographical listings, see the Martindale-Hubbell Law Directory

PORTLAND, * Cumberland Co.

BENNETT AND ASSOCIATES, P.A. (AV)

Suite 300, 121 Middle Street, P.O. Box 7799, 04112-7799
Telephone: 207-773-4775
Telecopier: 207-774-2366
Email: 104142.2363@compuserve.com

Herbert H. Bennett (1928-1992)	Frederick B. Finberg
Peter Bennett	Melinda J. Caterine
Jeffrey Bennett	Clare S. Benedict

Counsel for: Associated Grocers of New England; Coca Cola Bottling Company of Northern New England, Inc.; General Star Indemnity Company; Northern Utilities/Bay State Gas; Pratt & Whitney (Division of United Technologies); Primerica Financial Services (The Travelers); Sprague Energy (C.H. Sprague & Son); Perrier Group of America, Inc.; Lepage Bakeries, Inc. (Country Kitchen); Texaco, Inc.

For full biographical listings, see the Martindale-Hubbell Law Directory

---

MOON, MOSS, MCGILL & BACHELDER, P.A. (AV)

Ten Free Street, P.O. Box 7250, 04112-7250
Telephone: 207-775-6001
Facsimile: 207-775-6407; 207-775-6441

Richard G. Moon	Stephan G. Bachelder
Philip J. Moss	Robert M. Hayes
Linda D. McGill	Timothy J. O'Brien
	Thomas H. Somers

Jonathan Shapiro	Eric John Uhl
James P. Bailinson	Terrence J. Briggs

SPECIAL COUNSEL

Julie A. Boesky (Not admitted in ME)

For full biographical listings, see the Martindale-Hubbell Law Directory

---

PETRUCCELLI & MARTIN (AV)

50 Monument Square, P.O. Box 9733, 04104-5033
Telephone: 207-775-0200
Telecopier: 207-775-2360

MEMBERS OF FIRM

Joel C. Martin	Daniel W. Bates
	James B. Haddow

Representative Clients: Coopers & Lybrand; Epilogue Technology Corp.; Goodwill of Maine, Inc.; K-D Wood, Inc.; Senior Spectrum; Systems Consulting, Inc.

For full biographical listings, see the Martindale-Hubbell Law Directory

---

PIERCE ATWOOD (AV)

One Monument Square, 04101
Telephone: 207-791-1100
Fax: 207-791-1350
Email: info@PierceAtwood.com
Augusta, Maine Office: 77 Winthrop Street.
Telephone: 207-622-6311.
Fax: 207-623-9367.
Newburyport, Massachusetts Office: 6 Harris Street.
Telephone: 508-465-9599.
Fax: 508-465-9945.

MEMBERS OF FIRM

S. Mason Pratt, Jr.	James R. Erwin, II
Charles S. Einsiedler, Jr.	William H. Nichols
Peter H. Jacobs	Anthony R. Derosby

OF COUNSEL

Margaret Coughlin LePage

ASSOCIATES

Eric D. Altholz	Allan M. Muir
	Fall Ferguson

For Complete List of Firm Personnel, See General Section

For full biographical listings, see the Martindale-Hubbell Law Directory

---

PRETI, FLAHERTY, BELIVEAU & PACHIOS (AV)

A Limited Liability Company
443 Congress Street, P.O. Box 11410, 04104-7410
Telephone: 207-791-3000
Telecopier: 207-791-3111
Email: admin@pfbpnet.com
Augusta, Maine Office: 45 Memorial Circle, P.O. Box 1058, 04332-1058.
Telephone: 207-623-5300.
Telecopier: 207-623-2914.

(See Next Column)

PRETI, FLAHERTY, BELIVEAU & PACHIOS—*Continued*

MEMBERS OF FIRM

Keith A. Powers	Evan M. Hansen
Daniel Rapaport	Geoffrey K. Cummings
Michael G. Messerschmidt	Stephen E. F. Langsdorf
Randall B. Weill	(Augusta Office)

Elizabeth A. Olivier

OF COUNSEL

Albert J. Beliveau, Jr.

ASSOCIATE

Nelson J. Larkins

Representative Clients: Bronze Craft Corp.; Northern New England Benefit Trust; Maine Turnpike Authority; Maine Maritime Academy; Guy Gannett Publishing Co.

For Complete List of Firm Personnel, See General Section

For full biographical listings, see the Martindale-Hubbell Law Directory

TROUBH, HEISLER & PIAMPIANO, P.C. (AV)

511 Congress Street, P.O. Box 9711, 04104-5011
Telephone: 207-780-6789
Fax: 207-774-2339

William B. Troubh	Thomas E. Getchell
Edwin A. Heisler	Michael Richards
Robert J. Piampiano	William K. McKinley
Kevin M. Gillis	Daniel F. Gilligan
Michael P. Boyd	Paul S. Bulger

John G. Richardson	Linda L. Sears

Daniel R. Felkel

For full biographical listings, see the Martindale-Hubbell Law Directory

WRIGHT, COON & CUNNINGHAM, P.A. (AV)

377 Fore Street, P.O. Box 7526, 04112
Telephone: 207-775-7722
Fax: 207-772-7045
Email: lexfori@lexfori.com

Steven F. Wright	John R. Coon

Gregory M. Cunningham

For full biographical listings, see the Martindale-Hubbell Law Directory

MARYLAND

BALTIMORE,* (Independent City)

GENDLER & SINGLETON, P.A. (AV)

Ten East Eager Street, 21202-2592
Telephone: 410-727-2425
Fax: 410-685-4232

Craig Marshall Gendler	Danae Christina Velis
John S. Singleton	Andrew Hermann

For full biographical listings, see the Martindale-Hubbell Law Directory

KAHN, SMITH & COLLINS, P.A. (AV)

110 Saint Paul Street, 6th Floor, 21202
Telephone: 410-244-1010
Fax: 410-244-8001
Email: incourt@ari.net *URL:* http://www.interbit.com/ksc

Andrew H. Kahn	Francis J. Collins
Joel A. Smith	David V. Diggs

Christyne L. Neff

Sarah Pazourek Harlan	Leslie A. Pladna

For full biographical listings, see the Martindale-Hubbell Law Directory

KOLLMAN & SHEEHAN, P.A. (AV)

Sun Life Building, 20 South Charles Street, 21201
Telephone: 410-727-4300
Telecopier: 410-727-4391

Frank L. Kollman	Peter S. Saucier
David M. Sheehan	Francis R. Laws

Darrell R. VanDeusen

Bruce M. Luchansky	Jonathan J. Biedron
Clifford B. Geiger	Randi A. Klein

Charles J. Kresslein

For full biographical listings, see the Martindale-Hubbell Law Directory

PIPER & MARBURY L.L.P. (AV)

Charles Center South, 36 South Charles Street, 21201-3018
Telephone: 410-539-2530
FAX: 410-539-0489
Email: lawfirm@pipermar.com
Washington, D.C. Office: 1200 Nineteenth Street, N.W., 20036-2430.
Telephone: 202-861-3900.
FAX: 202-223-2085.
Easton, Maryland Office: 117 Bay Street, 21601-2703.
Telephone: 410-820-4460.
FAX: 410-820-4463.
New York, N.Y. Office: 1251 Avenue of the Americas, 10020-1104.
Telephone: 212-835-6000.
FAX: 212-835-6001.
Philadelphia, Pennsylvania Office: 3400 Two Logan Square, 18th & Arch Streets, 19103-2762.
Telephone: 215-656-3300.
FAX: 215-656-3301.

MEMBERS OF FIRM

Leonard E. Cohen	Richard J. Hafets
Russell H. Gardner	Emmett F. McGee, Jr.

Eric Paltell

ASSOCIATES

Lynette M. Phillips (Resident, New York, N.Y. Office)	Ann L. Lamdin

For Complete List of Firm Personnel, See General Section

For full biographical listings, see the Martindale-Hubbell Law Directory

SHAWE & ROSENTHAL (AV)

Sun Life Building, 20 South Charles Street, 21201
Telephone: 410-752-1040
Telecopier: 410-752-8861
Email: srmail@Shawe.com *URL:* http://www.shawe.com

MEMBERS OF FIRM

Earle K. Shawe	Eric Hemmendinger
William J. Rosenthal	J. Michael McGuire
Carrol Hament (Retired)	Mark J. Swerdlin
Stephen D. Shawe	Gary L. Simpler
Arthur M. Brewer	R. Michael Smith
Bruce S. Harrison	Robert H. Ingle, III
Patrick M. Pilachowski	Elizabeth I. Torphy-Donzella

Francis W. Connolly

Representative Clients: Amdahl Corp.; Baltimore Gas & Electric Co.; Bethlehem Steel Corp.; Black & Decker (U.S.) Inc.; Federal Reserve Bank of Richmond; The May Department Stores Co. (Hecht's, Washington, D.C.; Filene's); McDonald's Corp.; Thiokol Corp.; United States Fidelity & Guaranty Co.; Geico.

For full biographical listings, see the Martindale-Hubbell Law Directory

VENABLE ATTORNEYS AT LAW VENABLE, BAETJER AND HOWARD, LLP (AV)

A Partnership including Professional Corporations
1800 Mercantile Bank & Trust Building, 2 Hopkins Plaza, 21201
Telephone: 410-244-7400
Email: INFO@Venable.win.net
Washington, D.C. Office: Venable, Baetjer, Howard & Civiletti LLP. Suite 1000, 1201 New York Avenue, N.W.
Telephone: 202-962-4800.
McLean, Virginia Office: Suite 400, 2010 Corporate Ridge.
Telephone: 703-760-1600.
Rockville, Maryland Office: Suite 500, One Church Street, P. O. Box 1906.
Telephone: 301-217-5600.
Towson, Maryland Office: 210 Allegheny Avenue, P. O. Box 5517.
Telephone: 410-494-6200.

MEMBERS OF FIRM

John Henry Lewin, Jr. (P.C.)	Sondra Harans Block (Resident, Rockville, Maryland Office)
Stanley Mazaroff (P.C.)	
Roger W. Titus (Resident, Rockville, Maryland Office)	Craig E. Smith
Douglas D. Connah, Jr. (P.C.) (Also at Washington, D.C. Office)	Robert G. Ames (Also at Washington, D.C. Office)
	Nell B. Strachan
Kenneth C. Bass, III (Not admitted in MD; Washington, D.C. and McLean, Virginia Offices)	Barbara E. Schlaff
	L. Paige Marvel
	G. Stewart Webb, Jr.
	George W. Johnston (P.C.)
John H. Zink, III (Resident, Towson, Maryland Office)	Jana Howard Carey (P.C.)
	Jeffrey A. Dunn (also at Washington, D.C. Office)
Paul T. Glasgow (Resident, Rockville, Maryland Office)	George F. Pappas (Also at Washington, D.C. Office)
Joseph C. Wich, Jr. (Resident, Towson, Maryland Office)	James L. Shea (Also at Washington, D.C. Office)
Joseph G. Block (Not admitted in MD; Resident, Washington, D.C. Office)	Jeffrey P. Ayres (P.C.)
	Maurice Baskin (Resident, Washington, D.C. Office)

(See Next Column)

VENABLE ATTORNEYS AT LAW VENABLE, BAETJER AND HOWARD, LLP,
Baltimore—Continued

MEMBERS OF FIRM (Continued)

C. Carey Deeley, Jr. (Also at Towson, Maryland Office)
Christopher R. Mellott
James A. Dunbar (Also at Washington, D.C. Office)
Ronald W. Taylor
Robert L. Waldman
John A. Roberts (Also at Rockville, Maryland Office)

Patrick J. Stewart (Also at Washington, D.C. Office)
Gary M. Hnath (Resident, Washington, D.C. Office)
Mitchell Y. Mirviss
Michael W. Robinson (Resident, McLean, Virginia Office)
Elizabeth Marzo Borinsky

OF COUNSEL

A. Samuel Cook (P.C.) (Resident, Towson, Maryland Office)

ASSOCIATES

Scharon L. Ball
Paul D. Barker, Jr.
Patrick L. Clancy (Resident, Rockville, Maryland Office)
Patricia Gillis Cousins (Resident, Rockville, Maryland Office)
David W. Goewey (Not admitted in MD; Resident, Washington, D.C. Office)
E. Anne Hamel
John C. Hardwick, Jr. (Resident, Washington, D.C. Office)
Todd J. Horn
Gregory L. Laubach (Resident, Rockville, Maryland Office)

Vicki Margolis (Also at Washington, D.C. Office)
Christine M. McAnney (Not admitted in MD; Resident, McLean, Virginia Office)
John A. McCauley
Traci H. Mundy (Not admitted in MD; Resident, McLean, Virginia Office)
John T. Prisbe
Larry Robert Seegull
Thomas H. Strong
Linda Marotta Thomas
Karen D. Woodard (Resident, Washington, D.C. Office)

For Complete List of Firm Personnel, See General Section

For full biographical listings, see the Martindale-Hubbell Law Directory

WHITEFORD, TAYLOR & PRESTON L.L.P. (AV)

7 Saint Paul Street, 21202-1626
Telephone: 410-347-8700
Telex: 5101012334
Fax: 410-752-7092
Email: 2019267@mcimail.com *URL:* http://www.wtplaw.com
Towson, Maryland Office: 210 West Pennsylvania Avenue.
Telephone: 410-832-2000.
Fax: 410-832-2015.
Washington, D.C. Office: 1025 Connecticut Avenue, N.W.
Telephone: 202-659-6800.
Fax: 202-331-0573.
Columbia, Maryland Office: 10440 Little Patuxent Parkway.
Telephone: 410-884-0700.
Fax: 410-884-0719.
Alexandria, Virginia Office: 1317 King Street.
Telephone: 703-836-5742.
Fax: 703-836-0265.

MEMBERS OF FIRM

Larry M. Wolf
Arthur P. Rogers (Resident Washington, D.C. Office)
Joseph K. Pokempner

Robert S. Hillman
Steven E. Bers
Jeanne M. Phelan
Kevin C. McCormick

Peter D. Guattery

ASSOCIATE

Melissa L. Menkel

For Complete List of Firm Personnel, See General Section

For full biographical listings, see the Martindale-Hubbell Law Directory

BETHESDA, Montgomery Co.

PALEY, ROTHMAN, GOLDSTEIN, ROSENBERG & COOPER, CHARTERED (AV)

Seventh Floor, One Bethesda Center, 4800 Hampden Lane, 20814
Telephone: 301-656-7603
Telecopier: 301-654-7354
Email: prg@paleyrothman.com

Glenn M. Cooper
Victor J. Rosenberg
Mark S. Goldstein
Mark S. Rothman
Stephen H. Paley
Paula A. Calimafde
Ronald A. Dweck
Arthur H. Blitz
Robert H. Maclay
Steven A. Widdes

Hope Eastman
Dennis L. Sharp
R. Thomas Hoffmann
Albert D. Pailet
Diane A. Fox
Theodore P. Stein
Jeffrey A. Kolender
Wendelin I. Lipp
Robert B. Bowytz
Mark A. Binstock

Patricia M. Weaver
Alan D. Eisler
David M. Rothenstein

Brent M. Goldstein
Jeffrey D. Olster
Kathleen M. Dumais

(See Next Column)

SENIOR COUNSEL

Alan S. Mark   Daniel S. Koch

For full biographical listings, see the Martindale-Hubbell Law Directory

COCKEYSVILLE, Baltimore Co.

LAW OFFICES OF MARCY M. ENGELBRECHT, P.A. (AV)

19 Hillsyde Court, 21030
Telephone: 410-628-0040
FAX: 410-628-1112

Marcy M. Engelbrecht

Representative Clients: Norwest Financial; Farberware; John Hopkins Hospital; Broadway Services, Inc.; W.R. Berkley & Co.
Reference: Signet Bank.

For full biographical listings, see the Martindale-Hubbell Law Directory

*ROCKVILLE,** Montgomery Co.

STEIN, SPERLING, BENNETT, DE JONG, DRISCOLL, GREENFEIG & METRO, P.A. (AV)

25 West Middle Lane, 20850
Telephone: 301-340-2020; 800-435-5230
Telecopier: 301-340-8217

David C. Driscoll, Jr.
Jack A. Garson

A. Howard Metro
Jeffrey M. Schwaber

Donald N. Sperling

For Complete List of Firm Personnel, See General Section

For full biographical listings, see the Martindale-Hubbell Law Directory

VENABLE ATTORNEYS AT LAW VENABLE, BAETJER AND HOWARD, LLP (AV)

A Partnership including Professional Corporations
Suite 500, One Church Street, P.O. Box 1906, 20850-4129
Telephone: 301-217-5600
FAX: 301-217-5617
Baltimore, Maryland Office: 1800 Mercantile Bank & Trust Building, 2 Hopkins Plaza.
Telephone: 410-244-7400.
Washington, D.C. Office: Venable, Baetjer, Howard & Civiletti LLP, Suite 1000, 1201 New York Avenue, N.W.
Telephone: 202-962-4800.
McLean, Virginia Office: Suite 400, 2010 Corporate Ridge.
Telephone: 703-760-1600.
Towson, Maryland, Office: 210 Allegheny Avenue, P. O. Box 5517.
Telephone: 410-494-6200.

MEMBERS OF FIRM

Roger W. Titus
Paul T. Glasgow

Sondra Harans Block
John A. Roberts (Also at Baltimore, Maryland Office)

ASSOCIATES

Patrick L. Clancy
Patricia Gillis Cousins

Gregory L. Laubach

For Complete List of Firm Personnel, See General Section

For full biographical listings, see the Martindale-Hubbell Law Directory

SILVER SPRING, Montgomery Co.

ALEXANDER, BEARDEN, HAIRSTON & MARKS, LLP (AV)

(Formerly, Alexander, Aponte & Marks, LLP)
Lee Plaza-Suite 805, 8601 Georgia Avenue, 20910
Telephone: 301-589-2222
Facsimile: 301-589-2523
Washington, D.C. Office: 2021 L Street, N.W., Suite 300, 20036.
Telephone: 202-293-3700.
Fax: 202-293-7359.
New York, New York Office: 330 Madison Avenue, 36th Floor.
Telephone: 212-808-0008.
Fax: 212-599-1028.

Abbey G. Hairston

Bridnetta D. Edwards   Adrian Van Nelson II

Reference: Riggs National Bank of Washington, D.C.

For full biographical listings, see the Martindale-Hubbell Law Directory

*TOWSON,** Baltimore Co.

KRUCHKO & FRIES (AV)

600 Washington Avenue, Suite 305, 21204
Telephone: 410-321-7310
Telecopier: 410-821-7918
McLean, Virginia Office: Suite 202, 7929 Westpark Drive.
Telephone: 703-734-0554.

(See Next Column)

KRUCHKO & FRIES—*Continued*

Washington, D.C. Office: 601 Pennsylvania Avenue, Suite 900.
Telephone: 202-347-6550.

MEMBERS OF FIRM

John G. Kruchko	Steven W. Ray (Not admitted in
Jay R. Fries	MD; Resident, McLean,
Paul M. Lusky	Virginia Office)

ASSOCIATES

Kathleen A. Talty	Joan E. Book
Edward Lee Isler (Not admitted	Jason M. Branciforte (Not
in MD; Resident, McLean,	admitted in MD; Resident,
Virginia Office)	McLean, Virginia Office)
Susan Tahernia (Resident,	
McLean, Virginia Office)	

OF COUNSEL
Frank S. Astroth

For full biographical listings, see the Martindale-Hubbell Law Directory

VENABLE ATTORNEYS AT LAW VENABLE, BAETJER AND HOWARD, LLP (AV)

A Partnership including Professional Corporations
210 Allegheny Avenue, P.O. Box 5517, 21204
Telephone: 410-494-6200
FAX: 410-821-0147
Baltimore, Maryland Office: 1800 Mercantile Bank & Trust Building, 2 Hopkins Plaza.
Telephone: 410-244-7400.
Washington, D.C. Office: Venable, Baetjer, Howard & Civiletti LLP, Suite 1000, 1201 New York Avenue, N.W.
Telephone: 202-962-4800.
McLean, Virginia Office: Suite 400, 2010 Corporate Ridge.
Telephone: 703-760-1600.
Rockville, Maryland Office: Suite 500, One Church Street, P. O. Box 1906.
Telephone: 301-217-5600.

PARTNERS

John H. Zink, III	C. Carey Deeley, Jr. (Also at
Joseph C. Wich, Jr.	Baltimore, Maryland Office)

OF COUNSEL
A. Samuel Cook (P.C.)

For Complete List of Firm Personnel, See General Section

For full biographical listings, see the Martindale-Hubbell Law Directory

MASSACHUSETTS

*BOSTON,** Suffolk Co.

FOLEY, HOAG & ELIOT LLP (AV)

One Post Office Square, 02109
Telephone: 617-832-1000
Cable Address: "Foleyhoag"
Telex: 94-0693
Telecopier: 617-832-7000
Email: fhe@fhe.com *URL:* http://www.fhe.com
Washington, D.C. Office: 1615 L Street, N.W.
Telephone: 202-775-0600.
Telecopier: 202-857-0140.

MEMBERS OF FIRM

David B. Ellis	Stephen B. Deutsch
Peter B. Ellis	William B. Koffel
Philip Burling	Kevin J. Fitzgerald
Paul V. Lyons	James T. Montgomery, Jr.
Arthur G. Telegen	(Resident at Washington,
	D.C. Office)

ASSOCIATES

Pamela B. Blatte	Lisa C. Hay
James W. Bucking	Amy B. G. Katz
Marie E. Burke	Jonathan A. Keselenko
Brian D. Carlson	Gerald A. Mc Donough
Jeffrey S. Follett	Michael L. Rosen
	Michele A. Whitham

For Complete List of Firm Personnel, See General Section

For full biographical listings, see the Martindale-Hubbell Law Directory

GLOVSKY, TARLOW & MILBERG (AV)

Suite 810, 31 Milk Street, 02109-5104
Telephone: 617-423-7100
Telecopier: 617-482-8034
Washington, D.C. Office: 1090 Vermont Avenue, N.W.
Telephone: 202-659-1971.

(See Next Column)

Richard D. Glovsky	Melinda Milberg
	Daniel S. Tarlow

ASSOCIATES

Peter M. Kelley	John F. Tocci
	Debra L. Feldstein

OF COUNSEL

Harry M. Carey, Jr.	Lynne K. Zusman (Not
Paul S. Davis	admitted in MA; Resident,
Barry H. Field	Washington, D.C. Office)

For full biographical listings, see the Martindale-Hubbell Law Directory

HANIFY & KING, PROFESSIONAL CORPORATION (AV)

One Federal Street, 02110-2007
Telephone: 617-423-0400
Telefax: 617-423-0498

James Coyne King	Daniel J. Lyne
John D. Hanify	Donald F. Farrell, Jr.
Harold B. Murphy	Barbara Wegener Pfirrman
David Lee Evans	Gerard P. Richer
	Timothy P. O'Neill

Jean A. Musiker	Joseph F. Cortellini
Ann M. Chiacchieri	Eddirland Duncan
Melissa J. Cassedy	Andrew G. Lizotte
Jeffrey J. Upton	Karen A. Whitley
Michael R. Perry	Christopher K. Barry-Smith
Charles A. Dale, III	William T. Harrington
Kathleen E. Cross	Matthew McCue
David M. Wright	Robyn J. Bartlett
	Owen P. Kane

For full biographical listings, see the Martindale-Hubbell Law Directory

MENARD, MURPHY & WALSH (AV)

One Financial Center, 02111
Telephone: 617-832-2500
Telecopier: 617-832-2550

Arthur P. Menard	John E. Coyne
Paul J. Murphy	John S. Leonard
Joseph H. Walsh	Theodore E. Daiber
	Kevin G. Mahoney

For full biographical listings, see the Martindale-Hubbell Law Directory

MORGAN, BROWN & JOY (AV)

One Boston Place, 02108
Telephone: 617-523-6666
Facsimile: 617-367-3125
Email: MORGbrwn@shore.net

MEMBERS OF FIRM

John W. Morgan (1898-1974)	William F. Joy, Jr.
William F. Joy	Robert P. Joy
Alan I. Kaplan	Nathan L. Kaitz
James M. Paulson	Keith H. McCown
Nicholas DiGiovanni, Jr.	Keith B. Muntyan
	Laurence J. Donoghue

ASSOCIATES

Robert P. Morris	Jaclyn L. Kugell
Allison B. Kaplan	Richard J. Joy
Susan L. Lipsitz	Joseph P. McConnell
James J. Rooney	Diane M. Saunders
Anne Kinnane	Patricia Lim

OF COUNSEL

Harold N. Mack	Murray Brown

Representative Clients: Acushnet Company; American Telephone & Telegraph; Boston Edison Co.; Combustion Engineering; Data General Corp.; Federated Department Stores; General Electric; John Hancock Mutual Life Insurance Co.; Kraft Foods, Inc.

For full biographical listings, see the Martindale-Hubbell Law Directory

PALMER & DODGE LLP (AV)

One Beacon Street, 02108
Telephone: 617-573-0100
Facsimile: 617-227-4420

MEMBERS OF FIRM

Michael R. Brown	Judith A. Malone
Andrew L. Eisenberg	Henry G. Stewart

For Complete List of Firm Personnel, See General Section

For full biographical listings, see the Martindale-Hubbell Law Directory

Boston—Continued

SHERBURNE, POWERS & NEEDHAM, P.C. (AV)

One Beacon Street, 02108
Telephone: 617-523-2700
Fax: 617-523-6850
Email: @SHERBURNE.COM

William D. Weeks	Benjamin Volinski
John T. Collins	Mark Schonfeld
Allan J. Landau	James D. Smeallie
Stephen A. Hopkins	Paul Killeen
Alan I. Falk	Gordon P. Katz
C. Thomas Swaim	Joseph B. Darby, III
James Pollock	Richard M Yanofsky
William V. Tripp III	James E. McDermott
Stephen S. Young	Kenneth P. Brier
William F. Machen	Robert V. Lizza
W. Robert Allison	Miriam Goldstein Altman
Philip J. Notopoulos	John J. Monaghan
Richard J. Hindlian	Margaret J. Palladino
Paul E. Troy	Mark C. Michalowski
Harold W. Potter, Jr.	David Scott Sloan
Philip S. Lapatin	M. Chrysa Long
Pamela A. Duckworth	Lawrence D. Bradley

Miriam J. McKendall

Cynthia A. Brown	Amy J. Mastrobattista
Cynthia M. Hern	Leslie A. Sprinkle
Meredeth A. Beers	Douglas W. Clapp
Dianne R. Phillips	Jeffrey A. Huebschmann
Paul M. James	Tamara E. Goulston
Theodore F. Hanselman	Paul G. Lannon, Jr.
Joshua C. Krumholz	Nicholas J. Psyhogeos
Ieuan G. Mahony	Edward J. Naughton
Jeffrey J. Nix	Kathaleen Kelly Cutone
(Not admitted in MA)	Laurie A. Tribble
Kenneth L. Harvey	Neil C. Higgins
Christopher J. Trombetta	Deborah Paige Stone
Elise N. Zoli	Brian R. Popiel

COUNSEL

Haig Der Manuelian	Karl J. Hirshman
Mason M. Taber, Jr.	Dale R. Johnson

For full biographical listings, see the Martindale-Hubbell Law Directory

WARNER & STACKPOLE LLP (AV)

75 State Street, 02109
Telephone: 617-951-9000
Telecopier: 617-951-9151
Email: w&s@warstack.com

MEMBERS OF FIRM

Judith G. Dein	Ronald F. Kehoe
Henry T. Goldman	Stephen E. Moore

ASSOCIATE

Anne T. Mitchell

For Complete List of Firm Personnel, See General Section

For full biographical listings, see the Martindale-Hubbell Law Directory

PITTSFIELD,* Berkshire Co.

CAIN, HIBBARD, MYERS & COOK, A PROFESSIONAL CORPORATION (AV)

66 West Street, 01201
Telephone: 413-443-4771
Telecopier: 413-443-7694
Great Barrington, Massachusetts Office: 309 Main Street, 01230.
Telephone: 413-528-4771.
Fax: 413-528-5553.

C. Jeffrey Cook	Michael E. MacDonald
John F. Rogers	John A. Agostini

Diane M. DeGiacomo

Nancy A. Lyon	Kevin M. Kinne
Benjamin Smith	Lee D. Flournoy

Representative Clients: Bank of Boston/First Agricultural Bank; Great Barrington Savings Bank; Greylock Credit Union; The Berkshire Gas Company; Berkshire Health Systems, Inc.; Berkshire Physicians & Surgeons, P.C. *Local Counsel for:* General Electric Co.; Boston Symphony Orchestra; Statewide Funding Corporation.

For full biographical listings, see the Martindale-Hubbell Law Directory

SPRINGFIELD,* Hampden Co.

COOLEY, SHRAIR P.C. (AV)

5th Floor, 1380 Main Street, 01103
Telephone: 413-781-0750
Telecopier: 413-733-3042

David A. Shrair	Rona S. Fingold
Irving D. Labovitz	Peter W. Shrair
Robert L. Dambrov	Norman C. Michaels
Alan S. Dambrov	Mark A. NeJame
Alice E. Zaft	Mark D. Mason

Daniel E. Bruso

Representative Clients: Peter Pan Bus Lines, Inc.; Buxton Co.; State Line Potato Chip Co.; Park West Bank and Trust Company; Westfield Savings Bank; Merrill, Lynch, Pierce, Fenner and Smith; City of Springfield, Mass.; Dairy Mart; Western Region; Town of Longmeadow, Mass.; Springfield College.

For full biographical listings, see the Martindale-Hubbell Law Directory

SKOLER, ABBOTT & PRESSER, P.C. (AV)

Suite 2000, One Monarch Place, 01144
Telephone: 413-737-4753
Fax: 413-787-1941
Email: skoler@wca.com
Worcester, Massachusetts Office: 30 Park Avenue.
Telephone: 508-757-5335.

Martin E. Skoler (1932-1991)	Jay M. Presser
Ralph F. Abbott, Jr.	John H. Glenn

Rosemary J. Nevins

Richard U. Stubbs, Jr.	Jeffrey C. Hummel

Marylou Fabbo

OF COUNSEL

Martin Fleisher

LEGAL SUPPORT PERSONNEL

Chelsey Ugolik

Representative Clients: Baystate Medical Center; Erving Paper Mills; Hanover Insurance Company; Monarch Life Insurance Company; Monsanto Co.; Smith & Wesson; Spalding & Evenflo; The Waltham-Weston Hospital & Medical Center.

For full biographical listings, see the Martindale-Hubbell Law Directory

WORCESTER,* Worcester Co.

MOUNTAIN, DEARBORN & WHITING (AV)

370 Main Street, 01608
Telephone: 508-756-2423
Fax: 508-755-6640

MEMBERS OF FIRM

Alfred N. Whiting (1920-1989)	Francis J. Russell
Thomas R. Mountain	Dale R. Harger
Richard W. Dearborn	Mark W. Bloom
Samuel R. DeSimone	Donald J. O'Neil
Henry W. Beth	Lawrence S. Delaney

Ann K. Molloy

ASSOCIATE

Richard M. Freije

For full biographical listings, see the Martindale-Hubbell Law Directory

SKOLER, ABBOTT & PRESSER, P.C. (AV)

30 Park Avenue, 01605
Telephone: 508-757-5335
Email: skoler@wca.com
Springfield, Massachusetts Office: Suite 2000, One Monarch Place.
Telephone: 413-737-4753.
Fax: 413-787-1941.

Martin E. Skoler (1932-1991)	Jay M. Presser
Ralph F. Abbott, Jr.	John H. Glenn

Rosemary J. Nevins

Richard U. Stubbs, Jr.	Jeffrey C. Hummel

Marylou Fabbo

OF COUNSEL

Martin Fleisher

LEGAL SUPPORT PERSONNEL

Chelsey Ugolik

Representative Clients: Baystate Medical Center; Erving Paper Mills; Hanover Insurance Company; Monsanto Company; National Envelope Co.; Smith & Wesson; Spalding & Evenflo; The Waltham-Weston Hospital & Medical Center.

For full biographical listings, see the Martindale-Hubbell Law Directory

MICHIGAN

ANN ARBOR, * Washtenaw Co.

BRAUN KENDRICK FINKBEINER PLC (AV)

700 First National Building, 48104
Telephone: 313-995-4100
Telecopier: 313-995-4798
URL: http://www.bkf-law.com
Bay City, Michigan Office: 201 Phoenix Building, P.O. Box 2039.
Telephone: 517-895-8505.
Telecopier: 517-895-8437.
Saginaw, Michigan Office: 101 N. Washington, Suite 812.
Telephone: 517-753-3461.
Telecopier: 517-753-3951.

Barry M. Levine

Representative Clients: The Dow Chemical Co.; General Motors Corp.; Lobdell Emery Manufacturing Co.; Merrill, Lynch, Inc.; Saginaw General Hospital; Saginaw News; The Wickes Foundation.

For full biographical listings, see the Martindale-Hubbell Law Directory

ELLMANN & ELLMANN, P.C. (AV)

206 South Fifth, Suite 200, 48104
Telephone: 313-668-4800
Facsimile: 313-662-3893
Email: ELLMANN@AOL.COM
Farmington Hills, Michigan Office: 28000 Weymouth.
Telephone: 313-851-0737.
Fax: 313-851-0738.

James I. Ellmann (1887-1969)   Douglas S. Ellmann
Claudia Roberts Ellmann
OF COUNSEL
William M. Ellmann   Robert L. Ellmann
                                (Not admitted in MI)

For full biographical listings, see the Martindale-Hubbell Law Directory

HOOPER, HATHAWAY, PRICE, BEUCHE & WALLACE (AV)

126 South Main Street, 48104
Telephone: 313-662-4426
Fax: 313-662-9559

Joseph C. Hooper (1899-1980)   Gregory A. Spaly
Alan E. Price   Robert W. Southard
James R. Beuche   William J. Stapleton
Bruce T. Wallace   Bruce C. Conybeare, Jr.
Charles W. Borgsdorf   Anthony P. Patti
Mark R. Daane   Marcia J. Major
OF COUNSEL
James A. Evashevski   Roderick K. Daane

Representative Clients: Michigan Livestock Exchange; Michigan Livestock Credit Corporation; City of Ann Arbor; Glacier Hill; Cimage Corporation; Domtar Gypsum, Inc.

For Complete List of Firm Personnel, See General Section

For full biographical listings, see the Martindale-Hubbell Law Directory

MILLER, CANFIELD, PADDOCK AND STONE, P.L.C. (AV)

A Professional Limited Liability Company
Founded in 1852 by Sidney Davy Miller
101 North Main Street, Seventh Floor, 48104-1400
Telephone: 313-663-2445
Fax: 313-747-7147
Detroit, Michigan Office: 150 West Jefferson, Suite 2500, 48226-4415.
Telephone: 313-963-6420.
Fax: 313-496-7500.
Cable Address: "Stem Detroit."
Bloomfield Hills, Michigan Office: Suite 100, Pinehurst Office Center, 1400 North Woodward, 48303-2014.
Telephone: 313-645-5000.
Fax: 313-645-1917.
Grand Rapids, Michigan Office: 1200 Campau Square Plaza, 99 Monroe, N.W., 49503-2639.
Telephone: 616-454-8656.
Fax: 616-776-6322.
Howell, Michigan Office: 121 South Barnard Street, Suite 4, 48843-2305.
Telephone: 517-546-7600.
Telecopier: 517-546-6974.
Kalamazoo, Michigan Office: 444 West Michigan Avenue, 49007-3752.
Telephone: 616-381-7030.
Fax: 616-382-0244.
Lansing, Michigan Office: One Michigan Avenue, Suite 900, 48933-1609.
Telephone: 517-487-2070.
Fax: 517-374-6304.

(See Next Column)

Monroe, Michigan Office: The Executive Centre, 214 East Elm Avenue, 48161-2682.
Telephone: 313-243-2000.
Fax: 313-243-0901.
Washington, D.C. Office: 1225 Nineteenth Street, N.W., Suite 400. 20036.
Telephone: 202-429-5575; 785-0600.
Fax: 202-331-1118; 785-1234.
Pensacola, Florida Office: 25 West Cedar, 32501.
Telephone: 904-469-1088.
Fax: 904-432-0677.
St. Petersburg, Florida Office: 100 Second Avenue S., Suite 7045, 33701.
Telephone: 813-982-6000.
Fax: 813-892-6002.
New York, New York Office: Eleventh Floor, 135 East 57th Street, 10022-2087.
Telephone: 212-754-5400.
Fax: 212-754-5401.
Gdansk, Poland Office: Suite 322, Dom Technika Building, UI. Rajska 6, 80-850.
Telephone: 011-485-831-2808.
Fax: 011-485-831-4719.
Warsaw, Poland Office: UI. Marszalkowska 82, Suite 561, 00-517.
Telephone: 011-482-623-6457 and 6458.
Fax: 011-482-623-6459.

RESIDENT PRINCIPALS
Robert E. Gilbert   Charles A. Duerr, Jr.

Representative Firm Clients: Chrysler Corporation; Comerica, Incorporated; City of Detroit, Michigan; Detroit Tigers, Inc.; First of Michigan; Ford Motor Company; Ford Motor Credit Company; Great Lakes Bancorp; Henry Ford Hospital; INVETECH Company.

For Complete List of Firm Personnel, See General Section

For full biographical listings, see the Martindale-Hubbell Law Directory

PEAR SPERLING EGGAN & MUSKOVITZ, P.C. (AV)

Domino's Farms, 24 Frank Lloyd Wright Drive, 48105
Telephone: 313-665-4441
Fax: 313-665-8788
Ypsilanti, Michigan Offices: 5 South Washington Street.
Telephone: 313-483-3626 and 2164 Bellevue at Washtenaw.
Telephone: 313-483-7177.

Melvin J. Muskovitz   Francyne Stacey
Thomas E. Daniels   Helen Conklin Vick
Paul R. Fransway   David E. Kempner

Counsel for: Domino's Pizza, Inc.; Townsend and Bottum, Inc.; Dynamation, Inc.; Citizens Banking Corporation; Thomas Design and Engineering Services, Inc.; Mechanical Dynamics, Inc.; Meadowbrook Insurance Group; City of Wixom; City of Ypsilanti; Ann Arbor Transportation Authority.

For Complete List of Firm Personnel, See General Section

For full biographical listings, see the Martindale-Hubbell Law Directory

BAY CITY, * Bay Co.

BRAUN KENDRICK FINKBEINER PLC (AV)

201 Phoenix Building, P.O. Box 2039, 48708
Telephone: 517-895-8505
Telecopier: 517-895-8437
URL: http://www.bkf-law.com
Saginaw, Michigan Office: 101 N. Washington, Suite 812. 8th Floor Second National Bank Building.
Telephone: 517-753-3461.
Telecopier: 517-753-3951.
Ann Arbor, Michigan Office: 700 First National Building.
Telephone: 313-995-4100.
Telecopier: 313-995-4798.

Ralph J. Isackson   Gregory E. Meter
George F. Gronewold, Jr.   Daniel S. Opperman
Frank M. Quinn   Gregory T. Demers
OF COUNSEL
Patrick D. Neering

Representative Clients: APV Chemical Machinery, Inc.; Bay Health Systems; Catholic Federal Credit Union; City of Saginaw; City of Vassar; City of Milwaukee; Corporate Service; Cox Cable.

For Complete List of Firm Personnel, See General Section

For full biographical listings, see the Martindale-Hubbell Law Directory

BINGHAM FARMS, Oakland Co.

KORNEY & HELDT (AV)

30700 Telegraph Road, Suite 1551, 48025
Telephone: 810-646-1050
Fax: 810-646-1054

J. Douglas Korney   Jeffrey A. Heldt

For full biographical listings, see the Martindale-Hubbell Law Directory

Bingham Farms—Continued

SOTIROFF ABRAMCZYK & RAUSS, P.C. (AV)

30400 Telegraph Road, Suite 444, 48025-4541
Telephone: 810-642-6000
Facsimile: 810-642-9001

Philip Sotiroff	Lawrence A. Tower
Lawrence R. Abramczyk	Robert B. Goldi
Dennis M. Rauss	Keith A. Sotiroff

For full biographical listings, see the Martindale-Hubbell Law Directory

BIRMINGHAM, Oakland Co.

MACDONALD AND GOREN, P.C. (AV)

Suite 200, 260 East Brown Street, 48009
Telephone: 810-645-5940
Fax: 810-645-2490

Harold C. MacDonald   Kalman G. Goren
Cindy Rhodes Victor

Amy L. Glenn	Lawrence C. Atorthy
David D. Marsh	Miriam Blanks-Smart
Glenn G. Ross	John T. Klees

Rose Marie Karadsheh
OF COUNSEL
Robert L. Biederman

Representative Clients: Beaudin, Gallanis; Beaudin, Incorporated; Orlandi Gear Co., Inc.; Bing Steel, Inc.; Superb Manufacturing, Inc.; Spring Engineering, Inc.; Adrian Steel Co.; Southfield Radiology Associates, P.C.; HDS Services, Inc.; TGI Friday's Inc.; Quality Gold of Cincinnati, Inc.

For full biographical listings, see the Martindale-Hubbell Law Directory

BLOOMFIELD HILLS, Oakland Co.

DAWDA, MANN, MULCAHY & SADLER, P.L.C. (AV)

1533 North Woodward Avenue Suite 200, 48304
Telephone: 810-642-3700
Fax: 810-642-7791
Email: EMail@DMMS.Com

Suanne Tiberio Trimmer	Amy Bateson
John Mucha, III	Keith James

Joseph K. Hart, Jr.

Representative Clients: Bally's Total Fitness Corp.; Cardell Corporation; Career Systems Development Corp.; Saturn Electronics & Engineering, Inc.; Dow Corning Corp.; Ford Motor Company; Ladbroke Racing Corporation; La-Z-Boy, Inc.; Smith, Hinchman & Grylls; Walker Wire & Steel Corp.

For full biographical listings, see the Martindale-Hubbell Law Directory

HOWARD & HOWARD ATTORNEYS, P.C. (AV)

The Pinehurst Office Center, Suite 101, 1400 North Woodward Avenue, 48304-2856
Telephone: 810-645-1483
Telecopier: 810-645-1568
Kalamazoo, Michigan Office: The Kalamazoo Building, Suite 400, 107 West Michigan Avenue.
Telephone: 616-382-1483.
Telecopier: 616-382-1568.
Lansing, Michigan Office: The Phoenix Building, Suite 500, 222 Washington Square, North.
Telephone: 517-485-1483.
Telecopier: 517-485-1568.
Peoria, Illinois Office: The Creve Coeur Building, Suite 200, 321 Liberty Street.
Telephone: 309-672-1483.
Telecopier: 309-672-1568.
Tampa, Florida Office: First of America Plaza, Suite 2000, 201 East Kennedy Boulevard.
Telephone: 813-229-1483.
Telecopier: 813-229-1568.

Carol A. Friend   Robert B. Johnston
Brad A. Rayle

Representative Clients: For Representative Client list, see General Practice, Bloomfield Hills, MI.

For Complete List of Firm Personnel, See General Section

For full biographical listings, see the Martindale-Hubbell Law Directory

DAVID D. PATTON & ASSOCIATES, P.C. (AV)

100 Bloomfield Hills Parkway, Suite 110, 48304
Telephone: 810-258-6020
Fax: 810-258-6052
Email: Litigation@Aol.Com

David D. Patton

(See Next Column)

Ellen Bartman Jannette   Patricia C. White
David H. Patton (1912-1993)

For full biographical listings, see the Martindale-Hubbell Law Directory

VAN SUILICHEM & BROWN, P.C. (AV)

525 North Woodward Avenue, Suite 1000, 48304
Telephone: 810-642-0900
Fax: 810-642-7123

Donald A. Van Suilichem   Malcolm D. Brown

Robert C. Tice	Scott T. Patterson
Valerie L. MacFarlane	Gary C. Ankers
Christina M. Brookshire	Jeffrey T. Harrison

For full biographical listings, see the Martindale-Hubbell Law Directory

DETROIT,* Wayne Co.

ABBOTT, NICHOLSON, QUILTER, ESSHAKI & YOUNGBLOOD, P.C. (AV)

19th Floor, One Woodward Avenue, 48226
Telephone: 313-963-2500
Telecopier: 313-963-7882

C. Richard Abbott	Carl F. Jarboe
John R. Nicholson	Jay A. Kennedy
Thomas R. Quilter III	Timothy A. Stoepker
Gene J. Esshaki	Timothy J. Kramer
John F. Youngblood	Norbert T. Madison, Jr.
James B. Perry	William D. Gilbride, Jr.

Mary P. Nelson	Kathryn L. Ritchie
Michael R. Blum	Jill A. Bankey
Thomas F. Hatch	Dawn M. Macaddino
Anne Warren Bagno	Casimir J. Swastek
Eric J. Girdler	Daniel G. Kielczewski

George M. Mesrey
OF COUNSEL
Thomas C. Shumaker   Karen Smith Kienbaum

For full biographical listings, see the Martindale-Hubbell Law Directory

BODMAN, LONGLEY & DAHLING LLP (AV)

34th Floor 100 Renaissance Center, 48243
Telephone: 313-259-7777
Fax: 313-393-7579
Email: 2080194@mcimail.com
Troy, Michigan Office: Suite 2020, 755 West Big Beaver Road.
Telephone: 810-362-2110.
Fax: 810-244-0780.
Ann Arbor, Michigan Office: 110 Miller, Suite 300.
Telephone: 313-761-3780.
Fax: 313-930-2494.
Northern Michigan Office: 229 Court Street, P.O. Box 405, Cheboygan.
Telephone: 616-627-4351.
Fax: 616-627-2802.

MEMBERS OF FIRM

Richard D. Rohr	Kathleen A. Lieder
James T. Heimbuch	(Northern Michigan Office)
James J. Walsh	Karen L. Piper
John C. Cashen (Troy Office)	R. Craig Hupp
Lloyd C. Fell	Henry N. Carnaby (Troy Office)
(Northern Michigan Office)	

For Representative Client List, See General Section

For Complete List of Firm Personnel, See General Section

For full biographical listings, see the Martindale-Hubbell Law Directory

BRADY HATHAWAY, PROFESSIONAL CORPORATION (AV)

1330 Buhl Building, 48226-3602
Telephone: 313-965-3700
Telecopier: 313-965-2830

John F. Brady	Daniel J. Bretz
Thomas M. J. Hathaway	Liliana A. Ciccodicola
Thomas P. Brady	Connie M. Cessante

OF COUNSEL
Ingrid K. Brey

Representative Clients: Beam Stream, Inc.; Bundy Tubing Company; Energy Conversion Devices, Inc.; Schering Corporation; Warner-Lambert; Wolverine Technologies; ABB Environmental Services; GMIS, Inc.; Marriott Corp.

For Complete List of Firm Personnel, See General Section

For full biographical listings, see the Martindale-Hubbell Law Directory

Detroit—Continued

BUTZEL LONG, A PROFESSIONAL CORPORATION (AV)

Suite 900, 150 West Jefferson, 48226
Telephone: 313-225-7000
Telecopier: 313-225-7080
Email: melnick@butzel.com *URL:* http://www.butzel.com
Birmingham, Michigan Office: Suite 200, 32270 Telegraph Road.
Telephone: 810-258-1616.
Telecopier: 810-258-1439.
Lansing, Michigan Office: 118 West Ottawa Street.
Telephone: 517-372-6622.
Telecopier: 517-372-6672.
Ann Arbor, Michigan Office: Suite 300, 350 South Main Street.
Telephone: 313-995-3110.
Telecopier: 313-995-1777.
Grosse Pointe Farms, Michigan Office: Suite 260, 21 Kercheval.
Telephone: 313-886-5446.
Telecopier: 313-886-2114.

William M. Saxton	Lynne E. Deitch
Robert J. Battista	Daniel B. Tukel
John H. Dudley, Jr.	Carey A. DeWitt
Donald B. Miller	Robert A. Boonin
John P. Hancock, Jr.	Andrea Roumell Dickson
Mark T. Nelson	James S. Rosenfeld
Bruce L. Sendek	Jordan S. Schreier (Ann Arbor)

OF COUNSEL
David M. Gaskin (Grosse Pointe Farms)

David K. Tillman	Susan Hartmus Hiser
Nicholas J. Stasevich	Sherri A. Krause

Antoinette M. Pilzner

Representative Clients: Associated General Contractors; Central Michigan University; Detroit Diesel Corp.; Michigan Road Builders Assn.; Stroh Brewery Co.; Teledyne, Inc.; Tishken Products, Inc.; United Parcel Services of America, Inc.; The University of Michigan; William Beaumont Hospital.

For Complete List of Firm Personnel, See General Section

For full biographical listings, see the Martindale-Hubbell Law Directory

CHARFOOS, REITER, PETERSON, HOLMQUIST & PILCHAK, P.C. (AV)

476 State of Michigan Plaza Building, 1200 Sixth Street, 48226
Telephone: 313-961-7011
Email: CRPHP@ix.netcom.com
Farmington Hills, Michigan Office: 30500 Northwestern Highway, Suite 400.
Telephone: 810-626-7300.
Fax: 810-626-7305.

Myron B. Charfoos	Kenneth E. Jones
James A. Reiter	Marianne G. Talon
Daniel Peterson	Deborah S. Dorland
C. John Holmquist, Jr.	Daniel G. Cohen
William E. Pilchak	Danial J. Hébert

Representative Clients: Advanced Technology Laboratories, Inc.; Active Transportation Co.; Dallas & Mavis Forwarding Co.; Fabristeel Products; Fidelity Bank; Key International; Modern Engineering, Inc.; Multifastener Spring Division; Richfield Hotel Management Co,; 46th, 47th and 48th District Courts.

For full biographical listings, see the Martindale-Hubbell Law Directory

CLARK HILL P.L.C. (AV)

500 Woodward Avenue, Suite 3500, 48226
Telephone: 313-965-8300
Facsimile: 313-962-4348
Oakland County, Michigan Office: Third Floor, 255 South Woodward Avenue, Birmingham.
Telephone: 810-642-9692.
Facsimile: 810-642-2174.
Lansing, Michigan Office: Suite 600, 200 North Capitol Avenue.
Telephone: 517-484-4481.
Facsimile: 517-484-1246.
Minneapolis, Minnesota Office: Suite 1000, One Financial Plaza, 120 South Sixth Street.
Telephone: 612-332-0102.
Facsimile: 612-332-3225.
Kansas City, Missouri Office: Suite 1400, Bryant Building, 1102 Grand Avenue.
Telephone: 816-221-5578.
Facsimile: 816-221-0303.

(See Next Column)

David P. Wood	Frank T. Mamat
J. Walker Henry	William A. Moore
Ralph H. Houghton, Jr.	Rachelle G. Silberberg
Fred W. Batten	Margaret Carroll Alli (Resident, Oakland County Office)
Robert W. Morgan	
David H. Paruch (Resident, Oakland County Office)	Dorothy Hanigan Basmaji (Resident, Oakland County Office)

SENIOR ATTORNEY
A. David Baumhart, III (Resident, Oakland County Office)

OF COUNSEL
Dwight H. Vincent

Kay Rivest Butler	Marsha Kay Nettles
Patricia Bordman	Michael F. Smith

Representative Clients: American Red Cross; Bechtel Eastern Power Corp.; The Budd Company; Canteen Corporation; First Federal of Michigan; Dow Corning Corporation; La-Z-Boy Chair Company; Rouge Steel Company.

For Complete List of Firm Personnel, See General Section

For full biographical listings, see the Martindale-Hubbell Law Directory

DICKINSON, WRIGHT, MOON, VAN DUSEN & FREEMAN (AV)

500 Woodward Avenue, Suite 4000, 48226-3425
Telephone: 313-223-3500
Facsimile: 313-223-3598
Bloomfield Hills, Michigan Office: 525 North Woodward Avenue, Suite 2000.
Telephone: 810-433-7200.
Facsimile: 810-433-7274.
Grand Rapids, Michigan Office: 200 Ottawa Avenue, N.W., Suite 900.
Telephone: 616-458-1300.
Facsimile: 616-458-6753.
Lansing, Michigan Office: Suite 200, 215 South Washington Square.
Telephone: 517-371-1730.
Facsimile: 517-487-4700.
Washington, D.C. Office: Suite 800, 1901 L Street, N.W.
Telephone: 202-457-0160.
Facsimile: 202-659-1559.
Chicago, Illinois Office: 225 West Washington, Suite 400.
Telephone: 312-220-0300.
Facsimile: 312-220-0021.

MEMBERS OF FIRM

Johanna H. Armstrong (Bloomfield Hills Office)	Timothy H. Howlett
George R. Ashford	Maurice G. Jenkins
William C. Bertrand, Jr. (Lansing Office)	Thomas G. Kienbaum
	Joseph C. Marshall, III
Robert E. Carr (Bloomfield Hills Office)	Noel D. Massie
	Richard D McNulty (Lansing Office)
David R. Deromedi	Theodore R. Opperwall
Sherisse Eddy Fiorvento (Bloomfield Hills Office)	Eric J. Pelton (Bloomfield Hills Office)
Elizabeth Phelps Hardy (Bloomfield Hills Office)	Elizabeth M. Pezzetti (Bloomfield Hills Office)

Jennifer A. Zinn

OF COUNSEL
Thomas D. McLennan (Bloomfield Hills Office)

ASSOCIATES

Julia Turner Baumhart (Bloomfield Hills Office)	Kelli L. Kerbawy (Bloomfield Hills Office)
Peter G. Golden (Bloomfield Hills Office)	Jeffery M. Peterson
	Louis Theros (Chicago, Illinois Office)

For Representative Client list, see General Section.

For Complete List of Firm Personnel, See General Section

For full biographical listings, see the Martindale-Hubbell Law Directory

DYKEMA GOSSETT PLLC (AV)

400 Renaissance Center, 48243-1668
Telephone: 313-568-6800
Cable Address: "Dyke-Detroit"
Telex: 23-0121
Fax: 313-568-6594
Email: 2084153@mcimail.com
Ann Arbor, Michigan Office: 315 East Eisenhower Parkway, Suite 100, 48108-3306.
Telephone: 313-747-7660.
Fax: 313-747-7696.
Bloomfield Hills, Michigan Office: 1577 North Woodward Avenue, Suite 300, 48304-2820.
Telephone: 810-540-0700.
Fax: 810-540-0763.
Chicago, Illinois Office: 55 East Monroe Street, Suite 3250, 60603-5709.
Telephone: 312-551-4900.
Fax: 312-551-4919.

(See Next Column)

DYKEMA GOSSETT PLLC, *Detroit—Continued*

Grand Rapids, Michigan Office: 200 Oldtown Riverfront Building, 248
Louis Campau Promenade, N.W., 49503-2668.
Telephone: 616-776-7500.
Fax: 616-776-7573.
Lansing, Michigan Office: 800 Michigan National Tower, 48933-1707.
Telephone: 517-374-9100.
Fax: 517-374-9191.
Washington, D.C. Office: Franklin Square, Suite 300 West, 1300 I Street,
N.W., 20005-3306.
Telephone: 202-522-8600.
Fax: 202-522-8669.

MEMBERS OF FIRM

Timothy K. Carroll	Patrick F. Hickey
Bruce G. Davis (Resident at Ann Arbor Office)	Seth M. Lloyd
	Debra M. McCulloch
Robert L. Duty (Resident at Bloomfield Hills Office)	Derek I. Meier
	Joseph A. Ritok, Jr.
John A. Entenman	Ronald J. Santo
Martin Jay Galvin	Paul H. Townsend, Jr.
James P. Greene (Resident at Ann Arbor Office)	

ASSOCIATES

John F. Birmingham, Jr.	Rosemary G. Schikora
Elizabeth M. Donovan	Todd J. Shoudy
Kiffi Y. Ford	Jeffrey N. Silveri (Resident at Ann Arbor Office)
James F. Hermon	
Jennifer J. Howe (Resident at Chicago, Illinois Office)	Alethea Wilson
Kasandra L. Richardson (Resident at Ann Arbor Office)	

For Complete List of Firm Personnel, See General Section

For full biographical listings, see the Martindale-Hubbell Law Directory

---

EGGENBERGER, EGGENBERGER, McKINNEY, WEBER & HOFMEISTER, P.C. (AV)

42nd Floor Penobscot Building, 48226
Telephone: 313-961-9722

William J. Eggenberger (1900-1984)	John P. McKinney
	Stephen L. Weber
William D. Eggenberger	Paul D. Hofmeister
Robert E. Eggenberger	Thomas R. Paxton

Mary T. Humbert	James B. Eggenberger

Representative Clients: Central National Insurance Group of Omaha; Great
Central Insurance Co.; Preferred Risk Mutual Insurance Company of Des
Moines, Iowa; State Automobile and Casualty Underwriters; State Farm Fire
and Casualty Co.
Reference: Comerica Bank-Detroit.

For full biographical listings, see the Martindale-Hubbell Law Directory

---

FEIKENS, VANDER MALE, STEVENS, BELLAMY & GILCHRIST, P.C. (AV)

One Detroit Center Suite 3400, 500 Woodward Avenue, 48226-3406
Telephone: 313-962-5909
Fax: 313-962-3125
Email: FEIKENS@COUNSEL.COM

Robert E. Dice (1922-1983)	Lee A. Stevens
Jon Feikens	William C. Hurley
Jack E. Vander Male	Linda M. Galbraith
Frederick B. Bellamy	Michael S. Cafferty
Alan Gordon Gilchrist	Robert H. Feikens
L. Neal Kennedy	Gerald W. Van Wyke
Bruce A. VandeVusse	Roger L. Wolcott
	Sharon McPhail

Richard G. Koefod	Keith J. Soltis
Joseph E. Kozely, Jr.	Michael B. Barey
Jeffrey Feikens	Renee T. VanderHagen
	Michael P. Citrin

OF COUNSEL

Sam W. Thomas (P.C.)	Walter Vincent Bernard III

LEGAL SUPPORT PERSONNEL
PARALEGALS

Robert Westveer	Linda Barthlow

For full biographical listings, see the Martindale-Hubbell Law Directory

---

FOSTER, MEADOWS & BALLARD, P.C. (AV)

3200 Penobscot Building, 48226
Telephone: 313-961-3234
Cable Address: "Foster"
Telex: 23-5823
Facsimile: 313-961-6184

(See Next Column)

Sparkman D. Foster (1897-1967)	Richard A. Dietz
Charles R. Hrdlicka	Robert H. Fortunate
Paul D. Galea	Robert G. Lahiff
	Camille A. Raffa-Dietz

Michael J. Liddane	Paul A. Kettunen

OF COUNSEL

John L. Foster	John F. Langs
	John A. Mundell, Jr.

For full biographical listings, see the Martindale-Hubbell Law Directory

---

HONIGMAN MILLER SCHWARTZ AND COHN (AV)

A Partnership including Professional Corporations
2290 First National Building, 48226
Telephone: 313-256-7800
Telecopier: 313-962-0176
Telex: 235705
URL: http://law.honigman.com
Lansing, Michigan Office: Phoenix Building, 222 North Washington
Square, Suite 400, 48933-1800.
Telephone: 517-484-8282.
West Palm Beach, Florida Office: Suite 800 Esperante Building, 222
Lakeview Avenue, 33401-6112.
Telephone: 561-838-4500.
Tampa, Florida Office: 2700 SunTrust Financial Centre, 401 E. Jackson
Street, 33602-5226.
Telephone: 813-221-6600.

MEMBERS OF FIRM

Norman D. Hawkins	William D. Sargent
Linn A. Hynds	Samina R. Schey
A. David Mikesell	Stuart H. Teger

ASSOCIATES

Ann L. Andrews (Lansing, Michigan Office)	Cameron J. Evans
	Russell S. Linden
	Barbara A. Van Zanten

Representative Clients: White Castle System, Inc.; Koepplinger's Bakery,
Inc.; Handleman Co.; Gantos, Inc.; Guardian Industries, Inc.; Detroit Edi-
son Company; General Motors Corporation; Delta Dental of Michigan, Inc.
; Frank's Nursery and Crafts; Children's Hospital of Michigan.

For Complete List of Firm Personnel, See General Section

For full biographical listings, see the Martindale-Hubbell Law Directory

---

KELLER, THOMA, SCHWARZE, SCHWARZE, DuBAY & KATZ, P.C. (AV)

440 East Congress, 5th Floor, 48226
Telephone: 313-965-7610
Bloomfield Hills, Michigan Office: Suite 122, 100 West Long Lake Road.
Telephone: 810-642-5218.

Leonard A. Keller (1906-1970)	Terrence J. Miglio
Frederick B. Schwarze	Gary P. King
Thomas H. Schwarze	Robert A. Lusk
Dennis B. DuBay	Linda M. Foster
James R. Miller	Bruce M. Bagdady
Stewart J. Katz	Carl F. Schwarze
Anthony J. Heckemeyer	George P. Butler, III
Thomas L. Fleury	Brian A. Kreucher
	Kenneth C. Howell

OF COUNSEL

Richard J. Thoma	Charles E. Keller

Counsel for: Livonia Public Schools; Ludington News Co., Inc.
Representative Clients: Borg-Warner Corp.; E & L Transport Co.; The Kro-
ger Co.; Holnam, Inc.
Public Employer Clients: City of Farmington Hills; City of Flint; City of
Grosse Pointe Woods; Saginaw Public Schools.

For Complete List of Firm Personnel, See General Section

For full biographical listings, see the Martindale-Hubbell Law Directory

---

LAW OFFICES OF THOMAS E. MARSHALL (AV)

Ford Building, Suite 1805, 615 Griswold, 48226-3583
Telephone: 313-963-4483
Telecopier: 313-963-4736

ASSOCIATES

Phyllis Leah Hurks-Hill	Alejandro Navarro

OF COUNSEL

Andrew J. Bean

For full biographical listings, see the Martindale-Hubbell Law Directory

Detroit—Continued

MILLER, CANFIELD, PADDOCK AND STONE, P.L.C. (AV)

A Professional Limited Liability Company
Founded in 1852 by Sidney Davy Miller
150 West Jefferson, Suite 2500, 48226-4415
Telephone: 313-963-6420
Fax: 313-496-7500
Cable Address: "Stem Detroit"
Detroit, Michigan Office: 150 West Jefferson, Suite 2500, 48226-4415.
Telephone: 313-963-6420.
Fax: 313-496-7500.
Cable Address: "Stem Detroit."
Ann Arbor, Michigan Office: 101 North Main Street, 7th Floor, 48104-1400.
Telephone: 313-663-2445.
Fax: 313-747-7147.
Bloomfield Hills, Michigan Office: Suite 100, Pinehurst Office Center, 1400 North Woodward, 48303-2014.
Telephone: 313-645-5000.
Fax: 313-645-1917.
Grand Rapids, Michigan Office: 1200 Campau Square Plaza, 99 Monroe, N.W., 49503-2639.
Telephone: 616-454-8656.
Fax: 616-776-6322.
Howell, Michigan Office: 121 South Barnard Street, Suite 4, 48843-2305.
Telephone: 517-546-7600.
Telecopier: 517-546-6974.
Kalamazoo, Michigan Office: 444 West Michigan Avenue, 49007-3752.
Telephone: 616-381-7030.
Fax: 616-382-0244.
Lansing, Michigan Office: One Michigan Avenue, Suite 900, 48933-1609.
Telephone: 517-487-2070.
Fax: 517-374-6304.
Monroe, Michigan Office: The Executive Centre, 214 East Elm Avenue, 48161-2682.
Telephone: 313-243-2000.
Fax: 313-243-0901.
Washington, D.C. Office: 1225 Nineteenth Street, N.W., Suite 400. 20036.
Telephone: 202-429-5575; 785-0600.
Fax: 202-331-1118; 785-1234.
Pensacola, Florida Office: 25 West Cedar, 32501.
Telephone: 904-469-1088.
Fax: 904-432-0677.
St. Petersburg, Florida Office: 100 Second Avenue S., Suite 7045, 33701.
Telephone: 813-982-6000.
Fax: 813-892-6002.
New York, New York Office: Eleventh Floor, 135 East 57th Street, 10022-2087.
Telephone: 212-754-5400.
Fax: 212-754-5401.
Gdansk, Poland Office: Suite 322, Dom Technika Building, UI. Rajska 6, 80-850.
Telephone: 011-485-831-2808.
Fax: 011-485-831-4719.
Warsaw, Poland Office: UI. Marszalkowska 82, Suite 561, 00-517.
Telephone: 011-482-623-6457 and 6458.
Fax: 011-482-623-6459.

PRINCIPALS OF FIRM

Leonard D. Givens
Thomas P. Hustoles (Kalamazoo Office)
Jerome R. Watson
Donna J. Donati
Richard J. Seryak
Kevin M. McCarthy (Kalamazoo Office)
Beverly Hall Burns
Charles S. Mishkind (Grand Rapids, Lansing and Kalamazoo Offices)

Walter Briggs Connolly, Jr.
Alison B. Marshall (Washington, D.C. Office)
Megan P. Norris
Charles A. Duerr, Jr. (Ann Arbor Office)
Kurt N. Sherwood (Kalamazoo Office)

OF COUNSEL
James E. Tobin
SENIOR ATTORNEY
George D. Mesritz
ASSOCIATES

John H. Willems
Joseph G. Sullivan

Yvonne R. Haddad
Robbi L. Sackville

Representative Firm Clients: Chrysler Corporation; Comerica, Incorporated; City of Detroit, Michigan; Detroit Tigers, Inc.; First of Michigan; Ford Motor Company; Ford Motor Credit Company; Great Lakes Bancorp; Henry Ford Hospital; INVETECH Company.

For Complete List of Firm Personnel, See General Section

For full biographical listings, see the Martindale-Hubbell Law Directory

PATTERSON, PHIFER & PHILLIPS, P.C. (AV)

L. B. King Building, 1274 Library Street, Suite 500, 48226
Telephone: 313-964-2360

(See Next Column)

Michael D. Patterson
Dwight W. Phillips

Randolph D. Phifer

Joseph M. White
Lisa A. Cylar

Eugene M. Holmes

Representative Clients: Certainteed Corp.; Children's Aid Society of Detroit; Chrysler Corp.; Citizens Insurance Cos.; City of Detroit; County of Wayne; Detroit Board of Education; Detroit Neighborhood Housing Services; General Mills Restaurant, Inc.; General Motors Corp.

For full biographical listings, see the Martindale-Hubbell Law Directory

RILEY AND ROUMELL, P.C. (AV)

7th Floor, Ford Building, 48226-3986
Telephone: 313-962-8255
Telefax: 313-962-2937

Wallace D. Riley
George T. Roumell, Jr.
William F. Dennis
Steven M. Zarowny

Amy E. Newberg
Alfred John Eppens
Wilber M. Brucker III
Allen J. Lippitt

Gregory T. Schultz

OF COUNSEL
William D. Cohan

Emmet E. Tracy, Jr.

Representative Clients: Detroit Board of Education; Wayne County; City of Livonia; Lapeer County Road Commission; Manistee County Road Commission; Lake Superior State University; Village of Lake Orion; White Chapel Memorial Assn.

For full biographical listings, see the Martindale-Hubbell Law Directory

STEINBERG, O'CONNOR, PATON & BURNS, P.L.L.C. (AV)

1724 Ford Building, 615 Griswold Street, 48226-3901
Telephone: 313-962-3738
Telefax: 313-962-3779

Richard L. Steinberg
Doyle O'Connor

Alison L. Paton
Janice L. Burns

For full biographical listings, see the Martindale-Hubbell Law Directory

STRINGARI, FRITZ, KREGER, AHEARN & CRANDALL, P.C. (AV)

510 First National Building, 48226-3538
Telephone: 313-961-6474
Fax: 313-961-5688

Richard J. Fritz
Conrad W. Kreger
Brian S. Ahearn

Martin E. Crandall
Kenneth S. Wilson
Dallas G. Moon

John C. Dickinson
OF COUNSEL
Karl R. Bennett, Jr.

Representative Clients: Automotive Moulding Co.; American Sunroof Corp.; Erb Lumber Co.; City of Detroit; Children's Hospital of Michigan; City Management Corp.; Variety Foodservices, Inc.

For full biographical listings, see the Martindale-Hubbell Law Directory

TIMMIS & INMAN, L.L.P. (AV)

300 Talon Centre, 48207
Telephone: 313-396-4200
Telecopier: 313-396-4228

Michael T. Timmis
Robert E. Graziani
George A. Peck
Richard L. Levin

Henry J. Brennan, III
Mark W. Peyser
Richard M. Miettinen
Lisa R. Gorman

Bradley J. Knickerbocker

Michael F. Wais
OF COUNSEL
Wayne C. Inman

Representative Clients: Talon Inc.; Engineered Plastic Products, Inc.; Talon Automotive Group L.L.C.; Reflectolite Products Co., Inc.; North American Die Casting Corp.; Atlas Holding Company.

For Complete List of Firm Personnel, See General Section

For full biographical listings, see the Martindale-Hubbell Law Directory

FARMINGTON HILLS, Oakland Co.

CHARFOOS, REITER, PETERSON, HOLMQUIST & PILCHAK, P.C. (AV)

Suite 400, 30500 Northwestern Highway, 48334-3179
Telephone: 810-626-7300
Facsimile: 810-626-7305
Email: CRPHP@ix.netcom.com
Detroit, Michigan Office: 1200 Sixth Street.
Telephone: 313-961-7011.

Myron B. Charfoos	Kenneth E. Jones
James A. Reiter	Marianne G. Talon
Daniel Peterson	Deborah S. Dorland
C. John Holmquist, Jr.	Daniel G. Cohen
William E. Pilchak	Danial J. Hébert

Representative Clients: Advanced Technology Laboratories, Inc.; Active Transportation Co.; Dallas & Mavis Forwarding Co.; Fabristeel Products; Fidelity Bank; Key International; Modern Engineering, Inc.; Multifastener Spring Division; Richfield Hotel Management Co.; 46th, 47th and 48th District Courts.

For full biographical listings, see the Martindale-Hubbell Law Directory

---

FLINT, * Genesee Co.

GAULT DAVISON A PROFESSIONAL SERVICE CORPORATION (AV)

Tenth Floor, Northbank Center, 432 North Saginaw Street, 48502-2032
Telephone: 810-234-3633
Fax: 810-233-3387
Email: GLTDAV@tir.com

Frederick L. Schmoll, III	Kendall B. Williams
Edward B. Davison	

Gary Spinning Casey	Abner J. Tansil

Representative Clients: Shoney's, Inc.; City of Flint; Healthplus of Michigan; Genesee Packaging, Co.; Security Federal Credit Union; Mott Community College; Hurley Medical Center; American Red Cross; Flint Urban League.

For full biographical listings, see the Martindale-Hubbell Law Directory

---

LAW OFFICES OF PATRICK M. KIRBY A PROFESSIONAL CORPORATION (AV)

G1335 South Linden Road, Suite G, 48532
Telephone: 810-230-0833
Fax: 810-230-8222

Patrick M. Kirby

Todd O. Pope

Representative Clients: Brotherhood Mutual Insurance Co.; City of Flint; K&K Insurance Group; Merchants and Medical Credit Corp.; Nero Plastics; Rent-A-Center.

For full biographical listings, see the Martindale-Hubbell Law Directory

---

GRAND RAPIDS, * Kent Co.

LAW, WEATHERS & RICHARDSON, P.C. (AV)

Bridgewater Place, Suite 800, 333 Bridge Street, N.W., 49504
Telephone: 616-459-1171
Facsimile: 616-732-1740

William R. Hineline	John P. Schneider
Stephen D. Turner	Kevin B. Krauss
Bruce A. Courtade	

Representative Clients: F.D.I.C.; Ford Motor Credit Co.; Herman Miller, Inc.; Kent County Aeronautics Board; Marriott Corp.; The Procter & Gamble Co.; Peerless Insurance Co.; Ryder Systems, Inc.

For Complete List of Firm Personnel, See General Section

For full biographical listings, see the Martindale-Hubbell Law Directory

---

PATTERSON, KINNEY & RUGA (AV)

5075 Cascade Road S.E., 49546
Telephone: 616-285-9886
Fax: 616-285-5572

MEMBERS OF FIRM

Peter A. Patterson	Sheila Kinney
Barbara A. Ruga	

For full biographical listings, see the Martindale-Hubbell Law Directory

---

VARNUM, RIDDERING, SCHMIDT & HOWLETT LLP (AV)

A Limited Liability Partnership including Professional Corporations
Bridgewater Place, P.O. Box 352, 49501-0352
Telephone: 616-336-6000
800-262-0011
Facsimile: 616-336-7000
Telex: 1561593 VARN
Email: varnum@vrsh.com
Lansing, Michigan Office: The Victor Center, Suite 810, 210 North Washington Square, 48933.
Telephone: 517-482-6237.
Facsimile: 517-482-6937.
Kalamazoo, Michigan Office: 350 East Michigan Avenue, 49007.
Telephone: 616-382-2300.
Facsimile: 616-382-2382.
Grand Haven, Michigan Office: 321 Washington Street, P.O. Box 288, 49417.
Telephone: 616-846-7100.
Facsimile: 616-846-7101.
Battle Creek, Michigan Office: 4950 West Dickman Road, Suite B-1, 49015.
Telephone: 616-962-7144.
Bingham Farms, Michigan Office: 31600 Telegraph Road, Suite 230, 48025.
Telephone: 810-594-7330.
Facsimile: 810-594- 7331.

MEMBERS OF FIRM

Kent J. Vana	Paul M. Kara
Carl E. Ver Beek	Gregory M. Palmer
Gary P. Skinner	David E. Khorey
Thomas J. Barnes	Timothy J. Tornga
Larry J. Titley	David A. Rhem
Richard A. Hooker (Resident at Kalamazoo Office)	Donald P. Lawless
	Jeffrey J. Fraser
Joseph J. Vogan	Richard D. Fries
John Patrick White	James R. Stadler
Richard R. Symons	

OF COUNSEL

Eugene Alkema	H. Edward Paul

COUNSEL

James R. Viventi (Resident at Lansing Office)

ASSOCIATES

Eric J. Guerin (Resident at Kalamazoo Office)	Mary C. Bonnema
	Linda L. Bunge
Anthony R. Comden	

Counsel for: CMI International, Inc.; Donnelly Corporation; Excel Industries, Inc.; Georgia Pacific Corp.; Grand Valley State University; Holland Hitch; Knape & Vogt Manufacturing Co.; Meijer, Inc.; Mercy Health Services; Packaging Corporation of America.

For Complete List of Firm Personnel, See General Section

For full biographical listings, see the Martindale-Hubbell Law Directory

---

WARNER NORCROSS & JUDD LLP (AV)

900 Old Kent Building, 111 Lyon Street, N.W., 49503-2489
Telephone: 616-752-2000
Fax: 616-752-2500
Muskegon, Michigan Office: 400 Terrace Plaza, P.O. Box 900.
Telephone: 616-727-2600.
Fax: 616-727-2699.
Holland, Michigan Office: Curtis Center, Suite 300, 170 College Avenue.
Telephone: 616-396-9800.
Fax: 616-396-3656.

OF COUNSEL

Lawson E. Becker

MEMBERS OF FIRM

Donald J. Veldman (Resident at Muskegon Office)	Robert J. Chovanec
	Robert W. Sikkel (Muskegon and Holland Offices)
Jack B. Combs	
Joseph F. Martin	Louis C. Rabaut
Stephen B. Grow	

Representative Clients: Blodgett Memorial Center; Guardsman Products, Inc.; Kysor Industrial Corp.; Michigan Bankers Assn.; Old Kent Financial Corp.; Muskegon Community College; Michigan Civil Service Commission; Hart & Cooley Manufacturing.

For Complete List of Firm Personnel, See General Section

For full biographical listings, see the Martindale-Hubbell Law Directory

KALAMAZOO,* Kalamazoo Co.

HOWARD & HOWARD ATTORNEYS, P.C. (AV)

The Kalamazoo Building, Suite 400, 107 West Michigan
Avenue, 49007-3956
Telephone: 616-382-1483
Telecopier: 616-382-1568
Bloomfield Hills, Michigan Office: The Pinehurst Office Center, Suite 101,
1400 North Woodward Avenue.
Telephone: 810-645-1483.
Telecopier: 810-645-1568.
Lansing, Michigan Office: The Phoenix Building, Suite 500, 222
Washington Square North.
Telephone: 517-485-1483.
Telecopier: 517-485-1568.
Peoria, Illinois Office: The Creve Coeur Building, Suite 200, 321 Liberty
Street.
Telephone: 309-672-1483.
Telecopier: 309-672-1568.
Tampa, Florida Office: First of America Plaza, Suite 2000, 201 East
Kennedy Boulevard.
Telephone: 813-229-1483.
Telecopier: 813-229-1568.

John W. Allen	Robert C. Beck
Gerry Bartlett-McMahon	Lawrence J. Murphy

Representative Clients: For Representative Client list, see General Practice,
Kalamazoo, MI.

For Complete List of Firm Personnel, See General Section

For full biographical listings, see the Martindale-Hubbell Law Directory

KREIS, ENDERLE, CALLANDER & HUDGINS, A PROFESSIONAL CORPORATION (AV)

One Moorsbridge, P.O. Box 4010, 49003-4010
Telephone: 616-324-3000
Telecopier: 616-324-3010
Email: kech@sapien.net *URL:* http://www.kech.com/

Douglas L. Callander	John F. Koryto

For Complete List of Firm Personnel, See General Section

For full biographical listings, see the Martindale-Hubbell Law Directory

LILLY & LILLY, P.C. (AV)

505 South Park Street, 49007
Telephone: 616-381-7763
Fax: 616-344-6880

Charles M. Lilly (1903-1990)	Terrence J. Lilly

For full biographical listings, see the Martindale-Hubbell Law Directory

MILLER, CANFIELD, PADDOCK AND STONE, P.L.C. (AV)

A Professional Limited Liability Company
Founded in 1852 by Sidney Davy Miller
444 West Michigan Avenue, 49007-3752
Telephone: 616-381-7030
Fax: 616-382-0244
Detroit, Michigan Office: 150 West Jefferson, Suite 2500, 48226-4415.
Telephone: 313-963-6420.
Fax: 313-496-7500.
Cable Address: "Stem Detroit."
Ann Arbor, Michigan Office: 101 North Main Street, 7th Floor,
48104-1400.
Telephone: 313-663-2445.
Fax: 313-747-7147.
Bloomfield Hills, Michigan Office: Suite 100, Pinehurst Office Center, 1400
North Woodward, 48303-2014.
Telephone: 313-645-5000.
Fax: 313-645-1917.
Grand Rapids, Michigan Office: 1200 Campau Square Plaza, 99 Monroe,
N.W., 49503-2639.
Telephone: 616-454-8656.
Fax: 616-776-6322.
Howell, Michigan Office: 121 South Barnard Street, Suite 4, 48843-2305.
Telephone: 517-546-7600.
Telecopier: 517-546-6974.
Lansing, Michigan Office: One Michigan Avenue, Suite 900, 48933-1609.
Telephone: 517-487-2070.
Fax: 517-374-6304.
Monroe, Michigan Office: The Executive Centre, 214 East Elm Avenue,
48161-2682.
Telephone: 313-243-2000.
Fax: 313-243-0901.
Washington, D.C. Office: 1225 Nineteenth Street, N.W., Suite 400. 20036.
Telephone: 202-429-5575; 785-0600.
Fax: 202-331-1118; 785-1234.
Pensacola, Florida Office: 25 West Cedar, 32501.
Telephone: 904-469-1088.
Fax: 904-432-0677.

(See Next Column)

St. Petersburg, Florida Office: 100 Second Avenue S., Suite 7045, 33701.
Telephone: 813-982-6000.
Fax: 813-892-6002.
New York, New York Office: Eleventh Floor, 135 East 57th Street,
10022-2087.
Telephone: 212-754-5400.
Fax: 212-754-5401.
Gdansk, Poland Office: Suite 322, Dom Technika Building, UI. Rajska 6,
80-850.
Telephone: 011-485-831-2808.
Fax: 011-485-831-4719.
Warsaw, Poland Office: UI. Marszalkowska 82, Suite 561, 00-517.
Telephone: 011-482-623-6457 and 6458.
Fax: 011-482-623-6459.

PRINCIPALS OF FIRM

Eric V. Brown, Jr.	Kevin M. McCarthy
John A. Campbell	Pamela Chapman Enslen
Thomas P. Hustoles	Kurt N. Sherwood

ASSOCIATE
James B. Thelen

Representative Firm Clients: Chrysler Corporation; Comerica, Incorporated;
City of Detroit, Michigan; Detroit Tigers, Inc.; First of Michigan; Ford Mo-
tor Company; Ford Motor Credit Company; Great Lakes Bancorp; Henry
Ford Hospital; INVETECH Company.

For Complete List of Firm Personnel, See General Section

For full biographical listings, see the Martindale-Hubbell Law Directory

---

LANSING, Ingham Co.

DUNNINGS & FRAWLEY, P.C. (AV)

Duncan Building, 530 South Pine Street, 48933-2299
Telephone: 517-487-8222
Fax: 517-487-2026
Email: conrights@voyager.net

Stuart J. Dunnings, Jr.	John J. Frawley

Stuart J. Dunnings, III	Steven D. Dunnings
Shauna L. Dunnings	

Representative Clients: Lansing Board of Education; Lansing Housing Commission; Ford Motor Co.
References: First of America; Michigan National Bank.

For full biographical listings, see the Martindale-Hubbell Law Directory

FOSTER, SWIFT, COLLINS & SMITH, P.C. (AV)

313 South Washington Square, 48933-2193
Telephone: 517-371-8100
Telecopier: 517-371-8200
URL: http://www.fosterswift.com
Farmington Hills, Michigan Office: 32300 Northwestern Highway, Suite
230.
Telephone: 810-539-9900.
Fax: 810-851-7504.

Theodore W. Swift	David J. Houston
Stephen O. Schultz	Michael J. Bommarito
William R. Schulz	Melissa J. Jackson
Scott L. Mandel	Peter R. Albertins
Kathryn M. Niemer	Sheralee S. Hurwitz

General Counsel for: First American Bank-Central; Story, Inc.; Michigan
Milk Producers Assn.; Edward W. Sparrow Hospital; St. Lawrence Hospital;
Demmer Corp.; Michigan Financial Corp.
Local Counsel for: Shell Oil Co.; Michigan-Mutual Insurance Co.; Century
Telephone.

For Complete List of Firm Personnel, See General Section

For full biographical listings, see the Martindale-Hubbell Law Directory

FRASER TREBILCOCK DAVIS & FOSTER, P.C. (AV)

1000 Michigan National Tower, 48933
Telephone: 517-482-5800
Fax: 517-482-0887

Michael E. Cavanaugh	Brandon W. Zuk
John J. Loose	Sharon A. Bruner

Counsel for: Auto Owners Insurance Company; Dowleg Manufacturing;
Michigan Education Association; Michigan Non-Profit Homes; Tri-State
Hospital Supply Corporation.

For Complete List of Firm Personnel, See General Section

For full biographical listings, see the Martindale-Hubbell Law Directory

Lansing—Continued

HOWARD & HOWARD ATTORNEYS, P.C. (AV)

The Phoenix Building, Suite 500, 222 Washington Square,
North, 48933-1817
Telephone: 517-485-1483
Telecopier: 517-485-1568
Kalamazoo, Michigan Office: The Kalamazoo Building, Suite 400, 107
West Michigan Avenue.
Telephone: 616-382-1483.
Telecopier: 616-382-1568.
Bloomfield Hills, Michigan Office: The Pinehurst Office Center, Suite 101,
1400 North Woodward Avenue.
Telephone: 810-645-1483.
Telecopier: 810-645-1568.
Peoria, Illinois Office: The Creve Coeur Building, Suite 200, 321 Liberty
Street.
Telephone: 309-672-1483.
Telecopier: 309-672-1568.
Tampa, Florida Office: First of America Plaza, Suite 2000, 201 East
Kennedy Boulevard.
Telephone: 813-229-1483.
Telecopier: 813-229-1568.

Todd D. Chamberlain   C. Douglas Moran

Representative Clients: For Representative Client list, see General Practice,
Lansing, MI.

For Complete List of Firm Personnel, See General Section

For full biographical listings, see the Martindale-Hubbell Law Directory

MILLER, CANFIELD, PADDOCK AND STONE, P.L.C. (AV)

A Professional Limited Liability Company
Founded in 1852 by Sidney Davy Miller
Suite 900, One Michigan Avenue, 48933-1609
Telephone: 517-487-2070
Fax: 517-374-6304
Detroit, Michigan Office: 150 West Jefferson, Suite 2500, 48226-4415.
Telephone: 313-963-6420.
Fax: 313-496-7500.
Cable Address: "Stem Detroit."
Ann Arbor, Michigan Office: 101 North Main Street, 7th Floor,
48104-1400.
Telephone: 313-663-2445.
Fax: 313-747-7147.
Bloomfield Hills, Michigan Office: Suite 100, Pinehurst Office Center, 1400
North Woodward, 48303-2014.
Telephone: 313-645-5000.
Fax: 313-645-1917.
Grand Rapids, Michigan Office: 1200 Campau Square Plaza, 99 Monroe,
N.W., 49503-2639.
Telephone: 616-454-8656.
Fax: 616-776-6322.
Howell, Michigan Office: 121 South Barnard Street, Suite 4, 48843-2305.
Telephone: 517-546-7600.
Telecopier: 517-546-6974.
Kalamazoo, Michigan Office: 444 West Michigan Avenue, 49007-3752.
Telephone: 616-381-7030.
Fax: 616-382-0244.
Monroe, Michigan Office: The Executive Centre, 214 East Elm Avenue,
48161-2682.
Telephone: 313-243-2000.
Fax: 313-243-0901.
Washington, D.C. Office: 1225 Nineteenth Street, N.W., Suite 400. 20036.
Telephone: 202-429-5575; 785-0600.
Fax: 202-331-1118; 785-1234.
Pensacola, Florida Office: 25 West Cedar, 32501.
Telephone: 904-469-1088.
Fax: 904-432-0677.
St. Petersburg, Florida Office: 100 Second Avenue S., Suite 7045, 33701.
Telephone: 813-982-6000.
Fax: 813-892-6002.
New York, New York Office: Eleventh Floor, 135 East 57th Street,
10022-2087.
Telephone: 212-754-5400.
Fax: 212-754-5401.
Gdansk, Poland Office: Suite 322, Dom Technika Building, UI. Rajska 6,
80-850.
Telephone: 011-485-831-2808.
Fax: 011-485-831-4719.
Warsaw, Poland Office: UI. Marszalkowska 82, Suite 561, 00-517.
Telephone: 011-482-623-6457 and 6458.
Fax: 011-482-623-6459.

PRINCIPALS OF FIRM
William J. Danhof (Resident)

Representative Firm Clients: Chrysler Corporation; Comerica, Incorporated;
City of Detroit, Michigan; Detroit Tigers, Inc.; First of Michigan; Ford Mo-
tor Company; Ford Motor Credit Company; Great Lakes Bancorp; Henry
Ford Hospital; INVETECH Company.

(See Next Column)

For Complete List of Firm Personnel, See General Section

For full biographical listings, see the Martindale-Hubbell Law Directory

MONROE,* Monroe Co.

BRAUNLICH, RUSSOW & BRAUNLICH, A PROFESSIONAL CORPORATION (AV)

111 South Macomb Street, 48161
Telephone: 313-241-8300
Fax: 313-241-7715

William J. Braunlich, Jr.   Thomas P. Russow
(1924-1992)   William H. Braunlich

Philip A. Costello   Marie C. Kennedy
Patricia M. Poupard   Susan J. Mehregan
Ann L. Nickel   Robert Wetzel
                Michael G. Roehrig
LEGAL SUPPORT PERSONNEL
Ruth G. Flint

Representative Clients: State Farm Mutual Insurance Co.; Auto Club Insurance Assn.; Farm Bureau Insurance Co.; Home Mutual Insurance Co.; Cincinnati Insurance Co.; Board of Road Commissioners, Monroe County; Port
of Monroe; Monroe County Community College; City of Luna Pier; City of
Petersburg.

For full biographical listings, see the Martindale-Hubbell Law Directory

MOUNT CLEMENS,* Macomb Co.

PETERSON, HAY AND COMSA, P.C. (AV)

18 First Street, P.O. Box 688, 48046-0688
Telephone: 810-469-3600
Facsimile: 810-469-2537

James R. Peterson (1931-1991)   David A. Comsa
William L. Hay   Thomas S. Michael
                Lynn M. Capp

For full biographical listings, see the Martindale-Hubbell Law Directory

PONTIAC,* Oakland Co.

BOOTH PATTERSON, P.C. (AV)

1090 West Huron Street, 48328
Telephone: 810-681-1200
Fax: 810-681-1754

Douglas W. Booth (1918-1992)   David J. Lee
Calvin E. Patterson (1913-1987)   Allan T. Motzny
Parvin C. Lee, Jr.   Michael J. Hughes
J. Timothy Patterson   Michael D. Bishop
                Eric S. Meier

For full biographical listings, see the Martindale-Hubbell Law Directory

PORT HURON,* St. Clair Co.

FLETCHER DeGROW (AV)

522 Michigan Street, 48060-3893
Telephone: 810-987-8444
Facsimile: 810-987-8149

MEMBERS OF FIRM
Gary A. Fletcher   Mark G. Clark
ASSOCIATE
William L. Fealko, III

Representative Clients: Wirtz MFG.; Raymond Excavating; City of Port Hu-
ron; City of Marsville; St. Clair County; Port Huron Area School District;
Intermediate School District of St. Clair County; East China School District;
Marysville School District; Algonac School District.

For Complete List of Firm Personnel, See General Section

For full biographical listings, see the Martindale-Hubbell Law Directory

SAGINAW,* Saginaw Co.

BRAUN KENDRICK FINKBEINER PLC (AV)

101 N. Washington Suite 812, 48607-1297
Telephone: 517-753-3461
Telecopier: 517-753-3951
URL: http://www.bkf-law.com
Bay City, Michigan Office: 201 Phoenix Building, P.O. Box 2039.
Telephone: 517-895-8505.
Telecopier: 517-895-8437.
Ann Arbor, Michigan Office: 700 First National Building.
Telephone: 313-995-4100.
Telecopier: 313-995-4798.

James V. Finkbeiner   Robert A. Kendrick
E. Louis Ognisanti   John A. Decker

(See Next Column)

BRAUN KENDRICK FINKBEINER PLC—*Continued*

Irenna M. Garapetian
OF COUNSEL
J. Richard Kendrick

Representative Clients: The Dow Chemical Co.; General Motors Corp.; Lobdell Emery Manufacturing Co.; Merrill, Lynch, Inc.; Saginaw General Hospital; Saginaw News; The Wickes Foundation.

For Complete List of Firm Personnel, See General Section

For full biographical listings, see the Martindale-Hubbell Law Directory

---

MASUD, GILBERT & PATTERSON, P.C. (AV)

4449 Fashion Square Boulevard, 48603-1242
Telephone: 517-792-4499
Fax: 517-792-7725

David John Masud	Donald A. Gilbert
	Gary D. Patterson

Kraig M. Schutter	Paula R. Coffee
	Kathleen A. Eickholt

Representative Clients: Dow Corning Corp.; Boritz Health Care Facilities; Associated Builders & Contractors; Michigan Sugar Co.; Saginaw Charter Township; Saginaw Township Community School; Central Michigan Railway; St. Mary's Medical Center; Forward Corp.

For full biographical listings, see the Martindale-Hubbell Law Directory

---

SMITH & BROOKER, P.C. (AV)

The Gold Building, 4855 State Street, Suite 4, 48603
Telephone: 517-799-1891
Fax: 517-799-1145
Bay City, Michigan Office: 703 Washington Avenue.
Telephone: 517-892-2595.
Flint, Michigan Office: 1309 South Linden Road, Suite C, P.O. Box 315000.
Telephone: 810-733-0140.

RESIDENT ATTORNEYS

Francis B. Drinan	Michael J. Huffman

OF COUNSEL

Carl H. Smith, Jr.	Albert C. Hicks

Representative Clients: CIGNA; Citizens Insurance Co.; City of Saginaw; General Motors Corp.; Saginaw Township Community Schools; Saginaw Intermediate School District; State Farm Mutual Automobile Insurance Co.; Tri-City Airport Commission; CSX Transportation; Tittabawasee Township.

For full biographical listings, see the Martindale-Hubbell Law Directory

---

ST. JOSEPH, * Berrien Co.

BUTZBAUGH & DEWANE, P.L.C. (AV)

Law and Title Building, 811 Ship Street, P.O. Box 27, 49085
Telephone: 616-983-0191
Fax: 616-983-5078
Email: b-d-law@parrett.net.

MEMBERS OF FIRM

John E. Dewane	Michael J. Roberts

Representative Clients: Whirlpool Corp.; American Society of Agricultural Engineers; Imperial Printing Co.

For Complete List of Firm Personnel, See General Section

For full biographical listings, see the Martindale-Hubbell Law Directory

---

TROFF, PETZKE & AMMESON (AV)

Law and Title Building, 811 Ship Street, P.O. Box 67, 49085
Telephone: 616-983-0161
Facsimile: 616-983-0166

MEMBERS OF FIRM

Theodore E. Troff	Roger A. Petzke
	Charles F. Ammeson

ASSOCIATES

Bennett S. Schwartz	Daniel G. Lambrecht
	Deborah L. Berecz

For full biographical listings, see the Martindale-Hubbell Law Directory

---

SOUTHFIELD, Oakland Co.

MARK H. COUSENS (AV)

26261 Evergreen Road, Suite 110, 48076
Telephone: 810-355-2150
Fax: 810-355-2170
Email: laborlaw@mich.com

(See Next Column)

ASSOCIATE
John E. Eaton

For full biographical listings, see the Martindale-Hubbell Law Directory

---

HIGHLAND & ZANETTI (AV)

Suite 205, 24445 Northwestern Highway, 48075
Telephone: 810-352-9580

John N. Highland	J. R. Zanetti, Jr.
	R. Michael John

Duncan Hall Brown	Ronald D. Holton

For full biographical listings, see the Martindale-Hubbell Law Directory

---

SOMMERS, SCHWARTZ, SILVER & SCHWARTZ, P.C. (AV)

2000 Town Center, Suite 900, 48075
Telephone: 810-355-0300
Telecopier: 810-746-4001
Plymouth, Michigan Office: 747 South Main Street.
Telephone: 313-455-4250.

Donald J. Gasiorek	David A. Kotzian
Justin C. Ravitz	Patricia A. Stamler
Joseph A. Golden	Sam G. Morgan
Daniel D. Swanson	Gary E. Abeska
	David J Szymanski

OF COUNSEL
Marvin R. Stempien

Representative Clients: Automatic Data Processing; Vlasic & Co.; C. A. Muer Corp.; O/E Automation, Inc.; City of Taylor; Township of Van Buren; Vesco Oil Corp.; Royal Insurance Co.; Michigan Mutual/Amerisure Insurance Co.

For Complete List of Firm Personnel, See General Section

For full biographical listings, see the Martindale-Hubbell Law Directory

---

TRAVERSE CITY, * Grand Traverse Co.

MURCHIE, CALCUTT & BOYNTON (AV)

109 East Front Street, Suite 300, 49684
Telephone: 616-947-7190
Fax: 616-947-4341

Robert B. Murchie (1894-1975)	William B. Calcutt
Harry Calcutt	Mark A. Burnheimer
Jack E. Boynton	Dawn M. Rogers

ASSOCIATE
Ralph J. Dilley (Not admitted in MI)

General Counsel for: Old Kent Bank-Grand Traverse; Northwestern Savings Bank & Trust; Central-State Bancorp; Traverse City Record Eagle; WPNB-7 & WTOM-4; Emergency Consultants, Inc.; National Guardian Risk Retention Group, Inc.; Farmers Mutual Insurance Co.; Environmental Solutions, Inc.
Local Counsel for: Consumers Power Co.

For full biographical listings, see the Martindale-Hubbell Law Directory

---

TROY, Oakland Co.

BARLOW & LANGE, P.C. (AV)

3290 West Big Beaver Road Suite 310, 48084
Telephone: 810-649-3150
Facsimile: 810-649-3175

Thomas W. H. Barlow	Craig S. Schwartz
Craig W. Lange	Matthew S. Derby
Paul W. Coughenour	Gary S. Fealk

LEGAL SUPPORT PERSONNEL
Laura L. Russell

For full biographical listings, see the Martindale-Hubbell Law Directory

---

HAINER, DEMOREST & BERMAN, P.C. (AV)

888 West Big Beaver, Suite 1400, 48084
Telephone: 810-244-8424
Fax: 810-244-8455

Michael J. Hainer	Mark S. Demorest
	Leonard K. Berman

James D. Zazakis	Paul S. Miller
	Rae Ann LaFrance

OF COUNSEL

John P. Charters	Michael A. Kus
Michael A. Heck	Douglas W. Mires

Representative Clients: American Empire Surplus Lines Insurance Co.; Central Distributors of Beer, Inc.; City Management Corp.; Clarklift of Detroit, Inc.; Federal Reserve Bank of Chicago; Hotel Investment Services, Inc.;

(See Next Column)

HAINER, DEMOREST & BERMAN P.C., *Troy—Continued*

Michigan Pumping Service; Mid-West Instrument, Inc.; Rockwell International Corp.; Zurich Insurance Co.

For full biographical listings, see the Martindale-Hubbell Law Directory

KEYWELL AND ROSENFELD (AV)

Suite 600, 2301 West Big Beaver Road, 48084
Telephone: 810-649-3200
Fax: 810-649-0454

MEMBER OF FIRM
Gary W. Klotz
ASSOCIATES

Miriam R. Rosen	Christopher P. Mazzoli
	Laura W. Johnston

OF COUNSEL
Robert S. Rosenfeld

Reference: National Bank of Detroit.

For full biographical listings, see the Martindale-Hubbell Law Directory

MATHESON, PARR, SCHULER, EWALD & JOLLY, L.L.P. (AV)

2555 Crooks Road, Suite 200, 48084
Telephone: 810-643-7900
Telecopier: 810-643-0417

MEMBERS OF FIRM

Robert Alan Parr	Terence K. Jolly
	James D. Osmer

Representative Clients: National Automobile Transporters Labor Division; Brink's Inc.; Expertec, Inc.; Advance Technology, Inc.; Frito-Lay, Inc.
Reference: Comerica Bank.

For Complete List of Firm Personnel, See General Section

For full biographical listings, see the Martindale-Hubbell Law Directory

VALENTINE & ASSOCIATES, P.C.

(See West Bloomfield)

WEST BLOOMFIELD, Oakland Co.

VALENTINE & ASSOCIATES, P.C. (AV)

5767 West Maple Road, Suite 400, 48322
Telephone: 810-851-3010

Stephen K. Valentine, Jr.
OF COUNSEL
Philip G. Meyer

For full biographical listings, see the Martindale-Hubbell Law Directory

LAND USE LAW

ALABAMA

BIRMINGHAM, * Jefferson Co.

BRADLEY, ARANT, ROSE & WHITE (AV)

2001 Park Place, Suite 1400, P.O. Box 830709, 35283-0709
Telephone: 205-521-8000
Facsimile: 205-252-0264
Facsimile (SouthTrust Tower Office): 205-251-9915
URL: http://www.BARW.COM
Huntsville, Alabama Office: 200 Clinton Avenue West, Suite 900, 35801.
Telephone: 205-517-5100.
Facsimile: 205-533-5069.

MEMBER OF FIRM
Charles A. J. Beavers, Jr.

ASSOCIATE
Frank C. Galloway, III

For Complete List of Firm Personnel, See General Section

For full biographical listings, see the Martindale-Hubbell Law Directory

ARIZONA

PHOENIX, * Maricopa Co.

EARL, CURLEY & LAGARDE (AV)

3101 N. Central Avenue, Suite 1090, 85012
Telephone: 602-265-0094
Fax: 602-265-2195

MEMBERS OF FIRM
Stephen C. Earl   Michael J. Curley
Lynne A. Lagarde

Representative Clients: Del Webb Corporation; American Express Travel Related Services; Sinclair Oil Corporation; Mobil Land Development (Southwest) Corporation; Desert Mountain Properties; Opus Southwest; Scottsdale Princess Hotel; Westcor Partners; Grossman Company Properties; Trammell Crow Residential.

For full biographical listings, see the Martindale-Hubbell Law Directory

ZEITLIN & ZEITLIN, P.C. (AV)

A Partnership including a Professional Corporation
Camel Headquarters, 3900 East Camelback Road Suite 406, 85018
Telephone: 602-234-8905
Fax: 602-285-5589
Annapolis, Maryland Office: 2007 Tidewater Colony Drive, Suite 2B, 21401-8686.
Telephone: 410-266-9500.
Facsimile: 410-266-9522.

Dale S. Zeitlin   Dawn Stoll Zeitlin (P.C.)

For full biographical listings, see the Martindale-Hubbell Law Directory

CALIFORNIA

BEVERLY HILLS, Los Angeles Co.

DAPEER, ROSENBLIT & LITVAK, LLP (AV)

9460 Wilshire Boulevard, Fifth Floor, 90212
Telephone: 310-203-8200; 310-777-6676
Fax: 310-203-8213; 310-777-6675
Metropolitan Cities Office: 2770 East Slauson Avenue, P.O. Box 2067, Huntington Park, 90255.
Telephone: 213-587-5221.
Fax: 213-587-4190.

William Litvak   Steven H. Rosenblit
Kenneth B. Dapeer

For full biographical listings, see the Martindale-Hubbell Law Directory

CLAREMONT, Los Angeles Co.

C. ROBERT FERGUSON (AV)

237 West Fourth Street, 91711
Telephone: 909-482-0782; 818-795-4181
Fax: 909-624-7291

COSTA MESA, Orange Co.

RUTAN & TUCKER, LLP (AV)

A Partnership including Professional Corporations
611 Anton Boulevard, Suite 1400, P.O. Box 1950, 92626
Telephone: 714-641-5100; 213-625-7586
Telecopier: 714-546-9035
Email: rutan&tucker@mcimail.com *URL:* http://www.rutan.com

MEMBERS OF FIRM
Leonard A. Hampel, Jr.   Elizabeth L. Martyn
Michael D. Rubin   Kim D. Thompson
Jeffrey M. Oderman (P.C.)   Hans Van Ligten
David J. Aleshire   Robert Owen
Philip D. Kohn   Jeffrey A. Goldfarb
Joel D. Kuperberg   F. Kevin Brazil
M. Katherine Jenson   Layne H. Melzer

ASSOCIATES
Dan Slater   Julia L. Bond
A. Patrick Muñoz   Jennifer White-Sperling
S. Daniel Harbottle   Steven M. Coleman

For Complete List of Firm Personnel, See General Section

For full biographical listings, see the Martindale-Hubbell Law Directory

LONG BEACH, Los Angeles Co.

CAMERON, MADDEN, PEARLSON, GALE & SELLARS (AV)

One World Trade Center Suite 1600, 90831-1600
Telephone: 310-436-3888
Telecopier: 310-437-1967

MEMBERS OF THE FIRM
Timothy C. Cameron   Patrick T. Madden
Charles M. Gale   Paul R. Pearlson
James D. Sellars

ASSOCIATE
Lillian D. Salinger

For full biographical listings, see the Martindale-Hubbell Law Directory

LOS ANGELES, * Los Angeles Co.

BRAND FARRAR DZIUBLA FREILICH & KOLSTAD, LLP (AV)

Counsellors at Law
515 South Flower Street, Suite 3500, 90071-2201
Telephone: 213-228-0288
Facsimile: 213-426-6222
Correspondent Offices: Hong Kong, Shanghai, Beijing, Guangzhou, Xiamen, Shenzhen, Ulaanbaatar, New York and San Francisco.

Michael A. Brand   Amy E. Freilich
David W. Farrar   Charles K. Kolstad
Robert W. Dziubla   Margaret G. Graf

OF COUNSEL
H. Bennett Arnberger   Julia Marie Shymansky
David C. Buxbaum   Yelena Yeruhim
Sherry L. Geyer   Norman A. Chernin
Manender M. Grewal (Not   Joan M. Marquardt
   admitted in the United States)

For full biographical listings, see the Martindale-Hubbell Law Directory

OLIVER, VOSE, SANDIFER, MURPHY & LEE, A PROFESSIONAL CORPORATION (AV)

The Park, Second Floor, 281 South Figueroa Street, 90012
Telephone: 213-621-2000
Telecopier: 213-621-2211

Charles S. Vose   James Duff Murphy
Connie Cooke Sandifer   Edward W. Lee
Roger W. Springer

Mary L. McMaster   Bradley E. Wohlenberg
Arthur J. Hazarabedian   Timothy J. Chung
Kristin B. Mendenhall

OF COUNSEL
William B. Barr

Representative Clients: Cities of Covina, Hermosa Beach, South Pasadena and Calabasas; Los Angeles County North Valley Building Corp.; Los Angeles County Coroner's Building Corp.; Los Angeles County Montrose Sheriff's Station Corp.

(See Next Column)

OLIVER, VOSE, SANDIFER, MURPHY & LEE A PROFESSIONAL CORPORATION, Los Angeles—Continued

Special Counsel: Anaheim Redevelopment Agency; Arcadia Redevelopment Agency; City of Brea; Brea Redevelopment Agency; Calleguas Municipal Water District; City of Anaheim.

For full biographical listings, see the Martindale-Hubbell Law Directory

SHEPPARD, MULLIN, RICHTER & HAMPTON LLP (AV)

A Limited Liability Partnership including Professional Corporations
Forty-Eighth Floor, 333 South Hope Street, 90071-1448
Telephone: 213-620-1780
Telecopier: 213-620-1398
Cable Address: "Sheplaw"
Email: info@smrh.com URL: http://www.smrh.com
Orange County, California Office: 650 Town Center Drive, 4th Floor, Costa Mesa.
Telephone: 714-513-5100.
Telecopier: 714-513-5130. Home Page Address: http://www.smrh.com.
San Francisco, California Office: Seventeenth Floor, Four Embarcadero Center.
Telephone: 415-434-9100.
Telecopier: 415-434-3947. Home Page Address: http://www.smrh.com.
San Diego, California Office: Nineteenth Floor, 501 West Broadway.
Telephone: 619-338-6500.
Telecopier: 619-234-3815. Home Page Address: http://www.smrh.com.

MEMBERS OF FIRM

Joseph A. Darrell (San Francisco Office)	Robert H. Philibosian
Domenic C. Drago (San Diego Office)	Jack H. Rubens
	Theodore A. Russell
James Blythe Hodge * (San Francisco Office)	Richard L. Stone
	Timothy B. Taylor (San Diego Office)
M. Elizabeth McDaniel	Robert A. Thompson (San Francisco Office)
Christopher B. Neils (San Diego Office)	Robert E. Williams
Stephen J. O'Neil	William R. Wyatt (San Francisco Office)
Joseph E. Petrillo (San Francisco Office)	

*Professional Corporation

For full biographical listings, see the Martindale-Hubbell Law Directory

MENLO PARK, San Mateo Co.

ROBIN D. FAISANT (AV)

1550 El Camino Real, Suite 220, 94025
Telephone: 415-328-6333
Telecopier: 415-324-1031

For full biographical listings, see the Martindale-Hubbell Law Directory

NAPA,* Napa Co.

DICKENSON, PEATMAN & FOGARTY, A PROFESSIONAL LAW CORPORATION (AV)

809 Coombs Street, 94559-2977
Telephone: 707-252-7122
Telecopier: 707-255-6876

Joseph G. Peatman	Joseph M. Keebler
David W. Meyers	Cathy A. Roche
David B. Gilbreth	Linda Emerson
Richard P. Mendelson	Thomas F. Carey

For Complete List of Firm Personnel, See General Section

For full biographical listings, see the Martindale-Hubbell Law Directory

PALO ALTO, Santa Clara Co.

HANNA & VAN ATTA (AV)

A Partnership of Professional Corporations
525 University Avenue, Suite 705, 94301
Telephone: 415-321-5700
Fax: 415-321-5639

John Paul Hanna   David M. Van Atta

For full biographical listings, see the Martindale-Hubbell Law Directory

ROSEVILLE, Placer Co.

ROBBINS & LIVINGSTON (AV)

3300 Douglas Boulevard, Suite 365, 95661
Telephone: 916-773-4700
Facsimile: 916-773-4747
Email: plazolaw@aol.com

(See Next Column)

MEMBERS OF FIRM

Stephen Robbins   J. Cleve Livingston

Representative Clients: Ahmanson Developments, Inc.; Balcor Property Management Inc.; The Coker-Ewing Companies; Morrison Homes of Northern California (a division of George Wimpey, Inc.); Grove Investment Company, Inc.; Trammell Crow Residential; Richland Properties; Rancho Murieta Community Services District; California Environmental Associates; Cresleigh Homes; S.H. Cowell Foundation.

For full biographical listings, see the Martindale-Hubbell Law Directory

SACRAMENTO,* Sacramento Co.

HUNTER RICHEY DI BENEDETTO & BREWER, LLP (AV)

A Limited Liability Partnership
Renaissance Tower, 801 K Street, 23rd Floor, 95814-3525
Telephone: 916-491-3000
Facsimile: 916-491-3080
Email: hrdb@hrdb.com URL: http://www.hrdb.com

MEMBERS OF FIRM

William S. Hunter	James F. Geary
Win R. Richey	Janet C. Eisenbeis
Florence L. Di Benedetto	Jeffery D. Harris
Roy E. Brewer	Stephen C. Ruehmann
Anne E. Ferguson	Ralph T. Ferguson
Judith J. Citko	Sharon K. Sandeen
Kathryn T. Papalia	

LEGAL SUPPORT PERSONNEL

Lori J. Kelly (Paralegal)	Michele L. Nickell (Legal Assistant)
Deborah M. Romero (Paralegal)	
Linda Jane Hall (Legal Assistant)	Dawn Krein (Legal Assistant)
Jennifer E. Mueller (Legal Assistant)	Stephanie L. Neumann (Legal Assistant)

For full biographical listings, see the Martindale-Hubbell Law Directory

SAN DIEGO,* San Diego Co.

SPARBER, FERGUSON, PONDER & RYAN, A PROFESSIONAL LAW CORPORATION (AV)

Imperial Bank Building, 701 "B" Street, Tenth Floor, 92101-8103
Telephone: 619-239-3600
Facsimile: 619-239-5601

Richard E. Sparber	Greg J. Ryan
James P. Ferguson	Richard J. Annen
John E. Ponder	Daniel F. Morrin
Gary B. Rudolph	

Todd R. Gabriel	William P. Fennell
Carol R. McGinnis	James E. Highsmith

OF COUNSEL
Mark P. Mandell

LEGAL SUPPORT PERSONNEL
LEGAL ADMINISTRATOR
Beverly K. Driscoll

For full biographical listings, see the Martindale-Hubbell Law Directory

STEPHENSON WORLEY GARRATT SCHWARTZ HEIDEL & PRAIRIE (AV)

A Limited Liability Partnership
101 West Broadway, Suite 1300, 92101-8214
Telephone: 619-696-3500
Fax: 619-696-3555
Email: SDLAW@swgshp.com

MEMBERS OF FIRM

Gary J. Stephenson	Michael W. Prairie
Donald R. Worley	Timothy K. Garfield
Gregory C. M. Garratt	Lori A. Chamberlain
William J. Schwartz, Jr.	Jennifer Treese Wilson
Lynne L. Heidel	Amy Rosen
James B. MacRobbie	

OF COUNSEL

Kent H. Foster   Elaine L. Chan

Reference: Bank of Commerce.

For full biographical listings, see the Martindale-Hubbell Law Directory

SAN FRANCISCO,* San Francisco Co.

CASSIDY & VERGES, A PROFESSIONAL CORPORATION (AV)

20 California Street, Suite 500, 94111
Telephone: 415-788-2020
Fax: 415-788-2039

(See Next Column)

CASSIDY & VERGES A PROFESSIONAL CORPORATION—*Continued*

Stephen K. Cassidy	Kenneth Steven Taymor
Scott C. Verges	Deirdre M. Dawson
Thomas E. Panelli	Paul M. Kawakami
Wylie R. Sheldon	Jon L. Mangus
Anna C. Shimko	Eric L. Laurence

LEGAL SUPPORT PERSONNEL
Loretta T. MacDonald

For full biographical listings, see the Martindale-Hubbell Law Directory

ELLMAN, BURKE, HOFFMAN & JOHNSON, A PROFESSIONAL CORPORATION (AV)

One Ecker, Suite 200, 94105
Telephone: 415-777-2727
Fax: 415-495-7587
Email: managingdirector@ellman-burke.com *URL:*
http://www.ellman-burke.com

Howard N. Ellman	Thomas Paine
Michael J. Burke	Jay L. Paxton
Kenneth N. Burns	Thomas M. Sherwood
John D. Hoffman	Leslie M. Browne
Jeffrey W. Johnson	David H. Blackwell
Jodi Billehus Fedor	

For full biographical listings, see the Martindale-Hubbell Law Directory

SAN JOSE,* Santa Clara Co.

McMANIS, FAULKNER & MORGAN (AV)

160 West Santa Clara Street, 10th Floor, 95113
Telephone: 408-279-8700
Fax: 408-279-3244; 408-279-0494
Email: mfm@mfmlaw.com

MEMBERS OF FIRM
James McManis	William Faulkner
Donelle Morgan	

ASSOCIATES
Nora Rousso	Michael Reedy
Lisa Herrick	Douglas Watanabe
Kelly McHaffie	

For full biographical listings, see the Martindale-Hubbell Law Directory

SAN RAFAEL,* Marin Co.

RAGGHIANTI • FREITAS • MONTOBBIO • WALLACE LLP (AV)

874 Fourth Street, Suite D, 94901
Telephone: 415-453-9433
Fax: 415-453-8269

Gary T. Ragghianti	J. Randolph Wallace
David P. Freitas	Patrick M. Macias
J. Mark Montobbio	Robert F. Epstein
John Ralph Thomas	

For full biographical listings, see the Martindale-Hubbell Law Directory

COLORADO

ASPEN,* Pitkin Co.

OATES, HUGHES, KNEZEVICH & GARDENSWARTZ, P.C. (AV)

Aspen Plaza Building, 3rd Floor, 533 East Hopkins Avenue, 81611
Telephone: 970-920-1700
Telecopier: 970-920-1121
Email: ohkg@rof.net

Leonard M. Oates	Richard A. Knezevich
Ted D. Gardenswartz	

David B. Kelly	Rich Orman

OF COUNSEL
Robert W. Hughes	John Thomas Kelly

Counsel for: Stapleton Insurance Agency; Pitkin County Title, Inc.

For full biographical listings, see the Martindale-Hubbell Law Directory

DENVER,* Denver Co.

BROWNSTEIN HYATT FARBER & STRICKLAND, P.C. (AV)

Twenty-Second Floor, 410 Seventeenth Street, 80202-4437
Telephone: 303-534-6335
Telecopier: 303-623-1956
Washington, D.C. Office: 601 Pennsylvania Avenue, N.W., Suite 900.
Telephone: 202-434-8377.
Telecopier: 202-393-7864.

(See Next Column)

Thomas L. Strickland	Wayne F. Forman
Andrew W. Loewi	Bruce A. James
Cole Finegan	

Mark J. Mathews	Beth Doherty Quinn

Representative Clients: The Anschutz Corporation; Mission Viejo Company; The Prudential Insurance Company of America; Schmidt Construction Company; The Taubman Company, Inc.; Trammell Crow Company; Trillium Corporation; Vail Associates, Inc.; Western Wireless Corporation.

For Complete List of Firm Personnel, See General Section

For full biographical listings, see the Martindale-Hubbell Law Directory

OTTEN, JOHNSON, ROBINSON, NEFF & RAGONETTI, P.C. (AV)

950 Seventeenth Street, 16th Floor, 80202
Telephone: 303-825-8400
Telecopier: 303-825-6525

Thomas J. Ragonetti	Brad W. Schacht
Darrell G. Waas	R. Michael Shomo
Kevin A. Gliwa	Alex Iskenderian
Kenneth K. Skogg	William H. Brierly
J. Bart Johnson	

Representative Clients: Aetna Life Insurance Co.; The Broe Companies; Inc.; Colorado National Bank; Connecticut General Life Insurance Co.; First Nationwide Bank; Homart Development Co.; Land Title Guarantee Co.; Trizec Corporation Ltd.; U.S. West Communications, Inc.; The Western Sugar Co.

For Complete List of Firm Personnel, See General Section

For full biographical listings, see the Martindale-Hubbell Law Directory

GOLDEN,* Jefferson Co.

HOLLEY, ALBERTSON & POLK, P.C. (AV)

Suite 100, 1667 Cole Boulevard, 80401
Telephone: 303-233-7838
Fax: 303-233-2860

George Alan Holley	Scott D. Albertson
Dennis B. Polk	

Eric E. Torgersen	Thomas A. Walsh
Howard R. Stone	

Reference: First Bank of Wheat Ridge.

For full biographical listings, see the Martindale-Hubbell Law Directory

CONNECTICUT

GREENWICH, Fairfield Co.

BENTLEY, MOSHER, BABSON & LAMBERT, P.C. (AV)

20 Dayton Avenue, P.O. Box 788, 06836-0788
Telephone: 203-629-2424
Telecopier: 203-629-2545

Charles E. Mosher	M. Dean Montgomery
Richard J. Slagle	

For full biographical listings, see the Martindale-Hubbell Law Directory

IVEY, BARNUM & O'MARA, LLC (AV)

Meridian Building, 170 Mason Street, P.O. Box 1689, 06830
Telephone: 203-661-6000
Telecopier: 203-661-9462

MEMBERS OF FIRM
Michael J. Allen	Donat C. Marchand
Robert C. Barnum, Jr.	Miles F. McDonald, Jr.
Edward D. Cosden, Jr.	Edwin J. O'Mara, Jr.
Wilmot L. Harris, Jr.	Remy A. Rodas
William I. Haslun II	Gregory A. Saum
Michael J. Jones	Lorraine Slavin
Edward T. Krumeich, Jr.	Steven B. Steinmetz

ASSOCIATES
Paul G. Amicucci	Melissa Townsend Klauberg
Stephan B. Grozinger	Cristin L. Rothfuss
Juerg A. Heim	Alan S. Rubenstein
Jennifer B. Kallenbach	Sheryl L. Sensale
	(Not admitted in CT)

OF COUNSEL
James W. Cuminale	Jennifer D. Port
Philip R. McKnight	(Not admitted in CT)

For full biographical listings, see the Martindale-Hubbell Law Directory

MILFORD, New Haven Co.

HURWITZ & SAGARIN, P.C. (AV)

147 North Broad Street, P.O. Box 112, 06460
Telephone: 203-877-8000
Fax: 203-878-9800

Lewis A. Hurwitz

Andrew C. Kruger   John W. Knuff
Julie M. Cashin

For full biographical listings, see the Martindale-Hubbell Law Directory

FLORIDA

BRADENTON, * Manatee Co.

GRIMES GOEBEL GRIMES HAWKINS & GLADFELTER, P.A. (AV)

The Professional Building, 1023 Manatee Avenue West, P.O. Box
   1550, 34206
Telephone: 941-748-0151
Fax: 941-748-0158

William C. Grimes   Leslie Horton Gladfelter
Caleb J. Grimes   William S. Galvano

Counsel for: Schroeder Manatee Inc. (Agriculture and Land Development);
Pursley, Inc., (Horticulture, Retail and Land Development); Lombardo &
Skipper, Inc. (Civil Engineers); CCI Environmental Services, Inc. (Environ-
mental Consultants); Creekwood Investors, Ltd.; Old Hyde Park Village
Center, Ltd.; First Federal Savings & Loan Association of Florida.
Approved Attorneys for: Lawyers Title Insurance Corp.; Chicago Title Insur-
ance Co.; Attorneys Title Insurance Fund.

For Complete List of Firm Personnel, See General Section

For full biographical listings, see the Martindale-Hubbell Law Directory

**HARLLEE, PORGES, HAMLIN, KNOWLES, BALD & PROUTY,
P.A.** (AV)

1205 Manatee Avenue, West, 34205
Telephone: 941-748-3770
Telecopier: 941-748-4160
Email: Law@HarlleePorges.com

John P. Harllee, III   Kimberly Alario Bald
Gregory J. Porges   Steven W. Prouty
Curtis D. Hamlin   Mark A. Nelson
Timothy A. Knowles   Stephen W. Thompson

Joseph L. Najmy   Barrett S. Bell
Shelly A. Gallagher

For full biographical listings, see the Martindale-Hubbell Law Directory

FORT PIERCE, * St. Lucie Co.

GONANO & HARRELL, CHARTERED (AV)

Riverside National Bank Building, 1600 South Federal Highway, Suite
   200, 34950-5194
Telephone: 561-464-1032
FAX: 561-464-0282

Douglas E. Gonano   Daniel B. Harrell

Johnathan A. Ferguson   John J. Campione

General Counsel: School Board of St. Lucie County; Reserve Community
Development District; St. Lucie West Services District.
Representative Clients: East Coast Lumber & Supply Co.; Riverside National
Bank of Florida; Superior Title Services, Inc.
Approved Attorneys for: Attorneys' Title Insurance Fund; Commonwealth
Land Title Insurance Co.
References: Riverside National Bank of Florida; SunTrust, Treasure Coast,
N.A.

For full biographical listings, see the Martindale-Hubbell Law Directory

MIAMI, * Dade Co.

MILLEDGE IDEN & HELD (AV)

Suite 600, 2100 Ponce de Leon Boulevard (Coral Gables), 33134
Telephone: 305-445-1500
Facsimile: 305-446-9972

MEMBERS OF FIRM
Allan Milledge   Bruce F. Iden
Gary M. Held
ASSOCIATE
Dana J. McElroy

(See Next Column)

OF COUNSEL
John M. Milledge   Patricia Fields Anderson
Reference: Northern Trust Bank.

For full biographical listings, see the Martindale-Hubbell Law Directory

NAPLES, * Collier Co.

QUARLES & BRADY (AV)

Barnett Center, 4501 Tamiami Trail North Suite 300, 33940-3060
Telephone: 941-262-5959
Fax: 941-434-4999
Milwaukee, Wisconsin Office: 411 East Wisconsin Avenue, 53202-4497.
Telephone: 414-277-5000.
Fax: 414-271-3552.
Madison, Wisconsin Office: Firstar Plaza, One South Pinckney Street, P.O.
Box 2113, 53701-2113.
Telephone: 608-251-5000.
Fax: 608-251-9166.
West Palm Beach, Florida Office: 222 Lakeview Avenue, 4th Floor, 33401.
Telephone: 561-653-5000.
Fax: 561-653-5333.
Phoenix, Arizona Office: One Camelback Building, One East Camelback
Road, Suite 400, 85012-1649.
Telephone: 602-230-5500.
Fax: 602-230-5598.

PARTNERS
Thomas E. Maloney   Timothy G. Hains
F. Joseph McMackin, III   Leo J. Salvatori
ASSOCIATES
John D. Humphreville   Kevin A. Denti

For Complete List of Firm Personnel, See General Section

For full biographical listings, see the Martindale-Hubbell Law Directory

ST. AUGUSTINE, * St. Johns Co.

UPCHURCH, BAILEY & UPCHURCH, P.A. (AV)

780 North Ponce de Leon Boulevard, P.O. Drawer 3007, 32085-3007
Telephone: 904-829-9066
Facsimile: 904-825-4862

John D. Bailey, Jr.   Frank D. Upchurch, III
Katherine Gaertner Jones
OF COUNSEL
Hamilton D. Upchurch

Representative Clients: Aero Sport, Inc.; American Culinary Federation, Inc.;
Barnett Bank, N.A. Penney Retirement Community, Inc.; St. Augustine Alli-
gator Farm, Inc.; St. Augustine-St. Johns County Board of Realtors, Inc.
General Counsel: Flagler College; Flagler Hospital, Inc.; Prosperity Bank of
St. Augustine; St. Johns County School Board.

For Complete List of Firm Personnel, See General Section

For full biographical listings, see the Martindale-Hubbell Law Directory

STUART, * Martin Co.

**McCARTHY, SUMMERS, BOBKO, McKEY, WOOD & SAWYER,
P.A.** (AV)

2081 East Ocean Boulevard, Suite 2-A, 34996
Telephone: 561-286-1700
Fax: 561-283-1803
Email: mcsumm@gate.net *URL:* http://www.gate.net/~mcsumm/

Terence P. McCarthy   John D. McKey, Jr.
Robert P. Summers   Steven J. Wood
Noel A. Bobko   Thomas R. Sawyer

Representative Clients: American Bank of Martin County; First National
Bank and Trust Company of the Treasure Coast; Great Western Bank; Hy-
dratech Utilities; Lost Lake at Hobe Sound; Taylor Creek Marina, Inc.; GBS
Excavating, Inc.; Seaboard Savings Bank; Gary Player Design Group.

For full biographical listings, see the Martindale-Hubbell Law Directory

TAMPA, * Hillsborough Co.

BRICKLEMYER SMOLKER & BOLVES, P.A. (AV)

400 North Tampa Street, Suite 2400, 33602-4708
Telephone: 813-223-3888
Fax: 813-228-6422

Keith W. Bricklemyer   Brian A. Bolves
David Smolker   Jay J. Bartlett
Robert E. V. Kelley, Jr.

David M. Corry   I. Ed Pantaleon
Jeff D. Jackson   William D. Shepherd
Douglas C. Roland

For full biographical listings, see the Martindale-Hubbell Law Directory

Tampa—Continued

SMITH, WILLIAMS & HUMPHRIES, P.A. (AV)

Old Hyde Park, 712 South Oregon Avenue, 33606
Telephone: 813-253-5400
Fax: 813-254-3459
Orlando, Florida Office: Southeast Bank Building, Suite 701, 201 East Pine
Street.
Telephone: 407-849-5151.
Fax: 407-843-4076.

David Lisle Smith
Gregory L. Williams
J. Gregory Humphries
(Resident, Orlando Office)
Robert L. Harding
(Resident, Orlando Office)
Gregory E. Mierzwinski
Carole Taylor Kirkwood
Daniel William King

For full biographical listings, see the Martindale-Hubbell Law Directory

WEST PALM BEACH,* Palm Beach Co.

QUARLES & BRADY (AV)

222 Lakeview Avenue, 4th Floor, 33401
Telephone: 561-653-5000
Fax: 561-653-5333
Milwaukee, Wisconsin Office: 411 East Wisconsin Avenue, 53202-4497.
Telephone: 414-277-5000.
Fax: 414-271-3552.
Madison, Wisconsin Office: Firstar Plaza, One South Pinckney Street, P.O.
Box 2113, 53701-2113.
Telephone: 608-251-5000.
Fax: 608-251-9166.
Naples, Florida Office: Barnett Center, 4501 Tamiami Trail North, Suite
300, 33940-3060.
Telephone: 941-262-5959.
Fax: 941-434-4999.
Phoenix, Arizona Office: One Camelback Building, One East Camelback
Road, Suite 400, 85012-1649.
Telephone: 602-230-5500.
Fax: 602-230-5598.

PARTNERS

John S. Sammond   David L. Petersen

ASSOCIATE

Nancy Berz Colman

For Complete List of Firm Personnel, See General Section

For full biographical listings, see the Martindale-Hubbell Law Directory

GEORGIA

ATLANTA,* Fulton Co.

JOHNSON & MONTGOMERY (AV)

One Buckhead Plaza, 3060 Peachtree Road, N.W., Suite 400, 30305
Telephone: 404-262-1000
Telecopier: 404-262-1222

MEMBER OF FIRM

Albert Sidney Johnson

For full biographical listings, see the Martindale-Hubbell Law Directory

WILSON, BROCK & IRBY, L.L.C. (AV)

999 Peachtree Street, N.E., Suite 2000, 30309
Telephone: 404-853-5050
Fax: 404-853-1812

MEMBERS OF FIRM

Richard W. Wilson, Jr.
Frank L. Wilson, III
Lethco H. Brock, Jr.
John H. Irby

ASSOCIATES

Jerry D. Gerald   James Stuart Teague, Jr.
Paul Schillawski

OF COUNSEL

L. Robert Lovett

For full biographical listings, see the Martindale-Hubbell Law Directory

HAWAII

HONOLULU,* Honolulu Co.

CARLSMITH BALL WICHMAN CASE & ICHIKI (AV)

A Partnership including Law Corporations
Suite 2200, Pacific Tower, 1001 Bishop Street, P.O. Box 656, 96809-3402
Telephone: 808-523-2500
Cable Address: "CWCMI"
Telecopier: 808-523-0842
Telex: 723-8770 CWCMI HR
Kapolei, Hawaii Office: Kapolei Building, Suite 318, 1001 Kamokila
Boulevard.
Telephone: 808-523-2500.
Wailuku, Maui Hawaii Office: One Main Plaza, Suite 400, 2200 Main
Street, P.O. Box 1086.
Telephone: 808-242-4535.
Kailua-Kona, Hawaii Office: Second Floor, Bank of Hawaii Annex
Building, P.O. Box 1720.
Telephone: 808-329-6464.
Hilo, Hawaii Office: 121 Waianuenue Avenue, P.O. Box 686.
Telephone: 808-935-6644.
Agana, Guam Office: 4th Floor, Bank of Hawaii Building, P.O. Box BF.
Telephone: 671-472-6813.
Saipan, Commonwealth of the Northern Mariana Islands Office: Carlsmith
Building, Capitol Hill, P.O. Box 5241.
Telephone: (011) 670-322-3455.
Los Angeles, California Office: 555 South Flower Street, 25th Floor.
Telephone: 213-955-1200.
Washington, D.C. Office: 700 14th Street, N.W., 9th Floor.
Telephone: 202-508-1025.
Mexico City, Mexico Office: Monte Pelvous 111, Piso 1, Col. Lomas de
Chapultepec 11000, Mexico, D.F.
Telephone: (011-52-5) 520-8514.
Fax: (011-52-5) 540-1545.
*Mexico, D.F. Office of Carlsmith Ball Garcia Cacho y Asociados, S.C.
(Authorized to practice Mexican Law):* Monte Pelvoux 111, Piso 1, Col.
Lomas de Chapultepec, 11000 Mexico, D.F.
Telephone: (011-52-5) 520-8514.
Fax: (011-52-5) 540-1545.

MEMBERS OF FIRM

Edward E. Case
Grant Y. M. Chun
(Resident at Maui Office)
Patricia Devlin
Eric A. James (Resident at
Kapolei, Hawaii Office)
Karl K. Kobayashi
Steven S. C. Lim (Resident,
Hilo, Hawaii Office)
Tim Lui-Kwan
B. Martin Luna
(Resident at Maui Office)
Mark K. Murakami (Resident at
Kapolei, Hawaii Office)
David R. Nevitt
(Resident at Saipan Office)
Sylvester V. Quitiquit (Resident
at Kona, Hawaii Office)
Robert Edward Strand
Robert D. Triantos (Resident at
Kailua-Kona Office)
Paul M. Ueoka
(Resident at Maui Office)
Jon T. Yamamura

ASSOCIATES

Kristen S. Armstrong (Resident,
Agana, Guam Office)
Richard J Kiefer
Kevin E. Moore
(Resident at Saipan Office)

Representative Clients: Ala Moana Shopping Center; Bank of Hawaii; The
Estate of James of James Campbell; Kaluakoi Resort; The Myers Corporation; Nippon Shinpan U.S.A. Inc.; Outrigger Hotels; Queen Emma Foundation; Servco Pacific.

For Complete List of Firm Personnel, See General Section

For full biographical listings, see the Martindale-Hubbell Law Directory

ILLINOIS

MATTOON, Coles Co.

CRAIG & CRAIG (AV)

1807 Broadway, P.O. Box 689, 61938-0689
Telephone: 217-234-6481
Telecopier: 217-234-6486
Mount Vernon, Illinois Office: 227 1/2 South 9th Street.
Telephone: 618-244-7511.

MEMBERS OF FIRM

Craig Van Meter (1895-1981)
Fred H. Kelly (1894-1971)
Robert M. Werden (1908-1969)
George N. Gilkerson
(1911-1985)
John H. Armstrong
John P. Ewart
Richard F. Record, Jr.
Stephen L. Corn
Richard Charles Hayden
Robert G. Grierson
Gregory C. Ray
Paul R. Lynch (Resident, Mount
Vernon Office)
Kenneth F. Werts (Resident,
Mount Vernon Office)
John L. Barger

(See Next Column)

CRAIG & CRAIG, *Mattoon—Continued*

ASSOCIATES

Joshua N. Rosen (Resident,
 Mount Vernon Office)
Kathleen M. Stockwell

Theresa M. Thomson
Kristine M. Tuttle
Henry P. Villani (Resident,
 Mount Vernon Office)

OF COUNSEL

Jack E. Horsley

Counsel for: Monterey Coal Co., a Division of Exxon Coal USA, Inc.; Marathon Oil Co.; Illinois Central R.R. Co.; Okaw Building & Loan Assn., Mattoon, Illinois; The Medical Protective Insurance Co.; Consolidated Communications, Inc.; Lloyds Underwriters at London; Hartford Insurance Co.; Coles Together, a Not-For-Profit Corp.; Coles Building Corporation.

For full biographical listings, see the Martindale-Hubbell Law Directory

---

VERNON HILLS, Lake Co.

RICHARDS, RALPH & SCHWAB, CHTD. (AV)

Suite 345, One Hawthorn Place, 175 East Hawthorn Parkway, 60061
Telephone: 708-367-9699
FAX: 708-367-9621

Michael L. Ralph
David J. Schwab

Alan E. Richards

For full biographical listings, see the Martindale-Hubbell Law Directory

---

INDIANA

ELKHART, Elkhart Co.

CHESTER, PFAFF & BROTHERSON (AV)

317 West Franklin Street, P.O. Box 507, 46515-0507
Telephone: 219-294-5421
Fax: 219-522-1476

MEMBER OF FIRM

Robert A. Pfaff

For Complete List of Firm Personnel, See General Section

For full biographical listings, see the Martindale-Hubbell Law Directory

---

*EVANSVILLE,** Vanderburgh Co.

BOWERS, HARRISON, KENT & MILLER, LLP (AV)

25 N.W. Riverside Drive, P.O. Box 1287, 47706-1287
Telephone: 812-426-1231
Fax: 812-464-3676

MEMBERS OF FIRM

F. Wesley Bowers
Joseph H. Harrison
David V. Miller
Paul E. Black
Gary R. Case
Arthur D. Rutkowski
George C. Barnett, Jr.
Terry Noffsinger

Paul J. Wallace
David E. Gray
Gregory A. Kahre
Timothy J. Hubert
James P. Casey
Thomas A. Massey
Greg A. Granger
Joseph H. Harrison, Jr.

Lawrence L. Grimes

ASSOCIATES

Cedric Hustace
Christopher E. Carl
Michelle Agostino Cox
Sara Harrison Zeidler

Elizabeth Healy Campbell
Douglas K. Briody
Holly H. Wilhelmus
J. Edward Wicht

Paul Bernard Greif

OF COUNSEL

Addison M. Beavers
William G. Greif

K. Wayne Kent

Division Counsel in Indiana for: Southern Railway Co.
Representative Clients: Permanent Federal Savings Bank; Citizens Realty & Insurance, Inc.

For full biographical listings, see the Martindale-Hubbell Law Directory

---

*FORT WAYNE,** Allen Co.

BECKMAN, LAWSON, SANDLER, SNYDER & FEDEROFF (AV)

800 Standard Federal Plaza, 46802
Telephone: 219-422-0800
Facsimile: 219-420-1013
Syracuse, Indiana Office: 200 West Main Street.
Telephone: 219-457-5727.
Facsimile: 219-457-2056.

(See Next Column)

MEMBERS OF FIRM

Jack W. Lawson
Frank J. Gray
Howard B. Sandler
Stephen R. Snyder
James A. Federoff

William L. Sweet, Jr.
John H. Brandt
Jeffrey L. Gage
Thomas J. Goeglein
Jon A. Bragalone

Brian J. T'Kindt

ASSOCIATES

Douglas R. Adelsperger
Travis S. Friend
Jack C. Birch
Robert L. Nicholson
W. Randall Kammeyer

David D. Cornwell
Craig R. Patterson
Edward J. Ormsby
Daniel B. Starr
Laurie A. Singh

OF COUNSEL

Frederick A. Beckman
Douglas E. Miller

Neil F. Sandler

Reference: NBD, N.A.

For full biographical listings, see the Martindale-Hubbell Law Directory

---

*INDIANAPOLIS,** Marion Co.

BAKER & DANIELS (AV)

300 North Meridian Street, 46204
Telephone: 317-237-0300
FAX: 317-237-1000
Fort Wayne, Indiana Office: 111 East Wayne Street, Suite 800.
Telephone: 219-424-8000.
South Bend, Indiana Office: First Bank Building, 205 West Jefferson Boulevard.
Telephone: 219-234-4149.
Elkhart, Indiana Office: 301 B South Main Street, Suite 307,
Telephone: 219-296-6000.
Washington, D.C. Office: 1701 K Street, N.W., Suite 400.
Telephone: 202-785-1565.

MEMBER OF FIRM

Joseph M. Scimia

ASSOCIATE

Andrew Z. Soshnick

LEGAL SUPPORT PERSONNEL

Eugene Valanzano (Land Use Consultant)

Representative Clients: Anthem Insurance Companies, Inc.; AT&T Corp.; Bank One, Indianapolis, N.A.; Borg-Warner Corp.; City of Indianapolis; Cummins Engine Co.; Eli Lilly and Co.; General Motors Corp.; Indianapolis Public Schools; United Airlines.

For Complete List of Firm Personnel, See General Section

For full biographical listings, see the Martindale-Hubbell Law Directory

---

CLARK, QUINN, MOSES & CLARK (AV)

One Indiana Square, Suite 2200, 46204-2011
Telephone: 317-637-1321
Fax: 317-687-2344

MEMBERS OF FIRM

Thomas Michael Quinn

J. Murray Clark

ASSOCIATES

Michael D. Keele

Cameron F. Clark

LAND USE CONSULTANT

Elizabeth Bentz Williams (Land Use Consultant)

Representative Clients: Justus; The Shorewood Corporation; Marina Limited Partnership; Lafarge Corporation; Meijer Realty, Inc.; Lowe's; Kite Development; U-Stor Self Storage Warehouses; Mechanic's Laundry; Davis Homes.

For full biographical listings, see the Martindale-Hubbell Law Directory

---

DANN PECAR NEWMAN & KLEIMAN, PROFESSIONAL CORPORATION (AV)

Suite 2300, One American Square Box 82008, 46282
Telephone: 317-632-3232; Indiana: 800-622-4799
Telecopy: 317-632-2962

Theodore R. Dann (1907-1993)
Joel Yonover (1932-1995)
Philip D. Pecar
Norman R. Newman
David H. Kleiman
Jon B. Abels
Melvin R. Daniel
Lawrence F. Dorocke
Jeffrey A. Abrams
James H. Schwarz
Robert A. Rose

Walter E. Wolf, Jr.
Barry E. Beldin
Robert D. Swhier, Jr.
James P. Moloy
Robert J. Schuckit
Andrew A. Kleiman
Michael J. Gabovitch
Steven M. Pecar
Benjamin A. Pecar
Richard O. Kissel, II
Joseph D. Calderon

OF COUNSEL

Linda E. Cantor

Anthony J. Rose

(See Next Column)

DANN PECAR NEWMAN & KLEIMAN PROFESSIONAL CORPORATION—
Continued

Ellen C. Siakotos   Angela L. Mansfield
Stacy L. Hill   Martha M. K. Baird
             Karin L. Veatch

Attorneys for: Indianapolis Machinery Co., Inc.; Melvin Simon & Associates, Inc.; Pacers Basketball Corp.; Universal Fire & Casualty Co., Inc.; Bank One, Indianapolis, NA; INB National Bank; Nachi Technology, Inc.; Pharmaceutical Corporation of America; Logo 7, Inc.

For full biographical listings, see the Martindale-Hubbell Law Directory

---

LAFAYETTE,* Tippecanoe Co.

STUART & BRANIGIN (AV)

The Life Building, 300 Main Street, Suite 800, 47902
Telephone: 317-423-1561
Telecopier: 317-742-8175

MEMBERS OF FIRM

Allison Ellsworth Stuart   Stephen R. Pennell
   (1886-1950)   Anthony S. Benton
Roger D. Branigin (1902-1975)   Erik D. Spykman
Russell H. Hart   William E. Emerick
Roger D. Branigin, Jr.   John C. Duffey
Thomas L. Ryan   Mark E. DeYoung
James V. McGlone   Thomas B. Parent
Carl W. Kloepfer   Laura L. Bowker
Thomas R. McCully   Kevin D. Nicoson
Larry R. Fisher   Susan K. Roberts
Nina B. Kirkpatrick   John M. Stuckey
Mark Lillianfeld   Deborah B. Trice

COUNSEL
John F. Bodle

ASSOCIATES

Brent W. Huber   David A. Starkweather
William P. Kealey   Geoffrey Blazi
            A. James Chareq

General Counsel for: The Lafayette Life Insurance Co.; INB National Bank, N.W.; Lafayette Home Hospital, Inc.
State Counsel for: Norfolk & Western Railway Co.
Mr. Ryan is Counsel to: The Trustees of Purdue University.
Representative Clients: Aluminum Company of America; Liberty Mutual Insurance Group.

For full biographical listings, see the Martindale-Hubbell Law Directory

---

MERRILLVILLE, Lake Co.

BURKE, MURPHY, COSTANZA & CUPPY (AV)

Suite 600 8585 Broadway, 46410-7064
Telephone: 219-769-1313
Telecopier: 219-769-6806
East Chicago, Indiana Office: First National Bank Building. 720 West Chicago Avenue.
Telephone: 219-397-2401.
Telecopier: 219-397-0508.
Valparaiso, Indiana Office: 15 North Franklin Street, Suite 200.
Telephone: 219-531-0134.
Telecopier: 219-531-0507.
Palm Harbor, Florida Office: Suite 280, 33920 U.S. Highway 19 North.
Telephone: 813-787-7799.
Telecopier: 813-787-7237.

MEMBERS OF FIRM

Joseph E. Costanza   Gerald K. Hrebec
Frederick M. Cuppy   David K. Ranich
          Demetri J. Retson

ASSOCIATES

Todd A. Etzler   Philip C. Spahn

Representative Clients: Whiteco Industries; Continental Machine & Engineering Co., Inc.; Gary Steel Products Corp.; Superior Construction Co., Inc.; Federal National Mortgage Association; Morrison Construction Co.; St. Catherine Hospital of East Chicago, Indiana.

For Complete List of Firm Personnel, See General Section

For full biographical listings, see the Martindale-Hubbell Law Directory

---

KENTUCKY

LEXINGTON,* Fayette Co.

MARTIN, OCKERMAN & BRABANT (AV)

200 North Upper Street, 40507
Telephone: 606-254-4401
Fax: 606-231-7367
Email: ockerman@counsel.com

MEMBERS OF FIRM

Hogan Yancey (1881-1960)   Thomas C. Brabant
William B. Martin (1895-1975)   Foster Ockerman, Jr.
        Madeleine T. Baugh

OF COUNSEL
Foster Ockerman

Counsel for: Lexington Federal Savings Bank; Good Samaritan Foundation, Inc.; Equity Property and Development Co.; Park Communications of KY (WTVQ); AAA Blue Grass/Kentucky; Turfland Mall.
Reference: Bank One, Lexington, N.A.

For full biographical listings, see the Martindale-Hubbell Law Directory

RICHARD V. MURPHY (AV)

1010 First National Building, 167 West Main Street, 40507
Telephone: 606-233-9811
FAX: 606-255-9199

For full biographical listings, see the Martindale-Hubbell Law Directory

---

LOUISIANA

MONROE,* Ouachita Parish

THOMPSON, SPARKS, DEAN & MORRIS (AV)

A Partnership including a Professional Corporation
1401 Royal Street, P.O. Box 2867, 71207
Telephone: 318-388-1440
Fax: 318-322-0887

MEMBERS OF FIRM

M. C. Thompson (1885-1970)   George B. Dean, Jr., (P.C.)
James D. Sparks (1910-1987)   Wood T. Sparks
        John C. Morris, III

Representative Clients: South Central Bell Telephone Co.; Greater Ouachita Water Company; PHH Homequity Corp.; Commonwealth Relocation Services, Inc.; Remax, Monroe; Bell South Advertising & Publishing Corp.; Premier Mortgage Corp.; Countrywide Funding Corp.
Approved Attorneys for: Central Bank; Federal Land Bank.

For full biographical listings, see the Martindale-Hubbell Law Directory

NEW ORLEANS,* Orleans Parish

LAMOTHE & HAMILTON, A PROFESSIONAL LAW CORPORATION (AV)

Pan American Life Center, 601 Poydras Street, Suite 2750, 70130
Telephone: 504-566-1805
Telecopier: 504-566-1569
MCI Mail: 382-4472
Email: lhplc@neosoft.com

Frank E. Lamothe, III   Galen S. Brown
Charles E. Hamilton, III   M. Lizebeth Talbott
Karen Edginton Milner   Thomas J. Cortazzo

Reference: Jefferson Guaranty Bank, New Orleans, Louisiana.

For full biographical listings, see the Martindale-Hubbell Law Directory

SHREVEPORT,* Caddo Parish

BARLOW AND HARDTNER L.C. (AV)

Tenth Floor, Louisiana Tower, 401 Edwards Street, 71101-3289
Telephone: 318-227-1131
Telecopier: 318-227-1141
Mailing Address: P.O. Box 8, Shreveport, Louisiana, 71161-0008

Quintin T. Hardtner, III   Clair F. White
Malcolm S. Murchison   Stephen E. Ramey
Kay Cowden Medlin   Philip E. Downer, III
Joseph L. Shea, Jr.   Michael B. Donald
David R. Taggart   Jay A. Greenleaf

OF COUNSEL

Cecil E. Ramey, Jr.   Paula Hazelrig Hickman

Representative Clients: NorAm Energy Corp. (formerly Arkla, Inc.); Central and South West Corporation; Panhandle Eastern Corp.; Pennzoil Producing Co.; Ashland Oil, Inc.; Southwestern Electric Power Company; Energy Man-

(See Next Column)

BARLOW AND HARDTNER L.C., *Shreveport—Continued*

agement Corporation; TE Products Pipeline Company; Concorde Gas Marketing Company; General Electric Co.

For Complete List of Firm Personnel, See General Section

For full biographical listings, see the Martindale-Hubbell Law Directory

MAINE

*PORTLAND,** Cumberland Co.

VERRILL & DANA (AV)

One Portland Square, P.O. Box 586, 04112-0586
Telephone: 207-774-4000
Fax: 207-774-7499
Email: advice@verdan.com *URL:* http://www.verdan.com
Augusta, Maine Office: 45 Memorial Circle, P.O. Box 957.
Telephone: 207-623-3889.
Fax: 207-622-3117.
Kennebunk, Maine Office: Lafayette Center, P.O. Box 266.
Telephone: 207-985-7193.
Fax: 207-985-3957.
Washington, D.C. Office: 400 North Capitol Street, Suite 585.
Telephone: 202-624-9733.
Fax: 202-393-5218.

MEMBERS OF FIRM

Charles R. Oestreicher   Robert E. Cleaves, IV

For Complete List of Firm Personnel, See General Section

For full biographical listings, see the Martindale-Hubbell Law Directory

MASSACHUSETTS

*BOSTON,** Suffolk Co.

PALMER & DODGE LLP (AV)

One Beacon Street, 02108
Telephone: 617-573-0100
Facsimile: 617-227-4420

MEMBERS OF FIRM

Acheson H. Callaghan, Jr.   William L. Lahey
Norman P. Cohen   James M. Whalen

For Complete List of Firm Personnel, See General Section

For full biographical listings, see the Martindale-Hubbell Law Directory

WARNER & STACKPOLE LLP (AV)

75 State Street, 02109
Telephone: 617-951-9000
Telecopier: 617-951-9151
Email: w&s@warstack.com

MEMBERS OF FIRM

Paul C. Bauer   Howard A. Levine
Michael A. Leon   James G. Ward

ASSOCIATES

Michael E. Scott   Patricia Yung Wong

For Complete List of Firm Personnel, See General Section

For full biographical listings, see the Martindale-Hubbell Law Directory

MICHIGAN

BLOOMFIELD HILLS, Oakland Co.

ADKISON NEED (AV)

1533 North Woodward Avenue, Suite 210, 48304
Telephone: 810-540-7400
Fax: 810-540-7401
Email: AdkisNeed@aol.com

MEMBERS OF FIRM

Phillip G. Adkison   Paul Green
Gregory K. Need   Kelly A. Allen
Deborah M. Schneider

ASSOCIATES

Richard D. Kuhn, Jr.   Ann D. Christ
Kathryn N. Nichols   Laura B. Andoni

For full biographical listings, see the Martindale-Hubbell Law Directory

*KALAMAZOO,** Kalamazoo Co.

KREIS, ENDERLE, CALLANDER & HUDGINS, A PROFESSIONAL CORPORATION (AV)

One Moorsbridge, P.O. Box 4010, 49003-4010
Telephone: 616-324-3000
Telecopier: 616-324-3010
Email: kech@sapien.net *URL:* http://www.kech.com/

Alan G. Enderle   Thomas G. King
Jeffrey D. Swenarton

For Complete List of Firm Personnel, See General Section

For full biographical listings, see the Martindale-Hubbell Law Directory

SOUTHFIELD, Oakland Co.

MASON, STEINHARDT, JACOBS & PERLMAN, PROFESSIONAL CORPORATION (AV)

Suite 1500, 4000 Town Center, 48075-1415
Telephone: 810-358-2090
Fax: 810-358-3599

Gordon I. Ginsberg   Michael B. Perlman
Irving I. Boigon   Jerome P. Pesick
Jack Schon   Richard A. Polk
Walter B. Mason, Jr.   Jay W. Tower
Frederick D. Steinhardt   Jonathan B. Frank
John E. Jacobs   Neil S. Silver
L. Jeffrey Zauberman

Diane Flagg Goldstein   H. Adam Cohen

OF COUNSEL

Erwin B. Ellmann   Marvin C. Daitch
Randolph J. Friedman   John M. Roche

Representative Clients: Citibank, N.A.; City of Dearborn; DeMattia Development Co.; Forest City Enterprises; Michigan Wholesale Drug Assn.; Mortgage Bankers Association of Michigan; Nationwide Insurance Co.; City of Taylor; Union Labor Life Insurance Co.; Yellow Freight Systems, Inc.

For Complete List of Firm Personnel, See General Section

For full biographical listings, see the Martindale-Hubbell Law Directory

PROVIZER, LICHTENSTEIN & PHILLIPS, P.C. (AV)

4000 Town Center, Suite 1800, 48075
Telephone: 810-352-9080
Facsimile: 810-352-1491

Harold M. Provizer   David S. Lichtenstein
Robert I. Brown

Representative Clients: Grand Sakwa Development Co.; Plaza Management Corp.

For full biographical listings, see the Martindale-Hubbell Law Directory

MEDICAL MALPRACTICE

ALABAMA

BIRMINGHAM,* Jefferson Co.

HARE, WYNN, NEWELL AND NEWTON (AV)

A Partnership including Professional Corporations
Suite 800 Massey Building, 290 21st Street North, 35203
Telephone: 205-328-5330
FAX: 205-324-2165

MEMBERS OF FIRM

Francis H. Hare (1904-1983)	John W. Haley (P.C.)
Carlton T. Wynn	D. Leon Ashford (P.C.)
Neal C. Newell	Scott A. Powell
Alex W. Newton	James R. Pratt, III
Terrell Wynn, Jr.	S. Shay Samples
James J. Thompson, Jr.	Bruce J. McKee
Alva C. Caine	Michael D. Ermert
Ray O. Noojin, Jr., (P.C.)	Robert R. Riley, Jr.

Nolan Edward Awbrey

COUNSEL

Francis H. Hare, Jr., (P.C.)	James O. Haley

James K. Baker

References: AmSouth Bank of Birmingham; First Commercial Bank of Birmingham.

For full biographical listings, see the Martindale-Hubbell Law Directory

HARRIS, CLECKLER, BERG & ROGERS, P.C. (AV)

Historic 2007 Building, 2007 Third Avenue North, 35203-2366
Telephone: 205-328-2366
Telecopier: 205-328-0013
Email: hcbr@bham.mindspring.com

Lyman H. Harris	Lonette Lamb Berg
Michael H. Cleckler	Susan Rogers

Matthew J. Dougherty	Jeffrey K. Hollis

Brock G. Murphy

For full biographical listings, see the Martindale-Hubbell Law Directory

HOGAN, SMITH & ALSPAUGH, P.C. (AV)

2323 Second Avenue, North, 35203
Telephone: 205-324-5635
Telecopier: 205-324-5637

M. Clay Alspaugh	Richard D. Stratton
Ronald R. Crook	Jack Lee Roberts, Jr.

Reference: First Alabama Bank.

For full biographical listings, see the Martindale-Hubbell Law Directory

HUIE, FERNAMBUCQ AND STEWART (AV)

Suite 800 First Alabama Bank Building, 35203
Telephone: 205-251-1193
Telecopy: 205-251-1256

MEMBERS OF FIRM

Stanley A. Cash	M. Keith Gann
Robert M. Girardeau	J. Allen Sydnor, Jr.

ASSOCIATE

H. Lanier Brown, III

Representative Clients: Hunana, Inc.; Living Centers of America, Inc.; Cigna Insurance Co's.; CNS Insurance (medical mal practice group); Employers of Wausau (medical mal practice group); Home Health Care, Inc.; Columbia Hospital Corp.

For full biographical listings, see the Martindale-Hubbell Law Directory

LONDON & YANCEY (AV)

1000 Park Place Tower, 2001 Park Place, 35203
Telephone: 205-251-2531
FAX: 205-251-8929

MEMBERS OF FIRM

Alex T. London (1847-1908)	Thomas R. Elliott, Jr.
John London (1848-1935)	Bert S. Nettles
George W. Yancey (1883-1962)	Richard W. Lewis

ASSOCIATES

Allen R. Trippeer, Jr.	Laura Ellison Proctor
Mark David Hess	Paige Elliott-Pinson
Lisa Wright Borden	F. Daniel Wood, Jr.
A. David Fawal	C. Dennis Hughes

Michael J. Velezis

(See Next Column)

OF COUNSEL
Robert W. Norris

Representative Clients: State of Alabama; Cincinnati Ins. Co.; Lloyd's of London; Blue Cross/Blue Shield; Attorney's Mutual of Alabama; State Farm; CIGNA; Royal Ins. Co. of America; Paul Revere Ins. Co.; Chubb Group.

For full biographical listings, see the Martindale-Hubbell Law Directory

PITTMAN, HOOKS, DUTTON & HOLLIS, P.C. (AV)

1100 Park Place Tower, 35203
Telephone: 205-322-8880
Telecopier: 205-328-2711

W. Lee Pittman	L. Andrew Hollis, Jr.
Kenneth W. Hooks	Jeffrey C. Kirby
Tom Dutton	Ralph Bohanan, Jr.

Nat Bryan

Chris T. Hellums	Emily H. Nelson
Adam P. Morel	John Robert Potter

OF COUNSEL

James H. Davis	Myra B. Staggs
(Not admitted in AL)	

For full biographical listings, see the Martindale-Hubbell Law Directory

PORTERFIELD, HARPER & MILLS, P.A. (AV)

22 Inverness Center Parkway, Suite 600, P.O. Box 530790, 35253-0790
Telephone: 205-980-5000
Fax: 205-980-5001

Larry W. Harper	William Dudley Motlow, Jr.
William T. Mills, II	Philip F. Hutcheson

H. C. "Trey" Ireland, III

Representative Clients: CIGNA; St. Paul Insurance Co.; The Travelers; Figge International; White Consolidated Industries; Terex Corp.; Wausau Insurance; Baptist Health Systems, Inc.; Bruno's, Inc.; Harley Davidson, Inc.

For full biographical listings, see the Martindale-Hubbell Law Directory

STARNES & ATCHISON (AV)

100 Brookwood Place, P.O. Box 598512, 35259-8512
Telephone: 205-868-6000
Telecopier: 205-868-6099

MEMBERS OF FIRM

W. Stancil Starnes	Walter William Bates
W. Michael Atchison	Michael K. Wright
Michael A. Florie	Robert P. Mackenzie, III
Randal H. Sellers	Laura Howard Peck

Mark Christopher Eagan

ASSOCIATES

Sybil Vogtle Abbot	Scott M. Salter
Joseph S. Miller	Ashley E. Watkins

Elizabeth S. Webb

Representative Clients: Mutual Assurance, Inc.; AMI Brookwood Medical Center; American Medical International; Medical Care International; Mobile Infirmary Medical Center; CNA Insurance Co.

For full biographical listings, see the Martindale-Hubbell Law Directory

DECATUR,* Morgan Co.

EYSTER, KEY, TUBB, WEAVER & ROTH (AV)

Eyster Building, 402 East Moulton Street, S.E., P.O. Box 1607, 35602
Telephone: 205-353-6761
Fax: 205-353-6767

John C. Eyster (1863-1926)	Wm. B. Eyster (1921-1995)
Charles H. Eyster, Sr. (1888-1964)	

MEMBERS OF FIRM

John S. Key	Nicholas B. Roth
J. Glynn Tubb	J. Witty Allen
Laurence C. Weaver	William L. Middleton, III

James G. Adams, Jr.

ASSOCIATES

Jenny L. Mcleroy	John R. Baggette, Jr.

General Counsel for: Alabama Farmers Cooperative.
Regional Counsel for: AmSouth Bank.
Local Counsel for: Allstate Insurance Co.; Liberty Mutual Insurance Co.; Maryland Casualty Co.; Saginaw Steering Gear Division, General Motors Corp.; State Farm Mutual Automobile Insurance Co.; The Travelers.

For full biographical listings, see the Martindale-Hubbell Law Directory

ALABAMA—FLORENCE

FLORENCE, Lauderdale Co.

JONES & TROUSDALE (AV)

115 Helton Court, Suite B, P.O. Box 367, 35631-0367
Telephone: 205-767-0333
Telefax: 205-767-0331

MEMBERS OF FIRM

Robert E. Jones, III   Preston S. Trousdale, Jr.

A. DeLoach Stewart

For full biographical listings, see the Martindale-Hubbell Law Directory

GADSDEN, Etowah Co.

DORTCH, WRIGHT & WRIGHT (AV)

239 College Street, P.O. Box 405, 35902
Telephone: 205-546-4616

MEMBERS OF FIRM

Walter R. Dortch (1847-1926)   William B. Dortch (1892-1983)
G. C. Allen (1872-1935)   Curtis Wright
Curtis Wright, II

Attorneys for: St. Paul Insurance Cos.; Employers Insurance of Wausau; Mutual Assurance Society of Alabama; State Farm Insurance Cos.; Alabama Hospital Association Trust; Mutual Savings Life Insurance Co.; Lawyers Title Insurance Corp.; Nationwide Mutual Insurance Co.; Government Employees Insurance Co.; CSX Transportation Systems.

For full biographical listings, see the Martindale-Hubbell Law Directory

HUNTSVILLE, Madison Co.

THE LAW FIRM OF SINIARD, LAMAR & McKINNEY (AV)

125 Holmes Avenue, P.O. Box 2767, 35804
Telephone: 205-536-0770
Facsimile: 205-539-0540

MEMBERS OF FIRM

Tommy H. Siniard   Patrick M. Lamar
Jeffery W. McKinney

ASSOCIATE

M. Roy Braswell

For full biographical listings, see the Martindale-Hubbell Law Directory

MOBILE, Mobile Co.

BROWN, HUDGENS, P.C. (AV)

1495 University Boulevard, P.O. Box 16818, 36616-0818
Telephone: 334-344-7744
Fax: 334-343-9629

Alton R. Brown, Jr.   Vincent A. Noletto, Jr.
A. Neil Hudgens   William H. Sisson
Philip H. Partridge   R. Alan Alexander
Andrew L. Smith   Weyman W. McCranie, Jr.
David Scott Wright   Thomas N. Nolan, Jr.
James P. Green   Craig W. Goolsby

OF COUNSEL

Robert P. Denniston

D. Gavin Austill (1958-1989)   Winston R. Grow
Timothy A. Clarke   A. Edwin Stuardi, III

Representative Client: Alabama Hospital Association Trust.

For full biographical listings, see the Martindale-Hubbell Law Directory

MONTGOMERY, Montgomery Co.

MELTON, ESPY, WILLIAMS & HAYES, P.C. (AV)

301 Adams Avenue, P.O. Drawer 5130, 36103-5130
Telephone: 334-263-6621
Telecopier: 334-263-7252

Oakley Melton, Jr.   James E. Williams
Joseph C. Espy, III   Armstead Lester Hayes III

For full biographical listings, see the Martindale-Hubbell Law Directory

ALASKA

ANCHORAGE, Third Judicial District

DELANEY, WILES, HAYES, GERETY & ELLIS, INC. (AV)

1007 West Third Avenue, Suite 400, 99501
Telephone: 907-279-3581
Fax: 907-277-1331

(See Next Column)

Daniel A. Gerety   Howard A. Lazar
Timothy J. Lamb

Representative Clients: The Doctors Company; Norcal Mutual Insurance Co.; HealthCare Indemnity Co.; Medical Insurance Exchange of California; Lutheran Health Systems; Continental Insurance Co.; Liberty Northwest; Maryland Insurance Group; Royal Globe Insurance Co.

For Complete List of Firm Personnel, See General Section

For full biographical listings, see the Martindale-Hubbell Law Directory

ARIZONA

FLAGSTAFF, Coconino Co.

ASPEY, WATKINS & DIESEL, P.L.L.C. (AV)

123 North San Francisco, 3rd Floor, 86001
Telephone: 520-774-1478
Facsimile: 520-774-8404
Sedona, Arizona Office: 120 Soldier Pass Road.
Telephone: 520-282-5955.
Facsimile: 520-282-5962.
Page, Arizona Office: 904 North Navajo.
Telephone: 520-645-9694.
Cottonwood, Arizona Office: 2400 E. Highway 89A, Suite C.
Telephone: 520-639-1881.
Facsimile: 520-639-0272.

MEMBERS OF FIRM

Frederick M. Fritz Aspey   Donald H. Bayles, Jr.
Harold L. Watkins   Kaign N. Christy
Louis M. Diesel   John J. Dempsey
Bruce S. Griffen   Zachary J. Markham

James E. Ledbetter   Roger M. Baeurle
Whitney Cunningham   Amy E. Mabius
Pernell Whynn McGuire   Stephen A. Thompson
Joel E. Sannes

LEGAL SUPPORT PERSONNEL

Karla H. Falls, CLAS   Dominic M. Marino, Jr,
  (Legal Assistant)   (Paralegal Assistant)
Rocky C. Nissen (Paralegal   Carrie R. Flynn (Litigation
  Assistant, Sedona, Arizona   Paralegal, Cottonwood,
  Office)   Arizona Office)
Deborah D. Roberts, CLA
  (Legal Assistant)

Representative Clients: Farmer's Insurance Company of Arizona; Pepsi-Cola Bottling Company of Northern Arizona; Bill Luke's Chrysler-Plymouth, Inc.; First American Title Insurance Company; Transnation Title Insurance Co.; Page Electric Utility; Comprehensive Access Health Plan, Inc.; Northern Arizona Healthcare Corporation.
Reference: First Interstate Bank-Arizona, N.A., Flagstaff, Arizona.

For full biographical listings, see the Martindale-Hubbell Law Directory

PHOENIX, Maricopa Co.

BEGAM, LEWIS, MARKS & WOLFE A PROFESSIONAL ASSOCIATION OF LAWYERS (AV)

111 West Monroe Street, Suite 1400, 85003-1787
Telephone: 602-254-6071
Fax: 602-252-0042

Robert G. Begam   Daniel J. Adelman
Frank Lewis   Lisa Kurtz
Stanley J. Marks   Dena Rosen Epstein
Elliot G. Wolfe   Steven M. Friedman
Kelly J. McDonald   Richard P. Traulsen

Reference: National Bank of Arizona.

For full biographical listings, see the Martindale-Hubbell Law Directory

MICHAEL E. BRADFORD (AV)

4131 North 24th Street Building C Suite 201, 85016
Telephone: 602-955-0088
FAX: 602-955-6445

LEGAL SUPPORT PERSONNEL

Sandra M. Simcox

OF COUNSEL

Jerry Steele

For full biographical listings, see the Martindale-Hubbell Law Directory

Phoenix—Continued

BURCH & CRACCHIOLO, P.A. (AV)

702 East Osborn Road, Suite 200, 85014
Telephone: 602-274-7611
Fax: 602-234-0341
Mailing Address: P.O. Box 16882, Phoenix, AZ, 85011

Daniel Cracchiolo   Linda A. Finnegan
David G. Derickson   Jess A. Lorona

Representative Clients: Bashas' Inc.; Farmers Insurance Group; U-Haul International, Inc.

For Complete List of Firm Personnel, See General Section

For full biographical listings, see the Martindale-Hubbell Law Directory

DOYLE, WINTHROP, OBERBILLIG & WEST, P.C. (AV)

2800 North Central Avenue Suite 1550, 85004
Telephone: 602-240-6711
Fax: 602-240-6951
Mailing Address: P.O. Box 10417, Phoenix, Arizona, 85064-0417

Lawrence F. Winthrop   Robert H. Oberbillig
William H. Doyle   John C. West
               Beverly A. Bailey

For full biographical listings, see the Martindale-Hubbell Law Directory

FENNEMORE CRAIG, A PROFESSIONAL CORPORATION (AV)

Two North Central, Suite 2200, 85004
Telephone: 602-257-8700
Fax: 602-257-8527
Scottsdale, Arizona Office: 6263 North Scottsdale Road, Suite 290, 85250.
Telephone: 602-257-5400.
Fax: 602-257-5409.
Tucson, Arizona Office: One South Church Avenue, Suite 1030, 85701.
Telephone: 520-791-6800.
Fax: 520-791-6820.

John D. Everroad   Scott M. Finical
Phillip F. Fargotstein   Andrew M. Federhar

Jean Marie Sullivan

For Complete List of Firm Personnel, See General Section

For full biographical listings, see the Martindale-Hubbell Law Directory

GOLDSTEIN & McGRODER, LTD. A PROFESSIONAL CORPORATION (AV)

2200 East Camelback Road, Suite 221, 85016-3456
Telephone: 602-957-1500
Fax: 602-956-9294

Philip T. Goldstein   Patrick J. McGroder, III
               Suzanne P. Clarke

Jane E. Evans   Serena C. Montague
LEGAL SUPPORT PERSONNEL
Kevan S. DeWitt (Paralegal)

For full biographical listings, see the Martindale-Hubbell Law Directory

HARRIS & PALUMBO, A PROFESSIONAL CORPORATION (AV)

361 East Coronado, Suite 101, P.O. Box 13568, 85002-3568
Telephone: 602-271-9344
Fax: 602-252-2099

John David Harris   Gene M. Cullan
Kevin W. Keenan   Frank I. Powers
            Shawn M. Cunningham
OF COUNSEL
Anthony J. Palumbo

For full biographical listings, see the Martindale-Hubbell Law Directory

JENNINGS, STROUSS AND SALMON, P.L.C. (AV)

A Professional Limited Liability Company
One Renaissance Square, Two North Central, 85004-2393
Telephone: 602-262-5911
Fax: 602-253-3255

W. Michael Flood   Jay A. Fradkin
Gary L. Stuart   Jon D. Schneider
Barry E. Lewin   Michael J. O'Connor

For Complete List of Firm Personnel, See General Section

For full biographical listings, see the Martindale-Hubbell Law Directory

MARK & PEARLSTEIN, P.A. (AV)

Suite 150 The Brookstone, 2025 North Third Street, 85004
Telephone: 602-257-0200
Fax: 602-271-4711

Leonard J. Mark   Mr. Lynn M. Pearlstein
OF COUNSEL
Stephen G. Campbell

For full biographical listings, see the Martindale-Hubbell Law Directory

MITTEN, GOODWIN & RAUP, A PROFESSIONAL CORPORATION (AV)

One Columbus Plaza, 3636 North Central, Suite 1200, 85012
Telephone: 602-650-2000
Fax: 602-264-7033
Email: mgr@starlink.com

Roger C. Mitten   Stephen C. Yost
Calvin L. Raup   Scott J. Hergenroether

Steven P. Kramer   Jeffery S. Slater
Sharon Elizabeth Ravenscroft   Gary Beren
            Jeffrey J. Campbell

For full biographical listings, see the Martindale-Hubbell Law Directory

STUART J. REILLY, P.C. (AV)

2425 East Camelback Road, Suite 450, 85016
Telephone: 602-912-8544
FAX: 602-912-8541

Stuart J. Reilly

For full biographical listings, see the Martindale-Hubbell Law Directory

RENAUD, COOK & DRURY, P.A. (AV)

617 North 2nd Avenue, 85003
Telephone: 602-253-5101
Fax: 602-254-1448
Email: rcdlaw@rcdlaw.com
Scottsdale, Arizona Office: 6991 East Camelback Road, #D-103, 85251.
Telephone: 602-874-9000.
Fax: 602-874-9866.

J. Gordon Cook   Steven G. Mesaros
William W. Drury, Jr.   Charles A. Struble

Wade R. Causey   Charles S. Hover, III
Richard N. Crenshaw   Diane Mihalsky
David E. Gustafson   Tamara D. Nydell

For full biographical listings, see the Martindale-Hubbell Law Directory

LAW OFFICES OF RAYMOND J. SLOMSKI, P.C. (AV)

2901 North Central Avenue, Suite 1150, 85012
Telephone: 602-230-8777
Fax: 602-230-8707

Raymond J. Slomski

Kevin L. Beckwith   James M. Abernethy
LEGAL SUPPORT PERSONNEL
PARALEGALS
Patti A. Hibbeler   Diana G. Weeks
            Karen Kay Rush

For full biographical listings, see the Martindale-Hubbell Law Directory

LAW OFFICES OF RICHARD L. STROHM, P.C. (AV)

1136 East Campbell, 85014
Telephone: 602-279-6316
Mobile: 602-616-7094
Facsimile: 602-279-7102
Email: 102442.1444@compuserve.com

Richard L. Strohm
OF COUNSEL
Brad K. Keogh   Nedra J. Bates
LEGAL SUPPORT PERSONNEL
Mindy L. Raymond   Barbara A. Shore
  (Legal Assistant)   (Nurse Paralegal)
Richard M. Knaeble
  (Licensed Private Investigator)

For full biographical listings, see the Martindale-Hubbell Law Directory

Phoenix—Continued

KENNETH L. TUCKER, P.C. (AV)

1136 East Campbell, 85014
Telephone: 602-279-3660
Fax: 602-279-2162
Email: KTucker@futureone.com

Kenneth L. Tucker

Daniel P. J. Miller　　　　　　Kevin J. Tucker
LEGAL SUPPORT PERSONNEL
Mary Toniazzo Moock　　　　Toni R. Hoffman (Paralegal)
(Paralegal)

For full biographical listings, see the Martindale-Hubbell Law Directory

TURLEY & SWAN, P.C. (AV)

The Brookstone Office Complex, 2025 North Third Street, Suite
350, 85004-1471
Telephone: 602-254-1444
Fax: 602-229-1936

Albert R. Vermeire (1947-1988)　　Christopher J. Bork
Kent E. Turley　　　　　　　Christopher M. O'Donnell
Joseph B. Swan, Jr.　　　　　Elizabeth Savoini Fitch
　　　　Thomas J. Howard

For full biographical listings, see the Martindale-Hubbell Law Directory

VALDER LAW OFFICES, P.C. (AV)

Thompson House, 850 North Second Avenue, 85003
Telephone: 602-258-1899
Fax: 602-271-7071

Michael J. Valder

For full biographical listings, see the Martindale-Hubbell Law Directory

---

SCOTTSDALE, Maricopa Co.

RALPH E. MAHOWALD A PROFESSIONAL ASSOCIATION (AV)

6750 East Camelback Road Suite #104, 85251
Telephone: 602-481-0500
Fax: 602-481-0555

Ralph E. Mahowald

For full biographical listings, see the Martindale-Hubbell Law Directory

---

TUCSON,* Pima Co.

BEAL, SCHMIDT & DYER, P.C. (AV)

Suite 6000, West Tower, 5255 East Williams Circle, 85711
Telephone: 520-790-5600
Fax: 520-790-1163

Robert L. Beal　　　　　　James H. Dyer
Ted A. Schmidt　　　　　　Gary JD Dean

For full biographical listings, see the Martindale-Hubbell Law Directory

GOERING, ROBERTS, BERKMAN, RUBIN & BROGNA, P.C. (AV)

Suite 302, 1840 East River Road, 85718
Telephone: 520-577-9300
Fax: 520-577-0848

Scott Goering　　　　　　David L. Berkman
Howard T. Roberts, Jr.　　　William L. Rubin
　　　　Carmine A. Brogna

Christopher L. Enos

Representative Clients: Fireman's Fund Insurance; Safeco Insurance; Royal Insurance; Sentry Insurance; American International Group; Farmers Insurance; USAA; Country Companies; Cigna.
Reference: Bank One.

For full biographical listings, see the Martindale-Hubbell Law Directory

HARALSON, KINERK & MOREY (AV)

82 South Stone Avenue, 85701
Telephone: 520-792-4330
Fax: 520-623-9568

Bob Barber (1903-1978)　　　Burton J. Kinerk
Dale Haralson　　　　　　Carter Morey

Kenneth Lee　　　　　　Linda S. Sherrill
Gregory G. Wasley　　　　Colleen L. Kinerk
Daniel C. Gloria　　　　　Barry L. Entrekin
　　　　Thomas D. Welch

Reference: The National Bank of Arizona.

For full biographical listings, see the Martindale-Hubbell Law Directory

HAZLETT & WILKES (AV)

310 South Williams Boulevard, Suite 305, 85711
Telephone: 520-790-9663
Fax: 520-790-9616

MEMBERS OF FIRM
Carl E. Hazlett　　　　　　James M. Wilkes
ASSOCIATE
Thomas M. Bayham

For full biographical listings, see the Martindale-Hubbell Law Directory

HEALY LAW FIRM (AV)

Williams Centre, 5210 East Williams Circle Suite 730, 85711
Telephone: 520-790-1400

MEMBER OF FIRM
William T. Healy

References: Bank of America; Merrill Lynch.

For full biographical listings, see the Martindale-Hubbell Law Directory

KIMBLE, GOTHREAU & NELSON, P.C. (AV)

5285 East Williams Circle, Suite 3500, 85711-7411
Telephone: 520-748-2440
Fax: 520-748-2469

Michael J. Gothreau (1943-1990)　　David F. Toone
Darwin J. Nelson　　　　　　Michelle T. Lopez
Daryl A. Audilett　　　　　　Negatu Molla
Lawrence McDonough　　　　Michael E. Medina
　　　　Andrew J. Petersen
OF COUNSEL
William Kimble

Representative Clients: State of Arizona; General Motors Corp.; Procter & Gamble Co.; St. Paul Fire and Marine Insurance Co.; City of Tucson; Tucson Electric Power Co.; United States Fidelity & Guaranty Co.; Coriegis Co.; Allstate Insurance Co.

For full biographical listings, see the Martindale-Hubbell Law Directory

RONALD D. MERCALDO, LTD. (AV)

376 South Stone Avenue, 85701
Telephone: 520-624-1400
FAX: 520-624-1955

Ronald D. Mercaldo

Anthony J. Wiggins

Reference: Arizona Bank.

For full biographical listings, see the Martindale-Hubbell Law Directory

RABINOVITZ & ASSOCIATES, P.C. (AV)

721 North 4th Avenue, P.O. Box 41600, 85717
Telephone: 520-624-5526
Toll Free: 1-800-365-0821
Fax: 520-622-3776

Bernard I. Rabinovitz

John D. Ellis
OF COUNSEL
Clark J. Sloan (Not admitted in AZ)
LEGAL SUPPORT PERSONNEL
Michael Nelson (Paralegal)　　　Lisa Busciglio (Paralegal)
　　　　Ruth Polizz

Representative Client: Firemans Fund Insurance Co.

For full biographical listings, see the Martindale-Hubbell Law Directory

STOMPOLY, STROUD, GIDDINGS & GLICKSMAN, P.C. (AV)

1820 Citibank Tower, One South Church Avenue, 85702
Telephone: 520-628-8300
Telefax: 520-628-9948
Mailing Address: P.O. Box 190, Tucson, AZ, 85702-0190

John G. Stompoly

For Complete List of Firm Personnel, See General Section

For full biographical listings, see the Martindale-Hubbell Law Directory

STRICKLAND & STRICKLAND, P.C. (AV)

4400 E. Broadway, Suite 700, 85711-3517
Telephone: 520-795-8727
Fax: 520-795-5649

(See Next Column)

STRICKLAND & STRICKLAND P.C.—*Continued*

William E. Strickland   William E. Strickland, Jr.
Robert F. Palmquist

Representative Client: AkChin Indian Community.
Reference: Bank One (formerly Valley National Bank).

ARKANSAS

FORT SMITH, * Sebastian Co.

GILBREATH LAW FIRM (AV)

7000 Rogers Avenue, 72903
Telephone: 501-452-1181
Fax: 501-452-8652
Email: attysatlaw@aol.com

E. C. Gilbreath   Daniel W. Gilbreath

For full biographical listings, see the Martindale-Hubbell Law Directory

SHAW, LEDBETTER, HORNBERGER, COGBILL & ARNOLD (AV)

South Seventh and Parker, P.O. Box 185, 72902-0185
Telephone: 501-782-7294
FAX: 501-782-1493

Bruce H. Shaw (1904-1990)   Richard B. Shaw (1927-1988)

MEMBERS OF FIRM

Charles R. Ledbetter   James A. Arnold, II
Robert E. Hornberger   Ronald D. Harrison
J. Michael Cogbill   E. Diane Graham
R. Ray Fulmer, II

ASSOCIATE

Rebecca D. Hattabaugh

OF COUNSEL

J. Michael Shaw

Representative Clients: General: First National Bank of Fort Smith; Bank of Mansfield; Commercial Bank at Alma; Mid-South Dredging Co.
Local Attorneys for: St Paul Insurance Cos.; American Physician Insurance Exchange; Medical Protective Co.

For full biographical listings, see the Martindale-Hubbell Law Directory

---

LITTLE ROCK, * Pulaski Co.

ANDERSON & KILPATRICK (AV)

The First Commercial Building, 400 West Capitol Avenue, Suite 2640, 72201
Telephone: 501-372-1887
Fax: 501-372-7706
Email: ande@cei.net

MEMBERS OF FIRM

Overton S. Anderson, II   Aylmer Gene Williams
Mariam T. Hopkins

ASSOCIATES

Michael P. Vanderford   Penny Brown Wilbourn
C. Timothy Spainhour

For full biographical listings, see the Martindale-Hubbell Law Directory

BARBER, McCASKILL, AMSLER, JONES & HALE, P.A. (AV)

2700 First Commercial Building, 400 West Capitol Avenue, 72201-3414
Telephone: 501-372-6175
Telecopier: 501-375-2802

Azro L. Barber (1885-1979)   Richard C. Kalkbrenner
Elbert A. Henry (1889-1966)   G. Spence Fricke
John B. Thurman (1912-1971)   Gail Ponder Gaines
Austin McCaskill, Sr.   Michael J. Emerson
Guy Amsler, Jr.   R. Kenny McCulloch
Glenn W. Jones   Tim A. Cheatham
Michael E. Hale   Joseph F. Kolb
John S. Cherry, Jr.   Scott Michael Strauss
Robert L. Henry, III   Derek J. Edwards
Micheal L. Alexander   Thomas E. Osment, Jr.
William H. Edwards, Jr.   Christopher Gomlicker

Attorneys for: Associated Aviation Underwriters; Canal Insurance Co.; Fireman's Fund Insurance Co.; General Motors Corp.; General Motors Acceptance Corp.; Hanover Insurance Co.; Home Insurance Co.; Royal Insurance; United States Fidelity & Guaranty Co.; Universal Underwriters Insurance Co.

For full biographical listings, see the Martindale-Hubbell Law Directory

GARY EUBANKS & ASSOCIATES, P.A. (AV)

708 West Second Street, 72201
Telephone: 501-372-0266

(See Next Column)

Gary L. Eubanks   Hugh F. Spinks

William Gary Holt   Jack D. Files
James G. Schulze   Jason Files
Herman W. Eubanks   Matthew Hartness

For full biographical listings, see the Martindale-Hubbell Law Directory

HUCKABAY, MUNSON, ROWLETT & TILLEY, P.A. (AV)

First Commercial Building, Suite 1900, 400 West Capitol, 72201
Telephone: 501-374-6535
Fax: 501-374-5906

Mike Huckabay   John E. Moore
Bruce E. Munson   Tim Boone
Beverly A. Rowlett   Rick Runnells
James W. Tilley   Sarah Ann Presson
Edward T. Oglesby

D. Michael Huckabay, Jr.   Elizabeth Fletcher Rogers
Carol Lockard Worley   Julia L. Busfield
Mark S. Breeding   Jane M. Yocum
Terry D. Dugger

Representative Clients: Columbia/HCA Healthcare Corporation; Sisters of Charity of Nazareth Health System d/b/a St. Vincent Infirmary Medical Center; Tenet Healthcare Corp.

For full biographical listings, see the Martindale-Hubbell Law Directory

LASER, WILSON, BUFFORD & WATTS, P.A. (AV)

101 S. Spring Street, Suite 300, 72201-2488
Telephone: 501-376-2981
Telecopier: 501-376-2417

Sam Laser   J. Kendal "Ken" Cook
Richard N. Watts   David M. Donovan

Representative Clients: Allstate Insurance Co.; American International Insurance Group; Continental Insurance Cos.; Farm Bureau Insurance Cos. (Casualty & Fire); Farmers Insurance Group; GAB Business Services, Inc.; St. Paul Insurance Cos.; Scottsdale Insurance Co.; State Farm Auto (Fire) Insurance Cos.

For Complete List of Firm Personnel, See General Section

For full biographical listings, see the Martindale-Hubbell Law Directory

ROBERT McHENRY, P.A. (AV)

124 West Capitol Avenue Suite 1500, 72201
Telephone: 501-372-3425
Fax: 501-372-3428

Robert M. McHenry, Jr.   Donna J. Wolfe

References: First Commercial Bank, N.A., Little Rock, Arkansas; Boatmen's Bank & Trust, Little Rock, Ark.

For full biographical listings, see the Martindale-Hubbell Law Directory

THE McMATH LAW FIRM, P.A. (AV)

711 West Third Street, P.O. Box 3457, 72203
Telephone: 501-376-3021
Fax: 501-374-5118

Sidney S. McMath   Mart Vehik
Sandy S. McMath   Winslow Drummond
Phillip H. McMath   Paul E. Harrison
James Bruce McMath   Sandra L. Sanders

For full biographical listings, see the Martindale-Hubbell Law Directory

---

TEXARKANA, * Miller Co.

DUNN, NUTTER, MORGAN & SHAW (AV)

State Line Plaza, Box 8030, 71854-5945
Telephone: 501-773-5651
Telecopier: 501-772-2037
Email: law@clover.cleaf.com

MEMBERS OF FIRM

Winford L. Dunn, Jr.   R. Gary Nutter
W. David Carter

LEGAL SUPPORT PERSONNEL

LEGAL ASSISTANTS

Myra Conaway Wells

Representative Clients: CNA Insurance Cos.; Cigna Insurance Cos.; St. Michael Hospital.

For Complete List of Firm Personnel, See General Section

For full biographical listings, see the Martindale-Hubbell Law Directory

CALIFORNIA

APTOS, Santa Cruz Co.

RUMMONDS, WALTZ & MAIR (AV)

311 Bonita Drive, P.O. Box 1870, 95001
Telephone: 408-688-2911
Sacramento, California Office: 6991 Garden Highway. 95837.
Telephone: 916-927-4610.

MEMBERS OF FIRM

James S. Rummonds Peter K. Mair
Patrick J. Waltz
 (Resident, Sacramento Office)

For full biographical listings, see the Martindale-Hubbell Law Directory

COSTA MESA, Orange Co.

LAW OFFICES OF W. DOUGLAS EASTON (AV)

3200 Park Center Drive, Suite 1000, 92626
Telephone: 714-850-4590
Fax: 714-850-4500

Anderson L. Washburn Russel W. Jones
 Brian W. Easton

For full biographical listings, see the Martindale-Hubbell Law Directory

DANVILLE, Contra Costa Co.

CRADDICK, CANDLAND & CONTI, PROFESSIONAL CORPORATION (AV)

Danville-San Ramon Medical Center, 915 San Ramon Valley Boulevard, Suite 260, 94526-0810
Telephone: 510-838-1100
Fax: 510-743-0729

Marrs A. Craddick Judy S. Craddick
D. Stuart Candland Robert W. Hodges
Richard J. Conti W. David Walker
 Robert W. Lamson

Phillip J. Maddux Michael J. Garvin
Jean Louise Perry Diane C. Miller
 Steven L. Brown, Jr.

For full biographical listings, see the Martindale-Hubbell Law Directory

*FRESNO,** Fresno Co.

LANG, RICHERT & PATCH, A PROFESSIONAL CORPORATION (AV)

Fig Garden Financial Center, 5200 North Palm Avenue, 4th Floor, P.O. Box 40012, 93755
Telephone: 209-228-6700
Fax: 209-228-6727

Frank H. Lang Victoria J. Salisch
William T. Richert (1937-1993) Bradley A. Silva
Robert L. Patch, II Charles Trudrung Taylor
Val W. Saldaña Mark L. Creede
Douglas E. Noll Peter N. Zeitler
Michael T. Hertz Charles L. Doerksen

Laurie L. Quigley Nabil E. Zumout
Douglas E. Griffin Shawn H. Alikian
 Thomas E. Gauthier

References: Wells Fargo Bank (Fresno Main Office).

For full biographical listings, see the Martindale-Hubbell Law Directory

MILES, SEARS & EANNI, A PROFESSIONAL CORPORATION (AV)

2844 Fresno Street, P.O. Box 1432, 93716
Telephone: 209-486-5200
Fax: 209-486-5240

Wm. M. Miles (1909-1991) Richard C. Watters
Robert E. Sears (1918-1992) Gerald J. Maglio
Carmen A. Eanni William J. Seiler
 Douglas L. Gordon

For full biographical listings, see the Martindale-Hubbell Law Directory

GLENDALE, Los Angeles Co.

HAGENBAUGH & MURPHY (AV)

A Partnership including Professional Corporations
700 North Central Avenue, Suite 500, 91203
Telephone: 818-240-2600
Fax: 818-240-1253
Email: hmurphy@interserv.com *URL:* http://www.seamless.com/hm/
Orange County, California Office: 701 South Parker Street, Suite 8200, Orange.
Telephone: 714-835-5406.
Fax: 714-835-5949.
San Bernardino, California Office: 301 Vanderbilt Way, Suite 220.
Telephone: 909-884-5331.
FAX: 909-889-1250.

Van A. Hagenbaugh (1914-1980) Daniel A. Leipold (Resident, Orange County Office)
Sigurd E. Murphy (1903-1976)
William D. Stewart (A P.C.) Craig D. Aronson
John J. Tary (A P.C.) Paul G. Szumiak
Raymond R. Moore (A P.C.) Robert F. Donohue (Resident, Orange County Office)
Neil R. Gunny (Resident, Orange County Office) Katharine L. Spaniac (Resident, San Bernardino Office)
Alan R. Zuckerman
David L. Winter Alan H. Boon (Resident, Orange County Office)
Mary E. Porter
 Jamie B. Skebba

Raymond T. Gail (Resident, San Bernardino Office) Cathy L. Shipe (Resident, Orange County Office)
Kirk G. Neiberger Keri Lynn Bush
Meredith A. Musicant Michael A. Tonya
David M. Chute (Resident, Orange County Office) Laura C. McLennan
 Graciela L. Freixes
Luanne Walsh Melinda W. Ebelhar
Rhonda L. Etzwiler Kirk N. Sullivan
Steven M. Schuetze Gary P. Simonian
Thomas J. Heatly Mark Habeeb
Matthew R. Rungaitis Howard J. Hirsch (Resident, Orange County Office)
Stephen Barry
Julie M. DeRose Michelle Mann
Randal A. Whitecotton
 (Resident, San Bernardino Office)

Representative Clients: Farmers Insurance Group; Truck Insurance Exchange; Fire Insurance Exchange.

For full biographical listings, see the Martindale-Hubbell Law Directory

HEMER, BARKUS & CLARK (AV)

550 North Brand Boulevard, Suite 1800, P.O. Box 293, 91202
Telephone: 818-241-8999
Fax: 818-241-2014
Email: Kallwyr@aol.com
Ontario, California Office: 3401 Centrelake Drive, Suite 400.
Telephone: 714-467-0660.
Fax: 909-390-3628.

Ralph S. Hemer Ramune E. Barkus
 Bradley C. Clark
ASSOCIATES
Cathy L. Patrenos David A. Arkuss
Laurence Y. Wong Tom M Allen
Kristen L. Chesnut Richard I. Gonzalez
John P. Freeman Joann G. Housman
 Jack Rosenbaum

Reference: Sterling Bank.

For full biographical listings, see the Martindale-Hubbell Law Directory

THOMAS & PRICE (AV)

535 North Brand Boulevard, 7th Floor, 91203
Telephone: 213-387-4800; 818-500-4800
FAX: 818-500-4822
Ventura, California Office: 1655 Mesa Verde Avenue, Suite 230.
Telephone: 805-642-6255.
Fax: 805-642-4580.

MEMBERS OF FIRM
Michael Thomas Craig R. Donahue
Bonnie R. Louis Maureen F. Thomas
ASSOCIATES
John P. DeGomez Christian E. Sanne
Timothy A. Hodge Benjimin M. Brees
Linda B. Hurevitz Janet L. Keuper
 Kevin M. McCormick
OF COUNSEL
Lawrence E. Price

For full biographical listings, see the Martindale-Hubbell Law Directory

IRVINE, Orange Co.

PIVO & HALBREICH (AV)

1920 Main Street, Suite 800, 92714
Telephone: 714-253-2000

Kenneth R. Pivo	Douglas A. Amo
Eva S. Halbreich	Richard O. Schwartz

Mona Z. Hanna
ASSOCIATES

Charles A. Palmer	Michael A. Brodie
William J. Mall, III	Lance Gordon Greene
Kathleen E. Wilcox	Annie Glass Henshel
Timothy J. Lippert	Jennifer Batliner

Representative Clients: Physicians and Surgeons Underwriters Corp.; Fremont Indemnity; American Continental Insurance Co.; AKROS Medico Enterprises; Kaiser Foundation Healthplan, Inc.; Caronia Corp.; The Doctor's Co.; Harbor Regional Center; Developmental Disabilities Regional Center; South Central Los Angeles Regional Center.

For full biographical listings, see the Martindale-Hubbell Law Directory

LARKSPUR, Marin Co.

WEINBERG, HOFFMAN & CASEY (AV)

A Partnership including a Professional Corporation
900 Larkspur Landing Circle, Suite 155, 94939
Telephone: 415-461-9666
Fax: 415-461-9681

Ivan Weinberg	Joseph Hoffman

A. Michael Casey
OF COUNSEL
Mark Ropers

For full biographical listings, see the Martindale-Hubbell Law Directory

LONG BEACH, Los Angeles Co.

BURNS, AMMIRATO, PALUMBO, MILAM & BARONIAN, A PROFESSIONAL LAW CORPORATION (AV)

One World Trade Center, Suite 1200, 90831-1200
Telephone: 310-436-8338; 714-952-1047
Fax: 310-432-6049
Pasadena, California Office: 65 North Raymond Avenue, 2nd Floor.
Telephone: 818-796-5053; 213-258-8282.
Fax: 818-792-3078.

Vincent A. Ammirato

Grace C. Mori	Michael P. Vicencia

Michael E. Wenzel

For full biographical listings, see the Martindale-Hubbell Law Directory

LOS ANGELES, * Los Angeles Co.

AGNEW & BRUSAVICH

(See Torrance)

BONNE, BRIDGES, MUELLER, O'KEEFE & NICHOLS, PROFESSIONAL CORPORATION (AV)

3699 Wilshire Boulevard, 10th Floor, 90010-2719
Telephone: 213-480-1900
Fax: 213-738-5888
Santa Ana, California Office: 1750 East Fourth Street, Suite 450, P.O. Box 22018, 92702-2018.
Telephone: 714-835-1157.
Fax: 714-480-2585.
Santa Barbara, California Office: 801 Garden Street, Suite 300, 93101-5502.
Telephone: 805-965-2992.
Fax: 805-962-6509.
Riverside, California Office: 3403 Tenth Street, Suite 800, 92501-0749.
Telephone: 909-788-1944.
Fax: 909-683-7827.
San Luis Obispo, California Office: 1060 Palm Street, 93401-3221.
Telephone: 805-541-8350.
Fax: 805-541-6817.

Ried Bridges	Jeffrey C. Moffat
Kenneth N. Mueller	N. Denise Taylor
David J. O'Keefe	Patricia K. Ramsey (Resident in
James D. Nichols	Santa Barbara Office)
George E. Peterson	Theodore H. O'Leary
Joel Bruce Douglas	Michael D. Lubrani
Alexander B. T. Cobb	(Resident in Riverside Office)
Peter R. Osinoff	Christopher B. Marshall
Margaret Manton Holm	(Resident in Riverside Office)
(Resident in Santa Ana Office)	Thomas M. O'Neil

(See Next Column)

Mark B. Connely (Resident in Santa Luis Obispo Office)	Thomas R. Bradford (Also in Santa Barbara Office)
Peter G. Bertling (Resident in Santa Barbara Office)	

Louis W. Pappas	Jennifer L. Sturges
Yuk Kwong Law	Andrew S. Levey
Mary A. Seliger	Brian H. Clausen (Resident in
Thomas G. Scully	Santa Barbara Office)
(Resident in Santa Ana Office)	Patricia M. Egan
Janice B. Lee	Russell M. Mortyn
Martha A. H. Berman	Robert A. Mosier
Carmen Vigil	(Resident in Santa Ana Office)
Kathryn S. Pyke	Cynthia M. Herrera
Robert W. Bates	(Resident in Riverside Office)
(Resident in Riverside Office)	John A. Haughton
Douglas C. Smith	Melanie C. Butts
(Resident in Riverside Office)	Paul F. Arentz
Henry Yekikian	Jeannette Lynne Van Horst
(Resident in Riverside Office)	Robert A. Madison
Donna Bruce Koch	Barbara Kamenir Frankel
Julianne M. DeMarco	Raymond J. Mc Mahon
John H. Dodd	Mitzie L. Dobson
Kippy L. Wroten	Diana L. Kreinman
(Resident in Santa Ana Office)	Raymond L. Blessey
Sara E. Hersh	Jo Lynn Valoff
Heather J. Higson	(Resident in Santa Ana Office)
(Resident in Santa Ana Office)	Yoshiaki C. Kubota
Barbara Springe Kilroy	(Resident in Riverside Office)
(Resident in Santa Barbara Office)	Kimberly Netta
	(Resident in Riverside Office)
Mary Lawrence Test	Holly H. McGregor
Gregory Reyna Bunch	(Resident in Riverside Office)
George E. Nowotny, III	Mark S. Salz
(Resident in Santa Ana Office)	James A. Keens
Marie E. Colmey	Michael L. Bazzo
Gregory D. Werre	(Resident in Riverside Office)
Brian L. Hoffman	Kevin A. Duffis
Alison J. Vitacolonna	Marta A. Alcumbrac
(Resident in Santa Ana Office)	Cynthia C. Miller
Kathleen M. Walker	Melanie M. Frayer

Nana Nakano
OF COUNSEL
Bruce J. Bonne

Representative Clients: Southern California Physicians Insurance Exchange, Doctor's Co.; Cooperative of American Physicians; Norcal Mutual Insurance Co.

For full biographical listings, see the Martindale-Hubbell Law Directory

BOTTUM & FELITON, A PROFESSIONAL CORPORATION (AV)

Suite 1500, South Tower, 3200 Wilshire Boulevard, 90010
Telephone: 213-487-0402
Fax: 213-386-9803
San Diego, California Office: Suite 400 Emerald Plaza, 402 West Broadway.
Telephone: 619-595-4857.
Fax: 619-595-4863.

John R. Feliton, Jr.	Steve Johnson
Robert A. Wooten, Jr.	Mark A. Oertel

Alexander F. Giovanniello

Brian E. Cooper	Karl R. Loureiro

For full biographical listings, see the Martindale-Hubbell Law Directory

WILLIAM J. GARGARO, JR. A PROFESSIONAL CORPORATION (AV)

Suite 1800, 2049 Century Park East, 90067
Telephone: 310-552-0633
Fax: 310-552-9760

William J. Gargaro, Jr.

Reference: Wells Fargo Bank.

For full biographical listings, see the Martindale-Hubbell Law Directory

GORDON, EDELSTEIN, KREPACK, GRANT, FELTON & GOLDSTEIN (AV)

A Partnership including a Professional Corporation
Suite 1800, 3580 Wilshire Boulevard, 90010
Telephone: 213-739-7000
Fax: 213-386-1671

Roger L. Gordon	Richard I. Felton
Mark Edelstein	Irwin L. Goldstein (A
Howard D. Krepack	Professional Corporation)
Sherry E. Grant	Steven J. Kleifield

(See Next Column)

GORDON, EDELSTEIN, KREPACK, GRANT, FELTON & GOLDSTEIN, *Los Angeles—Continued*

ASSOCIATES

Joshua M. Merliss

David A. Goldstein

Eugenia L. Steele

For full biographical listings, see the Martindale-Hubbell Law Directory

HARNEY LAW OFFICES A LEGAL CORPORATION (AV)

Suite 1300 Figueroa Plaza, 201 North Figueroa Street, 90012-2636
Telephone: 213-482-0881
Fax: 213-250-4042

David M. Harney

David T. Harney

Julie A. Harney

Andrew J. Nocas

Vincent McGowan

Thomas A. Schultz

Reference: Bank of America.

For full biographical listings, see the Martindale-Hubbell Law Directory

KERN, STREETER & GONZALEZ (AV)

601 West 5th Street, Suite 1100, 90071
Telephone: 213-629-8100
Facsimile: 213-627-8765

MEMBERS OF FIRM

René J. Kern, Jr.

John W. Streeter

Michael D. Gonzalez

ASSOCIATES

Tina L. Gentile

Claudia T. Beightol

Angela J. Armitage

Christina L. Young

Representative Clients: Fremont Indemnity; Norcal Mutual Insurance Co.; Summit Health, Ltd.; Tristar Risk Management.

For full biographical listings, see the Martindale-Hubbell Law Directory

KUSSMAN & WHITEHILL (AV)

A Partnership including a Professional Corporation
Suite 1470, 10866 Wilshire Boulevard, 90024
Telephone: 310-474-4411
Fax: 310-474-6530

Russell S. Kussman (A
Professional Corporation)

Michael H. Whitehill

Steven G. Mehta

For full biographical listings, see the Martindale-Hubbell Law Directory

ROBERT L. LUTY A PROFESSIONAL CORPORATION (AV)

Suite 303, 11661 San Vicente Boulevard, 90049
Telephone: 310-207-4342
Fax: 310-207-5035

Robert L. Luty

Reference: Brentwood Savings Bank (Brentwood Branch).

For full biographical listings, see the Martindale-Hubbell Law Directory

PETER J. MCNULTY (AV)

827 Moraga Drive (Bel Air), 90049
Telephone: 310-471-2707
Fax: 310-472-7014
Gilroy, California Office: Suite F-2, 8352 Church Street.
Telephone: 408-848-5900.
Fax: 408-848-1391.
Aurora, Illinois Office: 8 East Galena Street.

ASSOCIATE

Michael L. Oran (A Professional Corporation)

OF COUNSEL

John A. Alvarez
(Resident, Gilroy Office)
Robert M. Foote
(Not admitted in CA)

Robert P. Friedman

Carl A. McMahan

Reference: City National Bank (Beverly Hills, California).

For full biographical listings, see the Martindale-Hubbell Law Directory

PIERRY & MOORHEAD, LLP (AV)

A Partnership including a Professional Corporation
301 North Avalon Boulevard, 90744-5888
Telephone: 310-834-2691, 213-775-8348, 714-636-2970
FAX: 310-518-5814

MEMBERS OF FIRM

Thomas J. Pierry, Sr.

Michael D. Moorhead (P.C.)

(See Next Column)

James M. McAdams

F. Joseph Ford, Jr.

Robert W. Ford

F. Javier Trujillo

Thomas J. Pierry, III

Joseph P. Pierry

For full biographical listings, see the Martindale-Hubbell Law Directory

ROBERT S. SCHLIFKIN (AV)

1925 Century Park East, Suite 1250, 90067-2713
Telephone: 310-553-5151
FAX: 310-553-7204

Reference: First Los Angeles Bank.

For full biographical listings, see the Martindale-Hubbell Law Directory

VEATCH, CARLSON, GROGAN & NELSON (AV)

A Partnership including a Professional Corporation
3926 Wilshire Boulevard, 90010
Telephone: 213-381-2861
Telefax: 213-383-6370

MEMBERS OF FIRM

James C. Galloway, Jr. (A
Professional Corporation)
Anthony D. Seine
Mark A. Weinstein
John A. Peterson

Gordon F. Sausser
Thomas M. Phillips
Amy W. Lyons
Michael Eric Wasserman
Michael A. Kramer

ASSOCIATES

Hollis O. Dyer
Mark M. Rudy
D. Michael Bush
André S. Goodchild
Kevin L. Henderson
Gilbert A. Garcia
William G. Lieb

Dawn M. Costello
Daniel R. Brown
Stephen D. Enerle
John J. Nolan, III
Steven W. Sedach
Joan E. Hewitt
Joanne M. Andrew

OF COUNSEL

David J. Aisenson
(Judge Retired)

Lyn A. Woodward

For full biographical listings, see the Martindale-Hubbell Law Directory

ROBERT D. WALKER A PROFESSIONAL CORPORATION (AV)

Suite 1208, One Park Plaza, 3250 Wilshire Boulevard, 90010-1606
Telephone: 213-382-8010
Fax: 213-388-1033

Robert D. Walker

Delia Flores

Reference: Bank of America (Los Angeles Main Office)

For full biographical listings, see the Martindale-Hubbell Law Directory

MENLO PARK, San Mateo Co.

O'REILLY & COLLINS, A PROFESSIONAL CORPORATION (AV)

2500 Sand Hill Road, Suite 201, 94025
Telephone: 415-854-7700
Fax: 415-854-8350

Terry O'Reilly

James P. Collins

James P. Tessier

Michael Danko

For full biographical listings, see the Martindale-Hubbell Law Directory

OAKLAND,* Alameda Co.

ANTHONY & CARLSON (AV)

1999 Harrison Street, Suite 1750, 94612
Telephone: 510-835-8400
Fax: 510-835-5566

MEMBERS OF FIRM

Steven R. Anthony

Richard H. Carlson

ASSOCIATE

Barbara L. Vankoll

OF COUNSEL

Jane L. Trigero

For full biographical listings, see the Martindale-Hubbell Law Directory

RANKIN, SPROAT, MIRES, TRAPANI & REISER, A PROFESSIONAL CORPORATION (AV)

Suite 1616, 1800 Harrison Street, 94612
Telephone: 510-465-3922
Fax: 510-452-3006
Email: rankin@best.com *URL:* http://www.rankinlaw.com

(See Next Column)

RANKIN, SPROAT, MIRES, TRAPANI & REISER A PROFESSIONAL
CORPORATION—*Continued*

Joseph F. Rankin (-1977)	Geoffrey A. Mires
Patrick T. Rankin (1943-1990)	Thomas A. Trapani
Ronald G. Sproat	Michael J. Reiser

David T. Shuey	Eugene G. Ashley
G. Trent Morrow	Kevin R. Mintz

Maribel Delgado Osborne

LEGAL SUPPORT PERSONNEL

Jennifer L. Rankin	Sue Perata (Medical Paralegal)
(Administrator)	Trish J. Fuzesy (Paralegal)
Betty E. Evans (Nurse Paralegal)	Sally J. Attia
	(Medical Paralegal)

Reference: Union Bank.

For full biographical listings, see the Martindale-Hubbell Law Directory

VAN BLOIS, KNOWLES, SCHWARTZ & BASKIN (AV)

Suite 2245 Ordway Building, One Kaiser Plaza, 94612
Telephone: 510-444-1906
Contra Costa County 510-947-1055
Fax: 510-444-1294

MEMBERS OF FIRM

R. Lewis Van Blois	Ellen R. Schwartz
Thomas C. Knowles	Richard J. Baskin

OF COUNSEL

Charles E. Farnsworth

For full biographical listings, see the Martindale-Hubbell Law Directory

---

ONTARIO, San Bernardino Co.

HEMER, BARKUS & CLARK (AV)

3401 Centre Lake Drive, Suite 400, 91764
Telephone: 909-467-0660
Fax: 909-390-3628
Glendale, California Office: 550 N. Brand, Suite 1800, 91202-6002.
Telephone: 818-241-8999.
Fax: 818-241-2014.

Ralph S. Hemer	Ramune E. Barkus

Bradley C. Clark

ASSOCIATES

Kristen L. Chesnut	Tom M Allen

Richard I. Gonzalez

For full biographical listings, see the Martindale-Hubbell Law Directory

---

PALM DESERT, Riverside Co.

BERMAN & WEISS (AV)

73-710 Fred Waring Drive, Suite 100, 92260
Telephone: 619-773-6677
Fax: 619-346-7779
Email: rw1224@aol.com *URL:*
http://www.lawinfo.com/law/ca/berman.html
Encino, California Office: 16055 Ventura Boulevard, Suite 900, 91436.
Telephone: 818-986-8000.
Facsimile: 818-986-3162.
Palm Springs, California Office: 1111 Tahquitz Canyon Way, Suite 203, 92262.
Telephone: 619-327-1777.
Fax: 619-346-7779.

MEMBERS OF FIRM

Richard B. Weiss	Martin M. Berman

For full biographical listings, see the Martindale-Hubbell Law Directory

---

PASADENA, Los Angeles Co.

BURNS, AMMIRATO, PALUMBO, MILAM & BARONIAN, A PROFESSIONAL LAW CORPORATION (AV)

65 North Raymond Avenue, 2nd Floor, 91103-3919
Telephone: 818-796-5053; 213-258-8282
Fax: 818-792-3078
Long Beach, California Office: One World Trade Center, Suite 1200.
Telephone: 310-436-8338; 714-952-1047.
Fax: 310-432-6049.

Michael A. Burns	Bruce Palumbo
Vincent A. Ammirato,	Jeffrey L. Milam
Resident, Long Bch	Robert H. Baronian

Normand A. Ayotte	Michael P. Vicencia,
Colleen Clark	Resident, LOng Bch
Valerie Julien-Peto	Michael E. Wenzel,
Susan E. Luhring	Resident, Long Bch
Grace C. Mori,	
Resident, Long Bch	

(See Next Column)

Reference: First Los Angeles Bank.

For full biographical listings, see the Martindale-Hubbell Law Directory

BURTON & NORRIS (AV)

35 South Raymond Avenue, Fourth Floor, 91105
Telephone: 818-449-8300
Fax: 818-449-4417

John C. Burton	Donald G. Norris

Victoria E. King

Reference: Bank of America (Pasadena).

For full biographical listings, see the Martindale-Hubbell Law Directory

FREEBURG, JUDY & NETTELS (AV)

600 South Lake Avenue, 91106
Telephone: 818-585-4150
FAX: 818-585-0718
Santa Ana, California Office: Xerox Centre. 1851 East First Street, Suite 120. 92705-4017.
Telephone: 714-569-0950.
Facsimile: 714-569-0955.

Steven J. Freeburg	J. Lawrence Judy

Charles F. Nettels

ASSOCIATES

Ingall W. Bull, Jr.	Holly A. McNulty
Richard B. Castle	Karen S. Freeburg
Cynthia B. Schaldenbrand	Jennifer D. Helsel
(Resident, Santa Ana Office)	William R. Francis
Robert S. Brody	Fred W. Brandt

Carla Crochet

For full biographical listings, see the Martindale-Hubbell Law Directory

HAMMOND, ZUETEL & CAHILL (AV)

Suite 540, 180 South Lake Avenue, 91101
Telephone: 818-449-5144; 213-684-2898
FAX: 213-684-1275

MEMBERS OF FIRM

Kenneth R. Zuetel, Jr.	Richard F. Cahill

ASSOCIATES

Cynthia L.K. Steele	Victoria K. Torigian

OF COUNSEL

John C. Cushman	P. Theodore Hammond

For full biographical listings, see the Martindale-Hubbell Law Directory

GEORGE E. MOORE A PROFESSIONAL LAW CORPORATION (AV)

Wells Fargo Building, 350 West Colorado Boulevard Suite 400, 91105-1894
Telephone: 818-440-1111
Fax: 818-440-9456

George E. Moore

For full biographical listings, see the Martindale-Hubbell Law Directory

---

*REDWOOD CITY,** San Mateo Co.

LOW, BALL & LYNCH, A PROFESSIONAL CORPORATION (AV)

10 Twin Dolphin, Suite B-500, 94065
Telephone: 415-591-8822
Fax: 415-591-8884
San Francisco, California Office: 601 California Street, Suite 2100, 94108.
Telephone: 415-981-6630.
Monterey, California Office: 10 Ragsdale Drive, Suite 175, 93940.
Telephone: 408-655-8822.

Raymond Coates	David L. Blinn
Chester G. Moore, III	Janet Kulig
James D. Miller	Thomas E. Mulvihill
William H. Holsinger	Jennifer Elizabeth Acheson

John R. Baumann	Joseph M. Fenech

Michael E. Sandgren

For full biographical listings, see the Martindale-Hubbell Law Directory

---

*SACRAMENTO,** Sacramento Co.

HARDY ERICH BROWN & WILSON, A PROFESSIONAL CORPORATION (AV)

1000 G Street, 95814
Telephone: 916-449-3800
Fax: 916-449-3888
Mailing Address: P.O. Box 13530, Sacramento, California, 95853-4530

(See Next Column)

HARDY ERICH BROWN & WILSON A PROFESSIONAL CORPORATION, Sacramento—Continued

John Quincy Brown, Jr.
Thomas C. Richards
L. Thomas Wagner

David L. Perrault
John Quincy Brown, III
Bruce E. Salenko

Sara A. Clark

Representative Clients: Norcal; Charter Behavioral Health; Mercy Health-care; Sierra Nevada Memorial Hospital; Zurich American Insurance Company.

For full biographical listings, see the Martindale-Hubbell Law Directory

PORTER, SCOTT, WEIBERG & DELEHANT, A PROFESSIONAL CORPORATION (AV)

350 University Avenue, Suite 200, 95825
Telephone: 916-929-1481
Fax: 916-927-3706

Russell G. Porter
A. Irving Scott, Jr.
Edwin T. Weiberg
John W. Delehant
Anthony S. Warburg
Ned P. Telford
James K. Mirabell
Craig A. Caldwell

Terence J. Cassidy
Tom H. Bailey
Carl J. Calnero
Russ J. Wunderli
Nancy J. Sheehan
Norman V. Prior
Timothy M. Blaine
Stephen E. Horan

Amanda R. Lowe
Clay A. Jackson
Elisa Ungerman
John Carl Padrick
Erik Z. Revai
Karen Beth Ebel
Carl L. Fessenden
Grant Collins Woodruff
James W. Walter, Jr.
Michael J. Baytosh
David A. Melton

Alysa Erdman Meyer
Richard Joseph Corbo, Jr.
Bruce A. Monfross
Marcos Kropf
Valerie Mercier
Jennifer E. Duggan
Vanessa W. Whang
Dennis C. Huie
Stephanie A. Sahakian
Kristin M. Engstom
Jeffrey S. Kravitz

For full biographical listings, see the Martindale-Hubbell Law Directory

SCHUERING ZIMMERMAN & SCULLY, LLP (AV)

400 University Avenue, 95825
Telephone: 916-567-0400
Fax: 916-568-0400

MEMBERS OF FIRM

Steven T. Scully (1948-1994)
Leo H. Schuering, Jr.
Robert H. Zimmerman
Thomas J. Doyle

Lawrence S. Giardina
Anthony D. Lauria
Keith D. Chidlaw
John J. Sillis

Regina A. Favors
Raymond R. Gates
Christian Koster
Scott A. Linn

Donna W. Low
Dominique A. Pollara
Theodore D. Poppinga
John P. Rhode

Douglas L. Smith

For full biographical listings, see the Martindale-Hubbell Law Directory

WILCOXEN, MONTGOMERY & HARBISON (AV)

A Partnership including a Professional Corporation
2114 K Street, 95816
Telephone: 916-442-2777

Daniel E. Wilcoxen (Inc.)   James R. Montgomery
Joseph F. Harbison, III

Patrick L. Hinrichsen
David E. Smith

Joanne M. Merry
Cindy L. Robbins

Reference: First Interstate Bank.

For full biographical listings, see the Martindale-Hubbell Law Directory

SAN DIEGO,* San Diego Co.

GEORGE P. ANDREOS A PROFESSIONAL LAW CORPORATION (AV)

401 West "A" Street Suite 1400, 92101
Telephone: 619-233-1077
Fax: 619-236-1518

George P. Andreos

For full biographical listings, see the Martindale-Hubbell Law Directory

BELSKY & ASSOCIATES (AV)

610 West Ash Street, Suite 700, 92101
Telephone: 619-232-8300
Fax: 619-338-0066

Daniel S. Belsky

Gabriel M. Benrubi
Lisa L. Hillan
Vincent J. Iuliano

Cynthia Brack McGrew
Timothy J. Tatro
Peter A. Zamoyski

References: Centre For Health Care Medical Associates; The Doctor's Company; Grossmont Bank; Graybill Medical Group, Inc.; Kaiser Foundation HealthPlan, Inc.; Norcal Mutual Insurance Co.; Sharp Mission Park Medical Group; Sharp Rees-Stealy Medical Group; Southern California Physician Insurance Exchange; Unifirst.

For full biographical listings, see the Martindale-Hubbell Law Directory

BOUDREAU & TRENTACOSTA, A PROFESSIONAL LAW CORPORATION (AV)

401 West "A" Street, Suite 1850, 92101-9773
Telephone: 619-238-1553
Fax: 619-238-8181
Email: AEGISLAW@AOL.COM

Steven M. Boudreau   Robert J. Trentacosta

Jon R. Williams

For full biographical listings, see the Martindale-Hubbell Law Directory

LAW OFFICES OF ROBERT S. KILBORNE IV (AV)

First National Bank Building, 401 West "A' Street, Suite 1850, 92101
Telephone: 619-237-1047
Fax: 619-237-1096

ASSOCIATE
David Arbogast
OF COUNSEL
Russell B. Wagner

For full biographical listings, see the Martindale-Hubbell Law Directory

NEIL, DYMOTT, PERKINS, BROWN & FRANK, A PROFESSIONAL CORPORATION (AV)

1010 Second Avenue, Suite 2500, 92101-4959
Telephone: 619-238-1712
Fax: 619-238-1562

Michael I. Neil
David G. Brown

Robert W. Frank
Robert W. Harrison

Sheila S. Trexler

Reference: Scripps Bank.

For full biographical listings, see the Martindale-Hubbell Law Directory

SAN FRANCISCO,* San Francisco Co.

BAILEY & KORNBLUM (AV)

1388 Sutter Street, Suite 820, 94109
Telephone: 415-440-7800
Fax: 415-440-7898

Don E. Bailey

For full biographical listings, see the Martindale-Hubbell Law Directory

BOKELMAN & BENJAMIN, A PROFESSIONAL LAW CORPORATION (AV)

Two Embarcadero Center Suite 1050, 94111-3823
Telephone: 415-398-3660
Facsimile: 415-788-0161

Robert U. Bokelman   Anglia Benjamin

For full biographical listings, see the Martindale-Hubbell Law Directory

JOHN GARDENAL A PROFESSIONAL CORPORATION (AV)

Suite 800 Cathedral Hill Office Building, 1255 Post Street, 94109
Telephone: 415-771-2700
FAX: 415-771-2072

John Gardenal

For full biographical listings, see the Martindale-Hubbell Law Directory

San Francisco—Continued

McGLYNN, McLORG & RITCHIE (AV)

Bayside Plaza, 177 Steuart Street, Suite 200, 94105
Telephone: 415-543-9000
Fax: 415-543-8300
Sacramento, California Office: 980 Ninth Street, 19th Floor, 95814.
Telephone: 916-446-6979.
Facsimile: 916-444-0826.

MEMBERS OF FIRM

John P. McGlynn	Daniel J. Meagher, Jr.
Vincent B. McLorg	Dane T. Jones
James R. Ritchie	Robyn Schanzenbach
Susan L. Penney	Wallace M. Tice

Karen E. Kirby

ASSOCIATES

Michele A. Perussina	Andrew A. Vandeveld
Michael C. Scanlon, Jr.	Cynthia L. Leahy
Allison K. West	Sandra A. Milligan

For full biographical listings, see the Martindale-Hubbell Law Directory

MOLLIGAN, COX & MOYER, A PROFESSIONAL CORPORATION (AV)

703 Market Street, Suite 1800, 94103
Telephone: 415-543-9464
Fax: 415-777-1828
Email: mocoxmoy@aol.com

Ingemar E. Hoberg (1903-1971)	Peter N. Molligan
John H. Finger (1913-1991)	Stephen T. Cox
Phillip E. Brown (Retired)	David W. Moyer

John C. Hentschel

OF COUNSEL

Kenneth W. Rosenthal	Barbara A. Zuras

For full biographical listings, see the Martindale-Hubbell Law Directory

MURPHY, PEARSON, BRADLEY & FEENEY, A PROFESSIONAL CORPORATION (AV)

88 Kearny Street, 11th Floor, 94108
Telephone: 415-788-1900
Telecopier: 415-393-8087
Sacramento, California Office: Suite 200, 3600 American River Drive, 95864.
Telephone: 916-483-6074.
Telecopier: 916-483-6088.

Arthur V. Pearson	Timothy J. Halloran

For Complete List of Firm Personnel, See General Section

For full biographical listings, see the Martindale-Hubbell Law Directory

O'CONNOR, COHN, DILLON & BARR, A LAW CORPORATION (AV)

The Folger Coffee Building, 101 Howard Street, Fifth Floor, 94105-1619
Telephone: 415-281-8888
Fax: 415-281-8890
Email: ocdb@slip.net

Joseph T. O'Connor (Deceased, 1959)	Janet L. Grove
	Mark Oium
Harold H. Cohn (1910-1992)	Lisa T. Ungerer
James L. Dillon	Joel C. Lamp
Duncan Barr	Michael J. FitzSimons

Dexter B. Louie

Thomas G. Manning	Karen K. Smith
Susan Reifel Goins	Daniel J. Herp
Deborah L. Panter	James A. Beltzer
Marirose Piciucco	(Not admitted in CA)
Keith Reyen	M. Elizabeth Bootle

For full biographical listings, see the Martindale-Hubbell Law Directory

TEHIN + PARTNERS, A PROFESSIONAL CORPORATION (AV)

Bank of America Center, 555 California Street, 33rd Floor, 94104-1609
Telephone: 415-951-8800
Fax: 415-951-8808

Nikolai Tehin (Professional Corporation)	Reilly Atkinson, IV
	Michael E. Brown
Pamela J. Stevens	Marcia A. Pollioni

For full biographical listings, see the Martindale-Hubbell Law Directory

WALKUP, MELODIA, KELLY & ECHEVERRIA, A PROFESSIONAL CORPORATION (AV)

30th Floor, 650 California Street, 94108
Telephone: 415-981-7210
Fax: 415-391-6965

Paul V. Melodia	Michael A. Kelly
Daniel J. Kelly	Kevin L. Domecus
John Echeverria	Jeffrey P. Holl
Ronald H. Wecht	Daniel Dell'Osso

Richard H. Schoenberger

Cynthia F. Newton	Michael J. Recupero
Erik Brunkal	Kenneth H. Facter

OF COUNSEL

John D. Link	Wesley Sokolosky

Reference: Bank of California, San Francisco Main Office, 400 California Street, San Francisco, Calif. 94104.

For full biographical listings, see the Martindale-Hubbell Law Directory

---

SAN JOSE, * Santa Clara Co.

THE BOCCARDO LAW FIRM (AV)

Eleventh Floor, 111 West St. John Street, 95115-0001
Telephone: 408-298-5678
Fax: 408-298-7503

MEMBERS OF FIRM

James F. Boccardo	John C. Stein
John W. McDonald	Richard L. Bowers
Brian N. Lawther	Russell L. Moore, Jr.

ASSOCIATES

Stephen Foster	Victor F. Stefan
David P. Moyles	Robert W. Thayer
Byron C. Foster	Richard Gregg

For full biographical listings, see the Martindale-Hubbell Law Directory

JAN CHAMPION (AV)

Ten Almaden Boulevard, Tenth Floor, 95113-2233
Telephone: 408-286-5550
Fax: 408-270-6777

For full biographical listings, see the Martindale-Hubbell Law Directory

COLLINS & SCHLOTHAUER (AV)

An Association of Attorneys including a Professional Corporation
60 South Market Street, Suite 1100, 95113-2369
Telephone: 408-298-5161
Fax: 408-297-5766
Affiliated Los Angeles, California Office: Schlothauer, Collins & Macaluso, 11661 San Vicente Boulevard, Suite 303.
Telephone: 310-820-8606.
Fax: 310-820-7057.

Mark Scott Collins (Inc.)	Linda L. Duiven
David N. Poll	Jovita Prestoza

OF COUNSEL

Thomas L. Schlothauer	Todd E. Macaluso

Representative Clients: Unigard Insurance; Farmers Insurance Co.; Fire Insurance Exchange; National American Insurance Co.; ABAG (Association of Bay Area Governmental Entities).

For full biographical listings, see the Martindale-Hubbell Law Directory

HINSHAW, WINKLER, DRAA, MARSH & STILL (AV)

152 North Third Street, Suite 300, P.O. Box 15030, 95115-0030
Telephone: 408-293-5959
Fax: 408-280-0966
Email: hinshaw-law.com

MEMBERS OF FIRM

Edward A. Hinshaw	Gerhard O. Winkler
Tyler G. Draa	Barry C. Marsh

Thomas E. Still

ASSOCIATES

Lynne Thaxter Brown	Jennifer H. Still
Bradford J. Hinshaw	Megan A. Smith

For full biographical listings, see the Martindale-Hubbell Law Directory

SAUCEDO & CORSIGLIA, A LAW CORPORATION (AV)

50 West San Fernando Street, Suite 425, 95113
Telephone: 408-289-1417
Fax: 408-289-8127

Norman W. Saucedo	Bradley M. Corsiglia

For full biographical listings, see the Martindale-Hubbell Law Directory

San Jose—Continued

TYNDALL & CAHNERS (AV)

An Association of Attorneys including a Professional Corporation
96 North Third Street, Suite 580, 95112
Telephone: 408-297-3700
Fax: 408-297-3721

John G. Tyndall III (P.C.)   John D. Cahners

Michael Francis Brown

For full biographical listings, see the Martindale-Hubbell Law Directory

SAN RAFAEL,* Marin Co.

RAGGHIANTI • FREITAS • MONTOBBIO • WALLACE LLP (AV)

874 Fourth Street, Suite D, 94901
Telephone: 415-453-9433
Fax: 415-453-8269

Gary T. Ragghianti   J. Randolph Wallace
David P. Freitas   Patrick M. Macias
J. Mark Montobbio   Robert F. Epstein
            John Ralph Thomas

For full biographical listings, see the Martindale-Hubbell Law Directory

SANTA ANA,* Orange Co.

BEAM, BROBECK & WEST (AV)

600 West Santa Ana Boulevard, Suite 1000, 92701
Telephone: 714-558-3944
Fax: 714-568-0129

MEMBERS OF FIRM

Byron J. Beam   Kirk H. Nakamura
David J. Brobeck, Jr.   Robert H. McMillan
John E. West   Daniel R. Sullivan

ASSOCIATES

Betsey J. Jeffery   Donald S. Zalewski
Charles W. Matheis, Jr.   Geralyn L. Skapik
Robert C. Hastie   David R. Rosenberg
Gregory L. Rippetoe   Louise M. Douville
Jennifer J. Miller   Kermit D. Marsh

Representative Clients: Aetna Insurance Co.; American General Life Insurance Co.; American Hospital Supply; Carl Warren & Co.; Casualty Insurance Co.; City of Anaheim; City of Fullerton; City of Newport Beach; Empire Insurance Cos.; Physicians Interindemnity.

For full biographical listings, see the Martindale-Hubbell Law Directory

HORTON BARBARO & REILLY (AV)

A Partnership including Professional Corporations
Second Floor, 200 North Main Street, 92701
Telephone: 714-835-2122
Fax: 714-973-4892
Email: HBR@Hortonetal.com *URL:* http://www.Hortonetal.com
MEMBERS OF FIRM

Jay Cordell Horton (A   Geoffrey S. Gray
  Professional Corporation)   John R. Hanna
Frank P. Barbaro (A   William O. Humphreys
  Professional Corporation)   Karen L. Karavatos
Ned P. Reilly (A Professional John E. O'Brien, Jr.
  Corporation)

ASSOCIATES

Malena R. LeClair   Timothy V. Kassouni
Robert J. Younger   Richard E. Donahoo

For full biographical listings, see the Martindale-Hubbell Law Directory

MARTIN, WILSON, ERICKSON & MACDOWELL, A PROFESSIONAL CORPORATION (AV)

6 Hutton Centre, Suite 500, 92707
Telephone: 714-972-1200
Facsimile: 714-972-1283

Scott A. Martin   Mary Fingal Erickson
Thomas L. Wilson   John R. MacDowell

Douglas M. Carasso   Wendy A. Weber
            Kevin F. Cahill

For full biographical listings, see the Martindale-Hubbell Law Directory

MCNEIL AND SUSSON, A PROFESSIONAL CORPORATION (AV)

2100 North Broadway, Suite 103, 92706-2624
Telephone: 714-835-1922
Facsimile: 714-835-2720

(See Next Column)

Joseph D. McNeil   Dana E. Susson

Kathryn Arnold   Edward A. Stumpp
            James R. Parrett

For full biographical listings, see the Martindale-Hubbell Law Directory

SANTA MONICA, Los Angeles Co.

LAW OFFICES OF DAVID J. WEISS (AV)

120 Broadway, Suite 301, P.O. Box 2102, 90407-2102
Telephone: 310-319-5470
Telecopier: 310-394-6223

ASSOCIATES

David M. Hillings   Marilyn R. Victor
            Joel D. Schwartz

For full biographical listings, see the Martindale-Hubbell Law Directory

SANTA ROSA,* Sonoma Co.

BELDEN, ABBEY, WEITZENBERG & KELLY, A PROFESSIONAL CORPORATION (AV)

1105 North Dutton Avenue, P.O. Box 1566, 95402
Telephone: 707-542-5050
Telecopier: 707-542-2589

W. Barton Weitzenberg   Wayne R. Wolski

Representative Clients: Exchange Bank of Santa Rosa; Westamerica Bank; North Bay Title Co.; Northwestern Title Security Co.; Geyser Peak Winery; Santa Rosa City School District; Sonoma National Bank; Arrowood Vineyards & Winery; Arthur & DeVincenzi Concrete; Friedman Bros. Hardware, Inc.

For Complete List of Firm Personnel, See General Section

For full biographical listings, see the Martindale-Hubbell Law Directory

TORRANCE, Los Angeles Co.

AGNEW & BRUSAVICH (AV)

20355 Hawthorne Boulevard, 90503
Telephone: 310-793-1400
Facsimile: 310-793-1499
Email: agnewbru@ix.netcom.com

Gerald E. Agnew, Jr.   Bruce M. Brusavich
            ASSOCIATES
Susan E. Hargrove   Christopher A. Kall
            Mark J. Peacock

For full biographical listings, see the Martindale-Hubbell Law Directory

TUSTIN, Orange Co.

MADORY, ZELL AND PLEISS, A PROFESSIONAL CORPORATION (AV)

The Centre Building, Meredith Financial Centre, 17822 East 17th Street, Suite 205, 92780-2183
Telephone: 714-832-3772
Telecopier: 714-832-7163
Mailing Address: P.O. Box 11120, Santa Ana, California, 92711-1120

George L. Moore (1926-1993)   Stephen H. Zell
Robert J. Graves (1921-1983) Larry T. Pleiss
Richard E. Madory   Mark G. McGrath
            Stephen J. Martino, R.N.

Patricia N. Scidmore, R.N.   Kathryn A. Madlock
            Brent S. Clemmer

Representative Client: Farmers Insurance Group of Companies.
Reference: Union Bank, Orange County Regional Office.

For full biographical listings, see the Martindale-Hubbell Law Directory

VENTURA,* Ventura Co.

LAW OFFICES OF FREDERICK H. BYSSHE, JR. (AV)

10 South California Street, 93001
Telephone: 805-648-3224
Fax: 805-653-0267

Terence Geoghegan

For full biographical listings, see the Martindale-Hubbell Law Directory

ENGLE & BRIDE (AV)

353 San Jon Road, 93001
Telephone: 805-643-2200
Fax: 805-643-3062

MEMBERS OF FIRM

Benjamin J. Engle   Robert F. Bride

(See Next Column)

ENGLE & BRIDE—*Continued*

ASSOCIATE
Daniel J. Carobine

For Complete List of Firm Personnel, See General Section

For full biographical listings, see the Martindale-Hubbell Law Directory

---

WALNUT CREEK, Contra Costa Co.

ANDERSON, GALLOWAY & LUCCHESE, A PROFESSIONAL CORPORATION (AV)

1676 North California Boulevard, Suite 500, 94596-4183
Telephone: 510-943-6383
Facsimile: 510-943-7542

Robert L. Anderson	Stephen J. Brooks
George Patrick Galloway	Joseph S. Picchi
David R. Lucchese	Coleen L. Welch
Martin J. Everson	Deborah C. Moritz-Farr
Thomas J. Donnelly	Marc G. Cowden
Ralph J. Smith	Erin Ruddy Sabey
James M. Nelson	Lea K. McMahan
Scott E. Murray	Michael E. Brewer
David A. Depolo	Sonja M. Dahl
Karen A. Sparks	Thomas J. Tarkoff

For full biographical listings, see the Martindale-Hubbell Law Directory

COLORADO

ASPEN,* Pitkin Co.

FREEMAN & JENNER, P.C. (AVⓣ)

215 South Monarch Street, Suite 202, 81611
Telephone: 970-925-3400
FAX: 970-925-4043
Bethesda, Maryland Office: 3 Bethesda Metro Center, Suite 1410.
Telephone: 301-907-7747.
FAX: 301-907-9877.
Washington, D.C. Office: 1000 16th Street, N.W., Suite 300.
Telephone: 301-907-7747.

Martin H. Freeman

BOULDER,* Boulder Co.

COOK & LEE, P.C. (AV)

5390 Manhattan Circle, 2nd Floor, 80303
Telephone: 303-543-1000
Fax: 303-543-8582

Stephen H. Cook	Larry D. Lee

Deborah R. Kirschman

For full biographical listings, see the Martindale-Hubbell Law Directory

WILLIAMS & TRINE, P.C. (AV)

1435 Arapahoe Avenue, 80302-6390
Telephone: 303-442-0173
Fax: 303-443-7677

William A. Trine	J. Conard Metcalf
Joel H. Greenstein (1933-1984)	Mari C. Bush

Michael A. Patrick
OF COUNSEL
Charles E. Williams

Reference: Norwest Bank of Boulder.

For full biographical listings, see the Martindale-Hubbell Law Directory

---

DENVER,* Denver Co.

CHALAT • JUSTINO, P.C. (AV)

1900 Grant Street, Suite 1050, 80203
Telephone: 303-861-1042
Toll Free in Colorado: 800-221-5526
Facsimile: 303-861-0506
Email: Jchalat@aol.com *URL:* http://www.chalat-justino.com

James H. Chalat	Stephen A. Justino
Linda J. Chalat	

Elliott L. Schoen

For full biographical listings, see the Martindale-Hubbell Law Directory

KENNEDY & CHRISTOPHER, P.C. (AV)

1660 Wynkoop Street, Suite 900, 80202
Telephone: 303-825-2700
Fax: 303-825-0434

Frank R. Kennedy	Lisa B. Heintz
Daniel R. Christopher	Ronald H. Nemirow
Kim B. Childs	Barbara H. Glogiewicz
Elizabeth A. Starrs	Dawn E. Mitzner
Richard B. Caschette	John R. Mann
Mark A. Fogg	Daniel R. McCune
Michael T. Mihm	Dean A. McConnell
Charles R. Ledbetter	Edward D. Bronfin

OF COUNSEL
Paul E. Scott

Matthew S. Feigenbaum	Christopher K. Miller
Catherine O'Brien-Crum	Carolyn Sprinthall Knaut
Steven J. Picardi	David B. Gelman
Theresa A. Dettling	Gary W. Flanagan

Representative Clients: AETNA Casualty and Surety Co.; American Medical International; Blue Cross/Blue Shield of Colorado; COPIC; The Doctors Co.; Hartford Insurance Co.; Home Insurance Co.; St. Paul Fire and Marine Insurance Co.; PRMS, Colorado Insurance Guaranty Association.

For full biographical listings, see the Martindale-Hubbell Law Directory

LEVENTHAL AND BOGUE, P.C. (AV)

950 South Cherry Street, Suite 600, 80222
Telephone: 303-759-9945
Fax: 303-759-9692
Email: LEVENBOG@AOL.COM

Jim Leventhal	Natalie Brown
Jeffrey A. Bogue	Victoria J. Koury
Bruce J. Kaye	Kelly P. Roberts

Grant Marylander

Reference: Southwest State Bank.

For full biographical listings, see the Martindale-Hubbell Law Directory

LONG & JAUDON, P.C. (AV)

The Bailey Mansion, 1600 Ogden Street, 80218-1414
Telephone: 303-832-1122
FAX: 303-832-1348

Joseph C. Jaudon, Jr.	Walter N. Houghtaling
Gary B. Blum	Carla M. LaRosa
Michael T. McConnell	Thomas C. Kearns, Jr.
Alan D. Avery	David H. Yun

Representative Clients: St. Joseph Hospital; Aetna Life & Casualty Company; The Doctors Company; Home Insurance Company; Baxter Healthcare.

For Complete List of Firm Personnel, See General Section

For full biographical listings, see the Martindale-Hubbell Law Directory

MILLER, McCARREN & HELMS, P.C. (AV)

410 Seventeenth Street, Suite 1200, 80202
Telephone: 303-436-1163
Telecopier: 303-436-1143

William J. McCarren	J. Kent Miller
	Thomas J. Helms

For full biographical listings, see the Martindale-Hubbell Law Directory

MYERS, BRADLEY AND DEVITT, P.C. (AV)

Suite 420, 4704 Harlan Street, 80212
Telephone: 303-433-8527
Fax: 303-433-8219

Frederick J. Myers	Jerald J. Devitt
Jon T. Bradley	Randall C. Arp

OF COUNSEL
Kent E. Hanson

Reference: Bank One Lakeside Banking Center.

For full biographical listings, see the Martindale-Hubbell Law Directory

RICHMAN & HENSEN, P.C. (AV)

Mellon Financial Center, Suite 1717, 1775 Sherman Street, 80203
Telephone: 303-830-1717
Facsimile: 303-830-1746

Alan E. Richman	Stephen J. Hensen

Steven Robert Kabler

For full biographical listings, see the Martindale-Hubbell Law Directory

Denver—Continued

TREECE, ALFREY, MUSAT & BOSWORTH, P.C. (AV)

Denver Place, 999 18th Street, Suite 1600, 80202
Telephone: 303-292-2700
Facsimile: 303-295-0414
Email: 73507.2446@compuserve.com

Thomas N. Alfrey	Timothy J. Judson
June Baker Laird	Victor M. Morales

For full biographical listings, see the Martindale-Hubbell Law Directory

---

ENGLEWOOD, Arapahoe Co.

SALMON, GODSMAN & NICHOLSON, PROFESSIONAL CORPORATION (AV)

Salmon Law Building, (I-25 at East Belleview) 7450 East Progress
Place, 80111
Telephone: 303-771-9900
Toll Free in Colorado: 1-800-547-9055
Fax: 303-773-6843
Breckenridge, Colorado Office: Briar Rose House, 213 Briar Rose Lane.
Telephone: 1-800-547-9055

John G. Salmon	William P. Godsman
	P. Randolph Nicholson
Francine R. Salazar	Penelope Clor

OF COUNSEL
Joseph M. Epstein

For full biographical listings, see the Martindale-Hubbell Law Directory

---

THOMAS J. TOMAZIN, P.C. (AV)

Suite 200, 5655 South Yosemite, 80111
Telephone: 303-771-1900
FAX: 303-793-0923

Thomas J. Tomazin

Representative Clients: Sheridan, Inc. (Leasing Division); Sovran Leasing; The Leasing Group; Contract Design Services, Inc.; American Natural Gas Corp.; Sonex Enterprises, Inc.; Am West Energy, Inc.; Mountain States Asphalt Paving, Inc.
Reference: Key Bank.

For full biographical listings, see the Martindale-Hubbell Law Directory

---

CONNECTICUT

BRIDGEPORT,* Fairfield Co.

BAI, POLLOCK AND COYNE, P.C. (AV)

Park City Plaza, 10 Middle Street, P.O. Box 1978, 06604
Telephone: 203-366-7991
Fax: 203-366-4723
Email: bpc@snet.net

Arnold J. Bai (1931-1992)	Garie J. Mulcahey
Paul E. Pollock	Raymond J. Plouffe, Jr.
James E. Coyne	Philip F. von Kuhn
Jeffrey A. Blueweiss	Madonna A. Sacco
	Michael S. Lynch
David J. Robertson	Colleen D. Fries
Edward P. Brady III	Neal P. Rogan
Andrew S. Turret	Jacquelyn Conlon
Gaileen A. Kaufman	Janine M. Savarese
Kevin S. Coyne	Louis A. Annecchino
	Kristin Beth Comstock

For full biographical listings, see the Martindale-Hubbell Law Directory

KOSKOFF, KOSKOFF & BIEDER, P.C. (AV)

350 Fairfield Avenue, 06604
Telephone: 203-336-4421
Fax: 203-368-3244
Stamford, Connecticut Office: 1172 Bedford Street.
Telephone: 203-325-3686.
Danbury, Connecticut Office: 1 Moss Avenue.
Telephone: 203-792-7100.

(See Next Column)

Theodore I. Koskoff (1913-1989)	Elizabeth Koskoff
Richard A. Fuchs (1945-1995)	Christopher D. Bernard
Michael P. Koskoff	Rosalind J. Koskoff
Richard A. Bieder	Karen E. Koskoff
Joel H. Lichtenstein	Carey B. Reilly
John D. Jessep	James D. Horwitz
(Resident at Danbury Office)	Vincent M. Musto
Angela C. Robinson	Gertrude A. Kiaunis
Michael A. Stratton	Joshua D. Koskoff
Lillian C. Gustilo	Susan B. Fink
Joel Thomas Faxon	

OF COUNSEL
Paul V. McNamara

For full biographical listings, see the Martindale-Hubbell Law Directory

---

WILLIAMS, COONEY & SHEEHY (AV)

One Lafayette Circle, 06604
Telephone: 203-331-0888
Telecopier: 203-331-0896

MEMBERS OF FIRM

Ronald D. Williams	Peter J. Dauk
Robert J. Cooney	Dion W. Moore
Edward Maum Sheehy	Ronald D. Williams, Jr.
Peter D. Clark	Francis A. Smith, Jr.
	(1951-1989)
Michael P. Bowler	Paul Sean Curtin
Michael Cuff Deakin	Suzannah Kim Nigro

Representative Clients: Aetna Life & Casualty Co.; Nationwide Insurance Co.; Connecticut Medical Insurance Co.; Zimmer Manufacturing Co.; The Travelers; Preferred Physicians Mutual; Podiatry Insurance Company of America; Medical Liability Mutual Insurance Company.

For full biographical listings, see the Martindale-Hubbell Law Directory

---

CHESHIRE, New Haven Co.

MOORE, O'BRIEN & JACQUES (AV)

700 West Johnson Avenue Suite 207, 06410
Telephone: 203-272-5881
Fax: 203-272-9273

MEMBERS OF FIRM

Garrett M. Moore	Stephen L. Jacques
Gregory E. O'Brien	Lisa Marie Ferraro

For full biographical listings, see the Martindale-Hubbell Law Directory

---

FAIRFIELD, Fairfield Co.

FRIEDMAN, MELLITZ & NEWMAN, P.C. (AV)

Successor to: Friedman & Friedman; Mellitz Krentzman & Newman
One Eliot Place, 06430
Telephone: 203-259-5300
Fax: 203-259-2996

Arthur D. Friedman	Joanne Patricia Sheehan
Noel R. Newman	Cheryl Ann Carolan
Steven A. Levy	Arthur Levy, Jr.

For full biographical listings, see the Martindale-Hubbell Law Directory

---

HARTFORD,* Hartford Co.

GORDON, MUIR AND FOLEY (AV)

Hartford Square North, Ten Columbus Boulevard, 06106-5123
Telephone: 860-525-5361
Telecopier: 860-525-4849

MEMBERS OF FIRM

William S. Gordon, Jr.	William J. Gallitto
(1946-1956)	Gerald R. Swirsky
George Muir (1939-1976)	Robert J. O'Brien
Edward J. Foley (1955-1983)	Philip J. O'Connor
Peter C. Schwartz	Kenneth G. Williams
John J. Reid	Chester J. Bukowski
John H. Goodrich, Jr.	Mary Ann Santacroce
R. Bradley Wolfe	J. Lawrence Price
Jon Stephen Berk	Mary Anne Alicia Charron
	James G. Kelly

ASSOCIATES

Kevin F. Morin	Andrew J. Hern
Claudia A. Baio	Eileen McCarthy Geel
Patrick T. Treacy	Christopher L. Slack
	Renee W. Dwyer

(See Next Column)

GORDON, MUIR AND FOLEY—*Continued*

OF COUNSEL

Stephen M. Riley

Reference: Fleet Bank.

For full biographical listings, see the Martindale-Hubbell Law Directory

JACKSON, O'KEEFE AND PHELAN (AV)

36 Russ Street, 06106-1571
Telephone: 860-278-4040
Fax: 860-527-2500
West Hartford, Connecticut Office: 62 LaSalle Road.
Telephone: 860-521-7500.
Fax: 860-561-5399.
Bethlehem, Connecticut Office: 423 Munger Lane. Telephone/
Fax: 203-266-5255.

MEMBERS OF FIRM

Jay W. Jackson	Michael E. Riley
Andrew J. O'Keefe	Peter K. O'Keefe
Denise Martino Phelan	Philip R. Dunn, Jr.
Matthew J. O'Keefe	Kathryn M. Cunningham
Joseph M. Busher, Jr.	

Representative Clients: Travelers Aetna Property Casualty Co.; ITT Hartford; Liberty Mutual Insurance Co.; Connecticut Medical Insurance Co.

For full biographical listings, see the Martindale-Hubbell Law Directory

KENNY, BRIMMER, MELLEY & MAHONEY (AV)

5 Grand Street, 06106
Telephone: 860-527-4226
FAX: 860-527-0214

Joseph P. Kenny (1920-1993)

MEMBERS OF FIRM

Leslie R. Brimmer	William J. Melley, III
Richard C. Mahoney	

ASSOCIATES

Anita M. Varunes	Beverly Johns
Dennis F. McCarthy	Edward J. Fitzgerald

For full biographical listings, see the Martindale-Hubbell Law Directory

O'BRIEN, TANSKI, TANZER & YOUNG (AV)

CityPlace II, 06103
Telephone: 860-525-2700
Telefax: 860-247-7861

MEMBERS OF FIRM

Donald W. O'Brien	Roland F. Young, III
James M. Tanski	Robert E. Kiley
Lois B. Tanzer	Thomas O. Anderson
Nancy Phillips Maxwell	

OF COUNSEL

Hilary Fisher Nelson	Donna R. Zito

ASSOCIATES

Caroline Schnog	P. Jo Anne Burgh
Robert D. Silva	Jennifer L. Cox
Albert G. Danker, Jr.	Tanya Feliciano

References: Shawmut National Bank; New England Bank.

For full biographical listings, see the Martindale-Hubbell Law Directory

NEW HAVEN,* New Haven Co.

JACOBS & JACOBS (AV)

700 State Street, 3rd Floor, 06511
Telephone: 203-777-2300
Fax: 203-787-5628

MEMBERS OF FIRM

Israel J. Jacobs (1918-1963)	Bruce D. Jacobs
Stanley A. Jacobs	Carol Wolven
Irene Prosky Jacobs	

Reference: Center Bank/First Union.

For full biographical listings, see the Martindale-Hubbell Law Directory

LYNCH, TRAUB, KEEFE AND ERRANTE, A PROFESSIONAL CORPORATION (AV)

52 Trumbull Street, P.O. Box 1612, 06506
Telephone: 203-787-0275
Fax: 203-782-0278
Email: ltke@snet.com *URL:* http://www.ltke.com

(See Next Column)

Stephen I. Traub	Donn A. Swift
Hugh F. Keefe	Charles E. Tiernan, III
Steven J. Errante	Robert W. Lynch
John J. Keefe, Jr.	Richard W. Lynch
John M. Walsh, Jr.	

Suzanne L. McAlpine	Lee Kennedy Tiernan
Christopher M. Licari	William F. Clark
Eric P. Smith	James A. Mongillo

OF COUNSEL

William C. Lynch

Local Counsel for: Transport Insurance Co., Dallas, Texas; American Trucking Associations; Roadway Express, Inc., Akron, Ohio; A.R.A. Philadelphia, Penn.; Consolidated Freightways, Menlo Park, California; Ogden Corp. *Labor Counsel:* Coca-Cola, U.S.A., Atlanta, Georgia (Private Truck Operation); The Dow Chemical Co.; Cincinnati Milacron.

For full biographical listings, see the Martindale-Hubbell Law Directory

NEW LONDON, New London Co.

THE REARDON LAW FIRM, P.C. (AV)

160 Hempstead Street, Drawer 1430, 06320
Telephone: 860-442-0444
Telecopier: 860-444-6445

Robert I. Reardon, Jr.	Angelo A. Ziotas

Wayne W. Lambert, Jr.	Scott D. Camassar

LEGAL SUPPORT PERSONNEL

Bette B. Beam	Jillene E. Bennett (Paralegal)
(Legal Administrator)	Kimberly A. McGinnis
Kelly G. MacDonald (Paralegal)	(Paralegal)
Sharon M. Burdsall (Paralegal)	

For full biographical listings, see the Martindale-Hubbell Law Directory

STAMFORD, Fairfield Co.

ROSENBLUM & FILAN (AV ⊤)

One Landmark Square, 06901
Telephone: 203-358-9200
Fax: 203-969-6140
Email: JBR@counsel.com
White Plains, New York Office: 50 Main Street. 10606.
Telephone: 914-686-6100.
Fax: 914-686-6140.
New York, New York Office: 400 Madison Avenue. 10017.
Telephone: 212-888-8001.
Fax: 212-888-3331.

MEMBERS OF FIRM

Patrick J. Filan	James B. Rosenblum

James S. Newfield	Theodore J. Greene
Michelle L. Youtz	Christina M. Casagrande
Brian M. Rosen	JoAnn Provetto

For full biographical listings, see the Martindale-Hubbell Law Directory

SILVER, GOLUB & TEITELL (AV)

184 Atlantic Street, P.O. Box 389, 06904
Telephone: 203-325-4491
Fax: 203-325-3769

MEMBERS OF FIRM

Richard A. Silver	Patricia M. Haugh (1942-1988)
David S. Golub	Elaine T. Silver
Ernest F. Teitell	John D. Josel

Mario DiNatale	Jonathan L. Mannina
Jonathan M. Levine	Jennifer Cohen Goldstein
Marilyn J. Ramos	J. Michael Lewis

For full biographical listings, see the Martindale-Hubbell Law Directory

WESTPORT, Fairfield Co.

LAW OFFICES OF PAUL J. PACIFICO (AV)

25 Ford Road, Suite 2, 06880
Telephone: 203-221-8066
Fax: 203-222-4833

For full biographical listings, see the Martindale-Hubbell Law Directory

DELAWARE

WILMINGTON, New Castle Co.

WARREN B. BURT & ASSOCIATES (AV)

1700 Mellon Bank Center, 919 Market Street, 19801-3023
Telephone: 302-429-9430
Fax: 302-429-9427

ASSOCIATES
Richard D. Abrams   Michael F. Duggan

For full biographical listings, see the Martindale-Hubbell Law Directory

DALEY, ERISMAN & VAN OGTROP (AV)

1224 King Street, 19801
Telephone: 302-658-4000
Fax: 302-652-8975
Email: jerisman@devolaw.com *URL:* http://www.devolaw.com
Newark, Delaware Office: 206 East Delaware Avenue.
Telephone: 302-368-0133.
FAX: 302-368-4587.

MEMBERS OF FIRM
Robert E. Daley   James A. Erisman
Piet H. van Ogtrop

References: Wilmington Trust Co.; Beneficial National Bank.

For full biographical listings, see the Martindale-Hubbell Law Directory

SMITH, KATZENSTEIN & FURLOW (AV)

The Corporate Plaza, 800 Delaware Avenue, P.O. Box 410, 19899
Telephone: 302-652-8400
Fax: 302-652-8405

MEMBERS OF FIRM
Robert J. Katzenstein   Susan L. Parker

Kathleen M. Miller

For Complete List of Firm Personnel, See General Section

For full biographical listings, see the Martindale-Hubbell Law Directory

TRZUSKOWSKI, KIPP, KELLEHER & PEARCE, P.A. (AV)

1020 North Bancroft Parkway, P.O. Box 429, 19899-0429
Telephone: 302-571-1782
Fax: 302-571-1638

Francis J. Trzuskowski   Robert K. Pearce
James F. Kipp   Edward F. Kafader
Daniel F. Kelleher   Francis J. Schanne

For full biographical listings, see the Martindale-Hubbell Law Directory

DISTRICT OF COLUMBIA

WASHINGTON, D.C. Co.

THE ABELSON LAW FIRM (AV)

Suite 300, 1000 Sixteenth Street, N.W., 20036
Telephone: 202-331-0600
Fax: 202-429-9088

Michael A. Abelson

For full biographical listings, see the Martindale-Hubbell Law Directory

THE FALK LAW FIRM (AV)

A Professional Limited Company
Suite 260 One Westin Center, 2445 M Street, N.W., 20037
Telephone: 202-833-8700
Telecopier: 202-872-1725
Email: FalkLaw@erols.com

James H. Falk, Sr.   John M. Falk
James H. Falk, Jr.   Robert K. Tompkins
OF COUNSEL
Pierre E. Murphy   Elizabeth C. Collins

For full biographical listings, see the Martindale-Hubbell Law Directory

KENNETH R. FEINBERG & ASSOCIATES (AV)

1120 20th Street, N.W. Suite 740 South, 20036
Telephone: 202-371-1110
Fax: 202-962-9290
New York, N.Y. Office: 780 3rd Avenue, Suite 2202.
Telephone: 212-527-9600.
Fax: 212-527-9611.

(See Next Column)

ASSOCIATES
Deborah E. Greenspan   Peter H. Woodin
Michael K. Rozen   (Not admitted in DC)
(Not admitted in DC)   M. Catherine Faint
OF COUNSEL
Jacqueline E. Zins

For full biographical listings, see the Martindale-Hubbell Law Directory

JACK H. OLENDER AND ASSOCIATES, P.C. (AV)

888 17th Street, N.W., 4th Floor, 20006
Telephone: 202-879-7777
Fax: 202-393-2245

Jack H. Olender

Harlow R. Case   Kim M. Keenan
Gary S. Freeman   Dan L. Gray, Jr.
Sandra H. Robinson   Marian K. Riedy
Narda M. Newby

For full biographical listings, see the Martindale-Hubbell Law Directory

PAULSON, NACE & NORWIND (AV)

1814 N Street, N.W., 20036
Telephone: 202-463-1999
Fax: 202-223-6824
Email: pnn@lawtort.com

MEMBERS OF FIRM
Richard S. Paulson (1928-1986)   Barry J. Nace
Edward L. Norwind
ASSOCIATES
Gloria A. Worch   James A. Ferguson
OF COUNSEL
Irving R. M. Panzer

For full biographical listings, see the Martindale-Hubbell Law Directory

SWARTZ & REED (AV)

1321 Connecticut Avenue, N.W., 20036
Telephone: 202-429-0429
Fax: 202-429-0109

MEMBERS OF FIRM
Dean E. Swartz   Barry S. Reed
ASSOCIATE
Elizabeth A. Karasik
OF COUNSEL
Allan W. Steinhorn

For full biographical listings, see the Martindale-Hubbell Law Directory

FLORIDA

BARTOW, Polk Co.

FROST, O'TOOLE & SAUNDERS, P.A. (AV)

395 South Central Avenue, P.O. Box 2188, 33830
Telephone: 941-533-0314; 800-533-0967
Telecopier: 941-533-8985

John W. Frost, II   Robert A. Carr
Neal L. O'Toole   Robert H. Van Hart
Thomas C. Saunders   John Marc Tamayo
Richard E. "Rick" Dantzler   Mark A. Sessums
Robert J. Aranda

Reference: Community National Bank, Bartow.

For full biographical listings, see the Martindale-Hubbell Law Directory

BOCA RATON, Palm Beach Co.

MICHAUD, BUSCHMANN, FOX, FERRARA & MITTELMARK, P.A. (AV)

33 Southeast 8th Street, 33432
Telephone: 561-392-0540
Fax: 561-392-0582
Email: Bocalaw@MBFFM.com

Scott H. Michaud   Brian S. Fox
Paul Buschmann   James T. Ferrara
Michael K. Mittelmark

Marc T. Millian

For full biographical listings, see the Martindale-Hubbell Law Directory

*BRADENTON,*** Manatee Co.

MULOCK, THOMPSON & LITTLE (AV)

A Partnership of Professional Associations
519 13th Street West, 34205
Telephone: 941-748-2104
Fax: 941-748-6588

Edwin T. Mulock (P.A.) W. Wade Thompson (P.A.)
Melton H. Little (P.A.)

Donald E. Grieco

Representative Client: Clerk of Circuit Court of Manatee County.
Approved Attorneys for: Attorneys' Title Insurance Fund.

For full biographical listings, see the Martindale-Hubbell Law Directory

---

CORAL GABLES, Dade Co.

GEORGE V. LANZA, P.A. (AV)

La Palma Building, 116 Alhambra Circle, 33134
Telephone: 305-448-4441
Fax: 305-445-9898

George V. Lanza

Reference: Consolidated Bank N.A.

For full biographical listings, see the Martindale-Hubbell Law Directory

---

PARENTI, FALK & WAAS, P.A. (AV)

113 Almeria Avenue, 33134
Telephone: 305-447-6500
Fax: 305-447-1777

Michael J. Parenti, III	Edward Hernandez
Glenn P. Falk	Armando Cortina
Norman M. Waas	Gail Leverett Parenti

Scott Solomon	Michael Patrick Bonner
	Michael A. Sastre

For full biographical listings, see the Martindale-Hubbell Law Directory

---

CRYSTAL RIVER, Citrus Co.

BEST & ANDERSON, P.A. (AV)

7655 West Gulf to Lake Highway, Suite 6, 34429
Telephone: 352-795-1107
Orlando, Florida Office: 20 North Orange Avenue, Suite 505.
Telephone: 407-425-2985.
Melbourne, Florida Office: Marina Towers, 709 South Harbor City
Boulevard, Suite 220, 32901.
Telephone: 407-727-9923.

David R. Best	Lawrence I. Hauser
George H. "Dutch" Anderson, III	

G. Clay Morris	Angela O'Neil
	Natt O. Reifler

For full biographical listings, see the Martindale-Hubbell Law Directory

---

DAYTONA BEACH, Volusia Co.

EUBANK, HASSELL & ASSOC., P.A. (AV)

Suite 301, 149 South Ridgewood Avenue, P.O. Box 2229, 32115-2229
Telephone: 904-238-1357
Telecopier: 904-258-7406

James O. Eubank, II	F. Bradley Hassell

M. Jennifer Moorhead	K. Judith Lane
Timothy A. Traster	Wiley S. Boston
Perette M. Lawrence	C. Richard Penalta

For full biographical listings, see the Martindale-Hubbell Law Directory

---

SMITH, SCHODER & BOUCK, P.A. (AV)

605 South Ridgewood Avenue, 32014
Telephone: 904-255-0505
FAX: 904-252-4794
Other Daytona Beach Office: 214 Loomis Avenue.
Telephone: 904-255-6711.

James W. Smith	Kim E. Bouck
C. Anthony Schoder, Jr.	Todd Michael Cranshaw
M. Kathleen Roddenberry	

For full biographical listings, see the Martindale-Hubbell Law Directory

---

*FORT LAUDERDALE,*** Broward Co.

CONRAD, SCHERER & JENNE (AV)

A Partnership of Professional Associations
Eighth Floor, 633 South Federal Highway, P.O. Box 14723, 33302
Telephone: 954-462-5500
Facsimile: 954-463-9244
Miami, Florida Office: International Place. 100 Southeast 2nd Street. Suite 2800. 33131.
Telephone: 305-856-9920.
Facsimile: 305-374-4408.

MEMBERS OF FIRM

William R. Scherer, Jr., (P.A.)	William V. Carcioppolo (P.A.)
Kenneth C. Jenne, II (P.A.)	James M. Eckhart (P.A.)
Gary S. Genovese (P.A.)	Lynn Futch Cooney (P.A.)

OF COUNSEL

Rex Conrad	Paul R. Larkin, Jr.

ASSOCIATES

Linda Rae Spaulding	Willie Earl Hall
Kimberly A. Kisslan	Derick J. Roulhac
Reid A. Cocalis	William R. Scherer, III
Albert L. Frevola, Jr.	Vanessa A. Reynolds

Local Counsel for: American Home Assurance Group; Caterpillar Tractor Co.; Division of Risk Management, State of Florida; Florida East Coast Railway; Fort Motor Co.; Liberty Mutual Insurance Co.; Ryder Truck Lines; Unigard Insurance Group.
Approved Attorneys for: Attorneys' Title Insurance Fund.
Reference: Barnett Bank of Fort Lauderdale.

For full biographical listings, see the Martindale-Hubbell Law Directory

---

COONEY, MATTSON, LANCE, BLACKBURN, RICHARDS & O'CONNOR, P.A. (AV)

301 East Las Olas Boulevard, P.O. Box 14546, 33302
Telephone: Telephone: 954-779-1900
WATS: 1-800-745-3864
Telecopier: 954-779-1910
Orlando, Florida Office: Nations Bank Tower, 111 N. Orange Avenue, Suite 1020.
Telephone: 407-843-2100.
Fax: 407-843-2061.

David F. Cooney	Walter C. Wyatt
Michael C. Mattson	Kieran F. O'Connor (Resident, Orlando, Florida Office)
Victor Lance (1956-1995)	
Ace J. Blackburn, Jr.	Pamela R. Kittrell
John H. Richards	Stephanie Arma Kraft
Dennis R. O'Connor (Resident, Orlando, Florida Office)	Andrea B. Chirls
	Michele Brigid McCaul
Bruce Michael Trybus	Daniel F. Tordella
Mary T. Szeluga	

For full biographical listings, see the Martindale-Hubbell Law Directory

---

HALICZER, PETTIS & WHITE, P.A. (AV)

101 Northeast Third Avenue, Sixth Floor, 33301
Telephone: 954-523-9922
Fax: 954-522-2512
Orlando, Florida Office: NationsBank Building. Suite 1275. 111 North Orange Avenue. 32801.
Telephone: 407-841-9866.
Fax: 407-841-9915.

James S. Haliczer	Kenneth E. White
Eugene K. Pettis	Lorna E. Brown-Burton

Amy B. Talisman	Margaret A. Benenati
Dean A. Robertson	Gina E. Caruso

For full biographical listings, see the Martindale-Hubbell Law Directory

---

McINTOSH, SAWRAN & CRAVEN, P.A. (AV)

Broward Financial Centre, Suite 1800, 500 East Broward Boulevard, P.O. Box 029008, 33302-9008
Telephone: 954-765-1001
Facsimile: 954-765-1005
Email: MCDEFENLAW@AOL.COM
West Palm Beach, Florida Office: Northridge Centre, 515 North Flagler Drive , Third Floor Pavillion, 33401.
Telephone: 561-802-4110.

Douglas M. McIntosh	Robert A. Craven
James C. Sawran	Carmen Y. Cartaya

Karina P. Gonzalez	Michael A. Petruccelli
	Jacqueline J. Porth

For full biographical listings, see the Martindale-Hubbell Law Directory

FORT MYERS,* Lee Co.

SMOOT ADAMS EDWARDS & GREEN, P.A. (AV)

One University Park Suite 600, 12800 University Drive, P.O. Box 60259, 33906-6259
Telephone: 941-489-1776
(800) 226-1777 (in Florida)
Fax: 941-489-2444
Email: 71600.2745@compuserve.com

J. Tom Smoot, Jr.	Bruce D. Green
Hal Adams	Steven I. Winer
Franklyn A. (Chip) Johnson	Mark R. Komray
(1947-1991)	Clayton W. Crevasse
Charles B. Edwards	M. Brian Cheffer

Robert S. Forman	C. Berk Edwards, Jr.
Kathleen W. McBride	Melville G. Brinson, III
Lowell Schoenfeld	Samuel J. Hagan, IV

For full biographical listings, see the Martindale-Hubbell Law Directory

JACKSONVILLE,* Duval Co.

GLENN K. ALLEN A PROFESSIONAL ASSOCIATION (AV)

The Plaza Building, 353 East Forsyth Street, 32202
Telephone: 904-355-7506
Facsimile: 904-353-8814

Glenn K. Allen

For full biographical listings, see the Martindale-Hubbell Law Directory

BROWN, TERRELL, HOGAN, ELLIS, McCLAMMA & YEGELWEL, P.A. (AV)

Suite 804 Blackstone Building, 233 East Bay Street, 32202
Telephone: 904-632-2424

Thomas R. Brown	T. Edward McClamma
James T. Terrell	Evan J. Yegelwel
Wayne Hogan	Thomas E. Duffy, Jr.
Timothy D. Ellis	Christopher G. Burns

Annette J. Ritter	Carroll Cayer
Anita Pryor	Michael S. Sharrit
	Alan M. Pickert

Reference: NCNB.

For full biographical listings, see the Martindale-Hubbell Law Directory

COKER, MYERS, SCHICKEL & SORENSON, P.A. (AV)

136 East Bay Street, P.O. Box 1860, 32201
Telephone: 904-356-6071
Fax: 904-353-2425

Howard C. Coker	R. Daniel Noey
M. Wayne Myers	Tonya Jo Wade
John J. Schickel	Ronald M. Owen
Charles A. Sorenson	John Moffitt Howell
Mark M. Green	Stephen M. Armstrong
Samuel H. Lanier	Corinne L. Heller
J. Thomas McKeel	Paul H. McLester
Wm. Earl Higginbotham	James H. Daniel

For full biographical listings, see the Martindale-Hubbell Law Directory

LILES, GAVIN & COSTANTINO (AV)

One Enterprise Center, Suite 1500, 225 Water Street, 32202
Telephone: 904-634-1100
Fax: 904-634-1234

Rutledge R. Liles	R. Kyle Gavin
	R. Scott Costantino

ASSOCIATE
Niels P. Murphy

For full biographical listings, see the Martindale-Hubbell Law Directory

PAJCIC & PAJCIC, P.A. (AV)

1900 Independent Square, 32202
Telephone: 904-358-8881
Fax: 904-354-1180

Gary Pajcic	Robert J. Link
Stephen J. Pajcic, III	Lee T. Griffin
Katherine Brown	Christine A. Clark
William S. Burns, Jr.	Thomas F. Slater

Reference: Barnett Bank of Jacksonville, N.A.

For full biographical listings, see the Martindale-Hubbell Law Directory

SMITH HULSEY & BUSEY (AV)

1800 First Union National Bank Tower, 225 Water Street, P.O. Box 53315, 32201-3315
Telephone: 904-359-7700
Facsimile: 904-359-7708; 353-9908

Lloyd Smith (1915-1987)
MEMBERS OF FIRM

Dennis L. Blackburn	E. Owen McCuller, Jr.
Stephen D. Busey	James H. Post
Douglas D. Chunn	Bryan L. Putnal
Earl E. Googe, Jr.	E. Lanny Russell
Jeanne E. Helton	Joel Settembrini, Jr.
Cynthia C. Jackson	Tim E. Sleeth
G. Preston Keyes	John R. Smith, Jr.
William E. Kuntz	James J. Taylor, Jr.
M. Richard Lewis, Jr.	Timothy W. Volpe
John F. MacLennan	Waddell A. Wallace, III
Raymond R. Magley	Harry M. Wilson, III

Michael M. Bajalia	R. Leanne McKnight
James A. Bolling, Jr.	Mary E. McManus
E. Lanier Drew	Jeanne M. Miller
Diana Salama Farhat	Stephen D. Moore, Jr.
Martin A. Fitzpatrick	Howard J. Smith
Michael R. Freed	Steven G. Spears
Lee G. Kellison	Melissa Smith Turra
Lauren P. Langham	Herschel T. Vinyard, Jr
Marjorie Conner Makar	Leslie A. Wickes
Bradley R. Markey	Karl A. Zillgitt

OF COUNSEL

Mark Hulsey	John E. Thrasher

Representative Clients: Baptist/St. Vincent's Health System, Inc.; Browning-Ferris Industries, Inc.; Champion Realty Corp. (Florida); First Union National Bank of Florida; Florida Rock Industries, Inc.; PGA Tour, Inc.; KPMG Peat Marwick; The Regency Group, Inc.; The Ritz-Carlton Hotel Co.; University of Florida.

For full biographical listings, see the Martindale-Hubbell Law Directory

JUPITER, Palm Beach Co.

THOMAS J. SCHULTE, P.A. (AV)

Suite 500, 1001 North U.S. Highway One, 33477
Telephone: 561-746-8600
Fax: 561-744-0670

Thomas J. Schulte

Representative Clients: Firemens' Fund Insurance Co.; Liberty Mutual Insurance, Co.; CIGNA; Professional Risk Management Services, Inc.; Florida Out-Patient Self Insurance Co.; Florida Physicians Insurance Trust; Catholic Diocese of Palm Beach; Gallagher & Bassett Services, Inc.; Anesthesiologists Professional Insurance Co.; Charter Bank.

For full biographical listings, see the Martindale-Hubbell Law Directory

LARGO, Pinellas Co.

WILLIAM S. JONASSEN, P.A. (AV)

10785 Ulmerton Road, 34648
Telephone: 813-586-1484
Fax: 813-585-9818
Mailing Address: P.O. Box 366, Indian Rocks Beach, 34635

William S. Jonassen

Representative Clients: Florida Lawyers Indemnity Group; Florida Podiatrist Trust; Gulf Atlantic Insurance Co.; Osteopathic Mutual Insurance Co.
General Counsel for: Indian Rocks State Bank.

For full biographical listings, see the Martindale-Hubbell Law Directory

MELBOURNE, Brevard Co.

BEST & ANDERSON, P.A. (AV)

Marina Towers, 709 South Harbor City Boulevard, Suite 220, 32901
Telephone: 407-727-9923
Orlando, Florida Office: 20 North Orange Avenue, Suite 505, 32801.
Telephone: 407-425-2985.
Crystal River, Florida Office: 7655 West Gulf to Lake Highway, Suite 6.
Telephone: 352-795-1107.

David R. Best	Lawrence I. Hauser
George H. "Dutch" Anderson, III	

G. Clay Morris	Angela O'Neil
	Natt O. Reifler

For full biographical listings, see the Martindale-Hubbell Law Directory

MIAMI, Dade Co.

ANGONES, HUNTER, McCLURE, LYNCH & WILLIAMS, P.A. (AV)

Ninth Floor-Concord Building, 66 West Flagler Street, 33130
Telephone: 305-371-5000
Fort Lauderdale: 954-728-9112
FAX: 305-371-3948

Frank R. Angones	Christopher J. Lynch
Steven Kent Hunter	Stewart D. Williams
John McClure	B. Scott Hunter
Leopoldo Garcia, Jr.	

Thomas W. Paradise	Lourdes Alfonsin Ruiz
Donna Joy Hunter	Kara D. Phinney

Insurance Clients: Allstate Insurance Co.; Prudential Property & Casualty Insurance Co.; Travelers Insurance Co.; Rollins Hudig Hall Healthcare Risk, Inc.

For Complete List of Firm Personnel, See General Section

For full biographical listings, see the Martindale-Hubbell Law Directory

DEUTSCH & BLUMBERG, P.A. (AV)

Suite 2802 New World Tower, 100 North Biscayne Boulevard, 33132
Telephone: 305-358-6329
Fax: 305-358-9304

Steven K. Deutsch	James C. Blecke
Edward R. Blumberg	Louis Thaler

For full biographical listings, see the Martindale-Hubbell Law Directory

EVERSOLE & RUDD, P.A. (AV)

Suite 106, Grove Forest Plaza, 2937 SW 27th Avenue, 33133
Telephone: 305-444-2255
Facsimile: 305-444-7288
Fort Lauderdale, Florida Office: 3511 Northeast 22nd Avenue, Suite 100.
Telephone: 954-563-4199.
Fax: 954-563-4030. Boca Raton Office: 2500 North Military Trail, Suite 102.
Telephone: 407-998-9900.
Fax: 407-998-4995.

John F. Eversole, III	James D. Rudd

For full biographical listings, see the Martindale-Hubbell Law Directory

FERRO & LEHR, P.A. (AV)

1401 Brickell, Suite 1040, 33131
Telephone: 305-377-1777
Fax: 305-377-0087

Henry G. Ferro	Bruce H. Lehr

For full biographical listings, see the Martindale-Hubbell Law Directory

FORD, DOMNICK, WOLF & LOPEZ-ALBEAR, P.A. (AV)

Penthouse 1-C, Two Datran Center, 9130 South Dadeland Boulevard, 33156
Telephone: 305-670-2000
Facsimile: 305-670-1353

T. Patrick Ford, Jr.	David A. Wolf
Sean C. Domnick	Carlos A. Lopez-Albear

For full biographical listings, see the Martindale-Hubbell Law Directory

THEODORE J. FOURNARIS PROFESSIONAL ASSOCIATION (AV)

145 Almeria Avenue (Coral Gables), 33134
Telephone: 305-448-7333
Telefax: 305-448-7394

Theodore J. Fournaris	Jose M. Cañas

OF COUNSEL
Morton J. Sanet

For full biographical listings, see the Martindale-Hubbell Law Directory

GEORGE, HARTZ, LUNDEEN, FLAGG & FULMER (AV)

4800 LeJeune Road (Coral Gables), 33146
Telephone: 305-662-4800
Fax: 305-667-8015
Fort Lauderdale, Florida Office: Suite 333 Justice Building East, 524 South Andrews Avenue, 33301.
Telephone: 954-462-1620.
Fax: 954-462-3629.
Fort Myers, Florida Office: Suite 402, Barnett Centre, 2000 Main Street, 33901.
Telephone: 941-337-7787.
Fax: 941-337-4303.

(See Next Column)

Tallahassee, Florida Office: Suite 900, Highpoint Center, 106 East College Avenue, 32302.
Telephone: 904-224-5252.
Fax: 904-222-3082.
West Palm Beach, Florida Office: Brandywine Centre 11, 560 Village Blvd., Suite 380, 33409.
Telephone: 561-478-8880.
Fax: 561-478-8838.
Orlando, Florida Office: 225 East Robinson Street, Suite 505, 32801.
Telephone: 407-843-4646.
Fax: 407-843-4264.

Charles K. George	Stanley V. Buky (Resident, West Palm Beach Office)
Charles Michael Hartz	
Mitchell L. Lundeen	Crane A. Johnstone (Resident, Fort Lauderdale Office)
Clinton D. Flagg	
Liana C. Silsby (Resident, Fort Lauderdale Office)	Douglas W. Barnes (Resident, Fort Lauderdale Office)
C. Richard Fulmer, Jr. (Resident, Fort Lauderdale Office)	Craig R. Stevens (Resident at Ft. Myers Office)
A. Scott Lundeen	Lynne E. Denneler (Resident, Fort Myers Office)
David V. King (Resident, Fort Lauderdale Office)	

ASSOCIATES

John R. Buchholz	Douglas Brent Steier (Resident, Fort Myers Office)
Maria A. Santoro (Resident, Tallahassee Office)	Matthew S. Nelles (Resident, Fort Lauderdale Office)
Esther E. Galicia (Resident, Fort Lauderdale Office)	Misty Merri Catherine Taylor
Matthew F. Minno (Resident, Tallahassee Office)	George A. Sarduy
Michael H. Imber (Resident, West Palm Beach Office)	Michael W. LeRoy (Resident, Fort Lauderdale Office)
Peter K. Spillis	Jack R. Simmons (Resident, Fort Lauderdale Office)
Loren Sonesen	R. David de Armas (Resident, Orlando Office)
Susan Bernhardt Rogers (Resident at Ft. Lauderdale Office)	Jennifer L. Bushey (Resident, West Palm Beach Office)
Timothy Dunbrack (Resident, Orlando Office)	Scott B. Albee (Resident, Fort Myers Office)
Charles M.P. George	Darin J. Lentner (Resident, Fort Lauderdale Office)
Frank Angione, Jr. (Resident, Fort Lauderdale Office)	

For full biographical listings, see the Martindale-Hubbell Law Directory

HADDAD, JOSEPHS, JACK, GAEBE & MARKARIAN (AV)

1493 Sunset Drive (Coral Gables), P.O. Box 345118, 33114
Telephone: Dade County: 305-666-6006
Telecopier: 305-662-9931
URL: http://www.haddadjosephs.com

MEMBERS OF FIRM

Gil Haddad	Lewis N. Jack, Jr.
Michael R. Josephs	John S. Gaebe
David K. Markarian	

ASSOCIATES

Elisabeth M. Allen	Lauren M. Ilvento
Helen Leen Miranda	Clifford A. Wolff
John William Gautier	

Representative Clients: U-Haul Corporation; ITT Sheraton; Zurich-American Insurance Company; Republic Claims Service Company; Southern Fire Insurance Adjusters.

For full biographical listings, see the Martindale-Hubbell Law Directory

PROENZA & ROBERTS, P.A. (AV)

Grove Plaza, 2900 Middle Street, 33133
Telephone: 305-442-1700
Telecopier: 305-442-2559

Morris C. Proenza (1940-1995)	H. Clay Roberts

Michael A. Vazquez
OF COUNSEL
Thomas L. Hurst

For full biographical listings, see the Martindale-Hubbell Law Directory

RUSSO & CULMO, P.A. (AV)

Suite 2000, 2601 South Bayshore Drive (Coconut Grove), 33133
Telephone: 305-854-3100
Fax: 305-854-5949

Don Russo	Thomas A. Culmo
Deborah J. Gander	

For full biographical listings, see the Martindale-Hubbell Law Directory

NICEVILLE, Okaloosa Co.

STANLEY BRUCE POWELL, P.A. (AV)

107 North Partin Drive, P.O. Box 400, 32588-0400
Telephone: 904-678-2118
Fax: 904-678-8336
Destin, Florida Office: Suite 21 Commerce Row, 225 Main Street.
Telephone: 904-837-9099.

Stanley Bruce Powell   David R. Swanick III

Representative Clients: Peoples National Bank of Niceville; Destin Bank; D&H Oil Co.
References: Peoples National Bank of Niceville; Destin Bank; Barnett Bank of Northwest Florida; Vanguard Bank and Trust Co.

For full biographical listings, see the Martindale-Hubbell Law Directory

ORLANDO,* Orange Co.

ADAMS, HILL, REIS, ADAMS, HALL & SCHIEFFELIN (AV)

1417 East Concord Street, 32803
Telephone: 407-896-0425
Fax: 407-896-9236

MEMBERS OF FIRM

George E. Adams   Janet W. Adams
G. Bruce Hill   Larry D. Hall
Gregory F. Reis   Thomas L. Schieffelin, Jr.

ASSOCIATES

William W. Large   William H. Olney
Matthew P. Bartolomei   Richard Coaxum, Jr
Christopher E. Butler

Representative Clients: Everglades Regional Medical Center; The Florida Hospital Trust Fund; The Florida Hospital Excess Trust Fund; Florida Hospital Workers Compensation/Self Insurance Trust Fund; Bartow Memorial Hospital; Bay Medical Center; Brooksville Regional Hospital; Cape Canaveral Hospital; Cape Coral Hospital; Desoto Memorial Hospital.

For full biographical listings, see the Martindale-Hubbell Law Directory

BEST & ANDERSON, P.A. (AV)

20 North Orange Avenue, Suite 505, 32801
Telephone: 407-425-2985
Crystal River, Florida Office: 7655 West Gulf to Lake Highway, Suite 6.
Telephone: 352-795-1107.
Melbourne, Florida Office: Marina Towers, 709 South Harbor City Boulevard, Suite 220, 32901.
Telephone: 407-727-9923.

David R. Best   Lawrence I. Hauser
George H. "Dutch" Anderson, III

G. Clay Morris   Angela O'Neil
Natt O. Reifler

For full biographical listings, see the Martindale-Hubbell Law Directory

BILLINGS, CUNNINGHAM, MORGAN & BOATWRIGHT, PROFESSIONAL ASSOCIATION (AV)

330 East Central Boulevard, 32801
Telephone: 407-425-2000
Fax: 407-843-8274

James Owen Cunningham   Joseph E. Boatwright, Jr.
Mary Ann Morgan   John T. Stemberger
Tracy L. Troutman-Cheek

OF COUNSEL

Jared M. Billings

For full biographical listings, see the Martindale-Hubbell Law Directory

BOBO, SPICER, CIOTOLI, FULFORD, BOCCHINO, DEBEVOISE & LE CLAINCHE, P.A. (AV)

Landmark Center One, Suite 510, 315 East Robinson Street, 32801-1949
Telephone: 407-849-1060
Fax: 407-843-4751
West Palm Beach, Florida Office: Esperante, Sixth Floor, 222 Lakeview Avenue, 33401.
Telephone: 407-684-6600.
FAX: 407-684-3828.

John W. Bocchino   D. Andrew DeBevoise
Patti A. Haber

Gregorio A. Francis   Ingrid A. de Graaff
Thomas W. Poulton

For full biographical listings, see the Martindale-Hubbell Law Directory

NOLAN CARTER, P.A. (AV)

Suite 1245 Eola Park Centre, 200 East Robinson Street, P.O. Box 2229, 32802
Telephone: 407-425-1621
Fax: 407-425-3322

Nolan Carter

Nathan P. Carter

For full biographical listings, see the Martindale-Hubbell Law Directory

LAW OFFICES OF DURIE & LAWSON, P.A. (AV)

1000 East Robinson Street, 32801
Telephone: 407-841-6000; 1-800-940-0442
Fax: 407-841-2425

Jack F. (Jay) Durie, Jr.   C. Alan Lawson

For full biographical listings, see the Martindale-Hubbell Law Directory

KELAHER, WIELAND AND HILADO, P.A. (AV)

Barnett Bank Center, 390 North Orange Avenue, Suite 1500, P.O. Box 944, 32802
Telephone: 407-841-7698; Brevard County: 407-639-4777
Fax: 407-841-2084

James P. Kelaher   Glen D. Wieland
Alfred J. Hilado

Paul A. Kelley   Robert J. Egan

Reference: First Union National Bank.

For full biographical listings, see the Martindale-Hubbell Law Directory

KARL O. KOEPKE (AV)

801 North Magnolia Avenue, Suite 107, 32803
Telephone: 407-841-0023
Fax: 407-425-4761
Email: klawfl@aol.com *URL:* http://www.klawfl.com

ASSOCIATE

Michael H. Truax

For full biographical listings, see the Martindale-Hubbell Law Directory

MAHER, GIBSON AND GUILEY A PROFESSIONAL ASSOCIATION OF LAWYERS (AV)

Suite 200, 90 East Livingston Street, 32801
Telephone: 407-839-0866
Fax: 407-425-7958

Michael Maher   Patricia M. Gibson
David D. Guiley

Steven R. Maher   Robin M. Orosz
Monique M. Edwards

OF COUNSEL

John Edward Jones (P.A.)

LEGAL SUPPORT PERSONNEL

INSURANCE CLAIM COORDINATOR

Charles R. Simpson

For full biographical listings, see the Martindale-Hubbell Law Directory

MARTINEZ, DALTON, DELLECKER & WILSON, PROFESSIONAL ASSOCIATION (AV)

719 Vassar Street, 32804
Telephone: 407-425-0712
Fax: 407-425-1856
URL: http://www.pixelstorm.com/mddw

Mel R. Martinez   Robert H. Dellecker
Roy B. Dalton, Jr.   Brian T. Wilson

Leticia Marques

For full biographical listings, see the Martindale-Hubbell Law Directory

McMILLEN & REINHART, P.A. (AV)

Sun Bank Center, Suite 1410, 200 South Orange Avenue, 32801
Telephone: 407-843-0126
Facsimile: 407-849-1267

Scott R. McMillen   Richard P. Reinhart

For full biographical listings, see the Martindale-Hubbell Law Directory

Orlando—Continued

PARRISH, BAILEY & MORSCH, P.A. (AV)

116 America Street, 32801
Telephone: 407-849-1776

Sidney H. Parrish   Michael K. Bailey
Mark V. Morsch

Donald A. Myers, Jr.

For full biographical listings, see the Martindale-Hubbell Law Directory

PEED & MITNIK, P.A. (AV)

1127 Edgewater Drive, 32804
Telephone: 407-422-2474
Fax: 407-843-8638

Fred M. Peed   Keith R. Mitnik

For full biographical listings, see the Martindale-Hubbell Law Directory

SANDERS, McEWAN, MARTINEZ, LUFF & DUKES, P.A. (AV)

108 East Central Boulevard, P.O. Box 753, 32801
Telephone: 407-423-8571
FAX: 407-423-8637
Email: smmld2@aol.com
Email: smmld@aol.com

Warren B. Parks (1879-1949)   Rafael E. "Ralph" Martinez
Wilson Sanders (1911-1981)   H. David Luff
O. Beverley McEwan   Thomas E. Dukes, III
   (1913-1995)   William E. Ruffier
John S. McEwan, II   Pierre Seacord
          Jeffrey Scott Badgley

Stephanie Ann Cunningham   Tyler S. McClay

Representative Clients: Auto Owners Insurance Co.; Bankers and Shippers Insurance Company of New York; Bridgestone/Firestone, Inc.; City Cab of Orlando, Inc.; CNA Insurance Company; Dependable Protective Mutual; Florida Physicians Insurance Co.; Gulf Atlantic Insurance Co.; Marine Office of America; M.C.I. Telecommunications Corporation.

For full biographical listings, see the Martindale-Hubbell Law Directory

---

PENSACOLA, * Escambia Co.

BELL, SCHUSTER & WHEELER, P.A. (AV)

119 West Garden Street, P.O. Box 12564, 32573-2564
Telephone: 904-438-1691
Fax: 904-438-3641

Robert D. Bell   Thomas E. Wheeler, Jr.
Charles A. Schuster   David W. Hiers

For full biographical listings, see the Martindale-Hubbell Law Directory

KERRIGAN, ESTESS, RANKIN & McLEOD (AV)

400 East Government Street, 32501
Telephone: 904-444-4444
Watts No.: 1-800-444-4404
FAX: 904-444-4495
Email: kerrigan@olis.com *URL:* http://www.kerrigan.com
Fort Walton Beach, Florida Office: 212 SE Eglin Parkway, Suite C.
Telephone: 904-244-1111.
Century, Florida Courtesy Office: 8210 North Century Boulevard.
Telephone: 800- 256-1120.
Gulf Breeze, Florida Courtesy Office: 50 Fort Pickens Road.
Telephone: 800-433-7777.
Panama City, Florida Office: 836 Jenks Avenue.
Telephone: 904-871-5000.
FAX: 904-872-2148.
Tallahassee, Florida Courtesy Office: 217 South Adams Street, First Floor.
Telephone: 904-671-5000.

MEMBERS OF FIRM

Robert G. Kerrigan   T. Michael McLeod
George W. Estess   Randle D. Thompson
William Rankin   Marcus J. Michles II
          Kristin L. Stewart
LEGAL SUPPORT PERSONNEL
Sam R. Peebles   James Michael Kerrigan, Ph.D.
          Renée J. Miller

Reference: 1st American Bank of Pensacola.

For full biographical listings, see the Martindale-Hubbell Law Directory

---

SARASOTA, * Sarasota Co.

DICKINSON & GIBBONS, P.A. (AV)

1750 Ringling Boulevard, P.O. Box 3979, 34230
Telephone: 941-366-4680
FAX: 941-953-3136

(See Next Column)

G. Hunter Gibbons   Burwell J. Jones
Ralph L. Marchbank, Jr.   Stephen G. Brannan

Representative Clients: Venice Hospital; Physicians Protective Trust Fund; Florida Physicians Insurance Co.; Lee Memorial Hospital; Manatee Memorial Hospital; Sarasota Memorial Hospital; Columbia Hospital Corp.; Florida Physicians Trust; Alexis; Squibb Corp.

For Complete List of Firm Personnel, See General Section

For full biographical listings, see the Martindale-Hubbell Law Directory

MATTHEWS, HUTTON & EASTMOORE (AV)

Suite 500, 1777 Main Street, P.O. Box 49377, 34230-6377
Telephone: 941-366-8888
Fax: 941-954-7777

MEMBERS OF FIRM

A. Lamar Matthews, Jr.   Jeanne S. Medawar
Steven D. Hutton   Arthur S. Hardy
Theodore C. Eastmoore   Martin Garcia
ASSOCIATE
          Edward K. DuBose

For full biographical listings, see the Martindale-Hubbell Law Directory

---

TALLAHASSEE, * Leon Co.

FONVIELLE & HINKLE (AV)

3375-A Capital Circle Northeast, 32308
Telephone: 904-422-7773
Fax: 904-422-3449
Email: lawyers@fonhink.com *URL:* http://www.fonhink.com
MEMBERS OF FIRM
C. David Fonvielle   Halley B. Lewis, III
Donald M. Hinkle   William H. Garvin III
          John H. Foote
LEGAL SUPPORT PERSONNEL
          Sandra M. Tate

For full biographical listings, see the Martindale-Hubbell Law Directory

---

TAMPA, * Hillsborough Co.

BAVOL, BUSH & SISCO, P.A. (AV)

100 South Ashley, Suite 2100, P.O. Box 3423, 33601-3423
Telephone: 813-228-7000
Telefax: 813-273-0091

Charles D. Bavol   Dale R. Sisco
Ronald E. Bush   Ricardo A. Fernandez

Audrey B. Rauchway   Edward M. Rooks
Andrew L. Rosenkranz   Harold L. Sebring, III

For full biographical listings, see the Martindale-Hubbell Law Directory

CUNNINGHAM LAW GROUP, P.A. (AV)

100 Ashley Drive, South, Suite 100, 33602
Telephone: 813-228-0505
Telefax: 813-229-7982

Anthony W. Cunningham   James D. Clark
Donald G. Greiwe   Dana Solin Kanfer

For full biographical listings, see the Martindale-Hubbell Law Directory

PATRICK H. DEKLE, P.A. (AV)

808 Landmark Building, 412 Madison Street, 33602-4640
Telephone: 813-223-2300

Patrick H. Dekle

For full biographical listings, see the Martindale-Hubbell Law Directory

RYWANT, ALVAREZ, JONES & RUSSO, PROFESSIONAL ASSOCIATION (AV)

Suite 500 Perry Paint & Glass Building, 109 North Brush Street, P.O. Box 3283, 33601
Telephone: 813-229-7007
Fax: 813-223-6544
Ocala, Florida Office: 3300 S.W. 34th Avenue, Suite 124C, 32674.
Telephone: 904-237-8810.
FAX: 904-237-2022.

Manuel J. Alvarez   Steven D. Lehner
Jill Diziel Emerson   Burke G. Lopez
Darrell D. Dirks   Kerry C. McGuinn, Jr.
Matthew D. Emerson   Andrew F. Russo
John A.C. Guyton, III   Michael S. Rywant
Gregory D. Jones   James R. Wilson

(See Next Column)

RYWANT, ALVAREZ, JONES & RUSSO PROFESSIONAL ASSOCIATION, *Tampa—Continued*

LEGAL SUPPORT PERSONNEL
Bradley Hugh Holt

Representative Clients: Peerless Insurance Co.; Gulf Insurance Group; Employers Casualty Co.; Landmark Insurance Co.

For full biographical listings, see the Martindale-Hubbell Law Directory

---

SOMERS & ASSOCIATES (AV)

3242 Henderson Boulevard, Suite 301, 33609-3056
Telephone: 813-872-7322
Fax: 813-872-8614

MEMBERS OF FIRM

Clifford L. Somers
Barbara B. Somers
Diane Ilene Zuckerman
John N. Jenkins

Representative Clients: Florida Physicians Insurance Co.; The Hartford Insurance Group; Cubic Corp.; AIG; CNA.

For full biographical listings, see the Martindale-Hubbell Law Directory

---

VERO BEACH,* Indian River Co.

MOSS, HENDERSON, BLANTON, KOVAL & LANIER, P.A. (AV)

817 Beachland Boulevard, P.O. Box 3406, 32964-3406
Telephone: 561-231-1900
Fax: 561-231-4387

George H. Moss, II
Steve L. Henderson
Robin A. Blanton
Thomas A. Koval
Clinton W. Lanier
Fred L. Kretschmer, Jr.
Lisa D. Harpring

Lewis W. Murphy, Jr.
Judith Goodman Hill
Kelly Cambron
Lawrence Y. Leonard
David F. Mancini

OF COUNSEL

Charles E. Garris
Ford J. Fegert
Everett J. Van Gaasbeck

Representative Clients: Aetna Life & Casualty; Alcoa Florida, Inc.; Florida Power & Light Co.; Insurance Company of North America; Liberty Mutual Insurance Co.; Sears, Roebuck & Co.; Sugar Cane Growers Cooperative of Florida; Norfolk Southern Corporation/North American Van Lines, Inc.

For full biographical listings, see the Martindale-Hubbell Law Directory

---

WEST PALM BEACH,* Palm Beach Co.

BOBO, SPICER, CIOTOLI, FULFORD, BOCCHINO, DeBEVOISE & LE CLAINCHE, P.A. (AV)

Esperante, Sixth Floor, 222 Lakeview Avenue, 33401
Telephone: 407-684-6600
Fax: 407-684-3828
Orlando, Florida Office: Landmark Center One, Suite 510, 315 East Robinson Street, 32801-1949.
Telephone: 407-849-1060.
Fax: 407-843-4751.

A. Russell Bobo
David W. Spicer
Eugene L. Ciotoli
Jeffrey C. Fulford
John W. Bocchino
  (Resident, Orlando Office)
D. Andrew DeBevoise
  (Resident, Orlando Office)
Stephan A. Le Clainche
Patti A. Haber
  (Resident, Orlando Office)
Joseph A. Osborne

Mark Alan Glassman
Michael S. Smith
Neil A. Deleon
Gregorio A. Francis
  (Resident, Orlando Office)
Michael D. Burt
Casey D. Shomo
Armando T. Lauritano
Ingrid A. de Graaff
  (Resident, Orlando Office)
Thomas W. Poulton
  (Resident, Orlando Office)

For full biographical listings, see the Martindale-Hubbell Law Directory

---

GAMOT & FREEMAN (AV)

315 Fifth Street, 33401-3709
Telephone: 561-655-6025
Fax: 561-655-5759
Palatka, Florida Office: 415 St. Johns Avenue.
Telephone: 904-325-6239.
Fax: 904-329-9626.

Melinda Penney Gamot
Terry N. Freeman
Albert J. Gamot, Jr.

For full biographical listings, see the Martindale-Hubbell Law Directory

---

STUART E. KOCHA, P.A. (AV)

118 Clematis Street, P.O. Box 1427, 33402
Telephone: 561-659-5611
Fax: 561-659-5636

Stuart E. Kocha
LEGAL SUPPORT PERSONNEL
David L. Halderman (Chief Investigator)

References: Admiralty Bank.

For full biographical listings, see the Martindale-Hubbell Law Directory

---

LYTAL, REITER, CLARK, SHARPE, ROCA, FOUNTAIN & WILLIAMS (AV)

A Partnership of Professional Associations
Tenth Floor, 515 North Flagler Drive, 33401
Telephone: 561-655-1990
Fax: 561-832-2932
Mailing Address: P.O. Box 4056, 33402

Lake Lytal, Jr. (P.A.)
Joseph J. Reiter (P.A.)
Mark W. Clark (P.A.)
Tracy R. Sharpe (P.A.)
Rafael J. Roca (P.A.)
Donald R. Fountain, Jr. (P.A.)
William S. Williams (P.A.)

Michael J. Overbeck
Yvette Trelles Murray
Kevin C. Smith
David M. Gaspari
Julie H. Littky-Rubin
Nancy L. La Vista
David C. Prather

Reference: United National Bank.

For full biographical listings, see the Martindale-Hubbell Law Directory

---

GARY ROBERTS & ASSOCIATES, P.A. (AV)

1675 Palm Beach Lakes Boulevard Seventh Floor, 33401
Telephone: 561-686-1800
FAX: 561-686-1533
Mailing Address: P.O. Drawer 4178, West Palm Beach, 33402
New Port Richey, Florida Office: Roberts, Sojka & Associates, P.A., 5841 Main Street, 34652.
Telephone: 813-847-1103.

Gary W. Roberts

For full biographical listings, see the Martindale-Hubbell Law Directory

---

SEARCY DENNEY SCAROLA BARNHART & SHIPLEY, PROFESSIONAL ASSOCIATION (AV)

2139 Palm Beach Lakes Boulevard, P.O. Drawer 3626, 33402-3626
Telephone: 407-686-6300
800-780-8607
800-220-7006 (Spanish)
Fax: 407-478-0754

Christian D. Searcy, Sr.
Earl L. Denney, Jr.
John Scarola
F. Gregory Barnhart
John A. Shipley
David K. Kelley, Jr.
Lawrence J. Block, Jr.
C. Calvin Warriner, III
William A. Norton
David J. Sales
Christopher K. Speed
William B. King

Karen E. Terry
Katherine Ann Martinez
T. Michael Kennedy
Todd S. Stewart
Laurie J. Briggs

LEGAL SUPPORT PERSONNEL

Deane L. Cady
  (Paralegal/Investigator)
James E. Cook
  (Paralegal/Investigator)
Emilio Diamantis
  (Paralegal/Investigator)
David W. Gilmore
  (Paralegal/Investigator)
Thaddeus E. Kulesa
  (Paralegal/Investigator)
J. Peter Love
  (Paralegal/Investigator)
Marjorie A. Morgan (Paralegal)
William H. Seabold
  (Paralegal/Investigator)
Kathleen Simon (Paralegal)
Steve M. Smith
  (Paralegal/Investigator)
Judson Whitehorn
  (Paralegal/Investigator)

For full biographical listings, see the Martindale-Hubbell Law Directory

---

GEORGIA

ATHENS,* Clarke Co.

COOK, NOELL, TOLLEY & WIGGINS (AV)

304 East Washington Street, P.O. Box 1927, 30603
Telephone: 706-549-6111
Fax: 706-548-0956

(See Next Column)

COOK, NOELL, TOLLEY & WIGGINS—*Continued*

MEMBERS OF FIRM

J. Vincent Cook	Morton M. Wiggins, III
John S. Noell, Jr.	Robert B. Bates
Edward D. Tolley	M. Kim Michael

For full biographical listings, see the Martindale-Hubbell Law Directory

---

ATLANTA,* Fulton Co.

BEDFORD, KIRSCHNER AND VENKER, P.C. (AV)

Suite 450, 600 West Peachtree Street, N.W., 30308
Telephone: 404-872-6646

T. Jackson Bedford, Jr.   Andrew R. Kirschner
Thomas J. Venker

For full biographical listings, see the Martindale-Hubbell Law Directory

BIRD, BALLARD & STILL (AV)

14 Seventeenth Street, Suite 5, P.O. Box 7009, 30357
Telephone: 404-873-4696
Fax: 404-872-3745

William Q. Bird

For full biographical listings, see the Martindale-Hubbell Law Directory

DAVID WM. BOONE, P.C. (AV)

3155 Roswell Road Suite 100, The Cotton Exchange, 30305
Telephone: 404-239-0305
FAX: 404-239-0520

David William Boone

For full biographical listings, see the Martindale-Hubbell Law Directory

BUTLER, WOOTEN, OVERBY, CHEELEY, PEARSON & FRYHOFER (AV)

2719 Buford Highway, 30324
Telephone: 404-321-1700
WATS 1-800-242-2962
Fax: 404-321-1713
Columbus, Georgia Office: 1500 Second Avenue, P.O. Box 2766.
Telephone: 706-322-1990; National Wats: 1-800-233-4086.
Fax: 706-323-2962.

MEMBERS OF FIRM

James E. Butler, Jr.	Albert M. Pearson, III
Joel O. Wooten, Jr.	George W. Fryhofer III
C. Frederick Overby	Peter J. Daughtery
Robert D. Cheeley	J. Frank Myers, III
	Lee Tarte Wallace

ASSOCIATES

Jason L. Crawford	Joshua Sacks
Keith A. Pittman	Teresa Thomas Abell
	Cale H. Conley

Reference: Columbus Bank and Trust, Columbus, Ga.

For full biographical listings, see the Martindale-Hubbell Law Directory

DREW ECKL & FARNHAM (AV)

880 West Peachtree Street, P.O. Box 7600, 30357
Telephone: 404-885-1400
Facsimile: 404-876-0992
Email: drew@igc.apc.org

MEMBERS OF FIRM

W. Wray Eckl	James M. Poe
	Hall F. McKinley III

ASSOCIATES

Suzanne VonHarten Sanders	Beverly Powell Sisk
Julianne L. Swilley	Nancy L. Pasterz
B. Greg Cline	Scott P. Archer
	(Not admitted in GA)

OF COUNSEL

Anne M. Landrum

Representative Clients: CNA Insurance Companies; OUM Corporation; Beverly Enterprises; Church Mutual Insurance Co.; CNA HealthPro; Prison Health Services, Inc.; Community Health Services, Inc.; Fannin Regional Hospital; Scottsdale Insurance Company; Henry General Hospital.

For Complete List of Firm Personnel, See General Section

For full biographical listings, see the Martindale-Hubbell Law Directory

DWYER, WHITE & SAPP (AV)

A Partnership including a Professional Corporation
Suite 700, 2100 Riveredge Parkway, 30328-4654
Telephone: 770-956-1984
Fax: 770-956-1381

(See Next Column)

MEMBERS

J. Matthew Dwyer, Jr. (P.C.)   Anne Woolf Sapp

ASSOCIATE

Carmen D. Smith

For full biographical listings, see the Martindale-Hubbell Law Directory

ENGLAND & McKNIGHT (AV)

Suite 410 River Ridge, 9040 Roswell Road, 30350
Telephone: 770-641-6010
FAX: 770-641-6003

MEMBERS OF FIRM

J. Melvin England   Robert H. McKnight, Jr.
Reference: Nations Bank N.A.

For full biographical listings, see the Martindale-Hubbell Law Directory

GARLAND, SAMUEL & LOEB, P.C. (AV)

3151 Maple Drive, N.E., 30305
Telephone: 404-262-2225
Fax: 404-365-5041
Email: TrialLaw@aol.com

Edward T. M. Garland   Donald F. Samuel
Robin N. Loeb

For full biographical listings, see the Martindale-Hubbell Law Directory

GOLDNER, SOMMERS, SCRUDDER & BASS (AV)

900 Circle 75 Parkway Suite 850, 30339
Telephone: 770-612-9200
Facsimile: 770-612-9201

Stephen L. Goldner   Susan V. Sommers

Benjamin David Ladner   Tammy Spivack Skinner

For Complete List of Firm Personnel, See General Section

For full biographical listings, see the Martindale-Hubbell Law Directory

HART & McINTYRE (AV)

Promenade Two Suite 3775, 1230 Peachtree Street, N.E., 30309
Telephone: 800-521-3775 (Nationwide); 404-876-3775
Fax: 404-873-3799

MEMBERS OF FIRM

George W. Hart   John C. McIntyre, Jr.
Reference: Nations Bank.

For full biographical listings, see the Martindale-Hubbell Law Directory

HILL AND BLEIBERG (AV)

Suite 200, 47 Perimeter Center East, 30346
Telephone: 770-394-7800
Fax: 770-394-7802

MEMBERS OF FIRM

Robert P. Bleiberg   Gary Hill

For full biographical listings, see the Martindale-Hubbell Law Directory

THOMAS E. MADDOX, JR., P.C. (AV)

3521 Habersham at Northlake (Tucker), 30084-4001
Telephone: 770-414-8055
Telecopier: 770-414-8755

Thomas E. Maddox, Jr.

LEGAL SUPPORT PERSONNEL

Matthew K. Johnson, Jr.

For full biographical listings, see the Martindale-Hubbell Law Directory

MILLS & MORAITAKIS (AV)

Resurgens Plaza, Suite 2515 945 East Paces Ferry Road, Northeast, 30326
Telephone: 404-261-0016
Facsimile: 404-261-0024

Roger Mills   Nicholas C. Moraitakis
Glenn E. Kushel

For full biographical listings, see the Martindale-Hubbell Law Directory

NALL, MILLER, OWENS, HOCUTT & HOWARD (AV)

Suite 200 Peachtree & Broad Building, 66 Luckie Street, 30303
Telephone: 404-522-2200
Fax: 404-522-2208

(See Next Column)

NALL, MILLER, OWENS, HOCUTT & HOWARD, *Atlanta—Continued*

MEMBERS OF FIRM

A. Walton Nall (1908-1984)	James R. Howard
James W. Dorsey (1914-1978)	George Robert Neuhauser
Edward S. White (1913-1992)	Robert L. Goldstucker
James S. Owens, Jr.	Kenneth P. McDuffie
Robert B. Hocutt	Kelly Eulenfeld Malone
Michael D. Hostetter	

COUNSEL
Samuel A. Miller

ASSOCIATES

Charles Richard Carson	Paul Jay Pontrelli
Mary Anne Palma	

LEGAL SUPPORT PERSONNEL

W. Gary Bush (Registered Nurse, Legal Assistant)	Michelle McGhee (Paralegal)
	Sheri L. Jordan (Paralegal)

Representative Clients: Adventist Health Systems; Charter Behavioral Health Systems of Atlanta at Peachford; The Doctor's Company; Em-Care, Inc.; Fisher Mangold; Georgia Osteopathic Hospital, Inc.; National Emergency Services, Inc.; Podiatry Insurance Company of America.

For full biographical listings, see the Martindale-Hubbell Law Directory

SAMUEL P. PIERCE, JR., P.C. (AV)

One Buckhead Plaza, Suite 850, 3060 Peachtree Road, N.W., 30305
Telephone: 404-364-2890
Fax: 404-240-0232

Samuel P. Pierce, Jr.

For full biographical listings, see the Martindale-Hubbell Law Directory

PIERCE & YOUNG (AV)

Building 1700, 2255 Cumberland Parkway Northwest, 30339-4575
Telephone: 770-435-0500
Telecopier: 770-435-0362

MEMBERS OF FIRM

J. Wayne Pierce	Richard M. Young

ASSOCIATE
Christy A. Dunkelberger

For full biographical listings, see the Martindale-Hubbell Law Directory

POPE, MCGLAMRY, KILPATRICK & MORRISON (AV)

A Partnership including Professional Corporations
83 Walton Street, N.W., P.O. Box 1733, 30303
Telephone: 404-523-7706;
Phenix City, Alabama: 334-298-7354
Columbus, Georgia Office: 318 11th Street, 2nd Floor, P.O. Box 2128, 31902-2128.
Telephone: 706-324-0050.

MEMBERS OF FIRM

C. Neal Pope (P.C.)	R. Timothy Morrison
Max R. McGlamry (P.C.) (Resident, Columbus, Georgia Office)	Michael L. McGlamry
	Earle F. Lasseter
	William Usher Norwood, III
Paul V. Kilpatrick, Jr. (Resident, Columbus, Georgia Office)	William J. Cornwell
	Jay F. Hirsch
Wade H. Tomlinson, III	

RESIDENT ASSOCIATE
C. Elizabeth Pope

Reference: Columbus Bank & Trust Co.

For full biographical listings, see the Martindale-Hubbell Law Directory

REYNOLDS & MCARTHUR (AV)

A Partnership including a Professional Corporation
Suite 1080, One Buckhead Plaza, 3060 Peachtree Road, N.W., 30305
Telephone: 404-240-0265
Fax: 404-262-3557
Macon, Georgia Office: 850 Walnut Street.
Telephone: 912-741-6000.
Fax: 912-742-0750.
Asheville, North Carolina Office: The Jackson Building, 22 South Pack Square, Suite 1200.
Telephone: 704-254-8523.
Fax: 704-254-3038.

MEMBERS OF FIRM

W. Carl Reynolds (P.C.)	O. Wendell Horne, III
Katherine L. McArthur	Bradley J. Survant
Charles M. Cork, III	Steve Ray Warren (Not admitted in GA)

For full biographical listings, see the Martindale-Hubbell Law Directory

ANDREW M. SCHERFFIUS, P.C. (AV)

3166 Mathieson Drive, P.O. Box 53299, 30355
Telephone: 404-261-3562; 1-800-521-2867
Fax: 404-841-0861

Andrew M. Scherffius

Tamara McDowell Ayres

For full biographical listings, see the Martindale-Hubbell Law Directory

THOMAS, KENNEDY, SAMPSON & PATTERSON (AV)

55 Marietta Street, N.W., Suite 1600, 30303
Telephone: 404-688-4503
Telecopier: 404-681-2950

MEMBERS OF FIRM

John Loren Kennedy (1942-1994)	P. Andrew Patterson
	Myra H. Dixon
Thomas G. Sampson	Jeffrey E. Tompkins

ASSOCIATES

Rosalind T. Drakeford	Adam L. Smith
Melynee C. Leftridge	Thomas G. Sampson, II
La'Sean M. Zilton	Ceasar C. Mitchell, II.
R. E. Thomas, Jr. (1911-1996)	

LEGAL SUPPORT PERSONNEL

Gwendolyn C.H. Dixon	Yvonne Torrence
Elbetha (Beth) Martin	Priscilla Yolanda Kelly
Nancy Allen-Haskell	Lureece D. Lewis (Paralegal)

For full biographical listings, see the Martindale-Hubbell Law Directory

WILLIAMS & HENRY (AV)

Suite 2020, 1100 Peachtree Street, N.E., 30309-4520
Telephone: 404-873-3000
Fax: 404-873-4508

MEMBERS OF FIRM

Benjamin S. Williams	Philip C. Henry
Harvey R. Spiegel	

ASSOCIATE
Joseph A. Fried

OF COUNSEL
Robert L. Callahan, III

Reference: Trust Company Bank.

For full biographical listings, see the Martindale-Hubbell Law Directory

---

AUGUSTA, * Richmond Co.

WILEY S. OBENSHAIN, III, P.C. (AV)

511 Courthouse Lane, 30901
Telephone: 706-722-1789
Fax: 706-722-3934

Wiley S. Obenshain, III

For full biographical listings, see the Martindale-Hubbell Law Directory

---

CARROLLTON, * Carroll Co.

TISINGER, TISINGER, VANCE & GREER, A PROFESSIONAL CORPORATION (AV)

100 Wagon Yard Plaza, P.O. Box 2069, 30117
Telephone: 770-834-4467
Fax: 770-834-5426

David H. Tisinger	Kevin B. Buice
David F. Miceli	

Representative Clients: CNA; MMI Companies, Inc.; St. Paul Fire and Marine Insurance Company.

For Complete List of Firm Personnel, See General Section

For full biographical listings, see the Martindale-Hubbell Law Directory

---

COLUMBUS, * Muscogee Co.

BUTLER, WOOTEN, OVERBY, CHEELEY, PEARSON & FRYHOFER (AV)

1500 Second Avenue, P.O. Box 2766, 31902
Telephone: 706-322-1990;
National Wats: 1-800-233-4086
Fax: 706-323-2962
Atlanta, Georgia Office: 2719 Buford Highway, 30324.
Telephone: 404-321-1700.
Fax: 404-321-1713. Wats Line: 1-800-242-2962.

(See Next Column)

BUTLER, WOOTEN, OVERBY, CHEELEY, PEARSON & FRYHOFER—*Continued*

MEMBERS OF FIRM

James E. Butler, Jr.	Albert M. Pearson, III
Joel O. Wooten, Jr.	George W. Fryhofer III
C. Frederick Overby	Peter J. Daughtery
Robert D. Cheeley	J. Frank Myers, III
Lee Tarte Wallace	

ASSOCIATES

Jason L. Crawford	Joshua Sacks
Keith A. Pittman	Teresa Thomas Abell
Cale H. Conley	

For full biographical listings, see the Martindale-Hubbell Law Directory

POPE, McGLAMRY, KILPATRICK & MORRISON (AV)

A Partnership including Professional Corporations
318 11th Street, 2nd Floor, P.O. Box 2128, 31902-2128
Telephone: 706-324-0050;
Phenix City, Alabama: 334-298-7354
Atlanta, Georgia Office: 83 Walton Street, N.W., P.O. Box 1733, 30303.
Telephone: 404-523-7706.

MEMBERS OF FIRM

C. Neal Pope (P.C.)	Michael L. McGlamry
Max R. McGlamry (P.C.)	Earle F. Lasseter
(Resident)	William Usher Norwood, III
Paul V. Kilpatrick, Jr.	(Resident, Atlanta Office)
(Resident)	William J. Cornwell
R. Timothy Morrison	Jay F. Hirsch
Wade H. Tomlinson, III	

RESIDENT ASSOCIATES

Joan S. Redmond	Teresa Pike Majors
Matthew N. Pope	

Reference: Columbus Bank & Trust Co.

For full biographical listings, see the Martindale-Hubbell Law Directory

DECATUR, * De Kalb Co.

ORR AND EDWARDS, ATTORNEYS AT LAW, P.C. (AV)

Suite 540, One West Court Square, 30030
Telephone: 404-377-1786
Telecopier: 404-377-1615

W. Fred Orr II	James G. Edwards II

Approved Attorneys for: Lawyers Title Insurance Corp.
Reference: SouthTrust Bank of Georgia, N.A.

For full biographical listings, see the Martindale-Hubbell Law Directory

PARKERSON, SHELFER & GROFF (AV)

715 First Union Plaza of Decatur, 250 East Ponce de Leon Avenue, 30030-3490
Telephone: 404-377-8143
Telecopier: 404-373-6829

MEMBERS OF FIRM

William S. Shelfer (1900-1975)	William S. Shelfer, Jr.
I. J. Parkerson	David B. Groff

Reference: Nations Bank of Georgia.

For full biographical listings, see the Martindale-Hubbell Law Directory

MACON, * Bibb Co.

BUZZELL & PINKSTON (AV)

Suite A, 175 New Street, 31201
Telephone: 912-742-8820
Telecopier: 912-742-3088

MEMBERS OF FIRM

R. William Buzzell, II	Loretta L. Pinkston

For full biographical listings, see the Martindale-Hubbell Law Directory

CHAMBLESS, HIGDON & CARSON (AV)

Suite 200 Ambrose Baber Building, 577 Walnut Street, P.O. Box 246, 31298-5399
Telephone: 912-745-1181
Telecopier: 912-746-9479

MEMBERS OF FIRM

Joseph H. Davis	Thomas F. Richardson
Joseph H. Chambless	Mary Mendel Katz
David B. Higdon	Emmitte H. Griggs
James F. Carson, Jr.	Marc T. Treadwell

ASSOCIATES

Kim H. Stroup	Jon Christopher Wolfe
James D. Tolliver	

(See Next Column)

(See Next Column)

LEGAL SUPPORT PERSONNEL

Angie Horton	Erie Reed

Local Counsel for: Atlanta Gas Light Co.; First Union National Bank of Georgia; Security National Bank.

For full biographical listings, see the Martindale-Hubbell Law Directory

REYNOLDS & McARTHUR (AV)

A Partnership including a Professional Corporation
850 Walnut Street, 31201
Telephone: 912-741-6000
Fax: 912-742-0750
Atlanta, Georgia Office: Suite 1080, One Buckhead Plaza, 3060 Peachtree Road, N.W.
Telephone: 404-240-0265.
Fax: 404-262-3557.
Asheville, North Carolina Office: The Jackson Building, 22 South Pack Square, Suite 1200.
Telephone: 704-254-8523.
Fax: 704-254-3038.

MEMBERS OF FIRM

W. Carl Reynolds (P.C.)	O. Wendell Horne, III
Katherine L. McArthur	Bradley J. Survant
Charles M. Cork, III	Steve Ray Warren
	(Not admitted in GA)

For full biographical listings, see the Martindale-Hubbell Law Directory

MARIETTA, * Cobb Co.

BARNES, BROWNING, TANKSLEY & CASURELLA (AV)

Suite 225, 166 Anderson Street, 30060
Telephone: 770-424-1500
Fax: 770-424-1740

MEMBERS OF FIRM

Roy E. Barnes	Jerry A. Landers, Jr.
Thomas J. Browning	Jeffrey G. Casurella
Charles B. Tanksley	Benny C. Priest

For full biographical listings, see the Martindale-Hubbell Law Directory

DOWNEY & CLEVELAND (AV)

288 Washington Avenue, 30060
Telephone: 770-422-3233
Fax: 770-423-4199

OF COUNSEL

Lynn A. Downey

MEMBERS OF FIRM

Robert H. Cleveland	Y. Kevin Williams
(1940-1989)	Russell B. Davis
Joseph C. Parker	G. Lee Welborn
Rodney S. Shockley	

ASSOCIATES

W. Curtis Anderson	Todd E. Hatcher
Scott D. Clay	Richard A. Griggs
Tara M. Waller	

Representative Clients: Allstate Insurance Co.; St. Paul Insurance Cos.; Georgia Farm Bureau Mutual Insurance Co.; State Farm Insurance Cos.; Cotton States Mutual Insurance Co.; Colonial Insurance Co. of California; Progressive Insurance Company; Auto Owners Insurance Company; Deep South Surplus, Inc.; Ed Voyles Oldsmobile, Honda and Chrysler-Plymouth.

For full biographical listings, see the Martindale-Hubbell Law Directory

HAWAII

HONOLULU, * Honolulu Co.

AYABE, CHONG, NISHIMOTO, SIA & NAKAMURA (AV)

A Partnership including a Professional Corporation
Pauahi Tower, Suite 2500, 1001 Bishop Street, 96813
Telephone: 808-537-6119
Telecopier: 808-526-3491

MEMBERS OF FIRM

Sidney K. Ayabe (P.C.)	Jeffrey H. K. Sia
John S. Nishimoto	Rhonda A. Nishimura

Representative Clients: Travelers Insurance Co.; St. Paul Fire and Marine Insurance Co.; The Employers Group of Insurance Companies; TIG Insurance Co.; Pacific Insurance Co.; Hartford Accident and Indemnity Co.; Continental Casualty Co.; CNA Insurance, Medical Insurance Exchange of California; The Doctors Company.

For Complete List of Firm Personnel, See General Section

For full biographical listings, see the Martindale-Hubbell Law Directory

Honolulu—Continued

CRONIN, FRIED, SEKIYA, KEKINA & FAIRBANKS ATTORNEYS AT LAW, A LAW CORPORATION (AV)

1900 Davies Pacific Center, 841 Bishop Street, 96813
Telephone: 808-524-1433
Fax: 808-536-2073

Paul F. Cronin	John D. Thomas, Jr.
L. Richard Fried, Jr.	Stuart A. Kaneko
Gerald Y. Sekiya	Bert S. Sakuda
Wayne K. Kekina	Allen K. Williams
David L. Fairbanks	Keith K. H. Young

Patrick W. Border	Clarence S.K. Kekina
Gregory L. Lui-Kwan	Sylvia E.J. Luke
Patrick F. McTernan	Geoffrey K.S. Komeya

For full biographical listings, see the Martindale-Hubbell Law Directory

LEE, KIM, WONG, YEE & LAU ATTORNEYS AT LAW, A LAW CORPORATION (AV)

Suite 700 Media Five Plaza, 345 Queen Street, 96813
Telephone: 808-536-4421
Telecopier: 808-521-3566

Douglas T. Y. Lee	Edmund K. U. Yee
Wayson W. S. Wong	Eric T. W. Kim
	Gene K. Lau

Arthur H. Kuwahara	Kendall J. Moser

OF COUNSEL
Steven H. Lee

For full biographical listings, see the Martindale-Hubbell Law Directory

PRICE OKAMOTO HIMENO & LUM ATTORNEYS AT LAW, A LAW CORPORATION (AV)

Suite 728, Ocean View Center, 707 Richards Street, 96813
Telephone: 808-538-1113
Fax: 808-533-0549

Warren Price, III	Sharon R. Himeno
Kenneth T. Okamoto	Bettina W. J. Lum
	Terence S. Yamamoto

Robert Kohn
OF COUNSEL

Stuart M. Cowan	Lawrence R. Cohen
	Michael K. Kaneshiro

For full biographical listings, see the Martindale-Hubbell Law Directory

ROBBINS & RHODES ATTORNEYS AT LAW, A LAW CORPORATION (AV)

Suite 2200 Davies Pacific Center, 841 Bishop Street, 96813
Telephone: 808-524-2355
Fax: 808-526-0290

Kenneth S. Robbins	Vincent A. Rhodes
	Shinken Naitoh

Representative Clients: CNA Insurance Co.; Farmers Insurance Group; Hilo Medical Center; Kahi Mohala Hospital; Kapiolani Medical Center for Women and Children; Kona Hospital; Maui Memorial Hospital; Podiatry Insurance Company of America; State of Hawaii; Wilcox Memorial Hospital.

For full biographical listings, see the Martindale-Hubbell Law Directory

TRECKER & FRITZ (AV)

820 Mililani Street, Suite 701, 96813
Telephone: 808-528-3900
Fax: 808-533-3684

MEMBERS OF FIRM

Steven J. Trecker	Magali V. Sunderland
Collin (Marty) Fritz	Hilary Benson Gangnes

For full biographical listings, see the Martindale-Hubbell Law Directory

WAILUKU,* Maui Co.

KRUEGER & CAHILL (AV)

2065 Main Street, 96793
Telephone: 808-244-7444; Honolulu: 536-7474
Facsimile: 808-244-4177
Email: maulaw@maui.net

MEMBERS OF FIRM

James Krueger	Peter T. Cahill
	John M. O'Neill

(See Next Column)

LEGAL SUPPORT PERSONNEL
LEGAL ASSISTANTS

Sharon O'Shaughnessy	Theresa N. Coletti

A List of Representative Clients and References will be furnished upon request.

For full biographical listings, see the Martindale-Hubbell Law Directory

ILLINOIS

CARBONDALE, Jackson Co.

BRANDON & SCHMIDT (AV)

916 West Main Street, P.O. Box 3898, 62902-3898
Telephone: 618-549-0777
Telecopier: 618-457-4691

MEMBERS OF FIRM

Wm. Kent Brandon	Charles E. Schmidt

ASSOCIATES

Jeffrey A. Goffinet	Christy W. Solverson
	Reona J. Jack

Representative Clients: State Farm Mutual Automobile Insurance Co.; State Farm Fire & Casualty Co.; Milwaukee Insurance Co.; Pekin Insurance Co.; Grinnel Mutual Reinsurance Co.; Western Casualty & Surety Co. (The Western Insurance Cos.); Illinois State Medical Ins. Services; Associated Physicians Ins. Co.; Hartford Ins. Co.
Reference: First National Bank of Carbondale.

For full biographical listings, see the Martindale-Hubbell Law Directory

CHICAGO,* Cook Co.

BURKE & BURKE, LTD. (AV)

2 First National Plaza, Suite 2200, 60603
Telephone: 312-726-6630
FAX: 312-726-1554
Downers Grove, Illinois Office: 5120 Forest, 60515.
Telephone: 708-852-9197.

John M. Burke	Dennis J. Burke
Edmund P. Burke	Molly C. Mason
	Karen Krajcir White

For full biographical listings, see the Martindale-Hubbell Law Directory

CLIFFORD LAW OFFICES, P.C. (AV)

120 North La Salle Street, 31st Floor, 60602
Telephone: 312-899-9090
1-800-899-0410
Fax: 312-251-1160
Email: 102554.2453@compuserve.com

Robert A. Clifford	Keith A. Hebeisen
	Kevin P. Durkin

Robert P. Walsh, Jr.	Richard L. Pullano
Susan A. Capra	Patricia C. Durkin
Jeffrey J. Kroll	Matthew I. Baker
Thomas K. Prindable	Timothy P. Rhatigan
Richard F. Burke, Jr.	Isobel S. Thomas

OF COUNSEL
Robert P. Sheridan

For full biographical listings, see the Martindale-Hubbell Law Directory

CONNELLY & SCHROEDER (AV)

One North Franklin Street, Suite 1200, 60606
Telephone: 312-251-9600
FAX: 312-251-9601
Geneva, Illinois Office: 1250 Executive Place, Suite 201.
Telephone: 708-232-6440.
FAX: 708-232-6450

MEMBERS OF FIRM

Michael P. Connelly	Charles H. Cole
John L. Schroeder	Daniel F. Konicek
(Resident, Geneva Office)	(Resident, Geneva Office)
Thomas F. Tobin	Eugene S. Kraus
Raymond E. Stachnik	Patrick G. Donnelly

OF COUNSEL
John W. Hough

(See Next Column)

CONNELLY & SCHROEDER—*Continued*

ASSOCIATES

Michelle L. Adams	Colleen Konicek
(Resident, Geneva Office)	Charina de los Reyes
Matthew Patrick Connelly	Abbey Fishman Romanek
Thomas W. Dillon	Martha Swatek
(Resident, Geneva Office)	(Resident, Geneva Office)
Mary Lisa Kamins	Carla A. Summers
John Michael Kelly	(Resident, Geneva Office)

For full biographical listings, see the Martindale-Hubbell Law Directory

CORBOY & DEMETRIO, P.C. (AV)

33 North Dearborn Street 21st Floor, 60602
Telephone: 312-346-3191
FAX: 312-346-5562
TDD: 312-236-3191
Email: phcorboy@aol.com

Philip H. Corboy	Thomas A. Demetrio
Susan J. Schwartz	Kevin G. Burke
Barry R. Chafetz	Kenneth T. Lumb
Mary E. Doherty	Margaret M. Power

Reference: The American National Bank & Trust Company, Chicago, Illinois.

For full biographical listings, see the Martindale-Hubbell Law Directory

GESSLER, HUGHES & SOCOL, LTD. (AV)

Three First National Plaza, Suite 2200, 60602
Telephone: 312-580-0100
Telecopy: 312-580-1994

Mark S. Dym	Terence J. Moran
George W. Gessler	Mark D. Olson
John K. Hughes	Matthew J. Piers
William P. Jones	David J. Pritchard
Peter M. Katsaros	Kalman D. Resnick
Mark A. LaRose	Frederick S. Rhine
Kimberley Marsh	Jonathan A. Rothstein
	Donna Kaner Socol

Benjamin P. Beringer	Alex W. Miller
Darilyn W. Bock	Belkis Cervantes Muldoon
Gary Chodorow	Jonathan D. Rosenblum
Anjali Dayal	Marci S. Sperling
Ruth M. Dunning	Dana H. Sukenik
Adam D. Ingber	J. Eric Vander Arend
Michael J. Klein	Maria L. Vertuno
Laura C. Liu	Mark B. Weiner
	Charles H. Wintersteen

OF COUNSEL

James T. Derico, Jr.	Darius S. Francescatti, M.D.
	Susan R. Gzesh

For full biographical listings, see the Martindale-Hubbell Law Directory

JEFFREY M. GOLDBERG & ASSOCIATES, LTD. (AV)

20 North Clark Street, Suite 3100, 60602
Telephone: 312-236-4146
Fax: 312-236-5913

Jeffrey M. Goldberg

Mark N. Pera	Suzanne Bonds
Lawrence R. Kream	Mark T. Solmor
Geoffrey Johnson	Barry I. Mortge

For full biographical listings, see the Martindale-Hubbell Law Directory

JOHNSON & BELL, LTD. (AV)

Suite 2200, 222 North La Salle Street, 60601
Telephone: 312-372-0770
Facsimile: 312-372-9818
Wheaton, Illinois Office: Suite 1640, 2100 Manchester Road.
Telephone: 630-510-0880.
Facsimile: 630-510-0939.

Brian C. Fetzer	Charles W. Planek
Timothy J. McKay	Kathryn K. Loft
Marilyn McCabe Reidy	Terry Takash

References available upon request.

For full biographical listings, see the Martindale-Hubbell Law Directory

KANE OBBISH PROPES & GARIPPO (AV)

19th Floor, 100 West Monroe Street, 60603
Telephone: 312-346-8355
Fax: 312-346-6549

MEMBERS OF FIRM

Michael J. Kane	Lorna E. Propes
James M. Obbish	Louis B. Garippo
	Susan G. Feibus

For full biographical listings, see the Martindale-Hubbell Law Directory

PETER D. KASDIN, LTD. (AV)

Suite 1960, 135 South La Salle Street, 60603
Telephone: 312-630-1990
Facsimile: 312-630-1103

Peter D. Kasdin

David W. Hepplewhite	Regina Picone Etherton

OF COUNSEL

David W. Horan

For full biographical listings, see the Martindale-Hubbell Law Directory

LANE & LANE (AV)

33 North Dearborn Street, Suite 2300, 60602
Telephone: 312-332-1400
Fax: 312-899-8003

MEMBERS OF FIRM

Fred Lane	Stephen I. Lane
	Scott D. Lane

ASSOCIATE

Joseph M. Dooley, III

OF COUNSEL

John F. Sandner	Nicholas V. Loizzi
Daniel M. Cullan	
(Not admitted in IL)	

For full biographical listings, see the Martindale-Hubbell Law Directory

LOGGANS AND COX (AV)

Suite 2850, 200 West Madison Street, 60606
Telephone: 312-201-8600
Telecopier: 312-201-1180
Email: loggans@aol.com

Susan E. Loggans	Michael J. Cox
Miles M. Dore	Ian Robert Alexander

For full biographical listings, see the Martindale-Hubbell Law Directory

THE LAW OFFICES OF MUNDAY & NATHAN (AV)

33 North Dearborn Street, Suite 2220, 60602
Telephone: 312-346-5678
Fax: 312-346-8394

John J. Munday	Thomas J. Nathan
James A. Tobin	Lisa Pach

For full biographical listings, see the Martindale-Hubbell Law Directory

STEPHEN M. PASSEN, LTD. (AV)

Suite 2900, 120 North La Salle Street, 60602
Telephone: 312-236-5878
Facsimile: 312-236-1162

Stephen M. Passen

Adam H. Fleischer

For full biographical listings, see the Martindale-Hubbell Law Directory

PAVALON & GIFFORD (AV)

Two North La Salle Street, Suite 1600, 60602
Telephone: 312-419-7400
Fax: 312-419-7408
Rockford, Illinois Office: 501 Seventh Street, Suite 501, 61104.
Telephone: 815-968-5100.

MEMBERS OF FIRM

Eugene I. Pavalon	Gary K. Laatsch
Geoffrey L. Gifford	Frank C. Marino
	Henry Phillip Gruss

(See Next Column)

PAVALON & GIFFORD, *Chicago—Continued*

Kathleen A. Russell   Christine Walsh Donnelly
        Christopher B. Meister

For full biographical listings, see the Martindale-Hubbell Law Directory

POWER ROGERS & SMITH, P.C. (AV)

35 West Wacker Drive, Suite 3700, 60601
Telephone: 312-236-9381
Fax: 312-236-0920

Joseph A. Power, Jr.   Thomas G. Siracusa
Larry R. Rogers   Paul L. Salzetta
Todd A. Smith   Thomas M. Power

Larry R. Rogers, Jr.   Ruth M. Degnan
        Devon C. Bruce

For full biographical listings, see the Martindale-Hubbell Law Directory

LAW OFFICES OF EDMUND J. SCANLAN, LTD. (AV)

134 North La Salle-Suite 220, 60602
Telephone: 312-372-0020
Fax: 312-372-1211

Edmund J. Scanlan   Richard C. Gleason

For full biographical listings, see the Martindale-Hubbell Law Directory

JOHN B. SCHWARTZ & ASSOCIATES (AV)

Suite 408, Thirty-Nine South La Salle Street, 60603
Telephone: 312-332-1586
Fax: 312-332-7009
Email: JSCHW888@aol.com

John B. Schwartz
ASSOCIATES
David J. Spira   Jami L. Sharfman
OF COUNSEL
Thomas W. Duda

For full biographical listings, see the Martindale-Hubbell Law Directory

SWANSON, MARTIN & BELL (AV)

One IBM Plaza, Suite 2900, 60611
Telephone: 312-321-9100
Fax: 312-321-0990
Wheaton, Illinois Office: 2100 Manchester Road, C-1420.
Telephone: 708-653-2266.
Fax: 708-653-2292.

MEMBERS OF FIRM
Lenard C. Swanson   Lawrence Helms
Kevin T. Martin   Joseph P. Switzer
Brian W. Bell   David E. Kawala
Stanley V. Boychuck   Bruce S. Terlep
Kay L. Schichtel   (Resident, Wheaton Office)
David J. Cahill   Robert J. Meyer
    (Resident, Wheaton Office)

ASSOCIATES
Kevin V. Boyle   Sheryl A. Pethers
Matthew D. Jacobson   Barbara N. Petrungaro
    (Resident, Wheaton Office) Aaron T. Shepley
Joseph P. Kincaid   André Martin Thapedi
Patricia S. Kocour   William Blake Weiler

For full biographical listings, see the Martindale-Hubbell Law Directory

JOHN C. WUNSCH, P.C. (AV)

77 West Washington Street, Suite 1420, 60602
Telephone: 312-977-9900
Fax: 312-236-2573

John C. Wunsch   Daniel J. Arnett

Reference: The Northern Trust Co.

For full biographical listings, see the Martindale-Hubbell Law Directory

EAST ST. LOUIS, St. Clair Co.

CARR, KOREIN, TILLERY, KUNIN, MONTROY & GLASS (AV)

412 Missouri Avenue, 62201
Telephone: 618-274-0434
Telecopier: 618-274-8369
St. Louis, Missouri Office: 701 Market Street, Suite 300.
Telephone: 314-241-4844.
Telecopier: 314-241-3525.
Belleville, Illinois Office: 5520 West Main.
Telephone: 618-277-1180.

(See Next Column)

MEMBERS OF FIRM
Rex Carr   Stephen M. Tillery
        Gerald L. Montroy
ASSOCIATES
Martin L. Perron   Robert L. King

References: Union Bank; First National Bank.

For Complete List of Firm Personnel, See General Section

For full biographical listings, see the Martindale-Hubbell Law Directory

EDWARDSVILLE,* Madison Co.

ARMSTRONG LAW OFFICES (AV)

South Main & Schwarz Street, P.O. Box 565, 62025
Telephone: 618-656-6770
Facsimile: 618-656-6808
Collinsville, Illinois Office: 103 South Morrison.
Telephone: 618-345-9258.

Benton Tad Armstrong   Stephen B. Evans

For full biographical listings, see the Martindale-Hubbell Law Directory

KANKAKEE,* Kankakee Co.

ACKMAN, MAREK, BOYD AND WOODRUFF, LTD. (AV)

Suite 400, One Dearborn Square, 60901
Telephone: 815-933-6681
Fax: 815-933-9985
Watseka, Illinois Office: 200 East Walnut Street.
Telephone: 815-432-5215.
Fax: 815-432-3186.
Manteno, Illinois Office: 10 North Locust Street.
Telephone: 815-468-7751.

J. Dennis Marek

Representative Clients: Illinois State Medical Insurance Exchange; Medical Protective; Preferred Physicians Mutual.

For Complete List of Firm Personnel, See General Section

For full biographical listings, see the Martindale-Hubbell Law Directory

MATTOON, Coles Co.

CRAIG & CRAIG (AV)

1807 Broadway, P.O. Box 689, 61938-0689
Telephone: 217-234-6481
Telecopier: 217-234-6486
Mount Vernon, Illinois Office: 227 1/2 South 9th Street.
Telephone: 618-244-7511.

MEMBERS OF FIRM
Craig Van Meter (1895-1981)   Stephen L. Corn
Fred H. Kelly (1894-1971)   Richard Charles Hayden
Robert M. Werden (1908-1969)   Robert G. Grierson
George N. Gilkerson   Gregory C. Ray
    (1911-1985)   Paul R. Lynch (Resident, Mount
John H. Armstrong   Vernon Office)
John P. Ewart   Kenneth F. Werts (Resident,
Richard F. Record, Jr.   Mount Vernon Office)
        John L. Barger
ASSOCIATES
Joshua N. Rosen (Resident,   Theresa M. Thomson
    Mount Vernon Office)   Kristine M. Tuttle
Kathleen M. Stockwell   Henry P. Villani (Resident,
                                   Mount Vernon Office)
OF COUNSEL
Jack E. Horsley

Counsel for: Monterey Coal Co., a Division of Exxon Coal USA, Inc.; Marathon Oil Co.; Illinois Central R.R. Co.; Okaw Building & Loan Assn., Mattoon, Illinois; The Medical Protective Insurance Co.; Consolidated Communications, Inc.; Lloyds Underwriters at London; Hartford Insurance Co.; Coles Together, a Not-For-Profit Corp.; Coles Building Corporation.

For full biographical listings, see the Martindale-Hubbell Law Directory

PERU, La Salle Co.

ANTHONY C. RACCUGLIA & ASSOCIATES (AV)

1200 Maple Drive, 61354
Telephone: 815-223-0230
Ottawa, Illinois Office: 633 La Salle Street.
Telephone: 815-434-2003.

ASSOCIATES
James A. McPhedran   Louis L. Bertrand

References: La Salle National Bank; Citizens First National Bank of Peru, Illinois.

For full biographical listings, see the Martindale-Hubbell Law Directory

WAUKEGAN, Lake Co.

LAW OFFICES OF PATRICK A. SALVI, P.C. (AV)

218 North Utica Street, 60085
Telephone: 847-249-1227
Telefax: 847-249-0138

Patrick A. Salvi

Michael P. Schostok　　　　　Paul R. Borth
John Andrew Kornak　　　　　Thomas J. Popovich
J. Matthew Dudley
OF COUNSEL
Bernard E. Grysen

References: First Midwest Bank, Waukegan, Illinois; Northern Trust Bank, Lake Forest, Illinois.

For full biographical listings, see the Martindale-Hubbell Law Directory

WHEATON, Du Page Co.

LAW OFFICES OF ROGER KEVIN O'REILLY (AV)

1776 South Naperville Road, Suite 206-A, 60189-5039
Telephone: 708-665-4444
Telecopier: 708-665-4442

Molly M. O'Reilly

For full biographical listings, see the Martindale-Hubbell Law Directory

INDIANA

EVANSVILLE, Vanderburgh Co.

GERLING LAW OFFICES, PROFESSIONAL CORPORATION (AV)

519 Main Street Walkway, P.O. Box 3203, 47731
Telephone: 812-423-5251
Fax: 812-423-9928

Gary L. Gerling　　　　　Christian M. Lenn
Edward B. Anderson　　　Gayle Gerling Pettinga
David G. Hatfield　　　　 Stephen Hensleigh Thomas

For full biographical listings, see the Martindale-Hubbell Law Directory

FORT WAYNE, Allen Co.

STANLEY A. LEVINE (AV)

Fort Wayne National Bank Building, Suite 2008, 110 West Berry
　Street, 46802
Telephone: 219-422-7431
Facsimile: 219-422-7433

For full biographical listings, see the Martindale-Hubbell Law Directory

HAMMOND, Lake Co.

GALVIN, GALVIN & LEENEY (AV)

5231 Hohman Avenue, 46320
Telephone: 219-933-0380
Fax: 219-933-0471

MEMBERS OF FIRM

Edmond J. Leeney (1897-1978)　　Carl N. Carpenter
Timothy P. Galvin, Sr.　　　　　John E. Chevigny
　(1894-1993)　　　　　　　　Timothy P. Galvin, Jr.
Francis J. Galvin, Sr.　　　　　Patrick J. Galvin
　(1902-1995)　　　　　　　　W. Patrick Downes

William G. Crabtree II　　　　Julie A. Rosenwinkel
John H. Lloyd, IV　　　　　　Amy Galvin Grogan

Attorneys For: CIGNA; St. Margaret Mercy Healthcare Centers, Inc.; St. Anthony Hospital and Health Centers (Michigan City); St. Elizabeth Hospital (LaFayette, IN).

For full biographical listings, see the Martindale-Hubbell Law Directory

INDIANAPOLIS, Marion Co.

CONOUR • DOEHRMAN (AV)

Suite 1725, One Indiana Square, 46204
Telephone: 317-269-3550
Fax: 317-269-3564
Toll Free: 800-269-3443

MEMBERS OF FIRM

William F. Conour　　　　　Thomas C. Doehrman

(See Next Column)

ASSOCIATES

Rex E. Baker　　　　　　　Daniel S. Chamberlain

For full biographical listings, see the Martindale-Hubbell Law Directory

HALL, RENDER, KILLIAN, HEATH & LYMAN, PROFESSIONAL CORPORATION (AV)

Suite 2000, One American Square Box 82064, 46282
Telephone: 317-633-4884
Fax: 317-633-4878
Email: hrkhl@hrkhl.com
Indianapolis North Office: Suite 820, 8402 Harcourt Road, 46260.
Telephone: 317-871-6222.
Fax: 317-338-3946.
Louisville, Kentucky Office: Providian Center, Suite 1530, 400 West
Market Street, 40202.
Telephone: 502-568-1890.
Fax: 502-568-4878.

William S. Hall　　　　　　N. Kent Smith
Timothy W. Kennedy　　　　Kevin P. Speer
　　　　　　Richard W. McMinn

Christopher L. Riegler
A. Courtney Guild, Jr. (Not
　admitted in IN; Resident,
　Louisville, Kentucky Office)

For Complete List of Firm Personnel, See General Section

For full biographical listings, see the Martindale-Hubbell Law Directory

ICE MILLER DONADIO & RYAN (AV)

One American Square Box 82001, 46282-0002
Telephone: 317-236-2100
Fax: 317-236-2219
Email: leel@imdr.com *URL:* http://www.imdr.com
South Bend, Indiana Office: 211 West Washington Street, Suite 2420.
Telephone: 219-234-7933.
Fax: 219-234-7965. Internet E-mail: leel@imdr.com. Web Site Address:
http://www.imdr.com.

MEMBERS OF FIRM

James V. Donadio　　　　　L. Alan Whaley
David J. Mallon, Jr.　　　　Bonnie L. Gallivan
Mary Nold Larimore　　　　Sherry A. Fabina-Abney
OF COUNSEL
Nancy Menard Riddle　　　　Kelly Bauman Pitcher
STAFF ATTORNEY
Michele Johnson Calderon
ASSOCIATES
Laure V. Flaniken　　　　　Kevin R. Knight
　　　　Christopher S. Sears

Representative Clients: Indiana University; PHICO Insurance Co.; St. Paul Insurance Co.; MultiMutual Insurance; Physicians Insurance Company of Indiana; St. Francis Hospital; St. Vincent's Hospital; Ophthalmic Mutual Insurance Company.

For Complete List of Firm Personnel, See General Section

For full biographical listings, see the Martindale-Hubbell Law Directory

LOCKE REYNOLDS BOYD & WEISELL (AV)

1000 Capital Center South, 201 North Illinois Street, 46204
Telephone: 317-237-3800
Telecopier: 317-237-3900

David S. Allen　　　　　　Karl M. Koons, III
Kevin Charles Murray　　　Todd J. Kaiser

Peter H. Pogue　　　　　　Susan E. Cline
Jon M. Pinnick　　　　　　Jerrilyn Powers Ramsey
Joyce A. Dietz　　　　　　Mary Margaret Ruth Feldhake
　　　　　James D. Shircliff
OF COUNSEL
Robert C. Riddell

Representative Clients: Charter Medical Corporation; Kentucky Medical Insurance Company; MMI Companies, Inc.; Methodist Hospital of Indiana, Inc.; PHICO Insurance Company; Physicians Insurance Company of Indiana, Inc.; Riverview Hospital; St. Francis Hospital Center; Wishard Memorial Hospital; Columbia/HCA (The Women's Hospital-Indianapolis).

For Complete List of Firm Personnel, See General Section

For full biographical listings, see the Martindale-Hubbell Law Directory

MILLER MULLER MENDELSON & KENNEDY (AV)

8900 Keystone Crossing Suite 1250, 46240
Telephone: 317-574-4500
1-800-394-3094
Fax: 317-574-4501

(See Next Column)

MILLER MULLER MENDELSON & KENNEDY, *Indianapolis—Continued*

MEMBERS OF FIRM

Michael S. Miller　　　　　　Tilden Mendelson
John Muller　　　　　　　　Timothy J. Kennedy

ASSOCIATE

Catherine A. Kling

For full biographical listings, see the Martindale-Hubbell Law Directory

---

MITCHELL HURST JACOBS & DICK (AV)

152 East Washington Street, 46204
Telephone: 317-636-0808
1-800-636-0808
Fax: 317-633-7680

MEMBERS OF FIRM

William W. Hurst　　　　　　Marshall S. Hanley
Samuel L. Jacobs　　　　　　Robert W. Strohmeyer, Jr.

ASSOCIATES

Danielle A. Takla　　　　　　Kimberly H. Danforth
John M. Reames　　　　　　Jennifer Levin Sinder

For full biographical listings, see the Martindale-Hubbell Law Directory

---

PARDIECK, GILL & VARGO, A PROFESSIONAL CORPORATION (AV)

The Old Bailey Building, 244 North College Avenue, 46202
Telephone: 317-639-3321
Fax: 317-639-3318
Email: pgv@pgvlaw.com
Seymour, Indiana Office: 100 North Chestnut Street. P.O. Box 608.
Telephone: 812-523-8686.

Roger L. Pardieck　　　　　　W. Brent Gill
　　　　　　John F. Vargo

Thomas L. Landwerlen　　　　　　Janet O. Vargo

OF COUNSEL

Robert C. Rothkopf

For full biographical listings, see the Martindale-Hubbell Law Directory

---

PRICE & BARKER (AV)

The Hammond Block Building, 301 Massachusetts Avenue, 46204
Telephone: 317-633-8787
Telecopier: 317-633-8797
New Albany, Indiana Office: 409 Bank Street, P.O. Box 785.
Telephone: 812-945-9151.
Fax: 812-945-6131.

PARTNERS

Henry J. Price　　　　　　Barbara J. Germano
Mary Arlien Findling　　　　Deborah K. Pennington

For full biographical listings, see the Martindale-Hubbell Law Directory

---

TABBERT HAHN EARNEST & STARKEY, P.C. (AV)

Suite 2100, One Indiana Square, 46204
Telephone: 317-639-5444
Fax: 317-639-5232

Don A. Tabbert　　　　　　Lorie A. Brown
Gregory F. Hahn　　　　　　Mark K. Sullivan
Lante K. Earnest　　　　　　Judy M. Tyrrell
Martha T. Starkey　　　　　Susan L. Abel

OF COUNSEL

James J. Nocon　　　　　　William D. Lalley
　　　　Douglas E. Cregor

For full biographical listings, see the Martindale-Hubbell Law Directory

---

TOWNSEND, HOVDE & MONTROSS (AV)

230 East Ohio Street, 46204
Telephone: 317-264-4444
FAX: 317-264-2080

F. Boyd Hovde　　　　　　W. Scott Montross
　　　　Frederick R. Hovde

Reference: N.B.D. Bank, N.A.

For full biographical listings, see the Martindale-Hubbell Law Directory

---

TOWNSEND & TOWNSEND (AV)

151 East Market Street, 46204
Telephone: 317-631-7777; 800-272-5720
FAX: 317-686-4449

Earl C. Townsend, Jr.　　　　　Earl C. Townsend, III

For full biographical listings, see the Martindale-Hubbell Law Directory

---

WILSON, KEHOE & WININGHAM (AV)

2859 North Meridian, 46208
Telephone: 317-920-6400
Fax: 317-920-6405
Richmond, Indiana Office: 42 South 9th Street, 47374.
Telephone: 317-962-9113.
Connersville, Indiana Office: 118 West 30th Street, 47331.
Telephone: 317-827-1100.
Muncie, Indiana Office: 3310 West Fox Ridge Lane, 47304.
Telephone: 317-284-2474.

MEMBERS OF FIRM

Harry A. Wilson, Jr.　　　　　D. Bruce Kehoe
　　　William E. Winingham, Jr.

ASSOCIATES

Ralph E. Dowling　　　　　Gerald A. Griffin, M.D.

Reference: The Indiana National Bank.

For full biographical listings, see the Martindale-Hubbell Law Directory

---

YOSHA LADENDORF KRAHULIK & WEDDLE (AV)

Pyramid II, First Floor, 3500 West DePauw Boulevard, Suite 2015, P.O. Box 68979, 46268
Telephone: 317-334-9200
FAX: 317-228-3355

MEMBERS OF FIRM

Louis Buddy Yosha　　　　　Mark C. Ladendorf
William Levy　　　　　　　Jon D. Krahulik
　　　　Robert G. Weddle

ASSOCIATES

David C. Krahulik　　　　　Angela M. Smith
Timothy C. Caress　　　　　Jeff D. Oliphant

SENIOR COUNSEL

Jeffrey A. Modisett

OF COUNSEL

Irwin J. Prince　　　　　　Irving L. Fink

Reference: National Bank of Indianapolis.

For full biographical listings, see the Martindale-Hubbell Law Directory

---

KOKOMO,* Howard Co.

RUSSELL, McINTYRE, HILLIGOSS & WELKE (AV)

116 North Main Street, P.O. Box 1047, 46901
Telephone: 317-456-3827
Telecopier: 317-456-3839

MEMBERS OF FIRM

Richard L. Russell　　　　　Thomas J. Hilligoss, Jr.
James B. McIntyre　　　　　Curtis C. Welke

ASSOCIATE

Andrew J. Vandenbosch

For full biographical listings, see the Martindale-Hubbell Law Directory

---

LAFAYETTE,* Tippecanoe Co.

STUART & BRANIGIN (AV)

The Life Building, 300 Main Street, Suite 800, 47902
Telephone: 317-423-1561
Telecopier: 317-742-8175

MEMBERS OF FIRM

Allison Ellsworth Stuart　　　Stephen R. Pennell
　　(1886-1950)　　　　　Anthony S. Benton
Roger D. Branigin (1902-1975)　Erik D. Spykman
Russell H. Hart　　　　　　William E. Emerick
Roger D. Branigin, Jr.　　　　John C. Duffey
Thomas L. Ryan　　　　　　Mark E. DeYoung
James V. McGlone　　　　　Thomas B. Parent
Carl W. Kloepfer　　　　　Laura L. Bowker
Thomas R. McCully　　　　Kevin D. Nicoson
Larry R. Fisher　　　　　　Susan K. Roberts
Nina B. Kirkpatrick　　　　John M. Stuckey
Mark Lillianfeld　　　　　Deborah B. Trice

COUNSEL

John F. Bodle

ASSOCIATES

Brent W. Huber　　　　　　David A. Starkweather
William P. Kealey　　　　　Geoffrey Blazi
　　　　A. James Chareq

General Counsel for: The Lafayette Life Insurance Co.; INB National Bank, N.W.; Lafayette Home Hospital, Inc.
State Counsel for: Norfolk & Western Railway Co.
Mr. Ryan is Counsel to: The Trustees of Purdue University.
Representative Clients: Aluminum Company of America; Liberty Mutual Insurance Group.

For full biographical listings, see the Martindale-Hubbell Law Directory

MUNSTER, Lake Co.

LAW OFFICES OF TIMOTHY F. KELLY (AV)

Suite 2A, 9250 Columbia Avenue, 46321
Telephone: 219-836-4062
Telecopier: 219-836-0167
Email: 76325.1505@Compuserve.Com

MEMBERS OF FIRM

Timothy F. Kelly   Karl K. Vanzo

ASSOCIATES

Harvey Karlovac   Steven J. Sersic

For Complete List of Firm Personnel, See General Section

For full biographical listings, see the Martindale-Hubbell Law Directory

---

NEW ALBANY, * Floyd Co.

MATTOX & MATTOX (AV)

Suite 420 Elsby Building, P.O. Box 1203, 47151-1203
Telephone: 812-944-8005
Facsimile: 812-944-2255
Email: mattox@ntr.net

MEMBERS OF FIRM

Richard L. Mattox   S. Frank Mattox

ASSOCIATES

Linda A. Mattox   Derrick H. Wilson
Karen R. Goodwell

Representative Clients: AAOMS National Insurance; Cablelink, Inc.; Floyd Memorial Hospital; John Deere Co.; Kimball International, Inc.; The Medical Protective Co.; Papa Johns Intl., Inc.; PHICO Insurance Co.; Physicians Group, Inc.; Robinson Nugent, Inc.

For full biographical listings, see the Martindale-Hubbell Law Directory

---

SEYMOUR, Jackson Co.

PARDIECK, GILL & VARGO, A PROFESSIONAL CORPORATION (AV)

100 North Chestnut Street, P.O. Box 608, 47274
Telephone: 812-523-8686
Fax: 812-522-4199
Email: pgv@pgylaw.com
Indianapolis, Indiana Office: The Old Bailey Building, 244 North College Avenue.
Telephone: 317-639-3321.

Roger L. Pardieck   W. Brent Gill

Bruce A. MacTavish   Karen J. Mellencamp Davis
Andrew M. Pardieck

References: Home Federal Savings Bank, Seymour, Indiana.

For full biographical listings, see the Martindale-Hubbell Law Directory

---

SOUTH BEND, * St. Joseph Co.

HARDIG, LEE AND GROVES, PROFESSIONAL ASSOCIATION (AV)

Suite 502, First Bank Building, 205 West Jefferson Boulevard, 46601
Telephone: 219-232-5923
Fax: 219-232-5942

James F. Groves

Representative Client: South Bend-Mishawaka New Car Dealers Assn.
Reference: First Interstate Bank of South Bend.

For full biographical listings, see the Martindale-Hubbell Law Directory

ROWE, ROWE & MAHER (AV)

Suite 900 Keybank Building, 46601
Telephone: 219-233-8200
Fax: 219-234-5987

R. Kent Rowe   R. Kent Rowe, III
Timothy J. Maher

ASSOCIATES

Gregory J. Haines   Steven D. Groth
Lee Korzan   Marie Anne Hendrie

Representative Clients: Amerisure Cos.; American Family and Cigna Cos.; Central Insurance Cos.; Professional Mutual; Michigan Mutual Liability Co.; Meridian Mutual Insurance Co.; Sentry Insurance, Inc.; Standard Mutual Insurance Co.; Vernon Insurance Cos.; American States Insurance Co.

For full biographical listings, see the Martindale-Hubbell Law Directory

---

IOWA

DES MOINES, * Polk Co.

ROXANNE B. CONLIN AND ASSOCIATES, P.C. (AV)

The Plaza, 300 Walnut Street - Suite 5, 50309-2239
Telephone: 515-282-3333
Fax: 515-282-0318

Roxanne B. Conlin

Melinda Kaye Ellwanger   Thomas J. Duff

For full biographical listings, see the Martindale-Hubbell Law Directory

FINLEY, ALT, SMITH, SCHARNBERG, MAY & CRAIG, P.C. (AV)

604 Locust Street, Fourth Floor Equitable Building, 50309
Telephone: 515-288-0145
Telecopier: 515-288-2724

Thomas A. Finley   Steven K. Scharnberg
John D. (Jack) Hilmes

Kerry A. Finley

Representative Clients: Aetna Casualty & Surety Co.; Aetna Life Insurance Co.; ALAS; American Society of Composers, Authors and Publishers; Equitable Life Assurance Society of the U.S.; Federated Insurance Co.; Meredith Corp.; Catholic Health Corp.; Iowa Methodist Medical Center.
Iowa Attorneys for: Midwest Medical Insurance Co.

For Complete List of Firm Personnel, See General Section

For full biographical listings, see the Martindale-Hubbell Law Directory

GALLIGAN, TULLY, DOYLE & REID, P.C. (AV)

Suite 5 The Plaza, 300 Walnut, 50309-2239
Telephone: 515-282-3333
Fax: 515-282-0318
Email: gallig29@ecity.net

Michael J. Galligan   Timm W. Reid
Robert G. Tully   Richard H. Doyle

OF COUNSEL

James A. Albert

Reference: Hawkeye Bank of Des Moines.

For full biographical listings, see the Martindale-Hubbell Law Directory

THE JAMES LAW FIRM, P.C. (AV)

630 Equitable Building, 604 Locust Street, 50309
Telephone: 515-246-8484
Fax: 515-246-8767

Dwight W. James   Frederick W. James

Reference: Norwest Bank.

For full biographical listings, see the Martindale-Hubbell Law Directory

---

OSKALOOSA, * Mahaska Co.

POTHOVEN, BLOMGREN & STRAVERS (AV)

1201 High Avenue West, P.O. Box 1066, 52577
Telephone: 515-673-4438
Fax: 515-673-5177
Email: PBSLAW@KDSI.NET

MEMBERS OF FIRM

Marion H. Pothoven   James Q. Blomgren
Randall C. Stravers

ASSOCIATE

Julie Bond Fisher

For full biographical listings, see the Martindale-Hubbell Law Directory

---

WEST DES MOINES, Polk Co.

LaMARCA & LANDRY, P.C. (AV)

1300 50th Street, 50266
Telephone: 515-225-2600
Fax: 515-225-8581

George A. LaMarca   Gregory W. Landry
Robert K. DuPuy

Gary G. Mattson

OF COUNSEL

Martin R. Anderson   Samuel S. Duffey

For full biographical listings, see the Martindale-Hubbell Law Directory

KANSAS

OVERLAND PARK, Johnson Co.

FISHER, PATTERSON, SAYLER & SMITH, L.L.P. (AV)

11050 Roe Avenue, Suite 210, 66211
Telephone: 913-339-6757
FAX: 913-339-6187
Topeka, Kansas Office: 534 South Kansas Avenue, Suite 400, P.O. Box 949, 66601.
Telephone: 913-232-7761.
Fax: 913-232-6604.

MEMBERS OF FIRM
Edwin Dudley Smith (Resident)   Michael K. Seck (Resident)
David P. Madden (Resident)
ASSOCIATE
Patrick G. Reavey (Resident)

For full biographical listings, see the Martindale-Hubbell Law Directory

---

SHAMBERG, JOHNSON & BERGMAN, CHARTERED (AV)

Suite 355, 4551 West 107th Street, 66207
Telephone: 913-642-0600
Fax: 913-642-9629
Kansas City, Kansas Office: Suite 860, New Brotherhood Building, 8th and State Streets.
Telephone: 913-281-1900.
Kansas City, Missouri Office: Suite 205, Scarritt Arcade Building, 819 Walnut.
Telephone: 816-556-9431.

Lynn R. Johnson	Victor A. Bergman
	John M. Parisi

Steven G. Brown	Anthony L. DeWitt
Steve N. Six	(Not admitted in KS)
	Patrick A. Hamilton

OF COUNSEL
John E. Shamberg

For full biographical listings, see the Martindale-Hubbell Law Directory

---

TOPEKA, * Shawnee Co.

BENNETT & DILLON, L.L.P. (AV)

1605 Southwest 37th Street, 66611
Telephone: 913-267-5063
Fax: 913-267-2652

MEMBERS OF FIRM
Mark L. Bennett, Jr.   Wilburn Dillon, Jr.
Ann L. Hoover

Jeffrey D. Jackson

References: Commerce Bank and Trust; Columbian National Bank and Trust; Silver Lake State Bank.

For full biographical listings, see the Martindale-Hubbell Law Directory

---

PALMER & LOWRY (AV)

Suite 102 Columbian Building, 112 West Sixth, 66603-3862
Telephone: 913-233-1836
Fax: 913-233-3703

MEMBERS OF FIRM
Jerry R. Palmer   Kirk W. Lowry
ASSOCIATE
L J Leatherman

References: Commerce State Bank; Merchants National Bank.

For full biographical listings, see the Martindale-Hubbell Law Directory

---

EUGENE B. RALSTON & ASSOCIATES, P.A. (AV)

2913 Southwest Maupin Lane, 66614-4139
Telephone: 913-273-8002
FAX: 913-273-0744
Email: ERalston@AOL.Com

Eugene B. Ralston

Kevin L. Diehl	Ronald P. Pope

LEGAL SUPPORT PERSONNEL
PARALEGALS
Barbara Cobuluis	Katrina Windholz
Teresa McLinn	Corri Wecker
	Bonnie Price

(See Next Column)

PRIVATE INVESTIGATOR
Jack L. Grant

For full biographical listings, see the Martindale-Hubbell Law Directory

WRIGHT, HENSON, SOMERS, SEBELIUS, CLARK & BAKER, LLP (AV)

Commerce Bank Building, 100 Southeast Ninth Street, 2nd Floor, P.O. Box 3555, 66601-3555
Telephone: 913-232-2200
FAX: 913-232-3344

MEMBERS OF FIRM
Thomas E. Wright   Anne Lamborn Baker
Evelyn Zabel Wilson
ASSOCIATES
Michael M. Walker   Donald Sutsu Lee

For Complete List of Firm Personnel, See General Section

For full biographical listings, see the Martindale-Hubbell Law Directory

---

WICHITA, * Sedgwick Co.

FOULSTON & SIEFKIN L.L.P. (AV)

700 Fourth Financial Center, 67202
Telephone: 316-267-6371
Facsimile: 316-267-6345
Topeka, Kansas Office: 1515 Bank IV Tower, 534 Kansas Avenue, 66603.
Telephone: 913-233-3600.
Fax: 913-233-1610.
Dodge City, Kansas Office: 810 Frontview, P.O. Box 1147, 67801.
Telephone: 316-227-8126.
Fax: 316-227-8451.
Member: Lex Mundi, A Global Association of 126 Independent Firms.

MEMBERS OF FIRM
Jay F. Fowler   Amy S. Lemley
Craig W. West

For Complete List of Firm Personnel, See General Section

For full biographical listings, see the Martindale-Hubbell Law Directory

---

KENTUCKY

BOWLING GREEN, * Warren Co.

ENGLISH, LUCAS, PRIEST & OWSLEY (AV)

1101 College Street, P.O. Box 770, 42102-0770
Telephone: 502-781-6500
Telecopier: 502-782-7782
Email: inquiry@elpo.com

MEMBERS OF FIRM
James H. Lucas	Murry A. Raines
Keith M. Carwell	Charles E. English, Jr.

ASSOCIATES
Robert A. Young	W. Cravens Priest, III
	Marc Allen Lovell

For Complete List of Firm Personnel, See General Section

For full biographical listings, see the Martindale-Hubbell Law Directory

---

HARLIN & PARKER, P.S.C. (AV)

519 East Tenth Street, P.O. Box 390, 42102-0390
Telephone: 502-842-5611
Telefax: 502-842-2607

William Jerry Parker   Jerry A. Burns

Insurance Clients: CNA Insurance Companies; Maryland Casualty Co.; American International Group.
Railroad and Utilities Clients: District Attorneys for BellSouth Telecommunications, Inc.; CSX Transportation, Inc.
Local Counsel for: General Motors Corp.
Representative Clients: Graves Gilbert Clinic.

For Complete List of Firm Personnel, See General Section

For full biographical listings, see the Martindale-Hubbell Law Directory

---

KERRICK, GRISE & STIVERS (AV)

1025 State Street, P.O. Box 9547, 42102-9547
Telephone: 502-782-8160
Fax: 502-782-5856
Elizabethtown, Kentucky Office: 2935 Dolphin Drive, Suite 102.
Telephone: 502-769-5788.
Fax: 502-737-9285.

(See Next Column)

KERRICK, GRISE & STIVERS—*Continued*
MEMBERS OF FIRM
Thomas N. Kerrick   Gregory N. Stivers
John R. Grise   H. Brent Brennenstuhl
ASSOCIATES
Lanna Martin Kilgore   Shawn Rosso Alcott
Laura M. Hagan (Resident,   Jason B. Bell
   Elizabethtown Office)

Representative Clients: Columbia Greenview Regional Hospital; Riverdell Hospital; Hospital Corporation of America; Russell County Hospital; Wayne County Hospital; Hardin Memorial Hospital; Kentucky Hospital Association Trust.

For full biographical listings, see the Martindale-Hubbell Law Directory

MILLIKEN LAW FIRM (AV)

426 East Main Street, P.O. Box 1640, 42102-1640
Telephone: 502-843-0800
Fax: 502-842-1237

W. Currie Milliken   Wesley V. Milliken

Reference: Trans Financial Bank, Bowling Green, Kentucky.

For full biographical listings, see the Martindale-Hubbell Law Directory

COVINGTON, Kenton Co.

ROBERT E. SANDERS AND ASSOCIATES, P.S.C. (AV)

The Charles H. Fisk House, 1017 Russell Street, 41011
Telephone: 606-491-3000
Fax: 606-655-4642
Email: 74762.3055@compuserve.com

Robert E. Sanders

Julie Lippert Duncan   Peggy A. Murphy
Lisa Pruitt Thorner
LEGAL SUPPORT PERSONNEL
Shirley L. Sanders   Sandra A. Head
Sheila D. Rachal

For full biographical listings, see the Martindale-Hubbell Law Directory

LEXINGTON,* Fayette Co.

LYNN, FULKERSON AND NICHOLS (AV)

267 West Short Street, 40507
Telephone: 606-253-0523
Telefax: 606-254-2098
MEMBERS OF FIRM
Deddo G. Lynn   Calvin R. Fulkerson
Mark E. Nichols
ASSOCIATE
Allen E. Grimes, III
OF COUNSEL
Edward R. Hays   Gordon W. Moss

Representative Clients: United States Fidelity & Guaranty Co.; The Travelers Insurance Co.

For full biographical listings, see the Martindale-Hubbell Law Directory

SAVAGE, GARMER & ELLIOTT, P.S.C. (AV)

Opera House Office Building, 141 North Broadway, 40507
Telephone: 606-254-9351
Fax: 606-233-9769

Joe C. Savage   William R. Garmer
Robert L. Elliott

For full biographical listings, see the Martindale-Hubbell Law Directory

LONDON,* Laurel Co.

FARMER, FARMER, KELLEY AND BROWN (AV)

502 West Fifth Street, Drawer 490, 40743
Telephone: 606-878-7640
Fax: 606-878-2364
Lexington, Kentucky Office: 121 Prosperous Place, Suite 13 B, 40509-1834.
Telephone: 606: 263-2567.
Facsimile: 606: 263-2567.
MEMBERS OF FIRM
F. Preston Farmer   Michael P. Farmer
John F. Kelley, Jr.   Martha L. Brown
ASSOCIATES
Suzanne S. Farmer   Bradford L. Breeding
Jason E. Williams   Estill D. Banks, II

For full biographical listings, see the Martindale-Hubbell Law Directory

LOUISVILLE,* Jefferson Co.

FRANKLIN AND HANCE, P.S.C. (AV)

The Speed House, 505 West Ormsby Avenue, 40203
Telephone: 502-637-6000
Fax: 502-637-1413

Larry B. Franklin   Michael R. Hance

David B. Gray   Hope Kathleen Fitzpatrick

Reference: First National Bank.

For full biographical listings, see the Martindale-Hubbell Law Directory

GARDNER, EWING & SOUZA (AV)

1600 Meidinger Tower, 462 South 4th Street, 40202-3467
Telephone: 502-585-5800
Fax: 502-585-5858
MEMBERS OF FIRM
Gary L. Gardner   C. David Ewing
Joseph C. Souza
ASSOCIATE
Anne Milton McMillin

References: PNC; National City Bank & Trust Co.

For full biographical listings, see the Martindale-Hubbell Law Directory

O'BRYAN, BROWN & TONER (AV)

Suite 1500 Starks Building, 40202
Telephone: 502-585-4700
Fax: 502-585-4703
Email: OBTLAW@aol.com
MEMBERS OF FIRM
Donald K. Brown, Jr.   David Scott Strite
Christopher P. O'Bryan   Andrew N. Clooney
Gerald R. Toner   Cathleen Charters Palmer
John L. Dotson   Clay Edwards
Emily A. Hoffman   Eric A. Paine
James P. Grohmann   Beth H. McMasters
OF COUNSEL
Joseph C. O'Bryan

For full biographical listings, see the Martindale-Hubbell Law Directory

OLDFATHER & MORRIS (AV)

1330 South Third Street, 40208
Telephone: 502-637-7200
Fax: 502-637-3999
Email: om@ntr.net

Ann B. Oldfather   James Barrett
Douglas H. Morris, II   Jennifer Jordan Hall

For full biographical listings, see the Martindale-Hubbell Law Directory

TAUSTINE, POST, SOTSKY, BERMAN, FINEMAN & KOHN (AV)

8th Floor Marion E. Taylor Building, 40202
Telephone: 502-589-5760
FAX: 502-584-5927
Email: 73344.624@compuserve.com
MEMBERS OF FIRM
Jerome D. Berman   H. Philip Grossman
ASSOCIATE
Kathleen A. Pakes

For full biographical listings, see the Martindale-Hubbell Law Directory

WEISS & FREDERICK (AV)

1425 Citizens Plaza, 40202
Telephone: 502-583-1000
FAX: 502-583-4478

Gary M. Weiss   Janice M. Weiss
Carl D. Frederick   William T. Haynes, Jr.
OF COUNSEL
Henry M. Burt   Karla W. Katakis

For full biographical listings, see the Martindale-Hubbell Law Directory

PIKEVILLE,* Pike Co.

PRUITT AND DE BOURBON LAW FIRM (AV)

The Call Building, Second Street, P.O. Box 339, 41502
Telephone: 606-437-7366; 437-7367; 237-1280
Fax: 606-432-2367

(See Next Column)

PRUITT AND DE BOURBON LAW FIRM, *Pikeville—Continued*

MEMBERS OF FIRM

James P. Pruitt, Jr.   P. Michael de Bourbon

Reference: The Citizen's Bank of Pikeville.

For full biographical listings, see the Martindale-Hubbell Law Directory

LOUISIANA

BATON ROUGE,* East Baton Rouge Parish

KEAN, MILLER, HAWTHORNE, D'ARMOND, McCOWAN & JARMAN, L.L.P. (AV)

22nd Floor, One American Place, P.O. Box 3513, 70821
Telephone: 504-387-0999
Fax: 504-388-9133
New Orleans, Louisiana Office: Energy Centre, Suite 1470, 1100 Poydras Street.
Telephone: 504-585-3050.
Fax: 504-585-3051.
Plaquemine, Louisiana Office: Suite 10, 23425 Railroad Avenue.
Telephone: 504-687-9845.
Fax: 504-382-3445.

MEMBERS OF FIRM

Charles S. McCowan, Jr.   Vance A. Gibbs
G. William Jarman   Bradley C. Myers

Linda G. Rodrigue   Gary P. Graphia
John F. Jakuback   Connor B. Eglin

Representative Clients: Anesthesiology Group, Baton Rouge, LA; Baton Rouge Clinic, Baton Rouge, LA; Bone & Joint Clinic, Baton Rouge, LA; Capitol Home Health, Baton Rouge, LA; Insurance Corporation of America, Houston, TX; Louisiana Medical Mutual Insurance Company, Metairie, LA.; The Paradigin Insurance Company, Louisville, KY.

For Complete List of Firm Personnel, See General Section

For full biographical listings, see the Martindale-Hubbell Law Directory

LANE, FERTITTA, LANE, JANNEY & THOMAS (AV)

435 Louisiana Avenue, P.O. Box 3335, 70821
Telephone: 504-387-0241
Fax: 504-387-1238

MEMBERS OF FIRM

Horace C. Lane (1921-1989)   Thomas A. Lane
Frank A. Fertitta   William F. Janney
Richard S. Thomas

ASSOCIATE

Margaret T. Lane

Representative Clients: State Farm Mutual Automobile Insurance Co.; State Farm Fire & Casualty Co.; United States Fidelity & Guaranty Co.; Aetna Casualty & Surety Co.; Employers Liability Assurance Corp., Ltd.; Allstate Insurance Co.; St. Paul Fire and Marine Insurance Co.; The Medical Protective Co.; Safeco Insurance Co. of America; Horace Mann Insurance Co.

For full biographical listings, see the Martindale-Hubbell Law Directory

WATSON, BLANCHE, WILSON & POSNER (AV)

505 North Boulevard, P.O. Drawer 2995, 70821-2995
Telephone: 504-387-5511
Fax: 504-387-5972

Peter T. Dazzio   Michael M. Remson
Felix R. Weill   P. Chauvin Wilkinson, Jr.
William E. Scott, III   Randall L. Champagne
René J. Pfefferle

ASSOCIATE

P. Scott Jolly

Representative Clients: Baton Rouge General Medical Center; Louisiana Hospital Association; Woman's Hospital.

For full biographical listings, see the Martindale-Hubbell Law Directory

---

LAFAYETTE,* Lafayette Parish

ROY, BIVINS, JUDICE & HENKE, A PROFESSIONAL LAW CORPORATION (AV)

600 Jefferson Street, Suite 800, P.O. Drawer Z, 70502
Telephone: 318-233-7430
Telecopier: 318-233-8403

(See Next Column)

Harmon F. Roy   Kenneth M. Henke
John A. Bivins   W. Alan Lilley
Ronald J. Judice   Philip E. Roberts
Patrick M. Wartelle

Representative Clients: Employers Insurance of Wausau; Louisiana Medical Mutual Ins. Co.; St. Paul Fire & Marine Ins. Co.; Our Lady of Lourdes Regional Medical Center, Inc.; Midwest Medical Ins. Co.; Olsten Home Health Care Services.

For full biographical listings, see the Martindale-Hubbell Law Directory

---

MONROE,* Ouachita Parish

HAYES, HARKEY, SMITH & CASCIO, L.L.P. (AV)

2811 Kilpatrick Boulevard, P.O. Box 8032, 71211-8032
Telephone: 318-387-2422
FAX: 318-388-5809

Thomas M. Hayes, Jr.   Charles S. Smith
  (1915-1994)   Thomas M. Hayes, III
Louis D. Smith   Bruce McKamy Mintz
Joseph D. Cascio, Jr.   C. Joseph Roberts, III
John B. Saye

OF COUNSEL

Haynes L. Harkey, Jr.

Karen L. Hayes   Elizabeth D. Bogan
Harry McClellan Moffett, IV

Representative Clients: Cigna, Inc.; CNA; Continental Insurance Healthcare; St. Francis Medical Center, Inc.; St. Paul Insurance Group; Travelers Ins. Co.

For full biographical listings, see the Martindale-Hubbell Law Directory

McLEOD VERLANDER (AV)

A Partnership including Professional Law Corporations
1900 North 18th Street, Suite 610, P.O. Box 2270, 71207-2270
Telephone: 318-325-7000
Telecopier: 318-324-0580
Email: mvlaw@iamerica.net

MEMBERS OF FIRM

Robert P. McLeod (P.L.C.)   Rick W. Duplissey
David E. Verlander, III (P.L.C.)   Pamela G. Nathan
Laurie J. Burkett

Representative Clients: Columbia Health Systems; Columbia North Monroe Hospital; Louisiana Medical Mutual Insurance Co.; The Orthopaedic Clinic of Monroe; Evanston Insurance Company; Extacorporeal Technologies, Inc.; Daig Corporation.

For full biographical listings, see the Martindale-Hubbell Law Directory

---

NEW ORLEANS,* Orleans Parish

BOGGS, LOEHN & RODRIGUE (AV)

A Partnership including Law Corporations
Suite 1800 Lykes Center, 300 Poydras Street, 70130-3597
Telephone: 504-523-7090
Fax: 504-581-6822

Charles A. Boggs (A Law   Edward A. Rodrigue, Jr., (A
  Corporation)   Law Corporation)
Thomas E. Loehn (A Law   Robert I. Baudouin
  Corporation)   Jedd S. Malish

Reference: First National Bank of Commerce, New Orleans, La.

For full biographical listings, see the Martindale-Hubbell Law Directory

CAPITELLI & WICKER (AV)

2950 Energy Centre, 1100 Poydras Street, 70163-2950
Telephone: 504-582-2425
FAX: 504-582-2422

Ralph Capitelli   T. Carey Wicker, III
Paul Michael Elvir, Jr.

OF COUNSEL

Terry Q. Alarcon

For full biographical listings, see the Martindale-Hubbell Law Directory

EMMETT, COBB, WAITS & KESSENICH, A PROFESSIONAL LAW CORPORATION (AV)

Suite 1950, 1515 Poydras Street, 70112
Telephone: 504-581-1301
Telex: 58-4430
Telecopier: 504-581-6020

(See Next Column)

EMMETT, COBB, WAITS & KESSENICH A PROFESSIONAL LAW CORPORATION—
Continued

Francis Emmett	John F. Emmett
Randolph J. Waits	Susan E. Henning
J. Fredrick Kessenich	Michael G. Helm
James A. Cobb, Jr.	Jack C. Benjamin, Jr.

Eugene W. Policastri

Reference: First National Bank of Commerce, New Orleans.

For full biographical listings, see the Martindale-Hubbell Law Directory

GAINSBURGH, BENJAMIN, DAVID, MEUNIER, NORIEA & WARSHAUER (AV)

2800 Energy Centre, 1100 Poydras, 70163-2800
Telephone: 504-522-2304
Telecopier: 504-528-9973
Email: GAINSBEN@IAMERICA.NET

OF COUNSEL

Jack C. Benjamin (P.L.C.)

MEMBERS OF FIRM

Robert J. David	Irving J. Warshauer
Gerald E. Meunier	Stevan C. Dittman
Nick F. Noriea, Jr.	Madeleine M. Landrieu

Darryl M. Phillips

ASSOCIATES

Michael G. Calogero	Jeffrey A. Mitchell

For full biographical listings, see the Martindale-Hubbell Law Directory

---

SHREVEPORT, Caddo Parish

TROY E. BAIN (AV)

1540 Irving Place, 71101
Telephone: 318-221-0076
Fax: 318-227-8290

Reference: Commercial National Bank of Shreveport.

For full biographical listings, see the Martindale-Hubbell Law Directory

---

MAYER, SMITH & ROBERTS, L.L.P. (AV)

1550 Creswell, 71101
Telephone: 318-222-2135, 222-2268
Fax: 318-222-6420
Email: (Attorney's First Name)@MSRLAW.COM

MEMBERS OF FIRM

Caldwell Roberts	David Butterfield
Walter O. Hunter, Jr.	Henry N. Bellamy
Mark A. Goodwin	John C. Turnage
Ben Marshall, Jr.	Paul R. Mayer, Jr.
Alexander S. Lyons	Steven E. Soileau
Kim Purdy Thomas	Deborah Shea Baukman

Caldwell Roberts, Jr.

ASSOCIATES

Frank K. Carroll	Dalton Roberts Ross

OF COUNSEL

Charles L. Mayer	Paul R. Mayer

Representative Clients: CNA Insurance Companies; Liberty Mutual Insurance Company; The St. Paul Companies; United States Fidelity and Guaranty Company; Schumpert Medical Center; Travelers Insurance Company; Great American Insurance Company; Insurance Corporation of America; Highlands Insurance Company.

For full biographical listings, see the Martindale-Hubbell Law Directory

MAINE

---

*AUGUSTA,** Kennebec Co.

* indicates certain Bar Register subscribers whose principal office is located elsewhere in the state and who have arranged for representation as a part of the state capital listings that follow

*** PIERCE ATWOOD (AV)**

77 Winthrop Street, 04330
Telephone: 207-622-6311
Fax: 207-623-9367
Email: info@PierceAtwood.com
Portland, Maine Office: One Monument Square.
Telephone: 207-791-1100.
Fax: 207-791-1350.
Newburyport, Massachusetts Office: 6 Harris Street.
Telephone: 508-465-9599.
Fax: 508-465-9945.

(See Next Column)

MEMBERS OF FIRM

Malcolm L. Lyons	John C. Nivison

For Complete List of Firm Personnel, See General Section

For full biographical listings, see the Martindale-Hubbell Law Directory

---

*PORTLAND,** Cumberland Co.

PRETI, FLAHERTY, BELIVEAU & PACHIOS (AV)

A Limited Liability Company
443 Congress Street, P.O. Box 11410, 04104-7410
Telephone: 207-791-3000
Telecopier: 207-791-3111
Email: admin@pfbpnet.com
Augusta, Maine Office: 45 Memorial Circle, P.O. Box 1058, 04332-1058.
Telephone: 207-623-5300.
Telecopier: 207-623-2914.

MEMBERS OF FIRM

Christopher D. Nyhan	Daniel Rapaport

Elizabeth A. Olivier

ASSOCIATE

Kevin J. Beal

Representative Clients: St. Paul Fire and Marine Insurance Co.; PHICO Insurance Co.

For Complete List of Firm Personnel, See General Section

For full biographical listings, see the Martindale-Hubbell Law Directory

---

SMITH ELLIOTT SMITH & GARMEY, P.A. (AV)

100 Commercial Street, Suite 304, 04101
Telephone: 207-774-3199
Telefax: 207-774-2235
Kennebunk, Maine Office: Route One South, 9 York Street.
Telephone: 207-985-4464.
Telefax: 207-985-3946.
Saco, Maine Office: 199 Main Street, P.O. Box 1179.
Telephone: 207-282-1527.
Telefax: 207-283-4412. Sanford
Telephone: 207-324-1560. Wells
Telephone: 207-646-0970.

Randall E. Smith	Terrence D. Garmey

Representative Clients: Town of Waterboro, Maine; City of Biddeford; Saco and Biddeford Savings Institution; Ocean Communities Federal Credit Union.
Local Counsel for: East Guard Insurance Co.
Reference: Saco & Biddeford Savings Institution.

For Complete List of Firm Personnel, See General Section

For full biographical listings, see the Martindale-Hubbell Law Directory

---

THOMPSON & BOWIE (AV)

Three Canal Plaza, P.O. Box 4630, 04112
Telephone: 207-774-2500
Telecopier: 207-774-3591

MEMBERS OF FIRM

Roy E. Thompson, Jr.	Frank W. DeLong, III
James M. Bowie	Michael E. Saucier
Daniel R. Mawhinney	Mark V. Franco
Rebecca H. Farnum	Elizabeth Knox Peck
Glenn H. Robinson	Cathy S. Roberts

ASSOCIATE

Paul C. Catsos

For full biographical listings, see the Martindale-Hubbell Law Directory

---

SACO, York Co.

SMITH ELLIOTT SMITH & GARMEY, P.A. (AV)

199 Main Street, P.O. Box 1179, 04072
Telephone: 207-282-1527
Telefax: 207-283-4412
Sanford *Telephone:* 207-324-1560
Portland *Telephone:* 207-774-3199
Wells *Telephone:* 207-646-0970
Kennebunk, Maine Office: Route One South, 9 York Street.
Telephone: 207-985-4464.
Telefax: 207-985-3946.
Portland, Maine Office: 100 Commercial Street, Suite 304.
Telephone: 207-774-3199.
Telefax: 207-774-2235.

Randall E. Smith	Terrence D. Garmey

John H. O'Neil, Jr.

Representative Clients: City of Biddeford; Town of Waterboro, Maine; Saco and Biddeford Savings Institution; Ocean Communities Federal Credit Union.

(See Next Column)

SMITH ELLIOTT SMITH & GARMEY P.A., *Saco—Continued*

Local Counsel for: East Guard Insurance Co.
Reference: Saco & Biddeford Savings Institution.

For Complete List of Firm Personnel, See General Section

For full biographical listings, see the Martindale-Hubbell Law Directory

MARYLAND

*BALTIMORE,** (Independent City)

ELLIN AND BAKER (AV)

Second Floor, 1101 St. Paul Street, 21202
Telephone: 410-727-1787
FAX: 410-547-1787
1-800-237-1787

MEMBER OF FIRM

Marvin Ellin   LaVonna Lee Vice

Michael P. Smith

For full biographical listings, see the Martindale-Hubbell Law Directory

GOODELL, DeVRIES, LEECH & GRAY, LLP (AV)

Suite 2000, One South Street, 21202
Telephone: 410-783-4000
Telecopy: 410-783-4040
Email: GDLG@GDLG.COM

MEMBERS OF FIRM

Bruce R. Parker   Craig B. Merkle
Thomas V. Monahan, Jr.   Bonnie J. Beavan
Susan T. Preston   Amy B. Heinrich

For full biographical listings, see the Martindale-Hubbell Law Directory

ISRAELSON, SALSBURY, CLEMENTS & BEKMAN (AV)

300 West Pratt Street Suite 450, 21201
Telephone: 410-539-6633
FAX: 410-625-9554

MEMBERS OF FIRM

Stuart Marshall Salsbury   Daniel M. Clements
Paul D. Bekman   Matthew Zimmerman
Laurence A. Marder

Scott R. Scherr   Lauren R. Calia
Carol J. Glover   Andrew David Alpert

COUNSEL TO THE FIRM
Max R. Israelson

OF COUNSEL
Samuel Omar Jackson, Jr. (Semi-Retired)

For full biographical listings, see the Martindale-Hubbell Law Directory

JANET, WILLOUGHBY & GERSHON, LLC (AV)

Executive Centre at Hooks Lane, 8 Reservoir Circle, Suite 200, 21208
Telephone: 410-653-3200
Toll Free: 888-4-MED-LAW
Fax: 410-653-9030

MEMBERS OF FIRM

Howard Alan Janet (P.C.)   Wayne M. Willoughby (P.A.)
Zev T. Gershon

ASSOCIATES
Randal D. Getz   Robin R. Smith
Anne Michele Crook

LEGAL SUPPORT PERSONNEL
Joan Hunter Green   Sharon Marie Schmidt
(Registered Nurse/Paralegal)   (Paralegal)

For full biographical listings, see the Martindale-Hubbell Law Directory

KAHN, SMITH & COLLINS, P.A. (AV)

110 Saint Paul Street, 6th Floor, 21202
Telephone: 410-244-1010
Fax: 410-244-8001
Email: incourt@ari.net *URL:* http://www.interbit.com/ksc

Andrew H. Kahn   Francis J. Collins
Joel A. Smith   David V. Diggs
Christyne L. Neff

Sarah Pazourek Harlan   Leslie A. Pladna

For full biographical listings, see the Martindale-Hubbell Law Directory

MEHLMAN & GREENBLATT, LLC (AV)

4 Reservoir Circle, Suite 100, 21208
Telephone: 410-486-4790
Fax: 410-486-4360

Gerson B. Mehlman   Frank W. Spector
Gary R. Greenblatt   Francis X. Leary
Wendy Lozinsky Shiff   Constance M. Hare

LEGAL SUPPORT PERSONNEL
Stephanie A. Ristvey (Paralegal)   Ruth P. Stein

For full biographical listings, see the Martindale-Hubbell Law Directory

ROBINETTE, DUGAN & JAKUBOWSKI, P.A. (AV)

The Robinette-Dugan Building, 801 St. Paul Street, 21202
Telephone: 410-659-6700
FAX: 410-752-0456

Gilbert H. Robinette   Ruth A. Jakubowski
Henry E. Dugan, Jr.   Bruce J. Babij

Pamela S. Foresman   George S. Tolley, III

OF COUNSEL
Marian V. Fleming

For full biographical listings, see the Martindale-Hubbell Law Directory

SCANLAN & ROSEN, P.A. (AV)

26 South Street, 21202-3399
Telephone: 410-244-1155
FAX: 410-244-1157

Alfred L. Scanlan, Jr.   Marc Seldin Rosen

Michael Stuart Warshaw   Colleen A. Cavanaugh

OF COUNSEL
James Lee Katz

For full biographical listings, see the Martindale-Hubbell Law Directory

SCHOCHOR, FEDERICO AND STATON, P.A. (AV)

The Paulton, 1211 St. Paul Street, 21202
Telephone: 410-234-1000
Toll Free: 888-234-0001
Facsimile: 410-234-1010
URL: http://www.sfspa.com
Washington D.C. Office: 750 First Street, N.E., Suite 905.
Telephone: 202-408-3300.

Jonathan Schochor   Philip C. Federico
                                Kerry D. Staton

Louis G. Close, III   Christopher P. Kennedy

For full biographical listings, see the Martindale-Hubbell Law Directory

BETHESDA, Montgomery Co.

FREEMAN & JENNER, P.C. (AV)

3 Bethesda Metro Center, Suite 1410, 20814
Telephone: 301-907-7747
FAX: 301-907-9877
Washington, D.C. Office: 1000 16th Street, N.W., Suite 300.
Telephone: 301-907-7747.
Aspen, Colorado Office: 215 South Monarch Street, Suite 202.
Telephone: 970-925-3400.
FAX: 970-925-4043.

Martin H. Freeman   Robert K. Jenner

Barbara E. Hirsch   Mark Allan Freeman

Reference: Crestar Bank of Maryland.

For full biographical listings, see the Martindale-Hubbell Law Directory

*ROCKVILLE,** Montgomery Co.

ARMSTRONG, DONOHUE & CEPPOS, CHARTERED (AV)

Suite 101, 204 Monroe Street, 20850
Telephone: 301-251-0440
Telecopier: 301-279-5929

Larry A. Ceppos   H. Kenneth Armstrong
                                Benjamin S. Vaughan

Oya S. Oner   Sharon A. Marcial
Pamela Barrow Kincheloe   J. Eric Rhoades

For full biographical listings, see the Martindale-Hubbell Law Directory

Rockville—Continued

BRAULT, GRAHAM, SCOTT & BRAULT (AV)

101 South Washington Street, 20850
Telephone: 301-424-1060
Fax: 301-424-7991
Washington, D.C. Office: 1906 Sunderland Place, N.W.
Telephone: 202-785-1200.
FAX: 202-785-4301.
Arlington, Virginia Office: Suite 1201, 2300 North Clarendon Boulevard, Courthouse Plaza.
Telephone: 703-358-9200.

OF COUNSEL

Laurence T. Scott   Janet S. Zigler (Resident)

MEMBERS OF FIRM

Denver H. Graham (1922-1987)   Daniel L. Shea (Resident)
Albert E. Brault (Retired)   M. Kathleen Parker (Resident)
Albert D. Brault (Resident)   David G. Mulquin (Resident)
Leo A. Roth, Jr.   James M. Brault (Resident)
James S. Wilson (Resident)   Regina Ann Casey (Resident)
Ronald G. Guziak   Sanford A. Friedman

ASSOCIATES

Holly D. Shupert (Resident)   Joan F. Brault (Resident)
Rhonda Ann Hurwitz (Resident)   Joseph P. Morra (Resident)
                   Michael A. Carlo

Representative Clients: American Oil Co.; Crum & Forster Group; Fireman's Fund American Insurance Cos.; Kemper Group; Reliance Insurance Cos.; Safeco Group; Government Employees Insurance Co.; Medical Mutual Insurance Society of Maryland; Legal Mutual Liability Insurance Society of Maryland.

For full biographical listings, see the Martindale-Hubbell Law Directory

MICHAEL S. MORGENSTERN & ASSOCIATES, P.C. (AV)

Fifth Floor, 110 North Washington Street, P.O. Box 4690, 20850
Telephone: 301-217-9500
FAX: 301-217-9579

Michael S. Morgenstern

Sheila Lowery Ferguson

OF COUNSEL

Carl Morgenstern   Lawrence S. Jacobs
  (Not admitted in MD)

For full biographical listings, see the Martindale-Hubbell Law Directory

MASSACHUSETTS

BOSTON, * Suffolk Co.

CORNELL AND GOLLUB (AV)

75 Federal Street, 02110
Telephone: 617-482-8100
Telecopier: 617-482-3917

MEMBERS OF FIRM

Robert W. Cornell (1910-1988)   Peter M. Durney
Karl L. Gollub (1934-1985)   Paul F. Lynch
David H. Sempert   Jane Treen Brand
Philip J. Foley   Janet J. Bobit

ASSOCIATES

Hugh M. Coxe   Thomas H. Dolan
Thomas A. Pursley   Eric B. Goldberg
David W. McGough   Kelly L. Wilkins
Susan Donaldson Novins   James P. Kerr
Marie Chadeayne Chafe   Patricia A. Hartnett

For full biographical listings, see the Martindale-Hubbell Law Directory

LAW OFFICES OF LEONARD GLAZER, P.C. & ASSOCIATES (AV)

One Longfellow Place Suite 3408, 02114
Telephone: 617-523-4411
Fax: 617-523-7433

Leonard Glazer

Frank E. Glazer   Anthony R. Orlando, III

For full biographical listings, see the Martindale-Hubbell Law Directory

SWARTZ & SWARTZ (AV)

10 Marshall Street, 02108
Telephone: 617-742-1900
Fax: 617-367-7193

(See Next Column)

Edward M. Swartz   Joan E. Swartz
Alan L. Cantor   James A. Swartz
Joseph A. Swartz   Harold David Levine
Victor A. Denaro   David P. Angueira

OF COUNSEL

Fredric A. Swartz

For full biographical listings, see the Martindale-Hubbell Law Directory

SPRINGFIELD, * Hampden Co.

LAW OFFICES OF THOMAS A. KENEFICK, III, P.C. (AV)

73 Chestnut Street, 01103
Telephone: 413-734-7000
Fax: 413-731-1302

Thomas A. Kenefick, III

For full biographical listings, see the Martindale-Hubbell Law Directory

WORCESTER, * Worcester Co.

CHRISTOPHER, HAYS, WOJCIK & MAVRICOS (AV)

370 Main Street, 01608
Telephone: 508-792-2800
FAX: 508-792-6224

MEMBERS OF FIRM

William W. Hays   David A. Wojcik
              John A. Mavricos

OF COUNSEL

Christopher Christopher   William C. Perrin, Jr.

Reference: Flagship Bank & Trust Co.

For full biographical listings, see the Martindale-Hubbell Law Directory

MICHIGAN

ANN ARBOR, * Washtenaw Co.

BOOTHMAN, HEBERT & ELLER, P.C. (AV)

300 N. Fifth Avenue, Suite 140, 48108
Telephone: 313-995-9050
Fax: 313-995-8966
Detroit, Michigan Office: Marquette Building, 243 West Congress, Suite 950.
Telephone: 313-964-0150.
Fax: 313-964-2226.

Richard C. Boothman (Resident)

For full biographical listings, see the Martindale-Hubbell Law Directory

HOOPER, HATHAWAY, PRICE, BEUCHE & WALLACE (AV)

126 South Main Street, 48104
Telephone: 313-662-4426
Fax: 313-662-9559

Joseph C. Hooper (1899-1980)   Gregory A. Spaly
John R. Hathaway (Retired)   Robert W. Southard
Alan E. Price   William J. Stapleton
James R. Beuche   Bruce C. Conybeare, Jr.
Bruce T. Wallace   Anthony P. Patti
Charles W. Borgsdorf   Marcia J. Major
Mark R. Daane   Angela L. Jackson

OF COUNSEL

James A. Evashevski   Roderick K. Daane

Representative Clients: Chem-Trend, Inc.; Dundee Cement Co.; Ervin Industries, Inc.; First Martin Corp.; Group 243 Design, Inc.; Honeywell; Microwave Sensors, Inc.; Shearson Lehman Hutton; O'Neal Construction Co.; Pittsfield Products, Inc.

For full biographical listings, see the Martindale-Hubbell Law Directory

BINGHAM FARMS, Oakland Co.

SMALL, TOTH, BALDRIDGE & VAN BELKUM, P.C. (AV)

30100 Telegraph Road Suite 250, 48025-4516
Telephone: 810-647-9595
Facsimile: 810-647-9599

Richard L. Small   David M. Baldridge
John M. Toth   Thomas G. Van Belkum
              Keith P. Felty

Representative Clients: The Medical Protective Co.; Michigan Physicians Mutual Liability Insurance Co.; Physicians Insurance Company of Michigan; AAMOS National; CNA Insurance Group; Anthem Insurance Co.; Oakwood United Hospitals; The Detroit Medical Center Affiliated Hospital.

For full biographical listings, see the Martindale-Hubbell Law Directory

BIRMINGHAM, Oakland Co.

CARSON FISCHER, P.L.C. (AV)

Third Floor, 300 East Maple Road, 48009-6317
Telephone: 810-644-4840
Facsimile: 810-644-1832

Robert M. Carson   Kathleen A. Stibich

For full biographical listings, see the Martindale-Hubbell Law Directory

GOREN & GOREN, P.C. (AV)

Suite 470, 30400 Telegraph Road, 48025
Telephone: 810-540-3100

Robert Goren   Steven E. Goren

Reference: Michigan National Bank-Oakland.

KELL & LYNCH, P.C. (AV)

300 East Maple Road, Suite 200, 48009
Telephone: 810-647-2333
Telefax: 810-647-2781

Michael V. Kell   Margaret A. Lynch

Jennifer T. Gilhool   Steven M. Ribiat
  (Not admitted in MI)

OF COUNSEL
M. Andrea Vaughn

Representative Clients: AlliedSignal, Inc.; AMP Inc.; Dow Corning Corp.; Hatteras Yachts; Lectron Products, Inc.; Metromedia Steakhouses, Inc.; Sybron Corp.; Michigan Consolidated Gas Co.; American Natural Resources.

For full biographical listings, see the Martindale-Hubbell Law Directory

BLOOMFIELD HILLS, Oakland Co.

THE GOOGASIAN FIRM, P.C. (AV)

6895 Telegraph Road, 48301-3138
Telephone: 810-540-3333
Fax: 810-540-7213

George A. Googasian   Craig Weber
          Steven G. Googasian

For full biographical listings, see the Martindale-Hubbell Law Directory

O'CONNOR, DEGRAZIA & TAMM, P.C. (AV)

4111 Andover East, 48302
Telephone: 810-433-2000
Fax: 810-433-2001

Richard M. O'Connor   Lorraine M. Knapp
James I. DeGrazia   Christopher T. Koch
James E. Tamm   Amy Hobbs Iannone
Julie McCann-O'Connor   Jay Dilday Gardner
Audrey J. Forbush   Thomas H. Schram

Representative Clients: Regents of the University of Michigan; William Beaumont Hospital; Michigan Physicians Mutual Liability Co.; Botsford General Hospital; Michigan Municipal League; Michigan Municipal Liability and Property Pool; Select Insured Risk Services; St. Paul Insurance Cos.; Physicians Insurance Company of Michigan; National Chiropractic Mutual.

For full biographical listings, see the Martindale-Hubbell Law Directory

DAVID D. PATTON & ASSOCIATES, P.C. (AV)

100 Bloomfield Hills Parkway, Suite 110, 48304
Telephone: 810-258-6020
Fax: 810-258-6052
Email: Litigation@Aol.Com

David D. Patton

Ellen Bartman Jannette   Patricia C. White
          David H. Patton (1912-1993)

For full biographical listings, see the Martindale-Hubbell Law Directory

PORTNOY, PIDGEON & ROTH, P.C. (AV)

3883 Telegraph, Suite 103, 48302
Telephone: 810-647-4242
Fax: 810-647-8251
Email: DWINNIE103@AOL.COM

Bernard N. Portnoy   Marc S. Berlin
James M. Pidgeon   Berton K. May
Robert P. Roth   Sheila Connor-Heath
          Charles A. Harrison III

(See Next Column)

Representative Clients: North Oakland Medical Center, Pontiac General Hospital Division; Hurly Medical Center, Flint, Michigan; McLaren Regional Medical Center, Flint, Michigan; William Beaumont Hospital, Royal Oak, Michigan; Detroit Osteopathic Hospital; Horizon Health Systems; Bi-County Community Hospital; Riverside Osteopathic; Lapeer Regional Hospital; OUM Group.

For full biographical listings, see the Martindale-Hubbell Law Directory

*DETROIT,** Wayne Co.

BLAKE, KIRCHNER, SYMONDS, MACFARLANE, LARSON & SMITH, P.C. (AV)

1432 Buhl Building, 48226
Telephone: 313-961-7321
Fax: 313-961-5972

F. Peter Blake   Meria E. Larson
Arthur G. Kirchner   Richard P. Smith
Daniel C. Symonds   Kevin T. Kennedy
Bruce F. MacFarlane   Jane P. Garrett
          Christopher G. Manolis

David B. Klein   Michael P. Donnelly
          Kim Leslie Kretzschmar

Reference: Comerica Bank.

For full biographical listings, see the Martindale-Hubbell Law Directory

BOOTHMAN, HEBERT & ELLER, P.C. (AV)

Marquette Building, 243 West Congress, Suite 950, 48226
Telephone: 313-964-0150
Fax: 313-964-2226
Ann Arbor, Michigan Office: 300 N. Fifth Avenue, Suite 140.
Telephone: 313-995-9050.
Fax: 313-995-8966.

Dale L. Hebert   Gary S. Eller
Richard C. Boothman
  (Resident, Ann Arbor Office)

George D. Moustakas   Marta J. Hoffman
Roy A. Luttmann   Sharon E. Hollins
          Joyce E. Taylor
OF COUNSEL
L. Stewart Hastings, Jr.   Kathryn A. Kerka

Representative Clients: University of Michigan; Michigan Physicians Mutual Liability Co.; Emergency Physicians Medical Group; Kaiser Permanente; Physicians Insurance Co. of Michigan.
Reference: Comerica Bank-Detroit.

For full biographical listings, see the Martindale-Hubbell Law Directory

FEIKENS, VANDER MALE, STEVENS, BELLAMY & GILCHRIST, P.C. (AV)

One Detroit Center Suite 3400, 500 Woodward Avenue, 48226-3406
Telephone: 313-962-5909
Fax: 313-962-3125
Email: FEIKENS@COUNSEL.COM

Jack E. Vander Male   Bruce A. VandeVusse
L. Neal Kennedy   William C. Hurley
          Linda M. Galbraith

Richard G. Koefod   Jeffrey Feikens
Joseph E. Kozely, Jr.   Michael B. Barey

For Complete List of Firm Personnel, See General Section

For full biographical listings, see the Martindale-Hubbell Law Directory

GLEICHER & REYNOLDS, P.C. (AV)

1500 Buhl Building, 48226
Telephone: 313-964-6900
Fax: 313-964-8976

Elizabeth Gleicher   Edward C. Reynolds, Jr.
LEGAL SUPPORT PERSONNEL
Laura Bocchini (Legal Coordinator)

For full biographical listings, see the Martindale-Hubbell Law Directory

MEGANCK & COTHORN, P.C. (AV)

Suite 950, 400 Renaissance Center, 48243-1509
Telephone: 313-259-6330
Fax: 313-259-7037

Allan G. Meganck   John A. Cothorn
          Suzanne C. Stanczyk

Thomas Myers   William G. Oldford, Jr.

(See Next Column)

MEGANCK & COTHORN P.C.—Continued

OF COUNSEL
David M. Thoms

Representative Clients: Ford Motor Company; Norton Co.; K-Mart Corp.; The Stanley Works; Textron; Figgie International; Phone-Poulenc Rorer Pharmaceuticals, Inc.; National Chiropractic Mutual Insurance Co.; Kellermeyer Building Services, Inc.; Tokio Marine Management Co.

For full biographical listings, see the Martindale-Hubbell Law Directory

MILLER, CANFIELD, PADDOCK AND STONE, P.L.C. (AV)

A Professional Limited Liability Company
Founded in 1852 by Sidney Davy Miller
150 West Jefferson, Suite 2500, 48226-4415
Telephone: 313-963-6420
Fax: 313-496-7500
Cable Address: "Stem Detroit"
Detroit, Michigan Office: 150 West Jefferson, Suite 2500, 48226-4415.
Telephone: 313-963-6420.
Fax: 313-496-7500.
Cable Address: "Stem Detroit."
Ann Arbor, Michigan Office: 101 North Main Street, 7th Floor, 48104-1400.
Telephone: 313-663-2445.
Fax: 313-747-7147.
Bloomfield Hills, Michigan Office: Suite 100, Pinehurst Office Center, 1400 North Woodward, 48303-2014.
Telephone: 313-645-5000.
Fax: 313-645-1917.
Grand Rapids, Michigan Office: 1200 Campau Square Plaza, 99 Monroe, N.W., 49503-2639.
Telephone: 616-454-8656.
Fax: 616-776-6322.
Howell, Michigan Office: 121 South Barnard Street, Suite 4, 48843-2305.
Telephone: 517-546-7600.
Telecopier: 517-546-6974.
Kalamazoo, Michigan Office: 444 West Michigan Avenue, 49007-3752.
Telephone: 616-381-7030.
Fax: 616-382-0244.
Lansing, Michigan Office: One Michigan Avenue, Suite 900, 48933-1609.
Telephone: 517-487-2070.
Fax: 517-374-6304.
Monroe, Michigan Office: The Executive Centre, 214 East Elm Avenue, 48161-2682.
Telephone: 313-243-2000.
Fax: 313-243-0901.
Washington, D.C. Office: 1225 Nineteenth Street, N.W., Suite 400. 20036.
Telephone: 202-429-5575; 785-0600.
Fax: 202-331-1118; 785-1234.
Pensacola, Florida Office: 25 West Cedar, 32501.
Telephone: 904-469-1088.
Fax: 904-432-0677.
St. Petersburg, Florida Office: 100 Second Avenue S., Suite 7045, 33701.
Telephone: 813-982-6000.
Fax: 813-892-6002.
New York, New York Office: Eleventh Floor, 135 East 57th Street, 10022-2087.
Telephone: 212-754-5400.
Fax: 212-754-5401.
Gdansk, Poland Office: Suite 322, Dom Technika Building, UI. Rajska 6, 80-850.
Telephone: 011-485-831-2808.
Fax: 011-485-831-4719.
Warsaw, Poland Office: UI. Marszalkowska 82, Suite 561, 00-517.
Telephone: 011-482-623-6457 and 6458.
Fax: 011-482-623-6459.

PRINCIPALS OF FIRM

Charles E. Ritter	James C. Foresman
(Kalamazoo Office)	Leland D. Barringer
Thomas G. Parachini	Brian J. Doren

Irene Bruce Hathaway

Representative Firm Clients: Chrysler Corporation; Comerica, Incorporated; City of Detroit, Michigan; Detroit Tigers, Inc.; First of Michigan; Ford Motor Company; Ford Motor Credit Company; Great Lakes Bancorp; Henry Ford Hospital; INVETECH Company.

For Complete List of Firm Personnel, See General Section

For full biographical listings, see the Martindale-Hubbell Law Directory

ROSEN & LOVELL, P.C. (AV)

Penobscot Building, 645 Griswold Street, Suite 3080, 48226-4224
Telephone: 313-961-7510
Fax: 313-961-2905

Paul A. Rosen	Joan Lovell

For full biographical listings, see the Martindale-Hubbell Law Directory

SCHUREMAN, FRAKES, GLASS & WULFMEIER (AV)

440 East Congress, Fourth Floor, 48226
Telephone: 313-961-1500
Telecopier: 313-961-1087
Harbor Springs, Michigan Office: One Spring Street Sq., 49740.
Telephone: 616-526-1145.
Telecopier: 616-526-9343.

MEMBERS OF FIRM

Jeptha W. Schureman	LeRoy H. Wulfmeier, III
John C. Frakes, Jr.	Cheryl L. Chandler
Charles F. Glass	David M. Ottenwess

ASSOCIATES

Daniel J. Dulworth	John J. Moran
	Paul A. Salyers

Reference: Comerica.

For full biographical listings, see the Martindale-Hubbell Law Directory

EAST LANSING, Ingham Co.

FARHAT, STORY & KRAUS, P.C. (AV)

Beacon Place, 4572 South Hagadorn Road, Suite 3, 48823
Telephone: 517-351-3700
Fax: 517-332-4122
Email: rkraus@sojourn.com

Leo A. Farhat	Chris A. Bergstrom
James E. Burns (1925-1979)	Kitty L. Groh
Monte R. Story	Charles R. Toy
Richard C. Kraus	David M. Platt
Max R. Hoffman Jr.	Thomas L. Sparks

Lawrence P. Schweitzer	Daniel B. Morgan
Debra A. Geroux	Mary K. Robbins-Kralapp

Reference: City Bank, St. Johns.

For full biographical listings, see the Martindale-Hubbell Law Directory

SMITH HAUGHEY RICE & ROEGGE, P.C. (AV)

1301 North Hagadorn Road, 48823-2320
Telephone: 517-332-3030
Facsimile: 517-332-3468
Grand Rapids, Michigan Office: 200 Calder Plaza Building, 250 Monroe Avenue, N.W., 49503-2251.
Telephone: 616-774-8000.
Facsimile: 616-774-2461.
Traverse City, Michigan Office: 241 East State Street, P.O. Box 848, 49685-0848.
Telephone: 616-929-4878.
Facsimile: 616-929-4182.

Douglas G. Powe

Daniel N. Stephens	James R. Duby, Jr.
	Veronica A. Marsich

For full biographical listings, see the Martindale-Hubbell Law Directory

FARMINGTON HILLS, Oakland Co.

NEMIER, TOLARI, LANDRY, MAZZEO & JOHNSON, P.C. (AV)

37000 Grand River, Suite 300, 48335
Telephone: 810-476-6900
Fax: 810-476-6564

Craig L. Nemier	David B. Landry
Jeffrey L. Tolari	Rik Mazzeo
	Mark R. Johnson

Michelle E. Mathieu	Kathy Contos Nash
Christopher A. Todd	Douglas S. Loomer
Thomas S. McLeod	Gregory A. Light

OF COUNSEL

William R. Still	Terry E. Pietryga

LEGAL SUPPORT PERSONNEL
Veeder Ann Willey (Support Staff)

For full biographical listings, see the Martindale-Hubbell Law Directory

FLINT,* Genesee Co.

MAX DEAN (AV)

Suite 1616 120 East 1st Street, 48502
Telephone: 810-235-5631
Fax: 810-235-8983

For full biographical listings, see the Martindale-Hubbell Law Directory

GRAND RAPIDS,* Kent Co.

BREMER, WADE, NELSON, LOHR & COREY, LLP (AV)

600 3 Mile Road, N.W., 49544-1601
Telephone: 616-784-4434
Fax: 616-784-7322

MEMBERS OF FIRM

William M. Bremer	Phillip J. Nelson
Michael D. Wade	James H. Lohr
	Michael J. Corey

ASSOCIATES

Barbara L. Olafsson	Olafur A. Olafsson

LEGAL SUPPORT PERSONNEL

Kathleen A. Fitzpatrick

For full biographical listings, see the Martindale-Hubbell Law Directory

BUCHANAN, SILVER & BECKERING, P.L.C. (AV)

300 Ottawa N.W., Suite 800, 49503
Telephone: 616-458-2464
Fax: 616-458-0608

MEMBERS OF FIRM

John C. Buchanan	Robert J. Buchanan
Lee T. Silver	Jane M. Beckering

For full biographical listings, see the Martindale-Hubbell Law Directory

GRUEL, MILLS, NIMS AND PYLMAN (AV)

50 Monroe Place, Suite 700 West, 49503
Telephone: 616-235-5500
Fax: 616-235-5550

MEMBERS OF FIRM

Grant J. Gruel	Scott R. Melton
William F. Mills	Brion J. Brooks
J. Clarke Nims	Thomas R. Behm
Norman H. Pylman, II	J. Paul Janes

Representative Clients: Aquinas College; Bell Helmet Co.; Blodgett Memorial Medical Center; Butterworth Hospital; Chem Central, Inc.; Cook Pump Co.; Grove, Inc.; NBDC; Heim Corp.

For full biographical listings, see the Martindale-Hubbell Law Directory

GARY J. MCINERNEY, P.C. (AV)

330 East Fulton, 49503
Telephone: 616-458-6111; 800-819-2332
Telecopier: 616-458-6446

Gary J. McInerney

Michael A. McInerney	Adna H. Underhill

For full biographical listings, see the Martindale-Hubbell Law Directory

SMITH HAUGHEY RICE & ROEGGE, P.C. (AV)

200 Calder Plaza Building, 250 Monroe Avenue, N.W., 49503-2251
Telephone: 616-774-8000
Facsimile: 616-774-2461
East Lansing, Michigan Office: 1301 North Hagadorn Road, 48823-2320.
Telephone: 517-332-3030.
Facsimile: 517-332-3468.
Traverse City, Michigan Office: 241 East State Street, P.O. Box 848, 49685-0848.
Telephone: 616-929-4878.
Facsimile: 616-929-4182.

Clifford A. Mitts (1902-1962)	Thomas R. Wurst
Laurence D. Smith (1913-1980)	Craig R. Noland
Robert V.V. Rice (1899-1982)	Paul M. Oleniczak
Michael S. Barnes (1944-1989)	Craig S. Neckers
L. Roland Roegge	Thomas E. Kent
Thomas F. Blackwell	Leonard M. Hickey
P. Laurence Mulvihill	John C. O'Loughlin
Lawrence P. Mulligan	Anthony J. Quarto
Thomas R. Tasker	Bruce P. Rissi
Paul H. Reinhardt	John M. Kruis
Lance R. Mather	Paul Van Oostenburg
Charles F. Behler	Dale Ann Iverson
John R. Sparks	William R. Jewell
Gary A. Rowe	Jon D. Vander Ploeg
William W. Jack, Jr.	Patrick F. Geary
William J. Hondorp	Terence J. Ackert
Thomas M. Weibel	Brian J. Kilbane
James G. Black	Dan C. Porter
E. Thomas Mc Carthy, Jr.	Phillip K. Mowers
Glenn W. House, Jr.	Carol D. Carlson
	Christopher R. Genther

(See Next Column)

Kay L. Griffith Hammond	Elizabeth Roberts VerHey
Marilyn S. Nickell	Jennifer Jane Nasser
Beth Suzanne Kromer	Ginny Kaye Mikita
Robert M. Kruse	Karl Werner Butterer, Jr.
John B. Combs	Susan Soon Im
Aileen M. Simet	J. Joseph Rossi
Matthew L. Meyer	Stacie R. Seitz
	Dwight K. Hamilton

OF COUNSEL

A. B. Smith, Jr.	Susan Bradley Jakubowski
David O. Haughey	Thomas P. Scholler

For full biographical listings, see the Martindale-Hubbell Law Directory

KALAMAZOO,* Kalamazoo Co.

MILLER, CANFIELD, PADDOCK AND STONE, P.L.C. (AV)

A Professional Limited Liability Company
Founded in 1852 by Sidney Davy Miller
444 West Michigan Avenue, 49007-3752
Telephone: 616-381-7030
Fax: 616-382-0244
Detroit, Michigan Office: 150 West Jefferson, Suite 2500, 48226-4415.
Telephone: 313-963-6420.
Fax: 313-496-7500.
Cable Address: "Stem Detroit."
Ann Arbor, Michigan Office: 101 North Main Street, 7th Floor, 48104-1400.
Telephone: 313-663-2445.
Fax: 313-747-7147.
Bloomfield Hills, Michigan Office: Suite 100, Pinehurst Office Center, 1400 North Woodward, 48303-2014.
Telephone: 313-645-5000.
Fax: 313-645-1917.
Grand Rapids, Michigan Office: 1200 Campau Square Plaza, 99 Monroe, N.W., 49503-2639.
Telephone: 616-454-8656.
Fax: 616-776-6322.
Howell, Michigan Office: 121 South Barnard Street, Suite 4, 48843-2305.
Telephone: 517-546-7600.
Telecopier: 517-546-6974.
Lansing, Michigan Office: One Michigan Avenue, Suite 900, 48933-1609.
Telephone: 517-487-2070.
Fax: 517-374-6304.
Monroe, Michigan Office: The Executive Centre, 214 East Elm Avenue, 48161-2682.
Telephone: 313-243-2000.
Fax: 313-243-0901.
Washington, D.C. Office: 1225 Nineteenth Street, N.W., Suite 400. 20036.
Telephone: 202-429-5575; 785-0600.
Fax: 202-331-1118; 785-1234.
Pensacola, Florida Office: 25 West Cedar, 32501.
Telephone: 904-469-1088.
Fax: 904-432-0677.
St. Petersburg, Florida Office: 100 Second Avenue S., Suite 7045, 33701.
Telephone: 813-982-6000.
Fax: 813-892-6002.
New York, New York Office: Eleventh Floor, 135 East 57th Street, 10022-2087.
Telephone: 212-754-5400.
Fax: 212-754-5401.
Gdansk, Poland Office: Suite 322, Dom Technika Building, Ul. Rajska 6, 80-850.
Telephone: 011-485-831-2808.
Fax: 011-485-831-4719.
Warsaw, Poland Office: Ul. Marszalkowska 82, Suite 561, 00-517.
Telephone: 011-482-623-6457 and 6458.
Fax: 011-482-623-6459.

PRINCIPALS OF FIRM

Charles E. Ritter

Representative Firm Clients: Chrysler Corporation; Comerica, Incorporated; City of Detroit, Michigan; Detroit Tigers, Inc.; First of Michigan; Ford Motor Company; Ford Motor Credit Company; Great Lakes Bancorp; Henry Ford Hospital; INVETECH Company.

For Complete List of Firm Personnel, See General Section

For full biographical listings, see the Martindale-Hubbell Law Directory

LANSING, Ingham Co.

FRASER TREBILCOCK DAVIS & FOSTER, P.C. (AV)

1000 Michigan National Tower, 48933
Telephone: 517-482-5800
Fax: 517-482-0887

C. Mark Hoover	Mark A. Bush

Charyn K. Hain	Marcy R. Meyer

Representative Clients: Michigan Physicians Mutual Liability Co.; Physicians Insurance Company of Michigan.

(See Next Column)

FRASER TREBILCOCK DAVIS & FOSTER P.C.—*Continued*

For Complete List of Firm Personnel, See General Section

For full biographical listings, see the Martindale-Hubbell Law Directory

SMITH HAUGHEY RICE & ROEGGE, P.C.

(See East Lansing)

TIMMER, JAMO & O'LEARY (AV)

521 Seymour Avenue, 48933
Telephone: 517-371-3500
Fax: 517-371-4514

MEMBERS OF FIRM

James A. Timmer
James S. Jamo

James S. O'Leary
Kathleen A. Lopilato

Representative Clients: Auto-Owners Insurance Co.; National Indemnity Insurance Co.; Travelers Insurance Co.; Ohio Farmers Insurance Co.; Bankers Life & Casualty Co.; Western Casualty & Surety Co.; Indiana Insurance Group; Western Surety Co.; Michigan Municipal League; Preston Trucking.

For full biographical listings, see the Martindale-Hubbell Law Directory

MOUNT CLEMENS,* Macomb Co.

MARTIN, BACON & MARTIN, P.C. (AV)

44 First Street, 48043
Telephone: 810-979-6500
Fax: 810-468-7016

James N. Martin
Jonathan E. Martin
Paul R. VanTol
Victor T. Van Camp

Michael R. Janes
Kevin L. Moffatt
John W. Crimando

Patrick D. Ball

Amy M. Chauvin

Reference: Old Kent Bank - Mt. Clemens.

For full biographical listings, see the Martindale-Hubbell Law Directory

MOUNT PLEASANT,* Isabella Co.

GRAY, SOWLE & IACCO, A PROFESSIONAL CORPORATION (AV)

600 East Broadway, 48858
Telephone: 517-772-5932
Fax: 517-773-0538

Loren E. Gray
Donald N. Sowle

Daniel A. Iacco
Cheryl E. Gray

References: Isabella Bank & Trust; First of America of Mount Pleasant.

For full biographical listings, see the Martindale-Hubbell Law Directory

MUSKEGON,* Muskegon Co.

LAGUE, NEWMAN & IRISH, A PROFESSIONAL CORPORATION (AV)

600 Terrace Plaza, P.O. Box 389, 49443
Telephone: 616-725-8148
Telecopier: 616-726-3404
Email: firm@lnilaw.com

William M. Newman

Alvin D. Treado

General Counsel: Hackley Hospital & Medical Center.

For Complete List of Firm Personnel, See General Section

For full biographical listings, see the Martindale-Hubbell Law Directory

SAGINAW,* Saginaw Co.

FORDNEY, DUST & PRINE (AV)

An Association of Professional Corporations
Suite 410 B Plaza North, 4800 Fashion Square Boulevard, P.O. Box 5289, 48603-0289
Telephone: 517-791-7060
Fax: 517-791-8009

MEMBERS OF FIRM

J. Michael Fordney
Tobin H. Dust

Andrew W. Prine
Matthew J. Coffey

For full biographical listings, see the Martindale-Hubbell Law Directory

ST. CLAIR SHORES, Macomb Co.

SAURBIER, PARADISO & DAVIS, P.L.C. (AV)

Suite 402, 400 Maple Park Boulevard, 48081
Telephone: 810-447-3700
Fax: 810-447-3755
Email: SAURBIR@IBM.NET
Detroit, Office: 1028 Buhl Building.
Telephone: 313-965-2220.

Scott A. Saurbier

Anthony J. Paradiso
Kevin L. Davis

ASSOCIATES

Joel A. Sanfield
Marc D. Saurbier
David Steiger
John M. Perrin

Amy A. Baranski
Jennifer A. Mazzuchi
Cheryl L. Ronk
Lawrence T Garcia

Gwendolyn M. Cook Jones

For full biographical listings, see the Martindale-Hubbell Law Directory

ST. JOSEPH,* Berrien Co.

GLOBENSKY, GLEISS, BITTNER & HYRNS, P.C. (AV)

610 Ship Street, P.O. Box 290, 49085
Telephone: 616-983-0551
Fax: 616-983-5858

H. S. Gray (1867-1961)
Luman H. Gray (1902-1952)
John L. Globensky
Henry W. Gleiss

Rodger V. Bittner
Randy S. Hyrns
J. Joseph Daly
Charles T. LaSata

James J. Riemland

General Counsel for: Shoreline Bank; Hanson Cold Storage Co.; Pearson Construction Co., Inc.
Approved Attorneys for: Lawyers Title Insurance Corp.
Reference: Shoreline Bank of Benton Harbor.

For full biographical listings, see the Martindale-Hubbell Law Directory

SOUTHFIELD, Oakland Co.

FIEGER, FIEGER & SCHWARTZ, A PROFESSIONAL CORPORATION (AV)

19390 West Ten Mile Road, 48075-2463
Telephone: 810-355-5555
Fax: 810-355-5148

Bernard J. Fieger (1922-1988)
Geoffrey N. Fieger
Michael Alan Schwartz

Todd J. Weglarz
Rebecca S. Eaton
Ven R. Johnson

William J. McHenry

OF COUNSEL

Barry Fayne

Beverly Hires Brode
Keitha Kay Cowen

For full biographical listings, see the Martindale-Hubbell Law Directory

HIGHLAND & ZANETTI (AV)

Suite 205, 24445 Northwestern Highway, 48075
Telephone: 810-352-9580

John N. Highland

J. R. Zanetti, Jr.
R. Michael John

Duncan Hall Brown

Ronald D. Holton

For full biographical listings, see the Martindale-Hubbell Law Directory

O'LEARY, O'LEARY, JACOBS, MATTSON, PERRY & MASON, P.C. (AV)

26777 Central Park Boulevard, Suite 275, 48076
Telephone: 810-948-1000
Fax: 810-799-8265
Email: olearyjacobs@michbar.org

John Patrick O'Leary
Thomas M. O'Leary
John P. Jacobs
Kenneth M. Mattson

C. Kenneth Perry, Jr.
Larry G. Mason
D. Jennifer Andreou
Kevin P. Hanbury

Alice A. Zetusky

For full biographical listings, see the Martindale-Hubbell Law Directory

PROVIZER, LICHTENSTEIN & PHILLIPS, P.C. (AV)

4000 Town Center, Suite 1800, 48075
Telephone: 810-352-9080
Facsimile: 810-352-1491

(See Next Column)

PROVIZER, LICHTENSTEIN & PHILLIPS P.C., *Southfield—Continued*

Randall E. Phillips	Noel F. Beck
Marilyn A. Madorsky	William J. Selinsky

Representative Clients: Reliance National Ins. Co.; Dr. Sampson Inwald; Dr. Saul Shapiro.

For full biographical listings, see the Martindale-Hubbell Law Directory

SCHWARTZ & JALKANEN, P.C. (AV)

Suite 200, 24400 Northwestern Highway, 48075
Telephone: 810-352-2555
Facsimile: 810-352-5963

Melvin R. Schwartz	Arthur W. Jalkanen
	Karl Eric Hannum
Deborah L. Laura	Lori A. Barker

For full biographical listings, see the Martindale-Hubbell Law Directory

SOMMERS, SCHWARTZ, SILVER & SCHWARTZ, P.C. (AV)

2000 Town Center, Suite 900, 48075
Telephone: 810-355-0300
Telecopier: 810-746-4001
Plymouth, Michigan Office: 747 South Main Street.
Telephone: 313-455-4250.

Stanley S. Schwartz	B. A. Tyler
Jeffrey N. Shillman	Michael J. Cunningham
Jeremy L. Winer	Matthew G. Curtis
David R. Getto	Helen K. Joyner
Norman D. Tucker	John L. Runco
Paul W. Hines	Susanne Pryce
Stephen N. Leuchtman	David J. Shea
Richard D. Fox	Anne M. Schoepfle
Frank Mafrice	Gary D. Dodds
Richard L. Groffsky	Jabran G. Yasso
David J. Winter	Kenneth T. Watkins
	Craig E. Feringa

OF COUNSEL
Howard Silver

General Counsel for: City of Taylor; Foodland Distributors; C.A. Muer Corporation; Vlasic & Company; Nederlander Corporation; Midwest Health Centers, P.C.
Representative Clients: Crum & Forster Insurance Company; City of Pontiac; Michigan National Bank.

For Complete List of Firm Personnel, See General Section

For full biographical listings, see the Martindale-Hubbell Law Directory

TRAVERSE CITY,* Grand Traverse Co.

SMITH HAUGHEY RICE & ROEGGE, P.C. (AV)

241 East State Street, P.O. Box 848, 49685-0848
Telephone: 616-929-4878
Facsimile: 616-929-4182
Grand Rapids, Michigan Office: 200 Calder Plaza Building, 250 Monroe Avenue, N.W., 49503-2251.
Telephone: 616-774-8000.
Facsimile: 616-774-2461.
East Lansing, Michigan Office: 1301 North Hagadorn Road, 48823-2320.
Telephone: 517-332-3030.
Facsimile: 517-332-3468.

George Frederick Bearup	Charles B. Judson
Mark P. Bickel	Robert W. Tubbs
P. David Vinocur	Robert M. Faulkner
R. Jay Hardin	Thomas C. Kates
John R. Vander Veen	Jeffrey R. Wonacott
Mark D. Williams	Todd W. Millar
	Erin Eileen Gerrity

For full biographical listings, see the Martindale-Hubbell Law Directory

THOMPSON & O'NEIL, P.C. (AV)

309 East Front Street, P.O. Box 429, 49685
Telephone: 616-929-9700; 1-800-678-1307
Fax: 616-929-7262

George R. Thompson	Daniel P. O'Neil
	William J. Brooks

For full biographical listings, see the Martindale-Hubbell Law Directory

TROY, Oakland Co.

HOLAHAN, MALLOY, MAYBAUGH & MONNICH (AV)

Suite 100, 2690 Crooks Road, 48084-4700
Telephone: 810-362-4747
Fax: 810-362-4779
East Tawas, Michigan Office: 910 East Bay Street.
Telephone: 517-362-4747.
Fax: 517-362-7331.

MEMBERS OF FIRM

J. Michael Malloy, III	David L. Delie, Jr.
James D. Maybaugh	William J. Kliffel
John R. Monnich	Ingrid Rosvold Kliffel

OF COUNSEL

Thomas H. O'Connor	Maureen Holahan (Retired; Resident, East Tawas Office)

For full biographical listings, see the Martindale-Hubbell Law Directory

WEST BLOOMFIELD, Oakland Co.

CHEATHAM & ACKER, P.C. (AV)

5777 West Maple Road, Suite 130, P.O. Box 255002, 48325-5002
Telephone: 810-932-2000
Fax: 810-932-2008

Charles C. Cheatham	Lawrence J. Acker
Tracy A. Leahy	Mary E. Hollman
	Christopher P. Jelinek

COUNSEL
Lynn L. Lower

For full biographical listings, see the Martindale-Hubbell Law Directory

LAW OFFICES OF DAVID J. COOPER A PROFESSIONAL CORPORATION (AV)

5777 West Maple, Suite 130, P.O. Box 255002, 48325-5002
Telephone: 810-932-8582
Fax: 810-932-2166
Email: AXDEF@aol.com

David J. Cooper

For full biographical listings, see the Martindale-Hubbell Law Directory

MERGERS AND ACQUISITIONS

ALABAMA

DOTHAN, * Houston Co.

JOHNSTON, HINESLEY, FLOWERS & CLENNEY, P.C., A PROFESSIONAL CORPORATION (AV)

291 North Oates Street, 36303
Telephone: 334-793-1115
Fax: 334-793-6603

G. David Johnston	William T. Flowers
William W. Hinesley	R. Eugene Clenney, Jr.

J. Ken Thompson

For full biographical listings, see the Martindale-Hubbell Law Directory

---

MOBILE, * Mobile Co.

ZIEMAN, SPEEGLE, OLDWEILER & JACKSON, L.L.C. (AV)

Suite 3200, First National Bank Building, P.O. Box 11, 36601
Telephone: 334-694-1700
Facsimile: 334-694-1998

MEMBERS OF THE FIRM

Thomas Troy Zieman, Jr.	Thomas P. Oldweiler
Jerome E. Speegle	Robert G. Jackson, Jr.

ASSOCIATE
Anthony Michael Hoffman

For full biographical listings, see the Martindale-Hubbell Law Directory

ARIZONA

PHOENIX, * Maricopa Co.

PHILIP T. PARIS (AV)

2929 North 44th Street, Suite 120, 85018
Telephone: 602-994-5813
Telecopier: 602-840-2771

For full biographical listings, see the Martindale-Hubbell Law Directory

CALIFORNIA

HERMOSA BEACH, Los Angeles Co.

NASH & EDGERTON (AV)

A Limited Liability Partnership
2615 Pacific Coast Highway, Suite 322, 90254
Telephone: 310-937-2066
Fax: 310-937-2063
Torrance, California Office: 3625 Del Amo Boulevard, suite 360.
Telephone: 310-370-8272.
Fax: 310-214-9677.

Savery L. Nash	Shelley Nash
Samuel Y. Edgerton, III	David Maurer

Damon Rubin

For full biographical listings, see the Martindale-Hubbell Law Directory

---

LOS ANGELES, * Los Angeles Co.

INGLIS, LEDBETTER & GOWER (AV)

500 South Grand Avenue, 18th Floor, 90071-2612
Telephone: 213-627-6800
Facsimile: 213-622-2857

MEMBERS OF FIRM

Michael K. Inglis	Richard G. Ritchie
Steven K. Ledbetter	Gregory H. Gocke
Richard S. Gower	John E. Hope

ASSOCIATES

Timothy E. Kearns	James W. Holchin
	Nancy B. Gonzalez

(See Next Column)

LEGAL SUPPORT PERSONNEL
Kevin Watkins

Representative Clients: Barnes-Dyer; Brehm Communications, Inc.; Inter-Insurance Exchange of the Automobile Club of Southern California; Presto Food Products, Inc.; Prudential Property and Casualty Insurance Co.; Safariland Ltd., Inc.; Cecil Saydah Co.

For full biographical listings, see the Martindale-Hubbell Law Directory

---

KONOWIECKI & RANK (AV)

A Partnership including a Professional Corporation
First Interstate World Center, 633 West 5th Street, Suite 3500, 90071-2007
Telephone: 213-229-0990
Telefax: 213-229-0992

Peter C. Rank	Kevin B. Kroeker
Joseph S. Konowiecki	Peter Roan
Michael C. Foster	Peter R. Mason
Jon N. Manzanares	Denise E. Hanna

ASSOCIATES

Cynthia J. Billey	Phillip R. Maltin
Edna M. Chism	Scott J. Moore
Ronan Cohen	John A. Mueller
Rosa Kwon Easton	Leslie Overfelt
Robert C. Hayden	Catherine M. Polisoto

Harold C. Pope

LEGAL SUPPORT PERSONNEL
Curtis J. Bergeron

Representative Clients: PacifiCare Health Systems, Inc.; UniHealth America; Columbia General Life Insurance Co.; Santa Clarita Health Care Assoc.; College Health Enterprises; Granada Hills Community Hospital; Redlands Community Hospital; Bay Shores Medical Group.
Reference: Bank of America.

For full biographical listings, see the Martindale-Hubbell Law Directory

---

MATTHIAS & BERG LLP (AV)

Seventh Floor, 515 South Flower Street, 90071
Telephone: 213-895-4200
Telecopier: 213-895-4058

Michael R. Matthias	Stuart R. Singer
Jeffrey P. Berg	Kenneth M. H. Hoff

Michael D. Berger

Representative Clients: Synagro Technologies, Inc.; Mexalit, S.A.; Maxitile, Inc.; Allstar Inns; Chatsworth Products, Inc.; International Meta Systems, Inc.; Residential Resources, Inc.; AVIC Group International, Inc.; AutoBitter Group, Inc. National Quality Care, Inc.; Greater China Corp.; HBO Ole.
Reference: First Professional Bank.

For full biographical listings, see the Martindale-Hubbell Law Directory

---

OSTROVE, KRANTZ & OSTROVE, A PROFESSIONAL CORPORATION (AV)

(Successor To: Ostrove and Lancer, A Professional Corporation; David Ostrove, A Professional Corporation)
5757 Wilshire Boulevard, Suite 535, 90036-3600
Telephone: 213-939-3400
Fax: 213-939-3500
Email: OSTROVE@AOL.COM

David Ostrove	David S. Krantz
	Kenneth E. Ostrove

Reference: First Business Bank.

For full biographical listings, see the Martindale-Hubbell Law Directory

---

SACRAMENTO, * Sacramento Co.

HUNTER RICHEY DI BENEDETTO & BREWER, LLP (AV)

A Limited Liability Partnership
Renaissance Tower, 801 K Street, 23rd Floor, 95814-3525
Telephone: 916-491-3000
Facsimile: 916-491-3080
Email: hrdb@hrdb.com *URL:* http://www.hrdb.com

MEMBERS OF FIRM

William S. Hunter	James F. Geary
Win R. Richey	Janet C. Eisenbeis
Florence L. Di Benedetto	Jeffery D. Harris
Roy E. Brewer	Stephen C. Ruehmann
Anne E. Ferguson	Ralph T. Ferguson
Judith J. Citko	Sharon K. Sandeen

Kathryn T. Papalia

(See Next Column)

HUNTER RICHEY DI BENEDETTO & BREWER LLP, *Sacramento—Continued*

LEGAL SUPPORT PERSONNEL

Lori J. Kelly (Paralegal)
Deborah M. Romero (Paralegal)
Linda Jane Hall
  (Legal Assistant)
Jennifer E. Mueller
  (Legal Assistant)

Michele L. Nickell
  (Legal Assistant)
Dawn Krein (Legal Assistant)
Stephanie L. Neumann
  (Legal Assistant)

For full biographical listings, see the Martindale-Hubbell Law Directory

---

*SAN JOSE,** Santa Clara Co.

MILLER, MORTON, CAILLAT & NEVIS (AV)

50 West San Fernando Street, Suite 1300, 95113-2413
Telephone: 408-292-1765
Telecopier: 408-292-4484

Richard W. Morton (1916-1975)   Charles V. Caillat (1920-1990)
Harvey C. Miller (1906-1993)

MEMBERS OF FIRM

David L. Nevis
Francis J. Hughes
Peter A. Kline
Stevan C. Adelman

Joseph A. Scanlan, Jr.
Carolyn Tobiason Stuart
William K. Hurley
Peter V. Dessau

Eric Mogensen

OF COUNSEL

Nancy F. Symons
Pamela J. Silberstein

Susan L. Sutton

ASSOCIATES

Kathryn E. Barrett
Katherine S. Pak

David I. Kornbluh
Kimberly Holtz MacMillan

Representative Clients: Trammell Crow Residential Services; Joe Kerley Lincoln Mercury Co.; Milligan News Co.; Joseph George Distributors; The Frozen Food Employees Pension Trust; Santa Clara Dental Society; New West Foods; Bay Apartment Communities; Guy F. Atkinson Company; A. Hathaway Co.

For full biographical listings, see the Martindale-Hubbell Law Directory

---

COLORADO

---

*DENVER,** Denver Co.

BRENMAN KEY & BROMBERG, P.C. (AV)

Mellon Financial Center Suite 1001, 1775 Sherman Street, 80203
Telephone: 303-894-0234
Fax: 303-839-1633

Albert Brenman
Thomas R. Bromberg

Donna A. Key
Steven W. McDonald

Theresa M. Mehringer

George D. Kreye

OF COUNSEL

Heather H. S. Sander
D. Elizabeth Wills

A. Thomas Tenenbaum
Edmund L. Epstein (Inactive)

For full biographical listings, see the Martindale-Hubbell Law Directory

---

JOHN G. HERBERT, P.C. (AV)

Larimer Corporate Plaza, Suite 310, 1675 Larimer Street, 80202
Telephone: 303-534-0522
Telefax: 303-534-3638

John G. Herbert

For full biographical listings, see the Martindale-Hubbell Law Directory

---

FLORIDA

---

*FORT MYERS,** Lee Co.

SMOOT ADAMS EDWARDS & GREEN, P.A. (AV)

One University Park Suite 600, 12800 University Drive, P.O. Box 60259, 33906-6259
Telephone: 941-489-1776
(800) 226-1777 (in Florida)
Fax: 941-489-2444
Email: 71600.2745@compuserve.com

(See Next Column)

J. Tom Smoot, Jr.
Hal Adams
Franklyn A. (Chip) Johnson
  (1947-1991)
Charles B. Edwards

Bruce D. Green
Steven I. Winer
Mark R. Komray
Clayton W. Crevasse
M. Brian Cheffer

Robert S. Forman
Kathleen W. McBride
Lowell Schoenfeld

C. Berk Edwards, Jr.
Melville G. Brinson, III
Samuel J. Hagan, IV.

For full biographical listings, see the Martindale-Hubbell Law Directory

---

*JACKSONVILLE,** Duval Co.

KIRSCHNER, MAIN, GRAHAM, TANNER & DEMONT, PROFESSIONAL ASSOCIATION (AV)

One Independent Drive, Suite 2000, P.O. Box 1559, 32201-1559
Telephone: 904-354-4141
Telecopier: 904-358-2199

Barry C. Averitt
Babette L. Fletcher
T. Malcolm Graham
Lee Stathis Haramis

Kenneth M. Kirschner
James L. Main
John T. Rogerson, III
Michael G. Tanner

Howard L. Alford
Robin C. Barco
John F. Germany, Jr.
Eric S. Kolar

Judy Ossi Marko
Charles S. McCall
Beth E. Weitzman
  (Not admitted in FL)

OF COUNSEL

Michael E. Demont
G. Stephen Manning

Wyman R. Duggan
Reese J. Henderson, Jr.

Representative Clients: The Maryland Insurance Group; NationsBank; The Suddath Cos.; Wickes Lumber Co.; BFI, Inc.

For full biographical listings, see the Martindale-Hubbell Law Directory

---

ILLINOIS

---

*CHICAGO,** Cook Co.

SUGAR, FRIEDBERG & FELSENTHAL (AV)

30 North La Salle Street, Suite 2600, 60602
Telephone: 312-704-9400
Telecopier: 312-372-7951
Cable: "SUGARFREE"

MEMBERS OF FIRM

Richard A. Sugar
Michael R. Friedberg
Steven A. Felsenthal
Andrew B. David
Leslie J. Weiss

Ira S. Neiman
Jonathan L. Mills
Etahn M. Cohen
Howard M. Helsinger
Robert F. Simon

Martin M. Weinstein

ASSOCIATES

Kathryn A. Erickson
Norman J. Ginsparg

Jay R. Hoffman
Sophia Stergianis

Jonathan W. Michael

For full biographical listings, see the Martindale-Hubbell Law Directory

---

*DECATUR,** Macon Co.

TIETZ & RICHARDSON (AV)

444 Millikin Court Building, P.O. Box 1664, 62525
Telephone: 217-425-1515
Telecopier: 217-425-4077

Christopher M. Tietz

Jeffrey D. Richardson

Representative Clients: Industrial Process Control Engineering Company; Dectra, Ltd.; Custom Computer Services, Inc.; Dover Elevator Co.; Craftmasters, Inc.; ICAL, Inc.; Farmers Insurance Group, Standard Mutual Insurance Co.; American Investment Bank; AgriBank, FCB.

For full biographical listings, see the Martindale-Hubbell Law Directory

---

*QUINCY,** Adams Co.

SCHMIEDESKAMP, ROBERTSON, NEU & MITCHELL (AV)

525 Jersey, P.O. Box 1069, 62306
Telephone: 217-223-3030
Telecopier: 217-223-1005

(See Next Column)

SCHMIEDESKAMP, ROBERTSON, NEU & MITCHELL—*Continued*
MEMBERS OF FIRM

Delmer R. Mitchell, Jr.   William G. Keller, Jr.
William M. McCleery, Jr.

Representative Clients: Mercantile Trust & Savings Bank; Moorman Manufacturing Co.; Knapheide Mfg. Co.; Harris Corp.; Quincy Compressor Division of Colt Industries, Inc.; Norfolk & Western R.R.; Quincy Soybean Co.; Better Bank Group; Marine Trust Co. of Carthage; Perry State Bank.

For Complete List of Firm Personnel, See General Section

For full biographical listings, see the Martindale-Hubbell Law Directory

INDIANA

INDIANAPOLIS, * Marion Co.

DANN PECAR NEWMAN & KLEIMAN, PROFESSIONAL CORPORATION (AV)

Suite 2300, One American Square Box 82008, 46282
Telephone: 317-632-3232; Indiana: 800-622-4799
Telecopy: 317-632-2962

Theodore R. Dann (1907-1993)   Walter E. Wolf, Jr.
Joel Yonover (1932-1995)   Barry E. Beldin
Philip D. Pecar   Robert D. Swhier, Jr.
Norman R. Newman   James P. Moloy
David H. Kleiman   Robert J. Schuckit
Jon B. Abels   Andrew A. Kleiman
Melvin R. Daniel   Michael J. Gabovitch
Lawrence F. Dorocke   Steven M. Pecar
Jeffrey A. Abrams   Benjamin A. Pecar
James H. Schwarz   Richard O. Kissel, II
Robert A. Rose   Joseph D. Calderon

OF COUNSEL

Linda E. Cantor   Anthony J. Rose

Ellen C. Siakotos   Angela L. Mansfield
Stacy L. Hill   Martha M. K. Baird
Karin L. Veatch

Attorneys for: Indianapolis Machinery Co., Inc.; Melvin Simon & Associates, Inc.; Pacers Basketball Corp.; Universal Fire & Casualty Co., Inc.; Bank One, Indianapolis, NA; INB National Bank; Nachi Technology, Inc.; Pharmaceutical Corporation of America; Logo 7, Inc.

For full biographical listings, see the Martindale-Hubbell Law Directory

KENTUCKY

PIKEVILLE, * Pike Co.

PRUITT AND DE BOURBON LAW FIRM (AV)

The Call Building, Second Street, P.O. Box 339, 41502
Telephone: 606-437-7366; 437-7367; 237-1280
Fax: 606-432-2367

MEMBERS OF FIRM

James P. Pruitt, Jr.   P. Michael de Bourbon

Reference: The Citizen's Bank of Pikeville.

For full biographical listings, see the Martindale-Hubbell Law Directory

LOUISIANA

LAFAYETTE, * Lafayette Parish

WILLIAM STUBBS FIRM (AV)

1018 Harding Street, Suite 102, 70503
Telephone: 318-233-9755
Fax: 318-233-9771

William P. Stubbs, Jr.
ASSOCIATES

J. Kevin Stelly   Julie A. Steed

For full biographical listings, see the Martindale-Hubbell Law Directory

NEW ORLEANS, * Orleans Parish

MICHAEL L. ECKSTEIN ATTORNEY AT LAW A PROFESSIONAL CORPORATION (AV)

1515 Poydras Street, Suite 2195, 70112
Telephone: 504-527-0701
Telecopier: 504-566-0040
VMX: 504-889-8876

Michael L. Eckstein   David Coleman Raphael, Jr.

Representative Clients: Anserphone of New Orleans, Inc.; Dixie Webb Graphic Corporations; Kencoil, Inc.; Life Point Systems, Inc.; Meeks Petroleum Company; Int-Oil Ventures, Ltd.; Dan-Gulf Shipping, Inc.; Action, Inc.; TCB Industries, Inc.

For full biographical listings, see the Martindale-Hubbell Law Directory

MICHIGAN

BIRMINGHAM, Oakland Co.

HYMAN AND LIPPITT, P.C. (AV)

185 Oakland Avenue, Suite 300, P.O. Box 1750, 48009
Telephone: 810-646-8292
Facsimile: 810-646-8375

J. Leonard Hyman   Kenneth F. Neuman
Norman L. Lippitt   Terry S. Givens
Douglas A. Hyman   Paul J. Fischer
Brian D. O'Keefe   John A. Sellers
H. Joel Newman   Robert H. Lippitt
Nazli G. Sater   Roger L. Myers
David N. Morrell, Jr.

For full biographical listings, see the Martindale-Hubbell Law Directory

BLOOMFIELD HILLS, Oakland Co.

DAWDA, MANN, MULCAHY & SADLER, P.L.C. (AV)

1533 North Woodward Avenue Suite 200, 48304
Telephone: 810-642-3700
Fax: 810-642-7791
Email: EMail@DMMS.Com

Michael D. Mulcahy   Curtis J. Mann
Edward C. Dawda   William L. Rosin

Todd A. Schafer   Tara E. Barr
Paul C. Apap
OF COUNSEL
Sidney W. Smith, Jr.

Representative Clients: AEGON USA Realty Advisors, Inc.; AMB Institutional Realty Advisors, Inc.; Bally's Total Fitness Corp.; BASF Corporation; Cardell Corporation; Cargill, Inc.; CB Commercial Real Estate; City Management; Ford Motor Company; G.E. Capital Realty Group.

For full biographical listings, see the Martindale-Hubbell Law Directory

DETROIT, * Wayne Co.

BUTZEL LONG, A PROFESSIONAL CORPORATION (AV)

Suite 900, 150 West Jefferson, 48226
Telephone: 313-225-7000
Telecopier: 313-225-7080
Email: melnick@butzel.com *URL:* http://www.butzel.com
Birmingham, Michigan Office: Suite 200, 32270 Telegraph Road.
Telephone: 810-258-1616.
Telecopier: 810-258-1439.
Lansing, Michigan Office: 118 West Ottawa Street.
Telephone: 517-372-6622.
Telecopier: 517-372-6672.
Ann Arbor, Michigan Office: Suite 300, 350 South Main Street.
Telephone: 313-995-3110.
Telecopier: 313-995-1777.
Grosse Pointe Farms, Michigan Office: Suite 260, 21 Kercheval.
Telephone: 313-886-5446.
Telecopier: 313-886-2114.

Morris Milmet (Birmingham)   Justin G. Klimko
Frank B. Vecchio (Birmingham)   Michael F. Golab (Birmingham)
William R. Ralls (Lansing)   James L. Hughes
C. Peter Theut   Arthur Dudley II
Richard E. Rassel   Gordon W. Didier (Birmingham)
Thomas E. Sizemore   Terry O. Lang
James C. Bruno   Melvin J. Hollowell, Jr.

(See Next Column)

BUTZEL LONG A PROFESSIONAL CORPORATION, *Detroit—Continued*

Nicholas J. Stasevich　　　　　Lois Elizabeth Bingham

Representative Clients: William Beaumont Hospital; The Detroit News, Inc.; General Fasteners Co.; Infinity Broadcasting; Kelsey-Hayes Co.; McKechnie PLC; New Venture Gear; Ricardo Group PLC; Stroh Brewery Co.; Takata, Inc.

For Complete List of Firm Personnel, See General Section

For full biographical listings, see the Martindale-Hubbell Law Directory

TIMMIS & INMAN, L.L.P. (AV)

300 Talon Centre, 48207
Telephone: 313-396-4200
Telecopier: 313-396-4228

Michael T. Timmis	Henry J. Brennan, III
Robert E. Graziani	Mark W. Peyser
George A. Peck	Richard M. Miettinen
Charles W. Royer	Lisa R. Gorman
Richard L. Levin	Bradley J. Knickerbocker

George M. Malis

Michael F. Wais	Patrick B. Carey
John P. Kanan	Erich J. D'Andrea

Shannon M. Nichols

OF COUNSEL

Wayne C. Inman	William B. Fitzgerald

W. Clark Durant, III

Representative Clients: Stylecraft Printing Co.; Stylerite Label Corp.; Retail Resources, Inc.; Deneb Robotics, Inc.; Applied Process, Inc.; Insilco Corp.; Variety Foods, Inc.; Certain Underwriters at Lloyds of London; Eastpointe Radiologists, P.C.; Talon Automotive Group L.L.C.

For full biographical listings, see the Martindale-Hubbell Law Directory

SOUTHFIELD, Oakland Co.

PROVIZER, LICHTENSTEIN & PHILLIPS, P.C. (AV)

4000 Town Center, Suite 1800, 48075
Telephone: 810-352-9080
Facsimile: 810-352-1491

David S. Lichtenstein	Marilyn A. Madorsky
Randall E. Phillips	Robert I. Brown

For full biographical listings, see the Martindale-Hubbell Law Directory

TROY, Oakland Co.

POLING, McGAW & POLING, P.C. (AV)

Suite 275, 5435 Corporate Drive, 48098
Telephone: 810-641-0500
Telecopier: 810-641-0506

Benson T. Buck (1926-1989)	Richard B. Poling, Jr.
Richard B. Poling	Gregory C. Hamilton
D. Douglas McGaw	Veronica B. O'Haro

James R. Parker

OF COUNSEL

Ralph S. Moore

Representative Clients: County of Oakland; City of Troy; United States Fidelity & Guaranty Co.; Sentry Insurance Co.; Admiral Insurance; DeMaria Construction Co.; Leo Corporation; Aetna Casualty and Surety Co.; Concord Design; Pneumo-Abex.

For full biographical listings, see the Martindale-Hubbell Law Directory

MUNICIPAL AND ZONING LAW

ALABAMA

BIRMINGHAM,* Jefferson Co.

BRADLEY, ARANT, ROSE & WHITE (AV)

2001 Park Place, Suite 1400, P.O. Box 830709, 35283-0709
Telephone: 205-521-8000
Facsimile: 205-252-0264
Facsimile (SouthTrust Tower Office): 205-251-9915
URL: http://www.BARW.COM
Huntsville, Alabama Office: 200 Clinton Avenue West, Suite 900, 35801.
Telephone: 205-517-5100.
Facsimile: 205-533-5069.

MEMBERS OF FIRM

Thad Gladden Long   Charles A. J. Beavers, Jr.

ASSOCIATE

Frank C. Galloway, III

For Complete List of Firm Personnel, See General Section

For full biographical listings, see the Martindale-Hubbell Law Directory

PARSONS, LEE & JULIANO, P.C. (AV)

2200 AmSouth/Harbert Plaza, 1901 Sixth Avenue, North, P.O. Box 371088, 35237-1088
Telephone: 205-326-6600
Fax: 205-324-7097

Robert E. Parsons   David A. Lee
Jasper P. Juliano   John M. Bergquist
Marcus W. Lee   Paul J. DeMarco
Marda W. Sydnor   Deborah Ann Payne
Tracy Toussaint

OF COUNSEL

Dorothy A. Powell

For full biographical listings, see the Martindale-Hubbell Law Directory

MOBILE,* Mobile Co.

FINKBOHNER AND LAWLER, L.L.C. (AV)

169 Dauphin Street Suite 300, P.O. Box 3085, 36652
Telephone: 334-438-5871
Fax: 334-432-8052

MEMBERS OF FIRM

George W. Finkbohner, Jr.   George W. Finkbohner, III
John L. Lawler   Royce A. Ray, III

For full biographical listings, see the Martindale-Hubbell Law Directory

OPELIKA,* Lee Co.

WALKER, HILL, ADAMS, UMBACH, MEADOWS & WALTON (AV)

Walker Building, 205 South 9th Street, P.O. Box 2069, 36803
Telephone: 334-745-6466
Fax: 334-749-2800

MEMBERS OF FIRM

Jacob A. Walker (1889-1973)   Robert T. Meadows, III
Phillip E. Adams, Jr.   Will O. (Trip) Walton, III
Arnold W. Umbach, Jr.   Jacob A. Walker, III

ASSOCIATES

Russell K. Bush   Robbie A. Hyde

OF COUNSEL

Jacob Walker   Hoyt W. Hill

For full biographical listings, see the Martindale-Hubbell Law Directory

ARIZONA

FLAGSTAFF,* Coconino Co.

HUFFORD, HORSTMAN, McCULLOUGH & MONGINI, P.C. (AV)

323 North Leroux Street, P.O. Box B, 86002-0808
Telephone: 520-774-1453
Fax: 520-779-3621

C. Benson Hufford   Margaret A. McCullough
Patrice M. Horstman   Michael E.J. Mongini
Eve A. Parnell

Philip (Jay) McCarthy, Jr.

(See Next Column)

LEGAL SUPPORT PERSONNEL

Doris Utzinger   Amy Klein (Legal Assistant)

Reference: First Interstate Bank of Arizona, N.A.

For full biographical listings, see the Martindale-Hubbell Law Directory

PHOENIX,* Maricopa Co.

BONNETT, FAIRBOURN, FRIEDMAN & BALINT, P.C. (AV)

4041 North Central Avenue Suite 1100, 85012
Telephone: 602-274-1100
Fax: 602-274-1199

Jerry C. Bonnett   Tara L. Jackson
William G. Fairbourn   Wendy J. Harrison
Andrew S. Friedman   Scott A. Erickson
Francis J. Balint, Jr.   Guy A. Hanson
H. Sullivan Bunch   Thomas B. Dixon
Michael N. Widener   Martin E. Latz
Robert J. Spurlock   Gina M. DeVito
C. Kevin Dykstra   Robert D. Ryan
Elaine A. Ryan   Guy P. Roll

OF COUNSEL

James Duke Cameron

For full biographical listings, see the Martindale-Hubbell Law Directory

DUSHOFF & McCALL, A PROFESSIONAL CORPORATION (AV)

Two Renaissance Square, Suite 1000, 40 North Central, 85004
Telephone: 602-254-3800
Fax: 602-258-2551
URL: http://www.dushoff@neta.com

Jay Dushoff   Robert H. Kreutzer
Jack E. McCall (1942-1995)   Michael Riikola
Denise J. Henslee

LEGAL SUPPORT PERSONNEL

Thomas M. Flynn   Roger L. Dunlap
Brad D. Larson   (Certified Legal Assistant)

For full biographical listings, see the Martindale-Hubbell Law Directory

EARL, CURLEY & LAGARDE (AV)

3101 N. Central Avenue, Suite 1090, 85012
Telephone: 602-265-0094
Fax: 602-265-2195

MEMBERS OF FIRM

Stephen C. Earl   Michael J. Curley
Lynne A. Lagarde

Representative Clients: Del Webb Corporation; American Express Travel Related Services; Sinclair Oil Corporation; Mobil Land Development (Southwest) Corporation; Desert Mountain Properties; Opus Southwest; Scottsdale Princess Hotel; Westcor Partners; Grossman Company Properties; Trammell Crow Residential.

For full biographical listings, see the Martindale-Hubbell Law Directory

FENNEMORE CRAIG, A PROFESSIONAL CORPORATION (AV)

Two North Central, Suite 2200, 85004
Telephone: 602-257-8700
Fax: 602-257-5409.
Scottsdale, Arizona Office: 6263 North Scottsdale Road, Suite 290, 85250.
Telephone: 602-257-5400.
Fax: 602-945-4932.
Tucson, Arizona Office: One South Church Avenue, Suite 1030, 85701.
Telephone: 520-791-6800.
Fax: 520-791-6820.

Michael Preston Green   Graeme E. M. Hancock
Andrew M. Federhar

For Complete List of Firm Personnel, See General Section

For full biographical listings, see the Martindale-Hubbell Law Directory

GAMMAGE & BURNHAM, P.L.C. (AV)

One Renaissance Square, Two North Central Avenue, Suite 1800, 85004
Telephone: 602-256-0566
Fax: 602-256-4475

MEMBERS OF FIRM

Grady Gammage, Jr.   Michael B. Withey
Stephen W. Anderson

Representative Clients: Kaufman & Broad of Arizona, Inc.; Viehmann Martin & Associates; Homes by Dave Brown; Evans Withycombe, Inc.; Waste Management, Inc.; Opus Southwest; Samaritan Health System; W.M. Grace Development Co.

For Complete List of Firm Personnel, See General Section

For full biographical listings, see the Martindale-Hubbell Law Directory

Phoenix—Continued

LAZARUS & ASSOCIATES, A PROFESSIONAL CORPORATION (AV)

One Arizona Center, 400 East Van Buren, Suite 980, 85004
Telephone: 602-340-0900
Facsimile: 602-340-8955

Larry S. Lazarus
OF COUNSEL
David K. Jones, P.C.

For full biographical listings, see the Martindale-Hubbell Law Directory

ULRICH, KESSLER & ANGER, P.C. (AV)

Suite 1000, 3030 North Central Avenue, 85012-2717
Telephone: 602-248-9465
Fax: 602-248-0165
Email: ukapc@aol.com

Paul G. Ulrich   Donn G. Kessler
William H. Anger

For full biographical listings, see the Martindale-Hubbell Law Directory

CALIFORNIA

BEVERLY HILLS, Los Angeles Co.

DAPEER, ROSENBLIT & LITVAK, LLP (AV)

9460 Wilshire Boulevard, Fifth Floor, 90212
Telephone: 310-203-8200; 310-777-6676
Fax: 310-203-8213; 310-777-6675
Metropolitan Cities Office: 2770 East Slauson Avenue, P.O. Box 2067,
Huntington Park, 90255.
Telephone: 213-587-5221.
Fax: 213-587-4190.

William Litvak   Steven H. Rosenblit
Kenneth B. Dapeer

For full biographical listings, see the Martindale-Hubbell Law Directory

COSTA MESA, Orange Co.

RUTAN & TUCKER, LLP (AV)

A Partnership including Professional Corporations
611 Anton Boulevard, Suite 1400, P.O. Box 1950, 92626
Telephone: 714-641-5100; 213-625-7586
Telecopier: 714-546-9035
Email: rutan&tucker@mcimail.com *URL:* http://www.rutan.com

MEMBERS OF FIRM

Michael D. Rubin   M. Katherine Jenson
Jeffrey M. Oderman (P.C.)   Richard Montevideo
Stan Wolcott (P.C.)   Elizabeth L. Martyn
Robert S. Bower   David B. Cosgrove
David J. Aleshire   Hans Van Ligten
Anne Nelson Lanphar   Robert Owen
Philip D. Kohn   Jeffrey A. Goldfarb
Joel D. Kuperberg   Layne H. Melzer
William W. Wynder   Lien Ski Harrison

ASSOCIATES

Dan Slater   Julia L. Bond
A. Patrick Muñoz   Jennifer White-Sperling
Steven M. Coleman

For Complete List of Firm Personnel, See General Section

For full biographical listings, see the Martindale-Hubbell Law Directory

EL MONTE, Los Angeles Co.

MICHAEL B. MONTGOMERY A LAW CORPORATION (AV)

10501 Valley Boulevard, Suite 121, 91731
Telephone: 818-452-1222
Fax: 818-452-8323
Ft. Lauderdale, Florida Office: Justice Building, 524 S. Andrews Avenue,
Suite 320 N.
Telephone: 954-522-9441.
Fax: 954-522-2076.

Michael B. Montgomery

Reference: Bank of America (San Marino Branch).

For full biographical listings, see the Martindale-Hubbell Law Directory

GLENDALE, Los Angeles Co.

LASKIN & GRAHAM (AV)

Suite 840, 800 North Brand Boulevard, 91203
Telephone: 213-665-6955; 818-547-4800; 714-957-3031
Telecopier: 818-547-3100

OF COUNSEL
Richard Laskin
MEMBERS OF FIRM

Arnold K. Graham   Michael Anthony Cisneros
Susan L. Vaage   Gregson M. Perry
John S. Peterson   Lynn I. Ibara

For full biographical listings, see the Martindale-Hubbell Law Directory

LOS ANGELES,* Los Angeles Co.

BARBOSA GARCIA & BARNES (AV)

A Partnership including a Professional Corporation
Suite 390, 500 Citadel Drive, 90040
Telephone: 213-889-6600
FAX: 213-889-6605

Henry S. Barbosa (P.C.)   Peter E. Langsfeld
Bonifacio Bonny Garcia   Kenneth T. Fong
Douglas D. Barnes   Jonathan B. Stone

Augustin R. Jimenez   Lorie A. Campos
Rajeev M. Talwani   Charisma T. Tan-Sanchez
Erick L. Solares   Diana M. Carbajal
Sylvia J. Trujillo
OF COUNSEL
Norman Lieberman   John F. Lagle

For full biographical listings, see the Martindale-Hubbell Law Directory

OLIVER, VOSE, SANDIFER, MURPHY & LEE, A PROFESSIONAL CORPORATION (AV)

The Park, Second Floor, 281 South Figueroa Street, 90012
Telephone: 213-621-2000
Telecopier: 213-621-2211

Charles S. Vose   James Duff Murphy
Connie Cooke Sandifer   Edward W. Lee
Roger W. Springer

Mary L. McMaster   Bradley E. Wohlenberg
Arthur J. Hazarabedian   Timothy J. Chung
Kristin B. Mendenhall
OF COUNSEL
William B. Barr

Representative Clients: Cities of Covina, Hermosa Beach, South Pasadena and Calabasas; Los Angeles County North Valley Building Corp.; Los Angeles County Coroner's Building Corp.; Los Angeles County Montrose Sheriff's Station Corp.
Special Counsel: Anaheim Redevelopment Agency; Arcadia Redevelopment Agency; City of Brea; Brea Redevelopment Agency; Calleguas Municipal Water District; City of Anaheim.

For full biographical listings, see the Martindale-Hubbell Law Directory

O'MELVENY & MYERS LLP (AV)

400 South Hope Street, 90071-2899
Telephone: 213-669-6000
Cable Address: "Moms"
Facsimile: 213-669-6407
Email: omminfo@omm.com
Century City, California Office: 1999 Avenue of the Stars, 90067-6035.
Telephone: 310-553-6700.
Facsimile: 310-246-6779.
Newport Beach, California Office: 610 Newport Center Drive, 92660-6429.
Telephone: 714-760-9600.
Cable Address: "Moms".
Facsimile: 714-669-6994.
San Francisco, California Office: Embarcadero Center West Tower, 275 Battery Street, 94111-3305.
Telephone: 415-984-8700.
Facsimile: 415-984-8701.
New York, New York Office: Citicorp Center, 153 East 53rd Street, 10022-4611.
Telephone: 212-326-2000.
Facsimile: 212-326-2061.
Washington, D.C. Office: 555 13th Street, N.W., 20004-1109.
Telephone: 202-383-5300.
Cable Address: "Moms".
Facsimile: 202-383-5414.
London, England Office: 10 Finsbury Square, London, EC2A 1LA.
Telephone: 0171-256-8451.
Facsimile: 0171-638-8205.

(See Next Column)

O'MELVENY & MYERS LLP—Continued

Tokyo, Japan Office: Sanbancho KB-6 Building, 6 Sanbancho, Chiyoda-ku, Tokyo 102, Japan.
Telephone: 03-3239-2900.
Facsimile: 03-3239-2432.
Hong Kong Office: Suite 1905, Peregrine Tower, Lippo Centre, 89 Queensway, Central, Hong Kong.
Telephone: 852-2523-8266.
Facsimile: 852-2522-1760.
Shanghai, Peoples Republic of China Office: Shanghai International Trade Centre, Suite 2011, 2200 Yan An Road West, Shanghai, 200335, PRC.
Telephone: 86-21-6219-5363.
Facsimile: 86-21-6275-4949.

PARTNER
Richard M. Jones

For Complete List of Firm Personnel, See General Section

For full biographical listings, see the Martindale-Hubbell Law Directory

---

ANDREW RUSSELL WILLING (AV)

Promenade West, 880 West First Street Suite 302, 90012
Telephone: 213-626-6600
Facsimile: 213-626-0488

Reference: Wells Fargo Bank (Pasadena Main Office).

For full biographical listings, see the Martindale-Hubbell Law Directory

---

MENLO PARK, San Mateo Co.

ROBIN D. FAISANT (AV)

1550 El Camino Real, Suite 220, 94025
Telephone: 415-328-6333
Telecopier: 415-324-1031

For full biographical listings, see the Martindale-Hubbell Law Directory

---

PASADENA, Los Angeles Co.

LAGERLOF, SENECAL, BRADLEY & SWIFT, LLP (AV)

301 North Lake Avenue, 10th Floor, 91101-4108
Telephone: 818-793-9400
FAX: 818-793-5900

MEMBERS OF FIRM

Joseph J. Burris (1913-1980)
Stanley C. Lagerlof (Retired)
H. Melvin Swift, Jr.
H. Jess Senecal
Jack T. Swafford
John F. Bradley
Timothy J. Gosney
William F. Kruse
Thomas S. Bunn, III
Andrew D. Turner
Rebecca J. Thyne

ASSOCIATES

James D. Ciampa
Robert W. Renken

Representative Clients: Anchor Glass Container Corp.; Bethlehem Steel Corp.; Orthopaedic Hospital; Palmdale Water District; Public Water Agencies Group; Ventura Port District; Walnut Valley Water District; Metric Construction Co., Inc.

For full biographical listings, see the Martindale-Hubbell Law Directory

---

SAN DIEGO, San Diego Co.

HOVEY, KIRBY, THORNTON & HAHN, A PROFESSIONAL CORPORATION (AV)

101 West Broadway, Suite 1100, 92101-8297
Telephone: 619-685-4000
Fax: 619-685-4004
Email: 74754.3143@compuserve.com

Gregg B. Hovey

For full biographical listings, see the Martindale-Hubbell Law Directory

---

SAN FRANCISCO, San Francisco Co.

ELLMAN, BURKE, HOFFMAN & JOHNSON, A PROFESSIONAL CORPORATION (AV)

One Ecker, Suite 200, 94105
Telephone: 415-777-2727
Fax: 415-495-7587
Email: managingdirector@ellman-burke.com *URL:* http://www.ellman-burke.com

Howard N. Ellman
Michael J. Burke
Kenneth N. Burns
John D. Hoffman
Jeffrey W. Johnson
Thomas Paine
Jay L. Paxton
Thomas M. Sherwood
Leslie M. Browne
David H. Blackwell
Jodi Billehus Fedor

For full biographical listings, see the Martindale-Hubbell Law Directory

---

SAN RAFAEL, Marin Co.

RAGGHIANTI • FREITAS • MONTOBBIO • WALLACE LLP (AV)

874 Fourth Street, Suite D, 94901
Telephone: 415-453-9433
Fax: 415-453-8269

Gary T. Ragghianti
David P. Freitas
J. Mark Montobbio
J. Randolph Wallace
Patrick M. Macias
Robert F. Epstein
John Ralph Thomas

For full biographical listings, see the Martindale-Hubbell Law Directory

---

COLORADO

ASPEN, Pitkin Co.

AUSTIN, PEIRCE & SMITH, P.C. (AV)

Suite 205, 600 East Hopkins Avenue, 81611
Telephone: 970-925-2600
FAX: 970-925-4720
Email: apspc@rof.net

Ronald D. Austin
Frederick F. Peirce
Thomas Fenton Smith

Michael P. Fossenier

Counsel for: Chase Manhattan of Colorado, Inc.; Clark's Market; Cootes, Reid & Waldron Property Management, Inc.; Crystal Palace Corp.; Snowmass Shopping Center; Coldwell Banker The Aspen Brokers, Ltd.; William Poss & Assoc., Architects; Snowmass Resort Association; Aspen/Pitkin County Housing Authority; Nations Title Insurance, Inc.

For full biographical listings, see the Martindale-Hubbell Law Directory

---

CASTLE ROCK, Douglas Co.

FOLKESTAD & FAZEKAS, P.C. (AV)

316 Wilcox Street, 80104-2495
Telephone: 303-688-3045
FAX: 303-688-3189

James B. Folkestad
Ernest F. Fazekas, II

Susan B. Shoemaker

Representative Clients: Bank of Douglas County; Johnson & Sons Construction, Inc.; B & W Construction Co.; Proto Construction & Paving, Inc.; Grimm Construction Co.; Ashcroft Homes of Denver LLC.
References: Bank of Douglas County; First National Bank of Castle Rock; First Bank of Castle Rock; Colorado National Bank.

For full biographical listings, see the Martindale-Hubbell Law Directory

---

DENVER, Denver Co.

ANKELE, ICENOGLE, NORTON, WHITE & SETER, A PROFESSIONAL CORPORATION (AV)

5690 DTC Boulevard (Greenwood Village) Suite 300, 80111
Telephone: 303-773-1666
Fax: 303-773-1883

William P. Ankele, Jr.
T. Edward Icenogle
Charles E. Norton
Gary R. White
Kim J. Seter
Mary A. Hupp
Barbara K. Tenney
Tamara K. Gilida
Kristen D. Bear

OF COUNSEL

C. Michael Sayre

For full biographical listings, see the Martindale-Hubbell Law Directory

---

HAYES, PHILLIPS & MALONEY, P.C. (AV)

Suite 450, The Market Center, 1350 Seventeenth Street, 80202-1517
Telephone: 303-825-6444
Fax: 303-825-1269

John E. Hayes
Herbert C. Phillips
James S. Maloney
M. Susan Lombardi
Bradley N. Shefrin
Corey Y. Hoffmann

Representative Clients: City of Northglenn; City of Sheridan; Metropolitan Denver Water Authority; Parker Water and Sanitation District; Town of Winter Park; City of Black Hawk; Town of Hudson; Town of Parker; Town of Alma; Greenwood Village.

For full biographical listings, see the Martindale-Hubbell Law Directory

Denver—Continued

MYERS, BRADLEY AND DEVITT, P.C. (AV)

Suite 420, 4704 Harlan Street, 80212
Telephone: 303-433-8527
Fax: 303-433-8219

Frederick J. Myers	Jerald J. Devitt
Jon T. Bradley	Randall C. Arp

OF COUNSEL
Kent E. Hanson

Reference: Bank One Lakeside Banking Center.

For full biographical listings, see the Martindale-Hubbell Law Directory

CONNECTICUT

CHESHIRE, New Haven Co.

JOHN K. KNOTT, JR. (AV)

325 South Main Street, 06410
Telephone: 203-271-3031

ASSOCIATE
Priscilla C. Mulvaney

For full biographical listings, see the Martindale-Hubbell Law Directory

GREENWICH, Fairfield Co.

ALBERT, WARD & JOHNSON, P.C. (AV)

125 Mason Street, P.O. Box 1668, 06836
Telephone: 203-661-8600
Telecopier: 203-661-8051

OF COUNSEL

David Albert	C. Robton Perelli-Minetti

Tom S. Ward, Jr.	Howard R. Wolfe
Scott R. Johnson	Christopher A. Kristoff
Jane D. Hogeman	Vicki K. Comberiati

For full biographical listings, see the Martindale-Hubbell Law Directory

NEW LONDON, New London Co.

WALLER, SMITH & PALMER, P.C. (AV)

52 Eugene O'Neill Drive, P.O. Box 88, 06320
Telephone: 860-442-0367
Telecopier: 860-447-9915
Old Lyme, Connecticut Office: 103-A Halls Road.
Telephone: 860-434-8063.
Telecopier: 860-434-9452.

Birdsey G. Palmer (Retired)	Hughes Griffis
William W. Miner	Edward B. O'Connell
Robert P. Anderson, Jr.	Frederick B. Gahagan
Robert W. Marrion	Mary E. Driscoll

Tracy M. Collins	Valerie Ann Votto
David P. Condon	Charles C. Anderson

General Counsel For: Town of East Lyme; Town of Lebanon.
Counsel For: Citizens Savings Bank; Sonoco/Northeastern, Inc.; The Nature Conservancy; Fleet Bank.
Local Counsel For: McCue Mortgage Co.; Citicorp Mortgage; U.S. Department of Housing and Urban Development.

For Complete List of Firm Personnel, See General Section

For full biographical listings, see the Martindale-Hubbell Law Directory

STAMFORD, Fairfield Co.

CACACE, TUSCH & SANTAGATA (AV)

777 Summer Street, P.O. Box 15859, 06901-0859
Telephone: 203-327-2000
Telecopier: 203-353-3392

MEMBERS OF FIRM

Michael J. Cacace	Mark P. Santagata
	Paul T. Tusch

ASSOCIATES

Edward F. Nemchek	Ronald E. Kowalski, II
Alice Ann Fitzpatrick	Pierrette A. Newman
	Russell A. Green

For full biographical listings, see the Martindale-Hubbell Law Directory

WESTPORT, Fairfield Co.

WILLIAM L. SCHEFFLER & ASSOCIATES (AV⊤)

P.O. Box 2773, 06880-0773
Telephone: 203-226-6600; 1-800-429-4480
Telecopier: 203-227-1873

For full biographical listings, see the Martindale-Hubbell Law Directory

WEISMAN & LUBELL (AV)

5 Sylvan Road South, P.O. Box 3184, 06880
Telephone: 203-226-8307
Telecopier: 203-221-7279

MEMBERS OF FIRM

Lawrence P. Weisman	Ellen B. Lubell

Debra B. Wolfert-Marino

For full biographical listings, see the Martindale-Hubbell Law Directory

DISTRICT OF COLUMBIA

WASHINGTON, D.C. Co.

ALEXANDER, BEARDEN, HAIRSTON & MARKS, LLP (AV)

Limited Liability Partnership
2021 L Street, N.W., Suite 300, 20036
Telephone: 202-293-3700
Fax: 202-293-7359
Silver Spring, Maryland Office: Lee Plaza, Suite 805, 8601 Georgia Avenue, 20910.
Telephone: 301-589-2222.
Facsimile: 301-539-2523.
New York, New York Office: 330 Madison Avenue, 36th Floor.
Telephone: 212-808-0008.
Fax: 212-599-1028.

Koteles Alexander	James L. Bearden
	Michelle C. Clay

Reference: Riggs National Bank of Washington, D.C.

For full biographical listings, see the Martindale-Hubbell Law Directory

CUTLER & STANFIELD, L.L.P. (AV)

700 Fourteenth Street, N.W., 20005-2010
Telephone: 202-624-8400
Fax: 202-624-8410
Denver, Colorado Office: 1675 Broadway, 80202.
Telephone: 303-825-7000.
FAX: 303-825-7005.

MEMBERS OF FIRM

Eliot R. Cutler	Peter J. Kirsch
Jeffrey L. Stanfield	Barry Conaty
Sheila D. Jones	Stephen H. Kaplan
Perry M. Rosen	(Not admitted in DC)

OF COUNSEL

Byron Keith Huffman, Jr.	Sarah M. Rockwell
	(Not admitted in DC)

ASSOCIATES

Katherine Boonin Andrus	Dana C. Nifosi
Françoise M. Carrier	Barbara Paley
Christopher M. Kamper	W. Eric Pilsk
(Not admitted in DC)	Timothy A. Pohle
William G. Malley	Thomas D. Roth

For full biographical listings, see the Martindale-Hubbell Law Directory

FRANK W. FRISK, JR., P.C. (AV)

Suite 125, Canal Square, 1054 Thirty-First Street, N.W., 20007
Telephone: 202-333-8433
Fax: 202-333-8431

Frank W. Frisk, Jr.

For full biographical listings, see the Martindale-Hubbell Law Directory

FLORIDA

BRADENTON,* Manatee Co.

McGUIRE, PRATT, MASIO & FARRANCE, P.A. (AV)

Suite 600, 1001 3rd Avenue West, P.O. Box 1866, 34206
Telephone: 941-748-7076
Fax: 941-747-9774

Hugh E. McGuire, Jr.	Carol A. Masio
Charles J. Pratt, Jr.	Robert A. Farrance

John W. Kaklis
OF COUNSEL
Carter H. Parry

Reference: Barnett Bank of Manatee County.

For full biographical listings, see the Martindale-Hubbell Law Directory

KISSIMMEE,* Osceola Co.

POHL & SHORT, P.A.

(See Winter Park)

MIAMI,* Dade Co.

MILLEDGE IDEN & HELD (AV)

Suite 600, 2100 Ponce de Leon Boulevard (Coral Gables), 33134
Telephone: 305-445-1500
Facsimile: 305-446-9972

MEMBERS OF FIRM

Allan Milledge	Bruce F. Iden

Gary M. Held
ASSOCIATE
Dana J. McElroy
OF COUNSEL

John M. Milledge	Patricia Fields Anderson

Reference: Northern Trust Bank.

For full biographical listings, see the Martindale-Hubbell Law Directory

NAPLES,* Collier Co.

VEGA, STANLEY, ZELMAN & HANLON, P.A. (AV)

2660 Airport Road South, 34112
Telephone: 941-774-3333
Fax: 941-776-6420

George Vega, Jr.	John F. Stanley

Thomas J. Wood

General Counsel for: Lely Estates; Naples Community Hospital.
Local Counsel: Quail Creek Developments.

For full biographical listings, see the Martindale-Hubbell Law Directory

ORLANDO,* Orange Co.

POHL & SHORT, P.A.

(See Winter Park)

ST. AUGUSTINE,* St. Johns Co.

UPCHURCH, BAILEY & UPCHURCH, P.A. (AV)

780 North Ponce de Leon Boulevard, P.O. Drawer 3007, 32085-3007
Telephone: 904-829-9066
Facsimile: 904-825-4862

John D. Bailey, Jr.	Frank D. Upchurch, III

Katherine Gaertner Jones
OF COUNSEL
Hamilton D. Upchurch

Representative Clients: Aero Sport, Inc.; American Culinary Federation, Inc.; Barnett Bank, N.A. Penney Retirement Community, Inc.; St. Augustine Alligator Farm, Inc.; St. Augustine-St. Johns County Board of Realtors, Inc. *General Counsel:* Flagler College; Flagler Hospital, Inc.; Prosperity Bank of St. Augustine; St. Johns County School Board.

For Complete List of Firm Personnel, See General Section

For full biographical listings, see the Martindale-Hubbell Law Directory

TALLAHASSEE,* Leon Co.

HOPPING GREEN SAMS & SMITH, PROFESSIONAL ASSOCIATION (AV)

123 South Calhoun Street, P.O. Box 6526, 32314
Telephone: 904-222-7500
Fax: 904-224-8551

(See Next Column)

James S. Alves	Wade L. Hopping
Brian H. Bibeau	Frank E. Matthews
Kathleen L. Blizzard	Richard D. Melson
Elizabeth C. Bowman	David L. Powell
Richard S. Brightman	William D. Preston
Peter C. Cunningham	Carolyn S. Raepple
Ralph A. DeMeo	Douglas S. Roberts
Thomas M. DeRose	Gary P. Sams
William H. Green	Robert P. Smith

Cheryl G. Stuart

Gary K. Hunter, Jr.	Karen Peterson
Jonathan T. Johnson	Michael P. Petrovich
Robert A. Manning	R. Scott Ruth
Angela R. Morrison	W. Steve Sykes
Gary V. Perko	T. Kent Wetherell, II

OF COUNSEL
W. Robert Fokes

Representative Clients: Atlantic Gulf Communities; Dunes and Viera East Community Development Districts; Florida Electric Power Coordinating Group; Florida Power & Light Co.; MCI Telecommunications; Seminole Electric Co.; Sugar Cane Growers Cooperative of Florida; UPS; Waste Management, Inc.; Wheelabrator.

For full biographical listings, see the Martindale-Hubbell Law Directory

TAMPA,* Hillsborough Co.

MORRISON, MORRISON & MILLS, P.A. (AV)

1200 West Platt Street Suite 100, 33606
Telephone: 813-258-3311
Telecopier: 813-258-3209

Thomas K. Morrison	Frederick J. Mills
Susan B. Morrison	James E. Holmes, Jr.

Representative Clients: SouthTrust Bank of West Florida; SouthTrust Bank of Alabama, National Association; NationsBank of Florida, N.A.; Mercantile Bank; Barnett Banks, Inc.; Southern Commerce Bank; Sun Bank of Pasco County; Hillsborough County Industrial Development Authority; Automation Packaging, Inc.; Medical Data Management, Inc.

For full biographical listings, see the Martindale-Hubbell Law Directory

RYDBERG & GOLDSTEIN, P.A. (AV)

Suite 200, 500 East Kennedy Boulevard, 33602
Telephone: 813-229-3900
Telecopier: 813-229-6101

Marsha Griffin Rydberg	Bruce S. Goldstein

Peter Baker	Tammy N. Giroux
Brian T. FitzGerald	Cynthia L. Bulan

Susan Greco Tuttle

For full biographical listings, see the Martindale-Hubbell Law Directory

WINTER PARK, Orange Co.

POHL & SHORT, P.A. (AV)

280 West Canton Avenue, Suite 410, P.O. Box 3208, 32790
Telephone: 407-647-7645; 407-647-POHL
Telefax: 407-647-2314

Frank L. Pohl	C. Teresa de Arrigoitia
Houston E. Short	George A. Golder
Dwight I. Cool	Norma Stanley
James Everett Shepherd V	Mark W. Garrett

John R. Simpson, Jr.

Representative Clients: American Pioneer Title Insurance Company; Institute of Internal Auditors, Inc.; Thompson Steel, Inc.; SunTrust, N.A.; The Bank of Winter Park; Bekins Moving and Storage Co., Inc.; Champion Boats, Inc.; KeyCom Telephone Systems, Inc.

For full biographical listings, see the Martindale-Hubbell Law Directory

GEORGIA

ATLANTA,* Fulton Co.

HAWKINS & PARNELL (AV)

4000 SunTrust Plaza, 303 Peachtree Street, N.E., 30308-3243
Telephone: 404-614-7400
Fax: 404-614-7500
Email: 73541.1626@compuserve.com

MEMBERS OF FIRM

Michael J. Goldman	T. Ryan Mock, Jr.
H. Lane Young, II	Robert U. Wright
Joseph R. Cullens	Kimberly Houston Ridley

(See Next Column)

HAWKINS & PARNELL, *Atlanta—Continued*
ASSOCIATES
Charles R. Beans   Stephen M. Brooks
Cullen Christie Wilkerson, Jr.   Allen L. Broughton

Representative Clients: ACCG-IRMA; GIRMA; Willis Corroon Corporation of Georgia; Titan Insurance Co.; American International Group; Gallagher Bassett Services, Inc.

For Complete List of Firm Personnel, See General Section

For full biographical listings, see the Martindale-Hubbell Law Directory

---

HOLT, NEY, ZATCOFF & WASSERMAN (AV)

A Partnership including Professional Corporations
100 Galleria Parkway, Suite 600, 30339
Telephone: 770-956-9600
Facsimile Number: 770-956-1490
MEMBERS OF FIRM
James M. Ney (P.C.)   J. Scott Jacobson
ASSOCIATE
Jay Frank Castle

Representative Clients: Equitable Real Estate Investment Management, Inc.; Gables Residential Trust; Georgia Scientific & Technical Research Foundation, Inc.; NationsBank, N.A. (South); Trammell Crow Residential; John Weiland Homes, Inc.; Childress Klein Properties; Genuine Parts Co.

For Complete List of Firm Personnel, See General Section

For full biographical listings, see the Martindale-Hubbell Law Directory

---

JOHNSON & MONTGOMERY (AV)

One Buckhead Plaza, 3060 Peachtree Road, N.W., Suite 400, 30305
Telephone: 404-262-1000
Telecopier: 404-262-1222
MEMBER OF FIRM
Albert Sidney Johnson

For full biographical listings, see the Martindale-Hubbell Law Directory

---

PETERSON DILLARD YOUNG ASSELIN & POWELL LLP (AV)

Suite 1100, 230 Peachtree Street, N.W., 30303
Telephone: 404-523-3300
Telecopier: 404-522-6000
MEMBERS OF FIRM
G. Douglas Dillard   William Woodson Galloway
Carl E. Westmoreland, Jr.   Larry M. Dingle

For full biographical listings, see the Martindale-Hubbell Law Directory

---

MCDONOUGH,* Henry Co.

SMITH, WELCH, STUDDARD & BRITTAIN (AV)

200 The Commerce Building, 235 Keys Ferry Street, P.O. Box 31, 30253
Telephone: 770-957-3937
Fax: 770-957-9165
Stockbridge, Georgia Office: 1231-A Eagle's Landing Parkway.
Telephone: 770-389-4864.
Fax: 770-389-5157.
MEMBERS OF FIRM
Ernest M. Smith (1911-1992)   Ben W. Studdard, III
A. J. Welch, Jr.   J. Mark Brittain
                     (Resident, Stockbridge Office)
ASSOCIATES
Patrick D. Jaugstetter   Shawn Marie Story
E. Gilmore Maxwell   Arthur Scully Barbee

Representative Clients: Alliance Corp.; Atlanta Motor Speedway, Inc.; Bellamy-Strickland Chevrolet, Inc.; Ceramic and Metal Coatings Corp.; City of Hampton; City of Locust Grove; City of Stockbridge; Henry County Board of Education; Henry County Water and Sewerage Authority.

For full biographical listings, see the Martindale-Hubbell Law Directory

---

NEWNAN,* Coweta Co.

GLOVER & DAVIS, P.A. (AV)

10 Brown Street, P.O. Box 1038, 30264
Telephone: 770-253-4330
Fax: 770-251-7152
Peachtree City, Georgia Office: Suite 130, 200 Westpark Drive.
Telephone: 770-487-5834.
Fax: 770-487-3492.

J. Littleton Glover, Jr.   Asa M. Powell, Jr.
Jerry Ann Conner

Representative Clients: Newnan Savings Bank; Pike Transfer Co.; Batson-Cook Company, General Corporate and Construction Divisions; Coweta County, Georgia; Heard County, Georgia.
Local Counsel for: International Latex Corp.; First Union National Bank of Georgia; West Georgia Farm Credit, ACA.

(See Next Column)

For Complete List of Firm Personnel, See General Section

For full biographical listings, see the Martindale-Hubbell Law Directory

HAWAII

HONOLULU,* Honolulu Co.

DWYER IMANAKA SCHRAFF KUDO MEYER & FUJIMOTO ATTORNEYS AT LAW, A LAW CORPORATION (AV)

1800 Pioneer Plaza, 900 Fort Street Mall, 96813
Telephone: 808-524-8000
Telecopier: 808-526-1419
Mailing Address: P.O. Box 2727, 96803
Email: hawaiilaw@dwyer-imanaka.com *URL:* http://www.dwyer-imanaka.com

John R. Dwyer, Jr.   William G. Meyer, III
Mitchell A. Imanaka   Wesley M. Fujimoto
Paul A. Schraff   Ronald Van Grant
Benjamin A. Kudo (Atty. at   Jon M. H. Pang
     Law, A Law Corp.)   Blake W. Bushnell
               Adelbert Green

Richard T. Asato, Jr.   Jeffery S. Werbelow
Scott W. Settle   Lori Ann K. Koseki
Darcie S. Yoshinaga   Troy T. Fukuhara
Lawrence I. Kawasaki   Katy Y. Chen
Stacy E. Uehara   Naomi S. Uyeno
Kris N. Nakagawa   Roger B. McKeague
OF COUNSEL
Randall Y. Iwase   R. Brian Tsujimura

For full biographical listings, see the Martindale-Hubbell Law Directory

ILLINOIS

BOLINGBROOK, Will Co.

MOSS AND BLOOMBERG, LTD. (AV)

305 West Briarcliff Road, Suite 201, P.O. Box 1158, 60440-0858
Telephone: 630-759-0800
Telecopier: 630-759-8504

Barry L. Moss   Steven P. Bloomberg
         George A. Marchetti

David J. Freeman   Daniel C Shapiro
Norma J. Guess   Judson L. Strain

For full biographical listings, see the Martindale-Hubbell Law Directory

---

CHICAGO,* Cook Co.

CHERRY & FLYNN (AV)

30 North La Salle Street, Suite 2300, 60602
Telephone: 312-372-2100
Telecopier: 312-853-0279

Myron M. Cherry   William R. Coulson
Peter Flynn   David D. Merritt
         Adam J. Levitt

For full biographical listings, see the Martindale-Hubbell Law Directory

---

SCARIANO, KULA, ELLCH AND HIMES, CHARTERED (AV)

Two Prudential Plaza 180 North Stetson Suite 3100, 60601-6224
Telephone: 312-565-3100
Facsimile: 312-565-0000
Chicago Heights, Illinois Office: 1450 Aberdeen.
Telephone: 708-755-1900.
Facsimile: 708-755-0000.

Anthony G. Scariano   Kathleen Field Orr
David P. Kula   John M. Izzo
Robert H. Ellch   Raymond A. Hauser
Alan T. Sraga   Kathleen Roche Hirsman
A. Lynn Himes   Joanne W. Schochat
Justino D. Petrarca   Anthony Ficarelli
Lawrence Jay Weiner   G. Robb Cooper
         Daniel M. Boyle
OF COUNSEL
Max A. Bailey   John B. Kralovec

(See Next Column)

SCARIANO, KULA, ELLCH AND HIMES CHARTERED—*Continued*

Patrick J. Broncato	Kelly A. Hayden
Rosanne Ciambrone	Todd K. Hayden
Jon G. Crawford	David A. Hemenway
Joel R. DeTella	Sarah E. Joyce
Teri E. Engler	Christopher L. Petrarca
Andrew C. Eulass	Shelia C. Riley

Janet L. Schwieters

For full biographical listings, see the Martindale-Hubbell Law Directory

CRYSTAL LAKE, McHenry Co.

ZUKOWSKI, ROGERS, FLOOD & MCARDLE (AV)

50 Virginia Street, 60014
Telephone: 815-459-2050
Facsimile: 815-459-9057
Chicago, Illinois Office: 100 South Wacker Drive, Suite 1502.
Telephone: 312-407-7700.
Facsimile: 312-332-1901.

PARTNERS

H. David Rogers	David W. McArdle
Richard G. Flood	Jeannine A. Thoms

Stuart D. Gordon

ASSOCIATES

William P. Stanton	Michael J. Chmiel
Melissa J. Cooney	Maureen T. Murphy
Kelly A. Cahill	E. Regan Shepley
Michael J. Smoron	Stuart M. Nagel

Kevin J. O'Brien

OF COUNSEL

Timothy J. Curran	Francis S. Lorenz

Representative Clients: Village of Algonquin; Village of Lake in the Hills; Village of Johnsburg; Village of Lakewood; Village of Bull Valley; Village of Hebron; City of Harvard; Village of Richmond; City of McHenry; Village of West Dundee.

For full biographical listings, see the Martindale-Hubbell Law Directory

GENEVA,* Kane Co.

SMITH, LANDMEIER & SKAAR, P.C. (AV)

15 North Second Street, 60134
Telephone: 708-232-2880
Fax: 708-232-2889

Howard E. Smith, Jr.	Allen L. Landmeier

Representative Clients: City of St. Charles; Cog Hill Golf & Country Club; Wasco Sanitary District; Testing Service Corp.

For Complete List of Firm Personnel, See General Section

For full biographical listings, see the Martindale-Hubbell Law Directory

JOLIET,* Will Co.

HERSCHBACH, TRACY, JOHNSON, BERTANI & WILSON (AV)

Two Rialto Square, 116 North Chicago Street, Sixth Floor, 60432
Telephone: 815-723-8500
Fax: 815-727-4846

Thomas R. Wilson	Raymond E. Meader
George F. Mahoney, III	David J. Silverman

Kerry Anne Weber

General Counsel For: First National Bank of Joliet; First National Bancorp.
Representative Clients: Villages of Channahon, Frankfort, Romeoville and Shorewood; City of Wilmington; Gallagher & Henry; Tope Corporation; Vulcan Materials; Waste Management, Inc.; Crosfield Chemicals, Inc.

For Complete List of Firm Personnel, See General Section

For full biographical listings, see the Martindale-Hubbell Law Directory

INDIANA

AUBURN,* De Kalb Co.

MEFFORD AND CARPENTER, A PROFESSIONAL CORPORATION (AV)

130 East Seventh Street, P.O. Box 667, 46706-0667
Telephone: 219-925-2300
Facsimile: 219-925-2610
URL: http://www.lawmc.com

(See Next Column)

Donald T. Mefford	Kirk D. Carpenter

J. Bryan Nugen

For full biographical listings, see the Martindale-Hubbell Law Directory

CRAWFORDSVILLE,* Montgomery Co.

BERRY, CAPPER, DONALDSON & TULLEY (AV)

131 North Green Street, P.O. Box 429, 47933
Telephone: 317-362-7340
Fax: 317-362-5023

Andrew N. Foley (1909-1963)	Richard G. Tulley
John R. Berry (1907-1986)	John S. Capper, IV

S. Bryan Donaldson

Representative Clients: Elston Bank & Trust Co.; R. R. Donnelley & Sons Co. (Crawfordsville Division); Linden State Bank; City of Crawfordsville, Ind.

For full biographical listings, see the Martindale-Hubbell Law Directory

ELKHART, Elkhart Co.

CHESTER, PFAFF & BROTHERSON (AV)

317 West Franklin Street, P.O. Box 507, 46515-0507
Telephone: 219-294-5421
Fax: 219-522-1476

MEMBER OF FIRM
Robert A. Pfaff

For Complete List of Firm Personnel, See General Section

For full biographical listings, see the Martindale-Hubbell Law Directory

FORT WAYNE,* Allen Co.

HELMKE, BEAMS, BOYER & WAGNER (AV)

300 Metro Building, Berry & Harrison Streets, 46802-2242
Telephone: 219-422-7422
Telecopier: 219-422-6764

MEMBERS OF FIRM

Walter E. Helmke (1901-1976)	Robert A. Wagner
Walter P. Helmke	J. Timothy McCaulay
R. David Boyer	Daniel J. Borgmann

Trina Glusenkamp Gould

OF COUNSEL

Glen J. Beams	John G. Reiber

Representative Clients: Aalco Distributing Co., Inc.; Brotherhood Mutual Insurance Co.; Fremont Community Schools; Teco, Inc.; Air-O-Mat, Inc.; Leo Distributors, Inc.; The City of Fort Wayne, Indiana; Foellinger Foundation, Inc.

For full biographical listings, see the Martindale-Hubbell Law Directory

STANLEY A. LEVINE (AV)

Fort Wayne National Bank Building, Suite 2008, 110 West Berry
Street, 46802
Telephone: 219-422-7431
Facsimile: 219-422-7433

For full biographical listings, see the Martindale-Hubbell Law Directory

SWIFT & FINLAYSON (AV)

803 South Calhoun Street Suite 500, 46802-2480
Telephone: 219-423-4422
Fax: 219-423-4427
Affiliated Law Firm: Leeuw, Plopper & Beeman-Poland, First Indiana Plaza, Suite 2000, 135 North Pennsylvania Street, Indianapolis, Indiana, 46204-2456.

MEMBERS OF FIRM

Frank A. Higgins (1925-1976)	William D. Swift

Craig R. Finlayson

ASSOCIATE
Charles D. Bash

OF COUNSEL

Gene R. Leeuw	Craig D. Doyle
Joseph W. Murphy	Charleyne L. Gabriel

John Michael Mead

For full biographical listings, see the Martindale-Hubbell Law Directory

INDIANAPOLIS,* Marion Co.

CLARK, QUINN, MOSES & CLARK (AV)

One Indiana Square, Suite 2200, 46204-2011
Telephone: 317-637-1321
Fax: 317-687-2344

MEMBERS OF FIRM

Thomas Michael Quinn	J. Murray Clark

Matthew R. Clark

(See Next Column)

CLARK, QUINN, MOSES & CLARK, *Indianapolis—Continued*

ASSOCIATES

Michael D. Keele   Cameron F. Clark

LAND USE CONSULTANT

Elizabeth Bentz Williams   (Land Use Consultant)

Representative Clients: Justus; The Shorewood Corporation; Marina Limited Partnership; Lafarge Corporation; Meijer Realty, Inc.; Lowe's; Kite Development; U-Stor Self Storage Warehouses; Mechanic's Laundry; Davis Homes.

For full biographical listings, see the Martindale-Hubbell Law Directory

DANN PECAR NEWMAN & KLEIMAN, PROFESSIONAL CORPORATION (AV)

Suite 2300, One American Square Box 82008, 46282
Telephone: 317-632-3232; Indiana: 800-622-4799
Telecopy: 317-632-2962

Theodore R. Dann (1907-1993)	Walter E. Wolf, Jr.
Joel Yonover (1932-1995)	Barry E. Beldin
Philip D. Pecar	Robert D. Swhier, Jr.
Norman R. Newman	James P. Moloy
David H. Kleiman	Robert J. Schuckit
Jon B. Abels	Andrew A. Kleiman
Melvin R. Daniel	Michael J. Gabovitch
Lawrence F. Dorocke	Steven M. Pecar
Jeffrey A. Abrams	Benjamin A. Pecar
James H. Schwarz	Richard O. Kissel, II
Robert A. Rose	Joseph D. Calderon

OF COUNSEL

Linda E. Cantor   Anthony J. Rose

Ellen C. Siakotos   Angela L. Mansfield
Stacy L. Hill   Martha M. K. Baird
        Karin L. Veatch

Attorneys for: Indianapolis Machinery Co., Inc.; Melvin Simon & Associates, Inc.; Pacers Basketball Corp.; Universal Fire & Casualty Co., Inc.; Bank One, Indianapolis, NA; INB National Bank; Nachi Technology, Inc.; Pharmaceutical Corporation of America; Logo 7, Inc.

For full biographical listings, see the Martindale-Hubbell Law Directory

LAFAYETTE,* Tippecanoe Co.

BALL, EGGLESTON, BUMBLEBURG & McBRIDE (AV)

810 Bank One Building, P.O. Box 1535, 47902
Telephone: 317-742-9046
Fax: 317-742-1966

Cable G. Ball (1904-1981)	Warren N. Eggleston
Owen Crook (1908-1977)	(1923-1991)

MEMBERS OF FIRM

Joseph T. Bumbleburg	Jeffrey J. Newell
John K. McBride	James T. Hodson
Jack L. Walkey	Brian Wade Walker
Michael J. Stapleton	Cheryl M. Knodle
	Randy J. Williams

General Counsel for: The Lafayette Union Railway Co.; Bank One, Lafayette, N.A.
Representative Clients: Farmers Insurance Group; General Accident Fire & Life Assurance Corp.; City of Lafayette Board of Parks and Recreation; West Lafayette Community School Corp.; Travelers Insurance Co.; Trustees, West Lafayette Public Library.

For full biographical listings, see the Martindale-Hubbell Law Directory

HANNA & GERDE (AV)

Fifth Floor Bank & Trust Building, P.O. Box 1098, 47902
Telephone: 317-742-5005
Fax: 317-742-6490

Charles H. Robertson   (1902-1982)

MEMBERS OF FIRM

George L. Hanna   Cy Gerde

OF COUNSEL

Eric H. Burns

ASSOCIATE

Mary A. Russell

Representative Client: City of Lafayette.
Reference: Lafayette Bank & Trust Co.; Salin Bank & Trust Co.

For full biographical listings, see the Martindale-Hubbell Law Directory

MERRILLVILLE, Lake Co.

BURKE, MURPHY, COSTANZA & CUPPY (AV)

Suite 600 8585 Broadway, 46410-7064
Telephone: 219-769-1313
Telecopier: 219-769-6806
East Chicago, Indiana Office: First National Bank Building. 720 West Chicago Avenue.
Telephone: 219-397-2401.
Telecopier: 219-397-0508.
Valparaiso, Indiana Office: 15 North Franklin Street, Suite 200.
Telephone: 219-531-0134.
Telecopier: 219-531-0507.
Palm Harbor, Florida Office: Suite 280, 33920 U.S. Highway 19 North.
Telephone: 813-787-7799.
Telecopier: 813-787-7237.

MEMBERS OF FIRM

Joseph E. Costanza	Gerald K. Hrebec
Frederick M. Cuppy	David K. Ranich
	Demetri J. Retson

ASSOCIATES

Todd A. Etzler   Philip C. Spahn

Representative Clients: Whiteco Industries; Continental Machine & Engineering Co., Inc.; Gary Steel Products Corp.; Superior Construction Co., Inc.; Federal National Mortgage Association; Morrison Construction Co.; St. Catherine Hospital of East Chicago, Indiana.

For Complete List of Firm Personnel, See General Section

For full biographical listings, see the Martindale-Hubbell Law Directory

MUNSTER, Lake Co.

LAW OFFICES OF EUGENE M. FEINGOLD (AV)

625 Ridge Road, Suite A, 46321
Telephone: 219-836-8800
Fax: 219-836-8944

ASSOCIATE

Steven P. Kennedy

For full biographical listings, see the Martindale-Hubbell Law Directory

WARSAW,* Kosciusko Co.

ROCKHILL, PINNICK, PEQUIGNOT, HELM, LANDIS & RIGDON (AV)

105 East Main Street, 46580-2742
Telephone: 219-267-6116
Telecopier: 219-269-9264

MEMBERS OF FIRM

Morrison A. Rockhill (1895-1961)	Brooks C. Pinnick
Donald Vanderveer (1892-1965)	Stanley E. Pequignot
Herbert H. Bent (1913-1984)	Richard K. Helm
Byron C. Kennedy (1907-1987)	Vern K. Landis
	Jay A. Rigdon
Jamelyn E. Freeman	

OF COUNSEL

Alvin T. Rockhill

Representative Clients: First National Bank of Warsaw, Warsaw, Indiana; Warsaw Times-Union Newspaper and WRSW Radio and Broadcast Station; State Farm Insurance Cos.; Warsaw Chemical Co., Inc.; Little Crow Milling Co., Inc.; Farmers State Bank; C & D Foods, Inc.; Maple Leaf Farms, Inc.; United Farm Bureau Mutual Insurance Co.

For full biographical listings, see the Martindale-Hubbell Law Directory

IOWA

IOWA CITY,* Johnson Co.

MEARDON, SUEPPEL, DOWNER & HAYES P.L.C. (AV)

122 South Linn Street, 52240
Telephone: 319-338-9222
Fax: 319-338-7250

William L. Meardon	Thomas D. Hobart
William F. Sueppel	William J. Sueppel

Representative Clients: United Technologies-Automotive; Perpetual Savings Bank; Economy Advertising Company; Metro Pavers, Inc.; League of Iowa Municipalities; Hills Bank and Trust Co.; J.M. Swank Co.; City of Muscatine; McComas-Lacina Construction Co., Inc.; Diamond Dave's Taco Company, Inc.

For Complete List of Firm Personnel, See General Section

For full biographical listings, see the Martindale-Hubbell Law Directory

KENTUCKY

---

*LEXINGTON,** Fayette Co.

RICHARD V. MURPHY (AV)

1010 First National Building, 167 West Main Street, 40507
Telephone: 606-233-9811
FAX: 606-255-9199

For full biographical listings, see the Martindale-Hubbell Law Directory

---

STOLL, KEENON & PARK, LLP (AV)

201 E. Main Street, Suite 1000, 40507-1380
Telephone: 606-231-3000
Telecopier: 606-253-1093; 606-253-1027
Frankfort, Kentucky Office: 307 Washington Street, 40601.
Telephone: 502-875-6220.
Telecopier: 502-875-6235.
Louisville, Kentucky Office: 400 West Market Street, Suite 2650,
40202-3377.
Telephone: 502-568-9100.
Telecopier: 502-568-5700.

MEMBERS OF FIRM

Samuel D. Hinkle IV	Herbert A. Miller, Jr.
William M. Lear, Jr.	Rena Gardner Wiseman
Lea Pauley Goff	

ASSOCIATE
Steven B. Loy

Representative Clients: Ball Homes, Inc.; McDonalds Corp.; National Development Council, Inc.; Super America, Inc.

For Complete List of Firm Personnel, See General Section

For full biographical listings, see the Martindale-Hubbell Law Directory

---

LOUISIANA

---

*NEW ORLEANS,** Orleans Parish

LAMOTHE & HAMILTON, A PROFESSIONAL LAW CORPORATION (AV)

Pan American Life Center, 601 Poydras Street, Suite 2750, 70130
Telephone: 504-566-1805
Telecopier: 504-566-1569
MCI Mail: 382-4472
Email: lhplc@neosoft.com

Frank E. Lamothe, III	Galen S. Brown
Charles E. Hamilton, III	M. Lizabeth Talbott
Karen Edginton Milner	Thomas J. Cortazzo

Reference: Jefferson Guaranty Bank, New Orleans, Louisiana.

For full biographical listings, see the Martindale-Hubbell Law Directory

---

MAINE

---

*BANGOR,** Penobscot Co.

EATON, PEABODY, BRADFORD & VEAGUE, P.A. (AV)

Fleet Center-Exchange Street, P.O. Box 1210, 04402-1210
Telephone: 207-947-0111
Telecopier: 207-942-3040
Email: epbv@aol.com
Augusta, Maine Office: 2 Central Plaza.
Telephone: 207-622-3747.
Telecopier: 207-622-9732.
Blue Hill, Maine Office: One East Blue Hill Road.
Telephone: 207-374-2812.
Telecopier: 207-374-2548.
Brunswick, Maine Office: 167 Park Row.
Telephone: 207-729-1144.
Telecopier: 207-729-1140.
Camden, Maine Office: 7-9 Washington Street.
Telephone: 207-236-3325.
Telecopier: 207-236-8611.
Dover-Foxcroft, Maine Office: 30 East Main Street.
Telephone: 207-564-8378.
Telecopier: 207-564-7059.

(See Next Column)

Michael B. Trainor
A List of Representative Clients available upon request.

For Complete List of Firm Personnel, See General Section

For full biographical listings, see the Martindale-Hubbell Law Directory

---

*PORTLAND,** Cumberland Co.

PIERCE ATWOOD (AV)

One Monument Square, 04101
Telephone: 207-791-1100
Fax: 207-791-1350
Email: info@PierceAtwood.com
Augusta, Maine Office: 77 Winthrop Street.
Telephone: 207-622-6311.
Fax: 207-623-9367.
Newburyport, Massachusetts Office: 6 Harris Street.
Telephone: 508-465-9599.
Fax: 508-465-9945.

MEMBERS OF FIRM

Dennis C. Keeler	Elaine S. Falender

ASSOCIATES

James M. Saffian	Christopher M. Dawe
David P. Littell	Helen L. Edmonds
Marcia A. Metcalf	(Not admitted in ME)

COUNSEL
Judith A. Fletcher Woodbury

For Complete List of Firm Personnel, See General Section

For full biographical listings, see the Martindale-Hubbell Law Directory

---

MARYLAND

---

*BALTIMORE,** (Independent City)

VENABLE ATTORNEYS AT LAW VENABLE, BAETJER AND HOWARD, LLP (AV)

A Partnership including Professional Corporations
1800 Mercantile Bank & Trust Building, 2 Hopkins Plaza, 21201
Telephone: 410-244-7400
Email: INFO@Venable.win.net
Washington, D.C. Office: Venable, Baetjer, Howard & Civiletti LLP. Suite 1000, 1201 New York Avenue, N.W.
Telephone: 202-962-4800.
McLean, Virginia Office: Suite 400, 2010 Corporate Ridge.
Telephone: 703-760-1600.
Rockville, Maryland Office: Suite 500, One Church Street, P. O. Box 1906.
Telephone: 301-217-5600.
Towson, Maryland Office: 210 Allegheny Avenue, P. O. Box 5517.
Telephone: 410-494-6200.

MEMBERS OF FIRM

Thomas P. Perkins, III (P.C.)	Cynthia M. Hahn (Resident,
John B. Howard (Resident,	Towson, Maryland Office)
Towson, Maryland Office)	Robert A. Hoffman (Resident,
John G. Milliken (Not admitted	Towson, Maryland Office)
in MD; Washington, D.C. and	
McLean, Virginia Offices)	

OF COUNSEL
Judith A. Armold

For Complete List of Firm Personnel, See General Section

For full biographical listings, see the Martindale-Hubbell Law Directory

---

*BEL AIR,** Harford Co.

STARK & KEENAN, A PROFESSIONAL ASSOCIATION (AV)

30 Office Street, 21014
Telephone: 410-838-5522
Baltimore: 410-879-2222
Fax: 410-879-0688

Elwood V. Stark, Jr.	Judith Cline-Silverstein
Charles B. Keenan, Jr.	Gregory A. Szoka
Edwin G. Carson	Robert S. Lynch

Claire Prin Blomquist	Paul W. Ishak
Kimberly Kahoe Muenter	Lawrence F. Kreis, Jr.

For full biographical listings, see the Martindale-Hubbell Law Directory

MARYLAND

EASTON, Talbot Co.

HENRY & PRICE LLC (AV)

117 Bay Street, P.O. Box 838, 21601
Telephone: 410-822-2600
Fax: 410-822-2626

MEMBERS OF FIRM

T. Hughlett Henry (1879-1966)	W. Thomas Fountain
T. Hughlett Henry, Jr.	David C. Bryan
(1910-1994)	Suzanne L. Hood

John G. Billmyre

ASSOCIATES

Sharon J. Ritter   Nannette G. Grimes

OF COUNSEL

William H. Price, II

Attorneys for: Talbot County Board of Appeals; Town of Preston; Chicago Title Insurance Co. of Maryland; Lawyers Title Insurance Corp.; Delmarva Power & Light Co.; John Hancock Mutual Life Insurance Co.; Metropolitan Life Insurance Co.

For full biographical listings, see the Martindale-Hubbell Law Directory

SALISBURY, Wicomico Co.

ADKINS, POTTS & SMETHURST, L.L.P. (AV)

Suite 600, One Plaza East, P.O. Box 4247, 21803-4247
Telephone: 410-749-0161
Fax: 410-749-5021

MEMBERS OF FIRM

Raymond Stevens Smethurst, Jr.   Robert B. Taylor

Representative Clients: Atlantic Wood Industries, Inc.; Campbell Soup Company; Delmarva Power & Light Co.; G. E. Capital Mortgage Services, Inc.; Lawyers' Title Insurance Corp.; Mellon Bank (DE); PNC Bank; Proko Industries, Inc.; Shopco Group; WBOC-TV.

For full biographical listings, see the Martindale-Hubbell Law Directory

MASSACHUSETTS

BOSTON, Suffolk Co.

KOPELMAN AND PAIGE, P.C. (AV)

Park Square Building, 31 St. James Avenue, 7th Floor, 02116
Telephone: 617-556-0007
Fax: 617-654-1735

Leonard Kopelman	John W. Giorgio
Donald G. Paige	Barbara J. Saint Andre
Elizabeth A. Lane	Joel B. Bard
Joyce F. Frank	Everett Joseph Marder

Patrick J. Costello

For Complete List of Firm Personnel, See General Section

For full biographical listings, see the Martindale-Hubbell Law Directory

SHERBURNE, POWERS & NEEDHAM, P.C. (AV)

One Beacon Street, 02108
Telephone: 617-523-2700
Fax: 617-523-6850
Email: @SHERBURNE.COM

William D. Weeks	Benjamin Volinski
John T. Collins	Mark Schonfeld
Allan J. Landau	James D. Smeallie
Stephen A. Hopkins	Paul Killeen
Alan I. Falk	Gordon P. Katz
C. Thomas Swaim	Joseph B. Darby, III
James Pollock	Richard M Yanofsky
William V. Tripp III	James E. McDermott
Stephen S. Young	Kenneth P. Brier
William F. Machen	Robert V. Lizza
W. Robert Allison	Miriam Goldstein Altman
Philip J. Notopoulos	John J. Monaghan
Richard J. Hindlian	Margaret J. Palladino
Paul E. Troy	Mark C. Michalowski
Harold W. Potter, Jr.	David Scott Sloan
Philip S. Lapatin	M. Chrysa Long
Pamela A. Duckworth	Lawrence D. Bradley

Miriam J. McKendall

Cynthia A. Brown	Joshua C. Krumholz
Cynthia M. Hern	Ieuan G. Mahony
Meredeth A. Beers	Jeffrey J. Nix
Dianne R. Phillips	(Not admitted in MA)
Paul M. James	Kenneth L. Harvey
Theodore F. Hanselman	Christopher J. Trombetta

(See Next Column)

Elise N. Zoli	Nicholas J. Psyhogeos
Amy J. Mastrobattista	Edward J. Naughton
Leslie A. Sprinkle	Kathaleen Kelly Cutone
Douglas W. Clapp	Laurie A. Tribble
Jeffrey A. Huebschmann	Neil C. Higgins
Tamara E. Goulston	Deborah Paige Stone
Paul G. Lannon, Jr.	Brian R. Popiel

COUNSEL

Haig Der Manuelian	Karl J. Hirshman
Mason M. Taber, Jr.	Dale R. Johnson

For full biographical listings, see the Martindale-Hubbell Law Directory

FRANKLIN, Norfolk Co.

ROCHE AND MURPHY (AV)

Franklin Office Park West, 38 Pond Street, Suite 308, P.O. Box 267, 02038
Telephone: 508-528-8300
FAX: 508-528-8889

MEMBERS OF FIRM

Neil J. Roche   Paul G. Murphy

ASSOCIATE

John J. Roche

For full biographical listings, see the Martindale-Hubbell Law Directory

SPRINGFIELD, Hampden Co.

FRATAR & KERN (AV)

1391 Main Street, Suite 500, 01103
Telephone: 413-734-3119
Telecopier: 413-736-0670

MEMBERS OF FIRM

Robert N. Fratar   William F. Kern

For full biographical listings, see the Martindale-Hubbell Law Directory

WORCESTER, Worcester Co.

MOUNTAIN, DEARBORN & WHITING (AV)

370 Main Street, 01608
Telephone: 508-756-2423
Fax: 508-755-6640

MEMBERS OF FIRM

Alfred N. Whiting (1920-1989)	Francis J. Russell
Thomas R. Mountain	Dale R. Harger
Richard W. Dearborn	Mark W. Bloom
Samuel R. DeSimone	Donald J. O'Neil
Henry W. Beth	Lawrence S. Delaney

Ann K. Molloy

ASSOCIATE

Richard M. Freije

For full biographical listings, see the Martindale-Hubbell Law Directory

MICHIGAN

BIRMINGHAM, Oakland Co.

CARSON FISCHER, P.L.C. (AV)

Third Floor, 300 East Maple Road, 48009-6317
Telephone: 810-644-4840
Facsimile: 810-644-1832

Robert M. Carson   Peter L. Wanger

For full biographical listings, see the Martindale-Hubbell Law Directory

WILLIAMS, SCHAEFER, RUBY & WILLIAMS, PROFESSIONAL CORPORATION (AV)

Suite 300, 380 North Woodward Avenue, 48009
Telephone: 810-642-0333
Telecopy: 810-642-0856

James A. Williams   Thomas G. Plunkett

Richard D. Rattner

OF COUNSEL

Robert A. Jacobs

Representative Clients: Beachum & Roeser Development Corporation; Groveland Township; Marriott Corporation; McDonald's Corporation; KinderCare Learning Centers; Michigan National Bank; Morgan-Mitsubishi Development Corporation; Sanilac County; Walmart; Western Development Company.

For full biographical listings, see the Martindale-Hubbell Law Directory

BLOOMFIELD HILLS, Oakland Co.

ADKISON NEED (AV)

1533 North Woodward Avenue, Suite 210, 48304
Telephone: 810-540-7400
Fax: 810-540-7401
Email: AdkisNeed@aol.com

MEMBERS OF FIRM

Phillip G. Adkison	Paul Green
Gregory K. Need	Kelly A. Allen
Deborah M. Schneider	

ASSOCIATES

Richard D. Kuhn, Jr.	Ann D. Christ
Kathryn N. Nichols	Laura B. Andoni

For full biographical listings, see the Martindale-Hubbell Law Directory

O'CONNOR, DeGRAZIA & TAMM, P.C. (AV)

4111 Andover East, 48302
Telephone: 810-433-2000
Fax: 810-433-2001

Richard M. O'Connor	Lorraine M. Knapp
James I. DeGrazia	Christopher T. Koch
James E. Tamm	Amy Hobbs Iannone
Julie McCann-O'Connor	Jay Dilday Gardner
Audrey J. Forbush	Thomas H. Schram

Representative Clients: Regents of the University of Michigan; William Beaumont Hospital; Michigan Physicians Mutual Liability Co.; Botsford General Hospital; Michigan Municipal League; Michigan Municipal Liability and Property Pool; Select Insured Risk Services; St. Paul Insurance Cos.; Physicians Insurance Company of Michigan; National Chiropractic Mutual.

For full biographical listings, see the Martindale-Hubbell Law Directory

*DETROIT,** Wayne Co.

ABBOTT, NICHOLSON, QUILTER, ESSHAKI & YOUNGBLOOD, P.C. (AV)

19th Floor, One Woodward Avenue, 48226
Telephone: 313-963-2500
Telecopier: 313-963-7882

C. Richard Abbott	Carl F. Jarboe
John R. Nicholson	Jay A. Kennedy
Thomas R. Quilter III	Timothy A. Stoepker
Gene J. Esshaki	Timothy J. Kramer
John F. Youngblood	Norbert T. Madison, Jr.
James B. Perry	William D. Gilbride, Jr.

Mary P. Nelson	Kathryn L. Ritchie
Michael R. Blum	Jill A. Bankey
Thomas F. Hatch	Dawn M. Macaddino
Anne Warren Bagno	Casimir J. Swastek
Eric J. Girdler	Daniel G. Kielczewski

George M. Mesrey

OF COUNSEL

Thomas C. Shumaker	Karen Smith Kienbaum

For full biographical listings, see the Martindale-Hubbell Law Directory

BODMAN, LONGLEY & DAHLING LLP (AV)

34th Floor 100 Renaissance Center, 48243
Telephone: 313-259-7777
Fax: 313-393-7579
Email: 2080194@mcimail.com
Troy, Michigan Office: Suite 2020, 755 West Big Beaver Road.
Telephone: 810-362-2110.
Fax: 810-244-0780.
Ann Arbor, Michigan Office: 110 Miller, Suite 300.
Telephone: 313-761-3780.
Fax: 313-930-2494.
Northern Michigan Office: 229 Court Street, P.O. Box 405, Cheboygan.
Telephone: 616-627-4351.
Fax: 616-627-2802.

MEMBERS OF FIRM

Thomas A. Roach (Ann Arbor Office)	F. Thomas Lewand
Herold McC. Deason	Michael A. Stack (Northern Michigan Office)
James A. Smith	Harvey W. Berman (Ann Arbor Office)
Joseph N. Brown	
Randolph S. Perry	Jerold Lax (Ann Arbor Office)
James J. Walsh	Sandra L. Sorini (Ann Arbor Office)

COUNSEL

John S. Dobson (Ann Arbor Office)

For Representative Client List, See General Section

(See Next Column)

For Complete List of Firm Personnel, See General Section

For full biographical listings, see the Martindale-Hubbell Law Directory

BUTZEL LONG, A PROFESSIONAL CORPORATION (AV)

Suite 900, 150 West Jefferson, 48226
Telephone: 313-225-7000
Telecopier: 313-225-7080
Email: melnick@butzel.com *URL:* http://www.butzel.com
Birmingham, Michigan Office: Suite 200, 32270 Telegraph Road.
Telephone: 810-258-1616.
Telecopier: 810-258-1439.
Lansing, Michigan Office: 118 West Ottawa Street.
Telephone: 517-372-6622.
Telecopier: 517-372-6672.
Ann Arbor, Michigan Office: Suite 300, 350 South Main Street.
Telephone: 313-995-3110.
Telecopier: 313-995-1777.
Grosse Pointe Farms, Michigan Office: Suite 260, 21 Kercheval.
Telephone: 313-886-5446.
Telecopier: 313-886-2114.

William R. Ralls (Lansing)	Steven D. Weyhing (Lansing)
John P. Hancock, Jr.	Leonard M. Niehoff
David W. Berry (Birmingham)	(Ann Arbor)
Carl Rashid, Jr.	Ronald E. Reynolds
Gordon W. Didier (Birmingham)	(Birmingham)

Susan Klein Friedlaender (Birmingham)

Representative Clients: Canton Township; Grosse Pointe Shores; Plymouth Township; Northville Township.

For Complete List of Firm Personnel, See General Section

For full biographical listings, see the Martindale-Hubbell Law Directory

JAFFE, RAITT, HEUER & WEISS, PROFESSIONAL CORPORATION (AV)

One Woodward Avenue, Suite 2400, 48226
Telephone: 313-961-8380
Telecopier: 313-961-8358
Cable Address: "Jafsni"
Southfield, Michigan Office: Travelers Tower, Suite 1520.
Telephone: 313-961-8380.
Monroe, Michigan Office: 214 East Elm Avenue, Suite 208,
Telephone: 313-241-6470.
Telefacsimile: 313-241-3849.

Julia Blakeslee	Robert S. Bolton

Kerry Gross-Bondy (Resident, Monroe, Michigan Office)

Representative Clients: Berlin Township; Frenchtown Charter Township.

For Complete List of Firm Personnel, See General Section

For full biographical listings, see the Martindale-Hubbell Law Directory

LAW OFFICES OF THOMAS E. MARSHALL (AV)

Ford Building, Suite 1805, 615 Griswold, 48226-3583
Telephone: 313-963-4483
Telecopier: 313-963-4736

ASSOCIATES

Phyllis Leah Hurks-Hill	Alejandro Navarro

OF COUNSEL

Andrew J. Bean

For full biographical listings, see the Martindale-Hubbell Law Directory

VANDEVEER GARZIA, PROFESSIONAL CORPORATION (AV)

Suite 1600, 333 West Fort Street, 48226
Telephone: 313-961-4880
Fax: 313-961-3822
Oakland County Office: 220 Park Street, Suite 300, Birmingham, Michigan.
Telephone: 810-645-0100.
Fax: 810-645-2430.
Macomb County Office: 50 Crocker Boulevard, Mount Clemens, Michigan.
Telephone: 810-468-4880.
Fax: 810-465-7159.
West Michigan Office: 1121 Ottawa Beach Road, Suite 140, Holland Michigan.
Telephone: 616-399-8600.
Fax: 616-786-9095.

John J. Lynch, III (Resident, Oakland County Office)	Thomas M. Peters

Dawn Twydell Gladhill

Representative Clients: Aetna Casualty and Surety Co.; Bic Corp.; CNA Insurance Group; Travelers Insurance Co.; United States Aviation Underwriters; Goodyear Tire & Rubber Co.

(See Next Column)

VANDEVEER GARZIA PROFESSIONAL CORPORATION, *Detroit—Continued*

For Complete List of Firm Personnel, See General Section

For full biographical listings, see the Martindale-Hubbell Law Directory

---

FARMINGTON HILLS, Oakland Co.

FINK ZAUSMER, P.C. (AV)

31700 Middlebelt Road, Suite 150, 48334
Telephone: 810-851-4111
Telefax: 810-851-0100
Detroit, Michigan Office: 1917 Penobscot Building.
Telephone: 313-963-3873.
Telefax: 313-961-6879.
Lansing, Michigan Office: One Michigan Avenue, Suite 1050.
Telephone: 517-372-2020.
Telefax: 517-371-3207.

David H. Fink	Mark J. Zausmer
	Avery K. Williams

Ruben Acosta	Karen Libertiny Ludden
Michael L. Caldwell	Amy M. Sitner

OF COUNSEL

John T. Peters, Jr.	Alan D. Wasserman

For full biographical listings, see the Martindale-Hubbell Law Directory

JOHNSON, ROSATI, GALICA, LABARGE, ASELTYNE, SUGAMELI & FIELD, P.C. (AV)

34405 W. Twelve Mile Road, Suite 200, 48331-5627
Telephone: 810-489-4100
Fax: 810-489-1726
Bay City, Michigan Office: 420 Shearer Building, 311 Center Avenue, 48708.
Telephone: 517-894-2600; 517-894-7191.
Fax: 517-894-7177.
Lansing, Michigan Office: 303 S. Waverly Road, 48917.
Telephone: 517-886-3800.
Fax: 517-886-9154.
St. Clair Shores, Michigan Office: 19900 E. 10 Mile Road, 48080.
Telephone: 313-777-3377.

Christopher J. Johnson	Laura Amtsbuechler
Carol A. Rosati	Marcia L. Howe
Kenneth G. Galica	Edward M. Olson
S. Randall Field	Daniel P. Dalton
Michael E. Rosati	Margaret T. Debler
Michael J. Sugameli	Marcelyn A. Stepanski
Kenneth A. Slusser	Andrey T. Tomkiw
	Linda B. Taylor

Representative Clients: Michigan Municipal Risk Management Authority; Metropolitan Association for Improved School Legislation Risk Management Trust; Indiana Insurance Co.; County of Lapeer; County of Van Buren; County of Otsego; City of Romulus; City of Harper Woods; City of Hazel Park; Chirco Realty.

For full biographical listings, see the Martindale-Hubbell Law Directory

---

GRAND RAPIDS,* Kent Co.

LAW, WEATHERS & RICHARDSON, P.C. (AV)

Bridgewater Place, Suite 800, 333 Bridge Street, N.W., 49504
Telephone: 616-459-1171
Facsimile: 616-732-1740

OF COUNSEL

Niel A. Weathers (Retired)	Robert W. Richardson
Jerome Van H. Sluggett (Retired)	Walter B. Freihofer
	John R. Nichols
W. Fred Hunting, Jr.	

William R. Hineline	Kurt G. Yost
Robert P. Cooper	Anthony P. Gauthier
Alan C. Bennett	Clifford H. Bloom
James L. Wernstrom	Scott G. Smith
Stephen D. Turner	Douglas W. Van Essen
John P. Schneider	Ingrid A. Jensen
Christopher L. Edgar	Ellen S. Carmody
John M. Huff	James A. Ens
Kevin B. Krauss	Bruce A. Courtade
Robert A. Buchanan	Mary Jane Rhoades
John H. Gretzinger	Jeffrey J. Van Winkle
Henry G. Swain	Jeffrey VanHorne Sluggett

David W. Centner	Terry E. Tobias
Roger A. Swets	M. Bridget Gleason
James T. Polonczyk	Michael J. Roth
Ronald M. Stella	Brian S. Fleetham

(See Next Column)

Representative Clients: F.D.I.C.; Ford Motor Credit Co.; Herman Miller, Inc.; Kent County Aeronautics Board; Marriott Corp.; The Procter & Gamble Co.; Peerless Insurance Co.; Ryder Systems, Inc.

For full biographical listings, see the Martindale-Hubbell Law Directory

---

KALAMAZOO,* Kalamazoo Co.

KREIS, ENDERLE, CALLANDER & HUDGINS, A PROFESSIONAL CORPORATION (AV)

One Moorsbridge, P.O. Box 4010, 49003-4010
Telephone: 616-324-3000
Telecopier: 616-324-3010
Email: kech@sapien.net *URL:* http://www.kech.com.

Alan G. Enderle	Douglas L. Callander
	Thomas G. King

For Complete List of Firm Personnel, See General Section

For full biographical listings, see the Martindale-Hubbell Law Directory

---

MONROE,* Monroe Co.

BRAUNLICH, RUSSOW & BRAUNLICH, A PROFESSIONAL CORPORATION (AV)

111 South Macomb Street, 48161
Telephone: 313-241-8300
Fax: 313-241-7715

William J. Braunlich, Jr. (1924-1992)	Thomas P. Russow
	William H. Braunlich

Philip A. Costello	Marie C. Kennedy
Patricia M. Poupard	Susan J. Mehregan
Ann L. Nickel	Robert Wetzel
	Michael G. Roehrig

LEGAL SUPPORT PERSONNEL

Ruth G. Flint

Representative Clients: State Farm Mutual Insurance Co.; Auto Club Insurance Assn.; Farm Bureau Insurance Co.; Home Mutual Insurance Co.; Cincinnati Insurance Co.; Board of Road Commissioners, Monroe County; Port of Monroe; Monroe County Community College; City of Luna Pier; City of Petersburg.

For full biographical listings, see the Martindale-Hubbell Law Directory

JAFFE, RAITT, HEUER & WEISS, PROFESSIONAL CORPORATION (AV)

214 East Elm Avenue, Suite 208, 48161
Telephone: 313-241-6470
Telefacsimile: 313-241-3849
Detroit, Michigan Office: One Woodward Avenue, Suite 2400.
Telephone: 313-961-8380.
Telecopier: 313-961-8358.
Southfield, Michigan Office: Suite 1520, Travelers Tower.
Telephone: 313-961-8380.

John A. Hohman, Jr. (Resident)

Kerry Gross-Bondy (Resident)

Representative Clients: Berlin Township; Frenchtown Charter Township.

For Complete List of Firm Personnel, See General Section

For full biographical listings, see the Martindale-Hubbell Law Directory

---

MOUNT CLEMENS,* Macomb Co.

ANTHONY, SEIBERT AND DLOSKI (AV)

Professional Limited Liability Company
202 Vicant Building, 59 North Walnut Street, 48043
Telephone: 810-469-3800
Fax: 810-469-2443

MEMBERS OF FIRM

Gary S. Anthony	Lawrence W. Dloski
Robert J. Seibert	Christine D. Anderson

Representative Clients: Townships of Chesterfield, Bruce, Washington and Ray.
Reference: Huntington Banks; First National Bank in Mount Clemens.

For full biographical listings, see the Martindale-Hubbell Law Directory

PETERSON, HAY AND COMSA, P.C. (AV)

18 First Street, P.O. Box 688, 48046-0688
Telephone: 810-469-3600
Facsimile: 810-469-2537

(See Next Column)

PETERSON, HAY AND COMSA P.C.—*Continued*

James R. Peterson (1931-1991)	David A. Comsa
William L. Hay	Thomas S. Michael
	Lynn M. Capp

For full biographical listings, see the Martindale-Hubbell Law Directory

WELCH, MacALPINE, BAHORSKI, BIEGLECKI & FARRELL, P.C. (AV)

71 North Avenue, 48043-5543
Telephone: 810-469-1111; 1-800-252-1654
Facsimile: 810-469-1609

Terry S. Welch	Thomas R. Bieglecki
Robert F. MacAlpine	Thaddeus M. Dombrowski
Timothy A. Bahorski	Marc P. Shaberman
John B. Farrell	Michael W. Sickles
	Christopher R. Baratta

For full biographical listings, see the Martindale-Hubbell Law Directory

PONTIAC,* Oakland Co.

BOOTH PATTERSON, P.C. (AV)

1090 West Huron Street, 48328
Telephone: 810-681-1200
Fax: 810-681-1754

Douglas W. Booth (1918-1992)	David J. Lee
Calvin E. Patterson (1913-1987)	Allan T. Motzny
Parvin C. Lee, Jr.	Michael J. Hughes
J. Timothy Patterson	Michael D. Bishop
	Eric S. Meier

Representative Clients: City of South Lyon; Holly Township; Charter Township of Orion; Township of Rose.

For full biographical listings, see the Martindale-Hubbell Law Directory

PORT HURON,* St. Clair Co.

FLETCHER DeGROW (AV)

522 Michigan Street, 48060-3893
Telephone: 810-987-8444
Facsimile: 810-987-8149

MEMBERS OF FIRM

Gary A. Fletcher	Mark G. Clark

ASSOCIATE
John D. Tomlinson

Representative Clients: Clay Township; City of Memphis; City of Port Huron; City of Marysville; Port Huron Area School District; Marysville Public Schools; Relleum Real Estate Development Co.

For Complete List of Firm Personnel, See General Section

For full biographical listings, see the Martindale-Hubbell Law Directory

ST. JOSEPH,* Berrien Co.

GLOBENSKY, GLEISS, BITTNER & HYRNS, P.C. (AV)

610 Ship Street, P.O. Box 290, 49085
Telephone: 616-983-0551
Fax: 616-983-5858

H. S. Gray (1867-1961)	Rodger V. Bittner
Luman H. Gray (1902-1952)	Randy S. Hyrns
John L. Globensky	J. Joseph Daly
Henry W. Gleiss	Charles T. LaSata
	James J. Riemland

General Counsel for: Shoreline Bank; Hanson Cold Storage Co.; Pearson Construction Co., Inc.
Approved Attorneys for: Lawyers Title Insurance Corp.
Reference: Shoreline Bank of Benton Harbor.

For full biographical listings, see the Martindale-Hubbell Law Directory

SOUTHFIELD, Oakland Co.

MASON, STEINHARDT, JACOBS & PERLMAN, PROFESSIONAL CORPORATION (AV)

Suite 1500, 4000 Town Center, 48075-1415
Telephone: 810-358-2090
Fax: 810-358-3599

Gordon I. Ginsberg	Michael B. Perlman
Irving I. Boigon	Jerome P. Pesick
Jack Schon	Richard A. Polk
Walter B. Mason, Jr.	Jay W. Tower
Frederick D. Steinhardt	Jonathan B. Frank
John E. Jacobs	Neil S. Silver
	L. Jeffrey Zauberman

Diane Flagg Goldstein	H. Adam Cohen

OF COUNSEL

Erwin B. Ellmann	Marvin C. Daitch
Randolph J. Friedman	John M. Roche

Representative Clients: Citibank, N.A.; City of Dearborn; DeMattia Development Co.; Forest City Enterprises; Michigan Wholesale Drug Assn.; Mortgage Bankers Association of Michigan; Nationwide Insurance Co.; City of Taylor; Union Labor Life Insurance Co.; Yellow Freight Systems, Inc.

For Complete List of Firm Personnel, See General Section

For full biographical listings, see the Martindale-Hubbell Law Directory

STERLING HEIGHTS, Macomb Co.

O'REILLY, RANCILIO, NITZ, ANDREWS & TURNBULL, P.C. (AV)

One Sterling Town Center, 12900 Hall Road, Suite 350, 48313-1151
Telephone: 810-726-1000
Fax: 810-726-1560

Paul J. O'Reilly	Bert T. Ross
Kenneth L. Rancilio	Michael J. Piatek
John A. Nitz	Pauline Stoey Baleda
Clark A. Andrews	Christopher P. Baker
Charles E. Turnbull	David B. Viar
Neil J. Lehto	Susan A. Rancilio
Craig S. Schoenherr, Sr.	Michael F. Goethals
	Danon D. Goodrum

OF COUNSEL
Gary J. Collins

Representative Clients: ACE Finishing, Inc.; Central Building Co.; Century Telecommunications Services, Inc.; Chivas Products, Ltd.; City of Harper Woods; City of Sterling Heights; Delta Fuels, Inc.; DJR Development Co.; First of America Bank Michigan, N.A.; First Optometry Eye Care Centers, Inc.

For full biographical listings, see the Martindale-Hubbell Law Directory

TRAVERSE CITY,* Grand Traverse Co.

RUNNING, WISE, WILSON, FORD AND PHILLIPS, P.L.C. (AV)

326 State Street, P.O. Box 686, 49684
Telephone: 616-946-2700
Tele-Fax: 616-946-0857

Harry T. Running (Deceased)	William L. Wise (Retired)

MEMBERS OF FIRM

Patrick J. Wilson	James C. Adams
Richard W. Ford	Sandra P. Howard
Thomas J. Phillips	Kent E. Gerberding

ASSOCIATES

Shelley A. Kester	Bradley L. Putney

OF COUNSEL

J. Bruce Donaldson	Douglas J. Donaldson

Representative Clients: Grand Traverse County Road Commission; Townships of Peninsula, East Bay, Garfield, Almira, Homestead, Glen Arbor, Lake Township; Grand Traverse Title Co.; Villages of Lake Ann and Honor.

For full biographical listings, see the Martindale-Hubbell Law Directory

ROBERT P. TREMP, P.C. (AV)

3939 M-72 East (Williamsburg), P.O. Box 3019, 49685-3019
Telephone: 616-938-2888
Telefax: 616-938-2988
Email: rptpc@traverse.com
Marquette, Michigan Office: 307 South Front Street, Suite 202.
Telephone: 906-228-8263.
Telefax: 906-228-5282.

Robert P. Tremp
LEGAL SUPPORT PERSONNEL
Paul Joseph Tremp (Private Investigator)

For full biographical listings, see the Martindale-Hubbell Law Directory

MUNICIPAL BOND/PUBLIC AUTHORITY FINANCING

ALABAMA

ALBERTVILLE, Marshall Co.

GULLAHORN & HARE, P.C. (AV)

310 West Main Street, P.O. Box 1669, 35950
Telephone: 205-878-1891
Fax: 205-878-1965

Charles R. Hare, Jr.   John C. Gullahorn

Jeffrey B. Carr

Representative Clients: First Bank of Boaz; The Home Bank; Peoples Independent Bank of Boaz; AmSouth Bank; Compass Bank; Albertville Industrial Development Board; Boaz Industrial Development Board; Marshall-Dekalb Electric Cooperative; Olympia Construction, Inc.

For full biographical listings, see the Martindale-Hubbell Law Directory

*BIRMINGHAM,** Jefferson Co.

BRADLEY, ARANT, ROSE & WHITE (AV)

2001 Park Place, Suite 1400, P.O. Box 830709, 35283-0709
Telephone: 205-521-8000
Facsimile: 205-252-0264
Facsimile (SouthTrust Tower Office): 205-251-9915
URL: http://www.BARW.COM
Huntsville, Alabama Office: 200 Clinton Avenue West, Suite 900, 35801.
Telephone: 205-517-5100.
Facsimile: 205-533-5069.

MEMBERS OF FIRM

John P. Adams   Alan K. Zeigler
John G. Harrell   John K. Molen
P. Nicholas Greenwood   Stephen K. Greene

Representative Transactional Clients: Alabama Water Pollution Control Authority; Auburn University; City of Huntsville; City of Mobile; Decatur General Hospital; Foley Utilities Board; Huntsville-Madison County Airport Authority; Mobile Airport Authority; University of Alabama; University of Alabama at Birmingham.

For Complete List of Firm Personnel, See General Section

For full biographical listings, see the Martindale-Hubbell Law Directory

BURR & FORMAN (AV)

3100 SouthTrust Tower, 420 North 20th Street, 35203
Telephone: 205-251-3000
Telecopier: 205-458-5100
Huntsville, Alabama Office: Suite 204, Regency Center, 400 Meridian Street.
Telephone: 205-551-0010.
Atlanta, Georgia Office: Suite 1800, One Georgia Center, 600 West Peachtree Street, 30308.
Telephone: 404-817-3536.
Facsimile: 404-817-3244.

MEMBERS OF FIRM

Joseph G. Stewart   George M. Taylor, III
Eric L. Carlton   Dwight L. Mixson, Jr.

For Complete List of Firm Personnel, See General Section

For full biographical listings, see the Martindale-Hubbell Law Directory

HASKELL SLAUGHTER & YOUNG, L.L.C. (AV)

1200 AmSouth/Harbert Plaza, 1901 Sixth Avenue North, 35203
Telephone: 205-251-1000
Facsimile: 205-324-1133
Montgomery, Alabama Office: 305 South Lawrence Street, P.O. Box 4660. 36103-4660.
Telephone: 334-265-8573.
Facsimile: 334-264-7945.

Wyatt Rushton Haskell   Robert D. Shattuck, Jr.
William M. Slaughter   E. Alston Ray
Benjamin B. Spratling III   Mark Edward Ezell
Beverly P. Baker

Paula B. Carroll

For Complete List of Firm Personnel, See General Section

For full biographical listings, see the Martindale-Hubbell Law Directory

SPAIN & GILLON, L.L.C. (AV)

The Zinszer Building, 2117 2nd Avenue North, 35203
Telephone: 205-328-4100
Telecopier: 205-324-8866

MEMBERS OF FIRM

John P. McKleroy, Jr.   Samuel H. Frazier
Glenn E. Estess, Jr.

General Counsel for: Liberty National Life Insurance Co.; Piggly Wiggly Alabama Distributing Co.; Alabama Insurance Guaranty Association; Alabama Life and Disability Insurance Guaranty Association; Alabama Insurance Underwriters Association.
Counsel for: The Minnesota Mutual Insurance Company of America; Government Employees Insurance Co.; Massachusetts Mutual Life Insurance Co.

For Complete List of Firm Personnel, See General Section

For full biographical listings, see the Martindale-Hubbell Law Directory

*MOBILE,** Mobile Co.

JOHNSTON, WILKINS & DRUHAN (AV)

Hannah Houses, 157-159 North Conception Street, P.O. Box 154, 36601
Telephone: 334-432-0738
Telecopier: 334-432-4874

MEMBERS OF FIRM

Samuel M. Johnston, Jr.   J. Michael Druhan, Jr.
(1919-1993)   James C. Johnston
Robert B. Wilkins (1922-1992)   Joseph S. Johnston

ASSOCIATE

Robert B. Stewart

Representative Clients: International Paper Co.; Morrison's, Inc.; SouthTrust Bank of Mobile; Employers Casualty Insurance Co.; Fidelity & Deposit Company of Maryland; General Accident Insurance Co.

For full biographical listings, see the Martindale-Hubbell Law Directory

LYONS, PIPES & COOK, P.C. (AV)

2 North Royal Street, P.O. Box 2727, 36652-2727
Telephone: 334-432-4481
Cable Address: "Lysea"
Telecopier: 334-433-1820

Wesley Pipes   W. David Johnson, Jr.

Representative Clients: Industrial Development Board of the City of Mobile; Mobile Airport Authority.

For Complete List of Firm Personnel, See General Section

For full biographical listings, see the Martindale-Hubbell Law Directory

ARIZONA

*PHOENIX,** Maricopa Co.

JENNINGS, STROUSS AND SALMON, P.L.C. (AV)

A Professional Limited Liability Company
One Renaissance Square, Two North Central, 85004-2393
Telephone: 602-262-5911
Fax: 602-253-3255

George C. Spilsbury   Anne L. Kleindienst

For Complete List of Firm Personnel, See General Section

For full biographical listings, see the Martindale-Hubbell Law Directory

MEYERS LAW FIRM (AV)

Suite 900, 2398 East Camelback Road, 85016
Telephone: 602-468-8900
Telecopier: 602-468-8910

Donald D. Meyers

Charles W. Lotzar   James F. Wees
Donald L. Meyers   Jason A. Donkersley

Reference: Bank of America, Arizona.

For full biographical listings, see the Martindale-Hubbell Law Directory

Phoenix—Continued

QUARLES & BRADY (AV)

One Camelback Building, One East Camelback Road, Suite 400, 85012-1649
Telephone: 602-230-5500
Fax: 602-230-5598
Milwaukee, Wisconsin Office: 411 East Wisconsin Avenue.
Telephone: 414-277-5000.
Fax: 414-271-3552.
Madison, Wisconsin Office: First Wisconsin Plaza, One South Pinckney Street, P.O. Box 2113.
Telephone: 608-251-5000.
Fax: 608-251-9166.
West Palm Beach, Florida Office: 222 Lakeview Ave., 4th Floor.
Telephone: 407-653-5000.
Fax: 407-653-5333.
Naples, Florida Office: Barnett Center, 4501 Tamiami Trail North, Suite 300.
Telephone: 813-262-5959.
Fax: 813-434-4999.

MEMBERS OF THE FIRM

P. Robert Moya   Judith M. Bailey

For Complete List of Firm Personnel, See General Section

For full biographical listings, see the Martindale-Hubbell Law Directory

SNELL & WILMER, L.L.P. (AV)

One Arizona Center, 85004-0001
Telephone: 602-382-6000
Fax: 602-382-6070
Tucson, Arizona Office: 1500 Norwest Tower, One South Church Avenue 85701-1612.
Telephone: 520-882-1200.
Fax: 520-884-1294.
Orange County Office: 1920 Main Street, Suite 1200, P.O. Box 57062, Irvine, California, 92619-7062.
Telephone: 714-253-2700.
Fax: 714-955-2507.
Salt Lake City, Utah Office: Broadway Centre, 111 East Broadway, Suite 900, 84111-1004.
Telephone: 801-237-1900.
Fax: 801-237-1950.

MEMBERS OF FIRM

William A. Hicks, III   Richard W. Sheffield
Charles E. James, Jr.

Representative Clients: State of Arizona; Arizona Board of Regents; Arizona Health Facilities Authority; Arizona Educational Loan Marketing Corporation; Pima County; Maricopa County Stadium District; City of Tucson; City of Scottsdale; Roosevelt Elementary School District.

For Complete List of Firm Personnel, See General Section

For full biographical listings, see the Martindale-Hubbell Law Directory

---

TUCSON, * Pima Co.

RAVEN, KIRSCHNER & NORELL, P.C. (AV)

Suite 1600, One South Church Avenue, 85701-1612
Telephone: 520-628-8700
Telefax: 520-798-5200

Mark B. Raven

Representative Clients: Continental Medical Systems, Inc.; El Paso Natural Gas Co.; Norwest Bank Arizona; El Rio-Santa Cruz Neighborhood Health Center, Inc.; Resolution Trust Corp.; Sierra Vista Community Hospital; Southern Arizona Rehabilitation Hospital; Northern Cochise Community Hospital.

For Complete List of Firm Personnel, See General Section

For full biographical listings, see the Martindale-Hubbell Law Directory

---

ARKANSAS

LITTLE ROCK, * Pulaski Co.

FRIDAY, ELDREDGE & CLARK (AV)

A Partnership including Professional Associations
Formerly, Smith, Williams, Friday, Eldredge & Clark
2000 First Commercial Building, 400 West Capitol Avenue, 72201-3493
Telephone: 501-376-2011
Telecopier: 501-376-2147; 376-6369
Email: fecmh@fec.sprint.com

MEMBERS OF FIRM

John C. Echols (P.A.)   Thomas P. Leggett, (P.A.)
James A. Buttry (P.A.)   J. Shepherd Russell, III, (P.A.)
Robert B. Beach, Jr., (P.A.)

(See Next Column)

ASSOCIATE

R. Christopher Lawson

COUNSEL

William L. Patton, Jr.

Counsel for: Union Pacific System; St. Paul Insurance Co.; Liberty Mutual Insurance Co.; Cigna Property & Casualty Co.; Arkansas Power & Light Co.; Dillard Department Stores, Inc.; First Commercial Corp.; Browning Arms Co.; Phillips Petroleum Co.; Aetna Casualty & Surety Co.

For Complete List of Firm Personnel, See General Section

For full biographical listings, see the Martindale-Hubbell Law Directory

---

GILL LAW FIRM, A PROFESSIONAL ASSOCIATION (AV)

3801 TCBY Tower, Capitol and Broadway, 72201
Telephone: 501-376-3800
Fax: 501-372-3359

John P. Gill   W. W. Elrod, II
Charles C. Owen (P.A.)   Heartsill Ragon III, (P.A.)

C. Tad Bohannon

For Complete List of Firm Personnel, See General Section

For full biographical listings, see the Martindale-Hubbell Law Directory

---

ROSE LAW FIRM, A PROFESSIONAL ASSOCIATION (AV)

120 East Fourth Street, 72201
Telephone: 501-375-9131
Telecopy: 501-375-1309

George E. Campbell   Les R. Baledge
M. Jane Dickey   Gordon M. Wilbourn

Franklin M. Faust

Representative Clients: Arkansas Development Finance Authority; Arkansas Soil and Water Conservation Commission; Arkansas Department of Pollution Control and Ecology; Crews & Associates, Inc.; City of Little Rock, Arkansas Airport Commission, Wastewater Commission and Residential Housing and Public Facilities Board; Llama Co.; PaineWebber Incorporated; Stephens Inc.

For Complete List of Firm Personnel, See General Section

For full biographical listings, see the Martindale-Hubbell Law Directory

---

WILLIAMS & ANDERSON (AV)

Twenty-Second Floor, 111 Center Street, 72201
Telephone: 501-372-0800
FAX: 501-372-6453

MEMBERS OF FIRM

W. Jackson Williams   James E. Hathaway III
David F. Menz   Rush B. Deacon

Jeanne L. Seewald

Representative Clients: Arkansas Development Finance Authority; Dean Witter Reynolds Inc.; Entergy Power, Inc.; Little Rock Newspapers, Inc. d/b/a/ Arkansas Democrat-Gazette; Metrocentre Improvement District No. 1 of the City of Little Rock; Potlatch Corporation; Texaco, Inc.; Wal-Mart Stores, Inc.

For Complete List of Firm Personnel, See General Section

For full biographical listings, see the Martindale-Hubbell Law Directory

---

WRIGHT, LINDSEY & JENNINGS (AV)

200 West Capitol Avenue, Suite 2200, 72201
Telephone: 501-371-0808
Fax: 501-376-9442
Email: tgraves@wlj.com *URL:* http://www.wlj.com/
Fayetteville, Arkansas Office: 101 West Mountain Street, Suite 206, 72701.
Telephone: 501-575-0808.
Fax: 501-575-0999.
Russellville, Arkansas Office: Suite E, 1110 West B Street.
Telephone: 501-968-7995.

John R. Tisdale   Walter E. May
John William Spivey III   Walter McSpadden
Charles C. Price   Kevin W. Kennedy
Fred M. Perkins III

Representative Clients: Arkansas Development Finance Authority; Pulaski County, Arkansas; City of Little Rock, Arkansas; Arkansas Industrial Development Commission; Arkansas Soil and Water Conservation Commission; Garland County Community College; Red River Technical College.

For full biographical listings, see the Martindale-Hubbell Law Directory

CALIFORNIA

COSTA MESA, Orange Co.

RUTAN & TUCKER, LLP (AV)

A Partnership including Professional Corporations
611 Anton Boulevard, Suite 1400, P.O. Box 1950, 92626
Telephone: 714-641-5100; 213-625-7586
Telecopier: 714-546-9035
Email: rutan&tucker@mcimail.com *URL:* http://www.rutan.com

MEMBERS OF FIRM

Stan Wolcott (P.C.)   William M. Marticorena

For Complete List of Firm Personnel, See General Section

For full biographical listings, see the Martindale-Hubbell Law Directory

EL MONTE, Los Angeles Co.

MICHAEL B. MONTGOMERY A LAW CORPORATION (AV)

10501 Valley Boulevard, Suite 121, 91731
Telephone: 818-452-1222
Fax: 818-452-8323
Ft. Lauderdale, Florida Office: Justice Building, 524 S. Andrews Avenue, Suite 320 N.
Telephone: 954-522-9441.
Fax: 954-522-2076.

Michael B. Montgomery

Reference: Bank of America (San Marino Branch).

For full biographical listings, see the Martindale-Hubbell Law Directory

LOS ANGELES,* Los Angeles Co.

JONES, DAY, REAVIS & POGUE (AV)

555 West Fifth Street Suite 4600, 90013-1025
Telephone: 213-489-3939
Telex: 181439 UD
Telecopier: 213-243-2539
In Irvine, California: 2603 Main Street, Suite 900.
Telephone: 714-851-3939.
Telex: 194911 Lawyers LSA.
Telecopier: 714-553-7539.
In Atlanta, Georgia: 3500 One Peachtree Center, 303 Peachtree Street, N.E.
Telephone: 404-521-3939.
Cable Address: "Attorneys Atlanta".
Telex: 54-2711.
Telecopier: 404-581-8330.
In Brussels, Belgium: Avenue Louise 480, 7th Floor, B-1050 Brussels.
Telephone: 32-2-645-14-11.
Telecopier: 32-2-645-14-45.
In Chicago, Illinois: 77 West Wacker.
Telephone: 312-782-3939.
Telecopier: 312-782-8585.
In Cleveland, Ohio: North Point, 901 Lakeside Avenue.
Telephone: 216-586-3939.
Cable Address: "Attorneys Cleveland."
Telex: 980389.
Telecopier: 216-579-0212.
In Columbus, Ohio: 1900 Huntington Center.
Telephone: 614-469-3939.
Cable Address: "Attorneys Columbus."
Telecopier: 614-461-4198.
In Dallas, Texas: 2300 Trammell Crow Center, 2001 Ross Avenue.
Telephone: 214-220-3939.
Cable Address: "Attorneys Dallas."
Telex: 730852.
Telecopier: 214-969-5100.
In Frankfurt, Germany: Triton Haus, Bockenheimer Landstrasse 42, 60323 Frankfurt am Main.
Telephone: 49-69-9726-3939.
Telecopier: 49-69-9726-3993.
In Geneva, Switzerland: 20, rue de Candolle.
Telephone: 41-22-320-2339.
Telecopier: 41-22-320-1232.
In Hong Kong: 29th Floor, Entertainment Building, 30 Queen's Road Central.
Telephone: 852-2526-6895.
Telecopier: 852-2868-5871.
In London England: Bucklersbury House, 3 Queen Victoria Street.
Telephone: 44-171-236-3939.
Telecopier: 44-171-236-1113.
In New Delhi, India: Pathak & Associates, 13th Floor, Dr. Gopal Das Bhaven, 28 Barakhamba Road.
Telephone: 91-11-373-8793.
Telecopier: 91-11-335-3761.

(See Next Column)

In New York, New York: 599 Lexington Avenue.
Telephone: 212-326-3939.
Cable Address: "JONESDAY NEWYORK."
Telex: 237013 JDRP UR.
Telecopier: 212-755-7306.
In Paris, France: 62, rue du Faubourg Saint-Honore.
Telephone: 33-1-44-71-3939.
Telex: 290156 Surgoe.
Telecopier: 33-1-49-24-0471.
In Pittsburgh, Pennsylvania: 500 Grant Street, 31st Floor.
Telephone: 412-391-3939.
Cable Address: "Attorneys Pittsburgh".
Telecopier: 412-394-7959.
In Riyadh, Saudi Arabia: The International Law Firm, Sulaymaniyah Center, Tahlia Street, P.O. Box 22166.
Telephone: (966-1) 462-8866.
Telecopier: (966-1) 462-9001.
In Taipei, Taiwan: 8th Floor, 2 Tun Hwa South Road, Section 2.
Telephone: (886-2) 704-6808.
Telecopier: (886-2) 704-6791.
In Tokyo, Japan: Toranomon MT Building, 4th Floor, 10-3, Toranomon 3-Chome, Minato-ku, Tokyo 105, Japan.
Telephone: 81-3-3433-3939.
Telecopier: 81-3-5401-2725.
In Washington, D.C.: Metropolitan Square, 1450 G Street, N.W.
Telephone: 202-879-3939.
Cable Address: "Attorneys Washington."
Telex: 89-2410 ATTORNEYS WASH.
Telecopier: 202-737-2832.

MEMBERS OF FIRM IN LOS ANGELES

Robert Dean Avery   James L. Baumoel
          Thomas R. Mueller

ASSOCIATES

Catherine A. Ehrgott   Kathryn Blagden
Valerie A. Brown   Ashley S.H. Sim

For Complete List of Firm Personnel, See General Section

For full biographical listings, see the Martindale-Hubbell Law Directory

OCHOA & SILLAS (AV)

444 South, Flower Street, 18th Floor, 90071
Telephone: 213-362-1400
Fax: 213-622-0162
Sacramento, California Office: Wells Fargo Center, 400 Capitol Mall, Suite 1850.
Telephone: 916-447-3383.
FAX: 916-447-3495.
Mexico City, Mexico Office: Bosques de Duraznos, No. 65-507-B, Bosques de Las Lomas, 11700 Mexico, D.F.
Telephone: 905-596-68-48.

MEMBERS OF FIRM

Ralph M. Ochoa   Herman Sillas
          Jacqueline Rich Moore

ASSOCIATES

Jack T. Molodanof   Rita A. Reyes
          Evan F. Hadnot

OF COUNSEL

Cochran & Lotkin, , Washington, D.C.

LEGAL SUPPORT PERSONNEL

Manuel Tejeda (Paralegal)   Jeanette M. Palma (Paralegal)
          Lori Lee Marino (Paralegal)

For full biographical listings, see the Martindale-Hubbell Law Directory

SAN FRANCISCO,* San Francisco Co.

JONES HALL HILL & WHITE, A PROFESSIONAL LAW CORPORATION (AV)

Four Embarcadero Center, Nineteenth Floor, 94111
Telephone: 415-391-5780
Telecopier: 415-391-5784
Email: info@jhhw.com *URL:* http://www.jhhw.com

Andrew C. Hall, Jr.   Brian D. Quint
Sharon Stanton White   Thomas A. Downey
Charles F. Adams   David J. Oster
Stephen R. Casaleggio   Michael D. Castelli
William H. Madison   David A. Walton
Paul J. Thimmig   Christopher K. Lynch

OF COUNSEL

Kenneth I. Jones

For full biographical listings, see the Martindale-Hubbell Law Directory

SAN MATEO, San Mateo Co.

G. A. LASTER (AV)

The Wilson Building, 630 North San Mateo Drive, P.O. Box
152, 94401-2328
Telephone: 415-342-3523
Telecopier: 415-342-6392

Gerald A. Laster

Representative Clients: Cities of Colma; King City; Mt. Shasta; Plymouth;
Redwood City; Castroville Water District; Franklin County Water District;
Quartz Hill Water District; Granada Sanitary District; Montara Sanitary
District.

For full biographical listings, see the Martindale-Hubbell Law Directory

COLORADO

DENVER,* Denver Co.

BALLARD SPAHR ANDREWS & INGERSOLL (AV)

Seventeenth Street Plaza Building, Suite 2300, 1225 17th
Street, 80202-5596
Telephone: 303-292-2400
Fax: 303-296-3956
Philadelphia, Pennsylvania Office: 1735 Market Street, 51st Floor.
Telephone: 215-665-8500.
Fax: 215-864-8999.
Harrisburg, Pennsylvania Office: 105 North Front Street.
Telephone: 717-236-3333.
Fax: 717-236-3884.
Salt Lake City, Utah Office: One Utah Center, 201 South Main Street,
Suite 1200.
Telephone: 801-531-3000.
Fax: 801-531-3001.
Washington, D.C. Office: Suite 900 East, 555 13th Street, N.W.
Telephone: 202-383-8800.
Fax: 202-383-8877; 383-8893.
Baltimore, Maryland Office: 300 East Lombard Street, 19th Floor.
Telephone: 410-528-5600.
Fax: 410-528-5650.
Camden, New Jersey Office: 800 Hudson Square, 5th Floor.
Telephone: 609-541-5577.
Fax: 609-541-8272.

Loring E. Harkness III

Matthew J. Hogan

For Complete List of Firm Personnel, See General Section

For full biographical listings, see the Martindale-Hubbell Law Directory

BROWNSTEIN HYATT FARBER & STRICKLAND, P.C. (AV)

Twenty-Second Floor, 410 Seventeenth Street, 80202-4437
Telephone: 303-534-6335
Telecopier: 303-623-1956
Washington, D.C. Office: 601 Pennsylvania Avenue, N.W., Suite 900.
Telephone: 202-434-8377.
Telecopier: 202-393-7864.

Michael R. McGinnis	Thomas J. Mancuso
Brent T. Slosky	Gregory W. Berger

Representative Clients: A.G. Edwards & Sons, Inc.; Arrowhead Metropolitan
District; Bachelor Gulch Metropolitan District; George K. Baum & Com-
pany; Beaver Creek Metropolitan District; Coughlin & Company, Inc.;
Hanifen, Imhoff Inc.; Kirkpatrick Pettis; Norwest Investment Services, Inc.;
Smith Barney Inc.

For Complete List of Firm Personnel, See General Section

For full biographical listings, see the Martindale-Hubbell Law Directory

HOLME ROBERTS & OWEN LLP (AV)

Suite 4100, 1700 Lincoln, 80203
Telephone: 303-861-7000
Telecopier: 303-866-0200
Email: hro@hro.com *URL:* http://www.hro.com
Boulder, Colorado Office: Suite 400, 1401 Pearl Street.
Telephone: 303-444-5955.
Telecopier: 303-444-1063.
Colorado Springs, Colorado Office: Suite 1300, 90 South Cascade Avenue.
Telephone: 719-473-3800.
Telecopier: 719-633-1518.
Salt Lake City, Utah Office: Suite 1100, 111 East Broadway.
Telephone: 801-521-5800.
Telecopier: 801-521-9639.

(See Next Column)

London, England Office: Mellier House, 26a Albemarle Street.
Telephone: 44-171-499-8776.
Telecopier: 44-171-499-7769.
Moscow, Russia Office: Kosmodamianskaya Nab. #52/1, Suite 9100,
113054.
Telephone: 7095-961-3000.
Telecopier: 7095-961-3001.
Kiev, Ukraine Office: Terestchenkovskaya #19, Suite 2, 252004.
Telephone: 380-44-224-1348.
Telecopier: 380-44-224-4986.

PARTNERS OF FIRM

Nick Nimmo	Mary L. Groves
Steve L. Gaines	Patricia C. Tisdale
(Colorado Springs Office)	David Harold Little
R. Bruce Johnson	(Salt Lake City Office)
(Salt Lake City Office)	

SPECIAL COUNSEL
Diane S. Barrett

SENIOR COUNSEL

Kathryn Stoker Worford	Erin Marie Smith

ASSOCIATE
Maria Mashenka Lundberg

For Complete List of Firm Personnel, See General Section

For full biographical listings, see the Martindale-Hubbell Law Directory

SHERMAN & HOWARD L.L.C. (AV)

Attorneys and Counselors at Law
633 Seventeenth Street, Suite 3000, 80202
Telephone: 303-297-2900
Telecopier: 303-298-0940
Colorado Springs, Colorado Office: Suite 1500, 90 South Cascade Avenue,
80903.
Telephone: 719-475-2440.
Las Vegas, Nevada Office: Swendseid & Stern a member in Sherman &
Howard L.L.C., 317 Sixth Street, 89101.
Telephone: 702-387-6073.
Reno, Nevada Office: Swendseid & Stern, a member in Sherman &
Howard L.L.C., 50 West Liberty Street, Suite 660, 89501.
Telephone: 702-323-1980.

Robert P. Mitchell	Jennifer Stern (Las Vegas and
John O. Swendseid (Las Vegas	Reno, Nevada Offices)
and Reno, Nevada Offices)	Ann Marie (Amy) Kennedy
Dee P. Wisor	Calvin T. Hanson
Stanley M. Raine	Maria L. Prevedel

COUNSEL

Michael D. Groshek	Amy L. Hirter
Carolyn Lubchenco	

James T. Giel (Not admitted in CO)

Representative Clients: Colorado Health Facilities Authority; Colorado Stu-
dent Obligation Bond Authority; Jefferson County, Colorado; Platte River
Power Authority; Clark County, Nevada; Farmington, New Mexico.; City of
Thornton, Colorado; Colorado Housing and Finance Authority.

For Complete List of Firm Personnel, See General Section

For full biographical listings, see the Martindale-Hubbell Law Directory

CONNECTICUT

WESTPORT, Fairfield Co.

WEISMAN & LUBELL (AV)

5 Sylvan Road South, P.O. Box 3184, 06880
Telephone: 203-226-8307
Telecopier: 203-221-7279

MEMBERS OF FIRM

Lawrence P. Weisman	Ellen B. Lubell

Debra B. Wolfert-Marino

For full biographical listings, see the Martindale-Hubbell Law Directory

DELAWARE

WILMINGTON, * New Castle Co.

POTTER ANDERSON & CORROON (AV)

350 Delaware Trust Building, P.O. Box 951, 19899-0951
Telephone: 302-984-6000
FAX: 302-658-1192
URL: HTTP://ATTYS.PACDELAWARE.COM
MEMBERS OF FIRM
Charles S. McDowell   Harold I. Salmons, III
OF COUNSEL
Richard L. McMahon
ASSOCIATE
Scott E. Waxman

Counsel for: The State of Delaware; Delaware Transportation Authority; DE Health Facilities Authority; New Castle County; Kent County; Sussex County; City of Dover; Delaware Trust Capital Management, Inc.; Delmarva Power & Light Co.; Hercules Inc.; General Motors Corp.

For Complete List of Firm Personnel, See General Section

For full biographical listings, see the Martindale-Hubbell Law Directory

DISTRICT OF COLUMBIA

WASHINGTON, D.C. Co.

* indicates certain Bar Register subscribers, in cities of comparable size and importance, who maintain an additional office in Washington, D.C. and who have arranged for representation as a part of the Washington, D.C. listings that follow

ALEXANDER, BEARDEN, HAIRSTON & MARKS, LLP (AV)

Limited Liability Partnership
2021 L Street, N.W., Suite 300, 20036
Telephone: 202-293-3700
Fax: 202-293-7359
Silver Spring, Maryland Office: Lee Plaza, Suite 805, 8601 Georgia Avenue, 20910.
Telephone: 301-589-2222.
Facsimile: 301-539-2523.
New York, New York Office: 330 Madison Avenue, 36th Floor.
Telephone: 212-808-0008.
Fax: 212-599-1028.

Kenneth H. Marks, Jr.   James L. Bearden
Kenneth S. Barr

Reference: Riggs National Bank of Washington, D.C.

For full biographical listings, see the Martindale-Hubbell Law Directory

* BALLARD SPAHR ANDREWS & INGERSOLL (AV)

Suite 900 East, 555 13th Street, N.W., 20004-1112
Telephone: 202-383-8800
Fax: 202-383-8877
Philadelphia, Pennsylvania Office: 1735 Market Street, 51st Floor.
Telephone: 215-665-8500.
Fax: 215-864-8999.
Harrisburg, Pennsylvania Office: 105 North Front Street.
Telephone: 717-236-3333.
Fax: 717-236-3884.
Denver, Colorado Office: Seventeenth Street Plaza Building, Suite 2300, 1225 17th Street.
Telephone: 303-292-2400.
Fax: 303-296-3956.
Salt Lake City, Utah Office: One Utah Center, 201 South Main Street, Suite 1200.
Telephone: 801-531-3000.
Fax: 801-531-3001.
Baltimore, Maryland Office: 300 East Lombard Street, 19th Floor.
Telephone: 410-528-5600.
Fax: 410-528-5650.
Camden, New Jersey Office: 800 Hudson Square, 5th Floor.
Telephone: 609-541-5577.
Fax: 609-541-8272.

Frederic L. Ballard, Jr.   Joseph A. Fanone
Charles S. Henck

John A. Washington, Jr.   Deborah A. Wisnowski
(Not admitted in DC)

For Complete List of Firm Personnel, See General Section

For full biographical listings, see the Martindale-Hubbell Law Directory

* JONES, DAY, REAVIS & POGUE (AV)

Metropolitan Square, 1450 G Street, N.W., 20005-2088
Telephone: 202-879-3939
Cable Address: "Attorneys Washington"
Telex: W.U. (Domestic) 89-2410 ATTORNEYS WASH (International) 64363 ATTORNEYS WASH
Telecopier: 202-737-2832
In Atlanta, Georgia: 3500 One Peachtree Center, 303 Peachtree Street, N.E
.
Telephone: 404-521-3939.
Cable Address: "Attorneys Atlanta".
Telex: 54-2711.
Telecopier: 404-581-8330.
In Brussels, Belgium: Avenue Louise 480, 7th Floor, B-1050 Brussels.
Telephone: 32-2-645-14-11.
Telecopier: 32-2-645-14-45.
In Chicago, Illinois: 77 West Wacker.
Telephone: 312-782-3939.
Telecopier: 312-782-8585.
In Cleveland, Ohio: North Point, 901 Lakeside Avenue.
Telephone: 216-586-3939.
Cable Address: "Attorneys Cleveland."
Telex: 980389.
Telecopier: 216-579-0212.
In Columbus, Ohio: 1900 Huntington Center.
Telephone: 614-469-3939.
Cable Address: "Attorneys Columbus."
Telecopier: 614-461-4198.
In Dallas, Texas: 2300 Trammell Crow Center, 2001 Ross Avenue.
Telephone: 214-220-3939.
Cable Address: "Attorneys Dallas."
Telex: 730852.
Telecopier: 214-969-5100.
In Frankfurt, Germany: Triton Haus, Bockenheimer Landstrasse 42, 60323 Frankfurt am Main.
Telephone: 49-69-9726-3939.
Telecopier: 49-69-9726-3993.
In Geneva, Switzerland: 20, rue de Candolle.
Telephone: 41-22-320-2339.
Telecopier: 41-22-320-1232.
In Hong Kong: 29th Floor, Entertainment Building, 30 Queen's Road Central.
Telephone: 852-2526-6895.
Telecopier: 852-2868-5871.
In Irvine, California: 2603 Main Street, Suite 900 .
Telephone: 714-851-3939.
Telex: 194911 Lawyers LSA.
Telecopier: 714-553-7539.
In London, England: One Mount Street.
Telephone: 44-71-493-9361.
Cable Address: "Surgoe London WI."
Telecopier: 44-71-493-9666.
In Los Angeles, California: 555 West Fifth Street, Suite 4600.
Telephone: 213-489-3939.
Telex: 181439 UD.
Telecopier: 213-243-2539.
In New Delhi, India: Pathak & Associates, 13th Floor, Dr. Gopal Das Bhaven, 28 Barakhamba Road.
Telephone: 91-11-373-8793.
Telecopier: 91-11-335-3761.
In New York, New York: 599 Lexington Avenue.
Telephone: 212-326-3939.
Cable Address: "JONESDAY NEWYORK."
Telex: 237013 JDRP UR.
Telecopier: 212-755-7306.
In Paris, France: 62, rue du Faubourg Saint-Honore.
Telephone: 33-1-44-71-3939.
Cable Address: "Surgoe Paris."
Telex: 290156 Surgoe.
Telecopier: 33-1-49-24-0471.
In Pittsburgh, Pennsylvania: 500 Grant Street, 31st Floor.
Telephone: 412-391-3939.
Cable Address: "Attorneys Pittsburgh".
Telecopier: 412-394-7959.
In Riyadh, Saudi Arabia: Law Offices of Saud M.A. Shawwaf, P.O. Box 22166.
Telephone: (966-1) 462-8866.
Telex: 401831 SAUCON SJ.
Telecopier: (966-1) 462-9001.
In Taipai, Taiwan: 8th Floor, 2 Tun Hwa South Road, Section 2.
Telephone: (886-2) 704-6808.
Telecopier: (886-2) 704-6791.
In Tokyo, Japan: Toranomon MT Building, 4th Floor, 10-3, Toranomon 3-Chome, Minato-Ku, Tokyo 105, Japan.
Telephone: 81-3-3433-3939.
Telecopier: 81-3-5401-2725.

MEMBERS OF FIRM IN WASHINGTON, D.C.
Frieda K. Wallison   Mark K. Sisitsky

(See Next Column)

JONES, DAY, REAVIS & POGUE, *Washington—Continued*
ASSOCIATES

Dennis D. Dillon   Richard J. Caplan
(Not admitted in DC)

For Complete List of Firm Personnel, See General Section

For full biographical listings, see the Martindale-Hubbell Law Directory

* LEWIS, CLAY & MUNDAY, A PROFESSIONAL CORPORATION (AV)

(Formerly Lewis, White & Clay, P.C.)
1000 16th Street, N.W., Suite 401, 20036
Telephone: 202-835-0616
Fax: 202-833-3316
Detroit, Michigan Office: 1300 First National Building, 660 Woodward Avenue. 48226-3531.
Telephone: 313-961-2550.
Troy, Michigan Office: Liberty Center, Suite 200. 100 West Big Beaver Road, 48084.
Telephone: 810-680-6702.
Fax: 810-680-6703.
Boston, Massachusetts Office: 10 Post Office Square. 02109.
Telephone: 617-422-8646.
Fax: 617-338-5693.

Karen Kendrick Brown (Resident)

For full biographical listings, see the Martindale-Hubbell Law Directory

* O'CONNOR & HANNAN (AV)

Suite 800, 1919 Pennsylvania Avenue, N.W., 20006-3483
Telephone: 202-887-1400
Telecopy: 202-466-2198
Minneapolis, Minnesota Office: 700 Baker Building, 706 South Second Avenue.
Telephone: 612-343-1200.
Telecopy: 612-343-1256.

MEMBERS OF FIRM

Patrick J. O'Connor   James W. Symington
Edward W. Brooke   Donald R. Dinan
Thomas H. Quinn   Michael Colopy
David R. Melincoff   Thomas J. Corcoran
Hope S. Foster   Robert M. Adler
Patrick E. O'Donnell   Peter M. Kazon
F. Gordon Lee   Christina W. Fleps
George J. Mannina, Jr.   Timothy W. Jenkins
John J. McDermott   Gary C. Adler
John M. Himmelberg

Craig A. Koenigs
OF COUNSEL

Joseph H. Blatchford   William W. Nickerson
E. William Crotty   Audrey P. Rasmussen
David L. Hill   H. George Schweitzer
Charles R. McCarthy, Jr.   Thomas J. Schneider
Moshe Schuldinger

For full biographical listings, see the Martindale-Hubbell Law Directory

RITTER EICHNER & NORRIS (AV)

The Jefferson Building, 1225 19th Street, N.W., 7th Floor, 20036
Telephone: 202-973-0100
Fax: 202-296-6990

MEMBERS OF FIRM

C. Willis Ritter   R. Wade Norris
Richard A. Eichner   (Not admitted in DC)

ASSOCIATE

Mary N. Simpkins

For full biographical listings, see the Martindale-Hubbell Law Directory

FLORIDA

*FORT LAUDERDALE,** Broward Co.

DOUMAR, CURTIS, CROSS, LAYSTROM & PERLOFF (AV)

A Partnership of Professional Corporations
1177 Southeast Third Avenue, 33316
Telephone: 954-525-3441
Fax: 954-525-3423
Direct Miami Line: 305-945-3172

(See Next Column)

MEMBERS OF FIRM

Raymond A. Doumar (P.C.)   John W. Perloff (P.C.)
Charles L. Curtis (P.C.)   E. Scott Allsworth (P.C.)
William S. Cross (P.C.)   John D. Voigt (P.C.)
C. William Laystrom, Jr. (P.C.)   Jeffrey S. Wachs (P.C.)
Mark E. Allsworth

Representative Clients: Albertson's, Inc.; Robinson-Humphrey/American Express; Deutsch-Ireland Properties; Massey-Yardley Chrysler Plymouth, Inc.; Waste Management, Inc.; Planned Development Corp.; Toys-R-Us Inc.; Lumbermans Mutual Casualty Co.; Melvin Simon and Associates.

For Complete List of Firm Personnel, See General Section

For full biographical listings, see the Martindale-Hubbell Law Directory

*ORLANDO,** Orange Co.

BAKER & HOSTETLER (AV)

SunBank Center, Suite 2300, 200 South Orange Avenue, 32802-3432
Telephone: 407-649-4000
In Cleveland, Ohio: 3200 National City Center, 1900 East Ninth Street.
Telephone: 216-621-0200.
In Columbus, Ohio: Capitol Square, Suite 2100, 65 East State Street.
Telephone: 614-228-1541.
In Denver, Colorado: 303 East 17th Avenue, Suite 1100.
Telephone: 303-861-0600.
In Houston, Texas: 1000 Louisiana, Suite 2000.
Telephone: 713-751-1600.
In Long Beach, California: 300 Oceangate, Suite 620.
Telephone: 310-432-2827.
In Los Angeles, California: 600 Wilshire Boulevard.
Telephone: 213-624-2400.
In Washington, D.C.: Washington Square, Suite 1100, 1050 Connecticut Avenue, N.W., Suite 1100.
Telephone: 202-861-1500.
In College Park, Maryland: 9658 Baltimore Boulevard, Suite 206.
Telephone: 301-441-2781.
In Alexandria, Virginia: 437 North Lee Street.
Telephone: 703-549-1294.
In San Francisco, California: One Sansome Street, Suite 2000.
Telephone: 415-951-4705.

PARTNER

Jerry R. Linscott

For Complete List of Firm Personnel, See General Section

For full biographical listings, see the Martindale-Hubbell Law Directory

PALM BEACH, Palm Beach Co.

CALDWELL & PACETTI (AV)

324 Royal Palm Way, P.O. Box 2775, 33480-2775
Telephone: 561-655-0620
Fax: 561-655-3775

MEMBERS OF FIRM

Manley P. Caldwell (1901-1971)   Charles F. Schoech
Madison F. Pacetti (1914-1994)   Elizabeth S. (Betsy) Burden
Manley P. Caldwell, Jr.   William E. Corley, III
Kenneth W. Edwards   Nicole Julianne Monsees
Mary M. Viator   John A. Weig

OF COUNSEL

Arthur E. Barrow (Retired)

Representative Clients: Shawano Drainage District; Acme Improvement District; Northern Palm Beach County Improvement District; Indian Trail Water Control District; Siemens Information Systems; Town Of Hypoluxo; Everglades Agricultural Area Environmental Protection District; Town of Lake Clarke Shores.

For full biographical listings, see the Martindale-Hubbell Law Directory

*SARASOTA,** Sarasota Co.

WILLIAMS, PARKER, HARRISON, DIETZ & GETZEN, PROFESSIONAL ASSOCIATION (AV)

200 South Orange Avenue, 34236-6749
Telephone: 941-366-4800
Telecopier: 941-366-5109
Mailing Address: P.O. Box 3258, Sarasota, Florida, 34230-3258
Email: wphdg.law@netsrg.com *URL:* http://www.sarasota-online.com/williamspa-w

J.J. Williams, Jr. (1886-1968)   J. Michael Hartenstine
W. Davis Parker (1920-1982)   Michele Boardman Grimes
William T. Harrison, Jr.   James L. Turner
George A. Dietz   William M. Seider
Monte K. Marshall   Elizabeth C. Marshall
James L. Ritchey   Robert W. Benjamin
William G. Lambrecht   Frank Strelec
John T. Berteau   Terri Salt Costa
John V. Cannon, III   David A. Wallace
Charles D. Bailey, Jr.   Mark A. Schwartz

(See Next Column)

WILLIAMS, PARKER, HARRISON, DIETZ & GETZEN PROFESSIONAL ASSOCIATION—*Continued*

Ric Gregoria	Carol Ann Kalish
Elvin W. Phillips	Linda R. Getzen
Jeffrey A. Grebe	Kimberly J. Page
John L. Moore	Phillip D. Eck
Morgan R. Bentley	J. Hugh Middlebrooks
Susan A. Barrett	Robert A. Warram

OF COUNSEL

William E. Getzen	Frazer F. Hilder

Hugh McPheeters, Jr.

LEGAL SUPPORT PERSONNEL

Mark Loveridge (Land Planner)

General Counsel for: Sarasota County Public Hospital Board; Sarasota-Manatee Airport Authority; Taylor Woodrow Homes Ltd.; FCCI Mutual Insurance Co.

Local Counsel for: NationsBank of Florida; Barnett Bank of Southwest Florida; Northern Trust Bank of Florida; SunTrust Bank, Gulfcoast.

For full biographical listings, see the Martindale-Hubbell Law Directory

---

TAMPA,* Hillsborough Co.

MORRISON, MORRISON & MILLS, P.A. (AV)

1200 West Platt Street Suite 100, 33606
Telephone: 813-258-3311
Telecopier: 813-258-3209

Thomas K. Morrison	Frederick J. Mills
Susan B. Morrison	James E. Holmes, Jr.

Representative Clients: SouthTrust Bank of West Florida; SouthTrust Bank of Alabama, National Association; NationsBank of Florida, N.A.; Mercantile Bank; Barnett Banks, Inc.; Southern Commerce Bank; Sun Bank of Pasco County; Hillsborough County Industrial Development Authority; Automation Packaging, Inc.; Medical Data Management, Inc.

For full biographical listings, see the Martindale-Hubbell Law Directory

---

GEORGIA

ATLANTA,* Fulton Co.

ALSTON & BIRD (AV)

A Partnership including Professional Corporations
One Atlantic Center, 1201 West Peachtree Street, 30309-3424
Telephone: 404-881-7000
Telecopier: 404-881-7777
Cable Address: AMGRAM GA
Telex: 54-2996
Easylink: 62985848
Washington, D.C. Office: 601 Pennsylvania Ave., N.W., North Building, Suite 250 20004.
Telephone: 202-508-3300.
Telecopier: 202-508-3333.

MEMBERS OF FIRM

L. Clifford Adams, Jr.	Terence J. Greene
Peter M. Wright	Karol V. Mason
Glenn R. Thomson	Della Wager Wells

SENIOR COUNSEL

Pierre Howard

ASSOCIATE

Christopher D. Ford

Representative Clients: A.G. Edwards & Sons, Inc.; First Union; The Fulton-DeKalb Hospital Authority; Municipal Electric Authority of GA; Municipal Gas Authority of GA; NationsBank.

For Complete List of Firm Personnel, See General Section

For full biographical listings, see the Martindale-Hubbell Law Directory

---

JONES, DAY, REAVIS & POGUE (AV)

3500 One Peachtree Center, 303 Peachtree Street, N.E., 30308-3242
Telephone: 404-521-3939
Cable Address: "Attorneys Atlanta"
Telex: 54-2711
Telecopier: 404-581-8330
In Brussels, Belgium: Avenue Louise 480, 7th Floor, B-1050 Brussels.
Telephone: 32-2-645-14-11.
Telecopier: 32-2-645-14-45.
In Chicago, Illinois: 77 West Wacker.
Telephone: 312-782-3939.
Telecopier: 312-782-8585.

(See Next Column)

In Cleveland, Ohio: North Point. 901 Lakeside Avenue.
Telephone: 216-586-3939.
Cable Address: "Attorneys Cleveland".
Telex: 980389.
Telecopier: 216-579-0212.
In Columbus, Ohio: 1900 Huntington Center.
Telephone: 614-469-3939.
Cable Address: "Attorneys Columbus".
Telecopier: 614-461-4198.
In Dallas, Texas: 2300 Trammell Crow Center, 2001 Ross Avenue.
Telephone: 214-220-3939.
Cable Address: "Attorneys Dallas."
Telex: 730852.
Telecopier: 214-969-5100.
In Frankfurt, Germany: Triton Haus, Bockenheimer Landstrasse 42, 60323 Frankfurt am Main.
Telephone: 49-69-9726-3939.
Telecopier: 49-69-9726-3993.
In Geneva, Switzerland: 20, rue de Candolle.
Telephone: 41-22-320-2339.
Telecopier: 41-22-320-1232.
In Hong Kong: 29th Floor, Entertainment Building, 30 Queen's Road Central.
Telephone. 852-2526-6895.
Telecopier: 852-2868-5871 or 852-2868-5699.
In Irvine, California: 2603 Main Street, Suite 900.
Telephone: 714-851-3939.
Telex: 194911 Lawyers LSA.
Telecopier: 714-553-7539.
In London, England: One Mount Street.
Telephone: 44-71-493-9361.
Cable Address: "Surgoe London WI."
Telecopier: 44-71-493-9666.
In Los Angeles, California: 555 West Fifth Street, Suite 4600.
Telephone: 213-489-3939.
Telex: 181439 UD.
Telecopier: 213-243-2539.
In New Delhi, India: Pathak & Associates, 9th Floor, Dr. Gopal Das Bhaven, 28 Barakhamba Road.
Telephone: 91-11-331-9719.
Telecopier: 91-11-331-7802.
In New York, New York: 599 Lexington Avenue.
Telephone: 212-326-3939.
Cable Address: "JONESDAY NEWYORK."
Telex: 237013 JDRP UR.
Telecopier: 212-755-7306.
In Paris, France: 62, rue du Faubourg Saint-Honore.
Telephone: 33-1-44-71-3939.
Cable Address: "Surgoe Paris."
Telex: 290156 Surgoe.
Telecopier: 33-1-49-24-0471.
In Pittsburgh, Pennsylvania: 500 Grant Street, 31st Floor.
Telephone: 412-391-3939.
Cable Address: "Attorneys Pittsburgh".
Telecopier: 412-394-7959.
In Riyadh, Saudi Arabia: Law Offices of Saud M.A. Shawwaf, P.O. Box 22166.
Telephone: (966-1) 462-8866.
Telex: 401831 SAUCON SJ.
Telecopier: (966-1) 462-9001.
In Taipei, Taiwan: 8th Floor, 2 Tun Hwa South Road, Section 2.
Telephone: (886-2) 704-6808.
Telecopier: (886-2) 704-6791.
In Tokyo, Japan: Toranomon MT Building, 4th Floor, 10-3, Toranomon 3-Chome, Minato-ku, Tokyo 105, Japan.
Telephone: 81-3-3433-3939.
Telecopier: 81-3-5401-2725.
In Washington, D.C.: Metropolitan Square, 1450 G Street, N.W.
Telephone: 202-879-3939.
Cable Address: "Attorneys Washington."
Telex: 89-2410 ATTORNEYS WASH.
Telecopier: 202-737-2832.

MEMBERS OF FIRM IN ATLANTA

William S. Paddock	John E. Zamer

Lizanne Thomas

OF COUNSEL

Dom H. Wyant

For Complete List of Firm Personnel, See General Section

For full biographical listings, see the Martindale-Hubbell Law Directory

---

LONG ALDRIDGE & NORMAN, LLP (AV)

A Limited Liability Partnership including Professional Corporations
One Peachtree Center, Suite 5300, 303 Peachtree Street, 30308
Telephone: 404-527-4000
Telecopier: 404-527-4198
Washington, D.C. Office: Suite 600, 701 Pennsylvania Avenue, N.W., 20004.
Telephone: 202-624-1200.
FAX: 202-624-1298.

(See Next Column)

LONG ALDRIDGE & NORMAN LLP, *Atlanta—Continued*

MEMBERS OF FIRM

Barbara L. Blackford	Edgar H. Sims, Jr. (P.C.)
R. William Ide III	Jesse J. Spikes
Margaret M. Joslin	John E. Theberge (Resident,
Mark S. Lange	Washington, D.C. Office)

ASSOCIATES

Robert E. DeWitt	Lynn Gavin
	Kenneth B. Pollock

For Complete List of Firm Personnel, See General Section

For full biographical listings, see the Martindale-Hubbell Law Directory

POWELL, GOLDSTEIN, FRAZER & MURPHY (AV)

A Partnership including a Professional Corporation
191 Peachtree Street, N.E., Sixteenth Floor, 30303
Telephone: 404-572-6600
Telex: 542864
Telecopier: 404-572-6999
Cable Address: "Pgfm"
Washington, D.C. Office: Sixth Floor, 1001 Pennsylvania Avenue, N.W., 20004.
Telephone: 202-347-0066.

MEMBERS OF FIRM

Lewis C. Horne, Jr.	Robert C. Lewinson
	Ronald D. Stallings

ASSOCIATE

Debra L. Skal

For Complete List of Firm Personnel, See General Section

For full biographical listings, see the Martindale-Hubbell Law Directory

SUTHERLAND, ASBILL & BRENNAN, L.L.P. (AV)

999 Peachtree Street, N.E., 30309-3996
Telephone: 404-853-8000
Facsimile: 404-853-8806
Email: postmaster@sablaw.com
Washington, D.C. Office: 1275 Pennsylvania Avenue, N.W., 20004-2404.
Telephone: 202-383-0100.
New York, N.Y. Office: 600 Madison Avenue, 11th Floor, 10022-1615.
Telephone: 212-605-6400.
Austin, Texas Office: 111 Congress Avenue, 23rd Floor, 78701-4079.
Telephone: 512-469-3350.

James L. Henderson, III	John H. Mobley, II

For Complete List of Firm Personnel, See General Section

For full biographical listings, see the Martindale-Hubbell Law Directory

THOMAS, KENNEDY, SAMPSON & PATTERSON (AV)

55 Marietta Street, N.W., Suite 1600, 30303
Telephone: 404-688-4503
Telecopier: 404-681-2950

MEMBERS OF FIRM

John Loren Kennedy (1942-1994)	P. Andrew Patterson
	Myra H. Dixon
Thomas G. Sampson	Jeffrey E. Tompkins

ASSOCIATES

Rosalind T. Drakeford	Adam L. Smith
Melynee C. Leftridge	Thomas G. Sampson, II
La'Sean M. Zilton	Ceasar C. Mitchell, II.
R. E. Thomas, Jr. (1911-1996)	

LEGAL SUPPORT PERSONNEL

Gwendolyn C.H. Dixon	Yvonne Torrence
Elbetha (Beth) Martin	Priscilla Yolanda Kelly
Nancy Allen-Haskell	Lureece D. Lewis (Paralegal)

For full biographical listings, see the Martindale-Hubbell Law Directory

WILSON, BROCK & IRBY, L.L.C. (AV)

999 Peachtree Street, N.E., Suite 2000, 30309
Telephone: 404-853-5050
Fax: 404-853-1812

MEMBERS OF FIRM

Richard W. Wilson, Jr.	Lethco H. Brock, Jr.
Frank L. Wilson, III	John H. Irby

ASSOCIATES

Jerry D. Gerald	James Stuart Teague, Jr.
	Paul Schillawski

OF COUNSEL

L. Robert Lovett

For full biographical listings, see the Martindale-Hubbell Law Directory

---

COLUMBUS, * Muscogee Co.

HATCHER, STUBBS, LAND, HOLLIS & ROTHSCHILD (AV)

A Limited Liability Partnership
Suite 500 The Corporate Center, 233 12th Street, P.O. Box 2707, 31902-2707
Telephone: 706-324-0201
Telecopier: 706-322-7747

MEMBERS OF FIRM

J. Barrington Vaught	John M. Tanzine, III
James E. Humes, II	Mote W. Andrews III

General Counsel for: SunTrust Bank, West Georgia, N.A.; TOM'S Foods Inc.; Muscogee County Board of Education; Columbus Georgia Water Board; St. Francis Hospital, Inc.
Local Counsel for: First Union National Bank of Georgia.

For Complete List of Firm Personnel, See General Section

For full biographical listings, see the Martindale-Hubbell Law Directory

---

MACON, * Bibb Co.

SELL & MELTON (AV)

A Partnership including a Professional Corporation
14th Floor, Charter Medical Building, P.O. Box 229, 31297-2899
Telephone: 912-746-8521
Telecopier: 912-745-6426

Buckner F. Melton	R. (Chix) Miller

General Counsel for: Macon Telegraph Publishing Co. (The Macon Telegraph); Macon-Bibb County Hospital Authority; County of Bibb; County of Twiggs; Smith & Sons Foods, Inc. (S & S Cafeterias); Macon Bibb County Industrial Authority; Burgess Pigment Co.

For Complete List of Firm Personnel, See General Section

For full biographical listings, see the Martindale-Hubbell Law Directory

---

MARIETTA, * Cobb Co.

AWTREY AND PARKER, P.C. (AV)

211 Roswell Street, P.O. Box 997, 30061
Telephone: 770-424-8000
Fax: 770-424-1594

L. M. Awtrey, Jr. (1915-1986)	Donald A. Mangerie (1924-1988)
George L. Dozier, Jr.	Barbara H. Martin
Harvey D. Harkness	A. Sidney Parker
Mike Harrison	Robert B. Silliman

General Counsel for: Kennesaw Finance Co.; Cobb Electric Membership Corporation; Development Authority of Cobb County.
Local Counsel for: Coats & Clark; Bell South Mobility; Lockheed-Georgia Corp.; Post Properties, Inc.; CSX Transportation, Inc.

For full biographical listings, see the Martindale-Hubbell Law Directory

---

IDAHO

BOISE, * Ada Co.

ELAM & BURKE, A PROFESSIONAL ASSOCIATION (AV)

Key Financial Center, 702 West Idaho Street, P.O. Box 1539, 83701
Telephone: 208-343-5454
Telecopier: 208-384-5844
Email: eblaw@elamburke.com

Ryan P. Armbruster

Representative Clients: City of Boise; Capital City Development Co.; Idaho Falls Redevelopment Agency; Ammon Urban Renewal Agency; Rigby Urban Renewal Agency; Rexburg Redevelopment Agency.

For Complete List of Firm Personnel, See General Section

For full biographical listings, see the Martindale-Hubbell Law Directory

ILLINOIS

CHICAGO,* Cook Co.

BELL, BOYD & LLOYD (AV)

Three First National Plaza Suite 3300, 70 West Madison Street, 60602
Telephone: 312-372-1121
FAX: 312-372-2098
Email: bbl@bbl.com
Washington, D.C. Office: 1615 L Street, N.W.
Telephone: 202-466-6300.
FAX: 202-463-0678.

MEMBERS OF FIRM

Lawrence C. Eppley	Paul T. Metzger
Jeffrey R. Ladd	William S. Price

For Complete List of Firm Personnel, See General Section

For full biographical listings, see the Martindale-Hubbell Law Directory

CHAPMAN AND CUTLER (AV)

111 West Monroe Street, 60603
Telephone: 312-845-3000
Fax: 312-701-2361
Salt Lake City, Utah Office: Suite 800, Key Bank Tower, 50 South Main Street.
Telephone: 801-533-0066.
Fax: 801-533-9595.
Phoenix, Arizona Office: Suite 1100, One Renaissance Square, 2 North Central Avenue.
Telephone: 602-256-4060.
Fax: 602-256-4099.

Daniel J. Bacastow	Kelly K. Kost
Andrea G. Bacon	Darrell R. Larsen, Jr.
Deborah Thomas Boye	Matthew R. Lewin
Lee A. Boye	William M. Libit
James C. Burr (Resident, Salt Lake City Office)	James E. Luebchow
	Timothy V. McGree
George D. Buzard, III	Robert W. Ollis, Jr.
Steven L. Clark	John S. Overdorff (Resident, Phoenix Office)
William E. Corbin, Jr.	
Richard A. Cosgrove	James R. Richardson
Patricia M. Curtner	Richard J. Scott (Resident, Salt Lake City Office)
William R. DeHaan (Resident, Phoenix Office)	
	M. John Trofa
C. Robert Foltz	John L. Tuohy
Lynda K. Given	John A. Ward
Charles L. Jarik	David G. Williams
Daniel L. Johnson	Steven N. Wohl

Erin P. Bartholomy	Jane E. Nagle
James M. Broeking	Susan E. Rollins
Nancy A. Burke	Frederick M. Snow
Marie I. Jordan	David J. Stevens (Resident, Salt Lake City Office)
Mark E. Laughman	
Mark T. Lee (Resident, Phoenix Office)	Christopher F. Walrath
	Rodney G. Wendt (Resident, Salt Lake City Office)
Simon C. J. Maple	
Marie-Anne Zabrocki	

For Complete List of Firm Personnel, See General Section

For full biographical listings, see the Martindale-Hubbell Law Directory

JONES, DAY, REAVIS & POGUE (AV)

77 West Wacker, 60601-1692
Telephone: 312-782-3939
Telecopier: 312-782-8585
In Atlanta, Georgia: 3500 One Peachtree Center, 303 Peachtree Street, N.E.
Telephone: 404-521-3939.
Cable Address: "Attorneys Atlanta".
Telex: 54-2711.
Telecopier: 404-581-8330.
In Brussels, Belgium: Avenue Louise 480, 7th Floor, B-1050 Brussels.
Telephone: 32-2-645-14-11.
Telecopier: 32-2-645-14-45.
In Cleveland, Ohio: North Point, 901 Lakeside Avenue.
Telephone: 216-586-3939.
Cable Address: "Attorneys Cleveland."
Telex: 980389.
Telecopier: 216-579-0212.
In Columbus, Ohio: 1900 Huntington Center.
Telephone: 614-469-3939.
Cable Address: "Attorneys Columbus."
Telecopier: 614-461-4198.
In Dallas, Texas: 2300 Trammell Crow Center, 2001 Ross Avenue.
Telephone: 214-220-3939.
Cable Address: "Attorneys Dallas."
Telex: 730852.
Telecopier: 214-969-5100.

(See Next Column)

In Frankfurt, Germany: Triton Haus, Bockenheimer Landstrasse 42, 60323 Frankfurt am Main.
Telephone: 49-69-9726-3939.
Telecopier: 49-69-9726-3993.
In Geneva, Switzerland: 20, rue de Candolle.
Telephone: 41-22-320-2339.
Telecopier: 41-22-320-1232.
In Hong Kong: 29th Floor, Entertainment Building, 30 Queen's Road Central.
Telephone: 852-2526-6895.
Telecopier: 852-2868-5871 or 852-2868-5699.
In Irvine, California: 2603 Main Street, Suite 900.
Telephone: 714-851-3939.
Telex: 194911 Lawyers LSA.
Telecopier: 714-553-7539.
In London, England: One Mount Street.
Telephone: 44-71-493-9361.
Cable Address: "Surgoe London WI."
Telecopier: 44-71-493-9666.
In Los Angeles, California: 555 West Fifth Street, Suite 4600.
Telephone: 213-489-3939.
Telex: 181439 UD.
Telecopier: 213-243-2539.
In New Delhi, India: Pathak & Associates, 9th Floor, Dr. Gopal Das Bhaven, 28 Barakhamba Road.
Telephone: 91-11-331-9719.
Telecopier: 91-11-331-7802.
In New York, New York: 599 Lexington Avenue.
Telephone: 212-326-3939.
Cable Address: "JONESDAY NEWYORK."
Telex: 237013 JDRP UR.
Telecopier: 212-755-7306.
In Paris, France: 62, rue du Faubourg Saint-Honore.
Telephone: 33-1-44-71-3939.
Cable Address: "Surgoe Paris."
Telex: 290156 Surgoe.
Telecopier: 33-1-49-24-0471.
In Pittsburgh, Pennsylvania: 500 Grant Street, 31st Floor.
Telephone: 412-391-3939.
Cable Address: "Attorneys Pittsburgh."
Telecopier: 412-394-7959.
In Riyadh, Saudi Arabia: Law Offices of Saud M.A. Shawwaf, P.O. Box 22166.
Telephone: (966-1) 462-8866.
Telex: 401831 SAUCON SJ.
Telecopier: (966-1) 462-9001.
In Taipei, Taiwan: 8th Floor, 2 Tun Hwa South Road, Section 2.
Telephone: (886-2) 704-6808.
Telecopier: (886-2) 704-6791.
In Tokyo, Japan: Toranomon MT Building, 4th Floor, 10-3, Toranomon 3-Chome, Minato-ku, Tokyo 105, Japan.
Telephone: 81-3-3433-3939.
Telecopier: 81-3-5401-2725.
In Washington, D.C.: Metropolitan Square, 1450 G Street, N.W.
Telephone: 202-879-3939.
Cable Address: "Attorneys Washington."
Telex: 89-2410 ATTORNEYS WASH.
Telecopier: 202-737-2832.

MEMBERS OF FIRM IN CHICAGO

Robert A. Yolles	Michael J. Mitchell
Robert H. Baker	Harold C. Sutter
Lynn Leland Coe	S. Louise Rankin

OF COUNSEL

William J. Harmon

ASSOCIATES

Timothy J. Melton	John F. Bibby, Jr.
Richard K. Tomei	Kathleen L. Brennan De Jesus
Mary Jo Quinn	David J. Kates

For Complete List of Firm Personnel, See General Section

For full biographical listings, see the Martindale-Hubbell Law Directory

SCARIANO, KULA, ELLCH AND HIMES, CHARTERED (AV)

Two Prudential Plaza 180 North Stetson Suite 3100, 60601-6224
Telephone: 312-565-3100
Facsimile: 312-565-0000
Chicago Heights, Illinois Office: 1450 Aberdeen.
Telephone: 708-755-1900.
Facsimile: 708-755-0000.

Anthony G. Scariano	Kathleen Field Orr
David P. Kula	John M. Izzo
Robert H. Ellch	Raymond A. Hauser
Alan T. Sraga	Kathleen Roche Hirsman
A. Lynn Himes	Joanne W. Schochat
Justino D. Petrarca	Anthony Ficarelli
Lawrence Jay Weiner	G. Robb Cooper
Daniel M. Boyle	

OF COUNSEL

Max A. Bailey	John B. Kralovec

(See Next Column)

SCARIANO, KULA, ELLCH AND HIMES CHARTERED, *Chicago—Continued*

Patrick J. Broncato	Kelly A. Hayden
Rosanne Ciambrone	Todd K. Hayden
Jon G. Crawford	David A. Hemenway
Joel R. DeTella	Sarah E. Joyce
Teri E. Engler	Christopher L. Petrarca
Andrew C. Eulass	Shelia C. Riley
	Janet L. Schwieters

For full biographical listings, see the Martindale-Hubbell Law Directory

VEDDER, PRICE, KAUFMAN & KAMMHOLZ (AV)

A Partnership including Vedder, Price, Kaufman & Kammholz, P.C.
222 North La Salle Street, 60601-1003
Telephone: 312-609-7500
Fax: 312-609-5005
New York, New York Office: Vedder, Price, Kaufman, Kammholz & Day, 805 Third Avenue.
Telephone: 212-407-7700.

MEMBERS OF FIRM

Michael L. Igoe, Jr.	John R. Obiala
Robert J. Stucker	James A. Spizzo
Robert J. Moran	Dalius F. Vasys
Daniel O'Rourke	Daniel T. Sherlock
Lawrence J. Casazza	Jennifer R. Evans
Michael W. Sculnick	Drew J. Scott
E. Wayne Robinson	Michael A. Nemeroff

ASSOCIATE
Paula K. DeAngelo

For Complete List of Firm Personnel, See General Section

For full biographical listings, see the Martindale-Hubbell Law Directory

PEORIA,* Peoria Co.

HOWARD & HOWARD ATTORNEYS, P.C. (AV)

The Creve Coeur Building, Suite 200, 321 Liberty Street, 61602-1403
Telephone: 309-672-1483
Telecopier: 309-672-1568
Kalamazoo, Michigan Office: The Kalamazoo Building, Suite 400, 107 West Michigan Avenue.
Telephone: 616-382-1483.
Telecopier: 616-382-1568.
Bloomfield Hills, Michigan Office: The Pinehurst Office Center, Suite 101, 1400 North Woodward Avenue.
Telephone: 810-645-1483.
Telecopier: 810-645-1568.
Lansing, Michigan Office: Suite 500, The Phoenix Building, 222 Washington Square, North.
Telephone: 517-485-1483.
Telecopier: 517-485-1568.
Tampa, Florida Office: First of America Plaza, Suite 2000, 201 East Kennedy Boulevard.
Telephone: 813-229-1483.
Telecopier: 813-229-1568.

Frederick G. Hoffman

Representative Clients: For Representative Client list, see General Practice, Peoria, IL.

For Complete List of Firm Personnel, See General Section

For full biographical listings, see the Martindale-Hubbell Law Directory

INDIANA

INDIANAPOLIS,* Marion Co.

BAKER & DANIELS (AV)

300 North Meridian Street, 46204
Telephone: 317-237-0300
FAX: 317-237-1000
Fort Wayne, Indiana Office: 111 East Wayne Street, Suite 800.
Telephone: 219-424-8000.
South Bend, Indiana Office: First Bank Building, 205 West Jefferson Boulevard.
Telephone: 219-234-4149.
Elkhart, Indiana Office: 301 B South Main Street, Suite 307,
Telephone: 219-296-6000.
Washington, D.C. Office: 1701 K Street, N.W., Suite 400.
Telephone: 202-785-1565.

MEMBERS OF FIRM

Theodore J. Esping	Thomas A. Pitman
David Lawther Johnson	Jill Harris Tanner
	Richard C. Starkey

(See Next Column)

ASSOCIATES

Thomas C. Froehle Jr.	Amy E. Kosnoff
	Jennifer L. Brajkovich

Representative Clients: Anthem Insurance Companies, Inc.; AT&T Corp.; Bank One, Indianapolis, N.A.; Borg-Warner Corp.; City of Indianapolis; Cummins Engine Co.; Eli Lilly and Co.; General Motors Corp.; Indianapolis Public Schools; United Airlines.

For Complete List of Firm Personnel, See General Section

For full biographical listings, see the Martindale-Hubbell Law Directory

BOSE MCKINNEY & EVANS (AV)

2700 First Indiana Plaza, 135 North Pennsylvania Street, 46204
Telephone: 317-684-5000
Facsimile: 317-684-5173
Indianapolis North Office: Suite 1201, 8888 Keystone Crossing, 46240.
Telephone: 317-574-3700.
Facsimile: 317-574-3716.

MEMBERS OF FIRM

Lewis C. Bose	L. Parvin Price
David A. Travelstead	Jon M. Bailey
Ronald M. Soskin	Karl R. Sturbaum
	Roderick H. Morgan

Representative Clients: Indiana Health Facilities Financing Authority; Metropolitan School District of Wayne Township, Marion County, Indiana; Metropolitan School District of Lawrence Township; Kemper Securities, Inc.; Gibson County Water District; DeKalb County Jail Building Corp.; The Indianapolis Local Public Improvement Bond Bank; Hendricks County; Avon Community Schools; The Indiana Bond Bank.

For Complete List of Firm Personnel, See General Section

For full biographical listings, see the Martindale-Hubbell Law Directory

DANN PECAR NEWMAN & KLEIMAN, PROFESSIONAL CORPORATION (AV)

Suite 2300, One American Square Box 82008, 46282
Telephone: 317-632-3232; Indiana: 800-622-4799
Telecopy: 317-632-2962

Theodore R. Dann (1907-1993)	Walter E. Wolf, Jr.
Joel Yonover (1932-1995)	Barry E. Beldin
Philip D. Pecar	Robert D. Swhier, Jr.
Norman R. Newman	James P. Moloy
David H. Kleiman	Robert J. Schuckit
Jon B. Abels	Andrew A. Kleiman
Melvin R. Daniel	Michael J. Gabovitch
Lawrence F. Dorocke	Steven M. Pecar
Jeffrey A. Abrams	Benjamin A. Pecar
James H. Schwarz	Richard O. Kissel, II
Robert A. Rose	Joseph D. Calderon

OF COUNSEL

Linda E. Cantor	Anthony J. Rose

Ellen C. Siakotos	Angela L. Mansfield
Stacy L. Hill	Martha M. K. Baird
	Karin L. Veatch

Attorneys for: Indianapolis Machinery Co., Inc.; Melvin Simon & Associates, Inc.; Pacers Basketball Corp.; Universal Fire & Casualty Co., Inc.; Bank One, Indianapolis, NA; INB National Bank; Nachi Technology, Inc.; Pharmaceutical Corporation of America; Logo 7, Inc.

For full biographical listings, see the Martindale-Hubbell Law Directory

ICE MILLER DONADIO & RYAN (AV)

One American Square Box 82001, 46282-0002
Telephone: 317-236-2100
Fax: 317-236-2219
Email: leel@imdr.com *URL:* http://www.imdr.com
South Bend, Indiana Office: 211 West Washington Street, Suite 2420.
Telephone: 219-234-7933.
Fax: 219-234-7965. Internet E-mail: leel@imdr.com. Web Site Address: http://www.imdr.com.

MEMBERS OF FIRM

Bruce A. Polizotto	Brenda S. Horn
Philip C. Genetos	Todd W. Ponder
James A. Shanahan	Lucy A. Emison
Jeffrey O. Lewis	Thomas W. Peterson
Thomas K. Downs	Patricia A. Zelmer
	Jane Neuhauser Herndon

SENIOR COUNSEL
Mark S. Moore

OF COUNSEL

Karen L. Arland	Thomas C. Smith
	Daniel E. Fisher

STAFF ATTORNEYS

Sandra K. Bickel	John W. Rowings

(See Next Column)

ICE MILLER DONADIO & RYAN—*Continued*

ASSOCIATES

Michael J. Melliere   Amy Corsaro Merritt

Counsel for: Indiana University; Purdue University; Indiana Bond Bank; Indiana Municipal Power Agency; Indiana Housing Finance Authority; Indiana Health Facility Financing Authority; Indiana Development Finance Authority; Citizens Gas & Coke Utility; Indianapolis International Airport Authority; Indiana Association of Cities and Towns.

For Complete List of Firm Personnel, See General Section

For full biographical listings, see the Martindale-Hubbell Law Directory

LAFAYETTE,* Tippecanoe Co.

STUART & BRANIGIN (AV)

The Life Building, 300 Main Street, Suite 800, 47902
Telephone: 317-423-1561
Telecopier: 317-742-8175

MEMBERS OF FIRM

Allison Ellsworth Stuart (1886-1950)	Stephen R. Pennell
Roger D. Branigin (1902-1975)	Anthony S. Benton
Russell H. Hart	Erik D. Spykman
Roger D. Branigin, Jr.	William E. Emerick
Thomas L. Ryan	John C. Duffey
James V. McGlone	Mark E. DeYoung
Carl W. Kloepfer	Thomas B. Parent
Thomas R. McCully	Laura L. Bowker
Larry R. Fisher	Kevin D. Nicoson
Nina B. Kirkpatrick	Susan K. Roberts
Mark Lillianfeld	John M. Stuckey
	Deborah B. Trice

COUNSEL

John F. Bodle

ASSOCIATES

Brent W. Huber   David A. Starkweather
William P. Kealey   Geoffrey Blazi
A. James Chareq

General Counsel for: The Lafayette Life Insurance Co.; INB National Bank, N.W.; Lafayette Home Hospital, Inc.
State Counsel for: Norfolk & Western Railway Co.
Mr. Ryan is Counsel to: The Trustees of Purdue University.
Representative Clients: Aluminum Company of America; Liberty Mutual Insurance Group.

For full biographical listings, see the Martindale-Hubbell Law Directory

NOBLESVILLE,* Hamilton Co.

CHURCH, CHURCH, HITTLE & ANTRIM (AV)

938 Conner Street, P.O. Box 10, 46060-0010
Telephone: 317-773-2190
Telecopier: 317-773-5320
Email: cchadoug@msn.com

MEMBERS OF FIRM

Douglas D. Church	Bruce M. Bittner
Jack G. Hittle	Brian J. Zaiger
J. Michael Antrim	David Joseph Barker
Martin E. Risacher	Leslie Craig Henderzahs

OF COUNSEL

Manson E. Church

Representative Clients: Noblesville Schools; Westfield-Washington Schools; Indiana School Finance Corp.; Community Bank; Metrobank; Towns of Westfield, Fishers; Reynolds Farm Equipment Co.; Weihe Engineering; Historic Railroad Multijurisdictional Port Authority.

For full biographical listings, see the Martindale-Hubbell Law Directory

KENTUCKY

BOWLING GREEN,* Warren Co.

ENGLISH, LUCAS, PRIEST & OWSLEY (AV)

1101 College Street, P.O. Box 770, 42102-0770
Telephone: 502-781-6500
Telecopier: 502-782-7782
Email: inquiry@elpo.com

MEMBERS OF FIRM

Charles E. English   Whayne C. Priest, Jr.
Keith M. Carwell

ASSOCIATES

Marc Allen Lovell   Jason P. Wright

For Complete List of Firm Personnel, See General Section

For full biographical listings, see the Martindale-Hubbell Law Directory

LEXINGTON,* Fayette Co.

STOLL, KEENON & PARK, LLP (AV)

201 E. Main Street, Suite 1000, 40507-1380
Telephone: 606-231-3000
Telecopier: 606-253-1093; 606-253-1027
Frankfort, Kentucky Office: 307 Washington Street, 40601.
Telephone: 502-875-6220.
Telecopier: 502-875-6235.
Louisville, Kentucky Office: 400 West Market Street, Suite 2650, 40202-3377.
Telephone: 502-568-9100.
Telecopier: 502-568-5700.

MEMBERS OF FIRM

Gary L. Stage   Douglas P. Romaine
Herbert A. Miller, Jr.   J. David Smith, Jr.

ASSOCIATE

R. Douglas Martin

Representative Clients: Bank One, Lexington, NA; Kentucky Association of Counties; Smith Barney, Inc.

For Complete List of Firm Personnel, See General Section

For full biographical listings, see the Martindale-Hubbell Law Directory

LOUISVILLE,* Jefferson Co.

HARPER, FERGUSON & DAVIS (AV)

1730 Meidinger Tower, 40202
Telephone: 502-582-3871
Telecopier: 502-582-3905

MEMBERS OF FIRM

Spencer E. Harper, Jr.   William W. Davis

OF COUNSEL

Jo M. Ferguson (Retired)

Representative Clients: Kentucky Housing Corp.; Lexington-Fayette Urban County Government; Cities of Louisville and Covington; Kenton County Airport Board (Cincinnati/No. Kentucky International Airport); Regional Airport Authority of Louisville and Jefferson County; Toyota Motor Mfg., U.S.A., Inc.; Scott Paper Company; Delta Air Lines, Inc.; Kentucky Utilities Co.; Louisville Gas & Electric Co.

For full biographical listings, see the Martindale-Hubbell Law Directory

PEDLEY, ZIELKE & GORDINIER (AV)

1150 Starks Building, 455 South Fourth Avenue, 40202
Telephone: 502-589-4600
Fax: 502-584-0422

MEMBERS OF FIRM

Lawrence L. Pedley	William W. Stodghill
Laurence J. Zielke	P. Stephen Gordinier
John K. Gordinier	Schuyler J. Olt
Frank G. Simpson, III	

OF COUNSEL

Caroline George Meena

ASSOCIATE

John H. Dwyer, Jr.

For full biographical listings, see the Martindale-Hubbell Law Directory

RUBIN HAYS & FOLEY (AV)

First Trust Centre 200 South Fifth Street, 40202
Telephone: 502-569-7550
Telecopier: 502-569-7555

MEMBERS OF FIRM

Wm. Carl Fust	Lisa Koch Bryant
Harry Lee Meyer	Sharon C. Hardy
David W. Gray	Charles S. Musson
Irvin D. Foley	W. Randall Jones
Joseph R. Gathright, Jr.	K. Gail Russell

ASSOCIATES

Christian L. Juckett   Courtney Lynn McCall

OF COUNSEL

James E. Fahey   Newman T. Guthrie

Representative Clients: J.C. Bradford & Co., Inc.; J.J.B. Hilliard, W.L. Lyons, Inc.; Huntington National Bank; Liberty National Bank and Trust Company; National City Bank; PNC Bank; Prudential Bache & Co., Inc.; Prudential Securities, Inc.; Society Bank; Stock Yards Bank and Trust Co.

For full biographical listings, see the Martindale-Hubbell Law Directory

Louisville—Continued

STITES & HARBISON (AV)

Formerly Stites, McElwain & Fowler and Harbison, Kessinger, Lisle & Bush
400 West Market Street, Suite 1800, 40202
Telephone: 502-587-3400
Frankfort, Kentucky Office: 421 West Main Street.
Telephone: 502-223-3477.
Lexington, Kentucky Office: 2300 Lexington Financial Center.
Telephone: 606-226-2300.
Jeffersonville, Indiana Office: 323 East Court Avenue.
Telephone: 812-282-7566.

MEMBERS OF FIRM

Robert W. Lanum	William H. Haden, Jr.
(Jeffersonville, Indiana Office)	William E. Hellmann

Representative Clients: South Central Bell Telephone Co.; Glenmore Distilleries Co.; New York Life Insurance Co.; Chrysler Financial Corp.; ARCO Metals Co.; Aetna Life & Casualty Insurance Cos.; Illinois Central Railroad Co.

For Complete List of Firm Personnel, See General Section

For full biographical listings, see the Martindale-Hubbell Law Directory

---

LOUISIANA

BATON ROUGE, * East Baton Rouge Parish

BREAZEALE, SACHSE & WILSON, L.L.P. (AV)

Twenty-Third Floor, One American Place, P.O. Box 3197, 70821-3197
Telephone: 504-387-4000
Fax: 504-387-5397
New Orleans, Louisiana Office: LL&E Tower, Suite 2400, 909 Poydras Street.
Telephone: 504-582-1170.
Fax: 504-584-5452.

MEMBERS OF FIRM

Leonard R. Nachman, II	Richard D. Leibowitz

Counsel for: Hibernia National Bank; South Central Bell Telephone Co.; Allied-Signal Corp.; Reynolds Metal Co.; Illinois Central Railroad Co.; The Continental Insurance Cos.; Fireman's Fund American Group; Chicago Bridge & Iron Co.; Montgomery Ward & Co.

For Complete List of Firm Personnel, See General Section

For full biographical listings, see the Martindale-Hubbell Law Directory

---

LAKE CHARLES, * Calcasieu Parish

THE CARMOUCHE LAW FIRM A PROFESSIONAL CORPORATION (AV)

Bank One Tower, 901 Lakeshore Drive, Suite 900, P.O. Drawer 2001, 70601-5270
Telephone: 318-433-0355
Telecopier: 318-433-1274
Email: clf@carmouche.com

Edward M. Carmouche	John F. Robichaux
(1921-1990)	David R. Frohn
Virginia M. Carmouche	W. Joseph Mize
(inactive)	Scott J. Pias
Joseph A. Delafield	John F. Wadsack
	Terry Thibodeaux

Elizabeth B. Hollins	Robin A. Anderson

LEGAL SUPPORT PERSONNEL

PARALEGALS

C. Lynn Bengston	Susan Meado
	Susan Fontenot

For full biographical listings, see the Martindale-Hubbell Law Directory

---

NEW ORLEANS, * Orleans Parish

FOLEY & JUDELL, L.L.P. (AV)

One Canal Place, Suite 2600, 365 Canal Street, 70130-1138
Telephone: 504-568-1249
Fax: 504-565-3900
Email: foleyjudel@aol.com
Baton Rouge, Louisiana Office: Acadia Trace Office Building, 2237 South Acadian Thruway, Suite 610.
Telephone: 504-923-2476.
Fax: 504-923-2477.

(See Next Column)

MEMBERS OF FIRM

Harold B. Judell	O. Ray Cornelius
Lonnie L. Bewley	David M. Wolf
J. Hugh Martin	David E. Henderson (Resident,
C. Grant Schlueter	Baton Rouge Office)
Susan Weeks	Wayne J. Neveu
Jerry R. Osborne	Alan L. Offner
	Meredith L. Hathorn

OF COUNSEL

Dudley C. Foley, Jr.	John W. Cox
	William H. Beck, Jr.

For full biographical listings, see the Martindale-Hubbell Law Directory

---

THE GODFREY FIRM A PROFESSIONAL LAW CORPORATION (AV)

2500 Energy Centre, 1100 Poydras Street, 70163-2500
Telephone: 504-585-7538
Fax: 504-585-7535

Jarrell E. Godfrey, Jr.	Cloyd F. Van Hook
	Patrick M. Files

For full biographical listings, see the Martindale-Hubbell Law Directory

---

MAINE

BANGOR, * Penobscot Co.

EATON, PEABODY, BRADFORD & VEAGUE, P.A. (AV)

Fleet Center-Exchange Street, P.O. Box 1210, 04402-1210
Telephone: 207-947-0111
Telecopier: 207-942-3040
Email: epbv@aol.com
Augusta, Maine Office: 2 Central Plaza.
Telephone: 207-622-3747.
Telecopier: 207-622-9732.
Blue Hill, Maine Office: One East Blue Hill Road.
Telephone: 207-374-2812.
Telecopier: 207-374-2548.
Brunswick, Maine Office: 167 Park Row.
Telephone: 207-729-1144.
Telecopier: 207-729-1140.
Camden, Maine Office: 7-9 Washington Street.
Telephone: 207-236-3325.
Telecopier: 207-236-8611.
Dover-Foxcroft, Maine Office: 30 East Main Street.
Telephone: 207-564-8378.
Telecopier: 207-564-7059.

Michael B. Trainor

A List of Representative Clients available upon request.

For Complete List of Firm Personnel, See General Section

For full biographical listings, see the Martindale-Hubbell Law Directory

---

PORTLAND, * Cumberland Co.

PIERCE ATWOOD (AV)

One Monument Square, 04101
Telephone: 207-791-1100
Fax: 207-791-1350
Email: info@PierceAtwood.com
Augusta, Maine Office: 77 Winthrop Street.
Telephone: 207-622-6311.
Fax: 207-623-9367.
Newburyport, Massachusetts Office: 6 Harris Street.
Telephone: 508-465-9599.
Fax: 508-465-9945.

MEMBERS OF FIRM

Bruce A. Coggeshall	James B. Zimpritch
	Christopher E. Howard

OF COUNSEL

Charles W. Allen

ASSOCIATES

James M. Saffian	Marcia A. Metcalf

For Complete List of Firm Personnel, See General Section

For full biographical listings, see the Martindale-Hubbell Law Directory

Portland—Continued

PRETI, FLAHERTY, BELIVEAU & PACHIOS (AV)

A Limited Liability Company
443 Congress Street, P.O. Box 11410, 04104-7410
Telephone: 207-791-3000
Telecopier: 207-791-3111
Email: admin@pfbpnet.com
Augusta, Maine Office: 45 Memorial Circle, P.O. Box 1058, 04332-1058.
Telephone: 207-623-5300.
Telecopier: 207-623-2914.

MEMBERS OF FIRM

Severin M. Beliveau
(Augusta Office)
Michael J. Gentile
(Augusta Office)

Eric P. Stauffer
James C. Pitney, Jr.
(Augusta Office)

ASSOCIATE
James E. Phipps

Representative Clients: Prudential Securities Incorporated; Kidder, Peabody & Co., Inc.; Paine Webber Incorporated; State of Maine; Town of Jay, Maine; A. G. Edwards, Inc.; Merrill Lynch & Co.; Chemical Securities Inc.; Goldman, Sachs & Co.

For Complete List of Firm Personnel, See General Section

For full biographical listings, see the Martindale-Hubbell Law Directory

MARYLAND

BALTIMORE,* (Independent City)

FUNK & BOLTON, A PROFESSIONAL ASSOCIATION (AV)

USF&G Tower Building, Suite 900, 100 Light Street, 21202
Telephone: 410-659-7700
Facsimile: 410-659-7773
Email: FBLAW.COM

David M. Funk
Bryan D. Bolton
Timothy E. Dixon

Lindsey A. Rader
Steven Jared Troy
Derek B. Yarmis

OF COUNSEL
J. Frank Nayden

Bryson F. Popham
Deborah R. Rivkin

For full biographical listings, see the Martindale-Hubbell Law Directory

PIPER & MARBURY L.L.P. (AV)

Charles Center South, 36 South Charles Street, 21201-3018
Telephone: 410-539-2530
FAX: 410-539-0489
Email: lawfirm@pipermar.com
Washington, D.C. Office: 1200 Nineteenth Street, N.W., 20036-2430.
Telephone: 202-861-3900.
FAX: 202-223-2085.
Easton, Maryland Office: 117 Bay Street, 21601-2703.
Telephone: 410-820-4460.
FAX: 410-820-4463.
New York, N.Y. Office: 1251 Avenue of the Americas, 10020-1104.
Telephone: 212-835-6000.
FAX: 212-835-6001.
Philadelphia, Pennsylvania Office: 3400 Two Logan Square, 18th & Arch Streets, 19103-2762.
Telephone: 215-656-3300.
FAX: 215-656-3301.

MEMBERS OF FIRM

Donald P. McPherson, III
Mark Pollak
John P. Machen
Stewart K. Diana
Elizabeth A. McKennon

William L. Henn, Jr.
Paul A. Tiburzi
Paul D. Shelton
Kurt J. Fischer
Kristin H. R. Franceschi

For Complete List of Firm Personnel, See General Section

For full biographical listings, see the Martindale-Hubbell Law Directory

VENABLE ATTORNEYS AT LAW VENABLE, BAETJER AND HOWARD, LLP (AV)

A Partnership including Professional Corporations
1800 Mercantile Bank & Trust Building, 2 Hopkins Plaza, 21201
Telephone: 410-244-7400
Email: INFO@Venable.win.net
Washington, D.C. Office: Venable, Baetjer, Howard & Civiletti LLP. Suite 1000, 1201 New York Avenue, N.W.
Telephone: 202-962-4800.
McLean, Virginia Office: Suite 400, 2010 Corporate Ridge.
Telephone: 703-760-1600.
Rockville, Maryland Office: Suite 500, One Church Street, P. O. Box 1906.
Telephone: 301-217-5600.

(See Next Column)

Towson, Maryland Office: 210 Allegheny Avenue, P. O. Box 5517.
Telephone: 410-494-6200.

MEMBERS OF FIRM

Thomas P. Perkins, III (P.C.)
Lee M. Miller (P.C.)
Robert A. Shelton
Thomas J. Kenney, Jr. (P.C.)
(Also at Washington, D.C. Office)
David J. Levenson (Not admitted in MD; Resident, Washington, D.C. Office)
Lars E. Anderson (Not admitted in MD; Resident, McLean, Virginia Office)

Paul T. Glasgow (Resident, Rockville, Maryland Office)
Sondra Harans Block (Resident, Rockville, Maryland Office)
Edward L. Wender (P.C.)
Mitchell Kolkin
Peter P. Parvis
Bruce H. Jurist (Also at Washington, D.C. Office)
James E. Cumbie
Davis V. R. Sherman

For Complete List of Firm Personnel, See General Section

For full biographical listings, see the Martindale-Hubbell Law Directory

WHITEFORD, TAYLOR & PRESTON L.L.P. (AV)

7 Saint Paul Street, 21202-1626
Telephone: 410-347-8700
Telex: 5101012334
Fax: 410-752-7092
Email: 2019267@mcimail.com *URL:* http://www.wtplaw.com
Towson, Maryland Office: 210 West Pennsylvania Avenue.
Telephone: 410-832-2000.
Fax: 410-832-2015.
Washington, D.C. Office: 1025 Connecticut Avenue, N.W.
Telephone: 202-659-6800.
Fax: 202-331-0573.
Columbia, Maryland Office: 10440 Little Patuxent Parkway.
Telephone: 410-884-0700.
Fax: 410-884-0719.
Alexandria, Virginia Office: 1317 King Street.
Telephone: 703-836-5742.
Fax: 703-836-0265.

MEMBERS OF FIRM

James C. Holman
Herman B. Rosenthal

Deborah H. Diehl
William M. Davidow, Jr.

ASSOCIATES
D. Scott Freed

Jonathan Z. May

For Complete List of Firm Personnel, See General Section

For full biographical listings, see the Martindale-Hubbell Law Directory

RIVERDALE, Prince Georges Co.

MEYERS, BILLINGSLEY, RODBELL & ROSENBAUM, P.A. (AV)

Suite 400 Berkshire Building, 6801 Kenilworth Avenue, 20737-1385
Telephone: 301-699-5800
Fax: 301-779-5746

Lance W. Billingsley

Frederick Stichnoth

Reference: First National Bank of Maryland.

For Complete List of Firm Personnel, See General Section

For full biographical listings, see the Martindale-Hubbell Law Directory

TOWSON,* Baltimore Co.

VENABLE ATTORNEYS AT LAW VENABLE, BAETJER AND HOWARD, LLP (AV)

A Partnership including Professional Corporations
210 Allegheny Avenue, P.O. Box 5517, 21204
Telephone: 410-494-6200
FAX: 410-821-0147
Baltimore, Maryland Office: 1800 Mercantile Bank & Trust Building, 2 Hopkins Plaza.
Telephone: 410-244-7400.
Washington, D.C. Office: Venable, Baetjer, Howard & Civiletti LLP, Suite 1000, 1201 New York Avenue, N.W.
Telephone: 202-962-4800.
McLean, Virginia Office: Suite 400, 2010 Corporate Ridge.
Telephone: 703-760-1600.
Rockville, Maryland Office: Suite 500, One Church Street, P. O. Box 1906.
Telephone: 301-217-5600.

PARTNERS

John B. Howard

Cynthia M. Hahn
Robert A. Hoffman

For Complete List of Firm Personnel, See General Section

For full biographical listings, see the Martindale-Hubbell Law Directory

UPPER MARLBORO, Prince Georges Co.

KNIGHT, MANZI, BRENNAN, SHAY AND HAM, A PROFESSIONAL ASSOCIATION (AV)

14440 Old Mill Road, 20772
Telephone: 301-952-0100
Annapolis/Baltimore: 410-792-3786
Fax: 301-952-0221
Crofton, Maryland Office: 2411 Crofton Lane, # 26.
Telephone: 301-261-0808.
Fax: 301-261-6945.
Mitchellville, Maryland Office: 12164 Central Avenue, Suite 228.
Telephone: 301-390-0577.
Fax: 301-390-8464.

William E. Knight	John F. Shay, Jr.
Robert A. Manzi	Richard J. Ham
William C. Brennan, Jr.	Martin J. Shuham

Monica M. Haley-Pierson	Norman D. Rivera
Daniel F. Lynch III	Robert L. Lombardo

OF COUNSEL
Stuart R. Hammett

For full biographical listings, see the Martindale-Hubbell Law Directory

MASSACHUSETTS

BOSTON, Suffolk Co.

MINTZ, LEVIN, COHN, FERRIS, GLOVSKY AND POPEO, P.C. (AV)

One Financial Center, 02111
Telephone: 617-542-6000
FAX: 617-542-2241
Internet: Each Attorney's Internet Address takes the following form: first initial last name @mintz.com (e.g., rmintz@mintz.com)
Washington, D.C. Office: 701 Pennsylvania Avenue, N.W. Suite 900.
Telephone: 202-434-7300.
Fax: 202-434-7400.

Francis X. Meaney	Maxwell D. Solet
Gregory A. Sandomirsky	John R. Regier
Ann-Ellen Marcus Hornidge	

For Complete List of Firm Personnel, See General Section

For full biographical listings, see the Martindale-Hubbell Law Directory

PALMER & DODGE LLP (AV)

One Beacon Street, 02108
Telephone: 617-573-0100
Facsimile: 617-227-4420

MEMBERS OF FIRM

Neil P. Arkuss	Ruth E. Fitch
Robert W. Buck	Robert H. Hale
Norman P. Cohen	Thomas W. Merrill
Jean M. DeLuca	Walter J. St. Onge, III
Charles E. DeWitt, Jr.	John M. Thomas
John G. Faria	Roger P. Vacco
Donald F. Winter	

OF COUNSEL
James W. Perkins

For Complete List of Firm Personnel, See General Section

For full biographical listings, see the Martindale-Hubbell Law Directory

WARNER & STACKPOLE LLP (AV)

75 State Street, 02109
Telephone: 617-951-9000
Telecopier: 617-951-9151
Email: w&s@warstack.com

MEMBERS OF FIRM

Timothy B. Bancroft	John C. Hutchins
Willard G. McGraw, Jr.	

ASSOCIATES

Daniel M. Carroll	David J. Powers
Jill M. Pechacek	Kathleen B. Woodard

For Complete List of Firm Personnel, See General Section

For full biographical listings, see the Martindale-Hubbell Law Directory

MICHIGAN

BLOOMFIELD HILLS, Oakland Co.

HOWARD & HOWARD ATTORNEYS, P.C. (AV)

The Pinehurst Office Center, Suite 101, 1400 North Woodward Avenue, 48304-2856
Telephone: 810-645-1483
Telecopier: 810-645-1568
Kalamazoo, Michigan Office: The Kalamazoo Building, Suite 400, 107 West Michigan Avenue.
Telephone: 616-382-1483
Telecopier: 616-382-1568.
Lansing, Michigan Office: The Phoenix Building, Suite 500, 222 Washington Square, North.
Telephone: 517-485-1483
Telecopier: 517-485-1568.
Peoria, Illinois Office: The Creve Coeur Building, Suite 200, 321 Liberty Street.
Telephone: 309-672-1483.
Telecopier: 309-672-1568.
Tampa, Florida Office: First of America Plaza, Suite 2000, 201 East Kennedy Boulevard.
Telephone: 813-229-1483.
Telecopier: 813-229-1568.

Roshunda L. Price-Harper	Robert L. Schwartz
Melanie Mayo West	

Representative Clients: For Representative Client list, see General Practice, Bloomfield Hills, MI.

For Complete List of Firm Personnel, See General Section

For full biographical listings, see the Martindale-Hubbell Law Directory

DETROIT, Wayne Co.

BODMAN, LONGLEY & DAHLING LLP (AV)

34th Floor 100 Renaissance Center, 48243
Telephone: 313-259-7777
Fax: 313-393-7579
Email: 2080194@mcimail.com
Troy, Michigan Office: Suite 2020, 755 West Big Beaver Road.
Telephone: 810-362-2110.
Fax: 810-244-0780.
Ann Arbor, Michigan Office: 110 Miller, Suite 300.
Telephone: 313-761-3780.
Fax: 313-930-2494.
Northern Michigan Office: 229 Court Street, P.O. Box 405, Cheboygan.
Telephone: 616-627-4351.
Fax: 616-627-2802.

MEMBERS OF FIRM

Herold McC. Deason	Christopher J. Dine
Joseph N. Brown	(Troy Office)
F. Thomas Lewand	Jerold Lax (Ann Arbor Office)
Barbara Bowman Bluford	Patrick C. Cauley

For Representative Client List, See General Section

For Complete List of Firm Personnel, See General Section

For full biographical listings, see the Martindale-Hubbell Law Directory

DICKINSON, WRIGHT, MOON, VAN DUSEN & FREEMAN (AV)

500 Woodward Avenue, Suite 4000, 48226-3425
Telephone: 313-223-3500
Facsimile: 313-223-3598
Bloomfield Hills, Michigan Office: 525 North Woodward Avenue, Suite 2000.
Telephone: 810-433-7200.
Facsimile: 810-433-7274.
Grand Rapids, Michigan Office: 200 Ottawa Avenue, N.W., Suite 900.
Telephone: 616-458-1300.
Facsimile: 616-458-6753.
Lansing, Michigan Office: Suite 200, 215 South Washington Square.
Telephone: 517-371-1730.
Facsimile: 517-487-4700.
Washington, D.C. Office: Suite 800, 1901 L Street, N.W.
Telephone: 202-457-0160.
Facsimile: 202-659-1559.
Chicago, Illinois Office: 225 West Washington, Suite 400.
Telephone: 312-220-0300.
Facsimile: 312-220-0021.

MEMBERS OF FIRM

James W. Bliss (Lansing Office)	W. Anthony Jenkins
Terence M. Donnelly	Kester K. So (Lansing Office)
John A. Everhardus	Richard A. Wendt
Kirk E. Grable (Lansing Office)	Paul M. Wyzgoski
Craig W. Hammond	Thomas V. Yates

CONSULTING PARTNERS

Charles R. Moon	Judson Werbelow
	(Lansing Office)

(See Next Column)

DICKINSON, WRIGHT, MOON, VAN DUSEN & FREEMAN—*Continued*
ASSOCIATES
Kathryn Kraus Nunzio   Rhonda D. Welburn
(Grand Rapids Office)

For Representative Client list, see General Section.

For Complete List of Firm Personnel, See General Section

For full biographical listings, see the Martindale-Hubbell Law Directory

---

DYKEMA GOSSETT PLLC (AV)

400 Renaissance Center, 48243-1668
Telephone: 313-568-6800
Cable Address: "Dyke-Detroit"
Telex: 23-0121
Fax: 313-568-6594
Email: 2084153@mcimail.com
Ann Arbor, Michigan Office: 315 East Eisenhower Parkway, Suite 100, 48108-3306.
Telephone: 313-747-7660.
Fax: 313-747-7696.
Bloomfield Hills, Michigan Office: 1577 North Woodward Avenue, Suite 300, 48304-2820.
Telephone: 810-540-0700.
Fax: 810-540-0763.
Chicago, Illinois Office: 55 East Monroe Street, Suite 3250, 60603-5709.
Telephone: 312-551-4900.
Fax: 312-551-4919.
Grand Rapids, Michigan Office: 200 Oldtown Riverfront Building, 248 Louis Campau Promenade, N.W., 49503-2668.
Telephone: 616-776-7500.
Fax: 616-776-7573.
Lansing, Michigan Office: 800 Michigan National Tower, 48933-1707.
Telephone: 517-374-9100.
Fax: 517-374-9191.
Washington, D.C. Office: Franklin Square, Suite 300 West, 1300 I Street, N.W., 20005-3306.
Telephone: 202-522-8600.
Fax: 202-522-8669.

MEMBERS OF FIRM
Bowden V. Brown (Resident at   Kathrin E. Kudner
Bloomfield Hills Office)   Stewart L. Mandell
James P. Kiefer   Brian J. Page (Resident at
(Resident at Lansing Office)   Grand Rapids Office)

ASSOCIATES
Ann D. Fillingham   Nicole Yvette Lamb-Hale
(Resident at Lansing Office)

For Complete List of Firm Personnel, See General Section

For full biographical listings, see the Martindale-Hubbell Law Directory

---

HONIGMAN MILLER SCHWARTZ AND COHN (AV)

A Partnership including Professional Corporations
2290 First National Building, 48226
Telephone: 313-256-7800
Telecopier: 313-962-0176
Telex: 235705
URL: http://law.honigman.com
Lansing, Michigan Office: Phoenix Building, 222 North Washington Square, Suite 400, 48933-1800.
Telephone: 517-484-8282.
West Palm Beach, Florida Office: Suite 800 Esperante Building, 222 Lakeview Avenue, 33401-6112.
Telephone: 561-838-4500.
Tampa, Florida Office: 2700 SunTrust Financial Centre, 401 E. Jackson Street, 33602-5226.
Telephone: 813-221-6600.

MEMBERS OF FIRM
Maurice S. Binkow   Mitchell R. Meisner
William M. Cassetta   Alex L. Parrish
John M. Kamins   G. Scott Romney
Denise J. Lewis   Brad M. Tomtishen
Stuart M. Lockman   William C. Whitbeck
                                     (Lansing, Michigan Office)

Representative Clients: Michigan Municipal Bond Authority; City of Detroit, Michigan; Wayne County, Michigan; Merrill Lynch & Co.; Goldman, Sachs & Co.; PaineWebber Incorporated; Roney & Co.; Bear, Stearns & Co., Inc.; Merrill Lynch & Co.; Goldman, Sachs & Co.

For Complete List of Firm Personnel, See General Section

For full biographical listings, see the Martindale-Hubbell Law Directory

---

JAFFE, RAITT, HEUER & WEISS, PROFESSIONAL CORPORATION (AV)

One Woodward Avenue, Suite 2400, 48226
Telephone: 313-961-8380
Telecopier: 313-961-8358
Cable Address: "Jafsni"
Southfield, Michigan Office: Travelers Tower, Suite 1520.
Telephone: 313-961-8380.
Monroe, Michigan Office: 214 East Elm Avenue, Suite 208,
Telephone: 313-241-6470.
Telefacsimile: 313-241-3849.

Gail A. Anderson   Ralph R. Margulis
Robert S. Bolton   Lawrence C. Patrick, Jr.
Gary R. Glenn   David H. Raitt
Robert J. Gordon   Stephen G. Schafer
Larry K. Griffis   Susan M. Sutton

Representative Clients: Michigan State Hospital Finance Authority.

For Complete List of Firm Personnel, See General Section

For full biographical listings, see the Martindale-Hubbell Law Directory

---

LEWIS, CLAY & MUNDAY, A PROFESSIONAL CORPORATION (AV)

(Formerly Lewis, White & Clay, P.C.)
1300 First National Building, 660 Woodward Avenue, 48226-3531
Telephone: 313-961-2550
Troy, Michigan Office: Liberty Center, Suite 200. 100 West Big Beaver Road. 48084.
Telephone: 810-680-6702.
Fax: 810-680-6703.
Washington, D.C. Office: 1000 16th Street, N.W., Suite 401. 20036.
Telephone: 202-835-0616.
Fax: 202-833-3316.
Boston, Massachusetts Office: 10 Post Office Square.
Telephone: 617-422-8646.
Fax: 617-338-5693.

David Baker Lewis   Frank E. Barbee
Eric Lee Clay   Camille Stearns Miller
Reuben A. Munday   Michael T. Raymond
Ulysses Whittaker Boykin   Jacqueline H. Sellers
Carl F. Stafford   David N. Zacks
Helen Francine Strong   Thomas J. Guyer
                    Blair A. Person

Karen Kendrick Brown   Hans J. Massaquoi, Jr.
(Resident, Washington, D.C.   Nancy C. Borland
Office)   Tammy L. Terry
J. Taylor Teasdale   Lynn Westfall Gross
Wade Harper McCree   Suzanne P. Pope
Tyrone A. Powell   Matthew R. Halpin
Susan D. Hoffman   Donica Thomas Varner
John J. Walsh   Damon L. White
Andrea L. Powell   (Not admitted in MI)
Althea Lynn Foster   Kathleen L. Royal

COUNSEL
Otis M. Smith (1922-1994)   G. Allen Bass (Resident, Boston,
Herbert O. Reid, Sr. (1915-1991)   Massachusetts Office)

Representative Clients: Omnicare Health Plan; Aetna Life & Casualty Co.; Chrysler Motors Corp.; Chrysler Financial Corp.; MCI Communications Corp.; City of Detroit; City of Detroit Building Authority; City of Detroit Downtown Development Authority; Consolidated Rail Corp. (Conrail); Equitable Life Assurance Society of the United States.

For full biographical listings, see the Martindale-Hubbell Law Directory

---

MILLER, CANFIELD, PADDOCK AND STONE, P.L.C. (AV)

A Professional Limited Liability Company
Founded in 1852 by Sidney Davy Miller
150 West Jefferson, Suite 2500, 48226-4415
Telephone: 313-963-6420
Fax: 313-496-7500
Cable Address: "Stem Detroit"
Detroit, Michigan Office: 150 West Jefferson, Suite 2500, 48226-4415.
Telephone: 313-963-6420.
Fax: 313-496-7500.
Cable Address: "Stem Detroit."
Ann Arbor, Michigan Office: 101 North Main Street, 7th Floor, 48104-1400.
Telephone: 313-663-2445.
Fax: 313-747-7147.
Bloomfield Hills, Michigan Office: Suite 100, Pinehurst Office Center, 1400 North Woodward, 48303-2014.
Telephone: 313-645-5000.
Fax: 313-645-1917.
Grand Rapids, Michigan Office: 1200 Campau Square Plaza, 99 Monroe, N.W., 49503-2639.
Telephone: 616-454-8656.
Fax: 616-776-6322.

(See Next Column)

MILLER, CANFIELD, PADDOCK AND STONE P.L.C., *Detroit—Continued*

Howell, Michigan Office: 121 South Barnard Street, Suite 4, 48843-2305.
Telephone: 517-546-7600.
Telecopier: 517-546-6974.
Kalamazoo, Michigan Office: 444 West Michigan Avenue, 49007-3752.
Telephone: 616-381-7030.
Fax: 616-382-0244.
Lansing, Michigan Office: One Michigan Avenue, Suite 900, 48933-1609.
Telephone: 517-487-2070.
Fax: 517-374-6304.
Monroe, Michigan Office: The Executive Centre, 214 East Elm Avenue, 48161-2682.
Telephone: 313-243-2000.
Fax: 313-243-0901.
Washington, D.C. Office: 1225 Nineteenth Street, N.W., Suite 400. 20036.
Telephone: 202-429-5575; 785-0600.
Fax: 202-331-1118; 785-1234.
Pensacola, Florida Office: 25 West Cedar, 32501.
Telephone: 904-469-1088.
Fax: 904-432-0677.
St. Petersburg, Florida Office: 100 Second Avenue S., Suite 7045, 33701.
Telephone: 813-982-6000.
Fax: 813-892-6002.
New York, New York Office: Eleventh Floor, 135 East 57th Street, 10022-2087.
Telephone: 212-754-5400.
Fax: 212-754-5401.
Gdansk, Poland Office: Suite 322, Dom Technika Building, UI. Rajska 6, 80-850.
Telephone: 011-485-831-2808.
Fax: 011-485-831-4719.
Warsaw, Poland Office: UI. Marszalkowska 82, Suite 561, 00-517.
Telephone: 011-482-623-6457 and 6458.
Fax: 011-482-623-6459.

PRINCIPALS OF FIRM

Robert E. Hammell	Thomas W. Linn
Joel L. Piell	Donald W. Keim
Robert E. Gilbert	Christopher J. Dembowski
(Ann Arbor Office)	(Lansing Office)
Charles L. Burleigh, Jr.	Amanda Van Dusen
Dennis R. Neiman	Cynthia B. Faulhaber
William J. Danhof	(Lansing Office)
(Lansing Office)	Harold W. Bulger, Jr.
Jerry T. Rupley	Michael P. McGee

OF COUNSEL

Stratton S. Brown	Richard I. Lott
Richard B. Gushée	(Pensacola, Florida Office)

ASSOCIATES

Amy S. Davis	Patrick F. McGow
Thomas D. Colis	

Representative Firm Clients: Chrysler Corporation; Comerica, Incorporated; City of Detroit, Michigan; Detroit Tigers, Inc.; First of Michigan; Ford Motor Company; Ford Motor Credit Company; Great Lakes Bancorp; Henry Ford Hospital; INVETECH Company.

For Complete List of Firm Personnel, See General Section

For full biographical listings, see the Martindale-Hubbell Law Directory

GRAND RAPIDS,* Kent Co.

VARNUM, RIDDERING, SCHMIDT & HOWLETT LLP (AV)

A Limited Liability Partnership including Professional Corporations
Bridgewater Place, P.O. Box 352, 49501-0352
Telephone: 616-336-6000
800-262-0011
Facsimile: 616-336-7000
Telex: 1561593 VARN
Email: varnum@vrsh.com
Lansing, Michigan Office: The Victor Center, Suite 810, 210 North Washington Square, 48933.
Telephone: 517-482-6237.
Facsimile: 517-482-6937.
Kalamazoo, Michigan Office: 350 East Michigan Avenue, 49007.
Telephone: 616-382-2300.
Facsimile: 616-382-2382.
Grand Haven, Michigan Office: 321 Washington Street, P.O. Box 288, 49417.
Telephone: 616-846-7100.
Facsimile: 616-846-7101.
Battle Creek, Michigan Office: 4950 West Dickman Road, Suite B-1, 49015.
Telephone: 616-962-7144.
Bingham Farms, Michigan Office: 31600 Telegraph Road, Suite 230, 48025.
Telephone: 810-594-7330.
Facsimile: 810-594- 7331.

MEMBERS OF FIRM

Jon F. DeWitt	Randall W. Kraker
Jeffrey L. Schad	Susan M. Wyngaarden
John W. Pestle	Richard D. Fries

COUNSEL

Fred M. Woodruff, Jr. (Resident at Bingham Farms Office)

Counsel for: City of Evart Local Development Finance Authority; City of Grandville; City of Plainwell Tax Increment Finance Authority; City of Walker; City of Walker Downtown Development Authority; Charter Township of Grand Rapids Economic Development Corp.; County of Kent; Kent County Building Authority; Newaygo Public Schools; Township of Ada.

For Complete List of Firm Personnel, See General Section

For full biographical listings, see the Martindale-Hubbell Law Directory

GROSSE POINTE FARMS, Wayne Co.

JOHN R. AXE AND ASSOCIATES (AV)

Suite 360, 21 Kercheval Avenue, 48236
Telephone: 313-884-1550; 1-800-383-MFCI
Fax: 313-884-0626

ASSOCIATE
Peter S. Ecklund
OF COUNSEL
Robert P. Allen

Reference: First of America Bank.

For full biographical listings, see the Martindale-Hubbell Law Directory

LANSING, Ingham Co.

HOWARD & HOWARD ATTORNEYS, P.C. (AV)

The Phoenix Building, Suite 500, 222 Washington Square, North, 48933-1817
Telephone: 517-485-1483
Telecopier: 517-485-1568
Kalamazoo, Michigan Office: The Kalamazoo Building, Suite 400, 107 West Michigan Avenue.
Telephone: 616-382-1483.
Telecopier: 616-382-1568.
Bloomfield Hills, Michigan Office: The Pinehurst Office Center, Suite 101, 1400 North Woodward Avenue.
Telephone: 810-645-1483.
Telecopier: 810-645-1568.
Peoria, Illinois Office: The Creve Coeur Building, Suite 200, 321 Liberty Street.
Telephone: 309-672-1483.
Telecopier: 309-672-1568.
Tampa, Florida Office: First of America Plaza, Suite 2000, 201 East Kennedy Boulevard.
Telephone: 813-229-1483.
Telecopier: 813-229-1568.

Brad S. Rutledge	Gina M. Torielli

Representative Clients: For Representative Client list, see General Practice, Lansing, MI.

For Complete List of Firm Personnel, See General Section

For full biographical listings, see the Martindale-Hubbell Law Directory

NATURAL RESOURCES LAW

ALABAMA

BIRMINGHAM, * Jefferson Co.

BRADLEY, ARANT, ROSE & WHITE (AV)

2001 Park Place, Suite 1400, P.O. Box 830709, 35283-0709
Telephone: 205-521-8000
Facsimile: 205-252-0264
Facsimile (SouthTrust Tower Office): 205-251-9915
URL: http://www.BARW.COM
Huntsville, Alabama Office: 200 Clinton Avenue West, Suite 900, 35801.
Telephone: 205-517-5100.
Facsimile: 205-533-5069.

MEMBER OF FIRM
John E. Hagefstration, Jr.

Counsel for: SouthTrust Bank of Alabama, National Association; Energen, Corporation (formerly Alagasco, Inc.); Blount, Inc.; Coca-Cola Bottling Company; United, Inc.; The New York Times Co.; Russell Corp.; Ford Motor Co.; Volkswagen of America, Inc.; Rust International Corp.

For Complete List of Firm Personnel, See General Section

For full biographical listings, see the Martindale-Hubbell Law Directory

MOBILE, * Mobile Co.

ARMBRECHT, JACKSON, DeMOUY, CROWE, HOLMES & REEVES, L.L.C. (AV)

1300 AmSouth Center, P.O. Box 290, 36601
Telephone: 334-405-1300
Facsimile: 334-432-6843; 433-3821

MEMBERS OF FIRM
Wm. H. Armbrecht, III	Grover E. Asmus II
Conrad P. Armbrecht	Dabney Bragg Foshee
Edward G. Hawkins	David E. Hudgens
Duane A. Graham	

Representative Clients: Kimberly Clark Corporation; UNOCAL; Exxon Co. (USA); Texaco, Inc.; Mobil Oil Corp.; Pacific Enterprises Oil Co. (USA); Callon Petroleum Co.; BP Exploration, Inc.; Jim Walter Resources, Inc.; Champion International Corp.

For Complete List of Firm Personnel, See General Section

For full biographical listings, see the Martindale-Hubbell Law Directory

JOHNSTONE, ADAMS, BAILEY, GORDON AND HARRIS, L.L.C. (AV)

Royal St. Francis Building, 104 St. Francis Street, P.O. Box 1988, 36633
Telephone: 334-432-7682
Facsimile: 334-432-2800
Telex: 782040

MEMBERS OF FIRM
Charles B. Bailey, Jr.	William H. Hardie, Jr.
Brock B. Gordon	I. David Cherniak
Ben H. Harris, Jr.	Alan C. Christian

ASSOCIATE
W. Andrew Wing, II

Representative Clients: Exxon Corp.; Conoco Inc.; Amerada Hess; Wilmon Timberlands, Inc.

For Complete List of Firm Personnel, See General Section

For full biographical listings, see the Martindale-Hubbell Law Directory

LYONS, PIPES & COOK, P.C. (AV)

2 North Royal Street, P.O. Box 2727, 36652-2727
Telephone: 334-432-4481
Cable Address: "Lysea"
Telecopier: 334-433-1820

Wesley Pipes	John Patrick Courtney, III
Norton W. Brooker, Jr.	Caroline C. McCarthy

Representative Clients: Champion International Corp.; Chevron U.S.A., Inc.; Coastal Corp.; Conoco, Inc.; Shell Oil Co.; Sonat, Inc.; Phillips Petroleum Co.; Kerr McGee Corp.; The Nature Conservancy; Atlantic Richfield Co.

For Complete List of Firm Personnel, See General Section

For full biographical listings, see the Martindale-Hubbell Law Directory

TUSCALOOSA, * Tuscaloosa Co.

WATSON, HARRISON & DeGRAFFENRIED (AV)

1651 McFarland Boulevard North, 35406-2212
Telephone: 205-345-1577
Fax: 205-345-1583

William T. Watson	Steven F. Harrison
Thomas W. Holley	

OF COUNSEL
Ryan DeGraffenried, Jr.

Michael C. Cornwell	Ricky J. McKinney

Representative Clients: BTA Oil Producers; Black Warrior Methane Corp.; Chevron U.S.A. Inc.; Cobra Oil & Gas Corp.; CXY Energy, Inc.; Exxon Co., USA; Fina Oil & Chemical Co.; Legacy Resources; Meridian Oil Inc.; Mitchell Energy Corp.

For full biographical listings, see the Martindale-Hubbell Law Directory

ALASKA

ANCHORAGE, * Third Judicial District

DELANEY, WILES, HAYES, GERETY & ELLIS, INC. (AV)

1007 West Third Avenue, Suite 400, 99501
Telephone: 907-279-3581
Fax: 907-277-1331

Stephen M. Ellis	Jeffrey P. Stark
Marc D. Bond	Clyde E. Sniffen, Jr.

Representative Clients: Alyeska Pipeline Service Co.; Arco Alaska Inc.; Bering Straits Native Corporation; Chevron Corporation; Mobil Oil Company; Phillips Petroleum Company; Nana Regional Corporation; Seibu Alaska Inc.

For Complete List of Firm Personnel, See General Section

For full biographical listings, see the Martindale-Hubbell Law Directory

ARIZONA

PHOENIX, * Maricopa Co.

APKER, APKER, HAGGARD & KURTZ, P.C. (AV)

2111 East Highland Avenue, Suite 230, 85016
Telephone: 602-381-0085
Telecopier: 602-956-3457

Burton M. Apker	David B. Apker
Jerry L. Haggard	Gerrie Apker Kurtz

Kevin M. Moran

Representative Clients: ASARCO Incorporated; Douglas Land Corp.; Frito-Lay, Inc.; Nevada Power Company; The North West Life Assurance Co.; Phelps Dodge Corporation; Santa Fe Pacific Gold Corporation; Santa Fe Pacific Industrials; Western Federal Savings & Loan Assn.

For full biographical listings, see the Martindale-Hubbell Law Directory

FENNEMORE CRAIG, A PROFESSIONAL CORPORATION (AV)

Two North Central, Suite 2200, 85004
Telephone: 602-257-8700
Fax: 602-257-8527
Scottsdale, Arizona Office: 6263 North Scottsdale Road, Suite 290, 85250.
Telephone: 602-257-5400.
Fax: 602-257-5409.
Tucson, Arizona Office: One South Church Avenue, Suite 1030, 85701.
Telephone: 520-791-6800.
Fax: 520-791-6820.

Calvin H. Udall	Timothy Berg
James M. Bush	Margaret R. Gallogly
James W. Johnson	Robert D. Anderson
Lauren J. Caster	Robert J. Kramer

Douglas C. Northup	Jeffrey C. Thacker

For Complete List of Firm Personnel, See General Section

For full biographical listings, see the Martindale-Hubbell Law Directory

Phoenix—Continued

JENNINGS, STROUSS AND SALMON, P.L.C. (AV)

A Professional Limited Liability Company
One Renaissance Square, Two North Central, 85004-2393
Telephone: 602-262-5911
Fax: 602-253-3255

David J. Calverley   James M. Ackerman
Richard N. Morrison   George Esahak-Gage
Shiela B. Schmidt

For Complete List of Firm Personnel, See General Section

For full biographical listings, see the Martindale-Hubbell Law Directory

QUARLES & BRADY (AV)

One Camelback Building, One East Camelback Road, Suite
    400, 85012-1649
Telephone: 602-230-5500
Fax: 602-230-5598
Milwaukee, Wisconsin Office: 411 East Wisconsin Avenue.
Telephone: 414-277-5000.
Fax: 414-271-3552.
Madison, Wisconsin Office: First Wisconsin Plaza, One South Pinckney
Street, P.O. Box 2113.
Telephone: 608-251-5000.
Fax: 608-251-9166.
West Palm Beach, Florida Office: 222 Lakeview Ave., 4th Floor.
Telephone: 407-653-5000.
Fax: 407-653-5333.
Naples, Florida Office: Barnett Center, 4501 Tamiami Trail North, Suite
300.
Telephone: 813-262-5959.
Fax: 813-434-4999.

MEMBER OF THE FIRM
Daniel L. Muchow

For Complete List of Firm Personnel, See General Section

For full biographical listings, see the Martindale-Hubbell Law Directory

SNELL & WILMER, L.L.P. (AV)

One Arizona Center, 85004-0001
Telephone: 602-382-6000
Fax: 602-382-6070
Tucson, Arizona Office: 1500 Norwest Tower, One South Church Avenue
85701-1612.
Telephone: 520-882-1200.
Fax: 520-884-1294.
Orange County Office: 1920 Main Street, Suite 1200, P.O. Box 57062,
Irvine, California, 92619-7062.
Telephone: 714-253-2700.
Fax: 714-955-2507.
Salt Lake City, Utah Office: Broadway Centre, 111 East Broadway, Suite
900, 84111-1004.
Telephone: 801-237-1900.
Fax: 801-237-1950.

MEMBERS OF FIRM
George H. Lyons   Steven M. Wheeler
Robert B. Hoffman   Richard W. Shapiro
G. Van Velsor Wolf, Jr.   Martha E. Gibbs
E. Jeffrey Walsh

SENIOR ATTORNEY
Thomas L. Mumaw

ASSOCIATES
Jeffrey Webb Crockett   Robert Henry
Carlos D. Ronstadt   Lisa A. Schuh

Representative Clients: Arizona Public Service Company; Coca Cola Enter-
prises; El Paso Natural Gas Company; Hughes Aircraft; Magma Copper
Company; Metro Mobile CTS, Inc.; Mitsubishi Motor Sales of America;
Toyota Technical Center; Tucson Airport Authority; Bank One, Arizona,
NA.

For Complete List of Firm Personnel, See General Section

For full biographical listings, see the Martindale-Hubbell Law Directory

---

SCOTTSDALE, Maricopa Co.

SPARKS, TEHAN & RYLEY, P.C. (AV)

7503 First Street, 85251-4573
Telephone: 602-949-1339
Fax: 602-949-7587

Joe P. Sparks   John H. Ryley

References: Bank One, Arizona, Trust Department; Northern Trust Bank of
Arizona, N.A.; First Interstate Bank of Arizona.

For full biographical listings, see the Martindale-Hubbell Law Directory

---

TUCSON,* Pima Co.

CHANDLER, TULLAR, UDALL & REDHAIR (AV)

1700 Bank of America Plaza, 33 North Stone Avenue, 85701
Telephone: 520-623-4353
Telefax: 520-792-3426

MEMBERS OF FIRM
Thomas Chandler   Dwight M. Whitley, Jr.
D. B. Udall   E. Hardy Smith
Jack Redhair   John J. Brady
Joe F. Tarver, Jr.   Christopher J. Smith
Steven Weatherspoon   Charles V. Harrington
Edwin M. Gaines, Jr.   Bruce G. MacDonald

ASSOCIATES
Joel T. Ireland   Kurt Kroese
Mark Fredenberg   Sean C. Chapman
Mariann T. Shinoskie   Anne M. Fulton

Representative Clients: Arizona Electric Power Cooperative, Inc.; Atlantic
Richfield Co.; CNA Insurance; Farmers Insurance Exchange; MICA; Chubb
Insurance Group; Aetna Casualty; State Farm Mutual Insurance Companies;
Santa Cruz Valley Water Authority.
Reference: Arizona Bank.

For Complete List of Firm Personnel, See General Section

For full biographical listings, see the Martindale-Hubbell Law Directory

SNELL & WILMER, L.L.P. (AV)

1500 Norwest Tower, One South Church Avenue, 85701-1612
Telephone: 520-882-1200
Fax: 520-884-1294
Phoenix, Arizona Office: One Arizona Center, 85004-0001.
Telephone: 602-382-6000.
Fax: 602-382-6070.
Orange County Office: 1920 Main Street, Suite 1200, P.O. Box 57062,
Irvine, California, 92619-7062.
Telephone: 714-253-2700
Fax: 714-955-2507.
Salt Lake City, Utah Office: Broadway Centre, 111 East Broadway, Suite
900, 84111- 1004.
Telephone: 801-237-1900.
Fax: 801-237-1950.

MEMBERS OF FIRM
Michael S. Milroy   Marjorie R. Perry
Marc G. Simon   Tibor Nagy, Jr.
Curt D. Reimann   William N. Poorten, III
John A. Robertson   Timothy E. Pickrell
Sandra S. Froman   Kathleen Brown Corey
Patrick E. Broom

OF COUNSEL
Clague A. Van Slyke

ASSOCIATES
Steven Adamczyk   Annemarie Hennelly
Eric S. Baker   Todd V. Jones
Rolando Ballesteros   Mark E. Konrad
Dawn Brewer   James K. (Jim) Mackie
Joan S. Caplan   Regina L. Nassen
David R. Cohen   Kathryn B. Nelson
J. Matthew Derstine   Russell B. Stowers
Rosalind R. Greene   M. Roxanne Veliz

Representative Clients: Transit Management, Inc.; Tucson Airport Authority;
Allstate Insurance Co.; Bank One, Arizona, NA; Southern Pacific Railroad
Co.; Ford Motor Co.; Chrysler Motors Corp.; Toyota Motor Sales, U.S.A.,
Inc.; BHP Copper, Inc.; Pinnacle West Capital Corp.; Safeway Inc.; Honey-
well, Inc.; Wells Fargo Bank, N.A.

For full biographical listings, see the Martindale-Hubbell Law Directory

STRICKLAND & STRICKLAND, P.C. (AV)

4400 E. Broadway, Suite 700, 85711-3517
Telephone: 520-795-8727
Fax: 520-795-5649

William E. Strickland   William E. Strickland, Jr.
Robert F. Palmquist

Representative Client: AkChin Indian Community.
Reference: Bank One (formerly Valley National Bank).

ARKANSAS

FORT SMITH,* Sebastian Co.

HARDIN, DAWSON & TERRY (AV)

Suite 500, Superior Federal Tower, 5000 Rogers Avenue, P.O. Box 10127, 72917-0127
Telephone: 501-452-2200
FAX: 501-452-9097

MEMBERS OF FIRM

G. C. Hardin (1884-1964)	Robert M. Honea
P. H. Hardin	J. Leslie Evitts III
Robert T. Dawson	J. Rodney Mills
Rex M. Terry	Kirkman T. Dougherty
J. Gregory Magness	

Counsel for: Superior Federal Bank, FSB; The Kansas City Southern Railway Co.; KFSM-TV; Johnson & Johnson; Ortho Pharmaceutical Corp; ASARCO Inc.; Allstate Insurance Co.; Southern Farm Bureau Insurance Co.; Dodson Insurance Group.

For full biographical listings, see the Martindale-Hubbell Law Directory

TEXARKANA,* Miller Co.

DUNN, NUTTER, MORGAN & SHAW (AV)

State Line Plaza, Box 8030, 71854-5945
Telephone: 501-773-5651
Telecopier: 501-772-2037
Email: law@clover.cleaf.com

MEMBERS OF FIRM

Charles A. Morgan	Nelson V. Shaw

OF COUNSEL

Hayes C. McClerkin

LEGAL SUPPORT PERSONNEL

LEGAL ASSISTANTS

Myra Conaway Wells	Sonja L. Oliver

Representative Clients: North American Energy Corporation (NorAm); Southwest Arkansas Water District; Southwest Arkansas Electric Cooperative Corp.; Red River Commission of Arkansas; Mobil Oil Co.; Oryx Energy Co.; Ethyl Corp.; Miller County Levee District No. 2; Miller County Improvement and Drainage District; Oxy, USA, Inc.

For Complete List of Firm Personnel, See General Section

For full biographical listings, see the Martindale-Hubbell Law Directory

CALIFORNIA

BEVERLY HILLS, Los Angeles Co.

SAMUEL D. INGHAM, III (AV)

Suite 830, 8383 Wilshire Boulevard, 90211-2407
Telephone: 213-651-5980
FAX: 213-651-5725
Email: sdiesq@aol.com

For full biographical listings, see the Martindale-Hubbell Law Directory

COSTA MESA, Orange Co.

McCORMICK, KIDMAN & BEHRENS, LLP (AV)

A Partnership of Professional Corporations
Imperial Bank Building, 695 Town Center Drive Suite 1400, 92626-1924
Telephone: 714-755-3100
Fax: 714-755-3110; 1-800-755-3125
Email: mkb1@ix.netcom.com

MEMBERS OF FIRM

Homer L. (Mike) McCormick, Jr., (P.C.)	Russell G. Behrens (P.C.)
Arthur G. Kidman (P.C.)	Suzanne M. Tague (P.C.)
	Janet R. Morningstar (P.C.)
Keith E. McCullough (P.C.)	

ASSOCIATES

David D. Boyer	John O. Clune
Robert A. Johnson	Bradley D. Pierce

For full biographical listings, see the Martindale-Hubbell Law Directory

IRVINE, Orange Co.

BROWN, PISTONE, HURLEY & VAN VLEAR, A PROFESSIONAL CORPORATION (AV)

Suite 900 AT&T Building, 8001 Irvine Center Drive, 92618-2921
Telephone: 714-727-0559
Fax: 714-727-0656
Email: BPHVLAW@AOL.COM
Phoenix, Arizona Office: 2999 North 44th Street, Suite 300.
Telephone: 602-968-2427.
Fax: 602-840-0794.
San Diego, California Office: 4350 La Jolla Village Drive, Suite 300.
Telephone: 619-546-4368.
Fax: 619-453-2839.
Sacramento, California Office: 980 Ninth Street, 16th Floor.
Telephone: 916-449-9541.
Fax: 916-446-7104.

Ernest C. Brown	Gregory F. Hurley
Thomas A. Pistone	John E. Van Vlear
Michael K. Wolder	

Francis T. Donohue, III	Sheila I. Patterson
Robert C. Schneider (Resident, Phoenix, Arizona Office)	Michael R. Gandee
	Julia E. Kress

OF COUNSEL

Robert G. Mahan	Brian A. Runkel
Stephen M. Wontrobski	(Not admitted in CA)

For full biographical listings, see the Martindale-Hubbell Law Directory

SNELL & WILMER, L.L.P. (AV)

1920 Main Street, Suite 1200, 92614
Telephone: 714-253-2700
FAX: 714-955-2507
URL: http://www.swlaw.com
Phoenix, Arizona Office: One Arizona Center, 85004-0001.
Telephone: 602-382-6000.
Fax: 602-382-6070.
Tucson, Arizona Office: Norwest Tower, Suite 1500, One South Church Avenue, 85701-1612.
Telephone: 520-882-1200.
Fax: 520-884-1294.
Salt Lake City, Utah Office: Broadway Centre, 111 East Broadway, Suite 900, 84111-1004.
Telephone: 801-237-1900.
Fax: 801-237-1950.

MEMBER OF FIRM

Diane R. Smith (Resident)

ASSOCIATE

Sean Michael Sherlock

For Complete List of Firm Personnel, See General Section

For full biographical listings, see the Martindale-Hubbell Law Directory

LAW OFFICES OF SUSAN M. TRAGER A PROFESSIONAL CORPORATION (AV)

The Landmark Building, Suite 104, 2100 S. E. Main Street, 92614
Telephone: 714-752-8971
Telefax: 714-863-9804

Susan M. Trager

Michele A. Staples	Laura Pavloff Couch

Representative Client: San Luis Rey Municipal Water District.
Reference: Sanwa Bank California.

For full biographical listings, see the Martindale-Hubbell Law Directory

LOS ANGELES,* Los Angeles Co.

DEMETRIOU, DEL GUERCIO, SPRINGER & MOYER, LLP (AV)

801 South Grand Avenue, 10th Floor, 90017
Telephone: 213-624-8407
Telecopy: 213-624-0174
Email: ddsm@juno.com *URL:* http://www.ddsm.com

MEMBERS OF FIRM

Craig A. Moyer	Andrew J. Bracker
Michael A. Francis	Kimberly E. Lewand
Jennifer T. Taggart	

OF COUNSEL

Ronald J. Del Guercio

Reference: Bank of America, L.A. Main Office, Los Angeles, Calif.

For full biographical listings, see the Martindale-Hubbell Law Directory

Los Angeles—Continued

HANNA AND MORTON (AV)

A Partnership including Professional Corporations
Seventeenth Floor, Wilshire-Grand Building, 600 Wilshire
Boulevard, 90017
Telephone: 213-628-7131
Facsimile: 213-623-3379

MEMBERS OF FIRM

Edward S. Renwick (A Professional Corporation)	James P. Lower
	David A. Ossentjuk

ASSOCIATE
Robert J. Roche

Representative Clients: Atlantic Richfield Co.; Mobil Oil Corp.; Shell Oil Corp.; Texaco, Inc.; Unocal.

For Complete List of Firm Personnel, See General Section

For full biographical listings, see the Martindale-Hubbell Law Directory

O'MELVENY & MYERS LLP (AV)

400 South Hope Street, 90071-2899
Telephone: 213-669-6000
Cable Address: "Moms"
Facsimile: 213-669-6407
Email: omminfo@omm.com
Century City, California Office: 1999 Avenue of the Stars, 90067-6035.
Telephone: 310-553-6700.
Facsimile: 310-246-6779.
Newport Beach, California Office: 610 Newport Center Drive, 92660-6429.
Telephone: 714-760-9600.
Cable Address: "Moms".
Facsimile: 714-669-6994.
San Francisco, California Office: Embarcadero Center West Tower, 275 Battery Street, 94111-3305.
Telephone: 415-984-8700.
Facsimile: 415-984-8701.
New York, New York Office: Citicorp Center, 153 East 53rd Street, 10022-4611.
Telephone: 212-326-2000.
Facsimile: 212-326-2061.
Washington, D.C. Office: 555 13th Street, N.W., 20004-1109.
Telephone: 202-383-5300.
Cable Address: "Moms".
Facsimile: 202-383-5414.
London, England Office: 10 Finsbury Square, London, EC2A 1LA.
Telephone: 0171-256-8451.
Facsimile: 0171-638-8205.
Tokyo, Japan Office: Sanbancho KB-6 Building, 6 Sanbancho, Chiyoda-ku, Tokyo 102, Japan.
Telephone: 03-3239-2900.
Facsimile: 03-3239-2432.
Hong Kong Office: Suite 1905, Peregrine Tower, Lippo Centre, 89 Queensway, Central, Hong Kong.
Telephone: 852-2523-8266.
Facsimile: 852-2522-1760.
Shanghai, Peoples Republic of China Office: Shanghai International Trade Centre, Suite 2011, 2200 Yan An Road West, Shanghai, 200335, PRC.
Telephone: 86-21-6219-5363.
Facsimile: 86-21-6275-4949.

PARTNER
Gregory B. Thorpe

For Complete List of Firm Personnel, See General Section

For full biographical listings, see the Martindale-Hubbell Law Directory

---

NEWPORT BEACH, Orange Co.

FRANK B. MYERS (AV)

Suite 720, 4400 MacArthur Boulevard, 92660
Telephone: 714-752-2001
Facsimile: 714-955-3670

For full biographical listings, see the Martindale-Hubbell Law Directory

---

PALO ALTO, Santa Clara Co.

A. DUNCAN KING (AV)

Suite 501, 2471 East Bayshore Road, 94303
Telephone: 800-255-3636; 415-494-6000
FAX: 415-494-3012
Email: adking@ix.netcom.com

For full biographical listings, see the Martindale-Hubbell Law Directory

---

PASADENA, Los Angeles Co.

LAGERLOF, SENECAL, BRADLEY & SWIFT, LLP (AV)

301 North Lake Avenue, 10th Floor, 91101-4108
Telephone: 818-793-9400
FAX: 818-793-5900

(See Next Column)

MEMBERS OF FIRM

Joseph J. Burris (1913-1980)	John F. Bradley
Stanley C. Lagerlof (Retired)	Timothy J. Gosney
H. Melvin Swift, Jr.	William F. Kruse
H. Jess Senecal	Thomas S. Bunn, III
Jack T. Swafford	Andrew D. Turner
Rebecca J. Thyne	

ASSOCIATES

James D. Ciampa	Robert W. Renken

Representative Clients: Anchor Glass Container Corp.; Bethlehem Steel Corp.; Orthopaedic Hospital; Palmdale Water District; Public Water Agencies Group; Ventura Port District; Walnut Valley Water District; Metric Construction Co., Inc.

For full biographical listings, see the Martindale-Hubbell Law Directory

WILLSEY LAW OFFICES OWNED BY A PROFESSIONAL CORPORATION (AV)

553 S. Marengo Avenue, 91101
Telephone: 818-577-1086
Fax: 818-304-2959

Burke W. Willsey	Daniel P. Willsey (A Professional Corporation)

Reference: Sanwa Bank.

For full biographical listings, see the Martindale-Hubbell Law Directory

---

SACRAMENTO, * Sacramento Co.

DE CUIR & SOMACH, A PROFESSIONAL CORPORATION (AV)

400 Capitol Mall, Suite 1900, 95814
Telephone: 916-446-7979
Facsimile: 916-446-8199

Dennis W. De Cuir	Sandra K. Dunn
Stuart L. Somach	William E. Hvidsten
Paul S. Simmons	Timothy M. Taylor
John A. Mendez	

Michael E. Vergara	Donald B. Gilbert
Donald B. Mooney	Elizabeth W. Johnson
Andrew M. Hitchings	

OF COUNSEL
David S. Kaplan

For full biographical listings, see the Martindale-Hubbell Law Directory

---

DOWNEY, BRAND, SEYMOUR & ROHWER (AV)

Suite 1050, 555 Capitol Mall, 95814
Telephone: 916-441-0131
FAX: 916-441-4021
Email: downey@dbsr.com *URL:* http://www.dbsr.com

MEMBERS OF FIRM

George Basye	David E. Lindgren
Philip A. Stohr	Dan L. Carroll
Henry E. Rodegerdts	Steven P. Saxton
James M. Day, Jr.	Julie A. Carter
Kevin M. O'Brien	Steven H. Goldberg
Patrick G. Mitchell	

ASSOCIATES

David R.E. Aladjem	JudyAnne McGinley
Gordon B. Burns	Sean B. Murphy
Heather B. Lee	Scott L. Shapiro
Stacey H. Leong	Helen Singmaster-Hernández

Counsel for: Las Vegas Valley Water District; East Contra Costa Irrigation District; Enron Oil and Gas Co.; Benton Oil and Gas Co.; Sacramento Municipal Utility District; Reclamation District No. 1000; Amerada Hess; General Motors Corp.; Anheuser-Busch Cos.; Mobil Oil Corp.

For Complete List of Firm Personnel, See General Section

For full biographical listings, see the Martindale-Hubbell Law Directory

---

SAN FRANCISCO, * San Francisco Co.

LAW OFFICES OF WESLEY R. HIGBIE (AV)

425 California Street 19th Floor, 94104
Telephone: 415-434-1474
Fax: 415-434-1050
Email: SailorWes@aol.com

For full biographical listings, see the Martindale-Hubbell Law Directory

COLORADO

ASPEN,* Pitkin Co.

PATRICK & STOWELL, P.C. (AV)

Suite 300, 205 South Mill Street, 81611
Telephone: 970-920-1028
Fax: 970-925-6847
URL: http://www.waterlaw.com

Kevin L. Patrick   Brian L. Stowell

Scott Carpenter Miller   Thomas Edward Kinney

LEGAL SUPPORT PERSONNEL
Jennifer R. Santa Barbara (Paralegal)

Representative Clients: Aspcol Corp., N.V.; McCloskey Enterprises, Inc.; Snowmass Land Co., a joint venture of Heitman Financial, Ltd. and Golub & Co.; Aspen Highlands Ski Area/Hines Highlands Limited Partnership; Dallas Creek Water Co.; Fairway Pines Estates Golf Club/Loghill Village Investors, Ltd.; Telluride Regional Airport Authority; Town of Gypsum; B.C. Ziegler & Company.

For full biographical listings, see the Martindale-Hubbell Law Directory

BOULDER,* Boulder Co.

VRANESH AND RAISCH, L.L.C. (AV)

1720 14th Street, P.O. Box 871, 80306
Telephone: 303-443-6151
Telecopier: 303-443-9586

MEMBERS OF FIRM

Jerry W. Raisch   Eugene J. Riordan
John R. Henderson   Paul J. Zilis
Michael D. Shimmin   George Vranesh (Retired)

Thomas Morris   Margaret J. Woods

Representative Clients: Cyprus Climax Metals Co.; City of Fort Collins; Colorado Association of Commerce and Industry; County of Arapahoe; Eastman Kodak Company; Hendricks Mining Company; Horizon Gold Corporation, Inc.; Metro Wastewater Reclamation District; Phillips Petroleum Company; Waste Management of North America.

For full biographical listings, see the Martindale-Hubbell Law Directory

DENVER,* Denver Co.

BALLARD SPAHR ANDREWS & INGERSOLL (AV)

Seventeenth Street Plaza Building, Suite 2300, 1225 17th Street, 80202-5596
Telephone: 303-292-2400
Fax: 303-296-3956
Philadelphia, Pennsylvania Office: 1735 Market Street, 51st Floor.
Telephone: 215-665-8500.
Fax: 215-864-8999.
Harrisburg, Pennsylvania Office: 105 North Front Street.
Telephone: 717-236-3333.
Fax: 717-236-3884.
Salt Lake City, Utah Office: One Utah Center, 201 South Main Street, Suite 1200.
Telephone: 801-531-3000.
Fax: 801-531-3001.
Washington, D.C. Office: Suite 900 East, 555 13th Street, N.W.
Telephone: 202-383-8800.
Fax: 202-383-8877; 383-8893.
Baltimore, Maryland Office: 300 East Lombard Street, 19th Floor.
Telephone: 410-528-5600.
Fax: 410-528-5650.
Camden, New Jersey Office: 800 Hudson Square, 5th Floor.
Telephone: 609-541-5577.
Fax: 609-541-8272.

Scott W. Hardt

For Complete List of Firm Personnel, See General Section

For full biographical listings, see the Martindale-Hubbell Law Directory

ROBERT L. BARTHOLIC (AV)

Suite 500, 1600 Broadway, 80202
Telephone: 303-830-0500
Fax: 303-860-7855
(Also Of Counsel to Clarence L. Bartholic, Englewood, Colorado and Associate to Hamilton and Faatz, A Professional Corporation, Denver, Colorado)

OF COUNSEL
Clarence L. Bartholic

Approved Attorney for: Mid-South Title Insurance Corp; Lawyers Title Insurance Co.

(See Next Column)

Representative Clients: Anschutz Corp.; Denver and Rio Grande Western Railroad Co.; Johnson Anderson Mortgage Co.; Arco Environmental Affairs; Burlington Northern Railroad Co. and Subsidiaries; American Association of Private Railroad Car Owners, Inc.
References: Colorado National Bank; Colorado State Bank.

For full biographical listings, see the Martindale-Hubbell Law Directory

BURNS WALL SMITH AND MUELLER, A PROFESSIONAL CORPORATION (AV)

303 East Seventeenth Avenue Suite 800, 80203-1260
Telephone: 303-830-7000
Telecopier: 303-830-6708
Email: BWSM@MCIMAIL.COM

Peter J. Wall   James E. Bosik
Gregory J. Smith   Steven F. Mueller
George W. Mueller   Robert T. Cosgrove

Gretchen L. Aultman   Donald D. Farlow

OF COUNSEL
Thomas M. Burns   Darrell C. Miller
Frank H. Houck   Anthony van Westrum

SPECIAL COUNSEL
John D. Amen   Robert Neece
Jack M. Merritts

Representative Clients: Snyder Oil Corporation; Amoco Production Company; Cabot Oil & Gas Production Corp.; Mull Drilling Company, Inc.; Presidio Exploration, Inc.; Northern Geophysical of America Inc.; Bannon Energy Incorporated; Harvard Gold Mining Co.; St. Mary Parish Land & Exploration Company; Veritas Energy Services (US), Inc.

For full biographical listings, see the Martindale-Hubbell Law Directory

DUFFORD & BROWN, P.C. (AV)

1700 Broadway, Suite 1700, 80290-1701
Telephone: 303-861-8013
Facsimile: 303-832-3804
Affiliated Office: Solomon, Pearl, Blum & Quinn, L.L.P., New York, NY and Denver, Colorado.

Philip G. Dufford   Phillip D. Barber
William C. Robb   Jack F. Ross
Richard L. Fanyo   Eugene F. Megyesy, Jr.

Joanne Herlihy
OF COUNSEL
Morris B. Hecox, Jr.

Representative Clients: BHP-Minerals, Inc.; CF&I Steel Corp.; Chevron Shale Oil Company; Coors Brewing Company; Denver Water Department; Echo Bay-Sunnyside Gold; Powderhorn Coal Co.; Energy Fuels Coal, Inc.; Equitable Resources Energy Company (Balcron Oil Division); Howell Petroleum Company.

For Complete List of Firm Personnel, See General Section

For full biographical listings, see the Martindale-Hubbell Law Directory

FRIEDLOB SANDERSON RASKIN PAULSON & TOURTILLOTT, LLC (AV)

1400 Glenarm Place, 80202-5099
Telephone: 303-571-1400
Fax: 303-595-3159; 303-595-3970; 303-615-5472
Email: 72731.505@Compuserve.Com
Englewood, Colorado Office: 8400 East Prentice Avenue, 80111-2918.
Telephone: 303-571-1400.

James W. Sanderson   W. B. Tourtillott
Christopher R. Paulson   Herrick K. Lidstone, Jr.

For full biographical listings, see the Martindale-Hubbell Law Directory

HOLME ROBERTS & OWEN LLP (AV)

Suite 4100, 1700 Lincoln, 80203
Telephone: 303-861-7000
Telecopier: 303-866-0200
Email: hro@hro.com *URL:* http://www.hro.com
Boulder, Colorado Office: Suite 400, 1401 Pearl Street.
Telephone: 303-444-5955.
Telecopier: 303-444-1063.
Colorado Springs, Colorado Office: Suite 1300, 90 South Cascade Avenue.
Telephone: 719-473-3800.
Telecopier: 719-633-1518.
Salt Lake City, Utah Office: Suite 1100, 111 East Broadway.
Telephone: 801-521-5800.
Telecopier: 801-521-9639.
London, England Office: Mellier House, 26a Albemarle Street.
Telephone: 44-171-499-8776.
Telecopier: 44-171-499-7769.

(See Next Column)

HOLME ROBERTS & OWEN LLP, *Denver—Continued*

Moscow, Russia Office: Kosmodamianskaya Nab. #52/1, Suite 9100, 113054.
Telephone: 7095-961-3000.
Telecopier: 7095-961-3001.
Kiev, Ukraine Office: Terestchenkovskaya #19, Suite 2, 252004.
Telephone: 380-44-224-1348.
Telecopier: 380-44-224-4986.

PARTNERS OF FIRM

Paul D. Holleman	Thomas F. Cope
Frank Erisman	Lynn Parker Hendrix
William D. Watson	Jan N. Steiert
William R. Roberts (Managing	Marla J. Williams
Partner, Boulder Office)	Steven B. Richardson
David K. Detton	James F. Cress
(Salt Lake City Office)	Kevin P. Block (Managing
	Partner, Kiev Office)

OF COUNSEL

Ted P. Stockmar	A. Edgar Benton
Kay M. Small (Boulder Office)	

ASSOCIATES

Edward E. Abels, Jr.	Peter O. Hansen
Denise M. DeForest	J. Alison Shelton

For Complete List of Firm Personnel, See General Section

For full biographical listings, see the Martindale-Hubbell Law Directory

---

JONES & KELLER, A PROFESSIONAL CORPORATION (AV)

Suite 1600, 1625 Broadway, 80202
Telephone: 303-573-1600
Fax: 303-893-6506

Marion F. Jones (1898-1978)	Thomas J. Burke, Jr.
Alec J. Keller (1913-1995)	Samuel E. Wing
Alvin J. Meiklejohn, Jr.	Reid A. Godbolt
Leslie R. Kehl	Rodney D. Knutson
Edward T. Lyons, Jr.	Kevin L. Brown
David E. Driggers	Barry L. Wilkie

Howard R. Hertzberg	Brent Nicholls
David A. Thayer	Michael Brian Cavanaugh
	Nathan D. Simmons

Reference: Colorado State Bank; Union Bank & Trust.

For full biographical listings, see the Martindale-Hubbell Law Directory

---

LOHF, SHAIMAN & JACOBS, P.C. (AV)

950 South Cherry Street, Suite 900, 80222
Telephone: 303-753-9000
Telecopier: 303-753-9997

David G. Ebner	J. Michael Morgan

Reference: Professional Bank.

For full biographical listings, see the Martindale-Hubbell Law Directory

---

NETZORG & MCKEEVER, PROFESSIONAL CORPORATION (AV)

Republic Plaza, 370 Seventeenth Street, Suite 3590, 80202
Telephone: 303-892-7100
Fax: 303-446-0506

Gordon W. Netzorg	Peter G. Koclanes
Cecil E. Morris, Jr.	Joan M. Collopy

OF COUNSEL
J. Nicholas McKeever, Jr.

For full biographical listings, see the Martindale-Hubbell Law Directory

---

PARCEL, MAURO, HULTIN & SPAANSTRA, P.C. (AV)

Suite 3600, 1801 California Street, 80202
Telephone: 303-292-6400
Telecopier: 303-295-3040

James K. Aronstein	Dean R. Massey
Jeffrey H. Desautels	Brian E. McGee
William J. Duffy	Habib Nasrullah
William A. Hillhouse II	Randy L. Parcel
James M. King	Kenneth L. Salazar
William R. Marsh	Don H. Sherwood

OF COUNSEL
Peggy E. Montaño

Jeffrey K. Reeser	Jeffrey W. Schwarz

Reference: 1st Interstate, Denver, Colorado.

For Complete List of Firm Personnel, See General Section

For full biographical listings, see the Martindale-Hubbell Law Directory

---

POULSON, ODELL & PETERSON, LLC (AV)

Suite 1400, 1775 Sherman Street, 80203
Telephone: 303-861-4400
Telecopier: 303-861-1225

William G. Odell	Stephen M. Thompson
C. M. (Pete) Peterson (Retired)	Carleton L. Ekberg
Randall M. Case	Alan B. Cameron
	MaryBeth Sobel

OF COUNSEL

Robert D. Poulson	Robert D. Buettner
Arthur Thad Smith	James W. Campbell (Retired)

William F. Leonard	Scott M. Campbell
	Mark Andrew Schlageter

Representative Clients: Apache Corporation; Anadarko Petroleum Corp.; Burlington Resources Oil & Gas Company; Conoco, Inc.; Enron Oil and Gas Co.; Exxon Co., USA; Fort Collins Consolidated Royalties, Inc.; Mobil Oil Corp.; Samedan Oil Corp.

For full biographical listings, see the Martindale-Hubbell Law Directory

---

ROOT & SCHINDLER, P.C. (AV)

410 17th Street, Suite 840, 80202
Telephone: 303-572-1235
Fax: 303-572-1256
Email: rootschi@ix.netcom.com

Thomas E. Root	Ronald I. Schindler

OF COUNSEL
F. Alan Fletcher

For full biographical listings, see the Martindale-Hubbell Law Directory

---

SHERMAN & HOWARD L.L.C. (AV)

Attorneys and Counselors at Law
633 Seventeenth Street, Suite 3000, 80202
Telephone: 303-297-2900
Telecopier: 303-298-0940
Colorado Springs, Colorado Office: Suite 1500, 90 South Cascade Avenue, 80903.
Telephone: 719-475-2440.
Las Vegas, Nevada Office: Swendseid & Stern a member in Sherman & Howard L.L.C., 317 Sixth Street, 89101.
Telephone: 702-387-6073.
Reno, Nevada Office: Swendseid & Stern, a member in Sherman & Howard L.L.C., 50 West Liberty Street, Suite 660, 89501.
Telephone: 702-323-1980.

Alan J. Gilbert	Ronald M. Eddy

COUNSEL
Gary L. Greer

Representative Clients: Newmont Gold Corp.; Benson Mineral Co.

For Complete List of Firm Personnel, See General Section

For full biographical listings, see the Martindale-Hubbell Law Directory

---

WELBORN SULLIVAN MECK & TOOLEY, P.C. (AV)

1775 Sherman Street, Suite 1800, 80203-4318
Telephone: 303-830-2500
Facsimile: 303-832-2366
Email: wsmt.denver@mep-1.sprint.com
Republic of Kazakstan Branch Office: 480100 Almaty 38 Dostyk Prospect, Suite 703.
Telephone: +7-3272 617-422; 616-509; 616-642.
Fax: +7-3272 615-840. *Email:* wsmt.welborn@mep-1.sprint.com.

John F. Welborn	Marla E. Valdez
John F. Meck	Karen Ostrander-Krug

Scott L. Sells

For Complete List of Firm Personnel, See General Section

For full biographical listings, see the Martindale-Hubbell Law Directory

---

LOUISVILLE, Boulder Co.

STEPHEN T. WILLIAMSON (AV)

813 Main, P.O. Box 850, 80027
Telephone: 303-666-4060
Fax: 303-666-4426
Email: louislaw@netone.com *URL:*
http://www.home.netone.com/~louislaw

(See Next Column)

STEPHEN T. WILLIAMSON—*Continued*
ASSOCIATE
Alan G. Hill

For full biographical listings, see the Martindale-Hubbell Law Directory

DISTRICT OF COLUMBIA

WASHINGTON, D.C. Co.

* indicates certain Bar Register subscribers, in cities of comparable size and importance, who maintain an additional office in Washington, D.C. and who have arranged for representation as a part of the Washington, D.C. listings that follow

* BAKER & BOTTS, L.L.P. (AV)

A Registered Limited Liability Partnership
The Warner, 1299 Pennsylvania Avenue, N.W., 20004-2400
Telephone: 202-639-7700
Fax: 202-639-7832
Email: postmaster@bakerbotts.com
Houston, Texas Office: One Shell Plaza, 910 Louisiana.
Telephone: 713-229-1234.
Austin, Texas Office: 1600 San Jacinto Center, 98 San Jacinto Boulevard.
Telephone: 512-322-2500.
Dallas, Texas Office: 2001 Ross Avenue.
Telephone: 214-953-6500.
New York, New York Office: 599 Lexington Avenue.
Telephone: 212-705-5000.
Moscow, Russian Federation Office: 10 ul. Bolshaya Dmitrovka (formerly Pushkinskaya), 103031.
Telephone: 7095/921-5300 (Local); 7501/929-7070 (International).

MEMBERS OF FIRM

J. Patrick Berry	Steven R. Hunsicker
William M. Bumpers	Bruce F. Kiely
Charles M. Darling, IV	Steven L. Leifer
Thomas J. Eastment	Randolph Quaile McManus
	Hugh Tucker

ASSOCIATES

Debra Raggio Bolton	Jennifer S. Leete
Debra J. Jezouit	Mark K. Lewis

For Complete List of Firm Personnel, See General Section

For full biographical listings, see the Martindale-Hubbell Law Directory

BRICKFIELD, BURCHETTE & RITTS, P.C. (AV)

8th Floor, West Tower, 1025 Thomas Jefferson Street, N.W., 20007-0805
Telephone: 202-342-0800
Fax: 202-342-0807
Austin, Texas Office: Suite 1050, 1005 Congress Avenue.
Telephone: 512-472-1081.

Peter J. P. Brickfield	Michael N. McCarty
William H. Burchette	Frederick H. Ritts
Mark C. Davis (Not admitted in DC; Resident, Austin, Texas Office)	Fernando Rodriguez (Not admitted in DC; Resident, Austin, Texas Office)
Michael E. Kaufmann	Christine C. Ryan
Peter J. Mattheis	Garrett A. Stone

COUNSEL

James W. Brew (Not admitted in DC)	Robert L. McCarty A. Hewitt Rose

Dean S. Brockbank (Not admitted in DC)	Julie B. Greenisen
Elizabeth Grieco Cunningham (Resident, Austin, Texas Office)	Stephen J. Karina (Not admitted in DC)
	Christopher C. O'Hara
Vincent P. Duane	Sonnet C. Schmidt
	Damon E. Xenopoulos

For full biographical listings, see the Martindale-Hubbell Law Directory

COHEN, MILSTEIN, HAUSFELD & TOLL, P.L.L.C. (AV)

West Tower, Suite 500, 1100 New York Avenue, N.W., 20005-3964
Telephone: 202-408-4600
Facsimile: 202-408-4699

MEMBERS OF FIRM

Jerry S. Cohen (1925-1995)	Lisa M. Mezzetti
Herbert E. Milstein	Andrew N. Friedman
Michael D. Hausfeld	Richard S. Lewis
Steven J. Toll	Daniel S. Sommers
Ann C. Yahner	Daniel A. Small (Not admitted in DC)

(See Next Column)

ASSOCIATES

Gary E. Mason	Michael J. Flannery
Cyrus Mehri	Paul T. Gallagher
Sharon A. Snyder	Alexander E. Barnett
Mark S. Willis (Not admitted in DC)	Angeline G. Chen
	Victoria C. Arthaud
Lillian S. Hagen	(Not admitted in DC)

OF COUNSEL
Anthony Z. Roisman

For full biographical listings, see the Martindale-Hubbell Law Directory

CUTLER & STANFIELD, L.L.P. (AV)

700 Fourteenth Street, N.W., 20005-2010
Telephone: 202-624-8400
Fax: 202-624-8410
Denver, Colorado Office: 1675 Broadway, 80202.
Telephone: 303-825-7000.
FAX: 303-825-7005.

MEMBERS OF FIRM

Eliot R. Cutler	Peter J. Kirsch
Jeffrey L. Stanfield	Barry Conaty
Sheila D. Jones	Stephen H. Kaplan
Perry M. Rosen	(Not admitted in DC)

OF COUNSEL

Byron Keith Huffman, Jr.	Sarah M. Rockwell (Not admitted in DC)

ASSOCIATES

Katherine Boonin Andrus	Dana C. Nifosi
Françoise M. Carrier	Barbara Paley
Christopher M. Kamper (Not admitted in DC)	W. Eric Pilsk
	Timothy A. Pohle
William G. Malley	Thomas D. Roth

For full biographical listings, see the Martindale-Hubbell Law Directory

FREEDMAN, LEVY, KROLL & SIMONDS (AV)

Suite 825, 1050 Connecticut Avenue, N.W., 20036-5366
Telephone: 202-457-5100
Cable Address: "Attorneys"
Telecopier: 202-457-5151
Email: flks@flks.com *URL:* http://www.flks.com/home/flks

MEMBER OF FIRM
Lawrence G. McBride

OF COUNSEL

Arnold Levy	Jerome H. Simonds

For Complete List of Firm Personnel, See General Section

For full biographical listings, see the Martindale-Hubbell Law Directory

FRANK W. FRISK, JR., P.C. (AV)

Suite 125, Canal Square, 1054 Thirty-First Street, N.W., 20007
Telephone: 202-333-8433
Fax: 202-333-8431

Frank W. Frisk, Jr.

For full biographical listings, see the Martindale-Hubbell Law Directory

KROOTH & ALTMAN (AV)

Suite 400, 1850 M Street, N.W., 20036-5803
Telephone: 202-293-8200
Telecopier: 202-872-0145, 202-775-5872
Columbia, Maryland Office: 5401 Twin Knolls Road, Suite 7, 21045.
Telephone: 301-596-1140.
Sterling, Virginia Office: 45591 Shepard Drive, Suite 101J, 20164.
Telephone: 703-450-2755.

MEMBERS OF FIRM

David L. Krooth (1907-1978)	Daniel Randolph Cole, Jr.
Norman S. Altman (Retired)	Patrick J. Clancy
William S. Tennant	James F. Perna
William J. Delany	Harrison C. Smith
Donald F. Libretta	Mario Greszes
E. Joseph Knoll	David A. Barsky
Michael E. Mazer	John E. Vihstadt
	Bonnie Hochman Rothell

OF COUNSEL

Victor A. Altman	Michael J. Milton
J. Stephen Britt	Robert J. Siciliano

ASSOCIATES

Jon I. Opert	Stephen J. Krooth
Felicia M. Groner	(Not admitted in DC)

For full biographical listings, see the Martindale-Hubbell Law Directory

ROBERT E. LOSCH, P.C. (AV)

1716 New Hampshire Avenue, N.W., 20009
Telephone: 202-296-4222

(See Next Column)

ROBERT E. LOSCH, P.C., *Washington—Continued*

Robert E. Losch

MORLEY CASKIN (AV)

1225 Eye Street, N.W., Suite 402, 20005
Telephone: 202-789-1100
Facsimile: 202-289-3928

OF COUNSEL
Stanley M. Morley (1912-1991)

MEMBERS OF FIRM

Joel F. Zipp   William A. Mogel
George H. Williams, Jr.

ASSOCIATE
Rita L. Wecker (Not admitted in DC)

For full biographical listings, see the Martindale-Hubbell Law Directory

---

PIERSON SEMMES AND BEMIS (AV)

Canal Square, 1054 31st Street, N.W., 20007
Telephone: 202-333-4000
Telex: 248528 PSF UR;
Telecopier: 202-965-0100

MEMBERS OF FIRM

W. DeVier Pierson	William C. Lieblich
David H. Semmes	David J. Hill
Douglas Knox Bemis, Jr.	David F. B. Smith
Peter J. Levin	Paul Ryberg, Jr.
Mark E. Greenwold	Thomas S. Warrick

Gerard A. Clark

ASSOCIATES

Clinton E. Cameron   Tamara R. Gelboin

For Complete List of Firm Personnel, See General Section

For full biographical listings, see the Martindale-Hubbell Law Directory

---

* VENABLE ATTORNEYS AT LAW VENABLE, BAETJER, HOWARD & CIVILETTI, LLP (AV)

A Partnership including Professional Corporations
Suite 1000, 1201 New York Avenue, N.W., 20005
Telephone: 202-962-4800
Fax: 202-962-8300
Baltimore, Maryland Office: Venable, Baetjer and Howard LLP, 1800 Mercantile Bank & Trust Building, 2 Hopkins Plaza.
Telephone: 410-244-7400.
McLean, Virginia Office: Venable, Baetjer and Howard LLP, Suite 400, 2010 Corporate Ridge.
Telephone: 703-760-1600.
Rockville, Maryland Office: Venable, Baetjer and Howard LLP, Suite 500, One Church Street, P. O. Box 1906.
Telephone: 301-217-5600.
Towson, Maryland Office: Venable, Baetjer and Howard LLP, 210 Allegheny Avenue, P. O. Box 5517.
Telephone: 410-494-6200.

MEMBERS OF FIRM

Benjamin R. Civiletti (P.C.) (Also at Baltimore and Towson, Maryland Offices)	Judson W. Starr (Also at Baltimore and Towson, Maryland Offices)
Anthony M. Carey (Not admitted in DC; Also at Baltimore, Maryland Office)	Jeffrey A. Dunn (Also at Baltimore, Maryland Office)
John G. Milliken (Also at McLean, Virginia Office)	James L. Shea (Not admitted in DC; also at Baltimore, Maryland Office)
Joseph G. Block	John J. Pavlick, Jr.
Michael Schatzow (Also at Baltimore, Maryland Office)	James A. Dunbar (Also at Baltimore, Maryland Office)
John F. Cooney	Thomas J. Kelly, Jr.
James K. Archibald (Also at Baltimore, Maryland Office)	

ASSOCIATES

Gregory S. Braker   Andrew R. Herrup
Valerie K. Mann

For Complete List of Firm Personnel, See General Section

For full biographical listings, see the Martindale-Hubbell Law Directory

---

VERNER, LIIPFERT, BERNHARD, McPHERSON AND HAND, CHARTERED (AV)

901 15th Street, N.W., 20005-2301
Telephone: 202-371-6000
Cable Address: "Verlip"
Telex: 1561792 VERLIP UT
Fax: 202-371-6279
Email: verner.com
McLean, Virginia Office: Sixth Floor, 8280 Greensboro Drive, 22102.
Telephone: 703-749-6000.
Fax: 703-749-6027.

(See Next Column)

Houston, Texas Office: 2600 Texas Commerce Tower, 600 Travis, 77002.
Telephone: 713-237-9034.
Fax: 713-237-1216.
Honolulu, Hawaii Office: Hawaii Times Building, 928 Nuuanu Avenue, Suite 400, 96817.
Telephone: 808-566-0999.
Fax: 808-566-0995.
Austin, Texas Office: Suite 1440 San Jacinto Center, 98 San Jacinto Boulevard, 78701.
Telephone: 512-703-6000.
Fax: 512-703-6003.

Douglas Ochs Adler	Glen L. Ortman
J. Cathy Fogel	Clinton A. Vince
Andrea Jill Grant	Bernhardt K. Wruble
Gary J. Klein	John H. Zentay

For Complete List of Firm Personnel, See General Section

For full biographical listings, see the Martindale-Hubbell Law Directory

---

FLORIDA

MIAMI, * Dade Co.

EARL, BLANK, KAVANAUGH & STOTTS, PROFESSIONAL ASSOCIATION (AV)

Suite 3636, One Biscayne Tower, Two South Biscayne Boulevard, 33131
Telephone: 305-358-3000
FAX: 305-358-5079
Email: ebks@aol.com
Sarasota, Florida Office: 1800 Second Street.
Telephone: 941-366-1180.
Fax: 941-366-1183. E-Mail: ebkssrq@aol.com.

William L. Earl	Dennis M. Stotts
Robert H. Blank	Mark T. Kobelinski
Judith Smith Kavanaugh	Stephen R. Verbit

Reference: NationsBank, N.A.

For full biographical listings, see the Martindale-Hubbell Law Directory

---

THOMSON MURARO RAZOOK & HART, P.A. (AV)

17th Floor, One Southeast Third Avenue, 33131
Telephone: 305-350-7200
Telecopier: 305-374-1005

Parker Davidson Thomson	Sarah L. Schweitzer
Robert E. Muraro	Carol A. Licko

Representative Clients: State of Florida; United States Sugar Corporation.

For Complete List of Firm Personnel, See General Section

For full biographical listings, see the Martindale-Hubbell Law Directory

---

PALM BEACH GARDENS, Palm Beach Co.

SCOTT, ROYCE, HARRIS, BRYAN, BARRA & JORGENSEN, PROFESSIONAL ASSOCIATION (AV)

4400 PGA Boulevard, Suite 800, 33410
Telephone: 561-624-3900
Fax: 561-624-3533

Raymond W. Royce	John M. Jorgensen
J. Richard Harris	Richard K. Barra
John L. Bryan, Jr.	Barry B. Byrd

Representative Clients: John D. and Catherine T. MacArthur Foundation; First Union National Bank of Florida, N.A.; The Realtors Association of the Palm Beaches, Inc.; Lost Tree Village; Jupiter Hills, Pappalardo Contractors, Inc.; Art Moran Pontiac, Inc.; Wal-Mart Stores, Inc.; Whitworth Farms; DuBois Growers.

For Complete List of Firm Personnel, See General Section

For full biographical listings, see the Martindale-Hubbell Law Directory

---

SARASOTA, * Sarasota Co.

EARL, BLANK, KAVANAUGH & STOTTS, PROFESSIONAL ASSOCIATION (AV)

1800 Second Street, Suite 888, 34236
Telephone: 941-366-1180
FAX: 941-366-1183
Email: ebkssrq@aol.com
Miami, Florida Office: Suite 3636, One Biscayne Tower, Two South Biscayne Boulevard.
Telephone: 305-358-3000.
Fax: 305-358-5079. E-Mail: ebks@aol.com.

(See Next Column)

EARL, BLANK, KAVANAUGH & STOTTS PROFESSIONAL ASSOCIATION—
Continued

William L. Earl	Dennis M. Stotts
Robert H. Blank	Mark T. Kobelinski
Judith Smith Kavanaugh	Stephen R. Verbit

Reference: NationsBank, N.A.

For full biographical listings, see the Martindale-Hubbell Law Directory

---

TALLAHASSEE, Leon Co.

HOPPING GREEN SAMS & SMITH, PROFESSIONAL ASSOCIATION (AV)

123 South Calhoun Street, P.O. Box 6526, 32314
Telephone: 904-222-7500
Fax: 904-224-8551

James S. Alves	Wade L. Hopping
Brian H. Bibeau	Frank E. Matthews
Kathleen L. Blizzard	Richard D. Melson
Elizabeth C. Bowman	David L. Powell
Richard S. Brightman	William D. Preston
Peter C. Cunningham	Carolyn S. Raepple
Ralph A. DeMeo	Douglas S. Roberts
Thomas M. DeRose	Gary P. Sams
William H. Green	Robert P. Smith
	Cheryl G. Stuart

Gary K. Hunter, Jr.	Karen Peterson
Jonathan T. Johnson	Michael P. Petrovich
Robert A. Manning	R. Scott Ruth
Angela R. Morrison	W. Steve Sykes
Gary V. Perko	T. Kent Wetherell, II

OF COUNSEL
W. Robert Fokes

Representative Clients: Atlantic Gulf Communities; Dunes and Viera East Community Development Districts; Florida Electric Power Coordinating Group; Florida Power & Light Co.; MCI Telecommunications; Seminole Electric Co.; Sugar Cane Growers Cooperative of Florida; UPS; Waste Management, Inc.; Wheelabrator.

For full biographical listings, see the Martindale-Hubbell Law Directory

---

TAMPA, Hillsborough Co.

HONIGMAN MILLER SCHWARTZ AND COHN (AV)

A Partnership including Professional Associations
2700 SunTrust Financial Centre, 401 E. Jackson Street, 33602-5226
Telephone: 813-221-6600
Telecopier: 813-223-4410
URL: http://law.honigman.com
West Palm Beach, Florida Office: Suite 800 Esperante Building, 222 Lakeview Avenue, 33401-6112.
Telephone: 561-838-4500.
Detroit, Michigan Office: 2290 First National Building, 48226.
Telephone: 313-256-7800.
Lansing, Michigan Office: 222 North Washington Square, Suite 400, 48933-1800.
Telephone: 517-484-8282.

MEMBERS

Michael G. Cooke (P.A.)	John W. Voelpel

For Complete List of Firm Personnel, See General Section

For full biographical listings, see the Martindale-Hubbell Law Directory

---

WEST PALM BEACH, Palm Beach Co.

HONIGMAN MILLER SCHWARTZ AND COHN (AV)

A Partnership including Professional Associations
Suite 800 Esperante Building, 222 Lakeview Avenue, 33401-6112
Telephone: 561-838-4500
Telecopier: 561-832-3036; 832-2645
URL: http://law.honigman.com
Tampa, Florida Office: 2700 SunTrust Financial Centre, 401 E. Jackson Street, 33602-5226.
Telephone: 813-221-6600.
Detroit, Michigan Office: 2290 First National Building, 48226.
Telephone: 313-256-7800.
Lansing, Michigan Office: 222 North Washington Square, Suite 400, 48933-1800.
Telephone: 517-484-8282.

MEMBERS

Carla L. Brown (P.A.)	E. Lee Worsham (P.A.)

Representative Clients: Adler Group, Inc.; Chiquita Brands, Inc.; E. Llwyd Ecclestone, Jr.; Forbes/Cohen Properties; ITT-Rayonier, Inc.; National Advertising Company; Pulte Corporation (Pulte Home Corp.); Thos. J. White Development Corp.; Linpro, Inc.; Rubin Periodical Group-FEC News.

(See Next Column)

For Complete List of Firm Personnel, See General Section

For full biographical listings, see the Martindale-Hubbell Law Directory

---

JONES, FOSTER, JOHNSTON & STUBBS, P.A. (AV)

Flagler Center Tower, 505 South Flagler Drive, Suite 1100, P.O. Box 3475, 33402-3475
Telephone: 561-659-3000
Fax: 561-832-1454

Sidney A. Stubbs	Peter A. Sachs
John Blair McCracken	Michael T. Kranz
John C. Randolph	John S. Trimper
Herbert Adams Weaver, Jr.	Mark B. Kleinfeld
Larry B. Alexander	Scott Gardner Hawkins
Thornton M. Henry	Steven J. Rothman
Margaret L. Cooper	Rebecca G. Doane
D. Culver Smith, III	Carl Angeloff (P.A.)
Allen R. Tomlinson	H. Michael Easley
Peter S. Holton	Joyce A. Conway

Christopher S. Duke	Edward Diaz
Scott L. McMullen	David Pratt
M. Tracey Biagiotti	Brian K. Waxman
Clay C. Brooker	David E. Dreyer
	(Not admitted in FL)

Counsel for: U.S. Trust Co.; NationsBank of Florida, N.A.; Island National Bank; Bankers Trust Company of Florida; Sun Bank/South Florida, N.A.; General Motors Acceptance Corp.

For full biographical listings, see the Martindale-Hubbell Law Directory

---

HAWAII

HONOLULU, Honolulu Co.

DWYER IMANAKA SCHRAFF KUDO MEYER & FUJIMOTO ATTORNEYS AT LAW, A LAW CORPORATION (AV)

1800 Pioneer Plaza, 900 Fort Street Mall, 96813
Telephone: 808-524-8000
Telecopier: 808-526-1419
Mailing Address: P.O. Box 2727, 96803
Email: hawaiilaw@dwyer-imanaka.com *URL:* http://www.dwyer-imanaka.com

John R. Dwyer, Jr.	William G. Meyer, III
Mitchell A. Imanaka	Wesley M. Fujimoto
Paul A. Schraff	Ronald Van Grant
Benjamin A. Kudo (Atty. at Law, A Law Corp.)	Jon M. H. Pang
	Blake W. Bushnell
	Adelbert Green

Richard T. Asato, Jr.	Jeffery S. Werbelow
Scott W. Settle	Lori Ann K. Koseki
Darcie S. Yoshinaga	Troy T. Fukuhara
Lawrence I. Kawasaki	Katy Y. Chen
Stacy E. Uehara	Naomi S. Uyeno
Kris N. Nakagawa	Roger B. McKeague

OF COUNSEL

Randall Y. Iwase	R. Brian Tsujimura

For full biographical listings, see the Martindale-Hubbell Law Directory

---

IDAHO

BOISE, Ada Co.

EBERLE, BERLIN, KADING, TURNBOW & McKLVEEN, CHARTERED (AV)

Capitol Park Plaza, 300 North Sixth Street, P.O. Box 1368, 83701
Telephone: 208-344-8535
Facsimile: 208-344-8542

William J. McKlveen	Bradley G. Andrews
Scott D. Hess	Stephen A. Bradbury

Representative Clients: Idaho Timber Corporation; Canfor U.S.A. Corporation.

For Complete List of Firm Personnel, See General Section

For full biographical listings, see the Martindale-Hubbell Law Directory

Boise—Continued

ELAM & BURKE, A PROFESSIONAL ASSOCIATION (AV)

Key Financial Center, 702 West Idaho Street, P.O. Box 1539, 83701
Telephone: 208-343-5454
Telecopier: 208-384-5844
Email: eblaw@elamburke.com

Carl P. Burke	Scott L. Campbell
John Magel	Harry M. Lane, Jr.

Jeffrey W. Pusch

Representative Clients: Morrison-Knudsen, Inc.; Texas Instruments, Inc.; Pechiney Corp.; Dow Corning Corporation; State Farm Insurance Cos.; Sinclair Oil Co. d/b/a Sun Valley Co.; Farmers Insurance Group; MK Gold Co.; Thompson Creek Mining Company.

For Complete List of Firm Personnel, See General Section

For full biographical listings, see the Martindale-Hubbell Law Directory

KETCHUM, Blaine Co.

JAMES L. KENNEDY, JR. (AV)

340 Second Street East, P.O. Box 2165, 83340
Telephone: 208-726-8255

Reference: First Interstate Bank of Idaho, N.A. (Ketchum-Sun Valley Branch); First Security Bank of Idaho, N.A. (Ketchum Branch)

For full biographical listings, see the Martindale-Hubbell Law Directory

ILLINOIS

MATTOON, Coles Co.

CRAIG & CRAIG (AV)

1807 Broadway, P.O. Box 689, 61938-0689
Telephone: 217-234-6481
Telecopier: 217-234-6486
Mount Vernon, Illinois Office: 227 1/2 South 9th Street.
Telephone: 618-244-7511.

MEMBERS OF FIRM

Craig Van Meter (1895-1981)	Stephen L. Corn
Fred H. Kelly (1894-1971)	Richard Charles Hayden
Robert M. Werden (1908-1969)	Robert G. Grierson
George N. Gilkerson (1911-1985)	Gregory C. Ray
John H. Armstrong	Paul R. Lynch (Resident, Mount Vernon Office)
John P. Ewart	Kenneth F. Werts (Resident, Mount Vernon Office)
Richard F. Record, Jr.	

John L. Barger

ASSOCIATES

Joshua N. Rosen (Resident, Mount Vernon Office)	Theresa M. Thomson
Kathleen M. Stockwell	Kristine M. Tuttle
	Henry P. Villani (Resident, Mount Vernon Office)

OF COUNSEL

Jack E. Horsley

Counsel for: Monterey Coal Co., a Division of Exxon Coal USA, Inc.; Marathon Oil Co.; Illinois Central R.R. Co.; Okaw Building & Loan Assn., Mattoon, Illinois; The Medical Protective Insurance Co.; Consolidated Communications, Inc.; Lloyds Underwriters at London; Hartford Insurance Co.; Coles Together, a Not-For-Profit Corp.; Coles Building Corporation.

For full biographical listings, see the Martindale-Hubbell Law Directory

INDIANA

*EVANSVILLE,** Vanderburgh Co.

BUTHOD & BUTHOD (AV)

4962 Lincoln Avenue, P.O. Box 2298, 47728-0298
Telephone: 812-473-8500
Fax: 812-473-8505

MEMBERS OF FIRM

James M. Buthod	John J. Buthod

Representative Clients: Ashland Oil, Inc.; Big Seven Drilling; Butler Petroleum Corp.; Citizen's Gas & Coke Utility (Indianapolis); Downen Production Co.; Duke Resources Corp.; Farm Bureau Oil Co., Inc.; V. R. Gallagher (Oil Producer); Gallagher Drilling, Inc.; Mobil Oil Corp.

For full biographical listings, see the Martindale-Hubbell Law Directory

---

*INDIANAPOLIS,** Marion Co.

ICE MILLER DONADIO & RYAN (AV)

One American Square Box 82001, 46282-0002
Telephone: 317-236-2100
Fax: 317-236-2219
Email: leel@imdr.com *URL:* http://www.imdr.com
South Bend, Indiana Office: 211 West Washington Street, Suite 2420.
Telephone: 219-234-7933.
Fax: 219-234-7965. Internet E-mail: leel@imdr.com. Web Site Address: http://www.imdr.com.

MEMBERS OF FIRM

G. Daniel Kelley, Jr.	Phillip L. Bayt

For Complete List of Firm Personnel, See General Section

For full biographical listings, see the Martindale-Hubbell Law Directory

PLEWS SHADLEY RACHER & BRAUN (AV)

1346 North Delaware Street, 46202-2415
Telephone: 317-637-0700
Telecopier: 317-637-0710

MEMBERS OF FIRM

George M. Plews	Peter M. Racher
Sue A. Shadley	Christopher J. Braun
	Jeffrey D. Claflin

ASSOCIATES

Harinder Kaur	Jeffrey D. Featherstun
Leonardo D. Robinson	Donna C. Marron
Frederick D. Emhardt	Michael A. Myers
S. Curtis DeVoe	Julie E. Polizzotto

OF COUNSEL

Christine C. H. Plews	Timothy J. Paris

For full biographical listings, see the Martindale-Hubbell Law Directory

TABBERT HAHN EARNEST & STARKEY, P.C. (AV)

Suite 2100, One Indiana Square, 46204
Telephone: 317-639-5444
Fax: 317-639-5232

Mark K. Sullivan

OF COUNSEL

Douglas E. Cregor

For full biographical listings, see the Martindale-Hubbell Law Directory

*MT. VERNON,** Posey Co.

HAWLEY, HUDSON & HAWLEY (AV)

309 Main Street, P.O. Box 716, 47620
Telephone: 812-838-4495
Fax: 812-838-9445

MEMBERS OF FIRM

K. Richard Hawley	Henry C. Hudson
	Marc E. Hawley

Representative Clients: Sohio Supply Co.; Farm Bureau Oil Co.; Wade Oil Corp.; Conyers Oil Service, Inc.; Coy Oil, Inc.; Trey Exploration, Inc.; Jarvis Drilling, Inc.; K.C. Oil Corp.; Ecus Corp.; Quinn Energy Corp.

For full biographical listings, see the Martindale-Hubbell Law Directory

*PRINCETON,** Gibson Co.

HALL, PARTENHEIMER & KINKLE (AV)

219 North Hart Street, P.O. Box 313, 47670
Telephone: 812-386-0050
FAX: 812-385-2575

MEMBERS OF FIRM

Verner P. Partenheimer	J. Robert Kinkle
	R. Scott Partenheimer

Representative Clients: Interlake Inc.; Gibson County Bank; Old Ben Coal Co.
Approved Attorneys for: Lawyers Title Insurance; Ticor Title Insurance.

For full biographical listings, see the Martindale-Hubbell Law Directory

KANSAS

*WICHITA,** Sedgwick Co.

ADAMS, JONES, ROBINSON AND MALONE, CHARTERED (AV)

600 Market Centre, 155 North Market, P.O. Box 1034, 67201-1034
Telephone: 316-265-8591
Telecopier: 316-265-9719
Email: ajrm@southwind.net *URL:* http://www.southwind.net,~ajrm

(See Next Column)

ADAMS, JONES, ROBINSON AND MALONE CHARTERED—*Continued*

Clifford L. Malone   Donald W. Bostwick
Teresa J. James

Representative Clients: The Williams Companies, Inc.; Williams Natural Gas Co.; Oxy U.S.A., Inc.: BHP Petroleum (Americas) Inc.; Mesa Operating Limited Partnership.

For full biographical listings, see the Martindale-Hubbell Law Directory

FOULSTON & SIEFKIN L.L.P. (AV)

700 Fourth Financial Center, 67202
Telephone: 316-267-6371
Facsimile: 316-267-6345
Topeka, Kansas Office: 1515 Bank IV Tower, 534 Kansas Avenue, 66603.
Telephone: 913-233-3600.
Fax: 913-233-1610.
Dodge City, Kansas Office: 810 Frontview, P.O. Box 1147, 67801.
Telephone: 316-227-8126.
Fax: 316-227-8451.
Member: Lex Mundi, A Global Association of 126 Independent Firms.
MEMBERS OF FIRM

Charles J. Woodin   Jim H. Goering

For Complete List of Firm Personnel, See General Section

For full biographical listings, see the Martindale-Hubbell Law Directory

HERSHBERGER, PATTERSON, JONES & ROTH, L.C. (AV)

600 Hardage Center, 100 South Main, 67202-3779
Telephone: 316-263-7583
Fax: 316-263-7595

Jerome E. Jones   Robert J. Roth

Representative Clients: Anadarko Petroleum Corporation; Mobil Oil Co.; Murfin Drilling; J.M. Huber Corporation; Oxy Oil & Gas USA, Inc.; Panhandle Eastern Pipeline Co.; Rine Drilling & Exploration Company; Tesoro Petroleum Corp.; Triad Drilling Co.

For Complete List of Firm Personnel, See General Section

For full biographical listings, see the Martindale-Hubbell Law Directory

KAHRS, NELSON, FANNING, HITE & KELLOGG, L.L.P. (AV)

Suite 630, 200 West Douglas Street, 67202-3089
Telephone: 316-265-7761
Telecopier: 316-267-7803
MEMBERS OF FIRM

Richard C. Hite   John G. Pike
Steven D. Gough   Dennis V. Lacey
Donald N. Peterson, II
OF COUNSEL
Robert Hall

Representative Clients: Amoco Production Co.; Coastal Oil & Gas Corp.; Enron Oil & Gas Corp.; J.M. Huber Corp.; Marathon Oil Co.; Peoples Natural Gas Co.; Union Pacific Resources Co.

For Complete List of Firm Personnel, See General Section

For full biographical listings, see the Martindale-Hubbell Law Directory

MORRIS, LAING, EVANS, BROCK & KENNEDY, CHARTERED (AV)

Fourth Floor, 200 West Douglas, 67202-3084
Telephone: 316-262-2671
Fax: 316-262-6226; 262-5991
Topeka, Kansas Office: 800 S.W. Jackson, Suite 914, 66612-2214.
Telephone: 913-232-2662.
Fax: 913-232-9983.

Ralph R. Brock   Susan R. Schrag
Joseph W. Kennedy   Robert E. Nugent
Donald E. Schrag   Michael Lennen
Robert K. Anderson   Karl R. Swartz
Bruce A. Ney

References: The Emprise Banks of Kansas; Mercantile Bank of Topeka; Southwest National Bank; Twin Lakes National Bank.

For Complete List of Firm Personnel, See General Section

For full biographical listings, see the Martindale-Hubbell Law Directory

YOUNG, BOGLE, MCCAUSLAND, WELLS & CLARK, P.A. (AV)

106 West Douglas, Suite 923, 67202
Telephone: 316-265-7841
Facsimile: 316-265-3956

Glenn D. Young, Jr.   Paul S. McCausland
Mark R. Maloney

Representative Clients: Bridgestone/Firestone Inc.; Deere & Co.; Citibank; Metropolitan Life Insurance Co.; Equitable Life Assurance Society of the United States; New York Life Insurance Co.

(See Next Column)

For Complete List of Firm Personnel, See General Section

For full biographical listings, see the Martindale-Hubbell Law Directory

KENTUCKY

BOWLING GREEN,* Warren Co.

ENGLISH, LUCAS, PRIEST & OWSLEY (AV)

1101 College Street, P.O. Box 770, 42102-0770
Telephone: 502-781-6500
Telecopier: 502-782-7782
Email: inquiry@elpo.com
MEMBERS OF FIRM

Charles E. English   Keith M. Carwell
James H. Lucas   Murry A. Raines
Whayne C. Priest, Jr.   Kurt W. Maier
Michael A. Owsley   Charles E. English, Jr.
D. Gaines Penn
ASSOCIATE
Robert A. Young

General Counsel for: Medical Center at Bowling Green; Warren Rural Electric Cooperative Corporation; Trans Financial Bank, N.A.; Southern Sanitation, Inc.
Representative Clients: Commercial Union Insurance Cos.; Kemper Insurance Group; St. Paul Insurance Co.; Eaton Corp.; Desa International; Sumitomo Electric Wiring Systems, Inc.

For Complete List of Firm Personnel, See General Section

For full biographical listings, see the Martindale-Hubbell Law Directory

HAZARD,* Perry Co.

GULLETT & COMBS (AV)

109 Broadway, Second Floor, P.O. Box 1039, 41702-5039
Telephone: 606-439-1373
Fax: 606-439-4450
Email: pgullett@mis.net; rgcombs@mis.net
MEMBERS OF FIRM

Asa P. Gullett, III   Ronald G. Combs
ASSOCIATES
Teresa G. Combs Reed   Matthew Lawton Bowling
LEGAL SUPPORT PERSONNEL
Jacqueline E. Goodin   Jimmie Lynn Jones

Reference: Peoples Bank and Trust Co.

For full biographical listings, see the Martindale-Hubbell Law Directory

HENDERSON,* Henderson Co.

KING, DEEP AND BRANAMAN (AV)

127 North Main Street, P.O. Box 43, 42420
Telephone: 502-827-1852
FAX: 502-826-7729
MEMBERS OF FIRM

Leo King (1893-1982)   Harry L. Mathison, Jr.
William M. Deep (1920-1990)   W. Mitchell Deep, Jr.
William Branaman   H. Randall Redding
Dorin E. Luck
ASSOCIATES
Leslie M. Newman   Greg L. Gager

Counsel for: Reynolds Metals Co.; P B & S Chemical Co.; Jim R. Smith Coal Co.; Har-Ken Oil Co.; American Electric Power; Texas Gas Exploration; Ashland Oil, Inc.; Hercules Petroleum; Refuge Exploration Co., Inc.

For full biographical listings, see the Martindale-Hubbell Law Directory

LEXINGTON,* Fayette Co.

BUCHANAN INGERSOLL, PROFESSIONAL CORPORATION (AV)

Suite 600, PNC Bank Plaza, 200 West Vine Street, 40507
Telephone: 606-225-5333
Telecopier: 606-225-5334
Pittsburgh, Pennsylvania Office: One Oxford Centre, 301 Grant Street, 20th Floor.
Telephone: 412-562-8800.
Philadelphia, Pennsylvania Office: Two Logan Square, Twelfth Floor, 18th & Arch Streets.
Telephone: 215-665-8700.
Harrisburg, Pennsylvania Office: 30 North Third Street.
Telephone: 717-237-4800.
Tampa, Florida Office: 101 East Kennedy Boulevard, Suite 1030.
Telephone: 813-222-8180.
North Miami Beach, Florida Office: 19495 Biscayne Boulevard, Suite 606.
Telephone: 305-933-5600.

(See Next Column)

BUCHANAN INGERSOLL PROFESSIONAL CORPORATION, *Lexington—Continued*

Miami, Florida Office: Nationsbank Tower, 100 S.E. Second Street.
Telephone: 305-347-4080.
Princeton, New Jersey Office: Buchanan Ingersoll, A Partnership, College Centre, 500 College Road East.
Telephone: 609-987-6800.
Buffalo, New York Office: 1100 Main Place Tower, 350 Main Street.
Telephone: 716-854-4100.
Fax: 716-854-4227.

John R. Leathers

Stephen G. Allen

For full biographical listings, see the Martindale-Hubbell Law Directory

STITES & HARBISON (AV)

Formerly Stites, McElwain & Fowler and Harbison, Kessinger, Lisle & Bush
2300 Lexington Financial Center, 40507
Telephone: 606-226-2300
Louisville, Kentucky Office: 400 West Market Street, Suite 1800.
Telephone: 502-587-3400.
Frankfort, Kentucky Office: 421 West Main Street.
Telephone: 502-223-3477.
Jeffersonville, Indiana Office: 323 East Court Avenue.
Telephone: 812-282-7566.

MEMBERS OF FIRM

Thomas E. Meng   Laura D. Keller

COUNSEL

Calvert T. Roszell

For Complete List of Firm Personnel, See General Section

For full biographical listings, see the Martindale-Hubbell Law Directory

STOLL, KEENON & PARK, LLP (AV)

201 E. Main Street, Suite 1000, 40507-1380
Telephone: 606-231-3000
Telecopier: 606-253-1093; 606-253-1027
Frankfort, Kentucky Office: 307 Washington Street, 40601.
Telephone: 502-875-6220.
Telecopier: 502-875-6235.
Louisville, Kentucky Office: 400 West Market Street, Suite 2650, 40202-3377.
Telephone: 502-568-9100.
Telecopier: 502-568-5700.

MEMBERS OF FIRM

Lindsey W. Ingram, Jr.   Charles E. Shivel, Jr.
Spencer D. Noe   Diane M. Carlton
          J. Mel Camenisch, Jr.

Representative Clients: A. T. Massey Coal Co., Inc.; Cyprus Amax Mineral Co.; Delta Natural Gas Co., Inc.; Mapco, Inc.; Peabody Coal Co.; United Coal Co.; Western Pocahontas Corp.; Ziegler Coal Holding Co.

For Complete List of Firm Personnel, See General Section

For full biographical listings, see the Martindale-Hubbell Law Directory

PRESTONSBURG,* Floyd Co.

COMBS AND ISAAC (AV)

99 North Lake Drive, P.O. Box 189, 41653
Telephone: 606-886-2391; 886-2392
Fax: 606-886-2776

MEMBERS OF FIRM

James A. Combs   Gregory A. Isaac

For full biographical listings, see the Martindale-Hubbell Law Directory

KAZEE, KINNER & CHAFIN (AV)

119 East Court Street, P.O. Box 700, 41653
Telephone: 606-886-2361; 886-2362
FAX: 606-886-9603
Email: dbkazee@pcc-uky.campus.mci.net
Paintsville, Kentucky Office: Family Federal Building, Suite 202, P.O. Box 1275.
Telephone: 606-789-3059.

MEMBERS OF FIRM

D. B. Kazee   P. Franklin Heaberlin
Mitchell D. Kinner   Robert J. Patton
John T. Chafin   William C. Mullins

Representative Clients: Island Creek Coal Co.; The Elk Horn Coal Corp.; First Commonwealth Bank; Old Republic Insurance Co.; Zurich American Insurance Co.; Maryland Casualty Co.; Bituminous Casualty Corp.; Mack Financial Corp.; Nationwide Insurance; Kentucky May Coal Co., Inc.

For full biographical listings, see the Martindale-Hubbell Law Directory

LOUISIANA

*BATON ROUGE,** East Baton Rouge Parish

BREAZEALE, SACHSE & WILSON, L.L.P. (AV)

Twenty-Third Floor, One American Place, P.O. Box 3197, 70821-3197
Telephone: 504-387-4000
Fax: 504-387-5397
New Orleans, Louisiana Office: LL&E Tower, Suite 2400, 909 Poydras Street.
Telephone: 504-582-1170.
Fax: 504-584-5452.

MEMBERS OF FIRM

Victor A. Sachse, III   John W. Barton, Jr.
Emile C. Rolfs, III   Jude C. Bursavich

ASSOCIATES

Luis A. Leitzelar   Andrew J. Harrison, Jr.

Counsel for: Hibernia National Bank; South Central Bell Telephone Co.; Allied-Signal Corp.; Reynolds Metal Co.; Illinois Central Railroad Co.; The Continental Insurance Cos.; Fireman's Fund American Group; Chicago Bridge & Iron Co.; Montgomery Ward & Co.

For Complete List of Firm Personnel, See General Section

For full biographical listings, see the Martindale-Hubbell Law Directory

GORDON, ARATA, McCOLLAM & DUPLANTIS, L.L.P. (AV)

A Partnership including Professional Law Corporations
1420 One American Place, 70825-0012
Telephone: 504-381-9643
Fax: 504-336-9763
New Orleans, Louisiana Office: Place St. Charles, Suite 4000, 201 St. Charles Avenue.
Telephone: 504-582-1111.
Fax: 504-582-1121.
Lafayette, Louisiana Office: 625 East Kaliste Saloom Road.
Telephone: 318-237-0132.
Fax: 318-237-3451.

RESIDENT ASSOCIATES

Teanna West Neskora   Daniel J. Shapiro

Representative Clients: Amoco Production Co.; Bass Enterprises; BHP Petroleum (Americas); Chevron U.S.A. Inc.; CNG Producing Co.; Enron Corp.; Freeport-McMoran Oil & Gas Co.; Union Oil Company of California.

For full biographical listings, see the Martindale-Hubbell Law Directory

KEAN, MILLER, HAWTHORNE, D'ARMOND, McCOWAN & JARMAN, L.L.P. (AV)

22nd Floor, One American Place, P.O. Box 3513, 70821
Telephone: 504-387-0999
Fax: 504-388-9133
New Orleans, Louisiana Office: Energy Centre, Suite 1470, 1100 Poydras Street.
Telephone: 504-585-3050.
Fax: 504-585-3051.
Plaquemine, Louisiana Office: Suite 10, 23425 Railroad Avenue.
Telephone: 504-687-9845.
Fax: 504-382-3445.

MEMBERS OF FIRM

G. William Jarman   J. Carter Wilkinson
Leonard L. Kilgore III   Sandra L. Edwards
Gary A. Bezet   Linda Sarradet Akchin
Maureen N. Harbourt   James P. Doré
M. Dwayne Johnson   Katherine W. King
          Charles S. McCowan III

Kelly Wilkinson   Robert M. Hoyland
Esteban Herrera, Jr.   Murray A. Greene
Susan Knight Carter (Resident, Julie Parelman Silbert (Resident,
  New Orleans Office)   New Orleans Office)
          Troy J. Charpentier

Representative Clients: Amoco Production Company, Houston, TX; BASF Corporation, Parsippany, NJ; Exxon Company, U.S.A., Baton Rouge, LA; Freeport McMoRan, Inc., New Orleans, LA; Georgia-Pacific Corporation, Atlanta, GA; Mobil Oil Corporation, Fairfax, VA; Tenneco, Inc., Houston, TX; Transcontinental Gas Pipe Line Company, Houston, TX Willamette Industries, Inc., Portland, OR.

For Complete List of Firm Personnel, See General Section

For full biographical listings, see the Martindale-Hubbell Law Directory

LAFAYETTE,* Lafayette Parish

GORDON, ARATA, McCOLLAM & DUPLANTIS, L.L.P. (AV)

A Partnership including Professional Law Corporations
625 East Kaliste Saloom Road, 70508-2508
Telephone: 318-237-0132
Fax: 318-237-3451
New Orleans, Louisiana Office: Place St. Charles, Suite 4000, 201 St. Charles Avenue.
Telephone: 504-582-1111.
Fax: 504-582-1121.
Baton Rouge, Louisiana Office: 1420 One American Place.
Telephone: 504-381-9643.
Fax: 504-336-9763.

RESIDENT MEMBERS OF FIRM

B. J. Duplantis (A P.L.C.)	William F. Bailey
Benjamin B. Blanchet	James E. Slatten, III
Samuel E. Masur	

RESIDENT ASSOCIATE

Denis C. Swords

Representative Clients: Amoco Production Co.; Bass Enterprises; BHP Petroleum (Americas); Chevron U.S.A. Inc.; CNG Producing Co.; Enron Corp.; Freeport-McMoran Oil & Gas Co.; Union Oil Company of California.

For full biographical listings, see the Martindale-Hubbell Law Directory

LISKOW & LEWIS, A PROFESSIONAL LAW CORPORATION (AV)

822 Harding Street, P.O. Box 52008, 70505
Telephone: 318-232-7424
Telecopier: 318-267-2399
New Orleans, Louisiana Office: 50th Floor, One Shell Square.
Telephone: 504-581-7979.
Telecopier: 504-592-5108; 504-592-5109.

RESIDENT PERSONNEL

Thomas D. Hardeman	Patrick W. Gray
Lawrence P. Simon, Jr.	James N. Mansfield, III
Joseph C. Giglio, Jr.	Charles B. Griffis, III
Richard W. Revels, Jr.	

OF COUNSEL

Robert T. Jorden	James L. Pelletier

Matt Jones

Representative Clients: Amerada Hess Corp.; Amoco Corporation; Bank One; BP America Inc.; Hibernia National Bank; Hunt Oil Company; Louisiana Public Service Commission; Mobil Oil Corp.; OXY U.S.A. Inc.; Union Oil Company of California; Union Pacific Resources Company.

For Complete List of Firm Personnel, See General Section

For full biographical listings, see the Martindale-Hubbell Law Directory

MANGHAM AND DAVIS (AV)

Suite 1400 First National Bank Towers, 600 Jefferson Street, P.O. Box 93110, 70509-3110
Telephone: 318-233-6200
Fax: 318-233-6521

Michael R. Mangham	Louis R. Davis

ASSOCIATES

Dawn Mayeux Fuqua	Claire A. Fisher

SPECIAL COUNSEL

Michael J. O'Shee

Reference: Hibernia National Bank, Lafayette, Louisiana.

For full biographical listings, see the Martindale-Hubbell Law Directory

NEW ORLEANS,* Orleans Parish

BROOK, PIZZA & VAN LOON, L.L.P. (AV)

400 Poydras Street, Suite 2500, 70130
Telephone: 504-566-0600
Telecopier: 504-595-8715
Email: lawfirm@bpvl.com
Slidell, Louisiana Office: 1400 A Gause Boulevard.
Telephone: 504-641-9468.
Telecopier: 504-643-7631.
Baton Rouge, Louisiana Office: 9100 Bluebonnet Centre Boulevard, Suite 402.
Telephone: 504-291-7300.
Telecopier: 504-291-4524.

Jack Pierce Brook	Normand F. Pizza
Ernest N. Morial (1929-1989)	Jan T. Van Loon
Richard Ernest Santora	

(See Next Column)

David M. Latham	Christopher J. Shenfield
David Shaw	Douglas R. Kinler
Stephanie B. LaBorde (Resident, Baton Rouge Office)	

SPECIAL COUNSEL

Betty Jean George Ray (Resident, Baton Rouge Office)	Mark D. Hudak

OF COUNSEL

Nyda Brook Zelenka	Carlina Davila L. Shenfield (not admitted in the United States)
Herschel C. Adcock	

For full biographical listings, see the Martindale-Hubbell Law Directory

CHAFFE, McCALL, PHILLIPS, TOLER & SARPY, L.L.P. (AV)

A Partnership including a Professional Law Corporation
2300 Energy Centre, 1100 Poydras Street, 70163-2300
Telephone: 504-585-7000
Telecopier: 504-585-7075
Cable Address: "Denegre"
Telex: (AT&T) 460122 CMPTS
Email: cmptsno%2049698@mcimail.com *URL:* http://www.chaffe.com/
Baton Rouge, Louisiana Office: 202 Two United Plaza, 8550 United Plaza Boulevard.
Telephone: 504-922-4300.
Fax: 504-922-4304.
Miami, Florida Office: 2600 Brickell Bay Office Tower, 1001 South Bayshore Drive, 33131.
Telephone: 305-377-3770.
Fax: 305-377-0080.
Caracas, Venezuela Office: Edificio Exa, Piso 10, Oficina PH-10, Avenida Venezuela entre Calles EL Retiro y Alameda, El Rosal.
Telephone: 011-582-953-4136.
Fax: 011-582-953-6518.

MEMBERS OF FIRM

James A. Barton, III	Harry R. Holladay
David R. Richardson	

OF COUNSEL

Gordon O. Ewin

Representative Clients: Amoco Production Co.; Texaco, Inc.; Samedan Oil Co.; Phillips Petroleum Co.; Placid Oil Co.

For Complete List of Firm Personnel, See General Section

For full biographical listings, see the Martindale-Hubbell Law Directory

GORDON, ARATA, McCOLLAM & DUPLANTIS, L.L.P. (AV)

A Partnership including Professional Law Corporations
Place St. Charles, Suite 4000, 201 St. Charles Avenue, 70170-4000
Telephone: 504-582-1111
Fax: 504-582-1121
Lafayette, Louisiana Office: 625 East Kaliste Saloom Road.
Telephone: 318-237-0132.
Fax: 318-237-3451.
Baton Rouge, Louisiana Office: 1420 One American Place.
Telephone: 504-381-9643.
Fax: 504-336-9763.

MEMBERS OF FIRM

John A. Gordon (A P.L.C.)	Paul E. Bullington
Blake G. Arata (A P.L.C.)	James L. Weiss
John M. McCollam (A P.L.C.)	Jason A. T. Jumonville
Guy E. Wall	Martin E. Landrieu
Cynthia A. Nicholson	Scott A. O'Connor

ASSOCIATES

C. Peck Hayne Jr.	Elizabeth L. Gordon
Marcy V. Massengale	

LAFAYETTE OFFICE

RESIDENT MEMBERS OF FIRM

B. J. Duplantis (A P.L.C.)	William F. Bailey
Benjamin B. Blanchet	James E. Slatten, III
Samuel E. Masur	

RESIDENT ASSOCIATE

Denis C. Swords

BATON ROUGE OFFICE

RESIDENT ASSOCIATE

Teanna West Neskora

Representative Clients: Amoco Production Co.; Bass Enterprises; CNG Producing Co.; Enron Corp; BHP Petroleum (Americas); Chevron U.S.A. Inc.; Freeport-McMoran Oil & Gas Co.; Union Oil Company of California.

For Complete List of Firm Personnel, See General Section

For full biographical listings, see the Martindale-Hubbell Law Directory

New Orleans—Continued

LAPEYRE, TERRELL & RANDAZZO (AV)

A Partnership including Professional Law Corporations
400 Poydras Street, Suite 1980, 70130-3277
Telephone: 504-524-5152
Fax: 504-524-3321
Email: fhl@latera.attmail.com

F. Henri Lapeyre, Jr. (P.L.C.)	Matthew J. Randazzo, III
Vernon L. Terrell, Jr. (P.L.C.)	(P.L.C.)

Etienne C. Lapeyre
OF COUNSEL
Felix H. Lapeyre

Reference: Whitney National Bank of New Orleans, New Orleans, La.

For full biographical listings, see the Martindale-Hubbell Law Directory

LISKOW & LEWIS, A PROFESSIONAL LAW CORPORATION (AV)

50th Floor, One Shell Square, 70139
Telephone: 504-581-7979
Telecopier: 504-556-4108; 504-556-4109
Lafayette, Louisiana Office: 822 Harding Street, P.O. Box 52008.
Telephone: 318-232-7424.
Telecopier: 318-267-2399.

Billy H. Hines	Wm. Craig Wyman
John M. King	Stevia M. Walther
J. Berry St. John, Jr.	Robert L. Theriot
John M. Wilson	Jonathan A. Hunter
George J. Domas	Mary S. Johnson
Robert E. Holden	Scott C. Seiler
Joe B. Norman	Cheryl Mollere Kornick
Lambert M. Laperouse	Guenton C. Slawson, Jr.

OF COUNSEL
Charles C. Gremillion

Peter C. Muller
RESIDENT PERSONNEL AT LAFAYETTE OFFICE

Thomas D. Hardeman	Patrick W. Gray
Lawrence P. Simon, Jr.	James N. Mansfield, III
Joseph C. Giglio, Jr.	Charles B. Griffis, III

Richard W. Revels, Jr.
OF COUNSEL

Robert T. Jorden	James L. Pelletier

Matt Jones

Representative Clients: Atlantic Richfield Co.; BASF Corp.; Federal Deposit Insurance Corporation; First National Bank of Commerce; Hibernia National Bank; Legg Mason Wood Walker; Mobil Oil Corporation; Pennzoil Company; Prudential Securities Inc.; Texaco, Inc.

For Complete List of Firm Personnel, See General Section

For full biographical listings, see the Martindale-Hubbell Law Directory

MILLING, BENSON, WOODWARD, HILLYER, PIERSON & MILLER, L.L.P. (AV)

A Partnership including Professional Law Corporations
Suite Twenty-Three Hundred, 909 Poydras Street, 70112-1017
Telephone: 504-569-7000
Cable Address: "Milling"
Telex: 58-4211
Telecopier: 504-569-7001
ABA net: 15656
MCI Mail: "Milling"
Lafayette, Louisiana Office: 101 La Rue France, Suite 200.
Telephone: 318-232-3929.
Telecopier: 318-233-4957.

MEMBERS OF FIRM

Charles D. Marshall, Jr. (P.C.)	Mary L. Grier Holmes (P.C.)
David N. Schell, Jr. (P.C.)	Robert T. Lorio (P.C.)

PARTNERS EMERITUS

Haywood H. Hillyer, Jr., (P.C.)	Joseph B. Miller

ASSOCIATES

Jay Corenswet	Alanna S. Arnold

LAFAYETTE OFFICE
RESIDENT MEMBER OF FIRM
Robert L. Cabes (P.C.)
SPECIAL COUNSEL
Randall C Loewen
RESIDENT ASSOCIATE
Gregory M. Attrep

Counsel for: Arthur Andersen & Co.; Chevron U.S.A., Inc.; Chrysler Corp.; The Dow Chemical Co.; E.I. duPont de Nemours & Co., Inc.; Exxon Corp.; Louisiana & Arkansas Railway Co.; The Louisiana Land & Exploration Co.; McDermott Incorporated; Whitney National Bank of New Orleans.

(See Next Column)

For Complete List of Firm Personnel, See General Section

For full biographical listings, see the Martindale-Hubbell Law Directory

PHELPS DUNBAR, L.L.P. (AV)

Texaco Center, 400 Poydras Street, 70130-3245
Telephone: 504-566-1311
Telecopier: 504-568-9130, 504-568-9007
Cable Address: "Howspencer"
Telex: 584125 WU
Telex: 6821155 WUI
Email: info@phelps.com
Baton Rouge, Louisiana Office: Suite 701, City National Bank Building, P.O. Box 4412.
Telephone: 504-346-0285.
Telecopier: 504-381-9197.
Jackson, Mississippi Office: Suite 500, Mtel Centré, 200 South Lamar Street, P.O. Box 23066.
Telephone: 601-352-2300.
Telecopier: 601-360-9777.
Tupelo, Mississippi Office: Seventh Floor, One Mississippi Plaza, P.O. Box 1220.
Telephone: 601-842-7907.
Telecopier: 601-842-3873.
Houston, Texas Office: Suite 900, 3040 Post Oak Boulevard.
Telephone: 713-626-1386.
Telecopier: 713-626-1388.
London, England Office: Suite 731, Level 7, Lloyd's, 1 Lime Street, London EC3M 7DQ England.
Telephone: 011-44-171-929-4765.
Telecopier: 011-44-171-929-0046.
Telex: 987321.

MEMBERS OF FIRM

Robert U. Soniat	Edward B. Poitevent, II
Harvey D. Wagar, III	Bruce V. Schewe
Alan C. Wolf	James A. Stuckey

David M. Hunter
COUNSEL
Gary Meringer

Representative Clients: Acadian Gas Pipeline System; Central Louisiana Electric Company, Inc.; Columbia Gas Development Corp.; Energy Development Corp.; Laurel Operating Company, Inc.; Phibro Energy USA, Inc.; Sabine Royalty Trust; Texas Gas Transmission Corp.; Transco Energy Co.; Unocal Exploration Corp.

For Complete List of Firm Personnel, See General Section

For full biographical listings, see the Martindale-Hubbell Law Directory

SHREVEPORT,* Caddo Parish

BARLOW AND HARDTNER L.C. (AV)

Tenth Floor, Louisiana Tower, 401 Edwards Street, 71101-3289
Telephone: 318-227-1131
Telecopier: 318-227-1141
Mailing Address: P.O. Box 8, Shreveport, Louisiana, 71161-0008

Malcolm S. Murchison	Clair F. White
Kay Cowden Medlin	Stephen E. Ramey
Joseph L. Shea, Jr.	Philip E. Downer, III
David R. Taggart	Michael B. Donald

Jay A. Greenleaf

Representative Clients: Anderson Oil & Gas, Inc.; Bass Enterprises Production Co.; Central Louisiana Electric Co., Inc.; Grigsby Petroleum, Inc.; Hilliard Petroleum; Kelley Oil Corporation; NorAm Energy Corp. (formerly Arkla, Inc.); Concorde Gas Marketing Company; Nelson Energy; Texas Eastern Corp.

For Complete List of Firm Personnel, See General Section

For full biographical listings, see the Martindale-Hubbell Law Directory

HARGROVE, PESNELL & WYATT, A P.L.C. (AV)

400 Texas Street Suite 1102, 71101
Telephone: 318-429-7200
Fax: 318-429-7201
Mailing Address: P.O. Box 59, Shreveport, Louisiana, 71161-0059

Billy R. Pesnell	David L. Smelley
Thomas James Wyatt	A. L. Wedgeworth, III
Joseph L. Hargrove, Jr.	Paul A. Strickland

Scott C. Sinclair

For full biographical listings, see the Martindale-Hubbell Law Directory

MAINE

*PORTLAND,** Cumberland Co.

PIERCE ATWOOD (AV)

One Monument Square, 04101
Telephone: 207-791-1100
Fax: 207-791-1350
Email: info@PierceAtwood.com
Augusta, Maine Office: 77 Winthrop Street.
Telephone: 207-622-6311.
Fax: 207-623-9367.
Newburyport, Massachusetts Office: 6 Harris Street.
Telephone: 508-465-9599.
Fax: 508-465-9945.

MEMBERS OF FIRM

Daniel E. Boxer	Philip F. W. Ahrens, III
John O'Leary	Kenneth Fairbanks Gray
John D. Delahanty	William E. Taylor
Thomas R. Doyle	Dixon P. Pike

ASSOCIATES

Kate L. Geoffroy	David P. Littell
Matthew D. Manahan	Abigail M. Holman
Adam H. Steinman	Helen L. Edmonds
	(Not admitted in ME)

For Complete List of Firm Personnel, See General Section

For full biographical listings, see the Martindale-Hubbell Law Directory

MARYLAND

*BALTIMORE,** (Independent City)

VENABLE ATTORNEYS AT LAW VENABLE, BAETJER AND HOWARD, LLP (AV)

A Partnership including Professional Corporations
1800 Mercantile Bank & Trust Building, 2 Hopkins Plaza, 21201
Telephone: 410-244-7400
Email: INFO@Venable.win.net
Washington, D.C. Office: Venable, Baetjer, Howard & Civiletti LLP. Suite 1000, 1201 New York Avenue, N.W.
Telephone: 202-962-4800.
McLean, Virginia Office: Suite 400, 2010 Corporate Ridge.
Telephone: 703-760-1600.
Rockville, Maryland Office: Suite 500, One Church Street, P. O. Box 1906.
Telephone: 301-217-5600.
Towson, Maryland Office: 210 Allegheny Avenue, P. O. Box 5517.
Telephone: 410-494-6200.

MEMBERS OF FIRM

Benjamin R. Civiletti (P.C.) (Also at Washington, D.C. and Towson, Maryland Offices)	Jeffrey A. Dunn (also at Washington, D.C. Office)
Anthony M. Carey (Also at Washington, D.C. Office)	James L. Shea (Also at Washington, D.C. Office)
John Henry Lewin, Jr. (P.C.)	Brigid E. Kenney
Robert G. Smith (P.C.)	John J. Pavlick, Jr. (Not admitted in MD; Resident, Washington, D. C. Office)
John G. Milliken (Not admitted in MD; Washington, D.C. and McLean, Virginia Offices)	Kathleen Gallogly Cox (Resident, Towson, Maryland Office)
Joseph C. Wich, Jr. (Resident, Towson, Maryland Office)	Christopher R. Mellott
Joseph G. Block (Not admitted in MD; Resident, Washington, D.C. Office)	M. King Hill, III (Resident, Towson, Maryland Office)
Michael Schatzow (Also at Washington, D.C. Office)	James A. Dunbar (Also at Washington, D.C. Office)
John F. Cooney (Not admitted in MD; Resident, Washington, D.C. Office)	Thomas J. Kelly, Jr. (Not admitted in MD; Resident, Washington, D. C. Office)
James K. Archibald (Also at Washington, D.C. Office)	Kevin L. Shepherd
Judson W. Starr (Not admitted in MD; Also at Washington, D.C. and Towson, Maryland Offices)	Mitchell Y. Mirviss
	Thomas M. Lingan

OF COUNSEL

Judith A. Armold

(See Next Column)

ASSOCIATES

Gregory S. Braker (Resident, Washington, D.C. Office)	Mary-Dulany James (Resident, Towson, Maryland Office)
Andrew R. Herrup (Resident, Washington, D.C. Office)	Valerie K. Mann (Not admitted in MD; Resident, Washington, D.C. Office)

For Complete List of Firm Personnel, See General Section

For full biographical listings, see the Martindale-Hubbell Law Directory

MICHIGAN

*ANN ARBOR,** Washtenaw Co.

BRAUN KENDRICK FINKBEINER PLC (AV)

700 First National Building, 48104
Telephone: 313-995-4100
Telecopier: 313-995-4798
URL: http://www.bkf-law.com
Bay City, Michigan Office: 201 Phoenix Building, P.O. Box 2039.
Telephone: 517-895-8505.
Telecopier: 517-895-8437.
Saginaw, Michigan Office: 101 N. Washington, Suite 812.
Telephone: 517-753-3461.
Telecopier: 517-753-3951.

Barry M. Levine

Representative Clients: The Dow Chemical Co.; General Motors Corp.; Lobdell Emery Manufacturing Co.; Merrill, Lynch, Inc.; Saginaw General Hospital; Saginaw News; The Wickes Foundation.

For full biographical listings, see the Martindale-Hubbell Law Directory

MILLER, CANFIELD, PADDOCK AND STONE, P.L.C. (AV)

A Professional Limited Liability Company
Founded in 1852 by Sidney Davy Miller
101 North Main Street, Seventh Floor, 48104-1400
Telephone: 313-663-2445
Fax: 313-747-7147
Detroit, Michigan Office: 150 West Jefferson, Suite 2500, 48226-4415.
Telephone: 313-963-6420.
Fax: 313-496-7500.
Cable Address: "Stem Detroit."
Bloomfield Hills, Michigan Office: Suite 100, Pinehurst Office Center, 1400 North Woodward, 48303-2014.
Telephone: 313-645-5000.
Fax: 313-645-1917.
Grand Rapids, Michigan Office: 1200 Campau Square Plaza, 99 Monroe, N.W., 49503-2639.
Telephone: 616-454-8656.
Fax: 616-776-6322.
Howell, Michigan Office: 121 South Barnard Street, Suite 4, 48843-2305.
Telephone: 517-546-7600.
Telecopier: 517-546-6974.
Kalamazoo, Michigan Office: 444 West Michigan Avenue, 49007-3752.
Telephone: 616-381-7030.
Fax: 616-382-0244.
Lansing, Michigan Office: One Michigan Avenue, Suite 900, 48933-1609.
Telephone: 517-487-2070.
Fax: 517-374-6304.
Monroe, Michigan Office: The Executive Centre, 214 East Elm Avenue, 48161-2682.
Telephone: 313-243-2000.
Fax: 313-243-0901.
Washington, D.C. Office: 1225 Nineteenth Street, N.W., Suite 400. 20036.
Telephone: 202-429-5575; 785-0600.
Fax: 202-331-1118; 785-1234.
Pensacola, Florida Office: 25 West Cedar, 32501.
Telephone: 904-469-1088.
Fax: 904-432-0677.
St. Petersburg, Florida Office: 100 Second Avenue S., Suite 7045, 33701.
Telephone: 813-982-6000.
Fax: 813-892-6002.
New York, New York Office: Eleventh Floor, 135 East 57th Street, 10022-2087.
Telephone: 212-754-5400.
Fax: 212-754-5401.
Gdansk, Poland Office: Suite 322, Dom Technika Building, Ul. Rajska 6, 80-850.
Telephone: 011-485-831-2808.
Fax: 011-485-831-4719.
Warsaw, Poland Office: Ul. Marszalkowska 82, Suite 561, 00-517.
Telephone: 011-482-623-6457 and 6458.
Fax: 011-482-623-6459.

(See Next Column)

MILLER, CANFIELD, PADDOCK AND STONE P.L.C., *Ann Arbor—Continued*

RESIDENT PRINCIPALS
Robert E. Gilbert

Representative Firm Clients: Chrysler Corporation; Comerica, Incorporated; City of Detroit, Michigan; Detroit Tigers, Inc.; First of Michigan; Ford Motor Company; Ford Motor Credit Company; Great Lakes Bancorp; Henry Ford Hospital; INVETECH Company.

For Complete List of Firm Personnel, See General Section

For full biographical listings, see the Martindale-Hubbell Law Directory

---

BAY CITY,* Bay Co.

BRAUN KENDRICK FINKBEINER PLC (AV)

201 Phoenix Building, P.O. Box 2039, 48708
Telephone: 517-895-8505
Telecopier: 517-895-8437
URL: http://www.bkf-law.com
Saginaw, Michigan Office: 101 N. Washington, Suite 812. 8th Floor Second National Bank Building.
Telephone: 517-753-3461.
Telecopier: 517-753-3951.
Ann Arbor, Michigan Office: 700 First National Building.
Telephone: 313-995-4100.
Telecopier: 313-995-4798.

Ralph J. Isackson	Gregory E. Meter
George F. Gronewold, Jr.	Daniel S. Opperman
Frank M. Quinn	Gregory T. Demers

OF COUNSEL
Patrick D. Neering

Representative Clients: APV Chemical Machinery, Inc.; Bay Health Systems; Catholic Federal Credit Union; City of Saginaw; City of Vassar; City of Milwaukee; Corporate Service; Cox Cable.

For Complete List of Firm Personnel, See General Section

For full biographical listings, see the Martindale-Hubbell Law Directory

---

DETROIT,* Wayne Co.

BODMAN, LONGLEY & DAHLING LLP (AV)

34th Floor 100 Renaissance Center, 48243
Telephone: 313-259-7777
Fax: 313-393-7579
Email: 2080194@mcimail.com
Troy, Michigan Office: Suite 2020, 755 West Big Beaver Road.
Telephone: 810-362-2110.
Fax: 810-244-0780.
Ann Arbor, Michigan Office: 110 Miller, Suite 300.
Telephone: 313-761-3780.
Fax: 313-930-2494.
Northern Michigan Office: 229 Court Street, P.O. Box 405, Cheboygan.
Telephone: 616-627-4351.
Fax: 616-627-2802.

MEMBERS OF FIRM
Carson C. Grunewald	James A. Smith
	Robert G. Brower

For Representative Client List, See General Section

For Complete List of Firm Personnel, See General Section

For full biographical listings, see the Martindale-Hubbell Law Directory

---

HONIGMAN MILLER SCHWARTZ AND COHN (AV)

A Partnership including Professional Corporations
2290 First National Building, 48226
Telephone: 313-256-7800
Telecopier: 313-962-0176
Telex: 235705
URL: http://law.honigman.com
Lansing, Michigan Office: Phoenix Building, 222 North Washington Square, Suite 400, 48933-1800.
Telephone: 517-484-8282.
West Palm Beach, Florida Office: Suite 800 Esperante Building, 222 Lakeview Avenue, 33401-6112.
Telephone: 561-838-4500.
Tampa, Florida Office: 2700 SunTrust Financial Centre, 401 E. Jackson Street, 33602-5226.
Telephone: 813-221-6600.

MEMBERS OF FIRM
Sally J. Churchill	John D. Pirich
Christopher J. Dunsky	(Lansing, Michigan Office)
Kenneth C. Gold	Joseph M. Polito
Philip A. Grashoff, Jr.	Paul Revere, III
Robert A. Hykan	Gary A. Trepod
Norman Hyman	(Lansing, Michigan Office)
Brian J. Negele	Grant R. Trigger

(See Next Column)

William A. Wichers II	Ruth E. Zimmerman
Jeffrey L. Woolstrum	(Lansing, Michigan Office)

ASSOCIATES
S. Lee Johnson	Walter J. Kramarz

RESIDENT IN WEST PALM BEACH, FLORIDA OFFICE
MEMBER
E. Lee Worsham (P.A.)

RESIDENT IN TAMPA, FLORIDA OFFICE
MEMBERS
Michael G. Cooke (P.A.)	John W. Voelpel

Representative Clients: Auto Alliance International Inc. (formerly Mazda Motor Manufacturing (USA) Corporation); Consumers Power Company; The Detroit Edison Company; Ford Motor Company; General Motors Corporation; Edw. C. Levy Co.; Masco Corporation and its affiliates; McLouth Steel Products Corporation; Morton International, Inc.

For Complete List of Firm Personnel, See General Section

For full biographical listings, see the Martindale-Hubbell Law Directory

---

MILLER, CANFIELD, PADDOCK AND STONE, P.L.C. (AV)

A Professional Limited Liability Company
Founded in 1852 by Sidney Davy Miller
150 West Jefferson, Suite 2500, 48226-4415
Telephone: 313-963-6420
Fax: 313-496-7500
Cable Address: "Stem Detroit"
Detroit, Michigan Office: 150 West Jefferson, Suite 2500, 48226-4415.
Telephone: 313-963-6420.
Fax: 313-496-7500.
Cable Address: "Stem Detroit."
Ann Arbor, Michigan Office: 101 North Main Street, 7th Floor, 48104-1400.
Telephone: 313-663-2445.
Fax: 313-747-7147.
Bloomfield Hills, Michigan Office: Suite 100, Pinehurst Office Center, 1400 North Woodward, 48303-2014.
Telephone: 313-645-5000.
Fax: 313-645-1917.
Grand Rapids, Michigan Office: 1200 Campau Square Plaza, 99 Monroe, N.W., 49503-2639.
Telephone: 616-454-8656.
Fax: 616-776-6322.
Howell, Michigan Office: 121 South Barnard Street, Suite 4, 48843-2305.
Telephone: 517-546-7600.
Telecopier: 517-546-6974.
Kalamazoo, Michigan Office: 444 West Michigan Avenue, 49007-3752.
Telephone: 616-381-7030.
Fax: 616-382-0244.
Lansing, Michigan Office: One Michigan Avenue, Suite 900, 48933-1609.
Telephone: 517-487-2070.
Fax: 517-374-6304.
Monroe, Michigan Office: The Executive Centre, 214 East Elm Avenue, 48161-2682.
Telephone: 313-243-2000.
Fax: 313-243-0901.
Washington, D.C. Office: 1225 Nineteenth Street, N.W., Suite 400. 20036.
Telephone: 202-429-5575; 785-0600.
Fax: 202-331-1118; 785-1234.
Pensacola, Florida Office: 25 West Cedar, 32501.
Telephone: 904-469-1088.
Fax: 904-432-0677.
St. Petersburg, Florida Office: 100 Second Avenue S., Suite 7045, 33701.
Telephone: 813-982-6000.
Fax: 813-892-6002.
New York, New York Office: Eleventh Floor, 135 East 57th Street, 10022-2087.
Telephone: 212-754-5400.
Fax: 212-754-5401.
Gdansk, Poland Office: Suite 322, Dom Technika Building, UI. Rajska 6, 80-850.
Telephone: 011-485-831-2808.
Fax: 011-485-831-4719.
Warsaw, Poland Office: UI. Marszalkowska 82, Suite 561, 00-517.
Telephone: 011-482-623-6457 and 6458.
Fax: 011-482-623-6459.

PRINCIPALS OF FIRM
Frank L. Andrews (Detroit and Bloomfield Hills Offices)	Thomas C. Phillips (Lansing Office)

Representative Firm Clients: Chrysler Corporation; Comerica, Incorporated; City of Detroit, Michigan; Detroit Tigers, Inc.; First of Michigan; Ford Motor Company; Ford Motor Credit Company; Great Lakes Bancorp; Henry Ford Hospital; INVETECH Company.

For Complete List of Firm Personnel, See General Section

For full biographical listings, see the Martindale-Hubbell Law Directory

GRAND RAPIDS, * Kent Co.

WARNER NORCROSS & JUDD LLP (AV)

900 Old Kent Building, 111 Lyon Street, N.W., 49503-2489
Telephone: 616-752-2000
Fax: 616-752-2500
Muskegon, Michigan Office: 400 Terrace Plaza, P.O. Box 900.
Telephone: 616-727-2600.
Fax: 616-727-2699.
Holland, Michigan Office: Curtis Center, Suite 300, 170 College Avenue.
Telephone: 616-396-9800.
Fax: 616-396-3656.

MEMBERS OF FIRM

John D. Tully	Paul T. Sorensen
Peter L. Gustafson	John D. Dunn
Michael L. Robinson	John V. Byl
Eugene E. Smary	Tracy T. Larsen

General Counsel for: Bissell Inc.; Blodgett Memorial Medical Center; Guardsman Products, Inc.; Haworth, Inc.; Kysor Industrial Corp.; Michigan Bankers Assn.; Old Kent Financial Corp.; Steelcase, Inc.; Wolverine World Wide, Inc.

For Complete List of Firm Personnel, See General Section

For full biographical listings, see the Martindale-Hubbell Law Directory

---

LANSING, Ingham Co.

* indicates certain Bar Register subscribers whose principal office is located elsewhere in the state and who have arranged for representation as a part of the state capital listings that follow

* HONIGMAN MILLER SCHWARTZ AND COHN (AV)

A Partnership including Professional Corporations
222 North Washington Square, Suite 400, 48933-1800
Telephone: 517-484-8282
Telecopier: 517-484-8286
URL: http://law.honigman.com
Detroit, Michigan Office: 2290 First National Building, 48226.
Telephone: 313-256-7800.
West Palm Beach, Florida Office: Suite 800 Esperante Building, 222 Lakeview Avenue, 33401-6112.
Telephone: 561-838-4500.
Tampa, Florida Office: 2700 SunTrust Financial Centre, 401 E. Jackson Street, 33602-5226.
Telephone: 813-221-6600.

MEMBERS

Frederick M. Baker, Jr.	John D. Pirich
Mark Morton	Gary A. Trepod

Representative Clients: Central Wayne County Sanitation Authority; Granger Land Development Company; Greater Detroit Resource Recovery Authority; Landfill Management Company; Michigan Disposal Service Corporation; Republic Waste Industries; Wayne Disposal, Inc.

For Complete List of Firm Personnel, See General Section

For full biographical listings, see the Martindale-Hubbell Law Directory

---

SAGINAW, * Saginaw Co.

BRAUN KENDRICK FINKBEINER PLC (AV)

101 N. Washington Suite 812, 48607-1297
Telephone: 517-753-3461
Telecopier: 517-753-3951
URL: http://www.bkf-law.com
Bay City, Michigan Office: 201 Phoenix Building, P.O. Box 2039.
Telephone: 517-895-8505.
Telecopier: 517-895-8437.
Ann Arbor, Michigan Office: 700 First National Building.
Telephone: 313-995-4100.
Telecopier: 313-995-4798.

James V. Finkbeiner	John A. Decker
Thomas R. Luplow	Barry M. Levine

Brian S. Makaric	Glenn L. Fitkin

OF COUNSEL

J. Richard Kendrick

Representative Clients: The Dow Chemical Co.; General Motors Corp.; Lobdell Emery Manufacturing Co.; Merrill, Lynch, Inc.; Saginaw General Hospital; Saginaw News; The Wickes Foundation.

For Complete List of Firm Personnel, See General Section

For full biographical listings, see the Martindale-Hubbell Law Directory

---

SOUTHFIELD, Oakland Co.

LAWRENCE M. ELKUS (AV)

3000 Town Center, Suite 2990, 48075
Telephone: 810-358-5300
Fax: 810-355-5608

For full biographical listings, see the Martindale-Hubbell Law Directory

PATENT, TRADEMARK, COPYRIGHT
AND
UNFAIR COMPETITION
(See also listings under Trademark, Copyright and Unfair Competition)

ALABAMA

BIRMINGHAM,* Jefferson Co.

BRADLEY, ARANT, ROSE & WHITE (AV)

2001 Park Place, Suite 1400, P.O. Box 830709, 35283-0709
Telephone: 205-521-8000
Facsimile: 205-252-0264
Facsimile (SouthTrust Tower Office): 205-251-9915
URL: http://www.BARW.COM
Huntsville, Alabama Office: 200 Clinton Avenue West, Suite 900, 35801.
Telephone: 205-517-5100.
Facsimile: 205-533-5069.

MEMBERS OF FIRM
Thad Gladden Long   J. David Pugh
Susan Donovan Josey
ASSOCIATE
John W. Smith T

Counsel for: SouthTrust Bank of Alabama, National Association; Energen, Corporation (formerly Alagasco, Inc.); Blount, Inc; Coca-Cola Bottling Company United, Inc.; The New York Times Co.; Russell Corp.; Walter Industries, Inc.; ASCAP, Auburn University.

For Complete List of Firm Personnel, See General Section

For full biographical listings, see the Martindale-Hubbell Law Directory

---

ARIZONA

PHOENIX,* Maricopa Co.

ALLEN & PRICE, P.L.C. (AV)

2850 East Camelback Road, Suite 170, 85016-4380
Telephone: 602-381-0500
Fax: 602-381-8899
Email: price@aplaw.com
Email: allen@aplaw.com

Robert E. B. Allen   Charles S. Price

For full biographical listings, see the Martindale-Hubbell Law Directory

BROWN & BAIN, A PROFESSIONAL ASSOCIATION (AV)

2901 North Central Avenue, P.O. Box 400, 85001-0400
Telephone: 602-351-8000
Telecopier: 602-351-8516
Palo Alto, California Affiliated Office: Brown & Bain, 1755 Embarcadero Road, Suite 200.
Telephone: 415-856-9411.
Telecopier: 415-856-6061.
Tucson, Arizona Affiliated Office: Brown & Bain, A Professional Association. One South Church Avenue, Nineteenth Floor, P.O. Box 2265.
Telephone: 602-798-7900
Telecopier: 602-798-7945.

C. Randall Bain	Jonathan M. James
Charles A. Blanchard	Anthony L. Marks
Alan H. Blankenheimer	Michael F. McNulty
Jack E. Brown	(Resident at Tucson Office)
H. Michael Clyde	Lawrence G. D. Scarborough
Paul F. Eckstein	Craig W. Soland
Terry E. Fenzl	Antonio T. Viera
Patricia A. Hubbard	Kim E. Williamson

C. Mark Kittredge   Deborah Henscheid Lyon
COUNSEL
Ian C. Ballon (Resident at Palo Alto Office)

For Complete List of Firm Personnel, See General Section

For full biographical listings, see the Martindale-Hubbell Law Directory

FENNEMORE CRAIG, A PROFESSIONAL CORPORATION (AV)

Two North Central, Suite 2200, 85004
Telephone: 602-257-8700
Fax: 602-257-8527
Scottsdale, Arizona Office: 6263 North Scottsdale Road, Suite 290, 85250.
Telephone: 602-257-5400.
Fax: 602-257-5409.
Tucson, Arizona Office: One South Church Avenue, Suite 1030, 85701.
Telephone: 520-791-6800.
Fax: 520-791-6820.

C. Owen Paepke   Ray K. Harris
Lesa J. Storey

Stacie K. Smith   Pamela J. Crane

For Complete List of Firm Personnel, See General Section

For full biographical listings, see the Martindale-Hubbell Law Directory

O'CONNOR, CAVANAGH, ANDERSON, KILLINGSWORTH & BESHEARS, A PROFESSIONAL ASSOCIATION (AV)

One East Camelback Road, Suite 1100, 85012-1656
Telephone: 602-263-2400
FAX: 602-263-2900
Email: firminfo@arizlaw.com
Sun City, Arizona Office: 13250 North Del Webb Boulevard, Suite B, 85351.
Telephone: 602-263-2808.
FAX: 602-933-3100.
Tucson, Arizona Office: O'Connor Cavanagh Molloy Jones, 33 N. Stone, Suite 2100, 85701, P.O. Box 2268, 85702.
Telephone: 520-622-3531.
FAX: 520-624-2816.
Nogales, Arizona Office: 1891 North Mastick Way, 85621.
Telephone: 520-761-4215.
FAX: 520-761-3505.

Donald J. Lenkszus

John D. Titus

For Complete List of Firm Personnel, See General Section

For full biographical listings, see the Martindale-Hubbell Law Directory

QUARLES & BRADY (AV)

One Camelback Building, One East Camelback Road, Suite 400, 85012-1649
Telephone: 602-230-5500
Fax: 602-230-5598
Milwaukee, Wisconsin Office: 411 East Wisconsin Avenue.
Telephone: 414-277-5000.
Fax: 414-271-3552.
Madison, Wisconsin Office: First Wisconsin Plaza, One South Pinckney Street, P.O. Box 2113.
Telephone: 608-251-5000.
Fax: 608-251-9166.
West Palm Beach, Florida Office: 222 Lakeview Ave., 4th Floor.
Telephone: 407-653-5000.
Fax: 407-653-5333.
Naples, Florida Office: Barnett Center, 4501 Tamiami Trail North, Suite 300.
Telephone: 813-262-5959.
Fax: 813-434-4999.

MEMBERS OF THE FIRM
Judith M. Bailey   Glenn Spencer Bacal
ASSOCIATES
Sean D. Garrison   Jennifer B. Wuamett

For Complete List of Firm Personnel, See General Section

For full biographical listings, see the Martindale-Hubbell Law Directory

SCOTTSDALE, Maricopa Co.

CATES & HOLLOWAY (AV)

Suite D-218, 6991 East Camelback Road, 85251
Telephone: 602-248-0982
Fax: 602-234-3330

MEMBER OF FIRM
Charles E. Cates
OF COUNSEL
Frank T. Barber   Richard G. Harrer
(Not admitted in AZ)   (Not admitted in AZ)

Representative Clients: Albers Technologies Corporation; The Dial Corp.; Greyhound Lines, Inc.; Performance Industries, Inc.; SunCor Development Company; Tire Service Equipment Mfg. Co., Inc.

For full biographical listings, see the Martindale-Hubbell Law Directory

ARKANSAS

LITTLE ROCK, * Pulaski Co.

IVESTER, SKINNER & CAMP, P.A. (AV)

Suite 1200, 111 Center Street, 72201
Telephone: 501-376-7788
FAX: 501-376-8536

Hermann Ivester   Todd A. Lewellen

For Complete List of Firm Personnel, See General Section

For full biographical listings, see the Martindale-Hubbell Law Directory

ROSE LAW FIRM, A PROFESSIONAL ASSOCIATION (AV)

120 East Fourth Street, 72201
Telephone: 501-375-9131
Telecopy: 501-375-1309

William H. Kennedy, III   James H. Druff
Amy Lee Stewart
COUNSEL
John A. Davis, III

Kathryn Bennett Perkins

Counsel for: ALLTEL Corporation; Acxiom Corporation; Aluminum Company of America; Bridgestone/Firestone, Inc.; General Motors Corp.; The Prudential Insurance Company of America; Stephens Group Inc.; TCBY Enterprises, Inc.; Tyson Foods, Inc.

For Complete List of Firm Personnel, See General Section

For full biographical listings, see the Martindale-Hubbell Law Directory

CALIFORNIA

EL SEGUNDO, Los Angeles Co.

HOWARD B. MILLER (AV)

2101 Rosecrans Avenue, Suite 5252, 90245
Telephone: 310-607-0003
Fax: 310-607-0005
Email: hbm@netcom.com

Reference: Wells Fargo Bank (Beverly Hills).

For full biographical listings, see the Martindale-Hubbell Law Directory

FRESNO, * Fresno Co.

KIMBLE, MACMICHAEL & UPTON, A PROFESSIONAL CORPORATION (AV)

Fig Garden Financial Center, 5260 North Palm Avenue, Suite 221, P.O. Box 9489, 93792-9489
Telephone: 209-435-5500
Telecopier: 209-435-1500
Email: kmu@primenet.com

Joseph C. Kimble (1910-1972)   Robert H. Scribner
Thomas A. MacMichael   Michael E. Moss
  (1920-1990)   Mark D. Miller
Jon Wallace Upton   Michael F. Tatham
Robert E. Bergin   W. Richard Lee
Jeffrey G. Boswell   D. Tyler Tharpe
Steven D. McGee   Sylvia Halkousis Coyle
Robert E. Ward   S. Brett Sutton
John P. Eleazarian   Michael J. Jurkovich

Douglas V. Thornton   Susan King Hatmaker
Robert William Branch   Lawrence J. Salisbury
Donald J. Pool   Daniel R. Foster
    Meredith E. Allen
     OF COUNSEL
     Mary Ann Bluhm

For full biographical listings, see the Martindale-Hubbell Law Directory

WORREL & WORREL (AV)

Suite 130, Civic Center Square, 2444 Main Street, 93721-1984
Telephone: 209-486-4526
Fax: 209-486-6948

Richard M. Worrel (1913-1995)   Rodney K. Worrel

Representative Clients: Bank of America; California State University, Fresno; California State University, Bakersfield; Duncan Enterprises; Fresno Pacific College; J. G. Boswell Co.; The Vendo Co.; City of Visalia.

(See Next Column)

For full biographical listings, see the Martindale-Hubbell Law Directory

GLENDALE, Los Angeles Co.

HAGENBAUGH & MURPHY (AV)

A Partnership including Professional Corporations
700 North Central Avenue, Suite 500, 91203
Telephone: 818-240-2600
Fax: 818-240-1253
Email: hmurphy@interserv.com *URL:* http://www.seamless.com/hm/
Orange County, California Office: 701 South Parker Street, Suite 8200, Orange.
Telephone: 714-835-5406.
Fax: 714-835-5949.
San Bernardino, California Office: 301 Vanderbilt Way, Suite 220.
Telephone: 909-884-5331.
FAX: 909-889-1250.

Van A. Hagenbaugh (1914-1980)   Daniel A. Leipold (Resident,
Sigurd E. Murphy (1903-1976)   Orange County Office)
William D. Stewart (A P.C.)   Craig D. Aronson
John J. Tary (A P.C.)   Paul G. Szumiak
Raymond R. Moore (A P.C.)   Robert F. Donohue (Resident,
Neil R. Gunny (Resident,   Orange County Office)
  Orange County Office)   Katharine L. Spaniac (Resident,
Alan R. Zuckerman   San Bernardino Office)
David L. Winter   Alan H. Boon (Resident, Orange
Mary E. Porter   County Office)
    Jamie B. Skebba

Raymond T. Gail (Resident, San   Cathy L. Shipe (Resident,
  Bernardino Office)   Orange County Office)
Kirk G. Neiberger   Keri Lynn Bush
Meredith A. Musicant   Michael A. Tonya
David M. Chute (Resident,   Laura C. McLennan
  Orange County Office)   Graciela L. Freixes
Luanne Walsh   Melinda W. Ebelhar
Rhonda L. Etzwiler   Kirk N. Sullivan
Steven M. Schuetze   Gary P. Simonian
Thomas J. Heatly   Mark Habeeb
Matthew R. Rungaitis   Howard J. Hirsch (Resident,
Stephen Barry   Orange County Office)
Julie M. DeRose   Michelle Mann
Randal A. Whitecotton
  (Resident, San Bernardino
  Office)

Representative Clients: Farmers Insurance Group; Truck Insurance Exchange; Fire Insurance Exchange.

For full biographical listings, see the Martindale-Hubbell Law Directory

IRVINE, Orange Co.

CALLAHAN & BLAINE, A PROFESSIONAL LAW CORPORATION (AV)

Suite 800, 18500 Von Karman, 92612
Telephone: 714-553-1155
Fax: 714-553-0784
Email: info@callahan-law.com

Daniel J. Callahan (A   Stephen E. Blaine
  Professional Corporation)

Kathleen L. Dunham   Andrew A. Smits
Jim P. Mahacek   Gary S. Spitzer
Michael J. Sachs   Edward Susolik
    Graig R. Woodburn
     OF COUNSEL
Shelley M. Liberto   Walt D. Mahaffa

For full biographical listings, see the Martindale-Hubbell Law Directory

GAUNTLETT & ASSOCIATES (AV)

18400 Von Karman, Suite 300, 92612
Telephone: 714-553-1010
Fax: 714-553-2050
Email: ugauntlett@aol.com

David A. Gauntlett

David A. Stall   Elizabeth A. Gillis
Leo E. Lundberg, Jr.   (Not admitted in CA)
Michael Danton Richardson   Mark H. Plager
William P. Warden   (Not admitted in CA)
Stanley H. Shure   Jeffrey S. Allison
     OF COUNSEL
Gary L. Hinman   Jose Zorrilla, Jr.

For full biographical listings, see the Martindale-Hubbell Law Directory

Irvine—Continued

OPPENHEIMER POMS SMITH (AV)

1920 Main Street, Suite 1050, 92714
Telephone: 714-263-8250
FAX: 714-263-8260
Email: owdlaw.com
Los Angeles, California Office: 2029 Century Park East, 38th Floor, 90067.
Telephone: 310-788-5000.
FAX: 310-277-1297.
San Jose, California Office: 333 West Santa Clara Street, Suite 1000, 95113.
Telephone: 408-275-8790.
FAX: 408-275-8793.
Oppenheimer Wolff & Donnelly:
Brussels, Belgium Office: Avenue Louise 250, Box 31, 1050.
Telephone: 32-2-626-0500.
FAX: 32-2-626-0510.
Chicago, Illinois Office: Two Prudential Plaza, 45th Floor, 180 North Stetson Avenue, 60601.
Minneapolis, Minnesota Office: 3400 Plaza VII, 45 South Seventh Street, 55401.
Telephone: 612-344-9300.
FAX: 612-344-9376.
New York, N.Y. Office: Citicorp Center, 153 East 53rd Street, 10022.
Telephone: 212-826-5000.
Telecopier: 212-486-0708.
Paris, France Office: 53 Avenue Montaigne, 75008.
Telephone: (33/1) 44 95 03 50.
FAX: (33/1) 44 95 03 40.
St. Paul, Minnesota Office: 1700 First Bank Building, 55101.
Telephone: 612-223-2500.
FAX: 612-223-2596.
Washington, D.C. Office: 1020 Nineteenth Street, N.W., Suite 400, 20036.
Telephone: 202-293-6300.
FAX: 202-293-6200.
Detroit, Michigan Office: Timberland Office Park, Suite 250, 5445 Corporate Drive, 48098.
Telephone: 810-267-8500.
FAX: 810-267-8559.
Affiliated Offices:
Goudsmit & Branbergen, J.J. Viottastraat, 46 Amsterdam 1071. Telephone: 31-20-662-30-31.
FAX: 31-20-673-65-58.
Pisano, DeVito, Maiano & Catucci, Piazza Del Duomo, 20, Milan 20122.
Telephone: 39-2-878281.
FAX: 39-2-861275.
Pisano, DeVito, Maiano & Catucci, Via G. Borsi, 3, Rome 00197.
Telephone: 39-6-8079087.
FAX: 39-6-8078407.

Richard L. Gausewitz	Edward F. O'Connor
Kurt A. MacLean	Terry L. Miller
Michael A. Kondzella	

Reference: City National Bank (Century Plaza Office, Century City).

For full biographical listings, see the Martindale-Hubbell Law Directory

LAGUNA BEACH, Orange Co.

LEVIN & GLUCK (AV)

384 Forest Avenue, Suite 13, 92651
Telephone: 714-497-7676
Facsimile: 714-497-7679
URL: http://www.lagunalaw.com

MEMBERS OF FIRM

William E. Levin	Peter J. Gluck (Not admitted in CA)

ASSOCIATES

Owen J. Bates	Sergio A. Gutierrez

OF COUNSEL

James E. Hawes

LEGAL SUPPORT PERSONNEL

Patricia E. Anderson	Merritt L. McKeon
Robert Z. Evora	Manfred E. Wolff

For full biographical listings, see the Martindale-Hubbell Law Directory

LAGUNA HILLS, Orange Co.

STETINA BRUNDA & BUYAN, A PROFESSIONAL CORPORATION (AV)

Suite 401, 24221 Calle De La Louisa, 92653
Telephone: 714-855-1246
Telex: 704355
Facsimile: 714-855-6371
Email: 104052.1330@compuserve.com

Kit M. Stetina (Mr.)	Bruce B. Brunda
Robert Dean Buyan	

(See Next Column)

Mark B. Garred	Thomas C. Naber
William J. Brucker	(Not admitted in CA)
Matthew A. Newboles	Darren S. Rimer

LEGAL SUPPORT PERSONNEL

Norman E. Carte	Kristy Kay Moore

Representative Clients: Northrop-Grumman Corp.; No Fear, Inc.; Dunn-Edwards, Inc.; Arnette Optic Illusions, Inc.; Baxter Corp.; Pick Systems; Bird Products Corp.; Tyco Industries, Inc.; Century 400, Inc.; 3-Day Blinds, Inc.

For full biographical listings, see the Martindale-Hubbell Law Directory

LOS ANGELES,* Los Angeles Co.

ASHEN, GOLANT & LIPPMAN (AV)

2029 Century Park East, Suite 2610, 90067
Telephone: 310-203-0303
Fax: 310-203-8803
Beverly Hills, California Office: 1737 Franklin Canyon Drive, 90210.
Telephone: 310-274-8060.
Fax: 310-858-1922.
Chicago, Illinois Office: 70 West Madison Street, 1700, 60602.
Telephone: 312-422-0729.
Fax: 312-422-0730.
Montrose, California Office: 4385 Ocean View Boulevard.
Telephone: 818-249-5961.
Fax: 818-249-8384.

MEMBERS OF FIRM

Robert M. Ashen	Peter I. Lippman
Joseph H. Golant	Elizabeth L. Swanson

Reference: City National Bank (Beverly Hills Office).

For full biographical listings, see the Martindale-Hubbell Law Directory

BRIGHT & LORIG, A PROFESSIONAL CORPORATION (AV)

633 West Fifth Street, Suite 3330, 90071
Telephone: 213-627-7774
Telecopier: 213-627-8508

Frederick A. Lorig	Patrick F. Bright

Lois A. Stone	Edward C. Schewe
Sidford Lewis Brown	Bruce R. Zisser

Reference: Manufacturers Bank (Headquarters Office).

For full biographical listings, see the Martindale-Hubbell Law Directory

FREILICH, HORNBAKER & ROSEN, P.C. (AV)

Suite 1434, 10960 Wilshire Boulevard, 90024
Telephone: 310-477-0578
Telex: 298725 Patl Ur
Telecopy: 310-473-9277

Arthur Freilich	Timothy T. Tyson
Robert D. Hornbaker	Lawrence S. Cohen
Leon D. Rosen	Lee Jay Mandell

Reference: Bank of America (Wilshire-Westwood Branch).

For full biographical listings, see the Martindale-Hubbell Law Directory

FULWIDER PATTON LEE & UTECHT, LLP (AV)

10877 Wilshire Boulevard, 10th Floor, 90024
Telephone: 310-824-5555
FAX: 310-824-9696
Email: fulwidr@primenet.com
Email: fulwidr@aol.com
Long Beach, California Office: 200 Oceangate, Suite 1550.
Telephone: 310-432-0453.
Fax: 310-435-6014. Internet: fulwidrlb@aol.com.

MEMBERS OF FIRM

Robert W. Fulwider (1903-1979)	James W. Paul
John M. Lee (1921-1978)	Craig B. Bailey
Warren L. Patton (1912-1985)	John S. Nagy
Richard A. Bardin	Stephen J. Strauss
Gilbert G. Kovelman	Thomas H. Majcher
Vern Schooley (Long Beach Resident Partner)	Thomas A. Runk

ASSOCIATES

David G. Parkhurst	Paul T. LaVoie
Paul M. Stull	John K. Fitzgerald
Gunther D. Hanke (Long Beach Resident Associate)	James Juo (Not admitted in CA)
Gary M. Anderson (Long Beach Resident Associate)	Russell C. Pangborn (Long Beach Resident Associate)
Ronald E. Perez	Richard B. Cates
Robert L. Kovelman	Derrick W. Reed (Long Beach Resident Associate)
Pamela G. Maher	Paul Y. Feng
John V. Hanley	

(See Next Column)

FULWIDER PATTON LEE & UTECHT LLP, *Los Angeles—Continued*
ASSOCIATES (Continued)
JoAnne M. Ybaben (Long Beach　　Sean M. Casey (Long Beach
　　Resident Associate)　　　　　　Resident Associate)
Muriel C. Haritchabalet

OF COUNSEL
Francis A. Utecht (Resident, Of　　I. Morley Drucker (A
　Counsel, Long Beach Office)　　　Professional Corporation)
Howard N. Sommers

For full biographical listings, see the Martindale-Hubbell Law Directory

JONES, DAY, REAVIS & POGUE (AV)

555 West Fifth Street Suite 4600, 90013-1025
Telephone: 213-489-3939
Telex: 181439 UD
Telecopier: 213-243-2539
In Irvine, California: 2603 Main Street, Suite 900.
Telephone: 714-851-3939.
Telex: 194911 Lawyers LSA.
Telecopier: 714-553-7539.
In Atlanta, Georgia: 3500 One Peachtree Center, 303 Peachtree Street,
N.E.
Telephone: 404-521-3939.
Cable Address: "Attorneys Atlanta".
Telex: 54-2711.
Telecopier: 404-581-8330.
In Brussels, Belgium: Avenue Louise 480, 7th Floor, B-1050 Brussels.
Telephone: 32-2-645-14-11.
Telecopier: 32-2-645-14-45.
In Chicago, Illinois: 77 West Wacker.
Telephone: 312-782-3939.
Telecopier: 312-782-8585.
In Cleveland, Ohio: North Point, 901 Lakeside Avenue.
Telephone: 216-586-3939.
Cable Address: "Attorneys Cleveland."
Telex: 980389.
Telecopier: 216-579-0212.
In Columbus, Ohio: 1900 Huntington Center.
Telephone: 614-469-3939.
Cable Address: "Attorneys Columbus."
Telecopier: 614-461-4198.
In Dallas, Texas: 2300 Trammell Crow Center, 2001 Ross Avenue.
Telephone: 214-220-3939.
Cable Address: "Attorneys Dallas."
Telex: 730852.
Telecopier: 214-969-5100.
In Frankfurt, Germany: Triton Haus, Bockenheimer Landstrasse 42, 60323
Frankfurt am Main.
Telephone: 49-69-9726-3939.
Telecopier: 49-69-9726-3993.
In Geneva, Switzerland: 20, rue de Candolle.
Telephone: 41-22-320-2339.
Telecopier: 41-22-320-1232.
In Hong Kong: 29th Floor, Entertainment Building, 30 Queen's Road
Central.
Telephone: 852-2526-6895.
Telecopier: 852-2868-5871.
In London England: Bucklersbury House, 3 Queen Victoria Street.
Telephone: 44-171-236-3939.
Telecopier: 44-171-236-1113.
In New Delhi, India: Pathak & Associates, 13th Floor, Dr. Gopal Das
Bhaven, 28 Barakhamba Road.
Telephone: 91-11-373-8793.
Telecopier: 91-11-335-3761.
In New York, New York: 599 Lexington Avenue.
Telephone: 212-326-3939.
Cable Address: "JONESDAY NEWYORK."
Telex: 237013 JDRP UR.
Telecopier: 212-755-7306.
In Paris, France: 62, rue du Faubourg Saint-Honore.
Telephone: 33-1-44-71-3939.
Telex: 290156 Surgoe.
Telecopier: 33-1-49-24-0471.
In Pittsburgh, Pennsylvania: 500 Grant Street, 31st Floor.
Telephone: 412-391-3939.
Cable Address: "Attorneys Pittsburgh".
Telecopier: 412-394-7959.
In Riyadh, Saudi Arabia: The International Law Firm, Sulaymaniyah
Center, Tahlia Street, P.O. Box 22166.
Telephone: (966-1) 462-8866.
Telecopier: (966-1) 462-9001.
In Taipei, Taiwan: 8th Floor, 2 Tun Hwa South Road, Section 2.
Telephone: (886-2) 704-6808.
Telecopier: (886-2) 704-6791.
In Tokyo, Japan: Toranomon MT Building, 4th Floor, 10-3, Toranomon
3-Chome, Minato-ku, Tokyo 105, Japan.
Telephone: 81-3-3433-3939.
Telecopier: 81-3-5401-2725.

(See Next Column)

In Washington, D.C.: Metropolitan Square, 1450 G Street, N.W.
Telephone: 202-879-3939.
Cable Address: "Attorneys Washington."
Telex: 89-2410 ATTORNEYS WASH.
Telecopier: 202-737-2832.
MEMBER OF FIRM IN LOS ANGELES
Victor G. Savikas

For Complete List of Firm Personnel, See General Section

For full biographical listings, see the Martindale-Hubbell Law Directory

LYON & LYON LLP (AV)

A Limited Liability Partnership including Professional Corporations
First Interstate World Center, 47th Floor, 633 West Fifth
　Street, 90071-2066
Telephone: 213-489-1600
Fax: 213-955-0440
Email: lyon@lyonlyon.com *URL:* http://www.lyonlyon.com
Costa Mesa, California Office: Suite 1200, 3200 Park Center Drive.
Telephone: 714-751-6606.
Fax: 714-751-8209.
San Jose, California Office: Suite 1150, 303 Almaden Boulevard.
Telephone: 408-993-1555.
Fax: 408-287-2664.
La Jolla, California Office: Suite 660, 4250 Executive Square.
Telephone: 619-552-8400.
Fax: 619-552-0159.

MEMBERS OF FIRM
Roland N. Smoot　　　　　　　　Arnold Sklar
Conrad R. Solum, Jr.　　　　　　John M. Benassi
James W. Geriak (A Professional　　　(La Jolla Office)
　Corporation) (Costa Mesa　　　James H. Shalek
　Office)　　　　　　　　　　Allan W. Jansen
Robert M. Taylor, Jr.　　　　　　　(Costa Mesa Office)
　(Costa Mesa Office)　　　　　Robert W. Dickerson
Samuel B. Stone (A Professional　　Roy L. Anderson
　Corporation) (Costa Mesa　　　David B. Murphy
　Office)　　　　　　　　　　　(Costa Mesa Office)
Douglas E. Olson (A　　　　　　James C. Brooks
　Professional Corporation) (La　　Jeffrey M. Olson
　Jolla Office)　　　　　　　　Steven D. Hemminger
Robert E. Lyon (A Professional　　　(San Jose Office)
　Corporation)　　　　　　　　Jerrold B. Reilly
Robert C. Weiss (A Professional　　Paul H. Meier
　Corporation)　　　　　　　　John A. Rafter, Jr.
Richard E. Lyon, Jr., (A　　　　　Kenneth H. Ohriner
　Professional Corporation)　　　Mary S. Consalvi
John D. McConaghy (A　　　　　　(La Jolla Office)
　Professional Corporation)　　　Lois M. Kwasigroch
William C. Steffin (A　　　　　　Lawrence R. LaPorte
　Professional Corporation)　　　Robert C. Laurenson
Coe A. Bloomberg (A　　　　　　　(La Jolla Office)
　Professional Corporation)　　　Carol A. Schneider
J. Donald McCarthy (A
　Professional Corporation)

ASSOCIATES
Hope E. Melville　　　　　　　　Anthony C. Chen
Michael J. Wise　　　　　　　　　(La Jolla Office)
Kurt T. Mulville　　　　　　　　Kenneth S. Roberts
　(Costa Mesa Office)　　　　　　(Costa Mesa Office)
Theodore S. Maceiko　　　　　　Brent D. Sokol
Richard Warburg　　　　　　　　Clarke W. Neumann, Jr.
　(La Jolla Office)　　　　　　　(La Jolla Office)
James P. Brogan　　　　　　　　John C. Kappos
　(Costa Mesa Office)　　　　　　(Costa Mesa Office)
Jeffrey D. Tekanic　　　　　　　Thomas J. Brindisi
Corrine M. Freeman　　　　　　　Richard C. Hsu
　(Costa Mesa Office)　　　　　Catherine Joyce
David A. Randall　　　　　　　　Charles Calvin Fowler
Christopher A. Vanderlaan　　　　　(Costa Mesa Office)
Bruce G. Chapman　　　　　　　Lisa Ward Karmelich
David T. Burse (San Jose Office)　　Vicki Gee Norton
Charles R. Balgenorth　　　　　　　(La Jolla Office)
Wayne B. Brown　　　　　　　　Jonathan T. Losk
　(La Jolla Office)　　　　　　　Timothy J. Lithgow
Jeffrey A. Miller　　　　　　　　　(La Jolla Office)
　(San Jose Office)　　　　　　　Michael A. Tomasulo
Armand F. Ayazi　　　　　　　　Thomas R. Rouse
Jessica R. Wolff　　　　　　　　Edward M. Jordan
　(La Jolla Office)　　　　　　　Charles A. Kertell
Mark J. Carlozzi　　　　　　　　James K. Sakaguchi
　(Costa Mesa Office)　　　　　　(Costa Mesa Office)
Sheldon O. Heber　　　　　　　Gary H. Silverstein
　(La Jolla Office)　　　　　　　(La Jolla Office)
Jeffrey William Guise　　　　　　Amy Stark Hellenkamp
　(La Jolla Office)　　　　　　　(La Jolla Office)
Charles S. Berkman　　　　　　Richard H. Pagliery
　(La Jolla Office)　　　　　　　William J. Kolegraff
Sheryl Rubinstein Silverstein　　　　(La Jolla Office)
　(La Jolla Office)　　　　　　Andrei Iancu
David E. Wang

(See Next Column)

LYON & LYON LLP—*Continued*

ASSOCIATES (Continued)

Jonathan Hallman
(La Jolla Office)
Lynn Y. McKernan
(San Jose Office)
Michael Bolan (San Jose Office)
Farshad Farjami
Dmitry Milikovsy
(San Jose Office)

Gregory R. Stephenson
Howard N. Wisnia
(La Jolla Office)
Mary Agnes Tuck
Arlyn Alonzo
Neal Matthew Cohen
(Costa Mesa Office)

OF COUNSEL

Bradford J. Duft
(La Jolla Office)
Suzanne L. Biggs
(La Jolla Office)

F.T. Alexandra Mahaney
(La Jolla Office)
Stephen S. Korniczky
(La Jolla Office)

Representative Clients: Cedars-Sinai Medical Center; Genentech; Honda; Mag Instrument, Inc.; Mitsubishi; Panavision; Quantum Corporation; Spectra-Physics, Inc.

For full biographical listings, see the Martindale-Hubbell Law Directory

HOWARD B. MILLER

(See El Segundo)

O'MELVENY & MYERS LLP (AV)

400 South Hope Street, 90071-2899
Telephone: 213-669-6000
Cable Address: "Moms"
Facsimile: 213-669-6407
Email: omminfo@omm.com
Century City, California Office: 1999 Avenue of the Stars, 90067-6035.
Telephone: 310-553-6700.
Facsimile: 310-246-6779.
Newport Beach, California Office: 610 Newport Center Drive, 92660-6429.
Telephone: 714-760-9600.
Cable Address: "Moms".
Facsimile: 714-669-6994.
San Francisco, California Office: Embarcadero Center West Tower, 275 Battery Street, 94111-3305.
Telephone: 415-984-8700.
Facsimile: 415-984-8701.
New York, New York Office: Citicorp Center, 153 East 53rd Street, 10022-4611.
Telephone: 212-326-2000.
Facsimile: 212-326-2061.
Washington, D.C. Office: 555 13th Street, N.W., 20004-1109.
Telephone: 202-383-5300.
Cable Address: "Moms".
Facsimile: 202-383-5414.
London, England Office: 10 Finsbury Square, London, EC2A 1LA.
Telephone: 0171-256-8451.
Facsimile: 0171-638-8205.
Tokyo, Japan Office: Sanbancho KB-6 Building, 6 Sanbancho, Chiyoda-ku, Tokyo 102, Japan.
Telephone: 03-3239-2900.
Facsimile: 03-3239-2432.
Hong Kong Office: Suite 1905, Peregrine Tower, Lippo Centre, 89 Queensway, Central, Hong Kong.
Telephone: 852-2523-8266.
Facsimile: 852-2522-1760.
Shanghai, Peoples Republic of China Office: Shanghai International Trade Centre, Suite 2011, 2200 Yan An Road West, Shanghai, 200335, PRC.
Telephone: 86-21-6219-5363.
Facsimile: 86-21-6275-4949.

PARTNER
Patrick Lynch

For Complete List of Firm Personnel, See General Section

For full biographical listings, see the Martindale-Hubbell Law Directory

OPPENHEIMER POMS SMITH (AV)

2029 Century Park East, 38th Floor, 90067
Telephone: 310-788-5000
FAX: 310-277-1297
Email: owdlaw.com
Orange County Office: 1920 Main Street, Suite 1050, Irvine, California, 92714.
Telephone: 714-263-8250.
FAX: 714-263-8260.
San Jose, California Office: 333 West Santa Clara Street, Suite 1000, 95113.
Telephone: 408-275-8790.
FAX: 408-275-8793.
Oppenheimer Wolff & Donnelly:
Brussels, Belgium Office: Avenue Louise 250, Box 31, 1050.
Telephone: 32-2-626-0500.
FAX: 32-2-626-0510.
Chicago, Illinois Office: Two Prudential Plaza, 45th Floor, 180 North Stetson Avenue, 60601.

(See Next Column)

Minneapolis, Minnesota Office: 3400 Plaza VII, 45 South Seventh Street, 55401.
Telephone: 612-344-9300.
FAX: 612-344-9376.
New York, N.Y. Office: Citicorp Center, 153 East 53rd Street, 10022.
Telephone: 212-826-5000.
Telecopier: 212-486-0708.
Paris, France Office: 53 Avenue Montaigne, 75008.
Telephone: (33/1) 44 95 03 50.
FAX: (33/1) 44 95 03 40.
St. Paul, Minnesota Office: 1700 First Bank Building, 55101.
Telephone: 612-223-2500.
FAX: 612-223-2596.
Washington, D.C. Office: 1020 Nineteenth Street, N.W., Suite 400, 20036.
Telephone: 202-293-6300.
FAX: 202-293-6200.
Detroit, Michigan Office: Timberland Office Park, Suite 250, 5445 Corporate Drive, 48098.
Telephone: 810-267-8500.
FAX: 810-267-8559.
Affiliated Offices:
Goudsmit & Branbergen, J.J. Viottastraat, 46 Amsterdam 1071. Telephone: 31-20-662-30-31.
FAX: 31-20-673-65-58.
Pisano, DeVito, Maiano & Catucci, Piazza Del Duomo, 20, Milan 20122.
Telephone: 39-2-878281.
FAX: 39-2-861275.
Pisano, DeVito, Maiano & Catucci, Via G. Borsi, 3, Rome 00197.
Telephone: 39-6-8079087.
FAX: 39-6-8078407.

Richard L. Gausewitz
(Resident, Irvine Office)
Michael A. Kondzella
(Resident, Irvine Office)
Alan C. Rose
William Poms
Guy Porter Smith
Gary E. Lande
Louis J. Bovasso
Edward F. O'Connor
(Resident, Irvine Office)
Bernard R. Gans
Michael D. Harris
Jerry R. Potts
Mark P. Wine
(Not admitted in CA)
Christopher Darrow

Jane Shay Wald
Douglas N. Larson
David J. Oldenkamp
Marc E. Brown
Terry L. Miller
(Resident, Irvine Office)
Kurt A. MacLean
(Resident, Irvine Office)
J. Patrick Weir
Charles Rosenberg
James A. Henricks
Alan P. Block
James W. Inskeep
Steven W. Smyrski
Scott R. Hansen
Peter L. Holmes
Craig A. Slavin

Joel D. Voelzke

Reference: City National Bank (Century Plaza Office, Century City).

For full biographical listings, see the Martindale-Hubbell Law Directory

PRETTY, SCHROEDER & POPLAWSKI, A PROFESSIONAL CORPORATION (AV)

Suite 2000, 444 South Flower Street, 90071
Telephone: 213-622-7700
Telecopier: 213-489-4210

Laurence H. Pretty
Robert A. Schroeder
Edward G. Poplawski

Mark Garscia
Jeffrey F. Craft
Michael J. MacDermott

Suzanne R. Jones

COUNSEL
Richard A. Wallen

OF COUNSEL
Walton Eugene Tinsley

Paul D. Tripodi, II
Marc H. Cohen
Keith A. Newburry
Sharon M. Fujita
J. Chris James

John A. Griecci
Anne Wang
Jeanine L. Hayes
Marc E. Hankin
Jeffrey A. Finn

For full biographical listings, see the Martindale-Hubbell Law Directory

ROBBINS, BERLINER & CARSON (AV)

Fifth Floor, Figueroa Plaza, 201 North Figueroa Street, 90012-2628
Telephone: 213-977-1001
Telecopier: 213-977-1003

MEMBERS OF FIRM

Billy A. Robbins
Robert Berliner
John Carson

Michael S. Elkind
Leonard D. Messinger
John M. May

Clark D. Gross

ASSOCIATES

Ying-Kit Lau
Horacio A. Farach
Sharon Wong

Deborah M. Nesset
Pete A. Smits
Wean Khing Wong

Lisa N. Partain

(See Next Column)

ROBBINS, BERLINER & CARSON, *Los Angeles—Continued*

OF COUNSEL

John P. Spitals

For full biographical listings, see the Martindale-Hubbell Law Directory

SHAPIRO, ROSENFELD & CLOSE, A PROFESSIONAL CORPORATION (AV)

Suite 2600, One Century Plaza, 2029 Century Park East, 90067
Telephone: 310-277-1818
Telecopier: 310-201-4776
Email: src__law@ix.netcom.com

Mitchell S. Shapiro	Jonathan J. Panzer
Edward M. Rosenfeld	Cathryn S. Gawne
Richard H. Close	Lisa K. Skaist
Helmut F. Furth	Rhonda H. Mehlman
Rochelle Buchsbaum Spandorf	Marna F. Miller
Douglas L. Carden	Jennifer A. DeMarrais

OF COUNSEL

Alan D. Jacobson	Alan G. Dowling
	Barry Kurtz

For full biographical listings, see the Martindale-Hubbell Law Directory

SMALL LARKIN & KIDDÉ (AV)

10940 Wilshire Boulevard, Eighteenth Floor, 90024
Telephone: 310-209-4400
Fax: 310-209-4450
Cable Address: SLK MARK
Telex: 49616151
Email: SLK@SLKlaw.com *URL:* http://www.lainet.com/legal/

MEMBERS OF FIRM

Thomas M. Small	Christopher C. Larkin
Joan Kupersmith Larkin	Jon E. Hokanson
Thomas S. Kiddé	Janet A. Kobrin

Kenneth L. Wilton	Donald J. Cox, Jr.
Barry C. Seaton	Michelle A. Cooke
Karen E. Samuels	Sasha E. Farrah
	(Not admitted in CA)

LEGAL SUPPORT PERSONNEL

Susan Brady Blasco

For full biographical listings, see the Martindale-Hubbell Law Directory

MENLO PARK, San Mateo Co.

ARNOLD, WHITE & DURKEE, A PROFESSIONAL CORPORATION (AV)

155 Linfield Drive, 94025-3741
Telephone: 415-614-4500
Facsimile: 415-614-4599
Email: info@awd.com *URL:* http://www.awd.com
Houston, Texas Office: 750 Bering Drive, 77057-2198; P.O. Box 4433, 77210-4433.
Telephone: 713-787-1400.
Facsimile: 713-789-2679.
Telex: 79-0924.
Austin, Texas Office: 1900 One American Center, 600 Congress Avenue, 78701-3248.
Telephone: 512-418-3000.
Facsimile: 512-474-7577.
Arlington, Virginia Office: 2001 Jefferson Davis Highway, Suite 401, 22202-3604.
Telephone: 703-415-1720.
Facsimile: 703-415-1728.
Chicago, Illinois Office: 800 Quaker Tower, 321 North Clark Street, 60610-4714.
Telephone: 312-744-0090.
Facsimile: 312-755-4489.
Minneapolis, Minnesota Office: 4850 First Bank Place, 601 Second Avenue South, 55402-4320.
Telephone: 612-321-2800.
Facsimile: 612-321-9600.

Gerald P. Dodson	Karen J. Kramer
Glenn W. Rhodes	(Not admitted in CA)
Mark K. Dickson	John R. Moore
Emily A. Evans	(Not admitted in CA)
David L. Bilsker	Chun-Pok "Roger" Leung
James F. Valentine	David West
Erica D. Wilson	Daniel T. Shvodian

For full biographical listings, see the Martindale-Hubbell Law Directory

FISH & RICHARDSON P.C. (AV)

2200 Sand Hill Road Suite 100, 94025
Telephone: 415-322-5070
Fax: 415-854-0875
Email: info@fr.com *URL:* http://www.fr.com
Washington, D.C. Office: 601 13th Street, N.W.
Telephone: 202-783-5070.
Fax: 202-783-2331.
Houston, Texas Office: One Riverway, Suite 1200.
Telephone: 713-629-5070.
Fax: 713-629-7811.
Boston, Massachusetts Office: 225 Franklin Street.
Telephone: 617-542-5070.
Fax: 617-542-8906.
Telex: 200154.
Minneapolis, Minnesota Office: Fish & Richardson P.C., P.A., 60 South Sixth Street, Suite 3300.
Telephone: 612-335-5070.
Fax: 612-288-9696.
La Jolla, California Office: 4225 Executive Square, Suite 1400.
Telephone: 619-678-5070.
Fax: 619-678-5099.
New York, N.Y. Office: 45 Rockefeller Plaza, Suite 2800.
Telephone: 212-765-5070.
Fax: 212-258-2291.

Frederick P. Fish (1855-1930)	John R. Schiffhauer
W.K. Richardson (1859-1951)	Karl Bozicevic
James H. A. Pooley	Jack L. Slobodin
Hans R. Troesch	William J. Egan, III
John E. Gartman	Reginald J. Suyat
	Jodi L. Sutton

OF COUNSEL

Mark A. Lemley	Roger S. Borovoy

Frank E. Scherkenbach	David J. Goren
Shelley K. Wessels	David M. Barkan
Wayne P. Sobon	Mark D. Kirkland
Howard G. Pollack	Timothy A. Porter
David M. Shaw	Audrey M. Sugimura
(Not admitted in CA)	

For full biographical listings, see the Martindale-Hubbell Law Directory

NEWPORT BEACH, Orange Co.

DRUMMOND & DUCKWORTH (AV)

4590 MacArthur Boulevard, Suite 500, 92660
Telephone: 714-724-1255
Fax: 714-724-1139
Email: patent__lawyer@msn.com

William H. Drummond	David G. Duckworth

For full biographical listings, see the Martindale-Hubbell Law Directory

KNOBBE, MARTENS, OLSON & BEAR, LLP (AV)

A Limited Liability Partnership including Professional Corporations
620 Newport Center Drive, 16th Floor, 92660
Telephone: 714-760-0404
Fax: 714-760-9502
San Diego, California Office: 501 West Broadway, Suite 1400.
Telephone: 619-235-8550.
Fax: 619-235-0176.
Riverside, California Office: 3801 University Avenue, Suite 710.
Telephone: 909-781-9231.
Fax: 909-781-4507.

Louis J. Knobbe (P.C.)	Vito A. Canuso III
Don W. Martens (P.C.)	William H. Shreve
Gordon H. Olson (P.C.)	Lynda J. Zadra-Symes
James B. Bear	Steven J. Nataupsky
Darrell L. Olson (P.C.)	Paul A. Stewart
William B. Bunker	Joseph F. Jennings
William H. Nieman	Craig S. Summers
Lowell Anderson	Brenton R. Babcock
Arthur S. Rose	Diane M. Reed
James F. Lesniak	Johnathan A. Barney
Jerry T. Sewell	John R. King
John B. Sganga, Jr.	Ronald J. Schoenbaum
Edward A. Schlatter	Richard C. Gilmore
W. Gerard von Hoffmann, III	John P. Giezentanner
Joseph R. Re	Adeel S. Akhtar
Catherine J. Holland	Frederick S. Berretta
Karen J. Vogel	Christopher A. Colvin
(Not admitted in CA)	James T. Hagler
Andrew H. Simpson	Stephen M. Lobbin
Jeffrey L. Van Hoosear	Douglas G. Muehlhauser
Daniel E. Altman	David N. Weiss
Ernest A. Beutler, Jr.	Lori L. Yamato
Marguerite L. Gunn	Glenn R. Smith
Stephen C. Jensen	Ann A. Byun

(See Next Column)

KNOBBE, MARTENS, OLSON & BEAR LLP—*Continued*

Stacey R. Halpern	John C. Wilson
R. Scott Weide	Joseph J. Basista
Michael K. Friedland	Lee W. Henderson
Stephen C. Beuerle	Chad W. Miller

Lena A. Basile

Representative Clients: AST Research Inc., Irvine; ASM America-Phoenix; NIH Washington, D.C.; Microsoft Corp.

For full biographical listings, see the Martindale-Hubbell Law Directory

---

OAKLAND,* Alameda Co.

PEZZOLA & REINKE, A PROFESSIONAL CORPORATION (AV)

Suite 1300, Lake Merritt Plaza, 1999 Harrison Street, 94612
Telephone: 510-273-8750
Telecopier: 510-834-7440
San Francisco, California Office: 650 California Street, 32nd Floor, 94111.
Telephone: 415-989-9710.
Menlo Park, California Office: 3000 Sand Hill Road, Building 4, Suite 160, 94025.
Telephone: 415-854-8797.

Stephen P. Pezzola

OF COUNSEL

Robert E. Krebs

Representative Clients: Medlogic Global Corporation; Ultimate Media Enterprises; Vertisoft Systems, Inc.

For full biographical listings, see the Martindale-Hubbell Law Directory

---

ORINDA, Contra Costa Co.

GILLIN, JACOBSON, ELLIS, LARSEN & DOYLE (AV)

2 Theatre Square Suite 230, 94563
Telephone: 510-258-0800
Fax: 510-848-0266
Email: lawfirm@gjeld.com
San Francisco Office: One Sutter Street, 10th Floor.
Telephone: 415-986-4777.

Andrew R. Gillin	Richard P. Doyle, Jr.
Ralph L. Jacobson	Susan Hunt
Luke Ellis	Mitchell S. Rosenfeld
James Paul Larsen	Catherine T. Doyle

For full biographical listings, see the Martindale-Hubbell Law Directory

---

PALO ALTO, Santa Clara Co.

BROWN & BAIN (AV)

1755 Embarcadero Road, Suite 200, 94306
Telephone: 415-856-9411
Telecopier: 415-856-6061
Phoenix, Arizona Affiliated Office: Brown & Bain, A Professional Association, 2901 North Central Avenue, P.O. Box 400.
Telephone: 602-351-8000.
Telecopier: 602-351-8516.
Tucson, Arizona Affiliated Office: Brown & Bain, A Professional Association. One South Church Avenue, Nineteenth Floor, P.O. Box 2265.
Telephone: 602-798-7900
Telecopier: 602-798-7945.

COUNSEL

Lois W. Abraham	Ian C. Ballon

For Complete List of Firm Personnel, See General Section

For full biographical listings, see the Martindale-Hubbell Law Directory

---

FISH & NEAVE (AV⊤)

Fish, Richardson & Neave, New York (1916-1969)
525 University Avenue Suite 300, 94301
Telephone: 415-617-4000
Telecopier: 415-617-4090
New York, New York Office: 1251 Avenue of the Americas.
Telephone: 212-596-9000.
Telex: 14-8367.
Cable Address: Fishneave.
Telecopier: 212-596-9090.

RESIDENT MEMBERS

Edward F. Mullowney	Norman H. Beamer
Robert J. Goldman	Mark D. Rowland
(Not admitted in CA)	Edward J. DeFranco

(See Next Column)

RESIDENT ASSOCIATES

Vicki S. Veenker	Derek Minihane
Nicola A. Pisano	(Not admitted in CA)
Gabrielle E. Higgins	Kurtis D. MacFerrin
Kevin P.B. Johnson	Ann Marie Whitley
Petrina S. Hsi	(Not admitted in CA)
(Not admitted in CA)	

For full biographical listings, see the Martindale-Hubbell Law Directory

---

FTHENAKIS & COLVIN (AV)

540 University Avenue, Suite 300, 94301
Telephone: 415-326-1397
Telecopier: 415-326-3203

MEMBERS OF FIRM

Basil P. Fthenakis	Oliver P. Colvin

For full biographical listings, see the Martindale-Hubbell Law Directory

---

KOLISCH HARTWELL DICKINSON McCORMACK & HEUSER, A PROFESSIONAL CORPORATION (AV)

420 Florence Street, 94301
Telephone: 415-325-8673
Facsimile: 415-325-5076
Email: concepts@concepts-law.com
Portland, Oregon Office: 200 Pacific Building, 520 S.W. Yamhill Street.
Telephone: 503-224-6655.
Fax: 503-295-6679.
Boise, Idaho Office: 802 W. Bannock, Suite 403A.
Telephone: 208-384-9166.
Fax: 208-384-9169.

Jon M. Dickinson	Peter E. Heuser
(Not admitted in CA)	David A. Fanning
John M. McCormack	Pierre C. Van Rysselberghe

For full biographical listings, see the Martindale-Hubbell Law Directory

---

TOWNSEND AND TOWNSEND AND CREW LLP (AV)

A Limited Liability Partnership including a Professional Corporation
379 Lytton Avenue, 94301-1431
Telephone: 415-326-2400
Telecopier: 415-326-2422
Email: inquire@townsend.com *URL:* http://www.townsend.com
San Francisco, California Office: Two Embarcadero Center, Eighth Floor.
Telephone: 415-576-0200.
Facsimile: 415-576-0300.
Denver, Colorado Office: 1200 17th Street, Suite 2700.
Telephone: 303-571-4000.
Fax: 303-571-4321.
Seattle, Washington Office: 601 Union Street, Suite 5400.
Telephone: 206-467-9600.
Telecopier: 206-623-6793.

MEMBERS OF FIRM

Kenneth R. Allen	Gary T. Aka
Robert C. Colwell	William M. Smith
Daniel J. Furniss	Paul C. Haughey
David N. Slone	Theodore G. Brown, III
James F. Hann	William J. Bohler
James M. Heslin	Karen B. Dow

OF COUNSEL

Henry K. Woodward	Renée A. Fitts

ASSOCIATES

Joe Liebeschuetz	Margaret A. Powers
Joseph M. Villeneuve	Kenneth L. Johnson
William L. Shaffer	Stephen J. Akerley
Richard Takashi Ogawa	Alice L. Wong
Theodore T. Herhold	Michael A. Gelblum
Shailendra C. Bhumralkar	Sam G. Campbell, III
Stephen Y.F. Pang	Byron W. Cooper
Dan H. Lang	Scott William Hewett
Michael J. Ritter	R. Ted Apple
John Thomas Raffle	Chiahua George Yu
Matthew B. Murphy	Hao-Yuan Tung
Mark D. Barrish	Gregory Scott Bishop
Melvin D. Chan	Shane Horan Hunter

James F. Kurkowski

For full biographical listings, see the Martindale-Hubbell Law Directory

---

PASADENA, Los Angeles Co.

FREDERICK GOTHA (AV)

Suite 823, 80 South Lake Avenue, 91101
Telephone: 818-796-1849
Telecopier: 818-405-0952

For full biographical listings, see the Martindale-Hubbell Law Directory

Pasadena—Continued

JOSEPH E. MUETH A LAW CORPORATION (AV)

225 South Lake Avenue, Eighth Floor, 91101-1599
Telephone: 818-584-0396
Fax: 818-584-6862

Joseph E. Mueth

Reference: Bank of America, 333 South Hope Street, Los Angeles, California.

For full biographical listings, see the Martindale-Hubbell Law Directory

SACRAMENTO,* Sacramento Co.

BLOOM & KRETEN (AV⊤)

77 Cadillac Drive, 95825
Telephone: 916-921-6181
Fax: 916-921-9213
Towson, Maryland Office: 401 Washington Avenue.
Telephone: 410-337-2295.
Facsimile: 410-337-2296.
European Office: Rue Frans Merjay, 21 B-1060, Brussels, Belgium.
Hong Kong Office: 10/F Vogue Building, 67 Wyndham Street, Central Hong Kong.

MEMBERS OF FIRM

Bernhard Kreten

Leonard Bloom
(Not admitted in CA)

LEGAL SUPPORT PERSONNEL

Dennis A. DeBoo (Resident)

For full biographical listings, see the Martindale-Hubbell Law Directory

GERBER, RITCHEY & O'BANION (AV)

5441 Fair Oaks Boulevard, 95608
Telephone: 916-971-1010
Facsimile: 916-487-0706
URL: http://www.intellectual.com

MEMBERS OF FIRM

Joseph E. Gerber
John P. O'Banion

James M. Ritchey

For full biographical listings, see the Martindale-Hubbell Law Directory

HUNTER RICHEY DI BENEDETTO & BREWER, LLP (AV)

A Limited Liability Partnership
Renaissance Tower, 801 K Street, 23rd Floor, 95814-3525
Telephone: 916-491-3000
Facsimile: 916-491-3080
Email: hrdb@hrdb.com URL: http://www.hrdb.com

MEMBERS OF FIRM

William S. Hunter	James F. Geary
Win R. Richey	Janet C. Eisenbeis
Florence L. Di Benedetto	Jeffery D. Harris
Roy E. Brewer	Stephen C. Ruehmann
Anne E. Ferguson	Ralph T. Ferguson
Judith J. Citko	Sharon K. Sandeen
	Kathryn T. Papalia

LEGAL SUPPORT PERSONNEL

Lori J. Kelly (Paralegal)	Michele L. Nickell
Deborah M. Romero (Paralegal)	(Legal Assistant)
Linda Jane Hall	Dawn Krein (Legal Assistant)
(Legal Assistant)	Stephanie L. Neumann
Jennifer E. Mueller	(Legal Assistant)
(Legal Assistant)	

For full biographical listings, see the Martindale-Hubbell Law Directory

SAN DIEGO,* San Diego Co.

BAKER, MAXHAM, JESTER & MEADOR, A PROFESSIONAL CORPORATION (AV)

Symphony Towers, 750 B Street, Suite 3100, 92101
Telephone: 619-233-9004
Facsimile: 619-544-1246 (Groups I, II, III)
URL: http://www.bmjm.com

Freling E. Baker	Michael H. Jester
Lawrence A. Maxham	Terrance A. Meador
	David A. Hall

Dan L. Hubert	Bruce W. Greenhaus
	Kent D. Baker

OF COUNSEL

Ervin F. Johnston	Walter W. Duft

Reference: Peninsula Bank of San Diego.

For full biographical listings, see the Martindale-Hubbell Law Directory

BROWN, MARTIN, HALLER & McCLAIN (AV)

1660 Union Street, 92101-2926
Telephone: 619-238-0999
Telex: 4992789 BANDM
Fax: (Group I, II, III) 619-238-0062

Carl R. Brown	Eleanor M. Musick
Neil F. Martin	Kathleen A. Pasulka
John L. Haller	Stephanie L. Seidman
James W. McClain	(Not admitted in CA)

Lawrence D. Maxwell	R. Kevin Perkins
Barry F. Soalt	Gary L. Bastman

OF COUNSEL

Russell Ben Miller

LEGAL SUPPORT PERSONNEL

Katherine Proctor	Sheryl Doran
(Patent Agent)	(Technical Advisor)
Paula Schoeneck (Patent Agent)	Luisa Bigornia
Jeffrey W. Winnkelman	(Technical Advisor)
(Technical Advisor)	

Representative Clients: Cubic Corp.; U.S. Elevator Corp.

For full biographical listings, see the Martindale-Hubbell Law Directory

FITCH, EVEN, TABIN & FLANNERY (AV)

4250 Executive Square, Suite 510, 92037
Telephone: 619-552-1311
Telecopier: 619-552-0095
Chicago, Illinois Office: 135 South La Salle Street, Suite 900.
Telephone: 312-372-7842.
Cable Address: "Patlaw".
Telex: 20 6566 Patlaw Cgo.
Telecopier: 312-372-7848.
Washington, D.C. Office: 2305 Wilson Boulevard (Arlington, Virginia, 22201).
Telephone: 703-243-9236.
Telecopier: 703-243-9207.

MEMBERS OF FIRM

Julius Tabin	Bryant R. Gold (Resident)
James J. Schumann (Not admitted in CA; Resident)	

OF COUNSEL

Robert R. Meads (Resident)

Thomas F. Lebens (Resident)	Robroy R. Fawcett (Resident)
	Denise M. Hickey

For full biographical listings, see the Martindale-Hubbell Law Directory

SAN FRANCISCO,* San Francisco Co.

FLEHR, HOHBACH, TEST, ALBRITTON & HERBERT (AV)

Suite 3400, Four Embarcadero Center, 94111-4187
Telephone: 415-781-1989
Telefax: 415-398-3249
TWX: 910-372-6669 "FLEHR SFO"
Email: FLEHR-IPLAW.COM
Palo Alto, California Office: Suite 200, 850 Hansen Way.
Telephone: 415-494-8700.
Telefax: 415-494-8771.

MEMBERS OF FIRM

Paul D. Flehr (1898-1992)	Richard E. Backus
Elmer S. Albritton (1922-1988)	James A. Sheridan
Harold C. Hohbach	(Resident, Palo Alto Office)
(Resident, Palo Alto Office)	Robert B. Chickering
Aldo J. Test	Gary S. Williams
(Resident, Palo Alto Office)	(Resident, Palo Alto Office)
Thomas O. Herbert	Richard F. Trecartin
(Resident, Palo Alto Office)	C. Michael Zimmerman
Donald N. MacIntosh	Walter H. Dreger
Jerry G. Wright	Steven F. Caserza
Edward S. Wright	(Resident, Palo Alto Office)
(Resident, Palo Alto Office)	William S. Galliani
David J. Brezner	Laura L. Kulhanjian

ASSOCIATES

Karen S. Smith	Jan P. Brunelle
Michael A. Kaufman	Robin M. Silva
Janet Elizabeth Muller	David C. Ashby
(Resident, Palo Alto)	(Resident, Palo Alto Office)
Edward N. Bachand	Douglas J. Crisman
(Resident, Palo Alto Office)	Mark T. Kresnak
R. Michael Ananian	David R. Heckadon
(Resident, Palo Alto Office)	Maria S. Swiatek
Stephen M. Knauer	(Resident, Palo Alto Office)
	Dolly Vance

OF COUNSEL

Julian Caplan (Resident, Palo Alto Office)

(See Next Column)

FLEHR, HOHBACH, TEST, ALBRITTON & HERBERT—*Continued*

LEGAL SUPPORT PERSONNEL

Robert L. McCarthy	Cheryl Ann Hernandez
Wendy Dea	Holly A. Metz
Steven D. Dennison	Margaret B. Joyce

Representative Clients: Genentec; McKesson, Inc.; Safeway Stores, Inc.; Watkins-Johnson Co.

For full biographical listings, see the Martindale-Hubbell Law Directory

---

FLYNN, DELICH & WISE (AV)

Suite 1750, 580 California Street, 94104
Telephone: 415-693-5566
Fax: 415-693-0410
Long Beach, California Office: 1 World Trade Center, Suite 1800.
Telephone: 310-435-2626.
Fax: 310-437-7555.

Sam D. Delich

Representative Clients: American Hawaii Cruises; Holland America Line; Through Transport Mutual Insurance Association, Ltd.; The Britannia Steam Ship Insurance Association Limited; The Steamship Mutual Underwriting Association (Bermuda) Ltd.; General Steamship Corp., Ltd.; Commodore Cruise Line, Ltd.; Interocean Steamship Corporation; Sea-Land Service, Inc.; Hatteras Yachts.

For full biographical listings, see the Martindale-Hubbell Law Directory

---

GALLAGHER & LATHROP, A PROFESSIONAL CORPORATION (AV)

601 California Street, Suite 1111, 94108-2805
Telephone: 415-989-8080
Facsimile: 415-989-0910
Email: office@patentz.com

Thomas A. Gallagher	David N. Lathrop

For full biographical listings, see the Martindale-Hubbell Law Directory

---

LIMBACH & LIMBACH, L.L.P. (AV)

2001 Ferry Building, 94111
Telephone: 415-433-4150
Fax: 415-433-8716
Email: inquiry@limbach.com
San Jose, California Office: 10 Almaden, Suite 1400.
Telephone: 408-291-5225.

MEMBERS OF FIRM

Karl A. Limbach	Michael A. Stallman
George C. Limbach	Philip A. Girard
John K. Uilkema	Michael J. Pollock
J. William Wigert, Jr.	Stephen M. Everett
Philip M. Shaw, Jr.	Deborah A. Bailey-Wells
Neil A. Smith	Maria S. Cefalu
Veronica Colby Devitt	Alfred A. Equitz
Ronald L. Yin	W. Patrick Bengtsson
Gerald T. Sekimura	Mark A. Dalla Valle

Charles P. Sammut

ASSOCIATES

Richard A. Nebb	Patricia Coleman James
Richard E. Wawrzyniak	Alan A. Limbach
Alan D. Minsk	Heidi L. Keefe
Mark C. Pickering	Douglas C. Limbach
Kathleen A. Frost	Brian J. Keating
David B. Woycechowsky	Seong-Kun Oh
Alan S. Hodes	Cameron A. King

Kyla L. Harriel

OF COUNSEL

J. Thomas McCarthy	Ted Naccarella

LEGAL SUPPORT PERSONNEL
PATENT AGENTS

Michael R. Ward	Steven M. Santisi

For full biographical listings, see the Martindale-Hubbell Law Directory

---

MAJESTIC, PARSONS, SIEBERT & HSUE, A PROFESSIONAL CORPORATION (AV)

Four Embarcadero Center, Suite 1100, 94111-4121
Telephone: 415-362-5556
Telex: 278638 MGPS
Telecopier: 415-362-5418
Santa Clara, California Office: 2700 Augustine Drive, Suite 198.
Telephone: 415-362-5556.

Gerald P. Parsons	J. Suzanne Siebert
Martin F. Majestic	James S. Hsue

Victor Hayato Okumoto	Joseph P. O'Malley

K. Alison DeRuntz

OF COUNSEL

Keiichi Nishimura

(See Next Column)

LEGAL SUPPORT PERSONNEL

Philip Yau

For full biographical listings, see the Martindale-Hubbell Law Directory

MEDLEN & CARROLL, LLP (AV)

220 Montgomery Street, Suite 2200, 94104
Telephone: 415-705-8410
Facsimile: 415-397-8338
Redwood City, California Office: 702 Marshall St., Suite 600.
Telephone: 415-299-8120.
Facsimile: 415-299-8127.
Cambridge, Massachusetts Office: Five Cambridge Center, Second Floor.
Telephone: 617-354-5455.
Facsimile: 617-354-8132.
Toledo, Ohio Office: One Seagate, Suite 960.
Telephone: 419-247-1010.
Facsimile: 419-247-1011.

MEMBERS OF FIRM

Virginia Shaw Medlen	Peter G. Carroll

ASSOCIATES

Lisa K. Levine	Cynthia Soumoff

Todd A. Lorenz

INTERNATIONAL TRADEMARK DEPARTMENT

Daw Aye Cho (Manager)

For full biographical listings, see the Martindale-Hubbell Law Directory

---

PHILLIPS, MOORE, LEMPIO & FINLEY (AV)

455 Market Street, Suite 1940, 94105-2440
Telephone: 415-882-7024
Facsimile: 415-882-7034
Email: lawyers@sf-iplaw.com *URL:* http://www.sf-iplaw.com

MEMBERS OF FIRM

Leonard Phillips (1924-1985)	Paul S. Lempio (Retired, 1996)
Carlisle M. Moore	Hugh D. Finley
(Retired, 1995)	Michael N. Berg

ASSOCIATE

Susan M. Reid

Representative Clients: Barrier Systems, Inc.; Blentech Corp.

For full biographical listings, see the Martindale-Hubbell Law Directory

---

SKJERVEN, MORRILL, MacPHERSON, FRANKLIN & FRIEL LLP (AV)

Suite 800, 601 California Street, 94108
Telephone: 415-986-8383
Telecopier: 415-982-7372
San Jose, California Office: Suite 700, 25 Metro Drive.
Telephone: 408-453-9200.
Telecopier: 408-453-7979.
Austin, Texas Office: Suite 300 West, 9600 Great Hills Trail.
Telephone: 512-794-3600.
Telecopier: 512-794-3601.

MEMBERS OF FIRM

Richard H. Skjerven (At San Jose, California and Austin, Texas Offices)	Charles D. Chalmers (Also at San Jose and Austin, Texas Offices)
Robert B. Morrill (Also at San Jose Office)	Kenneth E. Leeds (Resident, San Jose Office)
Alan H. MacPherson (Resident, San Jose Office)	Brian D. Ogonowsky (Resident, San Jose Office)
Richard K. Franklin (Resident, San Jose Office)	David E. Steuber (Resident, San Jose Office)
Thomas J. Friel, Jr. (Also at San Jose Office)	Laura Terlizzi (Resident, San Jose Office)
Marc David Freed (Also at San Jose Office)	Edward V. Anderson (Resident, San Jose Office)
Anthony de Alcuaz (Resident, San Jose Office)	Edward C. Kwok (Resident, San Jose Office)
Justin T. Beck (Resident, San Jose Office)	Michelle G. Breit (Resident, San Jose Office)
Joseph A. Greco (Resident, San Jose Office)	Stephen A. Terrile (Resident, Austin, Texas Office)
David W. Heid (Resident, San Jose Office)	Russell L. Johnson (Resident, San Jose Office)
Forrest E. Gunnison (Resident, San Jose Office)	Kimberly Paul Zapata (Resident, San Jose Office)
Norman R. Klivans, Jr. (Resident, San Jose Office)	Ken J. Koestner (Resident, Austin, Texas Office)

ASSOCIATES

Michael Shenker (Resident, San Jose Office)	T. Lester Wallace (Resident, San Jose Office)
Scott R. Brown (Resident, San Jose Office)	Peter H. Kang (Resident, San Jose Office)
Patrick T. Bever (Resident, San Jose Office)	Alexandra J. Horne (Resident, San Jose Office)
James E. Parsons (Resident, San Jose Office)	David T. Millers (Resident, San Jose Office)

(See Next Column)

SKJERVEN, MORRILL, MACPHERSON, FRANKLIN & FRIEL LLP, *San Francisco—Continued*

ASSOCIATES (Continued)

E. Eric Hoffman
(Resident, San Jose Office)
Omkarmurthy K. Suryadevara
(Resident, San Jose Office)
Emily M. Haliday
(Resident, San Jose Office)
Elizabeth Ann Hemphill
(Resident, San Jose Office)
William L. Paradice III
(Resident, San Jose Office)
L. Scott Primak
(Resident, San Jose Office)
Thomas E. Rossmeissl
(Resident, San Jose Office)
Steven M. Levitan
(Resident, San Jose Office)
Arthur J. Behiel
(Resident, San Jose Office)
Michael J. Halbert
(Resident, San Jose Office)
Jennifer A. Ochs
(Resident, San Jose Office)

Serge J. Hodgson
(Resident, San Jose Office)
Edward S. Mao
(Resident, San Jose Office)
Scott D. Minden
(Resident, San Jose Office)
Lisa Lee Pate
(Resident, San Jose Office)
Matthew T. Powers
(Resident, San Jose Office)
Leanne Price
(Resident, San Jose Office)
Jeffrey C. Whitley
(Resident, San Jose Office)
Paul Yang
(Resident, San Jose Office)
Juergen Krause-Polstorff
(Resident, San Jose Office)
Bryan K. Anderson
(Resident, San Jose Office)
Kent B. Chambers (Resident,
Austin, Texas Office)

OF COUNSEL

Thomas S. MacDonald
(Resident, San Jose Office)

H. Donald Nelson
(Resident, San Jose Office)

TECHNICAL COUNSEL

Ronald J. Meetin (Resident, San Jose Office)

PATENT AGENT

Anthony G. Dervan (Resident, San Jose Office)

Reference: Bank of America.

For full biographical listings, see the Martindale-Hubbell Law Directory

---

TOWNSEND AND TOWNSEND AND CREW LLP (AV)

A Limited Liability Partnership including a Professional Corporation
Two Embarcadero Center, Eighth Floor, 94111-3834
Telephone: 415-576-0200
Facsimile: 415-576-0300
Email: inquire@townsend.com *URL:* http://www.townsend.com
Palo Alto, California Office: 379 Lytton Avenue.
Telephone: 415-326-2400.
Telecopier: 415-326-2422.
Denver, Colorado Office: 1200 17th Street, Suite 2700.
Telephone: 303-571-4000.
Fax: 303-571-4321.
Seattle, Washington Office: 601 Union Street, Suite 5400.
Telephone: 206-467-9600.
Telecopier: 206-623-6793.

MEMBERS OF FIRM

Charles E. Townsend
(1868-1944)
Eugene Crew
William M. Hynes (A
Professional Corporation)
Bruce W. Schwab
George M. Schwab
Kenneth R. Allen
(Resident, Palo Alto Office)
Daniel J. Furniss
(Resident, Palo Alto Office)
James F. Hann
(Resident, Palo Alto Office)
M. Henry Heines
Gary T. Aka
(Resident, Palo Alto Office)
James G. Gilliland, Jr.
Charles E. Krueger
Richard L. Grossman
Paul C. Haughey
(Resident, Palo Alto Office)
Guy W. Chambers
Kenneth A. Weber
William J. Bohler
(Resident, Palo Alto Office)
Karen B. Dow
(Resident, Palo Alto Office)
Michael E. Woods
Margaret C. McHugh

Stephen S. Townsend
(1917-1986)
Paul W. Vapnek
J. Georg Seka
Roger L. Cook
William L. Jaeger
Robert J. Bennett
Robert C. Colwell
(Resident, Palo Alto Office)
David N. Slone
(Resident, Palo Alto Office)
Joel Linzner
James M. Heslin
(Resident, Palo Alto Office)
William M. Smith (Palo Alto,
California and Seattle,
Washington Offices)
Mark A. Steiner
E. Lynn Perry
Theodore G. Brown, III
(Resident, Palo Alto Office)
Mark T. Jansen
Steven W. Parmelee
(Resident in Seattle)
Ellen Lauver Weber
Duane H. Mathiowetz
K. T. (Sunny) Cherian
Mark Lee Pettinari
John A. Hughes

Kevin L. Bastian

OF COUNSEL

Charles E. Townsend, Jr.
Albert J. Hillman
Henry K. Woodward
(Resident, Palo Alto Office)
Renée A. Fitts
(Resident, Palo Alto Office)

Anthony B. Diepenbrock
Dirks B. Foster
Edward J. Keeling
Lesley S. Craig
(Resident, Denver Office)

(See Next Column)

ASSOCIATES

Victoria M. Kalmanson
Susan M. Spaeth
Eugenia Garrett-Wackowski
Babak Sadegh Sani
Joseph M. Villeneuve
(Resident, Palo Alto Office)
Richard Takashi Ogawa
(Resident, Palo Alto Office)
Stephen J. Le Blanc
Tom Hunter
Darin J. Gibby
(Resident, Denver Office)
Larry Mendenhall
Stephen Y.F. Pang
(Resident, Palo Alto Office)
Michael J. Ritter
(Resident, Palo Alto Office)
David G. Beck
Roger Kennedy
Jonathan Alan Quine
Melvin D. Chan
(Resident, Palo Alto Office)
Margaret A. Powers
(Resident, Palo Alto Office)
John R. Storella
David B. Ran
(Not admitted in CA)
Hector A. Alicea
John T. Rigsbee, Jr.
Michael A. Gelblum
(Resident, Palo Alto Office)
Byron W. Cooper
(Resident, Palo Alto Office)
John C. Baum
Gerald T. Gray
Annette S. Parent
Timothy L. Smith
R. Ted Apple
(Resident, Palo Alto Office)
Susan Kay Faris
Hao-Yuan Tung
(Resident, Palo Alto Office)
Kevin T. LeMond
(Not admitted in CA)

Paul F. Kirsch
Philip H. Albert
R. Gwen Lipsey
Joe Liebeschuetz
(Resident, Palo Alto Office)
William L. Shaffer
(Resident, Palo Alto Office)
Theodore T. Herhold
(Resident, Palo Alto Office)
William B. Kezer
Shailendra C. Bhumralkar
(Resident, Palo Alto Office)
Marc M. Gorelnik
Dan H. Lang
(Resident, Palo Alto Office)
John Thomas Raffle
(Resident, Palo Alto Office)
Matthew B. Murphy
(Resident, Palo Alto Office)
Mark D. Barrish
(Resident, Palo Alto Office)
Rosa S. Kim
Kenneth L. Johnson
(Resident, Palo Alto Office)
William T. Gallagher
Stephen J. Akerley
(Resident, Palo Alto Office)
Alice L. Wong
(Resident, Palo Alto Office)
Sam G. Campbell, III
(Resident, Palo Alto Office)
Diane E. Eisenberg
Brian A. E. Smith
Roger T. Barrett
(Resident, Denver, Office)
Scott William Hewett
(Resident, Palo Alto Office)
Laurie H. van Löben Sels
Chiahua George Yu
(Resident, Palo Alto Office)
Gregory Scott Bishop
(Resident, Palo Alto Office)
Shane Horan Hunter
(Resident, Palo Alto Office)

ASSOCIATES (Continued)

Jennifer Y. Liu
James F. Kurkowski
(Resident, Palo Alto Office)

Jeffrey J. King
(Resident, Seattle Office)

For full biographical listings, see the Martindale-Hubbell Law Directory

---

SAN JOSE,* Santa Clara Co.

HOPKINS & CARLEY, A LAW CORPORATION (AV)

Fifteenth Floor, 150 Almaden Boulevard, 95113-2089
Telephone: 408-286-9800
Facsimile: 408-998-4790

Leon A. Carley (1908-1984)　　Jon Michaelson
　　　　　　Robert V. Hawn

OF COUNSEL

Donald J. Pagel

Christine Baddell Redfield　　　Suzanne F. Seavello
　　　　Linda Larson Usoz

For Complete List of Firm Personnel, See General Section

For full biographical listings, see the Martindale-Hubbell Law Directory

---

SKJERVEN, MORRILL, MACPHERSON, FRANKLIN & FRIEL LLP (AV)

Suite 700, 25 Metro Drive, 95110
Telephone: 408-453-9200
Telecopier: 408-453-7979
San Francisco, California Office: Suite 800, 601 California Street.
Telephone: 415-986-8383.
Telecopier: 415-982-7372.
Austin, Texas Office: Suite 300 West, 9600 Great Hills Trail.
Telephone: 512-794-3600.
Telecopier: 512-794-3601.

MEMBERS OF FIRM

Richard H. Skjerven
(Also at Austin, Texas Office)
Robert B. Morrill
Alan H. MacPherson
Richard K. Franklin
Thomas J. Friel, Jr.
Marc David Freed
Anthony de Alcuaz

Justin T. Beck
Joseph A. Greco
David W. Heid
Forrest E. Gunnison
Norman R. Klivans, Jr.
Charles D. Chalmers (Also at
San Francisco and Austin,
Texas Offices)

(See Next Column)

SKJERVEN, MORRILL, MACPHERSON, FRANKLIN & FRIEL LLP—*Continued*

MEMBERS OF FIRM (Continued)

Kenneth E. Leeds	Michelle G. Breit
Brian D. Ogonowsky	Stephen A. Terrile (Resident,
David E. Steuber	Austin, Texas Office)
Laura Terlizzi	Russell L. Johnson
Edward V. Anderson	Kimberly Paul Zapata
Edward C. Kwok	Ken J. Koestner (Resident,
	Austin, Texas Office)

ASSOCIATES

Michael Shenker	Thomas E. Rossmeissl
Scott R. Brown	Steven M. Levitan
Patrick T. Bever	Arthur J. Behiel
James E. Parsons	Michael J. Halbert
T. Lester Wallace	Jennifer A. Ochs
Peter H. Kang	Serge J. Hodgson
Alexandra J. Horne	Edward S. Mao
David T. Millers	Scott D. Minden
E. Eric Hoffman	Lisa Lee Pate
Omkarmurthy K. Suryadevara	Matthew T. Powers
Emily M. Haliday	Leanne Price
Elizabeth Ann Hemphill	Jeffrey C. Whitley
William L. Paradice III	Paul Yang
L. Scott Primak	Juergen Krause-Polstorff

Bryan K. Anderson

OF COUNSEL

Thomas S. MacDonald   H. Donald Nelson

TECHNICAL COUNSEL

Ronald J. Meetin

PATENT AGENT

Anthony G. Dervan

Reference: Bank of America.

For full biographical listings, see the Martindale-Hubbell Law Directory

---

TUSTIN, Orange Co.

JACKSON LAW CORPORATION (AV)

Irvine Law Building, 17592 Irvine Boulevard, Suite 100, 92780
Telephone: 714-832-2080
Telecopier: 714-731-3167
Email: JacksonLaw@aol.com

Harold L. Jackson

For full biographical listings, see the Martindale-Hubbell Law Directory

---

WOODLAND HILLS, Los Angeles Co.

KELLY, BAUERSFELD, LOWRY & KELLEY (AV)

6320 Canoga Avenue Suite 1650, 91367
Telephone: 818-347-7900
Fax: 818-340-2859
Email: swkelley@msn.com

John E. Kelly	John D. Bauersfeld
Stuart O. Lowry	Scott W. Kelley

ASSOCIATE

Kamran Fattahi

Representative Clients: Rain Bird Sprinkler Mfg. Corp.; Seagate Technology, Inc.; J. R. Simplot Co.; MiniMed Inc.; Ebco Mfg. Co.; Medical Packaging Corp.; Kelly-Moore Paint Co., Inc.; Mrs. Gooch's Natural Foods, Inc.; Everest & Jennings, Inc.; Hydrotechnology, Inc.

For full biographical listings, see the Martindale-Hubbell Law Directory

LAW OFFICES OF ELLIOTT N. KRAMSKY (AV)

5850 Canoga Avenue, Suite 400, 91367
Telephone: 818-992-5221
Fax: 818-703-6978

For full biographical listings, see the Martindale-Hubbell Law Directory

---

COLORADO

ASPEN, * Pitkin Co.

FREEMAN & JENNER, P.C. (AV(T))

215 South Monarch Street, Suite 202, 81611
Telephone: 970-925-3400
FAX: 970-925-4043
Bethesda, Maryland Office: 3 Bethesda Metro Center, Suite 1410.
Telephone: 301-907-7747.
FAX: 301-907-9877.
Washington, D.C. Office: 1000 16th Street, N.W., Suite 300.
Telephone: 301-907-7747.

(See Next Column)

Martin H. Freeman

BOULDER, * Boulder Co.

GREENLEE, WINNER AND SULLIVAN, P.C. (AV)

5370 Manhattan Circle, Suite 201, 80303
Telephone: 303-499-8080
Facsimile: 303-499-8089
Email: winner@greenwin.com *URL:* http://www.greenwin.com/website

Lorance L. Greenlee	Ellen P. Winner
	Sally A. Sullivan

LEGAL SUPPORT PERSONNEL
PATENT AGENTS

Jennie M. Caruthers	Alison A. Langford
Donna M. Ferber	G. William Van Cleave

Reference: Bank One.

For full biographical listings, see the Martindale-Hubbell Law Directory

---

COLORADO SPRINGS, * El Paso Co.

HANES & SCHUTZ, P.C. (AV)

7222 Commerce Center Drive Suite 243, 80919
Telephone: 719-260-7900
Denver Line: 303-740-9694
Fax: 719-260-7904
Email: hands@rmii.com

Richard W. Hanes	Tim Schutz

Mark D. Francis (Not admitted in CO)

Representative Clients: Colorado State University Research Foundation; Dieterich Standard; Beech Aircraft Corp.; Surevoid Products, Inc.; Pikes Peak National Bank; Western Filter Co.; Pacer Industries; El Paso County Medical Society; Dynamic Materials Corporation; Injection Research Specialists, Inc.

For full biographical listings, see the Martindale-Hubbell Law Directory

---

DENVER, * Denver Co.

DORR, CARSON, SLOAN & BIRNEY, P.C. (AV)

3010 East Sixth Avenue, 80206
Telephone: 303-333-3010
FAX: 303-333-1470
URL: http://www.patnet.com/dcsb

Robert C. Dorr	Jack C. Sloan
W. Scott Carson	Thomas S. Birney

Stuart Langley	Leslie P. Kramer

OF COUNSEL

Christopher H. Munch	Steve A. Mains
	Gary H. Peterson

Representative Clients: Winegard Co.; Hewlett Packard; Intercat, Inc.; Steam Way International; Big Sur Waterbeds; Taco John's International; Micron Technology; University of Denver; The Denver Post Co.; Dreyer's Grand Ice Cream.

For full biographical listings, see the Martindale-Hubbell Law Directory

---

HOLME ROBERTS & OWEN LLP (AV)

Suite 4100, 1700 Lincoln, 80203
Telephone: 303-861-7000
Telecopier: 303-866-0200
Email: hro@hro.com *URL:* http://www.hro.com
Boulder, Colorado Office: Suite 400, 1401 Pearl Street.
Telephone: 303-444-5955.
Telecopier: 303-444-1063.
Colorado Springs, Colorado Office: Suite 1300, 90 South Cascade Avenue.
Telephone: 719-473-3800.
Telecopier: 719-633-1518.
Salt Lake City, Utah Office: Suite 1100, 111 East Broadway.
Telephone: 801-521-5800.
Telecopier: 801-521-9639.
London, England Office: Mellier House, 26a Albemarle Street.
Telephone: 44-171-499-8776.
Telecopier: 44-171-499-7769.
Moscow, Russia Office: Kosmodamianskaya Nab. #52/1, Suite 9100, 113054.
Telephone: 7095-961-3000.
Telecopier: 7095-961-3001.
Kiev, Ukraine Office: Terestchenkovskaya #19, Suite 2, 252004.
Telephone: 380-44-224-1348.
Telecopier: 380-44-224-4986.

(See Next Column)

HOLME ROBERTS & OWEN LLP, *Denver—Continued*

PARTNERS OF FIRM

Lynn Parker Hendrix
Paul E. Smith (Boulder Office)
Boyd N. Boland
James R. Ghiselli
  (Boulder Office)

Richard L. Gabriel
Kevin P. Block (Managing
  Partner, Kiev Office)
George G. Matava
Patrick K. Perrin
  (Boulder Office)

SPECIAL COUNSEL

David H. Goldberg

ASSOCIATES

Christopher Boffey (Resident,
  Moscow, Russia Office)

Daniel P. Maguire
Steven B. Smith
  (Colorado Springs Office)

For Complete List of Firm Personnel, See General Section

For full biographical listings, see the Martindale-Hubbell Law Directory

---

CONNECTICUT

FAIRFIELD, Fairfield Co.

PERMAN & GREEN, LLP (AV)

425 Post Road, 06430-6232
Telephone: 203-259-1800
Facsimile: 203-255-5170
Email: PGPANT@aol.com

MANAGING PARTNER

Clarence A. Green

PARTNERS

Harry F. Smith

Mark F. Harrington

ASSOCIATES

David M. Warren
  (Not admitted in CT)
Albert W. Hilburger
Thomas L. Tully
Michael J. Tully
  (Not admitted in CT)

John J. Goodwin
  (Not admitted in CT)
Ralph D. Gelling
  (Not admitted in CT)
Thomas P. Dowd
  (Not admitted in CT)

OF COUNSEL

Donald C. Caulfield

For full biographical listings, see the Martindale-Hubbell Law Directory

---

MILFORD, New Haven Co.

MELVIN I. STOLTZ (AV)

51 Cherry Street, 06460
Telephone: 203-874-8183
Facsimile: 203-878-9607
Email: melstol@ziplink.net

For full biographical listings, see the Martindale-Hubbell Law Directory

---

*NEW HAVEN,** New Haven Co.

BACHMAN & LaPOINTE, P.C. (AV)

900 Chapel Street, Suite 1201, 06510
Telephone: 203-777-6628
Cable Address: "Balapat" New Haven
Telex: 710-465-4066
FAX: 203-865-0297
Email: bachlap@aol.com

Robert H. Bachman
  (Not admitted in CT)

Gregory P. LaPointe
Barry L. Kelmachter

Richard S. Strickler
  (Not admitted in CT)

George A. Coury

For full biographical listings, see the Martindale-Hubbell Law Directory

---

WIGGIN & DANA (AV)

One Century Tower, 06508-1832
Telephone: 203-498-4400
Telefax: 203-782-2889
Hartford, Connecticut Office: One CityPlace.
Telephone: 203-297-3700.
FAX: 203-525-9380.
Stamford, Connecticut Office: Three Stamford Plaza, 301 Tresser
Boulevard.
Telephone: 203-363-7600.
Telefax: 203-363-7676.

(See Next Column)

MEMBERS OF FIRM

Shaun S. Sullivan
J. Drake Turrentine
  (Resident at Stamford)

D. Terence Jones
Mary R. Norris
James F. Farrington, Jr.
  (Resident at Stamford)

COUNSEL

Sidney R. Bresnick
  (Not admitted in CT)
Dale L. Carlson

Gregory S. Rosenblatt
  (Not admitted in CT)
William A. Simons
  (Not admitted in CT)

ASSOCIATES

Thomas L. Casagrande
Francis J. Duffin
Todd E. Garabedian
  (Not admitted in CT)
Merton G. Gollaher

Robert S. Hauser
Patricia Kavee Melick
  (Resident at Stamford)
Laura Wright Wooton
  (Resident at Stamford)

For Complete List of Firm Personnel, See General Section

For full biographical listings, see the Martindale-Hubbell Law Directory

---

SIMSBURY, Hartford Co.

LAW OFFICE OF VICTOR E. LIBERT (AV)

3 Mill Pond Lane Powder Forest Business Park, P.O. Box
  538, 06070-0538
Telephone: 860-651-9321
Fax: 860-651-5735

Victor E. Libert

ASSOCIATES

Frederick A. Spaeth

David T. Shoneman

For full biographical listings, see the Martindale-Hubbell Law Directory

---

WESTPORT, Fairfield Co.

LEVETT, ROCKWOOD & SANDERS, PROFESSIONAL CORPORATION (AV)

33 Riverside Avenue, P.O. Box 5116, 06881
Telephone: 203-222-0885
Telecopier: 203-226-8025

David R. Levett
John Sanders
B. Lance Sauerteig
Madeleine F. Grossman
James M. Barton
Judy A. Rabkin
Dorit Schutzengel Heimer

Sharon M. Schweitzer
Barbara A. Young
Steven M. Siegelaub
Marc J. Kurzman
Suzanne B. Albani
Peter H. Struzzi
Edward B. Chansky

Cheryl L. Johnson

OF COUNSEL

William O. Rockwood, Jr.

Robin K. Higgins

Ernest C. Mysogland

Patricia D. Weitzman

Representative Clients: Bankers Trust Company; Cannondale Corp.; Caradon, Inc.; Electrolux Corporation; Exxon Chemical Corporation; HealthSouth Corp.; Heyman Properties; Hospital of Saint Raphael; Marketing Corporation of America; St. Vincent's Medical Center.

For full biographical listings, see the Martindale-Hubbell Law Directory

---

DELAWARE

---

*WILMINGTON,** New Castle Co.

CONNOLLY, BOVE, LODGE & HUTZ (AV)

1220 Market Street, P.O. Box 2207, 19899-2207
Telephone: 302-658-9141
Telecopier: 302-658-5614
URL: http://WWW.CBLHLAW.COM

Arthur G. Connolly (Emeritus)
James M. Mulligan, Jr.
Arthur G. Connolly, Jr.
Rudolf E. Hutz
Harold Pezzner
John D. Fairchild
  (Not admitted in DE)
Richard M. Beck
  (Not admitted in DE)
Paul E. Crawford
Stanley C. Macel, III
Thomas M. Meshbesher

George Pazuniak
N. Richard Powers
Jeffrey B. Bove
Collins J. Seitz, Jr.
Patricia Smink Rogowski
Mary W. Bourke
Robert G. McMorrow, Jr.
  (Not admitted in DE)
R. Eric Hutz
Ashley I. Pezzner
William E. McShane
  (Not admitted in DE)

Gerard M. O'Rourke

(See Next Column)

CONNOLLY, BOVE, LODGE & HUTZ—*Continued*

For Complete List of Firm Personnel, See General Section

For full biographical listings, see the Martindale-Hubbell Law Directory

POTTER ANDERSON & CORROON (AV)

350 Delaware Trust Building, P.O. Box 951, 19899-0951
Telephone: 302-984-6000
FAX: 302-658-1192
URL: HTTP://ATTYS.PACDELAWARE.COM

MEMBERS OF FIRM

Charles S. Crompton, Jr.   William J. Marsden, Jr.

ASSOCIATES

Joanne Ceballos   Michael S. McGinniss

Counsel for: Delaware Trust Capital Management, Inc.; Delmarva Power & Light Co.; Diamond State Telephone Co.; Hercules Inc.; Corporation Trust Co.; General Motors Corp.; Chrysler Corp.; Citicorp.

For Complete List of Firm Personnel, See General Section

For full biographical listings, see the Martindale-Hubbell Law Directory

DISTRICT OF COLUMBIA

WASHINGTON, D.C. Co.

* indicates certain Bar Register subscribers, in cities of comparable size and importance, who maintain an additional office in Washington, D.C. and who have arranged for representation as a part of the Washington, D.C. listings that follow

ADDUCI, MASTRIANI & SCHAUMBERG, L.L.P. (AV)

1140 Connecticut Avenue, N.W., Suite 250, 20036
Telephone: 202-467-6300
Telefax: 202-466-2006
Email: adduci.com

MEMBERS OF FIRM

V. James Adduci, II   James C. Lydon
Louis S. Mastriani   (Not admitted in DC)
Tom M. Schaumberg   David A. Guth
Ronald J. Kubovcik   Katherine S. Nucci
Barbara A. Murphy   Larry L. Shatzer, II
Timothy Sullivan   Marcela B. Stras

Anri Suzuki   Peter B. Martine
Gregory C. Anthes   Michael L. Doane
              Martin R. Fischer

A list of Representative Clients and References will be furnished upon request.

For full biographical listings, see the Martindale-Hubbell Law Directory

* BAKER & BOTTS, L.L.P. (AV)

A Registered Limited Liability Partnership
The Warner, 1299 Pennsylvania Avenue, N.W., 20004-2400
Telephone: 202-639-7700
Fax: 202-639-7832
Email: postmaster@bakerbotts.com
Houston, Texas Office: One Shell Plaza, 910 Louisiana.
Telephone: 713-229-1234.
Austin, Texas Office: 1600 San Jacinto Center, 98 San Jacinto Boulevard.
Telephone: 512-322-2500.
Dallas, Texas Office: 2001 Ross Avenue.
Telephone: 214-953-6500.
New York, New York Office: 599 Lexington Avenue.
Telephone: 212-705-5000.
Moscow, Russian Federation Office: 10 ul. Bolshaya Dmitrovka (formerly Pushkinskaya), 103031.
Telephone: 7095/921-5300 (Local); 7501/929-7070 (International).

MEMBERS OF FIRM

Scott F. Partridge   Rodger L. Tate

ASSOCIATES

James B. Arpin   James G. Gatto
Christopher C. Campbell   Stacy B. Margolies
              James Remenick

For Complete List of Firm Personnel, See General Section

For full biographical listings, see the Martindale-Hubbell Law Directory

BANNER & WITCOFF, LTD. (AV)

Established In 1920 - Predecessor Parent
1001 G Street, N.W., 20001-4597
Telephone: 202-508-9100
Facsimile: 202-508-9299
Email: skerpon@ba-iplaw.com *URL:* http://www.ba-iplaw.com
Chicago, Illinois Office: Ten South Wacker Drive.
Telephone: 312-715-1000.
Facsimile: 312-715-1234.
Boston, Massachusetts Office: 75 State Street.
Telephone: 617-345-9100.
Facsimile: 617-345-9111.

Robert F. Altherr, Jr.   Lance G. Johnson
Donald W. Banner   Sarah A. Kagan
Pamela I. Banner   Edward F. McKie, Jr.
Alan I. Cantor   Kathy J. McKnight
Alan S. Cooper   Nina L. Medlock
William J. Fisher   James A. Niegowski
Mary Gronlund   Thomas L. Peterson
Barry L. Grossman   Joseph M. Potenza
Dale H. Hoscheit   Steven P. Schad
Thomas H. Jackson   Joseph M. Skerpon

Scott M. Alter   Robert S. Katz
David J. Cho   Joanne Ludovici-Lint
  (Not admitted in DC)   Adriana S. Luedke
Gary D. Fedorochko   Victor W. Marton
  (Not admitted in DC)   (Not admitted in DC)
Eric T. Fingerhut   Kelly C. Maynard
Daniel E. Fisher   Christopher L. McKee
Updeep S. Gill (Mickey)   Frederic M. Meeker
  (Not admitted in DC)   Michael J. Shea
Christopher R. Glembocki   (Not admitted in DC)
  (Not admitted in DC)   Kenneth K.D. Vu
Brian E. Hanlon   (Not admitted in DC)
  (Not admitted in DC)   Wendi L. Weinstein
Patricia E. Hong   Susan A. Wolffe
              Bradley C. Wright
COUNSEL
William W. Beckett   Franklin D. Wolffe

For full biographical listings, see the Martindale-Hubbell Law Directory

* BELL, BOYD & LLOYD (AV)

1615 L Street, N.W., 20036
Telephone: 202-466-6300
FAX: 202-463-0678
Chicago, Illinois Office: Three First National Plaza, Suite 3300, 70 West Madison Street.
Telephone: 312-372-1121.
FAX: 312-372-2098.

RESIDENT PARTNERS

Dante J. Picciano   Watson T. Scott

For Complete List of Firm Personnel, See General Section

For full biographical listings, see the Martindale-Hubbell Law Directory

BEVERIDGE, DEGRANDI, WEILACHER & YOUNG, L.L.P. (AV)

Suite 800, 1850 M Street, N.W., 20036
Telephone: 202-659-2811
Cable Address: "Jemead"
Telex: WUI 64470; WU 89-2393;
Telecopier: 202-659-1462
Email: BEVERIDGE-DEGRANDI.COM

MEMBERS OF FIRM

Andrew B. Beveridge   Richard G. Young
  (1915-1972)   Michael A. Makuch
Joseph A. DeGrandi   Dennis C. Rodgers
Robert G. Weilacher   Helen Hill Minsker
              Maurice U. Cahn
ASSOCIATES
Helen M. McCarthy   George A. Metzenthin
Thomas L. Evans   (Not admitted in DC)
  (Not admitted in DC)

PATENT AGENTS
Frank C. Cimino   Carolyn A. Favorito
              Qixia Zhang
LEGAL SUPPORT PERSONNEL
Joseph E. Washington   Steven W. Collier

Reference: First American Bank, Washington, D.C.

For full biographical listings, see the Martindale-Hubbell Law Directory

Washington—Continued

BROWDY AND NEIMARK (AV)

419 Seventh Street, N.W., 20004
Telephone: 202-628-5197
Cable Address: "Overture"
Telecopier: 202-737- 3528
Email: BRWDYNMRK@NMAA.ORG

Sheridan Neimark　　　　　　　Roger L. Browdy

Anne M. Kornbau　　　　　　　Nick Bromer
Norman J. Latker　　　　　　　(Not admitted in DC)

OF COUNSEL
Iver P. Cooper

PATENT AGENT
Allen C. Yun

For full biographical listings, see the Martindale-Hubbell Law Directory

* DICKINSON, WRIGHT, MOON, VAN DUSEN & FREEMAN (AV)

Suite 800, 1901 L Street, N.W., 20036-3506
Telephone: 202-457-0160
Facsimile: 202-659-1559
Detroit, Michigan Office: 500 Woodward Avenue, Suite 4000.
Telephone: 313-223-3500.
Facsimile: 313-223-3598.
Bloomfield Hills, Michigan Office: 525 North Woodward Avenue, Suite 2000.
Telephone: 810-433-7200.
Facsimile: 810-433-7274.
Grand Rapids, Michigan Office: 200 Ottawa Avenue, N.W., Suite 900.
Telephone: 616-458-1300.
Facsimile: 616-458-6753.
Lansing, Michigan Office: Suite 200, 215 South Washington Square.
Telephone: 517-371-1730.
Facsimile: 517-487-4700.
Chicago, Illinois Office: 225 West Washington, Suite 400.
Telephone: 312-220-0300.
Facsimile: 312-220-0021.

RESIDENT PARTNERS
Conrad J. Clark　　　　　　Samuel D. Littlepage
William E. Elwood　　　　　Jeffrey M. Petrash
　　　　　Michael T. Platt

RESIDENT OF COUNSEL
Marc A. Bergsman　　　　　Lucien N. Nedzi
David R. Haarz　　　　　　Stephanie Karen Wade

RESIDENT ASSOCIATE
Paul L. Sharer

For Representative Clients, see biographical section, Detroit, Michigan.

For full biographical listings, see the Martindale-Hubbell Law Directory

KENNETH R. FEINBERG & ASSOCIATES (AV)

1120 20th Street, N.W. Suite 740 South, 20036
Telephone: 202-371-1110
Fax: 202-962-9290
New York, N.Y. Office: 780 3rd Avenue, Suite 2202.
Telephone: 212-527-9600.
Fax: 212-527-9611.

ASSOCIATES
Deborah E. Greenspan　　　Peter H. Woodin
Michael K. Rozen　　　　　(Not admitted in DC)
　(Not admitted in DC)　　M. Catherine Faint

OF COUNSEL
Jacqueline E. Zins

For full biographical listings, see the Martindale-Hubbell Law Directory

FINNEGAN, HENDERSON, FARABOW, GARRETT & DUNNER, L.L.P. (AV)

Suite 700, 1300 I Street, N.W., 20005-3315
Telephone: 202-408-4000
Cable Address: "Finderbow"
Telex: 440275 ITT; 248740 RCA;
Facsimile: 202-408-4400
Tokyo, Japan Office: Toranomon No. 45 Mori Building, Third Floor, 1-5, Toranomon 5-chome Minato-Ku.
Telephone: 0081-3-3431-6943.
Facsimile: 0081-3-3431-6945.
Brussels, Belgium Office: Avenue Louise 326, Box 37, 1050.
Telephone: 011-322-646-0353.
Facsimile: 011-322-646-2135.

MEMBERS OF FIRM
Marcus B. Finnegan (1927-1979)　Brian G. Brunsvold
Douglas B. Henderson　　　　Tipton D. Jennings IV
Ford F. Farabow Jr.　　　　　Jerry D. Voight
Arthur S. Garrett　　　　　　Laurence R. Hefter
Donald R. Dunner　　　　　　Kenneth E. Payne

(See Next Column)

MEMBERS OF FIRM (Continued)

Herbert H. Mintz　　　　　Clair X. Mullen Jr.
C. Larry O'Rourke　　　　Christopher P. Foley
Albert J. Santorelli　　　　John C. Paul
Michael C. Elmer　　　　　Griffith B. Price Jr.
Richard H. Smith　　　　　John F. Hornick
Stephen L. Peterson　　　　Robert D. Litowitz
John M. Romary　　　　　David M. Kelly
Bruce C. Zotter　　　　　Kenneth John Meyers
Dennis P. O'Reilley　　　　Carol P. Einaudi
Allen M. Sokal　　　　　　Walter Y. Boyd Jr.
Robert D. Bajefsky　　　　Steven M. Anzalone
Richard Lee Stroup　　　　Darrel C. Karl
David W. Hill　　　　　　　(Not admitted in DC)
Thomas L. Irving (Resident　Jean Burke Fordis
　Partner, Brussels, Belgium　Barbara Clarke McCurdy
　Office)　　　　　　　　James K. Hammond
Charles E. Lipsey　　　　　　(Not admitted in DC)
Thomas W. Winland　　　　Richard V. Burgujian
Basil J. Lewris　　　　　　John Michael Jakes
Martin I. Fuchs　　　　　　John C. Lowe
E. Robert Yoches　　　　　Dirk D. Thomas
Barry W. Graham　　　　　Thomas W. Banks
Susan Haberman Griffen　　Christopher P. Isaac
Richard B. Racine　　　　　Bryan C. Diner
Thomas H. Jenkins III　　　M. Paul Barker
Robert E. Converse Jr.　　　Mark S. Sommers
　　　　　Kenneth M. Frankel

COUNSEL
Arthur J. Levine　　　　　Ernest F. Chapman
George E. Hutchinson　　　　(Not admitted in DC)
Herbert W. Patterson　　　Wayne W. Herrington
William T. McClain　　　　Don O. Burley
Wilford L. Wisner　　　　　Robert A. Cahill
Robert F. Ziems　　　　　　(Not admitted in DC)
Robert J. Eichelburg　　　　Liam O'Grady
　　　　　　　　　　　(Not admitted in DC)

ASSOCIATES
William H. Pratt　　　　　Michael L. Leetzow
Gerson S. Panitch　　　　　David Avrum Manspeizer
David S. Forman　　　　　Linda A. Wadler
Vincent P. Kovalick　　　　Lori-Ann Johnson
James W. Edmondson　　　R. Bruce Bower
Michael R. McGurk　　　　Colleen Superko
Jeffrey A. Berkowitz　　　　(Not admitted in DC)
　(Not admitted in DC)　　Thomas H. Martin
Cheri M. Taylor　　　　　　(Not admitted in DC)
Joann M. Neth　　　　　　David L. Soltz
Michael R. Kelly (Resident　Lisa F. Peller
　Associate, Tokyo, Japan　Thalia V. Warnement
　Office)　　　　　　　　Michele C. Bosch
Judy Garcia Barrett　　　　　(Not admitted in DC)
Michael J. Bell　　　　　　Howard Warren Levine
Luke Andrew Kilyk　　　　Leslie I. Bookoff
　(Not admitted in DC)　　Linda S. Paine-Powell
James B. Monroe　　　　　John R. Alison
　(Not admitted in DC)　　Barbara R. Rudolph
Michael K. Kirschner　　　Jeff E. Schwartz
Jeffrey David Karceski　　　Anthony M. Gutowski
Glenn E. J. Murphy　　　　Sandra M. Pohlman
　(Not admitted in DC)　　Stephen G. Kalinchak
　　　　　Elizabeth J. Hecht

Reference: Crestar Bank, N.A., Washington, D.C.

For full biographical listings, see the Martindale-Hubbell Law Directory

FISH & RICHARDSON P.C. (AV)

601 13th Street N.W., 20005
Telephone: 202-783-5070
Fax: 202-783-2331
Email: info@fr.com *URL:* http://www.fr.com
Boston, Massachusetts Office: 225 Franklin Street.
Telephone: 617-542-5070.
Fax: 617-542-8906.
Houston, Texas Office: One Riverway, Suite 1200.
Telephone: 713-629-5070.
Fax: 713-629-7811.
Menlo Park, California Office: 2200 Sand Hill Road, Suite 100.
Telephone: 415-322-5070.
Fax: 415-854-0875.
Minneapolis, Minnesota Office: 60 South Sixth Street, Suite 3300.
Telephone: 612-335-5070.
Fax: 612-288-9696.
La Jolla, California Office: 4225 Executive Square, Suite 1400.
Telephone: 619-678-5070.
Fax: 619-678-5099.
New York, N.Y. Office: 45 Rockefeller Plaza, Suite 2800.
Telephone: 212-765-5070.
Fax: 212-258-2291.

(See Next Column)

FISH & RICHARDSON P.C.—*Continued*

Frederick P. Fish (1855-1930)	Barry E. Bretschneider
W. K. Richardson (1859-1951)	Terry G. Mahn
Ralph A. Mittelberger	Arnold P. Lutzker
	Ruffin B. Cordell

OF COUNSEL

Rene D. Tegtmeyer	Susan Ann Richards

Keith A. Barritt	William R. Johnson
John F. Hayden	(Not admitted in DC)
John C. Phillips	Linda Liu Kordziel
	Ami P. Shah

For full biographical listings, see the Martindale-Hubbell Law Directory

✱ FITZPATRICK, CELLA, HARPER & SCINTO (AV)

1001 Pennsylvania Avenue, N.W., 20004-2505
Telephone: 202-347-8100
Facsimile: 202-347-8136
New York, N.Y. Office: 277 Park Avenue.
Telephone: 212-758-2400. International-
Telex: FCHS 236262.
Cable Address: "Fitzcel New York".
Facsimile: 212-758-2982.
Orange County, California Office: 650 Town Center Drive, Suite 1800, Costa Mesa.
Telephone: 714-540-8700.
Facsimile: 714-540-9823.

RESIDENT PARTNERS

John W. Behringer	Richard P. Bauer
Lawrence A. Stahl	Scott D. Malpede
William M. Wannisky	(Not admitted in DC)
Warren E. Olsen	Thomas J. O'Connell

COUNSEL

Robert C. Kline

RESIDENT ASSOCIATES

Christopher Philip Wrist	William J. Zak, Jr.
Gary M. Jacobs	Daniel S. Glueck
Steven E. Warner	Brian L. Klock
Jack S. Cubert	(Not admitted in DC)
(Not admitted in DC)	T Tom C. Gellenthien
Mark A. Williamson	(Not admitted in DC)
Jean K. Dudek	Sean W. O'Brien
Anne M. Maher	(Not admitted in DC)
(Not admitted in DC)	

For full biographical listings, see the Martindale-Hubbell Law Directory

JACOBSON, PRICE, HOLMAN & STERN (AV)

The Jenifer Building, 400 Seventh Street, N.W., 20004
Telephone: 202-638-6666
Cable Address: "Lawpat"
Telefax: 202-393-5350; 202-393-5351; 202-393-5352
Email: 5028614@mcimail.com

MEMBERS OF FIRM

Harvey B. Jacobson, Jr.	Marsha G. Gentner
D. Douglas Price	Jonathan L. Scherer
John Clarke Holman	Stanford W. Berman
Simor L. Moskowitz	Irwin M. Aisenberg
Michael R. Slobasky	William E. Player

ASSOCIATES

Leesa N. Weiss	Peter Steven Weissman
Guillermo Enrique Baeza	(Not admitted in DC)
(Not admitted in DC)	Kasen Harvey Jacobson
Andrew J. Gray, IV	(Not admitted in DC)

LEGAL SUPPORT PERSONNEL
PATENT AGENT

Tania J. Keeble

OF COUNSEL

Marvin R. Stern	Thomas A. Mauro

For full biographical listings, see the Martindale-Hubbell Law Directory

KEIL & WEINKAUF (AV)

1101 Connecticut Avenue, N.W., 20036
Telephone: 202-659-0100
Telecopier: 202-659-0105

MEMBERS OF FIRM

Herbert B. Keil	Russell E. Weinkauf
	(Not admitted in DC)

SPECIAL COUNSEL

Gerald H. Bjorge	Norman G. Torchin

ASSOCIATES

Malcolm John MacDonald	Robert T. Barker
	(Not admitted in DC)

(See Next Column)

OF COUNSEL

Edward T. McCabe	George F. Helfrich
	(Not admitted in DC)

PATENT AGENT

Henry R. Jiles

For full biographical listings, see the Martindale-Hubbell Law Directory

✱ KENYON & KENYON (AV)

1025 Connecticut Avenue, N.W., 20036
Telephone: 202-429-1776
Telecopier: (202) 429-0796, Groups II & III
New York, N.Y. Office: One Broadway.
Telephone: 212-425-7200.
Frankfurt, Germany Office: Bockenheimer Landstrasse 97-99, 60325 Frankfurt am Main.
Telephone: (69) 97-58-050.
Telecopier: (69) 97-58-05-99.
San Jose, California Office: 333 West San Carlos Street.
Telephone: 408-995-2800.

RESIDENT PARTNERS

John C. Altmiller	Edward T. Colbert
Philip J. McCabe	William K. Wells, Jr.
	Frank Pietrantonio

RESIDENT COUNSEL

Donald Knox Duvall

RESIDENT OF COUNSEL

John M. Rommel

RESIDENT ASSOCIATES

Suzanne M. Parker	C. Kyle Musgrove
Robert D. Anderson	(Not admitted in DC)
Paul M. Richter, Jr.	Gary S. Morris
Mark M. Supko	Barry S. Goldsmith
William T. Enos	Colleen H. McDuffie
David B. Bonham	(Not admitted in DC)
Linda B. Blackburn	William M. Merone
(Not admitted in DC)	(Not admitted in DC)
Judith L. Toffenetti	John F. Kacvinsky
(Not admitted in DC)	John W. Bateman
Brian S. Mudge	(Not admitted in DC)
(Not admitted in DC)	R. Edward Brake

For full biographical listings, see the Martindale-Hubbell Law Directory

LANE, AITKEN & McCANN (AV)

Watergate Office Building, 2600 Virginia Avenue, N.W., 20037
Telephone: 202-337-5556
Telecopier: 202-337-8073
Email: lam@access.digex.net

MEMBERS OF FIRM

Richard L. Aitken	Laurence J. Marhoefer
Clifton E. McCann	(Not admitted in DC)
John P. Shannon, Jr.	Andrew C. Aitken
	(Not admitted in DC)

ASSOCIATE

David D'Zurilla

OF COUNSEL

Joseph M. Lane

For full biographical listings, see the Martindale-Hubbell Law Directory

LEWIS & TRATTNER (AV)

Suite 875, 1150 18th Street, N.W., 20036-3816
Telephone: 202-331-1416
800-333-2540
Telecopier: 202-331-1463
Email: lewistrat@aol.com

MEMBERS OF FIRM

Warren L. Lewis	Stephen M. Trattner

ASSOCIATES

Kathryn A. Rookes	Kay-Margaret Cronk
(Not admitted in DC)	

OF COUNSEL

Jeffrey E. Kolton

For full biographical listings, see the Martindale-Hubbell Law Directory

MORGAN & FINNEGAN, L.L.P. (AV)

A Registered Liability Partnership
1299 Pennsylvania Avenue, N.W., Suite 960, 20004
Telephone: 202-857-7887
Facsimile: 202-857-7929
New York, N.Y. Office: 345 Park Avenue.
Telephone: 212-758-4800.
Cable Address: "Findurpine".
Telecopier: (212) 751-6849.
Telex: ITT 421792.

(See Next Column)

MORGAN & FINNEGAN L.L.P., *Washington—Continued*
RESIDENT PARTNER
Edward A. Pennington
COUNSEL
John E. Hoel　　　　　　　　Joseph C. Redmond, Jr.
　(Not admitted in DC)

ASSOCIATES
Mark L. Hogge　　　　　　　Carla M. Krivak
Michael S. Marcus　　　　　　Joseph P. Curtin
Christopher J. Hamaty　　　　Michael A. Schwartz
　　　　　　　　　　　　　　　(Not admitted in DC)

For full biographical listings, see the Martindale-Hubbell Law Directory

---

* PENNIE & EDMONDS (AV)

1667 K Street, N.W., Suite 1000, 20006
Telephone: 202-496-4400
Facsimile: 202-495-4444
Email: pennie.com *URL:* http://www.pennie.com
New York, New York Office: 1155 Avenue of the Americas.
Telephone: 212-790-9090.
Telex: (WUI) 66141-Pennie.
Cable Address: "Penangold."
Facsimile: GI/GII/GIII (212) 869-9741, GIII (212) 869-8864.
Menlo Park, California Office: 2730 Sand Hill Road.
Telephone: 415-854-3660.
Facsimile: 415-854-3694.

John C. Pennie (1858-1921)　　Dean S. Edmonds (1879-1972)
PARTNERS
Harry C. Jones, III　　　　　Allan A. Fanucci
Stanton T. Lawrence, III　　　Marcia H. Sundeen
Joseph V. Colaianni　　　　　Paul J. Zegger
　　　　　　　　　　　　　　　(Not admitted in DC)
ASSOCIATES
Wilma F. Triebwasser　　　　Lorri W. Jones
　(Not admitted in DC)　　　　　(Not admitted in DC)
Troy R. Lester　　　　　　　Nancy H. Lutz
　(Not admitted in DC)　　　　Ajay S. Pathak
H.T. Than　　　　　　　　　　(Not admitted in DC)
Anthony M. Insogna　　　　　Thomas E. Coverstone
Nanda K. Alapati　　　　　　　(Not admitted in DC)
Jeffrey A. Wolfson　　　　　　Kevin G. Rooney
　　　　　　　　　　　　　　　(Not admitted in DC)

For full biographical listings, see the Martindale-Hubbell Law Directory

---

POLLOCK, VANDE SANDE & PRIDDY, R.L.L.P. (AV)

Eighth Floor, 1990 M Street, N.W., P.O. Box 19088, 20036
Telephone: 202-331-7111
Fax: 202-293-6229
Email: PVSP@PVSP.COM

MEMBERS OF FIRM
Elliott I. Pollock　　　　　　Morris Liss
George Vande Sande　　　　　Townsend M. Belser, Jr.
Robert R. Priddy　　　　　　Martin Abramson
Richard Wiener　　　　　　　George R. Pettit
Burton A. Amernick　　　　　Thomas J. Vande Sande
Stanley B. Green　　　　　　Louis Woo
　　　　　Elzbieta Chlopecka
ASSOCIATES
Eric John Franklin　　　　　Robert Scott Wales
　　　　　　　　　　　　　　　(Not admitted in DC)

For full biographical listings, see the Martindale-Hubbell Law Directory

---

ROTHWELL, FIGG, ERNST & KURZ, A PROFESSIONAL CORPORATION (AV)

555 Thirteenth Street, N.W., 20004
Telephone: 202-783-6040
Telecopier: 202-783-6031
International Telex: 64285
Cable Address: "Bnbpat"
Email: rfek@rfek.com
Omaha, Nebraska Office: 1125 South 103rd Street, Suite 720.
Telephone: 402-398-9400.
Fax: 402-398-1983.

G. Franklin Rothwell　　　　George R. Repper
E. Anthony Figg　　　　　　Bart G. Newland
Barbara G. Ernst　　　　　　Steven Lieberman
Raymond A. Kurz　　　　　　Vincent M. De Luca

Celine M. Jimenez　　　　　　Moon Soo Lee
Jeffrey Bayne McIntyre　　　　(Not admitted in DC)
Joseph A. Hynds　　　　　　Kenneth M. Fagin
Michael G. Sullivan　　　　　　(Not admitted in DC)
Mark I. Bowditch　　　　　　Stephen B. Parker

(See Next Column)

OF COUNSEL
Lawrence G. Norris　　　　　Robert J. Jondle (Resident,
　　　　　　　　　　　　　　　Omaha, Nebraska Office)

For full biographical listings, see the Martindale-Hubbell Law Directory

---

ROYLANCE, ABRAMS, BERDO & GOODMAN, L.L.P. (AV)

1225 Connecticut Avenue, N.W., 20036-2680
Telephone: 202-659-9076
Cable Address: "Roypat"
Telex: 64416
Facsimile: 202-659-9344
Email: RABG@roylance.com

D. C. Roylance (1920-1995)　　David L. Tarnoff
David S. Abrams　　　　　　Michael T. Murphy
Robert H. Berdo　　　　　　Garrett V. Davis
Alfred N. Goodman　　　　　Stacey J. Longanecker
Mark S. Bicks　　　　　　　　(Not admitted in DC)
Richard A. Flynt　　　　　　Thomas P. Hilliard
John E. Holmes　　　　　　　(Not admitted in DC)
SENIOR OF COUNSEL
Frank E. Robbins
OF COUNSEL
Susan Neuberger Weller

For full biographical listings, see the Martindale-Hubbell Law Directory

---

THE M.H. SEARS LAW FIRM (AV)

2300 N Street, N.W., Suite 600, 20037
Telephone: 202-663-9048
Facsimile: 202-223-1512

MEMBERS OF FIRM
Mary Helen Sears　　　　　　Thomas S. Hahn
ASSOCIATE
James L. Sears　(Not admitted in DC)

For full biographical listings, see the Martindale-Hubbell Law Directory

---

SPENCER & FRANK (AV)

1100 New York Avenue, N.W., Suite 300 East, 20005-3955
Telephone: 202-414-4000
Telefax: 202-414-4040
Telex: Spencer 64267
Email: spencerfrank@mcimail.com

George H. Spencer　　　　　Robert Kinberg
Norman N. Kunitz　　　　　John W. Schneller
Robert J. Frank　　　　　　Allen Wood
Gabor J. Kelemen　　　　　Ashley J. Wells
　(Not admitted in DC)　　　Frederick F. Calvetti
Mark B. Harrison　　　　　　Julie A. Petruzzelli
ASSOCIATES
Barbara Schmidt Twardzik　　Laleh Jalali
Robert H. Berdo, Jr.　　　　　(Not admitted in DC)
COUNSEL
Jay M. Cantor (P.C.)　　　　Michael A. Gollin
LEGAL SUPPORT PERSONNEL
Lauren L. Fuller
TRANSLATORS
Barbara Rosenbaum　　　　　Isolde U. Wasley
TECHNICAL CONSULTANT
Michael S. Tuscan

For full biographical listings, see the Martindale-Hubbell Law Directory

---

TREXLER, BUSHNELL, GIANGIORGI & BLACKSTONE, LTD. (AV)

3231 Reservoir Road, N.W., 20007
Telephone: 202-337-5723
Chicago, Illinois Office: 105 West Adams Street, 36th Floor.
Telephone: 312-704-1890.
Telex: 206991.
FAX: 312-704-8023.

Charles L. Sturtevant

---

* VENABLE ATTORNEYS AT LAW VENABLE, BAETJER, HOWARD & CIVILETTI, LLP (AV)

A Partnership including Professional Corporations
Suite 1000, 1201 New York Avenue, N.W., 20005
Telephone: 202-962-4800
Fax: 202-962-8300
Baltimore, Maryland Office: Venable, Baetjer and Howard LLP, 1800
Mercantile Bank & Trust Building, 2 Hopkins Plaza.
Telephone: 410-244-7400.
McLean, Virginia Office: Venable, Baetjer and Howard LLP, Suite 400,
2010 Corporate Ridge.
Telephone: 703-760-1600.

(See Next Column)

VENABLE ATTORNEYS AT LAW VENABLE, BAETJER, HOWARD & CIVILETTI, LLP—*Continued*

Rockville, Maryland Office: Venable, Baetjer and Howard LLP, Suite 500, One Church Street, P. O. Box 1906.
Telephone: 301-217-5600.
Towson, Maryland Office: Venable, Baetjer and Howard LLP, 210 Allegheny Avenue, P. O. Box 5517.
Telephone: 410-494-6200.

MEMBERS OF FIRM

Thomas J. Kenney, Jr. (P.C.) (Not admitted in DC; Also at Baltimore, Maryland Office)	George F. Pappas (Also at Baltimore, Maryland Office)
Douglas D. Connah, Jr. (P.C.) (Also at Baltimore, Maryland Office)	William D. Coston
	William D. Quarles (Also at Towson, Maryland Office)
Kenneth C. Bass, III (Also at McLean, Virginia Office)	Jeffrey L. Ihnen
	James A. Dunbar (Also at Baltimore, Maryland Office)
Edward F. Glynn, Jr.	Robert J. Bolger, Jr. (Not admitted in DC; Also at Baltimore, Maryland Office)
James R. Myers	
Jeffrey D. Knowles	
Jeffrey A. Dunn (Also at Baltimore, Maryland Office)	Gary M. Hnath

OF COUNSEL
Barbara L. Waite

ASSOCIATES

James Nicholas Czaban (Not admitted in DC)	Edward Brendan Magrab
David W. Goewey	Vicki Margolis (Also at Baltimore, Maryland Office)

For Complete List of Firm Personnel, See General Section

For full biographical listings, see the Martindale-Hubbell Law Directory

WENDEROTH, LIND & PONACK (AV)

Suite 700 Southern Building, 805 Fifteenth Street, N.W., 20005
Telephone: 202-371-8850
Fascimile: 202-371-8856 (G-III)
202-371-5681(G-III)
202-371-8310 (G-III)
202-646-1179 (G-IV)
Email: wlp@attmail.com

MEMBERS OF FIRM

E. F. Wenderoth (1886-1974)	Matthew M. Jacob
John E. Lind (1892-1983)	Jeffrey Nolton
A. Ponack (1900-1969)	Warren M. Cheek, Jr.
John T. Miller	Nils E. Pedersen
Michael R. Davis	Charles R. Watts

OF COUNSEL
Vincent M. Creedon

ASSOCIATES

Mary F. Love	Michael S. Huppert (Not admitted in DC)

For full biographical listings, see the Martindale-Hubbell Law Directory

WIGMAN, COHEN, LEITNER & MYERS, A PROFESSIONAL CORPORATION (AV)

Intellectual Property and International Trade Attorneys
The Farragut Building 10th Floor, 900 17th Street, N.W., 20006
Telephone: 202-463-7700
Facsimile: 202-463-6915
Email: iplaw@laser.net

Herbert Cohen	Saul Leitner
Victor M. Wigman	Edward J. Farrell
George C. Myers, Jr. (Not admitted in DC)	Michael C. Greenbaum

Jan Christensen	Suzanne F. Gisler Metzler (Not admitted in DC)
Dorothy H. Patterson	
Michael D. White	Karl O. Neidert (Not admitted in DC)
Jonathan M. Cohen (Not admitted in DC)	
	Joseph G. Seeber

OF COUNSEL
Donald R. Greene

For full biographical listings, see the Martindale-Hubbell Law Directory

JOHN F. WITHERSPOON (AV)

The Army and Navy Club Building, 1627 I Street, N.W., 20006
Telephone: 202-835-3700
Facsimile: 202-775-1168

For full biographical listings, see the Martindale-Hubbell Law Directory

FLORIDA

FORT LAUDERDALE,* Broward Co.

LAW PRACTICE OF J.B. GROSSMAN, P.A. (AV)

2300 East Las Olas Boulevard Fourth Floor, 33301
Telephone: 954-767-3345
Fax: 954-767-3347

J.B. Grossman	Kenneth J. Dunn
Gary Arnold Feder	Blaine H. Hibberd

LEGAL SUPPORT PERSONNEL
Scott L. Lampert

For full biographical listings, see the Martindale-Hubbell Law Directory

MALIN, HALEY, DiMAGGIO AND CROSBY, P.A. (AV)

Suite 1609, 1 East Broward Boulevard, 33301
Telephone: 954-763-3303
Fax: 954-522-6507
Miami, Florida Office: 2000 South Dixie Highway, Suite 203, 33133.
Telephone: 305-374-4082.
West Palm Beach, Florida Office: Suite 600, 500 South Australian Avenue, 33401.
Telephone: 561-832-6341.

Eugene F. Malin (1936-1990)	Dale Paul DiMaggio
Barry L. Haley	Kevin P. Crosby

Daniel S. Polley	Cristina Pinheiro-Palmer (Not admitted in FL)
David P. Lhota	
Mark David Bowen	Rick F. Comoglio

OF COUNSEL
John C. Black (Not admitted in FL)

Representative Clients: IBM; Motorola; Blockbuster Entertainment; Hughes Aircraft Co.; CAE Electronics; Nova Southeastern University; Sea Ray Boats, Inc.; American Hydro-Surgical Instruments, Inc.; News and Sun-Sentinel; Huron Machine Products, Inc.

For full biographical listings, see the Martindale-Hubbell Law Directory

OLTMAN, FLYNN AND KUBLER (AV)

415 Galleria Professional Building, 915 Middle River Drive, 33304-3585
Telephone: 954-563-4814
Facsimile: 954-563-1226
Miami, Florida Office: Suite 2750 Nations Bank Tower, 100 S.E. 2nd Street.
Telephone: 305-947-3888.
Boca Raton, Florida Office: Suite 801 The Plaza, 5355 Town Center Road.
Telephone: 407-391-4900.

John H. Oltman	Frank L. Kubler

OF COUNSEL
Brian S. Steinberger

Representative Clients: Clairson International Corp.; New York Institute of Technology; Jensen Corp.; M & W Pump Corp.; Hollywood Federal Savings and Loan Assn.; Adaptive Systems, Inc.; Oki Telecom, Division of Oki America, Inc.; Security Plastics, Inc.; Eaton Oil Co.
Reference: Nations Bank, Fort Lauderdale.

For full biographical listings, see the Martindale-Hubbell Law Directory

---

MIAMI,* Dade Co.

DOMINIK & STEIN (AV)

Suite 225, 6175 N.W. 153rd Street (Miami Lakes), 33014
Telephone: 305-556-7000
Fax: 305-556-6577
Tampa, Florida Office: 600 N. West Shore Boulevard, Suite 1000, 33609.
Telephone: 813-289-2966.
Fax: 813-289-2967.

Jack E. Dominik	John J. Snyder
Stefan V. Stein	Sara Anne Burmeister
Stephan A. Pendorf	Floyd Brantley Chapman
	William B. Lafferty

OF COUNSEL
Leon Chasan (Not admitted in FL)

For full biographical listings, see the Martindale-Hubbell Law Directory

LOTT & FRIEDLAND, P.A. (AV)

255 Alhambra Circle, Suite 555, 33134
Telephone: 305-448-7089
Facsimile: 305-446-6191

Leslie J. Lott	Mark E. Stein
David K. Friedland	Cathy J. Lichter

(See Next Column)

LOTT & FRIEDLAND P.A., *Miami—Continued*

James S. Finn　　　　　　　Hector E. Villamar, Jr.

For full biographical listings, see the Martindale-Hubbell Law Directory

MALIN, HALEY, DIMAGGIO AND CROSBY, P.A. (AV)

2000 South Dixie Highway, Suite 203, 33133
Telephone: 305-374-4082
Fort Lauderdale, Florida Office: Suite 1609, 1 East Broward Boulevard.
Telephone: 954-763-3303.
Fax: 954-522-6507.
West Palm Beach, Florida Office: Suite 600, 500 South Australian Avenue.
Telephone: 561-832-6341.

Eugene F. Malin (1936-1990)　　Dale Paul DiMaggio
Barry L. Haley　　　　　　　　Kevin P. Crosby

Daniel S. Polley　　　　　　　Cristina Pinheiro-Palmer
David P. Lhota　　　　　　　　　(Not admitted in FL)
Mark David Bowen　　　　　　　Rick F. Comoglio
OF COUNSEL
John C. Black (Not admitted in FL)

For full biographical listings, see the Martindale-Hubbell Law Directory

ORLANDO,* Orange Co.

ALLEN, DYER, DOPPELT, MILBRATH & GILCHRIST (AV)

255 South Orange Avenue, Suite 1401, P.O. Box 3791, 32802-3791
Telephone: 407-841-2330
Fax: 407-841-2343

Herbert L. Allen　　　　　　Virginia M. Zock
Robert Dyer　　　　　　　　Christopher F. Regan
Ava K. Doppelt　　　　　　　Jeffrey S. Whittle
Stephen D. Milbrath　　　　　　(Not admitted in FL)
Brian R. Gilchrist　　　　　　David L. Sigalow
　　　　　　　　　　　　　　(Not admitted in FL)

For full biographical listings, see the Martindale-Hubbell Law Directory

MAGUIRE, VOORHIS & WELLS, P.A. (AV)

Two South Orange Avenue and, 200 South Orange Avenue, Suite 3000,
　P.O. Box 633, 32802
Telephone: 407-244-1100
Telecopier: 407-423-8796
Email: mvw@mvw.com *URL:* http://www.mvw.com
Melbourne, Florida Office: 1499 South Harbor City Boulevard, Suite 303.
Telephone: 407-951-1776.
Fax: 407-951-1849.
Tallahassee, Florida Office: 2804 Remington Green Circle, Suite 4.
Telephone 904-386-6060.
Fax: 904-385-8220.

Robert W. Duckworth

Robert L. Wolter
OF COUNSEL
Terence F. Brennan

For full biographical listings, see the Martindale-Hubbell Law Directory

TAMPA,* Hillsborough Co.

DOMINIK & STEIN (AV)

600 N. West Shore Boulevard, 33609
Telephone: 813-289-2966
Fax: 813-289-2967
Miami, Florida Office: Suite 225, 6175 N.W. 153rd Street (Miami Lakes).
Telephone: 305-556-7000.
Fax: 305-556-6577.

Jack E. Dominik　　　　　　John J. Snyder
Stefan V. Stein　　　　　　Sara Anne Burmeister
Stephan A. Pendorf　　　　　Floyd Brantley Chapman
OF COUNSEL
Leon Chasan (Not admitted in FL)

For full biographical listings, see the Martindale-Hubbell Law Directory

FRIJOUF, RUST & PYLE, P.A. (AV)

201 East Davis Boulevard (Davis Islands), 33606-3787
Telephone: 813-254-5100
Telecopier: 813-254-5400
Email: Frijouf@ix.netcom.com

Robert F. Frijouf　　　　　　Charles R. Rust

For full biographical listings, see the Martindale-Hubbell Law Directory

C. DOUGLAS MCDONALD, JR. & ASSOCIATES, P.A. (AV)

Suite 700, 501 East Kennedy Boulevard, P.O. Box 1528, 33601-1528
Telephone: 813-229-8176
Facsimile: 813-229-8073
Email: mcpatlaw@gate.net

C. Douglas McDonald, Jr.

William S. Van Royen　　　　Gary J. Pitzer

For full biographical listings, see the Martindale-Hubbell Law Directory

WEST PALM BEACH,* Palm Beach Co.

MALIN, HALEY, DIMAGGIO AND CROSBY, P.A. (AV)

Suite 600, 500 South Australian Avenue, 33401
Telephone: 561-832-6341
Fort Lauderdale, Florida Office: Suite 1609, 1 East Broward Boulevard.
Telephone: 954-763-3303.
Miami, Florida Office: 2000 South Dixie Highway, Suite 203.
Telephone: 305-374-4082.

Eugene F. Malin (1936-1990)　　Dale Paul DiMaggio
Barry L. Haley　　　　　　　　Kevin P. Crosby

Daniel S. Polley　　　　　　　Cristina Pinheiro-Palmer
David P. Lhota　　　　　　　　　(Not admitted in FL)
Mark David Bowen　　　　　　　Rick F. Comoglio
OF COUNSEL
John C. Black (Not admitted in FL)

For full biographical listings, see the Martindale-Hubbell Law Directory

QUARLES & BRADY (AV)

222 Lakeview Avenue, 4th Floor, 33401
Telephone: 561-653-5000
Fax: 561-653-5333
Milwaukee, Wisconsin Office: 411 East Wisconsin Avenue, 53202-4497.
Telephone: 414-277-5000.
Fax: 414-271-3552.
Madison, Wisconsin Office: Firstar Plaza, One South Pinckney Street, P.O.
Box 2113, 53701-2113.
Telephone: 608-251-5000.
Fax: 608-251-9166.
Naples, Florida Office: Barnett Center, 4501 Tamiami Trail North, Suite
300, 33940-3060.
Telephone: 941-262-5959.
Fax: 941-434-4999.
Phoenix, Arizona Office: One Camelback Building, One East Camelback
Road, Suite 400, 85012-1649.
Telephone: 602-230-5500.
Fax: 602-230-5598.

PARTNERS
J. Rodman Steele, Jr.　　　　Gregory A. Nelson
ASSOCIATES
Joseph W. Bain　　　　　　Robert J. Sacco

For Complete List of Firm Personnel, See General Section

For full biographical listings, see the Martindale-Hubbell Law Directory

GEORGIA

ATLANTA,* Fulton Co.

DEVEAU, COLTON & MARQUIS (AV)

Two Midtown Plaza Suite 1400, 1360 Peachtree Street, N.E., 30309-3209
Telephone: 404-875-3555
Facsimile: 404-875-8505
Email: patlanta@iX.netcom.com
MEMBERS OF FIRM
Todd Deveau　　　　　　　Laurence P. Colton
　　　　Harold L. Marquis
ASSOCIATES
Kenneth Southall　　　　　Bradley K. Groff
Jennifer Williams Colton　　Daniel J. Santos
　　　　Robert J. Gorman, Jr.

For full biographical listings, see the Martindale-Hubbell Law Directory

LOUIS T. ISAF, P.C. (AV)

6445 Powers Ferry Road, Suite 230, 30339-2909
Telephone: 770-951-2623
Fax: 770-612-9713

Louis T. Isaf

(See Next Column)

LOUIS T. ISAF, P.C.—*Continued*

Jeffrey R. Kuester   R. Stevan Coursey

LEGAL SUPPORT PERSONNEL

Mason A. Gross (Registered   Binh Vien Dao
Patent Agent and Technical   (Technical Advisor)
Specialist)

For full biographical listings, see the Martindale-Hubbell Law Directory

KILPATRICK & CODY LLP (AV)

Suite 2800, 1100 Peachtree Street, 30309-4530
Telephone: 404-815-6500
Telephone Copier: 404-815-6555
Telex: 54-2307
Washington, D.C. Office: Suite 800, 700 13th Street, N.W., 20005.
Telephone: 202-508-5800. Telephone Copier: 202-508-5858.
Brussels, Belgium Office: Avenue Louise 65, BTE 3, 1050 Brussels.
Telephone: (32) (2) 533-03-00.
Telecopier: (32) (2) 534-86-38.
London, England Office: 68 Pall Mall, London, SW1Y 5ES, England.
Telephone: (44) (71) 321 0477.
Telecopier: (44) (71) 930 9733.
Augusta, Georgia Office: Suite 1400 First Union Bank Building, P.O. Box
2043, 30903. Telephone (706) 724-2622. Telecopier (706) 722-0219.

OF COUNSEL
Thomas C. Shelton

MEMBERS OF FIRM

Miles J. Alexander   Laurel J. Lucey
Joseph M. Beck   George T. Marcou
Michael D. Bednarek   (Not admitted in GA)
  (Not admitted in GA)   Matthew H. Patton
William H. Brewster   John S. Pratt
Christopher P. Bussert   Dean W. Russell
James L. Ewing, IV   Jerre B. Swann
Dale Curtis Hogue, Sr.   Virginia S. Taylor
  (Not admitted in GA)

ASSOCIATES

George C. Beck   Richard T. Peterson (Resident,
  (Washington, D.C. Office)   Washington, D.C. Office)
Richard A. Clegg   Robert A. Rosenbloom
  (Not admitted in GA)   Nagendra Setty
Elizabeth H. Cohen   Mitchell G. Stockwell
Theodore H. Davis, Jr.   Clark G. Sullivan
Michael P. Fortkort   Geoffrey L. Sutcliffe
  (Washington, D.C. Office)   James A. Trigg
Michael K. Heilbronner   (Not admitted in GA)
Michael F. Labbee   Mitchell G. Weatherly
  (Not admitted in GA)   Cheryl Knowles Zalesky

For Complete List of Firm Personnel, See General Section

For full biographical listings, see the Martindale-Hubbell Law Directory

SMITH, HOWARD & AJAX (AV)

A Partnership including a Professional Corporation
300 Atlanta Financial Center South, 3333 Peachtree Road, N.E., 30326
Telephone: 404-239-1900
Fax: 404-239-1930

OF COUNSEL
Donald R. Andersen

For full biographical listings, see the Martindale-Hubbell Law Directory

HAWAII

HONOLULU,* Honolulu Co.

CADES SCHUTTE FLEMING & WRIGHT (AV)

Formerly Smith, Wild, Beebe & Cades
1000 Bishop Street, P.O. Box 939, 96808
Telephone: 808-521-9200
Telecopier: 808-531-8738
Email: cades@cades.com
Affiliated Law Firm: Udom-Prok Associates Law Offices, 105/36 Tharinee
Mansion, Borom Raj Chananee Road Bangkoknoi, Bangkok, Thailand,
10700.
Telephone: 011 662 435-4146.
Kailua-Kona, Hawaii Office: Hualalai Center, Suite B-303, 75-170 Hualalai
Road.
Telephone: 808-329-5811.
Telecopier: 808-326-1175.

(See Next Column)

MEMBER OF FIRM
Martin E. Hsia

Counsel for: First Hawaiian Bank; Alexander & Baldwin, Inc.; Theo. H. Davies & Co., Ltd.; C. Brewer & Company, Ltd.; Bank of America, FSB; Fun Factory, Inc.

For Complete List of Firm Personnel, See General Section

For full biographical listings, see the Martindale-Hubbell Law Directory

ILLINOIS

BARRINGTON, Cook & Lake Cos.

VIGIL & HANRATH (AV)

Successor to Thomas R. Vigil & Associates 1975-1991
836 South Northwest Highway, 60010-4683
Telephone: 847-382-6500
Facsimile: 847-382-6895
Cable: USPATLAW

Thomas R. Vigil   James P. Hanrath

For full biographical listings, see the Martindale-Hubbell Law Directory

CHICAGO,* Cook Co.

ARNOLD, WHITE & DURKEE, A PROFESSIONAL CORPORATION (AV)

800 Quaker Tower, 321 North Clark Street, 60610-4714
Telephone: 312-744-0090
Facsimile: 312-755-4489
Email: info@awd.com *URL:* http://www.awd.com
Houston, Texas Office: 750 Bering Drive, 77057-2198, P.O. Box 4433,
77210-4433.
Telephone: 713-787-1400.
Facsimile: 713-789-2679.
Telex: 79-0924.
Austin, Texas Office: 1900 One American Center, 600 Congress Avenue,
78701-3248.
Telephone: 512-418-3000.
Facsimile: 512-474-7577.
Arlington, Virginia Office: 2001 Jefferson Davis Highway, Suite 401,
22202-3604.
Telephone: 703-415-1720.
Facsimile: 703-415-1728.
Menlo Park, California Office: 155 Linfield Drive, 94025-3741.
Telephone: 415-614-4500.
Facsimile: 415-614-4599.
Minneapolis, Minnesota Office: 4850 First Bank Place, 601 Second Avenue
South, 55402-4320.
Telephone: 612-321-2800.
Facsimile: 612-321-9600.

Stephen G. Rudisill   Mark A. Thomas
Ronald B. Coolley   Christine F. Martin
J. Bradford Leaheey   Mary Jo Boldingh
Michael J. Blankstein   Daniel J. Burnham
Julio A. Garceran   Timothy R. Baumann
Paul R. Kitch   Steven R. Santema

OF COUNSEL
Slawomir (Steve) Z. Szczepanski

For full biographical listings, see the Martindale-Hubbell Law Directory

BANNER & ALLEGRETTI, LTD. (AV)

Established In 1920 - Predecessor Parent
Ten South Wacker Drive, 60606-7407
Telephone: 312-715-1000
Facsimile: 312-715-1234
Email: callahan@ba-iplaw.com *URL:* http://www.ba-iplaw.com
Washington, D.C. Office: 1001 G Street, N.W.
Telephone: 202-508-9100.
Facsimile: 202-508-9299.
Boston, Massachusetts Office: 75 State Street.
Telephone: 617-345-9100.
Facsimile: 617-345-9111.

D. Dennis Allegretti   Grantland G. Drutchas
Donald W. Banner   David M. Frischkorn
Mark T. Banner   James C. Gumina
Paul H. Berghoff   Bradley J. Hulbert
Denis A. Berntsen   Kyle K. Kappes
Daniel A. Boehnen   John J. McDonnell
James V. Callahan   Jon O. Nelson
Marc S. Cooperman   Edward W. Remus

(See Next Column)

BANNER & ALLEGRETTI LTD., *Chicago—Continued*

Christopher J. Renk	Seymour Rothstein
Robert H. Resis	Charles W. Shifley
	Jamie S. Smith

Lawrence H. Aaronson	Robert J. Irvine, III
Laura J. DeMoor	Kevin E. Noonan
Thomas A. Fairhall	Thomas K. Pratt
Michael S. Greenfield	Kenneth J. Rudofski
Barbara A. Heaphy	Matthew J. Sampson
A. Blair Hughes	Steven J. Sarussi
	J. Pieter Van Es

OF COUNSEL

W. Dennis Drehkoff	Charles F. Pigott
	Sheldon W. Witcoff

PATENT AGENTS

Mark Chao	Emily Miao

For full biographical listings, see the Martindale-Hubbell Law Directory

BELL, BOYD & LLOYD (AV)

Three First National Plaza Suite 3300, 70 West Madison Street, 60602
Telephone: 312-372-1121
FAX: 312-372-2098
Email: bbl@bbl.com
Washington, D.C. Office: 1615 L Street, N.W.
Telephone: 202-466-6300.
FAX: 202-463-0678.

MEMBERS OF FIRM

Christopher A. Bloom	Robert T. Johnson, Jr.
Carol A. Genis	Cornelius J. Tanis

ASSOCIATES

Sana Hakim	Heather C. Steinmeyer

For Complete List of Firm Personnel, See General Section

For full biographical listings, see the Martindale-Hubbell Law Directory

DICK AND HARRIS (AV)

Suite 3800, 181 West Madison Street, 60602
Telephone: 312-726-4000
Telecopier: 312-726-5834

MEMBERS OF FIRM

Richard Eugene Dick	Howard E. Silverman
Richard D. Harris	John S. Pacocha
Max Shaftal	Jody L. Factor

ASSOCIATES

Douglas B. Teaney	Jovan N. Jovanovic
Herbert H. Finn	Stevem Wayne Hays
Jordan A. Sigale	(Not admitted in IL)

For full biographical listings, see the Martindale-Hubbell Law Directory

DRESSLER, GOLDSMITH, MILNAMOW & KATZ, LTD. (AV)

Two Prudential Plaza, Suite 4700, 60601
Telephone: 312-616-5400
Facsimile: 312-616-5460
Arlington, Virginia Office: 2001 Jefferson Davis Highway.
Telephone: 703-415-0880.
Facsimile: 703-415-0883.

Max Dressler	John P. Milnamow
James E. Gauger, Jr.	Lisa von Bargen Mueller
Stephen D. Geimer	Thomas E. Northrup
Allen J. Hoover	Paul M. Odell
Martin L. Katz	Jack Shore
Annette M. McGarry	Joel E. Siegel
	Paul M. Vargo

OF COUNSEL

David D. Kaufman

For full biographical listings, see the Martindale-Hubbell Law Directory

FITCH, EVEN, TABIN & FLANNERY (AV)

135 South La Salle Street, Suite 900, 60603-4277
Telephone: 312-372-7842
Cable Address: "Patlaw"
Telex: 20 6566 Patlaw Cgo
Telecopier: 312-372-7848
San Diego, California Office: 4250 Executive Square, Suite 510.
Telephone: 619-552-1311.
Telecopier: 619-552-0095.
Washington, D.C. Office: 2305 Wilson Boulevard (Arlington, Virginia, 22201).
Telephone: 703-243-9236.
Telecopier: 703-243-9207.

(See Next Column)

MEMBERS OF FIRM

Morgan L. Fitch, Jr.	Philip T. Petti
Francis A. Even	John S. Paniaguas
Julius Tabin	Joseph T. Nabor
John F. Flannery	Donald A. Peterson
Robert B. Jones	John J. Cavanaugh (Retired)
James J. Schumann (Resident, San Diego, California Office)	James R. McBride
	James A. Sprowl
R. Steven Pinkstaff	Bruce R. Mansfield
James J. Hamill	Richard P. Beem
Timothy E. Levstik	James E. Turner, Jr.
Joseph E. Shipley	Richard A. Kaba
Bryant R. Gold (Resident, San Diego, California, Office)	(Not admitted in IL)
	Karl R. Fink
Robert J. Fox	Steven C. Schroer
Kenneth H. Samples	(Not admitted in IL)

OF COUNSEL

Louis Bernat	Edward W. Gray, Jr. (Resident, Arlington, Virginia Office)
Robert R. Meads (Resident, San Diego, California Office)	

Mark A. Hamill	Kathleen A. Ranney
Perry Jay Hoffman	Stephen S. Favakeh
James P. Krueger	R. Matthew Pipke
Mark W. Hetzler	Romi N. Bose
Timothy P. Maloney	Roberta L. Hastreiter
Jay A. Saltzman	Robroy R. Fawcett (Resident, San Diego, California Office)
Thomas F. Lebens (Resident, San Diego, California Office)	

For full biographical listings, see the Martindale-Hubbell Law Directory

GREER, BURNS & CRAIN, LTD. (AV)

Sears Tower, Suite 8660, 233 South Wacker Drive, 60606
Telephone: 312-993-0080
Facsimile: 312-993-0633
Email: GBC@interaccess.com

Roger D. Greer	Patrick G. Burns
	Lawrence J. Crain

Christopher J. Reckamp	B. Joe Kim
Steven P. Fallon	Timothy L. Harney
	Walter M. Douglas

For full biographical listings, see the Martindale-Hubbell Law Directory

KEGAN & KEGAN, LTD. (AV)

79 West Monroe Street, Suite 1320, 60603-4969
Telephone: 312-782-6495
Telecopier: (fax) 312-782-6494
Email: ElanKegan@aol.com

Albert I. Kegan (1908-1963)	Esther O. Kegan
	Daniel L. Kegan

Cynthia L. Scott	Diane Lidman Prendiville

OF COUNSEL

Marvin N. Benn

For full biographical listings, see the Martindale-Hubbell Law Directory

LAFF, WHITESEL, CONTE & SARET, LTD., A PROFESSIONAL CORPORATION (AV)

Suite 1700, 401 North Michigan Avenue, 60611-4212
Telephone: 312-661-2100
Cable Address: "Lawyer"
Telex: 20-6024
Telecopiers: 312-661-0029 312-527-3001
Email: lwcs@lwcs.com

Charles A. Laff	Louis Altman
J. Warren Whitesel	Joseph F. Schmidt
Robert F. I. Conte	Barry W. Sufrin
Larry L. Saret	Marshall W. Sutker
Martin L. Stern	Judith L. Grubner
	John T. Gabrielides

Jennifer A. Dunner	James B. Conte
Neil R. Ormos	Kelly L. Cummings
Kevin C. Trock	Tim Meece
Diana Flynn	William A. Meunier
John W. Hayes	Scott B. Feder

OF COUNSEL

Jack R. Halvorsen

For full biographical listings, see the Martindale-Hubbell Law Directory

Chicago—Continued

LEYDIG, VOIT & MAYER, LTD. (AV)

Two Prudential Plaza, 180 North Stetson Avenue, Suite 4900, 60601-6780
Telephone: 312-616-5600
Telecopier: 312-616-5700
Telex: 25-3533
Rockford, Illinois Office: 815 North Church Street.
Telephone: 815-963-7661.
Telecopier: 815-963-7664.
Telex: 25-3533.
Washington, D.C. Office: 700 Thirteenth Street, N.W., Suite 300.
Telephone: 202-737-6770.
Telecopier: 202-737-6776.
Telex: 25-3533.

Berton Scott Sheppard	Herbert C. Rose (Not admitted
James B. Muskal	in IL; Washington, D.C.
Dennis R. Schlemmer	Office)
Gordon R. Coons	Brett A. Hesterberg
John E. Rosenquist	Jeffrey S. Ward
John W. Kozak	Jeffrey A. Wyand (Not admitted
Mark E. Phelps	in IL; Washington, D.C.
H. Michael Hartmann	Office)
Lawrence S. Wick	Richard M. Johnson
Bruce M. Gagala	Paul J. Korniczky
Charles H. Mottier	Pamela J. Ruschau
John Kilyk, Jr.	Steven P. Petersen
Robert F. Green	John M. Augustyn
John B. Conklin	Theodore W. Anderson
James D. Zalewa	Noel I. Smith
Mark J. Liss	Christopher T. Griffith
John M. Belz	
(Washington, D.C. Office)	

Amy N. Cohen	Xavier Pillai
Lynn A. Tannehill	G. Russell Thill
Frederick N. Samuels (Not	Amir N. Penn
admitted in IL; Washington,	Carl J. Evens (Not admitted in
D.C. Office)	IL; Washington, D.C. Office)
Wesley O. Mueller	David J. Serbin
Jeremy M. Jay (Not admitted in	(Washington, D.C. Office)
IL; Washington, D.C. Office)	Audrey L. Bartnicki
Jeffrey B. Burgan	Gregory C. Bays
Eley O. Thompson	Darryl C. Salas
Mark Joy	David M. Thimmig
Regina M. Anderson	Ralph R. Veseli (Not admitted
James A. Flight	in IL; Resident, Washington,
Albert S. Michalik	D.C. Office)
Allen E. Hoover	Carol Larcher
David M. Airan	Thomas A. Miller
Michael H. Tobias (Not	(Resident, Rockford Office)
admitted in IL; Washington,	
D.C. Office)	

OF COUNSEL

C. Frederick Leydig	Arthur G. Gilkes
John P. Bundock, Jr.	John D. Foster
(Washington, D.C. Office)	(Washington, D.C. Office)
Paul L. Ahern	William J. Birmingham
Phillip H. Mayer	Ralph C. Medhurst

For full biographical listings, see the Martindale-Hubbell Law Directory

NIRO, SCAVONE, HALLER & NIRO (AV)

181 West Madison, Suite 4600, 60602-4515
Telephone: 312-236-0733
Facsimile: 312-236-3137

Raymond P. Niro	Joseph N. Hosteny, III
Thomas G. Scavone	Robert A. Vitale, Jr.
Timothy J. Haller	John C. Janka
William L. Niro	Richard B. Megley

Michael P. Mazza

Dean D. Niro	Christopher J. Lee
Raymond P. Niro, Jr.	James P. Murphy
Keith A. Vogt	David J. Sheikh
Arthur A. Gasey	Lawrence Cruz

Robert P. Greenspoon

For full biographical listings, see the Martindale-Hubbell Law Directory

PATTISHALL, MCAULIFFE, NEWBURY, HILLIARD & GERALDSON (AV)

Suite 5000, 311 South Wacker Drive, 60606
Telephone: 312-554-8000
Facsimile: 312-554-8015
Washington, D.C. Office: 320 Watergate, Six Hundred, 20037.
Telephone: 202-338-1300.
Facsimile: 202-338-9349.

(See Next Column)

MEMBERS OF FIRM

Beverly W. Pattishall	Robert W. Sacoff
Jeremiah D. McAuliffe	Mark V. B. Partridge
Robert M. Newbury	Joseph N. Welch II
Benjamin S. Warren III	Mark H. Hellmann
(Resident Partner,	Jean Marie R. Pechette
Washington, D.C. Office)	Daniel D. Frohling
Raymond I. Geraldson, Jr.	John Thompson Brown
David Craig Hilliard	Mary E. Innis
Edward G. Wierzbicki	Douglas N. Masters

Brett A. August	Kevin T. Conroy
Jonathan S. Jennings	Mark F. Schultz
John Michael Murphy	Bradley L. Cohn
Maxine Lans Retsky	Susan D. Hanaway
Nancy L. Clarke	Victor F. DeFrancis

For full biographical listings, see the Martindale-Hubbell Law Directory

PATULA & ASSOCIATES (AV)

A Professional Partnership
116 South Michigan Avenue 14th Floor, 60603
Telephone: 312-201-8220
Fax: 312-372-8681
Email: patula@worldnet.ATT.NET

Timothy T. Patula

ASSOCIATE

Charles T. Riggs Jr.

LEGAL SUPPORT PERSONNEL

Julia L. Spoor

For full biographical listings, see the Martindale-Hubbell Law Directory

ROCKEY, RIFKIN AND RYTHER (AV)

Two First National Plaza 20 South Clark Street Suite 2900, 60603
Telephone: 312-704-5600
Facsimile: 312-704-5616

MEMBERS OF FIRM

Keith V. Rockey	Thomas C. Elliott, Jr.
James P. Ryther	Kathleen A. Lyons
William T. Rifkin	Mary Spalding Burns

ASSOCIATE

John F. Rollins

OF COUNSEL

H. Vincent Harsha	Stanley M. Parmerter

For full biographical listings, see the Martindale-Hubbell Law Directory

ROPER & QUIGG (AV)

200 South Michigan Avenue Suite 1000, 60604
Telephone: 312-408-0855
Facsimile: 312-408-0865
Washington, D.C. Area Office: Three Crystal Park, 2231 Crystal Drive, Suite 410, Arlington, Virginia, 22202.
Telephone: 703-920-8910.

MEMBERS OF FIRM

Harry J. Roper	William P. Oberhardt
Donald J. Quigg (Not admitted	Raymond N. Nimrod
in IL; Resident, Arlington,	Steven R. Trybus
Virginia Office)	Archie W. Umphlett (Resident,
George S. Bosy	Arlington, Virginia Office)

ASSOCIATES

Aaron A. Barlow	John E. Titus
Ellen D. Law	Greg H. Gardella
(Not admitted in IL)	Frank J. Nuzzi
Sarah L. Taylor	Joseph M. Kuo

OF COUNSEL

E. Eugene Innis (Not admitted in IL)

For full biographical listings, see the Martindale-Hubbell Law Directory

STACK & FILPI, CHARTERED (AV)

Suite 411, 140 South Dearborn Street, 60603-5298
Telephone: 312-782-0690; 236-5032
Telecopier: 312-782-0936

Paul F. Stack	Robert A. Filpi

Christine R. Norgle-Loewer

OF COUNSEL

John H. Shurtleff	James A. McGurk

For full biographical listings, see the Martindale-Hubbell Law Directory

Chicago—Continued

TREXLER, BUSHNELL, GIANGIORGI & BLACKSTONE, LTD. (AV)

105 West Adams Street 36th Floor, 60603-6299
Telephone: 312-704-1890
FAX: 312-704-8023
Washington, D.C. Office: 3231 Reservoir Road, N.W.
Telephone: 202-337-5723.

Richard R. Trexler (1906-1995)	David J. Marr
Richard Bushnell	Grant H. Peters
Richard A. Giangiorgi	Geoffrey M. Novelli
Raiford A. Blackstone, Jr.	Linda L. Palomar

OF COUNSEL
Cynthia Bushnell Stevens

WASHINGTON, D.C. RESIDENT
Charles L. Sturtevant

For full biographical listings, see the Martindale-Hubbell Law Directory

WALLENSTEIN & WAGNER, LTD. (AV)

Suite 5300 311 South Wacker Drive, 60606-6604
Telephone: 312-554-3300
Facsimile: 312-554-3301

Robert E. Wagner	Daniel N. Christus
Alan L. Barry	Thomas K. Stine
Linda A. Kuczma	Micheal D. Lake
	Roger H. Stein

OF COUNSEL
Sidney Wallenstein

Joseph A. Fuchs	Michael G. Kelber
Jeffrey R. Gargano	Michael S. Leonard
Amy J. Gast	Monique Ann Morneault
David P. Gloekler	James P. Muraff
Tejpal S. Hansra	Paul Joseph Nykaza
Richard C. Himelhoch	Bradley F. Rademaker
James J. Jagoda	Marina N. Saito

For full biographical listings, see the Martindale-Hubbell Law Directory

WILDMAN, HARROLD, ALLEN & DIXON (AV)

225 West Wacker Drive, 30th Floor, 60606-1229
Telephone: 312-201-2000
Cable Address: "Whad"
Fax: 312-201-2555
URL: http://www.whad.com
Aurora, Illinois Office: 1851 W. Galena Boulevard, Suite 210.
Telephone: 630-892-7021.
Fax: 630-892-7158.
Waukegan, Illinois Office: 404 West Water, P. O. Box 890.
Telephone: 847-623-0700.
Fax: 847-244-5273.
Lisle, Illinois Office: 4300 Commerce Court.
Telephone: 630-955-0555.
New York, New York Office: Wildman, Harrold, Allen, Dixon & Smith.
The International Building, 45 Rockefeller Plaza, Suite 353.
Telephone: 212-632-3850.
Fax: 212-632-3858.
Toronto, Ontario affiliated Office: Keel Cottrelle. 36 Toronto Street, Ninth Floor, Suite 920.
Telephone: 416-367-2900.
Telefax: 416-367-2791.
Telex: 062-18660.
Mississauga, Ontario affiliated Office: Keel Cottrelle. 100 Matatson Avenue East, Suite 104.
Telephone: 416-890-7700.
Fax: 416-890-8006.

MEMBERS OF FIRM
John J. Arado	Craig Steven Fochler
Michael Dockterman	Bernard Harrold
Donald Flayton	Robert E. Kehoe, Jr.
	Charles R. Mandly, Jr.

COUNSEL
Diane G. Elder

Kathryn S. Bedward	Paul A. Slager
Jill A. Cuba	Lauren S. Tashma
Kevin B. Reid	Joleen S. Willis

For Complete List of Firm Personnel, See General Section

For full biographical listings, see the Martindale-Hubbell Law Directory

ROCKFORD, Winnebago Co.

LEYDIG, VOIT & MAYER, LTD. (AV)

815 North Church Street, 61103
Telephone: 815-963-7661
Telecopier: 815-963-7664.
Telex: 25-3533.
Chicago, Illinois Office: Two Prudential Plaza, 180 North Stetson Avenue, Suite 4900.
Telephone: 312-616-5600.
Telecopier: 312-616-5700.
Telex: 25-3533.
Washington, D.C. Office: 700 Thirteenth Street, N.W., Suite 300.
Telephone: 202-737-6770.
Telecopier: 202-737-6776.
Telex: 25-3533.

Charles S. Oslakovic	Thomas A. Miller

INDIANA

FORT WAYNE, Allen Co.

BAKER & DANIELS (AV)

111 East Wayne Street, Suite 800, 46802
Telephone: 219-424-8000
FAX: (219) 460-1700
Indianapolis, Indiana Office: 300 North Meridian Street.
Telephone: 317-237-0300.
South Bend, Indiana Office: First Bank Building, 205 West Jefferson Boulevard.
Telephone: 219-234-4149.
Elkhart, Indiana Office: 301 B South Main Street, Suite 307.
Telephone: 219-296-6000.
Washington, D.C. Office: 1701 K Street, N.W. Suite 400.
Telephone: 202-785-1565.

MEMBERS OF FIRM
John F. Hoffman	Anthony Niewyk
	Kevin R. Erdman

ASSOCIATES
Jeffrey O. Davidson	Debra L. Schroeder
(Not admitted in IN)	Kevin T. Duncan
David B. Kagan	Paul P. Kiel
(Not admitted in IN)	Brian C. Pauls

Representative Clients: Central Soya Co., Inc.; Essex Group, Inc.; ITT Corp.; Lincoln National Corp.; Lutheran Hospital of Indiana; Norwest Bank, Indiana, NA; Tokheim Corp.; Shambaugh & Son, Inc.; General Motors Corp.; Eli Lilly and Co.

For Complete List of Firm Personnel, See General Section

For full biographical listings, see the Martindale-Hubbell Law Directory

LUNDY & ASSOCIATES, P.C. (AV)

825 Anthony Wayne Building, 203 East Berry Street, 46802-2715
Telephone: 219-422-1534
Telecopier: 219-423-1590
Indianapolis, Indiana Office: 233 Circle Tower Building. 55 Monument Circle.
Telephone: 317-634-5552.

David A. Lundy

Reference: Fort Wayne National Bank.

For full biographical listings, see the Martindale-Hubbell Law Directory

INDIANAPOLIS, Marion Co.

BAKER & DANIELS (AV)

300 North Meridian Street, 46204
Telephone: 317-237-0300
FAX: 317-237-1000
Fort Wayne, Indiana Office: 111 East Wayne Street, Suite 800.
Telephone: 219-424-8000.
South Bend, Indiana Office: First Bank Building, 205 West Jefferson Boulevard.
Telephone: 219-234-4149.
Elkhart, Indiana Office: 301 B South Main Street, Suite 307,
Telephone: 219-296-6000.
Washington, D.C. Office: 1701 K Street, N.W., Suite 400.
Telephone: 202-785-1565.

MEMBERS OF FIRM
Lawrence A. Steward	John B. Swarbrick, Jr.
	John R. Schaibley, III

COUNSEL
Arthur R. Whale

(See Next Column)

BAKER & DANIELS—*Continued*

ASSOCIATES

Nancy G. Tinsley
Edward J. Prein

Representative Clients: Anthem Insurance Companies, Inc.; AT&T Corp.; Bank One, Indianapolis, N.A.; Borg-Warner Corp.; City of Indianapolis; Cummins Engine Co.; Eli Lilly and Co.; General Motors Corp.; Indianapolis Public Schools; United Airlines.

For Complete List of Firm Personnel, See General Section

For full biographical listings, see the Martindale-Hubbell Law Directory

LOCKE REYNOLDS BOYD & WEISELL (AV)

1000 Capital Center South, 201 North Illinois Street, 46204
Telephone: 317-237-3800
Telecopier: 317-237-3900

Stephen J. Dutton
David Elliott Jose
Richard A. Huser
Burton M. Harris
Charles B. Baldwin
Andrew James Richardson

Jeffrey R. Gaither

Craig A. Wood
Jeffrey S. Dible
Stephen L. Vaughan
David S. Klinestiver

Salim A. Hasan

Representative Clients: Boehringer Mannheim Corp.; Constar Plastics, Inc.; DowElanco; Electra Form, Inc.; Indiana University; Monon Corporation; National Wine & Spirits, Inc.; Noble Romans, Inc.; The Spaghetti Shop, Inc.; VonDuprin, Inc.

For Complete List of Firm Personnel, See General Section

For full biographical listings, see the Martindale-Hubbell Law Directory

LUNDY & ASSOCIATES, P.C. (AV)

233 Circle Tower Building, 55 Monument Circle, 46204-5901
Telephone: 317-634-5552
Telecopier: 219-423-1590
Fort Wayne, Indiana Office: 825 Anthony Wayne Building, 203 East Berry Street.
Telephone: 219-422-1534.

David A. Lundy

Reference: Fort Wayne National Bank.

For full biographical listings, see the Martindale-Hubbell Law Directory

WOODARD, EMHARDT, NAUGHTON, MORIARTY & McNETT (AV)

Bank One Center/Tower, 111 Monument Circle, Suite 3700, 46204-5137
Telephone: 317-634-3456
Telecopier: 317-637-7561
Telex: 810-341-3283
Cable Address: "Patents Ind"

MEMBERS OF FIRM

Harold R. Woodard
C. David Emhardt
Joseph A. Naughton, Jr.
John V. Moriarty
John C. McNett
Thomas Q. Henry
James M. Durlacher
Charles R. Reeves
Vincent O. Wagner
Stephen E. Zlatos
Spiro Bereveskos
William F. Bahret
Clifford W. Browning
R. Randall Frisk
Daniel J. Lueders
Michael D. Beck
Kenneth A. Gandy
Timothy N. Thomas

ASSOCIATES

Kerry Pauline Sisselman
Kurt N. Jones
John H. Allie
Jeffrey A. Michael
Deborah Rae Knoll
Holiday W. Banta
Troy J. Cole
L. Scott Paynter
J. Andrew Lowes
Charles J. Meyer
Darrin W. Harris
Matthew R. Schantz
Gregory B. Coy
Lisa H. Johnston

John V. Daniluck

STAFF ATTORNEY

Linda C. Shelby

OF COUNSEL

James L. Rowe

For full biographical listings, see the Martindale-Hubbell Law Directory

SOUTH BEND,* St. Joseph Co.

BAKER & DANIELS (AV)

First Bank Building, 205 West Jefferson Boulevard, 46601
Telephone: 219-234-4149
Fax: 219-239-1900
Indianapolis, Indiana Office: 300 North Meridian Street.
Telephone: 317-237-0300.
Fort Wayne, Indiana Office: 111 East Wayne Street, Suite 800.
Telephone: 219-424-8000.

(See Next Column)

Elkhart, Indiana Office: 301 B South Main Street, Suite 307.
Telephone: 219-296-6000.
Washington, D.C. Office: 1701 K Street, N.W., Suite 400.
Telephone: 202-785-1565.

MEMBER OF FIRM

James D. Hall

OF COUNSEL

Ken C. Decker

ASSOCIATES

David C. Read
Robert D. Null

Representative Clients: City of South Bend; 1st Source Bank; Jack-Post Corp.; Society Corp.; South Bend Drug Co.; WSBT, Inc.; General Motors Corp.; Eli Lilly and Company; Borg-Warner Corporation.

For Complete List of Firm Personnel, See General Section

For full biographical listings, see the Martindale-Hubbell Law Directory

IOWA

CEDAR RAPIDS,* Linn Co.

SHUTTLEWORTH & INGERSOLL, P.C. (AV)

500 Firstar Bank Building, P.O. Box 2107, 52406-2107
Telephone: 319-365-9461
Fax: 319-365-8443
Email: si-law@inav.net

James C. Nemmers
Glenn L. Johnson

Representative Clients: Aegon USA, Inc.; IES Industries; Met-Coil Systems Corporation; Parsons Technology, Inc.

For Complete List of Firm Personnel, See General Section

For full biographical listings, see the Martindale-Hubbell Law Directory

DAVENPORT,* Scott Co.

HENDERSON & STURM (AV)

204 Northwest Bank Building-Downtown, 101 West Second Street, 52801-1813
Telephone: 319-323-9731
Fax: 319-323-9709
Other Offices: Washington, D.C.; Des Moines, Iowa; Omaha, Nebraska.

MEMBERS OF FIRM

H. Robert Henderson
John E. Cepican

For full biographical listings, see the Martindale-Hubbell Law Directory

DES MOINES,* Polk Co.

DAVIS, BROWN, KOEHN, SHORS & ROBERTS, P.C. (AV)

(Formerly Davis, Hockenberg, Wine, Brown, Koehn & Shors, P.C.)
The Financial Center, 666 Walnut Street, Suite 2500, 50309-3993
Telephone: 515-288-2500
Cable: Davis Law
Facsimile: 515-243-0654
Affiliated London, England Office: Vizards, Solicitors, 42 Bedford Row. London WC1R 4JL England.
Telephone: 071-405-6302.
Facsimile: 071-405-6248.

Kent A. Herink
Brian J. Laurenzo

James R. Foley

For Complete List of Firm Personnel, See General Section

For full biographical listings, see the Martindale-Hubbell Law Directory

ZARLEY, McKEE, THOMTE, VOORHEES & SEASE (AV)

801 Grand, Suite 3200, 50309-2721
Telephone: 515-288-3667
Telex: 706625
Telecopier: 515-288-1338
Email: Patatty@Zarley.com *URL:* http://www.raccoon.com/~zarley
Omaha, Nebraska Office: 1111 Commercial Federal Tower, 2120 South 72nd Street.
Telephone: 402-392-2280.
Telecopier: 402-392-0734.
Toronto, Ontario, Canada Office: 40 King Street West, Suite 4300.
Telephone: 416-367-1576.
Telecopier: 416-367-6749.

MEMBERS OF FIRM

Donald H. Zarley
Bruce W. McKee
Dennis L. Thomte
Michael G. Voorhees
Edmund J. Sease
Mark D. Hansing
Kirk M. Hartung
Mark D. Frederiksen

(See Next Column)

ZARLEY, MCKEE, THOMTE, VOORHEES & SEASE, *Des Moines—Continued*
ASSOCIATES

Denise C. Mazour	Michael R. Crabb
(Not admitted in IA)	Bruce A. Johnson
Daniel J. Cosgrove	Wendy K. Hartung
Heidi Sease Nebel	Jeffrey D. Harty

Reference: Boatmen's National Bank of Des Moines (Des Moines, Iowa).

For full biographical listings, see the Martindale-Hubbell Law Directory

KANSAS

TOPEKA, * Shawnee Co.

WRIGHT, HENSON, SOMERS, SEBELIUS, CLARK & BAKER, LLP (AV)

Commerce Bank Building, 100 Southeast Ninth Street, 2nd Floor, P.O.
  Box 3555, 66601-3555
Telephone: 913-232-2200
FAX: 913-232-3344

MEMBERS OF FIRM

Thomas E. Wright	Bruce J. Clark

Representative Client: Newtek, Inc.

For Complete List of Firm Personnel, See General Section

For full biographical listings, see the Martindale-Hubbell Law Directory

KENTUCKY

COVINGTON, Kenton Co.

TALIAFERRO AND MEHLING (AV)

1005 Madison Avenue, P.O. Box 468, 41012-0468
Telephone: 606-291-9900
Fax: 606-291-3014

MEMBERS OF FIRM

Philip Taliaferro, III	Christopher J. Mehling
Lucinda C. Shirooni	

ASSOCIATES

C. Houston Ebert	Howard L. Tankersley
Alice G. Keys	

OF COUNSEL

Robert W. Carran	Norbert J. Bischoff
F. Edward Worland, Jr.	

For full biographical listings, see the Martindale-Hubbell Law Directory

LEXINGTON, * Fayette Co.

KING AND SCHICKLI (AV)

Corporate Gateway, Suite 210, 3070 Harrodsburg Road, 40503
Telephone: 606-223-4050
Telecopier: 606-224-9445

J. Ralph King	Warren D. Schickli
Charles Foster Moore	

For full biographical listings, see the Martindale-Hubbell Law Directory

LOUISVILLE, * Jefferson Co.

MIDDLETON & REUTLINGER, P.S.C. (AV)

2500 Brown and Williamson Tower, 40202-3410
Telephone: 502-584-1135
Fax: 502-561-0442
New Albany, Indiana Office: 2623 Charlestown Road, 47150.
Telephone: 812-944-7215.

James R. Higgins, Jr.	Charles G. Lamb

Amy B. Berge	James C. Eaves, Jr.
David W. Carrithers	John F. Salazar

Representative Clients: Brown & Williamson Tobacco Co., Inc.; Campbell
Tobacco Rehandling Co., Inc.; Corhart Refractories Corp.; DeTer Co., Inc.;
Porcelain Metals Corp.; Rosalco, Inc.; Tube Turns, Inc.; Universal Denim
Services; Vermont American Corp.; Whip Mix, Inc.

For Complete List of Firm Personnel, See General Section

For full biographical listings, see the Martindale-Hubbell Law Directory

ROBERT & MILLER (AV)

10000 Shelbyville Road, Suite 112, 40223
Telephone: 502-245-7717
Fax: 502-245-7932

MEMBERS OF FIRM

Arthur F. Robert (1901-1985)	M. Larry Miller

For full biographical listings, see the Martindale-Hubbell Law Directory

LOUISIANA

LAFAYETTE, * Lafayette Parish

LISKOW & LEWIS, A PROFESSIONAL LAW CORPORATION (AV)

822 Harding Street, P.O. Box 52008, 70505
Telephone: 318-232-7424
Telecopier: 318-267-2399
New Orleans, Louisiana Office: 50th Floor, One Shell Square.
Telephone: 504-581-7979.
Telecopier: 504-592-5108; 504-592-5109.

RESIDENT PERSONNEL

George H. Robinson, Jr.	Patrick W. Gray

Representative Clients: First National Bank of Commerce; John H. Carter
Co., Inc.; BMW of North America Inc.; Overhead Door Corporation; Duck
Head Apparel Co.; Cafe Cola, Inc.; Eimco Process Equipment Company;
Amerada Hess Corporation; PG&E Resources; Top Tool Co. Inc.

For Complete List of Firm Personnel, See General Section

For full biographical listings, see the Martindale-Hubbell Law Directory

METAIRIE, Jefferson Parish

PRAVEL, HEWITT, KIMBALL & KRIEGER, A PROFESSIONAL CORPORATION (AV)

Three Lakeway Center Suite 3290, 3838 North Causeway
  Boulevard, 70002-1767
Telephone: 504-835-2000
FAX: 504-835-2070
Mailing Address: P.O. Box 247881, New Orleans, Louisiana, 70184-4788
Email: phkkdoc@aol.com
Houston, Texas Office: Tenth Floor, 1177 West Loop South.
Telephone: 713-850-0909.
FAX: 713-850-0165.
Memphis, Tennessee Office: 5100 Poplar Avenue, Suite 2715.
Telephone: 901-683-8757.
Telephone: 901-767-8757.

Bernarr Roe Pravel	Charles C. Garvey, Jr.
(Not admitted in LA)	Gregory C. Smith

Seth M. Nehrbass	David L. Fox

For full biographical listings, see the Martindale-Hubbell Law Directory

NEW ORLEANS, * Orleans Parish

LISKOW & LEWIS, A PROFESSIONAL LAW CORPORATION (AV)

50th Floor, One Shell Square, 70139
Telephone: 504-581-7979
Telecopier: 504-556-4108; 504-556-4109
Lafayette, Louisiana Office: 822 Harding Street, P.O. Box 52008.
Telephone: 318-232-7424.
Telecopier: 318-267-2399.

Marilyn C. Maloney	Cheryl V. Cunningham
R. Keith Jarrett	Marie Breaux
	Kathleen Friel Hobson

Patricia Campbell Smith	Karen Daniel Ancelet

RESIDENT PERSONNEL AT LAFAYETTE OFFICE

George H. Robinson, Jr.	Patrick W. Gray

Representative Clients: First National Bank of Commerce; John H. Carter
Co., Inc.; BMW of North America Inc.; Overhead Door Corporation; Duck
Head Apparel Co.; Cafe Cola, Inc.; Eimco Process Equipment Company;
Amerada Hess Corporation; PG&E Resources; Top Tool Co., Inc.

For Complete List of Firm Personnel, See General Section

For full biographical listings, see the Martindale-Hubbell Law Directory

NATIONAL LAW OFFICES OF PUGH/ASSOCIATES PATENT & TRADEMARK ATTORNEYS (AV)

4917 St. Charles Avenue, 70115-4927
Telephone: 504-587-0000
Telecopier: 504-899-5360;
Cable Address: Pat. Pend . New Orleans
Email: epugh@patentlaw.com

(See Next Column)

NATIONAL LAW OFFICES OF PUGH/ASSOCIATES PATENT & TRADEMARK ATTORNEYS—*Continued*

C. Emmett Pugh

For full biographical listings, see the Martindale-Hubbell Law Directory

MAINE

BAR HARBOR, Hancock Co.

FENTON, CHAPMAN, FENTON, SMITH & KANE, P.A. (AV)

109 Main Street, P.O. Box B, 04609
Telephone: 207-288-3331
FAX: 207-288-9326

William Fenton	Chadbourn H. Smith
Douglas B. Chapman	Daniel H. Kane (1940-1995)
Nathaniel R. Fenton	Hancock Griffin, Jr. (1912-1980)

Margaret A. Timothy   Eric Lindquist

OF COUNSEL
Edwin R. Smith

Reference: Bar Harbor Banking and Trust Co.

For full biographical listings, see the Martindale-Hubbell Law Directory

MARYLAND

BALTIMORE,* (Independent City)

VENABLE ATTORNEYS AT LAW VENABLE, BAETJER AND HOWARD, LLP (AV)

A Partnership including Professional Corporations
1800 Mercantile Bank & Trust Building, 2 Hopkins Plaza, 21201
Telephone: 410-244-7400
Email: INFO@Venable.win.net
Washington, D.C. Office: Venable, Baetjer, Howard & Civiletti LLP. Suite 1000, 1201 New York Avenue, N.W.
Telephone: 202-962-4800.
McLean, Virginia Office: Suite 400, 2010 Corporate Ridge.
Telephone: 703-760-1600.
Rockville, Maryland Office: Suite 500, One Church Street, P. O. Box 1906.
Telephone: 301-217-5600.
Towson, Maryland Office: 210 Allegheny Avenue, P. O. Box 5517.
Telephone: 410-494-6200.

MEMBERS OF FIRM

George Cochran Doub (P.C.)	Jeffrey A. Dunn (also at Washington, D.C. Office)
Thomas J. Kenney, Jr. (P.C.) (Also at Washington, D.C. Office)	George F. Pappas (Also at Washington, D.C. Office)
Douglas D. Connah, Jr. (P.C.) (Also at Washington, D.C. Office)	William D. Coston (Not admitted in MD; Resident, Washington, D.C. Office)
Kenneth C. Bass, III (Not admitted in MD; Washington, D.C. and McLean, Virginia Offices)	William D. Quarles (Also at Washington, D.C. and Towson, Maryland Offices)
Edward F. Glynn, Jr. (Resident, Washington, D.C. Office)	Jeffrey L. Ihnen (Not admitted in MD; Resident, Washington, D. C. Office)
G. Stewart Webb, Jr.	James A. Dunbar (Also at Washington, D.C. Office)
James R. Myers (Not admitted in MD; Resident, Washington, D.C. Office)	Robert J. Bolger, Jr. (Also at Washington, D.C. Office)
Jeffrey D. Knowles (Not admitted in MD; Resident, Washington, D.C. Office)	David J. Heubeck
	Gary M. Hnath (Resident, Washington, D.C. Office)

Newton B. Fowler, III

ASSOCIATES

Paul D. Barker, Jr.	Mary-Dulany James (Resident, Towson, Maryland Office)
James Nicholas Czaban (Not admitted in MD; Resident, Washington, D.C. Office)	Edward Brendan Magrab (Resident, Washington, D.C. Office)
David W. Goewey (Not admitted in MD; Resident, Washington, D.C. Office)	Vicki Margolis (Also at Washington, D.C. Office)

John T. Prisbe

For Complete List of Firm Personnel, See General Section

For full biographical listings, see the Martindale-Hubbell Law Directory

BETHESDA, Montgomery Co.

FREEMAN & JENNER, P.C. (AV)

3 Bethesda Metro Center, Suite 1410, 20814
Telephone: 301-907-7747
FAX: 301-907-9877
Washington, D.C. Office: 1000 16th Street, N.W., Suite 300.
Telephone: 301-907-7747.
Aspen, Colorado Office: 215 South Monarch Street, Suite 202.
Telephone: 970-925-3400.
FAX: 970-925-4043.

Martin H. Freeman	Robert K. Jenner
Barbara E. Hirsch	Mark Allan Freeman

Reference: Crestar Bank of Maryland.

For full biographical listings, see the Martindale-Hubbell Law Directory

TOWSON,* Baltimore Co.

BLOOM & KRETEN (AV)

401 Washington Avenue, 21204
Telephone: 410-337-2295
Facsimile: 410-337-2296
Sacramento, California Office: 77 Cadillac Drive.
Telephone: 916-921-6181.
Fax: 916-921-9213.
European Office: Rue Frans Merjay, 21 B-1060, Brussels, Belgium.
Hong Kong Office: 10/F Vogue Building, 67 Wyndham Street, Central Hong Kong

Leonard Bloom	Robert M. Gamson
Bernhard Kreten (Resident, Sacramento, California Office)	

OF COUNSEL

James R. Gaffey (Not admitted in MD)	Benjamin J. Goldfarb
Bruce L. Lamb (Not admitted in MD)	Sam Rosen

LEGAL SUPPORT PERSONNEL

Yeva Burdman	Dennis A. DeBoo (Resident at Sacramento, California Office)

For full biographical listings, see the Martindale-Hubbell Law Directory

MASSACHUSETTS

BOSTON,* Suffolk Co.

BROMBERG & SUNSTEIN (AV)

125 Summer Street, 11th Floor, 02110
Telephone: 617-443-9292
Fax: 617-443-0004
Email: IPLAW@BROMSUN.COM

MEMBERS OF FIRM

Bruce D. Sunstein	Robert L. Kann
	Timothy M. Murphy

ASSOCIATES

Julia Huston	Samuel J. Petuchowski (Not admitted in MA)

OF COUNSEL
Robert M. Asher

For full biographical listings, see the Martindale-Hubbell Law Directory

CESARI AND McKENNA (AV)

30 Rowes Wharf, 02110
Telephone: 617-951-2500
Fax: 617-951-3927

Robert A. Cesari	Joseph H. Born
John F. McKenna	Patricia A. Sheehan
Martin J. O'Donnell	Michael E. Attaya
Thomas C. O'Konski	Steven J. Frank

Charles J. Barbas

Patrick J. O'Shea	George J. Jakobsche
Michael R. Reinemann	William A. Loginov

Rita M. Rooney

LEGAL SUPPORT PERSONNEL

Dora V. Dodin (Patent Engineer)	Heather B. Shapiro (Technical Specialist)

For full biographical listings, see the Martindale-Hubbell Law Directory

Boston—Continued

DIKE, BRONSTEIN, ROBERTS & CUSHMAN, LLP (AV)

A Limited Liability Partnership including Professional Corporations
130 Water Street, 02109
Telephone: 617-523-3400
Telefax: 617-523-6440; 523-7318
Email: ipl@dbrc.com *URL:* http://www.dbrc.com

David G. Conlin (P.C.)	Ronald I. Eisenstein
George W. Neuner (P.C.)	Henry D. Pahl, Jr.
Ernest V. Linek	Peter J. Manus (P.C.)
Linda M. Buckley	David S. Resnick
Peter F. Corless	

Cara Zucker Lowen	William J. Daley, Jr.
Brian Michaelis	David D. Lowry

OF COUNSEL
Sewall P. Bronstein (P.C.)	John L. Welch
Milton M. Oliver	

LEGAL SUPPORT PERSONNEL
Robert L. Buchanan, Ph.D.

For full biographical listings, see the Martindale-Hubbell Law Directory

FISH & RICHARDSON P.C. (AV)

225 Franklin Street, 02110-2804
Telephone: 617-542-5070
Fax: 617-542-8906
Cable Address: "Fishrich, Boston"
Telex: RCA 2 00154 Fishr Ur
URL: http://www.fr.com
Washington, D.C. Office: 601 13th Street, N.W.
Telephone: 202-783-5070.
Fax: 202-783-2331.
Houston, Texas Office: One Riverway, Suite 1200.
Telephone: 713-629-5070.
Fax: 713-629-7811.
Menlo Park, California Office: 2200 Sand Hill Road, Suite 100.
Telephone: 415-322-5070.
Fax: 415-854-0875.
Minneapolis, Minnesota Office: Fish & Richardson P.C., P.A., 60 South Sixth Street, Suite 3300.
Telephone: 612-335-5070.
Fax: 612-288-9696.
La Jolla, California Office: 4225 Executive Square, Suite 1400.
Telephone: 619-678-5070.
Fax: 619-678-5099.
New York, New York Office: 45 Rockefeller Plaza, Suite 2800.
Telephone: 212-765-5070.
Fax: 212-258-2291.

Frederick P. Fish (1855-1930)	William E. Booth
W. K. Richardson (1859-1951)	Timothy A. French
John N. Williams	Eric L. Prahl
Charles C. Winchester	Robert C. Nabinger
Robert E. Hillman	Mark J. Hebert
Frank P. Porcelli	Peter J. Devlin
Gregory A. Madera	Ronald E. Myrick
David L. Feigenbaum	Gary A. Walpert
John M. Skenyon	Janis K. Fraser
G. Roger Lee	Richard M. Sharkansky
Paul T. Clark	Heidi E. Harvey
Charles Hieken	Y. Rocky Tsao
Gilbert H. Hennessey, III	Alan Dean Smith
John W. Freeman	J. Peter Fasse

OF COUNSEL
Willis M. Ertman	Blair L. Perry

Molly Mosley-Goren	Jeffrey L. Snow
James E. Mrose	Jonathan J. Wainer
Jennifer T. Miller	(Not admitted in MA)
Donna M. Weinstein	Elizabeth A. Hurley
John J. Gagel	Jason A. Reyes
Sandra E. Marxen	Howard J. Susser
Kurt L. Glitzenstein	(Not admitted in MA)
Jolynn M. Lussier	Frank R. Occhiuti
Gary L. Creason	Anita L. Meiklejohn
Celia H. Ketley	Sean F. Heneghan
Karen F. Lech	Ronald S. Hermenau
Evelyn D. Shen	(Not admitted in MA)
Lawrence K. Kolodney	

For full biographical listings, see the Martindale-Hubbell Law Directory

LAHIVE & COCKFIELD (AV)

Sixty State Street, 02109
Telephone: 617-227-7400
Fax: 617-227-5941
Email: LC@LAHCOC.COM

(See Next Column)

MEMBERS OF FIRM
John A. Lahive, Jr.	Thomas J. Engellenner
W. Hugo Liepmann	Giulio A. DeConti, Jr.
James E. Cockfield	Ann Lamport Hammitte
Thomas V. Smurzynski	Paul Louis Myers
Ralph A. Loren	Elizabeth A. Hanley

ASSOCIATES
Michael I. Falkoff	Mark A. Kurisko
John V. Bianco	Beth E. Arnold
Amy B. Mandragouras	Jean M. Silveri
Anthony A. Laurentano	Carolyn G. d'Agincourt
Jane E. Remillard	Peter J. Rainville

OF COUNSEL
Jeremiah Lynch	Lawrence E. Monks

LEGAL SUPPORT PERSONNEL
PATENT AGENTS
Matthew P. Vincent

TECHNICAL SPECIALISTS
Catherine J. Kara	Ivana Maravic-Magovcevic
Mark D. Russett	Megan E. Williams
Isabelle M. Clauss	Sonia K. Guterman
Diana M. Collazzo	

For full biographical listings, see the Martindale-Hubbell Law Directory

LORUSSO & LOUD (AV)

440 Commercial Street, 02109
Telephone: 617-227-0700
Telefax: 617-723-4609
Telex: 286853 (RCA)
Alexandria, Virginia Office: 3137 Mt. Vernon Avenue.
Telephone: 703-739-9393.
Fax: 703-739-9391.
Portsmouth, New Hampshire Office: 93 State Street.
Telephone: 603-427-0070.
Fax: 603-427-5530.

MEMBERS OF FIRM
Anthony M. Lorusso	Thomas M. Saunders
George A. Loud (Resident,	Philip X. Murray
Alexandria, Virginia Office)	Sarah L. Byrne
Barbara A. Barakat	Deborah U. Verga

ASSOCIATES
Michael R. Hanna	Mark D. Lorusso
Donald J. Perreault	

OF COUNSEL
George W. Crowley

For full biographical listings, see the Martindale-Hubbell Law Directory

MORSE, ALTMAN & BENSON (AV)

73 Tremont Street, 02108
Telephone: 617-523-3515
FAX: 617-523-1872

Gerald Altman	G. Eugene Dacey
Deborah L. Benson	

ASSOCIATES
Steven K. Martin	Susan M.G. von Struensee

For full biographical listings, see the Martindale-Hubbell Law Directory

SHERBURNE, POWERS & NEEDHAM, P.C. (AV)

One Beacon Street, 02108
Telephone: 617-523-2700
Fax: 617-523-6850
Email: @SHERBURNE.COM

William D. Weeks	Benjamin Volinski
John T. Collins	Mark Schonfeld
Allan J. Landau	James D. Smeallie
Stephen A. Hopkins	Paul Killeen
Alan I. Falk	Gordon P. Katz
C. Thomas Swaim	Joseph B. Darby, III
James Pollock	Richard M Yanofsky
William V. Tripp III	James E. McDermott
Stephen S. Young	Kenneth P. Brier
William F. Machen	Robert V. Lizza
W. Robert Allison	Miriam Goldstein Altman
Philip J. Notopoulos	John J. Monaghan
Richard J. Hindlian	Margaret J. Palladino
Paul E. Troy	Mark C. Michalowski
Harold W. Potter, Jr.	David Scott Sloan
Philip S. Lapatin	M. Chrysa Long
Pamela A. Duckworth	Lawrence D. Bradley
Miriam J. McKendall	

(See Next Column)

SHERBURNE, POWERS & NEEDHAM P.C.—*Continued*

Cynthia A. Brown	Amy J. Mastrobattista
Cynthia M. Hern	Leslie A. Sprinkle
Meredeth A. Beers	Douglas W. Clapp
Dianne R. Phillips	Jeffrey A. Huebschmann
Paul M. James	Tamara E. Goulston
Theodore F. Hanselman	Paul G. Lannon, Jr.
Joshua C. Krumholz	Nicholas J. Psyhogeos
Ieuan G. Mahony	Edward J. Naughton
Jeffrey J. Nix	Kathaleen Kelly Cutone
(Not admitted in MA)	Laurie A. Tribble
Kenneth L. Harvey	Neil C. Higgins
Christopher J. Trombetta	Deborah Paige Stone
Elise N. Zoli	Brian R. Popiel

COUNSEL

Haig Der Manuelian	Karl J. Hirshman
Mason M. Taber, Jr.	Dale R. Johnson

For full biographical listings, see the Martindale-Hubbell Law Directory

WEINGARTEN, SCHURGIN, GAGNEBIN & HAYES (AV)

Ten Post Office Square, 02109
Telephone: 617-542-2290
Cable Address: "Celinan"
Telex: 940675
Telecopier: 617-451-0313

MEMBERS OF FIRM

Joseph Weingarten (1919-1984)	Victor B. Lebovici
Stanley M. Schurgin	Dean G. Bostock
Charles L. Gagnebin, III	Eugene A. Feher
Paul J. Hayes	Beverly E. Hjorth

ASSOCIATES

Holliday C. Heine	Thomas E. Anderson
Gordon R. Moriarty	David W. Rouille
Judith C. Crowley	Paul D. Durkee
Holmes W. Anderson	Nicholas P. Triano, III

For full biographical listings, see the Martindale-Hubbell Law Directory

WILLCOX, PIROZZOLO AND McCARTHY, PROFESSIONAL CORPORATION (AV)

50 Federal Street, 02110
Telephone: 617-482-5470
Telecopier: 617-423-1572

Harold M. Willcox (1925-1975)	Jack R. Pirozzolo
	Richard F. McCarthy

Richard L. Binder	Richard E. Bennett
	Judith Seplowitz Ziss

OF COUNSEL

Richard P. Crowley

For full biographical listings, see the Martindale-Hubbell Law Directory

LEXINGTON, Middlesex Co.

HAMILTON, BROOK, SMITH & REYNOLDS, P.C. (AV)

2 Militia Drive, 02173
Telephone: 617-861-6240
Telecopier: 617-861-9540
Email: hbsr@aol.com

Munroe H. Hamilton	John L. DuPré
(1906-1984)	David J. Brody
David E. Brook	Mary Lou Wakimura
James M. Smith	Thomas O. Hoover
Leo R. Reynolds	Alice O. Carroll
Patricia Granahan	N. Scott Pierce

OF COUNSEL

Richard A. Wise	Susan G. L. Glovsky

Anne J. Collins	Timothy J. Meagher
Robert T. Conway	Anthony P. Onello, Jr.
Steven G. Davis	Nina L. Pearlmutter
Carol A. Egner	Scott D. Rothenberger
Doreen M. Hogle	Deirdre E. Sanders
J. Grant Houston	Jay Shim
Rodney D. Johnson	Richard W. Wagner
Helen Lee	Lisa Marie Warren
Elizabeth Wechsler Mata	Helen E. Wendler
	Darrell L. Wong

LEGAL SUPPORT PERSONNEL

PATENT AGENT

Carolyn S. Elmore

For full biographical listings, see the Martindale-Hubbell Law Directory

SPRINGFIELD,* Hampden Co.

DOHERTY, WALLACE, PILLSBURY AND MURPHY, P.C. (AV)

19th Floor, One Monarch Place, 1414 Main Street, 01144
Telephone: 413-733-3111
Telecopier: 413-734-3910
Email: DWPM@DWPM.COM

Dudley B. Wallace (1900-1987)	L. Jeffrey Meehan
Louis W. Doherty (1898-1990)	David J. Martel
Robert E. Murphy	John James McCarthy
Paul S. Doherty	Joan Ho Bond
Samuel A. Marsella	William P. Hadley
Philip J. Callan, Jr.	Barry M. Ryan
Gary P. Shannon	Deborah A. Basile
Robert L. Leonard	Paul M. Maleck
A. Craig Brown	Claire L. Thompson
	W. Garth Janes

Michael J. Rye	Kevin M. Walkowski
Michael K. Callan	William F. Sullivan, Jr.
	Steven M. Coyle

OF COUNSEL

Frederick S. Pillsbury	Matthew J. Ryan, Jr.
	Gregory A. Schmidt

Local Counsel for: Nationwide Mutual Insurance Co.; Liberty Mutual Insurance Co.; General Motors Corp.; Wausau Insurance Cos.; Royal Insurance; Metropolitan Property & Liability Insurance Co.
Representative Clients: Fontaine Bros.; F.L. Roberts and Company Inc.; Town of Longmeadow.

For full biographical listings, see the Martindale-Hubbell Law Directory

MICHIGAN

ANN ARBOR,* Washtenaw Co.

HARNESS, DICKEY & PIERCE, P.L.C. (AV)

Suite 555, 301 East Liberty Street, 48104
Telephone: 313-662-8000
Telex: 287637 HARNES UR
Telefacsimile: 313-662-7813
Email: info@hdp.com *URL:* http://www.hdp.com
Troy, Michigan Office: 5445 Corporate Drive, Suite 400.
Telephone: 810-641-1600. Telefacsimile (All Groups): 810-641-0270.
Washington, D.C. Office: 888 Sixteenth Street, N.W.
Telephone: 202-835-7480. Telefacsimile 202-835-7487.

MEMBERS OF FIRM

James E. Stephenson (Resident)	Steven L. Oberholtzer (Resident)
	Eric J. Sosenko (Resident)

RESIDENT ASSOCIATES

G. Peter Albert, Jr.	William B. Batzer
	Charles T. Graham

Representative Clients: Chrysler Corp.; The Black and Decker Manufacturing Co.; Thermos Co.; Monroe Auto Equipment Co.; La-Z-Boy Chair Co.; Hughes Aircraft; Budd Co.; Dow Chemical Co.; Procter & Gamble; Kmart Properties.

For full biographical listings, see the Martindale-Hubbell Law Directory

BLOOMFIELD HILLS, Oakland Co.

HOWARD & HOWARD ATTORNEYS, P.C. (AV)

The Pinehurst Office Center, Suite 101, 1400 North Woodward
  Avenue, 48304-2856
Telephone: 810-645-1483
Telecopier: 810-645-1568
Kalamazoo, Michigan Office: The Kalamazoo Building, Suite 400, 107
West Michigan Avenue.
Telephone: 616-382-1483.
Telecopier: 616-382-1568.
Lansing, Michigan Office: The Phoenix Building, Suite 500, 222
Washington Square, North.
Telephone: 517-485-1483.
Telecopier: 517-485-1568.
Peoria, Illinois Office: The Creve Coeur Building, Suite 200, 321 Liberty
Street.
Telephone: 309-672-1483.
Telecopier: 309-672-1568.
Tampa, Florida Office: First of America Plaza, Suite 2000, 201 East
Kennedy Boulevard.
Telephone: 813-229-1483.
Telecopier: 813-229-1568.

(See Next Column)

HOWARD & HOWARD ATTORNEYS P.C., *Bloomfield Hills—Continued*

Robin W. Asher
John E. Carlson
William J. Clemens
Sally Lee Foley
David J. Gaskey

William H. Honaker
Harold W. Milton, Jr.
Theodore W. Olds III
Jeffrey G. Raphelson
Raymond E. Scott

Jon E. Shackelford

Representative Clients: For Representative Client list, see General Practice, Bloomfield Hills, MI.

For Complete List of Firm Personnel, See General Section

For full biographical listings, see the Martindale-Hubbell Law Directory

LYON, P.C. (AV)

3883 Telegraph Road, Suite 207, 48302-1476
Telephone: 810-645-5200
Facsimile: 810-645-1016

Lyman R. Lyon

For full biographical listings, see the Martindale-Hubbell Law Directory

RADER, FISHMAN & GRAUER PLLC (AV)

1533 North Woodward, Suite 140, 48304
Telephone: 810-594-0600
Fax: 810-594-0610
Email: info@raderfishman.com *URL:* http://www.intelprop.com

Ralph Terrance Rader
Michael D. Fishman
Richard D. Grauer
Joseph V. Coppola, Sr.
Michael B. Stewart

George C. Summerfield, Jr.
Glenn E. Forbis
Cynthia B. Summerfield
Stefan V. Chmielewski
Kevin D. Rutherford

For full biographical listings, see the Martindale-Hubbell Law Directory

---

DETROIT, * Wayne Co.

BARNES, KISSELLE, RAISCH, CHOATE, WHITTEMORE & HULBERT, P.C. (AV)

3500 Penobscot Building, 48226
Telephone: 313-962-4790
Telecopier: 313-962-0158
Cable Address: "Barkl"

Stuart C. Barnes (1885-1968)
John M. Kisselle (1894-1980)
Arthur Raisch (1902-1991)
Lacey Laughlin (1896-1956)
Prescott M. Hulbert (1865-1961)
Laurence J. Whittemore (1871-1946)
William J. Belknap (1883-1941)

L. Gaylord Hulbert (1895-1980)
Basil C. Foussianes
William H. Griffith
William J. Waugaman
Chester L. Davis, Jr.
William H. Francis
Robert C. Collins
Linda M. Deschere

Randy W. Tung

OF COUNSEL

Robert A. Choate   Alfonse John D'Amico

Representative Clients: General Motors Corporation; Goodyear Tire & Rubber Co.; Henry Ford Hospital; Motor Wheel Corp.; Owens-Illinois, Inc.; SPX Corp.; Vickers, Inc., a subsidiary of Trinova Corp.; Walbro Corp.

For full biographical listings, see the Martindale-Hubbell Law Directory

DICKINSON, WRIGHT, MOON, VAN DUSEN & FREEMAN (AV)

500 Woodward Avenue, Suite 4000, 48226-3425
Telephone: 313-223-3500
Facsimile: 313-223-3598
Bloomfield Hills, Michigan Office: 525 North Woodward Avenue, Suite 2000.
Telephone: 810-433-7200.
Facsimile: 810-433-7274.
Grand Rapids, Michigan Office: 200 Ottawa Avenue, N.W., Suite 900.
Telephone: 616-458-1300.
Facsimile: 616-458-6753.
Lansing, Michigan Office: Suite 200, 215 South Washington Square.
Telephone: 517-371-1730.
Facsimile: 517-487-4700.
Washington, D.C. Office: Suite 800, 1901 L Street, N.W.
Telephone: 202-457-0160.
Facsimile: 202-659-1559.
Chicago, Illinois Office: 225 West Washington, Suite 400.
Telephone: 312-220-0300.
Facsimile: 312-220-0021.

MEMBERS OF FIRM

Conrad J. Clark
(Washington, D.C. Office)
William E. Elwood
(Washington, D.C. Office)
Samuel D. Littlepage
(Washington, D.C. Office)

Jeffrey M. Petrash
(Washington, D.C. Office)
Michael T. Platt
(Washington, D.C. Office)

(See Next Column)

OF COUNSEL

Marc A. Bergsman
(Washington, D.C. Office)
David R. Haarz
(Washington, D.C. Office)

Lucien N. Nedzi
(Washington, D.C. Office)
Stephanie Karen Wade
(Washington, D.C. Office)

For Representative Client list, see General Section.

For Complete List of Firm Personnel, See General Section

For full biographical listings, see the Martindale-Hubbell Law Directory

DYKEMA GOSSETT PLLC (AV)

400 Renaissance Center, 48243-1668
Telephone: 313-568-6800
Cable Address: "Dyke-Detroit"
Telex: 23-0121
Fax: 313-568-6594
Email: 2084153@mcimail.com
Ann Arbor, Michigan Office: 315 East Eisenhower Parkway, Suite 100, 48108-3306.
Telephone: 313-747-7660.
Fax: 313-747-7696.
Bloomfield Hills, Michigan Office: 1577 North Woodward Avenue, Suite 300, 48304-2820.
Telephone: 810-540-0700.
Fax: 810-540-0763.
Chicago, Illinois Office: 55 East Monroe Street, Suite 3250, 60603-5709.
Telephone: 312-551-4900.
Fax: 312-551-4919.
Grand Rapids, Michigan Office: 200 Oldtown Riverfront Building, 248 Louis Campau Promenade, N.W., 49503-2668.
Telephone: 616-776-7500.
Fax: 616-776-7573.
Lansing, Michigan Office: 800 Michigan National Tower, 48933-1707.
Telephone: 517-374-9100.
Fax: 517-374-9191.
Washington, D.C. Office: Franklin Square, Suite 300 West, 1300 I Street, N.W., 20005-3306.
Telephone: 202-522-8600.
Fax: 202-522-8669.

MEMBERS OF FIRM

Barbara L. Goldman (Resident at Bloomfield Hills Office)
J. Timothy Hobbs (Not admitted in MI; Resident at Washington, D.C. Office)
Robert L. Kelly (Resident at Bloomfield Hills Office)
Bruce A. McDonald (Not admitted in MI; Resident at Washington, D.C. Office)

Janet L. Neary (Resident at Ann Arbor Office)
Charles R. Rutherford (Resident at Bloomfield Hills Office)
Thomas B. Spillane, Jr. (Resident at Bloomfield Hills Office)

OF COUNSEL

Gerald R. Black (Resident at Bloomfield Hills Office)

Edward J. Chalfie (Not admitted in MI; Resident at Chicago, Illinois Office)

ASSOCIATES

Hugo A. Delevie (Resident at Bloomfield Hills Office)
Joseph H. Hickey (Resident at Bloomfield Hills Office)
Kevin M. Hinman (Resident at Bloomfield Hills Office)

Christopher Kelly (Not admitted in MI; Resident at Washington, D.C. Office)
Kevin G. Mierzwa (Resident at Bloomfield Hills Office)
John W. Rees (Resident at Bloomfield Hills Office)

For Complete List of Firm Personnel, See General Section

For full biographical listings, see the Martindale-Hubbell Law Directory

MILLER, CANFIELD, PADDOCK AND STONE, P.L.C. (AV)

A Professional Limited Liability Company
Founded in 1852 by Sidney Davy Miller
150 West Jefferson, Suite 2500, 48226-4415
Telephone: 313-963-6420
Fax: 313-496-7500
Cable Address: "Stem Detroit"
Detroit, Michigan Office: 150 West Jefferson, Suite 2500, 48226-4415.
Telephone: 313-963-6420.
Fax: 313-496-7500.
Cable Address: "Stem Detroit."
Ann Arbor, Michigan Office: 101 North Main Street, 7th Floor, 48104-1400.
Telephone: 313-663-2445.
Fax: 313-747-7147.
Bloomfield Hills, Michigan Office: Suite 100, Pinehurst Office Center, 1400 North Woodward, 48303-2014.
Telephone: 313-645-5000.
Fax: 313-645-1917.
Grand Rapids, Michigan Office: 1200 Campau Square Plaza, 99 Monroe, N.W., 49503-2639.
Telephone: 616-454-8656.
Fax: 616-776-6322.

(See Next Column)

MILLER, CANFIELD, PADDOCK AND STONE P.L.C.—*Continued*

Howell, Michigan Office: 121 South Barnard Street, Suite 4, 48843-2305.
Telephone: 517-546-7600.
Telecopier: 517-546-6974.
Kalamazoo, Michigan Office: 444 West Michigan Avenue, 49007-3752.
Telephone: 616-381-7030.
Fax: 616-382-0244.
Lansing, Michigan Office: One Michigan Avenue, Suite 900, 48933-1609.
Telephone: 517-487-2070.
Fax: 517-374-6304.
Monroe, Michigan Office: The Executive Centre, 214 East Elm Avenue, 48161-2682.
Telephone: 313-243-2000.
Fax: 313-243-0901.
Washington, D.C. Office: 1225 Nineteenth Street, N.W., Suite 400. 20036.
Telephone: 202-429-5575; 785-0600.
Fax: 202-331-1118; 785-1234.
Pensacola, Florida Office: 25 West Cedar, 32501.
Telephone: 904-469-1088.
Fax: 904-432-0677.
St. Petersburg, Florida Office: 100 Second Avenue S., Suite 7045, 33701.
Telephone: 813-982-6000.
Fax: 813-892-6002.
New York, New York Office: Eleventh Floor, 135 East 57th Street, 10022-2087.
Telephone: 212-754-5400.
Fax: 212-754-5401.
Gdansk, Poland Office: Suite 322, Dom Technika Building, UI. Rajska 6, 80-850.
Telephone: 011-485-831-2808.
Fax: 011-485-831-4719.
Warsaw, Poland Office: UI. Marszalkowska 82, Suite 561, 00-517.
Telephone: 011-482-623-6457 and 6458.
Fax: 011-482-623-6459.

PRINCIPALS OF FIRM

Marjory G. Basile   Richard A. Gaffin
                       (Grand Rapids Office)

OF COUNSEL

Edward F. Langs   Benita J. Rohm
Raphael A. Monsanto   (Not admitted in MI)
 (Not admitted in MI)

ASSOCIATE
Robert R. Lech

Representative Firm Clients: Chrysler Corporation; Comerica, Incorporated; City of Detroit, Michigan; Detroit Tigers, Inc.; First of Michigan; Ford Motor Company; Ford Motor Credit Company; Great Lakes Bancorp; Henry Ford Hospital; INVETECH Company.

For Complete List of Firm Personnel, See General Section

For full biographical listings, see the Martindale-Hubbell Law Directory

---

GRAND RAPIDS,* Kent Co.

PRICE, HENEVELD, COOPER, DEWITT & LITTON (AV)

695 Kenmoor, S.E., P.O. Box 2567, 49501
Telephone: 616-949-9610
Telecopier: 616-957-8196

MEMBERS OF FIRM

Peter P. Price (Retired)   Randall G. Litton
Lloyd A. Heneveld   James A. Mitchell
Richard C. Cooper   Harold W. Reick
William W. DeWitt   Carl S. Clark
          Daniel L. Girdwood

ASSOCIATES

Douglas H. Siegel   Gunther J. Evanina
 (Not admitted in MI)   Steven C. Wichmann
Barry C. Kane   Jay G. Durst
Terry S. Callaghan   (Not admitted in MI)

Representative Clients: Amway Corp.; Michigan State University; Dow Chemical Co.; Gerber Products Co.; Kysor Industrial Corp.; L. Perrigo Co.; Prince Corp.; Ralston Purina Co.; Steelcase, Inc.; Wolverine World Wide, Inc.

For full biographical listings, see the Martindale-Hubbell Law Directory

VARNUM, RIDDERING, SCHMIDT & HOWLETT LLP (AV)

A Limited Liability Partnership including Professional Corporations
Bridgewater Place, P.O. Box 352, 49501-0352
Telephone: 616-336-6000
800-262-0011
Facsimile: 616-336-7000
Telex: 1561593 VARN
Email: varnum@vrsh.com
Lansing, Michigan Office: The Victor Center, Suite 810, 210 North Washington Square, 48933.
Telephone: 517-482-6237.
Facsimile: 517-482-6937.

(See Next Column)

Kalamazoo, Michigan Office: 350 East Michigan Avenue, 49007.
Telephone: 616-382-2300.
Facsimile: 616-382-2382.
Grand Haven, Michigan Office: 321 Washington Street, P.O. Box 288, 49417.
Telephone: 616-846-7100.
Facsimile: 616-846-7101.
Battle Creek, Michigan Office: 4950 West Dickman Road, Suite B-1, 49015.
Telephone: 616-962-7144.
Bingham Farms, Michigan Office: 31600 Telegraph Road, Suite 230, 48025.
Telephone: 810-594-7330.
Facsimile: 810-594- 7331.

MEMBERS OF FIRM

John E. McGarry   Timothy E. Eagle
Thomas L. Lockhart   Joel E. Bair
          Richard J. McKenna

COUNSEL

H. Lawrence Smith   Peter Visserman

ASSOCIATE
G. Thomas Williams, III

Counsel for: Cadillac Rubber & Plastics, Inc.; Cascade Engineering; Herman Miller, Inc.; Medtronic, Inc.; Neway Anchorlok, Inc.; Smith's Industries; X-Rite, Inc.

For Complete List of Firm Personnel, See General Section

For full biographical listings, see the Martindale-Hubbell Law Directory

---

WARNER NORCROSS & JUDD LLP (AV)

900 Old Kent Building, 111 Lyon Street, N.W., 49503-2489
Telephone: 616-752-2000
Fax: 616-752-2500
Muskegon, Michigan Office: 400 Terrace Plaza, P.O. Box 900.
Telephone: 616-727-2600.
Fax: 616-727-2699.
Holland, Michigan Office: Curtis Center, Suite 300, 170 College Avenue.
Telephone: 616-396-9800.
Fax: 616-396-3656.

MEMBERS OF FIRM

James H. Breay   John G. Cameron, Jr.
Peter L. Gustafson   Stephen C. Waterbury
          Charles E. Burpee

Representative Clients: Amstore Corp; Guardsman Products; H.H. Cutler Co.; High Q Manufacturing Co.; Morbark Industries, Inc.; ODL Incorporated; Pandrol Jackson, Inc.; Plascore, Inc.; Rockford Corp.; The Zondervan Corp.

For Complete List of Firm Personnel, See General Section

For full biographical listings, see the Martindale-Hubbell Law Directory

---

HOLLAND, Ottawa Co.

McKINNON AND McKINNON (AV)

A Partnership including a Professional Corporation
305 Hoover Boulevard, 49423
Telephone: 616-393-6400
Fax: 616-393-4931
Williamston, Michigan Office: One Energy Center, 148 East Grand River, P.O. Box 102.
Telephone: 517-349-0780.
Fax: 517-349-0781.

Malcolm R. McKinnon (P.C.)   Malcolm L. McKinnon

For full biographical listings, see the Martindale-Hubbell Law Directory

---

LANSING, Ingham Co.

FOSTER, SWIFT, COLLINS & SMITH, P.C. (AV)

313 South Washington Square, 48933-2193
Telephone: 517-371-8100
Telecopier: 517-371-8200
URL: http://www.fosterswift.com
Farmington Hills, Michigan Office: 32300 Northwestern Highway, Suite 230.
Telephone: 810-539-9900.
Fax: 810-851-7504.

Gary J. McRay   Steven H. Lasher

General Counsel for: First American Bank-Central; Story, Inc.; Michigan Milk Producers Assn.; Edward W. Sparrow Hospital; St. Lawrence Hospital; Demmer Corp.; Michigan Financial Corp.
Local Counsel for: Shell Oil Co.; Michigan-Mutual Insurance Co.; Century Telephone.

For Complete List of Firm Personnel, See General Section

For full biographical listings, see the Martindale-Hubbell Law Directory

OKEMOS, Ingham Co.

IAN C. McLEOD, P.C. (AV)

2190 Commons Parkway, 48864
Telephone: 517-347-4100
Telecopier: 517-347-4103

Ian C. McLeod   Mary M. Moyne

Representative Clients: Ash Stevens, Inc., Detroit, Michigan; Quest International, Inc., Sarasota, Florida; Michigan State University, East Lansing, Michigan; Wayne State University, Detroit, Michigan; Technical Advisors, Inc., Wayne, Michigan; Unilever, Netherlands, Prototypes, England; Lumigen Inc., Detroit, Michigan.
References: Michigan National Bank; First of America; Bank of Lansing, Lansing, Michigan.

For full biographical listings, see the Martindale-Hubbell Law Directory

---

SAGINAW, * Saginaw Co.

LEARMAN & McCULLOCH AND REISING, ETHINGTON, BARNARD & PERRY (AV)

5291 Colony Drive, North, 48603
Telephone: 517-799-5300
Telecopier: 792-8585
Troy, Michigan Office: Reising, Ethington, Barnard & Perry and Learman & McCulloch. Suite 400, 201 West Big Beaver Road. P.O. Box 4390.
Telephone: 810-689-3500.

RESIDENT PARTNERS
John F. Learman   John K. McCulloch
RESIDENT ASSOCIATE
Robert L. Farris

For full biographical listings, see the Martindale-Hubbell Law Directory

---

TRAVERSE CITY, * Grand Traverse Co.

BISHOP & HEINTZ, P.C. (AV)

440 W. Front at Oak Street, P.O. Box 707, 49685
Telephone: 616-946-4100
Fax: 616-946-8543

Douglas S. Bishop

Representative Clients: Old Kent Bank-Grand Traverse; Old Kent Bank & Trust Co.; NBD Bank, N.A.; Ball Aircraft, Inc.; Power Play International Inc.; National Cherry Festival; PDM Industries, Inc.; Bolthouse Machine Corp.; Corrections Management, Inc.; Buck Wilder, Inc.

For full biographical listings, see the Martindale-Hubbell Law Directory

---

TROY, Oakland Co.

DINNIN & DUNN, P.C. (AV)

Top of Troy Building, 755 West Big Beaver Road, Suite 2100, 48084
Telephone: 810-362-2800
Facsimile: 810-362-2864
Email: dinnindunn@michbar.org

Michael R. Dinnin   Robert A. Dunn
            Michael T. Raggio

For full biographical listings, see the Martindale-Hubbell Law Directory

---

HARNESS, DICKEY & PIERCE, P.L.C. (AV)

5445 Corporate Drive, Suite 400, 48098
Telephone: 810-641-1600
Cable Address: "PATENTS TROYMICHIGAN"
Telex: 287637 HARNES UR
Telefacsimile (All Groups): 810-641-0270
Email: info@hdp.com *URL:* http://www.hdp.com
Ann Arbor, Michigan Office: 301 East Liberty Street, Suite 555.
Telephone: 313-662-8000.
Telefacsimile: 313-662-7813.
Washington, D.C. Office: 888 Sixteenth Street, N.W.
Telephone: 202-835-7480.
Telefacsimile: 202-835-7487.

MEMBERS OF FIRM

J. King Harness (1897-1977)	Ronald W. Wangerow
Arthur W. Dickey (1897-1964)	Gregory A. Stobbs
Hodgson S. Pierce (1896-1947)	Steven L. Oberholtzer (Resident
Charles H. Blair	at Ann Arbor Office)
Joseph R. Papp	Michael P. Brennan
H. Keith Miller	Gordon K. Harris, Jr.
James E. Stephenson (Resident	Stephen J. Foss
at Ann Arbor Office)	Gary L. Newtson
Bernard J. Cantor	W. R. Duke Taylor (Resident at
Christopher M. Brock	Washington Office)
Richard L. Carlson	Richard P. Vitek
Ronald L. Hofer	Robert S. Nolan
Jeffrey A. Sadowski	Philip R. Warn
Paul A. Keller	Thomas A. Hallin
G. Gregory Schivley	Philip E. Rettig

MEMBERS OF FIRM (Continued)

Eric M. Dobrusin	Lisabeth H. Coakley
Mark D. Elchuk	Eric J. Sosenko (Resident at
Michael J. Schmidt	Ann Arbor Office)

ASSOCIATES

G. Peter Albert, Jr.	Ryan W. Massey
(Resident, Ann Arbor Office)	David A. McClaughry
William B. Batzer	John A. Miller
(Resident, Ann Arbor Office)	Thomas Traian Moga
John V. Biernacki	Douglas A. Mullen
Scott M. Confer	Stephen T. Olson
Garrett C. Donley	David G. Posz
Stanley M. Erjavac	George T. Schooff
Monte Lee Falcoff	Robert M. Siminski
Charles T. Graham (Resident at	Anthony G. Sitko
Ann Arbor Office)	DeAnn Foran Smith
Kevin T. Grzelak	Jeffrey P. Thennisch
Robert R. Kirkman	David P. Utykanski
Joseph M. Lafata	Bryant E. Wade
Douglas P. LaLone	Richard W. Warner

COUNSEL
Robert J. Wallace, Sr.

Representative Clients: Chrysler Corp.; The Black and Decker Manufacturing Co.; King-Seeley Thermos Co.; Monroe Auto Equipment Co.; La-Z-Boy Chair Co.; Hughes Aircraft; Budd Co.; Dow Chemical Co.; Procter & Gamble.

For full biographical listings, see the Martindale-Hubbell Law Directory

---

REISING, ETHINGTON, BARNARD & PERRY, L.L.P. AND LEARMAN & McCULLOCH (AV)

Suite 400, 201 West Big Beaver, P.O. Box 4390, 48099
Telephone: 810-689-3500
Fax: 810-689-4071
Email: postmaster@reising.com
Saginaw, Michigan Office: Learman & McCulloch and Reising, Ethington, Barnard & Perry. 5291 Colony Drive North, Saginaw, Michigan, 48603.
Telephone: 517-799-5300.
FAX: 517-792-8585.

MEMBERS OF FIRM

Richard P. Barnard (1924-1993)	Jeanne-Marie Marshall
Paul J. Reising (1923-1993)	John K. McCulloch (Resident
Paul J. Ethington	Saginaw, Michigan Office)
John C. Evans	Steven L. Permut
Francis J. Fodale	Owen E. Perry
Richard W. Hoffmann	William J. Schramm
John F. Learman (Resident,	
Saginaw, Michigan Office)	

ASSOCIATES

Craig A. Baldwin	Eric T. Jones
Edward J. Biskup	John P. Moran
Robert L. Farris (Resident,	Robert L. Stearns
Saginaw, Michigan Office)	James D. Stevens
Andrew M. Grove	Charles R. White

OF COUNSEL

Donald R. Fraser	David A. Greenlee
(Not admitted in MI)	

Reference: Michigan National Bank of Detroit.

For full biographical listings, see the Martindale-Hubbell Law Directory

PERSONAL INJURY

ALABAMA

ALEXANDER CITY, Tallapoosa Co.

MORRIS, HAYNES, INGRAM & HORNSBY (AV)

131 Main Street, P.O. Box 1660, 35011-1660
Telephone: 205-329-2000
Fax: 205-329-2015

Larry W. Morris	Kenneth F. Ingram, Jr.
Randall Stark Haynes	Clay Hornsby

OF COUNSEL

John F. Dillon, IV	Jennie Lee Kelley

Representative Clients: First National Bank; City of Alexander City; Town of Wadley; Russell Corp.
Approved Attorneys for: Lawyers Title Insurance Corp.; Mississippi Valley Title Insurance Co.

For full biographical listings, see the Martindale-Hubbell Law Directory

BIRMINGHAM, * Jefferson Co.

BAXLEY, DILLARD, DAUPHIN & McKNIGHT (AV)

2000 Sixteenth Avenue South, 35205
Telephone: 205-939-0995
Telecopier: 205-939-5025

MEMBERS OF FIRM

William J. Baxley	Charles A. Dauphin
Joel E. Dillard	Stewart D. McKnight, III

ASSOCIATES

Donald R. James, Jr	Paul R. Ellis
Mary Margaret Bailey	

For full biographical listings, see the Martindale-Hubbell Law Directory

BRADLEY, ARANT, ROSE & WHITE (AV)

2001 Park Place, Suite 1400, P.O. Box 830709, 35283-0709
Telephone: 205-521-8000
Facsimile: 205-252-0264
Facsimile (SouthTrust Tower Office): 205-251-9915
URL: http://www.BARW.COM
Huntsville, Alabama Office: 200 Clinton Avenue West, Suite 900, 35801.
Telephone: 205-517-5100.
Facsimile: 205-533-5069.

MEMBERS OF FIRM

John H. Morrow	John D. Watson, III
Hobart A. McWhorter, Jr.	Michael D. McKibben
Gary C. Huckaby	David Glenn Hymer
(Resident, Huntsville Office)	G. Rick Hall
James W. Gewin	(Resident, Huntsville Office)
Brittin Turner Coleman	Sid J. Trant
E. Cutter Hughes, Jr.	Stewart M. Cox
(Resident, Huntsville Office)	Philip J. Carroll III
Walter J. Sears, III	John E. Goodman
Joseph B. Mays, Jr.	T. Michael Brown
Norman Jetmundsen, Jr.	Warne S. Heath
Joseph S. Bird, III	(Resident, Huntsville Office)

COUNSEL

Scott M. Phelps

ASSOCIATES

Michael S. Denniston	Kenneth M. Perry
Denise Avery Dodson	Charles K. Hamilton
Julie Scharfenberg Elmer	

For Complete List of Firm Personnel, See General Section

For full biographical listings, see the Martindale-Hubbell Law Directory

BURGE & WETTERMARK, P.C. (AV)

2300 SouthTrust Tower, 420 North 20th Street, 35203-3204
Telephone: 205-251-9729; 800-633-3733
Fax: 205-323-0512
Atlanta, Georgia Office: 2700 The Grand, 75 14th Street, N.E., 30309.
Telephone: 404-875-2500; 800-749-8687.
Fax: 404-875-5807.
Jacksonville, Florida Office: 3100 Independent Drive, 32202.
Telephone: 904-353-1555 or 1-800-498-6657.
Fax: 904-353-3905.
Ludlow, Kentucky Office: 243 Elm Street, P.O. Box 16167.
Telephone: 606-491-7000; 800-872-4671.
Fax: 606-491-7001.

(See Next Column)

Frank O. Burge, Jr.	Gregory T. Hughes
James H. Wettermark	(Not admitted in AL)
F. Tucker Burge	Monroe Dykes Barber, Jr.
Courtney Burge Brown	Van Kirk McCombs, II
Michael J. Warshauer	James R. Holland, II
(Not admitted in AL)	(Not admitted in AL)
Gary F. Easom	Lyle Griffin Woodruff
(Not admitted in AL)	

References: AmSouth Bank; First Alabama Bank, Birmingham, Alabama.

For full biographical listings, see the Martindale-Hubbell Law Directory

GORDON, SILBERMAN, WIGGINS & CHILDS, A PROFESSIONAL CORPORATION (AV)

1400 SouthTrust Tower, 420 North 20th Street, 35203
Telephone: 205-328-0640
Telecopier: 205-254-1500

Bruce L. Gordon	Ann C. Robertson
Byron R. Perkins	Gregory O. Wiggins
	Brian M. Clark

For Complete List of Firm Personnel, See General Section

For full biographical listings, see the Martindale-Hubbell Law Directory

HARE, WYNN, NEWELL AND NEWTON (AV)

A Partnership including Professional Corporations
Suite 800 Massey Building, 290 21st Street North, 35203
Telephone: 205-328-5330
FAX: 205-324-2165

MEMBERS OF FIRM

Francis H. Hare (1904-1983)	John W. Haley (P.C.)
Carlton T. Wynn	D. Leon Ashford (P.C.)
Neal C. Newell	Scott A. Powell
Alex W. Newton	James R. Pratt, III
Terrell Wynn, Jr.	S. Shay Samples
James J. Thompson, Jr.	Bruce J. McKee
Alva C. Caine	Michael D. Ermert
Ray O. Noojin, Jr., (P.C.)	Robert R. Riley, Jr.
Nolan Edward Awbrey	

COUNSEL

Francis H. Hare, Jr., (P.C.)	James O. Haley
James K. Baker	

References: AmSouth Bank of Birmingham; First Commercial Bank of Birmingham.

For full biographical listings, see the Martindale-Hubbell Law Directory

HOGAN, SMITH & ALSPAUGH, P.C. (AV)

2323 Second Avenue, North, 35203
Telephone: 205-324-5635
Telecopier: 205-324-5637

William W. Smith	David J. Guin
M. Clay Alspaugh	Ronald R. Crook
R. Benjamin Hogan, III	Richard D. Stratton
David R. Donaldson	Pamela D. Beard
Benjamin E. Baker, Jr.	

Reference: First Alabama Bank.

For full biographical listings, see the Martindale-Hubbell Law Directory

RICHARD S. JAFFE, P.C. (AV)

1905 Fourteenth Avenue South, 35205
Telephone: 205-930-9800
Telecopier: 205-930-9809

Richard S. Jaffe

Stephen A. Strickland	Cecilie Russell Beasley

For full biographical listings, see the Martindale-Hubbell Law Directory

DAVID CROMWELL JOHNSON (AV)

The Land Title Building, Suite 200, 600 20th Street, North, 35203
Telephone: 205-327-5223

ASSOCIATES

J. Flint Liddon	Barry R. Tuggle

For full biographical listings, see the Martindale-Hubbell Law Directory

LIGHTFOOT, FRANKLIN & WHITE, L.L.C. (AV)

300 Financial Center, 505 20th Street North, 35203-2706
Telephone: 205-581-0700
Facsimile: 205-581-0799

(See Next Column)

LIGHTFOOT, FRANKLIN & WHITE L.L.C., *Birmingham—Continued*

Warren B. Lightfoot	E. Glenn Waldrop, Jr.
Samuel H. Franklin	Adam K. Peck
Jere F. White, Jr.	Harlan I. Prater, IV
Mac M. Moorer	Michael L. Bell
John M. Johnson	William S. Cox, III
M. Christian King	William H. King, III

Sarah Bruce Jackson	Sabrina A. Simon
William H. Brooks	Madeline H. Haikala
J. Banks Sewell, III	Wynn M. Shuford
Lee M. Hollis	Charles L. Rice, Jr.

Counsel for: AT&T; Ford Motor Co.; Emerson Electric Co.; Monsanto Co.; Chrysler Corp.; Unocal Corp.; The Upjohn Co.; Bristol-Myers Squibb Co.; The Goodyear Tire & Rubber Co.; Mitsubishi Motor Sales of America, Inc.

For full biographical listings, see the Martindale-Hubbell Law Directory

PITTMAN, HOOKS, DUTTON & HOLLIS, P.C. (AV)

1100 Park Place Tower, 35203
Telephone: 205-322-8880
Telecopier: 205-328-2711

W. Lee Pittman	L. Andrew Hollis, Jr.
Kenneth W. Hooks	Jeffrey C. Kirby
Tom Dutton	Ralph Bohanan, Jr.

Nat Bryan

Chris T. Hellums	Emily H. Nelson
Adam P. Morel	John Robert Potter

OF COUNSEL

James H. Davis	Myra B. Staggs
(Not admitted in AL)	

For full biographical listings, see the Martindale-Hubbell Law Directory

REDDEN, MILLS & CLARK (AV)

940 First Alabama Bank Building, 417 North 20th Street, 35203
Telephone: 205-322-0457
Fax: 205-322-8481

MEMBERS OF FIRM

L. Drew Redden	William N. Clark
William H. Mills	Gerald L. Miller

Stephen W. Shaw

ASSOCIATE

Maxwell H. Pulliam, Jr.

References: SouthTrust Bank; First Alabama Bank.

For full biographical listings, see the Martindale-Hubbell Law Directory

SPAIN & GILLON, L.L.C. (AV)

The Zinszer Building, 2117 2nd Avenue North, 35203
Telephone: 205-328-4100
Telecopier: 205-324-8866

MEMBERS OF FIRM

Eugene P. Stutts	Paul L. Sotherland
Alton B. Parker, Jr.	W. Gregory Smith

General Counsel for: Liberty National Life Insurance Co.; Piggly Wiggly Alabama Distributing Co.; Alabama Insurance Guaranty Association; Alabama Life and Disability Insurance Guaranty Association; Alabama Insurance Underwriters Association; Liberty Mutual Insurance Co.
Counsel for: Government Employees Insurance Co.; Liberty Mutual Insurance Cos.; United National Insurance Co.

For Complete List of Firm Personnel, See General Section

For full biographical listings, see the Martindale-Hubbell Law Directory

STARNES & ATCHISON (AV)

100 Brookwood Place, P.O. Box 598512, 35259-8512
Telephone: 205-868-6000
Telecopier: 205-868-6099

MEMBERS OF FIRM

W. Stancil Starnes	J. Bentley Owens, III
W. Michael Atchison	Walter William Bates
William Anthony Davis, III	Robert P. Mackenzie, III
Michael A. Florie	Jeffrey E. Friedman

ASSOCIATES

Joe L. Leak	P. Thomas Dazzio, Jr.

Rik S. Tozzi

Representative Clients: Aetna Casualty & Surety Company; Harbert Construction Co.; AMI Brookwood Medical Center; International Playtex, Inc.; Kawasaki Motors Corp.; Honda North America, Inc.; Roadway, Inc.; Cigna Corp.; Travelers Ins. Co.; United States Fidelity and Guaranty Co.

For full biographical listings, see the Martindale-Hubbell Law Directory

---

CHATOM, * Washington Co.

TURNER, ONDERDONK, KIMBROUGH & HOWELL, P.A. (AV)

100 Central Avenue, P.O. Drawer 1389, 36518
Telephone: 334-847-2237
Fax: 334-847-3115
Mobile, Alabama Office: 1359 Dauphin Street.
Telephone: 334-432-2855.
Fax: 334-432-2863.

Edward P. Turner, Jr.	Gordon K. Howell
A. Michael Onderdonk	Marc E. Bradley
William A. Kimbrough, Jr.	(Resident, Mobile Office)
(Resident, Mobile Office)	

Halron W. Turner	David M. Huggins
Frank Woodson	(Resident, Mobile Office)
(Resident, Mobile Office)	E. Tatum Turner

For full biographical listings, see the Martindale-Hubbell Law Directory

CULLMAN, * Cullman Co.

DRAKE & DRAKE (AV)

Suite A, 419 Second Avenue, S.W., P.O. Box 1165, 35055-4106
Telephone: 205-734-7602
Fax: 205-734-7696

MEMBERS OF FIRM

Tom Drake	Christine McKoy Drake

ASSOCIATE

Thomas E. Drake, II

Representative Clients: Cullman Electric Corp.; Shaver Poultry Breeding Farm, a Division of Cargill.
References: First National Bank of Birmingham; Peoples Bank of Cullman County.

For full biographical listings, see the Martindale-Hubbell Law Directory

DOTHAN, * Houston Co.

FARMER, PRICE, HORNSBY & WEATHERFORD (AV)

115 West Adams Street, Drawer 2228, 36301
Telephone: 334-793-2424
Fax: 334-793-6624

MEMBERS OF FIRM

J. Hubert Farmer (1896-1976)	Joel W. Weatherford
Edward M. Price, Jr.	D. Lewis Terry, Jr.
Ernest H. Hornsby	Elizabeth B. Glasgow

Representative Clients: AmSouth Bank, N.A.; Pea River Electric Cooperative; Hollis & Spann, Inc.; Faulkner Construction Co., Inc.; Burnham Shoes, Inc.; Quality Inn Carousel; Sheraton Inn; Holiday Inn-Ozark; Holiday Inn-Crestview; Inn South-Montgomery.

For full biographical listings, see the Martindale-Hubbell Law Directory

ENTERPRISE, Coffee Co.

PITTMAN AND PITTMAN (AV)

304 South Edwards Street, P.O. Drawer 1180, 36330
Telephone: 334-347-2655
Fax: 334-347-2657

MEMBERS OF FIRM

Joe S. Pittman	Joseph Stafford Pittman, Jr.

Representative Clients: City of Enterprise; Industrial Development Board of City of Enterprise; Enco Engineering Corp.; E. L. Gibson Foundation.
Approved Attorneys for: Mississippi Valley Title Insurance Co.

For full biographical listings, see the Martindale-Hubbell Law Directory

FLORENCE, * Lauderdale Co.

JONES & TROUSDALE (AV)

115 Helton Court, Suite B, P.O. Box 367, 35631-0367
Telephone: 205-767-0333
Telefax: 205-767-0331

MEMBERS OF FIRM

Robert E. Jones, III	Preston S. Trousdale, Jr.

A. DeLoach Stewart

For full biographical listings, see the Martindale-Hubbell Law Directory

POTTS & YOUNG (AV)

107 East College Street, 35630
Telephone: 205-764-7142
Fax: 205-764-7717

OF COUNSEL

Doyle R. Young (Retired)	Robert L. Potts

(See Next Column)

POTTS & YOUNG—*Continued*

MEMBERS OF FIRM

Frank V. Potts   Frank B. Potts
ASSOCIATES
Robert W. Beasley   Debra H. Coble

Representative Clients: E. A. Nelson Co., Inc.; Nelco, Inc.; American Abrasive Air & Service Co., Inc.; Diversified Products, Inc.; Big Deli Stores, Inc.; Spry Funeral Homes of Russellville, Sheffield & Florence; Americans United for the Separation of Church & State; Colbert County Community Economic Development Corp.
Reference: Bank Independent.

For full biographical listings, see the Martindale-Hubbell Law Directory

---

SELF & SELF (AV)

408 West Dr. Hicks Boulevard, P.O. Box 1062, 35631
Telephone: 205-767-2570; 1-800-336-2574
Fax: 205 767-2632

MEMBERS OF FIRM

Henry (Hank) H. Self, Jr.   Gilbert P. Self

Reference: Bank Independent; AmSouth Bank; Compass Bank.

For full biographical listings, see the Martindale-Hubbell Law Directory

---

FORT PAYNE, De Kalb Co.

SCRUGGS, JORDAN, DODD & DODD, P.A. (AV)

207 Alabama Avenue, South, P.O. Box 1109, 35967
Telephone: 205-845-5932
Fax: 205-845-4325

William D. Scruggs, Jr.   David Dodd
Robert K. Jordan   E. Allen Dodd, Jr.

Representative Clients: State Farm Insurance Company; Allstate Insurance Co., Inc.; USF&G Insurance Co.; Nucor, Inc.; Ladd Engineering, Inc.; ALABAMA Band; First Federal Savings & Loan Association of Dekalb County; Fritz Structural Steel, Inc.; Williamson Oil Co., Inc.

For full biographical listings, see the Martindale-Hubbell Law Directory

---

HUNTSVILLE, Madison Co.

BERRY, ABLES, TATUM, BAXTER, PARKER & HALL, P.C. (AV)

Legal Building, 315 Franklin Street, S.E., P.O. Box 165, 35804-0165
Telephone: 205-533-3740
Facsimile: 205-533-3751
Email: BAXTERJ@ATTMAIL.COM

William H. Blanton (1889-1973)   James T. Tatum, Jr.
Joe M. Berry   James T. Baxter, III
L. Bruce Ables   Thomas E. Parker, Jr.
                    Bill G. Hall

James K. Brabston   Mark Rogers Hunter

Representative Clients: AmSouth Bank; First Alabama Bank; General Shale Products Co.; The Hertz Corp.; Litton Industries, Inc.; Farmers Tractor Co.; Colonial Bank; Farm Credit Bank of Texas; SouthBank; Regions Mortgage.
Reference: First Alabama Bank.

For full biographical listings, see the Martindale-Hubbell Law Directory

---

BRADLEY, ARANT, ROSE & WHITE (AV)

200 Clinton Avenue West, Suite 900, 35801
Telephone: 205-517-5100
Facsimile: 205-533-5069
URL: http://www.BARW.COM
Birmingham, Alabama Office: 2001 Park Place, Suite 1400, P.O. Box 830709.
Telephone: 205-521-8000.
Facsimile: 205-251-8611, 251-8665, 252-0264. Facsimile (SouthTrust Tower Office): 205-251-9915.

RESIDENT PARTNERS

Gary C. Huckaby   Patrick H. Graves, Jr.
E. Cutter Hughes, Jr.   G. Rick Hall
                    Warne S. Heath

For Complete List of Firm Personnel, See General Section

For full biographical listings, see the Martindale-Hubbell Law Directory

---

HORNSBY, WATSON & MEGINNISS (AV)

1110 Gleneagles Drive, 35801
Telephone: 205-650-5500
Fax: 205-650-5504

Ralph W. Hornsby   David H. Meginniss
S. A. "Bud" Watson, Jr.   Ralph W. Hornsby, Jr.

For full biographical listings, see the Martindale-Hubbell Law Directory

---

MORRIS, CLOUD AND CONCHIN, P.C. (AV)

521 Madison Street, P.O. Box 248, 35804
Telephone: 205-534-0065
Fax: 205-539-0741

Harvey B. Morris (P.C.)   Joseph M. Cloud
                    Gary V. Conchin

Maureen "Mike" K. Cooper   Daniel B. Banks, Jr.

For full biographical listings, see the Martindale-Hubbell Law Directory

---

THE LAW FIRM OF SINIARD, LAMAR & McKINNEY (AV)

125 Holmes Avenue, P.O. Box 2767, 35804
Telephone: 205-536-0770
Facsimile: 205-539-0540

MEMBERS OF FIRM

Tommy H. Siniard   Patrick M. Lamar
        Jeffery W. McKinney
ASSOCIATE
        M. Roy Braswell

For full biographical listings, see the Martindale-Hubbell Law Directory

---

MOBILE, Mobile Co.

BRISKMAN & BINION, P.C. (AV)

205 Church Street, P.O. Box 43, 36601
Telephone: 334-433-7600
Fax: 334-433-4485

Donald M. Briskman   Christ N. Coumanis
Mack B. Binion   Walter G. (Stoney) Chavers

A List of Representative Clients will be furnished upon request.
References: First Alabama Bank; AmSouth Bank, N.A.; Southtrust Bank of Mobile.

For full biographical listings, see the Martindale-Hubbell Law Directory

---

BURNS, CUNNINGHAM & MACKEY, P.C. (AV)

50 St. Emanuel Street, P.O. Box 1583, 36633
Telephone: 334-432-0612

Peter F. Burns   Peter S. Mackey
William M. Cunningham, Jr.   Gary W. Fillingim

For full biographical listings, see the Martindale-Hubbell Law Directory

---

CUNNINGHAM, BOUNDS, YANCE, CROWDER & BROWN (AV)

1601 Dauphin Street, P.O. Box 66705, 36660
Telephone: 334-471-6191
Fax: 334-479-1031

Richard Bounds   Joseph M. Brown, Jr.
James A. Yance   Gregory B. Breedlove
John T. Crowder, Jr.   Andrew T. Citrin
Robert T. Cunningham, Jr.   Michael A. Worel

David G. Wirtes, Jr.   Mitchell K. Shelly
Toby D. Brown   Kelli Denise Taylor
                    OF COUNSEL
Robert T. Cunningham   Valentino D. B. Mazzia

For full biographical listings, see the Martindale-Hubbell Law Directory

---

DIAMOND, HASSER & FROST (AV)

1325 Dauphin Street, P.O. Drawer 40600, 36640
Telephone: 334-432-3362
Fax: 334-432-3367

MEMBERS OF FIRM

Ross Diamond, Jr. (1919-1978)   James E. Hasser, Jr.
Ross M. Diamond, III   James H. Frost

References: First Alabama Bank, Mobile; AM South Bank, Mobile.

For full biographical listings, see the Martindale-Hubbell Law Directory

---

FINKBOHNER AND LAWLER, L.L.C. (AV)

169 Dauphin Street Suite 300, P.O. Box 3085, 36652
Telephone: 334-438-5871
Fax: 334-432-8052

MEMBERS OF FIRM

George W. Finkbohner, Jr.   George W. Finkbohner, III
John L. Lawler   Royce A. Ray, III

For full biographical listings, see the Martindale-Hubbell Law Directory

---

HELMSING, LYONS, SIMS & LEACH, P.C. (AV)

The Laclede Building, 150 Government Street, P.O. Box 2767, 36652
Telephone: 334-432-5521
Telecopy: 334-432-0633

(See Next Column)

HELMSING, LYONS, SIMS & LEACH P.C., *Mobile—Continued*

Larry U. Sims	Robert H. Rouse
Champ Lyons, Jr.	Charles H. Dodson, Jr.
Frederick G. Helmsing	Richard E. Davis
John N. Leach, Jr.	Joseph P. H. Babington
Warren C. Herlong, Jr.	John J. Crowley, Jr.
James B. Newman	Joseph D. Steadman

Todd S. Strohmeyer	John Townsend Dukes
William R. Lancaster	P. Bradley Murray
Robin Kilpatrick Fincher	Leslie T. Fields

For full biographical listings, see the Martindale-Hubbell Law Directory

HESS & ATCHISON (AV)

301 St. Joseph Street, P.O. Box 1706, 36633
Telephone: 334-432-4546
Fax: 334-433-6635

Barry Hess	Mona Ann Vivar
James E. Atchison	Donald C. Partridge
	Lori Brown Meadows

Reference: Bank of Mobile.

For full biographical listings, see the Martindale-Hubbell Law Directory

INGE, TWITTY & DUFFY (AV)

1410 First Alabama Bank Building, 56 St. Joseph Street, P.O. Box 1109, 36633
Telephone: 334-433-3200
Facsimile: 334-433-3444

MEMBERS OF FIRM

James J. Duffy, Jr.	James J. Duffy, III

Francis H. Inge (1902-1959)	Thos. E. Twitty (1901-1975)
	Richard H. Inge (1912-1980)

For full biographical listings, see the Martindale-Hubbell Law Directory

MONTGOMERY,* Montgomery Co.

BEASLEY, WILSON, ALLEN, MAIN & CROW, P.C. (AV)

218 Commerce Street, P.O. Box 4160, 36104
Telephone: 334-269-2343
Fax: 334-269-2371
Mailing Address: P.O. Box 4160, 36103-4160

Jere Locke Beasley	J. Greg Allen
Frank M. Wilson	Michael J. Crow

Julia Anne Beasley	Robert L. Pittman

For full biographical listings, see the Martindale-Hubbell Law Directory

BECK & TRAVIS, P.C. (AV)

22 Scott Street, P.O. Box 5019, 36103-5019
Telephone: 334-832-4878
Fax: 334-832-4704

George L. Beck, Jr.
OF COUNSEL
W. Terry Travis

David Bryson Byrne, III

For full biographical listings, see the Martindale-Hubbell Law Directory

J. PAUL LOWERY A PROFESSIONAL CORPORATION (AV)

4183 Carmichael Road, 36106-2889
Telephone: 334-271-0852

J. Paul Lowery

Evans H. Marshall

References: First Montgomery Bank; AmSouth Bank.

For full biographical listings, see the Martindale-Hubbell Law Directory

RIGGS & NESMITH, P.A. (AV)

Suite 205 Lawrence Building, 472 South Lawrence Street, P.O. Box 1047, 36102
Telephone: 334-834-6990
Fax: 334-834-4796

Frank W. Riggs	Stephen M. NeSmith

For full biographical listings, see the Martindale-Hubbell Law Directory

THOMAS, MEANS & GILLIS, P.C. (AV)

3121 Zelda Court, Drawer 5058, 36103-5058
Telephone: 334-270-1033
Fax: 334-260-9396
Birmingham, Alabama Office: 1100 Financial Center, 35203.
Telephone: 205-328-7915.
Fax: 205-328-9669.

Kenneth L. Thomas (Resident, Birmingham, Alabama Office)	Tyrone C. Means
	Henry Lewis Gillis

J. Mark Englehart	Launice P. Sills
Cynthia W. Clinton	Anita L. Kelly
	Milton J. Westry

For full biographical listings, see the Martindale-Hubbell Law Directory

TUSCALOOSA,* Tuscaloosa Co.

JOSEPH G. PIERCE (AV)

2207 River Road West Suite One, P.O. Box 20086, 35402-0086
Telephone: 205-759-1234
Fax: 205-758-0502

Representative Clients: Indian River Regional Mental Health Center; Deputy Sheriffs Association of Tuscaloosa County; Deputy Sheriffs Association of Mobile County; Greene Beverage Co.; Aliceville Manor Nursing Home.

For full biographical listings, see the Martindale-Hubbell Law Directory

ARIZONA

CASA GRANDE, Pinal Co.

FITZGIBBONS LAW OFFICES, P.L.C. (AV)

Suite E, 711 East Cottonwood Lane, P.O. Box 11208, 85230-1208
Telephone: 520-426-3824
Fax: 520-426-9355

David A. Fitzgibbons	David A. Fitzgibbons, III
	Denis M. Fitzgibbons

For Complete List of Firm Personnel, See General Section

For full biographical listings, see the Martindale-Hubbell Law Directory

FLAGSTAFF,* Coconino Co.

ASPEY, WATKINS & DIESEL, P.L.L.C. (AV)

123 North San Francisco, 3rd Floor, 86001
Telephone: 520-774-1478
Facsimile: 520-774-8404
Sedona, Arizona Office: 120 Soldier Pass Road.
Telephone: 520-282-5955.
Facsimile: 520-282-5962.
Page, Arizona Office: 904 North Navajo.
Telephone: 520-645-9694.
Cottonwood, Arizona Office: 2400 E. Highway 89A, Suite C.
Telephone: 520-639-1881.
Facsimile: 520-639-0272.

MEMBERS OF FIRM

Frederick M. Fritz Aspey	Donald H. Bayles, Jr.
Harold L. Watkins	Kaign N. Christy
Louis M. Diesel	John J. Dempsey
Bruce S. Griffen	Zachary J. Markham

James E. Ledbetter	Roger M. Baeurle
Whitney Cunningham	Amy E. Mabius
Pernell Whynn McGuire	Stephen A. Thompson
	Joel E. Sannes

LEGAL SUPPORT PERSONNEL

Karla H. Falls, CLAS (Legal Assistant)	Dominic M. Marino, Jr, (Paralegal Assistant)
Rocky C. Nissen (Paralegal Assistant, Sedona, Arizona Office)	Carrie R. Flynn (Litigation Paralegal, Cottonwood, Arizona Office)
Deborah D. Roberts, CLA (Legal Assistant)	

Representative Clients: Farmer's Insurance Company of Arizona; Pepsi-Cola Bottling Company of Northern Arizona; Bill Luke's Chrysler-Plymouth, Inc.; First American Title Insurance Company; Transnation Title Insurance Co.; Page Electric Utility; Comprehensive Access Health Plan, Inc.; Northern Arizona Healthcare Corporation.
Reference: First Interstate Bank-Arizona, N.A., Flagstaff, Arizona.

For full biographical listings, see the Martindale-Hubbell Law Directory

Flagstaff—Continued

MANGUM, WALL, STOOPS & WARDEN, P.L.L.C. (AV)

222 East Birch Avenue, P.O. Box 10, 86002
Telephone: 520-779-6951
Fax: 520-773-1312

H. Karl Mangum (1908-1993)

OF COUNSEL

Douglas J. Wall   Robert W. Warden

MEMBERS OF FIRM

Daniel J. Stoops   Stephen K. Smith
A. Dean Pickett   Melinda L. Garrahan

ASSOCIATES

Deborah M. Fine   David L. Anderson
Michael H. Hinson

Representative Clients: Northern Arizona University; Flagstaff Unified School District; Museum of Northern Arizona; City of Sedona; Arizona School Board Association.
Local Counsel for: Bank of America-Arizona; Arizona Public Service; U.S.-.A.A.; State Farm Fire & Casualty Ins. Co.; Insurance Company of the West.

For Complete List of Firm Personnel, See General Section

For full biographical listings, see the Martindale-Hubbell Law Directory

---

KINGMAN,* Mohave Co.

MURPHY, LUTEY, SCHMITT & BECK (AV)

Suite H8, 2601 Stockton Hill Road, 86401
Telephone: 520-718-0888; 1-800-281-0822

Michael R. Murphy

Northern Arizona Counsel for: State Farm Mutual Automobile Insurance Co.; Transamerica Title Insurance Co.; Allstate Insurance Co.
Local Counsel for: The Stockmen's Bank.
Representative Clients: Prescott College; North-Aire Aviation, Inc.; Goswick Cattle Co.; Galpin Ford, Inc.; Sedona-Oak Creek Airport Authority; Yavapai County Fair Association (Prescott Downs).

LAKE HAVASU CITY, Mohave Co.

WACHTEL, BIEHN & MALM (AV)

Suite A, 2240 McCulloch Boulevard, 86403
Telephone: 520-855-5115
Fax: 520-855-5211

MEMBERS OF FIRM

Don Biehn   Steven A. Biehn
Denis R. Malm   Rex L. Martin

For Complete List of Firm Personnel, See General Section

For full biographical listings, see the Martindale-Hubbell Law Directory

---

MESA, Maricopa Co.

SKOUSEN, SKOUSEN, GULBRANDSEN & PATIENCE, P.C. (AV)

414 East Southern Avenue, 85204
Telephone: 602-833-8800
FAX: 602-833-7146

William J. Skousen   Michael J. Skousen
Richard E. Skousen   John E. Skousen
Richard M. Gulbrandsen   David L. Abney
Steve Patience   Gary A. Porter

References: First Interstate Bank, Mesa, Arizona; United Bank of Arizona, Mesa, Arizona.

For full biographical listings, see the Martindale-Hubbell Law Directory

---

PHOENIX,* Maricopa Co.

BEGAM, LEWIS, MARKS & WOLFE A PROFESSIONAL ASSOCIATION OF LAWYERS (AV)

111 West Monroe Street, Suite 1400, 85003-1787
Telephone: 602-254-6071
Fax: 602-252-0042

Robert G. Begam   Daniel J. Adelman
Frank Lewis   Lisa Kurtz
Stanley J. Marks   Dena Rosen Epstein
Elliot G. Wolfe   Steven M. Friedman
Kelly J. McDonald   Richard P. Traulsen

Reference: National Bank of Arizona.

For full biographical listings, see the Martindale-Hubbell Law Directory

---

BESS & DYSART, P.C. (AV)

7210 North 16th Street, 82020-5201
Telephone: 602-331-4600
Telecopier: 602-331-8600

(See Next Column)

Leon D. Bess   Timothy R. Hyland
Robert L. Dysart   William M. Demlong
Donald R. Kunz   Matthew D. Kleifield

Stephanie L. Chilton   Donald J. Sapala

For full biographical listings, see the Martindale-Hubbell Law Directory

---

RICHARD A. BLACK, P.C. (AV)

125 East Coronado Road, 85004
Telephone: 602-253-4700
Fax: 602-253-8880

Richard A. Black

For full biographical listings, see the Martindale-Hubbell Law Directory

---

BONNETT, FAIRBOURN, FRIEDMAN & BALINT, P.C. (AV)

4041 North Central Avenue Suite 1100, 85012
Telephone: 602-274-1100
Fax: 602-274-1199

William G. Fairbourn   Robert J. Spurlock
C. Kevin Dykstra

For full biographical listings, see the Martindale-Hubbell Law Directory

---

MICHAEL E. BRADFORD (AV)

4131 North 24th Street Building C Suite 201, 85016
Telephone: 602-955-0088
FAX: 602-955-6445

LEGAL SUPPORT PERSONNEL

Sandra M. Simcox

OF COUNSEL

Jerry Steele

For full biographical listings, see the Martindale-Hubbell Law Directory

---

CHARLES M. BREWER, LTD. (AV)

Brewer Building, 5500 North 24th Street, P.O. Box 10720, 85064
Telephone: 602-381-8787
Fax: 602-381-1152

Charles M. Brewer

Mark S. O'Connor   Luis Pedro Guerra
Dane London Wood

For full biographical listings, see the Martindale-Hubbell Law Directory

---

BURCH & CRACCHIOLO, P.A. (AV)

702 East Osborn Road, Suite 200, 85014
Telephone: 602-274-7611
Fax: 602-234-0341
Mailing Address: P.O. Box 16882, Phoenix, AZ, 85011

Daniel Cracchiolo   Linda A. Finnegan
Brian Kaven   Daniel R. Malinski
Ian Neale   Jess A. Lorona

Theodore (Todd) Julian

Representative Clients: Bashas' Inc.; Farmers Insurance Group; U-Haul International, Inc.

For Complete List of Firm Personnel, See General Section

For full biographical listings, see the Martindale-Hubbell Law Directory

---

CARMICHAEL & POWELL, PROFESSIONAL CORPORATION (AV)

7301 North 16th Street, 85020-5224
Telephone: 602-861-0777
Facsimile: 602-870-0296

Ronald W. Carmichael   Donald W. Powell
Sid A. Horwitz

Stephen Manes   Brian A. Hatch
Richard C. Gramlich

For full biographical listings, see the Martindale-Hubbell Law Directory

---

CRONIN & STANEWICH (AV)

One Columbus Plaza, 3636 North Central Avenue, Suite 560, 85012
Telephone: 602-222-4646
Fax: 602-222-4656

MEMBERS OF FIRM

Robert S. Cronin, Jr.   Robert B. Stanewich

For full biographical listings, see the Martindale-Hubbell Law Directory

Phoenix—Continued

CUNNINGHAM LAW FIRM (AV)

330 North Second Avenue, 85003
Telephone: 602-257-1750
Fax: 602-252-3436

James P. Cunningham   Matthew B. Cunningham

For full biographical listings, see the Martindale-Hubbell Law Directory

DEBUS & KAZAN, LTD. (AV)

335 East Palm Lane, 85004
Telephone: 602-257-8900
Fax: 602-257-0723

Larry L. Debus   Lawrence Ian Kazan

Tracey Westerhausen

References: Firstar Metropolitan Bank; Citibank, Arizona.

For full biographical listings, see the Martindale-Hubbell Law Directory

FENNEMORE CRAIG, A PROFESSIONAL CORPORATION (AV)

Two North Central, Suite 2200, 85004
Telephone: 602-257-8700
Fax: 602-257-8527
Scottsdale, Arizona Office: 6263 North Scottsdale Road, Suite 290, 85250.
Telephone: 602-257-5400.
Fax: 602-257-5409.
Tucson, Arizona Office: One South Church Avenue, Suite 1030, 85701.
Telephone: 520-791-6800.
Fax: 520-791-6820.

John D. Everroad   Kaye L. McCarthy
F. Pendleton Gaines, III   Scott M. Finical
Roger T. Hargrove   William T. Burghart
William L. Thorpe   Andrew M. Federhar
Graeme E. M. Hancock   Christopher P. Staring

Jean Marie Sullivan   Marc H. Lamber

For Complete List of Firm Personnel, See General Section

For full biographical listings, see the Martindale-Hubbell Law Directory

FOGEL AND LAMBER, PROFESSIONAL ASSOCIATION (AV)

One Windsor Professional Building, 2627 North Third Street, 85004-1197
Telephone: 602-264-3330
Fax: 602-274-5117

Sherman D. Fogel   Dennis M. Lamber
            Rex P. Bronnenkant
Reference: Chase Bank of Arizona.

For full biographical listings, see the Martindale-Hubbell Law Directory

GOLDMAN & KAPLAN, LTD. (AV)

2930 North 7th Street, 85014
Telephone: 602-264-9323
FAX: 602-274-7006
Email: mkaplan0@counsel.com

Alan Goldman   Mark E. Meltzer
Morris A. Kaplan   Paul D. Friedman
References: Republic National Bank; Merrill Lynch.

For full biographical listings, see the Martindale-Hubbell Law Directory

GOLDSTEIN & McGRODER, LTD. A PROFESSIONAL CORPORATION (AV)

2200 East Camelback Road, Suite 221, 85016-3456
Telephone: 602-957-1500
Fax: 602-956-9294

Philip T. Goldstein   Patrick J. McGroder, III
            Suzanne P. Clarke

Jane E. Evans   Serena C. Montague
LEGAL SUPPORT PERSONNEL
Kevan S. DeWitt (Paralegal)

For full biographical listings, see the Martindale-Hubbell Law Directory

STUART GOLDSTEIN (AV)

2702 North Third Street, 85004
Telephone: 602-279-1666
Telecopier: 602-285-1907

(See Next Column)

Stuart W. Goldstein

Reference: First Interstate Bank, Park Central Office, Phoenix.

For full biographical listings, see the Martindale-Hubbell Law Directory

JOHN PHILIP GRACE, P.C. (AV)

4500 North 32nd Street, Suite 201, 85018
Telephone: 602-954-0464
Fax: 602-954-6316

John Philip Grace

For full biographical listings, see the Martindale-Hubbell Law Directory

HARRIS & PALUMBO, A PROFESSIONAL CORPORATION (AV)

361 East Coronado, Suite 101, P.O. Box 13568, 85002-3568
Telephone: 602-271-9344
Fax: 602-252-2099

John David Harris   Gene M. Cullan
Kevin W. Keenan   Frank I. Powers
            Shawn M. Cunningham
OF COUNSEL
Anthony J. Palumbo

For full biographical listings, see the Martindale-Hubbell Law Directory

HORNE, KAPLAN AND BISTROW, P.C. (AV)

Renaissance Two, 40 North Central, Suite 2800, 85004
Telephone: 602-253-9700
Fax: 602-258-4805

Thomas C. Horne   Eric J. Bistrow
Martha Bachner Kaplan   Michael S. Dulberg
            Kimball J. Corson

For full biographical listings, see the Martindale-Hubbell Law Directory

JENNINGS, STROUSS AND SALMON, P.L.C. (AV)

A Professional Limited Liability Company
One Renaissance Square, Two North Central, 85004-2393
Telephone: 602-262-5911
Fax: 602-253-3255

W. Michael Flood   Michael R. Palumbo
Gary L. Stuart   H. Christian Bode
Gerald W. Alston   Jon D. Schneider
Barry E. Lewin   Michael J. O'Connor
Jay A. Fradkin   Katherine M. Cooper

Jennifer M. Bligh   Kim D. Steinmetz

For Complete List of Firm Personnel, See General Section

For full biographical listings, see the Martindale-Hubbell Law Directory

WILLIAM T. KEANE, P.C. (AV)

803 North 3rd Street, 85004
Telephone: 602-257-1323
Fax: 602-257-1416

William T. Keane

Reference: First Interstate Bank of Arizona.

For full biographical listings, see the Martindale-Hubbell Law Directory

MARK & PEARLSTEIN, P.A. (AV)

Suite 150 The Brookstone, 2025 North Third Street, 85004
Telephone: 602-257-0200
Fax: 602-271-4711

Leonard J. Mark   Mr. Lynn M. Pearlstein
OF COUNSEL
Stephen G. Campbell

For full biographical listings, see the Martindale-Hubbell Law Directory

TERRENCE J. McGILLICUDDY, P.C. (AV)

5080 North 40th Street, Suite 335, 85018
Telephone: 602-957-1960
800-957-1960
Fax: 602-957-7015

Terrence J. McGillicuddy

For full biographical listings, see the Martindale-Hubbell Law Directory

MILLER & MILLER, LTD. (AV)

Suite 2250, 3200 North Central Avenue, 85012
Telephone: 602-266-8440
Fax: 602-266-8453

(See Next Column)

MILLER & MILLER LTD.—*Continued*

Murray Miller   Robert M. Miller
Marcus Westervelt

For full biographical listings, see the Martindale-Hubbell Law Directory

MITTEN, GOODWIN & RAUP, A PROFESSIONAL CORPORATION (AV)

One Columbus Plaza, 3636 North Central, Suite 1200, 85012
Telephone: 602-650-2000
Fax: 602-264-7033
Email: mgr@starlink.com

Brian M. Goodwin   Stephen C. Yost
Calvin L. Raup   Martin P. Clare
Scott J. Hergenroether

Steven P. Kramer   Gary Beren
Sharon Elizabeth Ravenscroft   Jeffrey J. Campbell
Jeffery S. Slater   Lori V. Berke

For full biographical listings, see the Martindale-Hubbell Law Directory

MUCHMORE & WALLWORK, A PROFESSIONAL CORPORATION (AV)

2700 North Central Avenue, Suite 1225, 85004-1165
Telephone: 602-240-6699
Data: 602-240-6698
Facsimile: 602-240-6697
Email: muchwork@mmww.com *URL:* http://www.mmww.com

Charles J. Muchmore   Nicholas J. Wallwork
COUNSEL
Margaret M. Dean   Fredric D. Bellamy
Kathy E. Shimpock

Bridget S. Bade   Carolina L. Carver
(Senior Associate)   Margaret Benny Hurst
LEGAL SUPPORT PERSONNEL
Gloria A. Torres (Administrator   Gale James (Finance Manager
and Senior Paralegal)   and Paralegal)
John A. Bennett
(Litigation Support Manager)

Representative Clients: AgrEvo USA Company; BHP Copper Inc.; City of Scottsdale; Cyprus Amax Minerals Company; General Electric Co.; Homes by Dave Brown, Inc.; National Indemnity Insurance Company; Standard Insurance Company; Washington Mills Electro Minerals Company.
Reference: M & I Thunderbird Bank.

For full biographical listings, see the Martindale-Hubbell Law Directory

PLATTNER VERDERAME, P.C. (AV)

333 East Osborn, Suite 315, 85012-2365
Telephone: 602-266-2002
Fax: 602-266-6908

Richard S. Plattner   Frank Verderame

Randall A. Hinsch   David A. Thomson
Laurence G. Tinsley, Jr.

Representative Clients: Paradigm Insurance Company.

For full biographical listings, see the Martindale-Hubbell Law Directory

QUARLES & BRADY (AV)

One Camelback Building, One East Camelback Road, Suite 400, 85012-1649
Telephone: 602-230-5500
Fax: 602-230-5598
Milwaukee, Wisconsin Office: 411 East Wisconsin Avenue.
Telephone: 414-277-5000.
Fax: 414-271-3552.
Madison, Wisconsin Office: First Wisconsin Plaza, One South Pinckney Street, P.O. Box 2113.
Telephone: 608-251-5000.
Fax: 608-251-9166.
West Palm Beach, Florida Office: 222 Lakeview Ave., 4th Floor.
Telephone: 407-653-5000.
Fax: 407-653-5333.
Naples, Florida Office: Barnett Center, 4501 Tamiami Trail North, Suite 300.
Telephone: 813-262-5959.
Fax: 813-434-4999.

MEMBER OF THE FIRM
William M. Shattuck

(See Next Column)

ASSOCIATE
Colleen A. Scherkenbach

For Complete List of Firm Personnel, See General Section

For full biographical listings, see the Martindale-Hubbell Law Directory

STUART J. REILLY, P.C. (AV)

2425 East Camelback Road, Suite 450, 85016
Telephone: 602-912-8544
FAX: 602-912-8541

Stuart J. Reilly

For full biographical listings, see the Martindale-Hubbell Law Directory

RENAUD, COOK & DRURY, P.A. (AV)

617 North 2nd Avenue, 85003
Telephone: 602-253-5101
Fax: 602-254-1448
Email: rcdlaw@rcdlaw.com
Scottsdale, Arizona Office: 6991 East Camelback Road, #D-103, 85251.
Telephone: 602-874-9000.
Fax: 602-874-9866.

J. Gordon Cook   James L. Blair
William W. Drury, Jr.   Steven G. Mesaros
Charles A. Struble

W. Lloyd Benner   David E. Gustafson
Wade R. Causey   Charles S. Hover, III
Diana L. Clarke   Diane Mihalsky
Richard N. Crenshaw   Tamara D. Nydell

For full biographical listings, see the Martindale-Hubbell Law Directory

ROBBINS & GREEN, A PROFESSIONAL ASSOCIATION (AV)

1800 Norwest Tower, 3300 North Central Avenue, 85012-9826
Telephone: 602-248-7600
Fax: 602-266-5369

Philip A. Robbins   William H. Sandweg III
Richard W. Abbuhl   Dwayne Ross

For Complete List of Firm Personnel, See General Section

For full biographical listings, see the Martindale-Hubbell Law Directory

SHERWOOD, KLEIN, DUDLEY & ABRAM, P.A. (AV)

2400 Bank One Center, 201 North Central Avenue, 85073
Telephone: 602-254-7041
Fax: 602-254-7540

Andrew G. Klein

For full biographical listings, see the Martindale-Hubbell Law Directory

LAW OFFICES OF RAYMOND J. SLOMSKI, P.C. (AV)

2901 North Central Avenue, Suite 1150, 85012
Telephone: 602-230-8777
Fax: 602-230-8707

Raymond J. Slomski

Kevin L. Beckwith   James M. Abernethy
LEGAL SUPPORT PERSONNEL
PARALEGALS
Patti A. Hibbeler   Diana G. Weeks
Karen Kay Rush

For full biographical listings, see the Martindale-Hubbell Law Directory

LAW OFFICES OF RICHARD L. STROHM, P.C. (AV)

1136 East Campbell, 85014
Telephone: 602-279-6316
Mobile: 602-616-7094
Facsimile: 602-279-7102
Email: 102442.1444@compuserve.com

Richard L. Strohm
OF COUNSEL
Brad K. Keogh   Nedra J. Bates
LEGAL SUPPORT PERSONNEL
Mindy L. Raymond   Barbara A. Shore
(Legal Assistant)   (Nurse Paralegal)
Richard M. Knaeble
(Licensed Private Investigator)

For full biographical listings, see the Martindale-Hubbell Law Directory

Phoenix—Continued

TIMBANARD & TOLMAN, L.L.P. (AV)

722 East Osborn Road, Suite 100, 85014
Telephone: 602-230-1234
Fax: 602-230-1374
Mesa, Arizona Office: 1201 South Alma School Road, Suite 3400.
Telephone: 602-962-1234.

Jeffrey R. Timbanard	J. Robert Tolman

ASSOCIATE
David J. Don

For full biographical listings, see the Martindale-Hubbell Law Directory

---

TOLES & ASSOCIATES, P.C. (AV)

1010 East Jefferson Street, 85034
Telephone: 602-253-1010
Fax: 602-253-1048

M. Jeremy Toles

Richard M. Gerry	Craig C. Gillespie
Rosann K. Johnson	M. L. (Les) Weatherly, Jr.

OF COUNSEL
Barbara A. Jarvis

For full biographical listings, see the Martindale-Hubbell Law Directory

---

TREON, STRICK, LUCIA & AGUIRRE A PROFESSIONAL ASSOCIATION OF LAWYERS (AV)

2700 North Central Avenue, Suite 1400, 85004-1133
Telephone: 602-285-4400
Telecopier: 602-285-4483

Richard T. Treon	Michael P. Stark
Gerald J. Strick	Linda B. Williamson
Anthony R. Lucia	Teri Kessel Raven
John Aguirre	Cindy Hansel Strickland
Arthur G. Newman, Jr.	Jennifer R. Barnes
William G. Vose	Sharon G. Slifko
	Scott F. Frerichs

Robert C. Warnicke	Michael T. DePaoli

For full biographical listings, see the Martindale-Hubbell Law Directory

---

KENNETH L. TUCKER, P.C. (AV)

1136 East Campbell, 85014
Telephone: 602-279-3660
Fax: 602-279-2162
Email: KTucker@futureone.com

Kenneth L. Tucker

Daniel P. J. Miller	Kevin J. Tucker

LEGAL SUPPORT PERSONNEL

Mary Toniazzo Moock (Paralegal)	Toni R. Hoffman (Paralegal)

For full biographical listings, see the Martindale-Hubbell Law Directory

---

TURLEY & SWAN, P.C. (AV)

The Brookstone Office Complex, 2025 North Third Street, Suite 350, 85004-1471
Telephone: 602-254-1444
Fax: 602-229-1936

Albert R. Vermeire (1947-1988)	Christopher J. Bork
Kent E. Turley	Christopher M. O'Donnell
Joseph B. Swan, Jr.	Elizabeth Savoini Fitch
	Thomas J. Howard

For full biographical listings, see the Martindale-Hubbell Law Directory

---

PRESCOTT,* Yavapai Co.

MURPHY, LUTEY, SCHMITT & BECK (AV)

Elks Building, 117 East Gurley Street, 86301
Telephone: 520-445-6860
Fax: 520-445-6488
Yuma, Arizona Office: Valley Professional Plaza, 1763 West Twenty-Fourth Street, Suite 200.
Telephone: 520-726-0314.
Fax: 520-341-1079.
Kingman, Arizona Office: 2601 Stockton Hill Road, Suite H8.
Telephone: 520-718-0888; 1-800-281-0822.

MEMBERS OF FIRM

Thelton D. Beck	Selmer D. Lutey
Michael R. Murphy	Robert E. Schmitt

(See Next Column)

ASSOCIATES

Dan A. Wilson	Bruce E. Rosenberg

OF COUNSEL
Keith F. Quail

Northern Arizona Counsel for: State Farm Mutual Automobile Insurance Co.; Transamerica Title Insurance Co.; Allstate Insurance Co.
Local Counsel for: Bank One, Arizona, NA; The Stockmen's Bank.
Representative Clients: Prescott College; North-Aire Aviation, Inc.; Goswick Cattle Co.; Galpin Ford, Inc.; Yavapai County Fair Association (Prescott Downs).

For full biographical listings, see the Martindale-Hubbell Law Directory

---

SCOTTSDALE, Maricopa Co.

GROSSMAN, O'GRADY & McGOLDRICK, P.C. (AV)

5040 East Shea Boulevard Suite 168, 85254
Telephone: 602-948-9424
Fax: 602-948-9425

Jill H. Grossman	Evan S. Goldstein
Paul J. McGoldrick	Keith B. Forsyth

Sanford K. Gerber
OF COUNSEL
Michael J. O'Grady

For full biographical listings, see the Martindale-Hubbell Law Directory

---

RALPH E. MAHOWALD A PROFESSIONAL ASSOCIATION (AV)

6750 East Camelback Road Suite #104, 85251
Telephone: 602-481-0500
Fax: 602-481-0555

Ralph E. Mahowald

For full biographical listings, see the Martindale-Hubbell Law Directory

---

TEMPE, Maricopa Co.

LAW OFFICES OF GLYNN W. GILCREASE, JR. (AV)

6601 South Rural Road, 85283
Telephone: 602-897-0990
Telecopier: 602-831-5966

ASSOCIATE
Gordon Clevenger

For full biographical listings, see the Martindale-Hubbell Law Directory

---

TUCSON,* Pima Co.

BEAL, SCHMIDT & DYER, P.C. (AV)

Suite 6000, West Tower, 5255 East Williams Circle, 85711
Telephone: 520-790-5600
Fax: 520-790-1163

Robert L. Beal	James H. Dyer
Ted A. Schmidt	Gary JD Dean

For full biographical listings, see the Martindale-Hubbell Law Directory

---

DUFFIELD, MILLER, YOUNG, ADAMSON & ALFRED, P.C. (AV)

Suite 711, Transamerica Building, 177 North Church Avenue, 85701
Telephone: 520-792-1181
FAX: 520-792-2859
Green Valley, Arizona Office: 101-65 South La Canada, Green Valley Mall.
Telephone: 520-625-4404.
Fax: 520-625-4453.
La Paloma Office: La Paloma Corporate Center, 3573 East Sunrise Drive, Suite 115, Tucson, Arizona.
Telephone: 520-577-1135.
Fax: 520-577-1079.

Philip Hawley Smith	Thomas R. Althaus
Arthur H. Miller (1935-1995)	Richard Duffield
Larry R. Adamson	Eugene C. Gieseler
Samuel D. Alfred	K. Alexander Hobson
	Michael C. Young

LEGAL SUPPORT PERSONNEL

Cynthia Sargent Althaus	Joan Shelton, CLA
Mary Jane Arnesen	Christine M. Smith
Katrina Hillman	Barbara L. Steimle
Elizabeth Kohl-Sturgeon	Elaine Webb

Representative Clients: San Xavier Rock & Materials; Community Water Company of Green Valley.
Insurance Company Clientele: State Farm Mutual Insurance Cos.; Automobile Club Insurance Co.; Colonial Penn Insurance Co.; Metropolitan Property & Liability Insurance Co.; National Indemnity Ins. Co.

For full biographical listings, see the Martindale-Hubbell Law Directory

Tucson—Continued

GABROY, ROLLMAN & BOSSÉ, P.C. (AV)

Suite 201, 2195 East River Road, 85718
Telephone: 520-577-1300
Telefax: 520-577-0717

Steven L. Bossé
Richard M. Rollman
John Gabroy
Ronna L. Fickbohm

Ronald M. Lehman
Fred A. Farsjo
Lyle D. Aldridge

Richard A. Brown

For full biographical listings, see the Martindale-Hubbell Law Directory

GOERING, ROBERTS, BERKMAN, RUBIN & BROGNA, P.C. (AV)

Suite 302, 1840 East River Road, 85718
Telephone: 520-577-9300
Fax: 520-577-0848

Scott Goering
Howard T. Roberts, Jr.

David L. Berkman
William L. Rubin

Carmine A. Brogna

Christopher L. Enos

Representative Clients: Fireman's Fund Insurance; Safeco Insurance; Royal Insurance; Sentry Insurance; American International Group; Farmers Insurance; USAA; Country Companies; Cigna.
Reference: Bank One.

For full biographical listings, see the Martindale-Hubbell Law Directory

HARALSON, KINERK & MOREY (AV)

82 South Stone Avenue, 85701
Telephone: 520-792-4330
Fax: 520-623-9568

Dale Haralson
Carter Morey

Burton J. Kinerk

Thomas D. Welch

Reference: The National Bank of Arizona.

For full biographical listings, see the Martindale-Hubbell Law Directory

HEALY LAW FIRM (AV)

Williams Centre, 5210 East Williams Circle Suite 730, 85711
Telephone: 520-790-1400

MEMBER OF FIRM
William T. Healy

References: Bank of America; Merrill Lynch.

For full biographical listings, see the Martindale-Hubbell Law Directory

RONALD D. MERCALDO, LTD. (AV)

376 South Stone Avenue, 85701
Telephone: 520-624-1400
FAX: 520-624-1955

Ronald D. Mercaldo

Anthony J. Wiggins

Reference: Arizona Bank.

For full biographical listings, see the Martindale-Hubbell Law Directory

MILLER, PITT & McANALLY, P.C. (AV)

111 South Church Avenue, 85701-1680
Telephone: 520-792-3836
Telecopier: 520-624-5080
Nogales, Arizona Office: 272 West View Point, 85621.
Telephone: 520-281-1361.
Correspondent Office: Lizarraga, Robles, Savinon & Tapia, S.C. Boulevard Hidalgo 64, Colonia Centenario. CP 83000 Hermosillo, Sonora, Mexico.
Telephone: (62) 17-27-28, 12-79-89, 13-47-10, 12-79-18, 13-33-25, 12-77-70.

Barry N. Akin (1939-1988)
Janice A. Wezelman
Philip J. Hall

Grace McIlvain
Thomas G. Cotter
Armando Rivera

Gus Aragón, Jr.

Carole A. Summers
OF COUNSEL
Richard L. McAnally

Representative Clients available upon request.

(See Next Column)

For Complete List of Firm Personnel, See General Section

For full biographical listings, see the Martindale-Hubbell Law Directory

RABINOVITZ & ASSOCIATES, P.C. (AV)

721 North 4th Avenue, P.O. Box 41600, 85717
Telephone: 520-624-5526
Toll Free: 1-800-365-0821
Fax: 520-622-3776

Bernard I. Rabinovitz

John D. Ellis
OF COUNSEL
Clark J. Sloan (Not admitted in AZ)
LEGAL SUPPORT PERSONNEL
Michael Nelson (Paralegal)   Lisa Busciglio (Paralegal)
Ruth Polizz

Representative Client: Firemans Fund Insurance Co.

For full biographical listings, see the Martindale-Hubbell Law Directory

SAMET & GAGE, P.C. (AV)

717 North Sixth Avenue, 85705
Telephone: 520-624-8595
Fax: 520-623-4560

Dee-Dee Samet   Arthur V. Gage

References: Bank of America; Norwest Bank.

For full biographical listings, see the Martindale-Hubbell Law Directory

SHULTZ & ROLLINS, LTD. (AV)

St. Philip's Plaza, 4280 North Campbell Avenue, Suite 214, 85718-6580
Telephone: 520-577-7777

Silas H. Shultz   Michael F. Rollins

Dora Fitzpatrick

For full biographical listings, see the Martindale-Hubbell Law Directory

STOMPOLY, STROUD, GIDDINGS & GLICKSMAN, P.C. (AV)

1820 Citibank Tower, One South Church Avenue, 85702
Telephone: 520-628-8300
Telefax: 520-628-9948
Mailing Address: P.O. Box 190, Tucson, AZ, 85702-0190

John G. Stompoly   Elliot A. Glicksman
George Erickson

For Complete List of Firm Personnel, See General Section

For full biographical listings, see the Martindale-Hubbell Law Directory

STRICKLAND & STRICKLAND, P.C. (AV)

4400 E. Broadway, Suite 700, 85711-3517
Telephone: 520-795-8727
Fax: 520-795-5649

William E. Strickland   William E. Strickland, Jr.
Robert F. Palmquist

Representative Client: AkChin Indian Community.
Reference: Bank One (formerly Valley National Bank).

YUMA, Yuma Co.

CLARK & CARTER (AV)

256 South Second Avenue, 85364
Telephone: 520-783-6233
Fax: 520-783-0533

MEMBERS OF FIRM
A. James Clark   Rick K. Carter
ASSOCIATE
Heather D. Burgess

For full biographical listings, see the Martindale-Hubbell Law Directory

MURPHY, LUTEY, SCHMITT & BECK (AV)

Valley Professional Plaza, 1763 West Twenty-Fourth Street Suite 200, 85364
Telephone: 520-726-0314
Fax: 520-341-1079
Prescott, Arizona Office: Elks Building, 117 East Gurley Street.
Telephone: 602-445-6860.
Fax: 602-445-6488.
Kingman, Arizona Office: 2601 Stockton Hill Road, Suite H8.
Telephone: 520-718-0888; 1-800-281-0822.

(See Next Column)

MURPHY, LUTEY, SCHMITT & BECK, *Yuma—Continued*

Robert E. Schmitt

Northern Arizona Counsel for: State Farm Mutual Automobile Insurance Co.; Transamerica Title Insurance Co.; Allstate Insurance Co.
Southern Arizona Counsel for: Allstate Insurance Co.; Farmers Insurance; Western Agricultural Insurance Co..
Local Counsel for: Bank One Arizona, N.A.; General Motors Corp.; The Stockmen's Bank.
Representative Clients: Chino Valley Irrigation District; Prescott College; Galpin Ford, Inc.; Yavapai Medical Center, P.C.; Sedona-Oak Creek Airport Authority; Yavapai County Fair Association (Prescott Downs).

For full biographical listings, see the Martindale-Hubbell Law Directory

THE BRIAN E. SMITH LAW FIRM (AV)

The Brian Smith Building, 301 South 2nd Avenue, 85364
Telephone: 520-783-8811

Brian E. Smith
William J. Kerekes

Frank A. Fila
Thomas W. Anderson

LEGAL SUPPORT PERSONNEL
Bridget M. Hughes

Reference: Bank of America.

For full biographical listings, see the Martindale-Hubbell Law Directory

ARKANSAS

FAYETTEVILLE,* Washington Co.

ODOM, ELLIOTT, WINBURN, WATSON, SMITH & ODOM (AV)

No. 1 East Mountain Street, P.O. Drawer 1868, 72702
Telephone: 501-442-7575
FAX: 501-442-9008

MEMBERS OF FIRM
Bobby Lee Odom
Don R. Elliott, Jr.
Russell B. Winburn

Jason L. Watson
J. Timothy Smith
Conrad T. Odom

Timothy J. Myers

Reference: Bank of Fayetteville, Fayetteville, Arkansas.

For full biographical listings, see the Martindale-Hubbell Law Directory

HOT SPRINGS NATIONAL PARK,* Garland Co.

LANE, MUSE, ARMAN & PULLEN (AV)

Chamber of Commerce Building, Grand and Ouachita Avenues, P.O. Box 758, 71902
Telephone: 501-623-3356
Facsimile: 501-624-1902

MEMBERS OF FIRM
Earl J. Lane (1912-1989)
Richard S. Muse

R. Keith Arman
Donald C. Pullen

ASSOCIATES
Shannon Muse Carroll   Jon Bradley Gann
LEGAL SUPPORT PERSONNEL
LEGAL ASSISTANTS
James C. Arman   James S. Street
Jeanene Ramsey

Reference: Boatmen's National Bank.

For full biographical listings, see the Martindale-Hubbell Law Directory

LITTLE ROCK,* Pulaski Co.

BARBER, MCCASKILL, AMSLER, JONES & HALE, P.A. (AV)

2700 First Commercial Building, 400 West Capitol Avenue, 72201-3414
Telephone: 501-372-6175
Telecopier: 501-375-2802

Azro L. Barber (1885-1979)
Elbert A. Henry (1889-1966)
John B. Thurman (1912-1971)
Austin McCaskill, Sr.
Guy Amsler, Jr.
Glenn W. Jones
Michael E. Hale
John S. Cherry, Jr.
Robert L. Henry, III
Micheal L. Alexander
William H. Edwards, Jr.

Richard C. Kalkbrenner
G. Spence Fricke
Gail Ponder Gaines
Michael J. Emerson
R. Kenny McCulloch
Tim A. Cheatham
Joseph F. Kolb
Scott Michael Strauss
Derek J. Edwards
Thomas E. Osment, Jr.
Christopher Gomlicker

Attorneys for: Associated Aviation Underwriters; Canal Insurance Co.; Fireman's Fund Insurance Co.; General Motors Corp.; General Motors Acceptance Corp.; Hanover Insurance Co.; Home Insurance Co.; Royal Insurance;

(See Next Column)

United States Fidelity & Guaranty Co.; Universal Underwriters Insurance Co.

For full biographical listings, see the Martindale-Hubbell Law Directory

DODDS, KIDD, RYAN & MOORE (AV)

313 West Second Street, 72201
Telephone: 501-375-9901
FAX: 501-376-0387

MEMBERS OF FIRM
J. B. Dodds (1909-1964)
J. L. Kidd, Jr.
Donald S. Ryan

Judson C. Kidd
Richard N. Moore, Jr.
Charles Gregory Alagood

ASSOCIATE
Robert T. James

Reference: First Commercial Bank in Little Rock.

For full biographical listings, see the Martindale-Hubbell Law Directory

DUNCAN & RAINWATER TRIAL LAWYERS A PROFESSIONAL ASSOCIATION (AV)

Suite 500 Three Financial Centre, 900 South Shackleford, P.O. Box 25938, 72221-5938
Telephone: 501-228-7600
FAX: 501-228-7664

Phillip J. Duncan (P.A.)
Michael R. Rainwater (P.A.)

Robert A. Russell, Jr.
Neil Ray Chamberlin

Michelle Banks Odum

For full biographical listings, see the Martindale-Hubbell Law Directory

GARY EUBANKS & ASSOCIATES, P.A. (AV)

708 West Second Street, 72201
Telephone: 501-372-0266

Gary L. Eubanks

Hugh F. Spinks

William Gary Holt
James G. Schulze
Herman W. Eubanks

Jack D. Files
Jason Files
Matthew Hartness

For full biographical listings, see the Martindale-Hubbell Law Directory

FRIDAY, ELDREDGE & CLARK (AV)

A Partnership including Professional Associations
Formerly, Smith, Williams, Friday, Eldredge & Clark
2000 First Commercial Building, 400 West Capitol Avenue, 72201-3493
Telephone: 501-376-2011
Telecopier: 501-376-2147; 376-6369
Email: fecmh@fec.sprint.com

MEMBERS OF FIRM
William H. Sutton (P.A.)
Frederick S. Ursery (P.A.)
John Dewey Watson (P.A.)
J. Phillip Malcom (P.A.)
James M. Simpson, Jr., (P.A.)
Donald H. Bacon (P.A.)
Barry E. Coplin (P.A.)
Elizabeth Robben Murray (P.A.)
Laura Hensley Smith (P.A.)

William Mell Griffin III, (P.A.)
Kevin A. Crass (P.A.)
William A. Waddell, Jr., (P.A.)
Scott J. Lancaster (P.A.)
James C. Baker (P.A.)
Scott H. Tucker (P.A.)
Guy Alton Wade (P.A.)
J. Michael Pickens (P.A.)
Tonia P. Jones (P.A.)

David D. Wilson (P.A.)

ASSOCIATES
Gregory D. Taylor
Fran C. Hickman

Betty J. Demory
Will Bond

Clifford W. Plunkett

Counsel for: Union Pacific System; St. Paul Insurance Co.; Liberty Mutual Insurance Co.; Cigna Property & Casualty Co.; Arkansas Power & Light Co.; Dillard Department Stores, Inc.; First Commercial Corp.; Browning Arms Co.; Phillips Petroleum Co.; Aetna Casualty & Surety Co.

For Complete List of Firm Personnel, See General Section

For full biographical listings, see the Martindale-Hubbell Law Directory

HUCKABAY, MUNSON, ROWLETT & TILLEY, P.A. (AV)

First Commercial Building, Suite 1900, 400 West Capitol, 72201
Telephone: 501-374-6535
Fax: 501-374-5906

Mike Huckabay
Bruce E. Munson
Beverly A. Rowlett
James W. Tilley

John E. Moore
Tim Boone
Rick Runnells
Sarah Ann Presson

Edward T. Oglesby

D. Michael Huckabay, Jr.
Carol Lockard Worley
Mark S. Breeding

Elizabeth Fletcher Rogers
Julia L. Busfield
Jane M. Yocum

Terry D. Dugger

(See Next Column)

HUCKABAY, MUNSON, ROWLETT & TILLEY P.A.—*Continued*

Representative Clients: Allstate Insurance Company; American International Group; Farmers Insurance Group; General Electric Company; Nationwide Insurance Group; Safeco Insurance Company; State Farm Mutual Automobile Insurance Company; State Farm Fire and Casualty Company; Tenet Healthcare Corp.; United States Fidelity and Guaranty Company.

For full biographical listings, see the Martindale-Hubbell Law Directory

ROSE LAW FIRM, A PROFESSIONAL ASSOCIATION (AV)

120 East Fourth Street, 72201
Telephone: 501-375-9131
Telecopy: 501-375-1309

Jerry C. Jones	Richard T. Donovan
David L. Williams	James H. Druff
James Hunter Birch	Amy Lee Stewart

COUNSEL
Phillip Carroll

Michael N. Shannon

Representative Clients: Kemper Insurance Group; Bridgestone/Firestone, Inc.; Aluminum Company of America; Baxter Healthcare Corporation; CIGNA Companies; J.A. Riggs Tractor Co.; General American Transportation Co.

For Complete List of Firm Personnel, See General Section

For full biographical listings, see the Martindale-Hubbell Law Directory

NEWPORT,* Jackson Co.

BOYCE LAW FIRM (AV)

307 Main, P.O. Box 38, 72112
Telephone: 501-523-3626; Jonesboro: 501-932-7189
Fax: 501-523-4839

Sam H. Boyce	Henry H. Boyce

LEGAL SUPPORT PERSONNEL
Betty Butler (Paralegal)

Reference: Merchants & Planters Bank, Newport, Arkansas.

For full biographical listings, see the Martindale-Hubbell Law Directory

CALIFORNIA

APTOS, Santa Cruz Co.

DENNIS J. KEHOE A LAW CORPORATION (AV)

311 Bonita Drive, 95003
Telephone: 408-662-8444
Fax: 408-662-0227

Dennis J. Kehoe

For full biographical listings, see the Martindale-Hubbell Law Directory

RUMMONDS, WALTZ & MAIR (AV)

311 Bonita Drive, P.O. Box 1870, 95001
Telephone: 408-688-2911
Sacramento, California Office: 6991 Garden Highway. 95837.
Telephone: 916-927-4610.

MEMBERS OF FIRM

James S. Rummonds	Peter K. Mair
Patrick J. Waltz	
(Resident, Sacramento Office)	

For full biographical listings, see the Martindale-Hubbell Law Directory

BAKERSFIELD,* Kern Co.

KLEIN, WEGIS, DeNATALE, GOLDNER & MUIR, LLP (AV)

A Partnership including Professional Corporations
(Formerly Di Giorgio, Davis, Klein, Wegis, Duggan & Friedman)
ARCO Tower, 4550 California Avenue, Second Floor, P.O. Box 11172, 93389-1172
Telephone: 805-395-1000
Telecopier: 805-326-0418
Email: kwdgm@kwdgm.com

MEMBERS OF FIRM

Anthony J. Klein (Inc.)	Ralph B. Wegis (Inc.)
Gregory A. Muir	

Representative Clients: Bank of America; Great Western Bank; Mojave Pipeline Co.; Transamerican Title Insurance Co.; Dean Whittier Reynolds, Inc.; California Republic Bank; San Joaquin Bank; Nahama & Weagant Energy Co.; Freymiller Trucking, Inc.; Westinghouse Electric Co.

(See Next Column)

For Complete List of Firm Personnel, See General Section

For full biographical listings, see the Martindale-Hubbell Law Directory

LAW OFFICES OF YOUNG WOOLDRIDGE (AV)

1800 30th Street, Fourth Floor, 93301
Telephone: 805-327-9661
Facsimile: 805-327-1087

MEMBERS OF FIRM

Joseph Wooldridge	Michael R. Young
A. Cameron Paulden (1927-1984)	Ernest A. Conant
	Steve W. Nichols
Robert J. Self	Larry R. Cox
G. Neil Farr	Scott K. Kuney
Michael A. Kaia	

ASSOCIATES

Russell B. Hicks	Vickie Y. Songer
Todd A. Gall	

OF COUNSEL

John B. Young	Edward M. Carpenter

Representative Clients: Arvin-Edison Water Storage District; Motor City Truck Sales and Service.
References: Wells Fargo Bank; First Interstate Bank; California Republic Bank.

For Complete List of Firm Personnel, See General Section

For full biographical listings, see the Martindale-Hubbell Law Directory

CHICO, Butte Co.

STEWART, HUMPHERYS, BURCHETT, SANDELMAN & MOLIN (AV)

Suite 6, 3120 Cohasset Road, P.O. Box 720, 95927
Telephone: 916-891-6111
Telecopier: 916-894-2103
Email: shbsm@sunset.net

MEMBERS OF FIRM

Ronald E. Stewart	Raymond L. Sandelman
Keith S. Humpherys	Richard J. Molin
Alan E. Burchett	Carol J. Tener
Stephen P. Trover	

Representative Clients: Special Risk Management Authority; North Valley Schools Insurance Group; Butte County School Self-Funded Medical Benefits Powers Authority; Shasta Trinity Health Joint Powers Authority; Northern California Community College Joint Powers Authority; Harbor Insurance Co.; Carolina Corp.; Hurst-Holme Insurance Co.; Zurich-American Insurance Co.

For full biographical listings, see the Martindale-Hubbell Law Directory

COSTA MESA, Orange Co.

LAW OFFICES OF W. DOUGLAS EASTON (AV)

3200 Park Center Drive, Suite 1000, 92626
Telephone: 714-850-4590
Fax: 714-850-4500

Anderson L. Washburn	Russel W. Jones
Brian W. Easton	

For full biographical listings, see the Martindale-Hubbell Law Directory

ELY, FRITZ & HOGAN (AV)

3100 Bristol Street #200, 92626
Telephone: 714-556-1480
Telecopier: 714-556-2863

MEMBERS OF FIRM

Thomas W. Ely	Michael G. Hogan
James H. Fritz	Jerome D. Rybarczyk

Charles A. Correia	Ronald F. Templer
Allen D. MacNeil	

OF COUNSEL
Gerald W. Mouzis

For full biographical listings, see the Martindale-Hubbell Law Directory

EL SEGUNDO, Los Angeles Co.

McGARRY & LAUFENBERG (AV)

300 North Sepulveda Boulevard, Suite 2294, 90245
Telephone: 310-335-1780
Fax: 310-335-1790

MEMBERS OF FIRM

James J. McGarry	Jeffrey J. Laufenberg
William Leamon Cummings	

(See Next Column)

McGARRY & LAUFENBERG, *El Segundo—Continued*

ASSOCIATES

Daniel D. Laufenberg　　　　John E. Zegel

For full biographical listings, see the Martindale-Hubbell Law Directory

---

ENCINO, Los Angeles Co.

STEPHEN H. HELLER A PROFESSIONAL CORPORATION (AV)

16830 Ventura Boulevard, Suite B, 91436-1714
Telephone: 818-995-4646

Stephen H. Heller

For full biographical listings, see the Martindale-Hubbell Law Directory

---

*FAIRFIELD,** Solano Co.

BARNETT • MATTICE (AV)

An Association of Sole Practitioners
712 Empire Street, 94533
Telephone: 707-425-0671
Fax: 707-425-4255

Robert E. Barnett　　　　Michael C. Mattice

For full biographical listings, see the Martindale-Hubbell Law Directory

---

*FRESNO,** Fresno Co.

LANG, RICHERT & PATCH, A PROFESSIONAL CORPORATION (AV)

Fig Garden Financial Center, 5200 North Palm Avenue, 4th Floor, P.O. Box 40012, 93755
Telephone: 209-228-6700
Fax: 209-228-6727

Frank H. Lang　　　　　　　　Victoria J. Salisch
William T. Richert (1937-1993)　Bradley A. Silva
Robert L. Patch, II　　　　　　Charles Trudrung Taylor
Val W. Saldaña　　　　　　　　Mark L. Creede
Douglas E. Noll　　　　　　　　Peter N. Zeitler
Michael T. Hertz　　　　　　　Charles L. Doerksen

Laurie L. Quigley　　　　　　　Nabil E. Zumout
Douglas E. Griffin　　　　　　　Shawn H. Alikian
　　　　　Thomas E. Gauthier

References: Wells Fargo Bank (Fresno Main Office).

For full biographical listings, see the Martindale-Hubbell Law Directory

MILES, SEARS & EANNI, A PROFESSIONAL CORPORATION (AV)

2844 Fresno Street, P.O. Box 1432, 93716
Telephone: 209-486-5200
Fax: 209-486-5240

Wm. M. Miles (1909-1991)　　Richard C. Watters
Robert E. Sears (1918-1992)　Gerald J. Maglio
Carmen A. Eanni　　　　　　　William J. Seiler
　　　　　Douglas L. Gordon

For full biographical listings, see the Martindale-Hubbell Law Directory

---

GLENDALE, Los Angeles Co.

FLANAGAN, BOOTH, UNGER & MOSES (AV)

1156 North Brand Boulevard, 91202-2582
Telephone: 818-244-8694
Fax: 818-244-1852
Santa Ana, California Office: 1851 East First Street, Suite 805, 92705.
Telephone: 714-835-2607.
Fax: 714-835-4825.

MEMBERS OF FIRM

J. Michael Flanagan　　　　Charles J. Unger
Douglas M. Booth　　　　　J. Barry Moses

ASSOCIATES

Michael T. Danis　　　　　James A. Grover

For full biographical listings, see the Martindale-Hubbell Law Directory

O'ROURKE, ALLAN & FONG (AV)

3rd Floor, 104 North Belmont, P.O. Box 10220, 91209-3220
Telephone: 818-247-4303
Fax: 818-247-1451

MEMBERS OF FIRM

Denis M. O'Rourke　　　　　Joan H. Allan
　　　　　Roderick D. Fong

ASSOCIATE

Denise Michelle O'Rourke

References: Verdugo Banking Co. (Glendale, California); Community Bank (Glendale, California).

(See Next Column)

For full biographical listings, see the Martindale-Hubbell Law Directory

THOMAS & PRICE (AV)

535 North Brand Boulevard, 7th Floor, 91203
Telephone: 213-387-4800; 818-500-4800
FAX: 818-500-4822
Ventura, California Office: 1655 Mesa Verde Avenue, Suite 230.
Telephone: 805-642-6255.
Fax: 805-642-4580.

MEMBERS OF FIRM

Michael Thomas　　　　　Craig R. Donahue
Bonnie R. Louis　　　　　Maureen F. Thomas

ASSOCIATES

John P. DeGomez　　　　Christian E. Sanne
Timothy A. Hodge　　　　Benjimin M. Brees
Linda B. Hurevitz　　　　Janet L. Keuper
　　　　　Kevin M. McCormick

OF COUNSEL

Lawrence E. Price

For full biographical listings, see the Martindale-Hubbell Law Directory

---

IRVINE, Orange Co.

CHRISTOPHER B. MEARS, A P.C. (AV)

Old Town Irvine, 14988 Sand Canyon Avenue, Suite 1-8, 92618
Telephone: 714-551-2250
Fax: 714-551-0887
Email: CMEARS1031@AOL.COM

Christopher B. Mears

For full biographical listings, see the Martindale-Hubbell Law Directory

---

LAGUNA BEACH, Orange Co.

THOMAS A. REILLY (AV)

1400 South Coast Highway, Penthouse Suite, 92651
Telephone: 714-494-8575

For full biographical listings, see the Martindale-Hubbell Law Directory

---

LAGUNA NIGUEL, Orange Co.

ROBINSON, PHILLIPS & CALCAGNIE, A PROFESSIONAL CORPORATION (AV)

Incorporated 1986
28202 Cabot Road Suite 200, 92677
Telephone: 714-347-8855
Fax: 714-347-8774
Email: rpc@robinson-pilaw.com
San Diego, California Office: 110 Laurel Street.
Telephone: 619-338-4060.
Fax: 619-338-0423.

Mark P. Robinson, Jr.　　　　Gordon G. Phillips, Jr.
　　　　　Kevin F. Calcagnie

Allan F. Davis　　　　　　　Susan Lee Guinn
　　　　　Jeoffrey L. Robinson

LEGAL SUPPORT PERSONNEL

Lin Moen　　　　　　　　　Darleen Perkins
Donna Hosea　　　　　　　Francine Teer
　　　　　Linda Audeoud

For full biographical listings, see the Martindale-Hubbell Law Directory

---

LARKSPUR, Marin Co.

KATZ, BIERER & BRADY, A PROFESSIONAL CORPORATION (AV)

101 Larkspur Landing Circle, Suite 223, 94939
Telephone: 415-925-1600
FAX: 415-925-0940

Richard L. Katz　　　　　Joel D. Bierer
　　　　Steven J. Brady

OF COUNSEL

Alvin J. Schifrin

For full biographical listings, see the Martindale-Hubbell Law Directory

WEINBERG, HOFFMAN & CASEY (AV)

A Partnership including a Professional Corporation
900 Larkspur Landing Circle, Suite 155, 94939
Telephone: 415-461-9666
Fax: 415-461-9681

Ivan Weinberg　　　　　Joseph Hoffman
　　　　A. Michael Casey

(See Next Column)

WEINBERG, HOFFMAN & CASEY—*Continued*

OF COUNSEL
Mark Ropers

For full biographical listings, see the Martindale-Hubbell Law Directory

LONG BEACH, Los Angeles Co.

EDWARD P. GEORGE, JR., INC. A PROFESSIONAL CORPORATION (AV)

Suite 430, 5000 East Spring Street, 90815
Telephone: 310-497-2900
Facsimile: 310-497-2904

Edward P. George, Jr.   Timothy L. O'Reilly
OF COUNSEL
Albert C. S. Ramsey

Reference: Harbor Bank, Long Beach.

For full biographical listings, see the Martindale-Hubbell Law Directory

PERONA, LANGER & BECK, A PROFESSIONAL CORPORATION (AV)

300 East San Antonio, 90807
Telephone: 310-426-6155
Facsimile: 310-490-9823
Los Angeles, California Office: 9255 Sunset Boulevard, Suite 920.
Telephone: 800-435-7542.

James T. Perona   Wayne M. Robertshaw
Major A. Langer   John C. Thornton
Ronald Beck   M. Lawrence Lallande
Ellen R. Serbin

Nelson L. Cohen   Edward T. Trumper
R. Paul Katrinak   Richard L. Stuhlbarg
Susan Graham   Rhonda Ann Visniski

For full biographical listings, see the Martindale-Hubbell Law Directory

RUSSELL & MIRKOVICH (AV)

One World Trade Center, Suite 1450, 90831-1450
Telephone: 310-436-9911
FAX: 310-436-1897

Carlton E. Russell   Joseph N. Mirkovich

For full biographical listings, see the Martindale-Hubbell Law Directory

STOLPMAN • KRISSMAN • ELBER • MANDEL & KATZMAN LLP (AV)

A Partnership including Professional Corporations
Nineteenth Floor, 111 West Ocean Boulevard, 90802-4649
Telephone: 310-435-8300
Telecopier: 310-435-8304
Los Angeles (Westwood) Office: Suite 1800, 10880 Wilshire Boulevard.
MEMBERS OF FIRM
Thomas G. Stolpman (Inc.)   Joel Krissman
Leonard H. Mandel   Mary Nielsen Abbott
Bernard Katzman (Inc.)   Donna Silver
Dennis M. Elber
ASSOCIATES
Edwin Silver   Lynne Rasmussen
Elaine Mandel

For full biographical listings, see the Martindale-Hubbell Law Directory

LOS ANGELES,* Los Angeles Co.

AGNEW & BRUSAVICH

(See Torrance)

BAUM, HEDLUND, ARISTEI, GUILFORD & DOWNEY, A PROFESSIONAL CORPORATION (AV)

Suite 950, 12100 Wilshire Boulevard, 90025
Telephone: 310-207-3233; 800-827-0087
Facsimile: 310-820-7444
Email: bhagd@bhagd.com *URL:* http://www.bhagd.com/attorneys/
Washington, D.C. Office: 1250 24th Street, N.W., Suite 300.
Telephone: 202-466-0513; 800-827-0097.
Facsimile: 202-466-0527.

Michael L. Baum   J. Clark Aristei
Paul J. Hedlund   Robert E. Guilford
William J. Downey III

John A. Greaves   Robert F. Foss
Cara L. Belle   Karen A. Barth
  (Not admitted in CA)   V. Neil Forn, II

(See Next Column)

Reference: Union Bank.

For full biographical listings, see the Martindale-Hubbell Law Directory

MATTHEW B. F. BIREN & ASSOCIATES (AV)

815 Moraga Drive, 90049-1633
Telephone: 310-476-3031; 381-5609
FAX: 310-471-3165
Email: mbfba@primenet.com

Marc J. Katzman   Debra J. Tauger
Edmont T. Barrett

Reference: First Los Angeles Bank (Century City, Los Angeles, Branch).

For full biographical listings, see the Martindale-Hubbell Law Directory

LAW OFFICES OF DAVID B. BLOOM A PROFESSIONAL CORPORATION (AV)

3325 Wilshire Boulevard, Ninth Floor, 90010
Telephone: 213-938-5248; 384-4088
Telecopier: 213-385-2009

David B. Bloom

Stephen S. Monroe (A   Susan Carole Jay
  Professional Corporation)   Edward Idell
Raphael A. Rosemblat   Sandra Kamenir
James E. Adler   Steven Wayne Lazarus
Bonni S. Mantovani   Andrew Edward Briseno
Roy A. Levun   Harold C. Klaskin
Cherie S. Raidy   Shelley M. Gould
Jonathan Udell   Peter O. Israel

For full biographical listings, see the Martindale-Hubbell Law Directory

BOTTUM & FELITON, A PROFESSIONAL CORPORATION (AV)

Suite 1500, South Tower, 3200 Wilshire Boulevard, 90010
Telephone: 213-487-0402
Fax: 213-386-9803
San Diego, California Office: Suite 400 Emerald Plaza, 402 West Broadway.
Telephone: 619-595-4857.
Fax: 619-595-4863.

John R. Feliton, Jr.   Steve Johnson
Robert A. Wooten, Jr.   Mark A. Oertel
Alexander F. Giovanniello

Kenneth C. Feldman   Julie A. Covell
Jerry Garcia   Karl R. Loureiro
Paul K. Schrieffer   Sean T. Hamada
Scott A. Hampton   Gary F. Werner
Gregg S. Garfinkel   Victor I. King
Brian E. Cooper   Andrea J. Lang
Linwood Warren, Jr.

For full biographical listings, see the Martindale-Hubbell Law Directory

GIRARDI AND KEESE (AV)

1126 Wilshire Boulevard, 90017-1904
Telephone: 213-977-0211
FAX: 213-481-1554
San Bernardino, California Office: 596 North Arrowhead.
Telephone: 714-381-1551.
FAX: 714-381-2566.

MEMBERS OF FIRM
Thomas V. Girardi   V. Andre Rekte (Resident, San
Robert M. Keese   Bernardino Office)
John A. Girardi   John K. Courtney
James B. Kropff   Amy Fisch Solomon
Robert W. Finnerty   Thomas C. Morgan
James G. O'Callahan   David N. Bigelow
Carrie J. Rognlien

References: Wells Fargo Bank (Los Angeles Head Office); Bank of Industry.

For full biographical listings, see the Martindale-Hubbell Law Directory

GORDON, EDELSTEIN, KREPACK, GRANT, FELTON & GOLDSTEIN (AV)

A Partnership including a Professional Corporation
Suite 1800, 3580 Wilshire Boulevard, 90010
Telephone: 213-739-7000
Fax: 213-386-1671

Roger L. Gordon   Richard I. Felton
Mark Edelstein   Irwin L. Goldstein (A
Howard D. Krepack   Professional Corporation)
Sherry E. Grant   Steven J. Kleifield

(See Next Column)

GORDON, EDELSTEIN, KREPACK, GRANT, FELTON & GOLDSTEIN, *Los Angeles—Continued*

ASSOCIATES

Joshua M. Merliss
David A. Goldstein
Eugenia L. Steele

For full biographical listings, see the Martindale-Hubbell Law Directory

HARNEY LAW OFFICES A LEGAL CORPORATION (AV)

Suite 1300 Figueroa Plaza, 201 North Figueroa Street, 90012-2636
Telephone: 213-482-0881
Fax: 213-250-4042

David M. Harney
David T. Harney
Julie A. Harney
Andrew J. Nocas
Vincent McGowan
Thomas A. Schultz

Reference: Bank of America.

For full biographical listings, see the Martindale-Hubbell Law Directory

KUSSMAN & WHITEHILL (AV)

A Partnership including a Professional Corporation
Suite 1470, 10866 Wilshire Boulevard, 90024
Telephone: 310-474-4411
Fax: 310-474-6530

Russell S. Kussman (A Professional Corporation)
Michael H. Whitehill

Steven G. Mehta

For full biographical listings, see the Martindale-Hubbell Law Directory

JOSÉ Y. LAUCHENGCO, JR. (AV)

3545 Wilshire Boulevard, Suite 247, 90010
Telephone: 213-380-9897

OF COUNSEL
Paul J. Estuar

For full biographical listings, see the Martindale-Hubbell Law Directory

LEBOVITS & DAVID, A PROFESSIONAL CORPORATION (AV)

Suite 3100, Two Century Plaza, 2049 Century Park East, 90067
Telephone: 310-277-0200
Fax: 310-552-1028

Moses Lebovits
Deborah A. David
OF COUNSEL
Joseph J. M. Lange

Reference: Imperial Bank (Main Office - Beverly Hills).

For full biographical listings, see the Martindale-Hubbell Law Directory

ROBERT L. LUTY A PROFESSIONAL CORPORATION (AV)

Suite 303, 11661 San Vicente Boulevard, 90049
Telephone: 310-207-4342
Fax: 310-207-5035

Robert L. Luty

Reference: Brentwood Savings Bank (Brentwood Branch).

For full biographical listings, see the Martindale-Hubbell Law Directory

MAGAÑA, CATHCART & MCCARTHY (AV)

A Partnership including Professional Corporations
Suite 810 Gateway West Building, 1801 Avenue of the Stars (Century City), 90067-5899
Telephone: 310-553-6630; 213-879-2531
Fax: 310-785-9143

Brian R. Magaña (Professional Corporation)
Peter T. Cathcart (Professional Corporation)
William H. Wimsatt (Professional Corporation)

Richard L. Bisetti
Deborah Mitzenmacher
Kathleen A. McCarthy
Daniel A. Cribbs
OF COUNSEL
Daniel C. Cathcart (Professional Corporation)
RETIRED
Raoul D. Magaña
James J. McCarthy

Reference: First Los Angeles Bank (1950 Avenue of the Stars, Los Angeles (Century City), California).

For full biographical listings, see the Martindale-Hubbell Law Directory

PETER J. MCNULTY (AV)

827 Moraga Drive (Bel Air), 90049
Telephone: 310-471-2707
Fax: 310-472-7014
Gilroy, California Office: Suite F-2, 8352 Church Street.
Telephone: 408-848-5900.
Fax: 408-848-1391.
Aurora, Illinois Office: 8 East Galena Street.
ASSOCIATE
Michael L. Oran (A Professional Corporation)
OF COUNSEL

John A. Alvarez
(Resident, Gilroy Office)
Robert M. Foote
(Not admitted in CA)
Robert P. Friedman
Carl A. McMahan

Reference: City National Bank (Beverly Hills, California).

For full biographical listings, see the Martindale-Hubbell Law Directory

PIERRY & MOORHEAD, LLP (AV)

A Partnership including a Professional Corporation
301 North Avalon Boulevard, 90744-5888
Telephone: 310-834-2691, 213-775-8348, 714-636-2970
FAX: 310-518-5814

MEMBERS OF FIRM
Thomas J. Pierry, Sr.
Michael D. Moorhead (P.C.)

James M. McAdams
F. Joseph Ford, Jr.
Robert W. Ford
F. Javier Trujillo
Thomas J. Pierry, III
Joseph P. Pierry

For full biographical listings, see the Martindale-Hubbell Law Directory

PRESTHOLT, KLEEGER, FIDONE & VILLASENOR (AV)

Suite 1600, 1055 West 7th Street, 90017
Telephone: 213-895-4811
FAX: 213-895-4817
San Francisco, California Office: 989 Market Street, 6th Floor.
Telephone: 415-267-6362.
Fax: 415-267-6275.

MEMBERS OF FIRM
David A. Prestholt
Kenneth S. Kleeger
Gary P. Fidone
Lisa A. Villasenor
Brian D. Holmberg
Willi H. Siepmann
David Crawford, III
Lisa L. Loveridge
Archie Chin
Robert J. Scott, Jr.
Avigal Horrow
Jamie Ann Louie
Robert S. Putnam
Arnie E. Goldstein
Brian J. Finn

For full biographical listings, see the Martindale-Hubbell Law Directory

SELMAN ● BREITMAN (AV)

11766 Wilshire Boulevard, Sixth Floor, 90025-6538
Telephone: 310-445-0800
Fax: 310-473-2525
San Diego, California Office: Emerald Plaza, 402 W. Broadway, Suite 400.
Telephone: 619-595-4880.
Facsimile: 619-595-4890.
San Francisco, California Office: Citicorp Center, One Sansome Street, Suite 1900.
Telephone: 415-951-4646.
Fax: 415-951-4676.

MEMBERS OF FIRM
Neil H. Selman
Craig R. Breitman
Robert A. Steller
(Partner, San Diego Office)
Alan B. Yuter
Nancy W. Shokohi
Jeffrey C. Segal
A. Scott Goldberg
Elaine K. Fresch
Nicholas Banko
Brad D. Bleichner
David L. Jones
Mark L. Jubelt
Monica Cruz Thornton
David T. Bamberger
Sterling Tao
(Partner, San Francisco Office)

Lynette Klawon
Ramon Z. Bacerdo (Resident, San Francisco Office)
John S. Knowlton
Murray M. Sinclair
Jeffrey A. Simmons
Mark S. Gruskin
Anthony L. Cione
Christopher J. Harrington
Sheryl W. Leichenger
Theresa Ann Loss
Jerry C. Popovich
Lisa Hannah Kahn
David H. Oken
Katy A. Nelson
Jan Long Pocaterra
Kim Karelis
Asim K. Desai
Pauline A. New
Dianne M. Costales
Eldon S. Edson
James B. Kamanski
Michael L. Mengoli
Rita H. Issagholian
Sarah F. Burke
(Resident, San Diego Office)
Darcy D. Jorgensen
Linda S. Wendell (Resident, San Francisco Office)
Jeffrey S. Bolender

(See Next Column)

SELMAN ● BREITMAN—*Continued*

Jeffrey T. Briggs	Kathleen T. Deeley
Marcie A. Keenan	Christopher A. Petrovic
Lisa M. Dyson (Resident, San Francisco Office)	Kimberly D. Allario (Resident, San Diego Office)
Aimee Y. Wong	Wendy Wen Yun Chang
Grace Horoupian	Jack M. Zakariaie

OF COUNSEL

Thomas A. Leary (Of Counsel, San Diego Office)

Reference: City National Bank (Beverly Hills Branch).

For full biographical listings, see the Martindale-Hubbell Law Directory

ROBERT D. WALKER A PROFESSIONAL CORPORATION (AV)

Suite 1208, One Park Plaza, 3250 Wilshire Boulevard, 90010-1606
Telephone: 213-382-8010
Fax: 213-388-1033

Robert D. Walker

Delia Flores

Reference: Bank of America (Los Angeles Main Office)

For full biographical listings, see the Martindale-Hubbell Law Directory

MENLO PARK, San Mateo Co.

DYER & WHITE (AV)

Suite 200, 800 Oak Grove Avenue, 94025
Telephone: 415-325-7000
Fax: 415-325-3116

MEMBERS OF FIRM

Charles A. Dyer	Rand N. White

For full biographical listings, see the Martindale-Hubbell Law Directory

O'REILLY & COLLINS, A PROFESSIONAL CORPORATION (AV)

2500 Sand Hill Road, Suite 201, 94025
Telephone: 415-854-7700
Fax: 415-854-8350

Terry O'Reilly	James P. Collins
James P. Tessier	Michael Danko

For full biographical listings, see the Martindale-Hubbell Law Directory

MODESTO,* Stanislaus Co.

CARDOZO & CARDOZO (AV)

1101 Sylvan Avenue, #B-4, 95350
Telephone: 209-571-3600
FAX: 209-571-1553

MEMBERS OF FIRM

A. A. Cardozo, Jr.	Richard A. Cardozo

LEGAL SUPPORT PERSONNEL

Patricia Bowers

For full biographical listings, see the Martindale-Hubbell Law Directory

MONTEREY, Monterey Co.

THE THOMPSON LAW FIRM (AV)

580 Calle Principal, First Floor, 93940-2818
Telephone: 408-646-1224
Fax: 408-646-1225

Ralph W. Thompson, III

For full biographical listings, see the Martindale-Hubbell Law Directory

NEWPORT BEACH, Orange Co.

KELEGIAN & THOMAS (AV)

4685 MacArthur Court, Suite 400, 92660
Telephone: 714-553-1200
Fax: 714-553-1013
Email: KelThomLaw@aol.com

Mark A. Kelegian	James P. Habel
Michael Paul Thomas	Jeri E. Tabback
Joseph P. Gallo	Dean H. McVay
Bruce A. Thomason	Erik R. Musurlian
Steven M. Hepps	William N. Villard

For full biographical listings, see the Martindale-Hubbell Law Directory

DONALD PETERS A LAW CORPORATION (AV)

1300 Dove Street, Suite 200, 92660
Telephone: 714-955-3818
Fax: 714-955-1341

(See Next Column)

Donald Peters

For full biographical listings, see the Martindale-Hubbell Law Directory

WENTWORTH & PAOLI, P.C. (AV)

4631 Teller Avenue, Suite 100, 92660
Telephone: 714-752-7711
Fax: 714-752-8339

Theodore S. Wentworth	Nancy Morse Knight
William M. Delli Paoli	Court Bryant Purdy

Reference: Wells Fargo Bank, Newport Beach, Calif.

For full biographical listings, see the Martindale-Hubbell Law Directory

NORWALK, Los Angeles Co.

CHARLES R. WELDON (AV)

Suite 104 Southeast Law Center, 12749 Norwalk Boulevard, P.O. Box 1110, 90651
Telephone: 310-864-3737
FAX: 310-863-9962

Jerry D. Turner	Paul R. Dixon
E. Neal Daley	Paul D. Brau
	Laila Havre Jacobsma

For full biographical listings, see the Martindale-Hubbell Law Directory

OAKLAND,* Alameda Co.

ANTHONY & CARLSON (AV)

1999 Harrison Street, Suite 1750, 94612
Telephone: 510-835-8400
Fax: 510-835-5566

MEMBERS OF FIRM

Steven R. Anthony	Richard H. Carlson

ASSOCIATE

Barbara L. Vankoll

OF COUNSEL

Jane L. Trigero

For full biographical listings, see the Martindale-Hubbell Law Directory

BENNETT, SAMUELSEN, REYNOLDS AND ALLARD, A PROFESSIONAL CORPORATION (AV)

1951 Webster Street, Suite 200, 94612
Telephone: 510-444-7688; 510-987-8001
Fax: 510-444-5849

Bryant M. Bennett (Retired)	Richard L. Reynolds
David J. Samuelsen	Anthony J. Allard
	John G. Cowperthwaite

Roger Blake Hohnsbeen	Frederick W. Gatt
Don Henry Schaefer	Rodney Ian Headington
Thomas S. Gelini	Candace Smith-Dabney

Representative Clients: Allstate Insurance Co.; California State Automobile Assn.; The Continental Insurance Cos.; County of Alameda.

For full biographical listings, see the Martindale-Hubbell Law Directory

GWILLIAM, IVARY, CHIOSSO, CAVALLI & BREWER, A PROFESSIONAL CORPORATION (AV)

1999 Harrison Street, Suite 1600, 94612-3528
Telephone: 510-832-5411
Fax: 510-832-1918
Mailing Address: P.O. Box 2079, 94604-2079
Email: Info@GICCB.com

J. Gary Gwilliam	James R. Chiosso
Eric H. Ivary	Steven R. Cavalli
	Steven J. Brewer

Marguerite E. Meade	Steven A. Reaves
	Molly Harrington

Reference: Civic Bank of Commerce, Oakland, California.

For full biographical listings, see the Martindale-Hubbell Law Directory

HAIMS, JOHNSON, MacGOWAN & McINERNEY (AV)

490 Grand Avenue, 94610
Telephone: 510-835-0500
Facsimile: 510-835-2833

(See Next Column)

HAIMS, JOHNSON, MACGOWAN & MCINERNEY, Oakland—Continued

MEMBERS OF FIRM

Arnold B. Haims	Randy M. Marmor
Gary R. Johnson	John K. Kirby
Clyde L. MacGowan	Robert J. Frassetto
Thomas McInerney	Caroline N. Valentino
Lawrence A. Baker	Dianne D. Peebles

ASSOCIATES

Joseph Y. Ahn	Anne M. Michaels
Edward D. Baldwin	Michelle Diane Perry
Marc P. Bouret	Edward C. Schroeder, Jr.

For full biographical listings, see the Martindale-Hubbell Law Directory

KAZAN, MCCLAIN, EDISES, SIMON & ABRAMS, A PROFESSIONAL LAW CORPORATION (AV)

171 Twelfth Street, Suite 300, 94607
Telephone: 510-465-7728; 893-7211
TDD: (510) 763-8808
Fax: 510-835-4913
Email: postmaster@kmes.com

Steven Kazan	Aaron H. Simon
David M. McClain	Denise Abrams

Francis E. Fernandez	Frances C. Schreiberg
Anne Michelle Burr	Simona A. Farrise
Dianna J. Lyons	Ronald J. Shingler

LEGAL SUPPORT PERSONNEL

Elizabeth C. Johnson (Director of Administration and Finance)

Reference: Union Bank (Oakland Main Branch).

For full biographical listings, see the Martindale-Hubbell Law Directory

VAN BLOIS, KNOWLES, SCHWARTZ & BASKIN (AV)

Suite 2245 Ordway Building, One Kaiser Plaza, 94612
Telephone: 510-444-1906
Contra Costa County 510-947-1055
Fax: 510-444-1294

MEMBERS OF FIRM

R. Lewis Van Blois	Ellen R. Schwartz
Thomas C. Knowles	Richard J. Baskin

OF COUNSEL

Charles E. Farnsworth

For full biographical listings, see the Martindale-Hubbell Law Directory

---

ORINDA, Contra Costa Co.

GILLIN, JACOBSON, ELLIS, LARSEN & DOYLE (AV)

2 Theatre Square Suite 230, 94563
Telephone: 510-258-0800
Fax: 510-848-0266
Email: lawfirm@gjeld.com
San Francisco Office: One Sutter Street, 10th Floor.
Telephone: 415-986-4777.

Andrew R. Gillin	Richard P. Doyle, Jr.
Ralph L. Jacobson	Susan Hunt
Luke Ellis	Mitchell S. Rosenfeld
James Paul Larsen	Catherine T. Doyle

For full biographical listings, see the Martindale-Hubbell Law Directory

---

PACIFIC PALISADES, Los Angeles Co.

WILLIAM A. SAMPSON II & ASSOCIATES (AV)

15332 Antioch Street, Suite 525, 90272
Telephone: 310-472-1839
Fax: 310-472-8670

For full biographical listings, see the Martindale-Hubbell Law Directory

---

PALM DESERT, Riverside Co.

BERMAN & WEISS (AV)

73-710 Fred Waring Drive, Suite 100, 92260
Telephone: 619-773-6677
Fax: 619-346-7779
Email: rw1224@aol.com *URL:*
http://www.lawinfo.com/law/ca/berman.html
Encino, California Office: 16055 Ventura Boulevard, Suite 900, 91436.
Telephone: 818-986-8000.
Facsimile: 818-986-3162.
Palm Springs, California Office: 1111 Tahquitz Canyon Way, Suite 203, 92262.
Telephone: 619-327-1777.
Fax: 619-346-7779.

(See Next Column)

MEMBERS OF FIRM

Richard B. Weiss	Martin M. Berman

For full biographical listings, see the Martindale-Hubbell Law Directory

---

PALO ALTO, Santa Clara Co.

HAWKINS, BLICK & FITZPATRICK (AV)

418 Florence Street, 94301
Telephone: 415-321-5656
Fax: 415-326-9636
San Jose, California Office: 96 North Third Street, Suite 300.
Telephone: 408-280-7111.
Fax: 408-292-7868.

Charles F. Hawkins	Stephen L. Blick
	Michael J. Fitzpatrick

ASSOCIATE

Mark F. Bernal

For full biographical listings, see the Martindale-Hubbell Law Directory

---

PASADENA, Los Angeles Co.

BURTON & NORRIS (AV)

35 South Raymond Avenue, Fourth Floor, 91105
Telephone: 818-449-8300
Fax: 818-449-4417

John C. Burton	Donald G. Norris
	Victoria E. King

Reference: Bank of America (Pasadena).

For full biographical listings, see the Martindale-Hubbell Law Directory

COLLINS, COLLINS, MUIR & TRAVER (AV)

Successor to Collins & Collins
Suite 300, 265 North Euclid, 91101
Telephone: 818-793-1163
FAX: 818-793-5982
Newport Beach, California Office: 333 Bayside Drive, 92660.
Telephone: 714-723-6284.
Fax: 714-723-7701.

MEMBERS OF FIRM

James E. Collins (1910-1987)	Robert J. Traver
John J. Collins	Frank J. D'Oro
Samuel J. Muir	Brian K. Stewart

ASSOCIATES

Paul L. Rupard	Christine E. Drage
Robert H. Stellwagen, Jr.	Peter L. Stacy
Tomas A. Guterres	Stephen W. Olson

For full biographical listings, see the Martindale-Hubbell Law Directory

FRANSCELL, STRICKLAND, ROBERTS & LAWRENCE, A PROFESSIONAL CORPORATION (AV)

Penthouse, 225 South Lake Avenue, 91101-3005
Telephone: 818-304-7830; 213-684-7830
Fax: 818-795-7460
Santa Ana, California Office: Suite 800, 401 Civic Center Drive West.
Telephone: 714-543-6511.
Fax: 714-543-6711.
Riverside, California Office: Suite 670, 3801 University Avenue.
Telephone: 909-686-1000.
Fax: 909-686-2565.

George J. Franscell	Donald C. McFarlane
Tracy Strickland	(Resident, Santa Ana Office)
(Resident, Santa Ana Office)	Libby Wong
Barbara E. Roberts	Cindy S. Lee
(Resident, Riverside Office)	Martin J. De Vries
David D. Lawrence	(Resident, Riverside Office)
Carol Ann Rohr	Ann Marie Sanders
Scott D. MacLatchie	Priscilla F. Slocum
S. Frank Harrell	Garth Matthew Drozin
(Resident, Santa Ana Office)	

For full biographical listings, see the Martindale-Hubbell Law Directory

KEVIN MEENAN (AV)

790 East Colorado Boulevard Ninth Floor Penthouse, 91101-2105
Telephone: 818-398-0000
FAX: 818-585-0999
Email: 73313.1624@compuserve.com

For full biographical listings, see the Martindale-Hubbell Law Directory

GEORGE E. MOORE A PROFESSIONAL LAW CORPORATION (AV)

Wells Fargo Building, 350 West Colorado Boulevard Suite 400, 91105-1894
Telephone: 818-440-1111
Fax: 818-440-9456

(See Next Column)

GEORGE E. MOORE A PROFESSIONAL LAW CORPORATION—*Continued*

George E. Moore

For full biographical listings, see the Martindale-Hubbell Law Directory

---

LAW OFFICES OF RICHARD R. REYES (AV)

1100 East Green Street, 91106
Telephone: 818-792-5672

For full biographical listings, see the Martindale-Hubbell Law Directory

---

THON, BECK, VANNI, PHILLIPI & NUTT, A PROFESSIONAL CORPORATION (AV)

1100 East Green Street, 91106-2506
Telephone: 818-795-8333
Fax: 818-449-9933

William M. Thon	Gregory R. Vanni
Thomas P. Beck	Steven V. Phillipi
	Brian C. Nutt

David M. Phillips
OF COUNSEL
Anthony de los Reyes

For full biographical listings, see the Martindale-Hubbell Law Directory

---

REDDING, * Shasta Co.

DUGAN BARR & ASSOCIATES (AV)

1824 Court Street, P.O. Box 994390, 96099-1648
Telephone: 916-243-8008
Fax: 916-243-1648
URL: http://www.CA-Lawyer.com/

Dugan Barr
ASSOCIATES

David L. Case	Douglas Mudford

Representative Clients: City of Redding; Mid Valley Bank; Scott Valley Bank; 3M; Enloe Hospital.
References: Scott Valley Bank, Redding Branch; Mid Valley Bank, Redding Branch.

For full biographical listings, see the Martindale-Hubbell Law Directory

---

MAIRE, MANSELL & BEASLEY, A LAW CORPORATION (AV)

2851 Park Marina Drive Suite 300, P.O. Drawer 994607, 96099-4607
Telephone: 916-246-6050
Fax: 916-246-6060
Email: MAIREMB@AOL.COM

Wayne H. Maire	Linda M. Carpenter
Patrick R. Beasley	David S. Perrine
Adam M. Pressman	Cynthia L. Cooper
	Eric R. Maire

For full biographical listings, see the Martindale-Hubbell Law Directory

---

G. NEIL TOCHER (AV)

833 Mistletoe Lane, Suite 102, 96002
Telephone: 916-221-1609
Fax: 916-221-1745

For full biographical listings, see the Martindale-Hubbell Law Directory

---

REDLANDS, San Bernardino Co.

WELEBIR & McCUNE, A PROFESSIONAL LAW CORPORATION (AV)

2068 Orange Tree Lane, Suite 215, 92374
Telephone: 909-335-0444
Fax: 909-335-0452
Mailing Address: P.O. Box 10488, San Bernardino, California, 92423
Email: WM__Law@MSN.COM

Douglas F. Welebir	Richard D. McCune, Jr.

George S. Theios	Jacqueline Carey-Wilson

OF COUNSEL
Arthur W. Kelly, Jr. (Retired)
LEGAL SUPPORT PERSONNEL

Renee Vargas	Deborah Marsh

For full biographical listings, see the Martindale-Hubbell Law Directory

---

REDWOOD CITY, * San Mateo Co.

LOW, BALL & LYNCH, A PROFESSIONAL CORPORATION (AV)

10 Twin Dolphin, Suite B-500, 94065
Telephone: 415-591-8822
Fax: 415-591-8884
San Francisco, California Office: 601 California Street, Suite 2100, 94108.
Telephone: 415-981-6630.
Monterey, California Office: 10 Ragsdale Drive, Suite 175, 93940.
Telephone: 408-655-8822.

Raymond Coates	David L. Blinn
Chester G. Moore, III	Janet Kulig
James D. Miller	Thomas E. Mulvihill
William H. Holsinger	Jennifer Elizabeth Acheson

John R. Baumann	Joseph M. Fenech
	Michael E. Sandgren

For full biographical listings, see the Martindale-Hubbell Law Directory

---

OWEN & MELBYE, A PROFESSIONAL CORPORATION (AV)

700 Jefferson Street, 94063
Telephone: 415-364-6500
Fax: 415-365-7036
Tahoe City, California Office: P.O. Box 1524.
Telephone: 916-546-2473.

William H. Owen	Edmund M. Scott
Richard B. Melbye	Pamela J. Helmer
Norman J. Roger	John S. Posthauer
	Paul R. Mangiantini

Albert P. Blake, Jr.	Conor A. Meyers
Dawn M. Patterson	Mary P. Derner

Representative Clients: Aetna Cravens Dargan Co.; Avco Lycoming; Beech Aircraft Corp.; California Casualty Indemnity Exchange; K & K Claims Service; Kemper Insurance Cos.; Mutual Service Insurance Co.; State Farm Mutual Insurance Cos.; Underwriters at Lloyds; United States Aviation Insurance Group.

For full biographical listings, see the Martindale-Hubbell Law Directory

---

M. GERALD SCHWARTZBACH (AV)

601 Brewster Avenue, P.O. Box 3389, 94103
Telephone: 415-367-6811
Fax: 415-368-0367

For full biographical listings, see the Martindale-Hubbell Law Directory

---

SACRAMENTO, * Sacramento Co.

CALLAHAN & DEACON (AV)

A Partnership including a Corporation
77 Cadillac Drive, Suite 240, 95825
Telephone: 916-929-1999
Fax: 916-929-1090
Email: gbc8esd@calweb.com

Gary B. Callahan (Inc.)	Edward S. Deacon

ASSOCIATE
Judith Clark Martin

For full biographical listings, see the Martindale-Hubbell Law Directory

---

CAULFIELD, DAVIES & DONAHUE (AV)

3500 American River Drive, Suite 100, 95864
Telephone: 916-487-7700
Fairfield, California Office: Fairfield West Plaza, 1455 Oliver Road, Suite 130.
Telephone: 707-426-0223.

MEMBERS OF FIRM

Richard Hyland Caulfield	James R. Donahue
Robert E. Davies	Bruce E. Leonard

ASSOCIATES

David N. Tedesco	Jennifer Gittisriboongul
Matthew Paul Donahue	John T. Stralen
Brian C. Haydon	David D. Poland
	Shannon Spellacy

For full biographical listings, see the Martindale-Hubbell Law Directory

---

DREYER, BABICH, BUCCOLA & CALLAHAM (AV)

715 University Avenue, 95825
Telephone: 916-920-2111
Fax: 916-920-5687

MEMBERS OF FIRM

Roger A. Dreyer	Robert A. Buccola
Joseph J. Babich	William C. Callaham

(See Next Column)

DREYER, BABICH, BUCCOLA & CALLAHAM, *Sacramento—Continued*

Craig C. Sheffer	Leland J. Aiken
Stephen F. Davids	Kevin G. Farnworth
John W. Jefferson	Eliot M. Reiner
Stanley P. Fleshman	Timothy J. O'Connor

For full biographical listings, see the Martindale-Hubbell Law Directory

FRIEDMAN, COLLARD, CUTTER & PANNETON, PROFESSIONAL CORPORATION (AV)

Suite 300, 7750 College Town Drive, 95826
Telephone: 916-381-9011
Telecopier: 916-381-7048

Morton L. Friedman	John Panneton
William H. Collard	Eric J. Ratinoff
C. Brooks Cutter	Ron Winters

For full biographical listings, see the Martindale-Hubbell Law Directory

HANSEN, BOYD, CULHANE & WATSON (AV)

A Partnership including Professional Corporations
Central City Centre, 1331 Twenty-First Street, 95814
Telephone: 916-444-2550
Telecopier: 916-444-2358

Hartley T. Hansen (Inc.)	Lawrence R. Watson
Kevin R. Culhane (Inc.)	John J. Rueda
David E. Boyd	James J. Banks

Lorraine M. Pavlovich
OF COUNSEL
Betsy S. Kimball

Thomas L. Riordan	Pamela B. Hooley
James O. Moses	Roger R. Billings

For full biographical listings, see the Martindale-Hubbell Law Directory

HARDY ERICH BROWN & WILSON, A PROFESSIONAL CORPORATION (AV)

1000 G Street, 95814
Telephone: 916-449-3800
Fax: 916-449-3888
Mailing Address: P.O. Box 13530, Sacramento, California, 95853-4530

John Quincy Brown, Jr.	Bruce E. Salenko
Anthony D. Osmundson	Daniel J. Coyle
Thomas C. Richards	Brian H. Charter
L. Thomas Wagner	Larry Caldwell
David L. Perrault	Richard L. Alley
John Quincy Brown, III	Whitney A. Davis
David S. Worthington	John C. Miller, Jr.

OF COUNSEL

Cavan Hardy	William A. Wilson
Norwood R. Erich	Richard M. Cunha

Sara A. Clark	Kelly F. Watson
Jay A. Resendez	Kristine E. Balough

Representative Clients: The Dial Corporation; General Motors Corporation; Goodyear Tire and Rubber Company; Little Caesar Enterprises, Inc.; Mobil Oil Corporation; Redman Industries, Inc.; Sacramento Municipal Utility District; Synnex Information Technologies, Inc.; Tri-Continent Scientific, Inc.; VIAD Corporation.

For full biographical listings, see the Martindale-Hubbell Law Directory

THOMAS F. LYTLE (AV)

Court Plaza Building, 901 H Street, Suite 609, 95814-1809
Telephone: 916-442-0701
Fax: 916-442-0780

For full biographical listings, see the Martindale-Hubbell Law Directory

MASON & THOMAS (AV)

2151 River Plaza Drive, Suite 100, P.O. Box 868, 95812-0868
Telephone: 916-567-8211
Fax: 916-567-8212

MEMBERS OF FIRM

Stephen A. Mason	Bradley S. Thomas

ASSOCIATES

Douglas W. Brown	Kevin L. Elder
Robert G. Kruse	Michele Raley
David S. Yost	David T. Ludington
Patrick J. Hehir	Timothy T. Wright

Anastasia Baskerville

For full biographical listings, see the Martindale-Hubbell Law Directory

MATHENY POIDMORE LINKERT & SEARS (AV)

3638 American River Drive, P.O. Box 13711, 95853-4711
Telephone: 916-978-3434
Fax: 916-978-3430
Email: mpls1@netcom.com

MEMBERS OF FIRM

Henry G. Matheny (1933-1984)	James C. Damir
Anthony J. Poidmore	Michael A. Bishop
Douglas A. Sears	Ernest A. Long
Richard S. Linkert	Joann Georgallis

Kent M. Luckey

ASSOCIATES

Matthew C. Jaime	Cathy A. Reynolds
Robert B. Berrigan	Eric R. Wiesel
Stephen J. Nardine	Reed R. Johnson
Ronald E. Enabnit	Danielle M. Guard

Andrea M. Croak

LEGAL SUPPORT PERSONNEL
PARALEGALS

Karen D. Fisher	Lynell Rae Steed
Fran Studer	Jennifer Bachman

Debbie Sue Miller

For full biographical listings, see the Martindale-Hubbell Law Directory

WILCOXEN, MONTGOMERY & HARBISON (AV)

A Partnership including a Professional Corporation
2114 K Street, 95816
Telephone: 916-442-2777

Daniel E. Wilcoxen (Inc.)	James R. Montgomery

Joseph F. Harbison, III

Patrick L. Hinrichsen	Joanne M. Merry
David E. Smith	Cindy L. Robbins

Reference: First Interstate Bank.

For full biographical listings, see the Martindale-Hubbell Law Directory

SAN BERNARDINO,* San Bernardino Co.

KASSEL & KASSEL (AV)

A Group of Independent Law Offices
Suite 207, Wells Fargo Bank Building, 334 West Third Street, 92401
Telephone: 909-884-6455
Fax: 909-884-8032

Philip Kassel	Gregory H. Kassel

References: Wells Fargo Bank; Bank of America; Bank of San Bernardino.

For full biographical listings, see the Martindale-Hubbell Law Directory

LAW OFFICES OF WILLIAM D. SHAPIRO (AV)

432 North Arrowhead Avenue, 92401
Telephone: 909-888-0102
Fax: 909-884-1767

For full biographical listings, see the Martindale-Hubbell Law Directory

SAN DIEGO,* San Diego Co.

GEORGE P. ANDREOS A PROFESSIONAL LAW CORPORATION (AV)

401 West "A" Street Suite 1400, 92101
Telephone: 619-233-1077
Fax: 619-236-1518

George P. Andreos

For full biographical listings, see the Martindale-Hubbell Law Directory

BELSKY & ASSOCIATES (AV)

610 West Ash Street, Suite 700, 92101
Telephone: 619-232-8300
Fax: 619-338-0066

Daniel S. Belsky

Gabriel M. Benrubi	Cynthia Brack McGrew
Lisa L. Hillan	Timothy J. Tatro
Vincent I. Iuliano	Peter A. Zamoyski

References: Centre For Health Care Medical Associates; The Doctor's Company; Grossmont Bank; Graybill Medical Group, Inc.; Kaiser Foundation HealthPlan, Inc.; Norcal Mutual Insurance Co.; Sharp Mission Park Medical Group; Sharp Rees-Stealy Medical Group; Southern California Physician Insurance Exchange; Unifirst.

For full biographical listings, see the Martindale-Hubbell Law Directory

San Diego—Continued

BOUDREAU & TRENTACOSTA, A PROFESSIONAL LAW CORPORATION (AV)

401 West "A" Street, Suite 1850, 92101-9773
Telephone: 619-238-1553
Fax: 619-238-8181
Email: AEGISLAW@AOL.COM

Steven M. Boudreau   Robert J. Trentacosta

Jon R. Williams

For full biographical listings, see the Martindale-Hubbell Law Directory

CASEY, GERRY, REED & SCHENK (AV)

110 Laurel Street, 92101
Telephone: 619-238-1811
Fax: 619-544-9232
Email: cglaw@cglaw.com

OF COUNSEL
David S. Casey   Richard F. Gerry
MEMBERS OF FIRM
David S. Casey, Jr.   T. Michael Reed
Frederick Schenk
ASSOCIATES
Robert J. Francavilla   Michael P. Montgomery
Gayle Meryl Blatt   Suzanne C. Etpison
Thomas D. Penfield   Bonnie E. Kane

Reference: San Diego National Bank.

For full biographical listings, see the Martindale-Hubbell Law Directory

DENNIS PAUL DORMAN & ASSOCIATES (AV)

1901 First Avenue, Suite 420, 92101
Telephone: 619-231-1430
Fax: 619-699-1173
Email: dorman@lawinfo.com *URL:*
http://www.lawinfo.com/law/ca/dorman
ASSOCIATE
Steven W. Siefert

For full biographical listings, see the Martindale-Hubbell Law Directory

DOUGHERTY & HILDRE (AV)

2550 Fifth Avenue, Suite 600, 92103-5624
Telephone: 619-232-9131
Telefax: 619-232-7317

William O. Dougherty   Fred M. Dudek
Donald F. Hildre   Mona H. Freedman

For full biographical listings, see the Martindale-Hubbell Law Directory

LAW OFFICES OF ROBERT S. KILBORNE IV (AV)

First National Bank Building, 401 West "A' Street, Suite 1850, 92101
Telephone: 619-237-1047
Fax: 619-237-1096

ASSOCIATE
David Arbogast
OF COUNSEL
Russell B. Wagner

For full biographical listings, see the Martindale-Hubbell Law Directory

LEVINE, STEINBERG & MILLER (AV)

550 West C Street, Suite 1810, 92101-8596
Telephone: 619-231-9449
Telecopier: 619-231-8638
MEMBERS OF FIRM
Harvey R. Levine   Craig A. Miller
Harris I. Steinberg   Jordan M. Cohen
Richard A. Huver

For full biographical listings, see the Martindale-Hubbell Law Directory

LUCE, FORWARD, HAMILTON & SCRIPPS LLP (AV)

A Partnership including Professional Corporations
600 West Broadway, Suite 2600, 92101
Telephone: 619-236-1414
Fax: 619-232-8311
URL: http://www.luce.com
La Jolla, California Office: 4275 Executive Square, Suite 800, 92037.
Telephone: 619-535-2639.
Fax: 619-453-2812.
Los Angeles, California Office: 777 South Figueroa, Suite 3600, 90017.
Telephone: 213-892-4992.
Fax: 213-892-7731.

(See Next Column)

San Francisco, California Office: 100 Bush Street, 20th Floor, 94104.
Telephone: 415-395-7900.
Fax: 415-395-7949.
New York, N.Y. Office: Citicorp Center, 153 East 53rd Street, 26th Floor, 10022.
Telephone: 212-754-1414.
Fax: 212-644-9727.
Chicago, Illinois Office: 180 North La Salle Street, Suite 1125, 60601.
Telephone: 312-641-0580.
Fax: 312-641-0380.
MEMBER OF FIRM
Gerald S. Davee

For Complete List of Firm Personnel, See General Section

For full biographical listings, see the Martindale-Hubbell Law Directory

McCLELLAN & BROWN, A PROFESSIONAL CORPORATION (AV)

1144 State Street, 92101
Telephone: 619-231-0505
Fax: 619-544-0540

Craig R. McClellan   LaMar B. Brown

For full biographical listings, see the Martindale-Hubbell Law Directory

OLINS, FOERSTER & HAYES (AV)

A Legal Liability Partnership including A Professional Corporation
2214 Second Avenue, 92101
Telephone: 619-238-1601
Fax: 619-238-1613
Email: ofh@cts.com
Santa Ana, California Office: 1314 West Fifth Street, Suite C, 92703.
Telephone: 714-836-9777.
Fax: 714-954-1156.
Riverside, California Office: 4361 Latham Street, Suite 240, 92501.
Telephone: 909-683-2485.
Fax: 909-683-1064.
MEMBERS OF FIRM
Douglas F. Olins   Barrett J. Foerster (A P.C.)
Dennis J. Hayes
ASSOCIATES
Laura H. Miller   Karen L. Cote
John C. Zucconi   (Resident, Riverside Office)
Barbara J. Ginsberg
  (Resident, Santa Ana Office)

For full biographical listings, see the Martindale-Hubbell Law Directory

*SAN FRANCISCO,** San Francisco Co.

BAILEY & KORNBLUM (AV)

1388 Sutter Street, Suite 820, 94109
Telephone: 415-440-7800
Fax: 415-440-7898

Don E. Bailey

For full biographical listings, see the Martindale-Hubbell Law Directory

STANLEY J. BELL A PROFESSIONAL CORPORATION (AV)

18th Floor, 505 Sansome Street, 94111
Telephone: 415-391-3700
San Diego, California Office: Suite 1200, 401 West A Street.
Telephone: 619-696-9445.
San Jose, California Office: Suite 830, 1735 Technology Drive.
Telephone: 408-295-1678.

Stanley J. Bell

Robert S. Arns (A Professional   Steven J. Bell
  Corporation)   John C. Dunn
Samuel Boyd McCullagh   M. Steven Parker
Sally G. Bechthold   Kirk Anthony Musacchio
Thomas K. Caselli   J. Kevin Morrison
Morgan C. Smith

For full biographical listings, see the Martindale-Hubbell Law Directory

BIANCO & MURPHY (AV)

44 Montgomery Street, Suite 4010, 94104
Telephone: 415-362-3344
Telecopier: 415-986-5271
Email: LAWRLB@AOL.COM
MEMBERS OF FIRM
Robert L. Bianco   Stephen M. Murphy
ASSOCIATES
Joseph P. Meyers   Gregory O. Bianco
Christopher M. Windle

For full biographical listings, see the Martindale-Hubbell Law Directory

San Francisco—Continued

BOKELMAN & BENJAMIN, A PROFESSIONAL LAW CORPORATION (AV)

Two Embarcadero Center Suite 1050, 94111-3823
Telephone: 415-398-3660
Facsimile: 415-788-0161

Robert U. Bokelman　　　　　　Anglia Benjamin

For full biographical listings, see the Martindale-Hubbell Law Directory

CARTWRIGHT & ALEXANDER, INC. (AV)

222 Front St., 5th Fl., 94111-4403
Telephone: 415-433-0440
Telecopier: 415-391-5845

Robert E. Cartwright　　　　Robert E. Cartwright, Jr.
(1925-1988)　　　　　　　　Mary E. Alexander

For full biographical listings, see the Martindale-Hubbell Law Directory

ANTHONY P. DAVID A PROFESSIONAL CORPORATION (AV)

One Montgomery Street, 15th Floor, 94104
Telephone: 415-981-0166
Fax: 415-433-3883

Anthony P. David

For full biographical listings, see the Martindale-Hubbell Law Directory

JOHN GARDENAL A PROFESSIONAL CORPORATION (AV)

Suite 800 Cathedral Hill Office Building, 1255 Post Street, 94109
Telephone: 415-771-2700
FAX: 415-771-2072

John Gardenal

For full biographical listings, see the Martindale-Hubbell Law Directory

J. KENNETH LYNCH (AV)

Citicorp Center, One Sansome, Suite 2100, 94104
Telephone: 415-951-4616
FAX: 415-951-4653

MOLLIGAN, COX & MOYER, A PROFESSIONAL CORPORATION (AV)

703 Market Street, Suite 1800, 94103
Telephone: 415-543-9464
Fax: 415-777-1828
Email: mocoxmoy@aol.com

Ingemar E. Hoberg (1903-1971)　　Peter N. Molligan
John H. Finger (1913-1991)　　　　Stephen T. Cox
Phillip E. Brown (Retired)　　　　David W. Moyer

John C. Hentschel
OF COUNSEL
Kenneth W. Rosenthal　　　　Barbara A. Zuras

For full biographical listings, see the Martindale-Hubbell Law Directory

MOORE & BROWNING (AV)

100 Bush Street, Suite 225, 94104
Telephone: 415-956-6500
Fax: 415-956-6580

Michael B. Moore　　　　　Charles A. Browning
LEGAL SUPPORT PERSONNEL
Pat Medina (Paralegal)

For full biographical listings, see the Martindale-Hubbell Law Directory

ROUDA, FEDER & TIETJEN (AV)

44 Montgomery, Suite 4000, 94104
Telephone: 415-398-5398
Fax: 415-398-8169

Ronald H. Rouda　　　　　John M. Feder
Timothy G. Tietjen

Mark J. Zanobini
LEGAL SUPPORT PERSONNEL
Cheryl Acree (Paralegal)

For full biographical listings, see the Martindale-Hubbell Law Directory

TEHIN + PARTNERS, A PROFESSIONAL CORPORATION (AV)

Bank of America Center, 555 California Street, 33rd Floor, 94104-1609
Telephone: 415-951-8800
Fax: 415-951-8808

Nikolai Tehin (Professional　　Reilly Atkinson, IV
Corporation)　　　　　　　Michael E. Brown
Pamela J. Stevens　　　　　Marcia A. Pollioni

For full biographical listings, see the Martindale-Hubbell Law Directory

WALKER & DURHAM (AV)

50 Francisco Street, Suite 160, 94133
Telephone: 415-986-3339
Fax: 415-986-1618

Walter H. Walker, III　　　　Dane J. Durham
ASSOCIATE
Lara L. Myers

For full biographical listings, see the Martindale-Hubbell Law Directory

WALKUP, MELODIA, KELLY & ECHEVERRIA, A PROFESSIONAL CORPORATION (AV)

30th Floor, 650 California Street, 94108
Telephone: 415-981-7210
Fax: 415-391-6965

Paul V. Melodia　　　　　　Michael A. Kelly
Daniel J. Kelly　　　　　　Kevin L. Domecus
John Echeverria　　　　　　Jeffrey P. Holl
Ronald H. Wecht　　　　　　Daniel Dell'Osso
Richard H. Schoenberger

Cynthia F. Newton　　　　　Michael J. Recupero
Erik Brunkal　　　　　　　Kenneth H. Facter
OF COUNSEL
John D. Link　　　　　　　Wesley Sokolosky

Reference: Bank of California, San Francisco Main Office, 400 California Street, San Francisco, Calif. 94104.

For full biographical listings, see the Martindale-Hubbell Law Directory

WARTNICK, CHABER, HAROWITZ, SMITH & TIGERMAN, A PROFESSIONAL CORPORATION (AV)

101 California Street, Suite 2200, 94111-5802
Telephone: 415-986-5566
Fax: 415-986-5896

Harry F. Wartnick　　　　　Steven M. Harowitz
Madelyn J. Chaber　　　　　Audrey A. Smith
Stephen M. Tigerman

Niromi L. Wijewantha　　　　Christopher C. Lamerdin
Phillip Scott Chan　　　　　Garry Cohen
Brenda D. Posada　　　　　Cheryl L. White
Gregory M. Sheffer

For full biographical listings, see the Martindale-Hubbell Law Directory

*SAN JOSE,** Santa Clara Co.

THE ALEXANDER LAW FIRM (AV)

55 South Market Street, Suite 1080, 95113
Telephone: 408-289-1776
Fax: 408-287-1776
Email: access@alexanderlaw.com *URL:* http://www.alexanderlaw.com/
Cincinnati, Ohio Office: The Alexander Law Firm, 1300 Mercantile Library Building, 414 Walnut Street.
Telephone: 513-723-1776.
Fax: 513-421-1776.

Richard Alexander
ASSOCIATES
Michael T. Alexander (Resident,　　Michael McShane
Cincinnati, Ohio Office)　　　　Amanda Hawes
Jonathan D. Pendleton　　　　Ann Saponara
Tyler A. Shaw
OF COUNSEL
William M. Audet

For full biographical listings, see the Martindale-Hubbell Law Directory

THE BOCCARDO LAW FIRM (AV)

Eleventh Floor, 111 West St. John Street, 95115-0001
Telephone: 408-298-5678
Fax: 408-298-7503

(See Next Column)

THE BOCCARDO LAW FIRM—*Continued*

MEMBERS OF FIRM

James F. Boccardo   John C. Stein
John W. McDonald   Richard L. Bowers
Brian N. Lawther   Russell L. Moore, Jr.

ASSOCIATES

Stephen Foster   Victor F. Stefan
David P. Moyles   Robert W. Thayer
Byron C. Foster   Richard Gregg

For full biographical listings, see the Martindale-Hubbell Law Directory

BOHN, BENNION & NILAND (AV)

Fairmont Plaza, 50 West San Fernando Street Suite 1020, 95113
Telephone: 408-279-4222
Fax: 408-295-2222

MEMBERS OF FIRM

Robert H. Bohn   David J. Bennion
Edward L. Niland

ASSOCIATE

Robert H. Bohn, Jr.

OF COUNSEL

Jeffrey W. Rickard

For full biographical listings, see the Martindale-Hubbell Law Directory

JAN CHAMPION (AV)

Ten Almaden Boulevard, Tenth Floor, 95113-2233
Telephone: 408-286-5550
Fax: 408-270-6777

For full biographical listings, see the Martindale-Hubbell Law Directory

COLLINS & SCHLOTHAUER (AV)

An Association of Attorneys including a Professional Corporation
60 South Market Street, Suite 1100, 95113-2369
Telephone: 408-298-5161
Fax: 408-297-5766
Affiliated Los Angeles, California Office: Schlothauer, Collins & Macaluso,
11661 San Vicente Boulevard, Suite 303.
Telephone: 310-820-8606.
Fax: 310-820-7057.

Mark Scott Collins (Inc.)   Linda L. Duiven
David N. Poll   Jovita Prestoza

OF COUNSEL

Thomas L. Schlothauer   Todd E. Macaluso

Representative Clients: Unigard Insurance; Farmers Insurance Co.; Fire Insurance Exchange; National American Insurance Co.; ABAG (Association of Bay Area Governmental Entities).

For full biographical listings, see the Martindale-Hubbell Law Directory

HAWKINS, BLICK & FITZPATRICK (AV)

96 North Third Street, Suite 300, 95112
Telephone: 408-280-7111
Fax: 408-292-7868
Palo Alto, California Office: 418 Florence Street.
Telephone: 415-321-5656.
Fax: 415-326-9636.

MEMBERS OF FIRM

Charles F. Hawkins   Stephen L. Blick
Michael J. Fitzpatrick

ASSOCIATE

Mark F. Bernal

For full biographical listings, see the Martindale-Hubbell Law Directory

LICCARDO, ROSSI, STURGES & McNEIL, A PROFESSIONAL LAW CORPORATION (AV)

1960 The Alameda, Suite 200, 95126
Telephone: 408-244-4570
Fax: 408-244-3294
Oakland, California Office: 1999 Harrison, Suite 1300.
Telephone: 415-834-2206.
Fax: 415-832-4432.

Salvador A. Liccardo   Craig Needham
Ronald R. Rossi   Gregory D. Hull
Robert S. Sturges   Martha Louise Caron
R. Donald McNeil   (Resident, Oakland Office)
David M. Hamerslough   Cynthia L. Chase
Susan R. Reischl   Laura Liccardo

(See Next Column)

Robert C. Colyar   Paul Salvatore Liccardo
Jeffery Lopez   Anne Jones
Wes Wagnon   Samuel A. Chuck
Richard B. Gullen   Laura M. Chiappe
Deborah T. Bjonerud   Daniel A. Hershkowitz
 (Resident, Oakland Office)   (Resident, Oakland Office)

For full biographical listings, see the Martindale-Hubbell Law Directory

DAVID MALNICK A PROFESSIONAL CORPORATION (AV)

10 Almaden Boulevard Tenth Floor, 95113-2233
Telephone: 408-292-5900
Fax: 408-292-5995

David E. Malnick

For full biographical listings, see the Martindale-Hubbell Law Directory

McMANIS, FAULKNER & MORGAN (AV)

160 West Santa Clara Street, 10th Floor, 95113
Telephone: 408-279-8700
Fax: 408-279-3244; 408-279-0494
Email: mfm@mfmlaw.com

MEMBERS OF FIRM

James McManis   William Faulkner
Donelle Morgan

ASSOCIATES

Nora Rousso   Michael Reedy
Lisa Herrick   Douglas Watanabe
Kelly McHaffie

For full biographical listings, see the Martindale-Hubbell Law Directory

SAUCEDO & CORSIGLIA, A LAW CORPORATION (AV)

50 West San Fernando Street, Suite 425, 95113
Telephone: 408-289-1417
Fax: 408-289-8127

Norman W. Saucedo   Bradley M. Corsiglia

For full biographical listings, see the Martindale-Hubbell Law Directory

SHEA & SHEA, A PROFESSIONAL LAW CORPORATION (AV)

The James Square Building, 255 North Market Street, Suite 190, 95110
Telephone: 408-292-2434
Fax: 408-292-1264

Michael M. Shea   Michael M. Shea, Jr.

Beth C. Watkins

For full biographical listings, see the Martindale-Hubbell Law Directory

SAN MARINO, Los Angeles Co.

JACK K. CONWAY (AV)

2460 Huntington Drive, 91108-2643
Telephone: 818-285-4333
Fax: 818-285-1526

For full biographical listings, see the Martindale-Hubbell Law Directory

SAN RAFAEL, Marin Co.

RAGGHIANTI • FREITAS • MONTOBBIO • WALLACE LLP (AV)

874 Fourth Street, Suite D, 94901
Telephone: 415-453-9433
Fax: 415-453-8269

Gary T. Ragghianti   J. Randolph Wallace
David P. Freitas   Patrick M. Macias
J. Mark Montobbio   Robert F. Epstein
John Ralph Thomas

For full biographical listings, see the Martindale-Hubbell Law Directory

SANTA ANA, Orange Co.

LAW OFFICES OF WYLIE A. AITKEN A LAW CORPORATION (AV)

3 Imperial Promenade, Suite 800, P.O. Box 2555, 92707-0555
Telephone: 714-434-1424
Fax: 714-434-3600

Wylie A. Aitken

David P. Crandall   Darren O'Leary Aitken
Richard A. Cohn   Annee M. Della Donna

Reference: Bank of America/Costa Mesa.

For full biographical listings, see the Martindale-Hubbell Law Directory

Santa Ana—Continued

GARRETT & JENSEN (AV)

433 Civic Center Drive, West, P.O. Box 22002, 92702-2002
Telephone: 714-550-0100
Fax: 714-550-0471
Riverside, California Office: 3403 10th Street, Suite 700.
Telephone: 909-781-0222.

MEMBERS OF FIRM

Boyd F. Jensen, II
Betty Fracisco

Mark S. Armijo
Jennifer Malone

Douglas M. Borthwick

OF COUNSEL

Kenneth R. Garrett

Representative Clients: Allstate Insurance Co.; Automobile Club of Southern California; Fireman's Fund American Insurance Co.; Government Employees Insurance Co.

For full biographical listings, see the Martindale-Hubbell Law Directory

HAIGHT, BROWN & BONESTEEL (AV)

A Partnership including Professional Corporations
Suite 900, 5 Hutton Centre Drive, 92707
Telephone: 714-754-1100
Telecopier: 714-754-0826
Santa Monica, California Office: 1620 26th Street, Suite 4000 North, P.O. Box 680.
Telephone: 310-449-6000.
Telecopier: 310-829-5117.
Telex: 705837.
Riverside, California Office: 3750 University Avenue, Suite 650.
Telephone: 909-341-8300.
Fax: 909-341-8309.
San Francisco, California Office: 20 Sansome Street, Suite 300.
Telephone: 415-986-7700.
Fax: 415-986-6954.

RESIDENT MEMBERS

Bruce L. Cleeland

Jay T. Thompson

ASSOCIATES

Laura M. Knox (Resident)

Jeffrey S. Gerardo (Resident)

Counsel for: Orange County: Aetna Casualty and Surety Co.; Zurich-American Insurance Cos.; Industrial Indemnity Co.; Professional Liability Claims Managers; Maryland Casualty Insurance Co.; Royal Insurance Company of America.

For Complete List of Firm Personnel, See General Section

For full biographical listings, see the Martindale-Hubbell Law Directory

HORTON BARBARO & REILLY (AV)

A Partnership including Professional Corporations
Second Floor, 200 North Main Street, 92701
Telephone: 714-835-2122
Fax: 714-973-4892
Email: HBR@Hortonetal.com URL: http://www.Hortonetal.com

MEMBERS OF FIRM

Jay Cordell Horton (A Professional Corporation)
Frank P. Barbaro (A Professional Corporation)
Ned P. Reilly (A Professional Corporation)

Geoffrey S. Gray
John R. Hanna
William O. Humphreys
Karen L. Karavatos
John E. O'Brien, Jr.

ASSOCIATES

Malena R. LeClair
Robert J. Younger

Timothy V. Kassouni
Richard E. Donahoo

For full biographical listings, see the Martindale-Hubbell Law Directory

HUNT, COLAW & ADAMS, INC. (AV)

615 Civic Center Drive West, Suite 300, 92701
Telephone: 714-558-9000
Fax: 714-558-0152

Vernon W. Hunt, Jr.

Thierry Patrick Colaw

John C. Adams, III

Reference: Wells Fargo Bank.

For full biographical listings, see the Martindale-Hubbell Law Directory

SANTA BARBARA,* Santa Barbara Co.

ANGLE, CARLSON, GOLDRICK & ROBERTS (AV)

A Partnership including a Professional Corporation
200 East Carrillo Street, Suite 310, 93101
Telephone: 805-963-7400
Fax: 805-963-7610

(See Next Column)

Robert O. Angle
Arthur W. Carlson (A P.C.)

Miles T. Goldrick
Paul A. Roberts

OF COUNSEL

Georgia C. McDermott

For full biographical listings, see the Martindale-Hubbell Law Directory

KINKLE, RODIGER AND SPRIGGS, PROFESSIONAL CORPORATION (AV)

125 East De La Guerra Street, 93101-2239
Telephone: 805-966-4700
Fax: 805-966-4120
Los Angeles, California Office: 600 North Grand Avenue.
Telephone: 213-629-1261.
Fax: 213-629-8382.
Santa Ana, California Office: 837 North Ross Street.
Telephone: 714-835-9011.
Fax: 714-667-7806.
Riverside, California Office: 3333 14th Street.
Telephone: 909-683-2410; 800-235-2039.
Fax: 909-683-7759.
San Diego, California Office: Suite 900 Driver Insurance Center, 1620 Fifth Avenue, P.O. Box 127900.
Telephone: 619-233-4566.
Fax: 619-233-8554.

John V. Hager
(Managing Attorney)
Edwin C. Mann

Joy L. Lim
Jeffery D. Lim
Chad M. Slack

Donna D. Geck

For full biographical listings, see the Martindale-Hubbell Law Directory

SANTA CRUZ,* Santa Cruz Co.

DUNLAP & BURDICK, A PROFESSIONAL LAW CORPORATION (AV)

121 Jewell Street, 95060
Telephone: 408-426-7040
Fax: 408-426-1095

Michael E. Dunlap

Paul P. Burdick

Garth V. Smith

For full biographical listings, see the Martindale-Hubbell Law Directory

SANTA MONICA, Los Angeles Co.

FOGEL, FELDMAN, OSTROV, RINGLER & KLEVENS, A LAW CORPORATION (AV)

1620 26th Street, Suite 100 South, 90404-4040
Telephone: 310-453-6711
Fax: 310-828-2191

Daniel Fogel (1923-1991)
Lester G. Ostrov
Larry R. Feldman

Joel N. Klevens
Robert M. Turner
Jerome L. Ringler

Richard L. Rosett

Stephen D. Rothschild
Leighanne Lake
Thomas H. Peters

Toni Martinson
David Bricker
Mark S. Eisenberg

OF COUNSEL

Carol S. May

Reference: Republic Bank of California, Beverly Hills, California.

For full biographical listings, see the Martindale-Hubbell Law Directory

GREENE, BROILLET, TAYLOR, WHEELER & PANISH (AV)

100 Wilshire Boulevard, 21st Floor, P.O. Box 2131, 90407-2131
Telephone: 310-576-1200

Bruce A. Broillet
Browne Greene

John C. Taylor
Timothy J. Wheeler

Brian J. Panish

Frank J. O'Kane Jr.
Mark T. Quigley
Christine D. Spagnoli

Scott H. Carr
Geoffrey S. Wells
Adam K. Shea

For full biographical listings, see the Martindale-Hubbell Law Directory

Santa Monica—Continued

HAIGHT, BROWN & BONESTEEL (AV)

A Partnership including Professional Corporations
1620 26th Street, Suite 4000 North, P.O. Box 680, 90404
Telephone: 310-449-6000
Telecopier: 310-829-5117
Telex: 705837
Santa Ana, California Office: Suite 900, 5 Hutton Centre Drive.
Telephone: 714-754-1100.
Telecopier: 714-754-0826.
Riverside, California Office: 3750 University Avenue, Suite 650.
Telephone: 909-341-8300.
Fax: 909-341-8309.
San Francisco, California Office: 201 Sansome Street, Suite 300.
Telephone: 415-986-7700.
Fax: 415-986-6954.

MEMBERS OF FIRM

Peter Q. Ezzell (A Professional Corporation)	Kevin R. Crisp
William G. Baumgaertner (A Professional Corporation)	Lee Marshall
	Steven E. Moyer
	Kenneth G. Anderson
Peter A. Dubrawski	William O. Martin, Jr.
J. R. Seashore	David C. McGovern

ASSOCIATES

Alicia E. Taylor	Michael J. Sipos
S. Christian Stouder	Michael H. Gottschlich

For Complete List of Firm Personnel, See General Section

For full biographical listings, see the Martindale-Hubbell Law Directory

---

SANTA ROSA,* Sonoma Co.

BELDEN, ABBEY, WEITZENBERG & KELLY, A PROFESSIONAL CORPORATION (AV)

1105 North Dutton Avenue, P.O. Box 1566, 95402
Telephone: 707-542-5050
Telecopier: 707-542-2589

W. Barton Weitzenberg　　　　Wayne R. Wolski

Representative Clients: Exchange Bank of Santa Rosa; Westamerica Bank; North Bay Title Co.; Northwestern Title Security Co.; Geyser Peak Winery; Santa Rosa City School District; Sonoma National Bank; Arrowood Vineyards & Winery; Arthur & DeVincenzi Concrete; Friedman Bros. Hardware, Inc.

For Complete List of Firm Personnel, See General Section

For full biographical listings, see the Martindale-Hubbell Law Directory

---

SAUSALITO, Marin Co.

WILLIAM C. GORDON A PROFESSIONAL CORPORATION (AV)

116 Caledonia Street, 94965
Telephone: 415-331-0200
Fax: 415-331-0252
Email: Williecg@aol.com

William C. Gordon

For full biographical listings, see the Martindale-Hubbell Law Directory

---

TORRANCE, Los Angeles Co.

AGNEW & BRUSAVICH (AV)

20355 Hawthorne Boulevard, 90503
Telephone: 310-793-1400
Facsimile: 310-793-1499
Email: agnewbru@ix.netcom.com

Gerald E. Agnew, Jr.　　　　Bruce M. Brusavich
ASSOCIATES
Susan E. Hargrove　　　　Christopher A. Kall
　　　　　Mark J. Peacock

For full biographical listings, see the Martindale-Hubbell Law Directory

---

VENTURA,* Ventura Co.

LAW OFFICES OF FREDERICK H. BYSSHE, JR. (AV)

10 South California Street, 93001
Telephone: 805-648-3224
Fax: 805-653-0267

Terence Geoghegan

For full biographical listings, see the Martindale-Hubbell Law Directory

---

ELLISON, HINKLE & BAYER, A PROFESSIONAL LAW CORPORATION (AV)

5550 Telegraph Road, P.O. Box 6130, 93006
Telephone: 805-656-4223
Fax: 805-656-4924

(See Next Column)

David R. Ellison　　　　Thomas L. Hinkle
　　Robert J. Bayer

　　　Jeffrey D. Johnsen

For full biographical listings, see the Martindale-Hubbell Law Directory

TAYLOR McCORD, A LAW CORPORATION (AV)

721 East Main Street, P.O. Box 1477, 93002
Telephone: 805-648-4700
Fax: 805-653-6124

Richard L. Taylor　　　　Robert L. McCord, Jr.
　　　David L. Praver

Patrick Cherry　　　　　Susan D. Siple
　　Rebbecca F. Calderwood
LEGAL SUPPORT PERSONNEL
PARALEGALS
Stephanie Gibson　　　　　Adele Rubino
　　　Diane Lovato

For full biographical listings, see the Martindale-Hubbell Law Directory

WHIPPLE AND VIELE, A PROFESSIONAL LAW CORPORATION (AV)

60 South California Street, 93001
Telephone: 805-643-8658; 643-8422
Fax: 805-653-6079

Edward A. Whipple

References: Wells Fargo Bank; American Commercial Bank.

For full biographical listings, see the Martindale-Hubbell Law Directory

---

WALNUT CREEK, Contra Costa Co.

HINTON & ALFERT, A PROFESSIONAL CORPORATION (AV)

Suite 600, 1646 North California Boulevard, 94596-4113
Telephone: 510-932-6006
Fax: 510-932-3412

Peter J. Hinton　　　　　Peter W. Alfert
　　　Michael P. Clark

Scott H. Z. Sumner　　　　Nancy A. Beninati

For full biographical listings, see the Martindale-Hubbell Law Directory

---

COLORADO

ASPEN,* Pitkin Co.

FREEMAN & JENNER, P.C. (AV⊤)

215 South Monarch Street, Suite 202, 81611
Telephone: 970-925-3400
FAX: 970-925-4043
Bethesda, Maryland Office: 3 Bethesda Metro Center, Suite 1410.
Telephone: 301-907-7747.
FAX: 301-907-9877.
Washington, D.C. Office: 1000 16th Street, N.W., Suite 300.
Telephone: 301-907-7747.

Martin H. Freeman

BOULDER,* Boulder Co.

COOK & LEE, P.C. (AV)

5390 Manhattan Circle, 2nd Floor, 80303
Telephone: 303-543-1000
Fax: 303-543-8582

Stephen H. Cook　　　　　Larry D. Lee

Deborah R. Kirschman

For full biographical listings, see the Martindale-Hubbell Law Directory

---

FRENCH & STONE, P.C. (AV)

720 Pearl Street, 80302
Telephone: 303-449-3891
Fax: 303-449-3992

Joseph C. French　　　　　David M. Haynes
　　　Mark M. Haynes

References: Bank One of Boulder; Boulder; Bank of Boulder.

For full biographical listings, see the Martindale-Hubbell Law Directory

Boulder—Continued

McCormick and Christoph, P.C. (AV)

1406 Pearl Street, Suite 200, 80302-5307
Telephone: 303-443-2281
Fax: 303-443-2862

G. Paul McCormick   James R. Christoph

For full biographical listings, see the Martindale-Hubbell Law Directory

Miller and Harrison, LLC (AV)

2305 Broadway, 80304-4106
Telephone: 303-449-2830
Fax: 303-449-2198

MEMBERS OF FIRM
Robert Bruce Miller   David B. Harrison
ASSOCIATE
Joan Clifford
OF COUNSEL
Steven Taffet

Reference: Norwest Bank.

For full biographical listings, see the Martindale-Hubbell Law Directory

Purvis, Gray, Schuetze & Gordon (AV)

The Exeter Building, Suite 501, 1050 Walnut Street, 80302
Telephone: 303-442-3366
Fax: 303-440-3688
Denver, Colorado Office: 303 East 17th Avenue, Suite 700.
Telephone: 303-860-1888.

MEMBERS OF FIRM
William R. Gray   Robert A. Schuetze
John A. Purvis   Glen F. Gordon

For full biographical listings, see the Martindale-Hubbell Law Directory

Peter Schild (AV)

1720 14th Street, #100, 80302
Telephone: 303-444-8720
Fax: 303-444-8720
Mailing Address: 259 E. Kelly Road, Boulder, CO, 80302

For full biographical listings, see the Martindale-Hubbell Law Directory

Williams & Trine, P.C. (AV)

1435 Arapahoe Avenue, 80302-6390
Telephone: 303-442-0173
Fax: 303-443-7677

William A. Trine   J. Conard Metcalf
Joel H. Greenstein (1933-1984)   Mari C. Bush
              Michael A. Patrick
OF COUNSEL
Charles E. Williams

Reference: Norwest Bank of Boulder.

For full biographical listings, see the Martindale-Hubbell Law Directory

BROOMFIELD, Boulder Co.

Schaden, Katzman & Lampert (AV)

11870 Airport Way, 80021
Telephone: 303-465-3663
Facsimile: 303-465-3884
Bloomfield Hills, Michigan Office: Schaden, Katzman & Lampert, 33 Bloomfield Hills Parkway, Suite 145, 48304.
Telephone: 810-258-4800.
Fax: 810-258-9212.
Ft. Lauderdale, Florida Office: 1700 E. Las Olas Boulevard, Suite 7, 33301-2408.
Telephone: 954-522-5154.
Facsimile: 954-522-5184.

Richard F. Schaden
ASSOCIATE
Kathleen M. Schaden

For full biographical listings, see the Martindale-Hubbell Law Directory

COLORADO SPRINGS,* El Paso Co.

Beltz, Edwards & Sabo, L.L.P. (AV)

729 South Cascade, 80903
Telephone: 719-473-4444; 719-634-6620
Fax: 719-444-0186

W. Thomas Beltz   Daniel P. Edwards
              John W. Sabo, III

(See Next Column)

Daniel A. West
Representative Clients: A.M.I. Industries, Inc.; Analytical Surveys, Inc.; A.C. Israel Enterprises, Inc.; Boddington Lumber Co., Inc.; Cardiovascular Surgeons of Colorado Springs, P.C.; Colorado Springs Radiologists, P.C.; Digital, Inc.; Music Semi-Conductors, Inc.; Schlage Lock Co.; Texas Instruments.

For full biographical listings, see the Martindale-Hubbell Law Directory

Gaddis, Kin & Herd, P.C. (AV)

118 South Wahsatch, Suite 100, 80903
Telephone: 719-471-3848
Fax: 719-471-0317

Larry R. Gaddis   Thomas J. Herd
James W. Kin   David L. Quicksall (1950-1991)
OF COUNSEL
James B. Turner

Reference: Norwest Bank of Colorado Springs.

For full biographical listings, see the Martindale-Hubbell Law Directory

Melat, Pressman, Ezell & Higbie (AV)

711 South Tejon Street, 80903-4041
Telephone: 719-475-0304
Fax: 719-475-0242

MEMBERS OF FIRM
Justin R. Melat   E. Steven Ezell
Glenn S. Pressman   Alanson Higbie
ASSOCIATE
Rebecca A. Lorenz
OF COUNSEL
Bernard R. Baker

References: Colorado Springs National Bank; Colorado Bank-Exchange.

For full biographical listings, see the Martindale-Hubbell Law Directory

The Tegtmeier Law Firm, P.C. (AV)

518 North Nevada, 80903
Telephone: 719-473-5757
Telefax: 719-473-6767

Richard L. Tegtmeier

Bradley S. Taylor

Reference: Norwest Bank of Colorado Springs and State Bank & Trust.

For full biographical listings, see the Martindale-Hubbell Law Directory

The Wills Law Firm (AV)

Holly Sugar Building, 2 North Cascade Avenue, Suite 1000, 80903-1651
Telephone: 719-633-8500
Telecopier: 719-471-7750

MEMBERS OF FIRM
Lee R. Wills   Wm. Andrew Wills, II

For full biographical listings, see the Martindale-Hubbell Law Directory

DENVER,* Denver Co.

Bragg & Baker, P.C. (AV)

Dominion Plaza, North Tower, Suite 1700N, 600 17th Street, 80202
Telephone: 303-571-4030
Fax: 303-893-9146

Douglas E. Bragg   John T. Baker

Christopher W. Jeffress
OF COUNSEL
John W. Hornbeck

For full biographical listings, see the Martindale-Hubbell Law Directory

Chalat • Justino, P.C. (AV)

1900 Grant Street, Suite 1050, 80203
Telephone: 303-861-1042
Toll Free in Colorado: 800-221-5526
Facsimile: 303-861-0506
Email: Jchalat@aol.com *URL:* http://www.chalat-justino.com

James H. Chalat   Stephen A. Justino
              Linda J. Chalat

Elliott L. Schoen

For full biographical listings, see the Martindale-Hubbell Law Directory

Denver—Continued

EWING & EWING, P.C. (AV)

8400 East Prentice Avenue, Suite 1115 (Englewood), 80111
Telephone: 303-771-3300
Fax: 303-793-3321

Robert Craig Ewing　　　　　　　　Mary Ewing

Julie A. Trent

For full biographical listings, see the Martindale-Hubbell Law Directory

LEVENTHAL AND BOGUE, P.C. (AV)

950 South Cherry Street, Suite 600, 80222
Telephone: 303-759-9945
Fax: 303-759-9692
Email: LEVENBOG@AOL.COM

Jim Leventhal　　　　　　　　Natalie Brown
Jeffrey A. Bogue　　　　　　　Victoria J. Koury
Bruce J. Kaye　　　　　　　　Kelly P. Roberts
　　　　　　Grant Marylander

Reference: Southwest State Bank.

For full biographical listings, see the Martindale-Hubbell Law Directory

MYERS, BRADLEY AND DEVITT, P.C. (AV)

Suite 420, 4704 Harlan Street, 80212
Telephone: 303-433-8527
Fax: 303-433-8219

Frederick J. Myers　　　　　　Jerald J. Devitt
Jon T. Bradley　　　　　　　　Randall C. Arp
　　　　　OF COUNSEL
　　　　　Kent E. Hanson

Reference: Bank One Lakeside Banking Center.

For full biographical listings, see the Martindale-Hubbell Law Directory

PURVIS, GRAY, SCHUETZE & GORDON (AV)

303 East 17th Avenue, Suite 700, 80203
Telephone: 303-860-1888
Boulder, Colorado Office: The Exeter Building, Suite 501, 1050 Walnut Street.
Telephone: 303-442-3366.
Fax: 303-440-3688.

MEMBERS OF FIRM
William R. Gray　　　　　　Robert A. Schuetze
John A. Purvis　　　　　　　Glen F. Gordon

For full biographical listings, see the Martindale-Hubbell Law Directory

RICHMAN & HENSEN, P.C. (AV)

Mellon Financial Center, Suite 1717, 1775 Sherman Street, 80203
Telephone: 303-830-1717
Facsimile: 303-830-1746

Alan E. Richman　　　　　　Stephen J. Hensen

Steven Robert Kabler

For full biographical listings, see the Martindale-Hubbell Law Directory

SPRINGER & STEINBERG, A PROFESSIONAL CORPORATION (AV)

Suite 1500, 1600 Broadway, 80202
Telephone: 303-861-2800
Fax: 303-832-7116

Jeffrey A. Springer　　　　　　Susan Fuller
Harvey A. Steinberg　　　　　　Amy Mandel Springer

Reference: Norwest Bank of Denver.

For full biographical listings, see the Martindale-Hubbell Law Directory

ENGLEWOOD, Arapahoe Co.

BRANNEY, HILLYARD AND BARNHART, L.L.P. (AV)

First Interstate Center, The Tenth Floor, 3333 South Bannock Street, 80110
Telephone: 303-761-5600
Fax: 303-761-9117

Joseph J. Branney　　　　　　W. Randolph Barnhart
Neil A. Hillyard　　　　　　　Michael J. Turner
　　　　　Angela L. Ekker

Reference: Key Bank.

For full biographical listings, see the Martindale-Hubbell Law Directory

KING ● PETERSON ● BROWN, LLC (AV)

Suite 1040 8400 East Prentice Avenue, P.O. Box 256, 80111
Telephone: 303-793-3400
Facsimile: 303-793-3678
Email: CEK5473@aol.com
Morrison, Colorado Office: 19423 North Turkey Creek Road, Suite G, 80465.
Telephone: 303-697-0575.
Facsimile: 303-697-5259.

Charles E. King　　　　　　Richard G. Peterson
　　　　　James L. Brown

Michael W. Reagor　　　　　Jeffrey N. Cole

For full biographical listings, see the Martindale-Hubbell Law Directory

SALMON, GODSMAN & NICHOLSON, PROFESSIONAL CORPORATION (AV)

Salmon Law Building, (I-25 at East Belleview) 7450 East Progress Place, 80111
Telephone: 303-771-9900
Toll Free in Colorado: 1-800-547-9055
Fax: 303-773-6843
Breckenridge, Colorado Office: Briar Rose House, 213 Briar Rose Lane.
Telephone: 1-800-547-9055

John G. Salmon　　　　　　William P. Godsman
　　　　　P. Randolph Nicholson

Francine R. Salazar　　　　　Penelope Clor
　　　　　OF COUNSEL
　　　　　Joseph M. Epstein

For full biographical listings, see the Martindale-Hubbell Law Directory

THOMAS J. TOMAZIN, P.C. (AV)

Suite 200, 5655 South Yosemite, 80111
Telephone: 303-771-1900
FAX: 303-793-0923

Thomas J. Tomazin

Representative Clients: Sheridan, Inc. (Leasing Division); Sovran Leasing; The Leasing Group; Contract Design Services, Inc.; American Natural Gas Corp.; Sonex Enterprises, Inc.; Am West Energy, Inc.; Mountain States Asphalt Paving, Inc.
Reference: Key Bank.

For full biographical listings, see the Martindale-Hubbell Law Directory

LAKEWOOD, Jefferson Co.

POLIDORI, GEROME, FRANKLIN AND JACOBSON, L.L.C. (AV)

Suite 300, 550 South Wadsworth Boulevard, 80226
Telephone: 303-936-3300
Fax: 303-936-0125

Gary L. Polidori　　　　　　Dennis J. Jacobson

For full biographical listings, see the Martindale-Hubbell Law Directory

LAMAR,* Prowers Co.

JOHN GEHLHAUSEN, P.C. (AV)

200 South Fifth Street, Drawer 1079, 81052
Telephone: 719-336-9071
Fax: Available Upon Request

John Gehlhausen

Darla Scranton Specht

For full biographical listings, see the Martindale-Hubbell Law Directory

STEAMBOAT SPRINGS,* Routt Co.

OLIPHANT, HAMMOND & O'HARA (AV)

A Law Partnership of Professional Corporations
919 Oak Street, P.O. Box 774425, 80477
Telephone: 970-879-6060
Fax: 970-879-5199

MEMBERS OF FIRM
James B. F. Oliphant, P.C.　　　Kristopher L. Hammond, P.C.
　　　Michael A. O'Hara, III, P.C.
　　　　　ASSOCIATE
Christopher D. Atwell　(Not admitted in CO)

For full biographical listings, see the Martindale-Hubbell Law Directory

CONNECTICUT

BRIDGEPORT,* Fairfield Co.

BAI, POLLOCK AND COYNE, P.C. (AV)

Park City Plaza, 10 Middle Street, P.O. Box 1978, 06604
Telephone: 203-366-7991
Fax: 203-366-4723
Email: bpc@snet.net

Arnold J. Bai (1931-1992)	Garie J. Mulcahey
Paul E. Pollock	Raymond J. Plouffe, Jr.
James E. Coyne	Philip F. von Kuhn
Jeffrey A. Blueweiss	Madonna A. Sacco
	Michael S. Lynch

David J. Robertson	Colleen D. Fries
Edward P. Brady III	Neal P. Rogan
Andrew S. Turret	Jacquelyn Conlon
Gaileen A. Kaufman	Janine M. Savarese
Kevin S. Coyne	Louis A. Annecchino
	Kristin Beth Comstock

For full biographical listings, see the Martindale-Hubbell Law Directory

ELSTEIN AND ELSTEIN, P.C. (AV)

Suite 400 1087 Broad Street, 06604-4231
Telephone: 203-367-4421
Telecopier: 203-366-8615

Henry Elstein	Bruce L. Elstein

For full biographical listings, see the Martindale-Hubbell Law Directory

GASTON & RUANE (AV)

Suite 403 350 Fairfield Avenue, 06604
Telephone: 203-334-1656
Fax: 203-333-4532

James O. Gaston	James J. Ruane
	JohnPatrick C. O'Brien

For full biographical listings, see the Martindale-Hubbell Law Directory

MEEHAN & MEEHAN (AV)

76 Lyon Terrace, 06604
Telephone: 203-333-1888
Fax: 203-331-0107

Richard T. Meehan, Sr.	Richard T. Meehan, Jr.
	Edward J. Gavin

For full biographical listings, see the Martindale-Hubbell Law Directory

WILLIAMS, COONEY & SHEEHY (AV)

One Lafayette Circle, 06604
Telephone: 203-331-0888
Telecopier: 203-331-0896

MEMBERS OF FIRM

Ronald D. Williams	Peter J. Dauk
Robert J. Cooney	Dion W. Moore
Edward Maum Sheehy	Ronald D. Williams, Jr.
Peter D. Clark	Francis A. Smith, Jr.
	(1951-1989)

Michael P. Bowler	Paul Sean Curtin
Michael Cuff Deakin	Suzannah Kim Nigro

Representative Clients: Aetna Life & Casualty Co.; Nationwide Insurance Co.; Connecticut Medical Insurance Co.; Zimmer Manufacturing Co.; Textron-Lycoming; The Stop & Shop Companies, Inc.; Shawmut Bank Connecticut, N.A.; Podiatry Insurance Company of America; Town of Easton, Conn.

For full biographical listings, see the Martindale-Hubbell Law Directory

YUDITSKI AND ZACKRISON, P.C. (AV)

105 Brooklawn Place, 06604
Telephone: 203-335-5996
Telefax: 203-336-5438

Thomas M. Yuditski	Mary K. Zackrison

Reference: First Union Bank of Connecticut.

For full biographical listings, see the Martindale-Hubbell Law Directory

FAIRFIELD, Fairfield Co.

FRIEDMAN, MELLITZ & NEWMAN, P.C. (AV)

Successor to: Friedman & Friedman; Mellitz Krentzman & Newman
One Eliot Place, 06430
Telephone: 203-259-5300
Fax: 203-259-2996

Arthur D. Friedman	Joanne Patricia Sheehan
Noel R. Newman	Cheryl Ann Carolan
Steven A. Levy	Arthur Levy, Jr.

For full biographical listings, see the Martindale-Hubbell Law Directory

GROTON, New London Co.

O'BRIEN, SHAFNER, STUART, KELLY & MORRIS, P.C. (AV)

475 Bridge Street, P.O. Drawer 929, 06340
Telephone: 860-445-2463
Fax: 860-445-4539
Norwich, Connecticut Office: 2 Courthouse Square.
Telephone: 860-889-3855.
Fax: 860-886-6352.

John C. O'Brien	Lloyd L. Langhammer
Matthew Shafner	Mark W. Oberlatz
Peter F. Stuart	Nathan J. Shafner
Carolyn P. Kelly	Richard J. Pascal
Granville R. Morris	Amy M. Stone
Frank N. Eppinger	Eric M. Janney
Mark E. Block	Katherine M. Dempski
(Resident at Norwich Office)	

For full biographical listings, see the Martindale-Hubbell Law Directory

HARTFORD,* Hartford Co.

JACKSON, O'KEEFE AND PHELAN (AV)

36 Russ Street, 06106-1571
Telephone: 860-278-4040
Fax: 860-527-2500
West Hartford, Connecticut Office: 62 LaSalle Road.
Telephone: 860-521-7500.
Fax: 860-561-5399.
Bethlehem, Connecticut Office: 423 Munger Lane. Telephone/
Fax: 203-266-5255.

MEMBERS OF FIRM

Jay W. Jackson	Michael E. Riley
Andrew J. O'Keefe	Peter K. O'Keefe
Denise Martino Phelan	Philip R. Dunn, Jr.
Matthew J. O'Keefe	Kathryn M. Cunningham
	Joseph M. Busher, Jr.

Representative Clients: Travelers Aetna Property Casualty Co.; ITT Hartford; Liberty Mutual Insurance Co.; Connecticut Medical Insurance Co.

For full biographical listings, see the Martindale-Hubbell Law Directory

KENNY, BRIMMER, MELLEY & MAHONEY (AV)

5 Grand Street, 06106
Telephone: 860-527-4226
FAX: 860-527-0214

Joseph P. Kenny (1920-1993)

MEMBERS OF FIRM

Leslie R. Brimmer	William J. Melley, III
	Richard C. Mahoney

ASSOCIATES

Anita M. Varunes	Beverly Johns
Dennis F. McCarthy	Edward J. Fitzgerald

For full biographical listings, see the Martindale-Hubbell Law Directory

REGNIER, TAYLOR, CURRAN & EDDY (AV)

CityPlace, 06103-4402
Telephone: 860-249-9121
FAX: 860-527-4343

MEMBERS OF FIRM

J. Ronald Regnier (1906-1987)	Ralph G. Eddy
Robert F. Taylor (1930-1994)	Jack D. Miller
Edmund T. Curran	Lawrence L. Connelli

ASSOCIATES

A. Patrick Alcarez	Frederick M. O'Brien
Robert B. McLaughlin	Keith Mccabe
A. Alan Sheffy	Beth D. Griffin
Robert A. Byers	Douglas E. Gilmore
Jay F. Huntington	Peter J. Casey
	Andrew W. Bray

(See Next Column)

REGNIER, TAYLOR, CURRAN & EDDY—*Continued*

Representative Clients: Atlantic Mutual Insurance Co.; Government Employees Insurance Co.; Hartford Accident & Indemnity Co.; Hartford Fire Insurance Co.; Pioneer Co-operative Fire; United Services Automobile Assn.; Vermont Mutual Insurance Co.

For full biographical listings, see the Martindale-Hubbell Law Directory

---

MILFORD, New Haven Co.

HURWITZ & SAGARIN, P.C. (AV)

147 North Broad Street, P.O. Box 112, 06460
Telephone: 203-877-8000
Fax: 203-878-9800

J. Daniel Sagarin

For full biographical listings, see the Martindale-Hubbell Law Directory

---

NEW HAVEN,* New Haven Co.

JONATHAN J. EINHORN (AV)

412 Orange Street, 06511
Telephone: 203-777-3777
Telecopier: 203-782-1721

LEGAL SUPPORT PERSONNEL
PARALEGALS

Gina R. Sack   Gail A. Berg

For full biographical listings, see the Martindale-Hubbell Law Directory

---

JACOBS & JACOBS (AV)

700 State Street, 3rd Floor, 06511
Telephone: 203-777-2300
Fax: 203-787-5628

MEMBERS OF FIRM

Israel J. Jacobs (1918-1963)   Bruce D. Jacobs
Stanley A. Jacobs   Carol Wolven
          Irene Prosky Jacobs

Reference: Center Bank / First Union.

For full biographical listings, see the Martindale-Hubbell Law Directory

---

JOSEPH R. MIRRIONE (AV)

55 Trumbull Street, P.O. Box 9444, 06534
Telephone: 203-562-4386
Fax: 203-785-0778

Reference: Bank of Boston, Connecticut.

For full biographical listings, see the Martindale-Hubbell Law Directory

---

ROSEN & DOLAN, P.C. (AV)

400 Orange Street, 06511
Telephone: 203-787-3513
Fax: 203-789-1605
Email: davidrosen@counsel.com
Email: spincus@counsel.com

David N. Rosen

Stephen M. Pincus

Reference: Peoples Bank.

For Complete List of Firm Personnel, See General Section

For full biographical listings, see the Martindale-Hubbell Law Directory

---

PAUL A. SCHOLDER ATTORNEY AT LAW, P.C. (AV)

2 Whitney Avenue, P.O. Box 1722, 06507
Telephone: 203-777-7218
Fax: 203-772-2672
Email: PaulA.Scholder,P.C. 102261.2673@CompuServe.com

Paul A. Scholder

John J. Morgan

References: Peoples Bank; Lafayette American Bank.

For full biographical listings, see the Martindale-Hubbell Law Directory

---

NEW LONDON, New London Co.

THE REARDON LAW FIRM, P.C. (AV)

160 Hempstead Street, Drawer 1430, 06320
Telephone: 860-442-0444
Telecopier: 860-444-6445

Robert I. Reardon, Jr.   Angelo A. Ziotas

Wayne W. Lambert, Jr.   Scott D. Camassar

(See Next Column)

LEGAL SUPPORT PERSONNEL

Bette B. Beam   Jillene E. Bennett (Paralegal)
  (Legal Administrator)   Kimberly A. McGinnis
Kelly G. MacDonald (Paralegal)   (Paralegal)
          Sharon M. Burdsall (Paralegal)

For full biographical listings, see the Martindale-Hubbell Law Directory

---

STAMFORD, Fairfield Co.

CASPER & DE TOLEDO LLC (AV)

1111 Summer Street, 06905
Telephone: 203-325-8600
Fax: 203-323-5970

Stewart M. Casper   Victoria de Toledo

Renée Mayerson Cannella   Melissa Balaban

For full biographical listings, see the Martindale-Hubbell Law Directory

---

PIAZZA & MELMED (AV)

112 Prospect Street, P.O. Box 15390, 06901
Telephone: 203-348-2465
Fax: 203-964-9509

MEMBERS OF FIRM

Anthony A. Piazza   Julian K. Melmed

Alan Scott Pickel   Angela M. Trombly
          Tara C. F. Ryan

For full biographical listings, see the Martindale-Hubbell Law Directory

---

SILVER, GOLUB & TEITELL (AV)

184 Atlantic Street, P.O. Box 389, 06904
Telephone: 203-325-4491
Fax: 203-325-3769

MEMBERS OF FIRM

Richard A. Silver   Patricia M. Haugh (1942-1988)
David S. Golub   Elaine T. Silver
Ernest F. Teitell   John D. Josel

Mario DiNatale   Jonathan L. Mannina
Jonathan M. Levine   Jennifer Cohen Goldstein
Marilyn J. Ramos   J. Michael Lewis

For full biographical listings, see the Martindale-Hubbell Law Directory

---

WOFSEY, ROSEN, KWESKIN & KURIANSKY (AV)

600 Summer Street, 06901
Telephone: 203-327-2300
Fax: 203-967-9273

MEMBERS OF FIRM

Abraham Wofsey (1915-1944)   Edward M. Kweskin
Michael Wofsey (1927-1951)   David M. Cohen
David M. Rosen (1926-1967)   Marshall Goldberg
Julius B. Kuriansky (1910-1992) Stephen A. Finn
Monroe Silverman   Judith Rosenberg
Emanuel Margolis   Mark H. Henderson
Howard C. Kaplan   Steven D. Grushkin
Anthony R. Lorenzo   Matthew J. Forstadt

OF COUNSEL

Saul Kwartin   Sydney C. Kweskin (Retired)

ASSOCIATES

Joseph Brachfeld   Eric M. Higgins
John J.L. Chobor   Valerie E. Maze
Steven M. Frederick   Randall M. Skigen
Joy A. Katz   Peter J. Schaffer
Galit Kierkut   Robert W. Finke

Representative Clients: Banque Paribas; Benenson Realty; Cellular Information Systems, Inc.; The Chase Manhattan Bank; First County Bank; Hartford Provision Co.; Louis Dreyfus Corp.; Norwalk Federation of Teachers; People's Bank; Ridgeway Shopping Center.

For full biographical listings, see the Martindale-Hubbell Law Directory

---

STRATFORD, Fairfield Co.

COUSINS AND JOHNSON, P.C. (AV)

2563 Main Street, 06497
Telephone: 203-386-1433
Fax: 203-386-9714

Donald C. Cousins   Albert E. Desrosiers
Norma S. Johnson   Michael A. Wolak, III
          Steven H. Cousins

(See Next Column)

COUSINS AND JOHNSON P.C., *Stratford—Continued*

Andrew V. O'Shea

Approved Attorneys for: Chicago Title Insurance Co.; Lawyers Title Insurance Corp.

For full biographical listings, see the Martindale-Hubbell Law Directory

*VERNON,*** Tolland Co.

FLAHERTY, MEISLER & COURTNEY (AV)

30 Lafayette Square, P.O. Box 508, 06066
Telephone: 860-872-7200
Fax: 860-875-6594
Email: FMACATTY@aol.com

MEMBERS OF FIRM
Leo B. Flaherty Jr.   Arthur P. Meisler
Joseph D. Courtney
ASSOCIATE
Elizabeth C. Foran

Reference: Savings Bank of Rockville.

For full biographical listings, see the Martindale-Hubbell Law Directory

WALLINGFORD, New Haven Co.

DELANEY, ZEMETIS, DONAHUE, DURHAM & NOONAN, P.C. (AV)

111 South Main Street, P.O. Box 747, 06492
Telephone: 203-269-1441
Fax: 203-284-9428

Joseph M. Delaney   Timothy W. Donahue
Terence A. Zemetis   Michael G. Durham
Patrick M. Noonan

Edward W. Mayer, Jr.   Edward T. Falsey, III
Thomas J. Flanagan   Mark Popolizio

For full biographical listings, see the Martindale-Hubbell Law Directory

FARRELL & LESLIE (AV)

375 Center Street, P.O. Box 369, 06492
Telephone: 203-269-7756
Fax: 203-269-1927

MEMBERS OF FIRM
Gerald E. Farrell   Ann Farrell Leslie
Gerald E. Farrell, Jr.   Brian J. Leslie

References: Dime Savings Bank of Wallingford; Shawmut Bank (Wallingford Office).

For full biographical listings, see the Martindale-Hubbell Law Directory

WESTPORT, Fairfield Co.

LAW OFFICES OF PAUL J. PACIFICO (AV)

25 Ford Road, Suite 2, 06880
Telephone: 203-221-8066
Fax: 203-222-4833

For full biographical listings, see the Martindale-Hubbell Law Directory

RUTKIN AND OLDHAM, L.L.C (AV)

323 Riverside Avenue, P.O. Box 295, 06881
Telephone: 203-227-7301
Fax: 203-222-9295

Arnold H. Rutkin   Sarah S. Oldham
OF COUNSEL
Kathleen A. Hogan

For full biographical listings, see the Martindale-Hubbell Law Directory

DELAWARE

*WILMINGTON,*** New Castle Co.

WARREN B. BURT & ASSOCIATES (AV)

1700 Mellon Bank Center, 919 Market Street, 19801-3023
Telephone: 302-429-9430
Fax: 302-429-9427

ASSOCIATES
Richard D. Abrams   Michael F. Duggan

For full biographical listings, see the Martindale-Hubbell Law Directory

CASARINO, CHRISTMAN & SHALK (AV)

Suite 1220, 222 Delaware Avenue, P.O. Box 1276, 19899
Telephone: 302-594-4500
Telecopier: 302-594-4509

MEMBERS OF FIRM
Stephen P. Casarino   Beth H. Christman
Colin M. Shalk   Donald M. Ransom
Patricia L. Peterson

Kenneth M. Doss   Diane M. Willette
Patricia Bartley Schwartz   Stacey L. Cummings

For full biographical listings, see the Martindale-Hubbell Law Directory

DALEY, ERISMAN & VAN OGTROP (AV)

1224 King Street, 19801
Telephone: 302-658-4000
Fax: 302-652-8975
Email: jerisman@devolaw.com *URL:* http://www.devolaw.com
Newark, Delaware Office: 206 East Delaware Avenue.
Telephone: 302-368-0133.
FAX: 302-368-4587.

MEMBERS OF FIRM
Robert E. Daley   James A. Erisman
Piet H. van Ogtrop

References: Wilmington Trust Co.; Beneficial National Bank.

For full biographical listings, see the Martindale-Hubbell Law Directory

KIMMEL, CARTER & ROMAN, P.A. (AV)

12th Floor, 913 Market Street, P.O. Box 272, 19899-0272
Telephone: 302-571-0800

Morton Richard Kimmel   Edward B. Carter, Jr.
Thomas J. Roman

William R. Peltz   Michael D. Bednash
Matthew M. Bartkowski

References: Wilmington Trust Co.; Delaware Trust Co.

For full biographical listings, see the Martindale-Hubbell Law Directory

EUGENE J. MAURER, JR., P.A. (AV)

1201-A King Street, 19801
Telephone: 302-652-7900
Fax: 302-652-2173

Eugene J. Maurer, Jr.
LEGAL SUPPORT PERSONNEL
Carol Rende (Paralegal)

For full biographical listings, see the Martindale-Hubbell Law Directory

POTTER ANDERSON & CORROON (AV)

350 Delaware Trust Building, P.O. Box 951, 19899-0951
Telephone: 302-984-6000
FAX: 302-658-1192
URL: http://www.ATTYS.PACDELAWARE.COM

MEMBERS OF FIRM
Daniel F. Wolcott, Jr.   Somers S. Price, Jr.
Kathleen Furey McDonough
COUNSEL
David L. Baumberger

Representative Clients: Conrail; National Railroad Passenger Corp.; General Motors Corp.; Chrysler Corp.; U.S. Mineral Products Co.; Boise Cascade Corp.; Mentor Corp.; Harley Davidson; Ford-New Holland, Inc.

For Complete List of Firm Personnel, See General Section

For full biographical listings, see the Martindale-Hubbell Law Directory

SMITH, KATZENSTEIN & FURLOW (AV)

The Corporate Plaza, 800 Delaware Avenue, P.O. Box 410, 19899
Telephone: 302-652-8400
Fax: 302-652-8405

MEMBERS OF FIRM
Robert J. Katzenstein   Susan L. Parker

Kathleen M. Miller

For Complete List of Firm Personnel, See General Section

For full biographical listings, see the Martindale-Hubbell Law Directory

Wilmington—Continued

THEISEN, LANK, MULFORD & GOLDBERG, P.A. (AV)

Ninth Floor, One Commerce Center, P.O. Box 1470, 19899
Telephone: 302-656-7712
Fax: 302-655-0923
Email: Theisen@delcorp.com *URL:* http://www.delcorp.theisen.com

Aubrey B. Lank	Steven D. Goldberg
John G. Mulford	Michael J. Goodrick
David S. Lank	

Richard L. Abbott

OF COUNSEL

Vincent A. Theisen (Retired)

References: Wilmington Trust Co.; PNC Bank.

For full biographical listings, see the Martindale-Hubbell Law Directory

TRZUSKOWSKI, KIPP, KELLEHER & PEARCE, P.A. (AV)

1020 North Bancroft Parkway, P.O. Box 429, 19899-0429
Telephone: 302-571-1782
Fax: 302-571-1638

Francis J. Trzuskowski	Robert K. Pearce
James F. Kipp	Edward F. Kafader
Daniel F. Kelleher	Francis J. Schanne

For full biographical listings, see the Martindale-Hubbell Law Directory

DISTRICT OF COLUMBIA

WASHINGTON, D.C. Co.

THE ABELSON LAW FIRM (AV)

Suite 300, 1000 Sixteenth Street, N.W., 20036
Telephone: 202-331-0600
Fax: 202-429-9088

Michael A. Abelson

For full biographical listings, see the Martindale-Hubbell Law Directory

BAUM, HEDLUND, ARISTEI, GUILFORD & DOWNEY A PROFESSIONAL CORPORATION (AV)

1250 24th Street, N.W., Suite 300, 20037
Telephone: 202-466-0513; 800-827-0097
Fax: 202-466-0527
Email: bhagd@bhagd.com *URL:* http://www.bhagd.com/attorneys/
Los Angeles, California Office: Suite 950, 12100 Wilshire Boulevard.
Telephones: 310-207-3233; 800-827-0087.
Facsimile: 310-820-7444.

Cara L. Belle

For full biographical listings, see the Martindale-Hubbell Law Directory

COALE & VAN SUSTEREN, A PROFESSIONAL CORPORATION (AV)

Chevy Chase Pavilion, 5335 Wisconsin Avenue N.W., Suite 720, 20015
Telephone: 202-686-6500
Facsimile: 202-686-9739

John P. Coale (A Professional Corporation)	Greta C. Van Susteren (Currently on leave)
Diane E. Cooley	Julia Wernett McInerny
David K. Lietz	Charlsa (Sandy) Broadus

For full biographical listings, see the Martindale-Hubbell Law Directory

KOONZ, MCKENNEY, JOHNSON, DEPAOLIS & LIGHTFOOT, P.C. (AV)

Suite 500, 2020 K Street, N.W., 20006
Telephone: 202-659-5500
Fax: 202-785-3719
Greenbelt, Maryland Office: 6411 Ivy Lane, Suite 204.
Telephone: 301-345-5700.
Fax: 301-474-5578.
Falls Church, Virginia Office: Suite 400, George Mason Square, 103 W. Broad Street.
Telephone: 703-237-9300.
Fax: 703-533-5974.

(See Next Column)

Joseph H. Koonz, Jr.	Paulette E. Chapman
Carolyn McKenney	John P. Zanelotti (Resident at Greenbelt, Maryland Office)
Roger C. Johnson	David M. Schloss
Peter C. DePaolis (Resident at Falls Church, Virginia Office)	Victor E. Long
Mark J. Brice	Keith W. Donahoe
William P. Lightfoot, Jr.	Jonathan E. Halperin
Marc Fiedler	William A. Musto (Not admitted in DC; Resident at Falls Church, Virginia Office)
Kenneth D. Bynum (Resident, Falls Church, Virginia Office)	
Karen A. Crist (Resident at Falls Church, Virginia Office)	Salvatore J. Zambri
	Harold E. Brazil
Jodi H. Blecker	

For full biographical listings, see the Martindale-Hubbell Law Directory

KUDER, SMOLLAR & FRIEDMAN, P.C. (AV)

Suite 200, 1925 K Street, N.W., 20006
Telephone: 202-331-7522
Fax: 202-331-0388
Email: ksflaw@lchange.com
Rockville, Maryland Office: 414 Hungerford Drive, Suite 456.
Telephone: 301-340-9090.

Armin U. Kuder	Susan Meyers Friedman
Paul R. Smollar	Theresa M. Mihalik

Jeffrey L. Poersch

OF COUNSEL

John V. Long

For full biographical listings, see the Martindale-Hubbell Law Directory

JACK H. OLENDER AND ASSOCIATES, P.C. (AV)

888 17th Street, N.W., 4th Floor, 20006
Telephone: 202-879-7777
Fax: 202-393-2245

Jack H. Olender

Harlow R. Case	Kim M. Keenan
Gary S. Freeman	Dan L. Gray, Jr.
Sandra H. Robinson	Marian K. Riedy
Narda M. Newby	

For full biographical listings, see the Martindale-Hubbell Law Directory

PAULSON, NACE & NORWIND (AV)

1814 N Street, N.W., 20036
Telephone: 202-463-1999
Fax: 202-223-6824
Email: pnn@lawtort.com

MEMBERS OF FIRM

Richard S. Paulson (1928-1986)	Barry J. Nace
Edward L. Norwind	

ASSOCIATES

Gloria A. Worch	James A. Ferguson

OF COUNSEL

Irving R. M. Panzer

For full biographical listings, see the Martindale-Hubbell Law Directory

FLORIDA

*BARTOW,** Polk Co.

FROST, O'TOOLE & SAUNDERS, P.A. (AV)

395 South Central Avenue, P.O. Box 2188, 33830
Telephone: 941-533-0314; 800-533-0967
Telecopier: 941-533-8985

John W. Frost, II	Robert A. Carr
Neal L. O'Toole	Robert H. Van Hart
Thomas C. Saunders	John Marc Tamayo
Richard E. "Rick" Dantzler	Mark A. Sessums
Robert J. Aranda	

Reference: Community National Bank, Bartow.

For full biographical listings, see the Martindale-Hubbell Law Directory

BOCA RATON, Palm Beach Co.

CARTER, CARLILE, NEALE & FRIEDMAN, P.A. (AV)

Suite 312, 1200 North Federal Highway, 33432
Telephone: 561-368-9900

(See Next Column)

CARTER, CARLILE, NEALE & FRIEDMAN P.A., *Boca Raton—Continued*

John E. Carter	Thomas E. Neale
Robert T. Carlile	Annette Friedman

For full biographical listings, see the Martindale-Hubbell Law Directory

WEISS & HANDLER, P.A. (AV)

Suite 218A, One Boca Place, 2255 Glades Road, 33431-7313
Telephone: 407-997-9995
Broward: 954-421-5101
Palm Beach: 407-734-8008
Telecopier: 407-997-5280

Howard I. Weiss	Henry B. Handler

Donald Feldman	Marissa I. Laakso
David K. Friedman	Mark R. Osherow
Carol A. Kartagener	Howard M. Rudolph (Resident, West Palm Beach Office)

OF COUNSEL

Malcolm L. Stein	Stanley E. Preiser
(Not admitted in FL)	(Not admitted in FL)
Raoul Lionel Felder	
(Not admitted in FL)	

For full biographical listings, see the Martindale-Hubbell Law Directory

BRADENTON,* Manatee Co.

GRIMES GOEBEL GRIMES HAWKINS & GLADFELTER, P.A. (AV)

The Professional Building, 1023 Manatee Avenue West, P.O. Box 1550, 34206
Telephone: 941-748-0151
Fax: 941-748-0158

William C. Grimes	John D. Hawkins
Caleb J. Grimes	William S. Galvano
	Douglas A. Peebles

For Complete List of Firm Personnel, See General Section

For full biographical listings, see the Martindale-Hubbell Law Directory

MULOCK, THOMPSON & LITTLE (AV)

A Partnership of Professional Associations
519 13th Street West, 34205
Telephone: 941-748-2104
Fax: 941-748-6588

Edwin T. Mulock (P.A.)	W. Wade Thompson (P.A.)
	Melton H. Little (P.A.)

Donald E. Grieco

Representative Client: Clerk of Circuit Court of Manatee County.
Approved Attorneys for: Attorneys' Title Insurance Fund.

For full biographical listings, see the Martindale-Hubbell Law Directory

CLEARWATER,* Pinellas Co.

JOHN D. FERNANDEZ, P.A. (AV)

918 Drew Street, 34615
Telephone: 813-461-4441
Email: fernand@gate.net

John D. Fernandez

Connie R. Stephens

For full biographical listings, see the Martindale-Hubbell Law Directory

CRYSTAL RIVER, Citrus Co.

BEST & ANDERSON, P.A. (AV)

7655 West Gulf to Lake Highway, Suite 6, 34429
Telephone: 352-795-1107
Orlando, Florida Office: 20 North Orange Avenue, Suite 505.
Telephone: 407-425-2985.
Melbourne, Florida Office: Marina Towers, 709 South Harbor City Boulevard, Suite 220, 32901.
Telephone: 407-727-9923.

David R. Best	Lawrence I. Hauser
George H. "Dutch" Anderson, III	

G. Clay Morris	Angela O'Neil
	Natt O. Reifler

For full biographical listings, see the Martindale-Hubbell Law Directory

DADE CITY,* Pasco Co.

GREENFELDER, MANDER, HANSON, MURPHY & DWYER (AV)

14217 Third Street, 33523
Telephone: 352-567-0411
Fax: 352-567-7758

MEMBERS OF FIRM

Albert R. Mander, III	T. Philip Hanson, Jr.

For full biographical listings, see the Martindale-Hubbell Law Directory

DAYTONA BEACH, Volusia Co.

CHANFRAU & CHANFRAU (AV)

A Partnership of Professional Associations
701 North Peninsula Drive, P.O. Box 265880, 32126-5880
Telephone: 904-258-7313
Telecopier: 904-238-1464
Email: pclaw@america.com

W. M. Chanfrau (P.A.)	Philip J. Chanfrau, Jr., (P.A.)

For full biographical listings, see the Martindale-Hubbell Law Directory

LANDIS, GRAHAM, FRENCH, HUSFELD, SHERMAN & FORD, P.A. (AV)

Formerly Hull, Landis, Graham & French
543 South Ridgewood Avenue, 32114
Telephone: 904-252-4717
Fax: 904-253-7352
De Land, Florida Office: 145 East Rich Avenue, P.O. Box 48.
Telephone: 904-734-3451.
Deltona, Florida Office: 204 Medical Arts Center, 1555 Saxon Boulevard.
Telephone: 407-574-1461.
Fax: 407-574-0242.

Erskine W. Landis (1900-1967)	Richard S. Graham
John L. Graham (1905-1978)	William E. Sherman
Thorwald J. Husfeld (1926-1995)	Sam N. Masters

OF COUNSEL

J. Compton French

Counsel for: Barnett Bank of Volusia County; State Farm Mutual Automobile Insurance Co.; West Volusia Hospital Authority; Central Florida Fern Cooperative, Inc.; General Motors Corp.; South Florida Natural Gas Co.; Florida Public Utilities Co.; Volusia County Industrial Development Authority; Florida United Methodist Children's Home: Volusia County Educational Facilities Authority.

For full biographical listings, see the Martindale-Hubbell Law Directory

LaRUE LAW FIRM (AV)

511 South Ridgewood Avenue, P.O. Box Box 1080, 32115
Telephone: 904-255-2783
Fax: 904-248-0724
Email: larue@america.com

Terrill J. LaRue

Reference: Barnett Bank.

For full biographical listings, see the Martindale-Hubbell Law Directory

SMITH, SCHODER & BOUCK, P.A. (AV)

605 South Ridgewood Avenue, 32014
Telephone: 904-255-0505
FAX: 904-252-4794
Other Daytona Beach Office: 214 Loomis Avenue.
Telephone: 904-255-6711.

James W. Smith	Kim E. Bouck
C. Anthony Schoder, Jr.	Todd Michael Cranshaw
	M. Kathleen Roddenberry

For full biographical listings, see the Martindale-Hubbell Law Directory

DE LAND,* Volusia Co.

LANDIS, GRAHAM, FRENCH, HUSFELD, SHERMAN & FORD, P.A. (AV)

Formerly Hull, Landis, Graham & French
145 East Rich Avenue, P.O. Box 48, 32721-0048
Telephone: 904-734-3451
Fax: 904-736-1350
Daytona Beach, Florida Office: 543 South Ridgewood Avenue, 32114.
Telephone: 904-252-4717.
Deltona, Florida Office: 204 Medical Arts Center, 1555 Saxon Boulevard.
Telephone: 407-574-1461.
Fax: 407-574-0242.

(See Next Column)

LANDIS, GRAHAM, FRENCH, HUSFELD, SHERMAN & FORD P.A.—*Continued*

Erskine W. Landis (1900-1967)	Joe G. Dykes, Jr.
John L. Graham (1905-1978)	Frank A. Ford, Jr.
Thorwald J. Husfeld (1926-1995)	Sam N. Masters
William E. Sherman	(Daytona Beach Office)
Richard S. Graham	Philip L. Partridge
(Daytona Beach Office)	Edwin Channing Coolidge, Jr.
William A. Ottinger	Kent A. Showalter, III
(Deltona Office)	

OF COUNSEL

J. Compton French	Frank A. Ford, Sr.
(Daytona Beach Office)	

Counsel for: Barnett Bank of Volusia County; State Farm Mutual Automobile Insurance Co.; West Volusia Hospital Authority; Central Florida Fern Cooperative, Inc.; General Motors Corp.; South Florida Natural Gas Co.; Florida Public Utilities Co.; Volusia County Industrial Development Authority; Florida United Methodist Children's Home; Volusia County Educational Facilities Authority.

For full biographical listings, see the Martindale-Hubbell Law Directory

FORT LAUDERDALE,* Broward Co.

E. HUGH CHAPPELL JR., P.A. (AV)

420 Northeast 3rd Street, 33301
Telephone: 954-467-2727
Fax: 954-523-3240

E. Hugh Chappell, Jr.

Reference: Sun Bank/Broward, N.A.; United National Bank.

For full biographical listings, see the Martindale-Hubbell Law Directory

CONRAD, SCHERER & JENNE (AV)

A Partnership of Professional Associations
Eighth Floor, 633 South Federal Highway, P.O. Box 14723, 33302
Telephone: 954-462-5500
Facsimile: 954-463-9244
Miami, Florida Office: International Place. 100 Southeast 2nd Street. Suite 2800. 33131.
Telephone: 305-856-9920.
Facsimile: 305-374-4408.

MEMBERS OF FIRM

William R. Scherer, Jr., (P.A.)	Gary S. Genovese (P.A.)
Kenneth C. Jenne, II (P.A.)	William V. Carcioppolo (P.A.)
Lynn Futch Cooney (P.A.)	

OF COUNSEL

Rex Conrad

ASSOCIATES

Linda Rae Spaulding	Reid A. Cocalis
Kimberly A. Kisslan	Albert L. Frevola, Jr.

Local Counsel for: American Home Assurance Group; Caterpillar Tractor Co.; Division of Risk Management, State of Florida; Florida East Coast Railway; Fort Motor Co.; Liberty Mutual Insurance Co.; Ryder Truck Lines; Unigard Insurance Group.
Approved Attorneys for: Attorneys' Title Insurance Fund.
Reference: Barnett Bank of Fort Lauderdale.

For Complete List of Firm Personnel, See General Section

For full biographical listings, see the Martindale-Hubbell Law Directory

COONEY, MATTSON, LANCE, BLACKBURN, RICHARDS & O'CONNOR, P.A. (AV)

301 East Las Olas Boulevard, P.O. Box 14546, 33302
Telephone: Telephone: 954-779-1900
WATS: 1-800-745-3864
Telecopier: 954-779-1910
Orlando, Florida Office: Nations Bank Tower, 111 N. Orange Avenue, Suite 1020.
Telephone: 407-843-2100.
Fax: 407-843-2061.

David F. Cooney	Walter C. Wyatt
Michael C. Mattson	Kieran F. O'Connor (Resident,
Victor Lance (1956-1995)	Orlando, Florida Office)
Ace J. Blackburn, Jr.	Pamela R. Kittrell
John H. Richards	Stephanie Arma Kraft
Dennis R. O'Connor (Resident,	Andrea B. Chirls
Orlando, Florida Office)	Michele Brigid McCaul
Bruce Michael Trybus	Daniel F. Tordella
Mary T. Szeluga	

For full biographical listings, see the Martindale-Hubbell Law Directory

ESLER, PETRIE & LINDIE, P.A. (AV)

Suite 300 The Advocate Building, 315 S.E. Seventh Street, 33301
Telephone: 954-764-5400
FAX: 954-764-5408

Gary A. Esler	C. Daniel Petrie, Jr.
	Beth G. Lindie

Representative Clients: The Chubb Group of Insurance Cos.; Fireman's Fund Insurance Co.; State of Florida-Department of Risk Management; Marriott Corp.; Gregson Furniture Industries, Inc.; Winsloew, Inc.; Richfield Hotel Management, Inc.; Mobile America Insurance Group, Inc.; Colonial Penn Insurance Co.
Reference: Capital Bank.

For full biographical listings, see the Martindale-Hubbell Law Directory

FERRERO, MIDDLEBROOKS & CARBO, P.A. (AV)

Sixth Floor Blackstone Building, 707 Southeast Third Avenue, P.O. Box 14604, 33302
Telephone: 954-462-4500
Miami: 949-2784
Telecopier: 954-462-6597

Ray Ferrero, Jr.	Michael J. Carbo
Ed Middlebrooks	Todd Middlebrooks

Reference: Barnett Bank of Broward County.

For full biographical listings, see the Martindale-Hubbell Law Directory

GILLESPIE & GOLDMAN (AV)

Port Royale Financial Center, 6550 North Federal Highway, 33308
Telephone: 954-761-8600
Facsimile: 954-525-2134

MEMBERS OF FIRM

John R. Gillespie, Jr.	Peter R. Goldman

For full biographical listings, see the Martindale-Hubbell Law Directory

HEINRICH GORDON HARGROVE WEIHE & JAMES, P.A. (AV)

500 East Broward Boulevard, Suite 1000, 33394-3092
Telephone: 954-527-2800
Facsimile: 954-524-9481
Email: heinrich-gordon.com
Palm Beach, Florida Office: 140 Royal Palm Way, Suite 206.
Telephone: 561-832-7600.
Facsimile: 561-833-0805.

Mark R. Boyd	Jeffrey A. O'Keefe
Richard G. Gordon	Gilbert E. Theissen
Eugene L. Heinrich	Kenneth W. Waterway

Representative Clients: Aetna Life Insurance Company; Allstate Insurance Company; Amerisure Companies; The BellSouth Companies; Blackfin Yacht Corporation, Inc.; First Westinghouse Equities Corporation; Schindler Elevator Corporation; Sears, Roebuck and Co.; Westinghouse Electric Corporation.

For Complete List of Firm Personnel, See General Section

For full biographical listings, see the Martindale-Hubbell Law Directory

KESSLER, MASSEY, CATRI, HOLTON & KESSLER, P.A. (AV)

110 Tower, Twentieth Floor, 110 Southeast Sixth Street, 33301
Telephone: 954-463-8593
Fax: 954-462-1303

Charles T. Kessler	Paula C. Kessler
Albert P. Massey, III	Gregory G. Coican
Wesley L. Catri	Andrea L. Kessler
Raymond O. Holton, Jr.	Edward D. Schuster

Gerard A. Tuzzio	Edwina V. Kessler

For full biographical listings, see the Martindale-Hubbell Law Directory

KRUPNICK CAMPBELL MALONE ROSELLI BUSER SLAMA & HANCOCK, P.A. (AV)

700 Southeast 3rd Avenue, 33316
Telephone: 954-763-8181
Fax: 954-763-8292

Jon E. Krupnick	Thomas E. Buser
Walter G. Campbell, Jr.	Joseph J. Slama
Kevin A. Malone	Kelly D. Hancock
Richard J. Roselli	Lisa A. McNelis

Louis R. Battista	Carol J. Healy
Ivan F. Cabrera	Elaine P. Krupnick
Robert D. Erben	Scott S. Liberman
Kelley Badger Gelb	Cinthia M. Manzano
Robert J. McKee	

(See Next Column)

KRUPNICK CAMPBELL MALONE ROSELLI BUSER SLAMA & HANCOCK P.A.,
Fort Lauderdale—Continued

OF COUNSEL

Ben J. Weaver   Dianne Jay Weaver

Reference: Nations Bank.

For full biographical listings, see the Martindale-Hubbell Law Directory

---

McGEE, GAINEY & HUSKEY, P.A. (AV)

2455 East Sunrise Boulevard, Penthouse West, 33304
Telephone: 954-563-8200
Fax: 954-566-7754

C. Edward McGee, Jr.   J. David Huskey, Jr.
James P. Gainey   Patricia J. Small

For full biographical listings, see the Martindale-Hubbell Law Directory

---

LAW OFFICES PRINCE, GLICK & McFARLANE, P.A. (AV)

1112 Southeast 3rd Avenue, 33316
Telephone: Broward: 954-525-1112
Dade: 305-940-6414
Fax: 954-462-1243

Charles M. Prince   Joseph Glick
William J. McFarlane, III

For full biographical listings, see the Martindale-Hubbell Law Directory

---

PURDY AND FLYNN, P.A. (AV)

1107 Southeast Fourth Avenue, 33316
Telephone: 954-356-0008

H. Mark Purdy   Rose Ann Flynn

ASSOCIATE

Patrick H. Gonyea

OF COUNSEL

Michael S. Insler

For full biographical listings, see the Martindale-Hubbell Law Directory

---

SHELDON J. SCHLESINGER, P.A. (AV)

1212 Southeast Third Avenue, 33335
Telephone: 954-467-8800

Sheldon J. Schlesinger   Robert W. Kelley
Scott P. Schlesinger   Sara C. Lindsey

For full biographical listings, see the Martindale-Hubbell Law Directory

---

FORT MYERS,* Lee Co.

BURKERT & HART (AV)

2205 McGregor Boulevard, P.O. Box 2485, 33902
Telephone: 941-337-4800
Fax: 941-337-5920

MEMBERS OF FIRM

Kim Patrick Hart   Peter C. Burkert

For full biographical listings, see the Martindale-Hubbell Law Directory

---

GARVIN & TRIPP, A PROFESSIONAL ASSOCIATION (AV)

2532 East First Street, P.O. Drawer 2040, 33902
Telephone: 941-334-1824
FAX: 941-334-6848

Jeffrey R. Garvin   Theodore L. Tripp, Jr.

Bruce M. Essen

Reference: Northern Trust Bank, Fort Myers, Florida.

For full biographical listings, see the Martindale-Hubbell Law Directory

---

PATRICK E. GERAGHTY A PROFESSIONAL ASSOCIATION (AV)

The Courtney Building, Suite 100, 2069 First Street, P.O. Box
1605, 33902-1605
Telephone: 941-334-9500
Fax: 941-334-8930

Patrick E. Geraghty   Thomas M. Dougherty

For full biographical listings, see the Martindale-Hubbell Law Directory

---

GOLDBERG, GOLDSTEIN & BUCKLEY, P.A. (AV)

1515 Broadway, P.O. Box 2366, 33901-2366
Telephone: 941-334-1146
Fax: 941-334-3039
Naples, Florida Office: 2150 Goodlette Road, Suite 105, Parkway
Financial Center, 34102.
Telephone: 941-262-4888.
Fax: 941-262-8716.

(See Next Column)

Port Charlotte, Florida Office: Emerald Square, Suite 1, 2852 Tamiami
Trail, 33952.
Telephone: 941-624-2393.
Fax: 941-624-2155.
Cape Coral, Florida Office: 1603 Hancock Bridge Parkway, 33990.
Telephone: 941-574-5575.
Fax: 941-574-9213.
Lehigh Acres, Florida Office: 1458 Lee Boulevard, Lee Boulevard Shopping
Center, 33936.
Telephone: 941-368-6101.
Fax: 941-368-2461.
South Fort Myers, Florida Office: Horizon Plaza, 16050 South Tamiami
Trail, Suite 101, 33908.
Telephone: 941-433-6777.
Fax: 941-433-0578.
Bonita Springs, Florida Office: 3431 Bonita Beach Road, Suite 208, 34134.
Telephone: 941-495-0003.
Fax: 941-495-0564.

Ray Goldstein   George J. Mitar
Stephen W. Buckley   Michael J. Ciccarone
Harvey B. Goldberg   Jay Cooper
John B. Cechman   Jonathan D. Conant
J. Jeffrey Rice   Raymond L. Racila
Richard Lee Purtz   Luis E. Insignares
Martin G. Arnowitz   Scot D. Goldberg

Approved Attorneys for: Attorneys' Title Insurance Fund.

For full biographical listings, see the Martindale-Hubbell Law Directory

---

HENDERSON, FRANKLIN, STARNES & HOLT, PROFESSIONAL ASSOCIATION (AV)

1715 Monroe Street, P.O. Box 280, 33902-0280
Telephone: 941-334-4121
Telecopier: 941-332-4494

Albert M. Frierson   Harold N. Hume, Jr.
Stephen L. Helgemo   Bruce M. Stanley
John A. Noland   Daniel W. Sheppard
Gerald W. Pierce   Steven G. Koeppel
J. Terrence Porter   Douglas B. Szabo
Michael J. Corso   Robert C. Shearman
Vicki L. Sproat   Andrew L. Ringers, Jr.
John W. Lewis   John F. Potanovic, Jr.
Craig Ferrante   Timothy J. Jesaitis
James L. Nulman   Jeffrey D. Kottkamp

Bridget A. Mast

Representative Clients: Aetna Property & Casualty Group; CIGNA Group;
CSX Transportation, Inc.; Fireman's Fund Insurance Cos.; Barnett Bank of
Lee County, N.A.; Northern Trust Bank of Florida, N.A.; The Hartford
Insurance Group; Travelers Group; United Telephone Company of Florida.

For Complete List of Firm Personnel, See General Section

For full biographical listings, see the Martindale-Hubbell Law Directory

---

FORT PIERCE,* St. Lucie Co.

NEILL GRIFFIN JEFFRIES & LLOYD, CHARTERED (AV)

311 South Second Street, P.O. Box 1270, 34954
Telephone: 561-464-8200
Fax: 561-464-2566

Richard V. Neill   J. Stephen Tierney, III
Michael Jeffries   Richard V. Neill, Jr.

Local Counsel for: Sun Trust Bank Treasure Coast, N.A., (Commercial and
Trust Departments); St. Paul Fire and Marine Insurance Co.; Chubb Group
of Insurances Cos.
Approved Attorneys for: Attorneys' Title Insurance Fund; Commonwealth
Land Title Insurance Co.
Reference: Sun Bank Treasure Coast, N.A., Fort Pierce, Florida (Commercial
and Trust Departments).

For full biographical listings, see the Martindale-Hubbell Law Directory

---

JACKSONVILLE,* Duval Co.

GLENN K. ALLEN A PROFESSIONAL ASSOCIATION (AV)

The Plaza Building, 353 East Forsyth Street, 32202
Telephone: 904-355-7506
Facsimile: 904-353-8814

Glenn K. Allen

For full biographical listings, see the Martindale-Hubbell Law Directory

---

BROWN, TERRELL, HOGAN, ELLIS, McCLAMMA & YEGELWEL, P.A. (AV)

Suite 804 Blackstone Building, 233 East Bay Street, 32202
Telephone: 904-632-2424

(See Next Column)

BROWN, TERRELL, HOGAN, ELLIS, McCLAMMA & YEGELWEL P.A.—
Continued

Thomas R. Brown	T. Edward McClamma
James T. Terrell	Evan J. Yegelwel
Wayne Hogan	Thomas E. Duffy, Jr.
Timothy D. Ellis	Christopher G. Burns

Annette J. Ritter	Carroll Cayer
Anita Pryor	Michael S. Sharrit
	Alan M. Pickert

Reference: NCNB.

For full biographical listings, see the Martindale-Hubbell Law Directory

COKER, MYERS, SCHICKEL & SORENSON, P.A. (AV)

136 East Bay Street, P.O. Box 1860, 32201
Telephone: 904-356-6071
Fax: 904-353-2425

Howard C. Coker	R. Daniel Noey
M. Wayne Myers	Tonya Jo Wade
John J. Schickel	Ronald M. Owen
Charles A. Sorenson	John Moffitt Howell
Mark M. Green	Stephen M. Armstrong
Samuel H. Lanier	Corinne L. Heller
J. Thomas McKeel	Paul H. McLester
Wm. Earl Higginbotham	James H. Daniel

For full biographical listings, see the Martindale-Hubbell Law Directory

HUGH COTNEY, P.A. (AV)

905 Blackstone Building, 233 East Bay Street, 32202
Telephone: 904-356-0162
FAX: 904-355-5170

Hugh Cotney

Representative Clients: First Insuramerica of Florida, Inc.; Deaf Services Center, Inc.

For full biographical listings, see the Martindale-Hubbell Law Directory

COWLES & SHAUGHNESSY, P.A. (AV)

Blackstone Building, Suite 901, 233 East Bay Street, 32202
Telephone: 904-359-9500
Fax: 904-359-9717

Robert L. Cowles	Daniel C. Shaughnessy
	Nancy E. Kemner

Eric C. Ragatz

For full biographical listings, see the Martindale-Hubbell Law Directory

LILES, GAVIN & COSTANTINO (AV)

One Enterprise Center, Suite 1500, 225 Water Street, 32202
Telephone: 904-634-1100
Fax: 904-634-1234

Rutledge R. Liles	R. Kyle Gavin
	R. Scott Costantino

ASSOCIATE
Niels P. Murphy

For full biographical listings, see the Martindale-Hubbell Law Directory

PAJCIC & PAJCIC, P.A. (AV)

1900 Independent Square, 32202
Telephone: 904-358-8881
Fax: 904-354-1180

Gary Pajcic	Robert J. Link
Stephen J. Pajcic, III	Lee T. Griffin
Katherine Brown	Christine A. Clark
William S. Burns, Jr.	Thomas F. Slater

Reference: Barnett Bank of Jacksonville, N.A.

For full biographical listings, see the Martindale-Hubbell Law Directory

TYGART AND SCHULER, P.A. (AV)

103 Barnett Regency Tower, 9550 Regency Square Boulevard, 32225-8164
Telephone: 904-721-0744
Facsimile: 904-721-5080

S. Thompson Tygart, Jr.	Carl Scott Schuler

Representative Client: Allstate Insurance Co.
Reference: Barnett Bank of Regency.

For full biographical listings, see the Martindale-Hubbell Law Directory

---

JUPITER, Palm Beach Co.

THOMAS J. SCHULTE, P.A. (AV)

Suite 500, 1001 North U.S. Highway One, 33477
Telephone: 561-746-8600
Fax: 561-744-0670

Thomas J. Schulte

Representative Clients: Firemens' Fund Insurance Co.; Liberty Mutual Insurance, Co.; CIGNA; Professional Risk Management Services, Inc.; Florida Out-Patient Self Insurance Co.; Florida Physicians Insurance Trust; Investors Insurance Group; Catholic Diocese of Palm Beach; Gallagher & Bassett Services, Inc.

For full biographical listings, see the Martindale-Hubbell Law Directory

LAKELAND, Polk Co.

BENEFIELD & CORDA (AV)

1715 Lakeland Hills Boulevard, 33805
Telephone: 941-665-8378

C. J. Benefield	William J. Corda

For full biographical listings, see the Martindale-Hubbell Law Directory

CRAWFORD & RODDENBERY, P.A. (AV)

Second Floor Citrus & Chemical Bank Building, 6150 South Florida Avenue, P.O. Box 5947, 33807
Telephone: 941-644-8929
Fax: 941-647-5331

Sidney M. Crawford	Neil A. Roddenbery

For full biographical listings, see the Martindale-Hubbell Law Directory

SMITH, CASSIDY, PLATT, HARRIS & RADABAUGH, P.A. (AV)

1920 South Florida Avenue, P.O. Box 1606, 33802
Telephone: 941-688-5440
Fax: 941-687-9046

J. Ron Smith	R. James Platt, Jr.
Thomas Cassidy	Eugene W. Harris
	John M. Radabaugh

For full biographical listings, see the Martindale-Hubbell Law Directory

LAKE WORTH, Palm Beach Co.

RICHARD H. WILLITS, P.A. (AV)

2290 10th Avenue, North Suite 404, 33461
Telephone: 1-800-870-0573
561-582-7600
Fax: 407-588-8819

Richard H. Willits, P.A.

For full biographical listings, see the Martindale-Hubbell Law Directory

LARGO, Pinellas Co.

WILLIAM S. JONASSEN, P.A. (AV)

10785 Ulmerton Road, 34648
Telephone: 813-586-1484
Fax: 813-585-9818
Mailing Address: P.O. Box 366, Indian Rocks Beach, 34635

William S. Jonassen

Representative Clients: Florida Lawyers Indemnity Group; Florida Podiatrist Trust; Gulf Atlantic Insurance Co.; Osteopathic Mutual Insurance Co.
General Counsel for: Indian Rocks State Bank.

For full biographical listings, see the Martindale-Hubbell Law Directory

MELBOURNE, Brevard Co.

BEST & ANDERSON, P.A. (AV)

Marina Towers, 709 South Harbor City Boulevard, Suite 220, 32901
Telephone: 407-727-9923
Orlando, Florida Office: 20 North Orange Avenue, Suite 505, 32801.
Telephone: 407-425-2985.
Crystal River, Florida Office: 7655 West Gulf to Lake Highway, Suite 6.
Telephone: 352-795-1107.

David R. Best	Lawrence I. Hauser
George H. "Dutch" Anderson, III	

G. Clay Morris	Angela O'Neil
	Natt O. Reifler

For full biographical listings, see the Martindale-Hubbell Law Directory

Melbourne—Continued

NANCE, CACCIATORE, SISSERSON, DURYEA AND HAMILTON (AV)

525 North Harbor City Boulevard, 32935
Telephone: 407-254-8416
Fax: 407-259-8243

MEMBERS OF FIRM

James H. Nance	John N. Hamilton
Sammy Cacciatore	Charles G. Barger, Jr.
Ronald G. Duryea	James N. Nance

OF COUNSEL
James A. Sisserson

Reference: First Union Bank.

For full biographical listings, see the Martindale-Hubbell Law Directory

---

MERRITT ISLAND, Brevard Co.

GRAHAM, MOLETTEIRE & TUTTLE, P.A. (AV)

775 East Merritt Island Causeway Suite 110, 32952
Telephone: 407-453-4081
Fax: 407-453-7252
Vero Beach, Florida Office: 5727 20th Street. Suite B.
Telephone: 561-563-0032.
Fax: 561-563-2134.

Andrew A. Graham	Douglas W. Tuttle
Robert M. Moletteire	Karla T. Torpy

For full biographical listings, see the Martindale-Hubbell Law Directory

---

MIAMI,* Dade Co.

ABRAMSON & MAGIDSON, P.A. (AV)

Suite 904, 800 Brickell Avenue, 33131
Telephone: 305-358-4400
Fax: 305-539-0477

John M. Abramson	David L. Magidson

For full biographical listings, see the Martindale-Hubbell Law Directory

CLARKE SILVERGLATE WILLIAMS & MONTGOMERY (AV)

A Partnership of Professional Corporations
100 North Biscayne Boulevard Suite 2401, 33132
Telephone: 305-377-0700
Facsimile: 305-377-3001
Chicago, Illinois Office: Williams & Montgomery, Ltd., 20 North Wacker Drive, Suite 2100.
Telephone: 312-443-3200.
Telex: 206598.
Facsimile: 312-443-1323.
Waukegan, Illinois Office: Williams & Montgomery, Ltd., 33 North County Street.
Telephone: 847-360-1220.
Wheaton, Illinois Office: Williams & Montgomery, Ltd., 310 S. County Farm Road.
Telephone: 708-690-3200.
Joliet, Illinois Office: Williams & Montgomery, Ltd., 81 North Chicago Avenue.
Telephone: 815-727-2653.

Mercer K. Clarke	Spencer H. Silverglate

OF COUNSEL
Henry H. Bolz, III

ASSOCIATES

Kelly Anne Luther	Eric L. Lundt
William C. Abruzzo	Carol A. Grant

For full biographical listings, see the Martindale-Hubbell Law Directory

COLSON, HICKS, EIDSON, COLSON & MATTHEWS (AV)

Floor 47 First Union Financial Center, 200 South Biscayne Boulevard, 33131-2351
Telephone: 305-373-5400

MEMBERS OF FIRM

Bill Colson	Tony Korvick
William M. Hicks	Enid Duany Mendoza
Mike Eidson	Newton P. Porter
Dean C. Colson	Julie Braman Kane
Joseph M. Matthews	Robb D. Steinberg
Brian Scott Yablonski	

Reference: Northern Trust Bank of Florida.

For full biographical listings, see the Martindale-Hubbell Law Directory

LAW OFFICES OF DAVID L. DEEHL (AV)

Suite 1575 Courthouse Tower, 44 West Flagler Street, 33130
Telephone: 305-358-9700
Telecopier: 305-358-4036
Email: DAVID@DEEHL.COM

(See Next Column)

ASSOCIATES

Susan Stanfill Carlson	Susan Guller

OF COUNSEL
Michele K. Feinzig

For full biographical listings, see the Martindale-Hubbell Law Directory

DEUTSCH & BLUMBERG, P.A. (AV)

Suite 2802 New World Tower, 100 North Biscayne Boulevard, 33132
Telephone: 305-358-6329
Fax: 305-358-9304

Steven K. Deutsch	James C. Blecke
Edward R. Blumberg	Louis Thaler

For full biographical listings, see the Martindale-Hubbell Law Directory

EVERSOLE & RUDD, P.A. (AV)

Suite 106, Grove Forest Plaza, 2937 SW 27th Avenue, 33133
Telephone: 305-444-2255
Facsimile: 305-444-7288
Fort Lauderdale, Florida Office: 3511 Northeast 22nd Avenue, Suite 100.
Telephone: 954-563-4199.
Fax: 954-563-4030. Boca Raton Office: 2500 North Military Trail, Suite 102.
Telephone: 407-998-9900.
Fax: 407-998-4995.

John F. Eversole, III	James D. Rudd

For full biographical listings, see the Martindale-Hubbell Law Directory

FERRO & LEHR, P.A. (AV)

1401 Brickell, Suite 1040, 33131
Telephone: 305-377-1777
Fax: 305-377-0087

Henry G. Ferro	Bruce H. Lehr

For full biographical listings, see the Martindale-Hubbell Law Directory

THEODORE J. FOURNARIS PROFESSIONAL ASSOCIATION (AV)

145 Almeria Avenue (Coral Gables), 33134
Telephone: 305-448-7333
Telefax: 305-448-7394

Theodore J. Fournaris	Jose M. Cañas

OF COUNSEL
Morton J. Sanet

For full biographical listings, see the Martindale-Hubbell Law Directory

ANDREW HALL AND ASSOCIATES, P.A. (AV)

Penthouse, 1428 Brickell Avenue, 33131
Telephone: 305-374-5030
Fax: 305-374-5033

Andrew C. Hall

Christopher M. David	William H. Strop
Christopher J. Dawes	Allan A. Joseph
Douglas M. Horn	

For full biographical listings, see the Martindale-Hubbell Law Directory

HARDY & BISSETT, P.A. (AV)

501 Northeast First Avenue, 33132
Telephone: 305-358-6200
Broward: 954-462-6377
Fax: 305-577-8230
Email: 102132.403@compuserve.com
Boca Raton, Florida Office: 2201 Corporate Boulevard, N.W., Suite 205.
Telephone: 407-998-9202.
Telecopier: 407-998-9693.

G. Jack Hardy	G. William Bissett

Howard K. Cherna	H. Dane Mottlau
Lee Philip Teichner	Jana Marie Yaw

Representative Clients: International Paper Co.; Masonite Corp.; Bridgestone/Firestone Inc.; American International Underwriters; American International Group, Inc.; Crown Equipment Corp.; The Coleman Co., Inc.; Brown & Williamson; Black & Decker (U.S.), Inc.; S-B Power Tool Company.

For full biographical listings, see the Martindale-Hubbell Law Directory

KAUFMAN MILLER DICKSTEIN & GRUNSPAN, P.A. (AV)

Suite 4650 First Union Financial Center, 200 South Biscayne Boulevard, 33131
Telephone: 305-372-5200
Telecopy: 305-374-3200

(See Next Column)

KAUFMAN MILLER DICKSTEIN & GRUNSPAN P.A.—*Continued*

Jeffrey W. Dickstein	Edward A. Kaufman
Alan M. Grunspan	Raymond V. Miller, Jr.

David James Smith   Niall T. McLachlan

For full biographical listings, see the Martindale-Hubbell Law Directory

PODHURST, ORSECK, JOSEFSBERG, EATON, MEADOW, OLIN & PERWIN, P.A. (AV)

Suite 800 City National Bank Building, 25 West Flagler
Street, 33130-1780
Telephone: 305-358-2800; Fort Lauderdale: 954-463-4346
Fax: 305-358-2382
Email: 76666.2340@COMPUSERVE.COM *URL:*
http://www.turbosales.com/"sfbj/podhurst.html

Aaron Podhurst	Michael S. Olin
Robert Orseck (1934-1978)	Joel S. Perwin
Robert C. Josefsberg	Steven C. Marks
Joel D. Eaton	Victor M. Diaz, Jr.
Barry L. Meadow	Katherine W. Ezell

Karen Podhurst Dern   Xavier Martínez
OF COUNSEL
Walter H. Beckham, Jr.

References: City National Bank of Miami; United National Bank of Miami.

For full biographical listings, see the Martindale-Hubbell Law Directory

PROENZA & ROBERTS, P.A. (AV)

Grove Plaza, 2900 Middle Street, 33133
Telephone: 305-442-1700
Telecopier: 305-442-2559

Morris C. Proenza (1940-1995)   H. Clay Roberts

Michael A. Vazquez
OF COUNSEL
Thomas L. Hurst

For full biographical listings, see the Martindale-Hubbell Law Directory

RUSSO & CULMO, P.A. (AV)

Suite 2000, 2601 South Bayshore Drive (Coconut Grove), 33133
Telephone: 305-854-3100
Fax: 305-854-5949

Don Russo   Thomas A. Culmo
Deborah J. Gander

For full biographical listings, see the Martindale-Hubbell Law Directory

SAMS & MARTIN, P.A. (AV)

The Atrium, Suite 200, 1500 San Remo Avenue (Coral Gables), 33146
Telephone: 305-666-3181
Fax: 305-666-5867
Miami Lakes, Florida Office: Sams, Spier & Hollon, 7975 Northwest
154th Street, 33016.
Telephone: 305-362-6222.
Fax: 305-362-0111.

Murray Sams, Jr.   Timothy M. Martin

Joseph I. Lipsky   Arthur B. Stark, P.A.
Lisa Fialkow Levine

For full biographical listings, see the Martindale-Hubbell Law Directory

LELAND E. STANSELL, JR., P.A. (AV)

903 Biscayne Building, 19 West Flagler Street, 33130
Telephone: 305-374-5911
Fax: 305-374-5337

Leland E. Stansell, Jr.

Roberto M. Ureta

For full biographical listings, see the Martindale-Hubbell Law Directory

NAPLES,* Collier Co.

HARDT LAW OFFICES, P.A. (AV)

Suite 705 SunTrust Building, 801 Laurel Oak Drive, 34108
Telephone: 941-598-2900
Fax: 941-598-3785

(See Next Column)

Frederick R. Hardt
References: Northern Trust Bank of Florida/Naples, N.A.; U.S. Trust Company of Florida; Sun Bank/Naples, N.A.

For full biographical listings, see the Martindale-Hubbell Law Directory

NEW PORT RICHEY, Pasco Co.

ROBERTS, SOJKA & ASSOCIATES, P.A. (AV)

5841 Main Street, 34652
Telephone: 813-847-1103
West Palm Beach, Florida Office: Roberts & Sojka, P.A., 1675 Palm
Beach Lakes Boulevard, Seventh Floor, P.O. Drawer 4178, 33402.
Telephone: 561-686-1800.
Fax: 561-686-1533.

Gary W. Roberts   Cindy A. Sojka

For full biographical listings, see the Martindale-Hubbell Law Directory

NICEVILLE, Okaloosa Co.

STANLEY BRUCE POWELL, P.A. (AV)

107 North Partin Drive, P.O. Box 400, 32588-0400
Telephone: 904-678-2118
Fax: 904-678-8336
Destin, Florida Office: Suite 21 Commerce Row, 225 Main Street.
Telephone: 904-837-9099.

Stanley Bruce Powell   David R. Swanick III

Representative Clients: Peoples National Bank of Niceville; Destin Bank;
D&H Oil Co.
References: Peoples National Bank of Niceville; Destin Bank; Barnett Bank
of Northwest Florida; Vanguard Bank and Trust Co.

For full biographical listings, see the Martindale-Hubbell Law Directory

NORTH PALM BEACH, Palm Beach Co.

LAW OFFICES OF PATRICK C. MASSA, P.A. (AV)

11891 U.S. Highway One, Suite 110, 33408-2864
Telephone: 407-694-1800
Facsimile: 407-694-1833

Patrick C. Massa

For full biographical listings, see the Martindale-Hubbell Law Directory

ORLANDO,* Orange Co.

BEST & ANDERSON, P.A. (AV)

20 North Orange Avenue, Suite 505, 32801
Telephone: 407-425-2985
Crystal River, Florida Office: 7655 West Gulf to Lake Highway, Suite 6.
Telephone: 352-795-1107.
Melbourne, Florida Office: Marina Towers, 709 South Harbor City
Boulevard, Suite 220, 32901.
Telephone: 407-727-9923.

David R. Best	Lawrence I. Hauser
George H. "Dutch" Anderson, III	

G. Clay Morris   Angela O'Neil
Natt O. Reifler

For full biographical listings, see the Martindale-Hubbell Law Directory

BILLINGS, CUNNINGHAM, MORGAN & BOATWRIGHT, PROFESSIONAL ASSOCIATION (AV)

330 East Central Boulevard, 32801
Telephone: 407-425-2000
Fax: 407-843-8274

James Owen Cunningham	Joseph E. Boatwright, Jr.
Mary Ann Morgan	John T. Stemberger

Tracy L. Troutman-Cheek
OF COUNSEL
Jared M. Billings

For full biographical listings, see the Martindale-Hubbell Law Directory

BOBO, SPICER, CIOTOLI, FULFORD, BOCCHINO, DEBEVOISE & LE CLAINCHE, P.A. (AV)

Landmark Center One, Suite 510, 315 East Robinson Street, 32801-1949
Telephone: 407-849-1060
Fax: 407-843-4751
West Palm Beach, Florida Office: Esperante, Sixth Floor, 222 Lakeview
Avenue, 33401.
Telephone: 407-684-6600.
FAX: 407-684-3828.

(See Next Column)

BOBO, SPICER, CIOTOLI, FULFORD, BOCCHINO, DEBEVOISE & LE CLAINCHE P.A., *Orlando—Continued*

John W. Bocchino	D. Andrew DeBevoise
	Patti A. Haber

Gregorio A. Francis	Ingrid A. de Graaff
	Thomas W. Poulton

For full biographical listings, see the Martindale-Hubbell Law Directory

NOLAN CARTER, P.A. (AV)

Suite 1245 Eola Park Centre, 200 East Robinson Street, P.O. Box 2229, 32802
Telephone: 407-425-1621
Fax: 407-425-3322

Nolan Carter

Nathan P. Carter

For full biographical listings, see the Martindale-Hubbell Law Directory

DEWOLF, WARD, O'DONNELL & GLATT, P.A. (AV)

Suite 1750, 111 North Orange Avenue, 32801-2399
Telephone: 407-841-7000
Telecopy: 407-843-6035

Thomas B. DeWolf	John H. Ward
	James E. Glatt, Jr.

Representative Clients: Walt Disney World Co.; The Walt Disney Co.; Fleetwood Enterprises, Inc.; Roadway Express; Massachusetts Mutual Life Insurance Co.; Employers Insurance of Wausau; World Transportation, Inc.; Marriott Corp.; Utah Home Fire Ins. Co.

For full biographical listings, see the Martindale-Hubbell Law Directory

LAW OFFICES OF DURIE & LAWSON, P.A. (AV)

1000 East Robinson Street, 32801
Telephone: 407-841-6000; 1-800-940-0442
Fax: 407-841-2425

Jack F. (Jay) Durie, Jr.	C. Alan Lawson

For full biographical listings, see the Martindale-Hubbell Law Directory

HILL AND PONTON, PROFESSIONAL ASSOCIATION (AV)

Suite 500, 605 East Robinson Street, P.O. Box 2673, 32801
Telephone: 407-422-4665

Brian D. Hill	Carol J. Ponton

Rebecca Jean Alexander	Shea A. Fugate
Maria T. Fabré	Karen M. Marcell
Maria D. Santana	
(Not admitted in FL)	

For full biographical listings, see the Martindale-Hubbell Law Directory

KELAHER, WIELAND AND HILADO, P.A. (AV)

Barnett Bank Center, 390 North Orange Avenue, Suite 1500, P.O. Box 944, 32802
Telephone: 407-841-7698; Brevard County: 407-639-4777
Fax: 407-841-2084

James P. Kelaher	Glen D. Wieland
	Alfred J. Hilado

Paul A. Kelley	Robert J. Egan

References: First Union Bank.

For full biographical listings, see the Martindale-Hubbell Law Directory

KING & BLACKWELL, P.A. (AV)

25 East Pine Street, P.O. Box 1631, 32802-1631
Telephone: 407-422-2472
Fax: 407-648-0161
Email: kbfirm@aol.com

David B. King	Bruce B. Blackwell
	Mayanne Downs

John F. Tannian	Thomas A. Zehnder

For full biographical listings, see the Martindale-Hubbell Law Directory

KARL O. KOEPKE (AV)

801 North Magnolia Avenue, Suite 107, 32803
Telephone: 407-841-0023
Fax: 407-425-4761
Email: klawfl@aol.com *URL:* http://www.klawfl.com

(See Next Column)

ASSOCIATE
Michael H. Truax

For full biographical listings, see the Martindale-Hubbell Law Directory

MAHER, GIBSON AND GUILEY A PROFESSIONAL ASSOCIATION OF LAWYERS (AV)

Suite 200, 90 East Livingston Street, 32801
Telephone: 407-839-0866
Fax: 407-425-7958

Michael Maher	Patricia M. Gibson
	David D. Guiley

Steven R. Maher	Robin M. Orosz
	Monique M. Edwards

OF COUNSEL
John Edward Jones (P.A.)
LEGAL SUPPORT PERSONNEL
INSURANCE CLAIM COORDINATOR
Charles R. Simpson

For full biographical listings, see the Martindale-Hubbell Law Directory

MARTINEZ, DALTON, DELLECKER & WILSON, PROFESSIONAL ASSOCIATION (AV)

719 Vassar Street, 32804
Telephone: 407-425-0712
Fax: 407-425-1856
URL: http://www.pixelstorm.com/mddw

Mel R. Martinez	Robert H. Dellecker
Roy B. Dalton, Jr.	Brian T. Wilson

Leticia Marques

For full biographical listings, see the Martindale-Hubbell Law Directory

McDONOUGH, O'DELL, BEERS, WIELAND, WILLIAMS AND KRAKAR (AV)

19 East Central Boulevard, P.O. Drawer 1991, 32802
Telephone: 407-425-7577
Fax: 407-423-0234

John R. McDonough	Donald N. Williams
Donald L. O'Dell	Michael J. Krakar
David C. Beers	A. Scott Toney
William J. Wieland	Nicholas a. Shannin
	Douglas K. Gartenlaub

For full biographical listings, see the Martindale-Hubbell Law Directory

WILLIAM G. OSBORNE, P.A. (AV)

538 East Washington Street, 32801-1996
Telephone: 407-422-5385
Fax: 407-422-5381

William G. Osborne
LEGAL SUPPORT PERSONNEL

Janet C. Pelletier (CLA)	Elizabeth I. Dunnigan
	(Office Manager)

For full biographical listings, see the Martindale-Hubbell Law Directory

OVERCHUCK & LANGA, P.A. (AV)

Suite 100, 90 East Livingston Street, 32801
Telephone: 407-839-0661
Fax: 407-839-4991

John R. Overchuck	Alan M. Schwerer
Ronald J. Langa	C. Richard Newsome

For full biographical listings, see the Martindale-Hubbell Law Directory

PARRISH, BAILEY & MORSCH, P.A. (AV)

116 America Street, 32801
Telephone: 407-849-1776

Sidney H. Parrish	Michael K. Bailey
	Mark V. Morsch

Donald A. Myers, Jr.

For full biographical listings, see the Martindale-Hubbell Law Directory

PEED & MITNIK, P.A. (AV)

1127 Edgewater Drive, 32804
Telephone: 407-422-2474
Fax: 407-843-8638

(See Next Column)

PEED & MITNIK P.A.—*Continued*

Fred M. Peed   Keith R. Mitnik

For full biographical listings, see the Martindale-Hubbell Law Directory

LAW OFFICE OF IRBY G. PUGH (AV)

218 Annie Street, 32806
Telephone: 407-843-5840
Reference: Upon Request.

For full biographical listings, see the Martindale-Hubbell Law Directory

RICHARD B. TROUTMAN, P.A.

(See Winter Park)

PALM BEACH GARDENS, Palm Beach Co.

SLAWSON & CUNNINGHAM (AV)

Harbour Financial Center, 2401 PGA Boulevard, Suite 140, 33410
Telephone: 407-625-6260
Facsimile: 407-625-6269

Richard W. Slawson (P.A.)   Fred A. Cunningham
Jeanmarie Whalen

For full biographical listings, see the Martindale-Hubbell Law Directory

*PENSACOLA,** Escambia Co.

KERRIGAN, ESTESS, RANKIN & McLEOD (AV)

400 East Government Street, 32501
Telephone: 904-444-4444
Watts No.: 1-800-444-4404
FAX: 904-444-4495
Email: kerrigan@olis.com *URL:* http://www.kerrigan.com
Fort Walton Beach, Florida Office: 212 SE Eglin Parkway, Suite C.
Telephone: 904-244-1111.
Century, Florida Courtesy Office: 8210 North Century Boulevard.
Telephone: 800- 256-1120.
Gulf Breeze, Florida Courtesy Office: 50 Fort Pickens Road.
Telephone: 800-433-7777.
Panama City, Florida Office: 836 Jenks Avenue.
Telephone: 904-871-5000.
FAX: 904-872-2148.
Tallahassee, Florida Courtesy Office: 217 South Adams Street, First Floor.
Telephone: 904-671-5000.

MEMBERS OF FIRM

Robert G. Kerrigan   T. Michael McLeod
George W. Estess   Randle D. Thompson
William Rankin   Marcus J. Michles II
              Kristin L. Stewart

LEGAL SUPPORT PERSONNEL

Sam R. Peebles   James Michael Kerrigan, Ph.D.
              Renée J. Miller

Reference: 1st American Bank of Pensacola.

For full biographical listings, see the Martindale-Hubbell Law Directory

PLANTATION, Broward Co.

FENSTER AND FAERBER, PROFESSIONAL ASSOCIATION (AV)

Suite 307, The Gulfstream Building, 8751 West Broward
  Boulevard, 33324
Telephone: 954-473-1500; Miami: 305-949-9998
Mailing Address: P.O. Box 16688, 33318

Jeffrey M. Fenster   Stacie L. Cohen
Jesse S. Faerber   Jene P. Williams

OF COUNSEL

Betty Anne Beavers

For full biographical listings, see the Martindale-Hubbell Law Directory

PORT CHARLOTTE, Charlotte Co.

WILKINS, FROHLICH, JONES, HEVIA, RUSSELL & SUTTER, P.A. (AV)

18501 Murdock Circle, Suite 601, 33948
Telephone: 941-625-0700
Telecopier: 941-625-9540

Gary L. Wilkins   Jesus M. Hevia
W. Cort Frohlich   W. Kevin Russell
Phillip J. Jones   Brian O. Sutter
Melissa Green Jones   Louise O. Hanaoka
              Victor G. Santiago

For full biographical listings, see the Martindale-Hubbell Law Directory

ST. PETERSBURG, Pinellas Co.

CHAMBERS, SALZMAN & BANNON, PROFESSIONAL ASSOCIATION (AV)

520 Fourth Street North, 33701
Telephone: 813-896-2167
Fax: 813-822-8981

Joseph H. Chambers   Rick G. Bannon
Barry M. Salzman   Joseph W. Chambers
              Jeffrey K. Chambers

Reference: NationsBank.

For full biographical listings, see the Martindale-Hubbell Law Directory

SKIPPER & DAY (AV)

2600 Ninth Street North Suite 500, 33704
Telephone: 813-821-2889
Fax: 813-823-7478

Chester L. Skipper   John W. Day
              Jesse L. Skipper

LEGAL SUPPORT PERSONNEL

Myrna A. Ballard (Legal Assistant)

Representative Clients: American Sign Co.; Bridgestone - Firestone; Warner Lambert Pharmaceuticals; A.M.F. Bowling, Inc.
Insurance Clients: Gulf Insurance; Prudential Insurance; Republic Insurance; A.I. Transport; Sedgewick James of Missouri; Federated Insurance Co.

For full biographical listings, see the Martindale-Hubbell Law Directory

*SARASOTA,** Sarasota Co.

MATTHEWS, HUTTON & EASTMOORE (AV)

Suite 500, 1777 Main Street, P.O. Box 49377, 34230-6377
Telephone: 941-366-8888
Fax: 941-954-7777

MEMBERS OF FIRM

A. Lamar Matthews, Jr.   Jeanne S. Medawar
Steven D. Hutton   Arthur S. Hardy
Theodore C. Eastmoore   Martin Garcia

ASSOCIATE

Edward K. DuBose

For full biographical listings, see the Martindale-Hubbell Law Directory

LAW OFFICES OF R. JACKSON McGILL (AV)

2033 Main Street, Suite 402, 34237
Telephone: 941-955-9942
Fax: 941-955-5347

Robert Jackson McGill

For full biographical listings, see the Martindale-Hubbell Law Directory

*STUART,** Martin Co.

FRIERSON & WATSON (AV)

A Partnership of Professional Associations
3601 S.E. Ocean Boulevard, Suite 4, 34996
Telephone: 561-288-1880
Fax: 561-288-1887
Port St. Lucie, Florida Office: 1920 S.E. Port St. Lucie Boulevard.
Telephone: 561-337-1203.
Fax: 561-337-1206.

Robert J. Watson (P.A.)
Robin Wesley Frierson (P.A.)
  (Resident, Port St. Lucie
  Office)

Reference: Sun Bank of Martin County.

For full biographical listings, see the Martindale-Hubbell Law Directory

*TALLAHASSEE,** Leon Co.

DAVIS & TAFF (AV)

210 East College Avenue, Suite 200, P.O. Box 37190, 32315-7190
Telephone: 904-222-6026
Telecopier: 904-224-1039

MEMBERS OF FIRM

Ken Davis   Angus Broward Taff, Jr.

For full biographical listings, see the Martindale-Hubbell Law Directory

FONVIELLE & HINKLE (AV)

3375-A Capital Circle Northeast, 32308
Telephone: 904-422-7773
Fax: 904-422-3449
Email: lawyers@fonhink.com *URL:* http://www.fonhink.com

(See Next Column)

FONVIELLE & HINKLE, *Tallahassee—Continued*

MEMBERS OF FIRM

C. David Fonvielle	Halley B. Lewis, III
Donald M. Hinkle	William H. Garvin III

John H. Foote

LEGAL SUPPORT PERSONNEL

Sandra M. Tate

For full biographical listings, see the Martindale-Hubbell Law Directory

MCFARLAIN, WILEY, CASSEDY & JONES, PROFESSIONAL ASSOCIATION (AV)

215 South Monroe Street, Suite 600, P.O. Box 2174, 32316-2174
Telephone: 904-222-2107
Telecopier: 904-222-8475

Richard C. McFarlain	Charles A. Stampelos
William B. Wiley	Linda McMullen
Marshall R. Cassedy	H. Darrell White, Jr.
Douglas P. Jones	Christopher Barkas

Harold R. Mardenborough, Jr.	Rogelio J. Fontela
Robert A. McNeely	Patrick John McGinley

For full biographical listings, see the Martindale-Hubbell Law Directory

TAMPA,* Hillsborough Co.

TIMOTHY G. ANDERSON, P.A. (AV)

213 South Brevard Avenue, 33606
Telephone: 813-251-0072

Timothy G. Anderson

Leslie L. Harley	Scott T. McCullough

For full biographical listings, see the Martindale-Hubbell Law Directory

BARR, MURMAN, TONELLI, HERZFELD & RUBIN (AV)

Enterprise Plaza, Suite 901, 201 East Kennedy Boulevard, P.O. Box 172669, 33672-0669
Telephone: 813-223-3951
Fax: 813-229-2254

James A. Murman	Ellen H. Lorenzen
Michael A. Tonelli	John R. Dixon
Daniel H. Sleet	Michael A. Connolly

Ashley J. McCorvey

OF COUNSEL

Billy R. Barr

Representative Client: CIGNA Insurance Co.

For full biographical listings, see the Martindale-Hubbell Law Directory

CLARK, CHARLTON & MARTINO, A PROFESSIONAL ASSOCIATION (AV)

Westshore Center, Suite 700, 1715 North Westshore Boulevard, P.O. Box 24268, 33623-4268
Telephone: 813-289-0700
Fax: 813-289-5498

Scott T. Borders	James W. Clark
Scott Charlton	Anthony T. Martino

Reference: Southtrust Bank of Tampa.

For full biographical listings, see the Martindale-Hubbell Law Directory

CUNNINGHAM LAW GROUP, P.A. (AV)

100 Ashley Drive, South, Suite 100, 33602
Telephone: 813-228-0505
Telefax: 813-229-7982

Anthony W. Cunningham	James D. Clark
Donald G. Greiwe	Dana Solin Kanfer

For full biographical listings, see the Martindale-Hubbell Law Directory

PATRICK H. DEKLE, P.A. (AV)

808 Landmark Building, 412 Madison Street, 33602-4640
Telephone: 813-223-2300

Patrick H. Dekle

For full biographical listings, see the Martindale-Hubbell Law Directory

ANTHONY J. LASPADA, P.A. (AV)

1802 North Morgan Street, 33602
Telephone: 813-223-6048
Pinellas Line: 813-894-1788
Fax: 813-228-9471

(See Next Column)

Anthony J. LaSpada

For full biographical listings, see the Martindale-Hubbell Law Directory

WILLIAM P. LEVENS (AV)

1907 West Kennedy Boulevard, 33606
Telephone: 813-251-5775
Toll Free: 1-800-395-0463

For full biographical listings, see the Martindale-Hubbell Law Directory

LEVINE, HIRSCH & SEGALL, P.A. (AV)

First Union Center, 100 South Ashley Drive, Suite 1600, P.O. Box 3429, 33601-3429
Telephone: 813-229-6585
Telecopier: 813-229-7210

Arnold D. Levine	Richard A. Hirsch
	Stephen L. Segall

Edward M. Brennan

For full biographical listings, see the Martindale-Hubbell Law Directory

PAUL G. MCDUFFEE, II (AV)

1211 West Fletcher Avenue, 33612-3363
Telephone: 813-265-3120
Fax: 813-265-3110

For full biographical listings, see the Martindale-Hubbell Law Directory

MILLER & OLSEN (AV)

Suite 310, 711 North Florida Avenue, 33602
Telephone: 813-223-3657
Fax: 813-225-1187

MEMBERS OF FIRM

E. Robert Miller, Jr.	Kenneth L. Olsen

ASSOCIATES

John G. Miller	Laura Lee Glass

OF COUNSEL

Edwin J. Bradley

Representative Clients: Liberty Mutual Insurance Co.; Ranger/Pan American Insurance Co.; Universal Underwriter Insurance Co.

For full biographical listings, see the Martindale-Hubbell Law Directory

MITZEL, MITZEL & GRAY, P.A. (AV)

100 North Tampa Street, Suite 3620, P.O. Box 3329, 33601-3329
Telephone: 813-223-9776
Fax: 813-223-6059

Richard M. Mitzel	John W. Mitzel

Frederick (Fritz) C. Gray

For full biographical listings, see the Martindale-Hubbell Law Directory

MURNAGHAN, FERGUSON & MAGUIRE, P.A. (AV)

Suite 2600, 100 North Tampa Street, P.O. Box 2937, 33601-2937
Telephone: 813-222-0123
Fax: 813-222-0124

Dennis R. Ferguson	E. Jeanne Maguire

Peter P. Murnaghan

For full biographical listings, see the Martindale-Hubbell Law Directory

CHARLES F. SANSONE (AV)

Suite 200, 701 North Franklin Street, 33602
Telephone: 813-223-9282
FAX: 813-229-0595

For full biographical listings, see the Martindale-Hubbell Law Directory

DALE M. SWOPE, P.A. (AV)

Suite 850, 777 South Harbour Island Boulevard, 33602
Telephone: 813-273-0017
Fax: 813-223-3678

Dale M. Swope

Matthew J. Cardillo	Lorraine E. Robinson

Rhonda L. Edwards

For full biographical listings, see the Martindale-Hubbell Law Directory

YERRID, KNOPIK & MUDANO, P.A. (AV)

Barnett Plaza, Suite 2160, 101 East Kennedy Boulevard, 33602
Telephone: 813-222-8222
Fax: 813-222-8224

(See Next Column)

YERRID, KNOPIK & MUDANO P.A.—*Continued*

C. Steven Yerrid   Christopher S. Knopik
Matthew S. Mudano

For full biographical listings, see the Martindale-Hubbell Law Directory

TAVARES,* Lake Co.

CAUTHEN, OLDHAM & KEOUGH, P.A. (AV)

131 West Main Street, 32778
Telephone: 352-343-3455
Fax: 352-343-8801

Gordon G. Oldham, Jr.   David E. Cauthen
Timothy S. Keough

References: First Union National Bank; First Federal Savings & Loan Association of Lake County.

For full biographical listings, see the Martindale-Hubbell Law Directory

VERO BEACH,* Indian River Co.

CLEM, POLACKWICH, VOCELLE & TAYLOR (AV)

A Partnership including Professional Associations
Univest Building-Suite 501, 2770 North Indian River Boulevard, 32960
Telephone: 561-562-8111
Fax: 561-562-2870

MEMBERS OF FIRM
Chester Clem (P.A.)   Louis B. Vocelle, Jr., (P.A.)
Alan S. Polackwich, Sr. (P.A.)   James A. Taylor, III
ASSOCIATE
Paul Richard Berg
OF COUNSEL
Robert Golden

References: Barnett Bank of The Treasure Coast; Northern Trust Bank of Vero Beach; Indian River National Bank; Riverside National Bank of Florida.

For full biographical listings, see the Martindale-Hubbell Law Directory

WEST PALM BEACH,* Palm Beach Co.

BOBO, SPICER, CIOTOLI, FULFORD, BOCCHINO, DeBEVOISE & LE CLAINCHE, P.A. (AV)

Esperante, Sixth Floor, 222 Lakeview Avenue, 33401
Telephone: 407-684-6600
Fax: 407-684-3828
Orlando, Florida Office: Landmark Center One, Suite 510, 315 East Robinson Street, 32801-1949.
Telephone: 407-849-1060.
Fax: 407-843-4751.

A. Russell Bobo   D. Andrew DeBevoise
David W. Spicer   (Resident, Orlando Office)
Eugene L. Ciotoli   Stephan A. Le Clainche
Jeffrey C. Fulford   Patti A. Haber
John W. Bocchino   (Resident, Orlando Office)
    (Resident, Orlando Office)   Joseph A. Osborne

Mark Alan Glassman   Casey D. Shomo
Michael S. Smith   Armando T. Lauritano
Neil A. Deleon   Ingrid A. de Graaff
Gregorio A. Francis   (Resident, Orlando Office)
    (Resident, Orlando Office)   Thomas W. Poulton
Michael D. Burt   (Resident, Orlando Office)

For full biographical listings, see the Martindale-Hubbell Law Directory

THE LAW OFFICE OF BILL BONE, P.A. (AV)

One Clearlake Centre Suite 1404, 250 Australian Avenue South, 33401
Telephone: 407-832-9400
Fax: 407-832-9445
Email: billbone@billbone.com

William Dudley "Bill" Bone
LEGAL SUPPORT PERSONNEL
Jeffrey F. Chapin   Richard E. Lopez

For full biographical listings, see the Martindale-Hubbell Law Directory

DAVIS, GORDON, DONER & CHANDLER, P.A. (AV)

515 North Flagler Drive, 7th Floor, 33401
Telephone: 561-659-7337
Facsimile: 561-659-0143
URL: http://www.dgdc.com

Zell Davis, Jr.   Adam S. Doner
Robert E. Gordon   Lawrence U. L. Chandler

Lawrence L. Klayman   Deirdre E. Brett

(See Next Column)

OF COUNSEL
Charles J. Oswald   Mikel D. Jones
                                     (Not admitted in FL)

For full biographical listings, see the Martindale-Hubbell Law Directory

ALAN C. ESPY, P.A. (AV)

Commerce Pointe, Suite 420, 1818 South Australian Avenue, 33409
Telephone: 561-478-4777
Fax: 561-478-0886

Alan C. Espy

Steven J. Cramer

For full biographical listings, see the Martindale-Hubbell Law Directory

FARISH, FARISH & ROMANI (AV)

316 Banyan Boulevard, P.O. Box 4118, 33402
Telephone: 561-659-3500
1-800-401-4LAW
Fax: 561-655-3158

MEMBERS OF FIRM
Joseph D. Farish (1892-1977)   Joseph D. Farish, Jr.
Robert V. Romani
ASSOCIATES
S. Emory Rogers   Peter M. Bassaline
Keith R. Taylor
LEGAL SUPPORT PERSONNEL
Ken P. Beelner

References: 1st Union Bank; Clewiston National Bank; Barnett Bank of Palm Beach County.

For full biographical listings, see the Martindale-Hubbell Law Directory

GAMOT & FREEMAN (AV)

315 Fifth Street, 33401-3709
Telephone: 561-655-6025
Fax: 561-655-5759
Palatka, Florida Office: 415 St. Johns Avenue.
Telephone: 904-325-6239.
Fax: 904-329-9626.

Melinda Penney Gamot   Terry N. Freeman
Albert J. Gamot, Jr.

For full biographical listings, see the Martindale-Hubbell Law Directory

STUART E. KOCHA, P.A. (AV)

118 Clematis Street, P.O. Box 1427, 33402
Telephone: 561-659-5611
Fax: 561-659-5636

Stuart E. Kocha
LEGAL SUPPORT PERSONNEL
David L. Halderman (Chief Investigator)

References: Admiralty Bank.

For full biographical listings, see the Martindale-Hubbell Law Directory

LEWIS, VEGOSEN, ROSENBACH & SILBER, P.A. (AV)

500 South Australian Avenue, P.O. Box 4388, 33402-4388
Telephone: 561-659-3300
Fax: 561-832-1991

Robert M. Lewis (1932-1982)   Cynthia J. Jackson
Dean Vegosen   Gary Walk
Dean J. Rosenbach   John B. Levitt
Louis M. Silber   Samuel A. Thomas
Gary M. Dunkel   Marshall J. Osofsky
Kenneth A. Treadwell   John R. Sheppard, Jr.
Cass Walker Christenson

For full biographical listings, see the Martindale-Hubbell Law Directory

JEFFREY M. LIGGIO, P.A. (AV)

213 Southern Boulevard, 33405
Telephone: 407-833-6604
Fax: 407-833-0870

Jeffrey M. Liggio
LEGAL SUPPORT PERSONNEL
Yara B. Vega (Paralegal)

For full biographical listings, see the Martindale-Hubbell Law Directory

West Palm Beach—Continued

LYTAL, REITER, CLARK, SHARPE, ROCA, FOUNTAIN & WILLIAMS (AV)

A Partnership of Professional Associations
Tenth Floor, 515 North Flagler Drive, 33401
Telephone: 561-655-1990
Fax: 561-832-2932
Mailing Address: P.O. Box 4056, 33402

Lake Lytal, Jr. (P.A.)	Tracy R. Sharpe (P.A.)
Joseph J. Reiter (P.A.)	Rafael J. Roca (P.A.)
Mark W. Clark (P.A.)	Donald R. Fountain, Jr. (P.A.)

William S. Williams (P.A.)

Michael J. Overbeck	David M. Gaspari
Yvette Trelles Murray	Julie H. Littky-Rubin
Kevin C. Smith	Nancy L. La Vista

David C. Prather

Reference: United National Bank.

For full biographical listings, see the Martindale-Hubbell Law Directory

CARL M. MATHISON, JR. (AV)

Northpoint Corporate Center, 701 Northpoint Parkway, Suite 208, 33407
Telephone: 561-471-4144
Fax: 407-471-3988

MONTGOMERY & LARMOYEUX (AV)

1016 Clearwater Place, Drawer 3086, 33402-3086
Telephone: 561-832-2880
Fax: 561-832-0887

MEMBERS OF FIRM

Robert M. Montgomery, Jr.	Christopher M. Larmoyeux

ASSOCIATES

Charles C. Powers	John B. Moores

Sharon Johnson Calix

For full biographical listings, see the Martindale-Hubbell Law Directory

PATRICK M. O'HARA, P.A. (AV)

Commerce Center, Suite 100, 324 Datura Street, 33401
Telephone: 561-659-3771
Fax: 561-659-4224

Patrick M. O'Hara

For full biographical listings, see the Martindale-Hubbell Law Directory

PRUITT & PRUITT, P.A. (AV)

Suite 400 Flagler Tower, 505 South Flagler Drive, 33401
Telephone: 407-655-8080
Fax: 407-655-4134

William H. Pruitt	William E. Pruitt

Reference: Flagler National Bank.

For full biographical listings, see the Martindale-Hubbell Law Directory

RICCI, HUBBARD, LEOPOLD & FRANKEL, P.A. (AV)

United National Bank Building, Suite 250, 1645 Palm Beach Lakes
Boulevard, P.O. Box 2946, 33402
Telephone: 561-684-6500
Fax: 651-697-2383
URL: http://www.PBOL.COM/RICCI

Edward M. Ricci	Theodore J. Leopold
James R. Hubbard	Lois J. Frankel

Scott C. Murray

For full biographical listings, see the Martindale-Hubbell Law Directory

ROBERTS & SOJKA, P.A. (AV)

1675 Palm Beach Lakes Boulevard, Seventh Floor P.O. Drawer
4178, 33401
Telephone: 561-686-1800
FAX: 561-686-1533
New Port Richey, Florida Office: Roberts, Sojka & Associates, P.A., 5841
Main Street, 34652.
Telephone: 813-847-1103.

Gary W. Roberts	Cindy A. Sojka

R. Edward Campbell

For full biographical listings, see the Martindale-Hubbell Law Directory

SEARCY DENNEY SCAROLA BARNHART & SHIPLEY, PROFESSIONAL ASSOCIATION (AV)

2139 Palm Beach Lakes Boulevard, P.O. Drawer 3626, 33402-3626
Telephone: 407-686-6300
800-780-8607
800-220-7006 (Spanish)
Fax: 407-478-0754

Christian D. Searcy, Sr.	Lawrence J. Block, Jr.
Earl L. Denney, Jr.	C. Calvin Warriner, III
John Scarola	William A. Norton
F. Gregory Barnhart	David J. Sales
John A. Shipley	Christopher K. Speed
David K. Kelley, Jr.	William B. King

Karen E. Terry	T. Michael Kennedy
Katherine Ann Martinez	Todd S. Stewart

Laurie J. Briggs

LEGAL SUPPORT PERSONNEL

Deane L. Cady	J. Peter Love
(Paralegal/Investigator)	(Paralegal/Investigator)
James E. Cook	Marjorie A. Morgan (Paralegal)
(Paralegal/Investigator)	William H. Seabold
Emilio Diamantis	(Paralegal/Investigator)
(Paralegal/Investigator)	Kathleen Simon (Paralegal)
David W. Gilmore	Steve M. Smith
(Paralegal/Investigator)	(Paralegal/Investigator)
Thaddeus E. Kulesa	Judson Whitehorn
(Paralegal/Investigator)	(Paralegal/Investigator)

For full biographical listings, see the Martindale-Hubbell Law Directory

WAGNER, JOHNSON & McAFEE, P.A. (AV)

Commerce Pointe, Suite 450, 1818 South Australian Avenue, P.O. Box
3466, 33402
Telephone: 561-686-5200; 1-800-899-5200
Fax: 561-686-6710
Email: macwjm@icanect.net

Ward Wagner, Jr.	Helen Wagner McAfee
Robert R. Johnson	William J. McAfee

Michael G. Bodik	Stacy D. Strolla

References: SunTrust Bank, South Florida, N.A.; Fidelity Federal Savings &
Loan Association of West Palm Beach.

For full biographical listings, see the Martindale-Hubbell Law Directory

MICHAEL P. WALSH, P.A. (AV)

501 South Flagler Drive, Suite 504, 33401
Telephone: 407-659-3989
Fax: 407-659-3822

Michael P. Walsh

For full biographical listings, see the Martindale-Hubbell Law Directory

WIEDERHOLD, MOSES, BULFIN & RUBIN, P.A. (AV)

Northbridge Centre, Suite 800, 515 North Flagler Drive, P.O. Box
3918, 33401
Telephone: 407-659-2296;
Broward: 954-763-5630
FAX: 407-659-2865

John P. Wiederhold	John J. Bulfin
Robert D. Moses	Kenneth M. Rubin

Lawrence I. Bass	Kay Seeber Hoff

Bruce R. Katzell

LEGAL SUPPORT PERSONNEL

Thomas M. Blinstrub

Reference: Barnett Bank of Palm Beach County.

For full biographical listings, see the Martindale-Hubbell Law Directory

---

WINTER HAVEN, Polk Co.

CURTIS ALEXANDER & VARNER (AV)

101 6th Street, N.W., P.O. Box 189, 33882-0189
Telephone: 941-297-5111
Telecopier: 941-293-4104

MEMBERS OF FIRM

Clinton A. Curtis	M. David Alexander, III

Joseph H. Varner, III

ASSOCIATE

Angela S. Klug

For full biographical listings, see the Martindale-Hubbell Law Directory

Winter Haven—Continued

THE STANLEY WINES LAW FIRM, P.A. (AV)

60 Second Street, S.E., P.O. Box 860, 33880
Telephone: 941-299-1263
Telecopier: 941-294-4397
Email: 76077.3453@compuserve.com

J. Mason Wines   Michael B. Murphy
Barry W. Bennett   Craig M. Spanjers
Larry S. Helms

Starlene D. McGory

References: SunTrust Bank/Mid-Florida, N.A.; Attorney's Title Insurance Fund; Jack M. Berry, Inc.; Berry-Cassidy, Inc.

For full biographical listings, see the Martindale-Hubbell Law Directory

---

WINTER PARK, Orange Co.

RICHARD B. TROUTMAN, P.A. (AV)

Suite 500 1245 West Fairbanks Avenue, 32789
Telephone: 407-647-5002
Fax: 407-647-2050

Richard B. Troutman   Brett M. Bressler

Stephen H. McNeill

For full biographical listings, see the Martindale-Hubbell Law Directory

---

GEORGIA

ALBANY,* Dougherty Co.

CANNON & MEYER VON BREMEN, LLP (AV)

2417 Westgate Drive, P.O. Box 70909, 31708-0909
Telephone: 912-435-1470
Telefax: 912-888-2156

MEMBERS OF FIRM
William E. Cannon, Jr.   Michael S. Meyer von Bremen
ASSOCIATES
Toysha M. Flowers   William H. Gregory, II
OF COUNSEL
Timothy O. Davis

For full biographical listings, see the Martindale-Hubbell Law Directory

---

ATHENS,* Clarke Co.

FOY S. HORNE, JR., P.C. (AV)

Suite 901, NationsBank Building, P.O. Box 706, 30603
Telephone: 706-549-6376
Fax: 706-613-2508

Foy S. Horne, Jr.
Bank Reference: NationsBank of Georgia, N.A.

For full biographical listings, see the Martindale-Hubbell Law Directory

---

HUDSON AND MONTGOMERY, P.C. (AV)

183 W. Clayton Street, P.O. Box 8068, 30603
Telephone: 706-549-9823
Fax: 706-353-3934

James E. Hudson   David R. Montgomery
Kenneth Kalivoda

References: NationsBank; Southern Heritage Savings Bank; Georgia National Bank.

For full biographical listings, see the Martindale-Hubbell Law Directory

---

ATLANTA,* Fulton Co.

WALTER H. BECKHAM, P.C. (AV)

2600 The Grand, 75 Fourteenth Street, 30309
Telephone: 404-873-8000
Fax: 404-873-8050

Walter H. Beckham, III

For full biographical listings, see the Martindale-Hubbell Law Directory

---

BEDFORD, KIRSCHNER AND VENKER, P.C. (AV)

Suite 450, 600 West Peachtree Street, N.W., 30308
Telephone: 404-872-6646

(See Next Column)

T. Jackson Bedford, Jr.   Andrew R. Kirschner
Thomas J. Venker

For full biographical listings, see the Martindale-Hubbell Law Directory

---

BIRD, BALLARD & STILL (AV)

14 Seventeenth Street, Suite 5, P.O. Box 7009, 30357
Telephone: 404-873-4696
Fax: 404-872-3745

William Q. Bird   William L. Ballard
Edward R. Still   John G. Mabrey
Karin L. Allen

For full biographical listings, see the Martindale-Hubbell Law Directory

---

BIVENS, HOFFMAN & FOWLER (AV)

A Partnership of Professional Corporations
5040 Roswell Road, N.E., 30342
Telephone: 404-256-6464
FAX: 404-256-1422

MEMBER OF FIRM
L. Brown Bivens (P.C.)

For full biographical listings, see the Martindale-Hubbell Law Directory

---

BLACKWOOD, MATTHEWS & STEEL (AV)

2695 Buford Highway Suite 100, 30324-3239
Telephone: 404-636-9797
Fax: 404-320-9790

MEMBERS OF FIRM
James B. Matthews, III   John B. Briggs
John D. Steel   H. Craig Stafford

For full biographical listings, see the Martindale-Hubbell Law Directory

---

BONDURANT, MIXSON & ELMORE, LLP (AV)

1201 W. Peachtree Street Suite 3900, 30309
Telephone: 404-881-4100
FAX: 404-881-4111

MEMBERS OF FIRM
Emmet J. Bondurant II   Dirk G. Christensen
H. Lamar Mixson   Jane E. Fahey
M. Jerome Elmore   John E. Floyd
Edward B. Krugman   Michael A. Sullivan
Jeffrey O. Bramlett   Michael B. Terry

Representative Clients: The Aetna Casualty and Surety Company; Blue Circle of America; Circle K; Conoco, Inc.; Delta Air Lines, Inc.; Queen Carpets, Inc.; Sanifill, Inc.; Ticketmaster; Trammell Crow Co.; Wyle Laboratories.

For full biographical listings, see the Martindale-Hubbell Law Directory

---

DAVID WM. BOONE, P.C. (AV)

3155 Roswell Road Suite 100, The Cotton Exchange, 30305
Telephone: 404-239-0305
FAX: 404-239-0520

David William Boone

For full biographical listings, see the Martindale-Hubbell Law Directory

---

BUTLER, WOOTEN, OVERBY, CHEELEY, PEARSON & FRYHOFER (AV)

2719 Buford Highway, 30324
Telephone: 404-321-1700
WATS 1-800-242-2962
Fax: 404-321-1713
Columbus, Georgia Office: 1500 Second Avenue, P.O. Box 2766.
Telephone: 706-322-1990; *National Wats:* 1-800-233-4086.
Fax: 706-323-2962.

MEMBERS OF FIRM
James E. Butler, Jr.   Albert M. Pearson, III
Joel O. Wooten, Jr.   George W. Fryhofer III
C. Frederick Overby   Peter J. Daughtery
Robert D. Cheeley   J. Frank Myers, III
Lee Tarte Wallace
ASSOCIATES
Jason L. Crawford   Joshua Sacks
Keith A. Pittman   Teresa Thomas Abell
Cale H. Conley

Reference: Columbus Bank and Trust, Columbus, Ga.

For full biographical listings, see the Martindale-Hubbell Law Directory

---

EDGAR L. CROSSETT, III, P.C. (AV)

5447 Roswell Road, Suite 200, 30342
Telephone: 404-843-1640
Telecopier: 404-847-0602

(See Next Column)

EDGAR L. CROSSETT, III, P.C., *Atlanta—Continued*

Edgar L. Crossett, III

For full biographical listings, see the Martindale-Hubbell Law Directory

DENNIS, CORRY, PORTER & GRAY (AV)

3300 One Atlanta Plaza, 950 East Paces Ferry Road, P.O. Box 18640, 30326
Telephone: 404-816-2800
Wats: 800-735-0838
Fax: 404-816-5656

MEMBERS OF FIRM

Robert E. Corry, Jr.	James S. Strawinski
R. Clay Porter	Grant B. Smith
William E. Gray, II	Frederick D. Evans, III

OF COUNSEL

Douglas Dennis

ASSOCIATES

Robert G. Ballard	Brian DeVoe Rogers
Matthew J. Jewell	Julia J. Yoffee
Pamela Jean Gray	Scott W. McMickle
J. Steven Fisher	Susan E. Cartwright
Thomas D. Trask	Christopher D. Pixley
Robert David Schoen	Raymond J. Kurey
Alison Roberts Solomon	Amber B. Shushan

Representative Clients: Schneider National, Inc.; Roadway Express, Inc.; Caliber System, Inc.

For full biographical listings, see the Martindale-Hubbell Law Directory

DOFFERMYRE, SHIELDS, CANFIELD, KNOWLES & DEVINE (AV)

Suite 1600, 1355 Peachtree Street, 30309
Telephone: 404-881-8900

Robert E. Shields	Kenneth S. Canfield
Ralph I. Knowles, Jr.	

ASSOCIATES

Leslie J. Bryan	Robert Hutton Brown, III
Georgiana Rizk	Laura M. Shamp
Samuel W. Wethern	

For full biographical listings, see the Martindale-Hubbell Law Directory

DREW ECKL & FARNHAM (AV)

880 West Peachtree Street, P.O. Box 7600, 30357
Telephone: 404-885-1400
Facsimile: 404-876-0992
Email: drew@igc.apc.org

MEMBERS OF FIRM

W. Wray Eckl	T. Bart Gary
Clayton H. Farnham	Kenneth A. Hindman
Arthur H. Glaser	Paul W. Burke
James M. Poe	Daniel C. Kniffen
John A. Ferguson, Jr.	John C. Bruffey, Jr.
Theodore Freeman	Benton J. Mathis, Jr.
John P. Reale	John G. Blackmon, Jr.
Stevan A. Miller	Gary R. Hurst
H. Michael Bagley	Dennis M. Hall
Hall F. McKinley III	J. William Haley
G. Randall Moody	Ann Bishop Byars
B. Holland Pritchard	Stephen W. Mooney

ASSOCIATES

Nicole D. Tifverman	Patricia R. Stevens
L. Lee Bennett, Jr.	C. Lawrence Meyer
Katherine D. Dixon	Philip G. Pompilio
William T. Mitchell	Robert J. Moye III
J. Robb Cruser	Sean W. Conley
Philip Wade Savrin	Mary Anne Ackourey
Lucian Gillis, Jr.	Beverly Powell Sisk
Peter H. Schmidt, II	Marion M. Handley
April Rich	Stuart B. Bagley
Maureen M. Middleton	Thomas L. Walker
Robert L. Welch	James P. Anderson
Suzanne VonHarten Sanders	Kathryn Blythe Offer
Leigh Lawson Reeves	Donald M. McManus, Jr.
Bruce A. Taylor, Jr.	Peter B. Barlow
Douglas M. Baker	Nancy L. Pasterz
David R. Bergquist	Gregory G. Schultz
Charles L. Norton, Jr.	Christopher R. Stovall
Nancy F. Rigby	Charles E. Symington, Jr.
Douglas G. Smith, Jr.	Kristian Knochel
Terrence T. Rock	(Not admitted in GA)
Phillip Comer Griffeth	Lewis P. Perling
Marian S. Singer	Scott P. Archer
Steven D. Prelutsky	(Not admitted in GA)
Julianne L. Swilley	Fred L. Hubbs Jr.
B. Greg Cline	W. Gregory Pope
Jennifer E. Moore	

(See Next Column)

SENIOR ATTORNEY

Richard Metzger

OF COUNSEL

Charles L. Drew	Anne M. Landrum
Christopher E. Parker	

Representative Clients: American International Group; Alexsis, Inc.; Church Mutual Insurance Company; CIGNA; Denman Tire Corporation; Scottsdale Insurance Co.; Cooper Tire and Rubber; CNA Insurance Company; Hanover Insurance Company; United States Fidelity and Guaranty.

For full biographical listings, see the Martindale-Hubbell Law Directory

DWYER, WHITE & SAPP (AV)

A Partnership including a Professional Corporation
Suite 700, 2100 Riveredge Parkway, 30328-4654
Telephone: 770-956-1984
Fax: 770-956-1381

MEMBERS

J. Matthew Dwyer, Jr. (P.C.)	William Woods White
Anne Woolf Sapp	

ASSOCIATES

Carmen D. Smith	Carmen S. Mills

For full biographical listings, see the Martindale-Hubbell Law Directory

ENGLAND & McKNIGHT (AV)

Suite 410 River Ridge, 9040 Roswell Road, 30350
Telephone: 770-641-6010
FAX: 770-641-6003

MEMBERS OF FIRM

J. Melvin England	Robert H. McKnight, Jr.

Reference: Nations Bank N.A.

For full biographical listings, see the Martindale-Hubbell Law Directory

GARLAND, SAMUEL & LOEB, P.C. (AV)

3151 Maple Drive, N.E., 30305
Telephone: 404-262-2225
Fax: 404-365-5041
Email: TrialLaw@aol.com

Edward T. M. Garland	Donald F. Samuel
Robin N. Loeb	

For full biographical listings, see the Martindale-Hubbell Law Directory

GOLDNER, SOMMERS, SCRUDDER & BASS (AV)

900 Circle 75 Parkway Suite 850, 30339
Telephone: 770-612-9200
Facsimile: 770-612-9201

Stephen L. Goldner	Henry E. Scrudder, Jr.

For Complete List of Firm Personnel, See General Section

For full biographical listings, see the Martindale-Hubbell Law Directory

HART & McINTYRE (AV)

Promenade Two Suite 3775, 1230 Peachtree Street, N.E., 30309
Telephone: 800-521-3775 (Nationwide); 404-876-3775
Fax: 404-873-3799

MEMBERS OF FIRM

George W. Hart	John C. McIntyre, Jr.

Reference: Nations Bank.

For full biographical listings, see the Martindale-Hubbell Law Directory

HILL AND BLEIBERG (AV)

Suite 200, 47 Perimeter Center East, 30346
Telephone: 770-394-7800
Fax: 770-394-7802

MEMBERS OF FIRM

Robert P. Bleiberg	Gary Hill

For full biographical listings, see the Martindale-Hubbell Law Directory

JOHNSON & WARD (AV)

2100 The Equitable Building, 100 Peachtree Street N.W., 30303-1962
Telephone: 404-524-5626
Facsimile: 404-524-1769

OF COUNSEL

D. Lake Rumsey, Jr.

(See Next Column)

JOHNSON & WARD—*Continued*

MEMBERS OF FIRM

William C. Lanham
Clark H. McGehee

John C. Dabney, Jr.
William D. deGolian

Bruce A. Maxwell

For Complete List of Firm Personnel, See General Section

For full biographical listings, see the Martindale-Hubbell Law Directory

KAUFMAN, CHAIKEN, RICKERTSEN, KREVOLIN, MILLER & HORST, A PROFESSIONAL CORPORATION (AV)

400 Perimeter Center Terrace, N.E., Suite 720, 30346-1234
Telephone: 770-390-9200
Facsimile: 770-395-6720
Email: rkaufm03@counsel.com

Robert J. Kaufman

Craig D. Miller

Michael G. Regas, II

References: Gulf States Mortgage Co., Inc.; Dyer & Dyer Volvo, Inc.; Trust Company Bank; Wachovia Bank of Georgia.

For Complete List of Firm Personnel, See General Section

For full biographical listings, see the Martindale-Hubbell Law Directory

THOMAS WILLIAM MALONE (AV)

Two Ravinia Drive Suite 300, 30346
Telephone: 770-390-7550
Fax: 770-390-7560

Lawrence J. Pond

J. Hoyt Young

ASSOCIATE

Deborah Haas Thaler

References: SunTrust Bank, Atlanta, Georgia; SunTrust Bank of South Georgia.

For full biographical listings, see the Martindale-Hubbell Law Directory

PIERCE & YOUNG (AV)

Building 1700, 2255 Cumberland Parkway Northwest, 30339-4575
Telephone: 770-435-0500
Telecopier: 770-435-0362

MEMBERS OF FIRM

J. Wayne Pierce

Richard M. Young

ASSOCIATE

Christy A. Dunkelberger

For full biographical listings, see the Martindale-Hubbell Law Directory

POPE, MCGLAMRY, KILPATRICK & MORRISON (AV)

A Partnership including Professional Corporations
83 Walton Street, N.W., P.O. Box 1733, 30303
Telephone: 404-523-7706;
Phenix City, Alabama: 334-298-7354
Columbus, Georgia Office: 318 11th Street, 2nd Floor, P.O. Box 2128, 31902-2128.
Telephone: 706-324-0050.

MEMBERS OF FIRM

C. Neal Pope (P.C.)
Max R. McGlamry (P.C.)
(Resident, Columbus, Georgia Office)
Paul V. Kilpatrick, Jr. (Resident, Columbus, Georgia Office)

R. Timothy Morrison
Michael L. McGlamry
Earle F. Lasseter
William Usher Norwood, III
William J. Cornwell
Jay F. Hirsch

Wade H. Tomlinson, III

RESIDENT ASSOCIATE

C. Elizabeth Pope

Reference: Columbus Bank & Trust Co.

For full biographical listings, see the Martindale-Hubbell Law Directory

REYNOLDS & MCARTHUR (AV)

A Partnership including a Professional Corporation
Suite 1080, One Buckhead Plaza, 3060 Peachtree Road, N.W., 30305
Telephone: 404-240-0265
Fax: 404-262-3557
Macon, Georgia Office: 850 Walnut Street.
Telephone: 912-741-6000.
Fax: 912-742-0750.
Asheville, North Carolina Office: The Jackson Building, 22 South Pack Square, Suite 1200.
Telephone: 704-254-8523.
Fax: 704-254-3038.

(See Next Column)

MEMBERS OF FIRM

W. Carl Reynolds (P.C.)
Katherine L. McArthur
Charles M. Cork, III

O. Wendell Horne, III
Bradley J. Survant
Steve Ray Warren
(Not admitted in GA)

For full biographical listings, see the Martindale-Hubbell Law Directory

ANDREW M. SCHERFFIUS, P.C. (AV)

3166 Mathieson Drive, P.O. Box 53299, 30355
Telephone: 404-261-3562; 1-800-521-2867
Fax: 404-841-0861

Andrew M. Scherffius

Tamara McDowell Ayres

For full biographical listings, see the Martindale-Hubbell Law Directory

KENNETH L. SHIGLEY (AV)

325 Hammond Drive, N.E. Suite 300, 30328-5028
Telephone: 404-252-1108
Fax: 404-843-3055
Email: kshigley@counsel.com *URL:* http://www.ga-law.com

For full biographical listings, see the Martindale-Hubbell Law Directory

THOMAS, KENNEDY, SAMPSON & PATTERSON (AV)

55 Marietta Street, N.W., Suite 1600, 30303
Telephone: 404-688-4503
Telecopier: 404-681-2950

MEMBERS OF FIRM

John Loren Kennedy
(1942-1994)
Thomas G. Sampson

P. Andrew Patterson
Myra H. Dixon
Jeffrey E. Tompkins

ASSOCIATES

Rosalind T. Drakeford
Melynee C. Leftridge
La'Sean M. Zilton

Adam L. Smith
Thomas G. Sampson, II
Ceasar C. Mitchell, II.

R. E. Thomas, Jr. (1911-1996)

LEGAL SUPPORT PERSONNEL

Gwendolyn C.H. Dixon
Elbetha (Beth) Martin
Nancy Allen-Haskell

Yvonne Torrence
Priscilla Yolanda Kelly
Lureece D. Lewis (Paralegal)

For full biographical listings, see the Martindale-Hubbell Law Directory

WILLIAMS & HENRY (AV)

Suite 2020, 1100 Peachtree Street, N.E., 30309-4520
Telephone: 404-873-3000
Fax: 404-873-4508

MEMBERS OF FIRM

Benjamin S. Williams

Philip C. Henry

Harvey R. Spiegel

ASSOCIATE

Joseph A. Fried

OF COUNSEL

Robert L. Callahan, III

Reference: Trust Company Bank.

For full biographical listings, see the Martindale-Hubbell Law Directory

---

AUGUSTA, * Richmond Co.

BURNSIDE, WALL, DANIEL, ELLISON & REVELL (AV)

A Partnership including Professional Corporations
454 Greene Street, P.O. Box 2125, 30903
Telephone: 706-722-0768
Fax: 706-722-5984

MEMBERS OF FIRM

Robert C. Daniel, Jr.
(1943-1993)
Thomas R. Burnside, Jr. (P.C.)

James B. Wall (P.C.)
James W. Ellison
Harry D. Revell

Thomas R. Burnside, III

ASSOCIATE

Lori S. D'Alessio

Representative Clients: Augusta-Richmond County Commission-Council; National Science Center Foundation, Inc.; CSRA Regional Development Center; City of Harlem, Georgia; Liquid Carbonic Corp.; Southern Machine & Tool Co.; Jefferson EMC; Southeastern Equipment Co.; SECO Aviation, Inc.; SECO Parts & Equipment, Inc.

For full biographical listings, see the Martindale-Hubbell Law Directory

Augusta—Continued

CAPERS, DUNBAR, SANDERS & BRUCKNER (AV)

Fifteenth Floor, First Union Bank Building, 30901-1454
Telephone: 706-722-7542
Telecopier: 706-724-7776

MEMBERS OF FIRM

John D. Capers   E. Frederick Sanders
Paul H. Dunbar, III   Ziva P. Bruckner

ASSOCIATE

Carl P. Dowling

For full biographical listings, see the Martindale-Hubbell Law Directory

STANLEY C. HOUSE (AV)

Suite 506 The Lamar Building, 753 Broad Street, P.O. Box
915, 30903-0915
Telephone: 706-722-3341
Fax: 706-722-0471
Email: schouse@counsel.com

Approved Attorney for: Lawyers Title Insurance Corp.
References: First Union Bank & Trust (Augusta); NationsBank (Augusta).

For full biographical listings, see the Martindale-Hubbell Law Directory

SAMUEL F. MAGUIRE (AV)

448 Telfair Street, 30901
Telephone: 706-722-4341
Fax: 706-724-8300

Representative Clients: Utilities of Augusta; Electrical Equipment Co.
Approved Attorney for: First American Title Insurance Co.

For full biographical listings, see the Martindale-Hubbell Law Directory

BLAKELY,* Early Co.

WILLIAM S. STONE, P.C. (AV)

Stone Building, 107 College Street, P.O. Box 70, 31723
Telephone: 912-723-3045
Fax: 912-723-4834

William S. Stone   William Lowrey Stone
                          (1894-1970)

Thomas E. Sasser, III   Kevin R. Dean
         T. Craig Earnest

For full biographical listings, see the Martindale-Hubbell Law Directory

BRUNSWICK,* Glynn Co.

KILLIAN AND BOYD (AV)

506 Monk Street, P.O. Box 1795, 31521
Telephone: 912-265-5063; 1-800-339-5063 (S.E. Georgia only)
Fax: 912-265-1209

MEMBERS OF FIRM

Robert P. Killian   Roy J. Boyd, Jr.

ASSOCIATE

Nathan P. Carter

For full biographical listings, see the Martindale-Hubbell Law Directory

BUFORD, Gwinnett Co.

JOSEPH E. CHEELEY, JR., P.C. (AV)

345 East Main Street, 30518-5718
Telephone: 770-945-1442
Fax: 770-945-1444

Joseph E. Cheeley, Jr.

For full biographical listings, see the Martindale-Hubbell Law Directory

CEDARTOWN,* Polk Co.

MUNDY & GAMMAGE, P.C. (AV)

216 Main Street, P.O. Box 930, 30125-0930
Telephone: 706-748-3870
Fax: 706-748-2489
Rome, Georgia Office: The Carnegie Building, 607 Broad Street.
Telephone: 706-290-5180.

Emil Lamar Gammage, Jr.   Miles L. Gammage
William D. Sparks   John S. Husser
(Mrs.) Gerry E. Holmes   B. Jean Crane
George E. Mundy   Kelly A. Benedict

For full biographical listings, see the Martindale-Hubbell Law Directory

COLUMBUS,* Muscogee Co.

BUTLER, WOOTEN, OVERBY, CHEELEY, PEARSON & FRYHOFER (AV)

1500 Second Avenue, P.O. Box 2766, 31902
Telephone: 706-322-1990;
National Wats: 1-800-233-4086
Fax: 706-323-2962
Atlanta, Georgia Office: 2719 Buford Highway, 30324.
Telephone: 404-321-1700.
Fax: 404-321-1713. Wats Line: 1-800-242-2962.

MEMBERS OF FIRM

James E. Butler, Jr.   Albert M. Pearson, III
Joel O. Wooten, Jr.   George W. Fryhofer III
C. Frederick Overby   Peter J. Daughtery
Robert D. Cheeley   J. Frank Myers, III
        Lee Tarte Wallace

ASSOCIATES

Jason L. Crawford   Joshua Sacks
Keith A. Pittman   Teresa Thomas Abell
        Cale H. Conley

For full biographical listings, see the Martindale-Hubbell Law Directory

POPE, McGLAMRY, KILPATRICK & MORRISON (AV)

A Partnership including Professional Corporations
318 11th Street, 2nd Floor, P.O. Box 2128, 31902-2128
Telephone: 706-324-0050;
Phenix City, Alabama: 334-298-7354
Atlanta, Georgia Office: 83 Walton Street, N.W., P.O. Box 1733, 30303.
Telephone: 404-523-7706.

MEMBERS OF FIRM

C. Neal Pope (P.C.)   Michael L. McGlamry
Max R. McGlamry (P.C.)   Earle F. Lasseter
 (Resident)   William Usher Norwood, III
Paul V. Kilpatrick, Jr.   (Resident, Atlanta Office)
 (Resident)   William J. Cornwell
R. Timothy Morrison   Jay F. Hirsch
       Wade H. Tomlinson, III

RESIDENT ASSOCIATES

Joan S. Redmond   Teresa Pike Majors
       Matthew N. Pope

Reference: Columbus Bank & Trust Co.

For full biographical listings, see the Martindale-Hubbell Law Directory

TAYLOR, HARP & CALLIER (AV)

Suite 900 The Corporate Center, P.O. Box 2645, 31902-2645
Telephone: 706-323-7711
National WATS: 1-800-422-3352
Fax: 706-323-7544

MEMBERS OF FIRM

J. Sherrod Taylor   J. Anderson Harp
      Jefferson C. Callier

For full biographical listings, see the Martindale-Hubbell Law Directory

CORNELIA, Habersham Co.

CATHEY & STRAIN (AV)

6 Irvin Street, P.O. Box 689, 30531
Telephone: 706-778-2601
Fax: 706-776-2899

MEMBERS OF FIRM

Dennis T. Cathey   Edward E. Strain, III

ASSOCIATES

J. Edward Staples   David A. Sleppy

For full biographical listings, see the Martindale-Hubbell Law Directory

DECATUR,* De Kalb Co.

HYATT & HYATT, P.C. (AV)

Suite 201, Trust Building, 545 North McDonough Street, 30030
Telephone: 404-378-3635
Fax: 404-377-8304

Charles H. Hyatt (1924-1995)   John M. Hyatt

For full biographical listings, see the Martindale-Hubbell Law Directory

PARKERSON, SHELFER & GROFF (AV)

715 First Union Plaza of Decatur, 250 East Ponce de Leon
Avenue, 30030-3490
Telephone: 404-377-8143
Telecopier: 404-373-6829

(See Next Column)

PARKERSON, SHELFER & GROFF—*Continued*
MEMBERS OF FIRM
William S. Shelfer (1900-1975)　　　William S. Shelfer, Jr.
I. J. Parkerson　　　　　　　　　　　David B. Groff

Reference: Nations Bank of Georgia.

For full biographical listings, see the Martindale-Hubbell Law Directory

HINESVILLE,* Liberty Co.

JONES, OSTEEN, JONES & ARNOLD (AV)

206 East Court Street, P.O. Box 800, 31313
Telephone: 912-876-0111
Cable Address: "JOJA"
Fax: 912-368-2979

MEMBERS OF FIRM
Charles M. Jones　　　　　　　　　Billy N. Jones
J. Noel Osteen　　　　　　　　　　Jeffery L. Arnold

ASSOCIATES
G. Brinson Williams, Jr.　　　　　　Mark W. Nickerson
Linnie L. Darden, III　　　　　　　L. Kelly Davis

General Counsel for: The Hinesville Bank; The Coastal Bank; Coastal Utilities, Inc.; Coastal Electric Membership Corp.; Liberty County Hospital Authority; Hinesville Area Board of Realtors; Liberty County Industrial Authority; Liberty County, Georgia; City of Riceboro.

For full biographical listings, see the Martindale-Hubbell Law Directory

JESUP,* Wayne Co.

ROBERT B. SMITH (AV)

356 East Cherry Street, P.O. Box 285, 31598
Telephone: 912-427-4779; 427-4629
FAX: 912-427-9203

References: Trust Company Bank of Southeast Georgia; Baxley Federal Savings Bank.

For full biographical listings, see the Martindale-Hubbell Law Directory

JONESBORO,* Clayton Co.

DRIEBE & DRIEBE, P.C. (AV)

6 Courthouse Way, P.O. Box 975, 30237
Telephone: 770-478-8894
Fax: 770-478-9606
Atlanta, Georgia Office: 152 Nassau Street, N.W.
Telephone: 404-524-0606.

Charles J. Driebe　　　　　　　　Charles J. Driebe, Jr.

For full biographical listings, see the Martindale-Hubbell Law Directory

LAWRENCEVILLE,* Gwinnett Co.

J. MICHAEL McGARITY, P.C. (AV)

229 W. Crogan Street, 30245
Telephone: 770-962-2656
Fax: 770-962-2412

J. Michael McGarity

Bridget Gauvin Moyer

For full biographical listings, see the Martindale-Hubbell Law Directory

WEBB, TANNER & POWELL (AV)

Suite 300 Gwinnett Federal Building, 750 South Perry Street, P.O. Box 27, 30246
Telephone: 770-962-8545; 963-3423
Fax: 770-963-3424

MEMBERS OF FIRM
Jones Webb　　　　　　　　　　　Anthony O. L. Powell
William G. Tanner　　　　　　　　Ralph L. Taylor, III
　　　　　　　　Andrew R. Mertz

Attorneys for: Brand Banking Co.; City of Lawrenceville, GA; Water and Sewer Authority of Gwinnett County; West Georgia Farm Credit, ACA; Georgia Power Co.; Lawyers Title Insurance Corp.; Young Harris College, Young Harris, Georgia; Chicago Title Insurance Co.; International Safety Instruments.

For Complete List of Firm Personnel, See General Section

For full biographical listings, see the Martindale-Hubbell Law Directory

MACON,* Bibb Co.

BUZZELL & PINKSTON (AV)

Suite A, 175 New Street, 31201
Telephone: 912-742-8820
Telecopier: 912-742-3088

(See Next Column)

MEMBERS OF FIRM
R. William Buzzell, II　　　　　　Loretta L. Pinkston

For full biographical listings, see the Martindale-Hubbell Law Directory

HALL, BLOCH, GARLAND & MEYER (AV)

1500 Charter Medical Building, P.O. Box 5088, 31213-3199
Telephone: 912-745-1625
Telecopier: 912-741-8822

MEMBERS OF FIRM
F. Kennedy Hall　　　　　　　　　J. Steven Stewart
Benjamin M. Garland　　　　　　　Mark E. Toth

ASSOCIATES
John Flanders Kennedy　　　　　　Todd C. Brooks
　　　　　　　Kimberly Cofer Harris

For Complete List of Firm Personnel, See General Section

For full biographical listings, see the Martindale-Hubbell Law Directory

O'NEAL, BROWN & SIZEMORE, A PROFESSIONAL CORPORATION (AV)

Suite 1001, American Federal Building, 544 Mulberry Street, 31201
Telephone: 912-742-8981
Telecopier: 912-743-5035
Atlanta, Georgia Office: Suite 2600, One Atlanta Plaza, 950 East Paces Ferry Road, N.E.
Telephone: 404-237-6701.
Telecopier: 404-233-1267.

H. T. O'Neal, Jr. (1924-1983)　　　Manley F. Brown
　　　　　　Lamar W. Sizemore, Jr.

For Complete List of Firm Personnel, See General Section

For full biographical listings, see the Martindale-Hubbell Law Directory

REYNOLDS & McARTHUR (AV)

A Partnership including a Professional Corporation
850 Walnut Street, 31201
Telephone: 912-741-6000
Fax: 912-742-0750
Atlanta, Georgia Office: Suite 1080, One Buckhead Plaza, 3060 Peachtree Road, N.W.
Telephone: 404-240-0265.
Fax: 404-262-3557.
Asheville, North Carolina Office: The Jackson Building, 22 South Pack Square, Suite 1200.
Telephone: 704-254-8523.
Fax: 704-254-3038.

MEMBERS OF FIRM
W. Carl Reynolds (P.C.)　　　　　O. Wendell Horne, III
Katherine L. McArthur　　　　　　Bradley J. Survant
Charles M. Cork, III　　　　　　　Steve Ray Warren
　　　　　　　　　　　　　　　　(Not admitted in GA)

For full biographical listings, see the Martindale-Hubbell Law Directory

SELL & MELTON (AV)

A Partnership including a Professional Corporation
14th Floor, Charter Medical Building, P.O. Box 229, 31297-2899
Telephone: 912-746-8521
Telecopier: 912-745-6426

Mitchel P. House, Jr.　　　　　　　John A. Draughon
Doye E. Green　　　　　　　　　　Russell M. Boston (P.C.)

ASSOCIATE
David M. Cusson

General Counsel for: Macon Telegraph Publishing Co. (The Macon Telegraph); Macon-Bibb County Hospital Authority; County of Bibb; County of Twiggs; Smith & Sons Foods, Inc. (S & S Cafeterias); Macon Bibb County Industrial Authority; Burgess Pigment Co.

For Complete List of Firm Personnel, See General Section

For full biographical listings, see the Martindale-Hubbell Law Directory

MARIETTA,* Cobb Co.

AWTREY AND PARKER, P.C. (AV)

211 Roswell Street, P.O. Box 997, 30061
Telephone: 770-424-8000
Fax: 770-424-1594

L. M. Awtrey, Jr. (1915-1986)　　　Donald A. Mangerie (1924-1988)
George L. Dozier, Jr.　　　　　　　Barbara H. Martin
Harvey D. Harkness　　　　　　　A. Sidney Parker
Mike Harrison　　　　　　　　　　Robert B. Silliman

General Counsel for: Kennesaw Finance Co.; Cobb Electric Membership Corporation; Development Authority of Cobb County.

(See Next Column)

AWTREY AND PARKER P.C., *Marietta—Continued*

Local Counsel for: Coats & Clark; Bell South Mobility; Lockheed-Georgia Corp.; Post Properties, Inc.; CSX Transportation, Inc.

For full biographical listings, see the Martindale-Hubbell Law Directory

---

BARNES, BROWNING, TANKSLEY & CASURELLA (AV)

Suite 225, 166 Anderson Street, 30060
Telephone: 770-424-1500
Fax: 770-424-1740

MEMBERS OF FIRM

Roy E. Barnes	Thomas J. Casurella (1956-1989)
Thomas J. Browning	Jerry A. Landers, Jr.
Charles B. Tanksley	Jeffrey G. Casurella

Benny C. Priest

OF COUNSEL

George T. Smith

For full biographical listings, see the Martindale-Hubbell Law Directory

---

STEVEN L. BEARD, P.C. (AV)

324 Cherokee Street, 30060
Telephone: 770-422-2642
Fax: 770-422-8954

Steven L. Beard

For full biographical listings, see the Martindale-Hubbell Law Directory

---

DOWNEY & CLEVELAND (AV)

288 Washington Avenue, 30060
Telephone: 770-422-3233
Fax: 770-423-4199

OF COUNSEL
Lynn A. Downey

MEMBERS OF FIRM

Robert H. Cleveland	Y. Kevin Williams
(1940-1989)	Russell B. Davis
Joseph C. Parker	G. Lee Welborn

Rodney S. Shockley

ASSOCIATES

W. Curtis Anderson	Todd E. Hatcher
Scott D. Clay	Richard A. Griggs

Tara M. Waller

Representative Clients: Allstate Insurance Co.; St. Paul Insurance Cos.; Georgia Farm Bureau Mutual Insurance Co.; State Farm Insurance Cos.; Cotton States Mutual Insurance Co.; Colonial Insurance Co. of California; Progressive Insurance Company; Auto Owners Insurance Company; Deep South Surplus, Inc.; Ed Voyles Oldsmobile, Honda and Chrysler-Plymouth.

For full biographical listings, see the Martindale-Hubbell Law Directory

---

RICHARD L. POWELL (AV)

142 Forest Avenue, P.O. Box 508, 30061
Telephone: 770-427-0266
Fax: 770-499-7883

LEGAL SUPPORT PERSONNEL
Richele L. Powell

MCDONOUGH, Henry Co.

SMITH, WELCH, STUDDARD & BRITTAIN (AV)

200 The Commerce Building, 235 Keys Ferry Street, P.O. Box 31, 30253
Telephone: 770-957-3937
Fax: 770-957-9165
Stockbridge, Georgia Office: 1231-A Eagle's Landing Parkway.
Telephone: 770-389-4864.
Fax: 770-389-5157.

MEMBERS OF FIRM

Ernest M. Smith (1911-1992)	Ben W. Studdard, III
A. J. Welch, Jr.	J. Mark Brittain
	(Resident, Stockbridge Office)

ASSOCIATES

Patrick D. Jaugstetter	Shawn Marie Story
E. Gilmore Maxwell	Arthur Scully Barbee

Representative Clients: Alliance Corp.; Atlanta Motor Speedway, Inc.; Bellamy-Strickland Chevrolet, Inc.; Ceramic and Metal Coatings Corp.; City of Hampton; City of Locust Grove; City of Stockbridge.

For full biographical listings, see the Martindale-Hubbell Law Directory

---

METTER, Candler Co.

JONES AND SMITH, P.C. (AV)

21 North Kennedy Street, P.O. Box 296, 30439
Telephone: 912-685-5763
Telecopier: 912-685-4902

(See Next Column)

Bobby Jones	Julian B. Smith, Jr.

David N. Nelson	Troy Marsh

Representative Clients: Metter Banking Co.; Wallace Business Forms, Inc.; Cal-Maine Foods, Inc.; Franklin Chevrolet; Federal Land Bank; Georgia Farm Bureau Mutual Insurance Co., Inc.; The Travelers Insurance Co.; Nationwide Insurance Co.; Candler County Board of Commissioners; Hospital Authority of Candler County.

NEWNAN, Coweta Co.

GLOVER & DAVIS, P.A. (AV)

10 Brown Street, P.O. Box 1038, 30264
Telephone: 770-253-4330
Fax: 770-251-7152
Peachtree City, Georgia Office: Suite 130, 200 Westpark Drive.
Telephone: 770-487-5834.
Fax: 770-487-3492.

J. Littleton Glover	W. Robert Hancock, Jr.
Welborn B. Davis, Jr.	(Resident, Peachtree Office)
(1922-1974)	Asa M. Powell, Jr.
J. Littleton Glover, Jr.	Jerry Ann Conner
Alan W. Jackson	Mark E. Dacy (Resident,
Randy E. Connell	Peachtree City Office)

Representative Clients: Newnan Savings Bank; Pike Transfer Co.; Batson-Cook Company, General Corporate and Construction Divisions; Coweta County, Georgia; Heard County, Georgia; Putnam-Greene Financial Corporation.
Local Counsel for: International Latex Corp.; First Union National Bank of Georgia; Wear Georgia; Farm Credit, ACA.

For full biographical listings, see the Martindale-Hubbell Law Directory

---

SAVANNAH, Chatham Co.

JOSEPH B. BERGEN AND FREDERICK S. BERGEN (AV)

Marist Place Lafayette Square, 123 Charlton Street, East, 31401
Telephone: 912-233-6600
Telecopy: 912-233-6660

MEMBERS OF FIRM

Joseph B. Bergen	Frederick S. Bergen

For full biographical listings, see the Martindale-Hubbell Law Directory

---

VALDOSTA, Lowndes Co.

J. CONVERSE BRIGHT (AV)

The McKey Building, 101 E. Central Avenue, P.O. Box 5889, 31603
Telephone: 912-247-7846
Telecopier: 912-245-0693

For full biographical listings, see the Martindale-Hubbell Law Directory

---

DODD AND DENNIS, P.C. (AV)

613 N. Patterson Street, P.O. Box 1066, 31603-1066
Telephone: 912-242-4470
Telefax: 912-245-7731
Email: doddlaw@mail.datasys.net *URL:* http://www.doddlaw.com

Roger J. Dodd	Sam D. Dennis

References: First Union Bank; First State Bank and Trust Co.; Park Avenue Bank.

For full biographical listings, see the Martindale-Hubbell Law Directory

---

HAWAII

HONOLULU, Honolulu Co.

GEORGE W. ASHFORD, JR. (AV)

2910 Pacific Tower, 1001 Bishop Street, 96813
Telephone: 808-528-0444
Telecopier: (808) 533-0761
Cable Address: Justlaw

Representative Clients: Lloyds of London; Baker Industries, Inc.; Burns International Security Services; Clark Equipment Co.; Great Lakes Chemical Corporation; California Union Insurance Co.; Great American Insurance Companies; Guaranty National Companies; Horace Mann Insurance Company; Marine Office of America Corp.

For full biographical listings, see the Martindale-Hubbell Law Directory

Honolulu—Continued

AYABE, CHONG, NISHIMOTO, SIA & NAKAMURA (AV)

A Partnership including a Professional Corporation
Pauahi Tower, Suite 2500, 1001 Bishop Street, 96813
Telephone: 808-537-6119
Telecopier: 808-526-3491

MEMBERS OF FIRM

Sidney K. Ayabe (P.C.)	Diane W. Wong
John S. Nishimoto	Rodney S. Nishida
Richard F. Nakamura	Patricia T. Fujii
Jeffrey H. K. Sia	Rhonda A. Nishimura
Francis M. Nakamoto	Gail M. Kang
Calvin E. Young	Ann H. Aratani

Ronald M. Shigekane	J. Thomas Weber
Robin R. Horner	Robert A. Mash
Virgil B. Prieto	Gary S. Miyamoto

Representative Clients: Travelers Insurance Co.; St. Paul Fire and Marine Insurance Co.; The Employers Group of Insurance Companies; TIG Insurance Co.; Pacific Insurance Co.; Hartford Accident and Indemnity Co.; Continental Casualty Co.; CNA Insurance Co.

For Complete List of Firm Personnel, See General Section

For full biographical listings, see the Martindale-Hubbell Law Directory

LAW OFFICES OF STUART M. COWAN (AV)

Ocean View Center, 707 Richards Street, Suite 728, 96813
Telephone: 808-533-1767
Fax: 808-533-0549
Kaneohe, Hawaii Office: Suite 202, 47-653 Kamehameha Highway.
Telephone: 808-533-1767.
Fax: 808-239-9175.
Reference: 1st Hawaiian Bank.

For full biographical listings, see the Martindale-Hubbell Law Directory

CRONIN, FRIED, SEKIYA, KEKINA & FAIRBANKS ATTORNEYS AT LAW, A LAW CORPORATION (AV)

1900 Davies Pacific Center, 841 Bishop Street, 96813
Telephone: 808-524-1433
Fax: 808-536-2073

Paul F. Cronin	John D. Thomas, Jr.
L. Richard Fried, Jr.	Stuart A. Kaneko
Gerald Y. Sekiya	Bert S. Sakuda
Wayne K. Kekina	Allen K. Williams
David L. Fairbanks	Keith K. H. Young

Patrick W. Border	Clarence S.K. Kekina
Gregory L. Lui-Kwan	Sylvia E.J. Luke
Patrick F. McTernan	Geoffrey K.S. Komeya

For full biographical listings, see the Martindale-Hubbell Law Directory

LYNCH & FARMER (AV)

Suite 2500, Mauka Tower Grosvenor Center, 737 Bishop Street, 96813
Telephone: 808-528-0100
Facsimile: 808-528-4997

Wesley W. Ichida	Steven J. Kim

Paul A. Lynch

LEGAL SUPPORT PERSONNEL

Sylvia M. Lee

For full biographical listings, see the Martindale-Hubbell Law Directory

IAN L. MATTOCH (AV)

Suite 1835 Grosvenor Center, 737 Bishop Street, 96813
Telephone: 808-523-2451
Cable Address: "Illnoncarb"
Fax: 808-531-2652
Hilo, Hawaii Office: 688 Kinoole Street, Suite 202.
Telephone: 808-969-3302.
Fax: 808-961-5599.
Kailua Kona, Hawaii Office: Hualalai Center, Suite D-211, 75-170 Hualalai Road.
Telephone: 808-326-1516.
Fax: 808-326-7416.
Kaneohe, Hawaii Office: 45-781 Kamehameha Highway.
Telephone: 808-247-8598.
Wailuku, Maui, Hawaii Office: 1 Main Plaza, Suite 500.
Telephone: 808-244-5007.
Fax: 808-242-2828.
Kamuela, Hawaii Office: Spencer House, Suite 236, Waimea Centers.
Telephone: 808-885-7727.
Fax: 808-885-1935.

(See Next Column)

William Copulos	Daniel P. Kirley
Rodger I. Hoffman	Jon Curtis Yoshimura
Virgil James Wilson, III	Daniel D. Ebihara

OF COUNSEL

Walter Davis

Reference: First Hawaiian Bank.

For full biographical listings, see the Martindale-Hubbell Law Directory

PERKIN & HOSODA (AV)

2440 Mauka Tower, Grosvenor Center, 737 Bishop Street, 96813
Telephone: 808-523-2300
Fax: 808-531-8898

MEMBERS OF FIRM

John Francis Perkin	Lyle S. Hosoda

For full biographical listings, see the Martindale-Hubbell Law Directory

DENNIS W. POTTS ATTORNEY AT LAW, A LAW CORPORATION (AV)

2700 Pacific Tower, 1001 Bishop Street, 96813
Telephone: 808-537-4575
Fax: 808-599-3524

Dennis W. Potts

For full biographical listings, see the Martindale-Hubbell Law Directory

PRICE OKAMOTO HIMENO & LUM ATTORNEYS AT LAW, A LAW CORPORATION (AV)

Suite 728, Ocean View Center, 707 Richards Street, 96813
Telephone: 808-538-1113
Fax: 808-533-0549

Warren Price, III	Sharon R. Himeno
Kenneth T. Okamoto	Bettina W. J. Lum

Terence S. Yamamoto

Robert Kohn

OF COUNSEL

Stuart M. Cowan	Lawrence R. Cohen

Michael K. Kaneshiro

For full biographical listings, see the Martindale-Hubbell Law Directory

TRECKER & FRITZ (AV)

820 Mililani Street, Suite 701, 96813
Telephone: 808-528-3900
Fax: 808-533-3684

MEMBERS OF FIRM

Steven J. Trecker	Magali V. Sunderland
Collin (Marty) Fritz	Hilary Benson Gangnes

For full biographical listings, see the Martindale-Hubbell Law Directory

LAW OFFICES OF RICHARD TURBIN A LAW CORPORATION (AV)

Suite 1850 Mauka Tower, Grosvenor Center, 737 Bishop Street, 96813
Telephone: 808-528-4000
FAX: 808-599-1984

Richard Turbin

Rai Saint Chu	Thomas M. Pico, Jr.

For full biographical listings, see the Martindale-Hubbell Law Directory

MICHAEL J. Y. WONG (AV)

2222 Central Pacific Plaza, 220 South King Street, 96813
Telephone: 808-536-1855
Fax: 808-536-1857

ASSOCIATE

R. Malia Taum

For full biographical listings, see the Martindale-Hubbell Law Directory

*WAILUKU,** Maui Co.

KRUEGER & CAHILL (AV)

2065 Main Street, 96793
Telephone: 808-244-7444; Honolulu: 536-7474
Facsimile: 808-244-4177
Email: maulaw@maui.net

MEMBERS OF FIRM

James Krueger	Peter T. Cahill

John M. O'Neill

(See Next Column)

KRUEGER & CAHILL, *Wailuku—Continued*

LEGAL SUPPORT PERSONNEL
LEGAL ASSISTANTS

Sharon O'Shaughnessy   Theresa N. Coletti

A List of Representative Clients and References will be furnished upon request.

For full biographical listings, see the Martindale-Hubbell Law Directory

---

ROST & GEIGER (AV)

610 One Main Plaza, 2200 Main Street, 96793
Telephone: 808-244-9044
Fax: 808-242-4195

Richard L. Rost   James W. Geiger

For full biographical listings, see the Martindale-Hubbell Law Directory

---

IDAHO

---

*LEWISTON,** Nez Perce Co.

AHERIN, RICE & ANEGON, A PROFESSIONAL ASSOCIATION (AV)

1212 Idaho Street, Drawer 698, 83501
Telephone: 208-746-3646

Darrel W. Aherin   Stephen C. Rice
Anthony C. Anegon

For full biographical listings, see the Martindale-Hubbell Law Directory

---

ILLINOIS

AURORA, Kane Co.

MURPHY, HUPP, FOOTE, MIELKE AND KINNALLY (AV)

North Island Center, P.O. Box 5030, 60507
Telephone: 708-844-0056
FAX: 708-844-1905

MEMBERS OF FIRM

William C. Murphy   Patrick M. Kinnally
Robert B. Hupp   Paul G. Krentz
Robert M. Foote   Joseph C. Loran
Craig S. Mielke   Gerald K. Hodge

Timothy D. O'Neil
OF COUNSEL
Robert T. Olson

Representative Clients: American Telephone & Telegraph Co.; Fox Valley Park District; Lyon Metal Products; Kane County Forest Preserve District; Hollywood Casino; Employers Mutual Insurance Co.; Forty-Eight Insulations, Inc.; UNR Asbestos Disease Trust; Richards-Wilcox Co.; National Bank & Trust Company of Syracuse.

For full biographical listings, see the Martindale-Hubbell Law Directory

---

*BELLEVILLE,** St. Clair Co.

HEILIGENSTEIN & BADGLEY, PROFESSIONAL CORPORATION (AV)

30 Public Square, 62220
Telephone: 618-235-1000
Fax: 618-235-1086

Christian E. Heiligenstein   Brad L. Badgley

B. Jay Dowling
Reference: Magna Bank, N.A.

For full biographical listings, see the Martindale-Hubbell Law Directory

---

*CHICAGO,** Cook Co.

ANESI, OZMON & RODIN, LTD. (AV)

161 North Clark Street, 21st Floor, 60601
Telephone: 312-372-3822
Fax: 312-372-3833

Nat P. Ozmon   Richard A. Kimnach
Charles E. Anesi (1912-1995)   Joseph J. Miroballi
Richard A. Lewin (1925-1985)   Douglas A. Colby
Curt N. Rodin   David J. Comeau
Mark Novak   James J. Morici, Jr.
Bruce M. Kohen   Alain Leval

(See Next Column)

Stephen S. Phalen   John M. Popelka
Marc A. Taxman   Telly C. Nakos
Scott H. Rudin   Michelle Dekalb
John A. Salzeider   Mark Murnane
David Figlioli   Richard B. Vaughn
Martin J. Lucas   Darius Bozorgi
Daniel V. O'Connor   R. Andrew Hahn
Paul W. Pasche   Ilonka E. Ulrich
Marc J. Cairo
OF COUNSEL
Noel C. Lindenmuth   Irving D. Fasman

For full biographical listings, see the Martindale-Hubbell Law Directory

---

BERMAN & YOTIS, A PROFESSIONAL ASSOCIATION (AV)

(A Professional Association comprised of Professional Corporations)
Suite 2215, 100 North La Salle Street, 60602
Telephone: 312-726-0531
Fax: 312-726-4928

Michael H. Berman (P.C.)   William W. Yotis, III, (P.C.)

Joy C. Airaudi   Dean J. Papadakis
Eric D. Kaplan   Dean Gournis
OF COUNSEL
Karen C. Yotis

For full biographical listings, see the Martindale-Hubbell Law Directory

---

CHARLES A. BOYLE & ASSOCIATES, LTD. (AV)

29 South La Salle Street, Suite 345, 60603
Telephone: 312-346-4944
FAX: 312-368-1061

Charles A. Boyle

Jennifer Leah Barron
Reference: Northern Trust of Chicago.

For full biographical listings, see the Martindale-Hubbell Law Directory

---

BRADLEY & BRADLEY (AV)

29 South La Salle Street Suite 950, 60603
Telephone: 312-372-5454
FAX: 312-372-5458

MEMBERS OF FIRM

Edward J. Bradley   Edward J. Bradley, Jr.

For full biographical listings, see the Martindale-Hubbell Law Directory

---

BRYDGES RISEBOROUGH PETERSON FRANKE AND MORRIS (AV)

A Partnership including Professional Corporations
28th Floor, 150 North Michigan Avenue, 60601
Telephone: 312-782-5042
FAX: 312-704-9107
Waukegan, Illinois Office: 110 North West Street.
Telephone: 847-249-0300.
FAX: 847-249-4755.
Phoenix, Arizona Office: 3030 North Central Avenue, Suite 408.
Telephone: 602-631-4400.
FAX: 602-631-4404.

MEMBERS OF FIRM

Louis W. Brydges, Sr.   Scott E. Nemanich
Allyn J. Franke   Reid S. Jacobson
George E. Riseborough (A   Donald M. Lonchar, Jr.
   Professional Corporation)   Peter J. Nordigian
J. V. Schaffenegger (1914-1986)   Robert L. Snook
Ralph Miller (1922-1988)   Stacey L. Seneczko
Donald G. Peterson   Rebecca Sarah Larson
Thomas A. Morris, Jr., (A   Neal T. Goldstein
   Professional Corporation)   Monica J. Conrad
Donald L. Sime   Gioconda (Jackie) V. Iannicelli
John H. Krackenberger   Jennifer M. Lundy
Jay Scott Nelson   Eleanor P. Cabreré
Michael A. Strom   Linda A. White
Louis W. Brydges, Jr.   William G. Berg
Leslie A. Peterson   John W. Dixon
Thomas K. Gerling   Thomas A. Kiepura

OF COUNSEL
Harry D. Strouse   Thomas J. Moran (1920-1995)
Jack L. Watson

For full biographical listings, see the Martindale-Hubbell Law Directory

Chicago—Continued

BURKE & BURKE, LTD. (AV)

2 First National Plaza, Suite 2200, 60603
Telephone: 312-726-6630
FAX: 312-726-1554
Downers Grove, Illinois Office: 5120 Forest, 60515.
Telephone: 708-852-9197.

John M. Burke	Dennis J. Burke
Edmund P. Burke	Molly C. Mason
	Karen Krajcir White

For full biographical listings, see the Martindale-Hubbell Law Directory

CLIFFORD LAW OFFICES, P.C. (AV)

120 North La Salle Street, 31st Floor, 60602
Telephone: 312-899-9090
1-800-899-0410
Fax: 312-251-1160
Email: 102554.2453@compuserve.com

Robert A. Clifford	Keith A. Hebeisen
	Kevin P. Durkin

Robert P. Walsh, Jr.	Richard L. Pullano
Susan A. Capra	Patricia C. Durkin
Jeffrey J. Kroll	Matthew I. Baker
Thomas K. Prindable	Timothy P. Rhatigan
Richard F. Burke, Jr.	Isobel S. Thomas

OF COUNSEL
Robert P. Sheridan

For full biographical listings, see the Martindale-Hubbell Law Directory

CORBOY & DEMETRIO, P.C. (AV)

33 North Dearborn Street 21st Floor, 60602
Telephone: 312-346-3191
FAX: 312-346-5562
TDD: 312-236-3191
Email: phcorboy@aol.com

Philip H. Corboy	Thomas A. Demetrio
	Philip Harnett Corboy, Jr.

Robert J. Bingle	Susan J. Schwartz
Francis Patrick Murphy	Michael K. Demetrio
	Kevin G. Burke

Renee Blahuta	Daniel M. Kotin
Thomas F. Boleky	Kenneth T. Lumb
Timothy J. Cavanagh	Michael G. Mahoney
Barry R. Chafetz	Michael K. Muldoon
G. Grant Dixon III	Mindy J. Nam
Mary E. Doherty	Margaret M. Power
Shawn S. Kasserman	Edward G. Willer
	David C. Wise

Reference: The American National Bank & Trust Company, Chicago, Illinois.

For full biographical listings, see the Martindale-Hubbell Law Directory

GESSLER, HUGHES & SOCOL, LTD. (AV)

Three First National Plaza, Suite 2200, 60602
Telephone: 312-580-0100
Telecopy: 312-580-1994

Mark S. Dym	Terence J. Moran
George W. Gessler	Mark D. Olson
John K. Hughes	Matthew J. Piers
William P. Jones	David J. Pritchard
Peter M. Katsaros	Kalman D. Resnick
Mark A. LaRose	Frederick S. Rhine
Kimberley Marsh	Jonathan A. Rothstein
	Donna Kaner Socol

Benjamin P. Beringer	Alex W. Miller
Darilyn W. Bock	Belkis Cervantes Muldoon
Gary Chodorow	Jonathan D. Rosenblum
Anjali Dayal	Marci S. Sperling
Ruth M. Dunning	Dana H. Sukenik
Adam D. Ingber	J. Eric Vander Arend
Michael J. Klein	Maria L. Vertuno
Laura C. Liu	Mark B. Weiner
	Charles H. Wintersteen

OF COUNSEL

James T. Derico, Jr.	Darius S. Francescatti, M.D.
	Susan R. Gzesh

For full biographical listings, see the Martindale-Hubbell Law Directory

HARRINGTON, THOMPSON, ACKER & HARRINGTON, LTD. (AV)

310 South Michigan Avenue Suite 2000, 60604
Telephone: 312-922-8833

Robert E. Harrington, Jr.	Kenneth J. Sophie, Jr.
Robert B. Thompson	Robert W. Coster
Laurence C. Acker	Stephen A. Murphy
Patrick J. Harrington	Monica A. Coscia
	Christy L. LeVan

Reference: American National Bank and Trust Co., Chicago, Illinois.

For full biographical listings, see the Martindale-Hubbell Law Directory

JOHN PATRICK HEALY (AV)

29 South La Salle - Suite 640, 60603
Telephone: 312-332-7950
Fax: 312-782-4502

ASSOCIATE
Sheryl E. Healy

For full biographical listings, see the Martindale-Hubbell Law Directory

KANE OBBISH PROPES & GARIPPO (AV)

19th Floor, 100 West Monroe Street, 60603
Telephone: 312-346-8355
Fax: 312-346-6549

MEMBERS OF FIRM

Michael J. Kane	Lorna E. Propes
James M. Obbish	Louis B. Garippo
	Susan G. Feibus

For full biographical listings, see the Martindale-Hubbell Law Directory

PETER D. KASDIN, LTD. (AV)

Suite 1960, 135 South La Salle Street, 60603
Telephone: 312-630-1990
Facsimile: 312-630-1103

Peter D. Kasdin

David W. Hepplewhite	Regina Picone Etherton

OF COUNSEL
David W. Horan

For full biographical listings, see the Martindale-Hubbell Law Directory

KREISMAN & RAKICH (AV)

An Association of Attorneys
33 North Dearborn Street Suite 2220, 60602-3109
Telephone: 312-346-0045
Fax: 312-346-2380
Email: RobertK233@AOL.COM
Matteson, Illinois Office: 21141 Governors Highway, Suite 200, 60443.
Telephone: 708-747-6700.
Fax: 708-481-6770.

Robert D. Kreisman (P.C.)	Steven D. Rakich

Edward L. Morrison, Jr.	James A. Haiser

For full biographical listings, see the Martindale-Hubbell Law Directory

LANE & LANE (AV)

33 North Dearborn Street, Suite 2300, 60602
Telephone: 312-332-1400
Fax: 312-899-8003

MEMBERS OF FIRM

Fred Lane	Stephen I. Lane
	Scott D. Lane

ASSOCIATE
Joseph M. Dooley, III
OF COUNSEL

John F. Sandner	Nicholas V. Loizzi
Daniel M. Cullan	
(Not admitted in IL)	

For full biographical listings, see the Martindale-Hubbell Law Directory

LOGGANS AND COX (AV)

Suite 2850, 200 West Madison Street, 60606
Telephone: 312-201-8600
Telecopier: 312-201-1180
Email: loggans@aol.com

Susan E. Loggans	Michael J. Cox

(See Next Column)

LOGGANS AND COX, *Chicago—Continued*

Miles M. Dore   Ian Robert Alexander

For full biographical listings, see the Martindale-Hubbell Law Directory

MULLEN & MINELLA (AV)

A Partnership including Professional Corporations
Three First National Plaza, Suite 2700, 60602
Telephone: 312-346-2998
Fax: 312-346-6024

MEMBERS OF FIRM

John C. Mullen (Ltd.)   Mary R. Minella
Christopher Mullen (P.C.)   Michael T. Mullen

For full biographical listings, see the Martindale-Hubbell Law Directory

THE LAW OFFICES OF MUNDAY & NATHAN (AV)

33 North Dearborn Street, Suite 2220, 60602
Telephone: 312-346-5678
Fax: 312-346-8394

John J. Munday   Thomas J. Nathan

James A. Tobin   Lisa Pach

For full biographical listings, see the Martindale-Hubbell Law Directory

BERNARD R. NEVORAL AND ASSOCIATES LTD. (AV)

150 North Wacker Drive, Suite 2450, 60606
Telephone: 312 263-7058
FAX: 312-263-4566

Bernard R. Nevoral

Maurice E. Dusky   Douglas C. Dorn

For full biographical listings, see the Martindale-Hubbell Law Directory

STEPHEN M. PASSEN, LTD. (AV)

Suite 2900, 120 North La Salle Street, 60602
Telephone: 312-236-5878
Facsimile: 312-236-1162

Stephen M. Passen

Adam H. Fleischer

For full biographical listings, see the Martindale-Hubbell Law Directory

LAW OFFICES OF ROBERT B. PATTERSON, LTD. (AV)

221 North La Salle Street, Suite 1050, 60601
Telephone: 312-236-0995
FAX: 312-984-5791

Robert B. Patterson

John F. Hedrich
LEGAL SUPPORT PERSONNEL
Marie E. DeRose   Jennifer A. Johnson (Paralegal)
(Legal Assistant)

For full biographical listings, see the Martindale-Hubbell Law Directory

PAVALON & GIFFORD (AV)

Two North La Salle Street, Suite 1600, 60602
Telephone: 312-419-7400
Fax: 312-419-7408
Rockford, Illinois Office: 501 Seventh Street, Suite 501, 61104.
Telephone: 815-968-5100.

MEMBERS OF FIRM

Eugene I. Pavalon   Gary K. Laatsch
Geoffrey L. Gifford   Frank C. Marino
    Henry Phillip Gruss

Kathleen A. Russell   Christine Walsh Donnelly
   Christopher B. Meister

For full biographical listings, see the Martindale-Hubbell Law Directory

POWER ROGERS & SMITH, P.C. (AV)

35 West Wacker Drive, Suite 3700, 60601
Telephone: 312-236-9381
Fax: 312-236-0920

(See Next Column)

Joseph A. Power, Jr.   Thomas G. Siracusa
Larry R. Rogers   Paul L. Salzetta
Todd A. Smith   Thomas M. Power

Larry R. Rogers, Jr.   Ruth M. Degnan
      Devon C. Bruce

For full biographical listings, see the Martindale-Hubbell Law Directory

LAW OFFICES OF EDMUND J. SCANLAN, LTD. (AV)

134 North La Salle-Suite 220, 60602
Telephone: 312-372-0020
Fax: 312-372-1211

Edmund J. Scanlan   Richard C. Gleason

For full biographical listings, see the Martindale-Hubbell Law Directory

LAW OFFICES DENNIS T. SCHOEN, P.C. (AV)

Suite 663, 221 North La Salle Street, 60601
Telephone: 312-558-9143
Facsimile: 312-558-5426

Dennis T. Schoen

James J. Seaberry, Jr.

For full biographical listings, see the Martindale-Hubbell Law Directory

JOHN B. SCHWARTZ & ASSOCIATES (AV)

Suite 408, Thirty-Nine South La Salle Street, 60603
Telephone: 312-332-1586
Fax: 312-332-7009
Email: JSCHW888@aol.com

John B. Schwartz
ASSOCIATES
David J. Spira   Jami L. Sharfman
OF COUNSEL
Thomas W. Duda

For full biographical listings, see the Martindale-Hubbell Law Directory

JOHN C. WUNSCH, P.C. (AV)

77 West Washington Street, Suite 1420, 60602
Telephone: 312-977-9900
Fax: 312-236-2573

John C. Wunsch   Daniel J. Arnett

Reference: The Northern Trust Co.

For full biographical listings, see the Martindale-Hubbell Law Directory

---

EDWARDSVILLE, Madison Co.

ARMSTRONG LAW OFFICES (AV)

South Main & Schwarz Street, P.O. Box 565, 62025
Telephone: 618-656-6770
Facsimile: 618-656-6808
Collinsville, Illinois Office: 103 South Morrison.
Telephone: 618-345-9258.

Benton Tad Armstrong   Stephen B. Evans

For full biographical listings, see the Martindale-Hubbell Law Directory

CARLSON WENDLER & SANDERSON, P.C. (AV)

90 Edwardsville Professional Park, P.O. Box 527, 62025
Telephone: 618-656-0066
Fax: 618-656-0009
St. Louis, Missouri Office: 1015 Locust, Suite 1024, 63101-1909.
Telephone: 314-241-8033.

Jon G. Carlson   Brian M. Wendler
    M. Melinda Sanderson

Charles W. Armbruster, III   Eric Jon Carlson
OF COUNSEL
Jonathan Isbell

For full biographical listings, see the Martindale-Hubbell Law Directory

---

GALESBURG, Knox Co.

MUSTAIN LINDSTROM & HENSON (AV)

1865 North Henderson Street, Suite 11B, 61401
Telephone: 309-344-5252
Telecopier: 309-344-3939

(See Next Column)

MUSTAIN LINDSTROM & HENSON—*Continued*

MEMBERS OF FIRM

Douglas D. Mustain
Robert Lindstrom
Carl E. Hawkinson
Ronald Henson
Christopher Henson

References: The Farmers and Mechanics Bank; Norwest Bank Illinois, N.A.; First Bank; First Financial Bank; Farmers State Bank of Western Illinois; McGladrey and Pullen.

For full biographical listings, see the Martindale-Hubbell Law Directory

---

JOLIET, * Will Co.

MCKEOWN, FITZGERALD, ZOLLNER, BUCK, HUTCHISON & RUTTLE (AV)

2455 Glenwood Avenue, 60435
Telephone: 815-729-4800
Fax: 815-729-4711
Frankfort, Illinois Office: 28 Kansas Street.
Telephone: 815-469-2176.
FAX: 815-469-0295.

MEMBERS OF FIRM

Charles J. McKeown (1908-1985)
Paul O. McKeown (1913-1982)
Richard T. Buck (1936-1992)
Joseph C. Fitzgerald
Max E. Zollner
Douglas P. Hutchison
David L. Ruttle
Theodore J. Jarz
Douglas J. McKeown
Timothy J. Rathbun
James B. Harvey
Kenneth A. Grey
Michael R. Lucas
Christopher N. Wise
Gary S. Mueller

ASSOCIATES

Frank S. Cservenyak, Jr.
Arthur J. Wilhelmi
Kurt J. Keller
Kelly Kathleen James

OF COUNSEL

George E. Sangmeister
Stewart C. Hutchison

Representative Clients: Caterpillar Tractor Co.; First National Bank of Lockport; Homart Development Co.; First Midwest Bank, N.A.; Silver Cross Hospital; Joliet Township High School District; Villages of: Plainfield and Mokena; Southwest Agency for Risk Management; Joliet Junior College Foundation; Health Service Systems, Inc.

For full biographical listings, see the Martindale-Hubbell Law Directory

---

SPESIA, AYERS, ARDAUGH & WUNDERLICH (AV)

Two Rialto Square, 116 North Chicago Street, Suite 200, 60431
Telephone: 815-726-4311
Fax: 815-726-6828

MEMBERS OF FIRM

Douglas F. Spesia
E. Kent Ayers
Dinah Lennon Archambeault
John R. Ardaugh
Gary L. Wunderlich

ASSOCIATES

John C. Roth
Christian G. Spesia
John M. Spesia

OF COUNSEL

Ralph C. Murphy
Arthur T. Lennon (1923-1988)
Kenneth E. Timm

Counsel For: Commonwealth Edison Co.; Illinois Bell Telephone Co.; Country Mutual Insurance Co.; Northern Illinois Gas Co.; Metropolitan Life Insurance Co.; Indiana Consolidated Insurance Cos.; A.N.R. Pipeline Co.; Amoco Chemical Corp.; Village of New Lenox; Peoples Gas Light & Coke Company.

For full biographical listings, see the Martindale-Hubbell Law Directory

---

MARION, * Williamson Co.

HARRIS, LAMBERT, HOWERTON & DORRIS (AV)

300 West Main Street, 62959
Telephone: 618-993-2616
Fax: 618-997-1845

MEMBERS OF FIRM

Ralph W. Harris (1904-1982)
Richard Gordon Lambert
Robert H. Howerton
Douglas N. Dorris

ASSOCIATE

Kelley Ray Phelps

For full biographical listings, see the Martindale-Hubbell Law Directory

---

NAPERVILLE, Du Page Co.

STEVEN B. LEVY, LTD. (AV)

40 Shuman Boulevard Suite 151, 60563
Telephone: 630-416-6300
Telefax: 630-416-6564
URL: http://www.sblevyltdlaw.com

(See Next Column)

Steven B. Levy

For full biographical listings, see the Martindale-Hubbell Law Directory

---

OTTAWA, * La Salle Co.

MYERS, DAUGHERITY, BERRY & O'CONOR, LTD. (AV)

130 East Madison Street, 61350
Telephone: 815-434-6206
Fax: 815-434-6203
Email: mdboc@TheRamp.net
Streator, Illinois Office: 7 North Point Drive.
Telephone: 815-672-3116.
Fax: 815-672-0738.

Eugene P. Daugherity
Richard J. Berry

Representative Clients: Auto Owners Insurance, Co.; Union Bank; First National Bank of Ottawa, Illinois; Union Bancorp Inc.; First State Bank; United States Fidelity & Guaranty Co.; St. Mary's Hospital; General Casualty Insurance, Co.

For Complete List of Firm Personnel, See General Section

For full biographical listings, see the Martindale-Hubbell Law Directory

---

PERU, La Salle Co.

ANTHONY C. RACCUGLIA & ASSOCIATES (AV)

1200 Maple Drive, 61354
Telephone: 815-223-0230
Ottawa, Illinois Office: 633 La Salle Street.
Telephone: 815-434-2003.

ASSOCIATES

James A. McPhedran
Louis L. Bertrand

References: La Salle National Bank; Citizens First National Bank of Peru, Illinois.

For full biographical listings, see the Martindale-Hubbell Law Directory

---

URBANA, * Champaign Co.

BECKETT & WEBBER, P.C. (AV)

508 South Broadway, P.O. Box 988, 61801-0988
Telephone: 217-328-0263
Fax: 217-328-0290

J. Steven Beckett
Roger B. Webber

Peter T. Borich
Brett N. Olmstead
Dedra L. Wright
Carol A. Dison
Gary A. Webber

For full biographical listings, see the Martindale-Hubbell Law Directory

---

WAUKEGAN, * Lake Co.

DIVER, GRACH, QUADE & MASINI (AV)

First Federal Savings and Loan Building, 111 North County Street, 60085
Telephone: 847-662-8611
FAX: 847-662-2960

MEMBERS OF FIRM

Clarence W. Diver (1883-1962)
Thomas W. Diver
Brian S. Grach
David R. Quade
Robert J. Masini
Sarah P. Lessman

Heidi J. Aavang
Paula Vincich Randall
Donna-Jo Rodden Vorderstrasse

OF COUNSEL

David L. Hazan

A list of Representative Clients will be furnished upon request.
Reference: First Midwest Bank of Waukegan.

For full biographical listings, see the Martindale-Hubbell Law Directory

---

LAW OFFICES OF PATRICK A. SALVI, P.C. (AV)

218 North Utica Street, 60085
Telephone: 847-249-1227
Telefax: 847-249-0138

Patrick A. Salvi

Michael P. Schostok
John Andrew Kornak
J. Matthew Dudley
Paul R. Borth
Thomas J. Popovich

OF COUNSEL

Bernard E. Grysen

References: First Midwest Bank, Waukegan, Illinois; Northern Trust Bank, Lake Forest, Illinois.

For full biographical listings, see the Martindale-Hubbell Law Directory

WEST FRANKFORT, Franklin Co.

SAM C. MITCHELL & ASSOCIATES (AV)

115 1/2 East Main Street, P.O. Box 280, 62896
Telephone: 618-932-2772; 937-2662
Telecopier: 618-932-3456

Sam C. Mitchell
ASSOCIATE
Bruce D. Irish

For full biographical listings, see the Martindale-Hubbell Law Directory

*WHEATON,** Du Page Co.

DONOVAN & ROBERTS, P.C. (AV)

104 East Roosevelt Road, Suite 202, P.O. Box 417, 60189-0417
Telephone: 630-668-4211
Fax: 630-668-2076

Keith E. Roberts, Sr.   Keith E. (Chuck) Roberts, Jr.
James J. Konetski

Marie F. Leach   Robert M. Skutt
Mark J. Lyons   Robert J. Lentz
Andrew L. Dryjanski   Rosemarie Calandra

For full biographical listings, see the Martindale-Hubbell Law Directory

STEVEN B. LEVY, LTD.

(See Naperville)

LAW OFFICES OF ROGER KEVIN O'REILLY (AV)

1776 South Naperville Road, Suite 206-A, 60189-5039
Telephone: 708-665-4444
Telecopier: 708-665-4442

Molly M. O'Reilly

For full biographical listings, see the Martindale-Hubbell Law Directory

SCHROEDER & HRUBY, LTD. (AV)

2100 Manchester Road, Suite 1015, P.O. Box 230, 60189
Telephone: 630-462-1400
Facsimile: 630-462-1665

Carl F. Schroeder   Ralph R. Hruby

For full biographical listings, see the Martindale-Hubbell Law Directory

INDIANA

*BLOOMINGTON,** Monroe Co.

BUNGER & ROBERTSON (AV)

226 South College Square, P.O. Box 910, 47402-0910
Telephone: 812-332-9295
Fax: 812-331-8808

MEMBERS OF FIRM
Don M. Robertson   Samuel R. Ardery
ASSOCIATES
William J. Beggs   John W. Richards

Representative Clients: Aetna Insurance Companies; Bloomington Hospital; Commercial Union Group; Indiana Insurance Co.; Liberty Mutual Insurance; Medical Protective Co.; Monroe County Community School Corp.; Professional Golf Car, Inc.; Prudential Insurance Company of America; State Farm Automobile Insurance Co.

For Complete List of Firm Personnel, See General Section

For full biographical listings, see the Martindale-Hubbell Law Directory

KELLEY, BELCHER & BROWN, A PROFESSIONAL CORPORATION (AV)

301 West Seventh Street, P.O. Box 3250, 47402-3250
Telephone: 812-336-9963
Telecopier: 812-336-4588

William H. Kelley   Thomas J. Belcher

Shannon L. Robinson   Darla Sue Brown
Jennifer A. Bauer

For full biographical listings, see the Martindale-Hubbell Law Directory

CLARKSVILLE, Clark Co.

MAYER, VOGT, SMITH & PALMQUIST (AV)

501 Eastern Boulevard, 47129
Telephone: 812-288-1235
Louisville, Kentucky: 502-584-5800
Fax: 812-288-1240

MEMBERS OF FIRM
John M. Mayer, Jr.   William E. Smith, III
Samuel H. Vogt, Jr.   Cara Wells Stigger
ASSOCIATES
Susan Wagner Hynes   Kerstin Ann Schuhmann

Representative Clients: First Savings Bank, FSB; PNC Bank Indiana, Inc.
Approved Attorneys for: Commonwealth Land Title Insurance Co.; Ticor Title Insurance Company; Old Republic National Title Insurance Company.
References: First Savings Bank, FSB; PNC Bank Indiana, Inc.

For Complete List of Firm Personnel, See General Section

For full biographical listings, see the Martindale-Hubbell Law Directory

*CRAWFORDSVILLE,** Montgomery Co.

BERRY, CAPPER, DONALDSON & TULLEY (AV)

131 North Green Street, P.O. Box 429, 47933
Telephone: 317-362-7340
Fax: 317-362-5023

Andrew N. Foley (1909-1963)   Richard G. Tulley
John R. Berry (1907-1986)   John S. Capper, IV
S. Bryan Donaldson

Representative Clients: Elston Bank & Trust Co.; R. R. Donnelley & Sons Co. (Crawfordsville Division); Linden State Bank; City of Crawfordsville, Ind.

For full biographical listings, see the Martindale-Hubbell Law Directory

*EVANSVILLE,** Vanderburgh Co.

BERGER AND BERGER (AV)

313 Main Street, 47708-1485
Telephone: 812-425-8101;
Indiana Only: 800-622-3604;
Outside Indiana: 800-327-0182
Fax: 812-421-5909

MEMBERS OF FIRM
Sydney L. Berger (1917-1988)   Sheila M. Corcoran
Charles L. Berger   Mark W. Rietman
Robert J. Pigman

References: Citizens National Bank of Evansville; Old National Bank in Evansville.

For full biographical listings, see the Martindale-Hubbell Law Directory

GERLING LAW OFFICES, PROFESSIONAL CORPORATION (AV)

519 Main Street Walkway, P.O. Box 3203, 47731
Telephone: 812-423-5251
Fax: 812-423-9928

Gary L. Gerling   Christian M. Lenn
Edward B. Anderson   Gayle Gerling Pettinga
David G. Hatfield   Stephen Hensleigh Thomas

For full biographical listings, see the Martindale-Hubbell Law Directory

*FORT WAYNE,** Allen Co.

STANLEY A. LEVINE (AV)

Fort Wayne National Bank Building, Suite 2008, 110 West Berry Street, 46802
Telephone: 219-422-7431
Facsimile: 219-422-7433

For full biographical listings, see the Martindale-Hubbell Law Directory

ROBY & HOOD (AV)

Standard Federal Plaza, Suite 520, 200 East Main, 46802
Telephone: 219-423-3366
Fax: 219-423-3367
Anderson, Indiana Office: One Citizens Plaza, Suite 305.
Telephone: 317-642-2402.

MEMBERS OF FIRM
Daniel A. Roby   Kathryn J. Roudebush
G. Stanley Hood   Thomas A. Manges
David Joseph Stach

References: Norwest Bank; NBD Bank.

For full biographical listings, see the Martindale-Hubbell Law Directory

GREENFIELD,* Hancock Co.

BRAND & ALLEN (AV)

Five Courthouse Plaza, P.O. Box 455, 46140
Telephone: 317-462-3455
Fax: 317-467-6109

Waldo C. Ging (1892-1971)   James L. Brand (1938-1996)
MEMBERS OF FIRM
Eric N. Allen   Dawn E. Wellman
James W. McNew
ASSOCIATES
Gregory A. Brand   Nicole A. Zelin
Mary G. Willis   Jeffrey W. Eakins

For full biographical listings, see the Martindale-Hubbell Law Directory

INDIANAPOLIS,* Marion Co.

CONOUR • DOEHRMAN (AV)

Suite 1725, One Indiana Square, 46204
Telephone: 317-269-3550
Fax: 317-269-3564
Toll Free: 800-269-3443

MEMBERS OF FIRM
William F. Conour   Thomas C. Doehrman
ASSOCIATES
Rex E. Baker   Daniel S. Chamberlain

For full biographical listings, see the Martindale-Hubbell Law Directory

DANN PECAR NEWMAN & KLEIMAN, PROFESSIONAL CORPORATION (AV)

Suite 2300, One American Square Box 82008, 46282
Telephone: 317-632-3232; Indiana: 800-622-4799
Telecopy: 317-632-2962

Theodore R. Dann (1907-1993)   Walter E. Wolf, Jr.
Joel Yonover (1932-1995)   Barry E. Beldin
Philip D. Pecar   Robert D. Swhier, Jr.
Norman R. Newman   James P. Moloy
David H. Kleiman   Robert J. Schuckit
Jon B. Abels   Andrew A. Kleiman
Melvin R. Daniel   Michael J. Gabovitch
Lawrence F. Dorocke   Steven M. Pecar
Jeffrey A. Abrams   Benjamin A. Pecar
James H. Schwarz   Richard O. Kissel, II
Robert A. Rose   Joseph D. Calderon
OF COUNSEL
Linda E. Cantor   Anthony J. Rose

Ellen C. Siakotos   Angela L. Mansfield
Stacy L. Hill   Martha M. K. Baird
Karin L. Veatch

Attorneys for: Indianapolis Machinery Co., Inc.; Melvin Simon & Associates, Inc.; Pacers Basketball Corp.; Universal Fire & Casualty Co., Inc.; Bank One, Indianapolis, NA; INB National Bank; Nachi Technology, Inc.; Pharmaceutical Corporation of America; Logo 7, Inc.

For full biographical listings, see the Martindale-Hubbell Law Directory

HOLLAND & HOLLAND (AV)

Two Market Square Center, Suite 1011, 251 East Ohio Street, 46204
Telephone: 317-637-4400
Fax: 317-262-9309

C. Warren Holland   Michael W. Holland
ASSOCIATE
Gretchen Holland Etling
OF COUNSEL
Charles G. Reeder

For full biographical listings, see the Martindale-Hubbell Law Directory

ICE MILLER DONADIO & RYAN (AV)

One American Square Box 82001, 46282-0002
Telephone: 317-236-2100
Fax: 317-236-2219
Email: leel@imdr.com *URL:* http://www.imdr.com
South Bend, Indiana Office: 211 West Washington Street, Suite 2420.
Telephone: 219-234-7933.
Fax: 219-234-7965. Internet E-mail: leel@imdr.com. Web Site Address: http://www.imdr.com.

MEMBERS OF FIRM
James R. Fisher   Debra Hanley Miller

For Complete List of Firm Personnel, See General Section

For full biographical listings, see the Martindale-Hubbell Law Directory

LOCKE REYNOLDS BOYD & WEISELL (AV)

1000 Capital Center South, 201 North Illinois Street, 46204
Telephone: 317-237-3800
Telecopier: 317-237-3900

Hugh E. Reynolds, Jr.   Julia Blackwell Gelinas
Lloyd H. Milliken, Jr.   Terrence L. Brookie
William V. Hutchens   Richard A. Huser
David S. Allen   Thomas J. Campbell
David M. Haskett   Diane Parsons Emswiller
Michael A. Bergin   Burton M. Harris
David T. Kasper   Thomas W. Farlow
Steven J. Strawbridge   Karl M. Koons, III
Thomas L. Davis   James Dimos
Robert A. Fanning   Kristen K. Rollison
Randall R. Riggs   Thomas R. Schultz
Alan S. Brown   Todd J. Kaiser
Mark J. Roberts   Eric A. Riegner
Kevin Charles Murray   Kevin C. Schiferl
Ariane Schallwig Johnson

Stephen L. Vaughan   Mary A. Schopper
Peter H. Pogue   Susan E. Cline
John H. Daerr   Jerrilyn Powers Ramsey
John K. McDavid   Katherine Coble Dassow
Robert W. Wright   Mary Margaret Ruth Feldhake
Jeffrey J. Mortier   Nelson D. Alexander
Nicholas C. Pappas   David Alexander Sorensen
OF COUNSEL
William H. Vobach   Robert C. Riddell

Representative Clients: American Honda Motor Co., Inc.; Associated Aviation Underwriters; Center for Claims Resolution; CNA Insurance Cos.; Citizens Insurance Co.; General Motors Corp.; Nationwide Insurance Co.; Siemens Corp.; St. Francis Hospital.

For Complete List of Firm Personnel, See General Section

For full biographical listings, see the Martindale-Hubbell Law Directory

MILLER MULLER MENDELSON & KENNEDY (AV)

8900 Keystone Crossing Suite 1250, 46240
Telephone: 317-574-4500
1-800-394-3094
Fax: 317-574-4501

MEMBERS OF FIRM
Michael S. Miller   Tilden Mendelson
John Muller   Timothy J. Kennedy
ASSOCIATE
Catherine A. Kling

For full biographical listings, see the Martindale-Hubbell Law Directory

MITCHELL HURST JACOBS & DICK (AV)

152 East Washington Street, 46204
Telephone: 317-636-0808
1-800-636-0808
Fax: 317-633-7680

MEMBERS OF FIRM
William W. Hurst   Marshall S. Hanley
Samuel L. Jacobs   Steven K. Huffer
Richard J. Dick   Robert W. Strohmeyer, Jr.
ASSOCIATES
Danielle A. Takla   Kimberly H. Danforth
John M. Reames   Jennifer Levin Sinder

General Counsel For: Dr. Tavel's Vision Center; Calderon Bros. Vending Machines, Inc.; Grocers Supply Co., Inc.; Power Train Services, Inc.; Frank E. Irish, Inc.; Bedding Liquidators; Galyan's Trading Co.; Harcourt Management Co., Inc.; Kosene & Kosene Mgt. & Dev. Co., Inc.; Hasten Bancorp.

For full biographical listings, see the Martindale-Hubbell Law Directory

OSBORN HINER LISHER & ORZESKE, P.C. (AV)

Suite 380, One Woodfield, 8330 Woodfield Crossing Boulevard, 46240
Telephone: 317-469-2100
Fax: 317-469-9011

John L. Lisher   Donald G. Orzeske

Donald K. Broad   Christopher Hamilton
OF COUNSEL
William M. Osborn   Edward A. Straith-Miller

For full biographical listings, see the Martindale-Hubbell Law Directory

Indianapolis—Continued

PARDIECK, GILL & VARGO, A PROFESSIONAL CORPORATION (AV)

The Old Bailey Building, 244 North College Avenue, 46202
Telephone: 317-639-3321
Fax: 317-639-3318
Email: pgv@pgvlaw.com
Seymour, Indiana Office: 100 North Chestnut Street. P.O. Box 608.
Telephone: 812-523-8686.

Roger L. Pardieck	W. Brent Gill
John F. Vargo	

Thomas L. Landwerlen	Janet O. Vargo

OF COUNSEL
Robert C. Rothkopf

For full biographical listings, see the Martindale-Hubbell Law Directory

PRICE & BARKER (AV)

The Hammond Block Building, 301 Massachusetts Avenue, 46204
Telephone: 317-633-8787
Telecopier: 317-633-8797
New Albany, Indiana Office: 409 Bank Street, P.O. Box 785.
Telephone: 812-945-9151.
Fax: 812-945-6131.

PARTNERS

Henry J. Price	Jerry A. Garau
Robert G. Barker	Barbara J. Germano
Mary Arlien Findling	Larry R. Jackson

For full biographical listings, see the Martindale-Hubbell Law Directory

DOUGLASS R. SHORTRIDGE (AV)

One Indiana Square, Suite 1700, 46204-2051
Telephone: 317-635-9535
Fax: 317-635-1061

For full biographical listings, see the Martindale-Hubbell Law Directory

TOWNSEND, HOVDE & MONTROSS (AV)

230 East Ohio Street, 46204
Telephone: 317-264-4444
FAX: 317-264-2080

F. Boyd Hovde	W. Scott Montross
John F. Townsend, Jr.	Frederick R. Hovde

OF COUNSEL
John F. Townsend

Reference: N.B.D. Bank, N.A.

For full biographical listings, see the Martindale-Hubbell Law Directory

TOWNSEND & TOWNSEND (AV)

151 East Market Street, 46204
Telephone: 317-631-7777; 800-272-5720
FAX: 317-686-4449

Earl C. Townsend, Jr.	Earl C. Townsend, III

For full biographical listings, see the Martindale-Hubbell Law Directory

WARD & WARD (AV)

1014 Circle Tower Building, 55 Monument Circle, 46204
Telephone: 317-639-9501
Fax: 317-637-1919

MEMBERS OF FIRM

Donald W. Ward	Charles P. Ward

For full biographical listings, see the Martindale-Hubbell Law Directory

WILSON, KEHOE & WININGHAM (AV)

2859 North Meridian, 46208
Telephone: 317-920-6400
Fax: 317-920-6405
Richmond, Indiana Office: 42 South 9th Street, 47374.
Telephone: 317-962-9113.
Connersville, Indiana Office: 118 West 30th Street, 47331.
Telephone: 317-827-1100.
Muncie, Indiana Office: 3310 West Fox Ridge Lane, 47304.
Telephone: 317-284-2474.

MEMBERS OF FIRM

Harry A. Wilson, Jr.	D. Bruce Kehoe
William E. Winingham, Jr.	

ASSOCIATES

Ralph E. Dowling	Gerald A. Griffin, M.D.

Reference: The Indiana National Bank.

For full biographical listings, see the Martindale-Hubbell Law Directory

YARLING, ROBINSON, HAMMEL & LAMB (AV)

151 North Delaware, Suite 1535, P.O. Box 44128, 46204
Telephone: 317-262-8800
Fax: 317-262-3046

MEMBERS OF FIRM

Richard W. Yarling	Edgar H. Lamb
Charles F. Robinson, Jr.	Douglas E. Rogers
John W. Hammel	Mark S. Gray
Linda Y. Hammel	Matthew C. Robinson

Representative Clients: Allstate Insurance Co.; American Family Mutual Insurance Company; Chrysler Credit Corporation; Fleet Financenter; General Motors Acceptance Corporation; Household Finance Corporation; Monroe Guaranty Insurance Company; Northbrook Property & Casualty Company; Pafco General Insurance Company; Security Pacific Finance Corporation.

For full biographical listings, see the Martindale-Hubbell Law Directory

YOSHA LADENDORF KRAHULIK & WEDDLE (AV)

Pyramid II, First Floor, 3500 West DePauw Boulevard, Suite 2015, P.O. Box 68979, 46268
Telephone: 317-334-9200
FAX: 317-228-3355

MEMBERS OF FIRM

Louis Buddy Yosha	Mark C. Ladendorf
William Levy	Jon D. Krahulik
	Robert G. Weddle

ASSOCIATES

David C. Krahulik	Angela M. Smith
Timothy C. Caress	Jeff D. Oliphant

SENIOR COUNSEL
Jeffrey A. Modisett

OF COUNSEL

Irwin J. Prince	Irving L. Fink

Reference: National Bank of Indianapolis.

For full biographical listings, see the Martindale-Hubbell Law Directory

YOUNG & RILEY (AV)

277 East 12th Street, 46202
Telephone: 317-639-2000
Fax: 317-639-2005

Thomas J. Young	William N. Riley

JEFFERSONVILLE,* Clark Co.

LAW OFFICE OF EDWIN S. SEDWICK (AV)

415 East Court Avenue, 47130
Telephone: 812-282-7200
Facsimile: 812-282-7393

For full biographical listings, see the Martindale-Hubbell Law Directory

KOKOMO,* Howard Co.

RUSSELL, MCINTYRE, HILLIGOSS & WELKE (AV)

116 North Main Street, P.O. Box 1047, 46901
Telephone: 317-456-3827
Telecopier: 317-456-3839

MEMBERS OF FIRM

Richard L. Russell	Thomas J. Hilligoss, Jr.
James B. McIntyre	Curtis C. Welke

ASSOCIATE
Andrew J. Vandenbosch

For full biographical listings, see the Martindale-Hubbell Law Directory

LAFAYETTE,* Tippecanoe Co.

BALL, EGGLESTON, BUMBLEBURG & MCBRIDE (AV)

810 Bank One Building, P.O. Box 1535, 47902
Telephone: 317-742-9046
Fax: 317-742-1966

Cable G. Ball (1904-1981)	Warren N. Eggleston
Owen Crook (1908-1977)	(1923-1991)

MEMBERS OF FIRM

Joseph T. Bumbleburg	Jeffrey J. Newell
John K. McBride	James T. Hodson
Jack L. Walkey	Brian Wade Walker
Michael J. Stapleton	Cheryl M. Knodle
Randy J. Williams	

Representative Clients: Available Upon Request.

For full biographical listings, see the Martindale-Hubbell Law Directory

Lafayette—Continued

HANNA & GERDE (AV)

Fifth Floor Bank & Trust Building, P.O. Box 1098, 47902
Telephone: 317-742-5005
Fax: 317-742-6490

Charles H. Robertson (1902-1982)
MEMBERS OF FIRM

George L. Hanna   Cy Gerde
OF COUNSEL
Eric H. Burns
ASSOCIATE
Mary A. Russell

Representative Client: City of Lafayette.
Reference: Lafayette Bank & Trust Co.; Salin Bank & Trust Co.

For full biographical listings, see the Martindale-Hubbell Law Directory

LOGANSPORT,* Cass Co.

MILLER, TOLBERT, MUEHLHAUSEN, MUEHLHAUSEN & GROFF, P.C. (AV)

216 Fourth Street Caller Box: 7010, 46947-7010
Telephone: 219-722-4343
FAX: 219-722-1936

Glenn L. Miller (1902-1992)   John C. Muehlhausen
George R. Wildman (1932-1994)   James K. Muehlhausen
Frank E. Tolbert   R. Tod Groff

John S. Damm

Counsel for: Area Five Council on Aging; ASCO Oil Company; Careage of Logansport, Inc.; Carter Concrete Block, Inc.; Hartford Insurance Co.; J&P Stores, Inc.; Logansport Memorial Hospital; Meridian Insurance Co.; Motorists Mutual Insurance Co.; Ohio Casualty Insurance Co.

For full biographical listings, see the Martindale-Hubbell Law Directory

MARION,* Grant Co.

KILEY, KILEY, HARKER, MICHAEL & CERTAIN (AV)

300 West Third Street, P.O. Box 899, 46952-0899
Telephone: 317-664-9041
Fax: 317-664-8119

MEMBERS OF FIRM

Robert Ralph Batton   David L. Kiley, Sr.
(1890-1963)   Michael J. Kiley
Albert L. Harker (1904-1965) Albert C. Harker
Albert Bonner Brown   Thomas W. Michael
(1911-1981)   Harry J. Certain
ASSOCIATE
Therese McCullough Pryor

Counsel for: Bank One, Marion, N.A.; Liniger Co., Inc.; Atlas Foundry Co.
Local Counsel for: GenCorp.; CPC Group; General Motors; Indiana Michigan Power Co./AEP; Indiana Bell Telephone Co.; Foster-Forbes, Division of American National Can Corp.

For full biographical listings, see the Martindale-Hubbell Law Directory

MERRILLVILLE, Lake Co.

SPANGLER, JENNINGS & DOUGHERTY, P.C. (AV)

8396 Mississippi Street, 46410-6398
Telephone: 219-769-2323
Facsimile: 219-769-5007
Valparaiso, Indiana Office: 150 Lincolnway, Suite 3001.
Telephone: 219-462-6151.
FAX: 219-477-4935.

Harry J. Jennings   David J. Hanson
Samuel J. Furlin   Robert P. Kennedy
Richard A. Mayer   James T. McNiece
Jay A. Charon   Daniel A. Gioia
John P. McQuillan   James D. McQuillan
Samuel J. Bernardi, Jr.   David L. Abel, II
(Valparaiso Office)   Harold G. Hagberg
Jon F. Schmoll   Gregory J. Tonner
Robert D. Hawk   Robert D. Brown

Robert J. Dignam   Anthony F. Tavitas
David R. Phillips   Lloyd P. Mullen
Kisti Good Risse

Representative Clients: Allstate Insurance Cos.; Bank One, Merriville, N.A.; First National Bank of Valparaiso; Ford Motor Credit Co.; Inland Steel Co.; Munster Calumet Shopping Center; School Town of Munster; St. Paul Insurance Cos.; State Farm Cos.; Volkswagen of America.

For Complete List of Firm Personnel, See General Section

For full biographical listings, see the Martindale-Hubbell Law Directory

MISHAWAKA, St. Joseph Co.

SCHINDLER AND OLSON (AV)

122 South Mill Street, P.O. Box 100, 46544
Telephone: 219-259-5461
Fax: 219-259-5462

OF COUNSEL
John W. Schindler (1884-1971)   John W. Schindler, Jr.
MEMBER OF FIRM
James J. Olson

A List of Representative Clients Will Be Furnished Upon Request.
Reference: 1st Source Bank of Mishawaka.

For full biographical listings, see the Martindale-Hubbell Law Directory

MUNCIE,* Delaware Co.

CANNON & BRUNS (AV)

119 North High Street, 47305
Telephone: 317-289-2161
FAX: 317-289-2162

MEMBERS OF FIRM

Thomas A. Cannon   William G. Bruns
Thomas A. Cannon, Jr.

References: First Merchants Bank, Muncie; American National Bank and Trust Company of Muncie.

For full biographical listings, see the Martindale-Hubbell Law Directory

MUNSTER, Lake Co.

LAW OFFICES OF TIMOTHY F. KELLY (AV)

Suite 2A, 9250 Columbia Avenue, 46321
Telephone: 219-836-4062
Telecopier: 219-836-0167
Email: 76325.1505@Compuserve.Com

MEMBERS OF FIRM

Timothy F. Kelly   Karl K. Vanzo
ASSOCIATES
Harvey Karlovac   Steven J. Sersic

For Complete List of Firm Personnel, See General Section

For full biographical listings, see the Martindale-Hubbell Law Directory

NEW ALBANY,* Floyd Co.

MATTOX & MATTOX (AV)

Suite 420 Elsby Building, P.O. Box 1203, 47151-1203
Telephone: 812-944-8005
Facsimile: 812-944-2255
Email: mattox@ntr.net

MEMBERS OF FIRM

Richard L. Mattox   S. Frank Mattox
ASSOCIATES
Linda A. Mattox   Derrick H. Wilson
Karen R. Goodwell

Representative Clients: AAOMS National Insurance; Cablelink, Inc.; Floyd Memorial Hospital; John Deere Co.; Kimball International, Inc.; The Medical Protective Co.; Papa Johns Intl., Inc.; PHICO Insurance Co.; Physicians Group, Inc.; Robinson Nugent, Inc.

For full biographical listings, see the Martindale-Hubbell Law Directory

NOBLESVILLE,* Hamilton Co.

CHURCH, CHURCH, HITTLE & ANTRIM (AV)

938 Conner Street, P.O. Box 10, 46060-0010
Telephone: 317-773-2190
Telecopier: 317-773-5320
Email: cchadoug@msn.com

MEMBERS OF FIRM

Douglas D. Church   Bruce M. Bittner
Jack G. Hittle   Brian J. Zaiger
J. Michael Antrim   David Joseph Barker
Martin E. Risacher   Leslie Craig Henderzahs
OF COUNSEL
Manson E. Church

Representative Clients: Noblesville Schools; Westfield-Washington Schools; Indiana School Finance Corp.; Community Bank; Metrobank; Towns of Westfield, Fishers; Reynolds Farm Equipment Co.; Weihe Engineering; Historic Railroad Multijurisdictional Port Authority.

For full biographical listings, see the Martindale-Hubbell Law Directory

RICHMOND, * Wayne Co.

HARRINGTON, MALEY, GARDNER & SAYRE (AV)

Third Floor, Harrington Bank Building, Two North Eighth, 47374-3090
Telephone: 317-966-6643
FAX: 317-966-6799

MEMBERS OF FIRM

Alonzo M. Gardner (1886-1941)	Robert J. Maley
Wilfred Jessup (1900-1944)	Gayle W. Gardner
Frank K. Chambers (1938-1955)	John M. Sayre, III
Floyd W. Gardner (1933-1965)	Kirk A. Weikart
Clifford M. Haworth (1923-1967)	

OF COUNSEL
John R. Harrington

General Counsel for: Harrington Bank, FSB.
Local Counsel for: Belden Manufacturing Co.; CIGNA.

For full biographical listings, see the Martindale-Hubbell Law Directory

SEYMOUR, Jackson Co.

PARDIECK, GILL & VARGO, A PROFESSIONAL CORPORATION (AV)

100 North Chestnut Street, P.O. Box 608, 47274
Telephone: 812-523-8686
Fax: 812-522-4199
Email: pgv@pgylaw.com
Indianapolis, Indiana Office: The Old Bailey Building, 244 North College Avenue.
Telephone: 317-639-3321.

Roger L. Pardieck	W. Brent Gill
Bruce A. MacTavish	Karen J. Mellencamp Davis
Andrew M. Pardieck	

References: Home Federal Savings Bank, Seymour, Indiana.

For full biographical listings, see the Martindale-Hubbell Law Directory

SOUTH BEND, * St. Joseph Co.

DORAN BLACKMOND READY HAMILTON & WILLIAMS (AV)

1700 Valley American Bank Building, 211 W. Washington Street, 46601
Telephone: 219-288-1800
Fax: 219-236-4265

MEMBERS OF FIRM

M. Edward Doran (1895-1982)	David T. Ready
John E. Doran	John C. Hamilton
Don G. Blackmond	A. Howard Williams

ASSOCIATE
Don Gregory Blackmond

For full biographical listings, see the Martindale-Hubbell Law Directory

HARDIG, LEE AND GROVES, PROFESSIONAL ASSOCIATION (AV)

Suite 502, First Bank Building, 205 West Jefferson Boulevard, 46601
Telephone: 219-232-5923
Fax: 219-232-5942

James F. Groves

Representative Client: South Bend-Mishawaka New Car Dealers Assn.
Reference: First Interstate Bank of South Bend.

For full biographical listings, see the Martindale-Hubbell Law Directory

EDWARD N. KALAMAROS & ASSOCIATES PROFESSIONAL CORPORATION (AV)

129 North Michigan Avenue, P.O. Box 4156, 46634
Telephone: 219-232-4801
Telecopier: 219-232-9736

Edward N. Kalamaros	Philip E. Kalamaros
Timothy J. Walsh	Sally P. Norton
Thomas F. Cohen	Kevin W. Kearney
Joseph M. Forte	Peter J. Bagiackas
Robert Deane Woods	David A. Wemhoff
Patrick J. Hinkle	Eric G. Ciesielski

Representative Clients: Liberty Mutual Insurance Co.; Employers Mutual of Wausau; Fireman's Fund American Insurance Group; St. Paul Insurance Companies; U.S.F. & G.; Cincinnati Insurance Co.; Kemper Group; Continental Loss Adjusting Services, Inc.; Orion Group.

For full biographical listings, see the Martindale-Hubbell Law Directory

ROWE, ROWE & MAHER (AV)

Suite 900 Keybank Building, 46601
Telephone: 219-233-8200
Fax: 219-234-5987

(See Next Column)

R. Kent Rowe	R. Kent Rowe, III
Timothy J. Maher	

ASSOCIATES

Gregory J. Haines	Steven D. Groth
Lee Korzan	Marie Anne Hendrie

For full biographical listings, see the Martindale-Hubbell Law Directory

SOPKO & FIRTH (AV)

Plaza Building, 5th Floor, 210 South Michigan Street, P.O. Box 300, 46624
Telephone: 219-234-3000
Telecopier: 219-234-4220

MEMBERS OF FIRM

Thomas C. Sopko	John C. Firth

ASSOCIATE
Brent E. Inabnit

OF COUNSEL
Ronald J. Jaicomo

References: 1st Source Bank; 1st Interstate Bank; Notre Dame Federal Credit Union.

For full biographical listings, see the Martindale-Hubbell Law Directory

VALPARAISO, * Porter Co.

BLACHLY, TABOR, BOZIK & HARTMAN (AV)

Suite 401 Indiana Federal Building, 46383
Telephone: 219-464-1041
Fax: 219-464-0927

MEMBERS OF FIRM

Glenn J. Tabor	David L. DeBoer
Duane W. Hartman	Thomas F. Macke

ASSOCIATES

Roger A. Weitgenant	Craig R. Van Schouwen

Reference: First National Bank.

For Complete List of Firm Personnel, See General Section

For full biographical listings, see the Martindale-Hubbell Law Directory

VINCENNES, * Knox Co.

PAUL B. LEDFORD PROFESSIONAL CORPORATION (AV)

707 Busseron Street, P.O. Box 535, 47591
Telephone: 812-882-1767
Fax: 812-882-1789

Paul B. Ledford

For full biographical listings, see the Martindale-Hubbell Law Directory

IOWA

CEDAR RAPIDS, * Linn Co.

TOM RILEY LAW FIRM, P.C. (AV)

4040 First Avenue N.E., P.O. Box 998, 52406-0998
Telephone: 319-363-4040
FAX: 319-363-9789
Iowa City, Iowa Office: 1220 Highway 6 West.
Telephone: 319-351-4996.
Burlington, Iowa Office: First National Bank Building, Second Floor, Main and Jefferson Streets, P.O. Box 1114.
Telephone: 319-753-5111.

Tom Riley	Thomas J. Currie
Peter C. Riley	James E. Bennett
T. Todd Becker	Gerald J. Kucera
Mark E. Liabo	Martin A. Diaz
Hugh G. Albrecht	Nestor Lobodiak
Sara Riley Brown	Susan A. Diehl
Charles C. Brown, Jr.	Andrew B. Prosser
Elmer M. Jones	

A list of Representative Clients will be furnished upon request.

For full biographical listings, see the Martindale-Hubbell Law Directory

COUNCIL BLUFFS, * Pottawattamie Co.

REILLY, PETERSEN & HANNAN, P.L.C. (AV)

215 South Main Street, P.O. Box 1016, 51502-1016
Telephone: 712-328-1575
Fax: 712-328-1562

(See Next Column)

REILLY, PETERSEN & HANNAN P.L.C.—*Continued*

C. R. Hannan   Michael G. Reilly
                Deborah L. Petersen

References: FirsTier; Firstar Bank of Council Bluffs.

For full biographical listings, see the Martindale-Hubbell Law Directory

---

DECORAH,* Winneshiek Co.

MILLER, PEARSON, GLOE, BURNS, BEATTY & COWIE, P.C. (AV)

301 West Broadway, 52101
Telephone: 319-382-4226
Fax: 319-382-3783

Frank R. Miller (1915-1977)   James Burns
Donald H. Gloe   Marion L. Beatty
                Robert J. Cowie, Jr.
                OF COUNSEL
                Floyd S. Pearson

Counsel for: Luther College; Decorah Community School District; Winneshiek County Memorial Hospital; Community First State Bank.
Local Counsel for: Iowa Mutual Insurance Cos.; Employers Mutual Liability Insurance Co. of Wisconsin; Continental Casualty Co.; Employers Mutual Casualty Co.; Grinnell Mutual Insurance Co.; Allied Mutual Insurance Co.

For full biographical listings, see the Martindale-Hubbell Law Directory

---

DES MOINES,* Polk Co.

ROXANNE B. CONLIN AND ASSOCIATES, P.C. (AV)

The Plaza, 300 Walnut Street - Suite 5, 50309-2239
Telephone: 515-282-3333
Fax: 515-282-0318

Roxanne B. Conlin

Melinda Kaye Ellwanger   Thomas J. Duff

For full biographical listings, see the Martindale-Hubbell Law Directory

FINLEY, ALT, SMITH, SCHARNBERG, MAY & CRAIG, P.C. (AV)

604 Locust Street, Fourth Floor Equitable Building, 50309
Telephone: 515-288-0145
Telecopier: 515-288-2724

Steven K. Scharnberg   John D. (Jack) Hilmes
Lorraine J. May   R. Todd Gaffney
                V. Glenn Goodwin, Jr.

Representative Clients: Aetna Casualty & Surety Co.; Aetna Life Insurance Co.; ALAS; American Society of Composers, Authors and Publishers; Equitable Life Assurance Society of the U.S.; Federated Insurance Co.; Meredith Corp.
Iowa Attorneys for: Midwest Medical Insurance Co.
District Attorneys for: Norfolk & Southern Railroad; Soo Line Railroad Company.

For Complete List of Firm Personnel, See General Section

For full biographical listings, see the Martindale-Hubbell Law Directory

THE JAMES LAW FIRM, P.C. (AV)

630 Equitable Building, 604 Locust Street, 50309
Telephone: 515-246-8484
Fax: 515-246-8767

Dwight W. James   Frederick W. James

Reference: Norwest Bank.

For full biographical listings, see the Martindale-Hubbell Law Directory

PATTERSON, LORENTZEN, DUFFIELD, TIMMONS, IRISH, BECKER & ORDWAY, L.L.P. (AV)

729 Insurance Exchange Building, 50309
Telephone: 515-283-2147
Fax: 515-283-1002

MEMBERS OF FIRM

G. O. Patterson (1914-1982)   Gregory J. Wilson
James A. Lorentzen   Jeffrey A. Boehlert
Theodore T. Duffield   Douglas A. Haag
William E. Timmons (Retired)   Charles E. Cutler
Roy M. Irish   Michael D. Huppert
F. H. Becker (Retired)   Martin C. Sprock
Gary D. Ordway   William A. Wickett
Robin L. Hermann   Frederick M. Haskins
Harry Perkins, III   Jeffrey A. Baker
Michael F. Lacey, Jr.   Janice M. Herfkens

(See Next Column)

ASSOCIATES

Coreen K. Bezdicek   Patrick V. Waldron
                Michael S Jones

Representative Clients: Allied Mutual Insurance Company; CNA Insurance Company; Chubb Insurance Group; Continental Western Insurance Co.; Farmers Insurance Group; Farmland Insurance Company; Grinnell Mutual Reinsurance Company; Hawkeye Security Insurance Company; Iowa Insurance Institute, St. Paul Fire & Marine Insurance Company.

For full biographical listings, see the Martindale-Hubbell Law Directory

THE ROSENBERG LAW FIRM (AV)

1010 Insurance Exchange Building, 505 Fifth Avenue, 50309
Telephone: 515-243-7600

MEMBERS OF FIRM

Raymond Rosenberg   Brent D. Rosenberg
Dean A. Stowers   Carole L. Hunt

Reference: Firstar Bank, Des Moines, Iowa.

For full biographical listings, see the Martindale-Hubbell Law Directory

WASKER, DORR, WIMMER & MARCOUILLER, P.C. (AV)

801 Grand Avenue, Suite 3100, 50309-8036
Telephone: 515-283-1801
Facsimile: 515-283-1802

Fred L. Dorr

Matthew D. Kern

For Complete List of Firm Personnel, See General Section

For full biographical listings, see the Martindale-Hubbell Law Directory

---

KEOKUK,* Lee Co.

LAW OFFICES OF JAMES P. HOFFMAN (AV)

Middle Road, P.O. Box 1087, 52632-1087
Telephone: 319-524-4441
Fax: 319-524-1638

For full biographical listings, see the Martindale-Hubbell Law Directory

---

WEST DES MOINES, Polk Co.

LaMARCA & LANDRY, P.C. (AV)

1300 50th Street, 50266
Telephone: 515-225-2600
Fax: 515-225-8581

George A. LaMarca   Gregory W. Landry
                Robert K. DuPuy

Gary G. Mattson
OF COUNSEL

Martin R. Anderson   Samuel S. Duffey

For full biographical listings, see the Martindale-Hubbell Law Directory

KANSAS

KANSAS CITY,* Wyandotte Co.

McANANY, VAN CLEAVE & PHILLIPS, P.A. (AV)

Fourth Floor, 707 Minnesota Avenue, P.O. Box 171300, 66117
Telephone: 913-371-3838
Facsimile: 913-371-4722
Lenexa, Kansas Office: Suite 200, 11900 West 87th Street Parkway.
Telephone: 913-888-9000.
Facsimile: 913-888-7049.
Kansas City, Missouri Office: Suite 304, 819 Walnut Street.
Telephone: 816-556-9417.

John J. Jurcyk, Jr.   Robert F. Rowe, Jr.
Robert D. Benham   (Resident, Lenexa Office)
Clifford T. Mueller   Douglas M. Greenwald
  (Resident, Lenexa Office)   Daniel F. Church
William P. Coates, Jr.
  (Resident, Lenexa Office)

OF COUNSEL
Frank D. Menghini

Reference: Guaranty Bank and Trust Co.

For Complete List of Firm Personnel, See General Section

For full biographical listings, see the Martindale-Hubbell Law Directory

OVERLAND PARK, Johnson Co.

RISJORD & JAMES, P.C. (AV)

Suite 100, 10680 Barkley, 66212
Telephone: 913-381-5151
Fax: 913-381-2569

Randy W. James   Aaron N. Woods
RETIRED
John C. Risjord

For full biographical listings, see the Martindale-Hubbell Law Directory

SHAMBERG, JOHNSON & BERGMAN, CHARTERED (AV)

Suite 355, 4551 West 107th Street, 66207
Telephone: 913-642-0600
Fax: 913-642-9629
Kansas City, Kansas Office: Suite 860, New Brotherhood Building, 8th and State Streets.
Telephone: 913-281-1900.
Kansas City, Missouri Office: Suite 205, Scarritt Arcade Building, 819 Walnut.
Telephone: 816-556-9431.

Lynn R. Johnson   Victor A. Bergman
John M. Parisi

Steven G. Brown   Anthony L. DeWitt
Steve N. Six   (Not admitted in KS)
Patrick A. Hamilton
OF COUNSEL
John E. Shamberg

For full biographical listings, see the Martindale-Hubbell Law Directory

---

TOPEKA,* Shawnee Co.

DAVIS, UNREIN, HUMMER & BUCK, L.L.P. (AV)

100 East Ninth Street, Third Floor, P.O. Box 3575, 66601-3575
Telephone: 913-354-1100
Fax: 913-354-1113

MEMBERS OF FIRM

Byron M. Gray (1901-1986)   J. Franklin Hummer
Maurice D. Freidberg   Mark A. Buck
  (1902-1965)   James B. Biggs
Charles L. Davis, Jr.   Christopher M. Rohrer
  (1921-1992)   Brenda L. Head
Michael J. Unrein   Eric I. Unrein

OF COUNSEL
Gary D. McCallister

For full biographical listings, see the Martindale-Hubbell Law Directory

FISHER, PATTERSON, SAYLER & SMITH, L.L.P. (AV)

534 South Kansas Avenue, Suite 400, P.O. Box 949, 66601
Telephone: 913-232-7761
Fax: 913-232-6604
Overland Park, Kansas Office: 11050 Roe Avenue, Suite 210, 66211.
Telephone: 913-339-6757.
Fax: 913-339-6187.

MEMBERS OF FIRM

Donald Patterson   Steve R. Fabert
Edwin Dudley Smith (Resident,   Ronald J. Laskowski
  Overland Park Office)   Michael K. Seck (Resident,
Larry G. Pepperdine   Overland Park Office)
James P. Nordstrom   David P. Madden (Resident,
Justice B. King   Overland Park Office)
J. Steven Pigg   Steven K. Johnson

ASSOCIATES

Kristine A. Larscheid   Billy E. Newman
Patrick G. Reavey (Resident,   David R. Cooper
  Overland Park Office)

OF COUNSEL
David H. Fisher
RETIRED
Charles Keith Sayler (Retired)

Representative Clients: Gage Shopping Center, Inc.; Fireman's Fund-American Insurance Cos.; United States Fidelity and Guaranty Co.; The Procter & Gamble Company; American Cyanamid Company; Commercial Union Insurance Companies; National Casualty/Scottsdale Insurance Co.; The Hartford; Berkshire Hathaway Companies.

For full biographical listings, see the Martindale-Hubbell Law Directory

PALMER & LOWRY (AV)

Suite 102 Columbian Building, 112 West Sixth, 66603-3862
Telephone: 913-233-1836
Fax: 913-233-3703

(See Next Column)

MEMBERS OF FIRM
Jerry R. Palmer   Kirk W. Lowry
ASSOCIATE
L J Leatherman

References: Commerce State Bank; Merchants National Bank.

For full biographical listings, see the Martindale-Hubbell Law Directory

EUGENE B. RALSTON & ASSOCIATES, P.A. (AV)

2913 Southwest Maupin Lane, 66614-4139
Telephone: 913-273-8002
FAX: 913-273-0744
Email: ERalston@AOL.Com

Eugene B. Ralston

Kevin L. Diehl   Ronald P. Pope
LEGAL SUPPORT PERSONNEL
PARALEGALS
Barbara Cobuluis   Katrina Windholz
Teresa McLinn   Corri Wecker
Bonnie Price
PRIVATE INVESTIGATOR
Jack L. Grant

For full biographical listings, see the Martindale-Hubbell Law Directory

WRIGHT, HENSON, SOMERS, SEBELIUS, CLARK & BAKER, LLP (AV)

Commerce Bank Building, 100 Southeast Ninth Street, 2nd Floor, P.O. Box 3555, 66601-3555
Telephone: 913-232-2200
FAX: 913-232-3344

MEMBERS OF FIRM
Thomas E. Wright   K. Gary Sebelius
Evelyn Zabel Wilson
ASSOCIATES
Michael M. Walker   Donald Sutsu Lee

For Complete List of Firm Personnel, See General Section

For full biographical listings, see the Martindale-Hubbell Law Directory

---

WICHITA,* Sedgwick Co.

DEPEW AND GILLEN, L.L.C. (AV)

151 North Main, Suite 700, 67202-1408
Telephone: 316-265-9621
Facsimile: 316-265-3819
Email: d-g@southwind.net

Spencer L. Depew   David W. Nickel
Dennis L. Gillen   Nicholas S. Daily
Randall K. Rathbun   David E. Rogers
Jack Scott McInteer   Charles C. Steincamp

For full biographical listings, see the Martindale-Hubbell Law Directory

FOULSTON & SIEFKIN L.L.P. (AV)

700 Fourth Financial Center, 67202
Telephone: 316-267-6371
Facsimile: 316-267-6345
Topeka, Kansas Office: 1515 Bank IV Tower, 534 Kansas Avenue, 66603.
Telephone: 913-233-3600.
Fax: 913-233-1610.
Dodge City, Kansas Office: 810 Frontview, P.O. Box 1147, 67801.
Telephone: 316-227-8126.
Fax: 316-227-8451.
Member: Lex Mundi, A Global Association of 126 Independent Firms.

MEMBERS OF FIRM
Mikel L. Stout   Jay F. Fowler
Darrell L. Warta   Amy S. Lemley
Craig W. West

For Complete List of Firm Personnel, See General Section

For full biographical listings, see the Martindale-Hubbell Law Directory

YOUNG, BOGLE, McCAUSLAND, WELLS & CLARK, P.A. (AV)

106 West Douglas, Suite 923, 67202
Telephone: 316-265-7841
Facsimile: 316-265-3956

Glenn D. Young, Jr.   Paul S. McCausland
Jerry D. Bogle   William A. Wells
Kenneth M. Clark

Representative Clients: Horace Mann Ins. Co.; Deere & Co.; Bridgestone/Firestone, Inc.; Massey-Ferguson, Inc.; Sears Roebuck & Co.; GAF Corp. (asbestos litigation).

(See Next Column)

YOUNG, BOGLE, MCCAUSLAND, WELLS & CLARK P.A.—*Continued*

For Complete List of Firm Personnel, See General Section

For full biographical listings, see the Martindale-Hubbell Law Directory

KENTUCKY

ASHLAND, Boyd Co.

MARTIN, PICKLESIMER, JUSTICE & VINCENT (AV)

431 Sixteenth Street, P.O. Box 2528, 41105-2528
Telephone: 606-329-8338
Fax: 606-325-8199

Richard W. Martin	David Justice
Max D. Picklesimer	John F. Vincent

ASSOCIATES

Thomas Wade Lavender, II	Brian Leslie Hewlett

Representative Clients: City of Ashland; FIVCO Area Development District; Boyd County Sanitation District No. 2; Mid-America Distributors, Inc. *Insurance Counsel for:* State Farm Mutual Automobile Insurance Co.; State Farm Fire and Casualty Co.; Aetna Casualty Insurance Co.; Grange Mutual Insurance Co.; Great American Insurance Co.

For full biographical listings, see the Martindale-Hubbell Law Directory

*BOWLING GREEN,** Warren Co.

ENGLISH, LUCAS, PRIEST & OWSLEY (AV)

1101 College Street, P.O. Box 770, 42102-0770
Telephone: 502-781-6500
Telecopier: 502-782-7782
Email: inquiry@elpo.com

MEMBERS OF FIRM

Kurt W. Maier	Charles E. English, Jr.

ASSOCIATES

Robert A. Young	W. Cravens Priest, III

For Complete List of Firm Personnel, See General Section

For full biographical listings, see the Martindale-Hubbell Law Directory

HARLIN & PARKER, P.S.C. (AV)

519 East Tenth Street, P.O. Box 390, 42102-0390
Telephone: 502-842-5611
Telefax: 502-842-2607

William Jerry Parker	Scott Charles Marks

Insurance Clients: CNA Insurance Companies; Maryland Casualty Co. *Railroad and Utilities Clients:* District Attorneys for BellSouth Telecommunications, Inc.; CSX Transportation, Inc. *Representative Clients:* Sears Roebuck & Company. *Local Counsel for:* General Motors Corp.; Ford Motor Co.; Chrysler Corp.

For Complete List of Firm Personnel, See General Section

For full biographical listings, see the Martindale-Hubbell Law Directory

KERRICK, GRISE & STIVERS (AV)

1025 State Street, P.O. Box 9547, 42102-9547
Telephone: 502-782-8160
Fax: 502-782-5856
Elizabethtown, Kentucky Office: 2935 Dolphin Drive, Suite 102.
Telephone: 502-769-5788.
Fax: 502-737-9285.

MEMBERS OF FIRM

Thomas N. Kerrick	Gregory N. Stivers
John R. Grise	H. Brent Brennenstuhl

ASSOCIATES

Lanna Martin Kilgore	Shawn Rosso Alcott
Laura M. Hagan (Resident, Elizabethtown Office)	Jason B. Bell

Representative Clients: Dollar General Corp.; Columbia Greenview Regional Hospital; Hospital Corporation of America; Hardin Memorial Hospital; Monarch Environmental, Inc.; Mid-South Management Group, Inc.; Trans Financial Bank; TKR Cable.

For full biographical listings, see the Martindale-Hubbell Law Directory

COVINGTON, Kenton Co.

ADAMS, BROOKING, STEPNER, WOLTERMANN & DUSING (AV)

421 Garrard Street, P.O. Box 861, 41012
Telephone: 606-291-7270
Fax: 606-291-7902
Florence, Kentucky Office: 8100 Burlington Pike, Suite 400, 41042.
Telephone: 606-371-6220.
Fax: 606-371-8341.

Donald L. Stepner	Gerald F. Dusing
James G. Woltermann	(Resident at Florence Office)
(Resident at Florence Office)	James R. Kruer
	Jeffrey C. Mando

ASSOCIATES

Marc D. Dietz	Stacey L. Graus
(Resident at Florence Office)	Chandra S. Baldwin
John S. "Brook" Brooking	
(Resident at Florence Office)	

Representative Clients: Balluff, Inc., Wampler, Inc., Kisters, Inc., Krauss-Maffei, Inc., A group of German companies; State Automobile Mutual Insurance Co.; Chevron of California; Great American Insurance Co.; Grange Mutual Insurance Co.; Meridian Mutual Insurance Co.; Fifth-Third Bank of Northern Ky.; Northern Kentucky University; ITT Hartford.

For Complete List of Firm Personnel, See General Section

For full biographical listings, see the Martindale-Hubbell Law Directory

ROBERT E. SANDERS AND ASSOCIATES, P.S.C. (AV)

The Charles H. Fisk House, 1017 Russell Street, 41011
Telephone: 606-491-3000
Fax: 606-655-4642
Email: 74762.3055@compuserve.com

Robert E. Sanders

Julie Lippert Duncan	Peggy A. Murphy
Lisa Pruitt Thorner	

LEGAL SUPPORT PERSONNEL

Shirley L. Sanders	Sandra A. Head
Sheila D. Rachal	

For full biographical listings, see the Martindale-Hubbell Law Directory

TALIAFERRO AND MEHLING (AV)

1005 Madison Avenue, P.O. Box 468, 41012-0468
Telephone: 606-291-9900
Fax: 606-291-3014

MEMBERS OF FIRM

Philip Taliaferro, III	Christopher J. Mehling
Lucinda C. Shirooni	

ASSOCIATES

C. Houston Ebert	Howard L. Tankersley
Alice G. Keys	

OF COUNSEL

Robert W. Carran	Norbert J. Bischoff
F. Edward Worland, Jr.	

For full biographical listings, see the Martindale-Hubbell Law Directory

*DANVILLE,** Boyle Co.

DEEDRA BENTHALL (AV)

326 West Main Street, P.O. Box 996, 40422
Telephone: 606-236-5791; 236-6940
Fax: 606-236-8254

Reference: Citizens National Bank.

For full biographical listings, see the Martindale-Hubbell Law Directory

SHEEHAN, BARNETT & HAYS, P.S.C. (AV)

114 South Fourth Street, P.O. Box 1517, 40423-1517
Telephone: 606-236-2641; 606-734-7552
FAX: 606-236-1483

James G. Sheehan, Jr.	Edward D. Hays
James William Barnett	Rebecca Lynn Rice

Representative Clients: Bank One; National City Bank; Great Financial Bank; Kentucky Farm Bureau Mutual Insurance Co.; Motorist Mutual Insurance Co.; R.R. Donnelley & Sons, Inc.; State Automobile Mutual Insurance Co.; City of Danville; Shelter Insurance Co.; Trim Masters, Inc.

For full biographical listings, see the Martindale-Hubbell Law Directory

FLORENCE, Boone Co.

ADAMS, BROOKING, STEPNER, WOLTERMANN & DUSING (AV)

8100 Burlington Pike, Suite 400, 41042-0576
Telephone: 606-371-6220
Fax: 606-371-8341
Covington, Kentucky Office: 421 Garrard Street.
Telephone: 606-291-7270.
Fax: 606-291-7902.

Donald L. Stepner	Gerald F. Dusing (Resident)
James G. Woltermann	Michael M. Sketch (Resident)
(Resident)	Dennis R. Williams (Resident)

Jeffrey C. Mando

ASSOCIATES

Marc D. Dietz (Resident)	Stacey L. Graus
John S. "Brook" Brooking	Chandra S. Baldwin
(Resident)	

Representative Clients: State Automobile Mutual Insurance Co.; Standard Oil Co. (Ky.); Great American Insurance Co.; Grange Mutual Insurance Co.; Meridian Mutual Insurance Co.; Fifth-Third Bank of Boone County; Northern Kentucky University.

For Complete List of Firm Personnel, See General Section

For full biographical listings, see the Martindale-Hubbell Law Directory

FRANKLIN,* Simpson Co.

STEERS & STEERS, P.S.C. (AV)

211 South College Street, P.O. Box 447, 42135-0447
Telephone: 502-586-4466
Telecopier: 502-586-4467

Roy L. Steers (1917-1980)	R. Lee Steers, Jr.

Kimberly J. Burns

For full biographical listings, see the Martindale-Hubbell Law Directory

HAZARD,* Perry Co.

GULLETT & COMBS (AV)

109 Broadway, Second Floor, P.O. Box 1039, 41702-5039
Telephone: 606-439-1373
Fax: 606-439-4450
Email: pgullett@mis.net; rgcombs@mis.net

MEMBERS OF FIRM

Asa P. Gullett, III	Ronald G. Combs

ASSOCIATES

Teresa G. Combs Reed	Matthew Lawton Bowling

LEGAL SUPPORT PERSONNEL

Jacqueline E. Goodin	Jimmie Lynn Jones

Reference: Peoples Bank and Trust Co.

For full biographical listings, see the Martindale-Hubbell Law Directory

HINDMAN,* Knott Co.

WEINBERG, CAMPBELL, SLONE & SLONE, P.S.C. (AV)

Main Street, P.O. Box 727, 41822
Telephone: 606-785-5048; 785-5049
Fax: 606-785-3021

William R. Weinberg	Jerry Wayne Slone
Randy A. Campbell	Randy G. Slone

Richard A. Counts

References: Bank of Hindman; Thacker & Grigsby Telephone Co.

For full biographical listings, see the Martindale-Hubbell Law Directory

HOPKINSVILLE,* Christian Co.

KEMP AND KEMP (AV)

608 South Main Street, P.O. Box 648, 42241
Telephone: 502-886-8272
Fax: 502-885-5207

MEMBERS OF FIRM

J. Daniel Kemp	Judy Hall Kemp

Counsel for: Pennyrile Rural Electric Cooperative Corp.; Southern States Cooperative.
Approved Attorneys for: Farm Credit Services; Commonwealth Land Title Insurance Co. (Agent).
References: NationsBank, Hopkinsville, Kentucky; First City Bank & Trust Co., Hopkinsville, Kentucky; United Southern Bank, Hopkinsville, Ky.

For full biographical listings, see the Martindale-Hubbell Law Directory

LEXINGTON,* Fayette Co.

LANDRUM & SHOUSE (AV)

106 West Vine Street, P.O. Box 951, 40588-0951
Telephone: 606-255-2424
Facsimile: 606-233-0308
Louisville, Kentucky Office: 400 West Market Street, Suite 1550, 40202.
Telephone: 502-589-7616.
Facsimile: 502-589-2119.

MEMBERS OF FIRM

John H. Burrus	Mark J. Hinkel
Thomas M. Cooper	Delores Hill Pregliasco
William C. Shouse	(Resident, Louisville Office)
Pierce W. Hamblin	John Garry McNeill
Mark L. Moseley	Jack E. Toliver
Leslie Patterson Vose	R. Kent Westberry
John R. Martin, Jr.	(Resident, Louisville Office)
(Resident, Louisville Office)	J. Denis Ogburn
Larry C. Deener	(Resident, Louisville Office)
Sandra Mendez Dawahare	Jane Durkin Samuel

Douglas L. Hoots

ASSOCIATES

Stephen D. Milner	Daniel E. Murner
Stephen R. Chappell	Courtney T. Baxter
Charles E. Christian	(Resident, Louisville Office)
Dave Whalin	Frank M. Jenkins, III
(Resident, Louisville Office)	

OF COUNSEL

Weldon Shouse

District Attorneys: CSX Transportation, Inc.
Special Trial Counsel: Ford Motor Co. and Affiliates (Eastern Kentucky); Clark Equipment Co.
Representative Clients: The Continental Insurance Cos.; U.S. Insurance Group; U.S. Fidelity & Guaranty Co.; Ohio Casualty Insurance Co.; CIGNA; Royal Insurance Cos.

For Complete List of Firm Personnel, See General Section

For full biographical listings, see the Martindale-Hubbell Law Directory

PETER PERLMAN LAW OFFICES, P.S.C. (AV)

388 South Broadway, 40508
Telephone: 606-253-3919
FAX: 606-259-0493

Peter Perlman

Bryce D. Franklin, Jr.	Pamela D. Perlman

For full biographical listings, see the Martindale-Hubbell Law Directory

PIPER, WELLMAN & BOWERS (AV)

200 North Upper Street, 40507
Telephone: 606-231-1012
Fax: 606-231-7367
Email: pwb200@uky.campus.mci.net

MEMBERS OF FIRM

George C. Piper	Dean T. Wellman

Barbara J. Bowers

ASSOCIATE

Johann F. Herklotz

For full biographical listings, see the Martindale-Hubbell Law Directory

ROBERTS & SMITH (AV)

167 West Main Street Suite 200, 40507
Telephone: 606-233-1104

MEMBERS OF FIRM

Larry S. Roberts	Kenneth W. Smith

For full biographical listings, see the Martindale-Hubbell Law Directory

SAVAGE, GARMER & ELLIOTT, P.S.C. (AV)

Opera House Office Building, 141 North Broadway, 40507
Telephone: 606-254-9351
Fax: 606-233-9769

Joe C. Savage	William R. Garmer

Robert L. Elliott

For full biographical listings, see the Martindale-Hubbell Law Directory

LOUISVILLE,* Jefferson Co.

THOMAS M. CRAWFORD, P.S.C. (AV)

200 Hart Block Building, 730 West Main, 40202-2640
Telephone: 502-589-6190
Fax: 502-584-1744

(See Next Column)

THOMAS M. CRAWFORD, P.S.C.—*Continued*

Thomas M. Crawford

For full biographical listings, see the Martindale-Hubbell Law Directory

FRANKLIN AND HANCE, P.S.C. (AV)

The Speed House, 505 West Ormsby Avenue, 40203
Telephone: 502-637-6000
Fax: 502-637-1413

Larry B. Franklin   Michael R. Hance

David B. Gray   Hope Kathleen Fitzpatrick
Reference: First National Bank.

For full biographical listings, see the Martindale-Hubbell Law Directory

HARGADON, LENIHAN, HARBOLT, & HERRINGTON (AV)

713 West Main Street, 40202
Telephone: 502-583-9701
FAX: 502-589-1144

MEMBERS OF FIRM

James B. Lenihan   A. Neal Herrington
Harry L. Hargadon, Jr.   Michael T. Cooper

ASSOCIATES

Mark A. Weis   Eric J. Haner

OF COUNSEL

John L. Harbolt

References: Liberty National Bank and Trust Co.; Citizens Fidelity Bank & Trust Co.

For full biographical listings, see the Martindale-Hubbell Law Directory

HUMMEL & COAN (AV)

Kentucky Home Life Building, The Seventeenth Floor, 239 South Fifth Street, 40202-3268
Telephone: 502-585-3084
Fax: 502-585-3548

OF COUNSEL

Washer Kaplan Rothschild Aberson & Miller

MEMBERS OF FIRM

Dennis J. Hummel   Marvin L. Coan

ASSOCIATE

David L. Sage II

Representative Clients: Georgia Pacific Corp.; Safeco Insurance Cos.; GRE Insurance Group; The Aetna Casualty & Surety Co.; Dr. Bizer's Vision World; Calvert Insurance Co.; Western Heritage Insurance Co.; Nobel Insurance Company.

For full biographical listings, see the Martindale-Hubbell Law Directory

LANDRUM & SHOUSE (AV)

400 West Market Street Suite 1550, 40202
Telephone: 502-589-7616
Facsimile: 502-589-2119
Lexington, Kentucky Office: 106 West Vine Street, P.O. Box 951.
Telephone: 606-255-2424.
Facsimile: 606-233-0308.

RESIDENT MEMBERS OF THE FIRM

John R. Martin, Jr.   R. Kent Westberry
Delores Hill Pregliasco   J. Denis Ogburn

RESIDENT ASSOCIATES

Dave Whalin   Courtney T. Baxter

For Complete List of Firm Personnel, See General Section

For full biographical listings, see the Martindale-Hubbell Law Directory

MIDDLETON & REUTLINGER, P.S.C. (AV)

2500 Brown and Williamson Tower, 40202-3410
Telephone: 502-584-1135
Fax: 502-561-0442
New Albany, Indiana Office: 2623 Charlestown Road, 47150.
Telephone: 812-944-7215.

O. Grant Bruton   Stewart L. Prather
Charles G. Middleton, III   G. Kennedy Hall, Jr.
Charles D. Greenwell   Mark S. Fenzel
John W. Bilby   Kathiejane Oehler
Timothy P. O'Mara   David J. Kellerman
                  Julie A. Gregory

(See Next Column)

Dennis D. Murrell   Augustus S. Herbert
Counsel for: Chevron USA; Logan Aluminum, Inc.; Louisville Gas & Electric Co.; MCI Telecommunications Corp.; Metropolitan Life Insurance Co.; Kosmos Cement Co.; Porcelain Metal Corp.; The Home Insurance Co.; The Kroger Co.; Demars Haka Development, Inc.

For Complete List of Firm Personnel, See General Section

For full biographical listings, see the Martindale-Hubbell Law Directory

OLDFATHER & MORRIS (AV)

1330 South Third Street, 40208
Telephone: 502-637-7200
Fax: 502-637-3999
Email: om@ntr.net

Ann B. Oldfather   James Barrett
Douglas H. Morris, II   Jennifer Jordan Hall

For full biographical listings, see the Martindale-Hubbell Law Directory

RUBIN HAYS & FOLEY (AV)

First Trust Centre 200 South Fifth Street, 40202
Telephone: 502-569-7550
Telecopier: 502-569-7555

MEMBERS OF FIRM

Wm. Carl Fust   Lisa Koch Bryant
Harry Lee Meyer   Sharon C. Hardy
David W. Gray   Charles S. Musson
Irvin D. Foley   W. Randall Jones
Joseph R. Gathright, Jr.   K. Gail Russell

ASSOCIATES

Christian L. Juckett   Courtney Lynn McCall

OF COUNSEL

James E. Fahey   Newman T. Guthrie

Representative Clients: J.C. Bradford & Co., Inc.; J.J.B. Hilliard, W.L. Lyons, Inc.; Huntington National Bank; Liberty National Bank and Trust Company; National City Bank; PNC Bank; Prudential Bache & Co., Inc.; Prudential Securities, Inc.; Society Bank; Stock Yards Bank and Trust Co.

For full biographical listings, see the Martindale-Hubbell Law Directory

SEILLER & HANDMAKER, LLP (AV)

2200 Meidinger Tower, 40202
Telephone: 502-584-7400
Telecopier: 502-583-2100
Paris, Kentucky Office: Seiller, Handmaker & Blevins, P.S.C., 1431 South Main Street.
Telephone: 606-987-3980.
Telecopier: 606-987-3982.
Cynthiana, Kentucky Office: Seiller, Handmaker & Blevins, P.S.C., 9 South Walnut.
Telephone: 606-234-2880.
New Albany, Indiana Office: 202 Pearl Street.
Telephone: 812-948-8307.
Telecopier: 812-948-8383.

Edward F. Seiller (1897-1990)

MEMBERS OF FIRM

Stuart Allen Handmaker   Maury D. Kommor
Bill V. Seiller   Cynthia Compton Stone
David M. Cantor   Glenn A. Cohen
Neil C. Bordy   Tomi Anne Blevins Pulliam
Kyle Anne Citrynell   (Paris and Cynthiana Offices)

ASSOCIATES

Pamela M. Greenwell   Donna F. Townsend
Michael C. Bratcher   Gregory A. Lindsey
John E. Brengle   Vicki L. Buba
Patrick R. Holland, II   Allen C. Platt III (Resident,
Edwin Jon Wolfe   New Albany, Indiana Office)

OF COUNSEL

Robert S. Frey

For full biographical listings, see the Martindale-Hubbell Law Directory

WEISS & FREDERICK (AV)

1425 Citizens Plaza, 40202
Telephone: 502-583-1000
FAX: 502-583-4478

Gary M. Weiss   Janice M. Weiss
Carl D. Frederick   William T. Haynes, Jr.

OF COUNSEL

Henry M. Burt   Karla W. Katakis

For full biographical listings, see the Martindale-Hubbell Law Directory

NEWPORT, Campbell Co.

DON JOHNSON, P.S.C. (AV)

20 North Grand Avenue, Suite 15, 41071
Telephone: 606-441-3900
Telecopier: 606-441-3018

Donald L. Johnson

Richard G. Johnson

Representative Clients: Provident Bank of Kentucky; Country Square (Super-Value) Market; Campbell Capital Development Group, Inc.; B&K Enterprises, Inc.; Yellow Cab of Newport, Inc.; Executive Transporation, Inc.; Airport Starter Systems, Inc.; Alexandria Capital Co.; M. Links Co., Inc; Hasco International Identification, Inc.

For full biographical listings, see the Martindale-Hubbell Law Directory

*OWENSBORO,** Daviess Co.

KAMUF, YEWELL, PACE & CONDON (AV)

Great Financial Federal Building, 322 Frederica Street, 42301
Telephone: 502-685-3901
Fax: 502-926-2005

MEMBERS OF FIRM

Charles J. Kamuf	Patrick D. Pace
David L. Yewell	David C. Condon

Representative Clients: Owensboro Municipal Utilities Commission; Lincoln Service Corp.; Hancock County Planning Commission; Daviess County Board of Education; Barmet Aluminum Corp.; Owensboro Sewer Commission; TICOR Title Insurance Co.; Chicago Title Insurance Co.; Owensboro Riverport Authority; Housing Authority of Owensboro.

For Complete List of Firm Personnel, See General Section

For full biographical listings, see the Martindale-Hubbell Law Directory

*PADUCAH,** McCracken Co.

LEN W. OGDEN, JR. (AV)

The Sinnott House, 228 North 9th Street, 42001-1850
Telephone: 502-444-0232
Fax: 502-444-0239

For full biographical listings, see the Martindale-Hubbell Law Directory

*PIKEVILLE,** Pike Co.

GARY C. JOHNSON, P.S.C. (AV)

104 Caroline Avenue, P.O. Box 231, 41502
Telephone: 606-437-4002
Telecopier: 606-437-0021
Hazard, Kentucky Office: 941 Memorial Drive, P.O. Box 509.
Telephone: 606-436-6059.
Fax: 606-436-4599.
Lexington, Kentucky Office: 101 Prosperous Place, Suite 100.
Telephone: 606-263-4002.

Gary C. Johnson

Anita Johnson	Jeffrey R. Morgan
Roy J. Downey	Jeremy R. Morgan
Timothy D. Belcher	Jimmie G. Orr, Jr.
Julie A. Butcher	Ray Stanley Jones, II
William Hickman, III	Masten Childers, II

For full biographical listings, see the Martindale-Hubbell Law Directory

PRUITT AND DE BOURBON LAW FIRM (AV)

The Call Building, Second Street, P.O. Box 339, 41502
Telephone: 606-437-7366; 437-7367; 237-1280
Fax: 606-432-2367

MEMBERS OF FIRM

James P. Pruitt, Jr.	P. Michael de Bourbon

Reference: The Citizen's Bank of Pikeville.

For full biographical listings, see the Martindale-Hubbell Law Directory

*VANCEBURG,** Lewis Co.

STANLEY AND BERTRAM, P.S.C. (AV)

P.O. Box 40, 41179-0040
Telephone: 606-796-3024; 796-3025
Fax: 606-796-2113

Avery L. Stanley	Thomas M. Bertram, II
Anita Esham Stanley	

A list of Representative Clients will be furnished upon request.

For full biographical listings, see the Martindale-Hubbell Law Directory

LOUISIANA

*BATON ROUGE,** East Baton Rouge Parish

deGRAVELLES, PALMINTIER & HOLTHAUS (AV)

628 St. Louis Street, 70802-0628
Telephone: 504-344-3735
Fax: 504-336-1146

MEMBERS OF FIRM

John W. deGravelles	Michael C. Palmintier
	Craig F. Holthaus

ASSOCIATES

Oliver Wendell Holmes, III	Michael L. Hebert

OF COUNSEL

David W. Robinson

LEGAL SUPPORT PERSONNEL

Jimmie W. Murvin (Paralegal)

For full biographical listings, see the Martindale-Hubbell Law Directory

DUÉ, CABALLERO, PERRY, PRICE & GUIDRY, (A PROFESSIONAL ASSOCIATION) (AV)

8201 Jefferson Highway, 70809
Telephone: 504-929-7481
Fax: 504-924-4519

Paul H. Dué	Donald W. Price
Rick A. Caballero	Kirk A. Guidry
John W. Perry, Jr.	Daniel J. Balhoff
	Randolph A. Piedrahita

OF COUNSEL

David W. Robertson

For full biographical listings, see the Martindale-Hubbell Law Directory

GEORGE AND GEORGE, LTD., A PROFESSIONAL LAW CORPORATION (AV)

8110 Summa Avenue, 70809
Telephone: 504-769-3064
Fax: 504-766-9974
Toll Free Numbers: 1-800-654-2335
Nationwide: 1-800-843-5702

James A. George

Reference: Hibernia National Bank of Baton Rouge.

For full biographical listings, see the Martindale-Hubbell Law Directory

LAW OFFICES OF ROBERT D. HOOVER, P.L.C. (AV)

533 Europe Street, P.O. Box 4248, 70821-4248
Telephone: 504-381-9386
Fax: 504-383-9147

Robert D. Hoover

For full biographical listings, see the Martindale-Hubbell Law Directory

LANE, FERTITTA, LANE, JANNEY & THOMAS (AV)

435 Louisiana Avenue, P.O. Box 3335, 70821
Telephone: 504-387-0241
Fax: 504-387-1238

MEMBERS OF FIRM

Horace C. Lane (1921-1989)	Thomas A. Lane
Frank A. Fertitta	William F. Janney
	Richard S. Thomas

ASSOCIATE

Margaret T. Lane

Representative Clients: State Farm Mutual Automobile Insurance Co.; State Farm Fire & Casualty Co.; United States Fidelity & Guaranty Co.; Aetna Casualty & Surety Co.; Employers Liability Assurance Corp., Ltd.; Allstate Insurance Co.; St. Paul Fire and Marine Insurance Co.; The Medical Protective Co.; Safeco Insurance Co. of America; Horace Mann Insurance Co.

For full biographical listings, see the Martindale-Hubbell Law Directory

SEALE, SMITH, ZUBER & BARNETTE (AV)

Two United Plaza, Suite 200, 8550 United Plaza Boulevard, 70809
Telephone: 504-924-1600
Telecopier: 504-924-6100

Armbrust Gordon Seale (1913-1989)	William C. Kaufman III
	John W. L. Swanner
Robert W. Smith (1922-1989)	James H. Morgan III
Donald S. Zuber	Ronald A. Seale
Kenneth E. Barnette	Brent E. Kinchen

(See Next Column)

SEALE, SMITH, ZUBER & BARNETTE—*Continued*

Charles K. Watts	William C. Rowe, Jr.
Myron A. Walker, Jr.	Lawrence R. Anderson, Jr.
Daniel A. Reed	Catherine S. Nobile

ASSOCIATES

Richard T. Reed	Anthony J. Russo, Jr.
Barbara G. Chatelain	Gregory D. Polozola

Representative Clients: Farmers Insurance Group; St. Paul Fire and Marine Insurance Company; United Services Automobile Association; General Motors Acceptance Corporation.
Reference: City National Bank, Baton Rouge, Louisiana.

For full biographical listings, see the Martindale-Hubbell Law Directory

---

WALTER LANDRY SMITH (AV)

12451 Highland Road, P.O. Box 82729, 70884-2729
Telephone: 504-769-0886
Facsimile: 504-769-9165

For full biographical listings, see the Martindale-Hubbell Law Directory

---

*HOUMA,** Terrebonne Parish

ST. MARTIN & LIRETTE, A PROFESSIONAL LAW CORPORATION (AV)

3373 Little Bayou Black Road, P.O. Box 2017, 70361-2017
Telephone: 504-876-3891;
Toll Free: 1-800-256-1533
Facsimile: 504-851-2219

Michael X. St. Martin	Conrad S. P. Williams, III
Danny J. Lirette	Michelle Mayne Davis
Joseph G. Jevic, III	

For full biographical listings, see the Martindale-Hubbell Law Directory

---

*LAFAYETTE,** Lafayette Parish

ALLEN LAW OFFICE (AV)

Suite 3-F, 224 St. Landry, P.O. Box 3204, 70502
Telephone: 318-232-9918
Toll Free: 800-232-1529

Raymond Morgan Allen	Aaron J. Allen

For full biographical listings, see the Martindale-Hubbell Law Directory

---

ANDERSON & BROUSSARD (AV)

A Partnership of Professional Law Corporations
600 Jefferson Street, Suite 700, P.O. Box 3524, 70502-3524
Telephone: 318-237-6100
Fax: 318-237-6107

Bennett Boyd Anderson, Jr., (A Professional Law Corporation)	Richard C. Broussard (A Professional Law Corporation)

For full biographical listings, see the Martindale-Hubbell Law Directory

---

BROUSSARD, DAVID & DAIGLE, A PROFESSIONAL LAW CORPORATION (AV)

557 Jefferson Street, P.O. Drawer 3308, 70502-3308
Telephone: 318-234-7000
Fax: 318-237-0344

Hal J. Broussard	Susan A. Daigle
Paul B. David	Bryan D. Scofield

Ped C. Kay, III	Todd G. Crawford
Richard J. Guidry	James T. Rivera

Representative Clients: Certain London Underwriters per individual approval of instructions; Lloyds of London Member Syndicates; Institute of London Underwriter Member Companies; Reliance Insurance Company of Pennsylvania; Reliance Insurance Company of Illinois; Reliance National Insurance Company; The Louisiana Insurance Guaranty Association; Louisiana Oilfield Legislative Committee, Inc. (Louisiana Association of Oilfield Casing Contractors; Association of Oilwell Servicing Contractors; Louisiana Pipeline Contractors Association; Offshore Pipeline Contractors Association; Louisiana Oilfield Contractor Association).

For full biographical listings, see the Martindale-Hubbell Law Directory

---

DOMENGEAUX WRIGHT MOROUX & ROY A PROFESSIONAL LAW CORPORATION (AV)

556 Jefferson Street, Suite 500, P.O. Box 3668, 70502-3668
Telephone: 318-233-3033; 1-800-375-3106
Fax: 318-232-8213

(See Next Column)

James Domengeaux (1907-1988)	Frank Edwards
Anthony D. Moroux (1948-1993)	James H. Domengeaux
Bob F. Wright (A Professional Law Corporation)	Gilbert Hennigan Dozier (A Professional Law Corporation)
James Parkerson Roy (A Professional Law Corporation)	Carla Marie Perron
	Vivian Veron Neumann
Thomas R. Edwards (A Professional Law Corporation)	Michael D. Goss

OF COUNSEL
Jerome E. Domengeaux

Reference: Mid-South National Bank; Advocate Financial, L.L.C.

For full biographical listings, see the Martindale-Hubbell Law Directory

---

RICHARD R. KENNEDY A PROFESSIONAL LAW CORPORATION (AV)

309 Polk Street, P.O. Box 3243, 70502-3243
Telephone: 318-232-1934
Fax: 318-232-9720
Email: kennedy@net-connect.net

Richard R. Kennedy

For full biographical listings, see the Martindale-Hubbell Law Directory

---

VOORHIES & LABBÉ, A PROFESSIONAL LAW CORPORATION (AV)

Fourth Floor, Acadiana National Bank Building, 700 St. John Street, P.O. Box 3527, 70502
Telephone: 318-232-9700
Telecopier: 318-235-4943

Bennett J. Voorhies (1901-1970)	John C. Jones
Donald Labbé (1900-1966)	Robert M. Francez
D. Mark Bienvenu (1931-1991)	Robert M. Kallam
H. Edwin McGlasson, Jr.	Elizabeth L. Guglielmo
W. Gerald Gaudet	Samuel R. Aucoin
Richard D. Chappuis, Jr.	James Allen Lochridge, Jr.
William M. Bass	Mary McCrory Hamilton
Robert A. Lecky	Bradley Joseph Haight
John N. Chappuis	Simone Chachere Dupre
Robert L. Ellender	George J. Armbruster, III
Cyd Sheree Page	Bradley J. Schlotterer

OF COUNSEL
John W. Hutchison

Representative Clients: Adams & Porter Associates; Aetna Casualty & Surety Insurance Co.; AIG Aviation, Inc.; American Home Assurance Co.; AMICA Mutual Insurance Co.; Appalachian Insurance Co.; Audubon/AIG Insurance Co.; Aviation Office of America; Bellefonte Insurance Co.; Chubb Group of Insurance Co. Co.

For full biographical listings, see the Martindale-Hubbell Law Directory

---

*LAKE CHARLES,** Calcasieu Parish

BAGGETT, McCALL & BURGESS, A PROFESSIONAL LAW CORPORATION (AV)

3006 Country Club Road, P.O. Drawer 7820, 70606-7820
Telephone: 318-478-8888
Fax: 318-478-8946
Email: bmblf@mail.maas.net

William B. Baggett	Jeffrey T. Gaughan
Robert C. McCall	Erin McCall Alley
William B. Baggett, Jr.	Christopher C. McCall
Roger G. Burgess	Nancy Jo Dougherty
Wells T. Watson	(Not admitted in LA)

For full biographical listings, see the Martindale-Hubbell Law Directory

---

LUNDY & DAVIS, L.L.P. (AV)

Calcasieu Marine Tower, One Lakeshore Drive, Suite 1600, P.O. Box 3010, 70602
Telephone: 318-439-0707
FAX: 318-439-1029
Jackson, Mississippi Office: 111 East Capitol Street, Suite 250.
Telephone: 601-948-3010.
Facsimile: 601-948-2143.
Houston, Texas Office: 1201 Louisiana, Suite 3179.
Telephone: 713-650-1204.
Facsimile: 713-650-1070.
Biloxi, Mississippi Office: 999 Howard Avenue.
Telephone: 601-435-7733.
Facsimile: 601-435-7737.

MEMBERS OF FIRM

Hunter W. Lundy	Jerry A. Johnson
Clayton A. L. Davis	David A. Bowers (Resident, Jackson, Mississippi Office)
Matthew E. Lundy (Resident, Houston, Texas Office)	

(See Next Column)

LUNDY & DAVIS L.L.P., *Lake Charles—Continued*

ASSOCIATES

Jackey W. South	Jody Brian Martin (Resident,
DeAnn Gibson	Jackson, Mississippi Office)
Samuel B. Gabb	Michael D. Carleton
James D. Cain, Jr.	Thomas P. LeBlanc

OF COUNSEL

Walter L. Nixon, Jr.

For full biographical listings, see the Martindale-Hubbell Law Directory

PLAUCHÉ SMITH & NIESET, A PROFESSIONAL LAW CORPORATION (AV)

1123 Pithon Street, P.O. Drawer 1705, 70602
Telephone: 318-436-0522
Facsimile: 318-436-9637

S. W. Plauché (1889-1952)	Jeffrey M. Cole
S. W. Plauché, Jr. (1915-1966)	Andrew R. Johnson, IV
A. Lane Plauché	Charles V. Musso, Jr.
Allen L. Smith, Jr.	Christopher P. Ieyoub
James R. Nieset	H. David Vaughan, II
Frank M. Walker, Jr.	Joseph R. Pousson, Jr.
Michael J. McNulty, III	Rebecca S. Young

Representative Clients: CIGNA; CNA Insurance Cos.; Commercial Union Insurance Cos.; Crum & Forster; General Motors Corp.; Reliance Insurance Cos.; Royal Insurance Group; State Farm; U.S. Insurance Group.

For full biographical listings, see the Martindale-Hubbell Law Directory

MONROE,* Ouachita Parish

MCLEOD VERLANDER (AV)

A Partnership including Professional Law Corporations
1900 North 18th Street, Suite 610, P.O. Box 2270, 71207-2270
Telephone: 318-325-7000
Telecopier: 318-324-0580
Email: mvlaw@iamerica.net

MEMBERS OF FIRM

Robert P. McLeod (P.L.C.)	Rick W. Duplissey
David E. Verlander, III (P.L.C.)	Pamela G. Nathan
Laurie J. Burkett	

For full biographical listings, see the Martindale-Hubbell Law Directory

MORGAN CITY, St. Mary Parish

LIPPMAN, MAHFOUZ & MARTIN (AV)

Inglewood Mall, 1025 Victor II Boulevard, P.O. Box 2526, 70381
Telephone: 504-384-1833
Fax: 504-385-4632

MEMBERS OF FIRM

Alfred S. Lippman	Thomas L. Mahfouz
Dale P. Martin	

ASSOCIATES

Brian M. Tranchina	David M. Thorguson

For full biographical listings, see the Martindale-Hubbell Law Directory

NATCHITOCHES,* Natchitoches Parish

A. J. GREGORY, JR. (AV)

714-B Third Street, P.O. Box 1131, 71457
Telephone: 318-352-9311
Fax: 318-352-8019
Shreveport, Louisiana Office: 1540 Irving Place.
Telephone: 318-221-0076.
Fax: 318-227-8290.

References: First Bank of Natchitoches; Bank One.

For full biographical listings, see the Martindale-Hubbell Law Directory

NEW ORLEANS,* Orleans Parish

THE BAGERT LAW FIRM (AV)

Suite 2055 Pan-American Life Center, 601 Poydras Street, 70130
Telephone: 504-523-1117
Facsimile: 504-522-5406
Email: bagertlf@ix.netcom.com

Bernard J. Bagert, Jr., (A P.L.C.)

For full biographical listings, see the Martindale-Hubbell Law Directory

BENCOMO & ASSOCIATES (AV)

Suite 2110 One Poydras Plaza, 639 Loyola Avenue, 70113
Telephone: 504-529-2929
Fax: 504-529-2018

Raul R. Bencomo

(See Next Column)

Todd Hebert

OF COUNSEL

Richard E. Anderson

For full biographical listings, see the Martindale-Hubbell Law Directory

CAPITELLI & WICKER (AV)

2950 Energy Centre, 1100 Poydras Street, 70163-2950
Telephone: 504-582-2425
FAX: 504-582-2422

Ralph Capitelli	T. Carey Wicker, III
Paul Michael Elvir, Jr.	

OF COUNSEL

Terry Q. Alarcon

For full biographical listings, see the Martindale-Hubbell Law Directory

GAINSBURGH, BENJAMIN, DAVID, MEUNIER, NORIEA & WARSHAUER (AV)

2800 Energy Centre, 1100 Poydras, 70163-2800
Telephone: 504-522-2304
Telecopier: 504-528-9973
Email: GAINSBEN@IAMERICA.NET

OF COUNSEL

Jack C. Benjamin (P.L.C.)

MEMBERS OF FIRM

Robert J. David	Irving J. Warshauer
Gerald E. Meunier	Stevan C. Dittman
Nick F. Noriea, Jr.	Madeleine M. Landrieu
Darryl M. Phillips	

ASSOCIATES

Michael G. Calogero	Jeffrey A. Mitchell

For full biographical listings, see the Martindale-Hubbell Law Directory

DARLEEN M. JACOBS A PROFESSIONAL LAW CORPORATION (AV)

823 St. Louis Street, 70112
Telephone: 504-522-3287; 522-0155
Cable Address: "Darjac."

Darleen M. Jacobs	Honorable S. Sanford Levy (1902-1989)

For full biographical listings, see the Martindale-Hubbell Law Directory

MARTZELL & BICKFORD (AV)

A Partnership including a Professional Corporation
338 Lafayette Street, 70130
Telephone: 504-581-9065
FAX: 504-581-7635

John R. Martzell (P.C.)	James P. Meyer
Scott R. Bickford	Duggan F. Ellis
Regina O. Matthews	M. Suzanne Montero

LEGAL SUPPORT PERSONNEL

Edie Koonce	Connie L. Cosse
Jane B. Daigle	Gailen L. Christian

For full biographical listings, see the Martindale-Hubbell Law Directory

MURRAY LAW FIRM (AV)

Suite 2550, LL&E Tower, 909 Poydras Street, 70112-4000
Telephone: 504-525-8100
Fax: 504-584-5249
1-800-467-8100

Stephen B. Murray

Charles R. Ward, Jr.	Richard L. West
Joseph A. Race	Edward N. Rodriguez
Perry Michael Nicosia	Stephen B. Murray, Jr.
Linda S. Harang	Julie A. Ardoin
Gano D. Lemoine III	Stephanie M. Lawrence

OF COUNSEL

Bonnie Schultz

For full biographical listings, see the Martindale-Hubbell Law Directory

SLATER LAW FIRM, A PROFESSIONAL CORPORATION (AV)

650 Poydras Street Suite 2600, 70130-6101
Telephone: 504-523-7333
Fax: 504-528-1080

(See Next Column)

SLATER LAW FIRM A PROFESSIONAL CORPORATION—*Continued*

Benjamin R. Slater, Jr.	Kevin M. Wheeler
Benjamin R. Slater, III	Anne Elise Brown
Mark E. Van Horn	Donald J. Miester, Jr.

Cory Rabin Cahn	James L. Bradford, III

SPECIAL COUNSEL

W. Malcolm Stevenson	Robert B. Acomb, III
Michael O. Waguespack	

Representative Clients: Norfolk Southern Corporation; The Quaker Oats Company; Electric Mutual Liability Insurance Company; Diversified Foods and Seasonings.

For full biographical listings, see the Martindale-Hubbell Law Directory

---

SHREVEPORT,* Caddo Parish

TROY E. BAIN (AV)

1540 Irving Place, 71101
Telephone: 318-221-0076
Fax: 318-227-8290

Reference: Commercial National Bank of Shreveport.

For full biographical listings, see the Martindale-Hubbell Law Directory

---

SAM N. GREGORIO A PROFESSIONAL LAW CORPORATION (AV)

1540 Irving Place, 71101
Telephone: 318-227-8282
Fax: 318-227-8290

Sam N. Gregorio

For full biographical listings, see the Martindale-Hubbell Law Directory

---

WELLBORN JACK, JR. (AV)

101 Milam Street, 71101
Telephone: 318-227-9637
Fax: 318-221-6076

For full biographical listings, see the Martindale-Hubbell Law Directory

---

MILLS, TIMMONS & FLOWERS, A PROFESSIONAL LAW CORPORATION (AV)

300 Law Center, 331 Milam Street, P.O. Box 1784, 71166-1784
Telephone: 318-222-0337
Fax: 318-222-5400

George H. Mills, Jr.	David C. Turansky
Wayne Timmons	J. Broocks Greer III
Peter R. Flowers	Sandra Lynn Walker

OF COUNSEL
William T. Allison

Reference: Hibernia National Bank.

For full biographical listings, see the Martindale-Hubbell Law Directory

---

SOCKRIDER, BOLIN & ANGLIN, A PROFESSIONAL LAW CORPORATION (AV)

327 Crockett Street, 71101
Telephone: 318-221-5503
Fax: 318-221-3849

John R. Pleasant (1905-1983)	James E. Bolin, Jr.
H. F. Sockrider, Jr.	D. Rex Anglin
Gregory H. Batte	

For full biographical listings, see the Martindale-Hubbell Law Directory

---

MAINE

AUGUSTA,* Kennebec Co.

* indicates certain Bar Register subscribers whose principal office is located elsewhere in the state and who have arranged for representation as a part of the state capital listings that follow

LIPMAN & KATZ, P.A. (AV)

227 Water Street, 04330
Telephone: 207-622-3711
Telecopier: 207-622-7415

Sumner H. Lipman	Robert J. Stolt
David M. Lipman	Keith R. Varner
Roger J. Katz	Ronald E. Colby, III

Laura J.R. Garcia	Walter F. McKee

(See Next Column)

OF COUNSEL
Joseph B. Campbell

For full biographical listings, see the Martindale-Hubbell Law Directory

* PIERCE ATWOOD (AV)

77 Winthrop Street, 04330
Telephone: 207-622-6311
Fax: 207-623-9367
Email: info@PierceAtwood.com
Portland, Maine Office: One Monument Square.
Telephone: 207-791-1100.
Fax: 207-791-1350.
Newburyport, Massachusetts Office: 6 Harris Street.
Telephone: 508-465-9599.
Fax: 508-465-9945.

MEMBERS OF FIRM

Malcolm L. Lyons	Michael D. Seitzinger
	John C. Nivison

ASSOCIATE
Daniel J. Stevens

For Complete List of Firm Personnel, See General Section

For full biographical listings, see the Martindale-Hubbell Law Directory

---

BANGOR,* Penobscot Co.

EATON, PEABODY, BRADFORD & VEAGUE, P.A. (AV)

Fleet Center-Exchange Street, P.O. Box 1210, 04402-1210
Telephone: 207-947-0111
Telecopier: 207-942-3040
Email: epbv@aol.com
Augusta, Maine Office: 2 Central Plaza.
Telephone: 207-622-3747.
Telecopier: 207-622-9732.
Blue Hill, Maine Office: One East Blue Hill Road.
Telephone: 207-374-2812.
Telecopier: 207-374-2548.
Brunswick, Maine Office: 167 Park Row.
Telephone: 207-729-1144.
Telecopier: 207-729-1140.
Camden, Maine Office: 7-9 Washington Street.
Telephone: 207-236-3325.
Telecopier: 207-236-8611.
Dover-Foxcroft, Maine Office: 30 East Main Street.
Telephone: 207-564-8378.
Telecopier: 207-564-7059.

Thomas M. Brown	William B. Devoe
Bernard J. Kubetz	Paul L. Gibbons
Douglas M. Smith	(Resident, Camden Office)
(Dover-Foxcroft and Augusta Offices)	Judy A.S. Metcalf
	(Resident, Brunswick Office)
Stephen G. Morrell	Jonathan B. Huntington
(Resident, Brunswick Office)	(Resident, Dover-Foxcroft Office)
Glen L. Porter	
Gordon H. S. Scott	Thad B. Zmistowski
(Resident, Augusta Office)	

A List of Representative Clients available upon request.

For Complete List of Firm Personnel, See General Section

For full biographical listings, see the Martindale-Hubbell Law Directory

---

VAFIADES, BROUNTAS & KOMINSKY (AV)

Key Plaza, 23 Water Street, P.O. Box 919, 04402-0919
Telephone: 207-947-6915
Telecopier: 207-941-0863

MEMBERS OF FIRM

Susan R. Kominsky	Eugene C. Coughlin, III
Marvin H. Glazier	Lisa Cohen Lunn

ASSOCIATES

Terence M. Harrigan	James C. Munch, III

OF COUNSEL
Lewis V. Vafiades

For Complete List of Firm Personnel, See General Section

For full biographical listings, see the Martindale-Hubbell Law Directory

---

BAR HARBOR, Hancock Co.

FENTON, CHAPMAN, FENTON, SMITH & KANE, P.A. (AV)

109 Main Street, P.O. Box B, 04609
Telephone: 207-288-3331
FAX: 207-288-9326

Douglas B. Chapman	Nathaniel R. Fenton
Chadbourn H. Smith	

(See Next Column)

FENTON, CHAPMAN, FENTON, SMITH & KANE P.A., *Bar Harbor—Continued*

Margaret A. Timothy　　　　　　Eric Lindquist

Reference: Bar Harbor Banking and Trust Co.

For Complete List of Firm Personnel, See General Section

For full biographical listings, see the Martindale-Hubbell Law Directory

---

*BATH,** Sagadahoc Co.

CONLEY & HALEY (AV)

Thirty Front Street, 04530
Telephone: 207-443-5576
Telefax: 207-443-6665

J. Michael Conley　　　　　　Laura M. O'Hanlon
Brian L. Champion　　　　　　Julie G. Martin

Representative Clients: Bath Iron Works Corporation; Central Maine Power Company; Saco Defense, Inc.; Sugarloaf Mountain Corporation.
References: Key Bank of Maine; First Federal Savings & Loan Association of Bath; Brunswick Federal Savings.

For Complete List of Firm Personnel, See General Section

For full biographical listings, see the Martindale-Hubbell Law Directory

---

*PORTLAND,** Cumberland Co.

BENNETT AND ASSOCIATES, P.A. (AV)

Suite 300, 121 Middle Street, P.O. Box 7799, 04112-7799
Telephone: 207-773-4775
Telecopier: 207-774-2366
Email: 104142.2363@compuserve.com

Herbert H. Bennett (1928-1992)　　Frederick B. Finberg
Peter Bennett　　　　　　　　　Melinda J. Caterine
Jeffrey Bennett　　　　　　　　Clare S. Benedict

Counsel for: Associated Grocers of New England; Coca Cola Bottling Company of Northern New England, Inc.; Generalstar Indemnity Company; Northern Utilities/Bay State Gas; Pratt & Whitney (Division of United Technologies); Primerica Financial Services (The Travelers); Sprague Energy (C.H. Sprague & Son); Perrier Group of America, Inc.; Lepage Bakeries, Inc. (Country Kitchen); Texaco, Inc.

For full biographical listings, see the Martindale-Hubbell Law Directory

---

FRIEDMAN & BABCOCK (AV)

Suite 400, Six City Center, P.O. Box 4726, 04112-4726
Telephone: 207-761-0900
Telecopier: 207-761-0186

MEMBERS OF FIRM

Harold J. Friedman　　　　　Thomas A. Cox
Ernest J. Babcock　　　　　　Karen Frink Wolf
Martha C. Gaythwaite　　　　Jennifer S. Begel
　　　　Laurence H. Leavitt

ASSOCIATES

Theodore H. Irwin, Jr.　　　Elizabeth A. Germani
Lee H. Bals　　　　　　　　Jonathan Marc Dunitz
Michelle Allott　　　　　　Darren Blaine Riggle
Arthur J. Lamothe　　　　　Tracy D. Hill
　　　　Bruce W. Hepler

For full biographical listings, see the Martindale-Hubbell Law Directory

---

PIERCE ATWOOD (AV)

One Monument Square, 04101
Telephone: 207-791-1100
Fax: 207-791-1350
Email: info@PierceAtwood.com
Augusta, Maine Office: 77 Winthrop Street.
Telephone: 207-622-6311.
Fax: 207-623-9367.
Newburyport, Massachusetts Office: 6 Harris Street.
Telephone: 508-465-9599.
Fax: 508-465-9945.

MEMBERS OF FIRM

Ralph I. Lancaster, Jr.　　　John C. Nivison
Peter W. Culley　　　　　　　(Resident, Augusta Office)
Daniel M. Snow　　　　　　　John J. Aromando
　　　　David E. Barry
ASSOCIATE
Daniel J. Stevens　(Resident, Augusta Office)

For Complete List of Firm Personnel, See General Section

For full biographical listings, see the Martindale-Hubbell Law Directory

---

RICHARDSON, WHITMAN, LARGE & BADGER, A PROFESSIONAL CORPORATION (AV)

465 Congress Street, 04101-3528
Telephone: 207-774-7474
Telecopier: 207-774-1343
Email: Portland@rwlb.com *URL:* http://wwwrwlb.com
Bangor, Maine Office: 82 Columbia Street, P.O. Box 2429.
Telephone: 207-945-5900.
Telecopier: 207-945-0758.

Harrison L. Richardson　　　Elizabeth G. Stouder
John S. Whitman　　　　　　Barri Bloom
Wendell G. Large　　　　　　Ann M. Murray
Frederick J. Badger, Jr.　　　(Resident, Bangor Maine)
　(Resident, Bangor Office)

Frederick F. Costlow　　　　Anne H. Cressey
　(Resident, Bangor Office)　Thomas R. McKeon
John B. Lucy　　　　　　　Carol I. Eisenberg
　(Resident, Bangor Office)

For full biographical listings, see the Martindale-Hubbell Law Directory

---

SMITH ELLIOTT SMITH & GARMEY, P.A. (AV)

100 Commercial Street, Suite 304, 04101
Telephone: 207-774-3199
Telefax: 207-774-2235
Kennebunk, Maine Office: Route One South, 9 York Street.
Telephone: 207-985-4464.
Telefax: 207-985-3946.
Saco, Maine Office: 199 Main Street, P.O. Box 1179.
Telephone: 207-282-1527.
Telefax: 207-283-4412. Sanford
Telephone: 207-324-1560. Wells
Telephone: 207-646-0970.

Randall E. Smith　　　　　Richard P. Romeo
Terrence D. Garmey　　　　Robert H. Furbish

Reference: Saco & Biddeford Savings Institution.

For full biographical listings, see the Martindale-Hubbell Law Directory

---

THOMPSON & BOWIE (AV)

Three Canal Plaza, P.O. Box 4630, 04112
Telephone: 207-774-2500
Telecopier: 207-774-3591

MEMBERS OF FIRM

Roy E. Thompson, Jr.　　　Frank W. DeLong, III
James M. Bowie　　　　　　Michael E. Saucier
Daniel R. Mawhinney　　　　Mark V. Franco
Rebecca H. Farnum　　　　　Elizabeth Knox Peck
Glenn H. Robinson　　　　　Cathy S. Roberts

ASSOCIATE
Paul C. Catsos

For full biographical listings, see the Martindale-Hubbell Law Directory

---

TROUBH, HEISLER & PIAMPIANO, P.C. (AV)

511 Congress Street, P.O. Box 9711, 04104-5011
Telephone: 207-780-6789
Fax: 207-774-2339

William B. Troubh　　　　Thomas E. Getchell
Edwin A. Heisler　　　　　Michael Richards
Robert J. Piampiano　　　　William K. McKinley
Kevin M. Gillis　　　　　　Daniel F. Gilligan
Michael P. Boyd　　　　　Paul S. Bulger

John G. Richardson　　　　Linda L. Sears
　　　　Daniel R. Felkel

For full biographical listings, see the Martindale-Hubbell Law Directory

---

SACO, York Co.

SMITH ELLIOTT SMITH & GARMEY, P.A. (AV)

199 Main Street, P.O. Box 1179, 04072
Telephone: 207-282-1527
Telefax: 207-283-4412
Sanford Telephone: 207-324-1560
Portland Telephone: 207-774-3199
Wells Telephone: 207-646-0970
Kennebunk, Maine Office: Route One South, 9 York Street.
Telephone: 207-985-4464.
Telefax: 207-985-3946.
Portland, Maine Office: 100 Commercial Street, Suite 304.
Telephone: 207-774-3199.
Telefax: 207-774-2235.

(See Next Column)

SMITH ELLIOTT SMITH & GARMEY P.A.—*Continued*

Randall E. Smith	Peter W. Schroeter
Charles W. Smith, Jr.	Robert H. Furbish
Terrence D. Garmey	John H. O'Neil, Jr.

References: Saco & Biddeford Savings Institution.

For Complete List of Firm Personnel, See General Section

For full biographical listings, see the Martindale-Hubbell Law Directory

---

SKOWHEGAN, * Somerset Co.

WRIGHT & MILLS, P.A. (AV)

218 Water Street, P.O. Box 9, 04976
Telephone: 207-474-3324
Telefax: 207-474-3609

Carl R. Wright	Paul P. Sumberg
S. Peter Mills	Janet T. Mills
	Kenneth A. Lexier

Representative Clients: Design Professionals Insurance Co., New Jersey; Solon Manufacturing Co., Solon, Maine; Kleinschmidt Associates-Engineers, Pittsfield, Maine; Acheron Engineering, Newport, Maine; E.W. Littlefield-Contractors, Hartland, Maine; WBRC-Architects, Bangor, Maine; Town of Skowhegan; Town of Norridgewock.

For full biographical listings, see the Martindale-Hubbell Law Directory

---

MARYLAND

ANNAPOLIS, * Anne Arundel Co.

COHEN, GREENE & WASSERMAN, P.A. (AV)

156 South Street, P.O. Box 909, 21404
Telephone: 410-268-4500
Baltimore: 410-269-0464
Washington, D.C: 301-261-1950
Telecopier: 410-269-6952

Allen W. Cohen	John R. Greene
	Harvey S. Wasserman

For full biographical listings, see the Martindale-Hubbell Law Directory

---

BALTIMORE, * (Independent City)

COOPER, BECKMAN & TUERK, L.L.P. (AV)

201 North Charles Street, Suite 2300, 21201
Telephone: 410-539-0300
FAX: 410-837-3923

MEMBERS OF FIRM

Gerald H. Cooper	Carl E. Tuerk, Jr.
A. Thomas Beckman	Larry E. Jordan

ASSOCIATES

Mary Rose E. Cook	Margaret R. Posa

For full biographical listings, see the Martindale-Hubbell Law Directory

ELLIN AND BAKER (AV)

Second Floor, 1101 St. Paul Street, 21202
Telephone: 410-727-1787
FAX: 410-547-1787
1-800-237-1787

MEMBER OF FIRM

Marvin Ellin	LaVonna Lee Vice

Michael P. Smith

For full biographical listings, see the Martindale-Hubbell Law Directory

ISRAELSON, SALSBURY, CLEMENTS & BEKMAN (AV)

300 West Pratt Street Suite 450, 21201
Telephone: 410-539-6633
FAX: 410-625-9554

MEMBERS OF FIRM

Stuart Marshall Salsbury	Daniel M. Clements
Paul D. Bekman	Matthew Zimmerman
	Laurence A. Marder

Scott R. Scherr	Lauren R. Calia
Carol J. Glover	Andrew David Alpert

COUNSEL TO THE FIRM

Max R. Israelson

(See Next Column)

OF COUNSEL

Samuel Omar Jackson, Jr. (Semi-Retired)

For full biographical listings, see the Martindale-Hubbell Law Directory

JANET, WILLOUGHBY & GERSHON, LLC (AV)

Executive Centre at Hooks Lane, 8 Reservoir Circle, Suite 200, 21208
Telephone: 410-653-3200
Toll Free: 888-4-MED-LAW
Fax: 410-653-9030

MEMBERS OF FIRM

Howard Alan Janet (P.C.)	Wayne M. Willoughby (P.A.)
	Zev T. Gershon

ASSOCIATES

Randal D. Getz	Robin R. Smith
	Anne Michele Crook

LEGAL SUPPORT PERSONNEL

Joan Hunter Green	Sharon Marie Schmidt
(Registered Nurse/Paralegal)	(Paralegal)

For full biographical listings, see the Martindale-Hubbell Law Directory

KAHN, SMITH & COLLINS, P.A. (AV)

110 Saint Paul Street, 6th Floor, 21202
Telephone: 410-244-1010
Fax: 410-244-8001
Email: incourt@ari.net *URL:* http://www.interbit.com/ksc

Andrew H. Kahn	Francis J. Collins
Joel A. Smith	David V. Diggs
	Christyne L. Neff

Sarah Pazourek Harlan	Leslie A. Pladna

For full biographical listings, see the Martindale-Hubbell Law Directory

PAUL R. KRAMER, P.A. (AV)

231 St. Paul Place, 21202-2003
Telephone: 410-727-5531
FAX: 410-727-2186

Paul R. Kramer

For full biographical listings, see the Martindale-Hubbell Law Directory

ROLLINS, SMALKIN, RICHARDS & MACKIE (AV)

401 North Charles Street, 21201
Telephone: 410-727-2443
Fax: 410-727-8390

MEMBERS OF FIRM

H. Beale Rollins (1898-1985)	John F. Linsenmeyer
Samuel S. Smalkin (1906-1982)	Thomas C. Gentner
T. Benjamin Weston (1913-1980)	Glenn W. Trimmer
Thomas G. Andrew (1910-1973)	Patrick G. Cullen
Edward C. Mackie	James P. O'Meara
	Dennis J. Sullivan

ASSOCIATES

Paul G. Donoghue	Donna Lynn Kolakowski-Hollen
Ralph E. Wilson III	Meg Bantley Whiteford
Kenneth G. Macleay	Anthony G. Lardieri

OF COUNSEL

Raymond A. Richards (Retired)	Hartman J. Miller

For full biographical listings, see the Martindale-Hubbell Law Directory

SCANLAN & ROSEN, P.A. (AV)

26 South Street, 21202-3399
Telephone: 410-244-1155
FAX: 410-244-1157

Alfred L. Scanlan, Jr.	Marc Seldin Rosen

Michael Stuart Warshaw	Colleen A. Cavanaugh

OF COUNSEL

James Lee Katz

For full biographical listings, see the Martindale-Hubbell Law Directory

SCHOCHOR, FEDERICO AND STATON, P.A. (AV)

The Paulton, 1211 St. Paul Street, 21202
Telephone: 410-234-1000
Toll Free: 888-234-0001
Facsimile: 410-234-1010
URL: http://www.sfspa.com
Washington D.C. Office: 750 First Street, N.E., Suite 905.
Telephone: 202-408-3300.

(See Next Column)

SCHOCHOR, FEDERICO AND STATON P.A., Baltimore—Continued

Jonathan Schochor   Philip C. Federico
          Kerry D. Staton

Louis G. Close, III   Christopher P. Kennedy

For full biographical listings, see the Martindale-Hubbell Law Directory

VENABLE ATTORNEYS AT LAW VENABLE, BAETJER AND HOWARD, LLP (AV)

A Partnership including Professional Corporations
1800 Mercantile Bank & Trust Building, 2 Hopkins Plaza, 21201
Telephone: 410-244-7400
Email: INFO@Venable.win.net
Washington, D.C. Office: Venable, Baetjer, Howard & Civiletti LLP. Suite 1000, 1201 New York Avenue, N.W.
Telephone: 202-962-4800.
McLean, Virginia Office: Suite 400, 2010 Corporate Ridge.
Telephone: 703-760-1600.
Rockville, Maryland Office: Suite 500, One Church Street, P. O. Box 1906.
Telephone: 301-217-5600.
Towson, Maryland Office: 210 Allegheny Avenue, P. O. Box 5517.
Telephone: 410-494-6200.

MEMBERS OF FIRM

Roger W. Titus (Resident, Rockville, Maryland Office)
Douglas D. Connah, Jr. (P.C.) (Also at Washington, D.C. Office)
John H. Zink, III (Resident, Towson, Maryland Office)
Bruce E. Titus (Resident, McLean, Virginia Office)
William D. Dolan, III (P.C.) (Not admitted in MD; Resident, McLean, Virginia Office)
Paul T. Glasgow (Resident, Rockville, Maryland Office)
Joseph C. Wich, Jr. (Resident, Towson, Maryland Office)
James K. Archibald (Also at Washington, D.C. Office)
Jeffrey A. Dunn (also at Washington, D.C. Office)
George F. Pappas (Also at Washington, D.C. Office)
James L. Shea (Also at Washington, D.C. Office)

Amy Berman Jackson (Not admitted in MD; Resident, Washington, D.C. Office)
William D. Quarles (Also at Washington, D.C. and Towson, Maryland Offices)
C. Carey Deeley, Jr. (Also at Towson, Maryland Office)
Kathleen Gallogly Cox (Resident, Towson, Maryland Office)
Christopher R. Mellott
Cynthia M. Hahn (Resident, Towson, Maryland Office)
M. King Hill, III (Resident, Towson, Maryland Office)
James A. Dunbar (Also at Washington, D.C. Office)
David J. Heubeck
Herbert G. Smith, II (Not admitted in MD; Resident, Washington, D.C. Office)
Terri L. Turner
Michael W. Robinson (Resident, McLean, Virginia Office)

ASSOCIATES

Paul D. Barker, Jr.
Daniel William China
Marina Lolley Dame (Resident, Towson, Maryland Office)
David W. Goewey (Not admitted in MD; Resident, Washington, D.C. Office)
E. Anne Hamel

Gregory L. Laubach (Resident, Rockville, Maryland Office)
Vicki Margolis (Also at Washington, D.C. Office)
Christine M. McAnney (Not admitted in MD; Resident, McLean, Virginia Office)
John A. McCauley

John T. Prisbe

For Complete List of Firm Personnel, See General Section

For full biographical listings, see the Martindale-Hubbell Law Directory

ROBIN PAGE WEST (AV)

110 St. Paul Street, Suite 301, 21202
Telephone: 410-244-0400
Fax: 410-244-0402
Email: robin.west.esq@counsel.com

For full biographical listings, see the Martindale-Hubbell Law Directory

BEL AIR,* Harford Co.

BROWN, BROWN & BROWN, A PROFESSIONAL ASSOCIATION (AV)

200 South Main Street, 21014
Telephone: 410-838-5500
Baltimore: 410-879-2220
Fax: 410-893-0402

A. Freeborn Brown   Augustus F. Brown
T. Carroll Brown   Albert J. A. Young

A. Frank Carven, III   Christopher R. vanRoden
Harold Douglas Norton   David E. Carey
          Ankur P. Dalal

(See Next Column)

Attorneys for: Baltimore Gas & Electric Co.; Chesapeake & Potomac Telephone Co.; Aberdeen Proving Ground Federal Credit Union; First Virginia Bank-Central Maryland; First National Bank of Maryland; Bell Atlantic Mobile Systems; First Harbor Securities; Maryland Portable Concrete, Inc.
Approved Counsel for: The Chicago Title Insurance Co. of Maryland, Inc.

For full biographical listings, see the Martindale-Hubbell Law Directory

STARK & KEENAN, A PROFESSIONAL ASSOCIATION (AV)

30 Office Street, 21014
Telephone: 410-838-5522
Baltimore: 410-879-2222
Fax: 410-879-0688

Elwood V. Stark, Jr.   Judith Cline-Silverstein
Charles B. Keenan, Jr.   Gregory A. Szoka
Edwin G. Carson   Robert S. Lynch

Claire Prin Blomquist   Paul W. Ishak
Kimberly Kahoe Muenter   Lawrence F. Kreis, Jr.

For full biographical listings, see the Martindale-Hubbell Law Directory

BETHESDA, Montgomery Co.

CHAIKIN & KARP, P.C. (AV)

7475 Wisconsin Avenue, Suite 800, 20814
Telephone: 301-654-8383
Fax: 301-654-7748
Washington, D.C. Office: The Law Building, 1232 Seventeenth Street, N.W.
Telephone: 202-659-8383.
Fax: 202-659-8680.

Donald J. Chaikin   John F. Mitchell (Not admitted in MD; Resident)
Ronald A. Karp
Ira Sherman   W. Michael Jacobs
Jeffrey A. Wigodsky   Donald C. Weinberg
Lawrence S. Lapidus   Jack A. Gold
J. Philip Kessel   Neil Florin
          Allan M. Siegel (Resident)

OF COUNSEL

Anthony G. Newman   Stanley A. First
Brian E. Frosh   (Not admitted in MD)
Silverio Coy
  (Not admitted in MD)

References: 1st American Bank; Security National Bank.

For full biographical listings, see the Martindale-Hubbell Law Directory

FREEMAN & JENNER, P.C. (AV)

3 Bethesda Metro Center, Suite 1410, 20814
Telephone: 301-907-7747
FAX: 301-907-9877
Washington, D.C. Office: 1000 16th Street, N.W., Suite 300.
Telephone: 301-907-7747.
Aspen, Colorado Office: 215 South Monarch Street, Suite 202.
Telephone: 970-925-3400.
FAX: 970-925-4043.

Martin H. Freeman   Robert K. Jenner

Barbara E. Hirsch   Mark Allan Freeman

Reference: Crestar Bank of Maryland.

For full biographical listings, see the Martindale-Hubbell Law Directory

LANHAM, Prince Georges Co.

McCARTHY, BACON & COSTELLO, L.L.P. (AV)

Washington Business Park, Suite 300, 4640 Forbes Boulevard, 20706-4323
Telephone: 301-306-1900
Fax: 301-306-1988
Email: mbc@erols.com *URL:* http://www.erols.com/mbc

MEMBERS OF FIRM

Kevin J. McCarthy   Michael McGowan
Edward C. Bacon   Patricia M. Thornton
John F. X. Costello   Mark D. Palmer
          Stan Derwin Brown

ASSOCIATES

John T. Bergin   Timothy Altemus
Michael O. Glynn, III   Heather Jean Kelly

OF COUNSEL

Charles E. Channing, Jr.

For full biographical listings, see the Martindale-Hubbell Law Directory

ROCKVILLE, Montgomery Co.

ANDERSON & QUINN (AV)

The Adams Law Center, 25 Wood Lane, 20850
Telephone: 301-762-3303
FAX: 301-762-3776
Other Rockville Maryland Office: 110 North West St., Suite 501, 20850.
Telephone: 301-340-0800.

MEMBERS OF FIRM

Charles C. Collins (1900-1973)	Donald P. Maiberger
Robert E. Anderson (Not	Robert P. Scanlon
admitted in MD; Retired)	James G. Healy
Francis X. Quinn	John A. Rego

ASSOCIATES

Alice Kelley Scanlon	Mary L. Fellin
Marnie E. Simon	Kelly Ann McInerney
Kerry Patricia Shanahan	Timothy J. Mulreany

Representative Clients: C & P Telephone; Commercial Union Insurance Cos.; Allstate Insurance Co.; State Farm Mutual Automobile Insurance Co.; Liberty Mutual Insurance Co.; Northbrook Insurance Cos.; Travelers Insurance Co.; National General Insurance Co.; American International Adjustment Co.; Marriott Corp.

For full biographical listings, see the Martindale-Hubbell Law Directory

ARMSTRONG, DONOHUE & CEPPOS, CHARTERED (AV)

Suite 101, 204 Monroe Street, 20850
Telephone: 301-251-0440
Telecopier: 301-279-5929

Larry A. Ceppos	H. Kenneth Armstrong
H. Patrick Donohue	Benjamin S. Vaughan
	John C. Monahan

Oya S. Oner	Sharon A. Marcial
Pamela Barrow Kincheloe	Garrett V. Williams
Richard S. Schrager	Andrew J. Marter

For full biographical listings, see the Martindale-Hubbell Law Directory

BRAULT, GRAHAM, SCOTT & BRAULT (AV)

101 South Washington Street, 20850
Telephone: 301-424-1060
Fax: 301-424-7991
Washington, D.C. Office: 1906 Sunderland Place, N.W.
Telephone: 202-785-1200.
FAX: 202-785-4301.
Arlington, Virginia Office: Suite 1201, 2300 North Clarendon Boulevard, Courthouse Plaza.
Telephone: 703-358-9200.

OF COUNSEL

Laurence T. Scott	Janet S. Zigler (Resident)

MEMBERS OF FIRM

Denver H. Graham (1922-1987)	Daniel L. Shea (Resident)
Albert E. Brault (Retired)	M. Kathleen Parker (Resident)
Albert D. Brault (Resident)	David G. Mulquin (Resident)
Leo A. Roth, Jr.	James M. Brault (Resident)
James S. Wilson (Resident)	Regina Ann Casey (Resident)
Ronald G. Guziak	Sanford A. Friedman

ASSOCIATES

Holly D. Shupert (Resident)	Joan F. Brault (Resident)
Rhonda Ann Hurwitz (Resident)	Joseph P. Morra (Resident)
	Michael A. Carlo

Representative Clients: American Oil Co.; Crum & Forster Group; Fireman's Fund American Insurance Cos.; Kemper Group; Reliance Insurance Cos.; Safeco Group; Government Employees Insurance Co.; Medical Mutual Insurance Society of Maryland; Legal Mutual Liability Insurance Society of Maryland.

For full biographical listings, see the Martindale-Hubbell Law Directory

MICHAEL S. MORGENSTERN & ASSOCIATES, P.C. (AV)

Fifth Floor, 110 North Washington Street, P.O. Box 4690, 20850
Telephone: 301-217-9500
FAX: 301-217-9579

Michael S. Morgenstern

Sheila Lowery Ferguson

OF COUNSEL

Carl Morgenstern	Lawrence S. Jacobs
(Not admitted in MD)	

For full biographical listings, see the Martindale-Hubbell Law Directory

STEIN, SPERLING, BENNETT, DE JONG, DRISCOLL, GREENFEIG & METRO, P.A. (AV)

25 West Middle Lane, 20850
Telephone: 301-340-2020; 800-435-5230
Telecopier: 301-340-8217

David C. Driscoll, Jr.	Donald N. Sperling
Stuart S. Greenfeig	Paul T. Stein

Fred A. Balkin	Darcy A. Shoop

For Complete List of Firm Personnel, See General Section

For full biographical listings, see the Martindale-Hubbell Law Directory

TOWSON, Baltimore Co.

NOLAN, PLUMHOFF & WILLIAMS, CHARTERED (AV)

Suite 700 Court Towers, 210 West Pennsylvania Avenue, 21204
Telephone: 410-823-7800
Fax: 410-296-2765

Stephen J. Nolan	Robert E. Cahill, Jr.
Robert L. Hanley, Jr.	Stuart Alan Schadt

Representative Clients: Injured Plaintiffs and Workers; Bituminous Insurance Companies; Carolina Freight Carriers Corporation; Keystone Insurance Company; Maryland Automobile Insurance Fund; Principal Casualty Insurance Company.

For Complete List of Firm Personnel, See General Section

For full biographical listings, see the Martindale-Hubbell Law Directory

VENABLE ATTORNEYS AT LAW VENABLE, BAETJER AND HOWARD, LLP (AV)

A Partnership including Professional Corporations
210 Allegheny Avenue, P.O. Box 5517, 21204
Telephone: 410-494-6200
FAX: 410-821-0147
Baltimore, Maryland Office: 1800 Mercantile Bank & Trust Building, 2 Hopkins Plaza.
Telephone: 410-244-7400.
Washington, D.C. Office: Venable, Baetjer, Howard & Civiletti LLP, Suite 1000, 1201 New York Avenue, N.W.
Telephone: 202-962-4800.
McLean, Virginia Office: Suite 400, 2010 Corporate Ridge.
Telephone: 703-760-1600.
Rockville, Maryland Office: Suite 500, One Church Street, P. O. Box 1906.
Telephone: 301-217-5600.

PARTNERS

John H. Zink, III	C. Carey Deeley, Jr. (Also at
Joseph C. Wich, Jr.	Baltimore, Maryland Office)
William D. Quarles (Also at	Kathleen Gallogly Cox
Washington, D.C. Office)	Cynthia M. Hahn
	M. King Hill, III

ASSOCIATES

Marina Lolley Dame	Mary-Dulany James

For Complete List of Firm Personnel, See General Section

For full biographical listings, see the Martindale-Hubbell Law Directory

UPPER MARLBORO, Prince Georges Co.

MENG & UREY (AV)

14507 Main Street, P.O. Box 549, 20773
Telephone: 301-627-1600
FAX: 301-627-2838

George E. Meng	Laura L. Greeves
Paul K. Urey, III	Ellen A. Marth

LEGAL SUPPORT PERSONNEL

Margaret Urey (Paralegal)

Representative Clients: State Farm Mutual Automobile Insurance Co.; State Farm Fire & Casualty Co.; Americlaim Adjustment Corp.; Old Line National Bank.

For full biographical listings, see the Martindale-Hubbell Law Directory

MASSACHUSETTS

AMESBURY, Essex Co.

HAMEL, DESHAIES & GAGLIARDI (AV)

Five Market Square, P.O. Box 198, 01913-0398
Telephone: 508-388-3558
Telecopier: 508-388-0441

(See Next Column)

HAMEL, DESHAIES & GAGLIARDI, *Amesbury—Continued*

MEMBER OF FIRM

Richard P. Hamel

ASSOCIATE

Roger D. Turgeon

Representative Clients: Essex County Gas Co., Amesbury, MA; First and Ocean National Bank, Newburyport, MA.
Approved Attorneys for: Chicago Title Insurance; Old Republic Title Insurance Co.

For Complete List of Firm Personnel, See General Section

For full biographical listings, see the Martindale-Hubbell Law Directory

---

BOSTON, * Suffolk Co.

BARRON & STADFELD, P.C. (AV)

Two Center Plaza, 02108
Telephone: 617-723-9800
Telecopier: 617-523-8359
Email: PUBLIC@BARRONSTAD.COM *URL:* HTTP://WWW.BARRONSTAD.COM
Hyannis, Massachusetts Office: 258 Winter Street.
Telephone: 617-778-6622.

Bernard A. Dwork	David P. Dwork
Enid M. Starr	Robert J. Hoffer
Edward E. Kelly	Rosemary Purtell

For Complete List of Firm Personnel, See General Section

For full biographical listings, see the Martindale-Hubbell Law Directory

DENNIS J. CURRAN (AV)

One State Street, Suite 410, 02109
Telephone: 617-742-3010
Fax: 617-742-1799

For full biographical listings, see the Martindale-Hubbell Law Directory

ESDAILE, BARRETT & ESDAILE (AV)

75 Federal Street, 02110
Telephone: 617-482-0333
Fax: 617-426-2978
Email: Esdaile@AOL.COM

MEMBERS OF FIRM

J. Newton Esdaile	Norman I. Jacobs
Charles W. Barrett, Jr.	Michael E. Mone
James N. Esdaile, Jr.	Patricia L. Kelly
Robert J. Rutecki	

ASSOCIATES

Shaun Spencer Forsyth	C. William Barrett
Rhonda Traver Maloney	Mary Moynihan Conneely
Steven J. Ryan	Jon M. Jacobs
Kathryn E. Hand	

OF COUNSEL

Charles J. Murray

For full biographical listings, see the Martindale-Hubbell Law Directory

LAW OFFICES OF LEONARD GLAZER, P.C. & ASSOCIATES (AV)

One Longfellow Place Suite 3408, 02114
Telephone: 617-523-4411
Fax: 617-523-7433

Leonard Glazer

Frank E. Glazer	Anthony R. Orlando, III

For full biographical listings, see the Martindale-Hubbell Law Directory

LAW OFFICES OF MARTIN KANTROVITZ (AV)

185 Devonshire Street, Suite 510, 02110
Telephone: 617-426-3050
FAX: 617-426-3640
Hudson, Massachusetts Office: 173 Washington Street. 01749.
Telephone: 508-562-3800.
New Bedford, Massachusetts Office: 60 Spring Street, Suite 12.
Telephone: 508-994-6010.

ASSOCIATE

Lisa Baer

For full biographical listings, see the Martindale-Hubbell Law Directory

McCORMACK & EPSTEIN (AV)

One International Place, 02110
Telephone: 617-951-2929
Telecopier: 617-951-2672
New York, N.Y. Office: 330 Madison Avenue, Twenty Seventh Floor.
Telephone: 212-935-0881.

(See Next Column)

MEMBERS OF FIRM

Robert D. Epstein	Mark E. Cohen
Michael J. McCormack	Joseph H. Aronson

Brian C. Duffey	Amy M. Soisson
George X. Pucci	Stephen D. Rosenberg
Marc L. LaCasse	Mary-Elise Connolly
Kjersten Johnsen	

Representative Clients: First State Insurance Co.; Crum & Forster Commercial Insurance; Liberty Mutual Insurance Co.; United States Fidelity & Guaranty Co.; Massachusetts Bay Transportation Authority; Technical Aid Corporation.

For full biographical listings, see the Martindale-Hubbell Law Directory

NATHANSON & GOLDBERG, A PROFESSIONAL CORPORATION (AV)

10 Union Wharf, 02109
Telephone: 617-742-9350
Fax: 617-742-3559

Alvin S. Nathanson	Valerie S. Carter
Arthur Goldberg	Shannon M. Fitzpatrick

Stuart J. Frank

For full biographical listings, see the Martindale-Hubbell Law Directory

PALMER & DODGE LLP (AV)

One Beacon Street, 02108
Telephone: 617-573-0100
Facsimile: 617-227-4420

MEMBERS OF FIRM

Jeffrey F. Jones	Francis C. Lynch
Daryl J. Lapp	Craig E. Stewart

For Complete List of Firm Personnel, See General Section

For full biographical listings, see the Martindale-Hubbell Law Directory

SARROUF, TARRICONE & FLEMMING (AV)

95 Commercial Wharf, 02110
Telephone: 617-227-5800
Fax: 617-227-5470

Camille Francis Sarrouf	Daniel J. Gibson
Anthony Tarricone	Sheryl M. Bourbeau
John B. Flemming	Camille F. Sarrouf, Jr.
George J. Leary, Jr.	Donald J. Savery

For full biographical listings, see the Martindale-Hubbell Law Directory

SHAPIRO & ASSOCIATES (AV)

One Beacon Street, 24th Floor, 02108
Telephone: 617-227-8100
Fax: 617-523-8100

Daniel B. Shapiro

ASSOCIATE

Bruce H. Norwell

Representative Clients: NLC Insurance Companies; Trust Insurance Co.; Liberty Mutual Insurance Co.

For full biographical listings, see the Martindale-Hubbell Law Directory

SHERBURNE, POWERS & NEEDHAM, P.C. (AV)

One Beacon Street, 02108
Telephone: 617-523-2700
Fax: 617-523-6850
Email: @SHERBURNE.COM

William D. Weeks	Benjamin Volinski
John T. Collins	Mark Schonfeld
Allan J. Landau	James D. Smeallie
Stephen A. Hopkins	Paul Killeen
Alan I. Falk	Gordon P. Katz
C. Thomas Swaim	Joseph B. Darby, III
James Pollock	Richard M Yanofsky
William V. Tripp III	James E. McDermott
Stephen S. Young	Kenneth P. Brier
William F. Machen	Robert V. Lizza
W. Robert Allison	Miriam Goldstein Altman
Philip J. Notopoulos	John J. Monaghan
Richard J. Hindlian	Margaret J. Palladino
Paul E. Troy	Mark C. Michalowski
Harold W. Potter, Jr.	David Scott Sloan
Philip S. Lapatin	M. Chrysa Long
Pamela A. Duckworth	Lawrence D. Bradley
Miriam J. McKendall	

(See Next Column)

SHERBURNE, POWERS & NEEDHAM P.C.—*Continued*

Cynthia A. Brown	Amy J. Mastrobattista
Cynthia M. Hern	Leslie A. Sprinkle
Meredeth A. Beers	Douglas W. Clapp
Dianne R. Phillips	Jeffrey A. Huebschmann
Paul M. James	Tamara E. Goulston
Theodore F. Hanselman	Paul G. Lannon, Jr.
Joshua C. Krumholz	Nicholas J. Psyhogeos
Ieuan G. Mahony	Edward J. Naughton
Jeffrey J. Nix	Kathaleen Kelly Cutone
(Not admitted in MA)	Laurie A. Tribble
Kenneth L. Harvey	Neil C. Higgins
Christopher J. Trombetta	Deborah Paige Stone
Elise N. Zoli	Brian R. Popiel

COUNSEL

Haig Der Manuelian	Karl J. Hirshman
Mason M. Taber, Jr.	Dale R. Johnson

For full biographical listings, see the Martindale-Hubbell Law Directory

SWARTZ & SWARTZ (AV)

10 Marshall Street, 02108
Telephone: 617-742-1900
Fax: 617-367-7193

Edward M. Swartz	Joan E. Swartz
Alan L. Cantor	James A. Swartz
Joseph A. Swartz	Harold David Levine
Victor A. Denaro	David P. Angueira

OF COUNSEL
Fredric A. Swartz

For full biographical listings, see the Martindale-Hubbell Law Directory

BROCKTON, Plymouth Co.

VINCENT P. CAHALANE, P.C. (AV)

478 Torrey Street, 02401
Telephone: 508-588-1222
Fax: 508-584-4748

Vincent P. Cahalane	Julie A. Cahalane Cahill
Robert J. Zullas	John E. Cahill

For full biographical listings, see the Martindale-Hubbell Law Directory

FITCHBURG, Worcester Co.

O'CONNOR AND RYAN, P.C. (AV)

61 Academy Street, 01420
Telephone: 508-345-4166
Fax: 508-343-8416

John M. O'Connor	Edward P. Ryan, Jr.

For full biographical listings, see the Martindale-Hubbell Law Directory

FRAMINGHAM, Middlesex Co.

DAVID I. SHORR (AV)

24 Union Avenue, 01701
Telephone: 508-879-4412
Fax: 508-872-2888

Marlene Kerble

References: Shawmut Bank; Framingham Savings Bank.

For full biographical listings, see the Martindale-Hubbell Law Directory

HAVERHILL, Essex Co.

FINBURY & SULLIVAN, P.C. (AV)

55 Ginty Boulevard, 01831
Telephone: 508-374-4736
Fax: 508-521-5307

Herbert W. Finbury	Daniel C. Finbury
John C. Sullivan	John A. Finbury

For full biographical listings, see the Martindale-Hubbell Law Directory

MILFORD, Worcester Co.

GREENWALD, GREENWALD & POWERS (AV)

409 Fortune Boulevard Granite Park, 01757-1746
Telephone: 508-478-8611
Fax: 508-634-3959; 478-5937

Alan Greenwald	Anne M. Givens
Steven A. Greenwald	Colleen B. Walker
John D. Powers	Kathleen R. Winsor

(See Next Column)

OF COUNSEL
Merek S. Rubin

For full biographical listings, see the Martindale-Hubbell Law Directory

SPRINGFIELD, * Hampden Co.

LAW OFFICES OF THOMAS A. KENEFICK, III, P.C. (AV)

73 Chestnut Street, 01103
Telephone: 413-734-7000
Fax: 413-731-1302

Thomas A. Kenefick, III

For full biographical listings, see the Martindale-Hubbell Law Directory

KEYES AND DONNELLAN, P.C. (AV)

1243 Main Street, 01103
Telephone: 413-781-6540
Fax: 413-739-3502
Email: keyes@wca.com

Daniel M. Keyes, Jr.	Deborah A. Bloom
Edward L. Donnellan	Michael K. Manning
Melinda M. Phelps	

Kevin C. Giordano	Mark D. Sullivan
Kathleen E. Sheehan	John M. Payne, Jr.

For full biographical listings, see the Martindale-Hubbell Law Directory

ROBINSON DONOVAN MADDEN & BARRY, P.C. (AV)

Suite 1600, BayBank Tower, 1500 Main Street, 01115
Telephone: 413-732-2301
Fax: 413-785-4658

Homans Robinson (1894-1973)	Milton J. Donovan (1906-1995)
Lawrence M. Sinclair (1942-1986)	

OF COUNSEL

John H. Madden, Jr.	Victor Rosenberg
Edward J. Barry	Richard S. Milstein

Gordon H. Wentworth	John C. Sikorski
James H. Tourtelotte	Nancy Frankel Pelletier
Charles K. Bergin, Jr.	Paul S. Weinberg
Ronald C. Kidd	Frederica H. McCarthy
Jeffrey W. Roberts	Matthew J. King
Jeffrey L. McCormick	Neva Kaufman Rohan
James F. Martin	Douglas F. Boyd
Robert P. Cunningham	James K. Bodurtha
Keith A. Minoff	

E. Paul Amata	Kimberly Davis Crear
(Not admitted in MA)	John W. Davis
James D. Chadwell	Edmund J. Gorman
Susan L. Cooper	Patricia M. Rapinchuk
Jonathan P. Rice	

Representative Clients: The First National Bank of Boston; United Cooperative Bank; Fleet Bank, N.A.; American Policyholders Insurance Co.; CNA; Commercial Union Insurance Co.; Hanover Insurance Group.

For full biographical listings, see the Martindale-Hubbell Law Directory

WORCESTER, * Worcester Co.

FULLER, ROSENBERG, PALMER & BELIVEAU (AV)

14 Harvard Street, P.O. Box 764, 01613
Telephone: 508-755-5225
Telecopier: 508-757-1039

MEMBERS OF FIRM

Albert E. Fuller	Peter A. Palmer
Kenneth F. Rosenberg	Thomas W. Beliveau

ASSOCIATES

Robert W. Towle	Michael I. Mutter
Julie Bednarz Russell	Brian F. Welsh
Timothy O. Ribley	John J. Finn
Mark W. Murphy	James C. Crowley, Jr.
Lisa R. Bertonazzi	John P. Donohue
Mark C. Darling	James F. Gettens
William J. Mason	John Arthur Johnson
Antoinette J. Yitchinsky	Ann F. Scannell

For full biographical listings, see the Martindale-Hubbell Law Directory

MICHIGAN

ANN ARBOR, Washtenaw Co.

BRAUN KENDRICK FINKBEINER PLC (AV)

700 First National Building, 48104
Telephone: 313-995-4100
Telecopier: 313-995-4798
URL: http://www.bkf-law.com
Bay City, Michigan Office: 201 Phoenix Building, P.O. Box 2039.
Telephone: 517-895-8505.
Telecopier: 517-895-8437.
Saginaw, Michigan Office: 101 N. Washington, Suite 812.
Telephone: 517-753-3461.
Telecopier: 517-753-3951.

Barry M. Levine

Representative Clients: The Dow Chemical Co.; General Motors Corp.; Lobdell Emery Manufacturing Co.; Merrill, Lynch, Inc.; Saginaw General Hospital; Saginaw News; The Wickes Foundation.

For full biographical listings, see the Martindale-Hubbell Law Directory

HURBIS & CLINTON (AV)

Fifth Floor, City Center Building, 48104
Telephone: 313-761-8358
Fax: 313-761-3134

Charles J. Hurbis	Mary F. Clinton
Robert Lipnik	Georgette E. David

Representative Clients: General Motors Corp.; ITT Hartford; Insurance Company of North America; The University of Michigan; North Oakland Medical Center; City of Pontiac; Sears Roebuck and Co.; Montgomery Ward and Co., Inc.; Sedjwick-James, Inc.

For full biographical listings, see the Martindale-Hubbell Law Directory

MAGILL AND RUMSEY, P.C. (AV)

Seventh Floor, First National Building, 201 South Main Street, 48104
Telephone: 313-995-2500
Fax: 313-995-4798

Robert F. Magill, Jr.	Ralph S. Rumsey

For full biographical listings, see the Martindale-Hubbell Law Directory

BINGHAM FARMS, Oakland Co.

HARNISCH & HOHAUSER, P.C. (AV)

30700 Telegraph Road, Suite 3475, 48025-4527
Telephone: 810-644-8600
Fax: 810-644-8344

Alan C. Harnisch	Michael S. Hohauser
Lawrence S. Gadd	William J. Yochim, Jr.

OF COUNSEL
Debra C. Holt

Representative Clients: Dealers Financial Service, Inc.; Eaton Corporation; Edgewood Electric, Inc.; ITT Commercial Finance; Jeffrey C. Harrell, Builder, Inc.; Johnson Controls, Inc.

For full biographical listings, see the Martindale-Hubbell Law Directory

BIRMINGHAM, Oakland Co.

CARSON FISCHER, P.L.C. (AV)

Third Floor, 300 East Maple Road, 48009-6317
Telephone: 810-644-4840
Facsimile: 810-644-1832

Robert M. Carson	Kathleen A. Stibich

For full biographical listings, see the Martindale-Hubbell Law Directory

GOREN & GOREN, P.C. (AV)

Suite 470, 30400 Telegraph Road, 48025
Telephone: 810-540-3100

Robert Goren	Steven E. Goren

Reference: Michigan National Bank-Oakland.

KELL & LYNCH, P.C. (AV)

300 East Maple Road, Suite 200, 48009
Telephone: 810-647-2333
Telefax: 810-647-2781

Michael V. Kell	Margaret A. Lynch

(See Next Column)

Jennifer T. Gilhool	Steven M. Ribiat
(Not admitted in MI)	

OF COUNSEL
M. Andrea Vaughn

Representative Clients: AlliedSignal, Inc.; AMP Inc.; Dow Corning Corp.; Hatteras Yachts; Lectron Products, Inc.; Metromedia Steakhouses, Inc.; Sybron Corp.; Michigan Consolidated Gas Co.; American Natural Resources.

For full biographical listings, see the Martindale-Hubbell Law Directory

MICHAEL B. SERLING, P.C. (AV)

280 North Woodward Avenue, Suite 406, 48009
Telephone: 810-647-6966

Michael B. Serling

Russell R. Beaudoen
OF COUNSEL
Philip J. Goodman

Reference: Comerica Bank, Birmingham, MI.

For full biographical listings, see the Martindale-Hubbell Law Directory

BLOOMFIELD HILLS, Oakland Co.

FEENEY KELLETT WIENNER & BUSH, PROFESSIONAL CORPORATION (AV)

950 North Hunter Boulevard, Second Floor, 48304-3927
Telephone: 810-258-1580
Fax: 810-258-0421

James P. Feeney	Cheryl A. Bush
S. Thomas Wienner	Deborah F. Collins
Peter M. Kellett	David N. Goltz

OF COUNSEL
Thomas J. Manganello

James J. Majernik	Seth D. Gould
G. Gregory Schuetz	Patrick G. Seyferth
Jeffrey A. Gallant	Mark A. Fisher
Bryan D. Cross	

For full biographical listings, see the Martindale-Hubbell Law Directory

THE GOOGASIAN FIRM, P.C. (AV)

6895 Telegraph Road, 48301-3138
Telephone: 810-540-3333
Fax: 810-540-7213

George A. Googasian	Craig Weber
	Steven G. Googasian

For full biographical listings, see the Martindale-Hubbell Law Directory

LISS AND ASSOCIATES, P.C. (AV)

The Pinehurst Building, 1400 North Woodward Avenue, Suite 200, 48304
Telephone: 810-647-9700
Facsimile: 810-647-5477; 810-647-0638

Arthur Y. Liss	Christine S. Reiner
Ronald S. Smith	Andrew M. Zack
	Karen E. Seder

For full biographical listings, see the Martindale-Hubbell Law Directory

DAVID D. PATTON & ASSOCIATES, P.C. (AV)

100 Bloomfield Hills Parkway, Suite 110, 48304
Telephone: 810-258-6020
Fax: 810-258-6052
Email: Litigation@Aol.Com

David D. Patton

Ellen Bartman Jannette	Patricia C. White
	David H. Patton (1912-1993)

For full biographical listings, see the Martindale-Hubbell Law Directory

PORTNOY, PIDGEON & ROTH, P.C. (AV)

3883 Telegraph, Suite 103, 48302
Telephone: 810-647-4242
Fax: 810-647-8251
Email: DWINNIE103@AOL.COM

(See Next Column)

PORTNOY, PIDGEON & ROTH P.C.—*Continued*

Bernard N. Portnoy	Marc S. Berlin
James M. Pidgeon	Berton K. May
Robert P. Roth	Sheila Connor-Heath

Charles A. Harrison III

Representative Clients: McLaren Regional Medical Center; Lapeer Regional Hospital; Hurley Medical Center; North Oakland Medical Center, Pontiac General Hospital Division.

For full biographical listings, see the Martindale-Hubbell Law Directory

---

SCHADEN, KATZMAN & LAMPERT (AV)

33 Bloomfield Hills Parkway, Suite 145, 48304
Telephone: 810-258-4800
Fax: 810-258-9212
Broomfield, Colorado Office: Schaden, Katzman & Lampert, 11870 Airport Way.
Telephone: 303-465-3663.
Facsimile: 303-465-3884.
Ft. Lauderdale, Florida Office: 1700 E. Las Olas Boulevard, Suite 7, 33301-2408.
Telephone: 954-522-5154.
Facsimile: 954-522-5184.

MEMBERS OF FIRM

Richard F. Schaden	David I. Katzman

Bruce A. Lampert

ASSOCIATES

Kathleen M. Schaden	John D. McClune

OF COUNSEL

Bruce O. Wilson

For full biographical listings, see the Martindale-Hubbell Law Directory

---

DETROIT,* Wayne Co.

DYKEMA GOSSETT PLLC (AV)

400 Renaissance Center, 48243-1668
Telephone: 313-568-6800
Cable Address: "Dyke-Detroit"
Telex: 23-0121
Fax: 313-568-6594
Email: 2084153@mcimail.com
Ann Arbor, Michigan Office: 315 East Eisenhower Parkway, Suite 100, 48108-3306.
Telephone: 313-747-7660.
Fax: 313-747-7696.
Bloomfield Hills, Michigan Office: 1577 North Woodward Avenue, Suite 300, 48304-2820.
Telephone: 810-540-0700.
Fax: 810-540-0763.
Chicago, Illinois Office: 55 East Monroe Street, Suite 3250, 60603-5709.
Telephone: 312-551-4900.
Fax: 312-551-4919.
Grand Rapids, Michigan Office: 200 Oldtown Riverfront Building, 248 Louis Campau Promenade, N.W., 49503-2668.
Telephone: 616-776-7500.
Fax: 616-776-7573.
Lansing, Michigan Office: 800 Michigan National Tower, 48933-1707.
Telephone: 517-374-9100.
Fax: 517-374-9191.
Washington, D.C. Office: Franklin Square, Suite 300 West, 1300 I Street, N.W., 20005-3306.
Telephone: 202-522-8600.
Fax: 202-522-8669.

MEMBERS OF FIRM

Ted T. Amsden	Craig L. John (Resident at Bloomfield Hills Office)
Susan Artinian	
Richard B. Baxter (Resident at Grand Rapids Office)	Sharon M. Kelly (Resident at Ann Arbor Office)
William J. Brennan (Resident at Grand Rapids Office)	Gregory M. Kopacz (Resident at Bloomfield Hills Office)
James M. Cameron, Jr. (Resident at Ann Arbor Office)	Richard J. Landau (Resident at Ann Arbor Office)
	Kathleen McCree Lewis
Laurence D. Connor	Bonnie L. Mayfield
Michael P. Cooney	Richard J. McClear
J. Terrance Dillon (Resident at Grand Rapids Office)	Derek I. Meier
	Stephen S. Muhich (Resident at Grand Rapids Office)
John A. Ferroli (Resident at Grand Rapids Office)	Howard E. O'Leary, Jr. (Resident at Washington, D.C. Office)
Robert J. Franzinger	
Barbara L. Goldman (Resident at Bloomfield Hills Office)	Marilyn A. Peters (Resident at Bloomfield Hills Office)
Dennis M. Haffey (Member in Charge of Bloomfield Hills Office)	Thomas W. B. Porter
	Jack C. Radcliffe, Jr. (Resident at Ann Arbor Office)
Mark E. Hauck	
E. Edward Hood (Member in Charge of Ann Arbor Office)	Jonathan D. Rowe (Resident at Ann Arbor Office)
Kathryn J. Humphrey	

(See Next Column)

MEMBERS OF FIRM (Continued)

Mary Elizabeth Royce (Resident at Bloomfield Hills Office)	Mark H. Sutton (Resident at Bloomfield Hills Office)
Suzanne Sahakian	Roger K. Timm
Lori M. Silsbury (Resident at Lansing Office)	Stephen D. Winter
	Daniel G. Wyllie
Daniel J. Stephenson (Resident at Ann Arbor Office)	Donald S. Young

ASSOCIATES

Laura M. Benitez (Resident at Ann Arbor Office)	Zora E. Johnson
	Steven Marchese (Resident at Ann Arbor Office)
Thomas S. Bishoff	
Kevin J. Bonner	Bryan D. Marcus
Michael J. Brown (Resident at Lansing Office)	Andrew W. Mayoras (Resident at Bloomfield Hills Office)
James R. Bruinsma (Resident at Grand Rapids Office)	Andrew J. McGuinness (Resident at Ann Arbor Office)
Margaret A. Costello	
Joseph K. Erhardt	Ava K. Ortner
Aren L. Fairchild	James C. Partridge
Cheryl Anne Fletcher	Ann Marie Ronchetto
Douglas J. Fryer (Resident at Bloomfield Hills Office)	Rosemary G. Schikora
	Bradley L. Smith (Resident at Ann Arbor Office)
Kevin P. Fularczyk	
Kimberly A. Gough (Resident at Bloomfield Hills Office)	Ronald J. Torbert
	Michael Tucker (Resident at Bloomfield Hills Office)
David G. Hagens (Resident at Grand Rapids Office)	Jill M. Wheaton
Joseph H. Hickey (Resident at Bloomfield Hills Office)	Marvin Douglas Wilder
	James Zavell
Robert M. Horwitz	Kevin M. Zielke

For Complete List of Firm Personnel, See General Section

For full biographical listings, see the Martindale-Hubbell Law Directory

---

EAMES WILCOX (AV)

1400 Buhl Building, 48226-3602
Telephone: 313-963-3750
Facsimile: 313-963-8485

MEMBERS OF FIRM

Leonard A. Wilcox, Jr.	Jerry R. Swift
Ronald J. Mastej	Neill T. Riddell
John W. Bryant	Kevin N. Summers
Robert E. Gesell	Keith M. Aretha

OF COUNSEL

Rex Eames	William B. McIntyre, Jr.

David R. Ritter

Representative Clients: ABF Freight System, Inc.; Chrysler Credit Corp.; City Transfer Co.; Engineered Heat Treat, Inc.; Fetz Engineering Co.; I E & E Industries, Inc.; Schneider Transport; Tank Carrier Employers Association of Michigan; TNT Transport Group, Inc.; Waste Management of Michigan.

For full biographical listings, see the Martindale-Hubbell Law Directory

---

EGGENBERGER, EGGENBERGER, McKINNEY, WEBER & HOFMEISTER, P.C. (AV)

42nd Floor Penobscot Building, 48226
Telephone: 313-961-9722

William J. Eggenberger (1900-1984)	John P. McKinney
	Stephen L. Weber
William D. Eggenberger	Paul D. Hofmeister
Robert E. Eggenberger	Thomas R. Paxton

Mary T. Humbert	James B. Eggenberger

Representative Clients: Central National Insurance Group of Omaha; Great Central Insurance Co.; Preferred Risk Mutual Insurance Company of Des Moines, Iowa; State Automobile and Casualty Underwriters; State Farm Fire and Casualty Co.
Reference: Comerica Bank-Detroit.

For full biographical listings, see the Martindale-Hubbell Law Directory

---

GLEICHER & REYNOLDS, P.C. (AV)

1500 Buhl Building, 48226
Telephone: 313-964-6900
Fax: 313-964-8976

Elizabeth Gleicher	Edward C. Reynolds, Jr.

LEGAL SUPPORT PERSONNEL

Laura Bocchini (Legal Coordinator)

For full biographical listings, see the Martindale-Hubbell Law Directory

---

GOODMAN, EDEN, MILLENDER & BEDROSIAN (AV)

30th Floor Cadillac Tower, 48226
Telephone: 313-965-0050
Fax: 313-965-4779

(See Next Column)

GOODMAN, EDEN, MILLENDER & BEDROSIAN, *Detroit—Continued*

Ernest Goodman	Barbara A. Patek
Morton A. Eden	Christopher R. Holliday
Robert L. Millender (1916-1978)	Victoria A. Roberts
George J. Bedrosian	Walid Y. Fakhoury
William H. Goodman	Michael J. Haddad
James A. Tuck (1942-1987)	Elizabeth A. Stafford
Richard A. Soble	Beatrice B. Logan
Robert A. Koory	Eric Isaac Frankie
Roderick V. MacNeal	Julia Sherwin
Edgar Jerome Dew	Marya V. Sieminski

For full biographical listings, see the Martindale-Hubbell Law Directory

MILLER, CANFIELD, PADDOCK AND STONE, P.L.C. (AV)

A Professional Limited Liability Company
Founded in 1852 by Sidney Davy Miller
150 West Jefferson, Suite 2500, 48226-4415
Telephone: 313-963-6420
Fax: 313-496-7500
Cable Address: "Stem Detroit"
Detroit, Michigan Office: 150 West Jefferson, Suite 2500, 48226-4415.
Telephone: 313-963-6420.
Fax: 313-496-7500.
Cable Address: "Stem Detroit."
Ann Arbor, Michigan Office: 101 North Main Street, 7th Floor, 48104-1400.
Telephone: 313-663-2445.
Fax: 313-747-7147.
Bloomfield Hills, Michigan Office: Suite 100, Pinehurst Office Center, 1400 North Woodward, 48303-2014.
Telephone: 313-645-5000.
Fax: 313-645-1917.
Grand Rapids, Michigan Office: 1200 Campau Square Plaza, 99 Monroe, N.W., 49503-2639.
Telephone: 616-454-8656.
Fax: 616-776-6322.
Howell, Michigan Office: 121 South Barnard Street, Suite 4, 48843-2305.
Telephone: 517-546-7600.
Telecopier: 517-546-6974.
Kalamazoo, Michigan Office: 444 West Michigan Avenue, 49007-3752.
Telephone: 616-381-7030.
Fax: 616-382-0244.
Lansing, Michigan Office: One Michigan Avenue, Suite 900, 48933-1609.
Telephone: 517-487-2070.
Fax: 517-374-6304.
Monroe, Michigan Office: The Executive Centre, 214 East Elm Avenue, 48161-2682.
Telephone: 313-243-2000.
Fax: 313-243-0901.
Washington, D.C. Office: 1225 Nineteenth Street, N.W., Suite 400. 20036.
Telephone: 202-429-5575; 785-0600.
Fax: 202-331-1118; 785-1234.
Pensacola, Florida Office: 25 West Cedar, 32501.
Telephone: 904-469-1088.
Fax: 904-432-0677.
St. Petersburg, Florida Office: 100 Second Avenue S., Suite 7045, 33701.
Telephone: 813-982-6000.
Fax: 813-892-6002.
New York, New York Office: Eleventh Floor, 135 East 57th Street, 10022-2087.
Telephone: 212-754-5400.
Fax: 212-754-5401.
Gdansk, Poland Office: Suite 322, Dom Technika Building, UI. Rajska 6, 80-850.
Telephone: 011-485-831-2808.
Fax: 011-485-831-4719.
Warsaw, Poland Office: UI. Marszalkowska 82, Suite 561, 00-517.
Telephone: 011-482-623-6457 and 6458.
Fax: 011-482-623-6459.

PRINCIPALS OF FIRM

Charles E. Ritter (Kalamazoo Office)	Stephen J. Ott
Thomas G. Parachini	Pamela Chapman Enslen (Kalamazoo Office)
W. Mack Faison	Richard F. X. Urisko
Leland D. Barringer	Brian J. Doren
Ronald E. Baylor (Kalamazoo Office)	Irene Bruce Hathaway

ASSOCIATES

Robert J. Haddad	Brian S. Westenberg

Representative Firm Clients: Chrysler Corporation; Comerica, Incorporated; City of Detroit, Michigan; Detroit Tigers, Inc.; First of Michigan; Ford Motor Company; Ford Motor Credit Company; Great Lakes Bancorp; Henry Ford Hospital; INVETECH Company.

For Complete List of Firm Personnel, See General Section

For full biographical listings, see the Martindale-Hubbell Law Directory

PATTERSON, PHIFER & PHILLIPS, P.C. (AV)

L. B. King Building, 1274 Library Street, Suite 500, 48226
Telephone: 313-964-2360

Michael D. Patterson	Randolph D. Phifer
	Dwight W. Phillips

Joseph M. White	Eugene M. Holmes
	Lisa A. Cylar

Representative Clients: Detroit Board of Education; Fireman's Fund Insurance Co.; General Motors Corp.; Home Federal Savings Bank; Liberty Mutual Insurance Co.; Metropolitan Life Insurance Co.; Michigan Basic Property Insurance Assn.; New York Life Insurance Co.; Wayne State University. *Reference:* First of American Bank-Detroit, N.A.

For full biographical listings, see the Martindale-Hubbell Law Directory

ROSEN & LOVELL, P.C. (AV)

Penobscot Building, 645 Griswold Street, Suite 3080, 48226-4224
Telephone: 313-961-7510
Fax: 313-961-2905

Paul A. Rosen	Joan Lovell

For full biographical listings, see the Martindale-Hubbell Law Directory

SCHUREMAN, FRAKES, GLASS & WULFMEIER (AV)

440 East Congress, Fourth Floor, 48226
Telephone: 313-961-1500
Telecopier: 313-961-1087
Harbor Springs, Michigan Office: One Spring Street Sq., 49740.
Telephone: 616-526-1145.
Telecopier: 616-526-9343.

MEMBERS OF FIRM

Jeptha W. Schureman	LeRoy H. Wulfmeier, III
John C. Frakes, Jr.	Cheryl L. Chandler
Charles F. Glass	David M. Ottenwess

ASSOCIATES

Daniel J. Dulworth	John J. Moran
	Paul A. Salyers

Reference: Comerica.

For full biographical listings, see the Martindale-Hubbell Law Directory

STEINBERG, O'CONNOR, PATON & BURNS, P.L.L.C. (AV)

1724 Ford Building, 615 Griswold Street, 48226-3901
Telephone: 313-962-3738
Telefax: 313-962-3779

Richard L. Steinberg	Alison L. Paton
Doyle O'Connor	Janice L. Burns

For full biographical listings, see the Martindale-Hubbell Law Directory

VANDEVEER GARZIA, PROFESSIONAL CORPORATION (AV)

Suite 1600, 333 West Fort Street, 48226
Telephone: 313-961-4880
Fax: 313-961-3822
Oakland County Office: 220 Park Street, Suite 300, Birmingham, Michigan.
Telephone: 810-645-0100.
Fax: 810-645-2430.
Macomb County Office: 50 Crocker Boulevard, Mount Clemens, Michigan.
Telephone: 810-468-4880.
Fax: 810-465-7159.
West Michigan Office: 1121 Ottawa Beach Road, Suite 140, Holland Michigan.
Telephone: 616-399-8600.
Fax: 616-786-9095.

Thomas P. Rockwell	Gary Alan Miller
James A. Sullivan	William L. Kiriazis
Michael M. Hathaway	Cynthia E. Merry
John J. Lynch, III (Resident, Oakland County Office)	Daniel P. Steele
Thomas M. Peters	Shelley K. Miller (Resident, Oakland County Office)
James K. Thome	Terrance P. Lynch
Ronald L. Cornell (Resident, Macomb County Office)	Dennis B. Cotter

For Complete List of Firm Personnel, See General Section

For full biographical listings, see the Martindale-Hubbell Law Directory

ZEFF AND ZEFF, P.C. (AV)

The Zeff Building, 607 Shelby, 48226
Telephone: 313-962-3825
Fax: 313-962-6007

Louis Zeff (1896-1966)	A. Robert Zeff

(See Next Column)

ZEFF AND ZEFF P.C.—*Continued*

Sheryl L. Berenbaum   Paul W. Broschay
                    Steven L. Berenbaum

For full biographical listings, see the Martindale-Hubbell Law Directory

EAST LANSING, Ingham Co.

FARHAT, STORY & KRAUS, P.C. (AV)

Beacon Place, 4572 South Hagadorn Road, Suite 3, 48823
Telephone: 517-351-3700
Fax: 517-332-4122
Email: rkraus@sojourn.com

Leo A. Farhat   Chris A. Bergstrom
James E. Burns (1925-1979)   Kitty L. Groh
Monte R. Story   Charles R. Toy
Richard C. Kraus   David M. Platt
Max R. Hoffman Jr.   Thomas L. Sparks

Lawrence P. Schweitzer   Daniel B. Morgan
Debra A. Geroux   Mary K. Robbins-Kralapp

Reference: City Bank, St. Johns.

For full biographical listings, see the Martindale-Hubbell Law Directory

FLINT,* Genesee Co.

MacDONALD, FITZGERALD & MacDONALD, P.C. (AV)

200 McKinnon Building, 48502
Telephone: 810-232-3184; 234-2204
Fax: 810-232-9632

Robert J. MacDonald   John J. FitzGerald (1919-1995)
(1914-1987)   R. Duncan MacDonald
                Timothy J. MacDonald

References: Michigan National Bank; Genesee Merchants Bank & Trust Co.

For full biographical listings, see the Martindale-Hubbell Law Directory

GRAND RAPIDS,* Kent Co.

ALLABEN, MASSIE, VANDER WEYDEN & TIMMER (AV)

Suite 850, Commerce Building, 5 Lyon Street, N.W., 49503
Telephone: 616-774-2182
Fax: 616-774-0602

MEMBERS OF FIRM

Fred Roland Allaben   Keith A. Vander Weyden
(1901-1985)   John J. Timmer
Sam F. Massie, Jr.   Robert W. Bandeen

John R. Allaben

Representative Clients: Auto Club Insurance Assn.; American States Insurance Co.; Michigan Mutual Liability Co.; Fidelity & Casualty Company of New York; U.S. Aircraft Insurance Group; Security Mutual Casualty Co.; Nationwide Mutual Insurance Co.; Security Mutual Casualty Co.; Nationwide Mutual Insurance Co.; Union Insurance Co.

For full biographical listings, see the Martindale-Hubbell Law Directory

BREMER, WADE, NELSON, LOHR & COREY, LLP (AV)

600 3 Mile Road, N.W., 49544-1601
Telephone: 616-784-4434
Fax: 616-784-7322

MEMBERS OF FIRM

William M. Bremer   Phillip J. Nelson
Michael D. Wade   James H. Lohr
                Michael J. Corey

ASSOCIATES

Barbara L. Olafsson   Olafur A. Olafsson

LEGAL SUPPORT PERSONNEL

Kathleen A. Fitzpatrick

For full biographical listings, see the Martindale-Hubbell Law Directory

BUCHANAN, SILVER & BECKERING, P.L.C. (AV)

300 Ottawa N.W., Suite 800, 49503
Telephone: 616-458-2464
Fax: 616-458-0608

MEMBERS OF FIRM

John C. Buchanan   Robert J. Buchanan
Lee T. Silver   Jane M. Beckering

For full biographical listings, see the Martindale-Hubbell Law Directory

DE GROOT, KELLER & VINCENT (AV)

300 Michigan Trust Building, 49503
Telephone: 616-459-6251
Fax: 616-459-6352

MEMBERS OF FIRM

Murray B. De Groot   Brian D. Vincent

For full biographical listings, see the Martindale-Hubbell Law Directory

DREW, COOPER & ANDING (AV)

Ledyard Building, Suite 300, 125 Ottawa Avenue, N.W., 49503-2898
Telephone: 616-454-8300

Stephen R. Drew   John E. Anding
Ann M. Cooper   Bridget C. Kehoe
                Brian K. Lawson

For full biographical listings, see the Martindale-Hubbell Law Directory

EARDLEY LAW OFFICES, P.C. (AV)

800 Monroe Avenue, N.W. Suite 312, 49503
Telephone: 616-458-2900
Fax: 616-458-3099

John F. Eardley   Eugenie B. Eardley

For full biographical listings, see the Martindale-Hubbell Law Directory

GRUEL, MILLS, NIMS AND PYLMAN (AV)

50 Monroe Place, Suite 700 West, 49503
Telephone: 616-235-5500
Fax: 616-235-5550

MEMBERS OF FIRM

Grant J. Gruel   Scott R. Melton
William F. Mills   Brion J. Brooks
J. Clarke Nims   Thomas R. Behm
Norman H. Pylman, II   J. Paul Janes

Representative Clients: Aquinas College; Bell Helmet Co.; Blodgett Memorial Medical Center; Butterworth Hospital; Chem Central, Inc.; Cook Pump Co.; Grove, Inc.; NBDC; Heim Corp.

For full biographical listings, see the Martindale-Hubbell Law Directory

GARY J. McINERNEY, P.C. (AV)

330 East Fulton, 49503
Telephone: 616-458-6111; 800-819-2332
Telecopier: 616-458-6446

Gary J. McInerney

Michael A. McInerney   Adna H. Underhill

For full biographical listings, see the Martindale-Hubbell Law Directory

MILLER, CANFIELD, PADDOCK AND STONE, P.L.C. (AV)

A Professional Limited Liability Company
Founded in 1852 by Sidney Davy Miller
1200 Campau Square Plaza, 99 Monroe, N.W., P.O. Box 329, 49503-2639
Telephone: 616-454-8656
Fax: 616-776-6322
Detroit, Michigan Office: 150 West Jefferson, Suite 2500, 48226-4415.
Telephone: 313-963-6420.
Fax: 313-496-7500.
Cable Address: "Stem Detroit."
Ann Arbor, Michigan Office: 101 North Main Street, 7th Floor, 48104-1400.
Telephone: 313-663-2445.
Fax: 313-747-7147.
Bloomfield Hills, Michigan Office: Suite 100, Pinehurst Office Center, 1400 North Woodward, 48303-2014.
Telephone: 313-645-5000.
Fax: 313-645-1917.
Howell, Michigan Office: 121 South Barnard Street, Suite 4, 48843-2305.
Telephone: 517-546-7600.
Telecopier: 517-546-6974.
Kalamazoo, Michigan Office: 444 West Michigan Avenue, 49007-3752.
Telephone: 616-381-7030.
Fax: 616-382-0244.
Lansing, Michigan Office: One Michigan Avenue, Suite 900, 48933-1609.
Telephone: 517-487-2070.
Fax: 517-374-6304.
Monroe, Michigan Office: The Executive Centre, 214 East Elm Avenue, 48161-2682.
Telephone: 313-243-2000.
Fax: 313-243-0901.
Washington, D.C. Office: 1225 Nineteenth Street, N.W., Suite 400. 20036.
Telephone: 202-429-5575; 785-0600.
Fax: 202-331-1118; 785-1234.
Pensacola, Florida Office: 25 West Cedar 32501.
Telephone: 904-469-1088.
Fax: 904-432-0677.

(See Next Column)

MILLER, CANFIELD, PADDOCK AND STONE P.L.C., *Grand Rapids—Continued*

St. Petersburg Florida Office: 100 Second Avenue S., Suite 7045, 33701.
Telephone: 813-982-6000.
Fax: 813-892-6002.
New York, New York Office: Eleventh Floor, 135 East 57th Street, 10022-2087.
Telephone: 212-754-5400.
Fax: 212-754-5401.
Gdansk, Poland Office: Suite 322, Dom Technika Building, UI. Rajska 6, 80-850.
Telephone: 011-485-831-2808.
Fax: 011-485-831-4719.
Warsaw, Poland Office: UI. Marszalkowska 82, Suite 561, 00-517.
Telephone: 011-482-623-6457 and 6458.
Fax: 011-482-623-6459.

PRINCIPALS OF FIRM

Mark E. Putney (Resident
　Director, Grand Rapids
　Office)
Richard A. Gaffin
Charles S. Mishkind (Detroit,
　Lansing and Kalamazoo
　Offices)

Michael G. Campbell
Robert E. Lee Wright
Vernon Bennett III
Douglas W. Crim

OF COUNSEL
David E. Hathaway
SENIOR ATTORNEYS

David J. Hasper

Stephen L. Elkins

ASSOCIATES

John C. Arndts
Bradley C. White

Daniel H. Roberts
John T. Stecco

Michael V. Camarota

Representative Firm Clients: Chrysler Corporation; Comerica, Incorporated; City of Detroit, Michigan; Detroit Tigers, Inc.; First of Michigan; Ford Motor Company; Ford Motor Credit Company; Great Lakes Bancorp; Henry Ford Hospital; INVETECH Company.

For full biographical listings, see the Martindale-Hubbell Law Directory

ROBERTS, BETZ & BLOSS, P.C. (AV)

555 Riverfront Plaza Building, 55 Campau, 49503
Telephone: 616-235-9955
Telecopier: 616-235-0404

Michael J. Roberts
Michael W. Betz
David J. Bloss
Gregory A. Block

Michael T. Small
Ralph M. Reisinger
Henry S. Emrich
Allan C. Vander Laan

George J. Quist

For full biographical listings, see the Martindale-Hubbell Law Directory

HANCOCK, Houghton Co.

WISTI & WISTI, P.C. (AV)

101 Quincy Street, 49930
Telephone: 906-482-5220
Fax: 906-482-8800
Iron Mountain, Michigan Office: 623 Stephenson Avenue.
Telephone: 906-779-1280.
Marquette, Michigan Office: 117 South Front Street.
Telephone: 906-228-8204.

Andrew H. Wisti

Mark Wisti
Daniel J. Wisti

Patricia A. Gotschalk

References: Superior National Bank & Trust Company of Hancock, Michigan; Houghton National Bank, Houghton, Michigan.

For full biographical listings, see the Martindale-Hubbell Law Directory

HOLLAND, Ottawa Co.

CUNNINGHAM DALMAN, P.C. (AV)

321 Settlers Road, P.O. Box 1767, 49422-1767
Telephone: 616-392-1821
Fax: 616-392-4769

Gordon H. Cunningham
Ronald L. Dalman
Max R. Murphy
James A. Bidol
Andrew J. Mulder
Joel G. Bouwens

Kenneth B. Breese
Jeffrey K. Helder
Ronald J. Vander Veen
David M. Zessin
Mark H. Zietlow
James W. Bouwens

Randall S. Schipper

Susan E. Vroegop

Melinda M. Abney

(See Next Column)

OF COUNSEL
Vernon D. Ten Cate　　　　　Kenneth B. Peirce, Jr.

Representative Clients: FMB-First Michigan Bank; First of America Bank-Holland, N.A.; Ottawa Savings Bank; City of Holland; Auto Club Insurance Assn. (AAA); American States Insurance Co.; Holland Economic Development Corp.; Hope College; Western Theological Seminary.
Reference: FMB-First Michigan Bank.

For full biographical listings, see the Martindale-Hubbell Law Directory

KALAMAZOO,* Kalamazoo Co.

FIELD & FIELD, P.C. (AV)

248 West Michigan Avenue, 49007
Telephone: 616-343-5581
Telecopy: 616-343-5560

Eugene Field (1916-1983)

Samuel T. Field

Reference: Old Kent Bank & Trust Company of Kalamazoo.

MILLER, CANFIELD, PADDOCK AND STONE, P.L.C. (AV)

A Professional Limited Liability Company
Founded in 1852 by Sidney Davy Miller
444 West Michigan Avenue, 49007-3752
Telephone: 616-381-7030
Fax: 616-382-0244
Detroit, Michigan Office: 150 West Jefferson, Suite 2500, 48226-4415.
Telephone: 313-963-6420.
Fax: 313-496-7500.
Cable Address: "Stem Detroit."
Ann Arbor, Michigan Office: 101 North Main Street, 7th Floor, 48104-1400.
Telephone: 313-663-2445.
Fax: 313-747-7147.
Bloomfield Hills, Michigan Office: Suite 100, Pinehurst Office Center, 1400 North Woodward, 48303-2014.
Telephone: 313-645-5000.
Fax: 313-645-1917.
Grand Rapids, Michigan Office: 1200 Campau Square Plaza, 99 Monroe, N.W., 49503-2639.
Telephone: 616-454-8656.
Fax: 616-776-6322.
Howell, Michigan Office: 121 South Barnard Street, Suite 4, 48843-2305.
Telephone: 517-546-7600.
Telecopier: 517-546-6974.
Lansing, Michigan Office: One Michigan Avenue, Suite 900, 48933-1609.
Telephone: 517-487-2070.
Fax: 517-374-6304.
Monroe, Michigan Office: The Executive Centre, 214 East Elm Avenue, 48161-2682.
Telephone: 313-243-2000.
Fax: 313-243-0901.
Washington, D.C. Office: 1225 Nineteenth Street, N.W., Suite 400. 20036.
Telephone: 202-429-5575; 785-0600.
Fax: 202-331-1118; 785-1234.
Pensacola, Florida Office: 25 West Cedar, 32501.
Telephone: 904-469-1088.
Fax: 904-432-0677.
St. Petersburg, Florida Office: 100 Second Avenue S., Suite 7045, 33701.
Telephone: 813-982-6000.
Fax: 813-892-6002.
New York, New York Office: Eleventh Floor, 135 East 57th Street, 10022-2087.
Telephone: 212-754-5400.
Fax: 212-754-5401.
Gdansk, Poland Office: Suite 322, Dom Technika Building, UI. Rajska 6, 80-850.
Telephone: 011-485-831-2808.
Fax: 011-485-831-4719.
Warsaw, Poland Office: UI. Marszalkowska 82, Suite 561, 00-517.
Telephone: 011-482-623-6457 and 6458.
Fax: 011-482-623-6459.

PRINCIPALS OF FIRM

Charles E. Ritter
Ronald E. Baylor

James E. Spurr
Pamela Chapman Enslen

ASSOCIATES

Kurt P. McCamman

Scott R. Sikkenga

Representative Firm Clients: Chrysler Corporation; Comerica, Incorporated; City of Detroit, Michigan; Detroit Tigers, Inc.; First of Michigan; Ford Motor Company; Ford Motor Credit Company; Great Lakes Bancorp; Henry Ford Hospital; INVETECH Company.

For Complete List of Firm Personnel, See General Section

For full biographical listings, see the Martindale-Hubbell Law Directory

LANSING, Ingham Co.

DUNNINGS & FRAWLEY, P.C. (AV)

Duncan Building, 530 South Pine Street, 48933-2299
Telephone: 517-487-8222
Fax: 517-487-2026
Email: conrights@voyager.net

Stuart J. Dunnings, Jr.	John J. Frawley

Stuart J. Dunnings, III	Steven D. Dunnings
Shauna L. Dunnings	

For full biographical listings, see the Martindale-Hubbell Law Directory

FOSTER, SWIFT, COLLINS & SMITH, P.C. (AV)

313 South Washington Square, 48933-2193
Telephone: 517-371-8100
Telecopier: 517-371-8200
URL: http://www.fosterswift.com
Farmington Hills, Michigan Office: 32300 Northwestern Highway, Suite 230.
Telephone: 810-539-9900.
Fax: 810-851-7504.

John L. Collins	Charles E. Barbieri
William R. Schulz	Scott L. Mandel
David H. Aldrich	Michael D. Sanders
Scott A. Storey	Kevin T. McGraw
Matthew W. Collins	

LEGAL SUPPORT PERSONNEL
LEGAL ASSISTANTS

Laurie A. Awad	Theresa G. Solberg

General Counsel for: First American Bank-Central; Story, Inc.; Michigan Milk Producers Assn.; Edward W. Sparrow Hospital; St. Lawrence Hospital; Demmer Corp.; Michigan Financial Corp.
Local Counsel for: Shell Oil Co.; Michigan-Mutual Insurance Co.; Century Telephone.

For Complete List of Firm Personnel, See General Section

For full biographical listings, see the Martindale-Hubbell Law Directory

TIMMER, JAMO & O'LEARY (AV)

521 Seymour Avenue, 48933
Telephone: 517-371-3500
Fax: 517-371-4514

MEMBERS OF FIRM

James A. Timmer	James S. O'Leary
James S. Jamo	Kathleen A. Lopilato

Representative Clients: Auto-Owners Insurance Co.; National Indemnity Insurance Co.; Travelers Insurance Co.; Ohio Farmers Insurance Co.; Bankers Life & Casualty Co.; Western Casualty & Surety Co.; Indiana Insurance Group; Western Surety Co.; Michigan Municipal League; Preston Trucking.

For full biographical listings, see the Martindale-Hubbell Law Directory

MONROE, Monroe Co.

BRAUNLICH, RUSSOW & BRAUNLICH, A PROFESSIONAL CORPORATION (AV)

111 South Macomb Street, 48161
Telephone: 313-241-8300
Fax: 313-241-7715

William J. Braunlich, Jr.	Thomas P. Russow
(1924-1992)	William H. Braunlich

Philip A. Costello	Marie C. Kennedy
Patricia M. Poupard	Susan J. Mehregan
Ann L. Nickel	Robert Wetzel
Michael G. Roehrig	

LEGAL SUPPORT PERSONNEL
Ruth G. Flint

Representative Clients: State Farm Mutual Insurance Co.; Auto Club Insurance Assn.; Farm Bureau Insurance Co.; Home Mutual Insurance Co.; Cincinnati Insurance Co.; Board of Road Commissioners, Monroe County; Port of Monroe; Monroe County Community College; City of Luna Pier; City of Petersburg.

For full biographical listings, see the Martindale-Hubbell Law Directory

MOUNT CLEMENS, Macomb Co.

MARTIN, BACON & MARTIN, P.C. (AV)

44 First Street, 48043
Telephone: 810-979-6500
Fax: 810-468-7016

(See Next Column)

James N. Martin	Michael R. Janes
Jonathan E. Martin	Kevin L. Moffatt
Paul R. VanTol	John W. Crimando
Victor T. Van Camp	

Patrick D. Ball	Amy M. Chauvin

Reference: Old Kent Bank - Mt. Clemens.

For full biographical listings, see the Martindale-Hubbell Law Directory

MOUNT PLEASANT, Isabella Co.

GRAY, SOWLE & IACCO, A PROFESSIONAL CORPORATION (AV)

600 East Broadway, 48858
Telephone: 517-772-5932
Fax: 517-773-0538

Loren E. Gray	Daniel A. Iacco
Donald N. Sowle	Cheryl E. Gray

References: Isabella Bank & Trust; First of America of Mount Pleasant.

For full biographical listings, see the Martindale-Hubbell Law Directory

PLYMOUTH, Wayne Co.

DRAUGELIS & ASHTON, L.L.P. (AV)

843 Penniman Avenue, 48170-1690
Telephone: 313-453-4044
Clawson, Michigan Office: 380 North Main Street.
Telephone: 810-588-7704.

MEMBERS OF FIRM

Edward F. Draugelis	Lamberto DiStefano
John A. Ashton	David T. Rogers
Donald S. Scully	Joseph R. Conte
Richard T. Haynes	Steven O. Ashton

ASSOCIATES

Dawn E. Clancy	Anne K. Mayer
Timothy M. O'Connor	Sally S. Stauffer
Floyd C. Virant	Darlene M. Germaine
Taras P. Jarema	Joel B. Ashton
Deborah A. Tonelli	Donald E. Walker
Timothy M. McKercher	Kathryn R. Mccool

For full biographical listings, see the Martindale-Hubbell Law Directory

PONTIAC, Oakland Co.

BOOTH PATTERSON, P.C. (AV)

1090 West Huron Street, 48328
Telephone: 810-681-1200
Fax: 810-681-1754

Douglas W. Booth (1918-1992)	David J. Lee
Calvin E. Patterson (1913-1987)	Allan T. Motzny
Parvin C. Lee, Jr.	Michael J. Hughes
J. Timothy Patterson	Michael D. Bishop
Eric S. Meier	

For full biographical listings, see the Martindale-Hubbell Law Directory

ROYAL OAK, Oakland Co.

CARDELLI, SCHAEFER & MASON, P.C. (AV)

322 West Lincoln, 48067
Telephone: 810-544-1100
Toll Free 1-800-411-7774
Telecopier: 810-544-1191

Thomas G. Cardelli	William C. Schaefer
Laura D. Mason	

Deborah A. Hebert	Tara Hanley Bratton
Mary Ann J. O'Neil	Diane T. Gorczyca
Lillian C. Pierce	Ronald E. Beier, II
John L. Weston	

Representative Clients: Allianz Insurance Company; Coltec Industries (Garlock Inc & Anchor Packing Company); Dana Corporation; Duchossois Industries, Inc.; Fruehauf Trailer Corporation; General Motors Corporation; Glaxo Wellcome, Inc.; Morton International, Inc.; Otis Elevator Company; Raymond Corporation; Robert Bosch Power Tool Corporation.

For full biographical listings, see the Martindale-Hubbell Law Directory

SAGINAW,* Saginaw Co.

BRAUN KENDRICK FINKBEINER PLC (AV)

101 N. Washington Suite 812, 48607-1297
Telephone: 517-753-3461
Telecopier: 517-753-3951
URL: http://www.bkf-law.com
Bay City, Michigan Office: 201 Phoenix Building, P.O. Box 2039.
Telephone: 517-895-8505.
Telecopier: 517-895-8437.
Ann Arbor, Michigan Office: 700 First National Building.
Telephone: 313-995-4100.
Telecopier: 313-995-4798.

Harold J. Blanchet, Jr.   Craig W. Horn

Representative Clients: The Dow Chemical Co.; General Motors Corp.; Lobdell Emery Manufacturing Co.; Merrill, Lynch, Inc.; Saginaw General Hospital; Saginaw News; The Wickes Foundation.

For Complete List of Firm Personnel, See General Section

For full biographical listings, see the Martindale-Hubbell Law Directory

ST. JOSEPH,* Berrien Co.

MICHAEL D. MARRS A PROFESSIONAL CORPORATION (AV)

421 Main Street, P.O. Box 124, 49085
Telephone: 616-982-4000
Fax: 616-982-0426
Email: MMarrsLaw@AOL.COM

Michael D. Marrs

For full biographical listings, see the Martindale-Hubbell Law Directory

TROFF, PETZKE & AMMESON (AV)

Law and Title Building, 811 Ship Street, P.O. Box 67, 49085
Telephone: 616-983-0161
Facsimile: 616-983-0166

MEMBERS OF FIRM
Theodore E. Troff   Roger A. Petzke
Charles F. Ammeson
ASSOCIATES
Bennett S. Schwartz   Daniel G. Lambrecht
Deborah L. Berecz

For full biographical listings, see the Martindale-Hubbell Law Directory

SAULT STE. MARIE,* Chippewa Co.

MOHER & CANNELLO, P.C. (AV)

150 Water Street, P.O. Box 538, 49783
Telephone: 906-632-3397
Fax: 906-632-0479
Newberry, Michigan Office: 200 East John.
Telephone: 906-293-3600.

Thomas G. Moher   Steven J. Cannello
Timothy S. Moher
LEGAL SUPPORT PERSONNEL
Bridgette A. Moher

For full biographical listings, see the Martindale-Hubbell Law Directory

SOUTHFIELD, Oakland Co.

FIEGER, FIEGER & SCHWARTZ, A PROFESSIONAL CORPORATION (AV)

19390 West Ten Mile Road, 48075-2463
Telephone: 810-355-5555
Fax: 810-355-5148

Bernard J. Fieger (1922-1988)   Todd J. Weglarz
Geoffrey N. Fieger   Rebecca S. Eaton
Michael Alan Schwartz   Ven R. Johnson
William J. McHenry
OF COUNSEL
Barry Fayne   Beverly Hires Brode
Keitha Kay Cowen

For full biographical listings, see the Martindale-Hubbell Law Directory

HIGHLAND & ZANETTI (AV)

Suite 205, 24445 Northwestern Highway, 48075
Telephone: 810-352-9580

John N. Highland   J. R. Zanetti, Jr.
R. Michael John

Duncan Hall Brown   Ronald D. Holton

For full biographical listings, see the Martindale-Hubbell Law Directory

---

PROVIZER, LICHTENSTEIN & PHILLIPS, P.C. (AV)

4000 Town Center, Suite 1800, 48075
Telephone: 810-352-9080
Facsimile: 810-352-1491

Harold M. Provizer   Deborah Molitz
David S. Lichtenstein   Constance S. Hall
Randall E. Phillips   Noel F. Beck
Marilyn A. Madorsky   William J. Selinsky
Evan A. Zagoria   Robert I. Brown
Jason Milstone

Representative Clients: Jefferson Ins. Co.; Reliance National Ins. Co.; Blackmoor Group; Thomas Howell Group; Fleming & Hall.

For full biographical listings, see the Martindale-Hubbell Law Directory

SCHWARTZ & JALKANEN, P.C. (AV)

Suite 200, 24400 Northwestern Highway, 48075
Telephone: 810-352-2555
Facsimile: 810-352-5963

Melvin R. Schwartz   Arthur W. Jalkanen
Karl Eric Hannum

Deborah L. Laura   Lori A. Barker

For full biographical listings, see the Martindale-Hubbell Law Directory

SOMMERS, SCHWARTZ, SILVER & SCHWARTZ, P.C. (AV)

2000 Town Center, Suite 900, 48075
Telephone: 810-355-0300
Telecopier: 810-746-4001
Plymouth, Michigan Office: 747 South Main Street.
Telephone: 313-455-4250.

Stanley S. Schwartz   Robert B. Sickels
Jeffrey N. Shillman   Michael J. Cunningham
Jeremy L. Winer   James D. Ledbetter
David R. Getto   Matthew G. Curtis
Norman D. Tucker   Helen K. Joyner
Robert H. Darling   John L. Runco
Paul W. Hines   Susanne Pryce
Stephen N. Leuchtman   David J. Shea
Richard D. Fox   Anne M. Schoepfle
Frank Mafrice   Gary D. Dodds
Richard L. Groffsky   Jabran G. Yasso
David J. Winter   Kenneth T. Watkins
B. A. Tyler   Craig E. Feringa
OF COUNSEL
Howard Silver   Marvin R. Stempien

General Counsel for: City of Taylor; Foodland Distributors; C.A. Muer Corporation; Vlasic & Company; Nederlander Corporation; Midwest Health Centers, P.C.
Representative Clients: Crum & Forster Insurance Company; City of Pontiac; Michigan National Bank.

For Complete List of Firm Personnel, See General Section

For full biographical listings, see the Martindale-Hubbell Law Directory

TRAVERSE CITY,* Grand Traverse Co.

MURCHIE, CALCUTT & BOYNTON (AV)

109 East Front Street, Suite 300, 49684
Telephone: 616-947-7190
Fax: 616-947-4341

Robert B. Murchie (1894-1975)   William B. Calcutt
Harry Calcutt   Mark A. Burnheimer
Jack E. Boynton   Dawn M. Rogers
ASSOCIATE
Ralph J. Dilley (Not admitted in MI)

General Counsel for: Old Kent Bank-Grand Traverse; Northwestern Savings Bank & Trust; Central-State Bancorp; Traverse City Record Eagle; WPNB-7 & WTOM-4; Emergency Consultants, Inc.; National Guardian Risk Retention Group, Inc.; Farmers Mutual Insurance Co.; Environmental Solutions, Inc.
Local Counsel for: Consumers Power Co.

For full biographical listings, see the Martindale-Hubbell Law Directory

RUNNING, WISE, WILSON, FORD AND PHILLIPS, P.L.C. (AV)

326 State Street, P.O. Box 686, 49684
Telephone: 616-946-2700
Tele-Fax: 616-946-0857

Harry T. Running (Deceased)   William L. Wise (Retired)
MEMBERS OF FIRM
Patrick J. Wilson   James C. Adams
Richard W. Ford   Sandra P. Howard
Thomas J. Phillips   Kent E. Gerberding

(See Next Column)

RUNNING, WISE, WILSON, FORD AND PHILLIPS P.L.C.—*Continued*

ASSOCIATES

Shelley A. Kester   Bradley L. Putney

OF COUNSEL

J. Bruce Donaldson   Douglas J. Donaldson

For full biographical listings, see the Martindale-Hubbell Law Directory

---

THOMPSON & O'NEIL, P.C. (AV)

309 East Front Street, P.O. Box 429, 49685
Telephone: 616-929-9700; 1-800-678-1307
Fax: 616-929-7262

George R. Thompson   Daniel P. O'Neil

William J. Brooks

For full biographical listings, see the Martindale-Hubbell Law Directory

---

WALTON, SMITH, PHILLIPS & DIXON, P.C. (AV)

216 Cass Street, P.O. Box 549, 49685
Telephone: 616-947-7410
Fax: 616-947-5112

Geoff G. Smith   L. Kent Walton
Thomas L. Phillips

OF COUNSEL

David S. Dixon

Representative Clients: The Travelers Insurance Cos.; Farm Bureau Insurance Group; First of America-Northern Michigan; State Farm Insurance.
Reference: First of America-Northern Michigan.

For full biographical listings, see the Martindale-Hubbell Law Directory

---

TROY, Oakland Co.

HOLAHAN, MALLOY, MAYBAUGH & MONNICH (AV)

Suite 100, 2690 Crooks Road, 48084-4700
Telephone: 810-362-4747
Fax: 810-362-4779
East Tawas, Michigan Office: 910 East Bay Street.
Telephone: 517-362-4747.
Fax: 517-362-7331.

MEMBERS OF FIRM

J. Michael Malloy, III   David L. Delie, Jr.
James D. Maybaugh   William J. Kliffel
John R. Monnich   Ingrid Rosvold Kliffel

OF COUNSEL

Thomas H. O'Connor   Maureen Holahan (Retired; Resident, East Tawas Office)

For full biographical listings, see the Martindale-Hubbell Law Directory

---

POLING, McGAW & POLING, P.C. (AV)

Suite 275, 5435 Corporate Drive, 48098
Telephone: 810-641-0500
Telecopier: 810-641-0506

Benson T. Buck (1926-1989)   Richard B. Poling, Jr.
Richard B. Poling   Gregory C. Hamilton
D. Douglas McGaw   Veronica B. O'Haro
James R. Parker

OF COUNSEL

Ralph S. Moore

Representative Clients: County of Oakland; City of Troy; United States Fidelity & Guaranty Co.; Sentry Insurance Co.; Admiral Insurance; DeMaria Construction Co.; Leo Corporation; Aetna Casualty and Surety Co.; Concord Design; Pneumo-Abex.

For full biographical listings, see the Martindale-Hubbell Law Directory

---

SCHIER, DENEWETH & PARFITT, P.C. (AV)

888 West Big Beaver Road, Suite 610, 48084-4737
Telephone: 810-362-5600
Telecopier: 810-362-0073

Carl F. Schier   Timothy P. Dugan
Ronald A. Deneweth   Janette E. Frank
Chris Parfitt   Mark D. Sassak

OF COUNSEL

Edward A. Ryder

Reference: Comerica Bank.

For full biographical listings, see the Martindale-Hubbell Law Directory

VALENTINE & ASSOCIATES, P.C.

(See West Bloomfield)

WEST BLOOMFIELD, Oakland Co.

VALENTINE & ASSOCIATES, P.C. (AV)

5767 West Maple Road, Suite 400, 48322
Telephone: 810-851-3010

Stephen K. Valentine, Jr.

OF COUNSEL

Philip G. Meyer

For full biographical listings, see the Martindale-Hubbell Law Directory

PROBATE, TRUSTS AND ESTATE PLANNING

ALABAMA

BIRMINGHAM, * Jefferson Co.

BERKOWITZ, LEFKOVITS, ISOM & KUSHNER, A PROFESSIONAL CORPORATION (AV)

1600 SouthTrust Tower, 420 North Twentieth Street, 35203
Telephone: 205-328-0480
Telecopier: 205-322-8007

Arnold K. Lefkovits	Thomas O. Kolb
Harold B. Kushner	Andrew J. Potts
Anne W. Mitchell	Nancy C. Hughes

For Complete List of Firm Personnel, See General Section

For full biographical listings, see the Martindale-Hubbell Law Directory

---

BRADLEY, ARANT, ROSE & WHITE (AV)

2001 Park Place, Suite 1400, P.O. Box 830709, 35283-0709
Telephone: 205-521-8000
Facsimile: 205-252-0264
Facsimile (SouthTrust Tower Office): 205-251-9915
URL: http://www.BARW.COM
Huntsville, Alabama Office: 200 Clinton Avenue West, Suite 900, 35801.
Telephone: 205-517-5100.
Facsimile: 205-533-5069.

MEMBERS OF FIRM

Thomas Neely Carruthers, Jr.	Ralph Howard Yeilding
William L. Hinds, Jr.	Scott E. Ludwig
	(Resident, Huntsville Office)

COUNSEL
John N. Wrinkle
ASSOCIATE
Jennifer Byers McLeod

For Complete List of Firm Personnel, See General Section

For full biographical listings, see the Martindale-Hubbell Law Directory

---

BURR & FORMAN (AV)

3100 SouthTrust Tower, 420 North 20th Street, 35203
Telephone: 205-251-3000
Telecopier: 205-458-5100
Huntsville, Alabama Office: Suite 204, Regency Center, 400 Meridian Street.
Telephone: 205-551-0010.
Atlanta, Georgia Office: Suite 1800, One Georgia Center, 600 West Peachtree Street, 30308.
Telephone: 404-817-3536.
Facsimile: 404-817-3244.

MEMBERS OF FIRM

Paul O. Woodall	Bruce A. Rawls
A. Brand Walton	Marvin Glenn Perry, Jr.

ASSOCIATE
Warren C. Matthews

For Complete List of Firm Personnel, See General Section

For full biographical listings, see the Martindale-Hubbell Law Directory

---

CORLEY, MONCUS & WARD, P.C. (AV)

400 Shades Creek Parkway, Suite 100, P.O. Box 59807, 35259
Telephone: 205-879-5959
Telecopier: 205-871-4411

Claude McCain Moncus

For Complete List of Firm Personnel, See General Section

For full biographical listings, see the Martindale-Hubbell Law Directory

---

FELD, HYDE, LYLE & WERTHEIMER, P.C. (AV)

2100 SouthBridge Parkway, Suite 590, 35209
Telephone: 205-802-7575
Facsimile: 205-802-7550

Louis B. Feld	Leonard Wertheimer, III
Gregory D. Hyde	Katherine Nowell Barr
John F. Lyle, III	J. Fred Kingren

OF COUNSEL
Edward K Wood, Jr

For full biographical listings, see the Martindale-Hubbell Law Directory

---

GORDON, SILBERMAN, WIGGINS & CHILDS, A PROFESSIONAL CORPORATION (AV)

1400 SouthTrust Tower, 420 North 20th Street, 35203
Telephone: 205-328-0640
Telecopier: 205-254-1500

Bruce L. Gordon	Augustus J. Beck, Jr.
Terrill W. Sanders	

For Complete List of Firm Personnel, See General Section

For full biographical listings, see the Martindale-Hubbell Law Directory

---

SPAIN & GILLON, L.L.C. (AV)

The Zinszer Building, 2117 2nd Avenue North, 35203
Telephone: 205-328-4100
Telecopier: 205-324-8866

MEMBERS OF FIRM

John P. McKleroy, Jr.	J. Birch Bowdre
Samuel H. Frazier	Glenn E. Estess, Jr.
J. Sanford Mullins, III	

General Counsel for: Liberty National Life Insurance Co.; Piggly Wiggly Alabama Distributing Co.; Alabama Insurance Guaranty Association; Alabama Life and Disability Insurance Guaranty Association; Alabama Insurance Underwriters Association.
Counsel for: The Minnesota Mutual Insurance Company of America; Government Employees Insurance Co.; Massachusetts Mutual Life Insurance Co.

For Complete List of Firm Personnel, See General Section

For full biographical listings, see the Martindale-Hubbell Law Directory

---

FLORENCE, * Lauderdale Co.

KELLER AND PAINE (AV)

An Association of Professional Corporations
212 South Cedar Street, P.O. Box 933, 35631
Telephone: 205-764-5822
Fax: 205-767-6360

MEMBERS OF FIRM

Jesse A. Keller	Michael T. Paine
Peter L. Paine	(Not admitted in AL)

LEGAL SUPPORT PERSONNEL

Carmel Sizemore	Gayle Blake

Counsel for: The American Road Insurance Co.; Lambert Transfer Co.

For full biographical listings, see the Martindale-Hubbell Law Directory

---

HUNTSVILLE, * Madison Co.

BERRY, ABLES, TATUM, BAXTER, PARKER & HALL, P.C. (AV)

Legal Building, 315 Franklin Street, S.E., P.O. Box 165, 35804-0165
Telephone: 205-533-3740
Facsimile: 205-533-3751
Email: BAXTERJ@ATTMAIL.COM

William H. Blanton (1889-1973)	James T. Tatum, Jr.
Joe M. Berry	James T. Baxter, III
L. Bruce Ables	Thomas E. Parker, Jr.
	Bill G. Hall

James K. Brabston	Mark Rogers Hunter

Representative Clients: AmSouth Bank; First Alabama Bank; General Shale Products Co.; The Hertz Corp.; Litton Industries, Inc.; Farmers Tractor Co.; Colonial Bank; Farm Credit Bank of Texas; SouthBank; Regions Mortgage.
Reference: First Alabama Bank.

For full biographical listings, see the Martindale-Hubbell Law Directory

---

BRADLEY, ARANT, ROSE & WHITE (AV)

200 Clinton Avenue West, Suite 900, 35801
Telephone: 205-517-5100
Facsimile: 205-533-5069
URL: http://www.BARW.COM
Birmingham, Alabama Office: 2001 Park Place, Suite 1400, P.O. Box 830709.
Telephone: 205-521-8000.
Facsimile: 205-251-8611, 251-8665, 252-0264. Facsimile (SouthTrust Tower Office): 205-251-9915.

RESIDENT PARTNERS

Charles R. Smith, Jr.	Scott E. Ludwig

For Complete List of Firm Personnel, See General Section

For full biographical listings, see the Martindale-Hubbell Law Directory

Huntsville—Continued

BURR & FORMAN (AV)

Suite 204, Regency Center, 400 Meridian Street, 35801
Telephone: 205-551-0010
Birmingham, Alabama Office: 3100 SouthTrust Tower, 420 North 20th
Street.
Telephone: 205-251-3000.
Telecopier: 205-458-5100.
Atlanta, Georgia Office: Suite 1800, One Georgia Center, 600 West
Peachtree Street, 30308.
Telephone: 404-817-3536.
Facsimile: 404-817-3244.

RESIDENT PARTNER
S. Dagnal Rowe

For full biographical listings, see the Martindale-Hubbell Law Directory

---

MOBILE,* Mobile Co.

JOHNSTONE, ADAMS, BAILEY, GORDON AND HARRIS, L.L.C. (AV)

Royal St. Francis Building, 104 St. Francis Street, P.O. Box 1988, 36633
Telephone: 334-432-7682
Facsimile: 334-432-2800
Telex: 782040

MEMBERS OF FIRM

Charles B. Bailey, Jr.	R. Gregory Watts
E. Watson Smith	Robert S. Frost

General Counsel for: First Alabama Bank, Mobile; Infirmary Health System/Mobile Infirmary Medical Center/Rotary Rehabilitation Hospital (Multi-Hospital System).
Counsel for: Oil and Gas: Exxon Corp. Business and Corporate: Bell South Telecommunications, Inc.; Aluminum Co. of America; Michelin North America, Inc.; Metropolitan Life Insurance Co.; Marine: The West of England Ship Owners Mutual Protection and Indemnity Association (Luxembourg); The Standard Steamship Owners' Protection and Indemnity Association (Bermuda) Ltd.

For Complete List of Firm Personnel, See General Section

For full biographical listings, see the Martindale-Hubbell Law Directory

---

LYONS, PIPES & COOK, P.C. (AV)

2 North Royal Street, P.O. Box 2727, 36652-2727
Telephone: 334-432-4481
Cable Address: "Lysea"
Telecopier: 334-433-1820

Thomas F. Garth	R. Mark Kirkpatrick
	John C. Bell

General Counsel: Inchcape Shipping Services.
Counsel: The Hertz Corp.; McKenzie Tank Lines, Inc.; SCNO Barge Lines, Inc.; Scott Paper Co.; Shell Oil Corp.
Trial Counsel: Aetna Life & Casualty Co.; Chubb Group of Insurance Companies.

For Complete List of Firm Personnel, See General Section

For full biographical listings, see the Martindale-Hubbell Law Directory

---

MONTGOMERY,* Montgomery Co.

VOLZ, PRESTWOOD & HANAN, P.C. (AV)

350 Adams Avenue, P.O. Box 1910, 36102-1910
Telephone: 334-264-6401
Fax: 334-834-4954

Charles H. Volz, Jr.	Charles H. Volz, III
Alvin T. Prestwood	Clinton Chadwell Carter
Ellis D. Hanan	Daniel Lewis Feinstein

LEGAL SUPPORT PERSONNEL
Mark A.W. Turpen

For full biographical listings, see the Martindale-Hubbell Law Directory

ARIZONA

CASA GRANDE, Pinal Co.

FITZGIBBONS LAW OFFICES, P.L.C. (AV)

Suite E, 711 East Cottonwood Lane, P.O. Box 11208, 85230-1208
Telephone: 520-426-3824
Fax: 520-426-9355

David A. Fitzgibbons	Robert M. Yates

For Complete List of Firm Personnel, See General Section

For full biographical listings, see the Martindale-Hubbell Law Directory

---

FLAGSTAFF,* Coconino Co.

ASPEY, WATKINS & DIESEL, P.L.L.C. (AV)

123 North San Francisco, 3rd Floor, 86001
Telephone: 520-774-1478
Facsimile: 520-774-8404
Sedona, Arizona Office: 120 Soldier Pass Road.
Telephone: 520-282-5955.
Facsimile: 520-282-5962.
Page, Arizona Office: 904 North Navajo.
Telephone: 520-645-9694.
Cottonwood, Arizona Office: 2400 E. Highway 89A, Suite C.
Telephone: 520-639-1881.
Facsimile: 520-639-0272.

MEMBERS OF FIRM

Frederick M. Fritz Aspey	Donald H. Bayles, Jr.
Harold L. Watkins	Kaign N. Christy
Louis M. Diesel	John J. Dempsey
Bruce S. Griffen	Zachary J. Markham

James E. Ledbetter	Roger M. Baeurle
Whitney Cunningham	Amy E. Mabius
Pernell Whynn McGuire	Stephen A. Thompson
	Joel E. Sannes

LEGAL SUPPORT PERSONNEL

Karla H. Falls, CLAS (Legal Assistant)	Dominic M. Marino, Jr, (Paralegal Assistant)
Rocky C. Nissen (Paralegal Assistant, Sedona, Arizona Office)	Carrie R. Flynn (Litigation Paralegal, Cottonwood, Arizona Office)
Deborah D. Roberts, CLA (Legal Assistant)	

Representative Clients: Farmer's Insurance Company of Arizona; Pepsi-Cola Bottling Company of Northern Arizona; Bill Luke's Chrysler-Plymouth, Inc.; First American Title Insurance Company; Transnation Title Insurance Co.; Page Electric Utility; Comprehensive Access Health Plan, Inc.; Northern Arizona Healthcare Corporation.
Reference: First Interstate Bank-Arizona, N.A., Flagstaff, Arizona.

For full biographical listings, see the Martindale-Hubbell Law Directory

---

MANGUM, WALL, STOOPS & WARDEN, P.L.L.C. (AV)

222 East Birch Avenue, P.O. Box 10, 86002
Telephone: 520-779-6951
Fax: 520-773-1312

OF COUNSEL
Douglas J. Wall

MEMBER OF FIRM
A. Dean Pickett

ASSOCIATE
Michael L. Transier

Representative Clients: Bank One; First Interstate Bank of Arizona; Nordstrom & Associates, CPA's.

For Complete List of Firm Personnel, See General Section

For full biographical listings, see the Martindale-Hubbell Law Directory

---

LAKE HAVASU CITY, Mohave Co.

WACHTEL, BIEHN & MALM (AV)

Suite A, 2240 McCulloch Boulevard, 86403
Telephone: 520-855-5115
Fax: 520-855-5211

MEMBERS OF FIRM

Don Biehn	Steven A. Biehn

For Complete List of Firm Personnel, See General Section

For full biographical listings, see the Martindale-Hubbell Law Directory

---

PHOENIX,* Maricopa Co.

BURCH & CRACCHIOLO, P.A. (AV)

702 East Osborn Road, Suite 200, 85014
Telephone: 602-274-7611
Fax: 602-234-0341
Mailing Address: P.O. Box 16882, Phoenix, AZ, 85011

Daniel Cracchiolo	Guadalupe Iniguez

Thomas A. Longfellow

Representative Clients: Bashas' Inc.; Farmers Insurance Group; U-Haul International, Inc.

For Complete List of Firm Personnel, See General Section

For full biographical listings, see the Martindale-Hubbell Law Directory

Phoenix—Continued

EHMANN & HILLER, P.C. (AV)

2525 East Camelback Road, Suite 720, 85016
Telephone: 602-956-5050
Telecopier: 602-468-9775
Email: NHillerO@counsel.com

Anthony V. Ehmann	John G. Pattullo
Neil H. Hiller	John F. Daniels, III

References: Valley National Bank of Arizona (Trust Department); First Interstate Bank of Arizona, N.A. (Trust Department); M & I Thunderbird Bank.

For full biographical listings, see the Martindale-Hubbell Law Directory

FENNEMORE CRAIG, A PROFESSIONAL CORPORATION (AV)

Two North Central, Suite 2200, 85004
Telephone: 602-257-8700
Fax: 602-257-8527
Scottsdale, Arizona Office: 6263 North Scottsdale Road, Suite 290, 85250.
Telephone: 602-257-5400.
Fax: 602-257-5409.
Tucson, Arizona Office: One South Church Avenue, Suite 1030, 85701.
Telephone: 520-791-6800.
Fax: 520-791-6820.

Neal Kurn	Louis F. Comus, Jr.
	Rita A. Eisenfeld

Karen A. Curosh	Stephen A. Good
	Susan Marie Ciupak

For Complete List of Firm Personnel, See General Section

For full biographical listings, see the Martindale-Hubbell Law Directory

GOLDMAN & KAPLAN, LTD. (AV)

2930 North 7th Street, 85014
Telephone: 602-264-9323
FAX: 602-274-7006
Email: mkaplan0@counsel.com

Alan Goldman	Mark E. Meltzer
Morris A. Kaplan	Paul D. Friedman

References: Republic National Bank; Merrill Lynch.

For full biographical listings, see the Martindale-Hubbell Law Directory

GOODSON, MANLEY & DURFEE, P.L.C. (AV)

The Brookstone Building, 2025 North 3rd Street, Suite 200, 85004-1471
Telephone: 602-252-5110
Fax: 602-257-1883

John F. Goodson	Colleen C. Manley
	Richard E. Durfee, Jr.

Lawrence F. Scaringelli	Bryan C. Moody

A list of Representative Clients will be furnished upon request.
Reference: First National Bank of Arizona.

For full biographical listings, see the Martindale-Hubbell Law Directory

JABURG & WILK, P.C. (AV)

Great American Bank Building, 3200 North Central Avenue, Suite 2000, 85012
Telephone: 602-248-1000
Fax: 602-248-0522

Gary J. Jaburg	Loren Molever
Alan H. Susman	Jeffrey H. Wolf
Lawrence E. Wilk	Michael J. McGivern
Roger L. Cohen	Mitchell Reichman
Randy Nussbaum	Beth S. Cohn

Marvin W. Manross	Timothy C. Dietz
Kathi Mann Sandweiss	Isabel M. Humphrey

Representative Clients: Wells Fargo Bank; Bank of America; Northern Trust Bank of America; Wells Fargo Realty Advisors Funding, Inc.; State of Arizona; FDIC; HFC; FNMA; FHLMC.

For full biographical listings, see the Martindale-Hubbell Law Directory

JENNINGS, STROUSS AND SALMON, P.L.C. (AV)

A Professional Limited Liability Company
One Renaissance Square, Two North Central, 85004-2393
Telephone: 602-262-5911
Fax: 602-253-3255

John R. Christian	I. Douglas Dunipace
Richard L. Lassen	Robert P. Solliday

(See Next Column)

For Complete List of Firm Personnel, See General Section

For full biographical listings, see the Martindale-Hubbell Law Directory

LANE & EHRLICH, LTD. (AV)

Fairmount Place, Suite 400, 4001 North Third Street, 85012
Telephone: 602-264-4442
Telecopier: 602-264-5006

Robert L. Lane	Gerald F. Ehrlich

References: Bank One Arizona; Harris Trust & Savings Bank; The Northern Trust Bank Arizona.

For full biographical listings, see the Martindale-Hubbell Law Directory

MacLean & Jacques, Ltd. (AV)

Suite 202, 40 East Virginia, 85004
Telephone: 602-263-5771
FAX: 602-279-5569

John H. MacLean (1932-1992)	Raoul T. Jacques

Cary T. Inabinet	Macre S. Inabinet

LEGAL SUPPORT PERSONNEL
Sharon Petterson

For full biographical listings, see the Martindale-Hubbell Law Directory

McCabe, O'Donnell & Wright, A Professional Association (AV)

3101 North Central Avenue Suite 700, 85012
Telephone: 602-264-0800
Facsimile: 602-274-0146
Email: mowphx@aol.com
Email: mowphx@mowphx.com

Joseph I. McCabe	Kathleen M. O'Donnell

A List of Representative Clients will be Furnished upon Request.

For full biographical listings, see the Martindale-Hubbell Law Directory

OLSEN-SMITH, LTD. (AV)

A Partnership of Professional Corporations and a Professional Limited Liability Company
3300 Virginia Financial Plaza, 301 East Virginia Avenue, 85004-1267
Telephone: 602-254-1040
Telecopier: 602-254-1041

Alfred J. Olsen	Susan K. Smith
	James J. Rossie, Jr.

References: The Northern Trust Bank of Arizona; Harris Trust Bank of Arizona; Arizona Community Foundation.

For full biographical listings, see the Martindale-Hubbell Law Directory

RENAUD, COOK & DRURY, P.A. (AV)

617 North 2nd Avenue, 85003
Telephone: 602-253-5101
Fax: 602-254-1448
Email: rcdlaw@rcdlaw.com
Scottsdale, Arizona Office: 6991 East Camelback Road, #D-103, 85251.
Telephone: 602-874-9000.
Fax: 602-874-9866.

J. Gordon Cook	Steven G. Mesaros
Cathey L. Joseph	Mark W. Roth

Diana L. Clarke

For full biographical listings, see the Martindale-Hubbell Law Directory

THOMAS J. SHUMARD (AV)

3550 North Central Avenue, Suite 1407, 85012
Telephone: 602-234-2247
Fax: 602-234-2420

For full biographical listings, see the Martindale-Hubbell Law Directory

SNELL & WILMER, L.L.P. (AV)

One Arizona Center, 85004-0001
Telephone: 602-382-6000
Fax: 602-382-6070
Tucson, Arizona Office: 1500 Norwest Tower, One South Church Avenue 85701-1612.
Telephone: 520-882-1200.
Fax: 520-884-1294.
Orange County Office: 1920 Main Street, Suite 1200, P.O. Box 57062, Irvine, California, 92619-7062.
Telephone: 714-253-2700.
Fax: 714-955-2507.

(See Next Column)

SNELL & WILMER L.L.P., *Phoenix—Continued*

Salt Lake City, Utah Office: Broadway Centre, 111 East Broadway, Suite 900, 84111-1004.
Telephone: 801-237-1900.
Fax: 801-237-1950.

MEMBERS OF FIRM

Joseph T. Melczer, III   David E. Weiss, Jr.

ASSOCIATE

Roger D. Curley

For Complete List of Firm Personnel, See General Section

For full biographical listings, see the Martindale-Hubbell Law Directory

---

PRESCOTT,* Yavapai Co.

FAVOUR, MOORE & WILHELMSEN, A PROFESSIONAL ASSOCIATION (AV)

1580 Plaza West Drive, P.O. Box 1391, 86302
Telephone: 520-445-2444
Fax: 520-771-0450

John M. Favour   Mark M. Moore
David K. Wilhelmsen

References: Bank of America; Northern Trust Bank of Arizona; Valley National Bank of Arizona; Citibank (Arizona); First Interstate Bank of Arizona; M & I Marshall & Ilsley Trust Company of Arizona.

For full biographical listings, see the Martindale-Hubbell Law Directory

MURPHY, LUTEY, SCHMITT & BECK (AV)

Elks Building, 117 East Gurley Street, 86301
Telephone: 520-445-6860
Fax: 520-445-6488
Yuma, Arizona Office: Valley Professional Plaza, 1763 West Twenty-Fourth Street, Suite 200.
Telephone: 520-726-0314.
Fax: 520-341-1079.
Kingman, Arizona Office: 2601 Stockton Hill Road, Suite H8.
Telephone: 520-718-0888; 1-800-281-0822.

MEMBERS OF FIRM

Thelton D. Beck   Selmer D. Lutey
Michael R. Murphy   Robert E. Schmitt

ASSOCIATES

Dan A. Wilson   Bruce E. Rosenberg

OF COUNSEL

Keith F. Quail

Counsel for: State Farm Mutual Automobile Insurance Co.; Allstate Insurance Co.; Farmers Insurance; Western Agricultural Insurance Co.
Local Counsel for: Bank One Arizona, NA; The Stockmen's Bank.
Representative Clients: Prescott College; Galpin Ford, Inc.; Sedona-Oak Creek Airport Authority; Yavapai County Fair Association (Prescott Downs).

For full biographical listings, see the Martindale-Hubbell Law Directory

---

SCOTTSDALE, Maricopa Co.

A. PAUL BLUNT, P.C. (AV)

6900 East Camelback Road, Suite 525, 85251
Telephone: 602-423-9500
Telecopier: 602-423-1936

A. Paul Blunt

Jay M. Polk

For full biographical listings, see the Martindale-Hubbell Law Directory

CASE & SILER, P.L.L.C. (AV)

Scottsdale Place, 5725 North Scottsdale Road Suite C 195, 85250
Telephone: 602-423-1113
Fax: 602-423-1119
Sun City, Arizona Office: 10220 West Bell Road, Suite 120, 85351.
Telephone: 602-972-9193.
Fax: 602-972-9258.

E. Dennis Siler   Stephen S. Case

ASSOCIATE

Andrea G. Somerville

OF COUNSEL

Bruce O. Bekkedahl

Representative Clients: M & I Marshall Ilsley Trust Company of Arizona; Northern Trust Bank of Arizona; Harris Trust Bank of Arizona; Bank One, Arizona, NA, Trust Dept.; First Interstate Bank of Arizona, Trust Dept.; Bank of America, Arizona, Trust Dept.

For full biographical listings, see the Martindale-Hubbell Law Directory

---

TAMARA L. DWORSKY (AV)

8655 East Via De Ventura Suite G-226, 85258
Telephone: 602-941-8337
Email: 72766.2742@compuserve.com

For full biographical listings, see the Martindale-Hubbell Law Directory

FENNEMORE CRAIG, A PROFESSIONAL CORPORATION (AV)

6263 North Scottsdale Road, Suite 290, 85250
Telephone: 602-257-5400
Fax: 602-945-4932
TWX: 910-950-4608
Phoenix, Arizona Office: Two North Central Avenue, Suite 2200, 85004.
Telephone: 602-257-8700.
Fax: 602-257-8527.
Tucson, Arizona Office: One South Church Avenue, Suite 1030, 85701.
Telephone: 520-791-6800.
Fax: 520-791-6820.

Philip A. Edlund

Susan Marie Ciupak

For Complete List of Firm Personnel, See General Section

For full biographical listings, see the Martindale-Hubbell Law Directory

ROSEPINK & ESTES (AV)

7373 North Scottsdale Road Suite D102, 85253
Telephone: 602-443-1280
Fax: 602-443-3664
Email: rosepink@syspac.com *URL:* http://www.syspac.com/~rosepink

MEMBERS OF FIRM

Robert J. Rosepink   David J. Estes

ASSOCIATES

Lynn F. Chandler   John R. Becker

References: Bank of America, Arizona; Biltmore Investors Bank; Chase Trust Company of Arizona; First Interstate Bank of Arizona, N.A.; Firstar Metropolitan Bank & Trust; M & I Marshall & Ilsley Trust Co. of Arizona; Northern Trust Bank of Arizona.

For full biographical listings, see the Martindale-Hubbell Law Directory

J. STEPHEN SIMON (AV)

Eldorado Square, Suite H-102, 6607 North Scottsdale Road, 85250
Telephone: 602-951-1536
Fax: 602-483-2699

References: Harris Trust Bank of Arizona; First Interstate Bank of Arizona, N.A.; Bank One, Arizona (N.A.).

For full biographical listings, see the Martindale-Hubbell Law Directory

SPARKS, TEHAN & RYLEY, P.C. (AV)

7503 First Street, 85251-4573
Telephone: 602-949-1339
Fax: 602-949-7587

Joe P. Sparks   Kevin T. Tehan
John H. Ryley

References: Bank One, Arizona, Trust Department; Northern Trust Bank of Arizona, N.A.; First Interstate Bank of Arizona.

For full biographical listings, see the Martindale-Hubbell Law Directory

STOCKTON & HING, P.A. (AV)

Deauville Building, 6609 North Scottsdale Road, 85253
Telephone: 602-951-0882
Telecopier: 602-483-7721

Henderson Stockton (1892-1978)   Robert Ong Hing
Gregory Ong Hing

Representative Clients: Alliance of American Insurers; American Council of Life Insurance; Amica Mutual Insurance Company; Arizona Conference Corporation of Seventh-Day Adventists; Arizona Life & Disability Insurance Guaranty Fund; Arizona Property and Casualty Insurance Guaranty Fund; Chubb Life Insurance Co.; Equitable Insurance Services; Globe Life & Accident Insurance Co.; Great Republic Life Insurance Co.

For full biographical listings, see the Martindale-Hubbell Law Directory

---

SUN CITY, Maricopa Co.

RONALD F. LARSON, P.C. (AV)

9899 West Bell Road, Bldg. A, 85351
Telephone: 602-933-4055
Fax: 602-972-9855
Email: rflpc@aol.com

(See Next Column)

RONALD F. LARSON, P.C.—*Continued*

Ronald F. Larson

Representative Clients: Moore Chrysler Plymouth, Inc.; El Dorado Condo Assn.; Phoenix Foundation, Inc.; Masonic Fellowship Center, Inc.; Northwest Valley Automotive Group, L.L.C.

For full biographical listings, see the Martindale-Hubbell Law Directory

O'CONNOR, CAVANAGH, ANDERSON, KILLINGSWORTH & BESHEARS, A PROFESSIONAL ASSOCIATION (AV)

13250 North Del Webb Boulevard, Suite B, 85351-3053
Telephone: 602-263-2808
FAX: 602-933-3100
Email: firminfo@arizlaw.com
Phoenix, Arizona Office: One East Camelback Road, Suite 1100, 85012.
Telephone: 602-263-2400.
FAX: 602-263-2900.
Tucson, Arizona Office: O'Connor Cavanagh Molloy Jones, 33 N. Stone, Suite 2100, 85701, P.O. Box 2268, 85702.
Telephone: 520-622-3531.
FAX: 520-624-2816.
Nogales, Arizona Office: 1891 North Mastick Way, 85621.
Telephone: 520-761-4215.
FAX: 520-761-3505.

William C. Wahl, Jr.

For full biographical listings, see the Martindale-Hubbell Law Directory

---

TUCSON, * Pima Co.

DUFFIELD, MILLER, YOUNG, ADAMSON & ALFRED, P.C. (AV)

Suite 711, Transamerica Building, 177 North Church Avenue, 85701
Telephone: 520-792-1181
FAX: 520-792-2859
Green Valley, Arizona Office: 101-65 South La Canada, Green Valley Mall.
Telephone: 520-625-4404.
Fax: 520-625-4453.
La Paloma Office: La Paloma Corporate Center, 3573 East Sunrise Drive, Suite 115, Tucson, Arizona.
Telephone: 520-577-1135.
Fax: 520-577-1079.

Philip Hawley Smith	Thomas R. Althaus
Arthur H. Miller (1935-1995)	Richard Duffield
Larry R. Adamson	Eugene C. Gieseler
Samuel D. Alfred	K. Alexander Hobson

Michael C. Young

LEGAL SUPPORT PERSONNEL

Cynthia Sargent Althaus	Joan Shelton, CLA
Mary Jane Arnesen	Christine M. Smith
Katrina Hillman	Barbara L. Steimle
Elizabeth Kohl-Sturgeon	Elaine Webb

Representative Clients: San Xavier Rock & Materials; Community Water Company of Green Valley.
Insurance Company Clientele: State Farm Mutual Insurance Cos.; Automobile Club Insurance Co.; Colonial Penn Insurance Co.; Metropolitan Property & Liability Insurance Co.; National Indemnity Ins. Co.

For full biographical listings, see the Martindale-Hubbell Law Directory

GABROY, ROLLMAN & BOSSÉ, P.C. (AV)

Suite 201, 2195 East River Road, 85718
Telephone: 520-577-1300
Telefax: 520-577-0717

Steven L. Bossé	Ronald M. Lehman
Richard M. Rollman	Fred A. Farsjo
John Gabroy	Lyle D. Aldridge
	Ronna L. Fickbohm

Richard A. Brown

For full biographical listings, see the Martindale-Hubbell Law Directory

MUNGER AND MUNGER, P.L.C. (AV)

333 North Wilmot, Suite 300, 85711
Telephone: 520-721-1900
Fax: 520-747-1550
Northwest Tucson Office: 6700 N. Oracle Road, Suite 411, Tucson 85704.
Telephone: 520-797-7173.
Fax: 520-797-7178.

John F. Munger	Clark W. Munger (Resident, Northwest Tucson Office)

(See Next Column)

Philip Kimble	Joy Athena
Karen S. Haller	Robert K. Lewis
Susan Gaylord Willis	Craig Wisnom (Resident,
Mark Edward Chadwick	Northwest Tucson Office)

Thomas A. Denker

OF COUNSEL

Doris Bates (Resident, Northwest Tucson Office)

Representative Clients: Jones Intercable; The Nature Conservancy; Tucson Greyhound Park; Tucson Realty and Trust; Associated Dermatologists; Red Rock Cattle Co.; U.S Rentals, Inc.; Nor-Tec Inc.; Grapevine Canyon Ranch; The Winters Co.

For full biographical listings, see the Martindale-Hubbell Law Directory

DANIEL H. O'CONNELL, P.C. (AV)

Suite 510, 6245 East Broadway, 85711
Telephone: 520-790-2535
Telefax: 520-571-8148

Daniel H. O'Connell

Benjamin J. Burnside

OF COUNSEL

Rosanne F. Lapan

Representative Clients: Empire West Cos.; Southwest Energy, Inc.; Alban Medical Associates; Industrial Motor & Control, Inc.; Allergy Asthma Associates, P.C.
Reference: Bank of America.

For full biographical listings, see the Martindale-Hubbell Law Directory

LAW OFFICES OF SLOSSER, HUDGINS & STRUSE, P.L.C. (AV)

Suite 125, 3573 East Sunrise Drive, 85718
Telephone: 520-529-3280
Fax: 520-529-1047

Paul D. Slosser	Richard S. Hudgins
	Robert M. Struse

Caryn I. Tate

For full biographical listings, see the Martindale-Hubbell Law Directory

SNELL & WILMER, L.L.P. (AV)

1500 Norwest Tower, One South Church Avenue, 85701-1612
Telephone: 520-882-1200
Fax: 520-884-1294
Phoenix, Arizona Office: One Arizona Center, 85004-0001.
Telephone: 602-382-6000.
Fax: 602-382-6070.
Orange County Office: 1920 Main Street, Suite 1200, P.O. Box 57062, Irvine, California, 92619-7062.
Telephone: 714-253-2700
Fax: 714-955-2507.
Salt Lake City, Utah Office: Broadway Centre, 111 East Broadway, Suite 900, 84111- 1004.
Telephone: 801-237-1900.
Fax: 801-237-1950.

MEMBERS OF FIRM

John A. Robertson	Sandra S. Froman

Representative Clients: Transit Management, Inc.; Tucson Airport Authority; Allstate Insurance Co.; Bank One, Arizona, NA; Southern Pacific Railroad Co.; Ford Motor Co.; Chrysler Motors Corp.; Toyota Motor Sales, U.S.A., Inc.; BHP Copper, Inc.; Pinnacle West Capital Corp.; Safeway Inc.; Honeywell, Inc.; Wells Fargo Bank, N.A.

For full biographical listings, see the Martindale-Hubbell Law Directory

STOMPOLY, STROUD, GIDDINGS & GLICKSMAN, P.C. (AV)

1820 Citibank Tower, One South Church Avenue, 85702
Telephone: 520-628-8300
Telefax: 520-628-9948
Mailing Address: P.O. Box 190, Tucson, AZ, 85702-0190

John G. Stompoly	James L. Stroud
	Charles E. Giddings

For Complete List of Firm Personnel, See General Section

For full biographical listings, see the Martindale-Hubbell Law Directory

ARKANSAS

FORREST CITY, St. Francis Co.

BUTLER, HICKY & LONG (AV)

2216 North Washington Street, P.O. Box 989, 72335
Telephone: 501-633-4611
FAX: 501-633-6848

MEMBERS OF FIRM

Philip Hicky   Fletcher Long, Jr.

ASSOCIATES

Gary J. Mitchusson   Rita Reed Harris

Representative Clients: First National Bank of Eastern Arkansas; Southern Farm Bureau Insurance Cos.; United States Aviation Underwriters Group; National Aviation Underwriters; Hartford Accident and Indemnity Co.; Peoples Implement Co.

For full biographical listings, see the Martindale-Hubbell Law Directory

---

LITTLE ROCK, Pulaski Co.

ARNOLD, GROBMYER & HALEY, A PROFESSIONAL ASSOCIATION (AV)

875 Union National Plaza, 124 West Capitol Avenue, P.O. Box 70, 72203
Telephone: 501-376-1171
Fax: 501-375-3548

Charles D. McDaniel   Joe A. Polk
Beth Ann Long

OF COUNSEL

John H. Haley

For Complete List of Firm Personnel, See General Section

For full biographical listings, see the Martindale-Hubbell Law Directory

BARBER, McCASKILL, AMSLER, JONES & HALE, P.A. (AV)

2700 First Commercial Building, 400 West Capitol Avenue, 72201-3414
Telephone: 501-372-6175
Telecopier: 501-375-2802

Azro L. Barber (1885-1979)	Richard C. Kalkbrenner
Elbert A. Henry (1889-1966)	G. Spence Fricke
John B. Thurman (1912-1971)	Gail Ponder Gaines
Austin McCaskill, Sr.	Michael J. Emerson
Guy Amsler, Jr.	R. Kenny McCulloch
Glenn W. Jones	Tim A. Cheatham
Michael E. Hale	Joseph F. Kolb
John S. Cherry, Jr.	Scott Michael Strauss
Robert L. Henry, III	Derek J. Edwards
Micheal L. Alexander	Thomas E. Osment, Jr.
William H. Edwards, Jr.	Christopher Gomlicker

Attorneys for: Associated Aviation Underwriters; Canal Insurance Co.; Fireman's Fund Insurance Co.; General Motors Corp.; General Motors Acceptance Corp.; Hanover Insurance Co.; Home Insurance Co.; Royal Insurance; United States Fidelity & Guaranty Co.; Universal Underwriters Insurance Co.

For full biographical listings, see the Martindale-Hubbell Law Directory

GILL LAW FIRM, A PROFESSIONAL ASSOCIATION (AV)

3801 TCBY Tower, Capitol and Broadway, 72201
Telephone: 501-376-3800
Fax: 501-372-3359

Charles C. Owen (P.A.)

C. Tad Bohannon

For Complete List of Firm Personnel, See General Section

For full biographical listings, see the Martindale-Hubbell Law Directory

HOOVER & KOOISTRA (AV)

111 Center Street, 11th Floor, 72201-4445
Telephone: 501-376-8500
Facsimile: 501-372-3255

MEMBERS OF FIRM

Paul W. Hoover, Jr.   John Kooistra, III
Max C. Mehlburger

For full biographical listings, see the Martindale-Hubbell Law Directory

---

PLASTIRAS, HYDEN & MIRON (AV)

A Partnership of Professional Associations
200 Louisiana, 72201
Telephone: 501-376-8222
Fax: 501-376-7047
1-800-467-8297
Hot Springs Village, Arkansas Office: Village Square, Suite "G", 4501 North Highway 7.
Telephone: 501-984-6366.
Fax: 501-984-6366. 1-800-467-8297.
Pine Bluff, Arkansas Office: 620 South Laurel.
Telephone: 501-536-8222. 1-800-467-8297.

MEMBERS OF FIRM

George N. Plastiras (P.A.)   James W. Hyden (P.A.)
Philip Miron (P.A.)

OF COUNSEL

James F. Goodhart

ASSOCIATES

Lyle D. Foster   Anthony A. Hilliard

For full biographical listings, see the Martindale-Hubbell Law Directory

ROSE LAW FIRM, A PROFESSIONAL ASSOCIATION (AV)

120 East Fourth Street, 72201
Telephone: 501-375-9131
Telecopy: 501-375-1309

W. Wilson Jones	Ronald M. Clark
William E. Bishop	David A. Smith
C. Brantly Buck	James L. Harris
	Clay H. Davis

COUNSEL

J. Gaston Williamson   W. Dane Clay

Bryant K. Cranford   Craig S. Lair

Representative Clients: ALLTEL Corporation; Acxiom Corporation; Arkansas Association of Bank Holding Cos.; Boatmen's Trust Company of Arkansas; Winthrop Rockefeller Foundation; Mercantile Bank of Central Arkansas; Tyson Foods, Inc.

For Complete List of Firm Personnel, See General Section

For full biographical listings, see the Martindale-Hubbell Law Directory

WALKER & BLACK (AV)

1000 West Third Street, P.O. Box 3780, 72203-3780
Telephone: 501-376-2382
Fax: 501-376-3352

MEMBERS OF FIRM

W. J. Walker   Kendell R. Black

Reference: First Commercial Bank.

For full biographical listings, see the Martindale-Hubbell Law Directory

---

CALIFORNIA

ARCADIA, Los Angeles Co.

HELMS, HANRAHAN & MYERS (AV)

Suite 685 Towne Centre Building, 150 North Santa Anita Avenue, 91006
Telephone: 818-445-1177
Email: helmsj@aol.com

James R. Helms, Jr.   James J. Hanrahan
Sterling E. Myers

LEGAL SUPPORT PERSONNEL

PARALEGALS

Michelle L. Upp   Josephine Phillips

Reference: Bank of America National Trust & Savings Assn. (Arcadia Branch).

For full biographical listings, see the Martindale-Hubbell Law Directory

---

BAKERSFIELD, Kern Co.

ELDON R. HUGIE (AV)

841 Mohawk Street, Suite 140, 93309
Telephone: 805-328-0200
Fax: 805-328-0204

Representative Clients: Tri-Fanucchi Farms, Inc.; Aquaculture Enterprises; Kern College Land Co.; Swanson Trusts.
References: Valliwide Bank (Bakersfield Main Branch).

For full biographical listings, see the Martindale-Hubbell Law Directory

Bakersfield—Continued

KLEIN, WEGIS, DeNATALE, GOLDNER & MUIR, LLP (AV)

A Partnership including Professional Corporations
(Formerly Di Giorgio, Davis, Klein, Wegis, Duggan & Friedman)
ARCO Tower, 4550 California Avenue, Second Floor, P.O. Box
11172, 93389-1172
Telephone: 805-395-1000
Telecopier: 805-326-0418
Email: kwdgm@kwdgm.com

MEMBERS OF FIRM
Anthony J. Klein (Inc.)   Claude P. Kimball
ASSOCIATE
Kevin C. Findley

Representative Clients: Bank of America; Great Western Bank; Mojave Pipeline Co.; Transamerican Title Insurance Co.; Dean Whittier Reynolds, Inc.; California Republic Bank; San Joaquin Bank; Nahama & Weagant Energy Co.; Freymiller Trucking, Inc.; Westinghouse Electric Co.

For Complete List of Firm Personnel, See General Section

For full biographical listings, see the Martindale-Hubbell Law Directory

---

BEVERLY HILLS, Los Angeles Co.

HOCHMAN, SALKIN AND DeROY, A PROFESSIONAL CORPORATION (AV)

9150 Wilshire Boulevard Suite 300, 90212-3414
Telephone: 310-281-3200; 273-1181
Fax: 310-859-1430

Bruce I. Hochman   Charles P. Rettig
Avram Salkin   Dennis Perez
          Steven R. Toscher
OF COUNSEL
George DeRoy

Stuart A. Simon   Michael W. Popoff
          Frederic J. Adam

Reference: Union Bank of California.

For full biographical listings, see the Martindale-Hubbell Law Directory

---

SAMUEL D. INGHAM, III (AV)

Suite 830, 8383 Wilshire Boulevard, 90211-2407
Telephone: 213-651-5980
FAX: 213-651-5725
Email: sdiesq@aol.com

For full biographical listings, see the Martindale-Hubbell Law Directory

---

TURNER, GERSTENFELD, WILK, AUBERT & YOUNG, LLP (AV)

Formerly Turner, Gerstenfeld, Wilk & Tigerman
Suite 510, 8383 Wilshire Boulevard, 90211
Telephone: 213-653-3900
Facsimile: 213-653-3021

MEMBERS OF FIRM
Gerald F. Gerstenfeld   Linda Wight Mazur
OF COUNSEL
Bert Z. Tigerman

For Complete List of Firm Personnel, See General Section

For full biographical listings, see the Martindale-Hubbell Law Directory

---

BURBANK, Los Angeles Co.

ALVIN N. LOSKAMP A LAW CORPORATION (AV)

290 East Verdugo Avenue, Suite 103, 91502
Telephone: 818-846-9000
Fax: 818-843-1441

Alvin N. Loskamp

References: Wells Fargo Bank, Glenoaks Branch, Burbank; Highland Savings & Loan, Burbank.

For full biographical listings, see the Martindale-Hubbell Law Directory

---

CARMEL, Monterey Co.

IAN D. McPHAIL A PROFESSIONAL CORPORATION (AV)

Villa Carmel, Suite 4, Mission at Fourth, P.O. Box 2734, 93921
Telephone: 408-625-4135
Telecopier: 408-625-4155
Santa Cruz, California Office: 331 Soquel Avenue, 95062.
Telephone: 408-427-2363.
Telecopier: 408-427-0511.

(See Next Column)

Ian D. McPhail

References: Comerica Bank; Home Savings; Coast Commercial Bank.

For full biographical listings, see the Martindale-Hubbell Law Directory

---

CHULA VISTA, San Diego Co.

ATHERTON & ALLEN (AV)

210 Towne Centre Professional Building, 345 "F" Street, 91910
Telephone: 619-420-6869

MEMBERS OF FIRM
Harvey H. Atherton (1881-1972)   Keith Atherton (Retired)
          David R. Allen

For full biographical listings, see the Martindale-Hubbell Law Directory

---

COSTA MESA, Orange Co.

HENRY J. COOPERSMITH (AV)

611 Anton Boulevard, Suite 1110, 92626
Telephone: 714-433-7340
Fax: 714-436-6109

For full biographical listings, see the Martindale-Hubbell Law Directory

---

RUTAN & TUCKER, LLP (AV)

A Partnership including Professional Corporations
611 Anton Boulevard, Suite 1400, P.O. Box 1950, 92626
Telephone: 714-641-5100; 213-625-7586
Telecopier: 714-546-9035
Email: rutan&tucker@mcimail.com *URL:* http://www.rutan.com

MEMBER OF FIRM
Paul Frederic Marx
ASSOCIATE
James S. Weisz
OF COUNSEL
David J. Garibaldi III

For Complete List of Firm Personnel, See General Section

For full biographical listings, see the Martindale-Hubbell Law Directory

---

ENCINO, Los Angeles Co.

ALPERT, BARR AND GROSS, A PROFESSIONAL LAW CORPORATION (AV)

Encino Office Park I, Suite 300, 6345 Balboa Boulevard, 91316-1523
Telephone: 818-881-5000
Fax: 818-881-1150

Lee Kanon Alpert   Mark S. Blackman
Gary L. Barr   Michael N. Balikian
Lisa W. Glazener   Judith R. Simon
Mark P. Gross   Jack S. Mack
          OF COUNSEL
Charles M. Hughes   Leonard S. Levy (A Professional
                            Corporation)

For full biographical listings, see the Martindale-Hubbell Law Directory

---

ESCONDIDO, San Diego Co.

DOROTHY A. COLE (AV)

Town View Professional Centre, 215 South Hickory Street, Suite 224, 92025-4361
Telephone: 619-745-6313

For full biographical listings, see the Martindale-Hubbell Law Directory

---

*FRESNO,** Fresno Co.

BRUCE D. BICKEL (AV)

470 E. Herndon Avenue, Suite 203, 93720-2929
Telephone: 209-435-7575
Facsimile: 209-435-1735
Email: brucebickel@earthlink.net

For full biographical listings, see the Martindale-Hubbell Law Directory

---

DOWLING, AARON & KEELER, INCORPORATED (AV)

Suite 200, 6051 North Fresno Street, 93710
Telephone: 209-432-4500
Fax: 209-432-4590
Email: dowling-law.com

Michael D. Dowling   William J. Keeler, Jr.
Richard M. Aaron   John C. Ganahl

(See Next Column)

DOWLING, AARON & KEELER INCORPORATED, *Fresno—Continued*

OF COUNSEL

Morris M. Sherr

Reference: Wells Fargo Bank (Main).

For Complete List of Firm Personnel, See General Section

For full biographical listings, see the Martindale-Hubbell Law Directory

KIMBLE, MacMICHAEL & UPTON, A PROFESSIONAL CORPORATION (AV)

Fig Garden Financial Center, 5260 North Palm Avenue, Suite 221, P.O. Box 9489, 93792-9489
Telephone: 209-435-5500
Telecopier: 209-435-1500
Email: kmu@primenet.com

Joseph C. Kimble (1910-1972)	Robert H. Scribner
Thomas A. MacMichael (1920-1990)	Michael E. Moss
	Mark D. Miller
Jon Wallace Upton	Michael F. Tatham
Robert E. Bergin	W. Richard Lee
Jeffrey G. Boswell	D. Tyler Tharpe
Steven D. McGee	Sylvia Halkousis Coyle
Robert E. Ward	S. Brett Sutton
John P. Eleazarian	Michael J. Jurkovich

Douglas V. Thornton	Susan King Hatmaker
Robert William Branch	Lawrence J. Salisbury
Donald J. Pool	Daniel R. Foster

Meredith E. Allen

OF COUNSEL

Mary Ann Bluhm

For full biographical listings, see the Martindale-Hubbell Law Directory

PARICHAN, RENBERG, CROSSMAN & HARVEY, LAW CORPORATION (AV)

Suite 130, 2350 West Shaw Avenue, P.O. Box 9950, 93794-0950
Telephone: 209-431-6300
Fax: 209-432-1018

Harold A. Parichan	Stephen T. Knudsen
Charles L. Renberg	Larry C. Gollmer
Richard C. Crossman	Robert G. Eliason
Ima Jean Harvey	Steven M. McQuillan

Deborah A. Coe	Karen L. Lynch
Maureen P. Holford	Michael L. Renberg

Reference: Bank of America, Commercial Banking Office, Fresno, California.

For full biographical listings, see the Martindale-Hubbell Law Directory

---

GLENDALE, Los Angeles Co.

BAKER, OLSON, LeCROY & DANIELIAN, A LAW CORPORATION (AV)

144 North Brand Boulevard, P.O. Box 29062, 91209-9062
Telephone: 818-502-5600
Facsimile: 818-241-2653

Sheldon S. Baker	Charles L. LeCroy, III
Eric Olson	Arsen Danielian

Michael S. Simon

OF COUNSEL

John J. Jacobson

For full biographical listings, see the Martindale-Hubbell Law Directory

GILL AND BALDWIN (AV)

130 North Brand Boulevard Fourth Floor, 91203
Telephone: 818-500-7755; 213-245-3131
Fax: 818-242-4305

MEMBERS OF FIRM

Samuel S. Gill (1912-1965)	Joseph C. Malpasuto
John M. Carmack	Kirk S. MacDonald

OF COUNSEL

Ernest R. Baldwin

Representative Clients: Kasler Corp.; Bireley Foundation.
Reference: American West Bank.

For full biographical listings, see the Martindale-Hubbell Law Directory

GREENWALD, HOFFMAN & MEYER (AV)

500 North Brand Boulevard, Suite 920, 91203-1904
Telephone: 818-507-8100; 213-381-1131
Fax: 818-507-8484

(See Next Column)

MEMBERS OF FIRM

Guy Preston Greenwald, Jr. (1914-1984)	Donald M. Hoffman
	Lawrence F. Meyer
Raul M. Montes	

ASSOCIATE

Jeanne Burns-Haindel

References: Bank of America (Los Angeles and Pasadena Trust Offices); Northern Trust of California (Headquarters Office); Bank of America (Glendale Main Branch).

For full biographical listings, see the Martindale-Hubbell Law Directory

IRSFELD, IRSFELD & YOUNGER LLP (AV)

A Partnership including Professional Corporations
Suite 900, 100 West Broadway, 91210-1296
Telephone: 818-242-6859
Fax: 818-240-7728
Email: 104736.1745@compuserver.com

MEMBERS OF FIRM

James B. Irsfeld (1880-1966)	Peter J. Irsfeld (P.C.)
Kenneth C. Younger (1922-1996)	James J. Waldorf (P.C.)
	C. Phillip Jackson (P.C.)
John H. Brink (P.C.)	Norman H. Green (P.C.)

Kathryn E. Van Houten

ASSOCIATES

Peter C. Wright	Diane L. Walker

RETIRED

James B. Irsfeld, Jr.

Representative Clients: Lear Sieglar, Inc.; Chrysler Credit Corp.
References: First Interstate Bank (Glendale Main Office); Bank of Hollywood.

For full biographical listings, see the Martindale-Hubbell Law Directory

O'ROURKE, ALLAN & FONG (AV)

3rd Floor, 104 North Belmont, P.O. Box 10220, 91209-3220
Telephone: 818-247-4303
Fax: 818-247-1451

MEMBERS OF FIRM

Denis M. O'Rourke	Joan H. Allan
Roderick D. Fong	

ASSOCIATE

Denise Michelle O'Rourke

References: Verdugo Banking Co. (Glendale, California); Community Bank (Glendale, California).

For full biographical listings, see the Martindale-Hubbell Law Directory

---

INDIAN WELLS, Riverside Co.

DOUGLAS MARTIN A LAW CORPORATION (AV)

Wall Street West, 74-785 Highway 111, Suite 201, 92210
Telephone: 619-776-1377
Fax: 619-776-1380

Douglas Martin

LEGAL SUPPORT PERSONNEL

Carol A. Moreno

For full biographical listings, see the Martindale-Hubbell Law Directory

---

IRVINE, Orange Co.

GRECO, MOLLIS & O'HARA, A PROFESSIONAL CORPORATION (AV)

18400 Von Karman, Suite 500, 92612-1514
Telephone: 714-263-0600
Fax: 714-263-1513

Thomas A. Greco	Kevin O'Hara
Ronald A. Mollis	Charles A. Mollis

For full biographical listings, see the Martindale-Hubbell Law Directory

JACQUELINE M. JENSEN, INC. (AV)

18006 Sky Park Circle, Suite 109, 92614
Telephone: 714-261-0100
Fax: 714-261-0176

Jacqueline M. Jensen

For full biographical listings, see the Martindale-Hubbell Law Directory

PIVO & HALBREICH (AV)

1920 Main Street, Suite 800, 92714
Telephone: 714-253-2000

(See Next Column)

PIVO & HALBREICH—*Continued*

Kenneth R. Pivo
Eva S. Halbreich
Richard O. Schwartz
Mona Z. Hanna

Representative Clients: Harbor Regional Center; Developmental Disabilities Regional Center; South Central Los Angeles Regional Center; North Los Angeles County Regional Center; Far Northern Regional Center; Kern Regional Center and Related Entities.

For full biographical listings, see the Martindale-Hubbell Law Directory

---

SNELL & WILMER, L.L.P. (AV)

1920 Main Street, Suite 1200, 92614
Telephone: 714-253-2700
FAX: 714-955-2507
URL: http://www.swlaw.com
Phoenix, Arizona Office: One Arizona Center, 85004-0001.
Telephone: 602-382-6000.
Fax: 602-382-6070.
Tucson, Arizona Office: Norwest Tower, Suite 1500, One South Church Avenue, 85701-1612.
Telephone: 520-882-1200.
Fax: 520-884-1294.
Salt Lake City, Utah Office: Broadway Centre, 111 East Broadway, Suite 900, 84111-1004.
Telephone: 801-237-1900.
Fax: 801-237-1950.

MEMBER OF FIRM
David W. Evans (Resident)

For Complete List of Firm Personnel, See General Section

For full biographical listings, see the Martindale-Hubbell Law Directory

---

LAGUNA BEACH, Orange Co.

DONALD L. DROZD (AV)

401 Glenneyre Street, Suite H, 92651-2401
Telephone: 714-497-2453
Fax: 714-376-2618
Email: DDROZD@aol.com

For full biographical listings, see the Martindale-Hubbell Law Directory

---

LAGUNA HILLS, Orange Co.

NANCY BOXLEY TEPPER A PROFESSIONAL CORPORATION (AV)

24031 El Toro Road, Suite 130, 92653
Telephone: 714-830-6660
Fax: 714-830-6123

Nancy Boxley Tepper

For full biographical listings, see the Martindale-Hubbell Law Directory

---

LA JOLLA, San Diego Co.

FERGUSON, NEWBURN & WESTON, A PROFESSIONAL CORPORATION (AV)

Suite 260, 7777 Fay Avenue, 92037
Telephone: 619-454-4233
Facsimile: 619-454-3052

Keith M. Ferguson (1903-1965)
John L. Newburn
(Retired, 1989)
William E. Ferguson
David Weston

References: Union Bank (La Jolla Office); Scripps Bank (La Jolla Office).

For full biographical listings, see the Martindale-Hubbell Law Directory

---

LUCE, FORWARD, HAMILTON & SCRIPPS LLP (AV)

A Partnership including Professional Corporations
La Jolla Golden Triangle, 4275 Executive Square, Suite 800, 92037
Telephone: 619-535-2639
Fax: 619-453-2812
URL: http://www.luce.com
San Diego, California Office: 600 West Broadway, Suite 2600, 92101.
Telephone: 619-236-1414.
Fax: 619-232-8311.
Los Angeles, California Office: 777 South Figueroa, Suite 3600, 90017.
Telephone: 213-892-4992.
Fax: 213-892-7731.
San Francisco, California Office: 100 Bush Street, 20th Floor, 94104.
Telephone: 415-395-7900.
Fax: 415-395-7949.
New York, N.Y. Office: Citicorp Center, 153 East 53rd Street, 26th Floor, 10022.
Telephone: 212-754-1414.
Fax: 212-644-9727.
Chicago, Illinois Office: 180 North La Salle Street, Suite 1125, 60601.
Telephone: 312-641-0580.
Fax: 312-641-0380.

(See Next Column)

MEMBERS OF FIRM
Jack G. Charney
Robert J. Durham, Jr.
Daniel N. Riesenberg
Frederick R. Vandeveer
Mary F. Gillick

ASSOCIATES
Carol K. Kao
Philip J. Sullivan

For full biographical listings, see the Martindale-Hubbell Law Directory

---

LANCASTER, Los Angeles Co.

MARK E. THOMPSON A PROFESSIONAL CORPORATION (AV)

857 West Lancaster Boulevard, 93534
Telephone: 805-945-5868
Fax: 805-723-7089

Mark E. Thompson

Cynthia R. Pollock

Reference: Antelope Valley Bank, Lancaster, California.

For full biographical listings, see the Martindale-Hubbell Law Directory

---

LONG BEACH, Los Angeles Co.

SIMON, MCKINSEY, MILLER, ZOMMICK, SANDOR & DUNDAS, A LAW CORPORATION (AV)

2750 Bellflower Boulevard, 90815
Telephone: 310-421-9354
Facsimile: 310-420-6455
Irvine, California Office: Suite 670, 4199 Campus Drive.
Telephone: 714-856-1916.
Facsimile: 714-856-3834.

Harry J. Simon (1922-1977)
Thomas W. McKinsey
(1920-1990)
Arthur W. Miller (Retired)
Kenneth Zommick

David L. Sandor
Geraldine G. Sandor
(Resident, Irvine Office)
David G. Dundas
(Resident, Irvine Office)

Robert M. Stone
Carrie Block
(Resident, Irvine Office)

For full biographical listings, see the Martindale-Hubbell Law Directory

---

LOS ALTOS, Santa Clara Co.

MALOVOS & KONEVICH (AV)

Los Altos Plaza, 5150 El Camino Real, Suite A-22, 94022
Telephone: 415-988-9700
Facsimile: 415-988-9639

Marian Malovos Konevich
Robert W. Konevich

RETIRED FOUNDING PARTNER
Kenneth R. Malovos

For full biographical listings, see the Martindale-Hubbell Law Directory

---

LOS ANGELES,* Los Angeles Co.

ANTIN & TAYLOR (AV)

1875 Century Park East, Suite 700, 90067
Telephone: 310-788-2733
Fax: 310-788-0754
Email: mantin@ix.netcom.com

MEMBERS OF FIRM
Michael Antin
Michael L. Taylor

For full biographical listings, see the Martindale-Hubbell Law Directory

---

BARTON, KLUGMAN & OETTING (AV)

A Partnership including Professional Corporations
37th Floor, 333 South Grand Avenue, 90071-1599
Telephone: 213-621-4000
Telecopier: 213-625-1832
Newport Beach Office: Suite 700, 4400 MacArthur Boulevard, P.O. Box 2350, 92660.
Telephone: 714-752-7551.
Telecopier: 714-752-0288.

COUNSEL TO FIRM
Robert M. Barton *
Robert H. Klugman *
Richard F. Oetting *

MEMBERS OF FIRM
David F. Morgan *
William D. Herz *
Charles J. Schufreider *
Robert Louis Fisher *
Gilbert D. Jensen *
David J. Cartano *
Martin J. Spear
Tod V. Beebe *
Ronald R. St. John
Mark A. Newton *
Margot I. McLeay

(See Next Column)

BARTON, KLUGMAN & OETTING, *Los Angeles—Continued*

ASSOCIATES

Barbara W. G. Crowley   Reiko L. Furuta
Jaleen Nelson

References: The Bank of California (Southern California Headquarters); Wells Fargo Bank, N.A. (Wells Fargo Center, Los Angeles).
*Denotes a lawyer whose Professional Corporation is a member of the partnership or is Counsel to the Firm

For full biographical listings, see the Martindale-Hubbell Law Directory

---

BERMAN, BLANCHARD, MAUSNER & RESSER, A LAW CORPORATION (AV)

4727 Wilshire Boulevard, Suite 500, 90010
Telephone: 213-965-1200
Telecopier: 213-965-1919
Email: BBMR@ix.netcom.com

Laurence M. Berman   Jeffrey N. Mausner
Lonnie C. Blanchard, III   Bernard M. Resser

Paul A. Hoffman   Cary P. Ocon
Eric Levinrad   Lisé Hamilton

For full biographical listings, see the Martindale-Hubbell Law Directory

---

MARTIN H. BLANK, JR. (AV)

11755 Wilshire Boulevard, Suite 1400, 90025-1520
Telephone: 310-477-5455
Fax: 310-444-9203
Email: marty@general.net

For full biographical listings, see the Martindale-Hubbell Law Directory

---

LAW OFFICES OF TOBI J. CHINSKI (AV)

1801 Century Park East, Suite 2500, 90067
Telephone: 310-286-6767
Fax: 310-286-1633

For full biographical listings, see the Martindale-Hubbell Law Directory

---

CLARK & TREVITHICK, A PROFESSIONAL CORPORATION (AV)

800 Wilshire Boulevard, 12th Floor, 90017
Telephone: 213-629-5700
Telecopier: 213-624-9441
San Francisco, California Office: 456 Montgomery Street, 20th Floor.
Telephone: 415-288-6520.
Fax: 415-398-2820.

Kevin P. Fiore   Dean I. Friedman

References: Wells Fargo Bank (Los Angeles Main Office); National Bank of California.

For Complete List of Firm Personnel, See General Section

For full biographical listings, see the Martindale-Hubbell Law Directory

---

DARLING, HALL & RAE (AV)

777 South Figueroa, 37th Floor, 90017
Telephone: 213-627-8104
Fax: 213-627-7795
Email: 71555.1466@Compuserve.com

MEMBERS OF FIRM

Hugh W. Darling (1901-1986)   Donald Keith Hall (1918-1984)
Edward S. Shattuck (1901-1965)   Matthew S. Rae, Jr.
George Gaylord Gute   Richard L. Stack
  (1922-1981)   Edwin Freston

OF COUNSEL

John L. Flowers

Reference: City National Bank (Pershing Square Office, Los Angeles, California).

For full biographical listings, see the Martindale-Hubbell Law Directory

---

DEMETRIOU, DEL GUERCIO, SPRINGER & MOYER, LLP (AV)

801 South Grand Avenue, 10th Floor, 90017
Telephone: 213-624-8407
Telecopy: 213-624-0174
Email: ddsm@juno.com *URL:* http://www.ddsm.com

MEMBER OF FIRM

Angela Shanahan

OF COUNSEL

Ronald J. Del Guercio

Reference: Bank of America, L.A. Main Office, Los Angeles, Calif.

For full biographical listings, see the Martindale-Hubbell Law Directory

---

KENNETH L. GOLDMAN PROFESSIONAL CORPORATION (AV)

1801 Century Park East, Suite 2222, 90067
Telephone: 310-552-1720
Fax: 312-552-7938

Kenneth L. Goldman

For full biographical listings, see the Martindale-Hubbell Law Directory

---

GREENBERG GLUSKER FIELDS CLAMAN & MACHTINGER LLP (AV)

21st Floor, 1900 Avenue of the Stars (Century City), 90067
Telephone: 310-553-3610
Fax: 310-553-0687

MEMBERS OF FIRM

Jon J. Gallo   Martin H. Webster
Robert E. Bennett, Jr.   Arnold D. Kahn

Reference: Wells Fargo Bank, 1801 Century Park East, Los Angeles, CA 90067.

For Complete List of Firm Personnel, See General Section

For full biographical listings, see the Martindale-Hubbell Law Directory

---

HANNA AND MORTON (AV)

A Partnership including Professional Corporations
Seventeenth Floor, Wilshire-Grand Building, 600 Wilshire
  Boulevard, 90017
Telephone: 213-628-7131
Facsimile: 213-623-3379

MEMBER OF FIRM

Michael I. Blaylock

OF COUNSEL

William N. Greene

For Complete List of Firm Personnel, See General Section

For full biographical listings, see the Martindale-Hubbell Law Directory

---

ROBERT M. HIMROD (AV)

1055 Wilshire Boulevard, Suite 1890, 90017
Telephone: 213-250-5722
Fax: 213-250-1894
Email: trhimrod@aol.com

ASSOCIATE

Thomas E. Himrod

Representative Clients: La Mirada Water Co.; Precision Coil Spring Co., Inc.

For full biographical listings, see the Martindale-Hubbell Law Directory

---

HOLLEY & GALEN (AV)

800 South Figueroa, Suite 1100, 90017
Telephone: 213-629-1880
Fax: 213-895-0363

MEMBERS OF FIRM

Albert J. Galen (Retired)   W. Michael Johnson
A. Steven Brown

ASSOCIATES

Debra Burchard Coffeen   Charles A. Jordan

For Complete List of Firm Personnel, See General Section

For full biographical listings, see the Martindale-Hubbell Law Directory

---

JOHNSON, POULSON, COONS & SLATER (AV)

10880 Wilshire Boulevard, Suite 1800, 90024
Telephone: 310-475-0611
Telecopier: 310-475-0143

MEMBERS OF FIRM

Jonathan E. Johnson   Lynn O. Poulson (Mr.)
Michael H. Coons

OF COUNSEL

Martin R. Slater

For full biographical listings, see the Martindale-Hubbell Law Directory

---

LOEB & LOEB LLP (AV)

A Limited Liability Partnership including Professional Corporations
Suite 1800, 1000 Wilshire Boulevard, 90017-2475
Telephone: 213-688-3400
Facsimile: 213-688-3460; 688-3461; 688-3462
Century City, California Office: Suite 2200, 10100 Santa Monica
Boulevard, Los Angeles, 90067-4164.
Telephone: 310-282-2000.
Facsimile: 310-282-2191; 282-2192.
New York, N.Y. Office: 345 Park Avenue, 10154-0037.
Telephone: 212-407-4000.
Facsimile: 212-407-4990.

(See Next Column)

LOEB & LOEB LLP—*Continued*

Washington, D.C. Office: Suite 601, 2100 M Street N.W., 20037-1207.
Telephone: 202-223-5700.
Facsimile: 202-223-5704.
Nashville, Tennessee Office: 45 Music Square West, 37203-3205.
Telephone: 615-749-8300;
Facsimile: 615-749-8308.
Rome, Italy Office: Piazza Digione 1, 00197.
Telephone: 011-396-808-8456.
Facsimile: 011-396-808-8288.

MEMBERS OF FIRM

Andrew S. Garb (A P.C.)	Stanford K. Rubin (A P.C.)
Jerome L. Levine	(Century City Office)
(New York City Office)	Bruce M. Stiglitz (A P.C.)
Jeffrey M. Loeb	William P. Wasserman (A P.C.)
David C. Nelson	Bruce J. Wexler
	(New York City Office)

OF COUNSEL

James R. Birnberg	Bernard M. Silbert
Abraham S. Guterman	(Century City Office)
(New York City Office)	Harvey L. Silbert
Arthur A. Segall	(Century City Office)
(New York City Office)	John S. Warren (A P.C.)
Alan D. Shulman	
(Century City Office)	

For Complete List of Firm Personnel, See General Section

For full biographical listings, see the Martindale-Hubbell Law Directory

LUND LAW CORPORATION (AV)

1901 Avenue of the Stars, Twentieth Floor, 90067
Telephone: 310-286-7485
Fax: 310-286-7486
Email: XLNT706@aol.com

Eric James Lund
OF COUNSEL
Theodore V. Kreps

For full biographical listings, see the Martindale-Hubbell Law Directory

MAHONEY, COPPENRATH, JAFFE & PEARSON LLP (AV)

A Partnership including Professional Corporations
2049 Century Park East, Suite 2480, 90067-3283
Telephone: 310-557-1919
Telecopier: 310-277-6536

MEMBERS OF FIRM

James E. Mahoney (P.C.)	Ronald C. Pearson
Walter G. Coppenrath, Jr.,	Daryl G. Parker
(P.C.)	Charles L. Grotts
Howard M. Jaffe (P.C.)	Arthur L. Martin

OF COUNSEL
Gerald Lee Tahajian

Reference: First Professional Bank, Santa Monica, California.

For full biographical listings, see the Martindale-Hubbell Law Directory

MINTON, MINTON AND RAND LLP (AV)

510 West Sixth Street, 90014
Telephone: 213-624-9394
Fax: 213-624-9323

MEMBERS OF FIRM
Carl W. Minton (1902-1974)	Carl Minton
	David E. Rand

Reference: Bank of America National Trust & Savings Assn. (Seventh & Flower Office, Los Angeles, Calif.).

For full biographical listings, see the Martindale-Hubbell Law Directory

MITCHELL, SILBERBERG & KNUPP LLP (AV)

A Partnership including Professional Corporations
11377 West Olympic Boulevard, 90064
Telephone: 310-312-2000
Fax: 310-312-3100

MEMBER OF FIRM
Allan B. Cutrow (A Professional Corporation)
OF COUNSEL
Jeffrey B. Wheeler
ASSOCIATES
Jeffrey K. Eisen	Jeannette Hahm
	Karl J. de Costa

References: Wells Fargo Bank, N.A.; Merrill, Lynch.

For Complete List of Firm Personnel, See General Section

For full biographical listings, see the Martindale-Hubbell Law Directory

FLOYD H. NORRIS (AV)

Suite 405 Norris Building, 714 South Hill Street, 90014
Telephone: 213-624-4088
FAX: 213-624-4080

References: Bank of America; Wells Fargo.

For full biographical listings, see the Martindale-Hubbell Law Directory

OLINCY & KARPEL (AV)

10960 Wilshire Boulevard, Suite 1111, 90024-3782
Telephone: 310-478-1213
FAX: 310-478-1215

MEMBERS OF FIRM
George R. Olincy (1904-1982)	J. Dan Olincy
	Philip Karpel

ASSOCIATE
Joyce Riley

For full biographical listings, see the Martindale-Hubbell Law Directory

O'MELVENY & MYERS LLP (AV)

400 South Hope Street, 90071-2899
Telephone: 213-669-6000
Cable Address: "Moms"
Facsimile: 213-669-6407
Email: omminfo@omm.com
Century City, California Office: 1999 Avenue of the Stars, 90067-6035.
Telephone: 310-553-6700.
Facsimile: 310-246-6779.
Newport Beach, California Office: 610 Newport Center Drive, 92660-6429.
Telephone: 714-760-9600.
Cable Address: "Moms".
Facsimile: 714-669-6994.
San Francisco, California Office: Embarcadero Center West Tower, 275 Battery Street, 94111-3305.
Telephone: 415-984-8700.
Facsimile: 415-984-8701.
New York, New York Office: Citicorp Center, 153 East 53rd Street, 10022-4611.
Telephone: 212-326-2000.
Facsimile: 212-326-2061.
Washington, D.C. Office: 555 13th Street, N.W., 20004-1109.
Telephone: 202-383-5300.
Cable Address: "Moms".
Facsimile: 202-383-5414.
London, England Office: 10 Finsbury Square, London, EC2A 1LA.
Telephone: 0171-256-8451.
Facsimile: 0171-638-8205.
Tokyo, Japan Office: Sanbancho KB-6 Building, 6 Sanbancho, Chiyoda-ku, Tokyo 102, Japan.
Telephone: 03-3239-2900.
Facsimile: 03-3239-2432.
Hong Kong Office: Suite 1905, Peregrine Tower, Lippo Centre, 89 Queensway, Central, Hong Kong.
Telephone: 852-2523-8266.
Facsimile: 852-2522-1760.
Shanghai, Peoples Republic of China Office: Shanghai International Trade Centre, Suite 2011, 2200 Yan An Road West, Shanghai, 200335, PRC.
Telephone: 86-21-6219-5363.
Facsimile: 86-21-6275-4949.

PARTNER
David D. Watts

For Complete List of Firm Personnel, See General Section

For full biographical listings, see the Martindale-Hubbell Law Directory

OSTROVE, KRANTZ & OSTROVE, A PROFESSIONAL CORPORATION (AV)

(Successor To: Ostrove and Lancer, A Professional Corporation; David Ostrove, A Professional Corporation)
5757 Wilshire Boulevard, Suite 535, 90036-3600
Telephone: 213-939-3400
Fax: 213-939-3500
Email: OSTROVE@AOL.COM

David Ostrove	David S. Krantz
	Kenneth E. Ostrove

Reference: First Business Bank.

For full biographical listings, see the Martindale-Hubbell Law Directory

POPKOFF & STERN (AV)

501 Shatto Place, Suite 100, 90020-1713
Telephone: 213-389-1358; 389-2174
Fax: 213-380-4154
Palm Springs, California Office: 225 South Civic Drive, Suite 212, 92262.
Telephone: 619-322-8041.

(See Next Column)

POPKOFF & STERN, *Los Angeles—Continued*

MEMBERS OF FIRM

Burton R. Popkoff   Gary N. Stern

RODI, POLLOCK, PETTKER, GALBRAITH & CAHILL, A LAW CORPORATION (AV)

Suite 400 801 South Grand Avenue, 90017
Telephone: 213-895-4900; 680-0823
Telecopiers: 213-895-4921; 895-4922; 895-4750

Karl B. Rodi (1908-1982)	Elizabeth B. Blakely
John D. Cahill	Robert C. Norton
John D. Pettker	John F. Cermak, Jr.
Daniel C. Bond (1942-1977)	Tim G. Ceperley
William R. Christian	Coralie Kupfer
Henry P. Pramov, Jr.	Cris K. O'Neall
Robert A. Yahiro	John S. Cha

Scott E. Adamson

Sonja A. Inglin	Richard Nessary
Thomas J. Yoo	Mark McCleary

OF COUNSEL

John P. Pollock   Margaret Rosenthal

For full biographical listings, see the Martindale-Hubbell Law Directory

SHIOTANI & INOUYE (AV)

11100 Santa Monica Boulevard, Suite 1820, 90025
Telephone: 310-575-3688
Telecopier: 310-575-4095

MEMBERS OF FIRM

Barney B. Shiotani   Lawrence G. Inouye

ASSOCIATE

Nicole Grattan Pearson

LEGAL SUPPORT PERSONNEL

Gabriela Velasquez (Paralegal)

References: First Los Angeles Bank (Airport Office); Bank of California.

For full biographical listings, see the Martindale-Hubbell Law Directory

SIMMONS, RITCHIE & SEGAL (AV)

555 South Flower Street Suite 4640, 90071
Telephone: 213-624-7391
FAX: 213-489-7559

MEMBERS OF FIRM

Frederick L. Simmons   Jonathan L. Simmons

William D. Segal

OF COUNSEL

Graham A. Ritchie   Lee E. Stark

Michael W. Roberts

Reference: South Bay Bank, Los Angeles.

For full biographical listings, see the Martindale-Hubbell Law Directory

STEPHENS, BERG & LASATER, A PROFESSIONAL CORPORATION (AV)

1055 West Seventh Street, Twenty-Ninth Floor, 90017
Telephone: 213-629-3111
Telecopy: 213-629-2302; 213-624-4734

Lawrence M. Berg (1947-1995)	Frederick A. Clark
R. Wicks Stephens II	Joel A. Goldman
Richard W. Lasater II	C. Stephen Davis
Mark G. Ancel	Kenneth A. Feinfield
Dudley M. Lang	Jean-Paul Menard
Joseph F. Butler	Michael J. Kaminsky

John A. Dragonette

OF COUNSEL

Louis R. Baker   J. Lane Tilson

For full biographical listings, see the Martindale-Hubbell Law Directory

WEINSTOCK, MANION, REISMAN, SHORE & NEUMANN, A LAW CORPORATION (AV)

Suite 800, 1888 Century Park East (Century City), 90067
Telephone: 310-553-8844
Los Angeles: 213-879-4481
Fax: 310-553-5165

Harold Weinstock	Martin A. Neumann
Louis A. Reisman	Marc L. Sallus
Sussan H. Shore	Robert E. Strauss

Susan Abraham

Gordon H. Einstein

(See Next Column)

OF COUNSEL

Gary M. Borofsky   M. Neil Solarz

References: City National Bank (Century City); Wells Fargo Bank (Beverly Hills Main Office); Security Pacific National Bank (Century Plaza Office); Sanwa Bank California.

For full biographical listings, see the Martindale-Hubbell Law Directory

WILLIAMS AND BALLAS (AV)

1800 Century Park East, Suite 510, 90067
Telephone: 310-557-8383
Fax: 310-557-8380
San Francisco, California Office: 160 Sansome Street, Suite 1200.
Telephone: 415-296-9904.
Fax: 415-981-0898.

MEMBERS OF FIRM

Lawrence D. Williams   Stephen B. Ballas

OF COUNSEL

Stanley P. Graham

ASSOCIATE

Melissa Hamilton

For full biographical listings, see the Martindale-Hubbell Law Directory

STUART D. ZIMRING (AV)

12650 Riverside Drive (North Hollywood), 91607-3492
Telephone: 818-755-4848
Fax: 818-508-0181

ASSOCIATE

Dena L. Klotz

Representative Clients: TransWorld Bank; Cytec Industries Inc.; Huntington Palisades Property Owners Assn.; Buff, Smith & Hensman Architects, Inc.

For full biographical listings, see the Martindale-Hubbell Law Directory

LOS OSOS, San Luis Obispo Co.

GEORGE, GALLO & SULLIVAN, A LAW CORPORATION (AV)

2238 Bayview Heights Drive, P.O. Box 6129, 93402
Telephone: 805-528-3351
Telecopier: 805-528-5598
Email: jgeorgeggs@aol.com
San Luis Obispo, California Office: 694 Santa Rosa, P.O. Box 12710.
Telephone: 805-544-3351.
Facsimile: 805-528-5598.

J. K. George

Anne C. Cyr

Reference: Mid State Bank, Los Osos, California.

For full biographical listings, see the Martindale-Hubbell Law Directory

MANHATTAN BEACH, Los Angeles Co.

STEINBERG BARNESS GLASGOW & FOSTER LLP (AV)

1334 Park View Avenue, Suite 100, 90266
Telephone: 310-546-5838
Telecopier: 310-546-5630
Email: SGBF@ix.netcom.com

MEMBERS OF FIRM

Alex Steinberg	Jordan G. Barness
Daniel I. Barness	Paul J. Laurin
Donna Glasgow	Shannon M. Foley
(Not admitted in CA)	Richard L. Weiner
Douglas B. Foster	William R. (Randy) Kirkpatrick

Jeffrey Michael Lee

OF COUNSEL

Roanld D. Harari (Not admitted in CA)

References: Home Bank; Imperial Bank; Citizens Commerical Trust & Savings Bank; Bank of America.

For full biographical listings, see the Martindale-Hubbell Law Directory

MENLO PARK, San Mateo Co.

ROBIN D. FAISANT (AV)

1550 El Camino Real, Suite 220, 94025
Telephone: 415-328-6333
Telecopier: 415-324-1031

For full biographical listings, see the Martindale-Hubbell Law Directory

MODESTO,* Stanislaus Co.

BRUNN & FLYNN, A PROFESSIONAL CORPORATION (AV)

928 12th Street, P.O. Box 3366, 95353
Telephone: 209-521-2133
Fax: 209-521-7584
Email: brunnfly@ix.netcom.com

Charles K. Brunn	Gerald E. Brunn
Timothy T. Flynn	Roger S. Matzkind

Michael G. Donovan   Andrew N. Eshoo

For full biographical listings, see the Martindale-Hubbell Law Directory

MONTEREY, Monterey Co.

GEORGE R. WALKER (AV)

5th Floor, Professional Building, 215 West Franklin Street, P.O. Box Law, 93942
Telephone: 408-649-1100
Fax: 408-649-6805

ASSOCIATES
Ute M. Isbill   Kathleen Llewellyn

Representative Clients: A. F. Victor Foundation, Carmel, California; The Carmel Foundation, Carmel, California; Robert Louis Stevenson School, Pebble Beach, California; Brintons Consolidated, Inc.; C & E Farms, Inc.; The Mildred Hitchcock Huff Charitable Trust.

For full biographical listings, see the Martindale-Hubbell Law Directory

MORRO BAY, San Luis Obispo Co.

OGLE & MERZON (AV)

A Partnership including a Professional Corporation
770 Morro Bay Boulevard, P.O. Box 720, 93443-0720
Telephone: 805-772-7353
Fax: 805-772-7713
San Luis Obispo, California Office: P.O. Box 1855, 93406.
Telephone: 805-543-0295.

Charles E. Ogle (A Professional   James B. Merzon
Corporation)

Charles G. Kirschner   Charles Patrick Ogle

For full biographical listings, see the Martindale-Hubbell Law Directory

MOUNTAIN VIEW, Santa Clara Co.

LUCE & QUILLINAN (AV)

444 Castro Street, Suite 900, 94041-2073
Telephone: 415-969-4000
FAX: 415-969-6953

MEMBERS OF FIRM
James G. Luce   James V. Quillinan
Melissa C. Johnson
ASSOCIATE
Sally F. Berry

For full biographical listings, see the Martindale-Hubbell Law Directory

NEWPORT BEACH, Orange Co.

PETER C. BRADFORD (AV)

Suite 1250, 610 Newport Center Drive, 92660
Telephone: 714-640-1800
FAX: 714-721-9923

References: Wells Fargo Bank; Bank of America, Trust Department.

For full biographical listings, see the Martindale-Hubbell Law Directory

THEODORE M. HANKIN (AV)

Suite 900, One Newport Place, 92660
Telephone: 714-752-8840
FAX: 714-851-1732

For full biographical listings, see the Martindale-Hubbell Law Directory

THOMAS W. HENDERSON (AV)

5030 Campus Drive, 92660
Telephone: 714-252-8544
Fax: 714-252-8548

Reference: Bank of America, Westcliff Branch, Newport Beach.

For full biographical listings, see the Martindale-Hubbell Law Directory

MILLAR, HODGES & BEMIS (AV)

One Newport Place, Suite 900, 1301 Dove Street, 92660-2448
Telephone: 714-752-7722
FAX: 714-752-6131

MEMBERS OF FIRM
Richard W. Millar, Jr.   Kenneth R. Hodges
Larry R. Bemis
ASSOCIATE
David A. St. Clair

Reference: Manufacturers Bank, Newport Beach, California.

For full biographical listings, see the Martindale-Hubbell Law Directory

EDWARD H. STONE, P.C. (AV)

270 Newport Center Drive, 92660-7535
Telephone: 714-640-2812
Fax: 714-640-9951

Edward H. Stone

For full biographical listings, see the Martindale-Hubbell Law Directory

MICHAEL V. VOLLMER (AV)

4340 Campus Drive, Suite 100, 92660-1892
Telephone: 714-852-0833
Fax: 714-852-8731
Email: mvollmer@aol.com

References: Bank of America NT&SA (Newport Beach, California); First American Trust Co. (Newport Beach, California).

For full biographical listings, see the Martindale-Hubbell Law Directory

NORTH HOLLYWOOD, Los Angeles Co.

F. BENTLEY MOONEY, JR. A LAW CORPORATION (AV)

4605 Lankershim Boulevard, Suite 718, 91602
Telephone: 818-769-4221
213-877-3902
FAX: 818-769-5002

F. Bentley Mooney, Jr.

For full biographical listings, see the Martindale-Hubbell Law Directory

OAKLAND,* Alameda Co.

AIKEN, KRAMER & CUMMINGS, INCORPORATED (AV)

Suite 550 Ordway Building, One Kaiser Plaza, 94612
Telephone: 510-834-6800
Fax: 510-834-9017
Email: aikenkrame@aol.com

Benj. R. Aiken (1879-1955)	John A. Harkavy
Bauer E. Kramer (Retired)	Elizabeth M. Engh
Benj. R. Aiken, Jr. (Retired)	Matthew F. Graham
Fred V. Cummings (Retired)	Steven J. Cramer
	Richard A. Sipos

OF COUNSEL
Russell L. Barlow   Bruce G. Herold
Michael A. Coan

Ellen Suzanne Wyatt   Michael S. Treppa

Reference: Union Bank of California, Oakland, California.

For full biographical listings, see the Martindale-Hubbell Law Directory

HARDIN, COOK, LOPER, ENGEL & BERGEZ (AV)

1999 Harrison Street, 18th Floor, 94612-3541
Telephone: 510-444-3131
Telecopier: 510-839-7940

MEMBERS OF FIRM
John C. Loper	George S. Peyton, Jr.
(Partner Emeritus)	Sandra F. Wagner
Barrie Engel	Linda C. Roodhouse

Representative Clients: Firemans Fund Insurance Cos.; City of Piedmont; The Dow Chemical Co.; Nissan Motor Corp.; Subaru of America; Weyerhauser Co.; Bay Area Rapid Transit District; Diamond Shamrock; Home Indemnity Co.; Rhone-Poulenc.

For Complete List of Firm Personnel, See General Section

For full biographical listings, see the Martindale-Hubbell Law Directory

NEAL & ASSOCIATES (AV)

Montclair Village, 6200 Antioch Street, Suite 202, P.O. Box 13314, 500, 94661-0314
Telephone: 510-339-0233
FAX: 510-339-6672
URL: http://www.seamless.com/hdn/hdn.html

Howard D. Neal

(See Next Column)

NEAL & ASSOCIATES, *Oakland—Continued*

Frank J. Gilbert   Steven S. Miyake

For full biographical listings, see the Martindale-Hubbell Law Directory

ORANGE, Orange Co.

JOHN A. DUNCAN A PROFESSIONAL CORPORATION (AV)

333 City Boulevard West, Suite 1420, 92668-2924
Telephone: 714-935-9800
FAX: 714-939-1485

John A. Duncan

For full biographical listings, see the Martindale-Hubbell Law Directory

PALM SPRINGS, Riverside Co.

SCHLECHT, SHEVLIN & SHOENBERGER, A LAW CORPORATION (AV)

Suite 100, 801 East Tahquitz Canyon Way, P.O. Box 2744, 92263-2744
Telephone: 619-320-7161
Facsimile: 619-323-1758; 619-325-4623

James M. Schlecht   John C. Shevlin

Representative Clients: Outdoor Resorts of America; The Escrow Connection; Wells Fargo Bank; Canyon Country Club; Waste Management Co.

For Complete List of Firm Personnel, See General Section

For full biographical listings, see the Martindale-Hubbell Law Directory

PALO ALTO, Santa Clara Co.

CRIST, GRIFFITHS, SCHULZ & BIORN, A PROFESSIONAL CORPORATION (AV)

550 Hamilton Avenue, Suite 300, 94301
Telephone: 415-321-5000
Fax: 415-326-2404

Robert E. Schulz   Kristofer W. Biorn
Robert A. Biorn   Mark R. Shepherd

OF COUNSEL

John R. Griffiths   Frank Lee Crist, Sr. (1898-1991)

Representative Clients: Peck & Hiller; Apple Computer, Inc.

For full biographical listings, see the Martindale-Hubbell Law Directory

FINCH, MONTGOMERY & WRIGHT (AV)

350 Cambridge Avenue, Suite 175, 94306
Telephone: 415-327-0888
Fax: 415-327-5316

MEMBERS OF FIRM

Toby F. Montgomery   Barbara P. Wright
Nathan C. Finch (1909-1990)

For full biographical listings, see the Martindale-Hubbell Law Directory

JOHN E. MILLER (AV)

250 Cambridge Avenue, Suite 102, 94306-1504
Telephone: 415-321-8886
Fax: 415-321-8998

ASSOCIATES

Annalisa C Wood   Kerre R. Dubinsky

Reference: Bank of the West.

For full biographical listings, see the Martindale-Hubbell Law Directory

PASADENA, Los Angeles Co.

LAGERLOF, SENECAL, BRADLEY & SWIFT, LLP (AV)

301 North Lake Avenue, 10th Floor, 91101-4108
Telephone: 818-793-9400
FAX: 818-793-5900

MEMBERS OF FIRM

Joseph J. Burris (1913-1980)   John F. Bradley
Stanley C. Lagerlof (Retired)   Timothy J. Gosney
H. Melvin Swift, Jr.   William F. Kruse
H. Jess Senecal   Thomas S. Bunn, III
Jack T. Swafford   Andrew D. Turner
Rebecca J. Thyne

ASSOCIATES

James D. Ciampa   Robert W. Renken

Representative Clients: Anchor Glass Container Corp.; Bethlehem Steel Corp.; Orthopaedic Hospital; Palmdale Water District; Public Water Agencies Group; Ventura Port District; Walnut Valley Water District; Metric Construction Co., Inc.

For full biographical listings, see the Martindale-Hubbell Law Directory

MARTIN & HUDSON (AV)

350 West Colorado Boulevard, Suite 320, 91105
Telephone: 818-793-8500
Telecopier: 818-793-8779

MEMBERS OF FIRM

Robert B. Martin, Jr.   Boyd D. Hudson

For full biographical listings, see the Martindale-Hubbell Law Directory

RICHARD F. MILLER A PROFESSIONAL CORPORATION (AV)

Suite 511, 199 South Los Robles Avenue, 91101
Telephone: 818-584-1400; 213-681-5400
Telecopier: 818-584-1447

Richard F. Miller

For full biographical listings, see the Martindale-Hubbell Law Directory

ALAN R. TALT (AV)

Suite 710, 790 East Colorado Boulevard, 91101
Telephone: 818-356-0853
Telecopier: 818-356-0731

Reference: U.S. Trust Company California.

For full biographical listings, see the Martindale-Hubbell Law Directory

WITTER AND HARPOLE (AV)

Wells Fargo Building, 350 W. Colorado Boulevard, Suite 400, 91105
Telephone: 213-624-1311, 818-440-1111
FAX: 213-620-0430
Email: 102444.2117@compuserve.com
Newport Beach, California Office: Suite 1050, 610 Newport Center Drive.
Telephone: 714-644-7600.
Fax: 714-759-1014.

MEMBERS OF FIRM

Myron E. Harpole   Eugene Harpole (1896-1987)
George G. Witter (1895-1978)   Debra M. Olsen (Resident, Newport Beach Office)

OF COUNSEL

James D. Harris (A Professional Corporation)

Reference: Union Bank (Newport Beach, Calif.).

For full biographical listings, see the Martindale-Hubbell Law Directory

PLEASANTON, Alameda Co.

JAMES J. PHILLIPS A PROFESSIONAL CORPORATION (AV)

4900 Hopyard Road, Suite 260, 94588
Telephone: 510-463-1980
Fax: 510-463-8656
Hayward, California Office: 1331 B Street, Suite 4.
Telephone: 510-886-2120.

James J. Phillips

For full biographical listings, see the Martindale-Hubbell Law Directory

RANCHO SANTA FE, San Diego Co.

COWLEY & CHIDESTER (AV)

6050 El Tordo, P.O. Box 2329, 92067
Telephone: 619-756-4410
Fax: 619-756-4386

MEMBERS

James M. Cowley   Steven J. Chidester
Ellen L. van Hoften

ASSOCIATES

Kristina A. Hancock   Nancy G. Henderson

OF COUNSEL

Lynn P. Hart

For full biographical listings, see the Martindale-Hubbell Law Directory

SACRAMENTO,* Sacramento Co.

TOSH G. YAMAMOTO A PROFESSIONAL CORPORATION (AV)

Greenhaven Professional Complex, 930 Florin Road, Suite 200, 95831
Telephone: 916-421-8455
Fax: 916-421-4312

Tosh G. Yamamoto   David James Richardson

For full biographical listings, see the Martindale-Hubbell Law Directory

SAN BERNARDINO,* San Bernardino Co.

WILSON, BORROR, DUNN & DAVIS (AV)

Suite 307, The Bank of California Building, 255 North D Street, 92401
Telephone: 909-884-8855
Fax: 909-884-5161

(See Next Column)

WILSON, BORROR, DUNN & DAVIS—*Continued*

MEMBERS OF FIRM

Fred A. Wilson (1886-1973)   James R. Dunn
Wm. H. Wilson (1915-1981)   Thomas M. Davis
Keith D. Davis

ASSOCIATES

Timothy P. Prince   Sarah L. Overton

OF COUNSEL

Caywood J. Borror

Representative Clients: Travelers Insurance Co.; Rockwell International; Westinghouse Air Brake Co.; Goodyear Tire and Rubber Co.; Home Insurance Co.; Cities of: Redlands, Chino, Colton, San Bernardino and Upland; The Canadian Insurance Co.

For full biographical listings, see the Martindale-Hubbell Law Directory

---

SAN CARLOS, San Mateo Co.

LAW OFFICE OF RICHARD W. HENSON (AV)

909 Laurel Street, 94070
Telephone: 415-591-7352
Fax: 415-591-9239
Email: rwhenson@best.com

For full biographical listings, see the Martindale-Hubbell Law Directory

---

SAN DIEGO,* San Diego Co.

BRIERTON & JONES (AV)

1010 Second Avenue, Suite 2300, 92101
Telephone: 619-696-7066
Fax: 619-696-6907

MEMBERS OF FIRM

B. James Brierton   Jerilyn S. Jones

For full biographical listings, see the Martindale-Hubbell Law Directory

---

CRABTREE & CRABTREE (AV)

3143 Fourth Avenue, 92103-5802
Telephone: 619-293-3403
Fax: 619-293-3405

MEMBERS OF FIRM

Brooks Crabtree   Daniel B. Crabtree

References: Union Bank; Bank of America National Trust & Savings Assn.; Northern Trust of California.

For full biographical listings, see the Martindale-Hubbell Law Directory

---

DAVID L. HICKSON (AV)

8910 University Center Lane Suite 230, 92122
Telephone: 619-457-1100
Facsimile: 619-457-0109

For full biographical listings, see the Martindale-Hubbell Law Directory

---

LINDLEY, LAZAR & SCALES, A PROFESSIONAL CORPORATION (AV)

One America Plaza, 600 West Broadway, Suite 1400, 92101-3302
Telephone: 619-234-9181
Fax: 619-234-8475
Email: 104413.1175@compuserve.com

William E. Johns   Raymond L. Heidemann
Stephen F. Treadgold   Elise Streicher Rogerson

OF COUNSEL

Maurice T. Watson   Philip P. Martin, Jr.

For Complete List of Firm Personnel, See General Section

For full biographical listings, see the Martindale-Hubbell Law Directory

---

LONNIE G. MCGEE (AV)

2470 Union Street, 92101-1320
Telephone: 619-696-5300
FAX: 619-696-7010
Email: lonmcgee@cts.com

For full biographical listings, see the Martindale-Hubbell Law Directory

---

SPARBER, FERGUSON, PONDER & RYAN, A PROFESSIONAL LAW CORPORATION (AV)

Imperial Bank Building, 701 "B" Street, Tenth Floor, 92101-8103
Telephone: 619-239-3600
Facsimile: 619-239-5601

(See Next Column)

Richard E. Sparber   Greg J. Ryan
James P. Ferguson   Richard J. Annen
John E. Ponder   Daniel F. Morrin
Gary B. Rudolph

Todd R. Gabriel   William P. Fennell
Carol R. McGinnis   James E. Highsmith

OF COUNSEL

Mark P. Mandell

LEGAL SUPPORT PERSONNEL

LEGAL ADMINISTRATOR

Beverly K. Driscoll

For full biographical listings, see the Martindale-Hubbell Law Directory

---

WALTERS & WARD, A PROFESSIONAL CORPORATION (AV)

Lakeview Professional Building, Rancho Bernardo, 11665 Avena Place, Suite 203, 92128-2403
Telephone: 619-485-9045; 566-1480
FAX: 619-485-0398

R. Michael Walters   Diane K. Ward

Robert N. Gary   Julie Ann Bowler

For full biographical listings, see the Martindale-Hubbell Law Directory

---

WINGERT, GREBING, ANELLO & BRUBAKER (AV)

A Partnership including Professional Corporations
One America Plaza, Seventh Floor, 600 West Broadway, 92101-3370
Telephone: 619-232-8151
Facsimile: 619-232-4665
Email: wgab@wgab.com
Las Vegas, Nevada Office: Ryan, Marks and Johnson, 317 South Sixth Street, 89101.
Telephone: 702-471-7270.
Facsimile: 702-471-1245.

MEMBERS OF FIRM

John R. Wingert (A Professional Corporation)   James Goodwin
Charles R. Grebing (A Professional Corporation)   Shawn D. Morris
Michael M. Anello (A Professional Corporation)   Robert M. Caietti
Alan K. Brubaker (A Professional Corporation)   Eileen Mulligan Marks (Resident, Las Vegas, Nevada Office)
Norman A. Ryan (Resident, Las Vegas, Nevada Office)   Christopher W. Todd
     Robert L. Johnson (Resident, Las Vegas, Nevada Office)
     Robert M. Juskie
John S. Addams

ASSOCIATES

Julie E. Saake   James J. Brown, Jr.
Michael Sullivan   Craig Gross
Carolyn P. Gallinghouse   Stephen C. Grebing
Kimberly I. Cary   Brian P. Worthington
Terie M. Theis   Melanie A. Jubelirer
James P. Broder (Resident, Las Vegas, Nevada Office)   Kimberly A. Davis
     Michael W. Vivoli

OF COUNSEL

William L. Todd, Jr.

Representative Clients: California Casualty Insurance Co.; Farmers Insurance Group; The Ohio Casualty Group; United Services Automobile Assn.; United States Fidelity & Guaranty Co.

For full biographical listings, see the Martindale-Hubbell Law Directory

---

SAN FRANCISCO,* San Francisco Co.

ADVICE & COUNSEL INCORPORATED (AV Ⓣ)

353 Sacramento Street, Suite 1500, 94111
Telephone: 415-955-5700
Fax: 415-388-5005
Email: willtrust@aol.com *URL:* http://www.adviceco.com/law
Marin County Office: 70 Lomita Drive, Suite 6, P. O. Box 1739, Mill Valley, 94942-1739.
Telephone: 415-388-5000.
Fax: 415-300-5005.

Gerry H. Goldsholle   Myra K. Levenson

For full biographical listings, see the Martindale-Hubbell Law Directory

---

AVERY & ASSOCIATES (AV)

49 Geary Street, Suite 202, 94108-5727
Telephone: 415-954-4800
Fax: 415-954-4810
Email: LJA@INFOARCH.COM

Luther J. Avery

(See Next Column)

AVERY & ASSOCIATES, *San Francisco—Continued*

OF COUNSEL

Mark J. Avery

LEGAL SUPPORT PERSONNEL

Matthew S. Avery

For full biographical listings, see the Martindale-Hubbell Law Directory

LAW OFFICES OF GARY D. BERGER (AV)

One Sansome Street, 19th Floor, 94104
Telephone: 415-731-2268
Fax: 415-239-5147

For full biographical listings, see the Martindale-Hubbell Law Directory

LAW OFFICES OF ELIZABETH ANNE BIRD (AV)

One Market Plaza, Spear Street Tower, Forty-First Floor, 94105
Telephone: 415-267-7200
Fax: 415-546-4962

Reference: The Bank of California.

For full biographical listings, see the Martindale-Hubbell Law Directory

BISHOP, BARRY, HOWE, HANEY & RYDER, A PROFESSIONAL CORPORATION (AV)

Embarcadero Center West, 12th Floor, 275 Battery Street, 94111-3333
Telephone: 415-421-8550
FAX: 415-362-4730

Ross R. Ryder (1940-1989)	Thomas O. Haran
Nelson C. Barry	Rebecca B. Aherne
Drayton F. Howe, Jr.	Michael W. Bolechowski
Jeffrey N. Haney	Mark C. Raskoff
	Patricia S. Lakner

William R. Brown	Stacey A. Kuch
J. Scott Wood	Marco R. Sumarriva
Mitchell J. Alward	Curtis A. Canfield
Lawrence S. Molton	Gregory R. de la Peña
Susan Knell Bumbalo	Paul Andrew Herp
Brook Bernard Bond	Rebecca E. Thomson
Marisa D'Amico	Jane E. Carey

OF COUNSEL

Woodrow W. Denney

Reference: The Redwood Bank.

For full biographical listings, see the Martindale-Hubbell Law Directory

FELDMAN, WALDMAN & KLINE, A PROFESSIONAL CORPORATION (AV)

3 Embarcadero Center, Suite 2800, 94111
Telephone: 415-981-1300
Fax: 415-981-1350
Email: info@fwk.com
Stockton, California Office: Sperry Building, 146-148 West Weber Avenue.
Telephone: 209-943-2004.
Fax: 209-943-0905.

Murry J. Waldman	Martha Jeanne Shaver
Leland R. Selna, Jr.	(Resident, Stockton Office)
Michael L. Korbholz	Robert Cedric Goodman
Howard M. Wexler	Laura Grad
Patricia S. Mar	William F. Adams
Kenneth W. Jones	Elizabeth A. Thompson
Paul J. Dion	Julie A. Jones
Vern S. Bothwell	David L. Kanel
L.J. Chris Martiniak	Abram S. Feuerstein
	Linda Sorensen

Laura J. Dawson	Dana A. Suntag
Joanne M. Lafreniere	(Resident, Stockton Office)
Paul A. Weiss	Danielle Ochs-Tillotson

OF COUNSEL

Richard L. Jaeger	Gerald A. Sherwin
	(Resident, Stockton Office)

For full biographical listings, see the Martindale-Hubbell Law Directory

FRIEDMAN, OLIVE, McCUBBIN, SPALDING, BILTER & ROOSEVELT, A PROFESSIONAL CORPORATION (AV)

22nd Floor, 425 California Street, 94104
Telephone: 415-434-1363
Facsimile: 415-434-1937

(See Next Column)

K. Bruce Friedman	D. Keith Bilter
Donald J. McCubbin	Michael A. Roosevelt
Philip F. Spalding	George F. Montgomery II

Helen Olive Milowe

OF COUNSEL

Jack H. Olive	William A. Seavey

For full biographical listings, see the Martindale-Hubbell Law Directory

IBERSHOF & DOLE (AV)

180 Montgomery Street Suite 1250, 94104
Telephone: 415-421-1144
FAX: 415-989-7359
Email: ibershof@aol.com

MEMBERS OF FIRM

William C. Ibershof	Stuart R. Dole

For full biographical listings, see the Martindale-Hubbell Law Directory

MacINNIS, DONNER & KOPLOWITZ (AV)

Suite 222, 465 California Street, 94104
Telephone: 415-434-2400
FAX: 415-433-1917

MEMBERS OF FIRM

James Martin MacInnis	Conrad Donner
(1914-1979)	Edward A. Koplowitz

For full biographical listings, see the Martindale-Hubbell Law Directory

SAN JOSE, * Santa Clara Co.

OWEN G. FIORE (AV)

Bank of America Building, 101 Park Center Plaza, Suite 1150, 95113
Telephone: 408-293-3616
Facsimile: 408-293-0430

John F. Ramsbacher	Leslie J. Daniels

For full biographical listings, see the Martindale-Hubbell Law Directory

HOPKINS & CARLEY, A LAW CORPORATION (AV)

Fifteenth Floor, 150 Almaden Boulevard, 95113-2089
Telephone: 408-286-9800
Facsimile: 408-998-4790

Leon A. Carley (1908-1984)	Dunham B. Sherer
John F. Hopkins	Anthony J. McCarthy
Robert D. Wenzel	James M. Hager
	Charles H. Packer

OF COUNSEL

Clarence A. Kellogg Jr.	Theodore J. Biagini

Jennifer M. Cunneen	H. Katerina Hertzog
Brian C. Finerty	Russell K. Smith
	Sharon L. Wong

For Complete List of Firm Personnel, See General Section

For full biographical listings, see the Martindale-Hubbell Law Directory

LICCARDO, ROSSI, STURGES & McNEIL, A PROFESSIONAL LAW CORPORATION (AV)

1960 The Alameda, Suite 200, 95126
Telephone: 408-244-4570
Fax: 408-244-3294
Oakland, California Office: 1999 Harrison, Suite 1300.
Telephone: 415-834-2206.
Fax: 415-832-4432.

Salvador A. Liccardo	Craig Needham
Ronald R. Rossi	Gregory D. Hull
Robert S. Sturges	Martha Louise Caron
R. Donald McNeil	(Resident, Oakland Office)
David M. Hamerslough	Cynthia L. Chase
Susan R. Reischl	Laura Liccardo

Robert C. Colyar	Paul Salvatore Liccardo
Jeffery Lopez	Anne Jones
Wes Wagnon	Samuel A. Chuck
Richard B. Gullen	Laura M. Chiappe
Deborah T. Bjonerud	Daniel A. Hershkowitz
(Resident, Oakland Office)	(Resident, Oakland Office)

For full biographical listings, see the Martindale-Hubbell Law Directory

San Jose—Continued

MILLER, MORTON, CAILLAT & NEVIS (AV)

50 West San Fernando Street, Suite 1300, 95113-2413
Telephone: 408-292-1765
Telecopier: 408-292-4484

Richard W. Morton (1916-1975)   Charles V. Caillat (1920-1990)
Harvey C. Miller (1906-1993)

MEMBERS OF FIRM

David L. Nevis	Joseph A. Scanlan, Jr.
Francis J. Hughes	Carolyn Tobiason Stuart
Peter A. Kline	William K. Hurley
Stevan C. Adelman	Peter V. Dessau

Eric Mogensen

OF COUNSEL

Nancy F. Symons	Susan L. Sutton

Pamela J. Silberstein

ASSOCIATES

Kathryn E. Barrett	David I. Kornbluh
Katherine S. Pak	Kimberly Holtz MacMillan

Representative Clients: Trammell Crow Residential Services; Joe Kerley Lincoln Mercury Co.; Milligan News Co.; Joseph George Distributors; The Frozen Food Employees Pension Trust; Santa Clara Dental Society; New West Foods; Bay Apartment Communities; Guy F. Atkinson Company; A. Hathaway Co.

For full biographical listings, see the Martindale-Hubbell Law Directory

---

SAN LUIS OBISPO, * San Luis Obispo Co.

GEORGE, GALLO & SULLIVAN, A LAW CORPORATION (AV)

694 Santa Rosa, P.O. Box 12710, 93406
Telephone: 805-544-3351
Facsimile: 805-528-5598
Email: jgeorgeggs@aol.com
Los Osos, California Office: 2238 Bayview Heights Drive, P.O. Box 6129.
Telephone: 805-528-3351.
Telecopier: 805-528-5598.

J. K. George

Anne C. Cyr

Reference: Mid State Bank, Los Osos, California.

For full biographical listings, see the Martindale-Hubbell Law Directory

---

SAN MATEO, San Mateo Co.

BASYE & GOLDEN (AV)

520 South El Camino Real, Suite 700, 94402
Telephone: 415-342-2500
Fax: 415-342-9560
Email: jpgolden@ix.netcom.com

MEMBERS OF FIRM

Paul E. Basye (1901-1991)	John P. Golden

For full biographical listings, see the Martindale-Hubbell Law Directory

STUBBS & STUBBS (AV)

Borel Estate Building, Suite 505, 1700 South El Camino Real, 94402-3051
Telephone: 415-345-4350
Telecopier: 415-345-6748
Email: stubbs__stubbs@msn.com

MEMBERS OF FIRM

Barry Stubbs	Brian P. Stubbs

Reference: Wells Fargo Bank.

For full biographical listings, see the Martindale-Hubbell Law Directory

THIRKELL & CRETAN (AV)

181 Second Avenue, Suite 625, P.O. Box 190, 94401
Telephone: 415-348-1016
Facsimile: 415-348-2968

MEMBERS OF FIRM

Edward D. Thirkell	Linda J. Ross
Clifford V. Cretan	Trent E. Wright

James B. Creighton

For full biographical listings, see the Martindale-Hubbell Law Directory

---

SAN RAFAEL, * Marin Co.

RAGGHIANTI • FREITAS • MONTOBBIO • WALLACE LLP (AV)

874 Fourth Street, Suite D, 94901
Telephone: 415-453-9433
Fax: 415-453-8269

(See Next Column)

Gary T. Ragghianti	J. Randolph Wallace
David P. Freitas	Patrick M. Macias
J. Mark Montobbio	Robert F. Epstein

John Ralph Thomas

For full biographical listings, see the Martindale-Hubbell Law Directory

---

SANTA ANA, * Orange Co.

JOHN G. BRADSHAW A PROFESSIONAL LAW CORPORATION (AV)

3 Imperial Promenade, Suite 800, 92707
Telephone: 714-641-1690
Fax: 714-641-1780

John G. Bradshaw

For full biographical listings, see the Martindale-Hubbell Law Directory

FERRUZZO & FERRUZZO (AV)

A Partnership of Professional Corporations
2114 North Broadway, 92706
Telephone: 714-834-9322
Telecopier: 714-834-9358

MEMBERS OF FIRM

Thomas G. Ferruzzo (A Professional Corporation)	James K. Leese (A Professional Corporation)
James J. Ferruzzo (A Professional Corporation)	

ASSOCIATES

John R. Pelle	Maria Ann Newkirk
Dirk E. Petchul	Paul A. Madruga
Gregory J. Ferruzzo	Lisa L. Schultz

OF COUNSEL

M. Susan Watson

For full biographical listings, see the Martindale-Hubbell Law Directory

JEFFREY R. MATSEN & ASSOCIATES (AV)

3 Imperial Promenade, Suite 445, 92707-5908
Telephone: 714-433-7850
Telecopier: 719-433-7815

Arlin P. Neser

For full biographical listings, see the Martindale-Hubbell Law Directory

---

SANTA BARBARA, * Santa Barbara Co.

ANGLE, CARLSON, GOLDRICK & ROBERTS (AV)

A Partnership including a Professional Corporation
200 East Carrillo Street, Suite 310, 93101
Telephone: 805-963-7400
Fax: 805-963-7610

Robert O. Angle	Miles T. Goldrick
Arthur W. Carlson (A P.C.)	Paul A. Roberts

OF COUNSEL

Georgia C. McDermott

For full biographical listings, see the Martindale-Hubbell Law Directory

MULLEN & HENZELL, L.L.P. (AV)

A California registered limited liability partnership
112 East Victoria Street, Post Office Drawer 789, 93102-0789
Telephone: 805-966-1501
FAX: 805-966-9204

MEMBERS OF FIRM

Thomas M. Mullen (1915-1991)	Robert A. Zeavin
Arthur A. Henzell (Retired)	Joseph F. Green
J. Robert Andrews	Gary W. Robinson
James W. Brown	Lawrence T. Sorensen
Dennis W. Reilly	Gregory F. Faulkner
Jeffrey C. Nelson	Richard G. Battles
Charles S. Bargiel	Edward C. Thoits
Jay L. Beckerman	William E. Degen

Michael E. Cage

OF COUNSEL

Kim A. Harley Seefeld

ASSOCIATES

Andrew M. Polinsky	Paul K. Wilcox
Catherine Perlman	Thomas Y. Chen

Richard E. Fogg

Representative Clients: Goleta Sanitary District; Interinsurance Exchange of the Automobile Club of Southern California; State Farm Fire & Casualty Co.; State Farm Mutual Automobile Insurance Co.

For full biographical listings, see the Martindale-Hubbell Law Directory

Santa Barbara—Continued

SEED, MACKALL & COLE LLP (AV)

1332 Anacapa Street, Suite 200, 93101
Telephone: 805-963-0669
Fax: 805-962-1404

MEMBERS OF FIRM

John R. Mackall	Christopher E. Hahn
Joseph L. Cole	Sandra Hitchens Thoits
Gregory Canova-Parker	David E. Reese
Thomas N. Harding	K. Andrew Kent
Peter A. Umoff	Alan D. Condren
Barton E. Clemens, Jr.	Nicholas J. Schneider

Representative Clients: City Commerce Bank; Montecito Bank & Trust; Santa Barbara Bank & Trust; Digital Instruments, Inc.; G & H Technology Inc.; Mission Research Corporation; Bermant Development Company; The Investec Real Estate Companies; STAR Telecommunications, Inc.; TELNET Communications Group.

For full biographical listings, see the Martindale-Hubbell Law Directory

GEORGE G. SHORT A PROFESSIONAL CORPORATION (AV)

1421 State Street, Suite A, 93101-2507
Telephone: 805-564-6644
Fax: 805-564-6646
Los Angeles, California Office: 815 Moraga Drive.
Telephone: 310-440-4299.
Telecopier: 805-564-6646.

George G. Short

For full biographical listings, see the Martindale-Hubbell Law Directory

*SANTA ROSA,** Sonoma Co.

BELDEN, ABBEY, WEITZENBERG & KELLY, A PROFESSIONAL CORPORATION (AV)

1105 North Dutton Avenue, P.O. Box 1566, 95402
Telephone: 707-542-5050
Telecopier: 707-542-2589

Thomas P. Kelly, Jr.

Representative Clients: Exchange Bank of Santa Rosa; Westamerica Bank; North Bay Title Co.; Northwestern Title Security Co.; Geyser Peak Winery; Santa Rosa City School District; Sonoma National Bank; Arrowood Vineyards & Winery; Arthur & DeVincenzi Concrete; Friedman Bros. Hardware, Inc.

For Complete List of Firm Personnel, See General Section

For full biographical listings, see the Martindale-Hubbell Law Directory

*STOCKTON,** San Joaquin Co.

RICHARD W. KONIG (AV)

6702 Inglewood Avenue, Suite A, 95207-3872
Telephone: 209-474-1251

TORRANCE, Los Angeles Co.

FINER, KIM & STEARNS (AV)

An Association of Professional Corporations
City National Bank Building, 3424 Carson Street, Suite 500, 90503
Telephone: 310-214-1477
Telecopier: 310-214-0764

W. A. Finer (A Professional Corporation)
LEGAL SUPPORT PERSONNEL
Marcia E. Talbert

For Complete List of Firm Personnel, See General Section

For full biographical listings, see the Martindale-Hubbell Law Directory

McGAUGHEY & SPIRITO (AV)

2377 Crenshaw Boulevard, Suite 310, 90501
Telephone: 310-787-8783
Fax: 310-787-9937

MEMBERS OF FIRM

Terence C. McGaughey	Joseph P. Spirito Jr.

ASSOCIATE
Steven Spitzer

Reference: Bay Cities National Bank.

For full biographical listings, see the Martindale-Hubbell Law Directory

CHRISTOPHER M. MOORE & ASSOCIATES A LAW CORPORATION (AV)

Suite 490 Union Bank Tower, 21515 Hawthorne Boulevard, 90503
Telephone: 310-540-8855
Fax: 310-316-1307
Email: chrismesq@aol.com

Christopher M. Moore

Sharon A. Bryan	Rebecca Lee Tomlinson Schroff
	Julia A. Stanton

For full biographical listings, see the Martindale-Hubbell Law Directory

UPLAND, San Bernardino Co.

ALTHOUSE & McDONOUGH (AV)

Second Floor, Metro Commerce Bank Building, 188 North Euclid Avenue, P.O. Box 698, 91785
Telephone: 909-985-9828
Telecopier: 909-985-3282

Charles S. Althouse	Elizabeth A. McDonough

References: Security Pacific National Bank, Upland Branch; First National Bank & Trust Company, Upland Branch.

For Complete List of Firm Personnel, See General Section

For full biographical listings, see the Martindale-Hubbell Law Directory

VINNEDGE, GAFNEY & GLADSON, INC. (AV)

255 West Foothill Boulevard, Suite 210, 91786
Telephone: 909-931-0879
Fax: 909-931-9219

George W. Vinnedge	Thomas J. Gafney
	Linda J. Gladson

LEGAL SUPPORT PERSONNEL

Linda A. Gooding	Sandra L. Lukens (Paralegal)
(Probate Assistant)	

For full biographical listings, see the Martindale-Hubbell Law Directory

*VENTURA,** Ventura Co.

BLEUEL & MUIRHEAD (AV)

2225 Sperry Avenue, Suite 1200, 93003
Telephone: 805-650-1818; 656-5711
Fax: 805-650-9071
Email: gavzdad@aol.com

MEMBERS OF FIRM

Bartley S. Bleuel	Michael L. Muirhead

For full biographical listings, see the Martindale-Hubbell Law Directory

TAYLOR McCORD, A LAW CORPORATION (AV)

721 East Main Street, P.O. Box 1477, 93002
Telephone: 805-648-4700
Fax: 805-653-6124

Richard L. Taylor	Robert L. McCord, Jr.
	David L. Praver

Patrick Cherry	Susan D. Siple
	Rebbecca F. Calderwood

LEGAL SUPPORT PERSONNEL
PARALEGALS

Stephanie Gibson	Adele Rubino
	Diane Lovato

For full biographical listings, see the Martindale-Hubbell Law Directory

VISTA, San Diego Co.

ERNEST L. HUNT, JR. (AV)

630 Alta Vista Drive, Suite 103, P.O. Box 640, 92085-0640
Telephone: 619-726-3839
Fax: 619-726-5491

For full biographical listings, see the Martindale-Hubbell Law Directory

WALNUT CREEK, Contra Costa Co.

STEWART, STEWART & O'NEIL (AV)

1908 Tice Valley Boulevard Rossmoor Shopping Center, 94595
Telephone: 510-932-8000
Fax: 510-932-4681

Thomas N. Stewart, Jr.	Jeannine O'Neil

For full biographical listings, see the Martindale-Hubbell Law Directory

WHITTIER, Los Angeles Co.

BEWLEY, LASSLEBEN & MILLER (AV)

13215 East Penn Street, Suite 510, 90602-1797
Telephone: 310-698-9771
Fax: 310-696-6357

MEMBERS OF FIRM

Thomas W. Bewley (1903-1986)
William M. Lassleben, Jr.
  (Retired)
Edward L. Miller
J. Terrence Mooschekian

Ernie Zachary Park
Robert H. Dewberry
Richard L. Dewberry
Jeffrey S. Baird
Kevin P. Duthoy

Joseph A. Vinatieri

ASSOCIATES

Jason C. Demille
Suzanne R. Kramer

John P. Godsil
Peter B. Fan

Representative Clients: Quaker City Federal Savings & Loan Assn.; Whittier College; Presbyterian Intercommunity Hospital; Bank of Whittier; Circuit Systems, Inc.; Lockhart Industries, Inc.; Subdivided Land, Inc.; United Ad-Label Co., Inc.
References: Bank of America National Trust & Savings Assn. (Whittier Main Office); Southern California Bank.

For full biographical listings, see the Martindale-Hubbell Law Directory

COLORADO

AURORA, Arapahoe & Adams Cos.

LEWIS W. DYMOND, JR. A PROFESSIONAL CORPORATION (AV)

Suite 212, 13900 East Harvard Avenue, 80014
Telephone: 303-695-8700
Fax: 303-696-0923
Email: lwdymond@ix.netcom.com

Lewis W. Dymond, Jr.

Reference: Norwest Bank of Aurora-City Center.

For full biographical listings, see the Martindale-Hubbell Law Directory

DAVID W. KIRCH, P.C. (AV)

14001 East Iliff Avenue, Suite 318, 80014
Telephone: 303-671-7726
Fax: 303-671-7679
Email: dkirch@lawyernet.com

David W. Kirch

For full biographical listings, see the Martindale-Hubbell Law Directory

BOULDER, * Boulder Co.

DOTY & SHAPIRO, P.C. (AV)

1720 Fourteenth Street, Suite 100, 80302-6353
Telephone: 303-443-3234
Telecopier: 303-443-3438

H. McGregor Doty, II
Mark R. Shapiro

For full biographical listings, see the Martindale-Hubbell Law Directory

COLORADO SPRINGS, * El Paso Co.

BELTZ, EDWARDS & SABO, L.L.P. (AV)

729 South Cascade, 80903
Telephone: 719-473-4444; 719-634-6620
Fax: 719-444-0186

W. Thomas Beltz
Daniel P. Edwards
John W. Sabo, III

Daniel A. West

For full biographical listings, see the Martindale-Hubbell Law Directory

WILTON W. COGSWELL, III (AV)

Suite 1020, Alamo Corporate Center, 102 South Tejon Street, 80903
Telephone: 719-473-1448
Facsimile: 719-473-1449
Email: wcogs3@aol.com
Denver, Colorado Office: Suite 2100, World Trade Center. 1675 Broadway.
Telephone: 303-592-4217.
Fax: 303-592-4223. E-Mail: WCOGSWELL@AOL.COM.

OF COUNSEL

Wilton W. Cogswell, IV (Resident, Denver Office)

For full biographical listings, see the Martindale-Hubbell Law Directory

GADDIS, KIN & HERD, P.C. (AV)

118 South Wahsatch, Suite 100, 80903
Telephone: 719-471-3848
Fax: 719-471-0317

Larry R. Gaddis
James W. Kin

Thomas J. Herd
David L. Quicksall (1950-1991)

OF COUNSEL

James B. Turner

Reference: Norwest Bank of Colorado Springs.

For full biographical listings, see the Martindale-Hubbell Law Directory

JAMES A. WEIR (AV)

Suite 510 Alamo Corporate Center, 102 South Tejon, 80903
Telephone: 719-473-9906
FAX: 719-473-8152

References: Bank One; Colorado National Bank/Exchange.

For full biographical listings, see the Martindale-Hubbell Law Directory

CRAIG, * Moffat Co.

WILLIAM V. LAWRENCE (AV)

510 Breeze Street, P.O. Box 1131, 81626
Telephone: 970-824-4730

Reference: Colorado Community First State Bank.

For full biographical listings, see the Martindale-Hubbell Law Directory

DENVER, * Denver Co.

HARRY L. ARKIN & ASSOCIATES, P.C. (AV)

Suite 2750 Lincoln Center, 1660 Lincoln Street, 80264
Telephone: 303-863-8400
Telefax: 303-832-4703
Email: harkin00@counsel.com
London, England Office: Verulam Chambers, Peer House, 8-14 Verulam Street, WCIX 8LZ.
Telephone: 071 813-2400.
Fax: 071 405-3870.

Harry L. Arkin

Sharon E. Smith
LEGAL SUPPORT PERSONNEL
Patricia A. Hanson

For full biographical listings, see the Martindale-Hubbell Law Directory

ATLASS PROFESSIONAL CORPORATION (AV)

2100 East Fourteenth Avenue, 80206-2106
Telephone: 303-377-0707
Fax: 303-321-2655
Email: atlass.com

Theodore B. Atlass

Carol Buchanan Lay

For full biographical listings, see the Martindale-Hubbell Law Directory

ROBERT L. BARTHOLIC (AV)

Suite 500, 1600 Broadway, 80202
Telephone: 303-830-0500
Fax: 303-860-7855

OF COUNSEL

Clarence L. Bartholic

Approved Attorney for: Mid-South Title Insurance Corp; Lawyers Title Insurance Co.
Representative Clients: Anschutz Corp.; Denver and Rio Grande Western Railroad Co.; Johnson Anderson Mortgage Co.; Arco Environmental Affairs; Burlington Northern Railroad Co. and Subsidiaries; American Association of Private Railroad Car Owners, Inc.
References: Colorado National Bank; Colorado State Bank.

For full biographical listings, see the Martindale-Hubbell Law Directory

JOHN DeBRUYN LAW OFFICES (AV)

2100 East Fourteenth Avenue, 80206
Telephone: 303-377-0707
Telecopier: 303-321-2655
Email: jdebruyn@usa.net

For full biographical listings, see the Martindale-Hubbell Law Directory

MICHAEL R. DICE AND COMPANY, L.L.C. (AV)

Suite 600, 3300 East First Avenue, 80206
Telephone: 303-321-6872
Fax: 303-321-3196

(See Next Column)

MICHAEL R. DICE AND COMPANY, L.L.C., Denver—Continued

Michael R. Dice

Ronald K. Ledgerwood
OF COUNSEL
John B. Carraher
LEGAL SUPPORT PERSONNEL
Sara M. Smith

For full biographical listings, see the Martindale-Hubbell Law Directory

ELROD, KATZ, PREEO, LOOK, MOISON & SILVERMAN, PROFESSIONAL CORPORATION (AV)

Suite 1100, 1120 Lincoln Street, 80203
Telephone: 303-832-1900
Fax: 303-863-0412

Richard B. Elrod	Harley K. Look, Jr.
Michael M. Katz	Peter R. Moison
Robert L. Preeo	Eldon E. Silverman

Jersey M. Green	Kathryn A. Reeves
Richard M. Hess, Jr.	Gilbert R. Egle
Martin J. Green	Timothy Kyle Jordan
Marilyn McWilliams	Brian E. Onorato

OF COUNSEL
Richard P. Rosen

For full biographical listings, see the Martindale-Hubbell Law Directory

GILL PROFESSIONAL CORPORATION (AV)

Suite 610, 5000 South Quebec, 80237-2705
Telephone: 303-770-3040
Facsimile: 303-770-3041

Lawrence D. Gill

Daniel K. Brady

For full biographical listings, see the Martindale-Hubbell Law Directory

GODDARD & GODDARD, P.C. (AV)

Suite 203, 1900 Wazee Street, 80202
Telephone: 303-292-3228
Fax: 303-292-1956

Susan B. Goddard	Jo Anna Goddard

LEGAL SUPPORT PERSONNEL

Theresa D. Cooley (Paralegal)	DeAnne Larrow (Paralegal)

For full biographical listings, see the Martindale-Hubbell Law Directory

HOLME ROBERTS & OWEN LLP (AV)

Suite 4100, 1700 Lincoln, 80203
Telephone: 303-861-7000
Telecopier: 303-866-0200
Email: hro@hro.com *URL:* http://www.hro.com
Boulder, Colorado Office: Suite 400, 1401 Pearl Street.
Telephone: 303-444-5955.
Telecopier: 303-444-1063.
Colorado Springs, Colorado Office: Suite 1300, 90 South Cascade Avenue.
Telephone: 719-473-3800.
Telecopier: 719-633-1518.
Salt Lake City, Utah Office: Suite 1100, 111 East Broadway.
Telephone: 801-521-5800.
Telecopier: 801-521-9639.
London, England Office: Mellier House, 26a Albemarle Street.
Telephone: 44-171-499-8776.
Telecopier: 44-171-499-7769.
Moscow, Russia Office: Kosmodamianskaya Nab. #52/1, Suite 9100, 113054.
Telephone: 7095-961-3000.
Telecopier: 7095-961-3001.
Kiev, Ukraine Office: Terestchenkovskaya #19, Suite 2, 252004.
Telephone: 380-44-224-1348.
Telecopier: 380-44-224-4986.

PARTNERS OF FIRM

James E. Bye	McKay Marsden
Judson W. Detrick	(Salt Lake City Office)
William S. Huff	Stephanie M. Tuthill
Donald J. Hopkins	James R. Ghiselli
Steve L. Gaines	(Boulder Office)
(Colorado Springs Office)	

ASSOCIATES

Charles B. Bruce, Jr.	Mary C. Gordon
Sherry A. Gonzales	(Salt Lake City Office)
Michelle M. Rose-Hughes	

(See Next Column)

For Complete List of Firm Personnel, See General Section

For full biographical listings, see the Martindale-Hubbell Law Directory

MYER, SWANSON, ADAMS & WOLF, P.C. (AV)

The Colorado State Bank Building, 1600 Broadway, Suite 1480, 80202-4915
Telephone: 303-866-9800
Facsimile: 303-866-9818

Rendle Myer	Robert K. Swanson
Allan B. Adams	Thomas J. Wolf

Philip T. Masterson
OF COUNSEL

Robert Swanson	Fred E. Neef (1910-1986)

Representative Clients: The Oppenheimer Funds; Daily Cash Accumulation Fund; The Centennial Trusts; Mile High Chapter of American Red Cross; Master Lease; Heartland Management Co.; Kan-Build of Colorado, Inc.
Reference: The Colorado State Bank of Denver.

For full biographical listings, see the Martindale-Hubbell Law Directory

MYERS, BRADLEY AND DEVITT, P.C. (AV)

Suite 420, 4704 Harlan Street, 80212
Telephone: 303-433-8527
Fax: 303-433-8219

Frederick J. Myers	Jerald J. Devitt
Jon T. Bradley	Randall C. Arp

OF COUNSEL
Kent E. Hanson

Reference: Bank One Lakeside Banking Center.

For full biographical listings, see the Martindale-Hubbell Law Directory

M. KENT OLSEN (AV)

3300 East First Avenue, Suite 600, 80206
Telephone: 303-321-6872
Facsimile: 303-321-3196

For full biographical listings, see the Martindale-Hubbell Law Directory

SHERMAN & HOWARD L.L.C. (AV)

Attorneys and Counselors at Law
633 Seventeenth Street, Suite 3000, 80202
Telephone: 303-297-2900
Telecopier: 303-298-0940
Colorado Springs, Colorado Office: Suite 1500, 90 South Cascade Avenue, 80903.
Telephone: 719-475-2440.
Las Vegas, Nevada Office: Swendseid & Stern a member in Sherman & Howard L.L.C., 317 Sixth Street, 89101.
Telephone: 702-387-6073.
Reno, Nevada Office: Swendseid & Stern, a member in Sherman & Howard L.L.C., 50 West Liberty Street, Suite 660, 89501.
Telephone: 702-323-1980.

Douglas M. Cain	David Thomas III
Duane F. Wurzer	Carol V. Berger

Bridget K. Sullivan	J. David Varley
Joseph M. Dencker	(Not admitted in CO)

Representative Clients: AT&T Corp.; Hathaway Corp.; Newmont Gold Corp.

For Complete List of Firm Personnel, See General Section

For full biographical listings, see the Martindale-Hubbell Law Directory

WADE ASH WOODS HILL & FARLEY, P.C. (AV)

Suite 400, 360 South Monroe Street, 80209
Telephone: 303-322-8943
Fax: 303-320-7501

James R. Wade	James W. Hill
Walter B. Ash	J. Michael Farley
	Steven R. Warden

Herbert E. Tucker, IV	Karen K. Hoiland
	David M. Swank

OF COUNSEL

Barbara Ruh	Lucius E. Woods (1921-1995)

Representative Clients: American Cancer Society (Colorado Division); Clayton College Foundation; Colorado National Bank of Denver (Trust Department); Drive Train Industries, Inc.; Investment Trust Co.; Kalcevic Farms, Inc.; Affiliated National Bank - Englewood (Trust Department); University of Colorado Foundation; Drive Train Industries.

For full biographical listings, see the Martindale-Hubbell Law Directory

Denver—Continued

ZISMAN AND INGRAHAM, P.C. (AV)

Suite 250, 3773 Cherry Creek Drive North, 80209
Telephone: 303-320-0023
Fax: 303-320-0034

Sanford Zisman   James F. Ingraham

For full biographical listings, see the Martindale-Hubbell Law Directory

GREELEY,* Weld Co.

BREGA & WINTERS, P.C. (AV)

1100 Tenth Street, Suite 402, 80631
Telephone: 970-352-4805
Fax: 970-352-6547
Denver, Colorado Office: One United Bank Center. 1700 Lincoln Street, Suite 2222 Street.
Telephone: 303-866-9400.
FAX: 303-861-9109.

Jerry D. Winters   Pamela A. Shaddock

Bradley D. Laue

For full biographical listings, see the Martindale-Hubbell Law Directory

LAKEWOOD, Jefferson Co.

POLIDORI, GEROME, FRANKLIN AND JACOBSON, L.L.C. (AV)

Suite 300, 550 South Wadsworth Boulevard, 80226
Telephone: 303-936-3300
Fax: 303-936-0125

R. Jerold Gerome

Representative Client: Colorado National Bank.

For full biographical listings, see the Martindale-Hubbell Law Directory

LAMAR,* Prowers Co.

SHINN LAWYERS (AV)

200 West Elm Street, P.O. Box 390, 81052
Telephone: 719-336-4313
Fax: 719-336-4315

MEMBERS OF FIRM
Carl M. Shinn   Wendy S. Shinn
ASSOCIATE
Donald L. Steerman

Counsel for: Amity Canal; Lamar Canal; District 67 Ditch Assn.; County of Cheyenne, Colorado; County of Kiowa, Colorado; Ragsdale Farms, Inc.; Sherler Farms; Hatcher Farms, Inc.; Young Bros. Equipment Co., Inc.; Buffalo Canal Co.

For full biographical listings, see the Martindale-Hubbell Law Directory

CONNECTICUT

CHESHIRE, New Haven Co.

WINTERS & FORTE (AV)

Waverly Professional Park, 315 Highland Avenue, Suite 102, P.O. Box 844, 06410
Telephone: 203-272-2927
Fax: 203-271-1222

MEMBERS OF FIRM
David Wayne Winters   Michael C. Forte

A List of Representative Clients will be furnished upon request.
References: Bank of Boston, Connecticut; Centerbank; LaFayette American Bank & Trust Co.

For full biographical listings, see the Martindale-Hubbell Law Directory

DARIEN, Fairfield Co.

MILLAR & AMBRETTE (AV)

23 Old King's Highway South, 06820-1267
Telephone: 203-655-7931
FAX: 203-656-2055

MEMBERS OF FIRM
Samuel D. B. Millar, Jr.   L. Conrad Ambrette
OF COUNSEL
Peter M. Ryan
ASSOCIATES
Patricia Moreland Gross   Carolyn C. Swiggart

For full biographical listings, see the Martindale-Hubbell Law Directory

RUCCI, BURNHAM, CARTA & EDELBERG (AV)

800 Post Road, P.O. Box 1107, 06820
Telephone: 203-655-7695
Facsimile: 203-655-4302
Email: rbce@netaxis.com

MEMBERS OF FIRM
Joseph J. Rucci, Jr.   Mark R. Carta
Paul H. Burnham   Paul B. Edelberg
Kevin C. Beuttenmuller
ASSOCIATES
Thomas C. Healey   Karen K. Linder
William M. Carello   John E. Seelert
Colette C. Symon   (Not admitted in CT)
OF COUNSEL
Ian R. Crawford   James C. Dempsey
George A. Reilly

For full biographical listings, see the Martindale-Hubbell Law Directory

FAIRFIELD, Fairfield Co.

BRAUNSTEIN & TODISCO, LLC (AV)

One Eliot Place, 06430
Telephone: 203-254-1118
Telecopier: 203-254-2453

Samuel L. Braunstein   Amy E. Todisco

Reference: People's Bank.

For full biographical listings, see the Martindale-Hubbell Law Directory

GREENWICH, Fairfield Co.

ALBERT, WARD & JOHNSON, P.C. (AV)

125 Mason Street, P.O. Box 1668, 06836
Telephone: 203-661-8600
Telecopier: 203-661-8051

OF COUNSEL
David Albert   C. Robton Perelli-Minetti

Tom S. Ward, Jr.   Howard R. Wolfe
Scott R. Johnson   Christopher A. Kristoff
Jane D. Hogeman   Vicki K. Comberiati

For full biographical listings, see the Martindale-Hubbell Law Directory

BENTLEY, MOSHER, BABSON & LAMBERT, P.C. (AV)

20 Dayton Avenue, P.O. Box 788, 06836-0788
Telephone: 203-629-2424
Telecopier: 203-629-2545

David F. Babson   Charles E. Mosher
Richard J. Slagle

For full biographical listings, see the Martindale-Hubbell Law Directory

HOLLAND KAUFMANN & BARTELS, LLC (AV)

289 Greenwich Avenue, 06830-6595
Telephone: 203-869-5600
Fax: 203-869-4648

Alexander J. Holland   Amy K. Wilfert
Charles B. Kaufmann, III   Harold R. Burke
Philip H. Bartels   Jean Mills Aranha
Beth K. Hansson   Lori E. Romano
John C. Fusco

For full biographical listings, see the Martindale-Hubbell Law Directory

IVEY, BARNUM & O'MARA, LLC (AV)

Meridian Building, 170 Mason Street, P.O. Box 1689, 06830
Telephone: 203-661-6000
Telecopier: 203-661-9462

MEMBERS OF FIRM
Michael J. Allen   Donat C. Marchand
Robert C. Barnum, Jr.   Miles F. McDonald, Jr.
Edward D. Cosden, Jr.   Edwin J. O'Mara, Jr.
Wilmot L. Harris, Jr.   Remy A. Rodas
William I. Haslun II   Gregory A. Saum
Michael J. Jones   Lorraine Slavin
Edward T. Krumeich, Jr.   Steven B. Steinmetz
ASSOCIATES
Paul G. Amicucci   Melissa Townsend Klauberg
Stephan B. Grozinger   Cristin L. Rothfuss
Juerg A. Heim   Alan S. Rubenstein
Jennifer B. Kallenbach   Sheryl L. Sensale
(Not admitted in CT)

(See Next Column)

IVEY, BARNUM & O'MARA LLC, *Greenwich—Continued*

OF COUNSEL

James W. Cuminale   Jennifer D. Port
Philip R. McKnight   (Not admitted in CT)

For full biographical listings, see the Martindale-Hubbell Law Directory

HARTFORD,* Hartford Co.

COPP & BERALL, LLP (AV)

55 Farmington Avenue, Suite 703, 06105
Telephone: 860-249-5261
Fax: 860-947-6382

MEMBERS OF FIRM

Frank S. Berall   Mark H. Neikrie
Suzanne Brown Walsh

OF COUNSEL

Belton A. Copp

References: Fleet Bank, N.A.; Union Trust Co.; Bank of Boston.

For full biographical listings, see the Martindale-Hubbell Law Directory

GORDON, MUIR AND FOLEY (AV)

Hartford Square North, Ten Columbus Boulevard, 06106-5123
Telephone: 860-525-5361
Telecopier: 860-525-4849

MEMBERS OF FIRM

William S. Gordon, Jr.   William J. Gallitto
  (1946-1956)   Gerald R. Swirsky
George Muir (1939-1976)   Robert J. O'Brien
Edward J. Foley (1955-1983)   Philip J. O'Connor
Peter C. Schwartz   Kenneth G. Williams
John J. Reid   Chester J. Bukowski
John H. Goodrich, Jr.   Mary Ann Santacroce
R. Bradley Wolfe   J. Lawrence Price
Jon Stephen Berk   Mary Anne Alicia Charron
              James G. Kelly

ASSOCIATES

Kevin F. Morin   Andrew J. Hern
Claudia A. Baio   Eileen McCarthy Geel
Patrick T. Treacy   Christopher L. Slack
              Renee W. Dwyer

OF COUNSEL

Stephen M. Riley

Reference: Fleet Bank.

For full biographical listings, see the Martindale-Hubbell Law Directory

GOULD, KILLIAN & WYNNE (AV)

One Commercial Plaza, 25th Floor, 06103-3595
Telephone: 860-278-1270
Telecopier: 860-244-9290

MEMBERS OF FIRM

Samuel Gould (1905-1994)   Mark W. Baronas
Robert K. Killian   William F. Healey
Francis J. Wynne   Nancy E. Gould
Martin A. Gould   Robert O. Wynne

For full biographical listings, see the Martindale-Hubbell Law Directory

SHIPMAN & GOODWIN LLP (AV)

One American Row, 06103-2819
Telephone: 860-251-5000
Telecopier: 860-251-5099
E-Mail: first initial last name @goodwin.com
Email: www@goodwin.com *URL:* http://shipman-goodwin.com
Lakeville, Connecticut Office: Porter Street.
Telephone: 203-435-2539.
Stamford, Connecticut Office: One Landmark Square.
Telephone: 203-324-8100.

MEMBERS OF FIRM

Stuyvesant K. Bearns   James T. Betts
  (Lakeville Office)   Coleman H. Casey
              Stephen K. Gellman

ASSOCIATE

Donna M. Mattiello

COUNSEL

Warren S. Randall   William H. Wood, Jr.
              Robert Ewing

For Complete List of Firm Personnel, See General Section

For full biographical listings, see the Martindale-Hubbell Law Directory

SOROKIN SOROKIN GROSS HYDE & WILLIAMS P.C. (AV)

One Corporate Center, 06103
Telephone: 860-525-6645
Fax: 860-522-1781
Simsbury, Connecticut Office: 730 Hopmeadow Street.
Telephone: 860-651-9348.
Rocky Hill, Connecticut Office: 2360 Main Street.
Telephone: 860-563-9305.
Fax: 860-529-6931.

Charles R. Moore, Jr.   Lewis Rabinovitz
              Barrie K. Wetstone

OF COUNSEL

Ethel Silver Sorokin

For Complete List of Firm Personnel, See General Section

For full biographical listings, see the Martindale-Hubbell Law Directory

NEW HAVEN,* New Haven Co.

BERGMAN, HOROWITZ & REYNOLDS, P.C. (AV)

157 Church Street, 19th Floor, P.O. Box 426, 06502
Telephone: 203-789-1320
Fax: 203-785-8127
Email: mailbox@taxlawyers.com *URL:* http://www.taxlawyers.com
New York, N.Y. Office: 499 Park Avenue, 26th Floor.
Telephone: 212-688-4150.

Stanley N. Bergman   James Russell Brockway
Robert H. Horowitz   Bruce I. Judelson
David L. Reynolds   David A. Ringold
Paul L. Behling   Kathryn Harner Smith
Kenneth N. Musen   Donald S. Hendel
William C. G. Swift, Jr.   Joy M. Miyasaki
Richard J. Klein   Paul M. Roy

Louis R. Piscatelli   Christopher J. Galuppo
James G. Dattaro   Jay H. Rubinstein
Edward A. Renn   (Not admitted in CT)
Tina E. Albright   David M. Hryck
Jay F. Krause   Margaret M. Murphy

For full biographical listings, see the Martindale-Hubbell Law Directory

NEW LONDON, New London Co.

WALLER, SMITH & PALMER, P.C. (AV)

52 Eugene O'Neill Drive, P.O. Box 88, 06320
Telephone: 860-442-0367
Telecopier: 860-447-9915
Old Lyme, Connecticut Office: 103-A Halls Road.
Telephone: 860-434-8063.
Telecopier: 860-434-9452.

Birdsey G. Palmer (Retired)   Hughes Griffis
William W. Miner   Edward B. O'Connell
Robert P. Anderson, Jr.   Frederick B. Gahagan
Robert W. Marrion   Mary E. Driscoll

Tracy M. Collins   Valerie Ann Votto
David P. Condon   Charles C. Anderson

General Counsel For: Town of East Lyme; Town of Lebanon.
Counsel For: Citizens Savings Bank; Sonoco/Northeastern, Inc.; The Nature Conservancy; Fleet Bank.
Local Counsel For: McCue Mortgage Co.; Citicorp Mortgage; U.S. Department of Housing and Urban Development.

For Complete List of Firm Personnel, See General Section

For full biographical listings, see the Martindale-Hubbell Law Directory

SOUTHPORT, Fairfield Co.

BRODY AND OBER, P.C. (AV)

135 Rennell Drive, P.O. Box 572, 06490-0572
Telephone: 203-259-7405
Fax: 203-255-8572

Charles S. Brody (1894-1976)   S. Giles Payne
Seth O. L. Brody   William J. Britt
Stanley B. Garrell   Barbara S. Miller
Frank F. Ober   Ronald B. Noren

Diane F. Martucci   Seth L. Cooper
              Douglas R. Brown

OF COUNSEL

James M. Thorburn   John F. Merchant

For full biographical listings, see the Martindale-Hubbell Law Directory

STAMFORD, Fairfield Co.

WOFSEY, ROSEN, KWESKIN & KURIANSKY (AV)

600 Summer Street, 06901
Telephone: 203-327-2300
Fax: 203-967-9273

MEMBERS OF FIRM

Abraham Wofsey (1915-1944)	Edward M. Kweskin
Michael Wofsey (1927-1951)	David M. Cohen
David M. Rosen (1926-1967)	Marshall Goldberg
Julius B. Kuriansky (1910-1992)	Stephen A. Finn
Monroe Silverman	Judith Rosenberg
Emanuel Margolis	Mark H. Henderson
Howard C. Kaplan	Steven D. Grushkin
Anthony R. Lorenzo	Matthew J. Forstadt

OF COUNSEL

Saul Kwartin   Sydney C. Kweskin (Retired)

ASSOCIATES

Joseph Brachfeld	Eric M. Higgins
John J.L. Chobor	Valerie E. Maze
Steven M. Frederick	Randall M. Skigen
Joy A. Katz	Peter J. Schaffer
Galit Kierkut	Robert W. Finke

Representative Clients: Banque Paribas; Benenson Realty; Cellular Information Systems, Inc.; The Chase Manhattan Bank; First County Bank; Hartford Provision Co.; Louis Dreyfus Corp.; Norwalk Federation of Teachers; People's Bank; Ridgeway Shopping Center.

For full biographical listings, see the Martindale-Hubbell Law Directory

---

WEST HARTFORD, Hartford Co.

BERMAN, BOURNS & CURRIE, LLC (AV)

970 Farmington Avenue, P.O. Box 271837, 06127-1837
Telephone: 860-232-4471
Fax: 860-523-4605

John A. Berman   Courtney B. Bourns
John K. Currie

Mary Beth Anderson   Robert W. Storm, Jr.

For full biographical listings, see the Martindale-Hubbell Law Directory

---

WESTPORT, Fairfield Co.

BLAZZARD, GRODD & HASENAUER, P.C. (AV)

943 Post Road East, P.O. Box 5108, 06881
Telephone: 203-226-7866
Telecopier: 203-454-4855
Hollywood, Florida Office: Suite 213, Oceanwalk Mall, 101 North Ocean Drive, 33019.
Telephone: 954-920-4864.
Facsimile: 954-920-6902. *E-Mail:* BGHFL@AOL.COM

Norse N. Blazzard	William E. Hasenauer
Leslie E. Grodd	Raymond A. O'Hara, III
Judith A. Hasenauer	Lynn Korman Stone
Maureen M. Murphy	

For full biographical listings, see the Martindale-Hubbell Law Directory

---

STUART A. McKEEVER (AV)

155 Post Road, East, 06880
Telephone: 203-227-4756
Fax: 203-454-2031

Reference: Fleet Bank.

For full biographical listings, see the Martindale-Hubbell Law Directory

---

RONALD L. SHEIMAN (AV)

1804 Post Road East, 06880
Telephone: 203-259-0599
Telecopier: 203-255-2570

For full biographical listings, see the Martindale-Hubbell Law Directory

---

DELAWARE

---

*WILMINGTON,** New Castle Co.

CONNOLLY, BOVE, LODGE & HUTZ (AV)

1220 Market Street, P.O. Box 2207, 19899-2207
Telephone: 302-658-9141
Telecopier: 302-658-5614
URL: http://WWW.CBLHLAW.COM

(See Next Column)

James M. Mulligan, Jr.	Charles J. Durante
Richard David Levin	Anne Love Barnett

For Complete List of Firm Personnel, See General Section

For full biographical listings, see the Martindale-Hubbell Law Directory

DALEY, ERISMAN & VAN OGTROP (AV)

1224 King Street, 19801
Telephone: 302-658-4000
Fax: 302-652-8975
Email: jerisman@devolaw.com *URL:* http://www.devolaw.com
Newark, Delaware Office: 206 East Delaware Avenue.
Telephone: 302-368-0133.
FAX: 302-368-4587.

MEMBERS OF FIRM

Robert E. Daley   James A. Erisman
Piet H. van Ogtrop

References: Wilmington Trust Co.; Beneficial National Bank.

For full biographical listings, see the Martindale-Hubbell Law Directory

HERDEG & ASSOCIATES, P.A. (AV)

Suite 500, One Commerce Center, Twelfth and Orange Streets, 19801
Telephone: 302-594-0665
Fax: 302-428-0369

John A. Herdeg

William B. du Pont, Jr.   William H. Lunger

For full biographical listings, see the Martindale-Hubbell Law Directory

POTTER ANDERSON & CORROON (AV)

350 Delaware Trust Building, P.O. Box 951, 19899-0951
Telephone: 302-984-6000
FAX: 302-658-1192
URL: HTTP://WWW.ATTYS.PACDELAWARE.COM

MEMBERS OF FIRM

Leonard S. Togman   David J. Garrett

ASSOCIATE

Scott E. Waxman

Representative Clients: Delaware Trust Capital Management, Inc.

For Complete List of Firm Personnel, See General Section

For full biographical listings, see the Martindale-Hubbell Law Directory

SCHLUSSER & REIVER, P.A. (AV)

1700 West 14th Street, 19806
Telephone: 302-655-8181
Fax: 302-655-8190

Robert E. Schlusser   Joanna Reiver

John A. Ciccarone

For full biographical listings, see the Martindale-Hubbell Law Directory

WILLIAMS, HERSHMAN & WISLER, P.A. (AV)

Suite 600, One Commerce Center, Twelfth and Orange Streets, P.O. Box 511, 19899-0511
Telephone: 302-575-0873
Telecopier: 302-575-1642

David Nicol Williams	Jeffrey C. Wisler
Douglas M. Hershman	Barbara Snapp Danberg

References: Wilmington Trust Co.; PNC Bank.

For full biographical listings, see the Martindale-Hubbell Law Directory

---

DISTRICT OF COLUMBIA

WASHINGTON, D.C. Co.

THE LAW OFFICES OF SHELTON M. BINSTOCK (AV)

1140 Connecticut Avenue, N.W., Suite 703, 20036
Telephone: 202-785-1111
Telecopier: 202-293-1471
Chevy Chase, Maryland Office: 5335 Wisconsin Avenue, Suite 440.
Telephone: 301-656-7646.

David B. Torchinsky
OF COUNSEL
James E. Secrist

For full biographical listings, see the Martindale-Hubbell Law Directory

Washington—Continued

CAPLIN & DRYSDALE, CHARTERED (AV)

One Thomas Circle, N.W., 20005
Telephone: 202-862-5000
Cable Address: "Capdale"
Telex: 904001 CAPL UR WSH
Fax: 202-429-3301
New York, N.Y. Office: 399 Park Avenue.
Telephone: 212-319-7125.
Fax: 212-644-6755.

Mortimer M. Caplin	Douglas D. Drysdale
Robert A. Klayman	Thomas A. Troyer
Ralph A. Muoio	David N. Webster
Elihu Inselbuch	H. David Rosenbloom
(Resident, New York Office)	Peter Van N. Lockwood
Ronald B. Lewis	Cono R. Namorato
Richard W. Skillman	Daniel B. Rosenbaum
Patricia G. Lewis	Richard E. Timbie
Bernard S. Bailor	Graeme W. Bush
Stafford Smiley	Albert G. Lauber, Jr.
Sally A. Regal	Scott D. Michel
Julie W. Davis	Kent A. Mason
Carl S. Kravitz	Trevor W. Swett III
Robert A. Boisture	Robert E. Culbertson
James Sottile, IV	Charles T. Plambeck
Harry J. Hicks, III	James E. Salles
Milton Cerny	Craig A. Sharon
Paul G. Cellupica	Matthew W. Frank
Michael T. Doran	Christian R. Pastore
Nathan D. Finch	(Not admitted in DC)
Jessica L. Goldstein	Elizabeth M. Sellers
Laura J. Kerrigan	Douglas N. Varley
	(Not admitted in DC)

OF COUNSEL

Robert H. Elliott, Jr.	Myron C. Baum
Vivian L. Cavalieri	C. Sanders McNew
Ann C. McMillan	(Resident, New York Office)
	Janne G. Gallagher

For full biographical listings, see the Martindale-Hubbell Law Directory

CRAIGHILL, MAYFIELD, FENWICK & CROMELIN (AV)

Suite 215, 4910 Massachusetts Avenue, N.W., 20016
Telephone: 202-364-4242
Facsimile: 202-966-1078

MEMBERS OF FIRM

G. Bowdoin Craighill, Jr.	Francis E. Fenwick
Richard H. Mayfield	Paul B. Cromelin, III
	Calvin H. Cobb, III

For full biographical listings, see the Martindale-Hubbell Law Directory

CROSS, MURPHY, SMUCK & HOUSTON (AV)

1350 Connecticut Avenue, N.W., Suite 300, 20036
Telephone: 202-393-8668
Telecopier: 202-833-2351
Email: anwalt1350@aol.com

MEMBERS OF FIRM

John W. Cross (1902-1971)	John C. Smuck
James Russell Murphy	Stuart E. Houston
(1905-1986)	

Reference: Crestar Bank, N.A.

For full biographical listings, see the Martindale-Hubbell Law Directory

THE FALK LAW FIRM (AV)

A Professional Limited Company
Suite 260 One Westin Center, 2445 M Street, N.W., 20037
Telephone: 202-833-8700
Telecopier: 202-872-1725
Email: FalkLaw@erols.com

James H. Falk, Sr.	John M. Falk
James H. Falk, Jr.	Robert K. Tompkins

OF COUNSEL

Pierre E. Murphy	Elizabeth C. Collins

For full biographical listings, see the Martindale-Hubbell Law Directory

IVINS, PHILLIPS & BARKER, CHARTERED (AV)

Suite 600, 1700 Pennsylvania Avenue, N.W., 20006
Telephone: 202-393-7600
Fax: 202-393-7601; 347-4256
Email: IPB@mindspring.com

(See Next Column)

H. Stewart Dunn, Jr.	Kevin P. O'Brien
Carroll J. Savage	Michael F. Solomon
Eric R. Fox	Daniel B. Stone
William L. Sollee	Patrick J. Smith
Carol K. Nickel	Michael R. Huffstetler
Leslie Jay Schneider	Laurie E. Keenan
Robert H. Wellen	Peter M. Daub
	Jeffrey E. Moeller

Steven H. Witmer	Robert P. Hanson
Rosina B. Barker	Sheryl E. McAfee
Claude B. Stansbury	Hamish P.M. Hume

OF COUNSEL

Jay W. Glasmann	Joseph E. McAndrews

For full biographical listings, see the Martindale-Hubbell Law Directory

QUINN, RACUSIN & GAZZOLA, CHARTERED (AV)

1401 H Street, N.W. Suite 510, 20005-2178
Telephone: 202-842-9300
Facsimile: 202-682-0148

John H. Quinn, Jr.	Joseph DiStefano
Robert A. Gazzola	Susan Yoder Torres
	Eric John Edwardson

RETIRED

Aaron J. Racusin (Retired)

LEGAL SUPPORT PERSONNEL

Mary G. Wheeler

For full biographical listings, see the Martindale-Hubbell Law Directory

THOMPSON, O'DONNELL, MARKHAM, NORTON & HANNON (AV)

The Southern Building, 805 Fifteenth Street, N.W., Suite 705, 20005
Telephone: 202-289-1133
Facsimile: 202-289-0275

John Jude O'Donnell	Randell Hunt Norton
Julian E. Markham, Jr.	J. Michael Hannon

ASSOCIATES

Kenneth G. Stallard	Brooke A. Pinkerton
	Matthew W Carlson

OF COUNSEL

J. Roy Thompson, Jr.	Henry F. Harding

Representative Clients: C. J. Langenfelder & Sons, Inc., Baltimore, Maryland; Bernard F. Locraft, Civil Engineers, Washington, D. C.; Security Trust, N.A. *References:* American Security Bank, N.A.; Franklin National Bank.

For full biographical listings, see the Martindale-Hubbell Law Directory

FLORIDA

AVENTURA, Dade Co.

BUCHANAN INGERSOLL, PROFESSIONAL CORPORATION (AV⊤)

One Turnberry Place, 19495 Biscayne Boulevard, Suite 606, 33180
Telephone: 305-933-5600
Telecopier: 305-933-2350
URL: http://www.bipc.com
Pittsburgh, Pennsylvania Office: One Oxford Centre, 301 Grant Street, 20th Floor.
Telephone: 412-562-8800.
Philadelphia, Pennsylvania Office: Two Logan Square, Twelfth Floor, 18th & Arch Streets.
Telephone: 215-665-8700.
Harrisburg, Pennsylvania Office: 30 North Third Street.
Telephone: 717-237-4800.
Miami, Florida Office: NationsBank Tower, 100 S.E. Second Street.
Telephone: 305-347-4080.
Tampa, Florida Office: Suite 2500, 401 East Jackson Street.
Telephone: 813-222-8180.
Princeton, New Jersey Office: Buchanan Ingersoll, A Partnership, College Centre, 500 College Road East.
Telephone: 609-987-6800.
Lexington, Kentucky Office: Suite 600, PNC Bank Plaza, 200 West Vine Street.
Telephone: 606-225-5333.
Buffalo, New York Office: 1100 Main Place Tower, 350 Main Street.
Telephone: 716-854-4100.
Fax: 816-854-4227.

Joshua L. Dubin	Mark J. Neuberger

SENIOR ATTORNEY

Ralph B. Bekkevold

(See Next Column)

BUCHANAN INGERSOLL PROFESSIONAL CORPORATION—*Continued*

Todd A. Bancroft	Randi S. Rothfield
Kevin Carmichael	Richard N. Schermer
Jeffrey M. Goodz	Rebecca S. Trinkler

For full biographical listings, see the Martindale-Hubbell Law Directory

BOCA RATON, Palm Beach Co.

PAUL A. BALDOVIN, JR., P.A. (AV)

Suite 405, Lake Wyman Plaza, 2424 North Federal Highway, 33431
Telephone: 561-361-0422
Fax: 561-361-0425

Paul A. Baldovin, Jr.
OF COUNSEL
Alexander L. Suto

For full biographical listings, see the Martindale-Hubbell Law Directory

CARTER, CARLILE, NEALE & FRIEDMAN, P.A. (AV)

Suite 312, 1200 North Federal Highway, 33432
Telephone: 561-368-9900

John E. Carter	Thomas E. Neale
Robert T. Carlile	Annette Friedman

For full biographical listings, see the Martindale-Hubbell Law Directory

DICKENSON, MURDOCH, REX AND SLOAN, CHARTERED (AV)

Suite 410 Compson Financial Center, 980 North Federal Highway, 33432
Telephone: 561-391-1900
Facsimile: 561-391-1933

David B. Dickenson	Robert H. Rex
Richard A. Murdoch	Barbara A. Sloan

Russell C. Silverglate

For full biographical listings, see the Martindale-Hubbell Law Directory

OSBORNE, OSBORNE & deCLAIRE, P.A. (AV)

Suite 100 Via Mizner Financial Plaza, 798 South Federal Highway, P.O. Drawer 40, 33429-9974
Telephone: 561-395-1000
Fax: 561-368-6930

Ray C. Osborne	George F. deClaire
R. Brady Osborne, Jr.	Ellen R. Itzler

Linda L. Snelling

Approved Attorneys for: First Union National Bank of Florida, N.A.; SunBank/South Florida, N.A.; Northern Trust Bank of Florida. NationsBank of Florida, N.A.

For full biographical listings, see the Martindale-Hubbell Law Directory

SCHROEDER & LARCHE, P.A. (AV)

One Boca Place, Suite 319-A, 2255 Glades Road, 33431-7313
Telephone: 561-241-0300
Broward: 954-421-0878
Telecopier: 561-241-0798

Michael A. Schroeder	W. Lawrence Larche

Alan Pellingra

For full biographical listings, see the Martindale-Hubbell Law Directory

BOYNTON BEACH, Palm Beach Co.

ROBERT M. ARLEN, P.A. (AV)

Suite 200, 1501 Corporate Drive, 33426
Telephone: 561-734-9977
Broward Line: 954-781-7822
Telefax: 561-734-7511

Robert M. Arlen

For full biographical listings, see the Martindale-Hubbell Law Directory

NICHOLAS H. HAGOORT, JR., P.A. (AV)

Woolbright Corporate Center, Suite 360, 1901 South Congress Avenue, 33426
Telephone: 561-369-1010
FAX: 561-369-1254
Email: nhagoort@aol.com

(See Next Column)

Nicholas H. Hagoort, Jr.

Reference: SunTrust.

For full biographical listings, see the Martindale-Hubbell Law Directory

BRADENTON,* Manatee Co.

BLALOCK, LANDERS, WALTERS AND VOGLER, P.A. (AV)

802 11th Street West, P.O. Box 469, 34205
Telephone: 941-748-0100
Fax: 941-745-2093

Robert G. Blalock	Edward Vogler, II
Clifford L. Walters, III	Barbara Ann Held

Dana C. Gentry	Michael D. Wyckoff
Charles F. Johnson, III	John E. Wickman
Lisbeth P. Bruce	Lisa E. Bagwell

James R. White

Representative Client: The Bradenton Herald, Inc.

For full biographical listings, see the Martindale-Hubbell Law Directory

GRIMES GOEBEL GRIMES HAWKINS & GLADFELTER, P.A. (AV)

The Professional Building, 1023 Manatee Avenue West, P.O. Box 1550, 34206
Telephone: 941-748-0151
Fax: 941-748-0158

William C. Grimes	Caleb J. Grimes

For Complete List of Firm Personnel, See General Section

For full biographical listings, see the Martindale-Hubbell Law Directory

HARLLEE, PORGES, HAMLIN, KNOWLES, BALD & PROUTY, P.A. (AV)

1205 Manatee Avenue, West, 34205
Telephone: 941-748-3770
Telecopier: 941-748-4160
Email: Law@HarlleePorges.com

John P. Harllee, III	Kimberly Alario Bald
Gregory J. Porges	Steven W. Prouty
Curtis D. Hamlin	Mark A. Nelson
Timothy A. Knowles	Stephen W. Thompson

Joseph L. Najmy	Barrett S. Bell

Shelly A. Gallagher

For full biographical listings, see the Martindale-Hubbell Law Directory

CLEARWATER,* Pinellas Co.

GASSMAN & CONETTA, P.A. (AV)

1245 Court Street Suite 102, 34616
Telephone: 813-442-1200
Fax: 813-443-5829

Alan S. Gassman	Tami F. Conetta

James F. Gulecas
LEGAL SUPPORT PERSONNEL

Shelley Weber	Dawn Shores

Dee Ann Moore

Representative Client: Techni-Car, Inc.
Reference: Republic Bank.

For full biographical listings, see the Martindale-Hubbell Law Directory

CORAL GABLES, Dade Co.

HENDRICKS & HENDRICKS (AV)

310 Alhambra Circle, 33134
Telephone: 305-445-3692
Fax: 305-446-8439

MEMBERS OF FIRM

R. A. Hendricks (1868-1963)	B. E. Hendricks (1904-1978)

Robert A. Hendricks

For full biographical listings, see the Martindale-Hubbell Law Directory

RICHARD H. HUNT & ASSOCIATES A PROFESSIONAL ASSOCIATION (AV)

2801 Ponce de Leon Boulevard Ninth Floor, 33134
Telephone: 305-569-9671
Telecopier: 305-445-7728
Email: huntmia@ix.netcom.com

Richard H. Hunt

Robert Scott Williams

(See Next Column)

RICHARD H. HUNT & ASSOCIATES A PROFESSIONAL ASSOCIATION, *Coral Gables—Continued*

SENIOR COUNSEL
George J. Baya (1900-1995)

For full biographical listings, see the Martindale-Hubbell Law Directory

---

DADE CITY,* Pasco Co.

ROBERT D. SUMNER, P.A. (AV)

14150 Sixth Street, P.O. Drawer 1047, 33526-1047
Telephone: 352-567-5658
Telecopier: 352-567-3928

Donna Sumner Cox (1958-1990)   Robert D. Sumner

General Counsel for: Pasco County Property Appraiser; St. Leo College, St. Leo, Florida.
Local Counsel for: The Four Score Corp.; Withlacoochee River Electric Cooperative, Inc.; Uradco, Inc.

For full biographical listings, see the Martindale-Hubbell Law Directory

---

DAVIE, Broward Co.

WILLIAM A. SNYDER (AV)

7931 S.W. 45th Street, 33328
Telephone: Broward: 954-475-1139

For full biographical listings, see the Martindale-Hubbell Law Directory

---

DAYTONA BEACH, Volusia Co.

DUNN, ABRAHAM & SWAIN (AV)

A Partnership of Professional Associations
347 South Ridgewood Avenue, P.O. Drawer 2600, 32115-2600
Telephone: 904-258-1222
Fax: 904-255-8521
Email: 71722.3430@compuserve.com

MEMBERS OF FIRM
Edgar M. Dunn, Jr., (P.A.)   Robert Abraham (P.A.)
Catherine G. Swain (P.A.)

ASSOCIATE
Suzanne A. Novak

For full biographical listings, see the Martindale-Hubbell Law Directory

LANDIS, GRAHAM, FRENCH, HUSFELD, SHERMAN & FORD, P.A. (AV)

Formerly Hull, Landis, Graham & French
543 South Ridgewood Avenue, 32114
Telephone: 904-252-4717
Fax: 904-253-7352
De Land, Florida Office: 145 East Rich Avenue, P.O. Box 48.
Telephone: 904-734-3451.
Deltona, Florida Office: 204 Medical Arts Center, 1555 Saxon Boulevard.
Telephone: 407-574-1461.
Fax: 407-574-0242.

Erskine W. Landis (1900-1967)   Richard S. Graham
John L. Graham (1905-1978)   William E. Sherman
Thorwald J. Husfeld (1926-1995)   Sam N. Masters

OF COUNSEL
J. Compton French

Counsel for: Barnett Bank of Volusia County; State Farm Mutual Automobile Insurance Co.; West Volusia Hospital Authority; Central Florida Fern Cooperative, Inc.; General Motors Corp.; South Florida Natural Gas Co.; Florida Public Utilities Co.; Volusia County Industrial Development Authority; Florida United Methodist Children's Home: Volusia County Educational Facilities Authority.

For full biographical listings, see the Martindale-Hubbell Law Directory

---

DEERFIELD BEACH, Broward Co.

PATTERSON & HARMON, P.A. (AV)

665 S.E. 10th Street, 33441
Telephone: 954-421-7700
Fax: 954-421-7956

George A. Patterson

Representative Clients: Butler Properties, Ltd.; Powerline Development, Inc.; Rivertown Apartments, Inc.; Rivertown Manor Condominium Association; Stainless, Inc.; Reliance Enterprises; Ransco Development, Inc.
Approved Attorneys for: Attorneys' Title Insurance Fund; Chicago Title Insurance Co.
Reference: Barnett Bank of Broward County, N.A.

For Complete List of Firm Personnel, See General Section

For full biographical listings, see the Martindale-Hubbell Law Directory

---

C. RICHARD SHAMEL, JR. (AV)

Hauser Building, 212 North Federal Highway, 33441
Telephone: 954-428-3700

Reference: Broward County Court Guardianship Program.

For full biographical listings, see the Martindale-Hubbell Law Directory

---

DE LAND,* Volusia Co.

LANDIS, GRAHAM, FRENCH, HUSFELD, SHERMAN & FORD, P.A. (AV)

Formerly Hull, Landis, Graham & French
145 East Rich Avenue, P.O. Box 48, 32721-0048
Telephone: 904-734-3451
Fax: 904-736-1350
Daytona Beach, Florida Office: 543 South Ridgewood Avenue, 32114.
Telephone: 904-252-4717.
Deltona, Florida Office: 204 Medical Arts Center, 1555 Saxon Boulevard.
Telephone: 407-574-1461.
Fax: 407-574-0242.

Erskine W. Landis (1900-1967)   Joe G. Dykes, Jr.
John L. Graham (1905-1978)   Frank A. Ford, Jr.
Thorwald J. Husfeld (1926-1995)   Sam N. Masters
William E. Sherman   (Daytona Beach Office)
Richard S. Graham   Philip L. Partridge
  (Daytona Beach Office)   Edwin Channing Coolidge, Jr.
William A. Ottinger   Kent A. Showalter, III
  (Deltona Office)

OF COUNSEL
J. Compton French   Frank A. Ford, Sr.
  (Daytona Beach Office)

Counsel for: Barnett Bank of Volusia County; State Farm Mutual Automobile Insurance Co.; West Volusia Hospital Authority; Central Florida Fern Cooperative, Inc.; General Motors Corp.; South Florida Natural Gas Co.; Florida Public Utilities Co.; Volusia County Industrial Development Authority; Florida United Methodist Children's Home; Volusia County Educational Facilities Authority.

For full biographical listings, see the Martindale-Hubbell Law Directory

---

DELRAY BEACH, Palm Beach Co.

DEVITT, THISTLE & DEVITT, P.A. (AV)

30 Southeast 4th Avenue, 33483
Telephone: 407-276-7436
Fax: 407-276-7522

Rhea Whitley (1903-1968)   Fred B. Devitt, Jr.
Calhoun Y. Byrd (1900-1985) J. Jeffrey Thistle
              Fred B. Devitt, III

Approved Attorneys for: Attorneys' Title Insurance Fund.
References: SunTrust/South Florida, N.A.; Barnett Banks Trust Co., N.A.

For full biographical listings, see the Martindale-Hubbell Law Directory

---

DELTONA, Volusia Co.

LANDIS, GRAHAM, FRENCH, HUSFELD, SHERMAN & FORD, P.A. (AV)

204 Medical Arts Center, 1555 Saxon Boulevard, 32725
Telephone: 407-574-1461
Fax: 407-574-0242
Daytona Beach, Florida Office: 543 South Ridgewood Avenue, 32114.
Telephone: 904-252-4717.
De Land, Florida Office: 145 East Rich Avenue, P.O. Box 48.
Telephone: 904-734-3451.

Erskine W. Landis (1900-1967)   Thorwald J. Husfeld (1926-1995)
John L. Graham (1905-1978)   William A. Ottinger

Counsel for: Barnett Bank of Volusia County; State Farm Mutual Automobile Insurance Co.; West Volusia Hospital Authority; Central Florida Fern Cooperative, Inc.; General Motors Corp.; South Florida Natural Gas Co.; Florida Public Utilities Co.; Volusia County Industrial Development Authority; Florida United Methodist Children's Home; Volusia County Educational Facilities Authority.

For full biographical listings, see the Martindale-Hubbell Law Directory

---

DESTIN, Okaloosa Co.

J. JEROME MILLER (AV)

Suite 3, 415 Mountain Drive, 32541
Telephone: 904-837-3860
Fax: 904-837-6158

Kevin M. Helmich

For full biographical listings, see the Martindale-Hubbell Law Directory

ENGLEWOOD, Sarasota & Charlotte Cos.

BATSEL, MCKINLEY, ITTERSAGEN, GUNDERSON & BERNTSSON, P.A. (AV)

Suite 204 Manor Pointe Professional Center, 1861 Placida Road, 34223
Telephone: 941-474-7713
Telecopier: 941-474-8276
Port Charlotte, Florida Office: 18401 Murdock Circle. 33948.
Telephone: 941-627-1000.
Telefax: 941-255-0684.

C. Guy Batsel	Scott D. Ittersagen
Michael R. McKinley (Resident, Port Charlotte Office)	Miko P. Gunderson
	Robert H. Berntsson (Resident, Port Charlotte Office)

Robert F. Koch (Resident, Port Charlotte Office)	Jerry Paul

For full biographical listings, see the Martindale-Hubbell Law Directory

WELLBAUM & MCLENNON, P.A. (AV)

1160 South McCall Road, Suite B, 34223
Telephone: 941-474-3241
Fax: 941-475-2927

Robert W. Wellbaum, Jr.	Thomas P. McLennon

Maurice L. Jemison

Reference: SouthTrust Bank.

For full biographical listings, see the Martindale-Hubbell Law Directory

FORT LAUDERDALE, * Broward Co.

CAMP & CAMP, P.A. (AV)

Sun Bank Center, Suite 1070, 515 East Las Olas Boulevard, 33301
Telephone: 954-524-8111
FAX: 954-524-2661

James D. Camp, Jr.	James D. Camp, III

General Counsel for: Sun Bank/South Florida, N.A., Trust Division, Broward Community College; Steel Fabricators, Inc.; Steel Joists, Inc.; Altman-Barry Construction, Inc.; LaGasse Pool Construction Co.; BRDG-Tndr Corp.
Representative Clients: Amp, Inc.; Ed Morse Chevrolet, Inc.; Gulfstream Pump and Equipment Co.

For full biographical listings, see the Martindale-Hubbell Law Directory

FRIEDRICH & FRIEDRICH, P.A. (AV)

Northern Trust Bank Building, Suite 202, 2601 East Oakland Park Boulevard, 33306
Telephone: 954-564-1245
Fax: 954-563-5079

J. Peter Friedrich	J. Peter Friedrich, Jr.

Approved Attorneys for: Northern Trust Bank of Florida; SunBank of S. Florida, NA.; Barnett Bank; NationsBank; Merrill Lynch.

For full biographical listings, see the Martindale-Hubbell Law Directory

THEODORE H. FULTON, JR. (AV)

321 Southeast 15th Avenue, P.O. Box 2427, 33303
Telephone: 954-467-2000
Telecopier: 954-467-2306

For full biographical listings, see the Martindale-Hubbell Law Directory

KELLEY, HERMAN & MILLS (AV)

Suite 206, 1401 East Broward Boulevard, 33301
Telephone: 954-462-7806
Fax: 954-522-0396

MEMBERS OF FIRM

Patrick G. Kelley	Richard A. Mills, III
Bruce K. Herman	Jeffrey B. Smith

Approved Attorneys for: Ticor Title Insurance Co.; Attorney's Title Insurance Fund.

For full biographical listings, see the Martindale-Hubbell Law Directory

WILLIAM A. ZEIHER, P.A. (AV)

2780 East Oakland Park Boulevard, 33306
Telephone: 954-561-8205
Fax: 954-561-8208

William A. Zeiher

For full biographical listings, see the Martindale-Hubbell Law Directory

FORT MYERS, * Lee Co.

ALLEN, KNUDSEN & DEBOEST, P.A. (AV)

1415 Hendry Street, P.O. Box 1480, 33902
Telephone: 941-334-1381
Telecopier: 941-334-0266
Naples, Florida Office: Park North Center, 5121 Castello Drive, Suite 1.
Telephone: 941-263-5040.
Fax: 941-263-6944.

George E. Allen (1916-1993)	Terrence F. Lenick
Arthur K. Knudsen, Jr.	William E. Stockman
Richard D. DeBoest	Tamela Eady Wiseman
Christopher N. Davies	Brenda A. Bayly
Robert H. Duckwall	Lori Westhrin Clifford
Richard D. DeBoest II	Dana M. Gallup
C. Michael Jackson	Thaddeus Dennis Kirkpatrick

P. Michael Villalobos

LEGAL SUPPORT PERSONNEL

Carolyn Fox Lambert (Paralegal)

Representative Clients: Lennar Homes, Inc.; Pulte Home Corp.; Cobb Theatres, Inc.; International Paper; Saxon Properties, Inc.; Scott's Hospitality, Inc.; WCN Communities, L.P.; Evelyn Jackman and Sons, Inc.; Pacificorp; Nite-Bright Sign Co.

For full biographical listings, see the Martindale-Hubbell Law Directory

AVERY, WHIGHAM & WINESETT, P.A. (AV)

Corner of First and Hendry Streets, 2248 First Street, P.O. Drawer 610, 33902-0610
Telephone: 941-334-7040
Fax: 941-334-6258

Richard W. Winesett	Dennis L. Avery
James M. Costello	

For full biographical listings, see the Martindale-Hubbell Law Directory

HENDERSON, FRANKLIN, STARNES & HOLT, PROFESSIONAL ASSOCIATION (AV)

1715 Monroe Street, P.O. Box 280, 33902-0280
Telephone: 941-334-4121
Telecopier: 941-332-4494

Ernest H. Hatch, Jr.

Representative Clients: Aetna Property & Casualty Group; CIGNA Group; CSX Transportation, Inc.; Fireman's Fund Insurance Cos.; Barnett Bank of Lee County, N.A.; Northern Trust Bank of Florida, N.A.; The Hartford Insurance Group; Travelers Group; United Telephone Company of Florida.

For Complete List of Firm Personnel, See General Section

For full biographical listings, see the Martindale-Hubbell Law Directory

LAW OFFICES OF LLOYD G. HENDRY, P.A. (AV)

Society First Federal Center, 2201 Second Street, Suite 502, P.O. Box 1509, 33902
Telephone: 941-332-7123
Fax: 941-332-5147

Lloyd G. Hendry	Mary Hendry Sonne
Harry O. Hendry	

For full biographical listings, see the Martindale-Hubbell Law Directory

SHEPPARD, BRETT, STEWART & HERSCH, P.A. (AV)

(Formerly Sheppard & Woolslair)
2121 West First Street, P.O. Drawer 400, 33902
Telephone: 941-334-1141
Fax: 941-334-3965

W. A. Sheppard (1898-1971)	Jay Andrew Brett
John K. Woolslair (1908-1968)	John F. Stewart
Craig R. Hersch	

OF COUNSEL

John Woolslair Sheppard

D. Hugh Kinsey, Jr.

Approved Attorneys for: Attorneys' Title Insurance Fund; Chicago Title Insurance Co.

For full biographical listings, see the Martindale-Hubbell Law Directory

SMOOT ADAMS EDWARDS & GREEN, P.A. (AV)

One University Park Suite 600, 12800 University Drive, P.O. Box 60259, 33906-6259
Telephone: 941-489-1776
(800) 226-1777 (in Florida)
Fax: 941-489-2444
Email: 71600.2745@compuserve.com

(See Next Column)

SMOOT ADAMS EDWARDS & GREEN P.A., *Fort Myers—Continued*

J. Tom Smoot, Jr.	Bruce D. Green
Hal Adams	Steven I. Winer
Franklyn A. (Chip) Johnson	Mark R. Komray
(1947-1991)	Clayton W. Crevasse
Charles B. Edwards	M. Brian Cheffer

Robert S. Forman	C. Berk Edwards, Jr.
Kathleen W. McBride	Melville G. Brinson, III
Lowell Schoenfeld	Samuel J. Hagan, IV.

For full biographical listings, see the Martindale-Hubbell Law Directory

FORT WALTON BEACH, Okaloosa Co.

JOHNNY FORTUNE, P.A. (AV)

92 Eglin Parkway N.E., P.O. Drawer 2167, 32549
Telephone: 904-243-7184
FAX: 904-244-2148

Johnny A. Fortune

Representative Client: Trust Department, Vanguard Bank & Trust Co.

For full biographical listings, see the Martindale-Hubbell Law Directory

GAINESVILLE,* Alachua Co.

WAYNE P. CASTELLO (AV)

Suite W, 2772 N.W. 43rd Street, 32606
Telephone: 352-377-4422
Telecopier: 352-373-5792
Email: GHWW53C@Prodigy.com

LEGAL SUPPORT PERSONNEL
Griffin Stegall (Legal Assistant)

For full biographical listings, see the Martindale-Hubbell Law Directory

JACKSONVILLE,* Duval Co.

KENNETH G. ANDERSON (AV)

Suite 2540, Riverplace Tower, 1301 Riverplace Boulevard, 32207-9039
Telephone: 904-399-8000
Telecopier: 904-346-3078

ASSOCIATES

James P. Stevens	Robert G. Hicks

For full biographical listings, see the Martindale-Hubbell Law Directory

WILLIAM R. BLACKARD, JR. (AV)

Suite 600, 100 Laura Street, 32202
Telephone: 904-354-4400

For full biographical listings, see the Martindale-Hubbell Law Directory

JEAN C. COKER, P.A. (AV)

Suite 160 Barnett Plaza, 6622 Southpoint Drive South, 32216
Telephone: 904-296-1100
Fax: 904-296-1200

Jean C. Coker

LEGAL SUPPORT PERSONNEL
Diana M. Len (Estate & Trust Administration Paralegal)

References: Barnett Banks Trust Company, National Association; First Union National Bank of Florida.

For full biographical listings, see the Martindale-Hubbell Law Directory

DONAHOO, DONAHOO & BALL, P.A. (AV)

(Incorporated in 1981)
2925 Barnett Center, 50 North Laura Street, 32202
Telephone: 904-354-8080
Fax: 904-791-9563

John W. Donahoo (1907-1993)	Haywood M. Ball
Thomas M. Donahoo	William B. McMenamy
Bruce D. Johnson	

Thomas M. Donahoo, Jr.

For full biographical listings, see the Martindale-Hubbell Law Directory

FRAZIER & FRAZIER, ATTORNEYS AT LAW, P.A. (AV)

Suite A 1515 Riverside Avenue, 32204
Telephone: 904-353-5616
Fax: 904-353-5619

(See Next Column)

William R. Frazier	W. Robinson Frazier

References: First Union National Bank of Florida; Barnett Bank of Jacksonville, N.A.; Enterprise National Bank of Jacksonville; First Guaranty Bank & Trust Co.

For full biographical listings, see the Martindale-Hubbell Law Directory

WILLIAM J. JOOS, P.A. (AV)

3030 Hartley Road Drive, Suite 5, 32257
Telephone: 904-724-6109
Fax: 904-724-6333

William J. Joos

SMITH HULSEY & BUSEY (AV)

1800 First Union National Bank Tower, 225 Water Street, P.O. Box 53315, 32201-3315
Telephone: 904-359-7700
Facsimile: 904-359-7708; 353-9908

Lloyd Smith (1915-1987)
MEMBERS OF FIRM

Dennis L. Blackburn	E. Owen McCuller, Jr.
Stephen D. Busey	James H. Post
Douglas D. Chunn	Bryan L. Putnal
Earl E. Googe, Jr.	E. Lanny Russell
Jeanne E. Helton	Joel Settembrini, Jr.
Cynthia C. Jackson	Tim E. Sleeth
G. Preston Keyes	John R. Smith, Jr.
William E. Kuntz	James J. Taylor, Jr.
M. Richard Lewis, Jr.	Timothy W. Volpe
John F. MacLennan	Waddell A. Wallace, III
Raymond R. Magley	Harry M. Wilson, III

Michael M. Bajalia	R. Leanne McKnight
James A. Bolling, Jr.	Mary E. McManus
E. Lanier Drew	Jeanne M. Miller
Diana Salama Farhat	Stephen D. Moore, Jr.
Martin A. Fitzpatrick	Howard J. Smith
Michael R. Freed	Steven G. Spears
Lee G. Kellison	Melissa Smith Turra
Lauren P. Langham	Herschel T. Vinyard, Jr
Marjorie Conner Makar	Leslie A. Wickes
Bradley R. Markey	Karl A. Zillgitt

OF COUNSEL

Mark Hulsey	John E. Thrasher

Representative Clients: Baptist/St. Vincent's Health System, Inc.; Browning-Ferris Industries, Inc.; Champion Realty Corp. (Florida); First Union National Bank of Florida; Florida Rock Industries, Inc.; PGA Tour, Inc.; KPMG Peat Marwick; The Regency Group, Inc.; The Ritz-Carlton Hotel Co.; University of Florida.

For full biographical listings, see the Martindale-Hubbell Law Directory

JUPITER, Palm Beach Co.

JOSEPH C. KEMPE PROFESSIONAL ASSOCIATION (AV)

Attorneys and Counselors at Law
America Plaza, Suite 400, 1070 East Indiantown Road, 33477-5111
Telephone: 561-747-7300
FAX: 561-747-7722
Email: JCKempe@msn.com
Stuart, Florida Office: Royal Palm Financial Center II, Suite 200, 789 South Federal Highway.
Telephone: 561-223-0700.
Fax: 561-223-0707.
Vero Beach, Florida Office: Suite B, 664 Azalea Lane.
Telephone: 561-562-4022.
Fax: 561-234-1422.

Joseph C. Kempe

Lesley Hogan	Sean L. Wilson
	Jane W. Bergacker

For full biographical listings, see the Martindale-Hubbell Law Directory

KISSIMMEE,* Osceola Co.

OVERSTREET RITCH & THACKER (AV)

100 Church Street, P.O. Box 420760, 34742
Telephone: 407-847-5151
FAX: 407-847-3353

MEMBERS OF FIRM

Murray Overstreet	John B. Ritch
	Jo Overstreet Thacker

Representative Client: Osceola County Tax Collector.
Approved Attorneys for: Attorneys' Title Insurance Fund.

For full biographical listings, see the Martindale-Hubbell Law Directory

Kissimmee—Continued

POHL & SHORT, P.A.

(See Winter Park)

LAKELAND, Polk Co.

HAHN, McCLURG, WATSON, GRIFFITH & BUSH, P.A. (AV)

101 South Florida Avenue, P.O. Box 38, 33802
Telephone: 941-688-7747
Telecopier: 941-683-4582

James P. Hahn	Stephen C. Watson
E.V. McClurg	John R. Griffith
	Philip H. Bush

General Counsel: Peoples Bank of Lakeland; First Federal of Florida; Publix Super Markets, Inc.
Approved Attorneys For: Attorneys' Title Insurance Fund; American Title Insurance Co.; Title & Trust Company of Florida; Federal Land Bank of Columbia, Columbia, S.C.
Reference: Peoples Bank of Lakeland.

For full biographical listings, see the Martindale-Hubbell Law Directory

---

LAKE WORTH, Palm Beach Co.

ALTMAN, GREER & DOUGHERTY (AV)

219 North Dixie Highway, 33460
Telephone: 407-588-3311
Fax: 407-588-3315

MEMBERS OF FIRM

Zell H. Altman	Bruce G. Greer
	Thomas H. Dougherty

For full biographical listings, see the Martindale-Hubbell Law Directory

---

MAITLAND, Orange Co.

DITTMER, WOHLUST & WILKINS, P.A. (AV)

Suite 100, 230 Lookout Place, P.O. Box 941690, 32794-1690
Telephone: 407-539-0009
Fax: 407-539-1995

Terrance H. Dittmer	G. Charles Wohlust
	Robert C. Wilkins, Jr.

OF COUNSEL

Richard F. Trismen	James A. McNabb, Jr.
	Bryan D. Austin

For full biographical listings, see the Martindale-Hubbell Law Directory

---

MELBOURNE, Brevard Co.

FRESE, NASH & TORPY, P.A. (AV)

Suite 505, 930 South Harbor City Boulevard, 32901
Telephone: 407-984-3300
FAX: 407-951-3741

Gary B. Frese	Vincent G. Torpy, Jr.
Charles Ian Nash	Gregory S. Hansen
	James Patrick Anderson

Laura L. Anderson	Stephen P. Heuston
	Patrick F. Roche

Reference: First Union National Bank of Florida.

For full biographical listings, see the Martindale-Hubbell Law Directory

---

KRASNY AND DETTMER (AV)

A Partnership of Professional Associations
780 South Apollo Boulevard, P.O. Box 428, 32902-0428
Telephone: 407-723-5646
Telecopier: 407-768-1147

Myron S. (Mike) Krasny (P.A.)	Dale A. Dettmer (P.A.)

Scott Krasny

Representative Client: Huntington National Bank of Florida.

For full biographical listings, see the Martindale-Hubbell Law Directory

---

MIAMI,* Dade Co.

PETER A. COHEN, P.A. (AV)

Penthouse One, 155 South Miami Avenue, 33130
Telephone: 305-358-9251
Fax: 305-358-3412

Peter A. Cohen

For full biographical listings, see the Martindale-Hubbell Law Directory

---

DUNWODY WHITE & LANDON, P.A. (AV)

550 Biltmore Way, Suite 810 (Coral Gables), 33134
Telephone: 305-529-1500
Fax: 305-529-8855
Naples, Florida Office: 4001 Tamiami Trail North, Suite 395, 34103.
Telephone: 941-263-5885.
Fax: 941-262-1442.
Palm Beach, Florida Office: 251 South County Road, P.O. Box 3165, 33480.
Telephone: 561-655-2120.
Fax: 561-655-2168.

Atwood Dunwody (1912-1996)	Thomas J. Matkov
Neil R. Chrystal	William T. Muir
Jack A. Falk, Jr.	Mitchell E. Silverstein
John J. Grundhauser	Robert A. White
Robert D. W. Landon, II	David L. Burg

For full biographical listings, see the Martindale-Hubbell Law Directory

---

NELSON C. KESHEN, P.A. (AV)

Two Datran Center, Suite 1511, 9130 South Dadeland Boulevard, 33156
Telephone: 305-670-7010
Facsimile: 305-670-6203

Nelson C. Keshen

Mindy D. Gerson

For full biographical listings, see the Martindale-Hubbell Law Directory

---

MARSHA G. MADORSKY (AV)

2665 South Bayshore Drive Suite 603, 33133
Telephone: 305-856-0879
Fax: 305-854-6093

OF COUNSEL
W. Tucker Gibbs
ASSOCIATE
Margaret C.F. Quinlivan

For full biographical listings, see the Martindale-Hubbell Law Directory

---

ZACK, SPARBER, KOSNITZKY, SPRATT & BROOKS, P.A. (AV)

International Place, 100 Southeast Second Street, Suite 2800, 33131-2144
Telephone: 305-539-8400
Facsimile: 305-539-1307

Byron L. Sparber	Deborah R. Mayo
Jorge A. Gonzalez	Roland Sanchez-Medina, Jr.
	Thomas O. Wells

For Complete List of Firm Personnel, See General Section

For full biographical listings, see the Martindale-Hubbell Law Directory

---

MIAMI BEACH, Dade Co.

STEINBERG, SLEWETT & YAFFE, P.A. (AV)

767 Arthur Godfrey Road, The Senator Law Center, 33140-9998
Telephone: Dade: 305-538-2344; Broward 954-462-2344
FAX: 305-538-0419
New York
New York, New York Office: 574 Fifth Avenue, 2nd Floor.
Telephone: 212-391-2080.

Paul B. Steinberg	Robert D. Slewett
	Robert H. Yaffe

For full biographical listings, see the Martindale-Hubbell Law Directory

---

NAPLES,* Collier Co.

DUNWODY WHITE & LANDON, P.A. (AV)

4001 Tamiami Trail North, Suite 395, 34103
Telephone: 941-263-5885
Fax: 941-262-1442
Miami, Florida Office: 550 Biltmore Way, Suite 810, 33134.
Telephone: 305-529-1500.
Fax: 305-529-8855.
Palm Beach, Florida Office: 251 South County Road, P.O. Box 3165, 33480.
Telephone: 561-655-2120.
Fax: 561-655-2168.

Jackson M. Bruce, Jr.	Ronald L. Fick
Neil R. Chrystal	Robert D. W. Landon, II
Jack A. Falk, Jr.	David M. Halpen

For full biographical listings, see the Martindale-Hubbell Law Directory

Naples—Continued

JAMES W. ELKINS, P.A. (AV)

Suite 303 The Fairway Building, 1000 Tamiami Trail North, 33940
Telephone: 941-263-0910
Fax: 941-263-6091

James W. Elkins

Approved Attorney for: Attorneys Title Insurance Fund.

For full biographical listings, see the Martindale-Hubbell Law Directory

GRANT, FRIDKIN & PEARSON, P.A. (AV)

Pelican Bay Corporate Centre, 5551 Ridgewood Drive, Suite 501, 34108
Telephone: 941-514-1000
Fax: 941-514-0377
Email: 76402.3516@compuserve.com
Key West, Florida Office: 422 Fleming Street, 33040.
Telephone: 305-296-4553.
Fax: 305-296-7049.

SHAREHOLDERS

G. Helen Athan	Jeffrey D. Fridkin
Michael A. Feldman	Richard C. Grant
William M. Pearson	

Thomas G. Norsworthy

For full biographical listings, see the Martindale-Hubbell Law Directory

MYERS KRAUSE & STEVENS, CHARTERED (AV)

5811 Pelican Bay Boulevard, Suite 600, 34108-2794
Telephone: 941-598-1221
Fax: 941-598-3499
URL: http://www.myerskrause.com

William H. Myers	Richard S. Franklin
Andrew J. Krause	David P. Browne
William K. Stevens	Robert J. Stommel
Jeffrey J. Beihoff	

References: NBD Bank; Northern Trust Bank of Florida, N.A.; SunTrust; U.S. Trust Company of Florida; Comerica Trust Company of Florida, N.A.; Chemical Bank Florida; Key Trust Company of Florida, N.A.; Bessemer Trust Company of Florida.

For full biographical listings, see the Martindale-Hubbell Law Directory

QUARLES & BRADY (AV)

Barnett Center, 4501 Tamiami Trail North Suite 300, 33940-3060
Telephone: 941-262-5959
Fax: 941-434-4999
Milwaukee, Wisconsin Office: 411 East Wisconsin Avenue, 53202-4497.
Telephone: 414-277-5000.
Fax: 414-271-3552.
Madison, Wisconsin Office: Firstar Plaza, One South Pinckney Street, P.O. Box 2113, 53701-2113.
Telephone: 608-251-5000.
Fax: 608-251-9166.
West Palm Beach, Florida Office: 222 Lakeview Avenue, 4th Floor, 33401.
Telephone: 561-653-5000.
Fax: 561-653-5333.
Phoenix, Arizona Office: One Camelback Building, One East Camelback Road, Suite 400, 85012-1649.
Telephone: 602-230-5500.
Fax: 602-230-5598.

PARTNERS

Thomas E. Maloney	Kimberly Leach Johnson

ASSOCIATES

Joseph D. Zaks	Samara S. Holland

For Complete List of Firm Personnel, See General Section

For full biographical listings, see the Martindale-Hubbell Law Directory

DENNIS R. WHITE, P.A. (AV)

Suite 300, Fifth Third Bank Building, 4099 Tamiami Trail North, 34103-3598
Telephone: 941-261-4700
Facsimile: 941-261-4721
Email: drw@whitelaw.com

Dennis R. White

For full biographical listings, see the Martindale-Hubbell Law Directory

NEW PORT RICHEY, Pasco Co.

JAMES J. ALTMAN (AV)

5628 Main Street, 34652
Telephone: 813-848-8435
Fax: 813-847-2750

(See Next Column)

ASSOCIATES

Robert N. Altman	Thomas P. Altman

Approved Attorney for: Attorneys' Title Insurance Fund.
Reference: NationsBank of Florida.

For full biographical listings, see the Martindale-Hubbell Law Directory

NORTH MIAMI BEACH, Dade Co.

NELSON & LAFEMINA, P.A. (AV)

One Turnberry Place 19495 Biscayne Boulevard, Suite 609, 33180-2320
Telephone: 505-932-2000
Telefax: 505-933-2350

Barry A. Nelson	Rose Marie LaFemina

For full biographical listings, see the Martindale-Hubbell Law Directory

ORLANDO,* Orange Co.

MORAN & SHAMS, P.A. (AV)

111 North Orange Avenue, Suite 1200, P.O. Box 472, 32802-0472
Telephone: 407-841-4141
Fax: 407-841-4148
Email: moran-shams@moran-shams.com

Thomas P. Moran	Robert S. MacDonald
Maurice Shams	Sidney H. Shams

References: NationsBank; Sun Bank; First Union National Bank.

For full biographical listings, see the Martindale-Hubbell Law Directory

POHL & SHORT, P.A.

(See Winter Park)

CRAIG B. WARD, P.A. (AV)

Suite 501, 105 East Robinson Street, 32801
Telephone: 407-839-0222
Fax: 407-839-0577

Craig B. Ward
OF COUNSEL
Charles D. Miner

Representative Clients: Hospitality Management Resources, Inc.; Lake of the Woods Homeowners Association, Inc.; Metro One, Inc. (Real Estate); National Ambulance Builders, Inc.; Poole Construction Co., Inc.; Power Concrete Products Co.; Richard Sibley Associates, Inc. (Advertising); Scientific-Atlanta, Inc.
Approved Agent For: First American Title Insurance Co.; Attorneys' Title Insurance Fund.

For full biographical listings, see the Martindale-Hubbell Law Directory

WINDERWEEDLE, HAINES, WARD & WOODMAN, P.A. (AV)

Barnett Bank Center, 390 North Orange Avenue, P.O. Box 1391, 32802-1391
Telephone: 407-423-4246
Telecopier: 407-423-7014
Winter Park, Florida Office: Barnett Bank Building 250 Park Avenue, South, P.O. Box 880.
Telephone: 407-423-4246.
Telecopier: 407-645-3728.

Harold A. Ward, III	William A. Walker II

References: Barnett Bank of Central Florida, N.A., Orlando, Florida; United American Bank; Seminole National Bank; Georgia Pacific Corp.; USX Corp.

For Complete List of Firm Personnel, See General Section

For full biographical listings, see the Martindale-Hubbell Law Directory

PALM BEACH, Palm Beach Co.

BAUGHER, METTLER & SHELTON (AV)

340 Royal Poinciana Plaza, P.O. Box 109, 33480
Telephone: 407-833-9631
Fax: 407-655-2835

MEMBERS OF FIRM

Thomas M. Mettler	John W. Shelton

ASSOCIATE
Francis X. J. Lynch

Reference: First National Bank in Palm Beach.

For full biographical listings, see the Martindale-Hubbell Law Directory

MINTMIRE & ASSOCIATES (AV)

265 Sunrise Avenue, Suite 204, 33480
Telephone: 561-832-5696
Fax: 561-659-5371

(See Next Column)

MINTMIRE & ASSOCIATES—Continuied

Donald F. Mintmire   Jeffrey A. Shaffer
Paul Safran, Jr.   Timothy D. Friedman

For full biographical listings, see the Martindale-Hubbell Law Directory

---

REID MOORE, JR. (AV)

115 Royal Ponciana Plaza, 50 Cocoanut Row, P.O. Box 2764, 33480
Telephone: 561-655-0400
Fax: 561-655-7063

For full biographical listings, see the Martindale-Hubbell Law Directory

---

MURPHY, REID, PILOTTE, ORD & AUSTIN (AV)

A Partnership of Professional Associations
Suite 100, 340 Royal Palm Way, 33480
Telephone: 561-655-4060
Facsimile: 561-832-5436
Vero Beach, Florida Office: Plantation Plaza, 6606-20th Street, P.O. Drawer M.
Telephone: 561-567-6480.
Facsimile: 561-562-0220.

Eugene W. Murphy Jr. (P.A.)   Frank T. Pilotte (P.A.)

For Complete List of Firm Personnel, See General Section

For full biographical listings, see the Martindale-Hubbell Law Directory

---

PALM BEACH GARDENS, Palm Beach Co.

MATHISON & MATHISON (AV)

5606 PGA Boulevard, Suite 211, 33418
Telephone: 561-624-2001
Facsimile: 561-624-0036

MEMBERS OF FIRM
Stephen S. Mathison   Carl M. Mathison, Jr.
ASSOCIATE
Frederic T. DeHon, Jr.

For full biographical listings, see the Martindale-Hubbell Law Directory

---

POMPANO BEACH, Broward Co.

JOHN L. KORTHALS (AV)

1401 East Atlantic Boulevard, 33060
Telephone: 954-783-2999
FAX: 954-783-9832

For full biographical listings, see the Martindale-Hubbell Law Directory

---

PORT RICHEY, Pasco Co.

THORNTON, TORRENCE & GONZALES, P.A. (AV)

6645 Ridge Road, 34668
Telephone: 813-845-6224
Telecopier: 813-845-7895

Ronald G. Thornton   Alfred W. Torrence, Jr.
Larry J. Gonzales

Mark A. Goettel

For full biographical listings, see the Martindale-Hubbell Law Directory

---

PUNTA GORDA, * Charlotte Co.

WOTITZKY, WOTITZKY, MIZELL & ROSS, P.A. (AV)

223 Taylor Street, 33950
Telephone: 941-639-2171
Telecopier: 941-639-8617

John B. Mizell   Edward L. Wotitzky
Warren R. Ross   Hal F. Wotitzky
OF COUNSEL
Frank Wotitzky   Leo Wotitzky

Jason B. Goldman

Representative Client: Punta Gorda Corp.
Approved Attorneys for: Attorneys' Title Insurance Fund, Orlando, Florida; Chicago Title Insurance Co.

For full biographical listings, see the Martindale-Hubbell Law Directory

---

ST. AUGUSTINE, * St. Johns Co.

UPCHURCH, BAILEY & UPCHURCH, P.A. (AV)

780 North Ponce de Leon Boulevard, P.O. Drawer 3007, 32085-3007
Telephone: 904-829-9066
Facsimile: 904-825-4862

(See Next Column)

John D. Bailey, Jr.   Tracy W. Upchurch
Michael A. Siragusa
OF COUNSEL
Hamilton D. Upchurch

Representative Clients: Aero Sport, Inc.; American Culinary Federation, Inc.; Barnett Bank, N.A. Penney Retirement Community, Inc.; St. Augustine Alligator Farm, Inc.; St. Augustine-St. Johns County Board of Realtors, Inc.
General Counsel: Flagler College; Flagler Hospital, Inc.; Prosperity Bank of St. Augustine; St. Johns County School Board.

For Complete List of Firm Personnel, See General Section

For full biographical listings, see the Martindale-Hubbell Law Directory

---

ST. PETERSBURG, Pinellas Co.

ALLAN & SHIPP, P.A. (AV)

6675 Thirteenth Avenue North, Suite 2C, 33710
Telephone: 813-381-9800
Fax: 813-381-1155
Clearwater, Florida Office: 2633 McCormick Drive, Suite 101, 34619.
Telephone: 813-381-9800.
Fax: 813-381-1155.

Linda R. Allan   Wayne E. Shipp

Stephen A. Baker   Terry J. Deeb
Carol E. Fant

For full biographical listings, see the Martindale-Hubbell Law Directory

---

RIDEN, EARLE & KIEFNER, P.A. (AV)

City Center, North Tower, 100 Second Avenue South, Suite 400, 33701-4336
Telephone: 813-822-6000
Telecopier: 813-821-3721

Thomas K. Riden   Christopher C. Ferguson
James T. Earle, Jr.   Timothy A. Miller
John R. Kiefner, Jr.   Gary E. Frazier
Paul Castagliola   James C. Rowe
Robert H. Crawford   Christopher B. Young
Neil G. Kiefer   Clifford J. Hunt
D. Jay Snyder   Benjamin Felder

M. Deanna Harris   Camille J. Iurillo
Michael Francis Bremer

For full biographical listings, see the Martindale-Hubbell Law Directory

---

WILLIAMSON, DIAMOND & CATON, P.A. (AV)

150 Second Avenue North, Suite 840, 33701
Telephone: 813-896-6900
Facsimile: 813-895-4552
Seminole, Florida Office: 7843 Seminole Boulevard, 33772.
Telephone: 813-398-3600.
Facsimile: 813-393-5458.

Richard P. Caton   Sandra Fascell Diamond
Douglas M. Williamson

For full biographical listings, see the Martindale-Hubbell Law Directory

---

SARASOTA, * Sarasota Co.

BOWMAN, GEORGE, SCHEB, TOALE & MARSHALL, P.A. (AV)

22 South Tuttle Avenue, Suite 3, 34237
Telephone: 941-366-5510
FAX: 941-951-0839
Other Sarasota, Florida Office: 1605 Main Street, Suite 705, 34236.
Telephone: 941-366-3290.
Fax: 941-957-4890.

David G. Bowman, Sr.   Robert P. Scheb
Eugene O. George   James E. Toale
David G. Bowman, Jr.
OF COUNSEL
James J. Drymon   I. W. Whitesell, Jr.
Reference: SouthTrust Bank.

For Complete List of Firm Personnel, See General Section

For full biographical listings, see the Martindale-Hubbell Law Directory

---

DICKINSON & GIBBONS, P.A. (AV)

1750 Ringling Boulevard, P.O. Box 3979, 34230
Telephone: 941-366-4680
FAX: 941-953-3136

(See Next Column)

DICKINSON & GIBBONS P.A., *Sarasota—Continued*

Francis C. Dart (1902-1972)	Burwell J. Jones
G. Hunter Gibbons	Richard R. Garland
Ward E. Dahlgren	Stephen G. Brannan
Lewis F. Collins, Jr.	Deborah J. Blue
Gary H. Larsen	Jeffrey D. Peairs
Camden T. French	Douglas R. Wight
Ralph L. Marchbank, Jr.	Stephen R. Kanzer
A. James Rolfes	David S. Preston

OF COUNSEL

Patrick H. Dickinson

LEGAL SUPPORT PERSONNEL

Christine C. Menzel	Janet E. Gadoury
Patricia L. Hunter	(Certified Legal Assistant)

Johanna H. Whitmire (Paralegal)

Representative Clients: Ford Motor Co.; Florida Power & Light Co.; Squibb Corp.
Insurance Clients: Liberty Mutual Insurance Co.; Allstate Insurance Co.; Nationwide Insurance Group; Ohio Casualty Insurance Co.; United States Fidelity & Guaranty Co.; State Farm Insurance Company.

For Complete List of Firm Personnel, See General Section

For full biographical listings, see the Martindale-Hubbell Law Directory

LYONS & BEAUDRY, P.A. (AV)

Suite 1111, Ellis Building, 1605 Main Street, 34236
Telephone: 941-366-3282
Fax: 941-954-1484

Robert W. Beaudry (1929-1991)	John J. Lyons

Carol Whitcher Wood	R. Craig Harrison

Reference: Nations Bank.

For full biographical listings, see the Martindale-Hubbell Law Directory

NAMACK, CLARK & KEENEY (AV)

1800 Second Street, Suite 855, 34236
Telephone: 941-365-0365
Fax: 941-954-4762

William H. Namack, III	James D. Keeney
James C. Clark	Clifford M. King

For full biographical listings, see the Martindale-Hubbell Law Directory

WIESNER ASSOCIATES, CHARTERED (AV)

1800 Second Street, Suite 870, 34236
Telephone: 941-365-9900
Fax: 941-365-4479
Email: Mrelderlaw@aol.com

Ira S. Wiesner

For full biographical listings, see the Martindale-Hubbell Law Directory

WILLIAMS, PARKER, HARRISON, DIETZ & GETZEN, PROFESSIONAL ASSOCIATION (AV)

200 South Orange Avenue, 34236-6749
Telephone: 941-366-4800
Telecopier: 941-366-5109
Mailing Address: P.O. Box 3258, Sarasota, Florida, 34230-3258
Email: wphdg.law@netsrg.com *URL:*
http://www.sarasota-online.com/williamspa-w

J.J. Williams, Jr. (1886-1968)	Frank Strelec
W. Davis Parker (1920-1982)	Terri Salt Costa
William T. Harrison, Jr.	David A. Wallace
George A. Dietz	Mark A. Schwartz
Monte K. Marshall	Ric Gregoria
James L. Ritchey	Elvin W. Phillips
William G. Lambrecht	Jeffrey A. Grebe
John T. Berteau	John L. Moore
John V. Cannon, III	Morgan R. Bentley
Charles D. Bailey, Jr.	Susan A. Barrett
J. Michael Hartenstine	Carol Ann Kalish
Michele Boardman Grimes	Linda R. Getzen
James L. Turner	Kimberly J. Page
William M. Seider	Phillip D. Eck
Elizabeth C. Marshall	J. Hugh Middlebrooks
Robert W. Benjamin	Robert A. Warram

OF COUNSEL

William E. Getzen	Frazer F. Hilder

Hugh McPheeters, Jr.

LEGAL SUPPORT PERSONNEL

Mark Loveridge (Land Planner)

General Counsel for: Sarasota County Public Hospital Board; Sarasota-Manatee Airport Authority; Taylor Woodrow Homes Ltd.; FCCI Mutual Insurance Co.

(See Next Column)

Local Counsel for: NationsBank of Florida; Barnett Bank of Southwest Florida; Northern Trust Bank of Florida; SunTrust Bank, Gulfcoast.

For full biographical listings, see the Martindale-Hubbell Law Directory

STUART,* Martin Co.

BRODIE & PAWLUC (AV)

Royal Palm Financial Center, 819 South Federal Highway, Suite 106, P.O. Box 2690, 34995
Telephone: 407-221-0110
Facsimile: 407-221-0113
Email: BPLAWFL@aol.com

Lawrence P. Brodie	Sonia M. Pawluc

For full biographical listings, see the Martindale-Hubbell Law Directory

JOSEPH C. KEMPE PROFESSIONAL ASSOCIATION (AV)

Attorneys and Counselors at Law
Royal Palm Financial Center II, Suite 200, 789 South Federal Highway, 34994
Telephone: 561-223-0700
FAX: 561-223-0707
Email: JCKempe@msn.com
Jupiter, Florida Office: America Plaza, Suite 400, 1070 East Indiantown Road. Telephone 561-747-7300.
Fax: 561-747-7722.
Vero Beach, Florida Office: 664 Azalea Lane, Suite B.
Telephone: 561-562-4022.
Fax: 561-234-1422.

Joseph C. Kempe

Lesley Hogan	Sean L. Wilson
	Jane W. Bergacker

For full biographical listings, see the Martindale-Hubbell Law Directory

McCARTHY, SUMMERS, BOBKO, McKEY, WOOD & SAWYER, P.A. (AV)

2081 East Ocean Boulevard, Suite 2-A, 34996
Telephone: 561-286-1700
Fax: 561-283-1803
Email: mcsumm@gate.net *URL:* http://www.gate.net/~mcsumm/

Terence P. McCarthy	John D. McKey, Jr.
Robert P. Summers	Steven J. Wood
Noel A. Bobko	Thomas R. Sawyer

Representative Clients: American Bank of Martin County; First National Bank and Trust Company of the Treasure Coast; Great Western Bank; Hydratech Utilities; Lost Lake at Hobe Sound; Taylor Creek Marina, Inc.; GBS Excavating, Inc.; Seaboard Savings Bank; Gary Player Design Group.

For full biographical listings, see the Martindale-Hubbell Law Directory

TAMPA,* Hillsborough Co.

SCOTT F. BARNETT (AV)

611 West Azeele Street, 33606-2205
Telephone: 813-251-1624
Fax: 813-254-8579
Email: SFBarnett@aol.com

For full biographical listings, see the Martindale-Hubbell Law Directory

FULLER, SWINDLE & HOLSONBACK, P.A. (AV)

100 North Tampa Street, Suite 2650, 33602
Telephone: 813-229-9119
Fax: Available Upon Request

Jeffery M. Fuller	John P. Holsonback
William R. Swindle	Christina C. Young

For full biographical listings, see the Martindale-Hubbell Law Directory

MANEY, DAMSKER, HARRIS & JONES, P.A. (AV)

606 Madison Street, P.O. Box 172009, 33672-0009
Telephone: 813-228-7371
Fax: 813-223-4846

David A. Maney	Karen Lynn Jones

For full biographical listings, see the Martindale-Hubbell Law Directory

PARIS & ASSOCIATES, P.A. (AV)

15310 Amberly Drive, Suite 300, 33647
Telephone: 813-975-1900
Fax: 813-975-1850

Deborah M. Paris

(See Next Column)

PARIS & ASSOCIATES P.A.—*Continued*

Francine L. Rackoff

For full biographical listings, see the Martindale-Hubbell Law Directory

PREVATT ENGLAND & TAYLOR (AV)

A Partnership of Professional Associations
One Tampa City Center, Suite 2505, P.O. Box 2920, 33602
Telephone: 813-273-9666
Telefax: 813-273-0414

Karen J. Prevatt   Lynne L. England
                    Mary L. Taylor

Representative Clients: Cone Constructors Inc.; Magic Wok International, Inc.; Dallas I. Construction & Development, Inc.; Bloomingdale Golfers Club; Central Florida Investments; Bioderm, Inc.; The Westerly Oceanus Co., Inc.

For full biographical listings, see the Martindale-Hubbell Law Directory

HARRY H. ROOT, III (AV)

903 Swann Avenue, 33606
Telephone: 813-251-8019
Fax: 813-251-1495

Approved Attorneys For: Attorneys Title Insurance Fund.
Reference: Barnett Bank, Tampa, Florida.

For full biographical listings, see the Martindale-Hubbell Law Directory

*TAVARES,** Lake Co.

CAUTHEN, OLDHAM & KEOUGH, P.A. (AV)

131 West Main Street, 32778
Telephone: 352-343-3455
Fax: 352-343-8801

Gordon G. Oldham, Jr.   David E. Cauthen
            Timothy S. Keough

References: First Union National Bank; First Federal Savings & Loan Association of Lake County.

For full biographical listings, see the Martindale-Hubbell Law Directory

*VERO BEACH,** Indian River Co.

JOSEPH C. KEMPE PROFESSIONAL ASSOCIATION (AV)

Attorneys and Counselors at Law
664 Azalea Lane, Suite B, 32963
Telephone: 561-562-4022
Fax: 561-234-1442
Email: JCKempe@msn.com
Jupiter, Florida Office: America Plaza, Suite 400, 1070 E. Indiantown Rd.
Telephone: 561-747-7300.
Fax: 561-747-7722.
Stuart, Florida Office: Royal Palm Financial Center II, Suite 200, 789 S. Federal Highway, Suite 200.
Telephone: 561-223-0700.
Fax: 561-223-0707.

Joseph C. Kempe   Sean L. Wilson
Lesley Hogan   Jane W. Bergacker

For full biographical listings, see the Martindale-Hubbell Law Directory

E. STEVEN LAUER, P.A. (AV)

612 Beachland Boulevard, 32963
Telephone: 407-234-4200
Fax: 407-234-4249

E. Steven Lauer

For full biographical listings, see the Martindale-Hubbell Law Directory

MOSS, HENDERSON, BLANTON, KOVAL & LANIER, P.A. (AV)

817 Beachland Boulevard, P.O. Box 3406, 32964-3406
Telephone: 561-231-1900
Fax: 561-231-4387

George H. Moss, II   Thomas A. Koval
Steve L. Henderson   Clinton W. Lanier
Robin A. Blanton   Fred L. Kretschmer, Jr.
            Lisa D. Harpring

Lewis W. Murphy, Jr.   Kelly Cambron
Judith Goodman Hill   Lawrence Y. Leonard
            David F. Mancini

(See Next Column)

OF COUNSEL
Charles E. Garris   Ford J. Fegert
            Everett J. Van Gaasbeck

Representative Clients: Aetna Life & Casualty; Alcoa Florida, Inc.; Florida Power & Light Co.; Insurance Company of North America; Liberty Mutual Insurance Co.; Sears, Roebuck & Co.; Sugar Cane Growers Cooperative of Florida; Norfolk Southern Corporation/North American Van Lines, Inc.

For full biographical listings, see the Martindale-Hubbell Law Directory

SMITH & SMITH (AV)

Citrus Financial Center, Suite 301, 1717 Indian River Boulevard, 32960
Telephone: 561-567-4351
Fax: 561-567-4298

MEMBERS OF FIRM
Sherman N. Smith, Jr.   Sherman N. Smith, III
            ASSOCIATE
            Anthony T. Golden

References: Citrus Bank, N.A.; Northern Trust Bank of Vero Beach.

For full biographical listings, see the Martindale-Hubbell Law Directory

STEWART & NALL, P.A. (AV)

3355 Ocean Drive, P.O. Box 3345, 32964-3345
Telephone: 561-231-3500
FAX: 561-231-9876

William J. Stewart   Cynthia L. Cambron
Robert C. Nall   Edith E. Collins
            Troy B. Hafner

Representative Clients: Harbor Branch Oceanographic Institution, Inc.; Indian River Memorial Hospital, Inc.
Approved Attorneys for: Attorneys' Title Insurance Fund; Commonwealth Land Title Insurance Co.
Reference: Northern Trust Bank Florida, N.A.

For full biographical listings, see the Martindale-Hubbell Law Directory

*WEST PALM BEACH,** Palm Beach Co.

AUGUST, COMITER, KULUNAS & SCHEPPS, P.A. (AV)

250 Australian Avenue South Suite 1100, 33401
Telephone: 407-835-9600
Fax: 407-835-9602
Washington, D.C. Office: 501 School Street, Suite 700.
Telephone: 202-646-5160.

Jerald David August   Joseph J. Kulunas
Richard B. Comiter   Mitchell D. Schepps
            OF COUNSEL
            James J. Freeland

For full biographical listings, see the Martindale-Hubbell Law Directory

BOYES & FARINA, PROFESSIONAL ASSOCIATION (AV)

Centurion Plaza, 1601 Forum Place, Suite 900, 33401
Telephone: 561-697-9393
Fax: 561-697-8980

William E. Boyes   John Farina

John Patrick Morrissey

For full biographical listings, see the Martindale-Hubbell Law Directory

PRESSLY & PRESSLY, P.A. (AV)

Esperante, Suite 910, 222 Lakeview Avenue, 33401-6112
Telephone: 561-659-4040
FAX: 561-655-6006

James G. Pressly, Jr.   David S. Pressly
            Trent S. Kiziah

For full biographical listings, see the Martindale-Hubbell Law Directory

QUARLES & BRADY (AV)

222 Lakeview Avenue, 4th Floor, 33401
Telephone: 561-653-5000
Fax: 561-653-5333
Milwaukee, Wisconsin Office: 411 East Wisconsin Avenue, 53202-4497.
Telephone: 414-277-5000.
Fax: 414-271-3552.
Madison, Wisconsin Office: Firstar Plaza, One South Pinckney Street, P.O. Box 2113, 53701-2113.
Telephone: 608-251-5000.
Fax: 608-251-9166.
Naples, Florida Office: Barnett Center, 4501 Tamiami Trail North, Suite 300, 33940-3060.
Telephone: 941-262-5959.
Fax: 941-434-4999.

(See Next Column)

QUARLES & BRADY, *West Palm Beach—Continued*

Phoenix, Arizona Office: One Camelback Building, One East Camelback Road, Suite 400, 85012-1649.
Telephone: 602-230-5500.
Fax: 602-230-5598.

PARTNER
John S. Sammond
ASSOCIATE
Elizabeth A. Dougherty

For Complete List of Firm Personnel, See General Section

For full biographical listings, see the Martindale-Hubbell Law Directory

---

JAMES E. WEBER, P.A. (AV)

Suite 502 The Flagler Center, 501 South Flagler Drive, 33401
Telephone: 407-832-2266
Fax: 407-833-3816

James E. Weber

For full biographical listings, see the Martindale-Hubbell Law Directory

---

WOOD & MURPHY (AV)

Suite 201, 400 Executive Center Drive, 33401
Telephone: 407-471-0555
Fax: 407-471-0588

Lawrence E. Murphy   Marshall B. Wood, Jr.

For full biographical listings, see the Martindale-Hubbell Law Directory

---

WINTER PARK, Orange Co.

POHL & SHORT, P.A. (AV)

280 West Canton Avenue, Suite 410, P.O. Box 3208, 32790
Telephone: 407-647-7645; 407-647-POHL
Telefax: 407-647-2314

Frank L. Pohl	C. Teresa de Arrigoitia
Houston E. Short	George A. Golder
Dwight I. Cool	Norma Stanley
James Everett Shepherd V	Mark W. Garrett

John R. Simpson, Jr.

Representative Clients: American Pioneer Title Insurance Company; Institute of Internal Auditors, Inc.; Thompson Steel, Inc.; SunTrust, N.A.; The Bank of Winter Park; Bekins Moving and Storage Co., Inc.; Champion Boats, Inc.; KeyCom Telephone Systems, Inc.

For full biographical listings, see the Martindale-Hubbell Law Directory

---

WINDERWEEDLE, HAINES, WARD & WOODMAN, P.A. (AV)

Barnett Bank Building, 250 Park Avenue, South, P.O. Box 880, 32790-0880
Telephone: 407-423-4246
Telecopier: 407-645-3728
Orlando, Florida Office: Barnett Bank Center, 390 North Orange Avenue, P.O. Box 1391.
Telephone: 407-423-4246.
Telecopier: 407-423-7014.

Harold A. Ward, III	C. Brent McCaghren
John D. Haines	Randolph J. Rush
William A. Walker II	W. Graham White

Nancy S. Freeman

References: Barnett Bank of Central Florida, N.A., Orlando, Florida; United American Bank; Seminole National Bank; Georgia Pacific Corp.; USX Corp.

For Complete List of Firm Personnel, See General Section

For full biographical listings, see the Martindale-Hubbell Law Directory

---

GEORGIA

ALBANY,* Dougherty Co.

PERRY & WALTERS (AV)

409-411 North Jackson Street, P.O. Box 469, 31702-0469
Telephone: 912-432-7438; 432-7481
Telecopier: 912-436-1417
Other Albany, Georgia Office: 503 North Jackson Street, P.O. Box 445, 31702-0445.
Telephone: 912-432-9960.

MEMBERS OF FIRM

R. Edgar Campbell	Samuel Brown Lippitt, Jr.
Keith T. Dorough	R. Kelly Raulerson
Richard W. Fields	James E. Reynolds, Jr.

Edgar B. Wilkin, Jr.

(See Next Column)

OF COUNSEL
H. H. Perry, Jr.   Jesse W. Walters

Division Counsel for: Seaboard Coast Line Railroad Co.
General Counsel for: First State Bank & Trust Co.; Carlton Co.; Bob's Candies, Inc.; Alcon Associates, Inc.; Albany-Dougherty County Hospital Authority.
Representative Clients: Merck & Co., Inc.; CNA Insurance; Chrysler Credit Corp.

For full biographical listings, see the Martindale-Hubbell Law Directory

---

ATLANTA,* Fulton Co.

FRANCIS M. BIRD, JR. (AV)

100 Galleria Parkway, N.W. Suite 1540, 30339
Telephone: 770-951-4720
Fax: 770-951-4723

For full biographical listings, see the Martindale-Hubbell Law Directory

---

BIVENS, HOFFMAN & FOWLER (AV)

A Partnership of Professional Corporations
5040 Roswell Road, N.E., 30342
Telephone: 404-256-6464
FAX: 404-256-1422

MEMBERS OF FIRM
Clifford G. Hoffman (P.C.)   Michael C. Fowler (P.C.)

For full biographical listings, see the Martindale-Hubbell Law Directory

---

BODKER, RAMSEY & ANDREWS, A PROFESSIONAL CORPORATION (AV)

Suite 615 1800 Peachtree Street, N.W., 30309-2507
Telephone: 404-351-1615
Telecopier: 404-352-1285

Brian D. Bodker	Stephen C. Andrews
Timothy J. Ramsey	Jon G. Blaustein

Harry J. Winograd

Thomas Rosseland	Kenneth L. Zirkman
David J. Maslia	Jessica J. Harper

Nicholas J. Cook

For full biographical listings, see the Martindale-Hubbell Law Directory

---

HARMON, SMITH, BRIDGES & WILBANKS (AV)

1795 Peachtree Street, N.E., 30309
Telephone: 404-881-1200
Fax: 404-881-8523

MEMBER OF FIRM
Tyrone M. Bridges

For full biographical listings, see the Martindale-Hubbell Law Directory

---

LEFKOFF, DUNCAN, MILLER, GRIMES, MILLER & BARWICK, P.C. (AV)

Suite 806, Eleven Piedmont Center, 3495 Piedmont Road, N.E., 30305
Telephone: 404-262-2000
Fax: 404-262-2897
Email: lawfirm@lefkoff-duncan.com

Douglas W. Duncan	Donna Gude Barwick
Joseph C. Miller	Patricia McHugh Thompson
Dora A. Miller	Rebekah G. Strickland

For full biographical listings, see the Martindale-Hubbell Law Directory

---

LONG ALDRIDGE & NORMAN, LLP (AV)

A Limited Liability Partnership including Professional Corporations
One Peachtree Center, Suite 5300, 303 Peachtree Street, 30308
Telephone: 404-527-4000
Telecopier: 404-527-4198
Washington, D.C. Office: Suite 600, 701 Pennsylvania Avenue, N.W., 20004.
Telephone: 202-624-1200.
FAX: 202-624-1298.

SENIOR COUNSEL
F. T. Davis, Jr., (P.C.)   W. Stell Huie

For Complete List of Firm Personnel, See General Section

For full biographical listings, see the Martindale-Hubbell Law Directory

---

RICHARD M. MORGAN, P.C. (AV)

One Midtown Plaza, Suite 1200, 1360 Peachtree Street, 30309
Telephone: 404-870-2251
Facsimile: 404-870-2213
Email: rmorgan@mindspring.com

(See Next Column)

RICHARD M. MORGAN, P.C.—*Continued*

Richard M. Morgan

For full biographical listings, see the Martindale-Hubbell Law Directory

---

SUTHERLAND, ASBILL & BRENNAN, L.L.P. (AV)

999 Peachtree Street, N.E., 30309-3996
Telephone: 404-853-8000
Facsimile: 404-853-8806
Email: postmaster@sablaw.com
Washington, D.C. Office: 1275 Pennsylvania Avenue, N.W., 20004-2404.
Telephone: 202-383-0100.
New York, N.Y. Office: 600 Madison Avenue, 11th Floor, 10022-1615.
Telephone: 212-605-6400.
Austin, Texas Office: 111 Congress Avenue, 23rd Floor, 78701-4079.
Telephone: 512-469-3350.

Michael J. Egan	Charles D. Hurt, Jr.

Larry J. White

Representative Clients: Trust Company Bank of Georgia; C & S/Sovran Trust Company (Georgia), N.A.; Wachovia Bank of Georgia, N.A.; First Union National Bank of Georgia.

For Complete List of Firm Personnel, See General Section

For full biographical listings, see the Martindale-Hubbell Law Directory

---

THRASHER, WHITLEY, HAMPTON & MORGAN, A PROFESSIONAL CORPORATION (AV)

Suite 2150, Five Concourse Parkway, 30328
Telephone: 770-804-8000
Telecopier: 770-804-5555

Charles J. Hampton

Representative Clients: First Southern Securities Group, Inc.; Georgia Dental Assn.; Kearney National, Inc.; Middle Bay Oil Company, Inc.; Perry & Co.; Smallwood, Reynolds, Stewart, Stewart & Assoc., Inc.; Sunchase Holdings, Ltd.; Touch Industries, Inc.

For full biographical listings, see the Martindale-Hubbell Law Directory

---

WILSON, STRICKLAND & BENSON, P.C. (AV)

1100 One Midtown Plaza, 1360 Peachtree Street, N.E., 30309
Telephone: 404-870-1800
Telecopier: 404-870-1808

R. Milton Crouch

For Complete List of Firm Personnel, See General Section

For full biographical listings, see the Martindale-Hubbell Law Directory

---

COLUMBUS, * Muscogee Co.

DAVIDSON, CALHOUN, MILLER & BUEHLER, P.C. (AV)

The Joseph House, 828 Broadway, P.O. Box 2828, 31902-2828
Telephone: 706-327-2552
Telecopier: 706-323-5838

J. Quentin Davidson, Jr.	Charles W. Miller

David A. Buehler

For Complete List of Firm Personnel, See General Section

For full biographical listings, see the Martindale-Hubbell Law Directory

---

HATCHER, STUBBS, LAND, HOLLIS & ROTHSCHILD (AV)

A Limited Liability Partnership
Suite 500 The Corporate Center, 233 12th Street, P.O. Box 2707, 31902-2707
Telephone: 706-324-0201
Telecopier: 706-322-7747

MEMBERS OF FIRM

Alan F. Rothschild	John M. Tanzine, III
Morton A. Harris	John McKay Sheftall
Charles T. Staples	Alan F. Rothschild, Jr.

Mote W. Andrews III

General Counsel for: SunTrust Bank, West Georgia, N.A.; TOM'S Foods Inc.; Kinnett Dairies, Inc.; St. Francis Hospital, Inc.; Bill Heard Enterprises, Inc.
Local Counsel for: First Union National Bank of Georgia; Equitable Life Assurance Society of the United States; Prudential Insurance Company of America; Metropolitan Life Insurance Co.

For Complete List of Firm Personnel, See General Section

For full biographical listings, see the Martindale-Hubbell Law Directory

---

DECATUR, * De Kalb Co.

McCONAUGHEY & GOFF (AV)

315 W. Ponce de Leon Avenue, #1070, 30030
Telephone: 404-378-3681
Fax: 404-378-3683

H. Stephen Goff, Jr.
OF COUNSEL
Dan E. McConaughey

For full biographical listings, see the Martindale-Hubbell Law Directory

---

GRIFFIN, * Spalding Co.

JOHN M. COGBURN, JR. (AV)

115 North Sixth Street, P.O. Box 907, 30224
Telephone: 770-228-2148
Telecopier: 770-228-5018

ASSOCIATE
Michael S. Evans

Representative Clients: Griffin-Spalding County Hospital Authority; Allstar Knitwear Co., Inc. (Textiles); Atlanta Tees, Inc. (Sportswear Distribution); Industrial Refrigeration Enterprises, Inc. (Refrigeration Engineers and Contractors).

For full biographical listings, see the Martindale-Hubbell Law Directory

---

MACON, * Bibb Co.

ANDERSON, WALKER & REICHERT, P.C. (AV)

Suite 404 SunTrust Bank Building, P.O. Box 6497, 31208-6497
Telephone: 912-743-8651
Telecopier: 912-743-9636

Albert P. Reichert	Albert P. Reichert, Jr.
Thomas L. Bass	John D. Reeves

Ramsey T. Way, Jr.

Representative Clients: Riverwood International USA, Inc.; Hospital Corporation of America; Pepsi-Cola Bottling Company of Macon; Radiology Associates of Macon, P.C.; Thiele Kaolin Company; SunTrust Bank of Middle Georgia, N.A.
General Insurance Clients: Liberty Mutual Insurance Co.; Alexis, Inc.

For Complete List of Firm Personnel, See General Section

For full biographical listings, see the Martindale-Hubbell Law Directory

---

MARIETTA, * Cobb Co.

AWTREY AND PARKER, P.C. (AV)

211 Roswell Street, P.O. Box 997, 30061
Telephone: 770-424-8000
Fax: 770-424-1594

L. M. Awtrey, Jr. (1915-1986)	Donald A. Mangerie (1924-1988)
George L. Dozier, Jr.	Barbara H. Martin
Harvey D. Harkness	A. Sidney Parker
Mike Harrison	Robert B. Silliman

General Counsel for: Kennesaw Finance Co.; Cobb Electric Membership Corporation; Development Authority of Cobb County.
Local Counsel for: Coats & Clark; Bell South Mobility; Lockheed-Georgia Corp.; Post Properties, Inc.; CSX Transportation, Inc.

For full biographical listings, see the Martindale-Hubbell Law Directory

---

BARNES, BROWNING, TANKSLEY & CASURELLA (AV)

Suite 225, 166 Anderson Street, 30060
Telephone: 770-424-1500
Fax: 770-424-1740

MEMBERS OF FIRM

Roy E. Barnes	Jerry A. Landers, Jr.

For full biographical listings, see the Martindale-Hubbell Law Directory

---

CUSTER & HILL, P.C. (AV)

241 Washington Avenue, P.O. Box 1224, 30061
Telephone: 770-429-8300
Fax: 770-429-8338

Lawrence B. Custer	Douglas A. Hill

Danna Lambert Wolfe

Reference: First Union National Bank.

For full biographical listings, see the Martindale-Hubbell Law Directory

Marietta—Continued

W. R. ROBERTSON, III (AV)

244 Roswell Street, Suite 600, 30060-2000
Telephone: 770-422-0200
Fax: 770-424-1322
Email: wrobert244@aol.com

For full biographical listings, see the Martindale-Hubbell Law Directory

W. ALLEN SEPARK (AV)

250 Church Street, Second Floor, P.O. Box 3475, 30061
Telephone: 770-422-3200
Fax: 770-514-1148

Reference: First Union National Bank, formerly Georgia State Bank.

For full biographical listings, see the Martindale-Hubbell Law Directory

*NEWNAN,** Coweta Co.

GLOVER & DAVIS, P.A. (AV)

10 Brown Street, P.O. Box 1038, 30264
Telephone: 770-253-4330
Fax: 770-251-7152
Peachtree City, Georgia Office: Suite 130, 200 Westpark Drive.
Telephone: 770-487-5834.
Fax: 770-487-3492.

J. Littleton Glover	W. Robert Hancock, Jr.
Welborn B. Davis, Jr.	(Resident, Peachtree Office)
(1922-1974)	Asa M. Powell, Jr.
J. Littleton Glover, Jr.	Jerry Ann Conner
Alan W. Jackson	Mark E. Dacy (Resident,
Randy E. Connell	Peachtree City Office)

Representative Clients: Newnan Savings Bank; Pike Transfer Co.; Batson-Cook Company, General Corporate and Construction Divisions; Coweta County, Georgia; Heard County, Georgia; Putnam-Greene Financial Corporation.
Local Counsel for: International Latex Corp.; First Union National Bank of Georgia; Wear Georgia; Farm Credit, ACA.

For full biographical listings, see the Martindale-Hubbell Law Directory

NORCROSS, Gwinnett Co.

THOMAS E. RAINES, P.C. (AV)

Suite 200, 3941 Holcomb Bridge Road, 30092
Telephone: 770-263-0093
Facsimile: 770-840-9725

Thomas E. Raines

Representative Clients: Linder Financial Corp.; Chris Motors, Inc.; Chris Imports, Inc.; Whirlpool Financial Corp.; Citizens Bank of Gwinnett; Textron Financial Corp.; SQL Financials International, Inc.

For full biographical listings, see the Martindale-Hubbell Law Directory

*SAVANNAH,** Chatham Co.

HUNTER, MACLEAN, EXLEY & DUNN, P.C. (AV)

200 East St. Julian Street, P.O. Box 9848, 31412
Telephone: 912-236-0261
Cable Address: "Ancan"
Telecopier: 912-236-4936
Telex: 54-6483
Atlanta, Georgia Office: The Peachtree, 1355 Peachtree Street, N.E., Suite 1050.
Telephone: 404-876-3611.
Fax: 404-870-2025.

Malcolm R. Maclean	Don L. Waters
John B. Miller	Wade W. Herring, II
Henry M. Dunn, Jr.	J. Reid Williamson, III
John M. Tatum	William E. Dillard, III
M. Lane Morrison	David M. Hirsberg

Steven J. Arsenault

Representative Clients: Savannah Foods & Industries, Inc.; SunTrust Bank, Savannah, N.A.; First Union Nations Bank of Georgia; Gulfstream Aerospace; Prudential Insurance Company of America; Historic Savannah Foundation, Inc.; John Hancock Mutual Life Insurance Co.; Norfolk Southern Corp.

For Complete List of Firm Personnel, See General Section

For full biographical listings, see the Martindale-Hubbell Law Directory

SILVERS, SIMPSON & CREASY, P.C. (AV)

Suite 102, AmeriBank Plaza, 7393 Hodgson Memorial Drive, 31406
Telephone: 912-925-7200
Facsimile: 912-925-0100

(See Next Column)

Mark M. Silvers, Jr.   K. Russell Simpson
          Neil A. Creasy

For full biographical listings, see the Martindale-Hubbell Law Directory

HAWAII

*HONOLULU,** Honolulu Co.

CADES SCHUTTE FLEMING & WRIGHT (AV)

Formerly Smith, Wild, Beebe & Cades
1000 Bishop Street, P.O. Box 939, 96808
Telephone: 808-521-9200
Telecopier: 808-531-8738
Email: cades@cades.com
Affiliated Law Firm: Udom-Prok Associates Law Offices, 105/36 Tharinee Mansion, Borom Raj Chananee Road Bangkoknoi, Bangkok, Thailand, 10700.
Telephone: 011 662 435-4146.
Kailua-Kona, Hawaii Office: Hualalai Center, Suite B-303, 75-170 Hualalai Road.
Telephone: 808-329-5811.
Telecopier: 808-326-1175.

MEMBERS OF FIRM

Robert B. Bunn	David C. Larsen
	Rhonda L. Griswold

ASSOCIATE
Eric S.T. Young

Counsel for: First Hawaiian Bank; Alexander & Baldwin, Inc.; Theo. H. Davies & Co., Ltd.; C. Brewer & Company, Ltd.; Bank of America, FSB.

For Complete List of Firm Personnel, See General Section

For full biographical listings, see the Martindale-Hubbell Law Directory

GERSON, GREKIN & WYNHOFF ATTORNEYS AT LAW, A LAW CORPORATION (AV)

Suite 780 Pacific Tower, 1001 Bishop Street, 96813
Telephone: 808-524-4800
Telecopier: 808-537-1420
Email: 102461.730@compuserve.com *URL:* ggwlaw@aloha.net

Mervyn S. Gerson	William J. Wynhoff
Nancy Nissen Grekin	Bruce D. Hieneman

For full biographical listings, see the Martindale-Hubbell Law Directory

REINWALD, O'CONNOR, MARRACK, HOSKINS & PLAYDON (AV)

(Formerly Anthony, Hoddick, Reinwald & O'Connor)
2400 PRI Tower, Grosvenor Center, P.O. Box 3199, 96801-3199
Telephone: 808-524-8350
Cable Address: "Hermes" Honolulu
Telecopier: 808-531-8628

MEMBER OF FIRM
Arthur B. Reinwald

For full biographical listings, see the Martindale-Hubbell Law Directory

IDAHO

*BOISE,** Ada Co.

ELAM & BURKE, A PROFESSIONAL ASSOCIATION (AV)

Key Financial Center, 702 West Idaho Street, P.O. Box 1539, 83701
Telephone: 208-343-5454
Telecopier: 208-384-5844
Email: eblaw@elamburke.com

Melville W. Fisher, II

Sandra L. Clapp

Representative Clients: West One Bank of Idaho, N.A.; First Security Bank of Idaho, N.A.; First Interstate Bank of Idaho, N.A.; Key Trust Company of the West.

For Complete List of Firm Personnel, See General Section

For full biographical listings, see the Martindale-Hubbell Law Directory

Boise—Continued

MARTIN, CHAPMAN, SCHILD & LASSAW, CHARTERED (AV)

216 West Jefferson Street, P.O. Box 2898, 83701
Telephone: 208-343-6485
Fax: 208-343-9819
Sun Valley, Idaho Office: P.O. Box 744.
Telephone: 208-788-2876.
Fax: 208-788-2818.
Twin Falls, Idaho Office: 834 Falls Avenue, Suite 1020A.
Telephone: 208-734-9629.

John S. Chapman

References: West One Bank, Idaho, N.A. (formerly Idaho First National Bank); First Security Bank of Idaho, N.A.

For Complete List of Firm Personnel, See General Section

For full biographical listings, see the Martindale-Hubbell Law Directory

POCATELLO,* Bannock Co.

MERRILL & MERRILL, CHARTERED (AV)

Key Bank Building, P.O. Box 991, 83204
Telephone: 208-232-2286
Fax: 208-232-2499

Wesley F. Merrill   Dave R. Gallafent
D. Russell Wight

For Complete List of Firm Personnel, See General Section

For full biographical listings, see the Martindale-Hubbell Law Directory

SUN VALLEY, Blaine Co.

MARTIN, CHAPMAN, SCHILD & LASSAW, CHARTERED (AV)

P.O. Box 744, 83303
Telephone: 208-788-2876
Fax: 208-788-2818
Boise, Idaho Office: 216 W. Jefferson P.O. Box 2989.
Telephone: 208-343-6485.
Fax: 208-343-9819.
Twin Falls, Idaho Office: 834 Falls Avenue, Suite 1020A.
Telephone: 208-734-9629.

John S. Chapman

References: First Security Bank of Idaho, N.A.; West One Bank, Idaho, N.A. (formerly Idaho First National Bank).

For full biographical listings, see the Martindale-Hubbell Law Directory

TWIN FALLS,* Twin Falls Co.

MARTIN, CHAPMAN, SCHILD & LASSAW, CHARTERED (AV)

834 Falls Avenue, Suite 1020A, 83301
Telephone: 208-734-9629
Boise, Idaho Office: 216 W. Jefferson St. P.O. Box 2898.
Telephone: 208-343-6485.
Fax: 208-343-9819.
Sun Valley, Idaho Office: P.O. Box 744.
Telephone: 208-788-2876.
Fax: 208-788-2818.

John S. Chapman

References: First Security Bank of Idaho, N.A.; West One Bank, Idaho, N.A. (formerly Idaho First National Bank).

For full biographical listings, see the Martindale-Hubbell Law Directory

ILLINOIS

BELLEVILLE,* St. Clair Co.

MATHIS, MARIFIAN, RICHTER & GRANDY, LTD. (AV)

720 West Main Street, 62220
Telephone: 618-234-9800; 314-421-2325
FAX: 618-234-9786

Patrick B. Mathis   Kevin J. Richter
George E. Marifian   Laura Koeneman Grandy
Kevin J. Stine

For full biographical listings, see the Martindale-Hubbell Law Directory

BLOOMINGTON,* McLean Co.

HARTWEG, MUELLER, TURNER, DRAZEWSKI & WOOD, P.C. (AV)

207 West Jefferson Street, Suite 400, P.O. Box 397, 61701-0397
Telephone: 309-827-0044
Telecopier: 309-829-0328

(See Next Column)

Darrell L. Hartweg   Ralph T. Turner
William A. Mueller, Jr.   Scott D. Drazewski
George C Wood

Michael J. Robak
OF COUNSEL
John R. Luedtke

Reference: Magna Bank of McLean County.

For full biographical listings, see the Martindale-Hubbell Law Directory

CHICAGO,* Cook Co.

ARONBERG GOLDGEHN DAVIS & GARMISA (AV)

Suite 3000 One IBM Plaza, 60611
Telephone: 312-828-9600
Telecopier: 312-828-9635

MEMBERS OF FIRM
James S. Jarvis   Ned S. Robertson
ASSOCIATE
Jacqueline Shim Bryant

For Complete List of Firm Personnel, See General Section

For full biographical listings, see the Martindale-Hubbell Law Directory

BRADLEY & BRADLEY (AV)

29 South La Salle Street Suite 950, 60603
Telephone: 312-372-5454
FAX: 312-372-5458

MEMBERS OF FIRM
Edward J. Bradley   Edward J. Bradley, Jr.

For full biographical listings, see the Martindale-Hubbell Law Directory

DEUTSCH, LEVY & ENGEL, CHARTERED (AV)

Suite 1700, 225 West Washington Street, 60606
Telephone: 312-346-1460
Wheaton, Illinois Office: Suite B2, 620 West Roosevelt Road.
Telephone: 708-665-9112.

Frank R. Cohen   Jerry I. Rudman

David I. Addis   Martin P. Ryan

For full biographical listings, see the Martindale-Hubbell Law Directory

McBRIDE BAKER & COLES (AV)

500 West Madison Street 40th Floor, 60661
Telephone: 312-715-5700
Cable Address: "Chilaw"
Telex: 270258
Telecopier: 312-993-9350
Email: lastname@mbc.com *URL:* http://www.mbc.com
Oakbrook Terrace, Illinois Office: Suite 1000, One Mid America Plaza, 60181-4710.
Telephone: 630-954-2100.
Telecopier: 630-954-2112.

MEMBERS OF FIRM
Andrew R. Gelman   Steven R. Lifson
David Shayne
OF COUNSEL
Robert O. Case
ASSOCIATES
Ruth Hill Bro   Edward J. Hannon

For Complete List of Firm Personnel, See General Section

For full biographical listings, see the Martindale-Hubbell Law Directory

NISEN & ELLIOTT (AV)

200 West Adams Street, Suite 2500, 60606
Telephone: 312-346-7800
Telecopier: 312-346-9316

MEMBERS OF FIRM
Paul F. Gerbosi   John Foster Lesch
Edward B. Mueller   John K. Kneafsey
Anthony Packard   Michael H. Moirano
Donald C. Shine   Robert O. Middleton
Mark F. Zaenger   William G. Daluga, Jr.
Michael J. Daley   Kenneth J. Rojc
Thomas V. McCauley

(See Next Column)

NISEN & ELLIOTT, *Chicago—Continued*

Robert Christie	Michael J. Pavlicek
Daniel P. Dawson	Brian D. Proctor
Donald F. Froehlke	Jeffrey S. Torosian
Helen M. Jensen	William A. Walker
Thomas K. Juffernbruch	Gregory C. Ward
Adam O. Kirwan	Eric R. Wilen
(Not admitted in IL)	

OF COUNSEL

Charles M. Nisen

For full biographical listings, see the Martindale-Hubbell Law Directory

POLLAK & HOFFMAN LTD. (AV)

Suite 1100, 150 North Wacker Drive, 60606
Telephone: 312-726-0001
FAX: 312-726-1098
Northbrook, Illinois Office: 1200 Shermer Road.
Telephone: 847-564-0130.
FAX: 847-564-0160.

Bertram L. Pollak	Michael E. Pollak
Jay M. Pollak	Bruce F. Hoffman
	Lee J. Lewin

For full biographical listings, see the Martindale-Hubbell Law Directory

SCHWARTZBERG, BARNETT & COHEN (AV)

55 West Monroe Street, 2400 Xerox Centre, 60603-5040
Telephone: 312-726-3555
Fax: 312-726-6299
Cable Address: "Justice"
Email: sb&c@twty.chi.il.us

MEMBERS OF FIRM

Ralph M. Schwartzberg	Mark T. Barnett (1939-1970)
(1939-1975)	Hugh J. Schwartzberg
	Benjamin H. Cohen

OF COUNSEL

Eugene P. Thomas Jr.

For full biographical listings, see the Martindale-Hubbell Law Directory

SUGAR, FRIEDBERG & FELSENTHAL (AV)

30 North La Salle Street, Suite 2600, 60602
Telephone: 312-704-9400
Telecopier: 312-372-7951
Cable: "SUGARFREE"

MEMBERS OF FIRM

Richard A. Sugar	Ira S. Neiman
Michael R. Friedberg	Jonathan L. Mills
Steven A. Felsenthal	Etahn M. Cohen
Andrew B. David	Howard M. Helsinger
Leslie J. Weiss	Robert F. Simon
	Martin M. Weinstein

ASSOCIATES

Kathryn A. Erickson	Jay R. Hoffman
Norman J. Ginsparg	Sophia Stergianis
	Jonathan W. Michael

For full biographical listings, see the Martindale-Hubbell Law Directory

WILSON & McILVAINE (AV)

500 West Madison, Suite 3700, 60661-2511
Telephone: 312-715-5000
Telecopier: 312-715-5155

PARTNERS

Walter W. Bell	Sarah M. Linsley
Jerry D. Jones	Thomas A. Polachek

ASSOCIATES

Patrick J. Bitterman	Susan M. Hughes
	Anne S. Quinn

For Complete List of Firm Personnel, See General Section

For full biographical listings, see the Martindale-Hubbell Law Directory

DECATUR,* Macon Co.

R. NICHOLAS BURTON (AV)

Suite 603 Millikin Court, 132 South Water Street, 62523
Telephone: 217-423-8861

References: The First National Bank of Decatur; First of America Bank-Illinois, N.A.; Magna Bank, N.A.; Soy Capital Bank & Trust Co.

For full biographical listings, see the Martindale-Hubbell Law Directory

EAST ST. LOUIS, St. Clair Co.

DUNHAM, BOMAN & LESKERA (AV)

520 First Illinois Bank Building, 327 Missouri Avenue, 62201
Telephone: 618-271-0535
Telecopier: 618-271-2800
Belleville, Illinois Office: 208 North High Street.
Telephone: 618-235-7222.
Telecopier: 618-397-2285.
Collinsville, Illinois Office: 300 West Clay Street.
Telephone: 618-344-7734.
Telecopier: 618-344-3853.

M.F. Oehmke (1887-1963)	Wm. C. Dunham (1893-1975)
	Howard Boman (1917-1985)

MEMBERS OF FIRM

John W. Leskera	Russell K. Scott
William L. Berry	Robert D. Francis
Eric C. Young	John L. Bitzer

Attorneys For: Collinsville School District #10; Hanover Insurance Co.;; Hartford Insurance Group; Home Indemnity Co.; State Farm Insurance Cos.; Transamerica Insurance Group; The Travelers Indemnity Co.; Wausau Insurance Cos.; Nationwide Insurance Co.; Atlantic Mutual Insurance Co..

For full biographical listings, see the Martindale-Hubbell Law Directory

EDWARDSVILLE,* Madison Co.

BURROUGHS, HEPLER, BROOM, MacDONALD & HEBRANK (AV)

Two Mark Twain Plaza, Suite 300, 103 West Vandalia Street, P.O. Box 510, 62025-0510
Telephone: 618-656-0184
Telecopier: 618-656-1364
Email: firm@ilmolaw.com

MEMBERS OF FIRM

George D. Burroughs	G. Gordon Burroughs
(1873-1977)	(Of Counsel)
William G. Burroughs	Larry E. Hepler
(1872-1952)	Gordon R. Broom
Mallory L. Burroughs	Theodore J. MacDonald, Jr.
(1884-1965)	Jeffrey S. Hebrank
Jesse L. Simpson (1884-1973)	Gary E. True
David L. Simpson (Retired)	Paul W. Johnson
	William J. Knapp

ASSOCIATES

Lisa K. Franke	Daniel W. Farroll
Jack H. Humes, Jr.	David J. Gerber
Melissa Griggs	Donald J. Ohl
L. David Green	D. Scott Rendleman
J. Todd Hayes	Gary A. Meadows
J. Robert Edmonds	T. Scott Stewart

Representative Clients: Ameritech; Travelers Insurance Co.; Fireman's Fund-American Insurance Group; CILCO; Employers Union Insurance Co.; The Hartford; Illinois Power Co.; W.R. Grace; Mark Twain Bank; Prairie Farms.

For full biographical listings, see the Martindale-Hubbell Law Directory

GALESBURG,* Knox Co.

MUSTAIN LINDSTROM & HENSON (AV)

1865 North Henderson Street, Suite 11B, 61401
Telephone: 309-344-5252
Telecopier: 309-344-3939

MEMBERS OF FIRM

Douglas D. Mustain	Ronald Henson
Robert Lindstrom	Christopher Henson
	Carl E. Hawkinson

References: The Farmers and Mechanics Bank; Norwest Bank Illinois, N.A.; First Bank; First Financial Bank; Farmers State Bank of Western Illinois; McGladrey and Pullen.

For full biographical listings, see the Martindale-Hubbell Law Directory

GENEVA,* Kane Co.

SMITH, LANDMEIER & SKAAR, P.C. (AV)

15 North Second Street, 60134
Telephone: 708-232-2880
Fax: 708-232-2889

Howard E. Smith, Jr.	Allen L. Landmeier
	James D. Skaar

Brian W. Baugh	Vincent J. Elders

References: Firstar Bank, Geneva, N.A., Geneva, Illinois; State Bank of Geneva, Geneva, Illinois.

For full biographical listings, see the Martindale-Hubbell Law Directory

HIGHLAND, Madison Co.

DONALD C. RIKLI (AV)

914 Broadway, 62249
Telephone: 618-654-2364
Fax: 618-654-4752

For full biographical listings, see the Martindale-Hubbell Law Directory

*JOLIET,** Will Co.

MCKEOWN, FITZGERALD, ZOLLNER, BUCK, HUTCHISON & RUTTLE (AV)

2455 Glenwood Avenue, 60435
Telephone: 815-729-4800
Fax: 815-729-4711
Frankfort, Illinois Office: 28 Kansas Street.
Telephone: 815-469-2176.
FAX: 815-469-0295.

MEMBERS OF FIRM

Charles J. McKeown (1908-1985)	Theodore J. Jarz
Paul O. McKeown (1913-1982)	Douglas J. McKeown
Richard T. Buck (1936-1992)	Timothy J. Rathbun
Joseph C. Fitzgerald	James B. Harvey
Max E. Zollner	Kenneth A. Grey
Douglas P. Hutchison	Michael R. Lucas
David L. Ruttle	Christopher N. Wise
	Gary S. Mueller

ASSOCIATES

Frank S. Cservenyak, Jr.	Kurt J. Keller
Arthur J. Wilhelmi	Kelly Kathleen James

OF COUNSEL

George E. Sangmeister   Stewart C. Hutchison

Representative Clients: Caterpillar Tractor Co.; First National Bank of Lockport; Homart Development Co.; First Midwest Bank, N.A.; Silver Cross Hospital; Joliet Township High School District; Villages of: Plainfield and Mokena; Southwest Agency for Risk Management; Joliet Junior College Foundation; Health Service Systems, Inc.

For full biographical listings, see the Martindale-Hubbell Law Directory

MATTOON, Coles Co.

CRAIG & CRAIG (AV)

1807 Broadway, P.O. Box 689, 61938-0689
Telephone: 217-234-6481
Telecopier: 217-234-6486
Mount Vernon, Illinois Office: 227 1/2 South 9th Street.
Telephone: 618-244-7511.

MEMBERS OF FIRM

Craig Van Meter (1895-1981)	Stephen L. Corn
Fred H. Kelly (1894-1971)	Richard Charles Hayden
Robert M. Werden (1908-1969)	Robert G. Grierson
George N. Gilkerson (1911-1985)	Gregory C. Ray
John H. Armstrong	Paul R. Lynch (Resident, Mount Vernon Office)
John P. Ewart	Kenneth F. Werts (Resident, Mount Vernon Office)
Richard F. Record, Jr.	
John L. Barger	

ASSOCIATES

Joshua N. Rosen (Resident, Mount Vernon Office)	Theresa M. Thomson
Kathleen M. Stockwell	Kristine M. Tuttle
	Henry P. Villani (Resident, Mount Vernon Office)

OF COUNSEL

Jack E. Horsley

Counsel for: Monterey Coal Co., a Division of Exxon Coal USA, Inc.; Marathon Oil Co.; Illinois Central R.R. Co.; Okaw Building & Loan Assn., Mattoon, Illinois; The Medical Protective Insurance Co.; Consolidated Communications, Inc.; Lloyds Underwriters at London; Hartford Insurance Co.; Coles Together, a Not-For-Profit Corp.; Coles Building Corporation.

For full biographical listings, see the Martindale-Hubbell Law Directory

NORTHBROOK, Cook Co.

OLSON, GRABILL & HOFFMAN (AV)

Suite 420, 707 Skokie Boulevard, 60062
Telephone: 847-564-8880; 564-9110
FAX: 847-564-8886
Chicago, Illinois Office: Olson, Grabill, Hoffman & Louis, 300 South Wacker Drive, Suite 2400.
Telephone: 312-332-6823.

MEMBERS OF FIRM

Norman L. Olson, Jr.	Fred Louis III
Edward M. Grabill, Jr.	Gregg A. Flitcraft
Thomas G. Hoffman	Kent J. Donewald

(See Next Column)

OF COUNSEL

G. Kent Yowell

For full biographical listings, see the Martindale-Hubbell Law Directory

OAK PARK, Cook Co.

GOEDERT & HUNTINGTON (AV)

6525 West North Avenue, 60302
Telephone: 708-848-6066
FAX: 708-848-6067

MEMBERS OF FIRM

John P. Goedert   Robert A. Huntington
            Michael J. DeBoer

For full biographical listings, see the Martindale-Hubbell Law Directory

*PEORIA,** Peoria Co.

JEROLD I. HORN (AV)

124 S.W. Adams Street, 61602-1320
Telephone: 309-676-2778
Fax: 309-676-2779

References: First of America Bank, Illinois, N.A.

For full biographical listings, see the Martindale-Hubbell Law Directory

*PONTIAC,** Livingston Co.

JOHNSON & TAYLOR (AV)

Formerly Ortman, Johnson & Taylor
109 North Mill Street, 61764
Telephone: 815-844-7151
FAX: 815-844-7539

MEMBERS OF FIRM

F. A. Ortman (1882-1955)   John A. Taylor
            Taylor F. Johnson

OF COUNSEL

J. Kenneth Johnson

Representative Clients: Flanagan State Bank; Flanagan School District; Flanagan-Graymont and Long Point Fire Districts; Hartford Steam Boiler Inspection Co.; Metro Life Insurance Co.; Good Samaritan Home of Flanagan; CAPS and Flanagan Park Districts; Evenglow Lodge; Livingston County Broadcasters; Albrecht and Oliver Trusts.

For full biographical listings, see the Martindale-Hubbell Law Directory

*ROCK ISLAND,** Rock Island Co.

NEPPLE, VAN DER KAMP & FLYNN, P.C. (AV)

Suite 202 American Bank Building, 1600 Fourth Avenue, P.O. Box 5408, 61204-5408
Telephone: 309-786-5700
Telecopier: 309-786-5745
Muscatine, Iowa Office: 216 Sycamore Street, P.O. Box 386, 52761-0386.
Telephone: 319-264-6840.

Roy W. Van Der Kamp   James A. Nepple
            Patrick J. Flynn

Milissa K. Hofmann

LEGAL SUPPORT PERSONNEL

Steven D. Perkins   Judy K. Freeman

For full biographical listings, see the Martindale-Hubbell Law Directory

*SPRINGFIELD,** Sangamon Co.

CHAPIN & CHAPIN (AV)

1000 First National Bank Building, 205 South Fifth Street, 62701
Telephone: 217-523-5611
Telecopier: 217-483-4789

MEMBERS OF FIRM

E.L. Chapin (1857-1934)	John R. Chapin
Roger E. Chapin (1890-1966)	Charles A. Chapin

References: First National Bank of Central Illinois; First of America Bank, Springfield; Bank One, Springfield.

For full biographical listings, see the Martindale-Hubbell Law Directory

*URBANA,** Champaign Co.

WEBBER & THIES, P.C. (AV)

202 Lincoln Square, P.O. Box 189, 61803-0189
Telephone: 217-367-1126
FAX: 217-367-3752

Richard L. Thies	Carl M. Webber
Craig R. Webber	David C. Thies
	Holten D. Summers

(See Next Column)

WEBBER & THIES P.C., *Urbana—Continued*

Tammy Koester Parks

For Complete List of Firm Personnel, See General Section

For full biographical listings, see the Martindale-Hubbell Law Directory

INDIANA

AUBURN,* De Kalb Co.

MEFFORD AND CARPENTER, A PROFESSIONAL CORPORATION (AV)

130 East Seventh Street, P.O. Box 667, 46706-0667
Telephone: 219-925-2300
Facsimile: 219-925-2610
URL: http://www.lawmc.com

Donald T. Mefford   Kirk D. Carpenter
J. Bryan Nugen

For full biographical listings, see the Martindale-Hubbell Law Directory

BLOOMINGTON,* Monroe Co.

BUNGER & ROBERTSON (AV)

226 South College Square, P.O. Box 910, 47402-0910
Telephone: 812-332-9295
Fax: 812-331-8808

MEMBERS OF FIRM
Don M. Robertson   Thomas Bunger
ASSOCIATE
Margaret M. Frisbie

Representative Clients: Aetna Insurance Companies; Bloomington Hospital; Commercial Union Group; Indiana Insurance Co.; Liberty Mutual Insurance; Medical Protective Co.; Monroe County Community School Corp.; Professional Golf Car, Inc.; Prudential Insurance Company of America; State Farm Automobile Insurance Co.

For Complete List of Firm Personnel, See General Section

For full biographical listings, see the Martindale-Hubbell Law Directory

CARMEL, Hamilton Co.

KNOWLES & ASSOCIATES (AV)

811 South Range Line Road, 46032
Telephone: 317-848-4360
Telecopier: 317-848-4363
URL: http://www.courts9@1x.netcom.com

William W. Knowles

D. Brandon Johnston   Tracy J. Follstad

For full biographical listings, see the Martindale-Hubbell Law Directory

CLARKSVILLE, Clark Co.

MAYER, VOGT, SMITH & PALMQUIST (AV)

501 Eastern Boulevard, 47129
Telephone: 812-288-1235
Louisville, Kentucky: 502-584-5800
Fax: 812-288-1240

MEMBERS OF FIRM
John M. Mayer, Jr.   Samuel H. Vogt, Jr.
ASSOCIATE
Susan Wagner Hynes

Representative Clients: First Savings Bank, FSB; PNC Bank Indiana, Inc.
Approved Attorneys for: Commonwealth Land Title Insurance Co.; Ticor Title Insurance Company; Old Republic National Title Insurance Company.
References: First Savings Bank, FSB; PNC Bank Indiana, Inc.

For Complete List of Firm Personnel, See General Section

For full biographical listings, see the Martindale-Hubbell Law Directory

COLUMBIA CITY,* Whitley Co.

GATES LAW OFFICE (AV)

407 Pinecrest Drive, P.O. Box 251, 46725-0251
Telephone: 219-244-5175
Fax: Available Upon Request

(See Next Column)

MEMBER OF FIRM
Benton E. Gates, Jr.
Attorneys for: Furnished upon request.

For full biographical listings, see the Martindale-Hubbell Law Directory

COLUMBUS,* Bartholomew Co.

SHARPNACK, BIGLEY, DAVID & RUMPLE (AV)

321 Washington Street, P.O. Box 310, 47202-0310
Telephone: 812-372-1553
Fax: 812-372-1567

MEMBERS OF FIRM
Thomas C. Bigley, Jr.   John R. Rumple
Jeffrey S. Washburn

For Complete List of Firm Personnel, See General Section

For full biographical listings, see the Martindale-Hubbell Law Directory

CRAWFORDSVILLE,* Montgomery Co.

BERRY, CAPPER, DONALDSON & TULLEY (AV)

131 North Green Street, P.O. Box 429, 47933
Telephone: 317-362-7340
Fax: 317-362-5023

Andrew N. Foley (1909-1963)   Richard G. Tulley
John R. Berry (1907-1986)   John S. Capper, IV
S. Bryan Donaldson

Representative Clients: Elston Bank & Trust Co.; R. R. Donnelley & Sons Co. (Crawfordsville Division); Linden State Bank; City of Crawfordsville, Ind.

For full biographical listings, see the Martindale-Hubbell Law Directory

ELKHART, Elkhart Co.

CHESTER, PFAFF & BROTHERSON (AV)

317 West Franklin Street, P.O. Box 507, 46515-0507
Telephone: 219-294-5421
Fax: 219-522-1476

MEMBERS OF FIRM
Robert A. Pfaff   Glenn E. Killoren
OF COUNSEL
Willard H. Chester   James R. Brotherson
LEGAL SUPPORT PERSONNEL
Wanda S. Wyrick (Paralegal)

For Complete List of Firm Personnel, See General Section

For full biographical listings, see the Martindale-Hubbell Law Directory

EVANSVILLE,* Vanderburgh Co.

LAW OFFICES OF RANDALL K. CRAIG (AV)

5000 East Virginia, Suite 1, 47715
Telephone: 812-477-3337
Telefax: 812-477-3658

For full biographical listings, see the Martindale-Hubbell Law Directory

FINE & HATFIELD (AV)

520 N.W. Second Street, P.O. Box 779, 47705-0779
Telephone: 812-425-3592
Telecopier: 812-421-4269
Email: Fine@Fine-Hatfield.com *URL:* http://www.Fine-Hatfield.com

MEMBERS OF FIRM
James E. Marchand   Thomas R. Fitzsimmons
William H. Mullis
ASSOCIATES
Debra S. McGowan   H. Linwood Shannon, III
Todd I. Glass

A List of Representative Clients Furnished Upon Request.

For full biographical listings, see the Martindale-Hubbell Law Directory

JACK A. STONE AND ASSOCIATES (AV)

1400 Old National Bank Building, 47708
Telephone: 812-423-2045
Fax: Available Upon Request

For full biographical listings, see the Martindale-Hubbell Law Directory

WRIGHT, EVANS AND DALY (AV)

425 Main Street, 47708
Telephone: 812-424-3300
Fax: 812-421-5588

(See Next Column)

WRIGHT, EVANS AND DALY—*Continued*

MEMBERS OF FIRM

Donald R. Wright   Gerald H. Evans
Christopher L. Lucas

Representative Clients: Browning-Ferris Industries of Indiana, Inc.; Castle Contracting Co., Inc.; Computing Solutions, Inc.; Happy China Trading Corporation; Manpower Incorporated of Evansville; Need-A-Nurse, Inc.; Mills-Wallace and Associates, Inc. Design Professionals; Servicemaster of Evansville, Inc.; Siemers Glass Company, Inc.; Southwestern Indiana Mental Health Center, Inc.

For Complete List of Firm Personnel, See General Section

For full biographical listings, see the Martindale-Hubbell Law Directory

---

FORT WAYNE,* Allen Co.

BEWLEY & KODAY (AV)

Fort Wayne National Bank Building, Suite 2006, 46802
Telephone: 219-424-0566
Telefax: 219-423-1325

George N. Bewley, Jr.   James Koday

For full biographical listings, see the Martindale-Hubbell Law Directory

---

BONAHOOM & BONAHOOM (AV)

110 W. Berry Street, Suite 1700, 46802
Telephone: 219-420-4055
Fax: 219-424-5311

Otto M. Bonahoom   Joseph G. Bonahoom

For full biographical listings, see the Martindale-Hubbell Law Directory

---

HELMKE, BEAMS, BOYER & WAGNER (AV)

300 Metro Building, Berry & Harrison Streets, 46802-2242
Telephone: 219-422-7422
Telecopier: 219-422-6764

MEMBERS OF FIRM

Walter E. Helmke (1901-1976)   Robert A. Wagner
Walter P. Helmke   J. Timothy McCaulay
R. David Boyer   Daniel J. Borgmann
Trina Glusenkamp Gould

OF COUNSEL

Glen J. Beams   John G. Reiber

Representative Clients: Aalco Distributing Co., Inc.; Brotherhood Mutual Insurance Co.; Fremont Community Schools; Teco, Inc.; Air-O-Mat, Inc.; Leo Distributors, Inc.; The City of Fort Wayne, Indiana; Foellinger Foundation, Inc.

For full biographical listings, see the Martindale-Hubbell Law Directory

---

SHAMBAUGH, KAST, BECK & WILLIAMS (AV)

600 Standard Federal Plaza, 46802-2405
Telephone: 219-423-1430
Fax: 219-422-9038

MEMBERS OF FIRM

Michael H. Kast   Daniel E. Serban
Stephen J. Williams   John B. Powell
Edward E. Beck   Timothy L. Claxton
James D. Streit

Counsel for: Hagerman Construction Corp.; Rogers Markets, Inc.; K & H Realty Corp.; Olive B. Cole Foundation; M. E. Raker Foundation, Inc.; Associates Financial Services Co., of Indiana, Inc.; Professional Federal Credit Union; Fort Wayne Education Association; American Ambassador Casualty Company; CBT Credit Services, Inc.

For Complete List of Firm Personnel, See General Section

For full biographical listings, see the Martindale-Hubbell Law Directory

---

SWIFT & FINLAYSON (AV)

803 South Calhoun Street Suite 500, 46802-2480
Telephone: 219-423-4422
Fax: 219-423-4427
Affiliated Law Firm: Leeuw, Plopper & Beeman-Poland, First Indiana Plaza, Suite 2000, 135 North Pennsylvania Street, Indianapolis, Indiana, 46204-2456.

MEMBERS OF FIRM

Frank A. Higgins (1925-1976)   William D. Swift
Craig R. Finlayson

ASSOCIATE

Charles D. Bash

(See Next Column)

OF COUNSEL

Gene R. Leeuw   Craig D. Doyle
Joseph W. Murphy   Charleyne L. Gabriel
John Michael Mead

For full biographical listings, see the Martindale-Hubbell Law Directory

---

FOWLER,* Benton Co.

BARCE & RYAN (AV)

103 North Jackson Avenue, P.O. Box 252, 47944-0252
Telephone: 317-884-0383
Fax: 317-884-0445
Kentland, Indiana Office: 301 East Graham Street, P.O. Box 338, 47951-0338.
Telephone: 219-474-5158.
Fax: 219-474-6610.

MEMBER OF FIRM

John W. Barce   J. Edward Barce (Resident)

For full biographical listings, see the Martindale-Hubbell Law Directory

---

WEIST & KEPNER (AV)

Weist Building, P.O. Box 101, 47944
Telephone: 317-884-1840
Fax: Available Upon Request

William B. Weist   Rex W. Kepner

References: Fowler State Bank, Fowler, Indiana; Farmers and Merchants Bank, Boswell, Indiana.

For full biographical listings, see the Martindale-Hubbell Law Directory

---

GREENWOOD, Johnson Co.

WILLIAMS HEWITT & ROBBINS, LLP (AV)

Suite 400, National City Bank Building, 300 South Madison Avenue, P.O. Box 405, 46142
Telephone: 317-888-1121
Facsimile: 317-887-4069

PARTNERS

Jon E. Williams   Brian C. Hewitt
J. Lee Robbins

ASSOCIATES

John M. White   Mark E. Need
John P. Wilkowski

For full biographical listings, see the Martindale-Hubbell Law Directory

---

INDIANAPOLIS,* Marion Co.

ADINAMIS & ADINAMIS, ATTORNEYS, A PROFESSIONAL CORPORATION (AV)

8710 North Meridian Street, 46260
Telephone: 317-580-9000
Indianapolis Downtown Office, By Appointment: Chamber of Commerce Building, 320 North Meridian Street, 46204.

George P. Adinamis   Susan L. Adinamis
Carol M. Adinamis   Jeffrey A. Saunders

For full biographical listings, see the Martindale-Hubbell Law Directory

---

BACKER & BACKER, A PROFESSIONAL CORPORATION (AV)

101 West Ohio Street, Suite 1500, 46204
Telephone: 317-684-3000
Telecopier: 317-684-3004

Herbert J. Backer (1914-1995)   Stephen A. Backer
David J. Backer

Reference: Bank One, Indianapolis.

For full biographical listings, see the Martindale-Hubbell Law Directory

---

BOBERSCHMIDT, MILLER, O'BRYAN & TURNER, A PROFESSIONAL ASSOCIATION (AV)

Bank One Center/Circle, 111 Monument Circle, Suite 302, 46204-5169
Telephone: 317-632-5892
Telecopier: 317-686-3423

Philip F. Boberschmidt   Berton W. O'Bryan
L. Craig Turner

A List of Representative Clients will be furnished upon request.

For full biographical listings, see the Martindale-Hubbell Law Directory

---

DALE & EKE, PROFESSIONAL CORPORATION (AV)

Suite 400, 9100 Keystone Crossing, 46240
Telephone: 317-844-7400
Fax: 317-574-9426

(See Next Column)

DALE & EKE PROFESSIONAL CORPORATION, *Indianapolis—Continued*

William J. Dale, Jr.	Catherine Chambers Kennedy
Joseph W. Eke	Karen A. Hosack
Deborah J. Caruso	A. Robert Lasich, Jr.
	Dawn Michelle Snow

For full biographical listings, see the Martindale-Hubbell Law Directory

DANN PECAR NEWMAN & KLEIMAN, PROFESSIONAL CORPORATION (AV)

Suite 2300, One American Square Box 82008, 46282
Telephone: 317-632-3232; Indiana: 800-622-4799
Telecopy: 317-632-2962

Theodore R. Dann (1907-1993)	Walter E. Wolf, Jr.
Joel Yonover (1932-1995)	Barry E. Beldin
Philip D. Pecar	Robert D. Swhier, Jr.
Norman R. Newman	James P. Moloy
David H. Kleiman	Robert J. Schuckit
Jon B. Abels	Andrew A. Kleiman
Melvin R. Daniel	Michael J. Gabovitch
Lawrence F. Dorocke	Steven M. Pecar
Jeffrey A. Abrams	Benjamin A. Pecar
James H. Schwarz	Richard O. Kissel, II
Robert A. Rose	Joseph D. Calderon

OF COUNSEL

Linda E. Cantor	Anthony J. Rose

Ellen C. Siakotos	Angela L. Mansfield
Stacy L. Hill	Martha M. K. Baird
	Karin L. Veatch

Attorneys for: Indianapolis Machinery Co., Inc.; Melvin Simon & Associates, Inc.; Pacers Basketball Corp.; Universal Fire & Casualty Co., Inc.; Bank One, Indianapolis, NA; INB National Bank; Nachi Technology, Inc.; Pharmaceutical Corporation of America; Logo 7, Inc.

For full biographical listings, see the Martindale-Hubbell Law Directory

HALL, RENDER, KILLIAN, HEATH & LYMAN, PROFESSIONAL CORPORATION (AV)

Suite 2000, One American Square Box 82064, 46282
Telephone: 317-633-4884
Fax: 317-633-4878
Email: hrkhl@hrkhl.com
Indianapolis North Office: Suite 820, 8402 Harcourt Road, 46260.
Telephone: 317-871-6222.
Fax: 317-338-3946.
Louisville, Kentucky Office: Providian Center, Suite 1530, 400 West Market Street, 40202.
Telephone: 502-568-1890.
Fax: 502-568-4878.

William S. Hall	Douglas P. Long
R. Terry Heath	Fred J. Bachmann
Jeffrey Peek	D. David Freeman

Jon F. Spadorcia

For Complete List of Firm Personnel, See General Section

For full biographical listings, see the Martindale-Hubbell Law Directory

ICE MILLER DONADIO & RYAN (AV)

One American Square Box 82001, 46282-0002
Telephone: 317-236-2100
Fax: 317-236-2219
Email: leel@imdr.com *URL:* http://www.imdr.com
South Bend, Indiana Office: 211 West Washington Street, Suite 2420.
Telephone: 219-234-7933.
Fax: 219-234-7965. Internet E-mail: leel@imdr.com. Web Site Address: http://www.imdr.com.

MEMBERS OF FIRM

Gordon D. Wishard	Lisa Stone Sciscoe

SENIOR COUNSEL

Gene E. Wilkins

STAFF ATTORNEY

Raymond J. Schoettle

For Complete List of Firm Personnel, See General Section

For full biographical listings, see the Martindale-Hubbell Law Directory

ROBERT A. LICHTENAUER (AV)

Suite 110, 8140 Knue Road, 46250
Telephone: 317-845-1988

For full biographical listings, see the Martindale-Hubbell Law Directory

SANDIFER & SANDIFER, P.C. (AV)

Suite 201, 7351 Shadeland Station, 46256
Telephone: 317-842-4161
Fax: 317-842-4176

James E. Sandifer	J. Edward Sandifer

For full biographical listings, see the Martindale-Hubbell Law Directory

TABBERT HAHN EARNEST & STARKEY, P.C. (AV)

Suite 2100, One Indiana Square, 46204
Telephone: 317-639-5444
Fax: 317-639-5232

Don A. Tabbert	Lorie A. Brown
Gregory F. Hahn	Mark K. Sullivan
Lante K. Earnest	Judy M. Tyrrell
Martha T. Starkey	Susan L. Abel

OF COUNSEL

James J. Nocon	William D. Lalley
	Douglas E. Cregor

For full biographical listings, see the Martindale-Hubbell Law Directory

YARLING, ROBINSON, HAMMEL & LAMB (AV)

151 North Delaware, Suite 1535, P.O. Box 44128, 46204
Telephone: 317-262-8800
Fax: 317-262-3046

MEMBERS OF FIRM

Richard W. Yarling	Edgar H. Lamb
Charles F. Robinson, Jr.	Douglas E. Rogers
John W. Hammel	Mark S. Gray
Linda Y. Hammel	Matthew C. Robinson

For full biographical listings, see the Martindale-Hubbell Law Directory

JASONVILLE, Greene Co.

ROWE & HAWKINS (AV)

103 West Main Street, 47438
Telephone: 812-665-2268
Fax: 812-665-2817

John S. Rowe	Jeff R. Hawkins

For full biographical listings, see the Martindale-Hubbell Law Directory

KENTLAND,* Newton Co.

BARCE & RYAN (AV)

301 East Graham Street, P.O. Box 338, 47951-0338
Telephone: 219-474-5158
Fax: 219-474-6610
Fowler, Indiana Office: 103 North Jackson Avenue, P.O. Box 252, 47944-0252.
Telephone: 317-884-0383.
Fax: 317-884-0445.

MEMBERS OF FIRM

John W. Barce	J. Edward Barce
R. Steven Ryan	(Resident at Fowler Office)

Representative Clients: USX Corporation; Metropolitan Life Insurance Company; Goodland State Bank; State Bank of Oxford; DeMotte State Bank; Newton County Stone; Northern Indiana Public Service Company; DeMeter, Inc; Town of Boswell; Town of Brook.

For Complete List of Firm Personnel, See General Section

For full biographical listings, see the Martindale-Hubbell Law Directory

KOKOMO,* Howard Co.

FELL, McGARVEY, TRAURING & WILSON (AV)

515 West Sycamore Street, P.O. Box 958, 46903-0958
Telephone: 317-457-9321
Telecopier: 317-452-0882

MEMBERS OF FIRM

John E. Fell, Jr.	Eugene J. McGarvey, Jr.

Representative Clients: Big R Stores; Cellular One of Kokomo, Inc.; First National Bank, Kokomo; Haynes International, Inc.; Hospital Authority of the City of Kokomo; Kokomo City Hall Building Corp.; PPG Industries, Inc.; Star Building Supply, Inc.; Mervis Industries, Inc.; Taylor Community School Corp.

For Complete List of Firm Personnel, See General Section

For full biographical listings, see the Martindale-Hubbell Law Directory

LAFAYETTE,* Tippecanoe Co.

BALL, EGGLESTON, BUMBLEBURG & McBRIDE (AV)

810 Bank One Building, P.O. Box 1535, 47902
Telephone: 317-742-9046
Fax: 317-742-1966

(See Next Column)

BALL, EGGLESTON, BUMBLEBURG & MCBRIDE—*Continued*

Cable G. Ball (1904-1981)   Warren N. Eggleston
Owen Crook (1908-1977)   (1923-1991)

MEMBERS OF FIRM

Joseph T. Bumbleburg   Jeffrey J. Newell
John K. McBride   James T. Hodson
Jack L. Walkey   Brian Wade Walker
Michael J. Stapleton   Cheryl M. Knodle
Randy J. Williams

General Counsel for: The Lafayette Union Railway Co.; Bank One, Lafayette, N.A.
Representative Clients: Farmers Insurance Group; General Accident Fire & Life Assurance Corp.; City of Lafayette Board of Parks and Recreation; West Lafayette Community School Corp.; Travelers Insurance Co.; Trustees, West Lafayette Public Library.

For full biographical listings, see the Martindale-Hubbell Law Directory

MAYFIELD AND BROOKS (AV)

322 Main Street, P.O. Box 650, 47902
Telephone: 317-423-5454
FAX: 317-742-8666

MEMBER OF FIRM
Thomas L. Brooks

Representative Clients: DeFouw Chevrolet, Inc.; Kendrick Buick-Cadillac, Inc.; Lafayette Real Estate Marketing Corp.; Smith Office Equipment, Inc.; American Vending Corp.; Sun Industries, Inc.; National Attorneys' Title Insurance Fund, Inc.
Reference: NBD Bank, N.A.

For Complete List of Firm Personnel, See General Section

STUART & BRANIGIN (AV)

The Life Building, 300 Main Street, Suite 800, 47902
Telephone: 317-423-1561
Telecopier: 317-742-8175

MEMBERS OF FIRM

Allison Ellsworth Stuart   Stephen R. Pennell
(1886-1950)   Anthony S. Benton
Roger D. Branigin (1902-1975)   Erik D. Spykman
Russell H. Hart   William E. Emerick
Roger D. Branigin, Jr.   John C. Duffey
Thomas L. Ryan   Mark E. DeYoung
James V. McGlone   Thomas B. Parent
Carl W. Kloepfer   Laura L. Bowker
Thomas R. McCully   Kevin D. Nicoson
Larry R. Fisher   Susan K. Roberts
Nina B. Kirkpatrick   John M. Stuckey
Mark Lillianfeld   Deborah B. Trice

COUNSEL
John F. Bodle

ASSOCIATES

Brent W. Huber   David A. Starkweather
William P. Kealey   Geoffrey Blazi
A. James Chareq

General Counsel for: The Lafayette Life Insurance Co.; INB National Bank, N.W.; Lafayette Home Hospital, Inc.
State Counsel for: Norfolk & Western Railway Co.
Mr. Ryan is Counsel to: The Trustees of Purdue University.
Representative Clients: Aluminum Company of America; Liberty Mutual Insurance Group.

For full biographical listings, see the Martindale-Hubbell Law Directory

LOGANSPORT,* Cass Co.

MILLER, TOLBERT, MUEHLHAUSEN, MUEHLHAUSEN & GROFF, P.C. (AV)

216 Fourth Street Caller Box: 7010, 46947-7010
Telephone: 219-722-4343
FAX: 219-722-1936

Glenn L. Miller (1902-1992)   John C. Muehlhausen
George R. Wildman (1932-1994)   James K. Muehlhausen
Frank E. Tolbert   R. Tod Groff

John S. Damm

Counsel for: Area Five Council on Aging; ASCO Oil Company; Careage of Logansport, Inc.; Carter Concrete Block, Inc.; Hartford Insurance Co.; J&P Stores, Inc.; Logansport Memorial Hospital; Meridian Insurance Co.; Motorists Mutual Insurance Co.; Ohio Casualty Insurance Co.

For full biographical listings, see the Martindale-Hubbell Law Directory

MARION,* Grant Co.

KILEY, KILEY, HARKER, MICHAEL & CERTAIN (AV)

300 West Third Street, P.O. Box 899, 46952-0899
Telephone: 317-664-9041
Fax: 317-664-8119

MEMBERS OF FIRM

Robert Ralph Batton   David L. Kiley, Sr.
(1890-1963)   Michael J. Kiley
Albert L. Harker (1904-1965)   Albert C. Harker
Albert Bonner Brown   Thomas W. Michael
(1911-1981)   Harry J. Certain

ASSOCIATE
Therese McCullough Pryor

Counsel for: Bank One, Marion, N.A.; Liniger Co., Inc.; Atlas Foundry Co.
Local Counsel for: GenCorp.; CPC Group; General Motors; Indiana Michigan Power Co./AEP; Indiana Bell Telephone Co.; Foster-Forbes, Division of American National Can Corp.

For full biographical listings, see the Martindale-Hubbell Law Directory

MISHAWAKA, St. Joseph Co.

SCHINDLER AND OLSON (AV)

122 South Mill Street, P.O. Box 100, 46544
Telephone: 219-259-5461
Fax: 219-259-5462

OF COUNSEL
John W. Schindler (1884-1971)   John W. Schindler, Jr.

MEMBER OF FIRM
James J. Olson

A List of Representative Clients Will Be Furnished Upon Request.
Reference: 1st Source Bank of Mishawaka.

For full biographical listings, see the Martindale-Hubbell Law Directory

MUNCIE,* Delaware Co.

CANNON & BRUNS (AV)

119 North High Street, 47305
Telephone: 317-289-2161
FAX: 317-289-2162

MEMBERS OF FIRM
Thomas A. Cannon   William G. Bruns
Thomas A. Cannon, Jr.

References: First Merchants Bank, Muncie; American National Bank and Trust Company of Muncie.

For full biographical listings, see the Martindale-Hubbell Law Directory

MUNSTER, Lake Co.

PINKERTON AND FRIEDMAN, PROFESSIONAL CORPORATION (AV)

The Fairmont, 9245 Calumet Avenue Suite 201, 46321
Telephone: 219-836-3050
Fax: 219-836-2955

Milton Roth (1925-1996)   Jeffrey F. Gunning
Kirk A. Pinkerton   Gail Oosterhof
Stuart J. Friedman   Richard N. Shapiro

For full biographical listings, see the Martindale-Hubbell Law Directory

RICHMOND,* Wayne Co.

HARRINGTON, MALEY, GARDNER & SAYRE (AV)

Third Floor, Harrington Bank Building, Two North Eighth, 47374-3090
Telephone: 317-966-6643
FAX: 317-966-6799

MEMBERS OF FIRM
Alonzo M. Gardner (1886-1941)   Robert J. Maley
Wilfred Jessup (1900-1944)   Gayle W. Gardner
Frank K. Chambers (1938-1955)   John M. Sayre, III
Floyd W. Gardner (1933-1965)   Kirk A. Weikart
Clifford M. Haworth
(1923-1967)

OF COUNSEL
John R. Harrington

General Counsel for: Harrington Bank, FSB.
Local Counsel for: Belden Manufacturing Co.; CIGNA.

For full biographical listings, see the Martindale-Hubbell Law Directory

RUSHVILLE,* Rush Co.

EARNEST, FOSTER, EDER, LEVI & NORTHAM (AV)

114 West Third Street, P.O. Box 430, 46173
Telephone: 317-932-4118
Fax: 317-932-4486

(See Next Column)

EARNEST, FOSTER, EDER, LEVI & NORTHAM, *Rushville—Continued*

Kenneth L. Earnest (1916-1995)

OF COUNSEL

James S. Foster

MEMBERS OF FIRM

Robert J. Eder   Richard K. Levi

David E. Northam

Representative Clients: Rush County REMC; First Federal Savings and Loan Association of Rushville; Rush Memorial Hospital; Farm Bureau Insurance Co.; Farmers State Bank; The Sampler, Inc.; Ticor Title Insurance Co.

For full biographical listings, see the Martindale-Hubbell Law Directory

---

TERRE HAUTE,* Vigo Co.

COX, ZWERNER, GAMBILL & SULLIVAN (AV)

511 Wabash Avenue, P.O. Box 1625, 47808-1625
Telephone: 812-232-6003
Fax: 812-232-6567

MEMBERS OF FIRM

Ernest J. Zwerner (1918-1980)   David W. Sullivan
Benjamin G. Cox (1915-1988)   Robert L. Gowdy
Gilbert W. Gambill, Jr.   Louis F. Britton
James E. Sullivan   Carroll D. Smeltzer
Benjamin G. Cox, Jr.   Jeffry A. Lind

ASSOCIATE

Ronald E. Jumps

OF COUNSEL

Robert D. Hepburn

Counsel for: Terre Haute First National Bank; Farmers Insurance Group; Indiana-American Water Co.; Indiana State University; Merchants National Bank of Terre Haute; Rose-Hulman Institute of Technology; Tribune-Star Publishing Co., Inc.; Weston Paper & Manufacturing Co.

For full biographical listings, see the Martindale-Hubbell Law Directory

WILKINSON, GOELLER, MODESITT, WILKINSON & DRUMMY (AV)

333 Ohio Street, P.O. Box 800, 47808-0800
Telephone: 812-232-4311
Fax: 812-235-5107

MEMBERS OF FIRM

Myrl O. Wilkinson   Kelvin L. Roots
David H. Goeller   John C. Wall
Raymond H. Modesitt   William M. Olah
B. Curtis Wilkinson   Craig M. McKee

Representative Corporate Clients: Merchants National Bank; Old National Trust Co.; Old National Bank.

For Complete List of Firm Personnel, See General Section

For full biographical listings, see the Martindale-Hubbell Law Directory

---

VALPARAISO,* Porter Co.

BLACHLY, TABOR, BOZIK & HARTMAN (AV)

Suite 401 Indiana Federal Building, 46383
Telephone: 219-464-1041
Fax: 219-464-0927

MEMBERS OF FIRM

Quentin A. Blachly   David L. Hollenbeck
Glenn J. Tabor   David L. DeBoer
James S. Bozik   Thomas F. Macke
Duane W. Hartman   Randall J. Zromkoski

Richard J. Rupcich

ASSOCIATES

Roger A. Weitgenant   Craig R. Van Schouwen

Reference: First National Bank.

For Complete List of Firm Personnel, See General Section

For full biographical listings, see the Martindale-Hubbell Law Directory

---

WARSAW,* Kosciusko Co.

LEMON, ARMEY, HEARN & LEININGER (AV)

210 North Buffalo Street, P.O. Box 770, 46581-0770
Telephone: 219-268-9111
Telecopier: 219-267-8647

MEMBERS OF FIRM

Thomas R. Lemon   Daniel K. Leininger
Michael E. Armey   Jane L. Kauffman
R. Steven Hearn   Ronald B. Cassidente

ASSOCIATE

Andrea E. Halpin

(See Next Column)

OF COUNSEL

Robert L. Rasor

Representative Clients: Lake City Bank; Zimmer Inc.; The Dalton Foundries, Inc.; Grace Schools, Inc.; Kosciusko Community Hospital, Inc.

For full biographical listings, see the Martindale-Hubbell Law Directory

---

IOWA

CEDAR RAPIDS,* Linn Co.

SHUTTLEWORTH & INGERSOLL, P.C. (AV)

500 Firstar Bank Building, P.O. Box 2107, 52406-2107
Telephone: 319-365-9461
Fax: 319-365-8443
Email: si-law@inav.net

Thomas M. Collins   Carroll J. Reasoner
Michael O. McDermott   William P. Prowell
Gary J. Streit   William S. Hochstetler

Dean D. Carrington

OF COUNSEL

W. R. Shuttleworth

Representative Clients: Firstar Bank Cedar Rapids, N.A.; First National Bank of Cedar Rapids; Norwest Bank Iowa, N.A.

For Complete List of Firm Personnel, See General Section

For full biographical listings, see the Martindale-Hubbell Law Directory

---

COUNCIL BLUFFS,* Pottawattamie Co.

SMITH PETERSON LAW FIRM (AV)

35 Main Place, Suite 300, P.O. Box 249, 51502
Telephone: 712-328-1833
Fax: 712-328-8320
Omaha, Nebraska Office: 9290 West Dodge Road, Suite 205.
Telephone: 402-397-8500.
Fax: 402-397-5519.

MEMBERS OF FIRM

Raymond A. Smith (1892-1977)   Lawrence J. Beckman
John LeRoy Peterson   Gregory G. Barntsen
  (1895-1969)   W. Curtis Hewett
Harold T. Beckman   Steven H. Krohn
Robert J. Laubenthal   Randy R. Ewing
Richard A. Heininger   Joseph D. Thornton

ASSOCIATES

T. J. Pattermann   Paul M. Shotkoski
Daniel Fretheim   (Not admitted in IA)

Representative Clients: Redland Insurance Group; Iowa Western Community College; Farm Credit Bank of Omaha; Demma Fruit Co.; Peoples National Bank; Council Bluffs Board of Water Works Trustee.

For full biographical listings, see the Martindale-Hubbell Law Directory

---

DAVENPORT,* Scott Co.

NOYES & GOSMA, L.L.P. (AV)

400 North Main Street, Suite 106, 52801
Telephone: 319-322-8223
Fax: 319-322-8234

MEMBERS OF FIRM

Michael L. Noyes   John S. Gosma

ASSOCIATE

Marie R. Rolling-Tarbox

OF COUNSEL

Clay LeGrand   Charles G. Rehling

Reference: Quad City Bank and Trust Company.

For full biographical listings, see the Martindale-Hubbell Law Directory

---

DES MOINES,* Polk Co.

CONNOLLY, O'MALLEY, LILLIS, HANSEN & OLSON, L.L.P. (AV)

820 Liberty Building, 6th & Grand Avenue, 50309
Telephone: 515-243-8157
Fax: 515-243-3919

MEMBERS OF FIRM

William J. Lillis   Peter S. Cannon
Russell J. Hansen   Streetar Cameron
Michael W. O'Malley   Douglas A. Fulton
Eugene E. Olson   Daniel L. Manning

Christopher R. Pose

(See Next Column)

CONNOLLY, O'MALLEY, LILLIS, HANSEN & OLSON L.L.P.—*Continued*
OF COUNSEL
John Connolly, III
A list of Representative Clients will be furnished upon request.
References will be furnished upon request.

For full biographical listings, see the Martindale-Hubbell Law Directory

---

DICKINSON, MACKAMAN, TYLER & HAGEN, P.C. (AV)

Suite 1600 Hub Tower, 699 Walnut Street, 50309-3986
Telephone: 515-244-2600
Telecopier: 515-246-4550

Barbara G. Barrett	David R. Rhein
Jeffrey T. Ramsey	(Not admitted in IA)
David M. Repp	Paul R. Tyler

Representative Clients: Board of Waterworks Trustees, Des Moines, Iowa; Merchants Bonding Co. (Mutual); Norwest Bank, N.A.

For Complete List of Firm Personnel, See General Section

For full biographical listings, see the Martindale-Hubbell Law Directory

---

FINLEY, ALT, SMITH, SCHARNBERG, MAY & CRAIG, P.C. (AV)

604 Locust Street, Fourth Floor Equitable Building, 50309
Telephone: 515-288-0145
Telecopier: 515-288-2724

David C. Craig

Representative Clients: Aetna Casualty & Surety Co.; Aetna Life Insurance Co.; ALAS; American Society of Composers, Authors and Publishers; Equitable Life Assurance Society of the U.S.; Federated Insurance Co.; Meredith Corp.
Iowa Attorneys for: Midwest Medical Insurance Co.
District Attorneys for: Norfolk & Southern Railroad; Soo Line Railroad Company.

For Complete List of Firm Personnel, See General Section

For full biographical listings, see the Martindale-Hubbell Law Directory

---

GREFE & SIDNEY, P.L.C. (AV)

2222 Grand Avenue, P.O. Box 10434, 50306
Telephone: 515-245-4300
Fax: 515-245-4452
Email: GRANDFIRM@AOL.COM

Rolland E. Grefe	Robert C. Thomson
Thomas W. Carpenter	Craig S. Shannon
Mary E. Kiener	

Representative Clients: Boatmen's National Bank of Des Moines; Easter Enterprises, Inc.; Freeman Decorating Co.; Pella Corp.

For Complete List of Firm Personnel, See General Section

For full biographical listings, see the Martindale-Hubbell Law Directory

---

MASON CITY, * Cerro Gordo Co.

WINSTON & BYRNE, LAWYERS, A PROFESSIONAL CORPORATION (AV)

119 Second Street, N.W., 50401
Telephone: 515-423-1913
Fax: 515-423-8998

Harold R. Winston	Michael G. Byrne

Representative Clients: Woodharbor Molding & Millworks, Inc.; Winkleman Farms, Inc.; Sparboe Iowa Corporation; Schmidt Family Farms, Inc.; First Citizen's National Bank of Mason City; Norwest Bank Iowa, N.A.

For full biographical listings, see the Martindale-Hubbell Law Directory

---

ROCKWELL CITY, * Calhoun Co.

LEWIS S. HENDRICKS (AV)

408 Fifth Street, P.O. Box 111, 50579
Telephone: 712-297-7567
Fax: 712-297-5407

Reference: National Bank of Rockwell City.

For full biographical listings, see the Martindale-Hubbell Law Directory

---

SIOUX CITY, * Woodbury Co.

BERENSTEIN, MOORE, MOSER, BERENSTEIN & HEFFERNAN (AV)

300 Commerce Building, P.O. Box 3207, 51102
Telephone: 712-252-0020
Fax: 712-252-0656

(See Next Column)

MEMBER OF FIRM
Marvin S. Berenstein

Representative Clients: Aalfs Manufacturing, Inc.; Boatmen's Bank; Beef Products, Inc.; Briar Cliff College; Canal Capital Corp.- Sioux City Stockyards; Firstar Bank Iowa, N.A.; Metropolitan Life Insurance Co.; Sioux Tools, Inc.- Snap-On-Tools; Marian Health Center, a division of Mercy Health Services; Wells Dairy & Blue Bunny Ice Cream.

For Complete List of Firm Personnel, See General Section

For full biographical listings, see the Martindale-Hubbell Law Directory

---

SHULL, COSGROVE, HELLIGE & LUNDBERG (AV)

700 Frances Building, 505 Fifth Street, P.O. Box 1828, 51102
Telephone: 712-255-4444
Telecopier: 712-255-4465

MEMBERS OF FIRM

James M. Cosgrove	Robert F. Meis
Michael R. Hellige	Scott A. Hindman
Paul D. Lundberg	James W. Radig

ASSOCIATES

Leif D. Erickson	Michael J. Frey
Stephen E. Doohen	

RETIRED
D. Carlton Shull

Representative Clients: Burlington Northern Inc.; Employers Mutual Cos.; Ford Motor Co.; The Hartford; Liberty Mutual Insurance Co.; Prince Manufacturing Corp.; Sioux City Journal; The Travelers; Western Iowa Tech Community College.

For full biographical listings, see the Martindale-Hubbell Law Directory

---

KANSAS

DODGE CITY, * Ford Co.

FOULSTON & SIEFKIN L.L.P. (AV)

810 Frontview, P.O. Box 1147, 67801
Telephone: 316-227-8126
Fax: 316-227-8451
Wichita, Kansas Office: 100 North Broadway, 700 Fourth Financial Center, 67202.
Telephone: 316-267-6371.
FAX: 316-267-6345.
Topeka, Kansas Office: 1515 Bank IV Tower, 534 Kansas Avenue, 66603.
Telephone: 913-233-3600.
FAX: 913-233-1610.
Member: Lex Mundi, A Global Association of 126 Independent Firms.

MEMBERS OF FIRM

William P. Trenkle, Jr.	David J. Rebein

For Complete List of Firm Personnel, See General Section

For full biographical listings, see the Martindale-Hubbell Law Directory

---

SALINA, * Saline Co.

NORTON, WASSERMAN, JONES & KELLY (AV)

215 South Santa Fe, P.O. Box 2388, 67402-2388
Telephone: 913-827-3646
Fax: 913-827-0538

MEMBERS OF FIRM

Frank C. Norton	Robert S. Jones
Kenneth W. Wasserman	Norman R. Kelly

ASSOCIATE
Robert A. Martin

Reference: Gypsum Valley Bank.

For full biographical listings, see the Martindale-Hubbell Law Directory

---

TOPEKA, * Shawnee Co.

GOODELL, STRATTON, EDMONDS & PALMER, L.L.P. (AV)

515 South Kansas Avenue, 66603-3999
Telephone: 913-233-0593
Telecopier: 913-233-8870
Email: GSEP@CJNETWORKS.COM

MEMBERS OF FIRM

Gerald L. Goodell	H. Philip Elwood
Gerald J. Letourneau	

OF COUNSEL

Robert A. McClure	John A. Bausch

(See Next Column)

GOODELL, STRATTON, EDMONDS & PALMER L.L.P., *Topeka—Continued*

SPECIAL COUNSEL

Joseph E. McKinney

Counsel for: American Home Life Insurance Co.

For Complete List of Firm Personnel, See General Section

For full biographical listings, see the Martindale-Hubbell Law Directory

---

WICHITA,* Sedgwick Co.

BEVER, DYE, MUSTARD & BELIN, L.C. (AV)

106 W. Douglas, Suite 700, 67202-3390
Telephone: 316-263-8294
Fax: 316-263-3142
Email: beverdye@feist.com

Ellis D. Bever (Retired)	R. Chris Robe
James D. Dye (1908-1995)	Eric J. Larson
Thomas D. Mustard (1909-1979)	Robert M. Hughes
Oscar F. Belin	Gregory L. Franken
Don B. Stahr	David B. Sutton
William M. Cobb	R. Eric Ireland
Jack D. Flesher	Hellen L. Haag

Karla R. Kerschen

Representative Clients: INTRUST Bank (NA); Commerce Bank, N.A.; Dwane L. Wallace Trust; Greater Wichita Community Foundation; Dane G. Hansen Trust.

For full biographical listings, see the Martindale-Hubbell Law Directory

---

FOULSTON & SIEFKIN L.L.P. (AV)

700 Fourth Financial Center, 67202
Telephone: 316-267-6371
Facsimile: 316-267-6345
Topeka, Kansas Office: 1515 Bank IV Tower, 534 Kansas Avenue, 66603.
Telephone: 913-233-3600.
Fax: 913-233-1610.
Dodge City, Kansas Office: 810 Frontview, P.O. Box 1147, 67801.
Telephone: 316-227-8126.
Fax: 316-227-8451.
Member: Lex Mundi, A Global Association of 126 Independent Firms.

MEMBERS OF FIRM

Stanley G. Andeel	Jim H. Goering

OF COUNSEL

Richard C. Harris

For Complete List of Firm Personnel, See General Section

For full biographical listings, see the Martindale-Hubbell Law Directory

---

HERSHBERGER, PATTERSON, JONES & ROTH, L.C. (AV)

600 Hardage Center, 100 South Main, 67202-3779
Telephone: 316-263-7583
Fax: 316-263-7595

Jerome E. Jones	Ken W. Dannenberg
John A. Vetter	Tracy A. Applegate

Counsel for: First National Bank in Wichita; Anadarko Petroleum Corporation; Chinese Industries; Mobil Oil Corp.; CNA Insurance; Royal Exchange Group; Central National Insurance Group; Transamerica Insurance Group; Northwestern National Insurance Group.

For Complete List of Firm Personnel, See General Section

For full biographical listings, see the Martindale-Hubbell Law Directory

---

YOUNG, BOGLE, MCCAUSLAND, WELLS & CLARK, P.A. (AV)

106 West Douglas, Suite 923, 67202
Telephone: 316-265-7841
Facsimile: 316-265-3956

Jerry D. Bogle	William A. Wells

Patrick C. Blanchard

References provided upon request.

For Complete List of Firm Personnel, See General Section

For full biographical listings, see the Martindale-Hubbell Law Directory

---

KENTUCKY

BOWLING GREEN,* Warren Co.

ENGLISH, LUCAS, PRIEST & OWSLEY (AV)

1101 College Street, P.O. Box 770, 42102-0770
Telephone: 502-781-6500
Telecopier: 502-782-7782
Email: inquiry@elpo.com

(See Next Column)

MEMBERS OF FIRM

Charles E. English	Wade T. Markham, II

ASSOCIATES

Vance Cook	Elizabeth J. McKinney

For Complete List of Firm Personnel, See General Section

For full biographical listings, see the Martindale-Hubbell Law Directory

---

HARLIN & PARKER, P.S.C. (AV)

519 East Tenth Street, P.O. Box 390, 42102-0390
Telephone: 502-842-5611
Telefax: 502-842-2607

William Jerry Parker	James David Bryant

Insurance Clients: American Hardware Mutual Insurance Co.; American International Group; CNA Insurance Companies; Government Employees Insurance Co.; Meridian Mutual Insurance Co.
Railroad and Utilities Clients: District Attorneys for BellSouth Telecommunications, Inc.; CSX Transportation, Inc.
Local Counsel for: General Motors Corp.; Ford Motor Corp.; Chrysler Corp.

For Complete List of Firm Personnel, See General Section

For full biographical listings, see the Martindale-Hubbell Law Directory

---

KERRICK, GRISE & STIVERS (AV)

1025 State Street, P.O. Box 9547, 42102-9547
Telephone: 502-782-8160
Fax: 502-782-5856
Elizabethtown, Kentucky Office: 2935 Dolphin Drive, Suite 102.
Telephone: 502-769-5788.
Fax: 502-737-9285.

MEMBERS OF FIRM

Thomas N. Kerrick	Gregory N. Stivers
John R. Grise	H. Brent Brennenstuhl

ASSOCIATES

Lanna Martin Kilgore	Shawn Rosso Alcott
Laura M. Hagan (Resident,	Jason B. Bell
Elizabethtown Office)	

Representative Clients: Dollar General Corp.; Columbia Greenview Regional Hospital; Hospital Corporation of America; Hardin Memorial Hospital; Monarch Environmental, Inc.; Mid-South Management Group, Inc.; Trans Financial Bank; TKR Cable.

For full biographical listings, see the Martindale-Hubbell Law Directory

---

CATLETTSBURG,* Boyd Co.

ADKINS & ADKINS (AV)

Adkins Building, 2813 Louisa Street, P.O. Box 653, 41129
Telephone: 606-739-4151
Fax: Available Upon Request

James E. Adkins	James E. Adkins, II

General Counsel for: Catlettsburg Federal Savings & Loan Assn.; Kentucky-Farmers Bank.
Local Counsel for: Federal National Mortgage Assn.
Approved Attorneys for: Farmers Home Administration.
Agents for: Commonwealth Land Title Insurance Co.

COVINGTON, Kenton Co.

ADAMS, BROOKING, STEPNER, WOLTERMANN & DUSING (AV)

421 Garrard Street, P.O. Box 861, 41012
Telephone: 606-291-7270
Fax: 606-291-7902
Florence, Kentucky Office: 8100 Burlington Pike, Suite 400, 41042.
Telephone: 606-371-6220.
Fax: 606-371-8341.

John R. S. Brooking	Michael M. Sketch
Donald L. Stepner	(Resident at Florence Office)
James G. Woltermann	Dennis R. Williams
(Resident at Florence Office)	(Resident at Florence Office)
Gerald F. Dusing	James R. Kruer
(Resident at Florence Office)	R. Jeffrey Schlosser

ASSOCIATES

Gregory S. Shumate	Paul J. Darpel
John S. "Brook" Brooking	(Resident, Florence Office)
(Resident at Florence Office)	Lori A. Schlarman
Stacey L. Graus	(Resident, Florence Office)

Chandra S. Baldwin

Representative Clients: Balluff, Inc., Wampler, Inc., Kisters, Inc., Krauss-Maffei, Inc., A group of German companies; State Automobile Mutual Insurance Co.; Chevron of California; Great American Insurance Co.; Grange Mutual Insurance Co.; Meridian Mutual Insurance Co.; Fifth-Third Bank of Northern Ky.; Northern Kentucky University; ITT Hartford.

For Complete List of Firm Personnel, See General Section

For full biographical listings, see the Martindale-Hubbell Law Directory

FLORENCE, Boone Co.

ADAMS, BROOKING, STEPNER, WOLTERMANN & DUSING (AV)

8100 Burlington Pike, Suite 400, 41042-0576
Telephone: 606-371-6220
Fax: 606-371-8341
Covington, Kentucky Office: 421 Garrard Street.
Telephone: 606-291-7270.
Fax: 606-291-7902.

John R. S. Brooking	Gerald F. Dusing (Resident)
Donald L. Stepner	Michael M. Sketch (Resident)
James G. Woltermann	Dennis R. Williams (Resident)
(Resident)	

ASSOCIATES

Marc D. Dietz (Resident)	John S. "Brook" Brooking
Gregory S. Shumate	(Resident)
Paul J. Darpel	

Representative Clients: State Automobile Mutual Insurance Co.; Standard Oil Co. (Ky.); Great American Insurance Co.; Grange Mutual Insurance Co.; Meridian Mutual Insurance Co.; Fifth-Third Bank of Boone County; Northern Kentucky University.

For Complete List of Firm Personnel, See General Section

For full biographical listings, see the Martindale-Hubbell Law Directory

GEORGETOWN,* Scott Co.

E. DURWARD WELDON (AV)

217 East Main Street, 40324
Telephone: 502-863-1285

Approved Attorney for: Lawyers Title Insurance Corporation of Richmond, Virginia; Louisville Title Division of Commonwealth Land Title Insurance Co. (Binder Agent); The Equitable Life Assurance Society of the United States.

For full biographical listings, see the Martindale-Hubbell Law Directory

LEXINGTON,* Fayette Co.

BROCK, BROCK & BAGBY (AV)

190 Market Street, P.O. Box 1630, 40592-1630
Telephone: 606-255-7000
Fax: 606-255-6198

MEMBERS OF FIRM

Walter L. Brock, Jr. (1918-1995)	Glen S. Bagby
Daniel N. Brock	J. Robert Lyons, Jr.

ASSOCIATES

Bruce A. Rector	Jane Hampton Herrick

LEGAL SUPPORT PERSONNEL

PARALEGALS

Pamela H. Brown	Freda Greer Grubbs

For full biographical listings, see the Martindale-Hubbell Law Directory

LANDRUM & SHOUSE (AV)

106 West Vine Street, P.O. Box 951, 40588-0951
Telephone: 606-255-2424
Facsimile: 606-233-0308
Louisville, Kentucky Office: 400 West Market Street, Suite 1550, 40202.
Telephone: 502-589-7616.
Facsimile: 502-589-2119.

MEMBERS OF FIRM

John H. Burrus	William C. Shouse
Mark L. Moseley	

ASSOCIATE

Charles E. Christian

District Attorneys: CSX Transportation, Inc.
Special Trial Counsel: Ford Motor Co. and Affiliates (Eastern Kentucky); Clark Equipment Co.
Representative Clients: The Continental Insurance Cos.; U.S. Insurance Group; U.S. Fidelity & Guaranty Co.; Ohio Casualty Insurance Co.; CIGNA; Royal Insurance Cos.

For Complete List of Firm Personnel, See General Section

For full biographical listings, see the Martindale-Hubbell Law Directory

MILLER, GRIFFIN & MARKS, P.S.C. (AV)

Suite 700 Security Trust Building, 271 West Short Street, 40507-1292
Telephone: 606-255-6676
Telecopier: 606-259-1562
URL: http://www.mis.net/mgm/

(See Next Column)

Harry B. Miller, Jr.	Michael D. Meuser
James M. Marks (1928-1963)	Thomas C. Marks
Robert S. Miller	Theodore E. Cowen
Thomas W. Miller	Judith K. Jones
Catesby Woodford	Stephen G. Amato
Donald R. Rose	Carroll M. Redford, III
Frank T. Becker	Helen M. Marks

Representative Clients: Central Kentucky Anesthesia, PSC.; Central Radiology Associates; Fifth Third Bank; Citicorp; Equine Capital Corp.; Anderson National Bank; Farmers Bank of Owingsville; C.V. Whitney Farm; Castleton Farm, Inc.; Equity Services, Inc.
Reference: Bank One Lexington, N.A.

For full biographical listings, see the Martindale-Hubbell Law Directory

STOLL, KEENON & PARK, LLP (AV)

201 E. Main Street, Suite 1000, 40507-1380
Telephone: 606-231-3000
Telecopier: 606-253-1093; 606-253-1027
Frankfort, Kentucky Office: 307 Washington Street, 40601.
Telephone: 502-875-6220.
Telecopier: 502-875-6235.
Louisville, Kentucky Office: 400 West Market Street, Suite 2650, 40202-3377.
Telephone: 502-568-9100.
Telecopier: 502-568-5700.

MEMBERS OF FIRM

William T. Bishop, III	Herbert A. Miller, Jr.
Douglas P. Romaine	

ASSOCIATES

Melissa Anne Stewart	Roger W. Madden

For Complete List of Firm Personnel, See General Section

For full biographical listings, see the Martindale-Hubbell Law Directory

LOUISVILLE,* Jefferson Co.

CONLIFFE, SANDMANN & SULLIVAN (AV)

621 West Main Street, 40202
Telephone: 502-587-7711
Telecopier: 502-587-7756
Other Louisville Office: 4169 Westport Road, Suite 111, 40207.
Telephone: 502-896-2966.
Jeffersonville, Indiana Office: 141 E. Spring Street, 47150.
Telephone: 812-949-7711.

Charles I. Sandmann (1936-1992)

MEMBERS OF FIRM

I. G. Spencer, Jr.	Sally Hardin Lambert
Karl N. Victor, Jr.	Edwin J. Lowry, Jr.
Michael E. Conliffe	Olivia Morris Fuchs
Richard M. Sullivan	James A. Babbitz
Sam Deeb	Kenneth A. Bohnert
Jack R. Underwood, Jr.	James T. Mitchell
E. Bruce Neikirk	Wm. Dennis Sims
Victoria Ann Ogden	Edward F. Busch
Robert A. Donald, III	Richard B. Taylor
Edward Lee Lasley	

OF COUNSEL

Allen P. Dodd, III	Alan R. Miller

For full biographical listings, see the Martindale-Hubbell Law Directory

LAWRENCE AND LAWRENCE (AV)

Suite 300, 200 South Seventh Street, 40202
Telephone: 502-583-4484
Fax: 502-583-4486

William W. Lawrence

Reference: PNC Bank & Trust Co.

For full biographical listings, see the Martindale-Hubbell Law Directory

MACKENZIE & PEDEN, P.S.C. (AV)

650 Starks Building, 455 South Fourth Avenue, 40202-2509
Telephone: 502-589-1110
Fax: 502-589-1117
Other Louisville, Kentucky Office: 8311 Shelbyville Road.
Telephone: 502-426-6688.
Fax: 502-425-0561.

William B. Peden (Retired)	Robert W. Dickey
Thomas G. Mooney (1939-1991)	William B. Bardenwerper
Wm. A. MacKenzie (Resident)	(Resident)
John G. Crutchfield	James T. Lobb
Wayne J. Carroll	Valerie T. Mayer (Resident)
James C. Hickey	Edward H. Bartenstein
B. Carlton Neat, III	Judith B. Hoge

(See Next Column)

MacKenzie & Peden P.S.C., *Louisville—Continued*

Sidney L. Hymson   Charles T. Baxter
Lee Ann Risner   John Patrick Hamm

OF COUNSEL

Walker C. Cunningham, Jr.   Robert W. Riley (Resident)
Lawrence J. Phillips   Stephen A. Schwager

Representative Clients: Allstate Insurance Co.; American States Insurance Co.; The Fund Insurance Companies; State Automobile Mutual Insurance Co..

For full biographical listings, see the Martindale-Hubbell Law Directory

HENRY B. MANN (AV)

22nd Floor Citizens Plaza, 40202
Telephone: 502-587-6544

References: Bank One; PNC Bank, Kentucky; Bank of Louisville; National City Bank, Kentucky.

MIDDLETON & REUTLINGER, P.S.C. (AV)

2500 Brown and Williamson Tower, 40202-3410
Telephone: 502-584-1135
Fax: 502-561-0442
New Albany, Indiana Office: 2623 Charlestown Road, 47150.
Telephone: 812-944-7215.

Ian Y. Henderson   Brooks Alexander
Charles G. Middleton, III   Kipley J. McNally

Clayton R. Hume

Counsel for: Chevron USA; Logan Aluminum, Inc.; Louisville Gas & Electric Co.; MCI Telecommunications Corp.; Metropolitan Life Insurance Co.; Kosmos Cement Co.; Porcelain Metal Corp.; The Home Insurance Co.; The Kroger Co.; Demars Haka Development, Inc.

For Complete List of Firm Personnel, See General Section

For full biographical listings, see the Martindale-Hubbell Law Directory

MORGAN & POTTINGER, P.S.C. (AV)

601 West Main Street, 40202
Telephone: 502-589-2780
Telecopier: 502-585-3498
Lexington, Kentucky Office: 133 West Short Street.
Telephone: 606-253-1900.
Telecopier: 606-255-2038.
New Albany, Indiana Office: 400 Pearl Street, Suite 100.
Telephone: 812-948-0008.
Telecopier: 812-944-6215.

Patrick E. Morgan   C. Edward Hastie
                (Resident, Lexington Office)

For Complete List of Firm Personnel, See General Section

For full biographical listings, see the Martindale-Hubbell Law Directory

RUBIN HAYS & FOLEY (AV)

First Trust Centre 200 South Fifth Street, 40202
Telephone: 502-569-7550
Telecopier: 502-569-7555

MEMBERS OF FIRM

Wm. Carl Fust   Lisa Koch Bryant
Harry Lee Meyer   Sharon C. Hardy
David W. Gray   Charles S. Musson
Irvin D. Foley   W. Randall Jones
Joseph R. Gathright, Jr.   K. Gail Russell

ASSOCIATES

Christian L. Juckett   Courtney Lynn McCall

OF COUNSEL

James E. Fahey   Newman T. Guthrie

Representative Clients: J.C. Bradford & Co., Inc.; J.J.B. Hilliard, W.L. Lyons, Inc.; Huntington National Bank; Liberty National Bank and Trust Company; National City Bank; PNC Bank; Prudential Bache & Co., Inc.; Prudential Securities, Inc.; Society Bank; Stock Yards Bank and Trust Co.

For full biographical listings, see the Martindale-Hubbell Law Directory

*MOREHEAD,** Rowan Co.

DEHNER & ELLIS (AV)

206 East Main Street, 40351
Telephone: 606-783-1504
FAX: 606-784-2744

Truman L. Dehner   John J. Ellis

For full biographical listings, see the Martindale-Hubbell Law Directory

---

*OWINGSVILLE,** Bath Co.

BYRON & ROBERTS (AV)

25 S. Court Street, 40360
Telephone: 606-674-2911

MEMBERS OF FIRM

Roger A. Byron   Winifred Byron Roberts

General Counsel for: Farmers Bank, Owingsville, Kentucky.
Local Counsel for: Delta Natural Gas Co.
Approved Attorneys for: Lawyers Title Insurance Corp.

For full biographical listings, see the Martindale-Hubbell Law Directory

*VANCEBURG,** Lewis Co.

STANLEY AND BERTRAM, P.S.C. (AV)

P.O. Box 40, 41179-0040
Telephone: 606-796-3024; 796-3025
Fax: 606-796-2113

Avery L. Stanley   Thomas M. Bertram, II
         Anita Esham Stanley

A list of Representative Clients will be furnished upon request.

For full biographical listings, see the Martindale-Hubbell Law Directory

LOUISIANA

*BATON ROUGE,** East Baton Rouge Parish

KANTROW, SPAHT, WEAVER & BLITZER, A PROFESSIONAL LAW CORPORATION (AV)

Suite 300, City Plaza, 445 North Boulevard, P.O. Box 2997, 70821-2997
Telephone: 504-383-4703
Fax: 504-343-0630; 343-0637

Byron R. Kantrow   Vincent P. Fornias
Carlos G. Spaht   David S. Rubin
Geraldine B. Weaver   Diane L. Crochet
Sidney M. Blitzer, Jr.   Richard F. Zimmerman, Jr.
Paul H. Spaht   Bob D. Tucker
Lee C. Kantrow   Martin E. Golden
John C. Miller   Joseph A. Schittone, Jr.

S. Layne Lee   Connell L. Archey
J. Michael Robinson, Jr.   Randal J. Robert

Representative Clients: CNA Insurance Cos.; Federal Deposit Insurance Corp.; Hartford Insurance Group; Air Products and Chemicals, Inc.; CF Industries, Inc.; AT&T; United Companies Financial Corp.

For full biographical listings, see the Martindale-Hubbell Law Directory

KEAN, MILLER, HAWTHORNE, D'ARMOND, McCOWAN & JARMAN, L.L.P. (AV)

22nd Floor, One American Place, P.O. Box 3513, 70821
Telephone: 504-387-0999
Fax: 504-388-9133
New Orleans, Louisiana Office: Energy Centre, Suite 1470, 1100 Poydras Street.
Telephone: 504-585-3050.
Fax: 504-585-3051.
Plaquemine, Louisiana Office: Suite 10, 23425 Railroad Avenue.
Telephone: 504-687-9845.
Fax: 504-382-3445.

MEMBERS OF FIRM

Ben R. Miller, Jr.   Carey J. Messina
Robert A. Hawthorne, Jr.   Isaac M. Gregorie, Jr.
         Todd A. Rossi

Kevin C. Curry

SPECIAL COUNSEL

Gerald Le Van

For Complete List of Firm Personnel, See General Section

For full biographical listings, see the Martindale-Hubbell Law Directory

GREGORY A. PLETSCH & ASSOCIATES A PROFESSIONAL LAW CORPORATION (AV)

Suite 301, Four United Plaza, 8555 United Plaza Boulevard, 70809
Telephone: 504-929-8525
Telecopier: 504-929-8520

Gregory A. Pletsch

For full biographical listings, see the Martindale-Hubbell Law Directory

LAKE CHARLES,* Calcasieu Parish

JONES, TÊTE, NOLEN, HANCHEY, SWIFT, SPEARS & FONTI, L.L.P. (AV)

First Federal Building, P.O. Box 910, 70602
Telephone: 318-439-8315
Telefax: 436-5606; 433-5536

MEMBERS OF FIRM

Sam H. Jones (1897-1978)	Kenneth R. Spears
William R. Tête	Edward J. Fonti
William M. Nolen	Charles N. Harper
James C. Hanchey	Gregory W. Belfour
Carl H. Hanchey	Robert J. Tête
William B. Swift	Yul D. Lorio

OF COUNSEL

John A. Patin   Edward D. Myrick

ASSOCIATE

Lilynn A. Cutrer

General Counsel for: First Federal Savings & Loan Association of Lake Charles; Beauregard Electric Cooperative, Inc.
Representative Clients: Atlantic Richfield Company; CITGO Petroleum Corp.; Conoco Inc.; MONTELL U.S.A., Inc.; ITT Hartford; Olin Corporation; OXY USA Inc.; Premier Bank, National Association; W.R. Grace & Co.

For full biographical listings, see the Martindale-Hubbell Law Directory

METAIRIE, Jefferson Parish

WEIR AND WALLEY (AV)

2721 Division Street, 70002-7084
Telephone: 504-455-7264
Fax: 504-455-7266

Andrew M. Weir   James M. Walley

ASSOCIATE

Mark Needham

References: The Whitney National Bank; First National Bank of Commerce.

For full biographical listings, see the Martindale-Hubbell Law Directory

MONROE,* Ouachita Parish

THOMPSON, SPARKS, DEAN & MORRIS (AV)

A Partnership including a Professional Corporation
1401 Royal Street, P.O. Box 2867, 71207
Telephone: 318-388-1440
Fax: 318-322-0887

MEMBERS OF FIRM

M. C. Thompson (1885-1970)	George B. Dean, Jr., (P.C.)
James D. Sparks (1910-1987)	Wood T. Sparks
John C. Morris, III	

Representative Clients: South Central Bell Telephone Co.; Greater Ouachita Water Company; PHH Homequity Corp.; Commonwealth Relocation Services, Inc.; Remax, Monroe; Bell South Advertising & Publishing Corp.; Premier Mortgage Corp.; Countrywide Funding Corp.
Approved Attorneys for: Central Bank; Federal Land Bank.

For full biographical listings, see the Martindale-Hubbell Law Directory

NEW ORLEANS,* Orleans Parish

MICHAEL L. ECKSTEIN ATTORNEY AT LAW A PROFESSIONAL CORPORATION (AV)

1515 Poydras Street, Suite 2195, 70112
Telephone: 504-527-0701
Telecopier: 504-566-0040
VMX: 504-889-8876

Michael L. Eckstein   David Coleman Raphael, Jr.

Representative Clients: Anserphone of New Orleans, Inc.; Dixie Webb Graphic Corporations; Kencoil, Inc.; Life Point Systems, Inc.; Meeks Petroleum Company; Int-Oil Ventures, Ltd.; Dan-Gulf Shipping, Inc.; Action, Inc.; TCB Industries, Inc.

For full biographical listings, see the Martindale-Hubbell Law Directory

LISKOW & LEWIS, A PROFESSIONAL LAW CORPORATION (AV)

50th Floor, One Shell Square, 70139
Telephone: 504-581-7979
Telecopier: 504-556-4108; 504-556-4109
Lafayette, Louisiana Office: 822 Harding Street, P.O. Box 52008.
Telephone: 318-232-7424.
Telecopier: 318-267-2399.

Leon J. Reymond, Jr.   Marguerite A. Noonan

(See Next Column)

Julia M. Pearce

Representative Clients: Atlantic Richfield Co.; BASF Corp.; Federal Deposit Insurance Corporation; First National Bank of Commerce; Hibernia National Bank; Legg Mason Wood Walker; Mobil Oil Corporation; Pennzoil Company; Prudential Securities Inc.; Texaco, Inc.

For Complete List of Firm Personnel, See General Section

For full biographical listings, see the Martindale-Hubbell Law Directory

ROBERT E. TARCZA (AV)

Thirteen Ten Whitney Building, Two Twenty Eight St. Charles Avenue, 70130
Telephone: 504-525-6696
Fax: 504-525-6701

ASSOCIATE

Juliet Puissegur Bland

OF COUNSEL

G. Anthony Gelderman, III

For full biographical listings, see the Martindale-Hubbell Law Directory

SHREVEPORT,* Caddo Parish

BARLOW AND HARDTNER L.C. (AV)

Tenth Floor, Louisiana Tower, 401 Edwards Street, 71101-3289
Telephone: 318-227-1131
Telecopier: 318-227-1141
Mailing Address: P.O. Box 8, Shreveport, Louisiana, 71161-0008

Quintin T. Hardtner, III   Stephen E. Ramey

OF COUNSEL

Cecil E. Ramey, Jr.   Paula Hazelrig Hickman

Representative Clients: Kelley Oil Corporation; NorAm Energy Corp. (formerly Arkla, Inc.); Panhandle Eastern Corp.; Pennzoil Producing Co.; Johnson Controls, Inc.; Ashland Oil, Inc.; Southwestern Electric Power Company; General Electric Co.

For Complete List of Firm Personnel, See General Section

For full biographical listings, see the Martindale-Hubbell Law Directory

MILLS, TIMMONS & FLOWERS, A PROFESSIONAL LAW CORPORATION (AV)

300 Law Center, 331 Milam Street, P.O. Box 1784, 71166-1784
Telephone: 318-222-0337
Fax: 318-222-5400

George H. Mills, Jr.	David C. Turansky
Wayne Timmons	J. Broocks Greer III
Peter R. Flowers	Sandra Lynn Walker

OF COUNSEL

William T. Allison

Reference: Hibernia National Bank.

For full biographical listings, see the Martindale-Hubbell Law Directory

SOCKRIDER, BOLIN & ANGLIN, A PROFESSIONAL LAW CORPORATION (AV)

327 Crockett Street, 71101
Telephone: 318-221-5503
Fax: 318-221-3849

John R. Pleasant (1905-1983)	James E. Bolin, Jr.
H. F. Sockrider, Jr.	D. Rex Anglin
	Gregory H. Batte

For full biographical listings, see the Martindale-Hubbell Law Directory

WINNFIELD,* Winn Parish

SIMMONS AND DERR (AV)

Simmons Building, Church Street, P.O. Box 525, 71483
Telephone: 318-628-3951

MEMBERS OF FIRM

Kermit M. Simmons   Jacque D. Derr

Reference: Bank of Winnfield & Trust Co.

For full biographical listings, see the Martindale-Hubbell Law Directory

MAINE

AUGUSTA,* Kennebec Co.

DOYLE & NELSON (AV)

150 Capitol Street, 04330
Telephone: 207-622-6124
Telefax: 207-623-1358
Toll Free: 800-639-3165

MEMBERS OF FIRM

Jon R. Doyle   Craig H. Nelson

ASSOCIATES

Daniel P. Riley, Jr.   Andrew B. MacLean

Local Counsel for: Citicorp and its subsidiaries; R.J. Reynolds Tobacco Co.; British Consulate General.
Counsel for: Financial Institutions Service Corp.; Miles Memorial Hospital; Maine Medical Records Assn.; Citicorp Acceptance Corp.; Citicorp Home-owners, Inc.

For full biographical listings, see the Martindale-Hubbell Law Directory

---

BANGOR,* Penobscot Co.

EATON, PEABODY, BRADFORD & VEAGUE, P.A. (AV)

Fleet Center-Exchange Street, P.O. Box 1210, 04402-1210
Telephone: 207-947-0111
Telecopier: 207-942-3040
Email: epbv@aol.com
Augusta, Maine Office: 2 Central Plaza.
Telephone: 207-622-3747.
Telecopier: 207-622-9732.
Blue Hill, Maine Office: One East Blue Hill Road.
Telephone: 207-374-2812.
Telecopier: 207-374-2548.
Brunswick, Maine Office: 167 Park Row.
Telephone: 207-729-1144.
Telecopier: 207-729-1140.
Camden, Maine Office: 7-9 Washington Street.
Telephone: 207-236-3325.
Telecopier: 207-236-8611.
Dover-Foxcroft, Maine Office: 30 East Main Street.
Telephone: 207-564-8378.
Telecopier: 207-564-7059.

Calvin E. True   John A. Cunningham
Clarissa B. Edelston   (Resident, Brunswick Office)
Douglas M. Smith   R. Lee Ivy
   (Dover-Foxcroft and Augusta
   Offices)

David W. Kesner

A List of Representative Clients available upon request.

For Complete List of Firm Personnel, See General Section

For full biographical listings, see the Martindale-Hubbell Law Directory

---

GROSS, MINSKY, MOGUL & SINGAL, P.A. (AV)

Key Plaza, 23 Water Street, P.O. Box 917, 04402-0917
Telephone: 207-942-4644
Telecopier: 207-942-3699
Email: gmm&s-law@atlsysnet.com *URL:*
http://www.atlsysnet.com/gmms

Edward I. Gross (Retired)   George C. Schelling
Jules L. Mogul (1930-1994)   Edward W. Gould
Norman Minsky   Steven J. Mogul
George Z. Singal   James R. Wholly
Louis H. Kornreich   Daniel A. Pileggi
        Philip K. Clarke

Wayne P. Libhart (Retired)   James S. Nixon
Sandra L. Rothera   F. Todd Lowell

Representative Client: Dahl Chase Pathology Associates.
Local Counsel for: The St. Paul Insurance Cos.; Aetna Life & Casualty Co.; Imperial Casualty & Indemnity Co.

For full biographical listings, see the Martindale-Hubbell Law Directory

---

VAFIADES, BROUNTAS & KOMINSKY (AV)

Key Plaza, 23 Water Street, P.O. Box 919, 04402-0919
Telephone: 207-947-6915
Telecopier: 207-941-0863

MEMBER OF FIRM
Susan R. Kominsky

ASSOCIATE
Paul R. Brown

(See Next Column)

OF COUNSEL
Nicholas P. Brountas

For Complete List of Firm Personnel, See General Section

For full biographical listings, see the Martindale-Hubbell Law Directory

---

BAR HARBOR, Hancock Co.

FENTON, CHAPMAN, FENTON, SMITH & KANE, P.A. (AV)

109 Main Street, P.O. Box B, 04609
Telephone: 207-288-3331
FAX: 207-288-9326

William Fenton   Chadbourn H. Smith
Douglas B. Chapman   Daniel H. Kane (1940-1995)
Nathaniel R. Fenton   Hancock Griffin, Jr. (1912-1980)

Margaret A. Timothy   Eric Lindquist

OF COUNSEL
Edwin R. Smith

Reference: Bar Harbor Banking and Trust Co.

For full biographical listings, see the Martindale-Hubbell Law Directory

---

ELLSWORTH,* Hancock Co.

HALE & HAMLIN (AV)

10 State Street, P.O. Box 729, 04605
Telephone: 207-667-2561
Telefax: 207-667-8790
Email: http://www.halehaml.com

Eugene Hale (1836-1918)   Philip R. Lovell (1899-1961)
Hannibal E. Hamlin (1858-1938)   Charles J. Hurley (1908-1981)
      Atherton Fuller (Retired)

MEMBERS OF FIRM
Barry K. Mills   Jeffrey W. Jones
Dale L. Worthen   Melissa Moll

ASSOCIATE
Laura Yustak Smith

Approved Attorneys for: Lawyers Title Insurance Corp.

For full biographical listings, see the Martindale-Hubbell Law Directory

---

KENNEBUNK, York Co.

REAGAN, ADAMS & CADIGAN (AV)

Eleven Main Street, P.O. Box 709, 04043
Telephone: 207-985-7181
Telecopier: 207-985-7003

MEMBERS OF FIRM
Thomas J. Reagan   Wayne T. Adams
      Paul W. Cadigan

Counsel for: Kennebunk Savings Bank.

For full biographical listings, see the Martindale-Hubbell Law Directory

---

PORTLAND,* Cumberland Co.

JENSEN BAIRD GARDNER & HENRY (AV)

Ten Free Street, P.O. Box 4510, 04112
Telephone: 207-775-7271
Telecopier: 207-775-7935
York County Office: 419 Alfred Street, Biddeford, Maine.
Telephone: 207-282-5107.
Telecopier: 207-282-6301.

OF COUNSEL
Merton G. Henry   John D. Bradford (Resident,
                 York County Office)

MEMBERS OF FIRM
Frank H. Frye   Elizabeth T. High

ASSOCIATES
Milda A. Castner (Resident,   Barry P. Fernald
  York County Office)

Representative Clients: Key Trust of Maine; Margaret Chase Smith Foundation.

For Complete List of Firm Personnel, See General Section

For full biographical listings, see the Martindale-Hubbell Law Directory

---

LeBLANC & YOUNG (AV)

183 Middle Street, P.O. Box 7950, 04112-7950
Telephone: 207-772-2800
Facsimile: 207-772-2822
Email: firm@leblancyoung.com *URL:* http://www.leblancyoung.com

(See Next Column)

LeBlanc & Young—*Continued*

Richard P. LeBlanc   James H. Young, II
              Abigail King Diggins

For full biographical listings, see the Martindale-Hubbell Law Directory

McCandless & Hunt (AV)

57 Exchange Street, 04101
Telephone: 207-772-4100
Telecopier: 207-772-1300

MEMBERS OF FIRM
Eileen M. L. Epstein   David E. Hunt
       Elizabeth T. McCandless
ASSOCIATE
Dennis J. O'Donovan

For full biographical listings, see the Martindale-Hubbell Law Directory

Pierce Atwood (AV)

One Monument Square, 04101
Telephone: 207-791-1100
Fax: 207-791-1350
Email: info@PierceAtwood.com
Augusta, Maine Office: 77 Winthrop Street.
Telephone: 207-622-6311.
Fax: 207-623-9367.
Newburyport, Massachusetts Office: 6 Harris Street.
Telephone: 508-465-9599.
Fax: 508-465-9945.

MEMBERS OF FIRM
Fred C. Scribner, Jr. (1908-1994)   Everett P. Ingalls
Warren E. Winslow, Jr.   Michael R. Currie
  (Resident, Augusta Office)   Barbara K. Wheaton
OF COUNSEL
Sigrid E. Tompkins   William C. Smith
ASSOCIATE
Mary McQuillen

For Complete List of Firm Personnel, See General Section

For full biographical listings, see the Martindale-Hubbell Law Directory

Preti, Flaherty, Beliveau & Pachios (AV)

A Limited Liability Company
443 Congress Street, P.O. Box 11410, 04104-7410
Telephone: 207-791-3000
Telecopier: 207-791-3111
Email: admin@pfbpnet.com
Augusta, Maine Office: 45 Memorial Circle, P.O. Box 1058, 04332-1058.
Telephone: 207-623-5300.
Telecopier: 207-623-2914.

MEMBERS OF FIRM
Estelle A. Lavoie   Michael L. Sheehan
OF COUNSEL
Robert F. Preti   Albert J. Beliveau, Jr.
       Robert W. Smith

For Complete List of Firm Personnel, See General Section

For full biographical listings, see the Martindale-Hubbell Law Directory

SKOWHEGAN,* Somerset Co.

Donald E. Eames (AV)

65 Cross Street, P.O. Box 959, 04976-0959
Telephone: 207-474-8105; 474-2626
Telefax: 207-474-8106
Representative Clients: Farrin Bros. & Smith, Contractors; Towns of Madison, Bingham, Canaan, Palmyra, Solon, New Portland; Moose River Lumber Co., Inc.; Lowell & Co.; The Bray Agency; Skowhegan State Fair; Hight-Chevrolet Buick, Inc.; Cadle Company; Redington-Fairview General Hospital; Redington Medical Associates.

For full biographical listings, see the Martindale-Hubbell Law Directory

YORK, York Co.

Erwin, Ott, Clark & Campbell (AV)

16A Woodbridge Road, P.O. Box 545, 03909
Telephone: 207-363-5208
Facsimile: 207-363-5322
MEMBERS OF FIRM
Frank E. Hancock (1923-1988)   John P. Campbell
James S. Erwin   David N. Ott
              Jeffery J. Clark

For full biographical listings, see the Martindale-Hubbell Law Directory

MARYLAND

BALTIMORE, * (Independent City)

Ferguson, Schetelich, Heffernan & Murdock, P.A. (AV)

1300 NationsBank Center 1, 100 South Charles Street, 21201

Telephone: 410-837-2200
Fax: 410-837-1188
Email: fshm@ix.netcom

Robert L. Ferguson, Jr.   Christopher J. Heffernan
Thomas J. Schetelich   M. Brooke Murdock

Michael N. Russo, Jr.   Peter Joseph Basile
Jodi K. Ebersole   Ann D. Ware

For full biographical listings, see the Martindale-Hubbell Law Directory

McKenney, Thomsen and Burke, LLP (AV)

Suite 400, One North Charles Street, 21201

Telephone: 410-539-2595
FAX: 410-783-0710
Washington, D.C. Office: Suite 500, 1225 Eye Street, N.W.
Telephone: 202-682-4741.
FAX: 202-547-3713.

OF COUNSEL
W. Gibbs McKenney
MEMBERS OF FIRM
George E. Thomsen   Paul E. Burke, Jr.
       Roszel C. Thomsen, II
ASSOCIATES
Hedley A. Clark   Robin McDaniel Hough

References: NationsBank; Mercantile-Safe Deposit & Trust Co.; Carroll County Bank and Trust Co.

For full biographical listings, see the Martindale-Hubbell Law Directory

Richard T. Stansbury A Professional Association (AV)

Suite 920, The B & O Building, Two North Charles Street, 21201-3754

Telephone: 410-727-6200
Facsimile: 410-385-2939

Annapolis, Maryland Office: 5th Floor, The Conte Building, 116 Defense Highway.
Telephone: 410-974-6007.
Facsimile: 410-974-6019.

Richard T. Stansbury

For full biographical listings, see the Martindale-Hubbell Law Directory

Stewart, Plant & Blumenthal, LLC (AV)

Suite 910 7 St. Paul Street, 21202

Telephone: 410-347-0506
FAX: 410-347-0513

MEMBERS OF FIRM
C. Van Leuven Stewart   Max E. Blumenthal
A. MacDonough Plant   Hugh A. ("Jay") Mitchell, Jr.
ASSOCIATES
Katherine W. Plant   Jonathan G. Lasley
       Lisa J. McGrath
OF COUNSEL
Adena W. Testa

For full biographical listings, see the Martindale-Hubbell Law Directory

Thieblot, Ryan, Martin & Miller, P.A. (AV)

4th Floor, The World Trade Center, 21202-3091
Telephone: 410-837-1140
Washington, D.C. Line: 202-628-8223
Fax: 410-837-3282
Towson, Maryland Office: Atlantic Federal Building. Suite 400. 100 West Road. 21204.
Telephone: 410-828-5900.

(See Next Column)

THIEBLOT, RYAN, MARTIN & MILLER P.A., *Baltimore—Continued*

Robert J. Thieblot	Robert D. Harwick, Jr.
Anthony W. Ryan	Anne M. Hrehorovich
J. Edward Martin, Jr.	Donna Marie Raffaele
Bruce R. Miller	Hamilton Fisk Tyler
Samuel S. Field III	

Representative Clients: R&I Worldwide; Living Trust Information Systems; Jubilee Year, Inc.; Chesapeake Charitable Trust Services.

For full biographical listings, see the Martindale-Hubbell Law Directory

VENABLE ATTORNEYS AT LAW VENABLE, BAETJER AND HOWARD, LLP (AV)

A Partnership including Professional Corporations
1800 Mercantile Bank & Trust Building, 2 Hopkins Plaza, 21201
Telephone: 410-244-7400
Email: INFO@Venable.win.net
Washington, D.C. Office: Venable, Baetjer, Howard & Civiletti LLP. Suite 1000, 1201 New York Avenue, N.W.
Telephone: 202-962-4800.
McLean, Virginia Office: Suite 400, 2010 Corporate Ridge.
Telephone: 703-760-1600.
Rockville, Maryland Office: Suite 500, One Church Street, P. O. Box 1906.
Telephone: 301-217-5600.
Towson, Maryland Office: 210 Allegheny Avenue, P. O. Box 5517.
Telephone: 410-494-6200.

MEMBERS OF FIRM

Jacques T. Schlenger (P.C.)	Jeffrey J. Radowich
John Henry Lewin, Jr. (P.C.)	Nell B. Strachan
Roger W. Titus (Resident, Rockville, Maryland Office)	L. Paige Marvel
Douglas D. Connah, Jr. (P.C.) (Also at Washington, D.C. Office)	James K. Archibald (Also at Washington, D.C. Office)
Alexander I. Lewis, III (P.C.) (Also at Towson, Maryland Office)	Christopher R. Mellott
	M. King Hill, III (Resident, Towson, Maryland Office)
Paul T. Glasgow (Resident, Rockville, Maryland Office)	James A. Dunbar (Also at Washington, D.C. Office)
Joseph C. Wich, Jr. (Resident, Towson, Maryland Office)	Robert L. Waldman
	David J. Heubeck
	Jeffrey K. Gonya

OF COUNSEL

Robert M. Thomas (P.C.)	David D. Downes (Resident, Towson, Maryland Office)
Robert R. Bair (P.C.)	
Emried D. Cole, Jr.	

ASSOCIATE
John P. Edgar

For Complete List of Firm Personnel, See General Section

For full biographical listings, see the Martindale-Hubbell Law Directory

---

BEL AIR,* Harford Co.

BROWN, BROWN & BROWN, A PROFESSIONAL ASSOCIATION (AV)

200 South Main Street, 21014
Telephone: 410-838-5500
Baltimore: 410-879-2220
Fax: 410-893-0402

A. Freeborn Brown	Augustus F. Brown
T. Carroll Brown	Albert J. A. Young

A. Frank Carven, III	Christopher R. vanRoden
Harold Douglas Norton	David E. Carey
Ankur P. Dalal	

Attorneys for: Baltimore Gas & Electric Co.; Chesapeake & Potomac Telephone Co.; Aberdeen Proving Ground Federal Credit Union; First Virginia Bank-Central Maryland; First National Bank of Maryland; Bell Atlantic Mobile Systems; First Harbor Securities; Maryland Portable Concrete, Inc. *Approved Counsel for:* The Chicago Title Insurance Co. of Maryland, Inc.

For full biographical listings, see the Martindale-Hubbell Law Directory

STARK & KEENAN, A PROFESSIONAL ASSOCIATION (AV)

30 Office Street, 21014
Telephone: 410-838-5522
Baltimore: 410-879-2222
Fax: 410-879-0688

Elwood V. Stark, Jr.	Judith Cline-Silverstein
Charles B. Keenan, Jr.	Gregory A. Szoka
Edwin G. Carson	Robert S. Lynch

Claire Prin Blomquist	Paul W. Ishak
Kimberly Kahoe Muenter	Lawrence F. Kreis, Jr.

For full biographical listings, see the Martindale-Hubbell Law Directory

---

BETHESDA, Montgomery Co.

BAUERSFELD, BURTON, HENDRICKS & VANDERHOOF, L.L.C. (AV)

Suite 1011, 7101 Wisconsin Avenue, 20814-4805
Telephone: 301-986-8600
FAX: 301-907-6854

Robert Ash (1894-1981)	Charles H. Burton
Carl F. Bauersfeld	John C. Hendricks
Martha Gower Vanderhoof	

For full biographical listings, see the Martindale-Hubbell Law Directory

RON M. LANDSMAN, P.A. (AV)

4550 Montgomery Avenue, Suite 901N, 20814
Telephone: 301-652-5050
Fax: 301-961-8615
Email: RLANDS7369@AOL.COM

Ron M. Landsman

Erin Adele Mahony	Debra G. Kathman
	Richard I. Miller

OF COUNSEL
Morris Klein

For full biographical listings, see the Martindale-Hubbell Law Directory

---

EASTON,* Talbot Co.

HENRY & PRICE LLC (AV)

117 Bay Street, P.O. Box 838, 21601
Telephone: 410-822-2600
Fax: 410-822-2626

MEMBERS OF FIRM

T. Hughlett Henry (1879-1966)	W. Thomas Fountain
T. Hughlett Henry, Jr. (1910-1994)	David C. Bryan
	Suzanne L. Hood
John G. Billmyre	

ASSOCIATES

Sharon J. Ritter	Nannette G. Grimes

OF COUNSEL
William H. Price, II

Attorneys for: Talbot County Board of Appeals; Town of Preston; Chicago Title Insurance Co. of Maryland; Lawyers Title Insurance Corp.; Delmarva Power & Light Co.; John Hancock Mutual Life Insurance Co.; Metropolitan Life Insurance Co.

For full biographical listings, see the Martindale-Hubbell Law Directory

WHEELER, THOMPSON, PARKER & COUNTS (AV)

129 North Washington Street, P.O. Box 1209, 21601
Telephone: 410-822-1122
Fax: 410-822-3635

MEMBERS OF FIRM

Edward T. Miller (1895-1968)	Dorothy H. Thompson
Ernest M. Thompson (1921-1989)	Willard C. Parker, II
	Richard L. Counts, III
Charles E. Wheeler	Douglas A. Collison

ASSOCIATE
John Whitelaw Ong

OF COUNSEL

Donald H. Olson	Philip E. Nuttle, Jr.

Representative Clients: Nationwide Insurance Co.; Home Indemnity Co.; Chicago Title Insurance Company of Maryland; State Farm Mutual Insurance Co.; Chesapeake College; Habitat for Humanity of Talbot County; Talbot County Board of Education; Fuller Motor Sales, Inc.; St. Michaels Housing Authority.
Reference: Nationsbank, Easton Branch.

For full biographical listings, see the Martindale-Hubbell Law Directory

---

GREENBELT, Prince Georges Co.

STANLEY S. PICKETT (AV)

Suite 414 Capital Office Park, 6411 Ivy Lane, 20770
Telephone: 301-513-0613
Fax: 301-513-0618

Stanley Sinclair Pickett

ASSOCIATE
Gordon J. Brumback

(See Next Column)

STANLEY S. PICKETT—*Continued*

LEGAL SUPPORT PERSONNEL

Stacy S. Pickett (Law Clerk)   Vivian W. Wolfe (Paralegal)

Representative Clients: B.F. Saul Co.; McDonald and Eudy Printers, Inc.; Condominium Management, Inc.; Long & Foster Realtors; Mitron Systems Corp.; Coldwell Banker; Glenanden Housing Authority; Koones & Montgomery, Inc.; Community Associations, Inc.

For full biographical listings, see the Martindale-Hubbell Law Directory

---

*ROCKVILLE,** Montgomery Co.

STEVEN M. KATZ, P.A. (AV)

Suite 208 401 East Jefferson Street, 20850
Telephone: 301-738-8441
Fax: 301-251-8888

Steven M. Katz

For full biographical listings, see the Martindale-Hubbell Law Directory

---

STEIN, SPERLING, BENNETT, DE JONG, DRISCOLL, GREENFEIG & METRO, P.A. (AV)

25 West Middle Lane, 20850
Telephone: 301-340-2020; 800-435-5230
Telecopier: 301-340-8217

David S. De Jong   Ann G. Jakabcin

Ava L. Healy

For Complete List of Firm Personnel, See General Section

For full biographical listings, see the Martindale-Hubbell Law Directory

---

SILVER SPRING, Montgomery Co.

DENA C. FEENEY, P.A. (AV)

Suite 220, 1010 Wayne Avenue, 20910
Telephone: 301-587-2240
Fax: 301-589-5412

Dena C. Feeney

Mary Frances Rhodes

For full biographical listings, see the Martindale-Hubbell Law Directory

---

*TOWSON,** Baltimore Co.

NOLAN, PLUMHOFF & WILLIAMS, CHARTERED (AV)

Suite 700 Court Towers, 210 West Pennsylvania Avenue, 21204
Telephone: 410-823-7800
Fax: 410-296-2765

Thomas J. Renner   E. Bruce Jones

Representative Clients: Baltimore County, Maryland; Bituminous Insurance Companies; Board of Education of Anne Arundel County; Carolina Freight Carriers Corporation; Humane Society of Baltimore County, Inc.; Patapsco Federal Savings & Loan Association; Pulte Home Corporation; Royal Oak Federal Savings Bank, F.S.B.; Shelter Development Corporation; Summit Broadcasting Corporation.

For Complete List of Firm Personnel, See General Section

For full biographical listings, see the Martindale-Hubbell Law Directory

---

VENABLE ATTORNEYS AT LAW VENABLE, BAETJER AND HOWARD, LLP (AV)

A Partnership including Professional Corporations
210 Allegheny Avenue, P.O. Box 5517, 21204
Telephone: 410-494-6200
FAX: 410-821-0147
Baltimore, Maryland Office: 1800 Mercantile Bank & Trust Building, 2 Hopkins Plaza.
Telephone: 410-244-7400.
Washington, D.C. Office: Venable, Baetjer, Howard & Civiletti LLP, Suite 1000, 1201 New York Avenue, N.W.
Telephone: 202-962-4800.
McLean, Virginia Office: Suite 400, 2010 Corporate Ridge.
Telephone: 703-760-1600.
Rockville, Maryland Office: Suite 500, One Church Street, P. O. Box 1906.
Telephone: 301-217-5600.

PARTNERS

Alexander I. Lewis, III (P.C.)   Joseph C. Wich, Jr.
(Also at Baltimore, Maryland   M. King Hill, III
Office)

(See Next Column)

OF COUNSEL
David D. Downes

For Complete List of Firm Personnel, See General Section

For full biographical listings, see the Martindale-Hubbell Law Directory

---

MASSACHUSETTS

AMESBURY, Essex Co.

HAMEL, DESHAIES & GAGLIARDI (AV)

Five Market Square, P.O. Box 198, 01913-0398
Telephone: 508-388-3558
Telecopier: 508-388-0441

MEMBER OF FIRM
Richard P. Hamel

ASSOCIATE
Peter R. Ayer, Jr.

Representative Clients: Essex County Gas Co., Amesbury, MA; First and Ocean National Bank, Newburyport, MA.
Approved Attorneys for: Chicago Title Insurance; Old Republic Title Insurance Co.

For Complete List of Firm Personnel, See General Section

For full biographical listings, see the Martindale-Hubbell Law Directory

---

ARLINGTON, Middlesex Co.

GRANNAN & MALOY, P.C. (AV)

Suite 408, 22 Mill Street, 02174
Telephone: 617-646-3200
Fax: 617-643-1126

William J. Grannan   Paul F. Maloy

For full biographical listings, see the Martindale-Hubbell Law Directory

---

*BOSTON,** Suffolk Co.

CITY, HAYES, MEAGHER & DISSETTE, P.C. (AV)

50 Congress Street, 02109
Telephone: 617-523-3050
Telecopier: 617-523-5612

Robert D. City   Kieran B. Meagher
James P. Hayes   Michael J. Dissette

Martin R. Fisch   Lewis R. Lear
Philip B. Evans   Philip Di Domenico
          Michael N. O'Connell, Jr.

For full biographical listings, see the Martindale-Hubbell Law Directory

---

CUDDY BIXBY (AV)

One Financial Center, 02111
Telephone: 617-348-3600
Telecopier: 617-348-3643
Wellesley, Massachusetts Office: 60 Walnut Street.
Telephone: 617-235-1034.

Brian D. Bixby   Robert J. O'Regan

For Complete List of Firm Personnel, See General Section

For full biographical listings, see the Martindale-Hubbell Law Directory

---

HEMENWAY & BARNES (AV)

60 State Street, 02109
Telephone: 617-227-7940
Fax: 617-227-0781

MEMBERS OF FIRM

George H. Kidder   Timothy F. Fidgeon
David H. Morse   Michael J. Puzo
Roy A. Hammer   Deborah J. Hall
Lawrence T. Perera   Kurt F. Somerville
George T. Shaw   Brian C. Broderick

For Complete List of Firm Personnel, See General Section

For full biographical listings, see the Martindale-Hubbell Law Directory

---

PACKENHAM, SCHMIDT & FEDERICO, P.C. (AV)

Four Longfellow Place, 35th Floor, 02114-2832
Telephone: 617-742-6565
Fax: 617-742-0292

(See Next Column)

PACKENHAM, SCHMIDT & FEDERICO P.C., *Boston—Continued*

Richard D. Packenham   Mary H. Schmidt
Phyllis E. Federico

David A. Schwartz

For full biographical listings, see the Martindale-Hubbell Law Directory

PALMER & DODGE LLP (AV)

One Beacon Street, 02108
Telephone: 617-573-0100
Facsimile: 617-227-4420

MEMBERS OF FIRM

Lawrence B. Cohen	Arthur B. Page
Laurie J. Hall	R. Robert Woodburn, Jr.
Eric F. Menoyo	Jackson W. Wright, Jr.

COUNSEL

Rhonda G. Hollander   Pamela M. Veasy

For Complete List of Firm Personnel, See General Section

For full biographical listings, see the Martindale-Hubbell Law Directory

PEABODY & ARNOLD (AV)

A Partnership including Professional Corporations
50 Rowes Wharf, 02110-3342
Telephone: 617-951-2100
Telecopier: 617-951-2125
Providence, Rhode Island Office: One Citizens Plaza, Suite 840.
Telephone: 401-831-8330.
Fax: 401-831-8359.

MEMBERS OF FIRM

Jason M. Cotton	Peter B. Seamans
Linda S. Dalby	Peter M. Shapland
David W. Fitts	Robert A. Vigoda
Frank N. Ray (Resident,	Edward E. Watts, III
Providence, Rhode Island	Stephen Ziobrowski
Office)	

COUNSEL

John G. Brooks

ASSOCIATES

Glenn B. Asch   William J. Dellea
Ingrid Sorensen

For Complete List of Firm Personnel, See General Section

For full biographical listings, see the Martindale-Hubbell Law Directory

RACKEMANN, SAWYER & BREWSTER, PROFESSIONAL CORPORATION (AV)

One Financial Center, 02111
Telephone: 617-542-2300
Telecopier: 617-542-7437

William B. Tyler	Janet M. Smith
Henry H. Thayer	Peter Friedenberg
Stephen Carr Anderson	Richard S. Novak
Albert M. Fortier, Jr.	J. David Leslie
Michael F. O'Connell	Sanford M. Matathia
Stuart T. Freeland	Richard J. Gallogly
Alan B. Rubenstein	James A. Wachta
James R. Shea, Jr.	Hanson S. Reynolds
Brian M. Hurley	Donald R. Pinto, Jr.

COUNSEL

Ronald S. Duby	Gordon M. Orloff
Lucy West Behymer	Eric A. Smith

OF COUNSEL

Albert B. Wolfe	George V. Anastas
August R. Meyer	Edward M. Condit
Richard H. Lovell	Alexander H. Spaulding

Margaret L. Hayes	Peter A. Alpert
Daniel J. Ossoff	Ellen M. Harrington
Melissa Langer Ellis	Lauren D. Armstrong
Daniel J. Bailey, III	Robert B. Foster
Michael S. Giaimo	Andrew H. Butler
Maura E. Murphy	Gayle E. Parlee
Mary L. Gallant	Elizabeth A. Gibbons
	Melissa Fang

For full biographical listings, see the Martindale-Hubbell Law Directory

SHERBURNE, POWERS & NEEDHAM, P.C. (AV)

One Beacon Street, 02108
Telephone: 617-523-2700
Fax: 617-523-6850
Email: @SHERBURNE.COM

(See Next Column)

William D. Weeks	Benjamin Volinski
John T. Collins	Mark Schonfeld
Allan J. Landau	James D. Smeallie
Stephen A. Hopkins	Paul Killeen
Alan I. Falk	Gordon P. Katz
C. Thomas Swaim	Joseph B. Darby, III
James Pollock	Richard M Yanofsky
William V. Tripp III	James E. McDermott
Stephen S. Young	Kenneth P. Brier
William F. Machen	Robert V. Lizza
W. Robert Allison	Miriam Goldstein Altman
Philip J. Notopoulos	John J. Monaghan
Richard J. Hindlian	Margaret J. Palladino
Paul E. Troy	Mark C. Michalowski
Harold W. Potter, Jr.	David Scott Sloan
Philip S. Lapatin	M. Chrysa Long
Pamela A. Duckworth	Lawrence D. Bradley
Miriam J. McKendall	

Cynthia A. Brown	Amy J. Mastrobattista
Cynthia M. Hern	Leslie A. Sprinkle
Meredeth A. Beers	Douglas W. Clapp
Dianne R. Phillips	Jeffrey A. Huebschmann
Paul M. James	Tamara E. Goulston
Theodore F. Hanselman	Paul G. Lannon, Jr.
Joshua C. Krumholz	Nicholas J. Psyhogeos
Ieuan G. Mahony	Edward J. Naughton
Jeffrey J. Nix	Kathaleen Kelly Cutone
(Not admitted in MA)	Laurie A. Tribble
Kenneth L. Harvey	Neil C. Higgins
Christopher J. Trombetta	Deborah Paige Stone
Elise N. Zoli	Brian R. Popiel

COUNSEL

Haig Der Manuelian	Karl J. Hirshman
Mason M. Taber, Jr.	Dale R. Johnson

For full biographical listings, see the Martindale-Hubbell Law Directory

SIMONDS, WINSLOW, WILLIS & ABBOTT, A PROFESSIONAL ASSOCIATION (AV)

50 Congress Street, 02109
Telephone: 617-367-4747
Fax: 617-227-1961

Marc A. Elfman	Brenda G. Levy
Robert S. Gulick	Dudley H. Willis
John L. Worden III	

For Complete List of Firm Personnel, See General Section

For full biographical listings, see the Martindale-Hubbell Law Directory

ARNOLD L. SLAVET (AV)

Sixty State Street, Suite 700, 02109
Telephone: 617-371-2977; 617-894-1022
Telecopier: 617-647-1436

For full biographical listings, see the Martindale-Hubbell Law Directory

WARNER & STACKPOLE LLP (AV)

75 State Street, 02109
Telephone: 617-951-9000
Telecopier: 617-951-9151
Email: w&s@warstack.com

MEMBERS OF FIRM

Elizabeth F. Potter   Gordon M. Stevenson, Jr.

ASSOCIATES

Elizabeth W. Ho   Kevin M. Meuse
Jennifer S. Rako

COUNSEL

Andrew C. Bailey   David W. Lewis, Jr.

OF COUNSEL

Endicott Smith

For Complete List of Firm Personnel, See General Section

For full biographical listings, see the Martindale-Hubbell Law Directory

---

CAMBRIDGE, * Middlesex Co.

JOHN J. ROCHE & ASSOCIATES (AV)

One Cambridge Center, Suite 405, 02142
Telephone: 617-621-3100
Telecopier: 617-621-3140

ASSOCIATE

Mark L. Saperstein

For full biographical listings, see the Martindale-Hubbell Law Directory

Cambridge—Continued

MERVIN M. WILF, LTD. (AV)

2 Berkeley Place, 02138
Telephone: 617-876-5200
Philadelphia, Pennsylvania Office: 3901 Mellon Bank Center. 1735 Market Street.
Telephone: 215-994-1430. 215- 568-4842.
Facsimile: 215-994-1432.

Mervin M. Wilf

A list of Representative Clients and References will be furnished upon request.

For full biographical listings, see the Martindale-Hubbell Law Directory

FRANKLIN, Norfolk Co.

GILMORE, REES & CARLSON, P.C. (AV)

1000 Franklin Village Drive, 02038
Telephone: 508-520-2200
Fax: 508-520-2217
Wellesley, Massachusetts Office: 20 Walnut Street, 02181.
Telephone: 617-431-9788.
Fax: 617-431-1957.

Daniel J. Gilmore	Bruce J. Bettigole
Christopher T. Carlson	Michael P. Doherty
Craig A. Ciechanowski	

OF COUNSEL
William J. Rees

Katherine A. Botelho	James H. Goldsmith
Jane Fisher Carlson	Peter J. Paulousky
Brian L. Gaudet	

For full biographical listings, see the Martindale-Hubbell Law Directory

HYANNIS, Barnstable Co.

PHILIP M. BOUDREAU (AV)

Boudreau Building, 396 North Street, 02555
Telephone: 508-775-1085
Fax: 508-771-0722

ASSOCIATES
Philip Michael Boudreau	Mark H. Boudreau

For full biographical listings, see the Martindale-Hubbell Law Directory

BOYD & BOYD, P.C. (AV)

One Sentry Plaza, 1185 Falmouth Road (Rte 28), Suite 101, 02632
Telephone: 508-775-7800
Fax: 508-775-5666
Weston, Massachusetts Office: Riverside Office Park, 13 Riverside Road, Suite 101.
Telephone: 617-899-7100.

F. Keats Boyd, Jr.	F. Keats Boyd, III

For full biographical listings, see the Martindale-Hubbell Law Directory

HADDLETON & COLLINS, P.C. (AV)

251 South Street, P.O. Box 1298, 02601
Telephone: 508-771-3132
Fax: 508-790-3760

Russell E. Haddleton	Joyce M. Collins

Michael Toivo Lahti

For full biographical listings, see the Martindale-Hubbell Law Directory

NATICK, Middlesex Co.

ZALTAS, MEDOFF & RAIDER (AV)

74 West Central Street, 01760
Telephone: 508-655-1960, Boston: 617-235-0217
Fax: 508-655-4347

Arnold I. Zaltas	Irving I. Medoff
Mark H. Raider	

ASSOCIATES
Kathryn A. Sanderson	George E. Levoy, III
A. David Zaltas	

For full biographical listings, see the Martindale-Hubbell Law Directory

NORTHAMPTON,* Hampshire Co.

MORSE & SACKS (AV)

31 Trumbull Road, 01060
Telephone: 413-584-1287
Fax: 413-584-0453

(See Next Column)

MEMBERS OF FIRM
Alvertus J. Morse (1872-1949)	Alvertus D. Morse (1904-1982)
Harley M. Sacks	

ASSOCIATES
Debra L. Purrington	John M. McLaughlin

Representative Clients: Bill Willard, Inc.

For full biographical listings, see the Martindale-Hubbell Law Directory

SPRINGFIELD,* Hampden Co.

ROBERT G. AGNOLI (AV)

Formerly Novak & Agnoli
1391 Main Street, 01103
Telephone: 413-734-8229
Fax: 413-733-6301

ASSOCIATE
Jane G. Martel

For full biographical listings, see the Martindale-Hubbell Law Directory

FRATAR & KERN (AV)

1391 Main Street, Suite 500, 01103
Telephone: 413-734-3119
Telecopier: 413-736-0670

MEMBERS OF FIRM
Robert N. Fratar	William F. Kern

For full biographical listings, see the Martindale-Hubbell Law Directory

ROBINSON DONOVAN MADDEN & BARRY, P.C. (AV)

Suite 1600, BayBank Tower, 1500 Main Street, 01115
Telephone: 413-732-2301
Fax: 413-785-4658

Homans Robinson (1894-1973)	Milton J. Donovan (1906-1995)
Lawrence M. Sinclair (1942-1986)	

OF COUNSEL
John H. Madden, Jr.	Victor Rosenberg
Edward J. Barry	Richard S. Milstein

Gordon H. Wentworth	John C. Sikorski
James H. Tourtelotte	Nancy Frankel Pelletier
Charles K. Bergin, Jr.	Paul S. Weinberg
Ronald C. Kidd	Frederica H. McCarthy
Jeffrey W. Roberts	Matthew J. King
Jeffrey L. McCormick	Neva Kaufman Rohan
James F. Martin	Douglas F. Boyd
Robert P. Cunningham	James K. Bodurtha
Keith A. Minoff	

E. Paul Amata (Not admitted in MA)	Kimberly Davis Crear
James D. Chadwell	John W. Davis
Susan L. Cooper	Edmund J. Gorman
	Patricia M. Rapinchuk
Jonathan P. Rice	

Representative Clients: The First National Bank of Boston; United Cooperative Bank; Fleet Bank, N.A.; American Policyholders Insurance Co.; CNA; Commercial Union Insurance Co.; Hanover Insurance Group.

For full biographical listings, see the Martindale-Hubbell Law Directory

SHATZ, SCHWARTZ AND FENTIN, P.C. (AV)

Suite 1100, 1441 Main Street, 01103
Telephone: 413-737-1131
Telecopier: 413-736-0375

Steven J. Schwartz	James B. Sheils
Stephen A. Shatz	Ann I. Weber
Gary S. Fentin	Ellen W. Freyman
Timothy P. Mulhern	Steven Weiss

Susan E. Zak
OF COUNSEL
John H. Mitchell, Jr.	Mark H. Bluver

References: Shawmut Bank N.A. Title Services and Title Insurance; Springfield Institution For Savings; BayBank Valley Trust Co.; Fleet Bank of Massachusetts, N.A.

For full biographical listings, see the Martindale-Hubbell Law Directory

WALTHAM, Middlesex Co.

HARNISH, JENNEY, MITCHELL AND RESH (AV)

564 Main Street, 02154
Telephone: 617-894-0000
Telecopier: 617-893-8357

(See Next Column)

HARNISH, JENNEY, MITCHELL AND RESH, *Waltham—Continued*

MEMBERS OF FIRM

Francis E. Jenney	Robert C. Mann
David L. Mitchell	Margaret Manzon Skinner
Harvey J. Resh	Rhonda B. Fogel
Joseph Melone	Cynthia Spahl

For full biographical listings, see the Martindale-Hubbell Law Directory

---

WORCESTER,* Worcester Co.

ERSKINE & ERSKINE (AV)

30 Highland Street, 01609-2704
Telephone: 508-753-7100
Fax: 508-753-8088

William T. Forbes (1876-1931)	Linwood M. Erskine, Jr.
Linwood M. Erskine, Sr.	Matthew F. Erskine
(1909-1956)	

For full biographical listings, see the Martindale-Hubbell Law Directory

---

MOUNTAIN, DEARBORN & WHITING (AV)

370 Main Street, 01608
Telephone: 508-756-2423
Fax: 508-755-6640

MEMBERS OF FIRM

Alfred N. Whiting (1920-1989)	Francis J. Russell
Thomas R. Mountain	Dale R. Harger
Richard W. Dearborn	Mark W. Bloom
Samuel R. DeSimone	Donald J. O'Neil
Henry W. Beth	Lawrence S. Delaney

Ann K. Molloy

ASSOCIATE

Richard M. Freije

For full biographical listings, see the Martindale-Hubbell Law Directory

---

SEDER & CHANDLER (AV)

A Partnership including a Professional Corporation
Established 1918
Burnside Building, 339 Main Street, 01608
Telephone: 508-757-7721
Telecopiers: 508-798-1863; 508-831-0955

MEMBERS OF FIRM

Samuel Seder (1918-1964)	Marvin S. Silver, P.C.
Harold Seder (1934-1988)	John L. Pfeffer, Jr.
Burton Chandler	Robert S. Adler
J. Robert Seder	Dawn E. Caccavaro
Darragh K. Kasakoff	Kevin C. McGee

Kurt L. Binder

ASSOCIATES

Paul J. O'Riordan	Jeffrey P. Greenberg

Denise M. Tremblay

OF COUNSEL

Saul A. Seder	Gerald E. Norman

Philip C. Lombardo, Jr.

Reference: First National Bank of Boston; Safety Fund National Bank; Fleet National Bank.

For full biographical listings, see the Martindale-Hubbell Law Directory

---

MICHIGAN

ANN ARBOR,* Washtenaw Co.

BRAUN KENDRICK FINKBEINER PLC (AV)

700 First National Building, 48104
Telephone: 313-995-4100
Telecopier: 313-995-4798
URL: http://www.bkf-law.com
Bay City, Michigan Office: 201 Phoenix Building, P.O. Box 2039.
Telephone: 517-895-8505.
Telecopier: 517-895-8437.
Saginaw, Michigan Office: 101 N. Washington, Suite 812.
Telephone: 517-753-3461.
Telecopier: 517-753-3951.

Barry M. Levine

Representative Clients: The Dow Chemical Co.; General Motors Corp.; Lobdell Emery Manufacturing Co.; Merrill, Lynch, Inc.; Saginaw General Hospital; Saginaw News; The Wickes Foundation.

For full biographical listings, see the Martindale-Hubbell Law Directory

---

HOOPER, HATHAWAY, PRICE, BEUCHE & WALLACE (AV)

126 South Main Street, 48104
Telephone: 313-662-4426
Fax: 313-662-9559

Alan E. Price

Representative Clients: Chem-Trend, Inc.; Dundee Cement Co.; Ervin Industries, Inc.; First Martin Corp.; Group 243 Design, Inc.; Honeywell; Microwave Sensors, Inc.; Shearson Lehman Hutton; O'Neal Construction Co.; Pittsfield Products, Inc.

For Complete List of Firm Personnel, See General Section

For full biographical listings, see the Martindale-Hubbell Law Directory

---

MILLER, CANFIELD, PADDOCK AND STONE, P.L.C. (AV)

A Professional Limited Liability Company
Founded in 1852 by Sidney Davy Miller
101 North Main Street, Seventh Floor, 48104-1400
Telephone: 313-663-2445
Fax: 313-747-7147
Detroit, Michigan Office: 150 West Jefferson, Suite 2500, 48226-4415.
Telephone: 313-963-6420.
Fax: 313-496-7500.
Cable Address: "Stem Detroit."
Bloomfield Hills, Michigan Office: Suite 100, Pinehurst Office Center, 1400 North Woodward, 48303-2014.
Telephone: 313-645-5000.
Fax: 313-645-1917.
Grand Rapids, Michigan Office: 1200 Campau Square Plaza, 99 Monroe, N.W., 49503-2639.
Telephone: 616-454-8656.
Fax: 616-776-6322.
Howell, Michigan Office: 121 South Barnard Street, Suite 4, 48843-2305.
Telephone: 517-546-7600.
Telecopier: 517-546-6974.
Kalamazoo, Michigan Office: 444 West Michigan Avenue, 49007-3752.
Telephone: 616-381-7030.
Fax: 616-382-0244.
Lansing, Michigan Office: One Michigan Avenue, Suite 900, 48933-1609.
Telephone: 517-487-2070.
Fax: 517-374-6304.
Monroe, Michigan Office: The Executive Centre, 214 East Elm Avenue, 48161-2682.
Telephone: 313-243-2000.
Fax: 313-243-0901.
Washington, D.C. Office: 1225 Nineteenth Street, N.W., Suite 400. 20036.
Telephone: 202-429-5575; 785-0600.
Fax: 202-331-1118; 785-1234.
Pensacola, Florida Office: 25 West Cedar, 32501.
Telephone: 904-469-1088.
Fax: 904-432-0677.
St. Petersburg, Florida Office: 100 Second Avenue S., Suite 7045, 33701.
Telephone: 813-982-6000.
Fax: 813-892-6002.
New York, New York Office: Eleventh Floor, 135 East 57th Street, 10022-2087.
Telephone: 212-754-5400.
Fax: 212-754-5401.
Gdansk, Poland Office: Suite 322, Dom Technika Building, UI. Rajska 6, 80-850.
Telephone: 011-485-831-2808.
Fax: 011-485-831-4719.
Warsaw, Poland Office: UI. Marszalkowska 82, Suite 561, 00-517.
Telephone: 011-482-623-6457 and 6458.
Fax: 011-482-623-6459.

RESIDENT PRINCIPALS

Robert E. Gilbert

SENIOR ATTORNEY

Ronald D. Gardner

Representative Firm Clients: Chrysler Corporation; Comerica, Incorporated; City of Detroit, Michigan; Detroit Tigers, Inc.; First of Michigan; Ford Motor Company; Ford Motor Credit Company; Great Lakes Bancorp; Henry Ford Hospital; INVETECH Company.

For Complete List of Firm Personnel, See General Section

For full biographical listings, see the Martindale-Hubbell Law Directory

---

PEAR SPERLING EGGAN & MUSKOVITZ, P.C. (AV)

Domino's Farms, 24 Frank Lloyd Wright Drive, 48105
Telephone: 313-665-4441
Fax: 313-665-8788
Ypsilanti, Michigan Offices: 5 South Washington Street.
Telephone: 313-483-3626 and 2164 Bellevue at Washtenaw.
Telephone: 313-483-7177.

Edwin L. Pear	Andrew M. Eggan

For Complete List of Firm Personnel, See General Section

For full biographical listings, see the Martindale-Hubbell Law Directory

Ann Arbor—Continued

WESTERMAN & ASSOCIATES, P.C. (AV)

345 South Division, 48104
Telephone: 313-995-9731
Facsimile: 313-995-9738

Susan S. Westerman

Susan M. Friedland

For full biographical listings, see the Martindale-Hubbell Law Directory

BIRMINGHAM, Oakland Co.

CARSON FISCHER, P.L.C. (AV)

Third Floor, 300 East Maple Road, 48009-6317
Telephone: 810-644-4840
Facsimile: 810-644-1832

Robert M. Carson   William C. Edmunds

For full biographical listings, see the Martindale-Hubbell Law Directory

HYMAN AND LIPPITT, P.C. (AV)

185 Oakland Avenue, Suite 300, P.O. Box 1750, 48009
Telephone: 810-646-8292
Facsimile: 810-646-8375

J. Leonard Hyman	Kenneth F. Neuman
Norman L. Lippitt	Terry S. Givens
Douglas A. Hyman	Paul J. Fischer
Brian D. O'Keefe	John A. Sellers
H. Joel Newman	Robert H. Lippitt
Nazli G. Sater	Roger L. Myers

David N. Morrell, Jr.

For full biographical listings, see the Martindale-Hubbell Law Directory

MacDONALD AND GOREN, P.C. (AV)

Suite 200, 260 East Brown Street, 48009
Telephone: 810-645-5940
Fax: 810-645-2490

Harold C. MacDonald   Kalman G. Goren
Cindy Rhodes Victor

Amy L. Glenn	Lawrence C. Atorthy
David D. Marsh	Miriam Blanks-Smart
Glenn G. Ross	John T. Klees

Rose Marie Karadsheh
OF COUNSEL
Robert L. Biederman

Representative Clients: Beaudin, Gallanis; Beaudin, Incorporated; Orlandi Gear Co., Inc.; Bing Steel, Inc.; Superb Manufacturing, Inc.; Spring Engineering, Inc.; Adrian Steel Co.; Southfield Radiology Associates, P.C.; HDS Services, Inc.; TGI Friday's Inc.; Quality Gold of Cincinnati, Inc.

For full biographical listings, see the Martindale-Hubbell Law Directory

WEINGARDEN & HAUER, P.C. (AV)

30100 Telegraph Road, Suite 221, 48025
Telephone: 810-258-0800
Telecopier: 810-258-2750

Larry A. Weingarden

Reference: Security Bank & Trust.

For full biographical listings, see the Martindale-Hubbell Law Directory

WILLIAMS, SCHAEFER, RUBY & WILLIAMS, PROFESSIONAL CORPORATION (AV)

Suite 300, 380 North Woodward Avenue, 48009
Telephone: 810-642-0333
Telecopy: 810-642-0856

James A. Williams	R. Jamison Williams, Jr.
Edward L. Ruby	Richard D. Rattner

James J. Williams

For full biographical listings, see the Martindale-Hubbell Law Directory

BLOOMFIELD HILLS, Oakland Co.

BEIER HOWLETT, PROFESSIONAL CORPORATION (AV)

200 East Long Lake Road, Suite 110, 48304-2361
Telephone: 810-645-9400
Fax: 810-645-9344

(See Next Column)

Dean G. Beier	Thomas J. Trenta
James L. Howlett	Mark W. Hafeli
Daniel C. Devine	Timothy J. Currier
Gerald G. White	Mary T. Schmitt Smith
Lawrence R. Ternan	Robert R. Shuman
Stephen W. Jones	John D. Staran
Frank S. Galgan	Joseph F. Yamin
Kenneth J. Sorensen	Phyllis Aiuto Zimmerman

P. Daniel Christ	Amy D. Comito
Richard A. Joslin, Jr.	Michael C. Gibbons
Lauren M. Underwood	George S. Fish

Nicole D. Bogard
OF COUNSEL
Robert G. Waddell

Representative Clients: Automobile Club Insurance Association (AAA); City of Birmingham; City of Lake Angelus; City of Rochester Hills; C.J. Edwards, Inc.; Dundee Community Schools; First of America Bank; Lake States Insurance Company; MAC Values; Troy School District.

For full biographical listings, see the Martindale-Hubbell Law Directory

DAWDA, MANN, MULCAHY & SADLER, P.L.C. (AV)

1533 North Woodward Avenue Suite 200, 48304
Telephone: 810-642-3700
Fax: 810-642-7791
Email: EMail@DMMS.Com

Edward C. Dawda   Curtis J. Mann

Paul C. Apap

For full biographical listings, see the Martindale-Hubbell Law Directory

MEYER, KIRK, SNYDER & SAFFORD, PLLC (AV)

Suite 100, 100 West Long Lake Road, 48304
Telephone: 810-647-5111
Telecopier: 810-647-6079
Detroit, Michigan Office: 2500 Penobscot Building.
Telephone: 313-961-1261.

George H. Meyer   John M. Kirk
Donald H. Baker, Jr.

Representative Clients: Available Upon Request.

For Complete List of Firm Personnel, See General Section

For full biographical listings, see the Martindale-Hubbell Law Directory

DAVID M. THOMS & ASSOCIATES, P.C. (AV)

1500 Woodward Avenue, Suite 100, 48304
Telephone: 313-259-6333
Facsimile: 313-259-7037
Detroit, Michigan Office: 400 Renaissance Center, Suite 950.
Telephone: 313-259-6333.
Fax: 313-259-7037.

David M. Thoms

Representative Clients: Fowler Agency Corp.; Gibbs World Wide Wines, Inc.; deBary Travel, Inc.; North Management, Inc.; RG & GR Harris Funeral Home, Inc.; St. Jude Children's Research Hospital; The Salvation Army.
References: Comerica Bank-Detroit; National Bank of Detroit.

For full biographical listings, see the Martindale-Hubbell Law Directory

*DETROIT,** Wayne Co.

ABBOTT, NICHOLSON, QUILTER, ESSHAKI & YOUNGBLOOD, P.C. (AV)

19th Floor, One Woodward Avenue, 48226
Telephone: 313-963-2500
Telecopier: 313-963-7882

C. Richard Abbott	Carl F. Jarboe
John R. Nicholson	Jay A. Kennedy
Thomas R. Quilter III	Timothy A. Stoepker
Gene J. Esshaki	Timothy J. Kramer
John F. Youngblood	Norbert T. Madison, Jr.
James B. Perry	William D. Gilbride, Jr.

Mary P. Nelson	Kathryn L. Ritchie
Michael R. Blum	Jill A. Bankey
Thomas F. Hatch	Dawn M. Macaddino
Anne Warren Bagno	Casimir J. Swastek
Eric J. Girdler	Daniel G. Kielczewski

George M. Mesrey
OF COUNSEL

Thomas C. Shumaker   Karen Smith Kienbaum

For full biographical listings, see the Martindale-Hubbell Law Directory

Detroit—Continued

BODMAN, LONGLEY & DAHLING LLP (AV)

34th Floor 100 Renaissance Center, 48243
Telephone: 313-259-7777
Fax: 313-393-7579
Email: 2080194@mcimail.com
Troy, Michigan Office: Suite 2020, 755 West Big Beaver Road.
Telephone: 810-362-2110.
Fax: 810-244-0780.
Ann Arbor, Michigan Office: 110 Miller, Suite 300.
Telephone: 313-761-3780.
Fax: 313-930-2494.
Northern Michigan Office: 229 Court Street, P.O. Box 405, Cheboygan.
Telephone: 616-627-4351.
Fax: 616-627-2802.

MEMBERS OF FIRM

George D. Miller, Jr.	Christopher J. Dine
Mark W. Griffin	(Troy Office)
(Ann Arbor Office)	Patrick C. Cauley
Kenneth R. Lango (Troy Office)	David P. Larsen
David M. Hempstead	Barnett Jay Colvin

COUNSEL
John S. Dobson (Ann Arbor Office)

For Representative Client List, See General Section

For Complete List of Firm Personnel, See General Section

For full biographical listings, see the Martindale-Hubbell Law Directory

CLARK HILL P.L.C. (AV)

500 Woodward Avenue, Suite 3500, 48226
Telephone: 313-965-8300
Facsimile: 313-962-4348
Oakland County, Michigan Office: Third Floor, 255 South Woodward Avenue, Birmingham.
Telephone: 810-642-9692.
Facsimile: 810-642-2174.
Lansing, Michigan Office: Suite 600, 200 North Capitol Avenue.
Telephone: 517-484-4481.
Facsimile: 517-484-1246.
Minneapolis, Minnesota Office: Suite 1000, One Financial Plaza, 120 South Sixth Street.
Telephone: 612-332-0102.
Facsimile: 612-332-3225.
Kansas City, Missouri Office: Suite 1400, Bryant Building, 1102 Grand Avenue.
Telephone: 816-221-5578.
Facsimile: 816-221-0303.

Douglas J. Rasmussen	Kevin M. Bernys (Resident,
Thomas F. Sweeney (Resident,	Oakland County Office)
Oakland County Office)	J. Thomas MacFarlane
Thomas S. Nowinski	(Resident, Oakland County
Joseph A. Bonventre	Office)
Michael G. Cumming	Andrea M. Kanski

Robin D. Ferriby	Jennifer Crawford
Christopher A. McMican	

Representative Clients: Booth Communications, Inc.; The Budd Co.; Coopers & Lybrand; Dow Corning Corp.; First Federal of Michigan; The Prudential Insurance Companies of America; R.P. Scherer Corp.

For Complete List of Firm Personnel, See General Section

For full biographical listings, see the Martindale-Hubbell Law Directory

EAMES WILCOX (AV)

1400 Buhl Building, 48226-3602
Telephone: 313-963-3750
Facsimile: 313-963-8485

MEMBERS OF FIRM

Leonard A. Wilcox, Jr.	Jerry R. Swift
Ronald J. Mastej	Neill T. Riddell
John W. Bryant	Kevin N. Summers
Robert E. Gesell	Keith M. Aretha

OF COUNSEL

Rex Eames	William B. McIntyre, Jr.
David R. Ritter	

Representative Clients: ABF Freight System, Inc.; Chrysler Credit Corp.; City Transfer Co.; Engineered Heat Treat, Inc.; Fetz Engineering Co.; I E & E Industries, Inc.; Schneider Transport; Tank Carrier Employers Association of Michigan; TNT Transport Group, Inc.; Waste Management of Michigan.

For full biographical listings, see the Martindale-Hubbell Law Directory

EGGENBERGER, EGGENBERGER, MCKINNEY, WEBER & HOFMEISTER, P.C. (AV)

42nd Floor Penobscot Building, 48226
Telephone: 313-961-9722

(See Next Column)

William J. Eggenberger	John P. McKinney
(1900-1984)	Stephen L. Weber
William D. Eggenberger	Paul D. Hofmeister
Robert E. Eggenberger	Thomas R. Paxton

Mary T. Humbert	James B. Eggenberger

Representative Clients: Central National Insurance Group of Omaha; Great Central Insurance Co.; Preferred Risk Mutual Insurance Company of Des Moines, Iowa; State Automobile and Casualty Underwriters; State Farm Fire and Casualty Co.
Reference: Comerica Bank-Detroit.

For full biographical listings, see the Martindale-Hubbell Law Directory

FEIKENS, VANDER MALE, STEVENS, BELLAMY & GILCHRIST, P.C. (AV)

One Detroit Center Suite 3400, 500 Woodward Avenue, 48226-3406
Telephone: 313-962-5909
Fax: 313-962-3125
Email: FEIKENS@COUNSEL.COM

Robert E. Dice (1922-1983)	Lee A. Stevens
Jon Feikens	William C. Hurley
Jack E. Vander Male	Linda M. Galbraith
Frederick B. Bellamy	Michael S. Cafferty
Alan Gordon Gilchrist	Robert H. Feikens
L. Neal Kennedy	Gerald W. Van Wyke
Bruce A. VandeVusse	Roger L. Wolcott

Sharon McPhail

Richard G. Koefod	Keith J. Soltis
Joseph E. Kozely, Jr.	Michael B. Barey
Jeffrey Feikens	Renee T. VanderHagen

Michael P. Citrin

OF COUNSEL

Sam W. Thomas (P.C.)	Walter Vincent Bernard III

LEGAL SUPPORT PERSONNEL
PARALEGALS

Robert Westveer	Linda Barthlow

For full biographical listings, see the Martindale-Hubbell Law Directory

FOSTER, MEADOWS & BALLARD, P.C. (AV)

3200 Penobscot Building, 48226
Telephone: 313-961-3234
Cable Address: "Foster"
Telex: 23-5823
Facsimile: 313-961-6184

Sparkman D. Foster (1897-1967)	Richard A. Dietz
Charles R. Hrdlicka	Robert H. Fortunate
Paul D. Galea	Robert G. Lahiff

Camille A. Raffa-Dietz

Michael J. Liddane	Paul A. Kettunen

OF COUNSEL

John L. Foster	John F. Langs

John A. Mundell, Jr.

For full biographical listings, see the Martindale-Hubbell Law Directory

HAYDUK, ANDREWS & HYPNAR, P.C. (AV)

1700 Buhl Building, 535 Griswold, 48226
Telephone: 313-962-4500
Fax: 313-964-6577

Mark S. Hayduk	Robin K. Andrews

Mark A. Hypnar

Sean Angus McPhillips	Lynn E. Radke

Representative Clients: Farmers Insurance Group; GameTime, Inc.; Admiral Insurance Co.; Heritage Ins. Alexis; Meijer, Inc.; Condon & Forsyth; Pinkerton's Inc.; Vik Brothers Ins.; Investors Ins. Group; Scibal Ins. Co.

For full biographical listings, see the Martindale-Hubbell Law Directory

JAFFE, RAITT, HEUER & WEISS, PROFESSIONAL CORPORATION (AV)

One Woodward Avenue, Suite 2400, 48226
Telephone: 313-961-8380
Telecopier: 313-961-8358
Cable Address: "Jafsni"
Southfield, Michigan Office: Travelers Tower, Suite 1520.
Telephone: 313-961-8380.
Monroe, Michigan Office: 214 East Elm Avenue, Suite 208,
Telephone: 313-241-6470.
Telefacsimile: 313-241-3849.

(See Next Column)

JAFFE, RAITT, HEUER & WEISS PROFESSIONAL CORPORATION—*Continued*

Penny L. Carolan   Joel S. Golden

Derek S. Adolf   Lesley A. Gaber

For Complete List of Firm Personnel, See General Section

For full biographical listings, see the Martindale-Hubbell Law Directory

JOHNSON & VALENTINE (AV)

4372 Penobscot Building, 48226
Telephone: 313-961-4700

MEMBERS OF FIRM

Edward C. Johnson   Glenn L. Valentine

ASSOCIATE

Dale T. McPherson

OF COUNSEL

Jarvis J. Schmidt

References: First of America Bank; Southeast Michigan, N.A.

For full biographical listings, see the Martindale-Hubbell Law Directory

JOSLYN KEYDEL & WALLACE (AV)

A Partnership of Professional Corporations
211 West Fort Street, Suite 2211, 48226-3270
Telephone: 313-964-4181
Fax: 313-964-4996

MEMBERS OF FIRM

Lee E. Joslyn (1864-1936)   Alan W. Joslyn (1899-1990)
Lee E. Joslyn, Jr. (1895-1955)   Frederick R. Keydel (P.C.)
             Harvey B. Wallace II (P.C.)

ASSOCIATE

Patrice M. Ticknor   Andrew W. MacLeod

LEGAL SUPPORT PERSONNEL
PARALEGALS

Diane C. Simpson   Justine B. Gudritz
Ruth G. Spector   Alice M. Pricer

References: NBD Bank, N.A.; Comerica Bank.

For full biographical listings, see the Martindale-Hubbell Law Directory

KELLER, THOMA, SCHWARZE, SCHWARZE, DuBAY & KATZ, P.C. (AV)

440 East Congress, 5th Floor, 48226
Telephone: 313-965-7610
Bloomfield Hills, Michigan Office: Suite 122, 100 West Long Lake Road.
Telephone: 810-642-5218.

James R. Miller   Anthony J. Heckemeyer

Counsel for: Livonia Public Schools; Ludington News Co., Inc.
Representative Clients: Borg-Warner Corp.; E & L Transport Co.; The Kroger Co.; Holnam, Inc.
Public Employer Clients: City of Farmington Hills; City of Flint; City of Grosse Pointe Woods; Saginaw Public Schools.

For Complete List of Firm Personnel, See General Section

For full biographical listings, see the Martindale-Hubbell Law Directory

MAY AND MAY, PROFESSIONAL CORPORATION (AV)

5510 Woodward Avenue, 48202
Telephone: 810-358-3800
Southfield, Michigan Office: 3000 Town Center, Suite 2600.
Telephone: 810-358-3800.

Alan A. May

Lawrence G. Snyder   Laura M. Kystad
             Penny L. Deitch

For full biographical listings, see the Martindale-Hubbell Law Directory

MILLER, CANFIELD, PADDOCK AND STONE, P.L.C. (AV)

A Professional Limited Liability Company
Founded in 1852 by Sidney Davy Miller
150 West Jefferson, Suite 2500, 48226-4415
Telephone: 313-963-6420
Fax: 313-496-7500
Cable Address: "Stem Detroit"
Detroit, Michigan Office: 150 West Jefferson, Suite 2500, 48226-4415.
Telephone: 313-963-6420.
Fax: 313-496-7500.
Cable Address: "Stem Detroit."

(See Next Column)

Ann Arbor, Michigan Office: 101 North Main Street, 7th Floor, 48104-1400.
Telephone: 313-663-2445.
Fax: 313-747-7147.
Bloomfield Hills, Michigan Office: Suite 100, Pinehurst Office Center, 1400 North Woodward, 48303-2014.
Telephone: 313-645-5000.
Fax: 313-645-1917.
Grand Rapids, Michigan Office: 1200 Campau Square Plaza, 99 Monroe, N.W., 49503-2639.
Telephone: 616-454-8656.
Fax: 616-776-6322.
Howell, Michigan Office: 121 South Barnard Street, Suite 4, 48843-2305.
Telephone: 517-546-7600.
Telecopier: 517-546-6974.
Kalamazoo, Michigan Office: 444 West Michigan Avenue, 49007-3752.
Telephone: 616-381-7030.
Fax: 616-382-0244.
Lansing, Michigan Office: One Michigan Avenue, Suite 900, 48933-1609.
Telephone: 517-487-2070.
Fax: 517-374-6304.
Monroe, Michigan Office: The Executive Centre, 214 East Elm Avenue, 48161-2682.
Telephone: 313-243-2000.
Fax: 313-243-0901.
Washington, D.C. Office: 1225 Nineteenth Street, N.W., Suite 400. 20036.
Telephone: 202-429-5575; 785-0600.
Fax: 202-331-1118; 785-1234.
Pensacola, Florida Office: 25 West Cedar, 32501.
Telephone: 904-469-1088.
Fax: 904-432-0677.
St. Petersburg, Florida Office: 100 Second Avenue S., Suite 7045, 33701.
Telephone: 813-982-6000.
Fax: 813-892-6002.
New York, New York Office: Eleventh Floor, 135 East 57th Street, 10022-2087.
Telephone: 212-754-5400.
Fax: 212-754-5401.
Gdansk, Poland Office: Suite 322, Dom Technika Building, UI. Rajska 6, 80-850.
Telephone: 011-485-831-2808.
Fax: 011-485-831-4719.
Warsaw, Poland Office: UI. Marszalkowska 82, Suite 561, 00-517.
Telephone: 011-482-623-6457 and 6458.
Fax: 011-482-623-6459.

PRINCIPALS OF FIRM

Lawrence A. King (P.C.)   James W. Williams
  (Bloomfield Hills Office)   (Bloomfield Hills Office)
George E. Parker, III   Gregory V. Di Censo
Kenneth E. Konop   (Bloomfield Hills Office)
  (Bloomfield Hills Office)

OF COUNSEL

William G. Butler   Peter P. Thurber

SENIOR ATTORNEYS

Ronald D. Gardner   Stephen L. Elkins
  (Ann Arbor Office)   (Grand Rapids Office)
John G. VanSlambrouck
  (Kalamazoo Office)

ASSOCIATE

Dawn M. Schluter (Bloomfield Hills Office)

Representative Firm Clients: Chrysler Corporation; Comerica, Incorporated; City of Detroit, Michigan; Detroit Tigers, Inc.; First of Michigan; Ford Motor Company; Ford Motor Credit Company; Great Lakes Bancorp; Henry Ford Hospital; INVETECH Company.

For Complete List of Firm Personnel, See General Section

For full biographical listings, see the Martindale-Hubbell Law Directory

R.H. PYTELL & ASSOCIATES, P.C. (AV)

18580 Mack Avenue, 48236
Telephone: 313-343-9200
Fax: 313-343-0207
Email: 103161.221@compuserve.com *URL:* http://lawinfo.com/law/mi/pytell.html

Robert H. Pytell   Henry C. Pytell (1903-1988)
             Paul E. Varchetti

Representative Clients: J & N Fabrications, Inc.; Walton-Pierce, Inc.; Yorkshire Market; U.S. Amada Ltd.; Hickeys Inc.; Midwest Underwriters Insurance Agency, Inc.; Cassens Transport Co.; Mr. B's Tire; Mr. B's Car Wash; New Roots Landscape, Inc.

For full biographical listings, see the Martindale-Hubbell Law Directory

Detroit—Continued

DAVID M. THOMS & ASSOCIATES, P.C. (AV)

400 Renaissance Center, Suite 950, 48243
Telephone: 313-259-6333
Facsimile: 313-259-7037
Bloomfield Hills, Michigan Office: 1500 Woodward Avenue, Suite 100.
Telephone: 313-259-6333.
Fax: 313-259-7037.

David M. Thoms

Audrey R. Holley   Duane B. Brown
OF COUNSEL
Allan G. Meganck   Thomas V. Trainer

Representative Clients: Avion Concepts, Inc.; Fowler Agency Corp.; Gibbs World Wide Wines, Inc.; deBary Travel, Inc.; North Management, Inc.; R.G. & G.R. Harris Funeral Home, Inc.; St. Jude Children's Research Hospital; The Salvation Army.
References: Comerica Bank-Detroit; National Bank of Detroit.

For full biographical listings, see the Martindale-Hubbell Law Directory

TIMMIS & INMAN, L.L.P. (AV)

300 Talon Centre, 48207
Telephone: 313-396-4200
Telecopier: 313-396-4228

Michael T. Timmis   Richard L. Levin
George A. Peck   George M. Malis

John P. Kanan   Erich J. D'Andrea
OF COUNSEL
Wayne C. Inman

Representative Clients: Stylecraft Printing Co.; Stylerite Label Corp.; Retail Resources, Inc.; Deneb Robotics, Inc.; Applied Process, Inc.; Insilco Corp.; Variety Foods, Inc.; Certain Underwriters at Lloyds of London; Eastpointe Radiologists, P.C.; Talon Automotive Group L.L.C.

For Complete List of Firm Personnel, See General Section

For full biographical listings, see the Martindale-Hubbell Law Directory

---

EAST LANSING, Ingham Co.

FARHAT, STORY & KRAUS, P.C. (AV)

Beacon Place, 4572 South Hagadorn Road, Suite 3, 48823
Telephone: 517-351-3700
Fax: 517-332-4122
Email: rkraus@sojourn.com

Leo A. Farhat   Chris A. Bergstrom
James E. Burns (1925-1979)   Kitty L. Groh
Monte R. Story   Charles R. Toy
Richard C. Kraus   David M. Platt
Max R. Hoffman Jr.   Thomas L. Sparks

Lawrence P. Schweitzer   Daniel B. Morgan
Debra A. Geroux   Mary K. Robbins-Kralapp

Representative Clients: Big L. Corp.; Michigan Automotive Wholesalers Association; Hartman-Fabco, Inc.; Lansing Electric Motors, Inc.; Mike Miller Lincoln Mercury; The John E. Fetzer Trust; The Ferris Foundation; Meijer Foundation.
Reference: City Bank, St. Johns.

For full biographical listings, see the Martindale-Hubbell Law Directory

---

FARMINGTON HILLS, Oakland Co.

COUZENS, LANSKY, FEALK, ELLIS, ROEDER & LAZAR, P.C. (AV)

33533 West Twelve Mile Road, Suite 150, P.O. Box 9057, 48333-9057
Telephone: 810-489-8600
Telecopier: 810-489-4156

Sheldon A. Fealk   Lisa J. Walters
Jack S. Couzens, II   Stephen Scapelliti
Jerry M. Ellis   Donald A. Wagner
Donald M. Lansky   Michael P. Witzke
Bruce J. Lazar   Cyrus Raamin Kashef
Alan C. Roeder   Gregg A. Nathanson
Renard J. Kolasa   Mark S. Frankel
Kathryn Gilson Sussman   Lynette M. Sheldon
Jeffrey A. Levine   Roger E. Winkelman
Phillip L. Sternberg   David B. Deutsch
Marc L. Prey   Monica Demko Moons

Representative Clients: Provided upon request.
Reference: Comerica Bank-Southfield.

For full biographical listings, see the Martindale-Hubbell Law Directory

---

HOROWITZ — GUDEMAN, P.C. (AV)

31700 Middlebelt, Suite 140, 48334
Telephone: 810-855-6020
Facsimile: 810-855-6025

Marvin I. Horowitz   Edward J. Gudeman
Stuart L. Sherman

Leslie I. Kollin
LEGAL SUPPORT PERSONNEL
Robin E. Cornell (Paralegal)

For full biographical listings, see the Martindale-Hubbell Law Directory

LAW OFFICE OF GARY POLLACK (AV)

30500 Northwestern Highway Suite 309, 48334-3178
Telephone: 810-932-0880
Facsimile: 810-932-8950

For full biographical listings, see the Martindale-Hubbell Law Directory

WRIGHT PENNING (AV)

27655 Middlebelt Road, Suite 170, 48334
Telephone: 810-477-6300
Fax: 810-477-7749

William M. Wright   LeClair L. Flaherty
Dan A. Penning   Dirk A. Beamer
Dale A. Anderson

For full biographical listings, see the Martindale-Hubbell Law Directory

---

FLINT, * Genesee Co.

GAULT DAVISON A PROFESSIONAL SERVICE CORPORATION (AV)

Tenth Floor, Northbank Center, 432 North Saginaw Street, 48502-2032
Telephone: 810-234-3633
Fax: 810-233-3387
Email: GLTDAV@tir.com

Russell E. Bowers   Kendall B. Williams
Bernard L. McAra   Edward B. Davison

Gary Spinning Casey   Abner J. Tansil
Christine A. Scherba

Representative Clients: NBD Bank; Citizens Banking Corporation.

For full biographical listings, see the Martindale-Hubbell Law Directory

---

GRAND RAPIDS, * Kent Co.

BORRE, PETERSON, FOWLER & REENS, P.C. (AV)

The Philo C. Fuller House, 44 Lafayette, N.E., P.O. Box 1767, 49501-1767
Telephone: 616-459-1971
Fax: 616-459-2393

Glen V. Borre   Ben A. Fowler
James B. Peterson   William G. Krupar

References: Old Kent Bank; NBD Bank; FMB-First Michigan Bank - Grand Rapids.

For Complete List of Firm Personnel, See General Section

For full biographical listings, see the Martindale-Hubbell Law Directory

HAYES, DAVIS & DELLENBUSCH (AV)

535 Fountain Street, N.E., 49503
Telephone: 616-459-6129
Fax: 619-458-8638

Kenneth T. Hayes (Retired)   Henry B. Davis, Jr.
Caroline M. Davis Dellenbusch

Reference: Old Kent Bank and Trust Co.

For full biographical listings, see the Martindale-Hubbell Law Directory

McSHANE & BOWIE, P.L.C. (AV)

1100 Campau Square Plaza, 99 Monroe Avenue, N.W., P.O. Box 360, 49501-0360
Telephone: 616-732-5000
Fax: 616-732-5099

MEMBERS OF FIRM
William H. Bowie   Keith P. Walker
John F. Shape

Representative Clients: Old Kent Bank; Amway Corp.; Hartger & Willard Mortgage Associates; Betten Dodge, Inc.; Randers Engineering, Inc.; BETA Design Group, Inc.; Wolverine Gas & Oil Co., Inc.; M. W. VanderVeen Co.

For Complete List of Firm Personnel, See General Section

For full biographical listings, see the Martindale-Hubbell Law Directory

Grand Rapids—Continued

RHOADES, McKEE, BOER, GOODRICH & TITTA (AV)

161 Ottawa N.W., Suite 600, 49503-2793
Telephone: 616-235-3500
Fax: 616-459-5102
Email: grlaw@grlaw.com *URL:* http://www.grlaw.com

Roger W. Boer	Mary Ann Cartwright
Edward B. Goodrich	Daniel L. Elve
Peter A. Titta	Thomas L. Saxe
Richard G. Leonard	James L. Schipper
Arthur C. Spalding	Laurie M. Strong
Bruce W. Neckers	Stephen A. Hilger
Robert J. Dugan	Gregory G. Timmer
Terrence L. Groesser	Mary Lynette Williams
Thomas P. Hogan	Scott J. Steiner
James M. Flaggert	Douglas P. Vanden Berge
	Robert C. Shaver

Jeff A. Moyer	Kenneth M. Horjus
Paul A. McCarthy	Randy J. Kolar
Todd Allen Hendricks	Molly M. McNamara

OF COUNSEL

Dale W. Rhoades	Jean McKee
F. William McKee	Charles T. Zimmerman
	Robert F. Williams

Reference: First Michigan Bank.

For full biographical listings, see the Martindale-Hubbell Law Directory

RUSSELL & BATCHELOR (AV)

Suite 411-S Waters Building, 161 Ottawa Avenue, N.W., 49503
Telephone: 616-774-8422
Fax: 616-774-0326

MEMBERS OF FIRM

Walter J. Russell	James W. Batchelor

Representative Clients: First National Acceptance Corp.; Trust Corp.; Equitable Insurance Co.; Chicago Title; D & N Savings Bank; Cowgern Miller Mortgage Co.; Federal National Mortgage Assn.; Department of Housing & Urban Development; Waterfield Mortgage Co.

For full biographical listings, see the Martindale-Hubbell Law Directory

VARNUM, RIDDERING, SCHMIDT & HOWLETT LLP (AV)

A Limited Liability Partnership including Professional Corporations
Bridgewater Place, P.O. Box 352, 49501-0352
Telephone: 616-336-6000
800-262-0011
Facsimile: 616-336-7000
Telex: 1561593 VARN
Email: varnum@vrsh.com
Lansing, Michigan Office: The Victor Center, Suite 810, 210 North Washington Square, 48933.
Telephone: 517-482-6237.
Facsimile: 517-482-6937.
Kalamazoo, Michigan Office: 350 East Michigan Avenue, 49007.
Telephone: 616-382-2300.
Facsimile: 616-382-2382.
Grand Haven, Michigan Office: 321 Washington Street, P.O. Box 288, 49417.
Telephone: 616-846-7100.
Facsimile: 616-846-7101.
Battle Creek, Michigan Office: 4950 West Dickman Road, Suite B-1, 49015.
Telephone: 616-962-7144.
Bingham Farms, Michigan Office: 31600 Telegraph Road, Suite 230, 48025.
Telephone: 810-594-7330.
Facsimile: 810-594- 7331.

MEMBERS OF FIRM

Hilary F. Snell	Dirk Hoffius
John C. Carlyle (Resident at	Fredric A. Sytsma
Grand Haven Office)	Marilyn A. Lankfer
Thomas T. Huff (Resident at	Jeffrey W. Beswick (Resident at
Kalamazoo Office)	Grand Haven Office)

OF COUNSEL
Gordon B. Boozer

ASSOCIATES

Thomas G. Kyros	Pamela J. Tyler

For Complete List of Firm Personnel, See General Section

For full biographical listings, see the Martindale-Hubbell Law Directory

WHEELER UPHAM, A PROFESSIONAL CORPORATION (AV)

Second Floor, Trust Building, 40 Pearl Street, N.W., 49503-3001
Telephone: 616-459-7100
Fax: 616-459-6366

(See Next Column)

Gordon B. Wheeler (1904-1986)	William H. Heritage, Jr.
Buford A. Upham (Retired)	Kenneth E. Tiews
Robert H. Gillette	Jack L. Hoffman
Geoffrey L. Gillis	Janet C. Baxter
John M. Roels	Peter Kladder, III
Gary A. Maximiuk	James M. Shade
Timothy J. Orlebeke	Thomas A. Kuiper

References: A List will be available upon request.

For full biographical listings, see the Martindale-Hubbell Law Directory

---

GROSSE POINTE, Wayne Co.

MARCO, WATKINS AND OWSIANY (AV)

20180 Mack Avenue, 48236
Telephone: 313-882-8800
Fax: 313-882-6211

MEMBERS OF FIRM

Paul Marco	Robert D. Watkins
	Michael J. Owsiany

OF COUNSEL
William E. Kennedy

For full biographical listings, see the Martindale-Hubbell Law Directory

---

GROSSE POINTE WOODS, Wayne Co.

JON B. GANDELOT, P.C. (AV)

19251 Mack Avenue, 48236
Telephone: 313-885-9100
Facsimile: 313-885-9152

Jon B. Gandelot

For full biographical listings, see the Martindale-Hubbell Law Directory

---

HARBOR SPRINGS, Emmet Co.

RAMER AND MOORE (AV)

One Spring Street Square, P.O. Box 5, 49740
Telephone: 616-526-6214
Fax: 616-526-9343

MEMBERS OF FIRM

James T. Ramer	Joel B. Moore

Representative Clients: City of Harbor Springs; Roaring Brook Assn.; Forest Beach Assn.; Birchwood Farms Property Owners Assn.; Pride Hunters & Jumpers, Inc.; Black Forest Farm.

For full biographical listings, see the Martindale-Hubbell Law Directory

---

HOLLAND, Ottawa Co.

CUNNINGHAM DALMAN, P.C. (AV)

321 Settlers Road, P.O. Box 1767, 49422-1767
Telephone: 616-392-1821
Fax: 616-392-4769

Gordon H. Cunningham	Kenneth B. Breese
Ronald L. Dalman	Jeffrey K. Helder
Max R. Murphy	Ronald J. Vander Veen
James A. Bidol	David M. Zessin
Andrew J. Mulder	Mark H. Zietlow
Joel G. Bouwens	James W. Bouwens
	Randall S. Schipper

Susan E. Vroegop	Melinda M. Abney

OF COUNSEL

Vernon D. Ten Cate	Kenneth B. Peirce, Jr.

Representative Clients: FMB-First Michigan Bank; First of America Bank-Holland, N.A.; Ottawa Savings Bank; City of Holland; Auto Club Insurance Assn. (AAA); American States Insurance Co.; Holland Economic Development Corp.; Hope College; Western Theological Seminary.
Reference: FMB-First Michigan Bank.

For full biographical listings, see the Martindale-Hubbell Law Directory

---

*KALAMAZOO,** Kalamazoo Co.

DeMENT AND MARQUARDT, P.L.C. (AV)

407 West Michigan Avenue, 49007
Telephone: 616-343-2106
Fax: 616-343-2107

Daniel L. DeMent	Michele C. Marquardt
	Catherine Contos Metzler

For full biographical listings, see the Martindale-Hubbell Law Directory

DIETRICH, ZODY, HOWARD & VANDERROEST, P.C. (AV)

834 King Highway, Suite 110, 49001
Telephone: 616-344-9236
Fax: 616-344-0412

(See Next Column)

DIETRICH, ZODY, HOWARD & VANDERROEST, P.C., *Kalamazoo—Continued*

G. Philip Dietrich   James W. Smith
Richard J. Howard   James E. VanderRoest
Philip W. Dietrich
OF COUNSEL
Brenda Wheeler Zody

For full biographical listings, see the Martindale-Hubbell Law Directory

---

EARLY, LENNON, PETERS & CROCKER, P.C. (AV)

900 Comerica Building, 49007-4752
Telephone: 616-381-8844
Fax: 616-349-8525

George H. Lennon, III   Gordon C. Miller
Robert M. Taylor

Attorneys for: General Motors Corp.; Wal-Mart Stores; Borgess Medical Center; Aetna Insurance: Kemper Group; Medical Protective Co.; Zurich Insurance; AAA; Liberty Mutual; Home Insurance.

For Complete List of Firm Personnel, See General Section

For full biographical listings, see the Martindale-Hubbell Law Directory

---

KREIS, ENDERLE, CALLANDER & HUDGINS, A PROFESSIONAL CORPORATION (AV)

One Moorsbridge, P.O. Box 4010, 49003-4010
Telephone: 616-324-3000
Telecopier: 616-324-3010
Email: kech@sapien.net *URL:* http://www.kech.com

Russell A. Kreis   Robert B. Borsos
C. Reid Hudgins III   Daniel P. McGlinn
Janice Roark Peters

For Complete List of Firm Personnel, See General Section

For full biographical listings, see the Martindale-Hubbell Law Directory

---

LEWIS & ALLEN, P.C. (AV)

Old Kent Bank Building, Suite 800, 136 East Michigan
Avenue, 49007-3946
Telephone: 616-388-7600
Fax: 616-349-3831

Dean S. Lewis   William A. Redmond
W. Fred Allen, Jr.   Stephen M. Denenfeld
Winfield J. Hollander   Gregory G. St. Arnauld
Bruce W. Martin   Anne McGregor Fries
Daniel L. Conklin   Thomas P. Lewis
Christopher T. Haenicke
LEGAL SUPPORT PERSONNEL
Dorothy B. Kelly

For full biographical listings, see the Martindale-Hubbell Law Directory

---

MILLER, CANFIELD, PADDOCK AND STONE, P.L.C. (AV)

A Professional Limited Liability Company
Founded in 1852 by Sidney Davy Miller
444 West Michigan Avenue, 49007-3752
Telephone: 616-381-7030
Fax: 616-382-0244
Detroit, Michigan Office: 150 West Jefferson, Suite 2500, 48226-4415.
Telephone: 313-963-6420.
Fax: 313-496-7500.
Cable Address: "Stem Detroit."
Ann Arbor, Michigan Office: 101 North Main Street, 7th Floor, 48104-1400.
Telephone: 313-663-2445.
Fax: 313-747-7147.
Bloomfield Hills, Michigan Office: Suite 100, Pinehurst Office Center, 1400 North Woodward, 48303-2014.
Telephone: 313-645-5000.
Fax: 313-645-1917.
Grand Rapids, Michigan Office: 1200 Campau Square Plaza, 99 Monroe, N.W., 49503-2639.
Telephone: 616-454-8656.
Fax: 616-776-6322.
Howell, Michigan Office: 121 South Barnard Street, Suite 4, 48843-2305.
Telephone: 517-546-7600.
Telecopier: 517-546-6974.
Lansing, Michigan Office: One Michigan Avenue, Suite 900, 48933-1609.
Telephone: 517-487-2070.
Fax: 517-374-6304.
Monroe, Michigan Office: The Executive Centre, 214 East Elm Avenue, 48161-2682.
Telephone: 313-243-2000.
Fax: 313-243-0901.

(See Next Column)

Washington, D.C. Office: 1225 Nineteenth Street, N.W., Suite 400. 20036.
Telephone: 202-429-5575; 785-0600.
Fax: 202-331-1118; 785-1234.
Pensacola, Florida Office: 25 West Cedar, 32501.
Telephone: 904-469-1088.
Fax: 904-432-0677.
St. Petersburg, Florida Office: 100 Second Avenue S., Suite 7045, 33701.
Telephone: 813-982-6000.
Fax: 813-892-6002.
New York, New York Office: Eleventh Floor, 135 East 57th Street, 10022-2087.
Telephone: 212-754-5400.
Fax: 212-754-5401.
Gdansk, Poland Office: Suite 322, Dom Technika Building, UI. Rajska 6, 80-850.
Telephone: 011-485-831-2808.
Fax: 011-485-831-4719.
Warsaw, Poland Office: UI. Marszalkowska 82, Suite 561, 00-517.
Telephone: 011-482-623-6457 and 6458.
Fax: 011-482-623-6459.

PRINCIPALS OF FIRM
Eric V. Brown, Jr.   John A. Campbell
OF COUNSEL
Gerard Thomas
SENIOR ATTORNEY
John G. VanSlambrouck

Representative Firm Clients: Chrysler Corporation; Comerica, Incorporated; City of Detroit, Michigan; Detroit Tigers, Inc.; First of Michigan; Ford Motor Company; Ford Motor Credit Company; Great Lakes Bancorp; Henry Ford Hospital; INVETECH Company.

For Complete List of Firm Personnel, See General Section

For full biographical listings, see the Martindale-Hubbell Law Directory

---

LANSING, Ingham Co.

FOSTER, SWIFT, COLLINS & SMITH, P.C. (AV)

313 South Washington Square, 48933-2193
Telephone: 517-371-8100
Telecopier: 517-371-8200
URL: http://www.fosterswift.com
Farmington Hills, Michigan Office: 32300 Northwestern Highway, Suite 230.
Telephone: 810-539-9900.
Fax: 810-851-7504.

Allan J. Claypool   Louis K. Nigg
Charles A. Janssen   Patricia A. Calore
Douglas A. Mielock
LEGAL SUPPORT PERSONNEL
LEGAL ASSISTANTS
Sandra L. De Santis   Kelly A. LaGrave, CLA

General Counsel for: First American Bank-Central; Story, Inc.; Michigan Milk Producers Assn.; Edward W. Sparrow Hospital; St. Lawrence Hospital; Demmer Corp.; Michigan Financial Corp.
Local Counsel for: Shell Oil Co.; Michigan-Mutual Insurance Co.; Century Telephone.

For Complete List of Firm Personnel, See General Section

For full biographical listings, see the Martindale-Hubbell Law Directory

---

FRASER TREBILCOCK DAVIS & FOSTER, P.C. (AV)

1000 Michigan National Tower, 48933
Telephone: 517-482-5800
Fax: 517-482-0887

Joe C. Foster, Jr.   Richard C. Lowe
Everett R. Zack   Nancy L. Little
Sharon A. Bruner

Counsel for: Bank One, East Lansing; Comerica Bank; First of America Bank-Central; Michigan National Bank; Old Kent Bank.

For Complete List of Firm Personnel, See General Section

For full biographical listings, see the Martindale-Hubbell Law Directory

---

MILLER, CANFIELD, PADDOCK AND STONE, P.L.C. (AV)

A Professional Limited Liability Company
Founded in 1852 by Sidney Davy Miller
Suite 900, One Michigan Avenue, 48933-1609
Telephone: 517-487-2070
Fax: 517-374-6304
Detroit, Michigan Office: 150 West Jefferson, Suite 2500, 48226-4415.
Telephone: 313-963-6420.
Fax: 313-496-7500.
Cable Address: "Stem Detroit."

(See Next Column)

MILLER, CANFIELD, PADDOCK AND STONE P.L.C.—*Continued*

Ann Arbor, Michigan Office: 101 North Main Street, 7th Floor, 48104-1400.
Telephone: 313-663-2445.
Fax: 313-747-7147.
Bloomfield Hills, Michigan Office: Suite 100, Pinehurst Office Center, 1400 North Woodward, 48303-2014.
Telephone: 313-645-5000.
Fax: 313-645-1917.
Grand Rapids, Michigan Office: 1200 Campau Square Plaza, 99 Monroe, N.W., 49503-2639.
Telephone: 616-454-8656.
Fax: 616-776-6322.
Howell, Michigan Office: 121 South Barnard Street, Suite 4, 48843-2305.
Telephone: 517-546-7600.
Telecopier: 517-546-6974.
Kalamazoo, Michigan Office: 444 West Michigan Avenue, 49007-3752.
Telephone: 616-381-7030.
Fax: 616-382-0244.
Monroe, Michigan Office: The Executive Centre, 214 East Elm Avenue, 48161-2682.
Telephone: 313-243-2000.
Fax: 313-243-0901.
Washington, D.C. Office: 1225 Nineteenth Street, N.W., Suite 400. 20036.
Telephone: 202-429-5575; 785-0600.
Fax: 202-331-1118; 785-1234.
Pensacola, Florida Office: 25 West Cedar, 32501.
Telephone: 904-469-1088.
Fax: 904-432-0677.
St. Petersburg Office: 100 Second Avenue S., Suite 7045, 33701.
Telephone: 813-982-6000.
Fax: 813-892-6002.
New York, New York Office: Eleventh Floor, 135 East 57th Street, 10022-2087.
Telephone: 212-754-5400.
Fax: 212-754-5401.
Gdansk, Poland Office: Suite 322, Dom Technika Building, UI. Rajska 6, 80-850.
Telephone: 011-485-831-2808.
Fax: 011-485-831-4719.
Warsaw, Poland Office: UI. Marszalkowska 82, Suite 561, 00-517.
Telephone: 011-482-623-6457 and 6458.
Fax: 011-482-623-6459.

PRINCIPALS OF FIRM
Michael R. Atkins (Resident)

Representative Firm Clients: Chrysler Corporation; Comerica, Incorporated; City of Detroit, Michigan; Detroit Tigers, Inc.; First of Michigan; Ford Motor Company; Ford Motor Credit Company; Great Lakes Bancorp; Henry Ford Hospital; INVETECH Company.

For Complete List of Firm Personnel, See General Section

For full biographical listings, see the Martindale-Hubbell Law Directory

---

LIVONIA, Wayne Co.

FRIED & ASSOCIATES, P.C. (AV)

32900 5 Mile Road, Suite 4, 48154
Telephone: 313-421-5055
Fax: 313-421-5591

William C. Fried

For full biographical listings, see the Martindale-Hubbell Law Directory

---

MIDLAND, * Midland Co.

RIECKER, VAN DAM, BARKER, BLACK & ZUBER, P.C. (AV)

414 Townsend Street, P.O. Box 632, 48640
Telephone: 517-631-1025
Facsimile: 517-631-9880

Philip Van Dam   Richard William Barker
R. Drummond Black

General Counsel for: Herbert H. and Grace A. Dow Foundation; Harry A. and Margaret D. Towsley Foundation; Midland Center for the Arts; Dow-Howell-Gilmore Associates, Inc.
Counsel for: Comerica Bank N.A.; Mid Michigan Regional Health System; Wolverine Bank, F.B.S.; Northern Star Companies; Midland County Growth and Economic Development Corp.; Bresnan Communications, Inc.

For Complete List of Firm Personnel, See General Section

For full biographical listings, see the Martindale-Hubbell Law Directory

---

MONROE, * Monroe Co.

BRAUNLICH, RUSSOW & BRAUNLICH, A PROFESSIONAL CORPORATION (AV)

111 South Macomb Street, 48161
Telephone: 313-241-8300
Fax: 313-241-7715

(See Next Column)

William J. Braunlich, Jr.   Thomas P. Russow
(1924-1992)   William H. Braunlich

Philip A. Costello   Marie C. Kennedy
Patricia M. Poupard   Susan J. Mehregan
Ann L. Nickel   Robert Wetzel
Michael G. Roehrig

LEGAL SUPPORT PERSONNEL
Ruth G. Flint

Representative Clients: State Farm Mutual Insurance Co.; Auto Club Insurance Assn.; Farm Bureau Insurance Co.; Home Mutual Insurance Co.; Cincinnati Insurance Co.; Board of Road Commissioners, Monroe County; Port of Monroe; Monroe County Community College; City of Luna Pier; City of Petersburg.

For full biographical listings, see the Martindale-Hubbell Law Directory

---

PONTIAC, * Oakland Co.

BOOTH PATTERSON, P.C. (AV)

1090 West Huron Street, 48328
Telephone: 810-681-1200
Fax: 810-681-1754

Douglas W. Booth (1918-1992)   David J. Lee
Calvin E. Patterson (1913-1987)   Allan T. Motzny
Parvin C. Lee, Jr.   Michael J. Hughes
J. Timothy Patterson   Michael D. Bishop
Eric S. Meier

For full biographical listings, see the Martindale-Hubbell Law Directory

---

SAGINAW, * Saginaw Co.

BRAUN KENDRICK FINKBEINER PLC (AV)

101 N. Washington Suite 812, 48607-1297
Telephone: 517-753-3461
Telecopier: 517-753-3951
URL: http://www.bkf-law.com
Bay City, Michigan Office: 201 Phoenix Building, P.O. Box 2039.
Telephone: 517-895-8505.
Telecopier: 517-895-8437.
Ann Arbor, Michigan Office: 700 First National Building.
Telephone: 313-995-4100.
Telecopier: 313-995-4798.

James V. Finkbeiner   Hugo E. Braun, Jr.
Thomas R. Luplow
OF COUNSEL
J. Richard Kendrick

Representative Clients: The Dow Chemical Co.; General Motors Corp.; Lobdell Emery Manufacturing Co.; Merrill, Lynch, Inc.; Saginaw General Hospital; Saginaw News; The Wickes Foundation.

For Complete List of Firm Personnel, See General Section

For full biographical listings, see the Martindale-Hubbell Law Directory

---

ST. JOSEPH, * Berrien Co.

BUTZBAUGH & DEWANE, P.L.C. (AV)

Law and Title Building, 811 Ship Street, P.O. Box 27, 49085
Telephone: 616-983-0191
Fax: 616-983-5078
Email: b__d__law@parrett.net

MEMBERS OF FIRM
Alfred M. Butzbaugh   Michael J. Roberts

Representative Clients: SJS Federal Savings Bank; American Society of Agricultural Engineers; Whirlpool Corp.; Transamerica Insurance Group; Automobile Club Insurance Assn.; Imperial Printing Co.

For Complete List of Firm Personnel, See General Section

For full biographical listings, see the Martindale-Hubbell Law Directory

---

FISHER LAW OFFICE (AV)

Law & Title Building, 811 Ship Street, P.O. Box 83, 49085-0083
Telephone: 616-983-5511
Telecopier: 616-893-5571

Vance A. Fisher

For full biographical listings, see the Martindale-Hubbell Law Directory

---

GLOBENSKY, GLEISS, BITTNER & HYRNS, P.C. (AV)

610 Ship Street, P.O. Box 290, 49085
Telephone: 616-983-0551
Fax: 616-983-5858

(See Next Column)

GLOBENSKY, GLEISS, BITTNER & HYRNS P.C., *St. Joseph—Continued*

H. S. Gray (1867-1961)	Rodger V. Bittner
Luman H. Gray (1902-1952)	Randy S. Hyrns
John L. Globensky	J. Joseph Daly
Henry W. Gleiss	Charles T. LaSata
James J. Riemland	

General Counsel for: Shoreline Bank; Hanson Cold Storage Co.; Pearson Construction Co., Inc.
Approved Attorneys for: Lawyers Title Insurance Corp.
Reference: Shoreline Bank of Benton Harbor.

For full biographical listings, see the Martindale-Hubbell Law Directory

---

TROFF, PETZKE & AMMESON (AV)

Law and Title Building, 811 Ship Street, P.O. Box 67, 49085
Telephone: 616-983-0161
Facsimile: 616-983-0166

MEMBERS OF FIRM

Theodore E. Troff	Roger A. Petzke
Charles F. Ammeson	

ASSOCIATES

Bennett S. Schwartz	Daniel G. Lambrecht
Deborah L. Berecz	

For full biographical listings, see the Martindale-Hubbell Law Directory

---

SOUTHFIELD, Oakland Co.

DE VINE & KOHN (AV)

29800 Telegraph Road, 48034
Telephone: 810-353-6500
Fax: 810-353-2514

Clifford J. De Vine	Sheldon B. Kohn

For full biographical listings, see the Martindale-Hubbell Law Directory

---

LAWRENCE M. ELKUS (AV)

3000 Town Center, Suite 2990, 48075
Telephone: 810-358-5300
Fax: 810-355-5608

For full biographical listings, see the Martindale-Hubbell Law Directory

---

ROBERT B. LABE, P.C. (AV)

2000 Town Center, Suite 1780, 48075
Telephone: 810-354-3100
Telecopier: 810-354-3926

Robert B. Labe	Heather Andrews Healy

Reference: Comercia Bank, N.A.; Dean Witter.

For full biographical listings, see the Martindale-Hubbell Law Directory

---

MADDIN, HAUSER, WARTELL, ROTH, HELLER & PESSES, P.C. (AV)

Third Floor Essex Center, 28400 Northwestern Highway, P.O. Box 215, 48037
Telephone: 810-354-4030, 355-5200
Telefax: 810-354-1422

Milton M. Maddin (1902-1984)	Robert D. Kaplow
Michael W. Maddin	William E. Sigler
Mark R. Hauser	Stewart C. W. Weiner
C. Robert Wartell	Charles M. Lax
Richard J. Maddin	Stuart M. Bordman
Richard F. Roth	Steven D. Sallen
Harvey R. Heller	Joseph M. Fazio
Ian D. Pesses	Gregory J. Gamalski
Michael S. Leib	Julie Chenot Mayer

Nathaniel H. Simpson	Lowell D. Salesin
Ronald A. Sollish	Marc J. Mendelson
Mark H. Fink	Joseph W. Girardot
Steven M. Wolock	Lori E. Talsky

OF COUNSEL

Joel D. Kellman

Reference: Comerica Bank.

For full biographical listings, see the Martindale-Hubbell Law Directory

---

MASON, STEINHARDT, JACOBS & PERLMAN, PROFESSIONAL CORPORATION (AV)

Suite 1500, 4000 Town Center, 48075-1415
Telephone: 810-358-2090
Fax: 810-358-3599

(See Next Column)

Gordon I. Ginsberg	Jerome P. Pesick
Irving I. Boigon	Robert G. Schuch (1943-1995)
Jack Schon	Richard A. Polk
Walter B. Mason, Jr.	Jay W. Tower
Frederick D. Steinhardt	Jonathan B. Frank
John E. Jacobs	Neil S. Silver
Michael B. Perlman	L. Jeffrey Zauberman

Diane Flagg Goldstein	H. Adam Cohen
David E. Nykanen	

OF COUNSEL

Erwin B. Ellmann	Marvin C. Daitch
Randolph J. Friedman	John M. Roche

Representative Clients: Citibank, N.A.; City of Dearborn; DeMattia Development Co.; Forest City Enterprises; Michigan Wholesale Drug Assn.; Mortgage Bankers Association of Michigan; Nationwide Insurance Co.; City of Taylor; Union Labor Life Insurance Co.; Yellow Freight Systems, Inc.

For full biographical listings, see the Martindale-Hubbell Law Directory

---

MAY AND MAY, PROFESSIONAL CORPORATION (AV)

3000 Town Center, Suite 2600, 48075
Telephone: 810-358-3800
Fax: 810-358-1627
Detroit, Michigan Office: 5510 Woodward Avenue.
Telephone: 810-358-3800.

Alan A. May

Lawrence G. Snyder	Laura M. Kystad
Penny L. Deitch	

For full biographical listings, see the Martindale-Hubbell Law Directory

---

PROVIZER, LICHTENSTEIN & PHILLIPS, P.C. (AV)

4000 Town Center, Suite 1800, 48075
Telephone: 810-352-9080
Facsimile: 810-352-1491

Harold M. Provizer	Marilyn A. Madorsky
David S. Lichtenstein	William J. Selinsky
Randall E. Phillips	Robert I. Brown

For full biographical listings, see the Martindale-Hubbell Law Directory

---

SOMMERS, SCHWARTZ, SILVER & SCHWARTZ, P.C. (AV)

2000 Town Center, Suite 900, 48075
Telephone: 810-355-0300
Telecopier: 810-746-4001
Plymouth, Michigan Office: 747 South Main Street.
Telephone: 313-455-4250.

Victor A. Coen	Tracy L. Allen
Scott C. Hess	

OF COUNSEL

Paul Groffsky	H. Rollin Allen

General Counsel for: City of Taylor; Foodland Distributors; C.A. Muer Corporation; Vlasic & Company; Nederlander Corporation; Midwest Health Centers, P.C.
Representative Clients: Crum & Forster Insurance Company; City of Pontiac; Michigan National Bank.

For Complete List of Firm Personnel, See General Section

For full biographical listings, see the Martindale-Hubbell Law Directory

---

TAWAS CITY,* Iosco Co.

LAW OFFICES OF MYLES AND TYLER (AV)

502 Lake Street, 48764-0518
Telephone: 517-362-4405
Telefax: 517-362-7840

Kenneth J. Myles	Ronald R. Tyler

For full biographical listings, see the Martindale-Hubbell Law Directory

---

TRAVERSE CITY,* Grand Traverse Co.

RUNNING, WISE, WILSON, FORD AND PHILLIPS, P.L.C. (AV)

326 State Street, P.O. Box 686, 49684
Telephone: 616-946-2700
Tele-Fax: 616-946-0857

Harry T. Running (Deceased)	William L. Wise (Retired)

MEMBERS OF FIRM

Patrick J. Wilson	James C. Adams
Richard W. Ford	Sandra P. Howard
Thomas J. Phillips	Kent E. Gerberding

ASSOCIATES

Shelley A. Kester	Bradley L. Putney

(See Next Column)

RUNNING, WISE, WILSON, FORD AND PHILLIPS P.L.C.—*Continued*
OF COUNSEL

J. Bruce Donaldson　　　　　　　Douglas J. Donaldson

For full biographical listings, see the Martindale-Hubbell Law Directory

---

TROY, Oakland Co.

BOOKHOLDER, BASSETT, GORNBEIN & COHEN, P.L.L.C. (AV)

Long Lake Crossings, 1301 West Long Lake Road, Suite 355, 48098
Telephone: 810-641-0100
Fax: 810-641-0109

Ronald M. Bookholder　　　　　Henry S. Gornbein
Scott Bassett　　　　　　　　　Susan E. Cohen

For full biographical listings, see the Martindale-Hubbell Law Directory

---

GRASSI & TOERING, P.L.C. (AV)

888 West Big Beaver, Suite 750, 48084
Telephone: 810-269-2020
Fax: 810-269-2025

Sebastian V. Grassi, Jr.　　　　　Douglas L. Toering

For full biographical listings, see the Martindale-Hubbell Law Directory

---

HOLAHAN, MALLOY, MAYBAUGH & MONNICH (AV)

Suite 100, 2690 Crooks Road, 48084-4700
Telephone: 810-362-4747
Fax: 810-362-4779
East Tawas, Michigan Office: 910 East Bay Street.
Telephone: 517-362-4747.
Fax: 517-362-7331.

MEMBERS OF FIRM

J. Michael Malloy, III　　　　　David L. Delie, Jr.
James D. Maybaugh　　　　　　William J. Kliffel
John R. Monnich　　　　　　　Ingrid Rosvold Kliffel

OF COUNSEL

Thomas H. O'Connor　　　　　Maureen Holahan (Retired;
　　　　　　　　　　　　　　　　Resident, East Tawas Office)

Representative Clients: Johnson & Higgens; Employers Reinsurance; Chubb Companies; American States Insurance Co.; Travelers Insurance; Pontiac Osteopathic Hospital; Michigan Health Care Corporation.

For full biographical listings, see the Martindale-Hubbell Law Directory

---

KEYWELL AND ROSENFELD (AV)

Suite 600, 2301 West Big Beaver Road, 48084
Telephone: 810-649-3200
Fax: 810-649-0454

MEMBERS OF FIRM

Gary A. Goldberg　　　　　　Lucy R. Benham
Norman E. Greenfield　　　　　Kelly M. Hayes
　　　　　Jeffrey B. Levine

ASSOCIATES

Robert A. Gross　　　　　　　David M. Elkin

Reference: National Bank of Detroit.

For full biographical listings, see the Martindale-Hubbell Law Directory

---

YPSILANTI, Washtenaw Co.

PEAR SPERLING EGGAN & MUSKOVITZ, P.C. (AV)

5 South Washington Street, 48197
Telephone: 313-483-3626
Fax: 313-483-1107
Ann Arbor, Michigan Office: Domino's Farms, 24 Frank Lloyd Wright Drive.
Telephone: 313-665-4441
Other Ypsilanti, Michigan Office: 2164 Bellevue at Washtenaw.
Telephone: 313-483-7177.

Lawrence W. Sperling　　　　　Thomas E. Daniels
Andrew M. Eggan　　　　　　　Helen Conklin Vick

Counsel for: Domino's Pizza, Inc.; Citizens Banking Corp.; Townsend and Bottum, Inc.; The Credit Bureau of Ypsilanti; City of Ypsilanti (Labor Counsel); Michigan Municipal Worker's Compensation; Self-Insurance Fund.
Approved Attorneys for: Lawyers Title Insurance Corp.

For full biographical listings, see the Martindale-Hubbell Law Directory

PRODUCT LIABILITY LAW

ALABAMA

ALEXANDER CITY, Tallapoosa Co.

MORRIS, HAYNES, INGRAM & HORNSBY (AV)

131 Main Street, P.O. Box 1660, 35011-1660
Telephone: 205-329-2000
Fax: 205-329-2015

Larry W. Morris	Kenneth F. Ingram, Jr.
Randall Stark Haynes	Clay Hornsby

OF COUNSEL

John F. Dillon, IV	Jennie Lee Kelley

Representative Clients: First National Bank; City of Alexander City; Town of Wadley; Russell Corp.
Approved Attorneys for: Lawyers Title Insurance Corp.; Mississippi Valley Title Insurance Co.

For full biographical listings, see the Martindale-Hubbell Law Directory

---

*BIRMINGHAM,** Jefferson Co.

BRADLEY, ARANT, ROSE & WHITE (AV)

2001 Park Place, Suite 1400, P.O. Box 830709, 35283-0709
Telephone: 205-521-8000
Facsimile: 205-252-0264
Facsimile (SouthTrust Tower Office): 205-251-9915
URL: http://www.BARW.COM
Huntsville, Alabama Office: 200 Clinton Avenue West, Suite 900, 35801.
Telephone: 205-517-5100.
Facsimile: 205-533-5069.

MEMBERS OF FIRM

Hobart A. McWhorter, Jr.	John D. Watson, III
Thad Gladden Long	Michael D. McKibben
Gary C. Huckaby	David Glenn Hymer
(Resident, Huntsville Office)	Sid J. Trant
Brittin Turner Coleman	Stewart M. Cox
Walter J. Sears, III	Philip J. Carroll III
	T. Michael Brown

ASSOCIATES

Denise Avery Dodson	James Tassin
John W. Smith T	(Resident, Huntsville Office)
	Charles K. Hamilton

For Complete List of Firm Personnel, See General Section

For full biographical listings, see the Martindale-Hubbell Law Directory

---

HARE, WYNN, NEWELL AND NEWTON (AV)

A Partnership including Professional Corporations
Suite 800 Massey Building, 290 21st Street North, 35203
Telephone: 205-328-5330
FAX: 205-324-2165

MEMBERS OF FIRM

Francis H. Hare (1904-1983)	John W. Haley (P.C.)
Carlton T. Wynn	D. Leon Ashford (P.C.)
Neal C. Newell	Scott A. Powell
Alex W. Newton	James R. Pratt, III
Terrell Wynn, Jr.	S. Shay Samples
James J. Thompson, Jr.	Bruce J. McKee
Alva C. Caine	Michael D. Ermert
Ray O. Noojin, Jr., (P.C.)	Robert R. Riley, Jr.
	Nolan Edward Awbrey

COUNSEL

Francis H. Hare, Jr., (P.C.)	James O. Haley
	James K. Baker

References: AmSouth Bank of Birmingham; First Commercial Bank of Birmingham.

For full biographical listings, see the Martindale-Hubbell Law Directory

---

HOGAN, SMITH & ALSPAUGH, P.C. (AV)

2323 Second Avenue, North, 35203
Telephone: 205-324-5635
Telecopier: 205-324-5637

William W. Smith	Ronald R. Crook
M. Clay Alspaugh	Richard D. Stratton
R. Benjamin Hogan, III	Pamela D. Beard
David R. Donaldson	Jack Lee Roberts, Jr.
David J. Guin	Benjamin E. Baker, Jr.

Reference: First Alabama Bank.

For full biographical listings, see the Martindale-Hubbell Law Directory

---

DAVID CROMWELL JOHNSON (AV)

The Land Title Building, Suite 200, 600 20th Street, North, 35203
Telephone: 205-327-5223

ASSOCIATES

J. Flint Liddon	Barry R. Tuggle

For full biographical listings, see the Martindale-Hubbell Law Directory

---

LONDON & YANCEY (AV)

1000 Park Place Tower, 2001 Park Place, 35203
Telephone: 205-251-2531
FAX: 205-251-8929

MEMBERS OF FIRM

Alex T. London (1847-1908)	Thomas R. Elliott, Jr.
John London (1848-1935)	Bert S. Nettles
George W. Yancey (1883-1962)	Richard W. Lewis

ASSOCIATES

Allen R. Trippeer, Jr.	Laura Ellison Proctor
Mark David Hess	Paige Elliott-Pinson
Lisa Wright Borden	F. Daniel Wood, Jr.
A. David Fawal	C. Dennis Hughes
	Michael J. Velezis

OF COUNSEL

Robert W. Norris

Representative Clients: State of Alabama; Cincinnati Ins. Co.; Lloyd's of London; Blue Cross/Blue Shield; Attorney's Mutual of Alabama; State Farm; CIGNA; Royal Ins. Co. of America; Paul Revere Ins. Co.; Chubb Group.

For full biographical listings, see the Martindale-Hubbell Law Directory

---

PARSONS, LEE & JULIANO, P.C. (AV)

2200 AmSouth/Harbert Plaza, 1901 Sixth Avenue, North, P.O. Box 371088, 35237-1088
Telephone: 205-326-6600
Fax: 205-324-7097

Robert E. Parsons	David A. Lee
Jasper P. Juliano	John M. Bergquist
Marcus W. Lee	Paul J. DeMarco
Marda W. Sydnor	Deborah Ann Payne
	Tracy Toussaint

OF COUNSEL

Dorothy A. Powell

For full biographical listings, see the Martindale-Hubbell Law Directory

---

PITTMAN, HOOKS, DUTTON & HOLLIS, P.C. (AV)

1100 Park Place Tower, 35203
Telephone: 205-322-8880
Telecopier: 205-328-2711

W. Lee Pittman	L. Andrew Hollis, Jr.
Kenneth W. Hooks	Jeffrey C. Kirby
Tom Dutton	Ralph Bohanan, Jr.
	Nat Bryan

Chris T. Hellums	Emily H. Nelson
Adam P. Morel	John Robert Potter

OF COUNSEL

James H. Davis	Myra B. Staggs
(Not admitted in AL)	

For full biographical listings, see the Martindale-Hubbell Law Directory

---

PORTERFIELD, HARPER & MILLS, P.A. (AV)

22 Inverness Center Parkway, Suite 600, P.O. Box 530790, 35253-0790
Telephone: 205-980-5000
Fax: 205-980-5001

Jack B. Porterfield, Jr.	Philip F. Hutcheson
Larry W. Harper	H. C. "Trey" Ireland, III
William T. Mills, II	Keith J. Pflaum
William Dudley Motlow, Jr.	Michael L. Haggard

Stephen Douglas Christie	Don L. Hall
Timothy W. Knight	W. Perry Webb
Mark E. King	Stephen Christopher Still
Karen Walker Casey	Eric Daniel Hoaglund
Kristin Daniels Horn	Michael Robert Lunsford

Representative Clients: CIGNA; St. Paul Insurance Co.; The Travelers; Figge International; White Consolidated Industries; Terex Corp.; Wausau Insurance; Baptist Health Systems, Inc.; Bruno's, Inc.; Harley Davidson, Inc.

For full biographical listings, see the Martindale-Hubbell Law Directory

---

SMITH, SPIRES & PEDDY (AV)

650 Financial Center, 505 North Twentieth Street, 35203-2662
Telephone: 205-251-5885

(See Next Column)

SMITH, SPIRES & PEDDY, *Birmingham—Continued*

Paul G. Smith	Michael B. Walls
Thomas S. Spires	Todd Hamilton
A. Joe Peddy	Scott M. Roberts

ASSOCIATES

Thomas Coleman, Jr.	Alan B. Lasseter
D. Gregory Dunagan	Reed R. Bates
David A. Hughes	

Representative Clients: Banker's & Shippers Insurance Co.; Alfa Insurance Co.; United States Fidelity & Guaranty Insurance Co.; R & D Trucking, Inc.; Racetrac Petroleum, Inc.; Transport South Inc.; Old Dominion Freight Line, Inc.; American States Insurance Co.; Trinity Industries, Inc.; Penn General.

For full biographical listings, see the Martindale-Hubbell Law Directory

STARNES & ATCHISON (AV)

100 Brookwood Place, P.O. Box 598512, 35259-8512
Telephone: 205-868-6000
Telecopier: 205-868-6099

MEMBERS OF FIRM

Stancil R. Starnes (1922-1983)	J. Bentley Owens, III
W. Stancil Starnes	Walter William Bates
W. Michael Atchison	Michael K. Wright
William Anthony Davis, III	Michael K. Beard
Michael A. Florie	Robert P. Mackenzie, III
L. Graves Stiff, III	Allan R. Wheeler
Carol A. Smith	Jeffrey E. Friedman
Randal H. Sellers	Laura Howard Peck
E. Martin Bloom	Thomas Lawson Selden
Mark Christopher Eagan	

ASSOCIATES

Sybil Vogtle Abbot	J. David Michaels
Steven T. McMeekin	Arthur Clair Brunson, III
Sharon A. Woodard	P. Thomas Dazzio, Jr.
Joe L. Leak	Kenneth Davis Graves
Joseph S. Miller	Elizabeth S. Webb
Scott M. Salter	Rik S. Tozzi
Jeannie Bugg Walston	Brenen Gene Ely
Ashley E. Watkins	Christopher John Zulanas

For full biographical listings, see the Martindale-Hubbell Law Directory

CHATOM,* Washington Co.

TURNER, ONDERDONK, KIMBROUGH & HOWELL, P.A. (AV)

100 Central Avenue, P.O. Drawer 1389, 36518
Telephone: 334-847-2237
Fax: 334-847-3115
Mobile, Alabama Office: 1359 Dauphin Street.
Telephone: 334-432-2855.
Fax: 334-432-2863.

Edward P. Turner, Jr.	Gordon K. Howell
A. Michael Onderdonk	Marc E. Bradley
William A. Kimbrough, Jr.	(Resident, Mobile Office)
(Resident, Mobile Office)	

Halron W. Turner	David M. Huggins
Frank Woodson	(Resident, Mobile Office)
(Resident, Mobile Office)	E. Tatum Turner

For full biographical listings, see the Martindale-Hubbell Law Directory

DECATUR,* Morgan Co.

HARRIS, CADDELL & SHANKS, P.C. (AV)

214 Johnston Street, S.E., P.O. Box 2688, 35602-2688
Telephone: 205-340-8000
Telecopier: 205-340-8040

Julian Harris (1904-1994)	Thomas A. Caddell
Norman W. Harris (P.C.)	William E. Shinn, Jr.
(Retired)	Gary A. Phillips
Philip T. Shanks (Retired)	Dow M. Perry, Jr.
Charles L. Murphree (Retired)	Barnes F. Lovelace, Jr.
John A. Caddell (P.A.)	Arthur W. Orr
Robert H. Harris	J. Noel King
Jon H. Moores	Jeffrey S. Brown

Attorneys for: The Industrial Development Board of the City of Decatur, Alabama; Amoco Chemical Co.; General Electric Co.; South Central Bell Telephone Co.; Trico Steel Co.; Auto-Owners Insurance Co.; ALFA Insurance Cos.; American General Life & Accident Insurance Co.; U.S.F. & G. Co.

For full biographical listings, see the Martindale-Hubbell Law Directory

DOTHAN,* Houston Co.

LEE & McINISH (AV)

238 West Main Street, P.O. Box 1665, 36302
Telephone: 334-792-4156
Facsimile: 334-794-8342

MEMBERS OF FIRM

W. L. Lee (1873-1944)	William C. Carn, III
Alto V. Lee, III (1915-1987)	Peter A. McInish
William L. Lee, III	Jerry M. White
Alan C. Livingston	William L. Lee, IV

OF COUNSEL
H. Dwight McInish

Counsel for: Seaboard Coast Line Railroad Co.; Atlanta & St. Andrews Bay Railroad Co.; ALFA; U. S. F. & G. Co.; Maryland Casualty Co.; Continental Insurance Cos.; Royal-Globe Group; Slocomb National Bank; The Federal Land Bank of Jackson; GTE South.

For full biographical listings, see the Martindale-Hubbell Law Directory

FLORENCE,* Lauderdale Co.

JONES & TROUSDALE (AV)

115 Helton Court, Suite B, P.O. Box 367, 35631-0367
Telephone: 205-767-0333
Telefax: 205-767-0331

MEMBERS OF FIRM

Robert E. Jones, III	Preston S. Trousdale, Jr.

A. DeLoach Stewart

For full biographical listings, see the Martindale-Hubbell Law Directory

GADSDEN,* Etowah Co.

SIMMONS, BRUNSON AND SASSER, ATTORNEYS, P.A. (AV)

1411 Rainbow Drive, P.O. Box 1189, 35902
Telephone: 205-546-9206
Telecopier: 205-546-8091

Clarence Simmons, Jr.	Steve P. Brunson
	James T. Sasser

Rebecca A. Walker	Jeff George Underwood
Jeffrey A. Brown	Scott C. Lloyd
	(Not admitted in AL)

Attorneys for: Preferred Risk Mutual Insurance Co.; ALFA Mutual Insurance Co.; Royal Insurance Cos.
Approved Attorneys for: Lawyers Title Insurance Corp.; Mississippi Valley Title Insurance Co.

For full biographical listings, see the Martindale-Hubbell Law Directory

HUNTSVILLE,* Madison Co.

HORNSBY, WATSON & MEGINNISS (AV)

1110 Gleneagles Drive, 35801
Telephone: 205-650-5500
Fax: 205-650-5504

Ralph W. Hornsby	David H. Meginniss
S. A. "Bud" Watson, Jr.	Ralph W. Hornsby, Jr.

For full biographical listings, see the Martindale-Hubbell Law Directory

MORRIS, CLOUD AND CONCHIN, P.C. (AV)

521 Madison Street, P.O. Box 248, 35804
Telephone: 205-534-0065
Fax: 205-539-0741

Harvey B. Morris (P.C.)	Joseph M. Cloud
	Gary V. Conchin

Maureen "Mike" K. Cooper	Daniel B. Banks, Jr.

For full biographical listings, see the Martindale-Hubbell Law Directory

MOBILE,* Mobile Co.

BROWN, HUDGENS, P.C. (AV)

1495 University Boulevard, P.O. Box 16818, 36616-0818
Telephone: 334-344-7744
Fax: 334-343-9629

Alton R. Brown, Jr.	Vincent A. Noletto, Jr.
A. Neil Hudgens	William H. Sisson
Philip H. Partridge	R. Alan Alexander
Andrew L. Smith	Weyman W. McCranie, Jr.
David Scott Wright	Thomas N. Nolan, Jr.
James P. Green	Craig W. Goolsby

(See Next Column)

BROWN, HUDGENS P.C.—*Continued*

OF COUNSEL
Robert P. Denniston

D. Gavin Austill (1958-1989)	Winston R. Grow
Timothy A. Clarke	A. Edwin Stuardi, III

Representative Client: CNA Insurance Group.

For full biographical listings, see the Martindale-Hubbell Law Directory

BURNS, CUNNINGHAM & MACKEY, P.C. (AV)

50 St. Emanuel Street, P.O. Box 1583, 36633
Telephone: 334-432-0612

Peter F. Burns	Peter S. Mackey
William M. Cunningham, Jr.	Gary W. Fillingim

For full biographical listings, see the Martindale-Hubbell Law Directory

CUNNINGHAM, BOUNDS, YANCE, CROWDER & BROWN (AV)

1601 Dauphin Street, P.O. Box 66705, 36660
Telephone: 334-471-6191
Fax: 334-479-1031

Richard Bounds	Joseph M. Brown, Jr.
James A. Yance	Gregory B. Breedlove
John T. Crowder, Jr.	Andrew T. Citrin
Robert T. Cunningham, Jr.	Michael A. Worel

David G. Wirtes, Jr.	Mitchell K. Shelly
Toby D. Brown	Kelli Denise Taylor

OF COUNSEL
Robert T. Cunningham	Valentino D. B. Mazzia

References: First Alabama Bank; AmSouth Bank, N.A.

For full biographical listings, see the Martindale-Hubbell Law Directory

DIAMOND, HASSER & FROST (AV)

1325 Dauphin Street, P.O. Drawer 40600, 36640
Telephone: 334-432-3362
Fax: 334-432-3367

MEMBERS OF FIRM
Ross Diamond, Jr. (1919-1978)	James E. Hasser, Jr.
Ross M. Diamond, III	James H. Frost

References: First Alabama Bank, Mobile; AM South Bank, Mobile.

For full biographical listings, see the Martindale-Hubbell Law Directory

FINKBOHNER AND LAWLER, L.L.C. (AV)

169 Dauphin Street Suite 300, P.O. Box 3085, 36652
Telephone: 334-438-5871
Fax: 334-432-8052

MEMBERS OF FIRM
George W. Finkbohner, Jr.	George W. Finkbohner, III
John L. Lawler	Royce A. Ray, III

For full biographical listings, see the Martindale-Hubbell Law Directory

INGE, TWITTY & DUFFY (AV)

1410 First Alabama Bank Building, 56 St. Joseph Street, P.O. Box 1109, 36633
Telephone: 334-433-3200
Facsimile: 334-433-3444

MEMBERS OF FIRM
James J. Duffy, Jr.	James J. Duffy, III

Francis H. Inge (1902-1959)	Thos. E. Twitty (1901-1975)
Richard H. Inge (1912-1980)	

For full biographical listings, see the Martindale-Hubbell Law Directory

LYONS, PIPES & COOK, P.C. (AV)

2 North Royal Street, P.O. Box 2727, 36652-2727
Telephone: 334-432-4481
Cable Address: "Lysea"
Telecopier: 334-433-1820

Joseph H. Lyons (1874-1957)	John Patrick Courtney, III
Sam W. Pipes, III (1916-1982)	W. David Johnson, Jr.
Walter M. Cook (1915-1988)	Joseph J. Minus, Jr.
Wesley Pipes	Caroline C. McCarthy
Norton W. Brooker, Jr.	William E. Shreve, Jr.
Cooper C. Thurber	R. Mark Kirkpatrick
Marion A. Quina, Jr.	Kenneth A. Nixon
Thomas F. Garth	Daniel S. Cushing
Claude D. Boone	Allen E. Graham
Walter M. Cook, Jr.	Michael C. Niemeyer

(See Next Column)

John C. Bell	M. Lauren Lemmon
M. Warren Butler	J. Murphy McMillan, III
Christopher Lee George	S. Wesley Pipes, V

General Counsel: Inchcape Shipping Services.
Counsel: The Hertz Corp.; McKenzie Tank Lines, Inc.; SCNO Barge Lines, Inc.; Scott Paper Co.; Shell Oil Corp.
Trial Counsel: Aetna Life & Casualty Co.; Chubb Group of Insurance Companies.

For full biographical listings, see the Martindale-Hubbell Law Directory

MONTGOMERY,* Montgomery Co.

BEASLEY, WILSON, ALLEN, MAIN & CROW, P.C. (AV)

218 Commerce Street, P.O. Box 4160, 36104
Telephone: 334-269-2343
Fax: 334-269-2371
Mailing Address: P.O. Box 4160, 36103-4160

Jere Locke Beasley	Frank M. Wilson
	J. Greg Allen

Blaine C. Stevens	J. Cole Portis
	LaBarron Nelson Boone

For full biographical listings, see the Martindale-Hubbell Law Directory

TUSCALOOSA,* Tuscaloosa Co.

JOSEPH G. PIERCE (AV)

2207 River Road West Suite One, P.O. Box 20086, 35402-0086
Telephone: 205-759-1234
Fax: 205-758-0502

Representative Clients: Indian River Regional Mental Health Center; Deputy Sheriffs Association of Tuscaloosa County; Deputy Sheriffs Association of Mobile County; Greene Beverage Co.; Aliceville Manor Nursing Home.

For full biographical listings, see the Martindale-Hubbell Law Directory

ALASKA

ANCHORAGE,* Third Judicial District

DELANEY, WILES, HAYES, GERETY & ELLIS, INC. (AV)

1007 West Third Avenue, Suite 400, 99501
Telephone: 907-279-3581
Fax: 907-277-1331

Daniel A. Gerety	James B. Friderici
Clay A. Young	Howard A. Lazar
William E. Moseley	Donald C. Thomas
	Timothy J. Lamb

Representative Clients: Crown Equipment Corporation; Ingersoll Rand Co.; J. C. Penney Co.; Gerber Products Co.; Grove Worldwide; Honda Motor Co.; Shasta Industries; Powermatic Inc.; R. D. Werner Co., Inc.; General Motors Corporation.

For Complete List of Firm Personnel, See General Section

For full biographical listings, see the Martindale-Hubbell Law Directory

ARIZONA

PHOENIX,* Maricopa Co.

BEGAM, LEWIS, MARKS & WOLFE A PROFESSIONAL ASSOCIATION OF LAWYERS (AV)

111 West Monroe Street, Suite 1400, 85003-1787
Telephone: 602-254-6071
Fax: 602-252-0042

Robert G. Begam	Daniel J. Adelman
Frank Lewis	Lisa Kurtz
Stanley J. Marks	Dena Rosen Epstein
Elliot G. Wolfe	Steven M. Friedman
Kelly J. McDonald	Richard P. Traulsen

Reference: National Bank of Arizona.

For full biographical listings, see the Martindale-Hubbell Law Directory

BESS & DYSART, P.C. (AV)

7210 North 16th Street, 82020-5201
Telephone: 602-331-4600
Telecopier: 602-331-8600

(See Next Column)

Bess & Dysart P.C., *Phoenix—Continued*

Leon D. Bess   Timothy R. Hyland
Robert L. Dysart   William M. Demlong
Donald R. Kunz   Matthew D. Kleifield

Stephanie L. Chilton   Donald J. Sapala

For full biographical listings, see the Martindale-Hubbell Law Directory

BROWN & BAIN, A PROFESSIONAL ASSOCIATION (AV)

2901 North Central Avenue, P.O. Box 400, 85001-0400
Telephone: 602-351-8000
Telecopier: 602-351-8516
Palo Alto, California Affiliated Office: Brown & Bain, 1755 Embarcadero
Road, Suite 200.
Telephone: 415-856-9411.
Telecopier: 415-856-6061.
Tucson, Arizona Affiliated Office: Brown & Bain, A Professional
Association. One South Church Avenue, Nineteenth Floor, P.O. Box
2265.
Telephone: 602-798-7900.
Telecopier: 602-798-7945.

C. Randall Bain   Howard Ross Cabot
John A. Buttrick   Joel W. Nomkin

For Complete List of Firm Personnel, See General Section

For full biographical listings, see the Martindale-Hubbell Law Directory

BURCH & CRACCHIOLO, P.A. (AV)

702 East Osborn Road, Suite 200, 85014
Telephone: 602-274-7611
Fax: 602-234-0341
Mailing Address: P.O. Box 16882, Phoenix, AZ, 85011

Ian Neale   Linda A. Finnegan

Representative Clients: Bashas' Inc.; Farmers Insurance Group; U-Haul International, Inc.

For Complete List of Firm Personnel, See General Section

For full biographical listings, see the Martindale-Hubbell Law Directory

CRONIN & STANEWICH (AV)

One Columbus Plaza, 3636 North Central Avenue, Suite 560, 85012
Telephone: 602-222-4646
Fax: 602-222-4656

MEMBERS OF FIRM
Robert S. Cronin, Jr.   Robert B. Stanewich

For full biographical listings, see the Martindale-Hubbell Law Directory

GOLDSTEIN & McGRODER, LTD. A PROFESSIONAL CORPORATION (AV)

2200 East Camelback Road, Suite 221, 85016-3456
Telephone: 602-957-1500
Fax: 602-956-9294

Philip T. Goldstein   Patrick J. McGroder, III
            Suzanne P. Clarke

Jane E. Evans   Serena C. Montague
LEGAL SUPPORT PERSONNEL
Kevan S. DeWitt (Paralegal)

For full biographical listings, see the Martindale-Hubbell Law Directory

MICHAEL L. McALLISTER, LTD. (AV)

2025 North Third Street Suite 100, 85004
Telephone: 602-253-8840
Telefax: 602-253-5526

Michael L. McAllister

Representative Clients: Continental AG; Continental General Tire, Inc.; The
Dometic Corporation; Michelin North America, Inc.; Montecito Homes;
Sears, Roebuck and Co.; Sulzermedica USA, Inc.; Uniroyal Goodrich Tire
Company, Inc.; White Consolidated Industries, Inc.; Yokohama Tire Corporation.

For full biographical listings, see the Martindale-Hubbell Law Directory

MITTEN, GOODWIN & RAUP, A PROFESSIONAL CORPORATION (AV)

One Columbus Plaza, 3636 North Central, Suite 1200, 85012
Telephone: 602-650-2000
Fax: 602-264-7033
Email: mgr@starlink.com

(See Next Column)

Roger C. Mitten   Edward R. Glady, Jr.
Brian M. Goodwin   Stephen C. Yost
            Martin P. Clare

Steven P. Kramer   Sharon Elizabeth Ravenscroft

For full biographical listings, see the Martindale-Hubbell Law Directory

MUCHMORE & WALLWORK, A PROFESSIONAL CORPORATION (AV)

2700 North Central Avenue, Suite 1225, 85004-1165
Telephone: 602-240-6699
Data: 602-240-6698
Facsimile: 602-240-6697
Email: muchwork@mmww.com *URL:* http://www.mmww.com

Charles J. Muchmore   Nicholas J. Wallwork
            COUNSEL
Margaret M. Dean   Fredric D. Bellamy
            Kathy E. Shimpock

Bridget S. Bade   Carolina L. Carver
(Senior Associate)   Margaret Benny Hurst
LEGAL SUPPORT PERSONNEL
Gloria A. Torres (Administrator   Gale James (Finance Manager
and Senior Paralegal)   and Paralegal)
John A. Bennett
(Litigation Support Manager)

Representative Clients: AgrEvo USA Company; BHP Copper Inc.; City of
Scottsdale; Cyprus Amax Minerals Company; General Electric Co.; Homes
by Dave Brown, Inc.; National Indemnity Insurance Company; Standard
Insurance Company; Washington Mills Electro Minerals Company.
Reference: M & I Thunderbird Bank.

For full biographical listings, see the Martindale-Hubbell Law Directory

O'CONNOR, CAVANAGH, ANDERSON, KILLINGSWORTH & BESHEARS, A PROFESSIONAL ASSOCIATION (AV)

One East Camelback Road, Suite 1100, 85012-1656
Telephone: 602-263-2400
FAX: 602-263-2900
Email: firminfo@arizlaw.com
Sun City, Arizona Office: 13250 North Del Webb Boulevard, Suite B,
85351.
Telephone: 602-263-2808.
FAX: 602-933-3100.
Tucson, Arizona Office: O'Connor Cavanagh Molloy Jones, 33 N. Stone,
Suite 2100, 85701, P.O. Box 2268, 85702.
Telephone: 520-622-3531.
FAX: 520-624-2816.
Nogales, Arizona Office: 1891 North Mastick Way, 85621.
Telephone: 520-761-4215.
FAX: 520-761-3505.

Ralph E. Hunsaker   Carol N. Cure
George H. Mitchell   Scott A. Salmon
Richard J. Woods   David L. Kurtz
Steven D. Smith   Paul J. Giancola
            Lisa M. Sommer

Ashley D. Adams   Mark D. Dillon

Representative Clients: Fleetwood Enterprises; Johnson & Johnson; Abbott
Laboratories; Keller Industries; Black & Decker Corp.; Arizona Elevator,
Inc.

For Complete List of Firm Personnel, See General Section

For full biographical listings, see the Martindale-Hubbell Law Directory

QUARLES & BRADY (AV)

One Camelback Building, One East Camelback Road, Suite
  400, 85012-1649
Telephone: 602-230-5500
Fax: 602-230-5598
Milwaukee, Wisconsin Office: 411 East Wisconsin Avenue.
Telephone: 414-277-5000.
Fax: 414-271-3552.
Madison, Wisconsin Office: First Wisconsin Plaza, One South Pinckney
Street, P.O. Box 2113.
Telephone: 608-251-5000.
Fax: 608-251-9166.
West Palm Beach, Florida Office: 222 Lakeview Ave., 4th Floor.
Telephone: 407-653-5000.
Fax: 407-653-5333.
Naples, Florida Office: Barnett Center, 4501 Tamiami Trail North, Suite
300.
Telephone: 813-262-5959.
Fax: 813-434-4999.

MEMBER OF THE FIRM
William M. Shattuck

(See Next Column)

QUARLES & BRADY—*Continued*

ASSOCIATE

Colleen A. Scherkenbach

For Complete List of Firm Personnel, See General Section

For full biographical listings, see the Martindale-Hubbell Law Directory

---

RENAUD, COOK & DRURY, P.A. (AV)

617 North 2nd Avenue, 85003
Telephone: 602-253-5101
Fax: 602-254-1448
Email: rcdlaw@rcdlaw.com
Scottsdale, Arizona Office: 6991 East Camelback Road, #D-103, 85251.
Telephone: 602-874-9000.
Fax: 602-874-9866.

J. Gordon Cook	William W. Drury, Jr.
Charles A. Struble	

Wade R. Causey	Charles S. Hover, III
Richard N. Crenshaw	Diane Mihalsky
Tamara D. Nydell	

For full biographical listings, see the Martindale-Hubbell Law Directory

---

SNELL & WILMER, L.L.P. (AV)

One Arizona Center, 85004-0001
Telephone: 602-382-6000
Fax: 602-382-6070
Tucson, Arizona Office: 1500 Norwest Tower, One South Church Avenue 85701-1612.
Telephone: 520-882-1200.
Fax: 520-884-1294.
Orange County Office: 1920 Main Street, Suite 1200, P.O. Box 57062, Irvine, California, 92619-7062.
Telephone: 714-253-2700.
Fax: 714-955-2507.
Salt Lake City, Utah Office: Broadway Centre, 111 East Broadway, Suite 900, 84111-1004.
Telephone: 801-237-1900.
Fax: 801-237-1950.

MEMBERS OF FIRM

Warren E. Platt	Donald D. Colburn
Douglas W. Seitz	Vaughn A. Crawford
Arthur P. Greenfield	Suzanne McCann
Arthur T. Anderson	Richard W. Shapiro
Timothy G. O'Neill	Martha E. Gibbs
Steven S. Guy	Patrick X. Fowler
Bob J. McCullough	Prithviraj S. Sivananthan

SENIOR ATTORNEY

Bruce P. White

ASSOCIATES

Lon A. Burke	Timothy J. Casey
Joseph C. Kreamer	

Representative Clients: Arizona Public Service Co.; Bank One, Arizona, NA.; First Security Bank of Utah, N.A.; Ford Motor Co.; Chrysler Motors Corp.; Toyota Motor Sales U.S.A.; BHP Copper, Inc.; U.S. Home Corp.; Pinnacle West Capital Corp.; Safeway, Inc.

For Complete List of Firm Personnel, See General Section

For full biographical listings, see the Martindale-Hubbell Law Directory

---

KENNETH L. TUCKER, P.C. (AV)

1136 East Campbell, 85014
Telephone: 602-279-3660
Fax: 602-279-2162
Email: KTucker@futureone.com

Kenneth L. Tucker

Daniel P. J. Miller	Kevin J. Tucker

LEGAL SUPPORT PERSONNEL

Mary Toniazzo Moock (Paralegal)	Toni R. Hoffman (Paralegal)

For full biographical listings, see the Martindale-Hubbell Law Directory

---

SCOTTSDALE, Maricopa Co.

RALPH E. MAHOWALD A PROFESSIONAL ASSOCIATION (AV)

6750 East Camelback Road Suite #104, 85251
Telephone: 602-481-0500
Fax: 602-481-0555

Ralph E. Mahowald

For full biographical listings, see the Martindale-Hubbell Law Directory

---

TUCSON, * Pima Co.

BEAL, SCHMIDT & DYER, P.C. (AV)

Suite 6000, West Tower, 5255 East Williams Circle, 85711
Telephone: 520-790-5600
Fax: 520-790-1163

Robert L. Beal	James H. Dyer
Ted A. Schmidt	Gary JD Dean

For full biographical listings, see the Martindale-Hubbell Law Directory

---

HEALY LAW FIRM (AV)

Williams Centre, 5210 East Williams Circle Suite 730, 85711
Telephone: 520-790-1400

MEMBER OF FIRM

William T. Healy

References: Bank of America; Merrill Lynch.

For full biographical listings, see the Martindale-Hubbell Law Directory

---

KIMBLE, GOTHREAU & NELSON, P.C. (AV)

5285 East Williams Circle, Suite 3500, 85711-7411
Telephone: 520-748-2440
Fax: 520-748-2469

Michael J. Gothreau (1943-1990)	David F. Toone
Darwin J. Nelson	Michelle T. Lopez
Daryl A. Audilett	Negatu Molla
Lawrence McDonough	Michael E. Medina
Andrew J. Petersen	

OF COUNSEL

William Kimble

Representative Clients: State of Arizona; General Motors Corp.; Procter & Gamble Co.; St. Paul Fire and Marine Insurance Co.; City of Tucson; Tucson Electric Power Co.; United States Fidelity & Guaranty Co.; Coriegis Co.; Allstate Insurance Co.

For full biographical listings, see the Martindale-Hubbell Law Directory

---

O'CONNOR CAVANAGH MOLLOY JONES, A PROFESSIONAL ASSOCIATION (AV)

Suite 2100 33 N. Stone, P.O. Box 2268, 85702
Telephone: 520-622-3531
FAX: 520-624-2816
Email: firminfo@arizlaw.com
Phoenix, Arizona Office: O'Connor, Cavanagh, Anderson, Killingsworth & Beshears, One East Camelback Road, Suite 1100, 85012.
Telephone: 602-263-2400.
FAX: 602-263-2900.
Sun City, Arizona Office: O'Connor, Cavanagh, Anderson, Killingsworth & Beshears, 13250 North Del Webb Boulevard, Suite B, 85351.
Telephone: 602-263-2808.
FAX: 602-933-3100.
Nogales, Arizona Office: O'Connor, Cavanagh, Anderson, Killingsworth & Beshears, 1891 North Mastick Way, 85621.
Telephone: 520-761-4215.
FAX: 520-761-3505.

Peter Akmajian

Amy M. Samberg	James D. Campbell

Representative Clients: Three-Five Systems; Main Street & Main; ITT Cannon; Bank of America; The Dial Corp; The Hartford; Dow Corning Corp.; Charles Schwab & Co., Inc.

For Complete List of Firm Personnel, See General Section

For full biographical listings, see the Martindale-Hubbell Law Directory

---

RABINOVITZ & ASSOCIATES, P.C. (AV)

721 North 4th Avenue, P.O. Box 41600, 85717
Telephone: 520-624-5526
Toll Free: 1-800-365-0821
Fax: 520-622-3776

Bernard I. Rabinovitz

John D. Ellis

OF COUNSEL

Clark J. Sloan (Not admitted in AZ)

LEGAL SUPPORT PERSONNEL

Michael Nelson (Paralegal)	Lisa Busciglio (Paralegal)
Ruth Polizz	

Representative Client: Firemans Fund Insurance Co.

For full biographical listings, see the Martindale-Hubbell Law Directory

Tucson—Continued

STOMPOLY, STROUD, GIDDINGS & GLICKSMAN, P.C. (AV)

1820 Citibank Tower, One South Church Avenue, 85702
Telephone: 520-628-8300
Telefax: 520-628-9948
Mailing Address: P.O. Box 190, Tucson, AZ, 85702-0190

John G. Stompoly

For Complete List of Firm Personnel, See General Section

For full biographical listings, see the Martindale-Hubbell Law Directory

YUMA, * Yuma Co.

THE BRIAN E. SMITH LAW FIRM (AV)

The Brian Smith Building, 301 South 2nd Avenue, 85364
Telephone: 520-783-8811

Brian E. Smith	Frank A. Fila
William J. Kerekes	Thomas W. Anderson

LEGAL SUPPORT PERSONNEL
Bridget M. Hughes

Reference: Bank of America.

For full biographical listings, see the Martindale-Hubbell Law Directory

ARKANSAS

FAYETTEVILLE, * Washington Co.

DAVIS, COX & WRIGHT, PLC (AV)

19 East Mountain Street, P.O. Drawer 1688, 72702-1688
Telephone: 501-521-7600
Fax: 501-521-7661

Sidney P. Davis, Jr.	William Jackson Butt, II
Walter B. Cox	Kelly P. Carithers
Tilden P. Wright, III	Tim E. Howell
Constance G. Clark	Don A. Taylor

Paul H. Taylor

John G. Trice	Mark W. Dossett
Laura J. Andress	David L. McCune

For full biographical listings, see the Martindale-Hubbell Law Directory

FORT SMITH, * Sebastian Co.

GILBREATH LAW FIRM (AV)

7000 Rogers Avenue, 72903
Telephone: 501-452-1181
Fax: 501-452-8652
Email: attysatlaw@aol.com

E. C. Gilbreath	Daniel W. Gilbreath

For full biographical listings, see the Martindale-Hubbell Law Directory

SHAW, LEDBETTER, HORNBERGER, COGBILL & ARNOLD (AV)

South Seventh and Parker, P.O. Box 185, 72902-0185
Telephone: 501-782-7294
FAX: 501-782-1493

Bruce H. Shaw (1904-1990)	Richard B. Shaw (1927-1988)

MEMBERS OF FIRM

Charles R. Ledbetter	James A. Arnold, II
Robert E. Hornberger	Ronald D. Harrison
J. Michael Cogbill	E. Diane Graham

R. Ray Fulmer, II

ASSOCIATE
Rebecca D. Hattabaugh

OF COUNSEL
J. Michael Shaw

Representative Clients: General: First National Bank of Fort Smith; Bank of Mansfield; Commercial Bank at Alma; Mid-South Dredging Co.
Local Attorneys for: Liberty Mutual Insurance Co.; St Paul Insurance Cos.; Black & Decker Inc.; Overhead Door Corp.; Coltec Industries, Inc.; A.W. Chesterton Co..

For full biographical listings, see the Martindale-Hubbell Law Directory

LITTLE ROCK, * Pulaski Co.

ANDERSON & KILPATRICK (AV)

The First Commercial Building, 400 West Capitol Avenue, Suite 2640, 72201
Telephone: 501-372-1887
Fax: 501-372-7706
Email: ande@cei.net

MEMBERS OF FIRM

Overton S. Anderson, II	Michael E. Aud
Joseph E. Kilpatrick, Jr.	Randy P. Murphy

ASSOCIATE
Michael P. Vanderford

For full biographical listings, see the Martindale-Hubbell Law Directory

BARBER, McCASKILL, AMSLER, JONES & HALE, P.A. (AV)

2700 First Commercial Building, 400 West Capitol Avenue, 72201-3414
Telephone: 501-372-6175
Telecopier: 501-375-2802

Azro L. Barber (1885-1979)	Richard C. Kalkbrenner
Elbert A. Henry (1889-1966)	G. Spence Fricke
John B. Thurman (1912-1971)	Gail Ponder Gaines
Austin McCaskill, Sr.	Michael J. Emerson
Guy Amsler, Jr.	R. Kenny McCulloch
Glenn W. Jones	Tim A. Cheatham
Michael E. Hale	Joseph F. Kolb
John S. Cherry, Jr.	Scott Michael Strauss
Robert L. Henry, III	Derek J. Edwards
Micheal L. Alexander	Thomas E. Osment, Jr.
William H. Edwards, Jr.	Christopher Gomlicker

Attorneys for: Associated Aviation Underwriters; Canal Insurance Co.; Fireman's Fund Insurance Co.; General Motors Corp.; General Motors Acceptance Corp.; Hanover Insurance Co.; Home Insurance Co.; Royal Insurance; United States Fidelity & Guaranty Co.; Universal Underwriters Insurance Co.

For full biographical listings, see the Martindale-Hubbell Law Directory

GARY EUBANKS & ASSOCIATES, P.A. (AV)

708 West Second Street, 72201
Telephone: 501-372-0266

Gary L. Eubanks	Hugh F. Spinks

William Gary Holt	Jack D. Files
James G. Schulze	Jason Files
Herman W. Eubanks	Matthew Hartness

For full biographical listings, see the Martindale-Hubbell Law Directory

HUCKABAY, MUNSON, ROWLETT & TILLEY, P.A. (AV)

First Commercial Building, Suite 1900, 400 West Capitol, 72201
Telephone: 501-374-6535
Fax: 501-374-5906

Mike Huckabay	John E. Moore
Bruce E. Munson	Tim Boone
Beverly A. Rowlett	Rick Runnells
James W. Tilley	Sarah Ann Presson

Edward T. Oglesby

D. Michael Huckabay, Jr.	Elizabeth Fletcher Rogers
Carol Lockard Worley	Julia L. Busfield
Mark S. Breeding	Jane M. Yocum

Terry D. Dugger

Representative Clients: The B.F. Goodrich Co.; Federal Cartridge Co.; General Electric Co.; Hayes Wheels; Massey-Ferguson, Inc.; Varity Corp.; Morbark Industries; Sears Roebuck & Co.; U-Haul International.

For full biographical listings, see the Martindale-Hubbell Law Directory

ROSE LAW FIRM, A PROFESSIONAL ASSOCIATION (AV)

120 East Fourth Street, 72201
Telephone: 501-375-9131
Telecopy: 501-375-1309

Jerry C. Jones	Richard T. Donovan
David L. Williams	James H. Druff
James Hunter Birch	Amy Lee Stewart

COUNSEL
Phillip Carroll

Kathryn Bennett Perkins	Michael N. Shannon

Counsel for: ALLTEL Corporation; Aluminum Company of America; Bridgestone/Firestone, Inc.; The Equitable Life Assurance Society of The United States; General Motors Corp.; The Prudential Insurance Company of America; Stephens Group Inc.; Tyson Foods, Inc.

(See Next Column)

ROSE LAW FIRM A PROFESSIONAL ASSOCIATION—*Continued*

For Complete List of Firm Personnel, See General Section

For full biographical listings, see the Martindale-Hubbell Law Directory

---

TEXARKANA,* Miller Co.

DUNN, NUTTER, MORGAN & SHAW (AV)

State Line Plaza, Box 8030, 71854-5945
Telephone: 501-773-5651
Telecopier: 501-772-2037
Email: law@clover.cleaf.com

MEMBERS OF FIRM

Winford L. Dunn, Jr.	Nelson V. Shaw
R. Gary Nutter	R. David Freeze
	W. David Carter

LEGAL SUPPORT PERSONNEL

LEGAL ASSISTANTS

Myra Conaway Wells	Sonja L. Oliver

For Complete List of Firm Personnel, See General Section

For full biographical listings, see the Martindale-Hubbell Law Directory

---

WEST MEMPHIS, Crittenden Co.

RIEVES & MAYTON (AV)

304 East Broadway, P.O. Box 1359, 72303
Telephone: 501-735-3420
Telecopier: 501-735-4678

MEMBERS OF FIRM

Elton A. Rieves, Jr. (1909-1984)	Michael R. Mayton
Elton A. Rieves, III	Elton A. Rieves, IV
	Martin W. Bowen

ASSOCIATES

William Terrell Smith, Jr.	David S. Wilson, III

For full biographical listings, see the Martindale-Hubbell Law Directory

---

CALIFORNIA

ALAMO, Contra Costa Co.

LAW OFFICES OF DAVID M. BIRKA-WHITE (AV)

3240 Stone Valley Road West, Suite 102, 94507
Telephone: 510-838-2090
Facsimile: 510-820-5592

For full biographical listings, see the Martindale-Hubbell Law Directory

---

COSTA MESA, Orange Co.

ELY, FRITZ & HOGAN (AV)

3100 Bristol Street #200, 92626
Telephone: 714-556-1480
Telecopier: 714-556-2863

MEMBERS OF FIRM

Thomas W. Ely	Michael G. Hogan
James H. Fritz	Jerome D. Rybarczyk

Charles A. Correia	Ronald F. Templer
	Allen D. MacNeil

OF COUNSEL

Gerald W. Mouzis

For full biographical listings, see the Martindale-Hubbell Law Directory

---

EL SEGUNDO, Los Angeles Co.

McGARRY & LAUFENBERG (AV)

300 North Sepulveda Boulevard, Suite 2294, 90245
Telephone: 310-335-1780
Fax: 310-335-1790

MEMBERS OF FIRM

James J. McGarry	Jeffrey J. Laufenberg
	William Leamon Cummings

ASSOCIATES

Daniel D. Laufenberg	John E. Zegel

For full biographical listings, see the Martindale-Hubbell Law Directory

---

FRESNO,* Fresno Co.

MILES, SEARS & EANNI, A PROFESSIONAL CORPORATION (AV)

2844 Fresno Street, P.O. Box 1432, 93716
Telephone: 209-486-5200
Fax: 209-486-5240

Wm. M. Miles (1909-1991)	Richard C. Watters
Robert E. Sears (1918-1992)	Gerald J. Maglio
Carmen A. Eanni	William J. Seiler
	Douglas L. Gordon

For full biographical listings, see the Martindale-Hubbell Law Directory

STAMMER, McKNIGHT, BARNUM & BAILEY (AV)

2540 West Shaw Lane, Suite 110, P.O. Box 9789, 93794-9789
Telephone: 209-449-0571
Fax: 209-432-2619

W. H. Stammer (1891-1969)	Frank D. Maul
James K. Barnum (1918-1987)	Craig M. Mortensen
Dean A. Bailey (1924-1995)	Jerry D. Jones
Galen McKnight (1904-1991)	Michael P. Mallery
James N. Hays	M. Bruce Smith
Carey H. Johnson	Thomas J. Georgouses

ASSOCIATES

Steven R. Stoker	Bruce J. Berger
M. Jaqueline Yates	Celene M.E. Boggs

Representative Clients: Pacific Bell; Chevron, U.S.A.; Fresno Irrigation District; The Travelers Insurance Group; State Farm Insurance Cos.;
Reference: Bank of America National Trust & Savings Assn. (Fresno Main Office).

For full biographical listings, see the Martindale-Hubbell Law Directory

---

GLENDALE, Los Angeles Co.

THOMAS & PRICE (AV)

535 North Brand Boulevard, 7th Floor, 91203
Telephone: 213-387-4800; 818-500-4800
FAX: 818-500-4822
Ventura, California Office: 1655 Mesa Verde Avenue, Suite 230.
Telephone: 805-642-6255.
Fax: 805-642-4580.

MEMBERS OF FIRM

Michael Thomas	Craig R. Donahue
Bonnie R. Louis	Maureen F. Thomas

ASSOCIATES

John P. DeGomez	Christian E. Sanne
Timothy A. Hodge	Benjimin M. Brees
Linda B. Hurevitz	Janet L. Keuper
	Kevin M. McCormick

OF COUNSEL

Lawrence E. Price

For full biographical listings, see the Martindale-Hubbell Law Directory

---

IRVINE, Orange Co.

SNELL & WILMER, L.L.P. (AV)

1920 Main Street, Suite 1200, 92614
Telephone: 714-253-2700
FAX: 714-955-2507
URL: http://www.swlaw.com
Phoenix, Arizona Office: One Arizona Center, 85004-0001.
Telephone: 602-382-6000.
Fax: 602-382-6070.
Tucson, Arizona Office: Norwest Tower, Suite 1500, One South Church Avenue, 85701-1612.
Telephone: 520-882-1200.
Fax: 520-884-1294.
Salt Lake City, Utah Office: Broadway Centre, 111 East Broadway, Suite 900, 84111-1004.
Telephone: 801-237-1900.
Fax: 801-237-1950.

MEMBERS OF FIRM

Robert J. Gibson (Resident)	Gary A. Wolensky (Resident)
Arthur P. Greenfield	Randolph T. Moore
	Luke A. Torres (Resident)

ASSOCIATES

Alexander L. Conti	Ronald T. Labriola
Ellen L. Darling	Jeffrey Scott Marks
	Daniel S. Rodman

For Complete List of Firm Personnel, See General Section

For full biographical listings, see the Martindale-Hubbell Law Directory

LARKSPUR, Marin Co.

WEINBERG, HOFFMAN & CASEY (AV)

A Partnership including a Professional Corporation
900 Larkspur Landing Circle, Suite 155, 94939
Telephone: 415-461-9666
Fax: 415-461-9681

Ivan Weinberg   Joseph Hoffman
                A. Michael Casey
            OF COUNSEL
            Mark Ropers

For full biographical listings, see the Martindale-Hubbell Law Directory

---

LONG BEACH, Los Angeles Co.

FISHER & PORTER, A LAW CORPORATION (AV)

110 Pine Avenue, 11th Floor, P.O. Box 22686, 90801-5686
Telephone: 310-435-5626
Telex: 284549 FPKLAW UR
Fax: 310-432-5399

Gerald M. Fisher   Therese G. Groff
David S. Porter   Michael W. Lodwick
            George P. Hassapis
            OF COUNSEL
Stephen C. Klausen   Stephen Chace Bass
            Anthony P. Lombardo

Vicki L. Hassman   Michael J. McLaughlin
Linda A. Mancini   Sandra L. Gryder
            Kenneth F. Mattfeld

For full biographical listings, see the Martindale-Hubbell Law Directory

FORD, WALKER, HAGGERTY & BEHAR, PROFESSIONAL LAW CORPORATION (AV)

One World Trade Center, Twenty Seventh Floor, 90831
Telephone: 310-983-2500
Telecopier: 310-983-2555

G. Richard Ford   Donna Rogers Kirby
Timothy L. Walker   Tina Ivankovic Mangarpan
William C. Haggerty   Susan D. Berger
Jeffrey S. Behar   Joseph A. Heath
Mark Steven Hennings   Robert J. Chavez
            J. Michael McClure

Arthur W. Schultz   Theodore A. Clapp
Jon T. Moseley   Stanley L. Scarlett
Maxine J. Lebowitz   Scott A. Ritsema
Timothy P. McDonald   Michael Guy Martin
K. Michele Williams   Colleen A. Strong
Stephen Ward Moore   Thomas L. Gourde
James D. Savage   Patrick J. Stark
Todd D. Pearl   Shayne L. Wulterin
Patrick J. Gibbs   Charles D. Jarrell
James O. Miller   Charles J. Schmitt
David Huchel   Kyle A. Ostergrad
Robert Reisinger   Todd L. Kessler
            OF COUNSEL
            Theodore P. Shield, P.L.C.

For full biographical listings, see the Martindale-Hubbell Law Directory

STOLPMAN • KRISSMAN • ELBER • MANDEL & KATZMAN LLP (AV)

A Partnership including Professional Corporations
Nineteenth Floor, 111 West Ocean Boulevard, 90802-4649
Telephone: 310-435-8300
Telecopier: 310-435-8304
Los Angeles (Westwood) Office: Suite 1800, 10880 Wilshire Boulevard.
            MEMBERS OF FIRM
Thomas G. Stolpman (Inc.)   Joel Krissman
Leonard H. Mandel   Mary Nielsen Abbott
Bernard Katzman (Inc.)   Donna Silver
            Dennis M. Elber
            ASSOCIATES
Edwin Silver   Lynne Rasmussen
            Elaine Mandel

For full biographical listings, see the Martindale-Hubbell Law Directory

WILLIAMS WOOLLEY COGSWELL NAKAZAWA & RUSSELL (AV)

111 West Ocean Boulevard, Suite 2000, 90802-4614
Telephone: 310-495-6000
Telecopier: 310-435-1359; 310-435-6812
Telex: ITT: 4933872; WU: 984929
Email: wwlaw@msn.com
Rancho Santa Fe, California Office: P.O. Box 9120, 16236 San Dieguito Road, Building 3, Suite 3-15, 92067.
Telephone: 619-497-0284.
Fax: 619-759-9938.
Port Hueneme, California Office: 237 E. Hueneme Road, Suite A, 93041.
Telephone: 805-488-8560.
Fax: 805-488-7896.

            MEMBERS OF FIRM
Reed M. Williams   Alan Nakazawa
David E. R. Woolley   Blake W. Larkin
Forrest R. Cogswell   Thomas A. Russell
            ASSOCIATES
Todd A. Valdes   Thomas G. Walsh
            Richard J. Nikas

For full biographical listings, see the Martindale-Hubbell Law Directory

---

LOS ANGELES, * Los Angeles Co.

AGNEW & BRUSAVICH

(See Torrance)

BELCHER, HENZIE & BIEGENZAHN, A PROFESSIONAL CORPORATION (AV)

333 South Hope Street, Suite 3650, 90071-1479
Telephone: 213-624-8293
Telecopier: 213-895-6082

Frank B. Belcher (1891-1979)   E. Lee Horton
David Bernard (1931-1978)   William T. DelHagen
John S. Curtis   Julia Azrael

Jeffrey L. Horwith   James C. Hildebrand
Georgette Renata Herget   Robert S. Cooper
David L. Bonar   Wun-ee Chelsea Chen
Raymond E. Hane, III   John Erin McOsker
            Mary E. Gram
            OF COUNSEL
George M. Henzie   Leo J. Biegenzahn
            James M. Derr

Reference: Bank of America (Los Angeles Main Office).

For full biographical listings, see the Martindale-Hubbell Law Directory

MATTHEW B. F. BIREN & ASSOCIATES (AV)

815 Moraga Drive, 90049-1633
Telephone: 310-476-3031; 381-5609
FAX: 310-471-3165
Email: mbfba@primenet.com

Marc J. Katzman   Debra J. Tauger
            Edmont T. Barrett

Reference: First Los Angeles Bank (Century City, Los Angeles, Branch).

For full biographical listings, see the Martindale-Hubbell Law Directory

CLARK & TREVITHICK, A PROFESSIONAL CORPORATION (AV)

800 Wilshire Boulevard, 12th Floor, 90017
Telephone: 213-629-5700
Telecopier: 213-624-9441
San Francisco, California Office: 456 Montgomery Street, 20th Floor.
Telephone: 415-288-6520.
Fax: 415-398-2820.

Philip W. Bartenetti   Leonard Brazil
Dolores Cordell   Arturo Santana Jr.
Vincent Tricarico   Kerry T. Ryan

References: Wells Fargo Bank (Los Angeles Main Office); National Bank of California.

For Complete List of Firm Personnel, See General Section

For full biographical listings, see the Martindale-Hubbell Law Directory

GIRARDI AND KEESE (AV)

1126 Wilshire Boulevard, 90017-1904
Telephone: 213-977-0211
FAX: 213-481-1554
San Bernardino, California Office: 596 North Arrowhead.
Telephone: 714-381-1551.
FAX: 714-381-2566.

(See Next Column)

GIRARDI AND KEESE—*Continued*

MEMBERS OF FIRM

Thomas V. Girardi	V. Andre Rekte (Resident, San
Robert M. Keese	Bernardino Office)
John A. Girardi	John K. Courtney
James B. Kropff	Amy Fisch Solomon
Robert W. Finnerty	Thomas C. Morgan
James G. O'Callahan	David N. Bigelow
	Carrie J. Rognlien

References: Wells Fargo Bank (Los Angeles Head Office); Bank of Industry.

For full biographical listings, see the Martindale-Hubbell Law Directory

GORDON, EDELSTEIN, KREPACK, GRANT, FELTON & GOLDSTEIN (AV)

A Partnership including a Professional Corporation
Suite 1800, 3580 Wilshire Boulevard, 90010
Telephone: 213-739-7000
Fax: 213-386-1671

Roger L. Gordon	Richard I. Felton
Mark Edelstein	Irwin L. Goldstein (A
Howard D. Krepack	Professional Corporation)
Sherry E. Grant	Steven J. Kleifield

ASSOCIATES

Joshua M. Merliss	David A. Goldstein
	Eugenia L. Steele

For full biographical listings, see the Martindale-Hubbell Law Directory

HARNEY LAW OFFICES A LEGAL CORPORATION (AV)

Suite 1300 Figueroa Plaza, 201 North Figueroa Street, 90012-2636
Telephone: 213-482-0881
Fax: 213-250-4042

David M. Harney	Andrew J. Nocas
David T. Harney	Vincent McGowan
Julie A. Harney	Thomas A. Schultz

Reference: Bank of America.

For full biographical listings, see the Martindale-Hubbell Law Directory

HORNBERGER & CRISWELL (AV)

444 South Flower, 31st Floor, 90071
Telephone: 213-488-1655
Facsimile: 213-488-1255
Email: kbranch0@counsel.com

MEMBERS OF FIRM

Nicholas W. Hornberger	Ann M. Ghazarians
Leslie E. Criswell	Michael A. Brewer
	Scott Alan Freedman

ASSOCIATES

Marlin E. Howes	James M. Slominski
Christopher T. Olsen	Michael C. Denlinger
Scott B. Cloud	Gayle L. Eskridge

OF COUNSEL

David E. Bower	William P. Driscoll

For full biographical listings, see the Martindale-Hubbell Law Directory

IVERSON, YOAKUM, PAPIANO & HATCH (AV)

One Wilshire Building, 27th Floor 624 South Grand Avenue, 90017
Telephone: 213-624-7444
Telecopier: 213 629-4563

Paul E. Iverson (1907-1975)	Frank B. Yoakum, Jr.
	(1906-1991)

MEMBERS OF FIRM

Patrick M. Mc Adam	Arnold D. Larson
	John M. Garrick

ASSOCIATES

Douglas C. Pease	Melissa A. Immel
Andrew K. Doty	Mary P. Lightfoot

OF COUNSEL

R. Noel Hatch

Representative Clients: Lockheed Corp.; International Paper; Bridgestone/-Firestone, Inc.
Reference: Security Pacific National Bank (Los Angeles Head Office).

For Complete List of Firm Personnel, See General Section

For full biographical listings, see the Martindale-Hubbell Law Directory

KERN, STREETER & GONZALEZ (AV)

601 West 5th Street, Suite 1100, 90071
Telephone: 213-629-8100
Facsimile: 213-627-8765

(See Next Column)

MEMBERS OF FIRM

René J. Kern, Jr.	John W. Streeter
	Michael D. Gonzalez

ASSOCIATES

Tina L. Gentile	Angela J. Armitage
Claudia T. Beightol	Christina L. Young

Representative Clients: Bridgestone/Firestone, Inc.; Hamada of America; Hasbro, Inc.; Honda Motor Co., Ltd.

For full biographical listings, see the Martindale-Hubbell Law Directory

KOSLOV & MEDLEN (AV)

30141 Agoura Road, Suite 200, 91301-4334
Telephone: 818-597-9996
FAX: 818-597-8848

MEMBERS OF FIRM

John Koslov	William P. Medlen

ASSOCIATE

Sabrina Simmons-Brill

For full biographical listings, see the Martindale-Hubbell Law Directory

KUSSMAN & WHITEHILL (AV)

A Partnership including a Professional Corporation
Suite 1470, 10866 Wilshire Boulevard, 90024
Telephone: 310-474-4411
Fax: 310-474-6530

Russell S. Kussman (A	Michael H. Whitehill
Professional Corporation)	

Steven G. Mehta

For full biographical listings, see the Martindale-Hubbell Law Directory

LANE POWELL SPEARS LUBERSKY LLP (AV)

A Partnership including Professional Corporations
333 South Hope Street, Suite 2400, 90071
Telephone: 213-680-1010
FAX: 213-680-1784
Other Offices at: Seattle, Washington; Portland, Oregon; Anchorage, Alaska; San Francisco, California; Olympia and Mount Vernon, Washington; Fairbanks, Alaska; London, England.

MEMBERS OF FIRM

Allan M. Bower	Ruth D. Kahn
John J. Geary, Jr.	Matthew P. Kesner
Kathryn R. Janssen	Lawrence P. Riff
Laurence F. Janssen	Carolyn J. Shields

ASSOCIATE

Daniel R. Blakey

Chevron Corp.; Exxon Company, U.S.A.; Shell Oil Co.; Monsanto Co.; Ashland Chemical Co.; Unocal Corp.; Texaco, Inc.; Mobil Oil Corp.; ARCO Chemical Co.; The Dow Chemical Co.

For full biographical listings, see the Martindale-Hubbell Law Directory

LEBOVITS & DAVID, A PROFESSIONAL CORPORATION (AV)

Suite 3100, Two Century Plaza, 2049 Century Park East, 90067
Telephone: 310-277-0200
Fax: 310-552-1028

Moses Lebovits	Deborah A. David

OF COUNSEL

Joseph J. M. Lange

Reference: Imperial Bank (Main Office - Beverly Hills).

For full biographical listings, see the Martindale-Hubbell Law Directory

ROBERT L. LUTY A PROFESSIONAL CORPORATION (AV)

Suite 303, 11661 San Vicente Boulevard, 90049
Telephone: 310-207-4342
Fax: 310-207-5035

Robert L. Luty

Reference: Brentwood Savings Bank (Brentwood Branch).

For full biographical listings, see the Martindale-Hubbell Law Directory

PETER J. MCNULTY (AV)

827 Moraga Drive (Bel Air), 90049
Telephone: 310-471-2707
Fax: 310-472-7014
Gilroy, California Office: Suite F-2, 8352 Church Street.
Telephone: 408-848-5900.
Fax: 408-848-1391.
Aurora, Illinois Office: 8 East Galena Street.

(See Next Column)

PETER J. McNULTY, *Los Angeles—Continued*

ASSOCIATES

Michael L. Oran (A Professional Corporation)

OF COUNSEL

John A. Alvarez
(Resident, Gilroy Office)
Robert M. Foote
(Not admitted in CA)

Robert P. Friedman
Carl A. McMahan

Reference: City National Bank (Beverly Hills, California).

For full biographical listings, see the Martindale-Hubbell Law Directory

PIERRY & MOORHEAD, LLP (AV)

A Partnership including a Professional Corporation
301 North Avalon Boulevard, 90744-5888
Telephone: 310-834-2691, 213-775-8348, 714-636-2970
FAX: 310-518-5814

MEMBERS OF FIRM

Thomas J. Pierry, Sr.

Michael D. Moorhead (P.C.)

James M. McAdams
F. Joseph Ford, Jr.
Robert W. Ford

F. Javier Trujillo
Thomas J. Pierry, III
Joseph P. Pierry

For full biographical listings, see the Martindale-Hubbell Law Directory

RADCLIFF, FRANDSEN & DONGELL (AV)

40th Floor, 777 South Figueroa Street, 90017
Telephone: 213-614-1990
Facsimile: 213-489-9263
San Francisco, California Office: 88 Kearny Street, Suite 1475.
Telephone: 415-399-8393.
Facsimile: 415-989-5465.
Rome, Italy Office: Via Tacito, 7.
Telephone: (39) 06-323-5588.
Facsimile: (39) 06-324-3392.

MEMBERS OF FIRM

Jules G. Radcliff, Jr.

Russell Mackay Frandsen

Richard A. Dongell

OF COUNSEL

Tal Clifton Finney

ASSOCIATES

Francis P. Aspessi
Ruben A. Castellon
William W. Funderburk, Jr.
Jeffrey A. Gagliardi
David K. Lee
Maria Anna Mancini

Jeffrey C. Mayes
Marisa A. Moret
Daniel E. Park
Scott D. Pinsky
Eric H. Saiki
Steve R. Segura

Glenn M. White

For full biographical listings, see the Martindale-Hubbell Law Directory

ROBIE & MATTHAI, A PROFESSIONAL CORPORATION (AV)

Biltmore Tower, 500 South Grand, Suite 1500, 90071
Telephone: 213-624-3062
Fax: 213-624-2563

James R. Robie
Edith R. Matthai
Michael J. O'Neill

Kyle Kveton
Maria Louise Cousineau
Pamela E. Dunn

Craig W. Brunet
Kim W. Sellars
Teresa J. Friederichs
Bernadine J. Stolar
Claudia Sokol

Karen R. Palmersheim
Brian D. Huben
Wendy L. Schneider
Natalie A. Kouyoumdjian
Gabrielle M. Jackson

Representative Clients: State Farm Fire & Casualty Co.; The Travelers; Fireman's Fund Ins. Co.; Lawyers Mutual Ins. Co.; Carrier Corp.
Reference: First Professional Bank.

For full biographical listings, see the Martindale-Hubbell Law Directory

SCHELL & DELAMER, LLP (AV)

A Partnership including Professional Corporations
865 South Figueroa Street Suite 2750, 90017
Telephone: 213-622-8181
Fax: 213-627-5252
Thousand Oaks, California Office: 100 East Thousand Oaks Boulevard, Suite 142.
Telephone: 805-496-9533.
Fax: 805-496-3424.

(See Next Column)

Gerald F. H. Delamer
(1892-1955)
Walter O. Schell (1895-1981)
Roland R. Kaspar (Professional Corporation)
Katherine B. Pene

Garrin James Shaw (Professional Corporation)
Robert S. Hamrick (Professional Corporation)
Jeffrey F. Briskin

ASSOCIATES

Candace E. Ahrens Kallberg
Denise A. Nardi
Randy A. Berg
Kenneth S. Markson
Joseph P. Sepikas
Gregory J. Amantia (Resident at Thousand Oaks Office)

John J. Latzanich, II. (Resident at Thousand Oaks Office)
Lori M. Levine
Sylvia Havens
Roman Y. Nykolyshyn

Representative Clients: Hartford Insurance Group; Liberty Mutual Group; Travelers Insurance Co.
References: Los Angeles: First Interstate Bank; Merrill-Lynch.

For full biographical listings, see the Martindale-Hubbell Law Directory

WOLF, RIFKIN & SHAPIRO, LLP (AV)

A Partnership including a Professional Corporation
11400 West Olympic Boulevard Ninth Floor, 90064-1565
Telephone: 310-478-4100
FAX: 310-479-1422

MEMBERS OF FIRM

Michael Wolf (A Professional Corporation)
Daniel C. Shapiro
Roy G. Rifkin
Michael T. Schulman
Leslie Steven Marks

Allan M. Rosenthal
Mindy Sheps
Norman S. Wisnicki
Barry T. Mitidiere
Marc E. Rohatiner
Charles H. Baren

Michael W. Rabkin

ASSOCIATES

Andrew S. Gelb
Matthew L. Grode
Matthew Fladell
Steven A. Silver
Mark J. Rosenbaum
Kelly Marie Allegra

Richard S. Grant
Karin E. Freeman
Lori A. Van Oosterhout
Paul W. Windust
Daniel Ng
Laura S. Blint

OF COUNSEL

Gerald Lloyd Friedman

Jeffrey R. Liebster

Denise M. Parga

For full biographical listings, see the Martindale-Hubbell Law Directory

MENLO PARK, San Mateo Co.

DYER & WHITE (AV)

Suite 200, 800 Oak Grove Avenue, 94025
Telephone: 415-325-7000
Fax: 415-325-3116

MEMBERS OF FIRM

Charles A. Dyer

Rand N. White

For full biographical listings, see the Martindale-Hubbell Law Directory

O'REILLY & COLLINS, A PROFESSIONAL CORPORATION (AV)

2500 Sand Hill Road, Suite 201, 94025
Telephone: 415-854-7700
Fax: 415-854-8350

Terry O'Reilly

James P. Collins

James P. Tessier

Michael Danko

For full biographical listings, see the Martindale-Hubbell Law Directory

NEWPORT BEACH, Orange Co.

KELEGIAN & THOMAS (AV)

4685 MacArthur Court, Suite 400, 92660
Telephone: 714-553-1200
Fax: 714-553-1013
Email: KelThomLaw@aol.com

Mark A. Kelegian
Michael Paul Thomas
Joseph P. Gallo
Bruce A. Thomason
Steven M. Hepps

James P. Habel
Jeri E. Tabback
Dean H. McVay
Erik R. Musurlian
William N. Villard

For full biographical listings, see the Martindale-Hubbell Law Directory

OAKLAND, Alameda Co.

GWILLIAM, IVARY, CHIOSSO, CAVALLI & BREWER, A PROFESSIONAL CORPORATION (AV)

1999 Harrison Street, Suite 1600, 94612-3528
Telephone: 510-832-5411
Fax: 510-832-1918
Mailing Address: P.O. Box 2079, 94604-2079
Email: Info@GICCB.com

J. Gary Gwilliam	James R. Chiosso
Eric H. Ivary	Steven R. Cavalli
	Steven J. Brewer

Marguerite E. Meade	Steven A. Reaves
	Molly Harrington

Reference: Civic Bank of Commerce, Oakland, California.

For full biographical listings, see the Martindale-Hubbell Law Directory

HAIMS, JOHNSON, MacGOWAN & McINERNEY (AV)

490 Grand Avenue, 94610
Telephone: 510-835-0500
Facsimile: 510-835-2833

MEMBERS OF FIRM

Arnold B. Haims	Randy M. Marmor
Gary R. Johnson	John K. Kirby
Clyde L. MacGowan	Robert J. Frassetto
Thomas McInerney	Caroline N. Valentino
Lawrence A. Baker	Dianne D. Peebles

ASSOCIATES

Joseph Y. Ahn	Anne M. Michaels
Edward D. Baldwin	Michelle Diane Perry
Marc P. Bouret	Edward C. Schroeder, Jr.

For full biographical listings, see the Martindale-Hubbell Law Directory

RANKIN, SPROAT, MIRES, TRAPANI & REISER, A PROFESSIONAL CORPORATION (AV)

Suite 1616, 1800 Harrison Street, 94612
Telephone: 510-465-3922
Fax: 510-452-3006
Email: rankin@best.com *URL:* http://www.rankinlaw.com

Joseph F. Rankin (-1977)	Geoffrey A. Mires
Patrick T. Rankin (1943-1990)	Thomas A. Trapani
Ronald G. Sproat	Michael J. Reiser

David T. Shuey	Eugene G. Ashley
G. Trent Morrow	Kevin R. Mintz
	Maribel Delgado Osborne

LEGAL SUPPORT PERSONNEL

Jennifer L. Rankin (Administrator)	Sue Perata (Medical Paralegal)
	Trish J. Fuzesy (Paralegal)
Betty E. Evans (Nurse Paralegal)	Sally J. Attia (Medical Paralegal)

Reference: Union Bank.

For full biographical listings, see the Martindale-Hubbell Law Directory

VAN BLOIS, KNOWLES, SCHWARTZ & BASKIN (AV)

Suite 2245 Ordway Building, One Kaiser Plaza, 94612
Telephone: 510-444-1906
Contra Costa County 510-947-1055
Fax: 510-444-1294

MEMBERS OF FIRM

R. Lewis Van Blois	Ellen R. Schwartz
Thomas C. Knowles	Richard J. Baskin

OF COUNSEL

Charles E. Farnsworth

For full biographical listings, see the Martindale-Hubbell Law Directory

PASADENA, Los Angeles Co.

BURNS, AMMIRATO, PALUMBO, MILAM & BARONIAN, A PROFESSIONAL LAW CORPORATION (AV)

65 North Raymond Avenue, 2nd Floor, 91103-3919
Telephone: 818-796-5053; 213-258-8282
Fax: 818-792-3078
Long Beach, California Office: One World Trade Center, Suite 1200.
Telephone: 310-436-8338; 714-952-1047.
Fax: 310-432-6049.

Michael A. Burns	Bruce Palumbo
Vincent A. Ammirato, Resident, Long Bch	Jeffrey L. Milam
	Robert H. Baronian

(See Next Column)

Normand A. Ayotte	Michael P. Vicencia,
Colleen Clark	Resident, LOng Bch
Valerie Julien-Peto	Michael E. Wenzel,
Susan E. Luhring	Resident, Long Bch
Grace C. Mori, Resident, Long Bch	

Reference: First Los Angeles Bank.

For full biographical listings, see the Martindale-Hubbell Law Directory

COLLINS, COLLINS, MUIR & TRAVER (AV)

Successor to Collins & Collins
Suite 300, 265 North Euclid, 91101
Telephone: 818-793-1163
FAX: 818-793-5982
Newport Beach, California Office: 333 Bayside Drive, 92660.
Telephone: 714-723-6284.
Fax: 714-723-7701.

MEMBERS OF FIRM

James E. Collins (1910-1987)	Robert J. Traver
John J. Collins	Frank J. D'Oro
Samuel J. Muir	Brian K. Stewart

ASSOCIATES

Paul L. Rupard	Christine E. Drage
Robert H. Stellwagen, Jr.	Peter L. Stacy
Tomas A. Guterres	Stephen W. Olson

For full biographical listings, see the Martindale-Hubbell Law Directory

KOLTS AND NAWA (AV)

The Walnut Plaza, Suite 195, 215 North Marengo Avenue, 91101
Telephone: 818-584-6968
FAX: 818-584-5718

MEMBERS OF FIRM

Raymond G. Kolts	Gary C. Nawa

ASSOCIATES

Lynn M. Johnson	Francis T. Kalinski, II
Linda M. Toutant	Diane L. Darvey
	Michael A. J. Nangano

OF COUNSEL

Kathlene Landgraf Kolts

For full biographical listings, see the Martindale-Hubbell Law Directory

KEVIN MEENAN (AV)

790 East Colorado Boulevard Ninth Floor Penthouse, 91101-2105
Telephone: 818-398-0000
FAX: 818-585-0999
Email: 73313.1624@compuserve.com

For full biographical listings, see the Martindale-Hubbell Law Directory

REDDING, Shasta Co.

DUGAN BARR & ASSOCIATES (AV)

1824 Court Street, P.O. Box 994390, 96099-1648
Telephone: 916-243-8008
Fax: 916-243-1648
URL: http://www.CA-Lawyer.com/

Dugan Barr

ASSOCIATES

David L. Case	Douglas Mudford

Representative Clients: City of Redding; Mid Valley Bank; Scott Valley Bank; 3M; Enloe Hospital.
References: Scott Valley Bank, Redding Branch; Mid Valley Bank, Redding Branch.

For full biographical listings, see the Martindale-Hubbell Law Directory

REDLANDS, San Bernardino Co.

WELEBIR & McCUNE, A PROFESSIONAL LAW CORPORATION (AV)

2068 Orange Tree Lane, Suite 215, 92374
Telephone: 909-335-0444
Fax: 909-335-0452
Mailing Address: P.O. Box 10488, San Bernardino, California, 92423
Email: WM__Law@MSN.COM

Douglas F. Welebir	Richard D. McCune, Jr.

George S. Theios	Jacqueline Carey-Wilson

OF COUNSEL

Arthur W. Kelly, Jr. (Retired)

(See Next Column)

WELEBIR & McCune A Professional Law Corporation, Redlands—Continued

LEGAL SUPPORT PERSONNEL

Renee Vargas   Deborah Marsh

For full biographical listings, see the Martindale-Hubbell Law Directory

REDWOOD CITY,* San Mateo Co.

Low, Ball & Lynch, A Professional Corporation (AV)

10 Twin Dolphin, Suite B-500, 94065
Telephone: 415-591-8822
Fax: 415-591-8884
San Francisco, California Office: 601 California Street, Suite 2100, 94108.
Telephone: 415-981-6630.
Monterey, California Office: 10 Ragsdale Drive, Suite 175, 93940.
Telephone: 408-655-8822.

Raymond Coates	David L. Blinn
Chester G. Moore, III	Janet Kulig
James D. Miller	Thomas E. Mulvihill
William H. Holsinger	Jennifer Elizabeth Acheson

John R. Baumann   Joseph M. Fenech
Michael E. Sandgren

For full biographical listings, see the Martindale-Hubbell Law Directory

Owen & Melbye, A Professional Corporation (AV)

700 Jefferson Street, 94063
Telephone: 415-364-6500
Fax: 415-365-7036
Tahoe City, California Office: P.O. Box 1524.
Telephone: 916-546-2473.

William H. Owen	Edmund M. Scott
Richard B. Melbye	Pamela J. Helmer
Norman J. Roger	John S. Posthauer
Paul R. Mangiantini	

Albert P. Blake, Jr.	Conor A. Meyers
Dawn M. Patterson	Mary P. Derner

Representative Clients: Aetna Cravens Dargan Co.; Avco Lycoming; Beech Aircraft Corp.; California Casualty Indemnity Exchange; K & K Claims Service; Kemper Insurance Cos.; Mutual Service Insurance Co.; State Farm Mutual Insurance Cos.; Underwriters at Lloyds; United States Aviation Insurance Group.

For full biographical listings, see the Martindale-Hubbell Law Directory

SACRAMENTO,* Sacramento Co.

Caulfield, Davies & Donahue (AV)

3500 American River Drive, Suite 100, 95864
Telephone: 916-487-7700
Fairfield, California Office: Fairfield West Plaza, 1455 Oliver Road, Suite 130.
Telephone: 707-426-0223.

MEMBERS OF FIRM

Richard Hyland Caulfield	James R. Donahue
Robert E. Davies	Bruce E. Leonard

ASSOCIATES

David N. Tedesco	Jennifer Gittisriboongul
Matthew Paul Donahue	John T. Stralen
Brian C. Haydon	David D. Poland
Shannon Spellacy	

For full biographical listings, see the Martindale-Hubbell Law Directory

Dreyer, Babich, Buccola & Callaham (AV)

715 University Avenue, 95825
Telephone: 916-920-2111
Fax: 916-920-5687

MEMBERS OF FIRM

Roger A. Dreyer	Robert A. Buccola
Joseph J. Babich	William C. Callaham

Craig C. Sheffer	Leland J. Aiken
Stephen F. Davids	Kevin G. Farnworth
John W. Jefferson	Eliot M. Reiner
Stanley P. Fleshman	Timothy J. O'Connor

For full biographical listings, see the Martindale-Hubbell Law Directory

Hardy Erich Brown & Wilson, A Professional Corporation (AV)

1000 G Street, 95814
Telephone: 916-449-3800
Fax: 916-449-3888
Mailing Address: P.O. Box 13530, Sacramento, California, 95853-4530

(See Next Column)

John Quincy Brown, Jr.	Bruce E. Salenko
Anthony D. Osmundson	Brian H. Charter
Thomas C. Richards	Larry Caldwell
L. Thomas Wagner	Richard L. Alley
John Quincy Brown, III	Whitney A. Davis
David S. Worthington	John C. Miller, Jr.

OF COUNSEL

Cavan Hardy	William A. Wilson
Norwood R. Erich	Richard M. Cunha

Sara A. Clark

Representative Clients: The Dial Corporation; General Motors Corporation; Goodyear Tire & Rubber Company; Mobil Oil Corporation; Sherwin-Williams Company; Synnex Information Technologies, Inc.; VIAD Corporation.

For full biographical listings, see the Martindale-Hubbell Law Directory

Johnson, Schachter & Collins, A Professional Corporation (AV)

701 University Avenue, Suite 150, 95825
Telephone: 916-921-5800
Telecopier: 916-921-0247
Email: 102514.3714@COMPUSERVE.COM

Robert H. Johnson	Alesa M. Schachter
	Kim H. Collins

George W. Holt	Carrie G. Pratt
Timothy P. Dailey	R. James Miller

OF COUNSEL

Ford R. Smith	Carolyn M. Wood
	Susanne M. Shelley

Representative Clients: Fireman's Fund Insurance Cos.; GAB Business Services; Jonsson Communications Corp.; McClatchy Newspapers and Broadcasting; State Farm Fire & Casualty Co.; State Farm Mutual Automobile Insurance Co.
Reference: Business & Professional Bank, Sacramento.

For full biographical listings, see the Martindale-Hubbell Law Directory

Nageley, Meredith & Ramsey, Inc. (AV)

8001 Folsom Boulevard, Suite 200, P.O. Box 276270, 95827-6270
Telephone: 916-386-8282
Fax: 916-386-8952

Sam R. Nageley	Gregory A. Meredith
	Joe Ramsey

Drew M. Johnson	Carole Sharples
Craig S. MacGlashan	L. Alan Warwick
Michael B. O'Harra	Janet M. Meredith
Lawrence N. Hensley	Debbie J. Vorous
	James C. Keowen

OF COUNSEL

Andrea M. Miller

For full biographical listings, see the Martindale-Hubbell Law Directory

Porter, Scott, Weiberg & Delehant, A Professional Corporation (AV)

350 University Avenue, Suite 200, 95825
Telephone: 916-929-1481
Fax: 916-927-3706

Russell G. Porter	Terence J. Cassidy
A. Irving Scott, Jr.	Tom H. Bailey
Edwin T. Weiberg	Carl J. Calnero
John W. Delehant	Russ J. Wunderli
Anthony S. Warburg	Nancy J. Sheehan
Ned P. Telford	Norman V. Prior
James K. Mirabell	Timothy M. Blaine
Craig A. Caldwell	Stephen E. Horan

Amanda R. Lowe	Alysa Erdman Meyer
Clay A. Jackson	Richard Joseph Corbo, Jr.
Elisa Ungerman	Bruce A. Monfross
John Carl Padrick	Marcos Kropf
Erik Z. Revai	Valerie Mercier
Karen Beth Ebel	Jennifer E. Duggan
Carl L. Fessenden	Vanessa W. Whang
Grant Collins Woodruff	Dennis C. Huie
James W. Walter, Jr.	Stephanie A. Sahakian
Michael J. Baytosh	Kristin M. Engstom
David A. Melton	Jeffrey S. Kravitz

For full biographical listings, see the Martindale-Hubbell Law Directory

Sacramento—Continued

SCHUERING ZIMMERMAN & SCULLY, LLP (AV)

400 University Avenue, 95825
Telephone: 916-567-0400
Fax: 916-568-0400

MEMBERS OF FIRM

Steven T. Scully (1948-1994)
Leo H. Schuering, Jr.
Robert H. Zimmerman
Thomas J. Doyle

Lawrence S. Giardina
Anthony D. Lauria
Keith D. Chidlaw
John J. Sillis

Regina A. Favors
Raymond R. Gates
Christian Koster
Scott A. Linn

Donna W. Low
Dominique A. Pollara
Theodore D. Poppinga
John P. Rhode

Douglas L. Smith

For full biographical listings, see the Martindale-Hubbell Law Directory

WILCOXEN, MONTGOMERY & HARBISON (AV)

A Partnership including a Professional Corporation
2114 K Street, 95816
Telephone: 916-442-2777

Daniel E. Wilcoxen (Inc.)
James R. Montgomery
Joseph F. Harbison, III

Patrick L. Hinrichsen
David E. Smith

Joanne M. Merry
Cindy L. Robbins

Reference: First Interstate Bank.

For full biographical listings, see the Martindale-Hubbell Law Directory

SAN DIEGO,* San Diego Co.

BOUDREAU & TRENTACOSTA, A PROFESSIONAL LAW CORPORATION (AV)

401 West "A" Street, Suite 1850, 92101-9773
Telephone: 619-238-1553
Fax: 619-238-8181
Email: AEGISLAW@AOL.COM

Steven M. Boudreau
Robert J. Trentacosta

Jon R. Williams

For full biographical listings, see the Martindale-Hubbell Law Directory

CASEY, GERRY, REED & SCHENK (AV)

110 Laurel Street, 92101
Telephone: 619-238-1811
Fax: 619-544-9232
Email: cglaw@cglaw.com

OF COUNSEL

David S. Casey
Richard F. Gerry

MEMBERS OF FIRM

David S. Casey, Jr.
Richard D. Westbrook, Jr.
(1944-1982)

T. Michael Reed
Frederick Schenk

ASSOCIATES

Robert J. Francavilla
Gayle Meryl Blatt
Thomas D. Penfield

Michael P. Montgomery
Suzanne C. Etpison
Bonnie E. Kane

Reference: San Diego National Bank.

For full biographical listings, see the Martindale-Hubbell Law Directory

CHAPIN, FLEMING & WINET, A PROFESSIONAL CORPORATION (AV)

Library, 501 West Broadway, 15th Floor, 92101
Telephone: 619-232-4261
Telefax: 619-232-4840
Email: cfwlaw@adnc.com *URL:* http://www.sandiego-online.com/cfwlaw
Vista, California Office: 410 South Melrose Drive, Suite 101.
Telephone: 619-758-4261.
Telefax: 619-758-6420.
Los Angeles, California Office: 12121 Wilshire Boulevard, Suite 401.
Telephone: 310-826-0133.
Telefax: 310-207-4236.
Palm Springs, California Office: 225 North El Cielo Road, Suite 470.
Telephone: 619-416-1400.
Telefax: 619-416-1405.

Victor M. Barr, Jr.
Craig H. Bell
  (Resident, Los Angeles Office)
Darryn L. Berner

Kelli Jean Brooks
Michael S. Burke
David H. Bushnell
  (Resident, Los Angeles Office)

(See Next Column)

Richard D. Carter
  (Resident, Los Angeles Office)
Dean G. Chandler
  (Resident, Vista Office)
Edward D. Chapin
Victoria Chen
George Chuang
  (Resident, Los Angeles Office)
Amber L. Eck
Robert Ehrenreich
  (Resident, Los Angeles Office)
Scott K. Endsley
George E. Fleming
Antonio Gastelum (Not
  admitted in United States)
Shirley A. Gauvin
Katherine M. Green
Terence L. Greene
Gregory Kevin Hansen
Howard L. Hoffenberg
  (Resident, Los Angeles Office)
Patrick M. Howe
Aaron H. Katz
Elizabeth J. Koumas
Traci Lynn Kuchta
Dana Marie Lawson
  (Resident, Los Angeles Office)
Jeffrey J. Leist
  (Resident, Los Angeles Office)

Tonya L. Morgan
  (Resident, Los Angeles Office)
David A. Myers
  (Resident, Los Angeles Office)
Brenda J. Pannell
  (Resident, Los Angeles Office)
Kennett L. Patrick
  (Resident, Vista Office)
Thomas V. Perea
  (Resident, Los Angeles Office)
Roger L. Popeney
Maria C. Roberts
Lawrence W. Shea, II
Douglas J. Simpson
Spencer C. Skeen
  (Resident, Los Angeles Office)
Howard Smith
  (Resident, Los Angeles Office)
Patricia L. Sullivan
Gregory S. Tavill
Frank L. Tobin
Grace I. Wang
  (Resident, Los Angeles Office)
Peter C. Ward
Jeffrey A. Weaver (Resident,
  Palm Springs Office)
Randall L. Winet
  (Resident, Vista Office)

OF COUNSEL

George F. Braun
Arthur D. Rutledge
  (Resident, Los Angeles Office)
Jeffrey C. Stodel
  (Resident, Los Angeles Office)

Irwin Waldman (A P.C.)
  (Resident, Los Angeles Office)
James Michael Zimmerman

For full biographical listings, see the Martindale-Hubbell Law Directory

DOUGHERTY & HILDRE (AV)

2550 Fifth Avenue, Suite 600, 92103-5624
Telephone: 619-232-9131
Telefax: 619-232-7317

William O. Dougherty
Donald F. Hildre

Fred M. Dudek
Mona H. Freedman

For full biographical listings, see the Martindale-Hubbell Law Directory

LUCE, FORWARD, HAMILTON & SCRIPPS LLP (AV)

A Partnership including Professional Corporations
600 West Broadway, Suite 2600, 92101
Telephone: 619-236-1414
Fax: 619-232-8311
URL: http://www.luce.com
La Jolla, California Office: 4275 Executive Square, Suite 800, 92037.
Telephone: 619-535-2639.
Fax: 619-453-2812.
Los Angeles, California Office: 777 South Figueroa, Suite 3600, 90017.
Telephone: 213-892-4992.
Fax: 213-892-7731.
San Francisco, California Office: 100 Bush Street, 20th Floor, 94104.
Telephone: 415-395-7900.
Fax: 415-395-7949.
New York, N.Y. Office: Citicorp Center, 153 East 53rd Street, 26th Floor, 10022.
Telephone: 212-754-1414.
Fax: 212-644-9727.
Chicago, Illinois Office: 180 North La Salle Street, Suite 1125, 60601.
Telephone: 312-641-0580.
Fax: 312-641-0380.

MEMBERS OF FIRM

Lawrence J. Kouns
Vickie E. Turner

R. Randal Crispen
Edward Patrick "Pat" Swan, Jr.

ASSOCIATES

Callie A. Bjurstrom
Michael L. Branch
Jane P. Bahnson

Marjorie A. Waltrip
David N. Ruben
  (Resident, Los Angeles Office)

For Complete List of Firm Personnel, See General Section

For full biographical listings, see the Martindale-Hubbell Law Directory

McCLELLAN & BROWN, A PROFESSIONAL CORPORATION (AV)

1144 State Street, 92101
Telephone: 619-231-0505
Fax: 619-544-0540

Craig R. McClellan
LaMar B. Brown

For full biographical listings, see the Martindale-Hubbell Law Directory

San Diego—Continued

NEIL, DYMOTT, PERKINS, BROWN & FRANK, A PROFESSIONAL CORPORATION (AV)

1010 Second Avenue, Suite 2500, 92101-4959
Telephone: 619-238-1712
Fax: 619-238-1562

Michael I. Neil   Thomas M. Dymott
              Roger G. Perkins

Reference: Scripps Bank.

For full biographical listings, see the Martindale-Hubbell Law Directory

THORSNES, BARTOLOTTA, McGUIRE & PADILLA (AV)

A Partnership including Professional Corporations
Fifth Avenue Financial Center, 11th Floor, 2550 Fifth Avenue, 92103
Telephone: 619-236-9363
Fax: 619-236-9653
Email: TBMP@lawinfo.com *URL:* http://www.tbmp.com

Michael T. Thorsnes (P.C.)   Mitchell S. Golub (P.C.)
Vincent J. Bartolotta, Jr., (P.C.)   Frederic L. Gordon (P.C.)
John F. McGuire (P.C.)   Palma Cesar Hooper (P.C.)
Michael D. Padilla (P.C.)   Neal H. Rockwood (P.C.)
Kevin F. Quinn (P.C.)   Daral B. Mazzarella (P.C.)
C. Brant Noziska (P.C.)   R. Christian Hulburt (P.C.)

ASSOCIATES

Jeffrey F. LaFave   John J. Rice
Stephen D. Lipkin   Robert E. Bright
Rhonda J. Thompson   Douglas J. Billings
Scott A. Kennedy   James T. Atkins
             Charles L. Stott

OF COUNSEL

Robert S. Kennedy

For full biographical listings, see the Martindale-Hubbell Law Directory

SAN FRANCISCO,* San Francisco Co.

BAILEY & KORNBLUM (AV)

1388 Sutter Street, Suite 820, 94109
Telephone: 415-440-7800
Fax: 415-440-7898

Don E. Bailey

For full biographical listings, see the Martindale-Hubbell Law Directory

CARTWRIGHT & ALEXANDER, INC. (AV)

222 Front St., 5th Fl., 94111-4403
Telephone: 415-433-0440
Telecopier: 415-391-5845

Robert E. Cartwright   Robert E. Cartwright, Jr.
(1925-1988)   Mary E. Alexander

For full biographical listings, see the Martindale-Hubbell Law Directory

CYRIL & CROWLEY (AV)

17th Floor, 456 Montgomery Street, 94104
Telephone: 415-989-1100
Facsimile: 415-421-6651
Email: candc@ix.netcom.com

MEMBERS OF FIRM

John W. Crowley   Michael W. Field
Robert B. Stringer   Carol P. Rohwer
David W. Gordon   Wendy J. Hannum

OF COUNSEL

Paul H. Cyril (A Professional Corporation)

ASSOCIATES

Elizabeth L. Dolter   Mark D. Fenske
Mark D. Skilling   Shannon M. Finnegan

For full biographical listings, see the Martindale-Hubbell Law Directory

JOHN GARDENAL A PROFESSIONAL CORPORATION (AV)

Suite 800 Cathedral Hill Office Building, 1255 Post Street, 94109
Telephone: 415-771-2700
FAX: 415-771-2072

John Gardenal

For full biographical listings, see the Martindale-Hubbell Law Directory

LAFAYETTE, KUMAGAI & CLARKE (AV)

100 Spear Street, Suite 400, 94105
Telephone: 415-357-4600
Facsimile: 415-357-4605

(See Next Column)

MEMBERS OF FIRM

Gary T. Lafayette   Kevin M. Clarke
            Susan T. Kumagai

ASSOCIATE

Valerie A. Andersen

For full biographical listings, see the Martindale-Hubbell Law Directory

LEACH, McGREEVY & BAUTISTA (AV)

1735 Pacific Avenue, 94109
Telephone: 415-775-4455
Telefax: 415-775-7435
Southern California Office: 13643 Fifth Street, Chino, CA. 91710.
Telephone: 909-590-2224.

Theodore Tamba (1900-1973)   Teresa A. Cunningham
John T. Harmon (1928-1993)   J. Curtis Cox
David G. Leach   Robert W. Shinnick
Richard E. McGreevy   Philip T. Kilduff
A. Marquez Bautista   Paul David Katerndahl

ASSOCIATE

John C. Connolly

OF COUNSEL

Roger G. Eliassen   Lloyd F. Postel

For full biographical listings, see the Martindale-Hubbell Law Directory

LIEFF, CABRASER, HEIMANN & BERNSTEIN, LLP (AV)

Embarcadero Center West, 30th Floor, 275 Battery Street, 94111
Telephone: 415-956-1000
Telecopier: 415-956-1008
Email: mail@lchb.com

Robert L. Lieff   Michael F. Ram
Elizabeth J. Cabraser   Joseph R. Saveri
Richard M. Heimann   Donald C. Arbitblit
William Bernstein   Robert J. Nelson
William B. Hirsch   Jacqueline E. Mottek
James M. Finberg   Morris A. Ratner
Karen E. Karpen   Melanie M. Piech

Richard L. Akel   Anthony K. Lee
Christine J. Anderson   Fabrice V. Nijhof
Kelly M. Dermody   Trina N. Parker
Eric B. Fastiff   Jonathan D. Selbin
Richard M. Franco   Mark N. Todzo
           Heather A. Woodard

For full biographical listings, see the Martindale-Hubbell Law Directory

J. KENNETH LYNCH (AV)

Citicorp Center, One Sansome, Suite 2100, 94104
Telephone: 415-951-4616
FAX: 415-951-4653

MOLLIGAN, COX & MOYER, A PROFESSIONAL CORPORATION (AV)

703 Market Street, Suite 1800, 94103
Telephone: 415-543-9464
Fax: 415-777-1828
Email: mocoxmoy@aol.com

Ingemar E. Hoberg (1903-1971)   Peter N. Molligan
John H. Finger (1913-1991)   Stephen T. Cox
Phillip E. Brown (Retired)   David W. Moyer

John C. Hentschel

OF COUNSEL

Kenneth W. Rosenthal   Barbara A. Zuras

For full biographical listings, see the Martindale-Hubbell Law Directory

MOORE & BROWNING (AV)

100 Bush Street, Suite 225, 94104
Telephone: 415-956-6500
Fax: 415-956-6580

Michael B. Moore   Charles A. Browning

LEGAL SUPPORT PERSONNEL

Pat Medina (Paralegal)

For full biographical listings, see the Martindale-Hubbell Law Directory

MORGENSTEIN & JUBELIRER, LLP (AV)

A Partnership including a Professional Corporation
One Market Plaza, Spear Street Tower, 32nd Floor, 94105
Telephone: 415-896-0666
Fax: 415-896-5592
Email: jubelirer@aol.com

(See Next Column)

MORGENSTEIN & JUBELIRER LLP—*Continued*

MEMBERS OF FIRM

Marvin D. Morgenstein (P.C.)	Rocky N. Unruh
Eliot S. Jubelirer	James L. McGinnis
Lee Ann Huntington	Charles W. LaGrave
Jean L. Bertrand	Wendi J. Berkowitz
Jeffrey R. Williams	John S. Worden
James R. Balich	Robert B. Mullen

OF COUNSEL

Laurie K. Anger

Lewis D. Barr	Natasha L. Golding
David H. Bromfield	Stephen M. Hankins
Michael "Cael" S. Davis	Simon E. Kisch
Roberta Nicol Dempster	John J. Petry
Bruce A. Wagman	

For full biographical listings, see the Martindale-Hubbell Law Directory

---

MURPHY, PEARSON, BRADLEY & FEENEY, A PROFESSIONAL CORPORATION (AV)

88 Kearny Street, 11th Floor, 94108
Telephone: 415-788-1900
Telecopier: 415-393-8087
Sacramento, California Office: Suite 200, 3600 American River Drive, 95864.
Telephone: 916-483-6074.
Telecopier: 916-483-6088.

John H. Feeney	Gregory A. Bastian (Resident, Sacramento Office)

For Complete List of Firm Personnel, See General Section

For full biographical listings, see the Martindale-Hubbell Law Directory

---

O'CONNOR, COHN, DILLON & BARR, A LAW CORPORATION (AV)

The Folger Coffee Building, 101 Howard Street, Fifth Floor, 94105-1619
Telephone: 415-281-8888
Fax: 415-281-8890
Email: ocdb@slip.net

Joseph T. O'Connor (Deceased, 1959)	Janet L. Grove
	Mark Oium
Harold H. Cohn (1910-1992)	Lisa T. Ungerer
James L. Dillon	Joel C. Lamp
Duncan Barr	Michael J. FitzSimons
Dexter B. Louie	

Thomas G. Manning	Karen K. Smith
Susan Reifel Goins	Daniel J. Herp
Deborah L. Panter	James A. Beltzer
Marirose Piciucco	(Not admitted in CA)
Keith Reyen	M. Elizabeth Bootle

For full biographical listings, see the Martindale-Hubbell Law Directory

---

PREUSS WALKER & SHANAGHER LLP (AV)

595 Market Street, 16th Floor, 94105
Telephone: 415-978-2600
Facsimile: 415-978-2613
Email: pws@pwsllp.com

MEMBERS OF FIRM

Charles F. Preuss	Donald F. Zimmer, Jr.
Gary T. Walker	Sheila Doyle Kelley
Denis F. Shanagher	Thomas W. Pulliam, Jr.
Vernon I. Zvoleff	Alan J. Lazarus
Michael J. Stortz	

John J. Powers	Constance D. Burton
Cynthia C. Roenisch	Paul S. Lecky
Kenneth P. Conour	Catherine M. Leon
Paula R. Lee	Elizabeth L. W. Ewert
Mel M. Negussie	

Representative Clients: Honda North America, Inc.; Johnson & Johnson; Merck & Co., Inc.; Minnesota Mining & Manufacturing Co. (3M); New United Motor Manufacturing; Nissan Motor Corporation; Plough Incorporated; Smith Kline Beecham; Toyota Motor Sales, U.S.A.

For full biographical listings, see the Martindale-Hubbell Law Directory

---

SARRAIL, LYNCH & HALL (AV)

44 Montgomery Street, 34th Floor, 94104
Telephone: 415-398-2404
Fax: 415-391-9076

(See Next Column)

Stephen W. Hall (1955-1993)	James A. Sarrail
	Linda J. Lynch

Michael J. Ruggles	Susan A. Byron
David Y. Wong	Ernest D. Faitos
Jonathan S. Larsen	Brian D. Harrison
Sheila M. Salomon	

OF COUNSEL

Jack A. Pollatsek

LEGAL SUPPORT PERSONNEL

Cynthia R. Benzerara

For full biographical listings, see the Martindale-Hubbell Law Directory

---

SCADDEN, HAMILTON & RYAN (AV)

580 California Street, Suite 1400, 94104
Telephone: 415-362-5116
Facsimile: 415-362-4214

James G. Scadden	Robert J. Ryan
Robert P. Hamilton	James P. Cunningham

James F. Hetherington	Eileen Santana Wright
Charles O. Thompson	Vincent C. Milani

LEGAL SUPPORT PERSONNEL

Laurie C. Meyer

For full biographical listings, see the Martindale-Hubbell Law Directory

---

TEHIN + PARTNERS, A PROFESSIONAL CORPORATION (AV)

Bank of America Center, 555 California Street, 33rd Floor, 94104-1609
Telephone: 415-951-8800
Fax: 415-951-8808

Nikolai Tehin (Professional Corporation)	Reilly Atkinson, IV
	Michael E. Brown
Pamela J. Stevens	Marcia A. Pollioni

For full biographical listings, see the Martindale-Hubbell Law Directory

---

WALKUP, MELODIA, KELLY & ECHEVERRIA, A PROFESSIONAL CORPORATION (AV)

30th Floor, 650 California Street, 94108
Telephone: 415-981-7210
Fax: 415-391-6965

Paul V. Melodia	Michael A. Kelly
Daniel J. Kelly	Kevin L. Domecus
John Echeverria	Jeffrey P. Holl
Ronald H. Wecht	Daniel Dell'Osso
Richard H. Schoenberger	

Cynthia F. Newton	Michael J. Recupero
Erik Brunkal	Kenneth H. Facter

OF COUNSEL

John D. Link	Wesley Sokolosky

Reference: Bank of California, San Francisco Main Office, 400 California Street, San Francisco, Calif. 94104.

For full biographical listings, see the Martindale-Hubbell Law Directory

---

WARTNICK, CHABER, HAROWITZ, SMITH & TIGERMAN, A PROFESSIONAL CORPORATION (AV)

101 California Street, Suite 2200, 94111-5802
Telephone: 415-986-5566
Fax: 415-986-5896

Harry F. Wartnick	Steven M. Harowitz
Madelyn J. Chaber	Audrey A. Smith
Stephen M. Tigerman	

Niromi L. Wijewantha	Christopher C. Lamerdin
Phillip Scott Chan	Garry Cohen
Brenda D. Posada	Cheryl L. White
Gregory M. Sheffer	

For full biographical listings, see the Martindale-Hubbell Law Directory

---

SAN JOSE, * Santa Clara Co.

THE ALEXANDER LAW FIRM (AV)

55 South Market Street, Suite 1080, 95113
Telephone: 408-289-1776
Fax: 408-287-1776
Email: access@alexanderlaw.com *URL:* http://www.alexanderlaw.com/
Cincinnati, Ohio Office: The Alexander Law Firm, 1300 Mercantile Library Building, 414 Walnut Street.
Telephone: 513-723-1776.
Fax: 513-421-1776.

(See Next Column)

THE ALEXANDER LAW FIRM, San Jose—Continued

Richard Alexander

ASSOCIATES

Michael T. Alexander (Resident,　Michael McShane
Cincinnati, Ohio Office)　　　　Amanda Hawes
Jonathan D. Pendleton　　　　　Ann Saponara

Tyler A. Shaw

OF COUNSEL

William M. Audet

For full biographical listings, see the Martindale-Hubbell Law Directory

THE BOCCARDO LAW FIRM (AV)

Eleventh Floor, 111 West St. John Street, 95115-0001
Telephone: 408-298-5678
Fax: 408-298-7503

MEMBERS OF FIRM

James F. Boccardo　　　　　John C. Stein
John W. McDonald　　　　　Richard L. Bowers
Brian N. Lawther　　　　　　Russell L. Moore, Jr.

ASSOCIATES

Stephen Foster　　　　　　　Victor F. Stefan
David P. Moyles　　　　　　　Robert W. Thayer
Byron C. Foster　　　　　　　Richard Gregg

For full biographical listings, see the Martindale-Hubbell Law Directory

BOHN, BENNION & NILAND (AV)

Fairmont Plaza, 50 West San Fernando Street Suite 1020, 95113
Telephone: 408-279-4222
Fax: 408-295-2222

MEMBERS OF FIRM

Robert H. Bohn　　　　　　　David J. Bennion
Edward L. Niland

ASSOCIATE

Robert H. Bohn, Jr.

OF COUNSEL

Jeffrey W. Rickard

For full biographical listings, see the Martindale-Hubbell Law Directory

JAN CHAMPION (AV)

Ten Almaden Boulevard, Tenth Floor, 95113-2233
Telephone: 408-286-5550
Fax: 408-270-6777

For full biographical listings, see the Martindale-Hubbell Law Directory

COLLINS & SCHLOTHAUER (AV)

An Association of Attorneys including a Professional Corporation
60 South Market Street, Suite 1100, 95113-2369
Telephone: 408-298-5161
Fax: 408-297-5766
Affiliated Los Angeles, California Office: Schlothauer, Collins & Macaluso,
11661 San Vicente Boulevard, Suite 303.
Telephone: 310-820-8606.
Fax: 310-820-7057.

Mark Scott Collins (Inc.)　　　Linda L. Duiven
David N. Poll　　　　　　　　Jovita Prestoza

OF COUNSEL

Thomas L. Schlothauer　　　　Todd E. Macaluso

Representative Clients: Unigard Insurance; Farmers Insurance Co.; Fire Insurance Exchange; National American Insurance Co.; ABAG (Association of Bay Area Governmental Entities).

For full biographical listings, see the Martindale-Hubbell Law Directory

LICCARDO, ROSSI, STURGES & McNEIL, A PROFESSIONAL LAW CORPORATION (AV)

1960 The Alameda, Suite 200, 95126
Telephone: 408-244-4570
Fax: 408-244-3294
Oakland, California Office: 1999 Harrison, Suite 1300.
Telephone: 415-834-2206.
Fax: 415-832-4432.

Salvador A. Liccardo　　　　　Craig Needham
Ronald R. Rossi　　　　　　　Gregory D. Hull
Robert S. Sturges　　　　　　Martha Louise Caron
R. Donald McNeil　　　　　　　(Resident, Oakland Office)
David M. Hamerslough　　　　Cynthia L. Chase
Susan R. Reischl　　　　　　　Laura Liccardo

(See Next Column)

Robert C. Colyar　　　　　　Paul Salvatore Liccardo
Jeffery Lopez　　　　　　　　Anne Jones
Wes Wagnon　　　　　　　　　Samuel A. Chuck
Richard B. Gullen　　　　　　Laura M. Chiappe
Deborah T. Bjonerud　　　　　Daniel A. Hershkowitz
(Resident, Oakland Office)　　　(Resident, Oakland Office)

For full biographical listings, see the Martindale-Hubbell Law Directory

DAVID MALNICK A PROFESSIONAL CORPORATION (AV)

10 Almaden Boulevard Tenth Floor, 95113-2233
Telephone: 408-292-5900
Fax: 408-292-5995

David E. Malnick

For full biographical listings, see the Martindale-Hubbell Law Directory

ROBINSON & WOOD, INC. (AV)

227 North First Street, 95113
Telephone: 408-298-7120
Fax: 408-298-0477
Email: rw@r-winc.com

Archie S. Robinson　　　　　Jonathan L. Lee
Weldon S. Wood　　　　　　　Jon B. Zimmerman
Thomas R. Fellows　　　　　　Mark B. Schellerup
David S. Henningsen　　　　　Andrew W. Olsson
Hugh F. Lennon　　　　　　　Erica R. Yew
Jesse F. Ruiz　　　　　　　　Arthur J. Casey
Christian B. Nielsen　　　　　Joseph C. Balestrieri

John L. Winchester, III　　　　Wendy Woolpert
Chadney C. Ankele　　　　　　Ann A. Nguyen
Robert A. Nakamae　　　　　　Kenneth I. Schumaker
Rebecca L. Moon　　　　　　　Anne C. Bailey
Wendy E. Flockhart　　　　　　Stephen D. Bays

For full biographical listings, see the Martindale-Hubbell Law Directory

SHEA & SHEA, A PROFESSIONAL LAW CORPORATION (AV)

The James Square Building, 255 North Market Street, Suite 190, 95110
Telephone: 408-292-2434
Fax: 408-292-1264

Michael M. Shea　　　　　　　Michael M. Shea, Jr.

Beth C. Watkins

For full biographical listings, see the Martindale-Hubbell Law Directory

SAN RAFAEL,* Marin Co.

RAGGHIANTI • FREITAS • MONTOBBIO • WALLACE LLP (AV)

874 Fourth Street, Suite D, 94901
Telephone: 415-453-9433
Fax: 415-453-8269

Gary T. Ragghianti　　　　　　J. Randolph Wallace
David P. Freitas　　　　　　　Patrick M. Macias
J. Mark Montobbio　　　　　　Robert F. Epstein
John Ralph Thomas

For full biographical listings, see the Martindale-Hubbell Law Directory

SANTA ANA,* Orange Co.

BEAM, BROBECK & WEST (AV)

600 West Santa Ana Boulevard, Suite 1000, 92701
Telephone: 714-558-3944
Fax: 714-568-0129

MEMBERS OF FIRM

Byron J. Beam　　　　　　　Kirk H. Nakamura
David J. Brobeck, Jr.　　　　Robert H. McMillan
John E. West　　　　　　　　Daniel R. Sullivan

ASSOCIATES

Betsey J. Jeffery　　　　　　Donald S. Zalewski
Charles W. Matheis, Jr.　　　Geralyn L. Skapik
Robert C. Hastie　　　　　　David R. Rosenberg
Gregory L. Rippetoe　　　　　Louise M. Douville
Jennifer J. Miller　　　　　　Kermit D. Marsh

Representative Clients: Aetna Insurance Co.; American General Life Insurance Co.; American Hospital Supply; Carl Warren & Co.; Casualty Insurance Co.; City of Anaheim; City of Fullerton; City of Newport Beach; Empire Insurance Cos.; Physicians Interindemnity.

For full biographical listings, see the Martindale-Hubbell Law Directory

Santa Ana—Continued

CASSIDY, WARNER, THURBER & LANE, A PROFESSIONAL CORPORATION (AV)

600 West Santa Ana Boulevard, Suite 700, 92701
Telephone: 714-835-9431
Fax: 714-835-5264

Alvin M. Cassidy	David K. Thurber
B. Kent Warner	Timothy X. Lane
	Bruce A. Winstead

Lloyd W. Felver	David C. Olson
	Glen A. Stebens

For full biographical listings, see the Martindale-Hubbell Law Directory

HORTON BARBARO & REILLY (AV)

A Partnership including Professional Corporations
Second Floor, 200 North Main Street, 92701
Telephone: 714-835-2122
Fax: 714-973-4892
Email: HBR@Hortonetal.com *URL:* http://www.Hortonetal.com

MEMBERS OF FIRM

Jay Cordell Horton (A Professional Corporation)	Geoffrey S. Gray
	John R. Hanna
Frank P. Barbaro (A Professional Corporation)	William O. Humphreys
	Karen L. Karavatos
Ned P. Reilly (A Professional Corporation)	John E. O'Brien, Jr.

ASSOCIATES

Malena R. LeClair	Timothy V. Kassouni
Robert J. Younger	Richard E. Donahoo

For full biographical listings, see the Martindale-Hubbell Law Directory

MARTIN, WILSON, ERICKSON & MACDOWELL, A PROFESSIONAL CORPORATION (AV)

6 Hutton Centre, Suite 500, 92707
Telephone: 714-972-1200
Facsimile: 714-972-1283

Scott A. Martin	Mary Fingal Erickson
Thomas L. Wilson	John R. MacDowell

Douglas M. Carasso	Wendy A. Weber
	Kevin F. Cahill

For full biographical listings, see the Martindale-Hubbell Law Directory

SANTA BARBARA,* Santa Barbara Co.

ARCHBALD & SPRAY (AV)

505 Bath Street, 93101
Telephone: 805-564-2070
Telecopier: 805-564-2081
Email: arch@silcom.com

MEMBERS OF FIRM

Malcolm Archbald (Retired)	Karen T. Burgett
Joseph L. Spray (1927-1985)	Edwin K. Loskamp
Kenneth L. Moes	Wm. Brennan Lynch
J. William McLafferty	Michael A. Colton
Douglas B. Large	Ann Gormican Anderson

SENIOR ATTORNEYS

Peri Maziarz	Katherine H. Bower

ASSOCIATE

Cheryl A. Shaw

OF COUNSEL

John W. Warnock

Representative Clients: Alexis Risk Management; Chevron, Inc.; CNA Insurance; The Flxible Corporation; Frankenmuth Mutual Insurance; Leinbach Machinery; Snap Products; Volvo GM Heavy Truck Corp.; Wisconsin Aluminum Foundry.

For full biographical listings, see the Martindale-Hubbell Law Directory

KINKLE, RODIGER AND SPRIGGS, PROFESSIONAL CORPORATION (AV)

125 East De La Guerra Street, 93101-2239
Telephone: 805-966-4700
Fax: 805-966-4120
Los Angeles, California Office: 600 North Grand Avenue.
Telephone: 213-629-1261.
Fax: 213-629-8382.
Santa Ana, California Office: 837 North Ross Street.
Telephone: 714-835-9011.
Fax: 714-667-7806.

(See Next Column)

Riverside, California Office: 3333 14th Street.
Telephone: 909-683-2410; 800-235-2039.
Fax: 909-683-7759.
San Diego, California Office: Suite 900 Driver Insurance Center, 1620 Fifth Avenue, P.O. Box 127900.
Telephone: 619-233-4566.
Fax: 619-233-8554.

John V. Hager (Managing Attorney)	Joy L. Lim
	Jeffery D. Lim
Edwin C. Mann	Chad M. Slack
	Donna D. Geck

For full biographical listings, see the Martindale-Hubbell Law Directory

SANTA CRUZ,* Santa Cruz Co.

DUNLAP & BURDICK, A PROFESSIONAL LAW CORPORATION (AV)

121 Jewell Street, 95060
Telephone: 408-426-7040
Fax: 408-426-1095

Michael E. Dunlap	Paul P. Burdick

Garth V. Smith

For full biographical listings, see the Martindale-Hubbell Law Directory

STOCKTON,* San Joaquin Co.

MAYALL, HURLEY, KNUTSEN, SMITH & GREEN, A PROFESSIONAL CORPORATION (AV)

2453 Grand Canal Boulevard, Second Floor, 95207-8253
Telephone: 209-477-3833
Fax: 209-473-4818

Edwin Mayall (1907-1980)	William W. Hale
John J. Hurley (Retired)	Mark Stephen Adams
Clarence D. Knutsen	J. Anthony Abbott
Alan E. Smith	Peter J. Whipple
Dennis J. Green	Kristen M. Hegge
	Vladimir F. Kozina

William L. Anderson	William J. Gorham, III
Donald W. West	Matthew Christopher Felix
Robert E. Laubengayer	Joseph A. Salazar, Jr.
Mark E. Berry	Steven A. Malcoun
	Lesley Solomon

Representative Clients: Allstate Insurance Co.; California State Automobile Assn.; Fireman's Fund Insurance Co.; General Motors Corp.; Texaco, Inc; State Farm Mutual Insurance Cos.; Beck Development, Inc; HD Arnaiz, Ltd; Vito Transporation; The Alpine Group.

For full biographical listings, see the Martindale-Hubbell Law Directory

TORRANCE, Los Angeles Co.

AGNEW & BRUSAVICH (AV)

20355 Hawthorne Boulevard, 90503
Telephone: 310-793-1400
Facsimile: 310-793-1499
Email: agnewbru@ix.netcom.com

Gerald E. Agnew, Jr.	Bruce M. Brusavich

ASSOCIATES

Susan E. Hargrove	Christopher A. Kall
	Mark J. Peacock

For full biographical listings, see the Martindale-Hubbell Law Directory

VENTURA,* Ventura Co.

LAW OFFICES OF FREDERICK H. BYSSHE, JR. (AV)

10 South California Street, 93001
Telephone: 805-648-3224
Fax: 805-653-0267

Terence Geoghegan

For full biographical listings, see the Martindale-Hubbell Law Directory

WALNUT CREEK, Contra Costa Co.

ANDERSON, GALLOWAY & LUCCHESE, A PROFESSIONAL CORPORATION (AV)

1676 North California Boulevard, Suite 500, 94596-4183
Telephone: 510-943-6383
Facsimile: 510-943-7542

(See Next Column)

ANDERSON, GALLOWAY & LUCCHESE A PROFESSIONAL CORPORATION, *Walnut Creek—Continued*

Robert L. Anderson	Stephen J. Brooks
George Patrick Galloway	Joseph S. Picchi
David R. Lucchese	Coleen L. Welch
Martin J. Everson	Deborah C. Moritz-Farr
Thomas J. Donnelly	Marc G. Cowden
Ralph J. Smith	Erin Ruddy Sabey
James M. Nelson	Lea K. McMahan
Scott E. Murray	Michael E. Brewer
David A. Depolo	Sonja M. Dahl
Karen A. Sparks	Thomas J. Tarkoff

For full biographical listings, see the Martindale-Hubbell Law Directory

HINTON & ALFERT, A PROFESSIONAL CORPORATION (AV)

Suite 600, 1646 North California Boulevard, 94596-4113
Telephone: 510-932-6006
Fax: 510-932-3412

Peter J. Hinton	Peter W. Alfert
	Michael P. Clark

Scott H. Z. Sumner	Nancy A. Beninati

For full biographical listings, see the Martindale-Hubbell Law Directory

COLORADO

BOULDER,* Boulder Co.

COOK & LEE, P.C. (AV)

5390 Manhattan Circle, 2nd Floor, 80303
Telephone: 303-543-1000
Fax: 303-543-8582

Stephen H. Cook	Larry D. Lee

Deborah R. Kirschman

For full biographical listings, see the Martindale-Hubbell Law Directory

WILLIAMS & TRINE, P.C. (AV)

1435 Arapahoe Avenue, 80302-6390
Telephone: 303-442-0173
Fax: 303-443-7677

William A. Trine	J. Conard Metcalf
Joel H. Greenstein (1933-1984)	Mari C. Bush
	Michael A. Patrick

OF COUNSEL
Charles E. Williams

Reference: Norwest Bank of Boulder.

For full biographical listings, see the Martindale-Hubbell Law Directory

BROOMFIELD, Boulder Co.

SCHADEN, KATZMAN & LAMPERT (AV)

11870 Airport Way, 80021
Telephone: 303-465-3663
Facsimile: 303-465-3884
Bloomfield Hills, Michigan Office: Schaden, Katzman & Lampert, 33 Bloomfield Hills Parkway, Suite 145, 48304.
Telephone: 810-258-4800.
Fax: 810-258-9212.
Ft. Lauderdale, Florida Office: 1700 E. Las Olas Boulevard, Suite 7, 33301-2408.
Telephone: 954-522-5154.
Facsimile: 954-522-5184.

Richard F. Schaden
ASSOCIATE
Kathleen M. Schaden

For full biographical listings, see the Martindale-Hubbell Law Directory

DENVER,* Denver Co.

GRUND & BRESLAU, P.C. (AV)

303 East Seventeenth Avenue, Suite 1030, 80203-1260
Telephone: 303-830-7770
Facsimile: 303-830-2313

(See Next Column)

John W. Grund	Della S. Nelson
Brad W. Breslau	Phillip Jeffrey Frazee

Representative Clients: Admiral Insurance Co.; Avco Corp.; Coca Cola Enterprises, Inc.; Denver Coca-Cola Bottling Co.; Essex Insurance Co.; Figgie International, Inc.; Homestead Insurance Co.; Safway Steel Products, Inc.

For full biographical listings, see the Martindale-Hubbell Law Directory

PARCEL, MAURO, HULTIN & SPAANSTRA, P.C. (AV)

Suite 3600, 1801 California Street, 80202
Telephone: 303-292-6400
Telecopier: 303-295-3040

Paul F. Hultin	John R. Trigg
Michael L. O'Donnell	Gary Wagner
Lori L. Roberts	Malcolm E. Wheeler

Angella K. Bond	Lee A. Mickus
	Edward C. Stewart

Reference: 1st Interstate, Denver, Colorado.

For Complete List of Firm Personnel, See General Section

For full biographical listings, see the Martindale-Hubbell Law Directory

WELLS, ANDERSON & RACE, LLC (AV)

1700 Broadway, Suite 1850, 80290
Telephone: 303-830-1212
Fax: 303-830-0898

Mary A. Wells	Geoffrey S. Race
Sheryl L. Anderson	Suanne M. Dell

Gregory E. Sopkin

Representative Clients: Associated Aviation Underwriters; Baxter Healthcare Corporation; Raytheon Aircraft Company; The Cessna Aircraft Co.; State Industries Inc.

For full biographical listings, see the Martindale-Hubbell Law Directory

WHITE AND STEELE, PROFESSIONAL CORPORATION (AV)

1225 17th Street, Suite 2800, 80202
Telephone: 303-296-2828
Telecopier: 303-296-3131
Email: law@wsteele.com
Cheyenne, Wyoming Office: 1912 Capital Avenue, Suite 416, 82003.
Telephone: 307-778-4160.
Telecopier: 307-778-7041.

R. Eric Peterson	John P. Craver
Michael W. Anderson	David J. Nowak
James M. Dieterich	Frederick W. Klann
	Thomas B. Quinn

Colorado Tort Counsel for: Goodyear Tire and Rubber Co.; The Dow Chemical Co.; Celotex.
Insurance Clients: Allied Insurance Co.; CNA; Kemper Insurance Group; Massachusetts Mutual Life Insurance Co.; U.S.A.A.; Underwriters at Lloyds; Farmers Insurance Group.

For Complete List of Firm Personnel, See General Section

For full biographical listings, see the Martindale-Hubbell Law Directory

ENGLEWOOD, Arapahoe Co.

SALMON, GODSMAN & NICHOLSON, PROFESSIONAL CORPORATION (AV)

Salmon Law Building, (I-25 at East Belleview) 7450 East Progress Place, 80111
Telephone: 303-771-9900
Toll Free in Colorado: 1-800-547-9055
Fax: 303-773-6843
Breckenridge, Colorado Office: Briar Rose House, 213 Briar Rose Lane.
Telephone: 1-800-547-9055

John G. Salmon	William P. Godsman
	P. Randolph Nicholson

Francine R. Salazar	Penelope Clor

OF COUNSEL
Joseph M. Epstein

For full biographical listings, see the Martindale-Hubbell Law Directory

CONNECTICUT

BRIDGEPORT,* Fairfield Co.

BAI, POLLOCK AND COYNE, P.C. (AV)

Park City Plaza, 10 Middle Street, P.O. Box 1978, 06604
Telephone: 203-366-7991
Fax: 203-366-4723
Email: bpc@snet.net

Arnold J. Bai (1931-1992)	Garie J. Mulcahey
Paul E. Pollock	Raymond J. Plouffe, Jr.
James E. Coyne	Philip F. von Kuhn
Jeffrey A. Blueweiss	Madonna A. Sacco
	Michael S. Lynch

David J. Robertson	Colleen D. Fries
Edward P. Brady III	Neal P. Rogan
Andrew S. Turret	Jacquelyn Conlon
Gaileen A. Kaufman	Janine M. Savarese
Kevin S. Coyne	Louis A. Annecchino
	Kristin Beth Comstock

For full biographical listings, see the Martindale-Hubbell Law Directory

WILLIAMS, COONEY & SHEEHY (AV)

One Lafayette Circle, 06604
Telephone: 203-331-0888
Telecopier: 203-331-0896

MEMBERS OF FIRM

Ronald D. Williams	Peter J. Dauk
Robert J. Cooney	Dion W. Moore
Edward Maum Sheehy	Ronald D. Williams, Jr.
Peter D. Clark	Francis A. Smith, Jr.
	(1951-1989)

Michael P. Bowler	Paul Sean Curtin
Michael Cuff Deakin	Suzannah Kim Nigro

Representative Clients: Aetna Life & Casualty Co.; Nationwide Insurance Co.; The Travelers; Zimmer Manufacturing Co.; Textron-Lycoming: The Stop & Shop Companies, Inc.; Shawmut Bank Connecticut, N.A.; Utica Mutual Insurance Co.; Royal Insurance; General Star Indemnity Company.

For full biographical listings, see the Martindale-Hubbell Law Directory

NEW HAVEN,* New Haven Co.

JACOBS & JACOBS (AV)

700 State Street, 3rd Floor, 06511
Telephone: 203-777-2300
Fax: 203-787-5628

MEMBERS OF FIRM

Israel J. Jacobs (1918-1963)	Bruce D. Jacobs
Stanley A. Jacobs	Carol Wolven
	Irene Prosky Jacobs

Reference: Center Bank/First Union.

For full biographical listings, see the Martindale-Hubbell Law Directory

LYNCH, TRAUB, KEEFE AND ERRANTE, A PROFESSIONAL CORPORATION (AV)

52 Trumbull Street, P.O. Box 1612, 06506
Telephone: 203-787-0275
Fax: 203-782-0278
Email: ltke@snet.com *URL:* http://www.ltke.com

Stephen I. Traub	Donn A. Swift
Hugh F. Keefe	Charles E. Tiernan, III
Steven J. Errante	Robert W. Lynch
John J. Keefe, Jr.	Richard W. Lynch
	John M. Walsh, Jr.

Suzanne L. McAlpine	Lee Kennedy Tiernan
Christopher M. Licari	William F. Clark
Eric P. Smith	James A. Mongillo

OF COUNSEL
William C. Lynch

Local Counsel for: Transport Insurance Co., Dallas, Texas; American Trucking Associations; Roadway Express, Inc., Akron, Ohio; A.R.A. Philadelphia, Penn.; Consolidated Freightways, Menlo Park, California; Ogden Corp.; Southern Connecticut Gas Co.
Labor Counsel: Coca-Cola, U.S.A., Atlanta, Georgia (Private Truck Operation); The Dow Chemical Co.; Cincinnati Milacron; Southern Connecticut Gas Co.

For full biographical listings, see the Martindale-Hubbell Law Directory

PAUL A. SCHOLDER ATTORNEY AT LAW, P.C. (AV)

2 Whitney Avenue, P.O. Box 1722, 06507
Telephone: 203-777-7218
Fax: 203-772-2672
Email: PaulA.Scholder,P.C.102261.2673@CompuServe.com

Paul A. Scholder

John J. Morgan

References: Peoples Bank; Lafayette American Bank.

For full biographical listings, see the Martindale-Hubbell Law Directory

NEW LONDON, New London Co.

THE REARDON LAW FIRM, P.C. (AV)

160 Hempstead Street, Drawer 1430, 06320
Telephone: 860-442-0444
Telecopier: 860-444-6445

Robert I. Reardon, Jr.	Angelo A. Ziotas

Wayne W. Lambert, Jr.	Scott D. Camassar

LEGAL SUPPORT PERSONNEL

Bette B. Beam	Jillene E. Bennett (Paralegal)
(Legal Administrator)	Kimberly A. McGinnis
Kelly G. MacDonald (Paralegal)	(Paralegal)
	Sharon M. Burdsall (Paralegal)

For full biographical listings, see the Martindale-Hubbell Law Directory

STAMFORD, Fairfield Co.

SILVER, GOLUB & TEITELL (AV)

184 Atlantic Street, P.O. Box 389, 06904
Telephone: 203-325-4491
Fax: 203-325-3769

MEMBERS OF FIRM

Richard A. Silver	Patricia M. Haugh (1942-1988)
David S. Golub	Elaine T. Silver
Ernest F. Teitell	John D. Josel

Mario DiNatale	Jonathan L. Mannina
Jonathan M. Levine	Jennifer Cohen Goldstein
Marilyn J. Ramos	J. Michael Lewis

For full biographical listings, see the Martindale-Hubbell Law Directory

WALLINGFORD, New Haven Co.

DELANEY, ZEMETIS, DONAHUE, DURHAM & NOONAN, P.C. (AV)

111 South Main Street, P.O. Box 747, 06492
Telephone: 203-269-1441
Fax: 203-284-9428

Joseph M. Delaney	Timothy W. Donahue
Terence A. Zemetis	Michael G. Durham
	Patrick M. Noonan

Edward W. Mayer, Jr.	Edward T. Falsey, III
Thomas J. Flanagan	Mark Popolizio

For full biographical listings, see the Martindale-Hubbell Law Directory

DELAWARE

WILMINGTON,* New Castle Co.

WARREN B. BURT & ASSOCIATES (AV)

1700 Mellon Bank Center, 919 Market Street, 19801-3023
Telephone: 302-429-9430
Fax: 302-429-9427

ASSOCIATES

Richard D. Abrams	Michael F. Duggan

For full biographical listings, see the Martindale-Hubbell Law Directory

CASARINO, CHRISTMAN & SHALK (AV)

Suite 1220, 222 Delaware Avenue, P.O. Box 1276, 19899
Telephone: 302-594-4500
Telecopier: 302-594-4509

MEMBERS OF FIRM

Stephen P. Casarino	Beth H. Christman
Colin M. Shalk	Donald M. Ransom
	Patricia L. Peterson

(See Next Column)

CASARINO, CHRISTMAN & SHALK, *Wilmington—Continued*

| Kenneth M. Doss | Diane M. Willette |
| Patricia Bartley Schwartz | Stacey L. Cummings |

For full biographical listings, see the Martindale-Hubbell Law Directory

---

SMITH, KATZENSTEIN & FURLOW (AV)

The Corporate Plaza, 800 Delaware Avenue, P.O. Box 410, 19899
Telephone: 302-652-8400
Fax: 302-652-8405

MEMBERS OF FIRM

| Robert J. Katzenstein | Susan L. Parker |
| Laurence V. Cronin | |

For Complete List of Firm Personnel, See General Section

For full biographical listings, see the Martindale-Hubbell Law Directory

---

DISTRICT OF COLUMBIA

WASHINGTON, D.C. Co.

---

* indicates certain Bar Register subscribers, in cities of comparable size and importance, who maintain an additional office in Washington, D.C. and who have arranged for representation as a part of the Washington, D.C. listings that follow

ALLEN, JOHNSON, ALEXANDER & KARP, P.A. (AV)

1707 L Street, N.W., Suite 1050, 20036
Telephone: 202-828-4141
Fax: 202-429-8798
Baltimore, Maryland Office: Suite 1540, 100 East Pratt Street.
Telephone: 410-727-5000.

D'Ana E. Johnson

Representative Clients: Scottsdale Insurance Co.; Nautilus Insurance Co.; Jefferson Insurance Co.; Liberty Mutual Insurance Co.; Avis Rent-A-Car; Otis Elevator Co.; Montgomery Elevator Co.; Admiral Insurance Co.; Local Government Insurance Trust; Lancer Insurance Co.

For Complete List of Firm Personnel, See General Section

For full biographical listings, see the Martindale-Hubbell Law Directory

---

COALE & VAN SUSTEREN, A PROFESSIONAL CORPORATION (AV)

Chevy Chase Pavilion, 5335 Wisconsin Avenue N.W., Suite 720, 20015
Telephone: 202-686-6500
Facsimile: 202-686-9739

| John P. Coale (A Professional Corporation) | Greta C. Van Susteren (Currently on leave) |

| Diane E. Cooley | Julia Wernett McInerny |
| David K. Lietz | Charlsa (Sandy) Broadus |

For full biographical listings, see the Martindale-Hubbell Law Directory

---

COHEN, MILSTEIN, HAUSFELD & TOLL, P.L.L.C. (AV)

West Tower, Suite 500, 1100 New York Avenue, N.W., 20005-3964
Telephone: 202-408-4600
Facsimile: 202-408-4699

MEMBERS OF FIRM

Jerry S. Cohen (1925-1995)	Lisa M. Mezzetti
Herbert E. Milstein	Andrew N. Friedman
Michael D. Hausfeld	Richard S. Lewis
Steven J. Toll	Daniel S. Sommers
Ann C. Yahner	Daniel A. Small (Not admitted in DC)

ASSOCIATES

Gary E. Mason	Michael J. Flannery
Cyrus Mehri	Paul T. Gallagher
Sharon A. Snyder	Alexander E. Barnett
Mark S. Willis (Not admitted in DC)	Angeline G. Chen
Lillian S. Hagen	Victoria C. Arthaud (Not admitted in DC)

OF COUNSEL

Anthony Z. Roisman

For full biographical listings, see the Martindale-Hubbell Law Directory

---

CONDON & FORSYTH (AV)

1016 Sixteenth Street, N.W., 20036
Telephone: 202-289-0500
Telecopier: 202-289-4524
Email: 103345.1077@compuserve.com
New York, N.Y. Office: 1251 Avenue of the Americas.
Telephone: 212-921-5100.
Telex: 426978.
Telecopier: 212-575-3638; 212-575-1298; 212-719-3638.
Los Angeles, California Office: 1900 Avenue of the Stars.
Telephone: 310-557-2030.
Telecopier: 310-557-1299.

RESIDENT PARTNERS

| Thomas J. Whalen | Timothy J. Lynes |

COUNSEL

Evelyn D. Sahr

SENIOR ATTORNEY

David G. Schryver

RESIDENT ASSOCIATES

| Thomas E. Healey | David F. Rifkind (Not admitted in DC) |

For full biographical listings, see the Martindale-Hubbell Law Directory

---

KENNETH R. FEINBERG & ASSOCIATES (AV)

1120 20th Street, N.W. Suite 740 South, 20036
Telephone: 202-371-1110
Fax: 202-962-9290
New York, N.Y. Office: 780 3rd Avenue, Suite 2202.
Telephone: 212-527-9600.
Fax: 212-527-9611.

ASSOCIATES

Deborah E. Greenspan	Peter H. Woodin
Michael K. Rozen (Not admitted in DC)	(Not admitted in DC)
	M. Catherine Faint

OF COUNSEL

Jacqueline E. Zins

For full biographical listings, see the Martindale-Hubbell Law Directory

---

* VENABLE ATTORNEYS AT LAW VENABLE, BAETJER, HOWARD & CIVILETTI, LLP (AV)

A Partnership including Professional Corporations
Suite 1000, 1201 New York Avenue, N.W., 20005
Telephone: 202-962-4800
Fax: 202-962-8300
Baltimore, Maryland Office: Venable, Baetjer and Howard LLP, 1800 Mercantile Bank & Trust Building, 2 Hopkins Plaza.
Telephone: 410-244-7400.
McLean, Virginia Office: Venable, Baetjer and Howard LLP, Suite 400, 2010 Corporate Ridge.
Telephone: 703-760-1600.
Rockville, Maryland Office: Venable, Baetjer and Howard LLP, Suite 500, One Church Street, P. O. Box 1906.
Telephone: 301-217-5600.
Towson, Maryland Office: Venable, Baetjer and Howard LLP, 210 Allegheny Avenue, P. O. Box 5517.
Telephone: 410-494-6200.

MEMBERS OF FIRM

Benjamin R. Civiletti (P.C.) (Also at Baltimore and Towson, Maryland Offices)	Jeffrey A. Dunn (Also at Baltimore, Maryland Office)
Douglas D. Connah, Jr. (P.C.) (Also at Baltimore, Maryland Office)	George F. Pappas (Also at Baltimore, Maryland Office)
James K. Archibald (Also at Baltimore, Maryland Office)	James L. Shea (Not admitted in DC; also at Baltimore, Maryland Office)
	Gary M. Hnath

ASSOCIATE

David W. Goewey

For Complete List of Firm Personnel, See General Section

For full biographical listings, see the Martindale-Hubbell Law Directory

---

FLORIDA

DAYTONA BEACH, Volusia Co.

EUBANK, HASSELL & ASSOC., P.A. (AV)

Suite 301, 149 South Ridgewood Avenue, P.O. Box 2229, 32115-2229
Telephone: 904-238-1357
Telecopier: 904-258-7406

| James O. Eubank, II | F. Bradley Hassell |

(See Next Column)

EUBANK, HASSELL & ASSOC. P.A.—*Continued*

M. Jennifer Moorhead	K. Judith Lane
Timothy A. Traster	Wiley S. Boston
Perette M. Lawrence	C. Richard Penalta

For full biographical listings, see the Martindale-Hubbell Law Directory

FORT LAUDERDALE,* Broward Co.

KESSLER, MASSEY, CATRI, HOLTON & KESSLER, P.A. (AV)

110 Tower, Twentieth Floor, 110 Southeast Sixth Street, 33301
Telephone: 954-463-8593
Fax: 954-462-1303

Charles T. Kessler	Paula C. Kessler
Albert P. Massey, III	Gregory G. Coican
Wesley L. Catri	Andrea L. Kessler
Raymond O. Holton, Jr.	Edward D. Schuster

Gerard A. Tuzzio	Edwina V. Kessler

For full biographical listings, see the Martindale-Hubbell Law Directory

FORT MYERS,* Lee Co.

SMOOT ADAMS EDWARDS & GREEN, P.A. (AV)

One University Park Suite 600, 12800 University Drive, P.O. Box
   60259, 33906-6259
Telephone: 941-489-1776
(800) 226-1777 (in Florida)
Fax: 941-489-2444
Email: 71600.2745@compuserve.com

J. Tom Smoot, Jr.	Bruce D. Green
Hal Adams	Steven I. Winer
Franklyn A. (Chip) Johnson	Mark R. Komray
(1947-1991)	Clayton W. Crevasse
Charles B. Edwards	M. Brian Cheffer

Robert S. Forman	C. Berk Edwards, Jr.
Kathleen W. McBride	Melville G. Brinson, III
Lowell Schoenfeld	Samuel J. Hagan, IV.

For full biographical listings, see the Martindale-Hubbell Law Directory

JACKSONVILLE,* Duval Co.

COWLES & SHAUGHNESSY, P.A. (AV)

Blackstone Building, Suite 901, 233 East Bay Street, 32202
Telephone: 904-359-9500
Fax: 904-359-9717

Robert L. Cowles	Daniel C. Shaughnessy
	Nancy E. Kemner

Eric C. Ragatz

Representative Clients: Mazda Motor of America; The Coca-Cola Co.; Genuine Parts Co.; Harley Davidson Motor Company; General Tire, Inc.; Bankhead Enterprises, Inc.; Fimez, Sp.A.

For full biographical listings, see the Martindale-Hubbell Law Directory

LILES, GAVIN & COSTANTINO (AV)

One Enterprise Center, Suite 1500, 225 Water Street, 32202
Telephone: 904-634-1100
Fax: 904-634-1234

Rutledge R. Liles	R. Kyle Gavin
	R. Scott Costantino

ASSOCIATE
Niels P. Murphy

For full biographical listings, see the Martindale-Hubbell Law Directory

PAJCIC & PAJCIC, P.A. (AV)

1900 Independent Square, 32202
Telephone: 904-358-8881
Fax: 904-354-1180

Gary Pajcic	Robert J. Link
Stephen J. Pajcic, III	Lee T. Griffin
Katherine Brown	Christine A. Clark
William S. Burns, Jr.	Thomas F. Slater

Reference: Barnett Bank of Jacksonville, N.A.

For full biographical listings, see the Martindale-Hubbell Law Directory

MIAMI,* Dade Co.

CLARKE SILVERGLATE WILLIAMS & MONTGOMERY (AV)

A Partnership of Professional Corporations
100 North Biscayne Boulevard Suite 2401, 33132
Telephone: 305-377-0700
Facsimile: 305-377-3001
Chicago, Illinois Office: Williams & Montgomery, Ltd., 20 North Wacker
Drive, Suite 2100.
Telephone: 312-443-3200.
Telex: 206598.
Facsimile: 312-443-1323.
Waukegan, Illinois Office: Williams & Montgomery, Ltd., 33 North
County Street.
Telephone: 847-360-1220.
Wheaton, Illinois Office: Williams & Montgomery, Ltd., 310 S. County
Farm Road.
Telephone: 708-690-3200.
Joliet, Illinois Office: Williams & Montgomery, Ltd., 81 North Chicago
Avenue.
Telephone: 815-727-2653.

Mercer K. Clarke	Spencer H. Silverglate

OF COUNSEL
Henry H. Bolz, III

ASSOCIATES

Kelly Anne Luther	Eric L. Lundt
William C. Abruzzo	Carol A. Grant

For full biographical listings, see the Martindale-Hubbell Law Directory

DEUTSCH & BLUMBERG, P.A. (AV)

Suite 2802 New World Tower, 100 North Biscayne Boulevard, 33132
Telephone: 305-358-6329
Fax: 305-358-9304

Steven K. Deutsch	James C. Blecke
Edward R. Blumberg	Louis Thaler

For full biographical listings, see the Martindale-Hubbell Law Directory

EVERSOLE & RUDD, P.A. (AV)

Suite 106, Grove Forest Plaza, 2937 SW 27th Avenue, 33133
Telephone: 305-444-2255
Facsimile: 305-444-7288
Fort Lauderdale, Florida Office: 3511 Northeast 22nd Avenue, Suite 100.
Telephone: 954-563-4199.
Fax: 954-563-4030. Boca Raton Office: 2500 North Military Trail, Suite
102.
Telephone: 407-998-9900.
Fax: 407-998-4995.

John F. Eversole, III	James D. Rudd

For full biographical listings, see the Martindale-Hubbell Law Directory

THEODORE J. FOURNARIS PROFESSIONAL ASSOCIATION (AV)

145 Almeria Avenue (Coral Gables), 33134
Telephone: 305-448-7333
Telefax: 305-448-7394

Theodore J. Fournaris	Jose M. Cañas

OF COUNSEL
Morton J. Sanet

For full biographical listings, see the Martindale-Hubbell Law Directory

HADDAD, JOSEPHS, JACK, GAEBE & MARKARIAN (AV)

1493 Sunset Drive (Coral Gables), P.O. Box 345118, 33114
Telephone: Dade County: 305-666-6006
Telecopier: 305-662-9931
URL: http://www.haddadjosephs.com

MEMBERS OF FIRM

Gil Haddad	Lewis N. Jack, Jr.
Michael R. Josephs	John S. Gaebe
	David K. Markarian

ASSOCIATES

Elisabeth M. Allen	Lauren M. Ilvento
Helen Leen Miranda	Clifford A. Wolff
	John William Gautier

Representative Clients: U-Haul Corporation; ITT Sheraton; Zurich-American Insurance Company; Republic Claims Service Company; Southern Fire Insurance Adjusters.

For full biographical listings, see the Martindale-Hubbell Law Directory

Miami—Continued

HARDY & BISSETT, P.A. (AV)

501 Northeast First Avenue, 33132
Telephone: 305-358-6200
Broward: 954-462-6377
Fax: 305-577-8230
Email: 102132.403@compuserve.com
Boca Raton, Florida Office: 2201 Corporate Boulevard, N.W., Suite 205.
Telephone: 407-998-9202.
Telecopier: 407-998-9693.

G. Jack Hardy   G. William Bissett

Howard K. Cherna   H. Dane Mottlau
Lee Philip Teichner   Jana Marie Yaw

Representative Clients: International Paper Co.; Masonite Corp.; Bridgestone/Firestone Inc.; American International Underwriters; American International Group, Inc.; Crown Equipment Corp.; The Coleman Co., Inc.; Brown & Williamson; Black & Decker (U.S.), Inc.; S-B Power Tool Company.

For full biographical listings, see the Martindale-Hubbell Law Directory

RUSSO & CULMO, P.A. (AV)

Suite 2000, 2601 South Bayshore Drive (Coconut Grove), 33133
Telephone: 305-854-3100
Fax: 305-854-5949

Don Russo   Thomas A. Culmo
              Deborah J. Gander

For full biographical listings, see the Martindale-Hubbell Law Directory

LELAND E. STANSELL, JR., P.A. (AV)

903 Biscayne Building, 19 West Flagler Street, 33130
Telephone: 305-374-5911
Fax: 305-374-5337

Leland E. Stansell, Jr.

Roberto M. Ureta

For full biographical listings, see the Martindale-Hubbell Law Directory

NICEVILLE, Okaloosa Co.

STANLEY BRUCE POWELL, P.A. (AV)

107 North Partin Drive, P.O. Box 400, 32588-0400
Telephone: 904-678-2118
Fax: 904-678-8336
Destin, Florida Office: Suite 21 Commerce Row, 225 Main Street.
Telephone: 904-837-9099.

Stanley Bruce Powell   David R. Swanick III

Representative Clients: Peoples National Bank of Niceville; Destin Bank; D&H Oil Co.
References: Peoples National Bank of Niceville; Destin Bank; Barnett Bank of Northwest Florida; Vanguard Bank and Trust Co.

For full biographical listings, see the Martindale-Hubbell Law Directory

ORLANDO,* Orange Co.

CABANISS & BURKE, P.A. (AV)

One Orlando Centre, Suite 1800, 800 North Magnolia Avenue, P.O. Box 2513, 32802-2513
Telephone: 407-246-1800
Fax: 407-246-1895
Tallahassee, Florida Office: 909 East Park Avenue, 32301.
Telephone: 904-561-6212.
Fax: 904-561-6214.

Ronald E. Cabaniss   Francis M. McDonald, Jr.
Thomas M. Burke   Larry D. Smith
Dean Bunch   Chris N. Kolos
  (Resident Tallahassee Office) J. Hood Roberts
              Michael J. Wiggins

Scott E. Damon   Michelle M. Perez-Sotolongo
Sarah A. Long   Winifred H. Quinlan
              F. Rand Wallis

For full biographical listings, see the Martindale-Hubbell Law Directory

LAW OFFICES OF DURIE & LAWSON, P.A. (AV)

1000 East Robinson Street, 32801
Telephone: 407-841-6000; 1-800-940-0442
Fax: 407-841-2425

(See Next Column)

Jack F. (Jay) Durie, Jr.   C. Alan Lawson

For full biographical listings, see the Martindale-Hubbell Law Directory

MAHER, GIBSON AND GUILEY A PROFESSIONAL ASSOCIATION OF LAWYERS (AV)

Suite 200, 90 East Livingston Street, 32801
Telephone: 407-839-0866
Fax: 407-425-7958

Michael Maher   Patricia M. Gibson
              David D. Guiley

Steven R. Maher   Robin M. Orosz
              Monique M. Edwards
                   OF COUNSEL
              John Edward Jones (P.A.)
         LEGAL SUPPORT PERSONNEL
       INSURANCE CLAIM COORDINATOR
              Charles R. Simpson

For full biographical listings, see the Martindale-Hubbell Law Directory

MARTINEZ, DALTON, DELLECKER & WILSON, PROFESSIONAL ASSOCIATION (AV)

719 Vassar Street, 32804
Telephone: 407-425-0712
Fax: 407-425-1856
URL: http://www.pixelstorm.com/mddw

Mel R. Martinez   Robert H. Dellecker
Roy B. Dalton, Jr.   Brian T. Wilson

Leticia Marques

For full biographical listings, see the Martindale-Hubbell Law Directory

OVERCHUCK & LANGA, P.A. (AV)

Suite 100, 90 East Livingston Street, 32801
Telephone: 407-839-0661
Fax: 407-839-4991

John R. Overchuck   Alan M. Schwerer
Ronald J. Langa   C. Richard Newsome

For full biographical listings, see the Martindale-Hubbell Law Directory

PARRISH, BAILEY & MORSCH, P.A. (AV)

116 America Street, 32801
Telephone: 407-849-1776

Sidney H. Parrish   Michael K. Bailey
              Mark V. Morsch

Donald A. Myers, Jr.

For full biographical listings, see the Martindale-Hubbell Law Directory

PENSACOLA,* Escambia Co.

BRIDGERS, GILL & HOLMAN (AV)

121 Palafox Place, 32501
Telephone: 904-432-6484
Fax: 904-432-6383

            MEMBERS OF FIRM
J. Dixon Bridgers, III   Stephen T. Holman
Jeffrey P. Gill   Tracey Scalfano Witt

For full biographical listings, see the Martindale-Hubbell Law Directory

FULLER, JOHNSON & FARRELL, P.A. (AV)

Quayside Quarters, 700 South Palafox, Suite 170, P.O. Box 12219, 32581
Telephone: 904-434-8845
Fax: 904-432-6667
Tallahassee, Florida Office: 111 North Calhoun Street, P.O. Box 1739, 32302-1739.
Telephone: 904-224-4663.
Fax: 904-561-8839.

Belinda Barnes deKozan   Alan R. Horky
Michael W. Kehoe   Christopher R. Johnson

Representative Clients: American Motors Corp.; Amoco Oil Co.; Black & Decker (U.S.), Inc.; Ford Motor Co.; Hitachi Power Tools USA, Ltd.; Hoffman-LaRoche, Inc.; Montgomery Ward and Company, Inc.; Robeson Industrial Corp.; Ryder Truck Lines, Inc.; Squibb, Inc.

For full biographical listings, see the Martindale-Hubbell Law Directory

Pensacola—Continued

B. RICHARD YOUNG, P.A. (AV)

309B South Palafox Place, 32501
Telephone: 904-432-2222
Fax: 904-432-1444

B. Richard Young
————————————

Penny L. Hendrix   Michael T. Bill

For full biographical listings, see the Martindale-Hubbell Law Directory

ST. PETERSBURG, Pinellas Co.

CHAMBERS, SALZMAN & BANNON, PROFESSIONAL ASSOCIATION (AV)

520 Fourth Street North, 33701
Telephone: 813-896-2167
Fax: 813-822-8981

Joseph H. Chambers   Rick G. Bannon
Barry M. Salzman   Joseph W. Chambers
        Jeffrey K. Chambers

Reference: NationsBank.

For full biographical listings, see the Martindale-Hubbell Law Directory

SARASOTA,* Sarasota Co.

NELSON ● HESSE (AV)

2070 Ringling Boulevard, P.O. Box 2524, 34230
Telephone: 941-366-7550
Fax: 941-955-3708

MEMBERS OF FIRM

Richard E. Nelson   Omer S. Causey
Ronald Alexander Cyril   William A. Dooley
  (1938-1988)   Michael S. Drews
Richard L. Smith   Frederick J. Elbrecht
F. Steven Herb   Gary W. Peal

ASSOCIATES

Philip Sypula   J. Neal Mobley
        Stephen M. Walker

General Counsel for: Enterprise National Bank; Dooley Mack Construction Co.
Representative Clients: Wellcraft Marine; Attorneys Title Insurance Fund; Travelers Insurance; SMH Radiology, Inc.; The Carlton Ranch, Inc.
References: Southtrust Bank; Enterprise National Bank.

For full biographical listings, see the Martindale-Hubbell Law Directory

TALLAHASSEE,* Leon Co.

FONVIELLE & HINKLE (AV)

3375-A Capital Circle Northeast, 32308
Telephone: 904-422-7773
Fax: 904-422-3449
Email: lawyers@fonhink.com *URL:* http://www.fonhink.com

MEMBERS OF FIRM

C. David Fonvielle   Halley B. Lewis, III
Donald M. Hinkle   William H. Garvin III
        John H. Foote

LEGAL SUPPORT PERSONNEL

Sandra M. Tate

For full biographical listings, see the Martindale-Hubbell Law Directory

FULLER, JOHNSON & FARRELL, P.A. (AV)

111 North Calhoun Street, P.O. Box 1739, 32302-1739
Telephone: 904-224-4663
Fax: 904-561-8839
Pensacola, Florida Office: Quayside Quarters, 700 South Palafox, Suite 170, P.O. Box 12219, 32581.
Telephone: 904-434-8845.
FAX: 904-432-6667.

Ben A. Andrews   Kathryn L. Johnson
Jeannette M. Andrews   Michael W. Kehoe
Wm. Stephen Black, II   (Resident, Pensacola Office)
Marjorie M. Cain   J. Craig Knox
Robert C. Crabtree   Belinda Barnes deKozan
Patrick J. Farrell, Jr.   (Resident, Pensacola Office)
S. William Fuller, Jr.   William R. Mabile, III
Alan R. Horky   P. Scott Mitchell
  (Resident, Pensacola Office) Steven Michael Puritz
Christopher R. Johnson   Paul A. Shapiro
  (Resident, Pensacola Office) Cynthia D. Simmons
Fred M. Johnson   Beverly H. Smith
        Michael J. Thomas

Representative Clients: Aetna Life & Casualty; American Continental Insurance Company; American International Group; American States Insurance Company; Amoco Oil Company; Anesthesiologists' Professional Assurance

(See Next Column)

Trust; Black & Decker (U.S.), Inc.; Bruno's, Inc.; CIGNA Companies; Coca-Cola Enterprises, Inc.

For full biographical listings, see the Martindale-Hubbell Law Directory

McFARLAIN, WILEY, CASSEDY & JONES, PROFESSIONAL ASSOCIATION (AV)

215 South Monroe Street, Suite 600, P.O. Box 2174, 32316-2174
Telephone: 904-222-2107
Telecopier: 904-222-8475

Richard C. McFarlain   Charles A. Stampelos
William B. Wiley   Linda McMullen
Marshall R. Cassedy   H. Darrell White, Jr.
Douglas P. Jones   Christopher Barkas
————————————
Harold R. Mardenborough, Jr.   Rogelio J. Fontela
Robert A. McNeely   Patrick John McGinley

For full biographical listings, see the Martindale-Hubbell Law Directory

TAMPA,* Hillsborough Co.

MICHAEL C. ADDISON (AV)

Suite 2175, 100 North Tampa Street, 33602-5145
Telephone: 813-223-2000
Facsimile: 813-228-6000
Mailing Address: P.O. Box 2175, Tampa, Florida, 33601-2175
Email: 72100.337@compuserve.com

For full biographical listings, see the Martindale-Hubbell Law Directory

TIMOTHY G. ANDERSON, P.A. (AV)

213 South Brevard Avenue, 33606
Telephone: 813-251-0072

Timothy G. Anderson
————————————

Leslie L. Harley   Scott T. McCullough

For full biographical listings, see the Martindale-Hubbell Law Directory

BAVOL, BUSH & SISCO, P.A. (AV)

100 South Ashley, Suite 2100, P.O. Box 3423, 33601-3423
Telephone: 813-228-7000
Telefax: 813-273-0091

Charles D. Bavol   Dale R. Sisco
Ronald E. Bush   Ricardo A. Fernandez
————————————
Audrey B. Rauchway   Edward M. Rooks
Andrew L. Rosenkranz   Harold L. Sebring, III

For full biographical listings, see the Martindale-Hubbell Law Directory

CUNNINGHAM LAW GROUP, P.A. (AV)

100 Ashley Drive, South, Suite 100, 33602
Telephone: 813-228-0505
Telefax: 813-229-7982

Anthony W. Cunningham   James D. Clark
Donald G. Greiwe   Dana Solin Kanfer

For full biographical listings, see the Martindale-Hubbell Law Directory

RYWANT, ALVAREZ, JONES & RUSSO, PROFESSIONAL ASSOCIATION (AV)

Suite 500 Perry Paint & Glass Building, 109 North Brush Street, P.O. Box 3283, 33601
Telephone: 813-229-7007
Fax: 813-223-6544
Ocala, Florida Office: 3300 S.W. 34th Avenue, Suite 124C, 32674.
Telephone: 904-237-8810.
FAX: 904-237-2022.

Manuel J. Alvarez   Steven D. Lehner
Jill Diziel Emerson   Burke G. Lopez
Darrell D. Dirks   Kerry C. McGuinn, Jr.
Matthew D. Emerson   Andrew F. Russo
John A.C. Guyton, III   Michael S. Rywant
Gregory D. Jones   James R. Wilson

LEGAL SUPPORT PERSONNEL

Bradley Hugh Holt

Representative Clients: Peerless Insurance Co.; Gulf Insurance Group; Employers Casualty Co.; Landmark Insurance Co.

For full biographical listings, see the Martindale-Hubbell Law Directory

Tampa—Continued

CHARLES F. SANSONE (AV)

Suite 200, 701 North Franklin Street, 33602
Telephone: 813-223-9282
FAX: 813-229-0595

For full biographical listings, see the Martindale-Hubbell Law Directory

YERRID, KNOPIK & MUDANO, P.A. (AV)

Barnett Plaza, Suite 2160, 101 East Kennedy Boulevard, 33602
Telephone: 813-222-8222
Fax: 813-222-8224

C. Steven Yerrid

For full biographical listings, see the Martindale-Hubbell Law Directory

WEST PALM BEACH, * Palm Beach Co.

DAVIS, GORDON, DONER & CHANDLER, P.A. (AV)

515 North Flagler Drive, 7th Floor, 33401
Telephone: 561-659-7337
Facsimile: 561-659-0143
URL: http//www.dgdc.com

Zell Davis, Jr.	Adam S. Doner
Robert E. Gordon	Lawrence U. L. Chandler

Lawrence L. Klayman	Deirdre E. Brett

OF COUNSEL

Charles J. Oswald	Mikel D. Jones
	(Not admitted in FL)

For full biographical listings, see the Martindale-Hubbell Law Directory

LYTAL, REITER, CLARK, SHARPE, ROCA, FOUNTAIN & WILLIAMS (AV)

A Partnership of Professional Associations
Tenth Floor, 515 North Flagler Drive, 33401
Telephone: 561-655-1990
Fax: 561-832-2932
Mailing Address: P.O. Box 4056, 33402

Lake Lytal, Jr. (P.A.)	Tracy R. Sharpe (P.A.)
Joseph J. Reiter (P.A.)	Rafael J. Roca (P.A.)
Mark W. Clark (P.A.)	Donald R. Fountain, Jr. (P.A.)
William S. Williams (P.A.)	

Michael J. Overbeck	David M. Gaspari
Yvette Trelles Murray	Julie H. Littky-Rubin
Kevin C. Smith	Nancy L. La Vista
David C. Prather	

Reference: United National Bank.

For full biographical listings, see the Martindale-Hubbell Law Directory

SEARCY DENNEY SCAROLA BARNHART & SHIPLEY, PROFESSIONAL ASSOCIATION (AV)

2139 Palm Beach Lakes Boulevard, P.O. Drawer 3626, 33402-3626
Telephone: 407-686-6300
800-780-8607
800-220-7006 (Spanish)
Fax: 407-478-0754

Christian D. Searcy, Sr.	Lawrence J. Block, Jr.
Earl L. Denney, Jr.	C. Calvin Warriner, III
John Scarola	William A. Norton
F. Gregory Barnhart	David J. Sales
John A. Shipley	Christopher K. Speed
David K. Kelley, Jr.	William B. King

Karen E. Terry	T. Michael Kennedy
Katherine Ann Martinez	Todd S. Stewart
Laurie J. Briggs	

LEGAL SUPPORT PERSONNEL

Deane L. Cady	J. Peter Love
(Paralegal/Investigator)	(Paralegal/Investigator)
James E. Cook	Marjorie A. Morgan (Paralegal)
(Paralegal/Investigator)	William H. Seabold
Emilio Diamantis	(Paralegal/Investigator)
(Paralegal/Investigator)	Kathleen Simon (Paralegal)
David W. Gilmore	Steve M. Smith
(Paralegal/Investigator)	(Paralegal/Investigator)
Thaddeus E. Kulesa	Judson Whitehorn
(Paralegal/Investigator)	(Paralegal/Investigator)

For full biographical listings, see the Martindale-Hubbell Law Directory

GEORGIA

ATHENS, * Clarke Co.

BLASINGAME, BURCH, GARRARD, BRYANT & ASHLEY, P.C. (AV)

440 College Avenue North, P.O. Box 832, 30603
Telephone: 706-354-4000
Telecopier: 706-353-0673
Greensboro, Georgia Office: 122 N. Main Street, P.O. Box 67, 30642.
Telephone: 706-453-7139.
Fax: 706-453-7842.

J. Ralph Beaird	Andrew J. Hill, III
Gary B. Blasingame	Michael A. Morris
E. Davison Burch	Thomas H. Rogers, Jr.
Henry G. Garrard, III	William D. Harvard
Everett Clay Bryant	Rikard L. Bridges
W. Seaborn Ashley, Jr.	Ivan A. Gustafson
M. Steven Heath	David S. Thomson

Richard W. Schmidt	Christopher G. Conley
Milton F. Eisenberg	Lloyd N. Bell
Stephen E.B. Smith	Kim T. Stephens
J. Branson Parker	Amy Lou Reynolds
J. David Felt, Jr.	C. Kathryn Hackney
Kathleen M. Timmons	

Representative Clients: NationsBank of Georgia, N.A.; Georgia Power Co.; Georgia Natural Gas Co.; Pittsburgh Corning Corp.; Downtown Athens Development Authority; Georgia National Bank; Fowler Products Co., Inc.; St. Paul Fire & Marine Insurance Co.; Athens Newspapers, Inc.; First Commerce Bancorp, Inc.

For full biographical listings, see the Martindale-Hubbell Law Directory

ATLANTA, * Fulton Co.

BIRD, BALLARD & STILL (AV)

14 Seventeenth Street, Suite 5, P.O. Box 7009, 30357
Telephone: 404-873-4696
Fax: 404-872-3745

William Q. Bird	William L. Ballard
Edward R. Still	John G. Mabrey
Karin L. Allen	

For full biographical listings, see the Martindale-Hubbell Law Directory

BLACKWOOD, MATTHEWS & STEEL (AV)

2695 Buford Highway Suite 100, 30324-3239
Telephone: 404-636-9797
Fax: 404-320-9790

MEMBERS OF FIRM

James B. Matthews, III	John D. Steel

For full biographical listings, see the Martindale-Hubbell Law Directory

BUTLER, WOOTEN, OVERBY, CHEELEY, PEARSON & FRYHOFER (AV)

2719 Buford Highway, 30324
Telephone: 404-321-1700
WATS 1-800-242-2962
Fax: 404-321-1713
Columbus, Georgia Office: 1500 Second Avenue, P.O. Box 2766.
Telephone: 706-322-1990; National Wats: 1-800-233-4086.
Fax: 706-323-2962.

MEMBERS OF FIRM

James E. Butler, Jr.	Albert M. Pearson, III
Joel O. Wooten, Jr.	George W. Fryhofer III
C. Frederick Overby	Peter J. Daughtery
Robert D. Cheeley	J. Frank Myers, III
Lee Tarte Wallace	

ASSOCIATES

Jason L. Crawford	Joshua Sacks
Keith A. Pittman	Teresa Thomas Abell
Cale H. Conley	

Reference: Columbus Bank and Trust, Columbus, Ga.

For full biographical listings, see the Martindale-Hubbell Law Directory

DOFFERMYRE, SHIELDS, CANFIELD, KNOWLES & DEVINE (AV)

Suite 1600, 1355 Peachtree Street, 30309
Telephone: 404-881-8900

Robert E. Shields	Kenneth S. Canfield
Ralph I. Knowles, Jr.	

(See Next Column)

DOFFERMYRE, SHIELDS, CANFIELD, KNOWLES & DEVINE—*Continued*

ASSOCIATES

Georgiana Rizk   Robert Hutton Brown, III
                    Laura M. Shamp

For full biographical listings, see the Martindale-Hubbell Law Directory

DREW ECKL & FARNHAM (AV)

880 West Peachtree Street, P.O. Box 7600, 30357
Telephone: 404-885-1400
Facsimile: 404-876-0992
Email: drew@igc.apc.org

MEMBERS OF FIRM

W. Wray Eckl	G. Randall Moody
Arthur H. Glaser	B. Holland Pritchard
James M. Poe	T. Bart Gary
Theodore Freeman	Kenneth A. Hindman
John P. Reale	Paul W. Burke
Stevan A. Miller	Daniel C. Kniffen
H. Michael Bagley	John C. Bruffey, Jr.
Hall F. McKinley III	John G. Blackmon, Jr.

Gary R. Hurst

ASSOCIATES

Nicole D. Tifverman	Terrence T. Rock
L. Lee Bennett, Jr.	Phillip Comer Griffeth
Katherine D. Dixon	Marian S. Singer
William T. Mitchell	Steven D. Prelutsky
J. Robb Cruser	Julianne L. Swilley
Philip Wade Savrin	B. Greg Cline
Lucian Gillis, Jr.	Patricia R. Stevens
Peter H. Schmidt, II	C. Lawrence Meyer
April Rich	Philip G. Pompilio
Maureen M. Middleton	Robert J. Moye III
Robert L. Welch	Sean W. Conley
Suzanne VonHarten Sanders	Mary Anne Ackourey
Leigh Lawson Reeves	Beverly Powell Sisk
Bruce A. Taylor, Jr.	Marion M. Handley
Douglas M. Baker	Donald M. McManus, Jr.
David R. Bergquist	Gregory G. Schultz
Charles L. Norton, Jr.	Christopher R. Stovall
Douglas G. Smith, Jr.	Scott P. Archer
	(Not admitted in GA)

OF COUNSEL

Charles L. Drew   Anne M. Landrum

Representative Clients: CNA Insurance Co.; Liberty Mutual Insurance Co.; Cooper Tire & Rubber Co.; Denman Tire Corp.; Warner Lambert Corp.; Advanced Hunting Equipment Co., Inc.; Garden Way, Inc.; Hanson Industries, Inc.; Vibroplant USA.

For Complete List of Firm Personnel, See General Section

For full biographical listings, see the Martindale-Hubbell Law Directory

ENGLAND & McKNIGHT (AV)

Suite 410 River Ridge, 9040 Roswell Road, 30350
Telephone: 770-641-6010
FAX: 770-641-6003

MEMBERS OF FIRM

J. Melvin England   Robert H. McKnight, Jr.

Reference: Nations Bank N.A.

For full biographical listings, see the Martindale-Hubbell Law Directory

GARLAND, SAMUEL & LOEB, P.C. (AV)

3151 Maple Drive, N.E., 30305
Telephone: 404-262-2225
Fax: 404-365-5041
Email: TrialLaw@aol.com

Edward T. M. Garland   Donald F. Samuel
                    Robin N. Loeb

For full biographical listings, see the Martindale-Hubbell Law Directory

GOLDNER, SOMMERS, SCRUDDER & BASS (AV)

900 Circle 75 Parkway Suite 850, 30339
Telephone: 770-612-9200
Facsimile: 770-612-9201

Stephen L. Goldner   Glenn S. Bass
Henry E. Scrudder, Jr.   C. G. Jester, Jr.

For Complete List of Firm Personnel, See General Section

For full biographical listings, see the Martindale-Hubbell Law Directory

HAWKINS & PARNELL (AV)

4000 SunTrust Plaza, 303 Peachtree Street, N.E., 30308-3243
Telephone: 404-614-7400
Fax: 404-614-7500
Email: 73541.1626@compuserve.com

MEMBERS OF FIRM

Albert H. Parnell	Stephen M. Lore
A. Timothy Jones	William H. Major, III
Alan F. Herman	T. Ryan Mock, Jr.
Michael J. Goldman	Lawrence J. Myers
H. Lane Young, II	Warner S. Fox
Joseph R. Cullens	Michael E. Hutchins
Julia Bennett Jagger	Ollie M. Harton

Kimberly Houston Ridley

ASSOCIATES

Edward C. Henderson, Jr.	Allen L. Broughton
Stephen M. Brooks	Kristine Berry Morain
	Jeb T. Branham

Representative Clients: The Coca-Cola Co.; Eli Lilly and Co.; Atlantic Richfield; Ericsson, Inc.; American Suzuki Motor Co.; Baxter Healthcare Corporation; MEDMARC; Suburban Manufacturing Company; Hoechst Celanese Corporation.

For Complete List of Firm Personnel, See General Section

For full biographical listings, see the Martindale-Hubbell Law Directory

HILL AND BLEIBERG (AV)

Suite 200, 47 Perimeter Center East, 30346
Telephone: 770-394-7800
Fax: 770-394-7802

MEMBERS OF FIRM

Robert P. Bleiberg   Gary Hill

For full biographical listings, see the Martindale-Hubbell Law Directory

JOHNSON & WARD (AV)

2100 The Equitable Building, 100 Peachtree Street N.W., 30303-1962
Telephone: 404-524-5626
Facsimile: 404-524-1769

MEMBERS OF FIRM

William C. Lanham   John C. Dabney, Jr.
Clark H. McGehee   Bruce A. Maxwell

For Complete List of Firm Personnel, See General Section

For full biographical listings, see the Martindale-Hubbell Law Directory

KILPATRICK & CODY LLP (AV)

Suite 2800, 1100 Peachtree Street, 30309-4530
Telephone: 404-815-6500
Telephone Copier: 404-815-6555
Telex: 54-2307
Washington, D.C. Office: Suite 800, 700 13th Street, N.W., 20005.
Telephone: 202-508-5800. Telephone Copier: 202-508-5858.
Brussels, Belgium Office: Avenue Louise 65, BTE 3, 1050 Brussels.
Telephone: (32) (2) 533-03-00.
Telecopier: (32) (2) 534-86-38.
London, England Office: 68 Pall Mall, London, SW1Y 5ES, England.
Telephone: (44) (71) 321 0477.
Telecopier: (44) (71) 930 9733.
Augusta, Georgia Office: Suite 1400 First Union Bank Building, P.O. Box 2043, 30903. Telephone (706) 724-2622. Telecopier (706) 722-0219.

MEMBERS OF FIRM

G. William Austin, III	A. Stephens Clay
Joseph M. Beck	Alan R. Perry, Jr.
Susan A. Cahoon	Caroline W. Spangenberg

For Complete List of Firm Personnel, See General Section

For full biographical listings, see the Martindale-Hubbell Law Directory

MILLS & MORAITAKIS (AV)

Resurgens Plaza, Suite 2515 945 East Paces Ferry Road, Northeast, 30326
Telephone: 404-261-0016
Facsimile: 404-261-0024

Roger Mills   Nicholas C. Moraitakis
                    Glenn E. Kushel

For full biographical listings, see the Martindale-Hubbell Law Directory

MOZLEY, FINLAYSON & LOGGINS LLP (AV)

A Limited Liability Partnership
One Premier Plaza Suite 900, 5605 Glenridge Drive, 30342
Telephone: 404-256-0700
Telecopier: 404-250-9355

(See Next Column)

MOZLEY, FINLAYSON & LOGGINS LLP, *Atlanta—Continued*

MEMBERS OF FIRM

J. Arthur Mozley	Eric D. Griffin, Jr.
Sewell K. Loggins	Richard D. Hall

Lawrence B. Domenico

ASSOCIATE

J. Marcus Howard

For full biographical listings, see the Martindale-Hubbell Law Directory

NALL, MILLER, OWENS, HOCUTT & HOWARD (AV)

Suite 200 Peachtree & Broad Building, 66 Luckie Street, 30303
Telephone: 404-522-2200
Fax: 404-522-2208

MEMBERS OF FIRM

A. Walton Nall (1908-1984)	James R. Howard
James W. Dorsey (1914-1978)	George Robert Neuhauser
Edward S. White (1913-1992)	Robert L. Goldstucker
James S. Owens, Jr.	Kenneth P. McDuffie
Robert B. Hocutt	Kelly Eulenfeld Malone

Michael D. Hostetter

COUNSEL

Samuel A. Miller

ASSOCIATES

Charles Richard Carson	Paul Jay Pontrelli

Mary Anne Palma

LEGAL SUPPORT PERSONNEL

W. Gary Bush (Registered	Michelle McGhee (Paralegal)
Nurse, Legal Assistant)	Sheri L. Jordan (Paralegal)

Representative Clients: GenCorp., Inc.; Hoover Treated Wood Products; Inter-City Products Corporation (U.S.A.); Lennox International, Inc.; Revco Discount Drug Centers, Inc.; Whirlpool Corporation; Winnebago Industries.

For full biographical listings, see the Martindale-Hubbell Law Directory

SAMUEL P. PIERCE, JR., P.C. (AV)

One Buckhead Plaza, Suite 850, 3060 Peachtree Road, N.W., 30305
Telephone: 404-364-2890
Fax: 404-240-0232

Samuel P. Pierce, Jr.

For full biographical listings, see the Martindale-Hubbell Law Directory

PIERCE & YOUNG (AV)

Building 1700, 2255 Cumberland Parkway Northwest, 30339-4575
Telephone: 770-435-0500
Telecopier: 770-435-0362

MEMBERS OF FIRM

J. Wayne Pierce	Richard M. Young

ASSOCIATE

Christy A. Dunkelberger

For full biographical listings, see the Martindale-Hubbell Law Directory

POPE, McGLAMRY, KILPATRICK & MORRISON (AV)

A Partnership including Professional Corporations
83 Walton Street, N.W., P.O. Box 1733, 30303
Telephone: 404-523-7706;
Phenix City, Alabama: 334-298-7354
Columbus, Georgia Office: 318 11th Street, 2nd Floor, P.O. Box 2128, 31902-2128.
Telephone: 706-324-0050.

MEMBERS OF FIRM

C. Neal Pope (P.C.)	R. Timothy Morrison
Max R. McGlamry (P.C.)	Michael L. McGlamry
(Resident, Columbus, Georgia	Earle F. Lasseter
Office)	William Usher Norwood, III
Paul V. Kilpatrick, Jr. (Resident,	William J. Cornwell
Columbus, Georgia Office)	Jay F. Hirsch

Wade H. Tomlinson, III

RESIDENT ASSOCIATE

C. Elizabeth Pope

Reference: Columbus Bank & Trust Co.

For full biographical listings, see the Martindale-Hubbell Law Directory

REYNOLDS & McARTHUR (AV)

A Partnership including a Professional Corporation
Suite 1080, One Buckhead Plaza, 3060 Peachtree Road, N.W., 30305
Telephone: 404-240-0265
Fax: 404-262-3557
Macon, Georgia Office: 850 Walnut Street.
Telephone: 912-741-6000.
Fax: 912-742-0750.

(See Next Column)

Asheville, North Carolina Office: The Jackson Building, 22 South Pack Square, Suite 1200.
Telephone: 704-254-8523.
Fax: 704-254-3038.

MEMBERS OF FIRM

W. Carl Reynolds (P.C.)	O. Wendell Horne, III
Katherine L. McArthur	Bradley J. Survant
Charles M. Cork, III	Steve Ray Warren
	(Not admitted in GA)

For full biographical listings, see the Martindale-Hubbell Law Directory

KENNETH L. SHIGLEY (AV)

325 Hammond Drive, N.E. Suite 300, 30328-5028
Telephone: 404-252-1108
Fax: 404-843-3055
Email: kshigley@counsel.com *URL:* http://www.ga-law.com

For full biographical listings, see the Martindale-Hubbell Law Directory

THOMAS, KENNEDY, SAMPSON & PATTERSON (AV)

55 Marietta Street, N.W., Suite 1600, 30303
Telephone: 404-688-4503
Telecopier: 404-681-2950

MEMBERS OF FIRM

John Loren Kennedy	P. Andrew Patterson
(1942-1994)	Myra H. Dixon
Thomas G. Sampson	Jeffrey E. Tompkins

ASSOCIATES

Rosalind T. Drakeford	Adam L. Smith
Melynee C. Leftridge	Thomas G. Sampson, II
La'Sean M. Zilton	Ceasar C. Mitchell, II.

R. E. Thomas, Jr. (1911-1996)

LEGAL SUPPORT PERSONNEL

Gwendolyn C.H. Dixon	Yvonne Torrence
Elbetha (Beth) Martin	Priscilla Yolanda Kelly
Nancy Allen-Haskell	Lureece D. Lewis (Paralegal)

For full biographical listings, see the Martindale-Hubbell Law Directory

---

AUGUSTA, * Richmond Co.

STANLEY C. HOUSE (AV)

Suite 506 The Lamar Building, 753 Broad Street, P.O. Box 915, 30903-0915
Telephone: 706-722-3341
Fax: 706-722-0471
Email: schouse@counsel.com

Approved Attorney for: Lawyers Title Insurance Corp.
References: First Union Bank & Trust (Augusta); NationsBank (Augusta).

For full biographical listings, see the Martindale-Hubbell Law Directory

---

BRUNSWICK, * Glynn Co.

FENDIG, McLEMORE, TAYLOR, WHITWORTH & DURHAM, P.C. (AV)

Suite 200 Suntrust Bank Building, P.O. Box 1996, 31521
Telephone: 912-264-4126
Telecopier: 912-264-0591

Albert Fendig, Jr.	Philip R. Taylor
Gilbert C. McLemore, Jr.	David T. Whitworth

James B. Durham

Donna L. Crossland	Beth M. Duncan

Counsel for: Suntrust Bank of S.E. Georgia, N.A.; First Federal Savings Bank; Sea Island Property Owners Assn.; Calsilite Manufacturing Co.; Continental Insurance Cos.; Crum & Forster; MIM Insurance Companies, Inc.; The Hertz Corp.; Insurance Company of North America; United States Fidelity & Guaranty Co.

For full biographical listings, see the Martindale-Hubbell Law Directory

---

COLUMBUS, * Muscogee Co.

BUTLER, WOOTEN, OVERBY, CHEELEY, PEARSON & FRYHOFER (AV)

1500 Second Avenue, P.O. Box 2766, 31902
Telephone: 706-322-1990;
National Wats: 1-800-233-4086
Fax: 706-323-2962
Atlanta, Georgia Office: 2719 Buford Highway, 30324.
Telephone: 404-321-1700.
Fax: 404-321-1713. Wats Line: 1-800-242-2962.

(See Next Column)

BUTLER, WOOTEN, OVERBY, CHEELEY, PEARSON & FRYHOFER—*Continued*

MEMBERS OF FIRM

James E. Butler, Jr.	Albert M. Pearson, III
Joel O. Wooten, Jr.	George W. Fryhofer III
C. Frederick Overby	Peter J. Daughtery
Robert D. Cheeley	J. Frank Myers, III
	Lee Tarte Wallace

ASSOCIATES

Jason L. Crawford	Joshua Sacks
Keith A. Pittman	Teresa Thomas Abell
	Cale H. Conley

For full biographical listings, see the Martindale-Hubbell Law Directory

POPE, McGLAMRY, KILPATRICK & MORRISON (AV)

A Partnership including Professional Corporations
318 11th Street, 2nd Floor, P.O. Box 2128, 31902-2128
Telephone: 706-324-0050;
Phenix City, Alabama: 334-298-7354
Atlanta, Georgia Office: 83 Walton Street, N.W., P.O. Box 1733, 30303.
Telephone: 404-523-7706.

MEMBERS OF FIRM

C. Neal Pope (P.C.)	Michael L. McGlamry
Max R. McGlamry (P.C.)	Earle F. Lasseter
(Resident)	William Usher Norwood, III
Paul V. Kilpatrick, Jr.	(Resident, Atlanta Office)
(Resident)	William J. Cornwell
R. Timothy Morrison	Jay F. Hirsch
	Wade H. Tomlinson, III

RESIDENT ASSOCIATES

Joan S. Redmond	Teresa Pike Majors
	Matthew N. Pope

Reference: Columbus Bank & Trust Co.

For full biographical listings, see the Martindale-Hubbell Law Directory

---

CORNELIA, Habersham Co.

CATHEY & STRAIN (AV)

6 Irvin Street, P.O. Box 689, 30531
Telephone: 706-778-2601
Fax: 706-776-2899

MEMBERS OF FIRM

Dennis T. Cathey	Edward E. Strain, III

ASSOCIATES

J. Edward Staples	David A. Sleppy

For full biographical listings, see the Martindale-Hubbell Law Directory

---

HINESVILLE,* Liberty Co.

JONES, OSTEEN, JONES & ARNOLD (AV)

206 East Court Street, P.O. Box 800, 31313
Telephone: 912-876-0111
Cable Address: "JOJA"
Fax: 912-368-2979

MEMBERS OF FIRM

Charles M. Jones	Billy N. Jones
J. Noel Osteen	Jeffery L. Arnold

ASSOCIATES

G. Brinson Williams, Jr.	Mark W. Nickerson
Linnie L. Darden, III	L. Kelly Davis

General Counsel for: The Hinesville Bank; The Coastal Bank; Coastal Utilities, Inc.; Coastal Electric Membership Corp.; Liberty County Hospital Authority; Hinesville Area Board of Realtors; Liberty County Industrial Authority; Liberty County, Georgia; City of Riceboro.

For full biographical listings, see the Martindale-Hubbell Law Directory

---

MACON,* Bibb Co.

REYNOLDS & McARTHUR (AV)

A Partnership including a Professional Corporation
850 Walnut Street, 31201
Telephone: 912-741-6000
Fax: 912-742-0750
Atlanta, Georgia Office: Suite 1080, One Buckhead Plaza, 3060 Peachtree Road, N.W.
Telephone: 404-240-0265.
Fax: 404-262-3557.
Asheville, North Carolina Office: The Jackson Building, 22 South Pack Square, Suite 1200.
Telephone: 704-254-8523.
Fax: 704-254-3038.

(See Next Column)

MEMBERS OF FIRM

W. Carl Reynolds (P.C.)	O. Wendell Horne, III
Katherine L. McArthur	Bradley J. Survant
Charles M. Cork, III	Steve Ray Warren
	(Not admitted in GA)

For full biographical listings, see the Martindale-Hubbell Law Directory

---

MARIETTA,* Cobb Co.

BARNES, BROWNING, TANKSLEY & CASURELLA (AV)

Suite 225, 166 Anderson Street, 30060
Telephone: 770-424-1500
Fax: 770-424-1740

MEMBERS OF FIRM

Roy E. Barnes	Jerry A. Landers, Jr.
Charles B. Tanksley	Jeffrey G. Casurella

For full biographical listings, see the Martindale-Hubbell Law Directory

---

ROME,* Floyd Co.

BRINSON, ASKEW, BERRY, SEIGLER, RICHARDSON & DAVIS (AV)

A Partnership including Professional Corporations
Omberg House, 615 West First Street, P.O. Box 5513, 30162-5513
Telephone: 706-291-8853;
Atlanta: 404-521-0908
Telecopier: 706-234-3574

MEMBERS OF FIRM

Robert M. Brinson (P.C.)	Hendrick L. Cromartie, III
C. King Askew (P.C.)	Wright W. Smith
Robert L. Berry	Mark M. J. Webb
Joseph M. Seigler, Jr.	Joseph B. Atkins
Thomas D. Richardson	I. Stewart Duggan, Jr.
J. Anderson Davis	James Daniel Blitch

Representative Clients: City of Rome; Georgia Power Co.; General Electric Company; News Publishing Company (Rome News Tribune); Redmond Regional Medical Center; Oglethorpe Power Corp.; Suhner Manufacturing, Inc.; The Federal Land Bank of Columbia; AmSouth Bank of Georgia; United States Fidelity & Guaranty Co.

For full biographical listings, see the Martindale-Hubbell Law Directory

---

SAVANNAH,* Chatham Co.

FORBES & BOWMAN (AV)

Park South D-14, 7505 Waters Avenue, P.O. Box 13929, 31416-0929
Telephone: 912-352-1190
FAX: 912-352-1471

Morton G. Forbes	John A. Foster
Catherine M. Bowman	Doris E. Brannon
	Scot V. Pool

Representative Clients: American International Group; AIG Claims Service; Continental Insurance Health Care; Cotton States Insurance Companies; Frito-Lay, Inc.; GAB Business Services, Inc.

For full biographical listings, see the Martindale-Hubbell Law Directory

KARSMAN, BROOKS & CALLAWAY, P.C. (AV)

301 West Congress Street, P.O. Box 9149, 31412
Telephone: 912-238-2750
Cable Address: "Karbro"
Telecopier: 912-238-2767

Stanley M. Karsman	R. Krannert Riddle
Charles C. Brooks	Edward M. Hughes
Timothy F. Callaway, III	Shari Sigman Miltiades
Stanley E. Harris, Jr.	D. Campbell Bowman, Jr.
James L. Drake, Jr.	Timothy J. Haeussler
Dana F. Braun	Tracie Grove Smith

For full biographical listings, see the Martindale-Hubbell Law Directory

HAWAII

*HONOLULU,** Honolulu Co.

ALCANTARA & FRAME ATTORNEYS AT LAW, A LAW CORPORATION (AV)

Suite 1100 Pioneer Plaza, 900 Fort Street Mall, 96813
Telephone: 808-536-6922
Fax: 808-521-8898
Telex: 650-225-8816
WUI: 101-650 225-8816
MCI ID: 225-8816
San Diego, California: 402 West Broadway, Suite 400.
Telephone: 619-595-3175.
Fax: 619-595-3176.

Leonard F. Alcantara	Robert G. Frame
	Bryan Y. Y. Ho

Joy Lee Cauble	Michael D. Formby
John O'Kane, Jr.	Eldon M. Ching
Evelyn J. Black	James W. Alcantara (Resident, San Diego, California)

Reference: City Bank, Honolulu.

For full biographical listings, see the Martindale-Hubbell Law Directory

GEORGE W. ASHFORD, JR. (AV)

2910 Pacific Tower, 1001 Bishop Street, 96813
Telephone: 808-528-0444
Telecopier: (808) 533-0761
Cable Address: Justlaw

Representative Clients: Lloyds of London; Baker Industries, Inc.; Burns International Security Services; Clark Equipment Co.; Great Lakes Chemical Corporation; California Union Insurance Co.; Great American Insurance Companies; Guaranty National Companies; Horace Mann Insurance Company; Marine Office of America Corp.

For full biographical listings, see the Martindale-Hubbell Law Directory

LAW OFFICES OF STUART M. COWAN (AV)

Ocean View Center, 707 Richards Street, Suite 728, 96813
Telephone: 808-533-1767
Fax: 808-533-0549
Kaneohe, Hawaii Office: Suite 202, 47-653 Kamehameha Highway.
Telephone: 808-533-1767.
Fax: 808-239-9175.

Reference: 1st Hawaiian Bank.

For full biographical listings, see the Martindale-Hubbell Law Directory

CRONIN, FRIED, SEKIYA, KEKINA & FAIRBANKS ATTORNEYS AT LAW, A LAW CORPORATION (AV)

1900 Davies Pacific Center, 841 Bishop Street, 96813
Telephone: 808-524-1433
Fax: 808-536-2073

Paul F. Cronin	John D. Thomas, Jr.
L. Richard Fried, Jr.	Stuart A. Kaneko
Gerald Y. Sekiya	Bert S. Sakuda
Wayne K. Kekina	Allen K. Williams
David L. Fairbanks	Keith K. H. Young

Patrick W. Border	Clarence S.K. Kekina
Gregory L. Lui-Kwan	Sylvia E.J. Luke
Patrick F. McTernan	Geoffrey K.S. Komeya

For full biographical listings, see the Martindale-Hubbell Law Directory

FUKUNAGA MATAYOSHI HERSHEY & CHING (AV)

A Partnership including a Law Corporation
City Center, Third Floor, 810 Richards Street, 96813
Telephone: 808-533-4300
Fax: 808-531-7585

PARTNERS

Kenneth K. Fukunaga	James H. Hershey
Jerold T. Matayoshi (A Law Corporation)	Wesley H. H. Ching
	Patricia Kehau Wall

ASSOCIATES

Lois H. Yamaguchi	Robert R. Sadaoka
	Lindai M. Dang

OF COUNSEL

Leighton K. Chong

Chrysler Corporation; Ford Motor Company; General Motors Corporation; Honda Motor Company, Ltd.; American Honda Motor Company; Isuzu Motors America, Inc.; Nissan Motor Co., Ltd.; Mitsubishi Motors Corporation; Owens-Illinois, Inc.; W.R. Grace & Co.-Conn.

(See Next Column)

For full biographical listings, see the Martindale-Hubbell Law Directory

KESSNER DUCA UMEBAYASHI BAIN & MATSUNAGA ATTORNEYS AT LAW, A LAW CORPORATION (AV)

19th Floor, Central Pacific Plaza, 220 South King Street, 96813
Telephone: 808-536-1900
Telecopier: 808-529-7177
Telex: 723 8616 OPAC IIR

Robert C. Kessner	Elton John Bain
James N. Duca	Emma S. Matsunaga
Clyde S. Umebayashi	Muriel M. Taira

Beverly S. K. Tom	Melanie S. Ono
Jacqueline W.S. Amai	Darin P. Wright
Dawn Jordan	Cori Ann C. Yokota

For full biographical listings, see the Martindale-Hubbell Law Directory

IAN L. MATTOCH (AV)

Suite 1835 Grosvenor Center, 737 Bishop Street, 96813
Telephone: 808-523-2451
Cable Address: "Illnoncarb"
Fax: 808-531-2652
Hilo, Hawaii Office: 688 Kinoole Street, Suite 202.
Telephone: 808-969-3302.
Fax: 808-961-5599.
Kailua Kona, Hawaii Office: Hualalai Center, Suite D-211, 75-170 Hualalai Road.
Telephone: 808-326-1516.
Fax: 808-326-7416.
Kaneohe, Hawaii Office: 45-781 Kamehameha Highway.
Telephone: 808-247-8598.
Wailuku, Maui, Hawaii Office: 1 Main Plaza, Suite 500.
Telephone: 808-244-5007.
Fax: 808-242-2828.
Kamuela, Hawaii Office: Spencer House, Suite 236, Waimea Centers.
Telephone: 808-885-7727.
Fax: 808-885-1935.

William Copulos	Daniel P. Kirley
Rodger I. Hoffman	Jon Curtis Yoshimura
Virgil James Wilson, III	Daniel D. Ebihara

OF COUNSEL

Walter Davis

Reference: First Hawaiian Bank.

For full biographical listings, see the Martindale-Hubbell Law Directory

ROBBINS & RHODES ATTORNEYS AT LAW, A LAW CORPORATION (AV)

Suite 2200 Davies Pacific Center, 841 Bishop Street, 96813
Telephone: 808-524-2355
Fax: 808-526-0290

Kenneth S. Robbins	Vincent A. Rhodes
	Shinken Naitoh

Representative Clients: American Reinsurance Co.; CNA Insurance Co.; Employers Reinsurance Co.; Textron, Inc.; Farmers Insurance Group; Industrial Underwriters Insurance Co.; Western Indemnity Co.

For full biographical listings, see the Martindale-Hubbell Law Directory

TRECKER & FRITZ (AV)

820 Mililani Street, Suite 701, 96813
Telephone: 808-528-3900
Fax: 808-533-3684

MEMBERS OF FIRM

Steven J. Trecker	Magali V. Sunderland
Collin (Marty) Fritz	Hilary Benson Gangnes

For full biographical listings, see the Martindale-Hubbell Law Directory

*WAILUKU,** Maui Co.

KRUEGER & CAHILL (AV)

2065 Main Street, 96793
Telephone: 808-244-7444; Honolulu: 536-7474
Facsimile: 808-244-4177
Email: maulaw@maui.net

MEMBERS OF FIRM

James Krueger	Peter T. Cahill
	John M. O'Neill

LEGAL SUPPORT PERSONNEL

LEGAL ASSISTANTS

Sharon O'Shaughnessy	Theresa N. Coletti

A List of Representative Clients and References will be furnished upon request.

(See Next Column)

KRUEGER & CAHILL—*Continued*

For full biographical listings, see the Martindale-Hubbell Law Directory

IDAHO

BOISE,* Ada Co.

LYNCH & ASSOCIATES, P.L.L.C. (AV)

West One Plaza, 101 S. Capitol Boulevard, Suite 1601, P.O. Box 739, 83701
Telephone: 208-331-5088
Fax: 208-331-0088

James B. Lynch

Penny L. Dykas   Mary L. McDougal
                Katherine M. Lynch

For full biographical listings, see the Martindale-Hubbell Law Directory

MOORE, BASKIN & PARKER (AV)

Washington Federal Plaza, 1001 West Idaho Street, Suite 400, P.O. Box 6756, 83707
Telephone: 208-336-6900
Facsimile: 208-336-7031

MEMBERS OF FIRM
Michael W. Moore   Thomas P. Baskin, III
                Paige Alan Parker
OF COUNSEL
Joseph M. Imhoff, Jr.

Representative Clients: Aetna Casualty & Surety, Co.; Capitol Indemnity Co.; Clarendon Insurance Co.; Crawford & Co.; Empire Fire & Marine Insurance Co.; Fireman's Fund Insurance Cos.; Idaho Counties Reciprocal Management Program; Idaho State Insurance Fund; Insurance Company of the West; Protective Insurance Co.

For full biographical listings, see the Martindale-Hubbell Law Directory

ILLINOIS

BELLEVILLE,* St. Clair Co.

CHURCHILL MCDONNELL & HATCH (AV)

10 East Washington Street, Suite 101, 62220
Telephone: 618-233-4525; 314-231-9961
Telecopier: 618-234-9826
St. Louis (Clayton), Missouri Office: Suite 1806, 7777 Bonhomme Avenue.
Telephone: 314-863-0220.

MEMBERS OF FIRM
Allen D. Churchill   Joseph B. McDonnell
                Mary Ann Hatch
ASSOCIATE
Paul J. Evans

Representative Clients: Cigna Insurance Co.; Agora Syndicate; ISBA Mutual Insurance Co.; Bridgestone/Firestone, Tire Sales Co.; The Travelers Insurance Co.; National Steel Corp., Granite City Steel Division; Coldwell Banker; Associated Physicians Insurance Co.; Combustion Engineering Company.
Reference: Magna Bank, N.A.

For full biographical listings, see the Martindale-Hubbell Law Directory

MCGLYNN & MCGLYNN (AV)

65 South 65th Street, 62223
Telephone: 618-398-5112; 314-381-5112
Telecopier: 618-398-5189

MEMBERS OF FIRM
Robert E. McGlynn   James McGlynn
                Joseph B. McGlynn, Jr.
ASSOCIATES
Michael L. McGlynn   Stephen P. McGlynn
                Maureen A. McGlynn
LEGAL SUPPORT PERSONNEL
Lawrence L. McGlynn

For full biographical listings, see the Martindale-Hubbell Law Directory

CHICAGO,* Cook Co.

BATES MECKLER BULGER & TILSON (AV)

8200 Sears Tower, 233 South Wacker, 60606
Telephone: 312-474-7900
Facsimile: 312-474-7898
URL: http://www.bmbt.com

MEMBERS OF FIRM
Patrick J. Foley   Mary F. Licari
Francis X. Grossi, Jr.   Bruce R. Meckler
Mari Henry Leigh   Steven D. Pearson
                Scott M. Seaman
ASSOCIATES
Dina L. Brantman   Robert C. Heist
John K. Daly   Darlene M. Jarzyna-Price
   (Not admitted in IL)   Charlene Kittredge
Robin Edelstein   Timothy A. Wolfe
OF COUNSEL
Joseph Frontino   Philip R. King
                Brian J. Williams

For full biographical listings, see the Martindale-Hubbell Law Directory

CHARLES A. BOYLE & ASSOCIATES, LTD. (AV)

29 South La Salle Street, Suite 345, 60603
Telephone: 312-346-4944
FAX: 312-368-1061

Charles A. Boyle

Jennifer Leah Barron

Reference: Northern Trust of Chicago.

For full biographical listings, see the Martindale-Hubbell Law Directory

BRYDGES RISEBOROUGH PETERSON FRANKE AND MORRIS (AV)

A Partnership including Professional Corporations
28th Floor, 150 North Michigan Avenue, 60601
Telephone: 312-782-5042
FAX: 312-704-9107
Waukegan, Illinois Office: 110 North West Street.
Telephone: 847-249-0300.
FAX: 847-249-4755.
Phoenix, Arizona Office: 3030 North Central Avenue, Suite 408.
Telephone: 602-631-4400.
FAX: 602-631-4404.

MEMBERS OF FIRM
Louis W. Brydges, Sr.   Scott E. Nemanich
Allyn J. Franke   Reid S. Jacobson
George E. Riseborough (A   Donald M. Lonchar, Jr.
   Professional Corporation)   Peter J. Nordigian
J. V. Schaffenegger (1914-1986)   Robert L. Snook
Ralph Miller (1922-1988)   Stacey L. Seneczko
Donald G. Peterson   Rebecca Sarah Larson
Thomas A. Morris, Jr., (A   Neal T. Goldstein
   Professional Corporation)   Monica J. Conrad
Donald L. Sime   Gioconda (Jackie) V. Iannicelli
John H. Krackenberger   Jennifer M. Lundy
Jay Scott Nelson   Eleanor P. Cabreré
Michael A. Strom   Linda A. White
Louis W. Brydges, Jr.   William G. Berg
Leslie A. Peterson   John W. Dixon
Thomas K. Gerling   Thomas A. Kiepura
OF COUNSEL
Harry D. Strouse   Thomas J. Moran (1920-1995)
                Jack L. Watson

For full biographical listings, see the Martindale-Hubbell Law Directory

BURKE & BURKE, LTD. (AV)

2 First National Plaza, Suite 2200, 60603
Telephone: 312-726-6630
FAX: 312-726-1554
Downers Grove, Illinois Office: 5120 Forest, 60515.
Telephone: 708-852-9197.

John M. Burke   Dennis J. Burke
Edmund P. Burke   Molly C. Mason
                Karen Krajcir White

For full biographical listings, see the Martindale-Hubbell Law Directory

CLIFFORD LAW OFFICES, P.C. (AV)

120 North La Salle Street, 31st Floor, 60602
Telephone: 312-899-9090
1-800-899-0410
Fax: 312-251-1160
Email: 102554.2453@compuserve.com

(See Next Column)

CLIFFORD LAW OFFICES P.C., *Chicago—Continued*

Robert A. Clifford	Keith A. Hebeisen
	Kevin P. Durkin

Robert P. Walsh, Jr.	Richard L. Pullano
Susan A. Capra	Patricia C. Durkin
Jeffrey J. Kroll	Matthew I. Baker
Thomas K. Prindable	Timothy P. Rhatigan
Richard F. Burke, Jr.	Isobel S. Thomas

OF COUNSEL

Robert P. Sheridan

For full biographical listings, see the Martindale-Hubbell Law Directory

CONNELLY & SCHROEDER (AV)

One North Franklin Street, Suite 1200, 60606
Telephone: 312-251-9600
FAX: 312-251-9601
Geneva, Illinois Office: 1250 Executive Place, Suite 201.
Telephone: 708-232-6440.
FAX: 708-232-6450

MEMBERS OF FIRM

Michael P. Connelly	Charles H. Cole
John L. Schroeder	Daniel F. Konicek
(Resident, Geneva Office)	(Resident, Geneva Office)
Thomas F. Tobin	Eugene S. Kraus
Raymond E. Stachnik	Patrick G. Donnelly

OF COUNSEL

John W. Hough

ASSOCIATES

Michelle L. Adams	Colleen Konicek
(Resident, Geneva Office)	Charina de los Reyes
Matthew Patrick Connelly	Abbey Fishman Romanek
Thomas W. Dillon	Martha Swatek
(Resident, Geneva Office)	(Resident, Geneva Office)
Mary Lisa Kamins	Carla A. Summers
John Michael Kelly	(Resident, Geneva Office)

For full biographical listings, see the Martindale-Hubbell Law Directory

DOWD & DOWD, LTD. (AV)

Suite 1000, 55 West Wacker Drive, 60601
Telephone: 312-704-4400
Telecopier: 312-704-4500

Joseph V. Dowd	Robert C. Yelton III
Michael E. Dowd	Patrick C. Dowd
Kenneth Gurber	Robert J. Golden
	Karen W. Worsek

S. Robert Depke	John M. McAndrews
Ryan J. Harrington	Edward W. McNabola
Jeffrey Edward Kehl	Martha A. Niles
Sarah A. Kennedy	Michael G. Patrizio
Richard B. Korn	Patrick J. Ruberry
Joseph J. Leonard	Anthony R. Rutkowski
Ronald J. Lukes	Jeffrey Scott Wrage

LEGAL SUPPORT PERSONNEL

Carol Barnes	Jill A. Weiseman

OF COUNSEL

Guenther Ahlf	John A. Garrity, III
	Joel S. Ostrow

For full biographical listings, see the Martindale-Hubbell Law Directory

JEFFREY M. GOLDBERG & ASSOCIATES, LTD. (AV)

20 North Clark Street, Suite 3100, 60602
Telephone: 312-236-4146
Fax: 312-236-5913

Jeffrey M. Goldberg

Mark N. Pera	Suzanne Bonds
Lawrence R. Kream	Mark T. Solmor
Geoffrey Johnson	Barry I. Mortge

For full biographical listings, see the Martindale-Hubbell Law Directory

GUNTY & McCARTHY (AV)

150 South Wacker Drive, Suite 1025, 60606
Telephone: 312-541-0022
Facsimile: 312-541-0033
St. Louis, Missouri Office: 1515 North Warson Road, Suite 137.
Telephone: 314-427-7262.
Facsimile: 314-427-7268.

Susan Gunty	James P. McCarthy

(See Next Column)

Stephen K. Milott	Kirk Austin
Paul D. Van Lysebettens	Karyn S. Glennon

For full biographical listings, see the Martindale-Hubbell Law Directory

KAPLAN & BEGY (AV)

One First National Plaza 51st Floor, 60603
Telephone: 312-345-3000
Fax: 312-345-3119

MEMBERS OF FIRM

Fred C. Begy, III	Joseph A. Bosco
Larry S. Kaplan	Martin K. LaPointe
James D. Solon	Richard A. Walker
Robert C. von Ohlen, Jr.	Mitchell J. Kanaan

ASSOCIATES

John B. Austin	Michael J. Vint
Donald F. Brosnan	Maritoni Derecho Kane
(Not admitted in IL)	Adriana Gardella
J. Peter Martin	Michael J. Frazier
Neal J. Moglin	John T. Midgett
Jeffrey E. Margulis	Keith S. Yamaguchi
Kevin R. Davis	Rose Jagust
Patrick J. Keating	Thomas C. Sokol
	Terrill Elise Pierce

For full biographical listings, see the Martindale-Hubbell Law Directory

LOGGANS AND COX (AV)

Suite 2850, 200 West Madison Street, 60606
Telephone: 312-201-8600
Telecopier: 312-201-1180
Email: loggans@aol.com

Susan E. Loggans	Michael J. Cox

Miles M. Dore	Ian Robert Alexander

For full biographical listings, see the Martindale-Hubbell Law Directory

MORRIS & STELLA (AV)

Suite 1200, 200 West Adams Street, 60606
Telephone: 312-782-2345
Telecopier: 312-750-0924

MEMBERS OF FIRM

William J. Morris	Joseph N. Stella
	Jeffrey W. Gunn

ASSOCIATES

Bruce J. Manos	Ronald Eric Bentsen
Z. John Balchunas	Martin J. Corn
William F. McDermott	Richard Burns Megley, Jr.

For full biographical listings, see the Martindale-Hubbell Law Directory

MULLEN & MINELLA (AV)

A Partnership including Professional Corporations
Three First National Plaza, Suite 2700, 60602
Telephone: 312-346-2998
Fax: 312-346-6024

MEMBERS OF FIRM

John C. Mullen (Ltd.)	Mary R. Minella
Christopher Mullen (P.C.)	Michael T. Mullen

For full biographical listings, see the Martindale-Hubbell Law Directory

BERNARD R. NEVORAL AND ASSOCIATES LTD. (AV)

150 North Wacker Drive, Suite 2450, 60606
Telephone: 312 263-7058
FAX: 312-263-4566

Bernard R. Nevoral

Maurice E. Dusky	Douglas C. Dorn

For full biographical listings, see the Martindale-Hubbell Law Directory

PAVALON & GIFFORD (AV)

Two North La Salle Street, Suite 1600, 60602
Telephone: 312-419-7400
Fax: 312-419-7408
Rockford, Illinois Office: 501 Seventh Street, Suite 501, 61104.
Telephone: 815-968-5100.

MEMBERS OF FIRM

Eugene I. Pavalon	Gary K. Laatsch
Geoffrey L. Gifford	Frank C. Marino
	Henry Phillip Gruss

(See Next Column)

PAVALON & GIFFORD—*Continued*

Kathleen A. Russell   Christine Walsh Donnelly
                  Christopher B. Meister

For full biographical listings, see the Martindale-Hubbell Law Directory

POWER ROGERS & SMITH, P.C. (AV)

35 West Wacker Drive, Suite 3700, 60601
Telephone: 312-236-9381
Fax: 312-236-0920

Joseph A. Power, Jr.   Thomas G. Siracusa
Larry R. Rogers   Paul L. Salzetta
Todd A. Smith   Thomas M. Power

Larry R. Rogers, Jr.   Ruth M. Degnan
                  Devon C. Bruce

For full biographical listings, see the Martindale-Hubbell Law Directory

SANCHEZ & DANIELS (AV)

Suite 500, 333 West Wacker Drive, 60606
Telephone: 312-641-1555
Fax: 312-641-3004
Wheaton, Illinois Office: 2100 Manchester Road, Suite 101.
Telephone: 708-871-6161.
Fax: 708-871-9771.
Boston, Massachusetts Office: Sanchez, Daniels & Fitch, 101 Federal Street, Suite 1934.
Telephone: 617-478-0547.
Fax: 617-478-0544.

MEMBERS OF FIRM

Manuel "Manny" Sanchez   Timothy V. Hoffman
John D. Daniels   Robert T. Varney
Lori S. Yokoyama   Franklin U. Valderrama
                  George L. Acosta

John J. Skawski   Vanessa L. Vargas
Lela D. Johnson   Marcelle R. Kott
Rebecca Morrissey   Yvette Rivas Diamond
Hugh C. O'Donnell   Stacey Sherr Michelon
Jane Solmor-Mordini   Julie F. Furer
Francine Stulac   Darryl Tom
Edward N. Robles   Susan K. Chae
Joseph P. Bonaccorsi   Edward M. Ordonez
Mark I. Fishbein   Paige Donaldson
Deborah L. Nico   Lesley A. Corey

For full biographical listings, see the Martindale-Hubbell Law Directory

SWANSON, MARTIN & BELL (AV)

One IBM Plaza, Suite 2900, 60611
Telephone: 312-321-9100
Fax: 312-321-0990
Wheaton, Illinois Office: 2100 Manchester Road, C-1420.
Telephone: 708-653-2266.
Fax: 708-653-2292.

MEMBERS OF FIRM

Lenard C. Swanson   Lawrence Helms
Kevin T. Martin   Joseph P. Switzer
Brian W. Bell   George F. Fitzpatrick, Jr.
Stanley V. Boychuck   David E. Kawala
Kay L. Schichtel   Bruce S. Terlep
David J. Cahill   (Resident, Wheaton Office)
  (Resident, Wheaton Office)   Robert J. Meyer

ASSOCIATES

Kevin V. Boyle   Patricia S. Kocour
Michael J. Hossack   A. Jay Koehler, III
Matthew D. Jacobson   Sheryl A. Pethers
  (Resident, Wheaton Office)   Barbara N. Petrungaro
Joseph P. Kincaid   Aaron T. Shepley
                  William Blake Weiler

OF COUNSEL

Edward T. Butt, Jr.   John C. Church

For full biographical listings, see the Martindale-Hubbell Law Directory

WILDMAN, HARROLD, ALLEN & DIXON (AV)

225 West Wacker Drive, 30th Floor, 60606-1229
Telephone: 312-201-2000
Cable Address: "Whad"
Fax: 312-201-2555
URL: http://www.whad.com
Aurora, Illinois Office: 1851 W. Galena Boulevard, Suite 210.
Telephone: 630-892-7021.
Fax: 630-892-7158.

(See Next Column)

Waukegan, Illinois Office: 404 West Water, P. O. Box 890.
Telephone: 847-623-0700.
Fax: 847-244-5273.
Lisle, Illinois Office: 4300 Commerce Court.
Telephone: 630-955-0555.
New York, New York Office: Wildman, Harrold, Allen, Dixon & Smith. The International Building, 45 Rockefeller Plaza, Suite 353.
Telephone: 212-632-3850.
Fax: 212-632-3858.
Toronto, Ontario affiliated Office: Keel Cottrelle. 36 Toronto Street, Ninth Floor, Suite 920.
Telephone: 416-367-2900.
Telefax: 416-367-2791.
Telex: 062-18660.
Mississauga, Ontario affiliated Office: Keel Cottrelle. 100 Matatson Avenue East, Suite 104.
Telephone: 416-890-7700.
Fax: 416-890-8006.

MEMBERS OF FIRM

Thomas D. Allen   Donald R. McGarrah
Richard C. Bartelt   Mark P. Miller
Cal R. Burnton   Timothy G. Nickels
Steven E. Danekas   Sarah L. Olson
Michael Dockterman   Richard C. Palmer
James P. Dorr   David F. Pardys
Robert E. Haley   (Waukegan Office)
Anthony G. Hopp   Douglas L. Prochnow
David A. Kanter   Fred E. Schulz
Anne Giddings Kimball   Robert L. Shuftan
Steven L. Larson   Robert A. Strelecky
  (Waukegan Office)   (Lisle Office)
Brian W. Lewis   Peter A. Tomaras
Michael L. McCluggage   James B. Vogts
                  Dale G. Wills

John T. Benz   Jill S. Miller
Eric P. Berlin   Stephanie B. Miller
Wendy L. Fink   Martha D. Owens
Shanthi V. Gaur   Kevin B. Reid
Michael A. Glackin   John A. Roberts
Adam J. Glazer   Ada Skyles
Scott Z. Hochfelder   Paul A. Slager
Michael J. Lotus   Lauren S. Tashma
Jeffrey A. McIntyre   Jeanne Walker

For Complete List of Firm Personnel, See General Section

For full biographical listings, see the Martindale-Hubbell Law Directory

JOHN C. WUNSCH, P.C. (AV)

77 West Washington Street, Suite 1420, 60602
Telephone: 312-977-9900
Fax: 312-236-2573

John C. Wunsch   Daniel J. Arnett

Reference: The Northern Trust Co.

For full biographical listings, see the Martindale-Hubbell Law Directory

EDWARDSVILLE,* Madison Co.

ARMSTRONG LAW OFFICES (AV)

South Main & Schwarz Street, P.O. Box 565, 62025
Telephone: 618-656-6770
Facsimile: 618-656-6808
Collinsville, Illinois Office: 103 South Morrison.
Telephone: 618-345-9258.

Benton Tad Armstrong   Stephen B. Evans

For full biographical listings, see the Martindale-Hubbell Law Directory

BURROUGHS, HEPLER, BROOM, MACDONALD & HEBRANK (AV)

Two Mark Twain Plaza, Suite 300, 103 West Vandalia Street, P.O. Box 510, 62025-0510
Telephone: 618-656-0184
Telecopier: 618-656-1364
Email: firm@ilmolaw.com

MEMBERS OF FIRM

George D. Burroughs   G. Gordon Burroughs
  (1873-1977)   (Of Counsel)
William G. Burroughs   Larry E. Hepler
  (1872-1952)   Gordon R. Broom
Mallory L. Burroughs   Theodore J. MacDonald, Jr.
  (1884-1965)   Jeffrey S. Hebrank
Jesse L. Simpson (1884-1973)   Gary E. True
David L. Simpson (Retired)   Paul W. Johnson
                  William J. Knapp

(See Next Column)

BURROUGHS, HEPLER, BROOM, MACDONALD & HEBRANK, *Edwardsville—Continued*

ASSOCIATES

Lisa K. Franke	Daniel W. Farroll
Jack H. Humes, Jr.	David J. Gerber
Melissa Griggs	Donald J. Ohl
L. David Green	D. Scott Rendleman
J. Todd Hayes	Gary A. Meadows
J. Robert Edmonds	T. Scott Stewart

Representative Clients: Ameritech; Travelers Insurance Co.; Fireman's Fund-American Insurance Group; CILCO; Employers Union Insurance Co.; The Hartford; Illinois Power Co.; W.R. Grace; Mark Twain Bank; Prairie Farms.

For full biographical listings, see the Martindale-Hubbell Law Directory

---

MATTOON, Coles Co.

CRAIG & CRAIG (AV)

1807 Broadway, P.O. Box 689, 61938-0689
Telephone: 217-234-6481
Telecopier: 217-234-6486
Mount Vernon, Illinois Office: 227 1/2 South 9th Street.
Telephone: 618-244-7511.

MEMBERS OF FIRM

Craig Van Meter (1895-1981)	Stephen L. Corn
Fred H. Kelly (1894-1971)	Richard Charles Hayden
Robert M. Werden (1908-1969)	Robert G. Grierson
George N. Gilkerson	Gregory C. Ray
(1911-1985)	Paul R. Lynch (Resident, Mount
John H. Armstrong	Vernon Office)
John P. Ewart	Kenneth F. Werts (Resident,
Richard F. Record, Jr.	Mount Vernon Office)

John L. Barger

ASSOCIATES

Joshua N. Rosen (Resident,	Theresa M. Thomson
Mount Vernon Office)	Kristine M. Tuttle
Kathleen M. Stockwell	Henry P. Villani (Resident,
	Mount Vernon Office)

OF COUNSEL
Jack E. Horsley

Counsel for: Monterey Coal Co., a Division of Exxon Coal USA, Inc.; Marathon Oil Co.; Illinois Central R.R. Co.; Okaw Building & Loan Assn., Mattoon, Illinois; The Medical Protective Insurance Co.; Consolidated Communications, Inc.; Lloyds Underwriters at London; Hartford Insurance Co.; Coles Together, a Not-For-Profit Corp.; Coles Building Corporation.

For full biographical listings, see the Martindale-Hubbell Law Directory

---

OAKBROOK TERRACE, Du Page Co.

GALLAGHER & JOSLYN (AV)

One Lincoln Centre, Suite 300, 60181
Telephone: 630-916-2600
FAX: 630-916-2606

MEMBERS OF FIRM

Gerard B. Gallagher	Barry E. Garley
David L. Joslyn	Ira E. Sussman

OF COUNSEL
Peter A. Bauer

For Complete List of Firm Personnel, See General Section

For full biographical listings, see the Martindale-Hubbell Law Directory

---

PERU, La Salle Co.

ANTHONY C. RACCUGLIA & ASSOCIATES (AV)

1200 Maple Drive, 61354
Telephone: 815-223-0230
Ottawa, Illinois Office: 633 La Salle Street.
Telephone: 815-434-2003.

ASSOCIATES

James A. McPhedran	Louis L. Bertrand

References: La Salle National Bank; Citizens First National Bank of Peru, Illinois.

For full biographical listings, see the Martindale-Hubbell Law Directory

---

INDIANA

---

*BLOOMINGTON,** Monroe Co.

KELLEY, BELCHER & BROWN, A PROFESSIONAL CORPORATION (AV)

301 West Seventh Street, P.O. Box 3250, 47402-3250
Telephone: 812-336-9963
Telecopier: 812-336-4588

William H. Kelley	Thomas J. Belcher
Shannon L. Robinson	Darla Sue Brown
	Jennifer A. Bauer

For full biographical listings, see the Martindale-Hubbell Law Directory

---

*EVANSVILLE,** Vanderburgh Co.

BERGER AND BERGER (AV)

313 Main Street, 47708-1485
Telephone: 812-425-8101;
Indiana Only: 800-622-3604;
Outside Indiana: 800-327-0182
Fax: 812-421-5909

MEMBERS OF FIRM

Charles L. Berger	Mark W. Rietman

References: Citizens National Bank of Evansville; Old National Bank in Evansville.

For full biographical listings, see the Martindale-Hubbell Law Directory

FINE & HATFIELD (AV)

520 N.W. Second Street, P.O. Box 779, 47705-0779
Telephone: 812-425-3592
Telecopier: 812-421-4269
Email: Fine@Fine-Hatfield.com *URL:* http://www.Fine-Hatfield.com

MEMBERS OF FIRM

Thomas H. Bryan	Patricia Kay Woodring
Danny E. Glass	William H. Mullis

ASSOCIATE
Todd I. Glass

A List of Representative Clients Furnished Upon Request.

For full biographical listings, see the Martindale-Hubbell Law Directory

GERLING LAW OFFICES, PROFESSIONAL CORPORATION (AV)

519 Main Street Walkway, P.O. Box 3203, 47731
Telephone: 812-423-5251
Fax: 812-423-9928

Gary L. Gerling	Christian M. Lenn
Edward B. Anderson	Gayle Gerling Pettinga
David G. Hatfield	Stephen Hensleigh Thomas

For full biographical listings, see the Martindale-Hubbell Law Directory

---

*FORT WAYNE,** Allen Co.

ROBY & HOOD (AV)

Standard Federal Plaza, Suite 520, 200 East Main, 46802
Telephone: 219-423-3366
Fax: 219-423-3367
Anderson, Indiana Office: One Citizens Plaza, Suite 305.
Telephone: 317-642-2402.

MEMBERS OF FIRM

Daniel A. Roby	Kathryn J. Roudebush
G. Stanley Hood	Thomas A. Manges
	David Joseph Stach

References: Norwest Bank; NBD Bank.

For full biographical listings, see the Martindale-Hubbell Law Directory

---

*INDIANAPOLIS,** Marion Co.

LOCKE REYNOLDS BOYD & WEISELL (AV)

1000 Capital Center South, 201 North Illinois Street, 46204
Telephone: 317-237-3800
Telecopier: 317-237-3900

Hugh E. Reynolds, Jr.	Randall R. Riggs
Lloyd H. Milliken, Jr.	Richard A. Huser
William V. Hutchens	Thomas J. Campbell
Michael A. Bergin	Burton M. Harris
Steven J. Strawbridge	Eric A. Riegner
	Kevin C. Schiferl
Stephen L. Vaughan	Nicholas C. Pappas
Jeffrey J. Mortier	Donald B. Kite, Sr.

(See Next Column)

LOCKE REYNOLDS BOYD & WEISELL—*Continued*
OF COUNSEL
William H. Vobach

Representative Clients: Allied Signal Inc.; American Honda Motor Co., Inc.; American Suzuki Motor Corporation; Black & Decker (U.S.) Inc.; Emerson Electric Company; General Motors Corporation; New United Motor Manufacturing; Siemens; Toyota Motor Sales, U.S.A., Inc.; White Consolidated Industries, Inc.

For Complete List of Firm Personnel, See General Section

For full biographical listings, see the Martindale-Hubbell Law Directory

MILLER MULLER MENDELSON & KENNEDY (AV)

8900 Keystone Crossing Suite 1250, 46240
Telephone: 317-574-4500
1-800-394-3094
Fax: 317-574-4501

MEMBERS OF FIRM

Michael S. Miller	Tilden Mendelson
John Muller	Timothy J. Kennedy

ASSOCIATE
Catherine A. Kling

For full biographical listings, see the Martindale-Hubbell Law Directory

MITCHELL HURST JACOBS & DICK (AV)

152 East Washington Street, 46204
Telephone: 317-636-0808
1-800-636-0808
Fax: 317-633-7680

MEMBERS OF FIRM

William W. Hurst	Marshall S. Hanley
Samuel L. Jacobs	Steven K. Huffer
Richard J. Dick	Robert W. Strohmeyer, Jr.

ASSOCIATES

Danielle A. Takla	Kimberly H. Danforth
John M. Reames	Jennifer Levin Sinder

For full biographical listings, see the Martindale-Hubbell Law Directory

OSBORN HINER LISHER & ORZESKE, P.C. (AV)

Suite 380, One Woodfield, 8330 Woodfield Crossing Boulevard, 46240
Telephone: 317-469-2100
Fax: 317-469-9011

John L. Lisher	Donald G. Orzeske
Donald K. Broad	Christopher Hamilton

OF COUNSEL

William M. Osborn	Edward A. Straith-Miller

For full biographical listings, see the Martindale-Hubbell Law Directory

PARDIECK, GILL & VARGO, A PROFESSIONAL CORPORATION (AV)

The Old Bailey Building, 244 North College Avenue, 46202
Telephone: 317-639-3321
Fax: 317-639-3318
Email: pgv@pgvlaw.com
Seymour, Indiana Office: 100 North Chestnut Street. P.O. Box 608.
Telephone: 812-523-8686.

Roger L. Pardieck	W. Brent Gill
	John F. Vargo
Thomas L. Landwerlen	Janet O. Vargo

OF COUNSEL
Robert C. Rothkopf

For full biographical listings, see the Martindale-Hubbell Law Directory

PRICE & BARKER (AV)

The Hammond Block Building, 301 Massachusetts Avenue, 46204
Telephone: 317-633-8787
Telecopier: 317-633-8797
New Albany, Indiana Office: 409 Bank Street, P.O. Box 785.
Telephone: 812-945-9151.
Fax: 812-945-6131.

PARTNERS

Henry J. Price	Robert G. Barker
	Jerry A. Garau

For full biographical listings, see the Martindale-Hubbell Law Directory

TOWNSEND, HOVDE & MONTROSS (AV)

230 East Ohio Street, 46204
Telephone: 317-264-4444
FAX: 317-264-2080

F. Boyd Hovde	W. Scott Montross
John F. Townsend, Jr.	Frederick R. Hovde

OF COUNSEL
John F. Townsend

Reference: N.B.D. Bank, N.A.

For full biographical listings, see the Martindale-Hubbell Law Directory

WARD & WARD (AV)

1014 Circle Tower Building, 55 Monument Circle, 46204
Telephone: 317-639-9501
Fax: 317-637-1919

MEMBERS OF FIRM

Donald W. Ward	Charles P. Ward

For full biographical listings, see the Martindale-Hubbell Law Directory

WILSON, KEHOE & WININGHAM (AV)

2859 North Meridian, 46208
Telephone: 317-920-6400
Fax: 317-920-6405
Richmond, Indiana Office: 42 South 9th Street, 47374.
Telephone: 317-962-9113.
Connersville, Indiana Office: 118 West 30th Street, 47331.
Telephone: 317-827-1100.
Muncie, Indiana Office: 3310 West Fox Ridge Lane, 47304.
Telephone: 317-284-2474.

MEMBERS OF FIRM

Harry A. Wilson, Jr.	D. Bruce Kehoe
	William E. Winingham, Jr.

ASSOCIATES

Ralph E. Dowling	Gerald A. Griffin, M.D.

Reference: The Indiana National Bank.

For full biographical listings, see the Martindale-Hubbell Law Directory

YARLING, ROBINSON, HAMMEL & LAMB (AV)

151 North Delaware, Suite 1535, P.O. Box 44128, 46204
Telephone: 317-262-8800
Fax: 317-262-3046

MEMBERS OF FIRM

Richard W. Yarling	Edgar H. Lamb
Charles F. Robinson, Jr.	Douglas E. Rogers
John W. Hammel	Mark S. Gray
Linda Y. Hammel	Matthew C. Robinson

For full biographical listings, see the Martindale-Hubbell Law Directory

YOSHA LADENDORF KRAHULIK & WEDDLE (AV)

Pyramid II, First Floor, 3500 West DePauw Boulevard, Suite 2015, P.O. Box 68979, 46268
Telephone: 317-334-9200
FAX: 317-228-3355

MEMBERS OF FIRM

Louis Buddy Yosha	Mark C. Ladendorf
William Levy	Jon D. Krahulik
	Robert G. Weddle

ASSOCIATES

David C. Krahulik	Angela M. Smith
Timothy C. Caress	Jeff D. Oliphant

SENIOR COUNSEL
Jeffrey A. Modisett

OF COUNSEL

Irwin J. Prince	Irving L. Fink

Reference: National Bank of Indianapolis.

For full biographical listings, see the Martindale-Hubbell Law Directory

---

*LA PORTE,** La Porte Co.

NEWBY, LEWIS, KAMINSKI & JONES (AV)

916 Lincoln Way, 46350
Telephone: 219-362-1577
Direct Line Michigan City: 219-879-6300
Fax: 219-362-2106
Mailing Address: P.O. Box 1816, La Porte, Indiana, 46352-1816

(See Next Column)

NEWBY, LEWIS, KAMINSKI & JONES, *La Porte—Continued*

MEMBERS OF FIRM

John E. Newby (1916-1990)	Edward L. Volk
Daniel E. Lewis, Jr.	Mark L. Phillips
Gene M. Jones	Martin W. Kus
John W. Newby	Marsha Schatz Volk
Perry F. Stump, Jr.	Mark A. Lienhoop
	James W. Kaminski

ASSOCIATES

William S. Kaminski	Christine A. Sulewski
	David P. Jones

SENIOR COUNSEL

Leon R. Kaminski

OF COUNSEL

Daniel E. Lewis

Counsel for: U. S. F. & G. Co.; State Farm Mutual Insurance Co.; Auto Owners Insurance Co.; Liberty Mutual Insurance Co.; Sullair Corp.; La Porte Community School Corp.; United Farm Bureau Mutual Insurance Co.; Physicians Insurance of Indiana; La Porte Hospital, Inc.; Norwest Bank.

For full biographical listings, see the Martindale-Hubbell Law Directory

---

MERRILLVILLE, Lake Co.

HOEPPNER WAGNER AND EVANS (AV)

Twin Towers, Suite 606 South, 1000 East 80th Place, 46410
Telephone: 219-769-6552; 800-263-1466 (IN,IL)
Fax: 219-738-2349
Valparaiso, Indiana Office: 103 East Lincolnway, P.O. Box 2357, 46384-2357.
Telephone: 219-464-4961; 800-879-2246 (IN,IL).
Fax: 219-465-0603.

RESIDENT MEMBER

John E. Hughes

For Complete List of Firm Personnel, See General Section

For full biographical listings, see the Martindale-Hubbell Law Directory

---

MUNSTER, Lake Co.

LAW OFFICES OF TIMOTHY F. KELLY (AV)

Suite 2A, 9250 Columbia Avenue, 46321
Telephone: 219-836-4062
Telecopier: 219-836-0167
Email: 76325.1505@Compuserve.Com

MEMBERS OF FIRM

Timothy F. Kelly	Karl K. Vanzo

ASSOCIATES

Harvey Karlovac	Steven J. Sersic

LEGAL SUPPORT PERSONNEL
LEGAL ASSISTANTS

Kristen Cook Faso	Kathleen E. Peek

For full biographical listings, see the Martindale-Hubbell Law Directory

---

*NEW ALBANY,** Floyd Co.

MATTOX & MATTOX (AV)

Suite 420 Elsby Building, P.O. Box 1203, 47151-1203
Telephone: 812-944-8005
Facsimile: 812-944-2255
Email: mattox@ntr.net

MEMBERS OF FIRM

Richard L. Mattox	S. Frank Mattox

ASSOCIATES

Linda A. Mattox	Derrick H. Wilson
	Karen R. Goodwell

Representative Clients: AAOMS National Insurance; Cablelink, Inc.; Floyd Memorial Hospital; John Deere Co.; Kimball International, Inc.; The Medical Protective Co.; Papa Johns Intl., Inc.; PHICO Insurance Co.; Physicians Group, Inc.; Robinson Nugent, Inc.

For full biographical listings, see the Martindale-Hubbell Law Directory

---

SEYMOUR, Jackson Co.

PARDIECK, GILL & VARGO, A PROFESSIONAL CORPORATION (AV)

100 North Chestnut Street, P.O. Box 608, 47274
Telephone: 812-523-8686
Fax: 812-522-4199
Email: pgv@pgylaw.com
Indianapolis, Indiana Office: The Old Bailey Building, 244 North College Avenue.
Telephone: 317-639-3321.

Roger L. Pardieck	W. Brent Gill

(See Next Column)

Bruce A. MacTavish	Karen J. Mellencamp Davis
	Andrew M. Pardieck

References: Home Federal Savings Bank, Seymour, Indiana.

For full biographical listings, see the Martindale-Hubbell Law Directory

---

*SOUTH BEND,** St. Joseph Co.

DORAN BLACKMOND READY HAMILTON & WILLIAMS (AV)

1700 Valley American Bank Building, 211 W. Washington Street, 46601
Telephone: 219-288-1800
Fax: 219-236-4265

MEMBERS OF FIRM

M. Edward Doran (1895-1982)	David T. Ready
John E. Doran	John C. Hamilton
Don G. Blackmond	A. Howard Williams

ASSOCIATE

Don Gregory Blackmond

For full biographical listings, see the Martindale-Hubbell Law Directory

---

EDWARD N. KALAMAROS & ASSOCIATES PROFESSIONAL CORPORATION (AV)

129 North Michigan Avenue, P.O. Box 4156, 46634
Telephone: 219-232-4801
Telecopier: 219-232-9736

Edward N. Kalamaros	Philip E. Kalamaros
Timothy J. Walsh	Sally P. Norton
Thomas F. Cohen	Kevin W. Kearney
Joseph M. Forte	Peter J. Bagiackas
Robert Deane Woods	David A. Wemhoff
Patrick J. Hinkle	Eric G. Ciesielski

Representative Clients: Liberty Mutual Insurance Co.; Employers Mutual of Wausau; Fireman's Fund American Insurance Group; St. Paul Insurance Companies; U.S.F. & G.; Cincinnati Insurance Co.; Kemper Group; Continental Loss Adjusting Services, Inc.; Orion Group.

For full biographical listings, see the Martindale-Hubbell Law Directory

---

ROWE, ROWE & MAHER (AV)

Suite 900 Keybank Building, 46601
Telephone: 219-233-8200
Fax: 219-234-5987

R. Kent Rowe	R. Kent Rowe, III
	Timothy J. Maher

ASSOCIATES

Gregory J. Haines	Steven D. Groth
Lee Korzan	Marie Anne Hendrie

For full biographical listings, see the Martindale-Hubbell Law Directory

---

*TERRE HAUTE,** Vigo Co.

WILKINSON, GOELLER, MODESITT, WILKINSON & DRUMMY (AV)

333 Ohio Street, P.O. Box 800, 47808-0800
Telephone: 812-232-4311
Fax: 812-235-5107

MEMBERS OF FIRM

Raymond H. Modesitt	William W. Drummy
	Scott M. Kyrouac

Representative Corporate Clients: Owens Corning Fiberglass; General Housewares Corp.; MAB Paints; PSI Energy, Inc.

For Complete List of Firm Personnel, See General Section

For full biographical listings, see the Martindale-Hubbell Law Directory

---

*VALPARAISO,** Porter Co.

HOEPPNER WAGNER AND EVANS (AV)

103 East Lincolnway, P.O. Box 2357, 46384-2357
Telephone: 219-464-4961; 800-879-2246 (IN,IL)
Fax: 219-465-0603
Merrillville, Indiana Office: Twin Towers, Suite 606 South, 1000 East 80th Place, 46410.
Telephone: 219-769-6552; 800-263-1466. (IN,IL,).
Fax: 219-738-2349.

RETIRED

Delmar R. Hoeppner

MEMBERS OF FIRM

William H. Wagner	Morris A. Sunkel
Larry G. Evans	James A. Cheslek
William F. Satterlee, III	James L. Jorgensen
Gordon A. Etzler	Ronald P. Kuker
John E. Hughes	Richard A. Browne
(Resident, Merrillville Office)	(Resident, Merrillville Office)

(See Next Column)

HOEPPNER WAGNER AND EVANS—*Continued*

MEMBERS OF FIRM (Continued)

F. Joseph Jaskowiak	Mark E. Schmidtke
(Resident, Merrillville Office)	Todd A. Leeth
Richard M. Davis	Michael P. Blaize

ASSOCIATES

Jonathan R. Hanson	Jeffrey W. Clymer
J. Brian Hittinger	Michael B. Miller
(Resident, Merrillville Office)	Jack A. Kramer
Lauren K. Kroeger	(Resident, Merrillville Office)

OF COUNSEL

Jim B. Brown (Resident, Merrillville Office)

Bethlehem Steel Corp.; Chester, Inc.; Hunt-Wesson Foods, Inc.; Owens-Corning Fiberglas Corp.; State Farm Insurance; Allstate Insurance Co.

For full biographical listings, see the Martindale-Hubbell Law Directory

---

WARSAW,* Kosciusko Co.

LEMON, ARMEY, HEARN & LEININGER (AV)

210 North Buffalo Street, P.O. Box 770, 46581-0770
Telephone: 219-268-9111
Telecopier: 219-267-8647

MEMBERS OF FIRM

Thomas R. Lemon	Daniel K. Leininger
Michael E. Armey	Jane L. Kauffman
R. Steven Hearn	Ronald B. Cassidente

ASSOCIATE

Andrea E. Halpin

OF COUNSEL

Robert L. Rasor

Representative Clients: Lake City Bank; Zimmer Inc.; The Dalton Foundries, Inc.; Grace Schools, Inc.; Kosciusko Community Hospital, Inc.; Othy, Inc.

For full biographical listings, see the Martindale-Hubbell Law Directory

---

IOWA

DES MOINES,* Polk Co.

FINLEY, ALT, SMITH, SCHARNBERG, MAY & CRAIG, P.C. (AV)

604 Locust Street, Fourth Floor Equitable Building, 50309
Telephone: 515-288-0145
Telecopier: 515-288-2724

Steven K. Scharnberg	John D. (Jack) Hilmes
	R. Todd Gaffney

Representative Clients: Aetna Casualty & Surety Co.; Aetna Life Insurance Co.; ALAS; American Society of Composers, Authors and Publishers; Equitable Life Assurance Society of the U.S.; Federated Insurance Co.; Meredith Corp.
Iowa Attorneys for: Midwest Medical Insurance Co.
District Attorneys for: Norfolk & Southern Railroad; Soo Line Railroad Company.

For Complete List of Firm Personnel, See General Section

For full biographical listings, see the Martindale-Hubbell Law Directory

---

PATTERSON, LORENTZEN, DUFFIELD, TIMMONS, IRISH, BECKER & ORDWAY, L.L.P. (AV)

729 Insurance Exchange Building, 50309
Telephone: 515-283-2147
Fax: 515-283-1002

MEMBERS OF FIRM

G. O. Patterson (1914-1982)	Gregory J. Wilson
James A. Lorentzen	Jeffrey A. Boehlert
Theodore T. Duffield	Douglas A. Haag
William E. Timmons (Retired)	Charles E. Cutler
Roy M. Irish	Michael D. Huppert
F. H. Becker (Retired)	Martin C. Sprock
Gary D. Ordway	William A. Wickett
Robin L. Hermann	Frederick M. Haskins
Harry Perkins, III	Jeffrey A. Baker
Michael F. Lacey, Jr.	Janice M. Herfkens

ASSOCIATES

Coreen K. Bezdicek	Patrick V. Waldron
	Michael S Jones

Representative Clients: Allied Mutual Insurance Company; CNA Insurance Company; Chubb Insurance Group; Continental Western Insurance Co.; Farmers Insurance Group; Farmland Insurance Company; Grinnell Mutual Reinsurance Company; Hawkeye Security Insurance Company; Iowa Insurance Institute, St. Paul Fire & Marine Insurance Company.

For full biographical listings, see the Martindale-Hubbell Law Directory

---

HARLAN,* Shelby Co.

KOHORST LAW FIRM (AV)

602 Market Street Building, P.O. Box 722, 51537-0722
Telephone: 712-755-3156
Fax: 712-755-7404

Robert Kohorst	Kathleen Schomer Kohorst

ASSOCIATES

William T. Early	Steven Elza Goodlow

Representative Clients: Employers Mutual Insurance Companies of Des Moines, Iowa; Farm Service Co-op., Harlan, Iowa; Thermogas Co., Tulsa, Oklahoma; Mid-America Pipeline Company, Inc., Tulsa, Oklahoma; United Fire & Casualty Co.; Farmers Mutual Telephone Co., Harlan, Iowa.

For full biographical listings, see the Martindale-Hubbell Law Directory

---

KANSAS

OVERLAND PARK, Johnson Co.

FISHER, PATTERSON, SAYLER & SMITH, L.L.P. (AV)

11050 Roe Avenue, Suite 210, 66211
Telephone: 913-339-6757
FAX: 913-339-6187
Topeka, Kansas Office: 534 South Kansas Avenue, Suite 400, P.O. Box 949, 66601.
Telephone: 913-232-7761.
Fax: 913-232-6604.

MEMBERS OF FIRM

Edwin Dudley Smith (Resident)	Michael K. Seck (Resident)
David P. Madden (Resident)	

ASSOCIATE

Patrick G. Reavey (Resident)

For full biographical listings, see the Martindale-Hubbell Law Directory

---

RISJORD & JAMES, P.C. (AV)

Suite 100, 10680 Barkley, 66212
Telephone: 913-381-5151
Fax: 913-381-2569

Randy W. James	Aaron N. Woods

RETIRED

John C. Risjord

For full biographical listings, see the Martindale-Hubbell Law Directory

---

SHAMBERG, JOHNSON & BERGMAN, CHARTERED (AV)

Suite 355, 4551 West 107th Street, 66207
Telephone: 913-642-0600
Fax: 913-642-9629
Kansas City, Kansas Office: Suite 860, New Brotherhood Building, 8th and State Streets.
Telephone: 913-281-1900.
Kansas City, Missouri Office: Suite 205, Scarritt Arcade Building, 819 Walnut.
Telephone: 816-556-9431.

Lynn R. Johnson	Victor A. Bergman
	John M. Parisi

Steven G. Brown	Anthony L. DeWitt
Steve N. Six	(Not admitted in KS)
	Patrick A. Hamilton

OF COUNSEL

John E. Shamberg

For full biographical listings, see the Martindale-Hubbell Law Directory

---

TOPEKA,* Shawnee Co.

FISHER, PATTERSON, SAYLER & SMITH, L.L.P. (AV)

534 South Kansas Avenue, Suite 400, P.O. Box 949, 66601
Telephone: 913-232-7761
Fax: 913-232-6604
Overland Park, Kansas Office: 11050 Roe Avenue, Suite 210, 66211.
Telephone: 913-339-6757.
Fax: 913-339-6187.

(See Next Column)

FISHER, PATTERSON, SAYLER & SMITH L.L.P., *Topeka—Continued*

MEMBERS OF FIRM

Donald Patterson	Steve R. Fabert
Edwin Dudley Smith (Resident, Overland Park Office)	Ronald J. Laskowski
	Michael K. Seck (Resident, Overland Park Office)
Larry G. Pepperdine	
James P. Nordstrom	David P. Madden (Resident, Overland Park Office)
Justice B. King	
J. Steven Pigg	Steven K. Johnson

ASSOCIATES

Kristine A. Larscheid	Billy E. Newman
Patrick G. Reavey (Resident, Overland Park Office)	David R. Cooper

OF COUNSEL
David H. Fisher

RETIRED
Charles Keith Sayler (Retired)

Representative Clients: Gage Shopping Center, Inc.; Fireman's Fund-American Insurance Cos.; United States Fidelity and Guaranty Co.; The Procter & Gamble Company; American Cyanamid Company; Commercial Union Insurance Companies; National Casualty/Scottsdale Insurance Co.; The Hartford; Berkshire Hathaway Companies.

For full biographical listings, see the Martindale-Hubbell Law Directory

---

PALMER & LOWRY (AV)

Suite 102 Columbian Building, 112 West Sixth, 66603-3862
Telephone: 913-233-1836
Fax: 913-233-3703

MEMBERS OF FIRM

Jerry R. Palmer	Kirk W. Lowry

ASSOCIATE
L J Leatherman

References: Commerce State Bank; Merchants National Bank.

For full biographical listings, see the Martindale-Hubbell Law Directory

---

EUGENE B. RALSTON & ASSOCIATES, P.A. (AV)

2913 Southwest Maupin Lane, 66614-4139
Telephone: 913-273-8002
FAX: 913-273-0744
Email: ERalston@AOL.Com

Eugene B. Ralston

Kevin L. Diehl	Ronald P. Pope

LEGAL SUPPORT PERSONNEL
PARALEGALS

Barbara Cobuluis	Katrina Windholz
Teresa McLinn	Corri Wecker
	Bonnie Price

PRIVATE INVESTIGATOR
Jack L. Grant

For full biographical listings, see the Martindale-Hubbell Law Directory

---

WICHITA,* Sedgwick Co.

KAHRS, NELSON, FANNING, HITE & KELLOGG, L.L.P. (AV)

Suite 630, 200 West Douglas Street, 67202-3089
Telephone: 316-265-7761
Telecopier: 316-267-7803

MEMBERS OF FIRM

Richard C. Hite	Marc A. Powell
Richard L. Honeyman	Forrest James Robinson, Jr.
Larry A. Withers	Don D. Gribble, II
Steven D. Gough	Vince P. Wheeler
Scott J. Gunderson	Alan R. Pfaff
Randy Troutt	Dennis V. Lacey
Arthur S. Chalmers	Donald N. Peterson, II

ASSOCIATES

J. Scott Pohl	Jeffrey R. Emerson
Lisa Adrian McPherson	

OF COUNSEL
H. W. Fanning

Representative Clients: American Telephone & Telegraph Co.; Chubb Group of Companies; Epson America, Inc.; Fuji Heavy Industries; Learjet Corp.; General Motors Corp.; Gulfstream Aerospace; Michelin Tire Corp.; Subaru of America, Inc.; Tokio Marine Insurance Cos.

For Complete List of Firm Personnel, See General Section

For full biographical listings, see the Martindale-Hubbell Law Directory

---

YOUNG, BOGLE, McCAUSLAND, WELLS & CLARK, P.A. (AV)

106 West Douglas, Suite 923, 67202
Telephone: 316-265-7841
Facsimile: 316-265-3956

Glenn D. Young, Jr.	William A. Wells
Jerry D. Bogle	Kenneth M. Clark
Paul S. McCausland	Patrick C. Blanchard
	Mark R. Maloney

OF COUNSEL
Orlin L. Wagner

Representative Clients: Bridgestone/Firestone Inc.; Deere & Co.; Sears Roebuck & Co.; White Consolidated Industries, Inc.; Straightline Mfg., Inc.

For full biographical listings, see the Martindale-Hubbell Law Directory

---

KENTUCKY

BOWLING GREEN,* Warren Co.

BELL, ORR, AYERS & MOORE, P.S.C. (AV)

1010 College Street, P.O. Box 738, 42102-0738
Telephone: 502-781-8111
Telecopier: 502-781-9027

Reginald L. Ayers	Barton D. Darrell
Timothy L. Mauldin	Timothy L. Edelen

General Counsel for: First American National Bank of Kentucky; Farm Credit Services of Mid-America, ACA.; Houchens Industries, Inc. (Food Markets and Shopping Centers); Warren County Board of Education; Bowling Green Municipal Utilities.
Representative Clients: Chicago Title Insurance Co.; Commonwealth Land Title Insurance Co.; Kentucky Farm Bureau Mutual Insurance Co.; Martin Automotive Group; Home Insurance Group.

For Complete List of Firm Personnel, See General Section

For full biographical listings, see the Martindale-Hubbell Law Directory

---

HARLIN & PARKER, P.S.C. (AV)

519 East Tenth Street, P.O. Box 390, 42102-0390
Telephone: 502-842-5611
Telefax: 502-842-2607

William Jerry Parker	Mark D. Alcott

Insurance Clients: CNA Insurance Co.; Maryland Casualty Co.
Railroad and Utilities Clients: District Attorneys for BellSouth Telecommunications, Inc.; CSX Transportation, Inc.
Representative Clients: Deere & Co.
Local Counsel for: General Motors Corp.; News Publishing Co.

For Complete List of Firm Personnel, See General Section

For full biographical listings, see the Martindale-Hubbell Law Directory

---

KERRICK, GRISE & STIVERS (AV)

1025 State Street, P.O. Box 9547, 42102-9547
Telephone: 502-782-8160
Fax: 502-782-5856
Elizabethtown, Kentucky Office: 2935 Dolphin Drive, Suite 102.
Telephone: 502-769-5788.
Fax: 502-737-9285.

MEMBERS OF FIRM

Thomas N. Kerrick	Gregory N. Stivers
John R. Grise	H. Brent Brennenstuhl

ASSOCIATES

Lanna Martin Kilgore	Shawn Rosso Alcott
Laura M. Hagan (Resident, Elizabethtown Office)	Jason B. Bell

Representative Clients: Dollar General Corp.; Columbia Greenview Regional Hospital; Hospital Corporation of America; Hardin Memorial Hospital; Monarch Environmental, Inc.; Mid-South Management Group, Inc.; Trans Financial Bank; TKR Cable.

For full biographical listings, see the Martindale-Hubbell Law Directory

---

COVINGTON, Kenton Co.

ROBERT E. SANDERS AND ASSOCIATES, P.S.C. (AV)

The Charles H. Fisk House, 1017 Russell Street, 41011
Telephone: 606-491-3000
Fax: 606-655-4642
Email: 74762.3055@compuserve.com

Robert E. Sanders

Julie Lippert Duncan	Peggy A. Murphy
	Lisa Pruitt Thorner

(See Next Column)

ROBERT E. SANDERS AND ASSOCIATES, P.S.C.—Continued

LEGAL SUPPORT PERSONNEL

Shirley L. Sanders   Sandra A. Head
Sheila D. Rachal

For full biographical listings, see the Martindale-Hubbell Law Directory

---

HINDMAN,* Knott Co.

WEINBERG, CAMPBELL, SLONE & SLONE, P.S.C. (AV)

Main Street, P.O. Box 727, 41822
Telephone: 606-785-5048; 785-5049
Fax: 606-785-3021

William R. Weinberg   Jerry Wayne Slone
Randy A. Campbell   Randy G. Slone
Richard A. Counts

References: Bank of Hindman; Thacker & Grigsby Telephone Co.

For full biographical listings, see the Martindale-Hubbell Law Directory

---

LEXINGTON,* Fayette Co.

PETER PERLMAN LAW OFFICES, P.S.C. (AV)

388 South Broadway, 40508
Telephone: 606-253-3919
FAX: 606-259-0493

Peter Perlman

Bryce D. Franklin, Jr.   Pamela D. Perlman

For full biographical listings, see the Martindale-Hubbell Law Directory

---

LONDON,* Laurel Co.

FARMER, FARMER, KELLEY AND BROWN (AV)

502 West Fifth Street, Drawer 490, 40743
Telephone: 606-878-7640
Fax: 606-878-2364
Lexington, Kentucky Office: 121 Prosperous Place, Suite 13 B, 40509-1834.
Telephone: 606: 263-2567.
Facsimile: 606: 263-2567.

MEMBERS OF FIRM

F. Preston Farmer   Michael P. Farmer
John F. Kelley, Jr.   Martha L. Brown

ASSOCIATES

Suzanne S. Farmer   Bradford L. Breeding
Jason E. Williams   Estill D. Banks, II

Representative Clients: Liberty Mutual Insurance Co.; American Sterilizer Co.; Line Power Inc.

For full biographical listings, see the Martindale-Hubbell Law Directory

---

LOUISVILLE,* Jefferson Co.

OLDFATHER & MORRIS (AV)

1330 South Third Street, 40208
Telephone: 502-637-7200
Fax: 502-637-3999
Email: om@ntr.net

Ann B. Oldfather   James Barrett
Douglas H. Morris, II   Jennifer Jordan Hall

For full biographical listings, see the Martindale-Hubbell Law Directory

WEISS & FREDERICK (AV)

1425 Citizens Plaza, 40202
Telephone: 502-583-1000
FAX: 502-583-4478

Gary M. Weiss   Janice M. Weiss
Carl D. Frederick   William T. Haynes, Jr.

OF COUNSEL

Henry M. Burt   Karla W. Katakis

For full biographical listings, see the Martindale-Hubbell Law Directory

WOODWARD, HOBSON & FULTON (AV)

2500 National City Tower, 101 South Fifth Street, 40202
Telephone: 502-581-8000
Fax: 502-581-8111
Lexington, Kentucky Office: PNC Bank Plaza, 200 West Vine Street, Suite 500.
Telephone: 606-244-7100.
Telecopier: 606-244-7111.
New Albany, Indiana Office: 611 East Spring Street, P.O. Box 288.
Telephone: 812-941-1800.
Telecopier: 812-941-1855.

(See Next Column)

MEMBERS OF FIRM

William D. Grubbs   Mary Jo Wetzel (Resident, New
Lionel A. Hawse (Resident,   Albany, Indiana Office)
   Lexington, Kentucky Office)   Gregory L. Smith
Harry K. Herren   Gregory A. Bölzle
David R. Monohan   Elizabeth Ullmer Mendel
Will H. Fulton   Jann B. Logsdon
Richard H. C. Clay   David T. Schaefer

ASSOCIATES

Benjamin Cowgill, Jr. (Resident,   L. Jay Gilbert
   Lexington, Kentucky Office)   William A. Green, III (Resident,
D. Craig York   Lexington, Kentucky Office)
Sandra Tremper O'Brien   Lydia Plamp Brownlow
Christopher R. Cashen
   (Resident, Lexington,
   Kentucky Office)

OF COUNSEL

Fielden Woodward

Representative Clients: Caterpillar Corp.; Clark Equipment Co.; Ford Motor Co.; General Motors Corp.; Nissan North America, Inc.; NUMMI; Snapper, Inc.; Toyota Motor Sales USA, Inc.; V.W.A.G.; Wyeth-Ayerst Laboratories, Inc., a division of American Home Products Corporation.

For Complete List of Firm Personnel, See General Section

For full biographical listings, see the Martindale-Hubbell Law Directory

---

LOUISIANA

ALEXANDRIA,* Rapides Parish

McLURE, PICKELS AND REICHMAN (AV)

901 Sixth Street, P.O. Box 1525, 71309-1525
Telephone: 318-445-5317
Fax: 318-442-3009

MEMBERS OF FIRM

Thomas C. McLure, Jr.   John G. McLure
   (1915-1984)   John C. Pickels
James B. Reichman

ASSOCIATES

Bonita K. Preuett   Ann E. Lowrey

Representative Clients: State Farm Mutual Automobile Insurance Company; USAA Group; State Farm Fire and Casualty Co.

For full biographical listings, see the Martindale-Hubbell Law Directory

---

BATON ROUGE,* East Baton Rouge Parish

LANE, FERTITTA, LANE, JANNEY & THOMAS (AV)

435 Louisiana Avenue, P.O. Box 3335, 70821
Telephone: 504-387-0241
Fax: 504-387-1238

MEMBERS OF FIRM

Horace C. Lane (1921-1989)   Thomas A. Lane
Frank A. Fertitta   William F. Janney
Richard S. Thomas

ASSOCIATE

Margaret T. Lane

Representative Clients: State Farm Mutual Automobile Insurance Co.; State Farm Fire & Casualty Co.; United States Fidelity & Guaranty Co.; Aetna Casualty & Surety Co.; Employers Liability Assurance Corp., Ltd.; Allstate Insurance Co.; St. Paul Fire and Marine Insurance Co.; The Medical Protective Co.; Safeco Insurance Co. of America; Horace Mann Insurance Co.

For full biographical listings, see the Martindale-Hubbell Law Directory

UNGLESBY & KOCH (AV)

246 Napoleon Street, 70802
Telephone: 504-387-0120
Fax: 504-336-4355
Email: unglkoch@premier.net

Lewis O. Unglesby   Deborah H. Baer
Karl J. Koch   Aidan C. Reynolds

For full biographical listings, see the Martindale-Hubbell Law Directory

WATSON, BLANCHE, WILSON & POSNER (AV)

505 North Boulevard, P.O. Drawer 2995, 70821-2995
Telephone: 504-387-5511
Fax: 504-387-5972

Peter T. Dazzio   William E. Scott, III
Felix R. Weill   P. Chauvin Wilkinson, Jr.
Randall L. Champagne

(See Next Column)

WATSON, BLANCHE, WILSON & POSNER, *Baton Rouge—Continued*

ASSOCIATE
P. Scott Jolly

Representative Clients: BP Chemicals, Inc.; Nutri/System, Inc.; Baton Rouge General Medical Center; Woman's Hospital; American International Group.

For full biographical listings, see the Martindale-Hubbell Law Directory

---

EUNICE, St. Landry Parish

I. JACKSON BURSON, JR. A PROFESSIONAL LAW CORPORATION (AV)

220 North Second Street, P.O. Box 985, 70535
Telephone: 318-457-1227
Fax: 318-457-8860

I. Jackson Burson, Jr.

For full biographical listings, see the Martindale-Hubbell Law Directory

---

*LAFAYETTE,** Lafayette Parish

DOMENGEAUX WRIGHT MOROUX & ROY A PROFESSIONAL LAW CORPORATION (AV)

556 Jefferson Street, Suite 500, P.O. Box 3668, 70502-3668
Telephone: 318-233-3033; 1-800-375-3106
Fax: 318-232-8213

James Domengeaux (1907-1988)	Frank Edwards
Anthony D. Moroux (1948-1993)	James H. Domengeaux
Bob F. Wright (A Professional	Gilbert Hennigan Dozier (A Professional Law Corporation)
Law Corporation)	Carla Marie Perron
James Parkerson Roy (A	Vivian Veron Neumann
Professional Law Corporation)	Michael D. Goss
Thomas R. Edwards (A Professional Law Corporation)	

OF COUNSEL
Jerome E. Domengeaux

Reference: Mid-South National Bank; Advocate Financial, L.L.C.

For full biographical listings, see the Martindale-Hubbell Law Directory

HILL & BEYER, A PROFESSIONAL LAW CORPORATION (AV)

101 LaRue France, Suite 502, P.O. Box 53006, 70505-3006
Telephone: 318-232-9733
Fax: 1-318-237-2566

John K. Hill, Jr.	Eugene P. Matherne (1962-1996)
Bret C. Beyer	Robert B. Purser
David R. Rabalais	Erin J. Sherburne
Marianna Broussard	

For full biographical listings, see the Martindale-Hubbell Law Directory

ROY, BIVINS, JUDICE & HENKE, A PROFESSIONAL LAW CORPORATION (AV)

600 Jefferson Street, Suite 800, P.O. Drawer Z, 70502
Telephone: 318-233-7430
Telecopier: 318-233-8403

Harmon F. Roy	Kenneth M. Henke
John A. Bivins	W. Alan Lilley
Ronald J. Judice	Philip E. Roberts
Patrick M. Wartelle	

Representative Clients: Employers Insurance of Wausau; Louisiana Medical Mutual Ins. Co.; C.N.A.; Aetna Casualty & Surety; Zurich Ins. Co.; Our Lady of Lourdes Regional Medical Center, Inc.; St Paul Fire & Marine Ins. Co.; First Financial Insurance Company; Great Lakes Chemical; OSCA.

For full biographical listings, see the Martindale-Hubbell Law Directory

---

*LAKE CHARLES,** Calcasieu Parish

THE CARMOUCHE LAW FIRM A PROFESSIONAL CORPORATION (AV)

Bank One Tower, 901 Lakeshore Drive, Suite 900, P.O. Drawer 2001, 70601-5270
Telephone: 318-433-0355
Telecopier: 318-433-1274
Email: clf@carmouche.com

David R. Frohn	Terry Thibodeaux

Robin A. Anderson

For full biographical listings, see the Martindale-Hubbell Law Directory

---

MANDEVILLE, St. Tammany Parish

BAILEY & DWYER (AV)

600 Mariner's Plaza, Suite 607, 70448
Telephone: 504-674-1105
Fax: 504-674-1966
Metairie Area Telephone: 504-833-8241
Fax: 504-837-4534

MEMBERS OF FIRM
B. Ralph Bailey	Frederick H. N. Dwyer
	Scott O. Gaspard

For full biographical listings, see the Martindale-Hubbell Law Directory

---

*NEW ORLEANS,** Orleans Parish

DEUTSCH, KERRIGAN & STILES, L.L.P. (AV)

A Partnership including Professional Law Corporations
755 Magazine Street, 70130-3672
Telephone: 504-581-5141
Cable Address: "Dekest"
Telex: 584358
Telecopier: 504-566-1201
Email: dks@dksno.com *URL:* http://www.dksno.com
St. Tammany Parish Office: 550 Pontchartrain Drive, Suite 200, Slidell, LA. 70458.
Telephone: 504-639-0555.
Fax: 504-639-0550

MEMBERS OF FIRM
Frederick R. Bott (P.L.C.)	Darrell K. Cherry (P.L.C.)
Robert E. Kerrigan, Jr., (P.L.C.)	Nancy J. Marshall
Raymon G. Jones (P.L.C.)	James G. Wyly, III
Francis J. Barry, Jr.	Janet L. MacDonell
Victor E. Stilwell, Jr., (P.L.C.)	Joseph L. McReynolds
Philip D. Lorio, III	Theodore L. White
A. Wendel Stout, III	William C. Harrison, Jr.
Terrence L. Brennan	Gary B. Roth
Marc J. Yellin (P.L.C.)	Lisa C. Winter
Howard L. Murphy	Karyn J. Vigh

ASSOCIATE
Pamela W. Carter

For Complete List of Firm Personnel, See General Section

For full biographical listings, see the Martindale-Hubbell Law Directory

FRILOT, PARTRIDGE, KOHNKE & CLEMENTS, L.C. (AV)

3600 Energy Centre, 1100 Poydras Street, 70163-3600
Telephone: 504-599-8000
Telecopier: 504-599-8100
Email: postmaster@fpkc.ccmail.compuserve.com *URL:* hhtp://www.fpkc.com

Sidney A. Backstrom	Douglas P. Matthews
C. William Belsom, Jr.	Stephanie Ann May
Francis H. Brown, III	Kenneth A. Mayeaux
James H. Brown, Jr.	Robert B. McNeal
George E. Cain, Jr.	Wayne K. McNeil
Michael T. Cali	Patrick J. McShane
Miles P. Clements	Joseph N. Mole
Andrew S. de Klerk	David A. Olson
George A. Frilot, III (A Professional Law Corp.)	Scott S. Partridge
	Greg A. Pellegrini
Frederick T. Greschner, Jr.	Michael R. Phillips
John J. Hainkel, III	James F. Shuey
Edward F. Kohnke, IV	James R. Silverstein
Allen J. Krouse, III	Peter E. Sperling
J. Dwight LeBlanc, III	Patrick A. Talley (P.C.)

For full biographical listings, see the Martindale-Hubbell Law Directory

GAINSBURGH, BENJAMIN, DAVID, MEUNIER, NORIEA & WARSHAUER (AV)

2800 Energy Centre, 1100 Poydras, 70163-2800
Telephone: 504-522-2304
Telecopier: 504-528-9973
Email: GAINSBEN@IAMERICA.NET

OF COUNSEL
Jack C. Benjamin (P.L.C.)

MEMBERS OF FIRM
Robert J. David	Irving J. Warshauer
Gerald E. Meunier	Stevan C. Dittman
Nick F. Noriea, Jr.	Madeleine M. Landrieu
Darryl M. Phillips	

ASSOCIATES
Michael G. Calogero	Jeffrey A. Mitchell

For full biographical listings, see the Martindale-Hubbell Law Directory

New Orleans—Continued

PULASKI, GIEGER & LABORDE, L.L.C. (AV)

Suite 4800, One Shell Square, 701 Poydras Street, 70139
Telephone: 504-561-0400
Telecopier: 504-561-1011

Michael T. Pulaski (P.C.)	Leo R. McAloon, III
Ernest P. Gieger, Jr., (P.C.)	John P. Gonzalez
Kenneth H. Laborde (P.C.)	J. Jeffery Raborn
Robert W. Maxwell (P.C.)	Lance Blake Williams
Keith W. McDaniel (P.C.)	James E. Swinnen
Sharon D. Smith (P.C.)	Gina S. Montgomery
Gary G. Hebert	Mary Beth Meyer

Julianne T. Echols

For full biographical listings, see the Martindale-Hubbell Law Directory

SLATER LAW FIRM, A PROFESSIONAL CORPORATION (AV)

650 Poydras Street Suite 2600, 70130-6101
Telephone: 504-523-7333
Fax: 504-528-1080

Benjamin R. Slater, Jr.	Kevin M. Wheeler
Benjamin R. Slater, III	Anne Elise Brown
Mark E. Van Horn	Donald J. Miester, Jr.

Cory Rabin Cahn	James L. Bradford, III

SPECIAL COUNSEL

W. Malcolm Stevenson	Robert B. Acomb, III

Michael O. Waguespack

Representative Clients: Anheuser-Busch, Incorporated; The Quaker Oats Company; Electric Mutual Liability Insurance Company; Diversified Foods and Seasonings.

For full biographical listings, see the Martindale-Hubbell Law Directory

*RUSTON,** Lincoln Parish

GOFF AND GOFF (AV)

612 North Vienna Street, P.O. Box 2050, 71270
Telephone: 318-255-1760
Fax: 318-255-7745
Email: giv@aol.com

A. Kennon Goff, III

Representative Clients: Ruston State Bank and Trust Co.; Community Trust Bank; South Central Bell Telephone Co.; Phillips Petroleum Co.; Aluminum Company of America; Society National Bank of Cleveland; Balboa Insurance Co.; Excalibur Insurance Co.; Shelter Insurance Co.; The Pyramid Life Insurance Co.;

For full biographical listings, see the Martindale-Hubbell Law Directory

*SHREVEPORT,** Caddo Parish

BARLOW AND HARDTNER L.C. (AV)

Tenth Floor, Louisiana Tower, 401 Edwards Street, 71101-3289
Telephone: 318-227-1131
Telecopier: 318-227-1141
Mailing Address: P.O. Box 8, Shreveport, Louisiana, 71161-0008

Joseph L. Shea, Jr.	Michael B. Donald

Representative Clients: Ashland Oil, Inc.; Beaird Industries, Inc.; Kelley Oil Corporation; NorAm Energy Corp. (formerly Arkla, Inc.); Panhandle Eastern Corp.; Pennzoil Producing Co.; Johnson Controls, Inc.; Ashland Oil, Inc.; Southwestern Electric Power Company.

For Complete List of Firm Personnel, See General Section

For full biographical listings, see the Martindale-Hubbell Law Directory

MAINE

*AUGUSTA,** Kennebec Co.

* indicates certain Bar Register subscribers whose principal office is located elsewhere in the state and who have arranged for representation as a part of the state capital listings that follow

* PIERCE ATWOOD (AV)

77 Winthrop Street, 04330
Telephone: 207-622-6311
Fax: 207-623-9367
Email: info@PierceAtwood.com
Portland, Maine Office: One Monument Square.
Telephone: 207-791-1100.
Fax: 207-791-1350.

(See Next Column)

Newburyport, Massachusetts Office: 6 Harris Street.
Telephone: 508-465-9599.
Fax: 508-465-9945.

MEMBERS OF FIRM

Malcolm L. Lyons	Michael D. Seitzinger
	John C. Nivison

ASSOCIATE

Daniel J. Stevens

For Complete List of Firm Personnel, See General Section

For full biographical listings, see the Martindale-Hubbell Law Directory

*PORTLAND,** Cumberland Co.

AMERLING & BURNS, A PROFESSIONAL ASSOCIATION (AV)

193 Middle Street, 04101
Telephone: 207-775-3581
Facsimile: 207-775-3814
Affiliated St. Croix Office: Coon & Sanford, P.O. Box 25918, Six Chandlers's Wharf, Suite 202, 00824-0918.

W. John Amerling	Arnold C. Macdonald
George F. Burns	Mary DeLano
David P. Ray	Joanne F. Cole

A. Robert Ruesch

OF COUNSEL

Bruce M. Jervis

Representative Clients: H.E. Sargent, Inc. (construction); Merrill Trust; J.M. Huber, Inc.; Jackson Laboratories; Hague International (engineering); Aetna Life & Casualty Co.; The Hartford; Great American Insurance Co.; Wausau Insurance Co.

For full biographical listings, see the Martindale-Hubbell Law Directory

FRIEDMAN & BABCOCK (AV)

Suite 400, Six City Center, P.O. Box 4726, 04112-4726
Telephone: 207-761-0900
Telecopier: 207-761-0186

MEMBERS OF FIRM

Harold J. Friedman	Thomas A. Cox
Ernest J. Babcock	Karen Frink Wolf
Martha C. Gaythwaite	Jennifer S. Begel

Laurence H. Leavitt

ASSOCIATES

Theodore H. Irwin, Jr.	Elizabeth A. Germani
Lee H. Bals	Jonathan Marc Dunitz
Michelle Allott	Darren Blaine Riggle
Arthur J. Lamothe	Tracy D. Hill

Bruce W. Hepler

For full biographical listings, see the Martindale-Hubbell Law Directory

THOMPSON & BOWIE (AV)

Three Canal Plaza, P.O. Box 4630, 04112
Telephone: 207-774-2500
Telecopier: 207-774-3591

MEMBERS OF FIRM

Roy E. Thompson, Jr.	Frank W. DeLong, III
James M. Bowie	Michael E. Saucier
Daniel R. Mawhinney	Mark V. Franco
Rebecca H. Farnum	Elizabeth Knox Peck
Glenn H. Robinson	Cathy S. Roberts

ASSOCIATE

Paul C. Catsos

For full biographical listings, see the Martindale-Hubbell Law Directory

WRIGHT, COON & CUNNINGHAM, P.A. (AV)

377 Fore Street, P.O. Box 7526, 04112
Telephone: 207-775-7722
Fax: 207-772-7045
Email: lexfori@lexfori.com

Steven F. Wright	John R. Coon

Gregory M. Cunningham

For full biographical listings, see the Martindale-Hubbell Law Directory

MARYLAND

BALTIMORE,* (Independent City)

ALLEN, JOHNSON, ALEXANDER & KARP, P.A. (AV)

Suite 1540, 100 East Pratt Street, 21202
Telephone: 410-727-5000
Fax: 410-727-0861
Washington, D.C. Office: 1707 L Street, N.W., Suite 1050.
Telephone: 202-828-4141.

Daniel Karp

Representative Clients: Scottsdale Insurance Co.; Nautilus Insurance Co.; Jefferson Insurance Co.; Liberty Mutual Insurance Co.; Avis Rent-A-Car; Otis Elevator Co.; Montgomery Elevator Co.; Admiral Insurance Co.; Local Government Insurance Trust; Lancer Insurance Co.

For Complete List of Firm Personnel, See General Section

For full biographical listings, see the Martindale-Hubbell Law Directory

---

ANDERSON, COE & KING, L.L.P. (AV)

201 North Charles Street, Suite 2000, 21201
Telephone: 410-752-1630
Cable Address: ABKO
Fax: 410-752 0085
Ocean City, Maryland Office: 7904 Coastal Highway, Suite 5, P.O. Box 535.
Telephone: 301-524-6411.
Fax: 301-524-9479.

COUNSEL

G. C. A. Anderson (1898-1985)	Frank J. Vecella
Ward B. Coe, Jr.	John F. King

MEMBERS OF FIRM

Robert H. Bouse, Jr.	G. Macy Nelson
E. Dale Adkins, III	E. Philip Franke, III
James A. Rothschild	Philip C. Jacobson
M. Bradley Hallwig	Lynn B. Malone
J. Michael Sloneker	Gregory L. Van Geison
Barbara McC. Stanley	

ASSOCIATES

Matthew T. Angotti	James S. Aist
Hugh Cropper, IV	Russell Sherlock Woodward
(Resident, Ocean City Office)	E. Scott Conover
H. Joy Sharp	

Representative Clients: Hartford Accident & Indemnity Co.; The St. Paul Insurance Cos.; Chrysler Corp.; Provident Life and Accident Insurance Co.; Emerson Electric Co.; Pennsylvania Hospital Ins. Co.; Maryland Association of Boards of Education Group Insurance Pool; Pittsburg Corning Corp.; Sierra Club; Hoover Treated Wood Products, Inc.

For full biographical listings, see the Martindale-Hubbell Law Directory

---

ELLIN AND BAKER (AV)

Second Floor, 1101 St. Paul Street, 21202
Telephone: 410-727-1787
FAX: 410-547-1787
1-800-237-1787

MEMBER OF FIRM

Marvin Ellin	LaVonna Lee Vice

Michael P. Smith

For full biographical listings, see the Martindale-Hubbell Law Directory

---

BERTRAM M. GOLDSTEIN & ASSOCIATES, P.A. (AV)

222 Blaustein Building, One North Charles Street, 21201-3710
Telephone: 410-539-2222
Fax: 410-539-8157

Bertram M. Goldstein

Dean Kasian	Jeffrey S. Goldstein
Andrea L. Saum	

For full biographical listings, see the Martindale-Hubbell Law Directory

---

GOODELL, DeVRIES, LEECH & GRAY, LLP (AV)

Suite 2000, One South Street, 21202
Telephone: 410-783-4000
Telecopy: 410-783-4040
Email: GDLG@GDLG.COM

MEMBERS OF FIRM

Charles P. Goodell, Jr.	Richard M. Barnes
Donald L. DeVries, Jr.	Thomas M. Goss
Sidney G. Leech	Bonnie J. Beavan
Susan T. Preston	Linda S. Woolf
Thomas J. Cullen, Jr.	

(See Next Column)

For full biographical listings, see the Martindale-Hubbell Law Directory

ISRAELSON, SALSBURY, CLEMENTS & BEKMAN (AV)

300 West Pratt Street Suite 450, 21201
Telephone: 410-539-6633
FAX: 410-625-9554

MEMBERS OF FIRM

Stuart Marshall Salsbury	Daniel M. Clements
Paul D. Bekman	Matthew Zimmerman
Laurence A. Marder	

Scott R. Scherr	Lauren R. Calia
Carol J. Glover	Andrew David Alpert

COUNSEL TO THE FIRM

Max R. Israelson

OF COUNSEL

Samuel Omar Jackson, Jr. (Semi-Retired)

For full biographical listings, see the Martindale-Hubbell Law Directory

---

JANET, WILLOUGHBY & GERSHON, LLC (AV)

Executive Centre at Hooks Lane, 8 Reservoir Circle, Suite 200, 21208
Telephone: 410-653-3200
Toll Free: 888-4-MED-LAW
Fax: 410-653-9030

MEMBERS OF FIRM

Howard Alan Janet (P.C.)	Wayne M. Willoughby (P.A.)
Zev T. Gershon	

ASSOCIATES

Randal D. Getz	Robin R. Smith
Anne Michele Crook	

LEGAL SUPPORT PERSONNEL

Joan Hunter Green	Sharon Marie Schmidt
(Registered Nurse/Paralegal)	(Paralegal)

For full biographical listings, see the Martindale-Hubbell Law Directory

---

ROBINETTE, DUGAN & JAKUBOWSKI, P.A. (AV)

The Robinette-Dugan Building, 801 St. Paul Street, 21202
Telephone: 410-659-6700
FAX: 410-752-0456

Gilbert H. Robinette	Ruth A. Jakubowski
Henry E. Dugan, Jr.	Bruce J. Babij

Pamela S. Foresman	George S. Tolley, III

OF COUNSEL

Marian V. Fleming

For full biographical listings, see the Martindale-Hubbell Law Directory

---

SCANLAN & ROSEN, P.A. (AV)

26 South Street, 21202-3399
Telephone: 410-244-1155
FAX: 410-244-1157

Alfred L. Scanlan, Jr.	Marc Seldin Rosen

Michael Stuart Warshaw	Colleen A. Cavanaugh

OF COUNSEL

James Lee Katz

For full biographical listings, see the Martindale-Hubbell Law Directory

---

SCHOCHOR, FEDERICO AND STATON, P.A. (AV)

The Paulton, 1211 St. Paul Street, 21202
Telephone: 410-234-1000
Toll Free: 888-234-0001
Facsimile: 410-234-1010
URL: http://www.sfspa.com
Washington D.C. Office: 750 First Street, N.E., Suite 905.
Telephone: 202-408-3300.

Jonathan Schochor	Philip C. Federico
Kerry D. Staton	

Louis G. Close, III	Christopher P. Kennedy

For full biographical listings, see the Martindale-Hubbell Law Directory

Baltimore—Continued

VENABLE ATTORNEYS AT LAW VENABLE, BAETJER AND HOWARD, LLP (AV)

A Partnership including Professional Corporations
1800 Mercantile Bank & Trust Building, 2 Hopkins Plaza, 21201
Telephone: 410-244-7400
Email: INFO@Venable.win.net
Washington, D.C. Office: Venable, Baetjer, Howard & Civiletti LLP. Suite 1000, 1201 New York Avenue, N.W.
Telephone: 202-962-4800.
McLean, Virginia Office: Suite 400, 2010 Corporate Ridge.
Telephone: 703-760-1600.
Rockville, Maryland Office: Suite 500, One Church Street, P. O. Box 1906.
Telephone: 301-217-5600.
Towson, Maryland Office: 210 Allegheny Avenue, P. O. Box 5517.
Telephone: 410-494-6200.

MEMBERS OF FIRM

Benjamin R. Civiletti (P.C.) (Also at Washington, D.C. and Towson, Maryland Offices)
George Cochran Doub (P.C.)
Roger W. Titus (Resident, Rockville, Maryland Office)
Douglas D. Connah, Jr. (P.C.) (Also at Washington, D.C. Office)
Robert G. Smith (P.C.)
John H. Zink, III (Resident, Towson, Maryland Office)
Paul F. Strain (P.C.)
Joseph C. Wich, Jr. (Resident, Towson, Maryland Office)
Nell B. Strachan
James K. Archibald (Also at Washington, D.C. Office)
Jeffrey A. Dunn (also at Washington, D.C. Office)

George F. Pappas (Also at Washington, D.C. Office)
James L. Shea (Also at Washington, D.C. Office)
Elizabeth C. Honeywell
William D. Quarles (Also at Washington, D.C. and Towson, Maryland Offices)
C. Carey Deeley, Jr. (Also at Towson, Maryland Office)
Kathleen Gallogly Cox (Resident, Towson, Maryland Office)
Christopher R. Mellott
M. King Hill, III (Resident, Towson, Maryland Office)
David J. Heubeck
Gary M. Hnath (Resident, Washington, D.C. Office)
Mitchell Y. Mirviss
Michael W. Robinson (Resident, McLean, Virginia Office)

ASSOCIATES

Paul D. Barker, Jr.
David W. Goewey (Not admitted in MD; Resident, Washington, D.C. Office)
Maria F. Howell
Mary-Dulany James (Resident, Towson, Maryland Office)
Gregory L. Laubach (Resident, Rockville, Maryland Office)

Vicki Margolis (Also at Washington, D.C. Office)
Christine M. McAnney (Not admitted in MD; Resident, McLean, Virginia Office)
John A. McCauley
John T. Prisbe

For Complete List of Firm Personnel, See General Section

For full biographical listings, see the Martindale-Hubbell Law Directory

ROBIN PAGE WEST (AV)

110 St. Paul Street, Suite 301, 21202
Telephone: 410-244-0400
Fax: 410-244-0402
Email: robin.west.esq@counsel.com

For full biographical listings, see the Martindale-Hubbell Law Directory

ROCKVILLE,* Montgomery Co.

ANDERSON & QUINN (AV)

The Adams Law Center, 25 Wood Lane, 20850
Telephone: 301-762-3303
FAX: 301-762-3776
Other Rockville Maryland Office: 110 North West St., Suite 501, 20850.
Telephone: 301-340-0800.

MEMBERS OF FIRM

Charles C. Collins (1900-1973)
Robert E. Anderson (Not admitted in MD; Retired)
Francis X. Quinn

Donald P. Maiberger
Robert P. Scanlon
James G. Healy
John A. Rego

ASSOCIATES

Alice Kelley Scanlon
Marnie E. Simon
Kerry Patricia Shanahan

Mary L. Fellin
Kelly Ann McInerney
Timothy J. Mulreany

Representative Clients: C & P Telephone; Commercial Union Insurance Cos.; Allstate Insurance Co.; State Farm Mutual Automobile Insurance Co.; Liberty Mutual Insurance Co.; Northbrook Insurance Cos.; Travelers Insurance Co.; National General Insurance Co.; American International Adjustment Co.; Marriott Corp.

For full biographical listings, see the Martindale-Hubbell Law Directory

BRAULT, GRAHAM, SCOTT & BRAULT (AV)

101 South Washington Street, 20850
Telephone: 301-424-1060
Fax: 301-424-7991
Washington, D.C. Office: 1906 Sunderland Place, N.W.
Telephone: 202-785-1200.
FAX: 202-785-4301.
Arlington, Virginia Office: Suite 1201, 2300 North Clarendon Boulevard, Courthouse Plaza.
Telephone: 703-358-9200.

ASSOCIATE

Michael A. Carlo

Representative Clients: American Oil Co.; Crum & Forster Group; Fireman's Fund American Insurance Cos.; Kemper Group; Reliance Insurance Cos.; Safeco Group; Government Employees Insurance Co.; Medical Mutual Insurance Society of Maryland; Legal Mutual Liability Insurance Society of Maryland.

For Complete List of Firm Personnel, See General Section

For full biographical listings, see the Martindale-Hubbell Law Directory

TOWSON,* Baltimore Co.

HOWELL, GATELY, WHITNEY & CARTER, LLP (AV)

401 Washington Avenue, Twelfth Floor, 21204
Telephone: 410-583-8000
Fax: 410-583-8031

MEMBERS OF FIRM

H. Thomas Howell
William F. Gately
Benjamin R. Goertemiller

Daniel W. Whitney
David A. Carter
William R. Levasseur

ASSOCIATES

Una M. Perez
George D. Bogris

Kathleen D. Leslie
Gerard Wm. Wittstadt, Jr.

Laura A. Gregory

For full biographical listings, see the Martindale-Hubbell Law Directory

VENABLE ATTORNEYS AT LAW VENABLE, BAETJER AND HOWARD, LLP (AV)

A Partnership including Professional Corporations
210 Allegheny Avenue, P.O. Box 5517, 21204
Telephone: 410-494-6200
FAX: 410-821-0147
Baltimore, Maryland Office: 1800 Mercantile Bank & Trust Building, 2 Hopkins Plaza.
Telephone: 410-244-7400.
Washington, D.C. Office: Venable, Baetjer, Howard & Civiletti LLP, Suite 1000, 1201 New York Avenue, N.W.
Telephone: 202-962-4800.
McLean, Virginia Office: Suite 400, 2010 Corporate Ridge.
Telephone: 703-760-1600.
Rockville, Maryland Office: Suite 500, One Church Street, P. O. Box 1906.
Telephone: 301-217-5600.

PARTNERS

Benjamin R. Civiletti (P.C.) (Also at Washington, D.C. and Baltimore, Maryland Offices)
John H. Zink, III

Joseph C. Wich, Jr.
C. Carey Deeley, Jr. (Also at Baltimore, Maryland Office)
Kathleen Gallogly Cox
M. King Hill, III

ASSOCIATE

Mary-Dulany James

For Complete List of Firm Personnel, See General Section

For full biographical listings, see the Martindale-Hubbell Law Directory

MASSACHUSETTS

BOSTON,* Suffolk Co.

BADGER, DOLAN, PARKER & COHEN (AV)

Formerly Badger, Sullivan, Kelley & Cole
2 Oliver Street, 02109
Telephone: 617-482-3030
Fax: 617-482-6919
Email: Badger@ma.ultranet.com

MEMBERS OF FIRM

Walter I. Badger (1885-1926)
John J. Sullivan (1926-1979)
David W. Kelley (1935-1986)

George F. Parker, III
James B. Dolan, Jr.
Lawrence J. Cohen

ASSOCIATES

Audrey LaRowe Nee
John J. Pentz

Paul J. Barresi

(See Next Column)

BADGER, DOLAN, PARKER & COHEN, *Boston—Continued*
OF COUNSEL
Joseph E. Rendini   G. Mitchell Eckel, III

For full biographical listings, see the Martindale-Hubbell Law Directory

FINNERTY & FINNERTY (AV)
Suite 230, 21 Custom House Street, 02110
Telephone: 617-737-3770
Fax: 617-737-0684

MEMBERS OF FIRM
John F. Finnerty (1917-1994)   Gail E. Finnerty
John F. Finnerty, Jr.   Brian P. Finnerty
Reference: Fleet Bank.

For full biographical listings, see the Martindale-Hubbell Law Directory

LAW OFFICES OF LEONARD GLAZER, P.C. & ASSOCIATES (AV)
One Longfellow Place Suite 3408, 02114
Telephone: 617-523-4411
Fax: 617-523-7433

Leonard Glazer

Frank E. Glazer   Anthony R. Orlando, III

For full biographical listings, see the Martindale-Hubbell Law Directory

HANIFY & KING, PROFESSIONAL CORPORATION (AV)
One Federal Street, 02110-2007
Telephone: 617-423-0400
Telefax: 617-423-0498

James Coyne King   Daniel J. Lyne
John D. Hanify   Donald F. Farrell, Jr.
Harold B. Murphy   Barbara Wegener Pfirrman
David Lee Evans   Gerard P. Richer
            Timothy P. O'Neill

Jean A. Musiker   Joseph F. Cortellini
Ann M. Chiacchieri   Eddirland Duncan
Melissa J. Cassedy   Andrew G. Lizotte
Jeffrey J. Upton   Karen A. Whitley
Michael R. Perry   Christopher K. Barry-Smith
Charles A. Dale, III   William T. Harrington
Kathleen E. Cross   Matthew McCue
David M. Wright   Robyn J. Bartlett
            Owen P. Kane

For full biographical listings, see the Martindale-Hubbell Law Directory

LAW OFFICES OF MARTIN KANTROVITZ (AV)
185 Devonshire Street, Suite 510, 02110
Telephone: 617-426-3050
FAX: 617-426-3640
Hudson, Massachusetts Office: 173 Washington Street. 01749.
Telephone: 508-562-3800.
New Bedford, Massachusetts Office: 60 Spring Street, Suite 12.
Telephone: 508-994-6010.

ASSOCIATE
Lisa Baer

For full biographical listings, see the Martindale-Hubbell Law Directory

PALMER & DODGE LLP (AV)
One Beacon Street, 02108
Telephone: 617-573-0100
Facsimile: 617-227-4420

MEMBERS OF FIRM
Michael T. Gass   Daryl J. Lapp
Jeffrey F. Jones   Francis C. Lynch
            Craig E. Stewart
COUNSEL
Cassandra Warshowsky

For Complete List of Firm Personnel, See General Section

For full biographical listings, see the Martindale-Hubbell Law Directory

SWARTZ & SWARTZ (AV)
10 Marshall Street, 02108
Telephone: 617-742-1900
Fax: 617-367-7193

Edward M. Swartz   Joan E. Swartz
Alan L. Cantor   James A. Swartz
Joseph A. Swartz   Harold David Levine
Victor A. Denaro   David P. Angueira

(See Next Column)

OF COUNSEL
Fredric A. Swartz

For full biographical listings, see the Martindale-Hubbell Law Directory

WARNER & STACKPOLE LLP (AV)
75 State Street, 02109
Telephone: 617-951-9000
Telecopier: 617-951-9151
Email: w&s@warstack.com

MEMBERS OF FIRM
Samuel Adams   Ralph T. Lepore, III
Michael DeMarco   Keith C. Long
Michael A. Hickey   Stephen L. Palmer
Antoinette D. Hubbard   Janice Kelley Rowan
Joseph J. Leghorn   Peter T. Wechsler
            Robert A. Whitney
ASSOCIATES
Alida M. Coo   Alexis Smith Hamdan
Kristine E. George   Christopher G. Lang
            Daniel E. Rosenfeld
OF COUNSEL
Norman A. Hubley

For Complete List of Firm Personnel, See General Section

For full biographical listings, see the Martindale-Hubbell Law Directory

BROCKTON, Plymouth Co.

VINCENT P. CAHALANE, P.C. (AV)
478 Torrey Street, 02401
Telephone: 508-588-1222
Fax: 508-584-4748

Vincent P. Cahalane   Julie A. Cahalane Cahill
Robert J. Zullas   John E. Cahill

For full biographical listings, see the Martindale-Hubbell Law Directory

PITTSFIELD,* Berkshire Co.

CAIN, HIBBARD, MYERS & COOK, A PROFESSIONAL CORPORATION (AV)
66 West Street, 01201
Telephone: 413-443-4771
Telecopier: 413-443-7694
Great Barrington, Massachusetts Office: 309 Main Street, 01230.
Telephone: 413-528-4771.
Fax: 413-528-5553.

Leonard H. Cohen   John A. Agostini
David O. Burbank   William A. Rota
            Diane M. DeGiacomo

Benjamin Smith   Kevin M. Kinne
            Lee D. Flournoy

Representative Clients: Bank of Boston/First Agricultural Bank; Great Barrington Savings Bank; Greylock Credit Union; The Berkshire Gas Company; Berkshire Health Systems, Inc.; Berkshire Physicians & Surgeons, P.C.
Local Counsel for: General Electric Co.; Boston Symphony Orchestra; Statewide Funding Corporation.

For full biographical listings, see the Martindale-Hubbell Law Directory

SPRINGFIELD,* Hampden Co.

MORIARTY, DONOGHUE & LEJA, P.C. (AV)
1331 Main Street, 01103
Telephone: 413-737-4319
Fax: 413-732-8767

James P. Moriarty (1878-1973)   Edward V. Leja
Thomas J. Donoghue   Patricia A. Barbalunga

Robert F. Connelly   John B. Stewart
            Bernard J. Romani III

Local Counsel for: Insurance Company of North America; United Community Insurance Company; Transamerica Insurance Co.; Preferred Mutual Insurance Co.; Utica Mutual Insurance Co.; Spalding & Evenflo Cos. Inc.; St. Paul Insurance Co.; Cigna Insurance Co.; Ina Pro; Ford Motor Co.

For full biographical listings, see the Martindale-Hubbell Law Directory

WORCESTER,* Worcester Co.

FULLER, ROSENBERG, PALMER & BELIVEAU (AV)
14 Harvard Street, P.O. Box 764, 01613
Telephone: 508-755-5225
Telecopier: 508-757-1039

(See Next Column)

FULLER, ROSENBERG, PALMER & BELIVEAU—*Continued*

MEMBERS OF FIRM

Albert E. Fuller	Peter A. Palmer
Kenneth F. Rosenberg	Thomas W. Beliveau

ASSOCIATES

Robert W. Towle	Michael I. Mutter
Julie Bednarz Russell	Brian F. Welsh
Timothy O. Ribley	John J. Finn
Mark W. Murphy	James C. Crowley, Jr.
Lisa R. Bertonazzi	John P. Donohue
Mark C. Darling	James F. Gettens
William J. Mason	John Arthur Johnson
Antoinette J. Yitchinsky	Ann F. Scannell

For full biographical listings, see the Martindale-Hubbell Law Directory

---

MICHIGAN

ANN ARBOR, * Washtenaw Co.

HURBIS & CLINTON (AV)

Fifth Floor, City Center Building, 48104
Telephone: 313-761-8358
Fax: 313-761-3134

Charles J. Hurbis	Mary F. Clinton

Robert Lipnik	Georgette E. David

Representative Clients: General Motors Corp.; ITT Hartford; Insurance Company of North America; The University of Michigan; North Oakland Medical Center; City of Pontiac; Sears Roebuck and Co.; Montgomery Ward and Co., Inc.; Sedjwick-James, Inc.

For full biographical listings, see the Martindale-Hubbell Law Directory

---

BIRMINGHAM, Oakland Co.

CARSON FISCHER, P.L.C. (AV)

Third Floor, 300 East Maple Road, 48009-6317
Telephone: 810-644-4840
Facsimile: 810-644-1832

Robert M. Carson	Kathleen A. Stibich

For full biographical listings, see the Martindale-Hubbell Law Directory

---

KELL & LYNCH, P.C. (AV)

300 East Maple Road, Suite 200, 48009
Telephone: 810-647-2333
Telefax: 810-647-2781

Michael V. Kell	Margaret A. Lynch

Jennifer T. Gilhool	Steven M. Ribiat
(Not admitted in MI)	

OF COUNSEL
M. Andrea Vaughn

Representative Clients: AlliedSignal, Inc.; AMP Inc.; Dow Corning Corp.; Hatteras Yachts; Lectron Products, Inc.; Metromedia Steakhouses, Inc.; Sybron Corp.; Michigan Consolidated Gas Co.; American Natural Resources.

For full biographical listings, see the Martindale-Hubbell Law Directory

---

BLOOMFIELD HILLS, Oakland Co.

FEENEY KELLETT WIENNER & BUSH, PROFESSIONAL CORPORATION (AV)

950 North Hunter Boulevard, Second Floor, 48304-3927
Telephone: 810-258-1580
Fax: 810-258-0421

James P. Feeney	Cheryl A. Bush
S. Thomas Wienner	Deborah F. Collins
Peter M. Kellett	David N. Goltz

OF COUNSEL
Thomas J. Manganello

James J. Majernik	Seth D. Gould
G. Gregory Schuetz	Patrick G. Seyferth
Jeffrey A. Gallant	Mark A. Fisher
	Bryan D. Cross

For full biographical listings, see the Martindale-Hubbell Law Directory

---

DAVID D. PATTON & ASSOCIATES, P.C. (AV)

100 Bloomfield Hills Parkway, Suite 110, 48304
Telephone: 810-258-6020
Fax: 810-258-6052
Email: Litigation@Aol.Com

David D. Patton

Ellen Bartman Jannette	Patricia C. White
David H. Patton (1912-1993)	

For full biographical listings, see the Martindale-Hubbell Law Directory

PORTNOY, PIDGEON & ROTH, P.C. (AV)

3883 Telegraph, Suite 103, 48302
Telephone: 810-647-4242
Fax: 810-647-8251
Email: DWINNIE103@AOL.COM

Bernard N. Portnoy	Robert P. Roth

Representative Clients: Honda North America; Honda Motor Co.

For full biographical listings, see the Martindale-Hubbell Law Directory

SCHADEN, KATZMAN & LAMPERT (AV)

33 Bloomfield Hills Parkway, Suite 145, 48304
Telephone: 810-258-4800
Fax: 810-258-9212
Broomfield, Colorado Office: Schaden, Katzman & Lampert, 11870 Airport Way.
Telephone: 303-465-3663.
Facsimile: 303-465-3884.
Ft. Lauderdale, Florida Office: 1700 E. Las Olas Boulevard, Suite 7, 33301-2408.
Telephone: 954-522-5154.
Facsimile: 954-522-5184.

MEMBERS OF FIRM

Richard F. Schaden	David I. Katzman
	Bruce A. Lampert

ASSOCIATES

Kathleen M. Schaden	John D. McClune

OF COUNSEL
Bruce O. Wilson

For full biographical listings, see the Martindale-Hubbell Law Directory

---

DETROIT, * Wayne Co.

BODMAN, LONGLEY & DAHLING LLP (AV)

34th Floor 100 Renaissance Center, 48243
Telephone: 313-259-7777
Fax: 313-393-7579
Email: 2080194@mcimail.com
Troy, Michigan Office: Suite 2020, 755 West Big Beaver Road.
Telephone: 810-362-2110.
Fax: 810-244-0780.
Ann Arbor, Michigan Office: 110 Miller, Suite 300.
Telephone: 313-761-3780.
Fax: 313-930-2494.
Northern Michigan Office: 229 Court Street, P.O. Box 405, Cheboygan.
Telephone: 616-627-4351.
Fax: 616-627-2802.

MEMBERS OF FIRM

Carson C. Grunewald	Lloyd C. Fell
James A. Smith	(Northern Michigan Office)
George G. Kemsley	Diane L. Akers
James J. Walsh	Gary D. Reeves (Troy Office)
David G. Chardavoyne	Stephen K. Postema
Robert G. Brower	(Ann Arbor Office)
Thomas Van Dusen	
(Troy Office)	

For Representative Client List, See General Section

For Complete List of Firm Personnel, See General Section

For full biographical listings, see the Martindale-Hubbell Law Directory

BUTZEL LONG, A PROFESSIONAL CORPORATION (AV)

Suite 900, 150 West Jefferson, 48226
Telephone: 313-225-7000
Telecopier: 313-225-7080
Email: melnick@butzel.com *URL:* http://www.butzel.com
Birmingham, Michigan Office: Suite 200, 32270 Telegraph Road.
Telephone: 810-258-1616.
Telecopier: 810-258-1439.
Lansing, Michigan Office: 118 West Ottawa Street.
Telephone: 517-372-6622.
Telecopier: 517-372-6672.
Ann Arbor, Michigan Office: Suite 300, 350 South Main Street.
Telephone: 313-995-3110.
Telecopier: 313-995-1777.

(See Next Column)

BUTZEL LONG A PROFESSIONAL CORPORATION, *Detroit—Continued*

Grosse Pointe Farms, Michigan Office: Suite 260, 21 Kercheval.
Telephone: 313-886-5446.
Telecopier: 313-886-2114.

Xhafer Orhan	Keefe A. Brooks
Edward M. Kronk	James E. Wynne
Philip J. Kessler	Bruce L. Sendek
Donald B. Miller	Lynn Abraham Sheehy
Daniel P. Malone	Sheldon H. Klein

Phillip C. Korovesis	Robert E. Norton II
Timothy M. Labadie	Barbara L. McQuade
	Herbert C. Donovan

Representative Clients: Bridgestone/Firestone, Inc.; Detroit Diesel Corp.; The Detroit News, Inc.; General Dynamics Corp.; General Tire Co.; Kelsey Hayes Co.; New Venture Gear; Sea Ray Boats; Stroh Brewery Co.; Takata Corp.

For Complete List of Firm Personnel, See General Section

For full biographical listings, see the Martindale-Hubbell Law Directory

CLARK HILL P.L.C. (AV)

500 Woodward Avenue, Suite 3500, 48226
Telephone: 313-965-8300
Facsimile: 313-962-4348
Oakland County, Michigan Office: Third Floor, 255 South Woodward Avenue, Birmingham.
Telephone: 810-642-9692.
Facsimile: 810-642-2174.
Lansing, Michigan Office: Suite 600, 200 North Capitol Avenue.
Telephone: 517-484-4481.
Facsimile: 517-484-1246.
Minneapolis, Minnesota Office: Suite 1000, One Financial Plaza, 120 South Sixth Street.
Telephone: 612-332-0102.
Facsimile: 612-332-3225.
Kansas City, Missouri Office: Suite 1400, Bryant Building, 1102 Grand Avenue.
Telephone: 816-221-5578.
Facsimile: 816-221-0303.

J. Thomas Lenga	Daniel J. Scully, Jr.
Dennis G. Bonucchi	Michael J. Sullivan
James E. Baiers	Cynthia L.M. Johnson

Katrina I. Crawley	Jeffrey A. Schultz

Representative Clients: The Budd Co.; Dow Corning Corporation; Kaiser Aluminum and Chemical Co.

For Complete List of Firm Personnel, See General Section

For full biographical listings, see the Martindale-Hubbell Law Directory

FEIKENS, VANDER MALE, STEVENS, BELLAMY & GILCHRIST, P.C. (AV)

One Detroit Center Suite 3400, 500 Woodward Avenue, 48226-3406
Telephone: 313-962-5909
Fax: 313-962-3125
Email: FEIKENS@COUNSEL.COM

Robert E. Dice (1922-1983)	Lee A. Stevens
Jon Feikens	William C. Hurley
Jack E. Vander Male	Linda M. Galbraith
Frederick B. Bellamy	Michael S. Cafferty
Alan Gordon Gilchrist	Robert H. Feikens
L. Neal Kennedy	Gerald W. Van Wyke
Bruce A. VandeVusse	Roger L. Wolcott
	Sharon McPhail

Richard G. Koefod	Keith J. Soltis
Joseph E. Kozely, Jr.	Michael B. Barey
Jeffrey Feikens	Renee T. VanderHagen
	Michael P. Citrin

OF COUNSEL

Sam W. Thomas (P.C.)	Walter Vincent Bernard III

LEGAL SUPPORT PERSONNEL

PARALEGALS

Robert Westveer	Linda Barthlow

For full biographical listings, see the Martindale-Hubbell Law Directory

FOSTER, MEADOWS & BALLARD, P.C. (AV)

3200 Penobscot Building, 48226
Telephone: 313-961-3234
Cable Address: "Foster"
Telex: 23-5823
Facsimile: 313-961-6184

(See Next Column)

Sparkman D. Foster (1897-1967)	Richard A. Dietz
Charles R. Hrdlicka	Robert H. Fortunate
Paul D. Galea	Robert G. Lahiff
	Camille A. Raffa-Dietz

Michael J. Liddane	Paul A. Kettunen

OF COUNSEL

John L. Foster	John F. Langs
	John A. Mundell, Jr.

Counsel For: Alexander and Alexander; Great American Ins. Co.; St. Paul Companies.

For full biographical listings, see the Martindale-Hubbell Law Directory

GLEICHER & REYNOLDS, P.C. (AV)

1500 Buhl Building, 48226
Telephone: 313-964-6900
Fax: 313-964-8976

Elizabeth Gleicher	Edward C. Reynolds, Jr.

LEGAL SUPPORT PERSONNEL

Laura Bocchini (Legal Coordinator)

For full biographical listings, see the Martindale-Hubbell Law Directory

HAYDUK, ANDREWS & HYPNAR, P.C. (AV)

1700 Buhl Building, 535 Griswold, 48226
Telephone: 313-962-4500
Fax: 313-964-6577

Mark S. Hayduk	Robin K. Andrews
	Mark A. Hypnar

Sean Angus McPhillips	Lynn E. Radke

Representative Clients: Farmers Insurance Group; GameTime, Inc.; Admiral Insurance Co.; Heritage Ins. Alexis; LMI; Meijer, Inc.; Condon & Forsyth; Pinkerton's Inc.; Vik Brothers Ins.; Investors Ins. Group.

For full biographical listings, see the Martindale-Hubbell Law Directory

LUPO & KOCZKUR, P.C. (AV)

1000 First National Building, 48226
Telephone: 313-964-0110
Fax: 313-964-3711

Dane A. Lupo	Paul S. Koczkur

Peter Kennedy Moody	Alexander B. Jarowyj

OF COUNSEL

Hulen R. Simpson	Dehai Tao

Representative Clients: Anheuser-Busch, Inc.; United Artists; ITT; Olsten; Thermadyne Industries; National Beverage; CIGNA/Insurance Company of North America; Michigan Millers; Walt Disney World; Vic Tanny International.

For full biographical listings, see the Martindale-Hubbell Law Directory

MEGANCK & COTHORN, P.C. (AV)

Suite 950, 400 Renaissance Center, 48243-1509
Telephone: 313-259-6330
Fax: 313-259-7037

Allan G. Meganck	John A. Cothorn
	Suzanne C. Stanczyk

Thomas Myers	William G. Oldford, Jr.

OF COUNSEL

David M. Thoms

Representative Clients: Ford Motor Company; Norton Co.; K-Mart Corp.; The Stanley Works; Textron; Figgie International; Phone-Poulenc Rorer Pharmaceuticals, Inc.; National Chiropractic Mutual Insurance Co.; Kellermeyer Building Services, Inc.; Tokio Marine Management Co.

For full biographical listings, see the Martindale-Hubbell Law Directory

ROSEN & LOVELL, P.C. (AV)

Penobscot Building, 645 Griswold Street, Suite 3080, 48226-4224
Telephone: 313-961-7510
Fax: 313-961-2905

Paul A. Rosen	Joan Lovell

For full biographical listings, see the Martindale-Hubbell Law Directory

TIMMIS & INMAN, L.L.P. (AV)

300 Talon Centre, 48207
Telephone: 313-396-4200
Telecopier: 313-396-4228

(See Next Column)

TIMMIS & INMAN L.L.P.—*Continued*

Michael T. Timmis	Henry J. Brennan, III
Robert E. Graziani	Mark W. Peyser
George A. Peck	Richard M. Miettinen
Charles W. Royer	Lisa R. Gorman
Richard L. Levin	Bradley J. Knickerbocker

George M. Malis

Michael F. Wais	Patrick B. Carey
John P. Kanan	Erich J. D'Andrea

Shannon M. Nichols

OF COUNSEL

Wayne C. Inman	William B. Fitzgerald

W. Clark Durant, III

Representative Clients: Stylecraft Printing Company; Stylerite Label Corporation; Retail Resources, Inc.; Deneb Robotics, Inc.; Applied Process, Inc.; Insilco Corporation; Variety Foods, Inc.; Certain Underwriters at Lloyds of London; Various Markets, Inc.; Fel-Pro, Inc.

For full biographical listings, see the Martindale-Hubbell Law Directory

ZEFF AND ZEFF, P.C. (AV)

The Zeff Building, 607 Shelby, 48226
Telephone: 313-962-3825
Fax: 313-962-6007

Louis Zeff (1896-1966)	A. Robert Zeff

Sheryl L. Berenbaum	Paul W. Broschay

Steven L. Berenbaum

For full biographical listings, see the Martindale-Hubbell Law Directory

FARMINGTON HILLS, Oakland Co.

NEMIER, TOLARI, LANDRY, MAZZEO & JOHNSON, P.C. (AV)

37000 Grand River, Suite 300, 48335
Telephone: 810-476-6900
Fax: 810-476-6564

Craig L. Nemier	David B. Landry
Jeffrey L. Tolari	Rik Mazzeo

Mark R. Johnson

Michelle E. Mathieu	Kathy Contos Nash
Christopher A. Todd	Douglas S. Loomer
Thomas S. McLeod	Gregory A. Light

OF COUNSEL

William R. Still	Terry E. Pietryga

LEGAL SUPPORT PERSONNEL

Veeder Ann Willey (Support Staff)

For full biographical listings, see the Martindale-Hubbell Law Directory

FLINT,* Genesee Co.

MACDONALD, FITZGERALD & MACDONALD, P.C. (AV)

200 McKinnon Building, 48502
Telephone: 810-232-3184; 234-2204
Fax: 810-232-9632

Robert J. MacDonald	John J. FitzGerald (1919-1995)
(1914-1987)	R. Duncan MacDonald

Timothy J. MacDonald

References: Michigan National Bank; Genesee Merchants Bank & Trust Co.

For full biographical listings, see the Martindale-Hubbell Law Directory

GRAND RAPIDS,* Kent Co.

BREMER, WADE, NELSON, LOHR & COREY, LLP (AV)

600 3 Mile Road, N.W., 49544-1601
Telephone: 616-784-4434
Fax: 616-784-7322

MEMBERS OF FIRM

William M. Bremer	Phillip J. Nelson
Michael D. Wade	James H. Lohr

Michael J. Corey

ASSOCIATES

Barbara L. Olafsson	Olafur A. Olafsson

LEGAL SUPPORT PERSONNEL

Kathleen A. Fitzpatrick

For full biographical listings, see the Martindale-Hubbell Law Directory

BUCHANAN, SILVER & BECKERING, P.L.C. (AV)

300 Ottawa N.W., Suite 800, 49503
Telephone: 616-458-2464
Fax: 616-458-0608

(See Next Column)

MEMBERS OF FIRM

John C. Buchanan	Robert J. Buchanan
Lee T. Silver	Jane M. Beckering

Representative Clients: Chrysler Corp.; Clark Equipment Co.; Colt's Manufacturing Company, Inc. (National Defense Counsel); Corning Glass; Montgomery KONE.

For full biographical listings, see the Martindale-Hubbell Law Directory

CHOLETTE, PERKINS & BUCHANAN (AV)

900 Campau Square Plaza Building, 99 Monroe Avenue, N.W., 49503
Telephone: 616-774-2131
Fax: 616-774-7016

MEMBERS OF FIRM

Calvin R. Danhof	Marc A. Kidder
Frederick W. Bleakley	Michael C. Mysliwiec
Reynolds A. Brander, Jr.	Evan L. MacFarlane
Edward Malinzak	John A. Quinn
Bruce M. Bieneman	Albert J. Engel, III
William J. Warren	Stephen C. Oldstrom
Donald C. Exelby	William E. McDonald, Jr.
Thomas H. Cypher	Mark E. Fatum
William A. Brengle	Richard K. Grover, Jr.
Alfred J. Parent	David J. DeGraw
Charles H. Worsfold	Martin W. Buschle
Michael P. McCasey	Miles J. Murphy, III

ASSOCIATES

Kenneth L. Block	Martha P. Forman
William J. Yob	Kathrine M. West
Robert E. Attmore	Ilse K. Masselink

John P. Lewis

Counsel for: Aetna Casualty & Surety Co.; Argonaut Insurance Co.; Auto-Owners Insurance Co.; Employers Mutual; Liberty Mutual Insurance Co.; Sentry Group; State Farm Insurance; Eastern Aviation and Marine Underwriters; Home Insurance Co.; Nationwide Insurance.

For Complete List of Firm Personnel, See General Section

For full biographical listings, see the Martindale-Hubbell Law Directory

WHEELER UPHAM, A PROFESSIONAL CORPORATION (AV)

Second Floor, Trust Building, 40 Pearl Street, N.W., 49503-3001
Telephone: 616-459-7100
Fax: 616-459-6366

Gordon B. Wheeler (1904-1986)	William H. Heritage, Jr.
Buford A. Upham (Retired)	Kenneth E. Tiews
Robert H. Gillette	Jack L. Hoffman
Geoffrey L. Gillis	Janet C. Baxter
John M. Roels	Peter Kladder, III
Gary A. Maximiuk	James M. Shade
Timothy J. Orlebeke	Thomas A. Kuiper

Counsel For: Prudential Ins. Co.; Travelers Ins. Co.; Auto-Owners Ins. Co.; Countrywide Services; Werner Co.; Cuprum S.A. de C.V.; Bridgestone/Firestone; Medtronic, Inc.; J.I. Case; Rockwell International.

For full biographical listings, see the Martindale-Hubbell Law Directory

LANSING, Ingham Co.

FRASER TREBILCOCK DAVIS & FOSTER, P.C. (AV)

1000 Michigan National Tower, 48933
Telephone: 517-482-5800
Fax: 517-482-0887

Joe C. Foster, Jr.	Ronald R. Sutton
Eugene Townsend (1926-1982)	Iris K. Socolofsky-Linder
Ronald R. Pentecost	Brett Jon Bean
Peter L. Dunlap	Richard C. Lowe
Everett R. Zack	Gary C. Rogers
Douglas J. Austin	Mark A. Bush
Robert W. Stocker, II	Michael H. Perry
Michael E. Cavanaugh	Brandon W. Zuk
John J. Loose	David D. Waddell
David E. S. Marvin	Thomas J. Waters
Stephen L. Burlingame	Mark R. Fox
C. Mark Hoover	Nancy L. Little
Darrell A. Lindman	Sharon A. Bruner

Michael C. Levine	Brian D. Herrington
Michael S. Ashton	David Brickey
Michael James Reilly	Marcy R. Meyer
Michelyn E. Pastuer	Wendy Mrazek Guilfoyle
Patrick K. Thornton	Graham K. Crabtree
Charyn K. Hain	Melinda A. Carlson

Kerry D. Hettinger

(See Next Column)

FRASER TREBILCOCK DAVIS & FOSTER P.C., *Lansing—Continued*

OF COUNSEL

Archie C. Fraser	James R. Davis
Everett R. Trebilcock	Donald A. Hines

Counsel for: Auto Club Insurance Assn. (ACIA); Auto Owners Insurance Co.; City of Mackinac Island; Federal Insurance Co.; Grand Trunk Railroad Co.; Prudential Insurance Company of America; State Farm Automobile Insurance Co.

For full biographical listings, see the Martindale-Hubbell Law Directory

---

RAYMOND JOSEPH (AV)

1602 Michigan National Tower, 48933
Telephone: 517-372-4410
Fax: 517-372-2137

OF COUNSEL

George R. Sidwell (1899-1983)	Michael Bowman
Bruce C. Blanton	

Representative Clients: Ashland Oil, Inc.; Complete Auto Transit, Inc.; Employers Insurance of Wausau; Evans Products Co.; Grain Dealers Mutl.; Harbor Insurance Co.; Interstate Motor Freight System; Lansing Symphony Assn., Inc.; Prudential LMI Insurance Co.

For full biographical listings, see the Martindale-Hubbell Law Directory

---

MOUNT CLEMENS,* Macomb Co.

MARTIN, BACON & MARTIN, P.C. (AV)

44 First Street, 48043
Telephone: 810-979-6500
Fax: 810-468-7016

James N. Martin	Michael R. Janes
Jonathan E. Martin	Kevin L. Moffatt
Paul R. VanTol	John W. Crimando
Victor T. Van Camp	

Patrick D. Ball	Amy M. Chauvin

Reference: Old Kent Bank - Mt. Clemens.

For full biographical listings, see the Martindale-Hubbell Law Directory

---

WELCH, MacALPINE, BAHORSKI, BIEGLECKI & FARRELL, P.C. (AV)

71 North Avenue, 48043-5543
Telephone: 810-469-1111; 1-800-252-1654
Facsimile: 810-469-1609

Terry S. Welch	Thomas R. Bieglecki
Robert F. MacAlpine	Thaddeus M. Dombrowski
Timothy A. Bahorski	Marc P. Shaberman
John B. Farrell	Michael W. Sickles
Christopher R. Baratta	

For full biographical listings, see the Martindale-Hubbell Law Directory

---

ROYAL OAK, Oakland Co.

CARDELLI, SCHAEFER & MASON, P.C. (AV)

322 West Lincoln, 48067
Telephone: 810-544-1100
Toll Free 1-800-411-7774
Telecopier: 810-544-1191

Thomas G. Cardelli	William C. Schaefer
Laura D. Mason	

Deborah A. Hebert	Tara Hanley Bratton
Mary Ann J. O'Neil	Diane T. Gorczyca
Lillian C. Pierce	Ronald E. Beier, II
John L. Weston	

Representative Clients: Allianz Insurance Company; Coltec Industries (Garlock Inc & Anchor Packing Company); Dana Corporation; Duchossois Industries, Inc.; Fruehauf Trailer Corporation; General Motors Corporation; Glaxo Wellcome, Inc.; Morton International, Inc.; Otis Elevator Company; Raymond Corporation; Robert Bosch Power Tool Corporation.

For full biographical listings, see the Martindale-Hubbell Law Directory

---

SOUTHFIELD, Oakland Co.

COLLINS, EINHORN, FARRELL & ULANOFF, A PROFESSIONAL CORPORATION (AV)

4000 Town Center, Suite 909, 48075-1473
Telephone: 810-355-4141
Facsimile: 810-355-2277

(See Next Column)

Morton H. Collins	Dale J. McLellan
Brian D. Einhorn	Kenneth C. Merritt
Clayton F. Farrell	Noreen L. Slank
Stuart A. Ulanoff	Michael J. Sullivan
Janice G. Hildenbrand	

Gerald A. Pawlak	Deborah A. Lujan
Neil W. MacCallum	Barbara H. Goldman
Timothy Orlando	Shannon M. Kos
Theresa M. Asoklis	Kevin P. Moloughney
Karen C. Liddle	Susan P. Saltzman
Lisa L. Fadler	Laura A. Ruckle

For full biographical listings, see the Martindale-Hubbell Law Directory

---

FIEGER, FIEGER & SCHWARTZ, A PROFESSIONAL CORPORATION (AV)

19390 West Ten Mile Road, 48075-2463
Telephone: 810-355-5555
Fax: 810-355-5148

Bernard J. Fieger (1922-1988)	Todd J. Weglarz
Geoffrey N. Fieger	Rebecca S. Eaton
Michael Alan Schwartz	Ven R. Johnson
William J. McHenry	

OF COUNSEL

Barry Fayne	Beverly Hires Brode
Keitha Kay Cowen	

For full biographical listings, see the Martindale-Hubbell Law Directory

---

HIGHLAND & ZANETTI (AV)

Suite 205, 24445 Northwestern Highway, 48075
Telephone: 810-352-9580

John N. Highland	J. R. Zanetti, Jr.
R. Michael John	

Duncan Hall Brown	Ronald D. Holton

For full biographical listings, see the Martindale-Hubbell Law Directory

---

PROVIZER, LICHTENSTEIN & PHILLIPS, P.C. (AV)

4000 Town Center, Suite 1800, 48075
Telephone: 810-352-9080
Facsimile: 810-352-1491

Harold M. Provizer	Constance S. Hall
Randall E. Phillips	Noel F. Beck
Marilyn A. Madorsky	William J. Selinsky
Deborah Molitz	Jason Milstone

Representative Clients: GAB; Coachman Industries; Reliance National Ins. Co.; Blackmoor Group.

For full biographical listings, see the Martindale-Hubbell Law Directory

---

SCHWARTZ & JALKANEN, P.C. (AV)

Suite 200, 24400 Northwestern Highway, 48075
Telephone: 810-352-2555
Facsimile: 810-352-5963

Melvin R. Schwartz	Arthur W. Jalkanen
Karl Eric Hannum	

Deborah L. Laura	Lori A. Barker

For full biographical listings, see the Martindale-Hubbell Law Directory

---

SOMMERS, SCHWARTZ, SILVER & SCHWARTZ, P.C. (AV)

2000 Town Center, Suite 900, 48075
Telephone: 810-355-0300
Telecopier: 810-746-4001
Plymouth, Michigan Office: 747 South Main Street.
Telephone: 313-455-4250.

Leonard B. Schwartz	Joseph E. Grinnan
Robert H. Darling	B. A. Tyler
James J. Vlasic	Robert B. Sickels

General Counsel for: City of Taylor; Foodland Distributors; C.A. Muer Corporation; Vlasic & Company; Nederlander Corporation; Midwest Health Centers, P.C.
Representative Clients: Crum & Forster Insurance Company; City of Pontiac; Michigan National Bank.

For Complete List of Firm Personnel, See General Section

For full biographical listings, see the Martindale-Hubbell Law Directory

TRAVERSE CITY,* Grand Traverse Co.

ROBB, MESSING, PALMER & DIGNAN, P.C. (AV)

420 East Front Street, P.O. Box 1132, 49684
Telephone: 616-929-1130
Fax: 616-929-7925
Wayne County, Michigan Office: The Annex, 20500 Eureka, Suite 313, Taylor, Michigan 48180.
Telephone: 313-284-5550.

Dean A. Robb	Charles W. Palmer (Resident,
Mark M. Messing	Taylor, Michigan Office)

Thomas J. Dignan

Merritt W. Green, II	Maura N. Brennan
Lucinda Keils	Kirk C. Waibel
(Resident, Taylor, Michigan)	

LEGAL SUPPORT PERSONNEL
Blair M. Robb

For full biographical listings, see the Martindale-Hubbell Law Directory

THOMPSON & O'NEIL, P.C. (AV)

309 East Front Street, P.O. Box 429, 49685
Telephone: 616-929-9700; 1-800-678-1307
Fax: 616-929-7262

George R. Thompson	Daniel P. O'Neil

William J. Brooks

For full biographical listings, see the Martindale-Hubbell Law Directory

TROY, Oakland Co.

POLING, McGAW & POLING, P.C. (AV)

Suite 275, 5435 Corporate Drive, 48098
Telephone: 810-641-0500
Telecopier: 810-641-0506

Benson T. Buck (1926-1989)	Richard B. Poling, Jr.
Richard B. Poling	Gregory C. Hamilton
D. Douglas McGaw	Veronica B. O'Haro

James R. Parker
OF COUNSEL
Ralph S. Moore

Representative Clients: County of Oakland; City of Troy; United States Fidelity & Guaranty Co.; Sentry Insurance Co.; Admiral Insurance; DeMaria Construction Co.; Leo Corporation; Aetna Casualty and Surety Co.; Concord Design; Pneumo-Abex.

For full biographical listings, see the Martindale-Hubbell Law Directory

REYNOLDS, BEEBY & MAGNUSON, P.C. (AV)

50 West Big Beaver Road Suite 400, 48084
Telephone: 810-740-9860
Fax: 810-740-9870
Detroit, Michigan Office: Ford Building, Suite 531.
Telephone: 313-961-2720.
Fax: 313-961-5930.

Thomas D. Beeby (Retired)	Kenneth M. Zorn
Gregory A. Reynolds	Thomas G. Grubba
Arnold N. Magnuson, Jr.	Frank K. Mandlebaum

Elizabeth A. Fellows	John A. Miller
Joseph J. Wright	William R. Huffman
Michael C. McKinnon	Michael V. Reynolds

Paul J. Haerens
OF COUNSEL
Adam A. Shakoor
LEGAL SUPPORT PERSONNEL
Lisa Slicker (Legal Assistant)

Representative Clients: American Contractors Insurance Group; American International Group; American Sterilizer Co.; American Suzuki Motor Corp.

For full biographical listings, see the Martindale-Hubbell Law Directory

WEST BLOOMFIELD, Oakland Co.

CHEATHAM & ACKER, P.C. (AV)

5777 West Maple Road, Suite 130, P.O. Box 255002, 48325-5002
Telephone: 810-932-2000
Fax: 810-932-2008

Charles C. Cheatham	Lawrence J. Acker

Tracy A. Leahy	Mary E. Hollman

Christopher P. Jelinek

COUNSEL
Lynn L. Lower
For full biographical listings, see the Martindale-Hubbell Law Directory

PUBLIC UTILITIES LAW

ALABAMA

BIRMINGHAM,* Jefferson Co.

BRADLEY, ARANT, ROSE & WHITE (AV)

2001 Park Place, Suite 1400, P.O. Box 830709, 35283-0709
Telephone: 205-521-8000
Facsimile: 205-252-0264
Facsimile (SouthTrust Tower Office): 205-251-9915
URL: http://www.BARW.COM
Huntsville, Alabama Office: 200 Clinton Avenue West, Suite 900, 35801.
Telephone: 205-517-5100.
Facsimile: 205-533-5069.

MEMBER OF FIRM
E. Cutter Hughes, Jr. (Resident, Huntsville Office)

For Complete List of Firm Personnel, See General Section

For full biographical listings, see the Martindale-Hubbell Law Directory

---

MONTGOMERY,* Montgomery Co.

BRANTLEY & WILKERSON, P.C. (AV)

405 South Hull Street, P.O. Box 830, 36101-0830
Telephone: 334-265-1500
Fax: 334-265-0319

Paul A. Brantley   Mark D. Wilkerson
Leah Snell Stephens

Representative Clients: Ala-Tenn Resources, Inc.; ALLTEL; Montgomery Cablevision; Southeastern Cellular; TDS.
Reference: SouthTrust Bank, N.A.

For full biographical listings, see the Martindale-Hubbell Law Directory

---

ARIZONA

PHOENIX,* Maricopa Co.

BROWN & BAIN, A PROFESSIONAL ASSOCIATION (AV)

2901 North Central Avenue, P.O. Box 400, 85001-0400
Telephone: 602-351-8000
Telecopier: 602-351-8516
Palo Alto, California Affiliated Office: Brown & Bain, 1755 Embarcadero Road, Suite 200.
Telephone: 415-856-9411.
Telecopier: 415-856-6061.
Tucson, Arizona Affiliated Office: Brown & Bain, A Professional Association. One South Church Avenue, Nineteenth Floor, P.O. Box 2265.
Telephone: 602-798-7900
Telecopier: 602-798-7945.

Philip R. Higdon   Michael F. McNulty
  (Resident at Tucson Office)   (Resident at Tucson Office)
Stephen E. Lee   Joel W. Nomkin
Joseph E. Mais   Michael W. Patten
Lex J. Smith

For Complete List of Firm Personnel, See General Section

For full biographical listings, see the Martindale-Hubbell Law Directory

---

ARKANSAS

LITTLE ROCK,* Pulaski Co.

GILL LAW FIRM, A PROFESSIONAL ASSOCIATION (AV)

3801 TCBY Tower, Capitol and Broadway, 72201
Telephone: 501-376-3800
Fax: 501-372-3359

John P. Gill   W. W. Elrod, II
Heartsill Ragon III, (P.A.)

For Complete List of Firm Personnel, See General Section

For full biographical listings, see the Martindale-Hubbell Law Directory

---

ROSE LAW FIRM, A PROFESSIONAL ASSOCIATION (AV)

120 East Fourth Street, 72201
Telephone: 501-375-9131
Telecopy: 501-375-1309

Herbert C. Rule, III   Brian Rosenthal
Stephen N. Joiner   J. Scott Schallhorn

Grant E. Fortson

Counsel for: ALLTEL Corporation; Aluminum Company of America; Bridgestone/Firestone, Inc.; The Equitable Life Assurance Society of The United States; General Motors Corp.; The Prudential Insurance Company of America; Stephens Group Inc.; Tyson Foods, Inc.

For Complete List of Firm Personnel, See General Section

For full biographical listings, see the Martindale-Hubbell Law Directory

---

CALIFORNIA

LOS ANGELES,* Los Angeles Co.

O'MELVENY & MYERS LLP (AV)

400 South Hope Street, 90071-2899
Telephone: 213-669-6000
Cable Address: "Moms"
Facsimile: 213-669-6407
Email: omminfo@omm.com
Century City, California Office: 1999 Avenue of the Stars, 90067-6035.
Telephone: 310-553-6700.
Facsimile: 310-246-6779.
Newport Beach, California Office: 610 Newport Center Drive, 92660-6429.
Telephone: 714-760-9600.
Cable Address: "Moms".
Facsimile: 714-669-6994.
San Francisco, California Office: Embarcadero Center West Tower, 275 Battery Street, 94111-3305.
Telephone: 415-984-8700.
Facsimile: 415-984-8701.
New York, New York Office: Citicorp Center, 153 East 53rd Street, 10022-4611.
Telephone: 212-326-2000.
Facsimile: 212-326-2061.
Washington, D.C. Office: 555 13th Street, N.W., 20004-1109.
Telephone: 202-383-5300.
Cable Address: "Moms".
Facsimile: 202-383-5414.
London, England Office: 10 Finsbury Square, London, EC2A 1LA.
Telephone: 0171-256-8451.
Facsimile: 0171-638-8205.
Tokyo, Japan Office: Sanbancho KB-6 Building, 6 Sanbancho, Chiyoda-ku, Tokyo 102, Japan.
Telephone: 03-3239-2900.
Facsimile: 03-3239-2432.
Hong Kong Office: Suite 1905, Peregrine Tower, Lippo Centre, 89 Queensway, Central, Hong Kong.
Telephone: 852-2523-8266.
Facsimile: 852-2522-1760.
Shanghai, Peoples Republic of China Office: Shanghai International Trade Centre, Suite 2011, 2200 Yan An Road West, Shanghai, 200335, PRC.
Telephone: 86-21-6219-5363.
Facsimile: 86-21-6275-4949.

PARTNER
Charles C. Read

For Complete List of Firm Personnel, See General Section

For full biographical listings, see the Martindale-Hubbell Law Directory

---

PALO ALTO, Santa Clara Co.

EARL NICHOLAS SELBY (AV)

420 Florence Street, Suite 200, 94301
Telephone: 415-323-0990
Fax: 415-325-9041
Email: nselby@well.com

Representative Clients: Nextel Communications, Inc.; ICG Access Services, Inc (IntelCom Group U.S.A., Inc., Denver, CO); Bay Area Teleport; Linkatel of California, L.P. (San Diego, Calif.); Shared Telecommunication Systems, Inc. (Hayward, Calif.).

For full biographical listings, see the Martindale-Hubbell Law Directory

COLORADO

DENVER, * Denver Co.

JONES & KELLER, A PROFESSIONAL CORPORATION (AV)

Suite 1600, 1625 Broadway, 80202
Telephone: 303-573-1600
Fax: 303-893-6506

Marion F. Jones (1898-1978)	Thomas J. Burke, Jr.
Alec J. Keller (1913-1995)	Samuel E. Wing
Alvin J. Meiklejohn, Jr.	Reid A. Godbolt
Leslie R. Kehl	Rodney D. Knutson
Edward T. Lyons, Jr.	Kevin L. Brown
David E. Driggers	Barry L. Wilkie

Howard R. Hertzberg	Brent Nicholls
David A. Thayer	Michael Brian Cavanaugh
Nathan D. Simmons	

Reference: Colorado State Bank; Union Bank & Trust.

For full biographical listings, see the Martindale-Hubbell Law Directory

WHITE AND STEELE, PROFESSIONAL CORPORATION (AV)

1225 17th Street, Suite 2800, 80202
Telephone: 303-296-2828
Telecopier: 303-296-3131
Email: law@wsteele.com
Cheyenne, Wyoming Office: 1912 Capital Avenue, Suite 416, 82003.
Telephone: 307-778-4160.
Telecopier: 307-778-7041.

Michael W. Anderson	Kurt A. Horton

OF COUNSEL

Fred L. Witsell	Kevin W. Hecht

Insurance Clients: Allied Insurance Co.; CNA; Kemper Insurance Group; Massachusetts Mutual Life Insurance Co.; U.S.A.A.; Underwriters at Lloyds; Farmers Insurance Group.

For Complete List of Firm Personnel, See General Section

For full biographical listings, see the Martindale-Hubbell Law Directory

DISTRICT OF COLUMBIA

WASHINGTON, D.C. Co.

BRICKFIELD, BURCHETTE & RITTS, P.C. (AV)

8th Floor, West Tower, 1025 Thomas Jefferson Street, N.W., 20007-0805
Telephone: 202-342-0800
Fax: 202-342-0807
Austin, Texas Office: Suite 1050, 1005 Congress Avenue.
Telephone: 512-472-1081.

Peter J. P. Brickfield	Michael N. McCarty
William H. Burchette	Frederick H. Ritts
Mark C. Davis (Not admitted in DC; Resident, Austin, Texas Office)	Fernando Rodriguez (Not admitted in DC; Resident, Austin, Texas Office)
Michael E. Kaufmann	Christine C. Ryan
Peter J. Mattheis	Garrett A. Stone

COUNSEL

James W. Brew (Not admitted in DC)	Robert L. McCarty
	A. Hewitt Rose

Dean S. Brockbank (Not admitted in DC)	Julie B. Greenisen
Elizabeth Grieco Cunningham (Resident, Austin, Texas Office)	Stephen J. Karina (Not admitted in DC)
	Christopher C. O'Hara
	Sonnet C. Schmidt
Vincent P. Duane	Damon E. Xenopoulos

For full biographical listings, see the Martindale-Hubbell Law Directory

BRUDER, GENTILE & MARCOUX, L.L.P. (AV)

1100 New York Avenue, N.W., Suite 510 East, 20005-3934
Telephone: 202-783-1350
Telecopiers: 202-737-9117; 347-2644
Email: brugen@ix.netcom.com

MEMBERS OF FIRM

George F. Bruder	David E. Goroff
Carmen L. Gentile	Gary E. Guy
Albert R. Simonds, Jr.	James H. McGrew
J. Michel Marcoux	Thomas L. Blackburn
Arlene Pianko Groner	

(See Next Column)

ASSOCIATE
Cheryl Lynn Belkowitz

For full biographical listings, see the Martindale-Hubbell Law Directory

MORLEY CASKIN (AV)

1225 Eye Street, N.W., Suite 402, 20005
Telephone: 202-789-1100
Facsimile: 202-289-3928

OF COUNSEL
Stanley M. Morley (1912-1991)
MEMBERS OF FIRM

Joel F. Zipp	William A. Mogel
George H. Williams, Jr.	

ASSOCIATE
Rita L. Wecker (Not admitted in DC)

For full biographical listings, see the Martindale-Hubbell Law Directory

TRAVIS & GOOCH (AV)

Suite 301, 1275 Pennsylvania Avenue, N.W., 20004
Telephone: 202-508-9000
Fax: 202-508-9033

MEMBERS OF FIRM

R. Gordon Gooch	Mark R. Haskell
Edmunds Travis, Jr. (Not admitted in DC)	Dena Eve Wiggins

ASSOCIATES

Glenn S. Benson	Jonya E. Wagner (Not admitted in DC)

For full biographical listings, see the Martindale-Hubbell Law Directory

FLORIDA

TALLAHASSEE, * Leon Co.

GATLIN, WOODS & CARLSON (AV)

A Partnership including a Professional Corporation
The Mahan Station, 1709-D Mahan Drive, 32308
Telephone: 904-877-7191
Telecopier: 904-877-9031

MEMBERS OF FIRM

B. Kenneth Gatlin (P.A.)	Thomas F. Woods
John D. Carlson	

ASSOCIATE
Wayne L. Schiefelbein

For full biographical listings, see the Martindale-Hubbell Law Directory

ROSE, SUNDSTROM & BENTLEY (AV)

A Partnership including Professional Associations
2548 Blairstone Pines Drive, P.O. Box 1567, 32302-1567
Telephone: 904-877-6555
Telecopier: 904-656-4029

MEMBERS OF FIRM

Chris H. Bentley (P.A.)	John R. Jenkins (P.A.)
F. Marshall Deterding	Robert M. C. Rose
Martin S. Friedman (P.A.)	William E. Sundstrom (P.A.)
John L. Wharton	

Representative Clients: Aloha Utilities, Inc.; East Central Florida Services, Inc.; Hydratech Utilities, Inc.; North Fort Myers Utility, Inc.; Utility Board of the City of Key West; Rotonda West Utilities Corp.

For full biographical listings, see the Martindale-Hubbell Law Directory

GEORGIA

ATLANTA, * Fulton Co.

LONG ALDRIDGE & NORMAN, LLP (AV)

A Limited Liability Partnership including Professional Corporations
One Peachtree Center, Suite 5300, 303 Peachtree Street, 30308
Telephone: 404-527-4000
Telecopier: 404-527-4198
Washington, D.C. Office: Suite 600, 701 Pennsylvania Avenue, N.W., 20004.
Telephone: 202-624-1200.
FAX: 202-624-1298.

(See Next Column)

LONG ALDRIDGE & NORMAN LLP—*Continued*

MEMBERS OF FIRM

Douglas L. Beresford (Resident, Washington, D.C. Office)
L. Craig Dowdy
Gordon D. Giffin
John E. Holtzinger, Jr. (Resident, Washington, D.C. Office)

Albert G. Norman, Jr.
Jacolyn A. Simmons (Resident, Washington, D.C. Office)
John T. Stough, Jr. (Resident, Washington, D.C. Office)
Robert I. White (Resident, Washington, D.C. Office)

ASSOCIATES

Kevin M. Downey (Resident, Washington, D.C. Office)
George F. Hobday, Jr. (Resident, Washington, D.C. Office)

Thadd A. Prisco (Resident, Washington, D.C. Office)
William E. Rice

OF COUNSEL

Matthew A. Towery

Nancy A. White (Resident, Washington, D.C. Office)

For Complete List of Firm Personnel, See General Section

For full biographical listings, see the Martindale-Hubbell Law Directory

WADE & CAMPBELL, LLP (AV)

Cumberland Center II, 3100 Cumberland Circle, Suite 1500, 30339
Telephone: 770-850-5000
FAX: 770-850-5075
Email: wadecamp@mindspring.com

MEMBERS OF FIRM

Allison Wade
Douglas N. Campbell
Michael S. Thwaites

ASSOCIATES

Nancy P. Parson
Edward H. Nicholson, Jr.
Walter Hamberg, III

Steven W. Hardy
Steven H. Jackman

Representative Clients: National Southwire Aluminium Co.; Southwire Co.

For full biographical listings, see the Martindale-Hubbell Law Directory

*CARROLLTON,** Carroll Co.

TISINGER, TISINGER, VANCE & GREER, A PROFESSIONAL CORPORATION (AV)

100 Wagon Yard Plaza, P.O. Box 2069, 30117
Telephone: 770-834-4467
Fax: 770-834-5426

Richard G. Tisinger, Sr.
C. David Mecklin, Jr.
Steven T. Minor

Representative Clients: Altamaha Electric Membership Corporation; Carroll Electric Membership Corporation; Excelsior Electric Membership Corporation; Georgia Electric Membership Corporation; Oglethorpe Power Corporation.

For Complete List of Firm Personnel, See General Section

For full biographical listings, see the Martindale-Hubbell Law Directory

IDAHO

*BOISE,** Ada Co.

MOFFATT, THOMAS, BARRETT, ROCK & FIELDS, CHARTERED (AV)

101 South Capitol Boulevard, P.O. Box 829, 83702
Telephone: 208-345-2000
FAX: 208-385-5384
Email: info@moffatt.com
Idaho Falls Office: 525 Park Avenue, Suite 2D, P.O. Box 1367, 83403.
Telephone: 208-522-6700.
FAX: 208-522-5111.
Pocatello, Idaho Office: 845 West Center, Suite C, P.O. Box 4941, 83201.
Telephone: 208-233-2001.

Eugene C. Thomas
Morgan W. Richards, Jr.

Representative Clients: BMC West Corporation; Chevron, U.S.A.; First Security Bank of Idaho, N.A.; General Motors Corp.; Idaho Potato Commission; Intermountain Gas Co.; John Alden Life Insurance Co.; Micron Technology, Inc.; Royal Insurance Cos.; St. Luke's Regional Medical Center & Mountain States Tumor Institute.

For Complete List of Firm Personnel, See General Section

For full biographical listings, see the Martindale-Hubbell Law Directory

*POCATELLO,** Bannock Co.

MERRILL & MERRILL, CHARTERED (AV)

Key Bank Building, P.O. Box 991, 83204
Telephone: 208-232-2286
Fax: 208-232-2499

Wesley F. Merrill
Stephen S. Dunn

Representative Client: Utah Power & Light Co. (PacifiCorp).

For Complete List of Firm Personnel, See General Section

For full biographical listings, see the Martindale-Hubbell Law Directory

ILLINOIS

*CHICAGO,** Cook Co.

SAUNDERS & MONROE (AV)

Suite 4201, 205 North Michigan Avenue, 60601
Telephone: 312-946-9000
Facsimile: 312-946-0528

MEMBERS OF FIRM

George L. Saunders, Jr.
Lee A. Monroe

Thomas F. Bush, Jr.
Matthew E. Van Tine
Thomas A. Doyle

Gwen A. Niedbalski

OF COUNSEL

Kenneth K. Howell
Victoria S. Kaplan

For full biographical listings, see the Martindale-Hubbell Law Directory

MATTOON, Coles Co.

CRAIG & CRAIG (AV)

1807 Broadway, P.O. Box 689, 61938-0689
Telephone: 217-234-6481
Telecopier: 217-234-6486
Mount Vernon, Illinois Office: 227 1/2 South 9th Street.
Telephone: 618-244-7511.

MEMBERS OF FIRM

Craig Van Meter (1895-1981)
Fred H. Kelly (1894-1971)
Robert M. Werden (1908-1969)
George N. Gilkerson (1911-1985)
John H. Armstrong
John P. Ewart
Richard F. Record, Jr.

Stephen L. Corn
Richard Charles Hayden
Robert G. Grierson
Gregory C. Ray
Paul R. Lynch (Resident, Mount Vernon Office)
Kenneth F. Werts (Resident, Mount Vernon Office)

John L. Barger

ASSOCIATES

Joshua N. Rosen (Resident, Mount Vernon Office)
Kathleen M. Stockwell

Theresa M. Thomson
Kristine M. Tuttle
Henry P. Villani (Resident, Mount Vernon Office)

OF COUNSEL

Jack E. Horsley

Counsel for: Monterey Coal Co., a Division of Exxon Coal USA, Inc.; Marathon Oil Co.; Illinois Central R.R. Co.; Okaw Building & Loan Assn., Mattoon, Illinois; The Medical Protective Insurance Co.; Consolidated Communications, Inc.; Lloyds Underwriters at London; Hartford Insurance Co.; Coles Together, a Not-For-Profit Corp.; Coles Building Corporation.

For full biographical listings, see the Martindale-Hubbell Law Directory

*PEORIA,** Peoria Co.

HOWARD & HOWARD ATTORNEYS, P.C. (AV)

The Creve Coeur Building, Suite 200, 321 Liberty Street, 61602-1403
Telephone: 309-672-1483
Telecopier: 309-672-1568
Kalamazoo, Michigan Office: The Kalamazoo Building, Suite 400, 107 West Michigan Avenue.
Telephone: 616-382-1483.
Telecopier: 616-382-1568.
Bloomfield Hills, Michigan Office: The Pinehurst Office Center, Suite 101, 1400 North Woodward Avenue.
Telephone: 810-645-1483.
Telecopier: 810-645-1568.
Lansing, Michigan Office: Suite 500, The Phoenix Building, 222 Washington Square, North.
Telephone: 517-485-1483.
Telecopier: 517-485-1568.

(See Next Column)

HOWARD & HOWARD ATTORNEYS, P.C., Peoria—Continued

Tampa, Florida Office: First of America Plaza, Suite 2000, 201 East Kennedy Boulevard.
Telephone: 813-229-1483.
Telecopier: 813-229-1568.

Frederick G. Hoffman   Diana M. Jagiella

Representative Clients: For Representative Client list, see General Practice, Peoria, IL.

For Complete List of Firm Personnel, See General Section

For full biographical listings, see the Martindale-Hubbell Law Directory

INDIANA

INDIANAPOLIS,* Marion Co.

BOSE MCKINNEY & EVANS (AV)

2700 First Indiana Plaza, 135 North Pennsylvania Street, 46204
Telephone: 317-684-5000
Facsimile: 317-684-5173
Indianapolis North Office: Suite 1201, 8888 Keystone Crossing, 46240.
Telephone: 317-574-3700.
Facsimile: 317-574-3716.

MEMBERS OF FIRM

L. Parvin Price   Robert K. Johnson

ASSOCIATES

J. Christopher Janak   J. Gregory Shelley
Jeffrey M. Reed

Representative Clients: Community Natural Gas Co.; Comptel MCI Indiana Water and Waste Water Assn.; German Township Water District; Midwest Natural Gas Co.; Hendricks County Regional Sewer District; Town of Schererville.

For Complete List of Firm Personnel, See General Section

For full biographical listings, see the Martindale-Hubbell Law Directory

CLARK, QUINN, MOSES & CLARK (AV)

One Indiana Square, Suite 2200, 46204-2011
Telephone: 317-637-1321
Fax: 317-687-2344

MEMBERS OF FIRM

Alex M. Clark (1916-1991)   John M. Moses
James C. Clark   J. Murray Clark
Thomas Michael Quinn   Matthew R. Clark

ASSOCIATES

Michael D. Keele   Cameron F. Clark
L. Michael Koch

OF COUNSEL

David M. Brooks   Robert C. Bruner

Representative Clients: Justus; The Shorewood Corporation; Marina Limited Partnership; Lafarge Corporation; Meijer Realty, Inc.; Lowe's; Kite Development; U-Stor Self Storage Warehouses; Mechanic's Laundry; Davis Homes.

For full biographical listings, see the Martindale-Hubbell Law Directory

IOWA

DES MOINES,* Polk Co.

MICHAEL R. MAY (AV)

Suite 935, Two Ruan Center, 601 Locust Street, 50309
Telephone: 515-245-3757
Fax: 515-245-5462

For full biographical listings, see the Martindale-Hubbell Law Directory

LOUISIANA

BATON ROUGE,* East Baton Rouge Parish

KEAN, MILLER, HAWTHORNE, D'ARMOND, MCCOWAN & JARMAN, L.L.P. (AV)

22nd Floor, One American Place, P.O. Box 3513, 70821
Telephone: 504-387-0999
Fax: 504-388-9133
New Orleans, Louisiana Office: Energy Centre, Suite 1470, 1100 Poydras Street.
Telephone: 504-585-3050.
Fax: 504-585-3051.
Plaquemine, Louisiana Office: Suite 10, 23425 Railroad Avenue.
Telephone: 504-687-9845.
Fax: 504-382-3445.

MEMBERS OF FIRM

G. William Jarman   Katherine W. King

J. Randy Young

Representative Clients: MCI Telecommunications Corporation, Washington, DC; Louisiana Energy Users Group.

For Complete List of Firm Personnel, See General Section

For full biographical listings, see the Martindale-Hubbell Law Directory

LAFAYETTE,* Lafayette Parish

ROY, BIVINS, JUDICE & HENKE, A PROFESSIONAL LAW CORPORATION (AV)

600 Jefferson Street, Suite 800, P.O. Drawer Z, 70502
Telephone: 318-233-7430
Telecopier: 318-233-8403

Ronald J. Judice

Representative Clients: Louisiana Energy and Power Authority; City of Kaplan, LA; Telecable Associates, Inc.

For Complete List of Firm Personnel, See General Section

For full biographical listings, see the Martindale-Hubbell Law Directory

NEW ORLEANS,* Orleans Parish

THE GODFREY FIRM A PROFESSIONAL LAW CORPORATION (AV)

2500 Energy Centre, 1100 Poydras Street, 70163-2500
Telephone: 504-585-7538
Fax: 504-585-7535

Jarrell E. Godfrey, Jr.   Cloyd F. Van Hook
Patrick M. Files

For full biographical listings, see the Martindale-Hubbell Law Directory

SHREVEPORT,* Caddo Parish

BARLOW AND HARDTNER L.C. (AV)

Tenth Floor, Louisiana Tower, 401 Edwards Street, 71101-3289
Telephone: 318-227-1131
Telecopier: 318-227-1141
Mailing Address: P.O. Box 8, Shreveport, Louisiana, 71161-0008

Malcolm S. Murchison   Clair F. White
David R. Taggart   Philip E. Downer, III
Michael B. Donald

Representative Clients: Central Louisiana Electric Co., Inc.; Central and South West Corporation; Louisiana Intrastate Gas Corp.; NorAm Energy Corp. (formerly Arkla, Inc.); Southwestern Electric Power Company; Public Service Co. of Oklahoma; Central Power and Light Co.; West Texas Utilities; Panhandle Eastern Corp.; Pennzoil Producing Co.

For Complete List of Firm Personnel, See General Section

For full biographical listings, see the Martindale-Hubbell Law Directory

WILKINSON, CARMODY & GILLIAM (AV)

1700 Beck Building, 400 Travis Street, P.O. Box 1707, 71166
Telephone: 318-221-4196
Telecopier: 318-221-3705

MEMBERS OF FIRM

John D. Wilkinson (1867-1929)   Bobby S. Gilliam
William Scott Wilkinson   Mark E. Gilliam
(1895-1985)   Penny D. Sellers
Arthur R. Carmody, Jr.   Patrick F. Robinson
Michael J. Ryan

Representative Clients: Farmers Insurance Group; Home Federal Savings & Loan Association of Shreveport; The Kansas City Southern Railway Co.; KTAL-TV; Lincoln National Life Insurance Co.; Mobil Oil Co.; Schumpert Medical Center; Sears, Roebuck & Co.; Southern Pacific Transportation Co.; Southwestern Electric Power Co.

(See Next Column)

WILKINSON, CARMODY & GILLIAM—*Continued*

For full biographical listings, see the Martindale-Hubbell Law Directory

MAINE

BATH, * Sagadahoc Co.

CONLEY & HALEY (AV)

Thirty Front Street, 04530
Telephone: 207-443-5576
Telefax: 207-443-6665

Mark L. Haley

Representative Clients: Bath Iron Works Corporation; Central Maine Power Company; Saco Defense, Inc.; Sugarloaf Mountain Corporation.
References: First Federal Savings & Loan Association of Bath; Key Bank of Maine; Brunswick Federal Savings.

For Complete List of Firm Personnel, See General Section

For full biographical listings, see the Martindale-Hubbell Law Directory

---

PORTLAND, * Cumberland Co.

PETRUCCELLI & MARTIN (AV)

50 Monument Square, P.O. Box 9733, 04104-5033
Telephone: 207-775-0200
Telecopier: 207-775-2360

MEMBERS OF FIRM

Gerald F. Petruccelli   Joel C. Martin

Representative Clients: Bangor Hydro-Electric Co.; Northeast Cellular Telephone Co., L.P.; Pine Tree Tel & Tel Co.

For full biographical listings, see the Martindale-Hubbell Law Directory

---

PIERCE ATWOOD (AV)

One Monument Square, 04101
Telephone: 207-791-1100
Fax: 207-791-1350
Email: info@PierceAtwood.com
Augusta, Maine Office: 77 Winthrop Street.
Telephone: 207-622-6311.
Fax: 207-623-9367.
Newburyport, Massachusetts Office: 6 Harris Street.
Telephone: 508-465-9599.
Fax: 508-465-9945.

MEMBERS OF FIRM

Gerald M. Amero   John W. Gulliver
Kevin F. Gordon

ASSOCIATE

Deborah L. Shaw

For Complete List of Firm Personnel, See General Section

For full biographical listings, see the Martindale-Hubbell Law Directory

---

MASSACHUSETTS

BOSTON, * Suffolk Co.

PALMER & DODGE LLP (AV)

One Beacon Street, 02108
Telephone: 617-573-0100
Facsimile: 617-227-4420

MEMBERS OF FIRM

Jeffrey F. Jones   Stanley Keller

COUNSEL

Jay E. Gruber

For Complete List of Firm Personnel, See General Section

For full biographical listings, see the Martindale-Hubbell Law Directory

REAL ESTATE LAW

ALABAMA

BIRMINGHAM, * Jefferson Co.

BERKOWITZ, LEFKOVITS, ISOM & KUSHNER, A PROFESSIONAL CORPORATION (AV)

1600 SouthTrust Tower, 420 North Twentieth Street, 35203
Telephone: 205-328-0480
Telecopier: 205-322-8007

Arnold K. Lefkovits	Chervis Isom
Denise W. Killebrew	

Lori L. Duwve

Representative Clients: Alabama Waste Services, Inc.; Bayer Properties, Inc.; Crest Realty Co.; Daniel Realty Corp.; Eason, Eyster & Sandner; Engel Realty Co., Inc.; McDonald's Corp.; Parisian, Inc.; Books-A-Million.

For Complete List of Firm Personnel, See General Section

For full biographical listings, see the Martindale-Hubbell Law Directory

BRADLEY, ARANT, ROSE & WHITE (AV)

2001 Park Place, Suite 1400, P.O. Box 830709, 35283-0709
Telephone: 205-521-8000
Facsimile: 205-252-0264
Facsimile (SouthTrust Tower Office): 205-251-9915
URL: http://www.BARW.COM
Huntsville, Alabama Office: 200 Clinton Avenue West, Suite 900, 35801.
Telephone: 205-517-5100.
Facsimile: 205-533-5069.

MEMBERS OF FIRM

Charles R. Smith, Jr.	Charles A. J. Beavers, Jr.
(Resident, Huntsville Office)	Lant B. Davis
Patrick H. Graves, Jr.	Bobby C. Underwood
(Resident, Huntsville Office)	John E. Hagefstration, Jr.
Axel Bolvig III	

COUNSEL

J. Robert Fleenor

ASSOCIATE

Frank C. Galloway, III

Counsel for: SouthTrust Bank of Alabama, National Association; Energen, Corporation; Blount, Inc.; Torchmark Corp.; Russell Corp.; Coca-Cola Bottling Company United, Inc.; Ford Motor Co.; Walter Industries, Inc.; The Birmingham Post Co. (Post-Herald); The New York Times Co.

For Complete List of Firm Personnel, See General Section

For full biographical listings, see the Martindale-Hubbell Law Directory

BURR & FORMAN (AV)

3100 SouthTrust Tower, 420 North 20th Street, 35203
Telephone: 205-251-3000
Telecopier: 205-458-5100
Huntsville, Alabama Office: Suite 204, Regency Center, 400 Meridian Street.
Telephone: 205-551-0010.
Atlanta, Georgia Office: Suite 1800, One Georgia Center, 600 West Peachtree Street, 30308.
Telephone: 404-817-3536.
Facsimile: 404-817-3244.

MEMBERS OF FIRM

J. Fred Powell	Carol H. Stewart
Joseph G. Stewart	Deborah P. Fisher
John F. DeBuys, Jr.	Gail Livingston Mills
Jack P. Stephenson, Jr.	W. Benjamin Johnson
Eric L. Carlton	Jeffrey T. Baker
Dwight L. Mixson, Jr.	Jill Verdeyen Deer

For Complete List of Firm Personnel, See General Section

For full biographical listings, see the Martindale-Hubbell Law Directory

CORLEY, MONCUS & WARD, P.C. (AV)

400 Shades Creek Parkway, Suite 100, P.O. Box 59807, 35259
Telephone: 205-879-5959
Telecopier: 205-871-4411

Claude McCain Moncus

Christopher P. Moseley

For Complete List of Firm Personnel, See General Section

For full biographical listings, see the Martindale-Hubbell Law Directory

DOMINICK, FLETCHER, YEILDING, WOOD & LLOYD, P.A. (AV)

2121 Highland Avenue, 35205
Telephone: 205-939-0033

Frank Dominick	Walter Fletcher
	Mary P. Thornton

Counsel for: Citizens Federal Savings Bank; St. Vincent's Hospital; Castle Mortgage Corporation; Thornton Construction Company, Inc.; Collateral Mortgage Corp.; Taylor Properties, L.L.C.

For Complete List of Firm Personnel, See General Section

For full biographical listings, see the Martindale-Hubbell Law Directory

GORDON, SILBERMAN, WIGGINS & CHILDS, A PROFESSIONAL CORPORATION (AV)

1400 SouthTrust Tower, 420 North 20th Street, 35203
Telephone: 205-328-0640
Telecopier: 205-254-1500

Bruce L. Gordon	Robert F. Childs, Jr.
	Ray D. Gibbons
Timothy D. Davis	Linda J. Peacock

For Complete List of Firm Personnel, See General Section

For full biographical listings, see the Martindale-Hubbell Law Directory

GORHAM & WALDREP, P.C. (AV)

2101 6th Avenue North, Suite 700, 35203
Telephone: 205-254-3216; 251-9166
Telecopier: 205-324-3802
Email: info@gorham-waldrep.com
Montgomery, Alabama Office: 250 Commerce Street, P.O. Box 4837, 36103-4837.
Telephone: 334-262-0777.
Telecopier: 334-262-0742.

Charles W. Gorham	LaVeeda Morgan Battle
Charlie D. Waldrep	John T. Natter
Thomas L. Stewart	Frank G. Alfano
Michael G. Kendrick	Kay L. McNabb Cason
William J. Bryant	Victor Kelley
	K. Mark Parnell

Victoria Franklin-Sisson	Leslie Miller Klasing
Karen Brown Evans	Brian Dennis Turner, Jr.
Mary H. Thompson	Anne D. Lamkin

Representative Clients: Jefferson County Personnel Board; Birmingham-Jefferson Civic Center Authority; The Water Works and Sewer Board of the City of Birmingham; City of Homewood; American Federation of Government Employees Local #1945; City of Pelham; Town of Kimberly; Alabama Tire Dealers Assn.; Southern States Body Shop Assn.

For full biographical listings, see the Martindale-Hubbell Law Directory

SPAIN & GILLON, L.L.C. (AV)

The Zinszer Building, 2117 2nd Avenue North, 35203
Telephone: 205-328-4100
Telecopier: 205-324-8866

MEMBERS OF FIRM

John P. McKleroy, Jr.	Samuel H. Frazier
	Harold H. Goings

General Counsel for: Liberty National Life Insurance Co.; Piggly Wiggly Alabama Distributing Co.; Alabama Insurance Guaranty Association; Alabama Life and Disability Insurance Guaranty Association; Alabama Insurance Underwriters Association.
Counsel for: SouthTrust Mortgage Corp.; Molton, Allen & Williams Corporation; Chase Manhattan Mortgage Corp.; Compass Bank.

For Complete List of Firm Personnel, See General Section

For full biographical listings, see the Martindale-Hubbell Law Directory

EUFAULA, Barbour Co.

WILLIAM V. NEVILLE, JR. (AV)

302 East Broad Street, P.O. Box 337, 36072-0337
Telephone: 334-687-5183
Fax: 334-687-6602

For full biographical listings, see the Martindale-Hubbell Law Directory

GUNTERSVILLE, * Marshall Co.

WRIGHT AND WRIGHT, A PROFESSIONAL CORPORATION (AV)

Worth Street, P.O. Box 70, 35976-0070
Telephone: 205-582-3721; 582-8590; 582-8411
Fax: 205-582-3733

(See Next Column)

WRIGHT AND WRIGHT A PROFESSIONAL CORPORATION, *Guntersville—Continued*

    T. Harvey Wright (1890-1972)   Harvey J. Wright
                    Wade K. Wright

Approved Attorneys for: Commonwealth Land Title Insurance Co.; Lawyers Title Insurance Corp.

HUNTSVILLE,* Madison Co.

BERRY, ABLES, TATUM, BAXTER, PARKER & HALL, P.C. (AV)

Legal Building, 315 Franklin Street, S.E., P.O. Box 165, 35804-0165
Telephone: 205-533-3740
Facsimile: 205-533-3751
Email: BAXTERJ@ATTMAIL.COM

William H. Blanton (1889-1973)	James T. Tatum, Jr.
Joe M. Berry	James T. Baxter, III
L. Bruce Ables	Thomas E. Parker, Jr.
	Bill G. Hall

James K. Brabston   Mark Rogers Hunter

Representative Clients: AmSouth Bank; First Alabama Bank; General Shale Products Co.; The Hertz Corp.; Litton Industries, Inc.; Farmers Tractor Co.; Colonial Bank; Farm Credit Bank of Texas; SouthBank; Regions Mortgage.
Reference: First Alabama Bank.

For full biographical listings, see the Martindale-Hubbell Law Directory

---

BRADLEY, ARANT, ROSE & WHITE (AV)

200 Clinton Avenue West, Suite 900, 35801
Telephone: 205-517-5100
Facsimile: 205-533-5069
URL: http://www.BARW.COM
Birmingham, Alabama Office: 2001 Park Place, Suite 1400, P.O. Box 830709.
Telephone: 205-521-8000.
Facsimile: 205-251-8611, 251-8665, 252-0264. Facsimile (SouthTrust Tower Office): 205-251-9915.

RESIDENT PARTNERS

Charles R. Smith, Jr.   Patrick H. Graves, Jr.

For Complete List of Firm Personnel, See General Section

For full biographical listings, see the Martindale-Hubbell Law Directory

---

BURR & FORMAN (AV)

Suite 204, Regency Center, 400 Meridian Street, 35801
Telephone: 205-551-0010
Birmingham, Alabama Office: 3100 SouthTrust Tower, 420 North 20th Street.
Telephone: 205-251-3000.
Telecopier: 205-458-5100.
Atlanta, Georgia Office: Suite 1800, One Georgia Center, 600 West Peachtree Street, 30308.
Telephone: 404-817-3536.
Facsimile: 404-817-3244.

RESIDENT PARTNER
L. Tennent Lee, III

For full biographical listings, see the Martindale-Hubbell Law Directory

---

STEPHENS, MILLIRONS, HARRISON & GAMMONS, P.C. (AV)

333 Franklin Street, P.O. Box 307, 35801
Telephone: 205-533-7711
Telecopier: 205-536-9388

Arthur M. Stephens	James G. Harrison
Paul L. Millirons	Robert C. Gammons

Attorneys for: Lomas Mortgage USA, Inc.; AmSouth Mortgage Co., Inc.

For full biographical listings, see the Martindale-Hubbell Law Directory

---

MOBILE,* Mobile Co.

JOHNSTONE, ADAMS, BAILEY, GORDON AND HARRIS, L.L.C. (AV)

Royal St. Francis Building, 104 St. Francis Street, P.O. Box 1988, 36633
Telephone: 334-432-7682
Facsimile: 334-432-2800
Telex: 782040

MEMBERS OF FIRM

I. David Cherniak   Robert S. Frost

General Counsel for: First Alabama Bank, Mobile; Infirmary Health System/Mobile Infirmary Medical Center/Rotary Rehabilitation Hospital (Multi-Hospital System).
Counsel for: Oil and Gas: Exxon Corp. Business and Corporate: Bell South Telecommunications, Inc.; Aluminum Co. of America; Michelin North America, Inc.; Metropolitan Life Insurance Co.; The Travelers Insurance Cos. Marine: The West of England Ship Owners Mutual Protection and In-

(See Next Column)

demnity Association (Luxembourg); The Standard Steamship Owners' Protection and Indemnity Association (Bermuda) Ltd.

For Complete List of Firm Personnel, See General Section

For full biographical listings, see the Martindale-Hubbell Law Directory

---

LYONS, PIPES & COOK, P.C. (AV)

2 North Royal Street, P.O. Box 2727, 36652-2727
Telephone: 334-432-4481
Cable Address: "Lysea"
Telecopier: 334-433-1820

Norton W. Brooker, Jr.	W. David Johnson, Jr.
Marion A. Quina, Jr.	R. Mark Kirkpatrick
Thomas F. Garth	John C. Bell

Representative Clients: James Graham Brown Foundation; Browning-Ferris Industries of Alabama, Inc.; Champion International Corporation; Inchcape Shipping Services, Inc.; SouthTrust Bank of Mobile.

For Complete List of Firm Personnel, See General Section

For full biographical listings, see the Martindale-Hubbell Law Directory

---

PIERCE, LEDYARD, LATTA & WASDEN, P.C. (AV)

Suite 900 Montlimar Place Office Building, 1110 Montlimar Drive, P.O. Box 16046, 36616
Telephone: 334-344-5151
Facsimile: 334-344-9696

Donald F. Pierce	Forrest S. Latta
Goodman G. Ledyard	H. William Wasden

OF COUNSEL
Caroline Wells Hinds

W. Pemble DeLashmet

Representative Clients: Associates Financial Services Company of Alabama, Inc.; BancBoston Mortgage Corporation; First Security Savings Bank, FSB; GeiBank Industrial Bank; Jim Walter Homes, Inc.; Merrill Lynch Credit Corp.; Oxford First; PHH US Mortgage Corp.; The Prudential Home Mortgage Company, Inc.; Unity Mortgage Corporation.

For full biographical listings, see the Martindale-Hubbell Law Directory

---

RAY G. RILEY, JR., P.C. (AV)

1110 Montlimar, Suite 200, 36609
Telephone: 334-343-5955
Fax: 334-342-4405

Ray G. Riley, Jr.

For full biographical listings, see the Martindale-Hubbell Law Directory

---

MONTGOMERY,* Montgomery Co.

KAUFMAN & ROTHFEDER, P.C. (AV)

2740 Zelda Road Post Office Drawer 4540, 36103-4540
Telephone: 334-244-1111
Fax: 334-244-1969

Samuel Kaufman	George W. Thomas
Richardson B. McKenzie, III	William B. Sellers

Counsel For: Alfa Builders, Inc.; Aronov Realty Company, Inc.; Ballard Realty Company, Inc.; First American Title Insurance Co.; Lawyers Title Insurance Co.; Liz Claiborne, Inc.; Alfa Mutual Fire Insurance Company; Palmer Wireless, Inc.

For full biographical listings, see the Martindale-Hubbell Law Directory

---

VOLZ, PRESTWOOD & HANAN, P.C. (AV)

350 Adams Avenue, P.O. Box 1910, 36102-1910
Telephone: 334-264-6401
Fax: 334-834-4954

Charles H. Volz, Jr.	Charles H. Volz, III
Alvin T. Prestwood	Clinton Chadwell Carter
Ellis D. Hanan	Daniel Lewis Feinstein

LEGAL SUPPORT PERSONNEL
Mark A.W. Turpen

For full biographical listings, see the Martindale-Hubbell Law Directory

---

TUSCALOOSA,* Tuscaloosa Co.

ZEANAH, HUST, SUMMERFORD, DAVIS & JONES, L.L.C. (AV)

Seventh Floor, AmSouth Bank Building, P.O. Box 1310, 35403
Telephone: 205-349-1383
Fax: 205-391-1319

MEMBERS OF FIRM

Olin W. Zeanah (1922-1987)	Kenneth D. Davis
Wilbor J. Hust, Jr.	Christopher H. Jones
E. Clark Summerford	Beverly A. Smith

(See Next Column)

ZEANAH, HUST, SUMMERFORD, DAVIS & JONES L.L.C.—*Continued*

OF COUNSEL

Marvin T. Ormond

Representative Clients: Alfa Insurance Cos.; Hartford Insurance Group; Home Insurance Co.; Nationwide Insurance Co.; Alabama Power Co.; Liberty Mutual Insurance Co.; The Uniroyal Goodrich Tire Co.

For full biographical listings, see the Martindale-Hubbell Law Directory

---

WETUMPKA, * Elmore Co.

ENSLEN, JOHNSTON & PINKSTON, L.L.C. (AV)

499 South Main Street, 36092
Telephone: 334-567-2545
Fax: 334-567-2547

John E. Enslen   Parker C. Johnston
Patrick D. Pinkston

References: Elmore County National Bank; First National Bank of Wetumpka.

For full biographical listings, see the Martindale-Hubbell Law Directory

---

ARIZONA

FLAGSTAFF, * Coconino Co.

ASPEY, WATKINS & DIESEL, P.L.L.C. (AV)

123 North San Francisco, 3rd Floor, 86001
Telephone: 520-774-1478
Facsimile: 520-774-8404
Sedona, Arizona Office: 120 Soldier Pass Road.
Telephone: 520-282-5955.
Facsimile: 520-282-5962.
Page, Arizona Office: 904 North Navajo.
Telephone: 520-645-9694.
Cottonwood, Arizona Office: 2400 E. Highway 89A, Suite C.
Telephone: 520-639-1881.
Facsimile: 520-639-0272.

MEMBERS OF FIRM

Frederick M. Fritz Aspey   Donald H. Bayles, Jr.
Harold L. Watkins   Kaign N. Christy
Louis M. Diesel   John J. Dempsey
Bruce S. Griffen   Zachary J. Markham

James E. Ledbetter   Roger M. Baeurle
Whitney Cunningham   Amy E. Mabius
Pernell Whynn McGuire   Stephen A. Thompson
Joel E. Sannes

LEGAL SUPPORT PERSONNEL

Karla H. Falls, CLAS   Dominic M. Marino, Jr,
(Legal Assistant)   (Paralegal Assistant)
Rocky C. Nissen (Paralegal   Carrie R. Flynn (Litigation
Assistant, Sedona, Arizona   Paralegal, Cottonwood,
Office)   Arizona Office)
Deborah D. Roberts, CLA
(Legal Assistant)

Representative Clients: Farmer's Insurance Company of Arizona; Pepsi-Cola Bottling Company of Northern Arizona; Bill Luke's Chrysler-Plymouth, Inc.; First American Title Insurance Company; Transnation Title Insurance Co.; Page Electric Utility; Comprehensive Access Health Plan, Inc.; Northern Arizona Healthcare Corporation.
Reference: First Interstate Bank-Arizona, N.A., Flagstaff, Arizona.

For full biographical listings, see the Martindale-Hubbell Law Directory

---

MESA, Maricopa Co.

JACKSON, WHITE, GARDNER & DECKER, P.C. (AV)

Suite 12000, 1201 S. Alma School Road, 85210
Telephone: 602-464-1111
Fax: 602-464-5692 *Statewide:* 800-243-1160
Email: JWGD@JWGDLAW.COM
Payson, Arizona Office: 260 Building C. Suite E, 108 E. Highway.
Telephone: 520-472-8878.

Roger C. Decker   Michael R. Pruitt
Wayne L. Gardner   Bradley D. Weech
Eric M. Jackson   David L. Weed
J. Grant Walker   Richard A. White
Roger R. Foote

(See Next Column)

William G. Rood   Hank E. Pearson
Eric K. MacDonald   Christine A. Wigton
Kelly G. Black

For full biographical listings, see the Martindale-Hubbell Law Directory

---

NOGALES, * Santa Cruz Co.

O'CONNOR, CAVANAGH, ANDERSON, KILLINGSWORTH & BESHEARS, A PROFESSIONAL ASSOCIATION (AV)

1891 North Mastick Way, 85621
Telephone: 520-761-4215
FAX: 520-761-3505
Email: firminfo@arizlaw.com
Phoenix, Arizona Office: One East Camelback Road, Suite 1100, 85012.
Telephone: 602-263-2400.
FAX: 602-263-2900.
Tucson, Arizona Office: O'Connor Cavanagh Molloy Jones, 33 N. Stone, Suite 2100, 85701, P.O. Box 2268, 85702.
Telephone: 520-622-3531.
FAX: 520-624-2816.
Sun City, Arizona Office: 13250 North Del Webb Boulevard, Suite B, 85351.
Telephone: 602-263-2808.
FAX: 602-933-3100.

Hector G. Arana   Kimberly A. Howard Arana

Representative Clients: Omega Produce Co.; Frank's Distributing, Inc.; City of Nogales; Collectron of Ariz., Inc.; James K. Wilson Produce Co.; Agricola Bon, S. de R.L. de C.V.; Angel Demerutis E.; Rene Carrillo C.; Arturo Lomeli; Theojary Crisantes E.

For Complete List of Firm Personnel, See General Section

For full biographical listings, see the Martindale-Hubbell Law Directory

---

PHOENIX, * Maricopa Co.

ANDERSON, BRODY, LEVINSON, WEISER & HORWITZ, P.A. (AV)

1112 West Camelback Road, 85013
Telephone: 602-234-0563
Fax: 602-234-2952

Donald E. Anderson   Ronald M. Horwitz
Jeffrey H. Levinson   Bradley D. Gardner
Paul M. Weiser   Alan M. Levinsky
Jamie A. Brody   Mark Bohn
Carrie M. Beasley

OF COUNSEL

Stephen A. Myers

For full biographical listings, see the Martindale-Hubbell Law Directory

---

APKER, APKER, HAGGARD & KURTZ, P.C. (AV)

2111 East Highland Avenue, Suite 230, 85016
Telephone: 602-381-0085
Telecopier: 602-956-3457

Burton M. Apker   David B. Apker
Jerry L. Haggard   Gerrie Apker Kurtz

Kevin M. Moran

Representative Clients: ASARCO Incorporated; Douglas Land Corp.; Frito-Lay, Inc.; Nevada Power Company; The North West Life Assurance Co.; Phelps Dodge Corporation; Santa Fe Pacific Gold Corporation; Santa Fe Pacific Industrials; Western Federal Savings & Loan Assn.

For full biographical listings, see the Martindale-Hubbell Law Directory

---

BONN, LUSCHER, PADDEN & WILKINS, CHARTERED (AV)

805 North Second Street, 85004
Telephone: 602-254-5557
Fax: 602-254-0656

Paul V. Bonn   Jeff C. Padden
Brian A. Luscher   Randall D. Wilkins

For full biographical listings, see the Martindale-Hubbell Law Directory

---

BONNETT, FAIRBOURN, FRIEDMAN & BALINT, P.C. (AV)

4041 North Central Avenue Suite 1100, 85012
Telephone: 602-274-1100
Fax: 602-274-1199

Jerry C. Bonnett   Robert J. Spurlock
William G. Fairbourn   C. Kevin Dykstra
Andrew S. Friedman   Elaine A. Ryan
Francis J. Balint, Jr.   Tara L. Jackson
H. Sullivan Bunch   Wendy J. Harrison
Michael N. Widener   Scott A. Erickson

(See Next Column)

BONNETT, FAIRBOURN, FRIEDMAN & BALINT P.C., *Phoenix—Continued*

Guy A. Hanson	Gina M. DeVito
Thomas B. Dixon	Robert D. Ryan
Martin E. Latz	Guy P. Roll

OF COUNSEL

James Duke Cameron

For full biographical listings, see the Martindale-Hubbell Law Directory

BROENING, OBERG, WOODS, WILSON & CASS, P.C. (AV)

1122 East Jefferson Street, P.O. Box 20527, 85036
Telephone: 602-271-7700
Telecopier: 602-258-7785
Email: aznvlaw@indirect.com *URL:* http://www.azlvlaw.com
Las Vegas, Nevada Office: 3930 Howard Hughes Parkway, Suite 200, 89109.
Telephone: 702-893-3383.
Fax: 702-893-3789.

James R. Broening	Cynthia van R. Cheney
Terrence P. Woods	Gary A. Fadell
John W. Oberg	Douglas G. Shook
Donald Wilson, Jr.	Mary B. Wilson
V. Andrew Cass	Bruce M. Preston
Kenneth C. Miller	Robert M. Moore
Neal B. Thomas	James G. McElwee, Jr.
Wesley S. Loy	David S. Shughart, III
Michael M. Haran	Marilyn D. Cage
Jerry T. Collen	John P. Robertson, II

David S. Cohen

Clark V. Vellis	Bethanne Klopp-Bryant
(Resident, Las Vegas, Nevada)	(Resident, Las Vegas, Nevada)
Katherine M. Barrett	Jeffrey H. Ballin
(Resident, Las Vegas, Nevada)	(Resident, Las Vegas, Nevada)
Mark G. Henness	Arleen N. Kaizer
(Resident, Las Vegas, Nevada)	(Resident, Las Vegas, Nevada)
Riley A. Clayton	Hayley B. Chambers
(Resident, Las Vegas, Nevada)	(Resident, Las Vegas, Nevada)

James W. Howard, Jr.

OF COUNSEL

Kevin T. Ahern	Richard E. Chambliss

Donald J. Newman

Representative Clients: Chubb Group of Insurance Cos.; Farmers Insurance Group; Home Insurance Co.; Ohio Casualty Insurance Group; St. Paul Fire and Marine Insurance Companies.

For full biographical listings, see the Martindale-Hubbell Law Directory

BROWN & BAIN, A PROFESSIONAL ASSOCIATION (AV)

2901 North Central Avenue, P.O. Box 400, 85001-0400
Telephone: 602-351-8000
Telecopier: 602-351-8516
Palo Alto, California Affiliated Office: Brown & Bain, 1755 Embarcadero Road, Suite 200.
Telephone: 415-856-9411.
Telecopier: 415-856-6061.
Tucson, Arizona Affiliated Office: Brown & Bain, A Professional Association. One South Church Avenue, Nineteenth Floor, P.O. Box 2265.
Telephone: 602-798-7900.
Telecopier: 602-798-7945.

Richard Calvin Cooledge	Michael F. McNulty
Kyle B. Hettinger	(Resident at Tucson Office)
Ronald E. Lowe	Sarah R. Simmons
	(Resident at Tucson Office)

Mala D. Clancey

For Complete List of Firm Personnel, See General Section

For full biographical listings, see the Martindale-Hubbell Law Directory

BURCH & CRACCHIOLO, P.A. (AV)

702 East Osborn Road, Suite 200, 85014
Telephone: 602-274-7611
Fax: 602-234-0341
Mailing Address: P.O. Box 16882, Phoenix, AZ, 85011

Jack D. Klausner	Andrew Abraham
Guadalupe Iniguez	Clare H. Abel
Daryl Manhart	Ralph D. Harris
Edwin C. Bull	David M. Villadolid

Marvin Davis	J. Brent Welker

Representative Clients: Bashas' Inc.; Farmers Insurance Group; U-Haul International, Inc.

For Complete List of Firm Personnel, See General Section

For full biographical listings, see the Martindale-Hubbell Law Directory

CARMICHAEL & POWELL, PROFESSIONAL CORPORATION (AV)

7301 North 16th Street, 85020-5224
Telephone: 602-861-0777
Facsimile: 602-870-0296

Ronald W. Carmichael

Stephen Manes	Brian A. Hatch

Representative Clients: Home Builders Association of Central Arizona: Ryland Homes.

For full biographical listings, see the Martindale-Hubbell Law Directory

COCHRAN & DAHL, P.C. (AV)

2999 North 44th Street, 85018
Telephone: 602-952-5300
Facsimile: 602-952-7010

Jerry L. Cochran	Larry J. Dahl

For full biographical listings, see the Martindale-Hubbell Law Directory

COHEN AND COTTON, P.C. A PROFESSIONAL CORPORATION (AV)

One Arizona Center, Suite 400, 400 East Van Buren Street, 85004
Telephone: 602-252-8400
FAX: 602-252-5339
Las Vegas, Nevada Office: 1001 First Interstate Bank Building, 302 East Carson Avenue, 89101.
Telephone: 702-387-7870.
Fax: 702-385-3331.

Ronald Jay Cohen	Joshua R. Woodard
John H. Cotton	Robert N. Mann
Laura H. Kennedy	John Maston O'Neal
Daniel G. Dowd	Jennifer Lynn Chutick
David W. Smith	Ed F. Hendricks, Jr.
Scott L. Long	Michael J. Ryan
	(Not admitted in AZ)

SPECIAL COUNSEL

Stacy J. Crouch	Paula M. DeMore

Representative Clients: Coopers & Lybrand; Del Webb Corp.; Grubb & Ellis Realty Co.; Talley Industries, Inc.; Accuvane Mortgage Co.; Express America Mortgage Co.

For full biographical listings, see the Martindale-Hubbell Law Directory

COPPERSMITH & GORDON P.L.C. (AV)

2633 East Indian School Road, Suite 300, 85016-6759
Telephone: 602-224-0999
Fax: 602-224-6020
Email: SAMnANDY@aol.com

Samuel G. Coppersmith

OF COUNSEL

M. Joyce Geyser	James J. Belanger

Reference: Norwest Bank Arizona, N.A.

For full biographical listings, see the Martindale-Hubbell Law Directory

CRUSE, FIRETAG & BOCK, P.C. (AV)

5611 North 16th Street, 85016
Telephone: 602-279-9411
Facsimile: 602-241-1260

Robert J. Cruse	Jules I. Firetag

Daniel A. Bock

John L. Stoss

OF COUNSEL

Stephen T. Meadow (P.C.)

Reference: Bank One (Sun City/Lakeview Office).

For full biographical listings, see the Martindale-Hubbell Law Directory

DUSHOFF & McCALL, A PROFESSIONAL CORPORATION (AV)

Two Renaissance Square, Suite 1000, 40 North Central, 85004
Telephone: 602-254-3800
Fax: 602-258-2551
URL: http://www.dushoff@neta.com

Jay Dushoff	Robert H. Kreutzer
Jack E. McCall (1942-1995)	Michael Riikola

Denise J. Henslee

LEGAL SUPPORT PERSONNEL

Thomas M. Flynn	Roger L. Dunlap
Brad D. Larson	(Certified Legal Assistant)

For full biographical listings, see the Martindale-Hubbell Law Directory

Phoenix—Continued

FENNEMORE CRAIG, A PROFESSIONAL CORPORATION (AV)

Two North Central, Suite 2200, 85004
Telephone: 602-257-8700
Fax: 602-257-8527
Scottsdale, Arizona Office: 6263 North Scottsdale Road, Suite 290, 85250.
Telephone: 602-257-5400.
Fax: 602-257-5409.
Tucson, Arizona Office: One South Church Avenue, Suite 1030, 85701.
Telephone: 520-791-6800.
Fax: 520-791-6820.

Robert P. Robinson	Leland M. Jones
Philip A. Edlund	Charles M. King
Ronald L. Ballard	Michael V. Mulchay
Stephen M. Savage	Margaret R. Gallogly
Mark A. Nesvig	Rebecca L. Burnham
James R. Huntwork	David E. Vieweg
George T. Cole	Lesa J. Storey

Selma F. Baharoglu	Brett L Hopper
Elizabeth M. Behnke	Alan S. Hall
Christopher W. Zaharis	William P. Wichterman
Susan L. Bostock	

For Complete List of Firm Personnel, See General Section

For full biographical listings, see the Martindale-Hubbell Law Directory

GALBUT & CONANT, A PROFESSIONAL CORPORATION (AV)

Camelback Esplanade, Suite 1020, 2425 East Camelback Road, 85016
Telephone: 602-955-1455
Fax: 602-955-1585

Martin R. Galbut	Paul A. Conant

John R. Augustine, Jr.

For full biographical listings, see the Martindale-Hubbell Law Directory

GAMMAGE & BURNHAM, P.L.C. (AV)

One Renaissance Square, Two North Central Avenue, Suite 1800, 85004
Telephone: 602-256-0566
Fax: 602-256-4475

MEMBERS OF FIRM

Grady Gammage, Jr.	Thomas J. McDonald
Shawn E. Tobin	Jeffrey J. Miller

Representative Clients: W.M. Grace Development; Viehmann, Martin & Associates; Evans-Withycombe, Inc.; Opus Southwest; Kaufman & Broad of Arizona, Inc.

For Complete List of Firm Personnel, See General Section

For full biographical listings, see the Martindale-Hubbell Law Directory

HIENTON, MINER, FRY & KURTZ, P.C. (AV)

3636 North Central Avenue, Suite 400, 85012-1997
Telephone: 602-240-6400
Fax: 602-240-6401

Gary H. Fry	William L. Kurtz
Joseph P. Hienton	Don J. Miner
Jeffrey S. Pitcher	

For full biographical listings, see the Martindale-Hubbell Law Directory

JENNINGS, STROUSS AND SALMON, P.L.C. (AV)

A Professional Limited Liability Company
One Renaissance Square, Two North Central, 85004-2393
Telephone: 602-262-5911
Fax: 602-253-3255

John R. Christian	Douglas G. Zimmerman
Gary G. Keltner	Philip J. MacDonnell
Lee E. Esch	Gerrit M. Steenblik
George Esahak-Gage	

Stephanie McRae

For Complete List of Firm Personnel, See General Section

For full biographical listings, see the Martindale-Hubbell Law Directory

JOHN S. LANCY & ASSOCIATES A PROFESSIONAL CORPORATION (AV)

Suite 390, 2425 East Camelback Road, 85016
Telephone: 602-381-6555
Fax: 602-381-6550

John S. Lancy

(See Next Column)

Steven W. Bienstock	Nina A. Ortega

For full biographical listings, see the Martindale-Hubbell Law Directory

LEWIS AND ROCA, LLP (AV)

A Limited Liability Partnership including a Professional Corporation
40 North Central Avenue, 85004-4429
Telephone: 602-262-5311
Fax: 602-262-5747
Email: mlp@lrlaw.com
Tucson, Arizona Office: One South Church Avenue, Suite 700, 86701-1620.
Telephone: 520-622-2090.
Fax: 520-622-3088. E-Mail: mlp@lrlaw.com.

MEMBERS OF FIRM

Douglas R. Chandler	D. Randall Stokes
Kenneth Van Winkle, Jr.	

ASSOCIATES

Thel W. Casper	Glenn D. Forcucci
	(Not admitted in AZ)

OF COUNSEL

Lyman A. Manser

Representative Clients: Bank One, Arizona, NA; Gosnell Development Corp.; Phoenix Memorial Hospital; The Prudential Insurance Company of America; Scottsdale Memorial Hospitals; UDC Homes, Inc.

For Complete List of Firm Personnel, See General Section

For full biographical listings, see the Martindale-Hubbell Law Directory

LIEBERMAN, DODGE, SENDROW & GERDING, LTD. (AV)

Valley Bank Tower, Suite 1801 3550 North Central Avenue, 85012-2114
Telephone: 602-277-3000
Fax: 602-277-7478
Chicago, Illinois Office: LaSalle Bank Building, Suite 1946, 135 South La Salle Street, 60603.
Telephone: 312-541-8510.
Fax: 312-541-2624.

David D. Dodge	Marc R. Lieberman
Paul S. Gerding	Susan G. Sendrow

Mary K. Farrington-Lorch
Paul S. Gerding, Jr. (Not admitted in AZ; Resident, Chicago, Illinois Office)

OF COUNSEL

Karen L. Kothe	Michael J. Fuller
Robert G. Anderson (P.C.)	Lawrence J. Buckley
John T. Callan	

Representative Clients: John Gardiner's Tennis Ranch; Arizona Education Association; Public Safety Personnel Retirement System; Wells Fargo Bank and Credit Corp.; Regency Savings Bank; Sears, Roebuck and Co.; Baxter Healthcare Corporation; Aetna Life Insurance Company; General Board of Pension and Health Benefits of the United Methodist Church; Anti-Defamation League of B'Nai B'Rith.

For full biographical listings, see the Martindale-Hubbell Law Directory

LINZER & DITSCH, P.C. (AV)

3242 North Sixteenth Street, 85016
Telephone: 602-956-2525
Fax: 602-241-9885

Stephen P. Linzer

Terry D. Warren

For full biographical listings, see the Martindale-Hubbell Law Directory

MACLEAN & JACQUES, LTD. (AV)

Suite 202, 40 East Virginia, 85004
Telephone: 602-263-5771
FAX: 602-279-5569

John H. MacLean (1932-1992)	Raoul T. Jacques

Cary T. Inabinet	Macre S. Inabinet

LEGAL SUPPORT PERSONNEL

Sharon Petterson

For full biographical listings, see the Martindale-Hubbell Law Directory

MARISCAL, WEEKS, McINTYRE & FRIEDLANDER, P.A. (AV)

2901 North Central Avenue Suite 200, 85012-2705
Telephone: 602-285-5000
Fax: 602-285-5100

(See Next Column)

MARISCAL, WEEKS, MCINTYRE & FRIEDLANDER P.A., *Phoenix—Continued*

Gary L. Birnbaum   Fred C. Fathe
Peter A. Winkler   Terry L. Tedesco

References: Northern Trust Bank of Arizona; National Bank of Arizona.

For Complete List of Firm Personnel, See General Section

For full biographical listings, see the Martindale-Hubbell Law Directory

MARTIN & PATTERSON, LTD. (AV)

Suite 1111, One Columbus Plaza, 3636 North Central Avenue, 85012
Telephone: 602-222-4700
Telecopier: 602-274-3984

James H. Patterson   Douglas G. Martin
OF COUNSEL
Richard H. Lee

For full biographical listings, see the Martindale-Hubbell Law Directory

McCABE, O'DONNELL & WRIGHT, A PROFESSIONAL ASSOCIATION (AV)

3101 North Central Avenue Suite 700, 85012
Telephone: 602-264-0800
Facsimile: 602-274-0146
Email: mowphx@aol.com
Email: mowphx@mowphx.com

Joseph I. McCabe   Kathleen M. O'Donnell
Jerry W. Lawson

For full biographical listings, see the Martindale-Hubbell Law Directory

MEYERS LAW FIRM (AV)

Suite 900, 2398 East Camelback Road, 85016
Telephone: 602-468-8900
Telecopier: 602-468-8910

Donald D. Meyers

Charles W. Lotzar   James F. Wees
Donald L. Meyers   Jason A. Donkersley

Reference: Bank of America, Arizona.

For full biographical listings, see the Martindale-Hubbell Law Directory

ROBERT J. NOVAK & ASSOCIATES (AV)

1440 E. Washington Street Suite 100, 85034
Telephone: 602-253-8000
Fax: 602-271-4733

ASSOCIATE
Herbert T. Swafford

Representative Clients: SouthTrust Mortgage, BancBoston; L.V. Associates, Ltd.; AEI Real Estate Fund Limited Partnership; Heron North American Property Trust; Tippmann Construction, Inc.; Sun World Corporation; G.B. Mannisto, Inc.; Phoenix Computer Systems, Inc.; Pasternack Architect, Inc.; Phoenix Plastics, Inc.

For full biographical listings, see the Martindale-Hubbell Law Directory

O'CONNOR, CAVANAGH, ANDERSON, KILLINGSWORTH & BESHEARS, A PROFESSIONAL ASSOCIATION (AV)

One East Camelback Road, Suite 1100, 85012-1656
Telephone: 602-263-2400
FAX: 602-263-2900
Email: firminfo@arizlaw.com
Sun City, Arizona Office: 13250 North Del Webb Boulevard, Suite B, 85351.
Telephone: 602-263-2808.
FAX: 602-933-3100.
Tucson, Arizona Office: O'Connor Cavanagh Molloy Jones, 33 N. Stone, Suite 2100, 85701, P.O. Box 2268, 85702.
Telephone: 520-622-3531.
FAX: 520-624-2816.
Nogales, Arizona Office: 1891 North Mastick Way, 85621.
Telephone: 520-761-4215.
FAX: 520-761-3505.

Gerald L. Jacobs   Steven L. Lisker
Mayor Shanken   Glenn M. Feldman
Michael E. Woolf   Gilbert L. Rudolph
Scott A. Rose   Daniel W. Peters
David L. Lansky

Mark W. Daliere   Robert H. Nagle
Jonathan R. Feldman

(See Next Column)

Barbara L. Bolin   Lisa R. Tsiolis

Representative Clients: Del Webb Corporation; The Dial Corp; Mobil Land Development Corporation; Johnson Wax Development Corporation; Connecticut General Life Insurance Company of America; Bankers Trust Company; The Equitable; Ameritech Pension Trust.

For Complete List of Firm Personnel, See General Section

For full biographical listings, see the Martindale-Hubbell Law Directory

PERRY, PIERSON & SILVER, P.L.C. (AV)

2901 North Central Avenue Suite 300, 85012
Telephone: 602-285-5165
Facsimile: 602-285-5100

Allan R. Perry   Timothy L. Pierson
Leon B. Silver

For full biographical listings, see the Martindale-Hubbell Law Directory

QUARLES & BRADY (AV)

One Camelback Building, One East Camelback Road, Suite 400, 85012-1649
Telephone: 602-230-5500
Fax: 602-230-5598
Milwaukee, Wisconsin Office: 411 East Wisconsin Avenue.
Telephone: 414-277-5000.
Fax: 414-271-3552.
Madison, Wisconsin Office: First Wisconsin Plaza, One South Pinckney Street, P.O. Box 2113.
Telephone: 608-251-5000.
Fax: 608-251-9166.
West Palm Beach, Florida Office: 222 Lakeview Ave., 4th Floor.
Telephone: 407-653-5000.
Fax: 407-653-5333.
Naples, Florida Office: Barnett Center, 4501 Tamiami Trail North, Suite 300.
Telephone: 813-262-5959.
Fax: 813-434-4999.

MEMBERS OF THE FIRM
Robert T. Bailes   David G. Beauchamp
Roger K. Spencer   Daniel L. Muchow
ASSOCIATES
Robert S. Bornhoft   Ronald M. Goldberg

For Complete List of Firm Personnel, See General Section

For full biographical listings, see the Martindale-Hubbell Law Directory

RENAUD, COOK & DRURY, P.A. (AV)

617 North 2nd Avenue, 85003
Telephone: 602-253-5101
Fax: 602-254-1448
Email: rcdlaw@rcdlaw.com
Scottsdale, Arizona Office: 6991 East Camelback Road, #D-103, 85251.
Telephone: 602-874-9000.
Fax: 602-874-9866.

J. Gordon Cook   Cathey L. Joseph

For full biographical listings, see the Martindale-Hubbell Law Directory

RIDENOUR, SWENSON, CLEERE & EVANS, P.C. (AV)

40 North Central Avenue, Suite 1400, 85004
Telephone: 602-254-2143
Fax: 602-254-8670

William G. Ridenour   William D. Fearnow
Gerard R. Cleere   Natalie P. Garth
Kurt A. Peterson

Representative Clients: American Arbitration Assn.; Biltmore Investors Bank; Citibank (Arizona); Federal Home Life Insurance Co.; Mellon Bank; Guarantee Mutual Life Co.; Indianapolis Life Insurance Co.; Kahler Corp.; Marriott Corp.; Farm Credit Services Southwest.

For full biographical listings, see the Martindale-Hubbell Law Directory

ROBBINS & GREEN, A PROFESSIONAL ASSOCIATION (AV)

1800 Norwest Tower, 3300 North Central Avenue, 85012-9826
Telephone: 602-248-7600
Fax: 602-266-5369

Wayne A. Smith   Jeffrey P. Boshes
Edmund F. Richardson   Janet B. Hutchison
Jack N. Rudel   Alfred W. Ricciardi

For Complete List of Firm Personnel, See General Section

For full biographical listings, see the Martindale-Hubbell Law Directory

Phoenix—Continued

SHIMMEL, HILL, BISHOP & GRUENDER, P.C. (AV)

3700 North 24th Street, 85016
Telephone: 602-224-9500
Telecopier: 602-955-6176

Daniel F. Gruender   Joseph Wm. Kruchek
            Margaret L. Steiner

Representative Clients: Talley Realty Group; Chrisitania Bank of Kredit-kasse; Farmers Insurance Group; Magellan Corporation; Harkins Amusement Enterprises, Inc.; Connecticut General Life; First Bank and Trust Flea Lacumbre Savings Bank; Mutual Trust Life Insurance Co.; Phoenix Newspapers, Inc.

For full biographical listings, see the Martindale-Hubbell Law Directory

SNELL & WILMER, L.L.P. (AV)

One Arizona Center, 85004-0001
Telephone: 602-382-6000
Fax: 602-382-6070
Tucson, Arizona Office: 1500 Norwest Tower, One South Church Avenue 85701-1612.
Telephone: 520-882-1200.
Fax: 520-884-1294.
Orange County Office: 1920 Main Street, Suite 1200, P.O. Box 57062, Irvine, California, 92619-7062.
Telephone: 714-253-2700.
Fax: 714-955-2507.
Salt Lake City, Utah Office: Broadway Centre, 111 East Broadway, Suite 900, 84111-1004.
Telephone: 801-237-1900.
Fax: 801-237-1950.

MEMBERS OF FIRM

Richard K. Mallery   Robert C. Bates
Jay D. Wiley   Joyce Kline Wright
        Jody Kathleen Pokorski

Representative Clients: American Newland Associates; Arizona Public Service; AZTAR Corp.; The Hewson Co.; Markland Properties, Inc.; Perini Land & Development Co.; SunCor Development Co.; Toyota Motor Corp.; Bank One, Arizona, NA.; Del Webb Corporation.

For Complete List of Firm Personnel, See General Section

For full biographical listings, see the Martindale-Hubbell Law Directory

WILENCHIK & BARTNESS, A PROFESSIONAL CORPORATION (AV)

2828 North Central Avenue, Thirteenth Floor, 85004
Telephone: 602-274-2828
Facsimile: 602-274-2822

Dennis I. Wilenchik   George H. Foster, Jr.
Becky Ann Bartness   Charles A. Grube
Craig T. Irish   Linda DuMars Bach
        Ann A. Scott Timmer

David N. Farren
OF COUNSEL
Allen D. Harnisch

Representative Clients: Alexander & Alexander, Inc.; The Chase Manhattan Bank, N.A.; Founders Bank of Arizona; Republic National Bank of Arizona; Richmond American Homes; Saddleback Homes; Geoffrey Edmunds & Associates; Home Depot U.S.A.; Scottsdale Racquet Club; International Surfacing, Inc.

For full biographical listings, see the Martindale-Hubbell Law Directory

ZEITLIN & ZEITLIN, P.C. (AV)

A Partnership including a Professional Corporation
Camel Headquarters, 3900 East Camelback Road Suite 406, 85018
Telephone: 602-234-8905
Fax: 602-285-5589
Annapolis, Maryland Office: 2007 Tidewater Colony Drive, Suite 2B, 21401-8686.
Telephone: 410-266-9500.
Facsimile: 410-266-9522.

Dale S. Zeitlin   Dawn Stoll Zeitlin (P.C.)

For full biographical listings, see the Martindale-Hubbell Law Directory

PRESCOTT,* Yavapai Co.

FAVOUR, MOORE & WILHELMSEN, A PROFESSIONAL ASSOCIATION (AV)

1580 Plaza West Drive, P.O. Box 1391, 86302
Telephone: 520-445-2444
Fax: 520-771-0450

(See Next Column)

John M. Favour   Mark M. Moore
        David K. Wilhelmsen

Representative Clients: Yavapai Title Co.; Hidden Valley Ranch; Glenn Straub Appraisers, Inc.; Lawyers Title Insurance Co.; Bullwacker Associates; The Ranch at Prescott Homeowner's Assn.; Sedona Brokers Ginny Hays Realty, Inc.; Village of Oak Creek Assn.

For full biographical listings, see the Martindale-Hubbell Law Directory

SCOTTSDALE, Maricopa Co.

FENNEMORE CRAIG, A PROFESSIONAL CORPORATION (AV)

6263 North Scottsdale Road, Suite 290, 85250
Telephone: 602-257-5400
Fax: 602-945-4932
TWX: 910-950-4608
Phoenix, Arizona Office: Two North Central Avenue, Suite 2200, 85004.
Telephone: 602-257-8700.
Fax: 602-257-8527.
Tucson, Arizona Office: One South Church Avenue, Suite 1030, 85701.
Telephone: 520-791-6800.
Fax: 520-791-6820.

Philip A. Edlund   George T. Cole

Alan S. Hall

For Complete List of Firm Personnel, See General Section

For full biographical listings, see the Martindale-Hubbell Law Directory

PESKIND HYMSON & GOLDSTEIN, P.C. (AV)

14595 North Scottsdale Road, Suite 14, 85254
Telephone: 602-991-9077
Fax: 602-443-8854

E. J. Peskind   Irving Hymson
        Marilee Miller Clarke

For full biographical listings, see the Martindale-Hubbell Law Directory

SPARKS, TEHAN & RYLEY, P.C. (AV)

7503 First Street, 85251-4573
Telephone: 602-949-1339
Fax: 602-949-7587

Joe P. Sparks   Kevin T. Tehan
        John H. Ryley

References: Bank One, Arizona, Trust Department; Northern Trust Bank of Arizona, N.A.; First Interstate Bank of Arizona.

For full biographical listings, see the Martindale-Hubbell Law Directory

STOCKTON & HING, P.A. (AV)

Deauville Building, 6609 North Scottsdale Road, 85253
Telephone: 602-951-0882
Telecopier: 602-483-7721

Henderson Stockton (1892-1978)   Robert Ong Hing
            Gregory Ong Hing

Representative Clients: Alliance of American Insurers; American Council of Life Insurance; Amica Mutual Insurance Company; Arizona Conference Corporation of Seventh-Day Adventists; Arizona Life & Disability Insurance Guaranty Fund; Arizona Property and Casualty Insurance Guaranty Fund; Chubb Life Insurance Co.; Equitable Insurance Services; Globe Life & Accident Insurance Co.; Great Republic Life Insurance Co.

For full biographical listings, see the Martindale-Hubbell Law Directory

TITUS, BRUECKNER & BERRY, P.C. (AV)

Scottsdale Centre Suite B-252, 7373 North Scottsdale Road, 85253-3527
Telephone: 602-483-9600
Fax: 602-483-3215
Email: TBandB@aol.com

Jon A. Titus   Charles R. Berry
Kurt M. Brueckner   Alex B. Vakula
        Garry S. O'Rafferty

David R. Jordan   K. Scott Reynolds
Scott K. Risley   Michael F. Patterson
        LEGAL SUPPORT PERSONNEL
Janice L. Innocenzi   Belle Taylor

Representative Clients: Arizona Department of Insurance; Dickinson & Co. Hancock Homes; McCallum Hill; Heritage Mint, Ltd.; Baukol Construction, Inc.; Office of Special Deputy Receiver, Illinois Department of Insurance; Peacock, Hislop, Staley & Given, Inc.; H.E.R.C. Products., Incorporated; Stewart Title and Trust of Phoenix, Inc.; Beazer Homes.

For full biographical listings, see the Martindale-Hubbell Law Directory

TUCSON, * Pima Co.

CHANDLER, TULLAR, UDALL & REDHAIR (AV)

1700 Bank of America Plaza, 33 North Stone Avenue, 85701
Telephone: 520-623-4353
Telefax: 520-792-3426

MEMBERS OF FIRM

Thomas Chandler	Dwight M. Whitley, Jr.
D. B. Udall	E. Hardy Smith
Jack Redhair	John J. Brady
Joe F. Tarver, Jr.	Christopher J. Smith
Steven Weatherspoon	Charles V. Harrington
Edwin M. Gaines, Jr.	Bruce G. MacDonald

ASSOCIATES

Joel T. Ireland	Kurt Kroese
Mark Fredenberg	Sean C. Chapman
Mariann T. Shinoskie	Anne M. Fulton

Representative Clients: Arizona Electric Cooperative Power, Inc.; Atlantic Richfield Co.; Northwestern Mutual Life Insurance; Preferred Risk Life Insurance Co.; Citizen Auto Stage; Starpass Properties.

For Complete List of Firm Personnel, See General Section

For full biographical listings, see the Martindale-Hubbell Law Directory

DUFFIELD, MILLER, YOUNG, ADAMSON & ALFRED, P.C. (AV)

Suite 711, Transamerica Building, 177 North Church Avenue, 85701
Telephone: 520-792-1181
FAX: 520-792-2859
Green Valley, Arizona Office: 101-65 South La Canada, Green Valley Mall.
Telephone: 520-625-4404.
Fax: 520-625-4453.
La Paloma Office: La Paloma Corporate Center, 3573 East Sunrise Drive, Suite 115, Tucson, Arizona.
Telephone: 520-577-1135.
Fax: 520-577-1079.

Philip Hawley Smith	Thomas R. Althaus
Arthur H. Miller (1935-1995)	Richard Duffield
Larry R. Adamson	Eugene C. Gieseler
Samuel D. Alfred	K. Alexander Hobson
	Michael C. Young

LEGAL SUPPORT PERSONNEL

Cynthia Sargent Althaus	Joan Shelton, CLA
Mary Jane Arnesen	Christine M. Smith
Katrina Hillman	Barbara L. Steimle
Elizabeth Kohl-Sturgeon	Elaine Webb

Representative Clients: San Xavier Rock & Materials; Community Water Company of Green Valley.
Insurance Company Clientele: State Farm Mutual Insurance Cos.; Automobile Club Insurance Co.; Colonial Penn Insurance Co.; Metropolitan Property & Liability Insurance Co.; National Indemnity Ins. Co.

For full biographical listings, see the Martindale-Hubbell Law Directory

ROBERT A. FORTUNO, P.C. (AV)

2200 East River Road, Suite 115, 85718
Telephone: 520-299-4610
Fax: 520-299-5602

Robert A. Fortuno

Elizabeth D. Bushell

Representative Clients: Diamond Management, Inc.; Rocking K Development Co.; Finger Canyon, L.L.C.; Foothills Resort Properties, Ltd.; Grubb & Ellis Commercial Real Estate; La Placita Partners, L.P.; Southwest Holdings, Ltd.; Tucson Realty and Trust Company.
Reference: Norwest Bank.

For full biographical listings, see the Martindale-Hubbell Law Directory

LEONARD FELKER ALTFELD & BATTAILE, P.C. (AV)

250 North Meyer Avenue, P.O. Box 191, 85702-0191
Telephone: 520-622-7733
Fax: 520-622-7967

David J. Leonard	Judith B. Leonard
Sidney L. Felker	Donna M. Aversa
Clifford B. Altfeld	Lynne M. Schwartz
John F. Battaile III	Edward O. Comitz
	Russell E. Krone

For full biographical listings, see the Martindale-Hubbell Law Directory

LEWIS AND ROCA, LLP (AV)

A Limited Liability Partnership including a Professional Corporation
One South Church Avenue Suite 700, 85701-1620
Telephone: 520-622-2090
Fax: 520-622-3088
Email: mlp@lrlaw.com
Phoenix, Arizona Office: 40 North Central Avenue, 85004-4429.
Telephone: 602-262-5311.
Fax: 602-262-5747. E-Mail: mlp@lrlaw.com.

RESIDENT MEMBERS

S. L. Schorr	Andrew Daru Schorr
Frank S. Bangs, Jr.	Lewis D. Schorr

Representative Clients: Advantage Health Network, Inc.; A.F. Sterling Builders; Arizona Bank; Capin Mercantile Corporation; Citibank (Arizona); Perini Land & Development Company; City of Scottsdale; Scotia Group Limited; Vistoso Partners.

For full biographical listings, see the Martindale-Hubbell Law Directory

MUNGER AND MUNGER, P.L.C. (AV)

333 North Wilmot, Suite 300, 85711
Telephone: 520-721-1900
Fax: 520-747-1550
Northwest Tucson Office: 6700 N. Oracle Road, Suite 411, Tucson 85704.
Telephone: 520-797-7173.
Fax: 520-797-7178.

John F. Munger	Clark W. Munger (Resident, Northwest Tucson Office)

Philip Kimble	Joy Athena
Karen S. Haller	Robert K. Lewis
Susan Gaylord Willis	Craig Wisnom (Resident,
Mark Edward Chadwick	Northwest Tucson Office)
	Thomas A. Denker

OF COUNSEL

Doris Bates (Resident, Northwest Tucson Office)

Representative Clients: Jones Intercable; The Nature Conservancy; Tucson Greyhound Park; Tucson Realty and Trust; Associated Dermatologists; Red Rock Cattle Co.; U.S Rentals, Inc.; Nor-Tec Inc.; Grapevine Canyon Ranch; The Winters Co.

For full biographical listings, see the Martindale-Hubbell Law Directory

DANIEL H. O'CONNELL, P.C. (AV)

Suite 510, 6245 East Broadway, 85711
Telephone: 520-790-2535
Telefax: 520-571-8148

Daniel H. O'Connell

Benjamin J. Burnside

OF COUNSEL

Rosanne F. Lapan

Representative Clients: Empire West Cos.; Southwest Energy, Inc.; Alban Medical Associates; Industrial Motor & Control, Inc.; Allergy Asthma Associates, P.C.
Reference: Bank of America.

For full biographical listings, see the Martindale-Hubbell Law Directory

O'CONNOR CAVANAGH MOLLOY JONES, A PROFESSIONAL ASSOCIATION (AV)

Suite 2100 33 N. Stone, P.O. Box 2268, 85702
Telephone: 520-622-3531
FAX: 520-624-2816
Email: firminfo@arizlaw.com
Phoenix, Arizona Office: O'Connor, Cavanagh, Anderson, Killingsworth & Beshears, One East Camelback Road, Suite 1100, 85012.
Telephone: 602-263-2400.
FAX: 602-263-2900.
Sun City, Arizona Office: O'Connor, Cavanagh, Anderson, Killingsworth & Beshears, 13250 North Del Webb Boulevard, Suite B, 85351.
Telephone: 602-263-2808.
FAX: 602-933-3100.
Nogales, Arizona Office: O'Connor, Cavanagh, Anderson, Killingsworth & Beshears, 1891 North Mastick Way, 85621.
Telephone: 520-761-4215.
FAX: 520-761-3505.

Drue A. Morgan-Birch

Representative Clients: Three-Five Systems; Main Street & Main; ITT Cannon; Bank of America; The Dial Corp; The Hartford; Dow Corning Corp.; Charles Schwab & Co., Inc.

For Complete List of Firm Personnel, See General Section

For full biographical listings, see the Martindale-Hubbell Law Directory

Tucson—Continued

RAVEN, KIRSCHNER & NORELL, P.C. (AV)

Suite 1600, One South Church Avenue, 85701-1612
Telephone: 520-628-8700
Telefax: 520-798-5200

Andrew Oldland Norell	S. Leonard Scheff
Mark B. Raven	Stephen A. Thomas

Representative Clients: Continental Medical Systems, Inc.; El Paso Natural Gas Co.; Norwest Bank Arizona; El Rio-Santa Cruz Neighborhood Health Center, Inc.; Resolution Trust Corp.; Sierra Vista Community Hospital; Southern Arizona Rehabilitation Hospital; Northern Cochise Community Hospital.

For Complete List of Firm Personnel, See General Section

For full biographical listings, see the Martindale-Hubbell Law Directory

SNELL & WILMER, L.L.P. (AV)

1500 Norwest Tower, One South Church Avenue, 85701-1612
Telephone: 520-882-1200
Fax: 520-884-1294
Phoenix, Arizona Office: One Arizona Center, 85004-0001.
Telephone: 602-382-6000.
Fax: 602-382-6070.
Orange County Office: 1920 Main Street, Suite 1200, P.O. Box 57062, Irvine, California, 92619-7062.
Telephone: 714-253-2700
Fax: 714-955-2507.
Salt Lake City, Utah Office: Broadway Centre, 111 East Broadway, Suite 900, 84111- 1004.
Telephone: 801-237-1900.
Fax: 801-237-1950.

MEMBERS OF FIRM

Michael S. Milroy	Curt D. Reimann

Representative Clients: The Estes Company; Perini Land and Development Company; Ramada, Inc. (now AZTAR Corporation); Rosehaugh/Montleigh Associates; The Symington Company; Talley Industries; Toyota Technical Center, Inc.; Tucson Airport Authority; Bank One, Arizona, NA.; Zev Bufman Sports, Entertainment and Facility Development Group.

For full biographical listings, see the Martindale-Hubbell Law Directory

YUMA,* Yuma Co.

BYRNE & BENESCH, P.C. (AV)

230 W. Morrison Street, P.O. Box 6446, 85364
Telephone: 520-782-1805
Fax: 520-782-1808

Peter C. Byrne (1916-1994)	Pamela Walsma
Wayne C. Benesch	Arturo I. Villarreal

For full biographical listings, see the Martindale-Hubbell Law Directory

ARKANSAS

LITTLE ROCK,* Pulaski Co.

ARNOLD, GROBMYER & HALEY, A PROFESSIONAL ASSOCIATION (AV)

875 Union National Plaza, 124 West Capitol Avenue, P.O. Box 70, 72203
Telephone: 501-376-1171
Fax: 501-375-3548

Benjamin F. Arnold	Richard L. Ramsay
Joe A. Polk	Robert R. Ross

OF COUNSEL
John H. Haley

For Complete List of Firm Personnel, See General Section

For full biographical listings, see the Martindale-Hubbell Law Directory

RICHARD C. DOWNING, P.A. (AV)

Lafayette Building, Suite 750, 523 South Louisiana, 72201
Telephone: 501-372-2066
FAX: 501-376-6420
Email: RCDown@aol.com

Richard C. Downing

For full biographical listings, see the Martindale-Hubbell Law Directory

HOOVER & KOOISTRA (AV)

111 Center Street, 11th Floor, 72201-4445
Telephone: 501-376-8500
Facsimile: 501-372-3255

(See Next Column)

MEMBERS OF FIRM

Paul W. Hoover, Jr.	John Kooistra, III
	Max C. Mehlburger

For full biographical listings, see the Martindale-Hubbell Law Directory

WILLIAM L. OWEN (AV)

The Fones House, 902 West Second, P.O. Box 989, 72203
Telephone: 501-372-1655
Fax: 501-372-7884

For full biographical listings, see the Martindale-Hubbell Law Directory

ROSE LAW FIRM, A PROFESSIONAL ASSOCIATION (AV)

120 East Fourth Street, 72201
Telephone: 501-375-9131
Telecopy: 501-375-1309

George E. Campbell	Kevin R. Burns
Herbert C. Rule, III	John T. Hardin
Garland J. Garrett	Stephen N. Joiner
Thomas P. Thrash	Brian Rosenthal
J. Scott Schallhorn	

Deanna J. Weisse

Representative Clients: ALLTEL Corporation; The Equitable Life Assurance Society of the United States; John Hancock Mutual Life Insurance Co.; Harvest Foods, Inc.; Massachusetts Mutual Life Assurance Co.; Mercantile Bank of Central Arkansas; Panhandle Eastern Corp.; Tramell Crow Companies; Tyson Foods, Inc.

For Complete List of Firm Personnel, See General Section

For full biographical listings, see the Martindale-Hubbell Law Directory

CALIFORNIA

ALISO VIEJO, Orange Co.

WORDES, WILSHIN, GOREN & CONNER (AV)

31 Journey Street, Suite 120, 92656-3334
Telephone: 714-643-1000
Telecopier: 714-643-2000
Email: firm@wwgc.com *URL:* http://www.wwgc.com

MEMBERS OF FIRM

Richard S. Wordes	Michael E. Goren
David B. Wilshin	Frank A. Conner

For full biographical listings, see the Martindale-Hubbell Law Directory

BAKERSFIELD,* Kern Co.

KLEIN, WEGIS, DeNATALE, GOLDNER & MUIR, LLP (AV)

A Partnership including Professional Corporations
(Formerly Di Giorgio, Davis, Klein, Wegis, Duggan & Friedman)
ARCO Tower, 4550 California Avenue, Second Floor, P.O. Box 11172, 93389-1172
Telephone: 805-395-1000
Telecopier: 805-326-0418
Email: kwdgm@kwdgm.com

MEMBERS OF FIRM

Anthony J. Klein (Inc.)	Barry L. Goldner
Thomas V. DeNatale, Jr.	David J. Cooper
Claude P. Kimball	

Representative Clients: World Title Company; Transamerica Title Insurance Company; The Prudential America West.

For Complete List of Firm Personnel, See General Section

For full biographical listings, see the Martindale-Hubbell Law Directory

BEVERLY HILLS, Los Angeles Co.

DAPEER, ROSENBLIT & LITVAK, LLP (AV)

9460 Wilshire Boulevard, Fifth Floor, 90212
Telephone: 310-203-8200; 310-777-6676
Fax: 310-203-8213; 310-777-6675
Metropolitan Cities Office: 2770 East Slauson Avenue, P.O. Box 2067, Huntington Park, 90255.
Telephone: 213-587-5221.
Fax: 213-587-4190.

William Litvak	Steven H. Rosenblit
	Kenneth B. Dapeer

For full biographical listings, see the Martindale-Hubbell Law Directory

SAMUEL D. INGHAM, III (AV)

Suite 830, 8383 Wilshire Boulevard, 90211-2407
Telephone: 213-651-5980
FAX: 213-651-5725
Email: sdiesq@aol.com

For full biographical listings, see the Martindale-Hubbell Law Directory

JACOBSON, SANDERS & BORDY, LLP (AV)

A Partnership including a Professional Corporation
9777 Wilshire Boulevard, Suite 718, 90212-1907
Telephone: 310-777-7488

MEMBERS OF FIRM

Lawrence H. Jacobson (A P.C.)   Michael J. Bordy
Michael R. E. Sanders

OF COUNSEL

David S. White   Patricia B. Kolber

For full biographical listings, see the Martindale-Hubbell Law Directory

SCHWARTZ, WISOT & WILSON, LLP (AV)

Suite 315, 315 South Beverly Drive, 90212
Telephone: 310-277-2323
Fax: 310-556-2308

Bruce Edward Schwartz   John D. Wilson
Valerie Wisot   Kathleen A. Calaway

OF COUNSEL
Paula Reddish Zinnemann

Reference: Great Western Bank (Century City Office, Los Angeles, California)

For full biographical listings, see the Martindale-Hubbell Law Directory

TURNER, GERSTENFELD, WILK, AUBERT & YOUNG, LLP (AV)

Formerly Turner, Gerstenfeld, Wilk & Tigerman
Suite 510, 8383 Wilshire Boulevard, 90211
Telephone: 213-653-3900
Facsimile: 213-653-3021

MEMBERS OF FIRM

Rubin M. Turner   Ronald D. Aubert
Gerald F. Gerstenfeld   Steven E. Young
Barry R. Wilk   Edward Friedman
Linda Wight Mazur

ASSOCIATES

Dortha Larene Pyles   Diane H. Pappas

OF COUNSEL
Bert Z. Tigerman

For Complete List of Firm Personnel, See General Section

For full biographical listings, see the Martindale-Hubbell Law Directory

WILNER, KLEIN & SIEGEL, A PROFESSIONAL CORPORATION (AV)

Suite 700, 9601 Wilshire Boulevard, 90210
Telephone: 213-272-8631; 310-550-4595
Facsimile: 213-272-4339
Brea, California Office: 3230 East Imperial Highway, Suite 309.
Telephone: 714-579-2600.
Facsimile: 714-579-2549.

Walter Klein   Wendy A. Goldberg
Samuel Wilner   Jodi Zucker Taksar
Leonard Siegel   Edward E. Wallace
Laura J. Snoke   Alan Goldberg
Joseph R. Serpico

Gary S. Kessler   Patrick M. Malone
Marc H. Goldsmith   Nora J. Hite
Floyd W. Cranmore   Mitchell S. Brachman
Teri E. Lawson   Stephen Coopersmith
Edwin J. Howard   Neil M. Popowitz
Thomas M. Ware, II   Jeffrey W. Deane
Joshua B. Bereny   Steven J. Parker
James P. Dexheimer   (Resident, Brea Office)
Eric S. Blum   Darrell J. Mariz
    (Resident, Brea Office)

OF COUNSEL

Allan E. Wilion, Inc.   Michael J. Grobaty
Richard B. Kott   (Resident, Brea Office)
    (Resident, Brea Office)

Reference: Mitsui Manufacturers Bank.

For full biographical listings, see the Martindale-Hubbell Law Directory

---

CARLSBAD, San Diego Co.

WEIL & WRIGHT (AV)

1921 Palomar Oaks Way, Suite 301, 92008
Telephone: 619-438-1214
Telefax: 619-438-2666

Paul M. Weil   David A. Ebersole
Archie T. Wright III   John F. Hilbert

For full biographical listings, see the Martindale-Hubbell Law Directory

CHICO, Butte Co.

STEWART, HUMPHERYS, BURCHETT, SANDELMAN & MOLIN (AV)

Suite 6, 3120 Cohasset Road, P.O. Box 720, 95927
Telephone: 916-891-6111
Telecopier: 916-894-2103
Email: shbsm@sunset.net

MEMBERS OF FIRM

Ronald E. Stewart   Raymond L. Sandelman
Keith S. Humpherys   Richard J. Molin
Alan E. Burchett   Carol J. Tener
Stephen P. Trover

Representative Clients: North State National Bank; Northern California Federal Land Bank; Northern California Production Credit Assn.; Drake Homes, Avag, Inc.; Meeks Building Center; Land's End Real Estate, Inc.

For full biographical listings, see the Martindale-Hubbell Law Directory

COSTA MESA, Orange Co.

ALBERT, WEILAND & GOLDEN (AV)

Center Tower, 650 Town Center Drive, Suite 1350, 92626
Telephone: 714-966-10000
FAX: 714-966-1002
Email: awglawyers@aol.com

Theodor C. Albert   Jennifer Ann Golison
Michael J. Weiland   Evan D. Smiley
Jeffrey I. Golden   Lei Lei Wang Ekvall
Philip E. Strok

For full biographical listings, see the Martindale-Hubbell Law Directory

COULOMBE & KOTTKE, A PROFESSIONAL CORPORATION (AV)

Comerica Bank Tower, 611 Anton Boulevard, Suite 1260, 92626
Telephone: 714-540-1234
Fax: 714-754-0808; 714-754-0707
Email: c-k@coulombe.com

Ronald B. Coulombe   Jon S. Kottke

COUNSEL
Roy B. Woolsey

LEGAL SUPPORT PERSONNEL

PARALEGALS

Vicky M. Pearson   Abeer F. Rider

LEGAL ADMINISTRATOR
Yvonne Mendoza

For full biographical listings, see the Martindale-Hubbell Law Directory

RUTAN & TUCKER, LLP (AV)

A Partnership including Professional Corporations
611 Anton Boulevard, Suite 1400, P.O. Box 1950, 92626
Telephone: 714-641-5100; 213-625-7586
Telecopier: 714-546-9035
Email: rutan&tucker@mcimail.com *URL:* http://www.rutan.com

MEMBERS OF FIRM

James R. Moore (P.C.)   Jeffrey M. Oderman (P.C.)
William R. Biel   Marcia A. Forsyth
Richard A. Curnutt   Anne Nelson Lanphar
John B. Hurlbut, Jr.   Randall M. Babbush
Michael W. Immell   Mary M. Green
Richard P. Sims   Mark B. Frazier
Edward D. Sybesma, Jr., (P.C.)   Lori Sarner Smith
Thomas S. Salinger (P.C.)   Kim D. Thompson
Michael D. Rubin   Stephen A. Ellis
Ira G. Rivin (P.C.)   Adam N. Volkert
F. Kevin Brazil

ASSOCIATES

Debra Dunn Steel   Paul J. Sievers
David H. Hochner   Joseph Louis Maga III
Patrick D. McCalla   Kraig C. Kilger
Robert Elliot Adel II

For Complete List of Firm Personnel, See General Section

For full biographical listings, see the Martindale-Hubbell Law Directory

EL MONTE, Los Angeles Co.

MICHAEL B. MONTGOMERY A LAW CORPORATION (AV)

10501 Valley Boulevard, Suite 121, 91731
Telephone: 818-452-1222
Fax: 818-452-8323
Ft. Lauderdale, Florida Office: Justice Building, 524 S. Andrews Avenue, Suite 320 N.
Telephone: 954-522-9441.
Fax: 954-522-2076.

Michael B. Montgomery

Reference: Bank of America (San Marino Branch).

For full biographical listings, see the Martindale-Hubbell Law Directory

---

ENCINO, Los Angeles Co.

AARONSON & AARONSON (AV)

16133 Ventura Boulevard, Suite 1080, 91436
Telephone: 818-783-3858; 818-783-0444
Fax: 818-783-3873; 818-783-3825

MEMBERS OF FIRM

Edward D. Aaronson   Arthur Aaronson

ASSOCIATE

Steven J. Berman

For full biographical listings, see the Martindale-Hubbell Law Directory

ALPERT, BARR AND GROSS, A PROFESSIONAL LAW CORPORATION (AV)

Encino Office Park I, Suite 300, 6345 Balboa Boulevard, 91316-1523
Telephone: 818-881-5000
Fax: 818-881-1150

Lee Kanon Alpert   Mark S. Blackman
Gary L. Barr   Michael N. Balikian
Lisa W. Glazener   Judith R. Simon
Mark P. Gross   Jack S. Mack

OF COUNSEL

Charles M. Hughes   Leonard S. Levy (A Professional Corporation)

For full biographical listings, see the Martindale-Hubbell Law Directory

---

FRESNO,* Fresno Co.

DOWLING, AARON & KEELER, INCORPORATED (AV)

Suite 200, 6051 North Fresno Street, 93710
Telephone: 209-432-4500
Fax: 209-432-4590
Email: dowling-law.com

Michael D. Dowling   Bruce S. Fraser
Richard M. Aaron   John C. Ganahl
Christopher A. Brown

OF COUNSEL

Morris M. Sherr

Reference: Wells Fargo Bank (Main).

For Complete List of Firm Personnel, See General Section

For full biographical listings, see the Martindale-Hubbell Law Directory

KIMBLE, MacMICHAEL & UPTON, A PROFESSIONAL CORPORATION (AV)

Fig Garden Financial Center, 5260 North Palm Avenue, Suite 221, P.O. Box 9489, 93792-9489
Telephone: 209-435-5500
Telecopier: 209-435-1500
Email: kmu@primenet.com

Joseph C. Kimble (1910-1972)   Robert H. Scribner
Thomas A. MacMichael   Michael E. Moss
 (1920-1990)   Mark D. Miller
Jon Wallace Upton   Michael F. Tatham
Robert E. Bergin   W. Richard Lee
Jeffrey G. Boswell   D. Tyler Tharpe
Steven D. McGee   Sylvia Halkousis Coyle
Robert E. Ward   S. Brett Sutton
John P. Eleazarian   Michael J. Jurkovich

Douglas V. Thornton   Susan King Hatmaker
Robert William Branch   Lawrence J. Salisbury
Donald J. Pool   Daniel R. Foster
Meredith E. Allen

OF COUNSEL

Mary Ann Bluhm

For full biographical listings, see the Martindale-Hubbell Law Directory

LANG, RICHERT & PATCH, A PROFESSIONAL CORPORATION (AV)

Fig Garden Financial Center, 5200 North Palm Avenue, 4th Floor, P.O. Box 40012, 93755
Telephone: 209-228-6700
Fax: 209-228-6727

Frank H. Lang   Victoria J. Salisch
William T. Richert (1937-1993) Bradley A. Silva
Robert L. Patch, II   Charles Trudrung Taylor
Val W. Saldaña   Mark L. Creede
Douglas E. Noll   Peter N. Zeitler
Michael T. Hertz   Charles L. Doerksen

Laurie L. Quigley   Nabil E. Zumout
Douglas E. Griffin   Shawn H. Alikian
Thomas E. Gauthier

References: Wells Fargo Bank (Fresno Main Office).

For full biographical listings, see the Martindale-Hubbell Law Directory

---

GLENDALE, Los Angeles Co.

BAKER, OLSON, LeCROY & DANIELIAN, A LAW CORPORATION (AV)

144 North Brand Boulevard, P.O. Box 29062, 91209-9062
Telephone: 818-502-5600
Facsimile: 818-241-2653

Sheldon S. Baker   Charles L. LeCroy, III
Eric Olson   Arsen Danielian

Michael S. Simon

OF COUNSEL

John J. Jacobson

For full biographical listings, see the Martindale-Hubbell Law Directory

GREENWALD, HOFFMAN & MEYER (AV)

500 North Brand Boulevard, Suite 920, 91203-1904
Telephone: 818-507-8100; 213-381-1131
Fax: 818-507-8484

MEMBERS OF FIRM

Guy Preston Greenwald, Jr.   Donald M. Hoffman
 (1914-1984)   Lawrence F. Meyer
Raul M. Montes

ASSOCIATE

Jeanne Burns-Haindel

References: Bank of America (Los Angeles and Pasadena Trust Offices); Northern Trust of California (Headquarters Office); Bank of America (Glendale Main Branch).

For full biographical listings, see the Martindale-Hubbell Law Directory

IRSFELD, IRSFELD & YOUNGER LLP (AV)

A Partnership including Professional Corporations
Suite 900, 100 West Broadway, 91210-1296
Telephone: 818-242-6859
Fax: 818-240-7728
Email: 104736.1745@compuserver.com

MEMBERS OF FIRM

James B. Irsfeld (1880-1966) Peter J. Irsfeld (P.C.)
Kenneth C. Younger   James J. Waldorf (P.C.)
 (1922-1996)   C. Phillip Jackson (P.C.)
John H. Brink (P.C.)   Norman H. Green (P.C.)
Kathryn E. Van Houten

ASSOCIATES

Peter C. Wright   Diane L. Walker

RETIRED

James B. Irsfeld, Jr.

Representative Clients: Lear Sieglar, Inc.; Chrysler Credit Corp.
References: First Interstate Bank (Glendale Main Office); Bank of Hollywood.

For full biographical listings, see the Martindale-Hubbell Law Directory

LASKIN & GRAHAM (AV)

Suite 840, 800 North Brand Boulevard, 91203
Telephone: 213-665-6955; 818-547-4800; 714-957-3031
Telecopier: 818-547-3100

OF COUNSEL

Richard Laskin

(See Next Column)

LASKIN & GRAHAM, *Glendale—Continued*

MEMBERS OF FIRM

Arnold K. Graham   Michael Anthony Cisneros
Susan L. Vaage   Gregson M. Perry
John S. Peterson   Lynn I. Ibara

For full biographical listings, see the Martindale-Hubbell Law Directory

O'ROURKE, ALLAN & FONG (AV)

3rd Floor, 104 North Belmont, P.O. Box 10220, 91209-3220
Telephone: 818-247-4303
Fax: 818-247-1451

MEMBERS OF FIRM

Denis M. O'Rourke   Joan H. Allan
Roderick D. Fong

ASSOCIATE

Denise Michelle O'Rourke

References: Verdugo Banking Co. (Glendale, California); Community Bank (Glendale, California).

For full biographical listings, see the Martindale-Hubbell Law Directory

INDIAN WELLS, Riverside Co.

DOUGLAS MARTIN A LAW CORPORATION (AV)

Wall Street West, 74-785 Highway 111, Suite 201, 92210
Telephone: 619-776-1377
Fax: 619-776-1380

Douglas Martin

LEGAL SUPPORT PERSONNEL

Carol A. Moreno

For full biographical listings, see the Martindale-Hubbell Law Directory

IRVINE, Orange Co.

BARNES, CROSBY, FITZGERALD & ZEMAN (AV)

2030 Main Street, Suite 1050, 92614
Telephone: 714-852-1100
Fax: 714-852-1501

MEMBERS OF FIRM

Robert Samuel Barnes   Larry S. Zeman
William M. Crosby   Mark H. Cheung
Michael J. FitzGerald   Alka N. Patel

OF COUNSEL

Frederick J. Stemmler

For full biographical listings, see the Martindale-Hubbell Law Directory

BARNETT & RUBIN, A PROFESSIONAL CORPORATION (AV)

2 Park Plaza, Suite 980, 92614
Telephone: 714-261-9700
Facsimile: 714-261-9799
Email: Lawyers@Pacbell.net

Richard L. Barnett   Jeffrey D. Rubin

Kathryn B. Salmond

For full biographical listings, see the Martindale-Hubbell Law Directory

BORCHARD & WILLOUGHBY, A PROFESSIONAL CORPORATION (AV)

18881 Von Karman Avenue, Suite 1400, 92612
Telephone: 714-644-6161
Fax: 714-263-1913

Michael D. Borchard   Michael L. Willoughby
Mark A. Rodriguez

Stephanie A. Pittaluga

For full biographical listings, see the Martindale-Hubbell Law Directory

CALLAHAN & BLAINE, A PROFESSIONAL LAW CORPORATION (AV)

Suite 800, 18500 Von Karman, 92612
Telephone: 714-553-1155
Fax: 714-553-0784
Email: info@callahan-law.com

Daniel J. Callahan (A   Stephen E. Blaine
Professional Corporation)

Kathleen L. Dunham   Andrew A. Smits
Jim P. Mahacek   Gary S. Spitzer
Michael J. Sachs   Edward Susolik
Graig R. Woodburn

(See Next Column)

OF COUNSEL

Shelley M. Liberto   Walt D. Mahaffa

For full biographical listings, see the Martindale-Hubbell Law Directory

JACKSON, DEMARCO & PECKENPAUGH, A LAW CORPORATION (AV)

4 Park Plaza, 16th Floor, P.O. Box 19704, 92714
Telephone: 714-752-8585
Fax: 714-752-0597

Lance A. Adair   Roger A. Grad
Marc D. Alexander   William Michael Hensley
Thomas D. Arnold   Darren L. Hereford
Diane P. Carey   Joan M. Huckabone
Brian W. Casserly   F. Scott Jackson
John W. Cochrane   Andrew V. Leitch
John C. Condas   Thomas D. Peckenpaugh
James R. DeMarco   John Petrasich
Steven J. Dzida   Andrew C. Schutz
Roger M. Franks   David C. Smith
Helene Z. Fransz   Douglas P. Smith
Edward A. Galloway   Jay R. Steinman
Michael L. Tidus

LEGAL SUPPORT PERSONNEL

Lavon DeGraw

For full biographical listings, see the Martindale-Hubbell Law Directory

MARK A. KOMPA (AV)

2603 Main Street, Suite 1170, 92714
Telephone: 714-250-9500
Facsimile: 714-250-9515

For full biographical listings, see the Martindale-Hubbell Law Directory

MCKENNA & STAHL (AV)

2603 Main Street, Suite 1010, 92614-6232
Telephone: 714-752-2800
Facsimile: 714-752-6723

Charles A. McKenna, Jr.   Harry S. Stahl

OF COUNSEL

Christopher E. Call

For full biographical listings, see the Martindale-Hubbell Law Directory

WATT, TIEDER & HOFFAR, L.L.P. (AV ⓣ)

3 Park Plaza, Suite 1530, 92714
Telephone: 714-852-6700
Telecopier: 714-261-0771
McLean Virginia Office: 7929 Westpark Drive, Suite 400,
Telephone: 703-749-1000.
Telecopier: 703-893-8029.
Washington, D.C. Office: 601 Pennsylvania Avenue, N.W. Suite 900,
Telephone: 202-462-4697.

MEMBERS OF FIRM

John B. Tieder, Jr.   Michael G. Long
(Not admitted in CA)   Christopher P. Pappas
Robert M. Fitzgerald
(Not admitted in CA)

ASSOCIATE

Gregory John Dukellis

For full biographical listings, see the Martindale-Hubbell Law Directory

LA JOLLA, San Diego Co.

LAW OFFICES OF MAURILE C. TREMBLAY A PROFESSIONAL CORPORATION (AV)

4180 La Jolla Village Drive, Suite 210, 92037
Telephone: 619-558-3030
FAX: 619-558-2502

Maurile C. Tremblay   Mark D. Estle

For full biographical listings, see the Martindale-Hubbell Law Directory

LONG BEACH, Los Angeles Co.

CAMERON, MADDEN, PEARLSON, GALE & SELLARS (AV)

One World Trade Center Suite 1600, 90831-1600
Telephone: 310-436-3888
Telecopier: 310-437-1967

MEMBERS OF THE FIRM

Timothy C. Cameron   Patrick T. Madden
Charles M. Gale   Paul R. Pearlson
James D. Sellars

(See Next Column)

CAMERON, MADDEN, PEARLSON, GALE & SELLARS—Continued
ASSOCIATE
Lillian D. Salinger

For full biographical listings, see the Martindale-Hubbell Law Directory

TAUBMAN, SIMPSON, YOUNG & SULENTOR (AV)

249 East Ocean Boulevard, Suite 700, P.O. Box 22670, 90801-5670
Telephone: 310-436-9201
FAX: 310-590-9695

E. C. Denio (1864-1952)	Richard G. Wilson (1928-1993)
Geo. A. Hart (1881-1967)	Roger W. Young
Geo. P. Taubman, Jr.	William J. Sulentor
(1897-1970)	Peter M. Williams
Matthew C. Simpson	Scott R. Magee
(1900-1988)	Maria M. Rohaidy

Stuart C. Talley

Attorneys for: Bixby Land Co.; Renick Cadillac, Inc.; Oil Operators Inc.
Local Counsel: Crown Cork & Seal Co., Inc.

For full biographical listings, see the Martindale-Hubbell Law Directory

LOS ALTOS, Santa Clara Co.

MALOVOS & KONEVICH (AV)

Los Altos Plaza, 5150 El Camino Real, Suite A-22, 94022
Telephone: 415-988-9700
Facsimile: 415-988-9639

Marian Malovos Konevich   Robert W. Konevich
RETIRED FOUNDING PARTNER
Kenneth R. Malovos

For full biographical listings, see the Martindale-Hubbell Law Directory

LOS ANGELES,* Los Angeles Co.

BAKER & HOSTETLER (AV)

600 Wilshire Boulevard, 90017-3212
Telephone: 213-624-2400
FAX: 213-975-1740
In Cleveland, Ohio: 3200 National City Center, 1900 East Ninth Street.
Telephone: 216-621-0200.
In Columbus, Ohio: Capitol Square, Suite 2100, 65 East State Street.
Telephone: 614-228-1541.
In Denver, Colorado: 303 East 17th Avenue, Suite 1100.
Telephone: 303-861-0600.
In Houston, Texas: 1000 Louisiana, Suite 2000.
Telephone: 713-236-0020.
In Long Beach, California: 300 Oceangate, Suite 620.
Telephone: 310-432-2827.
In Orlando, Florida: SunBank Center, Suite 2300, 200 South Orange Avenue.
Telephone: 407-649-4000.
In Washington, D. C.: Washington Square, Suite 1100, 1050 Connecticut Avenue, N. W.
Telephone: 202-861-1500.
In College Park, Maryland: 9658 Baltimore Boulevard, Suite 206.
Telephone: 301-441-2781.
In Alexandria, Virginia: 437 North Lee Street.
Telephone: 703-549-1294.
In San Francisco, California: One Sansome Street, Suite 2000.
Telephone: 415-951-4705.

PARTNERS
Byron Hayes, Jr.   Thomas G. Roberts
David C. Sampson

For Complete List of Firm Personnel, See General Section

For full biographical listings, see the Martindale-Hubbell Law Directory

BAKER AND JACOBSON, A PROFESSIONAL CORPORATION (AV)

Suite 500, 11377 West Olympic Boulevard, 90064-1683
Telephone: 310-914-7990
Fax: 310-914-7913

Robert P. Baker   Lawrence M. Jacobson

For full biographical listings, see the Martindale-Hubbell Law Directory

BERGMAN & WEDNER, INC. (AV)

Suite 900, 10880 Wilshire Boulevard, 90024
Telephone: 310-470-6110
Fax: Available on Request

Gregory M. Bergman	Robert M. Mason III
Gregory A. Wedner	Kristi Anne Sjoholm-Sierchio
Mark E. Fingerman	Keith A. Robinson
Alan Harvey Mittelman	John P. Dacey

(See Next Column)

John V. Tamborelli	Lisa S. Shukiar
Blithe Ann Smith	Daphne M. Humphreys

Suzanne Z. Shbaro
OF COUNSEL
Lloyd A. Bergman (1923-1994)   Jacob A. Wedner
SPECIAL COUNSEL
Richard V. Godino

For full biographical listings, see the Martindale-Hubbell Law Directory

MARTIN H. BLANK, JR. (AV)

11755 Wilshire Boulevard, Suite 1400, 90025-1520
Telephone: 310-477-5455
Fax: 310-444-9203
Email: marty@general.net

For full biographical listings, see the Martindale-Hubbell Law Directory

LAW OFFICES OF DAVID B. BLOOM A PROFESSIONAL CORPORATION (AV)

3325 Wilshire Boulevard, Ninth Floor, 90010
Telephone: 213-938-5248; 384-4088
Telecopier: 213-385-2009

David B. Bloom

Stephen S. Monroe (A	Susan Carole Jay
Professional Corporation)	Edward Idell
Raphael A. Rosemblat	Sandra Kamenir
James E. Adler	Steven Wayne Lazarus
Bonni S. Mantovani	Andrew Edward Briseno
Roy A. Levun	Harold C. Klaskin
Cherie S. Raidy	Shelley M. Gould
Jonathan Udell	Peter O. Israel

For full biographical listings, see the Martindale-Hubbell Law Directory

BRAND FARRAR DZIUBLA FREILICH & KOLSTAD, LLP (AV)

Counsellors at Law
515 South Flower Street, Suite 3500, 90071-2201
Telephone: 213-228-0288
Facsimile: 213-426-6222
Correspondent Offices: Hong Kong, Shanghai, Beijing, Guangzhou, Xiamen, Shenzhen, Ulaanbaatar, New York and San Francisco.

Michael A. Brand	Amy E. Freilich
David W. Farrar	Charles K. Kolstad
Robert W. Dziubla	Margaret G. Graf

OF COUNSEL

H. Bennett Arnberger	Julia Marie Shymansky
David C. Buxbaum	Yelena Yeruhim
Sherry L. Geyer	Norman A. Chernin
Manender M. Grewal (Not	Joan M. Marquardt
admitted in the United States)	

For full biographical listings, see the Martindale-Hubbell Law Directory

BUCHALTER, NEMER, FIELDS & YOUNGER, A PROFESSIONAL CORPORATION (AV)

24th Floor, 601 South Figueroa Street, 90017
Telephone: 213-891-0700
Fax: 213-896-0400
Email: buchalter@earthlink.net *URL:* http://www.buchalter.com
New York, New York Office: 15th Floor, 605 Third Avenue.
Telephone: 212-490-8600.
Fax: 212-490-6022.
San Francisco, California Office: 29th Floor, 333 Market Street.
Telephone: 415-227-0900.
Fax: 415-227-0770.
Newport Beach, California Office: Suite 1450, 620 Newport Center Drive.
Telephone: 714-760-1121.
Fax: 714-720-0182.

Gary A. York	Richard S. Angel
Kevin M. Brandt	Bryan Mashian

Dean Stackel	Shirley Sheau-Lih Lu
Mary LePique Dickson	Nicolas M. Kublicki

References: City National Bank; Wells Fargo Bank; Metrobank.

For Complete List of Firm Personnel, See General Section

For full biographical listings, see the Martindale-Hubbell Law Directory

J. T. CAIRNS & ASSOCIATES (AV)

200 North Larchmont Boulevard, 90004
Telephone: 213-962-5588
Telecopier: 213-463-4412

(See Next Column)

J. T. Cairns & Associates, *Los Angeles—Continued*
ASSOCIATE
Deann Hampton

For full biographical listings, see the Martindale-Hubbell Law Directory

CLARK & TREVITHICK, A PROFESSIONAL CORPORATION (AV)

800 Wilshire Boulevard, 12th Floor, 90017
Telephone: 213-629-5700
Telecopier: 213-624-9441
San Francisco, California Office: 456 Montgomery Street, 20th Floor.
Telephone: 415-288-6520.
Fax: 415-398-2820.

Donald P. Clark　　　　Kevin P. Fiore
Alexander C. McGilvray, Jr.　　James S. Arico
OF COUNSEL
John A. Tucker, Jr.

References: Wells Fargo Bank (Los Angeles Main Office); National Bank of California.

For Complete List of Firm Personnel, See General Section

For full biographical listings, see the Martindale-Hubbell Law Directory

PAUL N. CRANE (AV)

Suite 900, Two Century Plaza, 2049 Century Park East, 90067-3111
Telephone: 310-282-8118
FAX: 310-282-8077

For full biographical listings, see the Martindale-Hubbell Law Directory

DARLING, HALL & RAE (AV)

777 South Figueroa, 37th Floor, 90017
Telephone: 213-627-8104
Fax: 213-627-7795
Email: 71555.1466@Compuserve.com
MEMBERS OF FIRM
Hugh W. Darling (1901-1986)　　Donald Keith Hall (1918-1984)
Edward S. Shattuck (1901-1965)　Matthew S. Rae, Jr.
George Gaylord Gute　　　　Richard L. Stack
(1922-1981)　　　　　　Edwin Freston
OF COUNSEL
John L. Flowers

Reference: City National Bank (Pershing Square Office, Los Angeles, California).

For full biographical listings, see the Martindale-Hubbell Law Directory

DAVIS & FOX (AV)

1901 Avenue of the Stars, Suite 400, 90067
Telephone: 310-286-2915
Fax: 310-286-2916
MEMBERS OF FIRM
Calvin E. Davis　　　　Steven A. Fox
ASSOCIATES
Brian Aronson　　　　Amy L. Freisleben
Susan R. Peck
OF COUNSEL
Herbert D. Meyers

For full biographical listings, see the Martindale-Hubbell Law Directory

DEMETRIOU, DEL GUERCIO, SPRINGER & MOYER, LLP (AV)

801 South Grand Avenue, 10th Floor, 90017
Telephone: 213-624-8407
Telecopy: 213-624-0174
Email: ddsm@juno.com　*URL:* http://www.ddsm.com
MEMBERS OF FIRM
Jeffrey Z. B. Springer　　Stephen A. Del Guercio
Regina Liudzius Cobb
OF COUNSEL
Ronald J. Del Guercio

Reference: Bank of America, L.A. Main Office, Los Angeles, Calif.

For full biographical listings, see the Martindale-Hubbell Law Directory

FRIED, BIRD & CRUMPACKER, A PROFESSIONAL CORPORATION (AV)

10100 Santa Monica Boulevard, Suite 300, 90067-6031
Telephone: 310-551-7400
Facsimile: 310-556-4487

Jack Fried　　　　David W. Crumpacker, Jr.
Brian James Bird　　Nikki Wolontis
David M. Schachter

(See Next Column)

David K. Johnson

For full biographical listings, see the Martindale-Hubbell Law Directory

GOLDMAN & GORDON, L.L.P. (AV)

Suite 1920, 1801 Century Park East, 90067
Telephone: 310-277-7171
FAX: 310-277-1547
MEMBERS OF FIRM
A. S. Goldman (1895-1966)　　Leonard A. Goldman
Robert P. Gordon
ASSOCIATE
Melody G. Anderson

References: Bank of America, Fourth and Spring Branch, Los Angeles; Bank of America, Wilshire-San Vincente Branch, Beverly Hills.

For full biographical listings, see the Martindale-Hubbell Law Directory

GOLDMAN & KAGON, LAW CORPORATION (AV)

1801 Century Park East, Suite 2222, 90067
Telephone: 310-552-1707
Telecopier: 310-552-7938

Mark A. Goldman　　　Richard D. Goldman
Charles D. Meyer

For Complete List of Firm Personnel, See General Section

For full biographical listings, see the Martindale-Hubbell Law Directory

EARLE GARY GOODMAN (AV)

2934 1/2 Beverly Glenn Circle Suite 395, 90077
Telephone: 310-470-9033
Fax: 310-470-3494
Email: 23852@MSN.com

Reference: Bank of America, Westwood Village Office.

For full biographical listings, see the Martindale-Hubbell Law Directory

HANNA AND MORTON (AV)

A Partnership including Professional Corporations
Seventeenth Floor, Wilshire-Grand Building, 600 Wilshire Boulevard, 90017
Telephone: 213-628-7131
Facsimile: 213-623-3379
MEMBERS OF FIRM
James P. Modisette　　　Judith A. Lower
ASSOCIATE
Michael P. Wippler

For Complete List of Firm Personnel, See General Section

For full biographical listings, see the Martindale-Hubbell Law Directory

HILL, FARRER & BURRILL LLP (AV)

A Limited Liability Partnership including Professional Corporations
35th Floor, Union Bank Square, 445 South Figueroa Street, 90071
Telephone: 213-620-0460
Fax: 213-624-4840
MEMBERS OF FIRM
Wm. Harold Borthwick (P.C.)　　Alfred M. Clark, III
Michelle A. Meghrouni

For Complete List of Firm Personnel, See General Section

For full biographical listings, see the Martindale-Hubbell Law Directory

JONES, KAUFMAN & ACKERMAN LLP (AV)

10960 Wilshire Boulevard, Suite 1225, 90024
Telephone: 310-477-8575
Fax: 310-477-8768

Donald H. Jones　　　Michael S. Ackerman
Paul W. Kaufman　　　Marc H. Corman
Ellen Roth Nagler

For full biographical listings, see the Martindale-Hubbell Law Directory

KOSLOV & MEDLEN (AV)

30141 Agoura Road, Suite 200, 91301-4334
Telephone: 818-597-9996
FAX: 818-597-8848
MEMBERS OF FIRM
John Koslov　　　　William P. Medlen
ASSOCIATE
Sabrina Simmons-Brill

For full biographical listings, see the Martindale-Hubbell Law Directory

Los Angeles—Continued

KU, FONG, LARSEN & CHEN, LLP (AV)

523 West Sixth Street, Suite 528, 90014
Telephone: 213-488-1400
Telecopier: 213-236-9235

MEMBERS OF FIRM

H. G. Robert Fong   Paul A. Larsen
Frank W. Chen

OF COUNSEL
Edward Y. Ku

ASSOCIATES

Jack S. Yeh   Victor S. Sze

For full biographical listings, see the Martindale-Hubbell Law Directory

LOEB & LOEB LLP (AV)

A Limited Liability Partnership including Professional Corporations
Suite 1800, 1000 Wilshire Boulevard, 90017-2475
Telephone: 213-688-3400
Facsimile: 213-688-3460; 688-3461; 688-3462
Century City, California Office: Suite 2200, 10100 Santa Monica
Boulevard, Los Angeles, 90067-4164.
Telephone: 310-282-2000.
Facsimile: 310-282-2191; 282-2192.
New York, N.Y. Office: 345 Park Avenue, 10154-0037.
Telephone: 212-407-4000.
Facsimile: 212-407-4990.
Washington, D.C. Office: Suite 601, 2100 M Street N.W., 20037-1207.
Telephone: 202-223-5700.
Facsimile: 202-223-5704.
Nashville, Tennessee Office: 45 Music Square West, 37203-3205.
Telephone: 615-749-8300;
Facsimile: 615-749-8308.
Rome, Italy Office: Piazza Digione 1, 00197.
Telephone: 011-396-808-8456.
Facsimile: 011-396-808-8288.

MEMBERS OF FIRM

Michael D. Beck   James D. Friedman
   (New York City Office)   Joseph P. Heffernan (A P.C.)
Maribeth A. Borthwick   Irv Hepner
   (Century City Office)   (New York City Office)
Frank E. Feder (A P.C.)   Michael Bryce Kinney
   (Century City and New York   (New York City Office)
   Offices)   Michael Langs
David C. Fischer   Andrew E. Lippmann
   (New York City Office)   (New York City Office)
Kenneth D. Freeman   Susan V. Noonoo
   (New York City Office)   Jonathan P. Roth

OF COUNSEL
Gerald D. Kleinman (A P.C.) (Century City Office)

For Complete List of Firm Personnel, See General Section

For full biographical listings, see the Martindale-Hubbell Law Directory

MAHONEY, COPPENRATH, JAFFE & PEARSON LLP (AV)

A Partnership including Professional Corporations
2049 Century Park East, Suite 2480, 90067-3283
Telephone: 310-557-1919
Telecopier: 310-277-6536

MEMBERS OF FIRM

James E. Mahoney (P.C.)   Ronald C. Pearson
Walter G. Coppenrath, Jr.,   Daryl G. Parker
   (P.C.)   Charles L. Grotts
Howard M. Jaffe (P.C.)   Arthur L. Martin

OF COUNSEL
Gerald Lee Tahajian

Reference: First Professional Bank, Santa Monica, California.

For full biographical listings, see the Martindale-Hubbell Law Directory

MINTON, MINTON AND RAND LLP (AV)

510 West Sixth Street, 90014
Telephone: 213-624-9394
Fax: 213-624-9323

MEMBERS OF FIRM

Carl W. Minton (1902-1974)   Carl Minton
David E. Rand

Reference: Bank of America National Trust & Savings Assn. (Seventh & Flower Office, Los Angeles, Calif.).

For full biographical listings, see the Martindale-Hubbell Law Directory

MICHAEL M. MURPHY (AV)

555 South Flower Street, Suite 2850, 90071
Telephone: 213-488-3323
Fax: 213-689-0863

For full biographical listings, see the Martindale-Hubbell Law Directory

OLIVER, VOSE, SANDIFER, MURPHY & LEE, A PROFESSIONAL CORPORATION (AV)

The Park, Second Floor, 281 South Figueroa Street, 90012
Telephone: 213-621-2000
Telecopier: 213-621-2211

Charles S. Vose   James Duff Murphy
Connie Cooke Sandifer   Edward W. Lee
               Roger W. Springer

Mary L. McMaster   Bradley E. Wohlenberg
Arthur J. Hazarabedian   Timothy J. Chung
            Kristin B. Mendenhall

OF COUNSEL
William B. Barr

Representative Clients: Cities of Covina, Hermosa Beach, South Pasadena and Calabasas; Los Angeles County North Valley Building Corp.; Los Angeles County Coroner's Building Corp.; Los Angeles County Montrose Sheriff's Station Corp.
Special Counsel: Anaheim Redevelopment Agency; Arcadia Redevelopment Agency; City of Brea; Brea Redevelopment Agency; Calleguas Municipal Water District; City of Anaheim.

For full biographical listings, see the Martindale-Hubbell Law Directory

O'MELVENY & MYERS LLP (AV)

400 South Hope Street, 90071-2899
Telephone: 213-669-6000
Cable Address: "Moms"
Facsimile: 213-669-6407
Email: omminfo@omm.com
Century City, California Office: 1999 Avenue of the Stars, 90067-6035.
Telephone: 310-553-6700.
Facsimile: 310-246-6779.
Newport Beach, California Office: 610 Newport Center Drive, 92660-6429.
Telephone: 714-760-9600.
Cable Address: "Moms".
Facsimile: 714-669-6994.
San Francisco, California Office: Embarcadero Center West Tower, 275 Battery Street, 94111-3305.
Telephone: 415-984-8700.
Facsimile: 415-984-8701.
New York, New York Office: Citicorp Center, 153 East 53rd Street, 10022-4611.
Telephone: 212-326-2000.
Facsimile: 212-326-2061.
Washington, D.C. Office: 555 13th Street, N.W., 20004-1109.
Telephone: 202-383-5300.
Cable Address: "Moms".
Facsimile: 202-383-5414.
London, England Office: 10 Finsbury Square, London, EC2A 1LA.
Telephone: 0171-256-8451.
Facsimile: 0171-638-8205.
Tokyo, Japan Office: Sanbancho KB-6 Building, 6 Sanbancho, Chiyoda-ku, Tokyo 102, Japan.
Telephone: 03-3239-2900.
Facsimile: 03-3239-2432.
Hong Kong Office: Suite 1905, Peregrine Tower, Lippo Centre, 89 Queensway, Central, Hong Kong.
Telephone: 852-2523-8266.
Facsimile: 852-2522-1760.
Shanghai, Peoples Republic of China Office: Shanghai International Trade Centre, Suite 2011, 2200 Yan An Road West, Shanghai, 200335, PRC.
Telephone: 86-21-6219-5363.
Facsimile: 86-21-6275-4949.

PARTNER
Patricia Frobes (Newport Beach and Los Angeles Offices)

For Complete List of Firm Personnel, See General Section

For full biographical listings, see the Martindale-Hubbell Law Directory

RODI, POLLOCK, PETTKER, GALBRAITH & CAHILL, A LAW CORPORATION (AV)

Suite 400 801 South Grand Avenue, 90017
Telephone: 213-895-4900; 680-0823
Telecopiers: 213-895-4921; 895-4922; 895-4750

(See Next Column)

RODI, POLLOCK, PETTKER, GALBRAITH & CAHILL A LAW CORPORATION, *Los Angeles—Continued*

Karl B. Rodi (1908-1982)	Elizabeth B. Blakely
John D. Cahill	Robert C. Norton
John D. Pettker	John F. Cermak, Jr.
Daniel C. Bond (1942-1977)	Tim G. Ceperley
William R. Christian	Coralie Kupfer
Henry P. Pramov, Jr.	Cris K. O'Neall
Robert A. Yahiro	John S. Cha

Scott E. Adamson

Sonja A. Inglin	Richard Nessary
Thomas J. Yoo	Mark McCleary

OF COUNSEL

John P. Pollock   Margaret Rosenthal

For full biographical listings, see the Martindale-Hubbell Law Directory

ROSENFELD & WOLFF, A PROFESSIONAL CORPORATION (AV)

2049 Century Park East, Suite 600, 90067
Telephone: 310-556-1221
Fax: 310-556-0401

Morton M. Rosenfeld   Steven G. Wolff
Alan D. Aronson

For full biographical listings, see the Martindale-Hubbell Law Directory

SCHWARTZ, STEINSAPIR, DOHRMANN & SOMMERS (AV)

6300 Wilshire Boulevard, Suite 2000, 90048
Telephone: 213-655-4700
Fax: 213-655-4488
Pittsburgh, Pennsylvania Office: 3600 One Oxford Centre.
Telephone: 412-456-2008.
Fax: 412-456-2020.

MEMBERS OF FIRM

Laurence D. Steinsapir	Richard D. Sommers
Robert M. Dohrmann	Stuart Libicki

ASSOCIATE

Erika A. Zucker

For full biographical listings, see the Martindale-Hubbell Law Directory

SHEPPARD, MULLIN, RICHTER & HAMPTON LLP (AV)

A Limited Liability Partnership including Professional Corporations
Forty-Eighth Floor, 333 South Hope Street, 90071-1448
Telephone: 213-620-1780
Telecopier: 213-620-1398
Cable Address: "Sheplaw"
Email: info@smrh.com *URL:* http://www.smrh.com
Orange County, California Office: 650 Town Center Drive, 4th Floor, Costa Mesa.
Telephone: 714-513-5100.
Telecopier: 714-513-5130. Home Page Address: http://www.smrh.com.
San Francisco, California Office: Seventeenth Floor, Four Embarcadero Center.
Telephone: 415-434-9100.
Telecopier: 415-434-3947. Home Page Address: http://www.smrh.com.
San Diego, California Office: Nineteenth Floor, 501 West Broadway.
Telephone: 619-338-6500.
Telecopier: 619-234-3815. Home Page Address: http://www.smrh.com.

MEMBERS OF FIRM

Domenic C. Drago (San Diego Office)	Joseph E. Petrillo (San Francisco Office)
James Blythe Hodge * (San Francisco Office)	Jack H. Rubens
Brent R. Liljestrom (Orange County Office)	Thomas R. Sheppard *
James A. Lonergan	John R. Simon * (Orange County Office)
Christopher B. Neils (San Diego Office)	Joan H. Story (San Francisco Office)
Mark L. Nelson	Robert A. Thompson (San Francisco Office)
Mark T. Okuma	L. Kirk Wallace

Robert E. Williams

SPECIAL COUNSEL

Rebecca V. Hlebasko (San Francisco Office)	Ethna M. S. Piazza (San Diego Office)
Steven C. Nock (Orange County Office)	Brian G. Prentice

*Professional Corporation

For full biographical listings, see the Martindale-Hubbell Law Directory

SHERWOOD AND HARDGROVE (AV)

A Partnership including a Professional Corporation
Suite 240, 11990 San Vicente Boulevard, 90049-5004
Telephone: 310-826-2625
FAX: 310-826-6055

(See Next Column)

Don C. Sherwood (P.C.)	Kenneth M. Hardgrove

ASSOCIATES

Charles G. Brackins	Chet A. Cramin
Timothy S. Plum	Darlene R. David

For full biographical listings, see the Martindale-Hubbell Law Directory

SHIOTANI & INOUYE (AV)

11100 Santa Monica Boulevard, Suite 1820, 90025
Telephone: 310-575-3688
Telecopier: 310-575-4095

MEMBERS OF FIRM

Barney B. Shiotani   Lawrence G. Inouye

ASSOCIATE

Nicole Grattan Pearson

LEGAL SUPPORT PERSONNEL

Gabriela Velasquez (Paralegal)

References: First Los Angeles Bank (Airport Office); Bank of California.

For full biographical listings, see the Martindale-Hubbell Law Directory

RONALD P. SLATES A PROFESSIONAL CORPORATION (AV)

548 South Spring Street, Suite 1012, 90013-2309
Telephone: 213-624-1515; 213-654-1461
Fax: 213-624-7536; 213-654-1463

Ronald P. Slates

G. Michael Jackson

For full biographical listings, see the Martindale-Hubbell Law Directory

STEPHENS, BERG & LASATER, A PROFESSIONAL CORPORATION (AV)

1055 West Seventh Street, Twenty-Ninth Floor, 90017
Telephone: 213-629-3111
Telecopy: 213-629-2302; 213-624-4734

Lawrence M. Berg (1947-1995)	Frederick A. Clark
R. Wicks Stephens II	Joel A. Goldman
Richard W. Lasater II	C. Stephen Davis
Mark G. Ancel	Kenneth A. Feinfield
Dudley M. Lang	Jean-Paul Menard
Joseph F. Butler	Michael J. Kaminsky

John A. Dragonette

OF COUNSEL

Louis R. Baker   J. Lane Tilson

For full biographical listings, see the Martindale-Hubbell Law Directory

LAWRENCE C. TISTAERT (AV)

11766 Wilshire Boulevard, Suite 1580, 90025-6537
Telephone: 310-312-0874
Fax: 310-312-1034
Email: lctist@ix.netcom.com

Representative Clients: Bell Foundry Co.; Brendan Tours; Franklin Telecommunications Corp.; Munro Properties; United States Tour Operators Association.
Reference: Bank of America.

For full biographical listings, see the Martindale-Hubbell Law Directory

WEISS LAW CORPORATION (AV)

1901 Avenue of the Stars, 20th Floor, 90067
Telephone: 310-282-8600
Fax: 310-785-0010

Samuel H. Weiss

For full biographical listings, see the Martindale-Hubbell Law Directory

WOLF, RIFKIN & SHAPIRO, LLP (AV)

A Partnership including a Professional Corporation
11400 West Olympic Boulevard Ninth Floor, 90064-1565
Telephone: 310-478-4100
FAX: 310-479-1422

MEMBERS OF FIRM

Michael Wolf (A Professional Corporation)	Allan M. Rosenthal
Daniel C. Shapiro	Mindy Sheps
Roy G. Rifkin	Norman S. Wisnicki
Michael T. Schulman	Barry T. Mitidiere
Leslie Steven Marks	Marc E. Rohatiner
	Charles H. Baren

Michael W. Rabkin

(See Next Column)

WOLF, RIFKIN & SHAPIRO LLP—*Continued*

ASSOCIATES

Andrew S. Gelb	Richard S. Grant
Matthew L. Grode	Karin E. Freeman
Matthew Fladell	Lori A. Van Oosterhout
Steven A. Silver	Paul W. Windust
Mark J. Rosenbaum	Daniel Ng
Kelly Marie Allegra	Laura S. Blint

OF COUNSEL

Gerald Lloyd Friedman	Jeffrey R. Liebster
Denise M. Parga	

For full biographical listings, see the Martindale-Hubbell Law Directory

STUART D. ZIMRING (AV)

12650 Riverside Drive (North Hollywood), 91607-3492
Telephone: 818-755-4848
Fax: 818-508-0181

ASSOCIATE

Dena L. Klotz

Representative Clients: TransWorld Bank; Cytec Industries Inc.; Huntington Palisades Property Owners Assn.; Buff, Smith & Hensman Architects, Inc.

For full biographical listings, see the Martindale-Hubbell Law Directory

---

MANHATTAN BEACH, Los Angeles Co.

STEINBERG BARNESS GLASGOW & FOSTER LLP (AV)

1334 Park View Avenue, Suite 100, 90266
Telephone: 310-546-5838
Telecopier: 310-546-5630
Email: SGBF@ix.netcom.com

MEMBERS OF FIRM

Alex Steinberg	Jordan G. Barness
Daniel I. Barness	Paul J. Laurin
Donna Glasgow	Shannon M. Foley
(Not admitted in CA)	Richard L. Weiner
Douglas B. Foster	William R. (Randy) Kirkpatrick
Jeffrey Michael Lee	

OF COUNSEL

Roanld D. Harari (Not admitted in CA)

References: Home Bank; Imperial Bank; Citizens Commerical Trust & Savings Bank; Bank of America.

For full biographical listings, see the Martindale-Hubbell Law Directory

---

MISSION VIEJO, Orange Co.

THE BUCKLEY FIRM, P.C. (AV)

Suite 200, 26522 La Alameda, 92691
Telephone: 714-348-8300
Facsimile: 714-348-8310
Email: TBF__law@ix.netcom.com
Email: 73321.331@compuserve.com

Lawrence J. Buckley	John W. Klein
John Thomas Callan	Paula Scotland
Jeffrey W. Griffith	Edgar C. Smith, III
Stephen J. Kane	Adam H. Springel

OF COUNSEL

Timothy D. Carlyle	Jonathan C. Cavett

Reference: Bank of California.

For full biographical listings, see the Martindale-Hubbell Law Directory

---

MODESTO,* Stanislaus Co.

BRUNN & FLYNN, A PROFESSIONAL CORPORATION (AV)

928 12th Street, P.O. Box 3366, 95353
Telephone: 209-521-2133
Fax: 209-521-7584
Email: brunnfly@ix.netcom.com

Charles K. Brunn	Gerald E. Brunn
Timothy T. Flynn	Roger S. Matzkind

Michael G. Donovan	Andrew N. Eshoo

For full biographical listings, see the Martindale-Hubbell Law Directory

---

MORRO BAY, San Luis Obispo Co.

OGLE & MERZON (AV)

A Partnership including a Professional Corporation
770 Morro Bay Boulevard, P.O. Box 720, 93443-0720
Telephone: 805-772-7353
Fax: 805-772-7713
San Luis Obispo, California Office: P.O. Box 1855, 93406.
Telephone: 805-543-0295.

(See Next Column)

Charles E. Ogle (A Professional Corporation)	James B. Merzon

Charles G. Kirschner	Charles Patrick Ogle

For full biographical listings, see the Martindale-Hubbell Law Directory

---

MOUNTAIN VIEW, Santa Clara Co.

LUCE & QUILLINAN (AV)

444 Castro Street, Suite 900, 94041-2073
Telephone: 415-969-4000
FAX: 415-969-6953

MEMBERS OF FIRM

James G. Luce	James V. Quillinan
Melissa C. Johnson	

ASSOCIATE

Sally F. Berry

For full biographical listings, see the Martindale-Hubbell Law Directory

---

NEWPORT BEACH, Orange Co.

DAVIS, PUNELLI, KEATHLEY & WILLARD (AV)

610 Newport Center Drive, Suite 1000, P.O. Box 7920, 92658-7920
Telephone: 714-640-0700
Telecopier: 714-640-0714
San Diego, California Office: 501 West Broadway, Suite 900, 92101.
Telephone: 619-558-2581.

MEMBERS OF FIRM

Robert E. Willard	H. James Keathley
S. Eric Davis	Eric G. Anderson
Frank Punelli, Jr.	Katherine D. Keathley

OF COUNSEL

Lewis K. Uhler

For full biographical listings, see the Martindale-Hubbell Law Directory

MILLAR, HODGES & BEMIS (AV)

One Newport Place, Suite 900, 1301 Dove Street, 92660-2448
Telephone: 714-752-7722
FAX: 714-752-6131

MEMBERS OF FIRM

Richard W. Millar, Jr.	Kenneth R. Hodges
Larry R. Bemis	

ASSOCIATE

David A. St. Clair

Reference: Manufacturers Bank, Newport Beach, California.

For full biographical listings, see the Martindale-Hubbell Law Directory

JAMES M. PARKER (AV)

4695 MacArthur Court, Suite 1290, 92660
Telephone: 714-752-2408
Fax: 714-752-2464

For full biographical listings, see the Martindale-Hubbell Law Directory

WOLF & PFEIFER, A LAW CORPORATION (AV)

500 Newport Center Drive Suite 800, 92660
Telephone: 714-720-9200
Fax: 714-720-9250
URL: http://www.wolfpfeifer.com

Alan S. Wolf	Melissa L. Richards
Michael R. Pfeifer	Janice L. Celotti
Donald R. Davidson, III	

Roland P. Reynolds	C. Robert Simpson
Donna L. La Porte	Diane Weifenbach
James F. Lewin	

OF COUNSEL

Kay Virginia Gustafson

LEGAL SUPPORT PERSONNEL

Dona M. Harman

For full biographical listings, see the Martindale-Hubbell Law Directory

YOUNG & AMUNDSEN (AV)

620 Newport Center Drive, Suite 420, 92660
Telephone: 714-640-4400
Fax: 714-717-4862

MEMBERS OF FIRM

Steven R. Young	Roland J. Amundsen

For full biographical listings, see the Martindale-Hubbell Law Directory

OAKLAND, * Alameda Co.

AIKEN, KRAMER & CUMMINGS, INCORPORATED (AV)

Suite 550 Ordway Building, One Kaiser Plaza, 94612
Telephone: 510-834-6800
Fax: 510-834-9017
Email: aikenkrame@aol.com

Benj. R. Aiken (1879-1955)	John A. Harkavy
Bauer E. Kramer (Retired)	Elizabeth M. Engh
Benj. R. Aiken, Jr. (Retired)	Matthew F. Graham
Fred V. Cummings (Retired)	Steven J. Cramer
	Richard A. Sipos

OF COUNSEL

Russell L. Barlow	Bruce G. Herold
	Michael A. Coan

Ellen Suzanne Wyatt	Michael S. Treppa

Reference: Union Bank of California, Oakland, California.

For full biographical listings, see the Martindale-Hubbell Law Directory

PEZZOLA & REINKE, A PROFESSIONAL CORPORATION (AV)

Suite 1300, Lake Merritt Plaza, 1999 Harrison Street, 94612
Telephone: 510-273-8750
Telecopier: 510-834-7440
San Francisco, California Office: 650 California Street, 32nd Floor, 94111.
Telephone: 415-989-9710.
Menlo Park, California Office: 3000 Sand Hill Road, Building 4, Suite 160, 94025.
Telephone: 415-854-8797.

Stephen P. Pezzola	Thomas C. Armstrong

Representative Clients: Salesian Society; U.S. Ice Ventures; Young America Homes; Sky Meadows Homeowners Association.

For full biographical listings, see the Martindale-Hubbell Law Directory

ONTARIO, San Bernardino Co.

COVINGTON & CROWE (AV)

1131 West Sixth Street, P.O. Box 1515, 91762
Telephone: 909-983-9393
Fax: 909-391-6762
Email: covcrowe@ix.netcom.com

MEMBERS OF FIRM

Harold A. Bailin (1930-1988)	Stephen R. Wade
Samuel P. Crowe	Jette R. Anderson
George W. Porter	Audrey A. Perri
Robert E. Dougherty	Tracy L. Tibbals
Donald G. Haslam	Melanie Fisch
Robert F. Schauer	Robert H. Reeder
Edward A. Hopson	R. Doug Donesky
	Tammy S. Jager

ASSOCIATES

Howard S. Borenstein	Richard R. Muir
Denise Matthey	Kimberly A. Rohn
Katrina West	J. Michael Kaler
	Eric S. Vail

For full biographical listings, see the Martindale-Hubbell Law Directory

OXNARD, Ventura Co.

ENGLAND, WHITFIELD, SCHRÖEDER & TREDWAY, L.L.P. (AV)

300 Esplanade Drive, 6th Floor, 93030
Telephone: 805-485-9627
Ventura: 647-8237
Southern California Toll Free: 800-255-3485
Fax: 805-983-0297
URL: http://www.tsurf.com/ewst/
Thousand Oaks, California Office: Rolling Oaks Office Center, 351 Rolling Oaks Drive.
Telephone: Southern California Toll Free: 800-255-3485.

MEMBERS OF FIRM

Theodore J. England	Mark A. Nelson
Anson M. Whitfield	Eric J. Kananen
Robert W. Schröeder	Mary E. Schröeder
David W. Tredway	Oscar C. Gonzalez
Robert A. McSorley	Steven K. Perrin
Stuart A. Comis	Andrew S. Hughes
Mitchel B. Kahn	Madison M. Christian
	Kurt Edward Kananen

ASSOCIATES

William J. Kesatie	Linda Kathryn Ash
Melissa E. Cohen	Mark T. Barney

Representative Clients: Seneca Resources Corp. (oil & gas); Cal-Sun Produce Co.; Waste Management of California, Inc; Dah Chong Hong (Honda, Toyota, Mazda, Lexus, Acura, Saturn automobile dealerships); Willamette

(See Next Column)

Industries; Oxnard Harbor Association of Realtors; Port of Hueneme; Conejo Valley Association of Realtors; Power-One, Inc.

For full biographical listings, see the Martindale-Hubbell Law Directory

PALM DESERT, Riverside Co.

CRISTE, PIPPIN & GOLDS (AV)

Suite 200, 73-550 Alessandro Drive, 92260
Telephone: 619-862-1111
Fax: 619-776-4197
Email: cpgca@aol.com

MEMBERS OF FIRM

Michael A. Criste	Robert L. Pippin
	Irwin L. Golds

ASSOCIATE

Marie A. Bochnewich

For full biographical listings, see the Martindale-Hubbell Law Directory

PALM SPRINGS, Riverside Co.

SCHLECHT, SHEVLIN & SHOENBERGER, A LAW CORPORATION (AV)

Suite 100, 801 East Tahquitz Canyon Way, P.O. Box 2744, 92263-2744
Telephone: 619-320-7161
Facsimile: 619-323-1758; 619-325-4623

James M. Schlecht	Daniel T. Johnson

Representative Clients: Outdoor Resorts of America; The Escrow Connection; Wells Fargo Bank; Canyon Country Club; Waste Management Co.

For Complete List of Firm Personnel, See General Section

For full biographical listings, see the Martindale-Hubbell Law Directory

PALO ALTO, Santa Clara Co.

FLICKER & KERIN (AV)

Suite 460, 285 Hamilton, P.O. Box 840, 94302
Telephone: 415-321-0947
Fax: 415-326-9722

MEMBERS OF FIRM

Michael R. Flicker	Anthony J. Kerin, III

ASSOCIATES

Rhesa C. Rubin	Cheri A. Bell

For full biographical listings, see the Martindale-Hubbell Law Directory

HANNA & VAN ATTA (AV)

A Partnership of Professional Corporations
525 University Avenue, Suite 705, 94301
Telephone: 415-321-5700
Fax: 415-321-5639

John Paul Hanna	David M. Van Atta

Representative Clients: Bay Apartment Communities, Inc.; Calprop Corp; Classic Communities, Inc.; Diodati Development; DKB Homes; G.T.E. Reality; Haseko (California), Inc.; Hayman Homes; Kaufman and Broad; Lincoln Property Co.; Pacific Peninsula Group; Silicon Graphics Computer Systems; Sobrato Development Co.; Standard Pacific (Northern California); Sunstream Homes; Vintage Properties Development Corp.

For full biographical listings, see the Martindale-Hubbell Law Directory

A. DUNCAN KING (AV)

Suite 501, 2471 East Bayshore Road, 94303
Telephone: 800-255-3636; 415-494-6000
FAX: 415-494-3012
Email: adking@ix.netcom.com

For full biographical listings, see the Martindale-Hubbell Law Directory

PASADENA, Los Angeles Co.

BARKER & ROMNEY, A PROFESSIONAL CORPORATION (AV)

301 East Colorado Boulevard Suite 200, 91101-1977
Telephone: 818-578-1970; 213-617-3112
Facsimile: 818-578-0768

Lee Barker (1943-1996)	Timothy M. Howett
David T. Romney	Blaine Jay Wanke
	Cheryl A. Orr

Reference: City National Bank.

For full biographical listings, see the Martindale-Hubbell Law Directory

LAGERLOF, SENECAL, BRADLEY & SWIFT, LLP (AV)

301 North Lake Avenue, 10th Floor, 91101-4108
Telephone: 818-793-9400
FAX: 818-793-5900

(See Next Column)

LAGERLOF, SENECAL, BRADLEY & SWIFT LLP—*Continued*

MEMBERS OF FIRM

Joseph J. Burris (1913-1980)	John F. Bradley
Stanley C. Lagerlof (Retired)	Timothy J. Gosney
H. Melvin Swift, Jr.	William F. Kruse
H. Jess Senecal	Thomas S. Bunn, III
Jack T. Swafford	Andrew D. Turner
	Rebecca J. Thyne

ASSOCIATES

James D. Ciampa	Robert W. Renken

Representative Clients: Anchor Glass Container Corp.; Bethlehem Steel Corp.; Orthopaedic Hospital; Palmdale Water District; Public Water Agencies Group; Ventura Port District; Walnut Valley Water District; Metric Construction Co., Inc.

For full biographical listings, see the Martindale-Hubbell Law Directory

JAMES M. ORENDORFF (AV)

25 East Union Street, 91103
Telephone: 818-449-8200
FAX: 818-449-8370

For full biographical listings, see the Martindale-Hubbell Law Directory

WILLSEY LAW OFFICES OWNED BY A PROFESSIONAL CORPORATION (AV)

553 S. Marengo Avenue, 91101
Telephone: 818-577-1086
Fax: 818-304-2959

Burke W. Willsey	Daniel P. Willsey (A Professional Corporation)

Reference: Sanwa Bank.

For full biographical listings, see the Martindale-Hubbell Law Directory

WITTER AND HARPOLE (AV)

Wells Fargo Building, 350 W. Colorado Boulevard, Suite 400, 91105
Telephone: 213-624-1311, 818-440-1111
FAX: 213-620-0430
Email: 102444.2117@compuserve.com
Newport Beach, California Office: Suite 1050, 610 Newport Center Drive.
Telephone: 714-644-7600.
Fax: 714-759-1014.

MEMBERS OF FIRM

Myron E. Harpole	Eugene Harpole (1896-1987)
George G. Witter (1895-1978)	Debra M. Olsen (Resident, Newport Beach Office)

OF COUNSEL

James D. Harris (A Professional Corporation)

Reference: Union Bank (Newport Beach, Calif.).

For full biographical listings, see the Martindale-Hubbell Law Directory

PLEASANTON, Alameda Co.

GEOFFREY C. ETNIRE (AV)

4900 Hopyard Road, Suite 260, 94588
Telephone: 510-734-9950
Fax: 510-734-9170
Email: etnire@ricochet.net

For full biographical listings, see the Martindale-Hubbell Law Directory

REDWOOD CITY,* San Mateo Co.

LOW, BALL & LYNCH, A PROFESSIONAL CORPORATION (AV)

10 Twin Dolphin, Suite B-500, 94065
Telephone: 415-591-8822
Fax: 415-591-8884
San Francisco, California Office: 601 California Street, Suite 2100, 94108.
Telephone: 415-981-6630.
Monterey, California Office: 10 Ragsdale Drive, Suite 175, 93940.
Telephone: 408-655-8822.

Raymond Coates	David L. Blinn
Chester G. Moore, III	Janet Kulig
James D. Miller	Thomas E. Mulvihill
William H. Holsinger	Jennifer Elizabeth Acheson

John R. Baumann	Joseph M. Fenech
	Michael E. Sandgren

For full biographical listings, see the Martindale-Hubbell Law Directory

---

SACRAMENTO,* Sacramento Co.

THE BLEIER LAW FIRM (AV)

2100 21st Street, 95818-1708
Telephone: 916-454-2100
Fax: 916-454-2121
Email: tblf@bleier.com *URL:* http://www.bleier.com

Brenton A. Bleier

ASSOCIATES

Alan C. Campbell	Robert W. Hunt
Peter H. Mixon	Bradford A. Bleier

For full biographical listings, see the Martindale-Hubbell Law Directory

HANSEN, BOYD, CULHANE & WATSON (AV)

A Partnership including Professional Corporations
Central City Centre, 1331 Twenty-First Street, 95814
Telephone: 916-444-2550
Telecopier: 916-444-2358

Hartley T. Hansen (Inc.)	Lawrence R. Watson
Kevin R. Culhane (Inc.)	John J. Rueda
David E. Boyd	James J. Banks
	Lorraine M. Pavlovich

OF COUNSEL

Betsy S. Kimball

Thomas L. Riordan	Pamela B. Hooley
James O. Moses	Roger R. Billings

For full biographical listings, see the Martindale-Hubbell Law Directory

HARDY ERICH BROWN & WILSON, A PROFESSIONAL CORPORATION (AV)

1000 G Street, 95814
Telephone: 916-449-3800
Fax: 916-449-3888
Mailing Address: P.O. Box 13530, Sacramento, California, 95853-4530

John Quincy Brown, Jr.	Bruce E. Salenko
Anthony D. Osmundson	Daniel J. Coyle
Thomas C. Richards	Brian H. Charter
L. Thomas Wagner	Larry Caldwell
David L. Perrault	Richard L. Alley
John Quincy Brown, III	Glenda N. Reager
L. Kent Wyatt	Whitney A. Davis
	Michael J. Nelson

Linda Wilson Bloom

Representative Clients: American Promotional Events; Colliers Iliff Thorn & Company; Crain Industries, Inc.; Mather Federal Credit Union; Step Ahead Investments, Inc.; Woodmont Real Estate Services.

For full biographical listings, see the Martindale-Hubbell Law Directory

HUNTER RICHEY DI BENEDETTO & BREWER, LLP (AV)

A Limited Liability Partnership
Renaissance Tower, 801 K Street, 23rd Floor, 95814-3525
Telephone: 916-491-3000
Facsimile: 916-491-3080
Email: hrdb@hrdb.com *URL:* http://www.hrdb.com

MEMBERS OF FIRM

William S. Hunter	James F. Geary
Win R. Richey	Janet C. Eisenbeis
Florence L. Di Benedetto	Jeffery D. Harris
Roy E. Brewer	Stephen C. Ruehmann
Anne E. Ferguson	Ralph T. Ferguson
Judith J. Citko	Sharon K. Sandeen
	Kathryn T. Papalia

LEGAL SUPPORT PERSONNEL

Lori J. Kelly (Paralegal)	Michele L. Nickell
Deborah M. Romero (Paralegal)	(Legal Assistant)
Linda Jane Hall	Dawn Krein (Legal Assistant)
(Legal Assistant)	Stephanie L. Neumann
Jennifer E. Mueller	(Legal Assistant)
(Legal Assistant)	

For full biographical listings, see the Martindale-Hubbell Law Directory

LIVINGSTON & MATTESICH, LAW CORPORATION (AV)

1201 K Street, Suite 1100, 95814
Telephone: 916-442-1111
Fax: 916-448-1709
Email: liv-matt@gvn.net

Gene Livingston	Carol Livingston
James M. Mattesich	Rebecca M. Ceniceros

(See Next Column)

LIVINGSTON & MATTESICH LAW CORPORATION, *Sacramento—Continued*

Steven P. Belzer   Trisha M. McAlmond

Reference: Bank of California.

For full biographical listings, see the Martindale-Hubbell Law Directory

MATHENY POIDMORE LINKERT & SEARS (AV)

3638 American River Drive, P.O. Box 13711, 95853-4711
Telephone: 916-978-3434
Fax: 916-978-3430
Email: mpls1@netcom.com

MEMBERS OF FIRM

Henry G. Matheny (1933-1984)	James C. Damir
Anthony J. Poidmore	Michael A. Bishop
Douglas A. Sears	Ernest A. Long
Richard S. Linkert	Joann Georgallis
	Kent M. Luckey

ASSOCIATES

Matthew C. Jaime	Cathy A. Reynolds
Robert B. Berrigan	Eric R. Wiesel
Stephen J. Nardine	Reed R. Johnson
Ronald E. Enabnit	Danielle M. Guard
	Andrea M. Croak

LEGAL SUPPORT PERSONNEL
PARALEGALS

Karen D. Fisher	Lynell Rae Steed
Fran Studer	Jennifer Bachman
	Debbie Sue Miller

For full biographical listings, see the Martindale-Hubbell Law Directory

NAGELEY, MEREDITH & RAMSEY, INC. (AV)

8001 Folsom Boulevard, Suite 200, P.O. Box 276270, 95827-6270
Telephone: 916-386-8282
Fax: 916-386-8952

Sam R. Nageley   Gregory A. Meredith
Joe Ramsey

Drew M. Johnson	Carole Sharples
Craig S. MacGlashan	L. Alan Warwick
Michael B. O'Harra	Janet M. Meredith
Lawrence N. Hensley	Debbie J. Vorous
	James C. Keowen

OF COUNSEL

Andrea M. Miller

For full biographical listings, see the Martindale-Hubbell Law Directory

SAN DIEGO,* San Diego Co.

BROWN, MCDONNELL & ROMAKER, A PROFESSIONAL LAW CORPORATION (AV)

2390 Shelter Island Drive, Suite 210, 92106
Telephone: 619-221-9181
Fax: 619-221-9181

Sampson A. Brown   Michael B. McDonnell
John L. Romaker

Representative Clients: A to Z Marine Service; Knight & Carver Custom Yachts, Inc.; Lester & Lester Marine Survey, Inc.

For full biographical listings, see the Martindale-Hubbell Law Directory

FERRIS & BRITTON, A PROFESSIONAL CORPORATION (AV)

1600 First National Bank Center, 401 West A Street, 92101
Telephone: 619-233-3131
Fax: 619-232-9316

Alfred G. Ferris   Gary T. Moyer

Representative Clients: Agouron Pharmaceuticals, Inc.; Cox Communications, Inc.; Immuno Pharmaceutics, Inc.; Invitrogen Corporation; Peninsula Bank; Teleport Communications Group; Southwest Airlines.

For Complete List of Firm Personnel, See General Section

For full biographical listings, see the Martindale-Hubbell Law Directory

HOVEY, KIRBY, THORNTON & HAHN, A PROFESSIONAL CORPORATION (AV)

101 West Broadway, Suite 1100, 92101-8297
Telephone: 619-685-4000
Fax: 619-685-4004
Email: 74754.3143@compuserve.com

(See Next Column)

Gregg B. Hovey   M. Leslie Hovey
Dean T. Kirby, Jr.   Jane Hahn

For full biographical listings, see the Martindale-Hubbell Law Directory

HYDE AND WATERS (AV)

401 West "A" Street, Suite 1200, 92101
Telephone: 619-696-6911
Telecopier: 619-696-6919

MEMBERS OF FIRM

Laurel Lee Hyde   Timothy Doyle Waters

Representative Clients: Cardio Theatre, Inc.; C.W. Clark, Inc.; Foster Investment Corporation; Home Capital Corporation; Kmart Corporation; Midland Loan Services, L.P.; New World Communications Co.; The Regents of the University of California; San Diego Gas and Electric Company; Standard Process of Southern California.

For full biographical listings, see the Martindale-Hubbell Law Directory

LINDLEY, LAZAR & SCALES, A PROFESSIONAL CORPORATION (AV)

One America Plaza, 600 West Broadway, Suite 1400, 92101-3302
Telephone: 619-234-9181
Fax: 619-234-8475
Email: 104413.1175@compuserve.com

Luke R. Corbett	Stephen F. Treadgold
John M. Seitman	Michael H. Wexler
Robert M. McLeod	James Henry Fox
William E. Johns	R. Gordon Huckins
	Kenneth C. Jones

Representative Clients: Westana Builders-Developers; Chicago Title Insurance Company; Palomar Savings & Loan Association; George Wimpey, Inc.; Shapell Industries, Inc.; Pointe Builders; Morrison Homes, Inc.

For Complete List of Firm Personnel, See General Section

For full biographical listings, see the Martindale-Hubbell Law Directory

LUCE, FORWARD, HAMILTON & SCRIPPS LLP (AV)

A Partnership including Professional Corporations
600 West Broadway, Suite 2600, 92101
Telephone: 619-236-1414
Fax: 619-232-8311
URL: http://www.luce.com
La Jolla, California Office: 4275 Executive Square, Suite 800, 92037.
Telephone: 619-535-2639.
Fax: 619-453-2812.
Los Angeles, California Office: 777 South Figueroa, Suite 3600, 90017.
Telephone: 213-892-4992.
Fax: 213-892-7731.
San Francisco, California Office: 100 Bush Street, 20th Floor, 94104.
Telephone: 415-395-7900.
Fax: 415-395-7949.
New York, N.Y. Office: Citicorp Center, 153 East 53rd Street, 26th Floor, 10022.
Telephone: 212-754-1414.
Fax: 212-644-9727.
Chicago, Illinois Office: 180 North La Salle Street, Suite 1125, 60601.
Telephone: 312-641-0580.
Fax: 312-641-0380.

MEMBERS OF FIRM

Steven S. Wall	Stephen T. Toohill
Thomas M. Murray	Robert D. Buell
Ronald W. Rouse	Marjorie J. Burchett
Charles L. Hellerich	Valentine S. Hoy, VIII
Craig K. Beam	Timothy R. Pestotnik
Robert J. Bell	Christopher K. Barnette
Mark Hagarty	David M. Hymer
Nancy T. Scull	Jeffrey A. Chine
Thomas A. May	Roger C. Haerr

ASSOCIATES

Pamela Ewers Wagner	Michael G. Ramsey
Lynne D. Kaelin	Allan R. Gutkin
Christopher H. Findley	Jessica Hausknecht
Cindy Dobler Davis	(Not admitted in CA)

For Complete List of Firm Personnel, See General Section

For full biographical listings, see the Martindale-Hubbell Law Directory

SOLOMON WARD SEIDENWURM & SMITH, LLP (AV)

1200 Wells Fargo Plaza, 401 B Street, 92101
Telephone: 619-231-0303
Telecopier: 619-231-4755

(See Next Column)

SOLOMON WARD SEIDENWURM & SMITH LLP—*Continued*

MEMBERS OF FIRM

Michael D. Breslauer	Jeffrey A. Schneider
Cynthia L. Eldred	Richard L. Seidenwurm (P.C.)
Lawrence J. Kaplan	Jeffrey H. Silberman
Richard E. McCarthy	Miguel A. Smith
Edward J. McIntyre	Norman L. Smith
Paul S. Metsch	Gerald I. Solomon
Harry J. Proctor	Herbert J. Solomon

ASSOCIATES

A.Holland Denton	Michael A. Gardiner
Daniel E. Gardenswartz	Eric L. Gordon
Catherine L. Pierce	

OF COUNSEL

Keenan Behrle	Joseph M. Lesko

William O. Ward, III (Retired)

For full biographical listings, see the Martindale-Hubbell Law Directory

SPARBER, FERGUSON, PONDER & RYAN, A PROFESSIONAL LAW CORPORATION (AV)

Imperial Bank Building, 701 "B" Street, Tenth Floor, 92101-8103
Telephone: 619-239-3600
Facsimile: 619-239-5601

Richard E. Sparber	Greg J. Ryan
James P. Ferguson	Richard J. Annen
John E. Ponder	Daniel F. Morrin
Gary B. Rudolph	

Todd R. Gabriel	William P. Fennell
Carol R. McGinnis	James E. Highsmith

OF COUNSEL

Mark P. Mandell

LEGAL SUPPORT PERSONNEL

LEGAL ADMINISTRATOR

Beverly K. Driscoll

For full biographical listings, see the Martindale-Hubbell Law Directory

STEPHENSON WORLEY GARRATT SCHWARTZ HEIDEL & PRAIRIE (AV)

A Limited Liability Partnership
101 West Broadway, Suite 1300, 92101-8214
Telephone: 619-696-3500
Fax: 619-696-3555
Email: SDLAW@swgshp.com

MEMBERS OF FIRM

Gary J. Stephenson	Michael W. Prairie
Donald R. Worley	Timothy K. Garfield
Gregory C. M. Garratt	Lori A. Chamberlain
William J. Schwartz, Jr.	Jennifer Treese Wilson
Lynne L. Heidel	Amy Rosen
James B. MacRobbie	

OF COUNSEL

Kent H. Foster	Elaine L. Chan

Reference: Bank of Commerce.

For full biographical listings, see the Martindale-Hubbell Law Directory

ARTHUR M. WILCOX, JR. (AV)

Koll Center, 501 West Broadway, Suite 1600, 92101
Telephone: 619-696-6788
Fax: 619-696-8685
Email: amwilcox@ix.netcom.com

For full biographical listings, see the Martindale-Hubbell Law Directory

SAN FRANCISCO, * San Francisco Co.

BARTKO, ZANKEL, TARRANT & MILLER, PROFESSIONAL CORPORATION (AV)

900 Front Street, Suite 300, 94111
Telephone: 415-956-1900
Fax: 415-956-1152

John J. Bartko	Randall M. Faccinto
Martin I. Zankel	M. Manuel Fishman
Richard T. Tarrant	Christopher J. Hunt
Charles G. Miller	Theani Christine Louskos
Robert H. Bunzel	Brian McLaughlin
Kim A. Lambert	Howard L Pearlman
Michael D. Welch	C. Griffith Towle
Michael D. Abraham	Mary Elizabeth Trice
Glenn P. Zwang	

(See Next Column)

P. Craig Cardon	Carissa Shubb
Rita Maria Castro	Christopher D. Sullivan
Cynthia E. King	Ralph J. Sutton
Hussein M. Saffouri	Constance J. Yu

COUNSEL

Thomas A. Lee, Jr.

For full biographical listings, see the Martindale-Hubbell Law Directory

BERG, ZIEGLER, ANDERSON & PARKER, LLP (AV)

4 Embarcadero Center, Suite 1400, 94111
Telephone: 415-397-6000
Telecopier: 415-397-9449

MEMBERS OF FIRM

James M. Berg	Robert Ted Parker
William J. Ziegler	David B. Franklin
Robert L. Anderson	David L. Monetta
F. Gale Connor	

Douglas A. Applegate	Jennifer M. Malloy
Jeffrey B. Kirschenbaum	Patrick J. O'Brien

PARALEGALS

David A. Dunbar	Diane E. Gresham
Sharon L. Gostlin	

For full biographical listings, see the Martindale-Hubbell Law Directory

ALLAN M. BERLAND (AV)

601 California Street, Suite 2002, 94108
Telephone: 415-397-6711

For full biographical listings, see the Martindale-Hubbell Law Directory

BICKEL & ASSOCIATES (AV)

Four Embarcadero Center, Suite 3440, 94111
Telephone: 415-433-1200
Fax: 415-433-2985

Branden E. Bickel

ASSOCIATE

Dawn A. Silberstein

For full biographical listings, see the Martindale-Hubbell Law Directory

BISHOP, BARRY, HOWE, HANEY & RYDER, A PROFESSIONAL CORPORATION (AV)

Embarcadero Center West, 12th Floor, 275 Battery Street, 94111-3333
Telephone: 415-421-8550
FAX: 415-362-4730

Ross R. Ryder (1940-1989)	Thomas O. Haran
Nelson C. Barry	Rebecca B. Aherne
Drayton F. Howe, Jr.	Michael W. Bolechowski
Jeffrey N. Haney	Mark C. Raskoff
Patricia S. Lakner	

William R. Brown	Stacey A. Kuch
J. Scott Wood	Marco R. Sumarriva
Mitchell J. Alward	Curtis A. Canfield
Lawrence S. Molton	Gregory R. de la Peña
Susan Knell Bumbalo	Paul Andrew Herp
Brook Bernard Bond	Rebecca E. Thomson
Marisa D'Amico	Jane E. Carey

OF COUNSEL

Woodrow W. Denney

Reference: The Redwood Bank.

For full biographical listings, see the Martindale-Hubbell Law Directory

CASSIDY & VERGES, A PROFESSIONAL CORPORATION (AV)

20 California Street, Suite 500, 94111
Telephone: 415-788-2020
Fax: 415-788-2039

Stephen K. Cassidy	Kenneth Steven Taymor
Scott C. Verges	Deirdre M. Dawson
Thomas E. Panelli	Paul M. Kawakami
Wylie R. Sheldon	Jon L. Mangus
Anna C. Shimko	Eric L. Laurence

LEGAL SUPPORT PERSONNEL

Loretta T. MacDonald

For full biographical listings, see the Martindale-Hubbell Law Directory

San Francisco—Continued

ELLMAN, BURKE, HOFFMAN & JOHNSON, A PROFESSIONAL CORPORATION (AV)

One Ecker, Suite 200, 94105
Telephone: 415-777-2727
Fax: 415-495-7587
Email: managingdirector@ellman-burke.com *URL:*
http://www.ellman-burke.com

Howard N. Ellman	Thomas Paine
Michael J. Burke	Jay L. Paxton
Kenneth N. Burns	Thomas M. Sherwood
John D. Hoffman	Leslie M. Browne
Jeffrey W. Johnson	David H. Blackwell

Jodi Billehus Fedor

For full biographical listings, see the Martindale-Hubbell Law Directory

FELDMAN, WALDMAN & KLINE, A PROFESSIONAL CORPORATION (AV)

3 Embarcadero Center, Suite 2800, 94111
Telephone: 415-981-1300
Fax: 415-981-1350
Email: info@fwk.com
Stockton, California Office: Sperry Building, 146-148 West Weber Avenue.
Telephone: 209-943-2004.
Fax: 209-943-0905.

Murry J. Waldman	Martha Jeanne Shaver
Leland R. Selna, Jr.	(Resident, Stockton Office)
Michael L. Korbholz	Robert Cedric Goodman
Howard M. Wexler	Laura Grad
Patricia S. Mar	William F. Adams
Kenneth W. Jones	Elizabeth A. Thompson
Paul J. Dion	Julie A. Jones
Vern S. Bothwell	David L. Kanel
L.J. Chris Martiniak	Abram S. Feuerstein

Linda Sorensen

Laura J. Dawson	Dana A. Suntag
Joanne M. Lafreniere	(Resident, Stockton Office)
Paul A. Weiss	Danielle Ochs-Tillotson

OF COUNSEL

Richard L. Jaeger	Gerald A. Sherwin
	(Resident, Stockton Office)

For full biographical listings, see the Martindale-Hubbell Law Directory

GREENE RADOVSKY MALONEY & SHARE LLP (AV)

Four Embarcadero Center, Suite 4000, 94111
Telephone: 415-543-1400
Telecopier: 415-777-4961

Luke D. Bailey	Mark S. Hennigh
Thomas M. Feldstein	Graham Maloney
Ronald W. Garrity	Linda L. McCall
Rodney C. Gilmore	Russell D. Pollock
Richard L. Greene	Thomas L. Prestwich
Allen Grossman	Joseph S. Radovsky

Donald R. Share

OF COUNSEL

Lawrence B. Silver

James H. Abrams	Edward I. Kaplan
Stephen Anthony Bonovich	Davia M. Love
Gary R. Bruhns	Veronica K. Phillips
Joel S. Fisch	Dean A. Schlobohm
Giselle Sered Galper	Douglas P. Solomon
Rachel G. Hardie	Laird P. Steverango

Reference: The Bank of California, N.A.

For full biographical listings, see the Martindale-Hubbell Law Directory

MURPHY, PEARSON, BRADLEY & FEENEY, A PROFESSIONAL CORPORATION (AV)

88 Kearny Street, 11th Floor, 94108
Telephone: 415-788-1900
Telecopier: 415-393-8087
Sacramento, California Office: Suite 200, 3600 American River Drive, 95864.
Telephone: 916-483-6074.
Telecopier: 916-483-6088.

Karen M. Goodman	Mark S. Perelman
(Resident, Sacramento Office)	

For Complete List of Firm Personnel, See General Section

For full biographical listings, see the Martindale-Hubbell Law Directory

STUBBS, HITTIG & LEONE, A PROFESSIONAL CORPORATION (AV)

Fox Plaza, Suite 818, 1390 Market Street, 94102-5399
Telephone: 415-861-8200
Telecopier: 415-861-6700
Email: SHLSF@aol.com

Gregory E. Stubbs	Louis A. Leone
H. Christopher Hittig	Marina B. Pitts

For full biographical listings, see the Martindale-Hubbell Law Directory

LAW FIRM OF ROBERT A. SUSK (AV)

333 Bush Street, 26th Floor, 94104
Telephone: 415-982-3950
Fax: 415-982-6143

Robert A. Susk	Leslie J. Mann

ASSOCIATE

Jeffrey A. Glick

For full biographical listings, see the Martindale-Hubbell Law Directory

SAN JOSE,* Santa Clara Co.

HOPKINS & CARLEY, A LAW CORPORATION (AV)

Fifteenth Floor, 150 Almaden Boulevard, 95113-2089
Telephone: 408-286-9800
Facsimile: 408-998-4790

Leon A. Carley (1908-1984)	Stephen J. Kottmeier
John F. Hopkins	Ross G. Adler
Garth E. Pickett	Jeffrey E. Essner

Timothy H. Hopkins

H. Katerina Hertzog	Jay M. Ross

Sharon L. Wong

For Complete List of Firm Personnel, See General Section

For full biographical listings, see the Martindale-Hubbell Law Directory

LICCARDO, ROSSI, STURGES & McNEIL, A PROFESSIONAL LAW CORPORATION (AV)

1960 The Alameda, Suite 200, 95126
Telephone: 408-244-4570
Fax: 408-244-3294
Oakland, California Office: 1999 Harrison, Suite 1300.
Telephone: 415-834-2206.
Fax: 415-832-4432.

Salvador A. Liccardo	Craig Needham
Ronald R. Rossi	Gregory D. Hull
Robert S. Sturges	Martha Louise Caron
R. Donald McNeil	(Resident, Oakland Office)
David M. Hamerslough	Cynthia L. Chase
Susan R. Reischl	Laura Liccardo

Robert C. Colyar	Paul Salvatore Liccardo
Jeffery Lopez	Anne Jones
Wes Wagnon	Samuel A. Chuck
Richard B. Gullen	Laura M. Chiappe
Deborah T. Bjonerud	Daniel A. Hershkowitz
(Resident, Oakland Office)	(Resident, Oakland Office)

For full biographical listings, see the Martindale-Hubbell Law Directory

McPHARLIN, SPRINKLES & THOMAS, LLP (AV)

Ten Almaden Boulevard, Suite 1460, 95113
Telephone: 408-293-1900
Fax: 408-293-1999

MEMBERS OF FIRM

Linda Hendrix McPharlin	Mary Lee Malysz
Catherine C. Sprinkles	Paul M. Hogan
N. David Thomas	Paul S. Avilla

For full biographical listings, see the Martindale-Hubbell Law Directory

MILLER, MORTON, CAILLAT & NEVIS (AV)

50 West San Fernando Street, Suite 1300, 95113-2413
Telephone: 408-292-1765
Telecopier: 408-292-4484

Richard W. Morton (1916-1975)	Charles V. Caillat (1920-1990)

Harvey C. Miller (1906-1993)

MEMBERS OF FIRM

David L. Nevis	Joseph A. Scanlan, Jr.
Francis J. Hughes	Carolyn Tobiason Stuart
Peter A. Kline	William K. Hurley
Stevan C. Adelman	Peter V. Dessau

Eric Mogensen

(See Next Column)

MILLER, MORTON, CAILLAT & NEVIS—*Continued*

OF COUNSEL

Nancy F. Symons   Susan L. Sutton
Pamela J. Silberstein

ASSOCIATES

Kathryn E. Barrett   David I. Kornbluh
Katherine S. Pak   Kimberly Holtz MacMillan

Representative Clients: Trammell Crow Residential Services; Joe Kerley Lincoln Mercury Co.; Milligan News Co.; Joseph George Distributors; The Frozen Food Employees Pension Trust; Santa Clara Dental Society; New West Foods; Bay Apartment Communities; Guy F. Atkinson Company; A. Hathaway Co.

For full biographical listings, see the Martindale-Hubbell Law Directory

---

SAN RAFAEL,* Marin Co.

RAGGHIANTI • FREITAS • MONTOBBIO • WALLACE LLP (AV)

874 Fourth Street, Suite D, 94901
Telephone: 415-453-9433
Fax: 415-453-8269

Gary T. Ragghianti   J. Randolph Wallace
David P. Freitas   Patrick M. Macias
J. Mark Montobbio   Robert F. Epstein
John Ralph Thomas

For full biographical listings, see the Martindale-Hubbell Law Directory

---

SANTA ANA,* Orange Co.

SPERLING & PERGANDE (AV)

3 Hutton Centre, Suite 670, 92707
Telephone: 714-540-8500
Facsimile: 714-540-2599

MEMBERS OF FIRM

Dean P. Sperling   K. William Pergande

For full biographical listings, see the Martindale-Hubbell Law Directory

---

SANTA BARBARA,* Santa Barbara Co.

ANGLE, CARLSON, GOLDRICK & ROBERTS (AV)

A Partnership including a Professional Corporation
200 East Carrillo Street, Suite 310, 93101
Telephone: 805-963-7400
Fax: 805-963-7610

Robert O. Angle   Miles T. Goldrick
Arthur W. Carlson (A P.C.)   Paul A. Roberts

OF COUNSEL

Georgia C. McDermott

For full biographical listings, see the Martindale-Hubbell Law Directory

---

SEED, MACKALL & COLE LLP (AV)

1332 Anacapa Street, Suite 200, 93101
Telephone: 805-963-0669
Fax: 805-962-1404

MEMBERS OF FIRM

John R. Mackall   Christopher E. Hahn
Joseph L. Cole   Sandra Hitchens Thoits
Gregory Canova-Parker   David E. Reese
Thomas N. Harding   K. Andrew Kent
Peter A. Umoff   Alan D. Condren
Barton E. Clemens, Jr.   Nicholas J. Schneider

Representative Clients: City Commerce Bank; Montecito Bank & Trust; Santa Barbara Bank & Trust; Digital Instruments, Inc.; G & H Technology Inc.; Mission Research Corporation; Bermant Development Company; The Investec Real Estate Companies; STAR Telecommunications, Inc.; TELNET Communications Group.

For full biographical listings, see the Martindale-Hubbell Law Directory

---

SANTA MONICA, Los Angeles Co.

GILCHRIST & RUTTER, PROFESSIONAL CORPORATION (AV)

Wilshire Palisades Building, 1299 Ocean Avenue, Suite 900, 90401
Telephone: 310-393-4000
Facsimile: 310-394-4700
Los Angeles, California Office: 355 South Grand Avenue, Suite 4100.
Telephone: 213-617-8000.
Facsimile: 213-346-7973.

Frank Gooch, III   Susan Fowler McNally
Jonathan S. Gross   Thomas E. Stindt
Paul S. Rutter   Donald C. Nanney
James R. Andrews   Diana P. Scott

Michael E. Hagan   Sean T. Prosser

(See Next Column)

OF COUNSEL

Richard I. Gilchrist   Herbert Katz
Christine A. Page

For full biographical listings, see the Martindale-Hubbell Law Directory

---

RICHARD E. HODGE, INC. (AV)

The Water Garden East Tower, Suite 600, 2425 West Olympic Boulevard, 90404-4043
Telephone: 310-453-5344
Fax: 310-315-0051

Richard E. Hodge   Gary G. Kuist
Jefferson W. Gross

For full biographical listings, see the Martindale-Hubbell Law Directory

---

SACKS ZWEIG & BURRIS, LLP (AV)

100 Wilshire Building, Suite 1300, 100 Wilshire Boulevard, 90401
Telephone: 310-451-3113
Facsimile: 310-451-0089
San Francisco, California Office: 100 Pine Street, 21st Floor.
Telephone: 415-788-6794.
Facsimile: 415-788-7009.

MEMBERS

Donald S. Burris   Lee Sacks
Michael K. Zweig

ASSOCIATES

Les Bradford Hairrell   Filomena E. Meyer

OF COUNSEL

Dennis Holahan   Barton S. Selden

For full biographical listings, see the Martindale-Hubbell Law Directory

---

STEINBERG, NUTTER & BRENT, LAW CORPORATION (AV)

501 Colorado Avenue, Suite 300, 90401
Telephone: 310-451-9714
Telecopier: 310-451-0929
Woodland Hills, California Office: 21031 Ventura Boulevard, Suite 419.
Telephone: 818-703-6204.

Peter T. Steinberg   Guy B. Nutter
Paul M. Brent

James M. Buck

Reference: Santa Monica Bank.

For full biographical listings, see the Martindale-Hubbell Law Directory

---

GERALD T. YOSHIDA (AV)

100 Wilshire Boulevard, Suite 1000, 90401
Telephone: 310-393-9212
Telecopier: 310-395-2132

Representative Clients: Vido Artukovich & Sons Construction; McKean Construction; Spiess Construction; Gierlich-Mitchell, Inc.; Ullibarri Construction; Hill Crane Service, Inc.; ACI General Engineering Contractors; A.A. Portanova & Sons, Inc.; Rough Terraih, Inc.; Altfillisch Construction.

For full biographical listings, see the Martindale-Hubbell Law Directory

---

SANTA ROSA,* Sonoma Co.

BELDEN, ABBEY, WEITZENBERG & KELLY, A PROFESSIONAL CORPORATION (AV)

1105 North Dutton Avenue, P.O. Box 1566, 95402
Telephone: 707-542-5050
Telecopier: 707-542-2589

Thomas P. Kelly, Jr.   Candace H. Shirley
Richard W. Abbey   Lewis R. Warren

Peter J. Walls

Representative Clients: Exchange Bank of Santa Rosa; Westamerica Bank; North Bay Title Co.; Northwestern Title Security Co.; Geyser Peak Winery; Santa Rosa City School District; Sonoma National Bank; Arrowood Vineyards & Winery; Arthur & DeVincenzi Concrete; Friedman Bros. Hardware, Inc.

For Complete List of Firm Personnel, See General Section

For full biographical listings, see the Martindale-Hubbell Law Directory

---

TORRANCE, Los Angeles Co.

FINER, KIM & STEARNS (AV)

An Association of Professional Corporations
City National Bank Building, 3424 Carson Street, Suite 500, 90503
Telephone: 310-214-1477
Telecopier: 310-214-0764

(See Next Column)

FINER, KIM & STEARNS, *Torrance—Continued*

Harry J. Kim (A Professional Corporation)
W. A. Finer (A Professional Corporation)

Robert David Ciaccio
Robert B. Parsons

OF COUNSEL
Bennett A. Rheingold   Ryan E. Stearns

LEGAL SUPPORT PERSONNEL
Marcia E. Talbert

For Complete List of Firm Personnel, See General Section

For full biographical listings, see the Martindale-Hubbell Law Directory

---

VALENCIA, Los Angeles Co.

NAHIN AND NAHIN, LAW CORPORATION (AV)

23929 West Valencia Boulevard, Suite 411, 91355
Telephone: 805-287-3610
Fax: 805-287-3612
Email: nahin@aol.com
Los Angeles, California Office: 6500 Wilshire Boulevard, Suite 550.
Telephone: 213-651-0170.
Telecopier: 213-651-0158.

Bruce A. Nahin

For full biographical listings, see the Martindale-Hubbell Law Directory

---

VENTURA,* Ventura Co.

FERGUSON, CASE, ORR, PATERSON & CUNNINGHAM (AV)

1050 South Kimball Road, 93004
Telephone: 805-659-6800
Telecopier: 805-659-6818
Email: info@fcopc.com

Thomas R. Ferguson
Michael W. Case
John C. Orr
William E. Paterson
David L. Cunningham
Lou Carpiac

Joseph L. Strohman, Jr.
Robert L. Gallaway
Sandra M. Robertson
William B. Smith
Gisele Goetz
Ramon L. Guizar

Gregory W. Herring

Douglas E. Kulper
OF COUNSEL
Allen F. Camp

Representative Clients: First American Title Insurance Company; Wells Fargo Bank; The Hahn Company (Oaks Regional Shopping Center); Area Housing Authority of the County of Ventura; Buenaventura Medical Clinic, Inc.; Southern Pacific Milling Company; USA Petroleum Corporation; Cellular One.

For full biographical listings, see the Martindale-Hubbell Law Directory

LAW OFFICES OF MICHAEL R. SMENT (AV)

674 County Square Drive, Suite 108, 93003-5402
Telephone: 805-654-0311
Telecopier: 805-984-2399
Email: rockjr@aol.com
Los Angeles, California Office: 1800 Avenue of the Stars, Suite 1000.
Telephone: 310-277-6361; 277-6362.
Fax: 310-277-6517.

For full biographical listings, see the Martindale-Hubbell Law Directory

---

VISTA, San Diego Co.

ERNEST L. HUNT, JR. (AV)

630 Alta Vista Drive, Suite 103, P.O. Box 640, 92085-0640
Telephone: 619-726-3839
Fax: 619-726-5491

For full biographical listings, see the Martindale-Hubbell Law Directory

---

WALNUT CREEK, Contra Costa Co.

FIELD, RICHARDSON & WILHELMY (AV)

Peri Executive Centre, 2033 North Main Street, Suite 900, 94596-3729
Telephone: 510-934-7700
Telecopier: 510-934-6090

MEMBERS
Robert C. Field   Robert W. Richardson
Alan J. Wilhelmy

ASSOCIATE
Emelyn Jewett Carothers

(See Next Column)

OF COUNSEL
Donald L. Edgar

Reference: Civic Bank of Commerce (Walnut Creek Regional Office).

For full biographical listings, see the Martindale-Hubbell Law Directory

JACKL & KATZEN (AV)

2033 North Main Street, Suite 700, 94596
Telephone: 510-932-8500
Fax: 510-932-1961
Email: jklawfirm@aol.com

MEMBERS OF FIRM
V. James Jackl   Linda R. Katzen

Andrew N. Contopoulos

For full biographical listings, see the Martindale-Hubbell Law Directory

MORGAN, MILLER & BLAIR, PROFESSIONAL CORPORATION (AV)

1676 North California Boulevard, Suite 200, 94596-4137
Telephone: 510-937-3600
Telecopier: 510-943-1106
Email: info@mmb.law.com

Kenneth M. Miller
Richard G. Blair
Marilyn Morris
Bruce E. Ring
Darryl D. Ott
Ira J. Harris
Kathleen F. Carpenter
Michael K. Brown

Richard C. Vasquez
Smeeta S. Rishi
George S. Cabot
James M. Cady
Clifford R. Horner
Lance Burtis Smith
J. Bert Morgan, III (Retired)
Paula Keve Morgan (Retired)

For full biographical listings, see the Martindale-Hubbell Law Directory

---

COLORADO

ASPEN,* Pitkin Co.

AUSTIN, PEIRCE & SMITH, P.C. (AV)

Suite 205, 600 East Hopkins Avenue, 81611
Telephone: 970-925-2600
FAX: 970-925-4720
Email: apspc@rof.net

Ronald D. Austin   Frederick F. Peirce
Thomas Fenton Smith

Michael P. Fossenier

Counsel for: Chase Manhattan of Colorado, Inc.; Clark's Market; Cootes, Reid & Waldron Property Management, Inc.; Crystal Palace Corp.; Snowmass Shopping Center; Coldwell Banker The Aspen Brokers, Ltd.; William Poss & Assoc., Architects; Snowmass Resort Association; Aspen/Pitkin County Housing Authority; Nations Title Insurance, Inc.

For full biographical listings, see the Martindale-Hubbell Law Directory

J. NICHOLAS McGRATH, P.C. (AV)

Suite 203, 600 East Hopkins Avenue, 81611
Telephone: 970-925-2612
Telecopier: 970-925-4402
Email: nicklaw@csn.net *URL:* http://www.aspenlink.com/nicklaw

J. Nicholas McGrath

Susan W. Laatsch

Representative Clients: Alpine Surveys, Inc.; Aspen Alps Condominium Assn.; Aspen Center for Physics; Gant Condominium Assn.; Hotel Jerome Associates, Ltd. Partners; Redstone Investments, Inc. (Cleveholm Castle).

For Complete List of Firm Personnel, See General Section

For full biographical listings, see the Martindale-Hubbell Law Directory

---

BOULDER,* Boulder Co.

HOWARD BITTMAN (AV)

1406 Pearl Street, Suite 200, 80302
Telephone: 303-443-2281
Fax: 303-443-2862

For full biographical listings, see the Martindale-Hubbell Law Directory

Boulder—Continued

MARTIN & MEHAFFY (AV)

1655 Walnut Street, P.O. Box 1260, 80302
Telephone: 303-442-3375
Fax: 303-444-8398
Email: mmllc@aol.com *URL:* http://www.planetnetwork.com/law/

MEMBERS OF FIRM

James G. Martin (Retired)	Joel C. Maguire
John R. Mehaffy	Jeffrey L. Skovron
Lawrence C. Rider	Matthew S. Humphrey
Donald James Humphrey	Jonathan L. Miller

OF COUNSEL
Richard A. Tharp

Approved Attorneys for: Attorneys Title Guaranty Fund, Inc.

For full biographical listings, see the Martindale-Hubbell Law Directory

CASTLE ROCK,* Douglas Co.

FOLKESTAD & FAZEKAS, P.C. (AV)

316 Wilcox Street, 80104-2495
Telephone: 303-688-3045
FAX: 303-688-3189

James B. Folkestad   Ernest F. Fazekas, II

Susan B. Shoemaker

Representative Clients: Bank of Douglas County; Johnson & Sons Construction, Inc.; B & W Construction Co.; Proto Construction & Paving, Inc.; Grimm Construction Co.; Ashcroft Homes of Denver LLC.
References: Bank of Douglas County; First National Bank of Castle Rock; First Bank of Castle Rock; Colorado National Bank.

For full biographical listings, see the Martindale-Hubbell Law Directory

COLORADO SPRINGS,* El Paso Co.

BELTZ, EDWARDS & SABO, L.L.P. (AV)

729 South Cascade, 80903
Telephone: 719-473-4444; 719-634-6620
Fax: 719-444-0186

W. Thomas Beltz   Daniel P. Edwards
John W. Sabo, III

Daniel A. West

Representative Clients: Marth Taylor and Associates, Inc.; Martin Properties, Inc.; Phoenix Partners, LLC; Realtec Associates; WP Development Company.

For full biographical listings, see the Martindale-Hubbell Law Directory

FLYNN MCKENNA WRIGHT & KARSH (AV)

limited liability company
Plaza of the Rockies 111 South Tejon, Suite 202, 80903
Telephone: 719-578-8444
Fax: 719-578-8836

James T. Flynn	Randolph M. Karsh
R. Tim McKenna	Brian T. Murphy
Bruce M. Wright	Michael C. Potarf

Representative Clients: Peregrine Joint Venture; Nor'wood Development, Inc.; Vintage Development, Inc.; The Woziwodski Group (Consulting Architects); Wal-Mart Stores; Comito Custom Homes, Inc.; Colorado Springs Savings and Loan Association; Chase Manhattan Mortgage Corp.

For full biographical listings, see the Martindale-Hubbell Law Directory

GADDIS, KIN & HERD, P.C. (AV)

118 South Wahsatch, Suite 100, 80903
Telephone: 719-471-3848
Fax: 719-471-0317

Larry R. Gaddis	Thomas J. Herd
James W. Kin	David L. Quicksall (1950-1991)

OF COUNSEL
James B. Turner

Reference: Norwest Bank of Colorado Springs.

For full biographical listings, see the Martindale-Hubbell Law Directory

JAMES A. WEIR (AV)

Suite 510 Alamo Corporate Center, 102 South Tejon, 80903
Telephone: 719-473-9906
FAX: 719-473-8152

References: Bank One; Colorado National Bank/Exchange.

For full biographical listings, see the Martindale-Hubbell Law Directory

---

DENVER,* Denver Co.

BALLARD SPAHR ANDREWS & INGERSOLL (AV)

Seventeenth Street Plaza Building, Suite 2300, 1225 17th Street, 80202-5596
Telephone: 303-292-2400
Fax: 303-296-3956
Philadelphia, Pennsylvania Office: 1735 Market Street, 51st Floor.
Telephone: 215-665-8500.
Fax: 215-864-8999.
Harrisburg, Pennsylvania Office: 105 North Front Street.
Telephone: 717-236-3333.
Fax: 717-236-3884.
Salt Lake City, Utah Office: One Utah Center, 201 South Main Street, Suite 1200.
Telephone: 801-531-3000.
Fax: 801-531-3001.
Washington, D.C. Office: Suite 900 East, 555 13th Street, N.W.
Telephone: 202-383-8800.
Fax: 202-383-8877; 383-8893.
Baltimore, Maryland Office: 300 East Lombard Street, 19th Floor.
Telephone: 410-528-5600.
Fax: 410-528-5650.
Camden, New Jersey Office: 800 Hudson Square, 5th Floor.
Telephone: 609-541-5577.
Fax: 609-541-8272.

Beverly J. Quail

Anita Shakeh Agajanian   Karen Samuels Jones

For Complete List of Firm Personnel, See General Section

For full biographical listings, see the Martindale-Hubbell Law Directory

ROBERT L. BARTHOLIC (AV)

Suite 500, 1600 Broadway, 80202
Telephone: 303-830-0500
Fax: 303-860-7855

OF COUNSEL
Clarence L. Bartholic

Approved Attorney for: Mid-South Title Insurance Corp; Lawyers Title Insurance Co.
Representative Clients: Anschutz Corp.; Denver and Rio Grande Western Railroad Co.; Johnson Anderson Mortgage Co.; Arco Environmental Affairs; Burlington Northern Railroad Co. and Subsidiaries; American Association of Private Railroad Car Owners, Inc.
References: Colorado National Bank; Colorado State Bank.

For full biographical listings, see the Martindale-Hubbell Law Directory

BEARMAN TALESNICK & CLOWDUS, PROFESSIONAL CORPORATION (AV)

1200 Seventeenth Street, Suite 2600, 80202-5826
Telephone: 303-572-6500
Facsimile: 303-572-6511

W. Michael Clowdus   Martha S. Nachman
SPECIAL COUNSEL
Andrea Bloom

Representative Clients: Points of Colorado; Preferred Equities Corporation; Terrapark, Inc.; The Christie Lodge; Vacation Internationale, Inc.

For full biographical listings, see the Martindale-Hubbell Law Directory

BENJAMIN & ASSOCIATES, P.C. (AV)

5555 DTC Parkway Suite 4000-A (Englewood) 80111, P.O. Box 370509, 80237-0509
Telephone: 303-290-6600
Facsimile: 303-290-8323

James G. Benjamin

David M. Suhr

For full biographical listings, see the Martindale-Hubbell Law Directory

BERENBAUM, WEINSHIENK & EASON, P.C. (AV)

Suite 2600 Republic Plaza, 370 17th Street, 80202
Telephone: 303-825-0800
Facsimile: 303-629-7610
Durango, Colorado Office: 2815 Main.
Telephone: 303-247-1333.

Mandel Berenbaum (1914-1993)	Joseph S. Borus
Hubert T. Weinshienk (1931-1983)	Martin D. Buckley
Joseph Berenbaum	M. Frances Cetrulo
Charles A. Bewley	Daniel S. Duggan
	David R. Eason

(See Next Column)

BERENBAUM, WEINSHIENK & EASON, P.C., *Denver—Continued*

Richard L. Eason	Neil B. Oberfeld
Steven C. Hoth	Dean G. Panos
James A. Jacobson	Edwin G. Perlmutter
I. H. Kaiser	Barry M. Permut
Kenneth S. Kramer	Keith M. Pockross
James L. Kurtz-Phelan	Dan A. Sciullo
Charles P. Leder	Edward L. Sperry
A. Elizabeth Meyers	Eugene M. Sprague
H. Michael Miller	Robert G. Wilson, Jr.

Ronald I. Zall

J. Hunter Banbury	Amy L. Durfee
Patricia Bellac	Heather Scheel Hagemann

Stephen K. Schutte

SPECIAL COUNSEL

John E. Bush

Representative Clients: Stanley Works; Columbine Venture Funds; The Home Depot; Karman, Inc.; Lomas Mortgage; Southwest State Bank; The Bank of Boulder; Teamsters; Trinity Ventures; The David Johnson Group.

For full biographical listings, see the Martindale-Hubbell Law Directory

BRENMAN KEY & BROMBERG, P.C. (AV)

Mellon Financial Center Suite 1001, 1775 Sherman Street, 80203
Telephone: 303-894-0234
Fax: 303-839-1633

Albert Brenman	Donna A. Key
Thomas R. Bromberg	Steven W. McDonald

Theresa M. Mehringer	George D. Kreye

OF COUNSEL

Heather H. S. Sander	A. Thomas Tenenbaum
D. Elizabeth Wills	Edmund L. Epstein (Inactive)

For full biographical listings, see the Martindale-Hubbell Law Directory

BROWN, HARMON & ECKSTEIN, P.C. (AV)

Suite 3000 1700 Lincoln Street, 80203
Telephone: 303-293-3636
Fax: 303-830-2653
Email: eckstein@csn.org
Email: BHE@Lawyernet.com *URL:* http://eckstein.net/ecksteinlaw

James E. Brown

For full biographical listings, see the Martindale-Hubbell Law Directory

BROWNSTEIN HYATT FARBER & STRICKLAND, P.C. (AV)

Twenty-Second Floor, 410 Seventeenth Street, 80202-4437
Telephone: 303-534-6335
Telecopier: 303-623-1956
Washington, D.C. Office: 601 Pennsylvania Avenue, N.W., Suite 900.
Telephone: 202-434-8377.
Telecopier: 202-393-7864.

Norman Brownstein	Ronald B. Merrill
Steven W. Farber	Lynda A. McNeive
Edward N. Barad	Laura Jean Christman
John R. Call	Wayne H. Hykan
Steven M. Sommers	Bruce A. James

OF COUNSEL

Jack N. Hyatt	Ann B. Riley

Steven C. Demby

Robert Kaufmann	Jill E. Murray
Jay F. Kamlet	Howard J. Pollack
Ana Lazo Tenzer	Ellen O. Kauffmann
David M. Brown	Lea Ann T. Groesser

Representative Clients: Bank One; DPC Development Company; Nomura Asset Capital Corporation; Prime West Real Estate Services; The Republic Investment Fund, Inc.; SunAmerica Inc.; Trammell Crow Company; Transamerica Realty Services, Inc.; U.S. Home Corporation; Vail Associates, Inc.

For Complete List of Firm Personnel, See General Section

For full biographical listings, see the Martindale-Hubbell Law Directory

CARPENTER & KLATSKIN, P.C. (AV)

1500 Denver Club Building, 518 Seventeenth Street, 80202
Telephone: 303-534-6315
Telecopier: 303-534-0514

Willis V. Carpenter	Andrew S. Klatskin

Judith C. McNerny	Max A. Minnig, Jr.

(See Next Column)

LEGAL SUPPORT PERSONNEL
PARALEGAL
Holly S. Hoxeng

Reference: Colorado State Bank.

For full biographical listings, see the Martindale-Hubbell Law Directory

JON B. CLARKE, P.C. (AV)

Two DTC, Suite 150, 5290 DTC Parkway (Englewood), 80111-2721
Telephone: 303-779-0600
Fax: 303-850-7115
Email: jbclarke102421.2703@compuserve.com

Jon B. Clarke

For full biographical listings, see the Martindale-Hubbell Law Directory

DAVIS & WEINSTEIN (AV)

Suite 2600, 1600 Broadway, 80202
Telephone: 303-861-4166

Wendy W. Davis	Jo Ann Weinstein

For full biographical listings, see the Martindale-Hubbell Law Directory

DUFFORD & BROWN, P.C. (AV)

1700 Broadway, Suite 1700, 80290-1701
Telephone: 303-861-8013
Facsimile: 303-832-3804
Affiliated Office: Solomon, Pearl, Blum & Quinn, L.L.P., New York, NY and Denver, Colorado.

Thomas G. Brown	S. Kirk Ingebretsen
Randall J. Feuerstein	Edward D. White

Representative Clients: CF&I Steel, L.P.; IDS Life Insurance Company; Hall and Hall Mortgage Corporation; Reorganized CF&I Steel Corp.; Winding Brook Corporation.

For Complete List of Firm Personnel, See General Section

For full biographical listings, see the Martindale-Hubbell Law Directory

ELROD, KATZ, PREEO, LOOK, MOISON & SILVERMAN, PROFESSIONAL CORPORATION (AV)

Suite 1100, 1120 Lincoln Street, 80203
Telephone: 303-832-1900
Fax: 303-863-0412

Richard B. Elrod	Harley K. Look, Jr.
Michael M. Katz	Peter R. Moison
Robert L. Preeo	Eldon E. Silverman

Jersey M. Green	Kathryn A. Reeves
Richard M. Hess, Jr.	Gilbert R. Egle
Martin J. Green	Timothy Kyle Jordan
Marilyn McWilliams	Brian E. Onorato

OF COUNSEL

Richard P. Rosen

For full biographical listings, see the Martindale-Hubbell Law Directory

FAIRFIELD AND WOODS, P.C. (AV)

One Norwest Center, Suite 2400, 1700 Lincoln Street, 80203-4524
Telephone: 303-830-2400
Telecopier: 303-830-1033
Email: sseifert@fwlaw.com *URL:* http://www.fwlaw.com/

Peter F. Breitenstein	John J. Silver
Charlton H. Carpenter	Thomas P. Kearns
Howard Holme	Rocco A. Dodson
Robert S. Slosky	Mary E. Moser
James L. Stone	Brent T. Johnson
Michael M. McKinstry	Stephen H. Leonhardt
Robert L. Loeb, Jr.	Caroline C. Fuller
Daniel R. Frost	Gregory C. Smith
Stephen W. Seifert	John M. Tanner
Mary Jo Gross	Neil T. Duggan
Robert A. Holmes	Douglas J. Becker

SPECIAL COUNSEL

John S. Pfeiffer

Thomas M. Pierce	Jacalyn W. Peter
Suzanne R. Kalutkiewicz	David L. Joeris
Philip J. Roselli	Christine E. Payne

Sean D. Baker

Representative Clients: Bank of America; Bank of Montreal; Copper Mountain, Inc.; Crown Life Insurance Company; Denver Metropolitan Major League Baseball Stadium District; John Hancock Mutual Life Insurance Company; Norwest Bank Colorado, N.A.; Prime Retail, Inc.; Sun Life Assurance Company of Canada.

(See Next Column)

FAIRFIELD AND WOODS P.C.—*Continued*

For full biographical listings, see the Martindale-Hubbell Law Directory

MAURICE F. FOX (AV)

4465 Kipling Street (Wheat Ridge), 80033
Telephone: 303-424-4443
Fax: 303-421-4309

References: 1st Bank of Westland; 1st Bank of Wheat Ridge.

For full biographical listings, see the Martindale-Hubbell Law Directory

GRUND & BRESLAU, P.C. (AV)

303 East Seventeenth Avenue, Suite 1030, 80203-1260
Telephone: 303-830-7770
Facsimile: 303-830-2313

John W. Grund   Della S. Nelson
Brad W. Breslau   Phillip Jeffrey Frazee

Representative Clients: Basic Capital Management, Inc.; Colorado Farm Bureau Mutual Insurance Co.; Gallagher, Bassett Services, Inc.

For full biographical listings, see the Martindale-Hubbell Law Directory

HOLME ROBERTS & OWEN LLP (AV)

Suite 4100, 1700 Lincoln, 80203
Telephone: 303-861-7000
Telecopier: 303-866-0200
Email: hro@hro.com *URL:* http://www.hro.com
Boulder, Colorado Office: Suite 400, 1401 Pearl Street.
Telephone: 303-444-5955.
Telecopier: 303-444-1063.
Colorado Springs, Colorado Office: Suite 1300, 90 South Cascade Avenue.
Telephone: 719-473-3800.
Telecopier: 719-633-1518.
Salt Lake City, Utah Office: Suite 1100, 111 East Broadway.
Telephone: 801-521-5800.
Telecopier: 801-521-9639.
London, England Office: Mellier House, 26a Albemarle Street.
Telephone: 44-171-499-8776.
Telecopier: 44-171-499-7769.
Moscow, Russia Office: Kosmodamianskaya Nab. #52/1, Suite 9100, 113054.
Telephone: 7095-961-3000.
Telecopier: 7095-961-3001.
Kiev, Ukraine Office: Terestchenkovskaya #19, Suite 2, 252004.
Telephone: 380-44-224-1348.
Telecopier: 380-44-224-4986.

PARTNERS OF FIRM

Richard G. Wohlgenant   Robert H. Bach
G. Kevin Conwick   James R. Ghiselli
Bruce L. Likoff   (Boulder Office)
Martha Traudt Collins   Paul V. Timmins
Jill K. Rood (Boulder Office)   Patrick K. Perrin
     (Boulder Office)

SPECIAL COUNSEL

David H. Goldberg   John B. Wood (Boulder Office)
David W. Isbell
(Colorado Springs Office)

ASSOCIATES

Daron J. Arnold   Lisa Anne Hawkins
(Not admitted in CO)   Brent P. Karasiuk
Christopher Boffey (Resident,   (Colorado Springs Office)
Moscow, Russia Office)   William C. Letzsch, III
Rebecca Hall (Boulder Office)   Peter-Christian Olivo
     (Boulder Office)

For Complete List of Firm Personnel, See General Section

For full biographical listings, see the Martindale-Hubbell Law Directory

KARSH AND FULTON, PROFESSIONAL CORPORATION (AV)

Suite 710, 950 South Cherry Street, 80222
Telephone: 303-759-9669
Fax: 303-782-0902

Alan E. Karsh   Fred Gabler
Larry C. Fulton   J. Terry Wiggins
     Seymour Joseph

Antonio T. Ciccarelli

Representative Clients: Marcus and Millichap; Fidelity National Title Insurance; TransNation Title Insurance Company; The Travelers Insurance Company; Colorado Land Source, Ltd.; Zeff Properties; Lawyers Title Insurance Corp.; Commonwealth Land Title Insurance Corp.; First American Title Insurance Company; Old Republic National Title Insurance Co.

For full biographical listings, see the Martindale-Hubbell Law Directory

LOHF, SHAIMAN & JACOBS, P.C. (AV)

950 South Cherry Street, Suite 900, 80222
Telephone: 303-753-9000
Telecopier: 303-753-9997

Charles H. Jacobs   Robert Shaiman

Reference: Professional Bank.

For full biographical listings, see the Martindale-Hubbell Law Directory

MESSNER PAVEK & REEVES, LLC (AV)

600 Seventeenth Street, Suite 2800-South, 80202
Telephone: 303-623-1800
Facsimile: 303-623-0552
Evergreen, Colorado Office: 1202 Bergen Parkway, Suite 300.
Telephone: 303-670-1800.
Facsimile: 303-670-2606.

Bryant S. Messner   Ronald K. Reeves
David D. Pavek   (Resident, Evergreen Office)

SPECIAL COUNSEL

Robert W. Berry (Not admitted in CO)

OF COUNSEL

James R. Everson

John K. Shunk   Mary Jo Dougherty
David A. Reeves   Julia Griffith McVey
Heather Anne Hawker   Montgomery F. Moran

For full biographical listings, see the Martindale-Hubbell Law Directory

OTTEN, JOHNSON, ROBINSON, NEFF & RAGONETTI, P.C. (AV)

950 Seventeenth Street, 16th Floor, 80202
Telephone: 303-825-8400
Telecopier: 303-825-6525

Frank L. Robinson   Henry I. Lowe
Bruce B. Johnson   Kathleen M. Bottagaro
William R. Neff   R. Michael Shomo
Thomas J. Ragonetti   Michael C. Villano
Robert C. Fisher, Jr.   Alex Iskenderian
J. Thomas Macdonald   Victoria L. Hellmer
John D. Sternberg   Daniel J. Culhane
Michael Westover   Christopher T. Toll
Daniel M. Minzer   Richard C. Jennings
Kevin A. Gliwa   James C. Ellenberger

OF COUNSEL

Kenneth M. Robins

SPECIAL COUNSEL

Marguerite L. Sadler

Representative Clients: Aetna Life Insurance Co.; The Broe Companies; Inc.; Colorado National Bank; Connecticut General Life Insurance Co.; First Nationwide Bank; Homart Development Co.; Land Title Guarantee Co.; Trizec Corporation Ltd.; U.S. West Communications, Inc.; The Western Sugar Co.

For Complete List of Firm Personnel, See General Section

For full biographical listings, see the Martindale-Hubbell Law Directory

PARCEL, MAURO, HULTIN & SPAANSTRA, P.C. (AV)

Suite 3600, 1801 California Street, 80202
Telephone: 303-292-6400
Telecopier: 303-295-3040

Randall G. Alt   James M. King
     Michael M. Page

Reference: 1st Interstate, Denver, Colorado.

For Complete List of Firm Personnel, See General Section

For full biographical listings, see the Martindale-Hubbell Law Directory

SENN LEWIS VISCIANO & STRAHLE, PROFESSIONAL CORPORATION (AV)

Suite 4300, 1801 California Street, 80202
Telephone: 303-298-1122
Telecopier: 303-296-9101

Mark A. Senn   Wynn E. Strahle
Fredric J. Lewis   Stephen W. Arent

David C. Camp   Margie J. Titus
     Laura B. Redstone

OF COUNSEL

Lawrence A. Atler (P.C.)

(See Next Column)

SENN LEWIS VISCIANO & STRAHLE PROFESSIONAL CORPORATION, *Denver—Continued*

SPECIAL COUNSEL
Ellen Kirschenbaum

For Complete List of Firm Personnel, See General Section

For full biographical listings, see the Martindale-Hubbell Law Directory

WALTERS & JOYCE, P.C. (AV)

2015 York Street, 80205
Telephone: 303-322-1404
FAX: 303-377-5668

OF COUNSEL
Julia T. Waggener

Reference: Norwest Bank of Buckingham Square; Mountain States Bank.

For Complete List of Firm Personnel, See General Section

For full biographical listings, see the Martindale-Hubbell Law Directory

DURANGO,* La Plata Co.

FRANK J. ANESI (AV)

Suite 220, 835 East Second Avenue, P.O. Box 2185, 81302
Telephone: 970-247-9246
Fax: 970-259-2793

References: First National Bank of Durango; Burns Bank, Durango.

For full biographical listings, see the Martindale-Hubbell Law Directory

ENGLEWOOD, Arapahoe Co.

BANTA, HOYT, EVERALL & FARRINGTON, L.L.C. (AV)

Suite 240E, 5690 DTC Boulevard, 80111
Telephone: 303-220-8000
Fax: 303-220-0153

Richard J. Banta
OF COUNSEL
Craig E. Wagner

Representative Clients: American Institute of Timber Construction; Cherry Creek School District No. 5; City of Greenwood Village; Colorado School District Self Insurance Pool; Intermountain Rural Electric Association; Kiewit Western Co.; Littleton Public Schools; National Union Fire Insurance Co. (local); Southgate Sanitation and Water Districts.

For Complete List of Firm Personnel, See General Section

For full biographical listings, see the Martindale-Hubbell Law Directory

FORT COLLINS,* Larimer Co.

FISCHER, HOWARD & FRANCIS, LLP (AV)

125 South Howes, Suite 900, P.O. Box 506, 80522
Telephone: 970-482-4710
Fax: 970-482-4729

MEMBERS OF FIRM
Gene E. Fischer   Stephen E. Howard
Steven G. Francis

Approved Attorneys for: Attorney's Title Guaranty Fund, Inc.
Reference: First National Bank of Fort Collins, N.A.

For full biographical listings, see the Martindale-Hubbell Law Directory

GOLDEN,* Jefferson Co.

BRADLEY, CAMPBELL, CARNEY & MADSEN, PROFESSIONAL CORPORATION (AV)

1717 Washington Avenue, 80401-1994
Telephone: 303-278-3300
Fax: 303-278-3379
Email: firm@bccm.com

Leo N. Bradley

Counsel for: Coors Brewing Co.; Coors Ceramics Co.; Evergreen National Bank, Evergreen, Colorado; Clear Creek National Bank, Georgetown, Colorado; ASARCO, Inc.; Morrison-Knudsen; Westinghouse Electric Corp.
Local Counsel for: Public Service Company of Colorado.
Reference: Colorado National Bank, Denver, Colorado.

For Complete List of Firm Personnel, See General Section

For full biographical listings, see the Martindale-Hubbell Law Directory

HOLLEY, ALBERTSON & POLK, P.C. (AV)

Suite 100, 1667 Cole Boulevard, 80401
Telephone: 303-233-7838
Fax: 303-233-2860

(See Next Column)

George Alan Holley   Scott D. Albertson
Dennis B. Polk

Eric E. Torgersen   Thomas A. Walsh
Howard R. Stone

Reference: First Bank of Wheat Ridge.

For full biographical listings, see the Martindale-Hubbell Law Directory

GREELEY,* Weld Co.

BREGA & WINTERS, P.C. (AV)

1100 Tenth Street, Suite 402, 80631
Telephone: 970-352-4805
Fax: 970-352-6547
Denver, Colorado Office: One United Bank Center. 1700 Lincoln Street, Suite 2222 Street.
Telephone: 303-866-9400.
FAX: 303-861-9109.

Jerry D. Winters   Pamela A. Shaddock

Bradley D. Laue

For full biographical listings, see the Martindale-Hubbell Law Directory

VAIL, Eagle Co.

DUNN, ABPLANALP & CHRISTENSEN, P.C. (AV)

Suite 300 Vail Bank Building, 108 South Frontage Road
West, 81657-5087
Telephone: 970-476-0300
Telecopier: 970-476-4765

John W. Dunn   Arthur A. Abplanalp, Jr.
Randelle C. Stephenson

Representative Clients: Towns of Avon, Minturn and Red Cliff, Colorado.

For Complete List of Firm Personnel, See General Section

For full biographical listings, see the Martindale-Hubbell Law Directory

NORMAN R. HELWIG, P.C. (AV)

Suite 200-A, 1000 South Frontage Road West, 81657
Telephone: 970-479-9579
Telecopier: 970-479-9481
Email: helwig@csn.net

Norman R. Helwig

Representative Clients: RE/MAX Vail, Inc.; McInerney-McVey Real Estate, Inc.; Wescor Real Estate Development, Inc.; Canwest Ventures, Inc.; Camus Rental Mgt., Inc.; High Country Building Co.; Chateau at Beaver Creek Association; FirstBank Holding Company of Colorado, Inc. and subsidiary banks; Glen Eagle Townhome Ass'n.
Reference: FirstBank of Vail.

For full biographical listings, see the Martindale-Hubbell Law Directory

OTTO, PORTERFIELD & POST, LLC (AV)

51 Eagle Road, P.O. Box 3149, 81658-3149
Telephone: 970-949-5380
Fax: 970-845-9135

Frederick S. Otto   Wendell B. Porterfield, Jr.
William J. Post

References: 1st Bank of Vail; WestStar Bank.

For full biographical listings, see the Martindale-Hubbell Law Directory

CONNECTICUT

BRIDGEPORT,* Fairfield Co.

ELSTEIN AND ELSTEIN, P.C. (AV)

Suite 400 1087 Broad Street, 06604-4231
Telephone: 203-367-4421
Telecopier: 203-366-8615

Henry Elstein   Bruce L. Elstein

For full biographical listings, see the Martindale-Hubbell Law Directory

DARIEN, Fairfield Co.

MILLAR & AMBRETTE (AV)

23 Old King's Highway South, 06820-1267
Telephone: 203-655-7931
FAX: 203-656-2055

(See Next Column)

MILLAR & AMBRETTE—*Continued*

MEMBERS OF FIRM

Samuel D. B. Millar, Jr.   L. Conrad Ambrette

OF COUNSEL

Peter M. Ryan

ASSOCIATES

Patricia Moreland Gross   Carolyn C. Swiggart

For full biographical listings, see the Martindale-Hubbell Law Directory

---

RUCCI, BURNHAM, CARTA & EDELBERG (AV)

800 Post Road, P.O. Box 1107, 06820
Telephone: 203-655-7695
Facsimile: 203-655-4302
Email: rbce@netaxis.com

MEMBERS OF FIRM

Joseph J. Rucci, Jr.   Mark R. Carta
Paul H. Burnham   Paul B. Edelberg
          Kevin C. Beuttenmuller

ASSOCIATES

Thomas C. Healey   Karen K. Linder
William M. Carello   John E. Seelert
Colette C. Symon   (Not admitted in CT)

OF COUNSEL

Ian R. Crawford   James C. Dempsey
          George A. Reilly

For full biographical listings, see the Martindale-Hubbell Law Directory

---

GREENWICH, Fairfield Co.

ALBERT, WARD & JOHNSON, P.C. (AV)

125 Mason Street, P.O. Box 1668, 06836
Telephone: 203-661-8600
Telecopier: 203-661-8051

OF COUNSEL

David Albert   C. Robton Perelli-Minetti

Tom S. Ward, Jr.   Howard R. Wolfe
Scott R. Johnson   Christopher A. Kristoff
Jane D. Hogeman   Vicki K. Comberiati

For full biographical listings, see the Martindale-Hubbell Law Directory

---

HOLLAND KAUFMANN & BARTELS, LLC (AV)

289 Greenwich Avenue, 06830-6595
Telephone: 203-869-5600
Fax: 203-869-4648

Alexander J. Holland   Amy K. Wilfert
Charles B. Kaufmann, III   Harold R. Burke
Philip H. Bartels   Jean Mills Aranha
Beth K. Hansson   Lori E. Romano
          John C. Fusco

For full biographical listings, see the Martindale-Hubbell Law Directory

---

IVEY, BARNUM & O'MARA, LLC (AV)

Meridian Building, 170 Mason Street, P.O. Box 1689, 06830
Telephone: 203-661-6000
Telecopier: 203-661-9462

MEMBERS OF FIRM

Michael J. Allen   Donat C. Marchand
Robert C. Barnum, Jr.   Miles F. McDonald, Jr.
Edward D. Cosden, Jr.   Edwin J. O'Mara, Jr.
Wilmot L. Harris, Jr.   Remy A. Rodas
William I. Haslun II   Gregory A. Saum
Michael J. Jones   Lorraine Slavin
Edward T. Krumeich, Jr.   Steven B. Steinmetz

ASSOCIATES

Paul G. Amicucci   Melissa Townsend Klauberg
Stephan B. Grozinger   Cristin L. Rothfuss
Juerg A. Heim   Alan S. Rubenstein
Jennifer B. Kallenbach   Sheryl L. Sensale
          (Not admitted in CT)

OF COUNSEL

James W. Cuminale   Jennifer D. Port
Philip R. McKnight   (Not admitted in CT)

For full biographical listings, see the Martindale-Hubbell Law Directory

---

HARTFORD, * Hartford Co.

GORDON, MUIR AND FOLEY (AV)

Hartford Square North, Ten Columbus Boulevard, 06106-5123
Telephone: 860-525-5361
Telecopier: 860-525-4849

(See Next Column)

MEMBERS OF FIRM

William S. Gordon, Jr.   William J. Gallitto
  (1946-1956)   Gerald R. Swirsky
George Muir (1939-1976)   Robert J. O'Brien
Edward J. Foley (1955-1983)   Philip J. O'Connor
Peter C. Schwartz   Kenneth G. Williams
John J. Reid   Chester J. Bukowski
John H. Goodrich, Jr.   Mary Ann Santacroce
R. Bradley Wolfe   J. Lawrence Price
Jon Stephen Berk   Mary Anne Alicia Charron
          James G. Kelly

ASSOCIATES

Kevin F. Morin   Andrew J. Hern
Claudia A. Baio   Eileen McCarthy Geel
Patrick T. Treacy   Christopher L. Slack
          Renee W. Dwyer

OF COUNSEL

Stephen M. Riley

Reference: Fleet Bank.

For full biographical listings, see the Martindale-Hubbell Law Directory

---

SOROKIN SOROKIN GROSS HYDE & WILLIAMS P.C. (AV)

One Corporate Center, 06103
Telephone: 860-525-6645
Fax: 860-522-1781
Simsbury, Connecticut Office: 730 Hopmeadow Street.
Telephone: 860-651-9348.
Rocky Hill, Connecticut Office: 2360 Main Street.
Telephone: 860-563-9305.
Fax: 860-529-6931.

James G. Dowling, Jr.   Amelia M. Rugland
Barry D. Greene   Richard D. Tulisano
          (Resident, Rocky Hill Office)

For Complete List of Firm Personnel, See General Section

For full biographical listings, see the Martindale-Hubbell Law Directory

---

MILFORD, New Haven Co.

HARLOW, ADAMS & FRIEDMAN, P.C. (AV)

300 Bic Drive, 06460-3508
Telephone: 203-878-0661
Fax: 203-878-9568
Email: attorney@quidproquo.com

William D. Harlow (1921-1988)   Michael P. A. Williams
George W. Adams, III   Eric R. Gaynor
Dana Eric Friedman   Joseph A. Kubic
Theodore H. Shumaker   Elizabeth Stuckal
Stephen P. Wright   James M. Nugent

For full biographical listings, see the Martindale-Hubbell Law Directory

---

NEW HAVEN, * New Haven Co.

BERGMAN, HOROWITZ & REYNOLDS, P.C. (AV)

157 Church Street, 19th Floor, P.O. Box 426, 06502
Telephone: 203-789-1320
Fax: 203-785-8127
Email: mailbox@taxlawyers.com *URL:* http://www.taxlawyers.com
New York, N.Y. Office: 499 Park Avenue, 26th Floor.
Telephone: 212-688-4150.

Melvin Ditman   Jeremy A. Mellitz

Richard M. Porter   Paul J. Stankewich

For full biographical listings, see the Martindale-Hubbell Law Directory

---

GORMAN & ENRIGHT P.C. (AV)

59 Elm Street, P.O. Box 1961, 06509
Telephone: 203-865-1382
Telecopier: 203-776-7250

John R. Gorman   Brian G. Enright

OF COUNSEL

Patricia King   Earle Giovanniello

References: Bank of New Haven; AT&T Capital Corp.; McGladrey & Pullen.

For full biographical listings, see the Martindale-Hubbell Law Directory

---

SUSMAN, DUFFY & SEGALOFF, P.C. (AV)

55 Whitney Avenue, 06510-1300
Telephone: 203-624-9830
Telecopier: 203-562-8430
Mailing Address: P.O. Box 1684, New Haven, Connecticut, 06507-1684

(See Next Column)

SUSMAN, DUFFY & SEGALOFF P.C., *New Haven—Continued*

Allen H. Duffy (1931-1986)	Susan W. Wolfson
Michael Susman	Laura M. Sklaver
James H. Segaloff	Andrew R. Lubin
David A. Reif	James J. Perito
Joseph E. Faughnan	Matthew C. Susman
	Thomas E. Katon

Jennifer L. Schancupp	Peter G. Kruzynski
Donna Decker Morris	Joshua W. Cohen
	Vincent J. Candelora

OF COUNSEL

Diana C. Ballard	David P. Hambleton

For full biographical listings, see the Martindale-Hubbell Law Directory

---

NEW LONDON, New London Co.

WALLER, SMITH & PALMER, P.C. (AV)

52 Eugene O'Neill Drive, P.O. Box 88, 06320
Telephone: 860-442-0367
Telecopier: 860-447-9915
Old Lyme, Connecticut Office: 103-A Halls Road.
Telephone: 860-434-8063.
Telecopier: 860-434-9452.

William W. Miner	Hughes Griffis
Robert P. Anderson, Jr.	Edward B. O'Connell
Robert W. Marrion	Frederick B. Gahagan
	Mary E. Driscoll

Tracy M. Collins

General Counsel For: Town of East Lyme; Town of Lebanon.
Counsel For: Citizens Savings Bank; Sonoco/Northeastern, Inc.; The Nature Conservancy; Fleet Bank.
Local Counsel For: McCue Mortgage Co.; Citicorp Mortgage; U.S. Department of Housing and Urban Development.

For Complete List of Firm Personnel, See General Section

For full biographical listings, see the Martindale-Hubbell Law Directory

---

SOUTHPORT, Fairfield Co.

BRODY AND OBER, P.C. (AV)

135 Rennell Drive, P.O. Box 572, 06490-0572
Telephone: 203-259-7405
Fax: 203-255-8572

Charles S. Brody (1894-1976)	S. Giles Payne
Seth O. L. Brody	William J. Britt
Stanley B. Garrell	Barbara S. Miller
Frank F. Ober	Ronald B. Noren

Diane F. Martucci	Seth L. Cooper
	Douglas R. Brown

OF COUNSEL

James M. Thorburn	John F. Merchant

For full biographical listings, see the Martindale-Hubbell Law Directory

---

STAMFORD, Fairfield Co.

CACACE, TUSCH & SANTAGATA (AV)

777 Summer Street, P.O. Box 15859, 06901-0859
Telephone: 203-327-2000
Telecopier: 203-353-3392

MEMBERS OF FIRM

Michael J. Cacace	Mark P. Santagata
	Paul T. Tusch

ASSOCIATES

Edward F. Nemchek	Ronald E. Kowalski, II
Alice Ann Fitzpatrick	Pierrette A. Newman
	Russell A. Green

For full biographical listings, see the Martindale-Hubbell Law Directory

---

WALLINGFORD, New Haven Co.

FARRELL & LESLIE (AV)

375 Center Street, P.O. Box 369, 06492
Telephone: 203-269-7756
Fax: 203-269-1927

MEMBERS OF FIRM

Gerald E. Farrell	Ann Farrell Leslie
Gerald E. Farrell, Jr.	Brian J. Leslie

References: Dime Savings Bank of Wallingford; Shawmut Bank (Wallingford Office).

For full biographical listings, see the Martindale-Hubbell Law Directory

---

WEST HARTFORD, Hartford Co.

BERMAN, BOURNS & CURRIE, LLC (AV)

970 Farmington Avenue, P.O. Box 271837, 06127-1837
Telephone: 860-232-4471
Fax: 860-523-4605

John A. Berman	Courtney B. Bourns
	John K. Currie

Mary Beth Anderson	Robert W. Storm, Jr.

For full biographical listings, see the Martindale-Hubbell Law Directory

---

WESTPORT, Fairfield Co.

LESLIE BYELAS (AV)

1804 Post Road East, 06880
Telephone: 203-259-0599
Fax: 203-255-2570

For full biographical listings, see the Martindale-Hubbell Law Directory

STUART A. McKEEVER (AV)

155 Post Road, East, 06880
Telephone: 203-227-4756
Fax: 203-454-2031
Reference: Fleet Bank.

For full biographical listings, see the Martindale-Hubbell Law Directory

WILLIAM L. SCHEFFLER & ASSOCIATES (AV(T))

P.O. Box 2773, 06880-0773
Telephone: 203-226-6600; 1-800-429-4480
Telecopier: 203-227-1873

For full biographical listings, see the Martindale-Hubbell Law Directory

---

DELAWARE

DOVER,* Kent Co.

PARKOWSKI, NOBLE & GUERKE, PROFESSIONAL ASSOCIATION (AV)

116 West Water Street, P.O. Box 598, 19903
Telephone: 302-678-3262
Telecopier: 302-678-9415

F. Michael Parkowski	Jeremy W. Homer
John W. Noble	John C. Andrade
I. Barry Guerke	Jonathan Eisenberg
Clay T. Jester	Dana J. Schaefer
	Mark F. Dunkle

OF COUNSEL

George F. Gardner, III

Representative Clients: Delaware Solid Waste Authority; Cabe Associates (Consulting Engineers).
Approved Attorneys for: Ticor Title Insurance Co.
Reference: First National Bank of Wyoming.

For full biographical listings, see the Martindale-Hubbell Law Directory

---

WILMINGTON,* New Castle Co.

DALEY, ERISMAN & van OGTROP (AV)

1224 King Street, 19801
Telephone: 302-658-4000
Fax: 302-652-8975
Email: jerisman@devolaw.com *URL:* http://www.devolaw.com
Newark, Delaware Office: 206 East Delaware Avenue.
Telephone: 302-368-0133.
FAX: 302-368-4587.

MEMBERS OF FIRM

Robert E. Daley	James A. Erisman
	Piet H. van Ogtrop

References: Wilmington Trust Co.; Beneficial National Bank.

For full biographical listings, see the Martindale-Hubbell Law Directory

THEISEN, LANK, MULFORD & GOLDBERG, P.A. (AV)

Ninth Floor, One Commerce Center, P.O. Box 1470, 19899
Telephone: 302-656-7712
Fax: 302-655-0923
Email: Theisen@delcorp.com *URL:* http://www.delcorp.theisen.com

(See Next Column)

THEISEN, LANK, MULFORD & GOLDBERG P.A.—*Continued*

Aubrey B. Lank	Steven D. Goldberg
John G. Mulford	Michael J. Goodrick
	David S. Lank

Richard L. Abbott

OF COUNSEL

Vincent A. Theisen (Retired)

References: Wilmington Trust Co.; PNC Bank.

For full biographical listings, see the Martindale-Hubbell Law Directory

WILLIAMS, HERSHMAN & WISLER, P.A. (AV)

Suite 600, One Commerce Center, Twelfth and Orange Streets, P.O. Box 511, 19899-0511
Telephone: 302-575-0873
Telecopier: 302-575-1642

David Nicol Williams	Jeffrey C. Wisler
Douglas M. Hershman	Barbara Snapp Danberg

References: Wilmington Trust Co.; PNC Bank.

For full biographical listings, see the Martindale-Hubbell Law Directory

DISTRICT OF COLUMBIA

WASHINGTON, D.C. Co.

* indicates certain Bar Register subscribers, in cities of comparable size and importance, who maintain an additional office in Washington, D.C. and who have arranged for representation as a part of the Washington, D.C. listings that follow

ALEXANDER, BEARDEN, HAIRSTON & MARKS, LLP (AV)

Limited Liability Partnership
2021 L Street, N.W., Suite 300, 20036
Telephone: 202-293-3700
Fax: 202-293-7359
Silver Spring, Maryland Office: Lee Plaza, Suite 805, 8601 Georgia Avenue, 20910.
Telephone: 301-589-2222.
Facsimile: 301-539-2523.
New York, New York Office: 330 Madison Avenue, 36th Floor.
Telephone: 212-808-0008.
Fax: 212-599-1028.

Koteles Alexander

Reference: Riggs National Bank of Washington, D.C.

For full biographical listings, see the Martindale-Hubbell Law Directory

* BALLARD SPAHR ANDREWS & INGERSOLL (AV)

Suite 900 East, 555 13th Street, N.W., 20004-1112
Telephone: 202-383-8800
Fax: 202-383-8877
Philadelphia, Pennsylvania Office: 1735 Market Street, 51st Floor.
Telephone: 215-665-8500.
Fax: 215-864-8999.
Harrisburg, Pennsylvania Office: 105 North Front Street.
Telephone: 717-236-3333.
Fax: 717-236-3884.
Denver, Colorado Office: Seventeenth Street Plaza Building, Suite 2300, 1225 17th Street.
Telephone: 303-292-2400.
Fax: 303-296-3956.
Salt Lake City, Utah Office: One Utah Center, 201 South Main Street, Suite 1200.
Telephone: 801-531-3000.
Fax: 801-531-3001.
Baltimore, Maryland Office: 300 East Lombard Street, 19th Floor.
Telephone: 410-528-5600.
Fax: 410-528-5650.
Camden, New Jersey Office: 800 Hudson Square, 5th Floor.
Telephone: 609-541-5577.
Fax: 609-541-8272.

Paul K. Casey	Allan R. Winn
Mary Jo George	
(Not admitted in DC)	

COUNSEL

Kelly Mitchell Wrenn

(See Next Column)

C. Vaughan Gibson	David A. Pesel
(Not admitted in DC)	(Not admitted in DC)
Bryan Myers	
(Not admitted in DC)	

For Complete List of Firm Personnel, See General Section

For full biographical listings, see the Martindale-Hubbell Law Directory

LIOTTA, DRANITZKE & ENGEL (AV)

Suite 250, 1666 Connecticut Avenue, N.W., 20009
Telephone: 202-797-7700
Facsimile: 202-797-2354

MEMBERS OF FIRM

Alan Dranitzke	Robert Case Liotta
	Diana R. Engel

ASSOCIATE

Alisa A. Wilkins

For full biographical listings, see the Martindale-Hubbell Law Directory

* VENABLE ATTORNEYS AT LAW VENABLE, BAETJER, HOWARD & CIVILETTI, LLP (AV)

A Partnership including Professional Corporations
Suite 1000, 1201 New York Avenue, N.W., 20005
Telephone: 202-962-4800
Fax: 202-962-8300
Baltimore, Maryland Office: Venable, Baetjer and Howard LLP, 1800 Mercantile Bank & Trust Building, 2 Hopkins Plaza.
Telephone: 410-244-7400.
McLean, Virginia Office: Venable, Baetjer and Howard LLP, Suite 400, 2010 Corporate Ridge.
Telephone: 703-760-1600.
Rockville, Maryland Office: Venable, Baetjer and Howard LLP, Suite 500, One Church Street, P. O. Box 1906.
Telephone: 301-217-5600.
Towson, Maryland Office: Venable, Baetjer and Howard LLP, 210 Allegheny Avenue, P. O. Box 5517.
Telephone: 410-494-6200.

MEMBERS OF FIRM

Benjamin R. Civiletti (P.C.)	Thomas B. Hudson (Also at
(Also at Baltimore and	Baltimore, Maryland Office)
Towson, Maryland Offices)	James K. Archibald (Also at
Jan K. Guben (Not admitted in	Baltimore, Maryland Office)
DC; Also at Baltimore,	George F. Pappas (Also at
Maryland Office)	Baltimore, Maryland Office)
Thomas J. Madden	William D. Quarles (Also at
John G. Milliken (Also at	Towson, Maryland Office)
McLean, Virginia Office)	James A. Dunbar (Also at
	Baltimore, Maryland Office)

For Complete List of Firm Personnel, See General Section

For full biographical listings, see the Martindale-Hubbell Law Directory

WATT, TIEDER & HOFFAR, L.L.P. (AV)

601 Pennsylvania Avenue, N.W., Suite 900, 20004
Telephone: 202-462-4697
Telecopier: 703-893-8029
McLean Virginia Office: 7929 Westpark Drive, Suite 400,
Telephone: 703-749-1000.
Telecopier: 703-893-8029.
Irvine California Office: 3 Park Plaza, Suite 1530.
Telephone: 714-852-6700.

MEMBERS OF FIRM

John B. Tieder, Jr.	Robert K. Cox
	David C. Romm

For full biographical listings, see the Martindale-Hubbell Law Directory

WILKES, ARTIS, HEDRICK & LANE, CHARTERED (AV)

Suite 1100, 1666 K Street, N.W., 20006-2897
Telephone: 202-457-7800
Cable Address: "Wilan, Washington, D.C."
Annapolis, Maryland Office: Suite 400, 47 State Circle.
Telephone: 410-263-7800.
Bethesda, Maryland Office: Suite 800, 3 Bethesda Metro Center.
Telephone: 301-654-7800.
Greenbelt, Maryland Office: Suite 410, 6305 Ivy Lane.
Telephone: 301-345-7700.
Fairfax, Virginia Office: Suite 600, 11320 Random Hills Road.
Telephone: 703-385-8000.
Waldorf, Maryland Office: Suite 101, 1 Post Office Road.
Telephone: 301-645-2464; 301-843-7610 (Metro).

(See Next Column)

WILKES, ARTIS, HEDRICK & LANE CHARTERED, *Washington—Continued*

James C. Wilkes (1899-1968)	Allen Jones, Jr.
James E. Artis (1907-1978)	Eric S. Kassoff (Resident,
David M. Bond	Bethesda, Maryland Office)
Stephen J. Braun (Resident,	Jonathan I. Kipnis (Resident,
Waldorf, Maryland Office)	Greenbelt, Maryland Office)
Charles A. Camalier, III	William Kominers (Resident,
Jerald S. Cohn	Bethesda, Maryland Office)
Christopher H. Collins	John D. Lane
James P. Downey (Resident,	J. Carter McKaig
Fairfax, Virginia Office)	Gerard P. Panaro
Maureen Ellen Dwyer	Robert X. Perry, Jr.
John T. Epting	Allison Carney Prince
Jonathan L. Farmer	John E. Prominski, Jr.
Nancy G. Fax (Resident,	Whayne S. Quin
Bethesda, Maryland Office)	Richard K. Reed (Resident,
Phil T. Feola	Greenbelt, Maryland Office)
Stanley J. Fineman	Louis P. Robbins
David A. Fuss	David H. Saffern
Norman M. Glasgow	Kenneth L. Samuelson
Norman M. Glasgow, Jr.	Frank W. Stearns (Resident at
Larry A. Gordon (Resident,	Fairfax, Virginia Office)
Bethesda, Maryland Office)	Dana Brewington Stebbins
Robert L. Gorham	Lois J. Vermillion
Robert M. Gurss	Lorraine J. Webb (Resident,
Robert R. Harris (Resident,	Waldorf, Maryland Office)
Bethesda & Greenbelt,	Joseph B. Whitebread, Jr.
Maryland Offices)	Ramsey L. Woodworth

Matthew G. Ahrens (Resident,	Daniel G. Lloyd
Bethesda, Maryland Office)	Gail Prentiss Miller (Resident,
Ilene Baxt Campbell (Resident,	Fairfax, Virginia Office)
Fairfax, Virginia Office)	Matthew J. Murcko
Timothy Dugan (Resident,	(Not admitted in DC)
Bethesda, Maryland Office)	Mark S. Randall
Patricia Ann Harris (Resident,	Karin M. Ryan
Bethesda, Maryland Office)	Stuart A. Turow

For full biographical listings, see the Martindale-Hubbell Law Directory

FLORIDA

AVENTURA, Dade Co.

BUCHANAN INGERSOLL, PROFESSIONAL CORPORATION (AV⊤)

One Turnberry Place, 19495 Biscayne Boulevard, Suite 606, 33180
Telephone: 305-933-5600
Telecopier: 305-933-2350
URL: http://www.bipc.com
Pittsburgh, Pennsylvania Office: One Oxford Centre, 301 Grant Street, 20th Floor.
Telephone: 412-562-8800.
Philadelphia, Pennsylvania Office: Two Logan Square, Twelfth Floor, 18th & Arch Streets.
Telephone: 215-665-8700.
Harrisburg, Pennsylvania Office: 30 North Third Street.
Telephone: 717-237-4800.
Miami, Florida Office: NationsBank Tower, 100 S.E. Second Street.
Telephone: 305-347-4080.
Tampa, Florida Office: Suite 2500, 401 East Jackson Street.
Telephone: 813-222-8180.
Princeton, New Jersey Office: Buchanan Ingersoll, A Partnership, College Centre, 500 College Road East.
Telephone: 609-987-6800.
Lexington, Kentucky Office: Suite 600, PNC Bank Plaza, 200 West Vine Street.
Telephone: 606-225-5333.
Buffalo, New York Office: 1100 Main Place Tower, 350 Main Street.
Telephone: 716-854-4100.
Fax: 816-854-4227.

Richard N. Schermer

For Complete List of Firm Personnel, See General Section

For full biographical listings, see the Martindale-Hubbell Law Directory

BOCA RATON, Palm Beach Co.

CARTER, CARLILE, NEALE & FRIEDMAN, P.A. (AV)

Suite 312, 1200 North Federal Highway, 33432
Telephone: 561-368-9900

John E. Carter	Thomas E. Neale
Robert T. Carlile	Annette Friedman

For full biographical listings, see the Martindale-Hubbell Law Directory

DICKENSON, MURDOCH, REX AND SLOAN, CHARTERED (AV)

Suite 410 Compson Financial Center, 980 North Federal Highway, 33432
Telephone: 561-391-1900
Facsimile: 561-391-1933

David B. Dickenson	Robert H. Rex
Richard A. Murdoch	Barbara A. Sloan

Russell C. Silverglate

For full biographical listings, see the Martindale-Hubbell Law Directory

JOEL H. FELDMAN, P.A. (AV)

Suite 207, Tower D, Sanctuary Centre, 4800 North Federal Highway, 33431
Telephone: 561-392-4400
Fax: 561-392-1521

Joel H. Feldman

Andrew Merlo

For full biographical listings, see the Martindale-Hubbell Law Directory

STEVEN I. GREENWALD, P.A. (AV)

Boca Palm Professional Plaza, 6971 North Federal Highway, Suite 105, 33487
Telephone: 561-994-5560

Steven I. Greenwald

OF COUNSEL

Brandon J. Douglas

For full biographical listings, see the Martindale-Hubbell Law Directory

OSBORNE, OSBORNE & deCLAIRE, P.A. (AV)

Suite 100 Via Mizner Financial Plaza, 798 South Federal Highway, P.O. Drawer 40, 33429-9974
Telephone: 561-395-1000
Fax: 561-368-6930

Ray C. Osborne	George F. deClaire
R. Brady Osborne, Jr.	Ellen R. Itzler

Linda L. Snelling

Approved Attorneys for: First Union National Bank of Florida, N.A.; Sun-Bank/South Florida, N.A.; Northern Trust Bank of Florida. NationsBank of Florida, N.A.

For full biographical listings, see the Martindale-Hubbell Law Directory

SCHROEDER & LARCHE, P.A. (AV)

One Boca Place, Suite 319-A, 2255 Glades Road, 33431-7313
Telephone: 561-241-0300
Broward: 954-421-0878
Telecopier: 561-241-0798

Michael A. Schroeder	W. Lawrence Larche

Alan Pellingra

For full biographical listings, see the Martindale-Hubbell Law Directory

WEISS & HANDLER, P.A. (AV)

Suite 218A, One Boca Place, 2255 Glades Road, 33431-7313
Telephone: 407-997-9995
Broward: 954-421-5101
Palm Beach: 407-734-8008
Telecopier: 407-997-5280

Howard I. Weiss	Henry B. Handler

Donald Feldman	Marissa I. Laakso
David K. Friedman	Mark R. Osherow
Carol A. Kartagener	Howard M. Rudolph (Resident,
	West Palm Beach Office)

OF COUNSEL

Malcolm L. Stein	Stanley E. Preiser
(Not admitted in FL)	(Not admitted in FL)
Raoul Lionel Felder	
(Not admitted in FL)	

For full biographical listings, see the Martindale-Hubbell Law Directory

*BRADENTON,** Manatee Co.

BLALOCK, LANDERS, WALTERS AND VOGLER, P.A. (AV)

802 11th Street West, P.O. Box 469, 34205
Telephone: 941-748-0100
Fax: 941-745-2093

(See Next Column)

BLALOCK, LANDERS, WALTERS AND VOGLER P.A.—*Continued*

Robert G. Blalock	Edward Vogler, II
Clifford L. Walters, III	Barbara Ann Held

Dana C. Gentry	Michael D. Wyckoff
Charles F. Johnson, III	John E. Wickman
Lisbeth P. Bruce	Lisa E. Bagwell
	James R. White

Representative Client: The Bradenton Herald, Inc.

For full biographical listings, see the Martindale-Hubbell Law Directory

CONLEY & CLEARY (AV)

2401 Manatee Avenue West, 34205
Telephone: 941-748-8778
Telefax: 941-745-2572

Roger P. Conley   Kenneth W. Cleary

General Counsel for: Key Florida Bancorp. Inc. and all subsidiaries including Key Florida Bank, F.S.B.; Key Florida Funding Corp. and Key Financial Leasing, Inc.; Conley Subaru, Inc.; Warner Southern College; Suncoast Buick Dealers Association, Inc.; Florida Pontiac Dealers Association, Inc.; Conley Buick, Inc.; Conley Buick-Pontiac, Inc.; Racquet Club of El Conquistador, Inc.
Representative Clients: NationsBank.

For full biographical listings, see the Martindale-Hubbell Law Directory

GRIMES GOEBEL GRIMES HAWKINS & GLADFELTER, P.A. (AV)

The Professional Building, 1023 Manatee Avenue West, P.O. Box 1550, 34206
Telephone: 941-748-0151
Fax: 941-748-0158

William C. Grimes	Leslie Horton Gladfelter
Caleb J. Grimes	William S. Galvano

Counsel for: Schroeder Manatee Inc. (Agriculture and Land Development); Pursley, Inc., (Horticulture, Retail and Land Development); Lombardo & Skipper, Inc. (Civil Engineers); CCI Environmental Services, Inc. (Environmental Consultants); Creekwood Investors, Ltd.; Old Hyde Park Village Center, Ltd.; First Federal Savings & Loan Association of Florida.
Approved Attorneys for: Lawyers Title Insurance Corp.; Chicago Title Insurance Co.; Attorneys Title Insurance Fund.

For Complete List of Firm Personnel, See General Section

For full biographical listings, see the Martindale-Hubbell Law Directory

McGUIRE, PRATT, MASIO & FARRANCE, P.A. (AV)

Suite 600, 1001 3rd Avenue West, P.O. Box 1866, 34206
Telephone: 941-748-7076
Fax: 941-747-9774

Hugh E. McGuire, Jr.	Carol A. Masio
Charles J. Pratt, Jr.	Robert A. Farrance
	John W. Kaklis

OF COUNSEL
Carter H. Parry

Reference: Barnett Bank of Manatee County.

For full biographical listings, see the Martindale-Hubbell Law Directory

DAYTONA BEACH, Volusia Co.

DUNN, ABRAHAM & SWAIN (AV)

A Partnership of Professional Associations
347 South Ridgewood Avenue, P.O. Drawer 2600, 32115-2600
Telephone: 904-258-1222
Fax: 904-255-8521
Email: 71722.3430@compuserve.com
MEMBERS OF FIRM
Edgar M. Dunn, Jr., (P.A.)   Robert Abraham (P.A.)
Catherine G. Swain (P.A.)
ASSOCIATE
Suzanne A. Novak

For full biographical listings, see the Martindale-Hubbell Law Directory

ENGLEWOOD, Sarasota & Charlotte Cos.

BATSEL, McKINLEY, ITTERSAGEN, GUNDERSON & BERNTSSON, P.A. (AV)

Suite 204 Manor Pointe Professional Center, 1861 Placida Road, 34223
Telephone: 941-474-7713
Telecopier: 941-474-8276
Port Charlotte, Florida Office: 18401 Murdock Circle. 33948.
Telephone: 941-627-1000.
Telefax: 941-255-0684.

(See Next Column)

C. Guy Batsel	Scott D. Ittersagen
Michael R. McKinley (Resident, Port Charlotte Office)	Miko P. Gunderson
	Robert H. Berntsson (Resident, Port Charlotte Office)

Robert F. Koch (Resident, Port Charlotte Office)	Jerry Paul

For full biographical listings, see the Martindale-Hubbell Law Directory

WELLBAUM & McLENNON, P.A. (AV)

1160 South McCall Road, Suite B, 34223
Telephone: 941-474-3241
Fax: 941-475-2927

Robert W. Wellbaum, Jr.   Thomas P. McLennon

Maurice L. Jemison

Reference: SouthTrust Bank.

For full biographical listings, see the Martindale-Hubbell Law Directory

FORT LAUDERDALE,* Broward Co.

BERGER & DAVIS, P.A. (AV)

Suite 400, 100 N.E. 3rd Avenue, 33301
Telephone: 954-525-9900
Fax: 954-523-2872
Tallahassee, Florida Office: 215 South Monroe Street, Suite 804, 32301.
Telephone: 904-561-3010.
FAX: 904-561-3013.

Thomas L. Abrams	Manuel Kushner
James L. Berger	John D. C. Newton, II
Mitchell W. Berger	(Resident, Tallahassee Office)
Franklin H. Caplan	Leonard K. Samuels
James B. Davis	Laz L. Schneider
Nick Jovanovich	Daniel H. Thompson
Robert B. Judd	(Resident, Tallahassee Office)

Vincent J. Altino	Lisa D. MacClugage
Christine A. Butler	Dawn M. Meyers
Lawrence C. Callaway, III	Scott L. Pestcoe
Janice L. Griffin	Holiday Hunt Russell
	Jeffrey Scott Wertman

OF COUNSEL
Henry H. (Bucky) Fox

For full biographical listings, see the Martindale-Hubbell Law Directory

BRINKLEY, McNERNEY, MORGAN, SOLOMON & TATUM, LLP (AV)

Suite 1800, New River Center, 200 East Las Olas Boulevard, P.O. Box 522, 33301-2209
Telephone: Broward: 954-522-2200
Facsimile: 954-522-9123

MEMBERS OF FIRM

W. Michael Brinkley	Thomas R. Tatum
Michael J. McNerney	Stephen L. Ziegler
Philip J. Morgan	Kenneth E. Keechl
Harris K. Solomon	Donald J. Lunny, Jr.
	Roberta G. Stanley

ASSOCIATES

Christopher M. Trapani	Thomas J. Ansbro
Kenneth J. Joyce	David F. Hanley
	John A. Walker

OF COUNSEL
Amy R. Reeck

Approved Attorneys for: Attorneys' Title Insurance Fund; Chicago Title Insurance Co.; First American Title Insurance Co.

For full biographical listings, see the Martindale-Hubbell Law Directory

CLARK & SCHOLNIK (AV)

A Partnership of Professional Associations
Coastal Tower, 2400 East Commercial Boulevard, Suite 820, 33308
Telephone: 954-776-3800; 954-771-4790
Telecopier: 954-776-3825

MEMBER OF FIRM
Thomas M. Clark (P.A.)

Representative Clients: Suncoast Savings and Loan Association, F.S.A.; Sun-Trust Bank, South Florida, National Association; Midland Federal Savings and Loan Association; Haymarket Cooperative Bank; Colorado Federal Savings Bank; Northern Trust Bank of Florida, N.A.

For Complete List of Firm Personnel, See General Section

For full biographical listings, see the Martindale-Hubbell Law Directory

Fort Lauderdale—Continued

KELLEY, HERMAN & MILLS (AV)

Suite 206, 1401 East Broward Boulevard, 33301
Telephone: 954-462-7806
Fax: 954-522-0396

MEMBERS OF FIRM

Patrick G. Kelley	Richard A. Mills, III
Bruce K. Herman	Jeffrey B. Smith

Approved Attorneys for: Ticor Title Insurance Co.; Attorney's Title Insurance Fund.

For full biographical listings, see the Martindale-Hubbell Law Directory

MOSKOWITZ, MANDELL & SALIM, P.A. (AV)

Suite 510, 800 Corporate Drive, 33334
Telephone: 954-491-2000; Boca Raton Line: 407-750-7700
FAX: 954-491-2051

Michael W. Moskowitz	Craig J. Mandell
	William G. Salim, Jr.

Greg H. Rosenthal	Scott M. Zaslav

OF COUNSEL

Shirley D. Weisman (P.A.)	Monica I. Salis (P.A.)

Deborah Ann Byles

For full biographical listings, see the Martindale-Hubbell Law Directory

OPPENHEIM & PILELSKY, P.A. (AV)

1290 Weston Road, Suite 300, 33326
Telephone: 954-384-6114
Toll Free: 888-384-6114
Fax: 954-384-6115
Email: O&P@oppenheim.com *URL:* http://www.oppenheim.com

Monica B. Cunill

Representative Clients: Landmark Building & Design, Inc.; Nonstop City, Ltd.; Design 68, Inc.; Danro Homes, Inc.; Ambry Homes.

For full biographical listings, see the Martindale-Hubbell Law Directory

TRIPP, SCOTT, CONKLIN & SMITH (AV)

28th Floor, 110 Tower, 110 S.E. 6th Street, P.O. Box 14245, 33301
Telephone: 954-525-7500
Telecopier: 954-761-8475

Norman D. Tripp	Timothy J. McDermott
James A. Scott	Kimberly A. Gilmour
Howard L. Conklin	Richard D. Heller
Dennis Dustin Smith	Gregory A. McLaughlin
Peter G. Herman	Steven C. Elkin
Garry W. Johnson	Drake M. Batchelder

OF COUNSEL

Robert E. Huebner	Welcom H. Watson, Jr.

ASSOCIATES

O. Mason Hurst, II	Heidi E. Davis
Matthew Zifrony	Jeffrey S. Wood
Grant J. Smith	Scott J. Jordan
William J. Gross	Jason A. Diamond
Paul Octavio Lopez	Christopher L. Smith
Daniel E. Taylor	Angelia Maria Baldwin

Representative Clients: Commonwealth Land Title Insurance Co.; Northern Trust Bank of Florida, N.A.; Bank of North America; First Union National Bank of Florida; Norwest Mortgage, Inc.; Re/Max Lifestyles.

For full biographical listings, see the Martindale-Hubbell Law Directory

WILLIAM A. ZEIHER, P.A. (AV)

2780 East Oakland Park Boulevard, 33306
Telephone: 954-561-8205
Fax: 954-561-8208

William A. Zeiher

Representative Client: Mode Inc.; Ivanhoe Land Investments, Inc.
Approved Attorney for: Attorneys' Title Insurance Fund; Marrinson Group, Inc.; National Oil & Gas, Inc.; Pierwelders, Inc.

For full biographical listings, see the Martindale-Hubbell Law Directory

FORT MYERS,* Lee Co.

ALLEN, KNUDSEN & DeBOEST, P.A. (AV)

1415 Hendry Street, P.O. Box 1480, 33902
Telephone: 941-334-1381
Telecopier: 941-334-0266
Naples, Florida Office: Park North Center, 5121 Castello Drive, Suite 1.
Telephone: 941-263-5040.
Fax: 941-263-6944.

George E. Allen (1916-1993)	Terrence F. Lenick
Arthur K. Knudsen, Jr.	William E. Stockman
Richard D. DeBoest	Tamela Eady Wiseman
Christopher N. Davies	Brenda A. Bayly
Robert H. Duckwall	Lori Westhrin Clifford
Richard D. DeBoest II	Dana M. Gallup
C. Michael Jackson	Thaddeus Dennis Kirkpatrick
	P. Michael Villalobos

LEGAL SUPPORT PERSONNEL

Carolyn Fox Lambert (Paralegal)

Representative Clients: Lennar Homes, Inc.; Pulte Home Corp.; Cobb Theatres, Inc.; International Paper; Saxon Properties, Inc.; Scott's Hospitality, Inc.; WCN Communities, L.P.; Evelyn Jackman and Sons, Inc.; Pacificorp; Nite-Bright Sign Co.

For full biographical listings, see the Martindale-Hubbell Law Directory

HENDERSON, FRANKLIN, STARNES & HOLT, PROFESSIONAL ASSOCIATION (AV)

1715 Monroe Street, P.O. Box 280, 33902-0280
Telephone: 941-334-4121
Telecopier: 941-332-4494

Ronald W. Smalley	Charles J. Basinait
Denis H. Noah	Thomas H. Gunderson
Russell P. Schropp	David K. Fowler

Representative Clients: Aetna Property & Casualty Group; CIGNA Group; CSX Transportation, Inc.; Fireman's Fund Insurance Cos.; Barnett Bank of Lee County, N.A.; Northern Trust Bank of Florida, N.A.; The Hartford Insurance Group; Travelers Group; United Telephone Company of Florida.

For Complete List of Firm Personnel, See General Section

For full biographical listings, see the Martindale-Hubbell Law Directory

LAW OFFICES OF LLOYD G. HENDRY, P.A. (AV)

Society First Federal Center, 2201 Second Street, Suite 502, P.O. Box 1509, 33902
Telephone: 941-332-7123
Fax: 941-332-5147

Lloyd G. Hendry	Mary Hendry Sonne
	Harry O. Hendry

For full biographical listings, see the Martindale-Hubbell Law Directory

SHEPPARD, BRETT, STEWART & HERSCH, P.A. (AV)

(Formerly Sheppard & Woolslair)
2121 West First Street, P.O. Drawer 400, 33902
Telephone: 941-334-1141
Fax: 941-334-3965

W. A. Sheppard (1898-1971)	Jay Andrew Brett
John K. Woolslair (1908-1968)	John F. Stewart
	Craig R. Hersch

OF COUNSEL

John Woolslair Sheppard

D. Hugh Kinsey, Jr.

Approved Attorneys for: Attorneys' Title Insurance Fund; Chicago Title Insurance Co.

For full biographical listings, see the Martindale-Hubbell Law Directory

SMOOT ADAMS EDWARDS & GREEN, P.A. (AV)

One University Park Suite 600, 12800 University Drive, P.O. Box 60259, 33906-6259
Telephone: 941-489-1776
(800) 226-1777 (in Florida)
Fax: 941-489-2444
Email: 71600.2745@compuserve.com

J. Tom Smoot, Jr.	Bruce D. Green
Hal Adams	Steven I. Winer
Franklyn A. (Chip) Johnson	Mark R. Komray
(1947-1991)	Clayton W. Crevasse
Charles B. Edwards	M. Brian Cheffer

(See Next Column)

SMOOT ADAMS EDWARDS & GREEN P.A.—*Continued*

Robert S. Forman   C. Berk Edwards, Jr.
Kathleen W. McBride   Melville G. Brinson, III
Lowell Schoenfeld   Samuel J. Hagan, IV.

For full biographical listings, see the Martindale-Hubbell Law Directory

---

FORT PIERCE,* St. Lucie Co.

GONANO & HARRELL, CHARTERED (AV)

Riverside National Bank Building, 1600 South Federal Highway, Suite 200, 34950-5194
Telephone: 561-464-1032
FAX: 561-464-0282

Douglas E. Gonano   Daniel B. Harrell

Johnathan A. Ferguson   John J. Campione

General Counsel: School Board of St. Lucie County; Reserve Community Development District; St. Lucie West Services District.
Representative Clients: East Coast Lumber & Supply Co.; Riverside National Bank of Florida; Superior Title Services, Inc.
Approved Attorneys for: Attorneys' Title Insurance Fund; Commonwealth Land Title Insurance Co.
References: Riverside National Bank of Florida; SunTrust, Treasure Coast, N.A.

For full biographical listings, see the Martindale-Hubbell Law Directory

NEILL GRIFFIN JEFFRIES & LLOYD, CHARTERED (AV)

311 South Second Street, P.O. Box 1270, 34954
Telephone: 561-464-8200
Fax: 561-464-2566

Chester B. Griffin   Robert M. Lloyd
J. Stephen Tierney, III

Local Counsel for: Sun Trust Bank Treasure Coast, N.A., (Commercial and Trust Departments); St. Paul Fire and Marine Insurance Co.; Chubb Group of Insurances Cos.
Approved Attorneys for: Attorneys' Title Insurance Fund; Commonwealth Land Title Insurance Co.
Reference: Sun Bank Treasure Coast, N.A., Fort Pierce, Florida (Commercial and Trust Departments).

For full biographical listings, see the Martindale-Hubbell Law Directory

---

GAINESVILLE,* Alachua Co.

WAYNE P. CASTELLO (AV)

Suite W, 2772 N.W. 43rd Street, 32606
Telephone: 352-377-4422
Telecopier: 352-373-5792
Email: GHWW53C@Prodigy.com

LEGAL SUPPORT PERSONNEL
Griffin Stegall (Legal Assistant)

For full biographical listings, see the Martindale-Hubbell Law Directory

---

JACKSONVILLE,* Duval Co.

DONAHOO, DONAHOO & BALL, P.A. (AV)

(Incorporated in 1981)
2925 Barnett Center, 50 North Laura Street, 32202
Telephone: 904-354-8080
Fax: 904-791-9563

John W. Donahoo (1907-1993)   Haywood M. Ball
Thomas M. Donahoo   William B. McMenamy
Bruce D. Johnson

Thomas M. Donahoo, Jr.

For full biographical listings, see the Martindale-Hubbell Law Directory

WILLIAM J. JOOS, P.A. (AV)

3030 Hartley Road Drive, Suite 5, 32257
Telephone: 904-724-6109
Fax: 904-724-6333

William J. Joos

KIRSCHNER, MAIN, GRAHAM, TANNER & DEMONT, PROFESSIONAL ASSOCIATION (AV)

One Independent Drive, Suite 2000, P.O. Box 1559, 32201-1559
Telephone: 904-354-4141
Telecopier: 904-358-2199

(See Next Column)

Barry C. Averitt   Kenneth M. Kirschner
Babette L. Fletcher   James L. Main
T. Malcolm Graham   John T. Rogerson, III
Lee Stathis Haramis   Michael G. Tanner

Howard L. Alford   Judy Ossi Marko
Robin C. Barco   Charles S. McCall
John F. Germany, Jr.   Beth E. Weitzman
Eric S. Kolar   (Not admitted in FL)
OF COUNSEL
Michael E. Demont   Wyman R. Duggan
G. Stephen Manning   Reese J. Henderson, Jr.

Representative Clients: The Maryland Insurance Group; NationsBank; The Suddath Cos.; Wickes Lumber Co.; BFI, Inc.

For full biographical listings, see the Martindale-Hubbell Law Directory

SAMUEL L. LePRELL (AV)

901 Blackstone Building, 233 East Bay Street, 32202
Telephone: 904-353-3877
Fax: 904-359-9717

For full biographical listings, see the Martindale-Hubbell Law Directory

LOBRANO & KINCAID (AV)

Suite 1950 Independent Life Building, 1 Independent Drive, 32202
Telephone: 904-359-2100
Facsimile: 904-353-1332

Stephen D. Lobrano   Hope Adams Iseley
Wade McK. Hampton
OF COUNSEL
Harry G. Kincaid

Representative Clients: New York Life Insurance Co. (Real Estate and Claims Counsel); Fortis Benefits, Inc.; South Pine Associates, Inc.; Duplex Products, Inc.; The Washington Post Co.; Post-Newsweek Stations; Florida, Inc. (WJXT Television); International Effecten En Creditbank, N.V.; Hardage and Sons Estes-Krauss, Inc.; Watson Realty Corp.

For full biographical listings, see the Martindale-Hubbell Law Directory

SMITH HULSEY & BUSEY (AV)

1800 First Union National Bank Tower, 225 Water Street, P.O. Box 53315, 32201-3315
Telephone: 904-359-7700
Facsimile: 904-359-7708; 353-9908

Lloyd Smith (1915-1987)
MEMBERS OF FIRM
Dennis L. Blackburn   E. Owen McCuller, Jr.
Stephen D. Busey   James H. Post
Douglas D. Chunn   Bryan L. Putnal
Earl E. Googe, Jr.   E. Lanny Russell
Jeanne E. Helton   Joel Settembrini, Jr.
Cynthia C. Jackson   Tim E. Sleeth
G. Preston Keyes   John R. Smith, Jr.
William E. Kuntz   James J. Taylor, Jr.
M. Richard Lewis, Jr.   Timothy W. Volpe
John F. MacLennan   Waddell A. Wallace, III
Raymond R. Magley   Harry M. Wilson, III

Michael M. Bajalia   R. Leanne McKnight
James A. Bolling, Jr.   Mary E. McManus
E. Lanier Drew   Jeanne M. Miller
Diana Salama Farhat   Stephen D. Moore, Jr.
Martin A. Fitzpatrick   Howard J. Smith
Michael R. Freed   Steven G. Spears
Lee G. Kellison   Melissa Smith Turra
Lauren P. Langham   Herschel T. Vinyard, Jr
Marjorie Conner Makar   Leslie A. Wickes
Bradley R. Markey   Karl A. Zillgitt
OF COUNSEL
Mark Hulsey   John E. Thrasher

Representative Clients: Baptist/St. Vincent's Health System, Inc.; Browning-Ferris Industries, Inc.; Champion Realty Corp. (Florida); First Union National Bank of Florida; Florida Rock Industries, Inc.; PGA Tour, Inc.; KPMG Peat Marwick; The Regency Group, Inc.; The Ritz-Carlton Hotel Co.; University of Florida.

For full biographical listings, see the Martindale-Hubbell Law Directory

---

KISSIMMEE,* Osceola Co.

OVERSTREET RITCH & THACKER (AV)

100 Church Street, P.O. Box 420760, 34742
Telephone: 407-847-5151
FAX: 407-847-3353

(See Next Column)

OVERSTREET RITCH & THACKER, *Kissimmee—Continued*

MEMBERS OF FIRM

Murray Overstreet   John B. Ritch
Jo Overstreet Thacker

Representative Client: Osceola County Tax Collector.
Approved Attorneys for: Attorneys' Title Insurance Fund.

For full biographical listings, see the Martindale-Hubbell Law Directory

POHL & SHORT, P.A.

(See Winter Park)

LAKELAND, Polk Co.

HAHN, MCCLURG, WATSON, GRIFFITH & BUSH, P.A. (AV)

101 South Florida Avenue, P.O. Box 38, 33802
Telephone: 941-688-7747
Telecopier: 941-683-4582

James P. Hahn   Stephen C. Watson
E.V. McClurg   John R. Griffith
                    Philip H. Bush

General Counsel: Peoples Bank of Lakeland; First Federal of Florida; Publix Super Markets, Inc.
Approved Attorneys For: Attorneys' Title Insurance Fund; American Title Insurance Co.; Title & Trust Company of Florida; Federal Land Bank of Columbia, Columbia, S.C.
Reference: Peoples Bank of Lakeland.

For full biographical listings, see the Martindale-Hubbell Law Directory

PETERSON & MYERS, P.A. (AV)

100 East Main Street, P.O. Box 24628, 33802-4628
Telephone: 941-683-6511; 676-6934
Telecopier: 941-682-8031
Lake Wales, Florida Office: 130 East Central Avenue, P.O. Box 1079.
Telephones: 941-676-7611; 683-8942.
Winter Haven, Florida Office: Suite 300, 141 5th Street, N.W., P.O. Drawer 7608.
Telephone: 941-294-3360.

Philip O. Allen   Peter J. Munson
Jack P. Brandon   Corneal B. Myers
Beach A Brooks, Jr.   Cornelius B. Myers, III
Kristen Marie Buzzanca   E. Blake Paul
J. Davis Connor   Robert E. Puterbaugh
Michael S. Craig   Abel A. Putnam
Roy A. Craig, Jr.   Thomas B. Putnam, Jr.
Jacob C. Dykxhoorn   Deborah A. Ruster
Dennis P. Johnson   Stephen R. Senn
Kevin C. Knowlton   Andrea Teves Smith
Douglas A. Lockwood, III   Keith H. Wadsworth
M. Craig Massey   Kerry M. Wilson

General Counsel for: Barnett Bank of Polk County.
Representative Clients: Mutual Wholesale Co.; Barnett Banks, Inc.; Ben Hill Griffin, Inc.; Alcoma Association, Inc.
Approved Attorneys for: Equitable Life Assurance Society of the United States; Federal Land Bank, Columbia, South Carolina; Attorneys' Title Insurance Fund.

For full biographical listings, see the Martindale-Hubbell Law Directory

ROSS, WILLIAMS & DEAL, P.A. (AV)

230 South Florida Avenue Suite 501, 33801
Telephone: 941-688-6319
Fax: 941-683-1252

Dennis A. Ross   Gregory R. Deal
David J. Williams   Thomas Jason DeBari

Thomas P. Vecchio   Michael L. Davis

For full biographical listings, see the Martindale-Hubbell Law Directory

LAKE WALES, Polk Co.

PETERSON & MYERS, P.A. (AV)

130 East Central Avenue, P.O. Box 1079, 33853
Telephone: 941-676-7611; 683-8942
Telecopier: 941-676-0643
Lakeland, Florida Office: 100 East Main Street, P.O. Box 24628.
Telephones: 941-683-6511; 676-6934.
Winter Haven, Florida Office: Suite 300, 141 5th Street, N.W., P.O. Drawer 7608.
Telephone: 941-294-3360.

Philip O. Allen   J. Davis Connor
Jack P. Brandon   Michael S. Craig
Beach A Brooks, Jr.   Roy A. Craig, Jr.
Kristen Marie Buzzanca   Jacob C. Dykxhoorn

(See Next Column)

Dennis P. Johnson   Robert E. Puterbaugh
Kevin C. Knowlton   Abel A. Putnam
Douglas A. Lockwood, III   Thomas B. Putnam, Jr.
M. Craig Massey   Deborah A. Ruster
Peter J. Munson   Stephen R. Senn
Corneal B. Myers   Andrea Teves Smith
Cornelius B. Myers, III   Keith H. Wadsworth
E. Blake Paul   Kerry M. Wilson

General Counsel for: Barnett Bank of Polk County.
Representative Clients: Mutual Wholesale Co.; Barnett Banks, Inc.; Ben Hill Griffin, Inc.; Alcoma Association, Inc.
Approved Attorneys for: Equitable Life Assurance Society of the United States; Federal Land Bank, Columbia, South Carolina; Attorneys' Title Insurance Fund.

For full biographical listings, see the Martindale-Hubbell Law Directory

WEAVER & ASSOCIATES (AV)

240 Park Avenue, P.O. Box 466, 33859-0466
Telephone: 941-676-6000
Fax: 941-678-1515

James M. Weaver

Robin H. Stevenson
OF COUNSEL

George T. MacConnell   Susan A. Machata

For full biographical listings, see the Martindale-Hubbell Law Directory

LAKE WORTH, Palm Beach Co.

ALTMAN, GREER & DOUGHERTY (AV)

219 North Dixie Highway, 33460
Telephone: 407-588-3311
Fax: 407-588-3315

MEMBERS OF FIRM

Zell H. Altman   Bruce G. Greer
                Thomas H. Dougherty

For full biographical listings, see the Martindale-Hubbell Law Directory

MELBOURNE, Brevard Co.

GLEASON, BARLOW & BOHNE, P.A. (AV)

121-123 Fifth Avenue (Indialantic), P.O. Box 3648, 32903
Telephone: 407-723-5121
Fax: 407-984-5426

William H. Gleason   Karl W. Bohne, Jr.
T. Mitchell Barlow, Jr.
  (Resident)

Reference: First Union National Bank of Florida, Melbourne, Florida.

For full biographical listings, see the Martindale-Hubbell Law Directory

KRASNY AND DETTMER (AV)

A Partnership of Professional Associations
780 South Apollo Boulevard, P.O. Box 428, 32902-0428
Telephone: 407-723-5646
Telecopier: 407-768-1147

Myron S. (Mike) Krasny (P.A.)   Dale A. Dettmer (P.A.)

Scott Krasny

Representative Client: Huntington National Bank of Florida.

For full biographical listings, see the Martindale-Hubbell Law Directory

MIAMI,* Dade Co.

KEITH, MACK, LEWIS, COHEN & LUMPKIN (AV)

First Union Financial Center, Twentieth Floor, 200 South Biscayne Boulevard, 33131-2310
Telephone: 305-358-7605
Fax: 305-358-4755
Email: PREVAIL@KEITHMACK.COM

MEMBERS OF FIRM

Edgar Lewis   Jan Carson Cheezem
Robert A. Cohen   Loren S. Granoff
R. Hugh Lumpkin   Jack S. Lewis
Gregg S. Ahrens   Alan Rosenthal
                Norman S. Segall

ASSOCIATES

Michael J. Hogsten   Michele S. Primeau
Felix M. Lasarte   Cynthia Ramos
Dawn Marshall   Jack R. Reiter
Mercedes Padin   Karl J. Schumer
                Jeffrey P. Shapiro

(See Next Column)

KEITH, MACK, LEWIS, COHEN & LUMPKIN—*Continued*
OF COUNSEL
Seymour D. Keith   James L. Mack

Representative Clients: CitiBank, F.S.B.; Attorneys Title Insurance Fund, Inc.; Barnett Bank, N.A.
Approved Counsel: First American Title Insurance Co.; Attorneys Title Insurance Fund, Inc.; Commonwealth Title Insurance Co.
Reference: CitiBank, F.S.B.

For full biographical listings, see the Martindale-Hubbell Law Directory

LAW OFFICE OF WILLIAM P. McCAUGHAN (AV)

Suite 2803 World Trade Center, 80 S.W. Eighth Street, 33130
Telephone: 305-577-0058
Fax: 305-372-0526

For full biographical listings, see the Martindale-Hubbell Law Directory

MILLEDGE IDEN & HELD (AV)

Suite 600, 2100 Ponce de Leon Boulevard (Coral Gables), 33134
Telephone: 305-445-1500
Facsimile: 305-446-9972

MEMBERS OF FIRM
Allan Milledge   Bruce F. Iden
Gary M. Held
ASSOCIATE
Dana J. McElroy
OF COUNSEL
John M. Milledge   Patricia Fields Anderson
Reference: Northern Trust Bank.

For full biographical listings, see the Martindale-Hubbell Law Directory

PATTERSON & SWEENY (AV)

A Partnership of Professional Associations
Suite 2450, Courthouse Tower, 44 West Flagler Street, 33130
Telephone: 305-350-9000
Fax: 305-372-3940

John H. Patterson (P.A.)   John H. Patterson, Jr. (P.A.)
James H. Sweeny, III (P.A.)
OF COUNSEL
Cynthia Byrne Hall   Mark V. Silverio

For full biographical listings, see the Martindale-Hubbell Law Directory

RUBINSTEIN, KORNIK, BLOOM & MINSKER, A PROFESSIONAL ASSOCIATION (AV)

800 Brickell Avenue, Suite 1100, 33131
Telephone: 305-371-6800
Telecopier: 305-371-5760

Jeffrey D. Rubinstein   Kenneth M. Bloom
Gary H. Kornik   Joel N. Minsker (P.A.)

Nina Zuckerman Chepp   Stacey Schrage Goldstein
Rowena D. Reich
Reference: Sun Bank of Miami, N.A.

For full biographical listings, see the Martindale-Hubbell Law Directory

SIEGFRIED, RIVERA, LERNER DE LA TORRE & SOBEL, P.A. (AV)

Suite 1102, 201 Alhambra Circle (Coral Gables), 33134
Telephone: 305-442-3334
Fax: 305-443-3292

Steven M. Siegfried   Helio De La Torre
Oscar R. Rivera   Peter H. Edwards
Lisa A. Lerner   Stuart H. Sobel

Maria Victoria Arias   Elisabeth D. Kozlow
Gracian Celaya   Paul J. Layne
James F. Harrington   Samuel A. Persaud
Adrienne F. Promoff
OF COUNSEL
H. Hugh Mc Connell

For full biographical listings, see the Martindale-Hubbell Law Directory

WILLIAM C. SUSSMAN, P.A. (AV)

Suite 311, 1570 Madruga Avenue (Coral Gables), 33146
Telephone: 305-662-1991
Telefax: 305-661-6692
Email: WILLIAM@SUNSHINE-STATE.COM

(See Next Column)

William C. Sussman

For full biographical listings, see the Martindale-Hubbell Law Directory

ZACK, SPARBER, KOSNITZKY, SPRATT & BROOKS, P.A. (AV)

International Place, 100 Southeast Second Street, Suite 2800, 33131-2144
Telephone: 305-539-8400
Facsimile: 305-539-1307

Michael Kosnitzky   Heileen Sosa
Debra Weiss Goodstone   Jay A. Steinman

For Complete List of Firm Personnel, See General Section

For full biographical listings, see the Martindale-Hubbell Law Directory

---

*NAPLES,** Collier Co.

JAMES W. ELKINS, P.A. (AV)

Suite 303 The Fairway Building, 1000 Tamiami Trail North, 33940
Telephone: 941-263-0910
Fax: 941-263-6091

James W. Elkins

Approved Attorney for: Attorneys Title Insurance Fund.

For full biographical listings, see the Martindale-Hubbell Law Directory

GRANT, FRIDKIN & PEARSON, P.A. (AV)

Pelican Bay Corporate Centre, 5551 Ridgewood Drive, Suite 501, 34108
Telephone: 941-514-1000
Fax: 941-514-0377
Email: 76402.3516@compuserve.com
Key West, Florida Office: 422 Fleming Street, 33040.
Telephone: 305-296-4553.
Fax: 305-296-7049.

SHAREHOLDERS
G. Helen Athan   Jeffrey D. Fridkin
Michael A. Feldman   Richard C. Grant
William M. Pearson

Thomas G. Norsworthy

For full biographical listings, see the Martindale-Hubbell Law Directory

MYERS KRAUSE & STEVENS, CHARTERED (AV)

5811 Pelican Bay Boulevard, Suite 600, 34108-2794
Telephone: 941-598-1221
Fax: 941-598-3499
URL: http://www.myerskrause.com

William H. Myers   Richard S. Franklin
Andrew J. Krause   David P. Browne
William K. Stevens   Robert J. Stommel
Jeffrey J. Beihoff

References: NBD Bank; Northern Trust Bank of Florida, N.A.; SunTrust; U.S. Trust Company of Florida; Comerica Trust Company of Florida, N.A.; Chemical Bank Florida; Key Trust Company of Florida, N.A.; Bessemer Trust Company of Florida.

For full biographical listings, see the Martindale-Hubbell Law Directory

QUARLES & BRADY (AV)

Barnett Center, 4501 Tamiami Trail North Suite 300, 33940-3060
Telephone: 941-262-5959
Fax: 941-434-4999
Milwaukee, Wisconsin Office: 411 East Wisconsin Avenue, 53202-4497.
Telephone: 414-277-5000.
Fax: 414-271-3552.
Madison, Wisconsin Office: Firstar Plaza, One South Pinckney Street, P.O. Box 2113, 53701-2113.
Telephone: 608-251-5000.
Fax: 608-251-9166.
West Palm Beach, Florida Office: 222 Lakeview Avenue, 4th Floor, 33401.
Telephone: 561-653-5000.
Fax: 561-653-5333.
Phoenix, Arizona Office: One Camelback Building, One East Camelback Road, Suite 400, 85012-1649.
Telephone: 602-230-5500.
Fax: 602-230-5598.

PARTNERS
Thomas E. Maloney   Timothy G. Hains
F. Joseph McMackin, III   Leo J. Salvatori
ASSOCIATES
John D. Humphreville   Kevin A. Denti

For Complete List of Firm Personnel, See General Section

For full biographical listings, see the Martindale-Hubbell Law Directory

Naples—Continued

VEGA, STANLEY, ZELMAN & HANLON, P.A. (AV)

2660 Airport Road South, 34112
Telephone: 941-774-3333
Fax: 941-776-6420

George Vega, Jr.   John F. Stanley

John G. Vega
OF COUNSEL
Thomas R. Brown

Representative Clients: Lely Development; John Remington; Quail Creek.

For full biographical listings, see the Martindale-Hubbell Law Directory

NEW PORT RICHEY, Pasco Co.

DANIEL N. MARTIN, P.A. (AV)

Suite B-1, 8406 Massachusetts Avenue, P.O. Box 786, 34653
Telephone: 813-842-8439

Daniel N. Martin

Representative Clients: Regency Communities, Inc., formerly Minieri Communities of Florida, Inc.; Greene Builders, Inc.; Barnett Bank of Pasco County; Hospital Corporation of America.
Approved Attorneys for: Attorneys' Title Insurance Fund; First American Title Insurance Co.; Commonwealth Land Title Insurance Company.
Reference: Barnett Bank of Pasco County.

ORLANDO,* Orange Co.

ARNOLD, MATHENY & EAGAN, P.A. (AV)

801 North Magnolia Avenue, Suite 201, P.O. Box 2967, 32802
Telephone: 407-841-1550
Facsimile: 407-841-8746

William W. Arnold   Alexander J. Ombres
William L. Eagan   Arthur R. Louv
Lehn E. Abrams   R. Craig Cooley
          Barbara Anne Eagan

Representative Clients: Center Lake Properties, Ltd.; Chase Manhattan of Florida; Combustion Tec. Inc.; Commonwealth Land Title Insurance Com.; Contemporary Services; Dillard's Inc. of Florida; Doctor's Home Health Agency, Inc.; Electro-Science Invest Group, Ltd.; First Union National Bank; Forbes-Hamilton Management Co.

For full biographical listings, see the Martindale-Hubbell Law Directory

BAKER & HOSTETLER (AV)

SunBank Center, Suite 2300, 200 South Orange Avenue, 32802-3432
Telephone: 407-649-4000
In Cleveland, Ohio: 3200 National City Center, 1900 East Ninth Street.
Telephone: 216-621-0200.
In Columbus, Ohio: Capitol Square, Suite 2100, 65 East State Street.
Telephone: 614-228-1541.
In Denver, Colorado: 303 East 17th Avenue, Suite 1100.
Telephone: 303-861-0600.
In Houston, Texas: 1000 Louisiana, Suite 2000.
Telephone: 713-751-1600.
In Long Beach, California: 300 Oceangate, Suite 620.
Telephone: 310-432-2827.
In Los Angeles, California: 600 Wilshire Boulevard.
Telephone: 213-624-2400.
In Washington, D.C.: Washington Square, Suite 1100, 1050 Connecticut Avenue, N.W., Suite 1100.
Telephone: 202-861-1500.
In College Park, Maryland: 9658 Baltimore Boulevard, Suite 206.
Telephone: 301-441-2781.
In Alexandria, Virginia: 437 North Lee Street.
Telephone: 703-549-1294.
In San Francisco, California: One Sansome Street, Suite 2000.
Telephone: 415-951-4705.

MEMBER OF FIRM IN ORLANDO, FLORIDA
G. Thomas Ball (Managing Partner-Orlando Office)
PARTNERS

Stephen E. Cook   Kurt P. Gruber
Richard T. Fulton   Rosemary O'Shea
          Robert J. Webb
ASSOCIATES
Elise L. Bloom   Jacqueline Bozzuto
          Andrew T. Marcus

For Complete List of Firm Personnel, See General Section

For full biographical listings, see the Martindale-Hubbell Law Directory

HADDOCK PROFESSIONAL ASSOCIATION

(See Winter Park)
Email: edhaddock@aol.com

Approved Attorneys For: American Pioneer Title Insurance Co.
Reference: Southern Bank of Central Florida.

MORAN & SHAMS, P.A. (AV)

111 North Orange Avenue, Suite 1200, P.O. Box 472, 32802-0472
Telephone: 407-841-4141
Fax: 407-841-4148
Email: moran-shams@moran-shams.com

Thomas P. Moran   Robert S. MacDonald
Maurice Shams   Brian J. Moran
          Sidney H. Shams

Representative Clients: American Medical Associates, Inc.; Carse Oil Company; China Group, Inc.; Cruises Only, Inc.; Dayron, Inc.; R.C. Dunn Oil Company; Florida Pump, Inc.; Insurance Office of Florida; Photo Chemical Systems of Florida, Inc.; Whitehill Development Corporation.

For full biographical listings, see the Martindale-Hubbell Law Directory

POHL & SHORT, P.A.

(See Winter Park)

RUSSELL & HULL, P.A. (AV)

537 North Magnolia Avenue, P.O. Box 2751, 32802
Telephone: 407-422-1234
Telecopier: 407-423-2842

Rodney Laird Russell   Norman L. Hull

Reference: First Union National Bank, N.A.

For full biographical listings, see the Martindale-Hubbell Law Directory

CRAIG B. WARD, P.A. (AV)

Suite 501, 105 East Robinson Street, 32801
Telephone: 407-839-0222
Fax: 407-839-0577

Craig B. Ward
OF COUNSEL
Charles D. Miner

Representative Clients: Gladco, Inc. (American Gladiators); Lake of the Woods Homeowners Association, Inc.; Metro One, Inc. (Real Estate); National Ambulance Builders, Inc.; Poole Construction Co., Inc.; Power Concrete Products Co.; Richard Sibley Associates, Inc. (Advertising); Scientific-Atlanta, Inc.
Approved Agent for: First American Title Insurance Co.; Attorneys' Title Insurance Fund.

For full biographical listings, see the Martindale-Hubbell Law Directory

WILSON, LEAVITT & SMALL, P.A. (AV)

Nations Bank Tower, 111 North Orange Avenue, Suite 1575, 32801
Telephone: 407-843-4321
Fax: 407-423-1505

J. Christy Wilson, III   Jay W. Small
Mark R. Leavitt   Lauren B. Shapiro

Representative Clients: Circle K; Cumberland Farms; Hardee's Food Systems; Mobil Oil; Public Storage; Southland Corp.; NationsBank, N.A.; U.S.F.& G.; Oerther Foods; Seventh Day Adventists.

For full biographical listings, see the Martindale-Hubbell Law Directory

WINDERWEEDLE, HAINES, WARD & WOODMAN, P.A. (AV)

Barnett Bank Center, 390 North Orange Avenue, P.O. Box 1391, 32802-1391
Telephone: 407-423-4246
Telecopier: 407-423-7014
Winter Park, Florida Office: Barnett Bank Building 250 Park Avenue, South, P.O. Box 880.
Telephone: 407-423-4246.
Telecopier: 407-645-3728.

Victor E. Woodman   William A. Walker II
          Joseph Penn Carolan, III

Approved Attorneys For: Attorneys Title Insurance Fund, Inc.; Chicago Title Insurance Co.; Commonwealth Land Title Insurance Co.
Counsel for: Barnett Bank of Central Florida, N.A.
Representative Client: Whispering Waters Apartments.

For Complete List of Firm Personnel, See General Section

For full biographical listings, see the Martindale-Hubbell Law Directory

PALM BEACH, Palm Beach Co.

BAUGHER, METTLER & SHELTON (AV)

340 Royal Poinciana Plaza, P.O. Box 109, 33480
Telephone: 407-833-9631
Fax: 407-655-2835

MEMBERS OF FIRM

Thomas M. Mettler   John W. Shelton

ASSOCIATE

Francis X. J. Lynch

Reference: First National Bank in Palm Beach.

For full biographical listings, see the Martindale-Hubbell Law Directory

MURPHY, REID, PILOTTE, ORD & AUSTIN (AV)

A Partnership of Professional Associations
Suite 100, 340 Royal Palm Way, 33480
Telephone: 561-655-4060
Facsimile: 561-832-5436
Vero Beach, Florida Office: Plantation Plaza, 6606-20th Street, P.O. Drawer M.
Telephone: 561-567-6480.
Facsimile: 561-562-0220.

Eugene W. Murphy Jr. (P.A.)   Keith C. Austin, Jr. (P.A.)

For Complete List of Firm Personnel, See General Section

For full biographical listings, see the Martindale-Hubbell Law Directory

PALM BEACH GARDENS, Palm Beach Co.

HARRIS, KUKEY & HELGESEN, P.A. (AV)

Suite 201 Prosperity Gardens, 11380 Prosperity Farms Road, P.O. Box 31208, 33410
Telephone: 407-622-7755
Fax: 407-622-8422

George E. Harris   Andrew Helgesen
Lawrence M. Kukey

References: SunTrust; Attorneys Title Insurance Fund.

For full biographical listings, see the Martindale-Hubbell Law Directory

MATHISON & MATHISON (AV)

5606 PGA Boulevard, Suite 211, 33418
Telephone: 561-624-2001
Facsimile: 561-624-0036

MEMBERS OF FIRM

Stephen S. Mathison   Carl M. Mathison, Jr.

ASSOCIATE

Frederic T. DeHon, Jr.

For full biographical listings, see the Martindale-Hubbell Law Directory

POMPANO BEACH, Broward Co.

JOHN L. KORTHALS (AV)

1401 East Atlantic Boulevard, 33060
Telephone: 954-783-2999
FAX: 954-783-9832

For full biographical listings, see the Martindale-Hubbell Law Directory

PORT CHARLOTTE, Charlotte Co.

SCHWARZ & KAHLE, P.A. (AV)

21229 Olean Boulevard Suite B, 33952
Telephone: 941-625-4158
Facsimile: 941-625-5460

Gary A. Kahle   Stephen deH. Schwarz

Reference: SunTrust Bank / Gulf Coast.

For full biographical listings, see the Martindale-Hubbell Law Directory

PUNTA GORDA,* Charlotte Co.

WOTITZKY, WOTITZKY, MIZELL & ROSS, P.A. (AV)

223 Taylor Street, 33950
Telephone: 941-639-2171
Telecopier: 941-639-8617

John B. Mizell   Edward L. Wotitzky
Warren R. Ross   Hal F. Wotitzky

OF COUNSEL

Frank Wotitzky   Leo Wotitzky

(See Next Column)

Jason B. Goldman

Representative Client: Punta Gorda Corp.
Approved Attorneys for: Attorneys' Title Insurance Fund, Orlando, Florida; Chicago Title Insurance Co.

For full biographical listings, see the Martindale-Hubbell Law Directory

ST. AUGUSTINE,* St. Johns Co.

UPCHURCH, BAILEY & UPCHURCH, P.A. (AV)

780 North Ponce de Leon Boulevard, P.O. Drawer 3007, 32085-3007
Telephone: 904-829-9066
Facsimile: 904-825-4862

John D. Bailey, Jr.   Michael A. Siragusa

OF COUNSEL

Hamilton D. Upchurch

Representative Clients: Aero Sport, Inc.; American Culinary Federation, Inc.; Barnett Bank, N.A. Penney Retirement Community, Inc.; St. Augustine Alligator Farm, Inc.; St. Augustine-St. Johns County Board of Realtors, Inc.
General Counsel: Flagler College; Flagler Hospital, Inc.; Prosperity Bank of St. Augustine; St. Johns County School Board.

For Complete List of Firm Personnel, See General Section

For full biographical listings, see the Martindale-Hubbell Law Directory

ST. PETERSBURG, Pinellas Co.

STEIN, FORD, SCHAAF & TOWZEY, L.L.P. (AV)

501 First Avenue North, Suite 1000, 33701
Telephone: 813-894-4333
Fax: 813-894-0175; 813-822-7222

Henry A. Stein   Gary M. Schaaf
Harvey A. Ford   Phyllis J. Towzey
Paul A. Nelson   Sarah E. Williams

For full biographical listings, see the Martindale-Hubbell Law Directory

SANFORD,* Seminole Co.

STENSTROM, MCINTOSH, COLBERT, WHIGHAM & SIMMONS, P.A. (AV)

Suite 22 Sun Bank-Downtown, P.O. Box 4848, 32772-4848
Telephone: 407-322-2171
Fax: 407-330-2379
Email: stenstrom.com

Thomas E. Whigham   Franklin C. Whigham
(1952-1988)   Clayton D. Simmons
Douglas Stenstrom (Retired)   Robert K. McIntosh
William L. Colbert   Donna L. Surratt-McIntosh
William E. Reischmann, Jr.

Catherine D. Reischmann   James J. Partlow
Edgar J. Hedrick, III

OF COUNSEL

Kenneth W. McIntosh   S. Kirby Moncrief

Representative Clients: City of Sanford; City of Oviedo; City of Casselberry; Seminole Community College; City of Lake Mary; Sanford Housing Authority; City of DeBary; Seminole Soccer Club, Inc.; Tuskawilla Homeowners' Association; South Seminole-North Orange Wastewater Transmission Authority.

For full biographical listings, see the Martindale-Hubbell Law Directory

SARASOTA,* Sarasota Co.

DENT & COOK, P.A. (AV)

330 South Orange Avenue, P.O. Box 3269, 34230
Telephone: 941-952-1070
FAX: 941-952-1094

John C. Dent, Jr.   John F. Cook

Robert K. Robinson   John W. Chapman, Jr.

LEGAL SUPPORT PERSONNEL

Joyce Mintzer (CLA)

Representative Clients: The Rouse Company; CSX Realty; The Palmer Ranch; Joseph Cory Delivery Service; The State of Florida; Florida County Property Appraisers including Sarasota, Monroe, Hillsborough and Okaloosa Counties; Water Equipment Services, Inc.

For full biographical listings, see the Martindale-Hubbell Law Directory

DICKINSON & GIBBONS, P.A. (AV)

1750 Ringling Boulevard, P.O. Box 3979, 34230
Telephone: 941-366-4680
FAX: 941-953-3136

(See Next Column)

DICKINSON & GIBBONS P.A., *Sarasota—Continued*

Francis C. Dart (1902-1972)	Burwell J. Jones
G. Hunter Gibbons	Richard R. Garland
Ward E. Dahlgren	Stephen G. Brannan
Lewis F. Collins, Jr.	Deborah J. Blue
Gary H. Larsen	Jeffrey D. Peairs
Camden T. French	Douglas R. Wight
Ralph L. Marchbank, Jr.	Stephen R. Kanzer
A. James Rolfes	David S. Preston

OF COUNSEL

Patrick H. Dickinson

LEGAL SUPPORT PERSONNEL

Christine C. Menzel	Janet E. Gadoury
Patricia L. Hunter	(Certified Legal Assistant)

Johanna H. Whitmire (Paralegal)

Representative Clients: Ford Motor Co.; Florida Power & Light Co.; Squibb Corp.
Insurance Clients: Liberty Mutual Insurance Co.; Allstate Insurance Co.; Nationwide Insurance Group; Ohio Casualty Insurance Co.; United States Fidelity & Guaranty Co.; State Farm Insurance Company.

For Complete List of Firm Personnel, See General Section

For full biographical listings, see the Martindale-Hubbell Law Directory

---

KIRK PINKERTON, A PROFESSIONAL ASSOCIATION (AV)

720 South Orange Avenue, P.O. Box 3798, 34230
Telephone: 941-364-2400
Fax: 941-364-2490
Venice, Florida Office: 245 North Tamiami Trail, Suite A, 34285.
Telephone: 941-488-7811.
Fax: 941-488-2544.

Robert J. Carr	L. Norman Vaughan-Birch
William C. Strode	Timothy S. Shaw
L. Howard Payne	William E. Robertson, Jr.
Phillip A. Wolff	Michael A. Ortiz
David M. Silberstein	

Daniel A. Bechtold	David W. Payne
Anita J. Hanna	Michael E. Garlington

For full biographical listings, see the Martindale-Hubbell Law Directory

---

LYONS & BEAUDRY, P.A. (AV)

Suite 1111, Ellis Building, 1605 Main Street, 34236
Telephone: 941-366-3282
Fax: 941-954-1484

Robert W. Beaudry (1929-1991)	John J. Lyons

Carol Whitcher Wood	R. Craig Harrison

Reference: Nations Bank.

For full biographical listings, see the Martindale-Hubbell Law Directory

---

WILLIAMS, PARKER, HARRISON, DIETZ & GETZEN, PROFESSIONAL ASSOCIATION (AV)

200 South Orange Avenue, 34236-6749
Telephone: 941-366-4800
Telecopier: 941-366-5109
Mailing Address: P.O. Box 3258, Sarasota, Florida, 34230-3258
Email: wphdg.law@netsrg.com *URL:*
http://www.sarasota-online.com/williamspa-w

J.J. Williams, Jr. (1886-1968)	Frank Strelec
W. Davis Parker (1920-1982)	Terri Salt Costa
William T. Harrison, Jr.	David A. Wallace
George A. Dietz	Mark A. Schwartz
Monte K. Marshall	Ric Gregoria
James L. Ritchey	Elvin W. Phillips
William G. Lambrecht	Jeffrey A. Grebe
John T. Berteau	John L. Moore
John V. Cannon, III	Morgan R. Bentley
Charles D. Bailey, Jr.	Susan A. Barrett
J. Michael Hartenstine	Carol Ann Kalish
Michele Boardman Grimes	Linda R. Getzen
James L. Turner	Kimberly J. Page
William M. Seider	Phillip D. Eck
Elizabeth C. Marshall	J. Hugh Middlebrooks
Robert W. Benjamin	Robert A. Warram

OF COUNSEL

William E. Getzen	Frazer F. Hilder
Hugh McPheeters, Jr.	

LEGAL SUPPORT PERSONNEL

Mark Loveridge (Land Planner)

General Counsel for: Sarasota County Public Hospital Board; Sarasota-Manatee Airport Authority; Taylor Woodrow Homes Ltd.; FCCI Mutual Insurance Co.

(See Next Column)

Local Counsel for: NationsBank of Florida; Barnett Bank of Southwest Florida; Northern Trust Bank of Florida; SunTrust Bank, Gulfcoast.

For full biographical listings, see the Martindale-Hubbell Law Directory

---

STUART, * Martin Co.

McCARTHY, SUMMERS, BOBKO, McKEY, WOOD & SAWYER, P.A. (AV)

2081 East Ocean Boulevard, Suite 2-A, 34996
Telephone: 561-286-1700
Fax: 561-283-1803
Email: mcsumm@gate.net *URL:* http://www.gate.net/~mcsumm/

Terence P. McCarthy	John D. McKey, Jr.
Robert P. Summers	Steven J. Wood
Noel A. Bobko	Thomas R. Sawyer

Representative Clients: American Bank of Martin County; First National Bank and Trust Company of the Treasure Coast; Great Western Bank; Hydratech Utilities; Lost Lake at Hobe Sound; Taylor Creek Marina, Inc.; GBS Excavating, Inc.; Seaboard Savings Bank; Gary Player Design Group.

For full biographical listings, see the Martindale-Hubbell Law Directory

---

TALLAHASSEE, * Leon Co.

FIXEL & MAGUIRE (AV)

211 South Gadsden Street, 32301
Telephone: 904-681-1800
Fax: 904-681-9017
Orlando, Florida Office: 1250 Eola Park Centre, 200 East Robinson Street, 32801.
Telephone: 407-841-0443.
Fax: 407-841-9850.

Joe W. Fixel	Raymer F. Maguire, III

Representative Clients: Condemnees: Allen Morris Co.; Franklin Carriage Gate Shopping Center, Ltd.; Miccosukee Village Shopping Center, Ltd.; Nick Nicholas Ford, Inc.; Weaver Oil Co.; United Fuel Corp.; Majik Market Convenience Stores. Condemnors: Collier County Board of County Commissioners; Hillsborough County Board of County Commissioners.
Reference: Barnett Bank.

For full biographical listings, see the Martindale-Hubbell Law Directory

---

NOVEY, MENDELSON & ADAMSON (AV)

851 East Park Avenue, 32301
Telephone: 904-224-2000
FAX: 904-222-4951
Email: jmnovey@polaris.net

Jerome M. Novey	Robert D. Mendelson
Kristin Adamson	

For full biographical listings, see the Martindale-Hubbell Law Directory

---

ROSE, SUNDSTROM & BENTLEY (AV)

A Partnership including Professional Associations
2548 Blairstone Pines Drive, P.O. Box 1567, 32302-1567
Telephone: 904-877-6555
Telecopier: 904-656-4029

MEMBERS OF FIRM

Chris H. Bentley (P.A.)	Martin S. Friedman (P.A.)

Representative Clients: Aloha Utilities, Inc.; Bonita Springs Utility, Inc.; First American Title Insurance Company; North Fort Myers Utility, Inc.; Wise Realty Company.
Reference: Barnett Bank, Tallahassee.

For full biographical listings, see the Martindale-Hubbell Law Directory

---

TAMPA, * Hillsborough Co.

BRICKLEMYER SMOLKER & BOLVES, P.A. (AV)

400 North Tampa Street, Suite 2400, 33602-4708
Telephone: 813-223-3888
Fax: 813-228-6422

Keith W. Bricklemyer	Brian A. Bolves
David Smolker	Jay J. Bartlett
Robert E. V. Kelley, Jr.	

David M. Corry	I. Ed Pantaleon
Jeff D. Jackson	William D. Shepherd
Douglas C. Roland	

For full biographical listings, see the Martindale-Hubbell Law Directory

---

FUENTES AND KREISCHER (AV)

1407 West Busch Boulevard, 33612
Telephone: 813-933-6647
Fax: 813-932-8588

(See Next Column)

FUENTES AND KREISCHER—*Continued*
MEMBERS OF FIRM
Lawrence E. Fuentes   Albert C. Kreischer, Jr.

Reference: Northside Bank of Tampa.

For full biographical listings, see the Martindale-Hubbell Law Directory

---

GARCIA & FIELDS, P.A. (AV)

Suite 2560 Barnett Plaza, 101 East Kennedy Boulevard, 33602
Telephone: 813-222-8500
FAX: 813-222-8520

Joseph Garcia   Lesley J. Friedsam
Robert W. Fields   Victor D. Ines
     Kristina J. Jones

Reference: Barnett Bank of Tampa.

For full biographical listings, see the Martindale-Hubbell Law Directory

---

LAW OFFICE OF JOSEPH M. PANIELLO, P.A. (AV)

Suite 2720 One Tampa City Center, 201 North Franklin Street, P.O. Box 2347, 33601
Telephone: 813-228-7004
FAX: 813-221-2418

Joseph M. Paniello   J. Mackie Paniello

Gregory T. Hall   Clay A. Holtsinger

Representative Clients: J. I. Kislak Mortgage Corp.; Corinthian Mortgage Corp.; Knutson Mortgage Corp.; GE Capital Asset Mgt. Corp.; Source One Mortgage Services Corp.; Eastern Savings; Banc Plus Mortgage Co.; Bank of America.
Approved Attorney for: Attorney's Title Insurance Fund.

For full biographical listings, see the Martindale-Hubbell Law Directory

---

PARIS & ASSOCIATES, P.A. (AV)

15310 Amberly Drive, Suite 300, 33647
Telephone: 813-975-1900
Fax: 813-975-1850

Deborah M. Paris

Francine L. Rackoff

Representative Clients: NationsBank, N.A.; Michigan National Bank; Standard Federal Bank; Lloyds of London.

For full biographical listings, see the Martindale-Hubbell Law Directory

---

RYDBERG & GOLDSTEIN, P.A. (AV)

Suite 200, 500 East Kennedy Boulevard, 33602
Telephone: 813-229-3900
Telecopier: 813-229-6101

Marsha Griffin Rydberg   Bruce S. Goldstein

Peter Baker   Tammy N. Giroux
Brian T. FitzGerald   Cynthia L. Bulan
     Susan Greco Tuttle

For full biographical listings, see the Martindale-Hubbell Law Directory

---

SHEAR, NEWMAN, HAHN AND ROSENKRANZ, P.A. (AV)

Suite 1000, 201 East Kennedy Boulevard, 33602
Telephone: 813-228-8530
FAX: 813-221-9122

L. David Shear   Glenn M. Burton
Jerry L. Newman   Roland J. Lamb
William E. Hahn   Bruce Douglas Lamb
Stanley W. Rosenkranz   Jeffrey Drew Butt
James R. Freeman   Mark J. Ragusa
Rodney W. Morgan   Kelly Jo Schmedt

Marilyn Drivas Sandborn   Mildred D. Beam-Rucker
Scott P. Distasio   Joseph F. Diaco, Jr.
Thomas M. Hoeler   Elizabeth (Betsey) Taylor Herd
Christopher J. Schulte   Timothy M. Cerio
Kimberly D. Holladay   Mindy Paige Brostoff
Debra L. Boje   Carl A. Goldman
OF COUNSEL
Daniel J. Gibby   Leonard L. Kleinman

References: NationsBank; First National Bank.

For full biographical listings, see the Martindale-Hubbell Law Directory

---

SMITH, WILLIAMS & HUMPHRIES, P.A. (AV)

Old Hyde Park, 712 South Oregon Avenue, 33606
Telephone: 813-253-5400
Fax: 813-254-3459
Orlando, Florida Office: Southeast Bank Building, Suite 701, 201 East Pine Street.
Telephone: 407-849-5151.
Fax: 407-843-4076.

David Lisle Smith   Robert L. Harding
Gregory L. Williams   (Resident, Orlando Office)
J. Gregory Humphries   Gregory E. Mierzwinski
  (Resident, Orlando Office)   Carole Taylor Kirkwood
     Daniel William King

For full biographical listings, see the Martindale-Hubbell Law Directory

---

WILLIAMS, REED, WEINSTEIN, SCHIFINO & MANGIONE, P.A. (AV)

One Tampa City Center, 201 North Franklin Street, Suite 2600, P.O. Box 380, 33601
Telephone: 813-221-2626
Telefax: 813-221-7335

Robert V. Williams   Ralph P. Mangione
James M. Reed   Scott I. Steady
David B. Weinstein   R. Marshall Rainey
William J. Schifino, Jr.   David S. Jennis
     Russell S. Thomas

Kenneth G. Turkel   Robert R. Hearn
Aminie Mohip   John A. Schifino
Ricardo A. Roig   Jennifer A. Powers
V. Stephen Cohen   Elizabeth S. Hoskins
FIRM ADMINISTRATOR
Joseph C. Simmons

For full biographical listings, see the Martindale-Hubbell Law Directory

---

VERO BEACH,* Indian River Co.

CLEM, POLACKWICH, VOCELLE & TAYLOR (AV)

A Partnership including Professional Associations
Univest Building-Suite 501, 2770 North Indian River Boulevard, 32960
Telephone: 561-562-8111
Fax: 561-562-2870
MEMBERS OF FIRM
Chester Clem (P.A.)   Louis B. Vocelle, Jr., (P.A.)
Alan S. Polackwich, Sr. (P.A.)   James A. Taylor, III
ASSOCIATE
Paul Richard Berg
OF COUNSEL
Robert Golden

References: Barnett Bank of The Treasure Coast; Northern Trust Bank of Vero Beach; Indian River National Bank; Riverside National Bank of Florida.

For full biographical listings, see the Martindale-Hubbell Law Directory

---

COLLINS, BROWN, CALDWELL, BARKETT, ROSSWAY, GARAVAGLIA & MOORE, CHARTERED (AV)

756 Beachland Boulevard, P.O. Box 3686, 32964
Telephone: 561-231-4343
FAX: 561-234-5213

George G. Collins, Jr.   Bradley W. Rossway
Calvin B. Brown   Michael J. Garavaglia
William W. Caldwell   John E. Moore, III
Bruce D. Barkett   Lisa N. Thompson

Reference: First Union Bank of Indian River County, Vero Beach, Florida.

For full biographical listings, see the Martindale-Hubbell Law Directory

---

STEWART & NALL, P.A. (AV)

3355 Ocean Drive, P.O. Box 3345, 32964-3345
Telephone: 561-231-3500
FAX: 561-231-9876

William J. Stewart   Cynthia L. Cambron
Robert C. Nall   Edith E. Collins
     Troy B. Hafner

Representative Clients: Harbor Branch Oceanographic Institution, Inc.; Indian River Memorial Hospital, Inc.
Approved Attorneys for: Attorneys' Title Insurance Fund; Commonwealth Land Title Insurance Co.
Reference: Northern Trust Bank Florida, N.A.

For full biographical listings, see the Martindale-Hubbell Law Directory

WEST PALM BEACH,* Palm Beach Co.

HONIGMAN MILLER SCHWARTZ AND COHN (AV)

A Partnership including Professional Associations
Suite 800 Esperante Building, 222 Lakeview Avenue, 33401-6112
Telephone: 561-838-4500
Telecopier: 561-832-3036; 832-2645
URL: http://law.honigman.com
Tampa, Florida Office: 2700 SunTrust Financial Centre, 401 E. Jackson Street, 33602-5226.
Telephone: 813-221-6600.
Detroit, Michigan Office: 2290 First National Building, 48226.
Telephone: 313-256-7800.
Lansing, Michigan Office: 222 North Washington Square, Suite 400, 48933-1800.
Telephone: 517-484-8282.

MEMBERS

Steven R. Parson (P.A.)   Neil W. Platock (P.A.)
                 Marvin S. Rosen (P.A.)

For Complete List of Firm Personnel, See General Section

For full biographical listings, see the Martindale-Hubbell Law Directory

LEWIS, VEGOSEN, ROSENBACH & SILBER, P.A. (AV)

500 South Australian Avenue, P.O. Box 4388, 33402-4388
Telephone: 561-659-3300
Fax: 561-832-1991

Robert M. Lewis (1932-1982)	Cynthia J. Jackson
Dean Vegosen	Gary Walk
Dean J. Rosenbach	John B. Levitt
Louis M. Silber	Samuel A. Thomas
Gary M. Dunkel	Marshall J. Osofsky
Kenneth A. Treadwell	John R. Sheppard, Jr.

Cass Walker Christenson

For full biographical listings, see the Martindale-Hubbell Law Directory

NASON, GILDAN, YEAGER, GERSON & WHITE, P.A. (AV)

Penthouse Suite United National Bank Tower, 1645 Palm Beach Lakes Boulevard, 33401
Telephone: 561-686-3307
Fax: 561-686-5442

Herbert L. Gildan	Susan Fleischner Kornspan
Thomas J. Yeager	Alan I. Armour, II
Gary N. Gerson	Mark A. Pachman
John White, II	Elaine Johnson James
Phillip C. Gildan	Nathan E. Nason
Domenick R. Lioce	Gregory L. Scott

John M. McDivitt	Jeffrey B. Kahn

Craig S. Barnett

LEGAL SUPPORT PERSONNEL

Sandra R. Gronek	Constance Schiraldi
(Office Administrator)	(Real Estate Paralegal)
Kathy Pelly	Georgina J. Popham
(Litigation Paralegal)	(Corporate/Securities
Elsie T. Pollak	Paralegal)
(Litigation Paralegal)	

For full biographical listings, see the Martindale-Hubbell Law Directory

NEWBURGH, BALDWIN & GERSHMAN (AV)

1675 Palm Beach Lakes Boulevard, Suite 700, 33401
Telephone: 561-684-8898; 561-471-0470
Fax: 561-684-8820; 561-471-4222

MEMBERS OF FIRM

Steven S. Newburgh   Fletcher N. Baldwin, III
              Robert Scott Gershman

OF COUNSEL
Barry L. Clayton

For full biographical listings, see the Martindale-Hubbell Law Directory

PRESSLY & PRESSLY, P.A. (AV)

Esperante, Suite 910, 222 Lakeview Avenue, 33401-6112
Telephone: 561-659-4040
FAX: 561-655-6006

James G. Pressly, Jr.   David S. Pressly
                Trent S. Kiziah

For full biographical listings, see the Martindale-Hubbell Law Directory

QUARLES & BRADY (AV)

222 Lakeview Avenue, 4th Floor, 33401
Telephone: 561-653-5000
Fax: 561-653-5333
Milwaukee, Wisconsin Office: 411 East Wisconsin Avenue, 53202-4497.
Telephone: 414-277-5000.
Fax: 414-271-3552.
Madison, Wisconsin Office: Firstar Plaza, One South Pinckney Street, P.O. Box 2113, 53701-2113.
Telephone: 608-251-5000.
Fax: 608-251-9166.
Naples, Florida Office: Barnett Center, 4501 Tamiami Trail North, Suite 300, 33940-3060.
Telephone: 941-262-5959.
Fax: 941-434-4999.
Phoenix, Arizona Office: One Camelback Building, One East Camelback Road, Suite 400, 85012-1649.
Telephone: 602-230-5500.
Fax: 602-230-5598.

PARTNERS

John S. Sammond   David L. Petersen

ASSOCIATE
Nancy Berz Colman

For Complete List of Firm Personnel, See General Section

For full biographical listings, see the Martindale-Hubbell Law Directory

WOOD & MURPHY (AV)

Suite 201, 400 Executive Center Drive, 33401
Telephone: 407-471-0555
Fax: 407-471-0588

Lawrence E. Murphy   Marshall B. Wood, Jr.

For full biographical listings, see the Martindale-Hubbell Law Directory

WINTER HAVEN, Polk Co.

PETERSON & MYERS, P.A. (AV)

Suite 300, 141 5th Street N.W., P.O. Drawer 7608, 33883-7608
Telephone: 941-294-3360
Lake Wales, Florida Office: 130 East Central Avenue, P.O. Box 1079.
Telephones: 941-676-7611; 683-8942.
Lakeland, Florida Office: 100 East Main Street, P.O. Box 24628.
Telephones: 941-683-6511; 676-6934.

Philip O. Allen	Peter J. Munson
Jack P. Brandon	Corneal B. Myers
Beach A Brooks, Jr.	Cornelius B. Myers, III
Kristen Marie Buzzanca	E. Blake Paul
J. Davis Connor	Robert E. Puterbaugh
Michael S. Craig	Abel A. Putnam
Roy A. Craig, Jr.	Thomas B. Putnam, Jr.
Jacob C. Dykxhoorn	Deborah A. Ruster
Dennis P. Johnson	Stephen R. Senn
Kevin C. Knowlton	Andrea Teves Smith
Douglas A. Lockwood, III	Keith H. Wadsworth
M. Craig Massey	Kerry M. Wilson

General Counsel for: Barnett Bank of Polk County.
Representative Clients: Mutual Wholesale Co.; Barnett Banks, Inc.; Ben Hill Griffin, Inc.; Alcoma Association, Inc.
Approved Attorneys for: Attorneys' Title Insurance Fund; Federal Land Bank, Columbia, South Carolina; Equitable Life Assurance Society of the United States.

For full biographical listings, see the Martindale-Hubbell Law Directory

WINTER PARK, Orange Co.

GRAHAM, CLARK, JONES, BUILDER, PRATT & MARKS (AV)

Third Floor, NationsBank Building, 369 North New York Avenue, P.O. Drawer 1690, 32790
Telephone: 407-647-4455
Telefax: 407-740-7063

MEMBERS OF FIRM

Jesse E. Graham	Howard S. Marks
Scott D. Clark	Geoffrey D. Withers
Frederick W. Jones	Mary W. Christian
J. Lindsay Builder, Jr.	Jesse E. Graham, Jr.
James R. Pratt	Samuel M. Nelson

Jessica K. Hew

Approved Attorneys for: Chicago Title Insurance Co.
Reference: NationsBank of Florida.

For full biographical listings, see the Martindale-Hubbell Law Directory

Winter Park—Continued

HADDOCK PROFESSIONAL ASSOCIATION (AV)

3260 University Boulevard, Suite 210, 32792
Telephone: 407-679-6171
FAX: 407-679-8810
Mailing Address: P.O. Box 5148, Winter Park, FL, 32793-5148
Email: edhaddock@aol.com

Edward E. Haddock, Jr.

Approved Attorneys For: American Pioneer Title Insurance Co.
Reference: Southern Bank of Central Florida.

For full biographical listings, see the Martindale-Hubbell Law Directory

POHL & SHORT, P.A. (AV)

280 West Canton Avenue, Suite 410, P.O. Box 3208, 32790
Telephone: 407-647-7645; 407-647-POHL
Telefax: 407-647-2314

Frank L. Pohl	C. Teresa de Arrigoitia
Houston E. Short	George A. Golder
Dwight I. Cool	Norma Stanley
James Everett Shepherd V	Mark W. Garrett
John R. Simpson, Jr.	

Representative Clients: American Pioneer Title Insurance Company; Institute of Internal Auditors, Inc.; Thompson Steel, Inc.; SunTrust, N.A.; The Bank of Winter Park; Bekins Moving and Storage Co., Inc.; Champion Boats, Inc.; KeyCom Telephone Systems, Inc.

For full biographical listings, see the Martindale-Hubbell Law Directory

WINDERWEEDLE, HAINES, WARD & WOODMAN, P.A. (AV)

Barnett Bank Building, 250 Park Avenue, South, P.O. Box 880, 32790-0880
Telephone: 407-423-4246
Telecopier: 407-645-3728
Orlando, Florida Office: Barnett Bank Center, 390 North Orange Avenue, P.O. Box 1391.
Telephone: 407-423-4246.
Telecopier: 407-423-7014.

Victor E. Woodman	Randolph J. Rush
John D. Haines	Gregory L. Holzhauer
C. Brent McCaghren	Nancy S. Freeman

Approved Attorneys For: Attorneys Title Insurance Fund, Inc.; Chicago Title Insurance Co.; Commonwealth Land Title Insurance Co.
Counsel for: Barnett Bank of Central Florida, N.A.
Representative Client: Whispering Waters Apartments.

For Complete List of Firm Personnel, See General Section

For full biographical listings, see the Martindale-Hubbell Law Directory

GEORGIA

ALBANY,* Dougherty Co.

CANNON & MEYER VON BREMEN, LLP (AV)

2417 Westgate Drive, P.O. Box 70909, 31708-0909
Telephone: 912-435-1470
Telefax: 912-888-2156

MEMBERS OF FIRM

William E. Cannon, Jr.	Michael S. Meyer von Bremen

ASSOCIATES

Toysha M. Flowers	William H. Gregory, II

OF COUNSEL

Timothy O. Davis

For full biographical listings, see the Martindale-Hubbell Law Directory

ATLANTA,* Fulton Co.

ALEMBIK & ALEMBIK (AV)

3033 Maple Drive, N.E., 30305
Telephone: 404-261-7565
Fax: 404-264-0639

MEMBER OF FIRM

Aaron I. Alembik

References: Trust Company of Georgia; Wachovia Bank, Bank South.

For full biographical listings, see the Martindale-Hubbell Law Directory

ALEMBIK, FINE & CALLNER, P.A. (AV)

Marquis One Tower, Fourth Floor, 245 Peachtree Center Avenue, N.E., 30303
Telephone: 404-688-8800
Telecopier: 404-420-7191

(See Next Column)

Michael D. Alembik (1936-1993)	Ronald T. Gold
Lowell S. Fine	G. Michael Banick
Bruce W. Callner	Mark E. Bergeson
Kathy L. Portnoy	Russell P. Love

Z. Ileana Martinez	Janet Lichiello Franchi
Susan M. Lieppe	Heidi Koch Martin
Bruce R. Steinfeld	Janet Caroline Moja
John H. Zwald	

For full biographical listings, see the Martindale-Hubbell Law Directory

ALSTON & BIRD (AV)

A Partnership including Professional Corporations
One Atlantic Center, 1201 West Peachtree Street, 30309-3424
Telephone: 404-881-7000
Telecopier: 404-881-7777
Cable Address: AMGRAM GA
Telex: 54-2996
Easylink: 62985848
Washington, D.C. Office: 601 Pennsylvania Ave., N.W., North Building, Suite 250 20004.
Telephone: 202-508-3300.
Telecopier: 202-508-3333.

MEMBERS OF FIRM

Ralph Williams, Jr.	Christopher Glenn Sawyer
Walter W. Mitchell	Charles A. Brake, Jr.
Rawson Foreman	Albert E. Bender, Jr.
James F. Nellis, Jr.	Timothy J. Pakenham
T. Michael Tennant	William R. Klapp, Jr.
Michael R. Davis	Mark C. Rusche
Marci P. Schmerler	

ASSOCIATES

Christina K. Braisted	John S. Hetzel
James G. Farris, Jr.	J. Alan McNabb
Sandra L. Fitzgerald	Joseph P. L. Snyder
Daniel R. Weede	

COUNSEL

Leon Adams, Jr.	Glenda G. Bugg
Steven D. Collier	Homer Lee Walker

Representative Clients: First Union Corporation; Holiday Inn Worldwide; NationsBank Corporation; New York Life Insurance Company; Prudential Insurance Company of America; The Equitable Life Assurance Society of the United States; Watkins Associated Industries, Inc.

For Complete List of Firm Personnel, See General Section

For full biographical listings, see the Martindale-Hubbell Law Directory

CHOREY, TAYLOR & FEIL, A PROFESSIONAL CORPORATION (AV)

Suite 1700, The Lenox Building, 3399 Peachtree Road, N.E., 30326
Telephone: 404-841-3200
Facsimile: 404-841-3221

Eric D. Ranney	Susan Shivers Fink

For Complete List of Firm Personnel, See General Section

For full biographical listings, see the Martindale-Hubbell Law Directory

COHEN/DAVID & ASSOCIATES, P.C. (AV)

6000 Lake Forrest Drive, N.W. 100 Century Springs West, 30328-5902
Telephone: 404-256-7802
Fax: 404-255-0137
Tucker, Georgia Office: Suite 104, Building 12, 2193 Northlake Parkway, 30084.
Telephone: 770-493-8445.
Fax: 770-493-1831.
Roswell, Georgia Office: Suite 400, 1172 Grimes Bridge Road, 30075.
Telephone: 770-998-8100.
Fax: 770-998-6804.

Bruce P. Cohen	John H. David, Jr.
	(Resident, Roswell Office)

John M. Dugan	Robert G. Bennett III

OF COUNSEL

Annette Kerlin McBrayer

For full biographical listings, see the Martindale-Hubbell Law Directory

DAVID G. CROCKETT, P.C. (AV)

1950 Equitable Building, 100 Peachtree Street, N.W., 30303
Telephone: 404-522-4280
Telecopier: 404-589-9891

David G. Crockett

(See Next Column)

DAVID G. CROCKETT, P.C., *Atlanta—Continued*

Tait O. Norton

Approved Attorney for: Chicago Title Insurance Co.
Reference: NationsBank, N.A.

For full biographical listings, see the Martindale-Hubbell Law Directory

DAVIS, MATTHEWS & QUIGLEY, P.C. (AV)

Fourteenth Floor, Lenox Towers II, 3400 Peachtree Road, 30326
Telephone: 404-261-3900
Telecopier: 404-261-0159
Email: dmq@interserv.com

Ron L. Quigley   J. Michael Harrison

Approved Attorneys for: Lawyers Title Insurance Corp.

For Complete List of Firm Personnel, See General Section

For full biographical listings, see the Martindale-Hubbell Law Directory

GLASS, MCCULLOUGH, SHERRILL & HARROLD (AV)

1409 Peachtree Street, N.E., 30309
Telephone: 404-885-1500
Telecopier: 404-892-1801
Buckhead Office: Monarch Plaza, 3414 Peachtree Road, N.E., Suite 450,
Atlanta, Georgia, 30326-1162.
Telephone: 404-885-1500.
Telecopier: 404-231-1978.
Washington, D.C. Office: 1150 17th Street, N.W., Suite 605. Washington,
D.C., 20036.
Telephone: 202-785-8118.
Telecopier: 202-785-0128.
Knoxville, Tennessee Office: 606 West Main Avenue, Suite 205, P.O. Box
2543. Knoxville, Tennessee, 37901-2543.
Telephone: 423-971-5418.
Telecopier: 423-971-1706.

MEMBERS OF FIRM

Peter B. Glass	Paul P. Mattingly
Kenneth R. McCullough	Chester G. Rosenberg
Mark A. Block	Jerry A. Shaifer
William D. Brunstad	Bradley J. Taylor
Luther C. Curtis	Robert M. Trusty
James H. Kaminer, Jr.	Bradley E. Wahl

OF COUNSEL
Glee A. Triplett

ASSOCIATES

Terence G. Clark	Margaret A. McCue
Patrick J. Clarke	(Not admitted in GA)
D. Lynn Holliday	R. Bailey Teague
G. Wilson Horde, III	
(Not admitted in GA)	

For Complete List of Firm Personnel, See General Section

For full biographical listings, see the Martindale-Hubbell Law Directory

HOLT, NEY, ZATCOFF & WASSERMAN (AV)

A Partnership including Professional Corporations
100 Galleria Parkway, Suite 600, 30339
Telephone: 770-956-9600
Facsimile Number: 770-956-1490

MEMBERS OF FIRM

Robert G. Holt (P.C.)	Sanford H. Zatcoff (P.C.)
James M. Ney (P.C.)	Richard P. Vornholt
	Brian P. Cain

ASSOCIATE
Thomas K. Anderson

Representative Clients: Abrams Properties, Inc.; Citicorp Real Estate, Inc.;
Childress Klein Properties, Inc.; Confederation Life Insurance Co.; Trammell
Crow Residential; First American Title Insurance Co.; Gables Residential
Trust; Metric Realty; Old Republic National Title Insurance Co.; Roberts
Properties, Inc.

For Complete List of Firm Personnel, See General Section

For full biographical listings, see the Martindale-Hubbell Law Directory

KILPATRICK & CODY LLP (AV)

Suite 2800, 1100 Peachtree Street, 30309-4530
Telephone: 404-815-6500
Telephone Copier: 404-815-6555
Telex: 54-2307
Washington, D.C. Office: Suite 800, 700 13th Street, N.W., 20005.
Telephone: 202-508-5800. Telephone Copier: 202-508-5858.
Brussels, Belgium Office: Avenue Louise 65, BTE 3, 1050 Brussels.
Telephone: (32) (2) 533-03-00.
Telecopier: (32) (2) 534-86-38.

(See Next Column)

London, England Office: 68 Pall Mall, London, SW1Y 5ES, England.
Telephone: (44) (71) 321 0477.
Telecopier: (44) (71) 930 9733.
Augusta, Georgia Office: Suite 1400 First Union Bank Building, P.O. Box
2043, 30903. Telephone (706) 724-2622. Telecopier (706) 722-0219.

MEMBERS OF FIRM

Tim Carssow	Candace L. Fowler
Evelyn H. Coats	M. Andrew Kauss

ASSOCIATES

Lexie L. Craven	Mark A. Palmer
Nancy G. Gilreath	(Not admitted in GA)

For Complete List of Firm Personnel, See General Section

For full biographical listings, see the Martindale-Hubbell Law Directory

LIPSHUTZ, GREENBLATT & KING (AV)

2300 Harris Tower-Peachtree Center, 233 Peachtree Street, N.E., 30303
Telephone: 404-688-2300
Fax: 404-588-0648

MEMBERS OF FIRM

Robert J. Lipshutz	Edward L. Greenblatt
	Randall M. Lipshutz

OF COUNSEL

William R. King	Tito Mazzetta
	James V. Zito

ASSOCIATES

Paula B. Smith	Timothy L. S. Sitz

For full biographical listings, see the Martindale-Hubbell Law Directory

LONG ALDRIDGE & NORMAN, LLP (AV)

A Limited Liability Partnership including Professional Corporations
One Peachtree Center, Suite 5300, 303 Peachtree Street, 30308
Telephone: 404-527-4000
Telecopier: 404-527-4198
Washington, D.C. Office: Suite 600, 701 Pennsylvania Avenue, N.W.,
20004.
Telephone: 202-624-1200.
FAX: 202-624-1298.

MEMBERS OF FIRM

Clyde E. Click	W. Gregory Null
Robert D. Hancock, Jr.	William F. Stevens
	William F. Timmons

ASSOCIATES

James L. Barkin	Douglas D. Selph
Mindy S. Planer	Janice Nathanson Smith

For Complete List of Firm Personnel, See General Section

For full biographical listings, see the Martindale-Hubbell Law Directory

MACEY, WILENSKY, COHEN, WITTNER & KESSLER, LLP (AV)

285 Peachtree Center Avenue, Suite 600, 30303-1229
Telephone: 404-584-1200
Telecopier: 404-681-4355
Other Atlanta, Georgia Office: 5784 Lake Forrest Drive, Suite 214, 30328.

MEMBERS OF FIRM

Morris W. Macey	Frank B. Wilensky
	M. Todd Westfall

ASSOCIATE
Pamela Gronauer Hill

For Complete List of Firm Personnel, See General Section

For full biographical listings, see the Martindale-Hubbell Law Directory

PARKER, HUDSON, RAINER & DOBBS (AV)

1500 Marquis Two Tower, 285 Peachtree Center Avenue, N.E., 30303
Telephone: 404-523-5300
FAX: 404-522-8409
Tallahassee, Florida Office: The Perkins House, 118 North Gadsden
Street, 32301.
Telephone: 904-681-0191.
FAX: 904-681-9493.

MEMBER OF FIRM
Kenneth H. Kraft

For full biographical listings, see the Martindale-Hubbell Law Directory

PETERSON DILLARD YOUNG ASSELIN & POWELL LLP (AV)

Suite 1100, 230 Peachtree Street, N.W., 30303
Telephone: 404-523-3300
Telecopier: 404-522-6000

MEMBER OF FIRM
Malcolm D. Young, Jr.

For full biographical listings, see the Martindale-Hubbell Law Directory

Atlanta—Continued

RAMSAY & CALLOWAY (AV)

56 Perimeter Center East, N.E. Suite 400, 30346-2283
Telephone: 770-698-7960
Telecopier: 770-698-7990
Hilton Head, South Carolina Office: Suite 300 Professional Building.
Telephone: 803-686-4006.
Telecopier: 803-686-4494.

MEMBERS OF FIRM

Ernest C. Ramsay	N. H. Purvis
S. Marcus Calloway	Richard J. Beam, Jr.
J. F. Mixson, III	

ASSOCIATES

Donald J. Schliessmann, Jr.	Sebastian Sam Paxin
Christy B. Cheek	
Christine A. Hofmann (Resident, Hilton Head, South Carolina Office)	

Reference: NationsBank.

For full biographical listings, see the Martindale-Hubbell Law Directory

SLUTZKY, WOLFE AND BAILEY (AV)

2255 Cumberland Parkway, Building 1300, 30339
Telephone: 770-438-8000
Telecopier: 770-438-9657

MEMBERS OF FIRM

Stanley K. Slutzky	Bernard R. Wolfe
Danny C. Bailey	

ASSOCIATES

Ray S. Smith III	Barry M. Wolfe
William J. Lieberbaum	Brad M. Wolfe

For full biographical listings, see the Martindale-Hubbell Law Directory

SUTHERLAND, ASBILL & BRENNAN, L.L.P. (AV)

999 Peachtree Street, N.E., 30309-3996
Telephone: 404-853-8000
Facsimile: 404-853-8806
Email: postmaster@sablaw.com
Washington, D.C. Office: 1275 Pennsylvania Avenue, N.W., 20004-2404.
Telephone: 202-383-0100.
New York, N.Y. Office: 600 Madison Avenue, 11th Floor, 10022-1615.
Telephone: 212-605-6400.
Austin, Texas Office: 111 Congress Avenue, 23rd Floor, 78701-4079.
Telephone: 512-469-3350.

Alfred G. Adams, Jr.	James Bruce Jordan
H. Edward Hales, Jr.	William R. Patterson
J. Patton Hyman, III	James R. Paulk, Jr.
Haynes R. Roberts	

COUNSEL OF THE FIRM IN ATLANTA, GEORGIA

S. Perry Thomas, Jr.

For Complete List of Firm Personnel, See General Section
For full biographical listings, see the Martindale-Hubbell Law Directory

THOMAS, KENNEDY, SAMPSON & PATTERSON (AV)

55 Marietta Street, N.W., Suite 1600, 30303
Telephone: 404-688-4503
Telecopier: 404-681-2950

MEMBERS OF FIRM

John Loren Kennedy (1942-1994)	P. Andrew Patterson
	Myra H. Dixon
Thomas G. Sampson	Jeffrey E. Tompkins

ASSOCIATES

Rosalind T. Drakeford	Adam L. Smith
Melynee C. Leftridge	Thomas G. Sampson, II
La'Sean M. Zilton	Ceasar C. Mitchell, II.
R. E. Thomas, Jr. (1911-1996)	

LEGAL SUPPORT PERSONNEL

Gwendolyn C.H. Dixon	Yvonne Torrence
Elbetha (Beth) Martin	Priscilla Yolanda Kelly
Nancy Allen-Haskell	Lureece D. Lewis (Paralegal)

For full biographical listings, see the Martindale-Hubbell Law Directory

AUGUSTA,* Richmond Co.

CAPERS, DUNBAR, SANDERS & BRUCKNER (AV)

Fifteenth Floor, First Union Bank Building, 30901-1454
Telephone: 706-722-7542
Telecopier: 706-724-7776

MEMBERS OF FIRM

John D. Capers	E. Frederick Sanders
Paul H. Dunbar, III	Ziva P. Bruckner

(See Next Column)

ASSOCIATE

Carl P. Dowling

For full biographical listings, see the Martindale-Hubbell Law Directory

FULCHER, HAGLER, REED, HANKS & HARPER (AV)

A Partnership including Professional Corporations
520 Greene Street, P.O. Box 1477, 30903-1477
Telephone: 706-724-0171
Telecopier: 706-724-4573

MEMBERS OF FIRM

William M. Fulcher (1902-1993)	Michael B. Hagler (P.C.)
Gould B. Hagler (Retired)	James W. Purcell (P.C.)
William C. Reed (Retired)	J. Arthur Davison (P.C.)
David H. Hanks (P.C.)	Mark C. Wilby (P.C.)
John I. Harper (P.C.)	Ronald C. Griffeth
Robert C. Hagler (P.C.)	N. Staten Bitting, Jr. (P.C.)
David P. Dekle (P.C.)	

ASSOCIATES

Scott W. Kelly	Elizabeth A. McLeod
Cynthia A. Gray	Barry A. Fleming

General Counsel for: GIW Industries, Inc.
Division Counsel for: CSX Transportation; Textron, Inc. (E-Z Go Car Division).
Counsel for: NationsBank; Georgia Natural Gas Co. (a division of Atlanta Gas Light Co.); Champion International Corp.; Aetna Life and Casualty; Liberty Mutual Insurance Company; St. Paul Fire & Marine Insurance Co.; Kimberly Clark Corporation.

For full biographical listings, see the Martindale-Hubbell Law Directory

HUGGINS & ALLEN, P.C. (AV)

3529 Walton Way Ext., 30909
Telephone: 706-737-0014
Facsimile: 706-733-7556
Downtown Augusta Office: 457 Greene Street.
Telephone: 706-724-9654.
Facsimile: 706-724-5746.

C. Thomas Huggins	Frank W. Allen
Charles T. Huggins, Jr.	

For full biographical listings, see the Martindale-Hubbell Law Directory

HULL, TOWILL, NORMAN & BARRETT, A PROFESSIONAL CORPORATION (AV)

Seventh Floor, Trust Company Bank Building, P.O. Box 1564, 30903-1564
Telephone: 706-722-4481
Fax: 706-722-9779

James M. Hull (1885-1975)	Douglas D. Batchelor, Jr.
George B. Barrett (1894-1942)	David E. Hudson
Julian J. Willingham (1887-1963)	Neal W. Dickert
John Bell Towill (1907-1991)	John W. Gibson
Robert C. Norman (Retired, 1991)	William F. Hammond
	Mark S. Burgreen
W. Hale Barrett	George R. Hall
Lawton Jordan, Jr.	James B. Ellington
Patrick J. Rice	F. Michael Taylor

Robert A. Mullins	Michael S. Carlson
William J. Keogh, III	Ralph Emerson Hanna, III
Edward J. Tarver	Susan D. Barrett
J. Noel Schweers, III	Timothy E. Moses

Counsel for: Sun Trust Bank Augusta, N.A.; Georgia Federal Bank, FSB, Augusta Division; Southeastern Newspapers Corp.; Georgia Power Co.; Southern Bell Telephone & Telegraph Co.; St. Joseph Hospital, Augusta, Georgia, Inc.; Norfolk Southern Corp.; Merry Land & Investment Co., Inc.; Housing Authority of the City of Augusta; Georgia Press Association.

For full biographical listings, see the Martindale-Hubbell Law Directory

PAINE, McELREATH & HYDER, P.C. (AV)

301 Wheeler Executive Center, 3540 Wheeler Road, 30909
Telephone: 706-738-9710
Telecopier: 706-738-9761

Travers W. Paine, III	Benjamin F. McElreath
James D. Hyder, Jr.	

For full biographical listings, see the Martindale-Hubbell Law Directory

CARROLLTON,* Carroll Co.

TISINGER, TISINGER, VANCE & GREER, A PROFESSIONAL CORPORATION (AV)

100 Wagon Yard Plaza, P.O. Box 2069, 30117
Telephone: 770-834-4467
Fax: 770-834-5426

Richard G. Tisinger, Sr.　　　　Phillip D. Wilkins
　　　　　Stacey L. Blackmon

Representative Clients: Carrollton Center, Carrollton Federal Bank-FSB; Fairfield Communities, Inc.; William Hilton Parkway Retail Association.

For Complete List of Firm Personnel, See General Section

For full biographical listings, see the Martindale-Hubbell Law Directory

COLUMBUS,* Muscogee Co.

HATCHER, STUBBS, LAND, HOLLIS & ROTHSCHILD (AV)

A Limited Liability Partnership
Suite 500 The Corporate Center, 233 12th Street, P.O. Box 2707, 31902-2707
Telephone: 706-324-0201
Telecopier: 706-322-7747

MEMBERS OF FIRM

J. Barrington Vaught　　　　John M. Tanzine, III
Charles T. Staples　　　　　Alan F. Rothschild, Jr.
Joseph L. Waldrep　　　　　William C. Pound
George W. Mize, Jr.　　　　　Mote W. Andrews III

General Counsel for: SunTrust Bank, West Georgia, N.A.; TOM'S Foods Inc.; Muscogee County Board of Education; The Jordan Company; Flournoy Development Company; St. Francis Hospital, Inc.; Bill Heard Enterprises, Inc.
Assistant Division Counsel for: Norfolk Southern Corp.
Local Counsel for: First Union National Bank of Georgia.

For Complete List of Firm Personnel, See General Section

For full biographical listings, see the Martindale-Hubbell Law Directory

DECATUR,* De Kalb Co.

SIMMONS, WARREN, SZCZECKO & McFEE, PROFESSIONAL ASSOCIATION (AV)

315 West Ponce de Leon Avenue, Suite 850, 30030
Telephone: 404-378-1711
Fax: 404-377-6101

Wesley B. Warren, Jr.　　　　William C. McFee, Jr.

Representative Clients: David Hocker & Associates (Shopping Center Development); Julian LeCraw & Company (Real Estate); Intown Suites, Inc.; Preferred Lodging Systems, Inc.; Royal Oldsmobile; Cotter & Co.; Atlanta Neurosurgical Associates, P.A.; Troncalli Motors, Inc.

For Complete List of Firm Personnel, See General Section

For full biographical listings, see the Martindale-Hubbell Law Directory

GAINESVILLE,* Hall Co.

SMITH, GILLIAM AND WILLIAMS (AV)

200 Old Coca-Cola Building, 301 Green Street, N.W., P.O. Box 1098, 30503
Telephone: 770-536-3381
Fax: 770-531-1481

MEMBERS OF FIRM

R. Wilson Smith, Jr. (1906-1983)　　Jerry A. Williams
John H. Smith　　　　　　　　Kelly Anne Miles
Steven P. Gilliam　　　　　　　Bradley J. Patten

ASSOCIATES

M. Tyler Smith　　　　　　　Scott Arthur Ball

General Counsel for: Gainesville Industrial Electric Co.; Georgia Mutual Insurance, a Stock Company; L & R Farms; H. Wilson Manufacturing Co.; Goforth Electrical Supply; North Georgia Petroleum Co.; Gibbs Management Group, Inc.

For full biographical listings, see the Martindale-Hubbell Law Directory

GRIFFIN,* Spalding Co.

CUMMING, CUMMING & ESARY (AV)

322 South Sixth Street, P.O. Box 577, 30224
Telephone: 770-227-3746
Fax: 770-227-3891

MEMBERS OF FIRM

D. R. Cumming (1888-1970)　　W. Barron Cumming
Joseph R. Cumming (1906-1990)　Sidney R. Esary

Counsel for: First National Bank of Griffin; United Bank of Griffin; Rushton Cotton Mills.

(See Next Column)

Approved Attorneys for: Lawyers Title Insurance Corp.; Chicago Title Insurance Co.; Stewart Title Company.

For full biographical listings, see the Martindale-Hubbell Law Directory

HARTWELL,* Hart Co.

GORDON LAW FIRM (AV)

Gordon Building, P.O. Box 870, 30643
Telephone: 706-376-5418
FAX: 706-376-5416
Email: wgordon@counsel.com

Walter James Gordon

Eleanor Patat Cotton　　　　Kimberly A. Wilkerson
LEGAL SUPPORT PERSONNEL
Flo W. Brown

References: NationsBank of Georgia, N.A.; The Bank of Hartwell; Athens First Bank & Trust Company.

For full biographical listings, see the Martindale-Hubbell Law Directory

LAWRENCEVILLE,* Gwinnett Co.

ANDERSEN, DAVIDSON & TATE, P.C. (AV)

324 West Pike Street, Suite 200, P.O. Box 2000, 30246-2000
Telephone: 770-822-0900
Telecopier: 770-822-9680

Thomas J. Andersen　　　　Thomas T. Tate
Gerald Davidson, Jr.　　　　Jeffrey R. Mahaffey

Kathleen B. Guy

References: Sun Trust Bank; The Bank of Gwinnett County; Chicago Title Insurance Co.; Title Insurance Company of Minnesota.

For Complete List of Firm Personnel, See General Section

For full biographical listings, see the Martindale-Hubbell Law Directory

MARIETTA,* Cobb Co.

MOORE INGRAM JOHNSON & STEELE (AV)

A Limited Liability Company
192 Anderson Street, P.O. Box 3305, 30060
Telephone: 770-429-1499
Telecopier: 770-429-8631

MEMBERS OF FIRM

John H. Moore　　　　　　Eldon L. Basham
G. Phillip Beggs　　　　　　Sarah L. Bargo

ASSOCIATES

J. Kevin Moore　　　　　　Susan Withers Smith

Representative Clients: Traton Corp.; Oakleigh Development Corp.
Approved Attorneys For: Chicago Title Insurance Co.; First American Title Insurance Co.; Lawyers Title Insurance Corp.
References: Charter Bank and Trust Co.; First Alliance Bank.

For full biographical listings, see the Martindale-Hubbell Law Directory

SCHAAF & HODGES (AV)

An Association of Sole Practitioners
Suite 202, 1853 Piedmont Road, 30066
Telephone: 770-971-4312
Fax: 770-971-5106

Michael L. Schaaf　　　　　R.E. Hodges, Jr.
OF COUNSEL
James R. Gee

Reference: Wachovia Bank.

For full biographical listings, see the Martindale-Hubbell Law Directory

MCDONOUGH,* Henry Co.

SMITH, WELCH, STUDDARD & BRITTAIN (AV)

200 The Commerce Building, 235 Keys Ferry Street, P.O. Box 31, 30253
Telephone: 770-957-3937
Fax: 770-957-9165
Stockbridge, Georgia Office: 1231-A Eagle's Landing Parkway.
Telephone: 770-389-4864.
Fax: 770-389-5157.

MEMBERS OF FIRM

Ernest M. Smith (1911-1992)　　Ben W. Studdard, III
A. J. Welch, Jr.　　　　　　　J. Mark Brittain
　　　　　　　　　　　　　(Resident, Stockbridge Office)

(See Next Column)

SMITH, WELCH, STUDDARD & BRITTAIN—*Continued*

ASSOCIATES

Patrick D. Jaugstetter
E. Gilmore Maxwell

Shawn Marie Story
Arthur Scully Barbee

Representative Clients: Alliance Corp.; Atlanta Motor Speedway, Inc.; Bellamy-Strickland Chevrolet, Inc.; Ceramic and Metal Coatings Corp.; City of Hampton; City of Locust Grove; City of Stockbridge.

For full biographical listings, see the Martindale-Hubbell Law Directory

---

NEWNAN,* Coweta Co.

GLOVER & DAVIS, P.A. (AV)

10 Brown Street, P.O. Box 1038, 30264
Telephone: 770-253-4330
Fax: 770-251-7152
Peachtree City, Georgia Office: Suite 130, 200 Westpark Drive.
Telephone: 770-487-5834.
Fax: 770-487-3492.

J. Littleton Glover, Jr.
Alan W. Jackson
Randy E. Connell

W. Robert Hancock, Jr.
(Resident, Peachtree Office)
Mark E. Dacy (Resident, Peachtree City Office)

Representative Clients: Newnan Savings Bank; Pike Transfer Co.; Batson-Cook Company, General Corporate and Construction Divisions; Coweta County, Georgia.
Local Counsel for: International Latex Corp.; First Union National Bank of Georgia; West Georgia Farm Credit, ACA.

For Complete List of Firm Personnel, See General Section

For full biographical listings, see the Martindale-Hubbell Law Directory

---

ROSENZWEIG, JONES & MacNABB, P.C. (AV)

32 South Court Square, P.O. Box 220, 30264
Telephone: 770-253-3282
Fax: 770-251-7262

Sidney Pope Jones, Jr.

Charles C. Witcher

Approved Attorneys for: Lawyers Title Insurance Corp.; Chicago Title Insurance Co.

For Complete List of Firm Personnel, See General Section

For full biographical listings, see the Martindale-Hubbell Law Directory

---

SAVANNAH,* Chatham Co.

INGLESBY, FALLIGANT, HORNE, COURINGTON & NASH, A PROFESSIONAL CORPORATION (AV)

17 West McDonough Street, P.O. Box 1368, 31402-1368
Telephone: 912-232-7000
Telecopier: 912-232-7300

Sam P. Inglesby, Jr.
J. Daniel Falligant
Kathleen Horne

Dorothy W. Courington, II
Thomas A. Nash, Jr.
Dolly Chisholm

Representative Clients: NationsBank of Georgia, N.A.; Gulfstream Aerospace Corp.; Rotary Corp.; Atlanta Gas Light Co.; Ford Motor Credit Co.; Independent Insurance Agents of Savannah, Inc.; Savannah Christian Preparatory School; Savannah Mall; Continental Grain.

For Complete List of Firm Personnel, See General Section

For full biographical listings, see the Martindale-Hubbell Law Directory

---

TOCCOA,* Stephens Co.

McCLURE, RAMSAY & DICKERSON (AV)

400 Falls Road, P.O. Drawer 1408, 30577
Telephone: 706-886-3178
Fax: 706-886-1150

MEMBERS OF FIRM

Clyde M. McClure (1892-1976)
George B. Ramsay, Jr.

John A. Dickerson
Allan R. Ramsay

Marlin R. Escoe

ASSOCIATES

Alice D. Hayes

Elizabeth Felton Moore

Luther H. Beck, Jr.

OF COUNSEL

Knox Bynum

Counsel for: Coats and Clark, Inc.; Stephens Federal Savings & Loan Assn.; St. Paul Insurance Cos.; State Farm Insurance Cos.; Cotton States Insurance Cos.; City of Toccoa; Citizens Bank; Habersham Plantation Corp.; Patterson Pump Co; Georgia Farm Bureau Insurance Companies.

For full biographical listings, see the Martindale-Hubbell Law Directory

---

TUCKER, De Kalb Co.

ZION, TARLETON & SISKIN, P.C. (AV)

2191 Northlake Parkway Building 11, Suite 2, 30084
Telephone: 770-270-3800
Fax: 770-270-3811

Marvin H. Zion
John J. Tarleton

Mark J. Siskin
Mark D. Euster

Jonathan James Wade

Representative Clients: Wachovia Bank of Georgia, N.A.; Trust Company Mortgage; NationsBank of Georgia, N.A.; Wachovia Mortgage Company; HomeBanc Mortgage Corporation; Bank South Mortgage Corp.; BancBoston Mortgage Corporation; National Mortgage Investments Co., Inc.; Countrywide Funding Corporation; First Union Mortgage Corporation.

For full biographical listings, see the Martindale-Hubbell Law Directory

---

HAWAII

HONOLULU,* Honolulu Co.

AYABE, CHONG, NISHIMOTO, SIA & NAKAMURA (AV)

A Partnership including a Professional Corporation
Pauahi Tower, Suite 2500, 1001 Bishop Street, 96813
Telephone: 808-537-6119
Telecopier: 808-526-3491

MEMBERS OF FIRM

Sidney K. Ayabe (P.C.)
Jeffrey H. K. Sia

Rodney S. Nishida
Gail M. Kang

Representative Clients: Travelers Insurance Co.; St. Paul Fire and Marine Insurance Co.; The Employers Group of Insurance Companies; TIG Insurance Co.; Pacific Insurance Co.; Hartford Accident and Indemnity Co.; Continental Casualty Co.; CNA Insurance Co.

For Complete List of Firm Personnel, See General Section

For full biographical listings, see the Martindale-Hubbell Law Directory

---

BAYS, DEAVER, HIATT, LUNG & ROSE (AV)

A Partnership including Professional Corporations
16th Floor, Alii Place, 1099 Alakea Street, P.O. Box 1760, 96806
Telephone: 808-523-9000
Telecopier: 808-533-4184
Telex: RCA 7238976
Kamuela, Hawaii Office: Suite 204 Parker Square, 65-1280 Kawaihae Road.
Telephone: 808-885-3400.
Telecopier: 808-885-6765.

MEMBERS OF FIRM

A. Bernard Bays (A Law Corporation)
Phillip L. Deaver (A Law Corporation)
Jerry Michael Hiatt (A Law Corporation)
Harvey J. Lung (A Law Corporation)

Crystal K. Rose (A Law Corporation)
Jason N. Baba (A Law Corporation)
Carl H. Osaki (A Law Corporation)

ASSOCIATES

Michael W. Thomas
Karin L. Holma
Paul M. Saito
Mahilani Elizabeth Kellett
Donald E. Fisher

Wendy J. Utsumi
Bruce Voss
Robert E. Badger, Jr.
Edward J. Corwin
Ross N. Gushi

For full biographical listings, see the Martindale-Hubbell Law Directory

---

CADES SCHUTTE FLEMING & WRIGHT (AV)

Formerly Smith, Wild, Beebe & Cades
1000 Bishop Street, P.O. Box 939, 96808
Telephone: 808-521-9200
Telecopier: 808-531-8738
Email: cades@cades.com
Affiliated Law Firm: Udom-Prok Associates Law Offices, 105/36 Tharinee Mansion, Borom Raj Chananee Road Bangkoknoi, Bangkok, Thailand, 10700.
Telephone: 011 662 435-4146.
Kailua-Kona, Hawaii Office: Hualalai Center, Suite B-303, 75-170 Hualalai Road.
Telephone: 808-329-5811.
Telecopier: 808-326-1175.

(See Next Column)

CADES SCHUTTE FLEMING & WRIGHT, *Honolulu—Continued*

MEMBERS OF FIRM

Robert B. Bunn	Larry T. Takumi
Donald E. Scearce	Cary S. Matsushige
Richard A. Hicks	Gino L. Gabrio
Bernice Littman	Martin E. Hsia
Nicholas C. Dreher	Gail M. Tamashiro
Mark A. Hazlett	Grace Nihei Kido
Philip J. Leas	Donna Y. L. Leong

ASSOCIATES

Jeffrey D. Watts	Carlito P. Caliboso
Laurie A. Kuribayashi	Karen Wong
Michele M. Sunahara	Dean T. Yamamoto
Cynthia M. Johiro	Christopher T. Harrison

OF COUNSEL
Harold S. Wright

Counsel for: First Hawaiian Bank; Alexander & Baldwin, Inc.; Theo. H. Davies & Co., Ltd.; C. Brewer & Company, Ltd.; Bank of America, FSB; Kamehameha Schools/Bernice Pauahi Bishop Estate.

For Complete List of Firm Personnel, See General Section

For full biographical listings, see the Martindale-Hubbell Law Directory

---

CHING, YUEN & MORIKAWA (AV)

Pacific Tower, Suite 2700, 1001 Bishop Street, 96813
Telephone: 808-524-8880
Telecopier: 808-524-7664

MEMBERS OF FIRM

Russell L. Ching	William W. L. Yuen
	Randall I. Morikawa

ASSOCIATE
Joyce T. Tamanaha

Representative Clients: Finance Enterprises, Ltd.; Finance Factors, Ltd.; Finance Realty, Ltd.; Gentry Pacific, Ltd.; Goldman, Sachs & Co.; The Hertz Corporation; Kamehamela Schools Bernice Pauahi Bishop Estate; Merrill Lynch & Co.; The Sakura Bank, Ltd.; Sen Plex Corp.

For full biographical listings, see the Martindale-Hubbell Law Directory

---

DWYER IMANAKA SCHRAFF KUDO MEYER & FUJIMOTO ATTORNEYS AT LAW, A LAW CORPORATION (AV)

1800 Pioneer Plaza, 900 Fort Street Mall, 96813
Telephone: 808-524-8000
Telecopier: 808-526-1419
Mailing Address: P.O. Box 2727, 96803
Email: hawaiilaw@dwyer-imanaka.com *URL:*
http://www.dwyer-imanaka.com

John R. Dwyer, Jr.	William G. Meyer, III
Mitchell A. Imanaka	Wesley M. Fujimoto
Paul A. Schraff	Ronald Van Grant
Benjamin A. Kudo (Atty. at	Jon M. H. Pang
Law, A Law Corp.)	Blake W. Bushnell

Adelbert Green

Richard T. Asato, Jr.	Jeffery S. Werbelow
Scott W. Settle	Lori Ann K. Koseki
Darcie S. Yoshinaga	Troy T. Fukuhara
Lawrence I. Kawasaki	Katy Y. Chen
Stacy E. Uehara	Naomi S. Uyeno
Kris N. Nakagawa	Roger B. McKeague

OF COUNSEL

Randall Y. Iwase	R. Brian Tsujimura

For full biographical listings, see the Martindale-Hubbell Law Directory

---

LAW OFFICES OF MANUEL D. GARCIA (AV)

Makai Tower, Grosvenor Center, Suite 2550, 733 Bishop Street, 96813
Telephone: 808-522-0755
Facsimile: 808-522-0760

For full biographical listings, see the Martindale-Hubbell Law Directory

---

GERSON, GREKIN & WYNHOFF ATTORNEYS AT LAW, A LAW CORPORATION (AV)

Suite 780 Pacific Tower, 1001 Bishop Street, 96813
Telephone: 808-524-4800
Telecopier: 808-537-1420
Email: ggwlaw@aloha.net
Email: 102461.730@compuserve.com *URL:*
http://www.ggwlaw@aloha.net

Mervyn S. Gerson	William J. Wynhoff
Nancy Nissen Grekin	Bruce D. Hieneman

For full biographical listings, see the Martindale-Hubbell Law Directory

---

KOBAYASHI, SUGITA & GODA (AV)

A Partnership including Professional Corporations
8th Floor, Hawaii Tower, 745 Fort Street, 96813
Telephone: 808-539-8700
Telecopier: 808-539-8799
Telex: 6502396585 MCI
MCI Mail: 23 96585
ABA/Net: ABA2281

OF COUNSEL
Bert T. Kobayashi, Sr.

Reference: First Hawaiian Bank.

For Complete List of Firm Personnel, See General Section

For full biographical listings, see the Martindale-Hubbell Law Directory

---

LYNCH & FARMER (AV)

Suite 2500, Mauka Tower Grosvenor Center, 737 Bishop Street, 96813
Telephone: 808-528-0100
Facsimile: 808-528-4997

LEGAL SUPPORT PERSONNEL
Doreen C. Watanabe

For full biographical listings, see the Martindale-Hubbell Law Directory

---

McCORRISTON MIHO MILLER MUKAI (AV)

Five Waterfront Plaza, 4th Floor, 500 Ala Moana Boulevard, 96813
Telephone: 808-529-7300
Facsimile: 808-524-8293
Cable: Attorneys, Honolulu
Mailing Address: P.O. Box 2800, Honolulu, Hawaii, 96803-2800
Hilo, Hawaii Office: 56 Waianuenue Avenue, Suite 217, 96720.
Telephone: 808-935-6537.
Facsimile: 808-935-3398.

PARTNERS

Jon T. Miho	Patrick K. Lau
Clifford J. Miller	David N. Kuriyama
Franklin K. Mukai	Eric T. Kawatani
Stanley Y. Mukai	Keith K. Suzuka
D. Scott MacKinnon	Sharon H. Nishi
Kenneth B. Marcus	Randall F. Sakumoto
Kenneth G. K. Hoo	Andrew W. Char
	Alexander R. Jampel

OF COUNSEL
Robert E. Warner

COUNSEL
Charles E. Pear, Jr.

ASSOCIATES

Peter J. Hamasaki	Joel D. Kam
Darren Patrick Conley	Shulammite Kim
	Dean J. Myatt

Representative Clients: Nauru Phosphate Royalties Trust; Victoria Ward, Limited; Kamehameha Schools/Bishop Estate; Grand Wailea Resort; Mutual of New York; Long Term Credit Bank of Japan; Interval International, Inc.; Shell Group; The Walt Disney World Company.

For Complete List of Firm Personnel, See General Section

For full biographical listings, see the Martindale-Hubbell Law Directory

---

PITLUCK KIDO SATO & STONE (AV)

701 Bishop Street, 96813
Telephone: 808-523-5030
Telecopier: 808-545-4015
Email: reilly@aloha.net

MEMBERS OF FIRM

Wayne Marshall Pitluck	Dana Kiyomi Nalani Sato
Alan Takashi Kido	James Mauliola Keaka Stone, Jr.

OF COUNSEL
John W. Reilly

Reference: Bank of Hawaii.

For full biographical listings, see the Martindale-Hubbell Law Directory

---

PRICE OKAMOTO HIMENO & LUM ATTORNEYS AT LAW, A LAW CORPORATION (AV)

Suite 728, Ocean View Center, 707 Richards Street, 96813
Telephone: 808-538-1113
Fax: 808-533-0549

Warren Price, III	Sharon R. Himeno
Kenneth T. Okamoto	Bettina W. J. Lum
	Terence S. Yamamoto

Robert Kohn

(See Next Column)

PRICE OKAMOTO HIMENO & LUM ATTORNEYS AT LAW, A LAW
CORPORATION—*Continued*

OF COUNSEL

Stuart M. Cowan   Lawrence R. Cohen
Michael K. Kaneshiro

For full biographical listings, see the Martindale-Hubbell Law Directory

LAW OFFICES OF PETER STARN A LAW CORPORATION (AV)

Suite 1740 Grosvenor Center Mauka Tower, 737 Bishop Street, 96813
Telephone: 808-537-6100
Fax: 808-537-5434

Peter Starn   Duane R. Fisher

Sharon Valentine Lovejoy

For full biographical listings, see the Martindale-Hubbell Law Directory

STUBENBERG & DURRETT (AV)

1400 Pauahi Tower, 1001 Bishop Street, 96813
Telephone: 808-526-0892
Fax: 808-533-4399

James A. Stubenberg   Jonathan S. Durrett

Richard A. Kersenbrock, Jr.   Joseph L. Dwight, IV
Valerie J. Lam   Vivien Mia Weber
                    OF COUNSEL
Lorrie L. Stone   Russell W. Lousich
            James P. Clarke

For full biographical listings, see the Martindale-Hubbell Law Directory

IDAHO

BOISE,* Ada Co.

ELAM & BURKE, A PROFESSIONAL ASSOCIATION (AV)

Key Financial Center, 702 West Idaho Street, P.O. Box 1539, 83701

Telephone: 208-343-5454
Telecopier: 208-384-5844
Email: eblaw@elamburke.com

David B. Lincoln   Ryan P. Armbruster
            Harry M. Lane, Jr.

Representative Clients: Lincoln National Life Insurance Co.; Transamerica
Financial Services; State Farm Life Insurance Co.; West One Bank of Idaho;
U.S. Bancorp.

For Complete List of Firm Personnel, See General Section

For full biographical listings, see the Martindale-Hubbell Law Directory

KETCHUM, Blaine Co.

JAMES L. KENNEDY, JR. (AV)

340 Second Street East, P.O. Box 2165, 83340

Telephone: 208-726-8255

Reference: First Interstate Bank of Idaho, N.A. (Ketchum-Sun Valley
Branch); First Security Bank of Idaho, N.A. (Ketchum Branch)

For full biographical listings, see the Martindale-Hubbell Law Directory

POCATELLO,* Bannock Co.

MERRILL & MERRILL, CHARTERED (AV)

Key Bank Building, P.O. Box 991, 83204
Telephone: 208-232-2286
Fax: 208-232-2499

Dave R. Gallafent   Kent L. Hawkins

Representative Client: First American Title Insurance Co.

For Complete List of Firm Personnel, See General Section

For full biographical listings, see the Martindale-Hubbell Law Directory

ILLINOIS

BELLEVILLE,* St. Clair Co.

NEVILLE, RICHARDS, DEFRANCO & WULLER (AV)

5 Park Place, 62221
Telephone: 618-277-0900
Facsimile: 618-277-0970

MEMBERS OF FIRM

James E. Neville   James E. DeFranco
Timothy S. Richards   Robert G. Wuller, Jr.
                    ASSOCIATES
Shari M. Brunton   Ellen M. Edmonds
            Richard Thomas Roustio

For full biographical listings, see the Martindale-Hubbell Law Directory

BLOOMINGTON,* McLean Co.

HARTWEG, MUELLER, TURNER, DRAZEWSKI & WOOD, P.C. (AV)

207 West Jefferson Street, Suite 400, P.O. Box 397, 61701-0397
Telephone: 309-827-0044
Telecopier: 309-829-0328

Darrell L. Hartweg   Ralph T. Turner
William A. Mueller, Jr.   Scott D. Drazewski
            George C Wood

Michael J. Robak
                    OF COUNSEL
            John R. Luedtke

Reference: Magna Bank of McLean County.

For full biographical listings, see the Martindale-Hubbell Law Directory

BOLINGBROOK, Will Co.

MOSS AND BLOOMBERG, LTD. (AV)

305 West Briarcliff Road, Suite 201, P.O. Box 1158, 60440-0858
Telephone: 630-759-0800
Telecopier: 630-759-8504

Barry L. Moss   Steven P. Bloomberg
            George A. Marchetti

David J. Freeman   Daniel C Shapiro
Norma J. Guess   Judson L. Strain

For full biographical listings, see the Martindale-Hubbell Law Directory

CHAMPAIGN, Champaign Co.

HARRINGTON, PORTER, ERMENTROUT & TOCK (AV)

Suite 601 Huntington Towers, 201 West Springfield Avenue, P.O. Box
1550, 61824-1550
Telephone: 217-352-4167
Telecopier: 217-352-8707

MEMBERS OF FIRM

Earl C. Harrington (1895-1981)   Thomas E. Harrington
Louis A. Busch (1886-1946)   Daniel G. Harrington
Robert F. Busch (1914-1969)   J. C. Ermentrout
            Jeffrey W. Tock
                    ASSOCIATE
            Mary Ann Royse
                    OF COUNSEL
W. Kenneth Porter   Kip Randolph Pope

For full biographical listings, see the Martindale-Hubbell Law Directory

CHICAGO,* Cook Co.

ARONBERG GOLDGEHN DAVIS & GARMISA (AV)

Suite 3000 One IBM Plaza, 60611
Telephone: 312-828-9600
Telecopier: 312-828-9635

MEMBERS OF FIRM

Ronald J. Aronberg   Marc W. O'Brien
Steven P. Davis   Ned S. Robertson
William J. Garmisa   David H. Sachs
Young Kim   Robert N. Sodikoff
                    ASSOCIATES
Jacqueline Shim Bryant   Susan H. Mendelsohn

For Complete List of Firm Personnel, See General Section

For full biographical listings, see the Martindale-Hubbell Law Directory

Chicago—Continued

BELL, BOYD & LLOYD (AV)

Three First National Plaza Suite 3300, 70 West Madison Street, 60602
Telephone: 312-372-1121
FAX: 312-372-2098
Email: bbl@bbl.com
Washington, D.C. Office: 1615 L Street, N.W.
Telephone: 202-466-6300.
FAX: 202-463-0678.

MEMBERS OF FIRM

Gregory R. Andre	D. Scott Hargadon
Robert J. Best	Thomas Z. Hayward, Jr.
Terrence E. Budny	Thomas C. Homburger
Lawrence C. Eppley	Lawrence M. Mages
Sanford R. Gail	Matthew K. Phillips

David M. Saltiel

OF COUNSEL

Stanton H. Berlin	John C. York

ASSOCIATES

Michelle D, Bowers	Kathryn A. Finn

Maricel M. Mojares

For Complete List of Firm Personnel, See General Section

For full biographical listings, see the Martindale-Hubbell Law Directory

BERMAN & YOTIS, A PROFESSIONAL ASSOCIATION (AV)

(A Professional Association comprised of Professional Corporations)
Suite 2215, 100 North La Salle Street, 60602
Telephone: 312-726-0531
Fax: 312-726-4928

Michael H. Berman (P.C.)	William W. Yotis, III, (P.C.)

Joy C. Airaudi	Dean J. Papadakis
Eric D. Kaplan	Dean Gournis

OF COUNSEL

Karen C. Yotis

For full biographical listings, see the Martindale-Hubbell Law Directory

BOEHM, PEARLSTEIN & BRIGHT, LTD. (AV)

33 North La Salle Street Suite 3500, 60602
Telephone: 312-782-7474
Fax: 312-782-0380

Robert I. Boehm	Gary I. Blackman
Mark D. Pearlstein	Roy D. Kessel
Steven Bright	Donna Richman
Konstantinos Armiros	Bryan I. Schwartz

William Scott Schwartz

Representative Clients: First Bank; Cole Taylor Bank; LaSalle National Bank; LaSalle Bank N.I.; The Northern Trust Company; Firstar Bank of Illinois; First Union National Bank of North Carolina; CB Commerical; Merrill Lynch Business Financial Services, Inc.

For full biographical listings, see the Martindale-Hubbell Law Directory

CARNEY & BROTHERS, LTD. (AV)

30 North La Salle Street, Suite 3100, 60602
Telephone: 312-372-2909
Fax: 312-704-6693

Demetrius E. Carney	Ellen E. Douglass
Alan W. Brothers	Lori A. Owens
Hubert O. Thompson	James L. Bebley

Cheryl J Colston	Andre Gamble
Trasha A. Embry	Angela M. Williams

Oswald G. Lewis

OF COUNSEL

Joyce A. Hughes	Henry I. Thomas

Representative Clients: Allstate Life Insurance Co.; Amoco Oil Co.; Commonwealth Edison Co.; First National Bank of Chicago; General Motors Corp.; McDonald's Corp.; New York Life Insurance Co.; Pathway Financial; Seaway National Bank.

For full biographical listings, see the Martindale-Hubbell Law Directory

FAGEL & HABER (AV)

140 South Dearborn Street 14th Floor, 60603
Telephone: 312-346-7500
FAX: 312-580-2201
Telex No: 754542
Cable: "NOFLAWLAW"
URL: HTTP://WWW.FANDH.COM.

(See Next Column)

MEMBERS OF FIRM

Walter D. Cupkovic	John J. Cullerton
	Daniel G. Coman

ASSOCIATES

Christina Brotto	Victor A. Des Laurier
Patrick J. Cullerton	Thomas Bernard Golz

Ilyse D. Murman

For full biographical listings, see the Martindale-Hubbell Law Directory

GOLDBERG, KOHN, BELL, BLACK, ROSENBLOOM & MORITZ, LTD. (AV)

Suite 3700, 55 East Monroe Street, 60603
Telephone: 312-201-4000
Telecopier: 312-332-2196

Stephen B. Bell	Michael B. Manuel
Karen Ruth Bieber	David M. Mason
Dennis B. Black	William C. Meyers
Philip M. Blackman	Terry F. Moritz
Denise B. Caplan	Gerald F. Munitz
David L. Dranoff	Nora A. Naughton
Wayne S. Gilmartin	James B. Rosenbloom
Robert J. Goldberg	Gary N. Ruben
Gerald L. Jenkins	Daniel P. Shapiro
Michael D. Karpeles	Alan P. Solow
Frederic R. Klein	Douglas P. Taber
Richard M. Kohn	Carole K. Towne
Steven A. Levy	Kenneth S. Ulrich

Gary T. Zussman

Oscar L. Alcantara	William R. Loesch
Joel F. Brown	Kim Slotky Reich
Andrew R. Cardonick	Deborah Rzasnicki
David J. Chizewer	Robert E. Sarazen
Frederick H. Cohen	(Not admitted in IL)
Everett Cygal	Kristine M. Schuler
Michael B. Gray	Uli Widmaier
Darren M. Green	Amanda K. Williams
Lesley F. Kahlow	Lisa M. Young
Randall L. Klein	Melissa Lumberg Zagon

COUNSEL

Jeanne Boxer Ettelson	Patricia M. Relosky

For full biographical listings, see the Martindale-Hubbell Law Directory

GORDON & EINSTEIN, LTD. (AV)

224 East Ontario, 60611
Telephone: 312-280-7766
Telecopier: 312-280-9599

Raymond P. Gordon	Jean M. Einstein

LEGAL SUPPORT PERSONNEL

Laura A. Kozicki

For full biographical listings, see the Martindale-Hubbell Law Directory

HOWARD GORDON KAPLAN, LTD. (AV)

180 North La Salle Street, 28th Floor, 60601
Telephone: 312-641-2555
Facsimile No.: 312-641-6265
Email: howie641@aol.com

Howard Gordon Kaplan

Leonard J. Brenner	Rhonda D. Kaplan-Katz

For full biographical listings, see the Martindale-Hubbell Law Directory

McBRIDE BAKER & COLES (AV)

500 West Madison Street 40th Floor, 60661
Telephone: 312-715-5700
Cable Address: "Chilaw"
Telex: 270258
Telecopier: 312-993-9350
Email: lastname@mbc.com *URL:* http://www.mbc.com
Oakbrook Terrace, Illinois Office: Suite 1000, One Mid America Plaza, 60181-4710.
Telephone: 630-954-2100.
Telecopier: 630-954-2112.

MEMBERS OF FIRM

Steven B. Bashaw	Thomas J. Kinasz
John J. Cresto	David S. Mann
Anthony L. Frink	Elias N. Matsakis
Francis L. Keldermans	Michael L. Weissman

Larry M. Zanger

OF COUNSEL

Robert O. Case

(See Next Column)

McBRIDE BAKER & COLES—*Continued*

ASSOCIATES

Adam E. Berman   Joseph S. Messer
Thomas R. Stilp

For Complete List of Firm Personnel, See General Section

For full biographical listings, see the Martindale-Hubbell Law Directory

---

O'BRIEN, O'ROURKE & HOGAN (AV)

135 South La Salle Street Suite 830, 60603
Telephone: 312-372-1462
Fax: 312-372-8029
Orlando, Florida Office: Moye, O'Brien, O'Rourke, Hogan & Pickert, 201
East Pine Street, Suite 710.
Telephone: 407-843-3341.
Fax: 407-843-3048.
Atlanta, Georgia Office: Moye, O'Brien, O'Rourke, Hogan & Pickert, 999
Peachtree Street, Northeast, Suite 2020.
Telephone: 404-875-6300.

MEMBERS OF FIRM

William J. Cotter   Michael A. Gilman
W. Craig Fowler   Frederic G. Hogan

For full biographical listings, see the Martindale-Hubbell Law Directory

---

POLLAK & HOFFMAN LTD. (AV)

Suite 1100, 150 North Wacker Drive, 60606
Telephone: 312-726-0001
FAX: 312-726-1098
Northbrook, Illinois Office: 1200 Shermer Road.
Telephone: 847-564-0130.
FAX: 847-564-0160.

Bertram L. Pollak   Michael E. Pollak
Jay M. Pollak   Bruce F. Hoffman
Lee J. Lewin

For full biographical listings, see the Martindale-Hubbell Law Directory

---

SCHWARTZBERG, BARNETT & COHEN (AV)

55 West Monroe Street, 2400 Xerox Centre, 60603-5040
Telephone: 312-726-3555
Fax: 312-726-6299
Cable Address: "Justice"
Email: sb&c@twty.chi.il.us

MEMBERS OF FIRM

Ralph M. Schwartzberg   Mark T. Barnett (1939-1970)
(1939-1975)   Hugh J. Schwartzberg
Benjamin H. Cohen

OF COUNSEL

Eugene P. Thomas Jr.

For full biographical listings, see the Martindale-Hubbell Law Directory

---

SUGAR, FRIEDBERG & FELSENTHAL (AV)

30 North La Salle Street, Suite 2600, 60602
Telephone: 312-704-9400
Telecopier: 312-372-7951
Cable: "SUGARFREE"

MEMBERS OF FIRM

Richard A. Sugar   Ira S. Neiman
Michael R. Friedberg   Jonathan L. Mills
Steven A. Felsenthal   Etahn M. Cohen
Andrew B. David   Howard M. Helsinger
Leslie J. Weiss   Robert F. Simon
Martin M. Weinstein

ASSOCIATES

Kathryn A. Erickson   Jay R. Hoffman
Norman J. Ginsparg   Sophia Stergianis
Jonathan W. Michael

For full biographical listings, see the Martindale-Hubbell Law Directory

---

WILDMAN, HARROLD, ALLEN & DIXON (AV)

225 West Wacker Drive, 30th Floor, 60606-1229
Telephone: 312-201-2000
Cable Address: "Whad"
Fax: 312-201-2555
URL: http://www.whad.com
Aurora, Illinois Office: 1851 W. Galena Boulevard, Suite 210.
Telephone: 630-892-7021.
Fax: 630-892-7158.
Waukegan, Illinois Office: 404 West Water, P. O. Box 890.
Telephone: 847-623-0700.
Fax: 847-244-5273.
Lisle, Illinois Office: 4300 Commerce Court.
Telephone: 630-955-0555.

(See Next Column)

New York, New York Office: Wildman, Harrold, Allen, Dixon & Smith.
The International Building, 45 Rockefeller Plaza, Suite 353.
Telephone: 212-632-3850.
Fax: 212-632-3858.
Toronto, Ontario affiliated Office: Keel Cottrelle. 36 Toronto Street, Ninth
Floor, Suite 920.
Telephone: 416-367-2900.
Telefax: 416-367-2791.
Telex: 062-18660.
Mississauga, Ontario affiliated Office: Keel Cottrelle. 100 Matatson
Avenue East, Suite 104.
Telephone: 416-890-7700.
Fax: 416-890-8006.

MEMBERS OF FIRM

Bruce L. Boruszak   Mark W. Hianik
Paul S. Chervin   Richard C. Johnson
  (Waukegan Office)   (Lisle Office)
Thomas P. Duffy   Dean J. Leffelman (Lisle Office)
John L. Eisel   Sheldon P. Migdal
David J. Fischer   James R. Morrin
Peter H. Fritts   Robert W. Newman
Jeffrey P. Gray   Alan B. Roth
Robert E. Hamilton   Thomas H. Snyder
Ronald M. Hem (Aurora Office)   Sanford M. Stein
Louis P. Vitullo

COUNSEL

George W. Overton   Edwin A. Wahlen

Bruce M. Chanen   Christopher Kovach
Steven H. Klein   Beth S. Rubin
Ada Skyles

For Complete List of Firm Personnel, See General Section

For full biographical listings, see the Martindale-Hubbell Law Directory

---

WILSON & McILVAINE (AV)

500 West Madison, Suite 3700, 60661-2511
Telephone: 312-715-5000
Telecopier: 312-715-5155

PARTNERS

C. John Anderson   Marie K. Eitrheim
Cynthia A. Bergmann   Douglas R. Hoffman
Richard P. Blessen   Peter A. Sarasek
Michael F. Csar   Stephanie B. Shellenback

ASSOCIATES

Charles A. Lande   Mark A. Trager

For Complete List of Firm Personnel, See General Section

For full biographical listings, see the Martindale-Hubbell Law Directory

---

GALESBURG,* Knox Co.

MUSTAIN LINDSTROM & HENSON (AV)

1865 North Henderson Street, Suite 11B, 61401
Telephone: 309-344-5252
Telecopier: 309-344-3939

MEMBERS OF FIRM

Douglas D. Mustain   Ronald Henson
Robert Lindstrom   Christopher Henson
Carl E. Hawkinson

References: The Farmers and Mechanics Bank; Norwest Bank Illinois, N.A.;
First Bank; First Financial Bank; Farmers State Bank of Western Illinois;
McGladrey and Pullen.

For full biographical listings, see the Martindale-Hubbell Law Directory

---

JOLIET,* Will Co.

HERSCHBACH, TRACY, JOHNSON, BERTANI & WILSON (AV)

Two Rialto Square, 116 North Chicago Street, Sixth Floor, 60432
Telephone: 815-723-8500
Fax: 815-727-4846

Wayne R. Johnson   Kenneth A. Carlson
Thomas R. Wilson   David J. Silverman
Richard H. Teas   Roger D. Rickmon
George F. Mahoney, III   John S. Gallo
Raymond E. Meader   George M. Ferreti
A. Michael Wojtak   Richard E. Vogel
Kerry Anne Weber

OF COUNSEL

Donald J. Tracy   Louis R. Bertani
John L. O'Brien

General Counsel For: First National Bancorp.; First National Bank of Joliet.
Representative Clients: Chicago Title Insurance Co.; Vulcan Materials Company; Dow Chemical, U.S.A.; Marathon Oil Co.; Crosfield Chemicals, Inc.;
Waste Management, Inc.

(See Next Column)

HERSCHBACH, TRACY, JOHNSON, BERTANI & WILSON, *Joliet—Continued*

For Complete List of Firm Personnel, See General Section

For full biographical listings, see the Martindale-Hubbell Law Directory

LA SALLE, La Salle Co.

HERBOLSHEIMER, LANNON, HENSON, DUNCAN AND REAGAN, P.C. (AV)

State Bank Building, Suite 400, 654 First Street, P.O. Box 539, 61301
Telephone: 815-223-0111
FAX: 815-223-5829
Ottawa, Illinois Office: First Federal Savings Bank Building, 633 LaSalle Street, Suite 409.
Telephone: 815-434-1400.

George L. Herbolsheimer (1911-1992)	John S. Duncan, III
R. James Lannon, Jr.	Michael T. Reagan (Resident, Ottawa Office)
T. Donald Henson	Douglas A. Gift

Gary R. Eiten

Karen C. Eiten	Jill W. Klein
Michael C. Jansz (Resident, Ottawa Office)	Murl Tod Melton
	Lawrence M. Kaschak

Attorneys for: Aetna Insurance Group; St. Paul Fire and Marine Insurance Co.; State Farm Insurance Co.; The La Salle National Bank; La Salle State Bank; The Daily News Tribune Company, La Salle; Eureka Savings and Loan Assn.; Illinois Valley Community Hospital; Community Hospital of Ottawa; Commonwealth Edison, Co.

For full biographical listings, see the Martindale-Hubbell Law Directory

MATTOON, Coles Co.

CRAIG & CRAIG (AV)

1807 Broadway, P.O. Box 689, 61938-0689
Telephone: 217-234-6481
Telecopier: 217-234-6486
Mount Vernon, Illinois Office: 227 1/2 South 9th Street.
Telephone: 618-244-7511.

MEMBERS OF FIRM

Craig Van Meter (1895-1981)	Stephen L. Corn
Fred H. Kelly (1894-1971)	Richard Charles Hayden
Robert M. Werden (1908-1969)	Robert G. Grierson
George N. Gilkerson (1911-1985)	Gregory C. Ray
John H. Armstrong	Paul R. Lynch (Resident, Mount Vernon Office)
John P. Ewart	Kenneth F. Werts (Resident, Mount Vernon Office)
Richard F. Record, Jr.	

John L. Barger

ASSOCIATES

Joshua N. Rosen (Resident, Mount Vernon Office)	Theresa M. Thomson
Kathleen M. Stockwell	Kristine M. Tuttle
	Henry P. Villani (Resident, Mount Vernon Office)

OF COUNSEL

Jack E. Horsley

Counsel for: Monterey Coal Co., a Division of Exxon Coal USA, Inc.; Marathon Oil Co.; Illinois Central R.R. Co.; Okaw Building & Loan Assn., Mattoon, Illinois; The Medical Protective Insurance Co.; Consolidated Communications, Inc.; Lloyds Underwriters at London; Hartford Insurance Co.; Coles Together, a Not-For-Profit Corp.; Coles Building Corporation.

For full biographical listings, see the Martindale-Hubbell Law Directory

MOUNT VERNON,* Jefferson Co.

MITCHELL, NEUBAUER, SHAW & HANSON, P.C. (AV)

123 South 10th Street, Mercantile Bank Building, 6th Floor, P.O. Box 1088, 62864
Telephone: 618-242-0705
Telecopier: 618-242-4820

A. Ben Mitchell	Robert E. Shaw
Timothy R. Neubauer	Leslie James Hanson

Curtis W. Martin	T. David Purcell
Michael D. McHaney	David K. Overstreet

Attorneys For: Mercantile Bank of Mt. Vernon; Mt. Vernon Grade School District #80; Stewart Brothers Oil Producers; Illinois Super Foods, Inc.; Mt. Vernon Airport Authority; Henne Excavating & Construction.; J. M. Behimer Enterprises; Crossroads Community Hospital; Marion Ford-Mercury, Inc.

For full biographical listings, see the Martindale-Hubbell Law Directory

LAW OFFICE OF TERRY SHARP, P.C. (AV)

1115 Harrison Street, P.O. Box 906, 62864
Telephone: 618-242-0246
Fax: 618-242-1170
Benton, Illinois Office: 105 North Main Street.
Telephone: 618-435-5109.
FAX: 618-242-1170.

Terrell Lee Sharp

Brian Thomas McGovern

For full biographical listings, see the Martindale-Hubbell Law Directory

NORTHBROOK, Cook Co.

OLSON, GRABILL & HOFFMAN (AV)

Suite 420, 707 Skokie Boulevard, 60062
Telephone: 847-564-8880; 564-9110
FAX: 847-564-8886
Chicago, Illinois Office: Olson, Grabill, Hoffman & Louis, 300 South Wacker Drive, Suite 2400.
Telephone: 312-332-6823.

MEMBERS OF FIRM

Norman L. Olson, Jr.	Fred Louis III
Edward M. Grabill, Jr.	Gregg A. Flitcraft
Thomas G. Hoffman	Kent J. Donewald

OF COUNSEL

G. Kent Yowell

For full biographical listings, see the Martindale-Hubbell Law Directory

PONTIAC,* Livingston Co.

JOHNSON & TAYLOR (AV)

Formerly Ortman, Johnson & Taylor
109 North Mill Street, 61764
Telephone: 815-844-7151
FAX: 815-844-7539

MEMBERS OF FIRM

John A. Taylor	Taylor F. Johnson

Representative Clients: Flanagan State Bank; Flanagan and Long Point Fire; Protection Districts Flanagan School District; Hartford Steam Boiler Insp. Co.; Metropolitan Life Ins. Co.; Good Samaritan Home of Flanagan; CAPS & Flanagan Park Districts; Evenglow Lodge; Livingston County Broadcasters; Albrecht and Oliver Trusts.

For full biographical listings, see the Martindale-Hubbell Law Directory

SPRINGFIELD,* Sangamon Co.

MOHAN, ALEWELT, PRILLAMAN & ADAMI (AV)

First of America Center, Suite 325, 1 North Old Capitol Plaza, 62701-1323
Telephone: 217-528-2517
Telecopier: 217-528-2553
Email: fprillam@counsel.com.

MEMBERS

Edward J. Alewelt	Cheryl Stickel Neal

ASSOCIATES

Becky S. McCray	Patrick D. Shaw

Representative Clients: B & W Land Co.; Federal Deposit Insurance Corp.; McLaughlin Manufacturing Co.; Park Realty; Oak Park Subdivision Corp.

For Complete List of Firm Personnel, See General Section

For full biographical listings, see the Martindale-Hubbell Law Directory

VERNON HILLS, Lake Co.

RICHARDS, RALPH & SCHWAB, CHTD. (AV)

Suite 345, One Hawthorn Place, 175 East Hawthorn Parkway, 60061
Telephone: 708-367-9699
FAX: 708-367-9621

Michael L. Ralph	Alan E. Richards
	David J. Schwab

For full biographical listings, see the Martindale-Hubbell Law Directory

INDIANA

AUBURN,* De Kalb Co.

MEFFORD AND CARPENTER, A PROFESSIONAL CORPORATION (AV)

130 East Seventh Street, P.O. Box 667, 46706-0667
Telephone: 219-925-2300
Facsimile: 219-925-2610
URL: http://www.lawmc.com

Donald T. Mefford   Kirk D. Carpenter
J. Bryan Nugen

For full biographical listings, see the Martindale-Hubbell Law Directory

BLOOMINGTON,* Monroe Co.

BUNGER & ROBERTSON (AV)

226 South College Square, P.O. Box 910, 47402-0910
Telephone: 812-332-9295
Fax: 812-331-8808

MEMBERS OF FIRM
Don M. Robertson   Thomas Bunger
ASSOCIATE
William J. Beggs

Representative Clients: Aetna Insurance Companies; Bloomington Hospital; Commercial Union Group; Indiana Insurance Co.; Liberty Mutual Insurance; Medical Protective Co.; Monroe County Community School Corp.; Professional Golf Car, Inc.; Prudential Insurance Company of America; State Farm Automobile Insurance Co.

For Complete List of Firm Personnel, See General Section

For full biographical listings, see the Martindale-Hubbell Law Directory

CLARKSVILLE, Clark Co.

MAYER, VOGT, SMITH & PALMQUIST (AV)

501 Eastern Boulevard, 47129
Telephone: 812-288-1235
Louisville, Kentucky: 502-584-5800
Fax: 812-288-1240

MEMBERS OF FIRM
John M. Mayer, Jr.   Samuel H. Vogt, Jr.
Steven K. Palmquist
ASSOCIATE
Susan Wagner Hynes

Representative Clients: First Savings Bank, FSB; PNC Bank Indiana, Inc.
Approved Attorneys for: Commonwealth Land Title Insurance Co.; Ticor Title Insurance Company; Old Republic National Title Insurance Company.
References: First Savings Bank, FSB; PNC Bank Indiana, Inc.

For Complete List of Firm Personnel, See General Section

For full biographical listings, see the Martindale-Hubbell Law Directory

CRAWFORDSVILLE,* Montgomery Co.

BERRY, CAPPER, DONALDSON & TULLEY (AV)

131 North Green Street, P.O. Box 429, 47933
Telephone: 317-362-7340
Fax: 317-362-5023

Andrew N. Foley (1909-1963)   Richard G. Tulley
John R. Berry (1907-1986)   John S. Capper, IV
S. Bryan Donaldson

Representative Clients: Elston Bank & Trust Co.; R. R. Donnelley & Sons Co. (Crawfordsville Division); Linden State Bank; City of Crawfordsville, Ind.

For full biographical listings, see the Martindale-Hubbell Law Directory

ELKHART, Elkhart Co.

CHESTER, PFAFF & BROTHERSON (AV)

317 West Franklin Street, P.O. Box 507, 46515-0507
Telephone: 219-294-5421
Fax: 219-522-1476

MEMBERS OF FIRM
Robert A. Pfaff   Glenn E. Killoren
OF COUNSEL
James R. Brotherson
ASSOCIATE
Robert C. Whippo

(See Next Column)

LEGAL SUPPORT PERSONNEL
Wanda S. Wyrick (Paralegal)

For Complete List of Firm Personnel, See General Section

For full biographical listings, see the Martindale-Hubbell Law Directory

EVANSVILLE,* Vanderburgh Co.

BOWERS, HARRISON, KENT & MILLER, LLP (AV)

25 N.W. Riverside Drive, P.O. Box 1287, 47706-1287
Telephone: 812-426-1231
Fax: 812-464-3676

MEMBERS OF FIRM
Joseph H. Harrison   Gregory A. Kahre
Paul E. Black   Timothy J. Hubert
ASSOCIATES
Cedric Hustace   Sara Harrison Zeidler
OF COUNSEL
K. Wayne Kent

Representative Clients: Citizens Realty and Insurance, Inc.; General Growth Properties; Regency Associates, Ltd.; National Attorney's Title Assurance Fund, Inc.; Shell Mining Company; Commonwealth Land Title Insurance Company; American General Finance, Inc.

For Complete List of Firm Personnel, See General Section

For full biographical listings, see the Martindale-Hubbell Law Directory

FINE & HATFIELD (AV)

520 N.W. Second Street, P.O. Box 779, 47705-0779
Telephone: 812-425-3592
Telecopier: 812-421-4269
Email: Fine@Fine-Hatfield.com *URL:* http://www.Fine-Hatfield.com
MEMBER OF FIRM
James E. Marchand
A List of Representative Clients Furnished Upon Request.

For full biographical listings, see the Martindale-Hubbell Law Directory

KAHN, DEES, DONOVAN & KAHN (AV)

P.O. Box 3646, 47735-3646
Telephone: 812-423-3183
Fax: 812-423-3841
Email: evvlaw@k2d2.com

MEMBERS OF FIRM
Alan N. Shovers   G. Michael Schopmeyer
Jeffrey K. Helfrich
ASSOCIATES
Kent A. Brasseale, II   Martha J. Posey
Mark L. Boos

Representative Clients: Advance Transportation Company; D. Patrick, Inc.; Deaconess Hospital, Inc.; Keller-Crescent Co., Inc.; Kempf Group Inc.; O'-Daniel-Ranes, Inc.; Red Spot Paint & Varnish Co., Inc.; Rehabilitation Development Services, Inc.; J.H. Rudolph & Company, Inc.; J.E. Shekell, Inc.

For Complete List of Firm Personnel, See General Section

For full biographical listings, see the Martindale-Hubbell Law Directory

WRIGHT, EVANS AND DALY (AV)

425 Main Street, 47708
Telephone: 812-424-3300
Fax: 812-421-5588

MEMBERS OF FIRM
Claude B. Lynn (Retired)   Gerald H. Evans
Donald R. Wright   R. Lawrence Daly
Christopher L. Lucas

Representative Clients: Bosecker Construction Company; Castle Contracting Co., Inc.; Evansville Apartments, Inc.; Homehunters of Greater Evansville, Inc.; Huegel Realty, Inc.; Indian Woods Apartments, Ltd.; Indiana Realty Fund, Ltd.; Magnum Construction, Inc.; Mills-Wallace and Associates, Inc. Design Professionals; K & R Development Company.

For full biographical listings, see the Martindale-Hubbell Law Directory

FORT WAYNE,* Allen Co.

BECKMAN, LAWSON, SANDLER, SNYDER & FEDEROFF (AV)

800 Standard Federal Plaza, 46802
Telephone: 219-422-0800
Facsimile: 219-420-1013
Syracuse, Indiana Office: 200 West Main Street.
Telephone: 219-457-5727.
Facsimile: 219-457-2056.

(See Next Column)

BECKMAN, LAWSON, SANDLER, SNYDER & FEDEROFF, *Fort Wayne—Continued*

MEMBERS OF FIRM

Jack W. Lawson	William L. Sweet, Jr.
Frank J. Gray	John H. Brandt
Howard B. Sandler	Jeffrey L. Gage
Stephen R. Snyder	Thomas J. Goeglein
James A. Federoff	Jon A. Bragalone
	Brian J. T'Kindt

ASSOCIATES

Douglas R. Adelsperger	David D. Cornwell
Travis S. Friend	Craig R. Patterson
Jack C. Birch	Edward J. Ormsby
Robert L. Nicholson	Daniel B. Starr
W. Randall Kammeyer	Laurie A. Singh

OF COUNSEL

Frederick A. Beckman	Neil F. Sandler
	Douglas E. Miller

Reference: NBD, N.A.

For full biographical listings, see the Martindale-Hubbell Law Directory

---

BONAHOOM & BONAHOOM (AV)

110 W. Berry Street, Suite 1700, 46802
Telephone: 219-420-4055
Fax: 219-424-5311

Otto M. Bonahoom	Joseph G. Bonahoom

For full biographical listings, see the Martindale-Hubbell Law Directory

---

SWIFT & FINLAYSON (AV)

803 South Calhoun Street Suite 500, 46802-2480
Telephone: 219-423-4422
Fax: 219-423-4427
Affiliated Law Firm: Leeuw, Plopper & Beeman-Poland, First Indiana Plaza, Suite 2000, 135 North Pennsylvania Street, Indianapolis, Indiana, 46204-2456.

MEMBERS OF FIRM

Frank A. Higgins (1925-1976)	William D. Swift
	Craig R. Finlayson

ASSOCIATE

Charles D. Bash

OF COUNSEL

Gene R. Leeuw	Craig D. Doyle
Joseph W. Murphy	Charleyne L. Gabriel
	John Michael Mead

For full biographical listings, see the Martindale-Hubbell Law Directory

---

GREENWOOD, Johnson Co.

WILLIAMS HEWITT & ROBBINS, LLP (AV)

Suite 400, National City Bank Building, 300 South Madison Avenue, P.O. Box 405, 46142
Telephone: 317-888-1121
Facsimile: 317-887-4069

PARTNERS

Jon E. Williams	Brian C. Hewitt
	J. Lee Robbins

ASSOCIATES

John M. White	Mark E. Need
	John P. Wilkowski

For full biographical listings, see the Martindale-Hubbell Law Directory

---

INDIANAPOLIS,* Marion Co.

BACKER & BACKER, A PROFESSIONAL CORPORATION (AV)

101 West Ohio Street, Suite 1500, 46204
Telephone: 317-684-3000
Telecopier: 317-684-3004

Herbert J. Backer (1914-1995)	Stephen A. Backer
	David J. Backer

Reference: Bank One, Indianapolis.

For full biographical listings, see the Martindale-Hubbell Law Directory

---

BAKER & DANIELS (AV)

300 North Meridian Street, 46204
Telephone: 317-237-0300
FAX: 317-237-1000
Fort Wayne, Indiana Office: 111 East Wayne Street, Suite 800.
Telephone: 219-424-8000.
South Bend, Indiana Office: First Bank Building, 205 West Jefferson Boulevard.
Telephone: 219-234-4149.

(See Next Column)

Elkhart, Indiana Office: 301 B South Main Street, Suite 307,
Telephone: 219-296-6000.
Washington, D.C. Office: 1701 K Street, N.W., Suite 400.
Telephone: 202-785-1565.

MEMBERS OF FIRM

William F. Landers	Thomas A. Vogtner
Rory O'Bryan	George W. Somers
Mary Katherine Lisher	Karl P. Haas
	Joseph M. Scimia

ASSOCIATES

Mark C. Sausser	Andrew Z. Soshnick
	Mark E. Wright

Representative Clients: Anthem Insurance Companies, Inc.; AT&T Corp.; Bank One, Indianapolis, N.A.; Borg-Warner Corp.; City of Indianapolis; Cummins Engine Co.; Eli Lilly and Co.; General Motors Corp.; Indianapolis Public Schools; United Airlines.

For Complete List of Firm Personnel, See General Section

For full biographical listings, see the Martindale-Hubbell Law Directory

---

BOSE MCKINNEY & EVANS (AV)

2700 First Indiana Plaza, 135 North Pennsylvania Street, 46204
Telephone: 317-684-5000
Facsimile: 317-684-5173
Indianapolis North Office: Suite 1201, 8888 Keystone Crossing, 46240.
Telephone: 317-574-3700.
Facsimile: 317-574-3716.

MEMBERS OF FIRM

Philip A. Nicely	James C. Carlino
David L. Wills	Elizabeth Theobald Young
Jean S. Blackwell	Michael A. Trentadue

ASSOCIATES

Natalie J. Stucky	Robert C. Sproule
Tammy K. Haney	Jane A. Phillips

LEGAL SUPPORT PERSONNEL

Steven B. Granner (Zoning Consultant)

Representative Clients: Duke Realty Investments, Inc.; Carlstedt Dickman, Inc.; Citimark Development Cos.; Centex Homes; Ryland Homes; H. Emerson Young; HMI, Inc.; Skinner & Broadbent; The Inland Group, Inc.; The Travelers Insurance Co.

For Complete List of Firm Personnel, See General Section

For full biographical listings, see the Martindale-Hubbell Law Directory

---

CLARK, QUINN, MOSES & CLARK (AV)

One Indiana Square, Suite 2200, 46204-2011
Telephone: 317-637-1321
Fax: 317-687-2344

MEMBERS OF FIRM

Thomas Michael Quinn	J. Murray Clark

ASSOCIATES

Michael D. Keele	Cameron F. Clark

Representative Clients: Justus; The Shorewood Corporation; Marina Limited Partnership; Lafarge Corporation; Meijer Realty, Inc.; Lowe's; Kite Development; U-Stor Self Storage Warehouses; Mechanic's Laundry; Davis Homes.

For full biographical listings, see the Martindale-Hubbell Law Directory

---

DALE & EKE, PROFESSIONAL CORPORATION (AV)

Suite 400, 9100 Keystone Crossing, 46240
Telephone: 317-844-7400
Fax: 317-574-9426

William J. Dale, Jr.	Catherine Chambers Kennedy
Joseph W. Eke	A. Robert Lasich, Jr.
Deborah J. Caruso	Dawn Michelle Snow

For full biographical listings, see the Martindale-Hubbell Law Directory

---

DANN PECAR NEWMAN & KLEIMAN, PROFESSIONAL CORPORATION (AV)

Suite 2300, One American Square Box 82008, 46282
Telephone: 317-632-3232; Indiana: 800-622-4799
Telecopy: 317-632-2962

Theodore R. Dann (1907-1993)	James H. Schwarz
Joel Yonover (1932-1995)	Robert A. Rose
Philip D. Pecar	Walter E. Wolf, Jr.
Norman R. Newman	Barry E. Beldin
David H. Kleiman	Robert D. Swhier, Jr.
Jon B. Abels	James P. Moloy
Melvin R. Daniel	Robert J. Schuckit
Lawrence F. Dorocke	Andrew A. Kleiman
Jeffrey A. Abrams	Michael J. Gabovitch

(See Next Column)

DANN PECAR NEWMAN & KLEIMAN PROFESSIONAL CORPORATION— *Continued*

Steven M. Pecar	Richard O. Kissel, II
Benjamin A. Pecar	Joseph D. Calderon

OF COUNSEL

Linda E. Cantor	Anthony J. Rose

Ellen C. Siakotos	Angela L. Mansfield
Stacy L. Hill	Martha M. K. Baird
	Karin L. Veatch

Attorneys for: Indianapolis Machinery Co., Inc.; Melvin Simon & Associates, Inc.; Pacers Basketball Corp.; Universal Fire & Casualty Co., Inc.; Bank One, Indianapolis, NA; INB National Bank; Nachi Technology, Inc.; Pharmaceutical Corporation of America; Logo 7, Inc.

For full biographical listings, see the Martindale-Hubbell Law Directory

FEIWELL & HANNOY, PROFESSIONAL CORPORATION (AV)

251 North Illinois Street, Suite 1700, P.O. Box 44141, 46244-0141
Telephone: 317-237-2727
Facsimile: 317-237-2722

Murray J. Feiwell	Douglas J. Hannoy

John P. Sieger	Michael J. Feiwell
	Laura S. Carafiol

OF COUNSEL
Lisa Kay Decker

Representative Clients: Temple Inland Mortgage Corp.; United Companies Lending Corp.; GMAC Mortgage Corp.; NationsBanc Mortgage Corp.; Norwest Mortgage, Inc.; Meridian Real Estate Services, Inc.; Metro Realty Ltd. Partnership; Mathews, Click: Revel, Inc.

For full biographical listings, see the Martindale-Hubbell Law Directory

HACKMAN MCCLARNON HULETT & CRACRAFT (AV)

2400 One Indiana Square, 46204
Telephone: 317-636-5401
Facsimile: 317-686-3288
Email: hmhc@indy.net

MEMBERS OF FIRM

Marvin L. Hackman	Timothy K. Ryan
Robert S. Hulett	Philip B. McKiernan
Michael B. Cracraft	Vicki L. Anderson

ASSOCIATES

Thomas A. Dickey	Marci A. Reddick

OF COUNSEL

James R. McClarnon	John D. Cochran, Jr.
	Mark S. Alderfer

Representative Clients: F.C. Tucker Co., Inc.; Texas Eastern Products Pipeline Co.; The State Life Insurance Co.; NBD Bank, N.A.; Met Life International Real Estate Partners Limited Partnership; Manufacturers Life Insurance Company.

For full biographical listings, see the Martindale-Hubbell Law Directory

HUGHES AND SALLEE (AV)

(Not a Partnership)
Two Meridian Plaza, Suite 202, 10401 North Meridian Street, 46290
Telephone: 317-573-2255
Telecopier: 317-573-2266

David B. Hughes	Gary D. Sallee

For full biographical listings, see the Martindale-Hubbell Law Directory

ICE MILLER DONADIO & RYAN (AV)

One American Square Box 82001, 46282-0002
Telephone: 317-236-2100
Fax: 317-236-2219
Email: leel@imdr.com *URL:* http://www.imdr.com
South Bend, Indiana Office: 211 West Washington Street, Suite 2420.
Telephone: 219-234-7933.
Fax: 219-234-7965. Internet E-mail: leel@imdr.com. Web Site Address: http://www.imdr.com.

MEMBERS OF FIRM

Charles E. Wilson	Phillip L. Bayt
	Zeff A. Weiss

SENIOR COUNSEL
Timothy W. Sullivan

OF COUNSEL

James B. Burroughs	Mark D. Grant

RETIRED PARTNER
John A. Grayson

(See Next Column)

ASSOCIATES

Heather K. Olinger	Sarah K. Funke
Jared L. Burden	Allan S. Katz
	Gretchen W. Snelling

Representative Clients: The Sexton Cos.; Citicorp Real Estate, Inc.; Bank of America; Heitman Properties; Consolidated Products, Inc.; Ford Motor Credit Co.; SCM Real Estate Development Corp.; The Buckingham Companies; Pulte Homes; Mansur Development Corp.

For Complete List of Firm Personnel, See General Section
For full biographical listings, see the Martindale-Hubbell Law Directory

JOHNSON, SMITH, PENCE, DENSBORN, WRIGHT & HEATH (AV)

One Indiana Square Suite 1800, 46204
Telephone: 317-634-9777
Telecopier: 317-636-9061

MEMBERS OF FIRM

Sean Michael Clapp	Dennis A. Johnson
Peter D. Cleveland	Richard L. Johnson
	Michael J. Kaye

ASSOCIATES

Carolyn H. Andretti	Gretchen L. Doninger
Robert T. Buday	Stefany L. Mitlak

OF COUNSEL
John K. Smeltzer

For Complete List of Firm Personnel, See General Section
For full biographical listings, see the Martindale-Hubbell Law Directory

MITCHELL HURST JACOBS & DICK (AV)

152 East Washington Street, 46204
Telephone: 317-636-0808
1-800-636-0808
Fax: 317-633-7680

MEMBERS OF FIRM

Marvin H. Mitchell	Richard J. Dick
	Steven K. Huffer

ASSOCIATE
Michael T. McNelis

General Counsel For: Dr. Tavel's Vision Center; Calderon Bros. Vending Machines, Inc.; Grocers Supply Co., Inc.; Power Train Services, Inc.; Frank E. Irish, Inc.; Bedding Liquidators; Galyan's Trading Co.; Harcourt Management Co., Inc.; Kosene & Kosene Mgt. & Dev. Co., Inc.; Hasten Bancorp.

For full biographical listings, see the Martindale-Hubbell Law Directory

SOMMER & BARNARD, ATTORNEYS AT LAW, PC (AV)

4000 Bank One Tower, 111 Monument Circle, 46204-5140
Telephone: 317-630-4000
FAX: 317-236-9802
North Office: 8900 Keystone Crossing, Suite 1046, Indianapolis, Indiana, 46240-2134.
Telephone: 317-630-4000.
FAX: 317-844-4780.

Jerald I. Ancel	Marlene Reich
	Julianne S. Lis-Milam

Representative Clients: Comerica Bank; Excel Industries; Federal Express; New York Life; Renault Automation; Kimball International; Monsanto; TRW, Inc.

For Complete List of Firm Personnel, See General Section
For full biographical listings, see the Martindale-Hubbell Law Directory

STARK DONINGER & SMITH (AV)

Suite 700, 50 South Meridian Street, 46204
Telephone: 317-638-2400
Fax: 317-633-6618; 633-6619

MEMBERS OF FIRM

John C. Stark	Patricia Seasor Bailey
Bruce E. Smith	Brian J. Tuohy
John W. Van Buskirk	Mark A. Bailey
Richard W. Dyar	Lewis E. Willis, Jr.

ASSOCIATES

Thomas A. Brodnik	Richard B. Kaufman
Neil E. Lucas	Patrick J. Dietrick

COUNSEL

Clarence H. Doninger	Robert D. Maas
Gregory S. Fehribach	William K. Byrum

Representative Clients: American Consulting Engineers, Inc.; Ost Enterprises; The C.P. Morgan Co.; Nationwide Life Insurance Co.; Trinity Homes, Inc.

For full biographical listings, see the Martindale-Hubbell Law Directory

WALLACK & WALLACK, P.C. (AV)

One Indiana Square, Suite 2230, 46204
Telephone: 317-231-9000
FAX: 317-231-9900

Barry Z. Wallack	Michael S. Wallack

For full biographical listings, see the Martindale-Hubbell Law Directory

KOKOMO,* Howard Co.

FELL, McGARVEY, TRAURING & WILSON (AV)

515 West Sycamore Street, P.O. Box 958, 46903-0958
Telephone: 317-457-9321
Telecopier: 317-452-0882

MEMBERS OF FIRM

John E. Fell, Jr.   Eugene J. McGarvey, Jr.

Representative Clients: Big R Stores; Cellular One of Kokomo, Inc.; First National Bank, Kokomo; Haynes International, Inc.; Hospital Authority of the City of Kokomo; Kokomo City Hall Building Corp.; PPG Industries, Inc.; Star Building Supply, Inc.; Mervis Industries, Inc.; Taylor Community School Corp.

For Complete List of Firm Personnel, See General Section

For full biographical listings, see the Martindale-Hubbell Law Directory

LAFAYETTE,* Tippecanoe Co.

BALL, EGGLESTON, BUMBLEBURG & McBRIDE (AV)

810 Bank One Building, P.O. Box 1535, 47902
Telephone: 317-742-9046
Fax: 317-742-1966

Cable G. Ball (1904-1981)   Warren N. Eggleston
Owen Crook (1908-1977)   (1923-1991)

MEMBERS OF FIRM

Joseph T. Bumbleburg	Jeffrey J. Newell
John K. McBride	James T. Hodson
Jack L. Walkey	Brian Wade Walker
Michael J. Stapleton	Cheryl M. Knodle

Randy J. Williams

General Counsel for: The Lafayette Union Railway Co.; Bank One, Lafayette, N.A.

Representative Clients: Farmers Insurance Group; General Accident Fire & Life Assurance Corp.; City of Lafayette Board of Parks and Recreation; West Lafayette Community School Corp.; Travelers Insurance Co.; Trustees, West Lafayette Public Library.

For full biographical listings, see the Martindale-Hubbell Law Directory

STUART & BRANIGIN (AV)

The Life Building, 300 Main Street, Suite 800, 47902
Telephone: 317-423-1561
Telecopier: 317-742-8175

MEMBERS OF FIRM

Allison Ellsworth Stuart	Stephen R. Pennell
(1886-1950)	Anthony S. Benton
Roger D. Branigin (1902-1975)	Erik D. Spykman
Russell H. Hart	William E. Emerick
Roger D. Branigin, Jr.	John C. Duffey
Thomas L. Ryan	Mark E. DeYoung
James V. McGlone	Thomas B. Parent
Carl W. Kloepfer	Laura L. Bowker
Thomas R. McCully	Kevin D. Nicoson
Larry R. Fisher	Susan K. Roberts
Nina B. Kirkpatrick	John M. Stuckey
Mark Lillianfeld	Deborah B. Trice

COUNSEL

John F. Bodle

ASSOCIATES

Brent W. Huber	David A. Starkweather
William P. Kealey	Geoffrey Blazi

A. James Chareq

General Counsel for: The Lafayette Life Insurance Co.; INB National Bank, N.W.; Lafayette Home Hospital, Inc.
State Counsel for: Norfolk & Western Railway Co.
Mr. Ryan is Counsel to: The Trustees of Purdue University.
Representative Clients: Aluminum Company of America; Liberty Mutual Insurance Group.

For full biographical listings, see the Martindale-Hubbell Law Directory

MARION,* Grant Co.

KILEY, KILEY, HARKER, MICHAEL & CERTAIN (AV)

300 West Third Street, P.O. Box 899, 46952-0899
Telephone: 317-664-9041
Fax: 317-664-8119

MEMBERS OF FIRM

Robert Ralph Batton	David L. Kiley, Sr.
(1890-1963)	Michael J. Kiley
Albert L. Harker (1904-1965)	Albert C. Harker
Albert Bonner Brown	Thomas W. Michael
(1911-1981)	Harry J. Certain

ASSOCIATE

Therese McCullough Pryor

Counsel for: Bank One, Marion, N.A.; Liniger Co., Inc.; Atlas Foundry Co.
Local Counsel for: GenCorp.; CPC Group; General Motors; Indiana Michigan Power Co./AEP; Indiana Bell Telephone Co.; Foster-Forbes, Division of American National Can Corp.

For full biographical listings, see the Martindale-Hubbell Law Directory

MERRILLVILLE, Lake Co.

BURKE, MURPHY, COSTANZA & CUPPY (AV)

Suite 600 8585 Broadway, 46410-7064
Telephone: 219-769-1313
Telecopier: 219-769-6806
East Chicago, Indiana Office: First National Bank Building. 720 West Chicago Avenue.
Telephone: 219-397-2401.
Telecopier: 219-397-0508.
Valparaiso, Indiana Office: 15 North Franklin Street, Suite 200.
Telephone: 219-531-0134.
Telecopier: 219-531-0507.
Palm Harbor, Florida Office: Suite 280, 33920 U.S. Highway 19 North.
Telephone: 813-787-7799.
Telecopier: 813-787-7237.

MEMBERS OF FIRM

Edward L. Burke	George W. Carberry
Gerald K. Hrebec	Demetri J. Retson

ASSOCIATES

Todd A. Etzler	Philip C. Spahn

Representative Clients: NBD Bank, N.A.; Gough & Lesch Development Corporation; Whiteco Industries; Focus Group; Lehigh Portland Cement Company; City of East Chicago Department of Redevelopment; East Chicago Housing Authority.

For Complete List of Firm Personnel, See General Section

For full biographical listings, see the Martindale-Hubbell Law Directory

HODGES & DAVIS, P.C. (AV)

8700 Broadway, 46410
Telephone: 219-641-8700
Fax: 219-641-8710
Portage, Indiana Office: 6082 Lute Road. P.O. Box 1037.
Telephone: 219-762-9129.
Fax: 219-762-2826.

Clyde D. Compton	Bonnie C. Coleman
William B. Davis	Jill M. Madajczyk
Earle F. Hites	Laura B. Frost
R. Lawrence Steele	David H. Kreider
Gregory A. Sobkowski	Robert G. Vann

OF COUNSEL

Edward J. Hussey

Representative Clients: Lake Mortgage Co., Inc.; McDonald's Corporation; Walgreen Co.; Century 21 Heritage Realtors; D.G. Real Estate, Inc.

For Complete List of Firm Personnel, See General Section

For full biographical listings, see the Martindale-Hubbell Law Directory

MISHAWAKA, St. Joseph Co.

SCHINDLER AND OLSON (AV)

122 South Mill Street, P.O. Box 100, 46544
Telephone: 219-259-5461
Fax: 219-259-5462

OF COUNSEL

John W. Schindler (1884-1971)   John W. Schindler, Jr.

MEMBER OF FIRM

James J. Olson

Representative Clients: Penn-Harris-Madison School Corp.; All Star Realty Co.; School City of Mishawaka; Edward Rose & Sons.
Reference: 1st Source Bank of Mishawaka.

For full biographical listings, see the Martindale-Hubbell Law Directory

PORTAGE, Porter Co.

HODGES & DAVIS, P.C. (AV)

6082 Lute Road, P.O. Box 1037, 46368
Telephone: 219-762-9129
Fax: 219-762-2826
Merrillville, Indiana Office: 8700 Broadway.
Telephone: 219-641-8700.
Fax: 219-641-8710.

Clyde D. Compton	R. Lawrence Steele
Earle F. Hites	Gregory A. Sobkowski
	Bonnie C. Coleman

Representative Clients: Porter County Plan Commission; McDonald's Corporation; Walgreen Co.; Century 21 Heritage Realtors; D.G. Real Estate, Inc.; Lake Mortgage Co., Inc.

For full biographical listings, see the Martindale-Hubbell Law Directory

PRINCETON,* Gibson Co.

HALL, PARTENHEIMER & KINKLE (AV)

219 North Hart Street, P.O. Box 313, 47670
Telephone: 812-386-0050
FAX: 812-385-2575

MEMBERS OF FIRM

Verner P. Partenheimer   J. Robert Kinkle
R. Scott Partenheimer

Representative Clients: Interlake Inc.; Gibson County Bank; Old Ben Coal Co.
Approved Attorneys for: Lawyers Title Insurance; Ticor Title Insurance.

For full biographical listings, see the Martindale-Hubbell Law Directory

RICHMOND,* Wayne Co.

HARRINGTON, MALEY, GARDNER & SAYRE (AV)

Third Floor, Harrington Bank Building, Two North Eighth, 47374-3090
Telephone: 317-966-6643
FAX: 317-966-6799

MEMBERS OF FIRM

Alonzo M. Gardner (1886-1941)   Robert J. Maley
Wilfred Jessup (1900-1944)   Gayle W. Gardner
Frank K. Chambers (1938-1955)   John M. Sayre, III
Floyd W. Gardner (1933-1965)   Kirk A. Weikart
Clifford M. Haworth
(1923-1967)

OF COUNSEL

John R. Harrington

General Counsel for: Harrington Bank, FSB.
Local Counsel for: Belden Manufacturing Co.; CIGNA.

For full biographical listings, see the Martindale-Hubbell Law Directory

SOUTH BEND,* St. Joseph Co.

JONES, OBENCHAIN, FORD, PANKOW, LEWIS & WOODS (AV)

1800 Valley American Bank Building, P.O. Box 4577, 46634
Telephone: 219-233-1194
Fax: 233-8957; 233-9675

Vitus G. Jones (1879-1951)   Roland Obenchain (Retired)
Roland Obenchain (1890-1961)   Milton A. Johnson (Retired)
Francis Jones (1907-1988)   James H. Pankow (Retired)

MEMBERS OF FIRM

Thomas F. Lewis, Jr.   Robert M. Edwards, Jr.
Timothy W. Woods   John B. Ford
John R. Obenchain   Mark J. Phillipoff
Robert W. Mysliwiec   John W. Van Laere

ASSOCIATES

Edward P. Benchik   Robert S. Sanderson
Thomas F. Lewis, III

OF COUNSEL

G. Burt Ford

Attorneys For: Jack Hickey Homes; Portage Realty; Saint Joseph's Medical Center; The Equitable Life Assurance Society of the United States; Panzica Construction Co.

For full biographical listings, see the Martindale-Hubbell Law Directory

SOPKO & FIRTH (AV)

Plaza Building, 5th Floor, 210 South Michigan Street, P.O. Box 300, 46624
Telephone: 219-234-3000
Telecopier: 219-234-4220

MEMBERS OF FIRM

Thomas C. Sopko   John C. Firth

ASSOCIATE

Brent E. Inabnit

OF COUNSEL

Ronald J. Jaicomo

References: 1st Source Bank; 1st Interstate Bank; Notre Dame Federal Credit Union.

For full biographical listings, see the Martindale-Hubbell Law Directory

TERRE HAUTE,* Vigo Co.

COX, ZWERNER, GAMBILL & SULLIVAN (AV)

511 Wabash Avenue, P.O. Box 1625, 47808-1625
Telephone: 812-232-6003
Fax: 812-232-6567

(See Next Column)

MEMBERS OF FIRM

Ernest J. Zwerner (1918-1980)   David W. Sullivan
Benjamin G. Cox (1915-1988)   Robert L. Gowdy
Gilbert W. Gambill, Jr.   Louis F. Britton
James E. Sullivan   Carroll D. Smeltzer
Benjamin G. Cox, Jr.   Jeffry A. Lind

ASSOCIATE

Ronald E. Jumps

OF COUNSEL

Robert D. Hepburn

Counsel for: Terre Haute First National Bank; Farmers Insurance Group; Indiana-American Water Co.; Indiana State University; Merchants National Bank of Terre Haute; Rose-Hulman Institute of Technology; Tribune-Star Publishing Co., Inc.; Weston Paper & Manufacturing Co.

For full biographical listings, see the Martindale-Hubbell Law Directory

VALPARAISO,* Porter Co.

BLACHLY, TABOR, BOZIK & HARTMAN (AV)

Suite 401 Indiana Federal Building, 46383
Telephone: 219-464-1041
Fax: 219-464-0927

MEMBERS OF FIRM

Quentin A. Blachly   David L. Hollenbeck
Glenn J. Tabor   David L. DeBoer
James S. Bozik   Thomas F. Macke
Duane W. Hartman   Randall J. Zromkoski
Richard J. Rupcich

ASSOCIATES

Roger A. Weitgenant   Craig R. Van Schouwen

Reference: First National Bank.

For Complete List of Firm Personnel, See General Section

For full biographical listings, see the Martindale-Hubbell Law Directory

HOEPPNER WAGNER AND EVANS (AV)

103 East Lincolnway, P.O. Box 2357, 46384-2357
Telephone: 219-464-4961; 800-879-2246 (IN,IL)
Fax: 219-465-0603
Merrillville, Indiana Office: Twin Towers, Suite 606 South, 1000 East 80th Place, 46410.
Telephone: 219-769-6552; 800-263-1466. (IN,IL,).
Fax: 219-738-2349.

MEMBERS OF FIRM

William H. Wagner   Larry G. Evans
Todd A. Leeth

OF COUNSEL

Jim B. Brown (Resident, Merrillville Office)

Attorneys for: Bethlehem Steel Corp.; Chester, Inc.; Hunt-Wesson Foods, Inc.; NBD Bank, N.A.; Owens-Corning Fiberglas Corp.; Valparaiso University; State Farm Insurance; Allstate Insurance Co.; Indiana Federal Bank for Savings.

For Complete List of Firm Personnel, See General Section

For full biographical listings, see the Martindale-Hubbell Law Directory

IOWA

CEDAR RAPIDS,* Linn Co.

SHUTTLEWORTH & INGERSOLL, P.C. (AV)

500 Firstar Bank Building, P.O. Box 2107, 52406-2107
Telephone: 319-365-9461
Fax: 319-365-8443
Email: si-law@inav.net

James C. Nemmers   Thomas P. Peffer
Michael O. McDermott   William P. Prowell
Carroll J. Reasoner   William S. Hochstetler
LeeAnn M. Ferry

Dean D. Carrington

OF COUNSEL

W. R. Shuttleworth

COUNSEL

Joan Lipsky

Representative Clients: Amana Society; Archer-Daniels-Midland Co.; Cargill, Inc.; Cedar River Paper Company; Firstar Bank Cedar Rapids, N.A.; Lawyers Title Insurance Company; Met-Coil Systems Corporation; PMX Industries, Inc.; Ryan Construction Company; Shive-Hattery Engineers & Architects, Inc.

(See Next Column)

SHUTTLEWORTH & INGERSOLL P.C., *Cedar Rapids—Continued*

For Complete List of Firm Personnel, See General Section

For full biographical listings, see the Martindale-Hubbell Law Directory

---

COUNCIL BLUFFS,* Pottawattamie Co.

SMITH PETERSON LAW FIRM (AV)

35 Main Place, Suite 300, P.O. Box 249, 51502
Telephone: 712-328-1833
Fax: 712-328-8320
Omaha, Nebraska Office: 9290 West Dodge Road, Suite 205.
Telephone: 402-397-8500.
Fax: 402-397-5519.

MEMBERS OF FIRM

Raymond A. Smith (1892-1977)	Lawrence J. Beckman
John LeRoy Peterson (1895-1969)	Gregory G. Barntsen
	W. Curtis Hewett
Harold T. Beckman	Steven H. Krohn
Robert J. Laubenthal	Randy R. Ewing
Richard A. Heininger	Joseph D. Thornton

ASSOCIATES

T. J. Pattermann	Paul M. Shotkoski
Daniel Fretheim	(Not admitted in IA)

Representative Clients: Redland Insurance Group; Iowa Western Community College; Farm Credit Bank of Omaha; Demma Fruit Co.; Peoples National Bank; Council Bluffs Board of Water Works Trustee.

For full biographical listings, see the Martindale-Hubbell Law Directory

---

DAVENPORT,* Scott Co.

NOYES & GOSMA, L.L.P. (AV)

400 North Main Street, Suite 106, 52801
Telephone: 319-322-8223
Fax: 319-322-8234

MEMBERS OF FIRM

Michael L. Noyes	John S. Gosma

ASSOCIATE

Marie R. Rolling-Tarbox

OF COUNSEL

Clay LeGrand	Charles G. Rehling

Reference: Quad City Bank and Trust Company.

For full biographical listings, see the Martindale-Hubbell Law Directory

---

DES MOINES,* Polk Co.

CONNOLLY, O'MALLEY, LILLIS, HANSEN & OLSON, L.L.P. (AV)

820 Liberty Building, 6th & Grand Avenue, 50309
Telephone: 515-243-8157
Fax: 515-243-3919

MEMBERS OF FIRM

William J. Lillis	Eugene E. Olson
Russell J. Hansen	Streetar Cameron
Michael W. O'Malley	Christopher R. Pose

A list of Representative Clients will be furnished upon request. References will be furnished upon request.

For Complete List of Firm Personnel, See General Section

For full biographical listings, see the Martindale-Hubbell Law Directory

FINLEY, ALT, SMITH, SCHARNBERG, MAY & CRAIG, P.C. (AV)

604 Locust Street, Fourth Floor Equitable Building, 50309
Telephone: 515-288-0145
Telecopier: 515-288-2724

Jerry P. Alt

Representative Clients: Aetna Casualty & Surety Co.; Aetna Life Insurance Co.; ALAS; American Society of Composers, Authors and Publishers; Equitable Life Assurance Society of the U.S.; Federated Insurance Co.; Meredith Corp.
Iowa Attorneys for: Midwest Medical Insurance Co.
District Attorneys for: Norfolk & Southern Railroad; Soo Line Railroad Company.

For Complete List of Firm Personnel, See General Section

For full biographical listings, see the Martindale-Hubbell Law Directory

WASKER, DORR, WIMMER & MARCOUILLER, P.C. (AV)

801 Grand Avenue, Suite 3100, 50309-8036
Telephone: 515-283-1801
Facsimile: 515-283-1802

Charles F. Wasker	D. Mark Marcouiller
Fred L. Dorr	Robert A. Sims

(See Next Column)

Matthew D. Kern

For Complete List of Firm Personnel, See General Section

For full biographical listings, see the Martindale-Hubbell Law Directory

---

WATERLOO,* Black Hawk Co.

SWISHER & COHRT, P.L.C. (AV)

528 West Fourth Street, P.O. Box 1200, 50704
Telephone: 319-232-6555
FAX: 319-232-4835

Benjamin F. Swisher (1878-1959)	J. Douglas Oberman
L. J. Cohrt (1898-1974)	Stephen J. Powell
Charles F. Swisher (1919-1986)	Jim D. DeKoster
Jeffrey J. Greenwood (1953-1995)	Samuel C. Anderson
	Robert C. Griffin
Eldon R. McCann	Kevin R. Rogers
Steven A. Weidner	Beth E. Hansen
Larry J. Cohrt	Mark F. Conway

Natalie Williams Burris

Firm is Counsel for: Koehring Corp.; Clay Equipment; Chamberlain Manufacturing Co.; Waterloo Courier.
Local Counsel for: Allied Group; John Deere Insurance; Liberty Mutual Insurance Co.

For full biographical listings, see the Martindale-Hubbell Law Directory

---

KANSAS

WICHITA,* Sedgwick Co.

ADAMS, JONES, ROBINSON AND MALONE, CHARTERED (AV)

600 Market Centre, 155 North Market, P.O. Box 1034, 67201-1034
Telephone: 316-265-8591
Telecopier: 316-265-9719
Email: ajrm@southwind.net *URL:* http://www.southwind.net,~ajrm

Philip L. Bowman	Mert F. Buckley
	Laura L. Ice

Representative Clients: Mid Continent Federal Savings Bank; INTRUST Bank, NA; First Bank, fsb; Travelers Insurance Co; Williams Natural Gas Co.; City of Wichita, Sedgwick County, KS: A.O. Smith Corp.; Lease American Corp.

For full biographical listings, see the Martindale-Hubbell Law Directory

FOULSTON & SIEFKIN L.L.P. (AV)

700 Fourth Financial Center, 67202
Telephone: 316-267-6371
Facsimile: 316-267-6345
Topeka, Kansas Office: 1515 Bank IV Tower, 534 Kansas Avenue, 66603.
Telephone: 913-233-3600.
Fax: 913-233-1610.
Dodge City, Kansas Office: 810 Frontview, P.O. Box 1147, 67801.
Telephone: 316-227-8126.
Fax: 316-227-8451.
Member: Lex Mundi, A Global Association of 126 Independent Firms.

MEMBERS OF FIRM

Phillip S. Frick	Larry G. Rapp
James D. Oliver	Gary E. Knight

For Complete List of Firm Personnel, See General Section

For full biographical listings, see the Martindale-Hubbell Law Directory

HERSHBERGER, PATTERSON, JONES & ROTH, L.C. (AV)

600 Hardage Center, 100 South Main, 67202-3779
Telephone: 316-263-7583
Fax: 316-263-7595

Jerome E. Jones	John A. Vetter

OF COUNSEL

John L. Kratzer, Jr.

Counsel for: First National Bank in Wichita; Anadarko Petroleum Corporation; Chinese Industries; Mobil Oil Corp.; CNA Insurance; Royal Exchange Group; Central National Insurance Group; Transamerica Insurance Group; Northwestern National Insurance Group.

For Complete List of Firm Personnel, See General Section

For full biographical listings, see the Martindale-Hubbell Law Directory

Wichita—Continued

KAHRS, NELSON, FANNING, HITE & KELLOGG, L.L.P. (AV)

Suite 630, 200 West Douglas Street, 67202-3089
Telephone: 316-265-7761
Telecopier: 316-267-7803

MEMBERS OF FIRM

| Clark R. Nelson | Linda S. Parks |
| Steven D. Gough | John G. Pike |

ASSOCIATE
Todd M. Connell
OF COUNSEL
Robert Hall

Representative Clients: Garvey Center, L.C.; Maverick Development Corp.; Prairie Village Shopping Center, Inc.; The Ruffin Companies; Westway Shopping Center, Inc.

For Complete List of Firm Personnel, See General Section

For full biographical listings, see the Martindale-Hubbell Law Directory

YOUNG, BOGLE, McCAUSLAND, WELLS & CLARK, P.A. (AV)

106 West Douglas, Suite 923, 67202
Telephone: 316-265-7841
Facsimile: 316-265-3956

| William A. Wells | Kenneth M. Clark |
| Patrick C. Blanchard | |

Representative Clients: Equitable AgriBusiness, Inc.; 1st Nationwide Bank; Transamerica Financial Corp.; Citicorp., N.A.; Security Pacific Business Credit.

For Complete List of Firm Personnel, See General Section

For full biographical listings, see the Martindale-Hubbell Law Directory

KENTUCKY

ASHLAND, Boyd Co.

HOLBROOK & PITT (AV)

200 Home Federal Building, 1500 Carter Avenue, 41101
Telephone: 606-324-5136
Fax: 606-329-8998

Charles R. Holbrook, Jr.	Charles R. Holbrook III
(1909-1993)	Ernest M. Pitt, Jr.
Anna Holmes Ruth	

Reference: First American Bank.

For full biographical listings, see the Martindale-Hubbell Law Directory

BOWLING GREEN,* Warren Co.

BELL, ORR, AYERS & MOORE, P.S.C. (AV)

1010 College Street, P.O. Box 738, 42102-0738
Telephone: 502-781-8111
Telecopier: 502-781-9027

| Ray B. Buckberry, Jr. | Kevin C. Brooks |

General Counsel for: First American National Bank of Kentucky; Farm Credit Services of Mid-America, ACA.; Houchens Industries, Inc. (Food Markets and Shopping Centers); Warren County Board of Education; Bowling Green Municipal Utilities.
Representative Clients: Chicago Title Insurance Co.; Commonwealth Land Title Insurance Co.; Kentucky Farm Bureau Mutual Insurance Co.; Martin Automotive Group; Home Insurance Group.

For Complete List of Firm Personnel, See General Section

For full biographical listings, see the Martindale-Hubbell Law Directory

ENGLISH, LUCAS, PRIEST & OWSLEY (AV)

1101 College Street, P.O. Box 770, 42102-0770
Telephone: 502-781-6500
Telecopier: 502-782-7782
Email: inquiry@elpo.com

MEMBERS OF FIRM

| Whayne C. Priest, Jr. | Keith M. Carwell |

ASSOCIATE
Marc Allen Lovell

General Counsel for: Warren Rural Electric Cooperative Corporation; Trans Financial Bank, N.A.
Representative Clients: Commercial Union Insurance Cos.; Kemper Insurance Group; St. Paul Insurance Co.; Desa International; Sumitomo Electric Systems, Inc.
Agent For: First American Title Insurance Company; Chicago Title Insurance Company.

(See Next Column)

Approved Attorneys For: Commonwealth Land Title Insurance Co.

For Complete List of Firm Personnel, See General Section

For full biographical listings, see the Martindale-Hubbell Law Directory

HARLIN & PARKER, P.S.C. (AV)

519 East Tenth Street, P.O. Box 390, 42102-0390
Telephone: 502-842-5611
Telefax: 502-842-2607

| William Jerry Parker | Jerry A. Burns |
| | Scott Charles Marks |

Railroad and Utilities: District Attorney for BellSouth Telecommunications, Inc.; CSX Transportation, Inc.
Local Counsel For: General Motors Corp.; Ford Motor Co.; Chrysler Corp.
Approved Attorneys For: Commonwealth Land Title Insurance Co.
Representative Clients: Jim Walker Homes, Inc.; American General Insurance Group; American Diversified Development Co. (Bowling Green Mall); Equitable Life Assurance Society of the United States.

For Complete List of Firm Personnel, See General Section

For full biographical listings, see the Martindale-Hubbell Law Directory

KERRICK, GRISE & STIVERS (AV)

1025 State Street, P.O. Box 9547, 42102-9547
Telephone: 502-782-8160
Fax: 502-782-5856
Elizabethtown, Kentucky Office: 2935 Dolphin Drive, Suite 102.
Telephone: 502-769-5788.
Fax: 502-737-9285.

MEMBERS OF FIRM

| Thomas N. Kerrick | Gregory N. Stivers |
| John R. Grise | H. Brent Brennenstuhl |

ASSOCIATES

| Lanna Martin Kilgore | Shawn Rosso Alcott |
| Laura M. Hagan (Resident, Elizabethtown Office) | Jason B. Bell |

Representative Clients: Bowling Green Bank & Trust, N.A.; Huntington Mortgage Corp.; TransFinancial Bank; First American National Bank.

For full biographical listings, see the Martindale-Hubbell Law Directory

CATLETTSBURG,* Boyd Co.

ADKINS & ADKINS (AV)

Adkins Building, 2813 Louisa Street, P.O. Box 653, 41129
Telephone: 606-739-4151
Fax: Available Upon Request

| James E. Adkins | James E. Adkins, II |

General Counsel for: Catlettsburg Federal Savings & Loan Assn.; Kentucky-Farmers Bank.
Local Counsel for: Federal National Mortgage Assn.
Approved Attorneys for: Farmers Home Administration.
Agents for: Commonwealth Land Title Insurance Co.

COVINGTON, Kenton Co.

TALIAFERRO AND MEHLING (AV)

1005 Madison Avenue, P.O. Box 468, 41012-0468
Telephone: 606-291-9900
Fax: 606-291-3014

MEMBERS OF FIRM

| Philip Taliaferro, III | Christopher J. Mehling |
| | Lucinda C. Shirooni |

ASSOCIATES

| C. Houston Ebert | Howard L. Tankersley |
| | Alice G. Keys |

OF COUNSEL

| Robert W. Carran | Norbert J. Bischoff |
| | F. Edward Worland, Jr. |

For full biographical listings, see the Martindale-Hubbell Law Directory

DANVILLE,* Boyle Co.

SHEEHAN, BARNETT & HAYS, P.S.C. (AV)

114 South Fourth Street, P.O. Box 1517, 40423-1517
Telephone: 606-236-2641; 606-734-7552
FAX: 606-236-1483

| James G. Sheehan, Jr. | Edward D. Hays |
| James William Barnett | Rebecca Lynn Rice |

Representative Clients: Bank One; National City Bank; Great Financial Bank; Kentucky Farm Bureau Mutual Insurance Co.; Motorist Mutual Insurance Co.; R.R. Donnelley & Sons, Inc.; State Automobile Mutual Insurance Co.; City of Danville; Shelter Insurance Co.; Trim Masters, Inc.

For full biographical listings, see the Martindale-Hubbell Law Directory

FRANKFORT,* Franklin Co.

WILLIAM M. JOHNSON (AV)

Suite 3, Sower Building, 219 St. Clair Street, 40601
Telephone: 502-223-2322
FAX: 502-223-2666

ASSOCIATE
Geoffrey B. Greenawalt

Reference: Farmers Bank & Capital Trust Co.

For full biographical listings, see the Martindale-Hubbell Law Directory

GEORGETOWN,* Scott Co.

E. DURWARD WELDON (AV)

217 East Main Street, 40324
Telephone: 502-863-1285

Approved Attorney for: Lawyers Title Insurance Corporation of Richmond, Virginia; Louisville Title Division of Commonwealth Land Title Insurance Co. (Binder Agent); The Equitable Life Assurance Society of the United States.

For full biographical listings, see the Martindale-Hubbell Law Directory

GLASGOW,* Barren Co.

GARMON & GOODMAN (AV)

139 North Public Square, P.O. Box 663, 42142-0663
Telephone: 502-651-8812
Telecopier: 502-651-8846

MEMBERS OF FIRM

Larry D. Garmon   Charles A. Goodman III

Approved Attorneys for: Commonwealth Land Title Insurance Co. (agent); Chicago Title Insurance Co.
References: Trans Financial Bank, N.A., Glasgow, Ky; The New Farmers National Bank of Glasgow; South Central Bank of Barren County, Inc., Glasgow, Ky.; Farm Credit Services of Mid-America, ACA; Farmers Home Administration; Commonwealth Relocation Services.

For full biographical listings, see the Martindale-Hubbell Law Directory

HERBERT & HERBERT (AV)

135 North Public Square, P.O. Box 1000, 42141
Telephone: 502-651-9000
Fax: 502-651-3317
Email: h&hlaw@glasgow-ky.com

MEMBERS OF FIRM

H. Jefferson Herbert, Jr.   Betty Reece Herbert

Representative Clients: South Central Bank, South Broadway, Glasgow, Kentucky; Resort Financial Services, Inc., Park City, Kentucky; Commonwealth Land Title Insurance Co., Louisville, Kentucky; Pan-Osten Co.

For full biographical listings, see the Martindale-Hubbell Law Directory

HENDERSON,* Henderson Co.

KING, DEEP AND BRANAMAN (AV)

127 North Main Street, P.O. Box 43, 42420
Telephone: 502-827-1852
FAX: 502-826-7729

MEMBERS OF FIRM

Leo King (1893-1982)   Harry L. Mathison, Jr.
William M. Deep (1920-1990) W. Mitchell Deep, Jr.
William Branaman   H. Randall Redding
    Dorin E. Luck

ASSOCIATES

Leslie M. Newman   Greg L. Gager

Counsel for: Har-Ken Oil Co.; Equitable Resources Corp.; Farm Credit Services; Ohio Valley National Bank; Commonwealth Land Title Insurance Co.; Able Energy Co.; Lamar Properties; Hercules Petroleum; First Indiana Bank.

For full biographical listings, see the Martindale-Hubbell Law Directory

LEXINGTON,* Fayette Co.

GERALDS, MOLONEY & JONES (AV)

259 West Short Street, 40507
Telephone: 606-255-7946

R. P. Moloney (1902-1963) Billy W. Sherrow
Donald P. Moloney (1921-1972) John P. Schrader
Richard P. Moloney (1929-1972) E. Douglas Stephan
Oscar H. Geralds, Jr.   Robert L. Swisher
Michael R. Moloney   John G. Rice
Ernest H. Jones, II   Frances Geralds Rohlfing
    Gail Luhn Pyle

(See Next Column)

Representative Clients: Bank of the Bluegrass & Trust Co.; Norwest Mortgage Corporation; Waterfield Financial Corporation; PHH Homequity Corporation; Commonwealth Land Title Insurance Co. (Issuing Agent).
Reference: Bank of the Bluegrass & Trust Co.

For full biographical listings, see the Martindale-Hubbell Law Directory

LANDRUM & SHOUSE (AV)

106 West Vine Street, P.O. Box 951, 40588-0951
Telephone: 606-255-2424
Facsimile: 606-233-0308
Louisville, Kentucky Office: 400 West Market Street, Suite 1550, 40202.
Telephone: 502-589-7616.
Facsimile: 502-589-2119.

MEMBERS OF FIRM

John H. Burrus   William C. Shouse
   Mark L. Moseley

District Attorneys: CSX Transportation, Inc.
Special Trial Counsel: Ford Motor Co. and Affiliates (Eastern Kentucky); Clark Equipment Co.
Representative Clients: The Continental Insurance Cos.; U.S. Insurance Group; U.S. Fidelity & Guaranty Co.; Ohio Casualty Insurance Co.; CIGNA; Royal Insurance Cos.

For Complete List of Firm Personnel, See General Section

For full biographical listings, see the Martindale-Hubbell Law Directory

MARTIN, OCKERMAN & BRABANT (AV)

200 North Upper Street, 40507
Telephone: 606-254-4401
Fax: 606-231-7367
Email: ockerman@counsel.com

MEMBERS OF FIRM

Hogan Yancey (1881-1960) Thomas C. Brabant
William B. Martin (1895-1975) Foster Ockerman, Jr.
   Madeleine T. Baugh

OF COUNSEL

Foster Ockerman

Counsel for: Lexington Federal Savings Bank; Good Samaritan Foundation, Inc.; Equity Property and Development Co.; Park Communications of KY (WTVQ); AAA Blue Grass/Kentucky; Turfland Mall.
Reference: Bank One, Lexington, N.A.

For full biographical listings, see the Martindale-Hubbell Law Directory

MILLER, GRIFFIN & MARKS, P.S.C. (AV)

Suite 700 Security Trust Building, 271 West Short Street, 40507-1292
Telephone: 606-255-6676
Telecopier: 606-259-1562
URL: http://www.mis.net/mgm/

Harry B. Miller, Jr.   Michael D. Meuser
James M. Marks (1928-1963) Thomas C. Marks
Robert S. Miller   Theodore E. Cowen
Thomas W. Miller   Judith K. Jones
Catesby Woodford   Stephen G. Amato
Donald R. Rose   Carroll M. Redford, III
Frank T. Becker   Helen M. Marks

Representative Clients: Pierson-Trapp Co. (Real Estate Developers); Wiseman Homes, Inc.; Fountain Forestry, Inc.; Citicorp; Farmers Bank of Owingsville; Anderson National Bank; Radnor Homes, Inc.; Equity Services, Inc.; Profressive Mortgage Company; Fifth Third Bank.
Reference: Bank One Lexington, N.A.

For full biographical listings, see the Martindale-Hubbell Law Directory

STOLL, KEENON & PARK, LLP (AV)

201 E. Main Street, Suite 1000, 40507-1380
Telephone: 606-231-3000
Telecopier: 606-253-1093; 606-253-1027
Frankfort, Kentucky Office: 307 Washington Street, 40601.
Telephone: 502-875-6220.
Telecopier: 502-875-6235.
Louisville, Kentucky Office: 400 West Market Street, Suite 2650, 40202-3377.
Telephone: 502-568-9100.
Telecopier: 502-568-5700.

MEMBERS OF FIRM

William M. Lear, Jr.   Frank L. Wilford
Herbert A. Miller, Jr.   Robert W. Kellerman
Gary W. Barr   Rena Gardner Wiseman
   Dan M. Rose

ASSOCIATES

Richard A. Nunnelley   Steven B. Loy

Representative Clients: Ball Homes, Inc.; National Development Council; McDonalds Corp.; Kentucky River Coal Corp.; Super America, Inc.; Bank One.

(See Next Column)

STOLL, KEENON & PARK LLP—*Continued*

For Complete List of Firm Personnel, See General Section

For full biographical listings, see the Martindale-Hubbell Law Directory

VIMONT & WILLS (AV)

Suite 300, 155 East Main Street, 40507-1317
Telephone: 606-252-2202
Telecopier: 606-259-2927

MEMBERS OF FIRM

Richard E. Vimont	Bernard F. Lovely, Jr.

Richard M. Wehrle

ASSOCIATE

J. Thomas Rawlings

For full biographical listings, see the Martindale-Hubbell Law Directory

LOUISVILLE,* Jefferson Co.

JANE D. LOLLIS (AV)

Suite 400, Starks Building, 455 South Fourth Avenue, 40202
Telephone: 502-562-0760
Fax: 502-587-0231

For full biographical listings, see the Martindale-Hubbell Law Directory

MACKENZIE & PEDEN, P.S.C. (AV)

650 Starks Building, 455 South Fourth Avenue, 40202-2509
Telephone: 502-589-1110
Fax: 502-589-1117
Other Louisville, Kentucky Office: 8311 Shelbyville Road.
Telephone: 502-426-6688.
Fax: 502-425-0561.

William B. Peden (Retired)	James T. Lobb
Thomas G. Mooney (1939-1991)	Valerie T. Mayer (Resident)
Wm. A. MacKenzie (Resident)	Edward H. Bartenstein
John G. Crutchfield	Judith B. Hoge
Wayne J. Carroll	Sidney L. Hymson
James C. Hickey	Lee Ann Risner
B. Carlton Neat, III	Charles T. Baxter
Robert W. Dickey	John Patrick Hamm
William B. Bardenwerper (Resident)	

OF COUNSEL

Walker C. Cunningham, Jr.	Robert W. Riley (Resident)
Lawrence J. Phillips	Stephen A. Schwager

Representative Clients: Allstate Insurance Co.; American States Insurance Co.; The Fund Insurance Companies; State Automobile Mutual Insurance Co..

For full biographical listings, see the Martindale-Hubbell Law Directory

HENRY B. MANN (AV)

22nd Floor Citizens Plaza, 40202
Telephone: 502-587-6544

References: Bank One; PNC Bank, Kentucky; Bank of Louisville; National City Bank, Kentucky.

MAPOTHER & MAPOTHER (AV)

801 West Jefferson Street, 40202
Telephone: 502-587-5400
Fax: 502-587-5444
Email: 103210.1130@compuserve.com
Lexington, Kentucky Office: 177 North Upper Street.
Telephone: 606-253-0003.
Fax: 606-255-3961.
Jeffersonville, Indiana Office: 505 East Seventh Street.
Telephone: 812-288-5059.
Fax: 502-587-5444.
Cincinnati, Ohio Office: Kroger Building, Suite 2220, 1014 Vine Street.
Telephone: 513-381-4888.
Fax: 513-381-3117.
Huntington, West Virginia Office: Morris Building, Suite 701, 845 Fourth Avenue.
Telephone: 304-525-1185.
Fax: 304-529-3764.
Evansville, Indiana Office: 329 Main Street.
Telephone: 812-421-9108.
Fax: 812-421-9109.

MEMBERS OF FIRM

Thomas Cruise Mapother, Jr. (1907-1986)	William R. Mapother
	Thomas L. Canary, Jr.

Charles M. Friedman

Brian P. Conaty (Resident, Huntington, West Virginia Office)	Kathryn Pry Coryell (Resident, Jeffersonville, Indiana Office)
Andrea Fried Neichter	Roberta S. Dunlap (Resident, Evansville, Indiana Office)

(See Next Column)

Dean A. Langdon (Resident, Lexington Office)	Brian E. Chapman (Resident, Cincinnati, Ohio Office)
Lee W. Grace	T. Lawson McSwain, II
Roy Fugitt (Resident, Lexington Office)	Lisa A. Herndon
Susan E. Morton-Smith (Resident, Huntington, West Virginia Office)	

Representative Clients: General Electric Capital Corp; Bank One; National City Bank; PNC Bank; Huntington Mortgage Co.; Metmor Financial Inc.; Boatmen's National Mortgage Inc.; L&N Federal Credit Union; Mellon Mortgage Co.; Ford Motor Credit Co.; Ford Leasing Development Co.

For full biographical listings, see the Martindale-Hubbell Law Directory

MORGAN & POTTINGER, P.S.C. (AV)

601 West Main Street, 40202
Telephone: 502-589-2780
Telecopier: 502-585-3498
Lexington, Kentucky Office: 133 West Short Street.
Telephone: 606-253-1900.
Telecopier: 606-255-2038.
New Albany, Indiana Office: 400 Pearl Street, Suite 100.
Telephone: 812-948-0008.
Telecopier: 812-944-6215.

Patrick E. Morgan	James I. Murray (Resident, Lexington Office)
M. Deane Stewart	

Mark J. Sandlin

For Complete List of Firm Personnel, See General Section

For full biographical listings, see the Martindale-Hubbell Law Directory

RUBIN HAYS & FOLEY (AV)

First Trust Centre 200 South Fifth Street, 40202
Telephone: 502-569-7550
Telecopier: 502-569-7555

MEMBERS OF FIRM

Wm. Carl Fust	Lisa Koch Bryant
Harry Lee Meyer	Sharon C. Hardy
David W. Gray	Charles S. Musson
Irvin D. Foley	W. Randall Jones
Joseph R. Gathright, Jr.	K. Gail Russell

ASSOCIATES

Christian L. Juckett	Courtney Lynn McCall

OF COUNSEL

James E. Fahey	Newman T. Guthrie

Representative Clients: J.C. Bradford & Co., Inc.; J.J.B. Hilliard, W.L. Lyons, Inc.; Huntington National Bank; Liberty National Bank and Trust Company; National City Bank; PNC Bank; Prudential Bache & Co., Inc.; Prudential Securities, Inc.; Society Bank; Stock Yards Bank and Trust Co.

For full biographical listings, see the Martindale-Hubbell Law Directory

TAUSTINE, POST, SOTSKY, BERMAN, FINEMAN & KOHN (AV)

8th Floor Marion E. Taylor Building, 40202
Telephone: 502-589-5760
FAX: 502-584-5927
Email: 73344.624@compuserve.com

MEMBERS OF FIRM

Marvin M. Sotsky	Joseph E. Fineman
	Stanley W. Whetzel, Jr.

ASSOCIATE

Sandra Sotsky Harrison

For full biographical listings, see the Martindale-Hubbell Law Directory

TILFORD, DOBBINS, ALEXANDER, BUCKAWAY & BLACK (AV)

Suite 1400, One Riverfront Plaza, 40202
Telephone: 502-584-6137

MEMBERS OF FIRM

Charles W. Dobbins (1916-1992)	Charles W. Dobbins, Jr.
Henry J. Tilford (1880-1968)	Terrell L. Black
George S. Wetherby (1905-1954)	Mark Wesley Dobbins
Lawrence W. Wetherby (1908-1994)	Stuart E. Alexander, III
John T. Metcalf (1890-1974)	John M. Nader
Stuart E. Alexander	John A. Wilmes
William A. Buckaway, Jr.	Sandra F. Keene
	Thomas J.B. Hurst

David Dwight Cobb, Jr.

OF COUNSEL

Randolph Noe	Carolyn K. Balleisen

LEGAL SUPPORT PERSONNEL

Jennifer Olvey

For full biographical listings, see the Martindale-Hubbell Law Directory

OWENSBORO,* Daviess Co.

KAMUF, YEWELL, PACE & CONDON (AV)

Great Financial Federal Building, 322 Frederica Street, 42301
Telephone: 502-685-3901
Fax: 502-926-2005

MEMBER OF FIRM
Charles J. Kamuf

Representative Clients: Owensboro Municipal Utilities Commission; Lincoln Service Corp.; Hancock County Planning Commission; Daviess County Board of Education; Barmet Aluminum Corp.; Owensboro Sewer Commission; TICOR Title Insurance Co.; Chicago Title Insurance Co.; Owensboro Riverport Authority; Housing Authority of Owensboro.

For Complete List of Firm Personnel, See General Section

For full biographical listings, see the Martindale-Hubbell Law Directory

OWINGSVILLE,* Bath Co.

BYRON & ROBERTS (AV)

25 S. Court Street, 40360
Telephone: 606-674-2911

MEMBERS OF FIRM
Roger A. Byron   Winifred Byron Roberts

General Counsel for: Farmers Bank, Owingsville, Kentucky.
Local Counsel for: Delta Natural Gas Co.
Approved Attorneys for: Lawyers Title Insurance Corp.

For full biographical listings, see the Martindale-Hubbell Law Directory

PIKEVILLE,* Pike Co.

PRUITT AND DE BOURBON LAW FIRM (AV)

The Call Building, Second Street, P.O. Box 339, 41502
Telephone: 606-437-7366; 437-7367; 237-1280
Fax: 606-432-2367

MEMBERS OF FIRM
James P. Pruitt, Jr.   P. Michael de Bourbon

Reference: The Citizen's Bank of Pikeville.

For full biographical listings, see the Martindale-Hubbell Law Directory

SOMERSET,* Pulaski Co.

ADAMS & ADAMS (AV)

35 Public Square, P.O. Box 35, 42502-0035
Telephone: 606-679-6741; 678-4916
Fax: 606-679-3691

MEMBERS OF FIRM
Charles C. Adams   Norma B. Adams

ASSOCIATE
Jane Adams Venters

Counsel for: First and Farmers Bank of Somerset, Inc.; Aluminum Wheel Technology, Inc.
Representative Clients: Community Trust Bank, FSB; Aluminum Wheel Technology, Inc.; Food Fair Cos.; Kentucky Farm Bureau Mutual Insurance Cos.; Cumberland Valley Communications; Shamrock Coal Co.; Railum, Inc.; Hartco Flooring Co.

For full biographical listings, see the Martindale-Hubbell Law Directory

WILLIAMSTOWN,* Grant Co.

THRELKELD & THRELKELD, P.S.C. (AV)

144 N. Main Street, P.O. Box 277, 41097
Telephone: 606-824-3302
FAX: 606-824-3303

William F. Threlkeld   John Brent Threlkeld

Title Attorney for: Eagle Bank.
Approved Attorneys for: Lawyers Title Insurance Corp.; Chicago Title Insurance Co.; Commonwealth Land Title Insurance Co.

For full biographical listings, see the Martindale-Hubbell Law Directory

LOUISIANA

BATON ROUGE,* East Baton Rouge Parish

GUGLIELMO, MARKS, SCHUTTE, TERHOEVE & LOVE (AV)

(A Registered Limited Liability Partnership)
320 Somerulos Street, P.O. Box 3177, 70821-3177
Telephone: 504-387-6966
Fax: 504-387-8338

(See Next Column)

Carey J. Guglielmo   Glen Scott Love
Paul Marks, Jr.   Dawn T. Trabeau-Mire
Charles A. Schutte, Jr.   Joseph W. Mengis
Henry G. Terhoeve   Kevin P. Landreneau

Representative Clients: City National Bank; Greyhound Corp.; The Travelers Insurance Co.; Chrysler Corp.; State Farm Insurance Co's.; Travelers/Aetna Insurance Group; Aetna Life & Casualty Co.

For full biographical listings, see the Martindale-Hubbell Law Directory

KANTROW, SPAHT, WEAVER & BLITZER, A PROFESSIONAL LAW CORPORATION (AV)

Suite 300, City Plaza, 445 North Boulevard, P.O. Box 2997, 70821-2997
Telephone: 504-383-4703
Fax: 504-343-0630; 343-0637

Byron R. Kantrow   Vincent P. Fornias
Carlos G. Spaht   David S. Rubin
Geraldine B. Weaver   Diane L. Crochet
Sidney M. Blitzer, Jr.   Richard F. Zimmerman, Jr.
Paul H. Spaht   Bob D. Tucker
Lee C. Kantrow   Martin E. Golden
John C. Miller   Joseph A. Schittone, Jr.

S. Layne Lee   Connell L. Archey
J. Michael Robinson, Jr.   Randal J. Robert

Representative Clients: CNA Insurance Cos.; Federal Deposit Insurance Corp.; Hartford Insurance Group; Air Products and Chemicals, Inc.; CF Industries, Inc.; AT&T; United Companies Financial Corp.

For full biographical listings, see the Martindale-Hubbell Law Directory

KEAN, MILLER, HAWTHORNE, D'ARMOND, McCOWAN & JARMAN, L.L.P. (AV)

22nd Floor, One American Place, P.O. Box 3513, 70821
Telephone: 504-387-0999
Fax: 504-388-9133
New Orleans, Louisiana Office: Energy Centre, Suite 1470, 1100 Poydras Street.
Telephone: 504-585-3050.
Fax: 504-585-3051.
Plaquemine, Louisiana Office: Suite 10, 23425 Railroad Avenue.
Telephone: 504-687-9845.
Fax: 504-382-3445.

MEMBERS OF FIRM
Ben R. Miller, Jr.   Isaac M. Gregorie, Jr.
Robert A. Hawthorne, Jr.   G. Blane Clark, Jr.

Mark D. Mese   Dean Paul Cazenave

Representative Clients: American General Investment Corporation, Houston, TX; Commercial Properties Development Corporation, Baton Rouge, LA; DSM Copolymer, Inc., Baton Rouge, LA; Exxon Pipeline Company, Houston, TX; First American Title Insurance Company, Santa Anna, CA; Georgia Gulf Corporation, Atlanta, GA; Georgia-Pacific Corporation, Atlanta, GA; Greater Baton Rouge Association of Realtors, Inc., Baton Rouge, LA; Piccadilly Cafeterias, Inc., Baton Rouge, LA; Shell Pipe Line Company, Houston, TX.

For Complete List of Firm Personnel, See General Section

For full biographical listings, see the Martindale-Hubbell Law Directory

KIZER, HOOD & MORGAN, L.L.P. (AV)

A Partnership including a Professional Corporation
748 Main Street, 70802-5526
Telephone: 504-387-3121
Fax: 504-387-5611
Email: KHMLLP@AOL.COM

Roland C. Kizer (1899-1988)   Ralph E. Hood
Roland C. Kizer, Jr., (Ltd., A   J. Donald Morgan
  Law Corporation)   Walter N. O'Roark, III
         Stacy G. Butler

Representative Clients: Hibernia National Bank; Bank One, Louisiana, N.A.; The Dime Savings Bank of New York, FSB; G.E. Capital Asset Management Corp.; Bankers Systems, Inc.; United Companies Lending Corporation; Rabenhorst Life Insurance Co.; General Equipment, Inc. d/b/a Scott General; Old South Builders, Inc.; P.P.R., Inc.

For full biographical listings, see the Martindale-Hubbell Law Directory

JAMES — KEN– McCAY (AV)

10500 Coursey Boulevard, Suite 305, 70816-4039
Telephone: 504-292-9470
Fax: 504-295-1073
Watts: 1-800-495-7356

For full biographical listings, see the Martindale-Hubbell Law Directory

LAKE CHARLES,* Calcasieu Parish

BERGSTEDT & MOUNT (AV)

Second Floor, Magnolia Life Building, P.O. Drawer 3004, 70602-3004
Telephone: 318-433-3004
Facsimile: 318-433-8080

MEMBERS OF FIRM

Thomas M. Bergstedt   Benjamin W. Mount

ASSOCIATES

Van C. Seneca   Gregory P. Marceaux
Billy E. Loftin, Jr.

OF COUNSEL

Charles S. Ware

Representative Clients: Armstrong World Industries; Ashland Oil Co.; CIGNA Property & Casualty Companies; Homequity; Lake Area Medical Center; Leach Company; Olin Corporation; Terra Corporation; Town of Iowa; R. D. Werner Company.

For full biographical listings, see the Martindale-Hubbell Law Directory

THE CARMOUCHE LAW FIRM A PROFESSIONAL CORPORATION (AV)

Bank One Tower, 901 Lakeshore Drive, Suite 900, P.O. Drawer 2001, 70601-5270
Telephone: 318-433-0355
Telecopier: 318-433-1274
Email: clf@carmouche.com

John F. Robichaux   John F. Wadsack

Elizabeth B. Hollins

For full biographical listings, see the Martindale-Hubbell Law Directory

METAIRIE, Jefferson Parish

DWYER & CAMBRE, A PROFESSIONAL LAW CORPORATION (AV)

3421 N. Causeway Boulevard Suite 707, 70002
Telephone: 504-838-9090
Fax: 504-838-9187

Stephen I. Dwyer   Susanne M. Cambre
Gregory J. Charles

For full biographical listings, see the Martindale-Hubbell Law Directory

NEW ORLEANS,* Orleans Parish

BARRIOS, KINGSDORF & CASTEIX, L.L.P. (AV)

36th Floor, One Shell Square, 701 Poydras Street, 70139
Telephone: 504-524-3300
Fax: 504-524-3313

Dawn M. Barrios   Bruce S. Kingsdorf
Barbara Treuting Casteix

For full biographical listings, see the Martindale-Hubbell Law Directory

MIDDLEBERG, RIDDLE & GIANNA (AV)

31st Floor, Place St. Charles, 201 St. Charles Avenue, 70170-3100
Telephone: 504-525-7200
Telecopier: 504-581-5983
Dallas, Texas Office: 2323 Bryan Street, Suite 1600.
Telephone: 214-220-6300;
Telecopier: 214-220-2785.
Austin, Texas Office: 1300 South Mopac Expressway, First Floor.
Telephone: 512-434-8334.

MEMBERS OF FIRM

Ira Joel Middleberg   Dominic J. Gianna
Michael Lee Riddle
  (Austin and Dallas, Texas)

Paul J. Mirabile   Tina S. Clark
John D. Person   E. Ralph Lupin
Alan Dean Weinberger   A.J. Herbert, III
L. Marlene Quarles   Marshall J. Simien, Jr.
Ronald J. Vega   Wade P. Webster
Edward T. Suffern, Jr.   Brian G. Meissner
Rebecca J. King

For full biographical listings, see the Martindale-Hubbell Law Directory

STEEG AND O'CONNOR (AV)

Suite 3201 Place St. Charles, 201 St. Charles Avenue, 70170
Telephone: 504-582-1199
Fax: 504-582-1240

(See Next Column)

Moise S. Steeg, Jr.   Randy Opotowsky
Henry F. O'Connor, Jr.   Odom B. Heebe
Robert M. Steeg   Rose H. Delaney
Charles L. Stern, Jr.   Rose McCabe Le Breton
Odom B. Heebe, Jr.

OF COUNSEL

Bernhardt C. Heebe   Louis M. Jones

Reference: Whitney National Bank of New Orleans.

For full biographical listings, see the Martindale-Hubbell Law Directory

SHREVEPORT,* Caddo Parish

BARLOW AND HARDTNER L.C. (AV)

Tenth Floor, Louisiana Tower, 401 Edwards Street, 71101-3289
Telephone: 318-227-1131
Telecopier: 318-227-1141
Mailing Address: P.O. Box 8, Shreveport, Louisiana, 71161-0008

Quintin T. Hardtner, III   Stephen E. Ramey
Malcolm S. Murchison   Philip E. Downer, III
Jay A. Greenleaf

Representative Clients: The Brinkmann Corporation; General Electric Co.; Ivan Smith Furniture Company; Transcontinental Tower, L.C.; Kelley Oil Corporation; NorAm Energy Corp. (formerly Arkla, Inc.); Central and South West Company; Panhandle Eastern Corp.; Pennzoil Producing Co.; Ashland Oil, Inc.

For Complete List of Firm Personnel, See General Section

For full biographical listings, see the Martindale-Hubbell Law Directory

WEEMS, WRIGHT, SCHIMPF, HAYTER & CARMOUCHE, A PROFESSIONAL LAW CORPORATION (AV)

912 Kings Highway, 71104
Telephone: 318-222-2100
Fax: 318-226-5100

Ronald R. Weems   John O. Hayter, III
Kenneth P. Wright   John W. Pou

John C. Geyer

Representative Clients: First American Title Insurance Company; Lawyer's Title Insurance Company; Hibernia National Bank; Barksdale Federal Credit Union; Farm Credit Bank of Texas; Georgia-Pacific Corporation; Louisiana Title Company; Patterson Insurance; Stewart Title Guaranty Company.

For full biographical listings, see the Martindale-Hubbell Law Directory

WINNFIELD,* Winn Parish

SIMMONS AND DERR (AV)

Simmons Building, Church Street, P.O. Box 525, 71483
Telephone: 318-628-3951

MEMBERS OF FIRM

Kermit M. Simmons   Jacque D. Derr

Reference: Bank of Winnfield & Trust Co.

For full biographical listings, see the Martindale-Hubbell Law Directory

MAINE

AUBURN,* Androscoggin Co.

TRAFTON & MATZEN (AV)

Ten Minot Avenue (At Court Street), P.O. Box 470, 04212-0470
Telephone: 207-784-4531
Fax: 207-784-8738

Willis A. Trafton, Jr. (1918-1994)

MEMBERS OF FIRM

M. Kelly Matzen   Richard L. Trafton
Barbara L. Raimondi

Representative Clients: Peoples Heritage Savings Bank; Fleet Bank of Maine; Mid State College; Androscoggin Valley Council of Governments; Grace-lawn Memorial Park; Damon Refrigeration, Inc.

For full biographical listings, see the Martindale-Hubbell Law Directory

BANGOR, * Penobscot Co.

EATON, PEABODY, BRADFORD & VEAGUE, P.A. (AV)

Fleet Center-Exchange Street, P.O. Box 1210, 04402-1210
Telephone: 207-947-0111
Telecopier: 207-942-3040
Email: epbv@aol.com
Augusta, Maine Office: 2 Central Plaza.
Telephone: 207-622-3747.
Telecopier: 207-622-9732.
Blue Hill, Maine Office: One East Blue Hill Road.
Telephone: 207-374-2812.
Telecopier: 207-374-2548.
Brunswick, Maine Office: 167 Park Row.
Telephone: 207-729-1144.
Telecopier: 207-729-1140. .
Camden, Maine Office: 7-9 Washington Street.
Telephone: 207-236-3325.
Telecopier: 207-236-8611.
Dover-Foxcroft, Maine Office: 30 East Main Street.
Telephone: 207-564-8378.
Telecopier: 207-564-7059.

Edward D. Leonard, III	Terry W. Calderwood
Douglas M. Smith	(Resident, Camden Office)
(Dover-Foxcroft and Augusta	Paul L. Gibbons
Offices)	(Resident, Camden Office)
John A. Cunningham	Jonathan B. Huntington
(Resident, Brunswick Office)	(Resident, Dover-Foxcroft
Karen A. Huber	Office)

OF COUNSEL
Martin L. Wilk (Resident, Brunswick Office)

Lorena R. Rush
A List of Representative Clients available upon request.

For Complete List of Firm Personnel, See General Section

For full biographical listings, see the Martindale-Hubbell Law Directory

GROSS, MINSKY, MOGUL & SINGAL, P.A. (AV)

Key Plaza, 23 Water Street, P.O. Box 917, 04402-0917
Telephone: 207-942-4644
Telecopier: 207-942-3699
Email: gmm&s-law@atlsysnet.com *URL:*
http://www.atlsysnet.com/gmms

Edward I. Gross (Retired)	George C. Schelling
Jules L. Mogul (1930-1994)	Edward W. Gould
Norman Minsky	Steven J. Mogul
George Z. Singal	James R. Wholly
Louis H. Kornreich	Daniel A. Pileggi
	Philip K. Clarke

Wayne P. Libhart (Retired)	James S. Nixon
Sandra L. Rothera	F. Todd Lowell

Approved Attorneys For: First American Title Insurance Co.; Lawyers Title Insurance Co.
Agent For: First American Title Insurance Co.; Lawyers Title Insurance Co.

For full biographical listings, see the Martindale-Hubbell Law Directory

VAFIADES, BROUNTAS & KOMINSKY (AV)

Key Plaza, 23 Water Street, P.O. Box 919, 04402-0919
Telephone: 207-947-6915
Telecopier: 207-941-0863

MEMBER OF FIRM
Marvin H. Glazier
OF COUNSEL
Nicholas P. Brountas

Approved Attorneys For: Chicago Title Insurance Co.; Lawyers Title Insurance Corp.; New York TRW; Title Insurance, Inc.

For Complete List of Firm Personnel, See General Section

For full biographical listings, see the Martindale-Hubbell Law Directory

BAR HARBOR, Hancock Co.

FENTON, CHAPMAN, FENTON, SMITH & KANE, P.A. (AV)

109 Main Street, P.O. Box B, 04609
Telephone: 207-288-3331
FAX: 207-288-9326

William Fenton	Nathaniel R. Fenton
Douglas B. Chapman	Chadbourn H. Smith

Margaret A. Timothy
Reference: Bar Harbor Banking and Trust Co.

(See Next Column)

For Complete List of Firm Personnel, See General Section

For full biographical listings, see the Martindale-Hubbell Law Directory

ELLSWORTH, * Hancock Co.

HALE & HAMLIN (AV)

10 State Street, P.O. Box 729, 04605
Telephone: 207-667-2561
Telefax: 207-667-8790
URL: http://www.halehaml.com

Eugene Hale (1836-1918)	Philip R. Lovell (1899-1961)
Hannibal E. Hamlin (1858-1938)	Charles J. Hurley (1908-1981)
	Atherton Fuller (Retired)

MEMBERS OF FIRM
Barry K. Mills	Jeffrey W. Jones
Dale L. Worthen	Melissa Moll

ASSOCIATE
Laura Yustak Smith

Approved Attorneys for: Lawyers Title Insurance Corp.

For full biographical listings, see the Martindale-Hubbell Law Directory

KENNEBUNK, York Co.

REAGAN, ADAMS & CADIGAN (AV)

Eleven Main Street, P.O. Box 709, 04043
Telephone: 207-985-7181
Telecopier: 207-985-7003

MEMBERS OF FIRM
Thomas J. Reagan	Wayne T. Adams
	Paul W. Cadigan

Counsel for: Kennebunk Savings Bank.

For full biographical listings, see the Martindale-Hubbell Law Directory

PORTLAND, * Cumberland Co.

JENSEN BAIRD GARDNER & HENRY (AV)

Ten Free Street, P.O. Box 4510, 04112
Telephone: 207-775-7271
Telecopier: 207-775-7935
York County Office: 419 Alfred Street, Biddeford, Maine.
Telephone: 207-282-5107.
Telecopier: 207-282-6301.

OF COUNSEL
John D. Bradford (Resident, York County Office)
MEMBERS OF FIRM
Walter E. Webber	Ralph W. Austin (Resident,
Kenneth M. Cole, III	York County Office)
David J. Jones (Resident, York	Ronald A. Epstein
County Office)	Leslie E. Lowry, III

Representative Clients: General Motors Acceptance Corp.; York Insurance Co.; Maine Mall; Key Bank of Maine; Commonwealth Land Title Insurance Co.; Augusta Mall; Shaw's Supermarkets.

For Complete List of Firm Personnel, See General Section

For full biographical listings, see the Martindale-Hubbell Law Directory

PIERCE ATWOOD (AV)

One Monument Square, 04101
Telephone: 207-791-1100
Fax: 207-791-1350
Email: info@PierceAtwood.com
Augusta, Maine Office: 77 Winthrop Street.
Telephone: 207-622-6311.
Fax: 207-623-9367.
Newburyport, Massachusetts Office: 6 Harris Street.
Telephone: 508-465-9599.
Fax: 508-465-9945.

MEMBERS OF FIRM
Dennis C. Keeler	Elaine S. Falender

ASSOCIATES
James M. Saffian	Christopher M. Dawe
David P. Littell	Helen L. Edmonds
Marcia A. Metcalf	(Not admitted in ME)

COUNSEL
Judith A. Fletcher Woodbury

For Complete List of Firm Personnel, See General Section

For full biographical listings, see the Martindale-Hubbell Law Directory

Portland—Continued

PRETI, FLAHERTY, BELIVEAU & PACHIOS (AV)

A Limited Liability Company
443 Congress Street, P.O. Box 11410, 04104-7410
Telephone: 207-791-3000
Telecopier: 207-791-3111
Email: admin@pfbpnet.com
Augusta, Maine Office: 45 Memorial Circle, P.O. Box 1058, 04332-1058.
Telephone: 207-623-5300.
Telecopier: 207-623-2914.

MEMBERS OF FIRM

Michael J. Gentile (Augusta Office)	Dennis C. Sbrega
Eric P. Stauffer	Estelle A. Lavoie
James C. Pitney, Jr. (Augusta Office)	Susan E. LoGiudice
	Michael L. Sheehan

OF COUNSEL
Jeanne T. Cohn-Connor

Representative Clients: Guy Gannett Publishing Co.; Key Bank of Maine; RECOLL Management Corp.; Patten Corporation of Maine; Fleet Bank of Maine; Liberty Group.

For Complete List of Firm Personnel, See General Section

For full biographical listings, see the Martindale-Hubbell Law Directory

TROUBH, HEISLER & PIAMPIANO, P.C. (AV)

511 Congress Street, P.O. Box 9711, 04104-5011
Telephone: 207-780-6789
Fax: 207-774-2339

William B. Troubh	Thomas E. Getchell
Edwin A. Heisler	Michael Richards
Robert J. Piampiano	William K. McKinley
Kevin M. Gillis	Daniel F. Gilligan
Michael P. Boyd	Paul S. Bulger

John G. Richardson	Linda L. Sears
Daniel R. Felkel	

For full biographical listings, see the Martindale-Hubbell Law Directory

YORK, York Co.

ERWIN, OTT, CLARK & CAMPBELL (AV)

16A Woodbridge Road, P.O. Box 545, 03909
Telephone: 207-363-5208
Facsimile: 207-363-5322

MEMBERS OF FIRM

Frank E. Hancock (1923-1988)	John P. Campbell
James S. Erwin	David N. Ott
Jeffery J. Clark	

For full biographical listings, see the Martindale-Hubbell Law Directory

STRATER & STRATER, P.A. (AV)

266 York Street, P.O. Box 69, 03909
Telephone: 207-363-2900
Telefax: 207-363-2902

David Strater	Nicholas S. Strater

Representative Clients: Kennebunk Savings Bank; York Sewer District.
Approved Attorneys for: National Attorneys Title Insurance Co.; Lawyers Title Insurance Corp.; American Title Insurance Co.; Chicago Title Insurance Co.; Commonwealth Land Title Insurance Co.
References: Kennebunk Savings Bank; York Sewer District.

For full biographical listings, see the Martindale-Hubbell Law Directory

MARYLAND

ANNAPOLIS,* Anne Arundel Co.

BENJAMIN MICHAELSON, JR., P.A. (AV)

275 West Street, Suite 216, 21401
Telephone: 410-267-8178
Baltimore: 410-269-6966
Washington, D.C.: 301-261-2889
Fax: 410-267-8072

Benjamin Michaelson, Jr.

Representative Clients: Annapolis Banking and Trust Co.; First General Mortgage Co.

For full biographical listings, see the Martindale-Hubbell Law Directory

P. JAMES UNDERWOOD (AV)

9A Maryland Avenue, P.O. Box 2335, 21404
Telephone: 410-268-4247

Representative Clients: R D K & W Joint Venture; Kaufmann Limited Partnership; W K D & R Real Estate Company; Elanne Corporation.

BALTIMORE,* (Independent City)

ABRAMOFF, NEUBERGER AND LINDER, LLP (AV)

Suite 800, 250 West Pratt Street, 21201
Telephone: 410-539-8300
Fax: 410-539-8304

MEMBERS OF FIRM

David B. Abramoff	Rita A. Linder
Anilkumar J. Hoffberg	Richard S. Lehmann
Yaakov S. Neuberger	Steven M. Rosen
Nancy Haas	

OF COUNSEL
Stephen F. Bisbee

For full biographical listings, see the Martindale-Hubbell Law Directory

BALLARD SPAHR ANDREWS & INGERSOLL (AV)

300 East Lombard Street, 19th Floor, 21202-3268
Telephone: 410-528-5600
Fax: 410-528-5650
Philadelphia, Pennsylvania Office: 1735 Market Street, 51st Floor.
Telephone: 215-665-8500.
Fax: 215-864-8999.
Harrisburg, Pennsylvania Office: 105 North Front Street.
Telephone: 717-236-3333.
Fax: 717-236-3884.
Denver, Colorado Office: Seventeenth Street Plaza Building, Suite 2300, 1225 17th Street.
Telephone: 303-292-2400.
Fax: 303-296-3956.
Salt Lake City, Utah Office: One Utah Center, 201 South Main Street, Suite 1200.
Telephone: 801-531-3000.
Fax: 801-531-3001.
Washington, D.C. Office: Suite 900 East, 555 13th Street, N.W.
Telephone: 202-383-8800.
Fax: 202-383-8877; 383-8893.
Camden, New Jersey Office: 800 Hudson Square, 5th Floor.
Telephone: 609-541-5577.
Fax: 609-541-8272.

Ronald P. Fish	Gregory Reed
Morton P. Fisher, Jr.	Jane Ennis Sheehan
Sophie D. Goetz	Raymond G. Truitt
Charles R. Moran	Fred Wolf, III

Alan W. Adamson	Van Clinton Durrer, II
Athena Katcheves Alexandrides	Fran S. Glushakow-Smith
Jon M. Laria	

For full biographical listings, see the Martindale-Hubbell Law Directory

GALLAGHER, EVELIUS & JONES (AV)

Park Charles Suite 400, 218 North Charles Street, 21201
Telephone: 410-727-7702
Telecopier: 410-837-3079

MEMBERS OF FIRM

Francis X. Gallagher (1928-1972)	Linda H. Jones
C. Edward Jones (Retired)	Jack C. Tranter
John C. Evelius	Christopher J. Fritz
Richard O. Berndt	David E. Raderman
Thomas N. Biddison, Jr.	Peter E. Keith
Robert R. Kern, Jr.	Nita L. Schultz
Saul E. Gilstein	Michael W. Skojec
Thomas B. Lewis	Kathryn Kelley Hoskins
Bonnie Abrams Travieso	Mark P. Keener
Stephen A. Goldberg	Kevin J. Davidson
	Eileen M. Lunga
Lori A. Nicolle	

ASSOCIATES

Kenneth S. Gross	Matthew W. Oakey
Thomas C. Dame	Paula B. Grant
Mary Catherine Collins Gaver	Rebecca A. Weaver
Julie Ellen Squire	Michael J. Henigan
David W. Kinkopf	

LEGAL ASSISTANTS

Patricia C. Quayle	Iris T. H. Heath
Jeanmarie McGlynn	Cheryl J. Reinke

Representative Clients: Roman Catholic Archdiocese of Baltimore; Bozzuto & Associates, Inc.; The Enterprise Foundation; Mercy Medical Center, Inc.; First National Bank of Maryland.

For full biographical listings, see the Martindale-Hubbell Law Directory

Baltimore—Continued

MARTIN, JUNGHANS, SNYDER & BERNSTEIN, P.A. (AV)

Redwood Tower, Suite 2000, 217 East Redwood Street, 21202
Telephone: 410-547-7163
Facsimile: 410-547-1605

Gerard P. Martin	David L. Snyder
Paula M. Junghans	Gregg L. Bernstein

Kimberly Dunn Spelman   William S. Heyman

OF COUNSEL
Steven J. Sibel

LEGAL SUPPORT PERSONNEL
Linda S. Baker (Administrator)   Meg L. Zimmerman (Paralegal)

For full biographical listings, see the Martindale-Hubbell Law Directory

SOMMER & STEELE, L.L.C. (AV)

The B & O Building, Suite 930, Two North Charles Street, 21201
Telephone: 410-783-2790
Fax: 410-783-2797

Peter J. Sommer   Deborah Williams Steele

ASSOCIATE
Samuel Joseph Mangione

For Complete List of Firm Personnel, See General Section

For full biographical listings, see the Martindale-Hubbell Law Directory

VENABLE ATTORNEYS AT LAW VENABLE, BAETJER AND HOWARD, LLP (AV)

A Partnership including Professional Corporations
1800 Mercantile Bank & Trust Building, 2 Hopkins Plaza, 21201
Telephone: 410-244-7400
Email: INFO@Venable.win.net
Washington, D.C. Office: Venable, Baetjer, Howard & Civiletti LLP. Suite 1000, 1201 New York Avenue, N.W.
Telephone: 202-962-4800.
McLean, Virginia Office: Suite 400, 2010 Corporate Ridge.
Telephone: 703-760-1600.
Rockville, Maryland Office: Suite 500, One Church Street, P. O. Box 1906.
Telephone: 301-217-5600.
Towson, Maryland Office: 210 Allegheny Avenue, P. O. Box 5517.
Telephone: 410-494-6200.

MEMBERS OF FIRM

Russell Ronald Reno, Jr. (P.C.)	Sondra Harans Block (Resident,
Thomas P. Perkins, III (P.C.)	Rockville, Maryland Office)
James A. Cole	Thomas B. Hudson (Also at
Benjamin R. Civiletti (P.C.)	Washington, D.C. Office)
(Also at Washington, D.C.	David G. Lane (Resident,
and Towson, Maryland	McLean, Virginia Office)
Offices)	James K. Archibald (Also at
John B. Howard (Resident,	Washington, D.C. Office)
Towson, Maryland Office)	Edward L. Wender (P.C.)
David E. Belcher	George F. Pappas (Also at
Roger W. Titus (Resident,	Washington, D.C. Office)
Rockville, Maryland Office)	Ellen F. Dyke (Not admitted in
Daniel O'C. Tracy, Jr. (Also at	MD; Resident, McLean,
Rockville, Maryland Office)	Virginia Office)
Jan K. Guben (Also at	William D. Quarles (Also at
Washington, D. C Office)	Washington, D.C. and
James D. Wright (P.C.)	Towson, Maryland Offices)
John H. Zink, III (Resident,	Cynthia M. Hahn (Resident,
Towson, Maryland Office)	Towson, Maryland Office)
John G. Milliken (Not admitted	James A. Dunbar (Also at
in MD; Washington, D.C. and	Washington, D.C. Office)
McLean, Virginia Offices)	Robert A. Hoffman (Resident,
Bruce E. Titus (Resident,	Towson, Maryland Office)
McLean, Virginia Office)	J. Michael Brennan (Resident,
Paul T. Glasgow (Resident,	Towson, Maryland Office)
Rockville, Maryland Office)	Kevin L. Shepherd
Joseph C. Wich, Jr. (Resident,	Michael W. Robinson (Resident,
Towson, Maryland Office)	McLean, Virginia Office)

OF COUNSEL

David D. Downes (Resident,	Mary T. Flynn (Not admitted in
Towson, Maryland Office)	MD; Resident, McLean,
Judith A. Armold	Virginia Office)

ASSOCIATES

Courtney G. Capute	Patricia A. Malone (Resident,
Sandra Howard Darby	Towson, Maryland Office)
Mary-Dulany James (Resident,	Vicki Margolis (Also at
Towson, Maryland Office)	Washington, D.C. Office)
Michael S. Kosmas	John T. Prisbe
Christine J. Warren	

For Complete List of Firm Personnel, See General Section

For full biographical listings, see the Martindale-Hubbell Law Directory

---

BEL AIR, * Harford Co.

BROWN, BROWN & BROWN, A PROFESSIONAL ASSOCIATION (AV)

200 South Main Street, 21014
Telephone: 410-838-5500
Baltimore: 410-879-2220
Fax: 410-893-0402

A. Freeborn Brown	Augustus F. Brown
T. Carroll Brown	Albert J. A. Young

A. Frank Carven, III	Christopher R. vanRoden
Harold Douglas Norton	David E. Carey
Ankur P. Dalal	

Attorneys for: Baltimore Gas & Electric Co.; Chesapeake & Potomac Telephone Co.; Aberdeen Proving Ground Federal Credit Union; First Virginia Bank-Central Maryland; First National Bank of Maryland; Bell Atlantic Mobile Systems; First Harbor Securities; Maryland Portable Concrete, Inc. *Approved Counsel for:* The Chicago Title Insurance Co. of Maryland, Inc.

For full biographical listings, see the Martindale-Hubbell Law Directory

STARK & KEENAN, A PROFESSIONAL ASSOCIATION (AV)

30 Office Street, 21014
Telephone: 410-838-5522
Baltimore: 410-879-2222
Fax: 410-879-0688

Elwood V. Stark, Jr.	Judith Cline-Silverstein
Charles B. Keenan, Jr.	Gregory A. Szoka
Edwin G. Carson	Robert S. Lynch

Claire Prin Blomquist	Paul W. Ishak
Kimberly Kahoe Muenter	Lawrence F. Kreis, Jr.

For full biographical listings, see the Martindale-Hubbell Law Directory

---

EASTON, * Talbot Co.

HENRY & PRICE LLC (AV)

117 Bay Street, P.O. Box 838, 21601
Telephone: 410-822-2600
Fax: 410-822-2626

MEMBERS OF FIRM

T. Hughlett Henry (1879-1966)	W. Thomas Fountain
T. Hughlett Henry, Jr.	David C. Bryan
(1910-1994)	Suzanne L. Hood
John G. Billmyre	

ASSOCIATES
Sharon J. Ritter   Nannette G. Grimes

OF COUNSEL
William H. Price, II

Attorneys for: Talbot County Board of Appeals; Town of Preston; Chicago Title Insurance Co. of Maryland; Lawyers Title Insurance Corp.; Delmarva Power & Light Co.; John Hancock Mutual Life Insurance Co.; Metropolitan Life Insurance Co.

For full biographical listings, see the Martindale-Hubbell Law Directory

---

GREENBELT, Prince Georges Co.

STANLEY S. PICKETT (AV)

Suite 414 Capital Office Park, 6411 Ivy Lane, 20770
Telephone: 301-513-0613
Fax: 301-513-0618

Stanley Sinclair Pickett

ASSOCIATE
Gordon J. Brumback

LEGAL SUPPORT PERSONNEL
Stacy S. Pickett (Law Clerk)   Vivian W. Wolfe (Paralegal)

Representative Clients: B.F. Saul Co.; McDonald and Eudy Printers, Inc.; Condominium Management, Inc.; Long & Foster Realtors; Mitron Systems Corp.; Coldwell Banker; Glenanden Housing Authority; Koones & Montgomery, Inc.; Community Associations, Inc.

For full biographical listings, see the Martindale-Hubbell Law Directory

OCEAN CITY, Worcester Co.

WILLIAMS, HAMMOND, MOORE, SHOCKLEY & HARRISON, P.A. (AV)

3509 Coastal Highway, P.O. Box 739, 21842
Telephone: 410-289-3553
Fax: 410-289-4157
Email: whmsh@shore.intercom.net
Berlin, Maryland Office: 11070 Cathell Road, Suite 19.
Telephone: 410-641-8080.
Fax: 410-641-8282.

Marcus J. Williams (1923-1995)	Joseph E. Moore
Edward H. Hammond, Jr.	Raymond C. Shockley
Joseph G. Harrison, Jr.	

J. Richard Collins	Jeffrey A. Pilchard
Regan James Reno Smith	Brian D. Shockley

For full biographical listings, see the Martindale-Hubbell Law Directory

RIVERDALE, Prince Georges Co.

MEYERS, BILLINGSLEY, RODBELL & ROSENBAUM, P.A. (AV)

Suite 400 Berkshire Building, 6801 Kenilworth Avenue, 20737-1385
Telephone: 301-699-5800
Fax: 301-779-5746

William V. Meyers	Robert H. Rosenbaum

Reference: First National Bank of Maryland.

For Complete List of Firm Personnel, See General Section

For full biographical listings, see the Martindale-Hubbell Law Directory

ROCKVILLE,* Montgomery Co.

CHEN, WALSH, TECLER & McCABE (AV)

Suite 300, 200-A Monroe Street, 20850
Telephone: 301-279-9500
FAX: 301-294-5195

MEMBERS OF FIRM

William James Chen, Jr.	Kenneth B. Tecler
John Burgess Walsh, Jr.	John F. McCabe, Jr.

For full biographical listings, see the Martindale-Hubbell Law Directory

RIDGWAY AND GRIFFIN, CHARTERED (AV)

6177 Executive Boulevard, 20852
Telephone: 301-468-2545
Fax: 301-468-3538
Bethesda, Maryland Office: 7250 Woodmont Avenue, Suite 300.
Telephone: 301-654-2560.
Fax: 301-654-0325.
Oakton, Virginia Office: Ridgway, Griffin & Shreves, 2911 Hunter Mill Road, Suite 203.
Telephone: 703-242-2100.
Fax: 703-242-0725.

Richard C. Ridgway	Michael C. Ridgway
James M. Griffin	Robert A. Hickey
Frederick L. Shreves, II (Not admitted in MD; Resident, Oakton, Virginia Office)	

Vincent J. Keegan (Not admitted in MD; Resident, Oakton, Virginia Office)	Mark P. Kestner
	Colleen Smyth Cogan

For full biographical listings, see the Martindale-Hubbell Law Directory

STEIN, SPERLING, BENNETT, DE JONG, DRISCOLL, GREENFEIG & METRO, P.A. (AV)

25 West Middle Lane, 20850
Telephone: 301-340-2020; 800-435-5230
Telecopier: 301-340-8217

Jack A. Garson	Donald N. Sperling

Ann Marie M. Mehlert	Moia T. Gruber

For Complete List of Firm Personnel, See General Section

For full biographical listings, see the Martindale-Hubbell Law Directory

SALISBURY,* Wicomico Co.

ADKINS, POTTS & SMETHURST, L.L.P. (AV)

Suite 600, One Plaza East, P.O. Box 4247, 21803-4247
Telephone: 410-749-0161
Fax: 410-749-5021

(See Next Column)

MEMBERS OF FIRM

E. Dale Adkins, Jr. (1915-1982)	Raymond Stevens Smethurst, Jr.
Charles J. Potts (1910-1994)	Robert B. Taylor
L. Richard Phillips	

Representative Clients: Atlantic Wood Industries, Inc.; Campbell Soup Company; Delmarva Power & Light Co.; G. E. Capital Mortgage Services, Inc.; Lawyers' Title Insurance Corp.; Mellon Bank (DE); PNC Bank; Proko Industries, Inc.; Shopco Group; WBOC-TV.

For full biographical listings, see the Martindale-Hubbell Law Directory

SEABROOK, Prince Georges Co.

FOSSETT & BRUGGER, CHARTERED (AV)

The Aerospace Building, 10210 Greenbelt Road, 20706
Telephone: 301-794-6900
Telecopy: 301-794-7638
La Plata, Maryland Office: 105 LaGrange Avenue, P.O. Box F.
Telephone: 301-934-4200. Washington Line: 301-753-9600.
Fax: 301-870-2884.

George A. Brugger	William M. Shipp
Clarence L. Fossett	John C. Fredrickson
Nancy L. Slepicka	Garland H. Stillwell
Midgett S. Parker, Jr.	Mary A. Liano

LEGAL SUPPORT PERSONNEL

Dean Armstrong (Consulting Land Planner)

Representative Clients: Coscan Washington, Inc.; Citizens Bank & Trust Company of Maryland; The Edward J. DeBartolo Corp.; Ebenezer African Methodist Episcopal Church, Inc.; Greenhorne & O'Mara, Inc.; Kettler Brothers; Michael T. Rose Cos.; The Mutual Life Insurance Company of New York; RE/MAX International, Inc.; Richmond-American Homes; Winchester Homes, Inc.

For full biographical listings, see the Martindale-Hubbell Law Directory

TOWSON,* Baltimore Co.

VENABLE ATTORNEYS AT LAW VENABLE, BAETJER AND HOWARD, LLP (AV)

A Partnership including Professional Corporations
210 Allegheny Avenue, P.O. Box 5517, 21204
Telephone: 410-494-6200
FAX: 410-821-0147
Baltimore, Maryland Office: 1800 Mercantile Bank & Trust Building, 2 Hopkins Plaza.
Telephone: 410-244-7400.
Washington, D.C. Office: Venable, Baetjer, Howard & Civiletti LLP, Suite 1000, 1201 New York Avenue, N.W.
Telephone: 202-962-4800.
McLean, Virginia Office: Suite 400, 2010 Corporate Ridge.
Telephone: 703-760-1600.
Rockville, Maryland Office: Suite 500, One Church Street, P. O. Box 1906.
Telephone: 301-217-5600.

PARTNERS

Benjamin R. Civiletti (P.C.) (Also at Washington, D.C. and Baltimore, Maryland Offices)	Joseph C. Wich, Jr.
	William D. Quarles (Also at Washington, D.C. Office)
John B. Howard	Cynthia M. Hahn
John H. Zink, III	Robert A. Hoffman
	J. Michael Brennan

OF COUNSEL

David D. Downes

ASSOCIATES

Mary-Dulany James	Patricia A. Malone

For Complete List of Firm Personnel, See General Section

For full biographical listings, see the Martindale-Hubbell Law Directory

UPPER MARLBORO,* Prince Georges Co.

KNIGHT, MANZI, BRENNAN, SHAY AND HAM, A PROFESSIONAL ASSOCIATION (AV)

14440 Old Mill Road, 20772
Telephone: 301-952-0100
Annapolis/Baltimore: 410-792-3786
Fax: 301-952-0221
Crofton, Maryland Office: 2411 Crofton Lane, # 26.
Telephone: 301-261-0808.
Fax: 301-261-6945.
Mitchellville, Maryland Office: 12164 Central Avenue, Suite 228.
Telephone: 301-390-0577.
Fax: 301-390-8464.

William E. Knight	John F. Shay, Jr.
Robert A. Manzi	Richard J. Ham
William C. Brennan, Jr.	Martin J. Shuham

Monica M. Haley-Pierson	Norman D. Rivera
Daniel F. Lynch III	Robert L. Lombardo

(See Next Column)

KNIGHT, MANZI, BRENNAN, SHAY AND HAM A PROFESSIONAL ASSOCIATION, *Upper Marlboro—Continued*

OF COUNSEL

Stuart R. Hammett

For full biographical listings, see the Martindale-Hubbell Law Directory

MASSACHUSETTS

ARLINGTON, Middlesex Co.

GRANNAN & MALOY, P.C. (AV)

Suite 408, 22 Mill Street, 02174
Telephone: 617-646-3200
Fax: 617-643-1126

William J. Grannan   Paul F. Maloy

For full biographical listings, see the Martindale-Hubbell Law Directory

*BOSTON,*** Suffolk Co.

ADELSON, GOLDEN & LORIA, P.C. (AV)

Two Center Plaza, 02108
Telephone: 617-227-3730
Fax: 617-227-3353
Email: aglrelaw@pcix.com

Stephen M. Adelson	Leonard M. Simons
Neil D. Golden	Lisa S. Weisman
Martin A. Loria	Michael H. Arwe
Gary P. Sanginario	James A. Kelley

For full biographical listings, see the Martindale-Hubbell Law Directory

BARRON & STADFELD, P.C. (AV)

Two Center Plaza, 02108
Telephone: 617-723-9800
Telecopier: 617-523-8359
Email: PUBLIC@BARRONSTAD.COM *URL:*
HTTP://WWW.BARRONSTAD.COM
Hyannis, Massachusetts Office: 258 Winter Street.
Telephone: 617-778-6622.

Thomas V. Bennett   Julie Taylor Moran
Joseph G. Butler

For Complete List of Firm Personnel, See General Section

For full biographical listings, see the Martindale-Hubbell Law Directory

BERNKOPF, GOODMAN & BASEMAN LLP (AV)

125 Summer Street, 02110-1621
Telephone: 617-790-3000
Telecopier: 617-790-3300

MEMBERS OF FIRM

Abraham K. Cohen (1891-1957)	James B. Fox
Max E. Bernkopf (1919-1967)	Peter B. McGlynn
Sylvan A. Goodman (1935-1981)	Sheryl C. Starr
Harris I. Baseman	Richard B. Michaud
Kenneth M. Goldberg	Lydia G. Chesnick
Alan J. Grace	Martin C. Pomeroy
Marvin N. Geller	Eric R. Allon
Neil R. Markson	David L. Doyle
Gary P. Lilienthal	Barry S. Fischer

ASSOCIATES

John B. Harkavy	James M. Godec
James D. Friedman	Edward W. Wayland
Gwen P. Weisberg	Sharona Eliahou
Bruce D. Levin	Francis C. Morrissey
Richard P. Bennett	Todd D. Goldberg

For full biographical listings, see the Martindale-Hubbell Law Directory

CITY, HAYES, MEAGHER & DISSETTE, P.C. (AV)

50 Congress Street, 02109
Telephone: 617-523-3050
Telecopier: 617-523-5612

Robert D. City	Kieran B. Meagher
James P. Hayes	Michael J. Dissette

Martin R. Fisch	Lewis R. Lear
Philip B. Evans	Philip Di Domenico
	Michael N. O'Connell, Jr.

For full biographical listings, see the Martindale-Hubbell Law Directory

NATHANSON & GOLDBERG, A PROFESSIONAL CORPORATION (AV)

10 Union Wharf, 02109
Telephone: 617-742-9350
Fax: 617-742-3559

Alvin S. Nathanson	Valerie S. Carter
Arthur Goldberg	Shannon M. Fitzpatrick

Stuart J. Frank

For full biographical listings, see the Martindale-Hubbell Law Directory

PALMER & DODGE LLP (AV)

One Beacon Street, 02108
Telephone: 617-573-0100
Facsimile: 617-227-4420

MEMBERS OF FIRM

Raymond M. Murphy	David R. Rodgers
John E. Rattigan, Jr.	Thomas G. Schnorr
	James M. Whalen

COUNSEL

Kathryn Cochrane Murphy

For Complete List of Firm Personnel, See General Section

For full biographical listings, see the Martindale-Hubbell Law Directory

PEABODY & ARNOLD (AV)

A Partnership including Professional Corporations
50 Rowes Wharf, 02110-3342
Telephone: 617-951-2100
Telecopier: 617-951-2125
Providence, Rhode Island Office: One Citizens Plaza, Suite 840.
Telephone: 401-831-8330.
Fax: 401-831-8359.

MEMBERS OF FIRM

Paul J. Ayoub	Michael J. Glazerman
Jonathan Bangs	John R. Gowell, Jr. (Resident,
Michael F. Burke	Providence, Rhode Island
Jason M. Cotton	Office)
Amanda D. Darwin	John A. Kessler, Jr.
John K. Dineen	Suanne C. St. Charles
	Donald E. Vaughan

ASSOCIATES

Robert Payne Fox, Jr.	Mark W. McCarthy
John T. Smolak	John P. Dougherty
	Timothy J. Culver

For Complete List of Firm Personnel, See General Section

For full biographical listings, see the Martindale-Hubbell Law Directory

RACKEMANN, SAWYER & BREWSTER, PROFESSIONAL CORPORATION (AV)

One Financial Center, 02111
Telephone: 617-542-2300
Telecopier: 617-542-7437

William B. Tyler	Janet M. Smith
Henry H. Thayer	Peter Friedenberg
Stephen Carr Anderson	Richard S. Novak
Albert M. Fortier, Jr.	J. David Leslie
Michael F. O'Connell	Sanford M. Matathia
Stuart T. Freeland	Richard J. Gallogly
Alan B. Rubenstein	James A. Wachta
James R. Shea, Jr.	Hanson S. Reynolds
Brian M. Hurley	Donald R. Pinto, Jr.

COUNSEL

Ronald S. Duby	Gordon M. Orloff
Lucy West Behymer	Eric A. Smith

OF COUNSEL

Albert B. Wolfe	George V. Anastas
August R. Meyer	Edward M. Condit
Richard H. Lovell	Alexander H. Spaulding

Margaret L. Hayes	Peter A. Alpert
Daniel J. Ossoff	Ellen M. Harrington
Melissa Langer Ellis	Lauren D. Armstrong
Daniel J. Bailey, III	Robert B. Foster
Michael S. Giaimo	Andrew H. Butler
Maura E. Murphy	Gayle E. Parlee
Mary L. Gallant	Elizabeth A. Gibbons
	Melissa Fang

For full biographical listings, see the Martindale-Hubbell Law Directory

Boston—Continued

SHERBURNE, POWERS & NEEDHAM, P.C. (AV)

One Beacon Street, 02108
Telephone: 617-523-2700
Fax: 617-523-6850
Email: @SHERBURNE.COM

William D. Weeks	Benjamin Volinski
John T. Collins	Mark Schonfeld
Allan J. Landau	James D. Smeallie
Stephen A. Hopkins	Paul Killeen
Alan I. Falk	Gordon P. Katz
C. Thomas Swaim	Joseph B. Darby, III
James Pollock	Richard M Yanofsky
William V. Tripp III	James E. McDermott
Stephen S. Young	Kenneth P. Brier
William F. Machen	Robert V. Lizza
W. Robert Allison	Miriam Goldstein Altman
Philip J. Notopoulos	John J. Monaghan
Richard J. Hindlian	Margaret J. Palladino
Paul E. Troy	Mark C. Michalowski
Harold W. Potter, Jr.	David Scott Sloan
Philip S. Lapatin	M. Chrysa Long
Pamela A. Duckworth	Lawrence D. Bradley

Miriam J. McKendall

Cynthia A. Brown	Amy J. Mastrobattista
Cynthia M. Hern	Leslie A. Sprinkle
Meredeth A. Beers	Douglas W. Clapp
Dianne R. Phillips	Jeffrey A. Huebschmann
Paul M. James	Tamara E. Goulston
Theodore F. Hanselman	Paul G. Lannon, Jr.
Joshua C. Krumholz	Nicholas P. Psyhogeos
Ieuan G. Mahony	Edward J. Naughton
Jeffrey J. Nix	Kathaleen Kelly Cutone
(Not admitted in MA)	Laurie A. Tribble
Kenneth L. Harvey	Neil C. Higgins
Christopher J. Trombetta	Deborah Paige Stone
Elise N. Zoli	Brian R. Popiel

COUNSEL

Haig Der Manuelian	Karl J. Hirshman
Mason M. Taber, Jr.	Dale R. Johnson

For full biographical listings, see the Martindale-Hubbell Law Directory

SHERIN AND LODGEN LLP (AV)

100 Summer Street, 02110
Telephone: 617-426-5720
Fax: 617-542-5186
Email: lawyers@sherin.com
Los Angeles, California Office: 11300 W. Olympic Boulevard, Suite 700.
Telephone: 310-914-7891.
Fax: 310-552-5327.

MEMBERS OF FIRM

Arthur L. Sherin (1946-1964)	Mark A. Nowak
George E. Lodgen (1946-1971)	Ronald W. Ruth
Morton B. Brown	Steven D. Eimert
George Waldstein	Barbara A. O'Donnell
John M. Reed	A. Neil Hartzell
Robert J. Muldoon, Jr.	Kenneth J. Mickiewicz
Alette E. Reed	Craig M. Brown
Edward M. Bloom	Andrew Royce
Thomas J. Raftery	Daniel O. Gaquin
Joshua M. Alper	Thomas A. Hippler
Gary M. Markoff	Rhonda B. Parker
Bryan G. Killian	John J. Slater III
David A. Guberman	Philip G. Boyle
Kenneth R. Berman	Nereyda Garcia
Frank J. Bailey	John C. La Liberte
Thomas P. Gorman	Christopher A. Kenney
Dorothy Nelson Stookey	C. Forbes Sargent III

ASSOCIATES

Karen Elise Berman	Michael S. Bloom
Margaret H. Leeson	Carolyn M. Barker
Robert M. Carney	Karen O'Malley
Mary Ellen McDonough	Susanne M. Walsh
Caroline Woodward	Susan S. Sampson

Anne Marie Dowd

OF COUNSEL

Michael S. Strauss	David M. Franek

LEGAL SUPPORT PERSONNEL

Marilyn J. Stewart (Executive Director)

For full biographical listings, see the Martindale-Hubbell Law Directory

SIMONDS, WINSLOW, WILLIS & ABBOTT, A PROFESSIONAL ASSOCIATION (AV)

50 Congress Street, 02109
Telephone: 617-367-4747
Fax: 617-227-1961

(See Next Column)

William S. Abbott	Hugh V. A. Starkey
Robert S. Gulick	John L. Worden III
Robert Torrence Morrison	Edward J. Wynne III

For Complete List of Firm Personnel, See General Section

For full biographical listings, see the Martindale-Hubbell Law Directory

WARNER & STACKPOLE LLP (AV)

75 State Street, 02109
Telephone: 617-951-9000
Telecopier: 617-951-9151
Email: w&s@warstack.com

MEMBERS OF FIRM

Paul C. Bauer	Howard A. Levine
Michael A. Leon	Stanley V. Ragalevsky

James G. Ward

ASSOCIATES

Michael E. Scott	Patricia Yung Wong

For Complete List of Firm Personnel, See General Section

For full biographical listings, see the Martindale-Hubbell Law Directory

CAMBRIDGE,* Middlesex Co.

WILLIAM M. O'BRIEN (AV)

Suite 216, 186 Alewife Brook Parkway, 02138
Telephone: 617-661-2600
Fax: 617-864-0654

For full biographical listings, see the Martindale-Hubbell Law Directory

FRAMINGHAM, Middlesex Co.

GARRAHAN, BARBIERI & GARRAHAN, P.C. (AV)

1500 Worcester Road, P.O. Box 2482, 01701
Telephone: 508-626-9382
Facsimile: 508-626-1543

John P. Garrahan	Peter R. Barbieri

William C. Garrahan

Anna M. Corti

OF COUNSEL

Mark S. Bodner

For full biographical listings, see the Martindale-Hubbell Law Directory

STEWART T. HERRICK & ASSOCIATES (AV)

Suite 303, 1661 Worcester Road, 01701
Telephone: 508-875-0021
FAX: 508-875-0029

ASSOCIATE

Lauren P. Smith

For full biographical listings, see the Martindale-Hubbell Law Directory

FRANKLIN, Norfolk Co.

ROCHE AND MURPHY (AV)

Franklin Office Park West, 38 Pond Street, Suite 308, P.O. Box 267, 02038
Telephone: 508-528-8300
FAX: 508-528-8889

MEMBERS OF FIRM

Neil J. Roche	Paul G. Murphy

ASSOCIATE

John J. Roche

For full biographical listings, see the Martindale-Hubbell Law Directory

MILFORD, Worcester Co.

GREENWALD, GREENWALD & POWERS (AV)

409 Fortune Boulevard Granite Park, 01757-1746
Telephone: 508-478-8611
Fax: 508-634-3959; 478-5937

Alan Greenwald	Anne M. Givens
Steven A. Greenwald	Colleen B. Walker
John D. Powers	Kathleen R. Winsor

OF COUNSEL

Merek S. Rubin

For full biographical listings, see the Martindale-Hubbell Law Directory

NEWTON, Middlesex Co.

SCHLESINGER AND BUCHBINDER (AV)

1200 Walnut Street, 02161-1267
Telephone: 617-965-3500
Facsimile: 617-965-6824

MEMBERS OF FIRM

Stephen J. Buchbinder	Alan J. Schlesinger

Joanne E. Romanow

ASSOCIATES

James P. Berezin	Leonard M. Davidson

Heather G. Merrill

For full biographical listings, see the Martindale-Hubbell Law Directory

NORTHAMPTON, * Hampshire Co.

BOWEN & SIEGEL (AV)

40 Center Street, 01060
Telephone: 413-584-3384
Fax: 413-584-0139

MEMBERS OF FIRM

Kenneth B. Bowen	Andrew J. Siegel

Local Counsel for: First Pioneer Farm Credit, ACA.
Town Counsel for: Town of Williamsburg.

For full biographical listings, see the Martindale-Hubbell Law Directory

MORSE & SACKS (AV)

31 Trumbull Road, 01060
Telephone: 413-584-1287
Fax: 413-584-0453

MEMBERS OF FIRM

Alvertus J. Morse (1872-1949)	Alvertus D. Morse (1904-1982)

Harley M. Sacks

ASSOCIATES

Debra L. Purrington	John M. McLaughlin

Representative Clients: Bill Willard, Inc.

For full biographical listings, see the Martindale-Hubbell Law Directory

NORTH ATTLEBORO, Bristol Co.

CLAPP & MURPHY (AV)

12 Church Street, 02760
Telephone: 508-695-3554
Fax: 508-695-2523

MEMBERS OF FIRM

Stephen D. Clapp	Peter F. Murphy

OF COUNSEL

Daniel Del Vecchio

For full biographical listings, see the Martindale-Hubbell Law Directory

SPRINGFIELD, * Hampden Co.

FRATAR & KERN (AV)

1391 Main Street, Suite 500, 01103
Telephone: 413-734-3119
Telecopier: 413-736-0670

MEMBERS OF FIRM

Robert N. Fratar	William F. Kern

For full biographical listings, see the Martindale-Hubbell Law Directory

HENDEL, COLLINS & NEWTON, P.C. (AV)

101 State Street, 01103
Telephone: 413-734-6411
Fax: 413-734-8069

Philip J. Hendel	Joseph H. Reinhardt
Joseph B. Collins	Jonathan R. Goldsmith
Carla W. Newton	Henry E. Geberth, Jr.

George I. Roumeliotis

Representative Clients: Springfield Institution for Savings; United Cooperative Bank.
Approved Attorneys for: First American Title Insurance Co.; Commonwealth Land Title Ins. Co.
Reference: Shawmut Bank, N.A.

For full biographical listings, see the Martindale-Hubbell Law Directory

WALTHAM, Middlesex Co.

HARNISH, JENNEY, MITCHELL AND RESH (AV)

564 Main Street, 02154
Telephone: 617-894-0000
Telecopier: 617-893-8357

(See Next Column)

MEMBERS OF FIRM

Francis E. Jenney	Robert C. Mann
David L. Mitchell	Margaret Manzon Skinner
Harvey J. Resh	Rhonda B. Fogel
Joseph Melone	Cynthia Spahl

For full biographical listings, see the Martindale-Hubbell Law Directory

WORCESTER, * Worcester Co.

MOUNTAIN, DEARBORN & WHITING (AV)

370 Main Street, 01608
Telephone: 508-756-2423
Fax: 508-755-6640

MEMBERS OF FIRM

Alfred N. Whiting (1920-1989)	Francis J. Russell
Thomas R. Mountain	Dale R. Harger
Richard W. Dearborn	Mark W. Bloom
Samuel R. DeSimone	Donald J. O'Neil
Henry W. Beth	Lawrence S. Delaney

Ann K. Molloy

ASSOCIATE

Richard M. Freije

For full biographical listings, see the Martindale-Hubbell Law Directory

MICHIGAN

ADRIAN, * Lenawee Co.

WALKER, WATTS, JACKSON & McFARLAND (AV)

160 North Winter Street, 49221
Telephone: 517-265-8138
Fax: 517-265-8286

MEMBERS OF FIRM

William H. Walker	Mark A. Jackson
Prosser M. Watts, Jr.	Michael McFarland

Attorneys for: Bank of Lenawee; Consumers Power Co.; Norfolk & Western Railway Co.; Citizens Gas Fuel Co.; Auto Owners Insurance Co.; Amerisure Co.; Citizens Mutual Liability; State Farm Mutual Insurance Co.; Tower Insurance Co.

For full biographical listings, see the Martindale-Hubbell Law Directory

ANN ARBOR, * Washtenaw Co.

BRAUN KENDRICK FINKBEINER PLC (AV)

700 First National Building, 48104
Telephone: 313-995-4100
Telecopier: 313-995-4798
URL: http://www.bkf-law.com
Bay City, Michigan Office: 201 Phoenix Building, P.O. Box 2039.
Telephone: 517-895-8505.
Telecopier: 517-895-8437.
Saginaw, Michigan Office: 101 N. Washington, Suite 812.
Telephone: 517-753-3461.
Telecopier: 517-753-3951.

Barry M. Levine

Representative Clients: The Dow Chemical Co.; General Motors Corp.; Lobdell Emery Manufacturing Co.; Merrill, Lynch, Inc.; Saginaw General Hospital; Saginaw News; The Wickes Foundation.

For full biographical listings, see the Martindale-Hubbell Law Directory

CONLIN, McKENNEY & PHILBRICK, P.C. (AV)

350 South Main Street Suite 400, 48104-2131
Telephone: 313-761-9000
Fax: 313-761-9001

Edward F. Conlin (1902-1953)	Robert M. Brimacombe
John W. Conlin (1904-1972)	James A. Schriemer
Albert J. Parker (1901-1970)	William M. Sweet
Chris L. McKenney	Elizabeth M. Petoskey
Karl R. Frankena	Bradley J. MeLampy
Allen J. Philbrick	Joseph W. Phillips
Phillip J. Bowen	Lori A. Buiteweg
Michael D. Highfield	Douglas G. McClure
Bruce N. Elliott	Thomas B. Bourque
Neil J. Juliar	Marjorie M. Dixon

Kenneth L. Spencer

OF COUNSEL

John W. Conlin

Representative Clients: Fingerle Lumber Co.; Ann Arbor Area Board of Realtors; Borders, Inc.; Auto-Owners Insurance Co.; Key Bank.
Approved Attorneys for: Nations Title Insurance Co.; Ticor Title Insurance Co.

(See Next Column)

CONLIN, MCKENNEY & PHILBRICK P.C.—*Continued*

For full biographical listings, see the Martindale-Hubbell Law Directory

---

HOOPER, HATHAWAY, PRICE, BEUCHE & WALLACE (AV)

126 South Main Street, 48104
Telephone: 313-662-4426
Fax: 313-662-9559

Joseph C. Hooper (1899-1980)	Gregory A. Spaly
Alan E. Price	Robert W. Southard
James R. Beuche	William J. Stapleton
Bruce T. Wallace	Bruce C. Conybeare, Jr.
Charles W. Borgsdorf	Anthony P. Patti
Mark R. Daane	Marcia J. Major

OF COUNSEL

James A. Evashevski   Roderick K. Daane

Representative Clients: Chem-Trend, Inc.; Dundee Cement Co.; Ervin Industries, Inc.; First Martin Corp.; Group 243 Design, Inc.; Honeywell; Microwave Sensors, Inc.; Shearson Lehman Hutton; O'Neal Construction Co.; Pittsfield Products, Inc.

For Complete List of Firm Personnel, See General Section

For full biographical listings, see the Martindale-Hubbell Law Directory

---

MILLER, CANFIELD, PADDOCK AND STONE, P.L.C. (AV)

A Professional Limited Liability Company
Founded in 1852 by Sidney Davy Miller
101 North Main Street, Seventh Floor, 48104-1400
Telephone: 313-663-2445
Fax: 313-747-7147
Detroit, Michigan Office: 150 West Jefferson, Suite 2500, 48226-4415.
Telephone: 313-963-6420.
Fax: 313-496-7500.
Cable Address: "Stem Detroit."
Bloomfield Hills, Michigan Office: Suite 100, Pinehurst Office Center, 1400 North Woodward, 48303-2014.
Telephone: 313-645-5000.
Fax: 313-645-1917.
Grand Rapids, Michigan Office: 1200 Campau Square Plaza, 99 Monroe, N.W., 49503-2639.
Telephone: 616-454-8656.
Fax: 616-776-6322.
Howell, Michigan Office: 121 South Barnard Street, Suite 4, 48843-2305.
Telephone: 517-546-7600.
Telecopier: 517-546-6974.
Kalamazoo, Michigan Office: 444 West Michigan Avenue, 49007-3752.
Telephone: 616-381-7030.
Fax: 616-382-0244.
Lansing, Michigan Office: One Michigan Avenue, Suite 900, 48933-1609.
Telephone: 517-487-2070.
Fax: 517-374-6304.
Monroe, Michigan Office: The Executive Centre, 214 East Elm Avenue, 48161-2682.
Telephone: 313-243-2000.
Fax: 313-243-0901.
Washington, D.C. Office: 1225 Nineteenth Street, N.W., Suite 400. 20036.
Telephone: 202-429-5575; 785-0600.
Fax: 202-331-1118; 785-1234.
Pensacola, Florida Office: 25 West Cedar, 32501.
Telephone: 904-469-1088.
Fax: 904-432-0677.
St. Petersburg, Florida Office: 100 Second Avenue S., Suite 7045, 33701.
Telephone: 813-982-6000.
Fax: 813-892-6002.
New York, New York Office: Eleventh Floor, 135 East 57th Street, 10022-2087.
Telephone: 212-754-5400.
Fax: 212-754-5401.
Gdansk, Poland Office: Suite 322, Dom Technika Building, UI. Rajska 6, 80-850.
Telephone: 011-485-831-2808.
Fax: 011-485-831-4719.
Warsaw, Poland Office: UI. Marszalkowska 82, Suite 561, 00-517.
Telephone: 011-482-623-6457 and 6458.
Fax: 011-482-623-6459.

RESIDENT PRINCIPALS
Robert E. Gilbert

Representative Firm Clients: Chrysler Corporation; Comerica, Incorporated; City of Detroit, Michigan; Detroit Tigers, Inc.; First of Michigan; Ford Motor Company; Ford Motor Credit Company; Great Lakes Bancorp; Henry Ford Hospital; INVETECH Company.

For Complete List of Firm Personnel, See General Section

For full biographical listings, see the Martindale-Hubbell Law Directory

---

PEAR SPERLING EGGAN & MUSKOVITZ, P.C. (AV)

Domino's Farms, 24 Frank Lloyd Wright Drive, 48105
Telephone: 313-665-4441
Fax: 313-665-8788
Ypsilanti, Michigan Offices: 5 South Washington Street.
Telephone: 313-483-3626 and 2164 Bellevue at Washtenaw.
Telephone: 313-483-7177.

Edwin L. Pear	Thomas E. Daniels
Andrew M. Eggan	Joel F. Graziani
	Paul R. Fransway

Counsel For: Domino's Pizza, Inc.; Victory Lane Quick Oil Change, Inc.; Citizens Banking Corporation.

For Complete List of Firm Personnel, See General Section

For full biographical listings, see the Martindale-Hubbell Law Directory

---

BAY CITY,* Bay Co.

BRAUN KENDRICK FINKBEINER PLC (AV)

201 Phoenix Building, P.O. Box 2039, 48708
Telephone: 517-895-8505
Telecopier: 517-895-8437
URL: http://www.bkf-law.com
Saginaw, Michigan Office: 101 N. Washington, Suite 812. 8th Floor
Second National Bank Building.
Telephone: 517-753-3461.
Telecopier: 517-753-3951.
Ann Arbor, Michigan Office: 700 First National Building.
Telephone: 313-995-4100.
Telecopier: 313-995-4798.

Ralph J. Isackson	Daniel S. Opperman
George F. Gronewold, Jr.	Gregory T. Demers

OF COUNSEL
Patrick D. Neering

Representative Clients: APV Chemical Machinery, Inc.; Bay Health Systems; Catholic Federal Credit Union; City of Saginaw; City of Vassar; City of Milwaukee; Corporate Service; Cox Cable.

For Complete List of Firm Personnel, See General Section

For full biographical listings, see the Martindale-Hubbell Law Directory

---

BINGHAM FARMS, Oakland Co.

MEISNER & ASSOCIATES, P.C. (AV)

Suite 467, 30200 Telegraph Road, 48025-4506
Telephone: 810-644-4433

Robert M. Meisner

Robert R. Maxwell

For full biographical listings, see the Martindale-Hubbell Law Directory

---

SOTIROFF ABRAMCZYK & RAUSS, P.C. (AV)

30400 Telegraph Road, Suite 444, 48025-4541
Telephone: 810-642-6000
Facsimile: 810-642-9001

Philip Sotiroff	Lawrence A. Tower
Lawrence R. Abramczyk	Robert B. Goldi
Dennis M. Rauss	Keith A. Sotiroff

For full biographical listings, see the Martindale-Hubbell Law Directory

---

BIRMINGHAM, Oakland Co.

LOUIS J. BURNETT, P.C. (AV)

255 East Brown, Suite 210, 48009-6782
Telephone: 810-642-4345
Fax: 810-642-2005

Louis J. Burnett

Reference: Comerica, Detroit, Michigan.

For full biographical listings, see the Martindale-Hubbell Law Directory

---

CARSON FISCHER, P.L.C. (AV)

Third Floor, 300 East Maple Road, 48009-6317
Telephone: 810-644-4840
Facsimile: 810-644-1832

Robert M. Carson	William C. Edmunds
Peter L. Wanger	Todd M. Fink

For full biographical listings, see the Martindale-Hubbell Law Directory

---

HYMAN AND LIPPITT, P.C. (AV)

185 Oakland Avenue, Suite 300, P.O. Box 1750, 48009
Telephone: 810-646-8292
Facsimile: 810-646-8375

(See Next Column)

HYMAN AND LIPPITT P.C., *Birmingham—Continued*

J. Leonard Hyman	Kenneth F. Neuman
Norman L. Lippitt	Terry S. Givens
Douglas A. Hyman	Paul J. Fischer
Brian D. O'Keefe	John A. Sellers
H. Joel Newman	Robert H. Lippitt
Nazli G. Sater	Roger L. Myers
	David N. Morrell, Jr.

For full biographical listings, see the Martindale-Hubbell Law Directory

MACDONALD AND GOREN, P.C. (AV)

Suite 200, 260 East Brown Street, 48009
Telephone: 810-645-5940
Fax: 810-645-2490

Harold C. MacDonald	Kalman G. Goren
	Cindy Rhodes Victor

Amy L. Glenn	Lawrence C. Atorthy
David D. Marsh	Miriam Blanks-Smart
Glenn G. Ross	John T. Klees
	Rose Marie Karadsheh

OF COUNSEL

Robert L. Biederman

Representative Clients: Beaudin, Gallanis; Beaudin, Incorporated; Orlandi Gear Co., Inc.; Bing Steel, Inc.; Superb Manufacturing, Inc.; Spring Engineering, Inc.; Adrian Steel Co.; Southfield Radiology Associates, P.C.; HDS Services, Inc.; TGI Friday's Inc.; Quality Gold of Cincinnati, Inc.

For full biographical listings, see the Martindale-Hubbell Law Directory

WILLIAMS, SCHAEFER, RUBY & WILLIAMS, PROFESSIONAL CORPORATION (AV)

Suite 300, 380 North Woodward Avenue, 48009
Telephone: 810-642-0333
Telecopy: 810-642-0856

James A. Williams	Richard D. Rattner
Edward L. Ruby	William E. Hosler, III

OF COUNSEL

Robert A. Jacobs

Representative Clients: Amoco Oil Company; Beachum & Roeser Development Corporation; Biltmore Properties; Frankel Development Company; Jonna Construction Corporation; Lawyers Title Insurance Corp.; Michigan National Bank; Morgan-Mitsubishi Development Corporation; Sunderland Development Corporation; Western Development Company.

For full biographical listings, see the Martindale-Hubbell Law Directory

BLOOMFIELD HILLS, Oakland Co.

JON H. BERKEY, P.C. (AV)

1750 South Telegraph Road, Suite 107, 48302-0183
Telephone: 810-332-2100
Fax: 810-332-2190

Jon H. Berkey

Anthony A. Yezbick

For full biographical listings, see the Martindale-Hubbell Law Directory

DAWDA, MANN, MULCAHY & SADLER, P.L.C. (AV)

1533 North Woodward Avenue Suite 200, 48304
Telephone: 810-642-3700
Fax: 810-642-7791
Email: EMail@DMMS.Com

Michael D. Mulcahy	Edward C. Dawda
	William L. Rosin

Todd A. Schafer	Daniel M. Halprin
Tara E. Barr	Paul C. Apap

Representative Clients: AEGON USA Realty Advisors, Inc.; AMB Institutional Realty Advisors, Inc.; CB Commercial Real Estate; G.E. Capital Realty Group; Home Depot U.S.A., Inc.; Ladbroke Racing Corporation; Northwestern Mutual Life Insurance Company; Trammell Crow Company; Wal-Mart Stores, Inc.

For full biographical listings, see the Martindale-Hubbell Law Directory

DROLET, FREEMAN, COTTON, MACADDINO & NORRIS, P.C. (AV)

33 Bloomfield Hills Parkway, Suite 100, 48304
Telephone: 810-642-2255
Fax: 810-642-6460

(See Next Column)

David G. Barnett (1915-1989)	J. Kingsley Cotton, III
E. Peter Drolet	Kevin S. Macaddino
H. William Freeman	Matthew C. Norris

Scot A. Norris	Suzanne S. Reynolds
Brian P. Henry	Roger S. Helman
	Lauren D. Honet

OF COUNSEL

David M. Preston	John C. Earle

Representative Clients: Ajax Paving Industries, Inc.; American/SCI, Inc.; American Sun Roof Corporation; Angelo Iafrate Construction Co.; Beyster Lumber Co.; Boehle Chemicals, Inc.; Cambridge Homes, Inc.; Carroll Packaging, Inc.; Clawson Concrete Co.; Colwell Equipment Company, Inc.

For full biographical listings, see the Martindale-Hubbell Law Directory

MEYER, KIRK, SNYDER & SAFFORD, PLLC (AV)

Suite 100, 100 West Long Lake Road, 48304
Telephone: 810-647-5111
Telecopier: 810-647-6079
Detroit, Michigan Office: 2500 Penobscot Building.
Telephone: 313-961-1261.

George H. Meyer	John M. Kirk

Representative Clients: Available Upon Request.

For Complete List of Firm Personnel, See General Section

For full biographical listings, see the Martindale-Hubbell Law Directory

DETROIT,* Wayne Co.

ABBOTT, NICHOLSON, QUILTER, ESSHAKI & YOUNGBLOOD, P.C. (AV)

19th Floor, One Woodward Avenue, 48226
Telephone: 313-963-2500
Telecopier: 313-963-7882

C. Richard Abbott	Carl F. Jarboe
John R. Nicholson	Jay A. Kennedy
Thomas R. Quilter III	Timothy A. Stoepker
Gene J. Esshaki	Timothy J. Kramer
John F. Youngblood	Norbert T. Madison, Jr.
James B. Perry	William D. Gilbride, Jr.

Mary P. Nelson	Kathryn L. Ritchie
Michael R. Blum	Jill A. Bankey
Thomas F. Hatch	Dawn M. Macaddino
Anne Warren Bagno	Casimir J. Swastek
Eric J. Girdler	Daniel G. Kielczewski
	George M. Mesrey

OF COUNSEL

Thomas C. Shumaker	Karen Smith Kienbaum

For full biographical listings, see the Martindale-Hubbell Law Directory

BARRIS, SOTT, DENN & DRIKER, P.L.L.C. (AV)

211 West Fort Street, Fifteenth Floor, 48226-3281
Telephone: 313-965-9725
Telecopier: 313-965-2493
313-965-5398

Donald E. Barris	Robert E. Kass
Herbert Sott	Daniel M. Share
David L. Denn	Elaine Fieldman
Eugene Driker	Morley Witus
William G. Barris	John A. Libby
Sharon M. Woods	James S. Fontichiaro
Stephen E. Glazek	Daniel J. LaCombe
	Robert E. Epstein

COUNSEL

Leon S. Cohan

OF COUNSEL

Stanley M. Weingarden

Dennis M. Barnes	Monique K. Cirelli
Matthew J. Boettcher	Laura Suzanne Laurence
Thomas F. Cavalier	Molly Giles
C. David Bargamian	Eric S. Rosenthal
Michael J. Reynolds	Claudia D. Orr
Elizabeth A. Carrie	Alicia Monique Nails

Representative Clients: Avis Rent A Car System, Inc.; Borman's, Inc.; Consumers Power Co.; County of Wayne, Michigan; Ford Motor Co.; The Great Atlantic & Pacific Tea Company, Inc.; Henry Ford Health System; Michigan Consolidated Gas Co.; NBD Bank, N.A.; Textron, Inc.

For full biographical listings, see the Martindale-Hubbell Law Directory

Detroit—Continued

BIERI, BERNSTEIN & AMES (AV)

400 Renaissance Center, 35th Floor, 48243
Telephone: 313-567-4200
Fax: 313-567-2705
Email: bieri@rust.net *URL:* http://www.bieriandassoc.com
MEMBERS OF FIRM

James C. Bieri   Melvin S. Bernstein
                Stanley L. Ames

For full biographical listings, see the Martindale-Hubbell Law Directory

BODMAN, LONGLEY & DAHLING LLP (AV)

34th Floor 100 Renaissance Center, 48243
Telephone: 313-259-7777
Fax: 313-393-7579
Email: 2080194@mcimail.com
Troy, Michigan Office: Suite 2020, 755 West Big Beaver Road.
Telephone: 810-362-2110.
Fax: 810-244-0780.
Ann Arbor, Michigan Office: 110 Miller, Suite 300.
Telephone: 313-761-3780.
Fax: 313-930-2494.
Northern Michigan Office: 229 Court Street, P.O. Box 405, Cheboygan.
Telephone: 616-627-4351.
Fax: 616-627-2802.

MEMBERS OF FIRM

Alfred C. Wortley, Jr.   David W. Hipp
Michael B. Lewiston   Larry R. Shulman
Mark W. Griffin   Michael A. Stack
  (Ann Arbor Office)   (Northern Michigan Office)
Joseph J. Kochanek   Harvey W. Berman
                                  (Ann Arbor Office)

For Representative Client List, See General Section

For Complete List of Firm Personnel, See General Section

For full biographical listings, see the Martindale-Hubbell Law Directory

BRADY HATHAWAY, PROFESSIONAL CORPORATION (AV)

1330 Buhl Building, 48226-3602
Telephone: 313-965-3700
Telecopier: 313-965-2830

Thomas P. Brady   Daniel J. Bretz
                OF COUNSEL
            James A. Hathaway

Representative Clients: Beam Stream, Inc.; Bundy Tubing Company; Energy Conversion Devices, Inc.; The Hayman Co.; Schering Corporation; Warner-Lambert; Wolverine Technologies; ABB Environmental Services; Marriott Corp.

For Complete List of Firm Personnel, See General Section

For full biographical listings, see the Martindale-Hubbell Law Directory

BUTZEL LONG, A PROFESSIONAL CORPORATION (AV)

Suite 900, 150 West Jefferson, 48226
Telephone: 313-225-7000
Telecopier: 313-225-7080
Email: melnick@butzel.com *URL:* http://www.butzel.com
Birmingham, Michigan Office: Suite 200, 32270 Telegraph Road.
Telephone: 810-258-1616.
Telecopier: 810-258-1439.
Lansing, Michigan Office: 118 West Ottawa Street.
Telephone: 517-372-6622.
Telecopier: 517-372-6672.
Ann Arbor, Michigan Office: Suite 300, 350 South Main Street.
Telephone: 313-995-3110.
Telecopier: 313-995-1777.
Grosse Pointe Farms, Michigan Office: Suite 260, 21 Kercheval.
Telephone: 313-886-5446.
Telecopier: 313-886-2114.

Stephen A. Bromberg   Gordon W. Didier (Birmingham)
  (Birmingham)   Alan S. Levine (Birmingham)
Allan Nachman (Birmingham)   Anthony J. Saulino, Jr.
George H. Zinn, Jr.   (Birmingham)
Jack D. Shumate (Birmingham) Clara DeMatteis Mager
Leonard F. Charla   Patrick A. Karbowski
David W. Berry (Birmingham)   (Birmingham)
Carl Rashid, Jr.   Ronald E. Reynolds
D. Stewart Green (Birmingham) (Birmingham)

Susan Klein Friedlaender (Birmingham)

Representative Clients: Bank of New York; Besser Co.; Blue Cross/Blue Shield of Michigan; Chrysler First; Chrysler Motor Corp.; D & N Savings Bank; The Detroit News, Inc.; Dow Chemical Co.; First of America Bank Corp.; William Beaumont Hospital.

(See Next Column)

For Complete List of Firm Personnel, See General Section

For full biographical listings, see the Martindale-Hubbell Law Directory

CLARK HILL P.L.C. (AV)

500 Woodward Avenue, Suite 3500, 48226
Telephone: 313-965-8300
Facsimile: 313-962-4348
Oakland County, Michigan Office: Third Floor, 255 South Woodward Avenue, Birmingham.
Telephone: 810-642-9692.
Facsimile: 810-642-2174.
Lansing, Michigan Office: Suite 600, 200 North Capitol Avenue.
Telephone: 517-484-4481.
Facsimile: 517-484-1246.
Minneapolis, Minnesota Office: Suite 1000, One Financial Plaza, 120 South Sixth Street.
Telephone: 612-332-0102.
Facsimile: 612-332-3225.
Kansas City, Missouri Office: Suite 1400, Bryant Building, 1102 Grand Avenue.
Telephone: 816-221-5578.
Facsimile: 816-221-0303.

William B. Dunn   Timothy M. Koltun
Timothy W. Mast (Resident, Daniel H. Minkus (Resident,
  Oakland County Office)   Oakland County Office)
          Judith Greenstone Miller

Bernard T. Lourim   Georgette Borrego Dulworth
          Donald F. Berschback, II

Representative Clients: Metropolitan Life Insurance Company; The Prudential Insurance Company of America; J.E. Robert Companies; United States Fidelity and Guaranty Company; The Rouse Company.

For Complete List of Firm Personnel, See General Section

For full biographical listings, see the Martindale-Hubbell Law Directory

DYKEMA GOSSETT PLLC (AV)

400 Renaissance Center, 48243-1668
Telephone: 313-568-6800
Cable Address: "Dyke-Detroit"
Telex: 23-0121
Fax: 313-568-6594
Email: 2084153@mcimail.com
Ann Arbor, Michigan Office: 315 East Eisenhower Parkway, Suite 100, 48108-3306.
Telephone: 313-747-7660.
Fax: 313-747-7696.
Bloomfield Hills, Michigan Office: 1577 North Woodward Avenue, Suite 300, 48304-2820.
Telephone: 810-540-0700.
Fax: 810-540-0763.
Chicago, Illinois Office: 55 East Monroe Street, Suite 3250, 60603-5709.
Telephone: 312-551-4900.
Fax: 312-551-4919.
Grand Rapids, Michigan Office: 200 Oldtown Riverfront Building, 248 Louis Campau Promenade, N.W., 49503-2668.
Telephone: 616-776-7500.
Fax: 616-776-7573.
Lansing, Michigan Office: 800 Michigan National Tower, 48933-1707.
Telephone: 517-374-9100.
Fax: 517-374-9191.
Washington, D.C. Office: Franklin Square, Suite 300 West, 1300 I Street, N.W., 20005-3306.
Telephone: 202-522-8600.
Fax: 202-522-8669.

MEMBERS OF FIRM

David E. Doran (Resident at   Howard N. Luckoff (Resident at
  Grand Rapids Office)   Bloomfield Hills Office)
Fred J. Fechheimer (Resident at William T. Myers (Resident at
  Bloomfield Hills Office)   Bloomfield Hills Office)
Dennis M. Gannan (Resident at Robert L. Nelson (Member in
  Bloomfield Hills Office)   Charge of Grand Rapids
Alan M. Greene (Resident at   Office)
  Bloomfield Hills Office)   Brian J. Page (Resident at
Mary Steck Kershner   Grand Rapids Office)
Susan Allene Kovach   Cameron H. Piggott
Michael A. Lesha   Richard E. Rabbideau
          Wilfred A. Steiner, Jr.
          RETIRED PARTNER
            James W. Draper
            ASSOCIATES
Daniel J. Brondyk (Resident at Laurence D. Rich (Resident at
  Grand Rapids Office)   Bloomfield Hills Office)
Sean M. Carty   Catherine Kim Shierk (Resident
Karen R. Pifer (Resident at   at Bloomfield Hills Office)
  Bloomfield Hills Office)   Penny Brown Webster

(See Next Column)

DYKEMA GOSSETT PLLC, *Detroit—Continued*

For Complete List of Firm Personnel, See General Section

For full biographical listings, see the Martindale-Hubbell Law Directory

FILDEW HINKS, P.L.L.C. (AV)

3600 Penobscot Building, 645 Griswold Street, 48226-4291
Telephone: 313-961-9700
Telecopier: 313-961-0754

MEMBERS OF FIRM

Stanley L. Fildew (1896-1978)	Randall S. Wangen
Frank T. Hinks (1887-1974)	Mary Jane Ruffley
Richard E. Hinks (1916-1990)	Robert D. Welchli
John H. Fildew	William P. Thorpe
Alan C. Miller	Colleen A. Kramer
Charles D. Todd III	Stephen J. Pokoj

ASSOCIATES

Charles S. Kennedy, III	Walter B. Fisher, Jr.

References: First of America Bank-Detroit, N.A.; Comerica Bank-Detroit; National Bank of Detroit.

For full biographical listings, see the Martindale-Hubbell Law Directory

FOSTER, MEADOWS & BALLARD, P.C. (AV)

3200 Penobscot Building, 48226
Telephone: 313-961-3234
Cable Address: "Foster"
Telex: 23-5823
Facsimile: 313-961-6184

Sparkman D. Foster (1897-1967)	Richard A. Dietz
Charles R. Hrdlicka	Robert H. Fortunate
Paul D. Galea	Robert G. Lahiff

Camille A. Raffa-Dietz

Michael J. Liddane	Paul A. Kettunen

OF COUNSEL

John L. Foster	John F. Langs

John A. Mundell, Jr.

For full biographical listings, see the Martindale-Hubbell Law Directory

HONIGMAN MILLER SCHWARTZ AND COHN (AV)

A Partnership including Professional Corporations
2290 First National Building, 48226
Telephone: 313-256-7800
Telecopier: 313-962-0176
Telex: 235705
URL: http://www.law.honigman.com
Lansing, Michigan Office: Phoenix Building, 222 North Washington Square, Suite 400, 48933-1800.
Telephone: 517-484-8282.
West Palm Beach, Florida Office: Suite 800 Esperante Building, 222 Lakeview Avenue, 33401-6112.
Telephone: 561-838-4500.
Tampa, Florida Office: 2700 SunTrust Financial Centre, 401 E. Jackson Street, 33602-5226.
Telephone: 813-221-6600.

MEMBERS OF FIRM

Joel S. Adelman	Lawrence D. McLaughlin
John E. Amerman	Mitchell R. Meisner
C. Leslie Banas	Nancy M. Omichinski
Thomas J. Beale	J. Adam Rothstein
Maurice S. Binkow	Phyllis G. Rozof
Jonathan R. Borenstein	Roberta R. Russ
Richard J. Burstein	Jerome M. Salle
Gregory J. DeMars	Samina R. Schey
Frederick J. Frank	Laurence J. Schiff
H. Alan Gocha	Edward R. Schonberg
Margaret E. Greene	Michael B. Shapiro
Carl W. Herstein	Gary A. Trepod
Alan M. Hurvitz	(Lansing, Michigan Office)
Norman Hyman	Randall P. Whately
Edward F. Kickham	William C. Whitbeck
Kevin Kohls	(Lansing, Michigan Office)
Jeffrey R. Kravitz	Sheldon P. Winkelman
Denise J. Lewis	William J. Zousmer

ASSOCIATES

Jean-Vierre Adams	Amy M. Colton

Jill Mainster Menuck

RESIDENT IN WEST PALM BEACH, FLORIDA OFFICE
MEMBERS

Steven R. Parson (P.A.)	Neil W. Platock (P.A.)

Marvin S. Rosen (P.A.)

RESIDENT IN TAMPA, FLORIDA OFFICE
MEMBERS

Maria Maistrellis (P.A.)	James B. Soble (P.A.)

Counsel to: Forbes/Cohen Properties; General Motors Corporation Legal Staff (General Motors Corporation, General Motors Acceptance Corporation); The Hayman Company; Hines Interests Limited Partnership; Pulte Corporation; Schostak Brothers & Company, Inc.; The Sembler Company.

For Complete List of Firm Personnel, See General Section

For full biographical listings, see the Martindale-Hubbell Law Directory

JAFFE, RAITT, HEUER & WEISS, PROFESSIONAL CORPORATION (AV)

One Woodward Avenue, Suite 2400, 48226
Telephone: 313-961-8380
Telecopier: 313-961-8358
Cable Address: "Jafsni"
Southfield, Michigan Office: Travelers Tower, Suite 1520.
Telephone: 313-961-8380.
Monroe, Michigan Office: 214 East Elm Avenue, Suite 208,
Telephone: 313-241-6470.
Telefacsimile: 313-241-3849.

Gail A. Anderson	Mark P. Krysinski
Robert S. Bolton	Joel J. Morris
Penny L. Carolan	Cecil G. Raitt
Jeffrey L. Forman	Gerald F. Reinhart
Joel S. Golden	Mark D. Rubenfire
Blair B. Hysni	Lawrence R. Shoffner
Ira J. Jaffe	Arthur A. Weiss
Robin H. Krueger	Richard A. Zussman

Lesley A. Gaber	Jeffrey M. Weiss

OF COUNSEL
Nathan L. Milstein

Representative Clients: Edgemere Enterprises; Frankel Associates, Inc.; Somerset Inn & Apartments; Sosnick Development Co.; Uniprop, Inc.

For Complete List of Firm Personnel, See General Section

For full biographical listings, see the Martindale-Hubbell Law Directory

LEWIS, CLAY & MUNDAY, A PROFESSIONAL CORPORATION (AV)

(Formerly Lewis, White & Clay, P.C.)
1300 First National Building, 660 Woodward Avenue, 48226-3531
Telephone: 313-961-2550
Troy, Michigan Office: Liberty Center, Suite 200. 100 West Big Beaver Road. 48084.
Telephone: 810-680-6702.
Fax: 810-680-6703.
Washington, D.C. Office: 1000 16th Street, N.W., Suite 401. 20036.
Telephone: 202-835-0616.
Fax: 202-833-3316.
Boston, Massachusetts Office: 10 Post Office Square.
Telephone: 617-422-8646.
Fax: 617-338-5693.

David Baker Lewis	Frank E. Barbee
Eric Lee Clay	Camille Stearns Miller
Reuben A. Munday	Michael T. Raymond
Ulysses Whittaker Boykin	Jacqueline H. Sellers
Carl F. Stafford	David N. Zacks
Helen Francine Strong	Thomas J. Guyer

Blair A. Person

Karen Kendrick Brown (Resident, Washington, D.C. Office)	Hans J. Massaquoi, Jr.
	Nancy C. Borland
J. Taylor Teasdale	Tammy L. Terry
Wade Harper McCree	Lynn Westfall Gross
Tyrone A. Powell	Suzanne P. Pope
Susan D. Hoffman	Matthew R. Halpin
John J. Walsh	Donica Thomas Varner
Andrea L. Powell	Damon L. White
Althea Lynn Foster	(Not admitted in MI)
	Kathleen L. Royal

COUNSEL

Otis M. Smith (1922-1994)	G. Allen Bass (Resident, Boston,
Herbert O. Reid, Sr. (1915-1991)	Massachusetts Office)

Representative Clients: Omnicare Health Plan; Aetna Life & Casualty Co.; Chrysler Motors Corp.; Chrysler Financial Corp.; MCI Communications Corp.; City of Detroit; City of Detroit Building Authority; City of Detroit Downtown Development Authority; Consolidated Rail Corp. (Conrail); Equitable Life Assurance Society of the United States.

For full biographical listings, see the Martindale-Hubbell Law Directory

Detroit—Continued

MAGER, MERCER, SCOTT & ALBER, P.C. (AV)

500 Woodward Avenue Suite 3400, 48226
Telephone: 313-962-8212
Facsimile: 313-962-5413
Oakland County Office: Top of Troy Building, 755 West Big Beaver, Suite 1700, Troy, Michigan.
Telephone: 810-362-8212.
Facsimile: 810-362-6944.
Macomb County Office: 18285 Ten Mile Road, Suite 100, Roseville, Michigan.
Telephone: 810-771-1100.
Facsimile: 810-775-5170.

George J. Mager, Jr.

Representative Clients: ABB Flakt, Inc.; American States Insurance Co.; CEI Industries; Central Venture Corp.; CIGNA; Construction Management, Inc.

For full biographical listings, see the Martindale-Hubbell Law Directory

MILLER, CANFIELD, PADDOCK AND STONE, P.L.C. (AV)

A Professional Limited Liability Company
Founded in 1852 by Sidney Davy Miller
150 West Jefferson, Suite 2500, 48226-4415
Telephone: 313-963-6420
Fax: 313-496-7500
Cable Address: "Stem Detroit"
Detroit, Michigan Office: 150 West Jefferson, Suite 2500, 48226-4415.
Telephone: 313-963-6420.
Fax: 313-496-7500.
Cable Address: "Stem Detroit."
Ann Arbor, Michigan Office: 101 North Main Street, 7th Floor, 48104-1400.
Telephone: 313-663-2445.
Fax: 313-747-7147.
Bloomfield Hills, Michigan Office: Suite 100, Pinehurst Office Center, 1400 North Woodward, 48303-2014.
Telephone: 313-645-5000.
Fax: 313-645-1917.
Grand Rapids, Michigan Office: 1200 Campau Square Plaza, 99 Monroe, N.W., 49503-2639.
Telephone: 616-454-8656.
Fax: 616-776-6322.
Howell, Michigan Office: 121 South Barnard Street, Suite 4, 48843-2305.
Telephone: 517-546-7600.
Telecopier: 517-546-6974.
Kalamazoo, Michigan Office: 444 West Michigan Avenue, 49007-3752.
Telephone: 616-381-7030.
Fax: 616-382-0244.
Lansing, Michigan Office: One Michigan Avenue, Suite 900, 48933-1609.
Telephone: 517-487-2070.
Fax: 517-374-6304.
Monroe, Michigan Office: The Executive Centre, 214 East Elm Avenue, 48161-2682.
Telephone: 313-243-2000.
Fax: 313-243-0901.
Washington, D.C. Office: 1225 Nineteenth Street, N.W., Suite 400. 20036.
Telephone: 202-429-5575; 785-0600.
Fax: 202-331-1118; 785-1234.
Pensacola, Florida Office: 25 West Cedar, 32501.
Telephone: 904-469-1088.
Fax: 904-432-0677.
St. Petersburg, Florida Office: 100 Second Avenue S., Suite 7045, 33701.
Telephone: 813-982-6000.
Fax: 813-892-6002.
New York, New York Office: Eleventh Floor, 135 East 57th Street, 10022-2087.
Telephone: 212-754-5400.
Fax: 212-754-5401.
Gdansk, Poland Office: Suite 322, Dom Technika Building, Ul. Rajska 6, 80-850.
Telephone: 011-485-831-2808.
Fax: 011-485-831-4719.
Warsaw, Poland Office: Ul. Marszalkowska 82, Suite 561, 00-517.
Telephone: 011-482-623-6457 and 6458.
Fax: 011-482-623-6459.

PRINCIPALS OF FIRM

Robert E. Gilbert (Ann Arbor Office)	Frank L. Andrews (Detroit and Bloomfield Hills Offices)
Stephen G. Palms (Bloomfield Hills Office)	Michael A. Limauro

OF COUNSEL

Allen Schwartz	Anne H. Hiemstra

SENIOR ATTORNEY
David J. Hasper (Grand Rapids Office)

Representative Firm Clients: Chrysler Corporation; Comerica, Incorporated; City of Detroit, Michigan; Detroit Tigers, Inc.; First of Michigan; Ford Motor Company; Ford Motor Credit Company; Great Lakes Bancorp; Henry Ford Hospital; INVETECH Company.

(See Next Column)

For Complete List of Firm Personnel, See General Section

For full biographical listings, see the Martindale-Hubbell Law Directory

SHAHEEN, JACOBS & ROSS, P.C. (AV)

585 East Larned, Suite 200, 48226-4316
Telephone: 313-963-1301
Telecopier: 313-963-7123
Email: LAWSJR@AOL.COM

Joseph Shaheen (1920-1984)	Steven P. Ross
Michael A. Jacobs (1949-1992)	Michael J. Thomas
Thomas J. Wall, Jr.	

For full biographical listings, see the Martindale-Hubbell Law Directory

TIMMIS & INMAN, L.L.P. (AV)

300 Talon Centre, 48207
Telephone: 313-396-4200
Telecopier: 313-396-4228

Michael T. Timmis	Richard M. Miettinen
Charles W. Royer	Lisa R. Gorman
Henry J. Brennan, III	Bradley J. Knickerbocker
George M. Malis	

John P. Kanan	Patrick B. Carey

OF COUNSEL
Wayne C. Inman

Representative Clients: Talon Inc.; Talon Development Associates, Inc.; Franks Nursery & Crafts; Chateau Estates and/or CP Limited Partnership.

For Complete List of Firm Personnel, See General Section

For full biographical listings, see the Martindale-Hubbell Law Directory

---

EAST LANSING, Ingham Co.

FARHAT, STORY & KRAUS, P.C. (AV)

Beacon Place, 4572 South Hagadorn Road, Suite 3, 48823
Telephone: 517-351-3700
Fax: 517-332-4122
Email: rkraus@sojourn.com

Leo A. Farhat	Chris A. Bergstrom
James E. Burns (1925-1979)	Kitty L. Groh
Monte R. Story	Charles R. Toy
Richard C. Kraus	David M. Platt
Max R. Hoffman Jr.	Thomas L. Sparks

Lawrence P. Schweitzer	Daniel B. Morgan
Debra A. Geroux	Mary K. Robbins-Kralapp

Representative Clients: Big L. Corp.; Michigan Automotive Wholesalers Association; Hartman-Fabco, Inc.; Lansing Electric Motors, Inc.; Mike Miller Lincoln Mercury; Edward Rose Realty, Inc.
Reference: City Bank, St. Johns.

For full biographical listings, see the Martindale-Hubbell Law Directory

---

FARMINGTON HILLS, Oakland Co.

HOROWITZ — GUDEMAN, P.C. (AV)

31700 Middlebelt, Suite 140, 48334
Telephone: 810-855-6020
Facsimile: 810-855-6025

Marvin I. Horowitz	Edward J. Gudeman
Stuart L. Sherman	

Leslie I. Kollin
LEGAL SUPPORT PERSONNEL
Robin E. Cornell (Paralegal)

For full biographical listings, see the Martindale-Hubbell Law Directory

LAW OFFICE OF GARY POLLACK (AV)

30500 Northwestern Highway Suite 309, 48334-3178
Telephone: 810-932-0880
Facsimile: 810-932-8950

For full biographical listings, see the Martindale-Hubbell Law Directory

---

GRAND RAPIDS, Kent Co.

BORRE, PETERSON, FOWLER & REENS, P.C. (AV)

The Philo C. Fuller House, 44 Lafayette, N.E., P.O. Box 1767, 49501-1767
Telephone: 616-459-1971
Fax: 616-459-2393

(See Next Column)

BORRE, PETERSON, FOWLER & REENS P.C., *Grand Rapids—Continued*

Glen V. Borre	Frank H. Johnson
James B. Peterson	Mark D. Sevald
William C. Reens	William R. Vander Sluis
	William G. Krupar

References: Old Kent Bank; NBD Bank; FMB-First Michigan Bank - Grand Rapids.

For Complete List of Firm Personnel, See General Section

For full biographical listings, see the Martindale-Hubbell Law Directory

DAY & SAWDEY, A PROFESSIONAL CORPORATION (AV)

200 Monroe Avenue, Suite 500, 49503-2217
Telephone: 616-774-8121
Telefax: 616-774-0168

George B. Kingston (1889-1965)	James B. Frakie
John R. Porter (1915-1975)	Larry A. Ver Merris
Charles E. Day, Jr.	John Boyko, Jr.
Robert W. Sawdey	Jonathan F. Thoits
C. Mark Stoppels	John T. Piggins
	Thomas A. DeMeester

Representative Clients: American National Bank & Trust Company of Chicago; C.M.S. - North America, Inc.; Chemical Bank; National Westminster Bank; Old Kent Bank and Trust Co.

For full biographical listings, see the Martindale-Hubbell Law Directory

LAW, WEATHERS & RICHARDSON, P.C. (AV)

Bridgewater Place, Suite 800, 333 Bridge Street, N.W., 49504
Telephone: 616-459-1171
Facsimile: 616-732-1740

OF COUNSEL

Robert W. Richardson	Walter B. Freihofer

James L. Wernstrom	Clifford H. Bloom
Christopher L. Edgar	Ingrid A. Jensen
Robert A. Buchanan	James A. Ens
Henry G. Swain	Mary Jane Rhoades
Kurt G. Yost	Jeffrey J. Van Winkle

Representative Clients: Skinner & Broadbent; Perrigo Co.; Witmark, Inc.; Sligh Furniture Co.; Wolverine Gas & Oil Co., Inc.; Alpha Properties Investment Group.

For Complete List of Firm Personnel, See General Section

For full biographical listings, see the Martindale-Hubbell Law Directory

McSHANE & BOWIE, P.L.C. (AV)

1100 Campau Square Plaza, 99 Monroe Avenue, N.W., P.O. Box 360, 49501-0360
Telephone: 616-732-5000
Fax: 616-732-5099

OF COUNSEL

Jack M. Bowie (Retired)

MEMBERS OF FIRM

David L. Smith	Keith P. Walker
William H. Bowie	Dan M. Challa

Representative Clients: Old Kent; Metropolitan Life Insurance Co.; Hartger & Willard Mortgage Associates, Inc.; Fryling Construction Co.; Wolverine Builders, Inc.; Beta Design Group, Inc.; Ramblewood, Ltd.; M. W. VanderVeen Co.; Hefferan Property Management, Inc.; Dodgson Realty Co.

For Complete List of Firm Personnel, See General Section

For full biographical listings, see the Martindale-Hubbell Law Directory

RUSSELL & BATCHELOR (AV)

Suite 411-S Waters Building, 161 Ottawa Avenue, N.W., 49503
Telephone: 616-774-8422
Fax: 616-774-0326

MEMBERS OF FIRM

Walter J. Russell	James W. Batchelor

Representative Clients: First National Acceptance Company; Trust Corp.; Chicago Title; Cowger & Miller Mortgage Co.; Federal National Mortgage Association; Dept. of Veterans Affairs; Chrysler First Financial; Equitable Real Estate; Eastover Savings Bank; Commercial Federal Mortgage Corp.

For full biographical listings, see the Martindale-Hubbell Law Directory

TOLLEY, VANDENBOSCH & WALTON, P.C. (AV)

5650 Foremost Drive, S.E., 49546
Telephone: 616-942-8090
Facsimile: 616-942-4677

(See Next Column)

Peter R. Tolley	Michael C. Walton
Lynwood P. VandenBosch	James B. Doezema

For full biographical listings, see the Martindale-Hubbell Law Directory

VARNUM, RIDDERING, SCHMIDT & HOWLETT LLP (AV)

A Limited Liability Partnership including Professional Corporations
Bridgewater Place, P.O. Box 352, 49501-0352
Telephone: 616-336-6000
800-262-0011
Facsimile: 616-336-7000
Telex: 1561593 VARN
Email: varnum@vrsh.com
Lansing, Michigan Office: The Victor Center, Suite 810, 210 North Washington Square, 48933.
Telephone: 517-482-6237.
Facsimile: 517-482-6937.
Kalamazoo, Michigan Office: 350 East Michigan Avenue, 49007.
Telephone: 616-382-2300.
Facsimile: 616-382-2382.
Grand Haven, Michigan Office: 321 Washington Street, P.O. Box 288, 49417.
Telephone: 616-846-7100.
Facsimile: 616-846-7101.
Battle Creek, Michigan Office: 4950 West Dickman Road, Suite B-1, 49015.
Telephone: 616-962-7144.
Bingham Farms, Michigan Office: 31600 Telegraph Road, Suite 230, 48025.
Telephone: 810-594-7330.
Facsimile: 810-594- 7331.

MEMBERS OF FIRM

William K. Van't Hof	Mark C. Hanisch
Nyal D. Deems	Jonathan W. Anderson

COUNSEL

Fred M. Woodruff, Jr. (Resident at Bingham Farms Office)

Counsel for: Grooters Land Development; The Homestead Resort; A.C. Geenen Construction, Inc.; United Development Co.; Federal Home Loan Mortgage Corp.; Heartwell Mortgage Corp.; Chicago Title Insurance; First Michigan Bank Corp.; Michigan National Bank; Transnation Insurance.

For Complete List of Firm Personnel, See General Section

For full biographical listings, see the Martindale-Hubbell Law Directory

WARNER NORCROSS & JUDD LLP (AV)

900 Old Kent Building, 111 Lyon Street, N.W., 49503-2489
Telephone: 616-752-2000
Fax: 616-752-2500
Muskegon, Michigan Office: 400 Terrace Plaza, P.O. Box 900.
Telephone: 616-727-2600.
Fax: 616-727-2699.
Holland, Michigan Office: Curtis Center, Suite 300, 170 College Avenue.
Telephone: 616-396-9800.
Fax: 616-396-3656.

OF COUNSEL

Thomas R. Winquist

MEMBERS OF FIRM

John H. Logie	Jeffrey O. Birkhold
James H. Breay	John G. Cameron, Jr.
Ernest M. Sharpe	Richard E. Cassard
Hugh H. Makens	William W. Hall
Richard A. Durell	Sue O. Conway
Thomas H. Thornhill	Michael H. Schubert
(Resident at Muskegon Office)	(Resident at Muskegon Office)

Representative Clients: Bil Mar Foods; Steelcase Inc.; Haworth, Inc.; Guardsman Products, Inc.; Kessell Foods; Old Kent Financial Corporation; The Zondervan Corporation; Kysor Industrial Corporation; Whirlpool Corporation; Foremost Corporation of America.

For Complete List of Firm Personnel, See General Section

For full biographical listings, see the Martindale-Hubbell Law Directory

WHEELER UPHAM, A PROFESSIONAL CORPORATION (AV)

Second Floor, Trust Building, 40 Pearl Street, N.W., 49503-3001
Telephone: 616-459-7100
Fax: 616-459-6366

Gordon B. Wheeler (1904-1986)	William H. Heritage, Jr.
Buford A. Upham (Retired)	Kenneth E. Tiews
Robert H. Gillette	Jack L. Hoffman
Geoffrey L. Gillis	Janet C. Baxter
John M. Roels	Peter Kladder, III
Gary A. Maximiuk	James M. Shade
Timothy J. Orlebeke	Thomas A. Kuiper

Counsel For: Independent Cooperative Milk Producers Assn.; American Premier Underwriters, Inc.; The United Railroad Corp.; Westdale Better Homes and Gardens; Delta Properties, Inc.

(See Next Column)

WHEELER UPHAM A PROFESSIONAL CORPORATION—*Continued*

For full biographical listings, see the Martindale-Hubbell Law Directory

GROSSE POINTE, Wayne Co.

MARCO, WATKINS AND OWSIANY (AV)

20180 Mack Avenue, 48236
Telephone: 313-882-8800
Fax: 313-882-6211

MEMBERS OF FIRM

Paul Marco   Robert D. Watkins
Michael J. Owsiany

OF COUNSEL

William E. Kennedy

For full biographical listings, see the Martindale-Hubbell Law Directory

HOLLAND, Ottawa Co.

CUNNINGHAM DALMAN, P.C. (AV)

321 Settlers Road, P.O. Box 1767, 49422-1767
Telephone: 616-392-1821
Fax: 616-392-4769

Gordon H. Cunningham	Kenneth B. Breese
Ronald L. Dalman	Jeffrey K. Helder
Max R. Murphy	Ronald J. Vander Veen
James A. Bidol	David M. Zessin
Andrew J. Mulder	Mark H. Zietlow
Joel G. Bouwens	James W. Bouwens

Randall S. Schipper

Susan E. Vroegop   Melinda M. Abney

OF COUNSEL

Vernon D. Ten Cate   Kenneth B. Peirce, Jr.

Representative Clients: FMB-First Michigan Bank; First of America Bank-Holland, N.A.; Ottawa Savings Bank; City of Holland; Holland Economic Development Corp.

For full biographical listings, see the Martindale-Hubbell Law Directory

KALAMAZOO,* Kalamazoo Co.

EARLY, LENNON, PETERS & CROCKER, P.C. (AV)

900 Comerica Building, 49007-4752
Telephone: 616-381-8844
Fax: 616-349-8525

Lawrence M. Brenton   Robert M. Taylor
Blake D. Crocker   Patrick D. Crocker
Andrew J. Vorbrich

OF COUNSEL

Vincent T. Early

Attorneys for: General Motors Corp.; Wal-Mart Stores; Borgess Medical Center; Aetna Insurance: Kemper Group; Medical Protective Co.; Zurich Insurance; AAA; Liberty Mutual; Home Insurance.

For Complete List of Firm Personnel, See General Section

For full biographical listings, see the Martindale-Hubbell Law Directory

HOWARD & HOWARD ATTORNEYS, P.C. (AV)

The Kalamazoo Building, Suite 400, 107 West Michigan
Avenue, 49007-3956
Telephone: 616-382-1483
Telecopier: 616-382-1568
Bloomfield Hills, Michigan Office: The Pinehurst Office Center, Suite 101, 1400 North Woodward Avenue.
Telephone: 810-645-1483.
Telecopier: 810-645-1568.
Lansing, Michigan Office: The Phoenix Building, Suite 500, 222 Washington Square North.
Telephone: 517-485-1483.
Telecopier: 517-485-1568.
Peoria, Illinois Office: The Creve Coeur Building, Suite 200, 321 Liberty Street.
Telephone: 309-672-1483.
Telecopier: 309-672-1568.
Tampa, Florida Office: First of America Plaza, Suite 2000, 201 East Kennedy Boulevard.
Telephone: 813-229-1483.
Telecopier: 813-229-1568.

Stephen D. Bigelow   Michael L. Chojnowski
Jeffrey P. Chalmers   D. Craig Martin

Representative Clients: For Representative Client list, see General Practice, Kalamazoo, MI.

For Complete List of Firm Personnel, See General Section

For full biographical listings, see the Martindale-Hubbell Law Directory

KREIS, ENDERLE, CALLANDER & HUDGINS, A PROFESSIONAL CORPORATION (AV)

One Moorsbridge, P.O. Box 4010, 49003-4010
Telephone: 616-324-3000
Telecopier: 616-324-3010
Email: kech@sapien.net *URL:* http://www.kech.com

Russell A. Kreis   C. Reid Hudgins III
Alan G. Enderle   Jeffrey D. Swenarton

For Complete List of Firm Personnel, See General Section

For full biographical listings, see the Martindale-Hubbell Law Directory

LEWIS & ALLEN, P.C. (AV)

Old Kent Bank Building, Suite 800, 136 East Michigan
Avenue, 49007-3946
Telephone: 616-388-7600
Fax: 616-349-3831

Dean S. Lewis	William A. Redmond
W. Fred Allen, Jr.	Stephen M. Denenfeld
Winfield J. Hollander	Gregory G. St. Arnauld
Bruce W. Martin	Anne McGregor Fries
Daniel L. Conklin	Thomas P. Lewis

Christopher T. Haenicke

LEGAL SUPPORT PERSONNEL

Dorothy B. Kelly

For full biographical listings, see the Martindale-Hubbell Law Directory

MILLER, CANFIELD, PADDOCK AND STONE, P.L.C. (AV)

A Professional Limited Liability Company
Founded in 1852 by Sidney Davy Miller
444 West Michigan Avenue, 49007-3752
Telephone: 616-381-7030
Fax: 616-382-0244
Detroit, Michigan Office: 150 West Jefferson, Suite 2500, 48226-4415.
Telephone: 313-963-6420.
Fax: 313-496-7500.
Cable Address: "Stem Detroit."
Ann Arbor, Michigan Office: 101 North Main Street, 7th Floor, 48104-1400.
Telephone: 313-663-2445.
Fax: 313-747-7147.
Bloomfield Hills, Michigan Office: Suite 100, Pinehurst Office Center, 1400 North Woodward, 48303-2014.
Telephone: 313-645-5000.
Fax: 313-645-1917.
Grand Rapids, Michigan Office: 1200 Campau Square Plaza, 99 Monroe, N.W., 49503-2639.
Telephone: 616-454-8656.
Fax: 616-776-6322.
Howell, Michigan Office: 121 South Barnard Street, Suite 4, 48843-2305.
Telephone: 517-546-7600.
Telecopier: 517-546-6974.
Lansing, Michigan Office: One Michigan Avenue, Suite 900, 48933-1609.
Telephone: 517-487-2070.
Fax: 517-374-6304.
Monroe, Michigan Office: The Executive Centre, 214 East Elm Avenue, 48161-2682.
Telephone: 313-243-2000.
Fax: 313-243-0901.
Washington, D.C. Office: 1225 Nineteenth Street, N.W., Suite 400. 20036.
Telephone: 202-429-5575; 785-0600.
Fax: 202-331-1118; 785-1234.
Pensacola, Florida Office: 25 West Cedar, 32501.
Telephone: 904-469-1088.
Fax: 904-432-0677.
St. Petersburg, Florida Office: 100 Second Avenue S., Suite 7045, 33701.
Telephone: 813-982-6000.
Fax: 813-892-6002.
New York, New York Office: Eleventh Floor, 135 East 57th Street, 10022-2087.
Telephone: 212-754-5400.
Fax: 212-754-5401.
Gdansk, Poland Office: Suite 322, Dom Technika Building, UI. Rajska 6, 80-850.
Telephone: 011-485-831-2808.
Fax: 011-485-831-4719.
Warsaw, Poland Office: UI. Marszalkowska 82, Suite 561, 00-517.
Telephone: 011-482-623-6457 and 6458.
Fax: 011-482-623-6459.

PRINCIPALS OF FIRM

James E. Spurr   Steven M. Stankewicz

Representative Firm Clients: Chrysler Corporation; Comerica, Incorporated; City of Detroit, Michigan; Detroit Tigers, Inc.; First of Michigan; Ford Motor Company; Ford Motor Credit Company; Great Lakes Bancorp; Henry Ford Hospital; INVETECH Company.

(See Next Column)

MILLER, CANFIELD, PADDOCK AND STONE P.L.C., *Kalamazoo—Continued*

For Complete List of Firm Personnel, See General Section

For full biographical listings, see the Martindale-Hubbell Law Directory

---

LANSING, Ingham Co.

* indicates certain Bar Register subscribers whose principal office is located elsewhere in the state and who have arranged for representation as a part of the state capital listings that follow

FOSTER, SWIFT, COLLINS & SMITH, P.C. (AV)

313 South Washington Square, 48933-2193
Telephone: 517-371-8100
Telecopier: 517-371-8200
URL: http://www.fosterswift.com
Farmington Hills, Michigan Office: 32300 Northwestern Highway, Suite 230.
Telephone: 810-539-9900.
Fax: 810-851-7504.

Robert J. McCullen	Brent A. Titus
Steven L. Owen	Brian G. Goodenough

LEGAL SUPPORT PERSONNEL
LEGAL ASSISTANTS
Kelly A. LaGrave, CLA

General Counsel: First of America Bank - Central; Michigan Milk Producers Assn.; Story, Inc.; Edward W. Sparrow Hospital; St. Lawrence Hospital; Michigan Financial Corp.; The State Journal; Peninsular Products; Demmer Corp.

For Complete List of Firm Personnel, See General Section

For full biographical listings, see the Martindale-Hubbell Law Directory

---

FRASER TREBILCOCK DAVIS & FOSTER, P.C. (AV)

1000 Michigan National Tower, 48933
Telephone: 517-482-5800
Fax: 517-482-0887

Douglas J. Austin	Stephen L. Burlingame

Counsel for: Bank One Mortgage Company; Chanberg Construction Company; Delta Mills Estate Homeowners Association; Fleet Mortgage Co.; Frandorson Properties; Heron Creek Builders; Matin Commercial Properties.

For Complete List of Firm Personnel, See General Section

For full biographical listings, see the Martindale-Hubbell Law Directory

---

* HONIGMAN MILLER SCHWARTZ AND COHN (AV)

A Partnership including Professional Corporations
222 North Washington Square, Suite 400, 48933-1800
Telephone: 517-484-8282
Telecopier: 517-484-8286
URL: http://www.law.honigman.com
Detroit, Michigan Office: 2290 First National Building, 48226.
Telephone: 313-256-7800.
West Palm Beach, Florida Office: Suite 800 Esperante Building, 222 Lakeview Avenue, 33401-6112.
Telephone: 561-838-4500.
Tampa, Florida Office: 2700 SunTrust Financial Centre, 401 E. Jackson Street, 33602-5226.
Telephone: 813-221-6600.

MEMBERS
Gary A. Trepod	William C. Whitbeck

For Complete List of Firm Personnel, See General Section

For full biographical listings, see the Martindale-Hubbell Law Directory

---

HOWARD & HOWARD ATTORNEYS, P.C. (AV)

The Phoenix Building, Suite 500, 222 Washington Square, North, 48933-1817
Telephone: 517-485-1483
Telecopier: 517-485-1568
Kalamazoo, Michigan Office: The Kalamazoo Building, Suite 400, 107 West Michigan Avenue.
Telephone: 616-382-1483.
Telecopier: 616-382-1568.
Bloomfield Hills, Michigan Office: The Pinehurst Office Center, Suite 101, 1400 North Woodward Avenue.
Telephone: 810-645-1483.
Telecopier: 810-645-1568.
Peoria, Illinois Office: The Creve Coeur Building, Suite 200, 321 Liberty Street.
Telephone: 309-672-1483.
Telecopier: 309-672-1568.

(See Next Column)

Tampa, Florida Office: First of America Plaza, Suite 2000, 201 East Kennedy Boulevard.
Telephone: 813-229-1483.
Telecopier: 813-229-1568.

Todd D. Chamberlain	Christopher C. Cinnamon
	Patrick D. Hanes

Representative Clients: For Representative Client list, see General Practice, Lansing, MI.

For Complete List of Firm Personnel, See General Section

For full biographical listings, see the Martindale-Hubbell Law Directory

---

MILLER, CANFIELD, PADDOCK AND STONE, P.L.C. (AV)

A Professional Limited Liability Company
Founded in 1852 by Sidney Davy Miller
Suite 900, One Michigan Avenue, 48933-1609
Telephone: 517-487-2070
Fax: 517-374-6304
Detroit, Michigan Office: 150 West Jefferson, Suite 2500, 48226-4415.
Telephone: 313-963-6420.
Fax: 313-496-7500.
Cable Address: "Stem Detroit."
Ann Arbor, Michigan Office: 101 North Main Street, 7th Floor, 48104-1400.
Telephone: 313-663-2445.
Fax: 313-747-7147.
Bloomfield Hills, Michigan Office: Suite 100, Pinehurst Office Center, 1400 North Woodward, 48303-2014.
Telephone: 313-645-5000.
Fax: 313-645-1917.
Grand Rapids, Michigan Office: 1200 Campau Square Plaza, 99 Monroe, N.W., 49503-2639.
Telephone: 616-454-8656.
Fax: 616-776-6322.
Howell, Michigan Office: 121 South Barnard Street, Suite 4, 48843-2305.
Telephone: 517-546-7600.
Telecopier: 517-546-6974.
Kalamazoo, Michigan Office: 444 West Michigan Avenue, 49007-3752.
Telephone: 616-381-7030.
Fax: 616-382-0244.
Monroe, Michigan Office: The Executive Centre, 214 East Elm Avenue, 48161-2682.
Telephone: 313-243-2000.
Fax: 313-243-0901.
Washington, D.C. Office: 1225 Nineteenth Street, N.W., Suite 400. 20036.
Telephone: 202-429-5575; 785-0600.
Fax: 202-331-1118; 785-1234.
Pensacola, Florida Office: 25 West Cedar, 32501.
Telephone: 904-469-1088.
Fax: 904-432-0677.
St. Petersburg Office: 100 Second Avenue S., Suite 7045, 33701.
Telephone: 813-982-6000.
Fax: 813-892-6002.
New York, New York Office: Eleventh Floor, 135 East 57th Street, 10022-2087.
Telephone: 212-754-5400.
Fax: 212-754-5401.
Gdansk, Poland Office: Suite 322, Dom Technika Building, UI. Rajska 6, 80-850.
Telephone: 011-485-831-2808.
Fax: 011-485-831-4719.
Warsaw, Poland Office: UI. Marszalkowska 82, Suite 561, 00-517.
Telephone: 011-482-623-6457 and 6458.
Fax: 011-482-623-6459.

PRINCIPALS OF FIRM
William J. Danhof (Resident)

Representative Firm Clients: Chrysler Corporation; Comerica, Incorporated; City of Detroit, Michigan; Detroit Tigers, Inc.; First of Michigan; Ford Motor Company; Ford Motor Credit Company; Great Lakes Bancorp; Henry Ford Hospital; INVETECH Company.

For Complete List of Firm Personnel, See General Section

For full biographical listings, see the Martindale-Hubbell Law Directory

---

PLYMOUTH, Wayne Co.

SEMPLINER, THOMAS AND BOAK (AV)

711 West Ann Arbor Trail, 48170
Telephone: 313-453-6220, 455-4560

MEMBERS OF FIRM
William Sempliner (1908-1985)	John E. Thomas
	Stephen H. Boak

ASSOCIATES
Mark D. Lang	Tracy S. Thomas

OF COUNSEL
Robert P. Tiplady

For full biographical listings, see the Martindale-Hubbell Law Directory

*PONTIAC,** Oakland Co.

BOOTH PATTERSON, P.C. (AV)

1090 West Huron Street, 48328
Telephone: 810-681-1200
Fax: 810-681-1754

Douglas W. Booth (1918-1992)	David J. Lee
Calvin E. Patterson (1913-1987)	Allan T. Motzny
Parvin C. Lee, Jr.	Michael J. Hughes
J. Timothy Patterson	Michael D. Bishop

Eric S. Meier

For full biographical listings, see the Martindale-Hubbell Law Directory

*SAGINAW,** Saginaw Co.

BRAUN KENDRICK FINKBEINER PLC (AV)

101 N. Washington Suite 812, 48607-1297
Telephone: 517-753-3461
Telecopier: 517-753-3951
URL: http://www.bkf-law.com
Bay City, Michigan Office: 201 Phoenix Building, P.O. Box 2039.
Telephone: 517-895-8505.
Telecopier: 517-895-8437.
Ann Arbor, Michigan Office: 700 First National Building.
Telephone: 313-995-4100.
Telecopier: 313-995-4798.

James V. Finkbeiner	C. Patrick Kaltenbach
Hugo E. Braun, Jr.	Thomas R. Luplow

Brian F. Bauer
OF COUNSEL
J. Richard Kendrick

Representative Clients: The Dow Chemical Co.; General Motors Corp.; Lobdell Emery Manufacturing Co.; Merrill, Lynch, Inc.; Saginaw General Hospital; Saginaw News; The Wickes Foundation.

For Complete List of Firm Personnel, See General Section

For full biographical listings, see the Martindale-Hubbell Law Directory

*ST. JOSEPH,** Berrien Co.

BUTZBAUGH & DEWANE, P.L.C. (AV)

Law and Title Building, 811 Ship Street, P.O. Box 27, 49085
Telephone: 616-983-0191
Fax: 616-983-5078
Email: b__d__law@parrett.net

MEMBER OF FIRM
Alfred M. Butzbaugh

Representative Clients: F & M Bank; Old Kent Bank; SJS Federal Savings BAnk; Oronoko Township; Building Constructors, Inc.; Southwestern Michigan Abstract & Title Co.; Monte Package Co.; Reliable Disposal.

For Complete List of Firm Personnel, See General Section

For full biographical listings, see the Martindale-Hubbell Law Directory

FISHER LAW OFFICE (AV)

Law & Title Building, 811 Ship Street, P.O. Box 83, 49085-0083
Telephone: 616-983-5511
Telecopier: 616-893-5571

Vance A. Fisher

For full biographical listings, see the Martindale-Hubbell Law Directory

TROFF, PETZKE & AMMESON (AV)

Law and Title Building, 811 Ship Street, P.O. Box 67, 49085
Telephone: 616-983-0161
Facsimile: 616-983-0166

MEMBERS OF FIRM

Theodore E. Troff	Roger A. Petzke
Charles F. Ammeson	

ASSOCIATES

Bennett S. Schwartz	Daniel G. Lambrecht
Deborah L. Berecz	

For full biographical listings, see the Martindale-Hubbell Law Directory

SOUTHFIELD, Oakland Co.

MADDIN, HAUSER, WARTELL, ROTH, HELLER & PESSES, P.C. (AV)

Third Floor Essex Center, 28400 Northwestern Highway, P.O. Box 215, 48037
Telephone: 810-354-4030, 355-5200
Telefax: 810-354-1422

(See Next Column)

Milton M. Maddin (1902-1984)	Robert D. Kaplow
Michael W. Maddin	William E. Sigler
Mark R. Hauser	Stewart C. W. Weiner
C. Robert Wartell	Charles M. Lax
Richard J. Maddin	Stuart M. Bordman
Richard F. Roth	Steven D. Sallen
Harvey R. Heller	Joseph M. Fazio
Ian D. Pesses	Gregory J. Gamalski
Michael S. Leib	Julie Chenot Mayer

Nathaniel H. Simpson	Lowell D. Salesin
Ronald A. Sollish	Marc J. Mendelson
Mark H. Fink	Joseph W. Girardot
Steven M. Wolock	Lori E. Talsky

OF COUNSEL
Joel D. Kellman

Reference: Comerica Bank.

For full biographical listings, see the Martindale-Hubbell Law Directory

MASON, STEINHARDT, JACOBS & PERLMAN, PROFESSIONAL CORPORATION (AV)

Suite 1500, 4000 Town Center, 48075-1415
Telephone: 810-358-2090
Fax: 810-358-3599

John E. Jacobs	Neil S. Silver
Michael B. Perlman	L. Jeffrey Zauberman

Diane Flagg Goldstein

Representative Clients: Citibank, N.A.; City of Dearborn; DeMattia Development Co.; Forest City Enterprises; Michigan Wholesale Drug Assn.; Mortgage Bankers Association of Michigan; Nationwide Insurance Co.; City of Taylor; Union Labor Life Insurance Co.; Yellow Freight Systems, Inc.

For Complete List of Firm Personnel, See General Section

For full biographical listings, see the Martindale-Hubbell Law Directory

PROVIZER, LICHTENSTEIN & PHILLIPS, P.C. (AV)

4000 Town Center, Suite 1800, 48075
Telephone: 810-352-9080
Facsimile: 810-352-1491

Harold M. Provizer	Deborah Molitz
David S. Lichtenstein	Noel F. Beck
Randall E. Phillips	William J. Selinsky
Marilyn A. Madorsky	Robert I. Brown

Jason Milstone

For full biographical listings, see the Martindale-Hubbell Law Directory

SOMMERS, SCHWARTZ, SILVER & SCHWARTZ, P.C. (AV)

2000 Town Center, Suite 900, 48075
Telephone: 810-355-0300
Telecopier: 810-746-4001
Plymouth, Michigan Office: 747 South Main Street.
Telephone: 313-455-4250.

Steven J. Schwartz	David M. Black
Gary A. Taback	Joseph H. Bourgon

OF COUNSEL

Norman Samuel Sommers	Donald R. Epstein
Marvin R. Stempien	

General Counsel for: Michigan National Bank; Madison National Bank; Bank Hapoalim, B.M.; Beal Bank, S.A.; C.A. Muer Corporation; Kojaian Properties, Inc.; Vlasic & Company; Foodland Distributors; Nederlander Corporation.

For Complete List of Firm Personnel, See General Section

For full biographical listings, see the Martindale-Hubbell Law Directory

*TRAVERSE CITY,** Grand Traverse Co.

MURCHIE, CALCUTT & BOYNTON (AV)

109 East Front Street, Suite 300, 49684
Telephone: 616-947-7190
Fax: 616-947-4341

Robert B. Murchie (1894-1975)	William B. Calcutt
Harry Calcutt	Mark A. Burnheimer
Jack E. Boynton	Dawn M. Rogers

ASSOCIATE
Ralph J. Dilley (Not admitted in MI)

General Counsel for: Old Kent Bank-Grand Traverse; Northwestern Savings Bank & Trust; Central-State Bancorp; Traverse City Record Eagle; WPNB-7 & WTOM-4; Emergency Consultants, Inc.; National Guardian Risk Retention Group, Inc.; Farmers Mutual Insurance Co.; Environmental Solutions, Inc.

(See Next Column)

MURCHIE, CALCUTT & BOYNTON, *Traverse City—Continued*

Local Counsel for: Consumers Power Co.

For full biographical listings, see the Martindale-Hubbell Law Directory

RUNNING, WISE, WILSON, FORD AND PHILLIPS, P.L.C. (AV)

326 State Street, P.O. Box 686, 49684
Telephone: 616-946-2700
Tele-Fax: 616-946-0857

Harry T. Running (Deceased)   William L. Wise (Retired)
MEMBERS OF FIRM

Patrick J. Wilson	James C. Adams
Richard W. Ford	Sandra P. Howard
Thomas J. Phillips	Kent E. Gerberding

ASSOCIATES

Shelley A. Kester   Bradley L. Putney

OF COUNSEL

J. Bruce Donaldson   Douglas J. Donaldson

Representative Clients: Peninsula Fruit Exchange; Oleson Food Stores; Munson Healthcare; Munson Medical Center; Grand Traverse County Road Commission; Townships of Peninsula, East Bay, Garfield, Almira, Homestead.

For full biographical listings, see the Martindale-Hubbell Law Directory

---

TROY, Oakland Co.

AUSTIN HIRSCHHORN, P.C. (AV)

Suite 710 Columbia Center, 201 West Big Beaver Road, 48084-4152
Telephone: 810-680-1660
Fax: 810-680-1671

Austin Hirschhorn

For full biographical listings, see the Martindale-Hubbell Law Directory

---

JACOB & WEINGARTEN (AV)

2301 West Big Beaver Road, Suite 777, 48084
Telephone: 810-649-1900
Facsimile: 810-649-2920
West Palm Beach, Florida Office: 1555 Palm Beach Lake Boulevard, Suite 1510, 33401.
Telephone: 561-640-5600.
Facsimile: 561-683-0799.

Joel G. Jacob	Carole Crosby
Harry M. Eisenberg	Frank J. Badach
Peter A. Nathan (Resident, West	(Not admitted in MI)
Palm Beach, Florida Office)	Phillip J. Neuman
Steven P. Schubiner	Vicky Wood Kvicala

Michael B. Peterman

Representative Clients: Dean Witter Realty, Inc.; Franklin Group, Inc.; Kamin Realty Company; New Center Company; P.M. Realty Group; Ruby Tuesday, Inc.; Sunburst Properties, Inc.

For full biographical listings, see the Martindale-Hubbell Law Directory

---

POLING, McGAW & POLING, P.C. (AV)

Suite 275, 5435 Corporate Drive, 48098
Telephone: 810-641-0500
Telecopier: 810-641-0506

Benson T. Buck (1926-1989)	Richard B. Poling, Jr.
Richard B. Poling	Gregory C. Hamilton
D. Douglas McGaw	Veronica B. O'Haro

James R. Parker

OF COUNSEL

Ralph S. Moore

Representative Clients: County of Oakland; City of Troy; United States Fidelity & Guaranty Co.; Sentry Insurance Co.; Admital Insurance; DeMaria Construction Co.; Leo Corporation; Aetna Casualty and Surety Co.; Concord Design; Pneumo-Abex.

For full biographical listings, see the Martindale-Hubbell Law Directory

---

SCHIER, DENEWETH & PARFITT, P.C. (AV)

888 West Big Beaver Road, Suite 610, 48084-4737
Telephone: 810-362-5600
Telecopier: 810-362-0073

Carl F. Schier	Timothy P. Dugan
Ronald A. Deneweth	Janette E. Frank
Chris Parfitt	Mark D. Sassak

OF COUNSEL

Edward A. Ryder

References: Bosco Building Company; Horizon Development, Inc.; J. Socks Development Company; Mega Properties, Inc.; Metamora Golf and Country Club; Metamora Residential Land Company, LLC; Midwest Development

Company; Real Estate Equity Group; Trinity Land, Ltd.; Uznis-Deneweth Development Co.

For full biographical listings, see the Martindale-Hubbell Law Directory

---

WEST BLOOMFIELD, Oakland Co.

VALENTINE & ASSOCIATES, P.C. (AV)

5767 West Maple Road, Suite 400, 48322
Telephone: 810-851-3010

Stephen K. Valentine, Jr.
OF COUNSEL
Philip G. Meyer

For full biographical listings, see the Martindale-Hubbell Law Directory

SECURITIES LAW

ALABAMA

BIRMINGHAM,* Jefferson Co.

BERKOWITZ, LEFKOVITS, ISOM & KUSHNER, A PROFESSIONAL CORPORATION (AV)

1600 SouthTrust Tower, 420 North Twentieth Street, 35203
Telephone: 205-328-0480
Telecopier: 205-322-8007

B. G. Minisman, Jr.   W. Clark Goodwin

Representative Clients: AlaTenn Resources, Inc.; AlaTenn Natural Gas Co.; B.A.S.S., Inc.; Hanna Steel Co., Inc.; Liberty Trouser Co., Inc.; Parisian, Inc.; Southern Pipe & Supply Co., Inc.

For Complete List of Firm Personnel, See General Section

For full biographical listings, see the Martindale-Hubbell Law Directory

BRADLEY, ARANT, ROSE & WHITE (AV)

2001 Park Place, Suite 1400, P.O. Box 830709, 35283-0709
Telephone: 205-521-8000
Facsimile: 205-252-0264
Facsimile (SouthTrust Tower Office): 205-251-9915
URL: http://www.BARW.COM
Huntsville, Alabama Office: 200 Clinton Avenue West, Suite 900, 35801.
Telephone: 205-517-5100.
Facsimile: 205-533-5069.

MEMBERS OF FIRM

Edward M. Selfe   Michael R. Pennington
John P. Adams   Michael D. McKibben
Charles Larimore Whitaker   Paul S. Ware
John G. Harrell   Virginia Calvert Patterson
John K. Molen   Denson Nauls Franklin III
John B. Grenier   J. Paul Compton, Jr.

ASSOCIATES

Hall B, Bryant III   Dorothy C. Daigle
(Resident, Huntsville Office)   Joseph E. Smith
Paul D. Gilbert   Hugh Chester Boston, III
              Steven Austin King

For Complete List of Firm Personnel, See General Section

For full biographical listings, see the Martindale-Hubbell Law Directory

CORLEY, MONCUS & WARD, P.C. (AV)

400 Shades Creek Parkway, Suite 100, P.O. Box 59807, 35259
Telephone: 205-879-5959
Telecopier: 205-871-4411

Claude McCain Moncus   James S. Ward
              Ezra B. Perry, Jr.

For Complete List of Firm Personnel, See General Section

For full biographical listings, see the Martindale-Hubbell Law Directory

JOHNSTON, BARTON, PROCTOR & POWELL (AV)

2900 AmSouth/Harbert Plaza, 1901 Sixth Avenue North, 35203-2618
Telephone: 205-458-9400
Telecopier: 205-458-9500

MEMBERS OF FIRM

Harvey Deramus (1904-1970)   James C. Barton, Jr.
Alfred M. Naff (1923-1993)   Thomas E. Walker
Gilbert E. Johnston (1916-1994)   Anne P. Wheeler
G. Burns Proctor, Jr.   Barry V. Frederick
Sydney L. Lavender   Hollinger F. Barnard
Charles A. Powell, III   William D. Jones III
Jerome K. Lanning   David W. Proctor
Don B. Long, Jr.   Oscar M. Price III
Charles L. Robinson   W. Hill Sewell
J. William Rose, Jr.   Robert S. Vance, Jr.
Gilbert E. Johnston, Jr.   Richard J. Brockman
Ralph H. Smith II   Anthony A. Joseph
              William G. Somerville, III

COUNSEL

Josh Mullins, Jr.   Paul E. Toppins
              R. Marcus Givhan

OF COUNSEL

James C. Barton   Alfred Swedlaw
              Alan W. Heldman

(See Next Column)

ASSOCIATES

William K. Hancock   Helen Kathryn Downs
James P. Pewitt   Jennifer Fox Swain
Scott Wells Ford   Spencer A. Kinderman
David M. Hunt   Scott R. McLaughlin
Lee M. Pope   Pradley C. Mayhew
John W. Sheffield   W. Jonathan Daniel
Haskins W. Jones   J. Vincent Edge
Russell L. Irby, III   Allison Powell

General Counsel for: The Birmingham News Co.
Counsel for: General Motors Corp.; General Electric Capital Corp.; Goldome Credit Corp.

For full biographical listings, see the Martindale-Hubbell Law Directory

LIGHTFOOT, FRANKLIN & WHITE, L.L.C. (AV)

300 Financial Center, 505 20th Street North, 35203-2706
Telephone: 205-581-0700
Facsimile: 205-581-0799

Warren B. Lightfoot   Samuel H. Franklin
              Mac M. Moorer

Robin Hansen Graves

Counsel for: AT&T; Ford Motor Co.; Emerson Electric Co.; Monsanto Co.; Chrysler Corp.; Unocal Corp.; The Upjohn Co.; Bristol-Myers Squibb Co.; The Goodyear Tire & Rubber Co.; Mitsubishi Motor Sales of America, Inc.

For full biographical listings, see the Martindale-Hubbell Law Directory

PATRICK & LACY, P.C. (AV)

1201 Financial Center, 35203
Telephone: 205-323-5665
Telecopier: 205-324-6221

J. Vernon Patrick, Jr.   William M. Acker, III
Alex S. Lacy   Elizabeth N. Pitman

For full biographical listings, see the Martindale-Hubbell Law Directory

RITCHIE & REDIKER, L.L.C. (AV)

312 North 23rd Street, 35203
Telephone: 205-251-1288
Fax: 205-324-7830

Thomas A. Ritchie   Thomas L. Krebs
J. Michael Rediker   Steven P. Gregory
Carolyn L. Duncan   Christopher B. Harmon
              Patricia Diak Goodman

Representative Clients: Citation Corporation; Vesta Insurance Group, Inc.; Commerce Bank of Alabama; Heritage Bank; First Metro Bank; State Employees Retirement System of Alabama; Wall Street Deli, Inc.; Sterne, Agee & Leach, Inc.; National Office Buyers; Peoples Savings Life Insurance Co.

For full biographical listings, see the Martindale-Hubbell Law Directory

DOTHAN,* Houston Co.

JOHNSTON, HINESLEY, FLOWERS & CLENNEY, P.C., A PROFESSIONAL CORPORATION (AV)

291 North Oates Street, 36303
Telephone: 334-793-1115
Fax: 334-793-6603

G. David Johnston   William T. Flowers
William W. Hinesley   R. Eugene Clenney, Jr.
              J. Ken Thompson

For full biographical listings, see the Martindale-Hubbell Law Directory

MOBILE,* Mobile Co.

ARMBRECHT, JACKSON, DEMOUY, CROWE, HOLMES & REEVES, L.L.C. (AV)

1300 AmSouth Center, P.O. Box 290, 36601
Telephone: 334-405-1300
Facsimile: 334-432-6843; 433-3821

MEMBERS OF FIRM

E. B. Peebles III   James Dale Smith

Representative Clients: Cooper/T. Smith Stevedoring Co., Inc.; Dean Witter Reynolds, Inc.; Loyal American Life Insurance Co.; Mobile Gas Service Corp.; Prudential-Bache Securities, Inc.; United Bank Corporation of Alabama, Inc.; WKRG-TV, Inc.

For Complete List of Firm Personnel, See General Section

For full biographical listings, see the Martindale-Hubbell Law Directory

ARIZONA

PHOENIX, * Maricopa Co.

BONNETT, FAIRBOURN, FRIEDMAN & BALINT, P.C. (AV)

4041 North Central Avenue Suite 1100, 85012
Telephone: 602-274-1100
Fax: 602-274-1199

Jerry C. Bonnett	Tara L. Jackson
William G. Fairbourn	Wendy J. Harrison
Andrew S. Friedman	Scott A. Erickson
Francis J. Balint, Jr.	Guy A. Hanson
H. Sullivan Bunch	Thomas B. Dixon
Michael N. Widener	Martin E. Latz
Robert J. Spurlock	Gina M. DeVito
C. Kevin Dykstra	Robert D. Ryan
Elaine A. Ryan	Guy P. Roll

OF COUNSEL
James Duke Cameron

For full biographical listings, see the Martindale-Hubbell Law Directory

---

FENNEMORE CRAIG, A PROFESSIONAL CORPORATION (AV)

Two North Central, Suite 2200, 85004
Telephone: 602-257-8700
Fax: 602-257-8527
Scottsdale, Arizona Office: 6263 North Scottsdale Road, Suite 290, 85250.
Telephone: 602-257-5400.
Fax: 602-257-5409.
Tucson, Arizona Office: One South Church Avenue, Suite 1030, 85701.
Telephone: 520-791-6800.
Fax: 520-791-6820.

F. Pendleton Gaines, III	William L. Thorpe
Robert J. Hackett	Karen Ciupak McConnell
Mark A. Nesvig	Janet W. Lord

W. T. Eggleston, Jr.

For Complete List of Firm Personnel, See General Section

For full biographical listings, see the Martindale-Hubbell Law Directory

---

GALBUT & CONANT, A PROFESSIONAL CORPORATION (AV)

Camelback Esplanade, Suite 1020, 2425 East Camelback Road, 85016
Telephone: 602-955-1455
Fax: 602-955-1585

Martin R. Galbut	Paul A. Conant

John R. Augustine, Jr.

For full biographical listings, see the Martindale-Hubbell Law Directory

---

JENNINGS, STROUSS AND SALMON, P.L.C. (AV)

A Professional Limited Liability Company
One Renaissance Square, Two North Central, 85004-2393
Telephone: 602-262-5911
Fax: 602-253-3255

I. Douglas Dunipace	George C. Spilsbury

Anne L. Kleindienst

For Complete List of Firm Personnel, See General Section

For full biographical listings, see the Martindale-Hubbell Law Directory

---

JOHN S. LANCY & ASSOCIATES A PROFESSIONAL CORPORATION (AV)

Suite 390, 2425 East Camelback Road, 85016
Telephone: 602-381-6555
Fax: 602-381-6550

John S. Lancy

Steven W. Bienstock	Nina A. Ortega

For full biographical listings, see the Martindale-Hubbell Law Directory

---

LEWIS AND ROCA, LLP (AV)

A Limited Liability Partnership including a Professional Corporation
40 North Central Avenue, 85004-4429
Telephone: 602-262-5311
Fax: 602-262-5747
Email: mlp@lrlaw.com
Tucson, Arizona Office: One South Church Avenue, Suite 700, 86701-1620.
Telephone: 520-622-2090.
Fax: 520-622-3088. E-Mail: mlp@lrlaw.com.

(See Next Column)

MEMBERS OF FIRM

Kevin L. Olson	David M. Bixby
Scott DeWald	Bryant D. Barber

ASSOCIATES

Kevin G. Hunter	Julie M. Arvo MacKenzie

Representative Clients: MarkAir, Inc.; Rauscher Pierce Refsnes; Rockford Corp.; Samaritan Health System; Skymall, Inc.

For Complete List of Firm Personnel, See General Section

For full biographical listings, see the Martindale-Hubbell Law Directory

O'CONNOR, CAVANAGH, ANDERSON, KILLINGSWORTH & BESHEARS, A PROFESSIONAL ASSOCIATION (AV)

One East Camelback Road, Suite 1100, 85012-1656
Telephone: 602-263-2400
FAX: 602-263-2900
Email: firminfo@arizlaw.com
Sun City, Arizona Office: 13250 North Del Webb Boulevard, Suite B, 85351.
Telephone: 602-263-2808.
FAX: 602-933-3100.
Tucson, Arizona Office: O'Connor Cavanagh Molloy Jones, 33 N. Stone, Suite 2100, 85701, P.O. Box 2268, 85702.
Telephone: 520-622-3531.
FAX: 520-624-2816.
Nogales, Arizona Office: 1891 North Mastick Way, 85621.
Telephone: 520-761-4215.
FAX: 520-761-3505.

Robert S. Kant	Jean E. Harris
Richard B. Stagg	Michelle S. Monserez

Jere M. Friedman	Michael L. Kaplan

Brian P. Dolasinski

OF COUNSEL
Sara R. Ziskin

Representative Clients: SecurNet Mortgage Securities Corporation I; American Southwest Financial Corporation; Action Performance Companies; Cerprobe Corporation; Main Street and Main Incorporated; Homeplex Mortgage Investments Corporation; ASR Investments Corporation; Three-Five Systems, Inc.; Rural/Metro Corporation.

For Complete List of Firm Personnel, See General Section

For full biographical listings, see the Martindale-Hubbell Law Directory

---

QUARLES & BRADY (AV)

One Camelback Building, One East Camelback Road, Suite 400, 85012-1649
Telephone: 602-230-5500
Fax: 602-230-5598
Milwaukee, Wisconsin Office: 411 East Wisconsin Avenue.
Telephone: 414-277-5000.
Fax: 414-271-3552.
Madison, Wisconsin Office: First Wisconsin Plaza, One South Pinckney Street, P.O. Box 2113.
Telephone: 608-251-5000.
Fax: 608-251-9166.
West Palm Beach, Florida Office: 222 Lakeview Ave., 4th Floor.
Telephone: 407-653-5000.
Fax: 407-653-5333.
Naples, Florida Office: Barnett Center, 4501 Tamiami Trail North, Suite 300.
Telephone: 813-262-5959.
Fax: 813-434-4999.

MEMBERS OF THE FIRM

P. Robert Moya	Paul M. Gales

Steven P. Emerick

ASSOCIATES

Mary Beth Miller	Russell Mancuso
Mark N. Rogers	Mark K. Briggs

For Complete List of Firm Personnel, See General Section

For full biographical listings, see the Martindale-Hubbell Law Directory

---

SCOTTSDALE, Maricopa Co.

TITUS, BRUECKNER & BERRY, P.C. (AV)

Scottsdale Centre Suite B-252, 7373 North Scottsdale Road, 85253-3527
Telephone: 602-483-9600
Fax: 602-483-3215
Email: TBandB@aol.com

Jon A. Titus	Charles R. Berry
Kurt M. Brueckner	Alex B. Vakula

Garry S. O'Rafferty

David R. Jordan	K. Scott Reynolds
Scott K. Risley	Michael F. Patterson

(See Next Column)

TITUS, BRUECKNER & BERRY P.C.—*Continued*
LEGAL SUPPORT PERSONNEL
Janice L. Innocenzi   Belle Taylor

Representative Clients: Arizona Department of Insurance; Dickinson & Co.
Hancock Homes; McCallum Hill; Heritage Mint, Ltd.; Baukol Construction,
Inc.; Office of Special Deputy Receiver, Illinois Department of Insurance;
Peacock, Hislop, Staley & Given, Inc.; H.E.R.C. Products., Incorporated;
Stewart Title and Trust of Phoenix, Inc.; Beazer Homes.

For full biographical listings, see the Martindale-Hubbell Law Directory

TUCSON, * Pima Co.

O'CONNOR CAVANAGH MOLLOY JONES, A PROFESSIONAL ASSOCIATION (AV)

Suite 2100 33 N. Stone, P.O. Box 2268, 85702
Telephone: 520-622-3531
FAX: 520-624-2816
Email: firminfo@arizlaw.com
Phoenix, Arizona Office: O'Connor, Cavanagh, Anderson, Killingsworth &
Beshears, One East Camelback Road, Suite 1100, 85012.
Telephone: 602-263-2400.
FAX: 602-263-2900.
Sun City, Arizona Office: O'Connor, Cavanagh, Anderson, Killingsworth
& Beshears, 13250 North Del Webb Boulevard, Suite B, 85351.
Telephone: 602-263-2808.
FAX: 602-933-3100.
Nogales, Arizona Office: O'Connor, Cavanagh, Anderson, Killingsworth &
Beshears, 1891 North Mastick Way, 85621.
Telephone: 520-761-4215.
FAX: 520-761-3505.

Thomas E. Laursen

Reference: Citibank.

For Complete List of Firm Personnel, See General Section

For full biographical listings, see the Martindale-Hubbell Law Directory

ARKANSAS

LITTLE ROCK, * Pulaski Co.

ALLEN LAW FIRM, A PROFESSIONAL CORPORATION (AV)

950 Centre Place, 212 Center Street, 72201
Telephone: 501-374-7100
Telecopier: 501-374-1611
Email: hwallen@cei.net

H. William Allen

Sandra E. Jackson

Representative Clients: Boatmen's National Bank of Arkansas; Colonia Insurance Co.; Shoney's Inc.; Garlock, Inc.; National Bank of Commerce.

For full biographical listings, see the Martindale-Hubbell Law Directory

RICHARD C. DOWNING, P.A. (AV)

Lafayette Building, Suite 750, 523 South Louisiana, 72201
Telephone: 501-372-2066
FAX: 501-376-6420
Email: RCDown@aol.com

Richard C. Downing

For full biographical listings, see the Martindale-Hubbell Law Directory

FRIDAY, ELDREDGE & CLARK (AV)

A Partnership including Professional Associations
Formerly, Smith, Williams, Friday, Eldredge & Clark
2000 First Commercial Building, 400 West Capitol Avenue, 72201-3493
Telephone: 501-376-2011
Telecopier: 501-376-2147; 376-6369
Email: fecmh@fec.sprint.com
MEMBERS OF FIRM
Paul B. Benham, III, (P.A.)   Thomas N. Rose (P.A.)
Larry W. Burks (P.A.)   John Clayton Randolph (P.A.)
Robert S. Shafer (P.A.)   Jeffrey H. Moore (P.A.)
ASSOCIATE
Allison Graves

Representative Clients: Arkansas Power & Light Co.; Dillard Department
Stores, Inc.; Acxiom Corp.; First Commercial Corp.; Entergy Corp.; Union
Pacific Railroad; Browning Arms Co.; Phillips Cos., Inc.; Liberty Mutual
Ins. Co.; St. Paul Fire and Marine Ins. Co.

(See Next Column)

For Complete List of Firm Personnel, See General Section

For full biographical listings, see the Martindale-Hubbell Law Directory

HILBURN, CALHOON, HARPER, PRUNISKI & CALHOUN, LTD. (AV)

P.O. Box 1256, 72203-1256
Telephone: 501-372-0110
Fax: 501-372-2029
North Little Rock, Arkansas Office: Eighth Floor, Mercantile Bank
Building, One Riverfront Place, P.O. Box 5551, 72119.
Telephone: 501-372-0110.
Fax: 501-372-2029.

John E. Pruniski, III   Scott E. Daniel

Representative Clients: Mercantile Bank of Central Arkansas; Merrill Lynch
Pierce Fenner & Smith, Inc.; Smith Barney, Inc.; Prudential Securities Inc.

For Complete List of Firm Personnel, See General Section

For full biographical listings, see the Martindale-Hubbell Law Directory

HOOVER & KOOISTRA (AV)

111 Center Street, 11th Floor, 72201-4445
Telephone: 501-376-8500
Facsimile: 501-372-3255
MEMBERS OF FIRM
Paul W. Hoover, Jr.   John Kooistra, III
     Max C. Mehlburger

For full biographical listings, see the Martindale-Hubbell Law Directory

IVESTER, SKINNER & CAMP, P.A. (AV)

Suite 1200, 111 Center Street, 72201
Telephone: 501-376-7788
FAX: 501-376-8536

Hermann Ivester   Randal B. Frazier
H. Edward Skinner   Laura G. Wiltshire
Charles R. Camp   Todd A. Lewellen
     Stan D. Smith

For Complete List of Firm Personnel, See General Section

For full biographical listings, see the Martindale-Hubbell Law Directory

WILLIAMS & ANDERSON (AV)

Twenty-Second Floor, 111 Center Street, 72201
Telephone: 501-372-0800
FAX: 501-372-6453
MEMBERS OF FIRM
Peter G. Kumpe   J. Leon Holmes

Representative Clients: Arkansas Development Finance Authority; Dean Witter Reynolds Inc.; Entergy Power, Inc.; Little Rock Newspapers, Inc. d/b/a
Arkansas Democrat-Gazette; Potlatch Corporation; Texaco Inc.; Roman
Catholic Diocese of Little Rock; Wal-Mart Stores, Inc.

For Complete List of Firm Personnel, See General Section

For full biographical listings, see the Martindale-Hubbell Law Directory

WRIGHT, LINDSEY & JENNINGS (AV)

200 West Capitol Avenue, Suite 2200, 72201
Telephone: 501-371-0808
Fax: 501-376-9442
Email: tgraves@wlj.com *URL:* http://www.wlj.com/
Fayetteville, Arkansas Office: 101 West Mountain Street, Suite 206, 72701.
Telephone: 501-575-0808.
Fax: 501-575-0999.
Russellville, Arkansas Office: Suite E, 1110 West B Street.
Telephone: 501-968-7995.

C. Douglas Buford, Jr.   Anna Hirai Gibson
John William Spivey III   Walter McSpadden
Charles C. Price   Kevin W. Kennedy
Walter E. May   Fred M. Perkins III
     Michele L. Simmons

Representative Clients: Acxiom Corp.; Boatmen's National Bank of Arkansas; Brewer Personnel Services, Inc.; Hudson Foods, Inc.; J.B. Hunt Transport Services, Inc.; National Home Center, Inc.; Stephens Inc.

For full biographical listings, see the Martindale-Hubbell Law Directory

CALIFORNIA

COSTA MESA, Orange Co.

COULOMBE & KOTTKE, A PROFESSIONAL CORPORATION (AV)

Comerica Bank Tower, 611 Anton Boulevard, Suite 1260, 92626
Telephone: 714-540-1234
Fax: 714-754-0808; 714-754-0707
Email: c-k@coulombe.com

Ronald B. Coulombe   Jon S. Kottke
COUNSEL
Roy B. Woolsey
LEGAL SUPPORT PERSONNEL
PARALEGALS
Vicky M. Pearson   Abeer F. Rider
LEGAL ADMINISTRATOR
Yvonne Mendoza

For full biographical listings, see the Martindale-Hubbell Law Directory

RUTAN & TUCKER, LLP (AV)

A Partnership including Professional Corporations
611 Anton Boulevard, Suite 1400, P.O. Box 1950, 92626
Telephone: 714-641-5100; 213-625-7586
Telecopier: 714-546-9035
Email: rutan&tucker@mcimail.com *URL:* http://www.rutan.com
MEMBERS OF FIRM
Michael T. Hornak   Evridiki (Vicki) Dallas
Thomas G. Brockington   Thomas J. Crane
ASSOCIATES
James S. Weisz   Scott R. Santagata
Robert Elliot Adel II

For Complete List of Firm Personnel, See General Section

For full biographical listings, see the Martindale-Hubbell Law Directory

*FRESNO,** Fresno Co.

DOWLING, AARON & KEELER, INCORPORATED (AV)

Suite 200, 6051 North Fresno Street, 93710
Telephone: 209-432-4500
Fax: 209-432-4590
Email: dowling-law.com

Michael D. Dowling   Adolfo M. Corona
Richard M. Aaron   Philip David Kopp
Bruce S. Fraser   Rene Lastreto, II
William J. Keeler, Jr.   Francine Marie Kanne
John C. Ganahl   Christopher A. Brown

Richard E. Heatter   Michael P. Dowling
James C. Sherwood   Daniel T. Fitzpatrick
Mark D. Kruthers
OF COUNSEL
Daniel K. Whitehurst   Morris M. Sherr
Blaine Pettitt
Reference: Wells Fargo Bank (Main).

For full biographical listings, see the Martindale-Hubbell Law Directory

HERMOSA BEACH, Los Angeles Co.

NASH & EDGERTON (AV)

A Limited Liability Partnership
2615 Pacific Coast Highway, Suite 322, 90254
Telephone: 310-937-2066
Fax: 310-937-2063
Torrance, California Office: 3625 Del Amo Boulevard, suite 360.
Telephone: 310-370-8272.
Fax: 310-214-9677.

Savery L. Nash   Shelley Nash
Samuel Y. Edgerton, III   David Maurer
Damon Rubin

For full biographical listings, see the Martindale-Hubbell Law Directory

IRVINE, Orange Co.

BORCHARD & WILLOUGHBY, A PROFESSIONAL CORPORATION (AV)

18881 Von Karman Avenue, Suite 1400, 92612
Telephone: 714-644-6161
Fax: 714-263-1913

(See Next Column)

Michael D. Borchard   Michael L. Willoughby
Mark A. Rodriguez

Stephanie A. Pittaluga

For full biographical listings, see the Martindale-Hubbell Law Directory

GIBSON, HAGLUND & JOHNSON (AV)

2010 Main Street, Suite 400, 92714
Telephone: 714-752-1100
Fax: 714-752-1144
MEMBERS OF FIRM
Robert V. Gibson   Bruce H. Haglund
Paul H. Johnson

For full biographical listings, see the Martindale-Hubbell Law Directory

McKENNA & STAHL (AV)

2603 Main Street, Suite 1010, 92614-6232
Telephone: 714-752-2800
Facsimile: 714-752-6723

Charles A. McKenna, Jr.   Harry S. Stahl
OF COUNSEL
Christopher E. Call

For full biographical listings, see the Martindale-Hubbell Law Directory

LA JOLLA, San Diego Co.

FISHER THURBER LLP (AV)

La Jolla Executive Tower, 4225 Executive Square Suite 1600, 92037-1483
Telephone: 619-535-9400
Fax: 619-535-1616

David A. Fisher
OF COUNSEL
Marshall Thurber

Timothy J. Fitzpatrick   Nancy L. Mauriello
LEGAL SUPPORT PERSONNEL
Merrill R. Cannon

For full biographical listings, see the Martindale-Hubbell Law Directory

*LOS ANGELES,** Los Angeles Co.

CLARK & TREVITHICK, A PROFESSIONAL CORPORATION (AV)

800 Wilshire Boulevard, 12th Floor, 90017
Telephone: 213-629-5700
Telecopier: 213-624-9441
San Francisco, California Office: 456 Montgomery Street, 20th Floor.
Telephone: 415-288-6520.
Fax: 415-398-2820.

Donald P. Clark   Kevin P. Fiore
Alexander C. McGilvray, Jr.   Michael K. Wofford
Brent A. Reinke
References: Wells Fargo Bank (Los Angeles Main Office); National Bank of California.

For Complete List of Firm Personnel, See General Section

For full biographical listings, see the Martindale-Hubbell Law Directory

CORINBLIT & SELTZER, A PROFESSIONAL CORPORATION (AV)

Suite 820 Wilshire Park Place, 3700 Wilshire Boulevard, 90010-3085
Telephone: 213-380-4200
Telecopier: 213-385-7503; 385-4560
Email: mseltzer@AOL.com

Marc M. Seltzer   Christina A. Snyder
OF COUNSEL
Jack Corinblit, A Law   Earl P. Willens
Corporation

Gretchen M. Nelson   George A. Shohet
Moses Garcia

For full biographical listings, see the Martindale-Hubbell Law Directory

HENNIGAN, MERCER & BENNETT (AV)

601 South Figueroa Street, Suite 3300, 90017
Telephone: 213-694-1200
Fax: 213-694-1234
Email: Silverm@hmb.com

(See Next Column)

HENNIGAN, MERCER & BENNETT—*Continued*

J. Michael Hennigan
James W. Mercer
Bruce Bennett
John L. Amsden
C. Dana Hobart
Jeanne E. Irving
Pamala J. King

Laura Lindgren
Bruce R. MacLeod
Elizabeth D. Mann
Robert L. Palmer
Lauren A. Smith
Peter J. Most
Lee W. Potts

ASSOCIATES

Nichole M. Auden
Jacqueline Bendy
Mary H. Chu
A. Ann Hered
Gregory K. Jones
Ellen M. Keane

Linda A. Kontos
Jennifer Sulla
Michael Swartz
Shawna L. Ballard
Claudia Schweikert
David H. Martin

OF COUNSEL

Anthony Castanares

For full biographical listings, see the Martindale-Hubbell Law Directory

---

MATTHIAS & BERG LLP (AV)

Seventh Floor, 515 South Flower Street, 90071
Telephone: 213-895-4200
Telecopier: 213-895-4058

Michael R. Matthias
Jeffrey P. Berg

Stuart R. Singer
Kenneth M. H. Hoff

Michael D. Berger

Representative Clients: Synagro Technologies, Inc.; Mexalit, S.A.; Maxitile, Inc.; Allstar Inns; Chatsworth Products, Inc.; International Meta Systems, Inc.; Residential Resources, Inc.; AVIC Group International, Inc.; AutoBitter Group, Inc. National Quality Care, Inc.; Greater China Corp.; HBO Ole. *Reference:* First Professional Bank.

For full biographical listings, see the Martindale-Hubbell Law Directory

---

O'MELVENY & MYERS LLP (AV)

400 South Hope Street, 90071-2899
Telephone: 213-669-6000
Cable Address: "Moms"
Facsimile: 213-669-6407
Email: omminfo@omm.com
Century City, California Office: 1999 Avenue of the Stars, 90067-6035.
Telephone: 310-553-6700.
Facsimile: 310-246-6779.
Newport Beach, California Office: 610 Newport Center Drive, 92660-6429.
Telephone: 714-760-9600.
Cable Address: "Moms".
Facsimile: 714-669-6994.
San Francisco, California Office: Embarcadero Center West Tower, 275 Battery Street, 94111-3305.
Telephone: 415-984-8700.
Facsimile: 415-984-8701.
New York, New York Office: Citicorp Center, 153 East 53rd Street, 10022-4611.
Telephone: 212-326-2000.
Facsimile: 212-326-2061.
Washington, D.C. Office: 555 13th Street, N.W., 20004-1109.
Telephone: 202-383-5300.
Cable Address: "Moms".
Facsimile: 202-383-5414.
London, England Office: 10 Finsbury Square, London, EC2A 1LA.
Telephone: 0171-256-8451.
Facsimile: 0171-638-8205.
Tokyo, Japan Office: Sanbancho KB-6 Building, 6 Sanbancho, Chiyoda-ku, Tokyo 102, Japan.
Telephone: 03-3239-2900.
Facsimile: 03-3239-2432.
Hong Kong Office: Suite 1905, Peregrine Tower, Lippo Centre, 89 Queensway, Central, Hong Kong.
Telephone: 852-2523-8266.
Facsimile: 852-2522-1760.
Shanghai, Peoples Republic of China Office: Shanghai International Trade Centre, Suite 2011, 2200 Yan An Road West, Shanghai, 200335, PRC.
Telephone: 86-21-6219-5363.
Facsimile: 86-21-6275-4949.

PARTNER

John D. Hardy, Jr. (San Francisco Office and Los Angeles Office)

For Complete List of Firm Personnel, See General Section

For full biographical listings, see the Martindale-Hubbell Law Directory

---

ROSENFELD & WOLFF, A PROFESSIONAL CORPORATION (AV)

2049 Century Park East, Suite 600, 90067
Telephone: 310-556-1221
Fax: 310-556-0401

(See Next Column)

Morton M. Rosenfeld
Alan D. Aronson

Steven G. Wolff

For full biographical listings, see the Martindale-Hubbell Law Directory

---

SHAPIRO, ROSENFELD & CLOSE, A PROFESSIONAL CORPORATION (AV)

Suite 2600, One Century Plaza, 2029 Century Park East, 90067
Telephone: 310-277-1818
Telecopier: 310-201-4776
Email: src_law@ix.netcom.com

Mitchell S. Shapiro
Edward M. Rosenfeld
Richard H. Close
Helmut F. Furth
Rochelle Buchsbaum Spandorf
Douglas L. Carden

Jonathan J. Panzer
Cathryn S. Gawne
Lisa K. Skaist
Rhonda H. Mehlman
Marna F. Miller
Jennifer A. DeMarrais

OF COUNSEL

Alan D. Jacobson
Barry Kurtz

Alan G. Dowling

For full biographical listings, see the Martindale-Hubbell Law Directory

---

SHEPPARD, MULLIN, RICHTER & HAMPTON LLP (AV)

A Limited Liability Partnership including Professional Corporations
Forty-Eighth Floor, 333 South Hope Street, 90071-1448
Telephone: 213-620-1780
Telecopier: 213-620-1398
Cable Address: "Sheplaw"
Email: info@smrh.com *URL:* http://www.smrh.com
Orange County, California Office: 650 Town Center Drive, 4th Floor, Costa Mesa.
Telephone: 714-513-5100.
Telecopier: 714-513-5130. Home Page Address: http://www.smrh.com.
San Francisco, California Office: Seventeenth Floor, Four Embarcadero Center.
Telephone: 415-434-9100.
Telecopier: 415-434-3947. Home Page Address: http://www.smrh.com.
San Diego, California Office: Nineteenth Floor, 501 West Broadway.
Telephone: 619-338-6500.
Telecopier: 619-234-3815. Home Page Address: http://www.smrh.com.

COUNSEL

Myrl R. Scott *

MEMBERS OF FIRM

Anthony J. Bishop
John R. Bonn
    (San Diego Office)
Barbara L. Borden
    (San Diego Office)
David M. Bosko
    (Orange County Office)
Lawrence M. Braun
Arthur Wm. Brown, Jr.
John J. Giovannone
    (Orange County Office)

John D. Hussey *
Jon W. Newby
T. William Opdyke
Robert H. Philibosian
Randal B. Short
    (San Francisco Office)
James J. Slaby, Jr.
R. Marshall Tanner
    (Orange County Office)

*Professional Corporation

For full biographical listings, see the Martindale-Hubbell Law Directory

---

MOUNTAIN VIEW, Santa Clara Co.

LUCE & QUILLINAN (AV)

444 Castro Street, Suite 900, 94041-2073
Telephone: 415-969-4000
FAX: 415-969-6953

MEMBERS OF FIRM

James G. Luce
Melissa C. Johnson

James V. Quillinan

ASSOCIATE

Sally F. Berry

For full biographical listings, see the Martindale-Hubbell Law Directory

---

NEWPORT BEACH, Orange Co.

KRISTIN M. CANO (AV)

One Corporate Plaza, 92660
Telephone: 714-759-1505
FAX: 714-640-9535
Email: KristinCanoLawOffice@internetMCI.com

For full biographical listings, see the Martindale-Hubbell Law Directory

OAKLAND, * Alameda Co.

PEZZOLA & REINKE, A PROFESSIONAL CORPORATION (AV)

Suite 1300, Lake Merritt Plaza, 1999 Harrison Street, 94612
Telephone: 510-273-8750
Telecopier: 510-834-7440
San Francisco, California Office: 650 California Street, 32nd Floor, 94111.
Telephone: 415-989-9710.
Menlo Park, California Office: 3000 Sand Hill Road, Building 4, Suite
160, 94025.
Telephone: 415-854-8797.

Stephen P. Pezzola	Bruce P. Johnson
Donald C. Reinke	Gizelle A. Barany

LEGAL SUPPORT PERSONNEL
Gayle F. Detillion

Representative Clients: DSP Communications; Pacific Capital Partners, Inc.;
U.S. Electricar, Inc.; DSP Group, Inc.; California Medical Association; Summit Banshares, Inc.

For full biographical listings, see the Martindale-Hubbell Law Directory

PALO ALTO, Santa Clara Co.

CHRISTOPHER REAM (AV)

1717 Embarcadero Road, 94303
Telephone: 415-424-0821
Facsimile: 415-857-1288

For full biographical listings, see the Martindale-Hubbell Law Directory

SAN DIEGO, * San Diego Co.

DUCKOR SPRADLING & METZGER, A LAW CORPORATION (AV)

401 West A Street, Suite 2400, 92101-7909
Telephone: 619-231-3666
Telecopier: 619-231-6629
Email: dsm@dsmlaw.wanet.com

Michael J. Duckor	K. Michael Garrett
Gary J. Spradling	Patrick L. Prindle
Scott L. Metzger	Li-An C. Leonard
John C. Wynne	Stephen A. Bond
John W. Cutchin	R. Anthony Mahavier
Robert D. Rochelle	Robin Assaf Wofford
Robert L. Kenny	Leslie S. Akins
Laurie J. Orange	Jill Osmars Wolcott

Thomas R. Darton

Brian A. Barnhorst	Jamie M. Ryan
Catriona M. Cahill	Douglas A. Dube
Robert J. Solis	Gregory P. Olson
John J. Freni	Susan B. Hansen
Jessica M. Amgwerd	Julie D. Wiley

Laura B. Riesenberg

Representative Clients: Brookstreet Securities Corp.; City of Vista, California;
First Pacific National Bank; Invivo Research, Inc.; Leucadia National Corp.;
National Dispatch Center; County of Orange, California.

For full biographical listings, see the Martindale-Hubbell Law Directory

FERRIS & BRITTON, A PROFESSIONAL CORPORATION (AV)

1600 First National Bank Center, 401 West A Street, 92101
Telephone: 619-233-3131
Fax: 619-232-9316

Alfred G. Ferris

Representative Clients: Agouron Pharmaceuticals, Inc.; Immuno Pharmaceutics, Inc.; Invitrogen Corporation; Ad Com Information Systems; Global
Wireless Communications; Phase Metrics, Inc.; Receptors, Inc.

For Complete List of Firm Personnel, See General Section

For full biographical listings, see the Martindale-Hubbell Law Directory

MILLER MILOVE & KOB, A.P.C. (AV)

The Koll Center, 501 West Broadway, Suite 720, 92101
Telephone: 619-696-5200
Facsimile: 619-696-5393

Brian D. Miller	Jeffrey S. Kob
Bradd L. Milove	Cynthia M. Schleindl

OF COUNSEL
Mark A. Osman

Representative Clients: Broadcort Capital Corporation; First Wall Street;
Bank of Commerce; Personal Computers Products, Inc.; IDS Financial Services; Iowa Grain Company; JB Oxford & Company; Sentra Securities; Spelman & Co.; Vanguard Capital.

For full biographical listings, see the Martindale-Hubbell Law Directory

THE LAW OFFICES OF STEPHEN P. OGGEL, A P.C. (AV)

111 Elm Street, Suite 400, 92101
Telephone: 619-696-7500
Fax: 619-232-1065

Stephen P. Oggel

Brian J. McCormack

For full biographical listings, see the Martindale-Hubbell Law Directory

PAGE, POLIN & BUSCH, A PROFESSIONAL CORPORATION (AV)

350 West Ash Street, Suite 900, 92101-3436
Telephone: 619-231-1822
Fax: 619-231-1877
Fax: 619-231-1875
Email: pagepolin@pagepolin.com

Michael E. Busch	Richard W. Page
Kathleen A. Cashman-Kramer	Kenneth D. Polin
Richard L. Moskitis	Steven G. Rowles

Rod S. Fiori	Michael G. Rowles
Dorothy A. Johnson	(Not admitted in CA)
Jolene L. Parker	Barry M. Taira

For full biographical listings, see the Martindale-Hubbell Law Directory

SAN FRANCISCO, * San Francisco Co.

GOLD BENNETT & CERA LLP (AV)

595 Market Street, Suite 2300, 94105
Telephone: 415-777-2230
Fax: 415-777-5189
Email: gbc__law@ix.netcom.com *URL:*
http://www.netcom.com/~gbc__law/

Paul F. Bennett	Solomon B. Cera

George S. Trevor	Susan D. Resley
Patricia A. Szumowski	Rina Pedroza
Gregory C. Moore	Jeffrey D. Rosen

For full biographical listings, see the Martindale-Hubbell Law Directory

LIEFF, CABRASER, HEIMANN & BERNSTEIN, LLP (AV)

Embarcadero Center West, 30th Floor, 275 Battery Street, 94111
Telephone: 415-956-1000
Telecopier: 415-956-1008
Email: mail@lchb.com

Robert L. Lieff	Michael F. Ram
Elizabeth J. Cabraser	Joseph R. Saveri
Richard M. Heimann	Donald C. Arbitblit
William Bernstein	Robert J. Nelson
William B. Hirsch	Jacqueline E. Mottek
James M. Finberg	Morris A. Ratner
Karen E. Karpen	Melanie M. Piech

Richard L. Akel	Anthony K. Lee
Christine J. Anderson	Fabrice V. Nijhof
Kelly M. Dermody	Trina N. Parker
Eric B. Fastiff	Jonathan D. Selbin
Richard M. Franco	Mark N. Todzo

Heather A. Woodard

For full biographical listings, see the Martindale-Hubbell Law Directory

MANWELL & MILTON (AV)

20 California Street, Third Floor, 94111
Telephone: 415-362-2375
Telecopier: 415-362-1010
URL: HTTP://WWW.MM.LAWOFFICES.COM

Edmund R. Manwell	Denise B. Milton

ASSOCIATES

Mari C. Siebold	Ian R. Schwartz

Katayoon M. Cotto

For full biographical listings, see the Martindale-Hubbell Law Directory

ROSEN, BIEN & ASARO (AV)

Eighth Floor, 155 Montgomery Street, 94104
Telephone: 415-433-6830
Fax: 415-433-7104
Email: rba@rbalaw.com

Sanford Jay Rosen	Michael W. Bien

Andrea G. Asaro

(See Next Column)

ROSEN, BIEN & ASARO—*Continued*

Thomas Nolan	William H.D. Fernholz
Donna Petrine	Doris Y. Ng
M.J. Tony Paikeday	A. Marie Villafaña

For full biographical listings, see the Martindale-Hubbell Law Directory

SAVERI AND SAVERI, A PROFESSIONAL CORPORATION (AV)

41st Floor, Spear Street Tower, One Market Plaza, 94105-1001
Telephone: 415-243-4005
Fax: 415-243-4009

Richard Saveri	Guido Saveri

R. Alexander Saveri
OF COUNSEL
John A. Kithas

For full biographical listings, see the Martindale-Hubbell Law Directory

TORRANCE, Los Angeles Co.

PETILLON & HANSEN (AV)

An Association of Professional Corporations
1260 Union Bank Tower, 21515 Hawthorne Boulevard, 90503
Telephone: 310-543-0500
Fax: 310-543-0550
Email: PandHLaw@aol.com

Lee R. Petillon	Grant L. Simmons
Richard K. Hansen	Raymond J. Seto

Mark T. Hiraide

For full biographical listings, see the Martindale-Hubbell Law Directory

COLORADO

COLORADO SPRINGS,* El Paso Co.

BELTZ, EDWARDS & SABO, L.L.P. (AV)

729 South Cascade, 80903
Telephone: 719-473-4444; 719-634-6620
Fax: 719-444-0186

W. Thomas Beltz	Daniel P. Edwards

John W. Sabo, III

Daniel A. West

Representative Clients: A.M.I. Industries, Inc.; Analytical Surveys, Inc.; A.C. Israel Enterprises, Inc.; Boddington Lumber Co., Inc.; Cardiovascular Surgeons of Colorado Springs, P.C.; Colorado Springs Radiologists, P.C.; Digital, Inc.; Music Semi-Conductors, Inc.; Schlage Lock Co.; Texas Instruments.

For full biographical listings, see the Martindale-Hubbell Law Directory

DENVER,* Denver Co.

BALLARD SPAHR ANDREWS & INGERSOLL (AV)

Seventeenth Street Plaza Building, Suite 2300, 1225 17th Street, 80202-5596
Telephone: 303-292-2400
Fax: 303-296-3956
Philadelphia, Pennsylvania Office: 1735 Market Street, 51st Floor.
Telephone: 215-665-8500.
Fax: 215-864-8999.
Harrisburg, Pennsylvania Office: 105 North Front Street.
Telephone: 717-236-3333.
Fax: 717-236-3884.
Salt Lake City, Utah Office: One Utah Center, 201 South Main Street, Suite 1200.
Telephone: 801-531-3000.
Fax: 801-531-3001.
Washington, D.C. Office: Suite 900 East, 555 13th Street, N.W.
Telephone: 202-383-8800.
Fax: 202-383-8877; 383-8893.
Baltimore, Maryland Office: 300 East Lombard Street, 19th Floor.
Telephone: 410-528-5600.
Fax: 410-528-5650.
Camden, New Jersey Office: 800 Hudson Square, 5th Floor.
Telephone: 609-541-5577.
Fax: 609-541-8272.

Lyle B. Stewart
OF COUNSEL
Thomas H. Duncan

(See Next Column)

John E. Hayes, III	Darren R. Hensley
Alice Lim Rydberg	

For Complete List of Firm Personnel, See General Section

For full biographical listings, see the Martindale-Hubbell Law Directory

BEARMAN TALESNICK & CLOWDUS, PROFESSIONAL CORPORATION (AV)

1200 Seventeenth Street, Suite 2600, 80202-5826
Telephone: 303-572-6500
Facsimile: 303-572-6511

Alan L. Talesnick	Martha S. Nachman
Robert M. Bearman	Francis B. Barron

Representative Clients: Antennas America, Inc.; Barrett Resources Corporation; Chembio Diagnostic Systems, Inc.; Communications World International, Inc.; Specialized Computer Solutions, Inc.; USMX, Inc.

For full biographical listings, see the Martindale-Hubbell Law Directory

BERLINER ZISSER WALTER & GALLEGOS, P.C. (AV)

One Norwest Center, 1700 Lincoln Street, Suite 4700, 80203-4547
Telephone: 303-830-1700
Facsimile: 303-830-1705
Email: bzw&g.com

Martin M. Berliner	Larry D. Gallegos
David A. Zisser	David C. Roos
Robert W. Walter	Curt R. Foust

OF COUNSEL
Phillip C. Gans

For full biographical listings, see the Martindale-Hubbell Law Directory

BIRGE & MAYERS, P.C. (AV)

1700 Broadway, Suite 1501, 80290
Telephone: 303-860-7100
Facsimile: 303-860-7338

Thomas D. Birge	Cathryn B. Mayers

Representative Clients: Dean Witter Reynolds, Inc.; Walnut Street Securities.

For full biographical listings, see the Martindale-Hubbell Law Directory

BREGA & WINTERS, P.C. (AV)

One Norwest Center, 1700 Lincoln Street, Suite 2222, 80203
Telephone: 303-866-9400
Fax: 303-861-9109
Email: bwpc@indra.com
Greeley, Colorado Office: 1100 Tenth Street, Suite 402, 80631.
Telephone: 303-352-4805.
Fax: 303-352-6547.

James W. Bain	Brian A. Magoon
Stuart N. Bennett	Loren L. Mall
Charles F. Brega	Pamela A. Shaddock
Robert R. Dormer	(Resident, Greeley Office)
Robert C. Kaufman	Jay John Schnell
Ronald S. Loser	Jerry D. Winters
	(Resident, Greeley Office)
Peter A. Gergely	Bradley D. Laue
Wesley B. Howard, Jr.	(Resident, Greeley Office)
Yvonne Marie Kreye	Jack R. Luellen
S. Scott Lasher	(Not admitted in CO)

OF COUNSEL

Carolyn Jane Hariton	Mark Spitalnik

COUNSEL
Jay W. Enyart

For full biographical listings, see the Martindale-Hubbell Law Directory

BRENMAN KEY & BROMBERG, P.C. (AV)

Mellon Financial Center Suite 1001, 1775 Sherman Street, 80203
Telephone: 303-894-0234
Fax: 303-839-1633

Albert Brenman	Donna A. Key
Thomas R. Bromberg	Steven W. McDonald
Theresa M. Mehringer	George D. Kreye

OF COUNSEL

Heather H. S. Sander	A. Thomas Tenenbaum
D. Elizabeth Wills	Edmund L. Epstein (Inactive)

For full biographical listings, see the Martindale-Hubbell Law Directory

Denver—Continued

BROWN, HARMON & ECKSTEIN, P.C. (AV)

Suite 3000 1700 Lincoln Street, 80203
Telephone: 303-293-3636
Fax: 303-830-2653
Email: eckstein@csn.org
Email: BHE@Lawyernet.com *URL:* http://www.eckstein.net/ecksteinlaw

John A. Eckstein

For full biographical listings, see the Martindale-Hubbell Law Directory

BROWNSTEIN HYATT FARBER & STRICKLAND, P.C. (AV)

Twenty-Second Floor, 410 Seventeenth Street, 80202-4437
Telephone: 303-534-6335
Telecopier: 303-623-1956
Washington, D.C. Office: 601 Pennsylvania Avenue, N.W., Suite 900.
Telephone: 202-434-8377.
Telecopier: 202-393-7864.

Steven W. Farber	John R. Garrett
Jeffrey M. Knetsch	Steven S. Siegel

John L. Ruppert

Brent T. Slosky	David M. Brown

Representative Clients: ABT Building Products Corporation; Brothers Gourmet Coffees, Inc.; Capital Associates, Inc.; The Centennial Funds; Frontier Health Holdings, Inc.; Kohlberg & Co.; M.D.C. Holdings, Inc.; Renaissance Cosmetics, Inc.; Samsonite Corporation; Vail Associates, Inc.

For Complete List of Firm Personnel, See General Section

For full biographical listings, see the Martindale-Hubbell Law Directory

FRIEDLOB SANDERSON RASKIN PAULSON & TOURTILLOTT, LLC (AV)

1400 Glenarm Place, 80202-5099
Telephone: 303-571-1400
Fax: 303-595-3159; 303-595-3970; 303-615-5472
Email: 72731.505@Compuserve.Com
Englewood, Colorado Office: 8400 East Prentice Avenue, 80111-2918.
Telephone: 303-571-1400.

Raymond L. Friedlob	Herrick K. Lidstone, Jr.
Gerald Raskin	Mary M. Maikoetter

John W. Kellogg

For full biographical listings, see the Martindale-Hubbell Law Directory

JOHN G. HERBERT, P.C. (AV)

Larimer Corporate Plaza, Suite 310, 1675 Larimer Street, 80202
Telephone: 303-534-0522
Telefax: 303-534-3638

John G. Herbert

For full biographical listings, see the Martindale-Hubbell Law Directory

HOLME ROBERTS & OWEN LLP (AV)

Suite 4100, 1700 Lincoln, 80203
Telephone: 303-861-7000
Telecopier: 303-866-0200
Email: hro@hro.com *URL:* http://www.hro.com
Boulder, Colorado Office: Suite 400, 1401 Pearl Street.
Telephone: 303-444-5955.
Telecopier: 303-444-1063.
Colorado Springs, Colorado Office: Suite 1300, 90 South Cascade Avenue.
Telephone: 719-473-3800.
Telecopier: 719-633-1518.
Salt Lake City, Utah Office: Suite 1100, 111 East Broadway.
Telephone: 801-521-5800.
Telecopier: 801-521-9639.
London, England Office: Mellier House, 26a Albemarle Street.
Telephone: 44-171-499-8776.
Telecopier: 44-171-499-7769.
Moscow, Russia Office: Kosmodamianskaya Nab. #52/1, Suite 9100, 113054.
Telephone: 7095-961-3000.
Telecopier: 7095-961-3001.
Kiev, Ukraine Office: Terestchenkovskaya #19, Suite 2, 252004.
Telephone: 380-44-224-1348.
Telecopier: 380-44-224-4986.

PARTNERS OF FIRM

James C. Owen Jr.	Martha Dugan Rehm
Joseph W. Morrisey, Jr.	John F. Knoeckel
W. Dean Salter	Garth B. Jensen
Thomas A. Richardson	Paul G. Thompson
Francis R. Wheeler	Kevin P. Block (Managing
Nick Nimmo	Partner, Kiev Office)

(See Next Column)

OF COUNSEL
Harold S. Bloomenthal
SPECIAL COUNSEL
David H. Goldberg
SENIOR COUNSEL
Kathryn P. Beller
ASSOCIATES

Shuang Hu	Rashid Sharipov (Resident,
Neil F. O'Donnell	Moscow, Russia Office)
(Moscow Office)	Alexander Udovenko
Peter-Christian Olivo	(Moscow, Russia Office)
(Boulder Office)	Anna B. Veiksha (Kiev Office)
Maria V. Woods	

For Complete List of Firm Personnel, See General Section

For full biographical listings, see the Martindale-Hubbell Law Directory

JONES & KELLER, A PROFESSIONAL CORPORATION (AV)

Suite 1600, 1625 Broadway, 80202
Telephone: 303-573-1600
Fax: 303-893-6506

Marion F. Jones (1898-1978)	Thomas J. Burke, Jr.
Alec J. Keller (1913-1995)	Samuel E. Wing
Alvin J. Meiklejohn, Jr.	Reid A. Godbolt
Leslie R. Kehl	Rodney D. Knutson
Edward T. Lyons, Jr.	Kevin L. Brown
David E. Driggers	Barry L. Wilkie

Howard R. Hertzberg	Brent Nicholls
David A. Thayer	Michael Brian Cavanaugh
Nathan D. Simmons	

Reference: Colorado State Bank; Union Bank & Trust.

For full biographical listings, see the Martindale-Hubbell Law Directory

KRYS BOYLE GOLZ FREEDMAN & SCOTT, P.C. (AV)

Dominion Plaza, Suite 2700 South Tower 600 Seventeenth Street, 80202
Telephone: 303-893-2300
Facsimile: 303-893-2882

Thomas Boyle	Jeffrey J. Scott
Harold M. Golz	Fred S. Furst
Stanley F. Freedman (P.C.)	Andrew M. Schauer
Sharon M. Link	

RETIRED COUNSEL
Joseph F. Krys

For full biographical listings, see the Martindale-Hubbell Law Directory

NETZORG & McKEEVER, PROFESSIONAL CORPORATION (AV)

Republic Plaza, 370 Seventeenth Street, Suite 3590, 80202
Telephone: 303-892-7100
Fax: 303-446-0506

Gordon W. Netzorg	Peter G. Koclanes
Cecil E. Morris, Jr.	Joan M. Collopy

OF COUNSEL
J. Nicholas McKeever, Jr.

For full biographical listings, see the Martindale-Hubbell Law Directory

ALLEN G. REEVES, P.C. (AV)

900 Equitable Building, 730 17th Street, 80202
Telephone: 303-534-6278
Fax: 303-825-9147

Allen G. Reeves

REIMAN & BAYAZ, P.C. (AV)

1600 Broadway, Suite 1640, 80202
Telephone: 303-860-1500
Fax: 303-839-4380

Jeff Reiman	Marcie K. Bayaz
Darren E. Temkin-Nadel	Eric B. Liebman

For full biographical listings, see the Martindale-Hubbell Law Directory

SOLOMON PEARL BLUM & QUINN LLP (AV)

1700 Broadway, Suite 1820, 80290
Telephone: 303-832-6686
Fax: 303-832-6653
Email: SolPearl@aol.com
New York, New York Office: Woolworth Building, 37th Floor, 233 Broadway, 10007.

(See Next Column)

SOLOMON PEARL BLUM & QUINN LLP—*Continued*

Charlotte Amalie, St. Thomas, Virgin Islands Affiliated Office: Grunet Stout & Bruch, 24-25 Kongens Gade, P.O. Box 1030, 00804.
Telephone: 809-774-1320.
Fax: 809-774-7839.
Denver, Colorado Affiliated Office: Dufford & Brown, P.C., 1700 Broadway, Suite 1700, 80290.
Telephone: 303-861-8013.
Facsimile: 303-832-3804.

Robert A. Solomon   William L. Blum
Clifford R. Pearl   (Not admitted in CO)
            Thomas F. Quinn

For full biographical listings, see the Martindale-Hubbell Law Directory

---

JOHN B. WILLS (AV)

Suite 1940 410 Seventeenth Street, 80202
Telephone: 303-628-0747
Fax: 303-592-1846
Email: occ1940@aol.com

For full biographical listings, see the Martindale-Hubbell Law Directory

---

CONNECTICUT

HARTFORD, * Hartford Co.

SOROKIN SOROKIN GROSS HYDE & WILLIAMS P.C. (AV)

One Corporate Center, 06103
Telephone: 860-525-6645
Fax: 860-522-1781
Simsbury, Connecticut Office: 730 Hopmeadow Street.
Telephone: 860-651-9348.
Rocky Hill, Connecticut Office: 2360 Main Street.
Telephone: 860-563-9305.
Fax: 860-529-6931.

Morris W. Banks   Andrew C. Glassman

Sharon Kowal Freilich

For Complete List of Firm Personnel, See General Section

For full biographical listings, see the Martindale-Hubbell Law Directory

---

WEST HARTFORD, Hartford Co.

JOHN C. PETERS, P.C. (AV)

61 South Main Street, Suite 204, 06107
Telephone: 860-313-0255
Facsimile: 860-313-0257

John C. Peters

For full biographical listings, see the Martindale-Hubbell Law Directory

---

WESTPORT, Fairfield Co.

BLAZZARD, GRODD & HASENAUER, P.C. (AV)

943 Post Road East, P.O. Box 5108, 06881
Telephone: 203-226-7866
Telecopier: 203-454-4855
Hollywood, Florida Office: Suite 213, Oceanwalk Mall, 101 North Ocean Drive, 33019.
Telephone: 954-920-4864.
Facsimile: 954-920-6902. E-Mail: BGHFL@AOL.COM

Norse N. Blazzard   William E. Hasenauer
Leslie E. Grodd   Raymond A. O'Hara, III
Judith A. Hasenauer   Lynn Korman Stone
          Maureen M. Murphy

For full biographical listings, see the Martindale-Hubbell Law Directory

---

DELAWARE

WILMINGTON, * New Castle Co.

MORRIS AND MORRIS (AV)

Suite 1600, 1105 North Market Street, P.O. Box 2166, 19899-2166
Telephone: 302-426-0400
Facsimile: 302-426-0406

Irving Morris   Abraham Rappaport
Karen L. Morris   Patrick F. Morris

(See Next Column)

ASSOCIATES

Liam G. B. Murphy   Jacqueline L. Jenkin
Seth D. Rigrodsky   (Not admitted in DE)

For full biographical listings, see the Martindale-Hubbell Law Directory

---

SMITH, KATZENSTEIN & FURLOW (AV)

The Corporate Plaza, 800 Delaware Avenue, P.O. Box 410, 19899
Telephone: 302-652-8400
Fax: 302-652-8405

MEMBER OF FIRM
Craig B. Smith

For Complete List of Firm Personnel, See General Section

For full biographical listings, see the Martindale-Hubbell Law Directory

---

DISTRICT OF COLUMBIA

WASHINGTON, D.C. Co.

* indicates certain Bar Register subscribers, in cities of comparable size and importance, who maintain an additional office in Washington, D.C. and who have arranged for representation as a part of the Washington, D.C. listings that follow

COHEN, MILSTEIN, HAUSFELD & TOLL, P.L.L.C. (AV)

West Tower, Suite 500, 1100 New York Avenue, N.W., 20005-3964
Telephone: 202-408-4600
Facsimile: 202-408-4699

MEMBERS OF FIRM

Jerry S. Cohen (1925-1995)   Lisa M. Mezzetti
Herbert E. Milstein   Andrew N. Friedman
Michael D. Hausfeld   Richard S. Lewis
Steven J. Toll   Daniel S. Sommers
Ann C. Yahner   Daniel A. Small
                   (Not admitted in DC)

ASSOCIATES

Gary E. Mason   Michael J. Flannery
Cyrus Mehri   Paul T. Gallagher
Sharon A. Snyder   Alexander E. Barnett
Mark S. Willis   Angeline G. Chen
   (Not admitted in DC)   Victoria C. Arthaud
Lillian S. Hagen   (Not admitted in DC)

OF COUNSEL
Anthony Z. Roisman

For full biographical listings, see the Martindale-Hubbell Law Directory

---

DE MARTINO FINKELSTEIN ROSEN & VIRGA (AV)

A Partnership including Professional Corporations
Suite 400, 1818 N Street, N.W., 20036
Telephone: 202-659-0494
Telecopier: 202-659-1290
Email: DFRV90Brd@aol.com *URL:* http://www.dfrv.com
New York, N.Y. Office: Suite 1700, 90 Broad Street.
Telephone: 212-363-2500.
Telecopier: 212-363-2723.

MEMBERS OF FIRM

Kathleen L. Cerveny (Resident)   Jeffrey S. Rosen (Resident)
Ralph V. De Martino (Resident)   Gerard A. Virga (Not admitted
Steven R. Finkelstein (Not   in DC; Resident, New York,
   admitted in DC; Resident,   N.Y. Office)
   New York, N.Y. Office)

Keith H. Peterson (Not   Victoria A. Baylin (Not
   admitted in DC; Resident,   admitted in DC; Resident)
   New York, N.Y. Office)

LEGAL SUPPORT PERSONNEL

J. Keoni Robinson (Paralegal)   Patricia A. Lamm (Paralegal)
      Peter S. Cruttenden (Paralegal)

For full biographical listings, see the Martindale-Hubbell Law Directory

---

FREEDMAN, LEVY, KROLL & SIMONDS (AV)

Suite 825, 1050 Connecticut Avenue, N.W., 20036-5366
Telephone: 202-457-5100
Cable Address: "Attorneys"
Telecopier: 202-457-5151
Email: flks@flks.com *URL:* http://www.flks.com/home/flks

(See Next Column)

FREEDMAN, LEVY, KROLL & SIMONDS, *Washington—Continued*

MEMBERS OF FIRM

Walter Freedman	Arthur H. Bill
Peter E. Panarites	Thomas C. Lauerman
Gary O. Cohen	Marc B. Dorfman
Jay W. Freedman	Wayne M. Zell

Richard T. Choi

OF COUNSEL

Milton P. Kroll

SPECIAL TAX COUNSEL

Norman C. Bensley (Not admitted in DC)

ASSOCIATES

Philip Lawrence DeCamara, III   Bruce A. Rosenblum

For Complete List of Firm Personnel, See General Section

For full biographical listings, see the Martindale-Hubbell Law Directory

---

* LEWIS, CLAY & MUNDAY, A PROFESSIONAL CORPORATION (AV)

(Formerly Lewis, White & Clay, P.C.)
1000 16th Street, N.W., Suite 401, 20036
Telephone: 202-835-0616
Fax: 202-833-3316
Detroit, Michigan Office: 1300 First National Building, 660 Woodward Avenue. 48226-3531.
Telephone: 313-961-2550.
Troy, Michigan Office: Liberty Center, Suite 200. 100 West Big Beaver Road, 48084.
Telephone: 810-680-6702.
Fax: 810-680-6703.
Boston, Massachusetts Office: 10 Post Office Square. 02109.
Telephone: 617-422-8646.
Fax: 617-338-5693.

Karen Kendrick Brown (Resident)

For full biographical listings, see the Martindale-Hubbell Law Directory

---

MULDOON, MURPHY & FAUCETTE (AV)

5101 Wisconsin Avenue, N.W., 20016
Telephone: 202-362-0840
Telecopier: 202-966-9409; 202-363-5068

MEMBERS OF FIRM

Joseph A. Muldoon, Jr.	Richard V. Fitzgerald
George W. Murphy, Jr.	Joseph G. Passaic, Jr.
Douglas P. Faucette	Joseph P. Daly
John R. Hall	Mary M. Jackley Sjoquist
Thomas J. Haggerty	Lori M. Beresford
(Not admitted in DC)	Christina M. Gattuso

ASSOCIATES

Leslie Murphy	Kent M. Krudys
Ann E. Cox	Philip G. Feigen
Cynthia M. Krus	Marc Paul Levy
(Not admitted in DC)	Gwen Mulberry Morris
William E. Donnelly	Geoffrey W. Ryan
Lawrence M. F. Spaccasi	(Not admitted in DC)
(Not admitted in DC)	Thomas W. France
Patricia A. Murphy	(Not admitted in DC)
(Not admitted in DC)	

OF COUNSEL

Mary V. Harcar

For full biographical listings, see the Martindale-Hubbell Law Directory

---

* VENABLE ATTORNEYS AT LAW VENABLE, BAETJER, HOWARD & CIVILETTI, LLP (AV)

A Partnership including Professional Corporations
Suite 1000, 1201 New York Avenue, N.W., 20005
Telephone: 202-962-4800
Fax: 202-962-8300
Baltimore, Maryland Office: Venable, Baetjer and Howard LLP, 1800 Mercantile Bank & Trust Building, 2 Hopkins Plaza.
Telephone: 410-244-7400.
McLean, Virginia Office: Venable, Baetjer and Howard LLP, Suite 400, 2010 Corporate Ridge.
Telephone: 703-760-1600.
Rockville, Maryland Office: Venable, Baetjer and Howard LLP, Suite 500, One Church Street, P. O. Box 1906.
Telephone: 301-217-5600.
Towson, Maryland Office: Venable, Baetjer and Howard LLP, 210 Allegheny Avenue, P. O. Box 5517.
Telephone: 410-494-6200.

MEMBERS OF FIRM

Benjamin R. Civiletti (P.C.)	David J. Levenson
(Also at Baltimore and	Joe A. Shull
Towson, Maryland Offices)	Kenneth C. Bass, III (Also at
Ronald R. Glancz	McLean, Virginia Office)

(See Next Column)

MEMBERS OF FIRM (Continued)

Thomas B. Hudson (Also at Baltimore, Maryland Office)	William D. Quarles (Also at Towson, Maryland Office)
James K. Archibald (Also at Baltimore, Maryland Office)	Anita J. Finkelstein
James R. Myers	Gary M. Hnath
James L. Shea (Not admitted in DC; also at Baltimore, Maryland Office)	

ASSOCIATES

Pamela W. Carmody (Not admitted in DC; Also at Baltimore, Maryland Office)	Donald P. Creston
	David S. Darland
	John P. Fielding (Also at McLean, Virginia Office)

For Complete List of Firm Personnel, See General Section

For full biographical listings, see the Martindale-Hubbell Law Directory

---

WILMER, CUTLER & PICKERING (AV)

2445 M Street, N.W., 20037-1420
Telephone: 202-663-6000
Fax: 202-663-6363
Email: Law@Wilmer.Com
Baltimore, Maryland Office: 100 Light Street, 21202.
Telephone: 410-986-2800.
Fax: 410-986-2828.
European Offices:
4 Carlton Gardens, London, SW1Y 5AA, England. Telephone: +44 (171) 872-1000.
Fax: +44 (171) 839-3537.
Rue de la Loi 15Wetstraat, B-1040 Brussels, Belgium. Telephone: +32 (2) 285-4900.
Fax: +32 (2) 285-4949.
Friedrichstrasse 95, D-10117 Berlin, Germany. Telephone: +49 (30) 2022-6400.
Fax: +49 (30)2022-6500.

MEMBERS OF FIRM

Arthur F. Mathews	Harry J. Weiss
Louis R. Cohen	Brandon Becker
Michael R. Klein	Bruce E. Coolidge
Stephen F. Black	Andrew N. Vollmer
Robert B. McCaw	Charles E. Davidow
John Rounsaville, Jr.	Jeremy N. Rubenstein
Roger M. Witten	Joseph K. Brenner
David M. Becker	Stephen M. Cutler
Marianne K. Smythe	Eric R. Markus
Andrew B. Weissman	Eric J. Mogilnicki
George P. Stamas (Resident, Baltimore, Maryland Office)	Yoon-Young Lee

COUNSEL

Robert G. Bagnall

OF COUNSEL

Howard P. Willens

For Complete List of Firm Personnel, See General Section

For full biographical listings, see the Martindale-Hubbell Law Directory

---

FLORIDA

BOCA RATON, Palm Beach Co.

LAW OFFICES OF RICHARD H. LEVENSTEIN, P.A. (AV)

2101 Northwest 2nd Avenue Suite 2, 33431
Telephone: 561-392-7887
Fax: 561-392-3348
Stuart, Florida Office: 312 West Ocean Boulevard, 34994.
Telephone: 561-221-0521.
Fax: 561-221-0290.

Richard H. Levenstein

For full biographical listings, see the Martindale-Hubbell Law Directory

---

FORT LAUDERDALE, * Broward Co.

LAW PRACTICE OF J.B. GROSSMAN, P.A. (AV)

2300 East Las Olas Boulevard Fourth Floor, 33301
Telephone: 954-767-3345
Fax: 954-767-3347

J.B. Grossman	Kenneth J. Dunn
Gary Arnold Feder	Blaine H. Hibberd

LEGAL SUPPORT PERSONNEL

Scott L. Lampert

For full biographical listings, see the Martindale-Hubbell Law Directory

MIAMI, Dade Co.

BERMAN WOLFE & RENNERT, P.A. (AV)

35th Floor, International Place, 100 Southeast Second Street, 33131-2130
Telephone: 305-577-4177
Fax: 305-373-6036
Email: 76206.1400@compuserve.com.

Neil J. Berman	Howard J. Vogel
Leon J. Wolfe	Karen J. Orlin
Charles J. Rennert	Jill Nexon Berman

Sheila T. Lynch

For full biographical listings, see the Martindale-Hubbell Law Directory

CARLSON & BALES, A PROFESSIONAL ASSOCIATION (AV)

First Union Financial Center, 200 South Biscayne Boulevard, Suite 2770, 33131
Telephone: 305-372-9700
Fax: 305-372-8265

Curtis Carlson	Julie Anne Moxley
Richard M. Bales, Jr.	Ronald J. Lewittes

OF COUNSEL
Mara Beth Sommers

For full biographical listings, see the Martindale-Hubbell Law Directory

ZACK, SPARBER, KOSNITZKY, SPRATT & BROOKS, P.A. (AV)

International Place, 100 Southeast Second Street, Suite 2800, 33131-2144
Telephone: 305-539-8400
Facsimile: 305-539-1307

Michael Kosnitzky	Deborah R. Mayo
Marc H. Auerbach	Nancy E. McCarthy
Jorge A. Gonzalez	Roland Sanchez-Medina, Jr.
Thomas O. Wells	

For Complete List of Firm Personnel, See General Section

For full biographical listings, see the Martindale-Hubbell Law Directory

NAPLES, Collier Co.

GRADY & ASSOCIATES, LEGAL PROFESSIONAL ASSOCIATION (AV)

3411 Tamiami Trail North, Suite 200, 34103
Telephone: 941-261-6555
Fax: 941-261-1192

Thomas R. Grady

For full biographical listings, see the Martindale-Hubbell Law Directory

VEGA, STANLEY, ZELMAN & HANLON, P.A. (AV)

2660 Airport Road South, 34112
Telephone: 941-774-3333
Fax: 941-776-6420

George Vega, Jr.

John G. Vega

General Counsel for: Lely Estates; Naples Community Hospital.
Local Counsel: Quail Creek Developments.

For full biographical listings, see the Martindale-Hubbell Law Directory

ST. PETERSBURG, Pinellas Co.

ALLAN & SHIPP, P.A. (AV)

6675 Thirteenth Avenue North, Suite 2C, 33710
Telephone: 813-381-9800
Fax: 813-381-1155
Clearwater, Florida Office: 2633 McCormick Drive, Suite 101, 34619.
Telephone: 813-381-9800.
Fax: 813-381-1155.

Linda R. Allan	Wayne E. Shipp

Stephen A. Baker	Terry J. Deeb
Carol E. Fant	

For full biographical listings, see the Martindale-Hubbell Law Directory

RIDEN, EARLE & KIEFNER, P.A. (AV)

City Center, North Tower, 100 Second Avenue South, Suite 400, 33701-4336
Telephone: 813-822-6000
Telecopier: 813-821-3721

(See Next Column)

Thomas K. Riden	Christopher C. Ferguson
James T. Earle, Jr.	Timothy A. Miller
John R. Kiefner, Jr.	Gary E. Frazier
Paul Castagliola	James C. Rowe
Robert H. Crawford	Christopher B. Young
Neil G. Kiefer	Clifford J. Hunt
D. Jay Snyder	Benjamin Felder

M. Deanna Harris	Camille J. Iurillo
Michael Francis Bremer	

For full biographical listings, see the Martindale-Hubbell Law Directory

TAMPA, Hillsborough Co.

MICHAEL C. ADDISON (AV)

Suite 2175, 100 North Tampa Street, 33602-5145
Telephone: 813-223-2000
Facsimile: 813-228-6000
Mailing Address: P.O. Box 2175, Tampa, Florida, 33601-2175
Email: 72100.337@compuserve.com

For full biographical listings, see the Martindale-Hubbell Law Directory

ALPERT, BARKER & CALCUTT, P.A. (AV)

First Union Center, Suite 2000, 100 South Ashley Drive (33602), P.O. Box 3270, 33601-3270
Telephone: 813-223-4131
Fax: 813-228-9612

Jonathan L. Alpert	Chris A. Barker
Patrick B. Calcutt	

R. Christopher Rodems	William J. Cook
Gregory Joseph Blackburn	Emma Sleeth Hemness
David D. Ferrentino	Scott J. Flint
David A. Kessler	

Representative Clients: AABCO Mortgage & Investments, Inc.; Abbey/Foster, Inc.; Alexander & Alexander, Inc.; American International Group; American Risk Management Corp.; Atlantic Mutual Companies; The Clorox Co.; Colonia Insurance Co.; The Dow Chemical Co.; Gates McDonald and Company.

For full biographical listings, see the Martindale-Hubbell Law Directory

WILLIAMS, REED, WEINSTEIN, SCHIFINO & MANGIONE, P.A. (AV)

One Tampa City Center, 201 North Franklin Street, Suite 2600, P.O. Box 380, 33601
Telephone: 813-221-2626
Telefax: 813-221-7335

Robert V. Williams	Ralph P. Mangione
James M. Reed	Scott I. Steady
David B. Weinstein	R. Marshall Rainey
William J. Schifino, Jr.	David S. Jennis
Russell S. Thomas	

Kenneth G. Turkel	Robert R. Hearn
Aminie Mohip	John A. Schifino
Ricardo A. Roig	Jennifer A. Powers
V. Stephen Cohen	Elizabeth S. Hoskins

FIRM ADMINISTRATOR
Joseph C. Simmons

For full biographical listings, see the Martindale-Hubbell Law Directory

WEST PALM BEACH, Palm Beach Co.

BURT & PUCILLO (AV)

Esperanté, Suite 300 East, 222 Lakeview Avenue, 33401
Telephone: 407-835-9400
Telecopier: 407-835-0322

MEMBERS OF FIRM
C. Oliver Burt, III	Michael J. Pucillo
Wendy Hope Zoberman	

ASSOCIATE
Leo W. Desmond

OF COUNSEL
Carol McLean Brewer	Lauren S. Dadario

For full biographical listings, see the Martindale-Hubbell Law Directory

DAVIS, GORDON, DONER & CHANDLER, P.A. (AV)

515 North Flagler Drive, 7th Floor, 33401
Telephone: 561-659-7337
Facsimile: 561-659-0143
URL: http://www.dgdc.com

(See Next Column)

DAVIS, GORDON, DONER & CHANDLER P.A., *West Palm Beach—Continued*

Zell Davis, Jr.	Adam S. Doner
Robert E. Gordon	Lawrence U. L. Chandler

Lawrence L. Klayman	Deirdre E. Brett

OF COUNSEL

Charles J. Oswald	Mikel D. Jones
	(Not admitted in FL)

For full biographical listings, see the Martindale-Hubbell Law Directory

---

GEORGIA

ATLANTA,* Fulton Co.

APPEL, CHITWOOD & HARLEY (AV)

1400 Resurgens Plaza, 945 E. Paces Ferry Road, 30326
Telephone: 404-266-1650
Facsimile: 404-237-2150

MEMBERS OF FIRM

Martin D. Chitwood	Craig G. Harley

OF COUNSEL

Nick A. Dodys

For full biographical listings, see the Martindale-Hubbell Law Directory

---

HICKS, MALOOF & CAMPBELL, A PROFESSIONAL CORPORATION (AV)

Suite 2200 Marquis Two Tower, 285 Peachtree Center
    Avenue, 30303-1234
Telephone: 404-588-1100
Telecopy: 404-420-7474

Maurice Ted Maloof	Charles E. Wilson, III

For full biographical listings, see the Martindale-Hubbell Law Directory

---

HOLT, NEY, ZATCOFF & WASSERMAN (AV)

A Partnership including Professional Corporations
100 Galleria Parkway, Suite 600, 30339
Telephone: 770-956-9600
Facsimile Number: 770-956-1490

MEMBERS OF FIRM

Charles D. Vaughn	Barbara J. Schneider

Representative Clients: Champion Healthcare Corporation; Cummins South, Inc.; Roberts Realty Investors, Inc.; Sportslife, Inc.; The University Financing Foundation, Inc.; Trammell Crow Residential.

For Complete List of Firm Personnel, See General Section

For full biographical listings, see the Martindale-Hubbell Law Directory

---

KILPATRICK & CODY LLP (AV)

Suite 2800, 1100 Peachtree Street, 30309-4530
Telephone: 404-815-6500
Telephone Copier: 404-815-6555
Telex: 54-2307
Washington, D.C. Office: Suite 800, 700 13th Street, N.W., 20005.
Telephone: 202-508-5800. Telephone Copier: 202-508-5858.
Brussels, Belgium Office: Avenue Louise 65, BTE 3, 1050 Brussels.
Telephone: (32) (2) 533-03-00.
Telecopier: (32) (2) 534-86-38.
London, England Office: 68 Pall Mall, London, SW1Y 5ES, England.
Telephone: (44) (71) 321 0477.
Telecopier: (44) (71) 930 9733.
Augusta, Georgia Office: Suite 1400 First Union Bank Building, P.O. Box 2043, 30903. Telephone (706) 724-2622. Telecopier (706) 722-0219.

MEMBERS OF FIRM

Luis A. Aguilar	M. Andrew Kauss
Rupert M. Barkoff	Larry D. Ledbetter
Tim Carssow	Reinaldo Pascual
Jerome F. Connell, Jr.	Barry Phillips
W. Randy Eaddy	Martin R. Tilson, Jr.
F. Sheffield Hale	Michael H. Trotter

COUNSEL

Jan Meadows Davidson

(See Next Column)

ASSOCIATES

William B. Barkley	Jeffrey T. Skinner
Cecil L. Davis, Jr.	W. Craig Smith
Neil D. Falis	(Augusta, Georgia Office)
Randolph H. Houchins	James D. Steinberg
Stephanie K. Maffett	Whit F. Stolz

For Complete List of Firm Personnel, See General Section

For full biographical listings, see the Martindale-Hubbell Law Directory

LONG ALDRIDGE & NORMAN, LLP (AV)

A Limited Liability Partnership including Professional Corporations
One Peachtree Center, Suite 5300, 303 Peachtree Street, 30308
Telephone: 404-527-4000
Telecopier: 404-527-4198
Washington, D.C. Office: Suite 600, 701 Pennsylvania Avenue, N.W., 20004.
Telephone: 202-624-1200.
FAX: 202-624-1298.

MEMBERS OF FIRM

David M. Calhoun	Leonard A. Silverstein
William L. Floyd	Thomas R. B. Wardell

ASSOCIATES

Tania Louise Dyson	Virginia Ann Johnson
Janet Eifert Haury	Richard R. Willis

OF COUNSEL

William J. Carney

For Complete List of Firm Personnel, See General Section

For full biographical listings, see the Martindale-Hubbell Law Directory

---

PAGE & BACEK (AV)

3490 Piedmont Road, N.E., Suite 900, 30305-4801
Telephone: 404-365-9900
Telecopier: 404-264-0221

MEMBERS OF FIRM

J. Boyd Page	Brian N. Smiley
Donald A. Bacek	J. Michael Bishop
Steven J. Gard	Edward J. Dovin
	Sandra L. Malkin

ASSOCIATES

Peter J. Diskin	Michel V. Hurley

OF COUNSEL

Edward H. Saunders

For full biographical listings, see the Martindale-Hubbell Law Directory

---

PARKER, HUDSON, RAINER & DOBBS (AV)

1500 Marquis Two Tower, 285 Peachtree Center Avenue, N.E., 30303
Telephone: 404-523-5300
FAX: 404-522-8409
Tallahassee, Florida Office: The Perkins House, 118 North Gadsden Street, 32301.
Telephone: 904-681-0191.
FAX: 904-681-9493.

MEMBERS OF FIRM

David G. Russell	G. Wayne Hillis, Jr.
	William J. Holley, II

For full biographical listings, see the Martindale-Hubbell Law Directory

---

THRASHER, WHITLEY, HAMPTON & MORGAN, A PROFESSIONAL CORPORATION (AV)

Suite 2150, Five Concourse Parkway, 30328
Telephone: 770-804-8000
Telecopier: 770-804-5555

H. Grady Thrasher, III

Representative Clients: First Southern Securities Group, Inc.; Georgia Dental Assn.; Kearney National, Inc.; Middle Bay Oil Company, Inc.; Perry & Co.; Smallwood, Reynolds, Stewart, Stewart & Assoc., Inc.; Sunchase Holdings, Ltd.; Touch Industries, Inc.

For full biographical listings, see the Martindale-Hubbell Law Directory

---

WILSON, STRICKLAND & BENSON, P.C. (AV)

1100 One Midtown Plaza, 1360 Peachtree Street, N.E., 30309
Telephone: 404-870-1800
Telecopier: 404-870-1808

Daniel I. MacIntyre

For Complete List of Firm Personnel, See General Section

For full biographical listings, see the Martindale-Hubbell Law Directory

AUGUSTA, * Richmond Co.

HULL, TOWILL, NORMAN & BARRETT, A PROFESSIONAL CORPORATION (AV)

Seventh Floor, Trust Company Bank Building, P.O. Box 1564, 30903-1564
Telephone: 706-722-4481
Fax: 706-722-9779

James M. Hull (1885-1975)	Douglas D. Batchelor, Jr.
George B. Barrett (1894-1942)	David E. Hudson
Julian J. Willingham (1887-1963)	Neal W. Dickert
John Bell Towill (1907-1991)	John W. Gibson
Robert C. Norman	William F. Hammond
(Retired, 1991)	Mark S. Burgreen
W. Hale Barrett	George R. Hall
Lawton Jordan, Jr.	James B. Ellington
Patrick J. Rice	F. Michael Taylor

Robert A. Mullins	Michael S. Carlson
William J. Keogh, III	Ralph Emerson Hanna, III
Edward J. Tarver	Susan D. Barrett
J. Noel Schweers, III	Timothy E. Moses

Counsel for: Sun Trust Bank Augusta, N.A.; Georgia Federal Bank, FSB, Augusta Division; Southeastern Newspapers Corp.; Georgia Power Co.; Southern Bell Telephone & Telegraph Co.; St. Joseph Hospital, Augusta, Georgia, Inc.; Norfolk Southern Corp.; Merry Land & Investment Co., Inc.; Housing Authority of the City of Augusta; Georgia Press Association.

For full biographical listings, see the Martindale-Hubbell Law Directory

IDAHO

BOISE, * Ada Co.

EBERLE, BERLIN, KADING, TURNBOW & MCKLVEEN, CHARTERED (AV)

Capitol Park Plaza, 300 North Sixth Street, P.O. Box 1368, 83701
Telephone: 208-344-8535
Facsimile: 208-344-8542

R.M. Turnbow	Richard A. Riley
	Bradley G. Andrews

Representative Clients: Piper Jaffray, Inc.; Prudential Securities Inc.; Waddell & Reed Financial Services; Edward D. Jones & Co.; Hecla Mining Corp.

For Complete List of Firm Personnel, See General Section

For full biographical listings, see the Martindale-Hubbell Law Directory

ELAM & BURKE, A PROFESSIONAL ASSOCIATION (AV)

Key Financial Center, 702 West Idaho Street, P.O. Box 1539, 83701
Telephone: 208-343-5454
Telecopier: 208-384-5844
Email: eblaw@elamburke.com

Carl P. Burke	William J. Batt
	Jeffrey A. Thomson

Jeffrey W. Pusch

Representative Clients: Morrison-Knudsen, Inc.; Prudential Securities, Inc.; Sinclair Oil Co. d/b/a Sun Valley Co.; United Heritage Mutual Life Insurance Co.; United Heritage Financial Services, Inc.; Prudential Insurance Company of North America.

For Complete List of Firm Personnel, See General Section

For full biographical listings, see the Martindale-Hubbell Law Directory

ILLINOIS

CHICAGO, * Cook Co.

BELL, BOYD & LLOYD (AV)

Three First National Plaza Suite 3300, 70 West Madison Street, 60602
Telephone: 312-372-1121
FAX: 312-372-2098
Email: bbl@bbl.com
Washington, D.C. Office: 1615 L Street, N.W.
Telephone: 202-466-6300.
FAX: 202-463-0678.

(See Next Column)

MEMBERS OF FIRM

Cameron S. Avery	Patrick J. Maloney
John H. Bitner	John T. McCarthy
John C. Blew	D. Mark McMillan
William G. Brown	Janet D. Olsen
Steven E. Ducommun	William S. Price
Warren C. Haskin	John Craig Walker
(Managing Partner)	

ASSOCIATES

Randy A. Bridgeman	Ernest W. Torain, Jr.
Kevin J. McCarthy	Stacy H. Winick

For Complete List of Firm Personnel, See General Section

For full biographical listings, see the Martindale-Hubbell Law Directory

FAGEL & HABER (AV)

140 South Dearborn Street 14th Floor, 60603
Telephone: 312-346-7500
FAX: 312-580-2201
Telex No: 754542
Cable: "NOFLAWLAW"
URL: HTTP://WWW.FANDH.COM.

MEMBERS OF FIRM

Joel A. Haber	Robert B. Chapman

ASSOCIATE

Laura A. O'Neill

For full biographical listings, see the Martindale-Hubbell Law Directory

FREEMAN, FREEMAN & SALZMAN, P.C. (AV)

401 North Michigan Avenue, Suite 3200, 60611-4207
Telephone: 312-222-5100
Facsimile: 312-822-0870
Email: freeman@wwa.com

Lee A. Freeman (1909-1995)	James T. Malysiak
Lee A. Freeman, Jr.	Glynna W. Freeman
Jerrold E. Salzman	Phillip L. Stern
John F. Kinney	Albert F. Ettinger
	Chris C. Gair

Christopher M. Kelly	Michelle Reese Andrew
Derek J. Meyer	Kevin P. Kappock

For full biographical listings, see the Martindale-Hubbell Law Directory

WILLIAM J. HARTE, LTD. (AV)

Suite 1100, 111 West Washington Street, 60602
Telephone: 312-726-5015
Fax: 312-641-1288

William J. Harte

Sylvia A. Sotiras	Stephen L. Garcia
Erik D. Gruber	Joan M. Mannix
	Cynthia E. Cervini

OF COUNSEL

Daniel K. Schlorf	P. A. Sorrentino
David J. Walker	Irving R. Norman
	Robert L. Tucker

For full biographical listings, see the Martindale-Hubbell Law Directory

KAPLAN & BEGY (AV)

One First National Plaza 51st Floor, 60603
Telephone: 312-345-3000
Fax: 312-345-3119

MEMBERS OF FIRM

Fred C. Begy, III	Joseph A. Bosco
Larry S. Kaplan	Martin K. LaPointe
James D. Solon	Richard A. Walker
Robert C. von Ohlen, Jr.	Mitchell J. Kanaan

ASSOCIATES

John B. Austin	Michael J. Vint
Donald F. Brosnan	Maritoni Derecho Kane
(Not admitted in IL)	Adriana Gardella
J. Peter Martin	Michael J. Frazier
Neal J. Moglin	John T. Midgett
Jeffrey E. Margulis	Keith S. Yamaguchi
Kevin R. Davis	Rose Jagust
Patrick J. Keating	Thomas C. Sokol
	Terrill Elise Pierce

For full biographical listings, see the Martindale-Hubbell Law Directory

Chicago—Continued

KRISLOV & ASSOCIATES, LTD. (AV)

Suite 810, 222 North La Salle Street, 60601-1086
Telephone: 312-606-0500
Telecopier: 312-606-0207

Clinton A. Krislov

Jonathan Nachsin   Sara J. Weisenthal

For full biographical listings, see the Martindale-Hubbell Law Directory

LAWRENCE, KAMIN, SAUNDERS & UHLENHOP (AV)

208 South La Salle Street, Suite 1750, 60604
Telephone: 312-372-1947
Telecopier: 312-372-2389

MEMBERS OF FIRM

Paul B. Uhlenhop   Charles J. Risch
Kent Lawrence   Lawrence A. Rosen
          Michael Wise

Representative Clients: Dean Witter Reynolds Inc.; TransMarket Group, Inc.; Checkers, Simon & Rosner; A.G. Edwards & Sons, Inc.; Nash Weiss & Co.; Gofen & Glossberg, Inc.; Beacon Investment Co.

For full biographical listings, see the Martindale-Hubbell Law Directory

McBRIDE BAKER & COLES (AV)

500 West Madison Street 40th Floor, 60661
Telephone: 312-715-5700
Cable Address: "Chilaw"
Telex: 270258
Telecopier: 312-993-9350
Email: lastname@mbc.com *URL:* http://www.mbc.com
Oakbrook Terrace, Illinois Office: Suite 1000, One Mid America Plaza, 60181-4710.
Telephone: 630-954-2100.
Telecopier: 630-954-2112.

MEMBERS OF FIRM

Michael J. Boland   G. Gale Roberson, Jr.
William J. Cooney   Anne Hamblin Schiave
Lola Miranda Hale   Thomas P. Ward

SENIOR COUNSEL

Lawrence A. Coles, Jr.

OF COUNSEL

Robert O. Case

ASSOCIATE

Jerald Holisky

For Complete List of Firm Personnel, See General Section

For full biographical listings, see the Martindale-Hubbell Law Directory

McCONNELL & MENDELSON (AV)

140 South Dearborn Street, 9th Floor, 60603
Telephone: 312-263-1212
Telecopier: 312-263-0402

OF COUNSEL

Dennis A. Bell

Reference: The Northern Trust Co., Chicago, Illinois.

For full biographical listings, see the Martindale-Hubbell Law Directory

SAUNDERS & MONROE (AV)

Suite 4201, 205 North Michigan Avenue, 60601
Telephone: 312-946-9000
Facsimile: 312-946-0528

MEMBERS OF FIRM

George L. Saunders, Jr.   Thomas F. Bush, Jr.
Lee A. Monroe   Matthew E. Van Tine
          Thomas A. Doyle

Gwen A. Niedbalski

OF COUNSEL

Kenneth K. Howell   Victoria S. Kaplan

For full biographical listings, see the Martindale-Hubbell Law Directory

PETER R. SONDERBY, P.C. (AV)

135 South La Salle Street Suite 1424, 60603
Telephone: 312-201-0999
Fax: 312-201-0749;
Fax: 312-641-1930

Peter R. Sonderby

For full biographical listings, see the Martindale-Hubbell Law Directory

SUGAR, FRIEDBERG & FELSENTHAL (AV)

30 North La Salle Street, Suite 2600, 60602
Telephone: 312-704-9400
Telecopier: 312-372-7951
Cable: "SUGARFREE"

MEMBERS OF FIRM

Richard A. Sugar   Ira S. Neiman
Michael R. Friedberg   Jonathan L. Mills
Steven A. Felsenthal   Etahn M. Cohen
Andrew B. David   Howard M. Helsinger
Leslie J. Weiss   Robert F. Simon
          Martin M. Weinstein

ASSOCIATES

Kathryn A. Erickson   Jay R. Hoffman
Norman J. Ginsparg   Sophia Stergianis
          Jonathan W. Michael

For full biographical listings, see the Martindale-Hubbell Law Directory

*WHEATON,** Du Page Co.

JAMES E. BECKLEY & ASSOCIATES, P.C. (AV)

528 West Roosevelt Road, 60187
Telephone: 708-668-1335
Fax: 708-668-1342

James E. Beckley

Representative Clients: Bowater, Inc.; Oppenheimer & Co., Inc.; Capital Securities Investment Corp.

For full biographical listings, see the Martindale-Hubbell Law Directory

INDIANA

*INDIANAPOLIS,** Marion Co.

DANN PECAR NEWMAN & KLEIMAN, PROFESSIONAL CORPORATION (AV)

Suite 2300, One American Square Box 82008, 46282
Telephone: 317-632-3232; Indiana: 800-622-4799
Telecopy: 317-632-2962

Theodore R. Dann (1907-1993)   Walter E. Wolf, Jr.
Joel Yonover (1932-1995)   Barry E. Beldin
Philip D. Pecar   Robert D. Swhier, Jr.
Norman R. Newman   James P. Moloy
David H. Kleiman   Robert J. Schuckit
Jon B. Abels   Andrew A. Kleiman
Melvin R. Daniel   Michael J. Gabovitch
Lawrence F. Dorocke   Steven M. Pecar
Jeffrey A. Abrams   Benjamin A. Pecar
James H. Schwarz   Richard O. Kissel, II
Robert A. Rose   Joseph D. Calderon

OF COUNSEL

Linda E. Cantor   Anthony J. Rose

Ellen C. Siakotos   Angela L. Mansfield
Stacy L. Hill   Martha M. K. Baird
          Karin L. Veatch

Attorneys for: Indianapolis Machinery Co., Inc.; Melvin Simon & Associates, Inc.; Pacers Basketball Corp.; Universal Fire & Casualty Co., Inc.; Bank One, Indianapolis, NA; INB National Bank; Nachi Technology, Inc.; Pharmaceutical Corporation of America; Logo 7, Inc.

For full biographical listings, see the Martindale-Hubbell Law Directory

ICE MILLER DONADIO & RYAN (AV)

One American Square Box 82001, 46282-0002
Telephone: 317-236-2100
Fax: 317-236-2219
Email: leel@imdr.com *URL:* http://www.imdr.com
South Bend, Indiana Office: 211 West Washington Street, Suite 2420.
Telephone: 219-234-7933.
Fax: 219-234-7965. Internet E-mail: leel@imdr.com. Web Site Address: http://www.imdr.com.

MEMBERS OF FIRM

Berkley W. Duck   Stephen J. Hackman
Harry L. Gonso   Steven K. Humke
John R. Thornburgh   Elizabeth A. Smith

ASSOCIATES

Dean T. Burger   Brendan J. McKeough
Allan S. Katz   Kirstin Pace Salzman

For Complete List of Firm Personnel, See General Section

For full biographical listings, see the Martindale-Hubbell Law Directory

Indianapolis—Continued

JOHNSON, SMITH, PENCE, DENSBORN, WRIGHT & HEATH (AV)

One Indiana Square Suite 1800, 46204
Telephone: 317-634-9777
Telecopier: 317-636-9061

MEMBERS OF FIRM

James T. Crawford, Jr.
Donald K. Densborn
David Williams Russell

Thomas N. Eckerle
John R. Kirkwood

ASSOCIATE

Charles M. Freeland

For Complete List of Firm Personnel, See General Section

For full biographical listings, see the Martindale-Hubbell Law Directory

LOCKE REYNOLDS BOYD & WEISELL (AV)

1000 Capital Center South, 201 North Illinois Street, 46204
Telephone: 317-237-3800
Telecopier: 317-237-3900

Stephen J. Dutton
Jeffrey B. Bailey

Michael J. Schneider

David S. Klinestiver

Curt W. Hidde

Representative Clients: Baldwin & Lyons, Inc.; Dean Witter Reynolds, Inc.; Golden Rule Insurance Co.; Indy Connection Limousines, Inc.; Mantis Corporation; Paragon Medical, Inc.; Real Silk Investments, Inc.; Thurston Springer Miller Herd & Titak, Inc.; Traub & Company, Inc.

For Complete List of Firm Personnel, See General Section

For full biographical listings, see the Martindale-Hubbell Law Directory

McTURNAN & TURNER (AV)

2400 Market Tower, 10 West Market Street, 46204
Telephone: 317-464-8181
Telecopier: 317-464-8131

Lee B. McTurnan
Wayne C. Turner
Judy L. Woods

Jacqueline Bowman Ponder
Steven M. Badger
Matthew W. Foster

Matthew J. Salzman

For full biographical listings, see the Martindale-Hubbell Law Directory

SOMMER & BARNARD, ATTORNEYS AT LAW, PC (AV)

4000 Bank One Tower, 111 Monument Circle, 46204-5140
Telephone: 317-630-4000
FAX: 317-236-9802
North Office: 8900 Keystone Crossing, Suite 1046, Indianapolis, Indiana, 46240-2134.
Telephone: 317-630-4000.
FAX: 317-844-4780.

James K. Sommer
Julianne S. Lis-Milam

James A. Strain

OF COUNSEL

Philip L. McCool

Representative Clients: Comerica Bank; Excel Industries; Federal Express; Kimball International; Monsanto; Renault Automation; TRW, Inc.

For Complete List of Firm Personnel, See General Section

For full biographical listings, see the Martindale-Hubbell Law Directory

KANSAS

TOPEKA, * Shawnee Co.

GOODELL, STRATTON, EDMONDS & PALMER, L.L.P. (AV)

515 South Kansas Avenue, 66603-3999
Telephone: 913-233-0593
Telecopier: 913-233-8870
Email: GSEP@CJNETWORKS.COM

MEMBERS OF FIRM

Gerald L. Goodell
H. Philip Elwood
Gerald J. Letourneau

Michael W. Merriam
John H. Stauffer, Jr.
John D. Ensley

OF COUNSEL

Robert E. Edmonds (Retired)

Counsel for: St. Paul Fire & Marine Insurance Co.
General Counsel for: American Home Life Insurance Co.; Columbian National Title Insurance Co.; The Menninger Foundation; Stauffer Communications, Inc.; Kansas Medical Society; Kansas Hospital Association.

(See Next Column)

For Complete List of Firm Personnel, See General Section

For full biographical listings, see the Martindale-Hubbell Law Directory

WICHITA, * Sedgwick Co.

FOULSTON & SIEFKIN L.L.P. (AV)

700 Fourth Financial Center, 67202
Telephone: 316-267-6371
Facsimile: 316-267-6345
Topeka, Kansas Office: 1515 Bank IV Tower, 534 Kansas Avenue, 66603.
Telephone: 913-233-3600.
Fax: 913-233-1610.
Dodge City, Kansas Office: 810 Frontview, P.O. Box 1147, 67801.
Telephone: 316-227-8126.
Fax: 316-227-8451.
Member: Lex Mundi, A Global Association of 126 Independent Firms.

MEMBERS OF FIRM

Benjamin C. Langel
William R. Wood, II

James D. Oliver

For Complete List of Firm Personnel, See General Section

For full biographical listings, see the Martindale-Hubbell Law Directory

KENTUCKY

LEXINGTON, * Fayette Co.

STOLL, KEENON & PARK, LLP (AV)

201 E. Main Street, Suite 1000, 40507-1380
Telephone: 606-231-3000
Telecopier: 606-253-1093; 606-253-1027
Frankfort, Kentucky Office: 307 Washington Street, 40601.
Telephone: 502-875-6220.
Telecopier: 502-875-6235.
Louisville, Kentucky Office: 400 West Market Street, Suite 2650, 40202-3377.
Telephone: 502-568-9100.
Telecopier: 502-568-5700.

MEMBERS OF FIRM

Robert M. Watt, III
Gary L. Stage

Herbert A. Miller, Jr.
J. David Smith, Jr.

John W. Walters, Jr.

Representative Clients: Delta Natural Gas Co., Inc.; Farmers Capital Bank Corp.; Gamma One Laboratories, Inc.; Lexington Brewing Co.; Lexington Investment Co., Inc.; Medical Rehabilitation Centers, Inc.; MedPro, Inc.; Whitaker Bank Corporation of Kentucky.

For Complete List of Firm Personnel, See General Section

For full biographical listings, see the Martindale-Hubbell Law Directory

LOUISVILLE, * Jefferson Co.

GOLDBERG & SIMPSON, P.S.C. (AV)

3000 National City Tower, 40202
Telephone: 502-589-4440
Telefax: 502-581-1344
Washington, D.C. Office: 1200 G Street, N.W. - Suite 800, 20005.
Telephone: 202-434-8968.
Telefax: 202-737-5822.

Fred M. Goldberg
David B. Ratterman
Jonathan D. Goldberg
James S. Goldberg
Mitchell A. Charney
Steven A. Goodman
Edward L. Schoenbaechler
Cathy S. Pike
Stephen E. Smith
Cynthia Buss Maddox

William J. Hust, III
(Not admitted in KY)
Mary Alice Maple
Emily L. Lawrence
Douglas S. Haynes
Jan M. West
Charles H. Cassis
Robin Sylvester Craddock
John Joseph McLaughlin
Leslie E. Huber

Anthony J Elpers

OF COUNSEL

Ronald V. Simpson
David A. Brill

Kenneth G. Lee (Not admitted in KY; Resident, Washington, D.C. Office)

Representative Clients: National City Bank; Liberty Mutual Insurance Co.; Jewish Hospital Healthcare Services, Inc.; Louisville & Jefferson County Board of Health; Providian Corp.

For full biographical listings, see the Martindale-Hubbell Law Directory

Louisville—Continued

MIDDLETON & REUTLINGER, P.S.C. (AV)

2500 Brown and Williamson Tower, 40202-3410
Telephone: 502-584-1135
Fax: 502-561-0442
New Albany, Indiana Office: 2623 Charlestown Road, 47150.
Telephone: 812-944-7215.

C. Kent Hatfield   D. Randall Gibson
William Jay Hunter, Jr.

Counsel for: Chevron USA; Logan Aluminum, Inc.; Louisville Gas & Electric Co.; MCI Telecommunications Corp.; Metropolitan Life Insurance Co.; Kosmos Cement Co.; Porcelain Metal Corp.; The Home Insurance Co.; The Kroger Co.; Demars Haka Development, Inc.

For Complete List of Firm Personnel, See General Section

For full biographical listings, see the Martindale-Hubbell Law Directory

RUBIN HAYS & FOLEY (AV)

First Trust Centre 200 South Fifth Street, 40202
Telephone: 502-569-7550
Telecopier: 502-569-7555

MEMBERS OF FIRM

Wm. Carl Fust   Lisa Koch Bryant
Harry Lee Meyer   Sharon C. Hardy
David W. Gray   Charles S. Musson
Irvin D. Foley   W. Randall Jones
Joseph R. Gathright, Jr.   K. Gail Russell

ASSOCIATES

Christian L. Juckett   Courtney Lynn McCall

OF COUNSEL

James E. Fahey   Newman T. Guthrie

Representative Clients: J.C. Bradford & Co., Inc.; J.J.B. Hilliard, W.L. Lyons, Inc.; Huntington National Bank; Liberty National Bank and Trust Company; National City Bank; PNC Bank; Prudential Bache & Co., Inc.; Prudential Securities, Inc.; Society Bank; Stock Yards Bank and Trust Co.

For full biographical listings, see the Martindale-Hubbell Law Directory

LOUISIANA

*NEW ORLEANS,** Orleans Parish

LAMOTHE & HAMILTON, A PROFESSIONAL LAW CORPORATION (AV)

Pan American Life Center, 601 Poydras Street, Suite 2750, 70130
Telephone: 504-566-1805
Telecopier: 504-566-1569
MCI Mail: 382-4472
Email: lhplc@neosoft.com

Frank E. Lamothe, III   Galen S. Brown
Charles E. Hamilton, III   M. Lizabeth Talbott
Karen Edginton Milner   Thomas J. Cortazzo

Reference: Jefferson Guaranty Bank, New Orleans, Louisiana.

For full biographical listings, see the Martindale-Hubbell Law Directory

LISKOW & LEWIS, A PROFESSIONAL LAW CORPORATION (AV)

50th Floor, One Shell Square, 70139
Telephone: 504-581-7979
Telecopier: 504-556-4108; 504-556-4109
Lafayette, Louisiana Office: 822 Harding Street, P.O. Box 52008.
Telephone: 318-232-7424.
Telecopier: 318-267-2399.

Gene W. Lafitte   Marie Breaux
George Denegre, Jr.   John C. Anjier

Representative Clients: Prudential Securities Inc.; Rauscher, Pierce, Refsnes, Inc.; Howard, Weil, Labouisse, Friedrichs Inc.; Prudential Insurance Company of America.

For Complete List of Firm Personnel, See General Section

For full biographical listings, see the Martindale-Hubbell Law Directory

MARYLAND

*BALTIMORE,** (Independent City)

THOMAS & LIBOWITZ, A PROFESSIONAL ASSOCIATION (AV)

USF&G Tower, Suite 1100, 100 Light Street, 21202-1053
Telephone: 410-752-2468
Telecopier: 410-752-2046

Clinton R. Black, IV
OF COUNSEL
Susan M. Rittenhouse

For full biographical listings, see the Martindale-Hubbell Law Directory

VENABLE ATTORNEYS AT LAW VENABLE, BAETJER AND HOWARD, LLP (AV)

A Partnership including Professional Corporations
1800 Mercantile Bank & Trust Building, 2 Hopkins Plaza, 21201
Telephone: 410-244-7400
Email: INFO@Venable.win.net
Washington, D.C. Office: Venable, Baetjer, Howard & Civiletti LLP. Suite 1000, 1201 New York Avenue, N.W.
Telephone: 202-962-4800.
McLean, Virginia Office: Suite 400, 2010 Corporate Ridge.
Telephone: 703-760-1600.
Rockville, Maryland Office: Suite 500, One Church Street, P. O. Box 1906.
Telephone: 301-217-5600.
Towson, Maryland Office: 210 Allegheny Avenue, P. O. Box 5517.
Telephone: 410-494-6200.

MEMBERS OF FIRM

Benjamin R. Civiletti (P.C.)
  (Also at Washington, D.C.
  and Towson, Maryland
  Offices)
John Henry Lewin, Jr. (P.C.)
Lee M. Miller (P.C.)
Ronald R. Glancz (Not
  admitted in MD; Resident,
  Washington, D.C. Office)
David J. Levenson (Not
  admitted in MD; Resident,
  Washington, D.C. Office)
Joe A. Shull (Resident,
  Washington, D.C. Office)
Kenneth C. Bass, III (Not
  admitted in MD; Washington,
  D.C. and McLean, Virginia
  Offices)
John H. Zink, III (Resident,
  Towson, Maryland Office)
Joseph C. Wich, Jr. (Resident,
  Towson, Maryland Office)
Thomas B. Hudson (Also at
  Washington, D.C. Office)

Nell B. Strachan
G. Stewart Webb, Jr.
James K. Archibald (Also at
  Washington, D.C. Office)
James R. Myers (Not admitted
  in MD; Resident, Washington,
  D.C. Office)
James L. Shea (Also at
  Washington, D.C. Office)
William D. Quarles (Also at
  Washington, D.C. and
  Towson, Maryland Offices)
Christopher R. Mellott
John L. Sullivan, III (Not
  admitted in MD; Resident,
  McLean, Virginia Office)
Elizabeth R. Hughes
Anita J. Finkelstein (Not
  admitted in MD; Resident,
  Washington, D.C. Office)
Ariel Vannier
Gary M. Hnath (Resident,
  Washington, D.C. Office)
Francis X. Gallagher, Jr.
  (Not admitted in MD)

OF COUNSEL

Arthur W. Machen, Jr. (P.C.)
Herbert R. O'Conor, Jr.
  (Resident, Towson, Maryland
  Office)

ASSOCIATES

Pamela W. Carmody (Also at
  Washington, D.C. Office)
Michael W. Conron
Donald P. Creston (Not
  admitted in MD; Resident,
  Washington, D.C. Office)
David S. Darland (Not admitted
  in MD; Resident, Washington,
  D.C. Office)

John P. Fielding (Not admitted
  in MD; Washington, D.C. and
  McLean, Virginia Offices)
E. Anne Hamel
Mary-Dulany James (Resident,
  Towson, Maryland Office)
Wingrove S. Lynton
John T. Prisbe
Joseph C. Schmelter

Elizabeth M.S. Whaling

For Complete List of Firm Personnel, See General Section

For full biographical listings, see the Martindale-Hubbell Law Directory

MASSACHUSETTS

*BOSTON,** Suffolk Co.

GELB & GELB (AV)

20 Custom House Street, 02110
Telephone: 617-345-0010
Facsimile: 617-345-0009

(See Next Column)

GELB & GELB—*Continued*

MEMBER OF FIRM
Richard M. Gelb

For full biographical listings, see the Martindale-Hubbell Law Directory

NATHANSON & GOLDBERG, A PROFESSIONAL CORPORATION (AV)

10 Union Wharf, 02109
Telephone: 617-742-9350
Fax: 617-742-3559

Alvin S. Nathanson	Valerie S. Carter
Arthur Goldberg	Shannon M. Fitzpatrick

Stuart J. Frank

For full biographical listings, see the Martindale-Hubbell Law Directory

PALMER & DODGE LLP (AV)

One Beacon Street, 02108
Telephone: 617-573-0100
Facsimile: 617-227-4420

MEMBER OF FIRM
Stanley Keller

For Complete List of Firm Personnel, See General Section

For full biographical listings, see the Martindale-Hubbell Law Directory

PEABODY & ARNOLD (AV)

A Partnership including Professional Corporations
50 Rowes Wharf, 02110-3342
Telephone: 617-951-2100
Telecopier: 617-951-2125
Providence, Rhode Island Office: One Citizens Plaza, Suite 840.
Telephone: 401-831-8330.
Fax: 401-831-8359.

MEMBERS OF FIRM

John R. Gowell, Jr. (Resident, Providence, Rhode Island Office)	David F. Hendren
	Joseph D. S. Hinkley
	Anil Khosla
Ripley E. Hastings	Gregory L. White

ASSOCIATES

Frank S. Hamblett	Anna M. Magliocco-Chagnon
Amelia M. Charamba	Scott D. Karchmer

For Complete List of Firm Personnel, See General Section

For full biographical listings, see the Martindale-Hubbell Law Directory

LYNNFIELD, Essex Co.

WILLIAM M. PRIFTI (AV)

220 Broadway, Suite 204, 01940
Telephone: 617-593-4525
Fax: 617-598-5222

For full biographical listings, see the Martindale-Hubbell Law Directory

MICHIGAN

ANN ARBOR, * Washtenaw Co.

MILLER, CANFIELD, PADDOCK AND STONE, P.L.C. (AV)

A Professional Limited Liability Company
Founded in 1852 by Sidney Davy Miller
101 North Main Street, Seventh Floor, 48104-1400
Telephone: 313-663-2445
Fax: 313-747-7147
Detroit, Michigan Office: 150 West Jefferson, Suite 2500, 48226-4415.
Telephone: 313-963-6420.
Fax: 313-496-7500.
Cable Address: "Stem Detroit."
Bloomfield Hills, Michigan Office: Suite 100, Pinehurst Office Center, 1400 North Woodward, 48303-2014.
Telephone: 313-645-5000.
Fax: 313-645-1917.
Grand Rapids, Michigan Office: 1200 Campau Square Plaza, 99 Monroe, N.W., 49503-2639.
Telephone: 616-454-8656.
Fax: 616-776-6322.
Howell, Michigan Office: 121 South Barnard Street, Suite 4, 48843-2305.
Telephone: 517-546-7600.
Telecopier: 517-546-6974.

(See Next Column)

Kalamazoo, Michigan Office: 444 West Michigan Avenue, 49007-3752.
Telephone: 616-381-7030.
Fax: 616-382-0244.
Lansing, Michigan Office: One Michigan Avenue, Suite 900, 48933-1609.
Telephone: 517-487-2070.
Fax: 517-374-6304.
Monroe, Michigan Office: The Executive Centre, 214 East Elm Avenue, 48161-2682.
Telephone: 313-243-2000.
Fax: 313-243-0901.
Washington, D.C. Office: 1225 Nineteenth Street, N.W., Suite 400. 20036.
Telephone: 202-429-5575; 785-0600.
Fax: 202-331-1118; 785-1234.
Pensacola, Florida Office: 25 West Cedar, 32501.
Telephone: 904-469-1088.
Fax: 904-432-0677.
St. Petersburg, Florida Office: 100 Second Avenue S., Suite 7045, 33701.
Telephone: 813-982-6000.
Fax: 813-892-6002.
New York, New York Office: Eleventh Floor, 135 East 57th Street, 10022-2087.
Telephone: 212-754-5400.
Fax: 212-754-5401.
Gdansk, Poland Office: Suite 322, Dom Technika Building, UI. Rajska 6, 80-850.
Telephone: 011-485-831-2808.
Fax: 011-485-831-4719.
Warsaw, Poland Office: UI. Marszalkowska 82, Suite 561, 00-517.
Telephone: 011-482-623-6457 and 6458.
Fax: 011-482-623-6459.

RESIDENT PRINCIPALS

David N. Parsigian	Marta A. Manildi

OF COUNSEL
Edmond F. DeVine

RESIDENT ASSOCIATE
John O. Renken

Representative Firm Clients: Chrysler Corporation; Comerica, Incorporated; City of Detroit, Michigan; Detroit Tigers, Inc.; First of Michigan; Ford Motor Company; Ford Motor Credit Company; Great Lakes Bancorp; Henry Ford Hospital; INVETECH Company.

For Complete List of Firm Personnel, See General Section

For full biographical listings, see the Martindale-Hubbell Law Directory

BIRMINGHAM, Oakland Co.

CARSON FISCHER, P.L.C. (AV)

Third Floor, 300 East Maple Road, 48009-6317
Telephone: 810-644-4840
Facsimile: 810-644-1832

Robert M. Carson	Peter L. Wanger

For full biographical listings, see the Martindale-Hubbell Law Directory

BLOOMFIELD HILLS, Oakland Co.

FEENEY KELLETT WIENNER & BUSH, PROFESSIONAL CORPORATION (AV)

950 North Hunter Boulevard, Second Floor, 48304-3927
Telephone: 810-258-1580
Fax: 810-258-0421

James P. Feeney	Cheryl A. Bush
S. Thomas Wienner	Deborah F. Collins
Peter M. Kellett	David N. Goltz

OF COUNSEL
Thomas J. Manganello

James J. Majernik	Seth D. Gould
G. Gregory Schuetz	Patrick G. Seyferth
Jeffrey A. Gallant	Mark A. Fisher
	Bryan D. Cross

For full biographical listings, see the Martindale-Hubbell Law Directory

HOWARD & HOWARD ATTORNEYS, P.C. (AV)

The Pinehurst Office Center, Suite 101, 1400 North Woodward Avenue, 48304-2856
Telephone: 810-645-1483
Telecopier: 810-645-1568
Kalamazoo, Michigan Office: The Kalamazoo Building, Suite 400, 107 West Michigan Avenue.
Telephone: 616-382-1483.
Telecopier: 616-382-1568.
Lansing, Michigan Office: The Phoenix Building, Suite 500, 222 Washington Square, North.
Telephone: 517-485-1483.
Telecopier: 517-485-1568.

(See Next Column)

HOWARD & HOWARD ATTORNEYS P.C., *Bloomfield Hills—Continued*

Peoria, Illinois Office: The Creve Coeur Building, Suite 200, 321 Liberty Street.
Telephone: 309-672-1483.
Telecopier: 309-672-1568.
Tampa, Florida Office: First of America Plaza, Suite 2000, 201 East Kennedy Boulevard.
Telephone: 813-229-1483.
Telecopier: 813-229-1568.

Robert C. Rosselot   Robert L. Schwartz
(Not admitted in MI)   Melanie Mayo West

Representative Clients: For Representative Client list, see General Practice, Bloomfield Hills, MI.

For Complete List of Firm Personnel, See General Section

For full biographical listings, see the Martindale-Hubbell Law Directory

---

MILLER, CANFIELD, PADDOCK AND STONE, P.L.C. (AV)

A Professional Limited Liability Company
Founded in 1852 by Sidney Davy Miller
Suite 100 Pinehurst Office Center, 1400 North Woodward, P.O. Box 2014, 48303-2014
Telephone: 810-645-5000
Fax: 810-645-1917
Fax: 810-258-3036
Detroit, Michigan Office: 150 West Jefferson, Suite 2500, 48226-4415.
Telephone: 313-963-6420.
Fax: 313-496-7500.
Cable Address: "Stem Detroit."
Ann Arbor, Michigan Office: 101 North Main Street, 7th Floor, 48104-1400.
Telephone: 313-663-2445.
Fax: 313-747-7147.
Grand Rapids, Michigan Office: 1200 Campau Square Plaza, 99 Monroe, N.W., 49503-2639.
Telephone: 616-454-8656.
Fax: 616-776-6322.
Howell, Michigan Office: 121 South Barnard Street, Suite 4, 48843-2305.
Telephone: 517-546-7600.
Telecopier: 517-546-6974.
Kalamazoo, Michigan Office: 444 West Michigan Avenue, 49007-3752.
Telephone: 616-381-7030.
Fax: 616-382-0244.
Lansing, Michigan Office: One Michigan Avenue, Suite 900, 48933-1609.
Telephone: 517-487-2070.
Fax: 517-374-6304.
Monroe, Michigan Office: The Executive Centre, 214 East Elm Avenue, 48161-2682.
Telephone: 313-243-2000.
Fax: 313-243-0901.
Washington, D.C. Office: 1225 Nineteenth Street, N.W., Suite 400. 20036.
Telephone: 202-429-5575; 785-0600.
Fax: 202-331-1118; 785-1234.
Pensacola, Florida Office: 25 West Cedar, 32501.
Telephone: 904-469-1088.
Fax: 904-432-0677.
St. Petersburg, Florida Office: 100 Second Avenue S., Suite 7045, 33701.
Telephone: 813-982-6000.
Fax: 813-892-6002.
New York, New York Office: Eleventh Floor, 135 East 57th Street, 10022-2087.
Telephone: 212-754-5400.
Fax: 212-754-5401.
Gdansk, Poland Office: Suite 322, Dom Technika Building, UI. Rajska 6, 80-850.
Telephone: 011-485-831-2808.
Fax: 011-485-831-4719.
Warsaw, Poland Office: UI. Marszalkowska 82, Suite 561, 00-517.
Telephone: 011-482-623-6457 and 6458.
Fax: 011-482-623-6459.

RESIDENT PRINCIPALS

John A. Marxer (P.C.)   J. Kevin Trimmer
Brad B. Arbuckle

Representative Firm Clients: Chrysler Corporation; Comerica, Incorporated; City of Detroit, Michigan; Detroit Tigers, Inc.; First of Michigan; Ford Motor Company; Ford Motor Credit Company; Great Lakes Bancorp; Henry Ford Hospital; INVETECH Company.

For Complete List of Firm Personnel, See General Section

For full biographical listings, see the Martindale-Hubbell Law Directory

---

DETROIT, Wayne Co.

BODMAN, LONGLEY & DAHLING LLP (AV)

34th Floor 100 Renaissance Center, 48243
Telephone: 313-259-7777
Fax: 313-393-7579
Email: 2080194@mcimail.com
Troy, Michigan Office: Suite 2020, 755 West Big Beaver Road.
Telephone: 810-362-2110.
Fax: 810-244-0780.
Ann Arbor, Michigan Office: 110 Miller, Suite 300.
Telephone: 313-761-3780.
Fax: 313-930-2494.
Northern Michigan Office: 229 Court Street, P.O. Box 405, Cheboygan.
Telephone: 616-627-4351.
Fax: 616-627-2802.

MEMBERS OF FIRM

Richard D. Rohr   James R. Buschmann
Kenneth R. Lango (Troy Office)   Randolph S. Perry
Herold McC. Deason   Barbara Bowman Bluford

For Representative Client List, See General Section

For Complete List of Firm Personnel, See General Section

For full biographical listings, see the Martindale-Hubbell Law Directory

---

BUTZEL LONG, A PROFESSIONAL CORPORATION (AV)

Suite 900, 150 West Jefferson, 48226
Telephone: 313-225-7000
Telecopier: 313-225-7080
Email: melnick@butzel.com *URL:* http://www.butzel.com
Birmingham, Michigan Office: Suite 200, 32270 Telegraph Road.
Telephone: 810-258-1616.
Telecopier: 810-258-1439.
Lansing, Michigan Office: 118 West Ottawa Street.
Telephone: 517-372-6622.
Telecopier: 517-372-6672.
Ann Arbor, Michigan Office: Suite 300, 350 South Main Street.
Telephone: 313-995-3110.
Telecopier: 313-995-1777.
Grosse Pointe Farms, Michigan Office: Suite 260, 21 Kercheval.
Telephone: 313-886-5446.
Telecopier: 313-886-2114.

George H. Zinn, Jr.   Arthur Dudley II
Edward M. Kronk   Richard P. Saslow
Philip J. Kessler   Dennis K. Egan
Justin G. Klimko   Sheldon H. Klein
Michael F. Golab (Birmingham)   Ronald E. Reynolds
                     (Birmingham)

Phillip C. Korovesis

Representative Clients: American Investment Financial, N.A.; Bear Stearns; Drexel Burnham Lambert; The Evening News Assn.; Guardian Industries Co.; Jackson National Life Insurance Co.; Merrill Lynch Pierce Fenner & Smith, Inc.; Michigan Rivet Corp.; Paine Webber; Prudential Securities, Inc.

For Complete List of Firm Personnel, See General Section

For full biographical listings, see the Martindale-Hubbell Law Directory

---

CLARK HILL P.L.C. (AV)

500 Woodward Avenue, Suite 3500, 48226
Telephone: 313-965-8300
Facsimile: 313-962-4348
Oakland County, Michigan Office: Third Floor, 255 South Woodward Avenue, Birmingham.
Telephone: 810-642-9692.
Facsimile: 810-642-2174.
Lansing, Michigan Office: Suite 600, 200 North Capitol Avenue.
Telephone: 517-484-4481.
Facsimile: 517-484-1246.
Minneapolis, Minnesota Office: Suite 1000, One Financial Plaza, 120 South Sixth Street.
Telephone: 612-332-0102.
Facsimile: 612-332-3225.
Kansas City, Missouri Office: Suite 1400, Bryant Building, 1102 Grand Avenue.
Telephone: 816-221-5578.
Facsimile: 816-221-0303.

D. Kerry Crenshaw   Robert L. Weyhing, III
John F. Burns   John J. Hern, Jr.

Patrice Asimakis   John P. Hensien
Georgette Borrego Dulworth   Margery Siegel Klausner

Representative Clients: R.P. Scherer Corporation; LCI International; Rouge Steel Company; Code-Alarm, Inc.; Detrex Corporation; Eaton Corporation; Gerber Foundation; Frey Foundation; Bain Hogg Group plc; Equity Link, Ltd.

(See Next Column)

CLARK HILL P.L.C.—*Continued*

For Complete List of Firm Personnel, See General Section

For full biographical listings, see the Martindale-Hubbell Law Directory

JAFFE, RAITT, HEUER & WEISS, PROFESSIONAL CORPORATION (AV)

One Woodward Avenue, Suite 2400, 48226
Telephone: 313-961-8380
Telecopier: 313-961-8358
Cable Address: "Jafsni"
Southfield, Michigan Office: Travelers Tower, Suite 1520.
Telephone: 313-961-8380.
Monroe, Michigan Office: 214 East Elm Avenue, Suite 208,
Telephone: 313-241-6470.
Telefacsimile: 313-241-3849.

Penny L. Carolan	David D. Warner
Elliot A. Spoon	Janet G. Witkowski

Representative Clients: Edgemere Enterprises; Frankel Associates, Inc.; Somerset Inn & Apartments; Sosnick Development Co.; Uniprop, Inc.

For Complete List of Firm Personnel, See General Section

For full biographical listings, see the Martindale-Hubbell Law Directory

LEWIS, CLAY & MUNDAY, A PROFESSIONAL CORPORATION (AV)

(Formerly Lewis, White & Clay, P.C.)
1300 First National Building, 660 Woodward Avenue, 48226-3531
Telephone: 313-961-2550
Troy, Michigan Office: Liberty Center, Suite 200. 100 West Big Beaver Road. 48084.
Telephone: 810-680-6702.
Fax: 810-680-6703.
Washington, D.C. Office: 1000 16th Street, N.W., Suite 401. 20036.
Telephone: 202-835-0616.
Fax: 202-833-3316.
Boston, Massachusetts Office: 10 Post Office Square.
Telephone: 617-422-8646.
Fax: 617-338-5693.

David Baker Lewis	Frank E. Barbee
Eric Lee Clay	Camille Stearns Miller
Reuben A. Munday	Michael T. Raymond
Ulysses Whittaker Boykin	Jacqueline H. Sellers
Carl F. Stafford	David N. Zacks
Helen Francine Strong	Thomas J. Guyer
	Blair A. Person

Karen Kendrick Brown	Hans J. Massaquoi, Jr.
(Resident, Washington, D.C. Office)	Nancy C. Borland
	Tammy L. Terry
J. Taylor Teasdale	Lynn Westfall Gross
Wade Harper McCree	Suzanne P. Pope
Tyrone A. Powell	Matthew R. Halpin
Susan D. Hoffman	Donica Thomas Varner
John J. Walsh	Damon L. White
Andrea L. Powell	(Not admitted in MI)
Althea Lynn Foster	Kathleen L. Royal

COUNSEL

Otis M. Smith (1922-1994)	G. Allen Bass (Resident, Boston,
Herbert O. Reid, Sr. (1915-1991)	Massachusetts Office)

Representative Clients: Omnicare Health Plan; Aetna Life & Casualty Co.; Chrysler Motors Corp.; Chrysler Financial Corp.; MCI Communications Corp.; City of Detroit; City of Detroit Building Authority; City of Detroit Downtown Development Authority; Consolidated Rail Corp. (Conrail); Equitable Life Assurance Society of the United States.

For full biographical listings, see the Martindale-Hubbell Law Directory

MILLER, CANFIELD, PADDOCK AND STONE, P.L.C. (AV)

A Professional Limited Liability Company
Founded in 1852 by Sidney Davy Miller
150 West Jefferson, Suite 2500, 48226-4415
Telephone: 313-963-6420
Fax: 313-496-7500
Cable Address: "Stem Detroit"
Detroit, Michigan Office: 150 West Jefferson, Suite 2500, 48226-4415.
Telephone: 313-963-6420.
Fax: 313-496-7500.
Cable Address: "Stem Detroit."
Ann Arbor, Michigan Office: 101 North Main Street, 7th Floor, 48104-1400.
Telephone: 313-663-2445.
Fax: 313-747-7147.
Bloomfield Hills, Michigan Office: Suite 100, Pinehurst Office Center, 1400 North Woodward, 48303-2014.
Telephone: 313-645-5000.
Fax: 313-645-1917.

(See Next Column)

Grand Rapids, Michigan Office: 1200 Campau Square Plaza, 99 Monroe, N.W., 49503-2639.
Telephone: 616-454-8656.
Fax: 616-776-6322.
Howell, Michigan Office: 121 South Barnard Street, Suite 4, 48843-2305.
Telephone: 517-546-7600.
Telecopier: 517-546-6974.
Kalamazoo, Michigan Office: 444 West Michigan Avenue, 49007-3752.
Telephone: 616-381-7030.
Fax: 616-382-0244.
Lansing, Michigan Office: One Michigan Avenue, Suite 900, 48933-1609.
Telephone: 517-487-2070.
Fax: 517-374-6304.
Monroe, Michigan Office: The Executive Centre, 214 East Elm Avenue, 48161-2682.
Telephone: 313-243-2000.
Fax: 313-243-0901.
Washington, D.C. Office: 1225 Nineteenth Street, N.W., Suite 400. 20036.
Telephone: 202-429-5575; 785-0600.
Fax: 202-331-1118; 785-1234.
Pensacola, Florida Office: 25 West Cedar, 32501.
Telephone: 904-469-1088.
Fax: 904-432-0677.
St. Petersburg, Florida Office: 100 Second Avenue S., Suite 7045, 33701.
Telephone: 813-982-6000.
Fax: 813-892-6002.
New York, New York Office: Eleventh Floor, 135 East 57th Street, 10022-2087.
Telephone: 212-754-5400.
Fax: 212-754-5401.
Gdansk, Poland Office: Suite 322, Dom Technika Building, UI. Rajska 6, 80-850.
Telephone: 011-485-831-2808.
Fax: 011-485-831-4719.
Warsaw, Poland Office: UI. Marszalkowska 82, Suite 561, 00-517.
Telephone: 011-482-623-6457 and 6458.
Fax: 011-482-623-6459.

PRINCIPALS OF FIRM

Eric V. Brown, Jr.	Thomas H. Van Dis
(Kalamazoo Office)	(Kalamazoo Office)
Bruce D. Birgbauer	Brad B. Arbuckle
Carl H. von Ende	(Bloomfield Hills Office)
David D. Joswick (P.C.)	Mark T. Boonstra
John A. Marxer (P.C.)	Karen Ann McCoy
(Bloomfield Hills Office)	Steven M. Stankewicz
Clarence L. Pozza, Jr.	(Kalamazoo Office)
Jerry T. Rupley	David N. Parsigian
Kent E. Shafer	(Ann Arbor Office)
John R. Cook	Jay B. Rising (Lansing Office)
(Kalamazoo Office)	Marta A. Manildi
Thomas G. Appleman	(Ann Arbor Office)
(Bloomfield Hills Office)	

ASSOCIATES

Thomas R. Cox	John O. Renken (Ann Arbor
	and Washington, D.C. Offices)

Representative Firm Clients: Chrysler Corporation; Comerica, Incorporated; City of Detroit, Michigan; Detroit Tigers, Inc.; First of Michigan; Ford Motor Company; Ford Motor Credit Company; Great Lakes Bancorp; Henry Ford Hospital; INVETECH Company.

For Complete List of Firm Personnel, See General Section

For full biographical listings, see the Martindale-Hubbell Law Directory

TIMMIS & INMAN, L.L.P. (AV)

300 Talon Centre, 48207
Telephone: 313-396-4200
Telecopier: 313-396-4228

Michael T. Timmis	Henry J. Brennan, III
Robert E. Graziani	Mark W. Peyser
George A. Peck	Richard M. Miettinen
Charles W. Royer	Lisa R. Gorman
Richard L. Levin	Bradley J. Knickerbocker
	George M. Malis

Michael F. Wais	Patrick B. Carey
John P. Kanan	Erich J. D'Andrea
	Shannon M. Nichols

OF COUNSEL

Wayne C. Inman	William B. Fitzgerald
	W. Clark Durant, III

Representative Clients: Stylecraft Printing Company; Stylerite Label Corporation; Retail Resources, Inc.; Deneb Robotics, Inc.; Applied Process, Inc.; Insilco Corporation; Variety Foods, Inc.; Chateau Properties, Inc.

For full biographical listings, see the Martindale-Hubbell Law Directory

FARMINGTON HILLS, Oakland Co.

HOROWITZ — GUDEMAN, P.C. (AV)

31700 Middlebelt, Suite 140, 48334
Telephone: 810-855-6020
Facsimile: 810-855-6025

Marvin I. Horowitz   Edward J. Gudeman
Stuart L. Sherman

Leslie I. Kollin
LEGAL SUPPORT PERSONNEL
Robin E. Cornell (Paralegal)

For full biographical listings, see the Martindale-Hubbell Law Directory

---

GRAND RAPIDS,* Kent Co.

McSHANE & BOWIE, P.L.C. (AV)

1100 Campau Square Plaza, 99 Monroe Avenue, N.W., P.O. Box
360, 49501-0360
Telephone: 616-732-5000
Fax: 616-732-5099

OF COUNSEL
Jack M. Bowie (Retired)
MEMBERS OF FIRM

David L. Smith   William H. Bowie
John F. Shape

Representative Clients: M. W. VanderVeen Co.; Cambridge Development Co.

For Complete List of Firm Personnel, See General Section

For full biographical listings, see the Martindale-Hubbell Law Directory

---

MILLER, CANFIELD, PADDOCK AND STONE, P.L.C. (AV)

A Professional Limited Liability Company
Founded in 1852 by Sidney Davy Miller
1200 Campau Square Plaza, 99 Monroe, N.W., P.O. Box 329, 49503-2639
Telephone: 616-454-8656
Fax: 616-776-6322
Detroit, Michigan Office: 150 West Jefferson, Suite 2500, 48226-4415.
Telephone: 313-963-6420.
Fax: 313-496-7500.
Cable Address: "Stem Detroit."
Ann Arbor, Michigan Office: 101 North Main Street, 7th Floor,
48104-1400.
Telephone: 313-663-2445.
Fax: 313-747-7147.
Bloomfield Hills, Michigan Office: Suite 100, Pinehurst Office Center, 1400
North Woodward, 48303-2014.
Telephone: 313-645-5000.
Fax: 313-645-1917.
Howell, Michigan Office: 121 South Barnard Street, Suite 4, 48843-2305.
Telephone: 517-546-7600.
Telecopier: 517-546-6974.
Kalamazoo, Michigan Office: 444 West Michigan Avenue, 49007-3752.
Telephone: 616-381-7030.
Fax: 616-382-0244.
Lansing, Michigan Office: One Michigan Avenue, Suite 900, 48933-1609.
Telephone: 517-487-2070.
Fax: 517-374-6304.
Monroe, Michigan Office: The Executive Centre, 214 East Elm Avenue,
48161-2682.
Telephone: 313-243-2000.
Fax: 313-243-0901.
Washington, D.C. Office: 1225 Nineteenth Street, N.W., Suite 400. 20036.
Telephone: 202-429-5575; 785-0600.
Fax: 202-331-1118; 785-1234.
Pensacola, Florida Office: 25 West Cedar 32501.
Telephone: 904-469-1088.
Fax: 904-432-0677.
St. Petersburg Florida Office: 100 Second Avenue S., Suite 7045, 33701.
Telephone: 813-982-6000.
Fax: 813-892-6002.
New York, New York Office: Eleventh Floor, 135 East 57th Street,
10022-2087.
Telephone: 212-754-5400.
Fax: 212-754-5401.
Gdansk, Poland Office: Suite 322, Dom Technika Building, UI. Rajska 6,
80-850.
Telephone: 011-485-831-2808.
Fax: 011-485-831-4719.
Warsaw, Poland Office: UI. Marszalkowska 82, Suite 561, 00-517.
Telephone: 011-482-623-6457 and 6458.
Fax: 011-482-623-6459.

(See Next Column)

PRINCIPALS OF FIRM
Mark E. Putney (Resident Director, Grand Rapids Office)

Representative Firm Clients: Chrysler Corporation; Comerica, Incorporated;
City of Detroit, Michigan; Detroit Tigers, Inc.; First of Michigan; Ford Motor Company; Ford Motor Credit Company; Great Lakes Bancorp; Henry
Ford Hospital; INVETECH Company.

For Complete List of Firm Personnel, See General Section

For full biographical listings, see the Martindale-Hubbell Law Directory

WARNER NORCROSS & JUDD LLP (AV)

900 Old Kent Building, 111 Lyon Street, N.W., 49503-2489
Telephone: 616-752-2000
Fax: 616-752-2500
Muskegon, Michigan Office: 400 Terrace Plaza, P.O. Box 900.
Telephone: 616-727-2600.
Fax: 616-727-2699.
Holland, Michigan Office: Curtis Center, Suite 300, 170 College Avenue.
Telephone: 616-396-9800.
Fax: 616-396-3656.

OF COUNSEL

Lawson E. Becker	Harold F. Schumacher
Conrad A. Bradshaw	Charles C. Lundstrom

Thomas R. Winquist
MEMBERS OF FIRM

David A. Warner (1883-1966)	Thomas H. Thornhill
George S. Norcross (1889-1960)	(Resident at Muskegon Office)
Siegel W. Judd (1895-1982)	Jeffrey O. Birkhold
Platt W. Dockery (1906-1974)	Timothy Hillegonds
J. M. Neath, Jr. (1928-1974)	Blake W. Krueger
Leonard D. Verdier, Jr.	John G. Cameron, Jr.
(1915-1989)	John H. McKendry, Jr.
Thomas J. McNamara	(Resident at Muskegon Office)
(1936-1989)	Paul T. Sorensen
Phil R. Johnson (1908-1990)	Carl W. Dufendach
George L. Whitfield	Stephen C. Waterbury
Wallson G. Knack	Rodney D. Martin
Charles E. McCallum	Richard E. Cassard
Jerome M. Smith	Alex J. DeYonker
John D. Tully	Charles E. Burpee
R. Malcolm Cumming	John D. Dunn
William K. Holmes	William W. Hall
Roger M. Clark	Bruce C. Young
John H. Logie	Shane B. Hansen
Donald J. Veldman	F. William McKee
(Resident at Muskegon Office)	Louis C. Rabaut
I. John Snider, II	Paul R. Jackson
(Resident at Muskegon Office)	(Resident at Muskegon Office)
Jack B. Combs	Douglas A. Dozeman
Joseph F. Martin	John V. Byl
John R. Marquis	Janet Percy Knaus
(Resident at Holland Office)	Kathleen M. Hanenburg
John H. Martin	Tracy T. Larsen
(Resident at Muskegon Office)	Sue O. Conway
James H. Breay	Steven R. Heacock
Ernest M. Sharpe	Cameron S. DeLong
Vernon P. Saper	Jeffrey B. Power
Hugh H. Makens	Scott D. Hubbard
Joseph M. Sweeney	Stephen B. Grow
Gordon R. Lewis	Richard L. Bouma
Robert J. Chovanec	Daniel R. Gravelyn
Peter L. Gustafson	Robert J. Jonker
Roger H. Oetting	Devin S. Schindler
J. A. Cragwall, Jr.	Michael H. Schubert
Stephen R. Kretschman	(Resident at Muskegon Office)
W. Michael Van Haren	Valerie Pierre Simmons
Richard A. Durell	William C. Fulkerson
Michael L. Robinson	Anthony J. Kolenic, Jr.
Eugene E. Smary	James Moskal
Douglas E. Wagner	Mark K. Harder
Robert W. Sikkel (Muskegon	(Resident at Holland Office)
and Holland Offices)	

ASSOCIATES

Weldon H. Schwartz	Judith W. Hooyenga (Resident)
Kenneth W. Vermeulen	Gordon J. Toering
Mark E. Brouwer	Frank E. Berrodin
Jeffrey S. Battershall	Norbert F. Kugele
Jeffrey A. Ott	Shaun M. Murphy
Martha Walters Atwater	Kevin P. McDowell
Rodrick W. Lewis	(Resident at Holland Office)
Kevin G. Dougherty	Mark J. Wassink
Melvin G. Moseley, Jr.	Dennis J. Donohue
James J. Rabaut	Michael I. Kleaveland
James P. Enright	(Resident at Muskegon Office)
Timothy L. Horner	Elizabeth M. Topliffe
Richard D. Cornell, Jr.	Susan N. McFee
(Resident at Muskegon Office)	Julie H. Sullivan
R. Paul Guerre	Molly E. McFarlane
Loren M. Andrulis	William P. Dani
Karen J. Vanderwerff	Andrew D. Hakken
Susan Gell Meyers	Andrea J. Bernard

(See Next Column)

WARNER NORCROSS & JUDD LLP—*Continued*

ASSOCIATES (Continued)

Lori L. Gibson	Michael J. Puca
Mark T. Ostrowski	Robert Dubault
Daniel B. Ruble	(Resident at Muskegon Office)
Paul L. Winter	Tanya E. Buhk
(Resident at Muskegon Office)	(Resident at Holland Office)
Douglas W. Poland	James D. Zwiers
Michael P. Lunt	Edward J. Bardelli
Carin L. Ojala	Tashia L. Rivard
Daniel K. DeWitt	Daniel P. Ettinger
Michael K. Molitor	James L. Scott II
Melissa L. Collar	Steven W. Clark

General Counsel for: Bissell Inc.; Blodgett Memorial Medical Center; Guardsman Products, Inc.; Haworth, Inc.; Kysor Industrial Corp.; Michigan Bankers Assn.; Old Kent Financial Corp.; Steelcase Inc.; Wolverine World Wide, Inc.

For full biographical listings, see the Martindale-Hubbell Law Directory

---

KALAMAZOO,* Kalamazoo Co.

HOWARD & HOWARD ATTORNEYS, P.C. (AV)

The Kalamazoo Building, Suite 400, 107 West Michigan Avenue, 49007-3956
Telephone: 616-382-1483
Telecopier: 616-382-1568
Bloomfield Hills, Michigan Office: The Pinehurst Office Center, Suite 101, 1400 North Woodward Avenue.
Telephone: 810-645-1483.
Telecopier: 810-645-1568.
Lansing, Michigan Office: The Phoenix Building, Suite 500, 222 Washington Square North.
Telephone: 517-485-1483.
Telecopier: 517-485-1568.
Peoria, Illinois Office: The Creve Coeur Building, Suite 200, 321 Liberty Street.
Telephone: 309-672-1483.
Telecopier: 309-672-1568.
Tampa, Florida Office: First of America Plaza, Suite 2000, 201 East Kennedy Boulevard.
Telephone: 813-229-1483.
Telecopier: 813-229-1568.

Joseph B. Hemker   David E. Riggs

Representative Clients: For Representative Client list, see General Practice, Kalamazoo, MI.

For Complete List of Firm Personnel, See General Section

For full biographical listings, see the Martindale-Hubbell Law Directory

---

MILLER, CANFIELD, PADDOCK AND STONE, P.L.C. (AV)

A Professional Limited Liability Company
Founded in 1852 by Sidney Davy Miller
444 West Michigan Avenue, 49007-3752
Telephone: 616-381-7030
Fax: 616-382-0244
Detroit, Michigan Office: 150 West Jefferson, Suite 2500, 48226-4415.
Telephone: 313-963-6420.
Fax: 313-496-7500.
Cable Address: "Stem Detroit."
Ann Arbor, Michigan Office: 101 North Main Street, 7th Floor, 48104-1400.
Telephone: 313-663-2445.
Fax: 313-747-7147.
Bloomfield Hills, Michigan Office: Suite 100, Pinehurst Office Center, 1400 North Woodward, 48303-2014.
Telephone: 313-645-5000.
Fax: 313-645-1917.
Grand Rapids, Michigan Office: 1200 Campau Square Plaza, 99 Monroe, N.W., 49503-2639.
Telephone: 616-454-8656.
Fax: 616-776-6322.
Howell, Michigan Office: 121 South Barnard Street, Suite 4, 48843-2305.
Telephone: 517-546-7600.
Telecopier: 517-546-6974.
Lansing, Michigan Office: One Michigan Avenue, Suite 900, 48933-1609.
Telephone: 517-487-2070.
Fax: 517-374-6304.
Monroe, Michigan Office: The Executive Centre, 214 East Elm Avenue, 48161-2682.
Telephone: 313-243-2000.
Fax: 313-243-0901.
Washington, D.C. Office: 1225 Nineteenth Street, N.W., Suite 400. 20036.
Telephone: 202-429-5575; 785-0600.
Fax: 202-331-1118; 785-1234.
Pensacola, Florida Office: 25 West Cedar, 32501.
Telephone: 904-469-1088.
Fax: 904-432-0677.
St. Petersburg, Florida Office: 100 Second Avenue S., Suite 7045, 33701.
Telephone: 813-982-6000.
Fax: 813-892-6002.

New York, New York Office: Eleventh Floor, 135 East 57th Street, 10022-2087.
Telephone: 212-754-5400.
Fax: 212-754-5401.
Gdansk, Poland Office: Suite 322, Dom Technika Building, UI. Rajska 6, 80-850.
Telephone: 011-485-831-2808.
Fax: 011-485-831-4719.
Warsaw, Poland Office: UI. Marszalkowska 82, Suite 561, 00-517.
Telephone: 011-482-623-6457 and 6458.
Fax: 011-482-623-6459.

PRINCIPALS OF FIRM

Eric V. Brown, Jr.	James G. Vantine, Jr.
John R. Cook	Thomas H. Van Dis
	Steven M. Stankewicz

Representative Firm Clients: Chrysler Corporation; Comerica, Incorporated; City of Detroit, Michigan; Detroit Tigers, Inc.; First of Michigan; Ford Motor Company; Ford Motor Credit Company; Great Lakes Bancorp; Henry Ford Hospital; INVETECH Company.

For Complete List of Firm Personnel, See General Section

For full biographical listings, see the Martindale-Hubbell Law Directory

---

MONROE,* Monroe Co.

MILLER, CANFIELD, PADDOCK AND STONE, P.L.C. (AV)

A Professional Limited Liability Company
Founded in 1852 by Sidney Davy Miller
The Executive Centre, 214 East Elm Avenue, 48161-2682
Telephone: 313-243-2000
Fax: 313-243-0901
Detroit, Michigan Office: 150 West Jefferson, Suite 2500, 48226-4415.
Telephone: 313-963-6420.
Fax: 313-496-7500.
Cable Address: "Stem Detroit."
Ann Arbor, Michigan Office: 101 North Main Street, 7th Floor, 48104-1400.
Telephone: 313-663-2445.
Fax: 313-747-7147.
Bloomfield Hills, Michigan Office: Suite 100, Pinehurst Office Center, 1400 North Woodward, 48303-2014.
Telephone: 313-645-5000.
Fax: 313-645-1917.
Grand Rapids, Michigan Office: 1200 Campau Square Plaza, 99 Monroe, N.W., 49503-2639.
Telephone: 616-454-8656.
Fax: 616-776-6322.
Howell, Michigan Office: 121 South Barnard Street, Suite 4, 48843-2305.
Telephone: 517-546-7600.
Telecopier: 517-546-6974.
Kalamazoo, Michigan Office: 444 West Michigan Avenue, 49007-3752.
Telephone: 616-381-7030.
Fax: 616-382-0244.
Lansing, Michigan Office: One Michigan Avenue, Suite 900, 48933-1609.
Telephone: 517-487-2070.
Fax: 517-374-6304.
Washington, D.C. Office: 1225 Nineteenth Street, N.W., Suite 400. 20036.
Telephone: 202-429-5575; 785-0600.
Fax: 202-331-1118; 785-1234.
Pensacola, Florida Office: 25 West Cedar, 32501.
Telephone: 904-469-1088.
Fax: 904-432-0677.
St. Petersburg, Florida Office: 100 Second Avenue S., Suite 7045, 33701.
Telephone: 813-982-6000.
Fax: 813-892-6002.
Gdansk, Poland Office: Suite 322, Dom Technika Building, UI. Rajska 6, 80-850.
Telephone: 011-485-831-2808.
Fax: 011-485-831-4719.
Warsaw, Poland Office: UI. Marszalkowska 82, Suite 561, 00-517.
Telephone: 011-482-623-6457 and 6458.
Fax: 011-482-623-6459.

RESIDENT PRINCIPALS

Rocque E. Lipford (P.C.)

Representative Firm Clients: Chrysler Corporation; Comerica, Incorporated; City of Detroit, Michigan; Detroit Tigers, Inc.; First of Michigan; Ford Motor Company; Ford Motor Credit Company; Great Lakes Bancorp; Henry Ford Hospital; INVETECH Company.

For full biographical listings, see the Martindale-Hubbell Law Directory

SPORTS AND ENTERTAINMENT LAW

ARIZONA

PHOENIX,* Maricopa Co.

LAW OFFICES OF RICHARD L. STROHM, P.C. (AV)

1136 East Campbell, 85014
Telephone: 602-279-6316
Mobile: 602-616-7094
Facsimile: 602-279-7102
Email: 102442.1444@compuserve.com

Richard L. Strohm
OF COUNSEL

Brad K. Keogh   Nedra J. Bates
LEGAL SUPPORT PERSONNEL

Mindy L. Raymond   Barbara A. Shore
(Legal Assistant)   (Nurse Paralegal)
Richard M. Knaeble
(Licensed Private Investigator)

Representative Clients: Sean Young; Mel Weiser; Arigam Productions; Hummingbird Productions; Dock Ellis & Ari Clare Sports Management.

For full biographical listings, see the Martindale-Hubbell Law Directory

ARKANSAS

LITTLE ROCK,* Pulaski Co.

ROSE LAW FIRM, A PROFESSIONAL ASSOCIATION (AV)

120 East Fourth Street, 72201
Telephone: 501-375-9131
Telecopy: 501-375-1309

William H. Kennedy, III   Ronald M. Clark

Counsel for: ALLTEL Corporation; Aluminum Company of America; Bridgestone/Firestone, Inc.; The Equitable Life Assurance Society of The United States; General Motors Corp.; The Prudential Insurance Company of America; Stephens Group Inc.; Tyson Foods, Inc.

For Complete List of Firm Personnel, See General Section

For full biographical listings, see the Martindale-Hubbell Law Directory

CALIFORNIA

BEVERLY HILLS, Los Angeles Co.

PAUL D. SUPNIK (AV)

Suite 1200 Wells Fargo Bank Building, 433 North Camden Drive, 90210
Telephone: 310-205-2050
Telex: 292416
Facsimile: 310-205-2011
Email: ps@supnik.com *URL:* http://www.supnik.com

For full biographical listings, see the Martindale-Hubbell Law Directory

WEISSMANN, WOLFF, BERGMAN, COLEMAN & SILVERMAN (AV)

A Law Partnership including Professional Corporations
9665 Wilshire Boulevard, Suite 900, 90212-2316
Telephone: 310-858-7888
Facsimile: 310-550-7191
Email: WWBCS@EARTHLINK.NET
MEMBERS OF FIRM

Michael Bergman   Linda A. Kalm
Stewart S. Brookman   Steven Katleman
Stan Coleman   Alan G. Kirios (Law
Michael Lee Eidel   Corporation)
Mitchell Evall   Anjani Mandavia
Alan L. Grodin   Ronald J. Silverman (P.C.)
David J. Gullen (P.C.)   Todd M. Stern
Henry W. Holmes   Eric Weissmann (P.C.)
Daniel H. Wolff
ASSOCIATES

Lucy Noble Inman   Katharine Sabich-Robison
Melanie Grant Jones   Andrew J. Schmerzler
David B. Miercort   Robert M. Szymanski
Julie B. Waldman

(See Next Column)

OF COUNSEL
Ira S. Epstein   Lawrence B. Steinberg

For full biographical listings, see the Martindale-Hubbell Law Directory

FRESNO,* Fresno Co.

DOWLING, AARON & KEELER, INCORPORATED (AV)

Suite 200, 6051 North Fresno Street, 93710
Telephone: 209-432-4500
Fax: 209-432-4590
Email: dowling-law.com

Richard M. Aaron

Richard E. Heatter   Michael P. Dowling
Reference: Wells Fargo Bank (Main).

For Complete List of Firm Personnel, See General Section

For full biographical listings, see the Martindale-Hubbell Law Directory

GLENDALE, Los Angeles Co.

O'ROURKE, ALLAN & FONG (AV)

3rd Floor, 104 North Belmont, P.O. Box 10220, 91209-3220
Telephone: 818-247-4303
Fax: 818-247-1451
MEMBERS OF FIRM

Denis M. O'Rourke   Joan H. Allan
Roderick D. Fong
ASSOCIATE
Denise Michelle O'Rourke

References: Verdugo Banking Co. (Glendale, California); Community Bank (Glendale, California).

For full biographical listings, see the Martindale-Hubbell Law Directory

LOS ANGELES,* Los Angeles Co.

LAW OFFICES OF DAVID B. BLOOM A PROFESSIONAL CORPORATION (AV)

3325 Wilshire Boulevard, Ninth Floor, 90010
Telephone: 213-938-5248; 384-4088
Telecopier: 213-385-2009

David B. Bloom

Stephen S. Monroe (A   Susan Carole Jay
  Professional Corporation)   Edward Idell
Raphael A. Rosemblat   Sandra Kamenir
James E. Adler   Steven Wayne Lazarus
Bonni S. Mantovani   Andrew Edward Briseno
Roy A. Levun   Harold C. Klaskin
Cherie S. Raidy   Shelley M. Gould
Jonathan Udell   Peter O. Israel

For full biographical listings, see the Martindale-Hubbell Law Directory

LANGBERG, COHN & DROOZ (AV)

A Partnership including a Professional Corporation
12100 Wilshire Boulevard Suite 1650, 90025
Telephone: 310-979-3200
Telecopier: 310-979-3220

Barry B. Langberg (A   Beth F. Dumas
  Professional Corporation)   Mitchell J. Langberg
Eileen M. Cohn   Mary L. Muir
Deborah Drooz   Brian A. Murphy
OF COUNSEL

Peter C. Richards (A   Gilbert Gaynor
  Professional Corporation)   Polin Cohanne
Milton Segal
LEGAL SUPPORT PERSONNEL
PARALEGALS

Patricia Ann Essig   Jeanne A. Logé

For full biographical listings, see the Martindale-Hubbell Law Directory

MENES LAW CORPORATION (AV)

1801 Century Park East, Suite 1560, 90067
Telephone: 310-286-1313
Cable Address: "Showlaw"
Telex: 317948 MLC LSA
Fax: 310-556-5695

Barry A. Menes   Paul I. Menes

Marc M. Messineo

(See Next Column)

MENES LAW CORPORATION, *Los Angeles—Continued*

OF COUNSEL

John R. Climaco
(Not admitted in CA)

Edward M. Bernstein
(Not admitted in CA)

For full biographical listings, see the Martindale-Hubbell Law Directory

SIMKE CHODOS (AV)

A Partnership of Professional Corporation
Suite 1511, 1880 Century Park East, 90067
Telephone: 310-203-3888
Fax: 310-203-3866

Stuart A. Simke

David M. Chodos

Richard A. Fond

Ellen Resinski Rosen

James Robertson Martin

OF COUNSEL

James L. Keane

Reference: City National Bank (Wilshire-La Cienega Branch).

For full biographical listings, see the Martindale-Hubbell Law Directory

SLAFF, MOSK & RUDMAN (AV)

Suite 825, 9200 Sunset Boulevard, 90069
Telephone: 310-275-5351
Telecopier: 310-273-8706

George Slaff (1906-1989)

Edward Mosk (1916-1989)

MEMBERS OF FIRM

Norman G. Rudman

Marc R. Stein

Valerie V. Flugge

Reference: City National Bank.

For full biographical listings, see the Martindale-Hubbell Law Directory

WOLF, RIFKIN & SHAPIRO, LLP (AV)

A Partnership including a Professional Corporation
11400 West Olympic Boulevard Ninth Floor, 90064-1565
Telephone: 310-478-4100
FAX: 310-479-1422

MEMBERS OF FIRM

Michael Wolf (A Professional
Corporation)
Daniel C. Shapiro
Roy G. Rifkin
Michael T. Schulman
Leslie Steven Marks

Allan M. Rosenthal
Mindy Sheps
Norman S. Wisnicki
Barry T. Mitidiere
Marc E. Rohatiner
Charles H. Baren

Michael W. Rabkin

ASSOCIATES

Andrew S. Gelb
Matthew L. Grode
Matthew Fladell
Steven A. Silver
Mark J. Rosenbaum
Kelly Marie Allegra

Richard S. Grant
Karin E. Freeman
Lori A. Van Oosterhout
Paul W. Windust
Daniel Ng
Laura S. Blint

OF COUNSEL

Gerald Lloyd Friedman

Jeffrey R. Liebster

Denise M. Parga

For full biographical listings, see the Martindale-Hubbell Law Directory

ZIFFREN, BRITTENHAM, BRANCA & FISCHER (AV)

Thirty Second Floor, 2121 Avenue of the Stars, 90067
Telephone: 310-552-3388
Fax: 310-553-7068; 553-1648

MEMBERS OF FIRM

Kenneth Ziffren
Harry M. Brittenham
John G. Branca
Samuel N. Fischer
Paul L. Brindze
R. Dennis Luderer
David Nochimson
Gary S. Stiffelman

Clifford W. Gilbert-Lurie
Kathleen Hallberg
Jamie Young
Mitchell C. Tenzer
Kenneth A. August
Steven H. Burkow
David Lande
Jamey Cohen

For full biographical listings, see the Martindale-Hubbell Law Directory

---

SANTA MONICA, Los Angeles Co.

SACKS ZWEIG & BURRIS, LLP (AV)

100 Wilshire Building, Suite 1300, 100 Wilshire Boulevard, 90401
Telephone: 310-451-3113
Facsimile: 310-451-0089
San Francisco, California Office: 100 Pine Street, 21st Floor.
Telephone: 415-788-6794.
Facsimile: 415-788-7009.

(See Next Column)

MEMBERS

Donald S. Burris

Lee Sacks

Michael K. Zweig

ASSOCIATES

Les Bradford Hairrell

Filomena E. Meyer

OF COUNSEL

Dennis Holahan

Barton S. Selden

For full biographical listings, see the Martindale-Hubbell Law Directory

COLORADO

*DENVER,** Denver Co.

WHITE AND STEELE, PROFESSIONAL CORPORATION (AV)

1225 17th Street, Suite 2800, 80202
Telephone: 303-296-2828
Telecopier: 303-296-3131
Email: law@wsteele.com
Cheyenne, Wyoming Office: 1912 Capital Avenue, Suite 416, 82003.
Telephone: 307-778-4160.
Telecopier: 307-778-7041.

Stephen K. Gerdes
Glendon L. Laird

John P. Craver
Peter W. Rietz

Insurance Clients: Allied Insurance Co.; CNA; Kemper Insurance Group; Underwriters at Lloyds; U.S.A.A.; Breckenridge Colorado Ski Country USA; Copper Mountain; Crested Butte; Keystone; Vail; Winter Park.

For Complete List of Firm Personnel, See General Section

For full biographical listings, see the Martindale-Hubbell Law Directory

CONNECTICUT

WESTPORT, Fairfield Co.

ALAN NEIGHER (AV)

1804 Post Road East, 06880
Telephone: 203-259-0599
Fax: 203-255-2570

OF COUNSEL

Judith M. Trutt

For full biographical listings, see the Martindale-Hubbell Law Directory

DISTRICT OF COLUMBIA

WASHINGTON, D.C. Co.

ZEVNIK HORTON GUIBORD & McGOVERN, P.C. (AV)

Ninth Floor, 1299 Pennsylvania Avenue, N.W., 20004
Telephone: 202-824-0950
FAX: 202-824-0955
Chicago, Illinois Office: Suite 3300, 77 West Wacker Drive.
Telephone: 312-977-2500.
Telefax: 312-977-2560.
Los Angeles, California Office: 333 South Grand Avenue, Twenty First Floor.
Telephone: 213-437-5200.
Telefax: 213-437-5222.
New York, N.Y. Office: 745 Fifth Avenue, Twenty-Fifth Floor.
Telephone: 212-935-2735.
Telefax: 212-935-0614.
Palo Alto, California Office: 5 Palo Alto Square, 3000 El Camino Real.
Telephone: 415-842-5900.
Facsimile: 415-855-9226.
London, England Office: 4 Kings Bench Walk, Temple, London EC4Y 7DL.
Telephone: 071-353-0478.
Facsimile: 071-583-3549.
Norfolk, Virginia Office: Main Street Tower, 300 East Main Street, 13th Floor.
Telephone: 757-624-3480.
Fax: 757-624-3479.

(See Next Column)

ZEVNIK HORTON GUIBORD & McGOVERN P.C.—*Continued*

Paul Anton Zevnik
Michel Yves Horton
Barbara B. Guibord
(Not admitted in DC)
Patrick Michael McGovern
(Not admitted in DC)

Joseph G. Homsy
(Not admitted in DC)
John W. Roberts
(Not admitted in DC)
John K. Crossman
(Not admitted in DC)

Jonathan L. Osborne

Yolanda C. Griffin
(Not admitted in DC)

Michael J. Wilson

For full biographical listings, see the Martindale-Hubbell Law Directory

GEORGIA

ATLANTA,* Fulton Co.

HAWKINS & PARNELL (AV)

4000 SunTrust Plaza, 303 Peachtree Street, N.E., 30308-3243
Telephone: 404-614-7400
Fax: 404-614-7500
Email: 73541.1626@compuserve.com

MEMBERS OF FIRM

Albert H. Parnell
Jack N. Sibley
Thomas F. Wamsley, Jr.

ASSOCIATES

Edwin L. Hall, Jr.
Roger M. Goode

Allen W. Nelson
Thomas G. Tidwell

For Complete List of Firm Personnel, See General Section

For full biographical listings, see the Martindale-Hubbell Law Directory

LONG ALDRIDGE & NORMAN, LLP (AV)

A Limited Liability Partnership including Professional Corporations
One Peachtree Center, Suite 5300, 303 Peachtree Street, 30308
Telephone: 404-527-4000
Telecopier: 404-527-4198
Washington, D.C. Office: Suite 600, 701 Pennsylvania Avenue, N.W.,
20004.
Telephone: 202-624-1200.
FAX: 202-624-1298.

MEMBERS OF FIRM

Evan Appel
Jesse J. Spikes
James J. Thomas II

For Complete List of Firm Personnel, See General Section

For full biographical listings, see the Martindale-Hubbell Law Directory

PIERCE & YOUNG (AV)

Building 1700, 2255 Cumberland Parkway Northwest, 30339-4575
Telephone: 770-435-0500
Telecopier: 770-435-0362

MEMBER OF FIRM

Richard M. Young

For full biographical listings, see the Martindale-Hubbell Law Directory

THOMAS, KENNEDY, SAMPSON & PATTERSON (AV)

55 Marietta Street, N.W., Suite 1600, 30303
Telephone: 404-688-4503
Telecopier: 404-681-2950

MEMBERS OF FIRM

John Loren Kennedy
(1942-1994)
Thomas G. Sampson

P. Andrew Patterson
Myra H. Dixon
Jeffrey E. Tompkins

ASSOCIATES

Rosalind T. Drakeford
Melynee C. Leftridge
La'Sean M. Zilton

Adam L. Smith
Thomas G. Sampson, II
Ceasar C. Mitchell, II.

R. E. Thomas, Jr. (1911-1996)

LEGAL SUPPORT PERSONNEL

Gwendolyn C.H. Dixon
Elbetha (Beth) Martin
Nancy Allen-Haskell

Yvonne Torrence
Priscilla Yolanda Kelly
Lureece D. Lewis (Paralegal)

For full biographical listings, see the Martindale-Hubbell Law Directory

JONESBORO,* Clayton Co.

DRIEBE & DRIEBE, P.C. (AV)

6 Courthouse Way, P.O. Box 975, 30237
Telephone: 770-478-8894
Fax: 770-478-9606
Atlanta, Georgia Office: 152 Nassau Street, N.W.
Telephone: 404-524-0606.

Charles J. Driebe
Charles J. Driebe, Jr.

Approved Attorneys for: First American Title Insurance Co.; Attorney's Title
Guaranty Fund.
Representative Clients: Atlanta International Records, Inc.; Clayton News-
/Daily; Atlanta Beach Sports & Entertainment Park, Inc.; FlatTown Music
Co.; Odom Meaders Management.

For full biographical listings, see the Martindale-Hubbell Law Directory

ILLINOIS

CHICAGO,* Cook Co.

MICHAEL E. FOX & ASSOCIATES (AV)

500 North Dearborn, Suite 400, 60610
Telephone: 312-527-9600
Facsimile: 312-527-9606

ASSOCIATES

Julie A. Browning
Brian K. Abrams

For full biographical listings, see the Martindale-Hubbell Law Directory

GESSLER, HUGHES & SOCOL, LTD. (AV)

Three First National Plaza, Suite 2200, 60602
Telephone: 312-580-0100
Telecopy: 312-580-1994

Mark S. Dym
George W. Gessler
John K. Hughes
William P. Jones
Peter M. Katsaros
Mark A. LaRose
Kimberley Marsh

Terence J. Moran
Mark D. Olson
Matthew J. Piers
David J. Pritchard
Kalman D. Resnick
Frederick S. Rhine
Jonathan A. Rothstein

Donna Kaner Socol

Benjamin P. Beringer
Darilyn W. Bock
Gary Chodorow
Anjali Dayal
Ruth M. Dunning
Adam D. Ingber
Michael J. Klein
Laura C. Liu

Alex W. Miller
Belkis Cervantes Muldoon
Jonathan D. Rosenblum
Marci S. Sperling
Dana H. Sukenik
J. Eric Vander Arend
Maria L. Vertuno
Mark B. Weiner

Charles H. Wintersteen

OF COUNSEL

James T. Derico, Jr.

Darius S. Francescatti, M.D.

Susan R. Gzesh

For full biographical listings, see the Martindale-Hubbell Law Directory

INDIANA

INDIANAPOLIS,* Marion Co.

FEIWELL & HANNOY, PROFESSIONAL CORPORATION (AV)

251 North Illinois Street, Suite 1700, P.O. Box 44141, 46244-0141
Telephone: 317-237-2727
Facsimile: 317-237-2722

Murray J. Feiwell

Michael J. Feiwell

For full biographical listings, see the Martindale-Hubbell Law Directory

KENTUCKY

LOUISVILLE,* Jefferson Co.

Woodward, Hobson & Fulton (AV)

2500 National City Tower, 101 South Fifth Street, 40202
Telephone: 502-581-8000
Fax: 502-581-8111
Lexington, Kentucky Office: PNC Bank Plaza, 200 West Vine Street, Suite 500.
Telephone: 606-244-7100.
Telecopier: 606-244-7111.
New Albany, Indiana Office: 611 East Spring Street, P.O. Box 288.
Telephone: 812-941-1800.
Telecopier: 812-941-1855.

MEMBER OF FIRM
Robert L. Hallenberg
ASSOCIATE
William A. Green, III (Resident, Lexington, Kentucky Office)

Representative Clients: American Home Insurance Co.; Brown-Forman Corp.; CARITAS Health Services, Inc.; CSX Transportation, Inc.; Fischer Packing Company; Ford Motor Co.; Nationwide Insurance Co., Inc.; Ralston Purina Co.; Toyota Motor Corp.; Wal-Mart Stores, Inc.

For Complete List of Firm Personnel, See General Section

For full biographical listings, see the Martindale-Hubbell Law Directory

LOUISIANA

NEW ORLEANS,* Orleans Parish

Michael L. Eckstein Attorney at Law A Professional Corporation (AV)

1515 Poydras Street, Suite 2195, 70112
Telephone: 504-527-0701
Telecopier: 504-566-0040
VMX: 504-889-8876

Michael L. Eckstein

Representative Clients: Sam Mills; Renaldo Turnbull; Wesley Walls; William Roaf; Pat Swilling.

For full biographical listings, see the Martindale-Hubbell Law Directory

SHREVEPORT,* Caddo Parish

Wilkinson, Carmody & Gilliam (AV)

1700 Beck Building, 400 Travis Street, P.O. Box 1707, 71166
Telephone: 318-221-4196
Telecopier: 318-221-3705

MEMBERS OF FIRM

John D. Wilkinson (1867-1929)	Bobby S. Gilliam
William Scott Wilkinson	Mark E. Gilliam
(1895-1985)	Penny D. Sellers
Arthur R. Carmody, Jr.	Patrick F. Robinson
Michael J. Ryan	

Representative Clients: Farmers Insurance Group; Home Federal Savings & Loan Association of Shreveport; The Kansas City Southern Railway Co.; KTAL-TV; Lincoln National Life Insurance Co.; Mobil Oil Co.; Schumpert Medical Center; Sears, Roebuck & Co.; Southern Pacific Transportation Co.; Southwestern Electric Power Co.

For full biographical listings, see the Martindale-Hubbell Law Directory

MASSACHUSETTS

BOSTON,* Suffolk Co.

Bloom & Witkin (AV)

70 Franklin Street, 02110
Telephone: 617-443-4300
Fax: 617-443-4315

MEMBERS OF FIRM
Arnold Bloom   Mark J. Witkin

For full biographical listings, see the Martindale-Hubbell Law Directory

Palmer & Dodge LLP (AV)

One Beacon Street, 02108
Telephone: 617-573-0100
Facsimile: 617-227-4420

MEMBERS OF FIRM
Mark A. Fischer   John Taylor Williams

For Complete List of Firm Personnel, See General Section

For full biographical listings, see the Martindale-Hubbell Law Directory

MICHIGAN

BIRMINGHAM, Oakland Co.

Carson Fischer, P.L.C. (AV)

Third Floor, 300 East Maple Road, 48009-6317
Telephone: 810-644-4840
Facsimile: 810-644-1832

Robert M. Carson

For full biographical listings, see the Martindale-Hubbell Law Directory

MacDonald and Goren, P.C. (AV)

Suite 200, 260 East Brown Street, 48009
Telephone: 810-645-5940
Fax: 810-645-2490

Harold C. MacDonald	Kalman G. Goren
	Cindy Rhodes Victor

Amy L. Glenn	Lawrence C. Atorthy
David D. Marsh	Miriam Blanks-Smart
Glenn G. Ross	John T. Klees
	Rose Marie Karadsheh

OF COUNSEL
Robert L. Biederman

Representative Clients: Beaudin, Gallanis; Beaudin, Incorporated; Orlandi Gear Co., Inc.; Bing Steel, Inc.; Superb Manufacturing, Inc.; Spring Engineering, Inc.; Adrian Steel Co.; Southfield Radiology Associates, P.C.; HDS Services, Inc.; TGI Friday's Inc.; Quality Gold of Cincinnati, Inc.

For full biographical listings, see the Martindale-Hubbell Law Directory

SOUTHFIELD, Oakland Co.

Sommers, Schwartz, Silver & Schwartz, P.C. (AV)

2000 Town Center, Suite 900, 48075
Telephone: 810-355-0300
Telecopier: 810-746-4001
Plymouth, Michigan Office: 747 South Main Street.
Telephone: 313-455-4250.

Patrick B. McCauley	Kenneth T. Watkins
Justin C. Ravitz	Lenora R. Roland

General Counsel for: City of Taylor; Foodland Distributors; C.A. Muer Corporation; Vlasic & Company; Nederlander Corporation; Midwest Health Centers, P.C.
Representative Clients: Crum & Forster Insurance Company; City of Pontiac; Michigan National Bank.

For Complete List of Firm Personnel, See General Section

For full biographical listings, see the Martindale-Hubbell Law Directory

TAX LAW

ALABAMA

*BIRMINGHAM,** Jefferson Co.

BERKOWITZ, LEFKOVITS, ISOM & KUSHNER, A PROFESSIONAL CORPORATION (AV)

1600 SouthTrust Tower, 420 North Twentieth Street, 35203
Telephone: 205-328-0480
Telecopier: 205-322-8007

Arnold K. Lefkovits	Anne W. Mitchell
Harold B. Kushner	D. J. Simonetti
Henry I. Frohsin	W. Clark Goodwin
A. Lee Martin, Jr.	Thomas O. Kolb
Barry S. Marks	Thomas J. Mahoney, Jr.

Andrew J. Potts

Judy P. Hamer

Representative Clients: AlaTenn Resources, Inc.; AMI Brookwood Medical Center; B.A.S.S., Inc.; Eternal Word Television Network; Hanna Steel Co., Inc.; Liberty Trouser Co., Inc.; Parisian, Inc.; Southeast Health Plan, Inc.; Southern Pipe & Supply Co., Inc.

For Complete List of Firm Personnel, See General Section

For full biographical listings, see the Martindale-Hubbell Law Directory

BRADLEY, ARANT, ROSE & WHITE (AV)

2001 Park Place, Suite 1400, P.O. Box 830709, 35283-0709
Telephone: 205-521-8000
Facsimile: 205-252-0264
Facsimile (SouthTrust Tower Office): 205-251-9915
URL: http://www.BARW.COM
Huntsville, Alabama Office: 200 Clinton Avenue West, Suite 900, 35801.
Telephone: 205-517-5100.
Facsimile: 205-533-5069.

MEMBERS OF FIRM

Edward M. Selfe	Charles R. Smith, Jr.
Thomas Neely Carruthers, Jr.	(Resident, Huntsville Office)
William L. Hinds, Jr.	Scott E. Ludwig
Robert C. Walthall	(Resident, Huntsville Office)

Stuart Joseph Frentz

COUNSEL

Wm. Bew White, Jr. (Retired)   K. Wood Herren

ASSOCIATE

Dorothy C. Daigle

For Complete List of Firm Personnel, See General Section

For full biographical listings, see the Martindale-Hubbell Law Directory

BURR & FORMAN (AV)

3100 SouthTrust Tower, 420 North 20th Street, 35203
Telephone: 205-251-3000
Telecopier: 205-458-5100
Huntsville, Alabama Office: Suite 204, Regency Center, 400 Meridian Street.
Telephone: 205-551-0010.
Atlanta, Georgia Office: Suite 1800, One Georgia Center, 600 West Peachtree Street, 30308.
Telephone: 404-817-3536.
Facsimile: 404-817-3244.

MEMBERS OF FIRM

Paul O. Woodall	Jack P. Stephenson, Jr.
Louis H. Anders, Jr.	Bruce A. Rawls
A. Brand Walton	Henry Graham Beene

Marvin Glenn Perry, Jr.

ASSOCIATE

Warren C. Matthews

For Complete List of Firm Personnel, See General Section

For full biographical listings, see the Martindale-Hubbell Law Directory

DOMINICK, FLETCHER, YEILDING, WOOD & LLOYD, P.A. (AV)

2121 Highland Avenue, 35205
Telephone: 205-939-0033

C. Fred Daniels   Brian T. Williams

Jim G. McLaughlin

Counsel for: Citizens Federal Savings Bank; St. Vincent's Hospital; Birmingham-Southern College; Castle Mortgage Corporation; Methodist Homes for the Aging; Amerex.

(See Next Column)

For Complete List of Firm Personnel, See General Section

For full biographical listings, see the Martindale-Hubbell Law Directory

GORDON, SILBERMAN, WIGGINS & CHILDS, A PROFESSIONAL CORPORATION (AV)

1400 SouthTrust Tower, 420 North 20th Street, 35203
Telephone: 205-328-0640
Telecopier: 205-254-1500

Wilbur G. Silberman	C. Michael Quinn
Bruce L. Gordon	Dennis George Pantazis
Robert L. Wiggins, Jr.	Terrill W. Sanders
Robert F. Childs, Jr.	James Mendelsohn
Augustus J. Beck, Jr.	Richard J. Ebbinghouse
Harvey L. Wachsman	Ann K. Wiggins
Ray D. Gibbons	Samuel Fisher

Ann C. Robertson

Paul H. Webb	Byron R. Perkins
Mark P. Williams	Jon C. Goldfarb
Timothy C. Gann	Gregory O. Wiggins
Timothy D. Davis	Lee Winston
Joseph H. Calvin, III	Jon E. Lewis
Linda J. Peacock	Deborah A. Mattison
Elizabeth Evans Courtney	Rocco Calamusa, Jr.

OF COUNSEL

Robert H. Loeb

For Complete List of Firm Personnel, See General Section

For full biographical listings, see the Martindale-Hubbell Law Directory

GORHAM & WALDREP, P.C. (AV)

2101 6th Avenue North, Suite 700, 35203
Telephone: 205-254-3216; 251-9166
Telecopier: 205-324-3802
Email: info@gorham-waldrep.com
Montgomery, Alabama Office: 250 Commerce Street, P.O. Box 4837, 36103-4837.
Telephone: 334-262-0777.
Telecopier: 334-262-0742.

Charles W. Gorham	LaVeeda Morgan Battle
Charlie D. Waldrep	John T. Natter
Thomas L. Stewart	Frank G. Alfano
Michael G. Kendrick	Kay L. McNabb Cason
William J. Bryant	Victor Kelley

K. Mark Parnell

Victoria Franklin-Sisson	Leslie Miller Klasing
Karen Brown Evans	Brian Dennis Turner, Jr.
Mary H. Thompson	Anne D. Lamkin

Representative Clients: Jefferson County Personnel Board; Birmingham-Jefferson Civic Center Authority; The Water Works and Sewer Board of the City of Birmingham; City of Homewood; American Federation of Government Employees Local #1945; City of Pelham; Town of Kimberly; Alabama Tire Dealers Assn.; Southern States Body Shop Assn.

For full biographical listings, see the Martindale-Hubbell Law Directory

HASKELL SLAUGHTER & YOUNG, L.L.C. (AV)

1200 AmSouth/Harbert Plaza, 1901 Sixth Avenue North, 35203
Telephone: 205-251-1000
Facsimile: 205-324-1133
Montgomery, Alabama Office: 305 South Lawrence Street, P.O. Box 4660. 36103-4660.
Telephone: 334-265-8573.
Facsimile: 334-264-7945.

William M. Slaughter   Robert D. Shattuck, Jr.

Ross N. Cohen

Representative Clients: HEALTHSOUTH Corporation; USX Corporation; MedPartners, Inc.

For Complete List of Firm Personnel, See General Section

For full biographical listings, see the Martindale-Hubbell Law Directory

JOHNSTON, BARTON, PROCTOR & POWELL (AV)

2900 AmSouth/Harbert Plaza, 1901 Sixth Avenue North, 35203-2618
Telephone: 205-458-9400
Telecopier: 205-458-9500

MEMBERS OF FIRM

Harvey Deramus (1904-1970)	Don B. Long, Jr.
Alfred M. Naff (1923-1993)	Charles L. Robinson
Gilbert E. Johnston (1916-1994)	J. William Rose, Jr.
G. Burns Proctor, Jr.	Gilbert E. Johnston, Jr.
Sydney L. Lavender	Ralph H. Smith II
Charles A. Powell, III	James C. Barton, Jr.
Jerome K. Lanning	Thomas E. Walker

(See Next Column)

JOHNSTON, BARTON, PROCTOR & POWELL, *Birmingham—Continued*

Anne P. Wheeler	Oscar M. Price III
Barry V. Frederick	W. Hill Sewell
Hollinger F. Barnard	Robert S. Vance, Jr.
William D. Jones III	Richard J. Brockman
David W. Proctor	Anthony A. Joseph

William G. Somerville, III

COUNSEL

Josh Mullins, Jr.	Paul E. Toppins

R. Marcus Givhan

OF COUNSEL

James C. Barton	Alfred Swedlaw

Alan W. Heldman

ASSOCIATES

William K. Hancock	Helen Kathryn Downs
James P. Pewitt	Jennifer Fox Swain
Scott Wells Ford	Spencer A. Kinderman
David M. Hunt	Scott R. McLaughlin
Lee M. Pope	Bradley C. Mayhew
John W. Sheffield	W. Jonathan Daniel
Haskins W. Jones	J. Vincent Edge
Russell L. Irby, III	Allison Powell

General Counsel for: Anderson News Co.; The Baptist Medical Centers; The Birmingham News Co. (Publishers of the Birmingham News and owner of the Huntsville Times Co.); Southern Medical Association.
Counsel for: BellSouth Services, Inc.; General Motors Corp.; Jemison Inv. Co., Inc.; The Marmon Group; SouthTrust Bank of Alabama, N.A.

For full biographical listings, see the Martindale-Hubbell Law Directory

SPAIN & GILLON, L.L.C. (AV)

The Zinszer Building, 2117 2nd Avenue North, 35203
Telephone: 205-328-4100
Telecopier: 205-324-8866

MEMBERS OF FIRM

John P. McKleroy, Jr.	J. Birch Bowdre
Samuel H. Frazier	Glenn E. Estess, Jr.

Paul S. Leonard

Representative Clients: Golden Enterprises, Inc.; City of Birmingham; First Federal of Alabama, Federal Savings Bank; Housing Authority of the Birmingham District; Piggly Wiggly Alabama Distributing Co., Inc.; Golden Flake Snack Foods, Inc.; First General Lending Corporation; Alabama Health Plan; All-South Subcontractors, Inc.; Smith Barney, Harris Upham and Co., Inc.

For Complete List of Firm Personnel, See General Section

For full biographical listings, see the Martindale-Hubbell Law Directory

---

DECATUR,* Morgan Co.

EYSTER, KEY, TUBB, WEAVER & ROTH (AV)

Eyster Building, 402 East Moulton Street, S.E., P.O. Box 1607, 35602
Telephone: 205-353-6761
Fax: 205-353-6767

John C. Eyster (1863-1926)	Wm. B. Eyster (1921-1995)
Charles H. Eyster, Sr.	
(1888-1964)	

MEMBERS OF FIRM

John S. Key	Nicholas B. Roth
J. Glynn Tubb	J. Witty Allen
Laurence C. Weaver	William L. Middleton, III

James G. Adams, Jr.

ASSOCIATES

Jenny L. Mcleroy	John R. Baggette, Jr.

General Counsel for: Alabama Farmers Cooperative.
Regional Counsel for: AmSouth Bank.
Local Counsel for: Allstate Insurance Co.; Liberty Mutual Insurance Co.; Maryland Casualty Co.; Saginaw Steering Gear Division, General Motors Corp.; State Farm Mutual Automobile Insurance Co.; The Travelers.

For full biographical listings, see the Martindale-Hubbell Law Directory

---

HARRIS, CADDELL & SHANKS, P.C. (AV)

214 Johnston Street, S.E., P.O. Box 2688, 35602-2688
Telephone: 205-340-8000
Telecopier: 205-340-8040

Julian Harris (1904-1994)	Thomas A. Caddell
Norman W. Harris (P.C.)	William E. Shinn, Jr.
(Retired)	Gary A. Phillips
Philip T. Shanks (Retired)	Dow M. Perry, Jr.
Charles L. Murphree (Retired)	Barnes F. Lovelace, Jr.
John A. Caddell (P.A.)	Arthur W. Orr
Robert H. Harris	J. Noel King
Jon H. Moores	Jeffrey S. Brown

Attorneys for: First American Bank, Decatur, Alabama; SouthTrust Bank of Morgan County; Morgan County Commission; The Industrial Development Board of the City of Decatur, Alabama; Amoco Chemical Co.; South Central

(See Next Column)

Bell Telephone Co.; Trico Steel Co.; General Electric Co.; ConAgra, Inc.; Wolverine Tube, Inc.

For full biographical listings, see the Martindale-Hubbell Law Directory

---

DOTHAN,* Houston Co.

JOHNSTON, HINESLEY, FLOWERS & CLENNEY, P.C., A PROFESSIONAL CORPORATION (AV)

291 North Oates Street, 36303
Telephone: 334-793-1115
Fax: 334-793-6603

G. David Johnston	William T. Flowers
William W. Hinesley	R. Eugene Clenney, Jr.

J. Ken Thompson

For full biographical listings, see the Martindale-Hubbell Law Directory

---

FLORENCE,* Lauderdale Co.

KELLER AND PAINE (AV)

An Association of Professional Corporations
212 South Cedar Street, P.O. Box 933, 35631
Telephone: 205-764-5822
Fax: 205-767-6360

MEMBERS OF FIRM

Jesse A. Keller	Michael T. Paine
Peter L. Paine	(Not admitted in AL)

LEGAL SUPPORT PERSONNEL

Carmel Sizemore	Gayle Blake

Counsel for: The American Road Insurance Co.; Lambert Transfer Co.

For full biographical listings, see the Martindale-Hubbell Law Directory

---

HUNTSVILLE,* Madison Co.

BERRY, ABLES, TATUM, BAXTER, PARKER & HALL, P.C. (AV)

Legal Building, 315 Franklin Street, S.E., P.O. Box 165, 35804-0165
Telephone: 205-533-3740
Facsimile: 205-533-3751
Email: BAXTERJ@ATTMAIL.COM

William H. Blanton (1889-1973)	James T. Tatum, Jr.
Joe M. Berry	James T. Baxter, III
L. Bruce Ables	Thomas E. Parker, Jr.

Bill G. Hall

James K. Brabston	Mark Rogers Hunter

Representative Clients: AmSouth Bank; First Alabama Bank; General Shale Products Co.; The Hertz Corp.; Litton Industries, Inc.; Farmers Tractor Co.; Colonial Bank; Farm Credit Bank of Texas; SouthBank; Regions Mortgage.
Reference: First Alabama Bank.

For full biographical listings, see the Martindale-Hubbell Law Directory

---

BRADLEY, ARANT, ROSE & WHITE (AV)

200 Clinton Avenue West, Suite 900, 35801
Telephone: 205-517-5100
Facsimile: 205-533-5069
URL: http://www.BARW.COM
Birmingham, Alabama Office: 2001 Park Place, Suite 1400, P.O. Box 830709.
Telephone: 205-521-8000.
Facsimile: 205-251-8611, 251-8665, 252-0264. Facsimile (SouthTrust Tower Office): 205-251-9915.

RESIDENT PARTNERS

Charles R. Smith, Jr.	Scott E. Ludwig

For Complete List of Firm Personnel, See General Section

For full biographical listings, see the Martindale-Hubbell Law Directory

---

MOBILE,* Mobile Co.

ARMBRECHT, JACKSON, DeMOUY, CROWE, HOLMES & REEVES, L.L.C. (AV)

1300 AmSouth Center, P.O. Box 290, 36601
Telephone: 334-405-1300
Facsimile: 334-432-6843; 433-3821

MEMBERS OF FIRM

Marshall J. DeMouy	William B. Harvey

James Donald Hughes

Representative Clients: Cooper/T. Smith Co., Inc.; WKRG-TV, Inc.; United States Sports Academy; Smith's Bakery, Inc.; Taca International Airlines; Scott Paper Co.; Automation Technology, Inc.; Mobile Gas Service Corporation.

For Complete List of Firm Personnel, See General Section

For full biographical listings, see the Martindale-Hubbell Law Directory

Mobile—Continued

JOHNSTONE, ADAMS, BAILEY, GORDON AND HARRIS, L.L.C. (AV)

Royal St. Francis Building, 104 St. Francis Street, P.O. Box 1988, 36633
Telephone: 334-432-7682
Facsimile: 334-432-2800
Telex: 782040

MEMBERS OF FIRM

Charles B. Bailey, Jr.	R. Gregory Watts
E. Watson Smith	Robert S. Frost

Representative Clients: Commonwealth Land Title Insurance Co.; Delaney Development, Inc.; Exxon Corporation; First Alabama Bank; Infirmary Health System/Mobile Infirmary Medical Center/Rotary Rehabilitation Hospital (Multi-Hospital System); International Marine and Industrial Applicators; Lerio Corporation; Mobile Paint Manufacturing Co., Inc.

For Complete List of Firm Personnel, See General Section

For full biographical listings, see the Martindale-Hubbell Law Directory

---

LYONS, PIPES & COOK, P.C. (AV)

2 North Royal Street, P.O. Box 2727, 36652-2727
Telephone: 334-432-4481
Cable Address: "Lysea"
Telecopier: 334-433-1820

Wesley Pipes	R. Mark Kirkpatrick
Thomas F. Garth	Michael C. Niemeyer

Counsel: James Graham Brown Foundation, Inc.; Florence Foundation, Inc.; McKenzie Tank Lines, Inc.; SCNO Barge Lines, Inc.; Scott Paper Co.; Shell Oil Corp.

For Complete List of Firm Personnel, See General Section

For full biographical listings, see the Martindale-Hubbell Law Directory

---

VICKERS, RIIS, MURRAY AND CURRAN, L.L.C. (AV)

8th Floor, First Alabama Bank Building, 106 Saint Francis Street, P.O. Box 2568, 36652
Telephone: 334-432-9772
Fax: 334-432-9781

MEMBERS OF FIRM

J. Manson Murray	Zebulon M. P. Inge, Jr.
Ronald P. Davis	

For Complete List of Firm Personnel, See General Section

For full biographical listings, see the Martindale-Hubbell Law Directory

---

MONTGOMERY, * Montgomery Co.

KAUFMAN & ROTHFEDER, P.C. (AV)

2740 Zelda Road Post Office Drawer 4540, 36103-4540
Telephone: 334-244-1111
Fax: 334-244-1969

Alan E. Rothfeder	John Ward Weiss
Jo Karen Parr	Robert M. Ritchey
Richardson B. McKenzie, III	William B. Sellers
Robert E. L. Gilpin	J. Scott Pierce

Counsel For: Alfa Builders, Inc.; McInnis Corporation; The Russell Hospital Corporation; Med-South, Inc.; Russell Corporation; Sanders Lead Co., Inc.; Wiley Sanders Truck Lines, Inc.; Linden Lumber Company, Inc.; Aronov Realty Company, Inc.; K.W. Plastics Recycling.

For full biographical listings, see the Martindale-Hubbell Law Directory

---

VOLZ, PRESTWOOD & HANAN, P.C. (AV)

350 Adams Avenue, P.O. Box 1910, 36102-1910
Telephone: 334-264-6401
Fax: 334-834-4954

Charles H. Volz, Jr.	Charles H. Volz, III
Alvin T. Prestwood	Clinton Chadwell Carter
Ellis D. Hanan	Daniel Lewis Feinstein

LEGAL SUPPORT PERSONNEL
Mark A.W. Turpen

For full biographical listings, see the Martindale-Hubbell Law Directory

---

TUSCALOOSA, * Tuscaloosa Co.

PHELPS, JENKINS, GIBSON & FOWLER (AV)

1201 Greensboro Avenue, P.O. Box 020848, 35402-0848
Telephone: 205-345-5100
Fax: 205-758-4394
Fax: 205-391-6658

(See Next Column)

MEMBERS OF FIRM

Sam M. Phelps	Randolph M. Fowler
James J. Jenkins	Michael S. Burroughs
Johnson Russell Gibson, III	C. Barton Adcox
Farley A. Poellnitz	

ASSOCIATES

Karen C. Welborn	Stephen E. Snow
Sandra C. Guin	Thomas W. Davis
Lisa Paul Hodges	M. Kristi Wallace

LEGAL SUPPORT PERSONNEL

Alicia Suzanne Wilson	Ashley D. Sparks
Cathey Raye Hartline	Kimberly Susan Wright

Attorneys for: Aetna Insurance Co.; Allstate Insurance Co.; Carolina Casualty Insurance Co.; Continental Insurance Cos.; Fireman's Fund-American Insurance Cos.; Great American Insurance Co.; Hanover Insurance Co.

For full biographical listings, see the Martindale-Hubbell Law Directory

---

ARIZONA

NOGALES, * Santa Cruz Co.

O'CONNOR, CAVANAGH, ANDERSON, KILLINGSWORTH & BESHEARS, A PROFESSIONAL ASSOCIATION (AV)

1891 North Mastick Way, 85621
Telephone: 520-761-4215
FAX: 520-761-3505
Email: firminfo@arizlaw.com
Phoenix, Arizona Office: One East Camelback Road, Suite 1100, 85012.
Telephone: 602-263-2400.
FAX: 602-263-2900.
Tucson, Arizona Office: O'Connor Cavanagh Molloy Jones, 33 N. Stone, Suite 2100, 85701, P.O. Box 2268, 85702.
Telephone: 520-622-3531.
FAX: 520-624-2816.
Sun City, Arizona Office: 13250 North Del Webb Boulevard, Suite B, 85351.
Telephone: 602-263-2808.
FAX: 602-933-3100.

Hector G. Arana

Representative Clients: Omega Produce Co.; Frank's Distributing, Inc.; City of Nogales; Collectron of Ariz., Inc.; James K. Wilson Produce Co.; Agricola Bon, S. de R.L. de C.V.; Angel Demerutis E.; Rene Carrillo C.; Arturo Lomeli; Theojary Crisantes E.

For Complete List of Firm Personnel, See General Section

For full biographical listings, see the Martindale-Hubbell Law Directory

---

PHOENIX, * Maricopa Co.

BURCH & CRACCHIOLO, P.A. (AV)

702 East Osborn Road, Suite 200, 85014
Telephone: 602-274-7611
Fax: 602-234-0341
Mailing Address: P.O. Box 16882, Phoenix, AZ, 85011

Stephen E. Silver	Guadalupe Iniguez
	Brad S. Ostroff

Martha C. Patrick

Representative Clients: Bashas' Inc.; Farmers Insurance Group; U-Haul International, Inc.

For Complete List of Firm Personnel, See General Section

For full biographical listings, see the Martindale-Hubbell Law Directory

---

EHMANN & HILLER, P.C. (AV)

2525 East Camelback Road, Suite 720, 85016
Telephone: 602-956-5050
Telecopier: 602-468-9775
Email: NHiller0@counsel.com

Anthony V. Ehmann	John G. Pattullo
Neil H. Hiller	John F. Daniels, III

References: Valley National Bank of Arizona (Trust Department); First Interstate Bank of Arizona, N.A. (Trust Department); M & I Thunderbird Bank.

For full biographical listings, see the Martindale-Hubbell Law Directory

Phoenix—Continued

FENNEMORE CRAIG, A PROFESSIONAL CORPORATION (AV)

Two North Central, Suite 2200, 85004
Telephone: 602-257-8700
Fax: 602-257-8527
Scottsdale, Arizona Office: 6263 North Scottsdale Road, Suite 290, 85250.
Telephone: 602-257-5400.
Fax: 602-257-5409.
Tucson, Arizona Office: One South Church Avenue, Suite 1030, 85701.
Telephone: 520-791-6800.
Fax: 520-791-6820.

James Powers	Paul J. Mooney
Arthur D. Ehrenreich	David N. Heap
Neal Kurn	Ray K. Harris
David T. Cox	Gregg Hanks
Cynthia L. Shupe	Jim L. Wright

J. Barry Shelley

Marc L. Spitzer	Kendis K. Muscheid

Stephen A. Good

For Complete List of Firm Personnel, See General Section

For full biographical listings, see the Martindale-Hubbell Law Directory

GOLDMAN & KAPLAN, LTD. (AV)

2930 North 7th Street, 85014
Telephone: 602-264-9323
FAX: 602-274-7006
Email: mkaplan0@counsel.com

Alan Goldman	Mark E. Meltzer
Morris A. Kaplan	Paul D. Friedman

References: Republic National Bank; Merrill Lynch.

For full biographical listings, see the Martindale-Hubbell Law Directory

JABURG & WILK, P.C. (AV)

Great American Bank Building, 3200 North Central Avenue, Suite 2000, 85012
Telephone: 602-248-1000
Fax: 602-248-0522

Gary J. Jaburg	Loren Molever
Alan H. Susman	Jeffrey H. Wolf
Lawrence E. Wilk	Michael J. McGivern
Roger L. Cohen	Mitchell Reichman
Randy Nussbaum	Beth S. Cohn

Marvin W. Manross	Timothy C. Dietz
Kathi Mann Sandweiss	Isabel M. Humphrey

Representative Clients: Wells Fargo Bank; Bank of America; Northern Trust Bank of America; Wells Fargo Realty Advisors Funding, Inc.; State of Arizona; FDIC; HFC; FNMA; FHLMC.

For full biographical listings, see the Martindale-Hubbell Law Directory

JENNINGS, STROUSS AND SALMON, P.L.C. (AV)

A Professional Limited Liability Company
One Renaissance Square, Two North Central, 85004-2393
Telephone: 602-262-5911
Fax: 602-253-3255

John R. Christian	Robert J. Werner
Richard L. Lassen	Robert P. Solliday

For Complete List of Firm Personnel, See General Section

For full biographical listings, see the Martindale-Hubbell Law Directory

LANE & EHRLICH, LTD. (AV)

Fairmount Place, Suite 400, 4001 North Third Street, 85012
Telephone: 602-264-4442
Telecopier: 602-264-5006

Robert L. Lane	Gerald F. Ehrlich

References: Bank One Arizona; Harris Trust & Savings Bank; The Northern Trust Bank Arizona.

For full biographical listings, see the Martindale-Hubbell Law Directory

LEWIS AND ROCA, LLP (AV)

A Limited Liability Partnership including a Professional Corporation
40 North Central Avenue, 85004-4429
Telephone: 602-262-5311
Fax: 602-262-5747
Email: mlp@lrlaw.com
Tucson, Arizona Office: One South Church Avenue, Suite 700, 86701-1620.
Telephone: 520-622-2090.
Fax: 520-622-3088. *E-Mail:* mlp@lrlaw.com.

(See Next Column)

MEMBERS OF FIRM

David E. Manch	Patrick Derdenger
Hope Leibsohn	J. Tyler Haahr

ASSOCIATE

Anthony J. Blackwell

Representative Clients: Blood Systems, Inc.; General Motors Corp.; MCI Telecommunications Corp.; Mervyn's Stores; Samaritan Health System; Target Stores; Unisys Corp.

For Complete List of Firm Personnel, See General Section

For full biographical listings, see the Martindale-Hubbell Law Directory

MATHEW & MATHEW (AV)

2425 East Camelback Road, Suite 880, 85016
Telephone: 602-381-8556
Fax: 602-957-2137
Email: SATMATHEW@aol.com; IVANM5A@ad.com (IVANM5A@aol.com)

Ivan K. Mathew	Susan Turner Mathew

Reference: Biltmore Investors Bank.

For full biographical listings, see the Martindale-Hubbell Law Directory

McCABE, O'DONNELL & WRIGHT, A PROFESSIONAL ASSOCIATION (AV)

3101 North Central Avenue Suite 700, 85012
Telephone: 602-264-0800
Facsimile: 602-274-0146
Email: mowphx@aol.com
Email: mowphx@mowphx.com

Joseph I. McCabe	Kathleen M. O'Donnell

A List of Representative Clients will be Furnished upon Request.

For full biographical listings, see the Martindale-Hubbell Law Directory

NEWMARK IRVINE, P.A. (AV)

Suite 590 1419 North Third Street, 85004
Telephone: 602-230-8080
Fax: 602-230-0105

Stephen C. Newmark	Thomas K. Irvine

Jerry A. Fries

For full biographical listings, see the Martindale-Hubbell Law Directory

O'CONNOR, CAVANAGH, ANDERSON, KILLINGSWORTH & BESHEARS, A PROFESSIONAL ASSOCIATION (AV)

One East Camelback Road, Suite 1100, 85012-1656
Telephone: 602-263-2400
FAX: 602-263-2900
Email: firminfo@arizlaw.com
Sun City, Arizona Office: 13250 North Del Webb Boulevard, Suite B, 85351.
Telephone: 602-263-2808.
FAX: 602-933-3100.
Tucson, Arizona Office: O'Connor Cavanagh Molloy Jones, 33 N. Stone, Suite 2100, 85701, P.O. Box 2268, 85702.
Telephone: 520-622-3531.
FAX: 520-624-2816.
Nogales, Arizona Office: 1891 North Mastick Way, 85621.
Telephone: 520-761-4215.
FAX: 520-761-3505.

Richard C. Smith	Peter C. Guild
Charles F. Myers	Max K. Boyer

Leigh A. Kaylor

Thomas W. Bade

Representative Clients: Sun Health Corporation; Rural/Metro Corporation; Peabody Coal Co.; The P.G.A.; Del Webb Corporation; Hyatt Regency; Three-Five Systems, Inc.; Central Arizona Water Conservation District; Northern Trust Bank of Arizona.

For Complete List of Firm Personnel, See General Section

For full biographical listings, see the Martindale-Hubbell Law Directory

OLSEN-SMITH, LTD. (AV)

A Partnership of Professional Corporations and a Professional Limited Liability Company
3300 Virginia Financial Plaza, 301 East Virginia Avenue, 85004-1267
Telephone: 602-254-1040
Telecopier: 602-254-1041

(See Next Column)

OLSEN-SMITH LTD.—*Continued*

Alfred J. Olsen   Susan K. Smith
James J. Rossie, Jr.

References: The Northern Trust Bank of Arizona; Harris Trust Bank of Arizona; Arizona Community Foundation.

For full biographical listings, see the Martindale-Hubbell Law Directory

---

PLATTNER, SCHNEIDMAN & SCHNEIDER, P.C. (AV)

1707 East Highland, Suite 190, 85016
Telephone: 602-274-7955
Fax: 602-285-5589

Leslie A. Plattner   Gregory W. MacNabb
Jeff Schneidman   Sheila M. Rinder
John J. Schneider   Katherine M. Simmons

Laura M. Stover   Darrin C. Jeffries
I. Marshall Gan
OF COUNSEL
Robert M. Daudet

For full biographical listings, see the Martindale-Hubbell Law Directory

---

RIDENOUR, SWENSON, CLEERE & EVANS, P.C. (AV)

40 North Central Avenue, Suite 1400, 85004
Telephone: 602-254-2143
Fax: 602-254-8670

William G. Ridenour   William D. Fearnow
Gerard R. Cleere   Natalie P. Garth
James R. Hienton

For full biographical listings, see the Martindale-Hubbell Law Directory

---

SHIMMEL, HILL, BISHOP & GRUENDER, P.C. (AV)

3700 North 24th Street, 85016
Telephone: 602-224-9500
Telecopier: 602-955-6176

Daniel F. Gruender   Keith F. Overholt

James L. Person

Representative Clients: Dunn Del Re Steel; Keystone Graphics, Inc.; Original Apartment Movers.

For full biographical listings, see the Martindale-Hubbell Law Directory

---

SNELL & WILMER, L.L.P. (AV)

One Arizona Center, 85004-0001
Telephone: 602-382-6000
Fax: 602-382-6070
Tucson, Arizona Office: 1500 Norwest Tower, One South Church Avenue 85701-1612.
Telephone: 520-882-1200.
Fax: 520-884-1294.
Orange County Office: 1920 Main Street, Suite 1200, P.O. Box 57062, Irvine, California, 92619-7062.
Telephone: 714-253-2700.
Fax: 714-955-2507.
Salt Lake City, Utah Office: Broadway Centre, 111 East Broadway, Suite 900, 84111-1004.
Telephone: 801-237-1900.
Fax: 801-237-1950.
MEMBERS OF FIRM
Thomas R. Hoecker   Charles A. Pulaski, Jr.
Janet E. Barton   David E. Weiss, Jr.
Richard D. Blau   Marvin S. Swift, Jr.
OF COUNSEL
Edward Jacobson
ASSOCIATES
Nancy Kay Campbell   Moon Yung Kim
Catherine Wehling

Representative Clients: American Continental Creditors Committee; Arizona Public Service Company; Arizona Sports Foundation; Aztar Corporation; City of Phoenix; Magma Copper Company; Palo Verde Nuclear Generating Station; Talley Industries; Tucson Airport Authority; Bank One, Arizona, NA.

For Complete List of Firm Personnel, See General Section

For full biographical listings, see the Martindale-Hubbell Law Directory

---

SCOTTSDALE, Maricopa Co.

ROSEPINK & ESTES (AV)

7373 North Scottsdale Road Suite D102, 85253
Telephone: 602-443-1280
Fax: 602-443-3664
Email: rosepink@syspac.com *URL:* http://www.syspac.com/~rosepink
MEMBERS OF FIRM
Robert J. Rosepink   David J. Estes
ASSOCIATES
Lynn F. Chandler   John R. Becker

References: Bank of America, Arizona; Biltmore Investors Bank; Chase Trust Company of Arizona; First Interstate Bank of Arizona, N.A.; Firstar Metropolitan Bank & Trust; M & I Marshall & Ilsley Trust Co. of Arizona; Northern Trust Bank of Arizona.

For full biographical listings, see the Martindale-Hubbell Law Directory

---

*TUCSON,** Pima Co.

DUFFIELD, MILLER, YOUNG, ADAMSON & ALFRED, P.C. (AV)

Suite 711, Transamerica Building, 177 North Church Avenue, 85701
Telephone: 520-792-1181
FAX: 520-792-2859
Green Valley, Arizona Office: 101-65 South La Canada, Green Valley Mall.
Telephone: 520-625-4404.
Fax: 520-625-4453.
La Paloma Office: La Paloma Corporate Center, 3573 East Sunrise Drive, Suite 115, Tucson, Arizona.
Telephone: 520-577-1135.
Fax: 520-577-1079.

Philip Hawley Smith   Thomas R. Althaus
Arthur H. Miller (1935-1995)   Richard Duffield
Larry R. Adamson   Eugene C. Gieseler
Samuel D. Alfred   K. Alexander Hobson
Michael C. Young
LEGAL SUPPORT PERSONNEL
Cynthia Sargent Althaus   Joan Shelton, CLA
Mary Jane Arnesen   Christine M. Smith
Katrina Hillman   Barbara L. Steimle
Elizabeth Kohl-Sturgeon   Elaine Webb

Representative Clients: San Xavier Rock & Materials; Community Water Company of Green Valley.
Insurance Company Clientele: State Farm Mutual Insurance Cos.; Automobile Club Insurance Co.; Colonial Penn Insurance Co.; Metropolitan Property & Liability Insurance Co.; National Indemnity Ins. Co.

For full biographical listings, see the Martindale-Hubbell Law Directory

---

GABROY, ROLLMAN & BOSSÉ, P.C. (AV)

Suite 201, 2195 East River Road, 85718
Telephone: 520-577-1300
Telefax: 520-577-0717

Steven L. Bossé   Fred A. Farsjo

For Complete List of Firm Personnel, See General Section

For full biographical listings, see the Martindale-Hubbell Law Directory

---

HAWLEY, NYSTEDT & FLETCHER, P.C. (AV)

Old Farm Executive Park, 6075 East Grant Road, P.O. Box 31657, 85751-1657
Telephone: 520-886-3166
FAX: 520-886-5280

Gerald G. Hawley   Bradley Jon Nystedt
Gary L. Fletcher

Jill D. Wiley

Reference: Northern Trust Bank of Arizona.

For full biographical listings, see the Martindale-Hubbell Law Directory.

DANIEL H. O'CONNELL, P.C. (AV)

Suite 510, 6245 East Broadway, 85711
Telephone: 520-790-2535
Telefax: 520-571-8148

Daniel H. O'Connell

Benjamin J. Burnside
OF COUNSEL
Rosanne F. Lapan

Representative Clients: Empire West Cos.; Southwest Energy, Inc.; Alban Medical Associates; Industrial Motor & Control, Inc.; Allergy Asthma Associates, P.C.

(See Next Column)

DANIEL H. O'CONNELL, P.C., *Tucson—Continued*

Reference: Bank of America.

For full biographical listings, see the Martindale-Hubbell Law Directory

---

LAW OFFICES OF SLOSSER, HUDGINS & STRUSE, P.L.C. (AV)

Suite 125, 3573 East Sunrise Drive, 85718
Telephone: 520-529-3280
Fax: 520-529-1047

Paul D. Slosser	Richard S. Hudgins
Robert M. Struse	

Caryn I. Tate

For full biographical listings, see the Martindale-Hubbell Law Directory

---

SNELL & WILMER, L.L.P. (AV)

1500 Norwest Tower, One South Church Avenue, 85701-1612
Telephone: 520-882-1200
Fax: 520-884-1294
Phoenix, Arizona Office: One Arizona Center, 85004-0001.
Telephone: 602-382-6000.
Fax: 602-382-6070.
Orange County Office: 1920 Main Street, Suite 1200, P.O. Box 57062, Irvine, California, 92619-7062.
Telephone: 714-253-2700
Fax: 714-955-2507.
Salt Lake City, Utah Office: Broadway Centre, 111 East Broadway, Suite 900, 84111- 1004.
Telephone: 801-237-1900.
Fax: 801-237-1950.

MEMBER OF FIRM
Sandra S. Froman
ASSOCIATE
David R. Cohen

Representative Clients: Transit Management, Inc.; Tucson Airport Authority; Allstate Insurance Co.; Bank One, Arizona, NA; Southern Pacific Railroad Co.; Ford Motor Co.; Chrysler Motors Corp.; Toyota Motor Sales, U.S.A., Inc.; BHP Copper, Inc.; Pinnacle West Capital Corp.; Safeway Inc.; Honeywell, Inc.; Wells Fargo Bank, N.A.

For full biographical listings, see the Martindale-Hubbell Law Directory

---

ARKANSAS

---

*LITTLE ROCK,** Pulaski Co.

ARNOLD, GROBMYER & HALEY, A PROFESSIONAL ASSOCIATION (AV)

875 Union National Plaza, 124 West Capitol Avenue, P.O. Box 70, 72203
Telephone: 501-376-1171
Fax: 501-375-3548

Charles D. McDaniel	Joe A. Polk
	Beth Ann Long
	OF COUNSEL
	John H. Haley

For Complete List of Firm Personnel, See General Section

For full biographical listings, see the Martindale-Hubbell Law Directory

---

CATLETT & YANCEY, PLC (AV)

Eighteenth Floor, The Tower Building, 72201
Telephone: 501-372-2121
FAX: 501-372-5566;
TELEX: 6503414534
Moscow, Russia Office: Bolshoi Gnezdnykovsky Pereulok 10, Suite 624, 103009.
Telephone: (7-095) 229-6930.
Fax: 229-8234.

H. B. Stubblefield (1907-1991)	Terri S. Parnell
S. Graham Catlett	Sergey Chirkin (Not admitted in the United States)
H. Lawrence Yancey	
Evguiny V. Boureiko (Not admitted in the United States)	Nataliya V. Priezjaya (Not admitted in the United States)

Representative Clients: The Buffalo Co.; Catlett & Co.; Citizens Fidelity Insurance Co.; Frost and Company, CPA's; General Properties, Inc.; The Hathaway Group, Inc.; McKay and Company Residential Realtors; Midwest Lumber Co.; Motel Sleepers, Inc.; National Home Centers, Inc.

For full biographical listings, see the Martindale-Hubbell Law Directory

---

FRIDAY, ELDREDGE & CLARK (AV)

A Partnership including Professional Associations
Formerly, Smith, Williams, Friday, Eldredge & Clark
2000 First Commercial Building, 400 West Capitol Avenue, 72201-3493
Telephone: 501-376-2011
Telecopier: 501-376-2147; 376-6369
Email: fecmh@fec.sprint.com

MEMBERS OF FIRM

Byron M. Eiseman, Jr., (P.A.)	W. Thomas Baxter (P.A.)
H. T. Larzelere, Jr., (P.A.)	Joseph B. Hurst, Jr., (P.A.)
A. Wyckliff Nisbet, Jr., (P.A.)	Walter M. Ebel, III, (P.A.)
James E. Harris (P.A.)	J. Lee Brown (P.A.)
James M. Saxton (P.A.)	Price C. Gardner (P.A.)

ASSOCIATES

David M. Graf	Carla G. Spainhour
	James W. Smith

Counsel for: Union Pacific System; St. Paul Insurance Co.; Liberty Mutual Insurance Co.; Cigna Property & Casualty Co.; Arkansas Power & Light Co.; Dillard Department Stores, Inc.; First Commercial Corp.; Browning Arms Co.; Phillips Petroleum Co.; Aetna Casualty & Surety Co.

For Complete List of Firm Personnel, See General Section

For full biographical listings, see the Martindale-Hubbell Law Directory

---

GILL LAW FIRM, A PROFESSIONAL ASSOCIATION (AV)

3801 TCBY Tower, Capitol and Broadway, 72201
Telephone: 501-376-3800
Fax: 501-372-3359

Charles C. Owen (P.A.)

C. Tad Bohannon

For Complete List of Firm Personnel, See General Section

For full biographical listings, see the Martindale-Hubbell Law Directory

---

HATFIELD & LASSITER (AV)

401 West Capitol, Suite 502, 72201
Telephone: 501-374-9010
FAX: 501-374-8510

MEMBERS OF FIRM

Richard F. Hatfield	Jack T. Lassiter

Karen DeLayne Miller

For full biographical listings, see the Martindale-Hubbell Law Directory

---

HILBURN, CALHOON, HARPER, PRUNISKI & CALHOUN, LTD. (AV)

P.O. Box 1256, 72203-1256
Telephone: 501-372-0110
Fax: 501-372-2029
North Little Rock, Arkansas Office: Eighth Floor, Mercantile Bank Building, One Riverfront Place, P.O. Box 5551, 72119.
Telephone: 501-372-0110.
Fax: 501-372-2029.

Ken F. Calhoon	Carrold E. Ray

Michael E. Hartje, Jr.	Bruce D. Eddy

Representative Clients: Mercantile Bank of Central Arkansas; Merrill Lynch Pierce Fenner & Smith, Inc.; Central Arkansas Risk Management Association; Smith Barney, Inc.

For Complete List of Firm Personnel, See General Section

For full biographical listings, see the Martindale-Hubbell Law Directory

---

HOOVER & KOOISTRA (AV)

111 Center Street, 11th Floor, 72201-4445
Telephone: 501-376-8500
Facsimile: 501-372-3255

MEMBERS OF FIRM

Paul W. Hoover, Jr.	John Kooistra, III
	Max C. Mehlburger

For full biographical listings, see the Martindale-Hubbell Law Directory

Little Rock—Continued

PLASTIRAS, HYDEN & MIRON (AV)

A Partnership of Professional Associations
200 Louisiana, 72201
Telephone: 501-376-8222
Fax: 501-376-7047
1-800-467-8297
Hot Springs Village, Arkansas Office: Village Square, Suite "G", 4501
North Highway 7.
Telephone: 501-984-6366.
Fax: 501-984-6366. 1-800-467-8297.
Pine Bluff, Arkansas Office: 620 South Laurel.
Telephone: 501-536-8222. 1-800-467-8297.

MEMBERS OF FIRM
George N. Plastiras (P.A.)   James W. Hyden (P.A.)
Philip Miron (P.A.)
OF COUNSEL
James F. Goodhart
ASSOCIATES
Lyle D. Foster   Anthony A. Hilliard

For full biographical listings, see the Martindale-Hubbell Law Directory

ROSE LAW FIRM, A PROFESSIONAL ASSOCIATION (AV)

120 East Fourth Street, 72201
Telephone: 501-375-9131
Telecopy: 501-375-1309

W. Wilson Jones	Jackson Farrow Jr.
William E. Bishop	David A. Smith
C. Brantly Buck	James L. Harris
Ronald M. Clark	Clay H. Davis

Counsel for: ALLTEL Corporation; Aluminum Company of America; Donrey Media Group Inc.; Bridgestone/Firestone, Inc.; General Motors Corp.; Minnesota Mining and Manufacturing Co.; The Prudential Insurance Company of America; The Winthrop Rockefeller Foundation; Stephens Group Inc.; Tyson Foods, Inc.

For Complete List of Firm Personnel, See General Section

For full biographical listings, see the Martindale-Hubbell Law Directory

WILLIAMS & ANDERSON (AV)

Twenty-Second Floor, 111 Center Street, 72201
Telephone: 501-372-0800
FAX: 501-372-6453

MEMBERS OF FIRM
W. Jackson Williams   Rush B. Deacon

J. Cal McCastlain

Representative Clients: Arkansas Development Finance Authority; Dean Witter Reynolds Inc.; Entergy Power, Inc.; Little Rock Newspapers, Inc. d/b/a/ Arkansas Democrat-Gazette; Potlatch Corporation; Texaco, Inc.; Wal-Mart Stores, Inc.

For Complete List of Firm Personnel, See General Section

For full biographical listings, see the Martindale-Hubbell Law Directory

CALIFORNIA

BAKERSFIELD,* Kern Co.

BORTON, PETRINI & CONRON (AV)

The Borton, Petrini & Conron Building, 1600 Truxtun Avenue, P.O. Box 2026, 93303
Telephone: 805-322-3051
Voice Mail: 805-395-6700
Fax: 805-322-4628
Email: bpcbak@bpclaw.com
San Luis Obispo, California Office: 1114 Marsh Street.
Telephone: 805-541-4340.
Fax: 805-541-4558. Email: bpcslo@bpclaw.com.
Visalia, California Office: 206 South Mooney Boulevard, P.O. Box 1028.
Telephone: 209-627-5600.
Fax: 209-627-4309. Email: bpcvis@bpclaw.com.
Fresno, California Office: T. W. Patterson Building, 2014 Tulare Street, Suite 830.
Telephone: 209-268-0117.
Fax: 209-237-7995. Email: bpcfrs@bpclaw.com.
Sacramento, California Office: 2233 Watt Avenue, Suite 290.
Telephone: 916-484-3555.
Fax: 916-484-3550. Email: bpcsac@bpclaw.com.
Santa Barbara, California Office: 211 East Victoria Street, Suite D.
Telephone: 805-564-2404.
Fax: 805-564-2176. Email: bpcsb@bpclaw.com

(See Next Column)

Los Angeles, California Office: 707 Wilshire Boulevard, Suite 5100.
Telephone: 213-624-2869.
Fax: 213-489-3930. Email: bpcla@bpclaw.com.
San Diego, California Office: John Burnham Building, 610 West Ash Street, 9th Floor.
Telephone: 619-232-2424.
Fax: 619-531-0794. Email: bpcsd@bpclaw.com.
Newport Beach, California Office: 4675 MacArthur Court, Suite 1150.
Telephone: 714-752-2333.
Fax: 714-752-2854. Email: bpcnb@bpclaw.com.
Modesto, California Office: The Turner Building, 900 "H" Street, Suite D.
Telephone: 209-576-1701.
Fax: 209-527-9753. Email: bpcmod@bpclaw.com.
San Francisco, California Office: 111 Pine Street, Suite 730.
Telephone: 415-981-4415.
Fax: 415-391-5538. Email: bpcsf@bpclaw.com.
Redding, California Office: 280 Hemsted Drive, Suite 100.
Telephone: 916-222-1530.
Fax: 916-222-4498. Email: bpcred@bpclaw.com.
San Bernardino, California Office: 290 North "D" Street, Suite 500.
Telephone: 909-381-0527.
Fax: 909-381-0658. Email: bpcsbdo@bpclaw.com.
San Jose, California Office: 2 North Second Street.
Telephone: 408-298-3997.
Fax: 408-298-3365. Email: bpcsj@bpclaw.com.
Ventura, California Office: 1000 Hill Road, Suite 310.
Telephone: 805-650-9994.
Fax: 805-650-7125. Email: bpcvta@bpclaw.com.
Santa Rosa, California Office: 50 Santa Rosa Avenue, Suite 300.
Telephone: 707-527-9477.
Fax: 707-527-9488. Email: bpcsr@bpclaw.com.

MEMBER OF FIRM
Stephen M. Dake

Representative Clients: Castle and Cooke; Wells Fargo Bank; Pacific Gas & Electric.

For Complete List of Firm Personnel, See General Section

For full biographical listings, see the Martindale-Hubbell Law Directory

KLEIN, WEGIS, DENATALE, GOLDNER & MUIR, LLP (AV)

A Partnership including Professional Corporations
(Formerly Di Giorgio, Davis, Klein, Wegis, Duggan & Friedman)
ARCO Tower, 4550 California Avenue, Second Floor, P.O. Box 11172, 93389-1172
Telephone: 805-395-1000
Telecopier: 805-326-0418
Email: kwdgm@kwdgm.com

MEMBERS OF FIRM
Anthony J. Klein (Inc.)   Claude P. Kimball
ASSOCIATES
Kevin C. Findley   Stacy Henry Bowman

Representative Clients: Bank of America; Great Western Bank; Mojave Pipeline Co.; Transamerican Title Insurance Co.; Dean Whittier Reynolds, Inc.; California Republic Bank; San Joaquin Bank; Nahama & Weagant Energy Co.; Freymiller Trucking, Inc.; Westinghouse Electric Co.

For Complete List of Firm Personnel, See General Section

For full biographical listings, see the Martindale-Hubbell Law Directory

BEVERLY HILLS, Los Angeles Co.

ELI BLUMENFELD LAW CORPORATION (AV)

433 North Camden Drive, Suite 900, 90210
Telephone: 310-205-0800
FAX: 310-888-1120

Eli Blumenfeld

Reference: Union Bank (Century City Office).

For full biographical listings, see the Martindale-Hubbell Law Directory

HOCHMAN, SALKIN AND DEROY, A PROFESSIONAL CORPORATION (AV)

9150 Wilshire Boulevard Suite 300, 90212-3414
Telephone: 310-281-3200; 273-1181
Fax: 310-859-1430

Bruce I. Hochman	Charles P. Rettig
Avram Salkin	Dennis Perez
	Steven R. Toscher

OF COUNSEL
George DeRoy

Stuart A. Simon	Michael W. Popoff
	Frederic J. Adam

Reference: Union Bank of California.

For full biographical listings, see the Martindale-Hubbell Law Directory

Beverly Hills—Continued

SAMUEL D. INGHAM, III (AV)

Suite 830, 8383 Wilshire Boulevard, 90211-2407
Telephone: 213-651-5980
FAX: 213-651-5725
Email: sdiesq@aol.com

For full biographical listings, see the Martindale-Hubbell Law Directory

KAJAN MATHER AND BARISH, A PROFESSIONAL CORPORATION (AV)

Suite 805, 9777 Wilshire Boulevard, 90212
Telephone: 310-278-6080
Fax: 310-278-4805
Email: EHKKOTAX@PACBELL.NET

Elliott H. Kajan   Steven R. Mather
          Kenneth M. Barish

For full biographical listings, see the Martindale-Hubbell Law Directory

---

COSTA MESA, Orange Co.

RISLEY & ASSOCIATES (AV)

Suite 225, 3420 Bristol Street, 92626
Telephone: 714-557-9712
Fax: 714-557-9908
Email: Harviell@aol.com

Robert L. Risley
LEGAL SUPPORT PERSONNEL
Pamela D. Daguro (Paralegal)   Giselle E. Kavner (Paralegal)

Reference: Sanwa Bank, South Coast Office, Santa Ana; First American Trust Co., Newport Beach.

For full biographical listings, see the Martindale-Hubbell Law Directory

---

RUTAN & TUCKER, LLP (AV)

A Partnership including Professional Corporations
611 Anton Boulevard, Suite 1400, P.O. Box 1950, 92626
Telephone: 714-641-5100; 213-625-7586
Telecopier: 714-546-9035
Email: rutan&tucker@mcimail.com *URL:* http://www.rutan.com
MEMBERS OF FIRM
Paul Frederic Marx   Joseph D. Carruth
Edward D. Sybesma, Jr., (P.C.)   Evridiki (Vicki) Dallas
ASSOCIATE
James S. Weisz

For Complete List of Firm Personnel, See General Section

For full biographical listings, see the Martindale-Hubbell Law Directory

---

ESCONDIDO, San Diego Co.

GARTH O. REID, JR. A PROFESSIONAL LAW CORPORATION (AV)

319 East Second Avenue, 92025
Telephone: 619-746-6420

Garth O. Reid, Jr.

For full biographical listings, see the Martindale-Hubbell Law Directory

---

FRESNO,* Fresno Co.

DOWLING, AARON & KEELER, INCORPORATED (AV)

Suite 200, 6051 North Fresno Street, 93710
Telephone: 209-432-4500
Fax: 209-432-4590
Email: dowling-law.com

Michael D. Dowling   Bruce S. Fraser
Richard M. Aaron   William J. Keeler, Jr.
          John C. Ganahl
OF COUNSEL
Morris M. Sherr

Reference: Wells Fargo Bank (Main).

For Complete List of Firm Personnel, See General Section

For full biographical listings, see the Martindale-Hubbell Law Directory

KIMBLE, MacMICHAEL & UPTON, A PROFESSIONAL CORPORATION (AV)

Fig Garden Financial Center, 5260 North Palm Avenue, Suite 221, P.O.
  Box 9489, 93792-9489
Telephone: 209-435-5500
Telecopier: 209-435-1500
Email: kmu@primenet.com

(See Next Column)

Joseph C. Kimble (1910-1972)   Robert H. Scribner
Thomas A. MacMichael   Michael E. Moss
  (1920-1990)   Mark D. Miller
Jon Wallace Upton   Michael F. Tatham
Robert E. Bergin   W. Richard Lee
Jeffrey G. Boswell   D. Tyler Tharpe
Steven D. McGee   Sylvia Halkousis Coyle
Robert E. Ward   S. Brett Sutton
John P. Eleazarian   Michael J. Jurkovich

Douglas V. Thornton   Susan King Hatmaker
Robert William Branch   Lawrence J. Salisbury
Donald J. Pool   Daniel R. Foster
          Meredith E. Allen
OF COUNSEL
Mary Ann Bluhm

For full biographical listings, see the Martindale-Hubbell Law Directory

---

GLENDALE, Los Angeles Co.

BAKER, OLSON, LeCROY & DANIELIAN, A LAW CORPORATION (AV)

144 North Brand Boulevard, P.O. Box 29062, 91209-9062
Telephone: 818-502-5600
Facsimile: 818-241-2653

Sheldon S. Baker   Charles L. LeCroy, III
Eric Olson   Arsen Danielian

Michael S. Simon
OF COUNSEL
John J. Jacobson

For full biographical listings, see the Martindale-Hubbell Law Directory

---

IRSFELD, IRSFELD & YOUNGER LLP (AV)

A Partnership including Professional Corporations
Suite 900, 100 West Broadway, 91210-1296
Telephone: 818-242-6859
Fax: 818-240-7728
Email: 104736.1745@compuserver.com
MEMBERS OF FIRM
James B. Irsfeld (1880-1966)   Peter J. Irsfeld (P.C.)
Kenneth C. Younger   James J. Waldorf (P.C.)
  (1922-1996)   C. Phillip Jackson (P.C.)
John H. Brink (P.C.)   Norman H. Green (P.C.)
          Kathryn E. Van Houten
ASSOCIATES
Peter C. Wright   Diane L. Walker
RETIRED
James B. Irsfeld, Jr.

Representative Clients: Lear Sieglar, Inc.; Chrysler Credit Corp.
References: First Interstate Bank (Glendale Main Office); Bank of Hollywood.

For full biographical listings, see the Martindale-Hubbell Law Directory

---

IRVINE, Orange Co.

GRECO, MOLLIS & O'HARA, A PROFESSIONAL CORPORATION (AV)

18400 Von Karman, Suite 500, 92612-1514
Telephone: 714-263-0600
Fax: 714-263-1513

Thomas A. Greco   Kevin O'Hara
Ronald A. Mollis   Charles A. Mollis

For full biographical listings, see the Martindale-Hubbell Law Directory

JOSEPH E. MUDD, P.L.C. (AV)

8001 Irvine Center Drive, Suite 1170, 92618
Telephone: 714-453-1012
Fax: 714-453-1516

Joseph E. Mudd

Jeri L. Gartside   Dennis M. Sandoval
LEGAL SUPPORT PERSONNEL
Toni M. Storey

For full biographical listings, see the Martindale-Hubbell Law Directory

Irvine—Continued

STEPHEN J. SCHUMACHER (AV)

18201 Von Karman, Suite 220, 92612-1005
Telephone: 714-752-9425
Telecopier: 714-752-8170

Reference: Bank of America (Irvine Industrial Branch).

For full biographical listings, see the Martindale-Hubbell Law Directory

SNELL & WILMER, L.L.P. (AV)

1920 Main Street, Suite 1200, 92614
Telephone: 714-253-2700
FAX: 714-955-2507
URL: http://www.swlaw.com
Phoenix, Arizona Office: One Arizona Center, 85004-0001.
Telephone: 602-382-6000.
Fax: 602-382-6070.
Tucson, Arizona Office: Norwest Tower, Suite 1500, One South Church
Avenue, 85701-1612.
Telephone: 520-882-1200.
Fax: 520-884-1294.
Salt Lake City, Utah Office: Broadway Centre, 111 East Broadway, Suite
900, 84111-1004.
Telephone: 801-237-1900.
Fax: 801-237-1950.

MEMBER OF FIRM
David W. Evans (Resident)

For Complete List of Firm Personnel, See General Section

For full biographical listings, see the Martindale-Hubbell Law Directory

---

LONG BEACH, Los Angeles Co.

CAMERON, MADDEN, PEARLSON, GALE & SELLARS (AV)

One World Trade Center Suite 1600, 90831-1600
Telephone: 310-436-3888
Telecopier: 310-437-1967

MEMBERS OF THE FIRM
Timothy C. Cameron   Patrick T. Madden
Charles M. Gale   Paul R. Pearlson
             James D. Sellars
ASSOCIATE
Lillian D. Salinger

For full biographical listings, see the Martindale-Hubbell Law Directory

TAUBMAN, SIMPSON, YOUNG & SULENTOR (AV)

249 East Ocean Boulevard, Suite 700, P.O. Box 22670, 90801-5670
Telephone: 310-436-9201
FAX: 310-590-9695

E. C. Denio (1864-1952)   Richard G. Wilson (1928-1993)
Geo. A. Hart (1881-1967)   Roger W. Young
Geo. P. Taubman, Jr.   William J. Sulentor
  (1897-1970)   Peter M. Williams
Matthew C. Simpson   Scott R. Magee
  (1900-1988)   Maria M. Rohaidy
             Stuart C. Talley

Attorneys for: Bixby Land Co.; Renick Cadillac, Inc.; Oil Operators Inc.
Local Counsel: Crown Cork & Seal Co., Inc.

For full biographical listings, see the Martindale-Hubbell Law Directory

---

LOS ANGELES,* Los Angeles Co.

AJALAT, POLLEY & AYOOB (AV)

A Partnership including Professional Corporations
Suite 200, 643 South Olive Street, 90014
Telephone: 213-622-7400
Fax: 213-622-4738

MEMBERS OF FIRM
Charles R. Ajalat (A   Terry L. Polley (A Professional
  Professional Corporation)   Corporation)
             Richard J. Ayoob

Reference: Bank of America (Los Angeles Main Office).

For full biographical listings, see the Martindale-Hubbell Law Directory

ANTIN & TAYLOR (AV)

1875 Century Park East, Suite 700, 90067
Telephone: 310-788-2733
Fax: 310-788-0754
Email: mantin@ix.netcom.com

MEMBERS OF FIRM
Michael Antin   Michael L. Taylor

For full biographical listings, see the Martindale-Hubbell Law Directory

LAW OFFICES OF BRUCE R. BAILEY (AV)

1900 Avenue of the Stars, Suite 1630, 90067
Telephone: 310-286-9900
Telecopier: 310-286-9907
Email: brbailey@netcom.com *URL:* http://www.baileyfirm.com

ASSOCIATES
Gregory R. Schenz   John R. Denny
             Richard Charles Herman
OF COUNSEL
Claudio O. Wolff   Steven U. Ross

References: First Interstate Bank; Security Pacific National Bank.

For full biographical listings, see the Martindale-Hubbell Law Directory

---

BARTON, KLUGMAN & OETTING (AV)

A Partnership including Professional Corporations
37th Floor, 333 South Grand Avenue, 90071-1599
Telephone: 213-621-4000
Telecopier: 213-625-1832
Newport Beach Office: Suite 700, 4400 MacArthur Boulevard, P.O. Box
2350, 92660.
Telephone: 714-752-7551.
Telecopier: 714-752-0288.

COUNSEL TO FIRM
Robert M. Barton *   Robert H. Klugman *
             Richard F. Oetting *
MEMBERS OF FIRM
David F. Morgan *   David J. Cartano *
William D. Herz *   Martin J. Spear
Charles J. Schufreider *   Tod V. Beebe *
Robert Louis Fisher *   Ronald R. St. John
Gilbert D. Jensen *   Mark A. Newton *
             Margot I. McLeay
ASSOCIATES
Barbara W. G. Crowley   Reiko L. Furuta
             Jaleen Nelson

References: The Bank of California (Southern California Headquarters);
Wells Fargo Bank, N.A. (Wells Fargo Center, Los Angeles).
*Denotes a lawyer whose Professional Corporation is a member of the part-
nership or is Counsel to the Firm

For full biographical listings, see the Martindale-Hubbell Law Directory

BASILE & LANE, L.L.P. (AV)

11400 West Olympic Boulevard, 9th Floor, 90064-1565
Telephone: 310-478-2114
Fax: 310-478-0229

MEMBERS OF FIRM
Paul L. Basile, Jr.   Jeff W. Lane

For full biographical listings, see the Martindale-Hubbell Law Directory

BRAND FARRAR DZIUBLA FREILICH & KOLSTAD, LLP (AV)

Counsellors at Law
515 South Flower Street, Suite 3500, 90071-2201
Telephone: 213-228-0288
Facsimile: 213-426-6222
Correspondent Offices: Hong Kong, Shanghai, Beijing, Guangzhou,
Xiamen, Shenzhen, Ulaanbaatar, New York and San Francisco.

Michael A. Brand   Amy E. Freilich
David W. Farrar   Charles K. Kolstad
Robert W. Dziubla   Margaret G. Graf
OF COUNSEL
H. Bennett Arnberger   Julia Marie Shymansky
David C. Buxbaum   Yelena Yeruhim
Sherry L. Geyer   Norman A. Chernin
Manender M. Grewal (Not   Joan M. Marquardt
  admitted in the United States)

For full biographical listings, see the Martindale-Hubbell Law Directory

BUCHALTER, NEMER, FIELDS & YOUNGER, A PROFESSIONAL CORPORATION (AV)

24th Floor, 601 South Figueroa Street, 90017
Telephone: 213-891-0700
Fax: 213-896-0400
Email: buchalter@earthlink.net *URL:* http://www.buchalter.com
New York, New York Office: 15th Floor, 605 Third Avenue.
Telephone: 212-490-8600.
Fax: 212-490-6022.
San Francisco, California Office: 29th Floor, 333 Market Street.
Telephone: 415-227-0900.
Fax: 415-227-0770.
Newport Beach, California Office: Suite 1450, 620 Newport Center Drive.
Telephone: 714-760-1121.
Fax: 714-720-0182.

(See Next Column)

BUCHALTER, NEMER, FIELDS & YOUNGER A PROFESSIONAL CORPORATION,
Los Angeles—Continued

Gregory Keever   Philip J. Wolman

References: City National Bank; Wells Fargo Bank; Metrobank.

For Complete List of Firm Personnel, See General Section

For full biographical listings, see the Martindale-Hubbell Law Directory

---

CLARK & TREVITHICK, A PROFESSIONAL CORPORATION (AV)

800 Wilshire Boulevard, 12th Floor, 90017
Telephone: 213-629-5700
Telecopier: 213-624-9441
San Francisco, California Office: 456 Montgomery Street, 20th Floor.
Telephone: 415-288-6520.
Fax: 415-398-2820.

Kevin P. Fiore   Dean I. Friedman

References: Wells Fargo Bank (Los Angeles Main Office); National Bank of California.

For Complete List of Firm Personnel, See General Section

For full biographical listings, see the Martindale-Hubbell Law Directory

---

COHEN PRIMIANI & FOSTER, A PROFESSIONAL CORPORATION (AV)

2029 Century Park East, Suite 480, 90067
Telephone: 310-277-3963
Fax: 310-277-4351

Marc S. Primiani	Bernard Oster
Bradford S. Cohen	Samuel Israel
Michael D. Foster	Jeffrey Forer

Reference: Western Bank (Los Angeles, Calif.).

For full biographical listings, see the Martindale-Hubbell Law Directory

---

DEMETRIOU, DEL GUERCIO, SPRINGER & MOYER, LLP (AV)

801 South Grand Avenue, 10th Floor, 90017
Telephone: 213-624-8407
Telecopy: 213-624-0174
Email: ddsm@juno.com *URL:* http://www.ddsm.com

MEMBERS OF FIRM

Chris G. Demetriou (1915-1989)	Laurie E. Davis
Jeffrey Z. B. Springer	Gregory D. Trimarche
Craig A. Moyer	Karen McLaurin Chang
Angela Shanahan	Leslie M. Smario
Stephen A. Del Guercio	Andrew J. Bracker
Michael A. Francis	Kimberly E. Lewand
Regina Liudzius Cobb	Jennifer T. Taggart

Robert P. Silverstein

OF COUNSEL

Ronald J. Del Guercio   Richard A. Del Guercio
James P. Del Guercio

Reference: Bank of America, L.A. Main Office, Los Angeles, Calif.

For full biographical listings, see the Martindale-Hubbell Law Directory

---

GREENBERG GLUSKER FIELDS CLAMAN & MACHTINGER LLP (AV)

21st Floor, 1900 Avenue of the Stars (Century City), 90067
Telephone: 310-553-3610
Fax: 310-553-0687

MEMBERS OF FIRM

Sidney J. Machtinger   C. Bruce Levine
Gary L. Kaplan

Reference: Wells Fargo Bank, 1801 Century Park East, Los Angeles, CA 90067.

For Complete List of Firm Personnel, See General Section

For full biographical listings, see the Martindale-Hubbell Law Directory

---

HANNA AND MORTON (AV)

A Partnership including Professional Corporations
Seventeenth Floor, Wilshire-Grand Building, 600 Wilshire
Boulevard, 90017
Telephone: 213-628-7131
Facsimile: 213-623-3379

MEMBER OF FIRM
Michael I. Blaylock
OF COUNSEL
William N. Greene

For Complete List of Firm Personnel, See General Section

For full biographical listings, see the Martindale-Hubbell Law Directory

---

HILL, FARRER & BURRILL LLP (AV)

A Limited Liability Partnership including Professional Corporations
35th Floor, Union Bank Square, 445 South Figueroa Street, 90071
Telephone: 213-620-0460
Fax: 213-624-4840

MEMBERS OF FIRM
Leon S. Angvire (P.C.)   George Koide (P.C.)
Thomas F. Reed

For Complete List of Firm Personnel, See General Section

For full biographical listings, see the Martindale-Hubbell Law Directory

---

HOLLEY & GALEN (AV)

800 South Figueroa, Suite 1100, 90017
Telephone: 213-629-1880
Fax: 213-895-0363

MEMBERS OF FIRM
Albert J. Galen (Retired)   W. Michael Johnson

For Complete List of Firm Personnel, See General Section

For full biographical listings, see the Martindale-Hubbell Law Directory

---

JONES, DAY, REAVIS & POGUE (AV)

555 West Fifth Street Suite 4600, 90013-1025
Telephone: 213-489-3939
Telex: 181439 UD
Telecopier: 213-243-2539
In Irvine, California: 2603 Main Street, Suite 900.
Telephone: 714-851-3939.
Telex: 194911 Lawyers LSA.
Telecopier: 714-553-7539.
In Atlanta, Georgia: 3500 One Peachtree Center, 303 Peachtree Street, N.E.
Telephone: 404-521-3939.
Cable Address: "Attorneys Atlanta".
Telex: 54-2711.
Telecopier: 404-581-8330.
In Brussels, Belgium: Avenue Louise 480, 7th Floor, B-1050 Brussels.
Telephone: 32-2-645-14-11.
Telecopier: 32-2-645-14-45.
In Chicago, Illinois: 77 West Wacker.
Telephone: 312-782-3939.
Telecopier: 312-782-8585.
In Cleveland, Ohio: North Point, 901 Lakeside Avenue.
Telephone: 216-586-3939.
Cable Address: "Attorneys Cleveland."
Telex: 980389.
Telecopier: 216-579-0212.
In Columbus, Ohio: 1900 Huntington Center.
Telephone: 614-469-3939.
Cable Address: "Attorneys Columbus."
Telecopier: 614-461-4198.
In Dallas, Texas: 2300 Trammell Crow Center, 2001 Ross Avenue.
Telephone: 214-220-3939.
Cable Address: "Attorneys Dallas."
Telex: 730852.
Telecopier: 214-969-5100.
In Frankfurt, Germany: Triton Haus, Bockenheimer Landstrasse 42, 60323 Frankfurt am Main.
Telephone: 49-69-9726-3939.
Telecopier: 49-69-9726-3993.
In Geneva, Switzerland: 20, rue de Candolle.
Telephone: 41-22-320-2339.
Telecopier: 41-22-320-1232.
In Hong Kong: 29th Floor, Entertainment Building, 30 Queen's Road Central.
Telephone: 852-2526-6895.
Telecopier: 852-2868-5871.
In London England: Bucklersbury House, 3 Queen Victoria Street.
Telephone: 44-171-236-3939.
Telecopier: 44-171-236-1113.
In New Delhi, India: Pathak & Associates, 13th Floor, Dr. Gopal Das Bhaven, 28 Barakhamba Road.
Telephone: 91-11-373-8793.
Telecopier: 91-11-335-3761.
In New York, New York: 599 Lexington Avenue.
Telephone: 212-326-3939.
Cable Address: "JONESDAY NEWYORK."
Telex: 237013 JDRP UR.
Telecopier: 212-755-7306.
In Paris, France: 62, rue du Faubourg Saint-Honore.
Telephone: 33-1-44-71-3939.
Telex: 290156 Surgoe.
Telecopier: 33-1-49-24-0471.
In Pittsburgh, Pennsylvania: 500 Grant Street, 31st Floor.
Telephone: 412-391-3939.
Cable Address: "Attorneys Pittsburgh".
Telecopier: 412-394-7959.

(See Next Column)

JONES, DAY, REAVIS & POGUE—*Continued*

In Riyadh, Saudi Arabia: The International Law Firm, Sulaymaniyah Center, Tahlia Street, P.O. Box 22166.
Telephone: (966-1) 462-8866.
Telecopier: (966-1) 462-9001.
In Taipei, Taiwan: 8th Floor, 2 Tun Hwa South Road, Section 2.
Telephone: (886-2) 704-6808.
Telecopier: (886-2) 704-6791.
In Tokyo, Japan: Toranomon MT Building, 4th Floor, 10-3, Toranomon 3-Chome, Minato-ku, Tokyo 105, Japan.
Telephone: 81-3-3433-3939.
Telecopier: 81-3-5401-2725.
In Washington, D.C.: Metropolitan Square, 1450 G Street, N.W.
Telephone: 202-879-3939.
Cable Address: "Attorneys Washington."
Telex: 89-2410 ATTORNEYS WASH.
Telecopier: 202-737-2832.

MEMBERS OF FIRM IN LOS ANGELES

James F. Childs, Jr.   Elwood Lui
Ronald S. Rizzo   David S. Boyce
          Sarah Heck Griffin

SENIOR ATTORNEY
Lynn Leversen Kambe

ASSOCIATE
Kirstin D. Poirier-Whitley

For Complete List of Firm Personnel, See General Section

For full biographical listings, see the Martindale-Hubbell Law Directory

JONES, KAUFMAN & ACKERMAN LLP (AV)

10960 Wilshire Boulevard, Suite 1225, 90024
Telephone: 310-477-8575
Fax: 310-477-8768

Donald H. Jones   Michael S. Ackerman
Paul W. Kaufman   Marc H. Corman
          Ellen Roth Nagler

For full biographical listings, see the Martindale-Hubbell Law Directory

KOPPLE & KLINGER (AV)

A Law Partnership including a Professional Corporation
2029 Century Park East, Suite 1040, 90067
Telephone: 310-553-1444
Facsimile: 310-553-7335

MEMBERS OF FIRM
Robert C. Kopple (P.C.)   Leslie S. Klinger

OF COUNSEL
Richard P. Ayles

ASSOCIATES
Douglas W. Schwartz   Jeffrey A. Kaye
          Richard A. Marshall

For full biographical listings, see the Martindale-Hubbell Law Directory

LOEB & LOEB LLP (AV)

A Limited Liability Partnership including Professional Corporations
Suite 1800, 1000 Wilshire Boulevard, 90017-2475
Telephone: 213-688-3400
Facsimile: 213-688-3460; 688-3461; 688-3462
Century City, California Office: Suite 2200, 10100 Santa Monica Boulevard, Los Angeles, 90067-4164.
Telephone: 310-282-2000.
Facsimile: 310-282-2191; 282-2192.
New York, N.Y. Office: 345 Park Avenue, 10154-0037.
Telephone: 212-407-4000.
Facsimile: 212-407-4990.
Washington, D.C. Office: Suite 601, 2100 M Street N.W., 20037-1207.
Telephone: 202-223-5700.
Facsimile: 202-223-5704.
Nashville, Tennessee Office: 45 Music Square West, 37203-3205.
Telephone: 615-749-8300;
Facsimile: 615-749-8308.
Rome, Italy Office: Piazza Digione 1, 00197.
Telephone: 011-396-808-8456.
Facsimile: 011-396-808-8288.

MEMBERS OF FIRM
John Arao   Paul A. Sczudlo
Terence F. Cuff   Bruce M. Stiglitz (A P.C.)
Fredric M. Sanders   William P. Wasserman (A P.C.)
    (New York City Office)   William S. Woods, II

OF COUNSEL
Abraham S. Guterman   Harvey L. Silbert
    (New York City Office)   (Century City Office)
Jay Adams Knight   John S. Warren (A P.C.)
Arthur A. Segall
    (New York City Office)

(See Next Column)

ASSOCIATES
Paula G. Atkinson   Jay Fenster
                            (New York City Office)

For Complete List of Firm Personnel, See General Section

For full biographical listings, see the Martindale-Hubbell Law Directory

MAHONEY, COPPENRATH, JAFFE & PEARSON LLP (AV)

A Partnership including Professional Corporations
2049 Century Park East, Suite 2480, 90067-3283
Telephone: 310-557-1919
Telecopier: 310-277-6536

MEMBERS OF FIRM
James E. Mahoney (P.C.)   Ronald C. Pearson
Walter G. Coppenrath, Jr.,   Daryl G. Parker
    (P.C.)   Charles L. Grotts
Howard M. Jaffe (P.C.)   Arthur L. Martin

OF COUNSEL
Gerald Lee Tahajian

Reference: First Professional Bank, Santa Monica, California.

For full biographical listings, see the Martindale-Hubbell Law Directory

MATTHIAS & BERG LLP (AV)

Seventh Floor, 515 South Flower Street, 90071
Telephone: 213-895-4200
Telecopier: 213-895-4058

Michael R. Matthias   Stuart R. Singer
Jeffrey P. Berg   Kenneth M. H. Hoff
          Michael D. Berger

Representative Clients: Synagro Technologies, Inc.; Mexalit, S.A.; Maxitile, Inc.; Allstar Inns; Chatsworth Products, Inc.; International Meta Systems, Inc.; Residential Resources, Inc.; AVIC Group International, Inc.; AutoBitter Group, Inc. National Quality Care, Inc.; Greater China Corp.; HBO Ole.
Reference: First Professional Bank.

For full biographical listings, see the Martindale-Hubbell Law Directory

MITCHELL, SILBERBERG & KNUPP LLP (AV)

A Partnership including Professional Corporations
11377 West Olympic Boulevard, 90064
Telephone: 310-312-2000
Fax: 310-312-3100

MEMBERS OF FIRM
Allan E. Biblin (A Professional   Allan B. Cutrow (A Professional
    Corporation)   Corporation)
Eugene H. Veenhuis (A   Regina T. Shanney-Saborsky (A
    Professional Corporation)   Professional Corporation)
David Wheeler Newman (A
    Professional Corporation)

ASSOCIATES
Jeffrey D. Davine   Sheri E. Cohen

References: Wells Fargo Bank, N.A.; Merrill, Lynch.

For Complete List of Firm Personnel, See General Section

For full biographical listings, see the Martindale-Hubbell Law Directory

OLINCY & KARPEL (AV)

10960 Wilshire Boulevard, Suite 1111, 90024-3782
Telephone: 310-478-1213
FAX: 310-478-1215

MEMBERS OF FIRM
George R. Olincy (1904-1982)   J. Dan Olincy
          Philip Karpel

ASSOCIATE
Joyce Riley

For full biographical listings, see the Martindale-Hubbell Law Directory

O'MELVENY & MYERS LLP (AV)

400 South Hope Street, 90071-2899
Telephone: 213-669-6000
Cable Address: "Moms"
Facsimile: 213-669-6407
Email: omminfo@omm.com
Century City, California Office: 1999 Avenue of the Stars, 90067-6035.
Telephone: 310-553-6700.
Facsimile: 310-246-6779.
Newport Beach, California Office: 610 Newport Center Drive, 92660-6429.
Telephone: 714-760-9600.
Cable Address: "Moms".
Facsimile: 714-669-6994.

(See Next Column)

O'MELVENY & MYERS LLP, *Los Angeles—Continued*

San Francisco, California Office: Embarcadero Center West Tower, 275 Battery Street, 94111-3305.
Telephone: 415-984-8700.
Facsimile: 415-984-8701.
New York, New York Office: Citicorp Center, 153 East 53rd Street, 10022-4611.
Telephone: 212-326-2000.
Facsimile: 212-326-2061.
Washington, D.C. Office: 555 13th Street, N.W., 20004-1109.
Telephone: 202-383-5300.
Cable Address: "Moms".
Facsimile: 202-383-5414.
London, England Office: 10 Finsbury Square, London, EC2A 1LA.
Telephone: 0171-256-8451.
Facsimile: 0171-638-8205.
Tokyo, Japan Office: Sanbancho KB-6 Building, 6 Sanbancho, Chiyoda-ku, Tokyo 102, Japan.
Telephone: 03-3239-2900.
Facsimile: 03-3239-2432.
Hong Kong Office: Suite 1905, Peregrine Tower, Lippo Centre, 89 Queensway, Central, Hong Kong.
Telephone: 852-2523-8266.
Facsimile: 852-2522-1760.
Shanghai, Peoples Republic of China Office: Shanghai International Trade Centre, Suite 2011, 2200 Yan An Road West, Shanghai, 200335, PRC.
Telephone: 86-21-6219-5363.
Facsimile: 86-21-6275-4949.

PARTNER

Stuart P. Tobisman (Century City and Los Angeles Offices)

For Complete List of Firm Personnel, See General Section

For full biographical listings, see the Martindale-Hubbell Law Directory

---

PILLSBURY MADISON & SUTRO LLP (AV)

Citicorp Plaza, 725 South Figueroa Street, Suite 1200, 90017-2513
Telephone: 213-488-7100
Fax: 213-629-1033
Costa Mesa, California Office: Plaza Tower, Suite 1100, 600 Anton Boulevard, 92626.
Telephone: 714-436-6800.
Fax: 714-662-6999.
Silicon Valley Office: 2700 San Hill Road, Menlo Park, 94025.
Telephone: 415-233-4500.
Fax: 415-233-4545.
Sacramento, California Office: 400 Capitol Mall, Suite 1700, 95814.
Telephone: 916-329-4700.
Fax: 916-441-3583.
San Diego, California Office: 101 West Broadway, Suite 1800, 92101.
Telephone: 619-234-5000.
Fax: 619-236-1995.
San Francisco, California Office: 235 Montgomery Street, 94104.
Telephone: 415-983-1000.
Fax: 415-983-1200.
Washington, D.C. Office: 1100 New York Avenue, N.W., Ninth Floor, 20005.
Telephone: 202-861-3000.
Fax: 202-822-0944.
New York, New York Office: 520 Madison Avenue, 40th Floor, 10022.
Telephone: 212-328-4810.
Fax: 212-328-4824. One Liberty Plaza, 165 Broadway, 51st Floor.
Telephone: 212-374-1890.
Fax: 212-374-1852.
Hong Kong Office: 6/F Asia Pacific Finance Tower, Citibank Plaza, 3 Garden Road, Central.
Telephone: 011-852-2509-7100.
Fax: 011-852-2509-7188.
Tokyo, Japan Office: Pillsbury Madison & Sutro, Gaikokuho Jimu Bengoshi Jimusho, 5th Floor, Samon Eleven Building, 3-1, Samon-cho, Shinjuku-ku, Tokyo 160 Japan.
Telephone: 800-729-9830; 011-813-3354-3531.
Fax: 011-813-3354-3534.

MEMBERS OF FIRM

Anthon S. Cannon, Jr.	David L. Hayutin
Karl A. Schmidt	Don R. Weigandt

For Complete List of Firm Personnel, See General Section

For full biographical listings, see the Martindale-Hubbell Law Directory

---

RADCLIFF, FRANDSEN & DONGELL (AV)

40th Floor, 777 South Figueroa Street, 90017
Telephone: 213-614-1990
Facsimile: 213-489-9263
San Francisco, California Office: 88 Kearny Street, Suite 1475.
Telephone: 415-399-8393.
Facsimile: 415-989-5465.
Rome, Italy Office: Via Tacito, 7.
Telephone: (39) 06-323-5588.
Facsimile: (39) 06-324-3392.

(See Next Column)

MEMBERS OF FIRM

Jules G. Radcliff, Jr.	Russell Mackay Frandsen
Richard A. Dongell	

OF COUNSEL

Tal Clifton Finney

ASSOCIATES

Francis P. Aspessi	Jeffrey C. Mayes
Ruben A. Castellon	Marisa A. Moret
William W. Funderburk, Jr.	Daniel E. Park
Jeffrey A. Gagliardi	Scott D. Pinsky
David K. Lee	Eric H. Saiki
Maria Anna Mancini	Steve R. Segura
Glenn M. White	

For full biographical listings, see the Martindale-Hubbell Law Directory

---

RUFUS VON THÜLEN RHOADES (AV)

633 West Fifth Street, 20th Floor, 90071
Telephone: 213-896-2491
Fax: 213-362-2957
Email: rufustax@ix.netcom.com

Reference: City National Bank (3rd and Fairfax Branch).

For full biographical listings, see the Martindale-Hubbell Law Directory

---

RODI, POLLOCK, PETTKER, GALBRAITH & CAHILL, A LAW CORPORATION (AV)

Suite 400 801 South Grand Avenue, 90017
Telephone: 213-895-4900; 680-0823
Telecopiers: 213-895-4921; 895-4922; 895-4750

Karl B. Rodi (1908-1982)	Elizabeth B. Blakely
John D. Cahill	Robert C. Norton
John D. Pettker	John F. Cermak, Jr.
Daniel C. Bond (1942-1977)	Tim G. Ceperley
William R. Christian	Coralie Kupfer
Henry P. Pramov, Jr.	Cris K. O'Neall
Robert A. Yahiro	John S. Cha
Scott E. Adamson	

Sonja A. Inglin	Richard Nessary
Thomas J. Yoo	Mark McCleary

OF COUNSEL

John P. Pollock	Margaret Rosenthal

For full biographical listings, see the Martindale-Hubbell Law Directory

---

SHEPPARD, MULLIN, RICHTER & HAMPTON LLP (AV)

A Limited Liability Partnership including Professional Corporations
Forty-Eighth Floor, 333 South Hope Street, 90071-1448
Telephone: 213-620-1780
Telecopier: 213-620-1398
Cable Address: "Sheplaw"
Email: info@smrh.com *URL:* http://www.smrh.com
Orange County, California Office: 650 Town Center Drive, 4th Floor, Costa Mesa.
Telephone: 714-513-5100.
Telecopier: 714-513-5130. Home Page Address: http://www.smrh.com.
San Francisco, California Office: Seventeenth Floor, Four Embarcadero Center.
Telephone: 415-434-9100.
Telecopier: 415-434-3947. Home Page Address: http://www.smrh.com.
San Diego, California Office: Nineteenth Floor, 501 West Broadway.
Telephone: 619-338-6500.
Telecopier: 619-234-3815. Home Page Address: http://www.smrh.com.

COUNSEL

J. Stanley Mullin (Retired)

MEMBERS OF FIRM

Michael J. Changaris (San Diego Office)	Joseph G. Gorman, Jr. *
Randolph B. Godshall (Orange County Office)	Robert Joe Hull *
	James M. Lowy (San Francisco Office)
Martin J. Smith	

SPECIAL COUNSEL

Laurence K. Gould, Jr.

*Professional Corporation

For full biographical listings, see the Martindale-Hubbell Law Directory

---

SHIOTANI & INOUYE (AV)

11100 Santa Monica Boulevard, Suite 1820, 90025
Telephone: 310-575-3688
Telecopier: 310-575-4095

MEMBERS OF FIRM

Barney B. Shiotani	Lawrence G. Inouye

ASSOCIATE

Nicole Grattan Pearson

(See Next Column)

SHIOTANI & INOUYE—*Continued*

LEGAL SUPPORT PERSONNEL

Gabriela Velasquez (Paralegal)

References: First Los Angeles Bank (Airport Office); Bank of California.

For full biographical listings, see the Martindale-Hubbell Law Directory

---

SIMMONS, RITCHIE & SEGAL (AV)

555 South Flower Street Suite 4640, 90071
Telephone: 213-624-7391
FAX: 213-489-7559

MEMBERS OF FIRM

Frederick L. Simmons   Jonathan L. Simmons
William D. Segal

OF COUNSEL

Graham A. Ritchie   Lee E. Stark
Michael W. Roberts

Reference: South Bay Bank, Los Angeles.

For full biographical listings, see the Martindale-Hubbell Law Directory

---

STEPHEN E. SOLOMON (AV)

1801 Century Park East Suite 2400, 90067
Telephone: 310-556-0360
Fax: 310-556-0462

For full biographical listings, see the Martindale-Hubbell Law Directory

---

STEPHENS, BERG & LASATER, A PROFESSIONAL CORPORATION (AV)

1055 West Seventh Street, Twenty-Ninth Floor, 90017
Telephone: 213-629-3111
Telecopy: 213-629-2302; 213-624-4734

Lawrence M. Berg (1947-1995)   Frederick A. Clark
R. Wicks Stephens II   Joel A. Goldman
Richard W. Lasater II   C. Stephen Davis
Mark G. Ancel   Kenneth A. Feinfield
Dudley M. Lang   Jean-Paul Menard
Joseph F. Butler   Michael J. Kaminsky
                John A. Dragonette

OF COUNSEL

Louis R. Baker   J. Lane Tilson

For full biographical listings, see the Martindale-Hubbell Law Directory

---

WEINSTEIN, BOLDT, RACINE, HALFHIDE & CAMEL, PROFESSIONAL CORPORATION (AV)

1801 Century Park East, Suite 2200, 90067-2336
Telephone: 310-203-8466
Cable Address: "Swbrtax"
Telex: 701-793
Telecopy: 310-552-7938

David A. Weinstein   Roger G. Halfhide
Ronald M. Boldt   David J. Camel
Scott H. Racine   M. Katharine Davidson

OF COUNSEL

Thomas N. Lawson

Reference: City National Bank (Los Angeles, Calif.).

For full biographical listings, see the Martindale-Hubbell Law Directory

---

WEINSTOCK, MANION, REISMAN, SHORE & NEUMANN, A LAW CORPORATION (AV)

Suite 800, 1888 Century Park East (Century City), 90067
Telephone: 310-553-8844
Los Angeles: 213-879-4481
Fax: 310-553-5165

Harold Weinstock   Martin A. Neumann
Louis A. Reisman   Marc L. Sallus
Sussan H. Shore   Robert E. Strauss
            Susan Abraham

Gordon H. Einstein

OF COUNSEL

Gary M. Borofsky   M. Neil Solarz

References: City National Bank (Century City); Wells Fargo Bank (Beverly Hills Main Office); Security Pacific National Bank (Century Plaza Office); Sanwa Bank California.

For full biographical listings, see the Martindale-Hubbell Law Directory

---

WILLIAMS AND BALLAS (AV)

1800 Century Park East, Suite 510, 90067
Telephone: 310-557-8383
Fax: 310-557-8380
San Francisco, California Office: 160 Sansome Street, Suite 1200.
Telephone: 415-296-9904.
Fax: 415-981-0898.

MEMBERS OF FIRM

Lawrence D. Williams   Stephen B. Ballas

OF COUNSEL

Stanley P. Graham

ASSOCIATE

Melissa Hamilton

Representative Clients: Pre-Delivery Service Corp.; Simonson Mercedes; Rockview Dairies; Sun Meat Co.; Fonda, Garrard, Hilberman & Davis; Graphic Films, Inc.; M.P. Mountains of So. Cal., Inc.; ZB Industries Inc.; Coaster Co. of America.

For full biographical listings, see the Martindale-Hubbell Law Directory

---

MOUNTAIN VIEW, Santa Clara Co.

LUCE & QUILLINAN (AV)

444 Castro Street, Suite 900, 94041-2073
Telephone: 415-969-4000
FAX: 415-969-6953

MEMBERS OF FIRM

James G. Luce   James V. Quillinan
        Melissa C. Johnson

ASSOCIATE

Sally F. Berry

For full biographical listings, see the Martindale-Hubbell Law Directory

---

NEWPORT BEACH, Orange Co.

RONALD K. VAN WERT A PROFESSIONAL CORPORATION (AV)

One Newport Place, Suite 900, 1301 Dove Street, 92660
Telephone: 714-752-7964

Ronald K. Van Wert

For full biographical listings, see the Martindale-Hubbell Law Directory

---

OAKLAND,* Alameda Co.

PEZZOLA & REINKE, A PROFESSIONAL CORPORATION (AV)

Suite 1300, Lake Merritt Plaza, 1999 Harrison Street, 94612
Telephone: 510-273-8750
Telecopier: 510-834-7440
San Francisco, California Office: 650 California Street, 32nd Floor, 94111.
Telephone: 415-989-9710.
Menlo Park, California Office: 3000 Sand Hill Road, Building 4, Suite 160, 94025.
Telephone: 415-854-8797.

Stephen P. Pezzola   Thomas A. Maier
        Jeremy E. Wenokur

Representative Clients: U.S. Electricar; John Billington; Pacific Car Care, LLC; Zen Research, Inc.; Van Der Hunt & Brigagliano; Harold Robinson; Robert Tillman; Dantz Development Corp.

For full biographical listings, see the Martindale-Hubbell Law Directory

---

OXNARD, Ventura Co.

ENGLAND, WHITFIELD, SCHRÖEDER & TREDWAY, L.L.P. (AV)

300 Esplanade Drive, 6th Floor, 93030
Telephone: 805-485-9627
Ventura: 647-8237
Southern California Toll Free: 800-255-3485
Fax: 805-983-0297
URL: http://www.tsurf.com/ewst/
Thousand Oaks, California Office: Rolling Oaks Office Center, 351 Rolling Oaks Drive.
Telephone: Southern California Toll Free: 800-255-3485.

MEMBERS OF FIRM

Theodore J. England   Mark A. Nelson
Anson M. Whitfield   Eric J. Kananen
Robert W. Schröeder   Mary E. Schröeder
David W. Tredway   Oscar C. Gonzalez
Robert A. McSorley   Steven K. Perrin
Stuart A. Comis   Andrew S. Hughes
Mitchel B. Kahn   Madison M. Christian
            Kurt Edward Kananen

ASSOCIATES

William J. Kesatie   Linda Kathryn Ash
Melissa E. Cohen   Mark T. Barney

Representative Clients: Seneca Resources Corp. (oil & gas); Cal-Sun Produce Co.; Waste Management of California, Inc; Dah Chong Hong (Honda, Toyota, Mazda, Lexus, Acura, Saturn automobile dealerships); Willamette

(See Next Column)

ENGLAND, WHITFIELD, SCHRÖEDER & TREDWAY L.L.P., *Oxnard—Continued*

Industries; Oxnard Harbor Association of Realtors; Port of Hueneme; Conejo Valley Association of Realtors; Power-One, Inc.

For full biographical listings, see the Martindale-Hubbell Law Directory

---

PALM SPRINGS, Riverside Co.

LAW OFFICES OF HOWARD L. SANGER (AV)

Suite B-102, 400 South Farrell Drive, 92262
Telephone: 619-320-7421
Fax: 619-320-0351
Email: HOWARD@SMLAW.CCMAIL.COMPUSERVE.COM

ASSOCIATE
Christopher S. Manes

For full biographical listings, see the Martindale-Hubbell Law Directory

---

PALO ALTO, Santa Clara Co.

A. DUNCAN KING (AV)

Suite 501, 2471 East Bayshore Road, 94303
Telephone: 800-255-3636; 415-494-6000
FAX: 415-494-3012
Email: adking@ix.netcom.com

For full biographical listings, see the Martindale-Hubbell Law Directory

---

PASADENA, Los Angeles Co.

MARTIN & HUDSON (AV)

350 West Colorado Boulevard, Suite 320, 91105
Telephone: 818-793-8500
Telecopier: 818-793-8779

MEMBERS OF FIRM

Robert B. Martin, Jr.　　　　Boyd D. Hudson

For full biographical listings, see the Martindale-Hubbell Law Directory

---

WILLSEY LAW OFFICES OWNED BY A PROFESSIONAL CORPORATION (AV)

553 S. Marengo Avenue, 91101
Telephone: 818-577-1086
Fax: 818-304-2959

Burke W. Willsey　　　　Daniel P. Willsey (A
　　　　　　　　　　　　　Professional Corporation)

Reference: Sanwa Bank.

For full biographical listings, see the Martindale-Hubbell Law Directory

---

WITTER AND HARPOLE (AV)

Wells Fargo Building, 350 W. Colorado Boulevard, Suite 400, 91105
Telephone: 213-624-1311, 818-440-1111
FAX: 213-620-0430
Email: 102444.2117@compuserve.com
Newport Beach, California Office: Suite 1050, 610 Newport Center Drive.
Telephone: 714-644-7600.
Fax: 714-759-1014.

MEMBERS OF FIRM

Myron E. Harpole　　　　Eugene Harpole (1896-1987)
George G. Witter (1895-1978)　Debra M. Olsen (Resident,
　　　　　　　　　　　　　　　　Newport Beach Office)

OF COUNSEL
James D. Harris (A Professional Corporation)

Reference: Union Bank (Newport Beach, Calif.).

For full biographical listings, see the Martindale-Hubbell Law Directory

---

SACRAMENTO,* Sacramento Co.

LIVINGSTON & MATTESICH, LAW CORPORATION (AV)

1201 K Street, Suite 1100, 95814
Telephone: 916-442-1111
Fax: 916-448-1709
Email: liv-matt@gvn.net

Gene Livingston　　　　Carol Livingston
James M. Mattesich　　　Rebecca M. Ceniceros

Steven P. Belzer　　　　Trisha M. McAlmond

Reference: Bank of California.

For full biographical listings, see the Martindale-Hubbell Law Directory

---

SAN DIEGO,* San Diego Co.

GARRISON ARMSTRONG LAW CORPORATION (AV)

Suite 1300, 401 West A Street, 92101-7988
Telephone: 619-232-1811

Garrison R. Armstrong
LEGAL SUPPORT PERSONNEL
Iris R. Daniel (Legal Assistant)

For full biographical listings, see the Martindale-Hubbell Law Directory

---

FERRIS & BRITTON, A PROFESSIONAL CORPORATION (AV)

1600 First National Bank Center, 401 West A Street, 92101
Telephone: 619-233-3131
Fax: 619-232-9316

Alfred G. Ferris　　　　Tamara K. Fogg
　　　　　　Gary T. Moyer

Representative Clients: Agouron Pharmaceuticals, Inc.; Cox Communications, Inc.; Immuno Pharmaceutics, Inc.; Invitrogen Corporation; Peninsula Bank; Teleport Communications Group; Southwest Airlines.

For Complete List of Firm Personnel, See General Section

For full biographical listings, see the Martindale-Hubbell Law Directory

---

LINDLEY, LAZAR & SCALES, A PROFESSIONAL CORPORATION (AV)

One America Plaza, 600 West Broadway, Suite 1400, 92101-3302
Telephone: 619-234-9181
Fax: 619-234-8475
Email: 104413.1175@compuserve.com

Raymond L. Heidemann
OF COUNSEL
Maurice T. Watson

For Complete List of Firm Personnel, See General Section

For full biographical listings, see the Martindale-Hubbell Law Directory

---

LONNIE G. McGEE (AV)

2470 Union Street, 92101-1320
Telephone: 619-696-5300
FAX: 619-696-7010
Email: lonmcgee@cts.com

For full biographical listings, see the Martindale-Hubbell Law Directory

---

PAGE, POLIN & BUSCH, A PROFESSIONAL CORPORATION (AV)

350 West Ash Street, Suite 900, 92101-3436
Telephone: 619-231-1822
Fax: 619-231-1877
Fax: 619-231-1875
Email: pagepolin@pagepolin.com

Michael E. Busch　　　　Richard W. Page
Kathleen A. Cashman-Kramer　Kenneth D. Polin
Richard L. Moskitis　　　Steven G. Rowles

Rod S. Fiori　　　　　Michael G. Rowles
Dorothy A. Johnson　　　(Not admitted in CA)
Jolene L. Parker　　　　Barry M. Taira

For full biographical listings, see the Martindale-Hubbell Law Directory

---

SELTZER CAPLAN WILKINS & McMAHON, A PROFESSIONAL CORPORATION (AV)

2100 Symphony Towers, 750 B Street, 92101
Telephone: 619-685-3003
Fax: 619-685-3100

David J. Dorne　　　　John H. Alspaugh
　　　　Adrienne Jeffrey

Representative Clients: Chicago Title; Girard Savings Bank; Goodyear Tire & Rubber Co.; W.R. Grace & Co--Conn.; McDonnell-Douglas Corp.; McMillin Communities; Philip Morris Incorporated; Western Financial Savings Bank.

For Complete List of Firm Personnel, See General Section

For full biographical listings, see the Martindale-Hubbell Law Directory

---

LAW FIRM OF DAVID S. ZWEIG (AV)

Oceana Building, 4425 Bayard Street, Suite 200, 92109-4089
Telephone: 619-274-1818
Telefax: 619-274-8535

David S. Zweig

(See Next Column)

LAW FIRM OF DAVID S. ZWEIG—*Continued*

ASSOCIATE

Erin L. McCreary

Representative Clients: Tequila Sauza S.A. de C.V.; Dorians Tijuana S.A. de C.V.; Carlos 'N Charlies Enterprises, Inc.; Dupuis of California, Inc.; Commercial Mexicana S.A. de C.V.

References: Union Bank (San Diego); The RHB Trust Co., Ltd., Cayman Islands; Nevis Services Ltd.

For full biographical listings, see the Martindale-Hubbell Law Directory

---

SAN FRANCISCO,* San Francisco Co.

AVERY & ASSOCIATES (AV)

49 Geary Street, Suite 202, 94108-5727
Telephone: 415-954-4800
Fax: 415-954-4810
Email: LJA@INFOARCH.COM

Luther J. Avery

OF COUNSEL

Mark J. Avery

LEGAL SUPPORT PERSONNEL

Matthew S. Avery

For full biographical listings, see the Martindale-Hubbell Law Directory

---

LAWRENCE V. BROOKES (AV)

Two Rincon Center, 121 Spear Street Suite 301, 94105
Telephone: 415-777-9196
Fax: 415-777-9198

References in Tax Matters: Arkia, Shreveport, Louisiana; Automatic Data Processing, Clifton, New Jersey; Foster Enterprises, Foster City, Calif.; Willamette Industries, Portland, Oregon; U-Haul International, Phoenix, Arizona.

For full biographical listings, see the Martindale-Hubbell Law Directory

---

CHICKERING & GREGORY, A PROFESSIONAL CORPORATION (AV)

615 Battery Street, 94104
Telephone: 415-393-9000
FAX: 415-788-0596
Washington, D.C. Office: 1815 H Street, N.W., Suite 650.
Telephone: 202-463-7456.
Fax: 202-835-0663.

Donald M. Gregory (1897-1991)	Donald L. Field, Jr.
Sherman Chickering (1911-1993)	Putnam Livermore
C. Hayden Ames	Elvis J. Stahr, Jr.
	(Not admitted in CA)

For full biographical listings, see the Martindale-Hubbell Law Directory

---

FELDMAN, WALDMAN & KLINE, A PROFESSIONAL CORPORATION (AV)

3 Embarcadero Center, Suite 2800, 94111
Telephone: 415-981-1300
Fax: 415-981-1350
Email: info@fwk.com
Stockton, California Office: Sperry Building, 146-148 West Weber Avenue.
Telephone: 209-943-2004.
Fax: 209-943-0905.

Murry J. Waldman	Martha Jeanne Shaver
Leland R. Selna, Jr.	(Resident, Stockton Office)
Michael L. Korbholz	Robert Cedric Goodman
Howard M. Wexler	Laura Grad
Patricia S. Mar	William F. Adams
Kenneth W. Jones	Elizabeth A. Thompson
Paul J. Dion	Julie A. Jones
Vern S. Bothwell	David L. Kanel
L.J. Chris Martiniak	Abram S. Feuerstein
	Linda Sorensen

Laura J. Dawson	Dana A. Suntag
Joanne M. Lafreniere	(Resident, Stockton Office)
Paul A. Weiss	Danielle Ochs-Tillotson
	OF COUNSEL
Richard L. Jaeger	Gerald A. Sherwin
	(Resident, Stockton Office)

For full biographical listings, see the Martindale-Hubbell Law Directory

---

GREENE RADOVSKY MALONEY & SHARE LLP (AV)

Four Embarcadero Center, Suite 4000, 94111
Telephone: 415-543-1400
Telecopier: 415-777-4961

(See Next Column)

Luke D. Bailey	Mark S. Hennigh
Thomas M. Feldstein	Graham Maloney
Ronald W. Garrity	Linda L. McCall
Rodney C. Gilmore	Russell D. Pollock
Richard L. Greene	Thomas L. Prestwich
Allen Grossman	Joseph S. Radovsky
	Donald R. Share
	OF COUNSEL
	Lawrence B. Silver

James H. Abrams	Edward I. Kaplan
Stephen Anthony Bonovich	Davia M. Love
Gary R. Bruhns	Veronica K. Phillips
Joel S. Fisch	Dean A. Schlobohm
Giselle Sered Galper	Douglas P. Solomon
Rachel G. Hardie	Laird P. Steverango

Reference: The Bank of California, N.A.

For full biographical listings, see the Martindale-Hubbell Law Directory

---

LOSEY & ASSOCIATES (AV)

650 California Street, 12th Floor, 94108
Telephone: 415-421-3840
Telecopier: 415-421-0737

Michael J. Bollard (1961-1994)	F. Richard Losey
	ASSOCIATES
Daniel J. Leer	Mary L. Symons
	OF COUNSEL
Charles P. Teixeira	Alfred L. Rinaldo, Jr.
	Warren H. Rothman

For full biographical listings, see the Martindale-Hubbell Law Directory

---

MURPHY, PEARSON, BRADLEY & FEENEY, A PROFESSIONAL CORPORATION (AV)

88 Kearny Street, 11th Floor, 94108
Telephone: 415-788-1900
Telecopier: 415-393-8087
Sacramento, California Office: Suite 200, 3600 American River Drive, 95864.
Telephone: 916-483-6074.
Telecopier: 916-483-6088.

Arthur V. Pearson	Gregory A. Bastian
	(Resident, Sacramento Office)

For Complete List of Firm Personnel, See General Section

For full biographical listings, see the Martindale-Hubbell Law Directory

---

SILK, ADLER & COLVIN, A LAW CORPORATION (AV)

Russ Building, Suite 1120, 235 Montgomery Street, 94104
Telephone: 415-421-7555
Fax: 415-421-0712

Thomas Silk	Gregory L. Colvin
Elizabeth Buchalter Adler	Rosemary E. Fei
	Robert A. Wexler
	OF COUNSEL
	Erik D. Dryburgh

For full biographical listings, see the Martindale-Hubbell Law Directory

---

SIMPSON & GIGOUNAS (AV)

A Partnership including A Professional Corporation
One California Street, Suite 2750, 94111
Telephone: 415-391-4900
Fax: 415-296-7894
Sacramento, California Office: 915 University Avenue.
Telephone: 916-447-5152.
Tahoe City, California Office: 210 Grove Street, P.O. Box 5453.
Telephone: 916-583-4711.

MEMBERS OF FIRM

John Gigounas (A Professional Corporation)	Edward B. Simpson

For full biographical listings, see the Martindale-Hubbell Law Directory

---

TAYLOR & FAUST, A PROFESSIONAL CORPORATION (AV)

Suite 2525, One Montgomery Street, 94104
Telephone: 415-421-9535
Fax: 415-956-3231

Samuel Taylor (1906-1995)	Leland H. Faust
	Steven B. Kravitz

For full biographical listings, see the Martindale-Hubbell Law Directory

SAN JOSE, * Santa Clara Co.

OWEN G. FIORE (AV)

Bank of America Building, 101 Park Center Plaza, Suite 1150, 95113
Telephone: 408-293-3616
Facsimile: 408-293-0430

John F. Ramsbacher   Leslie J. Daniels

For full biographical listings, see the Martindale-Hubbell Law Directory

HOPKINS & CARLEY, A LAW CORPORATION (AV)

Fifteenth Floor, 150 Almaden Boulevard, 95113-2089
Telephone: 408-286-9800
Facsimile: 408-998-4790

Leon A. Carley (1908-1984)	Dunham B. Sherer
John F. Hopkins	Anthony J. McCarthy
Robert D. Wenzel	James M. Hager

Charles H. Packer

OF COUNSEL

Clarence A. Kellogg Jr.   Theodore J. Biagini

Jennifer M. Cunneen	Jessica M. Schwedner
H. Katerina Hertzog	Russell K. Smith

For Complete List of Firm Personnel, See General Section

For full biographical listings, see the Martindale-Hubbell Law Directory

MILLER, MORTON, CAILLAT & NEVIS (AV)

50 West San Fernando Street, Suite 1300, 95113-2413
Telephone: 408-292-1765
Telecopier: 408-292-4484

Richard W. Morton (1916-1975)   Charles V. Caillat (1920-1990)
Harvey C. Miller (1906-1993)

MEMBERS OF FIRM

David L. Nevis	Joseph A. Scanlan, Jr.
Francis J. Hughes	Carolyn Tobiason Stuart
Peter A. Kline	William K. Hurley
Stevan C. Adelman	Peter V. Dessau

Eric Mogensen

OF COUNSEL

Nancy F. Symons   Susan L. Sutton
Pamela J. Silberstein

ASSOCIATES

Kathryn E. Barrett	David I. Kornbluh
Katherine S. Pak	Kimberly Holtz MacMillan

Representative Clients: Trammell Crow Residential Services; Joe Kerley Lincoln Mercury Co.; Milligan News Co.; Joseph George Distributors; The Frozen Food Employees Pension Trust; Santa Clara Dental Society; New West Foods; Bay Apartment Communities; Guy F. Atkinson Company; A. Hathaway Co.

For full biographical listings, see the Martindale-Hubbell Law Directory

SANTA ANA, * Orange Co.

FERRUZZO & FERRUZZO (AV)

A Partnership of Professional Corporations
2114 North Broadway, 92706
Telephone: 714-834-9322
Telecopier: 714-834-9358

MEMBERS OF FIRM

Thomas G. Ferruzzo (A Professional Corporation)	James K. Leese (A Professional Corporation)
James J. Ferruzzo (A Professional Corporation)	

ASSOCIATES

John R. Pelle	Maria Ann Newkirk
Dirk E. Petchul	Paul A. Madruga
Gregory J. Ferruzzo	Lisa L. Schultz

OF COUNSEL

M. Susan Watson

For full biographical listings, see the Martindale-Hubbell Law Directory

SANTA BARBARA, * Santa Barbara Co.

GEORGE G. SHORT A PROFESSIONAL CORPORATION (AV)

1421 State Street, Suite A, 93101-2507
Telephone: 805-564-6644
Fax: 805-564-6646
Los Angeles, California Office: 815 Moraga Drive.
Telephone: 310-440-4299.
Telecopier: 805-564-6646.

(See Next Column)

George G. Short

For full biographical listings, see the Martindale-Hubbell Law Directory

VENTURA, * Ventura Co.

FAIRFIELD, STRAUSS, URITZ & KINIGSTEIN, A PROFESSIONAL CORPORATION (AV)

290 Maple Court, Suite 200, 93003
Telephone: 805-644-7458
Fax: 805-644-4325
Email: mail@venturalaw.com *URL:* http://www.venturalaw.com

William D. Fairfield	Curt W. Uritz
Anthony R. Strauss	Terry Kinigstein

Wilfred J. Freeman   Bruce P. Crary

For full biographical listings, see the Martindale-Hubbell Law Directory

COLORADO

COLORADO SPRINGS, * El Paso Co.

WILTON W. COGSWELL, III (AV)

Suite 1020, Alamo Corporate Center, 102 South Tejon Street, 80903
Telephone: 719-473-1448
Facsimile: 719-473-1449
Email: wcogs3@aol.com
Denver, Colorado Office: Suite 2100, World Trade Center. 1675 Broadway.
Telephone: 303-592-4217.
Fax: 303-592-4223. E-Mail: WCOGSWELL@AOL.COM.

OF COUNSEL

Wilton W. Cogswell, IV (Resident, Denver Office)

For full biographical listings, see the Martindale-Hubbell Law Directory

FLYNN MCKENNA WRIGHT & KARSH (AV)

limited liability company
Plaza of the Rockies 111 South Tejon, Suite 202, 80903
Telephone: 719-578-8444
Fax: 719-578-8836

James T. Flynn	Randolph M. Karsh
R. Tim McKenna	Brian T. Murphy
Bruce M. Wright	Michael C. Potarf

Representative Clients: Business News Network, Ic.; National Systems & Research, Inc.; Widefield Homes, Inc.

For full biographical listings, see the Martindale-Hubbell Law Directory

DENVER, * Denver Co.

ATLASS PROFESSIONAL CORPORATION (AV)

2100 East Fourteenth Avenue, 80206-2106
Telephone: 303-377-0707
Fax: 303-321-2655
Email: atlass.com

Theodore B. Atlass

Carol Buchanan Lay

For full biographical listings, see the Martindale-Hubbell Law Directory

BRENMAN KEY & BROMBERG, P.C. (AV)

Mellon Financial Center Suite 1001, 1775 Sherman Street, 80203
Telephone: 303-894-0234
Fax: 303-839-1633

Albert Brenman	Donna A. Key
Thomas R. Bromberg	Steven W. McDonald

Theresa M. Mehringer	George D. Kreye

OF COUNSEL

Heather H. S. Sander	A. Thomas Tenenbaum
D. Elizabeth Wills	Edmund L. Epstein (Inactive)

For full biographical listings, see the Martindale-Hubbell Law Directory

BROWNSTEIN HYATT FARBER & STRICKLAND, P.C. (AV)

Twenty-Second Floor, 410 Seventeenth Street, 80202-4437
Telephone: 303-534-6335
Telecopier: 303-623-1956
Washington, D.C. Office: 601 Pennsylvania Avenue, N.W., Suite 900.
Telephone: 202-434-8377.
Telecopier: 202-393-7864.

(See Next Column)

BROWNSTEIN HYATT FARBER & STRICKLAND P.C.—*Continued*

Michael J. Sternick   John L. Ruppert

Gregory W. Berger   Ellen O. Kauffmann

Representative Clients: Brothers Gourmet Coffees, Inc.; Capital Associates, Inc.; Corporate Express; Coughlin & Company, Inc.; Pacifica Holding Company; Renaissance Cosmetics, Inc.; SunAmerica Inc.; U.S. Home Corporation.

For Complete List of Firm Personnel, See General Section

For full biographical listings, see the Martindale-Hubbell Law Directory

JOHN DEBRUYN LAW OFFICES (AV)

2100 East Fourteenth Avenue, 80206
Telephone: 303-377-0707
Telecopier: 303-321-2655
Email: jdebruyn@usa.net

For full biographical listings, see the Martindale-Hubbell Law Directory

ELROD, KATZ, PREEO, LOOK, MOISON & SILVERMAN, PROFESSIONAL CORPORATION (AV)

Suite 1100, 1120 Lincoln Street, 80203
Telephone: 303-832-1900
Fax: 303-863-0412

Richard B. Elrod	Harley K. Look, Jr.
Michael M. Katz	Peter R. Moison
Robert L. Preeo	Eldon E. Silverman

Jersey M. Green	Kathryn A. Reeves
Richard M. Hess, Jr.	Gilbert R. Egle
Martin J. Green	Timothy Kyle Jordan
Marilyn McWilliams	Brian E. Onorato

OF COUNSEL
Richard P. Rosen

For full biographical listings, see the Martindale-Hubbell Law Directory

GUTHERY & RICKLES, P.C. (AV)

Cherry Creek Plaza II, 650 South Cherry Street Suite 1000, 80222
Telephone: 303-320-5889
Fax: 303-320-5890

Peter C. Guthery   Stephen P. Rickles

A list of Representative Clients that have provided written authorization will be furnished upon request.

For full biographical listings, see the Martindale-Hubbell Law Directory

HOLME ROBERTS & OWEN LLP (AV)

Suite 4100, 1700 Lincoln, 80203
Telephone: 303-861-7000
Telecopier: 303-866-0200
Email: hro@hro.com *URL:* http://www.hro.com
Boulder, Colorado Office: Suite 400, 1401 Pearl Street.
Telephone: 303-444-5955.
Telecopier: 303-444-1063.
Colorado Springs, Colorado Office: Suite 1300, 90 South Cascade Avenue.
Telephone: 719-473-3800.
Telecopier: 719-633-1518.
Salt Lake City, Utah Office: Suite 1100, 111 East Broadway.
Telephone: 801-521-5800.
Telecopier: 801-521-9639.
London, England Office: Mellier House, 26a Albemarle Street.
Telephone: 44-171-499-8776.
Telecopier: 44-171-499-7769.
Moscow, Russia Office: Kosmodamianskaya Nab. #52/1, Suite 9100, 113054.
Telephone: 7095-961-3000.
Telecopier: 7095-961-3001.
Kiev, Ukraine Office: Terestchenkovskaya #19, Suite 2, 252004.
Telephone: 380-44-224-1348.
Telecopier: 380-44-224-4986.

PARTNERS OF FIRM

James E. Bye	Judith L. L. Roberts
Robert J. Welter	(Co-Director, Moscow Office;
Judson W. Detrick	London Office)
Lawrence L. Levin	R. Bruce Johnson
David T. Mitzner	(Salt Lake City Office)
Charles A. Ramunno	Mark K. Buchi
William S. Huff	(Salt Lake City Office)
Donald J. Hopkins	Paul E. Smith (Boulder Office)
Carolyn E. Daniels	Thomas M. James
David K. Detton	(Colorado Springs Office)
(Salt Lake City Office)	McKay Marsden
Steve L. Gaines	(Salt Lake City Office)
(Colorado Springs Office)	David R. Child

(See Next Column)

PARTNERS OF FIRM (Continued)

John R. Wylie	Kevin P. Block (Managing
(Colorado Springs Office)	Partner, Kiev Office)
Stephanie M. Tuthill	Mark M. Hrenya

SPECIAL COUNSEL
Gary R. Thorup (Salt Lake City Office)

ASSOCIATES

Charles B. Bruce, Jr.	Alexander Udovenko
Valery Fedichin (Kiev Office)	(Moscow, Russia Office)
Sherry A. Gonzales	Thomas E. Yearout
Mary C. Gordon	Masahiro Max Yoshimura
(Salt Lake City Office)	Steven P. Young
Michelle M. Rose-Hughes	(Salt Lake City Office)
Nikita O. Sergeyev	
(Moscow, Russia Office)	

For Complete List of Firm Personnel, See General Section

For full biographical listings, see the Martindale-Hubbell Law Directory

JONES & KELLER, A PROFESSIONAL CORPORATION (AV)

Suite 1600, 1625 Broadway, 80202
Telephone: 303-573-1600
Fax: 303-893-6506

Marion F. Jones (1898-1978)	Thomas J. Burke, Jr.
Alec J. Keller (1913-1995)	Samuel E. Wing
Alvin J. Meiklejohn, Jr.	Reid A. Godbolt
Leslie R. Kehl	Rodney D. Knutson
Edward T. Lyons, Jr.	Kevin L. Brown
David E. Driggers	Barry L. Wilkie

Howard R. Hertzberg	Brent Nicholls
David A. Thayer	Michael Brian Cavanaugh
	Nathan D. Simmons

Reference: Colorado State Bank; Union Bank & Trust.

For full biographical listings, see the Martindale-Hubbell Law Directory

LOHF, SHAIMAN & JACOBS, P.C. (AV)

950 South Cherry Street, Suite 900, 80222
Telephone: 303-753-9000
Telecopier: 303-753-9997

Charles H. Jacobs   Moshe Luber
            Robert Shaiman

Reference: Professional Bank.

For full biographical listings, see the Martindale-Hubbell Law Directory

WILLIAM R. MCDONALD, P.C. (AV)

Suite 206, 155 South Madison, 80209-3013
Telephone: 303-321-3271
Fax: 303-320-1577

William R. McDonald

For full biographical listings, see the Martindale-Hubbell Law Directory

SHERMAN & HOWARD L.L.C. (AV)

Attorneys and Counselors at Law
633 Seventeenth Street, Suite 3000, 80202
Telephone: 303-297-2900
Telecopier: 303-298-0940
Colorado Springs, Colorado Office: Suite 1500, 90 South Cascade Avenue, 80903.
Telephone: 719-475-2440.
Las Vegas, Nevada Office: Swendseid & Stern a member in Sherman & Howard L.L.C., 317 Sixth Street, 89101.
Telephone: 702-387-6073.
Reno, Nevada Office: Swendseid & Stern, a member in Sherman & Howard L.L.C., 50 West Liberty Street, Suite 660, 89501.
Telephone: 702-323-1980.

Douglas M. Cain	Cynthia C. Benson
Duane F. Wurzer	Manuel D. Savage
R. Michael Sanchez	Carol V. Berger
David Thomas III	Kathleen A. Odle

Bridget K. Sullivan	J. David Varley
Joseph M. Dencker	(Not admitted in CO)

Representative Clients: Central Bank of Denver, N.A.; Tele-Communications, Inc.; VICORP Restaurants, Inc.; Public Employees' Retirement Assoc.

For Complete List of Firm Personnel, See General Section

For full biographical listings, see the Martindale-Hubbell Law Directory

Denver—Continued

SOLOMON PEARL BLUM & QUINN LLP (AV)

1700 Broadway, Suite 1820, 80290
Telephone: 303-832-6686
Fax: 303-832-6653
Email: SolPearl@aol.com
New York, New York Office: Woolworth Building, 37th Floor, 233 Broadway, 10007.
Charlotte Amalie, St. Thomas, Virgin Islands Affiliated Office: Grunet Stout & Bruch, 24-25 Kongens Gade, P.O. Box 1030, 00804.
Telephone: 809-774-1320.
Fax: 809-774-7839.
Denver, Colorado Affiliated Office: Dufford & Brown, P.C., 1700 Broadway, Suite 1700, 80290.
Telephone: 303-861-8013.
Facsimile: 303-832-3804.

Robert A. Solomon
Clifford R. Pearl
Thomas F. Quinn
William L. Blum
(Not admitted in CO)

For full biographical listings, see the Martindale-Hubbell Law Directory

LAW OFFICES OF JOSEPH H. THIBODEAU, P.C. (AV)

Suite 209, 155 South Madison Street, 80209
Telephone: 303-320-1250
Fax: 303-320-1577

Joseph H. Thibodeau

Kandace C. Gerdes　　　　　　Matthew T. Gehrke

For full biographical listings, see the Martindale-Hubbell Law Directory

ZISMAN AND INGRAHAM, P.C. (AV)

Suite 250, 3773 Cherry Creek Drive North, 80209
Telephone: 303-320-0023
Fax: 303-320-0034

Sanford Zisman　　　　　　James F. Ingraham

For full biographical listings, see the Martindale-Hubbell Law Directory

CONNECTICUT

CHESHIRE, New Haven Co.

WINTERS & FORTE (AV)

Waverly Professional Park, 315 Highland Avenue, Suite 102, P.O. Box 844, 06410
Telephone: 203-272-2927
Fax: 203-271-1222

MEMBERS OF FIRM

David Wayne Winters　　　　　　Michael C. Forte

A List of Representative Clients will be furnished upon request.
References: Bank of Boston, Connecticut; Centerbank; LaFayette American Bank & Trust Co.

For full biographical listings, see the Martindale-Hubbell Law Directory

FAIRFIELD, Fairfield Co.

BRAUNSTEIN & TODISCO, LLC (AV)

One Eliot Place, 06430
Telephone: 203-254-1118
Telecopier: 203-254-2453

Samuel L. Braunstein　　　　　　Amy E. Todisco

Reference: People's Bank.

For full biographical listings, see the Martindale-Hubbell Law Directory

GREENWICH, Fairfield Co.

IVEY, BARNUM & O'MARA, LLC (AV)

Meridian Building, 170 Mason Street, P.O. Box 1689, 06830
Telephone: 203-661-6000
Telecopier: 203-661-9462

MEMBERS OF FIRM

Michael J. Allen
Robert C. Barnum, Jr.
Edward D. Cosden, Jr.
Wilmot L. Harris, Jr.
William I. Haslun II
Michael J. Jones
Edward T. Krumeich, Jr.
Donat C. Marchand
Miles F. McDonald, Jr.
Edwin J. O'Mara, Jr.
Remy A. Rodas
Gregory A. Saum
Lorraine Slavin
Steven B. Steinmetz

(See Next Column)

ASSOCIATES

Paul G. Amicucci
Stephan B. Grozinger
Juerg A. Heim
Jennifer B. Kallenbach
Melissa Townsend Klauberg
Cristin L. Rothfuss
Alan S. Rubenstein
Sheryl L. Sensale
(Not admitted in CT)

OF COUNSEL

James W. Cuminale
Philip R. McKnight
Jennifer D. Port
(Not admitted in CT)

For full biographical listings, see the Martindale-Hubbell Law Directory

HARTFORD, * Hartford Co.

COPP & BERALL, LLP (AV)

55 Farmington Avenue, Suite 703, 06105
Telephone: 860-249-5261
Fax: 860-947-6382

MEMBERS OF FIRM

Frank S. Berall　　　　　　Mark H. Neikrie
Suzanne Brown Walsh

OF COUNSEL

Belton A. Copp

References: Fleet Bank, N.A.; Union Trust Co.; Bank of Boston.

For full biographical listings, see the Martindale-Hubbell Law Directory

SIEGEL, O'CONNOR, SCHIFF & ZANGARI, P.C. (AV)

150 Trumbull Street, 06103
Telephone: 860-727-8900
New Haven, Connecticut Office: 171 Orange Street, P.O. Drawer 906.
Telephone: 203-789-0001.

John W. Beck (Resident)
Gregory J. Bezz (Resident, New Haven, Connecticut Office)
Carole Williams Briggs (Resident)
Robert F. Cohn (Resident, New Haven, Connecticut Office)
Peter D. Hershman (Resident, New Haven, Connecticut Office)
Robert J. Percy (Resident)
Mario J. Zangari (Resident, New Haven, Connecticut Office)

Christine A. Barker (Resident, New Haven, Connecticut Office)
David G. Call (Resident)
Oscar M. Parente (Resident, New Haven, Connecticut Office)

For full biographical listings, see the Martindale-Hubbell Law Directory

SOROKIN SOROKIN GROSS HYDE & WILLIAMS P.C. (AV)

One Corporate Center, 06103
Telephone: 860-525-6645
Fax: 860-522-1781
Simsbury, Connecticut Office: 730 Hopmeadow Street.
Telephone: 860-651-9348.
Rocky Hill, Connecticut Office: 2360 Main Street.
Telephone: 860-563-9305.
Fax: 860-529-6931.

Morris W. Banks　　　　　　Charles R. Moore, Jr.
Barrie K. Wetstone

Sharon Kowal Freilich

For Complete List of Firm Personnel, See General Section

For full biographical listings, see the Martindale-Hubbell Law Directory

NEW HAVEN, * New Haven Co.

BERGMAN, HOROWITZ & REYNOLDS, P.C. (AV)

157 Church Street, 19th Floor, P.O. Box 426, 06502
Telephone: 203-789-1320
Fax: 203-785-8127
Email: mailbox@taxlawyers.com *URL:* http://www.taxlawyers.com
New York, N.Y. Office: 499 Park Avenue, 26th Floor.
Telephone: 212-688-4150.

Stanley N. Bergman
Robert H. Horowitz
David L. Reynolds
Paul L. Behling
Kenneth N. Musen
William C. G. Swift, Jr.
Richard J. Klein
James Russell Brockway
Bruce I. Judelson
David A. Ringold
Kathryn Harner Smith
Donald S. Hendel
Joy M. Miyasaki
Paul M. Roy

Louis R. Piscatelli
James G. Dattaro
Edward A. Renn
Tina E. Albright
Jay F. Krause
Christopher J. Galuppo
Jay H. Rubinstein
(Not admitted in CT)
David M. Hryck
Margaret M. Murphy

For full biographical listings, see the Martindale-Hubbell Law Directory

New Haven—Continued

SIEGEL, O'CONNOR, SCHIFF & ZANGARI, P.C. (AV)

171 Orange Street P.O. Drawer 906, 06510
Telephone: 203-789-0001
Hartford, Connecticut Office: 150 Trumbull Street.
Telephone: 860-727-8900.

John W. Beck (Resident, Hartford, Connecticut Office)	Robert F. Cohn (Resident)
Gregory J. Bezz (Resident)	Peter D. Hershman (Resident)
Carole Williams Briggs (Resident, Hartford, Connecticut Office)	Robert J. Percy (Resident, Hartford, Connecticut Office)
	Mario J. Zangari (Resident)

Christine A. Barker (Resident)	Oscar M. Parente (Resident)
David G. Call (Resident, Hartford, Connecticut Office)	

For full biographical listings, see the Martindale-Hubbell Law Directory

SOUTHPORT, Fairfield Co.

BRODY AND OBER, P.C. (AV)

135 Rennell Drive, P.O. Box 572, 06490-0572
Telephone: 203-259-7405
Fax: 203-255-8572

Charles S. Brody (1894-1976)	S. Giles Payne
Seth O. L. Brody	William J. Britt
Stanley B. Garrell	Barbara S. Miller
Frank F. Ober	Ronald B. Noren

Diane F. Martucci	Seth L. Cooper
	Douglas R. Brown

OF COUNSEL

James M. Thorburn	John F. Merchant

For full biographical listings, see the Martindale-Hubbell Law Directory

STAMFORD, Fairfield Co.

WOFSEY, ROSEN, KWESKIN & KURIANSKY (AV)

600 Summer Street, 06901
Telephone: 203-327-2300
Fax: 203-967-9273

MEMBERS OF FIRM

Abraham Wofsey (1915-1944)	Edward M. Kweskin
Michael Wofsey (1927-1951)	David M. Cohen
David M. Rosen (1926-1967)	Marshall Goldberg
Julius B. Kuriansky (1910-1992)	Stephen A. Finn
Monroe Silverman	Judith Rosenberg
Emanuel Margolis	Mark H. Henderson
Howard C. Kaplan	Steven D. Grushkin
Anthony R. Lorenzo	Matthew J. Forstadt

OF COUNSEL

Saul Kwartin	Sydney C. Kweskin (Retired)

ASSOCIATES

Joseph Brachfeld	Eric M. Higgins
John J.L. Chobor	Valerie E. Maze
Steven M. Frederick	Randall M. Skigen
Joy A. Katz	Peter J. Schaffer
Galit Kierkut	Robert W. Finke

Representative Clients: Banque Paribas; Benenson Realty; Cellular Information Systems, Inc.; The Chase Manhattan Bank; First County Bank; Hartford Provision Co.; Louis Dreyfus Corp.; Norwalk Federation of Teachers; People's Bank; Ridgeway Shopping Center.

For full biographical listings, see the Martindale-Hubbell Law Directory

WESTPORT, Fairfield Co.

BLAZZARD, GRODD & HASENAUER, P.C. (AV)

943 Post Road East, P.O. Box 5108, 06881
Telephone: 203-226-7866
Telecopier: 203-454-4855
Hollywood, Florida Office: Suite 213, Oceanwalk Mall, 101 North Ocean Drive, 33019.
Telephone: 954-920-4864.
Facsimile: 954-920-6902. E-Mail: BGHFL@AOL.COM

Norse N. Blazzard	William E. Hasenauer
Leslie E. Grodd	Raymond A. O'Hara, III
Judith A. Hasenauer	Lynn Korman Stone
	Maureen M. Murphy

For full biographical listings, see the Martindale-Hubbell Law Directory

LEVETT, ROCKWOOD & SANDERS, PROFESSIONAL CORPORATION (AV)

33 Riverside Avenue, P.O. Box 5116, 06881
Telephone: 203-222-0885
Telecopier: 203-226-8025

David R. Levett	Sharon M. Schweitzer
John Sanders	Barbara A. Young
B. Lance Sauerteig	Steven M. Siegelaub
Madeleine F. Grossman	Marc J. Kurzman
James M. Barton	Suzanne B. Albani
Judy A. Rabkin	Peter H. Struzzi
Dorit Schutzengel Heimer	Edward B. Chansky
	Cheryl L. Johnson

OF COUNSEL

William O. Rockwood, Jr.

Robin K. Higgins	Ernest C. Mysogland
	Patricia D. Weitzman

Representative Clients: Bankers Trust Company; Cannondale Corp.; Caradon, Inc.; Electrolux Corporation; Exxon Chemical Corporation; HealthSouth Corp.; Heyman Properties; Hospital of Saint Raphael; Marketing Corporation of America; St. Vincent's Medical Center.

For full biographical listings, see the Martindale-Hubbell Law Directory

STUART A. MCKEEVER (AV)

155 Post Road, East, 06880
Telephone: 203-227-4756
Fax: 203-454-2031

Reference: Fleet Bank.

For full biographical listings, see the Martindale-Hubbell Law Directory

RONALD L. SHEIMAN (AV)

1804 Post Road East, 06880
Telephone: 203-259-0599
Telecopier: 203-255-2570

For full biographical listings, see the Martindale-Hubbell Law Directory

DELAWARE

WILMINGTON,* New Castle Co.

MORRIS, NICHOLS, ARSHT & TUNNELL (AV)

1201 North Market Street, P.O. Box 1347, 19899-1347
Telephone: 302-658-9200
Telecopier: 302-658-3989

MEMBERS OF FIRM

Richard L. Sutton	Donald F. Parsons, Jr.
Johannes R. Krahmer	Jack B. Blumenfeld
O. Francis Biondi	Donald Nelson Isken
Lewis S. Black, Jr.	Donald E. Reid
Paul P. Welsh	Denison H. Hatch, Jr.
William O. LaMotte, III	Thomas C. Grimm
Douglas E. Whitney	Kenneth J. Nachbar
William H. Sudell, Jr.	Andrew M. Johnston
Martin P. Tully	Mary B. Graham
Thomas Reed Hunt, Jr.	Michael Houghton
A. Gilchrist Sparks, III	Matthew B. Lehr
Richard D. Allen	John S. McDaniel
David Ley Hamilton	Thomas R. Pulsifer
John F. Johnston	Jon E. Abramczyk
Walter C. Tuthill	Alan J. Stone
	Louis G. Hering

ASSOCIATES

Rachel A. Dwares	Jeffrey R. Wolters
Frederick H. Alexander	Kendra S. Baker
R. Judson Scaggs, Jr.	Maryellen Noreika
William M. Lafferty	David J. Teklits
Andrea L. Rocanelli	S. Mark Hurd
Karen Jacobs Louden	Lucinda Cole Cucuzzella
Karen L. Pascale	(Not admitted in DE)
Elaine C. Reilly	Lisa K. Crossland
Donna L. Culver	(Not admitted in DE)
Julia Heaney	Stanford L. Stevenson, III
Jonathan I. Lessner	Katherine Randolph
Lisa B. Baeurle	Witherspoon
Robert J. Dehney	J. Andrew Huffman
(Not admitted in DE)	(Not admitted in DE)
	Derek C. Abbott

(See Next Column)

MORRIS, NICHOLS, ARSHT & TUNNELL, *Wilmington—Continued*

COUNSEL

S. Samuel Arsht	Hugh M. Morris (1878-1966)
Andrew B. Kirkpatrick, Jr.	Alexander L. Nichols
David A. Drexler	(1906-1985)
Walter L. Pepperman, II	James M. Tunnell, Jr.
S. Maynard Turk	(1910-1986)

Representative Clients: The Coca Cola Co.; Delaware River and Bay Authority; Ford Motor Co.; J.P. Morgan Delaware; Longwood Foundation, Inc.; Rollins, Inc.; Texaco Inc.

For full biographical listings, see the Martindale-Hubbell Law Directory

---

POTTER ANDERSON & CORROON (AV)

350 Delaware Trust Building, P.O. Box 951, 19899-0951
Telephone: 302-984-6000
FAX: 302-658-1192
URL: HTTP://ATTYS.PACDELAWARE.COM

MEMBERS OF FIRM

Leonard S. Togman	David J. Garrett
	Mary E. Copper

ASSOCIATE

Scott E. Waxman

Representative Clients: Eastman Chemical Products, Inc.; Aramco Services Company; Republic New York Corporation.

For Complete List of Firm Personnel, See General Section

For full biographical listings, see the Martindale-Hubbell Law Directory

---

RICHARDS, LAYTON & FINGER, P.A. (AV)

One Rodney Square, P.O. Box 551, 19899
Telephone: 302-658-6541
Telecopier: 302-658-6548

Thomas P. Sweeney	Julian H. Baumann, Jr.
Richard G. Bacon	W. Donald Sparks, II

General Counsel for: Wilmington Trust Co.
Local Counsel for: General Motors Corp.; Shell Oil Co.; Aetna Group; Dean Witter Reynolds, Inc.; Gulf & Western Industries Inc.

For Complete List of Firm Personnel, See General Section

For full biographical listings, see the Martindale-Hubbell Law Directory

---

SCHLUSSER & REIVER, P.A. (AV)

1700 West 14th Street, 19806
Telephone: 302-655-8181
Fax: 302-655-8190

Robert E. Schlusser	Joanna Reiver

John A. Ciccarone

For full biographical listings, see the Martindale-Hubbell Law Directory

---

WILLIAMS, HERSHMAN & WISLER, P.A. (AV)

Suite 600, One Commerce Center, Twelfth and Orange Streets, P.O. Box 511, 19899-0511
Telephone: 302-575-0873
Telecopier: 302-575-1642

David Nicol Williams	Jeffrey C. Wisler
Douglas M. Hershman	Barbara Snapp Danberg

References: Wilmington Trust Co.; PNC Bank.

For full biographical listings, see the Martindale-Hubbell Law Directory

---

DISTRICT OF COLUMBIA

WASHINGTON, D.C. Co.

---

* indicates certain Bar Register subscribers, in cities of comparable size and importance, who maintain an additional office in Washington, D.C. and who have arranged for representation as a part of the Washington, D.C. listings that follow

---

ALEXANDER, BEARDEN, HAIRSTON & MARKS, LLP (AV)

Limited Liability Partnership
2021 L Street, N.W., Suite 300, 20036
Telephone: 202-293-3700
Fax: 202-293-7359
Silver Spring, Maryland Office: Lee Plaza, Suite 805, 8601 Georgia Avenue, 20910.
Telephone: 301-589-2222.
Facsimile: 301-539-2523.

(See Next Column)

New York, New York Office: 330 Madison Avenue, 36th Floor.
Telephone: 212-808-0008.
Fax: 212-599-1028.

Koteles Alexander

Reference: Riggs National Bank of Washington, D.C.

For full biographical listings, see the Martindale-Hubbell Law Directory

---

★ BAKER & BOTTS, L.L.P. (AV)

A Registered Limited Liability Partnership
The Warner, 1299 Pennsylvania Avenue, N.W., 20004-2400
Telephone: 202-639-7700
Fax: 202-639-7832
Email: postmaster @ bakerbotts.com
Houston, Texas Office: One Shell Plaza, 910 Louisiana.
Telephone: 713-229-1234.
Austin, Texas Office: 1600 San Jacinto Center, 98 San Jacinto Boulevard.
Telephone: 512-322-2500.
Dallas, Texas Office: 2001 Ross Avenue.
Telephone: 214-953-6500.
New York, New York Office: 599 Lexington Avenue.
Telephone: 212-705-5000.
Moscow, Russian Federation Office: 10 ul. Bolshaya Dmitrovka (formerly Pushkinskaya), 103031.
Telephone: 7095/921-5300 (Local); 7501/929-7070 (International).

MEMBERS OF FIRM

James A. Baker IV	O. Donaldson Chapoton
	(Not admitted in DC)

ASSOCIATES

Jane Boland Keough	Tamar C. Snyder

For Complete List of Firm Personnel, See General Section

For full biographical listings, see the Martindale-Hubbell Law Directory

---

BAKER & HOSTETLER (AV)

Washington Square, Suite 1100, 1050 Connecticut Avenue, N.W., 20036-5304
Telephone: 202-861-1500
In Cleveland, Ohio: 3200 National City Center, 1900 East Ninth Street.
Telephone: 216-621-0200.
In Columbus, Ohio: Capitol Square, Suite 2100, 65 East State Street.
Telephone: 614-228-1541.
In Denver, Colorado: 303 East 17th Avenue, Suite 1100.
Telephone: 303-861-0600.
In Houston, Texas: 1000 Louisiana, Suite 2000.
Telephone: 713-751-1600.
In Long Beach, California: 300 Oceangate, Suite 620.
Telephone: 310-432-2827.
In Los Angeles, California: 600 Wilshire Boulevard.
Telephone: 213-624-2400.
In Orlando, Florida: SunBank Center, Suite 2300, 200 South Orange Avenue.
Telephone: 305-841-1111.
In College Park, Maryland: 9658 Baltimore Boulevard, Suite 206.
Telephone: 301-441-2781.
In Alexandria, Virginia: 437 North Lee Street.
Telephone: 703-549-1294.
In San Francisco, California: One Sansome Street, Suite 2000.
Telephone: 415-951-4705.

PARTNERS

William F. Conroy	H. Karl Zeswitz, Jr.

RETIRED PARTNER

Harlan Pomeroy

For Complete List of Firm Personnel, See General Section

For full biographical listings, see the Martindale-Hubbell Law Directory

---

★ BALLARD SPAHR ANDREWS & INGERSOLL (AV)

Suite 900 East, 555 13th Street, N.W., 20004-1112
Telephone: 202-383-8800
Fax: 202-383-8877
Philadelphia, Pennsylvania Office: 1735 Market Street, 51st Floor.
Telephone: 215-665-8500.
Fax: 215-864-8999.
Harrisburg, Pennsylvania Office: 105 North Front Street.
Telephone: 717-236-3333.
Fax: 717-236-3884.
Denver, Colorado Office: Seventeenth Street Plaza Building, Suite 2300, 1225 17th Street.
Telephone: 303-292-2400.
Fax: 303-296-3956.
Salt Lake City, Utah Office: One Utah Center, 201 South Main Street, Suite 1200.
Telephone: 801-531-3000.
Fax: 801-531-3001.
Baltimore, Maryland Office: 300 East Lombard Street, 19th Floor.
Telephone: 410-528-5600.
Fax: 410-528-5650.

(See Next Column)

BALLARD SPAHR ANDREWS & INGERSOLL—*Continued*

Camden, New Jersey Office: 800 Hudson Square, 5th Floor.
Telephone: 609-541-5577.
Fax: 609-541-8272.

Frederic L. Ballard, Jr.   Charles S. Henck

Deborah A. Wisnowski

For Complete List of Firm Personnel, See General Section

For full biographical listings, see the Martindale-Hubbell Law Directory

THE LAW OFFICES OF SHELTON M. BINSTOCK (AV)

1140 Connecticut Avenue, N.W., Suite 703, 20036
Telephone: 202-785-1111
Telecopier: 202-293-1471
Chevy Chase, Maryland Office: 5335 Wisconsin Avenue, Suite 440.
Telephone: 301-656-7646.

David B. Torchinsky
OF COUNSEL
James E. Secrist

For full biographical listings, see the Martindale-Hubbell Law Directory

CAPLIN & DRYSDALE, CHARTERED (AV)

One Thomas Circle, N.W., 20005
Telephone: 202-862-5000
Cable Address: "Capdale"
Telex: 904001 CAPL UR WSH
Fax: 202-429-3301
New York, N.Y. Office: 399 Park Avenue.
Telephone: 212-319-7125.
Fax: 212-644-6755.

Mortimer M. Caplin	Douglas D. Drysdale
Robert A. Klayman	Thomas A. Troyer
Ralph A. Muoio	David N. Webster
Elihu Inselbuch	H. David Rosenbloom
(Resident, New York Office)	Peter Van N. Lockwood
Ronald B. Lewis	Cono R. Namorato
Richard W. Skillman	Daniel B. Rosenbaum
Patricia G. Lewis	Richard E. Timbie
Bernard S. Bailor	Graeme W. Bush
Stafford Smiley	Albert G. Lauber, Jr.
Sally A. Regal	Scott D. Michel
Julie W. Davis	Kent A. Mason
Carl S. Kravitz	Trevor W. Swett III
Robert A. Boisture	Robert E. Culbertson
James Sottile, IV	Charles T. Plambeck
Harry J. Hicks, III	James E. Salles
Milton Cerny	Craig A. Sharon
Paul G. Cellupica	Matthew W. Frank
Michael T. Doran	Christian R. Pastore
Nathan D. Finch	(Not admitted in DC)
Jessica L. Goldstein	Elizabeth M. Sellers
Laura J. Kerrigan	Douglas N. Varley
	(Not admitted in DC)

OF COUNSEL

Robert H. Elliott, Jr.	Myron C. Baum
Vivian L. Cavalieri	C. Sanders McNew
Ann C. McMillan	(Resident, New York Office)

Janne G. Gallagher

For full biographical listings, see the Martindale-Hubbell Law Directory

CROSS, MURPHY, SMUCK & HOUSTON (AV)

1350 Connecticut Avenue, N.W., Suite 300, 20036
Telephone: 202-393-8668
Telecopier: 202-833-2351
Email: anwalt1350@aol.com

MEMBERS OF FIRM

John W. Cross (1902-1971)	John C. Smuck
James Russell Murphy	Stuart E. Houston
(1905-1986)	

Reference: Crestar Bank, N.A.

For full biographical listings, see the Martindale-Hubbell Law Directory

DOW, LOHNES & ALBERTSON, PLLC (AV)

1200 New Hampshire Avenue, N.W. Suite 800, 20036-6802
Telephone: 202-776-2000
Facsimile: 202-776-2222
Email: postmaster@dla.com *URL:* http://www.dlalaw.com
Atlanta, Georgia Office: One Ravinia Drive, Suite 1600.
Telephone: 770-901-8800.
Telecopier: 770-901-8874.

(See Next Column)

MEMBERS OF THE FIRM

Corinne M. Antley	J. Michael Hines
Richard L. Braunstein	John C. Jost
Linda A. Fritts	Paul R. Lang
Joyce Trimble Gwadz	Bernard J. Long, Jr.
David A. Hildebrandt	Richard P. McHugh

John D. Ward

J. Clark Armitage	Michael A. Hepburn
Kevin P. Brandon	Stephen E. Lopez
Joan M. Corcoran	(Not admitted in DC)
(Not admitted in DC)	Stephanie M. Loughlin
Terri L. Evans	James R. Saxenian
(Not admitted in DC)	Karen M. Wheeler
	(Not admitted in DC)

For Complete List of Firm Personnel, See General Section

For full biographical listings, see the Martindale-Hubbell Law Directory

* FRIED, FRANK, HARRIS, SHRIVER & JACOBSON (AV)

A Partnership including Professional Corporations
Suite 800, 1001 Pennsylvania Avenue, N.W., 20004-2505
Telephone: 202-639-7000
Cable Address: "Steric Washington"
Telex: 892406
Telecopy Rapifax: 202-639-7008
Zap Mail: 202-338-0110
Email: postmaster@ffhsj.com
New York, New York Office: One New York Plaza.
Telephone: 212-859-8000.
Cable Address: "Steric New York." W.U. Int.
Telex: 620223. W.U. Int.
Telex: 662119. W.U. Domestic: 128173.
Telecopier: 212-859-4000 (Dex 6200).
Los Angeles, California Office: 725 South Figueroa Street.
Telephone: 213- 689-5800.
London, England Office: 4 Chiswell Street, London EC1Y 4UP.
Telephone: 011-44-171-972-9600.
Fax: 011-44-171-972-9602.
Paris, France Office: 7, Rue Royale, 75008.
Telephone: (+331) 40-17-04-04.
Fax: (+331) 40-17-08-30.

WASHINGTON, D.C. PARTNERS

Peter V. Z. Cobb	Alan S. Kaden
(Not admitted in DC)	

OF COUNSEL
Martin D. Ginsburg (P.C.)

For Complete List of Firm Personnel, See General Section

For full biographical listings, see the Martindale-Hubbell Law Directory

GROOM AND NORDBERG, CHARTERED (AV)

1701 Pennsylvania Avenue, N.W., Suite 1200, 20006
Telephone: 202-857-0620
Telecopier: 202-659-4503

Theodore R. Groom	William G. Schiffbauer
Carl A. Nordberg, Jr.	Charles W. Sherman, Jr.
Robert B. Harding	Thomas F. Fitzgerald
Louis T. Mazawey	William J. Flanagan
Michael F. Kelleher	Lonie Hassel
Irene Price	Linda K. Shore
Gary M. Ford	Thomas S. Gigot
Daniel Horowitz	Holly K. Hemphill
Robert P. Gallagher	Robin L. Greenhouse
Stephen M. Saxon	Ian D. Lanoff
Douglas W. Ell	Lynda Joy Striegel
William F. Hanrahan	Brenda R. Viehe-Naess
John P. McAllister	William M. Evans
Alan L. Fischl	Andrée M. St. Martin
(Not admitted in DC)	Jon W. Breyfogle
	(Not admitted in DC)

NON-ATTORNEY MEMBER
Peter E. Holmes
COUNSEL

John F. Murray	David W. Powell
Lincoln D. Weed	Edward B. Horahan III
Michael A. Thrasher	
(Not admitted in DC)	

Steven D. Jensen	Mark L. Lofgren
(Not admitted in DC)	(Not admitted in DC)
Regina M. Pizzonia	Maria O'Toole Jones
(Not admitted in DC)	Edward R. Horkan
Roberta J. Ufford	J. René Toadvine
Kevin M. O'Toole	Angela C. Montez
L. Richard Winchester	(Not admitted in DC)
(Not admitted in DC)	Brigen Lee Winters

(See Next Column)

GROOM AND NORDBERG CHARTERED, *Washington—Continued*

Mary Ann Dominy Edgar
Carl R. Erdmann
  (Not admitted in DC)
Kathryn A. English

Patrick J. Morgan
  (Not admitted in DC)
Elizabeth Thomas Dold
  (Not admitted in DC)

LEGAL SUPPORT PERSONNEL
CONSULTANTS
Jill Leonhardt

FINANCIAL ECONOMIST
Stephen C. Oakley

For full biographical listings, see the Martindale-Hubbell Law Directory

---

HOGAN & HARTSON L.L.P. (AV)

Columbia Square, 555 13th Street, N.W., 20004-1109
Telephone: 202-637-5600
Telex: 89-2757
Cable Address: "Hogander Washington"
Fax: 202-637-5910
Email: HHINFO@DC4.HHLAW.COM
Brussels, Belgium Office: Avenue des Arts 41, 1040.
Telephone: (32.2) 505.09.11.
Fax: (32.2) 505.09.96.
Budapest, Hungary Office: Bank Center, Granite Tower, 9th Floor, 1944 Budapest, Hungary.
Telephone: (36-1) 302-9050.
Fax: (36-1) 302-9060.
London, England Office: 21 Garlick Hill, EC4V 2AU.
Telephone: (44 171) 815 1200.
Fax: (44 171) 329 0299.
Moscow, Russia Office: 33/2 Usacheva Street, Building 3, 119048.
Telephone: (7095) 245-5190. Int'l
Telephone: (7501-907-0451).
Fax: (7095) 245-5192.
Fax: (7501) 907-0462 (International).
Paris, France (Affiliated Office): Cariddi, Mee, Rué, Avocats Associés à la Cour de Paris, 12, rue de la Paix, 75002.
Telephone: (33-1) 42.61.57.71.
Fax: (33-1) 42.61.79.21.
Prague, Czech Republic Office: Opletalova 37, 110 00.
Telephone: (42-2) 2422-9009.
Fax: (42-2) 2421-5105.
Warsaw, Poland Office: Marszalkowska 6/6, 00-590.
Telephone: (48 22) 628 0201; Int'l (48) 3912 1413.
Fax: (48 22) 628 7787; Int'l (48) 3912 1511.
Baltimore, Maryland Office: 111 South Calvert Street, 16th Floor.
Telephone: 410-659-2700.
Fax: 410-539-6981.
Bethesda, Maryland Office: Two Democracy Center, Suite 720, 6903 Rockledge Drive.
Telephone: 301-564-5000.
Fax: 301-493-5169.
Colorado Springs, Colorado Office: Two North Cascade Avenue, Suite 1300.
Telephone: 719-448-5900.
Fax: 719-448-5922.
Denver, Colorado Office: One Tabor Center, Suite 1500, 1200 Seventeenth Street.
Telephone: 303-899-7300.
Fax: 303-899-7333.
McLean, Virginia Office: 8300 Greensboro Drive.
Telephone: 703-848-2600.
Fax: 703-448-7650.

MEMBERS OF FIRM

Deborah Taylor Ashford
Sara-Ann Determan
Prentiss E. Feagles
Robert H. Kapp
Timothy A. Lloyd
H. Todd Miller
William L. Neff

Nancy Doerr O'Neil (Not admitted in DC; Washington, D.C. and Baltimore, Maryland Offices)
William C. Schmidt
Howard S. Silver
John S. Stanton

COUNSEL
Scott R. Lilienthal

OF COUNSEL
Seymour S. Mintz

ASSOCIATES

Edward S. Desmarais, Jr.
Robert Krasnodebski (Resident, Warsaw, Poland Office)
Mark L. Landis
  (Not admitted in DC)

Scott D. McClure
Lisa L. Poole
David A. Winter

For Complete List of Firm Personnel, See General Section

For full biographical listings, see the Martindale-Hubbell Law Directory

---

IVINS, PHILLIPS & BARKER, CHARTERED (AV)

Suite 600, 1700 Pennsylvania Avenue, N.W., 20006
Telephone: 202-393-7600
Fax: 202-393-7601; 347-4256
Email: IPB@mindspring.com

H. Stewart Dunn, Jr.
Carroll J. Savage
Eric R. Fox
William L. Sollee
Carol K. Nickel
Leslie Jay Schneider
Robert H. Wellen

Kevin P. O'Brien
Michael F. Solomon
Daniel B. Stone
Patrick J. Smith
Michael R. Huffstetler
Laurie E. Keenan
Peter M. Daub

Jeffrey E. Moeller

Steven H. Witmer
Rosina B. Barker
Claude B. Stansbury

Robert P. Hanson
Sheryl E. McAfee
Hamish P.M. Hume

OF COUNSEL

Jay W. Glasmann

Joseph E. McAndrews

For full biographical listings, see the Martindale-Hubbell Law Directory

---

★ JONES, DAY, REAVIS & POGUE (AV)

Metropolitan Square, 1450 G Street, N.W., 20005-2088
Telephone: 202-879-3939
Cable Address: "Attorneys Washington"
Telex: W.U. (Domestic) 89-2410 ATTORNEYS WASH (International) 64363 ATTORNEYS WASH
Telecopier: 202-737-2832
In Atlanta, Georgia: 3500 One Peachtree Center, 303 Peachtree Street, N.E.
Telephone: 404-521-3939.
Cable Address: "Attorneys Atlanta".
Telex: 54-2711.
Telecopier: 404-581-8330.
In Brussels, Belgium: Avenue Louise 480, 7th Floor, B-1050 Brussels.
Telephone: 32-2-645-14-11.
Telecopier: 32-2-645-14-45.
In Chicago, Illinois: 77 West Wacker.
Telephone: 312-782-3939.
Telecopier: 312-782-8585.
In Cleveland, Ohio: North Point, 901 Lakeside Avenue.
Telephone: 216-586-3939.
Cable Address: "Attorneys Cleveland."
Telex: 980389.
Telecopier: 216-579-0212.
In Columbus, Ohio: 1900 Huntington Center.
Telephone: 614-469-3939.
Cable Address: "Attorneys Columbus."
Telecopier: 614-461-4198.
In Dallas, Texas: 2300 Trammell Crow Center, 2001 Ross Avenue.
Telephone: 214-220-3939.
Cable Address: "Attorneys Dallas."
Telex: 730852.
Telecopier: 214-969-5100.
In Frankfurt, Germany: Triton Haus, Bockenheimer Landstrasse 42, 60323 Frankfurt am Main.
Telephone: 49-69-9726-3939.
Telecopier: 49-69-9726-3993.
In Geneva, Switzerland: 20, rue de Candolle.
Telephone: 41-22-320-2339.
Telecopier: 41-22-320-1232.
In Hong Kong: 29th Floor, Entertainment Building, 30 Queen's Road Central.
Telephone: 852-2526-6895.
Telecopier: 852-2868-5871.
In Irvine, California: 2603 Main Street, Suite 900 .
Telephone: 714-851-3939.
Telex: 194911 Lawyers LSA.
Telecopier: 714-553-7539.
In London, England: One Mount Street.
Telephone: 44-71-493-9361.
Cable Address: "Surgoe London WI."
Telecopier: 44-71-493-9666.
In Los Angeles, California: 555 West Fifth Street, Suite 4600.
Telephone: 213-489-3939.
Telex: 181439 UD.
Telecopier: 213-243-2539.
In New Delhi, India: Pathak & Associates, 13th Floor, Dr. Gopal Das Bhaven, 28 Barakhamba Road.
Telephone: 91-11-373-8793.
Telecopier: 91-11-335-3761.
In New York, New York: 599 Lexington Avenue.
Telephone: 212-326-3939.
Cable Address: "JONESDAY NEWYORK."
Telex: 237013 JDRP UR.
Telecopier: 212-755-7306.
In Paris, France: 62, rue du Faubourg Saint-Honore.
Telephone: 33-1-44-71-3939.
Cable Address: "Surgoe Paris."
Telex: 290156 Surgoe.
Telecopier: 33-1-49-24-0471.

(See Next Column)

JONES, DAY, REAVIS & POGUE—*Continued*

In Pittsburgh, Pennsylvania: 500 Grant Street, 31st Floor.
Telephone: 412-391-3939.
Cable Address: "Attorneys Pittsburgh".
Telecopier: 412-394-7959.
In Riyadh, Saudi Arabia: Law Offices of Saud M.A. Shawwaf, P.O. Box 22166.
Telephone: (966-1) 462-8866.
Telex: 401831 SAUCON SJ.
Telecopier: (966-1) 462-9001.
In Taipai, Taiwan: 8th Floor, 2 Tun Hwa South Road, Section 2.
Telephone: (886-2) 704-6808.
Telecopier: (886-2) 704-6791.
In Tokyo, Japan: Toranomon MT Building, 4th Floor, 10-3, Toranomon 3-Chome, Minato-Ku, Tokyo 105, Japan.
Telephone: 81-3-3433-3939.
Telecopier: 81-3-5401-2725.

MEMBERS OF FIRM IN WASHINGTON, D.C.

Joseph S. Iannucci	Lester W. Droller
James T. O'Hara	Raymond J. Wiacek

ASSOCIATES

Charles V. Stewart	Laura Sruggs Douglas
Candace A. Ridgway	Martin S. Rowley

For Complete List of Firm Personnel, See General Section

For full biographical listings, see the Martindale-Hubbell Law Directory

---

* McDERMOTT, WILL & EMERY (AV)

A Partnership including Professional Corporations
1850 K Street, N.W., 20006-2296
Telephone: 202-887-8000
Facsimile: 202-778-8087
URL: http://www.mwe.com
Chicago, Illinois Office: 227 West Monroe Street.
Telephone: 312-372-2000.
Facsimile: 312-984-7700.
Boston, Massachusetts Office: 75 State Street, Suite 1700.
Telephone: 617-345-5000.
Facsimile: 617-345-5077.
Miami, Florida Office: 201 South Biscayne Boulevard.
Telephone: 305-358-3500.
Facsimile: 305-347-6500.
Los Angeles, California Office: 2049 Century Park East.
Telephone: 310-277-4110.
Facsimile: 310-277-4730.
Newport Beach, California Office: 1301 Dove Street, Suite 500.
Telephone: 714-851-0633.
Facsimile: 714-851-9348.
New York, N.Y. Office: 50 Rockefeller Plaza.
Telephone: 212-547-5508.
Facsimile: 212-547-5444.
St. Petersburg, Russia Office: AOZT McDermott, Will & Emery, Griboyedova Canal 36, 191023, St. Petersburg, Russia.
Telephone: (7) (812) 310-52-44; 310-55-44; 310-59-44; 850-20-45.
Facsimile: (7) (812) 310-54-46; 325-84-50.
Vilnius, Lithuania Office: Smetonos 6, 2600 Vilnius, Lithuania.
Telephone: 370 2 61-43-08.
Facsimile: 370 2 22-79-55.

MEMBERS OF FIRM

Matthew T. Adams *	Gregory F. Jenner
James M. Boyle *	Christopher Kliefoth
Robert Feldgarden *	Philip A. McCarty *
David R. Fuller	J. Gary McDavid
(Not admitted in DC)	Evan M. Migdail
Jennifer Britt Giannattasio	James A. Riedy *
William L. Goldman *	Stephen E. Wells *
Thomas M. Ingoldsby	Jane E. Wilson

COUNSEL

Robert G. Kalik	Phoebe A. Mix

*Denotes a lawyer employed by a Professional Corporation which is a member of the Firm

For full biographical listings, see the Martindale-Hubbell Law Directory

---

MILLER & CHEVALIER, CHARTERED (AV)

Established 1920
655 Fifteenth Street, N.W., Suite 900, 20005-5701
Telephone: 202-626-5800
Fax: 202-628-0858
Email: inquiries@milchev.com

J. Bradford Anwyll	F. Scott Farmer
Ronald D. Aucutt	A. John Gabig
Dennis P. Bedell	Hal I. Gann
John Mourer Bixler	Lawrence B. Gibbs
Jay L. Carlson	Catherine Veihmeyer Hughes
Catherine L. Creech	Thomas D. Johnston
David B. Cubeta	Robert A. Katcher

(See Next Column)

Kevin L. Kenworthy	C. Frederick Oliphant III
Robert E. Liles, II	Jean A. Pawlow
John B. Magee	Catherine Tift Porter
Thomas W. Mahoney, Jr.	Frederick H. Robinson
Phillip L. Mann	Richard C. Stark
Robert L. Moore, II	Patricia J. Sweeney
Anne E. Moran	F. Brook Voght
John Stephan Nolan	Alexander Zakupowsky, Jr.

OF COUNSEL

Charles T. Akre	David W. Richmond
Numa L. Smith, Jr.	

Michael E. Baillif	Susan A. Maloney
David B. Blair	Frances B. Morgan
Rhonda Nesmith Crichlow	Lisa M. Robinson
Rocco V. Femia	(Not admitted in DC)
(Not admitted in DC)	Michael L. Schultz
Laura G. Ferguson	(Not admitted in DC)
Marc J. Gerson	Robert T. Smith
Carol Ann Johnson	(Not admitted in DC)
(Not admitted in DC)	Gary R. Vogel
Michael W. Wright	

For Complete List of Firm Personnel, See General Section

For full biographical listings, see the Martindale-Hubbell Law Directory

---

RITTER EICHNER & NORRIS (AV)

The Jefferson Building, 1225 19th Street, N.W., 7th Floor, 20036
Telephone: 202-973-0100
Fax: 202-296-6990

MEMBERS OF FIRM

C. Willis Ritter	R. Wade Norris
Richard A. Eichner	(Not admitted in DC)

ASSOCIATE

Mary N. Simpkins

For full biographical listings, see the Martindale-Hubbell Law Directory

---

SILVERSTEIN AND MULLENS, P.L.L.C. (AV)

1776 K Street, N.W., 20006
Telephone: 202-452-7900
Cable Address: "SILMUL WASH"
Telex: 64426
Telecopier: 202-452-7989
Email: silvmul@capcon.net

MEMBERS OF FIRM

Leonard L. Silverstein	Javed A. Khokhar
Gerald H. Sherman	Patrick G. Dooher
Stuart M. Lewis	David I. Kempler
Ronald D. Abramson	David H. Dickieson
John P. Warner	William M. Harvey
Donald B. Reynolds, Jr.	James J. Freedman
Diane J. Fuchs	Louis H. Diamond

ASSOCIATES

Patricia R. Lesser	James C. Diana
John S. Ross, III	Carmela T. Montesano
Richard S. Marshall	Deborah J. Israel
Carmen Irizarry-Díaz	Ruth C. Shaw

OF COUNSEL

Richard A. Mullens	Aen W. Webster
James C. Corman	Harrison B. McCawley
Deborah M. Beers	Haig V. Kalbian
Eric N. Miller	

For full biographical listings, see the Martindale-Hubbell Law Directory

---

STEPTOE & JOHNSON LLP (AV)

1330 Connecticut Avenue, N.W., 20036
Telephone: 202-429-3000
Cable Address: "Stepjohn"
Telex: 89-2503
Telecopier: 202-429-3902
Email: wbatterton@steptoe.com *URL:* http://www.steptoe.com
Phoenix, Arizona Office: Two Renaissance Square, 40 N. Central Avenue, Suite 2400, 85004.
Telephone: 602-257-5200.
Moscow, Russia Office: Steptoe & Johnson International AOZT. 25 Tsvetnoy Boulevard, Building 3 Moscow, Russia 103051.
Telephone: 011-7-501-258-5250.
Fax: 011-7-501-258-5251.
Almaty, Kazakhstan Office: Steptoe & Johnson Company Almaty. 84 Gogol Street, Suite 213, 480083.
Telephones: (3272) 50-11-25, (3272) 32-25-39.

(See Next Column)

STEPTOE & JOHNSON LLP, *Washington—Continued*

MEMBERS

James P. Holden	Susan H. Serling
Matthew J. Zinn	Blake D. Rubin
Theodore E. Rhodes	Melanie F. Nussdorf
Mark J. Silverman	J. Walker Johnson
Arthur L. Bailey	Carol A. Rhees
Paul J. Ondrasik, Jr.	Kevin M. Keyes

OF COUNSEL

Stanley Smilack	Ellen Kohn
Edward R. Mackiewicz	Matthew D. Lerner

ASSOCIATES

Eric Berger	Barbara Sloan
Cathie A. Jurgensmeyer	Steven B. Teplinsky
(Not admitted in DC)	Andrew Walker
Andrea R. Macintosh	Andrew J. Weinstein
Eric G. Serron	Lisa M. Zarlenga
(Not admitted in DC)	(Not admitted in DC)

For Complete List of Firm Personnel, See General Section

For full biographical listings, see the Martindale-Hubbell Law Directory

---

VINYARD & ASSOCIATES (AV)

Columbia Square, 555 13th Street, N.W., 20004-1109
Telephone: 202-637-6838
Facsimile: 202-637-5910
Telex: 248370 (RCA)

Walter Darnall Vinyard

For full biographical listings, see the Martindale-Hubbell Law Directory

---

WEBSTER, CHAMBERLAIN & BEAN (AV)

Suite 1000, 1747 Pennsylvania Avenue, N.W., 20006
Telephone: 202-785-9500

MEMBERS OF FIRM

Arthur L. Herold	Burkett Van Kirk
Alan P. Dye	Frank M. Northam
Edward D. Coleman	John W. Hazard, Jr.
Kent Masterson Brown	Hugh K. Webster
(Not admitted in DC)	

OF COUNSEL

Charles E. Chamberlain	J. Coleman Bean

ASSOCIATES

Charles M. Watkins	Brenley Locke Elias
David P. Goch	David L. Finch
	(Not admitted in DC)

For full biographical listings, see the Martindale-Hubbell Law Directory

---

WILLIAMS & CONNOLLY (AV)

725 Twelfth Street, N.W., 20005
Telephone: 202-434-5000

MEMBERS OF FIRM

Lewis H. Ferguson, III	Mary Greer Clark
James T. Fuller, III	Lon E. Musslewhite

S. Hollis M. Greenlaw

OF COUNSEL

Lyman G. Friedman

For Complete List of Firm Personnel, See General Section

For full biographical listings, see the Martindale-Hubbell Law Directory

---

WILMER, CUTLER & PICKERING (AV)

2445 M Street, N.W., 20037-1420
Telephone: 202-663-6000
Fax: 202-663-6363
Email: Law@Wilmer.Com
Baltimore, Maryland Office: 100 Light Street, 21202.
Telephone: 410-986-2800.
Fax: 410-986-2828.
European Offices:
4 Carlton Gardens, London, SW1Y 5AA, England. *Telephone:* +44 (171) 872-1000.
Fax: +44 (171) 839-3537.
Rue de la Loi 15Wetstraat, B-1040 Brussels, Belgium. Telephone: +32 (2) 285-4900.
Fax: +32 (2) 285-4949.
Friedrichstrasse 95, D-10117 Berlin, Germany. Telephone: +49 (30) 2022-6400.
Fax: +49 (30)2022-6500.

(See Next Column)

MEMBERS OF FIRM

F. David Lake, Jr.	Terrill A. Hyde
Kenneth W. Gideon	Bryan Slone (Resident,
William J. Wilkins	Baltimore, Maryland Office)

Robert B. Stack

COUNSEL

R. Scott Kilgore

For Complete List of Firm Personnel, See General Section

For full biographical listings, see the Martindale-Hubbell Law Directory

---

ZAPRUDER & ODELL (AV)

601 Thirteenth Street, N.W. Suite 720 North, 20005
Telephone: 202-508-9600
Fax: 202-508-9601
Bala Cynwyd, Pennsylvania Office: 401 City Avenue, Suite 415.
Telephone: 610-617-7500.
Fax: 610-617-7505.
London, England Office: Zapruder & Odell Thorsteinssons. 1 Fleet Place.
Telephone: 44 171 463-9650.
Fax: 44 171 463-9651.

WASHINGTON, D.C. OFFICE
MEMBERS OF FIRM

Henry G. Zapruder	Samuel M. Maruca
Roger A. Pies	David J. Fischer

Stuart E. Horwich

OF COUNSEL

Jeffrey L. Holden

ASSOCIATES

G. Frank Riley III	Daniel W. Luchsinger
(Not admitted in DC)	

BALA CYNWYD, PENNSYLVANIA OFFICE
MEMBERS OF THE FIRM

Herbert Odell	Joel C. Weiss

ASSOCIATE

Kevin Johnson

OF COUNSEL

Howard L. Gleit (Resident, Bala	Michael W. Freeland
Cynwyd, Pennsylvania Office)	

LEGAL SUPPORT PERSONNEL

Robert A. Ladig

For full biographical listings, see the Martindale-Hubbell Law Directory

---

FLORIDA

AVENTURA, Dade Co.

BUCHANAN INGERSOLL, PROFESSIONAL CORPORATION (AV Ⓣ)

One Turnberry Place, 19495 Biscayne Boulevard, Suite 606, 33180
Telephone: 305-933-5600
Telecopier: 305-933-2350
URL: http://www.bipc.com
Pittsburgh, Pennsylvania Office: One Oxford Centre, 301 Grant Street, 20th Floor.
Telephone: 412-562-8800.
Philadelphia, Pennsylvania Office: Two Logan Square, Twelfth Floor, 18th & Arch Streets.
Telephone: 215-665-8700.
Harrisburg, Pennsylvania Office: 30 North Third Street.
Telephone: 717-237-4800.
Miami, Florida Office: NationsBank Tower, 100 S.E. Second Street.
Telephone: 305-347-4080.
Tampa, Florida Office: Suite 2500, 401 East Jackson Street.
Telephone: 813-222-8180.
Princeton, New Jersey Office: Buchanan Ingersoll, A Partnership, College Centre, 500 College Road East.
Telephone: 609-987-6800.
Lexington, Kentucky Office: Suite 600, PNC Bank Plaza, 200 West Vine Street.
Telephone: 606-225-5333.
Buffalo, New York Office: 1100 Main Place Tower, 350 Main Street.
Telephone: 716-854-4100.
Fax: 816-854-4227.

Joshua L. Dubin	Mark J. Neuberger

SENIOR ATTORNEY

Ralph B. Bekkevold

Todd A. Bancroft	Randi S. Rothfield
Kevin Carmichael	Richard N. Schermer
Jeffrey M. Goodz	Rebecca S. Trinkler

For full biographical listings, see the Martindale-Hubbell Law Directory

BOCA RATON, Palm Beach Co.

RONALD T. MARTIN, P.A. (AV)

Suite 404, 7000 West Palmetto Park Road, 33433
Telephone: 561-338-4100
Fax: 561-338-9086

Ronald T. Martin
OF COUNSEL
Marcia E. Levine

For full biographical listings, see the Martindale-Hubbell Law Directory

BOYNTON BEACH, Palm Beach Co.

ROBERT M. ARLEN, P.A. (AV)

Suite 200, 1501 Corporate Drive, 33426
Telephone: 561-734-9977
Broward Line: 954-781-7822
Telefax: 561-734-7511

Robert M. Arlen

For full biographical listings, see the Martindale-Hubbell Law Directory

CORAL GABLES, Dade Co.

RICHARD H. HUNT & ASSOCIATES A PROFESSIONAL ASSOCIATION (AV)

2801 Ponce de Leon Boulevard Ninth Floor, 33134
Telephone: 305-569-9671
Telecopier: 305-445-7728
Email: huntmia@ix.netcom.com

Richard H. Hunt

Robert Scott Williams
SENIOR COUNSEL
George J. Baya (1900-1995)

For full biographical listings, see the Martindale-Hubbell Law Directory

FORT LAUDERDALE, * Broward Co.

BERGER & DAVIS, P.A. (AV)

Suite 400, 100 N.E. 3rd Avenue, 33301
Telephone: 954-525-9900
Fax: 954-523-2872
Tallahassee, Florida Office: 215 South Monroe Street, Suite 804, 32301.
Telephone: 904-561-3010.
FAX: 904-561-3013.

Thomas L. Abrams	Manuel Kushner
James L. Berger	John D. C. Newton, II
Mitchell W. Berger	(Resident, Tallahassee Office)
Franklin H. Caplan	Leonard K. Samuels
James B. Davis	Laz L. Schneider
Nick Jovanovich	Daniel H. Thompson
Robert B. Judd	(Resident, Tallahassee Office)

Vincent J. Altino	Lisa D. MacClugage
Christine A. Butler	Dawn M. Meyers
Lawrence C. Callaway, III	Scott L. Pestcoe
Janice L. Griffin	Holiday Hunt Russell

Jeffrey Scott Wertman
OF COUNSEL
Henry H. (Bucky) Fox

For full biographical listings, see the Martindale-Hubbell Law Directory

FORT MYERS, * Lee Co.

HENDERSON, FRANKLIN, STARNES & HOLT, PROFESSIONAL ASSOCIATION (AV)

1715 Monroe Street, P.O. Box 280, 33902-0280
Telephone: 941-334-4121
Telecopier: 941-332-4494

William N. Horowitz   Guy E. Whitesman

Representative Clients: Aetna Property & Casualty Group; CIGNA Group; CSX Transportation, Inc.; Fireman's Fund Insurance Cos.; Barnett Bank of Lee County, N.A.; Northern Trust Bank of Florida, N.A.; The Hartford Insurance Group; Travelers Group; United Telephone Company of Florida.

For Complete List of Firm Personnel, See General Section

For full biographical listings, see the Martindale-Hubbell Law Directory

SMOOT ADAMS EDWARDS & GREEN, P.A. (AV)

One University Park Suite 600, 12800 University Drive, P.O. Box 60259, 33906-6259
Telephone: 941-489-1776
(800) 226-1777 (in Florida)
Fax: 941-489-2444
Email: 71600.2745@compuserve.com

J. Tom Smoot, Jr.	Bruce D. Green
Hal Adams	Steven I. Winer
Franklyn A. (Chip) Johnson	Mark R. Komray
(1947-1991)	Clayton W. Crevasse
Charles B. Edwards	M. Brian Cheffer

Robert S. Forman	C. Berk Edwards, Jr.
Kathleen W. McBride	Melville G. Brinson, III
Lowell Schoenfeld	Samuel J. Hagan, IV.

For full biographical listings, see the Martindale-Hubbell Law Directory

JACKSONVILLE, * Duval Co.

KENNETH G. ANDERSON (AV)

Suite 2540, Riverplace Tower, 1301 Riverplace Boulevard, 32207-9039
Telephone: 904-399-8000
Telecopier: 904-346-3078

ASSOCIATES
James P. Stevens   Robert G. Hicks

For full biographical listings, see the Martindale-Hubbell Law Directory

WILLIAM R. BLACKARD, JR. (AV)

Suite 600, 100 Laura Street, 32202
Telephone: 904-354-4400

For full biographical listings, see the Martindale-Hubbell Law Directory

DONAHOO, DONAHOO & BALL, P.A. (AV)

(Incorporated in 1981)
2925 Barnett Center, 50 North Laura Street, 32202
Telephone: 904-354-8080
Fax: 904-791-9563

John W. Donahoo (1907-1993)	Haywood M. Ball
Thomas M. Donahoo	William B. McMenamy
	Bruce D. Johnson

Thomas M. Donahoo, Jr.

For full biographical listings, see the Martindale-Hubbell Law Directory

FRAZIER & FRAZIER, ATTORNEYS AT LAW, P.A. (AV)

Suite A 1515 Riverside Avenue, 32204
Telephone: 904-353-5616
Fax: 904-353-5619

William R. Frazier   W. Robinson Frazier

References: First Union National Bank of Florida; Barnett Bank of Jacksonville, N.A.; Enterprise National Bank of Jacksonville; First Guaranty Bank & Trust Co.

For full biographical listings, see the Martindale-Hubbell Law Directory

SMITH HULSEY & BUSEY (AV)

1800 First Union National Bank Tower, 225 Water Street, P.O. Box 53175, 32201-3315
Telephone: 904-359-7700
Facsimile: 904-359-7708; 353-9908

Lloyd Smith (1915-1987)
MEMBERS OF FIRM

Dennis L. Blackburn	E. Owen McCuller, Jr.
Stephen D. Busey	James H. Post
Douglas D. Chunn	Bryan L. Putnal
Earl E. Googe, Jr.	E. Lanny Russell
Jeanne E. Helton	Joel Settembrini, Jr.
Cynthia C. Jackson	Tim E. Sleeth
G. Preston Keyes	John R. Smith, Jr.
William E. Kuntz	James J. Taylor, Jr.
M. Richard Lewis, Jr.	Timothy W. Volpe
John F. MacLennan	Waddell A. Wallace, III
Raymond R. Magley	Harry M. Wilson, III

Michael M. Bajalia	Marjorie Conner Makar
James A. Bolling, Jr.	Bradley R. Markey
E. Lanier Drew	R. Leanne McKnight
Diana Salama Farhat	Mary E. McManus
Martin A. Fitzpatrick	Jeanne M. Miller
Michael R. Freed	Stephen D. Moore, Jr.
Lee G. Kellison	Howard J. Smith
Lauren P. Langham	Steven G. Spears

(See Next Column)

SMITH HULSEY & BUSEY, *Jacksonville—Continued*

Melissa Smith Turra	Leslie A. Wickes
Herschel T. Vinyard, Jr	Karl A. Zillgitt

OF COUNSEL

Mark Hulsey	John E. Thrasher

Representative Clients: Baptist/St. Vincent's Health System, Inc.; Browning-Ferris Industries, Inc.; Champion Realty Corp. (Florida); First Union National Bank of Florida; Florida Rock Industries, Inc.; PGA Tour, Inc.; KPMG Peat Marwick; The Regency Group, Inc.; The Ritz-Carlton Hotel Co.; University of Florida.

For full biographical listings, see the Martindale-Hubbell Law Directory

---

JUPITER, Palm Beach Co.

JOSEPH C. KEMPE PROFESSIONAL ASSOCIATION (AV)

Attorneys and Counselors at Law
America Plaza, Suite 400, 1070 East Indiantown Road, 33477-5111
Telephone: 561-747-7300
FAX: 561-747-7722
Email: JCKempe@msn.com
Stuart, Florida Office: Royal Palm Financial Center II, Suite 200, 789 South Federal Highway.
Telephone: 561-223-0700.
Fax: 561-223-0707.
Vero Beach, Florida Office: Suite B, 664 Azalea Lane.
Telephone: 561-562-4022.
Fax: 561-234-1422.

Joseph C. Kempe

Sean L. Wilson	Jane W. Bergacker

For full biographical listings, see the Martindale-Hubbell Law Directory

---

*KISSIMMEE,** Osceola Co.

POHL & SHORT, P.A.

(See Winter Park)

LAKELAND, Polk Co.

PETERSON & MYERS, P.A. (AV)

100 East Main Street, P.O. Box 24628, 33802-4628
Telephone: 941-683-6511; 676-6934
Telecopier: 941-682-8031
Lake Wales, Florida Office: 130 East Central Avenue, P.O. Box 1079.
Telephones: 941-676-7611; 683-8942.
Winter Haven, Florida Office: Suite 300, 141 5th Street, N.W., P.O. Drawer 7608.
Telephone: 941-294-3360.

Philip O. Allen	Peter J. Munson
Jack P. Brandon	Corneal B. Myers
Beach A Brooks, Jr.	Cornelius B. Myers, III
Kristen Marie Buzzanca	E. Blake Paul
J. Davis Connor	Robert E. Puterbaugh
Michael S. Craig	Abel A. Putnam
Roy A. Craig, Jr.	Thomas B. Putnam, Jr.
Jacob C. Dykxhoorn	Deborah A. Ruster
Dennis P. Johnson	Stephen R. Senn
Kevin C. Knowlton	Andrea Teves Smith
Douglas A. Lockwood, III	Keith H. Wadsworth
M. Craig Massey	Kerry M. Wilson

General Counsel for: Barnett Bank of Polk County.
Representative Clients: Mutual Wholesale Co.; Barnett Banks, Inc.; Ben Hill Griffin, Inc.
Approved Attorneys for: Equitable Life Assurance Society of the United States; Federal Land Bank, Columbia, South Carolina; Attorneys' Title Insurance Fund.

For full biographical listings, see the Martindale-Hubbell Law Directory

---

LAKE WALES, Polk Co.

PETERSON & MYERS, P.A. (AV)

130 East Central Avenue, P.O. Box 1079, 33853
Telephone: 941-676-7611; 683-8942
Telecopier: 941-676-0643
Lakeland, Florida Office: 100 East Main Street, P.O. Box 24628.
Telephones: 941-683-6511; 676-6934.
Winter Haven, Florida Office: Suite 300, 141 5th Street, N.W., P.O. Drawer 7608.
Telephone: 941-294-3360.

Philip O. Allen	Roy A. Craig, Jr.
Jack P. Brandon	Jacob C. Dykxhoorn
Beach A Brooks, Jr.	Dennis P. Johnson
Kristen Marie Buzzanca	Kevin C. Knowlton
J. Davis Connor	Douglas A. Lockwood, III
Michael S. Craig	M. Craig Massey

(See Next Column)

Peter J. Munson	Thomas B. Putnam, Jr.
Corneal B. Myers	Deborah A. Ruster
Cornelius B. Myers, III	Stephen R. Senn
E. Blake Paul	Andrea Teves Smith
Robert E. Puterbaugh	Keith H. Wadsworth
Abel A. Putnam	Kerry M. Wilson

General Counsel for: Barnett Bank of Polk County.
Representative Clients: Mutual Wholesale Co.; Barnett Banks, Inc.; Ben Hill Griffin, Inc.; Alcoma Association, Inc.
Approved Attorneys for: Equitable Life Assurance Society of the United States; Federal Land Bank, Columbia, South Carolina; Attorneys' Title Insurance Fund.

For full biographical listings, see the Martindale-Hubbell Law Directory

---

LAKE WORTH, Palm Beach Co.

RICHARD H. WILLITS, P.A. (AV)

2290 10th Avenue, North Suite 404, 33461
Telephone: 1-800-870-0573
561-582-7600
Fax: 407-588-8819

Richard H. Willits, P.A.

For full biographical listings, see the Martindale-Hubbell Law Directory

---

*MIAMI,** Dade Co.

DAVID M. GARVIN, P.A. (AV)

1401 Brickell Avenue, 33131
Telephone: 305-371-8101
Fax: 305-371-8848

David M. Garvin

For full biographical listings, see the Martindale-Hubbell Law Directory

---

SHUTTS & BOWEN (AV)

A Partnership including Professional Associations
1500 Miami Center, 201 South Biscayne Boulevard, 33131
Telephone: 305-358-6300
Telefax: 305-381-9982
URL: HTTP://WWW.LAWWORLD.COM/SHUTTS/
Orlando, Florida Office: 20 North Orange Avenue, Suite 1000.
Telephone: 407-423-3200.
Fax: 407-425-8316.
West Palm Beach, Florida Office: One Clearlake Centre, 250 Australian Avenue, Suite 500.
Telephone: 561-835-8500.
Fax: 561-650-8530.
Amsterdam, The Netherlands Office: Shutts & Bowen, B.V., Europa Boulevard 59, 1083 AD, Amsterdam.
Telephone: (31 20) 661-0969.
Fax: (31 20) 642-1475.
London, England Office: 43 Grosvenor Street, London W1X 9PG.
Telephone: 441-71-493-4840.
Telefax: 441-71-493-4299.

MEMBERS OF FIRM

Robert E. Gunn (P.A.) (Resident at West Palm Beach Office)	Louis Nostro
	Raul J. Salas
	John B. White (P.A.)

ASSOCIATE

Christopher W. Boyett

OF COUNSEL

Jordan Bittel (P.A.)	Stephen L. Perrone (P.A.)
Marshall J. Langer (P.A.) (Resident, London, England Office)	Rosemarie N. Sanderson Schade (P.A.) (Resident at Amsterdam, The Netherlands)

For Complete List of Firm Personnel, See General Section

For full biographical listings, see the Martindale-Hubbell Law Directory

---

SPENCER AND KLEIN, PROFESSIONAL ASSOCIATION (AV)

Suite 1901, 801 Brickell Avenue, 33131
Telephone: 305-374-7700
Telecopier: 305-374-4890

Brent D. Klein

Representative Clients: Aerocar Aviation, Inc.; America Publishing Group; American Association of Physicians and Surgeons; Coldwell Banker; Editorial Televisa; Grupo Anaya, S.A.; Independent Living Care, Inc.; Managed Care of America, Inc.; New Times, Inc.; Winn-Dixie Stores.

For Complete List of Firm Personnel, See General Section

For full biographical listings, see the Martindale-Hubbell Law Directory

Miami—Continued

THOMSON MURARO RAZOOK & HART, P.A. (AV)

17th Floor, One Southeast Third Avenue, 33131
Telephone: 305-350-7200
Telecopier: 305-374-1005

Robert E. Muraro   Richard J. Razook

Representative Clients: United States Sugar Corp.; Quotron Systems, Inc.; Bacardi; The Exotic Gardens, Inc.

For Complete List of Firm Personnel, See General Section

For full biographical listings, see the Martindale-Hubbell Law Directory

ZACK, SPARBER, KOSNITZKY, SPRATT & BROOKS, P.A. (AV)

International Place, 100 Southeast Second Street, Suite 2800, 33131-2144
Telephone: 305-539-8400
Facsimile: 305-539-1307

Byron L. Sparber	Deborah R. Mayo
Michael Kosnitzky	Nancy E. McCarthy
Marc H. Auerbach	Roland Sanchez-Medina, Jr.
Jorge A. Gonzalez	Thomas O. Wells

For Complete List of Firm Personnel, See General Section

For full biographical listings, see the Martindale-Hubbell Law Directory

---

MIAMI BEACH, Dade Co.

THERREL BAISDEN & MEYER WEISS (AV)

Suite 500, 1111 Lincoln Road Mall, 33139
Telephone: 305-672-1921
Telecopier: 305-674-0807

MEMBERS OF FIRM

Catchings Therrel (1890-1971)	Nicholas M. Daniels
Fred R. Baisden (1903-1971)	Ellen Rose
Baron De Hirsch Meyer (1899-1974)	Leo Rose, Jr.
	Fred R. Stanton
Milton Weiss (1913-1980)	Richard A. Wood

ASSOCIATES

Seth E. Ellis   Jonathan Feuerman
Peter M. Lopez

OF COUNSEL

David Darlow

General Counsel: Chase Federal Bank; Jefferson National Bank Trust Department; American Equity Site Developers.
Counsel for: City Planned Communities Corp.; Anthony Abraham Chevrolet.

For full biographical listings, see the Martindale-Hubbell Law Directory

---

NAPLES,* Collier Co.

JAMES W. ELKINS, P.A. (AV)

Suite 303 The Fairway Building, 1000 Tamiami Trail North, 33940
Telephone: 941-263-0910
Fax: 941-263-6091

James W. Elkins

Approved Attorney for: Attorneys Title Insurance Fund.

For full biographical listings, see the Martindale-Hubbell Law Directory

---

ORLANDO,* Orange Co.

BAKER & HOSTETLER (AV)

SunBank Center, Suite 2300, 200 South Orange Avenue, 32802-3432
Telephone: 407-649-4000
In Cleveland, Ohio: 3200 National City Center, 1900 East Ninth Street.
Telephone: 216-621-0200.
In Columbus, Ohio: Capitol Square, Suite 2100, 65 East State Street.
Telephone: 614-228-1541.
In Denver, Colorado: 303 East 17th Avenue, Suite 1100.
Telephone: 303-861-0600.
In Houston, Texas: 1000 Louisiana, Suite 2000.
Telephone: 713-751-1600.
In Long Beach, California: 300 Oceangate, Suite 620.
Telephone: 310-432-2827.
In Los Angeles, California: 600 Wilshire Boulevard.
Telephone: 213-624-2400.
In Washington, D.C.: Washington Square, Suite 1100, 1050 Connecticut Avenue, N.W., Suite 1100.
Telephone: 202-861-1500.
In College Park, Maryland: 9658 Baltimore Boulevard, Suite 206.
Telephone: 301-441-2781.
In Alexandria, Virginia: 437 North Lee Street.
Telephone: 703-549-1294.
In San Francisco, California: One Sansome Street, Suite 2000.
Telephone: 415-951-4705.

(See Next Column)

PARTNER

Joel H. Sharp, Jr.

For Complete List of Firm Personnel, See General Section

For full biographical listings, see the Martindale-Hubbell Law Directory

MORAN & SHAMS, P.A. (AV)

111 North Orange Avenue, Suite 1200, P.O. Box 472, 32802-0472
Telephone: 407-841-4141
Fax: 407-841-4148
Email: moran-shams@moran-shams.com

Maurice Shams   Robert S. MacDonald

Representative Clients: Adventist Health System Sunbelt Healthcare Corporation; American Medical Associates, Inc.; Carse Oil Company; China Group, Inc.; Cruises Only, Inc.; Dayron, Inc.; R.C. Dunn Oil Company; Insurance Office of Florida, Inc.; Manpower of Cedar Rapids and Central Florida; Photo Chemical Systems of Florida, Inc.

For full biographical listings, see the Martindale-Hubbell Law Directory

POHL & SHORT, P.A.

(See Winter Park)

PALM BEACH, Palm Beach Co.

BAUGHER, METTLER & SHELTON (AV)

340 Royal Poinciana Plaza, P.O. Box 109, 33480
Telephone: 407-833-9631
Fax: 407-655-2835

MEMBERS OF FIRM

Thomas M. Mettler   John W. Shelton

ASSOCIATE

Francis X. J. Lynch

Reference: First National Bank in Palm Beach.

For full biographical listings, see the Martindale-Hubbell Law Directory

PETER W. METTLER (AV)

140 Royal Palm Way Suite 202, 33480
Telephone: 407-832-7600
Fax: 407-833-0805

For full biographical listings, see the Martindale-Hubbell Law Directory

MURPHY, REID, PILOTTE, ORD & AUSTIN (AV)

A Partnership of Professional Associations
Suite 100, 340 Royal Palm Way, 33480
Telephone: 561-655-4060
Facsimile: 561-832-5436
Vero Beach, Florida Office: Plantation Plaza, 6606-20th Street, P.O. Drawer M.
Telephone: 561-567-6480.
Facsimile: 561-562-0220.

Frank T. Pilotte (P.A.)

For Complete List of Firm Personnel, See General Section

For full biographical listings, see the Martindale-Hubbell Law Directory

---

ST. PETERSBURG, Pinellas Co.

RIDEN, EARLE & KIEFNER, P.A. (AV)

City Center, North Tower, 100 Second Avenue South, Suite 400, 33701-4336
Telephone: 813-822-6000
Telecopier: 813-821-3721

Thomas K. Riden	Christopher C. Ferguson
James T. Earle, Jr.	Timothy A. Miller
John R. Kiefner, Jr.	Gary E. Frazier
Paul Castagliola	James C. Rowe
Robert H. Crawford	Christopher B. Young
Neil G. Kiefer	Clifford J. Hunt
D. Jay Snyder	Benjamin Felder

M. Deanna Harris	Camille J. Iurillo
	Michael Francis Bremer

For full biographical listings, see the Martindale-Hubbell Law Directory

SARASOTA,* Sarasota Co.

WILLIAMS, PARKER, HARRISON, DIETZ & GETZEN, PROFESSIONAL ASSOCIATION (AV)

200 South Orange Avenue, 34236-6749
Telephone: 941-366-4800
Telecopier: 941-366-5109
Mailing Address: P.O. Box 3258, Sarasota, Florida, 34230-3258
Email: wphdg.law@netsrg.com *URL:*
http://www.sarasota-online.com/williamspa-w

J.J. Williams, Jr. (1886-1968)	Frank Strelec
W. Davis Parker (1920-1982)	Terri Salt Costa
William T. Harrison, Jr.	David A. Wallace
George A. Dietz	Mark A. Schwartz
Monte K. Marshall	Ric Gregoria
James L. Ritchey	Elvin W. Phillips
William G. Lambrecht	Jeffrey A. Grebe
John T. Berteau	John L. Moore
John V. Cannon, III	Morgan R. Bentley
Charles D. Bailey, Jr.	Susan A. Barrett
J. Michael Hartenstine	Carol Ann Kalish
Michele Boardman Grimes	Linda R. Getzen
James L. Turner	Kimberly J. Page
William M. Seider	Phillip D. Eck
Elizabeth C. Marshall	J. Hugh Middlebrooks
Robert W. Benjamin	Robert A. Warram

OF COUNSEL

William E. Getzen   Frazer F. Hilder
Hugh McPheeters, Jr.

LEGAL SUPPORT PERSONNEL

Mark Loveridge (Land Planner)

General Counsel for: Sarasota County Public Hospital Board; Sarasota-Manatee Airport Authority; Taylor Woodrow Homes Ltd.; FCCI Mutual Insurance Co.
Local Counsel for: NationsBank of Florida; Barnett Bank of Southwest Florida; Northern Trust Bank of Florida; SunTrust Bank, Gulfcoast.

For full biographical listings, see the Martindale-Hubbell Law Directory

---

STUART,* Martin Co.

JOSEPH C. KEMPE PROFESSIONAL ASSOCIATION (AV)

Attorneys and Counselors at Law
Royal Palm Financial Center II, Suite 200, 789 South Federal
  Highway, 34994
Telephone: 561-223-0700
FAX: 561-223-0707
Email: JCKempe@msn.com
Jupiter, Florida Office: America Plaza, Suite 400, 1070 East Indiantown
Road. Telephone 561-747-7300.
Fax: 561-747-7722.
Vero Beach, Florida Office: 664 Azalea Lane, Suite B.
Telephone: 561-562-4022.
Fax: 561-234-1422.

Joseph C. Kempe

Sean L. Wilson   Jane W. Bergacker

For full biographical listings, see the Martindale-Hubbell Law Directory

---

TALLAHASSEE,* Leon Co.

THE PHIPPS FIRM (AV)

215 South Monroe Street, Suite 802, P.O. Box 1315
Telephone: 904-222-7000
FAX: 904-681-3998

Benjamin K. Phipps   George C. Hamm
References: Barnett Bank; Sun Trust Bank.

For full biographical listings, see the Martindale-Hubbell Law Directory

---

TAMPA,* Hillsborough Co.

MANEY, DAMSKER, HARRIS & JONES, P.A. (AV)

606 Madison Street, P.O. Box 172009, 33672-0009
Telephone: 813-228-7371
Fax: 813-223-4846

David A. Maney   Karen Lynn Jones

For full biographical listings, see the Martindale-Hubbell Law Directory

---

PREVATT ENGLAND & TAYLOR (AV)

A Partnership of Professional Associations
One Tampa City Center, Suite 2505, P.O. Box 2920, 33602
Telephone: 813-273-9666
Telefax: 813-273-0414

(See Next Column)

Karen J. Prevatt   Lynne L. England
Mary L. Taylor

Representative Clients: Cone Constructors Inc.; Magic Wok International, Inc.; Dallas I. Construction & Development, Inc.; Bloomingdale Golfers Club; Central Florida Investments; Bioderm, Inc.; The Westerly Oceanus Co., Inc.

For full biographical listings, see the Martindale-Hubbell Law Directory

---

SHARP & SMITH, P.A. (AV)

One Urban Centre, Suite 745, 4830 West Kennedy Boulevard, 33609
Telephone: 813-286-4199
FAX: 813-286-4197
Email: sharpsmith@earthlink.net

William M. Sharp, Sr.   Karen Rowley Smith
William T. Harrison, III

For full biographical listings, see the Martindale-Hubbell Law Directory

---

VERO BEACH,* Indian River Co.

JOSEPH C. KEMPE PROFESSIONAL ASSOCIATION (AV)

Attorneys and Counselors at Law
664 Azalea Lane, Suite B, 32963
Telephone: 561-562-4022
Fax: 561-234-1442
Email: JCKempe@msn.com
Jupiter, Florida Office: America Plaza, Suite 400, 1070 E. Indiantown Rd.
Telephone: 561-747-7300.
Fax: 561-747-7722.
Stuart, Florida Office: Royal Palm Financial Center II, Suite 200, 789 S. Federal Highway, Suite 200.
Telephone: 561-223-0700.
Fax: 561-223-0707.

Joseph C. Kempe   Sean L. Wilson
Jane W. Bergacker

For full biographical listings, see the Martindale-Hubbell Law Directory

---

E. STEVEN LAUER, P.A. (AV)

612 Beachland Boulevard, 32963
Telephone: 407-234-4200
Fax: 407-234-4249

E. Steven Lauer

For full biographical listings, see the Martindale-Hubbell Law Directory

---

WEST PALM BEACH,* Palm Beach Co.

AUGUST, COMITER, KULUNAS & SCHEPPS, P.A. (AV)

250 Australian Avenue South Suite 1100, 33401
Telephone: 407-835-9600
Fax: 407-835-9602
Washington, D.C. Office: 501 School Street, Suite 700.
Telephone: 202-646-5160.

Jerald David August   Joseph J. Kulunas
Richard B. Comiter   Mitchell D. Schepps
OF COUNSEL
James J. Freeland

For full biographical listings, see the Martindale-Hubbell Law Directory

---

JONES, FOSTER, JOHNSTON & STUBBS, P.A. (AV)

Flagler Center Tower, 505 South Flagler Drive, Suite 1100, P.O. Box 3475, 33402-3475
Telephone: 561-659-3000
Fax: 561-832-1454

Sidney A. Stubbs	Peter A. Sachs
John Blair McCracken	Michael T. Kranz
John C. Randolph	John S. Trimper
Herbert Adams Weaver, Jr.	Mark B. Kleinfeld
Larry B. Alexander	Scott Gardner Hawkins
Thornton M. Henry	Steven J. Rothman
Margaret L. Cooper	Rebecca G. Doane
D. Culver Smith, III	Carl Angeloff (P.A.)
Allen R. Tomlinson	H. Michael Easley
Peter S. Holton	Joyce A. Conway

Christopher S. Duke	Edward Diaz
Scott L. McMullen	David Pratt
M. Tracey Biagiotti	Brian K. Waxman
Clay C. Brooker	David E. Dreyer
	(Not admitted in FL)

Counsel for: U.S. Trust Co.; NationsBank of Florida, N.A.; Island National Bank; Bankers Trust Company of Florida; Sun Bank/South Florida, N.A.; General Motors Acceptance Corp.

For full biographical listings, see the Martindale-Hubbell Law Directory

West Palm Beach—Continued

ROGERS, BOWERS, DEMPSEY AND PALADINO (AV)

Flagler Center Tower, Suite 1330, 505 South Flagler Drive, 33401
Telephone: 407-655-8980
Fax: 407-655-9480

MEMBERS OF FIRM

Robert O. Rogers	W. Glenn Dempsey
David E. Bowers	Richard Paladino

For full biographical listings, see the Martindale-Hubbell Law Directory

---

WINTER PARK, Orange Co.

POHL & SHORT, P.A. (AV)

280 West Canton Avenue, Suite 410, P.O. Box 3208, 32790
Telephone: 407-647-7645; 407-647-POHL
Telefax: 407-647-2314

Frank L. Pohl	C. Teresa de Arrigoitia
Houston E. Short	George A. Golder
Dwight I. Cool	Norma Stanley
James Everett Shepherd V	Mark W. Garrett
	John R. Simpson, Jr.

Representative Clients: American Pioneer Title Insurance Company; Institute of Internal Auditors, Inc.; Thompson Steel, Inc.; SunTrust, N.A.; The Bank of Winter Park; Bekins Moving and Storage Co., Inc.; Champion Boats, Inc.; KeyCom Telephone Systems, Inc.

For full biographical listings, see the Martindale-Hubbell Law Directory

GEORGIA

ATLANTA,* Fulton Co.

ALSTON & BIRD (AV)

A Partnership including Professional Corporations
One Atlantic Center, 1201 West Peachtree Street, 30309-3424
Telephone: 404-881-7000
Telecopier: 404-881-7777
Cable Address: AMGRAM GA
Telex: 54-2996
Easylink: 62985848
Washington, D.C. Office: 601 Pennsylvania Ave., N.W., North Building, Suite 250 20004.
Telephone: 202-508-3300.
Telecopier: 202-508-3333.

MEMBERS OF FIRM

Frazer Durrett, Jr.	Terence J. Greene
Joe T. Taylor	John C. Sawyer
Philip C. Cook	Michael T. Petrik
Arnold L. Feinstein	Timothy J. Peaden
Pinney L. Allen	Sam K. Kaywood, Jr.

ASSOCIATES

Michelle M. Henkel	Gretchen D. Locy
	Ben E. Muraskin

Representative Clients: Atlantic Steel Industries, Inc.; Bank South Corporation; Charles Schwab Corporation; Genuine Parts Company; Gold Kist Inc.; National Data Corporation; NationsBank Corporation; Racetrac Petroleum, Inc.; Sears, Roebuck and Co.; Waffle House, Inc.

For Complete List of Firm Personnel, See General Section

For full biographical listings, see the Martindale-Hubbell Law Directory

---

BIVENS, HOFFMAN & FOWLER (AV)

A Partnership of Professional Corporations
5040 Roswell Road, N.E., 30342
Telephone: 404-256-6464
FAX: 404-256-1422

MEMBER OF FIRM

Clifford G. Hoffman (P.C.)

For full biographical listings, see the Martindale-Hubbell Law Directory

---

BODKER, RAMSEY & ANDREWS, A PROFESSIONAL CORPORATION (AV)

Suite 615 1800 Peachtree Street, N.W., 30309-2507
Telephone: 404-351-1615
Telecopier: 404-352-1285

Brian D. Bodker	Jon G. Blaustein
	Kenneth L. Zirkman

For full biographical listings, see the Martindale-Hubbell Law Directory

---

DAVIS, MATTHEWS & QUIGLEY, P.C. (AV)

Fourteenth Floor, Lenox Towers II, 3400 Peachtree Road, 30326
Telephone: 404-261-3900
Telecopier: 404-261-0159
Email: dmq@interserv.com

William M. Matthews	J. Michael Harrison
	Melvin L. Drake, Jr.

Chason Lash Harrison, Jr.	Bradley Jay Denson

Approved Attorneys for: Lawyers Title Insurance Corp.

For Complete List of Firm Personnel, See General Section

For full biographical listings, see the Martindale-Hubbell Law Directory

ROBERT W. FISHER, LLC (AV)

The Peachtree Suite 1700, 1355 Peachtree Street, 30309-3266
Telephone: 404-853-3500
Telecopier: 404-853-3501
Telex: 154210

Robert W. Fisher	John R. Jones, Jr.
Stephen C. Beeler	
(Not admitted in GA)	

For full biographical listings, see the Martindale-Hubbell Law Directory

THE HISHON FIRM, LLC (AV)

999 Peachtree Street N.E. Suite 1900, 30309
Telephone: 404-817-7791
Fax: 404-817-2486

Robert H. Hishon

Nancy R. Daspit

For full biographical listings, see the Martindale-Hubbell Law Directory

HOLT, NEY, ZATCOFF & WASSERMAN (AV)

A Partnership including Professional Corporations
100 Galleria Parkway, Suite 600, 30339
Telephone: 770-956-9600
Facsimile Number: 770-956-1490

MEMBER OF FIRM

Michael G. Wasserman (P.C.)

Representative Clients: Trammell Crow Residential; Roberts Properties, Inc.; The Sterling Group, Inc.; Novak Development Corp.

For Complete List of Firm Personnel, See General Section

For full biographical listings, see the Martindale-Hubbell Law Directory

JONES, DAY, REAVIS & POGUE (AV)

3500 One Peachtree Center, 303 Peachtree Street, N.E., 30308-3242
Telephone: 404-521-3939
Cable Address: "Attorneys Atlanta"
Telex: 54-2711
Telecopier: 404-581-8330
In Brussels, Belgium: Avenue Louise 480, 7th Floor, B-1050 Brussels.
Telephone: 32-2-645-14-11.
Telecopier: 32-2-645-14-45.
In Chicago, Illinois: 77 West Wacker.
Telephone: 312-782-3939.
Telecopier: 312-782-8585.
In Cleveland, Ohio: North Point. 901 Lakeside Avenue.
Telephone: 216-586-3939.
Cable Address: "Attorneys Cleveland".
Telex: 980389.
Telecopier: 216-579-0212.
In Columbus, Ohio: 1900 Huntington Center.
Telephone: 614-469-3939.
Cable Address: "Attorneys Columbus".
Telecopier: 614-461-4198.
In Dallas, Texas: 2300 Trammell Crow Center, 2001 Ross Avenue.
Telephone: 214-220-3939.
Cable Address: "Attorneys Dallas."
Telex: 730852.
Telecopier: 214-969-5100.
In Frankfurt, Germany: Triton Haus, Bockenheimer Landstrasse 42, 60323 Frankfurt am Main.
Telephone: 49-69-9726-3939.
Telecopier: 49-69-9726-3993.
In Geneva, Switzerland: 20, rue de Candolle.
Telephone: 41-22-320-2339.
Telecopier: 41-22-320-1232.
In Hong Kong: 29th Floor, Entertainment Building, 30 Queen's Road Central.
Telephone: 852-2526-6895.
Telecopier: 852-2868-5871 or 852-2868-5699.

(See Next Column)

JONES, DAY, REAVIS & POGUE, *Atlanta—Continued*

In Irvine, California: 2603 Main Street, Suite 900.
Telephone: 714-851-3939.
Telex: 194911 Lawyers LSA.
Telecopier: 714-553-7539.
In London, England: One Mount Street.
Telephone: 44-71-493-9361.
Cable Address: "Surgoe London WI."
Telecopier: 44-71-493-9666.
In Los Angeles, California: 555 West Fifth Street, Suite 4600.
Telephone: 213-489-3939.
Telex: 181439 UD.
Telecopier: 213-243-2539.
In New Delhi, India: Pathak & Associates, 9th Floor, Dr. Gopal Das
Bhaven, 28 Barakhamba Road.
Telephone: 91-11-331-9719.
Telecopier: 91-11-331-7802.
In New York, New York: 599 Lexington Avenue.
Telephone: 212-326-3939.
Cable Address: "JONESDAY NEWYORK."
Telex: 237013 JDRP UR.
Telecopier: 212-755-7306.
In Paris, France: 62, rue du Faubourg Saint-Honore.
Telephone: 33-1-44-71-3939.
Cable Address: "Surgoe Paris."
Telex: 290156 Surgoe.
Telecopier: 33-1-49-24-0471.
In Pittsburgh, Pennsylvania: 500 Grant Street, 31st Floor.
Telephone: 412-391-3939.
Cable Address: "Attorneys Pittsburgh".
Telecopier: 412-394-7959.
In Riyadh, Saudi Arabia: Law Offices of Saud M.A. Shawwaf, P.O. Box
22166.
Telephone: (966-1) 462-8866.
Telex: 401831 SAUCON SJ.
Telecopier: (966-1) 462-9001.
In Taipei, Taiwan: 8th Floor, 2 Tun Hwa South Road, Section 2.
Telephone: (886-2) 704-6808.
Telecopier: (886-2) 704-6791.
In Tokyo, Japan: Toranomon MT Building, 4th Floor, 10-3, Toranomon
3-Chome, Minato-ku, Tokyo 105, Japan.
Telephone: 81-3-3433-3939.
Telecopier: 81-3-5401-2725.
In Washington, D.C.: Metropolitan Square, 1450 G Street, N.W.
Telephone: 202-879-3939.
Cable Address: "Attorneys Washington."
Telex: 89-2410 ATTORNEYS WASH.
Telecopier: 202-737-2832.

MEMBERS OF FIRM IN ATLANTA

James H. Landon	Rory D. Lyons
Milford B. Hatcher, Jr.	Ralph R. Morrison

SENIOR ATTORNEY
Arthur G. Kent

ASSOCIATE
J. Olen Earl

For Complete List of Firm Personnel, See General Section

For full biographical listings, see the Martindale-Hubbell Law Directory

---

KILPATRICK & CODY LLP (AV)

Suite 2800, 1100 Peachtree Street, 30309-4530
Telephone: 404-815-6500
Telephone Copier: 404-815-6555
Telex: 54-2307
Washington, D.C. Office: Suite 800, 700 13th Street, N.W., 20005.
Telephone: 202-508-5800. *Telephone Copier:* 202-508-5858.
Brussels, Belgium Office: Avenue Louise 65, BTE 3, 1050 Brussels.
Telephone: (32) (2) 533-03-00.
Telecopier: (32) (2) 534-86-38.
London, England Office: 68 Pall Mall, London, SW1Y 5ES, England.
Telephone: (44) (71) 321 0477.
Telecopier: (44) (71) 930 9733.
Augusta, Georgia Office: Suite 1400 First Union Bank Building, P.O. Box
2043, 30903. Telephone (706) 724-2622. Telecopier (706) 722-0219.

MEMBERS OF FIRM

Harold E. Abrams	Lynn E. Fowler
R. Alexander Bransford, Jr.	Thompson H. Gooding, Jr.
A. Kimbrough Davis	James R. Kanner
Suzanne G. Mason	

COUNSEL
Scott M. Dayan

ASSOCIATES

David K. Anderson	Derek P. Richman
Mary Balent Long	Michael B. Rubenstein

For Complete List of Firm Personnel, See General Section

For full biographical listings, see the Martindale-Hubbell Law Directory

---

LEFKOFF, DUNCAN, MILLER, GRIMES, MILLER & BARWICK, P.C. (AV)

Suite 806, Eleven Piedmont Center, 3495 Piedmont Road, N.E., 30305
Telephone: 404-262-2000
Fax: 404-262-2897
Email: lawfirm@lefkoff-duncan.com

Joseph Lefkoff	Dora A. Miller
Douglas W. Duncan	Donna Gude Barwick
Joseph C. Miller	Patricia McHugh Thompson

For full biographical listings, see the Martindale-Hubbell Law Directory

---

LONG ALDRIDGE & NORMAN, LLP (AV)

A Limited Liability Partnership including Professional Corporations
One Peachtree Center, Suite 5300, 303 Peachtree Street, 30308
Telephone: 404-527-4000
Telecopier: 404-527-4198
Washington, D.C. Office: Suite 600, 701 Pennsylvania Avenue, N.W.,
20004.
Telephone: 202-624-1200.
FAX: 202-624-1298.

MEMBERS OF FIRM

Mark S. Lange	Bruce H. Wynn
Patricia E. Tate	Charles T. Zink

ASSOCIATE
Charles J. Middleton (Not admitted in GA)

For Complete List of Firm Personnel, See General Section

For full biographical listings, see the Martindale-Hubbell Law Directory

---

SUTHERLAND, ASBILL & BRENNAN, L.L.P. (AV)

999 Peachtree Street, N.E., 30309-3996
Telephone: 404-853-8000
Facsimile: 404-853-8806
Email: postmaster@sablaw.com
Washington, D.C. Office: 1275 Pennsylvania Avenue, N.W., 20004-2404.
Telephone: 202-383-0100.
New York, N.Y. Office: 600 Madison Avenue, 11th Floor, 10022-1615.
Telephone: 212-605-6400.
Austin, Texas Office: 111 Congress Avenue, 23rd Floor, 78701-4079.
Telephone: 512-469-3350.

William H. Bradley	Charles D. Hurt, Jr.
Reginald J. Clark	Mark D. Kaufman
Katherine Meyers Cohen	Bennett Lexon Kight
N. Jerold Cohen	M. Celeste Pickron
Michael J. Egan	Randolph W. Thrower
Stephen F. Gertzman	C. Christopher Trower
William M. Hames	Larry J. White
James K. Hasson, Jr.	Walter H. Wingfield
Walter Hellerstein	
(Not admitted in GA)	

COUNSEL OF THE FIRM
IN ATLANTA, GEORGIA
Donald M. Etheridge, Jr. (Not admitted in GA)

For Complete List of Firm Personnel, See General Section

For full biographical listings, see the Martindale-Hubbell Law Directory

---

WILSON, STRICKLAND & BENSON, P.C. (AV)

1100 One Midtown Plaza, 1360 Peachtree Street, N.E., 30309
Telephone: 404-870-1800
Telecopier: 404-870-1808

R. Milton Crouch

For Complete List of Firm Personnel, See General Section

For full biographical listings, see the Martindale-Hubbell Law Directory

---

AUGUSTA, * Richmond Co.

HULL, TOWILL, NORMAN & BARRETT, A PROFESSIONAL CORPORATION (AV)

Seventh Floor, Trust Company Bank Building, P.O. Box
1564, 30903-1564
Telephone: 706-722-4481
Fax: 706-722-9779

James M. Hull (1885-1975)	Douglas D. Batchelor, Jr.
George B. Barrett (1894-1942)	David E. Hudson
Julian J. Willingham (1887-1963)	Neal W. Dickert
John Bell Towill (1907-1991)	John W. Gibson
Robert C. Norman	William F. Hammond
(Retired, 1991)	Mark S. Burgreen
W. Hale Barrett	George R. Hall
Lawton Jordan, Jr.	James B. Ellington
Patrick J. Rice	F. Michael Taylor

(See Next Column)

HULL, TOWILL, NORMAN & BARRETT A PROFESSIONAL CORPORATION—
Continued

Robert A. Mullins	Michael S. Carlson
William J. Keogh, III	Ralph Emerson Hanna, III
Edward J. Tarver	Susan D. Barrett
J. Noel Schweers, III	Timothy E. Moses

Counsel for: Sun Trust Bank Augusta, N.A.; Georgia Federal Bank, FSB, Augusta Division; Southeastern Newspapers Corp.; Georgia Power Co.; Southern Bell Telephone & Telegraph Co.; St. Joseph Hospital, Augusta, Georgia, Inc.; Norfolk Southern Corp.; Merry Land & Investment Co., Inc.; Housing Authority of the City of Augusta; Georgia Press Association.

For full biographical listings, see the Martindale-Hubbell Law Directory

---

COLUMBUS,* Muscogee Co.

DAVIDSON, CALHOUN, MILLER & BUEHLER, P.C. (AV)

The Joseph House, 828 Broadway, P.O. Box 2828, 31902-2828
Telephone: 706-327-2552
Telecopier: 706-323-5838

J. Quentin Davidson, Jr.	Charles W. Miller
David A. Buehler	

For Complete List of Firm Personnel, See General Section

For full biographical listings, see the Martindale-Hubbell Law Directory

---

HATCHER, STUBBS, LAND, HOLLIS & ROTHSCHILD (AV)

A Limited Liability Partnership
Suite 500 The Corporate Center, 233 12th Street, P.O. Box 2707, 31902-2707
Telephone: 706-324-0201
Telecopier: 706-322-7747

MEMBERS OF FIRM

Alan F. Rothschild	John M. Tanzine, III
Morton A. Harris	Alan F. Rothschild, Jr.
Charles T. Staples	Mote W. Andrews III

ASSOCIATE
Theodore Darryl (Ted) Morgan

General Counsel for: SunTrust Bank, West Georgia, N.A.; TOM'S Foods Inc.; Muscogee County Board of Education; The Jordan Company; Georgia Crown Distributing Co.; Flournoy Development Company; Bill Heard Enterprises, Inc.; St. Francis Hospital, Inc.
Local Counsel for: First Union National Bank of Georgia.

For Complete List of Firm Personnel, See General Section

For full biographical listings, see the Martindale-Hubbell Law Directory

---

ROTHSCHILD & MORGAN (AV)

1030 First Avenue, P.O. Box 2788, 31902-2788
Telephone: 706-324-4167
FAX: 706-324-1969

MEMBER OF FIRM
Jerome M. Rothschild

Reference: Columbus Bank and Trust Company.

For Complete List of Firm Personnel, See General Section

For full biographical listings, see the Martindale-Hubbell Law Directory

---

DECATUR,* De Kalb Co.

SIMMONS, WARREN, SZCZECKO & McFEE, PROFESSIONAL ASSOCIATION (AV)

315 West Ponce de Leon Avenue, Suite 850, 30030
Telephone: 404-378-1711
Fax: 404-377-6101

M. T. Simmons, Jr.	Joseph Szczecko
Wesley B. Warren, Jr.	William C. McFee, Jr.

Representative Clients: David Hocker & Associates (Shopping Center Development); Julian LeCraw & Company (Real Estate); Intown Suites, Inc.; Preferred Lodging Systems, Inc.; Royal Oldsmobile; Cotter & Co.; Atlanta Neurosurgical Associates, P.A.; Troncalli Motors, Inc.

For full biographical listings, see the Martindale-Hubbell Law Directory

---

GAINESVILLE,* Hall Co.

SMITH, GILLIAM AND WILLIAMS (AV)

200 Old Coca-Cola Building, 301 Green Street, N.W., P.O. Box 1098, 30503
Telephone: 770-536-3381
Fax: 770-531-1481

(See Next Column)

MEMBERS OF FIRM

R. Wilson Smith, Jr. (1906-1983)	Jerry A. Williams
John H. Smith	Kelly Anne Miles
Steven P. Gilliam	Bradley J. Patten

ASSOCIATES

M. Tyler Smith	Scott Arthur Ball

General Counsel for: Gainesville Industrial Electric Co.; Georgia Mutual Insurance, a Stock Company; L & R Farms; H. Wilson Manufacturing Co.; Goforth Electrical Supply; North Georgia Petroleum Co.; Gibbs Management Group, Inc.

For full biographical listings, see the Martindale-Hubbell Law Directory

---

MACON,* Bibb Co.

ANDERSON, WALKER & REICHERT, P.C. (AV)

Suite 404 SunTrust Bank Building, P.O. Box 6497, 31208-6497
Telephone: 912-743-8651
Telecopier: 912-743-9636

Albert P. Reichert, Jr.	John D. Reeves

Ramsey T. Way, Jr.

Representative Clients: Riverwood International USA, Inc.; Hospital Corporation of America; Pepsi-Cola Bottling Company of Macon; Radiology Associates of Macon, P.C.; Thiele Kaolin Company; SunTrust Bank of Middle Georgia, N.A.
General Insurance Clients: Liberty Mutual Insurance Co.; Alexis, Inc.

For Complete List of Firm Personnel, See General Section

For full biographical listings, see the Martindale-Hubbell Law Directory

---

HALL, BLOCH, GARLAND & MEYER (AV)

1500 Charter Medical Building, P.O. Box 5088, 31213-3199
Telephone: 912-745-1625
Telecopier: 912-741-8822

MEMBER OF FIRM
J. Patrick Meyer, Jr.

For Complete List of Firm Personnel, See General Section

For full biographical listings, see the Martindale-Hubbell Law Directory

---

MARIETTA,* Cobb Co.

W. ALLEN SEPARK (AV)

250 Church Street, Second Floor, P.O. Box 3475, 30061
Telephone: 770-422-3200
Fax: 770-514-1148

Reference: First Union National Bank, formerly Georgia State Bank.

For full biographical listings, see the Martindale-Hubbell Law Directory

---

SAVANNAH,* Chatham Co.

HUNTER, MACLEAN, EXLEY & DUNN, P.C. (AV)

200 East St. Julian Street, P.O. Box 9848, 31412
Telephone: 912-236-0261
Cable Address: "Ancan"
Telecopier: 912-236-4936
Telex: 54-6483
Atlanta, Georgia Office: The Peachtree, 1355 Peachtree Street, N.E., Suite 1050.
Telephone: 404-876-3611.
Fax: 404-870-2025.

Henry M. Dunn, Jr.	David M. Hirsberg
Don L. Waters	Steven J. Arsenault
Caroline Louise Osborne	

Representative Clients: Memorial Medical Center, Inc.; Carson Products Co.

For Complete List of Firm Personnel, See General Section

For full biographical listings, see the Martindale-Hubbell Law Directory

---

SILVERS, SIMPSON & CREASY, P.C. (AV)

Suite 102, AmeriBank Plaza, 7393 Hodgson Memorial Drive, 31406
Telephone: 912-925-7200
Facsimile: 912-925-0100

Mark M. Silvers, Jr.	K. Russell Simpson
Neil A. Creasy	

For full biographical listings, see the Martindale-Hubbell Law Directory

HAWAII

HONOLULU, * Honolulu Co.

CHING, YUEN & MORIKAWA (AV)

Pacific Tower, Suite 2700, 1001 Bishop Street, 96813
Telephone: 808-524-8880
Telecopier: 808-524-7664

MEMBERS OF FIRM
Russell L. Ching   William W. L. Yuen
Randall I. Morikawa
ASSOCIATE
Joyce T. Tamanaha

Representative Clients: Finance Enterprises, Ltd.; Finance Factors, Ltd.; Finance Realty, Ltd.; Gentry Pacific, Ltd.; Goldman, Sachs & Co.; The Hertz Corporation; Kamehamela Schools Bernice Pauahi Bishop Estate; Merrill Lynch & Co.; The Sakura Bank, Ltd.; Sen Plex Corp.

For full biographical listings, see the Martindale-Hubbell Law Directory

LAW OFFICES OF MANUEL D. GARCIA (AV)

Makai Tower, Grosvenor Center, Suite 2550, 733 Bishop Street, 96813
Telephone: 808-522-0755
Facsimile: 808-522-0760

For full biographical listings, see the Martindale-Hubbell Law Directory

McCORRISTON MIHO MILLER MUKAI (AV)

Five Waterfront Plaza, 4th Floor, 500 Ala Moana Boulevard, 96813
Telephone: 808-529-7300
Facsimile: 808-524-8293
Cable: Attorneys, Honolulu
Mailing Address: P.O. Box 2800, Honolulu, Hawaii, 96803-2800
Hilo, Hawaii Office: 56 Waianuenue Avenue, Suite 217, 96720.
Telephone: 808-935-6537.
Facsimile: 808-935-3398.

PARTNERS
Franklin K. Mukai   Donald K. O. Wong
Stanley Y. Mukai   Michael J. O'Malley
Michael Rosenthal

Representative Clients: Classics Resorts Limited; TSA International Limited; Eaton Vance Management; Hawaii Dental Service; Jas. Glover Holding Company; PrimeCo Investors LLC; UGI Corporation; Kids Earth Fund; Sports Shinko (Hawaii) Co., Ltd.; DIA Pacific Corporation.

For Complete List of Firm Personnel, See General Section

For full biographical listings, see the Martindale-Hubbell Law Directory

REINWALD, O'CONNOR, MARRACK, HOSKINS & PLAYDON (AV)

(Formerly Anthony, Hoddick, Reinwald & O'Connor)
2400 PRI Tower, Grosvenor Center, P.O. Box 3199, 96801-3199
Telephone: 808-524-8350
Cable Address: "Hermes" Honolulu
Telecopier: 808-531-8628

MEMBER OF FIRM
Arthur B. Reinwald

For full biographical listings, see the Martindale-Hubbell Law Directory

IDAHO

BOISE, * Ada Co.

EBERLE, BERLIN, KADING, TURNBOW & McKLVEEN, CHARTERED (AV)

Capitol Park Plaza, 300 North Sixth Street, P.O. Box 1368, 83701
Telephone: 208-344-8535
Facsimile: 208-344-8542

William J. McKlveen   Joseph H. Uberuaga, II
Steven E. Alkire

Sarah E. Scott

Representative Clients: TJ International; Hecla Mining Company; Agri Beef Co.; Key Trust Company of The West.

For Complete List of Firm Personnel, See General Section

For full biographical listings, see the Martindale-Hubbell Law Directory

ELAM & BURKE, A PROFESSIONAL ASSOCIATION (AV)

Key Financial Center, 702 West Idaho Street, P.O. Box 1539, 83701
Telephone: 208-343-5454
Telecopier: 208-384-5844
Email: eblaw@elamburke.com

Melville W. Fisher, II   Peter C. K. Marshall

Sandra L. Clapp

Representative Clients: Morrison-Knudsen, Inc.; U.S. West Communications; Sinclair Oil Co. d/b/a Sun Valley Co.; IBM; Grand Metropolitan (Pillsbury); Rhone Poulenc.

For Complete List of Firm Personnel, See General Section

For full biographical listings, see the Martindale-Hubbell Law Directory

ILLINOIS

BELLEVILLE, * St. Clair Co.

MATHIS, MARIFIAN, RICHTER & GRANDY, LTD. (AV)

720 West Main Street, 62220
Telephone: 618-234-9800; 314-421-2325
FAX: 618-234-9786

Patrick B. Mathis   Kevin J. Richter
George E. Marifian   Laura Koeneman Grandy
Kevin J. Stine

For full biographical listings, see the Martindale-Hubbell Law Directory

THOMPSON COBURN (AV)

525 West Main Street, 62220
Telephone: 618-277-4700; 314-271-1800
Telecopier: 618-236-3434
St. Louis, Missouri Office: One Mercantile Center.
Telephone: 314-552-6000.
Telecopier: 314-552-7000.
St. Charles, Missouri Office: 200 North Third Street.
Telephone: 314-946-7717.
Telecopier: 314-946-4938.
Washington, D.C. Office: 700 14th Street, N.W., Suite 900.
Telephone: 202-508-1000.
Telecopier: 202-508-1010.
Houston, Texas Office: 2400 NationsBank Center, 700 Louisiana.
Telephone: 713-225-3800.
Telecopier: 713-225-3828.

MEMBERS OF FIRM
Joseph R. Lowery   Mark J. Stegman
Garrett C. Reuter   Kurt S. Schroeder

Representative Clients: First Illinois Bank; Harcros Pigments, Inc.; Illinois-American Water Co.; Illinois Bell Telephone Co.; Magna Group, Inc.; Magna Trust Co.; Marsh Company; Memorial Hospital of Belleville; Norfolk Southern Corp.; Union Electric Co.

For Complete List of Firm Personnel, See General Section

For full biographical listings, see the Martindale-Hubbell Law Directory

BLOOMINGTON, * McLean Co.

HARTWEG, MUELLER, TURNER, DRAZEWSKI & WOOD, P.C. (AV)

207 West Jefferson Street, Suite 400, P.O. Box 397, 61701-0397
Telephone: 309-827-0044
Telecopier: 309-829-0328

Darrell L. Hartweg   Ralph T. Turner
William A. Mueller, Jr.   Scott D. Drazewski
George C Wood

Michael J. Robak
OF COUNSEL
John R. Luedtke

Reference: Magna Bank of McLean County.

For full biographical listings, see the Martindale-Hubbell Law Directory

CHICAGO,* Cook Co.

BELL, BOYD & LLOYD (AV)

Three First National Plaza Suite 3300, 70 West Madison Street, 60602
Telephone: 312-372-1121
FAX: 312-372-2098
Email: bbl@bbl.com
Washington, D.C. Office: 1615 L Street, N.W.
Telephone: 202-466-6300.
FAX: 202-463-0678.

MEMBERS OF FIRM

Durward J. (James) Gehring	Paul T. Metzger
Thomas F. Joyce	Richard L. Sevcik
Alice S. Lonoff	Anita Medina Tyson
	Robert L. Wiesenthal

OF COUNSEL

Alan R. Brodie	Rollin C. Huggins, Jr.
William N. Haddad	Allen R. Smart

ASSOCIATES

Brian T. Gardner	Dawn M. Weber
(Not admitted in IL)	

For Complete List of Firm Personnel, See General Section

For full biographical listings, see the Martindale-Hubbell Law Directory

---

BURMAN & MANNING (AV)

135 South La Salle Street, Suite 2512, 60603
Telephone: 312-236-2994
312-346-4885

MEMBERS OF FIRM

Ira M. Burman	Richard L. Manning

OF COUNSEL

William E. Borenstein

Reference: La Salle National Bank, Chicago, Illinois.

For full biographical listings, see the Martindale-Hubbell Law Directory

---

DEUTSCH, LEVY & ENGEL, CHARTERED (AV)

Suite 1700, 225 West Washington Street, 60606
Telephone: 312-346-1460
Wheaton, Illinois Office: Suite B2, 620 West Roosevelt Road.
Telephone: 708-665-9112.

Terry L. Engel	Frank R. Cohen
	Jerry I. Rudman

David I. Addis	Martin P. Ryan

For full biographical listings, see the Martindale-Hubbell Law Directory

---

FAGEL & HABER (AV)

140 South Dearborn Street 14th Floor, 60603
Telephone: 312-346-7500
FAX: 312-580-2201
Telex No: 754542
Cable: "NOFLAWLAW"
URL: HTTP://WWW.FANDH.COM.

MEMBERS OF FIRM

Sherwin M. Lesk	Norton N. Gold
	Daniel G. Coman

ASSOCIATES

Gary H. Cole	Patrick J. Cullerton
	Michael P. Rhoades

For full biographical listings, see the Martindale-Hubbell Law Directory

---

GORDON & EINSTEIN, LTD. (AV)

224 East Ontario, 60611
Telephone: 312-280-7766
Telecopier: 312-280-9599

Raymond P. Gordon	Jean M. Einstein

LEGAL SUPPORT PERSONNEL

Laura A. Kozicki

For full biographical listings, see the Martindale-Hubbell Law Directory

---

JONES, DAY, REAVIS & POGUE (AV)

77 West Wacker, 60601-1692
Telephone: 312-782-3939
Telecopier: 312-782-8585
In Atlanta, Georgia: 3500 One Peachtree Center, 303 Peachtree Street, N.E.
Telephone: 404-521-3939.
Cable Address: "Attorneys Atlanta".
Telex: 54-2711.
Telecopier: 404-581-8330.

(See Next Column)

In Brussels, Belgium: Avenue Louise 480, 7th Floor, B-1050 Brussels.
Telephone: 32-2-645-14-11.
Telecopier: 32-2-645-14-45.
In Cleveland, Ohio: North Point, 901 Lakeside Avenue.
Telephone: 216-586-3939.
Cable Address: "Attorneys Cleveland."
Telex: 980389.
Telecopier: 216-579-0212.
In Columbus, Ohio: 1900 Huntington Center.
Telephone: 614-469-3939.
Cable Address: "Attorneys Columbus."
Telecopier: 614-461-4198.
In Dallas, Texas: 2300 Trammell Crow Center, 2001 Ross Avenue.
Telephone: 214-220-3939.
Cable Address: "Attorneys Dallas."
Telex: 730852.
Telecopier: 214-969-5100.
In Frankfurt, Germany: Triton Haus, Bockenheimer Landstrasse 42, 60323 Frankfurt am Main.
Telephone: 49-69-9726-3939.
Telecopier: 49-69-9726-3993.
In Geneva, Switzerland: 20, rue de Candolle.
Telephone: 41-22-320-2339.
Telecopier: 41-22-320-1232.
In Hong Kong: 29th Floor, Entertainment Building, 30 Queen's Road Central.
Telephone: 852-2526-6895.
Telecopier: 852-2868-5871 or 852-2868-5699.
In Irvine, California: 2603 Main Street, Suite 900.
Telephone: 714-851-3939.
Telex: 194911 Lawyers LSA.
Telecopier: 714-553-7539.
In London, England: One Mount Street.
Telephone: 44-71-493-9361.
Cable Address: "Surgoe London WI."
Telecopier: 44-71-493-9666.
In Los Angeles, California: 555 West Fifth Street, Suite 4600.
Telephone: 213-489-3939.
Telex: 181439 UD.
Telecopier: 213-243-2539.
In New Delhi, India: Pathak & Associates, 9th Floor, Dr. Gopal Das Bhaven, 28 Barakhamba Road.
Telephone: 91-11-331-9719.
Telecopier: 91-11-331-7802.
In New York, New York: 599 Lexington Avenue.
Telephone: 212-326-3939.
Cable Address: "JONESDAY NEWYORK."
Telex: 237013 JDRP UR.
Telecopier: 212-755-7306.
In Paris, France: 62, rue du Faubourg Saint-Honore.
Telephone: 33-1-44-71-3939.
Cable Address: "Surgoe Paris."
Telex: 290156 Surgoe.
Telecopier: 33-1-49-24-0471.
In Pittsburgh, Pennsylvania: 500 Grant Street, 31st Floor.
Telephone: 412-391-3939.
Cable Address: "Attorneys Pittsburgh."
Telecopier: 412-394-7959.
In Riyadh, Saudi Arabia: Law Offices of Saud M.A. Shawwaf, P.O. Box 22166.
Telephone: (966-1) 462-8866.
Telex: 401831 SAUCON SJ.
Telecopier: (966-1) 462-9001.
In Taipei, Taiwan: 8th Floor, 2 Tun Hwa South Road, Section 2.
Telephone: (886-2) 704-6808.
Telecopier: (886-2) 704-6791.
In Tokyo, Japan: Toranomon MT Building, 4th Floor, 10-3, Toranomon 3-Chome, Minato-ku, Tokyo 105, Japan.
Telephone: 81-3-3433-3939.
Telecopier: 81-3-5401-2725.
In Washington, D.C.: Metropolitan Square, 1450 G Street, N.W.
Telephone: 202-879-3939.
Cable Address: "Attorneys Washington."
Telex: 89-2410 ATTORNEYS WASH.
Telecopier: 202-737-2832.

MEMBERS OF FIRM IN CHICAGO

Ronald S. Rizzo	Douglas H. Walter
(Not admitted in IL)	Stephanie Balcerzak Graves

OF COUNSEL

William S. McKay, Jr.

ASSOCIATES

Joni L. Andrioff	Richard E. Aderman

For Complete List of Firm Personnel, See General Section

For full biographical listings, see the Martindale-Hubbell Law Directory

Chicago—Continued

THE LAW OFFICES OF MARC J. LANE A PROFESSIONAL CORPORATION (AV)

Suite 2100 180 North La Salle Street, 60601-2701
Telephone: 312-372-1040
800-372-1040
Fax: 312-346-1040
Email: success@marcjlane.com *URL:* http://www.marcjlane.com

Marc J. Lane

Gregory A. Papiernik

For full biographical listings, see the Martindale-Hubbell Law Directory

McBRIDE BAKER & COLES (AV)

500 West Madison Street 40th Floor, 60661
Telephone: 312-715-5700
Cable Address: "Chilaw"
Telex: 270258
Telecopier: 312-993-9350
Email: lastname@mbc.com *URL:* http://www.mbc.com
Oakbrook Terrace, Illinois Office: Suite 1000, One Mid America Plaza, 60181-4710.
Telephone: 630-954-2100.
Telecopier: 630-954-2112.

MEMBERS OF FIRM

David Ackerman	Morgan J. Ordman
Andrew R. Gelman	Robert I. Schwimmer
Thomas J. Kinasz	David Shayne
Steven R. Lifson	Larry M. Zanger

OF COUNSEL
Robert O. Case

ASSOCIATES
Edward J. Hannon   Jonathan E. Strouse

For Complete List of Firm Personnel, See General Section

For full biographical listings, see the Martindale-Hubbell Law Directory

McDERMOTT, WILL & EMERY (AV)

A Partnership including Professional Corporations
227 West Monroe Street, 60606-5096
Telephone: 312-372-2000
Facsimile: 312-984-7700
Boston, Massachusetts Office: 75 State Street, Suite 1700.
Telephone: 617-345-5000.
Facsimile: 617-345-5077.
Miami, Florida Office: 201 South Biscayne Boulevard.
Telephone: 305-358-3500.
Facsimile: 305-347-6500.
Washington, D.C. Office: 1850 K Street, N.W.
Telephone: 202-887-8000.
Facsimile: 202-778-8087.
Los Angeles, California Office: 2049 Century Park East.
Telephone: 310-277-4110.
Facsimile: 310-277-4730.
Newport Beach, California Office: 1301 Dove Street, Suite 500.
Telephone: 714-851-0633.
Facsimile: 714-851-9348.
New York, N.Y. Office: 1211 Avenue of the Americas.
Telephone: 212-768-5400.
Facsimile: 212-768-5444.
St. Petersburg, Russia Office: AOZT McDermott, Will & Emery, Griboyedova Canal 36, 191023 St. Petersburg, Russia.
Telephone: (7) (812) 310-52-44; 310-55-44; 310-59-44; 850-20-45.
Facsimile: (7) (812) 310-54-46; 325-84-50.
Vilnius, Lithuania Office: Smetonos 6, 2600 Vilnius, Lithuania.
Telephone: 370 2 61-43-08.
Facsimile: 370 2 22-79-55.

MEMBERS OF FIRM

George W. Benson	Lydia R. B. Kelley
Stuart M. Berkson *	Andrea S. Kramer
John A. Biek *	James L. Malone III *
Thomas C. Borders *	Sandra Parker McGill
Thomas H. Donohoe	Edward F. Michalak
David J. Duez *	Gail H. Morse *
Michael R. Fayhee *	Lonn W. Myers *
Kevin J. Feeley	Alan J. Olson *
John Edmund Gaggini *	Gregory G. Palmer
Richard A. Hanson *	William R. Pomierski
Kristen E. Hazel	Barry J. Quirke
Charles E. Hussey II	James M. Roche *
Thomas M. Jones *	David R. Ryder
Stanley R. Kaminski, Jr. *	Lowell D. Yoder
Gary C. Karch	Daniel N. Zucker

(See Next Column)

ASSOCIATES

Melissa A. Connell	Adam J. Narot
David A. Fruchtman	Courtney N. Stillman
Sheri L. Hurbanis	Rebecca E. Wacaser
Matthew P. Larvick	Jeffrey C. Wagner

*Denotes a lawyer employed by a Professional Corporation which is a member of the Firm.

For full biographical listings, see the Martindale-Hubbell Law Directory

SARNOFF & BACCASH (AV)

One North La Salle Street Suite 1701, 60602-3907
Telephone: 312-782-8310
Fax: 312-782-8635

MEMBERS OF FIRM
Michael F. Baccash   Robert M. Sarnoff

LEGAL SUPPORT PERSONNEL
REAL ESTATE APPRAISER (MAI) AND ENVIRONMENTAL ANALYST
James G. Frommeyer, III

CERTIFIED PUBLIC ACCOUNTANT
Michael Foley

PROPERTY TAX ADMINISTRATORS

Jeanine Marie Herzeg, Commercial, Industrial and Residential Property Tax Analyst.	Paula J. Wirth, Property Tax Analyst. Scott Herzeg, Computer and Systems Analyst. Residential Property Tax Analyst.
Milena K. Mesin, Property Tax Analyst.	

For full biographical listings, see the Martindale-Hubbell Law Directory

STONE, McGUIRE & BENJAMIN (AV)

Suite 3230, 55 East Monroe Street, 60603
Telephone: 312-372-4100
Fax: 312-372-9461
Northbrook, Illinois Office: 801 Skokie Boulevard.
Telephone: 847-205-9700.
FAX: 847-205-9492.

MEMBERS OF FIRM

Howard L. Stone	Lee E. Gussin
David A. McGuire	(Resident, Northbrook Office)
Marc A. Benjamin	Michael L. Siegel
(Resident, Northbrook Office)	Edward C. Richard

ASSOCIATES

Carl E. Poli	Michael A. Harsch
	(Resident, Northbrook Office)

For full biographical listings, see the Martindale-Hubbell Law Directory

SUGAR, FRIEDBERG & FELSENTHAL (AV)

30 North La Salle Street, Suite 2600, 60602
Telephone: 312-704-9400
Telecopier: 312-372-7951
Cable: "SUGARFREE"

MEMBERS OF FIRM

Richard A. Sugar	Ira S. Neiman
Michael R. Friedberg	Jonathan L. Mills
Steven A. Felsenthal	Etahn M. Cohen
Andrew B. David	Howard M. Helsinger
Leslie J. Weiss	Robert F. Simon
	Martin M. Weinstein

ASSOCIATES

Kathryn A. Erickson	Jay R. Hoffman
Norman J. Ginsparg	Sophia Stergianis
	Jonathan W. Michael

For full biographical listings, see the Martindale-Hubbell Law Directory

VEDDER, PRICE, KAUFMAN & KAMMHOLZ (AV)

A Partnership including Vedder, Price, Kaufman & Kammholz, P.C.
222 North La Salle Street, 60601-1003
Telephone: 312-609-7500
Fax: 312-609-5005
New York, New York Office: Vedder, Price, Kaufman, Kammholz & Day, 805 Third Avenue.
Telephone: 212-407-7700.

MEMBERS OF FIRM

Michael G. Beemer	Daniel T. Sherlock
William F. Walsh	Jonathan H. Bogaard
	Timothy W. O'Donnell

PARTNER AT NEW YORK CITY
Denise L. Blau

For Complete List of Firm Personnel, See General Section

For full biographical listings, see the Martindale-Hubbell Law Directory

DECATUR,* Macon Co.

R. NICHOLAS BURTON (AV)

Suite 603 Millikin Court, 132 South Water Street, 62523
Telephone: 217-423-8861

References: The First National Bank of Decatur; First of America Bank-Illinois, N.A.; Magna Bank, N.A.; Soy Capital Bank & Trust Co.

For full biographical listings, see the Martindale-Hubbell Law Directory

ROCKFORD,* Winnebago Co.

WILLIAMS & MCCARTHY, A PROFESSIONAL CORPORATION (AV)

321 West State Street, P.O. Box 219, 61105-0219
Telephone: 815-987-8900
Fax: 815-968-0019
URL: http://www.wilmac.com
Oregon, Illinois Office: 607 Washington Street. P.O. Box 339.
Telephone: 815-732-2101.
Fax: 815-732-2289.

John R. Kinley   Elmer C. Rudy
                   John E. Pfau

Representative Clients: Aircraft Gear Corp.; Anderson Industries, Inc.; Gallagher Bassett Insurance Co.; Liberty Mutual Insurance Co.; Atwood Industries, Inc.; The Travelers; American Mutual Insurance Co.; Rockford Health Systems; Chrysler Corp.; USF&G, West Bend.

For Complete List of Firm Personnel, See General Section

For full biographical listings, see the Martindale-Hubbell Law Directory

ROCK ISLAND,* Rock Island Co.

NEPPLE, VAN DER KAMP & FLYNN, P.C. (AV)

Suite 202 American Bank Building, 1600 Fourth Avenue, P.O. Box 5408, 61204-5408
Telephone: 309-786-5700
Telecopier: 309-786-5745
Muscatine, Iowa Office: 216 Sycamore Street, P.O. Box 386, 52761-0386.
Telephone: 319-264-6840.

Roy W. Van Der Kamp   James A. Nepple
                  Patrick J. Flynn

                  Milissa K. Hofmann

LEGAL SUPPORT PERSONNEL

Steven D. Perkins   Judy K. Freeman

For full biographical listings, see the Martindale-Hubbell Law Directory

SPRINGFIELD,* Sangamon Co.

MOHAN, ALEWELT, PRILLAMAN & ADAMI (AV)

First of America Center, Suite 325, 1 North Old Capitol Plaza, 62701-1323
Telephone: 217-528-2517
Telecopier: 217-528-2553
Email: fprillam@counsel.com.

MEMBERS

Edward J. Alewelt   Paul E. Adami
        Cheryl Stickel Neal

OF COUNSEL

James T. Mohan

For Complete List of Firm Personnel, See General Section

For full biographical listings, see the Martindale-Hubbell Law Directory

URBANA,* Champaign Co.

WEBBER & THIES, P.C. (AV)

202 Lincoln Square, P.O. Box 189, 61803-0189
Telephone: 217-367-1126
FAX: 217-367-3752

Richard L. Thies   Craig R. Webber
        Holten D. Summers

For Complete List of Firm Personnel, See General Section

For full biographical listings, see the Martindale-Hubbell Law Directory

INDIANA

EVANSVILLE,* Vanderburgh Co.

LAW OFFICES OF RANDALL K. CRAIG (AV)

5000 East Virginia, Suite 1, 47715
Telephone: 812-477-3337
Telefax: 812-477-3658

For full biographical listings, see the Martindale-Hubbell Law Directory

FINE & HATFIELD (AV)

520 N.W. Second Street, P.O. Box 779, 47705-0779
Telephone: 812-425-3592
Telecopier: 812-421-4269
Email: Fine@Fine-Hatfield.com URL: http://www.Fine-Hatfield.com

MEMBER OF FIRM

Thomas R. Fitzsimmons

A List of Representative Clients Furnished Upon Request.

For full biographical listings, see the Martindale-Hubbell Law Directory

KAHN, DEES, DONOVAN & KAHN (AV)

P.O. Box 3646, 47735-3646
Telephone: 812-423-3183
Fax: 812-423-3841
Email: evvlaw@k2d2.com

MEMBERS OF FIRM

Alan N. Shovers   John E. Hegeman
G. Michael Schopmeyer   Jeffrey K. Helfrich

ASSOCIATES

Marjorie J. Scharpf   Mark L. Boos

Representative Clients: Joe W. Morgan, Inc.; Intrametco Processing, Inc.; Crescent Plastics, Inc.; Elmer Buchta Trucking, Inc.; Schuttler Music; Deaconess Hospital, Inc.; Old National Bancorp; North Park Cinemas, Inc.; Red Spot Paint & Varnish Co.

For Complete List of Firm Personnel, See General Section

For full biographical listings, see the Martindale-Hubbell Law Directory

JACK A. STONE AND ASSOCIATES (AV)

1400 Old National Bank Building, 47708
Telephone: 812-423-2045
Fax: Available Upon Request

For full biographical listings, see the Martindale-Hubbell Law Directory

FORT WAYNE,* Allen Co.

SHAMBAUGH, KAST, BECK & WILLIAMS (AV)

600 Standard Federal Plaza, 46802-2405
Telephone: 219-423-1430
Fax: 219-422-9038

MEMBERS OF FIRM

Michael H. Kast   Daniel E. Serban
Stephen J. Williams   John B. Powell
Edward E. Beck   Timothy L. Claxton
                 James D. Streit

Counsel for: Hagerman Construction Corp.; Rogers Markets, Inc.; K & H Realty Corp.; Olive B. Cole Foundation; M. E. Raker Foundation, Inc.; Associates Financial Services Co., of Indiana, Inc.; Professional Federal Credit Union; Fort Wayne Education Association; American Ambassador Casualty Company; CBT Credit Services, Inc.

For Complete List of Firm Personnel, See General Section

For full biographical listings, see the Martindale-Hubbell Law Directory

INDIANAPOLIS,* Marion Co.

ADINAMIS & ADINAMIS, ATTORNEYS, A PROFESSIONAL CORPORATION (AV)

8710 North Meridian Street, 46260
Telephone: 317-580-9000
Indianapolis Downtown Office, By Appointment: Chamber of Commerce Building, 320 North Meridian Street, 46204.

George P. Adinamis   Susan L. Adinamis
Carol M. Adinamis   Jeffrey A. Saunders

For full biographical listings, see the Martindale-Hubbell Law Directory

BAKER & DANIELS (AV)

300 North Meridian Street, 46204
Telephone: 317-237-0300
FAX: 317-237-1000
Fort Wayne, Indiana Office: 111 East Wayne Street, Suite 800.
Telephone: 219-424-8000.

(See Next Column)

BAKER & DANIELS, *Indianapolis—Continued*

South Bend, Indiana Office: First Bank Building, 205 West Jefferson Boulevard.
Telephone: 219-234-4149.
Elkhart, Indiana Office: 301 B South Main Street, Suite 307,
Telephone: 219-296-6000.
Washington, D.C. Office: 1701 K Street, N.W., Suite 400.
Telephone: 202-785-1565.

MEMBERS OF FIRM

Stephen H. Paul	Francina A. Dlouhy
Donald P. Bennett	J. Daniel Ogren

ASSOCIATES

Robert M. Bond	Brian S. Fennerty
Janet Madden Charles	

Representative Clients: Anthem Insurance Companies, Inc.; AT&T Corp.; Bank One, Indianapolis, N.A.; Borg-Warner Corp.; City of Indianapolis; Cummins Engine Co.; Eli Lilly and Co.; General Motors Corp.; Indianapolis Public Schools; United Airlines.

For Complete List of Firm Personnel, See General Section

For full biographical listings, see the Martindale-Hubbell Law Directory

---

BOSE MCKINNEY & EVANS (AV)

2700 First Indiana Plaza, 135 North Pennsylvania Street, 46204
Telephone: 317-684-5000
Facsimile: 317-684-5173
Indianapolis North Office: Suite 1201, 8888 Keystone Crossing, 46240.
Telephone: 317-574-3700.
Facsimile: 317-574-3716.

MEMBERS OF FIRM

Robert P. Kassing	R. J. McConnell
G. Pearson Smith, Jr.	Gary L. Chapman
Ronald M. Soskin	Donald M. Meyer

ASSOCIATE

J. Gregory Shelley

Representative Clients: First Indiana Bank; Indiana League of Savings Institutions, Inc.; Indianapolis Life Insurance Co.; Duke Realty Investments, Inc.; Emmis Broadcasting Corp.; Young Automotive Group; USX Corp.; Columbia Management, Inc.; Indiana Supply Company; Collins Auto Group.

For Complete List of Firm Personnel, See General Section

For full biographical listings, see the Martindale-Hubbell Law Directory

---

DALE & EKE, PROFESSIONAL CORPORATION (AV)

Suite 400, 9100 Keystone Crossing, 46240
Telephone: 317-844-7400
Fax: 317-574-9426

William J. Dale, Jr.	Karen A. Hosack
Joseph W. Eke	Dawn Michelle Snow

For full biographical listings, see the Martindale-Hubbell Law Directory

---

DANN PECAR NEWMAN & KLEIMAN, PROFESSIONAL CORPORATION (AV)

Suite 2300, One American Square Box 82008, 46282
Telephone: 317-632-3232; Indiana: 800-622-4799
Telecopy: 317-632-2962

Theodore R. Dann (1907-1993)	Walter E. Wolf, Jr.
Joel Yonover (1932-1995)	Barry E. Beldin
Philip D. Pecar	Robert D. Swhier, Jr.
Norman R. Newman	James P. Moloy
David H. Kleiman	Robert J. Schuckit
Jon B. Abels	Andrew A. Kleiman
Melvin R. Daniel	Michael J. Gabovitch
Lawrence F. Dorocke	Steven M. Pecar
Jeffrey A. Abrams	Benjamin A. Pecar
James H. Schwarz	Richard O. Kissel, II
Robert A. Rose	Joseph D. Calderon

OF COUNSEL

Linda E. Cantor	Anthony J. Rose

Ellen C. Siakotos	Angela L. Mansfield
Stacy L. Hill	Martha M. K. Baird
	Karin L. Veatch

Attorneys for: Indianapolis Machinery Co., Inc.; Melvin Simon & Associates, Inc.; Pacers Basketball Corp.; Universal Fire & Casualty Co., Inc.; Bank One, Indianapolis, NA; INB National Bank; Nachi Technology, Inc.; Pharmaceutical Corporation of America; Logo 7, Inc.

For full biographical listings, see the Martindale-Hubbell Law Directory

---

JOSEPH D. GEESLIN, JR. (AV)

Suite 2530 One Indiana Square, 46204
Telephone: 317-632-4421
Fax: 317-637-9755

For full biographical listings, see the Martindale-Hubbell Law Directory

---

ICE MILLER DONADIO & RYAN (AV)

One American Square Box 82001, 46282-0002
Telephone: 317-236-2100
Fax: 317-236-2219
Email: leel@imdr.com *URL:* http://www.imdr.com
South Bend, Indiana Office: 211 West Washington Street, Suite 2420.
Telephone: 219-234-7933.
Fax: 219-234-7965. Internet E-mail: leel@imdr.com. Web Site Address: http://www.imdr.com.

MEMBERS OF FIRM

Donald G. Sutherland	Gregory L. Pemberton
Leonard J. Betley	Steven K. Humke
James D. Kemper	Mark J. Richards
Barton T. Sprunger	Daniel S. Corsaro

OF COUNSEL

Daniel E. Fisher

STAFF ATTORNEY

Raymond J. Schoettle

ASSOCIATES

Joseph E. Whitsett, Jr.	Dean T. Burger
Terrence J. Keusch	Gareth W. Kuhl
Kathleen S. Kiefer	Gina M. Giacone

Counsel for: Cummins Engine Company, Inc.; Indianapolis Motor Speedway Corp.; Biomet, Inc.; Bristol-Myers Squibb Co.; Aluminum Company of America; Amax, Inc.; Community Hospitals of Indiana, Inc.; Pension Fund of the Christian Church; Thomson Consumer Electronics, Inc.; Reilly Industries, Inc.

For Complete List of Firm Personnel, See General Section

For full biographical listings, see the Martindale-Hubbell Law Directory

---

ROBERT A. LICHTENAUER (AV)

Suite 110, 8140 Knue Road, 46250
Telephone: 317-845-1988

For full biographical listings, see the Martindale-Hubbell Law Directory

---

LOCKE REYNOLDS BOYD & WEISELL (AV)

1000 Capital Center South, 201 North Illinois Street, 46204
Telephone: 317-237-3800
Telecopier: 317-237-3900

James J. McGrath	Michael T. Bindner
	Michael J. Schneider

Jeffrey S. Dible

Counsel For: Bethlehem Steel Corp.; Caylor-Nickel Clinic, P.C.; Countrymark Cooperative, Inc.; Health & Hospital Corporation; IBM Corporation; Messenger Courier Association of America; Mid-America Capital Resources, Inc. (subsidiary of IPALCO, Inc.); National Wine & Spirits Corp.; Resort Condominiums International, Inc.

For Complete List of Firm Personnel, See General Section

For full biographical listings, see the Martindale-Hubbell Law Directory

---

*LAFAYETTE,** Tippecanoe Co.

STUART & BRANIGIN (AV)

The Life Building, 300 Main Street, Suite 800, 47902
Telephone: 317-423-1561
Telecopier: 317-742-8175

MEMBERS OF FIRM

Allison Ellsworth Stuart (1886-1950)	Stephen R. Pennell
Roger D. Branigin (1902-1975)	Anthony S. Benton
Russell H. Hart	Erik D. Spykman
Roger D. Branigin, Jr.	William E. Emerick
Thomas L. Ryan	John C. Duffey
James V. McGlone	Mark E. DeYoung
Carl W. Kloepfer	Thomas B. Parent
Thomas R. McCully	Laura L. Bowker
Larry R. Fisher	Kevin D. Nicoson
Nina B. Kirkpatrick	Susan K. Roberts
Mark Lillianfeld	John M. Stuckey
	Deborah B. Trice

COUNSEL

John F. Bodle

ASSOCIATES

Brent W. Huber	David A. Starkweather
William P. Kealey	Geoffrey Blazi
	A. James Chareq

(See Next Column)

STUART & BRANIGIN—*Continued*

General Counsel for: The Lafayette Life Insurance Co.; INB National Bank, N.W.; Lafayette Home Hospital, Inc.
State Counsel for: Norfolk & Western Railway Co.
Mr. Ryan is Counsel to: The Trustees of Purdue University.
Representative Clients: Aluminum Company of America; Liberty Mutual Insurance Group.

For full biographical listings, see the Martindale-Hubbell Law Directory

---

MUNSTER, Lake Co.

PINKERTON AND FRIEDMAN, PROFESSIONAL CORPORATION (AV)

The Fairmont, 9245 Calumet Avenue Suite 201, 46321
Telephone: 219-836-3050
Fax: 219-836-2955

Milton Roth (1925-1996)	Jeffrey F. Gunning
Kirk A. Pinkerton	Gail Oosterhof
Stuart J. Friedman	Richard N. Shapiro

For full biographical listings, see the Martindale-Hubbell Law Directory

---

TERRE HAUTE, * Vigo Co.

WILKINSON, GOELLER, MODESITT, WILKINSON & DRUMMY (AV)

333 Ohio Street, P.O. Box 800, 47808-0800
Telephone: 812-232-4311
Fax: 812-235-5107

MEMBERS OF FIRM

Myrl O. Wilkinson	David H. Goeller
	William M. Olah

Representative Corporate Clients: Merchants National Bank; General Housewares Corp.; MAB Paints; Union Hospital; Associated Physicians and Surgeons Clinic, LCC.; PSI Energy, Inc.; Old National Trust Company; Old National Bank.

For Complete List of Firm Personnel, See General Section

For full biographical listings, see the Martindale-Hubbell Law Directory

---

IOWA

CEDAR RAPIDS, * Linn Co.

SHUTTLEWORTH & INGERSOLL, P.C. (AV)

500 Firstar Bank Building, P.O. Box 2107, 52406-2107
Telephone: 319-365-9461
Fax: 319-365-8443
Email: si-law@inav.net

Michael O. McDermott	Gary J. Streit
	William S. Hochstetler

Dean D. Carrington

COUNSEL

Ann F. Hammond

Representative Clients: Amana Society; Archer-Daniels-Midland Co.; Coe College; Firstar Bank Cedar Rapids, N.A.; Hansen Lind Meyer, Inc.; McLeod Telecommunications Group, Inc.; Met-Coil Systems Corporation; SCI Financial Group, Inc.

For Complete List of Firm Personnel, See General Section

For full biographical listings, see the Martindale-Hubbell Law Directory

---

COUNCIL BLUFFS, * Pottawattamie Co.

SMITH PETERSON LAW FIRM (AV)

35 Main Place, Suite 300, P.O. Box 249, 51502
Telephone: 712-328-1833
Fax: 712-328-8320
Omaha, Nebraska Office: 9290 West Dodge Road, Suite 205.
Telephone: 402-397-8500.
Fax: 402-397-5519.

MEMBERS OF FIRM

Raymond A. Smith (1892-1977)	Lawrence J. Beckman
John LeRoy Peterson	Gregory G. Barntsen
(1895-1969)	W. Curtis Hewett
Harold T. Beckman	Steven H. Krohn
Robert J. Laubenthal	Randy R. Ewing
Richard A. Heininger	Joseph D. Thornton

(See Next Column)

ASSOCIATES

T. J. Pattermann	Paul M. Shotkoski
Daniel Fretheim	(Not admitted in IA)

Representative Clients: Redland Insurance Group; Iowa Western Community College; Farm Credit Bank of Omaha; Demma Fruit Co.; Peoples National Bank; Council Bluffs Board of Water Works Trustee.

For full biographical listings, see the Martindale-Hubbell Law Directory

---

DES MOINES, * Polk Co.

DAVIS, BROWN, KOEHN, SHORS & ROBERTS, P.C. (AV)

(Formerly Davis, Hockenberg, Wine, Brown, Koehn & Shors, P.C.)
The Financial Center, 666 Walnut Street, Suite 2500, 50309-3993
Telephone: 515-288-2500
Cable: Davis Law
Facsimile: 515-243-0654
Affiliated London, England Office: Vizards, Solicitors, 42 Bedford Row. London WC1R 4JL England.
Telephone: 071-405-6302.
Facsimile: 071-405-6248.

Donald J. Brown	Frank J. Carroll
Stephen W. Roberts	Bruce I. Campbell
Michael G. Kulik	David B. VanSickel
	Nicholas H. Roby

William A. Boatwright	Mark L. Stember

For Complete List of Firm Personnel, See General Section

For full biographical listings, see the Martindale-Hubbell Law Directory

---

DICKINSON, MACKAMAN, TYLER & HAGEN, P.C. (AV)

Suite 1600 Hub Tower, 699 Walnut Street, 50309-3986
Telephone: 515-244-2600
Telecopier: 515-246-4550

F. Richard Lyford	David R. Rhein
Jeffrey T. Ramsey	(Not admitted in IA)
David M. Repp	Linda S. Weindruch

Representative Clients: Iowa Taxpayers Association; Preferred Risk Life Insurance Co.; Williams Cos.

For Complete List of Firm Personnel, See General Section

For full biographical listings, see the Martindale-Hubbell Law Directory

---

FINLEY, ALT, SMITH, SCHARNBERG, MAY & CRAIG, P.C. (AV)

604 Locust Street, Fourth Floor Equitable Building, 50309
Telephone: 515-288-0145
Telecopier: 515-288-2724

David C. Craig

Representative Clients: Aetna Casualty & Surety Co.; Aetna Life Insurance Co.; ALAS; American Society of Composers, Authors and Publishers; Equitable Life Assurance Society of the U.S.; Federated Insurance Co.; Meredith Corp.
Iowa Attorneys for: Midwest Medical Insurance Co.
District Attorneys for: Norfolk & Southern Railroad; Soo Line Railroad Company.

For Complete List of Firm Personnel, See General Section

For full biographical listings, see the Martindale-Hubbell Law Directory

---

GREFE & SIDNEY, P.L.C. (AV)

2222 Grand Avenue, P.O. Box 10434, 50306
Telephone: 515-245-4300
Fax: 515-245-4452
Email: GRANDFIRM@AOL.COM

Rolland E. Grefe	Robert C. Thomson
Thomas W. Carpenter	Craig S. Shannon
	Mary E. Kiener

Representative Clients: Easter Enterprises, Inc.; Freeman Decorating Co.; Pella Windows.

For Complete List of Firm Personnel, See General Section

For full biographical listings, see the Martindale-Hubbell Law Directory

---

SIOUX CITY, * Woodbury Co.

BERENSTEIN, MOORE, MOSER, BERENSTEIN & HEFFERNAN (AV)

300 Commerce Building, P.O. Box 3207, 51102
Telephone: 712-252-0020
Fax: 712-252-0656

MEMBERS OF FIRM

Marvin S. Berenstein	Jeffrey A. Johnson

(See Next Column)

BERENSTEIN, MOORE, MOSER, BERENSTEIN & HEFFERNAN, *Sioux City—Continued*

ASSOCIATE
Mitchell A. Herigstad

Representative Clients: Aalfs Manufacturing, Inc.; Boatmen's Bank; Beef Products, Inc.; Briar Cliff College; Canal Capital Corp.- Sioux City Stockyards; Firstar Bank Iowa, N.A.; Metropolitan Life Insurance Co.; Sioux Tools, Inc.- Snap-On-Tools; Marian Health Center, a division of Mercy Health Services; Wells Dairy & Blue Bunny Ice Cream.

For Complete List of Firm Personnel, See General Section

For full biographical listings, see the Martindale-Hubbell Law Directory

---

KANSAS

DODGE CITY, * Ford Co.

FOULSTON & SIEFKIN L.L.P. (AV)

810 Frontview, P.O. Box 1147, 67801
Telephone: 316-227-8126
Fax: 316-227-8451
Wichita, Kansas Office: 100 North Broadway, 700 Fourth Financial Center, 67202.
Telephone: 316-267-6371.
FAX: 316-267-6345.
Topeka, Kansas Office: 1515 Bank IV Tower, 534 Kansas Avenue, 66603.
Telephone: 913-233-3600.
FAX: 913-233-1610.
Member: Lex Mundi, A Global Association of 126 Independent Firms.

MEMBER OF FIRM
William P. Trenkle, Jr.

For Complete List of Firm Personnel, See General Section

For full biographical listings, see the Martindale-Hubbell Law Directory

---

TOPEKA, * Shawnee Co.

COFFMAN, DEFRIES & NOTHERN, A PROFESSIONAL ASSOCIATION (AV)

534 S. Kansas Avenue, Suite 925, 66603-3407
Telephone: 913-234-3461
Fax: 913-234-3363

Harold R. Schroeder (1920-1986)	James Robert Groff (Retired)
Barney J. Heeney, Jr. (Retired)	H. Hurst Coffman
	S. Lucky DeFries
R. Austin Nothern	

Richard Harmon	Susan Krehbiel William
Jeffrey A. Wietharn	

Representative Clients: Texaco; General Dynamics; Cohen Esrey Real Estate Co.; Colgate-Palmolive Co.; Simon Property Group, LP.

For full biographical listings, see the Martindale-Hubbell Law Directory

FOULSTON & SIEFKIN L.L.P. (AV)

1515 Bank IV Tower, 534 Kansas Avenue, 66603
Telephone: 913-233-3600
Fax: 913-233-1610
Wichita, Kansas Office: 100 North Broadway, 700 Fourth Financial Center, 67202.
Telephone: 316-267-6371.
Fax: 316-267-6345.
Dodge City, Kansas Office: 810 Frontview, P.O. Box 1147, 67801.
Telephone: 316-227-8126.
Fax: 316-227-8451.
Member: Lex Mundi, A Global Association of 126 Independent Firms.

MEMBER OF FIRM
James P. Rankin

For full biographical listings, see the Martindale-Hubbell Law Directory

GOODELL, STRATTON, EDMONDS & PALMER, L.L.P. (AV)

515 South Kansas Avenue, 66603-3999
Telephone: 913-233-0593
Telecopier: 913-233-8870
Email: GSEP@CJNETWORKS.COM

MEMBERS OF FIRM
H. Philip Elwood   Gerald J. Letourneau

OF COUNSEL
Robert A. McClure

(See Next Column)

SPECIAL COUNSEL
Joseph E. McKinney

Counsel for: St. Paul Fire & Marine Insurance Co.
General Counsel for: American Home Life Insurance Co.; Columbian National Title Insurance Co.; The Menninger Foundation; Stauffer Communications, Inc.; Kansas Medical Society; Kansas Hospital Association.

For Complete List of Firm Personnel, See General Section

For full biographical listings, see the Martindale-Hubbell Law Directory

---

WICHITA, * Sedgwick Co.

BEVER, DYE, MUSTARD & BELIN, L.C. (AV)

106 W. Douglas, Suite 700, 67202-3390
Telephone: 316-263-8294
Fax: 316-263-3142
Email: beverdye@feist.com

Ellis D. Bever (Retired)	R. Chris Robe
James D. Dye (1908-1995)	Eric J. Larson
Thomas D. Mustard (1909-1979)	Robert M. Hughes
Oscar F. Belin	Gregory L. Franken
Don B. Stahr	David B. Sutton
William M. Cobb	R. Eric Ireland
Jack D. Flesher	Hellen L. Haag
Karla R. Kerschen	

Representative Clients: Borton, Inc.; City Publishing Co., Inc.; INTRUST Bank, NA; F.G. Holl Trust; Kansas Health Foundation; Klepper Oil Co.; Krause Plow Corp.; National Cooperative Refinery Assn.; Pickrell Drilling Co.; Vanier, Inc.

For full biographical listings, see the Martindale-Hubbell Law Directory

---

FOULSTON & SIEFKIN L.L.P. (AV)

700 Fourth Financial Center, 67202
Telephone: 316-267-6371
Facsimile: 316-267-6345
Topeka, Kansas Office: 1515 Bank IV Tower, 534 Kansas Avenue, 66603.
Telephone: 913-233-3600.
Fax: 913-233-1610.
Dodge City, Kansas Office: 810 Frontview, P.O. Box 1147, 67801.
Telephone: 316-227-8126.
Fax: 316-227-8451.
Member: Lex Mundi, A Global Association of 126 Independent Firms.

MEMBERS OF FIRM
Stanley G. Andeel	Eric F. Melgren
Harvey R. Sorensen	William P. Trenkle, Jr.
Christopher M. Hurst	(Resident, Dodge City Office)
James P. Rankin	
(Resident, Topeka Office)	

For Complete List of Firm Personnel, See General Section

For full biographical listings, see the Martindale-Hubbell Law Directory

---

KENTUCKY

BOWLING GREEN, * Warren Co.

ENGLISH, LUCAS, PRIEST & OWSLEY (AV)

1101 College Street, P.O. Box 770, 42102-0770
Telephone: 502-781-6500
Telecopier: 502-782-7782
Email: inquiry@elpo.com

MEMBERS OF FIRM
Charles E. English   Wade T. Markham, II

ASSOCIATES
Vance Cook   Elizabeth J. McKinney

For Complete List of Firm Personnel, See General Section

For full biographical listings, see the Martindale-Hubbell Law Directory

---

GEORGETOWN, * Scott Co.

E. DURWARD WELDON (AV)

217 East Main Street, 40324
Telephone: 502-863-1285

Approved Attorney for: Lawyers Title Insurance Corporation of Richmond, Virginia; Louisville Title Division of Commonwealth Land Title Insurance Co. (Binder Agent); The Equitable Life Assurance Society of the United States.

For full biographical listings, see the Martindale-Hubbell Law Directory

LEXINGTON,* Fayette Co.

WILLIAM R. BAGBY (AV)

1107 First National Building, 167 West Main Street, 40507
Telephone: 606-254-2321

Reference: Bank One.

For full biographical listings, see the Martindale-Hubbell Law Directory

---

STOLL, KEENON & PARK, LLP (AV)

201 E. Main Street, Suite 1000, 40507-1380
Telephone: 606-231-3000
Telecopier: 606-253-1093; 606-253-1027
Frankfort, Kentucky Office: 307 Washington Street, 40601.
Telephone: 502-875-6220.
Telecopier: 502-875-6235.
Louisville, Kentucky Office: 400 West Market Street, Suite 2650,
40202-3377.
Telephone: 502-568-9100.
Telecopier: 502-568-5700.

MEMBERS OF FIRM

William T. Bishop, III	Frank L. Wilford
Douglas P. Romaine	C. Joseph Beavin
John W. Walters, Jr.	

ASSOCIATE
Roger W. Madden

Representative Clients: A.T. Massey Coal Co., Inc.; Breeders Cup Ltd.; Claiborne Farm; Delta Airlines; Keeneland Assn., Inc.; Kentucky Thoroughbred Assn., Inc.; Mill Ridge Farm, Ltd.; Pathology & Cytology Laboratories, Inc.

For Complete List of Firm Personnel, See General Section

For full biographical listings, see the Martindale-Hubbell Law Directory

---

LOUISVILLE,* Jefferson Co.

MIDDLETON & REUTLINGER, P.S.C. (AV)

2500 Brown and Williamson Tower, 40202-3410
Telephone: 502-584-1135
Fax: 502-561-0442
New Albany, Indiana Office: 2623 Charlestown Road, 47150.
Telephone: 812-944-7215.

Brooks Alexander	D. Randall Gibson
Kipley J. McNally	

Clayton R. Hume

Representative Clients: The Kroger Co.; Campbell Tobacco Rehandling Co., Inc.; Chevron U.S.A., Inc.; Henderson Electric Co.; Cardinal Aluminum Co.; Porcelain Metal Corp.; EnTrade Corp.; Soltech, Inc.; Bluegrass Electronics, Inc.; Alexander & Alexander (SISCO).

For Complete List of Firm Personnel, See General Section

For full biographical listings, see the Martindale-Hubbell Law Directory

---

RUBIN HAYS & FOLEY (AV)

First Trust Centre 200 South Fifth Street, 40202
Telephone: 502-569-7550
Telecopier: 502-569-7555

MEMBERS OF FIRM

Wm. Carl Fust	Lisa Koch Bryant
Harry Lee Meyer	Sharon C. Hardy
David W. Gray	Charles S. Musson
Irvin D. Foley	W. Randall Jones
Joseph R. Gathright, Jr.	K. Gail Russell

ASSOCIATES

Christian L. Juckett	Courtney Lynn McCall

OF COUNSEL

James E. Fahey	Newman T. Guthrie

Representative Clients: J.C. Bradford & Co., Inc.; J.J.B. Hilliard, W.L. Lyons, Inc.; Huntington National Bank; Liberty National Bank and Trust Company; National City Bank; PNC Bank; Prudential Bache & Co., Inc.; Prudential Securities, Inc.; Society Bank; Stock Yards Bank and Trust Co.

For full biographical listings, see the Martindale-Hubbell Law Directory

---

TAUSTINE, POST, SOTSKY, BERMAN, FINEMAN & KOHN (AV)

8th Floor Marion E. Taylor Building, 40202
Telephone: 502-589-5760
FAX: 502-584-5927
Email: 73344.624@compuserve.com

MEMBERS OF FIRM

Robert A. Kohn	Maria A. Fernandez

For full biographical listings, see the Martindale-Hubbell Law Directory

---

LOUISIANA

ALEXANDRIA,* Rapides Parish

CROWELL & OWENS, L.L.C. (AV)

Hibernia National Bank Building Sixth Floor, P.O. Box 330, 71309-0330
Telephone: 318-445-1488
Fax: 318-445-9098

MEMBERS OF FIRM

William B. Owens	W. Brent Pearson

ASSOCIATE
W. Alan Pesnell

For full biographical listings, see the Martindale-Hubbell Law Directory

---

GOLD, WEEMS, BRUSER, SUES & RUNDELL, A PROFESSIONAL LAW CORPORATION (AV)

2001 MacArthur Drive, P.O. Box 6118, 71307-6118
Telephone: 318-445-6471
Telecopier: 318-445-6476

Charles S. Weems, III	Kenneth O. Ortego
	Dorrell Jarrell Brister

Representative Clients: Automated Prescription Systems, Inc.; Roy O. Martin Lumber Co., Inc.; Rapides Bank & Trust Company in Alexandria; Aetna Casualty Group; Allstate Insurance Co.; Texas Industries, Inc.; International Paper Company; Louisiana-Pacific Corporation.

For Complete List of Firm Personnel, See General Section

For full biographical listings, see the Martindale-Hubbell Law Directory

---

BATON ROUGE,* East Baton Rouge Parish

KEAN, MILLER, HAWTHORNE, D'ARMOND, McCOWAN & JARMAN, L.L.P. (AV)

22nd Floor, One American Place, P.O. Box 3513, 70821
Telephone: 504-387-0999
Fax: 504-388-9133
New Orleans, Louisiana Office: Energy Centre, Suite 1470, 1100 Poydras Street.
Telephone: 504-585-3050.
Fax: 504-585-3051.
Plaquemine, Louisiana Office: Suite 10, 23425 Railroad Avenue.
Telephone: 504-687-9845.
Fax: 504-382-3445.

MEMBERS OF FIRM

Ben R. Miller, Jr.	Isaac M. Gregorie, Jr.
Carey J. Messina	G. Blane Clark, Jr.
	Todd A. Rossi

Dean Paul Cazenave	Kevin C. Curry

Representative Clients: Arcadian Corporation, Geismar, LA; Copolymer Rubber and Chemical Corporation, Baton Rouge, LA; Dow Chemical Company, Midland, CO; Dowell Schlumberger, Houston, TX; Georgia Gulf Corporation, Atlanta, GA; ICI Americas, Wilmington, DE; The Lamar Advertising Co., Baton Rouge, LA; Riverwood International Corporation, West Monroe, LA; Rhone-Poulenc Basic Chemicals Company, Shelton, CT; Vulcan Materials Company, Birmingham, AL.

For Complete List of Firm Personnel, See General Section

For full biographical listings, see the Martindale-Hubbell Law Directory

---

GREGORY A. PLETSCH & ASSOCIATES A PROFESSIONAL LAW CORPORATION (AV)

Suite 301, Four United Plaza, 8555 United Plaza Boulevard, 70809
Telephone: 504-929-8525
Telecopier: 504-929-8520

Gregory A. Pletsch

For full biographical listings, see the Martindale-Hubbell Law Directory

---

SCHANEVILLE & BARINGER, L.L.C. (AV)

918 Government Street Second Floor, 70802
Telephone: 504-383-9953
Fax: 504-387-3198

Dan D. Schaneville	Dale R. Baringer
	Donald Meltzer

John C. Hopewell, III

OF COUNSEL
David O. Mooney

For full biographical listings, see the Martindale-Hubbell Law Directory

Baton Rouge—Continued

SCHMIDT & KUEHNE, A PROFESSIONAL LAW CORPORATION (AV)

10935 Perkins Road, P.O. Box 80317, 70898
Telephone: 504-767-7093
Telecopier: 504-767-7096

Robert C. Schmidt   G. Bruce Kuehne

For full biographical listings, see the Martindale-Hubbell Law Directory

WATSON, BLANCHE, WILSON & POSNER (AV)

505 North Boulevard, P.O. Drawer 2995, 70821-2995
Telephone: 504-387-5511
Fax: 504-387-5972

Harvey H. Posner   Robert L. Roland
                Richard S. Dunn

Representative Clients: Citizens Savings and Loan Association; Community Coffee Company, Inc.; Louisiana Hospital Association; Prudential Insurance Company of America (The).

For full biographical listings, see the Martindale-Hubbell Law Directory

MONROE,* Ouachita Parish

ARNOLD, PETTWAY & DIXON, L.L.P. (AV)

1603 Lamy Lane, 71201
Telephone: 318-388-1950
Telecopier: 318-323-7478

Forrest E. Arnold, III   James R. Pettway
                Joe H. Dixon, Jr.

Representative Clients: Bancroft Bag, Inc.; Bulk Pack, Inc.; Homeland Federal Savings Bank; Johnny's Pizza House, Inc.

For full biographical listings, see the Martindale-Hubbell Law Directory

JOHN L. LUFFEY, JR. (AV)

1101 Royal Avenue, Drawer 7580, 71211-7580
Telephone: 318-323-3800
Fax: 318-325-8357
Email: jluffey@iamerica.net

For full biographical listings, see the Martindale-Hubbell Law Directory

THOMPSON, SPARKS, DEAN & MORRIS (AV)

A Partnership including a Professional Corporation
1401 Royal Street, P.O. Box 2867, 71207
Telephone: 318-388-1440
Fax: 318-322-0887

MEMBERS OF FIRM

M. C. Thompson (1885-1970)   George B. Dean, Jr., (P.C.)
James D. Sparks (1910-1987)   Wood T. Sparks
                John C. Morris, III

Representative Clients: South Central Bell Telephone Co.; Greater Ouachita Water Company; PHH Homequity Corp.; Commonwealth Relocation Services, Inc.; Remax, Monroe; Bell South Advertising & Publishing Corp.; Premier Mortgage Corp.; Countrywide Funding Corp.
Approved Attorneys for: Central Bank; Federal Land Bank.

For full biographical listings, see the Martindale-Hubbell Law Directory

NEW ORLEANS,* Orleans Parish

DEUTSCH, KERRIGAN & STILES, L.L.P. (AV)

A Partnership including Professional Law Corporations
755 Magazine Street, 70130-3672
Telephone: 504-581-5141
Cable Address: "Dekest"
Telex: 584358
Telecopier: 504-566-1201
Email: dks@dksno.com *URL:* http://www.dksno.com
St. Tammany Parish Office: 550 Pontchartrain Drive, Suite 200, Slidell, LA. 70458.
Telephone: 504-639-0555.
Fax: 504-639-0550

MEMBERS OF FIRM

William W. Messersmith, III,   Daniel A. Smith
  (P.L.C.)   Richard B. Montgomery III
Peter J. Butler   Susan Whittington Leidner
                Peter J. Butler, Jr.

ASSOCIATES

Richard G. Passler   W. Christopher Beary

For Complete List of Firm Personnel, See General Section

For full biographical listings, see the Martindale-Hubbell Law Directory

MICHAEL L. ECKSTEIN ATTORNEY AT LAW A PROFESSIONAL CORPORATION (AV)

1515 Poydras Street, Suite 2195, 70112
Telephone: 504-527-0701
Telecopier: 504-566-0040
VMX: 504-889-8876

Michael L. Eckstein   David Coleman Raphael, Jr.

Representative Clients: Anserphone of New Orleans, Inc.; Dixie Web Graphic Corporation; Kencoil, Inc.; Life Point Systems, Inc.; Meeks Petroleum Company; Int-Oil Ventures, Ltd.; Dan-Gulf Shipping, Inc.; Axonn Corporation; Action Ink, Inc.; TCB Industries, Inc.

For full biographical listings, see the Martindale-Hubbell Law Directory

ELKINS & ASSOCIATES, A PROFESSIONAL LAW CORPORATION (AV)

201 St. Charles Avenue, Suite 3700, 70170
Telephone: 504-529-3600
Fax: 504-529-7163

Gary J. Elkins   Pamela W. Hammond
Yvonne Chalker   Scott D. Morgan
David B. Epstein   A. Kelton Longwell

OF COUNSEL
Jerry F. Palmer

Representative Clients: The Aetna Casualty and Surety Co.; Atlantis International, Inc.; Banque Indosuez; Chevron Land and Development, Inc.; Chrestia & Staub, Inc.; Circus Circus; CSLA, Inc.; Cross Marine, Inc.; Cucos Inc.; Desire Community Housing Corporation; Enertech Industries, Inc.

For full biographical listings, see the Martindale-Hubbell Law Directory

THE GODFREY FIRM A PROFESSIONAL LAW CORPORATION (AV)

2500 Energy Centre, 1100 Poydras Street, 70163-2500
Telephone: 504-585-7538
Fax: 504-585-7535

Jarrell E. Godfrey, Jr.   Cloyd F. Van Hook
                Patrick M. Files

For full biographical listings, see the Martindale-Hubbell Law Directory

LISKOW & LEWIS, A PROFESSIONAL LAW CORPORATION (AV)

50th Floor, One Shell Square, 70139
Telephone: 504-581-7979
Telecopier: 504-556-4108; 504-556-4109
Lafayette, Louisiana Office: 822 Harding Street, P.O. Box 52008.
Telephone: 318-232-7424.
Telecopier: 318-267-2399.

Leon J. Reymond, Jr.   Marguerite A. Noonan
                Robert S. Angelico

Julia M. Pearce

Representative Clients: BP Exploration Inc.; Chevron U.S.A.; Cooper Industries Inc.; Ingram Industries; OXY USA Inc.; Texaco Inc.; Unocal Corp.

For Complete List of Firm Personnel, See General Section

For full biographical listings, see the Martindale-Hubbell Law Directory

MILLING, BENSON, WOODWARD, HILLYER, PIERSON & MILLER, L.L.P. (AV)

A Partnership including Professional Law Corporations
Suite Twenty-Three Hundred, 909 Poydras Street, 70112-1017
Telephone: 504-569-7000
Cable Address: "Milling"
Telex: 58-4211
Telecopier: 504-569-7001
ABA net: 15656
MCI Mail: "Milling"
Lafayette, Louisiana Office: 101 La Rue France, Suite 200.
Telephone: 318-232-3929.
Telecopier: 318-233-4957.

MEMBERS OF FIRM

David J. Conroy (P.C.)   Richard A. Whann (P.C.)
William C. Gambel (P.C.)   Hilton S. Bell (P.C.)
Charles A. Snyder (P.C.)   John W. Colbert (P.C.)

PARTNERS EMERITUS

M. Truman Woodward, Jr.,   G. Henry Pierson, Jr., (P.C.)
  (P.C.)

ASSOCIATE
Lisa F. Talley

For List of Representative Clients and Complete List of Firm Personnel, See General Section.

For Complete List of Firm Personnel, See General Section

For full biographical listings, see the Martindale-Hubbell Law Directory

New Orleans—Continued

PHELPS DUNBAR, L.L.P. (AV)

Texaco Center, 400 Poydras Street, 70130-3245
Telephone: 504-566-1311
Telecopier: 504-568-9130, 504-568-9007
Cable Address: "Howspencer"
Telex: 584125 WU
Telex: 6821155 WUI
Email: info@phelps.com
Baton Rouge, Louisiana Office: Suite 701, City National Bank Building,
P.O. Box 4412.
Telephone: 504-346-0285.
Telecopier: 504-381-9197.
Jackson, Mississippi Office: Suite 500, Mtel Centré, 200 South Lamar
Street, P.O. Box 23066.
Telephone: 601-352-2300.
Telecopier: 601-360-9777.
Tupelo, Mississippi Office: Seventh Floor, One Mississippi Plaza, P.O. Box
1220.
Telephone: 601-842-7907.
Telecopier: 601-842-3873.
Houston, Texas Office: Suite 900, 3040 Post Oak Boulevard.
Telephone: 713-626-1386.
Telecopier: 713-626-1388.
London, England Office: Suite 731, Level 7, Lloyd's, 1 Lime Street,
London EC3M 7DQ England.
Telephone: 011-44-171-929-4765.
Telecopier: 011-44-171-929-0046.
Telex: 987321.

MEMBERS OF FIRM

F. M. Bush, III (Not admitted
in LA; Jackson and Tupelo,
Mississippi Offices)
C. Delbert Hosemann, Jr. (Not
admitted in LA; Resident,
Jackson, Mississippi Office)
Robert W. Nuzum
Glover A. Russell, Jr. (Not
admitted in LA; Resident,
Jackson, Mississippi Office)

Richard E. Matheny (Resident,
Baton Rouge, Louisiana
Office)
Deborah Shelby Nichols (Not
admitted in LA; Resident,
Jackson, Mississippi Office)
David P. Webb (Not admitted
in LA; Resident, Jackson,
Mississippi Office)

COUNSEL

Jane E. Armstrong
Linda Bounds Sherman (Not
admitted in LA; Resident,
Jackson, Mississippi Office)
Gregory D. Pirkle (Not admitted
in LA; Jackson and Tupelo,
Mississippi Offices)

John V. Eskrigge (Not admitted
in LA; Resident, Jackson,
Mississippi Office)

ASSOCIATES

John B. Beard (Not admitted in
LA; Resident, Jackson,
Mississippi Office)
John B. Landry, Jr. (Not
admitted in LA; Resident,
Jackson, Mississippi Office)

Stephen M. Wilson (Not
admitted in LA; Jackson and
Tupelo, Mississippi Offices)

Representative Clients: Bank of Mississippi; Dominion Resources, Inc.; Falco
Lime, Inc.; First National Bank of Commerce; First National Bank of Jefferson Parish; Hibernia National Bank; Louisiana General Services, Inc.; Pathology Laboratories, Inc. dba Puckett Labs; Rubicon Inc.

For Complete List of Firm Personnel, See General Section

For full biographical listings, see the Martindale-Hubbell Law Directory

---

SHREVEPORT, * Caddo Parish

BARLOW AND HARDTNER L.C. (AV)

Tenth Floor, Louisiana Tower, 401 Edwards Street, 71101-3289
Telephone: 318-227-1131
Telecopier: 318-227-1141
Mailing Address: P.O. Box 8, Shreveport, Louisiana, 71161-0008

Quintin T. Hardtner, III   Malcolm S. Murchison
                    David R. Taggart

OF COUNSEL

Cecil E. Ramey, Jr.   Paula Hazelrig Hickman

Representative Clients: Kelley Oil Corporation; NorAm Energy Corp. (formerly Arkla, Inc.); Central and South West Corporation; Panhandle Eastern
Corp.; Pennzoil Producing Co.; Johnson Controls, Inc.; Ashland Oil, Inc.;
Southwestern Electric Power Company; General Electric Co.

For Complete List of Firm Personnel, See General Section

For full biographical listings, see the Martindale-Hubbell Law Directory

---

MAINE

LEWISTON, Androscoggin Co.

BRANN & ISAACSON (AV)

184 Main Street, P.O. Box 3070, 04243-3070
Telephone: 207-786-3566
Telecopier: 207-783-9325
Email: JMTHO7A@Prodigy.COM

MEMBERS OF FIRM

Louis J. Brann (1876-1948)
Peter A. Isaacson (1895-1980)
Irving Isaacson
George S. Isaacson
Alfred C. Frawley, III

Martin I. Eisenstein
Martha E. Greene
David W. Bertoni
Peter D. Lowe
Benjamin W. Lund

ASSOCIATES

Daniel C. Stockford
Roy T. Pierce

David C. Pierson
Kevin R. Haley

Representative Clients: L.L. Bean, Inc.; Direct Marketing Assn.; Readers
Digest Assn.; The Sharper Image; Bantam Doubleday Dell, Inc.; Livermore
Falls Trust Co.; Dow Chemical Co.; United Egg Producers; Miller Hydro
Group.

For full biographical listings, see the Martindale-Hubbell Law Directory

---

PORTLAND, * Cumberland Co.

LeBLANC & YOUNG (AV)

183 Middle Street, P.O. Box 7950, 04112-7950
Telephone: 207-772-2800
Facsimile: 207-772-2822
Email: firm@leblancyoung.com *URL:* http:///www.leblancyoung.com

Richard P. LeBlanc   James H. Young, II
          Abigail King Diggins

For full biographical listings, see the Martindale-Hubbell Law Directory

McCANDLESS & HUNT (AV)

57 Exchange Street, 04101
Telephone: 207-772-4100
Telecopier: 207-772-1300

MEMBERS OF FIRM

Eileen M. L. Epstein   David E. Hunt
          Elizabeth T. McCandless

ASSOCIATE

Dennis J. O'Donovan

For full biographical listings, see the Martindale-Hubbell Law Directory

---

PIERCE ATWOOD (AV)

One Monument Square, 04101
Telephone: 207-791-1100
Fax: 207-791-1350
Email: info@PierceAtwood.com
Augusta, Maine Office: 77 Winthrop Street.
Telephone: 207-622-6311.
Fax: 207-623-9367.
Newburyport, Massachusetts Office: 6 Harris Street.
Telephone: 508-465-9599.
Fax: 508-465-9945.

MEMBERS OF FIRM

Fred C. Scribner, Jr. (1908-1994)
Everett P. Ingalls
James G. Good
Daniel M. Snow

Michael R. Currie
William H. Nichols
Sarah H. Beard
Barbara K. Wheaton

OF COUNSEL

William C. Smith

ASSOCIATES

Michael N. Ambler, Jr.
Eric D. Altholz

Mary McQuillen
Jonathan A. Block

COUNSEL

Michael S. Wilson

For Complete List of Firm Personnel, See General Section

For full biographical listings, see the Martindale-Hubbell Law Directory

---

PRETI, FLAHERTY, BELIVEAU & PACHIOS (AV)

A Limited Liability Company
443 Congress Street, P.O. Box 11410, 04104-7410
Telephone: 207-791-3000
Telecopier: 207-791-3111
Email: admin@pfbpnet.com
Augusta, Maine Office: 45 Memorial Circle, P.O. Box 1058, 04332-1058.
Telephone: 207-623-5300.
Telecopier: 207-623-2914.

(See Next Column)

PRETI, FLAHERTY, BELIVEAU & PACHIOS, *Portland—Continued*

MEMBERS OF FIRM

Severin M. Beliveau	James C. Pitney, Jr.
(Augusta Office)	(Augusta Office)

Michael L. Sheehan

ASSOCIATE

James E. Phipps

Representative Clients: IBM; IMB Credit Corp.; Bowater Inc./Great Northern Paper Inc.; UAH Hydro-Kennebec L.P.; Stratton Energy Associates; United Timber Corp.; Mount Desert Island Hospital; Maine Coast Memorial Hospital; Maine Auto Dealers Assn.; Maine Oil Dealers Assn.

For Complete List of Firm Personnel, See General Section

For full biographical listings, see the Martindale-Hubbell Law Directory

---

ROCKLAND,* Knox Co.

STROUT & PAYSON, P.A. (AV)

10 Masonic Street, P.O. Box 248, 04841-0248
Telephone: 207-594-8400
Fax: 207-594-2724

Arthur E. Strout	Esther R. Barnhart
Joseph B. Pellicani (1936-1988)	Carol Ann Lundquist
Robert J. Levine	Randal E. Watkinson

Elizabeth Biddle Jennings

OF COUNSEL

Curtis M. Payson	John Knight

Approved Attorneys for: First American Title Insurance Co.; Chicago Title Insurance Co.

For full biographical listings, see the Martindale-Hubbell Law Directory

---

SOUTH PORTLAND, Cumberland Co.

VAN MEER & BELANGER, P.A. (AV)

25 Long Creek Drive, 04106
Telephone: 207-871-7500
Fax: 207-871-7505

Thomas J. Van Meer	D. Kelley Young
Norman R. Belanger	Richard N. Bryant

Betts J. Gorsky

For full biographical listings, see the Martindale-Hubbell Law Directory

---

MARYLAND

BALTIMORE,* (Independent City)

FERGUSON, SCHETELICH, HEFFERNAN & MURDOCK, P.A. (AV)

1300 NationsBank Center 1, 100 South Charles Street, 21201
Telephone: 410-837-2200
Fax: 410-837-1188
Email: fshm@ix.netcom

Robert L. Ferguson, Jr.	Christopher J. Heffernan
Thomas J. Schetelich	M. Brooke Murdock

Michael N. Russo, Jr.	Peter Joseph Basile
Jodi K. Ebersole	Ann D. Ware

For full biographical listings, see the Martindale-Hubbell Law Directory

---

MCKENNEY, THOMSEN AND BURKE, LLP (AV)

Suite 400, One North Charles Street, 21201
Telephone: 410-539-2595
FAX: 410-783-0710
Washington, D.C. Office: Suite 500, 1225 Eye Street, N.W.
Telephone: 202-682-4741.
FAX: 202-547-3713.

OF COUNSEL

W. Gibbs McKenney

MEMBERS OF FIRM

George E. Thomsen	Paul E. Burke, Jr.

Roszel C. Thomsen, II

ASSOCIATES

Hedley A. Clark	Robin McDaniel Hough

References: NationsBank; Mercantile-Safe Deposit & Trust Co.; Carroll County Bank and Trust Co.

For full biographical listings, see the Martindale-Hubbell Law Directory

---

LOUISE Y. MELEDIN (AV)

406 Bosley Avenue, 21204-0901
Telephone: 410-494-8833
Fax: 410-583-9899

OF COUNSEL

Henry L. Meledin

For full biographical listings, see the Martindale-Hubbell Law Directory

---

PIPER & MARBURY L.L.P. (AV)

Charles Center South, 36 South Charles Street, 21201-3018
Telephone: 410-539-2530
FAX: 410-539-0489
Email: lawfirm@pipermar.com
Washington, D.C. Office: 1200 Nineteenth Street, N.W., 20036-2430.
Telephone: 202-861-3900.
FAX: 202-223-2085.
Easton, Maryland Office: 117 Bay Street, 21601-2703.
Telephone: 410-820-4460.
FAX: 410-820-4463.
New York, N.Y. Office: 1251 Avenue of the Americas, 10020-1104.
Telephone: 212-835-6000.
FAX: 212-835-6001.
Philadelphia, Pennsylvania Office: 3400 Two Logan Square, 18th & Arch Streets, 19103-2762.
Telephone: 215-656-3300.
FAX: 215-656-3301.

MEMBERS OF FIRM

Stuart A. Smith	Lawrence M. Katz
(Resident, New York Office)	Joseph H. Langhirt

Lee A. Sheller

ASSOCIATES

Stephen M. Sharkey	Jordan I. Bailowitz

For Complete List of Firm Personnel, See General Section

For full biographical listings, see the Martindale-Hubbell Law Directory

---

RICHARD T. STANSBURY A PROFESSIONAL ASSOCIATION (AV)

Suite 920, The B & O Building, Two North Charles Street, 21201-3754
Telephone: 410-727-6200
Facsimile: 410-385-2939
Annapolis, Maryland Office: 5th Floor, The Conte Building, 116 Defense Highway.
Telephone: 410-974-6007.
Facsimile: 410-974-6019.

Richard T. Stansbury

For full biographical listings, see the Martindale-Hubbell Law Directory

---

STEWART, PLANT & BLUMENTHAL, LLC (AV)

Suite 910 7 St. Paul Street, 21202
Telephone: 410-347-0506
FAX: 410-347-0513

MEMBERS OF FIRM

C. Van Leuven Stewart	Max E. Blumenthal
A. MacDonough Plant	Hugh A. ("Jay") Mitchell, Jr.

ASSOCIATES

Katherine W. Plant	Jonathan G. Lasley

Lisa J. McGrath

OF COUNSEL

Adena W. Testa

For full biographical listings, see the Martindale-Hubbell Law Directory

---

VENABLE ATTORNEYS AT LAW VENABLE, BAETJER AND HOWARD, LLP (AV)

A Partnership including Professional Corporations
1800 Mercantile Bank & Trust Building, 2 Hopkins Plaza, 21201
Telephone: 410-244-7400
Email: INFO@Venable.win.net
Washington, D.C. Office: Venable, Baetjer, Howard & Civiletti LLP. Suite 1000, 1201 New York Avenue, N.W.
Telephone: 202-962-4800.
McLean, Virginia Office: Suite 400, 2010 Corporate Ridge.
Telephone: 703-760-1600.
Rockville, Maryland Office: Suite 500, One Church Street, P. O. Box 1906.
Telephone: 301-217-5600.
Towson, Maryland Office: 210 Allegheny Avenue, P. O. Box 5517.
Telephone: 410-494-6200.

MEMBERS OF FIRM

Jacques T. Schlenger (P.C.)	Lars E. Anderson (Not admitted
Neal D. Borden (Also at	in MD; Resident, McLean,
Washington, D.C. Office)	Virginia Office)
Daniel O'C. Tracy, Jr. (Also at	Alexander I. Lewis, III (P.C.)
Rockville, Maryland Office)	(Also at Towson, Maryland
Jan K. Guben (Also at	Office)
Washington, D. C Office)	

(See Next Column)

VENABLE ATTORNEYS AT LAW VENABLE, BAETJER AND HOWARD, LLP— *Continued*

MEMBERS OF FIRM (Continued)

Michael Schatzow (Also at Washington, D.C. Office)
Bryson L. Cook (P.C.) (Also at Washington, D.C. Office)
Barbara E. Schlaff
L. Paige Marvel
Edward L. Wender (P.C.)
David M. Fleishman
Mitchell Kolkin
W. Robert Zinkham
Robert L. Waldman

John A. Roberts (Also at Rockville, Maryland Office)
Robert J. Bolger, Jr. (Also at Washington, D.C. Office)
Bruce H. Jurist (Also at Washington, D.C. Office)
James V. Bitonti (Resident, McLean, Virginia Office)
Newton B. Fowler, III
Michael J. Baader
Jeffrey K. Gonya

Robert H. Geis, Jr.

OF COUNSEL

Robert M. Thomas (P.C.)
Robert R. Bair (P.C.)
Emried D. Cole, Jr.

John A. Wilhelm (Not admitted in MD; Resident, McLean, Virginia Office)

Todd K. Snyder

ASSOCIATES

Louis B. Barr
Wallace E. Christner (Also at Washington, D.C. Office)
John P. Edgar
Gregory L. Laubach (Resident, Rockville, Maryland Office)
Traci H. Mundy (Not admitted in MD; Resident, McLean, Virginia Office)

Brian J. O'Connor (Not admitted in MD)
Neal H. Strum
Linda Marotta Thomas
Elizabeth M.S. Whaling
Robin L. Zimelman

For Complete List of Firm Personnel, See General Section

For full biographical listings, see the Martindale-Hubbell Law Directory

---

BETHESDA, Montgomery Co.

PALEY, ROTHMAN, GOLDSTEIN, ROSENBERG & COOPER, CHARTERED (AV)

Seventh Floor, One Bethesda Center, 4800 Hampden Lane, 20814
Telephone: 301-656-7603
Telecopier: 301-654-7354
Email: prg@paleyrothman.com

Victor J. Rosenberg
Mark S. Rothman
Stephen H. Paley
Ronald A. Dweck

Robert H. Maclay
Steven A. Widdes
Dennis L. Sharp
Jeffrey A. Kolender

For Complete List of Firm Personnel, See General Section

For full biographical listings, see the Martindale-Hubbell Law Directory

---

*ROCKVILLE,** Montgomery Co.

STEIN, SPERLING, BENNETT, DE JONG, DRISCOLL, GREENFEIG & METRO, P.A. (AV)

25 West Middle Lane, 20850
Telephone: 301-340-2020; 800-435-5230
Telecopier: 301-340-8217

David S. De Jong

Ann G. Jakabcin

Ava L. Healy

For Complete List of Firm Personnel, See General Section

For full biographical listings, see the Martindale-Hubbell Law Directory

---

MASSACHUSETTS

*BOSTON,** Suffolk Co.

BLOOM & WITKIN (AV)

70 Franklin Street, 02110
Telephone: 617-443-4300
Fax: 617-443-4315

MEMBERS OF FIRM

Arnold Bloom

Mark J. Witkin

For full biographical listings, see the Martindale-Hubbell Law Directory

BURNS & LEVINSON LLP (AV)

125 Summer Street, 02110-1624
Telephone: 617-345-3000
Telecopier: 617-345-3299
Email: firm@B-L.com
Rockland, Massachusetts Office: 1001 Hingham Street.
Telephone: 617-982-4100.
Telecopier: 617-982-4141.

MEMBERS OF FIRM

Howard D. Medwed

Melvin A. Warshaw
Evelyn A. Haralampu

For Complete List of Firm Personnel, See General Section

For full biographical listings, see the Martindale-Hubbell Law Directory

---

CITY, HAYES, MEAGHER & DISSETTE, P.C. (AV)

50 Congress Street, 02109
Telephone: 617-523-3050
Telecopier: 617-523-5612

Robert D. City
James P. Hayes

Kieran B. Meagher
Michael J. Dissette

Martin R. Fisch
Philip B. Evans

Lewis R. Lear
Philip Di Domenico

Michael N. O'Connell, Jr.

For full biographical listings, see the Martindale-Hubbell Law Directory

---

FOLEY, HOAG & ELIOT LLP (AV)

One Post Office Square, 02109
Telephone: 617-832-1000
Cable Address: "Foleyhoag"
Telex: 94-0693
Telecopier: 617-832-7000
Email: fhe@fhe.com *URL:* http://www.fhe.com
Washington, D.C. Office: 1615 L Street, N.W.
Telephone: 202-775-0600.
Telecopier: 202-857-0140.

MEMBERS OF FIRM

Robert L. Birnbaum
Leonard Schneidman
Paul E. Tsongas
Louis P. Georgantas
Deborah A. Willard
John L. Burke, Jr. (Resident, Washington, D.C. Office)

Stefanie D. Cantor
Bruce A. Kinn
James T. Montgomery, Jr. (Resident at Washington, D.C. Office)
Richard R. Schaul-Yoder

ASSOCIATE

Thomas N. Molins

For Complete List of Firm Personnel, See General Section

For full biographical listings, see the Martindale-Hubbell Law Directory

---

McDERMOTT, WILL & EMERY (AV)

A Partnership including Professional Corporations
75 State Street, Suite 1700, 02109-1807
Telephone: 617-345-5000
Facsimile: 617-345-5077
Chicago, Illinois Office: 227 West Monroe Street.
Telephone: 312-372-2000.
Facsimile: 312-984-7700.
Miami, Florida Office: 201 South Biscayne Boulevard.
Telephone: 305-358-3500.
Facsimile: 305-347-6500.
Washington, D.C. Office: 1850 K Street, N.W.
Telephone: 202-887-8000.
Facsimile: 202-778-8087.
Los Angeles, California Office: 2049 Century Park East.
Telephone: 310-277-4110.
Facsimile: 310-277-4730.
Newport Beach, California Office: 1301 Dove Street, Suite 500.
Telephone: 714-851-0633.
Facsimile: 714-851-9348.
New York, N.Y. Office: 1211 Avenue of the Americas.
Telephone: 212-768-5400.
Facsimile: 212-768-5444.
St. Petersburg, Russia Office: AOZT McDermott, Will & Emery, Griboyedova Canal 36, 191023 St. Petersburg, Russia.
Telephone: (7) (812) 310-52-44; 310-55-44; 310-59-44; 850-20-45.
Facsimile: (7) (812) 310-54-46; 325-84-50.
Vilnius, Lithuania Office: Smetonos 6, 2600 Vilnius, Lithuania.
Telephone: 370 2 61-43-08.
Facsimile: 370 2 22-79-55.

MEMBER OF FIRM

Steven L. Paul

For full biographical listings, see the Martindale-Hubbell Law Directory

Boston—Continued

PALMER & DODGE LLP (AV)

One Beacon Street, 02108
Telephone: 617-573-0100
Facsimile: 617-227-4420

MEMBERS OF FIRM

Neil P. Arkuss	Malcolm E. Hindin
Robert W. Buck	Eric F. Menoyo
Ralph C. Derbyshire	Arthur B. Page
Karl P. Fryzel	Thomas M. Spera

Jackson W. Wright, Jr.

For Complete List of Firm Personnel, See General Section

For full biographical listings, see the Martindale-Hubbell Law Directory

RACKEMANN, SAWYER & BREWSTER, PROFESSIONAL CORPORATION (AV)

One Financial Center, 02111
Telephone: 617-542-2300
Telecopier: 617-542-7437

William B. Tyler	Janet M. Smith
Henry H. Thayer	Peter Friedenberg
Stephen Carr Anderson	Richard S. Novak
Albert M. Fortier, Jr.	J. David Leslie
Michael F. O'Connell	Sanford M. Matathia
Stuart T. Freeland	Richard J. Gallogly
Alan B. Rubenstein	James A. Wachta
James R. Shea, Jr.	Hanson S. Reynolds
Brian M. Hurley	Donald R. Pinto, Jr.

COUNSEL

Ronald S. Duby	Gordon M. Orloff
Lucy West Behymer	Eric A. Smith

OF COUNSEL

Albert B. Wolfe	George V. Anastas
August R. Meyer	Edward M. Condit
Richard H. Lovell	Alexander H. Spaulding

Margaret L. Hayes	Peter A. Alpert
Daniel J. Ossoff	Ellen M. Harrington
Melissa Langer Ellis	Lauren D. Armstrong
Daniel J. Bailey, III	Robert B. Foster
Michael S. Giaimo	Andrew H. Butler
Maura E. Murphy	Gayle E. Parlee
Mary L. Gallant	Elizabeth A. Gibbons

Melissa Fang

For full biographical listings, see the Martindale-Hubbell Law Directory

ROPES & GRAY (AV)

One International Place, 02110
Telephone: 617-951-7000
Fax: 617-951-7050
Email: postmaster@ropesgray.com
Washington, D.C. Office: One Franklin Square, 1301 K Street, NW, Suite 800 East.
Telephone: 202-626-3900.
Telecopy: 202-626-3961.
Providence, Rhode Island Office: 30 Kennedy Plaza.
Telephone: 401-455-4400.
Telecopy: 401-455-4401.

MEMBERS OF FIRM

David J. Blattner, Jr.	Susan A. Johnston
Fred R. Becker	Eric M. Elfman
Ronald L. Groves	Adelbert L. Spitzer
Carolyn M. Osteen	Brett A. Robbins
Stephen E. Shay	Rom P. Watson
(Not admitted in MA)	

ASSOCIATES

Christopher M. Leich	Karen A. Johnson
Loretta R. Richard	James R. Brown, Jr.
Deborah J. Coleman	Christopher Ceruolo

Debra Brown Allen

OF COUNSEL

Wilson C. Piper	Harry K. Mansfield

For Complete List of Firm Personnel, See General Section

For full biographical listings, see the Martindale-Hubbell Law Directory

SHERBURNE, POWERS & NEEDHAM, P.C. (AV)

One Beacon Street, 02108
Telephone: 617-523-2700
Fax: 617-523-6850
Email: @SHERBURNE.COM

(See Next Column)

William D. Weeks	Benjamin Volinski
John T. Collins	Mark Schonfeld
Allan J. Landau	James D. Smeallie
Stephen A. Hopkins	Paul Killeen
Alan I. Falk	Gordon P. Katz
C. Thomas Swaim	Joseph B. Darby, III
James Pollock	Richard M Yanofsky
William V. Tripp III	James E. McDermott
Stephen S. Young	Kenneth P. Brier
William F. Machen	Robert V. Lizza
W. Robert Allison	Miriam Goldstein Altman
Philip J. Notopoulos	John J. Monaghan
Richard J. Hindlian	Margaret J. Palladino
Paul E. Troy	Mark C. Michalowski
Harold W. Potter, Jr.	David Scott Sloan
Philip S. Lapatin	M. Chrysa Long
Pamela A. Duckworth	Lawrence D. Bradley

Miriam J. McKendall

Cynthia A. Brown	Amy J. Mastrobattista
Cynthia M. Hern	Leslie A. Sprinkle
Meredeth A. Beers	Douglas W. Clapp
Dianne R. Phillips	Jeffrey A. Huebschmann
Paul M. James	Tamara E. Goulston
Theodore F. Hanselman	Paul G. Lannon, Jr.
Joshua C. Krumholz	Nicholas J. Psyhogeos
Ieuan G. Mahony	Edward J. Naughton
Jeffrey J. Nix	Kathaleen Kelly Cutone
(Not admitted in MA)	Laurie A. Tribble
Kenneth L. Harvey	Neil C. Higgins
Christopher J. Trombetta	Deborah Paige Stone
Elise N. Zoli	Brian R. Popiel

COUNSEL

Haig Der Manuelian	Karl J. Hirshman
Mason M. Taber, Jr.	Dale R. Johnson

For full biographical listings, see the Martindale-Hubbell Law Directory

WARNER & STACKPOLE LLP (AV)

75 State Street, 02109
Telephone: 617-951-9000
Telecopier: 617-951-9151
Email: w&s@warstack.com

MEMBERS OF FIRM

Robert W. Holmes, Jr.	Stephen E. Moore

Walter G. Van Dorn

ASSOCIATE

Elizabeth W. Ho

COUNSEL

Andrew C. Bailey

For Complete List of Firm Personnel, See General Section

For full biographical listings, see the Martindale-Hubbell Law Directory

CAMBRIDGE,* Middlesex Co.

MERVIN M. WILF, LTD. (AV)

2 Berkeley Place, 02138
Telephone: 617-876-5200
Philadelphia, Pennsylvania Office: 3901 Mellon Bank Center. 1735 Market Street.
Telephone: 215-994-1430. 215- 568-4842.
Facsimile: 215-994-1432.

Mervin M. Wilf

A list of Representative Clients and References will be furnished upon request.

For full biographical listings, see the Martindale-Hubbell Law Directory

NEWTON, Middlesex Co.

VACOVEC, MAYOTTE & SINGER (AV)

Two Newton Place, Suite 340, 255 Washington Street, 02158-1633
Telephone: 617-964-0500
Fax: 617-969-2002
Email: vacovec@aol.com

MEMBERS OF FIRM

Kenneth J. Vacovec	Paula N. Singer
Maureen C. Mayotte	Jeffrey M. Brown

Kenneth H. Light

ASSOCIATES

Angela M. Cox	Arthur R. Kerr, II

Sam J. Serbello

OF COUNSEL

Stephen P. Koster	John G. Ganick

For full biographical listings, see the Martindale-Hubbell Law Directory

WORCESTER,* Worcester Co.

MOUNTAIN, DEARBORN & WHITING (AV)

370 Main Street, 01608
Telephone: 508-756-2423
Fax: 508-755-6640

MEMBERS OF FIRM

Alfred N. Whiting (1920-1989)	Francis J. Russell
Thomas R. Mountain	Dale R. Harger
Richard W. Dearborn	Mark W. Bloom
Samuel R. DeSimone	Donald J. O'Neil
Henry W. Beth	Lawrence S. Delaney

Ann K. Molloy

ASSOCIATE

Richard M. Freije

For full biographical listings, see the Martindale-Hubbell Law Directory

SEDER & CHANDLER (AV)

A Partnership including a Professional Corporation
Established 1918
Burnside Building, 339 Main Street, 01608
Telephone: 508-757-7721
Telecopiers: 508-798-1863; 508-831-0955

MEMBERS OF FIRM

Samuel Seder (1918-1964)	Marvin S. Silver, P.C.
Harold Seder (1934-1988)	John L. Pfeffer, Jr.
Burton Chandler	Robert S. Adler
J. Robert Seder	Dawn E. Caccavaro
Darragh K. Kasakoff	Kevin C. McGee

Kurt L. Binder

ASSOCIATES

Paul J. O'Riordan	Jeffrey P. Greenberg

Denise M. Tremblay

OF COUNSEL

Saul A. Seder	Gerald E. Norman

Philip C. Lombardo, Jr.

Reference: First National Bank of Boston; Safety Fund National Bank; Fleet National Bank.

For full biographical listings, see the Martindale-Hubbell Law Directory

MICHIGAN

ANN ARBOR,* Washtenaw Co.

BRAUN KENDRICK FINKBEINER PLC (AV)

700 First National Building, 48104
Telephone: 313-995-4100
Telecopier: 313-995-4798
URL: http://www.bkf-law.com
Bay City, Michigan Office: 201 Phoenix Building, P.O. Box 2039.
Telephone: 517-895-8505.
Telecopier: 517-895-8437.
Saginaw, Michigan Office: 101 N. Washington, Suite 812.
Telephone: 517-753-3461.
Telecopier: 517-753-3951.

Barry M. Levine

Representative Clients: The Dow Chemical Co.; General Motors Corp.; Lobdell Emery Manufacturing Co.; Merrill, Lynch, Inc.; Saginaw General Hospital; Saginaw News; The Wickes Foundation.

For full biographical listings, see the Martindale-Hubbell Law Directory

MAGILL AND RUMSEY, P.C. (AV)

Seventh Floor, First National Building, 201 South Main Street, 48104
Telephone: 313-995-2500
Fax: 313-995-4798

Robert F. Magill, Jr.	Ralph S. Rumsey

For full biographical listings, see the Martindale-Hubbell Law Directory

MILLER, CANFIELD, PADDOCK AND STONE, P.L.C. (AV)

A Professional Limited Liability Company
Founded in 1852 by Sidney Davy Miller
101 North Main Street, Seventh Floor, 48104-1400
Telephone: 313-663-2445
Fax: 313-747-7147
Detroit, Michigan Office: 150 West Jefferson, Suite 2500, 48226-4415.
Telephone: 313-963-6420.
Fax: 313-496-7500.
Cable Address: "Stem Detroit."

(See Next Column)

Bloomfield Hills, Michigan Office: Suite 100, Pinehurst Office Center, 1400 North Woodward, 48303-2014.
Telephone: 313-645-5000.
Fax: 313-645-1917.
Grand Rapids, Michigan Office: 1200 Campau Square Plaza, 99 Monroe, N.W., 49503-2639.
Telephone: 616-454-8656.
Fax: 616-776-6322.
Howell, Michigan Office: 121 South Barnard Street, Suite 4, 48843-2305.
Telephone: 517-546-7600.
Telecopier: 517-546-6974.
Kalamazoo, Michigan Office: 444 West Michigan Avenue, 49007-3752.
Telephone: 616-381-7030.
Fax: 616-382-0244.
Lansing, Michigan Office: One Michigan Avenue, Suite 900, 48933-1609.
Telephone: 517-487-2070.
Fax: 517-374-6304.
Monroe, Michigan Office: The Executive Centre, 214 East Elm Avenue, 48161-2682.
Telephone: 313-243-2000.
Fax: 313-243-0901.
Washington, D.C. Office: 1225 Nineteenth Street, N.W., Suite 400. 20036.
Telephone: 202-429-5575; 785-0600.
Fax: 202-331-1118; 785-1234.
Pensacola, Florida Office: 25 West Cedar, 32501.
Telephone: 904-469-1088.
Fax: 904-432-0677.
St. Petersburg, Florida Office: 100 Second Avenue S., Suite 7045, 33701.
Telephone: 813-982-6000.
Fax: 813-892-6002.
New York, New York Office: Eleventh Floor, 135 East 57th Street, 10022-2087.
Telephone: 212-754-5400.
Fax: 212-754-5401.
Gdansk, Poland Office: Suite 322, Dom Technika Building, UI. Rajska 6, 80-850.
Telephone: 011-485-831-2808.
Fax: 011-485-831-4719.
Warsaw, Poland Office: UI. Marszalkowska 82, Suite 561, 00-517.
Telephone: 011-482-623-6457 and 6458.
Fax: 011-482-623-6459.

RESIDENT PRINCIPALS

Robert E. Gilbert	Orin D. Brustad

Deborah W. Thompson

SENIOR ATTORNEY

Ronald D. Gardner

Representative Firm Clients: Chrysler Corporation; Comerica, Incorporated; City of Detroit, Michigan; Detroit Tigers, Inc.; First of Michigan; Ford Motor Company; Ford Motor Credit Company; Great Lakes Bancorp; Henry Ford Hospital; INVETECH Company.

For Complete List of Firm Personnel, See General Section

For full biographical listings, see the Martindale-Hubbell Law Directory

WESTERMAN & ASSOCIATES, P.C. (AV)

345 South Division, 48104
Telephone: 313-995-9731
Facsimile: 313-995-9738

Susan S. Westerman

Susan M. Friedland

For full biographical listings, see the Martindale-Hubbell Law Directory

BAY CITY,* Bay Co.

BRAUN KENDRICK FINKBEINER PLC (AV)

201 Phoenix Building, P.O. Box 2039, 48708
Telephone: 517-895-8505
Telecopier: 517-895-8437
URL: http://www.bkf-law.com
Saginaw, Michigan Office: 101 N. Washington, Suite 812. 8th Floor Second National Bank Building.
Telephone: 517-753-3461.
Telecopier: 517-753-3951.
Ann Arbor, Michigan Office: 700 First National Building.
Telephone: 313-995-4100.
Telecopier: 313-995-4798.

Ralph J. Isackson	Daniel S. Opperman
George F. Gronewold, Jr.	Gregory T. Demers

OF COUNSEL

Patrick D. Neering

Representative Clients: APV Chemical Machinery, Inc.; Bay Health Systems; Catholic Federal Credit Union; City of Saginaw; City of Vassar; City of Milwaukee; Corporate Service; Cox Cable.

For Complete List of Firm Personnel, See General Section

For full biographical listings, see the Martindale-Hubbell Law Directory

BIRMINGHAM, Oakland Co.

CARSON FISCHER, P.L.C. (AV)

Third Floor, 300 East Maple Road, 48009-6317
Telephone: 810-644-4840
Facsimile: 810-644-1832

Robert M. Carson   William C. Edmunds

For full biographical listings, see the Martindale-Hubbell Law Directory

MACDONALD AND GOREN, P.C. (AV)

Suite 200, 260 East Brown Street, 48009
Telephone: 810-645-5940
Fax: 810-645-2490

Harold C. MacDonald   Kalman G. Goren
Cindy Rhodes Victor

Amy L. Glenn   Lawrence C. Atorthy
David D. Marsh   Miriam Blanks-Smart
Glenn G. Ross   John T. Klees
Rose Marie Karadsheh
OF COUNSEL
Robert L. Biederman

Representative Clients: Beaudin, Gallanis; Beaudin, Incorporated; Orlandi Gear Co., Inc.; Bing Steel, Inc.; Superb Manufacturing, Inc.; Spring Engineering, Inc.; Adrian Steel Co.; Southfield Radiology Associates, P.C.; HDS Services, Inc.; TGI Friday's Inc.; Quality Gold of Cincinnati, Inc.

For full biographical listings, see the Martindale-Hubbell Law Directory

WEINGARDEN & HAUER, P.C. (AV)

30100 Telegraph Road, Suite 221, 48025
Telephone: 810-258-0800
Telecopier: 810-258-2750

Larry A. Weingarden

Reference: Security Bank & Trust.

For full biographical listings, see the Martindale-Hubbell Law Directory

BLOOMFIELD HILLS, Oakland Co.

DAWDA, MANN, MULCAHY & SADLER, P.L.C. (AV)

1533 North Woodward Avenue Suite 200, 48304
Telephone: 810-642-3700
Fax: 810-642-7791
Email: EMail@DMMS.Com

Edward C. Dawda   Curtis J. Mann

Tara E. Barr   Paul C. Apap

For full biographical listings, see the Martindale-Hubbell Law Directory

HOWARD & HOWARD ATTORNEYS, P.C. (AV)

The Pinehurst Office Center, Suite 101, 1400 North Woodward Avenue, 48304-2856
Telephone: 810-645-1483
Telecopier: 810-645-1568
Kalamazoo, Michigan Office: The Kalamazoo Building, Suite 400, 107 West Michigan Avenue.
Telephone: 616-382-1483.
Telecopier: 616-382-1568.
Lansing, Michigan Office: The Phoenix Building, Suite 500, 222 Washington Square, North.
Telephone: 517-485-1483.
Telecopier: 517-485-1568.
Peoria, Illinois Office: The Creve Coeur Building, Suite 200, 321 Liberty Street.
Telephone: 309-672-1483.
Telecopier: 309-672-1568.
Tampa, Florida Office: First of America Plaza, Suite 2000, 201 East Kennedy Boulevard.
Telephone: 813-229-1483.
Telecopier: 813-229-1568.

Robert B. Johnston   James C. Wickens
John E. Young

Representative Clients: For Representative Client list, see General Practice, Bloomfield Hills, MI.

For Complete List of Firm Personnel, See General Section

For full biographical listings, see the Martindale-Hubbell Law Directory

DETROIT, Wayne Co.*

ALLARD & FISH, A PROFESSIONAL CORPORATION (AV)

2600 Buhl Building, 535 Griswold Avenue, 48226
Telephone: 313-961-6141
Facsimile: 313-961-6142
Email: afish@michbar.org

David W. Allard   Ralph R. McKee
Deborah L. Fish   Elias Themistocles Majoros

For full biographical listings, see the Martindale-Hubbell Law Directory

BENDURE & THOMAS (AV)

577 East Larned, Suite 210, 48226-4392
Telephone: 313-961-1525
Fax: 313-961-1553

MEMBERS OF FIRM
Mark R. Bendure   Marc E. Thomas
ASSOCIATES
J. Christopher Caldwell   Victor S. Valenti
Kevin P. Kavanagh
OF COUNSEL
John A. Lydick   Thomas R. Present

For full biographical listings, see the Martindale-Hubbell Law Directory

BODMAN, LONGLEY & DAHLING LLP (AV)

34th Floor 100 Renaissance Center, 48243
Telephone: 313-259-7777
Fax: 313-393-7579
Email: 2080194@mcimail.com
Troy, Michigan Office: Suite 2020, 755 West Big Beaver Road.
Telephone: 810-362-2110.
Fax: 810-244-0780.
Ann Arbor, Michigan Office: 110 Miller, Suite 300.
Telephone: 313-761-3780.
Fax: 313-930-2494.
Northern Michigan Office: 229 Court Street, P.O. Box 405, Cheboygan.
Telephone: 616-627-4351.
Fax: 616-627-2802.

MEMBERS OF FIRM
Pierre V. Heftler   Christopher J. Dine
George D. Miller, Jr.   (Troy Office)
David M. Hempstead   Patrick C. Cauley
John C. Cashen (Troy Office)   Barnett Jay Colvin

For Representative Client List, See General Section

For Complete List of Firm Personnel, See General Section

For full biographical listings, see the Martindale-Hubbell Law Directory

CLARK HILL P.L.C. (AV)

500 Woodward Avenue, Suite 3500, 48226
Telephone: 313-965-8300
Facsimile: 313-962-4348
Oakland County, Michigan Office: Third Floor, 255 South Woodward Avenue, Birmingham.
Telephone: 810-642-9692.
Facsimile: 810-642-2174.
Lansing, Michigan Office: Suite 600, 200 North Capitol Avenue.
Telephone: 517-484-4481.
Facsimile: 517-484-1246.
Minneapolis, Minnesota Office: Suite 1000, One Financial Plaza, 120 South Sixth Street.
Telephone: 612-332-0102.
Facsimile: 612-332-3225.
Kansas City, Missouri Office: Suite 1400, Bryant Building, 1102 Grand Avenue.
Telephone: 816-221-5578.
Facsimile: 816-221-0303.

Douglas J. Rasmussen   Michael G. Cumming
Thomas F. Sweeney (Resident,   Kevin M. Bernys (Resident,
   Oakland County Office)   Oakland County Office)
Robert G. Buydens   J. Thomas MacFarlane
Thomas S. Nowinski   (Resident, Oakland County
Joseph A. Bonventre   Office)
Andrea M. Kanski

Robin D. Ferriby   Jennifer Crawford
Christopher A. McMican

Representative Clients: Chrysler Corporation; Eagle Trailer Company; Merck & Co.; Michigan Manufacturers Association; Rouge Steel Company; Sidley Diamond Tool Co.; Thompson Transport.

For Complete List of Firm Personnel, See General Section

For full biographical listings, see the Martindale-Hubbell Law Directory

Detroit—Continued

DYKEMA GOSSETT PLLC (AV)

400 Renaissance Center, 48243-1668
Telephone: 313-568-6800
Cable Address: "Dyke-Detroit"
Telex: 23-0121
Fax: 313-568-6594
Email: 2084153@mcimail.com
Ann Arbor, Michigan Office: 315 East Eisenhower Parkway, Suite 100,
48108-3306.
Telephone: 313-747-7660.
Fax: 313-747-7696.
Bloomfield Hills, Michigan Office: 1577 North Woodward Avenue, Suite
300, 48304-2820.
Telephone: 810-540-0700.
Fax: 810-540-0763.
Chicago, Illinois Office: 55 East Monroe Street, Suite 3250, 60603-5709.
Telephone: 312-551-4900.
Fax: 312-551-4919.
Grand Rapids, Michigan Office: 200 Oldtown Riverfront Building, 248
Louis Campau Promenade, N.W., 49503-2668.
Telephone: 616-776-7500.
Fax: 616-776-7573.
Lansing, Michigan Office: 800 Michigan National Tower, 48933-1707.
Telephone: 517-374-9100.
Fax: 517-374-9191.
Washington, D.C. Office: Franklin Square, Suite 300 West, 1300 I Street,
N.W., 20005-3306.
Telephone: 202-522-8600.
Fax: 202-522-8669.

MEMBERS OF FIRM

Joseph F. Dillon	Louis W. Kasischke (Resident at
James M. Elsworth	Bloomfield Hills Office)
William E. Fisher	Mark C. Larson
Steven E. Grob	Stewart L. Mandell
Raymond T. Huetteman, Jr.	Thomas B. Spillane, Jr.
(Resident at Ann Arbor	(Resident at Bloomfield Hills
Office)	Office)

OF COUNSEL

Eugene A. Gargaro, Jr.

ASSOCIATES

Marie R. Deveney (Resident at	Mary T. Malpass
Ann Arbor Office)	Sherrill D. Wolford

For Complete List of Firm Personnel, See General Section

For full biographical listings, see the Martindale-Hubbell Law Directory

FILDEW HINKS, P.L.L.C. (AV)

3600 Penobscot Building, 645 Griswold Street, 48226-4291
Telephone: 313-961-9700
Telecopier: 313-961-0754

MEMBERS OF FIRM

Stanley L. Fildew (1896-1978)	Randall S. Wangen
Frank T. Hinks (1887-1974)	Mary Jane Ruffley
Richard E. Hinks (1916-1990)	Robert D. Welchli
John H. Fildew	William P. Thorpe
Alan C. Miller	Colleen A. Kramer
Charles D. Todd III	Stephen J. Pokoj

ASSOCIATES

Charles S. Kennedy, III	Walter B. Fisher, Jr.

References: First of America Bank-Detroit, N.A.; Comerica Bank-Detroit;
National Bank of Detroit.

For full biographical listings, see the Martindale-Hubbell Law Directory

HONIGMAN MILLER SCHWARTZ AND COHN (AV)

A Partnership including Professional Corporations
2290 First National Building, 48226
Telephone: 313-256-7800
Telecopier: 313-962-0176
Telex: 235705
URL: http://law.honigman.com
Lansing, Michigan Office: Phoenix Building, 222 North Washington
Square, Suite 400, 48933-1800.
Telephone: 517-484-8282.
West Palm Beach, Florida Office: Suite 800 Esperante Building, 222
Lakeview Avenue, 33401-6112.
Telephone: 561-838-4500.
Tampa, Florida Office: 2700 SunTrust Financial Centre, 401 E. Jackson
Street, 33602-5226.
Telephone: 813-221-6600.

MEMBERS OF FIRM

Keith B. Braun	Mary Jo Larson
Roger Cook	Marguerite Munson Lentz
John H. Eggertsen	Mark Morton
Michael J. Friedman	(Lansing, Michigan Office)
Gerald M. Griffith	Charles Nida
Jeffrey A. Hyman	James H. Novis

(See Next Column)

Benjamin O. Schwendener, Jr.	Brad M. Tomtishen
(Lansing, Michigan Office)	Alan M. Valade
Sherill Siebert	(Lansing, Michigan Office)
Richard S. Soble	Richard E. Zuckerman

ASSOCIATE

Mary Ann Taylor (Detroit and Lansing, Michigan Offices)

RESIDENT IN WEST PALM BEACH, FLORIDA OFFICE

MEMBERS

Ronald S. Kochman (P.A.)	Mark Nussbaum (P.A.)

Representative Clients: See General Section.

For Complete List of Firm Personnel, See General Section

For full biographical listings, see the Martindale-Hubbell Law Directory

JAFFE, RAITT, HEUER & WEISS, PROFESSIONAL CORPORATION (AV)

One Woodward Avenue, Suite 2400, 48226
Telephone: 313-961-8380
Telecopier: 313-961-8358
Cable Address: "Jafsni"
Southfield, Michigan Office: Travelers Tower, Suite 1520.
Telephone: 313-961-8380.
Monroe, Michigan Office: 214 East Elm Avenue, Suite 208,
Telephone: 313-241-6470.
Telefacsimile: 313-241-3849.

Alexander B. Bragdon	Joel J. Morris
Gary R. Glenn	David H. Raitt
Ira J. Jaffe	William E. Sider
Robert E. Lewis	Arthur A. Weiss
	Janet G. Witkowski

Representative Clients: Edgemere Enterprises; Frankel Associates, Inc.; Somerset Inn & Apartments; Sosnick Development Co.; Uniprop, Inc.

For Complete List of Firm Personnel, See General Section

For full biographical listings, see the Martindale-Hubbell Law Directory

JOSLYN KEYDEL & WALLACE (AV)

A Partnership of Professional Corporations
211 West Fort Street, Suite 2211, 48226-3270
Telephone: 313-964-4181
Fax: 313-964-4996

MEMBERS OF FIRM

Lee E. Joslyn (1864-1936)	Alan W. Joslyn (1899-1990)
Lee E. Joslyn, Jr. (1895-1955)	Frederick R. Keydel (P.C.)
	Harvey B. Wallace II (P.C.)

ASSOCIATE

Patrice M. Ticknor	Andrew W. MacLeod

LEGAL SUPPORT PERSONNEL

PARALEGALS

Diane C. Simpson	Justine B. Gudritz
Ruth G. Spector	Alice M. Pricer

References: NBD Bank, N.A.; Comerica Bank.

For full biographical listings, see the Martindale-Hubbell Law Directory

MILLER, CANFIELD, PADDOCK AND STONE, P.L.C. (AV)

A Professional Limited Liability Company
Founded in 1852 by Sidney Davy Miller
150 West Jefferson, Suite 2500, 48226-4415
Telephone: 313-963-6420
Fax: 313-496-7500
Cable Address: "Stem Detroit"
Detroit, Michigan Office: 150 West Jefferson, Suite 2500, 48226-4415.
Telephone: 313-963-6420.
Fax: 313-496-7500.
Cable Address: "Stem Detroit."
Ann Arbor, Michigan Office: 101 North Main Street, 7th Floor,
48104-1400.
Telephone: 313-663-2445.
Fax: 313-747-7147.
Bloomfield Hills, Michigan Office: Suite 100, Pinehurst Office Center, 1400
North Woodward, 48303-2014.
Telephone: 313-645-5000.
Fax: 313-645-1917.
Grand Rapids, Michigan Office: 1200 Campau Square Plaza, 99 Monroe,
N.W., 49503-2639.
Telephone: 616-454-8656.
Fax: 616-776-6322.
Howell, Michigan Office: 121 South Barnard Street, Suite 4, 48843-2305.
Telephone: 517-546-7600.
Telecopier: 517-546-6974.
Kalamazoo, Michigan Office: 444 West Michigan Avenue, 49007-3752.
Telephone: 616-381-7030.
Fax: 616-382-0244.

(See Next Column)

MILLER, CANFIELD, PADDOCK AND STONE P.L.C., *Detroit—Continued*

Lansing, Michigan Office: One Michigan Avenue, Suite 900, 48933-1609.
Telephone: 517-487-2070.
Fax: 517-374-6304.
Monroe, Michigan Office: The Executive Centre, 214 East Elm Avenue, 48161-2682.
Telephone: 313-243-2000.
Fax: 313-243-0901.
Washington, D.C. Office: 1225 Nineteenth Street, N.W., Suite 400. 20036.
Telephone: 202-429-5575; 785-0600.
Fax: 202-331-1118; 785-1234.
Pensacola, Florida Office: 25 West Cedar, 32501.
Telephone: 904-469-1088.
Fax: 904-432-0677.
St. Petersburg, Florida Office: 100 Second Avenue S., Suite 7045, 33701.
Telephone: 813-982-6000.
Fax: 813-892-6002.
New York, New York Office: Eleventh Floor, 135 East 57th Street, 10022-2087.
Telephone: 212-754-5400.
Fax: 212-754-5401.
Gdansk, Poland Office: Suite 322, Dom Technika Building, UI. Rajska 6, 80-850.
Telephone: 011-485-831-2808.
Fax: 011-485-831-4719.
Warsaw, Poland Office: UI. Marszalkowska 82, Suite 561, 00-517.
Telephone: 011-482-623-6457 and 6458.
Fax: 011-482-623-6459.

PRINCIPALS OF FIRM

Lawrence A. King (P.C.) (Bloomfield Hills Office)	James W. Williams (Bloomfield Hills Office)
George E. Parker, III	Michael R. Atkins (Lansing Office)
Stevan Uzelac (P.C.)	
Robert S. Ketchum	Jeffrey M. McHugh
Samuel J. McKim, III, (P.C.)	Robert F. Rhoades
Rocque E. Lipford (P.C.) (Monroe Office)	Gregory V. Di Censo (Bloomfield Hills Office)
John A. Thurber (P.C.) (Bloomfield Hills Office)	Michael A. Indenbaum
Orin D. Brustad	Vernon Bennett III (Grand Rapids and Kalamazoo Offices)
John A. Campbell (Kalamazoo Office)	Deborah W. Thompson
Kenneth E. Konop (Bloomfield Hills Office)	

OF COUNSEL

William G. Butler	Joseph F. Maycock, Jr.
Peter P. Thurber	Richard I. Loebl

SENIOR ATTORNEYS

Ronald D. Gardner (Ann Arbor Office)	Walter A. Payne, III

ASSOCIATES

Joanne B. Faycurry	Dawn M. Schluter (Bloomfield Hills Office)

Representative Firm Clients: Chrysler Corporation; Comerica, Incorporated; City of Detroit, Michigan; Detroit Tigers, Inc.; First of Michigan; Ford Motor Company; Ford Motor Credit Company; Great Lakes Bancorp; Henry Ford Hospital; INVETECH Company.

For Complete List of Firm Personnel, See General Section

For full biographical listings, see the Martindale-Hubbell Law Directory

---

DAVID M. THOMS & ASSOCIATES, P.C. (AV)

400 Renaissance Center, Suite 950, 48243
Telephone: 313-259-6333
Facsimile: 313-259-7037
Bloomfield Hills, Michigan Office: 1500 Woodward Avenue, Suite 100.
Telephone: 313-259-6333.
Fax: 313-259-7037.

David M. Thoms

Audrey R. Holley	Duane B. Brown

OF COUNSEL

Allan G. Meganck	Thomas V. Trainer

Representative Clients: Avion Concepts, Inc.; Fowler Agency Corp.; Gibbs World Wide Wines, Inc.; deBary Travel, Inc.; North Management, Inc.; R.G. & G.R. Harris Funeral Home, Inc.; St. Jude Children's Research Hospital; The Salvation Army.
References: Comerica Bank-Detroit; National Bank of Detroit.

For full biographical listings, see the Martindale-Hubbell Law Directory

---

TIMMIS & INMAN, L.L.P. (AV)

300 Talon Centre, 48207
Telephone: 313-396-4200
Telecopier: 313-396-4228

(See Next Column)

Michael T. Timmis	Richard L. Levin
George M. Malis	
John P. Kanan	Erich J. D'Andrea

OF COUNSEL
Wayne C. Inman

Representative Client: Talon Inc.; Chateau Properties, Inc.

For Complete List of Firm Personnel, See General Section

For full biographical listings, see the Martindale-Hubbell Law Directory

---

EAST LANSING, Ingham Co.

FARHAT, STORY & KRAUS, P.C. (AV)

Beacon Place, 4572 South Hagadorn Road, Suite 3, 48823
Telephone: 517-351-3700
Fax: 517-332-4122
Email: rkraus@sojourn.com

Leo A. Farhat	Chris A. Bergstrom
James E. Burns (1925-1979)	Kitty L. Groh
Monte R. Story	Charles R. Toy
Richard C. Kraus	David M. Platt
Max R. Hoffman Jr.	Thomas L. Sparks

Lawrence P. Schweitzer	Daniel B. Morgan
Debra A. Geroux	Mary K. Robbins-Kralapp

Representative Clients: Big L. Corp.; Michigan Automotive Wholesalers Association.; Hartman-Fabco, Inc.; Lansing Electric Motors, Inc.; Mike Miller Lincoln Mercury; GTE Sprint Communications Corp.; GTE Directories Services Corp.; The John E Fetzer Trust.
Reference: City Bank, St. Johns.

For full biographical listings, see the Martindale-Hubbell Law Directory

---

FARMINGTON HILLS, Oakland Co.

COUZENS, LANSKY, FEALK, ELLIS, ROEDER & LAZAR, P.C. (AV)

33533 West Twelve Mile Road, Suite 150, P.O. Box 9057, 48333-9057
Telephone: 810-489-8600
Telecopier: 810-489-4156

Sheldon A. Fealk	Lisa J. Walters
Jack S. Couzens, II	Stephen Scapelliti
Jerry M. Ellis	Donald A. Wagner
Donald M. Lansky	Michael P. Witzke
Bruce J. Lazar	Cyrus Raamin Kashef
Alan C. Roeder	Gregg A. Nathanson
Renard J. Kolasa	Mark S. Frankel
Kathryn Gilson Sussman	Lynette M. Sheldon
Jeffrey A. Levine	Roger E. Winkelman
Phillip L. Sternberg	David B. Deutsch
Marc L. Prey	Monica Demko Moons

Representative Clients: Provided upon request.
Reference: Comerica Bank-Southfield.

For full biographical listings, see the Martindale-Hubbell Law Directory

---

HOROWITZ — GUDEMAN, P.C. (AV)

31700 Middlebelt, Suite 140, 48334
Telephone: 810-855-6020
Facsimile: 810-855-6025

Marvin I. Horowitz	Edward J. Gudeman
Stuart L. Sherman	

Leslie I. Kollin

LEGAL SUPPORT PERSONNEL
Robin E. Cornell (Paralegal)

For full biographical listings, see the Martindale-Hubbell Law Directory

---

GRAND RAPIDS,* Kent Co.

BORRE, PETERSON, FOWLER & REENS, P.C. (AV)

The Philo C. Fuller House, 44 Lafayette, N.E., P.O. Box 1767, 49501-1767
Telephone: 616-459-1971
Fax: 616-459-2393

Glen V. Borre	Ben A. Fowler
James B. Peterson	William G. Krupar

Representative Clients: A.L. Truck Lines, Inc.; Beaver Island Boat Co.; Big Rapids Products, Inc.; Chadalee Farms, Inc.; Herbruck Poultry Ranch, Inc.; J&H Oil Co.; Master Finish Co.; Michigan Blueberry Growers Association; NBD Bank; Pfeiffer Lincoln Mercury, Inc.

For Complete List of Firm Personnel, See General Section

For full biographical listings, see the Martindale-Hubbell Law Directory

Grand Rapids—Continued

LAW, WEATHERS & RICHARDSON, P.C. (AV)

Bridgewater Place, Suite 800, 333 Bridge Street, N.W., 49504
Telephone: 616-459-1171
Facsimile: 616-732-1740

William R. Hineline
John P. Schneider

Christopher L. Edgar
John M. Huff

Kurt G. Yost

Representative Clients: F.D.I.C.; Ford Motor Credit Co.; Herman Miller, Inc.; Kent County Aeronautics Board; Marriott Corp.; The Procter & Gamble Co.; Peerless Insurance Co.; Ryder Systems, Inc.

For Complete List of Firm Personnel, See General Section

For full biographical listings, see the Martindale-Hubbell Law Directory

RUSSELL & BATCHELOR (AV)

Suite 411-S Waters Building, 161 Ottawa Avenue, N.W., 49503
Telephone: 616-774-8422
Fax: 616-774-0326

MEMBER OF FIRM
Walter J. Russell

Representative Clients: Progressive Architects/Engineers/Planners, Inc.; Quality Brass, Inc.; Shellcast, Inc.; Victor S. Barnes and Co.; Stovall Well Drilling; F. R. Neuman Co.; Start Advertising, Inc.; Tri-River Agency; Van. R. Kipka, Inc.; Wiltzer, Gerald R., Builder.

For full biographical listings, see the Martindale-Hubbell Law Directory

VARNUM, RIDDERING, SCHMIDT & HOWLETT LLP (AV)

A Limited Liability Partnership including Professional Corporations
Bridgewater Place, P.O. Box 352, 49501-0352
Telephone: 616-336-6000
800-262-0011
Facsimile: 616-336-7000
Telex: 1561593 VARN
Email: varnum@vrsh.com
Lansing, Michigan Office: The Victor Center, Suite 810, 210 North Washington Square, 48933.
Telephone: 517-482-6237.
Facsimile: 517-482-6937.
Kalamazoo, Michigan Office: 350 East Michigan Avenue, 49007.
Telephone: 616-382-2300.
Facsimile: 616-382-2382.
Grand Haven, Michigan Office: 321 Washington Street, P.O. Box 288, 49417.
Telephone: 616-846-7100.
Facsimile: 616-846-7101.
Battle Creek, Michigan Office: 4950 West Dickman Road, Suite B-1, 49015.
Telephone: 616-962-7144.
Bingham Farms, Michigan Office: 31600 Telegraph Road, Suite 230, 48025.
Telephone: 810-594-7330.
Facsimile: 810-594-7331.

MEMBERS OF FIRM

Hilary F. Snell
John C. Carlyle (Resident at Grand Haven Office)
Daniel C. Molhoek
Thomas T. Huff (Resident at Kalamazoo Office)
Dirk Hoffius

Larry J. Titley
Fredric A. Sytsma
Frank G. Dunten, P.C.
Marilyn A. Lankfer
Carl Oosterhouse, P.C.
Kaplin S. Jones, P.C.
Timothy J. Tornga

Scott A. Huizenga

ASSOCIATES

Thomas G. Kyros

Pamela J. Tyler

Joseph B. Levan

For Complete List of Firm Personnel, See General Section

For full biographical listings, see the Martindale-Hubbell Law Directory

WARNER NORCROSS & JUDD LLP (AV)

900 Old Kent Building, 111 Lyon Street, N.W., 49503-2489
Telephone: 616-752-2000
Fax: 616-752-2500
Muskegon, Michigan Office: 400 Terrace Plaza, P.O. Box 900.
Telephone: 616-727-2600.
Fax: 616-727-2699.
Holland, Michigan Office: Curtis Center, Suite 300, 170 College Avenue.
Telephone: 616-396-9800.
Fax: 616-396-3656.

OF COUNSEL

Charles C. Lundstrom

Thomas R. Winquist

(See Next Column)

MEMBERS OF FIRM

George L. Whitfield
Jerome M. Smith
Vernon P. Saper
Roger H. Oetting
Stephen R. Kretschman
W. Michael Van Haren

John H. McKendry, Jr.
(Resident at Muskegon Office)
Carl W. Dufendach
Sue O. Conway
Steven R. Heacock
Cameron S. DeLong

Jeffrey B. Power

Representative Clients: Bissell Inc.; Blodgett Memorial Medical Center; Guardsman Products, Inc.; Haworth, Inc.; Howard Miller Clock Company; Kysor Industrial Corp.; Michigan Bankers Assn.; Old Kent Financial Corp.; Steelcase Inc.; Wolverine World Wide, Inc.

For Complete List of Firm Personnel, See General Section

For full biographical listings, see the Martindale-Hubbell Law Directory

GROSSE POINTE FARMS, Wayne Co.

ALLAN NEEF (AV)

18580 Mack Avenue, 48236
Telephone: 313-343-9200
Fax: 313-343-0207

For full biographical listings, see the Martindale-Hubbell Law Directory

KALAMAZOO,* Kalamazoo Co.

EARLY, LENNON, PETERS & CROCKER, P.C. (AV)

900 Comerica Building, 49007-4752
Telephone: 616-381-8844
Fax: 616-349-8525

George H. Lennon, III

Robert M. Taylor

Attorneys for: General Motors Corp.; Wal-Mart Stores; Borgess Medical Center; Aetna Insurance: Kemper Group; Medical Protective Co.; Zurich Insurance; AAA; Liberty Mutual; Home Insurance.

For Complete List of Firm Personnel, See General Section

For full biographical listings, see the Martindale-Hubbell Law Directory

HOWARD & HOWARD ATTORNEYS, P.C. (AV)

The Kalamazoo Building, Suite 400, 107 West Michigan Avenue, 49007-3956
Telephone: 616-382-1483
Telecopier: 616-382-1568
Bloomfield Hills, Michigan Office: The Pinehurst Office Center, Suite 101, 1400 North Woodward Avenue.
Telephone: 810-645-1483.
Telecopier: 810-645-1568.
Lansing, Michigan Office: The Phoenix Building, Suite 500, 222 Washington Square North.
Telephone: 517-485-1483.
Telecopier: 517-485-1568.
Peoria, Illinois Office: The Creve Coeur Building, Suite 200, 321 Liberty Street.
Telephone: 309-672-1483.
Telecopier: 309-672-1568.
Tampa, Florida Office: First of America Plaza, Suite 2000, 201 East Kennedy Boulevard.
Telephone: 813-229-1483.
Telecopier: 813-229-1568.

Eric E. Breisach

Peter J. Livingston

D. Craig Martin

Representative Clients: For Representative Client list, see General Practice, Kalamazoo, MI.

For Complete List of Firm Personnel, See General Section

For full biographical listings, see the Martindale-Hubbell Law Directory

KREIS, ENDERLE, CALLANDER & HUDGINS, A PROFESSIONAL CORPORATION (AV)

One Moorsbridge, P.O. Box 4010, 49003-4010
Telephone: 616-324-3000
Telecopier: 616-324-3010
Email: kech@sapien.net *URL:* http://www.kech.com

Russell A. Kreis
C. Reid Hudgins III

Daniel P. McGlinn
Janice Roark Peters

Matthew S. DePerno

For Complete List of Firm Personnel, See General Section

For full biographical listings, see the Martindale-Hubbell Law Directory

Kalamazoo—Continued

MILLER, CANFIELD, PADDOCK AND STONE, P.L.C. (AV)

A Professional Limited Liability Company
Founded in 1852 by Sidney Davy Miller
444 West Michigan Avenue, 49007-3752
Telephone: 616-381-7030
Fax: 616-382-0244
Detroit, Michigan Office: 150 West Jefferson, Suite 2500, 48226-4415.
Telephone: 313-963-6420.
Fax: 313-496-7500.
Cable Address: "Stem Detroit."
Ann Arbor, Michigan Office: 101 North Main Street, 7th Floor,
48104-1400.
Telephone: 313-663-2445.
Fax: 313-747-7147.
Bloomfield Hills, Michigan Office: Suite 100, Pinehurst Office Center, 1400
North Woodward, 48303-2014.
Telephone: 313-645-5000.
Fax: 313-645-1917.
Grand Rapids, Michigan Office: 1200 Campau Square Plaza, 99 Monroe,
N.W., 49503-2639.
Telephone: 616-454-8656.
Fax: 616-776-6322.
Howell, Michigan Office: 121 South Barnard Street, Suite 4, 48843-2305.
Telephone: 517-546-7600.
Telecopier: 517-546-6974.
Lansing, Michigan Office: One Michigan Avenue, Suite 900, 48933-1609.
Telephone: 517-487-2070.
Fax: 517-374-6304.
Monroe, Michigan Office: The Executive Centre, 214 East Elm Avenue,
48161-2682.
Telephone: 313-243-2000.
Fax: 313-243-0901.
Washington, D.C. Office: 1225 Nineteenth Street, N.W., Suite 400. 20036.
Telephone: 202-429-5575; 785-0600.
Fax: 202-331-1118; 785-1234.
Pensacola, Florida Office: 25 West Cedar, 32501.
Telephone: 904-469-1088.
Fax: 904-432-0677.
St. Petersburg, Florida Office: 100 Second Avenue S., Suite 7045, 33701.
Telephone: 813-982-6000.
Fax: 813-892-6002.
New York, New York Office: Eleventh Floor, 135 East 57th Street,
10022-2087.
Telephone: 212-754-5400.
Fax: 212-754-5401.
Gdansk, Poland Office: Suite 322, Dom Technika Building, UI. Rajska 6,
80-850.
Telephone: 011-485-831-2808.
Fax: 011-485-831-4719.
Warsaw, Poland Office: UI. Marszalkowska 82, Suite 561, 00-517.
Telephone: 011-482-623-6457 and 6458.
Fax: 011-482-623-6459.

PRINCIPALS OF FIRM

John A. Campbell   Vernon Bennett III

Representative Firm Clients: Chrysler Corporation; Comerica, Incorporated;
City of Detroit, Michigan; Detroit Tigers, Inc.; First of Michigan; Ford Motor
Company; Ford Motor Credit Company; Great Lakes Bancorp; Henry
Ford Hospital; INVETECH Company.

For Complete List of Firm Personnel, See General Section

For full biographical listings, see the Martindale-Hubbell Law Directory

---

LANSING, Ingham Co.

* indicates certain Bar Register subscribers whose principal office is
located elsewhere in the state and who have arranged for representation
as a part of the state capital listings that follow

* HONIGMAN MILLER SCHWARTZ AND COHN (AV)

A Partnership including Professional Corporations
222 North Washington Square, Suite 400, 48933-1800
Telephone: 517-484-8282
Telecopier: 517-484-8286
URL: http://law.honigman.com
Detroit, Michigan Office: 2290 First National Building, 48226.
Telephone: 313-256-7800.
West Palm Beach, Florida Office: Suite 800 Esperante Building, 222
Lakeview Avenue, 33401-6112.
Telephone: 561-838-4500.
Tampa, Florida Office: 2700 SunTrust Financial Centre, 401 E. Jackson
Street, 33602-5226.
Telephone: 813-221-6600.

MEMBERS

Mark Morton   Benjamin O. Schwendener, Jr.
Alan M. Valade

(See Next Column)

ASSOCIATE
Mary Ann Taylor

For Complete List of Firm Personnel, See General Section

For full biographical listings, see the Martindale-Hubbell Law Directory

---

HOWARD & HOWARD ATTORNEYS, P.C. (AV)

The Phoenix Building, Suite 500, 222 Washington Square,
North, 48933-1817
Telephone: 517-485-1483
Telecopier: 517-485-1568
Kalamazoo, Michigan Office: The Kalamazoo Building, Suite 400, 107
West Michigan Avenue.
Telephone: 616-382-1483.
Telecopier: 616-382-1568.
Bloomfield Hills, Michigan Office: The Pinehurst Office Center, Suite 101,
1400 North Woodward Avenue.
Telephone: 810-645-1483.
Telecopier: 810-645-1568.
Peoria, Illinois Office: The Creve Coeur Building, Suite 200, 321 Liberty
Street.
Telephone: 309-672-1483.
Telecopier: 309-672-1568.
Tampa, Florida Office: First of America Plaza, Suite 2000, 201 East
Kennedy Boulevard.
Telephone: 813-229-1483.
Telecopier: 813-229-1568.

Kim D. Crooks   Gina M. Torielli
Michele LaForest Halloran   Patrick R. Van Tiflin

Representative Clients: For Representative Client list, see General Practice,
Lansing, MI.

For Complete List of Firm Personnel, See General Section

For full biographical listings, see the Martindale-Hubbell Law Directory

---

LIVONIA, Wayne Co.

FRIED & ASSOCIATES, P.C. (AV)

32900 5 Mile Road, Suite 4, 48154
Telephone: 313-421-5055
Fax: 313-421-5591

William C. Fried

For full biographical listings, see the Martindale-Hubbell Law Directory

---

*SAGINAW,** Saginaw Co.

BRAUN KENDRICK FINKBEINER PLC (AV)

101 N. Washington Suite 812, 48607-1297
Telephone: 517-753-3461
Telecopier: 517-753-3951
URL: http://www.bkf-law.com
Bay City, Michigan Office: 201 Phoenix Building, P.O. Box 2039.
Telephone: 517-895-8505.
Telecopier: 517-895-8437.
Ann Arbor, Michigan Office: 700 First National Building.
Telephone: 313-995-4100.
Telecopier: 313-995-4798.

David L. Turner

Representative Clients: The Dow Chemical Co.; General Motors Corp.; Lobdell
Emery Manufacturing Co.; Merrill, Lynch, Inc.; Saginaw General Hospital;
Saginaw News; The Wickes Foundation.

For Complete List of Firm Personnel, See General Section

For full biographical listings, see the Martindale-Hubbell Law Directory

---

*ST. JOSEPH,** Berrien Co.

BUTZBAUGH & DEWANE, P.L.C. (AV)

Law and Title Building, 811 Ship Street, P.O. Box 27, 49085
Telephone: 616-983-0191
Fax: 616-983-5078
Email: b⊗d⊗law@parrett.net

MEMBERS OF FIRM

Alfred M. Butzbaugh   Michael J. Roberts

Representative Clients: SJS Federal Savings Bank; American Society of Agricultural
Engineers; Whirlpool Corp.; Transamerica Insurance Group; Automobile
Club Insurance Assn.; Imperial Printing Co.

For Complete List of Firm Personnel, See General Section

For full biographical listings, see the Martindale-Hubbell Law Directory

---

SOUTHFIELD, Oakland Co.

DE VINE & KOHN (AV)

29800 Telegraph Road, 48034
Telephone: 810-353-6500
Fax: 810-353-2514

(See Next Column)

DE VINE & KOHN—*Continued*

Clifford J. De Vine   Sheldon B. Kohn

For full biographical listings, see the Martindale-Hubbell Law Directory

HOFFERT & ASSOCIATES, P.C. (AV)

3000 Town Center, Suite 2990, 48075-1365
Telephone: 810-355-5600
Facsimile: 810-355-5608

Myles B. Hoffert

Claris K. Cwirko   Frank M. Peraino
LEGAL SUPPORT PERSONNEL
Frederick W. Morgan   Robert A. Eckhardt
Ernest E. Beren   Kenneth W. Voss
(Property Tax Consultant)

Representative Clients: Toys "R" Us, Inc.; Chrysler Corp.; Tamaroff Group of Automotive Cos.; Aetna Realty; Village Green Management; IBM Corp.; Detroit Edison; Comerica Bank, Sun Life of Canada; Phoenix Mutual Insurance Co.

For full biographical listings, see the Martindale-Hubbell Law Directory

ROBERT B. LABE, P.C. (AV)

2000 Town Center, Suite 1780, 48075
Telephone: 810-354-3100
Telecopier: 810-354-3926

Robert B. Labe   Heather Andrews Healy

Reference: Comercia Bank, N.A.; Dean Witter.

For full biographical listings, see the Martindale-Hubbell Law Directory

MADDIN, HAUSER, WARTELL, ROTH, HELLER & PESSES, P.C. (AV)

Third Floor Essex Center, 28400 Northwestern Highway, P.O. Box 215, 48037
Telephone: 810-354-4030, 355-5200
Telefax: 810-354-1422

Milton M. Maddin (1902-1984)   Robert D. Kaplow
Michael W. Maddin   William E. Sigler
Mark R. Hauser   Stewart C. W. Weiner
C. Robert Wartell   Charles M. Lax
Richard J. Maddin   Stuart M. Bordman
Richard F. Roth   Steven D. Sallen
Harvey R. Heller   Joseph M. Fazio
Ian D. Pesses   Gregory J. Gamalski
Michael S. Leib   Julie Chenot Mayer

Nathaniel H. Simpson   Lowell D. Salesin
Ronald A. Sollish   Marc J. Mendelson
Mark H. Fink   Joseph W. Girardot
Steven M. Wolock   Lori E. Talsky
OF COUNSEL
Joel D. Kellman

Reference: Comerica Bank.

For full biographical listings, see the Martindale-Hubbell Law Directory

MASON, STEINHARDT, JACOBS & PERLMAN, PROFESSIONAL CORPORATION (AV)

Suite 1500, 4000 Town Center, 48075-1415
Telephone: 810-358-2090
Fax: 810-358-3599

Walter B. Mason, Jr.

Representative Clients: Citibank, N.A.; City of Dearborn; DeMattia Development Co.; Forest City Enterprises; Michigan Wholesale Drug Assn.; Mortgage Bankers Association of Michigan; Nationwide Insurance Co.; City of Taylor; Union Labor Life Insurance Co.; Yellow Freight Systems, Inc.

For Complete List of Firm Personnel, See General Section

For full biographical listings, see the Martindale-Hubbell Law Directory

JACK M. SCHULTZ, P.C. (AV)

3000 Town Center, Suite 2990, 48075-1365
Telephone: 810-354-3440
Facsimile: 810-355-5608

Jack M. Schultz

For full biographical listings, see the Martindale-Hubbell Law Directory

SOMMERS, SCHWARTZ, SILVER & SCHWARTZ, P.C. (AV)

2000 Town Center, Suite 900, 48075
Telephone: 810-355-0300
Telecopier: 810-746-4001
Plymouth, Michigan Office: 747 South Main Street.
Telephone: 313-455-4250.

Steven J. Schwartz   Lenora R. Roland
Scott C. Hess

Representative Clients: Foodland Distributors; C.A. Muer Corporation; Vlasic & Company; Nederlander Corporation; Midwest Health Centers, P.C.; Vesco Oil Corporation.

For Complete List of Firm Personnel, See General Section

For full biographical listings, see the Martindale-Hubbell Law Directory

TROY, Oakland Co.

MORRIS, ROWLAND, PREKEL, FREDERICK, LEWIS & LEWINSKI, P.L.C. (AV)

Suite 921, 2301 West Big Beaver Road, 48084
Telephone: 810-649-2910
Fax: 810-649-4679
MEMBERS OF FIRM
Donald E. Paquette (1932-1983)   Robert B. Frederick
George L. Morris, Jr.   Eugene W. Lewis, III
James W. Rowland   Richard R. Lewinski
Leonard J. Prekel   Gregory M. Frassrand

For full biographical listings, see the Martindale-Hubbell Law Directory

TRADEMARK, COPYRIGHT AND UNFAIR COMPETITION

(See also listings under Patent, Trademark, Copyright and Unfair Competition)

ALABAMA

BIRMINGHAM, * Jefferson Co.

BRADLEY, ARANT, ROSE & WHITE (AV)

2001 Park Place, Suite 1400, P.O. Box 830709, 35283-0709
Telephone: 205-521-8000
Facsimile: 205-252-0264
Facsimile (SouthTrust Tower Office): 205-251-9915
URL: http://www.BARW.COM
Huntsville, Alabama Office: 200 Clinton Avenue West, Suite 900, 35801.
Telephone: 205-517-5100.
Facsimile: 205-533-5069.

MEMBERS OF FIRM

Thad Gladden Long	Linda A. Friedman
James W. Gewin	Michael R. Pennington

ASSOCIATE
Michael S. Denniston

Counsel for: SouthTrust Bank of Alabama, National Association; Energen, Corporation (formerly Alagasco, Inc.); Blount, Inc.; Coca-Cola Bottling Company United, Inc.; The New York Times Col; Russell Corp.; Walter Industries, Inc.; ASCAP; Auburn University.

For Complete List of Firm Personnel, See General Section

For full biographical listings, see the Martindale-Hubbell Law Directory

---

ARIZONA

PHOENIX, * Maricopa Co.

HORNE, KAPLAN AND BISTROW, P.C. (AV)

Renaissance Two, 40 North Central, Suite 2800, 85004
Telephone: 602-253-9700
Fax: 602-258-4805

Kimball J. Corson

For full biographical listings, see the Martindale-Hubbell Law Directory

JENNINGS, STROUSS AND SALMON, P.L.C. (AV)

A Professional Limited Liability Company
One Renaissance Square, Two North Central, 85004-2393
Telephone: 602-262-5911
Fax: 602-253-3255

Anne L. Kleindienst

For Complete List of Firm Personnel, See General Section

For full biographical listings, see the Martindale-Hubbell Law Directory

LEWIS AND ROCA, LLP (AV)

A Limited Liability Partnership including a Professional Corporation
40 North Central Avenue, 85004-4429
Telephone: 602-262-5311
Fax: 602-262-5747
Email: mlp@lrlaw.com
Tucson, Arizona Office: One South Church Avenue, Suite 700, 86701-1620.
Telephone: 520-622-2090.
Fax: 520-622-3088. E-Mail: mlp@lrlaw.com.

MEMBERS OF FIRM

Peter D. Baird	Patricia K. Norris
Dale A. Danneman	Thomas H. Campbell
James T. Acuff, Jr.	Rosemarie Christofolo

ASSOCIATE
Jeff A. Shumway
OF COUNSEL
Lance J. Rose

Representative Clients: Del Webb Corp.; E & J Gallo Wineries; EMI Records Group; First Data Corp.; Jim Henson Productions; Next Base, Limited; Skymall, Inc.

For Complete List of Firm Personnel, See General Section

For full biographical listings, see the Martindale-Hubbell Law Directory

---

PERRY, PIERSON & SILVER, P.L.C. (AV)

2901 North Central Avenue Suite 300, 85012
Telephone: 602-285-5165
Facsimile: 602-285-5100

Allan R. Perry	Timothy L. Pierson
	Leon B. Silver

For full biographical listings, see the Martindale-Hubbell Law Directory

---

CALIFORNIA

BEVERLY HILLS, Los Angeles Co.

PAUL D. SUPNIK (AV)

Suite 1200 Wells Fargo Bank Building, 433 North Camden Drive, 90210
Telephone: 310-205-2050
Telex: 292416
Facsimile: 310-205-2011
Email: ps@supnik.com *URL:* http://www.supnik.com

For full biographical listings, see the Martindale-Hubbell Law Directory

---

COSTA MESA, Orange Co.

RUTAN & TUCKER, LLP (AV)

A Partnership including Professional Corporations
611 Anton Boulevard, Suite 1400, P.O. Box 1950, 92626
Telephone: 714-641-5100; 213-625-7586
Telecopier: 714-546-9035
Email: rutan&tucker@mcimail.com *URL:* http://www.rutan.com

MEMBERS OF FIRM

Edward D. Sybesma, Jr., (P.C.)	Michael T. Hornak
	Mark B. Frazier

ASSOCIATES

James S. Weisz	Robert Elliot Adel II

For Complete List of Firm Personnel, See General Section

For full biographical listings, see the Martindale-Hubbell Law Directory

---

FRESNO, * Fresno Co.

DOWLING, AARON & KEELER, INCORPORATED (AV)

Suite 200, 6051 North Fresno Street, 93710
Telephone: 209-432-4500
Fax: 209-432-4590
Email: dowling-law.com

Michael D. Dowling	John C. Ganahl

Richard E. Heatter

Reference: Wells Fargo Bank (Main).

For Complete List of Firm Personnel, See General Section

For full biographical listings, see the Martindale-Hubbell Law Directory

---

LOS ANGELES, * Los Angeles Co.

BAKER & HOSTETLER (AV)

600 Wilshire Boulevard, 90017-3212
Telephone: 213-624-2400
FAX: 213-975-1740
In Cleveland, Ohio: 3200 National City Center, 1900 East Ninth Street.
Telephone: 216-621-0200.
In Columbus, Ohio: Capitol Square, Suite 2100, 65 East State Street.
Telephone: 614-228-1541.
In Denver, Colorado: 303 East 17th Avenue, Suite 1100.
Telephone: 303-861-0600.
In Houston, Texas: 1000 Louisiana, Suite 2000.
Telephone: 713-236-0020.
In Long Beach, California: 300 Oceangate, Suite 620.
Telephone: 310-432-2827.
In Orlando, Florida: SunBank Center, Suite 2300, 200 South Orange Avenue.
Telephone: 407-649-4000.
In Washington, D. C.: Washington Square, Suite 1100, 1050 Connecticut Avenue, N. W.
Telephone: 202-861-1500.
In College Park, Maryland: 9658 Baltimore Boulevard, Suite 206.
Telephone: 301-441-2781.
In Alexandria, Virginia: 437 North Lee Street.
Telephone: 703-549-1294.
In San Francisco, California: One Sansome Street, Suite 2000.
Telephone: 415-951-4705.

PARTNER
Anthony M. Keats

(See Next Column)

BAKER & HOSTETLER, *Los Angeles—Continued*

ASSOCIATE

Steve W. Ackerman

For Complete List of Firm Personnel, See General Section

For full biographical listings, see the Martindale-Hubbell Law Directory

---

BERMAN, BLANCHARD, MAUSNER & RESSER, A LAW CORPORATION (AV)

4727 Wilshire Boulevard, Suite 500, 90010
Telephone: 213-965-1200
Telecopier: 213-965-1919
Email: BBMR@ix.netcom.com

Laurence M. Berman	Jeffrey N. Mausner
Lonnie C. Blanchard, III	Bernard M. Resser

Paul A. Hoffman	Cary P. Ocon
Eric Levinrad	Lisé Hamilton

For full biographical listings, see the Martindale-Hubbell Law Directory

---

BLECHER & COLLINS, A PROFESSIONAL CORPORATION (AV)

611 West Sixth Street, 20th Floor, 90017
Telephone: 213-622-4222
Telecopier: 213-622-1656

Maxwell M. Blecher	Ralph C. Hofer
Harold R. Collins, Jr.	William C. Hsu
John E. Andrews	James Robert Noblin
Florence F. Cameron	Donald R. Pepperman
Alicia G. Rosenberg	

For full biographical listings, see the Martindale-Hubbell Law Directory

---

JONES, DAY, REAVIS & POGUE (AV)

555 West Fifth Street Suite 4600, 90013-1025
Telephone: 213-489-3939
Telex: 181439 UD
Telecopier: 213-243-2539
In Irvine, California: 2603 Main Street, Suite 900.
Telephone: 714-851-3939.
Telex: 194911 Lawyers LSA.
Telecopier: 714-553-7539.
In Atlanta, Georgia: 3500 One Peachtree Center, 303 Peachtree Street, N.E.
Telephone: 404-521-3939.
Cable Address: "Attorneys Atlanta".
Telex: 54-2711.
Telecopier: 404-581-8330.
In Brussels, Belgium: Avenue Louise 480, 7th Floor, B-1050 Brussels.
Telephone: 32-2-645-14-11.
Telecopier: 32-2-645-14-45.
In Chicago, Illinois: 77 West Wacker.
Telephone: 312-782-3939.
Telecopier: 312-782-8585.
In Cleveland, Ohio: North Point, 901 Lakeside Avenue.
Telephone: 216-586-3939.
Cable Address: "Attorneys Cleveland."
Telex: 980389.
Telecopier: 216-579-0212.
In Columbus, Ohio: 1900 Huntington Center.
Telephone: 614-469-3939.
Cable Address: "Attorneys Columbus."
Telecopier: 614-461-4198.
In Dallas, Texas: 2300 Trammell Crow Center, 2001 Ross Avenue.
Telephone: 214-220-3939.
Cable Address: "Attorneys Dallas."
Telex: 730852.
Telecopier: 214-969-5100.
In Frankfurt, Germany: Triton Haus, Bockenheimer Landstrasse 42, 60323 Frankfurt am Main.
Telephone: 49-69-9726-3939.
Telecopier: 49-69-9726-3993.
In Geneva, Switzerland: 20, rue de Candolle.
Telephone: 41-22-320-2339.
Telecopier: 41-22-320-1232.
In Hong Kong: 29th Floor, Entertainment Building, 30 Queen's Road Central.
Telephone: 852-2526-6895.
Telecopier: 852-2868-5871.
In London England: Bucklersbury House, 3 Queen Victoria Street.
Telephone: 44-171-236-3939.
Telecopier: 44-171-236-1113.
In New Delhi, India: Pathak & Associates, 13th Floor, Dr. Gopal Das Bhaven, 28 Barakhamba Road.
Telephone: 91-11-373-8793.
Telecopier: 91-11-335-3761.

(See Next Column)

In New York, New York: 599 Lexington Avenue.
Telephone: 212-326-3939.
Cable Address: "JONESDAY NEWYORK."
Telex: 237013 JDRP UR.
Telecopier: 212-755-7306.
In Paris, France: 62, rue du Faubourg Saint-Honore.
Telephone: 33-1-44-71-3939.
Telex: 290156 Surgoe.
Telecopier: 33-1-49-24-0471.
In Pittsburgh, Pennsylvania: 500 Grant Street, 31st Floor.
Telephone: 412-391-3939.
Cable Address: "Attorneys Pittsburgh".
Telecopier: 412-394-7959.
In Riyadh, Saudi Arabia: The International Law Firm, Sulaymaniyah Center, Tahlia Street, P.O. Box 22166.
Telephone: (966-1) 462-8866.
Telecopier: (966-1) 462-9001.
In Taipei, Taiwan: 8th Floor, 2 Tun Hwa South Road, Section 2.
Telephone: (886-2) 704-6808.
Telecopier: (886-2) 704-6791.
In Tokyo, Japan: Toranomon MT Building, 4th Floor, 10-3, Toranomon 3-Chome, Minato-ku, Tokyo 105, Japan.
Telephone: 81-3-3433-3939.
Telecopier: 81-3-5401-2725.
In Washington, D.C.: Metropolitan Square, 1450 G Street, N.W.
Telephone: 202-879-3939.
Cable Address: "Attorneys Washington."
Telex: 89-2410 ATTORNEYS WASH.
Telecopier: 202-737-2832.

MEMBER OF FIRM IN LOS ANGELES

Victor G. Savikas

For Complete List of Firm Personnel, See General Section

For full biographical listings, see the Martindale-Hubbell Law Directory

---

KATZ, HOYT, SEIGEL & KAPOR LLP (AV)

A Partnership including a Professional Corporation
Suite 820, 11111 Santa Monica Boulevard, 90025-3342
Telephone: 310-473-1300
Telecopier: 310-473-7138

MEMBERS OF FIRM

Charles J. Katz (1905-1983)	William Schoenholz
Louis C. Hoyt (1905-1994)	Jack R. Lenack
Benjamin S. Seigel (P.C.)	Russell L. Allyn
Jeffrey H. Kapor	Douglas M. Lipstone
Scott H. Jacobs	Moira Doherty
Alan Jay Cohen	Marla Milner

For full biographical listings, see the Martindale-Hubbell Law Directory

---

KU, FONG, LARSEN & CHEN, LLP (AV)

523 West Sixth Street, Suite 528, 90014
Telephone: 213-488-1400
Telecopier: 213-236-9235

MEMBERS OF FIRM

H. G. Robert Fong	Paul A. Larsen
	Frank W. Chen

OF COUNSEL

Edward Y. Ku

ASSOCIATES

Jack S. Yeh	Victor S. Sze

For full biographical listings, see the Martindale-Hubbell Law Directory

---

LANGBERG, COHN & DROOZ (AV)

A Partnership including a Professional Corporation
12100 Wilshire Boulevard Suite 1650, 90025
Telephone: 310-979-3200
Telecopier: 310-979-3220

Barry B. Langberg (A Professional Corporation)	Beth F. Dumas
	Mitchell J. Langberg
Eileen M. Cohn	Mary L. Muir
Deborah Drooz	Brian A. Murphy

OF COUNSEL

Peter C. Richards (A Professional Corporation)	Gilbert Gaynor
	Polin Cohanne
Milton Segal	

LEGAL SUPPORT PERSONNEL

PARALEGALS

Patricia Ann Essig	Jeanne A. Logé

For full biographical listings, see the Martindale-Hubbell Law Directory

Los Angeles—Continued

LEOPOLD, PETRICH & SMITH, A PROFESSIONAL CORPORATION (AV)

(Formerly Youngman, Hungate & Leopold)
Suite 3110, 2049 Century Park East (Century City), 90067
Telephone: 310-277-3333
Telecopier: 310-277-7444

Gordon E. Youngman (1903-1983)	Edward A. Ruttenberg Vincent Cox
A. Fredric Leopold	Donald R. Gordon
Louis P. Petrich	Walter R. Sadler
Joel McCabe Smith	Daniel M. Mayeda

OF COUNSEL
Richard Hungate

Paul M. Krekorian	Gary M. Grossenbacher
David Aronoff	Robert S. Gutierrez

For full biographical listings, see the Martindale-Hubbell Law Directory

LOEB & LOEB LLP (AV)

A Limited Liability Partnership including Professional Corporations
Suite 1800, 1000 Wilshire Boulevard, 90017-2475
Telephone: 213-688-3400
Facsimile: 213-688-3460; 688-3461; 688-3462
Century City, California Office: Suite 2200, 10100 Santa Monica Boulevard, Los Angeles, 90067-4164.
Telephone: 310-282-2000.
Facsimile: 310-282-2191; 282-2192.
New York, N.Y. Office: 345 Park Avenue, 10154-0037.
Telephone: 212-407-4000.
Facsimile: 212-407-4990.
Washington, D.C. Office: Suite 601, 2100 M Street N.W., 20037-1207.
Telephone: 202-223-5700.
Facsimile: 202-223-5704.
Nashville, Tennessee Office: 45 Music Square West, 37203-3205.
Telephone: 615-749-8300;
Facsimile: 615-749-8308.
Rome, Italy Office: Piazza Digione 1, 00197.
Telephone: 011-396-808-8456.
Facsimile: 011-396-808-8288.

MEMBERS OF FIRM

Phillip E. Adler (A P.C.)	Stuart Lubitz (Century City Office)
Kenneth B. Anderson (New York City Office)	Gary D. Mann (Century City Office)
David H. Carlin (New York City Office)	William J. Marlow (New York City Office)
Marc Chamlin (New York City Office)	Stephen R. Mick
Alex Chartove (Washington, D.C. Office)	Charles H. Miller (New York City Office)
Richard J. Codding (Century City Office)	Douglas E. Mirell David M. Simon (Century City Office)
Kenneth R. Costello	
Martin D. Fern	Lee N. Steiner (New York City Office)
Evan Finkel (Century City Office)	James D. Taylor (New York City Office)
Jay M. Finkelstein (Washington, D.C. Office)	Roger R. Wise (Century City Office)
William K. Konrad (Century City Office)	Richard H. Zaitlen (Century City Office)
Don F. Livornese (Century City Office)	

ASSOCIATES

Paul H. Kovelman (Century City Office)	Ted Rittmaster (Century City Office)
David L. Lubitz	David W. Victor (Century City Office)
Paul G. Nagy (Century City Office)	Joseph F. von Sauers (Century City Office)
Chris P. Perque (Century City Office)	Weining Yang (Century City Office)

For Complete List of Firm Personnel, See General Section

For full biographical listings, see the Martindale-Hubbell Law Directory

MCDERMOTT, WILL & EMERY (AV)

A Partnership including Professional Corporations
2049 Century Park East, 90067-3208
Telephone: 310-277-4110
Facsimile: 310-277-4730
URL: http://www.mwe.com
Chicago, Illinois Office: 227 West Monroe Street.
Telephone: 312-372-2000.
Facsimile: 312-984-7700.
Boston, Massachusetts Office: 75 State Street, Suite 1700.
Telephone: 617-345-5000.
Facsimile: 617-345-5077.

(See Next Column)

Miami, Florida Office: 201 South Biscayne Boulevard.
Telephone: 305-358-3500.
Facsimile: 305-347-6500.
Washington, D.C. Office: 1850 K Street, N.W.
Telephone: 202-887-8000.
Facsimile: 202-778-8087.
Newport Beach, California Office: 1301 Dove Street, Suite 500.
Telephone: 714-851-0633.
Facsimile: 714-851-9348.
New York, N.Y. Office: 50 Rockefeller Plaza.
Telephone: 212-547-5508.
Facsimile: 212-547-5444.
St. Petersburg, Russia Office: AOZT McDermott, Will & Emery, Griboyedova Canal 36, 191023, St. Petersburg, Russia.
Telephone: (7) (812) 310-52-44; 310-55-44; 310-59-44; 850-20-45.
Facsimile: (7) (812) 310-54-46; 325-84-50.
Vilnius, Lithuania Office: Smetonos 6, 2600 Vilnius, Lithuania.
Telephone: 370 2 61-43-08.
Facsimile: 370 2 22-79-55.

MEMBERS OF FIRM

Stephen A. Kroft	Robert H. Rotstein
Robert P. Mallory	Allan L. Schare
Richard K. Simon	

For full biographical listings, see the Martindale-Hubbell Law Directory

O'MELVENY & MYERS LLP (AV)

400 South Hope Street, 90071-2899
Telephone: 213-669-6000
Cable Address: "Moms"
Facsimile: 213-669-6407
Email: omminfo@omm.com
Century City, California Office: 1999 Avenue of the Stars, 90067-6035.
Telephone: 310-553-6700.
Facsimile: 310-246-6779.
Newport Beach, California Office: 610 Newport Center Drive, 92660-6429.
Telephone: 714-760-9600.
Cable Address: "Moms".
Facsimile: 714-669-6994.
San Francisco, California Office: Embarcadero Center West Tower, 275 Battery Street, 94111-3305.
Telephone: 415-984-8700.
Facsimile: 415-984-8701.
New York, New York Office: Citicorp Center, 153 East 53rd Street, 10022-4611.
Telephone: 212-326-2000.
Facsimile: 212-326-2061.
Washington, D.C. Office: 555 13th Street, N.W., 20004-1109.
Telephone: 202-383-5300.
Cable Address: "Moms".
Facsimile: 202-383-5414.
London, England Office: 10 Finsbury Square, London, EC2A 1LA.
Telephone: 0171-256-8451.
Facsimile: 0171-638-8205.
Tokyo, Japan Office: Sanbancho KB-6 Building, 6 Sanbancho, Chiyoda-ku, Tokyo 102, Japan.
Telephone: 03-3239-2900.
Facsimile: 03-3239-2432.
Hong Kong Office: Suite 1905, Peregrine Tower, Lippo Centre, 89 Queensway, Central, Hong Kong.
Telephone: 852-2523-8266.
Facsimile: 852-2522-1760.
Shanghai, Peoples Republic of China Office: Shanghai International Trade Centre, Suite 2011, 2200 Yan An Road West, Shanghai, 200335, PRC.
Telephone: 86-21-6219-5363.
Facsimile: 86-21-6275-4949.

PARTNER
Patrick Lynch

For Complete List of Firm Personnel, See General Section

For full biographical listings, see the Martindale-Hubbell Law Directory

SLAFF, MOSK & RUDMAN (AV)

Suite 825, 9200 Sunset Boulevard, 90069
Telephone: 310-275-5351
Telecopier: 310-273-8706

George Slaff (1906-1989)	Edward Mosk (1916-1989)

MEMBERS OF FIRM

Norman G. Rudman	Marc R. Stein
	Valerie V. Flugge

Reference: City National Bank.

For full biographical listings, see the Martindale-Hubbell Law Directory

MODESTO, * Stanislaus Co.

RICHARD DOUGLAS BREW A PROFESSIONAL LAW CORPORATION (AV)

Suite 350 / Judge Frank C. Damrell Building, 1601 I Street, 95354-1110
Telephone: 209-572-3157
Telefax: 209-572-4641
Email: interleg.com

Richard Douglas Brew

For full biographical listings, see the Martindale-Hubbell Law Directory

SACRAMENTO, * Sacramento Co.

HUNTER RICHEY DI BENEDETTO & BREWER, LLP (AV)

A Limited Liability Partnership
Renaissance Tower, 801 K Street, 23rd Floor, 95814-3525
Telephone: 916-491-3000
Facsimile: 916-491-3080
Email: hrdb@hrdb.com *URL:* http://www.hrdb.com

MEMBERS OF FIRM

William S. Hunter	James F. Geary
Win R. Richey	Janet C. Eisenbeis
Florence L. Di Benedetto	Jeffery D. Harris
Roy E. Brewer	Stephen C. Ruehmann
Anne E. Ferguson	Ralph T. Ferguson
Judith J. Citko	Sharon K. Sandeen

Kathryn T. Papalia

LEGAL SUPPORT PERSONNEL

Lori J. Kelly (Paralegal)	Michele L. Nickell
Deborah M. Romero (Paralegal)	(Legal Assistant)
Linda Jane Hall	Dawn Krein (Legal Assistant)
(Legal Assistant)	Stephanie L. Neumann
Jennifer E. Mueller	(Legal Assistant)
(Legal Assistant)	

For full biographical listings, see the Martindale-Hubbell Law Directory

SAN DIEGO, * San Diego Co.

BROWN, MARTIN, HALLER & McCLAIN (AV)

1660 Union Street, 92101-2926
Telephone: 619-238-0999
Telex: 4992789 BANDM
Fax: (Group I, II, III) 619-238-0062

Carl R. Brown	Eleanor M. Musick
Neil F. Martin	Kathleen A. Pasulka
John L. Haller	Stephanie L. Seidman
James W. McClain	(Not admitted in CA)

Lawrence D. Maxwell	R. Kevin Perkins
Barry F. Soalt	Gary L. Bastman

OF COUNSEL

Russell Ben Miller

LEGAL SUPPORT PERSONNEL

Katherine Proctor	Sheryl Doran
(Patent Agent)	(Technical Advisor)
Paula Schoeneck (Patent Agent)	Luisa Bigornia
Jeffrey W. Winnkelman	(Technical Advisor)
(Technical Advisor)	

Representative Clients: Cubic Corp.; U.S. Elevator Corp.

For full biographical listings, see the Martindale-Hubbell Law Directory

FERRIS & BRITTON, A PROFESSIONAL CORPORATION (AV)

1600 First National Bank Center, 401 West A Street, 92101
Telephone: 619-233-3131
Fax: 619-232-9316

Christopher Q. Britton   Michael R. Weinstein

Representative Clients: Agouron Pharmaceuticals, Inc.; Cox Communications, Inc.; Peninsula Bank; Teleport Communications Group; Southwest Airlines; Structural Bioinformatics, Inc.

For Complete List of Firm Personnel, See General Section

For full biographical listings, see the Martindale-Hubbell Law Directory

SAN FRANCISCO, * San Francisco Co.

MURPHY, PEARSON, BRADLEY & FEENEY, A PROFESSIONAL CORPORATION (AV)

88 Kearny Street, 11th Floor, 94108
Telephone: 415-788-1900
Telecopier: 415-393-8087
Sacramento, California Office: Suite 200, 3600 American River Drive, 95864.
Telephone: 916-483-6074.
Telecopier: 916-483-6088.

James A. Murphy	Timothy J. Halloran
Arthur V. Pearson	Karen M. Goodman
Michael P. Bradley	(Resident, Sacramento Office)
John H. Feeney	Mark S. Perelman
Gregory A. Bastian	Mark Ellis
(Resident, Sacramento Office)	(Resident, Sacramento Office)

William S. Kronenberg

Gregg Anthony Thornton	Veronica E. Rendon
Anne F. Marchant	Mikel C. Deimler
Antoinette Waters Farrell	Erica Brachfeld
Michael K. Pazdernik	(Resident, Sacramento Office)
(Resident, Sacramento Office)	Kristina L. Thornton
Alexander J. Berline	(Resident, Sacramento Office)
Alec Hunter Boyd	Joan E. Low
Jane L. O'Hara Gamp	Dennis J. Priolo
Joseph E. Addiego, III	(Resident, Sacramento Office)
Maretta D. Ward	Anthony O. Ayeni
Brett M. Witter	(Resident, Sacramento Office)
Brad S. Parker	Farzad Tabatabai
Barbara A. Cotter	(Resident, Sacramento Office)
Margaret M. Schneck	Randall L. Thompson
Gregory W. McCracken	Maria S. Magaros
Steven L. Jawgiel	(Resident, Sacramento Office)

For full biographical listings, see the Martindale-Hubbell Law Directory

ROSEN, BIEN & ASARO (AV)

Eighth Floor, 155 Montgomery Street, 94104
Telephone: 415-433-6830
Fax: 415-433-7104
Email: rba@rbalaw.com

Sanford Jay Rosen	Michael W. Bien
	Andrea G. Asaro

Thomas Nolan	William H.D. Fernholz
Donna Petrine	Doris Y. Ng
M.J. Tony Paikeday	A. Marie Villafaña

For full biographical listings, see the Martindale-Hubbell Law Directory

LAWRENCE G. TOWNSEND (AV)

455 Market Street, 19th Floor, 94105
Telephone: 415-882-3288
FAX: 415-882-3299
Email: LGTOWNSEND@aol.com

For full biographical listings, see the Martindale-Hubbell Law Directory

SAN JOSE, * Santa Clara Co.

McMANIS, FAULKNER & MORGAN (AV)

160 West Santa Clara Street, 10th Floor, 95113
Telephone: 408-279-8700
Fax: 408-279-3244; 408-279-0494
Email: mfm@mfmlaw.com

MEMBERS OF FIRM

James McManis	William Faulkner
	Donelle Morgan

ASSOCIATES

Nora Rousso	Michael Reedy
Lisa Herrick	Douglas Watanabe

Kelly McHaffie

For full biographical listings, see the Martindale-Hubbell Law Directory

COLORADO

DENVER, * Denver Co.

BERENBAUM, WEINSHIENK & EASON, P.C. (AV)

Suite 2600 Republic Plaza, 370 17th Street, 80202
Telephone: 303-825-0800
Facsimile: 303-629-7610
Durango, Colorado Office: 2815 Main.
Telephone: 303-247-1333.

Mandel Berenbaum (1914-1993)	Kenneth S. Kramer
Hubert T. Weinshienk	James L. Kurtz-Phelan
(1931-1983)	Charles P. Leder
Joseph Berenbaum	A. Elizabeth Meyers
Charles A. Bewley	H. Michael Miller
Joseph S. Borus	Neil B. Oberfeld
Martin D. Buckley	Dean G. Panos
M. Frances Cetrulo	Edwin G. Perlmutter
Daniel S. Duggan	Barry M. Permut
David R. Eason	Keith M. Pockross
Richard L. Eason	Dan A. Sciullo
Steven C. Hoth	Edward L. Sperry
James A. Jacobson	Eugene M. Sprague
I. H. Kaiser	Robert G. Wilson, Jr.

Ronald I. Zall

J. Hunter Banbury	Amy L. Durfee
Patricia Bellac	Heather Scheel Hagemann

Stephen K. Schutte
SPECIAL COUNSEL
John E. Bush

Representative Clients: Stanley Works; Columbine Venture Funds; The Home Depot; Karman, Inc.; Lomas Mortgage; Southwest State Bank; The Bank of Boulder; Teamsters; Trinity Ventures; The David Johnson Group.

For full biographical listings, see the Martindale-Hubbell Law Directory

---

DORR, CARSON, SLOAN & BIRNEY, P.C. (AV)

3010 East Sixth Avenue, 80206
Telephone: 303-333-3010
FAX: 303-333-1470
URL: http://www.patnet.com/dcsb

Robert C. Dorr	Jack C. Sloan
W. Scott Carson	Thomas S. Birney

Stuart Langley	Leslie P. Kramer

OF COUNSEL

Christopher H. Munch	Steve A. Mains

Gary H. Peterson

Representative Clients: Winegard Co.; Hewlett Packard; Intercat, Inc.; Steam Way International; Big Sur Waterbeds; Taco John's International; Micron Technology.

For full biographical listings, see the Martindale-Hubbell Law Directory

---

DUFFORD & BROWN, P.C. (AV)

1700 Broadway, Suite 1700, 80290-1701
Telephone: 303-861-8013
Facsimile: 303-832-3804
Affiliated Office: Solomon, Pearl, Blum & Quinn, L.L.P., New York, NY and Denver, Colorado.

David W. Furgason	Edward D. White

Scott J. Mikulecky

Thomas E. J. Hazard

Representative Clients: Starbucks Coffee Company; Louis Vuitton, S.A.

For Complete List of Firm Personnel, See General Section

For full biographical listings, see the Martindale-Hubbell Law Directory

---

CONNECTICUT

FAIRFIELD, Fairfield Co.

PERMAN & GREEN, LLP (AV)

425 Post Road, 06430-6232
Telephone: 203-259-1800
Facsimile: 203-255-5170
Email: PGPANT@aol.com

MANAGING PARTNER
Clarence A. Green

(See Next Column)

PARTNERS

Harry F. Smith	Mark F. Harrington

ASSOCIATES

David M. Warren	John J. Goodwin
(Not admitted in CT)	(Not admitted in CT)
Albert W. Hilburger	Ralph D. Gelling
Thomas L. Tully	(Not admitted in CT)
Michael J. Tully	Thomas P. Dowd
(Not admitted in CT)	(Not admitted in CT)

OF COUNSEL
Donald C. Caulfield

For full biographical listings, see the Martindale-Hubbell Law Directory

---

DISTRICT OF COLUMBIA

WASHINGTON, D.C. Co.

* indicates certain Bar Register subscribers, in cities of comparable size and importance, who maintain an additional office in Washington, D.C. and who have arranged for representation as a part of the Washington, D.C. listings that follow

ALEXANDER, BEARDEN, HAIRSTON & MARKS, LLP (AV)

Limited Liability Partnership
2021 L Street, N.W., Suite 300, 20036
Telephone: 202-293-3700
Fax: 202-293-7359
Silver Spring, Maryland Office: Lee Plaza, Suite 805, 8601 Georgia Avenue, 20910.
Telephone: 301-589-2222.
Facsimile: 301-539-2523.
New York, New York Office: 330 Madison Avenue, 36th Floor.
Telephone: 212-808-0008.
Fax: 212-599-1028.

Koteles Alexander	James L. Bearden

Susan C. Lee

Reference: Riggs National Bank of Washington, D.C.

For full biographical listings, see the Martindale-Hubbell Law Directory

---

* BAKER & BOTTS, L.L.P. (AV)

A Registered Limited Liability Partnership
The Warner, 1299 Pennsylvania Avenue, N.W., 20004-2400
Telephone: 202-639-7700
Fax: 202-639-7832
Email: postmaster@bakerbotts.com
Houston, Texas Office: One Shell Plaza, 910 Louisiana.
Telephone: 713-229-1234.
Austin, Texas Office: 1600 San Jacinto Center, 98 San Jacinto Boulevard.
Telephone: 512-322-2500.
Dallas, Texas Office: 2001 Ross Avenue.
Telephone: 214-953-6500.
New York, New York Office: 599 Lexington Avenue.
Telephone: 212-705-5000.
Moscow, Russian Federation Office: 10 ul. Bolshaya Dmitrovka (formerly Pushkinskaya), 103031.
Telephone: 7095/921-5300 (Local); 7501/929-7070 (International).

MEMBERS OF FIRM

Scott F. Partridge	Rodger L. Tate

ASSOCIATES

James B. Arpin	James G. Gatto
Christopher C. Campbell	Stacy B. Margolies

James Remenick

For Complete List of Firm Personnel, See General Section

For full biographical listings, see the Martindale-Hubbell Law Directory

---

BAKER & HOSTETLER (AV)

Washington Square, Suite 1100, 1050 Connecticut Avenue, N.W., 20036-5304
Telephone: 202-861-1500
In Cleveland, Ohio: 3200 National City Center, 1900 East Ninth Street.
Telephone: 216-621-0200.
In Columbus, Ohio: Capitol Square, Suite 2100, 65 East State Street.
Telephone: 614-228-1541.
In Denver, Colorado: 303 East 17th Avenue, Suite 1100.
Telephone: 303-861-0600.
In Houston, Texas: 1000 Louisiana, Suite 2000.
Telephone: 713-751-1600.
In Long Beach, California: 300 Oceangate, Suite 620.
Telephone: 310-432-2827.

(See Next Column)

BAKER & HOSTETLER, *Washington—Continued*

In Los Angeles, California: 600 Wilshire Boulevard.
Telephone: 213-624-2400.
In Orlando, Florida: SunBank Center, Suite 2300, 200 South Orange
Avenue.
Telephone: 305-841-1111.
In College Park, Maryland: 9658 Baltimore Boulevard, Suite 206.
Telephone: 301-441-2781.
In Alexandria, Virginia: 437 North Lee Street.
Telephone: 703-549-1294.
In San Francisco, California: One Sansome Street, Suite 2000.
Telephone: 415-951-4705.

PARTNER
Belinda Jayne Scrimenti

For Complete List of Firm Personnel, See General Section

For full biographical listings, see the Martindale-Hubbell Law Directory

BANNER & WITCOFF, LTD. (AV)

Established In 1920 - Predecessor Parent
1001 G Street, N.W., 20001-4597
Telephone: 202-508-9100
Facsimile: 202-508-9299
Email: skerpon@ba-iplaw.com *URL:* http://www.ba-iplaw.com
Chicago, Illinois Office: Ten South Wacker Drive.
Telephone: 312-715-1000.
Facsimile: 312-715-1234.
Boston, Massachusetts Office: 75 State Street.
Telephone: 617-345-9100.
Facsimile: 617-345-9111.

Robert F. Altherr, Jr.	Lance G. Johnson
Donald W. Banner	Sarah A. Kagan
Pamela I. Banner	Edward F. McKie, Jr.
Alan I. Cantor	Kathy J. McKnight
Alan S. Cooper	Nina L. Medlock
William J. Fisher	James A. Niegowski
Mary Gronlund	Thomas L. Peterson
Barry L. Grossman	Joseph M. Potenza
Dale H. Hoscheit	Steven P. Schad
Thomas H. Jackson	Joseph M. Skerpon

Scott M. Alter	Robert S. Katz
David J. Cho	Joanne Ludovici-Lint
(Not admitted in DC)	Adriana S. Luedke
Gary D. Fedorochko	Victor W. Marton
(Not admitted in DC)	(Not admitted in DC)
Eric T. Fingerhut	Kelly C. Maynard
Daniel E. Fisher	Christopher L. McKee
Updeep S. Gill (Mickey)	Frederic M. Meeker
(Not admitted in DC)	Michael J. Shea
Christopher R. Glembocki	(Not admitted in DC)
(Not admitted in DC)	Kenneth K.D. Vu
Brian E. Hanlon	(Not admitted in DC)
(Not admitted in DC)	Wendi L. Weinstein
Patricia E. Hong	Susan A. Wolffe

Bradley C. Wright
COUNSEL

William W. Beckett	Franklin D. Wolffe

For full biographical listings, see the Martindale-Hubbell Law Directory

FINNEGAN, HENDERSON, FARABOW, GARRETT & DUNNER, L.L.P. (AV)

Suite 700, 1300 I Street, N.W., 20005-3315
Telephone: 202-408-4000
Cable Address: "Finderbow"
Telex: 440275 ITT; 248740 RCA;
Facsimile: 202-408-4400
Tokyo, Japan Office: Toranomon No. 45 Mori Building, Third Floor, 1-5,
Toranomon 5-chome Minato-Ku.
Telephone: 0081-3-3431-6943.
Facsimile: 0081-3-3431-6945.
Brussels, Belgium Office: Avenue Louise 326, Box 37, 1050.
Telephone: 011-322-646-0353.
Facsimile: 011-322-646-2135.

MEMBERS OF FIRM

Douglas B. Henderson	Thomas W. Winland
Ford F. Farabow Jr.	E. Robert Yoches
Arthur S. Garrett	Barry W. Graham
Donald R. Dunner	Susan Haberman Griffen
Tipton D. Jennings IV	Christopher P. Foley
Laurence R. Hefter	John C. Paul
Michael C. Elmer	Griffith B. Price Jr.
John M. Romary	John F. Hornick
Richard Lee Stroup	Robert D. Litowitz
David W. Hill	David M. Kelly

Mark S. Sommers
COUNSEL
Arthur J. Levine

(See Next Column)

ASSOCIATES

Jeffrey A. Berkowitz	Lisa F. Peller
(Not admitted in DC)	Linda S. Paine-Powell

John R. Alison

Reference: Crestar Bank, N.A., Washington, D.C.

For full biographical listings, see the Martindale-Hubbell Law Directory

LANE, AITKEN & McCANN (AV)

Watergate Office Building, 2600 Virginia Avenue, N.W., 20037
Telephone: 202-337-5556
Telecopier: 202-337-8073
Email: lam@access.digex.net

MEMBERS OF FIRM

Richard L. Aitken	Laurence J. Marhoefer
Clifton E. McCann	(Not admitted in DC)
John P. Shannon, Jr.	Andrew C. Aitken
	(Not admitted in DC)

ASSOCIATE
David D'Zurilla
OF COUNSEL
Joseph M. Lane

For full biographical listings, see the Martindale-Hubbell Law Directory

* McDERMOTT, WILL & EMERY (AV)

A Partnership including Professional Corporations
1850 K Street, N.W., 20006-2296
Telephone: 202-887-8000
Facsimile: 202-778-8087
URL: http://www.mwe.com
Chicago, Illinois Office: 227 West Monroe Street.
Telephone: 312-372-2000.
Facsimile: 312-984-7700.
Boston, Massachusetts Office: 75 State Street, Suite 1700.
Telephone: 617-345-5000.
Facsimile: 617-345-5077.
Miami, Florida Office: 201 South Biscayne Boulevard.
Telephone: 305-358-3500.
Facsimile: 305-347-6500.
Los Angeles, California Office: 2049 Century Park East.
Telephone: 310-277-4110.
Facsimile: 310-277-4730.
Newport Beach, California Office: 1301 Dove Street, Suite 500.
Telephone: 714-851-0633.
Facsimile: 714-851-9348.
New York, N.Y. Office: 50 Rockefeller Plaza.
Telephone: 212-547-5508.
Facsimile: 212-547-5444.
St. Petersburg, Russia Office: AOZT McDermott, Will & Emery,
Griboyedova Canal 36, 191023, St. Petersburg, Russia.
Telephone: (7) (812) 310-52-44; 310-55-44; 310-59-44; 850-20-45.
Facsimile: (7) (812) 310-54-46; 325-84-50.
Vilnius, Lithuania Office: Smetonos 6, 2600 Vilnius, Lithuania.
Telephone: 370 2 61-43-08.
Facsimile: 370 2 22-79-55.

MEMBERS OF FIRM

Stanislaus Aksman	Jack Q. Lever, Jr.
(Not admitted in DC)	Raphael V. Lupo
William H. Barrett	Susan Somers Neal
Melise R. Blakeslee	(Not admitted in DC)
Kenneth L. Cage	Robert S. Schwartz
Mark G. Davis	Carl W. Schwarz
Seth D. Greenstein	James H. Sneed

Donna M. Tanguay

For full biographical listings, see the Martindale-Hubbell Law Directory

JOHN H. MIDLEN, JR. CHARTERED (AV)

3238 Prospect Street, N.W., 20007-3214
Telephone: 202-333-1500
Facsimile: 202-333-6852
Email: john@midlen.com *URL:* http://www.midlen.com

John H. Midlen, Jr.

For full biographical listings, see the Martindale-Hubbell Law Directory

SHAWN, MANN & NIEDERMAYER, L.L.P. (AV)

1850 M Street, N.W., Suite 280, 20036-5803
Telephone: 202-331-7900
Fax: 202-331-0726
Washington, D.C., Government Affairs Office: 499 S. Capitol Street, S.W.,
Suite 420.
Telephone: 202-842-3000.
Fax: 202-547-7161.
Los Angeles, California Office: 2029 Century Park East, Suite 1690.
Telephone: 310-553-8065.
Fax: 310-557-0729.

(See Next Column)

SHAWN, MANN & NIEDERMAYER L.L.P.—*Continued*

San Diego, California Office: 401 West "A" Street, Suite 1850.
Telephone: 619-236-0303.
Fax: 619-238-8181.
San Francisco, California Office: The Fox Plaza, 1390 Market Street, Suite 1204.
Telephone: 415-982-0150.
Fax: 415-522-0513.
Bloomington, Minnesota Office: 2090 West 98th Street.
Telephone: 612-881-6577.
Fax: 612-881-6894.

MEMBERS OF FIRM

William H. Shawn	James E. King
Kim D. Mann	Gregory S. Abrams
Roy I. Niedermayer	James O'Neil Attridge
Joseph L. Steinfeld, Jr.	Robert N. Vohra

ASSOCIATES

Gary L. Stanley	Bryan D. Parker
John T. Siegler	(Not admitted in DC)
Joseph A. Hess	James R. Bruner

GOVERNMENT AFFAIRS PARTNERS

James A. DeChaine	Jon L. Boisclair

GOVERNMENT AFFAIRS ASSOCIATES

Jane E. Shey	Lynda M. Murphy
	Steven T. Kingsley

For full biographical listings, see the Martindale-Hubbell Law Directory

---

* VENABLE ATTORNEYS AT LAW VENABLE, BAETJER, HOWARD & CIVILETTI, LLP (AV)

A Partnership including Professional Corporations
Suite 1000, 1201 New York Avenue, N.W., 20005
Telephone: 202-962-4800
Fax: 202-962-8300
Baltimore, Maryland Office: Venable, Baetjer and Howard LLP, 1800 Mercantile Bank & Trust Building, 2 Hopkins Plaza.
Telephone: 410-244-7400.
McLean, Virginia Office: Venable, Baetjer and Howard LLP, Suite 400, 2010 Corporate Ridge.
Telephone: 703-760-1600.
Rockville, Maryland Office: Venable, Baetjer and Howard LLP, Suite 500, One Church Street, P. O. Box 1906.
Telephone: 301-217-5600.
Towson, Maryland Office: Venable, Baetjer and Howard LLP, 210 Allegheny Avenue, P. O. Box 5517.
Telephone: 410-494-6200.

MEMBERS OF FIRM

Thomas J. Kenney, Jr. (P.C.) (Not admitted in DC; Also at Baltimore, Maryland Office)	George F. Pappas (Also at Baltimore, Maryland Office)
Douglas D. Connah, Jr. (P.C.) (Also at Baltimore, Maryland Office)	William D. Coston
	William D. Quarles (Also at Towson, Maryland Office)
Kenneth C. Bass, III (Also at McLean, Virginia Office)	Jeffrey L. Ihnen
Edward F. Glynn, Jr.	James A. Dunbar (Also at Baltimore, Maryland Office)
James R. Myers	Robert J. Bolger, Jr. (Not admitted in DC; Also at Baltimore, Maryland Office)
Jeffrey D. Knowles	
Jeffrey A. Dunn (Also at Baltimore, Maryland Office)	Gary M. Hnath

OF COUNSEL

Barbara L. Waite

ASSOCIATES

James Nicholas Czaban (Not admitted in DC)	David W. Goewey
	Edward Brendan Magrab

For Complete List of Firm Personnel, See General Section

For full biographical listings, see the Martindale-Hubbell Law Directory

---

FLORIDA

MIAMI,* Dade Co.

ISICOFF & RAGATZ, P.A. (AV)

1101 Brickell Avenue, Suite 704, 33131
Telephone: 305-373-3232
Fax: 305-373-3233
Email: FIRM@IRLAW.COM

Eric D. Isicoff	Teresa Ragatz

Barbara J. Kaplan	Michael R. Evans

(See Next Column)

OF COUNSEL

Jay Koenigsberg

For full biographical listings, see the Martindale-Hubbell Law Directory

KENNY NACHWALTER SEYMOUR ARNOLD CRITCHLOW & SPECTOR, PROFESSIONAL ASSOCIATION (AV)

1100 Miami Center, 201 South Biscayne Boulevard, 33131-4327
Telephone: 305-373-1000
Facsimile: 305-372-1861
ABA/net: 18338
Email: 7502552@MCIMAIL.COM
Rogersville, Tennessee Office: 107 East Main Street, Suite 301, 37857-3347.
Telephone: 423-272-5300.
Facsimile: 423-272-4961.

James J. Kenny	Brian F. Spector
Michael Nachwalter	Kevin J. Murray
Richard Alan Arnold	Harry R. Schafer
	David H. Lichter

Representative Clients: Cartier, Inc.; GTE Directories Corp.; Macmillan, Inc.; Mont Blanc-Simplo Gmbh.; Rolex Watch, USA, Inc.; Pepe Jeans USA, Inc.; Louis Vuitton Malletier; Dooney & Burke, Inc.; Tommy Hilfiger USA, Inc.; Tommy Hilfiger Licensing, Inc.

For Complete List of Firm Personnel, See General Section

For full biographical listings, see the Martindale-Hubbell Law Directory

McDERMOTT, WILL & EMERY (AV)

A Partnership including Professional Corporations
201 South Biscayne Boulevard, 33131-4336
Telephone: 305-358-3500
Facsimile: 305-347-6500
URL: http://www.mwe.com
Chicago, Illinois Office: 227 West Monroe Street.
Telephone: 312-372-2000.
Facsimile: 312-984-7700.
Boston, Massachusetts Office: 75 State Street, Suite 1700.
Telephone: 617-345-5000.
Facsimile: 617-345-5077.
Washington, D.C. Office: 1850 K Street, N.W.
Telephone: 202-887-8000.
Facsimile: 202-778-8087.
Los Angeles, California Office: 2049 Century Park East.
Telephone: 310-277-4110.
Facsimile: 310-277-4730.
Newport Beach, California Office: 1301 Dove Street, Suite 500.
Telephone: 714-851-0633.
Facsimile: 714-851-9348.
New York, N.Y. Office: 50 Rockefeller Plaza.
Telephone: 212-547-5508.
Facsimile: 212-547-5444.
St. Petersburg, Russia Office: AOZT McDermott, Will & Emery, Griboyedova Canal 36, 191023 St. Petersburg, Russia.
Telephone: (7) (812) 310-52-44; 310-55-44; 310-59-44; 850-20-45.
Facsimile: (7) (812) 310-54-46; 325-84-50.
Vilnius, Lithuania Office: Smetonos 6, 2600 Vilnius, Lithuania.
Telephone: 370 2 61-43-08.
Facsimile: 370 2 22-79-55.

MEMBER OF FIRM

Steven E. Siff *

For full biographical listings, see the Martindale-Hubbell Law Directory

---

GEORGIA

ATLANTA,* Fulton Co.

ALSTON & BIRD (AV)

A Partnership including Professional Corporations
One Atlantic Center, 1201 West Peachtree Street, 30309-3424
Telephone: 404-881-7000
Telecopier: 404-881-7777
Cable Address: AMGRAM GA
Telex: 54-2996
Easylink: 62985848
Washington, D.C. Office: 601 Pennsylvania Ave., N.W., North Building, Suite 250 20004.
Telephone: 202-508-3300.
Telecopier: 202-508-3333.

MEMBERS OF FIRM

John K. Train III	Martin J. Elgison
William C. Humphreys, Jr.	H. Stephen Harris, Jr.
Peter Kontio	Michael P. Kenny
Kevin E. Grady	Randall L. Allen
Peter Q. Bassett	James J. Wolfson
Frank G. Smith III	Beth K. Toberman

(See Next Column)

ALSTON & BIRD, *Atlanta—Continued*
ASSOCIATES
John P. Fry James M. Jordan III
David J. Stewart
COUNSEL
Janet E. Witt

Representative Clients: Borden, Inc.; Genuine Parts Company; Houston's Restaurants, Inc.; Printpack, Inc.; Suntory Water Group, Inc.

For Complete List of Firm Personnel, See General Section

For full biographical listings, see the Martindale-Hubbell Law Directory

---

BONDURANT, MIXSON & ELMORE, LLP (AV)

1201 W. Peachtree Street Suite 3900, 30309
Telephone: 404-881-4100
FAX: 404-881-4111

MEMBERS OF FIRM
Emmet J. Bondurant II Dirk G. Christensen
H. Lamar Mixson Jane E. Fahey
M. Jerome Elmore John E. Floyd
Edward B. Krugman Michael A. Sullivan
Jeffrey O. Bramlett Michael B. Terry

Representative Clients: The Aetna Casualty and Surety Company; Blue Circle of America; Circle K; Conoco, Inc.; Delta Air Lines, Inc.; Queen Carpets, Inc.; Sanifill, Inc.; Ticketmaster; Trammell Crow Co.; Wylie Laboratories.

For full biographical listings, see the Martindale-Hubbell Law Directory

---

KAUFMAN, CHAIKEN, RICKERTSEN, KREVOLIN, MILLER & HORST, A PROFESSIONAL CORPORATION (AV)

400 Perimeter Center Terrace, N.E., Suite 720, 30346-1234
Telephone: 770-390-9200
Facsimile: 770-395-6720
Email: rkaufm03@counsel.com

Fredric Chaiken

References: Gulf States Mortgage Co., Inc.; Dyer & Dyer Volvo, Inc.; Trust Company Bank; Wachovia Bank of Georgia.

For Complete List of Firm Personnel, See General Section

For full biographical listings, see the Martindale-Hubbell Law Directory

---

SUTHERLAND, ASBILL & BRENNAN, L.L.P. (AV)

999 Peachtree Street, N.E., 30309-3996
Telephone: 404-853-8000
Facsimile: 404-853-8806
Email: postmaster@sablaw.com
Washington, D.C. Office: 1275 Pennsylvania Avenue, N.W., 20004-2404.
Telephone: 202-383-0100.
New York, N.Y. Office: 600 Madison Avenue, 11th Floor, 10022-1615.
Telephone: 212-605-6400.
Austin, Texas Office: 111 Congress Avenue, 23rd Floor, 78701-4079.
Telephone: 512-469-3350.

Thomas A. Cox J. D. Fleming, Jr.
Patricia Bayer Cunningham John H. Fleming
COUNSEL OF THE FIRM IN ATLANTA, GEORGIA
Edmund B. Burke
For Complete List of Firm Personnel, See General Section
For full biographical listings, see the Martindale-Hubbell Law Directory

---

HAWAII

HONOLULU, Honolulu Co.
DWYER IMANAKA SCHRAFF KUDO MEYER & FUJIMOTO ATTORNEYS AT LAW, A LAW CORPORATION (AV)

1800 Pioneer Plaza, 900 Fort Street Mall, 96813
Telephone: 808-524-8000
Telecopier: 808-526-1419
Mailing Address: P.O. Box 2727, 96803
Email: hawaiilaw@dwyer-imanaka.com *URL:*
http://www.dwyer-imanaka.com

John R. Dwyer, Jr. William G. Meyer, III
Mitchell A. Imanaka Wesley M. Fujimoto
Paul A. Schraff Ronald Van Grant
Benjamin A. Kudo (Atty. at Jon M. H. Pang
Law, A Law Corp.) Blake W. Bushnell
Adelbert Green

(See Next Column)

Richard T. Asato, Jr. Jeffery S. Werbelow
Scott W. Settle Lori Ann K. Koseki
Darcie S. Yoshinaga Troy T. Fukuhara
Lawrence I. Kawasaki Katy Y. Chen
Stacy E. Uehara Naomi S. Uyeno
Kris N. Nakagawa Roger B. McKeague
OF COUNSEL
Randall Y. Iwase R. Brian Tsujimura

For full biographical listings, see the Martindale-Hubbell Law Directory

---

IDAHO

BOISE, Ada Co.
MOFFATT, THOMAS, BARRETT, ROCK & FIELDS, CHARTERED (AV)

101 South Capitol Boulevard, P.O. Box 829, 83702
Telephone: 208-345-2000
FAX: 208-385-5384
Email: info@moffatt.com
Idaho Falls Office: 525 Park Avenue, Suite 2D, P.O. Box 1367, 83403.
Telephone: 208-522-6700.
FAX: 208-522-5111.
Pocatello, Idaho Office: 845 West Center, Suite C, P.O. Box 4941, 83201.
Telephone: 208-233-2001.

Paul S. Street Thomas C. Morris
Patrick J. Kole

Representative Clients: BMC West Corporation; Chevron, U.S.A.; First Security Bank of Idaho, N.A.; General Motors Corp.; Idaho Potato Commission; Intermountain Gas Co.; John Alden Life Insurance Co.; Micron Technology, Inc.; Royal Insurance Cos.; St. Luke's Regional Medical Center & Mountain States Tumor Institute.

For Complete List of Firm Personnel, See General Section

For full biographical listings, see the Martindale-Hubbell Law Directory

---

ILLINOIS

CHICAGO, Cook Co.
CHERRY & FLYNN (AV)

30 North La Salle Street, Suite 2300, 60602
Telephone: 312-372-2100
Telecopier: 312-853-0279

Myron M. Cherry William R. Coulson
Peter Flynn David D. Merritt
Adam J. Levitt

For full biographical listings, see the Martindale-Hubbell Law Directory

---

DAVIS, MANNIX & McGRATH (AV)

125 South Wacker Drive, Suite 1700, 60606
Telephone: 312-332-3033
Fax: 312-332-6376

David C. Bogan (1946-1995) Julia D. Mannix
Champ W. Davis, Jr. Gini S. Marziani
Marsha K. Hoover William T. McGrath

John B. Alsterda J. Thomas Warlick, IV
Richard R. Danis, Jr. (Not admitted in IL)
OF COUNSEL
Celeste Ebers Kralovec Margaret F. Woulfe

For full biographical listings, see the Martindale-Hubbell Law Directory

---

DICK AND HARRIS (AV)

Suite 3800, 181 West Madison Street, 60602
Telephone: 312-726-4000
Telecopier: 312-726-5834

MEMBERS OF FIRM
Richard Eugene Dick Howard E. Silverman
Richard D. Harris John S. Pacocha
Max Shaftal Jody L. Factor

(See Next Column)

DICK AND HARRIS—*Continued*

ASSOCIATES

Douglas B. Teaney	Jovan N. Jovanovic
Herbert H. Finn	Stevem Wayne Hays
Jordan A. Sigale	(Not admitted in IL)

For full biographical listings, see the Martindale-Hubbell Law Directory

FORAN & SCHULTZ (AV)

Suite 3000, 30 North La Salle Street, 60602
Telephone: 312-368-8330
Fax: 312-580-2600

MEMBERS OF FIRM

Thomas A. Foran	Jack J. Carriglio
Richard G. Schultz	Steven H. Gistenson
James R. Figliulo	Brooke R. Whitted
Stephen A. Gorman	Jeffrey C. Blumenthal
Jeff D. Harris	Carl A. Gigante
	Carmen D. Caruso

ASSOCIATES

Teresa F. Frisbie	Brian P. Liston
Peter A. Silverman	Paul A. Henmueller
Marla B. Wilneff	James J. Sipchen, Jr.
Daniel D. Kasten	Mitchell S. Chaban
Patrick R. Gabrione	Dana L. Romaniuk
	Jessica Dickstein

OF COUNSEL

Harry G. Comerford

For full biographical listings, see the Martindale-Hubbell Law Directory

McDERMOTT, WILL & EMERY (AV)

A Partnership including Professional Corporations
227 West Monroe Street, 60606-5096
Telephone: 312-372-2000
Facsimile: 312-984-7700
Boston, Massachusetts Office: 75 State Street, Suite 1700.
Telephone: 617-345-5000.
Facsimile: 617-345-5077.
Miami, Florida Office: 201 South Biscayne Boulevard.
Telephone: 305-358-3500.
Facsimile: 305-347-6500.
Washington, D.C. Office: 1850 K Street, N.W.
Telephone: 202-887-8000.
Facsimile: 202-778-8087.
Los Angeles, California Office: 2049 Century Park East.
Telephone: 310-277-4110.
Facsimile: 310-277-4730.
Newport Beach, California Office: 1301 Dove Street, Suite 500.
Telephone: 714-851-0633.
Facsimile: 714-851-9348.
New York, N.Y. Office: 1211 Avenue of the Americas.
Telephone: 212-768-5400.
Facsimile: 212-768-5444.
St. Petersburg, Russia Office: AOZT McDermott, Will & Emery, Griboyedova Canal 36, 191023 St. Petersburg, Russia.
Telephone: (7) (812) 310-52-44; 310-55-44; 310-59-44; 850-20-45.
Facsimile: (7) (812) 310-54-46; 325-84-50.
Vilnius, Lithuania Office: Smetonos 6, 2600 Vilnius, Lithuania.
Telephone: 370 2 61-43-08.
Facsimile: 370 2 22-79-55.

MEMBERS OF FIRM

Michelle C. Burke	Steven H. Hoeft *
Margaret M. Duncan	Kenneth J. Jurek
Rosanne J. Faraci	Paula J. Krasny
Byron L. Gregory *	Mercedes A. Laing
Steven P. Handler *	Joseph H. Paquin, Jr.
	Bruce H. Weitzman *

*Denotes a lawyer employed by a Professional Corporation which is a member of the Firm.

For full biographical listings, see the Martindale-Hubbell Law Directory

PATTISHALL, McAULIFFE, NEWBURY, HILLIARD & GERALDSON (AV)

Suite 5000, 311 South Wacker Drive, 60606
Telephone: 312-554-8000
Facsimile: 312-554-8015
Washington, D.C. Office: 320 Watergate, Six Hundred, 20037.
Telephone: 202-338-1300.
Facsimile: 202-338-9349.

MEMBERS OF FIRM

Beverly W. Pattishall	David Craig Hilliard
Jeremiah D. McAuliffe	Edward G. Wierzbicki
Robert M. Newbury	Robert W. Sacoff
Benjamin S. Warren III	Mark V. B. Partridge
(Resident Partner, Washington, D.C. Office)	Joseph N. Welch II
	Mark H. Hellmann
Raymond I. Geraldson, Jr.	Jean Marie R. Pechette

(See Next Column)

MEMBERS OF FIRM (Continued)

Daniel D. Frohling	Mary E. Innis
John Thompson Brown	Douglas N. Masters

Brett A. August	Kevin T. Conroy
Jonathan S. Jennings	Mark F. Schultz
John Michael Murphy	Bradley L. Cohn
Maxine Lans Retsky	Susan D. Hanaway
Nancy L. Clarke	Victor F. DeFrancis

For full biographical listings, see the Martindale-Hubbell Law Directory

*GENEVA,** Kane Co.

SMITH, LANDMEIER & SKAAR, P.C. (AV)

15 North Second Street, 60134
Telephone: 708-232-2880
Fax: 708-232-2889

Allen L. Landmeier

Vincent J. Elders

References: Firstar Bank, Geneva, N.A., Geneva, Illinois; State Bank of Geneva, Geneva, Illinois.

For Complete List of Firm Personnel, See General Section

For full biographical listings, see the Martindale-Hubbell Law Directory

INDIANA

*INDIANAPOLIS,** Marion Co.

ICE MILLER DONADIO & RYAN (AV)

One American Square Box 82001, 46282-0002
Telephone: 317-236-2100
Fax: 317-236-2219
Email: leel@imdr.com *URL:* http://www.imdr.com
South Bend, Indiana Office: 211 West Washington Street, Suite 2420.
Telephone: 219-234-7933.
Fax: 219-234-7965. Internet E-mail: leel@imdr.com. Web Site Address: http://www.imdr.com.

MEMBERS OF FIRM

Jack R. Snyder	Philip A. Whistler
Jay G. Taylor	John F. Prescott, Jr.
David M. Mattingly	Paul B. Overhauser

OF COUNSEL

Bradley L. Williams	Bruce W. Longbottom

ASSOCIATES

Doreen J. Gridley	Harold C. Moore
	Lynn M. Gagel

Counsel For: Delco Remey America; Thomson Consumer Electronics, Inc.; Reilly Industries, Inc.; Haynes International, Inc.; Powerway, Inc.; Software Solutions, Inc.; Wavetek, Inc.; Bioanalytical Systems, Inc.; Fairbanks Communications, Inc.; Nor-Cote International, Inc.; Wilhelm Environmental Technologies, Inc.; Biomet, Inc.; Indianapolis Motor Speedway; Southern Corp.

For Complete List of Firm Personnel, See General Section

For full biographical listings, see the Martindale-Hubbell Law Directory

*LAFAYETTE,** Tippecanoe Co.

STUART & BRANIGIN (AV)

The Life Building, 300 Main Street, Suite 800, 47902
Telephone: 317-423-1561
Telecopier: 317-742-8175

MEMBERS OF FIRM

Allison Ellsworth Stuart (1886-1950)	Stephen R. Pennell
Roger D. Branigin (1902-1975)	Anthony S. Benton
Russell H. Hart	Erik D. Spykman
Roger D. Branigin, Jr.	William E. Emerick
Thomas L. Ryan	John C. Duffey
James V. McGlone	Mark E. DeYoung
Carl W. Kloepfer	Thomas B. Parent
Thomas R. McCully	Laura L. Bowker
Larry R. Fisher	Kevin D. Nicoson
Nina B. Kirkpatrick	Susan K. Roberts
Mark Lillianfeld	John M. Stuckey
	Deborah B. Trice

COUNSEL

John F. Bodle

ASSOCIATES

Brent W. Huber	David A. Starkweather
William P. Kealey	Geoffrey Blazi
	A. James Chareq

(See Next Column)

STUART & BRANIGIN, *Lafayette—Continued*

General Counsel for: The Lafayette Life Insurance Co.; INB National Bank, N.W.; Lafayette Home Hospital, Inc.
State Counsel for: Norfolk & Western Railway Co.
Mr. Ryan is Counsel to: The Trustees of Purdue University.
Representative Clients: Aluminum Company of America; Liberty Mutual Insurance Group.

For full biographical listings, see the Martindale-Hubbell Law Directory

---

SOUTH BEND,* St. Joseph Co.

MAY, OBERFELL & LORBER (AV)

300 North Michigan Street, 46601
Telephone: 219-232-2031
Facsimile: 219-232-9789
Elkhart, Indiana Office: 307 South Main Street.
Telephone: 219-295-7281.
Facsimile: 219-295-7273.

MEMBER OF FIRM
John J. Lorber
ASSOCIATE
Christopher A. Nichols

Representative Clients: Keybank; Big C Lumber Co., Inc.; Penn Central Corporation; Orbitron Industries, Inc.; ITT Hartford, ASA Corporation.

For full biographical listings, see the Martindale-Hubbell Law Directory

---

KANSAS

WICHITA,* Sedgwick Co.

FOULSTON & SIEFKIN L.L.P. (AV)

700 Fourth Financial Center, 67202
Telephone: 316-267-6371
Facsimile: 316-267-6345
Topeka, Kansas Office: 1515 Bank IV Tower, 534 Kansas Avenue, 66603.
Telephone: 913-233-3600.
Fax: 913-233-1610.
Dodge City, Kansas Office: 810 Frontview, P.O. Box 1147, 67801.
Telephone: 316-227-8126.
Fax: 316-227-8451.
Member: Lex Mundi, A Global Association of 126 Independent Firms.
MEMBERS OF FIRM

James D. Oliver   R. Douglas Reagan
                         (Resident, Dodge City Office)

For Complete List of Firm Personnel, See General Section

For full biographical listings, see the Martindale-Hubbell Law Directory

---

KENTUCKY

LOUISVILLE,* Jefferson Co.

SEILLER & HANDMAKER, LLP (AV)

2200 Meidinger Tower, 40202
Telephone: 502-584-7400
Telecopier: 502-583-2100
Paris, Kentucky Office: Seiller, Handmaker & Blevins, P.S.C., 1431 South Main Street.
Telephone: 606-987-3980.
Telecopier: 606-987-3982.
Cynthiana, Kentucky Office: Seiller, Handmaker & Blevins, P.S.C., 9 South Walnut.
Telephone: 606-234-2880.
New Albany, Indiana Office: 202 Pearl Street.
Telephone: 812-948-8307.
Telecopier: 812-948-8383.

Edward F. Seiller (1897-1990)
MEMBERS OF FIRM

Stuart Allen Handmaker   Maury D. Kommor
Bill V. Seiller   Cynthia Compton Stone
David M. Cantor   Glenn A. Cohen
Neil C. Bordy   Tomi Anne Blevins Pulliam
Kyle Anne Citrynell   (Paris and Cynthiana Offices)
ASSOCIATES
Pamela M. Greenwell   Donna F. Townsend
Michael C. Bratcher   Gregory A. Lindsey
John E. Brengle   Vicki L. Buba
Patrick R. Holland, II   Allen C. Platt III (Resident,
Edwin Jon Wolfe   New Albany, Indiana Office)

(See Next Column)

OF COUNSEL
Robert S. Frey

For full biographical listings, see the Martindale-Hubbell Law Directory

---

MARYLAND

BALTIMORE,* (Independent City)

VENABLE ATTORNEYS AT LAW VENABLE, BAETJER AND HOWARD, LLP (AV)

A Partnership including Professional Corporations
1800 Mercantile Bank & Trust Building, 2 Hopkins Plaza, 21201
Telephone: 410-244-7400
Email: INFO@Venable.win.net
Washington, D.C. Office: Venable, Baetjer, Howard & Civiletti LLP. Suite 1000, 1201 New York Avenue, N.W.
Telephone: 202-962-4800.
McLean, Virginia Office: Suite 400, 2010 Corporate Ridge.
Telephone: 703-760-1600.
Rockville, Maryland Office: Suite 500, One Church Street, P. O. Box 1906.
Telephone: 301-217-5600.
Towson, Maryland Office: 210 Allegheny Avenue, P. O. Box 5517.
Telephone: 410-494-6200.

MEMBERS OF FIRM

George Cochran Doub (P.C.)	Jeffrey A. Dunn (also at Washington, D.C. Office)
Thomas J. Kenney, Jr. (P.C.) (Also at Washington, D.C. Office)	George F. Pappas (Also at Washington, D.C. Office)
Douglas D. Connah, Jr. (P.C.) (Also at Washington, D.C. Office)	William D. Coston (Not admitted in MD; Resident, Washington, D.C. Office)
Kenneth C. Bass, III (Not admitted in MD; Washington, D.C. and McLean, Virginia Offices)	William D. Quarles (Also at Washington, D.C. and Towson, Maryland Offices)
Edward F. Glynn, Jr. (Resident, Washington, D.C. Office)	Jeffrey L. Ihnen (Not admitted in MD; Resident, Washington, D. C. Office)
G. Stewart Webb, Jr.	James A. Dunbar (Also at Washington, D.C. Office)
James R. Myers (Not admitted in MD; Resident, Washington, D.C. Office)	Robert J. Bolger, Jr. (Also at Washington, D.C. Office)
Jeffrey D. Knowles (Not admitted in MD; Resident, Washington, D.C. Office)	David J. Heubeck
	Gary M. Hnath (Resident, Washington, D.C. Office)

Newton B. Fowler, III
ASSOCIATES

Paul D. Barker, Jr.	Edward Brendan Magrab (Resident, Washington, D.C. Office)
James Nicholas Czaban (Not admitted in MD; Resident, Washington, D.C. Office)	Vicki Margolis (Also at Washington, D.C. Office)
David W. Goewey (Not admitted in MD; Resident, Washington, D.C. Office)	John T. Prisbe

For Complete List of Firm Personnel, See General Section

For full biographical listings, see the Martindale-Hubbell Law Directory

---

WEINER, ASTRACHAN, GUNST, HILLMAN AND ALLEN, A PROFESSIONAL CORPORATION (AV)

120 East Baltimore Street Suite 2100, 21202
Telephone: 410-783-3500
FAX: 410-783-3510

Arnold M. Weiner   Allan P. Hillman
James B. Astrachan   Steven A. Allen
Peter H. Gunst   Thomas J. Zagami

Bruce L. Mann   Donna M.D. Thomas
         Heather H. Polzin-Vovakes

For full biographical listings, see the Martindale-Hubbell Law Directory

---

MASSACHUSETTS

BOSTON,* Suffolk Co.

CESARI AND McKENNA (AV)

30 Rowes Wharf, 02110
Telephone: 617-951-2500
Fax: 617-951-3927

(See Next Column)

CESARI AND McKENNA—*Continued*

Robert A. Cesari	Joseph H. Born
John F. McKenna	Patricia A. Sheehan
Martin J. O'Donnell	Michael E. Attaya
Thomas C. O'Konski	Steven J. Frank
Charles J. Barbas	

Patrick J. O'Shea	George J. Jakobsche
Michael R. Reinemann	William A. Loginov
Rita M. Rooney	

LEGAL SUPPORT PERSONNEL

Dora V. Dodin	Heather B. Shapiro
(Patent Engineer)	(Technical Specialist)

For full biographical listings, see the Martindale-Hubbell Law Directory

DIKE, BRONSTEIN, ROBERTS & CUSHMAN, LLP (AV)

A Limited Liability Partnership including Professional Corporations
130 Water Street, 02109
Telephone: 617-523-3400
Telefax: 617-523-6440; 523-7318
Email: ipl@dbrc.com *URL:* http://www.dbrc.com

David G. Conlin (P.C.)	Ronald I. Eisenstein
George W. Neuner (P.C.)	Henry D. Pahl, Jr.
Ernest V. Linek	Peter J. Manus (P.C.)
Linda M. Buckley	David S. Resnick
Peter F. Corless	

Cara Zucker Lowen	William J. Daley, Jr.
Brian Michaelis	David D. Lowry

OF COUNSEL

Sewall P. Bronstein (P.C.)	John L. Welch
Milton M. Oliver	

LEGAL SUPPORT PERSONNEL

Robert L. Buchanan, Ph.D.

For full biographical listings, see the Martindale-Hubbell Law Directory

McDERMOTT, WILL & EMERY (AV)

A Partnership including Professional Corporations
75 State Street, Suite 1700, 02109-1807
Telephone: 617-345-5000
Facsimile: 617-345-5077
Chicago, Illinois Office: 227 West Monroe Street.
Telephone: 312-372-2000.
Facsimile: 312-984-7700.
Miami, Florida Office: 201 South Biscayne Boulevard.
Telephone: 305-358-3500.
Facsimile: 305-347-6500.
Washington, D.C. Office: 1850 K Street, N.W.
Telephone: 202-887-8000.
Facsimile: 202-778-8087.
Los Angeles, California Office: 2049 Century Park East.
Telephone: 310-277-4110.
Facsimile: 310-277-4730.
Newport Beach, California Office: 1301 Dove Street, Suite 500.
Telephone: 714-851-0633.
Facsimile: 714-851-9348.
New York, N.Y. Office: 1211 Avenue of the Americas.
Telephone: 212-768-5400.
Facsimile: 212-768-5444.
St. Petersburg, Russia Office: AOZT McDermott, Will & Emery,
Griboyedova Canal 36, 191023 St. Petersburg, Russia.
Telephone: (7) (812) 310-52-44; 310-55-44; 310-59-44; 850-20-45.
Facsimile: (7) (812) 310-54-46; 325-84-50.
Vilnius, Lithuania Office: Smetonos 6, 2600 Vilnius, Lithuania.
Telephone: 370 2 61-43-08.
Facsimile: 370 2 22-79-55.

MEMBERS OF FIRM

Anthony A. Bongiorno	James J. Marcellino
Donald R. Frederico	Gordon T. Walker
Erich Luschei	Alicia M. V. Wyman *

*Denotes a lawyer employed by a Professional Corporation which is a member of the Firm.

For full biographical listings, see the Martindale-Hubbell Law Directory

MORSE, ALTMAN & BENSON (AV)

73 Tremont Street, 02108
Telephone: 617-523-3515
FAX: 617-523-1872

Gerald Altman	G. Eugene Dacey
Deborah L. Benson	

(See Next Column)

ASSOCIATES

Steven K. Martin	Susan M.G. von Struensee

For full biographical listings, see the Martindale-Hubbell Law Directory

PALMER & DODGE LLP (AV)

One Beacon Street, 02108
Telephone: 617-573-0100
Facsimile: 617-227-4420

MEMBERS OF FIRM

F. Andrew Anderson	Mark A. Fischer

ASSOCIATE

Richard B. Smith

For Complete List of Firm Personnel, See General Section

For full biographical listings, see the Martindale-Hubbell Law Directory

MICHIGAN

BLOOMFIELD HILLS, Oakland Co.

ADKISON NEED (AV)

1533 North Woodward Avenue, Suite 210, 48304
Telephone: 810-540-7400
Fax: 810-540-7401
Email: AdkisNeed@aol.com

MEMBERS OF FIRM

Phillip G. Adkison	Paul Green
Gregory K. Need	Kelly A. Allen
Deborah M. Schneider	

ASSOCIATES

Richard D. Kuhn, Jr.	Ann D. Christ
Kathryn N. Nichols	Laura B. Andoni

For full biographical listings, see the Martindale-Hubbell Law Directory

DETROIT,* Wayne Co.

BODMAN, LONGLEY & DAHLING LLP (AV)

34th Floor 100 Renaissance Center, 48243
Telephone: 313-259-7777
Fax: 313-393-7579
Email: 2080194@mcimail.com
Troy, Michigan Office: Suite 2020, 755 West Big Beaver Road.
Telephone: 810-362-2110.
Fax: 810-244-0780.
Ann Arbor, Michigan Office: 110 Miller, Suite 300.
Telephone: 313-761-3780.
Fax: 313-930-2494.
Northern Michigan Office: 229 Court Street, P.O. Box 405, Cheboygan.
Telephone: 616-627-4351.
Fax: 616-627-2802.

MEMBERS OF FIRM

Randolph S. Perry	Robert G. Brower
James J. Walsh	Fredrick J. Dindoffer
David G. Chardavoyne	Susan M. Kornfield
	(Ann Arbor Office)

For Representative Client List, See General Section

For Complete List of Firm Personnel, See General Section

For full biographical listings, see the Martindale-Hubbell Law Directory

BUTZEL LONG, A PROFESSIONAL CORPORATION (AV)

Suite 900, 150 West Jefferson, 48226
Telephone: 313-225-7000
Telecopier: 313-225-7080
Email: melnick@butzel.com *URL:* http://www.butzel.com
Birmingham, Michigan Office: Suite 200, 32270 Telegraph Road.
Telephone: 810-258-1616.
Telecopier: 810-258-1439.
Lansing, Michigan Office: 118 West Ottawa Street.
Telephone: 517-372-6622.
Telecopier: 517-372-6672.
Ann Arbor, Michigan Office: Suite 300, 350 South Main Street.
Telephone: 313-995-3110.
Telecopier: 313-995-1777.
Grosse Pointe Farms, Michigan Office: Suite 260, 21 Kercheval.
Telephone: 313-886-5446.
Telecopier: 313-886-2114.

Richard E. Rassel	Leonard M. Niehoff
Edward M. Kronk	(Ann Arbor)
Philip J. Kessler	J. Michael Huget (Ann Arbor)

(See Next Column)

BUTZEL LONG A PROFESSIONAL CORPORATION, *Detroit—Continued*

Robin K. Luce	Laurie J. Michelson
Barbara L. McQuade	John C. Blattner (Ann Arbor)

Representative Clients: Crain Communications, Inc.; Detroit Diesel Corp.; The Detroit News, Inc.; Ferndale Laboratories; General Dynamics Corp.; Kelly Services; Kelsey Hayes Co.; Stroh Brewery Co.; Takata Corp.; The University of Michigan.

For Complete List of Firm Personnel, See General Section

For full biographical listings, see the Martindale-Hubbell Law Directory

---

GRAND RAPIDS,* Kent Co.

PRICE, HENEVELD, COOPER, DeWITT & LITTON (AV)

695 Kenmoor, S.E., P.O. Box 2567, 49501
Telephone: 616-949-9610
Telecopier: 616-957-8196

MEMBERS OF FIRM

Peter P. Price (Retired)	Randall G. Litton
Lloyd A. Heneveld	James A. Mitchell
Richard C. Cooper	Harold W. Reick
William W. DeWitt	Carl S. Clark

Daniel L. Girdwood

ASSOCIATES

Douglas H. Siegel	Gunther J. Evanina
(Not admitted in MI)	Steven C. Wichmann
Barry C. Kane	Jay G. Durst
Terry S. Callaghan	(Not admitted in MI)

Representative Clients: Amway Corp.; Michigan State University; Dow Chemical Co.; Gerber Products Co.; Kysor Industrial Corp.; L. Perrigo Co.; Prince Corp.; Ralston Purina Co.; Steelcase, Inc.; Wolverine World Wide, Inc.

For full biographical listings, see the Martindale-Hubbell Law Directory

---

VARNUM, RIDDERING, SCHMIDT & HOWLETT LLP (AV)

A Limited Liability Partnership including Professional Corporations
Bridgewater Place, P.O. Box 352, 49501-0352
Telephone: 616-336-6000
800-262-0011
Facsimile: 616-336-7000
Telex: 1561593 VARN
Email: varnum@vrsh.com
Lansing, Michigan Office: The Victor Center, Suite 810, 210 North Washington Square, 48933.
Telephone: 517-482-6237.
Facsimile: 517-482-6937.
Kalamazoo, Michigan Office: 350 East Michigan Avenue, 49007.
Telephone: 616-382-2300.
Facsimile: 616-382-2382.
Grand Haven, Michigan Office: 321 Washington Street, P.O. Box 288, 49417.
Telephone: 616-846-7100.
Facsimile: 616-846-7101.
Battle Creek, Michigan Office: 4950 West Dickman Road, Suite B-1, 49015.
Telephone: 616-962-7144.
Bingham Farms, Michigan Office: 31600 Telegraph Road, Suite 230, 48025.
Telephone: 810-594-7330.
Facsimile: 810-594- 7331.

MEMBERS OF FIRM

John E. McGarry	Timothy E. Eagle
Thomas L. Lockhart	Joel E. Bair

Richard J. McKenna

COUNSEL

H. Lawrence Smith	Peter Visserman

ASSOCIATE

G. Thomas Williams, III

Counsel for: Cadillac Rubber & Plastics, Inc.; Cascade Engineering; Herman Miller, Inc.; Medtronic, Inc.; Neway Anchorlok, Inc.; Smith's Industries; X-Rite, Inc.

For Complete List of Firm Personnel, See General Section

For full biographical listings, see the Martindale-Hubbell Law Directory

---

SOUTHFIELD, Oakland Co.

BROOKS & KUSHMAN, P.C. (AV)

1000 Town Center, Twenty Second Floor, 48075
Telephone: 810-358-4400

Ernie L. Brooks	Ralph M. Burton
James A. Kushman	John A. Artz
David R. Syrowik	Robert C. J. Tuttle
Mark A. Cantor	Earl J. LaFontaine

Ronald M. Nabozny	Keith L. Zerschling
Thomas A. Lewry	Elizabeth F. Janda
John E. Nemazi	Robert C. Brandenburg
Kevin J. Heinl	A. Frank Duke
William G. Abbatt	Timothy G. Newman
Donald J. Harrington	John M. Halan
Paul M. Schwartz	Jeffrey M. Szuma
George R. Mosher	Maria Franek
Frederick M. Ritchie	James R. Ignatowski
John M. Sheridan	Frank A. Angileri

William G. Conger

Sangeeta G. Shah	Rhonda L. McCoy-Pfau
Christopher W. Quinn	Eric L. Doyle
Konstantine J. Diamond	John S. Artz

For full biographical listings, see the Martindale-Hubbell Law Directory

TRANSPORTATION LAW

ALABAMA

BIRMINGHAM,* Jefferson Co.

BRADLEY, ARANT, ROSE & WHITE (AV)

2001 Park Place, Suite 1400, P.O. Box 830709, 35283-0709
Telephone: 205-521-8000
Facsimile: 205-252-0264
Facsimile (SouthTrust Tower Office): 205-251-9915
URL: http://www.BARW.COM
Huntsville, Alabama Office: 200 Clinton Avenue West, Suite 900, 35801.
Telephone: 205-517-5100.
Facsimile: 205-533-5069.

MEMBERS OF FIRM

Hobart A. McWhorter, Jr.   Joseph B. Mays, Jr.
John D. Watson, III

For Complete List of Firm Personnel, See General Section

For full biographical listings, see the Martindale-Hubbell Law Directory

BURGE & WETTERMARK, P.C. (AV)

2300 SouthTrust Tower, 420 North 20th Street, 35203-3204
Telephone: 205-251-9729; 800-633-3733
Fax: 205-323-0512
Atlanta, Georgia Office: 2700 The Grand, 75 14th Street, N.E., 30309.
Telephone: 404-875-2500; 800-749-8687.
Fax: 404-875-5807.
Jacksonville, Florida Office: 3100 Independent Drive, 32202.
Telephone: 904-353-1555 or 1-800-498-6657.
Fax: 904-353-3905.
Ludlow, Kentucky Office: 243 Elm Street, P.O. Box 16167.
Telephone: 606-491-7000; 800-872-4671.
Fax: 606-491-7001.

Frank O. Burge, Jr.   Gregory T. Hughes
James H. Wettermark   (Not admitted in AL)
F. Tucker Burge   Monroe Dykes Barber, Jr.
Courtney Burge Brown   Van Kirk McCombs, II
Michael J. Warshauer   James R. Holland, II
   (Not admitted in AL)   (Not admitted in AL)
Gary F. Easom   Lyle Griffin Woodruff
   (Not admitted in AL)

References: AmSouth Bank; First Alabama Bank, Birmingham, Alabama.

For full biographical listings, see the Martindale-Hubbell Law Directory

ARIZONA

PHOENIX,* Maricopa Co.

FENNEMORE CRAIG, A PROFESSIONAL CORPORATION (AV)

Two North Central, Suite 2200, 85004
Telephone: 602-257-8700
Fax: 602-257-8527
Scottsdale, Arizona Office: 6263 North Scottsdale Road, Suite 290, 85250.
Telephone: 602-257-5400.
Fax: 602-257-5409.
Tucson, Arizona Office: One South Church Avenue, Suite 1030, 85701.
Telephone: 520-791-6800.
Fax: 520-791-6820.

C. Webb Crockett   F. Pendleton Gaines, III
Timothy Berg

For Complete List of Firm Personnel, See General Section

For full biographical listings, see the Martindale-Hubbell Law Directory

ARKANSAS

LITTLE ROCK,* Pulaski Co.

HILBURN, CALHOON, HARPER, PRUNISKI & CALHOUN, LTD. (AV)

P.O. Box 1256, 72203-1256
Telephone: 501-372-0110
Fax: 501-372-2029
North Little Rock, Arkansas Office: Eighth Floor, Mercantile Bank Building, One Riverfront Place, P.O. Box 5551, 72119.
Telephone: 501-372-0110.
Fax: 501-372-2029.

John C. Calhoun, Jr.   Scott E. Daniel

Representative Client: Mercantile Bank of Central Arkansas.

For Complete List of Firm Personnel, See General Section

For full biographical listings, see the Martindale-Hubbell Law Directory

CALIFORNIA

BEVERLY HILLS, Los Angeles Co.

MILES L. KAVALLER A PROFESSIONAL LAW CORPORATION (AV)

Suite 315, 315 South Beverly Drive, 90212
Telephone: 310-277-2323
Fax: 310-556-2308
Email: MKavaller@themall.net *URL:*
http://www.LA-Freight.com/Kavaller.htm

Miles L. Kavaller

Reference: City National Bank (6th & Olive Branch).

For full biographical listings, see the Martindale-Hubbell Law Directory

LONG BEACH, Los Angeles Co.

FISHER & PORTER, A LAW CORPORATION (AV)

110 Pine Avenue, 11th Floor, P.O. Box 22686, 90801-5686
Telephone: 310-435-5626
Telex: 284549 FPKLAW UR
Fax: 310-432-5399

Gerald M. Fisher   Therese G. Groff
David S. Porter   Michael W. Lodwick
        George P. Hassapis
          OF COUNSEL
Stephen C. Klausen   Stephen Chace Bass
       Anthony P. Lombardo

Vicki L. Hassman   Michael J. McLaughlin
Linda A. Mancini   Sandra L. Gryder
      Kenneth F. Mattfeld

For full biographical listings, see the Martindale-Hubbell Law Directory

RUSSELL & MIRKOVICH (AV)

One World Trade Center, Suite 1450, 90831-1450
Telephone: 310-436-9911
FAX: 310-436-1897

Carlton E. Russell   Joseph N. Mirkovich

For full biographical listings, see the Martindale-Hubbell Law Directory

WILLIAMS WOOLLEY COGSWELL NAKAZAWA & RUSSELL (AV)

111 West Ocean Boulevard, Suite 2000, 90802-4614
Telephone: 310-495-6000
Telecopier: 310-435-1359; 310-435-6812
Telex: ITT: 4933872; WU: 984929
Email: wwlaw@msn.com
Rancho Santa Fe, California Office: P.O. Box 9120, 16236 San Dieguito Road, Building 3, Suite 3-15, 92067.
Telephone: 619-497-0284.
Fax: 619-759-9938.
Port Hueneme, California Office: 237 E. Hueneme Road, Suite A, 93041.
Telephone: 805-488-8560.
Fax: 805-488-7896.

MEMBERS OF FIRM

Reed M. Williams   Alan Nakazawa
David E. R. Woolley   Blake W. Larkin
Forrest R. Cogswell   Thomas A. Russell

(See Next Column)

WILLIAMS WOOLLEY COGSWELL NAKAZAWA & RUSSELL, *Long Beach—Continued*

ASSOCIATES

Todd A. Valdes   Thomas G. Walsh
Richard J. Nikas

For full biographical listings, see the Martindale-Hubbell Law Directory

---

LOS ANGELES, * Los Angeles Co.

BOTTUM & FELITON, A PROFESSIONAL CORPORATION (AV)

Suite 1500, South Tower, 3200 Wilshire Boulevard, 90010
Telephone: 213-487-0402
Fax: 213-386-9803
San Diego, California Office: Suite 400 Emerald Plaza, 402 West Broadway.
Telephone: 619-595-4857.
Fax: 619-595-4863.

John R. Feliton, Jr.

Gregg S. Garfinkel   Julie A. Covell
Brian E. Cooper   Karl R. Loureiro

For full biographical listings, see the Martindale-Hubbell Law Directory

---

SAN FRANCISCO, * San Francisco Co.

MICHAEL S. RUBIN (AV)

88 Kearny Street, Suite 1700, 94108
Telephone: 415-986-0820
Fax: 415-986-7964
Email: mrubin@hooked.net

For full biographical listings, see the Martindale-Hubbell Law Directory

---

SAN MATEO, San Mateo Co.

MICHAEL L. DWORKIN (AV)

155 Bovet Road, Suite 455, 94402
Telephone: 415-577-1321
Fax: 415-372-1077
Email: law@avialex.com *URL:* http://www.avialex.com

For full biographical listings, see the Martindale-Hubbell Law Directory

COLORADO

DENVER, * Denver Co.

ROBERT L. BARTHOLIC (AV)

Suite 500, 1600 Broadway, 80202
Telephone: 303-830-0500
Fax: 303-860-7855

OF COUNSEL
Clarence L. Bartholic

Representative Clients: Anschutz Corp.; Denver and Rio Grande Western Railroad Co.; Burlington Northern Railroad Co. and Subsidiaries; American Association of Private Railroad Car Owners, Inc.

For full biographical listings, see the Martindale-Hubbell Law Directory

---

CUTLER & STANFIELD, L.L.P. (AV⊤)

1675 Broadway, 80202
Telephone: 303-825-7000
Fax: 303-825-7005
Washington, D.C. Office: 700 Fourteenth Street, N.W.
Telephone: 202-624-8400.
FAX: 202-624-8410.

MEMBERS OF FIRM

Eliot R. Cutler
  (Not admitted in CO)
Jeffrey L. Stanfield
  (Not admitted in CO)
Sheila D. Jones

Perry M. Rosen
Peter J. Kirsch
  (Not admitted in CO)
Barry Conaty
Stephen H. Kaplan

OF COUNSEL
Sarah M. Rockwell

ASSOCIATE
Christopher M. Kamper

For full biographical listings, see the Martindale-Hubbell Law Directory

---

JONES & KELLER, A PROFESSIONAL CORPORATION (AV)

Suite 1600, 1625 Broadway, 80202
Telephone: 303-573-1600
Fax: 303-893-6506

(See Next Column)

Marion F. Jones (1898-1978)   Thomas J. Burke, Jr.
Alec J. Keller (1913-1995)   Samuel E. Wing
Alvin J. Meiklejohn, Jr.   Reid A. Godbolt
Leslie R. Kehl   Rodney D. Knutson
Edward T. Lyons, Jr.   Kevin L. Brown
David E. Driggers   Barry L. Wilkie

Howard R. Hertzberg   Brent Nicholls
David A. Thayer   Michael Brian Cavanaugh
Nathan D. Simmons

Reference: Colorado State Bank; Union Bank & Trust.

For full biographical listings, see the Martindale-Hubbell Law Directory

CONNECTICUT

NEW HAVEN, * New Haven Co.

LYNCH, TRAUB, KEEFE AND ERRANTE, A PROFESSIONAL CORPORATION (AV)

52 Trumbull Street, P.O. Box 1612, 06506
Telephone: 203-787-0275
Fax: 203-782-0278
Email: ltke@snet.com *URL:* http://www.ltke.com

Stephen I. Traub
Hugh F. Keefe
Steven J. Errante
John J. Keefe, Jr.

Donn A. Swift
Charles E. Tiernan, III
Robert W. Lynch
Richard W. Lynch

John M. Walsh, Jr.

Suzanne L. McAlpine
Christopher M. Licari
Eric P. Smith

Lee Kennedy Tiernan
William F. Clark
James A. Mongillo

OF COUNSEL
William C. Lynch

Local Counsel for: Transport Insurance Co., Dallas, Texas; American Trucking Associations; Roadway Express, Inc., Akron, Ohio; A.R.A. Philadelphia, Penn.; Consolidated Freightways, Menlo Park, California; Ogden Corp.
Labor Counsel: Coca-Cola, U.S.A., Atlanta, Georgia (Private Truck Operation); The Dow Chemical Co.; Cincinnati Milacron; Southern Connecticut Gas Co.

For full biographical listings, see the Martindale-Hubbell Law Directory

DISTRICT OF COLUMBIA

WASHINGTON, D.C. Co.

* indicates certain Bar Register subscribers, in cities of comparable size and importance, who maintain an additional office in Washington, D.C. and who have arranged for representation as a part of the Washington, D.C. listings that follow

BAKER & HOSTETLER (AV)

Washington Square, Suite 1100, 1050 Connecticut Avenue, N.W., 20036-5304
Telephone: 202-861-1500
In Cleveland, Ohio: 3200 National City Center, 1900 East Ninth Street.
Telephone: 216-621-0200.
In Columbus, Ohio: Capitol Square, Suite 2100, 65 East State Street.
Telephone: 614-228-1541.
In Denver, Colorado: 303 East 17th Avenue, Suite 1100.
Telephone: 303-861-0600.
In Houston, Texas: 1000 Louisiana, Suite 2000.
Telephone: 713-751-1600.
In Long Beach, California: 300 Oceangate, Suite 620.
Telephone: 310-432-2827.
In Los Angeles, California: 600 Wilshire Boulevard.
Telephone: 213-624-2400.
In Orlando, Florida: SunBank Center, Suite 2300, 200 South Orange Avenue.
Telephone: 305-841-1111.
In College Park, Maryland: 9658 Baltimore Boulevard, Suite 206.
Telephone: 301-441-2781.
In Alexandria, Virginia: 437 North Lee Street.
Telephone: 703-549-1294.
In San Francisco, California: One Sansome Street, Suite 2000.
Telephone: 415-951-4705.

(See Next Column)

BAKER & HOSTETLER—*Continued*

PARTNER
Richard A. Hauser

For Complete List of Firm Personnel, See General Section

For full biographical listings, see the Martindale-Hubbell Law Directory

CUTLER & STANFIELD, L.L.P. (AV)

700 Fourteenth Street, N.W., 20005-2010
Telephone: 202-624-8400
Fax: 202-624-8410
Denver, Colorado Office: 1675 Broadway, 80202.
Telephone: 303-825-7000.
FAX: 303-825-7005.

MEMBERS OF FIRM
Eliot R. Cutler	Peter J. Kirsch
Jeffrey L. Stanfield	Barry Conaty
Sheila D. Jones	Stephen H. Kaplan
Perry M. Rosen	(Not admitted in DC)

OF COUNSEL
Byron Keith Huffman, Jr.   Sarah M. Rockwell
(Not admitted in DC)

ASSOCIATES
Katherine Boonin Andrus	Dana C. Nifosi
Françoise M. Carrier	Barbara Paley
Christopher M. Kamper	W. Eric Pilsk
(Not admitted in DC)	Timothy A. Pohle
William G. Malley	Thomas D. Roth

For full biographical listings, see the Martindale-Hubbell Law Directory

GILMAN & PANGIA (AV)

Suite 600 Federal Bar Building, 1815 H Street, N.W., 20006
Telephone: 202-466-5100
Facsimile: 202-331-8986
McLean, Virginia Office: Suite 1070, 8180 Greensboro Drive.
Telephone: 703-356-5070.
Fax: 703-356-5085.

MEMBERS OF FIRM
Nicholas Gilman	Barry C. Hansen
Michael J. Pangia	John J. Carlino (1946-1987)

Karla E. Saguil (Not admitted in DC)
OF COUNSEL
William J. Olson

For full biographical listings, see the Martindale-Hubbell Law Directory

GROVE, JASKIEWICZ AND COBERT (AV)

Suite 400, 1730 M Street, N.W., 20036
Telephone: 202-296-2900
Telecopier: 202-296-1370
Baltimore, Maryland Office: The Park Plaza, 800 North Charles Street, Suite 400.
Telephone: 301-727-7010.

MEMBERS OF FIRM
William J. Grove (1914-1988)	Joseph Michael Roberts
Ronald N. Cobert	Andrew M. Danas
Edward J. Kiley	Andrew M. Whitman
Robert L. Cope	(Not admitted in DC)

OF COUNSEL
Leonard A. Jaskiewicz	Lawrence E. Dubé, Jr.
James F. Flint	James K. Jeanblanc
Edmund M. Jaskiewicz	

For full biographical listings, see the Martindale-Hubbell Law Directory

LAROE, WINN, MOERMAN & DONOVAN (AV)

3506 Idaho Avenue, N.W., 20016
Telephone: 202-362-3010
Telecopier: 202-362-3050

MEMBERS OF FIRM
Wilbur LaRoe, Jr. (1921-1957)   Arthur L. Winn, Jr. (1928-1995)
Paul M. Donovan
SPECIAL COUNSEL
David A. Sutherlund
OF COUNSEL
Samuel H. Moerman

For full biographical listings, see the Martindale-Hubbell Law Directory

REA, CROSS & AUCHINCLOSS (AV)

Suite 420, 1920 N Street, N.W., 20036
Telephone: 202-785-3700
Fax: 202-659-4934

(See Next Column)

MEMBERS OF FIRM
Edgar Watkins (1903-1959)	Leo C. Franey
Bryce Rea, Jr.	Brian L. Troiano
Donald E. Cross (1923-1986)	Keith G. O'Brien
Thomas M. Auchincloss, Jr.	John D. Heffner
Robert A. Wimbish	

For full biographical listings, see the Martindale-Hubbell Law Directory

SHAWN, MANN & NIEDERMAYER, L.L.P. (AV)

1850 M Street, N.W., Suite 280, 20036-5803
Telephone: 202-331-7900
Fax: 202-331-0726
Washington, D.C., Government Affairs Office: 499 S. Capitol Street, S.W., Suite 420.
Telephone: 202-842-3000.
Fax: 202-547-7161.
Los Angeles, California Office: 2029 Century Park East, Suite 1690.
Telephone: 310-553-8065.
Fax: 310-557-0729.
San Diego, California Office: 401 West "A" Street, Suite 1850.
Telephone: 619-236-0303.
Fax: 619-238-8181.
San Francisco, California Office: The Fox Plaza, 1390 Market Street, Suite 1204.
Telephone: 415-982-0150.
Fax: 415-522-0513.
Bloomington, Minnesota Office: 2090 West 98th Street.
Telephone: 612-881-6577.
Fax: 612-881-6894.

MEMBERS OF FIRM
William H. Shawn   Kim D. Mann
Joseph L. Steinfeld, Jr.

For full biographical listings, see the Martindale-Hubbell Law Directory

STEPTOE & JOHNSON LLP (AV)

1330 Connecticut Avenue, N.W., 20036
Telephone: 202-429-3000
Cable Address: "Stepjohn"
Telex: 89-2503
Telecopier: 202-429-3902
Email: wbatterton@steptoe.com *URL:* http://www.steptoe.com
Phoenix, Arizona Office: Two Renaissance Square, 40 N. Central Avenue, Suite 2400, 85004.
Telephone: 602-257-5200.
Moscow, Russia Office: Steptoe & Johnson International AOZT. 25 Tsvetnoy Boulevard, Building 3 Moscow, Russia 103051.
Telephone: 011-7-501-258-5250.
Fax: 011-7-501-258-5251.
Almaty, Kazakhstan Office: Steptoe & Johnson Company Almaty. 84 Gogol Street, Suite 213, 480083.
Telephones: (3272) 50-11-25, (3272) 32-25-39.

MEMBERS
Richard P. Taylor	Timothy M. Walsh
Betty Jo Christian	Samuel M. Sipe, Jr.
William Karas	John D. Graubert
Charles G. Cole	David H. Coburn

For Complete List of Firm Personnel, See General Section

For full biographical listings, see the Martindale-Hubbell Law Directory

* VENABLE ATTORNEYS AT LAW VENABLE, BAETJER, HOWARD & CIVILETTI, LLP (AV)

A Partnership including Professional Corporations
Suite 1000, 1201 New York Avenue, N.W., 20005
Telephone: 202-962-4800
Fax: 202-962-8300
Baltimore, Maryland Office: Venable, Baetjer and Howard LLP, 1800 Mercantile Bank & Trust Building, 2 Hopkins Plaza.
Telephone: 410-244-7400.
McLean, Virginia Office: Venable, Baetjer and Howard LLP, Suite 400, 2010 Corporate Ridge.
Telephone: 703-760-1600.
Rockville, Maryland Office: Venable, Baetjer and Howard LLP, Suite 500, One Church Street, P. O. Box 1906.
Telephone: 301-217-5600.
Towson, Maryland Office: Venable, Baetjer and Howard LLP, 210 Allegheny Avenue, P. O. Box 5517.
Telephone: 410-494-6200.

MEMBERS OF FIRM
Jan K. Guben (Not admitted in DC; Also at Baltimore, Maryland Office)	Judson W. Starr (Also at Baltimore and Towson, Maryland Offices)
Joe A. Shull	James R. Myers
Robert G. Ames (Also at Baltimore, Maryland Office)	George F. Pappas (Also at Baltimore, Maryland Office)
James K. Archibald (Also at Baltimore, Maryland Office)	

(See Next Column)

VENABLE ATTORNEYS AT LAW VENABLE, BAETJER, HOWARD & CIVILETTI, LLP, *Washington—Continued*

For Complete List of Firm Personnel, See General Section

For full biographical listings, see the Martindale-Hubbell Law Directory

VERNER, LIIPFERT, BERNHARD, MCPHERSON AND HAND, CHARTERED (AV)

901 15th Street, N.W., 20005-2301
Telephone: 202-371-6000
Cable Address: "Verlip"
Telex: 1561792 VERLIP UT
Fax: 202-371-6279
Email: verner.com
McLean, Virginia Office: Sixth Floor, 8280 Greensboro Drive, 22102.
Telephone: 703-749-6000.
Fax: 703-749-6027.
Houston, Texas Office: 2600 Texas Commerce Tower, 600 Travis, 77002.
Telephone: 713-237-9034.
Fax: 713-237-1216.
Honolulu, Hawaii Office: Hawaii Times Building, 928 Nuuanu Avenue, Suite 400, 96817.
Telephone: 808-566-0999.
Fax: 808-566-0995.
Austin, Texas Office: Suite 1440 San Jacinto Center, 98 San Jacinto Boulevard, 78701.
Telephone: 512-703-6000.
Fax: 512-703-6003.

Douglas Ochs Adler	William C. Evans
Berl Bernhard	Joseph L. Manson, III
Roy G. Bowman	Ronald B. Natalie
Hopewell H. Darneille, III	Russell E. Pommer
Michael J. Roberts	

For Complete List of Firm Personnel, See General Section

For full biographical listings, see the Martindale-Hubbell Law Directory

WILMER, CUTLER & PICKERING (AV)

2445 M Street, N.W., 20037-1420
Telephone: 202-663-6000
Fax: 202-663-6363
Email: Law@Wilmer.Com
Baltimore, Maryland Office: 100 Light Street, 21202.
Telephone: 410-986-2800.
Fax: 410-986-2828.
European Offices:
4 Carlton Gardens, London, SW1Y 5AA, England. Telephone: +44 (171) 872-1000.
Fax: +44 (171) 839-3537.
Rue de la Loi 15Wetstraat, B-1040 Brussels, Belgium. Telephone: +32 (2) 285-4900.
Fax: +32 (2) 285-4949.
Friedrichstrasse 95, D-10117 Berlin, Germany. Telephone: +49 (30) 2022-6400.
Fax: +49 (30)2022-6500.

MEMBERS OF FIRM

James S. Campbell	Dr. Andreas Weitbrecht (Resident, European Office, Brussels, Belgium)
Jeffrey N. Shane	
Dieter G. F. Lange (Resident, European Office, London, England)	Paul A. von Hehn (Resident, European Office, Brussels, Belgium)
Stephen P. Doyle	
James S. Venit (Not admitted in DC; Resident, European Office, Brussels, Belgium)	

COUNSEL

Lester Nurick
John J. Kallaugher (Resident, European Office, London, England)

For Complete List of Firm Personnel, See General Section

For full biographical listings, see the Martindale-Hubbell Law Directory

FLORIDA

*JACKSONVILLE,** Duval Co.

MOSELEY, WARREN, PRICHARD & PARRISH, P.A. (AV)

501 West Bay Street, 32202
Telephone: 904-356-1306
Cable Address: "Ragland"
Telex: 5-6374
Telecopier: 904-354-0194

(See Next Column)

Reuben Ragland (1882-1954)	Joseph W. Prichard, Jr.
Louis Kurz (1891-1965)	Robert B. Parrish
E. Dale Joyner (1943-1993)	Andrew J. Knight II
James F. Moseley	Richard K. Jones
Robert E. Warren	James F. Moseley, Jr.

Phillip A. Buhler	Stanley M. Weston
Melanie E. Shepherd	Kimberly Held Israel
Victor J. Zambetti	Tracy A. Chesser
Mathew G. Nasrallah	Ivan A. Colao

OF COUNSEL

James E. Williams	Neil C. Taylor

Counsel for: CSX Transportation; Britannia Steam Ship Insurance Assn., Ltd.; The West of England Protection & Indemnity Assn. (Luxembourg); Crowley American Transport Services, Inc.; Howard Johnson Co.; United Kingdom Mutual Steamship Assurance Assn., Ltd. (Bermuda); General Food Corp.; The London Steam-Ship Owners' Mutual Insurance Assn., Ltd.

For full biographical listings, see the Martindale-Hubbell Law Directory

NORTH MIAMI BEACH, Dade Co.

BECKHAM & BECKHAM, P.A. (AV)

17071 West Dixie Highway, Suite B, 33160
Telephone: 305-945-1851
Fax: 305-940-8706
Email: Beckham-Beckham@worldnet.att.net

Pamela Beckham	Eugene G. Beckham
	Robert J. Beckham, Jr.

For full biographical listings, see the Martindale-Hubbell Law Directory

GEORGIA

*ATLANTA,** Fulton Co.

DENNIS, CORRY, PORTER & GRAY (AV)

3300 One Atlanta Plaza, 950 East Paces Ferry Road, P.O. Box 18640, 30326
Telephone: 404-816-2800
Wats: 800-735-0838
Fax: 404-816-5656

MEMBERS OF FIRM

Robert E. Corry, Jr.	James S. Strawinski
R. Clay Porter	Grant B. Smith
William E. Gray, II	Frederick D. Evans, III

OF COUNSEL

Douglas Dennis

ASSOCIATES

Robert G. Ballard	Brian DeVoe Rogers
Matthew J. Jewell	Julia J. Yoffee
Pamela Jean Gray	Scott W. McMickle
J. Steven Fisher	Susan E. Cartwright
Thomas D. Trask	Christopher D. Pixley
Robert David Schoen	Raymond J. Kurey
Alison Roberts Solomon	Amber B. Shushan

Representative Clients: Schneider National, Inc.; Roadway Express, Inc.; Caliber System, Inc.

For full biographical listings, see the Martindale-Hubbell Law Directory

HAWKINS & PARNELL (AV)

4000 SunTrust Plaza, 303 Peachtree Street, N.E., 30308-3243
Telephone: 404-614-7400
Fax: 404-614-7500
Email: 73541.1626@compuserve.com

MEMBERS OF FIRM

Alan F. Herman	William H. Major, III
	Warner S. Fox

ASSOCIATES

Edwin L. Hall, Jr.	Blanche Rose Miller
	Stephen M. Brooks

Representative Clients: J.B. Hunt; VanLiner Insurance Company; Crete Carriers Corporation; Reliance National Insurance Company; Watkins Motor Lines; Continental National Insurance Company; Global Van Lines; Saia Motor Freight; Carolina Freight; American President Lines.

For Complete List of Firm Personnel, See General Section

For full biographical listings, see the Martindale-Hubbell Law Directory

ILLINOIS

CHICAGO,* Cook Co.

BELGRADE AND O'DONNELL, A PROFESSIONAL CORPORATION (AV)

311 South Wacker Drive, Suite 2770, 60606
Telephone: 312-360-9500
Facsimile: 312-360-9550

Steven B. Belgrade	Kim Richard Kardas
John A. O'Donnell	Rachel A. Tindel
George M. Velcich	Daniel Donohue

For full biographical listings, see the Martindale-Hubbell Law Directory

PAVALON & GIFFORD (AV)

Two North La Salle Street, Suite 1600, 60602
Telephone: 312-419-7400
Fax: 312-419-7408
Rockford, Illinois Office: 501 Seventh Street, Suite 501, 61104.
Telephone: 815-968-5100.

MEMBERS OF FIRM

Eugene I. Pavalon	Gary K. Laatsch
Geoffrey L. Gifford	Frank C. Marino
Henry Phillip Gruss	

Kathleen A. Russell	Christine Walsh Donnelly
Christopher B. Meister	

For full biographical listings, see the Martindale-Hubbell Law Directory

INDIANA

FORT WAYNE,* Allen Co.

BARRETT & McNAGNY (AV)

215 East Berry Street, P.O. Box 2263, 46801-2263
Telephone: 219-423-9551
Telecopier: 219-423-8924

MEMBERS OF FIRM

Thomas A. Herr	Anthony M. Stites

ASSOCIATE

Cathleen M. Shrader

Counsel For: Overnite Transportation Co.; Lancer Insurance Co.
Representative Clients: Builder's Transport, Inc.; Consolidated Freightways, Inc.; Munson Transportation; Progressive Casualty Co.

For Complete List of Firm Personnel, See General Section

For full biographical listings, see the Martindale-Hubbell Law Directory

HAMMOND, Lake Co.

ABRAHAMSON, REED & ADLEY (AV)

200 Russell Street, 46320
Telephone: 219-937-1500
Fax: 219-937-3174

MEMBERS OF FIRM

Harold Abrahamson	Kenneth D. Reed
Michael C. Adley	

ASSOCIATES

Scott R. Bilse	Christopher R. Karsten

References: Calumet National Bank, Hammond; Mercantile National Bank, Hammond.

For full biographical listings, see the Martindale-Hubbell Law Directory

LAFAYETTE,* Tippecanoe Co.

STUART & BRANIGIN (AV)

The Life Building, 300 Main Street, Suite 800, 47902
Telephone: 317-423-1561
Telecopier: 317-742-8175

MEMBERS OF FIRM

Allison Ellsworth Stuart	Nina B. Kirkpatrick
(1886-1950)	Mark Lillianfeld
Roger D. Branigin (1902-1975)	Stephen R. Pennell
Russell H. Hart	Anthony S. Benton
Roger D. Branigin, Jr.	Erik D. Spykman
Thomas L. Ryan	William E. Emerick
James V. McGlone	John C. Duffey
Carl W. Kloepfer	Mark E. DeYoung
Thomas R. McCully	Thomas B. Parent
Larry R. Fisher	Laura L. Bowker

(See Next Column)

Kevin D. Nicoson	John M. Stuckey
Susan K. Roberts	Deborah B. Trice

COUNSEL

John F. Bodle

ASSOCIATES

Brent W. Huber	David A. Starkweather
William P. Kealey	Geoffrey Blazi
A. James Chareq	

General Counsel for: The Lafayette Life Insurance Co.; INB National Bank, N.W.; Lafayette Home Hospital, Inc.
State Counsel for: Norfolk & Western Railway Co.
Mr. Ryan is Counsel to: The Trustees of Purdue University.
Representative Clients: Aluminum Company of America; Liberty Mutual Insurance Group.

For full biographical listings, see the Martindale-Hubbell Law Directory

IOWA

DES MOINES,* Polk Co.

FINLEY, ALT, SMITH, SCHARNBERG, MAY & CRAIG, P.C. (AV)

604 Locust Street, Fourth Floor Equitable Building, 50309
Telephone: 515-288-0145
Telecopier: 515-288-2724

Jerry P. Alt	R. Todd Gaffney

Representative Clients: Aetna Casualty & Surety Co.; Aetna Life Insurance Co.; ALAS; American Society of Composers, Authors and Publishers; Equitable Life Assurance Society of the U.S.; Federated Insurance Co.; Meredith Corp.
Iowa Attorneys for: Midwest Medical Insurance Co.
District Attorneys for: Norfolk & Southern Railroad; Soo Line Railroad Company.

For Complete List of Firm Personnel, See General Section

For full biographical listings, see the Martindale-Hubbell Law Directory

KANSAS

TOPEKA,* Shawnee Co.

BENNETT & DILLON, L.L.P. (AV)

1605 Southwest 37th Street, 66611
Telephone: 913-267-5063
Fax: 913-267-2652

MEMBERS OF FIRM

Mark L. Bennett, Jr.	Wilburn Dillon, Jr.
Ann L. Hoover	

Jeffrey D. Jackson

References: Commerce Bank and Trust; Columbian National Bank and Trust; Silver Lake State Bank.

For full biographical listings, see the Martindale-Hubbell Law Directory

FOULSTON & SIEFKIN L.L.P. (AV)

1515 Bank IV Tower, 534 Kansas Avenue, 66603
Telephone: 913-233-3600
Fax: 913-233-1610
Wichita, Kansas Office: 100 North Broadway, 700 Fourth Financial Center, 67202.
Telephone: 316-267-6371.
Fax: 316-267-6345.
Dodge City, Kansas Office: 810 Frontview, P.O. Box 1147, 67801.
Telephone: 316-227-8126.
Fax: 316-227-8451.
Member: Lex Mundi, A Global Association of 126 Independent Firms.

SPECIAL COUNSEL

James L. Grimes, Jr.

For full biographical listings, see the Martindale-Hubbell Law Directory

LOUISIANA

NEW ORLEANS,* Orleans Parish

PULASKI, GIEGER & LABORDE, L.L.C. (AV)

Suite 4800, One Shell Square, 701 Poydras Street, 70139
Telephone: 504-561-0400
Telecopier: 504-561-1011

Michael T. Pulaski (P.C.)	Leo R. McAloon, III
Ernest P. Gieger, Jr., (P.C.)	John P. Gonzalez
Kenneth H. Laborde (P.C.)	J. Jeffery Raborn
Robert W. Maxwell (P.C.)	Lance Blake Williams
Keith W. McDaniel (P.C.)	James E. Swinnen
Sharon D. Smith (P.C.)	Gina S. Montgomery
Gary G. Hebert	Mary Beth Meyer

Julianne T. Echols

For full biographical listings, see the Martindale-Hubbell Law Directory

---

SLATER LAW FIRM, A PROFESSIONAL CORPORATION (AV)

650 Poydras Street Suite 2600, 70130-6101
Telephone: 504-523-7333
Fax: 504-528-1080

Benjamin R. Slater, Jr.	Kevin M. Wheeler
Benjamin R. Slater, III	Anne Elise Brown
Mark E. Van Horn	Donald J. Miester, Jr.

Cory Rabin Cahn	James L. Bradford, III

SPECIAL COUNSEL

W. Malcolm Stevenson	Robert B. Acomb, III

Michael O. Waguespack

Representative Clients: Norfolk Southern Corporation; The Alabama Great Southern Railroad Company; North American Van Lines; New Orleans Steamship Association; Fleet Transport Company, Inc.

For full biographical listings, see the Martindale-Hubbell Law Directory

---

SHREVEPORT,* Caddo Parish

BARLOW AND HARDTNER L.C. (AV)

Tenth Floor, Louisiana Tower, 401 Edwards Street, 71101-3289
Telephone: 318-227-1131
Telecopier: 318-227-1141
Mailing Address: P.O. Box 8, Shreveport, Louisiana, 71161-0008

Malcolm S. Murchison	David R. Taggart

Michael B. Donald

Representative Clients: Kelley Oil Corporation; NorAm Energy Corp. (formerly Arkla, Inc.); NorAm Gas Transmission Company; Central and South West Corporation; Panhandle Eastern Corp.; Pennzoil Producing Co.; Johnson Controls, Inc.; Ashland Oil, Inc.; Southwestern Electric Power Company; Brammer Engineering, Inc.

For Complete List of Firm Personnel, See General Section

For full biographical listings, see the Martindale-Hubbell Law Directory

---

WILKINSON, CARMODY & GILLIAM (AV)

1700 Beck Building, 400 Travis Street, P.O. Box 1707, 71166
Telephone: 318-221-4196
Telecopier: 318-221-3705

MEMBERS OF FIRM

John D. Wilkinson (1867-1929)	Bobby S. Gilliam
William Scott Wilkinson	Mark E. Gilliam
(1895-1985)	Penny D. Sellers
Arthur R. Carmody, Jr.	Patrick F. Robinson

Michael J. Ryan

Representative Clients: Farmers Insurance Group; Home Federal Savings & Loan Association of Shreveport; The Kansas City Southern Railway Co.; KTAL-TV; Lincoln National Life Insurance Co.; Mobil Oil Co.; Schumpert Medical Center; Sears, Roebuck & Co.; Southern Pacific Transportation Co.; Southwestern Electric Power Co.

For full biographical listings, see the Martindale-Hubbell Law Directory

---

MARYLAND

BALTIMORE,* (Independent City)

FERGUSON, SCHETELICH, HEFFERNAN & MURDOCK, P.A. (AV)

1300 NationsBank Center 1, 100 South Charles Street, 21201
Telephone: 410-837-2200
Fax: 410-837-1188
Email: fshm@ix.netcom

(See Next Column)

Robert L. Ferguson, Jr.	Christopher J. Heffernan
Thomas J. Schetelich	M. Brooke Murdock

Michael N. Russo, Jr.	Peter Joseph Basile
Jodi K. Ebersole	Ann D. Ware

For full biographical listings, see the Martindale-Hubbell Law Directory

---

VENABLE ATTORNEYS AT LAW VENABLE, BAETJER AND HOWARD, LLP (AV)

A Partnership including Professional Corporations
1800 Mercantile Bank & Trust Building, 2 Hopkins Plaza, 21201
Telephone: 410-244-7400
Email: INFO@Venable.win.net
Washington, D.C. Office: Venable, Baetjer, Howard & Civiletti LLP. Suite 1000, 1201 New York Avenue, N.W.
Telephone: 202-962-4800.
McLean, Virginia Office: Suite 400, 2010 Corporate Ridge.
Telephone: 703-760-1600.
Rockville, Maryland Office: Suite 500, One Church Street, P. O. Box 1906.
Telephone: 301-217-5600.
Towson, Maryland Office: 210 Allegheny Avenue, P. O. Box 5517.
Telephone: 410-494-6200.

MEMBERS OF FIRM

Stanley Mazaroff (P.C.)	George W. Johnston (P.C.)
Jan K. Guben (Also at Washington, D. C Office)	Judson W. Starr (Not admitted in MD; Also at Washington, D.C. and Towson, Maryland Offices)
James D. Wright (P.C.)	
John G. Milliken (Not admitted in MD; Washington, D.C. and McLean, Virginia Offices)	James R. Myers (Not admitted in MD; Resident, Washington, D.C. Office)
Joseph C. Wich, Jr. (Resident, Towson, Maryland Office)	Jana Howard Carey (P.C.)
Robert G. Ames (Also at Washington, D.C. Office)	Mitchell Kolkin
Richard L. Wasserman (P.C.)	George F. Pappas (Also at Washington, D.C. Office)
James K. Archibald (Also at Washington, D.C. Office)	Kevin L. Shepherd

OF COUNSEL

Emried D. Cole, Jr.

ASSOCIATE

Vicki Margolis (Also at Washington, D.C. Office)

For Complete List of Firm Personnel, See General Section

For full biographical listings, see the Martindale-Hubbell Law Directory

---

MASSACHUSETTS

BOSTON,* Suffolk Co.

PALMER & DODGE LLP (AV)

One Beacon Street, 02108
Telephone: 617-573-0100
Facsimile: 617-227-4420

MEMBERS OF FIRM

Jean M. DeLuca	Thomas W. Merrill
Charles E. DeWitt, Jr.	David R. Rodgers
William L. Lahey	Walter J. St. Onge, III
Scott P. Lewis	James M. Whalen

For Complete List of Firm Personnel, See General Section

For full biographical listings, see the Martindale-Hubbell Law Directory

---

MICHIGAN

ANN ARBOR,* Washtenaw Co.

MILLER, CANFIELD, PADDOCK AND STONE, P.L.C. (AV)

A Professional Limited Liability Company
Founded in 1852 by Sidney Davy Miller
101 North Main Street, Seventh Floor, 48104-1400
Telephone: 313-663-2445
Fax: 313-747-7147
Detroit, Michigan Office: 150 West Jefferson, Suite 2500, 48226-4415.
Telephone: 313-963-6420.
Fax: 313-496-7500.
Cable Address: "Stem Detroit."
Bloomfield Hills, Michigan Office: Suite 100, Pinehurst Office Center, 1400 North Woodward, 48303-2014.
Telephone: 313-645-5000.
Fax: 313-645-1917.

(See Next Column)

MILLER, CANFIELD, PADDOCK AND STONE P.L.C.—*Continued*

Grand Rapids, Michigan Office: 1200 Campau Square Plaza, 99 Monroe, N.W., 49503-2639.
Telephone: 616-454-8656.
Fax: 616-776-6322.
Howell, Michigan Office: 121 South Barnard Street, Suite 4, 48843-2305.
Telephone: 517-546-7600.
Telecopier: 517-546-6974.
Kalamazoo, Michigan Office: 444 West Michigan Avenue, 49007-3752.
Telephone: 616-381-7030.
Fax: 616-382-0244.
Lansing, Michigan Office: One Michigan Avenue, Suite 900, 48933-1609.
Telephone: 517-487-2070.
Fax: 517-374-6304.
Monroe, Michigan Office: The Executive Centre, 214 East Elm Avenue, 48161-2682.
Telephone: 313-243-2000.
Fax: 313-243-0901.
Washington, D.C. Office: 1225 Nineteenth Street, N.W., Suite 400. 20036.
Telephone: 202-429-5575; 785-0600.
Fax: 202-331-1118; 785-1234.
Pensacola, Florida Office: 25 West Cedar, 32501.
Telephone: 904-469-1088.
Fax: 904-432-0677.
St. Petersburg, Florida Office: 100 Second Avenue S., Suite 7045, 33701.
Telephone: 813-982-6000.
Fax: 813-892-6002.
New York, New York Office: Eleventh Floor, 135 East 57th Street, 10022-2087.
Telephone: 212-754-5400.
Fax: 212-754-5401.
Gdansk, Poland Office: Suite 322, Dom Technika Building, UI. Rajska 6, 80-850.
Telephone: 011-485-831-2808.
Fax: 011-485-831-4719.
Warsaw, Poland Office: UI. Marszalkowska 82, Suite 561, 00-517.
Telephone: 011-482-623-6457 and 6458.
Fax: 011-482-623-6459.

RESIDENT PRINCIPALS
Robert E. Gilbert

Representative Firm Clients: Chrysler Corporation; Comerica, Incorporated; City of Detroit, Michigan; Detroit Tigers, Inc.; First of Michigan; Ford Motor Company; Ford Motor Credit Company; Great Lakes Bancorp; Henry Ford Hospital; INVETECH Company.

For Complete List of Firm Personnel, See General Section

For full biographical listings, see the Martindale-Hubbell Law Directory

---

DETROIT,* Wayne Co.

CLARK HILL P.L.C. (AV)

500 Woodward Avenue, Suite 3500, 48226
Telephone: 313-965-8300
Facsimile: 313-962-4348
Oakland County, Michigan Office: Third Floor, 255 South Woodward Avenue, Birmingham.
Telephone: 810-642-9692.
Facsimile: 810-642-2174.
Lansing, Michigan Office: Suite 600, 200 North Capitol Avenue.
Telephone: 517-484-4481.
Facsimile: 517-484-1246.
Minneapolis, Minnesota Office: Suite 1000, One Financial Plaza, 120 South Sixth Street.
Telephone: 612-332-0102.
Facsimile: 612-332-3225.
Kansas City, Missouri Office: Suite 1400, Bryant Building, 1102 Grand Avenue.
Telephone: 816-221-5578.
Facsimile: 816-221-0303.

Richard C. Marsh   James E. Baiers

Representative Clients: Leaseway Transportation Corp.; Gra-Bell Truck Line, Inc.; Motor City Cartage Co.; Thompson Transport, Ltd.; Liquid Cargo Lines, Ltd.; Transportation Club of Detroit.

For Complete List of Firm Personnel, See General Section

For full biographical listings, see the Martindale-Hubbell Law Directory

---

EAMES WILCOX (AV)

1400 Buhl Building, 48226-3602
Telephone: 313-963-3750
Facsimile: 313-963-8485

MEMBERS OF FIRM

Leonard A. Wilcox, Jr.	Jerry R. Swift
Ronald J. Mastej	Neill T. Riddell
John W. Bryant	Kevin N. Summers
Robert E. Gesell	Keith M. Aretha

(See Next Column)

OF COUNSEL

Rex Eames	William B. McIntyre, Jr.
	David R. Ritter

Representative Clients: ABF Freight System, Inc.; ANR Freight System, Inc.; City Transfer Co.; Kingsway Transports Limited; Parker Motor Freight, Inc.; Robinson Cartage Co.; Rogers Cartage Co.; Schneider Transport; Tank Carrier Employers Association of Michigan; TNT Transport Group, Inc.

For full biographical listings, see the Martindale-Hubbell Law Directory

---

FOSTER, MEADOWS & BALLARD, P.C. (AV)

3200 Penobscot Building, 48226
Telephone: 313-961-3234
Cable Address: "Foster"
Telex: 23-5823
Facsimile: 313-961-6184

Sparkman D. Foster (1897-1967)	Richard A. Dietz
Charles R. Hrdlicka	Robert H. Fortunate
Paul D. Galea	Robert G. Lahiff
Camille A. Raffa-Dietz	

Michael J. Liddane	Paul A. Kettunen

OF COUNSEL

John L. Foster	John F. Langs
	John A. Mundell, Jr.

Representative Clients: Burlington Northern Railway; Canadian National Railways; Grand Trunk Western Railroad Co.; British Marine Mutual Insurance Association, Ltd.; Brittania Steam-Ship Insurance Association; Japan Ship Owners Mutual Protection & Indemnity Association; Liverpool and London Steamship Protection & Indemnity Association, Ltd.

For full biographical listings, see the Martindale-Hubbell Law Directory

---

LEWIS, CLAY & MUNDAY, A PROFESSIONAL CORPORATION (AV)

(Formerly Lewis, White & Clay, P.C.)
1300 First National Building, 660 Woodward Avenue, 48226-3531
Telephone: 313-961-2550
Troy, Michigan Office: Liberty Center, Suite 200. 100 West Big Beaver Road. 48084.
Telephone: 810-680-6702.
Fax: 810-680-6703.
Washington, D.C. Office: 1000 16th Street, N.W., Suite 401. 20036.
Telephone: 202-835-0616.
Fax: 202-833-3316.
Boston, Massachusetts Office: 10 Post Office Square.
Telephone: 617-422-8646.
Fax: 617-338-5693.

David Baker Lewis	Frank E. Barbee
Eric Lee Clay	Camille Stearns Miller
Reuben A. Munday	Michael T. Raymond
Ulysses Whittaker Boykin	Jacqueline H. Sellers
Carl F. Stafford	David N. Zacks
Helen Francine Strong	Thomas J. Guyer
Blair A. Person	

Karen Kendrick Brown (Resident, Washington, D.C. Office)	Hans J. Massaquoi, Jr.
	Nancy C. Borland
J. Taylor Teasdale	Tammy L. Terry
Wade Harper McCree	Lynn Westfall Gross
Tyrone A. Powell	Suzanne P. Pope
Susan D. Hoffman	Matthew R. Halpin
John J. Walsh	Donica Thomas Varner
Andrea L. Powell	Damon L. White (Not admitted in MI)
Althea Lynn Foster	Kathleen L. Royal

COUNSEL

Otis M. Smith (1922-1994)	G. Allen Bass (Resident, Boston, Massachusetts Office)
Herbert O. Reid, Sr. (1915-1991)	

Representative Clients: Omnicare Health Plan; Aetna Life & Casualty Co.; Chrysler Motors Corp.; Chrysler Financial Corp.; MCI Communications Corp.; City of Detroit; City of Detroit Building Authority; City of Detroit Downtown Development Authority; Consolidated Rail Corp. (Conrail); Equitable Life Assurance Society of the United States.

For full biographical listings, see the Martindale-Hubbell Law Directory

Detroit—Continued

MILLER, CANFIELD, PADDOCK AND STONE, P.L.C. (AV)

A Professional Limited Liability Company
Founded in 1852 by Sidney Davy Miller
150 West Jefferson, Suite 2500, 48226-4415
Telephone: 313-963-6420
Fax: 313-496-7500
Cable Address: "Stem Detroit"
Detroit, Michigan Office: 150 West Jefferson, Suite 2500, 48226-4415.
Telephone: 313-963-6420.
Fax: 313-496-7500.
Cable Address: "Stem Detroit."
Ann Arbor, Michigan Office: 101 North Main Street, 7th Floor, 48104-1400.
Telephone: 313-663-2445.
Fax: 313-747-7147.
Bloomfield Hills, Michigan Office: Suite 100, Pinehurst Office Center, 1400 North Woodward, 48303-2014.
Telephone: 313-645-5000.
Fax: 313-645-1917.
Grand Rapids, Michigan Office: 1200 Campau Square Plaza, 99 Monroe, N.W., 49503-2639.
Telephone: 616-454-8656.
Fax: 616-776-6322.
Howell, Michigan Office: 121 South Barnard Street, Suite 4, 48843-2305.
Telephone: 517-546-7600.
Telecopier: 517-546-6974.
Kalamazoo, Michigan Office: 444 West Michigan Avenue, 49007-3752.
Telephone: 616-381-7030.
Fax: 616-382-0244.
Lansing, Michigan Office: One Michigan Avenue, Suite 900, 48933-1609.
Telephone: 517-487-2070.
Fax: 517-374-6304.
Monroe, Michigan Office: The Executive Centre, 214 East Elm Avenue, 48161-2682.
Telephone: 313-243-2000.
Fax: 313-243-0901.
Washington, D.C. Office: 1225 Nineteenth Street, N.W., Suite 400. 20036.
Telephone: 202-429-5575; 785-0600.
Fax: 202-331-1118; 785-1234.
Pensacola, Florida Office: 25 West Cedar, 32501.
Telephone: 904-469-1088.
Fax: 904-432-0677.
St. Petersburg, Florida Office: 100 Second Avenue S., Suite 7045, 33701.
Telephone: 813-982-6000.
Fax: 813-892-6002.
New York, New York Office: Eleventh Floor, 135 East 57th Street, 10022-2087.
Telephone: 212-754-5400.
Fax: 212-754-5401.
Gdansk, Poland Office: Suite 322, Dom Technika Building, UI. Rajska 6, 80-850.
Telephone: 011-485-831-2808.
Fax: 011-485-831-4719.
Warsaw, Poland Office: UI. Marszalkowska 82, Suite 561, 00-517.
Telephone: 011-482-623-6457 and 6458.
Fax: 011-482-623-6459.

PRINCIPALS OF FIRM

Leonard D. Givens
John R. Cook
(Kalamazoo Office)

Ronald E. Baylor
(Kalamazoo Office)

OF COUNSEL
Lawrence D. Owen (Lansing Office)

Representative Firm Clients: Chrysler Corporation; Comerica, Incorporated; City of Detroit, Michigan; Detroit Tigers, Inc.; First of Michigan; Ford Motor Company; Ford Motor Credit Company; Great Lakes Bancorp; Henry Ford Hospital; INVETECH Company.

For Complete List of Firm Personnel, See General Section

For full biographical listings, see the Martindale-Hubbell Law Directory

---

GRAND RAPIDS,* Kent Co.

WARNER NORCROSS & JUDD LLP (AV)

900 Old Kent Building, 111 Lyon Street, N.W., 49503-2489
Telephone: 616-752-2000
Fax: 616-752-2500
Muskegon, Michigan Office: 400 Terrace Plaza, P.O. Box 900.
Telephone: 616-727-2600.
Fax: 616-727-2699.
Holland, Michigan Office: Curtis Center, Suite 300, 170 College Avenue.
Telephone: 616-396-9800.
Fax: 616-396-3656.

OF COUNSEL

Lawson E. Becker
Conrad A. Bradshaw
Thomas R. Winquist

Harold F. Schumacher
Charles C. Lundstrom

(See Next Column)

MEMBERS OF FIRM

David A. Warner (1883-1966)
George S. Norcross (1889-1960)
Siegel W. Judd (1895-1982)
Platt W. Dockery (1906-1974)
J. M. Neath, Jr. (1928-1974)
Leonard D. Verdier, Jr. (1915-1989)
Thomas J. McNamara (1936-1989)
Phil R. Johnson (1908-1990)
George L. Whitfield
Wallson G. Knack
Charles E. McCallum
Jerome M. Smith
John D. Tully
R. Malcolm Cumming
William K. Holmes
Roger M. Clark
John H. Logie
Donald J. Veldman
(Resident at Muskegon Office)
I. John Snider, II
(Resident at Muskegon Office)
Jack B. Combs
Joseph F. Martin
John R. Marquis
(Resident at Holland Office)
John H. Martin
(Resident at Muskegon Office)
James H. Breay
Ernest M. Sharpe
Vernon P. Saper
Hugh H. Makens
Joseph M. Sweeney
Gordon R. Lewis
Robert J. Chovanec
Peter L. Gustafson
Roger H. Oetting
J. A. Cragwall, Jr.
Stephen R. Kretschman
W. Michael Van Haren
Richard A. Durell
Michael L. Robinson
Eugene E. Smary
Douglas E. Wagner
Robert W. Sikkel (Muskegon and Holland Offices)

Thomas H. Thornhill
(Resident at Muskegon Office)
Jeffrey O. Birkhold
Timothy Hillegonds
Blake W. Krueger
John G. Cameron, Jr.
John H. McKendry, Jr.
(Resident at Muskegon Office)
Paul T. Sorensen
Carl W. Dufendach
Stephen C. Waterbury
Rodney D. Martin
Richard E. Cassard
Alex J. DeYonker
Charles E. Burpee
John D. Dunn
William W. Hall
Bruce C. Young
Shane B. Hansen
F. William McKee
Louis C. Rabaut
Paul R. Jackson
(Resident at Muskegon Office)
Douglas A. Dozeman
John V. Byl
Janet Percy Knaus
Kathleen M. Hanenburg
Tracy T. Larsen
Sue O. Conway
Steven R. Heacock
Cameron S. DeLong
Jeffrey B. Power
Scott D. Hubbard
Stephen B. Grow
Richard L. Bouma
Daniel R. Gravelyn
Robert J. Jonker
Devin S. Schindler
Michael H. Schubert
(Resident at Muskegon Office)
Valerie Pierre Simmons
William C. Fulkerson
Anthony J. Kolenic, Jr.
James Moskal
Mark K. Harder
(Resident at Holland Office)

ASSOCIATES

Weldon H. Schwartz
Kenneth W. Vermeulen
Mark E. Brouwer
Jeffrey S. Battershall
Jeffrey A. Ott
Martha Walters Atwater
Rodrick W. Lewis
Kevin G. Dougherty
Melvin G. Moseley, Jr.
James J. Rabaut
James P. Enright
Timothy L. Horner
Richard D. Cornell, Jr.
(Resident at Muskegon Office)
R. Paul Guerre
Loren M. Andrulis
Karen J. Vanderwerff
Susan Gell Meyers
Judith W. Hooyenga (Resident)
Gordon J. Toering
Frank E. Berrodin
Norbert F. Kugele
Shaun M. Murphy
Kevin P. McDowell
(Resident at Holland Office)
Mark J. Wassink
Dennis J. Donohue
Michael I. Kleaveland
(Resident at Muskegon Office)

Elizabeth M. Topliffe
Susan N. McFee
Julie H. Sullivan
Molly E. McFarlane
William P. Dani
Andrew D. Hakken
Andrea J. Bernard
Lori L. Gibson
Mark T. Ostrowski
Daniel B. Ruble
Paul L. Winter
(Resident at Muskegon Office)
Douglas W. Poland
Michael P. Lunt
Carin L. Ojala
Daniel K. DeWitt
Michael K. Molitor
Melissa L. Collar
Michael J. Puca
Robert Dubault
(Resident at Muskegon Office)
Tanya E. Buhk
(Resident at Holland Office)
James D. Zwiers
Edward J. Bardelli
Tashia L. Rivard
Daniel P. Ettinger
James L. Scott II
Steven W. Clark

Representative Clients: Ryder Truck Lines, Inc.; Bernea Trucking Co.; Ron Besteman Transport; Bulkmatic Transport Co.; Bestway Moving Bay Cartage; Davis Motor Express, Inc.; Equity Transportation, Inc.; Graff Trucking Co.; Grand Express Inc.; Lemmen Transportation Co.

For full biographical listings, see the Martindale-Hubbell Law Directory

WHEELER UPHAM, A PROFESSIONAL CORPORATION (AV)

Second Floor, Trust Building, 40 Pearl Street, N.W., 49503-3001
Telephone: 616-459-7100
Fax: 616-459-6366

(See Next Column)

WHEELER UPHAM A PROFESSIONAL CORPORATION—*Continued*

Gordon B. Wheeler (1904-1986)	William H. Heritage, Jr.
Buford A. Upham (Retired)	Kenneth E. Tiews
Robert H. Gillette	Jack L. Hoffman
Geoffrey L. Gillis	Janet C. Baxter
John M. Roels	Peter Kladder, III
Gary A. Maximiuk	James M. Shade
Timothy J. Orlebeke	Thomas A. Kuiper

Counsel for: Conrail; The United Railroad Corp.; American Premier Underwriters, Inc.; Navistar.

For full biographical listings, see the Martindale-Hubbell Law Directory

---

KALAMAZOO,* Kalamazoo Co.

MILLER, CANFIELD, PADDOCK AND STONE, P.L.C. (AV)

A Professional Limited Liability Company
Founded in 1852 by Sidney Davy Miller
444 West Michigan Avenue, 49007-3752
Telephone: 616-381-7030
Fax: 616-382-0244
Detroit, Michigan Office: 150 West Jefferson, Suite 2500, 48226-4415.
Telephone: 313-963-6420.
Fax: 313-496-7500.
Cable Address: "Stem Detroit."
Ann Arbor, Michigan Office: 101 North Main Street, 7th Floor, 48104-1400.
Telephone: 313-663-2445.
Fax: 313-747-7147.
Bloomfield Hills, Michigan Office: Suite 100, Pinehurst Office Center, 1400 North Woodward, 48303-2014.
Telephone: 313-645-5000.
Fax: 313-645-1917.
Grand Rapids, Michigan Office: 1200 Campau Square Plaza, 99 Monroe, N.W., 49503-2639.
Telephone: 616-454-8656.
Fax: 616-776-6322.
Howell, Michigan Office: 121 South Barnard Street, Suite 4, 48843-2305.
Telephone: 517-546-7600.
Telecopier: 517-546-6974.
Lansing, Michigan Office: One Michigan Avenue, Suite 900, 48933-1609.
Telephone: 517-487-2070.
Fax: 517-374-6304.
Monroe, Michigan Office: The Executive Centre, 214 East Elm Avenue, 48161-2682.
Telephone: 313-243-2000.
Fax: 313-243-0901.
Washington, D.C. Office: 1225 Nineteenth Street, N.W., Suite 400. 20036.
Telephone: 202-429-5575; 785-0600.
Fax: 202-331-1118; 785-1234.
Pensacola, Florida Office: 25 West Cedar, 32501.
Telephone: 904-469-1088.
Fax: 904-432-0677.
St. Petersburg, Florida Office: 100 Second Avenue S., Suite 7045, 33701.
Telephone: 813-982-6000.
Fax: 813-892-6002.
New York, New York Office: Eleventh Floor, 135 East 57th Street, 10022-2087.
Telephone: 212-754-5400.
Fax: 212-754-5401.
Gdansk, Poland Office: Suite 322, Dom Technika Building, UI. Rajska 6, 80-850.
Telephone: 011-485-831-2808.
Fax: 011-485-831-4719.
Warsaw, Poland Office: UI. Marszalkowska 82, Suite 561, 00-517.
Telephone: 011-482-623-6457 and 6458.
Fax: 011-482-623-6459.

PRINCIPALS OF FIRM

Eric V. Brown, Jr.	John R. Cook

Representative Firm Clients: Chrysler Corporation; Comerica, Incorporated; City of Detroit, Michigan; Detroit Tigers, Inc.; First of Michigan; Ford Motor Company; Ford Motor Credit Company; Great Lakes Bancorp; Henry Ford Hospital; INVETECH Company.

For Complete List of Firm Personnel, See General Section

For full biographical listings, see the Martindale-Hubbell Law Directory

---

LANSING, Ingham Co.

* indicates certain Bar Register subscribers whose principal office is located elsewhere in the state and who have arranged for representation as a part of the state capital listings that follow

---

FOSTER, SWIFT, COLLINS & SMITH, P.C. (AV)

313 South Washington Square, 48933-2193
Telephone: 517-371-8100
Telecopier: 517-371-8200
URL: http://www.fosterswift.com
Farmington Hills, Michigan Office: 32300 Northwestern Highway, Suite 230.
Telephone: 810-539-9900.
Fax: 810-851-7504.

Robert E. McFarland	Kathryn M. Niemer
	Rebecca S. Davies

OF COUNSEL
John W. Ester

Representative Clients: Central Transport, Inc.; Davis Cartage Co.; Pony Express Courier Corp.; Universal Am-Can Ltd.; Michigan Intra-State Motor Tariff Bureau, Inc.; O-J Transport Co.; Troy CAB Co.

For Complete List of Firm Personnel, See General Section

For full biographical listings, see the Martindale-Hubbell Law Directory

---

* HONIGMAN MILLER SCHWARTZ AND COHN (AV)

A Partnership including Professional Corporations
222 North Washington Square, Suite 400, 48933-1800
Telephone: 517-484-8282
Telecopier: 517-484-8286
URL: http://law.honigman.com
Detroit, Michigan Office: 2290 First National Building, 48226.
Telephone: 313-256-7800.
West Palm Beach, Florida Office: Suite 800 Esperante Building, 222 Lakeview Avenue, 33401-6112.
Telephone: 561-838-4500.
Tampa, Florida Office: 2700 SunTrust Financial Centre, 401 E. Jackson Street, 33602-5226.
Telephone: 813-221-6600.

MEMBERS

Frederick M. Baker, Jr.	Daniel J. Demlow
	Ruth E. Zimmerman

For Complete List of Firm Personnel, See General Section

For full biographical listings, see the Martindale-Hubbell Law Directory

---

NOVI, Oakland Co.

LAW OFFICES OF SULLIVAN & LEAVITT, P.C. (AV)

22375 Haggerty Road, 48375
Telephone: 810-349-3980
Fax: 810-349-2810
Mailing Address: P.O. Box 400, Northville, MI, 48167

Robert A. Sullivan (1917-1979)	Martin J. Leavitt

Paul E. Robinson	Michael J. Leavitt
	Barbara L. Watry

OF COUNSEL
David Loeffler

Representative Clients: Aggregate Carriers of Michigan, Inc.; National Association of Engineering Cos.; D & H Mack Kenworth Sales & Service, Inc.; Gordon F. Laramie Crane Co.; Premiere Video, Inc.; Palmer Moving & Storage, Inc.; McLouth Steel Products, Inc.; Menlo Tool; Storage and Transport; Highland Superstores.

For full biographical listings, see the Martindale-Hubbell Law Directory

---

SOUTHFIELD, Oakland Co.

O'LEARY, O'LEARY, JACOBS, MATTSON, PERRY & MASON, P.C. (AV)

26777 Central Park Boulevard, Suite 275, 48076
Telephone: 810-948-1000
Fax: 810-799-8265
Email: olearyjacobs@michbar.org

John Patrick O'Leary	C. Kenneth Perry, Jr.
Thomas M. O'Leary	Larry G. Mason
John P. Jacobs	D. Jennifer Andreou
Kenneth M. Mattson	Kevin P. Hanbury
	Alice A. Zetusky

For full biographical listings, see the Martindale-Hubbell Law Directory

TROY, Oakland Co.

HACKETT, MAXWELL & PHILLIPS, P.L.L.C. (AV)

City Center Building, Suite 1470, 888 West Big Beaver Road, 48084
Telephone: 810-362-2600
Fax: 810-362-3610
Email: hackmax@michbar.org

Patrick E. Hackett   Phillip B. Maxwell

Representative Clients: Lake State Railway Co.; Michigan Interstate Railway Co.; CSX Transportation; Michigan Railway Assn.; Norfolk Southern Corp.; Ann Arbor Railroad; North American Van Lines.

For full biographical listings, see the Martindale-Hubbell Law Directory

MATHESON, PARR, SCHULER, EWALD & JOLLY, L.L.P. (AV)

2555 Crooks Road, Suite 200, 48084
Telephone: 810-643-7900
Telecopier: 810-643-0417

MEMBERS OF FIRM

Eugene C. Ewald   Robert D. Schuler

Representative Clients: National Automobile Transporters Labor Division; Brink's Inc.; Expertec, Inc.; Advance Technology, Inc.; Frito-Lay, Inc. *Reference:* Comerica Bank.

For Complete List of Firm Personnel, See General Section

For full biographical listings, see the Martindale-Hubbell Law Directory

WORKERS COMPENSATION

ALABAMA

BIRMINGHAM, * Jefferson Co.

BRADLEY, ARANT, ROSE & WHITE (AV)

2001 Park Place, Suite 1400, P.O. Box 830709, 35283-0709
Telephone: 205-521-8000
Facsimile: 205-252-0264
Facsimile (SouthTrust Tower Office): 205-251-9915
URL: http://www.BARW.COM
Huntsville, Alabama Office: 200 Clinton Avenue West, Suite 900, 35801.
Telephone: 205-517-5100.
Facsimile: 205-533-5069.

MEMBERS OF FIRM

Jay D. St. Clair   John William Hargrove

ASSOCIATES

Amy K. Myers   T. Matthew Miller
John W. Smith T   David M. Lawson
James Tassin
(Resident, Huntsville Office)

For Complete List of Firm Personnel, See General Section

For full biographical listings, see the Martindale-Hubbell Law Directory

SMITH, SPIRES & PEDDY (AV)

650 Financial Center, 505 North Twentieth Street, 35203-2662
Telephone: 205-251-5885

Paul G. Smith   Michael B. Walls
Thomas S. Spires   Todd Hamilton
A. Joe Peddy   Scott M. Roberts

ASSOCIATES

Thomas Coleman, Jr.   Alan B. Lasseter
D. Gregory Dunagan   Reed R. Bates
David A. Hughes

Representative Clients: Banker's & Shippers Insurance Co.; Alfa Insurance Co.; United States Fidelity & Guaranty Insurance Co.; R & D Trucking, Inc.; Racetrac Petroleum, Inc.; Transport South Inc.; Old Dominion Freight Line, Inc.; American States Insurance Co.; Trinity Industries, Inc.; Penn General.

For full biographical listings, see the Martindale-Hubbell Law Directory

CHATOM, * Washington Co.

TURNER, ONDERDONK, KIMBROUGH & HOWELL, P.A. (AV)

100 Central Avenue, P.O. Drawer 1389, 36518
Telephone: 334-847-2237
Fax: 334-847-3115
Mobile, Alabama Office: 1359 Dauphin Street.
Telephone: 334-432-2855.
Fax: 334-432-2863.

Edward P. Turner, Jr.   Gordon K. Howell
A. Michael Onderdonk   Marc E. Bradley
William A. Kimbrough, Jr.   (Resident, Mobile Office)
(Resident, Mobile Office)

Halron W. Turner   David M. Huggins
Frank Woodson   (Resident, Mobile Office)
(Resident, Mobile Office)   E. Tatum Turner

For full biographical listings, see the Martindale-Hubbell Law Directory

CULLMAN, * Cullman Co.

DRAKE & DRAKE (AV)

Suite A, 419 Second Avenue, S.W., P.O. Box 1165, 35055-4106
Telephone: 205-734-7602
Fax: 205-734-7696

MEMBERS OF FIRM

Tom Drake   Christine McKoy Drake

ASSOCIATE

Thomas E. Drake, II

Representative Clients: Cullman Electric Corp.; Shaver Poultry Breeding Farm, a Division of Cargill.
References: First National Bank of Birmingham; Peoples Bank of Cullman County.

For full biographical listings, see the Martindale-Hubbell Law Directory

ST. JOHN & ST. JOHN (AV)

108 Third Street South East, P.O. Drawer K, 35055
Telephone: 205-734-3542
Fax: 205-734-3544

MEMBERS OF FIRM

F. E. St. John (1874-1943)   Juliet G. St. John
Finis E. St. John (1909-1984)   Finis E. St. John, IV
Finis E. St. John, III   Gaynor L. St. John
(1933-1984)   Wells Rutland Turner, III

Attorneys for: U.S. Fidelity & Guaranty Co.; Golden-Rod Broilers, Inc.; Travelers Insurance Cos.; Liberty Mutual Insurance Cos.; ALFA Mutual Insurance Co.; First Federal Savings & Loan; The Atlanta Casualty Companies; Auto-Owners Insurance Co.

For full biographical listings, see the Martindale-Hubbell Law Directory

HUNTSVILLE, * Madison Co.

HORNSBY, WATSON & MEGINNISS (AV)

1110 Gleneagles Drive, 35801
Telephone: 205-650-5500
Fax: 205-650-5504

Ralph W. Hornsby   David H. Meginniss
S. A. "Bud" Watson, Jr.   Ralph W. Hornsby, Jr.

For full biographical listings, see the Martindale-Hubbell Law Directory

MORRIS, CLOUD AND CONCHIN, P.C. (AV)

521 Madison Street, P.O. Box 248, 35804
Telephone: 205-534-0065
Fax: 205-539-0741

Harvey B. Morris (P.C.)   Joseph M. Cloud
Gary V. Conchin

Maureen "Mike" K. Cooper   Daniel B. Banks, Jr.

For full biographical listings, see the Martindale-Hubbell Law Directory

THE LAW FIRM OF SINIARD, LAMAR & McKINNEY (AV)

125 Holmes Avenue, P.O. Box 2767, 35804
Telephone: 205-536-0770
Facsimile: 205-539-0540

MEMBERS OF FIRM

Tommy H. Siniard   Patrick M. Lamar
Jeffery W. McKinney

ASSOCIATE

M. Roy Braswell

For full biographical listings, see the Martindale-Hubbell Law Directory

MONTGOMERY, * Montgomery Co.

NIX, HOLTSFORD & VERCELLI, P.C. (AV)

300 A Water Street, Suite 300, P.O. Box 4128, 36103
Telephone: 334-262-2006
Fax: 334-834-3616

H. E. Nix, Jr.   Charles E. Vercelli, Jr.
Alex L. Holtsford, Jr.   Floyd R. Gilliland
T. Randall Lyons

Marianne T. Cosse   Phil Collins
Steven A. Higgins   G. Gregory Locklier
David M. Anderson   David P. Stevens

Representative Clients: Kemper Group; Waffle House, Inc.; Sabel Industries, Inc.; Alfa Mutual Insurance Company; United States Fidelity & Guaranty Insurance Company.

For full biographical listings, see the Martindale-Hubbell Law Directory

ARIZONA

PHOENIX, * Maricopa Co.

DOHERTY & VENEZIA, A PROFESSIONAL CORPORATION (AV)

100 West Clarendon, Suite 1720, 85013
Telephone: 602-277-1585
Fax: 602-277-1182

Julie A. Doherty   Stephen M. Venezia

For full biographical listings, see the Martindale-Hubbell Law Directory

Phoenix—Continued

DON A. FENDON, P.C. (AV)

320 East McDowell, Suite 230, 85004
Telephone: 602-256-2000
AZ & Ontario, Santa Barbara, San Diego, CA only: 800-228-2300
Fax: 602-256-6383
Mailing Address: P.O. Box 36365, Phoenix, AZ, 85067-6365

Don A. Fendon
LEGAL SUPPORT PERSONNEL
Lynne Carmody (Paralegal)

For full biographical listings, see the Martindale-Hubbell Law Directory

LONG, LUNDMARK & POPPE, P.A. (AV)

100 West Clarendon, Suite 2180, P.O. Box 33997, 85013
Telephone: 602-279-9777
Fax: 602-279-0925

James B. Long   R. Todd Lundmark
Melinda K. Poppe

For full biographical listings, see the Martindale-Hubbell Law Directory

JOHN W. MAIN, P.C. (AV)

100 West Clarendon Suite 1250, 85013-3508
Telephone: 602-650-2220

John W. Main

Representative Clients: AlliedSignal Aerospace Company; ASARCO Incorporated; Bashas' Markets Inc.; Pennzoil Company; State Farm Fire and Casualty Company; U S West Communications.

For full biographical listings, see the Martindale-Hubbell Law Directory

MITTEN, GOODWIN & RAUP, A PROFESSIONAL CORPORATION (AV)

One Columbus Plaza, 3636 North Central, Suite 1200, 85012
Telephone: 602-650-2000
Fax: 602-264-7033
Email: mgr@starlink.com

Brian M. Goodwin   Martin P. Clare

For full biographical listings, see the Martindale-Hubbell Law Directory

LAWRENCE P. NICHOLLS, P.C. (AV)

722 East Osborn Road, Suite 120, 85014
Telephone: 602-234-2123
Fax: 602-264-9895

Lawrence P. Nicholls

For full biographical listings, see the Martindale-Hubbell Law Directory

CHARLES M. WILMER, P.C. (AV)

722 East Osborn Road, Suite 120, 85014-5215
Telephone: 602-241-9424
FAX: 602-264-9895

Charles M. Wilmer

For full biographical listings, see the Martindale-Hubbell Law Directory

TUCSON,* Pima Co.

RABINOVITZ & ASSOCIATES, P.C. (AV)

721 North 4th Avenue, P.O. Box 41600, 85717
Telephone: 520-624-5526
Toll Free: 1-800-365-0821
Fax: 520-622-3776

Bernard I. Rabinovitz

John D. Ellis
OF COUNSEL
Clark J. Sloan (Not admitted in AZ)
LEGAL SUPPORT PERSONNEL
Michael Nelson (Paralegal)   Lisa Busciglio (Paralegal)
Ruth Polizz

Representative Client: Firemans Fund Insurance Co.

For full biographical listings, see the Martindale-Hubbell Law Directory

SAMET & GAGE, P.C. (AV)

717 North Sixth Avenue, 85705
Telephone: 520-624-8595
Fax: 520-623-4560

(See Next Column)

Dee-Dee Samet   Arthur V. Gage
References: Bank of America; Norwest Bank.

For full biographical listings, see the Martindale-Hubbell Law Directory

ARKANSAS

FORT SMITH,* Sebastian Co.

SHAW, LEDBETTER, HORNBERGER, COGBILL & ARNOLD (AV)

South Seventh and Parker, P.O. Box 185, 72902-0185
Telephone: 501-782-7294
FAX: 501-782-1493

Bruce H. Shaw (1904-1990)   Richard B. Shaw (1927-1988)
MEMBERS OF FIRM
Charles R. Ledbetter   James A. Arnold, II
Robert E. Hornberger   Ronald D. Harrison
J. Michael Cogbill   E. Diane Graham
R. Ray Fulmer, II
ASSOCIATE
Rebecca D. Hattabaugh
OF COUNSEL
J. Michael Shaw

Representative Clients: Liberty Mutual Insurance Company; St. Paul Insurance Company; CIGNA; Houston General; Fireman's Fund; Alexsis, Inc.; Arkansas Nursing Home Self-Insured Trust; Gerber Products'; Franklin Electric; Consolidated Freightways.

For full biographical listings, see the Martindale-Hubbell Law Directory

LITTLE ROCK,* Pulaski Co.

ANDERSON & KILPATRICK (AV)

The First Commercial Building, 400 West Capitol Avenue, Suite 2640, 72201
Telephone: 501-372-1887
Fax: 501-372-7706
Email: ande@cei.net

MEMBERS OF FIRM
Joseph E. Kilpatrick, Jr.   Aylmer Gene Williams
Michael E. Aud   Randy P. Murphy
Mariam T. Hopkins
ASSOCIATES
Michael P. Vanderford   Penny Brown Wilbourn
C. Timothy Spainhour

For full biographical listings, see the Martindale-Hubbell Law Directory

BARBER, MCCASKILL, AMSLER, JONES & HALE, P.A. (AV)

2700 First Commercial Building, 400 West Capitol Avenue, 72201-3414
Telephone: 501-372-6175
Telecopier: 501-375-2802

Azro L. Barber (1885-1979)   Richard C. Kalkbrenner
Elbert A. Henry (1889-1966)   G. Spence Fricke
John B. Thurman (1912-1971)   Gail Ponder Gaines
Austin McCaskill, Sr.   Michael J. Emerson
Guy Amsler, Jr.   R. Kenny McCulloch
Glenn W. Jones   Tim A. Cheatham
Michael E. Hale   Joseph F. Kolb
John S. Cherry, Jr.   Scott Michael Strauss
Robert L. Henry, III   Derek J. Edwards
Micheal L. Alexander   Thomas E. Osment, Jr.
William H. Edwards, Jr.   Christopher Gomlicker

Attorneys for: Associated Aviation Underwriters; Canal Insurance Co.; Fireman's Fund Insurance Co.; General Motors Corp.; General Motors Acceptance Corp.; Hanover Insurance Co.; Home Insurance Co.; Royal Insurance; United States Fidelity & Guaranty Co.; Universal Underwriters Insurance Co.

For full biographical listings, see the Martindale-Hubbell Law Directory

HUCKABAY, MUNSON, ROWLETT & TILLEY, P.A. (AV)

First Commercial Building, Suite 1900, 400 West Capitol, 72201
Telephone: 501-374-6535
Fax: 501-374-5906

Mike Huckabay   John E. Moore
Bruce E. Munson   Tim Boone
Beverly A. Rowlett   Rick Runnells
James W. Tilley   Sarah Ann Presson
Edward T. Oglesby

(See Next Column)

HUCKABAY, MUNSON, ROWLETT & TILLEY P.A.—*Continued*

D. Michael Huckabay, Jr.	Elizabeth Fletcher Rogers
Carol Lockard Worley	Julia L. Busfield
Mark S. Breeding	Jane M. Yocum

Terry D. Dugger

Representative Clients: AIG Claims Services, Inc.; Crawford & Company; Employers Mutual Insurance Company; Farmers Insurance Group; General Adjustment Bureau; Hanover Insurance Company; Houston General Insurance Company; Lumber Mutual Insurance Co.; Lindsey Morden; Reliance Insurance Co.; State Farm Insurance Companies: United States Fidelity & Guaranty Company.

For full biographical listings, see the Martindale-Hubbell Law Directory

LASER, WILSON, BUFFORD & WATTS, P.A. (AV)

101 S. Spring Street, Suite 300, 72201-2488
Telephone: 501-376-2981
Telecopier: 501-376-2417

Keith Martin McPherson	Thomas J. Diaz

Frank B. Newell
OF COUNSEL
Ralph R. Wilson

Representative Clients: AIG Claim Services; Arkansas Insurance Adjusting, Inc.; Continental Loss Adjusting, Little Rock, AR, Metairie, LA, Dallas, TX, Fort Lauderdale, FL and Chicago, IL; Crawford & Co.; Gallagher Bassett Services, Inc.; The Silvey Cos.; State Farm Insurance Co.; Columbia Insurance Group; Farm Bureau Insurance; Great West Casualty Co.

For Complete List of Firm Personnel, See General Section

For full biographical listings, see the Martindale-Hubbell Law Directory

ROSE LAW FIRM, A PROFESSIONAL ASSOCIATION (AV)

120 East Fourth Street, 72201
Telephone: 501-375-9131
Telecopy: 501-375-1309

Tim Boe	James Hunter Birch

James M. Gary
COUNSEL
Phillip Carroll

Mark Alan Peoples	Kathryn Bennett Perkins
David P. Martin	Michael N. Shannon

Counsel for: Aluminum Company of America; Bridgestone/Firestone, Inc.; The Equitable Life Assurance Society of The United States; General Motors Corp.; Georgia-Pacific Corp.; The Prudential Insurance Company of America; Stephens Group Inc.; Tyson Foods, Inc.

For Complete List of Firm Personnel, See General Section

For full biographical listings, see the Martindale-Hubbell Law Directory

CALIFORNIA

COSTA MESA, Orange Co.

RUTAN & TUCKER, LLP (AV)

A Partnership including Professional Corporations
611 Anton Boulevard, Suite 1400, P.O. Box 1950, 92626
Telephone: 714-641-5100; 213-625-7586
Telecopier: 714-546-9035
Email: rutan&tucker@mcimail.com *URL:* http://www.rutan.com
MEMBER OF FIRM
David C. Larsen (P.C.)

For Complete List of Firm Personnel, See General Section

For full biographical listings, see the Martindale-Hubbell Law Directory

LOS ANGELES, * Los Angeles Co.

GORDON, EDELSTEIN, KREPACK, GRANT, FELTON & GOLDSTEIN (AV)

A Partnership including a Professional Corporation
Suite 1800, 3580 Wilshire Boulevard, 90010
Telephone: 213-739-7000
Fax: 213-386-1671

Roger L. Gordon	Richard I. Felton
Mark Edelstein	Irwin L. Goldstein (A
Howard D. Krepack	Professional Corporation)
Sherry E. Grant	Steven J. Kleifield

(See Next Column)

ASSOCIATES

Joshua M. Merliss	David A. Goldstein

Eugenia L. Steele

For full biographical listings, see the Martindale-Hubbell Law Directory

SAN BERNARDINO, * San Bernardino Co.

EGGER & HALLETT, PROFESSIONAL LAW CORPORATION (AV)

325 West Hospitality Lane, Suite 300, P.O. Box 5009, 92412
Telephone: 909-890-0403
Fax: 909-890-0503
Yorba Linda, California Office: 22800 Savi Ranch Parkway, Suite 218.
Telephone: 714-974-6299.
Fax: 714-974-7215.
San Diego, California Office: 600 B Street, Suite 2200.
Telephone: 619-236-9377.
Fax: 619-236-1329.
City of Industry, California Office: 13200 Crossroads Parkway North, Suite 400
Telephone: 310-695-4951.
Fax: 310-695-9647.
Salinas, California Office: 158 Central Avenue, Suite 3.
Telephone: 408-771-1414.
Fax: 408-771-1408.
Pleasant Hill, California Office: 3478 Buskirk Avenue, Suite 1025.
Telephone: 510-746-7187.
Fax: 510-937-1611.

Patrick R. Egger	Michael D. Barba
Eugene R. Hallett	John W. Belcher
Ronald M. McCormick	H. Neal Wells IV
Keith R. Talmadge	Michael G. McDonald
Bruce S. Emerick	(Resident, Pleasant Hill Office)

Representative Clients: County of San Bernardino; Pan American Underwriters/Paula Insurance Co.; City of Palm Springs; City of Riverside; Kemper Insurance Co.; Am. International Group; Republic Indemnity of America; County of Orange; Legion Ins. Co.; Travelers Aetna; Association of California Hospital Districts; California Hospital Affiliated Insurance Services; Care America; Federated Stores; Employers First Insurance; Pacific Rim.

For full biographical listings, see the Martindale-Hubbell Law Directory

MARK BOLSON KUNTZ & SEREMBE (AV)

600 North Arrowhead Avenue, Suite 215, 92401
Telephone: 909-889-0421
Fax: 909-889-6236

MEMBERS OF FIRM

Philip A. Mark	Stephen J. Serembe
John A. Kuntz	Janet Rice Kuntz

C. Robert Bakke
ASSOCIATES

W. Scott Plyler	Charles Gregory Johnson
Nadine E. Betsworth	Louis David Seaman
Myrle Rountree Petty	Joseph B. Holcombe

OF COUNSEL
John H. Bolson

For full biographical listings, see the Martindale-Hubbell Law Directory

SAN FRANCISCO, * San Francisco Co.

HARBINSON, CARLSON & TUNE, A PROFESSIONAL CORPORATION (AV)

Suite 618, 114 Sansome Street, 94104-3814
Telephone: 415-986-3992
Fax: 415-986-3995

Thomas J. Harbinson	Martha M. Mangold
Mark H. Tune	Lisa Erickson Kasselik

Joel D. Tondreau	Liliana C. Naficy

For full biographical listings, see the Martindale-Hubbell Law Directory

LEACH, McGREEVY & BAUTISTA (AV)

1735 Pacific Avenue, 94109
Telephone: 415-775-4455
Telefax: 415-775-7435
Southern California Office: 13643 Fifth Street, Chino, CA. 91710.
Telephone: 909-590-2224.

Theodore Tamba (1900-1973)	Teresa A. Cunningham
John T. Harmon (1928-1993)	J. Curtis Cox
David G. Leach	Robert W. Shinnick
Richard E. McGreevy	Philip T. Kilduff
A. Marquez Bautista	Paul David Katerndahl

ASSOCIATE
John C. Connolly

(See Next Column)

LEACH, MCGREEVY & BAUTISTA, *San Francisco—Continued*

OF COUNSEL

Roger G. Eliassen Lloyd F. Postel

For full biographical listings, see the Martindale-Hubbell Law Directory

LAW OFFICES OF WAYNE LUTTRINGER (AV)

311 California Street, Suite 500, 94104
Telephone: 415-421-2583
Fax: 415-421-2584

ASSOCIATE

James A. Glimme

OF COUNSEL

M. Francis Brass Patrick M.K. Richardson

For full biographical listings, see the Martindale-Hubbell Law Directory

COLORADO

*COLORADO SPRINGS,** El Paso Co.

BELTZ, EDWARDS & SABO, L.L.P. (AV)

729 South Cascade, 80903
Telephone: 719-473-4444; 719-634-6620
Fax: 719-444-0186

W. Thomas Beltz Daniel P. Edwards
John W. Sabo, III

Daniel A. West

Representative Clients: A.M.I. Industries, Inc.; Analytical Surveys, Inc.; A.C. Israel Enterprises, Inc.; Boddington Lumber Co., Inc.; Cardiovascular Surgeons of Colorado Springs, P.C.; Colorado Springs Radiologists, P.C.; Digital, Inc.; Music Semi-Conductors, Inc.; Schlage Lock Co.; Texas Instruments.

For full biographical listings, see the Martindale-Hubbell Law Directory

RETHERFORD, MULLEN, JOHNSON & BRUCE, L.L.C. (AV)

415 South Sahwatch, P.O. Box 1580, 80901
Telephone: 719-475-2014
Fax: 719-630-1267

MEMBERS OF FIRM

Jerry A. Retherford Neil C. Bruce
J. Stephen Mullen Patrick R. Salt
Anthony A. Johnson J. Ronald Voss
Lori M. Moore

ASSOCIATES

Amelia L. Klemme Debra A. Long
M. James Zendejas Patricia Richardson

OF COUNSEL

E. William Shaffer, Jr. Carla M. Albers

Reference: City of Colorado Springs.

For full biographical listings, see the Martindale-Hubbell Law Directory

*DENVER,** Denver Co.

WHITE AND STEELE, PROFESSIONAL CORPORATION (AV)

1225 17th Street, Suite 2800, 80202
Telephone: 303-296-2828
Telecopier: 303-296-3131
Email: law@wsteele.com
Cheyenne, Wyoming Office: 1912 Capital Avenue, Suite 416, 82003.
Telephone: 307-778-4160.
Telecopier: 307-778-7041.

Stephen G. Sparr David J. Nowak
John P. Craver Ted A. Krumreich

Robert H. Coate Kimberly A. Viergever
Michelle R. Magruder Matthew W. Tills
Frank D. Sledge Charles W. Yett

Colorado Tort Counsel for: Goodyear Tire and Rubber Co.; The Dow Chemical Co.; Firestone Tire and Rubber Co.
Insurance Clients: Allied Insurance Co.; American Compensation Insurance Company; Colorado Worker's Compensation Insurance Authority; CNA; Kemper Insurance Group.

For Complete List of Firm Personnel, See General Section

For full biographical listings, see the Martindale-Hubbell Law Directory

CONNECTICUT

*BRIDGEPORT,** Fairfield Co.

COTTER, COTTER AND SOHON, P.C. (AV)

P.O. Box 5660 Bayview Station, 06610
Telephone: 203-335-3131
Fax: 203-874-1983
Milford, Connecticut Office: 500 Boston Post Road, 06460.
Telephone: 203-882-7143.
Fax: 203-874-1983.

D. Harold Cotter (1893-1961) Ellen M. Costello
Thomas H. Cotter Kevin M. Blake
John J. Cotter Catherine A. Stewart
Kevin M. Tepas Michael V. Vocalina
Daniel H. Cotter James F Mullen
William L. Cotter James P. Mooney
Catherine N. Anderson Matthias J. DeAngelo

Representative Clients: Royal Globe Indemnity Co.; Covenant Group; United States Fidelity & Guaranty Co.; Commercial Union Insurance Co.; Transport Insurance Co.; Metropolitan Insurance Co.; CNA; Nationwide Insurance Co.; Employers of Wassau Insurance Co.; Peerless Insurance Co.

For full biographical listings, see the Martindale-Hubbell Law Directory

FAIRFIELD, Fairfield Co.

FRIEDMAN, MELLITZ & NEWMAN, P.C. (AV)

Successor to: Friedman & Friedman; Mellitz Krentzman & Newman
One Eliot Place, 06430
Telephone: 203-259-5300
Fax: 203-259-2996

Arthur D. Friedman Joanne Patricia Sheehan
Noel R. Newman Cheryl Ann Carolan
Steven A. Levy Arthur Levy, Jr.

For full biographical listings, see the Martindale-Hubbell Law Directory

GLASTONBURY, Hartford Co.

POMERANZ, DRAYTON & STABNICK (AV)

95 Glastonbury Boulevard, 06033-4412
Telephone: 860-657-8000; 800-246-5541
Fax: 860-657-9838

Douglas L. Drayton Jason M. Dodge
James L. Pomeranz Anne Kelly Zovas
Richard T. Stabnick Richard L. Aiken, Jr.
Lucas D. Strunk Margaret E. Corrigan

ASSOCIATES

Michael J. McAuliffe Stephen G. Ekern

For full biographical listings, see the Martindale-Hubbell Law Directory

STRATFORD, Fairfield Co.

COUSINS AND JOHNSON, P.C. (AV)

2563 Main Street, 06497
Telephone: 203-386-1433
Fax: 203-386-9714

Donald C. Cousins Albert E. Desrosiers
Norma S. Johnson Michael A. Wolak, III
Steven H. Cousins

Andrew V. O'Shea

Approved Attorneys for: Chicago Title Insurance Co.; Lawyers Title Insurance Corp.

For full biographical listings, see the Martindale-Hubbell Law Directory

DELAWARE

*WILMINGTON,** New Castle Co.

CASARINO, CHRISTMAN & SHALK (AV)

Suite 1220, 222 Delaware Avenue, P.O. Box 1276, 19899
Telephone: 302-594-4500
Telecopier: 302-594-4509

MEMBERS OF FIRM

Stephen P. Casarino Beth H. Christman
Colin M. Shalk Donald M. Ransom
Patricia L. Peterson

(See Next Column)

CASARINO, CHRISTMAN & SHALK—*Continued*

Kenneth M. Doss   Diane M. Willette
Patricia Bartley Schwartz   Stacey L. Cummings

For full biographical listings, see the Martindale-Hubbell Law Directory

KIMMEL, CARTER & ROMAN, P.A. (AV)

12th Floor, 913 Market Street, P.O. Box 272, 19899-0272
Telephone: 302-571-0800

Morton Richard Kimmel   Edward B. Carter, Jr.
Thomas J. Roman

William R. Peltz   Michael D. Bednash
Matthew M. Bartkowski

References: Wilmington Trust Co.; Delaware Trust Co.

For full biographical listings, see the Martindale-Hubbell Law Directory

ROBERT W. RALSTON (AV)

10 East 13th Street, P.O. Box 1396, 19899
Telephone: 302-429-0758
Fax: 302-429-0193

For full biographical listings, see the Martindale-Hubbell Law Directory

FLORIDA

DAYTONA BEACH, Volusia Co.

SMITH, SCHODER & BOUCK, P.A. (AV)

605 South Ridgewood Avenue, 32014
Telephone: 904-255-0505
FAX: 904-252-4794
Other Daytona Beach Office: 214 Loomis Avenue.
Telephone: 904-255-6711.

C. Anthony Schoder, Jr.

For full biographical listings, see the Martindale-Hubbell Law Directory

FORT LAUDERDALE,* Broward Co.

HALICZER, PETTIS & WHITE, P.A. (AV)

101 Northeast Third Avenue, Sixth Floor, 33301
Telephone: 954-523-9922
Fax: 954-522-2512
Orlando, Florida Office: NationsBank Building. Suite 1275. 111 North Orange Avenue. 32801.
Telephone: 407-841-9866.
Fax: 407-841-9915.

James S. Haliczer   Kenneth E. White
Eugene K. Pettis   Lorna E. Brown-Burton

Amy B. Talisman   Margaret A. Benenati
Dean A. Robertson   Gina E. Caruso

For full biographical listings, see the Martindale-Hubbell Law Directory

KESSLER, MASSEY, CATRI, HOLTON & KESSLER, P.A. (AV)

110 Tower, Twentieth Floor, 110 Southeast Sixth Street, 33301
Telephone: 954-463-8593
Fax: 954-462-1303

Charles T. Kessler   Paula C. Kessler
Albert P. Massey, III   Gregory G. Coican
Wesley L. Catri   Andrea L. Kessler
Raymond O. Holton, Jr.   Edward D. Schuster

Gerard A. Tuzzio   Edwina V. Kessler

For full biographical listings, see the Martindale-Hubbell Law Directory

JACKSONVILLE,* Duval Co.

GABEL & HAIR (AV)

76 South Laura Street, Suite 1600, 32202-3421
Telephone: 904-353-7329
Fax: 904-358-1637
Email: lawoffcs@gabelhair.com
MEMBERS OF FIRM

George D. Gabel, Jr.   Sheldon Boney Forte
Karen Harris Williams

(See Next Column)

ASSOCIATES
Robert Blaine Birthisel   Brooks Charles Rathet
Representative Clients: Southern Bell Telephone and Telegraph Company; Florida Hotel-Motel; Self-Insurer's Fund.

For Complete List of Firm Personnel, See General Section

For full biographical listings, see the Martindale-Hubbell Law Directory

LAKELAND, Polk Co.

ROSS, WILLIAMS & DEAL, P.A. (AV)

230 South Florida Avenue Suite 501, 33801
Telephone: 941-688-6319
Fax: 941-683-1252

Dennis A. Ross   Gregory R. Deal
David J. Williams   Thomas Jason DeBari

Thomas P. Vecchio   Michael L. Davis

For full biographical listings, see the Martindale-Hubbell Law Directory

SMITH, CASSIDY, PLATT, HARRIS & RADABAUGH, P.A. (AV)

1920 South Florida Avenue, P.O. Box 1606, 33802
Telephone: 941-688-5440
Fax: 941-687-9046

J. Ron Smith   R. James Platt, Jr.
Thomas Cassidy   Eugene W. Harris
John M. Radabaugh

For full biographical listings, see the Martindale-Hubbell Law Directory

ORLANDO,* Orange Co.

KELAHER, WIELAND AND HILADO, P.A. (AV)

Barnett Bank Center, 390 North Orange Avenue, Suite 1500, P.O. Box 944, 32802
Telephone: 407-841-7698; *Brevard County:* 407-639-4777
Fax: 407-841-2084

James P. Kelaher   Glen D. Wieland
Alfred J. Hilado

Paul A. Kelley   Robert J. Egan
Reference: First Union National Bank.

For full biographical listings, see the Martindale-Hubbell Law Directory

ZIMMERMAN, SHUFFIELD, KISER & SUTCLIFFE, P.A. (AV)

Landmark Center One, Suite 600, 315 East Robinson Street, P.O. Box 3000, 32802
Telephone: 407-425-7010
Telecopier: 407-425-2747

Bernard J. Zimmerman   Robert L. Dietz
W. Charles Shuffield   Stephen B. Hatcher
Wendell J. Kiser   Robert W. Peacock, Jr.
Roland A. Sutcliffe Jr.   Clement L. Hyland
Robert E. Mansbach, Jr.   J. Timothy Schulte
Pamela Lynn Foels
OF COUNSEL
Gerard J. Turner

Melissa Dubina Kaplan   Kevin G. Malchow
Eric P. Gibbs   Thomas Warren Sculco
Joseph C. L. Wettach   Kevin L. Lienard
Edward C. Duncan, III   Daniel R. Murphy
Charles H. Leo   Michael C. Tyson
Vivian M. Reeves   Lori A. Walsingham Smith
Kraig N. Johnson   Scot G. Nimmo
Gene E. Crick, Jr.   Lynne R. Wilson
Charles B. Costar III   Lori A. Newsome
Joanne Marie Toner
LEGAL SUPPORT PERSONNEL
PARALEGALS
Jeanne Ann Roper   Shannon E. Brooks
L. Darlene Riley

For full biographical listings, see the Martindale-Hubbell Law Directory

PENSACOLA,* Escambia Co.

BRIDGERS, GILL & HOLMAN (AV)

121 Palafox Place, 32501
Telephone: 904-432-6484
Fax: 904-432-6383

(See Next Column)

BRIDGERS, GILL & HOLMAN, *Pensacola—Continued*

MEMBERS OF FIRM

J. Dixon Bridgers, III	Stephen T. Holman
Jeffrey P. Gill	Tracey Scalfano Witt

For full biographical listings, see the Martindale-Hubbell Law Directory

---

ST. PETERSBURG, Pinellas Co.

CHAMBERS, SALZMAN & BANNON, PROFESSIONAL ASSOCIATION (AV)

520 Fourth Street North, 33701
Telephone: 813-896-2167
Fax: 813-822-8981

Barry M. Salzman

Reference: NationsBank.

For full biographical listings, see the Martindale-Hubbell Law Directory

---

RIDEN, EARLE & KIEFNER, P.A. (AV)

City Center, North Tower, 100 Second Avenue South, Suite 400, 33701-4336
Telephone: 813-822-6000
Telecopier: 813-821-3721

Thomas K. Riden	Christopher C. Ferguson
James T. Earle, Jr.	Timothy A. Miller
John R. Kiefner, Jr.	Gary E. Frazier
Paul Castagliola	James C. Rowe
Robert H. Crawford	Christopher B. Young
Neil G. Kiefer	Clifford J. Hunt
D. Jay Snyder	Benjamin Felder

M. Deanna Harris	Camille J. Iurillo
Michael Francis Bremer	

For full biographical listings, see the Martindale-Hubbell Law Directory

---

TAMPA,* Hillsborough Co.

BARBAS, WEED, MORGAN & WHEELEY (AV)

1802 West Cleveland Street, 33605
Telephone: 813-254-6575
FAX: 813-254-4690
Lakeland, Florida Office: 500 S. Florida Avenue, Suite 600, 38801.
Telephone: 941-680-2712.
Palm Harbor, Florida Office: 2708 Alternate 19 N. Suite 701, 34683.
Telephone: 813-443-5323.
New Port Richey, Florida Office: 6014 U.S. 19, Suite 101-4.
Telephone: 813-849-0592.

Martha-Irene Weed	Stephen M. Barbas
Matthew B. Wheeley	

ASSOCIATES

David F. Koenig	L. Gray Sanders
Kelly Barcia Nunez	Nilo J. Sanchez, Jr.
Jimmie Butler	

References: First Florida Bank, N.A.; Sun Bank.

For full biographical listings, see the Martindale-Hubbell Law Directory

---

ROSEN & OSBORNE, P.A. (AV)

4016 Henderson Boulevard, 33629
Telephone: 813-289-4009
Telefax: 813-289-7644

Stephen L. Rosen	Richard W. Osborne

Willa M. Russell

For full biographical listings, see the Martindale-Hubbell Law Directory

---

SHOFI, SMITH, HENNEN & GRAMOVOT, P.A. (AV)

One North Dale Mabry, Suite 800, P.O. Box 10430, 33679-0430
Telephone: 813-876-7796
FAX: 813-876-0509

John D. Shofi	Larry I. Gramovot
John S. Smith	Sandra L. Peacock
William E. Hennen	Matthew R. Danahy
James E. Bogos	

Jon A. McAuliffe	Rochelle L. Lefler
Frank Clark	Kenneth S. Takacs, Jr.

Reference: City Bank of Tampa.

For full biographical listings, see the Martindale-Hubbell Law Directory

---

VERO BEACH,* Indian River Co.

MOSS, HENDERSON, BLANTON, KOVAL & LANIER, P.A. (AV)

817 Beachland Boulevard, P.O. Box 3406, 32964-3406
Telephone: 561-231-1900
Fax: 561-231-4387

George H. Moss, II	Thomas A. Koval
Steve L. Henderson	Clinton W. Lanier
Robin A. Blanton	Fred L. Kretschmer, Jr.
Lisa D. Harpring	

Lewis W. Murphy, Jr.	Kelly Cambron
Judith Goodman Hill	Lawrence Y. Leonard
David F. Mancini	

OF COUNSEL

Charles E. Garris	Ford J. Fegert
Everett J. Van Gaasbeck	

Representative Clients: Aetna Life & Casualty; Alcoa Florida, Inc.; Florida Power & Light Co.; Insurance Company of North America; Liberty Mutual Insurance Co.; Sears, Roebuck & Co.; Sugar Cane Growers Cooperative of Florida; Norfolk Southern Corporation/North American Van Lines, Inc.

For full biographical listings, see the Martindale-Hubbell Law Directory

---

WINTER HAVEN, Polk Co.

THE STANLEY WINES LAW FIRM, P.A. (AV)

60 Second Street, S.E., P.O. Box 860, 33880
Telephone: 941-299-1263
Telecopier: 941-294-4397
Email: 76077.3453@compuserve.com

J. Mason Wines	Michael B. Murphy
Barry W. Bennett	Craig M. Spanjers
Larry S. Helms	

Starlene D. McGory

References: SunTrust Bank/Mid-Florida, N.A.; Attorney's Title Insurance Fund; Jack M. Berry, Inc.; Berry-Cassidy, Inc.

For full biographical listings, see the Martindale-Hubbell Law Directory

---

GEORGIA

ALBANY,* Dougherty Co.

PERRY & WALTERS (AV)

409-411 North Jackson Street, P.O. Box 469, 31702-0469
Telephone: 912-432-7438; 432-7481
Telecopier: 912-436-1417
Other Albany, Georgia Office: 503 North Jackson Street, P.O. Box 445, 31702-0445.
Telephone: 912-432-9960.

MEMBERS OF FIRM

R. Edgar Campbell	Samuel Brown Lippitt, Jr.
Keith T. Dorough	R. Kelly Raulerson
Richard W. Fields	James E. Reynolds, Jr.
Edgar B. Wilkin, Jr.	

OF COUNSEL

H. H. Perry, Jr.	Jesse W. Walters

Division Counsel for: Seaboard Coast Line Railroad Co.
General Counsel for: First State Bank & Trust Co.; Carlton Co.; Bob's Candies, Inc.; Alcon Associates, Inc.; Albany-Dougherty County Hospital Authority.
Representative Clients: Merck & Co., Inc.; CNA Insurance; Chrysler Credit Corp.

For full biographical listings, see the Martindale-Hubbell Law Directory

---

ATHENS,* Clarke Co.

FOY S. HORNE, JR., P.C. (AV)

Suite 901, NationsBank Building, P.O. Box 706, 30603
Telephone: 706-549-6376
Fax: 706-613-2508

Foy S. Horne, Jr.

Bank Reference: NationsBank of Georgia, N.A.

For full biographical listings, see the Martindale-Hubbell Law Directory

ATLANTA, * Fulton Co.

FAIN, MAJOR & WILEY, P.C. (AV)

The Hurt Building, 50 Hurt Plaza, Suite 300, 30303
Telephone: 404-688-6633
Telecopier: 404-420-1544

Gene A. Major	Thomas E. Brennan
Charles A. Wiley, Jr.	John K. Miles, Jr.
	Darryl G. Haynes

Brian Alligood	Kim Monroe Jackson
Derek A. Mendicino	Robert G. Mikell

OF COUNSEL
Donald M. Fain

Representative Clients: Allstate Insurance Co.; Budget Rent-A-Car; Arkansas Best Corp.; Chrysler Insurance Co.; Georgia Farm Bureau Mutual Insurance Co.; Hertz Corp.; Universal Underwriters Insurance Co.; Westfield Insurance co.; Winn-Dixie Stores, Inc.

For Complete List of Firm Personnel, See General Section

For full biographical listings, see the Martindale-Hubbell Law Directory

GOLDNER, SOMMERS, SCRUDDER & BASS (AV)

900 Circle 75 Parkway Suite 850, 30339
Telephone: 770-612-9200
Facsimile: 770-612-9201

Susan V. Sommers	Alfred A. Quillian, Jr.
	Sandra G. Chase

Linda Jacobsen Pollock	Tiffany T. Norman
Marci R. Weston	Jane Carol Taylor

For Complete List of Firm Personnel, See General Section

For full biographical listings, see the Martindale-Hubbell Law Directory

PIERCE & YOUNG (AV)

Building 1700, 2255 Cumberland Parkway Northwest, 30339-4575
Telephone: 770-435-0500
Telecopier: 770-435-0362

MEMBER OF FIRM
J. Wayne Pierce

For full biographical listings, see the Martindale-Hubbell Law Directory

WEBB, CARLOCK, COPELAND, SEMLER & STAIR (AV)

A Partnership including Professional Corporations
2600 Marquis Two Tower, 285 Peachtree Center Avenue, P.O. Box 56887, 30343-0887
Telephone: 404-522-8220
Fax: 404-523-2345

MEMBERS OF FIRM

Robert C. Semler (P.C.)	Johannes S. Kingma

ASSOCIATES

Philip P. Taylor	Lynn B. Olmert
Christopher A. Whitlock	Colleen P. O'Neill

For full biographical listings, see the Martindale-Hubbell Law Directory

WILSON, STRICKLAND & BENSON, P.C. (AV)

1100 One Midtown Plaza, 1360 Peachtree Street, N.E., 30309
Telephone: 404-870-1800
Telecopier: 404-870-1808

Warner R. Wilson, Jr.	Earl B. Benson, Jr.
	N. Sandy Epstein

Anne W. Lewis	F. Robert Slotkin, Jr.
Samuel T. Brannan	Sara L. Doyle

For Complete List of Firm Personnel, See General Section

For full biographical listings, see the Martindale-Hubbell Law Directory

AUGUSTA, * Richmond Co.

ALLGOOD, CHILDS, MEHRHOF AND MILLIANS, P.C. (AV)

615 Telfair Building, P.O. Box 1523, 30903
Telephone: 706-724-6526
Fax: 706-724-0043

T. Allen Childs, Jr.	Michael W. Millians
Richard R. Mehrhof, Jr.	Thomas F. Allgood, Jr.

(See Next Column)

OF COUNSEL
Thomas F. Allgood, Sr.

Representative Clients: Allstate Insurance Co.; Therman Ceramics.

For full biographical listings, see the Martindale-Hubbell Law Directory

FULCHER, HAGLER, REED, HANKS & HARPER (AV)

A Partnership including Professional Corporations
520 Greene Street, P.O. Box 1477, 30903-1477
Telephone: 706-724-0171
Telecopier: 706-724-4573

MEMBERS OF FIRM

William M. Fulcher (1902-1993)	Michael B. Hagler (P.C.)
Gould B. Hagler (Retired)	James W. Purcell (P.C.)
William C. Reed (Retired)	J. Arthur Davison (P.C.)
David H. Hanks (P.C.)	Mark C. Wilby (P.C.)
John I. Harper (P.C.)	Ronald C. Griffeth
Robert C. Hagler (P.C.)	N. Staten Bitting, Jr. (P.C.)
	David P. Dekle (P.C.)

ASSOCIATES

Scott W. Kelly	Elizabeth A. McLeod
Cynthia A. Gray	Barry A. Fleming

General Counsel for: GIW Industries, Inc.
Division Counsel for: CSX Transportation; Textron, Inc. (E-Z Go Car Division).
Counsel for: NationsBank; Georgia Natural Gas Co. (a division of Atlanta Gas Light Co.); Champion International Corp.; Aetna Life and Casualty; Liberty Mutual Insurance Company; St. Paul Fire & Marine Insurance Co.; Kimberly Clark Corporation.

For full biographical listings, see the Martindale-Hubbell Law Directory

DALTON, * Whitfield Co.

KINNEY, KEMP, PICKELL, SPONCLER & JOINER (AV)

A Partnership including a Professional Corporation
225 W. King Street, P.O. Box 398, 30722-0398
Telephone: 706-278-5211
FAX: 706-275-6566

MEMBERS OF FIRM

R. Carter Pittman (1898-1972)	Horace Greely Joiner, Jr.
L. Hugh Kemp (P.C.)	Henry C. Tharpe, Jr.
Charles L. Pickell	F. Gregory Melton
Maurice M. Sponcler, Jr.	Richard W. Andrews
	Timothy H. Allred

ASSOCIATES

Mark D. Newberry	Robert Adam Cowan

OF COUNSEL
Hinton Eugene Kinney

General Counsel for: North Georgia Electric Membership Cooperative; Queen Carpet Corp.; Hardwick Bank & Trust Company.
Representative Clients: Allstate Insurance Co.; Liberty Mutual Insurance Co.; State Farm Mutual Automobile Insurance Co.; Norfolk Southern Railway Company; General Motors Corporation and Dalton Board of Education.

For full biographical listings, see the Martindale-Hubbell Law Directory

DECATUR, * De Kalb Co.

HYATT & HYATT, P.C. (AV)

Suite 201, Trust Building, 545 North McDonough Street, 30030
Telephone: 404-378-3635
Fax: 404-377-8304

Charles H. Hyatt (1924-1995)	John M. Hyatt

For full biographical listings, see the Martindale-Hubbell Law Directory

MACON, * Bibb Co.

SELL & MELTON (AV)

A Partnership including a Professional Corporation
14th Floor, Charter Medical Building, P.O. Box 229, 31297-2899
Telephone: 912-746-8521
Telecopier: 912-745-6426

Doye E. Green	Russell M. Boston (P.C.)

General Counsel for: Macon Telegraph Publishing Co. (The Macon Telegraph); Macon-Bibb County Hospital Authority; County of Bibb; County of Twiggs; Smith & Sons Foods, Inc. (S & S Cafeterias); Macon Bibb County Industrial Authority; Burgess Pigment Co.

For Complete List of Firm Personnel, See General Section

For full biographical listings, see the Martindale-Hubbell Law Directory

ROSSVILLE, Walker Co.

HARRISS, HARTMAN, AARON, WHARTON, BOYD & SECORD, P.C. (AV)

200 McFarland Building, P.O. Drawer 220, 30741
Telephone: 706-861-0203

Robert J. Harriss	Robert A. Wharton, Jr.
James M. Aaron, Jr.	William G. Boyd
	James A. Secord

Richard S. Taliaferro

For full biographical listings, see the Martindale-Hubbell Law Directory

SAVANNAH, * Chatham Co.

GANNAM & GNANN (AV)

130 West Bay Street, P.O. Box 10085, 31412
Telephone: 912-232-1192
Fax: 912-238-9917

MEMBERS OF FIRM

Michael J. Gannam	J. Hamrick Gnann, Jr.
	Joseph M. Gannam

For full biographical listings, see the Martindale-Hubbell Law Directory

VALDOSTA, * Lowndes Co.

CLYATT, CLYATT, WALLACE & DEVAUGHN, P.C. (AV)

410 North Valdosta Road, P.O. Box 5799, 31603
Telephone: 912-241-9091
Fax: 912-245-1635

Robert M. Clyatt	Russell Cotter Wallace
Melissa M. Clyatt	C. Elizabeth DeVaughn
	Joni B. Parker

For full biographical listings, see the Martindale-Hubbell Law Directory

HAWAII

HONOLULU, * Honolulu Co.

KESSNER DUCA UMEBAYASHI BAIN & MATSUNAGA ATTORNEYS AT LAW, A LAW CORPORATION (AV)

19th Floor, Central Pacific Plaza, 220 South King Street, 96813
Telephone: 808-536-1900
Telecopier: 808-529-7177
Telex: 723 8616 OPAC IIR

Robert C. Kessner	Elton John Bain
James N. Duca	Emma S. Matsunaga
Clyde S. Umebayashi	Muriel M. Taira

Beverly S. K. Tom	Melanie S. Ono
Jacqueline W.S. Amai	Darin P. Wright
Dawn Jordan	Cori Ann C. Yokota

For full biographical listings, see the Martindale-Hubbell Law Directory

IDAHO

BOISE, * Ada Co.

ELAM & BURKE, A PROFESSIONAL ASSOCIATION (AV)

Key Financial Center, 702 West Idaho Street, P.O. Box 1539, 83701
Telephone: 208-343-5454
Telecopier: 208-384-5844
Email: eblaw@elamburke.com

Ryan P. Armbruster	James A. Ford

Rebecca A. Broadbent

Representative Client: Idaho State Insurance Fund.

For Complete List of Firm Personnel, See General Section

For full biographical listings, see the Martindale-Hubbell Law Directory

ELLIS, BROWN & SHEILS, CHARTERED (AV)

707 North 8th, P.O. Box 388, 83701
Telephone: 208-345-7832
Fax: 208-345-9564

(See Next Column)

Allen B. Ellis	Stephen C. Brown
	Max M. Sheils, Jr.

Representative Clients: Farm Credit Services Northwest, A.C.A.; Wausau Insurance Cos.; State Insurance Fund; Crawford & Company; Idaho Power Co.; Ada Planning Assn.; Consolidated Supply Co.; Finch-Brown Co.
References: West One Bank; First Interstate Bank.

For full biographical listings, see the Martindale-Hubbell Law Directory

ILLINOIS

CHICAGO, * Cook Co.

BRADLEY & BRADLEY (AV)

29 South La Salle Street Suite 950, 60603
Telephone: 312-372-5454
FAX: 312-372-5458

MEMBERS OF FIRM

Edward J. Bradley	Edward J. Bradley, Jr.

For full biographical listings, see the Martindale-Hubbell Law Directory

GAROFALO, HANSON, SCHREIBER & VANDLIK, CHARTERED (AV)

211 West Wacker Drive, 14th Floor, 60606-1217
Telephone: 312-670-2000
Facsimile: 312-419-1336

Joseph A. Garofalo	Robert G. Lammie
Alan V. Hanson	Bennett F. Hart
Scott T. Schreiber	Philip G. Brinckerhoff
Mark J. Vandlik	Gregory P. Sujack
David F. Buysse	Derek A. Storm
	Steven R. Scarlati, Jr.

Jonathan E. Barrish	Andrew L. Rane
Michael S. Purves	Kathleen M. Callahan
Kerrie A. Lethbridge	Kurt E. Hanson

For full biographical listings, see the Martindale-Hubbell Law Directory

JOHNSON, DROZDZIK, VAN DRISKA & ANDROS, LTD. A PROFESSIONAL CORPORATION (AV)

200 West Adams Street, Suite 1005, 60606
Telephone: 312-236-6006
FAX: 312-236-4731

Anita Senese-Johnson	George J. Andros
Ronald L. Drozdzik	Gail A. Galante
Rebecca Schneiderman (1940-1987)	Jack M. Shanahan
Terrance J. Van Driska (1932-1995)	Patrick D. Duffy

For full biographical listings, see the Martindale-Hubbell Law Directory

MURPHY, SMITH & POLK, A PROFESSIONAL CORPORATION (AV)

Twenty-Fifth Floor, Two First National Plaza 20 South Clark Street, 60603-1891
Telephone: 312-558-1220
Telecopier: 807-3619
Email: msp@pg.net

Charles E. Murphy

Julia A. Donnelly	Charles R. Marcordes

For full biographical listings, see the Martindale-Hubbell Law Directory

ROOKS, PITTS AND POUST (AV)

10 South Wacker Drive, Suite 2300, 60606
Telephone: 312-876-1700
Fax: 312-876-1155
Wheaton, Illinois Office: 201 Naperville Road.
Telephone: 708-690-8500.
Facsimile: 708-690-8553.
Joliet, Illinois Office: 111 North Ottawa Street.
Telephone: 815-727-4511.
Facsimile: 815-727-1586.
Winnetka, Illinois Office: 560 Green Bay Road.
Telephone: 847-441-5615.
Fax: 847-441-9367.

MEMBERS OF FIRM

Frank C. Rowland	Geoffrey A. Bryce
Ian M. Sherman	Michael Gahan
	J. Barrett Long

(See Next Column)

ROOKS, PITTS AND POUST—*Continued*

Glennon P. Dolan	Gerald T. Karr
Ellen D. Holzman	Daniel M. Noland

For Complete List of Firm Personnel, See General Section

For full biographical listings, see the Martindale-Hubbell Law Directory

STEVENSON, RUSIN AND FRIEDMAN, LTD. (AV)

Suite 1530 10 South Riverside Plaza, 60606
Telephone: 312-454-5110
Fax: 312-454-6166

OF COUNSEL

Douglas F. Stevenson	Larry J. Chilton
Michael E. Rusin	David William Porter
Stephen J. Friedman	Gregory G. Vacala
John A. Maciorowski	Jon Yambert
Kenneth N. Marshall	Daniel Arkin
Randall R. Stark	

Jean Marie Calcagno	Scott A. Labow
Brad A. Carder	Sharon M. Peart
Paul A. Coghlan	Theodore James Powers
P. Bartley Durham	Mark P. Rusin
Daniel R. Egan	Kevin A. Shaw
Frederick Scott Glassman	James J. Zahour

For full biographical listings, see the Martindale-Hubbell Law Directory

FAIRVIEW HEIGHTS, St. Clair Co.

KEEFE & DePAULI, P.C. (AV)

2 Executive Drive, P.O. Box 3190, 62208
Telephone: 618-624-2444
Fax: 618-624-6031

William L. Rogers	Thomas H. Kuergeleis
James K. Keefe	

William L. Hanks	Patrick M. Keefe
William Lemp	Richard H. Risse
Andrew T. Nalefski	Dennis O. Douglas
Kevin M. Hazlett	Scott A. White
Darren K. Short	

OF COUNSEL

Thomas Q. Keefe	Frank E. DePauli

Reference: Magna Bank.

For full biographical listings, see the Martindale-Hubbell Law Directory

GALESBURG,* Knox Co.

MUSTAIN LINDSTROM & HENSON (AV)

1865 North Henderson Street, Suite 11B, 61401
Telephone: 309-344-5252
Telecopier: 309-344-3939

MEMBERS OF FIRM

Douglas D. Mustain	Ronald Henson
Robert Lindstrom	Christopher Henson
Carl E. Hawkinson	

References: The Farmers and Mechanics Bank; Norwest Bank Illinois, N.A.; First Bank; First Financial Bank; Farmers State Bank of Western Illinois; McGladrey and Pullen.

For full biographical listings, see the Martindale-Hubbell Law Directory

HARRISBURG,* Saline Co.

JELLIFFE, FERRELL & MORRIS (AV)

108 East Walnut Street, 62946
Telephone: 618-253-7153; 253-7647
Telecopier: 618-252-1843

OF COUNSEL
Charles R. Jelliffe

MEMBERS OF FIRM

DeWitt Twente (1904-1976)	Donald V. Ferrell
Walden E. Morris	

ASSOCIATES

Michal Doerge	Thomas J. Foster

Representative Clients: Auto-Owners Insurance; Country Cos; Metropolitan Life Insurance; Ohio Casualty Group; Standard Mutual Insurance Co.; State Farm Cos; Redland Insurance Co.; Aetna Casualty & Surety Co.; Kerr-McGee Coal Corp.; Sahara Coal Co.

For full biographical listings, see the Martindale-Hubbell Law Directory

MATTOON, Coles Co.

CRAIG & CRAIG (AV)

1807 Broadway, P.O. Box 689, 61938-0689
Telephone: 217-234-6481
Telecopier: 217-234-6486
Mount Vernon, Illinois Office: 227 1/2 South 9th Street.
Telephone: 618-244-7511.

MEMBERS OF FIRM

Craig Van Meter (1895-1981)	Stephen L. Corn
Fred H. Kelly (1894-1971)	Richard Charles Hayden
Robert M. Werden (1908-1969)	Robert G. Grierson
George N. Gilkerson	Gregory C. Ray
(1911-1985)	Paul R. Lynch (Resident, Mount
John H. Armstrong	Vernon Office)
John P. Ewart	Kenneth F. Werts (Resident,
Richard F. Record, Jr.	Mount Vernon Office)
John L. Barger	

ASSOCIATES

Joshua N. Rosen (Resident,	Theresa M. Thomson
Mount Vernon Office)	Kristine M. Tuttle
Kathleen M. Stockwell	Henry P. Villani (Resident,
	Mount Vernon Office)

OF COUNSEL
Jack E. Horsley

Counsel for: Monterey Coal Co., a Division of Exxon Coal USA, Inc.; Marathon Oil Co.; Illinois Central R.R. Co.; Okaw Building & Loan Assn., Mattoon, Illinois; The Medical Protective Insurance Co.; Consolidated Communications, Inc.; Lloyds Underwriters at London; Hartford Insurance Co.; Coles Together, a Not-For-Profit Corp.; Coles Building Corporation.

For full biographical listings, see the Martindale-Hubbell Law Directory

ROCKFORD,* Winnebago Co.

PICHA & SALISBURY (AV)

Edgebrook Court Building, 1639 North Alpine, Suite 300, 61107-1449
Telephone: 815-227-4300
FAX: 815-227-4330

MEMBERS OF FIRM

George J. Picha	Jeffrey L. Salisbury
Lloyd R. McCumber	

ASSOCIATES

William A. Meister	Amy J. Szczepaniak

Representative Clients: Self-Insured Clients: A.O. Smith Automotive Products Co.; Atwood Industries, Inc.; Chrysler Corp.; Elco Textron; Estwing Manufacturing Company.
Insurance Carriers: American States Insurance Co.; Bituminous Insurance Companies; Casualty Insurance Company; Country Companies; General Casualty Companies.

For full biographical listings, see the Martindale-Hubbell Law Directory

VANDALIA,* Fayette Co.

BURNSIDE DEES JOHNSTON & CHOISSER (AV)

First National Bank Building, 62471
Telephone: 618-283-3260
Fax: 618-283-2851

MEMBERS OF FIRM

J. G. Burnside (1873-1969)	Joe Dees
Robert G. Burnside	Jack B. Johnston
Dale F. Choisser	

General Counsel for: First National Bank; The First State Bank of St. Peter; State Bank of Farina; South-Central Regional Planning And Development Commission; S&S Urethane, Inc.
Local Counsel for: Pekin Insurance Co.

For full biographical listings, see the Martindale-Hubbell Law Directory

INDIANA

EVANSVILLE,* Vanderburgh Co.

FINE & HATFIELD (AV)

520 N.W. Second Street, P.O. Box 779, 47705-0779
Telephone: 812-425-3592
Telecopier: 812-421-4269
Email: Fine@Fine-Hatfield.com *URL:* http://www.Fine-Hatfield.com

MEMBERS OF FIRM

Ronald R. Allen	Danny E. Glass
Patricia Kay Woodring	

(See Next Column)

FINE & HATFIELD, *Evansville—Continued*

ASSOCIATES

Debra S. McGowan   H. Linwood Shannon, III

A List of Representative Clients Furnished Upon Request.

For full biographical listings, see the Martindale-Hubbell Law Directory

---

MATTINGLY, RUDOLPH, FINE & PORTER (AV)

221 N.W. Fifth Street, Second Floor, P.O. Box 1507, 47706
Telephone: 812-422-9444
Fax: 812-421-7459
Email: mrfp@evansville.net

MEMBER OF FIRM
Ross E. Rudolph

ASSOCIATES

Jeffrey W. Henning   Keith A. Sermersheim

Reference: National City Bank of Evansville.

For full biographical listings, see the Martindale-Hubbell Law Directory

---

INDIANAPOLIS,* Marion Co.

BUSCHMANN, CARR & SHANKS, PROFESSIONAL CORPORATION (AV)

1020 Market Tower, 10 West Market Street, 46204-2963
Telephone: 317-636-5511
Fax: 317-636-3661
Email: bcs@indy.net *URL:* http://www.buschmann.com/bcs/

Stephen R. Buschmann   John N. Shanks II

Representative Clients: Archer-Daniels Midland Co.; Ball Corp.; Industrial Valley Title Insurance; Creative Risk Management, Inc.; Deflecto Corporation; Glenfed Mortgage Corp.; Gates McDonald; Merchants National Bank & Trust Company of Muncie; Monumental Life Insurance Co.; National Council on Compensation Insurance.

For full biographical listings, see the Martindale-Hubbell Law Directory

---

MARION,* Grant Co.

KILEY, KILEY, HARKER, MICHAEL & CERTAIN (AV)

300 West Third Street, P.O. Box 899, 46952-0899
Telephone: 317-664-9041
Fax: 317-664-8119

MEMBERS OF FIRM
Robert Ralph Batton   David L. Kiley, Sr.
(1890-1963)   Michael J. Kiley
Albert L. Harker (1904-1965) Albert C. Harker
Albert Bonner Brown   Thomas W. Michael
(1911-1981)   Harry J. Certain

ASSOCIATE
Therese McCullough Pryor

Counsel for: Bank One, Marion, N.A.; Liniger Co., Inc.; Atlas Foundry Co.
Local Counsel for: GenCorp.; CPC Group; General Motors; Indiana Michigan Power Co./AEP; Indiana Bell Telephone Co.; Foster-Forbes, Division of American National Can Corp.

For full biographical listings, see the Martindale-Hubbell Law Directory

---

SOUTH BEND,* St. Joseph Co.

EDWARD N. KALAMAROS & ASSOCIATES PROFESSIONAL CORPORATION (AV)

129 North Michigan Avenue, P.O. Box 4156, 46634
Telephone: 219-232-4801
Telecopier: 219-232-9736

Edward N. Kalamaros   Philip E. Kalamaros
Timothy J. Walsh   Sally P. Norton
Thomas F. Cohen   Kevin W. Kearney
Joseph M. Forte   Peter J. Bagiackas
Robert Deane Woods   David A. Wemhoff
Patrick J. Hinkle   Eric G. Ciesielski

Representative Clients: South Bend Medical Foundation, Inc.; Powell Tool Supply, Inc.; Cooper Industries/Anco Division; Orthopedic & Sports Medicine Center of Northern Indiana, Inc.; Edward J. DeBartolo Corporation; University Park Mall; Marriott Corporation; Employers Reinsurance Corporation; Orion Group.

For full biographical listings, see the Martindale-Hubbell Law Directory

---

IOWA

DES MOINES,* Polk Co.

FINLEY, ALT, SMITH, SCHARNBERG, MAY & CRAIG, P.C. (AV)

604 Locust Street, Fourth Floor Equitable Building, 50309
Telephone: 515-288-0145
Telecopier: 515-288-2724

Lorraine J. May   V. Glenn Goodwin, Jr.
              Dawn R. Siebert

Representative Clients: Aetna Casualty & Surety Co.; Aetna Life Insurance Co.; ALAS; American Society of Composers, Authors and Publishers; Equitable Life Assurance Society of the U.S.; Federated Insurance Co.; Meredith Corp.
Iowa Attorneys for: Midwest Medical Insurance Co.
District Attorneys for: Norfolk & Southern Railroad; Soo Line Railroad Company.

For Complete List of Firm Personnel, See General Section

For full biographical listings, see the Martindale-Hubbell Law Directory

---

LAW OFFICES OF MICHAEL R. HOFFMANN, P.L.C. (AV)

Breakwater Building, 3708 75th Street, 50322
Telephone: 515-270-8899
Fax: 515-270-0115
Email: MRHLaw@AOL.COM

Michael R. Hoffmann

Nathan R. McConkey   Jeffrey W. Lanz
              Randy Rose

For full biographical listings, see the Martindale-Hubbell Law Directory

---

PATTERSON, LORENTZEN, DUFFIELD, TIMMONS, IRISH, BECKER & ORDWAY, L.L.P. (AV)

729 Insurance Exchange Building, 50309
Telephone: 515-283-2147
Fax: 515-283-1002

MEMBERS OF FIRM
G. O. Patterson (1914-1982)   Gregory J. Wilson
James A. Lorentzen   Jeffrey A. Boehlert
Theodore T. Duffield   Douglas A. Haag
William E. Timmons (Retired) Charles E. Cutler
Roy M. Irish   Michael D. Huppert
F. H. Becker (Retired)   Martin C. Sprock
Gary D. Ordway   William A. Wickett
Robin L. Hermann   Frederick M. Haskins
Harry Perkins, III   Jeffrey A. Baker
Michael F. Lacey, Jr.   Janice M. Herfkens

ASSOCIATES
Coreen K. Bezdicek   Patrick V. Waldron
              Michael S Jones

Representative Clients: Allied Mutual Insurance Company; CNA Insurance Company; Chubb Insurance Group; Continental Western Insurance Co.; Farmers Insurance Group; Farmland Insurance Company; Grinnell Mutual Reinsurance Company; Hawkeye Security Insurance Company; Iowa Insurance Institute, St. Paul Fire & Marine Insurance Company.

For full biographical listings, see the Martindale-Hubbell Law Directory

---

KEOKUK,* Lee Co.

LAW OFFICES OF JAMES P. HOFFMAN (AV)

Middle Road, P.O. Box 1087, 52632-1087
Telephone: 319-524-4441
Fax: 319-524-1638

For full biographical listings, see the Martindale-Hubbell Law Directory

---

KENTUCKY

COVINGTON, Kenton Co.

TALIAFERRO AND MEHLING (AV)

1005 Madison Avenue, P.O. Box 468, 41012-0468
Telephone: 606-291-9900
Fax: 606-291-3014

MEMBERS OF FIRM
Philip Taliaferro, III   Christopher J. Mehling
Lucinda C. Shirooni
ASSOCIATES
C. Houston Ebert   Howard L. Tankersley
              Alice G. Keys

(See Next Column)

TALIAFERRO AND MEHLING—*Continued*

OF COUNSEL

Robert W. Carran   Norbert J. Bischoff
                F. Edward Worland, Jr.

For full biographical listings, see the Martindale-Hubbell Law Directory

WARE, BRYSON, WEST & KUMMER (AV)

157 Barnwood Drive, 41017
Telephone: 606-341-0255
FAX: 606-341-1876

MEMBERS OF FIRM

Rodney S. Bryson   Greg D. Voss
Larry C. West   Robert B. Cetrulo
John R. Kummer   Susanne M. Cetrulo
Mark W. Howard   David W. Martin

ASSOCIATES

W. L. (Skip) Hammons, Jr.   Orie S. Ware (1882-1974)
James M. West   William O. Ware (1908-1961)
                James C. Ware (1913-1991)

Attorneys for: First National Bank of Northern Ky.; State Farm Insurance Co.; Reliance Insurance Group; Maryland Casualty Insurance Co.; Kemper Insurance Co.; Prudential Insurance Co.; State Farm Fire & Casualty Insurance Co.; Shelby Mutual Insurance Co.; Cincinnati Insurance Co.

For full biographical listings, see the Martindale-Hubbell Law Directory

---

DANVILLE, * Boyle Co.

DEEDRA BENTHALL (AV)

326 West Main Street, P.O. Box 996, 40422
Telephone: 606-236-5791; 236-6940
Fax: 606-236-8254

Reference: Citizens National Bank.

For full biographical listings, see the Martindale-Hubbell Law Directory

---

HINDMAN, * Knott Co.

WEINBERG, CAMPBELL, SLONE & SLONE, P.S.C. (AV)

Main Street, P.O. Box 727, 41822
Telephone: 606-785-5048; 785-5049
Fax: 606-785-3021

William R. Weinberg   Jerry Wayne Slone
Randy A. Campbell   Randy G. Slone
                Richard A. Counts

References: Bank of Hindman; Thacker & Grigsby Telephone Co.

For full biographical listings, see the Martindale-Hubbell Law Directory

---

LEXINGTON, * Fayette Co.

BOEHL STOPHER & GRAVES (AV)

444 West Second Street, 40508
Telephone: 606-252-6721
FAX: 606-253-1445
Louisville, Kentucky Office: Suite 2300, Providian Center, 400 West Market Street.
Telephone: 502-589-5980.
Fax: 502-561-9400.
Paducah, Kentucky Office: Suite 340 Executive Inn Riverfront, One Executive Boulevard.
Telephone: 502-442-4369.
Fax: 502-442-4689.
Prestonsburg, Kentucky Office: 105 West Court Street.
Telephone: 606-886-8004.
Fax: 606-886-9579.
New Albany, Indiana Office: Elsby East, Suite 204, 400 Pearl Street.
Telephone: 812-948-5053.
Fax: 812-948-9233.

RESIDENT PARTNERS

W. T. Adkins   Steven G. Kinkel
Nolan Carter, Jr.   Kim Martin Wilkie
Gregory K. Jenkins   Guillermo A. Carlos
Ronald L. Green   James B. Cooper

RESIDENT ASSOCIATES

Steven R. Armstrong   Patrick J. Murphy, II
Michael J. Cox   Brennen C. Ragone
                Fredrick A. Bailey, Jr.

Counsel For: Amerisure Companies; Baptist Healthcare System; CIGNA Companies; CNA Insurance Companies; Ford Motor Co.; Kemper National Insurance Group; Levi Strauss & Co.; Monroe County Insurance Company; Old Republic Insurance; Peabody Coal Company.

For full biographical listings, see the Martindale-Hubbell Law Directory

FERRERI & FOGLE (AV)

500 Quality Place, 300 East Main Street, 40507
Telephone: 606-253-4700
Telefax: 606-253-4702
Louisville, Kentucky Office: 203 Speed Building, 333 Guthrie Green.
Telephone: 502-582-1381.
Telefax: 502-581-9887.

MEMBERS OF FIRM

Thomas L. Ferreri   Joel W. Aubrey
Ronald J. Pohl   Roberta K. Kiser
                Robert S. Jones

ASSOCIATES

Stanley S. Dawson   Marcus A. Roland
Sherri P. Brown   Cynthia Bibb Pectol
Hugh Brett Stonecipher   Stephanie Dawn Ross

For full biographical listings, see the Martindale-Hubbell Law Directory

LANDRUM & SHOUSE (AV)

106 West Vine Street, P.O. Box 951, 40588-0951
Telephone: 606-255-2424
Facsimile: 606-233-0308
Louisville, Kentucky Office: 400 West Market Street, Suite 1550, 40202.
Telephone: 502-589-7616.
Facsimile: 502-589-2119.

MEMBERS OF FIRM

Thomas M. Cooper   John Garry McNeill
John R. Martin, Jr.   J. Denis Ogburn
  (Resident, Louisville Office)   (Resident, Louisville Office)
Mark J. Hinkel   Jane Durkin Samuel
                Douglas L. Hoots

ASSOCIATES

Stephen R. Chappell   Frank M. Jenkins, III
Daniel E. Murner   Sheila P. Hiestand
                Cynthia K. Lowe

District Attorneys: CSX Transportation, Inc.
Special Trial Counsel: Ford Motor Co. and Affiliates (Eastern Kentucky); Clark Equipment Co.
Representative Clients: The Continental Insurance Cos.; U.S. Insurance Group; U.S. Fidelity & Guaranty Co.; Ohio Casualty Insurance Co.; CIGNA; Royal Insurance Cos.

For Complete List of Firm Personnel, See General Section

For full biographical listings, see the Martindale-Hubbell Law Directory

LYNN, FULKERSON AND NICHOLS (AV)

267 West Short Street, 40507
Telephone: 606-253-0523
Telefax: 606-254-2098

MEMBER OF FIRM

Calvin R. Fulkerson

ASSOCIATE

Jo Alice Van Nagell

OF COUNSEL

Gordon W. Moss

Representative Clients: United States Fidelity & Guaranty Co.; The Travelers Insurance Co.

For full biographical listings, see the Martindale-Hubbell Law Directory

VIMONT & WILLS (AV)

Suite 300, 155 East Main Street, 40507-1317
Telephone: 606-252-2202
Telecopier: 606-259-2927

MEMBER OF FIRM

Timothy C. Wills

ASSOCIATES

Barbara Booker Wills   Kimberly Lemmons Garrison

For full biographical listings, see the Martindale-Hubbell Law Directory

---

LONDON, * Laurel Co.

HAMM, MILBY & RIDINGS (AV)

120 North Main Street, 40741
Telephone: 606-864-4126
Fax: 606-878-8144

MEMBERS OF FIRM

Robert L. Milby   Marcia Milby Ridings
                Kenneth H. Gilliam

James A. Ridings   Gregory A. Lay
                LaDonna Lynn Koebel

Representative Clients: Acceleration National; Aetna Life & Casualty Ins. Co.; All Risk Claims Service, Inc.; Allstate Insurance Co.; Alexis; American Automobile Mutual Ins.; American Bankers; American Hardware Ins. Co.

(See Next Column)

HAMM, MILBY & RIDINGS, London—Continued

For full biographical listings, see the Martindale-Hubbell Law Directory

LOUISVILLE,* Jefferson Co.

BOEHL STOPHER & GRAVES (AV)

Suite 2300 Providian Center, 400 West Market Street, 40202-3354
Telephone: 502-589-5980
FAX: 502-561-9400
Lexington, Kentucky Office: 444 West Second Street.
Telephone: 606-252-6721.
Fax: 606-253-1445.
Paducah, Kentucky Office: Suite 340 Executive Inn Riverfront, One Executive Boulevard.
Telephone: 502-442-4369.
Fax: 502-442-4689.
Prestonsburg, Kentucky Office: 105 West Court Street.
Telephone: 606-886-8004.
Fax: 606-886-9579.
New Albany, Indiana Office: Elsby East, Suite 204, 400 Pearl Street.
Telephone: 812-948-5053.
Fax: 812-948-9233.

MEMBERS OF FIRM

Larry L. Johnson	Peter J. Glauber
Wesley G. Gatlin	Walter E. Harding
Philip J. Reverman, Jr.	Douglas A. U'Sellis

ASSOCIATES

Mary Ann Kiwala	John C. Talbott
William J. Crowe	David P. Haick
Denise Basford Askin	Thomas M. Edelen

Counsel For: Amerisure Companies; Baptist Healthcare System; CIGNA Companies; CNA Insurance Companies; Ford Motor Co.; Kemper National Insurance Group; Levi Strauss & Co.; Monroe County Insurance Company; Old Republic Insurance; Peabody Coal Company.

For Complete List of Firm Personnel, See General Section

For full biographical listings, see the Martindale-Hubbell Law Directory

FERRERI & FOGLE (AV)

203 Speed Building, 333 Guthrie Green, 40202
Telephone: 502-582-1381
Telefax: 502-581-9887
Lexington, Kentucky Office: 500 Quality Place, 300 East Main Street.
Telephone: 606-253-4700.
Telefax: 606-253-4702.

MEMBERS OF FIRM

Thomas L. Ferreri	C. Patrick Fulton
James G. Fogle	Phillipe W. Rich
Judson F. Devlin	Walter C. Jobson

ASSOCIATES

Brian Timothy Gannon	Lisa J. Sutton
John G. Grohmann	Dennis M. Ostrowski
William A. Lyons	Anthony Finaldi
	(Not admitted in KY)

OF COUNSEL

William A. Miller	Glenn L. Schilling

Representative Clients: Aetna Life and Casualty; Alexsis; American International Adjustment Co.; American Resources Insurance Co.; American States Insurance Co.; Bituminous Insurance Co.; Chubb Group of Insurance Cos.; Commercial Union Insurance Co.; Commonwealth of Kentucky; Compensation Hospital Association Trust.

For full biographical listings, see the Martindale-Hubbell Law Directory

SEILLER & HANDMAKER, LLP (AV)

2200 Meidinger Tower, 40202
Telephone: 502-584-7400
Telecopier: 502-583-2100
Paris, Kentucky Office: Seiller, Handmaker & Blevins, P.S.C., 1431 South Main Street.
Telephone: 606-987-3980.
Telecopier: 606-987-3982.
Cynthiana, Kentucky Office: Seiller, Handmaker & Blevins, P.S.C., 9 South Walnut.
Telephone: 606-234-2880.
New Albany, Indiana Office: 202 Pearl Street.
Telephone: 812-948-8307.
Telecopier: 812-948-8383.

Edward F. Seiller (1897-1990)

MEMBERS OF FIRM

Stuart Allen Handmaker	Maury D. Kommor
Bill V. Seiller	Cynthia Compton Stone
David M. Cantor	Glenn A. Cohen
Neil C. Bordy	Tomi Anne Blevins Pulliam
Kyle Anne Citrynell	(Paris and Cynthiana Offices)

(See Next Column)

ASSOCIATES

Pamela M. Greenwell	Donna F. Townsend
Michael C. Bratcher	Gregory A. Lindsey
John E. Brengle	Vicki L. Buba
Patrick R. Holland, II	Allen C. Platt III (Resident,
Edwin Jon Wolfe	New Albany, Indiana Office)

OF COUNSEL

Robert S. Frey

For full biographical listings, see the Martindale-Hubbell Law Directory

WILLIAMS & WAGONER (AV)

101 Bullitt Lane, Oxmoor Place, 40222
Telephone: 502-429-5700
Fax: 502-429-5720
Lexington, Kentucky Office: Lexington Financial Center, 250 West Main Street, Suite 710.
Telephone: 606-252-3669.
Telecopier: 606-252-3487.

MEMBERS OF FIRM

Philip Williams	C. Thomas Hectus
James R. Wagoner	L. J. (Todd) Hollenbach, IV
W. Kenneth Nevitt	Dennis L. Mattingly
Carole M. Pearlman	Carla Foreman Dallas

ASSOCIATES

Robert M. Beal	R. Scott Summers
R. Thad Keal	(Resident, Lexington Office)
David Scott Dupps	Sun S. Choy
James M. Burd	Craig Louis Johnson
Robert A. Button, Jr.	Jeffrey T. Sampson
M. Kathryn Manis	J. Key Schoen
(Resident, Lexington Office)	Annette C. Karem
Mary E. Schaffner	Jane Rice Williams
George T. T. Kitchen III	(Resident, Lexington Office)

For full biographical listings, see the Martindale-Hubbell Law Directory

MADISONVILLE,* Hopkins Co.

MITCHELL, JOINER, HARDESTY & LOWTHER (AV)

113 East Center Street, Drawer 659, 42431-0659
Telephone: 502-825-4455
Telefax: 502-825-9600

Thomas A. Mitchell	Richard M. Joiner
Charles E. Lowther	

For Complete List of Firm Personnel, See General Section

For full biographical listings, see the Martindale-Hubbell Law Directory

PADUCAH,* McCracken Co.

BOEHL STOPHER & GRAVES (AV)

Suite 340 Executive Inn Riverfront, One Executive Boulevard, 42001
Telephone: 502-442-4369
FAX: 502-442-4689
Louisville, Kentucky Office: Providian Center, Suite 2300, 400 West Market Street.
Telephone: 502-589-5980.
Fax: 502-561-9400.
Lexington, Kentucky Office: 444 West Second Street.
Telephone: 606-252-6721.
Fax: 606-253-1445.
Prestonsburg, Kentucky Office: 105 West Court Street.
Telephone: 606-886-8004.
Fax: 606-886-9579.
New Albany, Indiana Office: Elsby East, Suite 204, 400 Pearl Street.
Telephone: 812-948-5053.
Fax: 812-948-9233.

RESIDENT PARTNER

Jonathan Freed

Counsel for: Ford Motor Co.; Texas Eastern Transmission Corp.; Coca-Cola Bottling Co.; National Collegiate Athletic Assn.; Hartford Accident and Indemnity Co.; Continental Insurance Group; St. Paul Fire & Marine Insurance Co.; Lloyds of London; Old Republic Insurance Co.

For Complete List of Firm Personnel, See General Section

For full biographical listings, see the Martindale-Hubbell Law Directory

PAINTSVILLE,* Johnson Co.

WELLS, PORTER, SCHMITT & JONES (AV)

327 Main Street, 41240
Telephone: 606-789-3747; 789-3749; 789-3775
Fax: 606-789-3790

MEMBER OF FIRM

John V. Porter, Jr.

(See Next Column)

WELLS, PORTER, SCHMITT & JONES—*Continued*

ASSOCIATES

Johnny L. Griffith   Jon H. Johnson

Representative Clients: Wausau; Travelers; Fireman's Fund; Ladegast & Heffner; CNA.

For Complete List of Firm Personnel, See General Section

For full biographical listings, see the Martindale-Hubbell Law Directory

---

*PIKEVILLE,** Pike Co.

PRUITT AND DE BOURBON LAW FIRM (AV)

The Call Building, Second Street, P.O. Box 339, 41502
Telephone: 606-437-7366; 437-7367; 237-1280
Fax: 606-432-2367

MEMBERS OF FIRM

James P. Pruitt, Jr.   P. Michael de Bourbon

Reference: The Citizen's Bank of Pikeville.

For full biographical listings, see the Martindale-Hubbell Law Directory

---

LOUISIANA

---

*BATON ROUGE,** East Baton Rouge Parish

GUGLIELMO, MARKS, SCHUTTE, TERHOEVE & LOVE (AV)

(A Registered Limited Liability Partnership)
320 Somerulos Street, P.O. Box 3177, 70821-3177
Telephone: 504-387-6966
Fax: 504-387-8338

Carey J. Guglielmo   Glen Scott Love
Paul Marks, Jr.   Dawn T. Trabeau-Mire
Charles A. Schutte, Jr.   Joseph W. Mengis
Henry G. Terhoeve   Kevin P. Landreneau

Representative Clients: City National Bank; Greyhound Corp.; The Travelers Insurance Co.; Chrysler Corp.; State Farm Insurance Co's.; Travelers/Aetna Insurance Group; Aetna Life & Casualty Co.

For full biographical listings, see the Martindale-Hubbell Law Directory

SHOCKEY & ZIOBER, A PROFESSIONAL LAW CORPORATION (AV)

Suite 3-A, 5551 Corporate Boulevard, P.O. Box 80286, 70898-0286
Telephone: 504-929-8929
Telecopier: 504-928-7694

John David Ziober   William C. Shockey

Emily Phillips Ziober   Jennifer R. Treadway Morris
Douglas J. Cochran   James E. Moore, Jr.

For full biographical listings, see the Martindale-Hubbell Law Directory

---

*LAKE CHARLES,** Calcasieu Parish

THE CARMOUCHE LAW FIRM A PROFESSIONAL CORPORATION (AV)

Bank One Tower, 901 Lakeshore Drive, Suite 900, P.O. Drawer 2001, 70601-5270
Telephone: 318-433-0355
Telecopier: 318-433-1274
Email: clf@carmouche.com

David R. Frohn

For full biographical listings, see the Martindale-Hubbell Law Directory

---

MANDEVILLE, St. Tammany Parish

BAILEY & DWYER (AV)

600 Mariner's Plaza, Suite 607, 70448
Telephone: 504-674-1105
Fax: 504-674-1966
Metairie Area Telephone: 504-833-8241
Fax: 504-837-4534

MEMBERS OF FIRM

B. Ralph Bailey   Frederick H. N. Dwyer
Scott O. Gaspard

For full biographical listings, see the Martindale-Hubbell Law Directory

---

*NEW ORLEANS,** Orleans Parish

HEBERT, MOULEDOUX & BLAND, A PROFESSIONAL LAW CORPORATION (AV)

Pan-American Life Center, Suite 1650, 601 Poydras Street, 70130
Telephone: 504-525-3333
Cable Address: "HMBL"
Telex: 588-092;
Fax: 504-523-4224

Wilton E. Bland, III   Roch P. Poelman
Alan Guy Brackett

Representative Clients: Archer-Daniels Midland Company; Bisso Marine Company, Inc.; Carline Geismar Fleet, Inc.; Cooper/T. Smith Stevedoring Company, Inc.; Delta Queen Steamboat Co.; Diamond Offshore Drilling, Inc.; LOOP INC.; Marine Equipment Management Corporation; McDermott Incorporated; Olympic Marine Company.

For Complete List of Firm Personnel, See General Section

For full biographical listings, see the Martindale-Hubbell Law Directory

---

*SHREVEPORT,** Caddo Parish

MAYER, SMITH & ROBERTS, L.L.P. (AV)

1550 Creswell, 71101
Telephone: 318-222-2135, 222-2268
Fax: 318-222-6420
Email: (Attorney's First Name)@MSRLAW.COM

MEMBERS OF FIRM

Caldwell Roberts   David Butterfield
Walter O. Hunter, Jr.   Henry N. Bellamy
Mark A. Goodwin   John C. Turnage
Ben Marshall, Jr.   Paul R. Mayer, Jr.
Alexander S. Lyons   Steven E. Soileau
Kim Purdy Thomas   Deborah Shea Baukman
Caldwell Roberts, Jr.

ASSOCIATES

Frank K. Carroll   Dalton Roberts Ross

OF COUNSEL

Charles L. Mayer   Paul R. Mayer

Representative Clients: CNA Insurance Companies; Liberty Mutual Insurance Company; The St. Paul Companies; United States Fidelity and Guaranty Company; Schumpert Medical Center; Travelers Insurance Company; Great American Insurance Company; Insurance Corporation of America; Highlands Insurance Company.

For full biographical listings, see the Martindale-Hubbell Law Directory

MILLS, TIMMONS & FLOWERS, A PROFESSIONAL LAW CORPORATION (AV)

300 Law Center, 331 Milam Street, P.O. Box 1784, 71166-1784
Telephone: 318-222-0337
Fax: 318-222-5400

George H. Mills, Jr.   David C. Turansky
Wayne Timmons   J. Broocks Greer III
Peter R. Flowers   Sandra Lynn Walker

OF COUNSEL

William T. Allison

Reference: Hibernia National Bank.

For full biographical listings, see the Martindale-Hubbell Law Directory

---

MAINE

---

*PORTLAND,** Cumberland Co.

TROUBH, HEISLER & PIAMPIANO, P.C. (AV)

511 Congress Street, P.O. Box 9711, 04104-5011
Telephone: 207-780-6789
Fax: 207-774-2339

William B. Troubh   Thomas E. Getchell
Edwin A. Heisler   Michael Richards
Robert J. Piampiano   William K. McKinley
Kevin M. Gillis   Daniel F. Gilligan
Michael P. Boyd   Paul S. Bulger

John G. Richardson   Linda L. Sears
Daniel R. Felkel

For full biographical listings, see the Martindale-Hubbell Law Directory

MARYLAND

---

*BALTIMORE,** (Independent City)

ROLLINS, SMALKIN, RICHARDS & MACKIE (AV)

401 North Charles Street, 21201
Telephone: 410-727-2443
Fax: 410-727-8390

MEMBERS OF FIRM

H. Beale Rollins (1898-1985)	John F. Linsenmeyer
Samuel S. Smalkin (1906-1982)	Thomas C. Gentner
T. Benjamin Weston (1913-1980)	Glenn W. Trimmer
Thomas G. Andrew (1910-1973)	Patrick G. Cullen
Edward C. Mackie	James P. O'Meara

Dennis J. Sullivan

ASSOCIATES

Paul G. Donoghue	Donna Lynn Kolakowski-Hollen
Ralph E. Wilson III	Meg Bantley Whiteford
Kenneth G. Macleay	Anthony G. Lardieri

OF COUNSEL

Raymond A. Richards (Retired)   Hartman J. Miller

For full biographical listings, see the Martindale-Hubbell Law Directory

---

LARGO, Prince Georges Co.

SHIPLEY & HORNE, P.A. (AV)

1101 Mercantile Lane, Suite 240, 20774
Telephone: 301-925-1800
Fax: 301-925-1803

Russell W. Shipley   Arthur J. Horne, Jr.

For full biographical listings, see the Martindale-Hubbell Law Directory

---

*ROCKVILLE,** Montgomery Co.

ANDERSON & QUINN (AV)

The Adams Law Center, 25 Wood Lane, 20850
Telephone: 301-762-3303
FAX: 301-762-3776
Other Rockville Maryland Office: 110 North West St., Suite 501, 20850.
Telephone: 301-340-0800.

MEMBERS OF FIRM

Charles C. Collins (1900-1973)	Donald P. Maiberger
Robert E. Anderson (Not	Robert P. Scanlon
admitted in MD; Retired)	James G. Healy
Francis X. Quinn	John A. Rego

ASSOCIATES

Alice Kelley Scanlon	Mary L. Fellin
Marnie E. Simon	Kelly Ann McInerney
Kerry Patricia Shanahan	Timothy J. Mulreany

Representative Clients: C & P Telephone; Commercial Union Insurance Cos.; Allstate Insurance Co.; State Farm Mutual Automobile Insurance Co.; Liberty Mutual Insurance Co.; Northbrook Insurance Cos.; Travelers Insurance Co.; National General Insurance Co.; American International Adjustment Co.; Marriott Corp.

For full biographical listings, see the Martindale-Hubbell Law Directory

---

*TOWSON,** Baltimore Co.

HOWELL, GATELY, WHITNEY & CARTER, LLP (AV)

401 Washington Avenue, Twelfth Floor, 21204
Telephone: 410-583-8000
Fax: 410-583-8031

MEMBER OF FIRM

William R. Levasseur

For Complete List of Firm Personnel, See General Section

For full biographical listings, see the Martindale-Hubbell Law Directory

---

MASSACHUSETTS

---

*BOSTON,** Suffolk Co.

BURNS & LEVINSON LLP (AV)

125 Summer Street, 02110-1624
Telephone: 617-345-3000
Telecopier: 617-345-3299
Email: firm@B-L.com
Rockland, Massachusetts Office: 1001 Hingham Street.
Telephone: 617-982-4100.
Telecopier: 617-982-4141.

(See Next Column)

MEMBERS OF FIRM

William H. Clancy   Michael Weinberg

ASSOCIATES

Lawrence J. McNally, Jr.	Pamela G. Smith
Amy L. McDonald	

OF COUNSEL

Warren E. Tolman

Argonaut Ins. Co.; Kemper Ins. Group; Legion Ins. Group; TIG Ins. Co.; Crawford & Co.; Guaranty Fund Management Services; Teredyne.

For Complete List of Firm Personnel, See General Section

For full biographical listings, see the Martindale-Hubbell Law Directory

---

*SPRINGFIELD,** Hampden Co.

ROBINSON DONOVAN MADDEN & BARRY, P.C. (AV)

Suite 1600, BayBank Tower, 1500 Main Street, 01115
Telephone: 413-732-2301
Fax: 413-785-4658

Homans Robinson (1894-1973)	Milton J. Donovan (1906-1995)
Lawrence M. Sinclair (1942-1986)	

OF COUNSEL

John H. Madden, Jr.	Victor Rosenberg
Edward J. Barry	Richard S. Milstein

Gordon H. Wentworth	John C. Sikorski
James H. Tourtelotte	Nancy Frankel Pelletier
Charles K. Bergin, Jr.	Paul S. Weinberg
Ronald C. Kidd	Frederica H. McCarthy
Jeffrey W. Roberts	Matthew J. King
Jeffrey L. McCormick	Neva Kaufman Rohan
James F. Martin	Douglas F. Boyd
Robert P. Cunningham	James K. Bodurtha

Keith A. Minoff

E. Paul Amata	Kimberly Davis Crear
(Not admitted in MA)	John W. Davis
James D. Chadwell	Edmund J. Gorman
Susan L. Cooper	Patricia M. Rapinchuk

Jonathan P. Rice

Representative Clients: The First National Bank of Boston; United Cooperative Bank; Fleet Bank, N.A.; American Policyholders Insurance Co.; CNA; Commercial Union Insurance Co.; Hanover Insurance Group.

For full biographical listings, see the Martindale-Hubbell Law Directory

---

*WORCESTER,** Worcester Co.

FULLER, ROSENBERG, PALMER & BELIVEAU (AV)

14 Harvard Street, P.O. Box 764, 01613
Telephone: 508-755-5225
Telecopier: 508-757-1039

MEMBERS OF FIRM

Albert E. Fuller	Peter A. Palmer
Kenneth F. Rosenberg	Thomas W. Beliveau

ASSOCIATES

Robert W. Towle	Michael I. Mutter
Julie Bednarz Russell	Brian F. Welsh
Timothy O. Ribley	John J. Finn
Mark W. Murphy	James C. Crowley, Jr.
Lisa R. Bertonazzi	John P. Donohue
Mark C. Darling	James F. Gettens
William J. Mason	John Arthur Johnson
Antoinette J. Yitchinsky	Ann F. Scannell

For full biographical listings, see the Martindale-Hubbell Law Directory

---

MILTON, LAURENCE & DIXON (AV)

100 Front Street, Suite 825, 01608
Telephone: 508-791-6386
Fax: 508-799-4879

MEMBERS OF FIRM

Stanley B. Milton (1899-1992)	Karen A. Loughlin
Robert C. Milton (1932-1977)	Beth Anne Bagley
Gerard R. Laurence	Daniel M. Wrenn
Charles W. Dixon	William R. Trainor
Paul P. O'Connor	Karyn E. Polito

OF COUNSEL

John G. Preston

Reference: Shawmut Worcester County Bank N.A.

For full biographical listings, see the Martindale-Hubbell Law Directory

MICHIGAN

ANN ARBOR,* Washtenaw Co.

BRAUN KENDRICK FINKBEINER PLC (AV)

700 First National Building, 48104
Telephone: 313-995-4100
Telecopier: 313-995-4798
URL: http://www.bkf-law.com
Bay City, Michigan Office: 201 Phoenix Building, P.O. Box 2039.
Telephone: 517-895-8505.
Telecopier: 517-895-8437.
Saginaw, Michigan Office: 101 N. Washington, Suite 812.
Telephone: 517-753-3461.
Telecopier: 517-753-3951.

Barry M. Levine

Representative Client: General Motors Corporation.

For full biographical listings, see the Martindale-Hubbell Law Directory

HURBIS & CLINTON (AV)

Fifth Floor, City Center Building, 48104
Telephone: 313-761-8358
Fax: 313-761-3134

Charles J. Hurbis   Mary F. Clinton

Robert Lipnik   Georgette E. David

Representative Clients: General Motors Corp.; ITT Hartford; Insurance Company of North America; The University of Michigan; North Oakland Medical Center; City of Pontiac; Sears Roebuck and Co.; Montgomery Ward and Co., Inc.; Sedjwick-James, Inc.

For full biographical listings, see the Martindale-Hubbell Law Directory

BIRMINGHAM, Oakland Co.

LACEY & JONES (AV)

600 South Adams Road, Suite 300, 48009-6827
Telephone: 810-433-1414
Fax: 810-433-1241
Grand Rapids, Michigan Office: Suite 430, Ledyard Building, 125 Ottawa Avenue, N.W.
Telephone: 616-776-3641.
Fax: 616-776-3516.

Ralph B. Lacey (1885-1966)   Francis L. Sylvester (Retired)
William J. Jones (1908-1991)   Paul Van Hartesveldt (Retired)
Robert B. Lacey (1912-1976)   John A. Hilgendorf (Retired)

MEMBERS OF FIRM

Theodore A. Lughezzani   Dennis E. Zacharski
Steve N. Yardley   T. F. Felker, Jr.
John Hayes   Gerald M. Marcinkoski
Charles E. Mann   William A. Day
Larry P. Beidelman   Kathleen McNichol Behn
Bruce C. Roberts   Richard N. Lovernick
Lawrence G. Kozaruk   Peter M. Roggenbaum
David J. Duthie
  (Resident, Grand Rapids)

ASSOCIATES

Michael T. Reinholm   Timothy D. Finegan
Johnnie B. Rambus   Robert H. Orlowski, Jr.
Sean J. Powers   J. Patrick O'Neill
Timothy M. McAree   Dawn M. Sutkiewicz
  (Resident, Grand Rapids)   D. Michael McCann

OF COUNSEL

Thomas J. Sullivan   Robert L. Beardslee
               William G. Sinn

Representative Clients: Alexsis, Inc.; Ameritech; Chrysler Corporation; CIGNA; Liberty Mutual Insurance Company; Meijer, Inc.; Metropolitan Prop. & Casualty; Michigan Hospital Association; Travelers Insurance Company.

For full biographical listings, see the Martindale-Hubbell Law Directory

DETROIT,* Wayne Co.

BLAKE, KIRCHNER, SYMONDS, MACFARLANE, LARSON & SMITH, P.C. (AV)

1432 Buhl Building, 48226
Telephone: 313-961-7321
Fax: 313-961-5972

F. Peter Blake   Meria E. Larson
Arthur G. Kirchner   Richard P. Smith
Daniel C. Symonds   Kevin T. Kennedy
Bruce F. MacFarlane   Jane P. Garrett
            Christopher G. Manolis

(See Next Column)

David B. Klein   Michael P. Donnelly
            Kim Leslie Kretzschmar

Reference: Comerica Bank.

For full biographical listings, see the Martindale-Hubbell Law Directory

BRADY HATHAWAY, PROFESSIONAL CORPORATION (AV)

1330 Buhl Building, 48226-3602
Telephone: 313-965-3700
Telecopier: 313-965-2830

John F. Brady   Daniel J. Bretz
Thomas M. J. Hathaway   Liliana A. Ciccodicola
Thomas P. Brady   Connie M. Cessante

OF COUNSEL

James A. Hathaway   Ingrid K. Brey

Representative Clients: Beam Stream, Inc.; Bundy Tubing Company; Energy Conversion Devices, Inc.; Schering Corporation; Warner-Lambert; Wolverine Technologies; ABB Environmental Services; GMIS, Inc.; Marriott Corp.

For full biographical listings, see the Martindale-Hubbell Law Directory

CHARFOOS, REITER, PETERSON, HOLMQUIST & PILCHAK, P.C. (AV)

476 State of Michigan Plaza Building, 1200 Sixth Street, 48226
Telephone: 313-961-7011
Email: CRPHP@ix.netcom.com
Farmington Hills, Michigan Office: 30500 Northwestern Highway, Suite 400.
Telephone: 810-626-7300.
Fax: 810-626-7305.

Myron B. Charfoos   Kenneth E. Jones
James A. Reiter   Marianne G. Talon
Daniel Peterson   Deborah S. Dorland
C. John Holmquist, Jr.   Daniel G. Cohen
William E. Pilchak   Danial J. Hébert

Representative Clients: The Accident Fund Co.; CNA Insurance Co.; Detroit Board of Education; Frankenmuth Insurance Co.; Hyatt Regency; Meadowbrook Insurance Group; MAXCIS, Inc.; Michigan Auto Dealers' Self-Insured Fund; Michigan Health & Hospital Assn.; Sedgewick James of Mich.

For full biographical listings, see the Martindale-Hubbell Law Directory

CONKLIN, BENHAM, DUCEY, LISTMAN & CHUHRAN, P.C. (AV)

1740 First National Building, 48226
Telephone: 313-961-8690
Fax: 313-961-4786
Traverse City, Michigan Office: 415 East Front Street.
Telephone: 616-947-4300.
Fax: 616-947-3924.

S. Gerard Conklin (1903-1975)   David J. Watts
Donald G. Ducey   Martin L. Critchell
William R. Listman   Thomas A. Plagens
Thomas P. Chuhran   John S. Chapman
Thomas J. McNally   David J. Berge
            Dwight D. Labadie

Martin M. Summer

Representative Clients: General Motors Corp.; Great Lakes Division, National Steel Corp.; The Accident Fund Co.; Frankenmuth Mutual Insurance Co.; The Budd Co.; CIGNA/INA-Aetna; Michigan Health & Hospital Association; Oakwood Health Services Corp.; Chrysler Corp.; Sedgewick James of Michigan.

For full biographical listings, see the Martindale-Hubbell Law Directory

KELLER, THOMA, SCHWARZE, SCHWARZE, DuBAY & KATZ, P.C. (AV)

440 East Congress, 5th Floor, 48226
Telephone: 313-965-7610
Bloomfield Hills, Michigan Office: Suite 122, 100 West Long Lake Road.
Telephone: 810-642-5218.

Thomas L. Fleury   Patrice L. Baker
            John J. Rabaut

Counsel for: Livonia Public Schools; Ludington News Co., Inc.
Representative Clients: Borg-Warner Corp.; E & L Transport Co.; The Kroger Co.; Holnam, Inc.
Public Employer Clients: City of Farmington Hills; City of Flint; City of Grosse Pointe Woods; Saginaw Public Schools.

For Complete List of Firm Personnel, See General Section

For full biographical listings, see the Martindale-Hubbell Law Directory

PATTERSON, PHIFER & PHILLIPS, P.C. (AV)

L. B. King Building, 1274 Library Street, Suite 500, 48226
Telephone: 313-964-2360

(See Next Column)

PATTERSON, PHIFER & PHILLIPS P.C., *Detroit—Continued*

Michael D. Patterson　　　　　　Randolph D. Phifer
Dwight W. Phillips

Joseph M. White　　　　　　　　Eugene M. Holmes
Lisa A. Cylar

Representative Clients: Detroit Board of Education; Fireman's Fund Insurance Co.; General Motors Corp.; Home Federal Savings Bank; Liberty Mutual Insurance Co.; Metropolitan Life Insurance Co.; Michigan Basic Property Insurance Assn.; New York Life Insurance Co.; Wayne State University. *Reference:* First of American Bank-Detroit, N.A.

For full biographical listings, see the Martindale-Hubbell Law Directory

---

FARMINGTON HILLS, Oakland Co.

CHARFOOS, REITER, PETERSON, HOLMQUIST & PILCHAK, P.C. (AV)

Suite 400, 30500 Northwestern Highway, 48334-3179
Telephone: 810-626-7300
Facsimile: 810-626-7305
Email: CRPHP@ix.netcom.com
Detroit, Michigan Office: 1200 Sixth Street.
Telephone: 313-961-7011.

Myron B. Charfoos　　　　　　Kenneth E. Jones
James A. Reiter　　　　　　　　Marianne G. Talon
Daniel Peterson　　　　　　　　Deborah S. Dorland
C. John Holmquist, Jr.　　　　　Daniel G. Cohen
William E. Pilchak　　　　　　　Danial J. Hébert

Representative Clients: The Accident Fund Co.; CNA Insurance Co.; Detroit Board of Education; Frankenmuth Insurance Co.; Hyatt Regency; Meadowbrook Insurance Group; MAXCIS, Inc.; Michigan Auto Dealers' Self-Insured Fund; Michigan Health & Hospital Assn.; Sedgewick James of Mich.

For full biographical listings, see the Martindale-Hubbell Law Directory

---

*FLINT,** Genesee Co.

MacDONALD, FITZGERALD & MacDONALD, P.C. (AV)

200 McKinnon Building, 48502
Telephone: 810-232-3184; 234-2204
Fax: 810-232-9632

Robert J. MacDonald　　　　　John J. FitzGerald (1919-1995)
(1914-1987)　　　　　　　　　R. Duncan MacDonald
Timothy J. MacDonald

References: Michigan National Bank; Genesee Merchants Bank & Trust Co.

For full biographical listings, see the Martindale-Hubbell Law Directory

---

*KALAMAZOO,** Kalamazoo Co.

EARLY, LENNON, PETERS & CROCKER, P.C. (AV)

900 Comerica Building, 49007-4752
Telephone: 616-381-8844
Fax: 616-349-8525

John T. Peters, Jr.

Attorneys for: General Motors Corp.; Wal-Mart Stores; Borgess Medical Center; Aetna Insurance: Kemper Group; Medical Protective Co.; Zurich Insurance; AAA; Liberty Mutual; Home Insurance.

For Complete List of Firm Personnel, See General Section

For full biographical listings, see the Martindale-Hubbell Law Directory

---

LANSING, Ingham Co.

DUNNINGS & FRAWLEY, P.C. (AV)

Duncan Building, 530 South Pine Street, 48933-2299
Telephone: 517-487-8222
Fax: 517-487-2026
Email: conrights@voyager.net

Stuart J. Dunnings, Jr.　　　　　John J. Frawley

Stuart J. Dunnings, III　　　　　Steven D. Dunnings
Shauna L. Dunnings

Representative Clients: Lansing Board of Education; Lansing Housing Commission; Ford Motor Co.
References: First of America; Michigan National Bank.

For full biographical listings, see the Martindale-Hubbell Law Directory

---

*SAGINAW,** Saginaw Co.

BRAUN KENDRICK FINKBEINER PLC (AV)

101 N. Washington Suite 812, 48607-1297
Telephone: 517-753-3461
Telecopier: 517-753-3951
URL: http://www.bkf-law.com
Bay City, Michigan Office: 201 Phoenix Building, P.O. Box 2039.
Telephone: 517-895-8505.
Telecopier: 517-895-8437.
Ann Arbor, Michigan Office: 700 First National Building.
Telephone: 313-995-4100.
Telecopier: 313-995-4798.

Harold J. Blanchet, Jr.　　　　　Bruce L. Dalrymple
E. Louis Ognisanti　　　　　　　Charles A. Gilfeather

Representative Client: General Motors Corporation.

For Complete List of Firm Personnel, See General Section

For full biographical listings, see the Martindale-Hubbell Law Directory

---

SOUTHFIELD, Oakland Co.

PROVIZER, LICHTENSTEIN & PHILLIPS, P.C. (AV)

4000 Town Center, Suite 1800, 48075
Telephone: 810-352-9080
Facsimile: 810-352-1491

Harold M. Provizer　　　　　　David S. Lichtenstein
William J. Selinsky

For full biographical listings, see the Martindale-Hubbell Law Directory

---

*TRAVERSE CITY,** Grand Traverse Co.

CONKLIN, BENHAM, DUCEY, LISTMAN & CHUHRAN, P.C. (AV)

415 East Front Street, 49684
Telephone: 616-947-4300
Fax: 616-947-3924
Detroit, Michigan Office: 1740 First National Building.
Telephone: 313-961-8690.
Fax: 313-961-4786.

Michael J. Gillman　　　　　　　Jeffrey E. Gwillim

C. Bruce Taylor

Representative Clients: The Accident Fund Co.; Alexsis Risk Management Service; Amerisure Companies; American International Adjusting; Citizens Management, Inc.; Lake State Insurance Co.; Michigan Association of Counties; Michigan Construction Industry Self-Insurers' Fund; Michigan Health & Hospital Assn.; State of Michigan.

For full biographical listings, see the Martindale-Hubbell Law Directory